DICTIONARY
OF
INTERNATIONAL
BIOGRAPHY

31ST EDITION

PUBLISHER
Nicholas S. Law

EDITOR IN CHIEF
Jon Gifford

PRODUCTION/DESIGN
Bryan Carpenter
Scott Gwinnett

EDITORIAL ASSISTANTS
Ann Dewison
Sara Rains
Rebecca Partner

All communications to: International Biographical Centre
Cambridge CB2 3QP, England

DICTIONARY
OF
INTERNATIONAL
BIOGRAPHY

31ST EDITION

2004

International Biographical Centre
Cambridge, England

ISBN: 1 903986 08 7

Printed and bound in the United Kingdom by:
Antony Rowe Ltd
Bumper's Farm Industrial Estate
Chippenham, Wiltshire, England
SN14 6LH

FOREWORD BY THE PUBLISHER

I am delighted to offer the *Thirty First Edition* of the **Dictionary of International Biography,** the flagship publication of the International Biographical Centre of Cambridge, England, to its many readers or 'users' throughout the world.

The **Dictionary of International Biography** attempts to reflect contemporary achievement in every profession and field of interest within as many countries as possible. It is an ever growing reference source since very few biographical entries are repeated from one edition to the next and only then when they have been updated with relevant new material. In this way each new Edition adds thousands of new biographies to those already published in the series; to date more than 215,000 biographies have been presented from information supplied and checked by those individuals who are featured.

As with previous Editions of the Dictionary, the *Thirty First* has been dedicated to a number of individuals who have been chosen by our Editorial Board to represent the thousands whose lives and work have received notice in this title over the years. They are, in alphabetical order:

Anne Geert Bartelds

Daniel D. Brunda DDG LPIBA MOIF IOM AdVSci DO

Dr. David Donaldson MB ChB FRCP FRCPath CBiol FIBiol CChem FRSC EurClinChem

Peter Galliner AdVBus IOM

Prof. Dr. Kazuyosi Ikeda D.Sc D.Litt. LPIBA DDG IOM LFWLA MOIF CH DO

Roy O. Kendall

Owen William Loneragan DDG

Demetrios Zeno Pierides

Dr Kunitomo Sato MD PhD DDG CH MOIF DO AdVMed

Dr. Troy A. Smith

Betty Irene Parham Stines

Sonia Viktoria Wanner AdVAh

To those in the Dedication Section and to all who are mentioned in this *Thirty First Edition* I offer my congratulations and admiration.

I am often asked how we select individuals for inclusion in the **Dictionary of International Biography** and for that matter other titles published by the IBC. Readers and researchers should know that we publish only information which has been provided by those listed and in every case we have had their permission to publish it. Selection is made on the grounds of achievement and contribution on a professional, occupational, national or international level, as well as interest to the reader. An additional intention is to provide librarians of major libraries with a cumulative reference work consisting of Volumes published annually.

It cannot be emphasised too strongly that there is no charge or fee of any kind for inclusion in the Dictionary. Every entrant was sent at least one typescript for approval before publication in order to eliminate errors and to ensure accuracy and relevance. While great care has been taken by our Editors it is always possible that in a work of this size a few errors may have been made. If this is the case, my apologies in advance.

I would be grateful to hear from readers and researchers who feel that particular individuals should appear in future Volumes of the **Dictionary of International Biography** or any other relevant IBC works of reference. Such recommendations may be sent to the IBC's Research Department. Since our researchers have great difficulty in contacting some important figures it is always helpful to us to have addresses.

Nicholas S. Law
Editorial Director
International Biographical Centre
Cambridge CB2 3QP
England

July 2004

INTERNATIONAL BIOGRAPHICAL CENTRE RANGE OF REFERENCE TITLES

From one of the widest ranges of contemporary biographical reference works published under any one imprint, some IBC titles date back to the 1930's. Each edition is compiled from information supplied by those listed, who include leading personalities of particular countries or professions. Information offered usually includes date and place of birth; family details; qualifications; career histories; awards and honours received; books published or other creative work; other relevant information including postal address. Naturally there is no charge or fee for inclusion. New editions are freshly compiled and contain on average 80-90% new information. New titles are regularly added to the IBC reference library.

Titles include:

2000 Eminent Scientists of Today
Dictionary of International Biography
Who's Who in Asia and the Pacific Nations
2000 Outstanding People
Who's Who in the 21st Century
2000 Outstanding Scientists of the 21st Century
2000 Outstanding Scholars of the 21st Century
2000 Outstanding Intellectuals of the 21st Century
Living Science

Enquires to:
Editorial Offices
International Biographical Centre
St Thomas Place
Ely
Cambridgeshire
CB7 4GG
England

DEPUTY DIRECTORS GENERAL OF THE IBC

Ms Ji Young Kim DDG, Korea
Prof Pill Soo Kim LPIBA DDG IOM AdVSci CH, Korea
Prof Rev Dr Kim Kwang Tae LFIBA DDG, Korea
Prof Katsumi Kimura DDG, Japan
Dr Vihar Nikolov Kiskinov DDG, Bulgaria
Prof Hirohisa Kitano DDG, Japan
Dr Aggrey Kiyingi DDG, Australia
Mr Tor G Kjoelberg DDG, Norway
Dr Albert S Klainer MD DDG IOM, USA
Prof Eliezer I Klainman LPIBA IOM AdVMed DDG, Israel
Prof Vladimir V Klyuev DDG, Russia
Mr Dagfinn Andreas Knudsen DDG, Norway
Dr Edvard Kobal DDG, Slovenia
Mr Nikolai Mykola I Kobasko DDG, USA
Prof Toshiro Kobayashi MOIF DDG, Japan
Prof Yukio Kobayashi DDG LFIBA, Japan
Mr Charles Joseph Kocian DDG LFIBA AdVSci, USA
Dr Spincer Sih-Ping Koh DDG, Taiwan
Prof Oleg A Kolobov DDG, Russia
Prof Dr Hisatoki Komaki DDG IOM LFIBA, Japan
Prof Victor G Komar DDG, Russia
Prof Changduk Kong DDG, Korea
Prof Dr Toshihiko Kono DDG, USA
Dr Alfred V Kottek LFIBA DDG IOM, Canada
Prof Ryszard Kozlowski DDG, Poland
Dr Walter Kreyszig DDG, Canada
Dr Alexei Krivolutsky DDG, Russia
Bishop Navasard Ktshoyan CH DDG, Armenia
Dr Joy T Kunjappu DDG, USA
Prof Dr Chang-Yang Kuo DDG IOM, Taiwan
Dr Soji Kurimoto IOM AdVMed DDG, Japan
Marvin Z Kurlan MD FACS LFIBA DDG IOM, USA
Mr Kisho Kurokawa DDG LPIBA IOM, Japan
Prof Vladimir G Kuz DDG, Ukraine
Ms Tuulikki Kyllonen-Heikel DDG LFIBA IOM, Finland
Prof Bernhard Kytzler DDG, South Africa
Mr Joseph Anthony La Russa DDG, USA
Prof Tadeusz Z Lachowicz IOM CH AdVSci DDG, Poland
Prof Aris Lacis DDG, Latvia
Mrs Elly A Ladas DDG, Greece
Dr Armando Vicente Lago IOM DDG CH, Argentina
Dr Niki Laïopoulou DDG LFIBA, Greece
Mr Paul F Lalande MOIF DDG, France
Dr Lam Lai Sing LFIBA IOM DDG, Hong Kong
Mr Billy Lam LFIBA DDG, Hong Kong
Dr Luc Johan Lambrecht LPIBA DDG MOIF IOM, Belgium
Dr V Landers LPIBA LFWLA MOIF IOM, USA
Dr Ted Lane DDG, USA
Ms Lilly Katherine Lane DDG, USA
Dr Dale P Layman PhD MOIF DDG LPIBA AdVMed IOM, USA
Dr Harry C Layton DDG IOM LHD, USA
Prof Phan Le Xuan DSc DDG AdVMed, France
Dr Charles L Leavitt LPIBA DDG, USA
Prof Helmut Lechner LFIBA IOM DDG CH MOIF, Austria
Dr Anne W M Lee DDG, Hong Kong
Dr Don Yoon Lee PhD LFIBA DDG, USA
Dr Elhang Howard Lee DDG, Korea
Dr Irene Lee DDG, USA
Dr Shyh-Dye Lee DDG, Taiwan
Mr Andrew Siu-Woo Lee MOIF DDG LPIBA, Hong Kong
Ms Emily H M Kuo Lee DDG, USA
Ms Angela W Y Lee DDG, Hong Kong
Prof Jeong Y Lee DDG LFIBA, Korea
Dr Laurence A Lees LFIBA DDG, Australia
Miss Joy LeRoy LFIBA MOIF DDG IOM, USA
Prof Gorazd Lesnicar DDG, Slovenia
Prof Li Zhongying DDG, China
Prof Liang Dan-Fong LFIBA DDG, Taiwan
Dr Phillip K Lim LPIBA DDG, USA
Ms Joan Pek Bee Lim LFIBA IOM DDG, Malaysia

Prof Chen-Chong Lin LFIBA DDG, Taiwan
Prof Chung-sheng Lin DDG, Taiwan
Prof Ping-Wha Lin DDG MOIF, USA
Ms J C McKee Lindsay LPIBA IOM DDG MOIF, USA
Ms Joanne M Lindsey IOM DDG MOIF, USA
Mr Liu Guohui DDG, China
Prof Liu Chung Chu DDG, China
Prof Yanpei Liu DDG, China
Mr Chiu-Yuen Benson Lo LFIBA DDG, Hong Kong
Dr Pek Liong Loa LPIBA DDG MOIF IOM, Germany
Dr Otto-Robert Loesener DDG, USA
Dr Kheng Min Loi DDG, Malaysia
Mr Ho-Quang Long DDG, Vietnam
Mrs Julia M LoTempio DDG, USA
Prof Dr Ramon Lucas Lucas LFIBA DDG, Italy
Dr ing Drita Lulo LPIBA IOM DDG AdVSci MOIF, Albania
Prof Luo Yuanzheng DDG, China
Prof T Maghiar DDG AdVSci IOM LFIBA MOIF, Romania
Mr Russell J Maharaj IOM DDG, Trinidad & Tobago
Prof Abel Maharramov DDG, Azerbaijan
Dr Virendra B Mahesh LFIBA DDG IOM MOIF, USA
Dr Florence Omolara Mahoney DDG AdVAh, Gambia
Dr Moses Makayoto DDG, Kenya
Mr Vladimir G Makhankov DDG, USA
Mr Faramaz Maksudov DDG, Azerbaijan
Prof Lyubov T Malaya DDG, Ukraine
Mr Hamid A Malik DDG, Saudi Arabia
Dr H Malin LPIBA LFWLA IOM MOIF AdVMed CH, USA
Prof Efim M Malitikov FIBA DDG, Russia
Dr John J Manolakakis MD LPIBA DDG IOM, Zimbabwe
Ms Patricia J S Mapel DDG, USA
Mr Israel Arieh Mark DDG, Israel
Dr Louise Martin DDG, USA
Dr Koshi Maruyama DDG, Japan
Ms Mmaletshabo Cynthia Masolotate DDG, Botswana
The Hon John Ross Matheson DDG LFIBA, Canada
Mr Om Prakash Mathur DDG, India
Dr Clarice Chris Matteson PhD DDG, USA
Mr Giuseppe Mauri DDG, Italy
Dr Dmitry Mavlo MOIF DDG, Russia
Dr Patricia J Maybin IOM DDG, USA
Prof Dumitru I Mazilu DDG, Romania
Dr Ivan I Mazur DDG, UK
Ms Mabel Mazzini IOM DDG, Argentina
Dr Colette Grace Mazzucelli FIBA DDG, USA
Dr Lucie Mba DDG, Central Africa
Mr Tito Titus Mboweni DDG, South Africa
Dr Leland McClanahan DDG MOIF LFIBA, USA
Mr Gary Albert McConnell MOIF DDG, Norway
Prof Marianne McDonald LFIBA IOM CH AdVAh DDG, USA
Mr Paul McDonald Smith DDG MOIF, Australia
Prof Nasip Mecaj DDG, Albania
Mr Francis C Meddleton LFIBA DDG, USA
Prof Dr M A El-Fattah Mehaia LFIBA DDG, Saudi Arabia
Mr Ioannis Melissanidis DDG, Greece
Prof Dr Parakkat Ramakrishnan Menon DDG, India
Mr Paul J Meyer IOM LFIBA, USA
Dr Isaac L Mgemane LPIBA IOM DDG CH, South Africa
Prof Dr Alexandru Mica DDG, Romania
Mr Eustachy Michajlow IOM DDG, USA
Prof Dr H A Michalek MOIF DDG, Austria
Mr John Albert Middleton LFIBA DDG, USA
Dr P Mierzejewski Count of Calmont DDG, Poland
Prof Peter Mikhailenko DDG MOIF IOM, Ukraine
Dr Victor N Mikhailov LFIBA IOM DDG, Russia
Prof Alexander T Mikhailov DDG, Spain
Dr Yoshitsugu Miki LFIBA DDG IOM, Japan
His Excellency Mikkola DDG LDAF FAOE, Sweden
Dr Errol C Miller DDG LFIBA, Jamaica
Mr T E Miller LFIBA LFWLA DDG, USA

Dr Mariam Rajab DDG, Lebanon
Dr Srinivasa S Rajan LFIBA DDG, India
Mr Anumolu Ramakrishna DDG, India
Dr Sundaram Ramaswamy DDG, India
Mr Harold Radj Ramdhani DDG, Suriname
Dr Aspy Phiroze Rana DDG, India
Dr A Satyanarayana Rao DDG, India
Dr Usha Rao DDG, India
Dr Harun Ar Rashid DDG, Bangladesh
Dr Gerald Lee Ratliff DDG, USA
Dr Paul Ratnayake DDG, Switzerland
Dr Md Abdur Razzaque DDG, Bangladesh
Orlando M Recinos Arguello DDG, El Salvador
Reverend Heinrich Reinhardt PhD, Switzerland
Dr Harry Charles Reinl DDG, USA
Dr Milan Remko LPIBA MOIF DDG, Slovakia
Dr Jaidev Singh Retola DDG, India
Dr Lonnie Royce Rex DDG, USA
Madame Madeleine Rey-Brochard DDG, France
Prof Man Young Rhee DDG, Korea
Mr Eugene E Rhemann LPIBA DDG, USA
Dr Albert Edward Richardson DDG, USA
Ms Mary M Robben LPIBA MOIF DDG, USA
Dr A Robertson-Pearce DDG IOM, Sweden
Mrs Trudy Rodine-Wolfsehr DDG, USA
Dr Grayce M Roessler DDG, USA
Dr Belle Sara Rosenbaum IOM DDG, USA
Dr Yuriy A Rossikhin DDG, Russia
Ms C I Rouchdy LFIBA MOIF DDG, Saudi Arabia
Dr Seth Isaiah Rubin IOM DDG, USA
Dr P A Rubio MD PhD LPIBA DDG, USA
Mr Erik Yngvar Rudstrom FIBA DDG IOM, Norway
Mr Abdul Razzak Rumane LPIBA DDG IOM AdVSci, Kuwait
Prof Vladimir A Rusol LPIBA DDG MOIF, Russia
Dr Bindeshwar Sah DDG, India
Mrs Shikiko Saitoh LPIBA IOM DDG, Japan
Prof Ahmad Salahuddin DDG LFIBA MOIF, Zimbabwe
Mr Mohammad Abdul Saleem LFIBA DDG, United Arab Emirates
Dr Holem M Saliba DDG IOM AdVSci CH LFIBA, Lebanon
Dr Uday Salunkhe DDG, India
Mr Anatoly Samokhin DDG, Russia
Mr E F Sanguinetti DDG, Argentina
Ira S Saposnik MD JD PhD DDG DO, USA
Mr Masakazu Sarai DDG, Japan
Dr K N Saraswathy DDG, India
Dr Kazuo Sato DDG, Japan
Dr Kunitomo Sato MD PhD DDG CH MOIF FIBA, Japan
Dr Mitsuo Sato DDG, Japan
Mr Sagandyk Satubaldin DDG, Kazakhstan
Ms Mariann D Savilla, USA
Dr Martin H Savitz LFIBA DDG, USA
Mr Anton I Savvov DDG, Ukraine
Prof Akiko Sawaguchi DDG, Japan
Prof Dr Adolf E Schindler DDG LFIBA, Germany
Prof Dr Robert M Schmidt LFIBA DDG, USA
Prof Judith T Scholl LFIBA DDG, USA
Mr Jorg U Schroeder LFIBA MOIF DDG, Germany
Dr Adrijano Schwab IOM DDG, Slovenia
Mr Ainsworth D Scott LPIBA DDG IOM MOIF, Jamaica
Mr Dennis Screpetis LPIBA DDG, USA
HE A A Sedacca LFIBA MOIF OIA DDG DG SFO LDAF, USA
Prof Vasiliy Sedenko DDG, Russia
Prof Andrew Seim DDG, USA
Prof Baik Lin Seong DDG, Korea
Jukka Tapani Seppinen DDG, Finland
Dr Elsa C Servy DDG, Argentina
Dr Shirish Shah LFIBA DDG, USA
Prof Mrad Shahia DDG, South Africa
Prof Dr Alexei N Shamin DDG, Russia

Dr Isadore Shapiro DDG IOM, USA
Dr Hari Shanker Sharma DDG, Sweden
Mr Hamzeh Mohammed Shaweesh FIBA DDG, Jordan
Prof George V Shchokin DDG LFIBA MOIF, Ukraine
Dr Muhammad M Mukram Sheikh DDG HLFIBA IOM, Botswana
Dr Mohammad Shekari Yazdi LFIBA CH DDG, Austria
Dr Nimish Shelat LPIBA DDG, India
Master Ronger Shen DDG, USA
Dr Chai Cheng Sheng DDG, Singapore
Prof Dr Bat-Sheva Sheriff IOM LFWLA DDG, Israel
Ms Shi Bingxia DDG, China
Prof Tso-Min Shih DDG, Taiwan
Prof Chun-Jen Shih LFIBA DDG, Taiwan
Mr Tamaz Shilakadze IOM DDG, Georgia
Dr Sang-Tai Shim DDG, Korea
Mr Sadao Shimoji MOIF DDG, Japan
Prof Koki Shimoji DDG LFIBA, Japan
Ms Marina V Shitikova DDG, Russia
Dr Leonid Vassilievich Shmakov DDG, Russia
Prof Dr Jau-Ying Shyr (Stone) DDG, Taiwan
Ms Monique S Sidaross DDG, USA
Mr Robert D Siedle LPIBA DDG AdVBus IOM, USA
Prof G S Siklosi DDG LPIBA MOIF IOM CH, Hungary
Dr Velimir N Simicevic MD IOM DDG, Croatia
Dr Teja Singh LFIBA IOM DDG, Canada
Dr Navin Kumar Sinha DDG, India
Mr Aleksandre Sitnikov DDG, Russia
Dr Valery K Smirnov LFIBA MOIF DDG, Russia
Prof Dr Ion Socoteanu DDG, Romania
Prof Vladimir Solenov DDG, Russia
Dr (Mrs) Olatokunbo A Somolu DDG LFIBA, Nigeria
Dr Olateju Abiola Somorin DDG, Nigeria
Ms Anne-Marie A Sondakh DDG, Indonesia
Prof Song Zhongyue DDG, China
Dr Sanjay Sood DDG, USA
Dr Ranjit Sookdar DDG, Trinidad & Tobago
Dr Igor Sourovtzev DDG, Russia
Miss Callie J Spady FIBA DDG, USA
Mr Ion G Spanulescu DDG, Romania
Dr David A Spencer LFIBA AdVSci DDG LFWLA IOM MOIF, UK
Ms Linda Bushell Spencer DDG, USA
Mr Peter Stadler DDG LFIBA, Denmark
Ms Ursula Helena Stanescu DDG, Romania
Mrs Joan E Starr FWLA DDG, Australia
Dr Lindley Joseph Stiles IOM DDG FIBA AdVAh, USA
Ms Annette Michelle Stokes IOM DDG, USA
Mr Charles Bryan Streaker Sr DDG, USA
Prof Jovan Strikovic DDG MOIF FIBA, Yugoslavia
Prof Roman G Strongin LFIBA DDG, Russia
Dr H Chien-Fan Su LFIBA IOM MOIF DDG, USA
Dr T N Subba Rao DDG, India
Mr Fadil Sulejmani DDG, Macedonia
Prof Dr A Sun IOM MOIF LPIBA DDG CH AdVMed, China
Prof Qian Zhang Sun DDG MOIF, China
Mr Ulf L Sundblad DDG, Sweden
Dr E Sundermoorthy HPSM DHMS DDG, India
Mr Harta Susanto DDG, Indonesia
Mrs B Sutton LPIBA FWLA DDG, UK
Prof Dr Shin'ichi Suzuki DDG FIBA, Japan
Dr Srikanta M N Swamy LFIBA DDG IOM, Canada
Mr James E Sweeney LFIBA DDG, USA
Dr Nightingale C Syabballo DDG, Zambia
Dr Emmanuel H Tadross LPIBA DDG IOM, Canada
Dr Akira Takahashi DDG, Japan
Mr Norio Takeoka DDG, Japan
Prof Ichiro Taki DDG, Japan
Neva B Talley-Morris DDG, USA
Mr Charlie K L Tan LPIBA MOIF DO DDG, Singapore
Prof Hiroshige Tanaka DDG LFIBA AdVFin, Japan

ADVISERS TO THE DIRECTOR GENERAL

LIFETIME ACHIEVEMENT AWARD

Mrs Benigna G Able-Thomas IOM, The Gambia
Prof Antonio A Acosta IOM DDG, USA
Maitre Artist Afewerk Tekle IOM CH, Ethiopia
Dr Pius Anozie C Agwaramgbo, Nigeria
Dr Jagdish Chand Ahuja MA PhD LFIBA, USA
Ryoko Akamatsu, Japan
Prof E M Alahuhta IOM DDG LPIBA MOIF CH AdVAh, Finland
Dr Monica Albu, Romania
Mr Hans H Amtmann, USA
Dr Tae Lyong An, USA
Mr An Tae Ho LFIBA DDG, Korea
Prof John Joseph Ansbro IOM DDG AdVAh, USA
Prof Ioannis Konstantinos Argyros, USA
Mr Hans Gustaf Erik Astrom, Sweden
Dr Detlev Baller, Germany
Mr Melver Raymond Barnes, USA
Dr Leonard Octavius Barrett DDG, USA
Ms Juanita M Basham MOIF, USA
The Hon Dr Jack G Beale AO ME HonDSc HonLLD LPIBA DDG AdVSci MOIF, Australia
Prof Pier Franco Beatrice LPIBA AdVAh DDG, Italy
Sandra E Beguhn AdVAh LFIBA CH DDG DO, USA
Ms Marilyn A Bennett, USA
Dr (Sir) Moses Gordon Bestman DDG LFIBA CH, Nigeria
Prof Rodger Bick LFIBA, USA
Ms Barbara Sue Bolin, USA
Dr Lutgart Elizabeth Bonte IOM, Belgium
Prof Carlos Soares Borrego, Portugal
Dr Sandra Breitenbach LFIBA IOM DDG, Norway
Dr Werner A Breuer, USA
Mr Daniel D Brunda DDG LPIBA MOIF IOM AdVSci DO, USA
Dr Chang Wan-Hsi (Mo Jen) DDG, Taiwan
Dr Hyoun K Chang, Korea
Mr Valentinos Christou Charalambous, Cyprus
Dr Pang-Chi Chen DDG MOIF IOM LPIBA, Taiwan
Dr Yue Cheng LFIBA DDG, USA
Dr Cho Kwungsoo LFIBA, Korea
Dr Moo Jeh Cho LFIBA, Korea
Prof Chu Han-Shu, China
Ms Karen A Clarke LPIBA, USA
Ms Jacqueline Turner Copeland, USA
Mr Donald Mercer Cormie IOM, USA
Prof Ignacio Cornejo Aguirre FIBA IOM, Spain
Mr Ronald Lloyd Cox IOM LFIBA MOIF, USA
Dr Sami Namek Wafa Dajani AdVSci DDG, Jordan
Rev Dr Gommar A De Pauw, USA
Mrs Thaneswari De Silva LPIBA, Sri Lanka
Ms Handunnetti S V De Silva IOM FIBA, USA
Dr Shirley L Dixon LFIBA DDG CH AdVMed, USA
Dr Michael William Doll, USA
Mr Emmanuel C Duncan, Grenada
Mr Allen Broderick Edmundson, USA
Prof Mohammad H S El-Ahl DDG MOIF IOM, Egypt
Dr M F Elkady DDG IOM LFIBA, Saudi Arabia
Ms Eden P Espina, USA
Prof Margaret E Fahey, USA
Dr Brady J Fletcher LFIBA, USA
Prof Klaus D E Friedland IOM CH, Germany
Dr Hajime Fukazawa LFIBA MOIF DDG IOM CH, Japan
Dr T Funahashi LPIBA DDG IOM CH, Japan
Ms Ranka Pejovic Gajic, USA
Mr Joseph Francis Galluzzo, USA
Prof Dr Pedro Garaguso, Argentina
Prof Maurice P Gautier, France
Ms Susan Gibson, USA
Mr Bruce A Grindley LFIBA, Spain
Ms Margaret E Hamer, Australia

Prof E Hanaoka-Kawamura IOM AdVAh DDG LPIBA CH, Japan
Dr Raymond Kenneth Hart IOM, USA
Dr Daryl E Hartter, USA
Prof Dr Kazuyuki Hatada LFIBA DDG IOM, Japan
Prof Albert A Hayden LFIBA, USA
Pastor J B Hays Jr, USA
Dr Mahmoud H Hijazy AdVMed, Saudi Arabia
Dr Yoshitaka Hirooka LFIBA, Japan
Ms Alicia Hopkinson-Carter, USA
Dr Tohru Horiuchi LPIBA DDG IOM MOIF AdVMed, Japan
Prof John Wen-Chain Hsu DDG, Taiwan
Mr Chun Fang Huang, Taiwan
Mrs Stacy Huey, USA
Dr Samuel Wilson Hynd CBE, Swaziland
Prof Dr Kazuyosi Ikeda DSc DLitt DDG IOM LPIBA LFWLA MOIF CH, Japan
Prof S Itoh IOM DDG LPIBA AdVMed MOIF CH, Japan
Mr Neil H Jacoby Jr LPIBA IOM AdVSci CH DO DDG, USA
Mr John Eric Janke CH, USA
Dr Satish D Joglekar, India
Dr Roger Anthony Charles Jones IOM, Australia
Prof Gudrun Kalmbach H E, Germany
Dr Stefan Kassay, Slovakia
Dr Satish K Kaushik, Australia
Dr Hiroshi Kawamoto IOM AdVSci DDG MOIF, Japan
Mr John G Kellas IOM AdVSci CH DDG MOIF, Australia
Ms Maydra Jane Penisson Kennedy, USA
Mr James Sewell Kerr DDG FIBA, Jamaica
Dr Tawfik Khoja, Saudi Arabia
Ms Won Andrea Kim, Korea
Prof Pill Soo Kim LPIBA DDG IOM AdVSci CH, Korea
Dr Vladimir Kislik, Israel
Prof Kowan Young Ko AdVSci, Korea
Prof Changduk Kong DDG, Korea
Dr Helena Kucerova, Czech Republic
Mr Nickolay I Kuchersky IOM MOIF, Uzbekistan
Dr Soji Kurimoto IOM AdVMed DDG, Japan
Prof Tadeusz Z Lachowicz IOM CH AdVSci DDG, Poland
Dr Luc Johan Lambrecht LPIBA DDG MOIF IOM, Belgium
Mrs Clara Maria Laura Marrama Lanaro LFIBA, USA
Dr V Landers LPIBA LFWLA DDG MOIF IOM, USA
Mr Andy Lee Lang CH, Austria
Prof Dr Cecilia Popescu Latis, Romania
Dr Dale P Layman PhD MOIF DDG LPIBA AdVMed IOM, USA
Prof Carla Ann Bouska Lee IOM AdVMed FIBA, USA
Dr Hulbert Austin Lee, Canada
Dr Kenneth Bok Lee, USA
Prof Dr Hans Albert Paul Lenk, Germany
Miss Joy LeRoy LFIBA MOIF DDG IOM, USA
Dr Yu-Chu Maxwell Li, Taiwan
Mrs A List LFIBA IOM LFWLA MOIF HE, Germany
Dr Han-Shou Liu IOM, USA
J Antonio G Lopez MD, USA
Dr ing Drita Lulo LPIBA IOM DDG AdVSci, Albania
Mr Kenneth P Maas, USA
Prof T Maghiar DDG AdVSci IOM LFIBA MOIF, Romania
Dr Virendra B Mahesh LPIBA DDG IOM MOIF, USA
Dr Madhuri Majumder, Malaysia
Dr H Malin LPIBA LFWLA DDG IOM MOIF AdVMed CH, USA
Dr John J Manolakakis MD LPIBA DDG IOM, Zimbabwe
Prof James W Marchand, USA
Ms Laurabelle Martin MOIF, USA
Dean Towle Mason MD IOM, USA
Prof Marianne McDonald LFIBA IOM CH AdVAh DDG, USA
James Buckner McKinnon, USA
Mrs Rosaline Means IOM, USA

Dr Isaac L Mgemane LPIBA IOM DDG CH, South Africa
Dr William H Minshall IOM, Canada
Dr Pitabasa Misra FIBA, Saudi Arabia
Ms Marie Jocelyne Moise DDG, USA
Prof Chul So Moon IOM, USA
Prof Dr Emil Mosonyi LFIBA IOM, Germany
Dr Yukio Nagamachi DDG IOM, Japan
Mr Miklos Nagy, USA
Dr Xuan Cuong Nguyen LFIBA CH IOM, Vietnam
Mrs Angela C Nicols, USA
Prof Stig H M Nystrom IOM, Finland
Rev Prof Yusufu Ameh Obaje DDG IOM, Nigeria
Rev Prof Dr Elizabeth Mary Okelo, Kenya
Dr Imeh T Okopido DDG, Nigeria
Dr Claes G Orvell IOM DDG MOIF AdVMed FIBA, Sweden
Mr Ericson Omotayo Oyetibo, Nigeria
Mr Nick Pahys Jr DDG CH AdVAh FIBA, USA
Mr Panagiotis A Papadakis LFIBA DDG CH AdVFin, Greece
Dr Soo-Jin Park CH, Korea
Prof Dong Gon Park, Korea
Dr Norman Pearson LFIBA IOM MOIF CH, Canada
Mr Daniel A Phillips LPIBA CH AdVBus MOIF DO, USA
Prof Dr E N Pinguli CH LPIBA AdVSci IOM DDG DO, Albania
Mr Jozsef Pinter DDG, Hungary
Ms Marina Pirtskhalava, Georgia
Elmer Plischke PhD IOM, USA
Dr Sitaram Poddar IOM LFIBA, Jamaica
Commander Vernon S Poindexter IOM CH, USA
Dr Witold Poplawski, Canada
Prof Gavril Popov DO LFIBA, Russia
Ms Harriett Kinloch H Price, USA
Mr Eddie B Pue, USA
Dr Zvonimir Puretic DDG, Croatia
Mr Rhi Sang-Kyu, Korea
Dr Ronald George Ribble, USA
Dr Stuart Glen Rice, USA
Mr Herbert Ricketts, Peru
Dr Pierre Rioux LFIBA IOM, USA
Prof Ivar K Rossavik LFIBA, USA
Dr Gary S Roubin, USA
Dr Harry Rowe, Germany
Dr Seth Isaiah Rubin IOM DDG, USA
Mr Abdul Razzak Rumane LPIBA DDG IOM AdVSci, Kuwait
Dr Kazuo Sato DDG, Japan
Dr Kunitomo Sato PhD DDG CH MOIF, Japan
Mr Arthur V Savage, USA
Dr Joseph Martin Schor, USA
Dr Adrijano Schwab IOM DDG, Slovenia
Dr Isadore Shapiro DDG IOM, USA
Mr Alhaji Umaru Ali Shinkafi CH, Nigeria
Mr Taku Shirai, Japan
Mr Robert D Siedle LPIBA DDG AdVBus, USA
Mrs Lois Oliver Sigler, USA
Prof G S Siklosi DDG LPIBA MOIF IOM CH, Hungary
Dr Navin Kumar Sinha DDG, India
Prof Torstein Sjovold MOIF, Sweden
Dr Gregorio Skromne-Kadlubik IOM, Mexico
Mrs Mary Spencer, Spain
Mr Robert Steiner, Australia
Ms Margaret C Sticht, Nigeria
Dr Lindley Joseph Stiles IOM DDG FIBA AdVAh, USA
Prof Dr A Sun IOM MOIF LPIBA DDG CH AdVMed, Taiwwan
Dr Srikanta M N Swamy LFIBA DDG IOM, Canada
Dr Yasuo Tahama LPIBA IOM, Japan
Prof Paul C L Tang IOM CH MOIF LFIBA DDG DO, USA
Prof Albert Tezla CH, USA
Dr M Thiel IOM LPIBA DDG MOIF AAAS CH, Germany
Dr William Harold Thueme, USA
Mrs Anne Tooby CH, USA
Dr Zdzislawa Traczyk, Poland
Dr Jerry R Trevino, USA

Dr Gregory Vastatzidis LFIBA DDG, Greece
David Lynn Vesely MD PhD, USA
Ms Reba Faye Wade, USA
Dr Florence Muringi Wambugu, Kenya
Dr Jong Wang DDG, USA
Mr Henri T Werring MOIF DDG AdVBus FIBA, Norway
Mr Brooks Morris Whitehurst FIBA DDG, USA
Baron C K W Wong MD LFIBA MOIF DO DDG, USA
Prof Thomas S Woods, USA
Lt Gen John MacNair Wright Jr, USA
Prof Yun Xia, China
Dr Etsuo Yamamura MOIF DDG IOM, Japan
Mr Anson A Yeager Sr LFIBA, USA
Dr Gili Yen IOM DDG, Taiwan
Prof Dr K Yoshihara LPIBA DDG IOM MOIF AdVAh, Japan
Mr Watson T Yoshimoto LPIBA MOIF IOM, USA
Prof Yu Bao Ming MOIF DDG, China
Prof Yonggao Zhao, China
Prof Fulian Zhuang, China

VICE CONSULS OF THE IBC

Prof E M Alahuhta IOM DDG LPIBA MOIF CH AdVAh,
Finland
Mario Vernon Arroyo-Gomez LPIBA DDG LFWLA IOM
MOIF AdVAh, Gibraltar
Dr Sandra Breitenbach LFIBA IOM, Norway
Mr Craig Edward Burgess LFIBA MOIF IOM AdVAh, USA
Juseon Byun PhD, Korea
Ms Margot Cairnes LFIBA DDG, Australia
Dr Wen-Ying Chang LPIBA MOIF DDG IOM, China
Dr Yue Cheng LFIBA DDG, USA
Mr John Davies, Australia
Dr Shirley L Dixon LFIBA DDG CH AdVMed, USA
Dr M F Elkady DDG IOM LFIBA, Saudi Arabia
Dr James E Ewing DDG MOIF, USA
Mrs Elisabeth Anne Rooney-Ewing DDG MOIF, USA
Mr Joji Hagiwara LFIBA DDG MOIF, Japan
Prof E Hanaoka-Kawamura IOM AdVAh DDG LPIBA CH,
Japan
Dr Tohru Horiuchi LPIBA DDG IOM MOIF AdVMed, Japan
Professor Dr Kazuyosi Ikeda DSc DLitt DDG IOM LPIBA
LFWLA MOIF CH, Japan
Dr Seishi Isobe DDG, Japan
Mr John G Kellas IOM AdVSci CH DDG MOIF, Australia
Dr Rustom A Khatib DDG, Lebanon
Prof Pill Soo Kim LPIBA DDG IOM AdVSci CH, Korea
Mr Kong Hyung-Yun, Korea
Mr Nickolay I Kuchersky IOM, Uzbekistan
Mr Temirgali A Kuketaev, Kazakhstan
Mrs Elly A Ladas DDG, Greece
K Jameson Lawrence Esq, USA
Professor Jeong Y Lee DDG LFIBA, Korea
Miss Joy LeRoy LFIBA MOIF DDG IOM, USA
Ms Joanne M Lindsey IOM DDG MOIF, USA
Mr Liu Dao-shun, China
Dr H Malin LPIBA LFWLA DDG IOM MOIF AdVMed CH,
USA
Dr Clarice Chris Matteson PhD DDG, USA
Professor Vladimir Matvienko IOM, Ukraine
Professor Willibald Nagler DDG IOM LFIBA, USA
Professor Albert Nikolaevich Nikitin, Russia
Rev Prof Yusufu Ameh Obaje DDG IOM, Africa
Mr Shozo Ohtsuka LPIBA DDG, Japan
Professor Vladimir Okrepilov, Russia
Dr Gladys S Ostrom MOIF DDG, USA
Mr Nick Pahys Jr DDG CH AdVAh FIBA, USA
Professor Jeom K Paik PhD, Korea
Dr A Robertson-Pearce DDG IOM, Sweden
Professor Valery Sagaidatchny, Greece
Dr Kunitomo Sato DDG CH FIBA, Japan
Dr Isadore Shapiro DDG IOM, USA
Mr Tamaz Shilakadze IOM DDG, Georgia
Mr Herman de Somer, Belgium
Prof Dr A Sun IOM MOIF LPIBA DDG CH AdVMed, China
Prof Paul C L Tang IOM CH MOIF LFIBA DDG, USA
Mr Ioannis Tarnanas, Greece
Dr Isaac Willis MD DSc CH LFIBA AdVMed, USA
Mr Alexander Yakovitski, Belarus
Dr Vak Y Yoo MOIF DDG LPIBA AdVMed IOM, Korea

THE
WORLDWIDE HONOURS
LIST

PETER A ADUJA

FOR AN OUTSTANDING CONTRIBUTION TO

COMMUNITY, STATE AND NATION

INAUGURATED IN THE YEAR 2003

★ ★ ★ ★ ★

PROFESSOR AMOS ENIOLA AKINGBOHUNGBE

FOR AN OUTSTANDING CONTRIBUTION TO

ENTOMOLOGY

INAUGURATED IN THE YEAR 2003

★ ★ ★ ★ ★

JORDI BABOT AZOY

FOR AN OUTSTANDING CONTRIBUTION TO

CHEMISTRY

INAUGURATED IN THE YEAR 2003

★ ★ ★ ★ ★

DR YALLAPRAGADA RAMESH BABU

FOR AN OUTSTANDING CONTRIBUTION TO

INDUSTRIAL ENGINEERING

INAUGURATED IN THE YEAR 2003

★ ★ ★ ★ ★

DR RONNIE BARKHAN

FOR AN OUTSTANDING CONTRIBUTION TO

HYPNOTHERAPY AND PSYCHOTHERAPY

INAUGURATED IN THE YEAR 2003

★ ★ ★ ★ ★

MELVER R BARNES
FOR AN OUTSTANDING CONTRIBUTION TO

CHEMISTRY AND PARTICLE PHYSICS

INAUGURATED IN THE YEAR 2003

★ ★ ★ ★ ★

SANDRA E BEGUHN
FOR AN OUTSTANDING CONTRIBUTION TO

POETRY

INAUGURATED IN THE YEAR 2003

★ ★ ★ ★ ★

DR ALI BEHFAR

INAUGURATED IN THE YEAR 2004

★ ★ ★ ★ ★

PROFESSOR DR GUIDO BIMBERG
FOR AN OUTSTANDING CONTRIBUTION TO

MUSICOLOGY AND MEDIA ENTERTAINMENT BUSINESS

INAUGURATED IN THE YEAR 2003

★ ★ ★ ★ ★

DR JUDITH BRIGHAM
FOR AN OUTSTANDING CONTRIBUTION TO

CLASSICAL CHRISTIAN WESTERN CIVILISATION

INAUGURATED IN THE YEAR 2004

★ ★ ★ ★ ★

DANIEL DONALD BRUNDA
FOR AN OUTSTANDING CONTRIBUTION TO

AEROSPACE AND ELECTROMAGNETIC POWERLINE RADIATION ENGINEERING

INAUGURATED IN THE YEAR 2003

★ ★ ★ ★ ★

FLORIANA BULIC-JAKUS
FOR AN OUTSTANDING CONTRIBUTION TO

DIFFERENTAL EXPRESSION OF BB PROTEIN

INAUGURATED IN THE YEAR 2003

ZIHNI J BUZO
FOR AN OUTSTANDING CONTRIBUTION TO

CIVIL ENGINEERING

INAUGURATED IN THE YEAR 2003

★ ★ ★ ★ ★

PROFESSOR YUNG FRANK CHIANG
FOR AN OUTSTANDING CONTRIBUTION TO

LAW AND LEGAL EDUCATION

INAUGURATED IN THE YEAR 2003

★ ★ ★ ★ ★

DR C JULIANA CHING
FOR AN OUTSTANDING CONTRIBUTION TO

BUSINESS AND MEDICINE

INAUGURATED IN THE YEAR 2003

★ ★ ★ ★ ★

PROFESSOR HAN-SHU CHU
FOR AN OUTSTANDING CONTRIBUTION TO

RADIOASTRONOMY AND ASTROPHYSICS

INAUGURATED IN THE YEAR 2003

★ ★ ★ ★ ★

DR SARA CIAMPI
FOR AN OUTSTANDING CONTRIBUTION TO

LITERATURE AND PHILOSOPHY

INAUGURATED IN THE YEAR 2003

★ ★ ★ ★ ★

DONALD MERCER CORMIE
FOR AN OUTSTANDING CONTRIBUTION TO

ARTS AND LAW

INAUGURATED IN THE YEAR 2003

★ ★ ★ ★ ★

JASPER L. CUMMINGS
FOR AN OUTSTANDING CONTRIBUTION TO

EDUCATION

INAUGURATED IN THE YEAR 2003

★ ★ ★ ★ ★

PROFESSOR DR DONCHO DONEV
FOR AN OUTSTANDING CONTRIBUTION TO

SOCIAL MEDICINE & PUBLIC HEALTH

INAUGURATED IN THE YEAR 2002

★ ★ ★ ★ ★

DR MARY JOSEPHINE DRAYTON
FOR AN OUTSTANDING CONTRIBUTION TO

EDUCATION AND LOCAL AND REGIONAL GOVERNMENT

INAUGURATED IN THE YEAR 2003

★ ★ ★ ★ ★

PROFESSOR (HR) HARRY EDWARDS
FOR AN OUTSTANDING CONTRIBUTION TO

ECONOMICS, POLITICS AND THIRD-WORLD DEVELOPMENT

INAUGURATED IN THE YEAR 2003

★ ★ ★ ★ ★

FINN EGIL EIDE
FOR AN OUTSTANDING CONTRIBUTION TO

PHILOSOPHY AND ART

INAUGURATED IN THE YEAR 2004

★ ★ ★ ★ ★

DR M F ELKADY
FOR AN OUTSTANDING CONTRIBUTION TO

ECONOMIC, FINANCE AND BUSINESS ADMINISTRATION AND STRENGTHENING THE RELATION AMONG ENTERPRISES

INAUGURATED IN THE YEAR 2003

★ ★ ★ ★ ★

DAVID RAMSEY FOSTER
FOR AN OUTSTANDING CONTRIBUTION TO

WOMEN'S GOLF

INAUGURATED IN THE YEAR 2003

★ ★ ★ ★ ★

DR WILLIAM O FOYE
FOR AN OUTSTANDING CONTRIBUTION TO

RESEARCH AND SCHOLARSHIP

INAUGURATED IN THE YEAR 2003

★ ★ ★ ★ ★

DR HAJIME FUKIZAWA
FOR AN OUTSTANDING CONTRIBUTION TO

HEAD AND NECK CANCER THERAPY AND ORAL SURGERY

INAUGURATED IN THE YEAR 2004

★ ★ ★ ★ ★

DR JUVENAL GUTIERREZ-MOCTEZUMA
FOR AN OUTSTANDING CONTRIBUTION TO

PAEDIATRIC NEUROLOGY IN MEXICO

INAUGURATED IN THE YEAR 2003

★ ★ ★ ★ ★

PROFESSOR RAMI W HAMDALLAH

INAUGURATED IN THE YEAR 2004

★ ★ ★ ★ ★

PROFESSOR EIKO HANAOKA
FOR AN OUTSTANDING CONTRIBUTION TO

PHILOSOPHY OF RELIGION

INAUGURATED IN THE YEAR 2003

★ ★ ★ ★ ★

E R HANKS
FOR AN OUTSTANDING CONTRIBUTION TO

REAL ESTATE DEVELOPMENT IN THE 20TH CENTURY

INAUGURATED IN THE YEAR 2003

★ ★ ★ ★ ★

PROFESSOR DR KAZUYUKI HATADA
FOR AN OUTSTANDING CONTRIBUTION TO

NUMBER THEORY OF SIEGEL CUSP FORMS

INAUGURATED IN THE YEAR 2003

★ ★ ★ ★ ★

PROFESSOR ALBERT A HAYDEN
FOR AN OUTSTANDING CONTRIBUTION TO

HISTORY

INAUGURATED IN THE YEAR 2003

★ ★ ★ ★ ★

DR RODOLFO HERRERA-LLERANDI
FOR AN OUTSTANDING CONTRIBUTION TO

SURGERY AND MEDICAL EDUCATION

INAUGURATED IN THE YEAR 2003

★ ★ ★ ★ ★

PROFESSOR CHIAKI ITOH
FOR AN OUTSTANDING CONTRIBUTION TO

UNIFIED GAUGE THEORY OF WEAK, ELECTROMAGNETIC AND STRONG INTERACTIONS

INAUGURATED IN THE YEAR 2003

★ ★ ★ ★ ★

NEIL H JACOBY JR

FOR AN OUTSTANDING CONTRIBUTION TO

ASTRODYNAMICS AND ASTRONAUTICS

INAUGURATED IN THE YEAR 2003

★ ★ ★ ★ ★

DR SATISH D JOGLEKAR

FOR AN OUTSTANDING CONTRIBUTION TO

THEORETICAL HIGH ENERGY PHYSICS

INAUGURATED IN THE YEAR 2003

★ ★ ★ ★ ★

ROGER ANTHONY CHARLES JONES

FOR AN OUTSTANDING CONTRIBUTION TO

AGRICULTURAL SCIENCE - PLANT VIROLOGY

INAUGURATED IN THE YEAR 2004

★ ★ ★ ★ ★

SALLY D P JONES

FOR AN OUTSTANDING CONTRIBUTION TO

UNITED NATIONS ORGANISATIONS

INAUGURATED IN THE YEAR 2003

★ ★ ★ ★ ★

DR INDIRA YASHWANT JUNGHARE

FOR AN OUTSTANDING CONTRIBUTION TO

SOUTH ASIAN LANGUAGES AND CULTURES

INAUGURATED IN THE YEAR 2004

★ ★ ★ ★ ★

PROFESSOR DR GUDRUN KALMBACH HE
FOR AN OUTSTANDING CONTRIBUTION TO

SCIENCE AND SOCIETY

INAUGURATED IN THE YEAR 2003

★ ★ ★ ★ ★

DR HIROSHI KAWAMOTO
FOR AN OUTSTANDING CONTRIBUTION TO

THEORETICAL PHYSICS

INAUGURATED IN THE YEAR 2003

★ ★ ★ ★ ★

JOHN GORDON KELLAS
FOR AN OUTSTANDING CONTRIBUTION TO

PHARMACEUTICAL DISPENSING AND AS AN INVESTOR

INAUGURATED IN THE YEAR 2003

★ ★ ★ ★ ★

COMMODORE ANAND KHANDEKAR (RETD)
FOR AN OUTSTANDING CONTRIBUTION TO

INFORMATION TECHNOLOGY

INAUGURATED IN THE YEAR 2003

★ ★ ★ ★ ★

DR NORIYASU KIHARA
FOR AN OUTSTANDING CONTRIBUTION TO

HIBAKUSHA AS A MEMBER OF NGO TO THE U.N.

INAUGURATED IN THE YEAR 2003

★ ★ ★ ★ ★

DR SU GWAN KIM

FOR AN OUTSTANDING CONTRIBUTION TO

ORAL AND MAXILLOFACIAL SURGERY

INAUGURATED IN THE YEAR 2004

★ ★ ★ ★ ★

DR VLADIMIR KISLIK

FOR AN OUTSTANDING CONTRIBUTION TO

CHEMISTRY, SEPARATION SCIENCE

INAUGURATED IN THE YEAR 2003

★ ★ ★ ★ ★

JULIE ANN LAHOOD

FOR AN OUTSTANDING CONTRIBUTION TO

HISTORIC BUILDINGS AND POETRY

INAUGURATED IN THE YEAR 2004

★ ★ ★ ★ ★

BEULAH ENFIELD "BOO" LAW

FOR AN OUTSTANDING CONTRIBUTION TO

EDUCATION AND HELPING THE COMMUNITY

INAUGURATED IN THE YEAR 2004

★ ★ ★ ★ ★

MISS JOY LEROY

FOR AN OUTSTANDING CONTRIBUTION TO

LEADERSHIP AND THE ARTS

INAUGURATED IN THE YEAR 2003

★ ★ ★ ★ ★

CHEE-PENG LIM PHD

FOR AN OUTSTANDING CONTRIBUTION TO

ARTIFICIAL INTELLIGENCE

INAUGURATED IN THE YEAR 2004

★ ★ ★ ★ ★

DR ING DRITA LULO

FOR AN OUTSTANDING CONTRIBUTION TO

THE FIELD OF CONSTRUCTION ENGINEERING

INAUGURATED IN THE YEAR 2003

★ ★ ★ ★ ★

JAN MAEGAARD

FOR AN OUTSTANDING CONTRIBUTION TO

MUSICOLOGY

INAUGURATED IN THE YEAR 2002

★ ★ ★ ★ ★

DR JOHN J MANOLAKAKIS MD

FOR AN OUTSTANDING CONTRIBUTION TO

MEDICINE, HEALTHCARE AND LANGUAGES

INAUGURATED IN THE YEAR 2003

★ ★ ★ ★ ★

LAURABELLE MARTIN

FOR AN OUTSTANDING CONTRIBUTION TO

TEACHING AND COMMUNITY SERVICE

INAUGURATED IN THE YEAR 2003

★ ★ ★ ★ ★

DR AJAX MENEKRATIS

FOR AN OUTSTANDING CONTRIBUTION TO

ORAL RECONSTRUCTION

INAUGURATED IN THE YEAR 2002

★ ★ ★ ★ ★

PROFESSOR J W F MULDER

FOR AN OUTSTANDING CONTRIBUTION TO

LINGUISTICS

INAUGURATED IN THE YEAR 2002

★ ★ ★ ★ ★

DR IVKA MARIA MUNDA

FOR AN OUTSTANDING CONTRIBUTION TO

MARINE BIOLOGY - PHYCOLOGY

INAUGURATED IN THE YEAR 2003

★ ★ ★ ★ ★

PROFESSOR AKIRA NAGATOMI

FOR AN OUTSTANDING CONTRIBUTION TO

ENTOMOLOGY

INAUGURATED IN THE YEAR 2003

★ ★ ★ ★ ★

DR SHIGEHISA NAKAMURA

FOR AN OUTSTANDING CONTRIBUTION TO

GEOPHYSICAL SCIENCES

INAUGURATED IN THE YEAR 2002

★ ★ ★ ★ ★

DR BETTY NEFF BALCH
FOR AN OUTSTANDING CONTRIBUTION TO

OBSTETRICAL NURSING AND EDUCATION

INAUGURATED IN THE YEAR 2004

★ ★ ★ ★ ★

DR W R OGG
FOR AN OUTSTANDING CONTRIBUTION TO

THE ARTS, LAW AND PHILOSOPHY

INAUGURATED IN THE YEAR 2003

★ ★ ★ ★ ★

COLONEL MICHAEL ORLANDO U.S.A.F. RET
FOR AN OUTSTANDING CONTRIBUTION TO

IMPLEMENTING INTERNATIONAL PROGRAMS AND POLICIES

INAUGURATED IN THE YEAR 2003

★ ★ ★ ★ ★

EUGENE THOMAS OUZTS
FOR AN OUTSTANDING CONTRIBUTION TO

EDUCATION AND RELIGION

INAUGURATED IN THE YEAR 2003

★ ★ ★ ★ ★

PROFESSOR YOO HWAN PARK
FOR AN OUTSTANDING CONTRIBUTION TO

PDT, ONCOLOGY - HOMEOPATHY

INAUGURATED IN THE YEAR 2003

★ ★ ★ ★ ★

DR ARIE PEDDEMORS

FOR AN OUTSTANDING CONTRIBUTION TO

MUSIC AND ARCHAEOLOGY

INAUGURATED IN THE YEAR 2004

★ ★ ★ ★ ★

PROFESSOR DR RUDIGER PFEIFFER

FOR AN OUTSTANDING CONTRIBUTION TO

MUSICOLOGY AND MEDIA ENTERTAINMENT BUSINESS

INAUGURATED IN THE YEAR 2003

★ ★ ★ ★ ★

DANIEL A PHILLIPS

FOR AN OUTSTANDING CONTRIBUTION TO

BUSINESS AND COMMUNITY LEADERSHIP

INAUGURATED IN THE YEAR 2003

★ ★ ★ ★ ★

PROFESSOR DR E N K PINGULI

FOR AN OUTSTANDING CONTRIBUTION TO

THE FIELD OF CONSTRUCTION ENGINEERING

INAUGURATED IN THE YEAR 2003

★ ★ ★ ★ ★

PROFESSOR ELMER PLISCHKE

FOR AN OUTSTANDING CONTRIBUTION TO

GOVERNMENT AND POLITICS

INAUGURATED IN THE YEAR 2003

★ ★ ★ ★ ★

PROFESSOR DR ZDZISLAW W PUSLECKI
FOR AN OUTSTANDING CONTRIBUTION TO

ECONOMIC SCIENCE

INAUGURATED IN THE YEAR 2003

★ ★ ★ ★ ★

DR MARIA REVERTE BERNAL
FOR AN OUTSTANDING CONTRIBUTION TO

PHARMACOLOGY

INAUGURATED IN THE YEAR 2003

★ ★ ★ ★ ★

DR BHAGWAN SAHAY
FOR AN OUTSTANDING CONTRIBUTION TO

PETROLEUM GEOLOGICAL ENGINEERING

INAUGURATED IN THE YEAR 2002

★ ★ ★ ★ ★

DR SWAMI PRANAVANANDA SARASWATI
FOR AN OUTSTANDING CONTRIBUTION TO

WORKING FOR WORLD PEACE AND WELFARE OF HUMANITY FOR MORE THAN HALF A CENTURY

INAUGURATED IN THE YEAR 2003

★ ★ ★ ★ ★

HONORABLE KAZUO SATO
FOR AN OUTSTANDING CONTRIBUTION TO

MECHANICAL ENGINEERING AND INVENTING THE TWO CYCLE ENGINE

INAUGURATED IN THE YEAR 2003

★ ★ ★ ★ ★

PROFESSOR DR ROBERT M SCHMIDT
FOR AN OUTSTANDING CONTRIBUTION TO

MEDICAL RESEARCH, EDUCATION AND ADMINISTRATION

INAUGURATED IN THE YEAR 2003

★ ★ ★ ★ ★

DR DONG-KEUN SHIN
FOR AN OUTSTANDING CONTRIBUTION TO

COMPUTER SCIENCE

INAUGURATED IN THE YEAR 2003

★ ★ ★ ★ ★

TROY ALVIN SMITH
FOR AN OUTSTANDING CONTRIBUTION TO

NUMERICAL ANALYSIS OF SHELLS

INAUGURATED IN THE YEAR 2003

★ ★ ★ ★ ★

DR LINDLEY JOSEPH STILES
FOR AN OUTSTANDING CONTRIBUTION TO

THE CREATION OF THE SOCIAL WISDOM: THE BEST SHOULD TEACH

INAUGURATED IN THE YEAR 2003

★ ★ ★ ★ ★

SVEN STROMQVIST
FOR AN OUTSTANDING CONTRIBUTION TO

LINGUISTIC AND COGNITIVE SCIENCES

INAUGURATED IN THE YEAR 2003

★ ★ ★ ★ ★

PROFESSOR DR A SUN

FOR AN OUTSTANDING CONTRIBUTION TO

IMMUNOLOGY AND MEDICINE

INAUGURATED IN THE YEAR 2003

★ ★ ★ ★ ★

DR KATHLEEN DAS SUNEJA

FOR AN OUTSTANDING CONTRIBUTION TO

THE FIELD OF INTERNATIONAL RELATIONS

INAUGURATED IN THE YEAR 2003

★ ★ ★ ★ ★

CHARLIE K L TAN

FOR AN OUTSTANDING CONTRIBUTION TO

AEROSPACE AND GROUND SUPPORT SERVICES

INAUGURATED IN THE YEAR 2003

★ ★ ★ ★ ★

DR WILLIAM H THUEME

FOR AN OUTSTANDING CONTRIBUTION TO

PEACE THROUGH UNDERSTANDING

INAUGURATED IN THE YEAR 2003

★ ★ ★ ★ ★

DR GARNIK TONOYAN

INAUGURATED IN THE YEAR 2004

★ ★ ★ ★ ★

GLORIA VADUS
FOR AN OUTSTANDING CONTRIBUTION TO

SCIENTIFIC DOCUMENT EXAMINATION

INAUGURATED IN THE YEAR 2004

★ ★ ★ ★ ★

DR JONG WANG
FOR AN OUTSTANDING CONTRIBUTION TO

EDUCATION & LITERATURE

INAUGURATED IN THE YEAR 2003

★ ★ ★ ★ ★

BABATUNDE O WILLIAMS
FOR AN OUTSTANDING CONTRIBUTION TO

REFINERIES PROCESS DESIGN AND CONSTRUCTION

INAUGURATED IN THE YEAR 2003

★ ★ ★ ★ ★

DR ALAN WONG-YUN SANG
FOR AN OUTSTANDING CONTRIBUTION TO

ART AND LITERATURE

INAUGURATED IN THE YEAR 2004

★ ★ ★ ★ ★

DR ETSUO YAMAMURA
FOR AN OUTSTANDING CONTRIBUTION TO

MODEL REFERENCE ADAPTIVE ECONOMICS

INAUGURATED IN THE YEAR 2004

★ ★ ★ ★ ★

DR RAYMOND J YOUNG
FOR AN OUTSTANDING CONTRIBUTION TO

HIGHER EDUCATION - COMMUNITY COLLEGES

INAUGURATED IN THE YEAR 2003

★ ★ ★ ★ ★

VLADIMIR ZAKHAROV
FOR AN OUTSTANDING CONTRIBUTION TO

FLOURINE CHEMISTRY

INAUGURATED IN THE YEAR 2003

★ ★ ★ ★ ★

PROFESSOR URI ZEHAVI
FOR AN OUTSTANDING CONTRIBUTION TO

BIOCHEMISTRY

INAUGURATED IN THE YEAR 2003

★ ★ ★ ★ ★

DR WENDELL E ZEHEL
FOR AN OUTSTANDING CONTRIBUTION TO

BIOTECHNOLOGY

INAUGURATED IN THE YEAR 2003

★ ★ ★ ★ ★

DR YUMING ZHOU
FOR AN OUTSTANDING CONTRIBUTION TO

POETIC LITERATURE

INAUGURATED IN THE YEAR 2003

★ ★ ★ ★ ★

CONTENTS

Foreword by the Publisher   V - VI

Range of IBC Titles   VII

Deputy Directors General of the IBC   VIII - XIV

Advisers to the Director General   XV

Lifetime Achievement Award   XVI - XVII

Vice Consuls of the IBC   XVIII

The Worldwide Honours List   XIX - XXXVIII

Dedications   1 - 41

Biographies   43 - 1121

Honours Lists   1123 - 1162

Dedications

ANNE GEERT BARTELDS

For your Outstanding Contribution to Music

ANNE GEERT BARTELDS

Anne Geert Bartelds is a composer, arranger, conductor, trumpet player, teacher, publicist and translator (Dutch, English, German, French). He was born on 21 January 1966 in Assen, The Netherlands. Mr Bartelds studied trumpet at the Groningen Conservatory and went on to attend Groningen State University where he undertook studies in English Language and Literature and Musicology, specialising in 20th Century and American music, dialectology and comparative interpretation studies.

Mr Bartelds' career has included numerous appointments as conductor and composer/arranger, as well as working as a free-lance brass, clarinet and piano player since 1983 in the fields of symphonic, band and jazz music. As an arranger, composer and orchestrator of both serious and light music he has worked with 11 music publishers in The Netherlands, the United Kingdom and Germany. Mr Bartelds is also a private brass teacher and a private English teacher. He has been Artistic Director of the Noordenveld regional wind-band clinics and a conductor of Big Band Noordenveld in Paterswolde, The Netherlands. He was appointed music critic and journalist for the Dutch regional newspaper, Oostermoer Noordenveld, in 1994 and the following year began work as a translator and editor of Muzika Publishers Tzummarum. Mr Bartelds became conductor of the Northern Sym- and Swingphonic Brass based in Eelde, The Netherlands, in 1996, and since 1997 he has been an adjudicator for the Schoonebeek Music Festival and a free-lance translator for BS Translations in Groningen.

In 1998 Mr Bartelds took up the appointment of correspondent to Music en Show, Winds Magazine, and in 1999 he became a stand-in brass teacher at Delfzijl School of Music. He has also recently become a translator and editor for Gobelin Music Publications Akkrum, and a brass teacher for the Adorp Musical Society in The Netherlands. In 2001 Mr Bartelds was appointed conductor of the Fanfare Adorp Musical Society, the Folkloristic Band De Lindelanders, the Linde Youth Ensemble and the DES Musical Society of Linde. He added to this list in 2002 with the inclusion of The Eastermoor Singers Annen and the Kunst en Strijd Musical Society of Muntendam, and in 2003 also became conductor of the Christian Musical Society "Amicitia", Musselkanaal.

A prolific author, Mr Bartelds has published numerous articles in professional journals. They include most recently: "It don't mean a thing if it ain't got that swing: Aspects of the Big Band Era in American Music", 1990; "The Use of Transcriptions in wind-music", 1997; "63 Years of Christian Wind Music in Northern Drenthe", 1998; "Changes of Identity with Regard to Local Wind Bands in the Northern Part of the Dutch Province of Drenthe", 1998; and "The reflection of Elements of Afro-American Culture in George Gershwin's Opera "Porgy and Bess"", 2002. He has also published compositions for wind-band including: "Rhapsodic Essayette for Band"; "Travesuras Gatunas"; "The Launching"; "The Maiden Voyage"; "The Initial Quest"; "Northern Jubilee"; "Impromptu for Brass Band"; "Little Suite on Highland Folksongs, Festive Intrada"; and numerous arrangements.

In 1983 Mr Bartelds was invited by the German Foreign Office to a tour of the FGR because of exceptional achievements in the field of the German Language. He went on in 1997 to receive 2nd Prize at an International Composition Contest "connected with the Landes Musikfest Nordrhein Westfalen" in Brilon, Germany and in 2002 was a nominee for the Tynaarlo County Council Cultural Award 2002. The following year Mr Bartelds received 1st Prize from the Longridge Band Composers' Forum at Northwich. In 2003, Mr Bartelds was a nominee and finalist for the Fodens Richardson Award for Brass Band Composition and Arranging 2004 (final results to be announced in 2004). The IBC have recognised his achievements with the

DEDICATIONS

award of a Certificate of Merit for an outstanding contribution in the field of wind-music as well as his acceptance as a member of the International Order of Merit (IOM) for services to music. His works are also used as compulsory contest-pieces in The Netherlands, Belgium and Germany and were performed on Dutch national classical radio as well as twice at the Royal Concertgebouw in Amsterdam and at the 'Wereld Muziek Concours' (World Music Contest) at Kerkrade. Commentaries on Mr Bartelds' works (which range from marches, chorales, and original concert-pieces to transcriptions, paso dobles, and various works in 'lighter' idioms such as jazz, musical, latin american and rock), especially praise their 'fine and varied instrumentation' which was characterised as 'very transparent' and 'offering more variation in colour than is usual'.

In 2004, Mr Bartelds was voted International Musician of the Year 2003 for an outstanding contribution to wind- and brass band composition. He is a member of the World Association of Symphonic Bands and Ensembles, the British Association of Symphonic Bands and Wind Ensembles and the Royal Netherlands Federation of Musical Societies. He also belongs to the Netherlands Christian Federation of Musical Societies, the Flemish Wind-Music Association and the International Military Music Society, as well as the International Society for the Investigation and Promotion of Wind-Music and the Confédération Musicale de France. He also belongs to the Swiss Band-Music Association, Bundesvereinigung deutscher Musikverbände, the Australian Band and Orchestra Directors Association, the Union Grand-Duc Adolphe and the American Bandmaster Association.

A biography of Anne Geert Bartelds appears in the main section of this edition.

DANIEL D. BRUNDA DDG LPIBA
MOIF IOM AdVSci DO

*For your Outstanding Contribution to
Mechanical, Aerospace, Electromagnetic
Powerline Radiation and Science*

DANIEL DONALD BRUNDA, DDG, LPIBA, MOIF, IOM, AdVSci, DO

Registered as a Professional Engineer in the State of New Jersey, USA, Daniel Donald Brunda has had a long and successful career in aerospace engineering. Now retired, he continues to provide consulting services, parallel with pursuing his leisure interests as an inventor, author, investor and musician (accordion and dance). Apart from being the contributor of more than twenty articles to professional journals, he is an inventor and author of some stature, holding copyrights, as well as patents including one for a measurement system and method for determining the amount of electromagnetic radiation being absorbed by living beings.

The son of Michael Theodore and Ella Jurba Brunda, Daniel Brunda was born on 22 October 1930 in Lansford, Pennsylvania. Educated locally, he graduated from high school at the end of the 1940s, whereupon he entered Lehigh University, from which he earned a Bachelor of Science degree in Mechanical Engineering in 1952, followed by a Master of Science degree in Mechanical Engineering in 1953. He also carried out postgraduate studies at Johns Hopkins University in 1955, at Princeton University between 1958 and 1965, and finally at Drexel University in 1983.

Mr Brunda's first professional appointment was as an Aerodynamicist working for the Bell Aircraft Corp, then as a Performance Engineer with Glenn L Martin, based in Baltimore for three years. However, it was not long before the firm of Curtiss Wright was established in Princeton, New Jersey, where he spent one year as an Analytical Engineer in propulsion development, evaluation and performance. He left the firm in 1957 to join the US Naval Air Propulsion Center in Ewing, New Jersey, as an Aerospace Engineer engaged in research. In 1972 he was appointed local Manager of Independent Research and Development, a position he held until retiring in 1983. Meanwhile, in 1978 he commenced his present activity as a Consultant in powerline radiation energy engineering.

During his career Mr Brunda has gained a well-deserved reputation for his achievements. He provided the first scientific proof that powerline radiation is a cause of cancer and many other diseases. Following on from this, he determined for the first time the inductive impedance and radiation limits of human beings, as well as mathematically explaining the Electrophonic Effect discovered by Volta in 1800 AD. He himself is the discoverer of Brunda's Absorbance Law, the molecular weight of the average adult human being, and the absorbance of DNA. Notable is his copyrighted report entitled "Power Line Radiation, Your Genes, Hereditary Diseases, the Unified Nature of Electromagnetic Radiation Energy and Control and the Radiation Limits of Human Beings". The book will be published by Xlibris Book Publishing Co in the year 2004.

Mr Brunda is an Associate Fellow of the Bioelectromagnetic Society. Moreover, besides holding life membership in the American Society of Mechanical Engineers, he gained admission to the American Institute of Aeronautics and Astronautics, where he is a senior member. He is a Founder of the Order of the Electro-magnetic Powerline Radiation Engineers and also a Lifetime Deputy Governor of the American Biographical Institute Research Association. Among his many honours, Mr Brunda has been named an Outstanding Scientist of the 20th Century in the Field of Electro-magnetic Powerline Radiation and Control, in the year 2000 has become both a Deputy Director General and a Life Fellow of the IBC in the Americas, and is included in the 500 Founders of the 21st Century in Honour of an Outstanding Contribution in the Field of Engineering and Science by the IBC. More recently, in 2001, his work has been exhibited in the IBA Gallery of Excellence. Also in April of 2001 Mr Brunda was presented with a Certificate of Commendation from the Mayor of Ewing township, the President of the Council and council members, for services rendered since 1978. Mr Brunda has authored a book entitled "The

DEDICATIONS

Design of Safe Electric Transmission and Distribution Lines", which was copyrighted in the USA on 13 August 2001. The book is being published by Xlibris Book Publishing Co, Philadelphia, PA 19106, USA. He was also named "International Scientist of the Year 2001", listed among the "Outstanding Scientists of the 21st Century" and given the Lifetime Achievement Award for "Outstanding Contribution to the Design and Control of Safe Electrical Transmission, Distribution and Service Lines". He was elected a founder member of the Scientific Faculty as nominated by the Director General of the IBC, in recognition of his standing within the scientific community on 15 February 2002 and was included in the IBC On Line Hall of Fame on March 2002. Mr Brunda has been proclaimed an "Ambassador of Grand Eminence" and chosen as an USA representative of the American Biographical Institute (20 June 2002). The ABI also presented him with the World Lifetime Achievement Award in 2002 for outstanding achievements in electromagnetic powerline radiation. Mr Brunda is a founding cabinet member of the World Peace Diplomacy Forum (IBC, 2003) and is also included in the publications "Living Science" and "Living Legends" (IBC, 2003).

A biography of Daniel Donald Brunda, DDG, LPIBA, MOIF, IOM, AdVSci, DO appears in the main section of this edition.

DR. DAVID DONALDSON MB ChB FRCP FRCPath CBiol FIBiol CChem FRSC EurClinChem
For your Outstanding Contribution to Chemical Pathology

DR DAVID DONALDSON, MB, ChB, FRCP, FRCPath, CBiol, FIBiol, CChem, FRSC, EurClinChem

David Donaldson was born on 13 February 1936 in Birmingham, England. He currently works as Consultant Chemical Pathologist at Gatwick Park Hospital, Horley, Surrey, but was Consultant Chemical Pathologist at East Surrey Hospital, Redhill, Surrey and Crawley Hospital, Crawley, West Sussex from 1970-2001. Educated at King Edward's School in Birmingham, Dr Donaldson graduated in medicine from Birmingham University Medical School in 1959 and spent the next three years working in hospitals in Birmingham and Yorkshire. He became a member of the Royal College of Physicians, London in 1963 and then in 1964 Dr Donaldson joined the National Hospital for Nervous Diseases in London where he trained in chemical pathology becoming a member of the Royal College of Pathologists in 1969.

As an author, Dr Donaldson has over 100 publications in professional journals and chapters in books. His own books include "Essential Diagnostic Tests in Biochemistry and Haematology" (co-author, 1971), "Diagnostic Function Tests in Chemical Pathology" (co-author, 1989) and "Psychiatric Disorders with a Biochemical Basis" (1998). He also lectures extensively at home and abroad on many topics.

Dr Donaldson was elected to Fellowship of the Royal College of Pathologists in 1981. He became Fellow of the Royal Society of Health in 1989 and Fellow of the International College of Nutrition in 1997 and was then elected Fellow of the Royal College of Physicians in 1999. Dr Donaldson also holds membership of many professional organisations around the world such as the American Association for the Advancement of Science, the Association of Clinical Biochemists, the European Atherosclerosis Society and the British Atherosclerosis Society. He also belongs to the British Association for the Advancement of Science, the New York Academy of Sciences, the Faculty of History and Philosophy of Medicine and Pharmacy (Worshipful Society of Apothecaries of London) and the Harveian Society of London. In 2002 he was the recipient of the Mori Felicitation Award from the International College of Nutrition.

A biography of Dr David Donaldson, MB, ChB, FRCP, FRCPath, CBiol, FIBiol, CChem, FRSC, EurClinChem, appears in the main section of this edition.

PETER GALLINER AdVBus IOM

*For your Outstanding Contribution to
Press Freedom*

PETER GALLINER, AdVBus, IOM

Publisher Peter Galliner was born on 19 September 1920 in Berlin, Germany and educated in Berlin and London. With his first wife, Edith Marguerite Goldsmidt, he had one daughter, Nicola. He is now married to Helga Stenschke.

Mr Galliner began his career working for Reuters in London between 1944-47, before joining the Financial Times in London as Foreign Manager. He held this post until 1960. The following year, Mr Galliner was appointed Chairman of Board and Managing Director of the Ullstein Publishing Group in Berlin and then in 1965 he joined the British Printing Corporation, London, as vice-chairman and managing director of the Publishing Group remaining there for five years. Subsequently he worked as an International Publishing Consultant. Since 1970, Mr Galliner has been chairman of Peter Galliner Associates, and has also spent 18 years as a director of the International Press Institute (1975-93). He became chairman of International Encounters in 1995.

In recognition of his achievements, Mr Galliner has received many awards. In 1965 he received the Order of Merit 1st Class in Germany and in 1982 he was presented with the Ecomienda from the Orden de Isabel la Catolica, Spain. During the 1990s he was given the Commander's Cross of the Order of Merit, Germany, the Turkish Press Freedom Award, and the Media and Communication Award in Krakow, Poland.

A biography of Peter Galliner, AdVBus, IOM appears in the main section of this edition.

PROF. DR. KAZUYOSI IKEDA
D.Sc D.Litt. LPIBA DDG IOM
LFWLA MOIF CH DO

For your Outstanding Contribution to
Poetry and Science

PROFESSOR DR KAZUYOSI IKEDA, DSc, DLitt, LPIBA, DDG, IOM, LFWLA, MOIF, CH, DO

Kazuyosi Ikeda DSc, DLitt, is not only a professor of theoretical physics at Japan's Osaka University, but also a bilingual poet of renown. He was born on 15 July 1928, the eldest son of Yosikatu Ikeda and of Misao Ikeda. His birthplace was on Japan's coast, far distant from the busy quarters of Fukuoka City but within a ten minutes walk of Kyushu University. Thus, he spent his childhood surrounded by both the beauty of nature and an academic atmosphere. It was these circumstances that strongly stimulated him to become a scientist engaged in academic researches as well as a poet singing of the beauties of nature.

As a middle school student (1941-45), Dr Ikeda enjoyed both his scientific and literary subjects equally. Even after going up to Fukuoka High School's Science-A Course in 1945, and entering the Kyushu University Department of Physics in 1948, his interest in literature never wavered. He read many literary works and began composing his own poems while undertaking scientific research.

After graduating from the Faculty of Science of Kyushu University in 1951 (with the First Degree "Rigakusi"), Dr Ikeda enrolled in a Postgraduate Course of the University's Department of Physics. His first scientific paper, "On the Theory of Condensation" (dealing with the statistical mechanics of condensation of gasses and the mathematical analysis of the singular point representing condensation), was presented at the International Conference on Theoretical Physics in Kyoto in 1953. This was the first international scientific meeting held in Japan, and Dr Ikeda was its youngest lecturer. For this paper and his participation in the conference, he was highly praised by Professor J E Mayer of the University of Chicago (USA), as well as by other famous scholars involved in the field of theoretical physics. By virtue of this work (which became his doctoral dissertation), he received an award from the Yukawa Commemorative Scholarship Fund in 1954, and subsequently, this paper has formed an important basis for numerous future articles that Dr Ikeda has written.

On 20 November 1956, Dr Ikeda married Mieko Aikyama, daughter of Rokurobê (a university professor of German literature). Their daughter, Hiroko Yamaguti, holds Bachelor of Arts and Master of Arts degrees in the Italian language, and their son, Yosihumi Ikeda, studied with the Faculty of Literature at Kyushu University.

While continuing his studies at Kyushu University, Dr Ikeda was appointed to the post of assistant in the University's Department of Physics (1956). In 1957, he gained the degree of Doctor of Science, and in 1960, he became an associate professor in the Kyushu University Faculty of Science's Department of Physics. Five years later, he moved to Osaka University as an associate professor in the Department of Applied Physics of the Faculty of Engineering. He was then promoted, in 1968, to full professor, and in 1989, he transferred his work to the newly established Department of Mathematical Sciences, thus becoming a professor of theoretical physics and mathematical physics in the department. In 1992, he was named professor emeritus by Osaka University, at the same time becoming a professor at the International Earth Environment University of Japan (of which he was installed as President in 1995).

In the scientific realm, Dr Ikeda has made numerous outstanding accomplishments throughout his career, greatly contributing to the fields of theoretical physics, mathematical physics, and chemical physics, particularly as related to the (classical and quantum) statistical mechanics of the properties of matter and the phase transitions by investigation of an assembly of interacting molecules with the use of mathematical-analytical methods. His papers on the statistical-mechanical theory of the condensation phenomena of gases and the phase transitions in substances, with the full use of his unique original rigorous mathematical methods, have been widely noticed and have been very highly evaluated in the international academic world. His interests also extend to the celestial mechanics of comets, and he has theoretically investigated the orbit and motion of the comet whose appearance in 634 and 635 AD was recorded in the Japanese ancient history *Nihon Syoki* (in this research, he has referred to the Chinese history of the Tang Period). Additional research covers such subjects as the theory of the properties of matter as applications of the principles of classical and quantum mechanics, the quantum statistical mechanics of gases and liquids, the statistical-mechanical theory of condensation of gases, the theory of the thermodynamic properties of gases with the use of the cluster expansion, the theoretical research of phase transitions with the application of the theory of functions of a complex variable, the statistical-mechanical theory of (gaseous and liquid) helium, lattice gases, one-dimensional substances, solutions, and the theoretical-mechanical research on comets in ancient times. On these subjects, Dr Ikeda has produced over one hundred papers and monographs, including "On the Theory of Condensation" (1953), "Generalized Theory of Condensing Systems" (1961), "On the Yang-Lee Distribution of Zeros for a Gas Obeying van de Waals' Equation of State III – Calculations for Low Temperatures" (1974), "Volume-Dependent Cluster Sums for Lattice Gases I – Calculation of the Temperley Coefficients" (1975), "Statistical Mechanics of One-Dimensional Systems I – Phase Transitions of a van der Waals Gas" (1981), "Distribution of Zeros and the Equation of State IV – Ideal Bose-Einstein Gas" (1982), "Phase Transitions of Lattice Gases – Satisfaction of the G-Condition" (1984), "Statistical-Mechanical Theory of One-Dimensional Gases with Short-Range and Long-Range Intermolecular Forces II – Phase Transition at the Absolute Zero" (1985), "Statistical-Mechanical Theory of Osmotic Pressure of One-Dimensional Multicomponent Systems I – Expansion in Terms of the Molar Fractions of the Solutes" (1991), and "Thermodynamical Behavior of Liquid Water near the Triple Point" (1991).

In addition to his numerous journal articles, Dr Ikeda has published many books on theoretical physics, including *Statistical Thermodynamics* (1975), *Mechanics Without Use of Mathematical Formulae - from a Moving Stone to Halley's comet* (1980), *Invitation to Mechanics -from the Fundamentals of Calculus to the Motion of a Comet* (with appendix on a comet in ancient times, 1985), *Basic Mechanics* (1987), *Basic Thermodynamics - from Entropy to Osmotic Pressure* (1991), and *Graphical Theory of Relativity* (1998). Early in his career, he translated ter Haar's *Thermostatistics* (1960), and he contributed a chapter on "Statistical Thermodynamics of Imperfect Gases and Condensation Phenomena" to the volume *Modern Developments in Thermodynamics* (edited by B Gal-Or in 1974).

As a poet, Dr Ikeda asserts, with emphasis, that the true poem, essentially different from prose, should have the beauty of rhythm (or metre) as well as the beauty of sentiment, and he deplores the fact that many Japanese poets neglect the importance of rhythm in poetry and compose only free verse. Creating many poems of fixed form with beautiful rhythm, he has published the collection *Bansyô Hyakusi* (A Hundred Poems on All Creation) and has been serialising poems in *Chishiki* (Knowledge), one of the most famous monthly magazines in Japan, since 1989, and in the *Osaka University Newspaper* since 1979. He has also produced numerous essays on poetry and has published over 30 literary books, including *The World of God, Creation and Poetry* (1991), etc and over 16 collections of poems. He has also published over 60 literary articles, essays and reviews. His representative poems and his opinions on poetry have been included in the Olympic Anthology *The First 100* (Barcelona-92 Olympoetry), as well as in many other world-famous anthologies and journals, including *Samvedana, Metverse Muse,*

Parnassus of World Poets, Modern Poetry, World Poetry, Global Poetry, Poet, Contemporary Poets, The Brain Wave, The "O", Poets International, Kafla Inter-Continental, and *Dayspring.* His collection of English poems, *Poems on the Hearts of Creation,* was published in England in 1993, and his *Mountains* (World Poets Series of Ferdinandea, 1995) and *North, South, East and West* (World Poets Library of Olympoetry, 1996) have been published in Italy and the USA, respectively. Other volumes of English poems, *Hearts of Myriad Things in the Universe, Kazuyosi's Poetry on the Animate and Inanimate,* and *Poems on Love and Peace,* were published in 1998, while *Songs of the Soul* and *Hearts of Innumerous Things in Heaven and Earth* were published in 1999 and 2000, respectively. He has also published *The World of Hearts* (2002), *Peace Offerings* (2003), *Men and Nature* (2003), *Spring Rain* (2003) and numerous other books of poetry. He has also been serialising the translations of Shakespeare's Sonnets into Japanese poems of fixed form in the seven-and-five-syllable metre.

In his poetry, Dr Ikeda sings of the hearts and minds of many things of nature, on the basis of his sincere love for all creation. He follows the Japanese traditional seven-and-five-syllable metre (a very pleasing Japanese metre made popular in the 12th century). He indites numerous poems in this metre, not only in Japanese, but also in English. He is a bilingual poet, filling his poems with both lyric emotion and scientific lucidity, thus gaining many enthusiastic and admiring readers throughout the world. The aim of his making of poetry is the establishing of global brotherhood and world peace through people's genuine love for all creation; for it he sings of the hearts of things, animate, inanimate or man-made, which were created directly or indirectly by God and so have their own hearts as gifts of God. Besides the 7-and-5-syllable metre (sitigotyo in Japanese) poetry, he has made haiku, tanka and Chinese classical fixed-form poetry (originated in the Tang Period) with the same aim as above. He has introduced sitigotyo into English poetry for the first time in the history of English literature, in order to make his English poems soak deep in people's hearts. Included here are five of Dr Ikeda's poems in Romanised Japanese. The subject of the first poem is a lion who is king of the beasts, although old. He, having no enemy, is perfectly calm at his seat, and his heart is elevated to the state of spiritual awakening. In the second poem, the author sings of a seal, whose passionate love for a female brings about grim struggles against other males. The third poem is a song about a peregrine, a hero of the sky, whose heart becomes tender the moment he thinks of his love in his homeland. A fishing net, the subject of the fourth poem, symbolises a person who ardently endeavours to grasp his love's secret heart compared to the fish in the deep sea. The fifth poem depicts the lamentation of an octopus caught in a pot, noting that Japanese people catch octopuses, which are edibles in Japan, by setting up deceitful pots in the sea. The translated poems, by the author himself, are in the seven-and-five-syllable metre as are the original poems; thus in each poem a line consists of the first part (of seven syllables) and the second part (of five syllables). The translation is to the right of the original. These poems, in English and Japanese, are quoted from *Poems on the Hearts of Creation.*

Sisi	**A Lion**
Sisi tuyokereba Sisi no Za ni	The strongest of all the beasts, he is a lion.
Sizukani suwari mizirogazu.	On the throne is he seated stilly and calmly.
Siru ya, oitaru Sisi wa ima	Who knows the old lion's mind full of religion?
Sinnyo no Tuki ni akugaruru.	He admires the holy light of the moon deeply.

DEDICATIONS

Azarasi
Ayumu Sube naku Ti wo haedo,
Sakarite Tuma wo arasoeba,
Ranran to site Me zo hikaru.
Siru ya, hagesiki Koi-gokoro.

A Seal
On the land I can not walk; I proceed creeping.
In the exciting season I fight for a wife;
I glare at my enemy, with my eyes flaming.
Does one know my intense love burning out my life?

Hayabusa
Hayaki wo hokoru wa ga Tubasa.
Yamayama koete tobi-yukeba,
Huto omoi-izu, Hurusato no
Sayuri no Hana ya ware wo matu.

A Peregrine
Priding myself on my wing, very fast I fly.
Soaring over the mountains, reminded am I
Of my beloved lily in my home country
Waiting for my return home solitarily.

Gyomô
Kimi wa Watatumi, ware wa Ami.
Yogoto ni Uo wo kotogotoku
Morasazi tote zo Ami wo utu.
Uo koso kimi ga Kokoro nare.

A Fishing Net
Thou art the great and deep sea; I'm a fishing net.
Night after night I plunge down into thee deeply,
So that I may catch the fish in thee entirely,
Because the fish are thy heart, profound and secret.

Takotubo
Tanosiki Yado to omoisi ni,
Kono Kurusisa wo ikani semu.
Tumitoga nakute torawaresi
Hone naki wa ga Mi itoosi ya.

An Octopus Pot
Thinking it a happy inn, I have entered it.
But how distressing it is! A man's tricky pit!
Alas, I have been captured, although not guilty.
On myself, having no bone, do I take pity.

Professor Ikeda's sphere of pursuits is very wide. His achievements cover theoretical physics and poetry, and his scientific research ranges from the statistical theory of an assembly of molecules to the mechanical theory of the motion of a comet. Moreover, he has a wide variety of hobbies and interests, including such uncommon and rather unique pastimes as seeing Kabuki and Noh plays, seeing and performing Noh farces, chanting Noh songs, and reading Japanese classical literature and ancient history. He has appeared on stage in many Noh farces. Still, in all his fields of interest, his goals are essentially the same. The wholehearted pursuit of beauty, whether in the natural world or in the human world, is his lifelong goal, supported by his strong religious belief. He is convinced that the universe was created by God and from its origin has contained beauty given by the Creator, and that it is mankind's mission to discover, substantiate and polish such beauty. He has, with that sense of mission, been devoting himself to the pursuit of such beauty through his scientific and poetic work. In the field of theoretical physics, he zealously endeavours to research into nature by beautiful mathematical arguments based on logical rigour, and to find more and more beauty of mathematical orderliness in the natural phenomena. In the theoretical-mechanical research of comets, he has scientifically substantiated the ancient people's admiration for the beauty of comets. And in the field of poetry, he makes great efforts to construct a beautiful world consisting of aesthetic feelings and rhythmic words by employing the traditional metre in modern poetry.

Dr Ikeda shares his ideas with his colleagues through memberships in various professional organisations. He is an active member of the Physical Society of Japan, serving as a committee member since 1970 and holding the office of Chairman of the Osaka Branch during 1976-77 and 1983-84. He has also served on the Executive Committee of Centenary of the Physical Society of Japan (1976-77) and has been editor of the *Journal of the Physical Society of Japan* (1976-78). He is currently a member of the New York Academy of Sciences, he is director of the Kansai Branch of the Professors World Peace Academy, and he is chairman of both the Osaka Branch of the National Coalition for the Unification of North East West South (1988 to present) and of the Osaka University Branch of the Professors-Students Coalition for the Unification of North East West South (1987 to present). In addition, he is a life member of the World Institute of Achievement, a Life Fellow and Life Patron of the International Biographical Association, a Research Fellow, Deputy Director General, and Honorary Member of the Advisory Council of the International Biographical Centre, and a Life Fellow of the World Literary Academy. By the American Biographical Institute, he has been named a Life Fellow and Deputy Governor of the American Biographical Institute Research Association, an Honorary Advisor to the Board of Advisors, a Continental Governor, and Research Advisor of the Year for 1991. Away from the scientific world, Dr Ikeda is a Member of Merit for Life, as well as a member of the Grand Council of the Confederation of Chivalry. He is a life member of the Lifetime Achievement Academy and an honorary founder (representative of Japan) of the Olympoetry Movement. In addition, he has been named a Senator and Minister Plenipotentiary for Asian States of the Council of the States for Protection of Life and a Senator of the Maison Internationale des Intellectuels. He has been a life fellow of the United Writers' Association since 1990, a life member of the World Academy of Arts and Culture and the World Congress of Poets since 1992, a life fellow of the International Poets Academy, also since 1992, and an Academician of Honor of the Accademia Ferdinandea di Scienze, Lettere ed Arti since 1994. He is a charter member of the Order of International Fellowship, honorary director of the World Parnassians Guild International, a member of the board of the Modern Poets Society, a founding charter member of Leading Intellectuals of the World, a member of the Planetary Society, an editor of *Modern Poetry*, Litterateur Life Chief Patron of Metverse Muse, an Academician of Academia Argentina, an Academician of Merit of the Accademia Internazionale "Trinacria" Lettere-Arte-Scienze, and a Senator and Minister Plenipotentiary for Japan of the International Parliament for Safety and Peace. Furthermore, he is a board member of the Advisory Council of Ansted University, a founding member of the London Diplomatic Academy and the American Order of Excellence, an honorary life member of the Jagruthi Kiran Foundation, a founder member of the Scientific Faculty of Cambridge, a patron of Katha Kshetre, a patron of the Brain Wave English Lit-Q, a corresponding member (representative of Japan) of the Institut des Affaires Internationales, Chief Executive of the Michael Madhusudan Academy, a patron of the Karuna India Society, Patron-in-Chief of the Chetana Literary Group, Chief Patron of the Home of Letters, Patron-in-Chief of the Voice of Kolkata, and a founding member of the International Honour Society, an advisory board member of the Creative Writing and Criticism, an editorial board member of Titiksha, a director of the International Writers and Artists Association, an executive member of Commissione di Lettera Internationale, the regional co-ordinator of Japan and Asia Pacific of the International Poetry for Peace Association, a member of the Cyberwet Net, and Patron-in-Chief of the OMEGA Welfare Organisation.

DEDICATIONS

In recognition of his outstanding contributions as a theoretical physicist and poet, Dr Ikeda has been awarded the World Decoration of Excellence Award (1989), an International Cultural Diploma of Honor (1989), a Distinguished Leadership Award (1989), a Statesman's Award (1989), the title of Grand Ambassador of Achievement (1989), the International Order of Merit (1990), a Biographical Honor Award (1990), a Commemorative Medal of Honor (1990), the Professional Performance Key Award (1990), a Leader in Science Award (1990), and a Notable Author Award (1990). He has been inducted into the Hall of Fame of the American Biographical Institute, the World Biographical Hall of Fame, *The World Who's Who* Hall of Fame, the *Millennium Hall of Fame,* the Men's Inner Circle of Achievement, The International Governors Club of the American Biographical Institute, the *First Five Hundred at the New Millennium*, and the American Hall of Fame, and has been named to the International Biographical Centre's Honours List and the IBC Director General's Honours List, with biographical inclusion in over fifty international reference volumes, including *International Who's Who of Intellectuals, International Who's Who in Poetry, International Directory of Distinguished Leadership, Five Thousand Personalities of the World, Dictionary of International Biography, The First Five Hundred, International Book of Honor, International Leaders in Achievement, International Register of Profiles, Men of Achievement, Men and Women of Distinction, Who's Who in the World, Who's Who in Science and Engineering, Who's Who in America, Reference Asia, The Asia-Pacific Who's Who, 2000 Outstanding People of the 20th Century, International Who's Who of Contemporary Achievement, Five Hundred Leaders of Influence, The World Who's Who of Men and Women of Distinction, Who's Who in Australasia and the Pacific Nations, Asian./American Who's Who, Outstanding People of the 20th Century, 2000 Outstanding Scientists of the 20th Century,* and others. Furthermore, he has received the Chevalier Grand Cross (1991), the Golden Academy Award for Lifetime Achievement (1991), a One-in-a-Million Award (1991), a Twenty-Five Year Achievement Award (1992), the title of Most Admired Man of the Decade (1992), a Silver Shield of Valor (1992), and International Honors Cup (1992), a 20th Century Award for Achievement (1993), the Award of International Eminent Poet (1993), and Who's Who of the Year Award (1993), a Five-Star Leader Award (1993), and the Degree of Honorary Doctor of Environmental Science (1993). In 1994, he received a Gold Record of Achievement, Attestato di Merito of Accademia Ferdinandea, and the Prize Catania e il suo Vulcano; in 1995, he was awarded the Prize Catania Duomo, the Order of International Ambassadors, the Medalla al Merito of the International Parliament for Safety and Peace, and a Diploma of Honor of the Institute of International Affairs and the degree of Honorary Doctor of Science from the World Academy, as well as the degree of Honorary Doctor of Literature; in 1996, he received the International Artistic-Literary Prize of Athene, the Presidential Seal of Honor, a Platinum Record for Exceptional Performance, the Decree of International Letter for Cultural Achievement, the Order of Pegasus of Highest Degree, and a Gold Star Award; and in 1997, he was awarded an International Sash of Academia, an International Artistic-Literary Prize of Primavera Catanes, and a Golden Scroll of Excellence.

Along with his numerous awards and prizes, Dr Ikeda earned the titles of Knight of the Templar Order (1995), Knight of the Lofsensic Ursinius Order (1995), Knight of the Holy Grail Order (1995), Knight of the Universal Knights Order (1995), Knight of the San Ciriaco Order (1995), Knight of the Year of International Writers and Artists Association (1995), Man of the Year (1990, 1993, 1994, 1995, 1997, 1998, 1999, 2000), International Man of the Year (1991/92, 1996/97, 1998/99), Personality of the Year (1991, 1998), International Man of the Millennium (1999), Outstanding Man of the 20th Century (1999), and World Laureate (1999). In 1998 he was presented with the Albert Einstein Academy Award for Outstanding Achievement, as well as a 2000 Millennium Medal of Honor, and in 1999, he received the Pandit Prize, the World Lifetime Achievement Award, the Gold Medal of Outstanding Scientist, the World Award of Accomplishment, a Certificate of Mutual Loyalty for DDG, the Cultural Doctorate in Poetical Literature from the World University Roundtable (in USA), and the Best World Poet of the Year 1999. In 2000, he received Poet of the Millennium Award, the Torch of Global Inspiration, Who's Who Medal, the Prize Oscar 2000, Gran Premio d'Autore, International Commendation of Success in the Professions of Science and Poetry, and the New Millennium Michael Madhusudan Award. In 2001, conferred on him were the International Medal for Scientific Excellence, the International Literary Prize "Libro d'Oro", the Netaji Subhush Chandra Bose National Award for Excellence in the Field of Poetry and Environmental Science, Global Peace and Friendship Award, Outstanding Professional Award in Science and Literature, the Ivory Eagle 2001 Award, and the titles of International Scientist of the Year 2001, Knight Commander of Sovereign Order of Ambrosini's, International Intellectual of the Year 2001, Outstanding Man of the 21st Century, and Companion of Honour. In 2002, he received the American Medal of Honor, the Legacy of Honor, the Sphatica (India) International Poet Award, the International Peace Prize, the Mandakini Literary Award, and the Excellence in World Poetry Award, and the titles of World Citizen of the Year, Vice Consul of IBC, Ambassador of Grand Eminence, and Most Influential Scientist of the Decade. In 2003, he received the Voice of Kolkata Award, the Outstanding Academic Medal; the Contemporary Diamond Award, and the Golden Book International Prize for Sto Mikrokosmo. In 2004 he received the Order of Distinction as Specialist in Theoretical Physics and Poetry, the Great Mind of the 21st Century Medal, the Honour of Greatest Intellectual, the Outstanding Scientist Medal, the Award of Einstein Chair of Science, and the Master Diploma for Special Honours in Science and Poetry from the World Academy of Letters. In addition, more than twenty-five publications, including the following, have been dedicated to him: *International Who's Who of Intellectuals, International Book of Honor, Dictionary of International Biography, International Register of Profiles, International Directory of Distinguished Leadership, Five Thousand Personalities of the World, Men and Women of Distinction, Men of Achievement, International Who's Who of Contemporary Achievement, International Leaders of Achievement, International Who's Who of 20th Century Achievement, Five Hundred Leaders of Influence, Outstanding People of the 20th Century, The Millennium Hall of Fame, 2000 Outstanding People of the 20th Century, The First 500 at the New Millennium, 2000 Outstanding Scientists of the 20th Century, 2000 Outstanding Scholars of the 20th Century, 2000 Outstanding Intellectuals of the 20th Century,* and *2000 Outstanding Scientists of the 21st Century.* His biography is listed in more than 50 international famous Who's Who books in the world.

In ending this essay, five additional poems by Kazuyosi Ikeda, as well as translations by the author, are given below, for deeper appreciation of the sublime spirit of his poetry. The subject of the first poem is a tiger who grieves over his fateful sin of killing and eating his victim and swears to atone for his sin in the next world. A jaguar, the subject of the second poem, begins to search for his prey, running fiercely, while he shouts inwardly a warning at weak animals. The third poem is a song about an otter, who lives a serious and honest life in the river, particularly interested in educating his children. In the fourth poem, the author sings of a mine (ie, a mountain containing minerals) which laments over the misery of being plundered of its contents by men. And in the fifth poem, a fishing rod dreams of catching a great source of happiness from the fantastic submarine kingdom.

DEDICATIONS

Tora

Torite Kurawamu Ikimono wo
Ranran to site nerau nari.
Tomoni kanasimi tomoni nake.
Raise ni Tumi wo aganawamu.

A Tiger

I will now catch and eat thee, a poor living thing;
I am staring thee fixedly, my fierce eyes glaring.
Weep over our woeful fate together with me.
In the other world I will compensate to thee.

Zyagâ

Sika mo Masira mo Mi wo kakuse.
Yaora okitaru kono Kemono,
Kawa no Madara mo azayaka ni,
Araarasikumo No wo hasiru.

A Jaguar

Monkeys, deer and peccaries! Make yourselves hidden!
Never become my victims! I have just risen.
The spots of my skin are clear, showing my fierceness.
I am running in the field with great savageness.

Kawauso

Kawa ni sumituki oyogedomo,
Ware wa Kemono zo, Ko wo umite,
Uo toru Sube wo osietutu,
Sora-gokoro naku Yo wo wataru.

An Otter

Residing in the river, I swim every day;
But I am an animal, breeding my children.
Teaching them to catch fish and to bear life's burden,
I live without a false heart in a sincere way.

Kanayama

Kataki Yamahada ugatitewa
Nasake Yôsya mo Aragane no
Yama no Kokoro wo sainamite
Magane Akagane hori-idasu.

A Mine

People dig mine hard body, a mine's hard body;
And they rob me of mine ore very cruelly.
They torture mine heart sorely with their heartless picks
And take iron and copper with their iron picks.

Turizao

Tukisenu Sati wa Minasoko no
Ryûgûzyô no Uo no Mure.

Sao sinayaka ni tuyokereba,
Ooi naru Yume turi-agemu.

A Fishing Rod

Inexhaustible treasures at the sea bottom
Are large schools of fish swimming in Neptune's kingdom.
I am a fine fishing rod, strong and elastic.
So shall I catch a great dream, sweet and romantic.

A biography of Professor Dr Kazuyosi Ikeda, DSc, DLitt, LPIBA, DDG, IOM, LFWLA, MOIF, CH, DO appears in the main section of this edition.

ROY O. KENDALL

For your Outstanding Contribution to
Basic Biological Research of Lepidoptera

ROY O KENDALL

Roy Kendall is a retired US Federal Civil Service employee. He was born on 21 May 1912 in Gray County, Kansas, USA. He married Conway (Connie) Alford Montgomery and they had two sons. Sadly, Mrs Kendall and one of their sons are now deceased.

Roy Kendall studied at Louisiana State University between 1936-37 and at Trinity University from 1951 until 1956. In the course of his career he has held several honorary positions and worked as a Research Associate for the Welder Wildlife Foundation and Florida State College of Arthropods. He has also served as a technical consultant to the Texas Parks and Wildlife Department. Before his retirement Mr Kendall worked in administration, dealing with acquisitions, storage and distribution of military supplies and equipment. He currently continues his basic biological research of lepidoptera. As an author he has published 40 articles on lepidoptera life histories in professional journals and has contributed to the Lepidopterists' Society Commemorative Volume (xvii, 1945-73).

Reflecting his work on the study of butterflies, Mr Kendall is honoured to have nine Lepidoptera patronyms described honouring him and his late wife. There are also two books dedicated to him by the authors: "A Field Guide to Butterflies of Texas" by Raymond W Neck, 1996 and "Butterflies of West Texas Parks and Preserves" by Roland H Wauer, 2002. Mr Kendall was the recipient of the John Abbot Award in 1984 and the Floyd E Potter Jr Award in 1989. Texas A and M University gave him and his late wife an Honorary Leadership Recognition in 1994 with the unveiling of a Bronze Portrait Plaque on the entrance wall of their Entomology building. Mr Kendall is a member of the Lepidopterists' Society (international), the Southern Lepidopterists' Society and the Journal of Research on Lepidoptera.

A biography of Roy O Kendall appears in the main section of this edition.

**OWEN WILLIAM
LONERAGAN DDG**
*For your Outstanding Contribution to
Strategy For Sustainable Living*

OWEN WILLIAM LONERAGAN, DDG

Owen William Loneragan was born on 26 March 1924 in Maylands, Western Australia. He is married to Joan Edith Shaw and they have two sons and one daughter, with eight grandchildren between the ages of six and 22 years. Mr Loneragan has been employed in the regeneration and treatments, growth and ecology of Jarrah, Karri, Sandalwood in forests, forestry, forest parks and reserves for 33 years. He is a driving force for the adoption of Esperanto as a common language in education of inter-cultural communication in all schools, for the transfer of skills and of knowledge and of the development of all understanding, especially of harmony and peace for our children and for humanity.

Following 3½ years of war service and five years of academia, Mr Loneragan was privileged to study the gestalten pattern of the indigenous pristine jarrah and karri forests of southwest Western Australia. He observed the majestic aura of the observable ecological phenomena having, in addition to their separate parts, their integration into plant societies and of whole living habitat formations. Consequently and subsequently, he became dedicated to what is becoming known as a "Strategy for Sustainable Living". This is being developed from the World Conservation Strategy II 1990: Reference – Koeyers, J Snr (1993); (1992) – United Nations Association of Australia submission on Treaty on Alternative Economic Models of the International Forum of Non-Government Organisations and Social Movement, Rio de Janeiro, June 05. The environmental debts imposed by rich people and rich countries on Planet Earth still require outstanding payments for their solutions.

The World Conservation Strategy recognises the limitations of the resource base of spaceship Earth for sustaining healthy, life-supporting habitats. Ever-increasing rates of change being caused by the demands of the economy are being wrought in the effects upon the environment. People fall well behind the necessary price to pay for the management costs to prevent and cure their own abuse or pollution and effects upon others.

Healthy habitats in natural systems are sustained in equilibrium by Nature's regulatory mechanisms of checks and feedback, controlling the observed ecological balances and the unseen steady states of change (within and between societies in Nature's successions of surviving climax formations). When a limited value of one effective factor in a stable system is exceeded (by too much or by too little; Daubenmire, E F, 1947), a disorder occurs in the whole system. Examples in Australia include desertification and salination, following too much removal of tree cover. Thus we see that factors of the environment, which appear not to be limiting in the short term, become the limiting factors for sustaining a healthy ecosystem in the long-term period of management.

Steady-states of populations and of economics (Daly 1986; 1991), require valuation of the benefits and uses of the resources (UN General Assembly Doc A/CONF.151/PC/27, p17-20 IV Economic Value of Forests, 1991; Landquist, 1992) and limits to these values are identified and defined by a set of measurable indicators - the classification and measurement of these criteria systematically (as direct values and as indirect, optional, opportunity or replacement values). The desirable regulatory mechanisms to establish a conventional range of freedom of operations between the allowable limits of maxima and minima, will improve the existing situation. State boundaries in Australia, however, are obstacles to solution of problems. Organisation or re-organisation, with creation of centralised policies and of decentralised operations to achieve satisfactory performance of outcomes with change, require adequate feedback information data on the regulatory mechanisms.

DEDICATIONS

Policies created by decision-makers and specialists require strategies for their management by the local authorities. When advertising products for example, legislation could require for each dollar spent persuading people to buy, that it ought to be balanced by another dollar paid to a responsible local authority in order for it to provide environmental amenities in safety, health and occupation for the local community – and in addition, for when advertising health hazard products, an extra dollar for dollar ought to be paid towards hospital costs being borne by the community. Every person should be able to perceive for her/himself an opportunity to be a valuable contributing member of society; communication is the beginning of all understanding, intercultural communication the development of all understanding. There should be reasonable equity, not necessarily equality in goods, but equality in services and togetherness in satisfactory performance, as perceived by the majority of members of the society. Using a common language for inter-cultural communication will enhance vertical and lateral communication within and among communities and advance the transfer of skills and knowledge, and understanding, thus benefiting humanity.

The language we speak tends to unite us with those who speak it and divide us from those who do not - a common language (Esperanto) is a facilitator for peace (Aldridge et al, c1986). Esperanto is precise, has phonetic spelling (one letter, one sound) and having regular grammar is relatively easier to learn and understand than other languages. Although most of its vocabulary comes from European origin, the way it is put together has similarities with some major Asian languages. The Esperanto language lives as a mutual world aid network for inter-cultural communication and development of all understanding. To introduce intercultural communication and share understanding among people with the common language Esperanto will facilitate advancement of harmony and peace.

Its teachings, envisaged by the Baha'i Cause in seeking world unity, are summed up in a set of ten principles and offered as a basis for a new civilisation (Sohrab et al, 1962). As well as the spiritual solution of the economic problem (cited as principle 8) we now have creative outcomes of the principles of steady-state populations and of economics (generated by the then senior environmental economist of the World Bank, Herman E Daly, introduced above): these innovations, still being ignored by decision-makers in governments and industries (to conceal and perpetuate concealment of economic reality, Galbraith, 1991) are forever vital for prevention and suppression of mistreatment or abuse of people and of the environment in both peace and war (Kidron and Smith, 1983; Suter, 1985; Koeyers, 1993).

In conclusion, Mr Loneragan makes the recommendation for advancement of a vision and mission by means of a strategy, summarising the above requirements for our leaders, with courage, integrity and innovation, to achieve sustainable living and survival of our living planet Earth (Ferencz and Keyes Jr, 1988). Thinking how authorities might maximise society's welfare in the key areas of economics, politics, the law, training and education, (brought up in relation to motivation for innovation, and to diplomacy with integrity, for example), his summary on the theme of "A Strategy for Sustainable Living" reads –

1. Economics and development activities are degrading the world environment and currently, these processes and Planet Earth are not sustainable.
2. Sustainable activities will require governments and industries to agree to implementing and developing sustainable policies.
3. Regulatory mechanisms are required to establish a range of freedom of operations between the sustainable maximum and minimum production of goods and population, for sustainable living.

4. A common world auxiliary language (Esperanto) will facilitate all understanding of the development of sustainable policies and activities.
5. How changes might clarify decision-making and aid implementation is suggested.

References:

Aldridge, W R, Professor Adcock, C J and Dr Rogers, D E (c1986) – Esperanto in Peace Education, Wellington Pilot Scheme Proposal, New Zealand

Daly, H E (1986) – Population: Toward a new economic model, Bulletin of the Atomic Scientists, April

Daly, H E (1991) – Sustainable Development is possible only if we Forego Growth, United Nations Development Forum, Sep-Oct

Daubenmire, E F (1947) – "Plants and Environment", Wiley, NY, USA

Ferencz, B B and Keyes, K Jr (1988) – "PlanetHood: The key to your survival and prosperity" 190p, Vision Books, Coos Bay, California, USA

Galbraith, J K (1991) – Essay: The Sting of Truth, Scientific American p96, May

Kidron M and Smith D (1983) – "The War Atlas: Armed Conflict and Armed Peace", Pluto Press, (Dymocks Books)

Koeyers, J E Snr (1993) – The Rio Report, 46p, United Nations Association of Australia, Western Australia Inc, Perth

Landquist, S (1992) – Submission to Inquiry into Australia's Relationship with the World Bank and the International Money Fund, UNAA (WA) Perth, March 20

Sohrab M A and Miller J A (1962) – Baha'i Cause, "Collier's Encyclopaedia" p461/462, Cromwell-Collier Publishing Co, USA, GB

Suter, K D (1985) – Peaceworking: The United Nations and Disarmament, 188p, United Nations Association of Australia, Sydney

Recommendation for Advancement of a Vision, by Means of a Mission and a Strategy to Advance Concordance of Harmony and Peace:

A. Have a vision of Parliaments of Concordance, each having a majority of members, working in the same direction of benevolent goodwill and endeavour – as World Peace and Diplomacy Forum of the International Biographical Centre, Cambridge, England – for the advancement of democratic governments and of "we the peoples of the United Nations organisation".

B. Hope in Friendship/Fellowship, Harmony and Peace Foundation is a mission identified and defined in the systemised knowledge of the world language, Esperanto. Esperanto has an essential scientific significance for achieving easier understanding of languages and for advancement of enjoyment of harmonious interdependence towards peace in the long term, in service to our children in schools, communities and humanity: Reference Loneragan Owen (2003) – United Nations Association of Australia (Western Australia) Business and Development Plan Languages, UN Matters Issue 224 – Winter, P 1-3 Perth, Western Australia.

C. Aim to live by creative laws for advancement of healthy sustainable habitats, not subject to arbitrary and unpredictable whims of humans. This means that decision-makers and the law, with aid of education and training, have essential roles in the prevention and suppression of every kind of abuse, aiming towards a steady state of economics and of population, incorporating equity and justice, as well as the beneficial rights of personal freedom.

In conclusion, Mr Loneragan writes: "Instead of continuing a downward trend to world devastation, through insufficient insight and want of will to identify, define and achieve ecological dependent and interdependent laws of Nature for "Sustainable Living", we require to aspire to work together in a world auxiliary language towards a healthy, steady-state climax of creative evolution." He is dedicated to "we the peoples of the United Nations" living by creative laws for ecological sustainable habitats, and to the value-added skills of the essential scientific significance of the world auxiliary language, Esperanto, for the building of world peace as the ultimate outcome along future pathways, including human rights with acceptance of responsibilities for each other's well-being in social justice in service to the world's children, community and to humanity."

A biography of Owen William Loneragan, DDG appears in the main section of this edition.

DEMETRIOS ZENO PIERIDES
For your Outstanding Contribution to
Arts and Culture

DEMETRIOS ZENO PIERIDES

Demetrios Zeno Pierides is president of the Pierides Foundation. He was born on 30 June 1937 in Cyprus and is the father of one son.

Following his studies at the University of Lausanne, Switzerland between 1956-60, Mr Pierides earned his BSc in Economics. In the course of his career, he has held the position of companies chairman in a total of 38 shipping, travel, hotel and insurance companies, as well as his current position of president of the Pierides Foundation (responsible for 13 museums and art galleries in Cyprus and Greece). Mr Pierides is also vice president of the University of Cyprus and a director of the Bank of Cyprus in Nicosia and Athens.

Mr Pierides has won recognition for his work and as a result holds many honours and awards. He is a Knight First Class of the Royal Order of VASA and a Commander of the Royal Order of Polar Star of Sweden. He has also been awarded the Academy of Athens Highest Award, the Gold Medal of Republic of Cyprus and the title of Governor of the European Cultural Foundation. In France, Mr Pierides is a Commander of Arts and Letters and a Commander of National Order of Merit. He holds a Doctor Honoris Causa presented by the Faculty of Philosophy of the University of Athens and is a Commander of Order of Merit, Italy, has a Gold Medal from the Municipality of Larnaca, Cyprus and a Gold Cross Order of Honour, Greece.

A biography of Demetrios Zeno Pierides appears in the main section of this edition.

DR KUNITOMO SATO
MD PhD DDG CH MOIF
DO AdVMed
For your Outstanding Contribution to
Medicine, Peace, Arts and Welfare

DR KUNITOMO SATO, MD, PhD, DDG, CH, MOIF, DO, AdVMed

Kunitomo Sato was born on 19 August 1954 in Osaka, Japan. He was educated at the National University of Osaka, graduating the Medical Department in 1978.

Dr Sato joined the Cardiovascular division of the National Osaka University Hospital in 1978, and continues to work there today. The following year, 1979, Dr Sato became Chief "of the Sakurabashi-Watanabe Hospital", and then he was made the president of the North-Osaka Hospital and General Kanoh Hospital in 1980. Dr Sato has been both the chancellor and president of Kunitomo Hospital Cardiac Transplantation Centre in Kyusyu at the same time. He went ahead and researched cardiac transplantation during his 7 years in the USA.

As a professional author, Dr Sato has published numerous books including "Sudden Death Occurs at the Most Powerful and Fruitful Age" (1988). He has also written over 500 articles including: "Clinical Significance of Human Plasma ANP, BNP measurement medical – current and future prospectives", "The first discovery of the therapies of Blood-White-Garland syndrome after 200 years from the first publication in 1733", "To live or not to live depends on the selection of your doctor" and "There is a key to save your life in this book!". A winner of many honours and awards, the doctor has most recently won the Testimonial of Life Senator of the World Nations Congress, and been listed in both Leading Intellectuals of the World and 2000 Outstanding Intellectuals of the 21st Century. Dr Sato is a member of the Japan Medical Society, who have awarded him their Distinguished Service Medal. He also belongs to the SCTS-JC, PPSA-JC, ASH/AHA, WNC, PPG inner circle, the Japan Circulation Society, the Heart Rehabilitation Society, and the Japan Internal Medicine Society. In 2004 he was distinguished as an Honorary Citizen of the City of Kawanishi by the Mayor, Mr Susuma Shibao.

A biography of Dr Kunitomo Sato, MD, PhD,DDG, CH, MOIF, DO, AdVMed appears in the main section of this edition.

DR. TROY A. SMITH

For your Outstanding Contribution to
Numerical Analysis of Shells

DR TROY ALVIN SMITH

Troy Alvin Smith is an Aerospace Research Engineer. He was born the son of Wade Hampton and Augusta Mabel (Lindsey) Smith on 4 July 1922 in Sylvatus, Virginia, USA. He graduated from Sylvatus High School on 24 May 1940 as class valedictorian. On 24 November 1990 he married Grace Marie Peacock.

Dr Smith served in the US Navy Reserve in the Pacific Theatre of Operations between 1942-46. The naval unit with which he was serving was awarded the Presidential Unit Citation for naval action during the Battle of Leyte Gulf on 23-26 October 1944. At the end of World War II, he returned to his studies in engineering at the University of Virginia and was awarded the earned BCE degree by the University of Virginia in June 1948.

Dr Smith was employed as a civilian Structural Engineer with the Corps of Engineers of the US Army during the period from 1948-59. During the period from June 1951 to June 1952 he pursued graduate study at the University of Michigan from which he was awarded the MSE degree in June 1952. He was employed as Chief Structural Engineer of Brown Engineering Company Inc, Huntsville, Alabama for one year during 1959-60. He was employed as a Structural Research Engineer with the US Army Missile Command, Redstone Arsenal, Alabama from 1960-63, as an Aerospace Engineer from 1963-80, and as an Aerospace Research Engineer from 1980-96. Throughout his career, Dr Smith has continued his studies, earning his PhD degree in Engineering Mechanics at the University of Michigan, which was awarded in May 1970.

Since November 1996, Dr Smith has served as an Aerospace Engineer Emeritus with the US Army Aviation and Missile Command, Redstone Arsenal, Alabama. He has been a Registered Professional Engineer in Virginia since 1948 and in Alabama since 1959. Dr Smith has published 14 major US Army technical reports on analysis of shells and other structures as well as articles in the AIAA Journal and the Journal of Sound and Vibration on analysis of shells. His doctoral dissertation was entitled "Numerical Solution for the Dynamic Response of Rotationally Symmetric Shells of Revolution under Transient Loadings". Dr Smith is a member of Sigma Xi, the New York Academy of Sciences, and the Association of the US Army. He has received honours for his achievements, and in 1969 was awarded a Secretary of the Army Research and Study Fellowship for Graduate Study at the University of Michigan.

A biography of Dr Troy Alvin Smith appears in the main section of this edition.

BETTY IRENE PARHAM STINES

*For your Outstanding Contribution as a
Professional Artist and for Encouraging
Creativeness in Art in Young People*

BETTY IRENE (PARHAM) STINES

Betty Irene (Parham) Stines was born on 3 May 1918 in Stinesville, Indiana, USA. She is a professional artist. From her marriage to Willard Russell Elliott, Ms Stines has a son and two daughters. Following her first husband's death, she married Edmond Glen Stines.

During the 1940s and 1950s Ms Stines was a Brownie Scout leader and a Sunday School teacher in Ellettsville, Indiana, and then worked in the Unique Florist Shoppe as a floral designer between 1963-69. At this time, she also served as chairman and co-chairman of Art Exhibits at the Monroe County Fall Festival in Ellettsville. From 1964 until 1980, Ms Stines was an organiser and member of the Hoosier Hills Art Guild, serving as recording secretary, organiser of the Annual Student Art Exhibit, and on the Board of Directors.

Between 1952-2002, Ms Stines took part in many art exhibitions at Indiana University, Manchester College, Hoosier Hills Art Gallery, Owen County Art Guild and Swope Art Gallery. Numerous photographs and articles about her exhibitions and paintings have been published, such as her mural for the First Baptist Church in Ellettsville in the Bloomington Herald Telephone Newspaper (1949). News of her work has also been reported by the Ellettsville Journal (opening of First Fall Festival Art Show) and the Bloomington Herald Telephone (photograph and article of Officers and Directors of Hoosier Hills Art Guild planning for the Grand Opening of the new Art Gallery, 1964). The Ellettsville Journal also printed a photograph and article of the presentation of her painting to the Indiana Gas and Water Company by Ellettsville Chamber of Commerce.

In honour of her achievements, Ms Stines has received many first prizes in Juried Art Shows, as well as Best of Show and Champion Exhibitor awards. In 1967 she was presented with a Certificate of Award as an Exhibitor of Fine Arts at the State House Salon, Indianapolis. Her biographical details are listed in Who's Who publications and biographical dictionaries. Ms Stines is a member of the First Baptist Church in Ellettsville, Indiana and belongs to the National Museum of Women in the Arts, Washington DC.

A biography of Betty Irene (Parham) Stines appears in the main section of this edition.

SONIA VIKTORIA WANNER AdVAh
For your Outstanding Contribution to the Field of Fine Arts

PROFESSOR SONIA VIKTORIA WANNER, AdVAh

Artist in Fine Art, Sonia Wanner was born on 15 March 1931 in Gothenburg, Sweden, one of the largest harbours in Scandinavia. She is married to Sigvard Ulf and they have two sons.

Between 1976-94, Sonia Wanner worked at the Chalmers University of Technology and Architecture in Gothenburg. During her career she has taken part in more than 100 exhibitions in Sweden, Norway, Paris, Geneva, Vienna, Innsbrück, Seoul, Beirut, Monte Carlo, Los Angeles and New York.

At an early age Sonia Wanner came into contact with the sea and learnt to love and respect the majesty of the waves in the stormy surroundings of the harbour where she often found herself, and on board small sailing vessels owned by her family. Because of many challenges during her upbringing, she learnt early on how to stand on her own feet. This has proven to be a valuable quality in her fight for a top position as an artist. Another quality that has been an asset is her unbounded sense of humour, the kind by which the people of Gothenburg are well known. Although living in a modern world, she has been pleased to find that the classic style of art she represents is appealing to most art lovers. A sample of her work can be found at her website (www.wanner.net).

She has received many honours and awards including a scholarship by Eva Ljungqvist's Scholarship Fund in 1992 and a Diploma from International Professional Women. As a result of a successful career, Sonia Wanner has earned the right to be listed in national and international biographical publications. She is mentioned in "2000 Outstanding Artists and Designers in the 20th Century" and the "Dictionary of International Biography, 29th Edition". Her details also appear in the "Dictionary of Swedish Artists, Sweden", "Who's Who in International Art, Switzerland", "Who's Who in Professionals and Business Women" and Dizionario Enciclopedico Intenazionale d'Arte Moderna e Contemporanea. Sonia Wanner has received the honour of entry into the Hall of Fame for outstanding achievements in the Field of Fine Arts.

In her professional capacity, Sonia Wanner is a member of a number of organisations including West Sweden Chamber of Commerce and Industry, the Swedish Artist Association, the Swedish Artist Federation and the Linos School of New York and Verona, the Regional Resource Centre for Women's Work and Development in Western Sweden and the Women's Art Library in London. She also belongs to the Metropolitan Museum of Art, New York; the National Museum of Women in the Arts, Washington; the Federation Nationale de la Culture Francaise; and the Accademia Internazionale "Greci-Marino" Accademia del Verbano di Lettere, Arti, Scienze, Italy.

A biography of Professor Sonia Viktoria Wanner, AdVAh, appears in the main section of this edition.

Biographies

Dictionary of International Biography

A

AARFLOT Rolf Ove Bertil Andreas, b. 9 July 1919, Norrköping, Sweden. Headmaster; Captain. m. Ingrid Lyttkens, 16 December 1950, 1 son, 1 daughter. Education: MSc, Academy of War. Appointments: Second Lieutenant, 1943; Lieutenant, 1946; Captain, 1951; Master, secondary school, 1955; Headmaster, secondary school, 1964. Publications: Newspaper articles, Something About the Lundell Secondary School, 1984; The Jubilee Book of the Lundell School, 1992. Honour: Knight of the Order of Northern Star, 1972. Memberships: Southern Rotary Club of Uppsala; Tennis Club of Uppsala; Principal of the Road Association at Kolstad. Address: Tiundag 41, 75230 Uppsala, Sweden.

AARON Larry Gene, b. 10 October 1945, Danville, Virginia, USA. Teacher; Minister; Writer. m. Nancy Cody Ikenberry, 1 son, 2 daughters. Education: BSc, Virginia Tech, 1968; Bachelor of Religious Education, Midwestern Baptist College, 1974; Master of Divinity, Liberty University, 1986; Doctor of Ministry, Luther Rice Seminary, 1999. Appointments: Chairman, Science Department, Chatham High School, Tightsqueeze, Virginia; Adjunct Faculty, National College of Business and Technology, Danville Branch, Danville, Virginia. Publications: Race to the Dan, cover article for Sons of the American Revolution national magazine; Associate editor and writer, EVINCE magazine. Honours: First Place, Feature Writing Series, Virginia Press Association, 2001, 2003. Memberships: Society of Protozoologists; Danville Museum of Fine Arts and History. Address: 185 Martindale Drive, Danville, VA 24541, USA.

ABADJIEV Valentin Ivanov, b. 8 September 1946, Razgrad, Bulgaria. Associate Professor in Applied Mechanics. m. Evdokia Nikolova, 1 daughter. Education: MSc, Mechanical Engineering, University of Rousse, Rousse, 1970; PhD, Applied Mechanics, Bulgarian Academy of Sciences, Sofia, 1985. Appointments: Research Fellow, Institute Motors/Cars, Sofia, 1972-83; Assistant Professor, 1983-88, Associate Professor, 1988-, Institute of Mechanics, Bulgarian Academy of Sciences; Chairman of Board of Directors, Education/Science Co, Sofia, 1997-2000. Publications: Author, co-author, over 70 scientific publications of applied mechanics; 1 book; 19 Bulgarian patents. Honours: National Medal for Inventions, State Committee of Science, 1987; 3rd Competitive Session Science Award, Ministry of Education and Science, 1997. Memberships: Steering Committee of Bulgarian Union of Standardization, 2001-; National Technical Committee Standardization, 1993-; Science Council Institute Mechanics, 1993-; Regional Municipal Council, Sofia, 1994-99; High Testimonial Committee, Special Science Council, 1998-; Board of Directors, Education/Science Co, 1997-2002. Address: Institute of Mechanics, Bulgarian Academy of Sciences, Academic G Bonchev Str, Bl 4, 1113 Sofia, Bulgaria. E-mail: abadjiev@imbm.bas.bg

ABBADO Claudio, b. 26 June 1933, Milan, Italy. Conductor. Education: Giuseppe Verdi Conservatory, Milan; Academy of Music, Vienna, with Hans Swabarowsky. Debut: La Scala, Milan, 1960, in concert celebrating tercentenary of A Scarlatti; Salzburg Festival, 1965, local premiere of G Manzoni's opera Atomtod. Career: Conducted opening of La Scala season, 1967; Music Director, La Scala, 1968-86; Covent Garden debut, 1968 (Don Carlos); Has conducted the Vienna Philharmonic Orchestra from 1972; Tour of USA with Cleveland and Philadelphia Orchestras, 1972; Tour with La Scala company to Munich, 1972; USSR, 1974; London 1976 (Simon Boccanegra); USA, 1976; Japan, 1981; Tour with the Vienna Philharmonic to Japan and China, 1973; Founder, European Community Youth Orchestra, 1978; Musical Director, London Symphony Orchestra, 1979-88 (series of concerts, Mahler, Vienna and the 20th Century, 1985); Principal Conductor, Chamber Orchestra of Europe, 1981; Founder of La Filharmonica della Scala, 1982; Principal Guest Conductor of Chicago Symphony Orchestra, 1982-85; Debut at the Vienna State Opera, 1984; Director, 1986-91; Founder, Gustav Mahler Jugendorchester, Vienna, 1986; Conductor, New Year's Eve concerts, Vienna, 1988 and 1990; Appointed Musical Director and Principal Conductor, Berlin Philharmonic Orchestra, 1989-2002; Promenade Concerts, London, 1991, with the Gustav Mahler Jugendorchester (5th Symphony) and the Berlin Philharmonic (Brahms 2nd Piano Concerto and Mahler 4); Conductor, The House of the Dead, Salzburg Festival, 1992; Bruckner's 5th Symphony with the Gustav Mahler Youth Orchestra, Promenade Concerts, 1993; La Scala, 1994, Il Barbiere di Siviglia; Artistic Director, Salzburg Easter Festival, 1994; Engaged to conduct Tristan und Isolde at Salzburg, 1999; Founder, Lucern Festival Orchestra, 2001. Recordings include: Operas by Rossini and Verdi, Mussorgsky, Berg, Schubert (Fierabras); Music by Berg and Nono; Complete Symphonies of Mahler, Schubert, Mendelssohn, Beethoven and Tchaikovsky; Mozart Piano Concertos with Rudolf Serkin; Brahms Piano Concerto No 1, with Brendel and Vivaldi's Four Seasons, with Viktoria Mullova; Works of Haydn and Prokofiev, Bartók, Ravel, Debussy; currently working on cycle of complete Bruckner symphonies. Publication: La Casa Del Suoni: Book for Children about Music; Musica sopra Berlino, 1998, 2001; Suite Concertante from the Ballet Hawaii, 2000. Honours include: Mozart Medaille; Premio Abbiati; Officier of the French Légion d'Honneur; Koussevitzky Prize (Tanglewood); Winner, Mitropoulos Conducting Competition; Conductor of the Year, Opernwelt Review, 2000; Oscar della Lirica, 2001. Address: Berliner Philharmonisches Orchester, Matthäikirchstrasse 1, 10785 Berlin, Germany.

ABBAS Samir, b. 3 May 1947, Jeddah, Saudi Arabia. Director. m. Omayma, 2 sons, 2 daughters. Education: MBBCH, MS, Cairo, Egypt; FICS, FRCOG, England. Appointments: Professor, Obstetrics and Gynaecology, King Abdulaziz University, Jeddah; Pioneer of infertility treatment in the Middle East since 1984. Publications: Over 120 in professional journals. Memberships: President, Saudi Fertility Society; ESHRE; SDGS; MEFS. Address: Al-Iqtesad International Tower, Wali Al-Ahad Street, PO Box 12190, Jeddah 21473, Saudi Arabia. E-mail: samirabbas@yahoo.com

ABBASI Shahid Abbas, b. 6 June 1950, Khilchipur, India. University Professor. m. Naseema Abbasi, 3 daughters. Education: MS, Miami, 1972; PhD, 1976; DSc, 1987; Professional Engineer; Chartered Engineer; Diploma in Environmental Engineering, Tokyo. Appointments: Head, Water Quality and Environment Division, Centre for Water Resources, 1979-87; Visiting Professor, California State University, 1984-87; Senior Professor, Director, Centre for Pollution Control and Energy Technology, 1987-. Publications: 27 Books; 300 Technical Papers. Honours: $20000 Prize, International Desalination Association, New York; National Hydrology Award; Gold Medal, International Energy Conference; IPCL Award on Industrial Safety; IIChE National Award on Risk Assessment; S K Seth Prize; Nawab Zen Yar Jung Medal. Memberships: National Productivity Organisation; FIE; FIPHE; FIAH; FIEE; FIIChE. Address: Centre for Pollution Control and Energy Technology, Pondicherry University, Kalapet, Pondicherry 605 014, India.

ABBASS Isah Mohammed, b. 27 September 1957, Zaria, Nigeria. Political Economist. m. Binta, 5 daughters. Education: BA, History/Political Science, 1981, PGD Public Administration, 1984; MSc, Political Science, 1990, PhD, Political Economy, 1997, Ahmadu Bello University, Zaria, Nigeria. Appointments: Education

Officer, Ministry of Education, Bauchi State and Kaduna State, 1981-82; Master Grade II, 1982-85, Master Grade I, 1985-86, Barewa College Zaria, Kaduna State Ministry of Education; Lecturer II, 1986-88, Lecturer I, 1988-92, Senior Lecturer, 1992-96, Principal Lecturer, 1996-98, Chief Lecturer, 1998, Kaduna Polytechnic; Lecturer, Department of Political Science, Ahmadu Bello University, 1998; Registrar and Secretary to the Council, Petroleum Training Institute, Delta State, Nigeria, 1998-. Publications: 5 book chapters include: Towards a Rational Understanding of the Problems of Education in Zaria, 2003; ZEDA: A Decade of Challenge and Accomplishments 1992-2002, 2003; Gender Differential and the Role of Women in Irrigated Agriculture, forthcoming; Numerous seminar, conference and workshop papers and contributions to newspapers; Reports: The Demise of Education in Kaduna State, 1994; Memorandum on the Request for the Creation of Zazzau State. Honours include: Distinguished Merit Award, Society of Petroleum Engineers, 2002; Meritorious Award, Zeda Board of Trustees, 2002; Ashvale Challenge Certificate of Achievement, Aberdeen, Scotland, 2003; Highest and Most Distinguished Awards, Honorary fellowship, Fellowship Certificate, Award of Excellence, Institute of Administrative Management, Nigeria, 2003; Certificate of Academic Excellence Award, Electrical/Electronic Engineering Department, Petroleum Training Institute, 2003; Honorary Doctorate, The Marlborough University, USA, 2003. Memberships: Marlborough University Graduate Association; Institute of Administrative Management, Nigeria; Institute of Petroleum/Energy Institute, London; Institute of Management Consultants; Society of Educational Administrators of Nigeria; Nigerian Safety Association; Institute of Personnel Management of Nigeria; Nigeria Institute of Management. Address: Petroleum Training Institute, PMB 20, Effurun, Delta State, Nigeria.

ABBOTT Aloris, b. 22 July 1931, Maynard, Minnesota, USA. Nurse; Administrator. m. Roy L Abbott, 1987, 2 daughters. Education: Diploma, Broadlawns School Nursing, Des Moines, 1952; Certified Operating Room Nurse; Certified Nursing Administrator. Appointments: Head Nurse, Iowa Methodist Center, Des Moines; Private Scrub Nurse, Des Moines; Head Nurse, Operating Room and Recovery Room, Nursing Co-ordinator Operating Room, Operating Room and Recovery Room Co-ordinator, Virginia Medical Center, Des Moines; Retired, 1991. Memberships: Advisory Board, Des Moines Area Community College; Board of Directors, Council on Nursing Administration; ANA; Association Operating Room Nurses; Nurses Organisation, Virginia. Address: 3519 Crestmoor Pl, Des Moines, IA 50310-4322, USA.

ABD AL-MEGUID Ahmed Esmat, b. 22 March 1923, Alexandria, Egypt. Diplomatist. m. Eglal Abou-Hamda, 1950, 3 sons. Education: Faculty of Law, Alexandria; University of Paris; PhD. Appointments: Attaché, Secretary, Egyptian Embassy, London; Head, British Desk, 1954-56, Assistant Director, Legal Department, 1961-63, Head, Cultural and Technical Assistance Department, 1967-68, Ministry of Foreign Affairs, Cairo; Counsellor, Permanent Mission to United Nations European Office, Geneva, 1957-61; Minister Counsellor, Egyptian Embassy, Paris, 1963-67; Official Spokesman of Government and Head of Information Department, 1968-69; Ambassador to France, 1969-70; Minister of State for Cabinet Affairs, 1970-72; Head, Permanent Delegation to United Nations, 1972-82; Chairman, Cairo Preparatory Conference for Geneva Peace Conference, 1977; Minister of Foreign Affairs, 1984-91; Deputy Prime Minister, 1985-91; Secretary-General, League of Arab States, 1991-2001; Private law practice, 2001-; Director, Cairo International Arbitration Centre; Participant, United Nations Conferences on Law of the Sea, 1959, Consular Relations, 1963, Law of Treaties, 1969.

Publications: Several articles in Revue Egyptienne de Droit International. Honours: Decorated, 1967, Grand Croix, 1971, Ordre National du Mérite, Egypt; First Class Decoration, Arab Republic of Egypt, 1970; Numerous foreign decorations. Memberships: Politbureau; National Democratic Party; International Law Association; Advisory Council, Institute for International Studies. Address: 78 El Nile Street, Apt 23, Giza, Egypt.

ABD-ELMOTAAL Hussein, b. 7 October 1960, Cairo, Egypt. Professor. m. R Abd-Elkader, 1 son, 1 daughter. Education: BSc, Ain Shams University, Egypt, 1983; MSc, Ain Shams University, Egypt, 1987; PhD, Graz University of Technology, Austria, 1991. Appointments: Professor of Surveying and Geodesy & Head, Civil Engineering Department, Faculty of Engineering, Minia University. Honour: International Association of Geodesy, Best Paper Award, 1993. Membership: Member, International Association of Geodesy. Address: Civil Engineering Department, Faculty of Engineering, Minia University, 61111 Minia, Egypt.

ABDEL AZIZ Samir Fouad, b. 26 March 1957, Cairo, Egypt. Assistant Professor. m. Iman AbdelRhman Ismail, 1 son, 2 daughters. Education: MBBch, 1982, Master Ob/Gyn, 1986, Al Azhar Faculty of Medicine; Md, Al Azhar University, 1992. Appointments: Resident Ob/Gyn, 1984-87, Assistant Lecturer, 1987-92, Lecturer, consultant, 1993-98, Assistant Professor, 1998-, Assistant Professor, 1998-2003, Professor, 2003-, Al Azhar. Memberships: International Gynecologic Cancer Society; World Oncology Network; President, www.arubicobgyn.net. Address: 10 Shazly Street, El Naam, Helmiat El Zeitoun, Cairo, Egypt.

ABDEL-HALIM Ibrahim, b. 3 December 1946, Cairo, Egypt. Professor of Engineering. m. Ragaa Abdel-Kader Mahmoud. Education: BSc, Electric Power and Machines, Ain-Shams University, Cairo, Egypt, 1968; MSc, Electrical Engineering, Cairo University, Egypt, 1973; PhD, Electrical Engineering, Loughborough University of Technology, England, 1978. Appointments: Professor of Electric Machines, Power Electronics and Electric Drives, 1985, Head of Electrical Engineering Department, 1981-83, 1991-95, 2000-02, Vice Dean (Post Graduate Studies), 2002-, Consultant, Electric Drives, 1993-, Zagazig University, Benha Branch, Egypt. Consultant, Electric Drives. Publications: Over 53 scientific papers published in local Egypt and International Conferences and Journals. Honours: State Prize in Engineering, Egypt, 1992; Medal of Excellence, 1st Class from the President of Egypt, 1995. Listed in: Biographical Publications. Memberships: Fellow of the Institution of Electrical Engineers (FIEE), London, England. Address: 13 Ady (Ali Ismail), off El-Tahir Street, El-Dokki, Giza 12311, Egypt. E-mail: iamabd@link.net

ABDEL-MOGIB Mamdouh, b. 24 April 1959, Dakahlia, Egypt. Professor. m. Hanaa M Raghib, 2 sons, 1 daughter. Education: BSc Chemistry with distinction, 1981, MSc, Organic Chemistry, 1986, Mansoura University; PhD, Organic Chemistry through a Channel System between Technical University of Berlin and Mansoura University, awarded by Mansoura University, 1990. Appointments: Administrator, 1981-86, Assistant Lecturer, 1986-1990, Lecturer in Organic Chemistry, 1990-94, Chemistry Department, Faculty of Science, Mansoura University; On loan as Associate Professor, Chemistry Department, Faculty of Science, King Abdulaziz University, Saudi Arabia, 1994-2004. Publications: About 50 articles most of them in the field of isolation and structure elucidation of natural products; 2 reviews, 2 books. Honours: Channel System Scholarship between TU Berlin and Mansoura University 1988-90; One month award from Institute of Organic Chemistry, TU Berlin, 1992; Listed in Who's Who publications and biographical dictionaries. Memberships: Egyptian Scientificans' Syndicate, 1981; Club Member of Chemweb.com, 1999-; New York Academy of Sciences, 2000-. Address: Chemistry Department, Faculty of Science, Mansoura University, Mansoura 35516, Mansoura, Egypt. E-mail: mamdouh_m@hotmail.com

ABDEL-RAHIM Muddathir, b. 19 July 1932, Ad-Damar, Sudan. University Professor; Former Ambassador. m. Zaynab Muhammad Badri, 5 sons, 3 daughters. Education: BA, Economics, History and Arabic, University of London, England, 1955; BA (First Class Hons), Politics, University of Nottingham, England, 1958; PhD, Economic and Social Studies (Government), University of Manchester, England, 1964. Appointments: Lecturer in Government, Manchester University, 1960-65; Senior Lecturer then Professor, University of Khartoum, Sudan, 1965-70, 1980-88; Visiting Professor, Temple University, Philadelphia, USA, 1984-85; Vice Chancellor, Omdurman Islamic University, Sudan, 1988-91; Professor, International Institute of Islamic Thought and Civilization, Kuala Lumpur, Malaysia, 1997-. Publications include: Imperialism and Nationalism in the Sudan, 1969; The Problem of the Southern Sudan (in Arabic), 1970; Editor: Human Rights in Theory and Practice (in Arabic), 1968; Islam in The Sudan, 1988; Islam in Africa, 2001. Honours: Listed in Who's Who in the World. Memberships include: International Institute for Strategic Studies, London; Jordanian Royal Academy, Amman; Academy of Arabic Language, Khartoum; American Association of Sudanese Studies. Address: International Institute of Islamic Thought and Civilization, 205A, Jalan Damansara, Damansara Heights, 50480 Kuala Lumpur, Malaysia.

ABDEL-SALAM Omar E, b. 29 March 1947, Egypt. Professor. m. Amany M Rashaad, 1 son, 2 daughters. Education: BS, 1968, MS, 1973, Chemical Engineering, Cairo University; PhD, University of Missouri-Columbia, USA, 1976. Appointments: Faculty Member, 1968-, Professor, 1987-, Cairo University; Research Associate, University of Missouri-Columbia, 1976-78; Sabbatical to Al-Fateh University, Libya and University of Science and Technology, Jordan, 1983-84. Publications: Over 40 articles in journals and international conferences. Honours: State Award in Engineering Sciences, Academy of Scientific Research, 1984; Presidential Administration Medallion of 1st Degree in Arts and Science, 1985, Egypt. Memberships: Egyptian Engineering Syndicate; Egyptian Society of Chemical Engineers; Egyptian Society for Metallic Corrosion. Address: Chemical Engineering Department, Cairo University, Giza, Cairo, Egypt.

ABDOULAYE Souley, Politician; Business Executive. Appointments: Formerly Banker; Minister of Commerce, Transport and Tourism, Niger, 1993-94; Prime Minister of Niger, 1994-95; Minister of Transport, 1996. Memberships: Convention Démocratique et Social-Rahana. Address: c/o Ministry of Transport, Niamey, Niger.

ABDUL Paula, b. 19 June 1963, Los Angeles, California, USA. Singer; Dancer; Choreographer. Education: Television and Radio Studies, Cal State, Northridge College. Musical Education: Studied jazz and tap dance. Career: Choreographer, LA Laker basketball cheerleaders; Scenes in films: Bull Durham; Coming To America; The Waiting Game; Appeared in a Saturday Night Live sketch with David Duchovny. Choreographer, pop videos including: The Jacksons and Mick Jagger: Torture; George Michael: Monkey; with Janet Jackson: Nasty; When I Think Of You; What Have You Done For Me Lately; Fitness video, Cardio Dance. Worldwide performances as singer include: Tours throughout US, UK, Japan and Far East; Prince's Trust Rock Gala, London Palladium, 1989; America Has Heart (earthquake and hurricane benefit concert),

1989; LIFEbeat's Counteraid (AIDS benefit concert), 1993; Own dance company, Co Dance; Judge, American Idol, 2002-03. Recordings: Solo albums: Forever Your Girl (Number 1, US), 1989; Shut Up And Dance (The Dance Mixes), 1990; Spellbound (Number 1, US), 1991; Head Over Heels, 1995; Contributor, Disney charity album For Our Children, 1991; Greatest Hits, 2000; US Number 1 singles include: Straight Up; Forever Your Girl; Cold Hearted; Opposites Attract; Rush Rush; The Promise Of A New Day. Honours: MTV Video Award, Best Choreography, Janet Jackson's Nasty, 1987; Emmy, Best Choreography, for Tracey Ullman Show, 1989; Rolling Stone Awards, including Best Female Singer, 1989; American Music Awards include: Favourite Pop/ Rock Female Vocalist, 1989, 1992; Billboard Magazine, Top Female Pop Album, 1990; Grammy, Best Music Video, Opposites Attract, 1991; Star on Hollywood Walk Of Fame, 1993; Humanitarian of the Year, Starlight Foundation, Los Angeles, 1992; Numerous Gold and Platinum discs. Address: Third Rail Entertainment, Tri-Star Bldg, 10202 W Washington Avenue, Suite 26, Culver City, CA 90232, USA.

ABDUL GHANI Abdul Aziz, b. 4 July 1939, Haifan, Republic of Yemen. Politician; Speaker of Shoora Council. m. Aceya Hamza, 5 sons, 1 daughter. Education: BA, Economics, Colorado College, USA, 1962; MA, Economics, 1964, PhD (Hon), 1978, University of Colorado, USA. Appointments: Minister of Health, 1968-69; Minister of Economy, 1970-71; Prime Minister, Yemen Arab Republic, 1975-80; Vice president, Yemen Arab Republic, 1980-83; Prime Minister, 1983-90, 1994-97; Member of Presidential Council, 1990-94; Speaker of the Shoora Council, 2001-. Publications: Many articles in local and international newspapers. Honours: Sash of Mareb, Decoration of Unity, Sash of Al Fateh, Libya; Sash of King Abdul Aziz, Saudi Arabia; Decoration of Merit, Lebanon. Memberships: Yemen Economists Society; Arab Economics Union; Arab Thought Forum; Chairman, Fulbright Alumni Association, Yemen. Address: PO Box 9671, Sana'a, Republic of Yemen. E-mail: aghani@y.net.ye website: www.shoora.go.ye

ABDULLAH IBN AL HUSSEIN (HM King), b. 30 January 1962, Amman. King of Jordan; Head of State; Army Officer. m. Rania Yassin, 1993, 1 son, 1 daughter. Education: Islamic Education College; St Edmund's School, Surrey, England; Deerfield Academy, USA; Sandhurst Military Academy; Oxford University; Advanced Study, International Affairs, School of Foreign Service, Georgetown University, Washington, 1987-88; Attended Command and Staff College, Camberley, England, 1990. Appointments: Commissioned 2nd Lieutenant, 1981; Reconnaissance Troup Leader, 13th/18th Bn, Royal Hussars (British Army), Federal Republic of Germany and England; Rank of 1st Lieutenant, 1984; Platoon Commander and Co second-in-Command, 40th Armoured Brigade, Jordan; Commander, Tank Co 91st Armoured Brigade 1985-86 (rank of Captain); Tactics Instructor, Helicopter Anti-Tank Wing, 1986-87; Commander, Co 17th Tank Battalion, 2nd Guards Brigade then Battalion 2nd in Command (rank of Major), 1989; Armour Rep, Office of the Inspector General, 1991; Commander, 2nd Armoured Car Regiment, 40th Brigade (rank of Lieutenant Colonel), 1992; Rank of Colonel, 1993; Deputy Commander, Jordanian Special Forces, 1994; Rank of Brigadier, 1994; Assumed Command of Royal Jordanian Special Forces; Commander, Special Operations Command, 1997-; President, Jordan National Football Federation; President, International Tourism Golden Rudder Society; Head, National for Committee for Tourism and Archaeological Film Production, 1997-; Succeeded to the throne 7 February 1999. Address: Royal Hashemite Court, Amman, Jordan.

Dictionary of International Biography

ABEDI Saied, b. 12 July 1966, Salmas, Iran. Principal Research Engineer. m. Sanaz Noubakhti Afshar. Education: BSc, Telecommunications, Sharif University of Technology, Tehran, Iran, 1989; MSc, Artificial Intelligence and Signal Processing, 1996, PhD, Mobile Communications, 2000, University of Surrey, England. Appointments: Research and Development Engineer, Fajre Research Company, Tehran, Iran, 1990-95; Research Fellow, Centre for Communications Systems Research, University of Surrey, England, 1998-2001; Principal Research Engineer, Fujitsu Laboratories of Europe Ltd, Hayes, Middlesex, England, 2001-. Publications: Articles in scientific journals include most recently as first author: A Genetic Multiuser Receiver for Code Division Multiple Access Communications, 2000; A New CDMA Multiuser Detection Technique Using an Evolutionary Algorithm, 2001; Genetically Modified Multiuser Detection for Code Division Multiple Access Systems, 2002; A Genetic Approach for Downlink Packet Scheduling in HSDPA System, Accepted paper; 9 papers presented at conferences; 9 UK Patents. Honours: NTL Prize for Research Excellence, 1999; Vodaphone Airtouch Prize for Research Excellence, 2000; Both these prizes were jointly awarded by a board of scientists and experts from a group of companies including: Nokia, Vodaphone, NTL, Marconi, INMARSAT and CCSR, University of Surrey. Membership: Member, IEEE. Address: Mobile Radio Technology, Fujitsu Laboratories of Europe Ltd, Hayes Park Central, Hayes End Road, Hayes, Middlesex UB4 8FE, England. E-mail: s.abedi@fle.fujitsu.com

ABEL Donald Clement, b. 26 June 1948, Pomeroy, Washington, USA. Philosophy Educator. m. Diane, 6 August 1988. Education: BA, Gonzaga University, 1971; MA, Tulane University, 1973; Licentiate, St Michael's Institute, 1975; MDiv, Loyola University, Chicago, 1979; PhD, Northwest University, 1983. Appointments: Instructor, Gonzaga University, 1973-75; Northwest University, 1981-83; Editor, Great Books Foundation, 1983-84; Assistant Professor, St Norbert College, 1984-91; Associate Professor, 1991-2000; Professor, 2000-. Publications: Freud on Instinct and Morality, 1989; Theories of Human Nature, 1992; Fifty Readings in Philosophy, 1994; Discourses: A Database of Philosophy Readings, 1994-; Human Nature, Philosophy of Education, An Encyclopedia, 1996; Elements of Philosophy: An Introduction, co-author, 2002. Honours: University Fellowship, Northwest University; Dissertation Year Fellowship; W Earl Sasser Young Professor Award; Leonard Ledvina Award for Excellence in Teaching; Donald B King Distinguished Scholarship Award. Memberships: American Philosophical Association; American Catholic Philosophical Association; Society for Ancient Greek Philosophy; Society for Philosophy and Psychology. Address: Philosophy Department, St Norbert College, 100 Grant St, De Pere, WI 54115-2099, USA.

ABEL Rajaratnam, b. 11 September 1945, Prakasapuram, India. Physician. m. Jolly, 1 son, 1 daughter. Education: MBBS (Bachelor Medicine and Surgery), 1971; MPH (Master Public Health), 1981. Appointments: Staff Physician, Seventh Day Adventist Hospitals, Banepa Nepal, Ranchi, Bihar, Poona, Maharastra and Nuzvid AP, 1971-78; Chief Medical Officer, RUHSA Programme managing Primary and Secondary health care, 1978-84; Head of RUHSA Department, Christian Medical College, Vellore (managing Health and Development), 1984-; President, ASHUR Society, 1985; Board Member and Treasurer, Nav Jeevan Seva Mandal, 1985-99; Institutional Member, State Advisory Board on Biogas, 1889; Vice President, Tamil Nadu Voluntary Health Association, 1995-99. Publications: Over 80 articles in national and international journals as principal or co-author including books: Anemia in Pregnancy –Impact of Iron Deworming and IEC, 1999; Sustainable Health and Development: RUHSA's Development, 2003. Honours: Life Member, Delta Omega Society, Alpha Chapter, USA; Fellow International College of Nutrition. Memberships: Life Member: Tuberculosis Association of Tamil Nadu, Madras; Nutrition Society of India, Hyderbad; Indian Public Health Association, Calcutta. Address: RUHSA Department, RUHSA Campus PO, Vellore District – 632209, Tamil Nadu, S India.

ABELLAN José Luis, b. 19 May 1933, Madrid, Spain. Professor. 2 sons. Education: MA Humanities, University of Complutense, 1960; PhD, 1961. Appointments: Professor, University Rio Piedras, 1961-63, University of Belfast, Northern Ireland, 1963-65, University of Complutense, Madrid, Spain, 1966-. Publications: Erasmism in Spain, 1976; History of Spanish Thought 1979-92, 7 volumes. Honour: National Essay Prize, 1981; Honorary Fellow, Spanish and Spanish American Studies, Nebraska, USA. Memberships: North American Spanish Language Academy; Representative for Spain, Executive Board, UNESCO, 1983-85; President, Atheneum of Madrid, 2001. Address: Gravina 7, 28004 Madrid, Spain.

ABERCROMBIE Alex, b. 5 April 1951, Cape Town, South Africa. Attorney. m. Jenny, 2 sons, 2 daughters. Education: Attorneys Admission Diploma, 1973; Post Graduate Diploma in Company Law, 1991; Certificate in Sports Law, 1992. Appointments: Partner in Law Firm, Hofmeyer Herbstein Gihwala; Acting Judge, High Court, Cape Town. Honours: Special State Award for contribution to South African football, President Nelson Mandela. Memberships: Cape Law Society. Address: 11 Golden Grove, Rondebosch, Cape Town, South Africa.

ABERSON Michael Eliazar, b. 25 May 1932, Moscow, Russia. Electrical Engineer; Product Manager. m. Esther Kotlarov, 1 daughter. Education: MSc, Electrical Engineering, Moscow Russia, 1954; PhD, Power Distribution, Academy of Urban Economy, 1969; Management Consulting, Dorset Business School, 1989; Registered Professional Engineer, Israel. Appointments: Repair Foreman, Urban Electrical networks, Dnepropetrovsk, Ukraine, 1954-55; Project Engineer, Project Institute, Moscow, 1955-58; Senior Project Engineer, Electroproject Institute, 1958-64; Junior to Senior Scholar, Academy of Urban Economics, 1964-80; Refusnik, 1980-85; Senior Scholar, Israel Electrical Corporation, Ltd, Haifa, 1986-97; Manager, Research and Development Group dealing with digital data protocol, static stability, management probabilities and statistical analysis of voltage quality. Publications: Articles and reviews in professional scientific journals and books include the report: An object-oriented real-time open protocol, IEEE, Jerusalem, 1996; Monograph: Economic Behavior Model and Voltage Pattern, 2000; 3 US patents based on J von Neumann and N Wiener's classic works. Honour: Award: Certificate, Who's Who in the World, 2003, Marquis, USA. Membership: Planetary Society. Address: Brener Str 22-1, Haifa 32546, Israel.

ABIKO Seiya, b. 20 January 1942, Tokyo, Japan. Professor. m. Kazuko Tsunogae, 2 daughters. Education: BSc, Faculty of Science, 1964, MSc, 1970, PhD, 1981, Graduate School of Science, University of Tokyo. Appointments: Part time Lecturer, Kanagawa University, 1975-83; Part time Lecturer, University of Tokyo, 1982-84; Part time Lecturer, Nihon University, 1982-94; Professor, Seirei Christopher College, 1988-. Publications: On the Chemico-Thermal Origins of Special Relativity, 1991; What was it that Brought Forth the Succession of Fundamental Discoveries 1895-1897, 1996; Lessons from Nursing Theories: Towards the Humanisation of Technology, 1991; Einstein's Kyoto Address: How I Created the Theory of Relativity, 2000. Memberships: The History of Science Society; The History of Science Society of Japan; The Physical Society of Japan; Japanese Society for Science and Technology Studies. Address: 1-12-9 Minami-Town, Nishitokyo-City, Tokyo 188-0012, Japan. E-mail: abiko@ceres.dti.ne.jp

Dictionary of International Biography

ABLEY Mark, b. 13 May 1955, England. Poet; Journalist. m. Annie Beer, 15 August 1981, 2 daughters. Education: BA, Honours, English, University of Saskatchewan, 1975; BA, Honours, English, St John's College, Oxford, 1977; MA(Oxon), 1983. Appointments: Freelance Writer, 1978-87; Contributing Editor, Saturday Night, 1986-92; Literary Editor, Montreal Gazette, 1989-91; Feature Writer, Montreal Gazette, 1991-2003. Publications: Beyond Forget, 1986; Blue Sand, Blue Moon, 1988; Glasburyon, 1994; Stories From the Ice Storm, 1999; Ghost Cat, 2001; Spoken Here, 2003. Contributions to: Times Literary Supplement; Malahat Review; New Statesman; Encounter; The Listener; Brick; London Review of Books; Quarto; Outposts; Dandelion; Grain; Matrix; Border Crossings; Fiddlehead; Poetry Review. Honours: Eric Gregory Award, 1981; Shortlisted, QSpell Award, 1989, 1995; Mark Harrison Prize, 1992, 1997. Memberships: Writers' Union of Canada; Quebec Writers' Federation; PEN. Address: 52 Winston Circle, Pointe-Claire, Quebec H9S 4X6, Canada

ABRAHAM F Murray, b. 24 October 1939, Pittsburgh, Pennsylvania, USA. Actor. m. Kate Hannan, 1962, 2 children. Education: Texas University. Career: Professor, Brooklyn College, 1985-; Director, No Smoking Please; Appeared in numerous Broadway plays, musicals, on television, also films including: Amadeus, 1985; The Name of the Rose, Russicum, Slipstream, Hard Rain, Personal Choice, Eye of the Widow, 1989; An Innocent Man, 1990; Mobsters, 1991; Bonfire of the Vanities, 1991; By The Sword, 1992; Last Action Hero, 1993; Surviving the Game, Nostradamus, 1994; Mighty Aphrodite, 1995; Children of the Revolution, 1996; Mimic, 1997; Star Trek IX, 1998; Falcone, Esther, 1999; Finding Forrester, 2000; I cavaleieri che fecero l'impresa, 2001; 13 Ghosts, 2001; Joshua, 2002. Narrator, Herman Melville, Damned in Paradise, 1985. Honours: Obie Award, for Uncle Vanya, 1984; Golden Globe Award, 1985; Los Angeles Film Critics Award, 1985; Academy Award, for Amadeus, 1985. Address: c/o Paradigm, Santa Monica Boulevard # 2500, Los Angeles, CA 90067, USA.

ABRAM Joseph, b. 21 April 1951, Cairo, Egypt. Professor of Architecture; Painter. divorced, 2 daughters. Education: Architect DPLG, School of Architecture, Nancy, 1975; DEA, History of Art, Sorbonne, Paris, 1990. Appointments: Professor, Researcher, School of Architecture, Nancy, France, 1975-; Professor, School of Fine Arts, Metz, 1991-95; Painter, White Portraits of Vladimir Maiakovski, Quite Images of Industry, 10 exhibitions, 1983-93; Researcher, History Laboratory of Contemporary Architecture, Nancy, 1985-; Designer, cast-iron furniture, firm in Lorraine, 1986-88, prototypes exhibited Paris, 1987, New York, 1992; Professor, Institute of Architecture, Geneva, 1995-2004; Editorial Board Member, Faces, Geneva, 1995-; Lecturer, many European countries; Curator or Scientific Consultant, exhibitions at French Institute of Architecture, Cooper Union School, New York, Architecture Museum, Basel, Columbia University architecture galleries, Pompidou Centre, School of Arts, Metz, La Première Rue, Briey, Musée Malraux, Le Havre, galleria civica d'arte moderna, Turin. Publications: Author: Albert Flocon and the Curvilinear Perspective; The Reconstruction of Le Havre; Hugo Herdeg and the World of Objects; Contemporaneity at the limits; Political Will and Cultural Identity Crisis in late-twentieth-century French Architecture; Architecture in France after the World War II; Essays on Perret, Nitzchke, Nelson, Lagneau-Weill-Dimitrijevic, Diener and Diener, Vacchini, Devanthéry and Lamunière, Genzling; Beaudouin; Numerous essays for museum catalogues; Articles in various magazines. Honour: Winner with his Arkhitekton of Glass monument project, Inventer 89 Competition to commemorate French Revolution Bicentennial, 1987. Address: 59 Rue de la Mutualité, 54600 Villers-lès-Nancy, France.

ABRAMOVIC Biljana, b. 15 December 1952, Novi Sad. University Professor. m. Borislav Abramovic, 1 daughter. Education: BS 1975, MS 1979, PhD 1983, Faculty of Sciences, University of Novi Sad. Appointments: Assistant, 1976-84; Assistant Professor, 1984-90; Associate Professor, 1990-95; Professor, 1995-: all at the Faculty of Sciences, University of Novi Sad. Publications: About 75 articles; Catalytic Methods for the Determination of Noble Metals, Computer in Catalytic Analysis, Expert System for Catalytic Titrations, Carbon-based Electrodes in the Analysis of Pharmaceutical Preparations, Photomineralization of the Herbicide, Analysis of Mycotoxins, articles; Microanalysis, Practical Exercises in Microanalysis, Practical Exercises in Environmental Analysis, books. Honours: 200 Citations. Memberships: Serbian Chemical Society, 1974-; Chemical Society of Vojvodina, 1977-; President of Chemical Society of Vojvodina, 2001-; Vice-President, Serbian Chemical Society, 2002-; Member, Editorial Board, Journal of Serbian Chemical Society. Address: Fruskogorska 30, 21000 Novi Sad, Serbia and Montenegro.

ABRAMSKY Jennifer, b. 7 October 1946. Radio Producer and Editor. m. Alasdair Liddell, 1976, 1 son, 1 daughter. Education: BA, University of East Anglia. Appointments: Programme Operations Assistant, 1969, Producer, The World at One, 1973, Editor, PM, 1978, Producer, Radio Four Budget Programmes, 1979-86, Editor, Today Programme, 1986-87, Editor, News and Current Affairs Radio, 1987-93, established Radio Four News FM, 1991, Controller, Radio Five Live, 1993-96, Director, Continuous News, including Radio Five Live, BBC News 24, BBC World, BBC News Online, Ceefax, and Director, 1998-2000, BBC Radio and Music, 2000-, BBC Radio; News International Visiting Professor of Broadcast Media, 2002. Honours: Woman of Distinction, Jewish Care, 1990; Honorary Professor, Thames Valley University, 1994; Sony Radio Academy Award, 1995; Honorary MA, Salford University, 1997; Royal Academy Fellowship, 1998. Memberships: Member, Economic and Social Research Council, 1992-96; Editorial Board, British Journalism Review, 1993-; Member, Board of Governors, BFI, 2000-. Address: BBC, Broadcasting House, Portland Place, London W1A 1AA, England.

ABROSIMOV Anatoly, b. 14 October 1929, Moscow, Russia. Physicist. m. Margaret, 1 daughter. Education: Diploma of Physicist, Moscow State University, 1953; First degree, Candidate of Physics and Mathematics, 1966; Visitor Researcher, Imperial College, London University, 1968-69. Appointments: Director, Dubna Branch, Moscow State University, 1975-82; Senior Scientific Researcher, Nuclear Physics and Physics of Elementary Particles, 1985. Publications: 90 publications; Contributions to professional journals, mainly in field of Cosmic Rays and High Energy Physics; Book: From Estate to Communal Flat, 2001. Honour: Diploma of Discovery in Astrophysics, Priority, 1958, Moscow, 1971. Memberships: Physical Society of Russia, 1990; Honorary Member International Biographical Centre Advisory Council. Address: House 4, Building 4, Flat 57, 26 Bakinskikh Commissar Str, 119526 Moscow, Russia.

ABSE Dannie, b. 22 September 1923, Cardiff, Glamorgan, Wales. Physician; Poet; Writer; Dramatist. m. Joan Mercer, 4 Aug 1951, 1 son, 2 daughters. Education: St Illtyd's College, Cardiff; University of South Wales and Monmouthshire, Cardiff; King's College, London; MD, Westminster Hospital, London, 1950. Appointments: Manager, Chest Clinic, Central Medical Establishment, London, 1954-82; Senior Fellow in Humanities, Princeton University, New Jersey, 1973-74. Publications: Poetry: Funland and Other Poems, 1973; Lunchtime, 1974; Way Out in the Centre, 1981; White Coat, Purple Coat: Collected Poems, 1948-88, 1989; Remembrance of Crimes Past, 1990; On the Evening

Road, 1994; Intermittent Journals, 1994; Twentieth-Century Anglo-Welsh Poetry, 1997; A Welsh Retrospective, 1997; Arcadia, One Mile, 1998; Goodbye Twentieth Century, 2001; New and Collected Poems, 2002, many others. Editor: The Music Lover's Literary Companion, 1988; The Hutchinson Book of Post-War British Poets, 1989. Fiction: Ash on a Young Man's Sleeve, 1954; Some Corner of an English Field, 1956; O Jones, O Jones, 1970; Voices in the Gallery, 1986. Contributions to: BBC and various publications in UK and USA. Honours: Foyle Award, 1960; Welsh Arts Council Literature Prizes, 1971, 1987; Cholmondeley Award, 1985. Memberships: Poetry Society, president, 1979-92; Royal Society of Literature, fellow, 1983; Welsh Academy, fellow, 1990, president, 1995. Address: c/o Shiel Land Associates Ltd, 43 Doughty Street, London WC1N 2LF, England.

ABSOLON Karel B, b. 21 March 1926, Brno, Czechoslovakia. Professor of Surgery; Author. m. Mary Bendix, 2 sons, 2 daughters. Education: MD, Yale School of Medicine, 1952; Internship, University of Minnesota Hospitals, 1952; PhD, Surgery, MS, Physiology, 1963, University of Minnesota; PhD, Honorary, Masaryk University, Brno, Czech Republic. Appointments: Assistant Professor, University of Minnesota, Medical School, 1962-65; Assistant Clinical Professor of Surgery, Southwestern Medical School, 1965-72; Chief of Surgery, Washington Hospital Center, 1972-77; Associate Professor of Surgery, George Washington University Medical School; Professor, Academic Chairman of Surgery, Chief of Surgery, University of Illinois, VA Administration Medical Center, 1977-80; Special Expert Appointment, National Institutes of Health, 1980-83; President, Kabel Publishers, Rockville, MD, 1983-84; Visiting Professor of Surgery, Eastern Illinois University, 1985; Locum Tenens Chief, AMISAL, National Securities Hospital, Saudi Arabia, 1985; President, Kable Publishers, Rockville, Maryland, USA, 1983-. Publications: Over 500 publications; 10 books. Honours: Borden Price; James Hudson Brown Fellowship; Teaching Award; Comenius Medal Olomonc, Czech Republic, 1996; Palady Medal, Bratislava, Slovakia, 1996. Memberships: American College of Surgeons; International Surgical Society; Society of VA Surgeons; Academic Surgeons Society; Washington Metropolitan Thoratic and Cardiovascular Society; Society of the Arts and Science. Address: 11225 Huntover Drive, Rockville, MD 20852, USA.

ABU-ARAB Mahmoud, b. 3 September 1953, Majd El-Korum, Israel. Psychologist. (1) Zlatica Minichova, divorced, 2 daughters, (2) 1 son. Education: MA, Clinical Psychology, 1981; PhD, Psychology, 1985. Appointments: Psychology, City Council, Bratislava, Slovakia, 1982; Psychology, Pezinok Psychiatric Hospital, Slovakia, 1984; Lecturer, Ibrahimieh College, Jerusalem, 1985; Director, Palestinian Counseling Centre, Jerusalem, 1986; Research Officer, Arab Studies Society, Jerusalem, 1987; Counselor, Bankstown Technical College, Sydney, Australia, 1988; Counselor, Granville Technical College, Sydney, Australia, 1989; Head, Psychology Department, Al-Amal Hospital, Jeddah, Saudi Arabia, 1993; Psychology, Transcultural Mental Health Centre, Cumberland Hospital, Sydney, Australia, 1994; Psychology, Private Practice, Sydney, Australia, 1994. Publications: Laterality and Writing Directions, 1985; Some Personality Correlates in a Group of Alcoholics, 1985; Screening Methods and Their Applications, 1985; Standardization of the SCL-90-R on Palestinian Population, 1988; Relapse Cues and Relapse Risk Factors Among Saudi Drug Addicts, 1994; Sexuality and Eroticism Among Males in Moslem Society, 1994; Some Personality Correlates in a Group of Drug Addicts, 1995; Neuropsychology, 1996. Honour: Justice of the Peace, Ministry of Justice, New South Wales, Australia, 1992. Memberships: Australian Psychology Society; New South Wales Counselors Association; College of Counseling Psychologists; National Acupuncture Detoxification Association; College of

Independently Practicing Psychologists; Australian Association for Applied Psychophysiology and Biofeedback; Australian Pain Society; College of Health Psychologists. Address: PO Box 391, Granville, NSW 2142, Australia.

ABU-GHAZALEH Bayan, b. 1960, Riyadh. Microbiologist. Education: BSc, Biological Sciences, 1981; MSc, Microbiology, 1984; PhD, Microbiology, 1990. Appointments: Researcher, Royal Scientific Society, Jordan, 1991-94; Assistant Professor, Hashemite University, Jordan, 1996-. Publications: Several articles in professional journals. Memberships: American Society for Microbiology; Jordanian Society of Biology. Address: PO Box 926966, Amman, Jordan.

ABUBAKAR Abdulsalami (General), b. 13 June 1942, Minna, Nigeria. Head of State; Army Officer. Education: Kaduna. Appointments: Joined, 1963, with United Nations Peacekeeping Force, Lebanon, 1978-79, Chief of Defence Staff, Chairman, Joint Chiefs of Staff of the Armed Forces, 1993-98, Commander-in-Chief, 1998, Nigerian Army; Formerly active, Committee of West African Chiefs of Staff; Head of Nigerian Government, 1998-99; Appointed UN Special Envoy to Democratic Republic of the Congo, 2000; Head of Commonwealth Observer Mission to Oversee Zimbabwe's Parliamentary Elections, 2000; Mission to Monitor Presidential Elections in Zimbabwe, March 2002. Address: c/o UN Mission in the Democratic Republic of the Congo, United Nations Plaza, New York, NY 10017, USA.

ABURKHES Mohamed Lutfi, b. 17 May 1952, Tripoli, Libya. Molecular Biologist. m. Mufida, 3 sons, 1 daughter. Education: BSc, Faculty of Agriculture, University of Tripoli, 1974; AEA, Attestation di Virologie, University de Bordeaux II, Bordeaux, France, 1977; Doctorate, Molecular Biology, Pasteur University, Strasbourg, France, 1979; Professor by publications. Appointments: Director, Biotechnology Laboratory, Agricultural Research Centre, 1975-. Publications: 21 publications in biotechnology, Libyan Economic Plants. Address: Agricultural Research Centre, P O Box 12029, Tripoli, Libya.

ABUSSUUD Abdulaziz, b. 5 August, 1940, Qatif, Saudi Arabia. Company Executive. m. Sabiha Al-Sinan, 3 sons. Education: Bachelor of Business Administration, American University of Beirut, 1971; Various Diplomas in Management and Insurance. Appointments: Various positions in Arab Commercial Enterprises (Group of Companies), 1961-86; Senior Vice-President, Gulf and Eastern Province of Saudi Arabia, 1986-88, Senior Group Vice-President, 1988-89, President and Chief Executive Officer, 1989-, Arab Commercial Enterprises. Memberships: Chartered Insurance Institute, London; Board of Directors, Amex (Saudi Arabia) Ltd; Vice-Chairman, National Committee for Insurance Services, Riyadh, Saudi Arabia. Address: Arab Commercial Enterprises, PO Box 667, Riyadh 11421, Saudi Arabia. E-mail: aaa@ace-ins.com Website: www.ace-ins.com

ABYZOV Sabit S, b. 12 February 1928, Nizegorodskaia Region, Russia. Microbiologist. Education: Graduate, University in Gorky, 1952. Appointments: Doctor of Sciences, Senior Scientist, 1971. Publications: Over 90 publications on the Antarctic and related subjects, 1977-. Memberships: COSPAR; Scientific Commission F and Russian Committee for Antarctic Research. Address: RAS Institute of Microbiology, 117811 Moscow, Russia.

ACCARDO Salvatore, b. 26 September 1941, Turin, Italy. Violinist; Conductor. Education: Studied with Luigi d' Ambrosio at Naples Conservatory, diploma in 1956; Postgraduate study with Yvonne Astruc at the Accademia Chigiana, Sienna. Career: Has toured extensively as solo violinist and latterly as conductor in

Dictionary of International Biography

Europe and America; Founded the Turin L'Orchestra da Camera Italiana in 1968; Soloist with the ensemble Musici, 1972-77 and Semaines Musicales of Chamber Music at Naples; Repertory includes Bach, Vivaldi and Paganini; Works composed for him include Fantasia for Violin and Orchestra by Walter Piston, Argot for Solo Violin by Franco Donatoni, and Dikhtas by Iannis Xenakis, 1980; Conducted Rossini's opera L'Occasione fa il Ladro at the 1987 Pesaro Festival; Plays several Stradivarius violins and a Guarnerius del Gesu o 1733; Took part in a performance of Schoenberg's String Trio at the Elizabeth Hall in London in 1990; Recordings include: Paganini's 24 Caprices and the Six Concertos. Publications: L'Arte del Violino, 1987; Edn Paganini Sixth Concerto, Paganini; Variations on "Carmagnola". Address: c/o Agenzia Resia Srl Rappresentanze e Segreterie Internazionali Artistische, Via Manzoni 31, 20121 Milan, Italy.

ACERBI Antonio, b. 26 July 1935, Lodi, Italy. Theologian; Professor of the History of Christianity. Education: Doctor of Law, Catholic University, Milan, Italy, 1953-57; Doctor of Theology, Theological Faculty, Milan Italy, 1968-72. Appointments: Lecturer, Theological Faculty of Sicile, Palermo, Italy, 1972-75; Lecturer, State University , Lecce, Italy, 1976-79; Lecturer, Catholic University, Milan, Italy, 1980-90; Professor, 1990-94, Dean, Faculty of Arts, 1993-94, State University, Potenza, Italy; Professor, 1994-, Head of the Department of Religious Sciences, 1994-, Catholic University of Milan, Italy. Publications: Author: Two Ecclesiologies. A Juridical Ecclesiology and a Communion Ecclesiology in "Lumen Gentium", 1975; The Church in Time. Glimpses on Projects of Relationships between Church and Society in the Last Century, 1979; Church, Culture, Society. Moments and Personages from Vatican the Second to Paul VI, 1988; Isaiah's Ascension. Christology and Christian Prophetism in Syria at the Beginning of the Second Century, 1989; Church and Democracy from Leo XIII to the Second Vatican Council, 1991; Co-author: Studies in World Religions, 1996; Modern State and Political Thought of Catholicism , 1999; Editor: Crime and Punishment? Theology faced with the Criminal Question, 1998; The Ministry of the Pope in Ecumenical Perspective, 1999; Church and Italy. Contributions to a History of their Relationships during the last two Centuries, 2003; Editor, Journal, Annals of Religious Sciences, 1996-. Honours: City of Iglesias Prize, 1992. Memberships include: Fellow, Association pour l'Etude de la Littérature Apochrife Chrétienne, Lausanne, Switzerland, 1988-; Member of the Scientific Committee, Centre for Advanced Studies in Religious Sciences, Piacenza, Italy, 1999-; Member, Scientific Committee, Centre for Religious Sciences, Trento, Italy, 2000-; Member, Scientific Committee, Italian Centre of Higher Studies on Religions, Bologna, Italy, 2000-; Chairman, Executive Committee, Pirovano Prizes, Luigi Sturzo Institute, Rome, Italy, 2000-. Address: Via Magenta 51, 26900 Lodi, Italy. E-mail: dip.scienzereligiose@unicatt.it

ACEVEDO Roberto, b. 30 November 1950, Santiago, Chile. Chemist. m. Lucia Cecilia, 3 sons, 2 daughters. Education: MSc, Universidad de Chile, 1974; PhD, University of London, 1981. Appointments: Assistant Lecturer, 1971-74, Assistant Professor, 1974-83, Associate Professor, 1984-91, Full Professor, 1991-, Universidad de Chile; Editor, Ciencia Abierta (URL: http:// cabierta.uchile.cl). Publications: Books: Atoms and Molecules, 1996; Introductory Elements in Atomic and Molecular Spectroscopy. Applications to Systems of Spectroscopic Interest, 2000; Topic in Physical Chemistry, 2003; Co-Author: 88 national publications, 38 in international congresses, 16 in electronic journals, 64 in international publications. Honours: Honorary Research Fellow, University of London, England, 1984-85, 1990-91; Bursor of EC, 1991; Visiting Scholar, University of Virginia, USA, 1993; Visiting Professor, Institute for Low Temperature and Structure Research, Wroclaw, Poland, 2000-2001; Visiting Professor, Institute Applied Physics and Department of Computer Methods, Nicholas Copernicus University, Torun, Poland, 2000-2001. Memberships: American Association for the Advancement of Science; Editorial Board: Asian Journal of Spectroscopy and Ciencia Al Dia. Address: Froilan Roa 5833, Pasaje 1, Casa 2950, Macul Santiago, Chile.

ACEVEDO BLANCO Manuel, b. 17 December 1962, San José, Costa Rica. Medical Doctor. m. Sylvia Araya, 3 sons. Education: Bachelor in Medical Sciences, Cum Laude Probatus, 1983; Licensed in Medical Sciences, Cum Laude Probatus, 1984; Doctor in Medical Sciences, Bene Probatus, 1985; Specialist in Internal Medicine, 1990. Appointments: Founder and Chief of Pain Management Clinic and Palliative Care, Cañas, Guanacaste, Costa Rica (also known as Cañas Pain Clinic); Medical Chief of Emergency Room, Cañas Clinic (an institutional, non-private clinic), Guanacaste, Costa Rica. Publications: Papers presented at congresses: Endoscopic Diagnosis of Whipple Disease (Case Report); Co-Morbid Factors in Cancer Patients. Honour: Distinguished Leadership Award, American Biographical Institute. Memberships: International Association for the Study of Pain; Vice-President, Costa Rica Association for the Study of Pain; International Association for Hospice and Palliative Care. Address: Tilarán, Guanacaste, Costa Rica, Central America. E-mail: aceblanc@sol.racsa.co.cr

ACHEBE (Albert) Chinua (lumogu), b. 16 November 1930, Ogidi, Nigeria. Writer; Poet; Editor; Professor. m. Christie Okoli, 10 September 1961, 2 sons, 2 daughters. Education: University College, Ibadan, 1948-53; BA, London University, 1953; Received training in broadcasting, BBC, London, 1956. Appointments: Producer, 1954-58, Controller, Eastern Region, Enugu, Nigeria, 1958-61, Founder-Director, Voice of Nigeria, 1961-66, Nigerian Broadcasting Corp, Lagos; Senior Research Fellow, 1967-72, Professor of English, 1976-81, Professor Emeritus, 1985-, University of Nigeria, Nsukka; Founding Editor, Okike: A Nigerian Journal of New Writing, 1971-; Professor of English, University of Massachusetts, 1972-75; Director, Okike Arts Centre, Nsukka, 1984-; Founder-Publisher, Uwa Ndi Igbo: A Bilingual Journal of Igbo Life and Arts, 1984-; Pro-Chancellor and Chairman of the Council, Anambra State University of Technology, Enugu, 1986-88; Charles P Stevenson Professor, Bard College, New York, 1990-; Visiting Professor and Lecturer at universities in Canada and the US; Goodwill Ambassador, UN Population Fund, 1998-. Publications: Novels: Things Fall Apart, 1958; No Longer at Ease, 1960; Arrow of God, 1964; A Man of the People, 1966; Anthills of the Savannah, 1987. Other Fiction: The Sacrificial Egg and Other Stories, 1962; Girls at War (short stories), 1973. Juvenile Fiction: Chike and the River, 1966; How the Leopard Got His Claws (with John Iroaganachi), 1972; The Flute, 1978; The Drum, 1978. Poetry: Beware, Soul-Brother and Other Poems, 1971; Christmas in Biafra and Other Poems, 1973. Essays: Morning Yet on Creation Day, 1975; The Trouble With Nigeria, 1983; Hopes and Impediments, 1988; Editor: Don't Let Him Die: An Anthology of Memorial Poems for Christopher Okigbo (with Dubem Okafor), 1978; Aka Weta: An Anthology of Igbo Poetry (with Obiora Udechukwu), 1982; African Short Stories (with C L Innes), 1984; The Heinemann Book of Contemporary African Short Stories (with C L Innes), 1992; Another Africa (with R Lyons), 1998; Home and Exile, autobiographical essay, 2000. Contributions to: Periodicals. Honours: Margaret Wrong Memorial Prize, 1959; Nigerian National Trophy, 1961; Jock Campbell/New Statesman Award, 1965; Commonwealth Poetry Prize, 1972; Neil Gunn International Fellow, Scottish Arts Council, 1975; Lotus Award for Afro-Asian Writers, 1975; Nigerian National Order of Merit, 1979; Order of the Federal Republic of Nigeria, 1979; Commonwealth Foundation

Senior Visiting Practitioner Award, 1984; Booker Prize Nomination, 1987; 30 honorary doctorates, 1972-99; Campion Medal, 1996; National Creativity Award, Nigeria, 1999. Memberships: American Academy of Arts and Letters, honorary member; American Academy of Arts and Sciences, foreign honorary member; Association of Nigerian Authors, founder and president, 1981-86; Vice-president, Royal African Society, London, 1988; Commonwealth Arts Organization; Modern Language Association of America, honorary fellow; Royal Society of Literature, fellow, London, 1981; Writers and Scholars Educational Trust, London; Writers and Scholars International, London; Nigerian Academy of Letters, 1999. Address: Bard College, PO Box 41, Annandale-on-Hudson, NY 12504, USA.

ACHIDI ACHU Simon, b. 1934, Santa Mbu, Cameroon. Politician. Education: Yaoundé; University of Besançon, France; National School of Magistracy, Yaoundé. Appointments: Agricultural Assistant, Cameroon Development Corporation; Interpreter for Presidency, Yaoundé, Chief Accountant, Widikum Council, President, North-West Provincial Co-operative Union Ltd; Minister-delegate in charge of State Reforms, 1971; Minister of Justice, Keeper of the Seals, 1972-75; Private business, 1975-88; Elected Member of Parliament for Cameroon People's Democratic Movement, 1988; Prime Minister of Cameroon, 1992-96. Address: c/o Prime Minister's Office, Yaoundé, Cameroon.

ACKLAND Sidney Edmond Jocelyn (Joss), b. 29 February 1928, London, England. Actor. m. Rosemary Kirkcaldy, 18 August 1951, 2 sons, 1 deceased, 5 daughters. Education: Dame Alice Owens School; Central School of Speech Training and Dramatic Art. Career includes: Theatre work, 1945-; Member, Old Vic Theatre Company, 1958-61; Parts include: Toby Belch, Caliban, Pistol, Falstaff in Henry IV Part 1 and Merry Wives of Windsor; Artistic Director, Mermaid Theatre, 1961-63; West End Theatre roles include: Come as You Are; Hotel in Amsterdam; Clarence Darrow in Never the Sinner; Falstaff in Henry IV Parts 1 and 2; Captain Hook and Mr Darling in Peter Pan, Barbican Theatre; Sam in The Collaborators; Mitch in A Streetcar Named Desire; National tours include: Petruchio in The Taming of the Shrew; Sir in The Dresser; W End Musicals include: Justice Squeezum in Lock Up Your Daughters; Jorrocks in Jorrocks; Frederik in A Little Night Music; Peron in Evita; Captain Hook and Mr Darling in Peter Pan - The Musical; Chichester Festival Theatre, Ill in The Visit; John Tarleton in Misalliance; Over 300 TV appearances include: Barrett in The Barrets of Wimpole Street; C S Lewis in Shadowlands; Herman Goering in The Man Who Lived at the Ritz; Alan Holly in First and Last; Isaac in The Bible; Onassis in A Woman Named Jackie; The Captain in Deadly Voyage; Van de Furst in Heat of the Sun; Films include: Seven Days to Noon; The House That Dripped Blood; England Made Me; Royal Flash; A Zed and Two Noughts; The Godfather in The Sicilian; Broughton in White Mischief; Lethal Weapon 2; The Hunt for Red October; The Palermo Connection; Nowhere to Run; Object of Beauty; Miracle on 34th Street; Lord Clare in Firelight; The Monseigneur in My Giant; Gerald Carmody in Daisies in December; King Arthur in A Kid at King Arthur's Court; Mighty Ducks 1 and 3; Matisse in Surviving Picasso; Swaffer in Swept from the Sea; Mumbo Jumbo, 2000; Painting Faces, 2001; Othello, 2001; K19: The Widowmaker, 2001; No Good Deed, 2001; The House on Turk Street, 2002; I'll Be There, 2003. Publication: I Must Be in There Somewhere, autobiography, 1989. Memberships: Drug Helpline; Amnesty International; Covent Garden Community Association. Address: c/o Jonathan Altaras Associates, 2nd Floor, 13 Shorts Gardens, London, EC2H 9AT, England.

ADAM Antal, b. 14 February 1930, Janoshalma, Hungary. Professor of Public Law. m. Anna Babics, 1 son. Education: Law Student, Faculty of Law, University of Pécs, 1949-53; Doctoral Student, Hungarian Academy of Sciences, Budapest, 1954-1958. Appointments: Assistant Professor, Associate Professor, 1958-67; Professor of Public Law, Faculty of Law, University of Pécs, 1967-2000; Dean, Faculty of Law, Pécs, 1975-78; Judge of Constitutional Court, Budapest, 1990-98; Professor Emeritus, Editor in Chief, Jura, 2000-. Publications: Monographs: Presidential Council of People's Republic, 1958; Associations in the System of Civil Organisations, 1964; Co-Ordinational Activity of Council's Organisations, 1974; Governmental Activity in Hungary, 1979; Constitutional Values and Constitutional Jurisdiction, 1998; Theory of Public Law, 2001; Many others; More than 350 articles. Honours: Outstanding Worker in Education, 1965; Golden Medal of Work, 1972; Order of Star of Hungarian People's Republic, 1988; Eminent Professor, 1989; Middle Cross with Star of Hungarian Republic, 1999; Ministerial Recognition for Higher Education, 2000; Key to the City of Janoshalma, 2000. Memberships: Council of International Society of Constitutional Law; Administrative Committee of Hungarian Academy of Sciences; Hungarian Political Science Society; Hungarian Association of Constitutional Lawyers; Chairman, Scientific Committee of the Faculty of Law, University of Pécs; Chairman, For Youth Society. Address: 48-as ter 1, 7622 Pécs, Hungary. E-mail: eniko@ajk.pte.hu.

ADAM Gottfried W J, b. 1 December 1939, Treysa, Germany. Professor. 3 sons. Education: Dr Theol, University of Bonn, 1968; Dr Theol, Habil, University of Marburg, 1975. Appointments: Assistant, Theology Faculty, University of Bonn, 1966-67; Assistant, 1968-75, Lecturer, Professor, Practical Theology, 1976-77, 1980, University of Marburg; Professor, University of Goettingen, 1978-79; Professor, Protestant Theology, Chair, Philosophy Faculty, University of Wuerzburg, 1981-92; Professor, Religious Education, Chair, Faculty of Protestant Theology, Vienna, 1992; Dean, Faculty of Protestant Theology, University of Vienna, 1999. Publications: Author: 6 books; Editor, Co-editor: 20 books; 3 periodicals; 3 book series; 400 articles on theological and religious educational questions. Honours: Diploma of Theol h c, Sibiu, Romania, 1996; Károli Gáspar Reformatus University, Budapest, Hungary, 2000. Memberships: Wissenschaftliche Gesellschaft für Theologie; Rudolf-Buttmann-Gesellschaft für Hermenentische Theologie; Arbeitskreis für Religionspaedagogik; Religious Education Association, USA. Address: Chair of Religious Education, Faculty of Protestant Theology, Rooseveltplatz 10, A-1010 Wien, Austria. E-mail: gottfried.adam@univie.ac.at

ADAM Ken, b. 1921, Berlin, Germany. Film Designer. Education: London University. Career: Started as Junior Draughtsman on film set; Worked for films including Around the World in Eighty Days, 7 James Bond films, Dr Strangelove, Sleuth, Barry Lyndon, The Deceivers, The Freshman, Patriots, Chitty Chitty Bang Bang, The Madness of King George, Boys on the Side, Bogus, In and Out, The Out of Towners, The White Hotel, Taking Sides, Designed sets for La Fanciulla del West, Royal Opera House, London. Honours: Officer, Order of the British Empire; Academy Award for Barry Lyndon; Academy Award for The Madness of King George, 1994.

ADAM Theo, b. 1 August 1926, Dresden, Germany. Singer (Bass Baritone); Producer. Education: Sang in Dresden Kreuzchor and studied with Rudolf Dietrich in Dresden and in Weimar. Debut: Dresden in 1949 as the Hermit in Der Freischütz. Career includes: Berlin State Opera from 1952; Bayreuth debut in 1952 as Ortel in Meistersinger, later sang Wotan, Gurnemanz, King Henry, Pogner, Sachs and Amfortas; Covent Garden debut in 1967 as Wotan, Metropolitan Opera debut in 1969 as Sachs; Guest appearances include Hamburg, Vienna, Budapest and Chicago with roles including Berg's Wozzeck and Verdi's King Philip; Sang in and produced the premiere production of Dessau's Einstein at Berlin State Opera in 1974; Sang at Salzburg Festival, 1981, 1984 in premieres of Cerha's Baal and Berio's Un Re in Ascolto; In 1985 sang at reopened Semper Opera House, Dresden, in Der Freischütz and as Ochs in Der Rosenkavalier; Sang Don Alfonso at Tokyo in 1988 and La Roche in Capriccio at Munich Festival, 1990; Staged Graun's Cesare e Cleopatra for the 250th Anniversary of the Berlin State Opera, 1992; Sang Schigolch in Lulu at the Festival Hall in London, 1994 and at the Berlin Staatsoper, 1997; Sang in Henze's Bassarids at Dresden, 1997. Publication: Seht, hier ist Tinte, Feder, Papier..., autobiography, 1983. Recordings: Bach Cantatas; Freischütz; Parsifal; Meistersinger; Die Zauberflöte; Cosi fan tutte; Der Ring des Nibelungen; St Matthew Passion; Fidelio; Krenek's Karl V; Baal; Dantons Tod; Rosenkavalier; Die schweigsame Frau. Address: Schillerstrasse 14, 01326 Dresden, Germany.

ADAMO Joseph, b. 22 October 1938, Hoboken, New Jersey, USA. Professor of Biology. m. Connie, 1 son, 3 daughters. Education: BA, Biology, New Jersey City University, 1964; MS, Botany, Microbiology, Fairleigh Dickinson University, 1967; PhD, Nematology, Microbiology, Rutgers University, 1975. Appointments: Professor of Biology, Fairleigh Dickinson University, Teaneck, New Jersey, 1964-66; Professor of Biology, New Jersey City University, Jersey City, New Jersey, 1966-67; Professor of Biology, 1967-, Chairman, Science Department, 1981-90, Ocean County College; Professor of Biology, Georgian College, Lakewood , New Jersey, 1990-; Professor of Biology, Monmouth University, West Long Branch, New Jersey, 1997-. Publications: A Test System to Demonstrate Bacterial Conjugation, 1996; MIT Titration of Bacteriophage, 1996; New Techniques for Analysis of Microbial Gene Transfer, 1999; A Metabolic Inhibition Test to Detect the Cidal or Static Effects of Antimicrobial Agents, 2002. Honours: University Fellow, Fairleigh Dickinson University, 1965-67; Fulbright Scholar (Asia), 1973-74; Hammond Science Award, 1964; Visiting Professor, Rutgers University, 1986-88, Drexel University, 1992, 1994. Memberships: American Society for Microbiology; Theobald Smith Society; New Jersey Academy of Science; National Association of Biology Teachers; American Phytopathological Society. Address: 185 Maple Avenue, Toms River, NJ 08753, USA. E-mail: joadamo@aol.com

ADAMS Bryan, b. 5 November 1959, Kingston, Ontario, Canada. Singer; Songwriter; Musician. Career: International Recording Artist; Signed contract with A&M Records, 1979; 45 million albums sold world-wide, 1995; Numerous worldwide tours. Creative Works: Albums: Bryan Adams; Cuts Like A Knife, 1983; You Want It You Got It; Reckless, 1984; Into The Fire, 1987; Waking Up The Neighbours, 1991; Live! Live! Live!; 18 'Til I Die, 1996; The Best of Me, 2000. Singles: Kids Wanna Rock; Summer of 69; Heaven; Run To You; Can't Stop This Thing We've Started; It's Only Love; Everything I Do, I Do It For You; Have You Ever Really Loved A Woman; I Finally Found Someone; Soundtrack: Spirit: Stallion of the Cimarron. Photography exhibitions: Toronto; Montreal; Saatchi Gallery, London; Royal Jubilee Exhibition, Windsor Castle, 2002. Publications: Bryan Adams: The Officials Biography, 1995; Made in Canada; Photographs by Bryan Adams. Honour: Longest Standing No 1 in UK Singles Charts, 16 weeks, 1994; Diamond Sales Award; 12 Juno Awards; Recording Artist of the Decade; Order of Canada; Order of British Columbia. Address: c/o Press Department, A&M Records, 136-144 New King's Road, London, SW6 4LZ, England.

ADAMS Gerard (Gerry), b. 6 October 1948, Belfast, Ireland. Politician; Writer. m. Colette McArdle, 1971, 1 son. Appointments: Founder Member, Northern Ireland Civil Rights Association; Elected to Northern Ireland Assembly, 1982; MP, Sinn Fein, West Belfast, 1983-92, 1997-; Vice-President, Sinn Fein, 1978-83;

President, Sinn Fein, 1983-; Member, for Belfast West, Northern Ireland Assembly, 1998-2000. Publications: Books: Falls Memory, Politics of Irish Freedom, Pathway to Peace, 1988; Cage 11 (autobiography), 1990; The Street and Other Stories, 1992; Selected Writings, 1994; Our Day Will Come (autobiography), 1996; Before the Dawn (autobiography), 1996, An Irish Voice, 1997; An Irish Journal, 2001. Memberships: PEN; West Belfast Festival. Address: 51-55 Falls Road, Belfast, BT12 4PD, Northern Ireland.

ADAMS Pat, b. 8 July 1928, Stockton, California, USA. Artist; Educator. m. R Arnold Ricks, 24 June 1972, 2 sons. Education: Studies, California College of Arts and Crafts, 1945, Chicago Art Institute, 1947, Brooklyn Museum Art School, 1950-51; BA, University of California, Berkeley, 1949. Appointments: Art Faculty, Bennington College, Vermont, 1964-93; Visiting Critic of Painting, School of Art, Yale University, New Haven, 1971-72, 1976, 1979, 1982-83, Yale-Norfolk, Connecticut, 1987; Visiting Professor, Painting Fall Semesters, 1990-95; Distinguished Visiting Artist, American University, Washington DC, 2002; Visiting Lecturer, many universities and colleges. Creative Works: One-woman exhibitions include: Zabriskie Gallery, New York City, biannually, 1954-, Williams College Museum of Art, 1972, Rutgers University Art Museum, 1978, Contemporary Art Center, Cincinnati, 1979, Columbia Museum of Art and Science, South Carolina, 1982; Virginia Commonwealth University, 1982, Haggin Museum, Stockton, California, 1986, University of Virginia, 1986, New York Academy of Sciences, 1988, AAAS, Washington, 1988; Addison-Ripley Galleries, Washington, 1988; Berkshire Museum, 1988; Jaffe, Friede and Strauss Galleries, Dartmouth College, Hanover, New Hampshire, 1994; Tarrant Gallery, Flynn Centre, Burlington, 2001. Honours: Fulbright Scholarship, 1956; Award, National Council for Arts, 1968; National Endowment for the Arts, 1976, 1987; College Art Association, Distinguished Teaching of Art, 1984; Achievement Award, Stockton Arts Commission, 1985; Award in Art, American Academy and Institute of Arts and Letters, 1986; Vermont Governor's Excellence in Art, 1995; American Academy and Institute, Jimmy Ernst Award, 1996; Henry Ward Ranger Purchase Prize, National Academy of Design, 2003 . Memberships: Fellow, Vermont Academy of Arts and Sciences; College Art Association; National Association of Women Artists; Phi Beta Kappa; Delta Epsilon; Academician, National Academy of Design; Yaddo Corporation. Address: 370 Elm Street, Bennington, VT 05201-2214, USA.

ADAMS Richard, b. 9 May 1920. Author. m. Barbara Elizabeth Acland, 26 September 1949, 2 daughters. Education: Bradfield College, Berkshire, 1938; Worcester College, Oxford, 1938; MA, Modern History, Oxford University, 1948. Appointments: Army service, 1940-46; Civil Servant, 1948-74; Assistant Secretary, Department of the Environment, 1974; Writer-in-Residence, University of Florida, 1975; Writer-in-Residence, Hollins College, VA, 1976. Publications: Watership Down, 1972, 2nd edition, 1982; Shardik, 1974; Nature Through the Seasons, co-author Max Hooper, 1975; The Tyger Voyage (narrative poem), 1976; The Ship's Cat (narrative poem), 1977; The Plague Dogs, 1977; Nature Day and Night, (co-author Max Hooper), 1978; The Girl on a Swing, 1980; The Iron Wolf (short stories), 1980; Voyage Through the Antarctic (co-author Ronald Lockley), 1982; Maia, 1984; The Bureaucats, 1985; A Nature Diary, 1985; Occasional Poets, anthology, 1986; The Legend of Te Tuna, narrative poem, 1986; Traveller, 1988; The Day Gone By, autobiography, 1990; Tales from Watership Down, 1996; The Outlandish Knight, 2000. Honours: Carnegie Medal for Watership Down, 1972; Guardian Award for Children's Fiction for Watership Down, 1972. Memberships: President, RSPCA, 1980-82. Address: 26 Church Street, Whitchurch, Hampshire RG28 7AR, England.

Dictionary of International Biography

ADAMS Roy Joseph, b. 28 June 1940, Philadelphia, Pennsylvania, USA. Professor of Industrial Relations. m. Marilyn Whitaker, 2 daughters. Education: BA, Arts and Sciences, College of Liberal Arts, Pennsylvania State University, 1967; MA, Industrial Relations, University of Wisconsin, 1970; PhD, Comparative Industrial Relations, University of Wisconsin, 1973. Appointments: Industrial Relations Specialist, Chase Manhattan Bank, New York, 1967-68; Chairman, Human Resources and Labour Relations Area, McMaster University, 1976-78; Director, Theme School in International Justice and Human Rights, McMaster University, 1996-97; Assistant Professor, Associate Professor, Full Professor, Emeritus Professor, Industrial Relations, McMaster University, 1973-; Columnist, Hamilton Spectator, 1997-2002; New Democratic Party Candidate for Ontario Provincial Parliament, 2003. Publications: White Collar Union Growth in Britain and Sweden, 1975; Co-author, Education and Working Canadians, 1979; Skills Development Leave for Working Canadians: Towards a National Strategy, 1983; Editor, Comparative Industrial Relations, Contemporary Research and Theory, 1991; Co-editor, Industrial Relations Theory, its Nature, Scope and Pedagogy, 1993; Industrial Relations under Liberal Democracy, North America in Comparative Perspective, 1995; Co-author, Good Jobs, Bad Jobs, No Jobs, Tough Choices for Canadian Labour Law, 1995; Co-author, Labour and Employment Law, Cases, Materials and Commentary, 1998; Numerous book chapters and papers in refereed journals. Honours include: McMaster Student Union Certificate of Appreciation for Outstanding Contributions to Undergraduate Education, 1982-83, 1985-86, 1992-93, 1996-97; McMaster Student Union Undergraduate Teaching Award, 1984-85; Basu Outstanding Teaching Award, McMaster MBA Association, 1989-90; Canadian Pacific Distinguished Visiting Professor, University of Toronto, 1990; Distinguished Visiting Scholar, University of Western Australia, 1996; Gérard Dion Award for outstanding contributions to Canadian and International Industrial Relations, Canadian Industrial Relations Association, 1997; Co-recipient, President's Award for Resource Design, 1997. Memberships include: Society for the Promotion of Human Rights in Employment; International Industrial Relations Association; Canadian Industrial Relations Association; Industrial Relations Research Association; International Sociological Association. Address: 50 Whitton Road, Hamilton, L8S 4C7 Canada. E-mail: adamsr@mcmaster.ca

ADAMSON Donald, b. 30 March 1939, Culcheth, Cheshire, England. Critic; Biographer; Historian. m. Helen Freda Griffiths, 24 September 1966, 2 sons. Education: Magdalen College, Oxford, England, 1956-59; University of Paris, France, 1960-61; MA, MLitt, DPhil (Oxon). Appointment: Visiting Fellow, Wolfson College, Cambridge. Publications: T S Eliot: A Memoir, 1971; The House of Nell Gwyn, jointly, 1974; Les Romantiques Français Devant La Peinture Espagnole, 1989; Blaise Pascal: Mathematician, Physicist, And Thinker About God, 1995; Rides Round Britain, The Travel Journals of John Byng, 5th Viscount Torrington, 1996; The Curriers' Company: A Modern History, 2000; various translations of Balzac and Maupassant. Honour: JP, Cornwall, England, 1993. Membership: FSA, 1979; FRSL, 1983; FIL, 1989. Address: Dodmore House, Meopham, Kent, DA13 0AJ, Dodmore, England.

ADAMSON Donald, b. 15 June 1943, Dumfries, Scotland. Writer; Poet; Editor. Education: MA, English Literature, 1965, MLitt, Applied Linguistics, 1975, Edinburgh University. Appointments: EFL posts in France, Finland, Iran and Kuwait; Longman EFL Division, Research and Development Unit; Freelance EFL Writer and Editor. Contributions to: Lines Review; Orbis; New Writing Scotland. Honours: Glasgow University/Radio Clyde Poetry Prize, 1985; 2nd Prize, Northwords Competition, 1995; Winner, Herald Millennium Poem Competition, 1999; Scottish Arts Council Writer's Bursary, 1995. Address: 1 St Peter's Court, Dalbeattie, Scotland.

ADAMU Omokhogie, b. 14 February 1933, Ughiekha, Nigeria. Publisher. m. Uduone Rafat Enakele, 6 sons, 9 daughters. Education: BBA, MBA, PhD, Western States University for Professional Studies, Missouri, USA, 1986-88. Appointments: Accounts, Sales Clerk, United Africa Company Ltd, 1951-52; Store Clerk, Nigerian Army, 1952-58; Import Export Representative, Winter Detlefs and Company, 1958-60; Assistant Manager, Advertising Association Nigeria Ltd, 1960-62; Accounts Clerk, Union Trading Company, 1962-63; Secretary, Costain West Africa Ltd, 1964-65; Accountant, Philip Holzman Ltd, 1965-67; Accounts Clerk, Ukpilla Cement Company ltd, 1967-69; Personnel Manager, Monier Construction Company Ltd, 1969-74; Administration Manager, Horicon Ltd, 1981-82; Publicity Secretary, Bendel State Farmers Council, Benin City, 1984; Secretary, Nigerian Farmers and Peasants Organisation, Benin City, 1984; President, Afenmai Farmers Multi-Purpose Co-operative Society, 1984-85; Education Agent, London City College, 1986; Contributing Editor, Neutral Force Commission Ltd, 1991-92; Consultant, Guest Writer, The Afenmai News Magazine, 1996-98; Chairman, Chief Executive Officer, Adamu Farms Ltd, 1963-93, Adamu Livestock Feeds Ltd, 1980-93, Adamu Management International, 1981-93; Director General, Development Data Exchange, 1986-2002; Chairman, Managing Editor, Bookwork Co., 2002-. Publications: Several newspaper and magazine articles, papers, radio and TV scripts. Honours: Certificate, Meritorious Contribution to Agriculture in Nigeria, 1981; Runner Up Prize, Quarterly Writing Competition, 1988; Gold Medal, Trophy, Federation of International Youth Sports, 2000. Memberships include: Etsako West Local Government, South Ibie District Education Committee, 1995; Committee on Creation of Afenmesan State, Local Government Area and Boundary Adjustment, 1996; Iyerekhu Secondary School Board of Governors, 1997-99; Member, National Geographic Society, USA, 2004. Address: Adamu Farm Estate, PO Box 78, Auchi 312101, Edo State, Nigeria.

ADCOCK Fleur, b. 10 February 1934, Papakura, New Zealand. Poet. Education: MA Victoria University of Wellington, 1955. Publications: The Eye of the Hurricane, 1964; Tigers, 1967; High Tide in the Garden, 1971; The Scenic Route, 1974; The Inner Harbour, 1979; Below Loughrigg, 1979; Selected Poems, 1983; The Virgin and the Nightingale, 1983; The Incident Book, 1986; Time Zones, 1991; Looking Back, 1997; Poems 1960-2000, 2000; Editor: The Oxford Book of Contemporary New Zealand Poetry, 1982; The Faber Book of 20th Century Women's Poetry, 1987; Translator and Editor: Hugh Primas and the Archpoet, 1994. Honour: Order of the British Empire, 1996. Membership: Fellow, Royal Society of Literature. Address: 14 Lincoln Road, London N2 9DL, England.

ADDINGTON David John, b. 22 July 1947, London, England. Legal Executive; Arbitrator; Priest. m. (1) Moira Louise Meiklejohn, divorced, 2 daughters, (2) Mary Ann Mitchelson, 1989, 1 son, 1 daughter. Education: Polytechnic Central, London, 1963-64; Trained in mediation with Centre for Effective Dispute Resolution, 2002; Certificate in Christian Studies, 2003. Appointments: Management Clerk, Field Fisher Waterhouse, London, 1963-71; Litigation Manager, D Miles Griffiths Piercy & Co, London, 1971-73; Rubinstein Callingham, London, 1973-75; S Rutter & Co, London, 1975-77; Appleby, Spurling & Kempe, Bermuda, 1977-94; Law Reform Committee, Bermuda Supreme Court Rules, 1989-; Mello, Hollis, Jones & Martin, Bermuda, 1994-; Committee, Bermuda Mediation and Arbitration Centre, 1994-; Ordained Deacon, 2001 and Priest, 2003, licensed as NSM

Dictionary of International Biography

to St Mary the Virgin Church, Warwick Parish, Bermuda. Publications: Contributed articles to professional journals. Memberships: Fellow, Institute of Legal Executives, 1972, Chairman of Bermuda Branch, 1982; Chartered Management Institute, 1982; Bermuda Zone International Association Lions Club, chairman, 1992-93; Master Lodge Civil and Military, Bermuda, 1995-97; Secretary, Bermuda Sailors Home Inc, 1995-98; Fellow, Chartered Institute of Arbitrators, 1996; Secretary, Anglican Church Synod, Bermuda, 1996-2002; Diocesan Reader, 1995 and Ordinand, 1998; St John's College Nottingham, England Extension Studies, 1998-; Chairman of the Board of Management, The Bermuda Sailors' Home Inc, 2001-; Chaplain, Royal Naval Association, Bermuda Branch, 2002-; Mariners Club, Sandys Boat Club, Jubilee Sailing Trust. Address: Mello, Jones & Martin, Reid House, 31 Church St, Hamilton, HM 12, Bermuda.

ADDIS Richard James, b. 23 August 1956. Journalist. m. Eunice Minogue, 1983, 1 son, 2 daughters. Education: Downing College, Cambridge; MA Cantab. Appointments: With Evening Standard, 1985-89; Deputy Editor, Sunday Telegraph, 1989-91; Executive Editor, Daily Mail, 1991-95; Editor, The Express on Sunday, 1996-98; Consultant Editor, Mail on Sunday, 1998-99; Editor, The Globe and Mail, Toronto, Ontario, Canada, 1999-2002; Assistant Editor, Design Editor, Financial Times, 2002-; Appointed Honoary Governor, York University, Canada, 2002. Address: Financial Times, One Southwark Bridge, London SE1 9HL, England. Website: www.ft.com

ADDISON Mark Eric, b. 22 January 1956. Civil Servant. m. Lucinda Clare Booth, 1987. Education: St John's College, Cambridge; City University; Imperial College, London; MA Cantab; MSc; PhD. Appointments: With Department of Employment, 1978-95, including Private Secretary to Parliamentary Under-Secretary of State, 1982, Private Secretary to Prime Minister, 1985, Regional Director, London Training Agency, 1988-91, Director of Finance and Resource Management, 1991-94; Director of Safety Policy, Health and Safety Executive, 1994-98; Chief Executive, Crown Prosecution Service, 1998-2001; Director General, Operations and Service Delivery), Department for Environment, Food and Rural Affairs, 2001-. Address: Department for Environment, Food and Rural Affairs, 1a Page Street, London SW1P 4PQ, England. Website: www.defra.gov.uk

ADDO Francis Yaw, b. 26 February 1948, Koforidua, Ghana. Project Manager; Quantity Surveyor; Arbitrator. m. Akua F Addo. Education: BSc, Building Technology, Ghana, 1973; MSc, Project Management, Pretoria, 2001; Postgraduate Diploma, College of Estate Management, Reading, England, 2001. Appointment: Managing Director, Building Industry Consultants Limited, Accra, Ghana, 1980-. Publication: Construction Today, volume I, No 70. Memberships: Fellow, Ghana Institution of Surveyors; Fellow Association of Arbitrators, Southern Africa; Fellow, Chartered Institute of Arbitrators; Corporate Member, Association of South African Quantity Surveyors; Incorporate Member, Chartered Institute of Building, UK. Address: Post Office Box GP 3684, Accra, Ghana, West Africa. E-mail: bic@ghana.com

ADE Wolfgang Roland, b. 15 January 1947, Stuttgart, Germany. Physician. m. Shizuko Okawa, 22 November 1981, 1 daughter. Education: Applied Managerial Economics, Fachschule für Betriebswirtschaft, Stuttgart, 1972-74; Medical School Universities of Hohenheim, Heidelberg, Tübingen, 1975-81. Appointments: Research Fellow, 1982-87, Lecturer, 1987-89, Tokyo Women's Medical College, Japan; Medical Advisor, Nippon Roussel, Roussel Morishita, Hoechst Marion Roussel, Aventis Pharma, 1983-; Adjunct Staff, Research and Scientific Officer, Juro Wada Commemorative Heart and Lung Institute, 1987-. Publications:

Author: Autoregulated Extra and Intracorporeal Pump System for Perfusion, 1992; Several articles in professional journals. Memberships: Secretary General, World Society of Cardio-Thoracic Surgeons; Secretary, World Artificial Organ, Immunology and Transplantation Society. Address: 8-10 Nishimizumoto 1-chome, Katsushika-ku, Tokyo 125-0031, Japan.

ADE-FOSUDO Mary, b. 16 October 1960, Lagos, Nigeria. Business Consultant. m. Prince Abewale J Fosudo, 2 sons, 3 daughters. Education: Diploma, Secretarial Studies, Pitman's College, London, England, 1979. Appointments: Artist, Drama Department, Radio Nigeria, 1979-82; Administrator, Fifth Avenue Holdings, 1982; Business Support Consultant, Arthur Anderson, 1982-99; Principal Partner, FOSAD Holdings Limited, 1999-. Honours: Doctor of Philosophy, University of Malborough, USA, 2003; National Administrative Management Merit, 2003; Award of Excellence in Business Management, 2003. Memberships: Head, Committee on Tourism, Hotel and Catering Services, Nigerian-American Chamber of Commerce; Affiliate Member, African Chamber of Commerce, Houston, Texas, USA; Fellow, Institute of Administrative and Management of Nigeria. Address: FOSAD Consulting Ltd, Ladico House, 4th Floor, Plot 1661, Oylin Jolayemi Street, Victoria Island, Lagos, Nigeria. E-mail: fosad@skannet.com

ADEBAYO Williams Oluwole, b. 1 June 1963, Epe-Ekiti, Moba Lga, Nigeria. Lecturer. m. Mary Olaitan, 2 sons, 2 daughters. Education: BSc honours, Geography, Ado-Ekiti, 1987; MSc, 1991, PhD, 2000, Geography, Ibadan; Diploma, Computer Science, DCPS, Akure, 1993. Appointments: Staff Secretary, Geography, Examination Co-ordinator, 1990-96; Fieldwork Co-ordinator, 1992-99; Head of Department, Geography, 1999-2002; Co-ordinator, UNAD EDP, 2000-01. Publications: 20 articles in learned journals. Honours: Best Graduating Student in Geography, 1987. Memberships: Environment and Behaviour Association of Nigeria; RSM; Nigerian Geographical Association; Nigerian Meteor Society. Address: Department of Geography and Planning Science, University of Ado-Ekiti, PMB 5363, Ado-Ekiti, Nigeria.

ADELMAN Saul Joseph, b. 18 November 1944, Atlantic City, New York, USA. Astronomer; College Professor. m. Carol, 3 sons. Education: BS, Physics, University of Maryland, 1966; PhD, Astronomy, California Institute of Technology, 1972. Appointments: Postdoctorate, NASA Space Flight Center, 1972-74, 1984-86; Assistant Astronomer, Boston University, 1974-78; Assistant Professor, Associate Professor, Professor, The Citadel, 1978-. Publications: 292 papers; 5 articles; 1 book. Honours: Phi Beta Kappa; Phi Kappa Phi; Sigma Pi Sigma; Sigma Xi. Memberships: International Astronomical Union; American Astronomical Society; Astronomical Society of the Pacific; Canadian Astronomical Society. Address: The Citadel Department of Physics, 171 Moultrie St, Charleston, SC 29409, USA.

ADENEKAN Olutayo David, b. 10 October 1942, Abeokuta, Ogun State, Nigeria. 2 sons, 3 daughters. Education: Kingston Polytechnic, 1969-72; Fellow, Institute of Chartered Management Accountants; Fellow, Institute of Chartered Accountants of Nigeria. Accountant, Federal Ministry of Works and Housing, 1965-72; Accountant, Senior Accountant, Nigerian Provident Fund, 1972-73; Senior Accountant, Head, Internal Audit Section, Texaco Nigeria Limited, 1973-78; Chairman, Oast Industries Ltd, De Stallion Finance Ltd, Oasis Exploration Ltd, 1978-; Managing Partner, Olutayo Adenekan & Co, Chartered Accountants, 1983-. Publications: Contribution to National Economic Recovery; One Bullet, One Love. Honour: Grand Prix Master for European Quality, 1990; Memberships: Institute of Chartered Accountants of Nigeria; Nigerian Institute of Taxation. Address: 22 Agboola Street, Ijeshatedo, Surulere, Lagos State, Nigeria.

Dictionary of International Biography

ADER Robert, b. 20 February 1932, New York, USA. Psychologist. m. Gayle Simon, 4 daughters. Education: BS, Tulane University, New Orleans, USA, 1953; PhD, Cornell University, Ithaca, New York, USA, 1957. Appointments: Teaching and Research Assistantships, Department of Psychology, Cornell University, 1953-57; Research Instructor, Psychiatry, University of Rochester School of Medicine and Dentistry, 1957-59; Research Senior Instructor, 1959-61; Research Assistant Professor, 1961-64; Associate Professor, 1964-68; Professor, Department of Psychiatry, University of Rochester, 1968-; Visiting Professor, Rudolf Magnus Institute for Pharmacology, University of Utrecht, The Netherlands, 1970-71; Dean's Professor, University of Rochester School of Medicine and Dentistry, 1982-83; Professor of Medicine, 1983-; George L Engel Professor, Psychosocial Medicine, 1983-2002; Distinguished University Professor, 2002-; Fellow, Centre for Advanced Study in the Behavioural Sciences, 1992-93. Publications: Behaviourally conditioned immunosuppression; Behaviour and the Immune System; Psychoneuroimmunology; The role of conditioning in pharmacotherapy; Many other publications. Honours: Research Scientist Award; Institutional Training Grant; Editor-in-Chief, Brain Behaviour and Immunity; Honorary MD; Honorary ScD; Many other honours. Memberships: Academy of Behavioural Medicine Research, President, 1984-85; American Psychosomatic Society, President, 1979-80; International Society for Developmental Psychobiology, President, 1981-82; Psychoneuroimmunology Research Society, Founding President, 1993-94; Many other memberships. Address: 7 Moss Creek Ct, Pittsford, NY 14534-1071, USA.

ADESH Hari Shanker, b. 7 August 1936, Bharat, India. Scholar; Author (Mahakavi); World Laureate (Vishwakari); Poet; Musicologist; Philosophist; Astrologer; (Prophet) Journalist; Artiste. Education: Doctorate (Hon), 3 Master's Degrees in Hindi Literature, Sanskrit Literature, Music, Indian Philosophy, Sahitya Alankaar, Sahitya Ratna, Sangeet Visharad. Appointments: Cultural Representative ICCR, Government of India in Republic of Trinidad and Tobago (West Indies) for ten years; Founder, Life-Director, Bharatiya Vidya Sansthhaan Trinidad and Tobago (Institute of Indian Knowledge), in many countries and Shri Adesh Ashram, 1977; Principal, Ashram College, San Fernando; Minister of Religion, establishing Bharatiya Vidya Sansthhaan Canada, 1981; Vidya Mandir, Spiritual Preceptor, Music and Philosophy Professor, Toronto, 1985; Minister of Religion, USA; Founded, Antar Raashtreeya Bharatiya Vidya Sansthhaan, USA, 1978; AHINSA Inc (Antar Raashtreeya Hindu Samaj), 1998; 32 International Annual Training Camps in Trinidad on Indian Culture; International performing artiste of radio, television and stage. Publications: Great Epic Anuraag and Shakuntalaa including over 300 books in Hindi, English and Urdu; Author of 7 Saptashatee (700 couplets) and Pravaasee Kee Paatee Bhaarat Maataa Ke Naam; About 10,000 public discourses, seminars and lectures; Composed over 5500 lyrics and songs, 120 audio cassettes, several CDs and LPs; Author of bilingual Hindi and Music texts; Playwright, director of many dramas staged in auditoriums in India, Trinidad and Canada. Honours: Over 50 national and international awards and honours in the field of Hindi Literature, Music, Philosophy, Education and Culture include: Dr M Satyanarayan Award, Ministry of Education, Government of India (Certificate of Appreciation for the Most Outstanding Hindi Author and Poet out of India); Hummingbird Gold Medal, Government of Trinidad and Tobago; Honorary Lieutenant Award, State of Louisiana, USA; Shawl of Honour, Canada; World Hindi Honour, India; International Hindi Award, 5th World Hindi Conference, Trinidad; Ramayan Puraskaar, 2nd World Ramayan Conference, Thailand. Memberships: Director General, Bharatiya Vidya Sansthhaan, Institute of Indian Knowledge, Trinidad and Tobago, Canada, USA; Deputy Governor, ABI; International World Peace Prize, United Cultural Convention, USA; Foundation Member, World Peace and Diplomacy Forum, Founding Cabinet (IBCUK); World Laureate, ABI; Trustee, Vishwa Hindu Parishad International; Patron, Hindi Prachhaarinee Sabha Canada; Editor-in-Chief, The History of Hindi Literature, Naagaree Prachhaarinee Sabha Kaashee, India; Editor-in-Chief, Jyoti-Eng, Jeewan Jyoti Title, Rishi (Sage), Param Sant (Great Saint), Sangeet Aachaarya and Naad-Vidya-Vaaridhi (Ocean of Knowledge of Music). Address: 18 Sugarbush Square, West Hill, Ontario M1C 3M7, Canada.

ADETUNJI Nasiru Adewale, b. 10 February 1970, Abeokuta, Nigeria. Chemist. m. Rasidat Sade Akintunde, 1 son, 1 daughter. Education: Final Diploma in Science Laboratory Technology, Chemistry/Biochemistry Option, 1998; MBA, 2001; PGD, Analytical/Environmental Chemistry, 2002. Appointments: Laboratory Assistant, 1990-94, Laboratory Technician, 1995-98, Assistant Manager, Quality Control, 2001-, IPI (Nig.) Ltd; Quality Control Supervisor, 1998-2000. Publications: Comparative Studies of the Composition of Detergent in Nigerian Market, 1998; Financing Small and Medium Scale Enterprises in Nigeria, 2001; Physico-Chemical Properties and Antimicrobial Activities of Mondora Myristica (Calabash Nutmeg) Oil Extract, 2002. Honour: Commendation on Installation and Commissioning of Sulphonation Plant of Tudab Engineering (Nigeria), Limited. Memberships: Nigerian Institute of Science Technology; American Chemical Society. Address: 4 Sanni Street, Off Araromi Ayetoro Road, PO Box 3482, Abeokuta, Ogun State, Nigeria. E-mail: naadetunji2@yahoo.com

ADEY Christopher, b. 1943, Essex, England. Conductor. Education: Royal Academy of Music, London, principally as violinist with Manoug Parikian. Career: Violinist until 1973 mainly with Halle and London Philharmonic Orchestras; Debut as Conductor in 1973; Became Associate Conductor for BBC Scottish Symphony Orchestra, 1973-76; Frequent guest appearances throughout Britain and with the leading London orchestras; Associate Conductor with Ulster Orchestra, 1981-84; Has worked in most European countries, Middle and Far East, Canada and USA; Frequent broadcasts for BBC and abroad; Extensive repertoire covering symphonic and chamber orchestra works of all periods and including choral works and opera; Professor of Conducting at Royal College of Music, 1979-92; Orchestral Trainer in demand at conservatoires throughout Britain and maintains a large commitment to guest conducting with county, national and international youth orchestras; Cycle of the complete Martinu symphonies for BBC, 1992. Honours include: ARAM, 1979; Commemorative Medal of Czech Government, 1986; FRCM, 1989. Address: 137 Ansden Road, Willesden Green, London NW2 4AH, England.

ADHAM Fatma Kamel, b. 26 January 1938, Cairo, Egypt. University Professor. m. T Hefnawy, deceased, 2 daughters. Education: BSc, Distinction, 1963, MSc, Entomology, 1969. PhD, Entomology, 1974, Faculty of Science, Cairo University, Cairo, Egypt. Appointments include: Demonstrator, 1963-74, Lecturer, 1974-79, Assistant Professor, 1979-85, Professor of Medical Entomology, 1985-, Department of Entomology, Faculty of Science, Cairo University; Insect Psysiologist, NTH-Cairo University Project, Epidemiological and Biological Aspects of Tick Borne Infection in Egypt and Elsewhere, 1977-80; Associate Professor, 1983-85, Professor (on lease), 1985-88, Al Ain University, United Arab Emirates; Professor (on lease), Girls' College, Faculty of Science, El Dammam, Saudi Arabia, 1994-96. Publications: 37 articles in professional journals and presented at conferences as author and co-author include most recently: Seasonal incidence of the carrion breeding blowflies Lucilia sericata (Meigen) and Chrysomya albiceps (Wied.) (Diptera: Calliphoridae) in Abu-Rawash Farm-Giza, Egypt, 2001; Histopathological studies of sheep infested with Chrysomya albiceps (Wied.), 2001; Larval aggregation and competition for food in experimental populations of Chrysomya albiceps (Wied.) (Diptera: Calliphoridae) and Wohlfartia nuba (Wied.) (Diptera: Sarcophagidae, 2001; The effects of laboratory Hepatozoon gracilis infection on the fecundity, mortality and longevity of Culex (Culex) pipienc Linnaeus (Diptera: Culicidae) in Egypt, 2003 (in press). Honours: Outstanding Female Executive Award; Woman of the Year; Listed in Who's Who publications and biographical dictionaries. Memberships: Entomological Society of Egypt; Egyptian Society of Parasitology; Egyptian Society of Histology and Cytology; Egyptian Society of Biochemistry. Address: 9 Shafik Ghorbal, Roxy, Heliopolis, Cairo, Egypt.

ADIE Kathryn (Kate) b. 19 September 1945, England. Television News Correspondent. Education: Newcastle University. Appointments: Technician and Producer, BBC Radio, 1969-76; Reporter, BBC TVS, 1977-79; BBC TV News, 1979-81; Correspondent, 1982-; Chief Correspondent, 1989-2003; Freelance journalist, broadcaster and TV presenter, 2003-. Publication: The Kindness of Strangers, autobiography, 2002. Honours: RTS News Award, 1981, 1987; Monte Carlo International News Award, 1981, 1990; Honorary MA, Bath University, 1987; BAFTA Richard Dimbleby Award, 1989; Honorary DLitt, City University, 1989; Honorary MA, Newcastle University, 1990; Freeman of Sunderland, 1990; Honorary DLitt, Sunderland University, 1991; Loughborough University, 1991; Honorary Professor, Sunderland University, 1995. Address: c/o BBC Television, Wood Lane, London W12 7RJ, England.

ADIGUZEL Osman, b. 28 November 1952, Nigde, Turkey. Physicist; Researcher. m. Hatice, 2 sons, 1 daughter. Education: BSc, Ankara University, 1974; MSc, 1977, PhD, 1980, Diyarbakir University. Appointments: Assistant, Diyarbakir University, 1975-80; Lecturer, 1980-82, Assistant Professor, 1982-90, Associate Professor, 1990-96, Professor, 1996-, Department of Physics, Firat University. Publications: Numerous articles in professional scientific journals. Honours: Certificate in recognition of significant contribution of 2 patterns to the Powder Diffraction File, International Centre for Diffraction Data, 2000. Memberships: Turkish Physical Society; International Theoretical Physics Centre. Address: Department of Physics, Firat University, 23169 Elazig, Turkey. E-mail: oadiguzel@firat.edu.tr

ADISA Opal Plamer, b. 6 November 1954, Kingston, Jamaica. Writer. 1 son, 2 daughters. Honours: BA, Communications, Hunter College, CUNY, 1975; MA, English, San Francisco State University, 1981; MA, Drama, San Francisco State University, 1986; PhD, Ethnic Studies, Literature, University of California, Berkeley, 1992. Appointments include: Lecturer, University of California, Berkeley, African American Studies Department, 1978-93; Instructor, City College of San Francisco, 1980-84; Poet, Oakland Museum, California, 1986-92; Lecturer, San Francisco State University, Black Studies Department, 1981-87; Associate Professor and Chair of Ethnic Studies/Cultural Diversity Program, 1993, Professor, 1998- California College of Arts and Crafts; Coordinator, Lockwood after-school program, Each One, Teach One, 1997-99. Publications: Books: Pina The Many-Eyed Fruit, 1985; Bake-Face and Other Guava Stories, 1986, 1989; Traveling Women (poetry collection, co-author), 1989; Tamarind and Mango Women (poetry), 1992; It Begins With Tears (novel), 1997; Leaf-of-Life, Poetry Collection, 2000; CD, The Tongue is a Drum, 2002; Caribbean Passion (poetry collection), 2004; Essays, articles, stories, book reviews, interviews, poems. Honours: Fellowships, Grants, writer's awards; Phi Beta Kappa, 1991; Cave Canem Fellow, 1999, 2000, 2001; Distinguished Bay Area Woman Writer Award, National Women's Political Caucus, 1991; PEN Oakland/ Josephine Miles Literary Award for poetry collection Tamarind and Mango Women, 1992; Canute A Brodhurst Prize for story, The Brethren, University of the Virgin Isles, St Croix, 1996; Laureate, San Francisco Public Library, 2000; Storytelling Grant, Oakland Cultural Arts Division, 2002-03; Multi-Media Grant, California Arts Council, 2002-04. Memberships include: Association of Caribbean Women Writers and Scholars; National Writers Union; National Association for Ethnic Studies; World Conjurers, Northern Association of African American Storytellers; Caribbean Association for Feminist Research and Action. Address: PO Box 10625, Oakland, CA 94610, USA. E-mail: opalpro@aol.com

ADITYA Gora, b. 5 December 1940, India. Biochemist. m. Phyllis Sheila, 2 sons, 1 daughter. Education: Bachelor of Science; Diploma in Hospital Administration. Appointments: President and Chief Executive Officer, Med-Chem Laboratories Limited; President, ACT Health Group Corporation; Chief Executive Officer, Atfinc; President, Assure Health Inc; Chairman of the Board, Hayes Clinical Laboratory, Florida, USA. Honour: Hind Rattan Award, for outstanding services, Prime Minister of India, 1998. Memberships: Canadian Association of Rehab Professionals; Canadian Society of Clinical Chemists. Address: 3 Fiddlers Circle, Maple, Ontario, L6A 1E9 Canada. E-mail: gaditya@acthealth.com

ADJANI Isabelle, b. 27 June 1955, France. Actress. Education: Lycée de Courbevoie. Appointment: President, Commn d'avances sur recettes, 1986-88. Career: Films include: Faustine et le bel été, 1972, Barocco, 1977; Nosferatu, 1978; Possession, 1980; Quartet, 1981; l'Eté Meurtrier, 1983; Camille Claudel, 1988; La Reine Margot, 1994; Diabolique, 1996. Theatre includes: La Maison de Bernada Alba, 1970; l'Avare, 1972-73 Port-Royal, 1973; Ondine, 1974; TV includes: Le Petit Bougnat, 1969; l'Ecole des Femmes, 1973; Top á Sacha Distel, 1974; Princesse aux Petit Pois, 1986. Honours: Best Actress, Cannes, Possession, 1981; Best Actress, Cannes, Quartet, 1982; Best Actress César, Best Actress Award, Berlin Film Festival, Camille Claudel, 1989; Best Actress César, La Reine Margot, 1995. Address: c/o Phonogram, 89 Boulevard Auguste Blanqui, 75013 Paris, France.

ADJI Boukary, b. Niger. Politician; Economist. Appointments: Minister of Finance, Niger, 1983-87; Deputy Governor, Central Bank of West African States, to 1996, 1997-; Prime Minister of Niger, 1996. Address: Banque Centrale des Etats de l'Afrique de l'Ouest, avenue Abdoulaye Fadiga, BP 3108, Dakar, Senegal. E-mail: webmaster@bceao.int Website: www.bceao.int

ADLER Margot Susanna, b. 16 April 1946, Little Rock, Arkansas, USA. Journalist; Radio Producer; Talk Show Host. Education: BA, University of California, Berkeley, 1968; MS, Columbia School of Journalism, 1970; Nieman Fellow, Harvard University, 1982. Publications: Drawing Down the Moon: Witches, Druids, Goddess-Worshippers and Other Pagans in America Today, 1979, revised edition, 1986; Heretic's Heart: A Journey Through Spirit and Revolution, 1997. Memberships: Authors Guild; American Federation of Radio and Television Artists. Address: 333 Central Park West, New York, NY 10025, USA.

ADLER-KARLSSON Gunnar, b. 6 March 1933, Karlshamn, Sweden. Professor. m. Marianne Ehrnford. Education: Studies at Harvard University and Berkeley University, 1961-62; Dr of Law, 1962; Dr of Economics, 1968. Appointments: Collaborator of Gunnar Myrdal, Stockholm University, 1962-68; Professor, University of Roskilde, 1974-89; Director, Capri Institute for International Social Philosophy, 1979-; Opened Europe's first Philosophical Park in Capri, 2000. Publications: 15 books on social problems and numerous articles in professional journals. Memberships: Numerous. Address: Box 79, I-80071, Anacapri, Italy. E-mail: adler.karlsson@capri.it Website: www.capriinstitute.org

ADLERSHTEYN Leon, b. 28 October 1925, St Petersburg, Russia. Naval Architect; Researcher; Educator. m. Irina Bereznaya. Education: MS, Shipbuilding Institute, St Petersburg, Russia 1945-51; DSc, Central Research Institute for Shipbuilding Technology, St Petersburg, Russia, 1970. Appointments: Private, Soviet Army, 1943-45; Foreman, Deputy Chief, Hull Shop, Baltic Shipyard, St Petersburg, Russia, 1951-63; Chief Technologist, Team Leader, 1963-74, Chief Researcher, 1993-94, Central Research Institute for Shipbuilding Technology; Head of the Chair, Professor, Shipbuilding Academy, 1974-94; Retired 1994. Publications: Author or co-author of 11 books which include: Accuracy in Ship Hull Manufacturing; Mechanisation and Automation of Ship Manufacturing; Modular Shipbuilding; Ship Examiner (2 editions); Handbook of Ship Marking and Examining Works and over 160 brochures and scientific articles; 9 Russian Patents. Honours: Order of the Patriotic War, 1st Class; 12 Russian Military Medals; 3 Medals of American Legion; Medals of Russian Industrial Exhibition; Listed in numerous Who's Who and biographical publications. Memberships: Fellow, Institute of Marine Engineering, Science and Technology, UK; Society of Naval Architects and Marine Engineers, USA; American Association of Invalids and Veterans of WWII from the former Soviet Union. Address: 72 Montgomery Street, Apt 1510, Jersey City, NJ 07302-3827, USA. E-mail: berez@aol.com

ADO Yurii, b. 12 June 1927, Yalta, Crimea, USSR. Physicist. m. Gouskova Margarita, 2 February 1951, 2 daughters. Education: Engineer Diploma, 1950; Candidate of Physics and Mathematical Sciences Diploma, 1957; Dr of Physics and Mathematical Sciences Diploma, 1967. Appointments: Engineer, Postgraduate Student, Senior Scientist of Lebedev Physics Institute, Moscow, 1950-64; Head, Accelerator Department, Institute for High Energy Physics, Protvino, 1964-88; Professor, 1977; Principal Scientist, IHEP Protvino, 1988-. Publications: About 140 publications in scientific magazines, pre-prints and proceedings of international and national conferences on particle accelerators. Honours: Decoration, Friendship of Nations, USSR, 1986; State Prize, USSR, 1970. Membership: Head of Chair, Moscow State University Physics Department, 1987-. Address: Lenin Street 12, Flat 26, Protvino, Moscow Region 142284, Russia.

ADOBOLI Eugène Koffi, b. 1934. Politician. Appointments: Formerly with Mission to United Nations; Prime Minister of Togo, 1999-2000. Address: c/o Office of the Prime Minister, Lomé, Togo.

ADORJAN Carol (Madden), (Kate Kenyon), b. 17 August 1934, Chicago, Illinois, USA. Writer; Teacher. m. William W Adorjan, 17 August 1957, 2 sons, 2 daughters. Education: BA, English Literature, Magna Cum Laude, Mundelein College, 1956. Appointments: Fellow, Midwest Playwrights Lab, 1977; Writer-in-Residence, Illinois Arts Council, 1981-; National Radio Theatre, 1980-81. Publications: Someone I Know, 1968; The Cat Sitter Mystery, 1972; Eighth Grade to the Rescue (as Kate Kenyon), 1987; A Little Princess (abridgment), 1987; Those Crazy Eighth Grade Pictures (as Kate Kenyon), 1987; WKID: Easy Radio Plays (with Yuri Rasovsky), 1988; The Copy Cat Mystery, 1990; That's What Friends Are For, 1990. Radio and Stage Plays: Julian Theater, BBC, National Radio Theatre, etc. Contributions to: Redbook; Woman's Day; North American Review; Denver Quarterly; Four Quarters; Yankee. Honours: Josephine Lusk Fiction Award, Munderlein College, 1955; Earplay, 1972; Illinois Arts Council Completion Grant, 1977-78; Dubuque Fine Arts Society National

One-Act Playwriting Competition, 1978; Ohio State Award, 1980. Memberships: Society of Midland Authors; Society of Children's Book Writers and Illustrators; Author's Guild. Address: 1667 Winnetka Road, Glenview, IL 60025, USA.

ADRIANO Dino, b. 24 April 1943. m. Susan Rivett, 1996, 2 daughters. Education: Highgate College. Appointments: Articled clerk, George W Spencer & Co, 1959-64; Trainee, Accounting department, J Sainsbury plc, 1964-65; Financial Accounts Department, 1965-73, Branch Financial Control Manager, 1973-80, Area Director, Sainsbury's Central and Western Area, 1986-89, Assistant Managing Director, 1995-96, Deputy Chief Executive, 1996-97, Joint Group Chief Executive, 1997-98, Group Chief Executive, 1998-2000, Chair, Chief Executive, 1997-2000, Sainsbury's Supermarkets Ltd; General Manager, 1981-86, Managing Director, 1989-95, Deputy Chief Executive, 1996-97, Homebase; Director, Laura Ashley plc, 1996-98; Trustee, 1990-96, Adviser on Retail Matters, 1996-, Vice Chair, 2001-, Oxfam; Trustee, Women's Royal Voluntary Service, 2001-. Address: Stamford House, Stamford Street, London SE1 9LL, England.

ADU Aboagye Ohene, b. 5 August 1960, Accra, Ghana. Mining and Structural Geologist. m. Bosompemah Ohene Adu, 1 son, 1 daughter. Education: BSc (Hons), Geology/Physics, Legon, Ghana, 1984; MSc, DIC, Applied Structural Geology and Rock Mechanics, Imperial College, London, England, 1996; Postgraduate Certificate in Management, 2002, MBA in progress, Henley Management College, England. Appointments: Geologist, 1984, Sectional Geologist, 1989-93, Senior Geologist, 1993-97, Geology Superintendent, 1997-2003, Ashanti Goldfields Company Ltd, Ghana. Memberships: Ghana Institution of geologists; Society for Mining, Metallurgy and Exploration; IASTG; ISRM. Address: Ashanti Goldfields Company Ltd, Box 10, Obuasi, Ghana. E-mail: aboagye.ohene-adu@ashantigold.com

ADVANI Chanderban Ghanshamdas, b. 23 July 1924, Hyderbad Sind, India. Businessman. m. Veena Chandru, 1 son, 1 daughter. Education: BA. Appointments: Manager, Narain Advani & Co, Karachi; Manager, French Drugs Co, Karachi; Manager, Indo-French Traders, Pondicherry; General Manager, L L Mohnani & Co, Yokohama, Japan; Chief Executive Officer, Nephews' International Inc. Yokohama, Japan; Proprietor, Nephews' Commercial Corporation, Karachi, India. Publications: Articles to various magazines and newspapers including Bharat Ratna, Hong Kong; Indian, Hong Kong. Honours: Medals, Citations, Mayors of Mumbai (India), Yokohama (Japan), Key to Yokahama from the Mayor of Yokohama. Memberships: Indian Chamber of Commerce, Japan; Indian Merchants Association of Yokohama; Foreign Correspondents Club of Japan; India International Centre, New Delhi; Yokohama Chamber of Commerce and Industry, Yokohama; Sinnim Lodge, Shriners Club, Tokyo. Address: 502, New Port Building, 25/16 Yamashita Cho, Naka Ku, Port PO Box 216, Yokohama 231-86-91, Japan. E-mail: nephewsjapan@yahoo.com

AFFLECK Ben, b. 15 August 1972, Berkeley, California, USA. Actor. Career: Appeared in films including School Ties, 1992, Buffy the Vampire Slayer, 1995, Dazed and Confused, 1995, Mallrats, 1995, Glory Daze, 1997, Office Killer, 1997, Chasing Amy, 1997, Going All the Way, 1997, Good Will Hunting, film and screenplay, 1997, Phantoms, 1998, Armageddon, 1998, Shakespeare in Love, 1998, Reindeer Games, 1999, Forces of Nature, 1999, Dogma, 1999, Daddy and Them, 1999, The Boiler Room, 1999, 200 Cigarettes, 1999; Bounce, 2000; The Third Wheel (also producer), 2000; Pearl Harbor, 2001; The Sum of All Fear, 2002; Changing Lanes, 2002; Daredevil, 2003. Television appearances include: Voyage of the Mimi, Against the Grain,

Dictionary of International Biography

Lifetstories: Family in Crisis, Hands of a Stranger, Daddy. Honours: Academy Award for Good Will Hunting, 1997; Golden Globe for Best Original Screenplay, 1997. Address: c/o Creative Artists Agency, 9830 Wilshire Boulevard, Beverly Hills, CA 90212, USA.

AGA KHAN IV Karim (HH Prince), b. 13 December 1936, Creux-de-Genthod, Geneva, Switzerland. Spiritual Leader and Imam of Ismaili Muslims. m. (1) Sarah Frances Croker-Poole, 1969, div. 1995, 2 sons, 1 daughter, (2) Princess Gabriele zu Leiningen, 1998. Education: BA, Harvard University. Career: Became Aga Khan IV on death of Aga Khan III, 1957; Granted title of His Highness by Queen Elizabeth II, 1957, title of His Royal Highness by the Shah of Iran, 1959; Founder, Chairman, Aga Khan Foundation, 1967, Aga Khan Award for Architecture, 1977-, Institute of IsmailimStudies, 1977-; Founder, Chancellor, Aga Khan University, Pakisitan, 1983; Founder, Chairman, Aga Khan Trust for Culturre, 1988; Founder and Chancellor, University of Central Asia, 2001. Honours: Commandeur, Ordre du Mérite Mauritanien, 1960; Grand Croix, Ordre du Prince Henry du Gouvernement Portugais, 1960, Ordre National de la Côte d'Ivoire, 1965, Ordre de la Haute-Volta, 1965, Ordre National Malagache, 1966, Ordre du Croissant Vert des Comores, 1966; Grand Cordon, Ordre du Tadj de l'Empire d'Iran, 1967; Honorary LLD, Peshawar University, 1967, University of Sind, 1970; Grand Cordon, Nishan-i-Imtiaz, Pakistan, 1970; Cavaliere di Gran Croce, Ordine al Merito della Repubblica, Italy, 1977; Grand Officier, Ordre National du Lion, Senegal, 1982; Nishan-e-Pakistan, 1983; Honorary LLD, McGill University, Montreal, 1983; Thomas Jefferson Memorial Foundation Medal in Architecture, University of Virginia, 1984; Honor Award, American Institute of Architects, 1984; Grand Cordon of Ouissam-al Arch, Morocco, 1986; Gold Medal, Consejo Superior de Colegios de Arquitectos, Spain, 1987; Honorary LLD, McMaster University, 1987; Cavaliere del Lavaro, Italy, 1988; Honorary DLitt, London University, 1989; Commandeur, Légion d'Honneur, France, 1990; Gran Cruz, Orden del Mérito Civil, Spain, 1991; Silver Medal, Académie d'Architecture, Paris, 1991; Huésped de Honor de Granada, Spain, 1991; Honorary LLD, University of Wales, 1993, Brown University, 1996; Hadrian Award, World Monuments Fund, USA, 1996; Grand Croix, Order of Merit, Portugal, 1998, Order of Friendship, Tajikistan, 1998; Gold Medal, City of Granada, Spain, 1998; Insignia of Honour, Union Internationale des Architectes, 2001. Memberships: Royal Yacht Squadron, 1982-; Honorary Fellow, Royal Institute of British Architects, 1991; Honorary Member, American Institute of Architects, 1992; Founder President, Costa Smeralda Yacht Club, Sardinia. Address: Aiglemont, 60270 Gouvieux, France.

AGASSI Andre, b. 29 April 1970, Las Vegas. American Tennis Player. m. (1) Brooke Shields, 1997, divorced 1999; (2) Steffi Graf, 1 son. Education: Coached from age of 13 by Nick Bolletteri; Strength coach Gil Reyes. Appointments: Semi Finalist, French Open, 1988; US Open, 1988, 1989; Member, US Team which defeated Australia in Davis Cup Final, 1990; Defeated Stefan Edberg to win inaugural ATP World Championships, Frankfurt, 1991; Finalist, French Open, 1990, 1991; US Open, 1990, 1995; Australian Open, 1994; Wimbledon, 1999; Men's Singles Wimbledon Champion, 1992; Won, US Open, 1994; Canadian Open, 1995; Australian Open, 1995, 2000, 2001, 2003; Winner, Olympic Games Tennis Tournament, 1996; Association of Tennis Professionals World Champion, 1990. Address: International Management Group, 1 Brieview Plaza, Suite 1300, Cleveland, OH 44114, USA.

AGEENKO Alexandr Ivanovich, b. 1 December 1929, Krasnodar, Russia. Professor of Virology. 1 daughter. Education: Graduate with Honours, I M Sechenov Moscow Medical Academy, Moscow, Russia, 1953. Appointment: Head of the Laboratory of

Virology and Clinical Immunology, P A Gertsen Scientific Research Oncological Institute, Moscow, Russia. Publications: More than 300 publications including 17 monographs, 10 inventions and 7 patents: Co-author, New integrated theory of cancerogenesis and universal diagnostic method for malignant tumours, 2000; Theoretics and practical aspects of the new general theory of cancerogenesis, 2003; Monographs: Heterotransplantation of malignant tumours, 1961; Viral cancerogenesis, 1969; Molecular biology and immunology of viral cancerogenesis, 1974; Mechanisms of viral cancerogenesis, 1978; Immunology and therapy of experimental tumours, 1982; Immunostimulation of tumour growth, 1984; Oncogens and cancerogenesis, 1986; The face of cancer, 1994; New cancer diagnostic: theory, diagnostic, treatment, rehabilitation, 2004. Honours: Memorable Diploma, Russian Society of Oncology; I P Pavlov Silver Medal, Contribution to the Cause of Development of Medicine and Public Health, Russian Academy of Natural Sciences, 1999; Order for Merit in Development of Science and Russian Economics, Russian Academy of Natural Science, 2004. Membership: Russian Society of Oncology; Academician, Russian Academy of Natural Science. Address: Pribrejniy proezd 4, flat 115, 125445 Moscow, Russia. E-mail: jqi@yandex.ru

AGEE William J, b. 5 January 1938, Boise, Idaho, USA. m. (1) Diane Weaver, 1957, 1 son, 2 daughters, (2) Mary Cunningham, 1982, 1 daughter. Education: Stanford University; University of Idaho; Harvard University. Appointments: Boise Cascade Corporation, 1963-72; Senior Vice-President, Chief Financial Officer, 1972-76, President and COO, 1976-77, Chair and Chief Executive Officer, 1977-83, President, 1977-79, Bendix Corporation; Chief Executive Officer, 1983-; Chair, President, Chief Executive Officer, Morrison Knudsen Corporation, 1988-95, Semper Enterprises Inc, Massachusetts; Director, ASARCO, Equitable Life Assurance Society of US, Dow Jones & Co Inc, Economic Club of Detroit, Detroit Renaissance Inc, National Council for US-China Trade, General Foods Corporation, Detroit Economic Growth Corporation, 1978-, United Foundation, National Council for US-China Trade. Memberships: Conference Board, Council on Foreign Relations, Business Roundtable, American and other institutes of CPAs, Board of Directors, Associates of Harvard Business School, 1977-; United Negroes College Fund, 1977; Chair, Governor's Higher Education Capital Investment Advisory Committee; President's Industrial Advisory Sub Committee on Economy and Trade Policy, 1978-79; Advisory Council, Cranbrook Educational Community, 1978; Trustee, 1978; Trustee, Urban Institute, Committee for Economic Development, 1977; Citizen Research Council, Michigan, 1977; Numerous honorary degrees.

AGNEW John Broughton, b. 27 October 1933, Sydney, Australia. Chemical Engineer. m. Elizabeth, 3 sons. Education: BE, Sydney, 1955; PhD, Monash, 1966. Appointments: BP, 1955-61; University of Melbourne, 1961-64; Monash University, 1964-83; University of Adelaide, 1983-98. Publications: 120 papers in professional journals and conference proceedings. Honours: Chemeca Medal; Centenary Medal; ICI Award of Excellence; Emeritus Professor, Adelaide University; John A Brodie Medal; Honorary Fellow IE Australia; Fellow Australian Academy of Technological Sciences and Engineering. Memberships: Several. Address: 12 Fowlers Road, Glen Osmond, SA 5064, Australia.

AGNEW Jonathan Geoffrey William, b. 30 July 1941, Windsor, England. Investment Banker. m. (1) Honourable Joanna Campbell, 1966, divorced 1985, 1 son, 2 daughters, (2) Marie-Claire Dreesmann, 1990, 1 son, 1 daughter. Education: Trinity College, Cambridge; MA Cantab. Appointments: With The Economist, 1964-65, IBRD, 1965-67; Positions, 1967-73, Director, 1971, Hill

Dictionary of International Biography

Samuel and Co; Non-Executive Director, Thos Agnew and Sons Ltd, 1969-; Positions, 1973-82, Managing Director, 1977, Morgan Stanley and Co; With J G W Agnew and Co, 1983-86; Chief Executive, ISRO, 1986; Positions, 1987-93, Chief Executive, 1989-93, Kleinwort Benson Group PLC; Chairman, Limit PLC, 1993-; Member, Council, Lloyd's, 1995-98; Chairman, Henderson Geared Income and Growth Trust, PLC, 1995-2003; Non-Executive Director, 1997, Deputy Chairman, 1999-2002, Chair, 2002-, Nationwide Building Society; Chairman, Gerrard Group PLC, 1998-; Non Executive Director, Beazley Group PLC, 2002-; Director, Soditic Ltd, 2001-. Address: Flat E, 51 Eaton Square, London SW1W 9BE, England. E-mail: jonathan.agnew@limit.com.uk

AGNEW Morland Herbert Julian, b. 20 September 1943, London, England. Art Dealer. m. (1) Elizabeth Margaret Moncrieff Mitchell, 1973, divorced 1992, 1 son, 2 daughters. (2) Victoria Burn Callander, 1993, 1 son. Education: Trinity College, Cambridge; MA Cantab. Appointments: Joined, 1965, Director, 1968, Managing Director, 1987-92, Chairman, 1992-, Thos Agnew and Sons Ltd. Memberships: President, British Antique Dealers Association, 1079-81; Chairman, Society of London Art Dealers, 1986-90. Address: Egmere Farm House, Egmere, Nr Walsingham, Norfolk, England. E-mail: julianagnew@agnewsgallery.co.uk Website: www.agnewsgallery.co.uk

AGPALO Remigio Escalona, b. 10 June 1928, Philippines. Professor Emeritus. Education: BA, with highest honours, University Maine, 1952; MA, 1956, PhD, 1958, Indiana University. Appointments: Instructor, Political Science, 1953-59, Assistant Professor, 1959-63, Associate Professor, 1964-68, Professor of Political Science, 1969-84, Retired, 1984, University of the Philippines. Publications include: Adventures in Political Science; The Political Process and the Nationalization of the Retail Trade in the Philippines; The Political Elite and the People: A Study of the Politics of Occidental Mindoro; José P Laurel: National Leader and Political Philosopher. Memberships: Phi Beta Kappa; Phi Kappa Phi; Pi Sigma Alpha; Philippine Political Science Association; National Research Council of the Philippines; Nigerian Political Science Association. Honours: Visiting Professor of Political Science, University of Benin, Nigeria, 1977-78; Ohio University, USA, 1985; Professor Emeritus of Political Science, Life-time, University of the Philippines, starting in 1988; Awarded Plaque of Recognition as one of the Pillars of the College of Social Sciences and Philosophy, University of the Philippines, for political science; National Social Scientist Award, political science, Philippine Social Science Council, 1990. Listed in: Several biographical publications. Address: Department of Political Science, College of Social Sciences and Philosophy, University of the Philippines, Diliman, Quezon City, Philippines.

AGRAWAL Satish Chandra, b. 20 October 1955, Varanasi, India. University Teacher. m. Sushma, 1 son, 1 daughter. Education: BSc, 1974, MSc, 1976, PhD, 1980, Postdoctoral Fellow, 1980-82, Banaras Hindu University, Varanasi. Appointments: Lecturer Botany, 1983-88, Senior Lecturer, 1988-96, Reader Botany, 1996-, University Allahabad, India. Publications: Author: Limnology, 1999; Marine Plants Ecology, 2002; Chapter to book; Research papers in Journals. Honours: Grantee University Grants Commission, New Delhi, 1990, 1997; Listed in several biographical publications. Membership: Phycological Society of India. Address: Department of Botany, University of Allahabad, Allahabad, India.

AGUIRRE SALA Jorge Francisco, b. 13 October 1960, Mexico. Philosopher; Psychologist. m. Martha Heckel, 1 son, 1 daughter. Education: Honour Degree, 1978-82, PhD, 1988-94, Philosophy, Specialisation, Psychotherapeutic Psychology, 1997-2002,

Universidad Iberoamericana. Appointments: Philosophy Teacher, Universidad Nacional Autonoma de Mexico, 1984-86; Philosopher; Psychologist. Publications: 4 articles in professional journals. Honours: Diploma Mejor Estudiante de la Generacion, Otorgado por la Universidad Iberoamericana, 1982; Diploma al Mejor Estudiante de México Otorgado por el Diario de México, 1982; Mención Honorífica, Otorgado por la Universidad Iberoamericana el 8-11-85, por Estudios de Licenciatura; Mención Honorífica, Otorgado por la Universidad Iberoamericana el 10-11-94, por Estudios de Doctorado; Diploma al Merito Universitario, Universidad Iberoamericana, 2000. Memberships: National System of Researchers; American Association of Collegiate Registrars and Admission Officers; Mexican Association of Philosophy; International Platonic Society; International Society for Neoplatonic Studies. Address: Ave Ignacio Morones Prieto 4500 CP 66238, San Pedro Garza Garcia, Nuevo Leon, Mexico. E-mail: joaguirre@udem.net

AGUTTER Jenny, b. 20 December 1952, Taunton, Somerset, England. Actress; Dancer. m. Johan Tham, 1990, 1 son. Education: Elmhurst Ballet School. Career: Film debut East of Sudan, 1964; Appeared in numerous films for both cinema and TV, dramas, plays and series on stage; Plays include: Spring Awakening; Tempest; Betrayal; Breaking the Code; Love's Labour's Lost; Peter Pan, 1997-98; Films include: Ballerina, 1964; The Railway Children, 1969; Logan's Run, 1975; Equus, 1975; The Eagle has Landed, Sweet William, 1980; An American Werewolf in London, 1981; Secret Places, 1983; Dark Tower, 1987; King of the Wind, 1989; Child's Play 2, 1991; Freddie as Fro 7, 1993; Blue Juice, 1995; English Places, English Faces, 1996; TV includes: Amy, 1980; Not a Penny More, Not a Penny Less, 1990; The Good Guys, 1991; Love Hurts, Heartbreak, 1994; The Buccaneers, 1995; And the Beat Goes On, 1996; A Respectable Trade, 1997; Bramwell, 1998; The Railway Children, 2000; Spooks, 2002. Publication: Snap, 1983. Honour: BAFTA Award for Equus. Address: c/o Marmont Management, Langham House, 308 Regent Street, London W1B 3AT, England.

AHARONI Herzl, b. 20 February 1937, Haifa, Israel. Professor. m. Miriam, 2 sons, 2 daughters. Education: BSc, 1964, MSc, 1967, Dip Ing, 1970, DSc, 1972, Electrical Engineering Faculty, Technion, Israel Institute of Technology, Haifa, Israel; Research on Semiconductor devices breakdown mechanisms and C.V.D of Si-Ge hetroepitaxial layers. Appointments: Professor, Department of Electrical and Computer Engineering, specialising in new processing development in microelectrics, Ben Gurion University, 1973-; Sabbatical activities include: Visiting Associate Professor, University of California at San Diego, lectures on semiconductor technology and circuit analysis, 1978-79; Advanced Photovoltaic Development Group Jet Propulsion Laboratory, Pasadena, California, 1979-80; ITO/InP photovoltaic devices, Solar Energy Research Institute, Golden, Colorado, 1984-86; Light emission from Si devices, University of Pretoria, Pretoria, South Africa, 1993-94; Low temperature Si devices processing, Tohoku University, Sendai, Japan, 1994-96, 1999-2001. Publications: 10 patents which include: Indirect Bandgap Semiconductor Optoelectronic Device; Optoelectronic Device with Separately Controllable Injection Means; Over 180 scientific publications including 2 conference invited papers and a plenary paper: Temperature Dependence of Surface Morphology of Chemical Vapor Deposition Grown Ge on Ge Substrates, 1990; In-Situ Measurement of Crystalline-Amorphous Transition in single crystal Si Substrates During Ion Implantation, 1992; In-Situ Computerized Optical Reflectivity Measurement System for Ion Implantation, 1993; Visible Light From Guardring Avalanche Silicon Photodiodes at Different Current Levels, 1993; The Spatial Distribution of Light From Silicon LED's, 1996; Analysis of n+p Silicon Junctions with

Dictionary of International Biography

Varying Substrate Doping Concentrations Made Under Ultraclean Processing Technology, 1997; Thin Inter-Polyoxide Films for Flash Memories Grown at low Temperature (400°C) by Oxygen Radicals, 2001; Highly Reliable Gate Oxidation Using Ctalytic Water Vapor Generator for MOS Device Fabrication, 2002; Silicon LED's Fabricated in Standard VLSI Technology as Components for All Silicon Monolithic Optoelectronic Systems, 2002. Poetry: Poems in the Rain, 1989; Poems From Heaven and Earth, 1993. Honours: Award for Jet Propulsion Laboratory, Research Associateship by NASA, National Research Council, 1979-80; School of Engineering Best Teacher Awards, Ben Gurion University, 1987, 1988; Esteemed Teacher Citation, Student Association, Ben Gurion University, 1988-89; Distinguished Research Professor, Rand Afrikaans University, Johannesburg, South Africa, 1990; Ben-Gurion University Annual Prize in Applied Electronics, awarded by the Polish Jewish Ex-Servicemen's Association of London, 1998; Supervised and co-authored a student conference paper which received the Young Researcher Award, SSDM, 2001; Fellow, IEE, 2003; Distinguished Lecturer, IEEE, 2003. Memberships: Senior Member, IEEE; Member of the American Physical Society; Israel Association of Crystal Growth; The Israel Vacuum Society; The Israel Physical Society. Address: Department of Electrical & Computer Engineering, Ben Gurion University of the Negev, PO Box 653, Beer Sheva 84105, Israel.

AHERN Bertie, b. 12 September 1951, Dublin. Irish Politician. m. Miriam P Kelly, 1975, 2 daughters. Education: Rathmines College of Commerce, Dublin; University College, Dublin. Appointments: Formerly Accountant, Mater Hospital, Dublin; Member, Dail, 1977; Member, Dublin City Council, 1979-; Lord Mayor, 1986-87; Minister of State, Departments of the Taoiseach and of Defence, 1982; Minister for Labour, 1987-91; Minister for Finance, 1991-94; President, EC Council of Ministers for Social Affairs, 1990; Member, Fianna Fail, President, 1994-; Prime Minister, Ireland, 1997-; Former Member of the Board of Governors, IMF World Bank, European Investment Bank (chair 1991-92), European Bank for Reconstruction and Development, EU Council of Ministers for Economics and Finance (ECOFIN). Honours: Grand Cross, Order of Merit with Star and Sash, Germany. Address: Department of the Taoiseach Government Buildings, Upper Merrion Street, Dublin 2, Republic of Ireland.

AHLSEN Leopold, b. 12 January 1927, Munich, Germany. Author. m. Ruth Gehwald, 1964, 1 son, 1 daughter. Publications: 13 plays, 23 radio plays, 68 television plays, 7 novels. Honours: Gerhart Hauptmann Prize; Schiller-Förderungspreis; Goldener Bildschirm; Hörspielpreis der Kriegsblinden; Silver Nymph of Monte Carlo; Bundesverdienstkreuz. Address: Waldschulstrasse 58, 81827 Munich, Germany.

AHLSKOG John Eric, b. 14 September 1945, Chicago, Illinois, USA. Neurologist. m. Faye Wayland, 3 sons. Education: BA, Michigan State University, 1967; PhD, Princeton University, 1973; MD, Dartmouth Medical School, 1976. Appointments: Instructor of Neurology, 1981-86, Assistant Professor of Neurology, 1986-93, Associate Professor of Neurology, 1993-98, Professor of Neurology, 1998-, Mayo Medical School, Rochester; Chair, Division of Movement Disorders, Department of Neurology, Rochester, 1992-2001; Consultant and Chair, Section of Movement Disorders, Mayo Clinic, Rochester, 2002-. Publications: Numerous articles in professional journals. Honours: Honors College, Michigan State University, 1967; Alpha Omega Alpha, Dartmouth Medical School, 1975. Memberships: American Academy of Neurology; Movement Disorder Society. Address: Department of Neurology, Mayo Clinic, 200 First St SW, Rochester, MN 55905, USA.

AHMAD Amjad, b. 10 November 1952, Lahore, Pakistan. Journalist; Trade Show Manager. m. Nida, 3 sons. Education: Diploma, Designer, Masters Degree in Communication Science, Technical University, Darmstadt, Germany, 1981-86. Appointments: Sales and Purchase Supervisor, Horst Hiller, GmbH, Frankfurt, Germany, 1986-91; Manager, Orbis Pictus, Photo Agency, Frankfurt, Germany, 1990-92; Managing Director, World Press International, Frankfurt, Germany, 1992-95; Managing Director, Dolmetscherkanzlei Ahmad, Frankfurt, Germany (court-approved translation bureau), 1995-99; Area Sales Manager, Demat GmbH, for the international trade show EuroMold, 1999-; Chairman, Institute of Art as Therapy, Institute für Kunst und Therapie, Potsdam, Germany, 2003-; Researcher for fine arts, experimental photography (photo-paintings); Developed new technique called "photo-abstraction"; Freelance Journalist and Public Relations Advisor, for various German commercial and cultural organisation, film documentation, reporting for American Forces Network and others including German WDR, ARTE, Deutsche Welle, 1986-; Exhibitions: Art works exhibited world-wide, latest venue, Holiday Inn, Frankfurt. Publications: Pictures of the World, the West-Eastern Divan, with comments from Nobel Laureate Professor Abdus Salam and preface by former Minister President of Lower Saxony and present Federal Chancellor of Germany, 1993; 50 Years of Pakistan, 1998; German—English-Urdu Dictionary, 1999. Honours: Scholarship, Dr Arthur Pfungst Stiftung, Frankfurt, 1983; William Blake Prize, Town of Celle, Germany, 1990; Artist of the Year, Research Institute of Fine Arts, Nürnberg, Germany, 1992. Memberships: Union of German Journalists; Provincial Executive of Industrial Trade Union, Germany; Humboldt-Gesellschaft, Academy of Arts and Sciences, Germany; Professional Union of Artists, Germany.

AHMAD Riaz, b. 10 April 1962, Chiniot, Pakistan. Soil Environmental Scientist. m. Shabana, 1 son, 2 daughter. Education: BSc Hons, 1985, MSc Hons, 1987, The University of Agriculture, Faisalabad, Pakistan; DHMS, The Punjab Homoeopathic Medical College, Faisalabad, 1988; RHMP, National Council for Homoeopathy, Pakistan; PhD, The University of Adelaide, Australia, 2000. Appointments: Research Officer, Plant Protection Institute, Faisalabad, 1986-95; Lecturer, Hahnemann Homoeopathic Medical College, Faisalabad, 1994; World Bank Doctoral Research Fellow, The University of Adelaide, Australia, 1995-2000; Research Fellow, AgResearch Ruakura Research Centre, Hamilton, New Zealand, 2000-01; The New Zealand Science and Technology Post Doctoral Research Fellow, 2001-. Publications: 52 published research papers, book chapters and popular articles. Honours: The World Bank Doctoral Fellowship Award, 1995; The University of Adelaide Research Travel Award, 1996; The Best Student Research Presentation Award, The Australian Society of Soil Science, 1998; The University of Adelaide Research Abroad Scholarship, 1998; Commonwealth Science Council Research and Travel Award, 1998; Harold Woolhouse Prize for best PhD, The University of Adelaide, 2000; New Zealand Science and Technology Post Doctoral Fellowship Award, 2001; Invited speaker at various international conferences; Listed in numerous Who's Who and biographical publications. Memberships: Chartered Chemist (MRACI CChem), The Royal Australian Chemical Institute, Australia; Asian Institute of NanoBioscience and Technology, Korea; Australian Society of Soil Science; International Union of Soil Scientists; Society of Environmental Toxicology and Chemistry (SETAC). Address: AgResearch, Ruakura Research Centre, East Street, Private Bag 3123, Hamilton, New Zealand. E-mail: riaz.ahmad@agresearch.co.nz

Dictionary of International Biography

AHMADI Mahnaz, b. 26 June 1967, Tehran, Iran. Audiologist. Education: BSc, Audiology, 1991; MSc, Audiology, 1996. Appointments: Faculty Member, Tehran Medical Sciences University, 1997-; Secretary-General, Iranian Audiologists' Society, 1998-; Chairwoman, The Third Iranian Congress on Audiology, 1999. Publications: Determining of Hearing Loss Identification Age and Related Factors in Tehran, 1991; Designing and Evaluating of Auditory Perception Test for 6-7 Years Old Children in Farsi, 1996; Determining of Sound Pressure Level and Vibration Caused by Dental Drill Turbin for Patients, 1997; Designing a Software for Interpreting the Auditory Brain Stem Evoked Responses, 2000. Honours: Honour Student, BSc, 1991, MSc, 1996; Best Lecturer, 1st and 2nd Iranian Congress on Audiology, 1992, 1996. Memberships: Faculty Member, Tehran Medical Sciences University; Secretary-General, Iranian Audiologists' Society. Address: College of Rehabilitation, Enghelab Avenue, Pich Shemiran, Tehran 11998, Iran.

AHMED Iqbal, b. 12 May 1950, Bangladesh. Senior Scientist. m. Syeda Afsa, 2 sons. Education: BSc Honours, University of Chittagong, 1971; MSc, Applied Chemistry, University of Dakha, 1973; PhD, Polymer Chemistry, North East London Polytechnic, England, 1981. Appointments: Assistant Chemist, Natural Gas Fertilizer Factory, Fenchugong, Bangladesh, 1973-76; Senior Research Chemist, Phillips Petroleum Co, Bartlesville, Oklahoma, USA, 1987-99; Senior Scientist, Deguna Superabsorber, Greensboro, North Carolina, 1999-. Publications: Numerous research articles in professional journals; 44 US patents in polymer and catalysis. Honours: Graduate, Student Fellow, British Council, London. Memberships: American Chemical Society; Royal Society of Chemistry. Address: 3605 Chance Road, Greensboro, NC 27410, USA. E-mail: iqafsa@aol.com

AHMED Mohammed Mujtaba, b. 15 February 1951, Sokoto, Nigeria. Civil Servant. m. Maryam M Ahmed, 2 sons, 4 daughters. Education: Diploma in Journalism, London Film and Journalism School, London, England, 1972-74; BSc, Political Science, 1975-77, Masters in Public Administration, 1977-78, Ohio University, USA. Appointments: Press Officer, 1970, Head, Film Unit Department, 1973, Ministry of Information, Sokoto; Administrative Officer, Executive Office of the Governor, Sokoto, 1978; Principal Assistant Secretary, Ministry of Trade and Industry, Sokoto, 1978; Under Secretary, Ministry of Agriculture and Forestry, Sokoto, 1980; Under Secretary Finance, Ministry of Finance, Sokoto, 1980-82; Deputy Permanent Secretary, Acting Secretary, Government and Constitutional Matters, Governor's Office Sokoto, 1982-84; Secretary, State Hotels Management and Tourism Development Board, Sokoto, 1984-85; Secretary, 1985-88, Director, 1988, Sokoto State Executive Council; Director General, Government House, Sokoto, 1988-89; Comptroller of Customs, 1989, Comptroller Promotion, 1989-91, Customs Area Controller, Yobe State Area Command, 1991-98; Comptroller, Federal Operations Unit, 1998-99; Deputy Comptroller General of Customs, Excise and Industrial Incentive, 1999-2001; Deputy Comptroller General, Enforcement and Drugs Department, 2001-, Nigeria Customs Service. Publications: The Role of Nigeria Customs Service in the Manufacture-in-Bond Scheme; Restoration of excise duty on 1996/1997 de-excised goods - confectioneries and other selected luxury goods in the next millennium; The challenges on Nigeria customs in the next millennium; The imperative for the restoration of excise duty on luxury goods. Memberships: Current memberships include: National Committee on the Proliferation and Illicit Trafficking in Small and Light Weapons, 2001; Sub-committee on All African Games Sub-committee on Security. Address: Nigeria Customs Service, Abidjan Street, Wuse, Zone 3, Abuja, Nigeria. E-mail: ahmedmm@nigeriacustoms.org

AHN Byung-Ha, b. 2 December 1940, Gwangju, Korea. Professor. m. Seon-Ae Park, 1 son, 1 daughter. Education: BA, Korean Air Force Academy, 1965; MA, 1977, PhD, 1980, Korean Advanced Institute of Science and Technology. Appointments: Pilot, Korean Air Force, 1966-70; Fellow, Korea Institute of Defence Analyses, 1981-85; Visiting Researcher, RAND Corp, USA, 1986; Visiting Professor, University of Washington, USA, 1987; Director, Center for Weapon Systems Study, Korea Institute of Defence Analyses, 1988-94; Professor, Vice President, Gwangju Institute of Science and Technology, 1995-. Publications: 200 articles in professional journals. Honours: Order of Merit, Inhun; Order of Merit, Samil. Memberships: Korean Institute of Industrial Engineers; Korean Institute of CALS/EC. Address: #1, Oryong-Dong, Buk-Gu, Gwangju, 500-712, Korea. E-mail: bayhay@kjist.ac.kr

AHRENDS Peter, b. 30 April 1933, Berlin, Germany. Architect. m. Elizabeth Robertson, 1954, 2 daughters. Education: Diploma with Honours, Architectural Association, London; ARIBA. Appointments: Research, decoration in Islamic architecture, 1956; Visiting Critic, External Examiner, Kumasi University, Architectural Association School of Architecture, Nova Scotia Technical University, Strathclyde University; Steffen Ahrends and Partners, Johannesburg, South Africa, 1957-58; Denys Lasdun and Partners, 1959-60; Julian Keable and Partners; Teacher, Architectural Association School of Architecture, 1960-61; Partner, Director, Ahrends, Burton and Koralek architectural practice, London, 1961-; Visiting Professor, Kingston Polytechnic, 1983-84; Taught at workshops, Architectural Association School of Architecture, Canterbury Art School, Edinburgh University, Winter School, Edinburgh, Plymouth Polytechnic, Plymouth Art School; Professor, Bartlett School of Architecture and Planning, University College, London, 1986-89; Exhibited, Royal Institute of British Architects Heinz Gallery, 1980, Royal Architects Institute, Ireland, and Douglas Hyde Gallery, Dublin, 1981, Braunschweig Technical University, Hanover Technical University, Finnish Architecture Museum, Helsinki, Alvar Aalto Museum, Jyväskylä, 1982, Architectural Association, Oslo, 1983; Recipient, numerous commissions, including Trinity College Library, Dublin, 1961, Residential building, Chichester Theological College, Grade II listed, 1965, Templeton College, Oxford, Grade II listed, 1969, Residential building, Keble College, Oxford, Grade II listed, 1976, Poplar Footbridge, London Docklands, 1992; Techniquest Science Centre, Cardiff, 1995, Loughborough University Business School, 1998, Dublin Dental Hospital extension, 1998; New British Embassy, Moscow, 1999; Waterford Visitor Centre, 1999; Carrickmines Croquet and Lawn Tennis Club, 2000; Dublin Inner City Development Study 2000; Council Offices at Offaly, Tipperary, North Riding and Tullamore 2000-01. Publications: Ahrends, Burton and Koralek, monograph, 1991; Numerous articles in professional journals. Honours: Good Design in Housing Award, 1977, Architecture Awards, 1978, 1993, 1996, 1999, Structural Steel Design Award, 1980, Structural Steel Commendation, 1993; Gulbenkian Museum of the Year Award, 1999. Memberships: Associate, Royal Institute of British Architects; Design Council; Chairman, UK Architects Against Apartheid, 1988-93. Address: 16 Rochester Road, London NW1 9JH, England. E-mail: abk@abklondon.com

AHTIALA Pekka, b. 12 June 1935, Helsinki, Finland. m. Anna-Maija, 1 son, 2 daughters. Education: BBA, 1956, MBA, 1958, Helsinki School of Economics and Administration; PhD, Harvard University, USA, 1964. Appointments: Teaching Fellow, Instructor, Harvard, early 1960s; Professor of Economics, 1965-99, Dean, Faculty of Economics and Administration, 1969-71, University of Tampere; Minister of the Chancery responsible for Economic Policy, Finnish Government; Visiting Professor of Economics,

Dictionary of International Biography

Northwestern University and Princeton University. Publications: 4 books; Articles in several professional journals. Honours: Blue Cross of Finland; Earhart Prize, Harvard University; Knight Commander of the Order of the Lion of Finland; World Culture Prize: Statue of Victory, Centro Studi e Ricerche Delle Nazioni, Italy, 1985; Best Paper Award, Multinational Finance Journal, 1999; Honorary Member, Junior Chamber International; Honorary Member, Omicron Delta Epsilon. Memberships: Nomination College of the Nobel Prize Committee on Economics of the Finnish Economic Association; American Economic Association; European Economic Association. Address: Liutunkuja 3, 36240 Kangasala, Finland.

AIBONI Sam Amaize, b. 17 July 1941, Warri, Delta State of Nigeria. Lecturer; Barrister; Solicitor. m. Vicky F, 2 sons, 2 daughters. Education: LLM, Moscow, 1971; MA, 1972; LLB, Cantab, 1973; LLD, Uppsala, Sweden, 1978; (BL) Barrister at Law. Appointments: Regional Director, International University Exchange Fund, Geneva, Switzerland and Lusaka, Zambia; Company Secretary, Niger Agencies, Holborn, London, England; Legal Expert, Council of Europe, Strasbourg, France; Research Fellow, Swedish Institute of International Law, Uppsala, Sweden; Dean of Law, University of Jos, Bendel State University, Ekpoma, Nigeria. Publications: Protection of Refugees in Africa. Honours: Visiting Professor, Osgoode Hall Law School, York University, Toronto, Canada; Fellow, Institute of Economic and Social Research (ISESR), Memorial University, St Johns, Newfoundland, Canada; Federal Government of Nigeria Scholar; Scholar, Cambridge University, UK; Edvard Cassel Foundation Scholar, Uppsala University, Uppsala, Sweden. Memberships: Nigeria Bar Association; Association of Law Teachers of Nigeria; International Law Association; Nigerian Society of International Law. Address: Faculty of Law, Ambrose Alli University, PMB 14 Ekpoma, Nigeria.

AICHINGER Ilse, b. 1 November 1921, Vienna, Austria. Novelist; Playwright. Education: University of Vienna, 1945-48. Appointments: Member of Grupe 47, 1951-. Publications: Die Grössere Hoffnung, 1948; Rede Unter dem Galgen, 1953; Eliza, Eliza, 1965; Selected Short Stories and Dialogue, 1966; Nachricht und Tag: Erzählungen, 1970; Schlechte Worter, 1976; Meine Sprache und Ich Erzählungen, 1978; Spiegelesichte: Erzählungen und Dialoge, 1979. Plays, Zu Keiner Stunde, 1957, 1980; Besuch im Pfarrhaus, 1961; Auckland: 4 Horspiele, 1969; Knopfe, 1978; Weisse Chrysanthemum, 1979; Radio Plays, Selected Poetry and Prose of Ilse Aichinger, 1983; Collected Works, 8 volumes, 1991. Honours: Belgian Europe Festival Prize, 1987; Town of Solothurn Prize, 1991. Address: c/o Fischer Verlag, Postfach 700480, 6000 Frankfurt, Germany.

AIELLO Danny, b. 20 May 1933, New York City, New York, USA. Actor. m. Sandy Cohen, 1955, 3 sons, 1 daughter. Career: Numerous film appearances including Bang the Drum Slowly, 1973; The Godfather II, 1976; Once Upon a Time in America, 1984; The Purple Rose of Cairo, 1985; Moonstruck, 1987, Do the Right Thing, 1989, Harlem Nights, 1989, Jacob's Ladder, 1990, Once Around, 1991, Hudson Hawk, 1991, The Closer, 1991, 29th Street, 1991, Mistress, 1992, Ruby, 1992, The Pickle, 1992, The Cemetery Club, 1992, The Professional, 1994, Prêt-à-Porter, 1994, Léon, 1994, City Hall, 1995, Power of Attorney, 1995, Two Days in the Valley, 1996, Mojave Moon, 1996, Two Much, 1996, A Brooklyn State of Mind, 1997, Bring Me the Head of Mavis Davis, 1998, Dust, 1999, Prince of Central Park, 2000, Dinner Rush, 2000, Off Key, 2001, The Russian Job, 2002, Marcus Timberwolf, 2002, The Last Request, 2002; Theatre appearances including Lamppost Reunion, 1975, Gemini, 1977, Hurlyburly, 1985; Appeared in TV films including The Preppie Murder, 1989, A

Family of Strangers, 1993, The Last Don, mini-series, 1997, Dellaventura, series, 1997, The Last Don II, mini-series, 1998. Honours: Theatre World Award for Lamppost Reunion, 1975; Obie Award for Gemini, 1977; Boston Critics Award, Chicago Critics Award, Los Angeles Critics Award, all for Best Supporting Actor in Do the Right Thing, 1989; Emmy Award for A Family of Strangers, 1993. Address: William Morris Agency, 151 South El Camino Drive, Beverly Hills, CA 90212, USA.

AIFTINCĂ Marin, b. 19 September 1942, Unteni, District Botosani, Romania. Philosopher. m. Iulia (Lache) Aiftinca, 2 sons. Education: Faculty of Journalism, Bucharest, 1974; Faculty of Philosophy, Bucharest, 1981; Post-University Course, Bucharest, 1979; Doctoral degree in Philosophy (PhD), University of Bucharest, 1991. Appointments: Journalist, 1964-70, 1974-77; University Lecturer, Faculty of Journalism, Bucharest, 1977-81; Editor, Romanian Academy and Scientific Secretary, 1981-90; Scientific Secretary of Department of Philosophy of Romanian Academy, Professor of Philosophy, University of Spiru Haret, Bucharest, Senior Research Worker, Institute of Philosophy, Bucharest, 1990-. Publications: 9 books; Over 70 scientific papers about philosophy of value and culture, aesthetics, history of philosophy; Books include: The Information's Babylon, 1987; Value and Valuation, 1994; Descartes and Modern Scientific Mind, 1990; Embodied of Thought, 1996; Value and Culture, 1998; Culture and Liberty, Catholic University of America, Washington, 1999; Nietzsche – Being and Value, 2003; Time and Value, 2003. Honours: Prize, Mircea Florian of Romanian Academy, 1994; Prize, Petre Andrei, of Academic Endower, Petre Andrei (University), Iassy, 1998; The Greate Prize of the International Centre of Culture and Art "George Apostu", Bacău, 2002. Memberships: European Society for the History of Human Sciences, Groningen; International Society of Value Inquiry, Atlanta, USA. Address: Bucharest, District 6, Bd Timisoara 27, Bl H Sc A, et 5, Ap 17, Romania.

AIMÉE Anouk, (Françoise Dreyfus), b. 27 April 1932, Paris, France. Actress. m. (2) Nico Papataksi, 1951, 1 daughter, (3) Pierre Barouh, 1966, (4) Albert Finney, 1970, divorced 1978. Education: Institut de Megève; Cours Bauer-Therond. Career: Theatre appearances include Sud, 1954, Love Letters, 1990, 1994; Appeared in films including Les mauvaises rencontres, 1955, Tous peuvent me tuer, Pot bouille and Montparnasse 19, 1957, La tête contre les murs, 1958, Les drageurs, 1959, La dolce vita, Le farceur, Lola, Les amours de Paris, L'imprévu, Quai Notre Dame, 1960, Le jugement dernier, Sodome et Gomorrhe, 1961; Les grands Chemins, Education sentimentale, Huit et demi, 1962, Un homme et une femme, 1966, Un soir un train, 1967, The Appointment Shop, Model Shop, Justine, 1968, Si c'était à refaire, 1976, Mon premier amour, 1978, Salto nel vuoto, 1979, La tragédie d'un homme ridicule, 1981, Qu'est-ce qui fait courir David?, 1982, Le Général de l'armée morte, 1983, Vive la Vie, Le succès à tout prix, 1984, Un homme et une femme: vingt ans déjà, 1986, Docteur Norman Bethune, 1992, Les Marmottes, 1993, Les Cents et Une Nuits, 1995, Prêt-à-porter, 1995; Appeared on television in Une page d'amour, 1979, Des voix dans le jardin. Honours: Commandeur des Arts et des Lettres. Address: Bureau Georges Beaume, 3 Quai Malaquais, 75006 Paris, France.

AITMATOV Chingiz Torekulovich, b. 12 December 1928, Sheker Villaga, Kirghizia, USSR. Writer; Diplomatist. m. Maria Urmatova, 1974, 3 sons, 1 daughter. Education: Kirghiz Agricultural Institute. Appointments: Writer, 1952-; Former Correspondent, Pravda; Member, Soviet Union Communist Party, 1959-91; First Secretary, 1964-69, Chairman, 1969-86, Cinema Union of Kirghiz SSR; Deputy to USSR Supreme Soviet, 1966-89; Candidate Member, 1969-71, Member, 1971-90, Central

Dictionary of International Biography

Committee, Kirghiz SSR Communist Party; Vice-Chairman, Committee of Solidarity with Peoples of Asian and African Countries, 1974-89; Chairman, Union of Writers of Kyrgyzstan, 1986-; Chief Editor, Innostrannaya Literatura, 1988-90; Ppeople's Deputy of the USSR, 1989-91; Member, Presidential Council, 1990-91; USSR Ambassador to Luxembourg, 1990-92; Kyrgyzstan Ambassador to Belgium and Luxembourg, 1992-. Publications include: Short stories, novels; Djamilya, 1959; Mr Poplar in a Red Kerchief, 1960; Face to Face, Short Stories, Melody, 1961; Tales of the Hills and the Steppes, 1963; Camel's Eye, The First Teacher, Farewell Gulsary, Mother Earth, 1963; Stories, 1967; The White Steamship, English translation, 1972; The Lament of the Migrating Bird, English translation, 1972; The Ascent of Mount Fuji, co-author, 1973; Earth and Water, co-author, 1978; Works, 3 volumes, 1978; Early Storks, 1979; Stories, 1979; Piebald Dog, Running Along the Sea Shore, The Day Lasts More Than a Hundred Years, 1980; Executioner's Block, 1986, English translation, 1987; Mother Earth and Other Stories, 1989; The Place of the Skull, The White Cloud of Chingiz Khan, 1991; A Conversation at the Foothill of Fujiyama Mountain, co-author, 1992; The Brand of Cassandra, 1994. Honours: Lenin Prize for Tales of the Hills and the Steppes, 1963; People's Writer of Kirghiz SSR, 1968; State Prize in Literature, 1968, 1977, 1983; Hero of Socialist Labour, 1978; Austrian State Prize for European Literature, 1994; Others from Germany, India, Turkey, USA. Memberships: Kirghiz Academy of Science, 1974; European Academy of Arts, Science and Humanity, 1983; Chairman, Issyk-Kul Forum, 1986-; World Academy of Art and Science, 1987. Address: Toktogul str 98, Apt 9, 720000 Bishkek, Kyrgyzstan.

AJOSE Akinsanya Sunny, b. 10 February 1946, Zaria, Kaduna State, Nigeria. Public Administration. m. Arinola, 3 sons, 4 daughters. Education: Associate of Arts Degree, Liberal Arts, Kennedy-King College, Chicago, USA, 1971; Bachelor of Arts Degree, Liberal Arts and Science, University of Illinois, Chicago, 1973; Master of Arts Degree, Social Science, Governors State University, Illinois, 1974. Appointments: Personnel Programmes Administrator, IBM Nigeria Ltd, Lagos, 1975-78; Administrative Officer Grade (VI), Lagos State Civil Service Commission, Ikeja, 1979-81; Administrative Officer Grade (V), Lagos State Ministry of Employment and Civil Service Matters, Ikeja, 1981-83; Chief Management Service Officer, Office of the Establishment, Training and Pensions, State Civil Service, 1983-92; Assistant Director, Lands and Housing Office, 1992-93; Director, State Directorate of Rural Development, 1993-98; Permanent Secretary, Ministry of Rural Development, 1998-99; Permanent Secretary, Parastatal Monitoring Office, 1999-2000; Permanent Secretary, Office of the Chief of Staff, 2000-. Memberships: Fellow, Institute of Public Administration of Nigeria; Associate, Institute of Management Consultants, UK. Address: 1310B Abisogun Leigh Street, Ogbu Phase II, GRA, Ikeja, Nigeria.

AKAHOSHI Kazuya, b. 15 August 1960, Kitakyushu City, Fukuoka, Japan. Gastroenterologist. m. Akiko Haraguchi, 2 sons, 1 daughter. Education: MD, Kagoshima University, 1986; PhD, Kyushu University, 1993. Appointments: From Resident to Researcher, Kyushu University Hospital, Fukuoka, Japan, 1986-91; Physician, National Nakatsu Hospital, Japan, 1991-93; Fukuoka Prefectural Kaho Hospital, 1993-94; Assistant Professor, Kyushu University, 1994-97; Head of Gastroenterology, Aso Iizuka Hospital, Japan, 1997-. Publications: Author, research articles in medical journals including: Gut, 1991; Radiology, 1992; Gastrointestinal Endoscopy, 1995, 1998, 1999, 2000; Endoscopy, 1997; British Journal of Radiology, 1997, 1998, 2001. Memberships: Fellow, Japanese Society of Gastroenterology (Kyushu branch); Fellow, Japan Gastroenterological Endoscopy Society. Address: Aso Iizuka Hospital, 3-83 Yoshio Town, 820 Iizuka City, Japan.

AKALE Matt Alfa Gordon, b. 5 April 1947, Atte, Nigeria. Science Educator. m. Christine Zuyeali Funmi, 3 sons, 2 daughters. Education: Federal College of Education, Zaria, Nigeria, 1967-70; B Ed, M Ed, PhD, Ahmadu Bello University, Zaria, 1974-87; Institute of Education, University of London, London, England, 1982 King's College, London, 1990, 1994. Appointments: Senior Lecturer, Ahmadu Bello University Institute of Education; Chief Programmes Officer, National Commission for Colleges of Education; Director, Academic Programmes. National Commission for Colleges of Education, Abuja, Nigeria. Publications: Articles in professional journals include: Design, Organisation and Administration of Science Laboratory, 1981; Relationship between Psycho-Social Environment and Cognitive Achievement in Science, 1998; Funding Teacher Education, 2002. Honour: Fellow, Science Teachers' Association of Nigeria. Memberships: Science Teachers' Association of Nigeria; Nigeria Academy of Education. Address: c/o National Commission for Colleges of Education, Ralph Shodeinde Street, Cadastral Zone AO1, Garki, PMB 0394, Abuja, Nigeria. E-mail: info@ncce.edu.ng

AKASHI Yasushi, b. 19 January 1931, Akita, Japan. Head of Research Institute. m. Itsuko Akashi, 1 son, 1 daughter. Education: BA, University of Tokyo, 1954; MA, University of Virginia, 1956; Fletcher School of Law and Diplomacy, 1956-57; PhD, Ritsumeikan University, 1998. Appointments: Under-Secretary-General of the UN, 1979-92; Special Representative of the UN Secretary-General for Cambodia, 1992-93; Special Representative of the UN Secretary-General for the former Yugoslavia, 1994-95; Under-Secretary-General of the UN, 1996-97; President, Hiroshima Peace Institute, 1998-99; Chairman, The Japan Centre for Conflict Prevention, 1999-; Representative of the Government of Japan for Peace-Building in Sri Lanka, 2002-. Publications: The United Nations, 1965, revised, 1975, 1985; The World Seen From the United Nations, 1992; An Agenda for Hope, 1993; Perseverance and Hope – 560 Days in Cambodia, 1995. Honours: New York Japanese Chamber of Commerce Annual Award, 1994; The Yomiuri International Co-operation Award, 1996; Foreign Minister's Commendation, 1998. Memberships: President, The Japan Association for the Study of the United Nations; Chairman, City Club of Tokyo; Board Member, International Olympic Truce Foundation. Address: 106, 5-12-21 Roppong, Minato-ken, Tokyo 106 0032, Japan.

AKAVIA Miriam, b. 20 November 1927, Kraków, Poland. Novelist; Translator. m. 3 December 1946, 2 daughters. Appointments: Co-editor of some bulletins. Publications: Adolescence of Autumn, 1975; Ha mechir (The Price), 1978; Galia & Miklosh, 1982; Karmi Sheli (My Own Vineyard), 1984; Adventure on a Bus, 1986; Ma Vigne A Moi, 1992; The Other Way: The Story of a Group (in Hebrew), 1992; An End To Childhood (in English), 1995, (in Polish), 1996; Jurek and Ania, Israel, 2000; Lombullás, Hungary, 2000; Short Stories, Urojenia, Poland, 2000. Contributions to: Various literary magazines. Honours: Dvorsecki Prize; Korczak Prize, SEK Prize (Sociéte Européen de Culture); Amicus Polonie; Cracovians Prize; Golden Medal, President Walesa, Poland, 1991; Prime Minister Prize, I Rabin, 1993; Prize Wizo, Creative Woman in Literature, Tel-Aviv, 1998; For the Promotion of Tolerance, Poland, 2000. Address: PO 53050, 61530 Tel-Aviv, Israel.

AKCASU A Ziya, b. 26 August 1924, Aydin, Turkey. Nuclear Engineer; Statistical Mechanic. m. Melahat Turksal, 1954, 3 children. Education: MS, Technical University of Istanbul, 1948; Diploma, International School of Science and Engineering, Argonne National Laboratory, 1957; PhD, Nuclear Engineering, Michigan University, 1963. Appointments include: Assistant Professor of Electronics, Technical University of Istanbul, 1948-53; Associate Professor, 1954-59; Resident Associate in Nuclear

Dictionary of International Biography

Engineering, Argonne National Laboratory, 1959-61; Professor of Nuclear Engineering, University of Michigan at Ann Arbor, 1968-1995; Professor Emeritus, 1995-; Numerous visiting residencies and Guest Professorships. Honours: Glenn Murphy Award, American Society of Engineering Educators, 1986; Alexander von Humboldt Research Award for Senior US Scientist, 1991; Science Award, Research Council of Republic of Turkey, Science and Technology (TÜBITAK), 1992; Excellence in Research Award, CoE, Michigan University, 1995. Memberships: Fellow, American Physics Society; Fellow, American Nuclear Society; Turkish Physics Society; Sigma Xi. Address: 2820 Pebble Creek Drive, Ann Arbor, MI 48108, USA.

AKCAY Okan, b. 30 October 1943, Aydin, Turkey. Marketing Educator. m. Susan Akcay, 6 July 1978, 1 son, 1 daughter. Education: BSc, Business Administration, 1968; MBA, 1971; Dr, Business Administration, 1974. Appointments: Instructor, 1972-74, Assistant Professor, 1974-86, MBA Coordinator, Assistant Dean, 1979-80, Consultant, Researcher, 1972-80, Consultant, Board Director, 1978-80, Assistant Professor, 1986-92, Professor, Marketing and MBA Faculty, 1992-. Publications: Advertising; New Product Development in Manufacturing Companies; Marketing Mix Analysis in the Turkish Service Sector; 18 other articles in professional journals in the area of marketing. Honours: Scholarship, Agency of International Development, 1969-71; Fellowship, MSU, 1976; Award, Outstanding American Marketing Association Club Advisor, 1985-86; Award, Outstanding International Business Club Advisor, 1990-91. Memberships: American Marketing Association, 1982-88; Academy of Marketing Science, 1986-90; Western Decision Science Institute, 1994-95; International Management Development Association, 1995-96. Address: 51 Clearview Drive, Mertztown, PA 19539, USA.

AKERS Arthur, b. 24 March 1927, Smethwick, Staffordshire, England. Engineering Educator. m. Marcia, 1 son, 1 daughter (deceased). Education: BSc (Honours), Physics and Mathematics, London University, England, 1953; ACT, Associate of College of Technology, Birmingham, England, 1954; MSc, Aeronautical Science, Cranfield Institute of Technology, England, 1955; PhD, Mechanical Engineering, London University, England, 1969. Appointments: Senior Lecturer, Bath University, 1960-64; Principal Lecturer, Lords of the Britannic Admiralty, Whitehall, London, Royal Naval College, Greenwich, 1964-68; Principal Lecturer, Royal Military College of Science, Shrivenham, England (now a division of Cranfield University), 1968-73, 1974-75; Visiting Professor, Mechanical Engineering, University of Virginia, Charlottesville, VA, 1973-74; Professor of Aerospace Engineering and Engineering Mechanics, Iowa State University, Ames, Iowa, 1975-99; Professor Emeritus, 1999-. Publications: Numerous in archival and foreign journals; 3 Textbooks; Arthur Akers Outstanding Freshman Engineer Award, 1983-. Memberships: Fellow, Royal Aeronautical Society; Fellow, American Society of Mechanical Engineers, International. Address: 1519 Stone Brooke Road, Ames, IA 50010-4191, USA.

AKERS-JONES David (Sir), b. 14 April 1927. Civil Servant. m. Jane Spickernell, deceased 2002, 1 son, deceased, 1 daughter. Education: Brasenose College, Oxford; MA Oxon. Appointments: British India Steam Navigation Co, 1945-49; Malayan Civil Service, 1954-57; Hong Kong Civil Service, 1957-86, including Secretary for New Territories and for District Administration, 1973-85, Chief Secretary, 1985-86, Hong Kong Government; Acting Governor, Hong Kong, 1986-87; Chairman, National Mutual Asia Hong Kong, now AXA China Region, 1987-, Hong Kong Housing Authority, 1988-93, AXA Life Advisory Board, 2001-, Global Asset Management, Hong Kong; Hong Kong Affairs Advisor to China, 1993-97; Director, Sime Darby Hong Kong, Hysan

Development Co Ltd, The Mingly Corporation Ltd, Shui On Properties Ltd; Member, Council, Australian National Gallery. Honours: Knight Commander, Order of the British Empire; Companion, Order of St Michael and St George; Honorary Member, Royal Institute of Civil Servants; Honorary DCL, Kent University, 1987; Honorary LLD, Chinese University of Hong Kong, 1988; Honorary DScS, City University, Hong Kong, 1993. Memberships: President, Outward Bound Trust, Hong Kong, 1986; Vice-President, World Wildlife Fund Hong Kong, 1995-. Address: Dragon View, 128 Castle Peak Road, Tsing Lung Tau, New Territories, Hong Kong Special Administrative Region, China. E-mail:akersjon@pacific.net.hk

AKIHITO Emperor, b. 23 December 1933, Tokyo, Japan. Emperor of Japan. m. Michiko Shoda, 10 April 1959, 2 sons, 1 daughter. Education: Private Tutors; Graduate, Gakushin University, 1956. Appointments: Invested, Crown Prince of Japan, 1952; Succeeded late father Emperor Hirohito, 1989; Crowned Emperor of Japan, 1990-; Honorary President: 3rd Asian Games, 1958; International Sports Games for the Disabled, 1964; 11th Pacific Scientific Congress, 1966; University of Tokyo, 1967; Japan World Exhibition, Osaka, 1970; 2nd International Conference on Indo-Pacific Fish, 1985. Publications: Co-author, Fish of the Japanese Archipelago; Contributor, numerous articles to professional journals including 25 papers in journal of Ichthyological Society of Japan. Honours include: Collar of the Superior Order of the Chrysanthemum, 1989. Memberships: Ichthyological Society of Japan; Linnean Society of London (Honorary); Research Association of Austin Museum (Honorary). Address: The Imperial Palace, 1-1 Chiyoda, Chiyoda-ku, Tokyo 100, Japan.

AKINGBADE George Oluwasegun, b. 3 June 1946, Ogun State, Nigeria. Civil Engineer. m. Monisola Olutayo Akingbade, 4 sons, 2 daughters. Education: BSc Engineering, University of Lagos, Yaba, 1966-69; MSc, Highways and Traffic Engineering, 1977-78, University of Birmingham, England. FNSE; C.Eng; FICE; FIHT; MASCE; MAAPT. Appointments: Pupil Executive Engineer, 1970-72, Executive Engineer Grade II, 1972-75, Executive Engineer Grade I, 1975-76, Senior Executive Engineer, 1976-78, Principal Civil Engineer, 1982-89, Assistant Director, 1989-95, Deputy Director, 1995-, F.M.W.& H; Federal Controller of Works and Housing: Gongola State, 1990; Taraba State, 1991-93; Kebbi State, 1997-98; Deputy Director Highways (Planning and Design), 1998; Deputy Director Highways (North East Zone), 1999; Deputy Director Highways (South East Zone), 2001-. Honours: Honorary Chieftancy Titles of : Obajemu of Akutupa-Bunu; Iwayeni of Ile-Oluji; Traditional Title of Akogun of Ikanna-Abeokuta. Address: 43 Araromi Street, Onike, Yaba-Lagos, Nigeria.

AKINRELE Olusegun Olufemi, b. 29 April 1960, Lagos, Nigeria. Town and Regional Planner/Master in Environmental Management. m. Omolola Esther, 2 sons, 1 daughter. Education: Yaba College of Technology, 1990; Ondo State University Akungba-Akoko, 2000 session; OND, HND Town and Regional Planning, 1990; Master in Environmental Management. Appointments: Planning Officer, Federal Capital Development Authority Area, Garki-Abuya, Planning and Survey Department; 9 years working experience on the Profession. Honours: Planning and Environmental Management. Memberships: Graduate Membership. Address: Lollyseg Computers Investment Nigeria Ltd. Opp RCCO, Praise Worship Assembly, Karu Along FHA, Abuja, Nigeria. E-mail: lollyseg@yahoo.com

AKRAM Wasim, b. 3 June 1966, Lahore, Pakistan. Cricketer. Education: Islamia College. Appointments: Left-Hand Mid-Order Batsman, Left-Arm Fast Bowler; Played for Pakistan Automobile

Corporation, 1984-85, Lahore, 1985-86, Lancashire, 1988-98 (Captain 1998); only bowler to have captured more than 400 wickets in both Test and one-day cricket; played in 104 Tests for Pakistan, 1984-85 to 2003, 25 as Captain, scoring 2,898 runs (average 22.64) including 3 hundreds and taking 414 wickets (average 23.6); Has scored 7,106 runs (7 hundreds) and taken 1,022 wickets in first class cricket to 2001; Toured England, 1987, 1992, 1996 (Captain); 350 limited-overs internationals (109 as Captain) taking record 490 wickets to 2003; Wisden Cricketer of the Year, 1993. Publication: Wasim, autobiography. Address: c/o Pakistan Cricket Board, Gaddafi Stadium, Ferozepur Road, Lahore 54600, Pakistan.

AKWAOWO Akwaowo Obobo, b. 27 May 1946, Nung Obong, Nsit Ubium, LGA. Founder, Bishop Truth and Life Church International. m. Sandra Akwaowo, 6 sons, 4 daughters. Education: GCE A-Level; RSA London, A-Level, 1973; Diploma in Ministry, 1981; Doctor of Divinity, 1983. Appointments: School Teacher, 1965; Secretary in Cross River Government Service, 1973-79; Bible Teacher, Pastor, Evangelist, Missionary, Author, Chancellor Shield of Faith Bible Institute, Bishop, 1992-; Professor, 2001-. Publications: 22 books include: The New Birth; The Unfailing Love; Life of a Reborn Christian; Keys to Getting Your Prayers Answered; Dunamis of the Holy Ghost; Ministers of the New Testament; The Peace of God. Honours include: Doctor of Sacred Laws and Letters, 1986; Honour Plaque, National Christian Fellowship Conference, Philadelphia, 1988; Certificate of Honour, NASU, Polytechnic, Calabar, 1990; Ecclesiastical Doyen, Nigeria, 2000; Distinctive Pioneer Service Award, Goodnews Community International, Nigeria, 2000; Pentecostal Founding Father's Award, CRS, Nigeria, 2001. Memberships: National Christian Fellowship Conference International, Philadelphia; Apostolic World Christian Fellowship, USA; Pentecostal Fellowship of Nigeria (1st Cross River State President). Address: Truth and Life Church International Inc, 6 Usoro Street/New Airport Road, P O Box 944, Calabar, CRS, Nigeria.

AL ABOUD Khalid Mohammad Owain, b. 13 May 1970, Makkah, Saudi Arabia. Dermatologist. m. Samiah Al Nofie, 1 son. Education: MBBS, College of Medicine, King Abdul Aziz University, Jeddah, 1993; Arab Board in Dermatology, 1999; Jordanian Board in Dermatology, 2000; Saudi Board in Dermatology, 2001. Appointments: Internship, Al Noor Specialist Hospital, Makkah, Saudi Arabia; General Practitioner, King Faisal Hospital, Taif, Saudi Arabia, 1995; Arab Board Training Programme in Assir Central Hospital, Abha, 1995-99; Dermatology Specialist, King Faisal Hospital, Taif, Saudi Arabia, 1999-; Medical Director and Assistant Director, Taif Maternity Hospital, Taif, Saudi Arabia, 2000-; Scientific collaboration with Department of Medical Genetics, Antwerp, Belgium and with Dr Ervin Epstein, University of California, USA. Publications: 10 articles in international medical journals as author include most recently: Ectopic respiratory mucous in the skin associated with skeletal malformation and polydactyly, 2001; Vaginitis Emphysematosa, 2002; Contributions to dermatology web sites; Contributions to newspapers and magazines; Papers presented at national and international conferences. Memberships: Saudi Society of Dermatology; Society of Pediatric Dermatology; American Academy of Dermatology. Address: PO Box No 5440, Makkah, Saudi Arabia. E-mail: amoa65@hotmail.com

AL HAWSAWI Khalid Ali Eisa, b. 31 May 1970, Makkah, Saudi Arabia. Dermatologist. m. Reem Al Molad, 2 sons, 1 daughter. Education: MBBS, College of Medicine, King Abdul Aziz University, Jeddah, Saudi Arabia, 1993; Arab Board in Dermatology, 1999; Jordanian Board in Dermatology, 2000; Saudi Board in Dermatology, 2000. Appointments: King Khalid National Guard Hospital, Jeddah, 1994; General Practitioner, King Faisal

Hospital, Taif, Saudi Arabia, 1995; Arab Board Training Programme in Assir Central Hospital, Abha, 1995-99; Dermatology Specialist, King Faisal Hospital, Taif, 2000-; Assistant Director, Mental Hospital, Taif, 2000-; Scientific collaboration with Department of Medical Genetics, University of Antwerp, Belgium and with Dr Ervin Epstein, University of California, USA. Publications: 10 articles in national international medical journals as author include: Mammary Paget's Disease: A case report and review, 2000; Vaginitis Emphysematosa, 2002; Contributions to dermatology web sites; Contributions to newspapers and magazines; Papers presented at national and international conferences. Memberships: Saudi Society of Dermatology; Society of Pediatric Dermatology; American Academy of Dermatology. Address: PO Box No 5440, Mahkkah, Saudi Arabia. E-mail: khawasawi2002@yahoo.com.

AL SHARIFI Mamdouh, b. 6 March 1954, Gurayat, Saudi Arabia. Director of Forensic Laboratories. m. Hanan Al Rowaili, 1 son, 1 daughter. Education: BS, Pharmacy, King Saud University, Riyadh, Saudi Arabia; MS, Toxicology, Indiana University, USA. Appointments: Director, Criminalistic Institute; Director, Police Polyclinic; Director, Forensic Laboratories. Publication: Drug and Narcotics: Its Use and Identification which is Taught in Police Academy, Saudi Arabia. Honours: Many Awards and Honours from Saudi Police; Certificate of Honour, Who's Who, 2001. Memberships: American Academy of Forensic Science; American Society of Mass Spectrometry; Forensic Science Society; International Association for Identification. Address: PB No 52875, Riyadh-11573, Saudi Arabia. E-mail: alsharifi@hotmail.com

AL-AHMAR Abdullah, b. 6 June 1936, Altal, Damascus, Syria. General Secretary of Baath Arab Socialist Party. m. Ghada Abu Saad, 6 sons, 3 daughters. Education: Elementary Teaching Qualification Diploma, 1959; Bachelor of Laws, 1964. Appointments: Elementary School Teacher, 1959-64; Office of Labour Director, United Arab Council for Industry, 1965; Secretary, Baath Arab Socialist Party, Countryside Branch, 1964-67; Governor, Hama City and Edleb City, 1967; Member, Provisional Leadership, 1970; Assistant Secretary General, 1970-71, Member, Regional Leadership, 1970-,Baath Arab Socialist Party; Member, Central Leadership, National Progressive Front, 1972-. Publications: The Baath and the Renewed Revolution, 1990; Many articles, lectures and editorials. Address: The Baath Arab Socialist Party, National Leadership, PO Box 849, Damascus, Syria.

AL-ARRAYED Jalil Ebrahim, b. 26 January 1933. Emeritus Professor; University Administrator. Education: BA, Chemistry, American University, Beirut, Lebanon, 1954; MEd, Science Education, Leicester University, England, 1964; PhD, Comparative Science Education and Management of Curriculum Development, Bath University, England, 1974. Appointments: Teacher, Sciences, Maths, 1954-59, Science Inspector, 1959-66, Bahrain Government Department of Education; Principal, Bahrain Men's Teachers Training College, 1966-72; Under-Secretary, Bahrain Ministry of Education, 1974-82; Executive Council Member (Bahrain Rep), 1975-82, Deputy Chairman, 1978-79; Chairman, 1979-80, Arab Bureau of Education for the Gulf States; Member, Bahrain Representative, Council for Higher Education in the Gulf States, 1965-95; Member, Board of Trees, Bahrain University College of Arts, Science and Education, 1979-86; Member Founding Committee, Arabian Gulf University, 1980-85; Member, IIEP Council of Consultant Fellows, Paris, 1984-92; Rector, Bahrain University College of Arts, Science and Education, 1982-87; Professor of Education, Vice President, Academic Affairs, University of Bahrain, 1987-91, Acting President, 1991; Participant, various regional and international conferences on education reform, and Chair, several committees. Publications: Author of books: A Critical Analysis of Arab School Science Teaching, 1980, Development and Evaluation of University Faculty in Arab Gulf States, 1994, Some Aspects of Contemporary Management Thought, 1996; More than 50 articles on educational issues in general and science education in particular, 1956-78. Honours: Gold Medal for Academic Achievement, Bahrain Government Department of Education, 1969; Prize for Academic Achievement, Bahrain Ministry of Education, 1975; American Biographical Institute Commemorative Medal of Honour, 1988; State Award for Outstanding Citizens, Government of Bahrain, 1992; International Association of University Presidents Certificate for Outstanding Contributions, 1996. Memberships: Life Fellow, International Biographical Association; Life Member, Indian Institute of Public Administration; Various organizations including: Chartered Management Institute; Institute of Administrative Management, UK; International Association of University Presidents; Royal Society of Chemistry (UK); Listed in numerous biographical dictionaries. Address: PO Box 26165, Adlia, Manama, Bahrain.

AL-AZZAWI Ramadan, b. 3 March 1966, Egypt. Assistant Professor of Comparative Literature. m. Hoda Awad, 3 daughters. Education: BA, English, Egypt, 1988; Diploma in Teaching Methodology and Curriculum Development, Ohio, USA, 1992; MA, American Theatre (Drama), Egypt, 1998; PhD, Comparative Literature, Egypt and USA, 2003. Appointments: English Language Instructor, 1989-98; Assistant Lecturer, English Literature, 1998-2003; Assistant Professor, Comparative Literature, 2003-. Publications: The Impact of the Concept of "Strive and Succeed" on the Contemporary American Society as reflected in David Mamet's Major Plays (MA Thesis), 1998; The Theme of Violence in the Plays of J B Priestley and Sam Shephard: A Comparative Study (PhD Thesis), 2003. Honours: TSI, Fulbright Commission, Athens, Ohio, USA, 1992; PhD Scholarship (Joint-Supervision), IUP , Indiana, Pennsylvania, USA, 2000-2002; Listed in Who's Who publications and biographical dictionaries. Memberships: Modern Language Association; Teachers of English to Speakers of Other Languages. Address: Kafr El-Shoubaki, Al-Gadid, Abu-Kabeer, Sharkia, Egypt. E-mail: razzawi@yahoo.com

AL-BADR Hamoud A, b. 27 October 1939, Ezzilfi, Saudi Arabia. Educator. m. Thuraya Shaikh, 4 sons. Education: BS, Cairo University in Journalism, 1963; MSc, Educational Administration, 1969, PhD, Public Relations, 1972, Michigan State University. Appointments: Assistant Professor, 1972-74, Registrar, 1974-76, Vice-President, 1976-88, Riyadh University; Professor, KSU, 1988-93; Secretary General, Shura Council, 1993-. Publications: PR Activities at two Saudi-Arabian Universities; Essentials of PR (Arabic); 37 published papers. Memberships: AAUA; AACRAO; PRSA; IPRA. Address: PO Box 263, Riyadh, Saudi Arabia 11411.

AL-GELBAN Khalid S, b. 5 October 1967, Saudi Arabia. Physician. m. A Al-Shahrani, 2 sons. Education: MBBS, College of Medicine, King Saud University Abha Branch, Saudi Arabia, 1995; Arab Board in Family Medicine, 2003; Saudi Board in Family Medicine, 3003; Jordanian Board in Family and Community Medicine, 2003. Appointments include: Clinical: Intern, 1995-96, Resident, Department of Paediatrics, 1996-97 Asir Central Hospital, Abha, Saudi Arabia; Resident, 1998-2002, Board Eligible, 2002-2003, Board Certified, 2003, Department of Family and Community Medicine, King Abdul Aziz Medical City, Riyadh, Saudi Arabia; Consultant, Prince Khalid Postgraduate Centre, 2003-; Academic: Demonstrator, 1997-2003, Consultant in Family Medicine, 2003, Assistant Professor, 2003-, Chairman of the Department, 2003-, Department of Family and Community Medicine, College of Medicine and Medical Sciences, King Khalid University, Saudi Arabia. Publications: Author and co-author of 7 articles in medical journals; 6 abstracts; Participant and/or presenter at 18 conferences and symposia. Honours: Best Research Paper of the Year, 4th Residents Day, National Guard Health Affairs, 2001; Resident of the Year , 2001-2002, King Abdul Aziz Medical City, Riyadh, Saudi Arabia. Memberships: Saudi Society of Medical Education; Saudi Society of Family and Community Medicine; American Association of Family Medicine Teachers; Manuscript Reviewer, Saudi Medical Journal. Address: Department of Family and Community Medicine, College of Medicine and Medical Sciences, King Khalid University, PO Box 641, Abha, Kingdom of Saudi Arabia. E-mail: khalidgelban@hotmail.com

AL-GHAMDI Yousef, b. 1964, Saudi Arabia. Consultant Dermatologist; Cosmetic Surgeon. Education: MB.ChB, King Abdullah University, Saudi Arabia, 1980; FRCPC, Dermatology, 1997, American Board of Dermatology, 1997, American Board of Laser Surgery, 2002, McGill University, Montreal, Canada; Fellowship in Dermatologic, Cosmetic and Laser Surgery. Appointments: Consultant Dermatologist and Cosmetic Surgeon; Examiner for the American Board of Laser Surgery. Publications: Articles in medical journals including: What is new in Hair Restoration Surgery, 1999; Hair Transplantation, 2000; Tufted Hair Follicalitil, 2001. Honours: The Physicians Recognition Award, 1997, 2000; The American Academy of Dermatology, CMF Award, 1997, 2000; The Saudi Cultural Mission Merit Award, 1997, 1998. Memberships: FAAD; FASD; FAACS; FASLS; FASLMS; FASHRS; FISDS; FISHRS; FISCLS; FISD; FESDS. Address: PO Box 31270, Jeddah 21497, Saudi Arabia. E-mail: duyousefmd@yahoo.com

AL-KHARRAT Edwar, b. 16 March 1926, Alexandria, Egypt. Writer; Poet. 2 sons. Education: LLB, Alexandria University, 1946. Appointments: Editor, Gallery 68 Magazine, 1968, Afro Asian Writings Magazine, 1968, Special Issue, Egyptian Literature of AL Karmal Magazine, 1984. Publications: High Walls, 1959; Hours of Pride, 1972; Ramah and the Dragon, 1980; Suffocations of Love and Mornings, 1983; The Other Time, 1985; City of Saffron, 1986; Girls of Alexandria, 1990; Waves of Nights, 1991; Bobello's Ruins, 1992; Penetrations of Love and Perdition, 1993; My Alexandria, 1993; The New Sensibility, 1994; From Silence to Rebellion, 1994; Transgeneric Writing, 1994; Ripples of Salt Dreams, 1994; Fire of Phantasies, 1995; Hymn to Density, 1995; 7 Interpretations, 1996; Wings of Your Bird Struck Me, 1996; Why?: Extracts of a Love Poem, 1996; Soaring Edifices, 1997; The Certitude of Thirst, 1998; Cry of the Unicorn, 1998; Throes of Facts and Madness, 1998; Beyond Reality, 1998; Voices of Medernity in Arabic Fiction, 1999; Seven Clouds, 2000; Boulders of Heaven, 2001; Way of Eagle, 2002; Conflict of Passions, 2003. Contributions to: Many Arab literary magazines. Honours: Arts and Letters Medal, 1972; State Prize for Short Story, 1972; Franco Arab Friendship Award, 1989; UWAIS Award for Fiction, 1995; State Merit Award for Literature, 2000. Memberships: Egyptian Writers Union; Gezira Sporting Club; Egyptian PEN Club Rapporteur; Committee on Fiction, High Council of Culture. Address: 45 Ahmed Hishmat Street, Zamalak 11211, Cairo, Egypt.

AL-KODMANI Nasser, b. 1 January 1961, Damascus, Syria, Civil Engineer. m. Rima Haj Ibrahim, 2 sons. Education: First certificate in English, Cambridge University, British council, Damascus, 1980; Test of English as a foreign language, Princeton University, USA, TOEFL, American cultural centre, Damascus, 1984; Bachelor of Science in Civil Engineering, Damascus University, Syria, 1985; Course in projected evaluation and visibility study, Damascus, 1990; Course in Construction Management, Abu-Dhabi, UAE, 1993. Appointments: Lieutenant,

Dictionary of International Biography

Syrian Armed Forces; Site Engineer, General Company for Building, Presidential Palace project, Damascus, Syria, 1985-86; Structural Engineer, General Company for Engineering and Consulting, Damascus, Syria, 1986-91; Construction Manager, Arabian Construction Company, Abu-Dhabi, UAE, 1991-; Carried out projects HE Sheikh Mohammed Bin Khalifah Tower, Citi Bank Tower; HE Sheikh Surour City Complex, Liwa Center; HE Dr Manae Saeed Al-Otaiba Palace; Commercial building for HE Sheikh Nahyan Bin Hamdan al Nahyan; Lulu Island Development; Shuweihat Power and Water Project and lot-D; HE Sheikh Kalifa Bim Zayed, Khalidio Complex. Publications: Earthquake Effects on Soil – Foundation Systems. Listed in: Several biographical publications. Membership: Syrian Engineers Syndicate, 1986-; American Society of Civil Engineers, 1992-; UAE Society of Civil Engineers, 1992-. Address: P O Box 2113, Abu Dhabi, United Arab Emirates. E-mail: kodmani@hotmail.com Website: www.accsal.co

AL-MARAYATI Abid A, b. 14 October 1931, Iraq. Professor. Education: BA, 1952, MA, 1954, Bradley University; PhD, New York University, 1959. Appointments: Instructor, Department of Government, University of Massachusetts, 1960; Technical Assistance Officer, International Atomic Energy Agency, Austria, 1960-62; Associate Professor, State University College of New York, 1962-64; Research Fellow, Harvard University, 1964-65; Associate Professor, Arizona State University, 1965-68; Professor and Former Director, Center for International Studies, Department of Political Science, University of Toledo, 1968-; Visiting Professor, University of Kuwait, 1982-83; Visiting Professor, Institute for Public Administration, Riyadh, Saudi Arabia, 1985-86; Visiting Professor, Beijing Foreign Studies University, 1991; Asylum Officer, Immigration and Naturalization Service, Justice Department, 1998; Distinguished Scholar, National Endowment for the Humanities, Hawaii Pacific University, 2001. Publications: 5 books; Over 20 articles and papers; Reviews of books and articles; Research proposals. Memberships: International Studies Association; American Political Science Association; The Middle East Institute; The Middle East Studies Association of North America; Phi Kappa Phi. Address: University of Toledo, 2109 Terrace View West, Toledo, OH 43607, USA. E-mail: a_almarayati@yahoo.com

AL-NAJJAR Ibrahim M, b. 29 October 1944, Bany Sohyla, Saudi Arabia. Professor. m. Lamis Al-Essess, 3 sons, 2 daughters. Education: BSc, Chemistry, Baghdad University, Iraq, 1967; Diploma, Chemistry, College of Science, Tripoli, Libya, 1975; PhD, Chemistry, York University, England, 1978. Appointments: Lecturer, Department of Chemistry, Gar Younis University, Libya, 1978-80; Postdoctoral, Department of Chemistry, York University, England, 1978; Assistant Professor, 1981-83, Associate professor, 1983-91, Department of Chemistry, College of Science, King Saud University, Saudi Arabia; Research Professor, 1993-, Director of Petroleum and Petrochemicals Research Institute, 1992-96, King Abdulaziz City for Science and Technology, Saudi Arabia; Visiting Professor, Department of Chemistry, Stanford University, California, USA, 1999-2000. Publications: More than 60 scientific papers; Author of 5 books for university students; Supervised PhD and MSc theses. Honours: Fulbright Scholarship, 1999-2000. Memberships: American Chemical Society; Royal Chemical Society; Swiss Chemical Society; Saudi Chemical Society. Address: King Abdulaziz City for Science and Technology, Petroleum and Petrochemical Research Institute, PO Box 6086, Riyadh 11442, Saudi Arabia. E-mail: alnajjar@kacst.edu.sa

AL-RIFAI Khawla, b. 13 August 1963, Kuwait. Biologist; Microbiologist. m. Ali Alomari, 1 son, 2 daughters. Education: BSc Natural Sciences, Biology Analysis, 1986, Jordan University.

Appointments: Environmental Technician, Royal Science Society, 1986-89, Food Microbiologist, 1989-92, Water Microbiologist, 1992-94, Environmental Microbiologist, 1994-96, Clinical Analyst, 1996-98, Head of Water Microbiology Laboratory, Ministry of Health of Jordan; Trained a group with Global Environmental Facilities, US aid in microbiology field; Biologist at the Central Labs Directorate, 2001; Quality Assurance Officer in project between USAID and Ministry of Health, Environmental Health Department, 2003. Memberships: New York Academy of Sciences; Jordan Society of Biological Scientists. Address: Jabal Al-Hussein, PO Box 212113, Amman, Jordan.

AL-SALEH Ahmad Muhammad, b. 8 March 1964, Riyadh, Saudi Arabia. University Lecturer. Education: BSc, Geology, King Saud University, Saudi Arabia, 1985; MSc, Mining, Leicester University, England, 1988; PhD, Geology, Liverpool University, England, 1993. Appointments: Demonstrator, 1986-87, Assistant Professor, 1993-2003, Associate Professor, 2003-, King Saud University, Saudi Arabia. Publications: Metamorphism and Ar/Ar dating of the Halaban ophiolite and associated units, (co-author), 1998; Structural rejuvenation of the eastern Arabian Shield during continental collision (co-author), 2001. Honours: Scholarship to study at Leicester University, King Saud University; Scholarship to study at Liverpool University, King Saud University. Memberships: Geological Society of London; Association of Exploration Geochemists; Society of Economic Geologists; Saudi Geological Society. Address: PO Box 2009, Riyadh, Saudi Arabia. E-mail: alsaleh@ksu.edu.sa

AL-SEMMARI Fahd Abdullah, b. 29 December 1957, Riyddh, Saudi Arabia. General Director. Education: PhD, Modern History, University of California, Riverside, 1989. Appointments: Dean, Academic Research, Imam University; Deputy Minister, Cultural Relations; Ministry of Higher Education; General Director, King Abdulaziz Foundation for Research and Archive. Publications: Saudi-German Relation in the Inter-War Period; Bibliography of Saudi Arabia During the Reign of King Abdulaziz; King Abdulaziz Private Library; The Royal Visit to Aramco; Forever Friends. Memberships: Middle Eastern Studies Association; American Historical Association. Address: P O Box 90179, Riyadh 11613, Saudi Arabia.

AL-TALIQ Rashid, Artist; Writer; Composer. Education: Germany: Trained in Music, Multi Media Art with Ica Vilander, Hamburg; Visual Communication (Photography, Video, Cinamatography) and Painting under Professor Rudolf Hausner, co-founder of the Fantastic Realism School of Vienna; USA: Dramatic Arts with José Corrales, San Francisco; Dance Theatre and Directing with Eponine Cuervo Moll, San Francisco; Trained in New Consciousness Techniques; Spain: Scenic Space with Claudio de Girolama, National Centre for New Scenic Tendencies, Madrid; Alternative Therapies in Facinas, Andalusia; United Arab Emirates, Arabic and Islamic Studies in Al-Ain. Career: Co-Director, Project Al-Waha – Dar Ibn 'Arabi, Intercultural Foundation Turuq, Morocco; Designer with "Made in Marrakesh", Morocco; Freelance Artist, Writer and Composer; Worked in international film productions in Spain and Morocco; Freelance Editor and Translator, Corona Verlag, Hamburg, Germany; Multi-Media Artist and Film Director with Al-Kabbas, Dubai, UAE; Co-Director with Abdul Mati Flarwein, XTASIS Galeria de Arte, Deia, Mallorca, Spain; Researcher for a film project in Egypt; Director Duende Multi-Media Productions, San Francisco, USA; Dancer and Actor with Windolls Performing Arts Ensemble, San Francisco, USA; Stylist, Advertising Studio of the Emporium, San Francisco, USA; Designer in Peru and Brazil; Interior Decorator in Venezuela; Solo and group art exhibitions in: Australia, Egypt, England, France, Germany, Japan, Morocco, Peru, Portugal, Spain,

Dictionary of International Biography

Tunisia, UEA, USA, Venezuela. Membership: Spanish General Society of Authors and Editors. Lives and works in Marrakesh and Berlin. E-mail: raltaliq@yahoo.com

ALADANGADY Narendra, b. 21 September 1962. Consultant Neonatologist. Education: MBBS, 1986, DCH, 1988, MD, Paediatrics, 1990, Managalore University, India; Paediatric Advanced Life Support Course Certificate, Managalore, 1991; MCRP (UK), 1995; United States Medical Licensing Examination, 1998; ILTM, UK, 2002; PhD in progress, 2004. Appointments include: Resident Medical Officer, SM Charitable Hospital, Ullal, India, 1986; Senior House Officer, Paediatrics: Kasturba Hospital, Manipal, India, 1987, Wenlock Hospital and Kasturba Hospital, Mangalore, 1987-88, Lady Goschen Hospital, Mangalore, 1988; Registrar in Paediatrics, Kasturba Medical College Teaching Hospital, Mangalore, 1989-90; Resident Paediatrician, Colaco Charitable Hospital and Vijaya Hospital, Mangalore, 1990; Lecturer in Paediatrics with Honorary Registrar Status, Kasturba Medical College Teaching Hospital, Mangalore , 1990-92; Senior House Officer, Neonatology, 1992-92, Senior House Officer 3 (Registrar) in Paediatrics:, Bellshill Maternity Hospital, Scotland,1993-95, Monklands Hospital, Scotland, 1995-96, Southern General Hospital, Glasgow, Scotland, 1995-96; Clinical Research Fellow/Registrar in Neonatology, The Queen Mother's Hospital, Glasgow, 1996-99; Clinical Lecturer in Neonatal Paediatrics/SpR in Paediatrics – Neonatology, 1999-2002, Consultant Neonatologist, Honorary Senior Lecturer, 2003-, Barts and the London Queen Mary's School of Medicine and Dentistry/ The Homerton University Hospital, London. Publications: 7 published articles in medical journals as co-author; 22 papers presented at conferences and seminars. Memberships: Canara Paediatric Society, Mangolore, India; Indian Academy of Paediatrics, Karnataka State Chapter; Indian Association of Paediatrics; MPS; Neonatal Society, UK; British Association of Perinatal Medicine; Institute for Learning and Teaching in Higher Education, UK; East London and City Health Authority Research Ethics Committee, UK. Address: 4 Grovewood Place, Woodford Bridge, Essex IG8 8PX, England. E-mail: n.alangady@qmul.ac.uk

ALAGNA Roberto, b. 7 June 1963, Clichy-sur-Bois, France. Singer (Tenor). m. (2) Angela Gheorghiu, 1996. Education: Studied in France and Italy. Debut: Plymouth, 1988, as Alfredo in La Traviata for Glyndebourne Touring Opera. Career: Sang Rodolfo at Covent Garden (1990) and has returned for Gounod's Roméo and Don Carlos, 1994-96; sang Donizetti's Roberto Devereux at Monte Carlo (1992) and the Duke of Mantua at the Vienna Staatsoper (1995); Sang Don Carlos at the Théâtre du Châtelet, Paris, 1996; American appearances at Chicago and New York (debut at Met 1996, as Rodolfo); Alfredo at La Scala, Milan. Recordings include: video of Gounod's Roméo et Juliette (Pioneer); La Traviata, from La Scala (Sony) and Don Carlos, Paris; Duets and Arias (with Angela Gheorghiu), La Boheme 1996, Don Carlos 1996, La Rondine 1997. Honours include: Winner, Pavarotti Competition, 1988; Chevalier des Arts et des Lettres; Personalite Musicale de l'Annee, 1994; Laurence Olivier Award for Outstanding Achievement in Opera, 1995; Victor Award for Best Singer, 1997. Address: c/o Lévon Sayan, 9 chemin de Plonjon, Geneva, Switzerland.

ALAGOA Ebiegberi Joe, b. 14 April 1933, Nembe, Bayelsa State. Historian. m. Mercy, 1 son. Education: St Luke's School, 1943-48; Government College, Umuahia, 1948-54; Cambridge School Certificate, University College, Ibadan, (London University) 1954-59; BA, PhD, University of Wisconsin, Madison, Wisconsin, USA, 1962-65. Appointments: Archivist, Senior Archivist, National Archives of Nigeria, 1959-62; Lecturer, Professor of History, Universities of Lagos and Ibadan, 1965-77; Professor, Dean of Humanities, Deputy Vice-Chancellor, Vice-

Chancellor, University of Port Harcourt, 1977-82; Ro-Chancellor, Niger Delta University, 2001-. Publications: Communicating African History, 1989. Honours: Government Scholar/College Scholar- Ibadan, 1944-59, Fellow of the Historical Society of Nigeria, 1982; Officer of the Order of the Niger (OON). Memberships: Historical Society of Nigeria; Fellow, Nigerian Academy of Letters (FNAL), 2001. Address: 11 Orogbum Crecent, GRA Phase II, PO Box 8611, Port Harcourt, Rivers State, Nigeria. E-mail: kala_joe@yahoo.com

ALAHUHTA Eila Marjatta, b. 23 September 1926, Mikkeli, Finland. Special Needs Educator. Education: MA; Dphil; Training as Special Teacher. Appointments: Teacher in Primary School and School for the Handicapped, 1948-73; Chief Teacher, Finnish College of Speech, 1973-80; Associate Professor of Special Pedagogy, University of Jyväskylä, 1977-83; Academic Docent, Special Education, University of Helsinki, 1979-90; Professor of Logopedics, University of Oulu, 1983-93, Dean and Vice Dean, Faculty of Humanities, University of Oulu, 1988-90; Adjunct Professor of Speech Pathology, Faculty of Liberal Arts, Wayne State University, USA, 1989-92. Publications: On the Defects of Perception, Reasoning and Spatial Orientation Ability in Linguistically Handicapped Children, 1976; I Play and I Talk, I Move and I Read, 1990, 1995. Memberships include: World Association for Education Research; Nordic Association for the Study of Child Language. Address: Koivuhovintie 6A, FIN-02700 Kauniainen, Finland.

ALAINI Mohsen Ahmed al-, b. 20 October 1932, Bani Bahloul, North Yemen. Politician; Diplomatist. m. Aziza Abulahom, 1962, 2 sons, 2 daughters. Education: Faculty of Law, Cairo University; Sorbonne, Paris. Appointments: Schoolteacher, Aden, 1958-60; International Confederation of Arab Trade Unions, 1960-62; Minister of Foreign Affairs, Yemeni Republic, September-December 1962, May-July 1965, 1974-80; Permanent Representative to United Nations, 1962-65, 1965-66, 1967-69, 1980-81; Prime Minister, November-December 1967, 1974-80; Ambassador to USSR, 1968-70; Prime Minister, Minister of Foreign Affairs, February 1971, September 1971-December 1972, June 1974-January 1975; Ambassador to UK, 1973-74; Ambassador to France, August-September 1974, 1975-76; Ambassador to Federal Republic of Germany, 1981-84; Ambassador to USA, 1984- 97; Deputy Chair, Consultative Council, 1997-. Publications: Battles and Conspiracies against Yemen, 1957; Fifty Years of Mounting Sands, autobiography, 2000. Address: PO Box 7922, San'a, Yemen.

ALARCON RIVERA Fabián Ernesto, b. 1947, Quito, Ecuador. Politician. m. Lucía Peña, 2 sons, 1 daughter. Education: Pontifical Catholic University. Appointments: Councillor, Quito, 1969; Former Prefect of Pinchincha Province; Former Deputy to Congress (three times); Formerly Speaker of Congress (three times), Ecuador; Acting President of Ecuador, 6-10 February 1997; President of Ecuador, 1997-98; Arrested on charges of illegally hiring personnel, March 1999. Memberships: Frente Radical Alfarista. Address: c/o Office of the President, Palacio Nacional, García Moreno 1043, Quito, Ecuador.

ALBARN Damon, b. 23 March 1968, Whitechapel, London, England. Singer; Songwriter. Education: Drama School, Stratford East, 1 year. Musical Education: Part-time Music course, Goldsmith's College. Career: First solo concerts, Colchester Arts Centre; Member, Blur; Numerous television and radio appearances, include: Later With Jools Holland; Top Of The Pops; Loose Ends, Radio 4; Later With... Britpop Now; Extensive tours, concerts include: Alexandra Palace, Reading Festival, 1993; Glastonbury, 1994; Mile End, 1995; V97, 1997; UK Arena Tour, 1997;

Glastonbury, 1998; T in the Park, 1999; Reading and Leeds Festival, 1999; Actor, film, Face, 1997; Score for Ravenous, 1998; Score for Ordinary Decent Criminal, 1999; score for 101 Reykjavik (with Einar Benediktsson), 2000. Recordings: Albums: with Blur: Leisure, 1991; Modern Life Is Rubbish, 1993; Parklife, 1994; The Great Escape, 1995; Blur, 1997; 13, 1999; Best of 2000; (with Gorillaz) Gorillaz, 2001; G-Slides, 2002; Phase One Celebrity Take Down, 2002; Singles: She's So High, 1990; There's No Other Way, 1991; Bang, 1991; Popscene, 1992; For Tomorrow, 1993; Chemical World, 1993; Sunday Sunday, 1993; Girls And Boys, 1994; To The End, 1994; Parklife, 1994; End Of A Century, 1994; Country House, 1995; The Universal, 1995; Stereotypes, 1996; Beetlebum, 1997; Song 2, 1997; On Your Own, 1997; MOR, 1997; Tender, 1999; Coffee and TV, 1999; No Distance Left To Run, 1999; Music is My Radar, 2000; (with Gorillaz) Clint Eastwood, 2000; 19-2000, 2001; Rock the House, 2001; Tomorrow Comes Today, 2002; Solo: Original score for film Ravenous, directed by Antonia Bird, with Michael Nyman, 1998; Score for film Ordinary Decent Criminal, directed by Thasseus O'Sullivan, 1999; Mali Music, various contributors, 2002. Honours: Mercury Prize Nomination; Platinum album, Parklife; BRIT Awards: Best Single, Video, Album and Band, 1995; Q Awards, Best Album, 1994, 1995; Mercury Music Prize nomination, 1999; Platinum albums. Current Management: CMO Management, Unit 32, Ransome Dock, 35-37 Parkgate Road, London SW11 4NP, England.

ALBEE Edward (Franklin III), b. 12 March 1928, Virginia, USA. Playwright. Education: Trinity College, Hartford, Connecticut, 1946-47. Appointments: Lecturer at various US colleges and universities. Publications: Plays: The Zoo Story, 1958; The Death of Bessie Smith, 1959; The Sandbox, 1959; The American Dream, 1960; Who's Afraid of Virginia Woolf?, 1962; Tiny Alice, 1963; A Delicate Balance, 1966; Box, 1970; Quotations from Chairman Mao, 1970; All Over, 1971; Seascape, 1975; Counting the Ways, 1976; Listening, 1977; The Lady from Dubuque, 1979; Finding the Sun, 1982; The Man Who Had Three Arms, 1983; Marriage Play, 1987; Three Tall Women, 1991; Fragments, 1993; The Play about the Baby, 1996; The Goat, or, Who is Sylvia? 2000; Occupant, 2001. Adaptions of: Carson McCuller's The Ballad of the Sad Café, 1963; James Purdy's Malcolm, 1965; Giles Cooper's Everything in the Garden, 1967; Vladimir Nabokov's Lolita, 1980. Honours: Pulitzer Prizes in Drama, 1967, 1975, 1994; American Academy and Institute of Arts and Letters Gold Medal, 1980; Theater Hall of Fame, 1985. Memberships: Dramatists Guild Council; Edward F Albee Foundation, president. Address: 14 Harrison Street, New York, NY 10013, USA.

ALBERT Gábor, b. 30 October 1929, Hungary. Writer; Essayist. m. Zsuzsanna Marek, 30 October 1954, 1 son, 1 daughter. Education: Eötvös Lorand University, 1955. Appointments: Librarian, Széchényi National Library, 1955-64; Institute of Musicology, 1964-95; Editor-in-Chief, Új Magyarország, 1991-92, Magyarok Világlapja, 1992-96; Editor, The Pointer, 1994. Publications: Dragon and Octahedron, Short Stories; After Scattering, Essays; Where Are Those Columns, Novel; In a Shell, Novel; Book of Kings, Novel; Heroes of the Failures, Essays; Atheist, Short Stories; Final Settlement of a Wedding, Short Stories; Stephen King's Tart Wine, Essays, 1993; ...We Have Survived Him, Novel, 1996; The Stone Don't Feel It, Essays, 1998; I am Reading the Letters of B Szemere, Essay, 1999; The Old Dog is about to Cast His Coat, Essays, 2001; Vaults Gargoyles, Rosettes, Memoirs, 2002; In the Belly of the Fish, Novel; Initiation Ceremonies, Essays. Memberships: Association of Hungarian Writers, Member of Presidency, 1998-2001; Association of D Berzsenyi, Member of Presidency. Address: Erdő u 150, H 2092 Budakeszi, Hungary. E-mail: albert@vivamail.hu

ALBERT II, b. 6 June 1934, Belgium. King of Belgium. m. Donna Paola Ruffo Di Calabria, 1959, 2 sons, 1 daughter. Appointments: Formerly Prince of Liege; Former Vice Admiral of Navy; President, Caisse d'Epargne et de Retraite, 1954-92; President, Belgian Red Cross, 1958-93; President, Belgian Office of Foreign Trade, 1962; Appointed by Council of Europe as President of Conference of European Ministers responsible for protection of Cultural and Architectural Heritage, 1969; Participant in Numerous Conferences on environment including UN Conference, Stockholm, 1972; Chair, Belgian Olympic and Interfed Committee; Succeeded to the throne 9 August 1993 following death of his brother King Baudouin I. Address: Cabinet of the King, The Royal Place, rue Bréderode, 1000 Brussels, Belgium.

ALBERTI Kurt George Matthew Mayer (Sir), b. 27 September 1937, Germany. Professor of Medicine. m.(1) 1964, 3 sons, (2) Stephanie Amiel, 1988. Education: Balliol College, Oxford; MA; DPhil; FRCP; FRCPath; FRCPEd; FRCPGlas; FRCPI. Appointments: Research Fellow, Harvard University, USA, 1966-69; Research Officer, Oxford University, England, 1969-73; Professor of Chemical Pathology, Southampton University, 1973-78; Professor of Clinical Biochemistry, 1978-85, Professor of Medicine, 1985-2002, Dean of Medicine, 1995-97, University of Newcastle; Director of Research and Development, Northern and Yorkshire Region, 1992-95; President, Royal College of Physicians, 1997-2002; Professor of Metabolic Medicine, Imperial College, London, 1999-2002; Senior Research Fellow, London, 2002-; National Director for Emergency Access, Department of Health, 2002-. Publications: International Textbook of Diabetes Mellitus, 1st and 2nd editions, co-editor; Diabetes Annual, volumes 1-6, co-editor; Over 1,000 papers, reviews and edited books. Honours: Honorary MD, University of Aarhus, Denmark, 1998; Honorary Fellow, Balliol College, Oxford, 1999; DMed hc (University of Aarhus), (Southampton), 2000; Fellow, Academy of Medicine, Singapore, Hong Kong; Fellow, College of Physicians, Sri Lanka, Thailand. Address: Royal College of Physicians, 11 St Andrew's Place, Regents Park, London NW1 4LE, England. E-mail: professor.alberti@rcplondon.ac.uk

ALBINSKAYA Irina, b. 6 December 1962, Riga, Latvia. Computer Engineer. 2 sons. Education: System Engineer, Mathematician, Programmer, Riga Politechnic Institute, 1984; PhD, Moscow Experimental Scientific Research Institute Metal-Cutting Machine Tools, 1991. Appointments: Engineer-Programmer, State Design Enterprise Mechanization and Automation, Riga, 1984-92; Chief of Computer Science Department, Bank Baltica, 1992-97; Director of Methodology Department, Baltic Transit Bank, 1997-99; System Developer, Programmer, Eagleshade, 2001; System Manager, Moscow Consulting and Marketing, Tel Aviv, Israel, 2001-2003. Publications: Development of Mathematical Model for Definition of Efficient Characteristics of the Operation of a Flexible Manufacturing Module, 1990; Analysis of the Functioning of Flexible Manufacturing Modules by Simulation Modelling, 1991; and others. Memberships: Member, New York Academy of Sciences. Address: David Reznik 1/6, Netanya 42463, Israel. E-mail: ozmoscow@beregint.net

ALBONICO Marco, b. 29 October 1959, Torino, Italy. Medical Doctor; Parasitologist. m. Elena Ercole. Education: Medical Degree, Torino, 1984; Specialization in Infectious Diseases, University of Torino, 1988; Diploma in Tropical Medicine and Hygiene, University of Liverpool, 1991; PhD, London School of Hygiene and Tropical Medicine, 1997-2001. Appointments: Technical Advisor, Division of Communicable Diseases, World Health Organization, Geneva; Expert Parasitologist for Italian Cooperation Agency, Rome, Ministry of Foreign Affairs; Scientific Secretary, Ivo De Carneri Foundation, Milan, Italy; Adjunct

Dictionary of International Biography

Associate Professor, Johns Hopkins School of Public Health, Baltimore USA, 2000-2004. Publications include: Intestinal Helminth Prevalence and Hookworm Species Identification Among Pregnant women and Infants in the Rural Plains of Nepal, 1998; Association Between Multiple Geohelminth Species Infections in Schoolchildren from Pemba Island, 1997; Independent Evaluation of the Modified Kato-Katz According to Aginya, 1999; Clinical Pallor is Useful to Detect Severe Anaemia in Populations Where Anaemia is Prevalent and Severe, 1999; Control Strategies for Human Intestinal Nematodes Infection, 1999; Control of Epidemic Malaria on The Highlands of Madagascar, 1999; Methods To Sustain Drug Efficiency in Helminth Control Programmes, 2003. Memberships: Italian Society of Parasiology; Italian Society of Tropical Medicine; Royal Society of Tropical Medicine and Hygiene. Address: Via IV Marzo, 14 10122 Torino, Italy.

ALBRECHT Hans Joachim, b. 9 May 1931, Potsdam, Germany. Scientist. m. Angioletta Cavo. Education: University studies and research in Australia, 1950-57, Electronics Engineering, 1955; Dr-Ing (Dr in Engineering Science), Technical University of Aachen, Germany, 1972. Appointments: Consulting Engineer, Australia, 1955-57; Consulting Engineer, Research, International Geophysical Year, Italy, 1957; Laboratory and Project Head in Industry, Italy, 1958-61, Germany, 1961-65; Laboratory Head, 1965-67, Division Head, 1967-96, German Defence Research Establishment, FGAN; NATO appointments: Panel Member in AGARD (Scientific NATO Organisation), 1967-96; Chairman, NATO-TACSATCOM Committee (research and development in satellite communications), 1967-74; Director, AGARD study on communication systems, 1975-77; Chairman, AGARD panel of electromagnetic wave propagation, 1977-79; Director and Lecturer, AGARD Lecture Series, 1982; Director, studies in communications, command and control, 1980-87; German Research Ministry: Chairman, Planning Committee for Spacelab projects in communication and navigation, 1976-77. Publications: More than 100 scientific publications: Books: Planungssynthese fuer Spacelab-Projekte in Kommunikation & Navigation, 1978; Editor: Tropospheric Radio Wave Propagation, 1971; Artificial Modification of Propagation Media, 1977; Electromagnetic Propagation Characteristics of Surface Materials, 1977; Propagation Effects in Space/Earth Paths, 1980; Numerous articles in scientific journals. Honours: AGARD, von Kármán Medal 1994; Listed in Who's Who publications and biographical dictionaries. Memberships include: International Union of Radio Science, URSI, Vice-president, 1984-87, 1987-90, Member 1967, Chairman, 1978-93, National Committee in the Federal Republic of Germany; Corporate Member, 1955, Fellow, 1969, Institution of Radio and Electronics Engineers, Australia; Deutsches Museum; Armed Forces Communications and Electronics Association; German Aerospace Society; German Meteorological Society. Address: Boedikerweg 1, D-53498 Bad Breisig, Germany.

ALBRIGHT Carol Rausch, b. 20 March 1936, Evergreen Park, Illinois, USA. Writer; Editor; Retired Foundation Administrator. m. (1) Saul Gorski, 2 July 1961, deceased 22 June 1983, (2) John Albright, 26 October 1991, 2 sons. Education: BA, Augustana College, Rock Island, Illinois, 1956; Graduate Study, Lutheran Schools of Theology, Chicago, Berkeley, Washington University, St Louis. Appointments: Director, Lutheran Campus Ministry, Oregon State University, 1958-61; Publishing Consultant, 1966-70; Assistant Editor, World Book Encyclopaedia , 1970-75; Publishing Consultant, 1975-98; Contributing Editor, Doctor I've Read...., 1983-93; Executive Editor, Zygon: Journal of Religion and Science, 1989-98; Managing Editor, Science and Religion South, 1995-99; Publisher, Bridge Building, 1999; Co-Director, John Templeton Foundation Science and Religion Course Programme, Southern US, 1995-99; Co-Director, CTNS Science

and Religion course programme, Midwestern US,1999-2001. Publications: Beginning with the end; The Humanizing Brain; Where God Lives in the Human Brain; Growing in the Image of God; NeuroTheology. Honours: Academic Achievement Award, Institute for Religion in an Age of Science; Phi Beta Kappa; Chicago Women in Publishing; Award for Excellence in Periodical Writing. Memberships: Treasurer, Centre for Advanced Study in Religion and Science; Executive Council, American Theological Society, Midwest Division; Vice President for Religion, Institute for Religion in an Age of Science; Fellow, Zygon Center for Religion and Science; Society of Midland Authors. Address: 5415 S Hyde Park Blvd, Chicago, IL 60615, USA.

ALBRIGHT Lyle Frederick, b. 3 May 1921, Bay City, Michigan, USA. Chemical Engineer. m. Jeanette Van Belle, 2 daughters. Education: BSE, 1943, MS, 1944, PhD, 1950, University of Michigan. Appointments: Dow Chemical Company, Midland, 1939-41; E. I. DuPont de Nemours and Co, 1944-46; Colgate Palmolive Co, Research Chemical Engineer, 1950-51; University of Oklahoma, Assistant Professor, 1951-54, Associate Professor, 1954-55; University of Texas, Visiting Professor, 1952; Purdue University, Associate Professor, 1955-58, Professor, 1958-; Texas A & M University, Visiting Professor, 1985. Publications: 9 Books Including, Industrial and Laboratory Alkylation, 1977; Industrial and Laboratory Pyrolyses; Industrial and Laboratory Nitrations; Processes for Major Addition-Type Plastics And Their Monomers; Over 210 technical articles, book chapters and patents. Honours: Potter Award; Shreve Prize; F J and Dorothy Van Antwerpen Award, 2003. Memberships: American Institute of Chemical Engineers; American Chemical Society; Sigma Xi; Tau Beta Pi; Phi Lambda Upsilon; Omega Chi Epsilon; International Brotherhood Of Magicians. Address: Purdue University School of Chemical Engineering, Purdue University, West Lafayette IN 47907, USA.

ALBRIGHT Madeleine Korbel, b. 1938, Czechoslovakia. American Politician; Professor of International Affairs. m. Joseph Albright, divorced, 3 daughters. Education: Wellesley College; Columbia University. Appointments: Professor, International Affairs, Georgetown University, 1982-83; Head, Centre for National Policy, 1985-93; Former Legislative Aide to Democratic Senator Edmund Muskie; Former Member, National Security Council Staff in Carter Administration; Advisor, Democratic candidates, Geraldine Ferraro, 1984, Michael Dukakis, 1988; Permanent Representative to United Nations, 1993-97; Secretary of State, 1997-2001; Co-founder, The Albright Group, 2001-; Chair, National Democratic Institute, Washington DC, 2001-. Publications: Poland: the Role of the Press in Political Change, 1983; numerous articles. Memberships: Council on Foreign Relations; American Political Science Association; American Association for Advancement of Slavic Studies. Address: 901 15th Street, NW, Suite 1000, Washington, DC 20005, USA.

ALCARAZ Jose Luis, b. 3 July 1963, Hellin, Albacete, Spain. Engineering University Professor. Education: Bachelor, Murcia, Spain, 1981; Graduated in Industrial Engineering, Valencia, Spain, 1988; Doctor in Industrial Engineering, San Sebastian, Spain, 1993. Assistant Lecturer, Valencia, Spain, 1988-89, San Sebastian, Spain, 1989-93, Bilbao, Spain, 1993-94; Full Professor, Bilbao, Spain, 1994-. Publications: Books: Theory of Plasticity and Applications, 1993; Elasticity and Strength of Materials, 1995; Contributed papers to international journals. Honour: Graduation Special Award, 1988. Memberships: European Mechanics Society; New York Academy of Sciences; Spanish Association for Mechanical Engineering. Address: Dep Ingenieria Mecánica, Escuela Superior de Ingenieros, Alameda Urquijo, s/n, 48013 Bilbao, Spain.

ALDA Alan, b. 28 January 1936, New York, USA. Actor. m. Arlene Weiss, 3 daughters. Education: Fordham University. Appointments: Performed with Second City, 1963; Broadway roles in The Owl and the Pussycat, Purlie Victorious, Fair Game of Lovers, The Apple Tree, Our Town, London, 1991, Jake's Women, 1992. Creative Works: Films include: Gone are the Days, 1963; Paper Lion, 1968; The Extraordinary Seaman, 1968; The Moonshine War, 1970; Jenny, 1970; The Mephisto Waltz, 1971; To Kill a Clown, 1972; California Suite, 1978; Same Time Next Year, 1978; The Seduction of Joe Tynan, also wrote screenplay, 1979; Four Seasons, 1981; Sweet Liberty, 1986; A New Life, 1987; Crimes and Misdemeanours, 1989; Betsy's Wedding, 1990; Whispers in the Dark, 1992; And the Band Played On, 1993; Manhattan Murder Mystery, 1993; White Mile, 1994; Canadian Bacon, 1995; Everybody Says I Love You, 1996; Murder at 1600, 1997; Mad City, 1997; The Object of My Affection, 1998; Numerous TV includes: The Glass House, 1972; MASH, 1972-83. Honours: Theatre World Award; 5 Emmy Awards; 2 Directors Guild Awards; Writers Guild Award; 7 Peoples Choice Awards; Humanities Award for Writing; 5 Golden Globe Awards. Memberships: Trustee, Museum of TV and Radio; Rockefeller Foundation; President, National Commission for Observance of International Women's Year, 1976; Co-chair, National ERA Countdown Campaign, 1982. Address: c/o Martin Bregman Productions, 641 Lexington Avenue, NY 10022, USA.

ALDERMAN Minnis Amelia, b. 14 October 1928, Douglas, Georgia, USA. Counsellor; Psychologist, Business Woman, Executive. Education: AB, Music and Speech Dramatics, Georgia State College at Milledgeville, 1949; MA, Guidance, Counselling, Psychology, Supervision, Murray State University, Kentucky, 1960; PhD, Psychology and Performing Arts, ongoing. Appointments: Private music instructor, piano, violin, voice, organ 1981-; Band Director for Sacred Heart School 1982-98; Associate Dean, Professor and Head of Fine Arts Department, Wassuk College 1986-87; Academic Dean, Wassuk College 1987-90; Choir Director and Organist, Sacred Heart Church; Director, Ely Shoshone Tribal Child and Family Center and the Family and Community Center (ICWA and Social Services) 1988-93. Publications: Numerous articles, pamphlets, handbooks, journals and newsletters on guidance-counseling, functions and organisation in education, pupil personnel programs, music instruction and practice, social services programs, youth problems, mental health, problems of aging and geriatrics, tribal law; news articles and feature stories for newspapers and state organisations' publications. Honours include: Fellowship recipient to University of Utah in geriatric psychology 1974; Fellowship, University of Utah, 1975;American Biographical Institute, nominee for Most Admired Woman of the Decade, 1994; Delta Kappa Gamma Rose of Recognition Award 1994. Memberships include: Delta Kappa Gamma; International Platform Association; American Association of University Women; National Federation of Business and Professional Women; Eastern Nevada Child and Family Services Advisory Committee; Society of Descendents of Knights of the Most Noble Order of the Garter. Address: P O Box 150457, East Ely, NV 89315, USA.

ALDINGTON Charles Harold Stuart Low (Lord), b. 22 June 1948, London, England. Investment Banker. m. Regine von Csongrady-Schopf, 1989, 1 son, 2 daughters. Education: BA honours, New College, Oxford. Appointments: Citibank NA, New York , Hong Kong and Dusseldorf, 1971-77; Head of Ship Finance, Head of UK Corporate Lending, Director, Continental Europe, Grindlays Bank, 1978-86; Deutsche Bank AG: Director, Duisburg Branch, 1986-87; Managing Director, London, 1988-96; Managing Director, Investment Banking, 1996-; Chairman: European Vocational College, 1991-96; CENTEC, subsequently FOCUS Central

London, Central London TEC, 1995-99; Council Member, British-German Chamber of Commerce and Industry, 1995. Memberships: Oxford University Court of Benefactors, 1990-; Trustee, English International, 1979-86; Trustee, Whitechapel Art Gallery Foundation, 1991-96. Address: 59 Warwick Square, SW1V 2AL, London, England.

ALDISS Brian Wilson, b. 18 August 1925, East Dereham, England. Literary Editor; Writer; Critic. m. (2) Margaret Manson, 11 December 1965, 2 sons, 2 daughters. Appointments: President, British Science Fiction Association, 1960-64; Guest of Honour at World Science Fiction Convention, London, 1965, World Science Fiction Convention Brighton, 1979; Chairman, Committee of Management, Society of Authors, 1977-78; Arts Council Literature Panel, 1978-80; Booker McConnell Prize Judge, 1981; Fellow, Royal Society of Literature, 1990; Prix Utopia, 1999; Grand Master of Science Fiction, 2000. Publications: Novels include: Hothouse, 1962; Frankenstein Unbound, 1973; The Malacia Tapestry, 1976; Life in the West, 1980; The Helliconia Trilogy, 1982, 1983, 1985, 1996; Forgotten Life, 1988; Dracula Unbound, 1991; Remembrance Day, 1993; Somewhere East of Life, 1994; Story collections include: Seasons in Flight, 1984; Best SF Stories of Brian W Aldiss, 1988; A Romance of the Equator, Best Fantasy Stories, 1989; A Tupolev Too Far, 1993; The Secret of This book, 1995. Non-Fiction includes: Cities and Stones: A Traveller's Jugoslavia, 1966; Bury My Heart Heart at W H Smith's: A Writing Life, 1990; The Detached Retina (essays), 1995; At the Caligula Hotel (collected poems), 1995; Songs From the Steppes of Central Asia, 1996; The Twinkling of an Eye, My Life as a Englishman, 1998; When the Feast is Finished, 1998; White Mars (with Roger Penrose), 1999; Supertoys Last All Summer Long, 2001; The Cretan Teat, 2001; Super-State, 2002; Researches and Churches in Serbia, 2002; The Dark Sun Rises, poems, 2002; Affairs in Hampden Ferrers, 2003. Contributions to: Times Literary Supplement; Nature. Honours: Hugo Awards, 1962, 1987; Nebula Award, 1965; various British Science Fiction Association awards; Ferara Cometa d'Argento, 1977; Prix Jules Verne, Sweden, 1977; Science Fiction Research Association Pilgrim Awards, 1978; First International Association of the Fantastic in the Arts Distinguished Scholarship Award, 1986; J Lloyd Eaton Award, 1988; World Science Fiction President's Award, 1988. Hugo Nomination, 1991. Membership: Royal Society of Literature, fellow, honorary DLitt, 2000. Literary Agent: Michael Shaw, Curtis Brown. Address: Hambleden, 39 St Andrews Road, Old Headington, Oxford OX3 9DL, England.

ALDOUS Lucette, b. 26 September 1938, Auckland, New Zealand. Classical Ballet. m. Alan R Alder, 1 daughter. Education: Graduate, Royal Ballet School, London, England, 1956. Appointments: Prima Ballerina, Ballet Rambert, 1957-1961; Ballerina, London Festival Ballet, 1962-65; Ballerina, Royal Ballet, 1966-1971; Ballerina, Australian Ballet, 1971-76; Teacher, Australian Ballet School, 1978-82; Teacher, School of Dance, Victorian College of the Arts, 1982-83; Senior Lecturer in Dance, Western Australian Academy of Performing Arts, 1983-; Performances in BBC films including: Les Sylphides, Sleeping Beauty, The Nutcracker; Guest international appearances, 1959-72; Guest film appearances. Publications: Research video. Honours: Honorary Doctor of Letters, Edith Cowan University, Perth, WA; Award for Services to Dance, AusDance; Patron, Cecchetti Society of Australia; Honorary Member, Imperial Society of Teachers of Dancing; Councillor, Australia Council. Address: Dance Department, WAAPA@ECU, 2 Bradford Street, Mount Lawley, Perth, Western Australia.

ALDRIDGE (Harold Edward) James, b. 10 July 1918, England. Author; Journalist. m. Dina Mitchnik, 1942, 2 sons. Appointments: with Herald and Sun, Melbourne, Australia, 1937-38; Daily Sketch and Sunday Dispatch, London, 1939; Australian Newspaper Service, North American Newspaper Alliance (as war correspondent), Finland, Norway, Middle East, Greece, USSR, 1939-45; Correspondent, Time and Life, Tehran, 1944. Plays: 49th State, 1947; One Last Glimpse, 1981. Publications: Signed with Their Honour, 1942; The Sea Eagle, 1944; Of Many Men, 1946; The Diplomat. 1950; The Hunter, 1951; Heroes of the Empty View, 1954; Underwater Hunting for Inexperienced Englishmen, 1955; I Wish He Would Not Die, 1958; Gold and Sand, short stories, 1960; The Last Exile, 1961; A Captive in the Land, 1962; The Statesman's Game, 1966; My Brother Tom, 1966; The Flying 19, 1966; Living Egypt, with Paul Strand, 1969; Cairo: Biography of a City, 1970; A Sporting Proposition, 1973; The Marvellous Mongolian, 1974; Mockery in Arms, 1974; The Untouchable Juli, 1975; One Last Glimpse, 1977; Goodbye Un-America, 1979; The Broken Saddle, 1982; The True Story of Lilli Stubek, 1984; The True Story of Spit Mac Phee, 1985; The True Story of Lola MacKellar, 1993. Honours: Rhys Memorial Award, 1945; Lenin Peace Prize, 1972; Australian Childrens Book of the Year, 1985; Guardian Children's Fiction Prize. Address: c/o Curtis Brown, 28/29 Haymarket, London, SW1Y 4SP, England.

ALDRIN Buzz, b. 20 January 1930, Montclair, New Jersey. American Astronaut. m. (1) divorced 1978, (2) Lois Driggs-Cannon, 1988, 2 sons, 1 daughter. Education: US Military Academy; MA Institute of Technology. Appointments: Former Member, US Air Force; Completed Pilot Training, 1952; Flew Combat Mission during Korean War; Aerial Gunnery Instructor, Nellis Air Force Base, Nevada; Attended Squadron Officers School, Air University, Maswell Air Force Base, Alabama; Flight Commander, 36th Tectical Fighter Wing, Bitburg, Germany; Completed Astronautics Studies, MIT, 1963; Selected by NASA as Astronaut, 1963; Later assigned to Manned Spacecraft Centre, Houston, Texas; Pilot of Backup Crew for Gemini IX Mission, 1966; Pilot, Gemini XII, 1966; Backup Command module pilot for Apollo VIII; Lunar Module Pilot for Apollo XI; Landed on the moon, 20 July 1969; Commandant Aerospace Research Pilot School, 1971-72; Scientific Consultant, Beverly Hills Oil Co, Los Angeles; Chair, Starcraft Enterprises; Fellow, American Institute of Aeronautics and Astronautics; Retired from USAF, 1972; President, Research and Engineering Consultants Inc, 1972-; Consultant, JRW Jet Propulsion Laboratory. Publications: First on the Moon: A Voyage with Neil Armstrong, 1970; Return to Earth, 1973; Men from Earth, 1989; Encounter with the Tiber, 1996; Encounter with the Tiber – the Return, 2000. Honours: Honorary Member, Royal Astronautical Society; Several Honorary Degrees; Numerous Decorations and Awards. Address: 233 Emerald Bay, Laguna Beach, CA 92651, USA.

ALEINIKOV Gennady S, b. 10 November 1947, Minsk, Belarus. Banker. m. Olga Aleinikova, 3 sons. Education: Economy, Financing, Crediting, Belarussian State Institute of National Economy, 1977; International Economic Relations, Moscow Academy of Foreign Trade, 1985. Appointments: Chairman of the Board, Belvnesheconombank, Bank for Foreign Economic Affairs of the Republic of Belarus, 1992-97; Chairman, National Bank of the Republic of Belarus, 1997-98; Chairman, International Trade and Investment Bank (ITI Bank), Minsk, Belarus, 1999-. Honours: "Birmingham Torch" for Leadership in Business and Management, International Academy and the International Institute for Finance and Economic Partnerships, 1995; Honour Certificate of the European Market Research Centre, Brussels, Belgium, 1996; Recognised Economist of the Republic of Belarus. Memberships: International Academy of Leadership in Business and Management; Brussels International Banking Club. Address: ITI Bank, 12 Sovetskaya Street, 220030 Minsk, Belarus. E-mail: office@itibank.by

ALEKSANDROV Aleksandr Pavlovich, b. 20 February 1943, Moscow, Russia. Cosmonaut; Pilot. m. Natalia Valentinovna Aleksandrova, 1 son, 1 daughter. Education: Baumann Technical Institute, Moscow; PhD. Appointments: Served in Soviet Army; Space Programme, 1964-; Participant, elaboration of control system of spacecraft, Cosmonaut, from 1978; Participant, Soyuz-T and Salyut programmes; Successful completion of 149-day flight to Salyut-T orbital station, 1983; Spacewalk, July 1987; Return to Earth, 1987; Completed 160-day flight on Mir Space Station; Chief, Department of Crew Training and Extra Vehicular Activity, Energya design and production firm; Member, Extra Vehicular Activity Committee, IAF, 1994-. Honours: Hero of Soviet Union, 1983, 1987; Hero of Syria. Memberships: Academician, International Informatization Academy, 1997. Address: Khovanskaya Str 3-27, 129515 Moscow, Russia.

ALEMÁN LACAYO Arnoldo, b. 23 January 1946, Managua, Nicaragua. Politician. Education: National Autonomous University. Appointments: Former Leader, Pro-Somoza Liberal Student Youth Organization, 1960s; Imprisoned for alleged counter-revolutionary activity, 1980; Placed under house arrest, 1989; Mayor of Managua, 1990; President, Federation of Central American Municipalities, 1993-95; Leader, Liberal Party Alliance, 1996; President of Nicaragua, 1997-2001. Address: Oficina del Presidente, Managua, Nicaragua.

ALEMANY Gasper, b. 14 November 1959, Palma de Mallorca, Baleares. Pharmacologist. m. Amaia Ortiz, 1 son. Education: Licensed in Pharmacy, University of Barcelona, 1982; Graduated in Pharmacy, 1984; Chemist's, 1984; Specialist in Clinical Chemistry, 1990; Doctor in Pharmacy, University of Barcelona, 1991. Appointments: Clinical Chemistry Medical Doctor, Son Dureta National Health Service Hospital, 1987; Laboratory Medical Doctor, Juan March Balearic Government Hospital, 1991; Analytical and Clinical Chemistry Head of Laboratory, Andratx, 1994; Collaborator Professor, Department of Biology, University of Balearic Islands, 1996; NHS Pharmacy Inspector, 1997. Publications: Original articles for drug analysis in biological fluids by thin layer chromatography, in biomedical chromatography; Journal of A.O.A.C. Int. Honours: Juan March Foundation Grantee, 1978; Postdoctorate Balearic Government Grantee, 1992; Listed in: several biographical publications. Memberships: Spanish Association of Toxicology; International Association of Forensic Toxicology; American Association of Clinical Chemistry. Address: Plaza España 6, Andratx 07150, Spain. E-mail: galemany@infomail.lacaixa.es

ALEXANDER Anne A, b. 22 August 1927, Bartlesville, Oklahoma, USA. Artist; Salesperson. 3 sons, 2 daughters. Education: VAE, 1975, MA, 1980, University of Kansas. Appointments: Top Sales, Transworld Systems, Mission, KS; Artist; One Woman and Group Shows; Private Art Teacher; Elementary Art Teacher, Kemo, 1975-88. Publications: Restoring Historic Statues, Old St Mary's Church, Kemo; Award winning artist's show, Jefferson City, MO. Honours: Purchase Award, Art in Woods, Corp Woods, KS; Listed in Who's Who and biographical publications. Memberships: Kemo Mayors City Deal Commission; Planning Commission, Gladstone, MO. Address: Transworld Systems Inc, 5799 Broadmoor, Ste 312, Mission, KS 66202, USA.

ALEXANDER Bill, b. 23 February 1948, Hunstanton, Norfolk, England. Theatre Director. m. Juliet Harmer, 1978, 2 daughters. Education: Keele University. Appointments: Directed Shakespeare and classical and contemporary drama, Bristol Old Vic; Joined, 1977, Associate Director, 1984-91, Artistic Director, 1991-, Royal Shakespeare Company, productions including Tartuffe, Richard III, 1984, Volpone, The Accrington Pals, Clay, Captain Swing,

School of Night, A Midsummer Night's Dream, The Merry Wives of Windsor; Other theatre work, Nottingham Playhouse, Royal Court Theatre, Victory Theatre, New York and Shakespeare Theatre, Washington DC; Artistic Director, Birmingham Repertory Company, 1993-2000, productions including Othello, The Snowman, Macbeth, Dr Jekyll and Mr Hyde, The Alchemist, Awake and Sing, The Way of the World, Divine Right, The Merchant of Venice, Old Times, Frozen, Hamlet, The Tempest, The Four Alice Bakers, Jumpers, Nativity, 1999; Quarantine, 2000; Twelfth Night, 2000; An Enemy of the People, 2002; Frozen, 2002; Mappa Mundi, 2002; The Importance of Being Ernest, 2002. Publications: Film, The Snowman, 1998. Honours: Olivier Award for Director of the Year, 1986. Address: Rose Cottage, Tunley, Gloucestershire GL7 6LP, England.

ALEXANDER Connie, b. 1939, Hillsboro, Ohio, USA. Artist. Education: Graduate, Cincinnati Art Academy, 1961; Private studies with professional artists. Career: Exhibitions include: Group Show, Georgia Artist tours West Germany, 1978; Great Garden Sculpture Show, Piedmont Park, 1982; World's Fair, Knoxville, TN, 1982; Figurative Visions, group show, Ariel Gallery, Soho, New York, 1990; Echoes, 1993-94; The American Craft, group show, Trinity Gallery, 1994. Honours: Recipient, Artfest Award, Habitat for Humanity, 1998; 20 Year Anniversary, small works show, Trinity Gallery, 2002; Numerous for sculpture. Address: 351 Cherokee Street, Canton, GA 30114-3110, USA. E-mail: trinitygallery@mindspring.com

ALEXANDER Doris Muriel, b. 14 December 1922, Newark, New Jersey, USA. Professor; Writer. Education: BA, University of Missouri, 1944; MA, University of Pennsylvania, 1946; PhD, New York University, 1952. Appointments: Instructor, Rutgers University, 1950-56; Associate Professor, then Department Chairman, City University of New York, 1956-62. Publications: The Tempering of Eugene O'Neill, 1962; Creating Characters with Charles Dickens, 1991; Eugene O'Neill's Creative Struggle, 1992; Creating Literature Out of Life, 1996. Contributions to: Many journals. Honours: Penfield Fellowship, New York University, 1946; Fulbright Professor, University of Athens, 1966-67. Memberships: Association of Literary Scholars and Critics; Eugene O'Neill Society. Address: San Trovaso 1116, Dorsoduro, 30123 Venice, Italy.

ALEXANDER Sue, b. 20 August 1933, Tucson, Arizona, USA. Writer. m. 2 sons, 1 daughter. Education: Drake University, 1950-52; Northwestern University, 1952-53. Publications: Small Plays for You and a Friend, 1973; Nadir of the Streets, 1975; Peacocks Are Very Special, 1976; Witch, Goblin and Sometimes Ghost, 1976; Small Plays for Special Days, 1977; Marc the Magnificent, 1978; More Witch, Goblin and Ghost Stories, 1978; Seymour the Prince, 1979; Finding Your First Job, 1980; Whatever Happened to Uncle Albert? and Other Puzzling Plays, 1980; Witch, Goblin and Ghost in the Haunted Woods, 1981; Witch, Goblin and Ghost's Book of Things to Do, 1982; Nadia the Willful, 1983; Dear Phoebe, 1984; World Famous Muriel, 1984; Witch, Goblin and Ghost Are Back, 1985; World Famous Muriel and the Scary Dragon, 1985; America's Own Holidays, 1986; Lila on the Landing, 1987; There's More - Much More, 1987; World Famous Muriel and the Magic Mystery, 1990; Who Goes Out on Halloween?, 1990; Sara's City, 1995; What's Wrong Now, Millicent ?, 1996; One More Time, Mama, 1999; Behold the Trees, 2001. Contributions to: Short stories to Los Angeles Times. Honours: Many literary awards include Dorothy C McKenzie Award for distinguished contribution to the field of children's literature, 1980. Memberships: The Society of Children's Book Writers and Illustrators, Chairperson, Board of Directors; The Children's Literature Council of Southern California, Member of Board; Friends of Children and Libraries; California Readers Association. Address: 6846 McLaren, Canoga Park, CA 91307, USA.

ALEXANDROV Vladimir Vladimirovich, b. 4 February 1933, Leningrad, Russia. Professor of Geography-Oceanographer. m. Lydia Alexandrova, 2 sons. Education: Student, 1953-58, Diploma, 1958, Fulltime postgraduate, 1966-68, Doctorate, Hydrology, Water Resources, 1970, Geographical Faculty, St Petersburg State University; DSc, Physical Geography, Landscape Physics and Geochemistry, 1990; Senior Research Scientist Diploma, Sechenov Institute of Evolutionary Physiology and Biochemistry, Russian Academy of Sciences, 1997. Appointments: Scientist, Departments of Navy, Leningrad, 1958-65; Scientist, Institute of Limnology, Russian Academy of Sciences, Leningrad, 1968-86; Senior Research Scientist, Sechenov Institute of Evolutionary Physiology and Biochemistry, Russian Academy of Sciences, Leningrad, now St Petersburg, 1986-97; Expert, DS Council, Department of Geoecology, 1996, Professor, Department of Environmental Ecology, 1997-, St Petersburg State Poly technical University. Publications: Over 130 including: New own methods of measuring the movement in Fresh water, 1972; Electric interactions of polarized water masses and zooplankton in water bodies, 1982; Diurnal migration of hydrobionts as an indicator of connection between biological and geomagnetic rhythms of fluctuations in Solar-terrestrial system, 1985; Fresh Water Electrophysics, 1985; Current Problems in the Study and Preservation of Systems of the Biosphere, 1992; Electrokinetic fields of hydrobionts. Biorhythms of motional activity. Connection with Geomagnetism, 1996; Environmental Electromagnetic Fields and Motional Activity of Aquatic Organisms, 1998; Turbulent Water Processes in Lakes Indicated by Electrometric Method. Energetics, Hydrotechnics, 1998; Investigation of Low Level Electric and Magnetic Fields Disturbance on Living Organisms and Development of Measuring Methods and Equipment, including Computer-based video registration Systems, 2000. Honours: Honorary Diploma, Presidium, Russian Academy of Sciences for USSR Academy of Sciences 250-Year Jubilee, 1974; Honorary Diploma, Presidium, Leningrad Science Centre, 1981; Honorary Sign, Inhabitant of Leningrad Blockade, 1989; Jubilee Medal, 50 years Victory in World War II 1941-45, 1995; Jubilee Medal, 300 years of St Petersburg, 2003; Honorary Diploma, Minister of Education, 2003; Jubilee Medal, 60 years since the Facist Blocade of Leningrad, St Petersburg Government, 2003. Memberships: Geographical Society of Russia, 1966; St Petersburg Society of Natural Research, 1986; Hydrobiological Society of Russia, 1990; European Bioelectromagnetic Association, 1992; Union Deti Blokade-900, 1994; St Petersburg Scientists Home, St Petersburg State Poly Technical University, 1996; St Petersburg Scientists Home of Russian Academy of Sciences, 2001; International Academy of Ecology and Life Protection Sciences, academician, 2003. Address: 35/1 Thorez Ave, flat 5, Post box N35, 194223 St Petersburg, Russia. E-mail: alww@cef.spbstu.ru

ALEXEEV Boris, b. 2 May 1938, Orechovo-Zuevo, Moscow Region. Physicist; Educator. Divorcee, 1 daughter. Education: Degree in Physics, Engineering, 1961, PhD, 1964, Moscow Institute of Physics and Technology; DSc, Computer Centre of USSR Academy of Sciences, 1973; Professor of Physics, Higher Attestation Commission of USSR. Appointments: Senior Research Scientist, Computer Centre, USSR Academy of Sciences, 1964-73; Head of Physics Department, Moscow Aviation Institute, 1973-83; Head of Physics Department, Moscow Fine Chemical Technology Institute, 1983-; Visiting Professor, University of Provence (Marseilles), 1992-95, University of Alabama (Huntsville, USA), 1995, 1997. Publications: Over 250 scientific works including 17 books including: Mathematical Kinetics of

Reacting Gases (author), 1982; Transport Processes in Reacting Gases and Plasma (co-author), 1994, Generalized Boltzmann Physical Kinetics (2 volumes) (author), 1997. Honours: Meritorious Science and Technics Worker of Russia, 1989-; Presidents Stipend for Outstanding Russian Scientists, 1994-; Meritorious Worker, Higher Professional Education of Russia, 1998-; Man of the Year, Medal of Honor, ABI, 1999. Memberships: Russian National Committee on Theoretical and Applied Mechanics, 1987-; Organising Committee, Russian Academy of Sciences and Head of the Moscow Regional Committee, Moscow, 1991; Academician of the International Higher Education Academy of Sciences (General Physics and Astronomy) 1993-; New York Academy of Sciences, 1995-. Address: 3rd Frunzenskaya h 9, ap 130 Moscow 119270, Russia.

ALEXIADOU Genovefa, b. 19 March 1933, Volos, Greece. Cookbook Author; Publisher; TV Chef. m. Constantinos Alexiadis, 2 daughters. Education: Advanced Diploma, Violin, National Conservatory, Greece, 1949; BS, Chemistry, Aristotelian University, 1955; Nutrition Seminars, University of California, Berkeley; Workshops and seminars in food styling, food photography and other culinary arts at Oakland, California, 1984. Appointments: Chemist, N Kralis Chemistry Laboratories, Thessaloniki, Greece, 1956-69; Commercial Representative, Scientific Instruments Free-lance Agents, Thessaloniki, 1969-79; Publisher, Author, Editions Vefa Alexiadou, Thessaloniki, 1979-; TV Chef in ANT-1 TV, Athens, 1990-; Inventor of Vefa's House Franchise, 20 stores in Greece, 1994-. Publications: 11 self-published cookbooks in Greek; 4 translated into English; 40 booklets – 20 Best Recipes for.....series; Frequent Contributor to Greek and international magazines. Honours: Sorbon International du livre Gourmand, Best Merchandising, 40 booklet series with TV Magazine, 1998; Jacobs Creek Food Media Awards, South Australia, Silver Ladle for Best Photography of Sauced Sardines, 1999; World Cookbook Fair at Perigueux, Best Mediterranean Cookbook in Greek also Special Prize for Best Culinary Business Professional; Finalist, IACP Awards of Excellence for Lifetime Achievement; Nova Leaders of the Year Award, Business Woman of the Year, 2003. Memberships: Greek Publishers Association; International Association of Culinary Professionals; International Women's Organisation of Greece; Archestratos Centre for Preservation and Advancement of Traditional Greek Gastronomy. Address: 4 Leonidou Street, Metamorphosis 144 52 Athens, Greece. E-mail: vefa@vefa.gr

ALI Hassan, b. 30 November 1961, Damascus, Syria. Heart Surgeon. Education: Doctor of Medicine (MD), 1987; Doctor of Philosophy (PhD), 1995; Doctor of Medical Sciences (ScD), 1998; Clinical Professor of Cardiac Surgery, 1999. Appointments: Senior Cardiac Surgeon, 1994-98; Leading Cardiac Surgeon, 1999-2003; Major Cardiac Surgeon, 2003-. Publications: 106 scientific papers published in medical journals, 1991-2003; Co-author, 2 monographs. Honour: Diploma for best scientific work in cardiac sciences published by Russian Academy of Medical Sciences, 1996. Memberships: American Society of Thoracic Surgeons; European Association for Cardio-Thoracic Surgery; International Society for Heart and Lung Transplantation. Address: Flat 121, 1st Machinostroenia Street 6/A, Moscow 115088, Russia. E-mail: hali.gr@lycos.com

ALI Muhammad, b. 17 January 1942, Louisville, Kentucky. American Boxer. m. (1) Sonji Roi, divorced, (2) Belinda Boyd, divorced, (3) Veronica Porche, 1977, divorced, (4) Yolanda Williams, 2 sons, 7 daughters. Education: Louisville. Appointments: Amateur Boxer, 1954-60; Olympic Games Light-Heavyweight Champion, 1960; Professional Boxer, 1960-; Won World heavyweight title, 1964; Stripped of title after refusing to be drafted

into US Army, 1967; Returned to Professional Boxing, 1970; Regained World Heavyweight, 1974; Lost Title to Leon Spinks, 1978; Regained Title, Spinks, 1978; 56 victories in 61 fights, 1981; Lost to Larry Holmes, 1980; Acted in films, The Greatest; Freedom Road. Publications: The Greatest: My Own Story, 1975; Healing, 1996; More Than a Hero (with Hana Ali), 2000. Honours: Names Messenger of Peace, UN; Athlete of the Century, GQ Magazine; Lifetime Achievement Award, Amnesty International; Hon Consu General for Bangladesh in Chicago; named Messenger of Peace, UN, 1999. Memberships: Black Muslim Movement; Peace Corps Advisory Council. Address: P O Box 160, Berrien Springs, MI 49103, USA.

ALICIAS Eduardo R Jr, b. 10 August 1945, Vigan, Ilocos Sur Philippines. Professor. m. Teresita Raquepo, 1 son, 2 daughters. Education: BSc, Education, 1967; MA, Education, 1977; Doctor of Education, University of the Philippines, 1981; Diploma in Education, University of London Institute of Education, British Council Fellow, 1986. Appointments: Principal, Immaculate Conception Minor Seminary, Vigan, Ilocos Sur, the Philippines, 1972-77; Assistant Professor, 1981-88, Associate Professor, 1988-, College of Education, University of Philippines; Retired Professor, College of Education, University of The Philippines. Publications: (books) Data Organization and Analysis in a Computer Environment, 1995, 1997; Classroom Observation and Related Fallacies: Lessons for Educational Administration, 1996; Humor and Madness, 1997; Guinness World Record holder for the longest preface relative to the total book length. Honours: Melquiades Castro Professorial Chair Holder, College of Education, University of Philippines; Nominee for Poet of the Year, International Society of Poets, 2001, 2002; International Poet of Merit, International Society of Poets; Nominee for World Amateur Poet Champion, The International Society of Poets, Owings Mills, Maryland, USA, 2001, 2002. Memberships: Fellow, American Biographical Institute; Life Fellow, International Biographical Association; Distinguished Member, International Society of Poets. Address: Lot 20B & 21A Executive Homes, Hyacinth Street, Cainta Greenpark Village, Felix Avenue, Cainta, Rizal, The Philippines.

ALIOTH Gabrielle, b. 21 April 1955, Basel, Switzerland. Writer. m. Martin Alioth, 7 September 1979. Education: Master of Economics, Universities of Basel and Salzburg. Appointments: Economist, Prognos AG, Basel; Arbeitsgruppe für Konjunkturforschung, BAK; Assistant Lecturer, Operations Research, University of Basel. Publications: Novels: Der Narr, 1990; Wie ein kostbarer Stein, 1994; Die Arche der Frauen, 1996; Die stumme Reiterin, 1998; Die Erfindung von Liebe und Tod, 2003; Children's novels: Das Magische Licht, 2001; Im Tal der Schatten, 2002; Ach wie gut, dass niemand weiss, editor, 2004; Travel book: Irland – Eine Reise durchs Land der Regenbogen, 2003. Short stories and essays in various anthologies. Contributions to: Arts sections of Swiss and Austrian daily newspapers and periodicals; Features for German radio. Honour: Hamburger Literaturpreis für Der Narr, 1991. Memberships: PEN Centre for German-Speaking Writers Abroad; AdS. Address: Rosemount, Julianstown, Co Meath, Ireland.

ALISETTI Edwin Luis, b. 10 August 1969, Caracas, Venezuela. Engineer and Business Administrator. m. Saowapak Lynn Alisetti. Education: Bachelor of Science in Civil Engineering, Universidad Catolica Andres Bello, Caracas, 1993; Master of Science in Mechanical Engineering, 1998, Master of Business Administration, specialisation in Finance, Computer Information and International Business, 2001, University of Miami. Appointments: President and Director, Decoraciones Casa Bella, 1992-95; Data Analyst, University of Miami School of Architecture, 2000-01; E-Commerce, Latin America and Caribbean Division, Federal Express, 2000; Finance and Economics Tutor, University of

Miami's Economics Department, 2000-01; Business/Finance Internship, Merrill Lynch, 2001-02; Junior Analyst, Royal Bank of Canada, 2001-02; Finance and IT Consulting, The Financial Group, 2002; President, Director, Real Estate Investor, Katemi Group Inc, 2002-. Publications: Forced Convection Heat Transfer to Phase Change Material Slurries in Circular Ducts. Honours: MIBS Fellowship Award, University of Miami, 1999; Listed in national and international biographical dictionaries. Memberships: American Society of Mechanical Engineers, 1996-99. Address: 20300 West Country Club Dr #120, Aventura, FL 33180, USA. E-mail: ealisett@hotmail.com

ALKHATIB Burhan, b. 10 October 1944, Mosaib, Babel, Iraq. m. (1) 8 February 1978 - 9 February 1982, (2) 11 January 1987 - 27 April 1994, 2 sons, 1 daughter. Education: Engineering practice in Egypt, 1965; Degree in Engineering, BSME, Engineering College, Baghdad University, 1967; MA, The Gorky Literary Institute, 1975. Appointments: Engineer, 1968-69; Journalist, 1970-80; Stylist and Translator, 1975-86; Publisher, 1990-94. Publications: Khutwat ila Alufq Albaid (Steps Toward a Distant Horizon), 1967; Dabab fi Addahira (Mist at Midday), 1968; Shiqqatun fi Shari' Abi Nuwas (An Apartment on Abi Nuwas Street), 1972; Ajusur Azujajiyya (Bridges of Glass), 1975; Ashari 'aljadid (A New Street), 1980; Nujum Oldhuhr (Under the Heat of Midday), 1986; Suqut Sparta (The Fall of Sparta), 1992; Layla Baghdadia (A Baghdad Night), 1993; Babel alfaiha (The Aromatic Babylon), 1995; Thalik assaif fi Iskendria (That Summer in Alexandria), 1998; Aljanain Almuglaqa (The Closed Gardens), 2000. Contributions to: Translated 13 books, wrote number of essays and stories in Arab magazines and journals, between 1975-85. Membership: Sveriges författar förbund (The Writers Union of Sweden), 1998-. Address: Berg V 22 tr 3, 19631 Kungsangen, Sweden.

ALLADIN M Ibrahim, b. 11 May 1956, Mauritius. Professor; Director. m. Aisha, 2 sons. Education: BA(Hons), University of East London. 1982; M Ed, University of Alberta, Canada, 1984; PhD, La Trobe University, Australia, 1988. Appointments: Professor, Altai State University, 1993-; Director Cambrian International, 1995-; Advisor, 1996-. Publications: Several books including: Perspectives in Global Education, 1990; Teaching in Global Society, 1992; The Living Legend, 2000. Honours: Paul Harris Fellow; Citizenship Citation Award, Government of Canada. Memberships: Board Member, Sudbury Social Planning Council; Asia Pacific Research Network. Address: 3 Davenport Crescent, Sudbury, Ontario, Canada, P3A 5V2. E-mail: mialladin@hotmail.com

ALLADIN Saleh Mohammed, b. 3 March 1931, Secunderabad, India. Retired Professor of Astronomy. m. Farhat Akhtar, 2 sons, 3 daughters. Education: St Patrick's High School Senior, Cambridge, 1948; BSc, Nizam College, 1953; MSc, Physics, Osmania University, 1955; PhD, Astronomy and Astrophysics, University of Chicago, 1963. Appointments: Research Scholar, Osmania University, 1955-59; Research Assistant, Yerkes Observatory, USA, 1960-63; Lecturer, 1964-65; Senior Research Fellow, 1965-68, Reader, 1968-78, Professor, 1978-91, Osmania University; Senior Associate Inter University Centre for Astronomy and Astrophysics, Pune, 1990-96. Publications: Articles on: The Dynamics of Colliding Galaxies Ap J, 1965; Gravitational Interactions between Galaxies, with Narasimhan, Physics Reports, 1982; Views of Scientists on the Existence of God, 1991. Honours: Senior Visiting Fellow at the Universities of Oxford and Cambridge, 1980; Meghnad Saha Award for the Year 1981; University Grants Commission, India; Man of the Year, 2000; Listed in Several Biographical Publications. Memberships: International

Astronomical Union; Astronomical Society of India. Address: Alladin Building, 72 Sarojini Devi Road, Secunderabad 500 003, A P India.

ALLAHVERDI Ali, b. 14 May 1965, Van, Turkey, Professor. m. Hatice Altin, 2 daughters. Education: BS, Istanbul Technical University, 1986, MS, 1990, PhD, 1992, Rensselaer Polytechnic Institute. Appointments: Assistant Professor, Marmara University, Turkey, 1993-95; Assistant Professor, 1995-98, Associate Professor, 1998-2003, Professor, 2003-, Kuwait University, Safat, Kuwait. Publications: More than 40 articles in referred international journals and presented more than 30 papers at international conferences. Honours: Dissertation Prize, Rensselaer Polytechnic Institute, 1993; Doctoral Fellowship, Ministry of Education, Turkey, 1988-93. Memberships: Institute of Operations Research and Management Sciences; Institute of Industrial Engineers; Operational Research Society. Address: Department of Industrial Engineering, Kuwait University, PO Box 5969, Safat, Kuwait.

ALLAN Andrew Norman, b. 26 September 1943, Newcastle-upon-Tyne, England. Television Executive. m. (1) 2 daughters, (2) Joanna Forrest, 1978, 2 sons, 1 daughter. Education: BA, Birmingham University. Appointments: Presenter, ABC Television, 1965-66; Producer, Thames TV, 1966-69, 1971-75; Head of News, 1976-78; Producer, ITN, 1970; Director of Programmes, 1978-83, Deputy Managing Director, 1982-83, Managing Director, 1983-84, Tyne Tees TV; Director of Programmes, 1984-90, Managing Director, 1993-94, Central Independent TV; Managing Director, Central Broadcasting, 1990-93; Chief Executive, 1994-95, Director of Programmes, 1996-98, Carlton TV; Director, TV12, 1999-; Media Consultant, 1998-; Chair, Birmingham Repertory, 2000-; Chair, Route 4 PLC, 2001. Memberships: Fellow, Royal Television Society. Address: Wardington Lodge, Wardington, Banbury, Oxon OX17 1SE, England.

ALLASON Rupert William Simon, b. 8 November 1951, London, England. Author. m. Nicole Van Moppes, 15 June 1979, dissolved 1996, 1 son, 1 daughter. Education: Downside School, Bath, England; University of Grenoble, France; University of London, England. Appointments: Member of Parliament (Con) for Torbay, 1987-97; Editor, World Intelligence Review, 1985-. Publications: SPY!, with Richard Deacon, 1980; British Security Service Operations 1909-45, Bodley Head, 1981; A Matter of Trust: MI5 1945-72, 1982; MI6: British Secret Intelligence Service Operations 1909-45, 1983; The Branch: A History of the Metropolitan Police Special Branch, 1983; Unreliable Witness: Espionage Myths of the Second World War, 1984; GARBO, co-authored with Juan Pjujol, 1985; GCHQ: The Secret Wireless War, 1986; Molehunt, 1987; The Friends: Britain's Postwar Secret Intelligence Operations, 1988; Games of Intelligence, 1989; Seven Spies Who Changed the World, 1991; Secret War: The Story of SOE, 1992; The Faber Book of Espionage, 1993; The Illegals, 1993; The Faber Book of Treachery, 1995; The Secret War for the Falklands, 1997; Counterfeit Spies, 1998; Crown Jewels, 1998; Venona, 1999; The Third Secret, 2000. Address: Drury House, 34-43 Russell Street, London WC2B 5HA, England.

ALLEN Blair H, b. 2 July 1933, Los Angeles, California, USA. Writer; Poet; Editor; Artist. m. Juanita Aguilar Raya, 27 January 1968, 1 son, 1 daughter. Education: AA, San Diego City College, 1964; University of Washington, 1965-66; BA, San Diego State University, 1970. Appointments: Book Reviewer, Los Angeles Times, 1977-78; Special Feature Editor, Cerulean Press and Kent Publications, 1982-. Publications: Televisual Poems for Bloodshot Eyeballs, 1973; Malice in Blunderland, 1974; N/Z, 1979; The Atlantis Trilogy, 1982; Dreamwish of the Magician, 1983; Right Through the Silver Lined 1984 Looking Glass, 1984; The Magical

Dictionary of International Biography

World of David Cole (editor), 1984; Snow Summits in the Sun (anthology, editor), 1988; Trapped in a Cold War Travelogue, 1991; May Burning into August, 1992; The Subway Poems, 1993; Bonfire on the Beach, by John Brander (editor), 1993; The Cerulean Anthology of Sci-Fi/Outer Space/Fantasy/Poetry and Prose Poems (anthology, editor), 1995; When the Ghost of Cassandra Whispers in My Ears, 1996; Ashes Ashes All Fall Down, 1997; Around the World in 56 Days, 1998; Thunderclouds from the Door, 1999; Jabberbunglemerkeltoy, 1999; The Athens Café, 2000; The Day of the Jamberee Call, 2001; Assembled I Stand, 2002; Wine of Starlight, 2002; Snow Birds in Cloud Hands (anthology, editor), 2003; Trek into Yellowstone's Cascade Corner Wilderness, 2003. Contributions to: Numerous periodicals and anthologies. Honours: 1st Prize for Poetry, Pacificus Foundation Competition, 1992; Pacificus Foundation Literary Prize for Lifetime Achievement in Poetry, 2003; Various other honours and awards. Memberships: Association for Applied Poetry; Beyond Baroque Foundation; California State Poetry Society; Medina Foundation. Address: PO Box 162, 264 W. E. Street, Colton, CA 92324, USA.

ALLEN Geoffrey (Sir), b. 29 October 1928, Clay Cross, Derbyshire, England. Polymer Scientist; Administrator. m. Valerie Frances Duckworth, 1972, 1 daughter. Education: PhD, University of Leeds. Appointments: Postdoctoral Fellow, National Research Council, Canada, 1952-54; Lecturer, 1955-65, Professor of Chemical Physics, 1965-75, University of Manchester Institute of Science and Technology; Professor of Polymer Science, 1975-76, Professor of Chemical Technology, 1976-81, Imperial College of Science and Technology, University of London; Chair, Science Research Council, 1977-81; Visiting Fellow, Robinson College, Cambridge, 1980-; Head of Research, 1981-90, Director for Research and Engineering, 1982-90; Unilever PLC, 1981-90; Non-Executive Director, Courtaulds, 1987-93; President, Plastics and Rubber Institute, 1990-92; Executive Adviser, Kobe Steel Ltd, 1990-2000; Member, National Consumer Council, 1993-; Chancellor, University of East Anglia, 1994-. Honours: Honorary MSc, Manchester; Dr hc, Open University; Honorary DSc, Durham, East Anglia, 1984, Bath, Bradford, Keele, Loughborough, 1985, Essex, Leeds, 1986, Cranfield, 1988, Surrey, 1989, North London, 1999. Memberships: Fellow, Royal Society, Vice-President, 1991-93; Fellow, Institute of Physics; Fellow, Plastics and Rubber Institute. Address: 18 Oxford House, 52 Parkside, London SW19 5NE, England.

ALLEN Henry Lee, b. 7 July 1955, Joiner, Arkansas, USA. Professor. m. Juliet E A Cooper, 3 sons, 5 daughters. BA, Wheaton College, 1977; MA, 1979, PhD, 1988, University of Chicago. Appointments: Assistant to the President, Instructor in Sociology, Bethel College, 1982-87; Associate Professor of Sociology, Calvin College, 1987-91; Assistant Professor of Education, University of Rochester, New York, 1991-97; Associate Professor of Sociology, Rochester Institute of Technology, 1997-98; Associate Professor of Sociology, Wheaton College, 1998-2003. Publications: Numerous articles and papers. Honours: Danforth Graduate Fellow, Outstanding Young Man of America; Listed in national and international biographical dictionaries. Memberships: New York Academy of Sciences; Wilson Center Associates; North American Association of Computational Social and Organizational Science. Address: 111 West Lincoln Avenue, Wheaton, IL 60187, USA. E-mail: henry.l.allen@wheaton.edu

ALLEN Ronald John, b. 12 November 1940, Prince Albert, Canada. Astronomer. m. Janice Ruth Nielsen, 2 sons, 1 daughter. Education: Bachelor of Arts, Honours Physics, University of Saskatchewan, Canada, 1962; PhD, Physics, Massachusetts Institute of Technology, USA, 1967; Postdoctoral Fellow of the National Research Council of Canada, 1967, 1968; Observatoire

de Paris, France. Appointments: Research Associate, 1969, 1970, Research Supervisor, 1971, Lecturer in Radio Astronomy, 1972-80, Professor of Radio Astronomy, 1980-85, Chairman of the Astronomy Department and Dean of the Subfaculty of Astronomy, 1982-85, Kapteyn Astronomical Institute, University of Groningen, The Netherlands; Head, 1985-88, Professor of Astronomy, 1985-90, Department of Astronomy, University of Illinois at Urbana-Champaign; Astronomer (AURA), 1989-, Head of Science Computing and Research Support Division, 1989-95, Head of the Research Programs Office, 1995-99, Space Telescope Science Institute, Baltimore. Publications: 16 invited papers, 2 books co-edited; 72 refereed publications; Author and co-author of other publications. Honours: Numerous honours and awards; Invited Lecturer and Speaker on many conferences. Listed in: Several biographical publications. Memberships: Many memberships including Adjunct Professor, Department of Physics and Astronomy, The Johns Hopkins University, Baltimore, 1991-; Member, Commission J, International Radio Science Union, 1991-; Member, Science Team, NASA Space Interferometry Mission, 2000-. Address: Space Telescope Science Institute, 3700 San Martin Drive, Baltimore, MD 21218, USA.

ALLEN Suzanne, b. 31 May 1963, Santa Monica, California, USA. Financial Planning Executive; Insurance Agent; Writer. Education: BA, University of California, Santa Monica, 1986; MA, Education, California State University, Los Angeles, 1990; Postgraduate: Art Center School of Design, Pasadena, California, 1994-. Appointments: Certified Teacher, California; Licensed Real Estate Agent, California. Interviewer, Los Angeles Times Newspaper, 1986-88; Educator, Los Angeles Unified School District, 1987-90, Burbank Unified School District, 1990-94, 1994-; Partner, Financial Services, Roth & Associates/New York Life, Los Angeles, 1993-2000; Educator, Pasadena Unified School District, 2000-2002; Partner, Financial Services, Pacific Life Insurance Company, Vice-President, Jarvis & Mandell LLC Estate Planing Service, Massachusetts Mutual Insurance Company, 2001-; Agent Massachusetts Mutual Insurance, Beverley Hills, California, Partner, Retirement Educators Financial Services; Agent Consultant, Frasier Financial group, 2001-2002; Model, Actor, 1998-. Publications: End of Days, 2001; As Quinn Allen: I Will Serve You All My Days, Black Dahlia, Alone, 2002, I Miss Him, 2003, Waiting for Godot (poem), 2003. Honours include: 3 Silver Cups, International Poet of Merit; 5 Bronze Medals, International Poets Society; Silver Outstanding Achievement in Poetry Trophy, 2003; Piece of the Roof Award, New York. Memberships include: Civil War Trust; Volunteer, SPCA/Humane Society; Board member, Bungalow Heaven Neighborhood Association Life Member: NEA; Library of Congress; National Society for Historical preservation; Burbanks Teachers Union; International Hi IQ Society; Abraham Lincoln Association; Honorary Membership, International Society of Poets. Address: Jarvis & Mandell LLC, 1875 Century Park E # 1550, Los Angeles, CA 90067, USA

ALLEN Thomas (Sir), b. 10 September 1944, Seaham, County Durham, England. m. (1) Margaret Holley, 1968, divorced 1986, 1 son, (2) Jeannie Gordon Lascelles, 1988, 1 stepson, 1 stepdaughter. Education: Royal College of Music. Appointments: Principal Baritone: Welsh National Opera, 1968-72; Royal Opera House, Covent Garden, 1972-78; Glyndebourne Opera, 1973; Performances include: Die Zauberflote, 1973; Le Nozze di Figaro, 1974; Cosi fan Tutte, 1975; Don Giovanni, 1977; The Cunning Little Vixen, 1977; Simon Boccanegra, Billy Budd, La Boheme, L'Elisir d'Amore, Faust, Albert Herring, Die Fledermause, La Traviata, A Midsummer Night's Dream, Beckmesser, etc. Publications: Foreign Parts: A Singer's Journal, 1993; Art Exhibitions: Chelsea Festival, 2001; Salisbury Playhouse, 2001. Honours: Honorary Fellow, University of Sunderland; Queen's

Prize, 1967; Gulbenkian Fellow, 1968; MA Hon, Newcastle, 1984; RAM Hon, 1988; DMus Hon, Durham, 1988. Address: c/o Askonas Holt Ltd, Lonsdale Chambers, 27 Chancery Lane, London WC2A 1PF, England.

ALLEN Tim, b. 13 June 1953, Denver, USA. Education: West Michigan University; University of Detroit. Career: Creative Director, advertising agency; Comedian; Showtime Comedy Club All Stars, 1988; TV series include: Tim Allen: Men are Pigs, 1990; Home Improvement, 1991-; Tim Allen Rewrites America; Films include: Comedy's Dirtiest Dozen; The Santa Clause, 1994; Toy Story, 1995; Meet Wally Sparks, 1997; Jungle 2 Jungle, 1997; For Richer for Poorer, 1997; Galaxy Quest, 1999; Toy Story 2, 2000; Buzz Lightyear of Star Command: the Adventure Begins, 2000; Who is Cletis Tout?, 2001; Joe Somebody, 2001; Big Trouble, 2002; The Santa Clause 2, 2002. Publications: Don't Stand Too Close to a Naked Man, 1994; I'm Not Really Here, 1996. Honours: Favourite Comedy Actor, People's Choice Award, 1995, 1997-99. Address: c/o Commercial Unlimited, 8883 Wilshire Boulevard, Suite 850, Beverly Hills, CA 90211, USA.

ALLEN Woody (Allen Stewart Konigsberg), b. 1 December 1935, Brooklyn, New York. American Actor; Writer. m. (1) Harlene Rosen, divorced, (2) Louise Lasser, divorced, 1 son with Mia Farrow, (3) Soon-Yi Previn, 2 adopted daughters. Education: City College, New York; New York University. Career: Wrote for TV Performers: Herb Shriner, 1953; Sid Caesar, 1957; Art Carney, 1958-59; Jack Parr and Carol Channing; Also wrote for Tonight Show and the Gary Moore Show; Debut performance, Duplex, Greenwich Village, 1961; Performed in a variety of nightclubs across the US; Plays: Play It Again Sam; Don't Drink the Water, 1966; The Floating Light Bulb, 1981; Death Defying Acts, 1995; Films Include: What's New Pussycat?, 1965; Casino Royale, 1967; What's Up, Tiger Lily?, 1967; Take the Money and Run, 1969; Bananas, 1971; Everything You Always Wanted to Know About Sex, 1972; Play it Again Sam, 1972; Sleeper, 1973; Love and Death, 1976; The Front, 1976; Annie Hall, 1977; Interiors, 1978; Manhattan, 1979; Stardust Memories, 1980; A Midsummer Night's Sex Comedy, 1982; Zelig, 1983; Broadway Danny Rose, 1984; The Purple Rose of Cairo, 1985; Hannah and her Sister, 1985; Radio Days, 1987; September, 1987; Another Woman, 1988; Oedipus Wrecks, 1989; Crimes and Misdemeanors, 1989; Alice, 1990; Scenes from a Mall, Shadows and Fog, 1991; Husbands and Wives, 1992; Manhattan Murder Mystery, 1993; Bullets Over Broadway, 1995; Mighty Aphrodite, 1995; Everybody Says I Love You, 1997; Deconstructing Harry, 1997; Celebrity, 1998; Wild Man Blues, 1998; Stuck on You, 1998; Company Men, 1999; Sweet and Lowdown, 1999; Small Town Crooks, 2000; The Curse of the Jade Scorpion, 2001; Hail Sid Caesar! 2001; Hollywood Ending, 2002. Publications: Getting Even, 1971; Without Feathers, 1975; Side Effects, 1980; The Complete Prose, 1994; Contributions to Playboy and New Yorker. Honours: Academy Award for Best Director; Best Writer; D W Griffith Award, 1996. Address: 930 Fifth Avenue, New York, NY 10021, USA.

ALLENDE Isabel, b. 2 August 1942, Lima, Peru. Writer. m. (1) Miguel Frias, 1962, 1 son, 1 daughter, (2) William C Gordon, 17 July 1988. Appointments: Journalist, Paula Magazine, 1967-74; Mampato Magazine, 1969-74; Channel 13 World Hunger Campaign, 1964; Channel 7, various humourous programmes, 1970-74; Maga-Cine-Ellas, 1973; Administrator, Marroco School, Caracas, 1978-82; Freelance journalist, El Nacional newspaper, Caracas, 1976-83; Visiting teacher, Montclair State College, New Jersey, 1985, University of Virginia, Charlottesville, 1988, University of California, Berkeley, 1989; Writer, 1981-. Publications: The House of the Spirits, 1982; Of Love and Shadows, 1984; La Gorda de Porcelana, 1984; Eva Luna, 1989; Tales of Eva Luna, 1990; The Infinite Plan, 1992; Paula, 1995;

Aphrodite, a memoir of the senses, 1998; Daughter of Fortune, 1999; Portrait in Sepia, 2000. Honours: Novel of the Year, Panorama Literario, Chile, 1983; Point de Mire, Belgium, 1985; Author of the Year and Book of the Year, Germany, 1984; Grand Priz d'Evasion, France, 1984; Colima for Best Novel, Mexico, 1985; Author of the Year, Germany, 1986; Mulheres Best Novel, Portugal, 1987; Dorothy and Jillian Gish Prize, 1998; Sara Lee Frontrunner Award, 1998; GEMS Women of the Year Award, 1999; Donna Dell'Anno Award, Italy, 1999; Plays: Paula; Stories of Eva Luna; The House of the Spirits; Eva Luna. Address: 116 Caledonia Street, Sausalito, CA 94965, USA.

ALLEY Kirstie, b. Wichita, Kansas, USA. American Actress. m. Parker Stevenson, 1 son, 1 daughter. Education: University of Kansas. Appointments: Stage appearances include: Cat on a Hot Tin Roof; Answers; Regular TV Show Cheers, 1987-93; Other appearances in TV films and series: Star Trek II, The Wrath of Khan, 1982; One More Chance, Blind Date, Champions, 1983; Runaway, 1984; Summer School, 1987; Look Who's Talking Too, 1990; Madhouse, 1990; Look Who's Talking Now, 1993; David's Mother (TV Film), 1994; Village of the Damned, 1995; It Takes Two, 1995; Sticks and Stones, 1996; Nevada, 1996; For Richer or Poorer, 1997; Victoria's Closet, 1997; Deconstructing Harry, 1997; Toothless, 1997; Drop Dead Gorgeous, 1999; The Mao Game, 1999; Blonde, 2001; Salem Witch Trials, 2002; Back By Midnight, 2002. Address: Jason Weinberg and Associates, 122 East 25th Street, 2nd Floor, New York, NY 10010, USA.

ALLEY Wayne Edward, b. 16 May 1932, Portland, Oregon, USA. Senior United State District Judge. m. Marie L Alley, 1 son, 2 stepsons, 1 daughter. Education: AB with great distinction, Stanford University, 1952; JD, Stanford Law School, 1957; Diploma, US Army Command and General Staff College, 1970; Diploma, Industrial College of the Armed Forces, 1974. Appointments: US Army, 1953-51, 1957-81; Retired as Brigadier General; Dean and Professor of Law, University of Oklahoma College of Law, 1981-85; United States District Judge, 1985-. Publications: The Litigious Aftermath of Martial Law, 1962; The Overseas Commander's Power to Regulate the Private Life, 1967; Determinants of Military Judicial Decisions, 1974; Advocacy on Behalf of a Major Field Command, 1981. Honours: Phi Beta Kappa; Order of the Coif; Fellow, American Bar Association; Distinguished Service Medal; Legion of Merit Bronze Star; Meritorious Service Medal. Address: 4001 US Courthouse, Oklahoma City, OK 73120, USA. E-mail: judgewaynealley@okwd.uscourts.gov

ALLEYNE George (Sir), b. 7 October 1932, Barbados. Physician. m. Sylvan I Chen, 1958, 2 sons, 1 daughter. Education: MD, University of West Indies; Senior Resident, University Hospital of West Indies, 1963; FRCP. Appointments: Tropical Metabolism Research Unit, Jamaica, 1964-72; Professor of Medicine, 1972-81, Chair, Department of Medicine, 1976-81, University of West Indies; Head of Research Unit, 1981-83, Director of Health Programmes, 1982-90, Assistant Director, 1990-95, Director, 1995-, Pan American Health Organization, Washington DC, USA. Publications include: The Importance of Health: A Caribbean Perspective, 1989; Public Health for All, 1991; Health and Tourism, 1992; Over 100 articles in major scientific research journals. Honours: Honorary DSc, West Indies University, 1988; Order of the Caribbean Community, 2001. Address: Pan American Health Organization, 525 23rd Street NW, Washington, DC 20037, USA.

ALLI Waheed (Baron of Norbury in the London Borough of Croydon), b. 16 November 1964. Business Executive. Appointments: Co-Founder, Joint Managing Director, Planet 24

Dictionary of International Biography

Productions Ltd, formerly 24 Hour Productions, 1992-99; Managing Director, Production, Carlton Productions, 1988-2000; Director, Carlton TV, 1998-2000; Director, Chorion, 2002-. Memberships: Member, Teacher Training Agency, 1997-98; Panel 2000, Creative Industry Taskforce; Board member, English National Ballet, 2001-; Director, Shine Entertainment Ltd; Shine M; Castaway TV; Digital Radio Group Ltd. Address: House of Lords, London SW1A 0PW, England.

ALLIANCE David (Sir), b. June 1932. Business Executive. Appointments: 1st acquisition, Thomas Hoghton, Oswaldtwistle, 1956; Chair, N Brown Group, 1968-; Acquired Spirella, 1968, Vantona Ltd to form Vantona Group, 1975; Group Chief Executive, 1975-90, Chair, 1989-99, Coats Viyella; Acquired Carrington Viyella to form Vantona Viyella, 1983, Carrington Viyella to form Vantona Viyella, 1983, Nottingham Manufacturing, 1985, Coats Patons to form Coats Viyella, 1986; Chair, Tootal Group PLC, 1991-99. Honours: Commander, Order of the British Empire; Honorary Fellow, University of Manchester Institute of Science and Technology; Honorary LLD, Manchester, 1989; Honorary FCGI, 1991; Honorary DSc, Heriot-Watt, 1991; Honorary LLD, Liverpool, 1996. Memberships: Fellow, Royal Society of Arts; Companion, British Institute of Management. Address: N Brown Group, 53 Dale Street, Manchester M60 6ES, England.

ALLISON Jane Carey, b. 21 March 1959, Surrey, England. Portrait Painter. m. John T Freeman, 1 son. Education: Chelsea School of Art, 1977-80; Slade School of Fine Art, 1980-82. Career: Portrait Painter. Commissions: Professor P S Boulter, President, Royal College of Surgeons, Edinburgh; Professor Dorothy Geddes, President, Royal College of Surgeons, Edinburgh; Professor William Houston, Guy's Hospital; Professor Nairn Wilson, President, General Dental Council; Baroness Susan Greenfield, Neuroscientist, President, Royal Institute; Professor Daphne Jackson; Lord Mishcon; Lord Robens; Lord Nugent; Lord St Ostwald; Lt General Sir Michael Walker; Lt General Sir John Learmont; Lt General Sir Michael Willcocks, Black Road; Major General Stuart Watson; Major General Peter Bonnet; Sir Robert Clark, Chairman, United Biscuits; Mr David Fine, Chairman, Polydor; Mr Bruce Dawson, Chairman, KIO; Baron Jean Charles Velge, Chairman, Bekaert; Bishop George Reindorp; Bishop Ivor Watkins; Bishop Michael Adie; Bishop David Brown; Miss Enid Castle, Principal, Cheltenham Ladies College; Headmasters of: Wycliffe College, Kings School, Bruton, Worcester RGS, Christ's Hospital, Adams School, Bedford College, Dragon School, Oxford; Miss Suzannah York, Actress; Miss Viviana Durante, Principal Ballerina, Royal Ballet; The Court of Examiners, The Royal College of Surgeons; The London Board of Brewin Dolphin; Sir Christopher Collet, Lord Mayor of London. Address: 12 Sydney Road, Guildford, Surrey, GU1 3LJ, England.

ALLISON Michael John, b. 30 June 1940, Ipswich, Suffolk, England. Management Consultant. m. Janette Eaves Morse, 10 March 1967, 2 sons. Education: Ordinary Certificate in Mechanical Engineering, Ipswich Civic College, England, 1956-58; Higher National Diploma in Mechanical Engineering, North East Essex Technical College, England, 1958-61; Fellowship Diploma in Mechanical Engineering, 1974-76, Graduate Diploma in Quality Technology, 1976-79, RMIT University, Melbourne, Australia; Master of Business Systems, Monash University, Australia, 2002. Appointments include: Manufacturing Research Engineer, Boeing Co, Seattle, USA, 1967-70; Manufacturing Engineer, Aeronca Inc, Ohio, USA, 1970-71; Manager of Production Engineering and Quality Control, Flexdrive Industries Pty Ltd, 1971-78; Class 2 through to Principal Engineer, Teletraffic Forecasting, Switching Design, Transmission Design and Engineering Planning, Australian Telecommunications Corporation, 1978-88; Supervising Engineer,

TQM Development, TNE Metro, Australian Telecommunications Corporation, Melbourne, 1988-90; Consultant, Stockdales Pty Ltd, 1990-; Visiting Lecturer, Auckland Institute of Technology, Ballarat University, Deakin University. Publications include: Productivity Improvement Through Quality Planning, 1992; Management and Planning Tools in Quality Management, 1993; The Conversion Kit: The Guide to Problem Busting, 1994, 1996; Service Quality Systems, 1995; What is QS9000, 1996; The 20 Elements of ISO 9001: Clause 4/11 Control of Inspection, Measuring and Test Equipment, 1997; Business Process Reengineering or Quality Systems? Why Not Both?, 1997; Quality Management in Local Government, 1997. Honours: Managing Director's Prize, Ionides Cup, 1959; AOQ Prize, 1979; Shilkin Prize, 1994. Memberships: American Society for Quality - Certified Quality Engineer; Australian Organisation for Quality. Address: 8 Brixton Avenue, Eltham, Vic 3095, Australia.

ALLNER Walter, b. 2 January 1909, Dessau, Germany. Designer; Painter; Art Director. m. (1) Colette Vasselon, 1 son, (2) Jane Booth Pope, 1 son. Education: Student, Bauhaus-Dessau, 1927-30. Appointments: Designer, Gesellschafts-und Wirtschafts-Museum, Vienna, 1929; Assistant to Typographer Piet Zwart, Wassenaar, Holland, 1930; Editorial Painting and Advertising Designer, Paris, 1932-49; Partner, Omnium Graphique, Paris, 1933-36; Art Director, Formes, Editions d'Art Graphique et Photographique, Paris, 1933-36; Paris Editor, Swiss Art Magazine, Graphis, 1945-48; Founder, Editor, International Poster Annual, 1948-52; Co-Director, Editions Paralleles, Paris, 1948-51; Member, Staff Fortune Magazine, New York City, 1951-74, Art Director, 1962-74; Member, Faculty, Parsons School of Design, New York City, 1974-86; Visiting Critic, Member, Comite de Parrainage Ecole Superieure d'Arts Graphiques, Paris, 1979-; Freelance Designer, Design Consultant for Companies; Lecturer in Australia, 1983; Designer of Posters for Traffic Safety Campaign, Outdoor Advertising Association of America. Publications: Several articles in professional journals and magazines. Honours: Medal, Bauhaus-Dessau German Academy of Architecture, 1979; Recipient, AGI Henri Statuette for lifetime outstanding achievement in graphic design, 1998. Memberships: Alliance Graphique; American Institute of Graphic Arts; Associazione Italiana Creativi Comunicazione Visiva. Commissions and Creative Works: Exhibitions in Paris, Germany, Australia, USA, England, France, Holland, Switzerland, Latin America, Japan. Address: 110 Riverside Drive, New York, NY 10024, USA.

ALMAZAN Mauricio, b. 28 May 1943, Oaxaca, Mexico. Medical Doctor. m. Jacqueline Jean, 3 sons. Education: Certificate, Medical School, 1968; Diploma, American Board of Obstetrics and Gynaecology, 1976; Certificate, Accreditation Council for Gynaecologic Endoscopy, 1996. Appointments: Professor of Farmacology, University of Mexico, 1967; Professor, School of Nursery ABC Hospital, Mexico, 1966-86; Professor and Chief Endoscopy, Mexican Institute, 1974-1980; Medical Director, Assoc. Pro Maternal Health, Mexico, 1977-78; Chief of Research, Ministry of Health and Who, Mexico, 1981-82; Member of the Committee of Clinical Records, ABC Hospital, Mexico, 1968-92. Publications: 4 Creative works; 16 publications. Memberships: Fellow American College of Surgeons, 1973; Fellow American College of Obstetricians and Gynaecology, 1973; Associate The Royal Society of Medicine, London, England, 1974. Address: Ob-Gyn Office, 735 Ave Palmas Ste 801, 11000 Mexico City, Mexico.

ALMODÓVAR Pedro, b. 25 September 1951, La Mancha, Spain. Film Director. Career: Fronted a rock band; Worked at Telefónica, 10 years; Started film career with full-length super-8 films; Made 16mm short films, 1978-83, including Salome; Other films including Pepe, Luci, Bom y otras montón, Laberinto de pasiones,

1980, Dark Habits, 1983, What Have I Done to Deserve This?, 1985, Matador, 1986, Law of Desire, 1987, Women on the Verge of a Nervous Breakdown, 1988, Tie Me Up, Tie Me Down, 1990, Tacones Lejanos, 1991, Kika, 1993, The Flower of My Secret, 1996, Live Flesh, 1997, All About My Mother, 1991; Talk to Her, 2002. Publications: Fuego en las entrañas, 1982; The Patty Diphusa Stories and Other Writings, 1992. Honours: Felix Award, 1988; Academy Award for Best Foreign Language Film, 1999; BAFTA Award for Best Film not in the English Language, 2003; Academy Award for Best Original Screenplay, 2003. Address: c/o El Deseo SA, Ruiz Perelló 15, Madrid 28028, Spain.

ALMOHANDIS Ahmed A, b. 21 December 1949, Medina, Saudi Arabia. University Professor. m. Fayzah, 7 October 1973, 2 sons, 2 daughters. Education: BSc, 1970; MSc, 1974; PhD, 1977. Appointments: Vice-Dean, Students Affairs, 1983-85, Chairman, Geology Department, 1990-92, Chairman Astronomy Department, 1994-96, Vice Dean, 1992-95, College Science, Deputy Director, Translation Center, 1997-98, Director, Translation Center, 1998-, King Saud University, Riyadh. Publications: More than 100 papers and articles in geology and science in national and international journals. Honours: Numerous citations and medals from the King Saud University and Principality Youth Welfare, Saudi Arabia, 1980-97. Memberships: Mineralogical Society, UK; Mineralogical Society, USA. Address: Geology Department, College of Sciences, King Saud University, PO Box 2455, Riyadh 11451, Saudi Arabia.

ALMOND Andrew, b. 3 July 1972, Barnsley, England. Scientist. Education: BSc with first class honours, Physics, University of Edinburgh, Scotland, 1994; PhD, University of Manchester, England, 1997. Appointments: Wellcome Trust Prize Research Fellow, Department of Biochemistry, University of Manchester, 1997-99; Wellcome Trust Prize Travelling Research Fellow, Carlsberg Laboratory, Copenhagen, Denmark, 1999-2001, Department of Biochemistry, University of Oxford, England, 2001-02; BBSRC David Phillips Research Fellow, Department of Biochemistry, University of Oxford, 2002-. Publications: Numerous articles in professional scientific journals. Honours: Donald Fraser Bursary, 1993; Elected Chartered Physicist, CPhys, 1996. Memberships: Member, Institute of Physics, MInstP; British Society for Matrix Biology. Address: University of Oxford, South Parks Road, OX1 3QU, England. E-mail: andrew.almond@bioch.ox.ac.uk

ALMOND Ian, b. 21 September 1969, Skipton, Yorkshire, England. Lecturer. Education: Undergraduate, Warwick University, England/University of Illinois, USA, 1988-91; PhD, Edinburgh University, Scotland, 1995-99. Appointments: Tutor, Bari University, Italy, 1990-95; Lecturer, Erciyes University, Kayseri, Turkey, 1998-2000; Lecturer, Bosphorus University, Istanbul, Turkey, 2000-. Publications: Over 25 articles in journals including: Harvard Theological Review; New Literary History, Philosophy and Literature; Heythrop Journal; Author of book: Sufism and Deconstruction, 2004. Honours: Cited frequently in Philosophers' Index; Lewis Edward's Memorial Prize for Short Story, 1995, 1996. Memberships: JAAR; MLA. Address: Bogazici Universitesi, Bati Dilleri, Ingiliz Edebiyat, Boluma, Bebek 80815, Istanbul, Turkey. E-mail: mrianalmond@yahoo.co.uk

ALPERT Herb, b. 31 March 1935, Los Angeles, California, USA. Musician (trumpet); Songwriter; Arranger; Record Company Executive. m. Lani Hall, 1 son, 2 daughters. Education: University of Southern California. Career: 3 television specials; Leader, own group Tijuana Brass; Multiple world tours; Owner, Dore Records; Manager, Jan And Dean; Co-founder with Jerry Moss, A&M Records (formerly Carnival), 1962-89; Artists have included: The Carpenters; Captain And Tennille; Carole King; Cat Stevens; The

Police; Squeeze; Joe Jackson; Bryan Adams. Compositions include: Wonderful World, Sam Cooke (co-writer with Lou Adler). Recordings: The Lonely Bull; A Taste Of Honey; Spanish Flea; Tijuana Taxi; Casino Royale; This Guy's In Love With You (Number 1, UK and US), 1968; Rise (Number 1, US), 1979; Albums include: The Lonely Bull, 1963; Tijuana Brass, 1963; Tijuana Brass Vol 2, 1964; South Of The Border, 1965; Whipped Cream And Other Delights, 1965; Going Places, 1966; SRO, 1967; Sounds Like Us, 1967; Herb Alpert's 9th, 1968; The Best Of The Brass, 1968; Warm, 1969; Rise, 1979; Keep Your Eyes On Me, 1979; Magic Man, 1981; My Abstract Heart, 1989; Midnight Sun, 1992; Second Wind, 1996; Passion Dance, 1997; Colors, 1999. Honours: Numerous Grammy Awards. Address: c/o Kip Cohen, La Brea Tours, Inc., 1414 Sixth Street, Santa Monica, CA 90401, USA.

ALSAPIEDI Consuelo Veronica Karram, b. 9 November 1927, New York City, New York. Psychoanalytic Psychotherapist. m. John R Alsapiedi, 1 son, 1 daughter. Education: BA, Seton Hill College, 1949; MSW, Fordham University for Social Work, 1972; DSW, Institute of Psychoanalytic Psychotherapy for Clinical Social Work, 1985. Appointments: Catholic Charities, 1944-51; Case Aide I, II, III to SW and CC Court representative, Office of Mental Health, 1972-95; Therapy with patients and patients families, placements and out-patient services in communities, Manager of Drug and Alcohol Wards in Mental Heath Hospital, 1987-95; Senior Social Work Student Supervisor, 1985-94; Family Center Service, Therapy – All Ages (3 to 85), 1998-2000; Private Practice, 1975; Consultant, various insurance companies as required. Honours: Board Certification by AME, 1987; Commendations for outstanding work and results, workshops and conferences. Memberships: New York State Society for Clinical Social Workers; Menninger Society. Address: 71-36-110 St, Ste 1K, Forrest Hills, NY 11375-4838, USA.

ALSOP William Allen, b. 12 December 1947, Nottingham, England. Architect. m. Sheila Bean, 1972, 2 sons, 1 daughter. Education: Architectural Association. Career: Teacher of Sculpture, St Martin's College; Worked with Cedric Price; In practice with John Lyall; Designed ferry terminal, Hamburg; Design work on Cardiff barrage; Feasibility studies to recycle former De Lorean factory, Belfast; Designed government building, Marseilles; Established own practice, collaborates with Bruce Maclelan in producing architectural drawings; Principal, Alsop and Störmer Architects, 1979-2000; Principal, Director and Chair, Alsop Architects, 2001; Chair, Architecture Foundation, 2001-; Projects include: North Greenwich Station, 2000; Peckham Library and Media Centre, 2000; Commissioned to design Fourth Grace, Liverpool, 2002-. Publications: City of Objects, 1992; William Alsop Buildings and Projects, 1992; William Alsop Architect: Four Projects, 1993; Will Alsop and Jan Störmer, Architects, 1993; Le Grand Bleu-Marseille, 1994; Alsop and Störmer: Selected and Current Works. Honours: Officer, Order of the British Empire; Honorary LLD, Leicester; Stirling Prize, 2000. Memberships: Fellow, Royal Society of Arts. Address: 72 Pembroke Road, London W8 6NX, England. E-mail: walsop@alsopandstormer.co.uk Website: www.alsopandstormer.com

ALTARAC Silvio, b. 30 December 1958, Zagreb, Croatia. Urological Surgeon. m. Lidija Lopičić, 1 son, 1 daughter. Education: MD, 1983, PhD, 1989, School of Medicine, Zagreb. Appointments: Teaching Assistant, Department of Physiology and Immunology, Zagreb, 1985-89; Clinical Research Fellow, University Hospital Pittsburgh, 1990, Royal Hallamshire Hospital, Sheffield, 1993-94, University Hospital Innsbruck, 1995, Brigham and Women's Hospital, Harvard University, Boston, 1995-96;

Assistant Professor, School of Medicine, Zagreb, 1994-. Publications: Numerous articles in professional journals. Honours: Academician Drago Perović's Medal; Rector's Award for academic excellence; Listing in numerous biographical publications. Membership: European Association of Urology; American Urological Association. Address: Bukovačka cesta 229C, 10 000 Zagreb, Croatia.

ALTER Robert B(ernard), b. 2 April 1935, New York, USA. Professor; Literary Critic. m. Carol Cosman, 17 June 1974, 3 sons, 1 daughter. Education: BA, Columbia College, 1957; MA, 1958, PhD, 1962, Harvard University. Appointments: Instructor, Assistant Professor of English, Columbia University, 1962-66; Associate Professor of Hebrew and Comparative Literature, 1967-69, Professor of Hebrew and Comparative Literature, 1969-89, Class of 1937 Professor, 1989-, University of California, Berkeley. Publications: Partial Magic, 1975; Defenses of the Imagination, 1978; Stendhal: A Biography, 1979; The Art of Biblical Narrative, 1981; Motives for Fiction, 1984; The Art of Biblical Poetry, 1985; The Pleasures of Reading in an Ideological Age, 1989; Necessary Angels, 1991; The World of Biblical Literature, 1992; Hebrew and Modernity, 1994; Genesis: Translation and Commentary, 1996; The David Study: Translation and Commentary, 1999; Canon and Creativity, 2000. Contributions to: Commentary; New Republic; New York Times Book Review; London Review of Books; Times Literary Supplement. Honours: English Institute Essay Prize, 1965; National Jewish Book Award for Jewish Thought, 1982; Present Tense Award for Religious Thought, 1986; Award for Scholarship, National Foundation for Jewish Culture, 1995. Memberships: Association for Jewish Studies; Association of Literary Scholars and Critics; Council of Scholars of the Library of Congress; American Academy of Arts and Sciences; American Philosophical Society. Address: 1475 Le Roy Avenue, Berkeley, CA 94708, USA.

ALTHER Lisa, b. 23 July 1944, Tennessee, USA. Writer; Reviewer; University Professor. m. Richard Alther, 26 August 1966, divorced, 1 daughter. Education: BA, Wellesley College, 1966. Appointments: Staff Member, Atheneum Publishers, New York City, 1967-68; Freelance writer, 1968-; Lecturer, St Michael's College, Winooski, Vermont, 1980-81; Professor and Basler Chair, East Tennessee State University, 1999. Publications: Kinflicks, 1975; Original Sins, 1980; Other Women, 1984; Bedrock, 1990; Birdman and the Dancer, 1993; Five Minutes in Heaven, 1995. Contributions to: New York Times Magazine; New York Times Book Review; Natural History; New Society; Arts and Antiques; Boston Globe; Washington Post; Los Angeles Times; San Francisco Chronicle; Southern Living. Memberships: Authors Guild; National Writers Union; PEN. E-mail: lalther@aol.com

ALTHWAINI Sulayman Nasser, 31 December 1959, Ha'il City, Saudi Arabia. Assistant Dean. m. Nadia Alghelaigah, 4 sons. Education: BS, Science Education, 1982, MS, Curriculum and Instruction, 1991, King Saud University, Riyadh, Saudi Arabia; Ed D., Curriculum and Instruction. Montana State University, Bozeman, Montana, USA, 2000. Appointments: Science Teacher, Ministry of Education, Ha'il, Saudi Arabia, 1982-90; Science Teacher, Riyadh, Saudi Arabia, 1991-92; Arabic Class Teacher, Montana State University, Bozeman, Montana, USA, 2000; Assistant Dean, Ha'il Technical College, Ha'il, Saudi Arabia, 2000-2003. Honours: Honorary Citizenship of Bozeman, Montana, USA, 1998-99; Recognition from National Council on US-Arab Relations, Washington, USA, 1999; International Friendship and Understanding, Montana State University, Bozeman, Montana, USA, 2000; Listed in Who's Who publications and biographical dictionaries. Memberships: Ha'il Technical Education and Vocational Training Council, Ha'il, Saudi Arabia, 2000-; King

Abdulaziz Association, Ha'il, Saudi Arabia, 2001-; Saudi Psychological and Educational Association, Riyadh, Saudi Arabia, 2001-. Address: PO Box 1624, Ha'il City 81441, Saudi Arabia. E-mail: drsulayman@yahoo.com

ALTON Roger Martin, b. 20 December 1947, Oxford, England. Journalist. Divorced, 1 daughter. Education: Exeter College, Oxford. Appointments: Graduate Trainee, then General Reporter and Deputy Features Editor, Liverpool Post, 1969-73; Sub-Editor, News, 1973-76, Chief Sub-Editor, News, 1976-81, Deputy Sports Editor, 1981-85, Arts Editor, 1985-90, Weekend Magazine Editor, 1990-93, Features Editor, 1993-96, Assistant Editor, 1996-98, The Guardian; Editor, The Observer, 1998-. Honours: Editor of the Year, What the Papers Say Awards, 2000. Address: Office of the Editor, The Observer, 119 Farringdon Road, London EC1R 3ER, England. E-mail: editor@observer.co.uk Website: www.observer.co.uk

ALTSCHUL b j, b. 28 January 1948. Public Relations Counselor; Educator. Education: BA, University of South Florida, Tampa; MA, University of Maryland, College Park, 1995. Appointments: Public Relations Director, Valkyrie Press Inc, St Petersburg, Florida, 1974-77; Founding Editor, Bay Life and Tampa Bay Monthly, 1977-79; Public Relations Director, Florida Renaissance Festival, 1980; Managing Editor, Florida Tourist News, Clearwater, 1981; Public Relations Counselor, Freelance Writer-Editor, 1981-; Manager, Editorial and Information Services, Virginia Port Authority, 1985-88; Director, Office of Communication, Virginia Department of Agriculture and Consumer Services, 1988-93; Public Relations Director, University of Maryland Biotechnology Institute, 1997-99; Lecturer, University of Maryland, Department of Communication, 1999-2001; Assistant Professor, American University, 2001-. Publications include: Famous Florida! Cracker Cookin' & Other Favorites, 1984; Virginia: A Commonwealth Comes of Age, contributor, 1988; Book chapters contributed to learning to teach: What You Need to Know to Develop a Successful Career as a Public Relations Educator, 3rd edition, 2003; Case Studies in International Public Relations, 2nd edition, forthcoming; Numerous freelance articles for consumer, business and trade publications. Honours: Award of Excellence, Periodicals, American Association of Port Authorities, 1987; Presidential Citation, PRSA, 1989; Best of Show, State Fair of Virginia 1992; 2nd Place, Graduate Research Interaction Day, University of Maryland, 1994; Top 3 Teaching Paper, Association for Education in Journalism and Mass Communication, 2003; Mini-Grant, National Federation of Press Women, 1995; 1st Place, Journalism Research, Public Relations, National Federation of Press Women, 1995. Memberships include: Public Relations Society of America; Association for Education in Journalism and Mass Communication; National Association of Science Writers; International Association of Business Communicators; Virginia State Agency Public Affairs Association; Hadassah. Address: 14100 Beechvue Lane, Silver Spring, MD 20906, USA.

ALUKO Samuel Adepoju, b. 18 August 1929, Ode-Ekiti, Nigeria. Economist. m. Joyce Anomoghan Ofuya, 4 sons, 2 daughters. Education: BSc, Economics, 1954, MSc, Economics, 1957, PhD, Economics, 1959, London. Appointments: Lecturer, Economics, University of Ife, Nigeria, 1962-64, 1967-80; Senior Lecturer, Associate Professor, Economics, Nsukka, Nigeria, 1964-66; Professor of Economics, IFE, 1967-80; Dean of Faculty, Social Sciences, 1970-73; Visiting Professor, University of Birmingham Centre of West African Studies, 1973-74; Visiting Scholar, Massachusetts Institute of Technology, 1962; Visiting Professor, Harvard University, USA, 1974; Member, various Government Committees, Nigeria, 1960-; Chairman, National Economic Intelligence Committee, Federal Government of Nigeria, 1994-

99; Ondo State Government Advisor, 1980-83. Publications: Numerous publications on the subject of economics, federal finance and economic development of Nigeria, 1957-; Christianity and Communism, 1965; Economic Recovery of Nigeria 1996-98. Honours: Numerous academic scholarships, London University and others; Honorary DSc, Futa Akure University, 1992, Kano University, 1998; Commander, Federal Republic of Nigeria, 1998. Memberships: Fellow, Nigerian Economic Society, 1992-; Member, Christian Association of Nigeria, 1962-; World Council of Churches, Geneva, 1966-; International Economic Association, 1968-. Address: 30 Owo Avenue, Ijapo Housing Estate, PO Box 1594, Akure, Ondo State, Nigeria.

ALUKO Timothy Mofolorunso, b. 14 June 1918, Ilesha, Nigeria. Novelist. m. Janet Adebisi Fajemisin, 1950, deceased 1996, 6 children. Education: BSc, University of London, 1948; PhD in Public Health Engineering, University of Lagos, 1976. Appointments: Executive Engineer, Public Works, Nigeria, 1950-56; Town Engineer, Lagos Town Council, 1956-60; Controller of Works and Permanent Secretary, Ministry of Works, Western Nigeria, 1960-66; Senior Lecturer and Associate Professor, University of Lagos, 1966-78; Commissioner of Finance, Government of Western Nigeria, 1971-73. Publications: One Man, One Wife, 1959; One Man, One Matchet, 1964; Kinsman and Foreman, 1966; Chief the Honourable Minister, 1970; His Worshipful Majesty, 1973; Wrong Ones in the Dock, 1982; A State of Our Own, 1986; Conduct Unbecoming, 1993; My Years of Service, 1994; First Year at State College, 1999 Uncollected short story: The New Engineer, 1968. Honours: Officer of the Order of the British Empire, 1963; Officer of the Order of the Niger, 1964; Association of Nigerian Author's Award for the Best Novel of 1993; Memberships: Fellow, Nigerian Society of Engineers; Nigerian Town Planning Institute; Nigerian Academy of Engineering; Institution of Civil Engineers. Address: 53 Ladipo Oluwote Road, Apapa, Lagos, Nigeria.

ALVAREZ Roberto, b. 13 June 1957, Buenos Aries, Argentina. Teacher; Professor. m. 17 November 1997. Education: University of Buenos Aires. Appointments: Professor of Soil Sciences, Faculty of Agronomy, University of Buenos Aires, 1981-; Editor-in-Chief, 1994-98, Co-editor, 1998-2002, Ciencia del Suelo; Director, Technical Careers Gardening and Horticulture of the Faculty of Agronomy, University of Buenos Aires, 2000-2002. Publications: Several papers in professional journals. Memberships: American Association of Agronomy; Soil Science Society; Argentine Soil Science Society; Argentine Society of Microbiology; Soil Science Society America. Address: Faculty of Agronomy, University of Buenos Aires, Av San Martin 4453, Buenos Aires, Argentina.

AMANN Charles A, b. 21 April 1926, Minnesota, USA. Engineer. m. Marilynn Reis, 26 August 1950, 1 son, 3 daughters. Education: BS, 1946, MSME, 1948, University of Minnesota. Appointments: General Motors Research Laboratories, 1949-91; Research Fellow, Director, Engineering Research Council, 1989-91; Principal Engineer, KAB Engineering, 1991-. Publications: Several articles in professional journals. Honours include: James Clayton Prize, 1975; Arch T Colwell Merit Award, SAE, 1984; ASME ICE Division Woodbury Award, 1989; National Academy of Engineering, 1989; University of Minnesota Outstanding Achievement Award, 1991; Internal Combustion Engine Award, ASME, 2000; Forest R McFarland Award, SAE, 2001; Distinguished Lecturer, ASME, 2002. Memberships: Society of Automotive Engineers; American Society of Mechanical Engineers; Sigma Xi. Address: 984 Satterlee Road, Bloomfield Hills, MI 48304-3152, USA.

AMANPOUR Christiane, b. 12 January 1958, London, England. Broadcasting Correspondent. m. James Rubin, 1998, 1 son. Education: New Hall, Cambridge; University of Rhode Island, USA. Appointments: Radio Producer and Research Assistant, BBC Radio, London, 1980-82; Radio Reporter, WBRU, Brown University, USA, 1981-83; Electronic Graphics Designer, WJAR, Providence, Rhode Island, 1983; Assistant, CNN International Assignment Desk, Atlanta, Georgia, 1983; News Writer, CNN, Atlanta, 1984-86; Reporter, Producer, CNN, New York, 1987-90; International Correspondent, 1990, Senior International Correspondent, 1994, Chief International Correspondent, 1996, CNN; Assignments include Gulf War coverage, 1990-91, USSR break-up and subsequent war in Tbilisi, 1991, extensive reports on conflict in former Yugoslavia and civil unrest and crises coverage, Haiti, Algeria, Somalia and Rwanda. Honours: Dr hc, Rhode Island; 3 Dupont-Columbia Awards, 1986-96; 2 News and Documentary Emmy Awards, 1999; George Foster Peabody Award, 1999; George Polk Award, 1999; University of Missouri Award for Distinguished Service to Journalism, 1999. Memberships: Fellow, Society of Professional Journalists. Address: c/o CNN International, CNN House, 19-22 Rathbone Place, London W1P 1DF, England.

AMATO Giuliano, b. 13 May 1938, Turin, Italy. Appointments: Joined Italian Socialist Party, 1958; Member, Central Committee, 1978-; Assistant Secretary; elected Deputy for Turin-Novara-Vercelli, 1983, 1987; Former Under-Secretary of State; President and Vice-President, Council of Ministers; Minister of the Treasury, 1987-89; Professor, Italian and Comparative Constitutional Law, University of Rome; National Deputy Secretary, Italian Socialist Party, 1988-92; Foreign debt negotiator for Albanian government, 1991-92, Prime Minister of Italy, 1992-93, 2000-01; Minister for Treasury, 1999-2001; Vice President, EU Special Convention on a Pan-European Constitution, 2001-. Address: Special Convention on a European Constitution, European Union, 200 rue de la Loi, 1049 Brussels, Belgium.

AMBRUS Julian L, b. 29 November 1924, Budapest. Physician; University Professor. m. Clara M Ambrus, 4 sons, 3 daughters. Education: MD, 1949; PhD, 1954; ScD (hc); FACP. Appointments: Professor of Internal Medicine, School of Medicine, State University of New York at Buffalo, New York, 1955-; Director of Cancer Research, Roswell Park, Memorial Cancer Institute, 1955-92; Chairman, Department of Experimental Pathology, State University of New York at Buffalo, RPC, 1982-92. Publications: Over 500 publications; 67 books or book chapters. Honours include: ScD, honoris causa, Niagara University, 1987; Distinguished Alumnus Award, Jefferson Medical College, 1990; Knight Commander of the Holy Sepulchre, Vatican, 1991; Foreign Member, National Academy of Science, Hungary, 1993. Memberships: Fellow, American College of Physicians; Member, American Society for Cancer Research. Address: Buffalo General Hospital, Kaleida Health System, State University of New York at Buffalo, 100 High Street, Buffalo, NY 14203, USA.

AMBRUS Michael Johann, b. 10 May 1948, Glimboca, Romania. Surgeon. m. Denise D Ambrus, 3 sons. Education: Medical Doctor, University of Medicine, Cluj-Napoca, Romania, 1972; Specialist in Surgery, 1981, Specialist in Traumatology, 1982, Koblenz, Gemany. Appointments: Physician, Surgical University Clinic III, Cluj-Napoca, Romania, 1972-75; Physician, Petrosani Hospital, Romania, 1975-76; Internship, Surgical University Clinic, Bucharest, Romania, 1976-77; Residency, 1977-80, Fellowship, 1980-82, Idar-Oberstein Hospital, Germany, 1980-82l Chief of Surgery and Traumatology, Löningen Hospital, Germany, 1983-. Publications: 12 publications in Romanian professional journals,

1967-72. Membership: German Association of Surgeons. Address: Grüner Weg 15, D-49624 Löningen, Germany. E-mail: dambrus@web.de

AMEH Emmanuel Adoyi, b. 31 December 1965, Kano, Nigeria. Medicine (Paediatric Surgery). m. Dr Nkeiruka Ameh, 1 son. Education: MBBS, Ahmadu Bello University, Zaria, Nigeria, 1989; Fellow of West African College of Surgeons (FWACS), Ahmadu Bello University Teaching Hospital, Zaria, 1997. Appointments: Registrar in Surgery, ABU Teaching Hospital, Zaria, 1992-94; Senior Registrar in General and Paediatric Surgery, 1994-97, Consultant in Paediatric Surgery, 1997-, Lecturer in Paediatric Surgery, 1997-, Lecturer and Demonstrator, in Human Anatomy, 1992-94, Ahmadu Bello University; Associate Lecturer in Surgery, Bayero University, Kano, Nigeria, 1995-96; Examiner in physiology (primary examinations), Examiner in Part II examination in Paediatric Surgery, all of West African College of Surgeons' Examination, 2000-. Publications: 106 on Paediatric Surgery and other aspects of Surgery in professional journals; 36 papers presented at conferences. Honours: Numerous prizes as a student including, Paediatric Association of Nigeria prize and the Kunle Ijaiya family memorial prize for best overall student in paediatrics, 1989; George Edington Prize, best final year student in Pathology, 1989; Barau Dikko prize for final year student in Surgery and anatomy, 1989; Alba Medical Award for best final year medical student, 1989; International Society for Surgery Travel Scholar Award, 2001; International Guest Scholar, American College of Surgeons, 2003. Memberships: Nigerian Medical Association; Medical and Dental Consultant's Association of Nigeria; Nigerian Surgical Research Society; New York Academy of Science; Surgical Sciences Research Society, Zaria; Members, Association of Paediatric Surgeons of Nigeria (APSON); African Society of Toxicological Science (ASTS); British Association of Paediatric Surgeons, Pan African Paediatric Surgical Association; Association of Surgeons of Nigeria (ASON). Address: Paediatric Surgery Unit, Department of Surgery, Ahmadu Bello University Teaching Hospital, Zaria, Nigeria.

AMELING Elly, b. 1938, Rotterdam, Netherlands. Opera Singer. m. Arnold W Beider, 1964. Education: Studied Singing with Jo Bollekamp, Jacoba and Sam Dresden, Bodi Rapp; Studied French Art Song with Pierre Bernac. Career: Recitals, Europe, South Africa, Japan; US debut, 1968; Annual tours, USA and Canada, 1968-; Has sung with Concertgebouw, New Philharmonic Orchestra, BBC Symphony Orchestra, Berlin Philharmonic, Cincinnati Symphony, San Francisco Symphony, Toronto Symphony, Chicago Symphony; Appeared in Mozart Festival, Washington DC, 1974, Caramoor Festival, 1974, Art Song Festival, Princeton, New Jersey, 1974. Publications: Recordings including Mozart Concert; Handel Concert; Bach Cantatas; Wolf's Mörike Lieder; Aimez-vous Handel?; Aimez-vous Mozart?; Bach's Christmas Oratorio; Mahler's Symphony No 2; Bruckner's Te Deum; Wolf's Italienisches Liederbuch. Honours: 1st Prize, Concours International de Musique, Geneva; Grand Prix du Disque; Edison Prize; Preis der Deutschen Schallplattenkritik; Stereo Review Record of the Year Award; Knight, Order of Orange-Nassau.

AMES Lloyd Leroy, b. 23 August 1927, Norwich, Connecticut, USA. Geochemist. m. Joan Nilsine Romstad, 1 son, 3 daughters. Education: BA, University of New Mexico, 1952; MS, 1955, PhD, 1956, Post PhD, 1957, University of Utah. Appointments: Staff Scientist, Basalt Waste Isolation Program; Conducting research, Hanford; Performed studies of the hydrothermal synthesis and exchange kinetics of the zeolites, highly specific exchanger materials; Extensive role in X ray diffraction and electronmicroprobe studies of soil minerals, basalts, feldspars, calcite, clays and interbed sequences underlying the Hanford environs. Publications: Numerous journal articles. Honours: Authored 3 US patents. Memberships: American Mineralogy Society; Mineralogical Association of Canada. Address: 43703 East Austin Court, West Richland, WA 99353, USA.

AMICOLA José, b. 15 February 1942, Buenos Aires, Argentina. Professor; Writer. Education: Licenciado en Letras, Universidad de Buenos Aires, Argentina; Dr Philosophiae, Universität Göttingen, Germany, 1982. Publications: Sobre Cortazar, 1969; Astrologia y Fascismo en la Obra de Arlt, 1984; Manuel Puig y La Tela Que Atrapa Al Lector, 1992; Dostoievski, 1994; De La Forma a La Informacion, 1997; Camp y Postvanguardia, 2000; La Batalla de los Generos, 2003. Honour: Premio Banco Mercantil, 1992. Memberships: Instituto Intern Literatura Iberoamericana, Pittsburgh. Address: Las Heras, 3794 - 11A, 1425 Buenos Aires, Argentina.

AMIN Zubair, b. 29 March 1966, Mymensingh, Bangladesh. Paediatrician; Medical Educator. m. Sonia, 2 daughters. Education: MBBS, Dhaka Medical College, Bangladesh, 1992; Diplomate, The American Board of Pediatrics, 1997; Masters Degree, Health Profession Education, University of Illinois at Chicago, USA, 1998; Specialist in Paediatrics, Ministry of Health, Singapore, 2001. Appointments: Intern, Dhaka Medical College Hospital, 1992-93; Resident in Paediatrics, University of Illinois at Chicago, 1994-97; Registrar, 1998-2000, Associate Consultant, 2001-, KK Women's and Children's Hospital, Singapore. Publications: Book: Basics in Medical Education; Articles in journals; Associate Editor, Asian Medical Educators. Honours: Prime Minister's Gold Medal for Academic Achievement, Bangladesh, 1993; International Educational Partnership in Pediatrics, University of Illinois at Chicago, 1994-98. Address: K K Women's and Children's Hospital, 100 Bukit Timam Road, Singapore 229899. E-mail: zubairamin@hotmail.com

AMIN DADA Idi (Field Marshal), b. 1925, Kakwa Region, West Nile. Ugandan Former Head of State and Army Officer. Appointments: Joined King's African Rifles, 1946; Corporal, 1959, Major, 1963, Colonel, 1964; Deputy Commander, Ugandan Army, 1964; Commander, Uganda Army and Air Force, 1966-70; Brigadier-General, 1967, Major-General, 1968, Field Marshal, 1975; President, Chief of Armed Forces, 1971-79; Minister of Defence, 1971-75; Chair, Defence Council, 1972-79; Minister of Internal Affairs, 1973, 1978-79, of Information and Broadcasting, 1973, of Foreign Affairs, 1974-75, 1978, of Health, 1977-79, of Information, Broadcasting and Tourism, Game and Wildlife, 1978-79; Chief of Staff, Ugandan Army, 1974-79; Chair, OAU Association of Heads of State, 1975-76, presided Kampala Summit, 1975, Addis Ababa Summit, 1976. Honours: Heavyweight Boxing Champion of Uganda, 1951-60; 8 highest military decorations, Uganda; Honorary LLD, Kampala, 1976.

AMIRALI Evangelia-Lila, b. 28 November 1962. Medical Doctor; Psychiatrist. m. J Hadjinicolaou, 4 sons. Education: MD, University of Athens, Greece, 1986; MSc, in progress; Candidate, Canadian Institute of Psychoanalysis. Appointments: Research Fellow, McGill University, 1988-90, Clinical Fellow, 1990-92; Psychiatrist, Child Psychiatrist, 2001, Universite de Montreal. Honours: A S Onassis Scholarship, 1990-92; Berta Mizne Award, 1988-90; Best Promising Clinician Prize, Department of Psychiatry, McGill University, 1999-2000; American Psychiatric Association Women Fellowship, 2001. Memberships: APA; CPA; QMA; AMPQ. Address: 2875 Douglas Avenue, Montreal, QC H3R 2C7, Canada.

AMIRISETTY Venkateswara Rao, b. 15 February 1952, Chilumuru. Teacher; Researcher. m. Parvathy, 1 son. Education: BSc, Maths and Physics, Andhra University, 1972; MSc, Solid State Physics, Saradar Patel University, 1972; PhD, Crystal Growth and Gels, 1980. Appointments: Junior Research Fellow, UGC, 1975-79; Senior Research Fellow, CSIR, 1980; Post-Doctoral Fellow, CSIR, 1980-81; Lecturer, Physics, 1981-91; Post-Doctoral Fellow, Ecole Polytechnique, CNRS, France, 1984-85; Visiting Scientist, CIES, France, 1989; Reader, Physics, 1991-; Visiting Professor, University of Lyon, RRA, France, 1992; Invited Professor, ADL, France, 1995; Visiting Professor, 1996; Senior Scientist, ADEM, France, 1998; Guest Scientist, Norwegian University of Science and Technology, NRC, Norway, 1999. Publications: Nearly 60 research papers related to crystal growth in gels; Growth of Single Crystals in Gels; Development and Characterization of Silica Aerogels; Preparation and Characterization of CdS and PbS Nanocrystals in Silica Gels; Production of Low Density and Large Area Silica Aerogels; Room Temperature Production of Silica Aerogels. Honours: Materials Research Society of India, MRSI Medal. Memberships: Semiconductor Society; Indian Physics Association; Indian Association of Physics Teachers; Thermal Analysis Society of India; Materials Research Society of India. Address: Air Glass Laboratory, Department of Physics, Shivaji University, Kolhapur 416004, Maharashtra, India.

AMIRYANTS Gennady, b. 4 June 1937, Kokand, USSR. Aeroelasticity Scientist. m. Irina Mkrtchyan, 2 daughters. Education: Graduate, Aviation Institute, Moscow, 1960; PhD, Physical Technical Institute, Moscow, 1968; Professor, Central Aerohydrodynamic Institute, TSAGI, Moscow, 1980. Appointments: Engineer, 1960-65, Leading Engineer, 1965-68, Head of Division, 1968-80, Head of Department, 1980-98, Principal Research Scientist, 1998-, Central Aerohydrodynamic Institute, TSAGI, Moscow. Publications: Books: Grischenko, 1991; Test Pilots I, 1997; Test Pilots II, 2001; Articles in professional journals include: Scientific Notes of TSAGI X, 1979; Adaptive selectively-deformable structures, 1998; Some applications of active aeroelasticity concepts, 2001; Honours: Gold Medal, World Exhibition of Inventions, Brussels, 1996; Silver Medal, World Exhibition of Inventions, Geneva, 1997. Membership: Programme Committee, International Council of Aviation Science. Address: Moscowscaya ploschad 7-45, 140180 Zhukovsky, Russia. E-mail: amiryants@mail.ru

AMIS Martin Louis, b. 25 August 1949, Oxford, England. Author. Education: BA, Exeter College, Oxford. Appointments: Fiction and Poetry Editor, Times Literary Supplement, 1974; Literary Editor, New Statesman, 1977-79; Special Writer, Observer Newspaper, 1980-. Publications: The Rachel Papers, 1973; Dead Babies, 1975; Success, 1978; Other People: A Mystery Story, 1981; Invasion of the Space Invaders, 1982; Money: A Suicide Note, 1984; The Moronic Inferno and Other Visits to America, 1986; Einstein's Monsters: Five Stories, 1987; London Fields, 1989; Time's Arrow, 1991; Visiting Mrs Nabokov and Other Excursions,1993; The Information, 1995; Night Train, 1997; Heavy Water and Other Stories, 1999; Experience, 2000; The War Against Cliché, 2001; Koba the Dread: Laughter and the Twenty Million, 2002. Honour: Somerset Maugham Award, 1974. Address: c/o Peters Fraser & Dunlop, 5th Floor, The Chambers, Chelsea Harbour, Lots Road, London SW10 0XP, England.

AMMANN Jean-Christophe, b. 14 Janaury 1939, Berlin, Germany. Art Director. m. Judith. Education: PhD, University Fribourg, Switzerland, 1966. Appointments: Professor, University Frankfurt/M and Giessen, 1992-; University of Heidelberg Lecturer, 2001-02. Publications: Articles in professional journals. Honours:

Decorated Officier des Arts and des Lettres, 2000; Decorated Goethe-Medal, City of Frankfurt/M, 2003. Address: Klettenbergstrasse 11, D-60322, Frankfurt/M, Germany.

AMOYAL Pierre Alain Wilfred, b. 22 June‘ 1949, Paris, France. Violinist. Education: Studied at the Paris Conservatoire and with Jascha Heifetz between 1966 and 1971. Debut: Paris 1971, in the Berg Concerto, with the Orchestre de Paris. Career: Appearances with the BBC Symphony Orchestra, Hallé Orchestra, London Philharmonic, Philharmonia, Berlin Philharmonic, Boston Symphony, Cleveland Orchestra, Philadelphia Orchestra and Orchestras in Canada and France; Conductors include Karajan, Ozawa, Boulez, Dutoit, Sanderling, Maazel, Solti, Prêtre, Masur and Rozhdestvensky; Plays Concertos by Berg, Schoenberg and Dutilleux, in addition to the standard repertory; Played Brahms Concerto with the Royal Philharmonic Orchestra, 1995; Artist in Residence at Beaumaris Festival in Wales, 1995; Recitals at St John's Smith Square for the BBC; New York Carnegie Hall debut 1985; Professor at the Paris Conservatoire from 1977; Currently Professor at the Lausanne Conservatoire. Recordings: Concertos by Dutilleux, Respighi and Saint Saëns with the Orchestre National conducted by Charles Dutoit; Chamber music (sonatas by Brahms, Fauré and Franck) with Pascal Rogé; Schoenberg Concerto with the London Symphony Orchestra conducted by Boulez. Honours include: Ginette Neveu Prize, 1963; Paganini Prize, 1964; Enescu Prize, 1970. Address: c/o Jacques Thelen, 252 rue du Faubourg Saint-Honoré, 75008 Paris, France.

AMY Jean-Jacques, b. 20 September 1940, Antwerp. Medical Doctor. 2 sons. Education: MD, Université Libre de Bruxelles, 1965; Degree in Tropical Medicine, Institute of Tropical Medicine, Antwerp, 1966. Appointments: Resident, The Mount Sinai Hospital, New York, 1967-71; Lecturer, Makerere University Medical School, Kampala, Uganda, 1971-73; Research Associate, University Hospital, Ghent, 1973-75; Attending Obstetrician and Gynaecologist, University Hospital, St Pierre, Brussels, 1975-78; Professor and Head of Department, University Hospital AZ-VUB, Brussels, 1979-. Publications: 274 scientific publications in obstetrics and gynaecology; Editor of 15 books. Honours: Distinguished Humanist Award. Memberships: Royal Belgian Society of Gynaecology and Obstetrics, Past President; Flemish Society of Obstetrics and Gynaecology, Past President. Address: Department of Gynaecology, Andrology and Obstetrics, Academisch Ziekenhuis V U B, Laarbeeklaan 101 B 1090, Brussels, Belgium.

AMZA Gheorghe M, b. 3 December 1948, Popesti, Romania. Engineer. m. Anca Amza, 1 son, 1 daughter. Education: Theoretical Licée, Horezu; Technology of Machine Building Faculty, Politechnic University of Bucharest; Mechanical Mathematical Faculty, University of Bucharest; Doctor Engineer, Politechnic University. Appointments: Ultrasonics Applications; Technology of Materials; Nontraditional Manufacturing Processes. Publications: Over 160 articles and 32 books. Honours: Silver Medal, Invention Exhibition, Geneva, 1995; Gold Medal, Invention Exhibition, Geneva, 1996. Memberships: Romanian Scientists American Academy; General Association of Romanian Engineers. Address: 14 G D Mirea Street, Ap 1, Sector 1, Bucharest, Romania. E-mail: amza@amza.camis.pub.ro

AN Ou, b. 29 April 1932, Liaoyang, Liaoning, China. Science Research. m. Wang Peilan, 23 September 1959, 3 sons. Education: Graduate, Physics Department, Beijing Normal University, 1956; Advanced Study of X-Ray Physics, Crystal Plasticity, Optical Mineralogy, Institute of Physics, Institute of Geology, Chinese Academy of Sciences, 1956-59. Appointments: Researcher, Geodynamics and its application in Earthquake forecast, Rockmass

Dictionary of International Biography

Engineering and Petroleum Exploration, Institute of Geomechanics, Geology Ministry and Institute of Geocrustal Dynamics, Chinese Seismological Bureau; Research Professor, Director of Department, Postgraduate Tutor; Evaluating Committeeman of Learning, Degree and Senior Title, Editing Committeeman, 3 journals. Publications include: 115 pieces of treatises; Systematic monograph: Tectonic Stress Field, 1992; Oil Pool in Hidden Mountain, 1999; Geocrustal Dynamics, 2000; X-ray Geomechanics, 2001; Research achievement: Took charge of 5 state grade and 11 ministerial grade scientific research projects; Discovered Residual Stress Field in rockmass and finished its measurement in area of $50x10^4km^2$ as deep as over 7km; Discovered Comprehensive strength of rock and its sintered contacting surfaces under joint action of residual and present stresses. Honours: Deputy Director General, International Biographical Centre; Research Board of Advisors, Board of Governors, Research Association of American Biographical Institute; Senior Advisor on Technique, Hong Kong Patent Exchange Company; Advisor, Chinese Association of International Famous Persons; Geodynamics and Seismology Science Award, 1996; Ardisia Japonica Outstanding Contribution Award, 1997; Oriental Famous Person Achievement Award, 2000; Gold Award, International Fair of New Products and New Technology, 2001; National Earthquake Science Foundation Award, 1997; Science and Technology 2nd Award of Provincial Ministerial Grade, 1981; Enjoy Governmental Special Subsidy, Assue by the State Council. Memberships: Chinese Physical Society; Beijing Geology Society; Beijing Mechanics Society; Director, Chinese Seismological Society. Address: PO Box 2855, Beijing 100085, China.

ANAND Mulk Raj, b. 12 December 1905, Peshawar, India. Novelist; University Teacher. m. (2) Shirin Vajifdar, 1950, 1 daughter. Education: BA (Hons), Punjab University, 1924; PhD, University College, University of London, 1929; Cambridge University, 1929-30. Appointments: Director, Kutub publishers, Bombay, 1946-; Teacher, Universities of Punjab, Benares, and Rajasthan, Jaipur, 1948-66. Publications: Untouchable, 1935 The Coolie, 1936; Two Leaves and a Bud, 1937; The Village, 1939; Lament on the Death of a Master of Arts, 1939; Across the Black Waters, 1940; The Sword and the Sickle, 1942; The Big Heart, 1945; Seven Summers: The Story of an Indian Childhood, 1951; Private Life of an Indian Prince, 1953; The Old Woman and the Cow, 1960; The Road, 1961; Morning Face, 1968; Confession of a Lover, 1976; The Bubble, 1984; Death of a Hero, 1995; Also: Various short stories and other works. Honours: Padma Bhushan, 1967; Sahitya Academy Award, 1974; Fellow, National Academy of Art, New Delhi; Hon DLitt, Delhi, Benares, Andhra, Patiala, Shantiniketan; Laureate of International Peace Prize. Address: Jassim House, 25 Cuffe Parade, Colaba, Mumbai 400005, India.

ANANI Tarig, b. 22 January 1965, Riyadh, Saudi Arabia. Attorney. Education: BA cum laude, University of Houston, Texas, USA, 1988; JD, University of Houston Law School, 1991; MBA, Rice University, 1992; JSM, Stanford University, 1994. Appointments: Corporate Associate, Curtis, Mallet-Prevost, Colt & Mosle, 1997-97; General Counsel, SAP Arabia, 1998-2002; President, International Operations and General Counsel, P2 Energy Solutions, 2002-. Publication: Extraterritorial Application of US Employment Laws, 1995. Honour: Recipient, Best ERP Solution Award from former Vice-President Al Gore, 2002. Memberships: State Bar of Texas; State Bar of California, 1993; Bar of the US Supreme Court, 1995; District of Columbia Bar, 2002. Address: P2 Energy Solutions, 4 Houston Center, 1221 Lamar, Suite 1400, Houston, TX 77010, USA. E-mail: tanani@aol.com Website: www.tarig.com

ANCAR Virgiliu, b. 24 February 1944, Pitesti, Arges, Romania. Physician. m. Marcella, 1 son. Education: University of Medicine, "Carol Davila", Bucharest, Romania, 1962-68; Doctor of Medical Sciences, University of "Carol Davila", Bucharest, 1983. Appointments: Resident, Obstetrics and Gynaecology, Polieo Clinic, Bucharest, 1968-71; Specialist and University Assistant, 1971-83, Assistant Professor, 1983-92, Professor, Head of Department of Obstetrics and Gynaecology, 1992-, St Pantelimon Clinic, Bucharest. Publications: Study and research of the value of aminoacid perfusion in fetal hypotrophy, 1980; Fetal hypotrophy, 1996; Obstetrics, 1997; Gynaecology (national editor), 1999; Obstetrics (Romanian Academy editor), 2001. Honours: Gheorghe Marinescu Prize, Romanian Academy, 1980; Knight of Steaua Romaniei (Star of Romania) Order, President of Romania, 2000. Memberships: National Society for Obstetrics and Gynaecology of Romania; Balkanic Medical Union; New York Academy of Sciences; Romanian Medical Academy; Lions Clubs International. Address: St Pantelimon Hospital, 340 Pantelimon Avenue, Sect 2, Bucharest, Romania.

ANCRAM Earl of, Michael Andrew Foster Jude Kerr, b. 7 July 1945. Politician. m. Lady Jane Fitzalan-Howard, 1975, 2 daughters. Education: Ampleforth; Christ Church College, Oxford; Edinburgh University. Appointments: Formerly in business; Columnist, Daily Telegraph (Manchester edition); Partner, Tenanted Arable Farm; Called to Scottish Bar, 1970; Practised Law, 1970-79; MP, Berwickshire and East Lothian, 1974; Edinburgh South, 1979-87; Devizes, 1992-; Parliamentary, Under-Secretary of State, Scottish Office, 1983-87; Parliamentary, Under-Secretary, Northern Ireland Office, 1993-94; Minister of State, 1994-96; Shadow Cabinet Spokesman for Constitutional Affairs, 1997-98; Chair, Conservative Party, 1998-2001; Vice Chair, 1975-80, Chair, 1980-83, Conservative Party, Scotland; Chair, North Corporate Communications, 1989-91; Director, CSM Parliamentary Consultants, 1988-92; Member of Board Scottish Homes, 1988-90; D L Roxburgh, Ettrick and Lauderdale, 1990. Memberships: House of Commons Energy Select Committee, 1979-83. Address: House of Commons, London, SW1A 0AA, England.

ANDELSON Robert V, b. 19 February 1931, Los Angeles, California, USA. Professor of Philosophy Emeritus; Writer; Editor. m. Bonny Orange Johnson, 7 June 1964. Education: AB equivalent, University of Chicago, 1952; AM, 1954, PhD, 1960, University of Southern California. Appointments: Assistant Professor to Professor of Philosophy Emeritus, Auburn University, 1965-92; Distinguished Research Fellow, American Institute for Economic Research, 1993-. Publications: Imputed Rights: An Essay in Christian Social Theory, 1971; Critics of Henry George (editor and co-author), 1979, 2nd edition, 2003; Commons Without Tragedy (editor and co-author), 1991; From Wasteland to Promised Land (with J M Dawsey), 1992; Land-Value Taxation Around the World (editor and co-author), second edition, 1997, 3rd edition, 2000. Contributions to: Scholarly journals. Honours: Foundation for Social Research Award (research grant), 1959; Relm Foundation Award (research grant), 1967; George Washington Honor Medals, Freedoms Foundation, 1970, 1972. Memberships: International Union for Land-Value Taxation and Free Trade, president, 1997-2001; Robert Schalkenbach Foundation, corporation member and director, 1986-, vice-president, 1998-2001, executive committee member, 2000-; American Journal of Economics and Sociology, editorial board member, 1969-, corporation director, 1999-; Southern Society for Philosophy and Psychology; Alabama Philosophical Society, president, 1968-69, 1978-79. Address: 534 Cary Drive, Auburn, AL 36830, USA. E-mail: rvandelson@charter.net

Dictionary of International Biography

ANDERSEN Søren Sigfrid Lindgård, b. 23 June 1966, Glostrop. Scientist. Education: BSc, Chemical Engineering, 1989; MSc, Chemical Engineering, MS Bioingenierie, 1991;Dr rer nat, Cell Biology, 1996. Appointments: Graduate Studies, 1991-96, Postdoctoral Studies, 1996-97, EMBL, Heidelberg; Postdoctoral Studies, Princeton University, 1997-98; Postdoctoral Studies, University of California, San Diego, 1998-2000; Postdoctoral Studies, University of California, Berkeley, 2000-01; Postdoctoral Studies, Stanford University, 2002-03. Publications: Several articles in professional journals; Editor, MICS, 2003. Honours: HCM, EU, EMBO and HFSPO Fellowships. Memberships: American Society for Cell Biology; FEANI EUR ING; IDA; Marie Curie Fellowship Association; Order of International Fellowship. Address: 1717 Woodland Avenue #215, Palo Alto, CA 94303, USA.

ANDERSLAND Orlando B, b. 15 August 1929, Albert Lea, Minnesota, USA. Civil Engineering Educator. m. Phyllis Burgess, 2 sons, 1 daughter. Education: BCE, University of Minnesota, Minneapolis, 1952; MSCE, 1956, PhD, 1960, Purdue University at West Lafayette, Indiana. Appointments: 1st Lieutenant, US Army Corps of Engineers, 1952-55; Staff Engineer, National Academy of Science, American Association of State Highway Officials Road Test, Ottawa, Illinois, 1956-57; Research Engineer, Purdue University, 1957-59; Faculty, 1960, Professor, 1968, Professor Emeritus, 1994-, Michigan State University. Publications: Co-author, An Introduction to Frozen Ground Engineering, 1994, 2nd edition, 2004; Co-editor, Contributor, Geotechnical Engineering for Cold Regions, 1978; Chapter in Ground Engineers Handbook, 1987; Numerous articles in professional journals; Co-author, Geotechnical Engineering and Soil Testing, 1992; Patentee in field. Honours: Distinguished Faculty Award, Michigan State University, 1979; Norwegian Postdoctoral Fellowship, 1966; Best Paper Award, ASCE Journal of Cold Regions Engineering, 1991; Proceedings of the Association Asphalt Paving Technologists, 1956; National Defence Service Medal; United Nations Service Medal; Korean Service Medal. Memberships: Fellow, American Society of Civil Engineers; American Society for Testing Materials; International Society for Soil Mechanics and Foundation Engineering; American Society for Engineering Education; Chi Epsilon; Tau Beta Pi; Sigma Xi. Address: Department of Civil and Environmental Engineering, Michigan State University, East Lansing, MI 48824, USA.

ANDERSON Elizabeth Lang, b. 3 March 1960, Orange, New Jersey, USA. Composer; Professor. m. David S Baltuch. Education: BA, Music, Gettysburg College, Gettysburg, Pennsylvania, 1982; Master of Music in Composition, Peabody Institute, Baltimore, Maryland, 1987; Certificate, Composition, Royal Conservatory of Brussels, 1990; Diploma, Electronic Music Composition, Royal Conservatory, Antwerp, 1993; Premier Prix in Electroacoustic Music Composition, Royal Conservatory of Mons, 1997; Superior Diploma In Electroacoustic Music Composition, Royal Conservatory of Mons, 1998; PhD, Electroacoustic Music Composition, in progress, City University, London, 1998-. Appointments: Instructor of Musicianship (Creative Music Theory), Peabody Preparatory, Baltimore, Maryland, 1985-87; Professor, Electroacoustic Music Composition, Academy of Soignies, Belgium, 1994-2002; Appointed to the faculty of the electroacoustic music department, Royal Conservatory of Mons, 2003-. Publications: Perception in Electroacoustic Music: A Preliminary Investigation and Expansion of the Reception Behaviours Devised by François Delalande, to be published. Honours: Music honoured in several competitions specialising in electroacoustic music including: Ascap/Seamus, Bourges, Noroit, Sao Paulo, Stockholm; Commissions from Musiques & Recherches, Belgium and La Chambre d'Ecoute, Belgium; Numerous works frequently performed at international festivals; Overseas Research Students Award Scheme Grant funded by the Committee of Vice-Chancellors and Principals of the Universities of the United Kingdom; Grant, British Federation of Women Graduates Charitable Foundation; Grant, Foundation SPES. Memberships: International Computer Music Association; International Alliance for Women in Music; Sonic Arts Network; Society for Electro-Acoustic Music in the United States. Address: Avenue de Monte Carlo, 11, 1190 Brussels, Belgium. E-mail: e.anderson@skynet.be

ANDERSON Frank Gist Jr, b. 17 August 1928, College Station, Texas, USA. Ophthalmologist; Educator. m. Jane Nugent Hafner, 1 son, 1 daughter. Education: BS, Biology, Texas A&M University, 1950; MD, University of Texas Medical Branch, 1954; Internship, University of Kansas, 1954-55; Ophthalmology Residency, May Foundation, 1958-61. Appointments: Medical Officer (Captain), US Army, 1955-57; Ophthalmologist, Kelsey-Seybold Clinic, Houston, Texas, 1961-64; Private Practice, Bryan, Texas, 1964-93; Clinical Professor of Ophthalmology, 1981-2001, Professor, Humanities in Medicine, 1996-2001, Texas A&M University. Publications: Books: History of Track and Field at Texas A&M University, 1972; History of Medicine in Brazos County, 2001; Articles: Treatment of Myasthemia Gravis Ptosis and Extraocular Muscle Palsies, 1976; Repair of Marginal Furrow Perforation , 1977; Hyperbaric Oxygen and Corneal Incision Healing, 1978. Honours: Distinguished Student, Texas A&M University; Honorary Member, Texas Medical Association; Honorary Member, Saint Joseph Hospital Medical Staff. Memberships: Fellow, American College of Surgeons; Fellow, American Academy of Ophthalmology; American Medical Association; Chancellor's Council Texas A&M University System. Address: 743 South Rosemary Drive, Bryan, TX 77802, USA.

ANDERSON Gerry, b. 14 April 1929, England. Film Maker. m. (1) Betty Wrightman, 1952, 2 daughters, (2) Sylvia Thamm, 1961, divorced, 1 son, (3), Mary Robbins, 1981, 1 son. Appointments: Trainee, Colonial Film Unit, 1943; Assistant Editor, Gainsborough Pictures, 1945-47; Dubbing Editor, 1949-53; Film Director, Polytechnic Films, 1954-55; Co-founder: Pentagon Films, 1955, AP Films, 1956, AP Merchandising, 1961; Director of TV commercials, 1961, 1988-92; Chair, Century 21 Organisation, 1966-75. TV Series Include: Adventure of Twizzle (52 shows), 1956; Torchy the Battery Boy (26 shows), 1957; Four Feather Falls (52 shows), 1958; Supercar (39 shows), 1959; Fireball XL5 (39 shows), 1961; Stingray (39 shows), 1962-63; Thunderbirds (32 shows screened in 20 countries), 1964-66; Captain Scarlet (32 shows), 1967; Joe 90 (30 shows), 1968; The Secret Service (13 shows), 1968; UFO (26 shows), 1969-70; The Protectors (52 shows), 1971-72; Space 1999 (48 shows), 1973-76; Terrahawks (39 shows), 1982-83; Dick Spanner (26 shows), 1987; Space Precinct, 1993-95; Lavender Castle, 1997; Firestorm, 2002; Numerous TV commercials; Films: Thunderbirds are Go, 1966; Thunderbird 6, 1968; Doppelganger, 1969. Honours: Honorary Fellow, British Kinematograph Sound and TV Society; President, Thames Valley and Chiltern Air Ambulance; Silver Arrow Award.

ANDERSON Gillian, b. 9 August 1968, Chicago, USA. Actress. m. Errol Clyde Klotz, divorced, 1 daughter. Education: DePaul University, Chicago; Goodman Theatre School, Chicago. Appointments: Worked at National Theatre, London; Appeared in two off-broadway productions; Best Known Role as Special Agent Dana Scully in TV Series, The X Files (Feature Film 1998); Film, The House of Mirth, 2000; Plays include: Absent Friends, Manhattan Theater Club, 1991; The Philanthropist, Along Wharf Theater, 1992; What the Night is For, Comedy Theatre, London, 2002; TV Films include, Home Fire Burning, 1992; When Planes

Go Down, 1996; Presenter, Future Fantastic, BBC TV. Honours: Golden Globe Awards, 1995, 1997; Screen Actors' Guild Awards, 1996, 1997; Emmy Award, 1997. Address: William Morris Agency, 151 El Camino Drive, Beverly Hills, CA 90212, USA. Website: www.gillianderson.ws

ANDERSON John Anthony (Sir), b. 2 August 1945, Wellington, New Zealand. Banker. m. Carol M Anderson, 1970, 2 sons, 1 daughter. Education: Christ's College; Victoria University of Wellington; FCA. Appointments: Deloitte Haskins and Sells chartered accountants, Wellington, 1962-69; Guest and Bell sharebrokers, Melbourne, Victoria, Australia, 1969-72; Joined, 1972, Chief Executive, Director, 1979, South Pacific Merchant Finance Ltd, Wellington; Deputy Chief Executive, 1988, Chief Executive, Director, 1990-, National Bank of New Zealand; Chair, Petroleum Corporation of New Zealand Ltd, 1986-88; Director, New Zealand Steel Ltd, 1986-87, Lloyds Merchant Bank, London, 1986-92, Lloyds Bank NZA, Australia, 1989-97; New Zealand Bankers' Association, 1991-92, 1999-2000; President, New Zealand Bankers Institute, 1990-2001; Chair, New Zealand Cricket Board, 1995-, New Zealand Sports Foundation Inc, 1999-2002; Other professional and public appointments. Honours: Knight Commander, Order of the British Empire; 1990 Commemoration Medal. Memberships: Chair, New Zealand Merchant Banks Association, 1982-89; Chair, New Zealand Bankers Association, 1992-. Address: 5 Fancourt Street, Karori, Wellington 5, New Zealand.

ANDERSON Kenneth Lynn, b. 18 September 1945, Pineville, Louisiana, USA. Professor Emeritus of English. 2 daughters. Education: Master Degree, Twentieth Century American and British Literature, Indiana University, 1969. Publications: Someone Bought the House on the Island: A Novel; The Intense Lover: A Suite of Poems; Mattie Cushman: A Psychodrama: Hasty Hearts, The Dumb Heart Has To Speak In Signs, a collection of short stories. Contributions to: Chattahoochee Review; Lullwater Review; James White Review; Connecticut Poetry Review; Poem; International Poetry Review. Honours: Louisiana State University's Caffee Medal; Finalist, Independent Publishers Book Awards, 1999. Memberships: Poets & Writers; Associated Writing Programs. Address: 608 Wendan Drive, Decatur, GA 30033-5530, USA.

ANDERSON Michael, b. 30 January 1920, London, England. Film Director. 1 son. Education: France. Appointments: Co-Director with Peter Ustinov, film, Private Angelo, 1949; Director, films: Waterfront, 1950; Hell Is Sold Out, 1952; Night Was Our Friend; Dial 17; Will Any Gentleman?; The House of the Arrow, 1952; The Dam Busters, 1954; Around the World in Eighty Days, 1956; Yangtse Incident, 1957; Chase a Crooked Shadow, 1957; Shake Hands with the Devil, 1958; Wreck of the Mary Deare, 1959-60; All the Fine Young Cannibals, 1960; The Naked Edge, 1961; Flight from Ashiya, in Japan, 1962; Operation Crossbow, 1964; The Quiller Memorandum, 1966; Shoes of The Fisherman, 1969; Pope Joan, 1970-71; Doc Savage, in Hollywood, 1973; Conduct Unbecoming, 1974; Logan's Run, MGM Hollywood, 1975; Orca - Killer Whale, 1976; Dominique, 1977; The Martian Chronicles, 1978; Bells, 1979-80; Millenium; Murder by Phone; Second Time Lucky; Separate Vacations; Sword of Gideon; Jeweller's Shop; Young Catherine; Millennium; Summer of the Monkeys. Address: c/o Film Rights Ltd, 113-117 Wardour Street, London W1, England.

ANDERSON Robert Geoffrey William, b. 2 May 1944, London, England. Museum Director. m. Margaret Elizabeth Callis Lea, 1973, 2 sons. Education: St John's College, Oxford; MA, Oxon; DPhil. Appointments: Keeper, Science Museum, London, 1980-

84; Director, Royal Scottish Museum, 1984-85, National Museums of Scotland, 1985-92, British Museum, London, 1992-; Curator, School of Advanced Study, University of London, 1994-. Publications: The Playfair Collection, 1978; Science in India, 1982; Science, Medicine and Dissent, editor, 1987; A New Museum for Scotland, editor, 1990; Joseph Black: a Bibliography, co-editor, 1992; Making Instruments Count, joint editor, 1993; The Great Court at the British Museum, 2000. Honours: Dexter Award, American Chemical Society, 1986; Honorary Fellow, Society of Antiquaries, Scotland, 1991; Honorary DSc, Edinburgh, 1995; Honorary DSc, Durham, 1998. Memberships: Fellow, Royal Society of Edinburgh; President, British Society for the History of Science, 1988-80; President, Scientific Instrument Committee, International Union of the History and Philosophy of Science, 1982-97; President, British Society for the History of Science, 1988-90; Board, Boerhaave Museum, Leiden, Netherlands, 1995-99. Address: The British Museum, London WC1B 3DSG, England.

ANDERSON William P, b. 8 August 1946, Laurers, South Carolina, USA. Pastor; Businessman. m. Cheryl E Anderson, 3 daughters. Education: BA, East Texas Bible College, 1976-79; In Depth Bible Studies, Loving Grace Ministries, 1979-82; Deeper Life Fellowship Studies, 1980-81; Andersonville Baptist Seminary, 1998. Appointments: US Army, 1965-68; Evangelistic Ministerial Work, 1978-82; Community Chaplain, Teacher, New York State Department of Correctional Service, 1979-81; Pastor, 1982-; US Postal Service, 1988-95; Currently Pastor, Chicago Miracle Temple Church, Chicago Heights, Illinois, USA. Publications: Articles in newspapers including, Chicago Defender, Chicago Sun-Times, South Suburban Tribune; Seminars on Biblical black history, evangelism, soul winning, theology. Honours: Numerous awards include: Combine Federal Campaign Eagle Club giver twice; NCNW Humanitarian, Chicago Heights; Proclamations from the Mayor of Chicago Heights, Greater Chicago Food Depository, WGCI 1390 Achievement, Chicago Heights Crossroads Fest, Hope for Kids; Dr Martin Luther King Dream Maker Award; Appearances on TV and radio throughout the South Suburban and Chicago area; Listed in Who's Who publications and biographical dictionaries. Memberships: Pastor's Congress of Chicago; Christian Council of Urban Affairs of Chicago, Illinois; Evangelical Church Alliance; American Legion; Disabled American Veterans. Address: Chicago Miracle Temple Church, Inc., 34 E 16th Street, Chicago Heights, IL 60411, USA.

ANDERSON William Robert, b. 26 January 1929, Kittanning, Pennsylvania, USA. Physician; Pathologist. m. Carol J Tammen, 1 son, 1 daughter. Education: BA, University of Rochester, 1951; MD, University of Pennsylvania School of Medicine, 1958; Anatomic and Clinical Pathology Residencies, New York Hospital, Cornell Medical Centre, 1958-69, New York VA Hospital, 1960-62. Appointments: Neuropathology Fellowship, Duke University, 1962-64; Director, Anatomic Pathology, Hennepin County Medical Centre, 1967-97; Chief of Pathology, 1984-95; Professor, Department of Laboratory Medicine and Pathology, University of Minnesota School of Medicine, 1975-. Publications: Numerous scientific publications in national and international pathology journals. Honours: Phi Beta Kappa, University of Rochester, 1951; Sigma Xi, Duke University, 1963; Mentor Recognition, University of Minnesota, 1989. Memberships: College of American Pathologists; International Academy of Pathology; Society for Ultrastructural Pathology; President, Minnesota Society of Pathologists, 1980-81. Address: 5725 Merry Lane, Excelsior, MN 55331, USA.

ANDRADE GONZALEZ Virgilio Manuel, b. 24 May 1967, Medico City, Mexico. Business Administrator. m. Lorena E Bererra, 1 son. Education: Business Administration, Northwestern

University, 1991. Appointments: Manager, Human Resources Divertido, Mexico City, Mexico, 1993; Manager, Human resources, La Ferio, Mexico City, Mexico, 1993-94; Manager, Public Relations, Mexico, 1993-94; Manager, Recruitment Tribunal Superior Agrasio, Mexico, 1995-98; Manager, Human Resources Mexico, 1998-99; Vice-President, Andrade Palacios, Mexico City, 1990-99; President, VAG, SA, Mexico City; Vice-President, Human Resources Institute, Sve, Mexico City, 1990-99. Memberships: International Association of Amusement Parks and Attractions; Themed Entertainment Association. Address: Av Redorma 155 5° piso, Col Cuahutemoc, Mexico City 06500, Mexico. E-mail: virgilioa@prodigy.net.mex

ANDRADE RUIZ Mirna Amelia, b. 2 December 1966, Trujillo, Venezuela. Specialist in Internal Medicine. 1 son. Education: Specialist in Internal Medicine, Universidad de los Andes, Merida, Venezuela; Master in Administration of Health Institutions. Appointments: Assistant Professor and Main Investigator, AIDS Research Centre, Universidad de los Andes, Merida, Venezuela; Regional Specialist, AIDS Regional Unit. Publications: Many publications in Venezuelan and international journals including: Venezuelan Society of Internal Medicine Magazine; Intercontinental and Cardiology and Internal Medicine Congress. Honours: President, Venezuelan Atherosclerosys Association of Merida; Member, Scientific Committee, Friends of Health Around the World; Diploma of Honour, Venezuelan Atherosclerosys Association of Merida; Encouragement Award for Research. Address: Servicio Medicina Interna, Hospital de la Universidad de los Andes, Merida, Venezuela. E-mail: mirnaandrade@hotmail.com

ANDRÁSSY István, b. 5 May 1927, Szolnok, Hungary. University Professor; Zoologist. m. Nagy Etelka, 1 son, 2 daughters. Education: Eotvos Lorand University, Biology Faculty, Budapest, 1951. Appointments: University Dr, PhD, 1956; Academy Dr, 1972; University Professor, 1974; Main Researcher, 1970-. Publications: Nearly 200 science papers in zoology, taxonomy, soil biology, nematology; 5 books published at home and abroad on nematodes. Honours: Prize of Academy of Sciences, Hungary; Prize of Society of Biology, Hungary; Prize of Academy of Russia. Memberships: Numerous zoological societies. Address: Eotvos University, ELTE Pázmány Péter str 1/C, 1117 Budapest, Hungary.

ANDRÉ Maurice, b. 21 May 1933, Alès, Gard, France. Trumpeter. Education: Studied with his father and with Sabarich at the Paris Conservatoire. Career: Soloist with the Concerts Lamoureuz, 1953-60, L'Orchestre Philharmonique of ORTF (French Radio), 1953-62, and the orchestra of the Operé-Comique, Paris, 1962-67; Many concert performances in Europe; North American Professor at the Paris Conservatoire, 1967-78; Composers who have written for him include Boris Blacher (Concerto 1971), Charles Chaynes, Marcel Landowski, Jean-Claude Eloy, Harold Genzmer, Bernhard Krol, Jean Langlais (Chorals for trumpet and organ), Henri Tomasi and André Jolivet (Arioso barocco, 1968). Honours: Chevalier de la Légion d'honneur; Commandeur des Arts et des Lettres; First Prize, Geneva International Competition, 1955, Munich International Competition, 1963, Schallplattenpreis, Berlin, 1970, Victoire de la musique, 1987.

ANDRE Talona, b. 11 January 1945, Pekin, Illinois, USA. Disabled. 1 daughter. Education: 1 semester, Bradley University; Dr of Divinity, Church of Gospel Ministery, 1976. Publication: National Poets Society, 1994. Contributions to: Sunday Suitor. Membership: Sunday Suitor. Address: 2124 N Drury Lane, Peoria, IL 61604-3040, USA.

ANDREEV Rumen Dimov, b. 20 March 1955, Sofia, Bulgaria. Engineer. Education: Master of Science, 1980, PhD, 1987, Sofia Technical University, Sofia, Bulgaria. Appointments: Constructor, Institute of Computer Technique, 1980-82; Research Fellow, Central Institute of Computer Technique and Technology, 1982-88; Research Associate, Central Laboratory of Automation and Scientific Instrumentation, 1988-93; Associate Professor, Institute of Computer and Communication Systems, Bulgarian Academy of Sciences, 1994-. Publications: Monograph: Graphics Systems: Architecture and Realization, 1993; Articles in scientific journals including: Computer Graphics Forum; Computers and Graphics; Interacting with Computers. Honours: Medal, Ministry of Defence, Republic of Bulgaria, 1974; Listed in Who's Who publications and biographical dictionaries. Memberships: Bulgarian Union of Automation and Informatics, British Computer Society; New York Academy of Sciences. Address: Institute of Computer and Communication Systems, Bulgarian Academy of Sciences, str Acad. G Bonchev Bl 2, 1113 Sofia, Bulgaria. E-mail: rumen@agatha.iac.bg

ANDRES-BARQUIN Pedro Jose, b. 9 January 1964, Zaragoza, Spain. Neuroscientist; Veterinarian. m. Maria Clemencia Hernandez, 1 daughter. Education: DVM, 1987, PhD, 1992, University of Zaragoza, Spain; MPH, Spanish National School of Public Health, 1993. Appointments: Fellow: University of Zaragoza, 1982-92, INSERM, France, 1990-91, University of California, San Francisco, USA, 1994-98; Head of Laboratory, F Hoffmann-La Roche, Basel, Switzerland, 2000-. Publications: Contributor of articles to professional journals in the field of biomedical research and education. Honours: CAI Degree Prize, 1987, National Degree Prize, 1988, Spanish Ministry of Education and Science. Memberships: Society for Neuroscience; American Society for Cell Biology; Spanish Society for Biochemistry and Molecular Biology. Address: Claragraben 117, Basel 4057, Switzerland. E-mail: pjandres@datacomm.ch

ANDRETTI Mario Gabriele, b. 28 February 1940, Montona, Italy. American Racing Driver. m. Dee Ann Hoch, 1961, 2 sons, 1 daughter. Appointments: Began midget car racing in US, graduating to US Auto Club National Formula; Indy Car National Champion, 1965, 1966, 1969, 1984; USAC Champion, 1965, 1966, 1969, 1974; Winner, Indianapolis 500 Miles, 1969; Winner, Daytona 500 Miles NASCAR Stock Car Race, 1967; Began Formula 1 Racing in 1968; World Champion, 1978; Third, 1977; Winner, International Race of Champions, 1979; President, MA 500 Inc, 1968-; Newman/Haas Racing, 1983; Honours: Driver of the Year, 1967, 1978, 1984; Driver of the Quarter Century, 1992; Driver of the Century, 1999-2000; All Time Indy Car Lap Leader (7587); Grand Prix Wins: South African (Ferrari); Japanese (Lotus Ford), 1976; US (Lotus Ford), 1977; Spanish (Lotus Ford), 1977; French (Lotus Ford), 1977; Italian (Lotus Ford), 1977; Argentine (Lotus Ford), 1978; Belgian (Lotus Ford), 1978; Spanish (Lotus Ford), 1978; French (Lotus Ford, 1978; German (Lotus Ford), 1978; Dutch (Lotus Ford), 1978. Address: 475 Rose Inn Avenue, Nazareth, PA 18064, USA.

ANDREW Christopher Robert, b. 18 February 1963, Richmond, Yorks. British Rugby Football Player. m. Sara, 2 daughters. Education: Cambridge University. Appointments: Chartered Surveyor; Fly-half; Former Member, Middlesbrough, Cambridge University, Nottingham, Gordon, Sydney, Australia clubs; Member, 1987-91, 1992-96, Captain, 1989-90, Wasps Club; Toulouse, 1991-92; Barbarians, Newcastle, 1996-; International debut England versus Romania, 1985; Five nations debut, England Versus France, 1985; Captain, England Team, England versus Romania, Bucharest, 1989; Retired from International Rugby, 1995; Development Director, Newcastle Rugby Football Club, 1995-.

Dictionary of International Biography

Publications: A Game and a Half, 1995. Honours: Record Holder for Drop Goals in Internationals. Memberships: Grand Slam Winning Team. Address: c/o Newcastle Rugby Football Club, Newcastle upon Tyne, NE3 2DT, England.

ANDREWS Anthony, b. 1 December 1948, Hampstead, London, England. Actor. m. Georgina Simpson, 1 son, 2 daughters. Career: Started acting, 1967; TV appearances include Doomwatch, Woodstock, 1972, A Day Out, Follyfoot, Fortunes of Nigel, 1973, The Pallisers, David Copperfield, 1974, Upstairs Downstairs, 1975, French Without Tears, The Country Wife, Much Ado About Nothing, 1977, Danger UXB, 1978, Romeo and Juliet, 1979, Brideshead Revisited, 1980, Ivanhoe, 1982, The Scarlet Pimpernel, 1983, Colombo, 1988, The Strange Case of Dr Jekyll and Mr Hyde, 1989, Hands of a Murderer, 1990, Lost in Siberia, 1990, The Law Lord, 1991, Jewels, 1992, Ruth Rendell's Heartstones, Mothertime; Films include The Scarlet Pimpernel, Under the Volcano, A War of the Children, Take Me High, 1973, Operation Daybreak, 1975, Les Adolescents, 1976, The Holcroft Covenant, 1986, Second Victory, 1987, Woman He Loved, 1988, The Lighthorsemen, 1988, Hannah's War, 1988, Lost in Siberia, as actor and producer, 1990, Haunted, as actor and producer, 1995; Appeared in plays, 40 Years On, A Midsummer Night's Dream, Romeo and Juliet, One of Us, 1986, Coming into Land, 1986, Dragon Variation, Tima and the Conways. Address: c/o Peters Fraser and Dunlop Ltd, 503 The Chambers, Chelsea Harbour, London SW10 0XF, England.

ANDREWS Julie (Dame), b. 1 October 1935, Walton-on-Thames, Surrey, England. Singer; Actress. m. (1) Tony Walton, 10 May 1959, divorced, 1 daughter; (2) Blake Edwards, 1969. Musical Education: Voice lessons with Lillian Stiles-Allen. Career: As actress: Debut, Starlight Roof, London Hippodrome, 1947; Appeared: Royal Command Performance, 1948; Broadway production, The Boy Friend, NYC, 1954; My Fair Lady, 1956-60; Camelot, 1960-62; Putting It Together, 1993; Film appearances include: Mary Poppins, 1964; The Americanization Of Emily, 1964; Torn Curtain, 1966; The Sound Of Music, 1966; Hawaii, 1966; Thoroughly Modern Millie, 1967; Stark, 1968; Darling Lili, 1970; The Tamarind Seed, 1973; 10, 1979; Little Miss Marker, 1980; S.O.B., 1981; Victor/Victoria, 1982; The Man Who Loved Women, 1983; That's Life!, 1986; Duet For One, 1986; The Sound of Christmas, TV, 1987; Relative Values, 1999; The Princess Diaries, 2001; Television debut, 1956; Host, The Julie Andrews Hour, 1972-73; Julie (comedy series), ABC-TV, 1992; Television films include Our Sons, 1991. Recordings: Albums: A Christmas Treasure, 1968; The Secret Of Christmas, 1977; Love Me Tender, 1983; Broadway's Fair, 1984; Love Julie, 1989; Broadway: The Music Of Richard Rogers, 1994; Here I'll Stay, 1996; Nobody Sings It Better, 1996; with Carol Burnett: Julie And Carol At Carnegie Hall, 1962; At The Lincoln Center, 1989; Cast and film soundtracks: My Fair Lady (Broadway cast), 1956; Camelot (Broadway cast), 1961; Mary Poppins (film soundtrack), 1964; The Sound Of Music (film soundtrack), 1965; The King And I (studio cast), 1992. Publications: Mandy (as Julie Edwards), 1971; The Last Of The Really Great Whangdoodles, 1974. Honours: Oscar, Mary Poppins, 1964; Golden Globe Awards, Hollywood Foreign Press Association, 1964, 1965; BAFTA Silver Mask, 1989; Kennedy Center Honor, 2001. Address: c/o Triad Artists, 10100 Santa Monica Boulevard, 16th Floor, Los Angeles, CA 90067, USA.

ANDREWS Lyman Henry, b. 2 April 1938, Denver, Colorado, USA. Writer. Education: BA, Brandeis University, 1960. Appointments: Assistant Lecturer, University of Wales, Swansea, 1964-65; Lecturer, University of Leicester, 1965-88; Poetry Critic, Sunday Times, 1969-78; Visiting Professor, Indiana University,

1978-79. Publications: Ash Flowers; Fugitive Visions; The Death of Mayakovsky; Kaleidoscope. Contributions to: Times; Sunday Times; Times Higher Educational Supplement; British Book News; San Francisco Examiner; Denver Post; Partisan Review; Encounter; El Corno Empumado; Les Lettres Nouvelles; New Mexico Quarterly; Carolina Quarterly; Transatlantic Review; Anglo Welsh Review; Poetry Quarterly; Root and Branch; Evergreen Review. Honours: Fulbright Fellowship; James Phelan Travelling Fellowship; Woodrow Wilson National Fellowship. Address: Flat 4-32, Victoria Centre, Nottingham, NG1 3PA, England.

ANDREWS Richard Nigel Lyon, b. 6 December 1944, Newport, Rhode Island, USA. Professor. m. Hannah Page Wheeler, 1 son, 1 daughter. Education: AB, Yale University, 1966; MRP, University of North Carolina, Chapel Hill, 1970; PhD, University of North Carolina, 1972. Appointments: Peace Corps Volunteer, 1966-68; Natural Resource Planner Aid, New York State Department of Conservation, 1969; Budget Examiner, Water Resources Branch, US Office of Management and Budget, 1970-72; Research Associate, University of North Carolina, 1972; Assistant Professor, Natural Resource Policy, University of Michigan, Ann Arbor, 1972-75; Assistant Professor, Urban and Regional Planning, 1974-75; Associate Professor, Natural Resource Policy, Urban and Regional Planning, 1975-81; Acting Chairman, Regional Planning Curriculum, 1975-76; Chairman, Resource Policy, Management Program, 1978-81; Professor of Environmental Policy, University of North Carolina, 1981-; Director, Institute for Environmental Studies, 1981-91; Director, Environmental Management and Policy Program, 1990-94; Chair of the Faculty, 1997-2000; Thomas Willis Lambeth Distinguished Professor of Public Policy, 2004-. Publications: 5 Books; Numerous Articles. Honours: Honorary Member, Golden Key National Honour Society; Fellow, National Academy of Public Administration; Fellow, American Association for the Advancement of Science; Member, Sigma Xi; Member, Delta Omega. Memberships: American Association for the Advancement of Science; Association for Public Policy Analysis and Management. Address: 298 Azalea Drive, Chapel Hill, NC 27517, USA.

ANDREYEV Vitaliy, b. 3 January 1939, Saint Petersburg, Russia. Biotechnologist. m. Nadezhda Vladimirovna, 2 sons. Education: Physicist Degree, State University of St Petersburg, 1961; Candidate, Physics and Mathematics, Agrophysical Academy, 1967; Doctor of Technical Sciences, Biotechnology, State Research Institute for Synthesis of Proteins, 1987. Appointments: Board Member, State Research Institute Medical Laboratory of Technology, 1970-2000; Chief, Laboratory, State Research Institute of Medical Laboratory Technique, 1970-2000; Director General ISC Interbiotec, 1991-2000; President Elecotech Consortium, 1996-; Founded, Electroecotechnologies Inc, USA, 2000. Publications: 200 publications, books, papers, patents. Honours: Golden and Silver Medals; Awards, Several Professional Competitions; Governmental Awards. Memberships: International Information Academy; Association of Producers of Medical Products; Association of St Petersburg Contractors. Address: 9/13, 8 Sovetskaya ul, Apartment 10, St Petersburg 193 130, Russia.

ANDRUS Hyrum Leslie, b. 12 March 1924, Lewisville, Idaho, USA. Author. m. Helen Mae Hillman Andrus, 3 sons. Education: AA Agriculture, Ricks College, 1949; BS Political Science, Ricks College, 1951; MS Political Science and Scripture, Brigham Young University, 1952; PhD Political Science, History and American Citizenship, Syracuse University, 1955. Publications: Joseph Smith and World Government, 1958; Joseph Smith The Man and The Seer, 1960-99; Liberalism, Conservatism and Mormonism, 1965; Doctrinal Commentary on the Pearl of Great Price, 1967-2003; God, Man and the Universe, 1968, 1999; The Challenge and the

Choice, contributions, 1969; Principles of Perfection, 1970, 1999; Doctrines of the Kingdom, 1973, 1999; They Knew The Prophet, co-author with Helen Mae Andrus, 1974, 1999; GospelLink, contributions, CD-Rom, The Revolution called Liberty: New Views on the Roots and Nature of Anglo-American Life and Liberty, 6 volumes, forthcoming. Honours: Karl G Maeser Research Award, 1967; Master Teacher Award, 1972; Included in numerous biographical listings publications.

ANDSNES Leif Ove, b. 7 April 1970, Karmooy, Norway. Pianist. Education: Studied at the Music Conservatory of Bergen with Jiri Hlinka. Debut: Oslo, 1987; British debut, Edinburgh Festival with the Oslo Philharmonic, Mariss Jansons, 1989; US Debut, Cleveland Symphony, Neeme Järvi. Career: Appearances include: Schleswig-Holstein Festival and with orchestras such as Los Angeles Philharmonic, Japan Philharmonic, Berlin Philharmonic, London Philharmonic, Philharmonia, City of Birmingham Symphony Orchestra, Royal Scottish National Orchestra, BBC Philharmonic Orchestra for his debut at the Proms, 1992 and Chicago Symphony Orchestra; Soloist, Last Night of the Proms, 2002; Artistic Director, Risor Festival; Recitals at Teatro Communale, Bologna, Wigmore Hall, Barbican Hall, London, Herkulesaal, Munich, Concertgebouw, Amsterdam, Konzerthaus Vienna and Glasgow Royal Concert Hall. Recordings include: Grieg: A Mino and Liszt A Major concerti; Janacek, Solo Piano Music; Chopin, Sonatas and Grieg, Solo Piano Music; Brahmns and Schumann works for piano and viola with Lars Anders Tomter. Honours include: First Prize, Hindemith Competition, Frankfurt am Main; Levin Prize, Bergen, 1999; Norwegian Music Critics' Prize, 1988; Grieg Prize, Bergen, 1990; Dorothy B Chandler Performing Art Award, Los Angeles, 1992; Gilmore Prize, 1997; Instrumentalist Award, Royal Philharmonic Society, 2000; Gramophone Award, Best Concerto Recording, 2000; Best Instrumental Recording, 2002; Commander, Royal Norwegian Order of St Olav, 2002. Address: c/o Kathryn Enticott, IMG Artists (Europe), Media House, 3 Burlington Lane, Chiswick, London W4 2TH, England.

ANEER Gunnar, Environmentalist. Education: Undergraduate courses in Statistics, Botany, Zoology, Filosofie Kandidat Degree, 1969, PhD, Department of Zoology, 1979; Docent (Associate Professor), Zoology, Marine Ecology, 1984, University of Stockholm, Sweden. Appointments: Third Amanuensis, 1969, First Amanuensis, 1969-70, Department of Zoology, Research Associate, 1972-73, 1973-79, 1979-83, 1983-90, Askö Laboratory, Department of Zoology, University of Stockholm, Sweden; Environmental Investigator, County Administrative Board of Stockholm, 1990-; In charge of Information Office for the Baltic Proper, 1992-; Several consultancy positions in Sweden and abroad include: Swedish Expert in a Helsinki Commission Working Group, Baltic Early Warning Event Reporting System, 1998-; Marine Monitoring Expert in the preparation group of the Svealand Coastal Water Association, 1999-. Publications: Over 20 articles in scientific journals as author and co-author include most recently: Between-reader variation in herring otolith ages and effects on estimated population parameters, 2000; A Tagging experiment on spring-spawning Baltic herring (Clupea harengus membras) in Southwest Finland in 1990-98, 2001; 9 scientific reports; 8 conference papers; 13 popular science papers. Address: County Administrative Board of Stockholm, Section for Environmental Information, Box 22067, S-104 22 Stockholm, Sweden. E-mail: gunnar.aneer@ab.lst.se

ANEES Sarmad, b. 26 April 1954, Muzaffarabad, Azad Kashmir, Pakistan. Senior Projects Engineer. m. Raana Ashraf, 1 son, 1 daughter. Education, BSc, Mechanical Engineering, 1979. Appointments: Senior Projects Engineer, 1980-91; Construction Manager, 1991-93; Manager, Projects Monitoring and Controls, 1993-94; Senior Projects Engineer, 1994-. Membership: Pakistan

Engineering Council. Address: ADNOC Distribution, PO Box 4188, Abu Dhabi, United Arab Emirates. E-mail: rsarmad@emirates.net.ae

ANG Hooi Hoon, b. 11 January 1964, Ipoh Perak. Lecturer. Researcher. Education: BPharm (Hons), 1988, PhD, 1993, University of Science, Malaysia; Admitted to PHP Institute, awarded Gold Medal, Doctoral Fellow, PHP Institute of Asia, Japan, 1995. Appointments: Graduate Assistant, School of Pharmaceutical Sciences, University of Science, Malaysia, 1988-90; Assistant Quality Control Manager, private pharmaceutical company, Ipoh Perak, 1992-93; Lecturer, 1994-2002, Associate Professor, 2002-, School of Pharmaceutical Sciences, University of Science, Malaysia. Publications: total of 150 publications. Honours: Awards from scientific institutions, fellowships, grants include: Third World Academy of Science, Trieste and Chinese Academy of Science Visiting Professorship, Beijing, February to April 1998; Awards: Young Investigator, European Societies of Chemotherapy, Stockholm, Sweden, 1998; Young Investigator, Science Council of Japan and Japanese Society of Parasitology, 1998; UNESCO Regional Office of Southeast Asia, Jakarta, 1998; Young Scientist and Technologist, ASEAN Committee of Science and Technology, Vietnam, 1998; Gold Star Award, Certificate of Achievement, International Woman of the Year Award, International Biographical Centre, England, 1998; International Woman of the Millennium, IBC, Cambridge, 1999; Postdoctoral Fellowship for Foreign Researchers Awardee, Japan Society for the Promotion of Science, 1999-2000; American Medal of Honor, ABI, 2003. Memberships: Vice-Chairman, 1994-95, Honorary Secretary, 1995-, Malaysian Pharmaceutical Society, Penang; Malaysian Society of Parasitology and Tropical Medicine; Malaysian Microbiology Society; Japanese Society of Parasitology; Third World Academy of Science, Trieste; Institute of Biology, Queensberry, UK, 1998-. Address: School of Pharmaceutical Sciences, University of Science, Malaysia, Minden 11800, Penang, Malaysia.

ANG Lee, b. 1954, Taipei, Taiwan. Film Director. m. Jane Lin. Education: New York University. Moved to USA 1978. Films: Pushing Hands, 1992; The Wedding Banquet, 1993; Eat Drink Man Woman, 1995; Sense and Sensibility, 1996; The Ice Storm, 1998; Ride with the Devil, 1998; Crouching Tiger, Hidden Dragon, 1999; Chosen, 2001. Honours: Winner, National Script Writing Contest, Taiwanese Government, 1990; Academy Award for Best Foreign Film, 1999; David Lean Award for Best Director; BAFTA, 2001; Golden Globe for Best Director, 2001

ANGEL James Robert, b. 20 September 1935, Sydney, Australia. Academic. Education: BA 1959, MA 1965, DipEd, 1966, University of Sydney; PhD, Australian National University, 1970. Appointments: Colombo Plan Expert, Northern Borneo, 1959-65; Commonwealth Office of Education, Sydney, 1965; Research Scholar, Australian National University, 1966-70; Lecturer, History, 1970-75, Senior Lecturer, 1975-94, University of Sydney; Editor, Current Affairs Bulletin, University of Sydney, 1982-85; Vice Principal, Senior Fellow, St Andrews College, 1982-87; Senior Tutor, St Pauls College, 1990-97. Publications include: Independence and Alliance: Australia in World Affairs 1975-80 (co-editor), 1982; The Australian Club: The First 50 Years 1838-1888, 1988; Diplomacy in the Market Place: Australia in World Affairs 1981-1990 (co-editor), 1992. Memberships include: President, University Sydney Arts Association, 1972-75; President 1975-79, New South Wales Branch, Australian Institute of International Affairs; Research Chairman, Australian Institute of International Affairs, 1985-87; Patron, Savoy Arts Company, 1985-. Honour: OBE, 1979. Address: PO Box 815, Narrabeen, New South Wales 2101, Australia.

Dictionary of International Biography

ANGELOU Maya, b. 4 April 1928, St Louis, Missouri, USA. Author. Appointments: Associate editor, Arab Observer, 1961-62; Assistant administrator, teacher, School of Music and Drama, University of Ghana, 1963-66; Feature editor, African Review, Accra, 1964-66; Reynolds Professor of American Studies, Wake Forest University, 1981-; Teacher of modern dance, Rome Opera House, Hambina Theatre, Tel Aviv; Member, Board of Governors, Maya Angelou Institute for the Improvement of Child and Family Education, Winston-Salem State University, North Carolina, 1998-; Theatre appearances include: Porgy and Bess, 1954-55; Calypso, 1957; The Blacks, 1960; Mother Courage, 1964; Look Away, 1973; Roots, 1977; How to Make an American Quilt, 1995; Plays: Cabaret for Freedom, 1960; The Least of These, 1966; Getting' Up Stayed On My Mind, 1967; Ajax, 1974; And Still I Rise, 1976; Moon On a Rainbow Shawl (producer), 1988. Film: Down in the Delta (director), 1998. Publications include: I Know Why the Caged Bird Sings, 1970; Just Give Me A Cool Drink of Water 'Fore I Die, 1971; Georgia, Georgia (screenplay), 1972; Oh Pray My Wings Are Gonna Fit Me Well, 1975; Singin' and Swingin' and Gettin' Merry Like Christmas, 1976; And Still I Rise, 1976; The Heart of a Woman, 1981; Shaker, Why Don't You Sing, 1983; All God's Children Need Travelling Shoes, 1986; Now Sheba Sings the Song, 1987; I Shall Not Be Moved, 1990; Gathered Together in My Name, 1991; Wouldn't Take Nothing for my Journey Now, 1993; Life Doesn't Frighten Me, 1993; Collected Poems, 1994; My Painted House, My Friendly Chicken and Me, 1994; Phenomenal Woman, 1995; Kofi and His Magic, 1996; Even the Stars Look Lonesome, 1997; Making Magic in the World, 1998. Honours: Horatios Alger Award, 1992; Grammy Award Best Spoken Word or Non-Traditional Album, 1994; Honorary Ambassador to UNICEF, 1996-; Lifetime Achievement Award for Literature, 1999; National Medal of Arts; Distinguished visiting professor at several universities; Chubb Fellowship Award, Yale University; Nominated, National Book Award, I Know Why the Caged Bird Sings; Tony Award Nomination, Performances in Look Away; Honorary degrees, Smith College, Lawrence University; Golden Eagle Award; First Reynolds Professor; The Matrix Award; American Academy of Achievements Golden Plate Award; Distinguished Woman of North Carolina; Essence Woman of the Year; Many others. Memberships: The Directors Guild of America; Equity; AFTRA; Woman's Prison Association; Harlem Writers Guild; Horatio Alger Association of Distinguished Americans; National Society for the Prevention of Cruelty to Children. Address: Care Dave La Camera, Lordly and Dame Inc, 51 Church Street, Boston, MA 02116-5417, USA.

ANGHELAKI-ROOKE Katerina, b. 22 February 1939, Athens, Greece. Poet; Translator. Education: Universities of Nice, Athens, Geneva, 1957-63. Appointments: Freelance Translator, 1962-; Visiting Professor (Fulbright), Harvard University, 1980; Visiting Fellow, Princeton University, 1987. Publications: Wolves and Clouds, 1963; Poems, 1963-69, 1971; The Body is the Victory and the Defeat of Dreams, in English, 1975; The Scattered Papers of Penelope, 1977; The Triumph of Constant Loss, 1978; Counter Love, 1982; The Suitors, 1984; Beings and Things on Their Own, in English, 1986; When the Body, 1988; Wind Epilogue, 1990; Empty Nature, 1993; Tristiu, 1995; From Purple into Night, in English, 1997; The Flesh, beautiful desert, 1996, in French, 2001; Matter Alone, 2001; Translating into Love Life's End, 2003, a bilingual edition in English, 2004; Translations of Works by Shakespeare, Albee, Dylan Thomas, Beckett, Seamus Heaney and from Russian: Pushkin, Mayiakorski, Lermontov, J Brodski, V Pelevin. Honours: Greek National Poetry Prize, 1985; Greek Academy Ouranis Prize, 2000. Address: Synesiou Kyrenes 4, 114 71 Athens, Greece.

ANGUS Beverley Margaret, b. 18 November 1934, Lautoka, Fiji. Parasitologist. m. James Robert Angus, 1 son, 1 daughter. Education: BSc, 1979, PhD, 1994, University of Queensland, Australia; Graduate Diploma, Education, Queensland University of Technology, Australia. Appointments: Scientific Researcher, 1980-; Research Associate and Honorary Consultant, Queensland Museum, Australia, 1997-. Publications: Books: Tick Fever and Cattle Tick in Australia 1829-1996, 1998; Parasitology and the Queensland Museum. Memberships: Australian Society for Parasitology; Australian Society for History of Medicine; Australian Veterinary History Society; Professional Historians' Association of Australia, Queensland. Address: 96 Mallawa Drive, Palm Beach, Queensland 4221, Australia. E-mail: bmangus@bigpond.net.au Website: www.bovinetickfever.com

ANGUS John F, b. 1947, Montreal, Canada. Business Turnaround Management. m. Toni Cochand, 4 children. Appointments: Partner, K D Marine Ltd, 1966-69; Partner, Dominion Diving Ltd, 1966-70; Partner, Aquasport Ltd, 1966-70; Manager, Advertising, Marketing and Public Relations, Alcan Canada Products Ltd, 1970-82; Chairman, Brill Church Cemetery Corporation, 1970-; President, Forrest Campbell Investments Ltd, 1975-; John F Angus Marketing and Communications, 1974-86; Chairman, CEO, Ontario Multi Material Recycling Inc, 1983-86; Chairman, CEIA Canadian Environmental Industry Association, 1988-91; Executive Vice President, President, Eco Corporation, Environmental Consulting Services, 1986-91; President, CEO, Stonehenge Corporation, 1989-; President, Chairman, Metal Supermarkets (Canada) Ltd, 1992-99; Director, PEMAC Preventive Engineering & Maintenance Association, 1996-99; President, Deep Expedition Inc, 1997-2002; CEO, Smart Products Inc, 1997-; President, CEO, GCI International, 1998-2001; Director, UBS Bank, Canada and UBS Trust, Canada, 1998-; President, Senneville Golf Links Inc, 2002-; Chairman, LiquiCell Corporation, 2001-; Chairman, Delta Corporation, 2001-; President, HeavyLift Canada Inc, 2000-. Honours: UN Medal for environmental stewardship, 1984. Memberships: Toronto Club; Forest & Stream Club; Kingston Yacht Club; Caledon Ski Club; Orleans Fish & Game Club; Caledon Mountain Trout Club; Braeside Golf Club, Senneville, Quebec; Turnaround Management Association. Address: Stonehenge Corporation, 99 Woodland, Beaconsfield, Quebec H9W 4W2, Canada. E-mail: john_angus@stonehengecorp.biz Website: www.stonehengecorp.biz

ANGUS Michael Richardson (Sir), b. 5 May 1930, Ashford, Kent, England. Company Director. m. Eileen Isabel May Elliott, 1952, 2 sons, 1 daughter. Education: BSc, Bristol University. Appointments: Served RAF, 1951-54; Joined Unilever PLC, 1954; Marketing Director, 1962-65, Managing Director, Research Bureau, 1965-67, Thibaud Gibbs, Paris, France, 1962-65; Sales Director, Lever Brothers, UK, 1967-70; Director, Unilever PLC and Unilever NV, 1970-92, Toilet Preparations Co-ordinator, 1970-76, Chemicals Co-ordinator, 1976-80, Regional Director, North America, 1979-84, Chair, Chief Executive Officer, Unilever United States Inc, New York, 1980-84, Chair, Chief Executive Officer, Lever Brothers Co, New York, 1980-84, Vice-Chair, 1984-86, Chair, 1986-92, Unilever PLC, Vice-Chair, Unilever NV, 1986-92; Governor, 1974, Chair of Governors, 1991-2002, Ashridge Management College; Joint Chair, 1984-89, President, 1990-94, Netherlands British Chamber of Commerce; Director, Leverhulme Trust, 1984-; Member of Council, 1986-, President, 1998, British Executive Service Overseas; Non-Executive Director, 1986-, Deputy Chair, 1992, Chair, 1992-99, Whitbread PLC; Non-Executive Director, Thorn EMI PLC, 1988-93; Non-Executive Director, 1988-2000, Deputy Chair, 1989-2000, British Airways PLC; Director, 1991-, Deputy Chair, 1991-94, National

Westminster Bank PLC; Deputy President, 1991-92, 1994-95, President, 1992-94, Confederation of British Industry; Chair of Governors, Royal Agricultural College, Cirencester, 1992-; Director, 1994-2000, Chair, 1994-98, Deputy Chair, 1998-2000, The Boots Co PLC; Member, Council of Management, Ditchley Foundation, 1994-; D L Gloucestershire, 1997; Chair, RAC Holdings Ltd, 1999-. Honours: Holland Trade Award, 1990; Honorary DSc, Bristol, 1990; Commander, Order of Orange Nassau, 1992; Honorary DSc, Buckingham, 1994; Honorary LLD, Nottingham, 1966. Memberships: Companion, Institute of Management. Address: Cerney House, North Cerney, Cirencester, Gloucestershire GL7 7BX, England.

ANGYAL Stephen John, b. 21 November 1914, Budapest, Hungary. Organic Chemist. m. Helga Ellen Steininger, 1 son, 1 daughter. Education: PhD, University of Science, Budapest, 1937; DSc, University of New South Wales, 1964. Appointments: Research Chemist, Chinoin Pharmaceuticals, Budapest; Research Chemist, Nicholas Pty Ltd, Melbourne, 1942-46; Lecturer, University of Sydney, 1946-51; Assistant Professor, 1953, Professor, 1960, Dean of Science, 1970-79, Emeritus Professor, 1979-, University of New South Wales. Publications: About 200 articles in chemistry journals, chapters in books; Joint author: Conformational Analysis, 1967. Honours: Nuffield Dominion Travelling Fellow, 1952; H G Smith Memorial Medal, Royal Australian Chemistry Institute, 1959; Ollé Prize, Royal Australian Chemistry Institute, 1967; OBE, 1977; Haworth Memorial Medal, Chemistry Society, London, 1980; Hudson Award, American Chemical Society, 1987. Memberships: Fellow, Royal Australian Chemists Institute; Fellow, Australian Academy of Science; Foreign Fellow, Hungarian Academy of Science. Address: 304 Sailors Bay Road, Northbridge, NSW 2063, Australia.

ANIFANTIS Nikolaos, b. 12 February 1955, Samos, Greece. Professor. m. Vasso Velaora, 1 son. Education: Mechanical Engineering degree, 1978, PhD, Mechanical Engineering, 1985, University of Patras. Appointments: Research Assistant, 1978, Lecturer, 1986, Assistant Professor, 1990, Mechanical and Aero Engineering Dept, University of Patras. Publications: 20 articles in international journals; 14 in conference proceedings. Memberships: Technical Chamber of Greece; Greek Association of Mechanical Engineers; New York Academy of Sciences; IEEE Computer Society; American Association for the Advancement of Science. Address: 43 Sarantaporou St, 26223 Patras, Greece.

ANISMAN Philip, b. 12 September 1941, Toronto, Canada. Lawyer. Education: BA, 1964, LLB, 1967, University of Toronto, Canada; LLM, 1971, JSD, 1974, University of California, Berkley. Appointments include: Assistant Professor, Faculty of Law, University of Western Ontario, 1968-71; Research Officer, Law Reform Commission of Canada, 1971-73; Director, Corporate Research Branch, Department of Consumer and Corporate Affairs, Canada, 1973-78; Consultant, National Companies and Securities Commission, Australia, 1983-86; Visiting Professor, Faculties of Law and Economics, Monash University, Australia, 1983; Professor of Law, Osgoode Hall Law School, York University, 1978-85; Special Counsel on Corporation, Securities and Constitutional Law, Goodman and Carr, Toronto, 1985-87; Public Member, Investment Dealers Association of Canada, 1990-2000; Sole Practitioner, 1987-. Publications: Numerous publications in professional journals, books and government studies. Honour: Walter Perry Johnson Fellowship, Boalt Hall Law School, University of California, Berkley, 1967-68. Memberships include: Associate member, American Bar Association; Member, ABA Section on Corporation Banking and Business Law; OBCA Advisory Committee, Canadian Bar Association, Ontario Branch,

Commercial and Corporation Law Section; University College Committee, University of Toronto. Address: 1905, 80 Richmond Street West, Toronto, Ontario M4H 1A4, Canada.

ANISTON Jennifer, b. 11 February 1969, Sherman Oaks, California, USA. Actress. m. Brad Pitt, 2000. Education: New York High School of the Performing Arts. Appointments: Theatre includes: For Dear Life; Dancing on Checker's Grave; Films include: Leprechaun, 1993; She's The One, 1996; Dream for an Insomniac, 1996; 'Til There Was You, 1996; Picture Perfect, 1997; The Object of My Affection, 1998; Office Space, 1999; The Iron Giant, 1999; Rock Star, 2001; The Good Girl, 2002; TV includes, Molloy (series); 1989; The Edge; Ferris Bueller; Herman's Head; Friends, 1994-2004. Honours: Emmy Award for Best Actress, 2002; Golden Globe for Best TV Actress in a Comedy, 2003. Address: c/o CAA, 9830 Wilshire Boulevard, Beverly Hills, CA 90212, USA.

ANN-MARGARET, b. 1941, Stockholm, Sweden. Actress; Singer; Dancer. m. Roger Smith, 1967. Appointments: Film Debut, Pocketful of Miracles, 1961; Films include: State Fair; Bye Bye Birdie; Once a Thief; The Cincinnati Kid; Stagecoach; Murderer's Row; C C & Co; Carnal Knowledge; RPM; Train Robbers; Tommy; The Twist; Joseph Andrews; Last Remark of Beau Geste; Magic; Middle Age Crazy; Return of the Soldier; I Ought to be in Pictures; Looking to Get Out; Twice in a Lifetime; 52 Pick-Up, 1987; New Life, 1988; Something More; Newsies, 1992; Grumpy Old Men, 1993; Grumpier Old Men, 1995; Any Given Sunday, 1999; The Last Producer, 2000; A Woman's a Helluva Thing, 2000; TV includes: Who Will Love My Children?, 1983; A Streetcar Named Desire, 1984; The Two Mrs Grenvilles, 1987; Our Sons, 1991; Nobody's Children, 1994; Following her Heart; Seduced by Madness; The Diana Borchardt Story, 1996; Blue Rodeo, 1996; Pamela Hanniman, 1999; Happy Face Murders, 1999; Perfect Murder, Perfect Town, 2000; The Tenth Kingdom, 2000; Also appears in cabaret. Publications: (with Todd Gold) Ann-Margaret: My Story, 1994. Honours: Five Golden Globe Awards; Three Female Star of the Year Awards. Address: William Morris Agency, 151 S, El Camino Drive, Beverly Hills, CA 90212, USA.

ANNADURAI S, b. 13 July 1967, Vellore, Tamilnadu, India. Pharmacist; Teacher; Researcher. m. I A Tamizharas, 1 daughter. Education: DPharm, Christian Medical College, Vellore, 1986; BPharm, Madras Medical College, Madras, 1990; MPharm, 1993, PhD (Pharmacy), 1998, Jadavpur University, Calcutta. Appointments: Pharmacy Intern, Christian Medical College, 1986; Graduate Apprentice, Indian Drugs and Pharmaceuticals Ltd, Madras, 1991; Junior Research Fellow, UGC at Jadavpur University, 1991-93; Lecturer in Pharmacy, S B College of Pharmacy, Sivakasi, 1993-94; Senior Research Fellow, CSIR at Jadavpur University, 1994-97; Lecturer, 1998-2002, Central and State Government Approved Formulation and Manufacturing Chemist, 1999-, Senior Lecturer, PhD grade, 2002-, Reader in Pharmacy, 2004, Department of Pharmacy, Christian Medical College. Publications: Original scientific research papers in many national and international conferences; Articles in peer-reviewed journals, 8 international and 2 national; Co-author, text book. Honours: First Class First in Order of Merit; Gold Medals in DPharm and MPharm; University Rank holder in BPharm; Junior Research Fellowship, UGC; Senior Research Fellowship, CSIR. Memberships: Indian Pharmaceutical Association; Indian Graduates Pharmacy Association; Association of Pharmacy Teachers of India; Indian Institute of Chemists; State Pharmacy Council of India; Life Fellow Institution of Chemists (India), 2003-. Address: Department of Pharmacy, Christian Medical College and Hospital, Ida Scudder Road, Vellore 632 004, Vellore District, Tamilnadu State, India. E-mail: annadurai36@hotmail.com

Dictionary of International Biography

ANNAN Kofi A, b. 8 April 1938, Ghana. International Civil Servant. m. Nane Lagergren, 1 son, 2 daughters. Education: University of Science and Technology; Kumasi Macalester College, St Paul, Minnesota, USA; Institut des Hautes Etudes Internationales, Geneva, Switzerland; MA, Institute of Technology, USA. Appointments: Held posts in UN ECA; Addis Ababa; UN, New York; WHO, Geneva, 1962-71; Administrative Managing Officer, UN, Geneva, 1972-74; Chief Civillian Personnel Officer, UNEF, Cairo, 1974; Managing Director, Ghana Tourist Development Co, 1974-76; Deputy Chief of Staff Services, Office of Personnel Services, Office of UNHCR, Geneva, 1976-80; Deputy Director, Division of Administration, Head of Personnel Services, 1980-83; Director of Administrative Services, Director of Budget, Office of Financial Services, UN, New York, 1984-87; Assistant Secretary General, Office of Human Resources Management, 1987-90; Controller, Office of Programme Planning, Budget and Finance, 1990-92; Assistant Secretary General, Department of Peace Keeping Operations, 1992-93; Under-Secretary General, 1993-96; UN Special Envoy (a.i) to former Yugoslavia, 1995-96; Secretary General, UN, 1997-. Honours: Alfred P Sloan Fellow, MIT, 1971-72; Honorary DCL, Oxford, 2001; Philadelphia Liberty Medal, 2001; Nobel Peace Prize, 2001. Address: United Nations, United Nations Plaza, New York, NY 10017, USA. Website: www.un.org

ANNAUD Jean-Jacques, b. 1 October 1943, Juvisy, Orge, France. Film Director. m. (1) Monique Rossignol, 1970, divorced, 1980, 1 daughter, (2) Laurence Duval, 1982, 1 daughter. Education: Institut des Hautes Etudes Cinématographiques, Paris; L-ès-L, Sorbonne, University of Paris. Career: Freelance Commercial Film Director, 500 films, 1966-75; Director, feature films including Black and White in Colour, 1976; Hot Head, 1979; Quest for Fire, 1981; Name of the Rose, 1988; The Bear, 1988; The Lover, 1992; Wings of Courage, 1994; Seven years in Tibet, 1997; Enemy at the Gates, 2001. Honours: Academy Award for Best Foreign Film, 1976; César Award, 1981; 2 César Awards, 1988. Address: 9 rue Guénégard, 75006 Paris, France.

ANNESLEY Hugh (Sir), b. 22 June 1939, Dublin, Ireland. Police Officer. m. Elizabeth Ann MacPherson, 1970, 1 son, 1 daughter. Appointments: Joined Metropolitan Police, 1958; Assistant Chief Constable of Sussex with special responsibility for personnel and training, 1976; Deputy Assistant Commissioner, Assistant Commissioner, 1985, Metropolitan Police; Head, Operations Department, Scotland Yard, 1987-89; Chief Constable, Royal Ulster Constabulary, 1989-96. Honours: Queen's Police Medal. Memberships: National Executive Institute, Federal Bureau of Investigation, 1986; Executive Committee, Interpol, British Representative, 1987-90, 1993-94; Member, 1997, Chair, 2000-, Board of Governors, Hill School for Girls. Address: c/o Brooklyn, Knock Road, Belfast BT5 6LE, Northern Ireland.

ANNIS Francesca, b. 1945, Actress. 1 son, 2 daughters. Appointments: with Royal Shakespeare Company, 1975-78; Plays include: The Tempest; The Passion Flower Hotel; Hamlet; Troilus and Cressida; Comedy of Errors; The Heretic; Mrs Klein; Rosmersholm; Lady Windermere's Fan; Hamlet; Films include: Cleopatra; Saturday Night Out; Murder Most Foul; The Pleasure Girls; Run With the Wind; The Sky Pirates; The Walking Stick; Penny Gold; Macbeth; Krull; Dune; Under the Cherry Moon; Golden River; El Rio de Oro; The Debt Collector; the End of the Affair; TV includes: Great Expectations; Children in Uniform; Love Story; Danger Man; The Human Jungle; Lily Langtry (role of Lily); Madam Bovary; Partners in Crime; Coming Out of Ice; Why Didn't They Ask Evans?; Magnum PI; Inside Story; Onassis - The Richest Man in the World, 1990; Parnell and the Englishwoman, 1991; Absolute Hell, 1991; The Gravy Train, 1991; Weep No More My

Lady, 1991; Between the Lines, 1993; Reckless, 1997; Deadly Summer, 1997; Wives and Daughters, 1999; Milk, 1999; Deceit, 2000. Address: c/o ICM, 76 Oxford Street, London, W1N 0AX, England.

ANSARI S M Razaullah, b. 8 April 1932, Delhi, India. Physicist originally, presently Historian of Science. m. (1) Annemarie, (2) Shaukat Nihal, 1 son, 3 daughters. Education: BS (Honours), Physics, 1953, MSc, Physics, 1955, Delhi University; DSc (dr rer nat), Karl-Eberhardt University, Tübingen, Germany, 1966; Certificate in German, Goethe Institute, Munich, 1959; Certificate, Diploma in Russian Language, Aligarh Muslim University, 1981, 1982. Appointments: Retired Professor of Physics, Aligarh Muslim University, Aligarh; Historian of Science, especially History of Exact Science in Medieval India and Islamic Countries; Established Department of History of Medicine and Science, Hamdard Institute, New Delhi, Professor and Head, 1984-86; Editor, Studies in History of Medicine and Science, 1984-2000; President, IUHPS Commission for History of Ancient and Medieval Astronomy, 2001-2005; Indian Society for History of Astronomy; Present research fields: working on astronomical Zijes (tables) compiled in India and History of exact science in Medieval India. Publications: 1 monograph, Introduction of Modern Western Astronomy in India, 1985; 2 edited volumes: History of Oriental Astronomy, 2002; Science and Technology in the Islamic World, 2002; 75 papers in international and national journals; 22 conference reports; 3 research projects. Honours: Former Fellow, Alexander von Humboldt Foundation (Bonn), 1959-62; Former President, IAU-IUHPS Commission for History of Astronomy, 1997-2001; IUHPS Commission for Islamic Science & Technology, 1993-97; Former President, IAU Commission for History of Astronomy, 1994-97. Memberships: Editorial Board of Indian Journal of History of Science, New Delhi; International Academy of History of Science, Paris, 1997; International Astronomical Union (IAU), 1973-; Elected Fellow, Royal Astronomical Society, 1972; Life Member, Indian Astronomical Society; Life Member, Indian Society for History of Mathematics; IUHPS Council (Executive), elected 1989-93, 1994-97; Secretary, Ibn Sina Academy of Medieval Medicine and Sciences, Aligarh, India. Address: Roshan Villa, Muzammil Manzil Compound, Dodhpur, Aligarh 202002, India. E-mail: raza.ansari@gmx.net

ANSARIFAR Ali, b. 17 November 1955, Persia. Lecturer. m. Education: BSc, Materials Engineering, 1978-81, PhD, Fracture Mechanics, 1981-86, Queen Mary College, University of London. Appointments: Postdoctoral Research Assistant, Chemical Engineering Department, Imperial College, University of London, 1986-89; Postdoctoral Research Assistant, Cavendish Laboratory, University of Cambridge, 1989-90; Upper Senior Research Scientist, Engineering Research and Design, Tun Abdul Razak Laboratory, The Malaysian Rubber Producers' Research Association, 1990-96; Lecturer, Polymer Engineering, Institute for Polymer Technology and Materials Engineering, Loughborough University, 1996-. Publications include: 41 articles in numerous scientific journals. Memberships: Institute of Physics; Convocation of the University of London; Professional member, Institute of Materials, Minerals and Mining; Loughborough University Ethical Advisory Committee. Address: 45 Montague Road, Clarendon Park, Leicester, LE2 ITK, England.

ANSTEE Margaret Joan (Dame), b. 25 June 1926, Writtle, Essex, England. United Nations Official; Lecturer; Consultant; Author. Education: Modern and Medieval Languages, Newnham College, Cambridge, 1944-47; MA, Newnham College, 1955; BSc, Economics, London University, 1964. Appointments: Lecturer in Spanish, Queen's University, Belfast, 1947-48; Third Secretary,

Foreign Office, 1948-52; UN Technical Assistance Board, Manila, 1952-54; Spanish Supervisor, University of Cambridge, 1955-56; UN Technical Assistance Board, Bogota, 1956-57, Uruguay, 1957-59, Bolivia, 1960-65; Resident Reporter, UNDP Ethiopia and UNDP Liaison Officer, ECA, 1965-67; Senior Economic Adviser, Office of Prime Minister, London, 1967-68; Senior Assistant to Commissioner in charge of study of Capacity of UN Development System, 1968-69; Resident Reporter, UNDP, Morocco, 1969-72, Chile (also UNDP Liaison Officer with ECLA) 1972-74; Deputy to UN Under Secretary General in charge of UN Relief Operation to Bangladesh and Deputy Co-ordinator of UN Emergency Assistance to Zambia, 1973; with UNDP, New York, 1974-78; Assistant General-Secretary of UN, Department of Technical Co-operation for Development), 1978-87; Special Representative of Secretary-General to Bolivia, 1982-92, for co-ordination of earthquake relief assistance to Mexico, 1985-87; Under Secretary-General, UN, 1987-93, Director-General of UN office at Vienna, Head of Centre for Social Development and Humanitarian Affairs, 1987-92, Special Representative of Secretary-General for Angola and Head of Angolan Verification Mission, 1992-93; Adviser to UN Secretary-General on peacekeeping, post-conflict peacebuilding and training troops for UN peacekeeping missions, 1994-; Chair, Advisory Group of Lessons Learned Unit, Department of Peacekeeping Operations, UN, 1996-2002; Co-ordinator of UN Drug Control Related Activities, 1987-90, of International Co-operation for Chernobyl, 1991-92; Secretary-General, 8th UN Congress on Prevention of Crime and Treatment of Offenders, August 1990; Writer, lecturer, consultant and adviser (ad honorem) to Bolivian Government, 1993-. Publications: The Administration of International Development Aid, 1969; Gate of the Sun: A Prospect of Bolivia, 1970; Africa and the World, 1970; Orphan of the Cold War: The Inside Story of the Collapse of the Angolan Peace Process, 1992-93, 1996. Memberships: Member, Advisory Board, UN Studies at Yale University, 1996-; Member, Advisory Council, Oxford Research Group, 1997-; Member, Advisory Board, UN Intellectual History Project, 1999-; Trustee, Helpage International, 1994-97; Patron and Board Member, British Angola Forum, 1998-; Member, International Council for Conflict Resolution, 2001-; Vice President, UK UN Association, 2002-. Honours: Honorary Fellow, Newnham College, Cambridge, 1991; Dr h c (Essex), 1994; Honorary LLD (Westminster), 1996; Honorary DSc (Economics) (London), 1998; Reves Peace Prize, William & Mary College, USA, 1993; Commander, Ouissam Alaouite, Morocco, 1972; Dama Gran Cruz Condor of the Andes, Bolivia, 1986; Grosse Goldene Ehrenzeichen am Bande, Austria, 1993. Address: c/o PNUD, Casilla 9072, La Paz, Bolivia; c/o The Walled Garden, Knill, Nr Presteigne, Powys LD8 2PR, United Kingdom.

ANSTISS Richard Gordon, b. 18 June 1962, Auckland, New Zealand. Environmental Geochemist. m. Sabine Nathalie Anstiss, 1 son. Education: BSc (Hons), University of Auckland, 1985; PhD, Victoria University of Wellington, 1990. Appointments: Senior Lecturer, Director, Trace Element Research Group, Auckland University of Technology, 1996-; Arsenic Consultant, New Zealand Ministry of Foreign Affairs and Trade, Bangladesh, 1998-2002; Visiting Associate Professor, Rajshahi University, Bangladesh, 2000-; Arsenic Technical Advisor, UNICEF, Wateraid, 1998-2000; Water Quality, Health Technical Advisor, Government Agencies, Universities, NGO's, 2000-. Publications include: Author: Study of leakage of long-term radionuclides at Moruroa and Fangataufa atolls, French Polynesia, 1996; Co-author: A sustainable community based arsenic mitigation pilot project in Bangladesh, 2001; Author: Bridging science and technology with development, 2004. Honours: Senior Prize in Geology, University of Auckland, 1983; Scholar, New Zealand Government, 1985-89; Jacob Joseph Scholar, VUW, 1989; Chemistry Division Research Award, DSIR,

1989; Fellow: University of California, Berkeley, 1990-91, Stanford University, 1991-93, CNRS, France, 1993-95, University of Auckland, 1996; Grantee, AUT, 1997, NZMFAT, 1998-2001; Listed in Who's Who publications and biographical dictionaries. Memberships: Association of Chemistry and the Environment; EnHealth; Development Network; RSNZ Nuclear Tests Effects Forum, 1996; Voting Assembly Greenpeace, 1997; Amnesty International; Auckland Refugee Council, 2001-2003. Address: Auckland University of Technology, St Pauls Street, Auckland 1020, Private Bag 92006, New Zealand. E-mail: richard.anstiss@aut.ac.nz

ANTIA H M, b. 6 November 1955, Indore, India. Scientist. Education: BSc, University of Indore, 1973; MSc, Indian Institute of Technology, 1975; PhD, Bombay University, 1979. Appointment: Astrophysics Group, Tata Institute of Fundamental Research, Mumbai, 1979-. Publications: Numerical Methods for Scientists and Engineers, 1991; About 60 research papers in various scientific journals. Honour: Gold Medal, Indore University, 1973. Memberships: Fellow, Indian Academy of Science, Bangalore; International Astronomical Union; Astronomical Society of India. Address: Astrophysics Group, Tata Institute of Fundamental Research, Homi Bhabha Road, Mumbai 400005, India.

ANTONIONI Michelangelo, b. 29 September 1913, Ferrara, Italy. Film Director. m. (1) Letizia, 1942, (2) Enrica Fico, 1986. Education: University of Bologna. Appointments: Films include: Gente del Po, 1943-47; Amorosa Menzogna, 1949; NU, 1948; Sette Canne un Vestito; La Villa dei Mostri; Superstizione, 1949; Documentaries: Cronaca di un Amore, 1950; La Signora Senza Camelie, 1951-52; I Vinti, 1952; Amore in Citta, 1953; Le Amiche, 1955; Il Grido, 1957; L'Avventura, 1959; La Notte, 1961; L'Eclisse, 1962; Il Deserto Rosso, 1964; Blow Up, 1966; Zabriskie Point, 1970; Chung Kuo-China, 1972; The Passenger, 1974; Il Mistero di Oberwald, 1979; Identificazione di una Donna, 1982; Fumbha Mela, 1989; Roma 90, 1989; Beyond the Clouds, 1995. Honours: City of Munich Prize; Critics Award, Cannes, 1960; Silver Bear, Berlin Film Festival, 1961; Golden Lion, XXV Venice Film Festival, 1964; Golden Palm, Cannes Film Festival, 1967; Best Director, Annual Awards, National Society of Film Critics; Grand Prix, Cannes Film Festival, 1982; Knight Grand Cross; Order of Merit; Commander, Ordre des Arts et des Lettres, 1992; Legion d'honneur. Address: Via Flemming III, 00191, Rome, Italy.

ANTONOV Igor Nickolaevich, b. 17 September 1954, Saratov, Russia. Physicist. m. Natalia Shurigina, 1 son, 1 daughter. Education: Diploma, Physics, Saratov University, 1977; Doctor of Technical Sciences, 1990. Appointments: Scientific worker, Saratov Politechnical Institute, 1977-81; Head, Department of Design Office, Electronic Institute, Academy of Sciences, 1981-92; Assistant Professor, Technical University, Saratov, 1992-. Publications: Over 50 articles to professional journals; 4 patents in the field; 1 monograph. Honours: Doctor of Technical Sciences; Zvezda Vernadskogo, 2001. Memberships: Member, New York Academy of Sciences. Address: Mezhdunarodnaya Str 18, Apartment 17, 410052, Saratov, Russia. E-mail: aea@sstu.runnet.ru

ANYA Chinasa C (Chinny), b. 9 February 1956, Awlaw, Nigeria. Materials Scientist; Engineer. Divorced, 2 sons. Education: MSc, Metallurgy and Engineering Materials, Polytechnic University, Bucharest, Romania, 1976-81; PhD, Metallurgy, University of Strathclyde, Glasgow, Scotland, 1986-89. Appointments: Lecturer, Metallurgy and Materials Science, Member, Faculty Appointments and Promotion Committee, Enugu State University of Science and Technology, Enugu, Nigeria, 1982-86; Research Associate, Department of Metallurgy and Engineering Materials, University of Strathclyde, Glasgow, Scotland, 1990-94; Research Assistant, Department of Materials, University of Oxford, Oxford, England, 1994-96; Process Controller, Dairy Crest Plc, Kiddlington, Oxford, England, 1997-. Publications: Author and co-author of 23 scientific and engineering papers which include: Microcracking and its Toughening Effect in Al_2O_3-SiCp 'Nanocomposites', 1997; Wet Erosive Wear of Alumina and its Composites with SiC Nano-Particles, 1998; A more consistent explanation of the strength of Al_2O_3/SiC nanocomposite after grinding and annealing, 2000. Honours include: Nigerian Government Scholar to Romania, 1975; Distinction in MSc Examination, 1981; Commonwealth Scholar to UK, 1986; Petch Prize for best Doctoral Thesis, 1990; Listed in Who's Who publications and biographical dictionaries. Memberships: Associate Member, Institute of Materials, Minerals and Mining, UK; Associate Member, Market Research Society of UK. Address: 37 Beech Crescent, Kidlington, Oxfordshire OX5 1DP, England. E-mail: cc.anya@ntlworld.com

ANYANWU Chukwukre, b. 14 April 1943, Nigeria. Physician. m. Grace, 5 sons, 1 daughter. Education: BA, Biology and Chemistry, St Joseph's College, Philadelphia, 1971; Postdoctorate Fellowship, Department of Nuclear Medicine, Temple Hospital, Philadelphia, 1982; Doctor of Medicine, Centro de Estudio Universitario de Santo Domingo, 1981. Appointments: Chemical Engineer, Celanese Plastic Company, Summit, New Jersey, USA, 1971-73; Mental Health Technician, Norristown State Hospital, 1978-79; John F Kennedy Memorial Hospital, 1981-83; Department of Obstetrics and Gynaecology, Lagos University Teaching Hospital, Nigeria, 1983-85; Therapist, Guiffre Medical Center and Misericordia Hospital, Philadelphia, 1985-88; Executive Director, AB Associates Inc, 1989-98; Independent Instructor, Community College of Philadelphia and Temple University, 1989-98. Publications: Many articles and papers in professional and popular journals. Honours: Outstanding Microbiology Lab Instructor, St Joseph's, 1970; Trophy, Golden Poet Award, World of Poetry, 1989; Founder, Chairman and CEO, African Congress, USA, 1995; First African immigrant in late 20th Century to contest for City Council-at-Large, Philadelphia, 1999; First Chairman and CEO, African Community Organisations, to pursue and apply for Independent Charter School for Immigrant Children K-8th Grade, Philadelphia School District, 2001, 2003; First Chairman, African Community Organizations, to endorse mayoral candidate, Philadelphia, 2003. Memberships: American Association for the Advancement of Science; St Joseph's University Biology/Chemistry Alumni; St Joseph's University Medical Alumni; St Joseph's University Nighthawk; World Affair Council; African Congress USA; National Association of Nigerian Professionals; The American Journal of Medicine; Pennsylvania Certified Addiction Counselors. Address: PO Box 38127, Philadelphia, PA 19140, USA.

ANZRANNII Avikm Axim, (Vikram Mehta), b. 18 June 1947, Shimla, India. Lecturer in English; Poet. m. 5 May 1979, 1 son, 1 daughter. Education: BSc, Engineering, Delhi College of Engineering, 1966; BA, Economics, SDB College, Shimla, 1968; MA, English, Regional Centre for P G Studies, Shimla, 1970. Appointment: Lecturer in English, Head of Department of Applied Science and Humanities, Government Polytechnic College for Women, Kandaghat, India. Publications: General English for Polytechnic Students, 1974; The Lover (for private circulation), 1976; Lillian O Ranni: A Love Song, 1987; Prem Geet (Hindi verses), 1990; 55 Love Songs of Anzrannii, 1995. Contributions to: Poetcrit; Poet, Madras; Marande; Durst; Ranchi. Honours: DLitt, WAAC, USA, 1990; Diploma of Excellence in Poetry, International Poets Academy, Madras, 1990. Memberships: World

Poetry Society, Madras; Writer's Forum, Ranchi; World Congress of Poets, California, USA. Address: Roop Ankush, Jakko, Shimla, (HP)-171001, India.

APASOV M Alexander, b. 13 June 1950, Gorno-Altaisk, Russia. Physicist; Educator. m. Galina Vasilyevna Yemets, 1 son. Education: Engineer-Physicist, Tomsk Polytechnical Institute, 1967-73; Postgraduate, 1981-85; Candidate of Science, 1991; Associate Professor, 2000; Doctor of Science, 2002. Appointments: Laboratory Assistant, Joint Institute for Nuclear Research, Dubna, USSR, 1971-73; Senior Laboratory Assistant, Physical Energetic Institute, Obninsk, 1973-75; Engineer-Designer, Bolshevik Works, Leningrad, 1975-77; Chief of the Laboratory, Machine Works, Yurga, 1977-92; Chief of the Office, Abrasive Works, Yurga, 1992-95; Department Head, Dean, Tomsk Polytechnic University Branch, Yurga, Russia, 1995-2004. Publications: Welding Destruction (monograph), 2002; Special Electometallurgy (textbook), 2003; Physical Foundation of Non-Destructive Testing During Welding, 2004; Method to Analyse Failure of Welded Joints (Certificate); Method of Non-Melting Revealing (patent); Other patents and articles. Honours: Prize-Winner (Laureate) Nuclear Physics, Obninsk, 1974; Prize-Winner (Laureate), Technical Physics, Yurga, 1980. Memberships: Deputy, Town Soviet of People's Deputies, 1990-95, 1997-99. Address: Moskovskay str. 26, Apart. 4, Yurga, Kemerovo Region, Russia 652050. E-mail: mchm@ud.tpu.edu.ru

APELAND Svein Gisle, b. 21 December 1953, Haugesund, Norway. Medical Doctor; General Practitioner; Youth Leader. m. Kari Nilsen, 2 daughters. Education: MD, 1979; Specialist Family Medicine (General Practitioner), 1995. Appointments: Hospital Practice, Medical and Surgical, Hammerfest, Norway, 1980-81; General Practitioner, 1981-94; Hospital Practice, Psychology, Haugesund, Norway, 1995-95; General Practice, Haugesund, 1995-; Unpaid Youth Leader, YMCA/YMCA-Scouts, Local Leader, Regional Leader and at the National Level, 1970-. Honour: Gold Medal, Highest Award of the Norwegian YMCA-Scouts. Memberships: YMCA/YMCA-Scouts: Norwegian Astronomical Association; Norwegian Medical Association. Address: Kvevegen 19, N-5517 Haugesund, Norway. E-mail: kanape@online.no

APFEL Necia H(alpern), b. 31 July 1930, Mt Vernon, New York, USA. Science Writer. m. Donald A Apfel, 7 September 1952, deceased, 1 son, 1 daughter. Education: BA magna cum laude, Tufts University, 1952; Radcliffe College Graduate School, 1952-53; Northwestern University Graduate School, 1962-69. Publications: Astronomy One (with J Allen Hynek), 1972; Architecture of the Universe (with J Allen Hynek), 1979; It's All Relative; Einstein's Theory of Relativity, 1981; The Moon and Its Exploration, 1982; Stars and Galaxies, 1982; Astronomy and Planetology, 1983, soft-cover edition as Astronomy Projects for Young Scientists, 1984; Calendars, 1985; It's All Elementary From Atoms to the Quantum World of Quarks, Leptons, and Gluons, 1985; Space Station, 1987; Space Law, 1988; Nebulae: The Birth and Death of Stars, 1988; Voyager to the Planets, 1991; Orion the Hunter, 1995. Contributions to: Various articles to Odyssey magazine; Ask Ulysses, and I/O Port monthly columns. Honours: Phi Beta Kappa, 1952; Nebulae chosen as 1 of 100 Best Children's Books, 1988. Memberships: Society of Midland Authors; Society of Children's Book Writers; Astronomical Society of the Pacific; American Association for the Advancement of Science; Planetary Society. Address: 3461 University Avenue, Highland Park, IL 60035, USA.

APOSTOLOS-CAPPADONA Diane, b. 10 May 1948, Trenton, New Jersey, USA. Research Professor. Education: BA, Religion, George Washington University, 1970; MA, Religion, 1973; MA,

Religion and Culture, Catholic University of America, 1979; PhD, American Civilisation, George Washington University, 1988. Appointments: Lecturer, Religion and Art, Center for Community Education, Bellarmine College, 1974; Professor, Lecturer, Religion and Art, Georgetown University, SSCE, 1978-; Visiting Lecturer, Religion and Art, Institute of Religious Study, University of St Thomas, 1979; Lecturer, Religion and the Arts, Humanities Institute, 1979-80; Lecturer, Religion, Mount Vernon College, 1980-85; Lecturer, Religion, George Washington University, 1981-86; Visiting Lecturer, Religion and Arts, Catholic University of America, 1985, 1986, 1989; Adjunct Professor, Art and Culture, Liberal Study Program, Georgetown University, 1985-; Adjunct Faculty in Christianity and Art, Pacific School of Religion, 1985-86, 1988-; Teaching Fellow, Graduate Theology Foundation, 1989-93; Visiting Faculty, Irish Theological Workshops, Cooleen High School, 1992; Adjunct Professor, Center for Muslim-Christian Understanding, Georgetown University, 1996-; Visiting Professor, Sophia University, 1999. Publications: Dictionary of Christian Art, 1994; Isamu Noguchi: Essays and Conversations, 1994; The Spirit and the Vision: The Influence of Christian Romanticism on 19th Century American Art, 1995; Encyclopaedia of Women in Religious Art, 1996; In Search of Mary Magdalene: Images and Traditions, 2002. Honours: Honorary Member, Gamma Tau Chapter of Alpha Sigma Lambda, National Honor Society; College Art Association, Travel Grant; Grant in Aid of Research, American Council of Learned Societies, 1989; Research Grant, American Academy of Religion, 1990; Senior Fellowship, Center for the Study of World Religion, Harvard University, 1996-97; Excellence in Teaching Faculty Award, Georgetown University, 2000; Annual Award for Excellence in the Arts, The Newington-Cropsey Foundation, 2000; Vicennial Medical for Faculty Service, Georgetown University, 2003; Post-Doctoral Research Award, Cultural Studies Center, The Newington-Cropsey Foundation, 2003-04; Listed in numerous Who's Who publications. Memberships: American Academy of Religion; American Association of Museums; American Association of University Women; American Study Association; Associations for Religious and Intellectual Life; College Art Association; College Theological Society; Congress on Research in Dance; International Council on Museums; The Society for Art, Religion and Contemporary Culture. Address: Centre for Muslim-Christian Understanding, Georgetown University, ICC #260, Washington, DC 20057-1052, USA.

APPLEBY Malcolm Arthur, b. 6 January 1946, Beckenham, Kent, England. Artist. m. Philippa Swann, 1 daughter. Education: Beckenham School of Art; Ravensbourne College of Art; Central School of Arts and Crafts; Sir John Cass School of Art; Royal College of Art. Career: Artist, Designer and Engraver; Held one-man art exhibition, Aberdeen Art Gallery, 1998. Honours: Littledale Scholar, 1969; Liveryman, Worshipful Company of Goldsmiths, 1991; Hon D Litt, Heriot-Watt, 2000. Address: Aultbeag, Grandtully, by Aberfeldy, Perthshire PH15 2QU, Scotland.

APPLEDORN Mary Jeanne van, b. 2 October 1927, Holland, Michigan, USA. Music Composer. Education: BM, Piano, Eastman School of Music, University of Rochester, New York, 1948; MM, Music Theory, 1950; PhD, Music, 1966; Post doctoral, Computer Synthesised Sound, Massachusetts Institute of Technology, 1982. Appointments: Paul Whitfield Horn Professor, Music, School of Music, Texas Tech University, Lubbock, Texas, USA, 1950-. Publications: Concerto for trumpet and band; Passages for trombone and piano; Ayre for strings; Rhapsody for trumpet and harp; Postcards to John for guitar; Freedom of Youth; Rhapsody for violin and orchestra; Symphony for percussion orchestra, 2000; Meliora: Symphony for winds and percussion; Gestures for clarinet quartet; Miniatures for trombone quartet; Soundscapes for bassoon and string quintet; A Symphony of Celebration for orchestra, 2003; others. Honours: International Trumpet Guild Award for Trio Italiano; ASCAP Standard Panel Awards, 1980-2003; Premier Prix, World Carillon Federation, Dijon, France; Delta Kappa Gamma International Scholarship; IX Premio Ancona, Italy, for Liquid Gold; National Council of Alpha Chi Omega's Award. Listed in: New Grove's Dictionary of Music and Musicians, 2000. Memberships: Mu Phi Epsilon; Delta Kappa Gamma; ASCAP. Address: School of Music, P O Box 42033, Texas Tech University, Lubbock, TX 79409-2033, USA.

APPLEYARD Sir Raymond K, b. 5 October 1922, Birtley, England. Scientist. m. Joan Greenwood, 1947, 1 son, 1 daughter. Education: Trinity College, Cambridge. Appointments: Instructor, Physics and Biophysics, Tale University, 1949-51; Fellow, Natural Sciences, Rockerfeller Foundation, 1951-53; Associate Research Officer, Atomic Energy of Canada Ltd, 1953-56; Secretary, UN Science Committee on the Effects of Atomic Radiation, 1957-61; Director, Biology Services, European Atomic Energy Community (EURATOM), 1961-73; Executive Secretary, European Molecular Biology Organisation, 1965-73; Secretary, European Molecular Biology Conference, 1969-73; Director General, Science and Technical Information and Information Management Commission of European Communities, 1973-81; Information Market and Innovation, 1981-86; President, Institute of Information Sciences, 1981-82; Institute of Translation and Interpreting, 1989-94; Honorary Doctor of Medicine (Ulm), 1977.

APSELOFF Marilyn Fain, b. 18 March 1934, Attleboro, USA. Professor of English, retired. m. Stanford S Apseloff, 21 November 1956, 3 sons, 1 daughter. Education: Bryn Mawr College, 1952-54; BA, 1954-56, MA, 1957, University of Cincinnati. Appointment: Instructor, Professor, Kent State University, 1968-. Publications include: They Wrote For Children Too, 1989; Elizabeth George Speare, 1991; Co-author: Nonsense Literature For Children, 1989. Honours: Graduate Fellow, University of Cincinnati, 1956-57; Honor Book, Nons Lit, 1990. Membership: Children's Literature Association. Address: English Department, Kent State University, Satterfield Hall, Kent, OH 44242, USA.

APTED Michael, b. 10 February 1941, Aylesbury, England. Film Director. Education: Cambridge University. Career: Researcher, Granada TV, 1963; Investigative Reporter, World in Action; Director debut as feature film director, The Triple Echo, 1972; Other films include Stardust, 1975; The Squeeze, 1977; Agatha, 1979; Coal Miner's Daughter, 1980; Continental Divide, 1981; P'TangYang Kipperbang, Gorky Park, 1983; Firstborn, 1984; Critical Condition, Gorillas in the Mist, 1988; Class Action, 1990; Incident at Oglala, Thunderheart, 1992; Blink, Moving the Mountain, 1993; Nell, 1994; Extreme Measures, 1996; Enigma, 2001; Enough, 2002; Television direction includes Coronation Street episodes, The Lovers comedy series, Folly Foot children's series, Another Sunday and Sweet F A, Kisses at Fifty, Poor Girl, Jack Point, UP document series including 28 UP, 35 UP, 42 UP; Always Outnumbered. Address: Michael Apted Film Co, 1901 Avenue of the Stars, Suite 1245, Los Angeles, CA 90067, USA.

AQUARO Giovanni, b. 17 April 1920, Mottola, Italy. Professor Emeritus formerly Professor of Mathematical Analysis. m. Maria Laura, 1 son. Education: University Degree, 1945; Qualification for University Teaching, 1958; University Professor, 1963. Appointments: University Assistant, 1945-47; Lecturer of Mathematics, 1947-63; Professor of Mathematical Analysis, University of Bari, 1963-71, 1975-96 Professor of Mathematical Analysis, University of Rome, 1971-75; Retired, 1997. Publications: Publications in mathematics. Honour: Gold Medal of Società Italiana delle Science, 1993. Memberships: Accademia delle Scienze di Torino; Accademia Pugiese delle Scienze. Address: Viale Salandra, 10/c, Sc A, 70124 Bari, Italy.

AQUINO Corazon (Cory), BA, b. 25 January 1933. Politician. m. Benigno S Aquino Jnr, 1954, assassinated 1983, 1 son, 4 daughter. Education: Mount St Vincent College, NY; Lived in USA in exile with husband, 1980-83. Appointments: President, Philippines, post-Marcos, 1986-92. Membership: United Nationalist Democratic Organization, 1985-; William Fulbright Prize for International Peace, 1996; Ramon Magsaysay Award for International Understanding, 1998. Address: 25 Times Street, Quezon City, Philippines.

ARACI Emre, b. 22 December 1968. Music Director. Education: BMus Hons, 1994, PhD, 1999, Faculty of Music, University of Edinburgh. Appointments: Founder, Conductor, President, Edinburgh University String Orchestra, 1992-97; Instructor, Department of Islamic and Middle-Eastern Studies and Centre for Continuing Education, University of Edinburgh; Post-doctoral Research Associate, The Skilliter Centre for Ottoman Studies, University of Cambridge; Director, The London Academy Ottoman Court Music Ensemble, 2000-. Publications: Many journal and newspaper articles in English and Turkish; Musical compositions, books and CDs. Honours: University of Edinburgh, Faculty of Music Merit Bursary, 1992, 1993, 1994; Gwynn Clutterbuck Scholarship, 1993; PhD sponsored by the Lord Inchcape's Foundation and Lady Lucinda Mackay; 3 year post-doctoral research scholarship, Türk Ekonomi Bankas . Memberships: The Anglo-Turkish Society Incorporated Society of Musicians; Turkish Area Study Group; The Donizetti Society; The Byron Society; The Savile Club; Royal Over-Seas League. Address: Ivinghoe Suite, The Grand, The Leas, Folkestone, Kent CT20 2LR. E-mail: emrearaci@yahoo.com

ARAFAT Yasser (Pseudonym of Mohammed Abed Ar'ouf Arafat), b. 24 August 1929, Jerusalem. Palestinian Resistance Leader. m. Sulia Tawil, 1991. Education: Cairo University. Appointments: Joined League of Palestinian Students, 1944; Member, Executive Committee, 1950; President, 1952-56; Formed with others, Al Fatah Movement, 1956; Engineer, Egypt, 1956; Kuwait, 1957-65; President, Executive Committee of Palestines National Liberation Movement (Al Fatah), 1968-; Chair, Executive Committee, Palestine Libertation Organisation, 1968-; President, Central Committee; Head, Political Department, 1973-; Chair, Palestine National Authority (PNA); Minister of the Interior, 1994-96, (acting) 2001; President, Palestine Legislative Council, 1996-; General Commander, Palestinian Revolutionary Forces. Honours: Shared Nobel Peace Prize, 1994; Addressed UN General Assembly, 1974; Joluot Curie Gold Medal; World Peace Council, 1975. Address: Palestine National Authority, Jericho Area, West Bank.

ARAGALL GARRIGA Giacomo (Jaime), b. 6 June 1939, Barcelona, Spain. Tenor. Education: Studied with Francesco Puig in Barcelona and with Vladimir Badiali in Milan. Debut: La Fenice, Venice, 1963 in the first modern performance of Verdi's Jerusalem. Career: La Scala Milan in 1963 as Mascagni's Fritz; In 1965 sang in Haydn's Le Pescatrici with Netherlands Opera and at the Edinburgh Festival; Vienna Staatsoper debut in 1966 as Rodolfo in La Bohème; Covent Garden debut in 1966 as the Duke of Mantua; Metropolitan Opera debut in 1968; Guest appearances in Berlin, Italy, San Francisco and at the Lyric Opera Chicago; Sang at San Carlo Opera Naples in 1972 in a revival of Donizetti's Caterina Cornaro; Festival appearances at Bregenz and Orange in 1984 as Cavaradossi and Don Carlos; Sang Gabriele Adorno at Barcelona in 1990 and Don Carlos at the Orange Festival in 1990;

Sang Rodolfo at Barcelona in 1991 and Don Carlos at the Deutsche Opera Berlin, 1992; Sang Cavaradossi at the Opéra Bastille, 1994. Other roles include Pinkerton, Romeo in I Capuleti e i Montecchi, Werther and Gennaro in Lucrezia Borgia. Recordings: La Traviata; Lucrezia Borgia; Faust; Rigoletto; Simon Boccanegra; Madama Butterfly. Address: c/o Stafford Law Associates, 6 Barham Close, Weybridge, Surrey KT13 9PR, England.

ARAI Asao, b. 10 January 1954, Chichibu, Saitama. Mathematician; Mathematical Physicist; University Professor. m. Sayoko Anada, 1 daughter. Education: BS, Chiba University, 1976; MS, University of Tokyo, 1979; DS, Gakushuin University, 1986. Appointments: Assistant Professor, Tokyo Institute of Technology, 1980-86; Lecturer, 1986-92, Associate Professor, 1992-95, Professor, 1995-, Hokkaido University. Publications: Hilbert Space and Quantum Mechanics, Kyouritsu-shuppan, 1997, in Japanese; Fock Spaces and Quantum Fields, Nippon Hyouronsha, 2000, in Japanese; many articles in professional journals. Listed in: Biographical Publication. Memberships: New York Academy of Sciences; International Association of Mathematical Physics; The Mathematical Society of Japan. Address: Department of Mathematics, Hokkaido University, Sapporo 060 0810, Japan.

ARAIZA (Jose) Francisco, b. 4 October 1950, Mexico City, Mexico. Singer (Tenor). Divorced, 2 sons, 2 daughters. Education: University of Mexico City; Vocal studies with Irma Gonzalez and Erika Kubacsek (Repertory). Debut: As First Prisoner in Beethoven's Fidelio, Mexico City, 1970. Career: With Karlsruhe Opera, 1974-78; Permanent member of Zurich Opera House, 1978-; Guest appearances in Vienna, Munich, Hamburg, Berlin, Covent Garden London, Opera Bastille Paris, La Scala of Milan, Rome, Parma, Barcelona, Madrid, San Francisco, Chicago, Buenos Aires and Japan; Also at the international festivals of Aix-en-Provence, Orange, Bayreuth, Salzburg (debut in 1980 under Karajan), Edinburgh, Rossini Festival Pesaro, Schubert Festival Hohenems, Richard Strauss Festival, Garmisch; Operatic repertoire ranges from Mozart and Rossini in 1983 to dramatic Italian and French repertory to Wagner roles such as Lohengrin in Venice 1990 and Walther in Die Meistersinger von Nürnberg with Metropolitan Opera in New York, 1993; Renowned Lieder and Concert Singer. Recordings include: Die schöne Müllerin; All major Mozart roles including Tamino, Belmonte, Ferrando, Don Ottavio and Idomeneo; Il Barbiere di Siviglia, Faust, Les Contes d'Hoffmann, La Bohème, Hagenbach in La Wally, Der Freischütz; Das Lied von der Erde, Beethoven's 9th Symphony, Die Schöpfung and Mozart's Requiem; Arias and Lieder; Several videos including: La Cenerentola; The Abduction from the Seraglio. Honours: Deutscher Schallplattenpreis; Orphee d'Or; Mozart Medal, University of Mexico City; Otello d'Oro: Goldener Merkur, Best Performer's Award, Munich, 1996; Named Professor, Staatliche Musikhochschule, Stuttgart, Germany, 2003. Address: c/o Kunstlermanagement, M Kursidem, Tal 15, 80331 Munich, Germany.

ARAKI Huzihiro, b. 28 July 1932, Tokyo, Japan. University Professor of Mathematics. m. Chieko Kawaguchi, 2 sons. Education: BSc, 1955, MSc, 1957, DSc, 1961, Kyoto University; PhD, Princeton University, 1960. Appointments: Assistant, Faculty of Engineering, 1957-61, Lecturer, 1961-64, Associate Professor, Research Institute Mathematical Science, 1964-65, Professor, 1966-96, Director, Research Institute for Mathematical Science, 1993-96, Kyoto University; Professor, Department of Mathematics, Faculty of Science and Technology, Science University of Tokyo, 1996-2001; Retired, 2001; Professor Emeritus, Kyoto University, 1996-. Publications: About 150 articles in scientific journals. Honours: UAP Scientific Prize, Paris, France, 1990; Asahi Prize for 1996, Tokyo, Japan, 1997; Poincaré Prize, International

Association of Mathematical Physics, 2003. Memberships: International Association of Mathematical Physics; Mathematical Society of Japan; Physical Society of Japan; American Mathematical Society. Address: 8-4 Shimogamo-Yakocho, Sakyoku, Kyoto 606-0837, Japan.

ARBNORI Pjeter, b. 18 January 1935, Durrës, Albania. Academician; Writer; Member of International Informatization Academy in General Consultative Status of United Nations, New York, Geneve; Member of Parliament. m. Suzana Gjeluci, 16 June 1991, 1 son, 1 daughter. Education: Degree, Philology, 1960. Appointments: Teacher, 1953; Teacher of Literature, 1960-61; Founder, Social Democratic (illegal) Party, 1960; Sentenced to death and imprisoned, 28 years, 1961-89; Carpenter, 1989; Founder, Chairman, Democratic Party of Shkodra, 1990; MP, 1991; MP, Speaker of Parliament, 1992; MP, Speaker, 1996; MP, 1997 Commission on Human Rights; MP, 2001 Commission on Human Rights, 1997; Hunger strike, 20 days, August-September 1997; Supporter of Access of Opposition Parties in Electric Media, 1997. Publications include: Novels: Long Stories: Kur dynden vikingët; Bukuroshja me Hijen; Mugujt e Mesjetës; E bardha dhe e zeza; E panjohura; Vdekja e Gebelsit; Shtëpia e mbetur përgjysmë; Vorbulla; Nga jeta në burgjet komuniste; Letter from Prison; The Fight to Remain a Man: 10300 days and nights in the Prisons of Communism; The Martyrs, I Martiri, The New Martyrs in Albania (English); Translations: Histoire d'Angleterre, Andre Maurois; The Rise and Fall of the Third Reich, Willam Shirer. Honours: People's Teacher; Torch of Democracy; Grand Officier de L'Ordre de Pleiade; The Pride of Scutari; Citizen of Honor of Vaudejës; President of the Board, Institute for Political Research "Alcide De Gasperi". Address: Rruga "Emin Duraku", Pallati 10/b, Tirana, Albania.

ARBOLEDA-FLÓREZ Julio, b. 7 February 1939, Colombia. Psychiatrist; Epidemiologist. m. 1 son, 1 daughter. Education: MD, Universidad Nacional Colombia, 1964; D Psych, University of Ottawa, Canada, 1970; Fellowship in Forensics, University of Toronto, 1971; PhD, University of Calgary, 1994. Appointments: Instructor, Faculty of Medicine and Head, Forensic Psychiatry Service, Royal Ottawa Hospital, 1970-75; Clinical Director, Regional Psychiatric Centre, Abbotsford, British Columbia, 1975-77; Director, Department of Psychiatry, Calgary General Hospital, 1988-97; Director, Forensic Division, Faculty of Medicine, University of Calgary, 1977-98; Chair, Department of Psychiatry, Queen's University, Canada, 1998-; Professor, Department of Psychiatry and Community Health Science and Adjunct Professor of Law, University of Calgary; Consultant: Pan-American Health Organisation, World Health Organisation, Department of Justice, Alta; Director, WHO Calgary Collaborating Centre for Research and Training in Mental Health; Visiting Professor at various universities abroad. Publications: Author: Canada's Health, 1996; Co-author: Mental Health Laws and Practice, 1994; Principal Author: Ethical and Legal Issues in Mental Health, 1995; The Facts about Mental Illness and Violence 1996; Forensic Psychiatric Medicine, 1999; Over 150 peer reviewed articles. Honours: Honorary Member: World Psychiatric Association, 1993, Psychiatric Association of Ecuador, 1994; Member Emeritus, Department of Forensic Psychiatry, Brazilian Psychiatric Association; Recipient, Bruno Cormier Award, Canadian Academy of Psychiatry and the Law, 1997; Board Member of several psychiatric journals. Memberships: Canadian Medical Association; Canadian Psychiatric Association; World Psychiatric Association; American Psychiatric Association; Secretary General, International Council of Prison Medical Services; President, International Journal of Law and Mental Health. Address: Queen's University Kingston, ON K7L 3N6, Canada. E-mail: ja9@post.queensu.ca

ARCAND Jean-Louis Leslie, b. 4 October 1964, Ebolowa, Cameroon. Professor. m. Francesca Bassi, 2 daughters. Education: BA, high honours, Swarthmore College, 1985; MPhil, Cambridge University, 1986; PhD, MIT, 1991. Appointments: Assistant Professor, 1991-96, Associate Professor, 1996-97, CRDE, University of Montreal; Professor, CERDI-CNRS, Université d'Auvergne, 1997-. Publications: Numerous articles in professional journals. Honours: Founding Fellow, European Development Network. Memberships: Journal of African Economics; Revue d'economie du dévelopment. Address: CERDI-CNRS, Université d'Auvergne, 65 boulevard Francois Mitterand, Clement Ferrand, France. E-mail: arcandjl@alum.mit.edu Website: www.erdi.org

ARCHANGELSKY Sergio, b. 27 March 1931, Morocco. Palaeontologist. m. Jos Ballester, 1 son, 1 daughter. Education: PhD, Natural Sciences, Buenos Aires University, 1957. Appointments: Professor, La Plata University, 1961-78; Superior Researcher, National Research Council, Argentina, 1985-; Head, Paleobotany Division, Argentine Museum of Natural History, 1985-. Publications: Fundamentals of Palaeobotany, 1970; Fossil Flora of the Baqueró Group, Cretaceous, Patagonia, 2003. Honours: Visiting Professor, Ohio State University, USA, 1984; Corresponding Member, Botanical Society America, 1975; Academician, National Academy Sciences, Cordoba, 1990; Honorary Vice-President, XVI International Botanical Congress, St Louis, USA, 1999. Memberships: Argentine Geological Society; Argentine Palaeontological Society; British Palaeontological Association; Fellow, Paleobotanical Society, India. Address: Urquiza 1132 Vicente, Lopez B1638BWJ, Buenos Aires, Argentina.

ARCHER Jeffrey Howard (Lord Archer of Weston-Super-Mare), b. 15 April 1940, Mark, Somerset, England. Author; Politician. m. Mary Weeden, 2 sons. Education: Brasenose College, Oxford. Appointments: Member, GLC for Havering, 1966-70; Member of Parliament for Louth (Conservative), 1969-74; Deputy Chair, Conservative Party, 1985-86; Sentenced to four years imprisonment for perjury and perverting the course of justice, 2001. Publications: Plays: Not a Penny More, Not a Penny Less, 1975; Shall We Tell the President?, 1977; Kane & Abel, 1979; A Quiver Full of Arrows, 1980; The Prodigal Daughter, 1982; First Among Equals, 1984; A Matter of Honour, 1986; A Twist in the Tale, 1988; As The Crow Flies, 1991; Honour Among Thieves, 1993; Twelve Red Herrings, 1994; The Fourth Estate, 1995; Collected Short Stories, 1997; The Eleventh Commandment, 1998; To Cut a Long Story Short (short stories), 2000; A Prison Diary, 2002; Sons of Fortune, 2003; Plays: Beyond Reasonable Doubt, 1987; Exclusive, 1989; The Accused, 2000. Honours: Queen's Birthday Honours, 1992; Lord Archer of Western Super Mare. Address: Peninsula Heights, 93 Albert Embankment, London SE1 7TY, England.

ARCHIBALD Reginald MacGregor, b. 2 March 1910, Syracuse, New York, USA. Physician; Biochemist. m. Evelyn Stroh, 12 June 1948, 1 son, 1 daughter. Education: BA, University of British Columbia, Canada, 1930; MA, 1932; PhD, University of Toronto, 1934; MD, University of Toronto, Canada, 1939. Appointments: Teaching and Research Assistant, University of British Columbia, Canada, 1932-34; Intern, Pathology, Hospital for Sick Children, Toronto, 1936; Surgeon, 1937, Intern, 1939-40, Toronto General Hospital; Assistant Resident, Hospital of Rockefeller Institute for Medical Research, 1940-42; Professor of Biochemistry, Johns Hopkins University, 1946-48, Chairman of Department; Member, Rockefeller Institute for Medical Research, 1948-49; Professor, Rockefeller University, 1949-80; Professor Emeritus and Senior Physician Emeritus, 1980-. Publications: Publications in numerous scientific journals. Honours:

Dictionary of International Biography

Editorial Boards of Journal of Biological Chemistry, 1948-58; Journal Clinical Endocrinology Metabolism, 1952-60; Child Development, 1954-60. Membership: Lawson Wilkins Society for Pediatric Endocrinology; American Chemical Society; Fell, New York Academy of Sciences; Biochemical Society (UK); Society for Research in Child Development; Medical and Chirurgical Faculty of Maryland; Sigma Xi; Society of Adolescent Medicine; Life Member, Harvey Society; Emeritus Fellow, Non Resident, Explorers Club. Address: 211 Second St NW, Apt 1810, Rochester, MN 55901, USA.

ARCHIBONG Lemmy Gabriel, 12 October 1955, Mbiatok-Itam. Journalism; Public Relations. m. Mary, 4 sons, 4 daughters. Education: OND, Diploma, BA, London School of Journalism, London, England, 1986-88; Distinction (Professional) Certificate in Public Relations, Nigerian Institute of Journalism, Lagos, 1987. Appointments include: Public Relations, Journalistic Services, Freelancing for Magazines, Newspapers and Radio, 1979-1990; Managing Editor, The Option Newspaper, 1991-93; Managing Director, Arch Dimensions Company, 1993-97; Managing Editor, The Ultimate Newspaper, 2001-; Sub Editor, Sensor Newspapers, 2003-. Publications: Columnist – Barracks Road; Issues Revisited; The Nigerian Chronicle; Group of Newspapers – Martinet Columnist in The Ultimate Newspaper; Over 100 articles and papers; Author, Real promises; Mysteries of The Mermaid Exposed and others. Honours include: Best Christian Writers Award from Christian Writers Association of Nigeria, 1991, and others. Memberships include: ANIPR; MNIPR; NUJ, many others. Address: 18 College Road, Mbiatok, Itam – ITU LGA, AKS, Nigeria. E-mail: lemmyga20@yahoo.com

ARDEN-GRIFFITH Paul, b. 18 January 1952, Stockport, England. Singer (Tenor). Education: Royal Manchester and Colleges of Music; GRSM (Teachers), Piano, Singing; ARMCM (Teachers), Piano, Singing; ARMCM (Performers), Singing; Cantica Voice Studio, London; Current Vocal Coach, Anthony Hocking. Debut: Puck in Benjamin Britten's Midsummer Night's Dream, Sadler's Wells Theatre, London, 1973. Career includes: Has sung UK, abroad; Franz Lehar's Merry Widow with English National Opera, London Coliseum; World premiere, Henze's We Come to the River, Covent Garden, 1976; UK premiere, Britten's Paul Bunyan, Aldeburgh Festival, 1976; Carlisle Floyd's Of Mice and Men, Wexford Festival, 1980; Carl Orff's Carmina Burana, Singapore Festival of the Arts, 1984; World concert tours, Hong Kong, Singapore, Sydney, 1983, 1985; Greenwich Festival, 1986-87; World premiere, Phantom of the Opera, London, 1986; Mobil Concert Season; Founder Member, Arts Council Opera 80 UK Touring Company; Guest Soloist, Royal Artillery Orchestra; Prokofiev's The Duenna, Wexford Festival, 1989; Count Almaviva in Rossini Bicentennial UK Tour of Barber of Seville, 1992; Opera Gala Nights Series aboard Cunard QE2, 1993; Puccini's Il Tabarro, Barezzi Opera, 1993; Miami, 1994-95; Rossini's Count Ory, White Horse Opera, England, 1996; Lloyd Webber's Sunset Boulevard, Germany, 1997-98; Verdi's La Traviata, White Horse Opera, England, 1998; Mozart's Die Zauberflöte, White Horse Opera, England, 1999; Puccini's La Boheme, Somerset Opera, UK, 2003; Puccini's Madam Butterfly, White Horse Opera, England, 2003; Sondheim's Sweeney Todd, Covent Garder, London, 2004. Address: c/o Ken Spencer Personal Management, 138 Sandy Hill Road, Woolwich, London SE18 7BA, England.

ARDOVA Asya Lazarevna, b. 11 October 1972, St Petersburg, Russia. Musician; Philologist; Publisher. Education: Diploma with Honours, Music College, Rimsky-Korsakov State Conservatoire, St Petersburg, 1989-93; Diploma with Honours, Pedagogical Hertsen University, St Petersburg, 1994-99. Appointments: Pianist-Executant, 1994-; Concert Master at the University, 1994-;

Managing Secretary, Association of Modern Music, 1996-; Recording modern composers on CD, 1996-; Editorial Board Manager, Compozitor Publishers, St Petersburg, 1999-. Publications: Monographs about Firtich and Avante-garde, 1999; Annotations to Smorgonskaya, Slonimsky; Synopses to Patlayenko, Tchaikovsky; Translations into English of: Letters of Shostakovich to Tishchenko; Libretto by Ya. Gordin to Ivan Grozny by Slonimsky; Albums: Petersburg Music 18th Century; Petersburg Music, 19th Century; Petersburg Music, 20th Century; J S Bach Padilas, Flute Sonatas (introductions to editions). Honours: Diploma with Honours, Pedagogical University, 1999; Diploma for Merits in the Professional Sphere, International Biographical Centre, 2000. Membership: Professional Women's Advisory Board. Address: Serebristiy Blvd 26-230, 197227 St Petersburg, Russia. E-mail: office@compozitor.spb.ru Website: http://www.compozitor.spb.ru

AREM Joel Edward, b. 28 December 1943, New York, USA. Mineralogist; Gemologist. m. Deborah, 1 son, 1 daughter. Education: BS, Geology, Brooklyn College, 1964; MA, Geology, Harvard University, 1967; PhD, Mineralogy, 1970. Appointments include: Consultant, US Department of Commerce, 1975-76; Consultant, Encyclopaedia Britannica Educational Corp, 1975-76; Consultant, Jewellers Circular-Keystone, 1978-85; President, Accredited Gemologists Association, 1977-79; Co-Founder, Editorial Board, PreciouStones Newsletter, 1978-84. Publications: Crystal Chemistry and Structure of Idocrase, PhD Dissertation, 1970; Man-Made Crystals, 1973; Rocks and Minerals, 1973; Gems and Jewelry, 1975, 2nd edition, 1992; Color Encyclopedia of Gemstones, 1977, 2nd edition, 1987; Discovering Rocks and Minerals, 1991. Honours include: Harvard University Scholarships, 1964-66; National Science Foundation Scholarships, 1966-68; Sigma Xi; Phi Beta Kappa. Memberships: Fellow, Gemmological Association of Great Britain; Fellow, Canadian Gemmological Association; Mineralogical Society of America; American Association for Crystal Growth; Mineral Museums Advisory Council; Friends of Mineralogy. Address: PO 5056, Laytonsville, MD 20882, USA.

ARENAS Richard Botter, b. 21 September 1960, Pasay City, Philippines. Chief of Surgical Oncology; Associate Professor of Surgery; Associate Professor of Biology. m. Patricia M Boone. Education: BA, magna cum laude, Chemistry, Washington University, 1982; Doctorate of Medicine, UMDNJ, Robert Wood Johnson Medical School, 1986. Appointments: Intern and Resident in Surgery, Hospital of St Raphael, Connecticut, 1986-89; Resident in Surgery, UMDNJ University Hospital, 1989-91; Fellow, Surgical Oncology, University of Chicago, 1991-94; Attending Surgeon, University of Chicago Hospitals and Clinics, 1994-2001; Attending Surgeon, Louis A Weiss Memorial Hospital, 1997-2001; Assistant Professor of Surgery, University of Chicago, 1994-2001; Associate Investigator, University of Chicago Cancer Research Center, 2000-01; Chief of Surgical Oncology, Baystate Health Systems, Massachusetts, 2001-; Associate Professor of Surgery, Tufts University School of Medicine, 2001-; Associate Professor of Biology, University of Massachusetts at Amherst, 2001-. Publications: Numerous articles in professional journals; Abstracts, book chapters and scientific presentations. Honours: Young Investigator's Award, American Society of Clinical Oncology, 1994; Young Investigator's Award, 1995, Auxiliary Board Foundation Grant, 1996-99, University of Chicago Cancer Research Foundation; Faculty Research Award, University of Chicago, 1998; Top Doctors, Chicago Metro Area, 2001. Memberships: American College of Surgeons; American Society of Clinical Oncology; Society of Surgical Oncology; Society for

Surgery of the Alimentary Tract; Crohn's and Colitis Foundation. Address: Baystate Medical Center, 759 Chestnut Street, Springfield, MA 01199, USA. E-mail: richard. Arenas@bhs.org

ARGYROS Ioannis Konstantinos, b. 20 February 1956, Athens, Greece. (US Citizen). Professor of Mathematical Sciences. m. Diana Mihallaq Mina Argyros, 3 sons. Education: BSc, Mathematics, Athens University, 1979; MSc, 1982, PhD, 1984, Mathematics, University of Georgia, USA. Appointments: Technical Consultant, Greek Army, 1979-82; Teaching-Research Assistant, University of Georgia, 1982-84; Visiting Professor, University of Iowa, 1984-86; Assistant Professor, New Mexico State University, 1986 -1990; Associate Professor, 1990-93, Tenured Associate Professor, 1993-94, Full Professor of Mathematical Sciences, 1994-, Cameron University, Lawton, Oklahoma, USA; Research work into numerical analysis, applied analysis and fixed point theory, management science, wavelet and neural networks, mathematical economics and mathematical physics; Work on the solution to Chandrasekhar's Nonlinear Integral Equations Related to Relative Transfer. Publications: 400 peer-reviewed mathematical manuscripts; 13 textbooks in computational mathematics; 250 article reviews for 35 mathematical journals; 5 book reviews; Editor, 7 mathematical journals; Over 65 invited lectures at national and overseas universities. Honours include: Holder of record in University of Georgia for receiving 2 graduate degrees in 2 consecutive years; Nominated for the Distinguished Research Award, Cameron University, 1993, 1995, 2001; Nominated for Hall of Fame Award, Cameron University; Distinguished Research Award, Medal of Excellence, Southwest Oklahoma Advanced Technology Association, 2001; Listed in several biographical reference books. Memberships: American Mathematical Society, 1982-; Phi Mu Epsilon; SAF, World Co-ordinating Council of the Science and Academic Forum of Greek Scientists Living Abroad. Address: Cameron University, Department of Mathematical Sciences, 2800 West Gore Boulevard, Lawton, OK 73505, USA.

ARINZE Francis, b. 1 November 1932, Eziowelle, Nigeria. Cardinal. Education: Diploma, Philosophy in Bigard Memorial Seminary, Enugu, Nigeria, 1953-55; BD, 1957, MA, 1959, DD, 1960, Theology, Urban University, Rome; Diploma, Education, University of London Institute of Education, 1963-64. Appointments: Auxiliary Bishop of Onitsha, Nigeria, 1965-67; Archbishop of Onitsha, 1967-85; Cardinal President, Pontifical Council for Interreligious Dialogue, Vatican City, 1985-2002; Prefect, Congregation for Divine Worship and the Discipline of the Sacraments, 2002-. Publications: Books include: Sacrifice in Igbo Religion, 1970; Answering God's Call, 1983; Alone With God, 1987; Meeting Other Believers, 1997; Brücken Bauen, 2000; The Holy Eucharist, 2001; Religions for Peace, 2002; God's Invisible Hand, 2003; Collections of Writings: Living Our Faith, 1983; In Christ to Christ and for Christ, 1983; Church in Dialogue, 1990; Looking For Light (5 volumes), 1990; Annual pastoral letters, 1971-85. Honours: PhD, hc, University of Nigeria, 1986; PhD, hc, Catholic University of America, Washington DC, 1998; DD, hc, Wake Forest University, Winston-Salem, North Carolina; Doctor of Humanities, University of Santo Tomas, Manila, 2001; DD hc, University of Our Lady of the Lake, Mundelein, Illinois, 2003. Memberships: Congregations for Doctrine of the Faith, Causes of the Saints, Oriental Churches and Evangelization of Peoples. Address: Congregation for Divine Worship, 00120 Vatican City, Europe.

ARIPOV Mersaid, b. 20 September, Tashkent Region, Ukbekistan. Professor. m. Mynira Sadikova, 2 sons, 1 daughter. Education: PhD, 1971; Professor, 1992; Doctor of Science, 1995. Appointment: Head of Department of Informatics and Applied Programming, National University of Tashkent, Uzbekistan. Publications: More than 180 publications; 10 books on Informatics, Information technologies. Honour: Honorary Worker of High Education of Republic of Uzbekistan. Memberships: American Mathematical Society; European Mathematical Society; Gesellschaft für Angewandte Mathematik und Mechanik. Address: NUU, Vuzgorodok, 700174 Tashkent, Uzbekistan. E-mail: m.aripov@nuuz.uzsci.net Website http://nuu.uz/comtech/maripov

ARKHIPOV Andrei, b. 8 September 1946, Karaganda, Kazakhstan, USSR. Physicist. 2 sons. Education: Graduate, Leningrad State University, Russia, 1970; PhD, 1973, DSc, 1993, Institute of High Energy Physics, Russia. Appointments: Scientist of Theoretical Physics Division, 1973-1985, Senior Scientist, 1985-95, Principal Researcher, 1995-, Institute of High Energy Physics, Russia; Lecturer, Physics, Moscow State University, 1978-98. Publications: Articles in scientific journals including: Soviet Journal of Theoretical and Mathematical Physics, 1990; Nuclear Physics, 2001; Hadron Spectroscopy, 2002. Honours: Nominated for International Scientist of the Year, 2003. Address: Theoretical Physics Division, Institute for High Energy Physics, 142280 Protvino, Moscow Region, Russia. E-mail: arkhipov@mx.ihep.su

ARKIN Alan Wolf, b. 26 March 1934, USA. Actor; Director. m. (1) 2 sons, (2) Barbara Dana, 1 son. Education: Los Angeles City College; Los Angeles State Col; Bennington College, Appointments: Made professional theatre debut with the Compass Players, St Louis, 1959; Joined 2nd City Group, Chicago, 1960; NY debut, Roy, Revue from the 2nd city, 1961; Played David Kolvitz, Enter Laughing, 1963-64; Appeared, Revue A View Under The Bridge, 1964; Harry Berline, Luv; Director, Eh?, Circle in the Square, 1966; Hail Scrawdyke, 1966; Little Murders, 1969; White House Murder Case, 1970; Director, The Sunshine Boys, Eh?, 1972; Director, Molly, 1973; Joan Lorraine, 1974; Films Include: The Heart is a Lonely Hunter, 1968; Popi, 1969; Catch 22, 1970; Little Murders (also director), 1971; Last of the Red Hot Lovers, 1972; Freebie and the Bean, 1974; Rafferty and the Gold Dust Twins, 1975; Hearts of the W, 1975; The In-laws, 1979; The Magician of Lublin, 1979; Simon, 1980; Chu Chu and the Philly Flash, 1981; The Last Unicorn, 1982; Joshua Then and Now (also director), 1985; Coupe de Ville, 1989; Havana, 1990; Edward Scissorhands, 1990; The Rocketeer, 1990; Glengarry Glen Ross, 1992; Indian Summer, 1993; So I Married an Axe Murderer, 1993; Steal Big, Steal Little, 1995; Mother Night, 1995; Grosse Point Blank, 1997; Gattaca, 1998; The Slums of Beverly Hills, 1998; Jakob the Liar, 1999; Arigo, 2000; America's Sweethearts, 2001; Thirteen Conversations About One Thing, 2001; Counting Sheep, 2002. TV Appearances Include: The Other Side of Hell, 1978; The Defection of Simas Kudirka, 1978; Captain Kangaroo, A Deadly Business, 1986; Escape from Sobibor, Necessary Parties; Cooperstown; Taking the Heat; Doomsday Gun. Publications: Tony's Hard Work Day; The Lemming Condition; Halfway Through the Door; The Clearing, 1986; Some Fine Grampa, 1995. Honours: Theatre World Award; Award Best Supporting Actor. Address: c/o William Morris Agency, 151 El Camino Drive, Beverly Hills, CA 90212, USA.

ARLMAN Paul, b. 11 July 1946, Bussum. Securities Exchange Official. m. Kieke Wys, 28 May 1971, 1 son, 1 daughter. Education: Law, Economics and International Affairs, Universities of Rotterdam, Groningen and Nice. Appointments: Ministry of Finance, Director, International Affairs, The Hague, 1970-86; European Investment Bank Board Member, 1981-86; World Bank Board Member, 1986-90; Secretary General, Amsterdam Stock Exchange, 1991-97; Secretary General Federation of European Securities Exchanges, 1998-; Board Member, European Corporate Governance Institute; Board Member, European Capital Market

Dictionary of International Biography

Institute; Chairman, Industry Advisory Committee of European Parliamentary Forum on Financial Services. Address: 41 rue du Lombard, Brussels, B-1000, Belgium.

ARMAND Susanne Marie, b. 20 January 1952, Houston, Texas, USA. Quality Control Laboratory Manager. Divorced, 1 son, 1 daughter. Education: Biotechnology Degree, North Harris Montgomery College, Houston, 1994. Appointments: Pharmaceutical Industry Quality Specialist, 1994-2003; Quality Control Laboratory Manager, 2003-. Honours: Listed in national and international biographical dictionaries; Biological Impact Assessment Award, Biotechnology Materials Teaching Grant, 1992-93; Aronex, first to receive chairman's award, 1997. Memberships: Association of Texas Electrologists; International Guild of Electrologists; American Society of Quality; Gulf Association of Athletics; American Decorating Society; Rollerskating Professional of America. Address: 4129 Double Oak Drive, Bedford, TX 76021, USA. E-mail: aggierunner@aggies.com

ARMANI Giorgio, b. 11 July 1934, Piacenza, Italy. Fashion Designer. Education: University of Milan. Appointments: Window dresser; Assistant buyer for La Rinascente, Milan, 1957-64; Designer and Product Developer, Hitman (menswear co of Cerruti Group), 1964-70; Freelance designer for several firms, 1970; founded Giorgio Armani SpA with Sergio Galeotti, 1975; Appeared on cover of Time, 1982. Honours: Dr hc (Royal College of Art), 1991; Numerous awards including Cutty Sark, 1980, 1981, 1984, 1986, 1987; First Designer Laureate, 1985; Ambrogino D'Oro, Milan, 1982; International Designer Award, Council of Fashion Designer of America, 1983; L'Pacchio D'Oro, 1984, 1986, 1987, 1988; L'Occhiolino D'Oro, 1984, 1986, 1987, 1988; Time-Life Achievement Award, 1987; Cristobal Balenciaga Award, 1988; Woolmark Award, New York, 1989, 1992; Senken Award, Japan, 1989; Award from People for the Ethical Treatment of Animals, USA, 1990; Fiorino d'Oro, Florence, for promoting Made in Italy image, 1992; Honorary Nomination from Brera Academy, Milan, 1993; Aguja de Oro Award, Spain, for best International Designer, 1993; Grand'Uffciale dell'ordine al merito, 1986; Gran Cavaliere, 1987. Address: Via Borgonuovo 21, 20121, Milan, Italy.

ARMATRADING Joan b. 9 December 1950, Basseterre, St Kitts, West Indies. Singer; Songwriter; Musician (guitar). Musical Education: Self-taught piano and guitar. Career: Songwriting, performing partnership, with Pam Nestor, 1969-73; Solo artiste, 1973-; Appearances include: Regular international tours; Concerts include: Prince's Trust Gala, Wembley Arena, 1986; Nelson Mandela's 70th Birthday Tribute, Wembley Stadium, 1988; Numerous world tours, 1973-96. Compositions include: Down To Zero; Willow, 1977. Recordings: Singles: Love And Affection, 1976; Rosie, 1980; Me Myself I, 1980; All The Way From America, 1980; I'm Lucky, 1981; Drop The Pilot, 1983; Perfect Day, 1997; Albums include: Whatever's For Us, 1973; Joan Armatrading, 1976; Show Some Emotion, 1977; Stepping Out, 1979; Me Myself I, 1980; Walk Under Ladders, 1981; The Key, 1983; Track Record, 1983; The Shouting Stage, 1988; The Very Best Of..., 1991; What's Inside, 1995; Living For You; Greatest Hits, 1996; Love And Affection, 1997; Lover Speak, 2003; Also appears on: Listen To The Music:70's Females, 1996; Carols Of Christmas Vol 2, 1997; Prince's Trust 10th Anniversary Birthday, 1997; Film soundtrack, The Wild Geese, 1978. Honour: BASCA Ivor Novello Award for Outstanding Contemporary Collection, 1996; M.B.E, 2001. Address: c/o F Winter and Co, Ramillies House, 2 Ramillies Street, London W1V 1DF, England.

ARMSON Kenneth Avery, b. 19 February 1927, North York, Ontario, Canada. Forester. m. Marjorie McLeod, 1 son. Education: BScF, University of Toronto, Faculty of Forestry, 1951; Diploma,

Forestry, Oxford University, 1955. Appointments: Professor of Forestry, University of Toronto, 1952-78; Special Advisor, Forest Regeneration, 1978-80; Chief Forester, Ontario Ministry of Natural Resources, 1980-83; Executive Coordinator, Forest Resources, Ontario Ministry of Natural Resources, 1983-86; Forestry Consultant, 1989-. Publications: Co-author, Forest Tree Nursery Soil Management, 1974; Forest Soils: Properties and Processes, 1977; Forest Management in Ontario, 1976; Canadian Forests: A Primer, 1999; Ontario Forests: A Historical Perspective, 2001; More than 120 professional and scientific papers. Honours: Achievement Award Gold Medal, Canadian Institute of Forestry, 1978; Ontario Forestry Award, 1990; Honorary Doctor of Science, Lakehead University, 1991; Lifetime Achievement Award for Leadership in Sustainable Forestry, 2002; The Queen's Golden Jubilee Medal, 2003. Memberships: President, 1967-69, Councillor, 1992-94, Ontario Professional Foresters Association; Director, 1961-62, Canadian Institute of Foresters; Society of American Forestry; Soil Science Society of America; President, 1964-65, Ontario Forestry Association; President, 1982-84, Canadian Forestry Association; Forest History Society. Address: Apt 1107, 61 St Clair Avenue West, Toronto, Ontario M4V 2YB, Canada. E-mail: karmson@sympatico.ca

ARMSTRONG Hilary Jane, b. 30 November 1945, Sunderland, England. Member of Parliament. m. Paul Corrigan. Education: BSc Sociology, West Ham College of Technology, 1964-67; Diploma in Social Work, Birmingham University, 1969-70. Appointments: VSO (Voluntary Service Overseas), Murray Girls High School, Kenya, 1967-69; Social Worker, Newcastle Social Services Department, 1970-73; Community Worker, Southwick Neighbourhood Action Project, 1973-75; Lecturer in Community and Youth Work, Sunderland Polytechnic, 1975-86; Member of Parliament, North West Durham, 1987-; Minister of State, Local Government and Housing, 1997-99; Minister of State, Local Government and Regions, 1999-2001; Government Chief Whip, 2001-. Honours: Privy Councillor, 2000. Address: House of Commons, London SW1A 0AA, England.

ARMSTRONG Joe C W, b. 30 January, 1934, Toronto, Canada. Author; Historian. m. Barbara Anne Grace, 2 sons, 2 daughters. Education: BA, History and Philosophy, Bishop's University, 1958. Appointments: Investment Director, Charterhouse Canada Ltd, Investment Bankers: 11 directorships held, Canada, UK, USA, 1963-67; Executive Vice-President and Director, Canadian Manoir Industries, Montreal Quebec, Canada, 1968-69; Senior Industrial Development Officer, Government of Canada, 1972-96; Senior Industrial Development Officer for Canada at World's Fair, Expo '86, Vancouver, British Columbia, Canada, 1986; Director, Economic Development, Canadian Council for Native Business, 1987; Owner, Publicist, "Canadiana Collection: Art & Discovery Maps of Canada", 1978-93; National Speaker to 30 Canadian Clubs, 1997-98; Over 200 national and international radio and television broadcasts on history, heritage and politics, 1978-2003; Author, Historian, Heritage Publicist, 1978-2004. Publications: Books: From Sea unto Sea: Art & Discovery Maps of Canada, 1982; Champlain, 1987, French, 1988; Magna for Canada Scholarship Fund, Inaugural Invitational Author, As Prime Minister I Would..., Essay "Days of Our Lives", 1995; Farewell the Peaceful Kingdom: The Seduction and Rape of Canada, 1963-1994, 1995; Oral and written public presentations on Canada's constitution, heritage, cartography and politics. Honours: Honorary Director, Canadian Institute of Surveyors, 1983; Director, Ontario Heritage Foundation, 1986; Ontario Advisory Committee on Land Registry Records, History Committee, Archaeology Committee, 1989; Honorary Member, Le Mouvement Francité, 1990; Cartographic Film Consultant, 1991. Memberships: Fellow, Royal Geographic

Society, UK, 1980; Fellow, Royal Geographic Society, Canada, 1981; Freemason. Address: 347 Keewatin Avenue, Toronto, Ontario M4P 2A4, Canada.

ARMSTRONG Neil A, b. 5 August 1930, Wapakoneta, Ohio, USA. Astronaut; Professor of Engineering. m. Janet Shearon, 2 sons. Education: Purdue University; University of South California. Appointments: Naval Aviator, 1949-52; Flew Combat Miss during Korean War; Joined NASA Lewis Flight Propulsion Laboratory, 1955; Transferred to NASA High Speed Flight Station, Edwards, California; Aeronautical Research Pilot, X-15 Project Pilot Flying to over 200,000 ft and at approximately 4,000 mph; Or Flight Test Work Including X-1 Rocket Research Plane; F-100, F-101, F-104, F5D, B-47 and the Paraglider; Selected as Astronaut by NASA, 1962; Command Pilot for Gemini VIII, 1966; backup Pilot for Gemini V, 1965; Flew to moon, Apollo XI, 1969; First man to set foot on the moon, 1969; Chair, Peace Corps, National Advisory Council, 1969; Deputy Associate Administrator, Aeronautics, NASA, Washington, 1970-71; Professor of Engineering, University of Cincinnati, 1971-79; Chair, Cardwell International Ltd, 1979-81; Chair, CTA Inc, 1982-92; AIL Systems Inc, 1989-; Director of numerous companies. Memberships: President's Commission on Space Shuttle, 1986; National Commission on Space, 1985-86; National Academy of Engineering; Fellow, Society of Experimental Test Pilots; American Institute of Aeronautics and Astronautics; Royal Astronautical Society. Honours: Honorary Member, International Academy of Astronautics; Honorary Fellow, International Astronomical Federation; Numerous decorations and awards from 17 countries; Presidential Medal of Freedom, NASA Exceptional Service Award; Royal Geographic Society, Gold Medal and Harmon International Aviation Trophy, 1970. Address: EDO Corporation, 60 East 42nd Street, Suite 5010, New York, NY 10165, USA.

ARMSTRONG Patrick Hamilton, b. 10 October 1941, Leeds, Yorkshire, England. University Lecturer. m. Moyra E J Irvine, 8 August 1964, 2 sons. Education: BSc, 1963, Dip Ed, 1964, MA, 1966, University of Durham; PhD, 1970. Appointment: Faculty, Department of Geography, University of Western Australia, Head of Department, 1980-82; Deputy Chief Examiner in Environmental Systems, 1996-2000; Chief Examiner, 2000-2005, International Baccalaireate Organization. Publications: Discovering Ecology, 1973; Discovering Geology, 1974; The Changing Landscape, 1975; A Series of Children's Book for Ladybird Books, 1976-79; Ecology, 1977; Reading and Interpretation of Australian and New Zealand Maps, 1981; Living in the Environment, 1982; The Earth: Home of Humanity, 1984; Charles Darwin in Western Australia, 1985; A Sketch Map Geography of Australia, 1988; A Sketch Map Physical Geography for Australia, 1989; Darwin's Desolate Islands, 1992; The English Parson-Naturalist: A Companionship between Science and Religion, 2000. Contributions to: New Scientist; Geographical Magazine; East Anglian Magazine; Geography; Cambridgeshire Life; Eastern Daily Press; West Australian Newspaper; Weekly Telegraph, Australia. Address: School of Earth & Geographical Sciences, University of Western Australia, Nedlands, WA 6907, Australia.

ARMSTRONG Robin Louis, b. 14 May 1935, Galt, Ontario, Canada. Physicist. m. Karen Elisabeth, 1 son. Education: BA, 1958, MSc, 1959, PhD, 1961, University of Toronto; Postdoctoral Studies, Oxford, England, 1961-62. Appointments: Assistant Professor of Physics, 1962-68, Associate Professor, 1968-71, Professor of Physics, 1971-90, Associate Chairman, Department of Physics, 1969-73, Chairman, Department of Physics, 1974-82, Dean, Faculty of Arts and Science, 1982-90; Adjunct Professor of Physics, 1990-98, Professor Emeritus, 1998-, University of Toronto, Canada; President and Vice-Chancellor, University of New

Brunswick, Canada, 1990-96; Special Advisor to the President, Wilfred Laurier University, 1997-2000; Member, Research and Development Committee, Atomic Energy of Canada Limited, 1999, Vice Chair, 2004-; Chair, Board of Directors, Canadian Arthritis Network, 2003-. Publications: Approximately 200 referred research papers in the following journals: Physical Review Letters; Physical Review; Journal of Chemical Physics; Journal of Magnetic Resonance; Canadian Journal of Physics; Review of Scientific Instruments; Journal of Physics C; Magnetic Resonance in Medicine; Physics in Medicine and Biology; Journal of Low Temperature Physics; Cement and Concrete Research; Magnetic Resonance Imaging; Several review articles; Text books with J D King: Mechanics, Waves and Thermal Physics, 1970; The Electromagnetic Interaction, 1973. Honours include: Numerous scholarships, fellowships and prizes as an undergraduate and graduate student; Rutherford Memorial Fellow, 1961-62; Herzberg Medal, 1973, Medal of Achievement, 1990, Canadian Association of Physicists; Fellow, Royal Society of Canada, 1979; Commemorative Medal for the 125th Anniversary of Canadian Confederation, 1992; Honorary Doctor of Science Degree, University of New Brunswick, 2001. Memberships: Committee on Civic Awards of Merit, City of Toronto, 1985-90; Natural Science and Engineering Research Council of Canada, 1991-97; Canadian Association of Physicists; International Society of Magnetic Resonance. Address: University of Toronto, Department of Physics, 60 St George Street, Toronto, Ontario, Canada M5S 1A7. E-mail: robinl.armstrong@sympatico.ca

ARMSTRONG Terry Lee, (Terry Lee, Milo Rosebud), b. 23 December 1949, Elgin, Nebraska, USA. Carpenter; Poet. m. Chris Alvarez, 16 November 1991, 1 daughter. Education: Associate in Arts; San Antonio College; North Texas State University; University of Texas at San Antonio. Appointments: Editor and Publisher, Milo Rosebud, Lone Stars Magazine, Armstrong Publishing Company. Publications: Call It Love; When the Soul Speaks; Heart Thoughts and I Love Yous. Contributions to: National Library of Poetry; Omnific; Poetic Eloquence; My Legacy; Telstar; Moments in Time; Mobius; The Plowman. Honours: 1st Place, Grand Prize, North American Open Poetry Contest, 1990; Poet of the Year, Poetry Break Journal, 1991; Man of the Year, International Men of Achievement, 1992. Memberships: Library of Congress, Texas. Address: 4219 Flint Hill, San Antonio, TX 78230, USA.

ARNAUT Luk Raf Remi, b. 8 March 1966, Gent, Belgium. Research Scientist. m. Maria V Tsiplakova. Education: "First Prize" Degree in Music Theory and Solfège, Royal Conservatoire of Music, Gent, Belgium, 1982; Degree in Applied Physics and Electrical Engineering, University of Gent, Gent, Belgium, 1989; MSc, Communication Engineering and Digital Electronics, 1991; PhD, Electrical Engineering, 1994, UMIST, Manchester, England. Appointments: Associate Professor of Electrical Engineering, UMIST, Manchester, 1991-94; Postdoctoral Research Scientist, QinetiQ, Farnborough, England, 1994-95; Visiting Scientist, Naval Research Laboratories, Washington DC, USA, 1995; Consultant, Technical Manager, Russtech Project, MBDA, Bristol UK, 1995-96; Senior Research Scientist, manager, Complex Electromagnetics Team, Assistant Co-Ordinator of Centre for Mathematical Modelling National Physical Laboratory, Teddington, England, 1996-. Publications: Principal author of over 40 articles in professional journals including, Proceedings of IEE (SMT), IEEE Transactions on Electromagnetic Compatibility, IEEE Transactions on Antennas and Propagation; Archiv für Elektronik und Übertragungstechnik; Radio Science; Journal of Electromagnetic Waves and Applications; Numerous conference proceedings; Book Chapters: Progress in Electromagnetics Research, 1997; Advances in Complex Electromagnetic Materials, 1997; Advances in

Electromagnetics of Complex Materials and Metamaterials, 2003; 1 patent. Honours: Erasmus Scholarship, European Union, 1990; Peter Allen Scholarship, 1994; Numerous invited presentations at conferences and symposia on advanced electromagnetic materials and reverberation processes; Invited Lecturer, Southampton University, 1995; Winner Rayleigh Award, 2002 (runner-up 2001). Address: National Physical Laboratory, Centre for Electromagnetic and Time Metrology, F2-A11, Teddington, TW11 0LW, England.

ARNOLD David Charles, b. 30 December 1941, Atlanta, Georgia, USA. Opera and Concert Singer. Education: BA, MA, Indiana University, Bloomington, Indiana; Artist's Diploma, New England Conservatory of Music, Boston, Massachusetts. Appointments: Metropolitan Opera, New York City Opera Company, English National Opera; Komische Oper, Berlin; International Festivals: Spoleto in Italy and USA; Concertgebouw, The Netherlands; Significant associations: Performing as soloist with Sir Georg Solti and the Chicago Symphony; Leonard Bernstein in premiere of David Diamond's 9th Symphony; James Levine with the Metropolitan Opera. Honours: National Opera Institute Career Grant; New York City Opera Gold Debut Award, Sullivan Foundation Award; Shoshana Foundation Award; Invited to sing at: White House on 2 occasions. Address: Grant House, 309 Wood Street, Burlington, NJ 08016, USA. ·

ARNOLD David Michael, b. 21 April 1958, Maidstone, Kent, England. Singer; Composer. 1 son. Education: Technical School; Music, Hackney & Hastings Colleges. Appointments: Various radio appearances, 1980-94; Founder, Own Record Label; Meridian TV, 1993, 1995. Creative Works: Recordings: High Upon the Rhythm; Hallelujah; Valentine; National Health Tender. Publications: Various. Memberships: PRS; MCPS. Address: 3B Castledown Avenue, Hastings, East Sussex TN34 3RJ, England.

AROMOLARAN Adebayo Babtunde, b. 8 March 1963, Lagos, Nigeria. Development Economist. m. Simisola Abosede, 1 son, 3 daughters. Education: Certificate of Competence in Farm Management Survey Methods, International Institute of Tropical Agriculture, Ibadan, 1983; Bachelor of Agriculture, University of Nigeria, Nsukka, 1984; MSc, Agricultural Economics, 1987, PhD, Agricultural Economics, 1993, University of Ibadan, Nigeria; Certificate in Academic Writing, English Language Institute, 2002, Postdoctoral Training in Development Economics, 2001-03, Yale University, USA. Appointments: Class Teacher, Owhere Grammar School, Edo State, 1984-85; Teaching Assistant, Department of Agricultural Economics, University of Ibadan, 1987-91; Associate Consultant, Monitoring and Evaluation Unit, UNICEF, 1990-91; Junior Research Fellow, University of Ibadan, 1990-92; Field Supervisor, UNICEF Household Food Security and Nutrition, 1991; Research Fellow, Center for Econometric and Allied Research, University of Ibadan, 1992-2000; Part-time Lecturer, Agribusiness and Rural Development Department, University of Technology, Ogbomosho, 1991-92; Lecturer, 1993-96, Lecturer I, 1996-99, Senior Lecturer, 1999-2002, Reader, Associate Professor in Agricultural Economics, 2002-, Department of Agricultural Economics and Farm Management, University of Agriculture, Abeokuta; Research Consultant: World Bank, 1993-94, 2000-01; National Center for Economic Management and Administration, Ibadan, 1994-; UNDP, 1994-96; FAO, 1995-96, 1996-97, 1997-98; UNDP/NCEMA, 1997; UNEP, 2000-01; Reviewer for academic journals, 1999-; Member, Editorial Board, Farm Management Association of Nigeria, 2001-; Postdoctoral Research Fellow, Yale University, 2001-03; Visiting Research Fellow in Development Economics, Economic Growth Center, Yale University, 2003-04; Scientific Adviser, International Foundation for Science, Sweden, 2004-. Publications: 23 articles in professional journals; 3 research monographs and working papers;

8 publications in refereed conference proceedings; Numerous unpublished reports and papers. Honours: Zard Postgraduate Scholarship Award, Faculty of Agriculture and Forestry, University of Ibadan, 1987-88; Ford Foundation Research Scholarship Award, International Institute of Tropical Agriculture, 1987-88; 5th Round Research Grantee, African Rural Social Science Research Network, 1996-98; Rockefeller Post Doctoral Fellowship Award for Research in Economics of the Family in Developing Countries, Economic Growth Centre, Yale University, USA, 2001-03; Nominated Man of the Year, ABI, 2003. Memberships: American Economic Association; American Agricultural Economic Association; Association of Christian Economists; African Rural Policy Analysis Network; African Economic Research Consortium; Nigerian Economic Society; Nigerian Association of Agricultural Economists; Farm Management Association of Nigeria; Ecological Society of Nigeria; Presidential Prayer Team; President and Chairman, Board of Trustees, Jesus Army Prophetic, Helps and Teaching Ministries Nigeria Inc. Address: Department of Agricultural Economics & Farm Management, University of Agriculture, PMB 2240, Abeokuta, Ogun State, Nigeria E-mail: adebayo.aromolaran@yale.edu

ARQUETTE Patricia, b. 8 April 1968. Actress. m. Nicholas Cage, divorced. Appointments: Films Include: Pretty Smart, 1986; A Nightmare on Elm Street 3: Dream Warriors, 1987; Time Out, 1988; Far North, 1988; The Indian Runner, 1991; Prayer of the Rollerboys, 1991; Ethan Frome, 1993; Trouble Bound, 1993; Inside Monkey Zetterland, 1993; True Romance, 1993; Holy Matrimony, 1994; Ed Wood, 1994; Beyond Infinity, 1995; Infinity, 1995; Flirting with Disaster, 1996; The Secret Agent, 1996; Lost Highway, 1997; Nightwatch, 1998; In the Boom Boom Room, 1999; Goodbye Lover, 1999; Stigmata, 1999; Bringing Out the Dead, 1999; Little Nicky, 2000; Human Nature, 2001; Films for TV Include: Daddy, 1987; Dillinger, 1991; Wildflower, 1991; Betrayed by Love, 1994; Toby's Story, 1998; The Hi -Lo Country, 1998; The Badge, 2002. Address: c/o UTA, 9560 Wilshire Blvd, 5th Floor, Beverley Hills, CA 90212, USA.

ARQUETTE Rosanna, b. 10 August 1959, New York, USA. Actress. m. (1) divorced, (2) James N Howard, divorced, (3) John Sidel, 1993. Appointments: Actress; Founder, Flower Child Productions; Films include: Gorp, 1980; SOB, 1981; Off The Wall, 1983; The Aviator, 1985; Desperately Seeking Susan, 1985; 8 Million Ways to Die, 1986; After Hours, 1986; Nobody's Fool, 1986; The Big Blue, 1988; Life Lessons, Black Rainbow, 1989; Wendy Cracked a Walnut, 1989; Sweet Revenge, 1990; Baby, It's You, 1990; Flight of the Intruder, 1990; The Linguini Incident, 1992; Fathers and Sons, 1992; Nowhere to Run, 1993; Pulp Fiction, 1994; Search and Destroy, 1995; Crash, 1996; Liar, 1997; Gone Fishin', 1997; Buffalo '66, 1997; Palmer's Pick Up, 1998; I'm Losing You, 1998; Homeslice, 1998; Floating Away, 1998; Hope Floats, 1998; Fait Accompli, 1998; Sugar Town, 1999; Palmer's Pick Up, 1999; Pigeonholed, 1999; Interview with a Dead Man, 1999; The Whole Nine Yards, 2000; Too Much Flesh, 2000; Things Behind the Sun, 2001; Big Bad Love, 2001; Good Advice, 2001; Diary of a Sex Addict, 2001. TV Films include: Harvest Home; The Wall; The Long Way Home; The Executioner's Song; One Cooks, the Other Doesn't; The Parade; Survival Guide; A Family Tree; Promised a Miracle; Sweet Revenge; Separation; The Wrong Man; Nowhere to Hide; I Know What You Did. Address: 8033 West Sunset Boulevard, #16, Los Angeles, CA 90046, USA.

ARREDONDO ALVAREZ Victor A, b. 20 February 1949, Cordoba, Veracruz, Mexico. Psychologist. m. Estrella Dorantes, 1 son, 1 daughter. Education: BA, Psychology, Universidad Veracruzana, 1973; MA, Psychology, Western Michigan University, USA, 1974; PhD, Educational Psychology, West

Virginia University, USA, 1978. Appointments: University Development Director, 1989-91, Higher Education Director, 1992-97, Ministry of Public Education, Mexico; President of the Universidad Veracruzana, Mexico, 1997; President of the Interamerican Organisation for Higher Education (IOHE), 2003-2005. Publications: Author, editor or co-author of 13 books and 31 articles on higher education issues including: Evaluation, Financing and Quality Assurance in Mexico's Higher Education, 1995; Towards an Alternative University Paradigm, 2001; Foreign Debt Relief for University-Based Community Services: New perspectives for self-sustained development, 2003. Honours: 1999 Award of Distinction from the Consortium for North American Collaboration in Higher Education (CONAHEC); Gold medal of Merit, University of Quintana Roo, 2001; National Award in Psychology, CNEIP, 2003; "Ocho Columnas" Prize in Education, 2003. Memberships: Hispanic Association of Colleges and Universities (HACU); CONAHEC; Global Alliance for Tranactional Education (GATE); International Association of University Presidents (IAUP). Address: Lomas del Estadio s/n, Zona Universitaria Xalapa, Veracruz C.P. 91090 Mexico. E-mail: varredondo@uv.mx Website: www.uv.mx

ARSENE Melania-Liliana, b. 11 December 1956, Bucharest, Romania. Biochemist. Education: BSc, 1979, MSc, 1980, PhD, 1998, University of Bucharest. Appointments: Biochemist, Drugs Factory, Bucharest, 1980-83, Biosynthesis Factory, Calafat, 1983; Researcher, Chemistry and Biochemistry Energetics Institute, 1983-90; Senior Researcher, Chemical Research Institute, 1990-; Human Training Centre, BioTechnology, 2000-. Publications: Over 40 articles in professional journals; Over 80 scientific communications to national and international congresses and conferences. Honour: National Award for Young Scientists, 1985. Memberships: Romanian Biological Society, 1992-; Romanian Biotechnology and Bioengineering Society, 1993-; New York Academy of Sciences, 1995-. Address: Cozla nr 8, Bl A7, Ap 49, 03-2734 Bucharest, Romania.

ARSOV Yanko Boyanov, b. 12 June 1934, Pazardjik, Bulgaria. Engineer Metallurgist. m. Hristodoli Dikova, 2 sons. Education: Engineer Metallurgist, University of Chemistry and Chemical Technology, Sofia, Bulgaria, 1958; PhD, High Institute of Steels and Alloys, Moscow, Russia 1964; DSc, 1975; Professor, 1989-; Corresponding Member, Bulgarian Academy of Sciences. Appointments: Head, Production Shop, Railway Works, Sofia, 1958-60; Research Associate, Central Research Engineering Institute, Sofia, 1960-64; Senior Specialist, State Committee on Science and Technology Progress, Sofia, 1964-66; Deputy Director, 1966-89, Director, 1989-, Institute of Metal Science, Bulgarian Academy of Science, Sofia. Publications: Books: Steel Castings, 1974; Metal technology, 1981; Casting Properties of Alloys, 1984; 150 articles; 20 patents and inventions. Honours: Gold Medal, Institute of Metal Science, Bulgarian Government, 1968; Award for developing gas counter pressure method, Institute of Metal Science, 1991; Grand Prix, EUREKA, Brussels, 2001. Memberships: Society of Automobile Engineers; American Foundrymen Society; Bulgarian Academy of Science. Address: 34 Edisson St, 1111 Sofia, Bulgaria. E-mail: arsov@ims.bas.bg

ARTHUR Elizabeth Ann, b. 15 November 1953, New York, New York, USA. Writer. m. Steven Bauer, 19 June 1982. Education: BA, English, University of Victoria, 1978; Diploma, Education, 1979. Appointments: Visiting Instructor, Creative Writing, University of Cincinnati, 1983-84; Visiting Assistant Professor, English, Miami University, 1984-85; Assistant Professor, English, 1985-92, Associate Professor, 1992-96, Indiana University-Purdue University at Indianapolis; Visiting Associate Professor, English, Miami University, 1996. Publications: Island

Sojourn (memoir), 1980; Beyond the Mountain (novel), 1983; Bad Guys (novel), 1986; Binding Spell (novel), 1988; Looking for the Klondike Stone (memoir), 1993; Antarctic Navigation, (novel), 1995; Bring Deeps (novel), 2002. Contributions to: New York Times; Outside; Backpacker; Ski-XC; Shenandoah. Honours: William Sloane Fellowship, Bread Loaf Writers' Conference, 1980; Writing Fellowship, Ossabaw Island Project, 1981; Grant in Aid, Vermont Council on the Arts, 1982; Fellowship in Prose, National Endowment for the Arts, 1982-83; Master Artist Fellowship, Indiana Arts Commission, Indianapolis, 1988; Fellowship in Fiction, National Endowment for the Arts, 1989-90; Antarctic Artists and Writers Grant, National Science Foundation, 1990; Critics Choice Award for Antarctic Navigation, 1995; Notable Book, New York Times Book Review, 1995. Membership: Poets and Writers. Address: Bath, IN 47010, USA.

ARTHUR Herbert Henry Gascoign, b. 30 June 1920, Bristol, England. Libraries and Museums Administrator. m. Kathleen Joan Fuge, 19 December 1947, 1 son, 1 daughter. Education: Diploma, 1948, Fellow, Library Association. Appointments: Librarian and Curator, Buxton, 1949; Director of Libraries and Arts, Wigan, 1950-68; Borough Librarian and Curator, Birkenhead, 1969-74; Director of Libraries, Museums and Arts, Wirral Metropolitan Borough, 1974-80; Merseyside Tourist Guide, 1980-85; Liverpool WEA, Lecturer, 1980-89; WEA Branch Officer, 1989-98; Chairman, Liverpool WEA, 1998-. Publications: History of Haigh Hall, Wigan; Wigan Charters from 1246; Guides to the Williamson Art Gallery and Museum and the Wirral Maritime Museum; 32 papers on Liverpool History and People in Woolton Annual, 1984-94; Lee Tapestry Room. Honour: Queen's Jubilee Medal, 1977. Memberships: Fellow, Chartered Institute of Library and Information Professionals, 1948; Professional Member, Museums Association, 1949; Fellow, Royal Society of Arts, 1949; Fellow, Chartered Institute of Management, 1974 Address: 20 Christchurch Road, Prenton, Wirral M B, CH43 5SF, England.

ARZT Donna Elaine, b. 9 December 1954, Philadelphia, Pennsylvania, USA. International Law. Education: BA, Brandeis University, 1976; JD, Harvard Law School, 1979; LLM, Columbia University School of Law, 1988. Appointments: General Counsel, Soviet Jewry Legal Advocacy Centre, 1979-81, 1985-88; Assistant Attorney General, Commonwealth of Massachusetts, 1981-85; Bond, Schoeneck and King, Distinguished Professor of Law; Professor of Law, Director, Centre for Global Law and Practice, Syracuse University College of Law, 1988-; Director, Lockerbie Trial, Families Project, 1999-2002. Publications: Refugees Into Citizens: Palestinians and the End of the Arab-Israeli Conflict, 1997. Honour: Michael Tryson Award for Leadership and Excellence in Human Rights, 1989. Memberships: American Society of International Law; American Bar Association. Address: Syracuse University College of Law, Syracuse, NY 13244, USA.

AS-SALAAM Jamaal (William L Williams Jr), b. 20 April 1955, Albany, New York, USA. Actor; Writer; Poet; Director; Producer. m. (1) Veronica Foster, divorced, 1 son, 1 daughter, (2) Arlene Hooks, divorced, 1 son, (3) Terisita Ann Lopez, divorced, 1 daughter. Education: State University of New York, Film History, 1972-76; University of Northern Colorado, Accounting, 1984-86; National University, Encino, California, 1990-92; California Arts Partnership, 1995-98; MCSE, Ednet Career Institute, 1998. Appointments: Track Labourer, Burlington No RR, 1978-85; Computer Specialist, Denver Public School, 1980-86; Saks Consultant, Tom Hopkins Sales Training, Denver, 1984-86; Technical Support, Teleoptics, Los Angeles, 1988-94; Computer Technician, Los Angeles County Schools, California, 1987-94; Digital Video Editor, California Arts Community Partners, Los Angeles, 1994-99; Researcher, Sales Inc, Beverley Hills, California, 1996-97; Producer, Mile High Cable Co, Denver, 1983-

86; Radio Announcer, Station KUVO, Denver, 1984-85; Actor; Director; Writer; Producer. Publications: Facing East, 1995; Portraits of Life, 1997. Memberships: Inner City Cultural Center; Denver Black Arts Theater Company; Win/Win Business Forum, Denver; Telepoetics; Los Angeles in Support of Gang Truce; Black Radical Congress. Honours: California Arts Community Project Award, California Institute of Arts; 1st prize, Upstate Photography, New York. Address: PO Box 111072, Aurora, CO 80042-1072, USA. E-mail: jamaal21@hotmail.com

ASANOV Usen, b. 26 January 1934, Naryn, Kyrghyz Republic. Chemist. m. Mrs Baimbetova, 3 sons, 1 daughter. Education: Moscow Chemical Technology Institute, 1950-56; Postgraduate Student, Moscow Institute of Physical Chemistry, 1957-60. Appointments: Head of Laboratory, 1960-79; Deputy Director, 1979-87, Institute of Chemistry, Academy of Sciences, Kyrghyz Republic; President, Kyrghyz State National University, 1987-92; Deputy of the Parliament of the Kyrghyz Republic, 1989-95; Chairman, High Attestation Commission, 1987-92; Chairman, National Attestation Commission of the Kyrghyz Republic, 1992-; Chief Editor, Kyrghyz National Encyclopaedia, 2002. Publications: 270 publications; 18 books; 51 patents. Honours: Honorary Inventor, 1981; Honorary Scientist of Kyrghyz Republic, 1993; Medal Dank of the Kyrghyz Republic, 1995; Laureate of the Balasagun State Prize, Laureate of the State Prize in Science and Technology, 2000; Manas Order, 2004; Professor Emeritus of several Universities. Memberships: Kyrghyz National Academy of Sciences, 1983; International Academy of Ecology, Man and Nature Protection Sciences, 1998; New York Academy of Science, 1999; Listed in Outstanding People of the 20th Century. Address: National Attestation Commission, Pr Erkindik 2, Bishkek 720040, Kyrghyz Republic. E-mail: vak@online.kg

ASANTE Molefi Kete, b. 14 August 1942, Vaidosta, California, USA. Professor; Poet. m. Kariamu Welsh, 1981, 1 son, 1 daughter. Education: BA, Oklahoma Christian University, 1964; MA, Pepperdine University, 1965; PhD, University of California at Los Angeles, 1968. Appointments: Professor, University of California at Los Angeles, 1969-73, State University of New York at Buffalo, 1973-84, Temple University, 1984-. Publications: Break of Dawn, 1964; Epic in Search of African Kings, 1979; Afrocentricity, 1980; The Afrocentric Idea, 1987; Kemet, Afrocentricity and Knowledge, 1992; Classical Africa, 1992; African American History, 1995; African Intellectual Heritage, 1996; Love Dance, 1997; African American Atlas, 1998. Publications: 55 books; 300 articles. Honours: Over 100 awards. Membership: 17 professional organisations including: African Writers Union, vice president, 1994-. Address: PO Box 30004, Elkins Park, PA 19027, USA. Website: www.asante.net

ASH William, b. 30 November 1917, Dallas, Texas, USA. Author; Radio Drama Script Editor. m. Ranjana, 1 son, 1 daughter. Education: University of Texas, Austin, Texas; MA, Modern Greats, Balliol College, Oxford. Appointments: Fighter Pilot, Royal Canadian Airforce, WWII; Prisoner of War, 1942-45; Representative, India and Pakistan, BBC, External Services; Script Editor, BBC Radio Drama Department; Literary Manager, Soho Poly Theatre; Chairman, Writers' Guild of Great Britain; Lecturer and Workshop Presenter. Publications: Fiction: The Lotus in the Sky, 1961; Choice of Arms, 1962; The Longest Way Round, 1963; Ride a Paper Tiger, 1968; Take-Off, 1969; Incorporated, 1980; Right Side Up, 1984; She? 1986; Bold Riot, 1992; What's the Big Idea, 1993; But My Fist Is Free, 1997; Rise Like Lions, 1998; Non-fiction: Marxism and Moral Concepts, 1964; Pickaxe and Rifle: The Story of the Albanian People, 1974; Morals and Politics: The Ethics of Revolution, 1977; A Red Square: The Autobiography of an Unconventional Revolutionary, 1978; The Way to Write

Radio Drama, 1985; Marxist Morality, 1997. Honour: MBE (Military Division). Memberships: Writer's Guild; NATFHE. Address: Flat 9, 43 Moscow Road, London W2 4AH, England.

ASHCROFT Richard. Vocalist; Songwriter; Musician (guitar). Career: Vocalist, The Verve; Concerts include: Lollaplooza Tour, US, 1994; UK tours, 1994-95; Support to Oasis, Paris, 1995; Glastonbury Festival, 1995. Compositions include: On Your Own; Drive You Home; History; No Knock On My Door. Recordings: Albums: A Storm In Heaven, 1993; A Northern Soul, 1995; Urban Hymns, 1997; Singles: This Is Music, 1995; On Your Own, 1995; 1995; History, 1995; Bitter Sweet Symphony, 1997; The Drugs Don't Work, 1997; Sonnet, 1998; Lucky Man, 1998. Current Management: Larrikin Management, 8391 Beverly Blvd #298, Los Angeles, CA 90048, USA.

ASHDOWN Sir Jeremy John Durham (Paddy), Baron Ashdown of Norton Sub-Hamdon, b. 27 February 1941, New Delhi, India. Member of Parliament. m. Jane Courtenay, 1962, 1 son, 1 daughter. Appointments: Served RM and 42 Commando, 1959-71; Commanded 2 Special Boat Section; Captain, Royal Marines; HM Diplomatic Service, 1st Secretary, UK Mission to United Nations, Geneva, 1971-76; Commercial Managers Department, Westlands Group, 1976-78; Senior Manager, Morlands Ltd, 1978-81; Liberal Candidate, 1979; Dorset County Council, 1982-83; Spokesman for Trade and Industry, 1983-86; Liberal Member of Parliament for Yeovil, 1983-88; Liberal/SDP Alliance Spokesman on Education and Science, 1987; Liberal Democrat Member of Parliament for Yeovil, 1988-2001; Liberal Democrat Spokesman on Northern Ireland, 1988-; Leader, Liberal Democrats, 1988-99; Appointed Privy Counsellor, 1989; Appointed Non-Executive Director of Time Companies Ltd & Independent Newspapers Ltd, 1999; UN International High Representative to Bosnia and Herzegovina, 2002-. Publications: Citizen's Britain: A Radical Agenda for the 1990s, 1989; Beyond Westminster, 1994; Making Change our Ally, 1994; The Ashdown Diaries 1988-97, 2000; The Ashdown Diaries Vol II, 1997-99, 2001. Address: House of Commons, London SW1A 0AA, England.

ASHER Jane, b. 5 April 1946. Actress; Writer; Cook. m. Gerald Scarfe, 2 sons, 1 daughter. Career: As Cook: Owner Jane Asher's Party Cake Shop and Sugarcraft, 1990-; Cake Designer and Consultant for Sainsbury's, 1992-99; Actress: Films include: Greengage Summer; Masque of the Red Death; Alfie; Dreamchild; TV Appearances include: Murder Most Horrid, 1991; The Choir, 1995; Good Living, 1997-99; Tricks Of The Trade, 1999; Crossroads, 2003; Stage Appearances include: Making it Better, 1992; Things We Do for Love, 1998; Is Everybody Happy, 2000; House and Garden, 2000; What the Butler Saw, 2001. Publications include: The Moppy Stories, 1987; Calendar of Cakes, 1989; Eats for Treats, 1990; Time to Play, 1993; Jane Asher's Book of Decorations Ideas, 1993; The Longing, 1996; The Question, 1998; Losing It, novel, 2002. Address: c/o Actual Management, 7 Great Russell Street, London, WC1B 3NH, England.

ASHLEY J(ohn) R(andle), b. 18 January 1926, Northwich, Cheshire, England. Retired Personnel Manager; Poet. m. Freda Gittens, 13 February 1950, deceased, 1 son. Appointments: Chemical Works Personnel Manager, Management Development, Senior Staff Job Evaluation Manager, ICI Mond Division until retirement. Contributions to: Journals. Membership: Poetry Society. Address: Bodavon, Crows Nest Lane, Great Budworth, Northwich, Cheshire CW9 6HZ, England.

ASHLEY Leonard (Raymond Nelligan), b. 5 December 1928, Miami, Florida, USA. Professor Emeritus of English; Author; Editor. Education: BA, 1949, MA, 1950, McGill University; AM,

1953, PhD, 1956, Princeton University. Appointments: Instructor, University of Utah, 1953-56; Assistant to the Air Historian, Royal Canadian Air Force, 1956-58; Instructor, University of Rochester, 1958-61; Faculty, New School for Social Research (part-time), 1962-72; Faculty, Brooklyn College of the City University, New York, 1961-95. Publications: What's in a Name?; Elizabethan Popular Culture; Colley Cibber; Nineteenth-Century British Drama; Authorship and Evidence in Renaissance Drama; Mirrors for Man; Other People's Lives; The Complete Book of Superstition, Prophecy and Luck; The Complete Book of Magic and Witchcraft; The Complete Book of Devils and Demons; The Complete Book of the Devil's Disciples; The Complete Book of Spells, Curses and Magical Recipes; The Complete Book of Vampires; The Complete Book of Ghosts and Poltergeists; The Complete Book of Werewolves; The Complete Book of Dreams; The Complete Book of Sex Magic; The Complete Book of Numerology; What I know about You; Ripley's Believe It Or Not Book of the Military; The Air Defence of North America; George Alfred Henty and the Victorian Mind; Turkey: Names and Naming Practices; A Military History of Modern China (collaborator); Shakespeare's Jest Book; George Peele: The Man and His Work; Language in Contemporary Society (co-editor); Language in The Era of Globalization (co-author); Language and Identity (co-editor); Geolinguistic Perspectives (co-editor); Phantasms of the Living (editor); Language in Modern Society; Language in Action. Contributions to: Anthologies; Reference books; Encyclopaedias; DLB; New DNB; Numerous books on names and naming including: Names of Places, Names in Literature, Names in Popular Culture, Art Attack: Essays on Names in Satire, Cornish Names. Honours: Shakespeare Gold Medal, 1949; LHD (Columbia Theological) honoris causa, 1998; American Name Society Best Article Award; Fellowships and grants. Memberships: American Name Society, president 1979, 1987, long-time member editorial board, executive board; International Linguistics Association, Secretary, 1982-82; American Association of University Professors, former president, Brooklyn College Chapter; McGill Graduates Society of New York, President, 1970-75; American Society of Geolinguistics, president 1991-; Princeton Club of New York; New York Academy of Sciences; Modern Language Association; American Dialect Society. Address: Library Technical Services, Brooklyn College of the City University of New York, Brooklyn, NY 11210, USA.

ASHTON Steven John, b. Woking, Surrey, England. Government Minister. m. Hari Dimitrakopoulou, 1 son, 1 daughter. Education: BA Hons, Political Studies, University of Manitoba, Canada; MA, Economics, Lakehead University. Appointments: President, University of Manitoba Student Union, 1978-79; Member, Legislative Assembly, Manitoba, 1981-; Opposition House Leader, 1989-99; Minister of Transportation and Government Service, 1999-2002; Minister of Conservation, Manitoba, 2003; Minister of Labour and Immigration, Manitoba, 2003; Minister of Water Stewardship, Manitoba, 2003-. Honours: Canada 125 Medal; Queens Jubilee Medal. Memberships: New Democratic Party; Secretary, Canadian Committee for the Restitution of the Parthenon Marbles; Royal Canadian Legion. Address: 95 Pike Crescent, Thompson, Manitoba, R8N O24, Canada.

ASHWORTH James, b. 2 January 1955, Burnley, Lancashire, England. Former College Lecturer. Education: University of Wales, 1980-83; Huddersfield Polytechnic, 1984-85; Nottingham University, 1991-92. Appointments: Courtaulds, 1974-76; Works Study Officer, Nelson Public Library, 1977; Local Historian, Padiham Youth Centre, Youth Worker 1984; Lecturer, Keighley Technical College, 1984-87. Contributions to: Anthologies: Dreams and Reality, 1994; Joyful Harvest, 1994; Blue and Green, 1996; A Passage in Time, 1996; Whispering Winds, 1997; Gallery of Artistry, 1997; Book of Prayer, 1997. Contributions to: Various

publications. Honours: Editor's Choice Award, International Society of Poets, 1996; Poetry Prize, Poetry Today, 1997; Poet of Merit Award, International Society of Poets, 1997. Address: 3 Chapel Close, Trawden, Nr Colne BB8 8QZ, England.

ASKHABOV Sultan Nazhmudinovich, b. 23 March 1954, Uzun-Agatch, USSR. Mathematician. m. Luiza Aindievna (Azueva) Askhabova, 2 sons, 2 daughters. Education: Candidate of Physics and Mathematics, Rostov-on-Don, USSR, 1982; Associate Professor, Department of Mathematical Analysis, Moscow, USSR, 1987; Professor, Department of Mathematical Analysis, Grozny, Russia, 1998. Appointments: Instructor, Department of Mathematical Analysis, Grozny, USSR, 1977-84; Associate Professor, Department of Mathematical Analysis, 1984-98; Head, Department of Mathematical Analysis, Checheno-Ingush State University, 1991-; Professor, Department of Mathematical Analysis, Chechen State University, 1998-. Publications: Monograph: Integral equations of convolution type with power nonlinearity (in Russian), 2001; Book: Probability Theory and Mathematical Statistics (in Russian), 2002. Honour: Chechen Republic Prize in Science, 1992. Memberships: American Mathematical Society; Reviewer of journal: Mathematical Reviews, USA. Address: Maikop State Technological Institute, 191 Pervomayskaya St, 38500 Maikop, Republic Adygheya, Russia. E-mail: ashabov@aport2000.ru

ASPINALL Robert William, b. 19 May 1962, Manchester, England. University Professor. m. Naomi. Education: BA, University of Reading, England, 1983; MA, University of Manchester, 1984; PGCE, Kingston Polytechnic, England, 1985; MA, University of Essex, England, D Phil, University of Oxford, 1997. Appointments: School Teacher, Glyn School, Epsom, Surrey, England, 1985-89; English Teacher, Urawa High School, Japan, 1989-92; Visiting Lecturer, Faculty of Language and Culture, Nagoya University, Japan, 1998-2001; Associate Professor, Department of Social Systems, Shiga University, Japan, 2001-. Publications: Teachers' Unions and the Politics of Education in Japan, 2001; Numerous articles on education and politics in Japan. Honours: Economic and Social Research Council Scholarship for Postgraduate Study, UK, 1992-93, 1994-97. Memberships: Japan International Education Society; British Association of Japanese Studies; Association of Asian Studies. Address: Nakayoshi Building 4F, Chikusa 3-15-7, Chikusa-ku, Nogoya, Japan. E-mail: aspinall@biwako.shiga-u.ac.jp

ASPLER Tony, b. 12 May 1939, London, England. Writer. 1 son, 1 daughter. Education: BA, McGill University, Canada, 1959. Publications: Streets of Askelon, 1972; One of My Marionettes, 1973; Chain Reaction (with Gordon Pape), 1978; The Scorpion Sanction (with Gordon Pape), 1980; Vintage Canada, 1983, updated edition, 1992; The Music Wars (with Gordon Pape), 1983; Titanic (novel), 1989; Blood is Thicker than Beaujolais (novel), 1993; Cellar and Silver (with Rose Murray), 1993; Aligoté to Zinfandel, 1994; The Beast of Barbaresco (novel), 1996; Death on the Douro (novel); Travels With My Corkscrew (non-fiction); The Wine Lover Cooks (with Kathleen Sloan), 1999; Canadian Wine for Dummies, 2000; US editions of: Blood is Thicker than Beaujolais, The Beast of Barbaresco, Death on the Douro, 2000. Contributions to: Periodicals. Membership: Crime Writers of Canada, founding chairman, 1982-84; Wine Writers Circle of Canada; Co-founder, Charitable Foundation "Grapes for Humanity". Address: 53 Craighurst Avenue, Toronto, Ontario, M4R 1J9, Canada.

ASSMANN Jan, b. 7 July 1938, Langelsheim. Professor of Egyptology. m. Aleida nee Bornkamm, 2 sons, 3 daughters. Education: Dr phil, 1965; Dr habil, 1971; Dr theol h.c, 1998. Appointments: Professor of Egyptology, Heidelberg University since 1976; Visiting professorships at Jerusalem, Paris, Yale and Houston. Publications: Author, 30 books; Editor, 30 books; 300 articles. Honours: Max Planck Forschungspreis, 1996; Deutscher Historikerpreis, 1998. Memberships: Akademie der Wissenschaften, Heidelberg; Deutsche Archäologisches Institut. Address: Im Neulich 5, D 69121 Heidelberg, Germany. E-mail: jan@assmanns.de

ASTILLERO Carlito, b. 13 December 1940, Tangub City, Philippines. Doctor of Medicine. m. Elena Clador B Astillero, 2 sons, 3 daughters. Education: Preparatory Medicine Diploma, 1962; Doctor of Medicine Diploma, 1968. Appointment: Medical Director, Pathology and Laboratory medicine Department, Dr Abdulrahman Al-Mishari General Hospital, Riyadh, Saudi Arabia, 1987-. Publications: Education: Rizalian Way; Federal Form of Government for Filipinos; Elements of Education; Tears and Joy of Filipino Migrant Workers. Honours: Philippine Medical Board Examinations Topnotcher, 1968; Special Presidential Award, Malacañang Palace, Philippines, 1996; Listed in Who's Who publications and biographical dictionaries. Address: 759 Capistrano Street, Molave, Zamboanga del Sur, Philippines. E-mail: drastrillo@yahoo.com

ÅSTRÖM (Hans) Gustaf (Erik), b. 11 September 1918, Högsjö, Sweden. Managing Director. 1 son, 1 daughter. Education: Engineering Special Student at the University of Technology Stockholm, 1949-51. Appointments: Repairman, Engineering Workshop, Utansjö Cellulosa AB, Sweden, 1933-39; Chief Engineer for Methods and Manufacturing, Swedish Air Force, Malmslätt, Sweden, 1943-59; Director, Sundsvalls Verkstäder AB, Örebro, 1959-65; Travelling as a Managing Director and Rationalisation Expert for several Swedish companies, 1966-68; Director, Sundsvalla Verkstäder AB, Örebro, 1969-82; Managing Director, Emhart Corporation Singapore Pte Ltd, 1983-86. Publications: Several books on genealogical research. Honours: Chairman and Secretary, Sweden's Association of Manufacturing Companies, Örebro, 1959-82; Representative, Örebro Administrative Province, His Majesty the King's Swedish Education Department, 1963-76; Member, Örebro County School Officers, 1970-76 Managing Director, Örebro Health Care AB, 1974-80; Ministry of Justices Member of the County Court, Örebro Administrative Province, 1981-83. Memberships: Honorary Member, Örebro Technical Museum Society; Rotary, 1962-; Nordic Union Society; Honorary Member, Genealogical Research Association of Ådalen; Honorary Member, Society of Friends of the Mining Industry; Örebro Pistol Shooting Club. Address: Karlsgatan 32 P, 703 41 Örebro, Sweden.

ATAMAN Orol Sadrettin, b. 1 September 1945, Ankara, Turkey. Architect; Regional Planner. m. Hurmuz Ataman, 1 son, 1 daughter. Education: BArch, 1968, MA, Regional Planning, 1970, Middle East Technical University, Ankara, Turkey; Post Graduate Course, Project Planning, University of Bradford, England, 1972. Appointments: Town Planner and Chief Planner, Ministry of Construction and Resettlement, Ankara, 1970-77; General Director of Tourism Planning, Ministry of Tourism, Ankara, 1977-82; Chief Planner, Makkah Region Development and Planning Office, Saudi Arabia, 1982-85; Group Leader, World Bank Sponsored Cukurova Metropolitan Region Urban Development Project, Adana, 1985-87; Vice Chairman, President, Technical Services Bureau, Ankara, 1987-94; President, Hill and Knowlton, Turkey, International Public Relations, Ankara, 1991-92; Board Member and President, PBMI Engineering and Consultancy, Ankara, 1992-94; Secretary General, Turkish Chamber of Architects, Ankara, 1994-96; Vice Chairman, KAMP-TUR Tourism Inc, Kusadasi, Turkey, 1989-2001; Overseas Business Development Manager, TEPE Construction Industry Inc, Ankara, 1996-99; Vice Chairman and

President, New Towns Investments Inc, Ankara, 1999-2001; President, ALVENSA Building Products Inc, Izmir, 2001-2002; Chief Planner, Qatar-Bahrain Causeway project, Doha, Qatar, 2002-2003; Project Manager, Establishment of a National Planning Information System Project, Riyadh, Saudi Arabia, 2003-. Publications: Over 20 articles for professional journals. Honours: 1st Mention, Zonguldak Metropolitan Area Planning Competition, 1973; 1st Mention, Gaziantep Urban Area Planning Competition, 1974; Best Professional Service Award, Municipality of Iskenderun, 1987; 30-Years Service Award, Ankara Chamber of Architects, 1998; 30th Anniversary Medal, Middle East Technical University, 1998; Universal Award of Accomplishment, American Biographical Institute, 2001. Memberships: President, 1980-82, Secretary General, 1994-96, Union of Turkish Chambers of Architects; President, Chamber of Turkish City and Regional Planners, 1973-77; Horse Riding Club; Club Flipper. Address: Turan Gunes Bulvari, 43/41, Cankaya, Ankara, 06450, Turkey. E-mail: orolataman@hotmail.com

ATHANASIADOU Georgia, b. 2 February 1969, Tripoli, Greece. Professor. m. G Tsoulos, 1 son. Education: MEng, Technical University of Athens, Greece, 1992; PhD, University of Bristol, England, 1997. Appointments: Research Assistant, Research Fellow, University of Bristol, 1994-99; Adaptive Broadband Ltd, Cambridge, England, 1999-2001; University of Cambridge, England, 2001-02; University of Peloponnese, Greece, 2002-. Honours: Bakala Postgraduate Bursary. Memberships: IEEE; TCG. Address: Plateia Kolokotroni 2, Tripoli 22100, Greece. E-mail: gathanasiadou@hotmail.com

ATHERTON Michael Andrew, b. 23 March 1968, Manchester, England. Cricketer. Education: Manchester Grammar School; Downing College, Cambridge. Appointments: Right Hand Opening Batsman; Leg Spin Bowler; Played for Cambridge University, 1987-89 (captain 1988-89); Lancashire, 1987-2001; England debut, 1989; 115 tests to May 2000, 54 as captain; (England record) Scoring 7,728 runs (average 37.69) including 16 centuries (to 1 January 2002); Has scored 18,349 first class runs (47 centuries) to end of 2000-01 season, including 1,193 in debut season; Toured Australia, 1990-91, 1994-95 (captain); 54 limited-overs internationals (43 as captain), to 20 August 1998; Toured South Africa, 1995-96, Zimbabwe and New Zealand, 1996-97, West Indies, 1998; Member, touring team in Australia, 1998-99, South Africa, 1999-2000, Pakistan and Sri Lanka, 2000-01; Retired, 2001; Cricket Commentator for Channel 4. Publications: A Test of Cricket, 1995; Opening Up (autobiography), 2002. Address: c/o Lancashire County Cricket Club, Old Trafford, Manchester, M16 0PX, England.

ATKINS Hannah Moriah, b. 1 November 1923, Winston-Salem, North Carolina, USA. Political Scientist. m. (1) Charles N Atkins, 2 sons, 1 daughter, (2) Everett O'Neal. Education: BS, 1943; MPA, 1957; Honorary Doctorates, 1987, 1989. Appointments: Oklahoma Secretary of State; Oklahoma Cabinet Secretary of Human Resources. Honours: Oklahoma Hall of Fame; Oklahoma Women's Hall of Fame; Oklahoma Trailblazer Award. Memberships: Elected Member, Oklahoma State House of Representatives, 1968-80; National Conference of C and J. Address: 3701 International Drive, Apartment 601, Silver Spring, MD 20906, USA.

ATKINS John Alfred, b. 26 May 1916, Carshalton, Surrey, England. Retired Teacher; Poet. m. Dorothy Joan Grey, 24 May 1940, 2 daughters. Education: BA, Honours, History, University of Bristol, 1938. Appointments: Head of English Department, Higher Teacher Training Institute, Omdurman, Sudan, 1966-68; Senior Lecturer, English Department, Benghazi University, Libya, 1968-70; Docent in English Literature, Lodz, Poland, 1970-76. Publications: Experience of England, 1941; Today's New Poets,

1944; The Pleasure Ground (co-author), 1947; Co-Author, Triad (group of poems), 1947. Contributions to: New Poetry, PEN; New Poetry, Arts Council; Penguin New Writing; Windmill; Poems of this War; Life and Letters Today; New Saxon Pamphlets; Mercury; Oasis; Australian International Quarterly; Outposts; Writing Today; Gangrel; Variegation; Voices; Million; HPJ (Hartforde Poets Journal); Numerous small magazines; poems featured on www.poetry.com. Honour: Eastern Arts Association Bursary, 1991. Membership: Balkerne Writers, Colchester, 1986-89. Address: Braeside Cottage, Mill Lane, Birch, Colchester CO2 0NH, England.

ATKINS Ronald Dean, b. 8 March 1948, Bonham, Texas, USA. Construction Business Owner. m. Michelle Jeanett, 1 son, 1 daughter. Education: Business and Industrial Arts, North Texas State University, 1971; Business courses, Extended Education, Southern Methodist University. Appointments: Carpenter, Superintendent, Construction Manager, Vice President Construction, Vice President Director of Operations, Executive Vice President, Chief Operating Officer, Owner. Publications: Silver Warranty Book; Zale Warranty Book; Legacy Warranty Book; F&J Newspaper; Humor and Motivation. Honours: Service Awards: Bronze Star, Air Medal, Army Commendation Medal; Builder of the Year, 1999; Distinguished Membership Award; Home of Texas Production and Quality Awards; Home Builder Expert Panelist; Design McSam Award. Memberships: Texas Association of Builders; National Association of Home Builders; Greater Dallas Association of Builders; International Conference of Building Officials; International Code Council. Address: 5301 Heather Court, Flower Mound, TX 75022, USA. E-mail: stellarcustomhomes@comcast.net

ATKINS Russell, b. 25 February 1926, Cleveland, Ohio, USA. Composer; Poet. Education: Cleveland School of Art, 1943; Cleveland Institute of Music, 1945-46; Private music study in composition with J Harold Bron, 1950-54. Appointments: Editor, Free Lance Magazine, 1950-80; Publicity Office Manager, Sutphen Music School, 1957-60; Creative Writing Instructor, Karamu Theatre, 1972-86; Writer-in-Residence, Cuyahoga Community College, 1973; Instructor, Ohio Programme in Humanities, 1978. Publications: Phenomena, 1961; Objects, 1963; Heretofore, 1968; Podium Presentations, 1969; Here in The, 1976; Whichever, 1978; Beyond the Reef, 1991. Contributions to: View; Beloit Poetry Journal; New York Times; Western Review; Botteghe Oscure; Writers Forum; Poetry Now; Coventry Reader; Cornfield Review; Stagebill. Honours: Consultant to various conferences and workshops; Karamu Theatre Tribute Award, 1971; Honorary Doctorate, Cleveland State University, 1976; Individual Artists Fellowship, Ohio Arts Council, 1978. Memberships: Cleveland State University Poetry Forum; Poets League of Greater Cleveland. Address: 6005 Grand Avenue, Cleveland, OH 44104, USA.

ATKINSON James, b. 27 April 1914, Tynemouth, Northumberland, England. Retired Professor of Theology; Writer. m. Laura Jean Nutley, deceased 1967, 1 son, 1 daughter. Education: BA, 1936, MA, 1938, M Litt, 1950, University of Durham; DTh, University of Münster, Germany, 1955; Hon DD, University of Hull, 1997. Publications: Library of Christian Classics, volume XVI, 1962; Rome and Reformation, 1966; Luther's Works, Vol 44, 1967; Luther and the Birth of Protestantism, 1968; The Reformation, 1968; The Trial of Luther, 1971; Martin Luther, 1983; The Darkness of Faith, 1987. Contributions to: Books and learned journals. Memberships: President of the Society for the Study of Theology; Society of the Study of Ecclesiastical History; L'Academie Internationale des Sciences Religieuses. Address: Leach House, Hathersage, Hope Valley, S32 1BA, England.

ATKINSON Rowan Sebastian, b. 6 January 1955, Newcastle-upon-Tyne, England. Actor; Author. m. Sunetra Sastry, 1990. Education: Universities of Newcastle and Oxford. Appointments: Stage Appearances include: Beyond a Joke, Hampstead, 1978; Oxford University, Revues at Edinburgh Fringe, One Man Show, London, 1981; The Nerd, 1985; The New Revue, 1986; The Sneeze, 1988; TV Appearances: Not the Nine O'Clock News, 1979-82; Blackadder, 1983; Blackadder II, 1985; Blackadder the Third, 1987; Blackadder Goes Forth, 1989; Mr Bean (13 episodes), 1990-96; Rowan Atkinson on Location in Boston, 1993; Full Throttle, 1994; The Thin Blue Line, 1995; Films Include: Never Say Never Again; The Tall Guy, 1989; The Appointments of Dennis Jennings, 1989; The Witches, 1990; Four Weddings and a Funeral, 1994; Hot Shots - Part Deux, 1994; Bean: The Ultimate Disaster Movie, 1997; Blackadder – Back and Forth, 2000; Maybe Baby, 2000; Rat Race, 2002; Scooby Doo, 2002; Johnny English, 2003; Love Actually, 2003. Address: c/o PBJ Management Ltd, 7 Soho Street, London W1D 3DQ, England. E-mail: general@pbjmgt.co.uk

ATLAN Henri, b. 27 December 1931, Blida, Algeria. University Professor. m. Bela, Rachel Kohn, 1 son, 1 daughter. Education: MD, University of Paris Medical School, 1958; PhD, Sorbonne and University of Paris VI, 1973. Appointments: Professor of Biophysics, University of Paris VI and University of Jerusalem, 1975-2000; Head, Department of Biophysics, Hospital Hotel Dieu, Paris, 1990-99; Director, Human Biology Research Centre, Hadassah University Hospital, Jerusalem, 1992-; Director of Research, Ecole des Hautes Etudes en Sciences Sociales, Paris, 1995-. Publications: Over 200 articles and 10 books on theories of complexity and self-organisation, cell biology and immunology, artificial intelligence, philosophy and ethics of biology, Jewish studies. Honours: French Legion of Honour (Chevalier), 1984; Ordre des Arts et de Lettres (Officer), 1984; Ordre National du Mérite (Officer), 1992; Award of the Presidency of the Italian Senate (Pio Mazu International Research Centre), 1999; Doctorate Honoris Causa, University of Montreal, 2000. Memberships: New York Academy of Sciences; Universal Academy of Cultures; French National Bioethics Committee, 1984-2000. Address: EHESS 54 Boulevard Raspail, 75006-Paris, France.

ATTENBOROUGH David Frederick, b. 8 May 1926, London, England. Naturalist; Film-Maker; Author. Education: Zoology, Clare College, Cambridge, England. Appointments: Military Service, Royal Navy, 1947-49; Editorial Assistant, educational publishing; Joined BBC Television, Trainee Producer, 1952; First expedition to West Africa, 1954; Many trips to study wildlife and human cultures, 1954-64; TV series, Zoo Quest; Controller, BBC2 and BBC Television Service, 1965-68; Director of Television Programmes, BBC, 1969-72; Member, Board of Management; TV Series include: Life on Earth, 1979, The Living Planet, 1983, The Trials of Life, 1990; The Private life of Plants, 1995; The Life of Birds, 1998. Publications: Zoo Quest to Guiana, 1956; Zoo Quest for a Dragon, 1957; Zoo Quest in Paraguay, 1959; Quest in Paradise, 1960; Zoo Quest to Madagascar, 1961; Quest under Capricorn, 1963; The Tribal Eye, 1976; Life on Earth, 1979; The Living Planet, 1984; The First Eden, 1987; Atlas of the Living World; 1989; The Trials of Life, 1990; The Private Life of Plants, 1994; The Life of Birds, 1998; The Life of Mammals, 2002; Life on Air, autobiography, 2002. Honours include: Silver Medal , Zoological Society of London, 1966; Gold Medal Royal Geographical Society; Kalinga Prize, UNESCO; Honorary Degrees: Leicester, London, Birmingham, Liverpool, Heriot-Watt, Sussex, Bath, Ulter, Durham, Bristol, Glasgow, Essex, Cambridge, Oxford; Knighted, 1985; Encyclopaedia Britannica Award, 1987; Edinburgh Medal, Edinburgh Science Festival, 1998; BP Natural

World Book Prize, 1998. Memberships include: Fellow, Royal Society, Honorary Fellow, British Academy of Film and Television Arts. Address: 5 Park Road, Richmond, Surrey, England.

ATTENBOROUGH Richard (Baron Attenborough of Richmond-upon-Thames), b. 29 August 1923, Cambridge, England. Actor; Producer; Director. m. Sheila Beryl Grant Sim, 1945, 1 son, 2 daughters. Education: Royal Academy of Dramatic Art, London. Appointments: First Stage Appearance as Richard Miller in Ah! Wilderness, Palmers Green 1941; West End Debut, Awake and Sing, 1942; First Film Appearance, In Which We Serve, 1942; Joined RAF, 1943; Seconded to RAF Film Unit for Journey Together, 1944; Demobilised, 1946; Returned to Stage, 1949; Formed Beaver Films, with Bryan Forbes, 1959; Allied Film Makers, 1960; Goodwill Ambassador for UNICEF, 1987-; Director, Chelsea Football Club, 1969-82; Many stage appearances; Film Appearances: School for Secrets; The Man Within; Dancing With Crime; Brighton Rock; London Belongs to Me; The Guinea Pig; The Lost People; Boys in Brown; Morning Departure; The Magic Box; The Great Escape; Dr Doolittle; David Copperfield; Jurassic Park; Miracle on 34th Street; The Lost World: Jurassic Park; Elizabeth; Puckoon; Many others; Produced: Whistle Down the Wind, 1961; The L Shaped Room; Directed: Young Winston, 1972; A Bridge Too Far, 1976; Magic, 1978; A Chorus Line, 1985; Grey Owl, 2000; Produced and Directed: Oh! What a Lovely War, 1968; Gandhi, 1981; Cry Freedom!, 1987; Chaplin, 1992; Shadowlands, 1993; In Love and War, 1997; Grey Owl, 1998. Publications: In Search of Gandhi, 1982; Richard Attenborough's Chorus Line, 1986; Cry Freedom, A Pictorial Record, 1987. Honours: 8 Oscars; 5 BAFTA Awards; 5 Hollywood Golden Globes; Directors Guild of America Award; others. Memberships: Tate Foundation; Royal Academy of Dramatic Arts; Help a London Child; Others. Address: Old Friars, Richmond Green, Surrey, TW9 1NQ, England.

ATWOOD Margaret (Eleanor), b. 18 November 1939, Ottawa, Ontario, Canada. Poet; Author; Critic. m. Graeme Gibson, 1 daughter. Education: BA, Victoria College, University of Toronto, 1961; AM, Radcliffe College, Cambridge, Massachusetts, 1962; Harvard University, 1962-63, 1965-67. Appointments: Teacher, University of British Columbia, 1964-65, Sir George Williams University, Montreal, 1967-68, University of Alberta, 1969-70, York University, 1971-72; Writer-in-Residence, University of Toronto, 1972-73, University of Alabama, Tuscaloosa, 1985, Macquarie University, Australia, 1987; Berg Chair, New York University, 1986. Publications: Poetry: Double Persephone, 1961; The Circle Game, 1964; Kaleidoscopes Baroque, 1965; Talismans for Children, 1965; Speeches for Doctor Frankenstein, 1966; The Animals in That Country, 1968; The Journals of Susanna Moodie, 1970; Procedures for Underground, 1970; Oratorio for Sasquatch, Man and Two Androids, 1970; Power Politics, 1971; You Are Happy, 1974; Selected Poems, 1976; Marsh Hawk, 1977; Two-Headed Poems, 1978; True Stories, 1981; Notes Towards a Poem That Can Never Be Written, 1981; Snake Poems, 1983; Interlunar, 1984; Selected Poems II: Poems Selected and New, 1976-1986, 1986; Selected Poems 1966-1984, 1990; Margaret Atwood Poems 1965-1975, 1991; Morning in the Burned House, 1995. Fiction: The Edible Woman, 1969; Surfacing, 1972; Lady Oracle, 1976; Dancing Girls, 1977; Life Before Man, 1979; Bodily Harm, 1981; Encounters With the Element Man, 1982; Murder in the Dark, 1983; Bluebeard's Egg, 1983; Unearthing Suite, 1983; The Handmaid's Tale, 1985; Cat's Eye, 1988; Wilderness Tips, 1991; Good Bones, 1992; The Robber Bride, 1993; Alias Grace, 1996; The Blind Assassin, 2000; Oryx and Crake, 2003. Non-Fiction: Survival: A Thematic Guide to Canadian Literature, 1972; Days of The Rebels 1815-1840, 1977; Second Words: Selected Critical Prose, 1982; The Oxford Book of Canadian Verse in English

(editor), 1982; The Best American Short Stories (editor with Shannon Ravenel), 1989; Strange Things: The Malevolent North in Canadian Literature, 1995; Negotiating with the Dead, 2002. Contributions to: Books in Canada; Canadian Literature; Globe and Mail; Harvard Educational Review; The Nation; New York Times Book Review; Washington Post. Honours: Guggenheim Fellowship, 1981; Companion of the Order of Canada, 1981; Fellow, Royal Society of Canada; Foreign Honorary Member, American Academy of Arts and Sciences, 1988; Order of Ontario, 1990; Centennial Medal, Harvard University, 1990; Commemorative Medal, 125th Anniversary of Canadian Confederation, 1992; Giller Prize, 1996; Author of the Year, Canadian Book Industry Award, 1997; Marian McFadden Memorial Lecturer, Indianapolis-Marion County Public Library Foundation, 1998; Booker Prize, 2000; Honorary degrees. Memberships: Writers Union of Canada, president, 1981-82; PEN International, president, 1985-86. Address: McClelland & Stewart, 481 University Ave, Suite 900, Toronto, Ontario, Canada M5G 2E9.

AUCAMP Hendrik Christoffel Lourens, b. 20 January 1934, Dordrecht, South Africa. Retired Academician. Education: BA, 1955, MA, cum laude, 1958, D Ed, 1974, University of Stellenbosch, South Africa. Appointments: Member of the Faculty of Education, University of Stellenbosch, South Africa, 1964-94; Currently writing on a daily basis. Publications: Short stories, essays, full-scale cabarets, plays, poetry include: 'n Bruidsbed vir tant Nonnie, 1970; Kort voor lank (essays on shorter prose forms), 1978; Volmink, 1981; Wat bly oor van soene? 1986; Dalk gaan niks verlore nie, 1992; Gewis is alles net in grap, 1995. Honours: Tafelberg Prize, 1970; W A Hofmeyr Prize, 1974; ATKV Theatre Award, 1980; Hertzog Prize, 1982; Recht Malan Prize, 1997; Honorary Doctorate, University of Stellenbosch, 2000. Membership: South African Academy for Art and Science. Address: PO Box 21611, Kloofstreet Post Office (8008), Cape Town, South Africa.

AULIN-AHMAVAARA Arvid, b. 7 August 1929 Oulu, Finland. Professor of Theoretical Physics and Social Science. m. Pirkko Somervuori. Education: Masters Degree, 1950, Dr Phil, 1954, University of Helsinki, Finland. Appointments: Research Fellow, Nordic Institute for Atom Physics, Copenhagen, Denmark, 1957-60; Research Fellow, Atom Energy Commission, Helsinki, 1960-61; Lecturer, Theoretical Physics, University of Helsinki, 1962-63; Professor of Theoretical Physics, University of Turku, Finland, 1963-67; Consultant, Finnish State Broadcasting Company, 1968-70; Research Professor, Academy of Finland, Helsinki, 1971-74; Professor of Mathematics and Methodology in Social Sciences, University of Tampere, Finland, 1974-92. Publications: The Cybernetic Laws of Social Progress, 1982; Foundations of Mathematical System Dynamics, 1989; Foundations of Economic Development, 1992; The Origins of Economic Growth, 1997; Reminiscences on Sociocybernetics, in Feedback to the Future No 15, 2001; Lecturer Notes in Economics and Mathematical Systems (Series): No 431: Causal and Stochastic Elements in Business Cycles, 1996; No 464: The Impact of Science on Economic Growth and its Cycles, 1998; Taboos of the Welfare State, in Finnish only, 1998; The Introduction of Genes to Social Sciences, with Tatu Vanhanen, in Finnish only, 2001. Address: Oulunkyläntori 2 C 16, 00640 Helsinki, Finland. E-mail: aulin@nettilinja.fi

AUSLENDER Leland Irwin, b. 18 March 1925, Denver, Colorado, USA. Photographer. 1 son. Education: BS, California Institute of Technology, 1945; MBA, Stanford University, 1948. Appointments: Film Director, NBC TV affiliate, Salt Lake City, Utah, 1948-52; Program Manager, CBS TV affiliate, Salines/

Monterey, California, 1953; Television Production Instructor, UCLA, 1955; Project Engineer, Film Production/Technical Writing, Hughes Aircraft Co, 1960-81; Auslender Productions, Los Angeles, California, 1980-; Celestial Images, Owner, Photographer, Los Angeles, 1997-; Publications: Distortion techniques used in filming "The Birth of Aphrodite", American Cinematographer, 1971. Honours: Silver Phoenix, Atlanta International Film Festival; One of Ten Best, Professional Photographers of America; Official US entries at Cannes, Bergamo and Edinburgh Film Festivals. Memberships: Charter member, Academy of Television Arts and Sciences; Professional Photographers of California. Commissions and Creative Works: Films: The Sculpture of Ron Boise; Dear Little Lightbird; The Birth of Aphrodite; Photographs include: Celestial Images, Celestial Portraits; Book and website in preparation; Exhibitions include: Stanford University Art Gallery; Pasadena Civic Center; Gallery 825; Los Angeles Convention Center; Carter Gallery; Sponto Gallery; Galaxy Gallery; Professional Photographers of California. Address: Celestial Images, 6036 Comey Avenue, Los Angeles, CA 90034-2204, USA.

AUSTRIA Atanacio (Tam) P, b. 25 August 1943, Tanay, Rizal, Philippines. Artist; Author. m. Mary Divine, 1 son, 1 daughter. Education: BA, University of Sto Tomas, 1960-64; MA, PhD, Universities in Arts and Academic Philosophical Research. Appointments: Senior Artist, Illustrator, Museum of Philippine History and Iconographical Archives (Ayala Museum); Commissioned to paint religious murals for the St Anthony Chapel in Forbes Park Makati; Held various one-man exhibitions, both local and international, 1970-2003; Represented the Philippine Community in the International Arts Festival, Berkeley, California, USA, 1970; President, Tanay Cultural Arts Foundation, 1975; Commissioned a mural for the Development Bank of the Philippines, 1988; Tanay Exemplary Awardee, 1995; SIC outstanding Alumni Award Golden Jubilee, 1997; President, Antipolo Visual Art Association, 1986; Member (Vocational Director), Rotary Club on Antipolo, 1984-85; Member, Arts Association of the Philippines; Lectured in various universities and communities, 1990-2003. Publications: Books: Recremindoism Rena Philosophy: How to be Inspired, 1998; Rep's Isipism, Speculative Method Research and Philosophical Analysis: How to do it. Honours: Mobil Art Awardee, 1982; Included in books: Best of the Philippines in Visual Arts; Distinctive Citizen of Rizal, 1991; 2000 Intellectuals of the 21st Century Order of Excellence, International Biographical Centre, Cambridge, England. Memberships: Fine Arts Trade Guild, London, England, Membership Directors, 1990. Address: #53 Magsaysay Avenue, Phase 11 Bankers Village 111, Antipolo City, Philippines.

AUTIN Bruno, b. 1 April 1939, Rouen, France. Physicist. m. Françoise Pellerin, 3 sons, 3 daughters. Education: Engineer, Ecole Nationale Supérieure des Télécommunications, Paris, 1963; Doctorate of Theoretical Physics, Intstitut Henri Poincaré, Paris. Appointments: Compagnie Française Thomas Houston, Bagneux, France, 1964; Organisation Européenne pour la Recherche Nucléaire (CERN), Geneva, Switzerland, 1967; Visiting Scientist, Lawrence Berkeley Laboratory, 1976, 1987. Publications: Théorie Quantique du Solide (Translation into French of Quantum Theory of Solids by Charles Kittel); Lattice Perturbation, 1983; Non Linear Betatron Oscillations, 1985 and 1989; Lattices for Anriproton Rings and Proposal for the CERN Antiproton Collector in Antiprotons for Colliding Beam Facilities; Editor, Neutrino Factories based on Muon Storage Rings, 2000. Honour: Senior Physicist at CERN. Membership: European Physical Society. Address: Le Clot des Sources, F-26770 Montbrison-sur-Lez, France. E-mail: brunorautin@netscape.net

AVEDON Richard, b. 15 May 1923, New York, USA. Photographer. m. (1) Dorcas Nowell, 1944, (2) Evelyn Franklin, 1951, 1 son, 1 daughter. Education: Columbia. Appointments: Staff Photographer, Harper's Bazaar, 1945-65; Member, Editorial Staff Theatre Arts Magazine, 1952-53; Vogue magazine, 1966-90; Photographer, New Yorker, 1992-; One Man Exhibitions: Smithsonian Institute, 1962; Minneapolis Institute of Arts, 1970; Museum of Modern Art, 1974; Marlborough Gallery, New York, 1975; Metropolitan Museum of Art New York, 1978; University of Art Museum, Berkeley, California, 1980; Amon Carter Museum, Fort Worth, TX, 1985; American Tour, Retrospective Richard Avedon Evidence, 1944-94; Whitney Museum of American Art, New York, 1994; Visiting Artist, Harvard University, 1986-87. Publications: Observations, 1959; Nothing Personal, 1964; Alice in Wonderland, 1973; Portraits, 1976; Rolling Stones Magazine, The Family, 1976; Avedon, Photographs, 19447-77; In the American West, 1985; An Autobiography, 1993; Evidence. Honours: Fellow, Timothy Dwight College, Yale University, 1975; President's Fellow, Rhode Island School of Design, 1978; Highest Achievement Medal Awards, Art Directors Show, 1950; Popular Photography World's 10 Greatest Photographers; National Magazine Award for Visual Excellence; Citation of Dedication to Fashion Photography, Pratt Institute; Chans Citation, University of California; Art Directors Club Hall of Fame; American Society of Magazine Photographers Photographer of the Year; Best Photography Book of the Year Award; Maine Photography Workshop; Director of the Year, Adweek magazines; Dr hc; Lifetime Achievement Award, Council of Fashion Designers of America; Harvard University Certificate of Recognition, Priz Nadar. Mental Health Association of New York City Human Award; Lifetime Achievement Award, Columbia University Graduate School of Journalism, 2000; Berlin Photography Prize, Deutsches Centrum für Photography, 2000. Address: 407 East 75th Street, New York, NY 10021, USA.

ÁVILA-RIVERA Carlos (Charlie), b. 7 May 1950, Arecibo, Puerto Rico. Professor. m. Gladys E Rivera, 4 sons. Education: BEd, Chemistry, 1976; BA, Science, 1978; MEd, Science Education, New York University, 1986; Scientific Researcher, pure and clean energy to produce electricity, 1989-. Appointments: Science professor, integrated science, 25 years; Research in theory of Singunification; also postulated that the anti-gravity equilibrium Theory can maintain vehicles running in the atmosphere and in space as a transportation media also in space with no need of toxic fiels, only using the centrifugal and centripetal forces (kinetic energy of earth rotational movement) against gravity, obtaining zero gravity in earth and atmosphere; Atermoelectric battery to run a car, no more acid batteries needed; A device-pendulum shaped that can detect earthquakes at least 3 to 5 seconds ahead of time to impact; Inventor of the electrochemical battery, pendulum shaped, which if put in orbit or space (zero gravity) by NASA can produce electricity for spaceships, the whole planet Earth, Liberty space station, colonies on the moon and other planets, working for an indefinite period of time; Songwriter. Publications: 1 patent; 1 song, Man Should Understand; 2 books, Space the 5th state of matter, and the thermoelectric battery and pendulum pacemaker; Postulated that: Anti-Gravity Equilibrium Theory can maintain vehicles running in the atmosphere and in space as a transportation media; A thermoelectric battery to run a car, no more Pb and acid batteries needed; A pendulum-shaped device, that can detect earthquakes at least 3 to 5 seconds ahead of impact. Honours: Outstanding Science Professor of the Year, 2003; Nominated for International Peace Prize, United Cultural Convention; Nominated for Nobel Prize in Physics; Recognised by Governor of Puerto Rico; Adviser, American Biographical Institute. Address: PO Box 14, Angeles, Puerto Rico 00611-0014. Website: www.1stbooks.com

Dictionary of International Biography

AVNI Tzvi (Jacob), b. 7 September 1927, Saarbrucken, Germany (living in Israel since 1935). Composer; Music Educator. m. Hanna Avni, 26 August 1979, 1 son, 1 daughter. Education includes: Diploma in Theory and Composition, Israel Music Academy, Tel Aviv, 1958; Further studies in USA with Copland and Lukas Foss at Tanglewood, 1962-64. Career includes: Director, AMLI Central Music Library, Tel Aviv, 1961-75; Director, Electronic Music Studio, 1977-, Professor of Music Theory and Composition, Rubin Academy, Jerusalem, 1971-96; Retired but still teaching composition; Composer in Residence, North Eastern University, Boston, 1993-94; Queens College, New York, 1994-95. Compositions include: Two String Quartets, Wind Quintet, Five Pantomimes for 8 Players; Works for choir, various electronic pieces, works for ballet, art films and radio plays; Vitrage for Harp Solo, 1990; Desert Scenes, symphony in 3 Movements, 1990; Three Lyric Songs on P Celan Poems for Mezzo Soprano, English Horn and Harp, 1990; Fagotti Fugati for 2 Bassoons, 1991; Variations on a Sephardic Tune for Recorder Ensemble, 1992; Haleluyah for Mixed Choir, 1993; Triptych for Piano, 1994; The Three Legged Monster, musical legend, for Narrator, Piano and Small Orchestra with text by Hanna Avni, 1994; Anthropomorphic Landscapes, No 1 Flute Solo, No 2 Oboe Solo, No 3 Clarinet Solo; If This Is A Man, Five Orchestra Songs (Soprano) on Poems by Primo Levi, 1998; The Ship of Hours, Four Symphonic Sketches on Paintings by M Ardon, 1999; Concerto for Bassoon and Orchestra, 2001; Bassoon Concerto, 2002; Songs and Melodies for mixed choir: in memory of Itzhak Rabin, 1996-97. Recordings include: Love Under a Different Sun, CD of Chamber - Vocal Works; Program Music 1980 with Israel Philharmonic and Mehta CD; Piano Sonata No 1, CD; String Quartet No 1 (Summer Strings), Israeli String Quartet, CD; 5 Variations for Mr "K", for percussion and Tape, CD; Piano Sonata No 2 (Epitaph), CD. Honours include: Acum Prize, 1966; Lieberson Prize for String Quartet No 2, 1969; Engel - Tel Aviv Prize for Holiday Metaphors, 1973; Küstermeyer Prize, 1990; Israel Prime Minister's Prize for Life Achievements, 1998; Culture prize of the Saarland, Germany 1998; The Israel Prize, 2001. Memberships include: Israel Composers League, Chairman 1978-80; Chairman of Israel Jeunesses Musicales. Address: 54 Bourla Street, Tel Aviv 69364, Israel.

AVTANDILOV Georgy Gerasimovitch, b. 21 September 1922, Dagestan, Russia. Professor. m. Lilya Osipova, 16 August 1953, 1 son, 1 daughter. Education: Graduate, State Medical Institute, North Osetiya, 1951, Candidate of Science, 1959, DSc, 1966, Professor, 1971. Appointments: Served in Army, 1940-45; Physician, Head of Department, Republican Hospital, Karbardino-Balkaria, 1951-65; Head, Central Pathological Anatomy Laboratory, Institute of Human Morphology, USSR Academy of Medical Science, 1965-75; Professor, Head of Pathological Anatomy, Chairman, Russian Medical Academy for Postgraduate Education, Moscow, 1975. Publications include: Books: Vascular Plexuses of the Brain, 1962; Morphometry in Pathology, 1973; Systemic Stereometry in Studying the Pathological Process, 1982; Problems of Pathogenesis and Pathanatomical Diagnostics of Diseases in the Aspects of Morphometry, 1984; Medical Morphometry, 1990; Fundamentals of Pathologoanatomical Practice, 1994; The Computerised Microtelephotometry in Diagnostic Histocytopathology, 1996; Over 300 papers in professional journals; 10 inventions and 1 discovery. Honours: Medal for Courage; Patriotic War Order, 1941-45; Honorary Scientist of Russian Federation, 1990. Memberships: Academy of Natural Science of Russian Federation; International Society of Stereologists; European Society of Pathologists; Hungarian, Czech and German Societies of Pathologists. Address: Chair of Pathology, RMA Barrikdnaya St 2, 123995 Moscow, Russia.

AWDRY Christopher Vere, b. 2 July 1940, Devizes, Wiltshire, England. Writer; Author. m. Diana Wendy, 1 son, 1 daughter. Education: Worksop College, 1954-58. Appointments: Printing and publishing, 1958-67; Civil Service, 1967; Columnist, Cambs, Hunts and Peterborough Life, 1978-83; Writer, The Railway Series (Thomas the Tank Engine), 1983-; Lecturer, WEA, 1992-. Publications: Numerous titles in The Railway Series, 1983-; Encyclopaedia of British Railway Companies, 1990; Brunel's Broad Gauge Railway, 1992; Contributions to: Little Railways of Britain, 1992, Over the Summit, 1993; Forward to Explore Britain's Steam Railways, 1995; Awdry's Steam Railways, 1995; Railways Galore, 1996; Volume in the Past and Present Series: Blisworth-Peterbrough Branch Line, 2001; Numerous articles in newspapers, journals and magazines. Memberships: President: Talyllyn Railway Preservation Society, Corris Railway Society, Forest of Dean Railway Society, Barrow-in-Furness Model Railway Society; Patron: Joe Homan Charity, Wensleydale Railway; Railway Correspondence and Travel Society; Railway and Canal Historical Society. Address: The Old Station House, Oundle, Peterborough PE 8 5LA, England. E-mail: chris@sodor.uk

AXELOS Christos, b. 23 January 1928, Athens, Greece. Professor of Philosophy. m. Helli, 2 sons. Education: Studying Philosophy, History, Art, Basel, 1949-50; Studying, Freiburg, Breisgau, Doctor of Philosophy, Department of Philosophy, 1950-52. Appointments: Assistant Master, Berlin, 1962-67; Assistant Master, Hamburg, 1967-69; Lecturer Fellow, Department of Philosophy, University of Hamburg, 1969-; Professor, 1973-. Publications: The Ontological Presuppositions of the Freedom Theory of Leibniz; Criticism of the Modern Greek Ideology; The Three Marks of Democracy; The criticism of the abstract humanism and the so-called primary ethics. A re-examination of Martin Heidegger's treatise "About humanism"; Analysis and Thought. About 30 articles including: The elaboration of the self and of the will in the metapsychology of Leibniz. Address: Talweg 10, 21218 Seevetal, Germany.

AXFORD David Norman, b. 14 June 1934, Great Britain. Meteorologist. m. Diana Rosemary Joan, 1 son, 2 daughters, 3 stepsons, 1 stepdaughter. Education: BA, 1957, MA, 1959, St John's College Cambridge; PhD, Meteorology, University of Cambridge, 1973; MSc, Southampton University, 1963; Administrative Staff College, Henley-on-Thames, 1974; Chartered Engineer, 1975; Civil Service College, Sunningdale, 1977; Civil Service Top Management Programme, 1984. Appointments include: Various appointments, research, weather forecasting and information, Meteorological Office, 1960-76; Assistant Director of Operational Instrumentation, 1976-80, Assistant Director of Telecommunications, 1980-82, Deputy Director of Observational Services, 1982-84, Director of Services and Deputy to the Director-General, 1984-89, Meteorological Office, Bracknell, Berkshire, England; Deputy Secretary-General, World Meteorological Organisation, Geneva, Switzerland, 1989-95; Independent Meteorological Consultant, 1996-. Honours: Honorary Positions: Fellow, Royal Meteorological Society, 1960-, Honorary General Secretary, 1982-89, Vice-President, 1989-91, Chairman Accreditation Committee, 1999-2004; Chairman, Accreditation Committee, European Meteorological Society, 2001-, Vice-President and Treasurer, 2002-; Chairman, Executive Council, British Association of Former UN Civil Servants, 1999-2004, Vice-President, 2004-. Memberships: Fellow, Institution of Electrical Engineers; Chartered Engineer; Fellow, Royal Meteorological Society; Chartered Meteorologist; Chairman of the Trustees, Stanford in the Vale Public Purposes Charity, 2000-2002, Clerk/Correspondent, 2002-; Chairman, Stanford in the Vale Local History Society, 2004-. Address: Honey End, 14 Ock Meadow, Stanford in the Vale, Oxon SN7 8LN, England.

AXTON Florence Gotthelf, b. 6 March 1915, Colorado, USA. Civic Volunteer; Poet. m. T Axton, deceased, 1 son. Education: PhD, Evergreen Christian College. Appointments: Assistant Director, Drama Department, Finch College, 1935-36, Finch Alumnae Association; Public Relations, Denver University; Drama Department, Dance Library; English Speaking Union Board of Governors; Interior Design Historian; Research Scientist, 2001. Publications: Over 27. Honours: 5 Awards, American Cancer Society. Memberships: Denver Art Museum; Central Christian Church, 2001; Mother Cabrini Shrine, 2001; Endowment Fund. Address: 3131E Almeda Ave, No 701, Denver, CO 80209-3411, USA.

AYATOLLAHI Seyyed Mohammad Taghi, b. 6 January 1953, Shiraz, Iran. Professor. m. Sareh, 1 daughter. Education: BSc, Statistics, Shiraz University, School of Arts and Sciences, 1970-76; MSc, Biostatistics, School of Graduate Studies, 1976-78; MS, Biostatistics, Columbia University, School of Public Health, 1978-80; PhD, Medical Statistics, London University, School of Hygiene and Tropical Medicine, 1989-91; PDRA; FSS; CStat, Medical Statistics, Epidemiology, Newcastle University, The Medical School, UK, 1992-94. Appointments: Technician, 1975-76; Senior Teacher, High Schools of Shiraz; Statistician, Programmer, Shiraz University, 1976-78; Lecturer, Head, Department of Biostatistics, 1982-89; Associate Dean, School of Medicine, 1983-84; Chairman, Educational Planning Bureau, 1984-85; Vice Chancellor, Shiraz University, 1984-88; Chairman, Secretary, Cultural Council, Shiraz University of Medical Sciences, 1988-89; Visiting Lecturer, London School of Hygiene and Tropical Medicine, 1990-91; Computer Programmer, University College of London, 1990-91; Statistical Programmer, Oxford University, 1991-92; Research Associate, Newcastle University, 1992-94; Professor, Shiraz University of Medical Sciences, 1994-; Dean, School of Graduate Studies, Shiraz University of Medical Sciences, 1996-2000; Dean, School of Public Health, Shiraz University of Medical Sciences, 1998-2003. Publications: over 120 papers and 18 books published. Honours: Distinguished Graduate Student; Fellow, Royal Statistical Society; Chartered Statistician; International Man of the Year; Noble Prize Winner, 2001; many others. Memberships: New York Academy of Sciences; Society for the Study of Human Biology; Iran Statistical Society; others. Address: Department of Biostatistics and Epidemiology, P O Box 71345-1874, Shiraz, Islamic Republic, Iran.

AYAZ Iftikhar Ahmad, b. 18 January 1936, Tanzania. Educator. m. Amatul Basit, 5 daughters, 1 son. Education: BEd, University of Newcastle upon Tyne; Diploma of Comparative Education, Dip TEFL, MA, University of London; PhD, International University Foundation, USA. Appointments: Teacher, District Education Officer, Regional Inspector of Schools, Chairman, Teacher Education Panel, Head, Department of Education, Tanzania, 1960-78; Senior Curriculum Advisor, Institute of Education, University of Dar es Salaam, Tanzania, 1978-81; Publications Officer, Centre on Integrated Rural Development, Arusha, Tanzania, 1981-85; Education Advisor and Consultant, Commonwealth Secretariat, 1985-92; UNESCO Co-ordinator and Manager of Education For Life Programme, 1992-95; UN Human Rights Commission Workshop on Minority Group Rights, 1997-; Honorary Consul of Tuvalu in the UK, 1995-; Attended numerous international conferences including most recently: World Conference against Racism, Racial Discrimination, Xenophobia and related Intolerance, Durban, South Africa, 2001; World Peace Summit in South Korea, 2003; Poverty Alleviation in SE Asia Conference, New Delhi, 2004; Broadcaster, Education programmes for teachers, Tanzania, 1979-81, Tuvalu, 1985-88; Co-ordinator, Language Support for Immigrant Workers, 1989. Publications: Numerous publications on education theory, philosophy and sociology, linguistics, literature, curriculum development, HR development, culture in education, peace education, education in small states. Honours: OBE, 1998; Alfred Nobel Medal, 1991; Hind Ratan and Hind Ratan Gold Medal, India, 2002; Nav Ratan and Nav Ratan Gold Medal, India, 2003; Federation for World Peace, USA, Ambassador for Peace Award; D Ed, Emeritus International University Foundation, USA; International Education Fellow, Commonwealth Institute, London, 1976-77; Commonwealth Fellowship for Higher Education; Vice-President, India's International Conference of Intellectuals, 2004. Memberships include: Honorary Chairman, RSPCA Tanga, 1957-60; Honorary Chairman, Overseas Students Union, Newcastle upon Tyne, 1973-75; Honorary Founder and Secretary, Tanzania Commonwealth Society, 1979-84; Commonwealth Association; National President, Ahmadiyya Muslims, 1997-2001. Address: Tuvalu House, 230 Worple Road, London SW20 8RH, England. E-mail: tuvaluconsulate@netscape.net

AYCKBOURN Alan (Sir), b. 12 April 1939, London, England. Theatre Director; Playwright; Artistic Director. Plays: Mr Whatnot, 1963; Relatively Speaking, 1965; How The Other Half Loves, 1969; Time And Time Again, 1971; Absurd Person Singular, 1972; The Norman Conquests, 1973; Absent Friends, 1974; Confusions, 1974; Bedroom Farce, 1975; Just Between Ourselves, 1976; Ten Times Table, 1977; Joking Apart, 1978; Sisterly Feelings, 1979; Taking Steps, 1979; Season's Greetings, 1980; Way Upstream, 1981; Intimate Exchanges, 1982; A Chorus Of Disapproval, 1984; Woman In Mind, 1985; A Small Family Business, 1987; "Henceforward", 1987; Man Of The Moment, 1988; Mr A's Amazing Maze Plays, 1988; The Revengers' Comedies, 1989; Invisible Friends, 1989; Body Language, 1990; Wildest Dreams, 1991; Time Of My Life, 1992; Dreams From A Summer House, (music by John Pattison), 1992; Communicating Doors, 1994; Haunting Julia, 1994; By Jeeves (with Andrew Lloyd Webber), 1996; The Champion Of Paribanou, 1996; Things We Do For Love, 1997; Comic Potential, 1998; The Boy Who Fell Into A Book, 1998; House & Garden, 1999; Callisto #7, 1999; Whenever, 2000; GamePlan, 2001; FlatSpin, 2001; RolePlay, 2001; Snake In The Grass, 2002; The Jollies, 2002; Sugar Daddies, 2003; Orvin – Champion Of Champions, 2003. Honours: Hon DLitt, Hull, 1981, Keele, 1987, Leeds, 1987, York, 1992, Bradford, 1994, Cardiff University of Wales, 1996, Open University, 1998; Commander of the Order of the British Empire, 1987; Cameron Mackintosh Professor of Contemporary Theatre, 1992; Knighthood, 1997. Memberships: Garrick Club; Fellow, Royal Society of Arts. Address: c/o Casarotto Ramsay and Associates Ltd, National House, 60-66 Wardour Street, London W1V 4ND, England.

AYKROYD Daniel Edward, b. 1 July 1952, Ottawa, Canada. Actor. m. (1) Maureen Lewis, 1974, divorced, 3 sons, (2) Donna Dixon, 1984, 2 daughters. Education: Carleton University, Ottawa. Appointments: Started as stand up comedian and worked on Saturday Night Live, 1975-79; Created and performed as the Blues Brothers; Albums include: Made in America; Films include: 1941, 1979; Mr Mike's Mondo Video, 1979; The Blues Brothers, 1980; Neighbors, 1981; Doctor Detroit, 1983; Trading Places, 1983; Twilight Zone, 1983; Ghostbusters, 1984; Nothing Lasts for Ever, 1984; Into the Night, 1985; Spies Like Us, 1985; Dragnet, 1987; Caddyshack II, 1988; The Great Outdoors, 1988; My Stepmother is an Alien, 1988; Ghostbusters II, 1989; Driving Miss Daisy, 1990; My Girl; Loose Cannons; Valkemania; Nothing But Trouble, 1991; Coneheads, 1993; My Girl II, 1994; North; Casper, 1995; Sergeant Bilko, 1996; Grosse Point Blank, 1997; Blues Brothers 2000, 1997; The Arrow, 1997; Susan's Plan, 1998; Antz, 1999; Diamonds, 1999; The House of Mirth, 2000; Stardom, 2000; Dying to Get Rich, 2000; The Devil and Daniel Webster, Not A Girl, Pearl Harbour, 2001; Evolution, 2001; Crossroads, 2002; Who Shot

Dictionary of International Biography

Victor Fox, 2002; The Curse of the Jade Scorpion, 2002. Honours: Emmy Award, 1976-77. Address: c/o CAA, 9830 Wilshire Boulevard, Beverly Hills, CA 90212, USA.

AYLESWORTH Julie Ann, b. 11 April 1953, Cincinnati, Ohio, USA. Writer; Artist. Education: BA, Drama, Vassar College, 1974; Dale Carnegie Course with Honours, 1980. Appointments: Freelance Writer, Artist, Jesus' Art House, 1974-; Administrative Assistant, Joy Center, 1980-; Clerk, Marlowe Community Center, Mental Health Services, Northwest, 1984-87; Administrative Assistant, Places for the Heart Realtors, 1985-87. Publications include: Numerous poems and articles to professional journals and magazines; Composer, Lyricist, 3 songs; Several theatrical roles. Honour: Designer, Mary B Fernalding Award. Memberships: College Hill Presbyterian Church; Cincinnati Zoological and Botanical gardens; Alzheimer's Association; World Emergency Relief; International Society of Poets. Address: Jesus' Art House, 1673 Cedar Avenue, #409, Cincinnati, OH 45224-2851, USA.

AYOZIE Daniel Ogechukwu, b. 28 November 1964, Portharcourt, Nigeria. Marketing and Advertising Educator. m. Victoria Ayozie, 1 son, 1 daughter. Education: National Diploma in Marketing, 1987, Higher National Diploma in Marketing, 1990, The Federal Polytechnic, Ilaro, Nigeria; Certificate Course and all CIM International Diploma Subjects, 1991-93, Chartered Institute of Marketing, Moorhall, London; Postgraduate Diploma in Advertising, Nigeria Institute of Journalism, Ogba, Nigeria, 1993-94; International Diploma, Chartered, Registered Marketer Status, Chartered Institute of Marketing, London; MBA, Marketing Management, Ogun State University, Nigeria, 1995-98; MBA Marketing Management, 1997-98; PhD, Business Administration, Delta State University, Abraka, Nigeria in progress. Appointments include: Salesman, Danayo Inc Company, Umuahia, Nigeria, 1985-86; Salesman, Aristoplast Company Ltd, 1987-88; Head of Department, Consultant, Lecturer, School of Management and Technology, Aba, Nigeria, 1991-92; Lecturer, Course Adviser, Exam Officer, Class Tutor, Department of Marketing, Federal Polytechnic, Ilaro, Nigeria, 1992; Several part-time lecturing and consultancy positions in Nigerian universities and technical institutions, 1994- include: Lecturer and Consultant, The Chartered Institute of Marketing of Nigeria, 1997-; Lecturer and Consultant, Federal University of Technology, Akure, Nigeria, Lagos Centre, Ambrose Ali University, Owode Centre, University of Ado Ekiti Abeokute Centre, 1998-2001; President, Chairman of Council, National Institute of Marketing of Nigeria, 2003-; Member of several editorial boards. Publications: Articles in professional journals include most recently: Developing an effective marketing education in Nigeria in the 21st century. Issues to be considered and resolved, 1999; The power of the Internet. Why marketing practitioners must adopt and use it now, 2001; The Application of Quantitative Techniques in the Distribution System of Nigeria, 2003; Pricing of Petroleum Products in Nigeria, The masses vs Profitability and Deregulation, 2003; Privatisation and Deregulation in Nigeria: Matters Arising, 2003; Services Marketing in Nigeria, 2003; Books include: Marketing Communication volumes I and II; Buy And Read This Book, Integrated Marketing Communications (IMC), 2002; Successful Advertising; The only advertising technique for you, 1997; Numerous papers presented at conferences. Honours: Second Best Postgraduate Student, Nigerian Institute of Journalism, 1994; First Prize, Associateship Category Essay Competition, Advertising Practitioners Council of Nigeria, 1999; Listed in Who's Who publications and biographical dictionaries. Memberships: Nigeria Institute of Management; Fellow and Council Member, Chartered Institute of Marketing of Nigeria; Fellow, National Institute of Marketing of Nigeria (NIMN); Graduate Member, Nigerian Marketing Association; Certified Institute of Purchasing and Supply

Management; The Chartered Institute of Marketing, UK; Advertising Practitioners Council of Nigeria; President, National Institute of Marketing of Nigeria, 2003-. Address: Department of Marketing, The Federal Polytechnic, PO Box 652, Illaro, Ogun State, Nigeria 111002. E-mail: danayo2001@yahoo.com

AZAB Hassan Ahmed, b. 16 June 1950, Ismailia, Egypt. Professor of Chemistry. m. Naima Fouad, 1 son, 1 daughter. Education: BSc, Chemistry, 1972; MSc, Chemistry, 1976; PhD, Chemistry, 1983. Appointments: Professor of Analytical and Inorganic Chemistry, Head of Chemistry Department, Vice-Dean, Faculty of Science, Suez Canal University, Ismailia, Egypt. Publications: More than 70 international publications in the field of analytical and inorganic chemistry; Recent publication on biologically important DNA-protein-metal ions systems. Honours: TWAS Award, 1989; Peaceful Fellowship, 1990 DAAD Award, 1996, 2003; DGF Award, 2000. Memberships: American Chemical Society; American Association for the Advancement of Science. Address: Faculty of Science, Chemistry Department, Suez Canal University, Ismailia, Egypt. E-mail: azab2@yahoo.com

AZIM Ekram, b. 10 November 1970, Kushtia, Bangladesh. Researcher. m. Kanig Fwehana, 1 daughter. Education: BSc (Hons), Fisheries, 1995, MS, Fisheries Biology and Limnology, 1997, Bangladesh Agricultural University; PhD, Aquaculture, Wageningen University, Netherlands, 2001. Appointments: Scientific Officer, Bangladesh Fisheries Research Institute, 1996-2000; Postdoctoral Fellow, Wageningen University, Netherlands, 2001-2002; Postdoctoral Fellow, Saitama University, Japan, 2002-2004. Publications: 30 in refereed journals; 8 in professional magazines; 4 in daily newspapers. Honours: Marie Curie Scholarship, Japan Society for the Promotion of Science, Postdoctoral Scholarship. Memberships: World Aquaculture Society; International Society for Theoretical and Applied Limnology; Aquaculture Association of Canada; The Royal Netherlands Society for Agricultural Sciences. Address: Department of Applied Ecological Engineering, Saitama University, 255 Shimo-okubo, Sakwa-ku, Saitama 338-8570, Japan.

AZINGER Paul William, b. 6 January 1960, Holyoke, Massachusetts, USA. Golfer. m. Toni, 2 daughters. Education: Florida State University. Appointments: Started playing golf aged 5; Turned professional, 1981; Won Phoenix Open, 1987; Herz Bay Hill Classic, 1988; Canon Greater Hartford Open, 1989; MONY Tournament of Champions, 1990; AT and T Pebble Beach National Pro Am, 1991; TOUR Championship, 1992; BMW International Open, 1990; Memorial Tournament, New England Classic, PGA Championship, Inverness, 1993; GWAA Ben Hogan Trophy, 1995; Member, US Ryder Cup Team, 1989, 1991, 1993, 2001; Broadcasting debut as reporter for NBC, 1995; Ryder Cup. Publications: Zinger. Honours: PGA Tour Player of the Year, 1987. Address: PGA Tour, 112 Tpc Boulevard, Ponte Vedra Beach, FL 33082, USA.

AZNAR José Maria, b. 25 February 1953, Madrid, Spain. Lawyer; Politician. m. 3 children. Education: Licence in Law, Complutense University of Madrid. Appointments: State Finance Inspector; Secretary General, Logrono Popular Alliance Party, 1979; Secretary General, Popular Alliance Party, 1982-87; Avila Delegate, 1982-87; Castilla y León Regional President, Popular Alliance Party; National Vice-President, Popular Party, 1989; President, Autonomous Community of Castilla y León's Popular Alliance, 1987-89; Popular Party's Elected Candidate for Presidency of Government, 1989; National Delegate for Madrid in the 4th, 5th and 6th Legislature; President of the Popular Parliamentarian Group in the Congress of Delegates, 1991; Vice

President, European Popular Party; Vice President International Democratic Union; Vice President, European Democratic Union; Invested President of Government of Spain (Prime Minister), 1996-2004; President, International Democratic Centre (IDC), 2001. Address: Partido Popular, Genova 13, Madrid, Spain.

AZOURI Issam Jamil, b. 13 November 1963, Beirut, Lebanon. Media Consultant. m. Emily Joussef Al-Asmar, 1 son, 1 daughter. Education: Bachelor Degree in Communication (PR and Advertising), The Lebanese University, Communication and Documentation College, 1988; Crestcom Bullet-Proof Manager, 1999; Press Skills Workshop, Med-Media and BBC, 1994. Appointments: Poster Magazine, Lebanon, 1979-83; Journalist, Annahar Newspaper, Lebanon, 1984-96; TV Presenter, Antenne Plus, Lebanon, 1994-96; Media Consultant, Worldspace Corporation, USA, 1997-98; Journalist, Agence France Press and German News Agency, 1998-2000; UNEP Regional Information Officer, 2001; UN Arabic Media Trainer, Centre for Development Communication, 2001-2003; Media Consultant, Abu Dhabi Police Directorate, 2004; Sworn Expert in courts (advertising and communication),Lebanon. Publications: Evaluation of IEC Materials for UNICEF, 1999; Book Chapters: Monuments in Mount Lebanon; Code 19 of the right to good service in government offices; More than 200 articles in the press covering different topics; Several speeches. Memberships: International Association of Business Communicators, USA; Lebanese Foundation of Permanent Civil Peace, Lebanon; Journalism Education Association, USA; Press Club, Lebanon; Arab-US Association of Communication Educators, USA; Youth Association for Social Awareness, Lebanon; Environment Electronic Friends, Bahrain. Address: Mansourieh el Metn, New Road, Azouri Residence, Lebanon. E-mail: drazouri@yahoo.com

AZPITARTE ROUSSE Juan, (Juan Berekiz), b. 27 April 1959, Bilbao, Spain. Writer; Poet. Education: Graduated in Philosophy and Theology, University of Deurto, Bilbao. Appointments: President, Gerekiz Artistic Association; Founder-Member, Graphologic Association in Basque Country. Publications: La Armonia y El Vitalismo, 1985; El Poeta y el Payaso, 1986; Poemas Raros, 1987; Mi Poesia Para Ti, 1988; Meditaciones en el asfalto, 1988; Sentimentios y Sonidos, 1988; A la Pintura, 1990. Contributions to: Gemma; Clarin; Mensajero; Redención; Bilbocio; Club CCC. Honours: Prize, Proyecto Hombre de Bizkaia, 1990; Patrocinado por la Asociación Artistiva Vizcaina. Memberships: Centro Cultural, Literario e Artistico de Gazeta de Felgueiras, Portugal; International Poetry, USA; Asociación Mundial de Escritores y Centro Cultural, Literario y Artistico Agustin Garcia Alonso-La Penorra 8, Vizcaya, Spain; Asociación Artistica Vizcaina, Spain. Address: Avda Zumalacarregui 119-9a C, 48007 Bilbao, Spain.

Dictionary of International Biography

B

BAAS Danielle Josee, b. 20 February 1958, Brussels, Belgium. Composer. m. Gianniodis Nicolas, 12 December 1987, 1 son. Appointments: Walk on part, Macbeth, Verdi; Occasional forming of the choirs; Piano accompaniment for classical and variety repertoire; President of Jury. Creative Works: More than 90 compositions include: Solo Guitar, Mutatis Mutandis, 1996; Ragtime for carillon, 1997. Honour: 4th Prize, Composition Competition for Piano, USA, 1997. Memberships: Association of Belgian Composers; IAWM; Piano Trio Society; SABAM; NPMA J Strauss; WPMA Bach; NPMA Guitars; CEBEDEM, 2001; Leader of Choirs, Variety; Leader of Yolande Uyttenhove Sextuor, Belgian Contemporary Music. Address: Rue Saint Vincent de Paul 2 B, 1090 Brussels, Belgium.

BABA Motoyoshi, b. 5 February 1953, Tokyo, Japan. Education: BEng, 1976, MSc, 1978, DSc, 1981, University of Tokyo. Appointments: Professor, Institute for Solid State Physics, University of Tokyo. Memberships: Physical Society of Japan. Address: Institute for Solid State Physics, University of Tokyo, 5-1-5 Kashiwanoha, Kashiwa, Chiba 277-8581, Japan. E-mail: baba@issp.u-tokyo.ac.jp

BABICH Alexander, b. 12 November 1952, Donetsk, Ukraine. Metallurgist; Educator. m. Eugenia Goldstein, 1 son. Education: Metallurgy Engineering, Donetsk Polytechnic Institute, 1974; PhD (Tech), 1984; Associate Professor, 1989. Appointments: Furnace Worker, Foreman, Donetsk Steel Plant, 1974-76; Engineer, Scientific worker, Donetsk Polytechnic Institute, 1978-85; Associate Professor, Donetsk State University of Technology, 1985-96; Visiting Researcher, National Centre for Metallurgical Investigation, Madrid, 1997-98; Researcher, Aachen University of Technology, 1998-. Publications: Over 120 publications including a monograph, a textbook and 13 patents. Honours: Grant, Ministry of Education and Science, Spain; Who's Who in the World Diploma, 1999; Listed in several biographical publications, Address: Hauptstr 78, 52066 Aachen, Germany. E-mail: babich@iehk.rwth-aachen.de

BABINGTON Anthony Patrick, b. 4 April 1920, Cork, Ireland. Retired Judge; Writer. Education: Inns of Court Law School. Appointments: Called to Bar, 1948; Circuit Judge, London, 1972-90. Publications: For the Sake of Example; No Memorial; Military Intervention in Britain; A House in Bow Street; The Rule of Law in Britain; The Devil to Pay; The Power to Silence; The English Bastille; Shell-Shock; An Uncertain Voyage, 2000. Memberships: PEN; Society of Authors; Special Forces Club; Garrick. Address: Thydon Cottage, Chilham, Canterbury, Kent CT4 8BX, England.

BABST Dean V, b. 14 October 1921, USA. Research Scientist. m. G Wyone Whittaker, 5 April 1947, 1 son, 3 daughters. Education: BA, 1947, MA, 1950, Washington (Seattle) University. Appointments: Research Scientist, for Federal and State agencies, USA, 30 years in total; Research Scientist, Nuclear Age Peace Foundation, 17 years to date; Campaigner for nuclear arms reduction and active peace campaigner. Publications: 2 books and 1 booklet; over 100 scientific articles; Numerous articles and papers in the fields of nuclear arms reduction and war prevention. Honours: Alpha Kappa Delta, 1950; Listed in numerous international biographical reference books, including, 2000 Notable American Men, 1994, 1995, International Directory of distinguished Leadership, 1996, 1997, 500 Leaders of Influence, 1997, American Biographical Institute; Outstanding People of the 20th Century, 1998, 2000, International Biographical Centre, Cambridge, England; Peace Ambassador, 1992; Honorary Member, IBC

Advisory Committee, 1995. Memberships: Center of Defense Information; UNA-USA; International Physicians for the Prevention of Nuclear War; Peace Action; Population Communications International. Address: 4489 Juneberry Court, Concord, CA 94521, USA.

BABU Yallapragada Ramesh, b. 14 January 1952, Bhattiprolu, India. Engineer. Education: Graduate, Mechanical Department, College of Engineering, Jawaharlal Nehru Technological University, 1975; MEng, Industrial Engineering, College of Engineering, Sri Venkateswara University, 1979; PhD, Mechanical Department, College of Engineering, Andhra University, 1993. Appointments: Lecturer, Mechanical Department, Bapatla Engineering College, 1982-86; Faculty, College of Engineering, Gandhi Institute of Technology and Management, Visakhapatnam, 1986-. Publications: Several articles in professional journals. Honours: World Lifetime Achievement Award, 1997; 20th Century Award for Achievement, 1998; 2000 Millennium Medal of Honour, 1998; International Man of the Millennium, 1999; Outstanding Man of the 20th Century, 1999; International Personality of the Year 2001; International Scientist of the Year, 2001; International Man of the Year 2000-2001; Great Minds of the 21st Century; International Book of Honor; International Who's Who of Twentieth Century Achievement; 2000 Outstanding Scientists of the 20th Century; 2000 Outstanding Scientists of the 21st Century . Memberships: Indian Institution of Industrial Engineering; Institution of Engineers, India; Research Board of Advisors, ABI, USA; Advisory Council IBC, England; Listed in numerous biographical publications including Five Hundred Leaders of Influence. Address: Mechanical Department, College of Engineering, Gandhi Institute of Technology and Management, Visakhapatnam 530045, Andhra Pradesh, India.

BABULAK Eduard, b. 5 June 1957, Michalovce, Czechoslovakia. Canadian National. International Scholar; Computer Scientist; Educator; Researcher; Consultant. Education: BSc and MSc, Electrical Engineering, Technical University, Kosice, Czechoslovakia, 1977-82; MSc, Computer Science, University of East London, London, England, 1990-91; PhD Candidate, Computer Engineering, Polytechnic of Montreal, Canada, 1993-95; PhD Candidate, Electrical and Computer Engineering, University of Ottawa, Canada, 1996-2000; PhD, Computing Science, Staffordshire University, Stafford, England, 2001-2003; Chartered Engineer, UK, 2002-; European Engineer, Brussels, 2002-. Appointments: College Professor, College in Prague and Bratislava, Czechoslovakia, 1984-88; Instructor, Brighton College of Technology, Brighton, England, 1990-93; Researcher and Teaching Assistant, Polytechnic of Montreal, Canada, 1993-95; Researcher and Teaching Assistant 1996-99, Researcher and Lecturer, 1998-99, University of Ottawa, Canada; Researcher and Lecturer, Penn State Erie, Erie, Pennsylvania, USA, 1999-2000; Associate Professor, Azusa Pacific University, Azusa, California, USA, 2000-2001; Senior Lecturer, Staffordshire University, Stafford, England, 2001-; Consultant Expert, Phare European Commission, Brussels, Belgium, 1992-. Publications: Articles in professional journals and papers presented at conferences include: Session Mobility and Quality of Service Specifications for Distributed Multimedia Applications, 2000; The University Network Model for the Quality of Service Provision Analysis, 2002; Methodology to Assess the User's Perception of Quality of Service, 2003. Honours include: Honorary Member of Editorial Boards; Nominated Fellow British Computer Society; Listed in Who's Who publications and biographical dictionaries. Memberships include: Senior Member, IEEE; Professional Member, Association of Computer Machinery; IEE, UK; Mathematical Association of America; American Mathematical Society; Institution of Plant Engineers; Board of Trade of

Pennsylvania, USA; Corporate Directors in Toronto, Canada; Institute of Directors, London; Institute of Export, Peterborough, UK; American Management Association; Institute of Management, UK. Address: School of Computing, Staffordshire University, Stafford ST18 0DG, England. E-mail: e.babulak@staffs.ac.uk

BACALBAŞA-DOBROVICI Nicolae, b. 8 June 1916, Criuleni, Moldova. Professor. m. Veronica, 2 sons. Education: Engineering Agricultural Diploma, Polytechnic Institute of Bucharest, 1934-39; Specialisation in Hydrobiology, University of Bucharest, 1940-41; Specialisation in Fishery Engineering, Romanian Institute of Fishery Research, 1941; Doctor of Technical Sciences, University of Dunãrea de Jos, Gala?i, 1972-. Appointments: Assistant Professor, Fish Technology, Constantza, 1948-53; Assistant Professor, Fish Technology, Polytech Institute, Galaţi, 1953-73; Expert, Fish Technology, Rome & Niger, 1969-70; Professor, Fish Technology, University of Dunarea de Jos, Galaţi, 1974-81; Professor Consultant, University of Dunãrea de Jos, Gala?i, 1982-. Publications: 5 books; 135 articles. Memberships: SIL; International Research Association of Danube; Ichthyology/Fisheries Group; National Geographical Society; Sturgeon Species Group of the Species Survival Commission; IUCN; American Association for the Advancement of Science. Address: Reg 11 Siret Str 50, Bl G1/65, 6200- Galaţi, Romania.

BACALL Lauren, b. 16 September 1924, New York, USA. Actress. m. (1) Humphrey Bogart, 1945, died 1957, (2) Jason Robards, 1961, divorced, 2 sons, 1 daughter. Career: Films include: Two Guys from Milwaukee, 1946; The Big Sleep; Young Man with a Horn; How to Marry a Millionaire; Blood Alley, Sex and the Single Girl; Murder on the Orient Express, 1974; Appointment with Death, 1988; Misery, 1990; All I Want for Christmas, 1991; The Field, 1993; Pret á Porter, 1995. Publications: Lauren Bacall by Myself, 1978; Lauren Bacall Now, 1994. Honours: 2 Tony Awards, 1970, 1981; Woman of the Year Award, 1981. Address: c/o Johnnies Planco, William Morris Agency, 1325 Avenue of the Americas, New York, NY 10019, USA.

BACHARACH Burt, b. 12 May 1928, Kansas City, Missouri, USA. Composer; Arranger; Conductor; Musician (piano). m. (1) Paula Stewart, (2) Angie Dickinson, (3) Carole Bayer Sager, 1982, 1 son, 1 daughter. Musical Education: Composition and Theory, McGill University, Montreal; Music Academy West, Santa Barbara. Career: Jazz musician, 1940s; Accompanist, arranger, conductor, various artists including Vic Damone; Marlene Dietrich; Joel Gray; Steve Lawrence. Compositions: Popular songs, film music and stage musicals; Regular collaborations with Hal David, 1962-70; Carole Bayer Sager, 1981-; Numerous hit songs as co-writer include: with Hal David: The Story Of My Life, Marty Robbins; Magic Moments, Perry Como; Tower Of Strength, Frankie Vaughan; Wives And Lovers, Jack Jones; 24 Hours From Tulsa, Gene Pitney; What The World Needs Now Is Love, Jackie DeShannon; Walk On By; Trains And Boats And Planes; Do You Know The Way To San Jose?; Alfie (all by Dionne Warwick); Anyone Who Had A Heart, Cilla Black; There's Always Something There To Remind Me, Sandie Shaw; Make It Easy On Yourself, Walker Brothers; What's New Pussycat?, Tom Jones; This Guy's In Love With You, Herb Alpert; Raindrops Keep Fallin' On My Head, Sacha Distel; Close To You, The Carpenters; Numerous film scores include: The Man Who Shot Liberty Valence; Wives And Lovers; What's New Pussycat?; Alfie; Casino Royale; Butch Cassidy And The Sundance Kid; with Carole Bayer Sager: Making Love, Roberta Flack; Heartlight, Neil Diamond; That's What Friends Are For, Dionne Warwick And Friends (AIDs charity record); On My Own, Patti Labelle and Michael McDonald; with Carole Bayer Sager, Peter Allen and Christopher Cross: Arthur's Theme, Christopher Cross. Recordings: Albums include: Hit

Maker, 1965; Reach Out, 1967; Make It Easy On Yourself, 1969; Burt Bacharach, 1971; Portrait In Music, 1971; Living Together, 1973; Greatest Hits, 1974; Futures, 1977, 1999; Woman, 1979; Walk On By, 1989; Butch Cassidy And The Sundance Kid, 1989; Publications: Numerous songbooks. Honours: Entertainer of the Year, with Hal David, Cue Magazine, 1969; 3 Academy Awards; Several Academy Award Nominations; 4 Grammy Awards; 2 Emmy Awards; 1 Tony Award. Address: c/o McMullen And Co, Hollywood, CA, USA.

BACHTA Abdelkadur, b. 5 July 1945, Tozeur, Tunisia. Professor of Philosophy and History of Science. m. Hafida, 3 sons. Education: Tunisian General Certificate of Education, 1966; French General Certificate of Education, 1968; Professorship of French Letters, 1968; BPhil, Tunisia, 1972; MPhil, Tunisia, 1976; Highest grade of doctorate in France, Philosophy, Paris, 1983. Appointments: Professor of French in Secondary School; Professor of Philosophy in Secondary School, Tunisia; Seaker in France, Philosophy, Paris X; Professor of Philosophy in University of EAU; Professor of Philosophy in Tunis (the highest grade). Publications: Books including: (in French) L'espace et le temps chez Newton et Kant, 1991; (Arabic) What is the Epistemology?, 1995; Méthods in Islamic Science; Articles in journals on philosophy and history of science in Arabic and French. Memberships: Vice President, Arabic Society of Philosophy; CTHS French Section History of Science; French Society of 18th Century Studies; Society of History of Science, French. Address: BP 390 Pupliposte Nassr 1, Rianna 2037, Tunisia.

BACK Lloyd, b. 13 February 1933, San Francisco, USA. Mechanical Engineer. m. Carol Peterson, 1 son, 2 daughters. Education: BS, 1959, PhD, 1962, University of California at Berkeley. Appointments: Supervisor, Fluid Dynamics, Reactive Processes and Biomedical Research, Jet Propulsion Laboratory, California Institute of Technology, Pasadena, 1962-92; Clinical Assistant Professor of Medicine, University of Southern California, 1974-92; Volunteer Faculty Member, School of Medicine, University of Southern California, Los Angeles, 1992-. Publications: Over 150 experimental and analytical publications in technical journals including investigations in rocket propulsion and blood flow through diseased arteries. Honours: Exceptional Service Award, NASA, 1979; ASME Fellow, Heat Transfer Division; Distinguished Service Award, 1987; 50th Anniversary Award, 1988. Memberships: ASME; AIAA. Address: 16 Rushingwind, Irvine, CA 92614-7409, USA.

BACK Tobias, b. 11 May 1962, Erbach/Odenwald, West Germany. Neurologist; Researcher. m. Clarisse Dakouo. Education: Human Medicine, University of Heidelberg School of Medicine, with final year at the Institute of Neurology, London, 1981-88; German medical examination, 1988; American medical examination (ECFMG), 1989. Appointments: Intern, Resident, Department of Neurology and Neuroradiology, University of Heidelberg and Charité Hospital, Berlin, 1988-96; Resident, Lecturer, Department of Neurology, Ludwig-Maximilian-University, Munich, 1996-2000; Professor, Neurology/Stroke Medicine, University of Marburg, 2001-. Publications: Contributions in the field of stroke research and neurological sciences; 40 original research articles; 24 reviews; Many contributions to books. Honours: Stroke Award, German Society of Neurology, 1998; Award, European Neurological Society, 2000. Memberships: Groddeck Society of Frankfurt; International Society of Cerebral Blood Flow and Metabolism; European Neurological Society; Society for Neuroscience. Address: Department of Neurology, Philipps University, R-Bultmann-Str 8, 35039 Marburg, Germany.

Dictionary of International Biography

BACKLEY Steve, b. 12 February 1969, Sidcup, Kent, England. Athelete. Appointments: Specializes in Javelin; Coached by John Trower; Commonwealth record holder, 1992 (91,46m); Gold Medal European Junior Championships, 1987; Silver Medal, World Junior Championships, 1988; Gold Medal European Cup, 1989, 1997; Bronze Medal, 1995; Gold Medal World Student Games, 1989, 1991; Gold Medal World Cup, 1989, 1994, 1998; Gold Medal Commonwealth Games, 1990, 1994, 2002; Silver Medal, 1998; Gold Medal European Championships, 1990, 1994, 1998, 2002; Bronze Medal Olympic Games, 1992; Silver Medal, 1996, 2000; Silver Medal World Championships, 1995, 1997; Athlete of the Year, UK Athletics, 2000. Publication: The Winning Mind.

BACON Kevin, b. 8 July 1958, Philadelphia. American Actor. m. Kyra Sedgewick, 1 son, 1 daughter. Education: Manning St Actor's Theatre. Appointments: Stage appearances include: Getting On, 1978; Glad Tidings, 1979-80; Mary Barnes, 1980; Album, 1980; Forty-Deuce, 1981; Flux, 1982; Poor Little Lambs, 1982; Slab Boys, 1983; Men Without Dates, 1985; Loot, 1986; Loot, 1986; Road; Spike Heels; TV appearances include: The Gift, 1979; Enormous Changes at the Last Minute, 1982; The Demon Murder Case, 1983; Tender Age, Lemon Sky; Frasier; Happy Birthday Elizabeth: A Celebration of Life, 1997; Film appearances include: National Lampoon's Animal House, 1978; Starting Over, 1979; Hero at Large, 1980; Friday the 13th, 1980; Only When I Laugh, 1981; Diner, 1982; Footloose, 1984; Quicksilver, 1985; White Water Summer, 1987; Planes, Trains and Automobiles, 1987; End of the Line, 1988; She's having A Baby, 1988; Criminal Law, 1989; The Big Picture, 1989; Tremors, 1990; Flatliners, 1990; Queens Logic, 1991; He Said/She Said, 1991; Pyrates, 1991; JFK, 1992; A Few Good Men, 1992; The Air Up There, 1994; The River Wild, 1994; Murder in the First, 1995; Apollo 13, 1995; Sleepers, 1996; Telling Lies in America, 1997; Picture Perfect, 1997; Digging to China, 1997; Wild Things, 1998; My Dog Skip, 1999; The Hollow Man, 1999; Stir of Echoes, 1999; Novocain, 2000; We Married Margo, 2000; 24 Hours, 2001; Trapped, 2002. Address: c/o Kevin Huvane, Creative Artists Agency, 9830 Wilshire Boulevard, Beverley Hills, CA 90212, USA.

BADAL José Ignacio, b. 30 July 1945, Murcia, Spain. Professor of Physics of the Earth. m. Carmen Soriano, 1 son. Education: BSc, Physics, 1968, PhD, Physics, 1976, University of Zaragoza; Postgraduate, Department of Physics of the Earth. Appointments: Assistant Professor, 1971-76, Associate Professor, 1976-77, 1978-79, Senior Lecturer, 1979-84, Professor, Physics of the Earth, 1985-, University of Zaragoza; Head, Seismology Group, University of Zaragoza; Director, Research Projects, Referee, National Agency for Scientific Evaluation, Deputy-Director for Geodesy and Geophysics, National Geographic Institute of Spain, 1996-98; Titular Member, European Seismological Commission, 1996-2000; Referee, international scientific journals and European fellowship funding organisations; Guest Editor, Tectonophysics, Physics of the Earth and Planetary Interiors. Publications: Over 115 papers in international scientific journals; about 180 oral presentations at international meetings. Memberships: American Geophysical Union; Seismological Society of America; European Geosciences Union; Vice-President, Section of Seismology and Physics of the Earth's Interior, Spanish National Committee for Geodesy and Geophysics. Address: Physics of the Earth, University of Zaragoza, Building B, Floor 3, Pedro Cerbuna 12, 50009 Zaragoza, Spain.

BADAWI Mohamed Mustafa, b. 10 June 1925, Alexandria, Egypt. Lecturer; Writer. Education: BA, Alexandria University, 1946; BA, 1950, PhD, 1954, London University. Appointments: Research Fellow, 1947-54, Lecturer, 1954-60, Assistant Professor, 1960-64, Alexandria University, Egypt; Lecturer, Oxford University, and Brasenose College, 1964-92; Fellow, St Antony's College, Oxford, 1967-; Editor, Journal of Arabic Literature, Leiden, 1970; Advisory Board Member, Cambridge History of Arabic Literature. Publications: An Anthology of Modern Arabic Verse, 1970; Coleridge as Critic of Shakespeare, 1973; A Critical Introduction to Modern Arabic Poetry, 1975; Background to Shakespeare, 1981; Modern Arabic Literature and the West, 1985; Modern Arabic Drama in Egypt, 1987; Early Arabic Drama, 1988; Modern Arabic Literature: Cambridge History of Arabic literature (editor), 1992; A Short History of Modern Arabic Literature, 1993; Several books and volumes of verse in Arabic. Honour: King Faisal International Prize for Arabic Literature. Memberships: Ministry of Culture, Egypt; Unesco Expert on Modern Arabic Culture. Address: St Antony's College, Oxford, England.

BADCOCK Gary David, b. 13 January 1961, Bay Roberts, Canada. Assistant Professor. m. Susan Dorothy Greig, 21 December 1988, 2 daughters. Education: BA, 1981, MA, 1984, Memorial University of Newfoundland; BD, 1987, PhD, 1991, University of Edinburgh, Scotland. Appointments: Teaching Fellow, University of Aberdeen, 1991-92; Meldrum Lecturer in Dogmatic Theology, University of Edinburgh, 1993-99; Assistant Professor, Huron College, London, Ontario, 1999-. Publications: Edited with D F Wright, Disruption to Diversity: Edinburgh Divinity, 1846-1996; Theology After the Storm, by John McIntyre (editor), 1995; Light of Truth and Fire of Love, 1997; The Way of Life, 1998. Contributions to: Co-author, books and scholarly journals. Honour: Leslie Tarr Award, 1998. Address: Faculty of Theology, Huron College, London, Ontario, Canada, N6G 1H3.

BADIAN Ernst, b. 8 August 1925, Vienna, Austria. m. Nathlie A Wimsett, 1950, 1 son, 1 daughter. Education: BA, University of New Zealand, 1945; MA, 1946, BA, Oxford University, England, 1950, MA, 1954, DPhil, 1956, LitD, Victoria University, Wellington, New Zealand, 1962; LittD (Hon), Macquarie University 1993; LitD (Hon) University of Canterbury, 1999. Appointments: Junior Lecturer, Classics, Victoria University, 1947-48; Assistant Lecturer, Classics and Ancient History, University of Sheffield, England, 1952-54; Lecturer, Classics, University of Durham, England, 1954-65; Professor, Ancient History, University of Leeds, England, 1965-69; Professor, Classics and History, SUNY, Buffalo, 1969-71; Professor, History, Harvard, 1971-82; John Moors Cabot Professor of History, 1982-98, John Moors Cabot Professor Emeritus, 1998-; Visiting Professor, Universities of Colorado, Oregon, Washington, South Africa, Heidelberg, Tel-Aviv, University of California Los Angeles; Sather Professor, University of California, Berkeley, 1976; Visiting Member, Institute of Advanced Study, Princeton, Fall 1980, Fall 1992; National Humanities Centre, Fall 1988; Kommission für Alte Geschichte, Munich, May 1989. Publications: Author: Foreign Clientelae, 264-70 BC, 1958, Conington Prize Oxford University; Studies in Greek and Roman History, 1964; Roman Imperialism in the Late Republic, 1967; Publicans and Sinners, 1972; From Plataea to Potidaea: Studies in the History and Historiography of the Pentecontaetia, 1993; Zöllner und Sünder, 1997; Editor, Polybius, 1966; Ancient Society and Institutions, 1966; Sir Ronald Syme, Roman Papers Vols 1-2, 1979; American Journal of Ancient History, 1976-2001. Honours: Fellow, American Council Learned Societies, 1972-73, 1982-83, Leverhulme Fellow, England, 1973; Guggenheim Fellow, 1984; Honorary Fellow, University College, Oxford University, England; Fellow, British Academy; Fellow, American Academy of Arts and Sciences; American Numismatic Society; Honorary Member, Society for Promotion of Roman Studies; Corresponding Member, Austrian Academy of Sciences; Foreign Member, Finnish Academy of Sciences; Corresponding Member, German Archaeological Institute; Austrian Cross of Honour in Science and Art. Membership: American Philological Association; Association of Ancient Historians; Classical

Association of Canada; Australian Society for Classical Studies; UK Classical Association; Society for Promotion of Hellenic Studies; Virgil Society. Address: 101 Monroe Road, Quincy, MA 02169, USA.

BADREDDINE Yasser, b. 7 August 1942, Nabatie, Lebanon. Writer; Poet; Calligrapher. m. Faten El-Rawas, 1 daughter. Education: License in Law, Arab University of Beirut. Appointments: Secretary, Lebanese Parliamentary Work and Investigation Committee, 1972-73; Chief, Studies and Research Department, Lebanese Parliament, 1973-77; Secretary, Lebanese Parliamentary Initiative Committee, 1977-83; Lebanese Parliamentary Bodies, 1983; Chief, Art Department, Arab Development Institution, 1983-90. Publications: Writing on my Wounds, 1973; Birds after Deluge, 1978; Flowers as my Color, 1988; Sara, 1997; Separation from Home Land, 1999; Tenderness of the Soil, 2003. Honours: 1st Prize, Artistic Design, Arab and International Book Exhibition, Gold Medals 1997, 1999; Your Face and the Exile, 2001: The prize of artistic design, Arab and International Book Exhibition, 2001. Memberships: Lebanese Writers Union; South Lebanon Culture Council. Address: 2485 Terrace Georges Jutras, Apt 310, St Hubert, Quebec J3Y 7A9, Canada.

BAEK Kwang-Hyun, b. Suwon South Korea. Associate Professor. Education: BS, Biology, Kyung-Hee University, Seoul, Korea, 1987; MS, Biological Sciences, University of Southern Mississippi, Hattiesburg, Mississippi, USA, 1989; PhD, Zoology and Genetics, Iowa State University, Ames, Iowa, 1995. Appointments: Research Associate, Division of Genetics, Harvard Medical School, Howard Hughes Medical Institute, Brigham and Women's Hospital, 1996-97; Research Fellow, Division of Paediatric Oncology, Harvard Medical School, Dana-Farber Cancer Institute, 1997-99; Assistant Professor, Pochon CHA University, 1999-2002; Director, Laboratory of Molecular Reproductive Immunology, Infertility Medical Centre of CHA General Hospital, 1999-2001; Associate Professor, Pochon CHA University, 2002-; Director, Laboratory of Molecular Signal Transduction, Cell and Gene Therapy Research Institute, CHA General Hospital, 2002-. Publications: 30 articles in professional journals as author and co-author; Ad Hoc Reviewer for Bio Techniques, 1995 and Korean Journal of Genetics, 2000-2002. Honour: Grant Reviewer for US-Israel Binational Science Foundation, 2000. Address: Graduate School of Life Science and Biotechnology, Pochon CHA University, CHA General Hospital, 605 Yeoksam 1-dong, Kangnam-gu, Seoul 135-081 South Korea. E-mail: baek@cha.ac.kr

BAEK Rongmin, b. 12 April 1958, Busan, Korea. Plastic Surgeon. m. Nayoung K Baek, 1 son, 1 daughter. Education: MD, PhD, Seoul National University College of Medicine, 1984; Board Certified Plastic Surgeon, Korea, 1990. Appointments: Associate Professor and Chairman, Department of Plastic Surgery, Inje University College of Medicine. Publications: Problems in Aesthetic Contouring of the Facial Skeleton in Orientals; Profiloplasty of the Lower Face by Maxillary and Mandibular Anterior Segmental Osteotomies; Refinement in Reduction Malarplasty; A New Surgical Treatment of Keloid. Honours: First Clinical Paper Award, 1988; Letter of Appreciation from Minister of Foreign Affairs, 1998. Memberships: ASPS; ASMS; KSPRS; WSRM; ISPRS. Address: CPO Box 10948, Plastic Surgery, Inje University Medical Centre, Seoul 100-699, Korea. E-mail: ronbaek@hotmail.com

BAGGIO Roberto, b. 18 February 1967, Caldogno, Italy. Footballer. m. Andreina Fabbri, 2 daughters. Appointments: Vicenza, 1985; Florentina, 1985-90; Juventus, 1990-95; Milan,

1995-97; Bologna, 1997-98; Inter Milan, 1998-2000; Brescia, 2000-; 300 career goals to 15 December 2002; Played for Italian National Team in 1990, 1994 and 1998 World Cups. Honours: Golden Ball Award, France, 1993; FIFA World Player of the Year, 1993; European Footballer of the Year, 1993; European Player of the Year, 1994; World Player of the Year, 1994. Address: Bologna FC, Via Casteldebole 10, 40132 Bologna, Italy.

BAGSHAW Malcolm A, b. 24 June 1925, Adrian, Michigan, USA. Medical Doctor. Widower, 1 son, 2 daughters. Education: BA, Wesleyan University, Middletown, Connecticut, USA, 1946; MD, Yale University School of Medicine, 1950. Appointments include: Hospital Corps and V-12, USNR, 1943-45; Intern, 1950-51, Junior Assistant Resident, 1951-52, Assistant Resident, 1952, Grace-New Haven Community Hospital, Connecticut; Assistant Resident, Resident, Junior Clinical Instructor, Department of Radiology, University of Michigan School of Medicine, 1953-56; Instructor in Radiology, 1956-59, Assistant Professor of Radiology, 1959-62, Director, Division of Radiation Therapy, 1960-92, Associate Professor of Radiology, 1962-69, Professor of Radiology, 1969-92, First Catherine and Howard Avery Professor, 1983-92, First Henry S Kaplan and Harry Lebeson Professor in Cancer Biology, 1992, Emeritus, 1992-, Stanford University School of Medicine, Stanford, California. Publications: Book: Cancer of the Prostate. Oncologic Volume 18; Multidisciplinary Decisions on Oncology, 1983; Over 70 book chapters and symposia proceedings; Over 180 articles in medical journals as author and co-author include most recently: Effect of combined transient androgen deprivation and irradiation following radical prostatectomy for prostatic cancer, 1998; Outcomes for men with clinically nonmetastatic prostate carcinoma managed with radical prostatectomy, external beam radiotherapy, or expectant management: a retrospective analysis, 2001. Honours include: Gold Medal, Nihon University, Japan, 1984; Medal of Honor, American Cancer Society, 1984; Gold Medal American Society of Therapeutic Radiology, 1985; Distinguished Alumnus Award, Wesleyan University, 1996; Charles P Kettering Award Gold Medal, 1996; Gold Medal Radiological Society of North America, 1999; Gilbert Fletcher Gold Medal, American College of Radiology, 2002; Numerous Visiting Professorships; Listed in Who's Who publications and biographical dictionaries. Memberships include: American Association for Cancer Research; Fellow, American College of Radiology; American Medical Association; American Radium Society; American Society for Therapeutic Radiology and Oncology; California Medical Association. Address: Department of Radiation Oncology, Division of Radiation Therapy, Stanford University Medical Center, Stanford, CA 84305, USA.

BAHAA EL-DIN M Moursi, b. 30 January 1950, Beni Suef, Egypt. Professor. m. 4 sons. Education: BSc, 1972, MSc, 1978, PhD, 1985, Agricultural Economics. Appointments: Professor of Agricultural Economics, Faculty of Agriculture, 1999. Publications: 20 scientific research papers; 5 books in the field of farm management, finance, economics, investment analysis and management of small enterprises. Honours: Award for work in the field of sustainable development, High Institute of Environment. Memberships: Agricultural Syndicate; Egyptian Association of Agricultural Economists. Address: Quarter No 11, Section 7, House 17, 6 October City, Giza, Egypt. E-mail: moodyy25@hotmail.com

BAI Sang Wook, b. 19 December 1963, Seoul, Korea. Professor. m. Byung Hwa Jung, 1 son, 1 daughter. Education: MD, 1988, MS, 1994, PhD, 1999, Yonsei University, Korea. Appointments: Instructor, 1999-2000, Assistant Professor, 2000-2004, Associate Professor, 2004-, Department of Obstetrics and Gynaecology, Yonsei University, Korea. Publications: 34 articles in international

Dictionary of International Biography

journals; 80 articles in domestic journals. Honours: Academic Award, Korean Menopause Society, 2000; Distinguished Professor, Yonsei University, 2003. Memberships: American Urogynecology Society; International Urogynecological Association; International Continence Society. Address: Department of Obstetrics and Gynecology, College of Medicine, Seodal-mun gu, Shinchon-dong 124, Seoul 120-752, Korea. E-mail: swbai@yumc.yonsei.ac.kr

BAIGENT Beryl, b. 16 December 1937, Llay, Wrexham, North Wales. Teacher; Writer; Poet. m. Alan H Baigent, 19 January 1963, 3 daughters. Education: BA in Physical Education, MA in English Literature, University of Western Ontario, London, Canada. Publications: The Quiet Village, 1972; Pause, 1974; In Counterpoint, 1976; Ancestral Dreams, 1981; The Sacred Beech, 1985; Mystic Animals, 1988; Absorbing the Dark, 1990; Hiraeth: In Search of Celtic Origins, 1994; Triptych: Virgins, Victims, Votives, 1996; Celtic Tree Calendar, 1999; The Mary Poems, 2000; And a Branch Shall Grow: The Irish Connection, forthcoming. Contributions to: Various anthologies and periodicals including: Poetry and Spiritual Practice, 2003. Honours: Ontario Weekly Newspaper Award, 1979; Fritch Memorial, Canadian Authors Association, 1982; Ontario Arts Council Awards, 1983, 1985, 1987; Kent Writers Award, 1986; Black Mountain Award, 1986; Canada Council Touring Awards, 1990, 1992, 1993, 1994, 1998; Forest City Poetry Award, 1991; International Affairs Touring Award, 1991; Welsh Arts Council Awards, 1993, 1994, 1996, 1998, 1999, 2001, 2003, 2004; Muse Journal Award, 1994. Memberships: Celtic Arts Association; Canadian Poetry Association; League of Canadian Poets, Ontario Representative, 1994-96. Address: 137 Byron Avenue, Thamesford, Ontario N0M 2M0, Canada.

BAILEY Cecil Dewitt, b. 25 October 1921, Zama, Southeast Attala County, Mississippi, USA. Engineer; Educator. m. Myrtis Taylor, 3 daughters, 2 deceased. Education: Bachelor of Science, Aeronautical Engineering, Mississippi State University, 1950; Master of Science, Aeronautical Engineering, 1954, PhD, 1962, Purdue University. Appointments: Pilot, Various USAF Aircraft, World War II, 1943-47; Pilot, B-47 Six Engine Jet Powered Bomber and Instructor, High Speed Aerodynamics, McConnell Air Force Base, Kansas, USA, 1950-52; Assistant Professor, Air Force Institute of Technology, Wright-Patterson Air Force Base, Ohio, 1954-58; Chief, Air Force Systems Command Office, NASA Langley Research Center, Hampton, Virginia, 1959-63; Staff Engineer, Headquarters, Air Force Systems Command, Andrews Air Force Base, Maryland, 1963-65; Associate Professor, Air Force Institute of Technology, Wright-Patterson Air Force Base, Ohio, 1965-67; Professor, The Ohio State University, Columbus, Ohio, 1970-85; Professor Emeritus, 1985-. Publications: More than 20 technical papers in 8 archival journals include: A New Look at Hamilton's Principle, 1975; Vibration and Stability of Non-conservative Follower Force Systems, 1981; Further Remarks on the Law of Varying Action and Symbol δ, 1989; The Unifying Laws of Classical Mechanics, 2002. Honours: Commendation Medal, USAF Air Force Systems Command, 1962; Commendation Medal, USAF Institute of Technology, 1976; Charles E MacQuigg Award for Outstanding Teaching, 1976. Address: 4176 Ashmore Road, Upper Arlington, Ohio, USA. E-mail: cecildbailey@aol.com

BAILEY Colin B, b. 20 October 1955, London, England. Art Historian; Curator. Education: BA (Hons), Brasenose College, 1975-78, Diploma in the History of Art, 1978-79, D Phil, 1979-85, Oxford University. Appointments: Assistant Curator of European Painting, Philadelphia Museum of Art, USA,1985-89; Curator of European Painting and Sculpture, 1989-90, Senior Curator, 1990-94, Kimbell Art Museum, Fort Worth, Texas, USA; Chief Curator, 1995-98, Deputy Director and Chief Curator, 1998-

2000, National Gallery of Canada; Chief Curator, The Frick Collection, New York, New York, USA, 2000-. Publications: Books: Masterpieces of Impressionism and Post Impressionism: The Annenberg Collection (co-author with Joseph J Rishel), 1989; The Loves of the Gods: Mythological Painting from Watteau to David, 1991-92; Renoir's Portraits: Impressions of an Age, 1997; Jean-Baptiste Greuze, The Laundress, 2000; Gustav Klimt (1862-1910): Modernism in the Making (General editor of the catalogue and curator of the exhibition), 2001; Patriotic Taste: Collecting Modern Art in Pre-Revolutionary Paris, 2002; The Age of Watteau, Chardin and Fragonard: Masterpieces of French Eighteenth-Century Genre Painting, 2003; Numerous articles and essays in learned journals. Honours: Chevalier de l'Ordre des Arts et des Lettres, 1994; Paul Mellon Senior Visiting Fellow, CASVA, National Gallery of Art, Washington DC, 1994; Clark Fellow, Sterling and Francine Clark Institute, Williamstown, Massachusetts, 1999. Memberships: Arts Correspondent, CBC Midday, 1995-2000; Trustee and Vice-President, The American Association of Museum Curators, 2001-. Address: The Frick Collection, 1 East 70th Street, New York, NY 10021, USA.

BAILEY David, b. 2 January 1938, London, England. Photographer; Film Director. m. (1) Rosemary Bramble, 1960, (2) Catherine Deneuve, 1965; (3) Marie Helvin, divorced, (4) Catherine Dyer, 1986, 2 sons, 1 daughter. Appointments: Self taught photographer for Vogue, UK, USA, France, Italy; Advertising Photography, 1959-; Director, Commercials, 1966-; TV Documentaries, 1968-; Exhibition National Portrait Gallery, 1971; Photographers Gallery, 1973; Olympus Gallery, 1980, 1982, 1983; Victoria and Albert Museum, 1983; International Centre of Photography, New York, 1984; Hamilton Gallery, 1990, 1992; Director, Producer, TV Film Who Dealt?, 1993; Documentary: Models Close Up, 1998; Director, feature film, The Intruder, 1999. Publications: Box of Pinups, 1964; Goodbye Baby and Amen, 1969; Warhol, 1974; Beady Minces, 1974; Mixed Moments, 1976; Trouble and Strife, 1980; NW1, 1982; Black and White Memories, 1983; Nudes, 1981-84, 1984; Imagine, 1985; The Naked Eye: Great Photographers of the Nude (with Martin Harrison), 1988; If We Shadows, 1992; The Lady is a Tramp, 1995; Rock and Roll Heroes, 1997; Archive, 1999; Chasing Rainbows, 2001. Honours: Dr hc, Bradford University, 2001. Address: c/o Robert Montgomery and Partners, 3 Junction Mews, Sale Place, London, W2, England.

BAILEY D(avid) R(oy) Shackleton, b. 10 December 1917, Lancaster, England. Pope Professor Emeritus of Latin Language and Literature; Writer; Editor; Translator. m. (1) Hilary Ann Bardwell, 1967, dissolved 1974, (2) Kristine Zvirbulis, 1994. Education: BA, 1939, MA, 1943, LittD, 1957, Cambridge University. Appointments: Fellow, 1944-55, Praelector, 1954-55, Fellow and Deputy Bursar, 1964, Senior Bursar, 1965-68, Gonville and Caius College, Cambridge; University Lecturer in Tibetan, Cambridge University, 1948-68; Fellow and Director of Studies in Classics, Jesus College, Cambridge, 1955-64; Visiting Lecturer in Classics, Harvard College, 1963; Professor of Latin, 1968-74, Adjunct Professor, 1989-, University of Michigan; Andrew V Raymond Visiting Professor, State University of New York at Buffalo, 1973-74; Professor of Greek and Latin, 1975-82, Pope Professor of Latin Language and Literature, 1982-88, Professor Emeritus, 1988-, Harvard University; Editor, Harvard Studies in Classical Philology, 1978-84; Visiting Professor, Peterhouse, Cambridge, 1980-81. Publications: The Sátapañcásátka of Matrceta, 1951; Propertiana, 1956; Towards a Text of Cicero ad Atticum, 1960; Ciceronis Epistulae ad Atticum IX-XVI, 1961; Cicero's Letters to Atticus, vols I and II, 1965, vol V, 1966, vol VI, 1967, vols III and IV, 1968, vol VII, 1970; Cicero, 1971; Two Studies in Roman Nomenclature, 1976; Cicero: Epistulae ad

Familiares, 2 volumes, 1977; Cicero's Letters to Atticus, 1978; Cicero's Letters to His Friends, 2 volumes, 1978; Towards a Text of Anthologia Latina, 1979; Selected Letters of Cicero, 1980; Cicero: Epistulae ad Q Fratrem et M Brutum, 1981; Profile of Horace, 1982; Anthologia Latina I.l, 1982; Horatius, 1985; Cicero: Philippics, 1986; Ciceronis Epistulae, 4 volumes, 1987-88; Lucanus, 1988; Onomasticon to Cicero's Speeches, 1988; Quintilianus: Declamationes minores, 1989; Martialis, 1990; Back from Exile, 1991; Martial, 3 volumes, 1993; Homoeoteleuton in Latin Dactylic Verse, 1994; Onomasticon to Cicero's Letters, 1995; Onomasticon to Cicero's Treatises, 1996; Selected Classical Papers, 1997; Cicero: Letters to Atticus, 1999; Valerius Maximus, 2000; Cicero's Letters to Friends, 2000; Cicero's Letters to Quintus and Brutus, 2002; Statius Silvae, 2003; and others. Contributions to: Scholarly periodicals. Honours: Charles Goodwin Prize, American Philological Association, 1978; National Endowment for the Humanities Fellowship, 1980-81; Hon LittD, University of Dublin, 1984; Kenyon Medal, British Academy, 1985; Honorary Member, Society for Roman Studies, 1999; Honorary Fellow, Gonville and Caius College, 2000. Memberships: American Academy of Arts and Science, fellow, 1979-; American Philosophical Society; British Academy, fellow. Address: 303 North Division, Ann Arbor, MI 48104, USA.

BAILEY Donovan, b. 16 December 1967, Manchester, Jamaica. Canadian Athlete; Marketing Consultant. 1 daughter. Emigrated to Canada in 1981. Appointments: Member, Canada's Winning 4 x 100m team, Commonwealth Games, 1994; Olympic Games, 1996; World Indoor record holder for 50m, 1996; Canadian 100m record holder, 1995, 1996; World Commonwealth and Olympic 100m record holder, 1996; Retired from athletics, 2001; Founder, Donovan Bailey Foundation to assist Canadian amateur athletes. Honour: Sprinter of the Decade, Track and Field News, 1999. Address: c/o Flynn Sports Management, 606-1185, Eglinton Avenue East, Toronto, Ontario, M3C 3C6, Canada.

BAILEY-LATTY Veda Elizabeth, b. 2 June 1930, Clarendon, Jamaica, West Indies. Educator. m. Isaac Francisco Latty. Education: BA, Arts and General Studies, University of the West Indies, 1973-76; Teachers Diploma, Mico College, Jamaica, 1960-62. Appointments: Pupil Teacher, Assistant Teacher, -1960; Teacher, 1962-73; Senior Teacher, Secondary level, 1976-77; Lecturer, Senior Lecturer, Vice Principal, Teachers College, 1977-94; Principal, Private Preparatory School, 1994-99. Publications: Historical and sociological articles, not yet published. Honours: Christian Long and Faithful Service, Clarendon Baptist Association; Honours for Professional Performance, Bethlehem Teachers College; Golden Torch, Jamaica Teachers Association. Memberships: John Austin Baptist Church, Jamaica Baptist Union; Retired Jamaica Teachers Association. Address: 6 Inglewood Drive, Inglewood, Clarendon, Jamaica, West Indies.

BAILLIE Harold W, b. 13 February 1950, New Jersey, USA. Professor. m. Paula J Murray, 1 son, 3 daughters. Education: AB, Yale University, 1972; MA, 1976, PhD, 1978, Boston College. Appointments: Professor, Philosophy, University of Scranton, 1978-; Visiting Professor, Yale University, 1998; Visiting Professor, University Trnava, Republic of Slovakia, 1999-; Affiliated Faculty, Department of Public Health and Management, Tbilisi State Medical University, 2000-05. Publications: Book: Health Care Ethics: Principles and Problems, 2001; Book chapters and articles. Honours: PhD, Highest Honours, 1978; Teacher of the Year, University of Scranton, 1982; Dedicatee, Senior Class Yearbook, University of Scranton, 1997. Address: Department of Philosophy, University of Scranton, Scranton, PA 18510-4507, USA. E-mail: baillieh1@scranton.edu

BAILYN Bernard, b. 10 September 1922, Hartford, Connecticut, USA. Professor Emeritus of History; Writer. m. Lotte Lazarsfeld, 18 June 1952, 2 sons. Education: AB, Williams College, 1945; MA, 1947, PhD, 1953, Harvard University. Appointments: Instructor, 1953-54, Assistant Professor, 1954-58, Associate Professor, 1958-61, Professor of History, 1961-66, Winthrop Professor of History, 1966-81, Adams University Professor, 1981-93, Director, Charles Warren Center for Studies in American History, 1983-94, James Duncan Phillips Professor of Early American History, 1991-93, Professor Emeritus, 1993-, Harvard University; Trevelyan Lecturer, 1971, Pitt Professor of American History, 1986-87, Cambridge University; Fellow, British Academy, and Christ's College, Cambridge, 1991. Publications: The New England Merchants in the Seventeenth Century, 1955; Massachusetts Shipping, 1697-1714: A Statistical Study (with Lotte Bailyn), 1959; Education in the Forming of American Society: Needs and Opportunities for Study, 1960; Pamphlets of the American Revolution, 1750-1776, Vol 1 (editor), 1965; The Apologia of Robert Keayne: The Self-Portrait of a Puritan Merchant (editor), 1965; The Ideological Origins of the American Revolution, 1967, new edition, 1992; The Origins of American Politics, 1968; The Intellectual Migration: Europe and America, 1930-1960 (editor with Donald Fleming), 1969; Religion and Revolution: Three Biographical Studies, 1970; Law in American History (editor with Donald Fleming), 1972; The Ordeal of Thomas Hutchinson, 1974; The Great Republic: A History of the American People (with others), 1977, 4th edition, 1992; The Press and the American Revolution (editor with John B Hench), 1980; The Peopling of British North America: An Introduction, 1986; Voyagers to the West: A Passage in the Peopling of America on the Eve of the Revolution, 1986; Faces of Revolution: Personalities and Themes in the Struggle for American Independence, 1990; Strangers within the Realm: Cultural Margins of the First British Empire (editor with Philip B Morgan), 1991; The Debate on the Constitution: Federalist and Antifederalist Speeches, Articles and Letters during the Struggle over Ratification, 2 volumes, 1993. Contributions to: Scholarly journals. Honours: Bancroft Prize, 1968; Pulitzer Prizes in History, 1968, 1987; National Book Award in History, 1975; Thomas Jefferson Medal, American Philosophical Society, 1993; Honorary doctorates; Catton Prize, Society of American Historians, 2000. Memberships: American Academy of Arts and Sciences; American Historical Association, president, 1981; American Philosophical Society; National Academy of Education; Royal Historical Society. Address: 170 Clifton Street, Belmont, MA 02178, USA.

BAINBRIDGE Beryl Margaret (Dame), b. 21 November 1934, Liverpool, England. Appointments: Actress, Repertory Theatres in UK, 1949-60; Clerk, Gerald Duckworth & Co Ltd, London, 1971-73. Publications: A Weekend with Claude, 1967; Another Part of the Wood, 1968; Harriet Said, 1972; The Dressmaker, 1973; The Bottle Factory Outing, 1974; Sweet William, 1975; A Quiet Life, Injury Time, 1976; Young Adolf, 1978; Winter Garden, 1980; English Journey or the Road to Milton Keynes, 1984; Watson's Apology, 1984; Mum & Mr Amitage, 1985; Forever England, 1986; Filthy Lucre, 1986; An Awfully Big Adventure, 1989; The Birthday Boys, 1991; Every Man For Himself, 1996; Master Georgie, 1998 According to Queeney, 2001. Honours: Guardian Fiction Award, 1974; Whitbread Award, 1977; Fellow, Royal Society of Literature, 1978; DLitt, University of Liverpool, 1986; Whitbread Award, 1997; James Tate Black Award, 1998; W H Smith Fiction Award, 1998; Dame Commander of the Order of the British Empire, 2000; David Cohen Prize, 2003. Address: 42 Albert Street, London NW1 7NU, England.

BAJWA Gurmail Singh, b. 14 May 1965, Kapurthala, Punjab, India. Government Youth Officer. m. Balwinderjit Kaur, 1 daughter. Education: BA, MA, History, 1988, Punjabi University, Patiala,

Dictionary of International Biography

India; MBA, Regional Institute of Management and Administration, Chandigarh, India; Diploma in Youth in Development, sponsored by Commonwealth Youth Programme Asia Centre; MSc, Sustainable Development, ongoing 2003. Appointments include: Assistant Project Officer, National Literacy Mission, Faridkot, Pubjab, 1988-89; Youth Organiser, Department of Youth Services, Government of Punjab, Amritsar, 1990-91; Project Co-ordinator, Drug Counselling Centre, Gurdaspur District, 1991-92; Organised Vocational Training Programme for thousands of unemployed females; Established numerous youth welfare clubs; Held position of Sector Magistrate; Currently, District Youth Co-ordinator, Nehru Yuva Kendra, Chandigarh, Ministry of Youth Affairs and Sport, Government of India. Publications: Several articles on human survival values and social evils in newspapers; Participant in several TV and radio programmes as resource person. Honours: Shaheed-E-Azam-Bhagat Singh Award, 1988-89; National Youth Award, 1990-91; State Government's Appreciation Award, 1992; Commonwealth Youth Programme Asia Award, 2001-2002; Man of the Year Award, 2002; Bharet Excellence Award, 2003; American Medal of Honor, 2003; Eminent Personality of India, IBRF (Nagpur) India. Memberships: Fellow Member, Management Studies Institute New Delhi, 1990-91; Former Member, Punjab State Youth Board; Member, Secretary, District Advisory Committee on Youth Programmes; Fellow, FUWAI; Fellow, IBRF. Address: Village – Tajpur, PO Bhawani Pur, Kapurthala, Punjab, India, 144601.

BAKAŠUN Vjekoslav, b. 28 November 1929, Kostrena, Croatia. Physician. Education: Graduate, Medical Faculty, Zagreb, Croatia, 1956; Special, Epidemiololgy, 1965; Doctoral Degree, Medical Faculty, Rijeka, 1982. Appointments: Head, Department of Epidemiology, 1973-85, Director, Regional Institute of Public Health, Rijeka, 1985-97, Adviser, 1997-2001 (retired); Professor, Epidemiology Medical Faculty, Rijeka, 1982-99. Publications: Scombrotoxic fish poisioning in the Rijeka Region, 1986; Epidemic incidents of acute diarrhoeal syndrome in the tourist area of the region of Rijeka 1981-1990, 1992; A rubella outbreak in the region of Rijeka, Croatia, (co-author), 1995; Mumps in the region of Rijeka, Croatia, 1997; Social and Medical Aspects of Poisoning by Ingested Mushrooms Picked up in the Country, co-author, 1998. Honours: World Lifetime Achievement Award, ABI, 1996; Deputy Governor, ABI Research Association, 1996. Memberships: Croatian Medical Association, 1956; Croatian Epidemiological Association, 1965; American Public Health Association, 1984; Croatian Academy of Medical Sciences, 1985; LFIBA, 1996; International Society for Environmental Epidemiology, 1996. Address: Iva Sodica 15, Kostrena 51221, Croatia.

BAKDASH Mohammed Hisham, b. 9 August 1934, Damascus, Syria. Medicine. m. Mary Anne Robinson, 1 son, 1 daughter. Education: Certificate in Science, Damascus University, 1953; MD, 1959; ECFMG, USA, 1964; American Board of Neurosurgery, 1969; Intern, St Joseph Hospital, New York City, 1963; Resident in General Surgery, St Joseph's Infirmary, Atlanta, 1964; Resident in Neurosurgery, Barrow Neurology Institute, Phoenix, 1965-66; Harbor General Hospital, Torrence, 1967; Fellow, Chief Resident in Neurosurgery, UCLA, 1968-69. Appointments: Assistant Professor, 1969-74, Associate Professor, 1974-79, Professor, 1979-99, Chairman of Department, 1969-99, Professor Emeritus, 2000-, Neurosurgery, Damascus University College of Medicine; Chief Examiner in Neurosurgery, Syrian Ministry of Health, 1969-2000; Chief of Neurosurgery, Muassat University Hospital, Damascus, 1969-99; Secretary, Arab Board of Neurosurgeons, 1995-99. Publications: Author of numerous articles in professional medical journals. Honours: Citation of Merit, Syrian Supreme Council of Sciences, 1987; Syrian Medical Association, 1991; Certificate of Appreciation, Pan Arab Association of Surgeons,

1994. Memberships: American Association of Neurological Surgeons; Fellow, ACS; Syrian Society of Neuroscientists. Address: Jisr Abiad, Damascus, Syria.

BAKER Alan, b. 19 August 1939, London, England. Mathematician. Education: BSc, Mathematics, University of London, 1961; PhD, Cambridge University, 1964. Appointments: Research Fellow, 1964-68, Director of Studies, Mathematics, 1968-74, Trinity College, Cambridge; Professor of Pure Mathematics, Cambridge University, 1974; Numerous Visiting Professorships in the USA and Europe; First Turán Lecturer, János Bolyai Mathematical Society, Hungary, 1978; Research into transcendental numbers. Publications: Numerous papers; Transcendental Number Theory, 1975; A Concise Introduction to the Theory of Numbers, 1984; New Advances in Transcendence Theory, as editor, 1988. Memberships: Fellow, Royal Society, 1973; Honorary Fellow, Indian National Science Academy, 1980; European Academy, 1998; Doctor Honoris Causa, University of Louis Pasteur, Strasbourg, 1998; Honorary Member, Hungarian Academy of Sciences, 2001. Address: Department of Pure Mathematics and Mathematical Statistics, 16 Mill Lane, Cambridge, CB2 1SB, England.

BAKER Imogene S, b. 28 November 1918, Florence, Texas, USA. Photographic Company Owner. m. Coley Baker, 1 son, 1 daughter. Education: University of Texas, Austin, Texas. Appointments: Worked at University of Texas; Internal Revenue Service; Social Security Administration; Owner, Roosevelt-Baker Photo Company. Address: 1815 S Almeda, Corpus Christi, TX 78404, USA.

BAKER June Frankland, b. 27 May 1935, Schenectady, New York, USA. Teacher; Poet. m. David A Baker, 6 July 1962, 2 daughters. Education: AB, State University of New York, Albany, 1957; MA, University of Pennsylvania, 1958. Appointments: Teacher, 1958-64; Writer, 1964-; Substitute Teacher, Journalism, Columbia Basin College, 1987. Publication: Co-Editor: Sand Tracks (anthology), 1976. Contributions to: Christian Science Monitor; Bellingham Review; Berkeley Poetry Review; Blue Unicorn; Commonweal; Crab Creek Review; Crosscurrents, A Quarterly; Gulf Stream Magazine; Kaleidoscope; Kansas Quarterly; Louisville Review; Southern Poetry Review; Three Rivers Poetry Journal; Writers Forum; Poetry Northwest; Poet Lore; Hiram Poetry Review; Calliope; Flyway; Artful Dodge; Notre Dame Review; Woven on the Wind (anthology) Address: 614 Lynnwood Court, Richland, WA 99352, USA.

BAKER Margaret Joyce, b. 21 May 1918, Reading, Berkshire, England. Education: King's College, London, 1936-37. Publications: The Fighting Cocks, 1949; Four Farthings and a Thimble, 1950; A Castle and Sixpence, 1951; The Family That Grew and Grew, 1952; Lions in the Potting Shed, 1954; The Wonderful Wellington Boots, 1955; Anna Sewell and Black Beauty, 1956; The Birds of Thimblepins, 1960; Homer in Orbit, 1961; The Cats of Honeytown, 1962; Castaway Christmas, 1963; Cut off from Crumpets, 1964; The Shoe Shop Bears, 1964; Home from the Hill, 1968; Snail's Place, 1970; The Last Straw, 1971; Boots and the Ginger Bears, 1972; The Sand Bird, 1973; Lock, Stock and Barrel, 1974; Sand in Our Shoes, 1976; The Gift Horse, 1982; Catch as Catch Can, 1983; Beware of the Gnomes, 1985; The Waiting Room Doll, 1986; Fresh Fields for Daisy, 1987. Address: Prickets, Old Cleeve, Nr Minehead, Somerset TA24 6HW, England.

BAKER Paul Raymond, b. 28 September 1927, Everett, Washington, USA. Professor. m. Elizabeth Kemp, 1 child. Education: AB, Stanford University, 1949; MA, Columbia

University, 1951; PhD, Harvard University, 1960. Appointments: Professor of History, 1965-, Director of American Civilization Program, 1972-92, New York University. Publications: Views of Society and Manners in America, by Frances Wright D'Arusmont, 1963; The Fortunate Pilgrims: Americans in Italy 1800-1860, 1964; The Atomic Bomb: The Great Decision, 1968, 1976; The American Experience, 5 volumes, 1976-79; Richard Morris Hunt, 1980; Stanny: The Gilded Life of Stanford White, 1989. Contributions to: Around the Square, 1982; Master Builders, 1985; The Architecture of Richard Morris Hunt, 1986. Honour: The Turpie Award in American Studies, 1994. Address: c/o Department of History, New York University, 53 Washington Square South, New York, NY 10012 USA.

BAKER William, b. 6 July 1944, Shipston, Warwickshire, England. Professor. m. 16 November 1969, 2 daughters. Education: BA Hons, Sussex University, 1963-66; MPhil, London University, 1966-69; PhD, 1974; MLS, Loughborough, 1986. Appointments: Lecturer; Thurrock Technical College, 1969-71; Ben-Gurion University, 1971-77; University of Kent, 1977-78; West Midlands College, 1978-85; Professor, Pitzer College, Claremont, California, 1981-82; Housemaster, Clifton College, 1986-89; Professor, Northern Illinois University, 1989-; Presidential Research Professor (Distinguished Professor), Northern Illinois University, 2003-; Editor, The Year's Work in English Studies, 2000-; George Eliot – G.H. Lewes Studies, 1981-. Publications: Harold Pinter, 1973; George Eliot and Judaism, 1975; The Early History of the London Library, 1992; Literary Theories: A Case Study in Critical Performance, 1996; Nineteenth Century British Book Collectors and Bibliographers, 1997; Twentieth Century British Book Collectors and Bibliographers, 1999; Pre-Nineteenth Century British Book Collectors and Bibliographers, 1999; The Letters of Wilkie Collins, 1999; Twentieth Century Bibliography and Textual Criticism, 2000; George Eliot: A Bibliographical History, 2002. Other: Editions of letters by George Henry Lewes, George Eliot, and Wilkie Collins, 2000-. Honours: Ball Brothers Foundation Fellowship, Lilly Library, Indiana University, 1993; Bibliographical Society of America, Fellowship, 1994-95; American Philosophical Society Grant, 1997; Choice Outstanding Academic Book of the Year Award, 2000; National Endowment for the Humanities Senior Fellowship, 2002-03. Memberships: Bibliographical Society of America; ALA; MLA; SHARP. Address: Department of English, Northern Illinois University, DeKalb, Illinois, USA.

BAKER William "Buck", b. 1 September 1954, Texas, USA. Author; Actor; Lecturer. Education: Bachelor of Science, The College of the Ozarks, Missouri, USA, 1978; Graduate Teaching Assistantship, University of Hawaii, 1978-79; Postgraduate Diploma in Theatre Studies, University of Wales, Cardiff, Wales, 1980; Theatre Management Course, Royal Academy of Dramatic Art, London, England, 1981; PhD, Columbia Pacific University (UK/USA), Birmingham, England, 1988. Appointments: Associate Director, Beacon Hill Theatre, College of the Ozarks, 1979-81; Associate Professor, Chairman, Department of Theatre, Avila University, Kansas City Missouri, 1982-96 Managing Director, Goppert Theatre, 1984-85; Lecturer at numerous workshops and seminars; Currently Author and Screen Actor, films include most recently, Kansas City, 1996; Ride with the Devil, 1999; The Painting, 2002. Publications: Celtic Mythological Influences on American Theatre 1750-1875, 1993; The Director's Handbook (A Survival Guide for the Theatre Director), 1994; I Taught My Father How To Fish, 1995; A Solitary Frost, 1998; The Orphans of Carmarthen, 2001; Vault of the Griffin, 2003. Honours: Graduate Foreign Studentship, Rotary Foundation of Rotary International, 1978; Professor of the Year, Avila University, 1990, 1992; Listed in Who's Who publications and biographical dictionaries.

Memberships: American Federation of Television and Radio Artists; Screen Actors Guild. Address: 410 South Russell, Odessa, MO 65726, USA.

BAKEWELL Joan Dawson, b. 16 April 1933, Stockport. Broadcaster; Writer. m. (1)Michael Bakewell, 1955, 1 son, 1 daughter, (2) Jack Emery, 1975. Education: Newnham College, Cambridge. Appointments: TV Critic, The Times, 1978-81; Columnist, Sunday Times, 1988-90; Associate, Newnham College, Cambridge, 1980-91; Associate Fellow, 1984-87; Gov BFI, 1994-99; Chair, 1999-2003; TV Includes: Sunday Break, 1962; Home at 4.30 (writer and producer), 1964; Meeting Point, The Second Sex, 1964; Late Night Line Up, 1965-72; The Youthful Eve, 1968; Moviemakers, National Film Theatre, 1971; Film 72; Film 73; Holiday, 74, 75, 76, 77, 78 (series); Reports Action (series) 1976-78; Arts UK:OK?, 1980; Heart of the Matter, 1988-2000; My Generation, 2000; One Foot in the Past, 2000; Taboo (series), 2001; Radio includes: Artist of the Week, 1998-99; The Brains Trust, 1999-; Belief, 2000. Publications; The New Priesthood: British Television Today, 1970; A Fine and Private Place, 1977; The Complete Traveller, 1977; The Heart of the Heart of the Matter, 1996; Contributions to journals. Address: c/o Knight Ayton Management, 10 Argyll Street, London, W1V 1AB, England.

BAKHTIYAROV Sayavur, b. 18 May 1952, Baku, Azerbaijan. Educator; Researcher. m. Rasima Aliyeva, 1 son, 1 daughter. Education: Diploma, Petroleum Engineering, 1974; PhD, 1978; DSc, 1992. Appointments: Assistant Professor, 1978-83, Associate Professor, 1983-92, Professor, 1992-95, Department Head, 1992-94, Senior Research Fellow, 1995-. Publications: 12 books, 120 articles in professional journals. Honours: Outstanding Doctoral Award, Ministry of Education, Moscow, 1972; National Economy Development Award, Moscow, 1987. Memberships: ASME; AFS; British Society of Rheology; Russian Society of Rheology. Address: Mechanical Engineering Department, Auburn University, 202 Ross Hall, Auburn, AL 36849-5341, USA.

BAKLIT Gideon, b. 5 February 1956, Dungyel-Garram District, Plateau State, Nigeria. Researcher. m. Mary G Baklit, deceased, 2 sons, 2 daughters. Education: BA (Hons) Geography, 1984, MSc, Rural Development, 1991, Amada Bellu University, Zaria, Nigeria. Appointments: Master Grade II, 1980-85, Education Officer I, 1985-90, Principal Education Officer, 1992, Ministry of Education, Nigeria; Assistant Research Fellow, 1992-95, Research Fellow II, 1995-98, Research Fellow I, 1998-2001, 2001-, Member Biostaff, 2001, University of Jos, Nigeria; Member, Plateau State Industrial Development Authority, Pankshin LGA, 1996-; Consultant, First Reach Consortium, Abuja Ube Research at Taraba, 2001. Publications include: Production and Utilisation of Biomass Energy for Rural Industries in Nigeria. Towards a Policy Shift, 2000; Publications for the Social Science Academy of Nigeria. Honours: Winner of 3 year research linkage for Centre for Development Studies of the University of Jos, Higher Education Programme on Biomass Research with King's College London, 1999-2002. Memberships: Farm Management Association of Nigeria; Christian Rural and Urban Development Association of Nigeria. Address: University of Jos, Centre for Development Studies, PMB 2054, Jos, Nigeria. E-mail: baklitg@unijos.edu.ng

BALA'ZS András, b. 15 November 1949, Budapest, Hungary. Biophysicist. m. Mária Majoros, 1 son. Education: BA, Biology, 1974, MSc, Theoretical Chemistry, 1976, Eötvös L University; PhD (Candidate) Biology, Hungarian Academy of Sciences. Appointments: Research Assistant, 1974-81, Research Worker, 1981-95, Consultant, 1995-, Eötvös L University, Theoretical Chemistry Group, Departments of Atomic/Biological Physics. Publications: In professional journals. Honours: Listed in

Dictionary of International Biography

biographical publications. Memberships: European Cell Biology Organisation; Union of Hungarian Chemists; Hungarian Biochemical Society; Hungarian Theoretical Biological Society; Molecular Electronics and Biocomputing Society; Vienna Freud Museum; World Wild Fund. Address: Department of Biological Physics, Eötvös L University, Pa'zmány Sétány 1, H-1117 Budapest, Hungary.

BALCEROWICZ Leszek, b. 1947 Lipno, Poland. Politician; Economist; Banker. Education: Graduate with distinction, Foreign Trade Faculty, Central School of Planning and Statistics (now Warsaw School of Economics), Warsaw Poland, 1970; MBA, St John's University, New York, USA, 1975; PhD, Economics, Central School of Planning and Statistics; Visiting Fellow, University of Sussex, 1985; Visiting Fellow, Marburg University, 1988. Appointments: Deputy Prime Minister and Minister of Finance, 1989-91; President, Economic Committee of the Council of Ministers; Professor, 1993-, Director, Chair of International Comparative Studies, 1993-, Warsaw School of Economics; President, Freedom Union, 1995-2000; Deputy Prime Minister, Minister of Finance, President of the Economics Committee of the Council of Ministers, 1997-2000; President, National Bank of Poland, 2001-. Honours: Honorary Degrees: University of Aix-en-Provence, France; University of Sussex, UK; De Paul University, Chicago, USA; University of Szczecin, Poland; Staffordshire University, UK; Mikolaj Kopernik University of Torun, Poland; Dundee University, Scotland; Economic University, Bratislava, Slovakia; Viadrina European University, Frankfurt (Oder), Germany; University of the Pacific, Lima, Peru; Alexandru Ioan Cuza University, Iasi, Romania; Ludwig Erhard Prize, Ludwig Erhard Foundation, Germany, 1992; Finance Minister of the Year, Euromoney monthly magazine, 1998; Central European Award for the Finance Minister of the Year 1998 in Central and Eastern Europe; Transatlantic Leadership Award, European Institute of Washington, 1999; Friedrich von Hayek Prize, Germany, 2001; Carl Bertelsmann Prize, 2001; Prize, Fasel Foundation, 2002. Memberships: European Economic Association; Polish Association of Sociologists; Polish Association of Economists; Chairman, Center for Social and Economic Research, Warsaw, 1992-2000. Address: National Bank of Poland, 11/21 Swietokrzyska Street, 00-919 Warsaw, Poland.

BALDINI Edoardo, b. 22 December 1962, Piacenza, Italy. Surgeon. m. Paola Pareti. Education: Diploma di Maturita Scientifica, 1981; Diploma di Laurea in Medicina e Chirurgia, 1987; Specialisation in General Surgery, 1992; Diplome Universitaire de Laparoscopie Appliquee a La Chirurgie Digestive, Nice, Paris, 1994; Diplome Etudes Approfondies in Surgical Sciences, 1999. Appointments: Physician, Piacenza Military Hospital, 1988-90, Civil Hospital Guastalla, 1990, Civil Hospital Aosta, 1990-91; Surgeon, Centre Hospitalier Universitaire de Nice, France, 1991-99; Surgeon, G Da Saliceto Hospital, Piacenza, Italy, 2000-. Publications: Articles concerning liver transplantation, hepatobiliary surgery and laparoscopic surgery. Memberships: New York Academy of Sciences; European Association for Endoscopic Surgery; Association Française de Chirurgie. Address: Via Ricci Oddi 23, 29100 Piacenza, Italy. E-mail: ebaldini@inwind.it

BALDUZZI Fabio Edoardo, b. 24 April 1970, Tortona (AL), Italy. Technical Director, Manager; Professor. m. Claudia Zaccone. Education: Laurea, cum laude, Electronic Engineering (Honours), 1994, PhD, Computer and Systems Engineering, 1998, Polytechnic of Turin, Italy. Appointments: R&D Engineer, MJC² Ltd, Crowthorne, Berkshire, England, 1995-96; Assistant Professor, Polytechnic of Turin, Turin, Italy, 1998-2002; Technical Director Manager, ICTEAM, Torino, Turin, 2002-; Partner, Cogitek, Turin, 2001. Publications: First-Order Hybrid Petri Nets: A Model for

Optimization, 2000; Decidability Results in FOHPN, 2001. Honour: Best paper Award, IEEE International Conference on Robotics and Automation, Detroit, 1999. Memberships: Institute of Electrical and Electronic Engineers; Italian Automatic Control Group, Address: Via Verolengo 42/6/F, 10149 Torino, Italy. E-mail: fabio.balduzzi@icteam.it

BALDWIN Alec (Alexander Rae Baldwin III), b. 3 April 1958, Masapequa, New York, USA. Actor. m. Kim Basinger, 1993, 1 daughter. Education: George Washington University; NY University; Lee Strasberg Theatre Institute; Studied with Mira Rostova and Elaine Aiken. Appointments: Stage Appearances Include: Loot, 1986; Serious Money, 1988; Prelude to a Kiss, 1990; A Streetcar named Desire, 1992; TV Appearances Include: The Doctors, 1980-82; Cutter to Houston, 1982; Knot's Landing, 1984-85; Love on the Run, 1985; A Dress Gray, 1986; The Alamo: 13 Days to Glory, 1986; Sweet Revenge, 1990; Nuremberg, 2000; Path to War, 2000; Second Nature, 2002; Film Appearances Include: Forever Lulu, 1987; She's Having A baby, 1987; Beetlejuice, 1988; Married to the Mob, 1988; Talk Radio, 1988; Working Girl, 1988; Great Balls of Fire, 1989; The Hunt for Red October, 1990; Miami Blues, 1990; Alice, 1990; The Marrying Man, 1991; Prelude to a Kiss, 1992; Glengarry Glen Ross, 1992; Malice, 1993; The Getaway, 1994; The Shadow, 1994; Heaven's Prisoners, 1995; Looking for Richard, 1996; The Juror, 1996; Ghosts of Mississippi, 1996; Bookworm, 1997; The Edge, 1997; Thick as Thieves, 1998; Outside Providence, 1998; Mercury Rising (producer), 1998; The Confession, 1999; Notting Hill, 1999; Thomas and the Magic Railroad, 2000; State and Main, 2000; Pearl Harbor, 2001; Final Fantasy: The Spirit's Within, 2001; The Royal Tenenbaums, 2001; The Devil and Daniel Webster, 2001; Path to War, 2002; Dr Seuss' The Cat in the Hat, 2003; The Cooler, 2003; Along Came Polly, 2004. Honours: The World Award, 1986. Memberships: Screen Actors Guild; American Federation of TV and Radio Artists; Actors Equity Association.

BALDWIN Michael, b. 1 May 1930, Gravesend, Kent, England. Author; Poet. Education: Open Scholar, 1949, Senior Scholar, 1953, St Edmund Hall, Oxford, 1950-55. Appointments: Assistant Master, St Clement Danes Grammar School, 1955-59; Lecturer, Senior Lecturer, Principal Lecturer, Head of English and Drama Department, Whitelands College, 1959-78. Publications: The Silent Mirror, 1951; Voyage From Spring, 1956; Death on a Live Wire, 1962; How Chas Egget Lost His Way in a Creation Myth, 1967; Hob, 1972; Buried God, 1973; Snook, 1980; King Horn, 1983; The Rape of Oc, 1993. The First Mrs Wordsworth, 1996; Dark Lady, 1998. Contributions to: Listener; Encounter; New Statesman; Texas Review; BBC Wildlife Magazine; Outposts. Honours: Rediffusion Prize, 1970; Cholmondeley Award, 1984; Fellow, Royal Society of Literature, 1985. Memberships: Vice Chairman, Arvon Foundation, 1974-90; Chairman, Arvon Foundation at Lumb Bank, 1980-89; Crime Writer's Association. Address: 35 Gilbert Road, Bromley, Kent BR1 3QP, England.

BALFOUR Maria, Lady Balfour of Inchrye, b. 27 June 1934, London, England. Artist. m. Lord Balfour of Inchyre, 1 daughter. Education: American and England; Self-taught painter. Career: Exhibitions: Loggia Gallery, 1975, 1980, 1985; Paris Salon; Galerie Internationale, New York, USA; Chelsea Art Society; Kensington and Chelsea Artists; R I Galleries; Medici Galleries; Lloyds Bank, Pall Mall, London, in aid of the Mental Health Foundation, 1990; Group exhibition in Southwold, Suffolk, England in aid of British Diabetic Association, 1995; Works in private collections in New Zealand, South Africa, Belgium, Holland, USA, Great Britain, Israel and Italy; Commission: Crest for Bridal Kneeler in Guy's Chapel to celebrate the 250th year of the founding of Guy's Hospital, 1976. Publications: Works included in: Dictionary of

Artists in Britain since 1945; Artists at Walberswick (East Anglian Interlude 1880-2000). Honours: Twice Medal Winner, Internationale Academie de Lutece, Paris, 1977; Painting "Sutherland, Scotland" selected by the Arts Council for an 18 month tour including Darlington, Enfield, Lincoln, Sunderland, Westcliff-on-Sea, Chester and Derby; Listed in Who's Who publications and biographical dictionaries. Memberships: Former Member, The Free Painters and Sculptors; Former Fellow, The Royal Society of Arts. Address: 4 Marsh End, Ferry Road, Walberswick, Suffolk IP18 6TH, England.

BALINT-PERIC Ljiljana, b. 16 March 1946, Belgrade. Biologist. m. Zoltan Balint. Education: Graduate degree, 1969; MSc, 1973; Specialization in Molecular Endocrinology, 1982; PhD, Medicine, 1992; Research Associate, 1994; Senior Research Associate, 1997. Appointments: European Nuclear Medical Congress, 1980, 1981, 1982, 1983, 1984, 1985, 1987; Yugoslav Endocrine Congress, 1984, 1988; International Study Group Steroid Hormones, 1989; International Symposium Osteoporosis, 1987, 1989; International Congress on Menopause, 1990, 1996, 1999; British Society Endocrinology Meeting, 1993; Balkan Congress of Endocrinology, 1981, 1999, 2001; European Congress of Endocrinology, 1987, 1998; European Congress of Menopause, 1997; International Congress of Endocrinology, 1984, 1988, 1992; World Congress of Gynaecological Endocrinology, 1986, 1988, 1990, 1992, 1995, 1999, 2000; World Congress on Fertility and Sterility, 1992, 2001. Publications: Over 90 scientific articles in international and national science journals and books: Over 120 appearances at international and national meetings and congresses. Honours: For successful work and contributions to development of Zvezdara University Medical Centre, 1986; Award for science publications, Zvezdara University Medical Centre, 1995; Listed in numerous biographical dictionaries. Memberships: Serbian Biology Society, 1976; Serbian Medical Society, Belgrade, 1982; Yugoslav Biochemical Society, 1984; Yugoslav Nuclear Medicine Society, 1986; International Society of Gynaecological Endocrinology, 2000. Address: Zvezdara University Medical Centre, D Tucovica 161, 11000 Belgrade, Serbia.

BALL Georgiy Olexiyovych (Alexeyevich), b. 24 May 1936, Kyiv, Ukraine. Engineer; Psychologist. m. Bosova Iryna Pavlivna, 1 son. Education: Graduated, Kyiv Polytechnic Institute, 1957; Candidate of Technical Sciences, 1964; DSc, Psychology, 1991. Appointments: Research Institute of Psychology, Ukraine (now G S Kostiuk's Institute of Psychology, Academy of Pedagogic Sciences of Ukraine), 1958-; Head, Laboratory of Methodology and Theory of Psychology, 1992-. Publications include: The Apparature Correlational Analysis of Random Processes, 1968; The Theory of Learning Tasks, 1990; The Conception of Personal Self-Actualization in the Humanistic Psychology, 1993; The Psychological Contents of Personal Freedom, 1997; Personal Freedom and Humanization of Education, 2001; Today Humanism and Education, 2003. Memberships: International Academy of Humanization of Education, 1995-; Correspondent Member, Academy of Pedagogic Sciences of Ukraine, 2003-. Address: G S Kostiuk's Institute of Psychology, 2 Pankivska Street, Kyiv 01033, Ukraine. E-mail: georgbal@i.com.ua

BALL Richard Everett, b. 31 October 1937, California, USA. Professor. m. Charlotte Ann Wicks, 2 sons. Education: BA, Sociology, California State University, Long Beach, 1961; MA, Sociology, 1975, PhD, Sociology, 1980, University of Florida. Appointments: Professor, Sociology, Ferris State University, 1980-; Assistant Professor, Sociology, University of West Alabama, 1978-79; Assistant Professor, Sociology, Erskine College, 1977-78. Publications: Marital Status and Life Satisfaction Among Black Americans, 1986; Black Husbands' Satisfaction with Their Family

Life, 1986; Children and Marital Happiness of Black Americans, 1993; The American Family at the Millennium, 1998. Honours: Senior Fulbright Scholar, Japan, 1993-94, Korea, 1998-99; Distinguished Service Award, MI Sociological Association, 1996. Memberships: Michigan Sociological Association, Board of Directors, 1982-, President, 1986-87, Vice President, 1985-86, Treasurer, 1991-98; Michigan Academy, Sociology Section Chair, 1985-86; Michigan Council on Family Relations, Board of Directors, 1988-91; Japan Studies Association, Editorial Board, 2000-. Address: Department of Social Sciences, Ferris State University, Big Rapids, MI 49307-2225, USA.

BALLARD James Graham, b. 15 November 1930, Shanghai, China; British Novelist; Short Story Writer. m. Helen Mary Mathews, 1954, deceased 1964, 1 son, 2 daughters. Education: King's College, Cambridge. Publications: The Drowned World, 1963; The 4 Dimensional Nightmare, 1963; The Terminal Beach, 1964; The Drought, 1965; The Crystal World, 1966; The Disaster Area, 1967; The Atrocity Exhibition, 1970; Crash, 1973; Vermilion Sands, 1973; Concrete Island, 1974; High Rise, 1975; Low Flying Aircraft, 1976; The Unlimited Dream Company, 1979; Myths of the Near Future, 1982; Empire of the Sun, 1984; The Venus Hunters, 1986; The Day of Creation, 1987; Running Wild, 1988; Memories of the Space Age, 1988; War Fever, 1990; The Kindness of Women, 1991; The Terminal Beach (short stories), 1992; Rushing to Paradise, 1994; A User's Guide to the Millennium, 1996; Cocaine Nights, 1996; Super-Cannes, 2000; The Complete Short Stories, 2001. Address: 36 Old Charlton Road, Shepperton, Middx, TW17 8AT, England.

BALLER Detlev Georg, b. 28 October 1951, Celle, Germany. Cardiologist. m. Brigitte Diestel, 1 son. Education: Thesis Degree in Physiology, summa cum laude, 1979; PhD in Physiology, 1983; Internal Medicine, 1990; Cardiology, 1992. Appointments: Associate Professor of Physiology and Internal Medicine, 2003, Department of Cardiology, Heart Centre North Rhine-Westfalia, Ruhr University, Bochum. Publications: 100 overall. Honours: MD thesis in Physiology, summa cum laude, Georg-August University of Göttingen, 1979. Memberships: German Society of Physiology; German Society of Internal Medicine; German Society of Cardiology; Scientific Committee, European Society of Cardiology. Address: Department of Cardiology, Heart Centre North Rhine-Westfalia, Georgstr 11, D-32545 Bad Oeynhausen, Germany.

BALLESTEROS Severiano, b. 9 April 1957, Santander, Spain. Golfer. m. Carmen Botin, 1988, 2 sons, 1 daughter. Career: Professional Golfer, 1974-; Spanish Young Professional title, 1975, 1978; French Open, 1977, 1982, 1985, 1986; Japan Open, 1977, 1978; Swiss Open, 1977, 1978, 1989; German Open, 1978, 1988; Open Champ, Lytham St Anne's, 1979, 1988; St Andrews, 1984; US Masters, 1980, 1983; World Matchplay Champ, Wentworth, 1981, 1982, 1984, 1985; Australian PGA Championship, 1981; Spanish Open, 1985; Dutch Open, 1986; British Masters, 1991; PGA Championship, 1991; International Open, 1994; numerous other titles in Europe, US, Australia; Member, Ryder Cup team 1979, 1983, 1985, 1987, 1989, 1995. Publication: Trouble Shooting, 1996. Honours: Prince of Asturias prize for sport, 1989. Address: Fairway SA, Pasaje de Pena 2-4, 39008 Santander, Spain.

BALNAVE Derick, b. 17 June 1941, Lisburn, Northern Ireland. Academic. m. Maureen Dawson, 1 son, 1 daughter. Education: BSc, 1963, PhD, 1966, DSc, 1983, Queen's University, Belfast, Northern Ireland. Appointments: Scientific, 1966-69, Senior Scientific, 1969-73, Principal Scientific, 1973-77, Officer, Department of Agriculture, Northern Ireland; Assistant Lecturer, 1967-71, Lecturer, 1971-75, Senior Lecturer, 1975-77, Reader, 1977, Queen's University, Belfast; Senior Lecturer, 1978-81,

Associate Professor, 1981-2001, University of Sydney, Australia; Research Director, Poultry Research Foundation, University of Sydney, 1978-2001; Honorary Governor, Poultry Research Foundation, University of Sydney, 2001-; Adjunct Professor, North Carolina State University, 1995-; Visiting Fellow, Cornell University, 1989. Publications: Approximately 150 scientific papers in professional journals; Over 200 conference and trade publications. Honours: Recipient, World's Poultry Science Association Australia Poultry Award, 1998. Memberships: Fellow, Royal Society of Chemistry; World's Poultry Science Association; Poultry Science Association Inc. Address: 26 Valley View Drive, Narellan, New South Wales, 2567 Australia. E-mail: derick.balnave@bigpond.com

BALTAS Nicholas Constantinos, b. 20 August 1946, Kastania, Evrytania, Greece. Professor of Economics. m. Maria (Tsamboula) Balta, 1 son, 1 daughter. Education: Athens School of Economics and Business Science, Department of Economics, 1965-70; MSoc Sc, 1970-72, PhD, 1972-74, University of Birmingham. Appointments: Research Assistant, Department of Econometrics and Social Statistics, University of Birmingham, 1972; Lecturer, Economics, British Institute of Marketing, 1975-76; Lecturer, Econometrics, Department of Economics, Aristotelion University of Thessaloniki, 1976-79; Senior Economist, Research and Planning Division, Agricultural Bank of Greece, 1976-1986; Associate Professor of Economics, 1985-90, Professor of Economics, 1990-, Head of Department, 1999-2003, Athens University of Economics and Business, Department of Economics. Publications include: Books and Research Monographs: The Role of State Intervention in Fruit Production, 1977; Expert, European Commission (DGRTO and DGTREN), 2002-03; Expert, Ministry of Agriculture, Greece, 2002-03; Expert, Economic and Social Committee, Greece, 2003 and 2004; Financing Investment in the Agricultural Sector, 1983; Topics of Economic Policy of the European Communities, 1989; A Short Run Model for the Poultry Sector in Greece, 1991; Incorporating Environmental Valuation into Policy Analysis, 1996; Economic Interdependence and Cooperation in Europe, 1998; Development Strategy and Investment in the Processing and Marketing of Agricultural Products, 2001; Numerous journals, book and conference proceedings and articles including: Private Investment and the Demand for Loanable Funds in the Greek Agricultural Sector, 1999; Common Agricultural Policy: Past, Present and Future, 2001; Modelling Farmers Land Use Decisions, 2002; The Welfare Effects of the Berlin CAP Agreement on Greek Agriculture, 2002; The Economy of the European Union, 2004; Book review: The Greek Economy: Sources of Growth in the Postwar Era, 1993. Honours: Fulbright Scholarship, 1991; British Council Scholarship, 1993; Jean Monnet Chair: EU Institutions and Economic Policy, 1999. Memberships include: Hellenic University Association for European Studies, President, 1999-2000 and 2002-03; European Community Studies Association; The Agricultural Economics Society; Greek Agricultural Economic Society; Hellenic Economic Association, Hellenic Operational Research Society. Address: Athens University of Economics and Business, 76 Patission Str, 104 34 Athens, Greece. E-mail: baltas@aueb.gr

BALZER Leslie Alfred, b. 17 October 1944, Sydney, New South Wales, Australia. Professor of Finance. m. Jannette Elaine Balzer, 1 son, 1 daughter. Education: BSc, Mathematics, Physics, BE Honours, 1st Class, University of New South Wales; PhD, Control and Management Systems, University of Cambridge, England; Graduate Diploma, Applied Finance and Investment, Securities Institute of Australia. Appointments include: Senior Lecturer, University of Technology, Sydney, 1976-83; Manager, Advanced Technology Centre, New South Wales Department of Industrial Development, 1983-85; Dean, Faculty of Engineering, Royal

Melbourne Institute of Technology, 1985-86; Company Director, Technisearch Ltd, 1985-86; Senior Executive, Pring Dean Ltd, 1986-89; Associate Principal, 1989, Principal, 1990, William M Mercer Pty Ltd; Director, John Ford and Associates Pty Ltd, 1990-91; Investment Manager, Lend Lease Corporation, 1991-2001; Principal and Senior Portfolio Manager, State Street Global Advisors, Australia, 2001-2003; Director, ASX Settlements and Transfer Corporation Pty Ltd, 2000-2003; Adjunct Professor of Finance, 2002-2003, Professor of Finance, 2003-, School of Banking and Finance, University of New South Wales; Member, Investment Strategy Committee of Board, 2003- and Head of Research, 2004-, Hedge Funds of Australia, 2003-. Publications: Over 30 papers in international research journals and international and research conferences; Author, major chapter entitled Investment Risk: a unified approach to upside and downside returns in Managing Downside Risk in Financial Markets, Editors, F Sortino and S E Satchell 2001. Honours: Colonial Sugar Refining Prize, A E Goodwin Memorial Scholar, University of New South Wales; Outstanding Paper of the Year, Journal of Investing, New York, 1994; Halmstad Prize, American Actuarial Education and Research Foundation, 1982. Memberships: Former Charter Member, American Society for Engineering Management; Fellow, Securities Institute of Australia; Fellow, Australian Institute of Company Directors; Fellow, Institution of Engineers, Australia, National Committee on Control and Computer Systems Chairman, 1985-86; Fellow, Institute of Mathematics and Its Applications, UK; Associate Fellow, Australian Institute of Management, Small Business Group Chairman, 1984; Australian Secretary, Asian-Oceanian Computing Industry Organisation, 1984-85; Vice-President, 1990-95, President, 1995-97, Q-Group, Australia; Former Australian representative on various technical committees; International Federation of Automatic Control. Address: PO Box 785, Pymble, New South Wales 2073, Australia. E-mail: lbalzer@bigpond.net.au

BAM Anthony M, b. 26 June 1946, Umtata, South Africa. Professor of Economic Development Studies. m. Julia Bam, 2 sons, 5 daughters. Education: FIAC (SA), 1979; B Com (Hons), 1994; Master of Business Administration, 1995; Master of Science, 1997; Doctor of Philosophy, 2003. Appointments: Accountant, Auditor, 10 years; National Director of Education, 5 years; Management Consultant, 5 years; Professor of Economic Development Studies, Chief Executive Officer, 2 years. Publications: Problems of Changing Consumer Demand in South Africa, 1996; Development of a Training Strategy for Productivity, 1997; Role of Foreign Direct Investment in South African Foreign Policy, 1999; The Problem of Consistent Disequilibrium in South Africa's Economy, 2002. Honour: National Award, Certificate of Excellence in Administration and Management, Government of Republic of South Africa presented by the State President, 1996. Memberships: Black Management Forum; Executive Member, Free Market Foundation. Address: PO Box 1212, Cape Town 8000, South Africa. E-mail: profbam@breadempowerment.co.za

BANARASI Das, b. 16 October 1955, Akorhi, Mirzapur, India. Teacher; Poet. m. Vimala Devi, 10 March 1972, 1 son. Education: Sahityacharya (Equivalent to MA in Sanskrit), 1982; BTC, 1988; MA, Hindi Literature, 1993. Appointments: Assistant Teacher, Government Basic School, Mirzapur, India. Publications: Srihanumadvandana, 1982; Srivindhyavasinicharitamrit, 1989; Sriashtabhujakathamanjari, 1991; Paryavarankaumudi in Sanskrit, Hindi, English, 1993; Utsarg, 1995; Hymn to Lord (Hanuman), 1995; Gandhari, 1996; Silver Poems, 1998. Contributions to: Poet International, Anthologised in Poems 96, World Poetry, 1996-2000. Honours: Sanskrit Literature Award, Uttar Pradesh Government Sanskrit Academy, 1995; Gram Ratna Award by Gram Panchayat

Akorhi, Mirzapur, 1996; Winged Word Award, International Socio-Literary Foundation, 1997. Address: s/o Srimolai, Village-Post Akorhi, District, Mirzapur 231307, UP, India.

BANATVALA Jangu, b. 7 January 1934, London. Doctor of Medicine. m. Roshan Mugaseth, 3 sons, 1 daughter, deceased. Education: Gonville and Caius College, Cambridge; The London Hospital Medical College; Department of Epidemiology and Health, Yale University, USA. Appointments: Polio Fund Research Fellow, Department of Pathology, University of Cambridge, 1961-64; Research Fellow, Department of Epidemiology and Health, University of Yale, 1964-65; Senior Lecturer and Reader, 1965-75, Professor, Clinical Virology, Honorary Consultant to the Hospitals (NHS trusts), 1975-99, St Thomas' Hospital Medical School later United Medical and Dental Schools of Guy's and St Thomas' Hospitals; Honorary Consultant Microbiologist to the Army, 1992-97; Emeritus Professor, Clinical Virology, Guy's, King's and St Thomas' School of Medicine and Dentistry, 1999-. Publications include: About 230 peer reviewed original papers published in General Medical journals and specialist Medical Journals; 50 Editorials for Lancet and BMJ; 30 Chapters in books; Editor, 3 books including Editions 1-4 (5th in progress) of Principles and Practice of Clinical Virology (joint editor); Various reports on blood borne virus infections. Honours: Whitby Medal, University of Cambridge, 1964; Founder Member, Academy of Medical Sciences, 1998; CBE, 1999. Memberships: Council of Governors, Forrest School, London, Mill Hill School, London; Freeman, City of London, 1987; Liveryman, Society of Apothecaries, 1986; Athenaeum; MCC; Leander, Henley on Thames; Honorary member, Hawks, Cambridge. Address: Church End, Henham, Bishops Stortford, Herts, CM22 6AN, England. E-mail: jangu@church-end-henham.co.uk

BANCIU Desideriu Mircea, b. 19 August 1941, Hunedoara, Romania. Professor of Chemistry. m. Anca Adriana, 1 daughter. Education: Chemical Engineer, 1962; PhD, 1969; Postdoctoral Fellow, Cologne, Germany. Appointments: Assistant, 1962-72, Assistant Professor, 1972-80, Associate Professor, 1980-90, Full Professor, 1990-, University Politechnica. Publications: Over 145 original papers of organic chemistry in refereed journals; 11 books in Romania and USA. Honours: Knight of the National Order, Faithful Service, Ministry of Education Award, 1969; Gh Spacu Chemistry Award, Romanian Academy, 1982; Listed in numerous biographical publications. Memberships: Full Member, Romanian Academy, President of the Chemical Sciences Section; ACS; European Chemical Society; Romanian Chemical Society; IUPAC Affiliate. Address: Romanian Academy, Calea Victoriei 125, 71102 Bucharest, Romania.

BANCROFT Anne, b. 17 September 1931, New York, USA. Actress. m. (2) Mel Brooks, 1964, 1 son. Appointments: Theatre: Broadway debut in Two for the Seesaw, 1958; Played Anne Sullivan, The Miracle Worker, 1959-60; A Cry of Prayers, 1968; Golda, 1977; The Devils, 1977; Mystery of the Rose Bouquet, 1989; Films: The Miracle Worker; Don't Bother to Knock; Tonight We Sing; Demetrius and the Gladiators; The Pumpkin Eater; Seven Women; The Graduate, 1968; Young Winston, 1971; The Prisoner of Second Avenue, 1974; The Hindenburg, 1975; Lipstick, 1976; Silent Movie, 1976; The Turning Point, 1977; Silent Movie, The Elephant Man, 1980; To Be or Not to Be, 1984; Agnes of God, 1985; 84 Charing Cross Road, 1986; Torch Song Trilogy, 1989; Bert Rigby You're a Fool, 1989; Broadway Bound, 1992; How to Make An American Quilt, 1995; Home for the Holidays, 1995; The Homecoming, 1996; Sunchasers, 1997; Critical Care, 1997; Great Expectations, 1998; Twin's America in 3D, 1998; Up at the Villa, 1999; Deep in My Heart, 1999; Wrote, Directed, Acted, Fatso; Numerous TV Appearances. Honours: Academy Award, The Miracle Worker, 1962; Golden Globe Award, 1968; Emmy

Award, Annie, the Woman in the Life of A Man, 1970; Lifetime Achievement, Comedy Award; American Comedy Awards, 1996. Address: c/o The Culver Studios, 9336 W Washington Boulevard, Culver City, CA 90232, USA.

BANCROFT Anne, b. 17 April 1923, London, England. Author. 2 sons, 2 daughters. Education: Sidney Webb Teacher's Training College, 1961-63. Publications: Religions of the East, 1974; Twentieth Century Mystics and Sages, 1976, republished 1989; Zen: Direct Pointing to Reality, 1980; The Luminous Vision, 1980, republished 1989; Six Medieval Mystics, 1981; Chinse New Year, 1984; Festivals of the Buddha, 1984; The Buddhist World, 1984; The New Religious World, 1985; Origins of the Sacred: The Spiritual Way in Western Tradition, 1987; Weavers of Wisdom, 1989. Contributions to: The Middle Way; Everyman's Encyclopedia; Women in the World's Religions. Memberships: Society of Authors; Society of Women Writers and Journalists. Address: 1 Grange Villas, The Street, Charmouth, Bridport, Dorset DT6 6QQ, England.

BANDERAS Antonio, b. 1960, Malaga. Film Actor. m. (1) Anna Banderas, (2) Melanie Griffith, 1996, 1 child. Appointments: Began Acting aged 14; Performed with National Theatre, Madrid, 6 Years; Films Include: Labyrinth of Passion; El Senor Galindez; El Caso Almeria; The Stilts; 27 Hours; Law of Desire; Matador; Tie Me Up! Tie Me Down!; Woman on the Verge of a Nervous Breakdown; The House of Spirits; Interviews with the Vampire; Philadelphia; The Mambo King; Love and Shadow; Miami Rhapsody; Young Mussolini; Return of Mariaolu; Assassins; Desperado; Evita; Never Talk to Strangers; Crazy in Alabama (director); The 13th Warrior; Dancing in the Dark, 2000; The Body, 2000; Spy Kids, 2001; Femme Fatale, 2002; Frida, 2002; Spy Kids 2: Island of Lost Dreams, 2002; Spy Kids 3-D: Game Over, 2003; Once Upon a Time in Mexico, 2003; Imagining Argentina, 2003. Address: c/o CAA, 9830 Wilshire Boulevard, Beverley Hills, CA 90212, USA.

BANDI Tünde, b. 17 May 1964, Cluj Napoca, Romania. Dentist. m. András-Zsolt Bandi, 2 daughters (twins). Education: Diploma in Dentistry, Medical University of Timosoara, Romania, 1989; Examination of Secondary Dentistry, 1992; Specialist in General Dentistry, 2002. Appointments: Dentist, Clinic of Paediatric Dentistry, Timisoara, 1990-92; School Dentist, Timisoara, 1992-97; Private Practice, 1997-. Membership: National Union of Dentists, Romania. Address: Vacarescu 4, Timisoara, Romania. E-mail: bandiko2002@yahoo.com

BANDYOPADHYAY Prayag, (B Prayag), b. 19 April 1945, India. m. Mitali, 16 April 1984, 1 daughter. Education: MA. Appointments: Lecturer, 1969-74; Senior Assistant Professor, 1974-. Publications: Prelude; Summer Thoughts; Shadows in a Subway; Selected Poems; The Highway Penguins; The Blue Threads; The Voice of a Terror; The Words Upside Down. Contributions to: Youth Times; Illustrated Weekly of India; Asian Modern Poetry, 1982, 1984, 1988; Li Poetry, Taiwan, 1989. Honours: 1st Prize, 5th World Congress of Poets, 1981; Mentioned as Poet Extraordinary in Tokyo; Honorary DLitt. Membership: Asian Poetry Centre, chairman. Address: 357/1/12/1, Prince Anwar Shah Road, Calcutta 68, India.

BANGHAM Alec Douglas, b. 10 November 1921, Manchester, England. Medical Biophysicist. m. Rosalind Barbara Reiss, 3 sons, 1 daughter. Education: Chelsea Polytechnic, 1939-41; University College, London, 1941-42; University College Hospital, London, 1942-44; MRCS LRCP, 1944; MB.BS, 1946; MD (London), 1965. Appointments: National Service, Captain RAMC, 1947-49; Lecturer Pathology, University College Hospital, London, 1949-52; Principal Scientific Officer, 1952-62; Senior Principal Scientific Officer, Institute of Animal Physiology, Babraham, 1962-82;

Dictionary of International Biography

Retired, 1982. Publications: 124 publications on the subjects: Cortisone and inflammation, surfaces of blood cells, phospholipases, genetics of haemoglobins, structure/function of cell membranes, liposomes as model membrane, mechanisms of anaesthesia, geodesic planes and lung mechanics. Honour: Distinguished Fellow Royal College of Physicians. Memberships: Elected Fellow of the Royal Society, 1977; Elected Fellow, University College (London), 1980; Elected Member Royal Society of Chemistry. Address: 17 High Green, Great Shelford, Cambridge, CB2 5EG, England.

BANISTER Judith, b. 10 September 1943, Washington DC, USA. Demographer. m. Kim Woodard, 1 son, 1 daughter. Education: BA, Swarthmore College, 1965; PhD, Stanford University, 1978. Appointments: Postdoctoral Research Fellow, East West Population Institute, 1978-80; Analyst, US Bureau of the Census, 1980-82; Adjunct Professor, George Washington University, 1981-91; Chief, China Branch, US Bureau of the Census, 1982-92; Chief, Center for International Research, US Bureau of the Census, 1992-94; Chief, International Programs Center, US Bureau of the Census, 1994-97; Professor, Hong Kong University of Science And Technology, 1997-2001; Senior Consultant, Javelin Investments, 2001-; Honorary Professor, Hong Kong University, 2002-. Publications: China's Changing Population, 1987; Vietnam Population Dynamics and Prospects, 1993; Articles, Conference Papers on China, Korea, Indochina, South Asia. Memberships: International Union for the Scientific Study of Population; Population Association of America; Association of Asian Studies; American Chamber of Commerce, Beijing. Address: Beijing Javelin Investment Consulting Company, Guan Cheng Yuan (Citichamp Place), Building 16, Suite 21-A, Madian, Haidian District, Beijing 100088, China.

BANKAVS Andrejs, b. 13 January 1945, Latvia. Linguist. m. Rota Tambaka, 1 son, 1 daughter. Education: Faculty of Foreign Languages, University of Latvia, 1968; PhDr, Linguistics, State Pedagogical Institute of Foreign Languages, Minsk, Belarus, 1978; Dr habil philol, University of Latvia, Riga, Latvia, 1993. Appointments: Lecturer, Associate Professor, 1968-93, Dean, 1979-86, Faculty of Foreign Languages, Professor, 1994-, Head of Romance Languages, Department of Faculty of Modern Languages, 1995-, University of Latvia; Chairman, Latvian Council of Science, Expert Committee for Linguistics, Literature and Arts, 1991-2000; Member, Scientific Council, Institute of Latvian Linguistics, 1993-; Guest Professor, University of Sauliai, Lithuania, 1999-2001. Publications: Approximately 110 articles in professional journals. Memberships: President, Latvian Teachers Council; Vice President, Canadian Studies in Latvia. Address: Visvalza 4a, Riga, LV 1050, Latvia. E-mail: anbank@lanet.lv

BANKS Iain, b. 1954, Fife, Scotland. Author. Education: Stirling University. Appointments: Technician, British Steel, 1976; IBM, Greenock, 1978. Publications: The Wasp Factory, 1984; Walking on Glass, 1985; The Bridge, 1986; Espedair Street, 1987; Canal Dreams, 1989; The Crow Road (adapted as TV series, 1996), 1992; Complicity, 1993; Whit, 1995; Science Fiction: Consider Phlebas, 1987; The Player of Games, 1988; Use of Weapons, 1990; The State of the Art, 1991; Against a Dark Background, 1993; Feersum Endjinn, 1994; Excession, 1996; A Song of Stone, 1998; Inversions, 1998; The Business, 1999; Windward, 2000; Dead Air, 2002. Address: c/o Little, Brown, Brettenham House, Lancaster Place, London, WC2E 7EN, England.

BANKS Russell, b. 28 March 1940, Barnstead. Author. m. (1) Darlene Bennett, divorced, 1962, 1 daughter, (2) Mary Gunst, divorced 1977, 3 daughters, (3) Kathy Walton, divorced 1988, (4) Chase Twichell. Education: Colgate University; University of North

Carolina, Chapel Hill. Appointments: Teacher, Creative Writing, Emerson College, Boston; University of New Hampshire, Durham; University of Alabama; New England College; Teacher, Creative Writing, Princeton University, 1982-. Publications: Waiting to Freeze, 1967; 30/6, 1969; Snow; Meditation of a Cautious Man in Winter, 1974; Novels: Family Life, 1975; Hamilton Stark, 1978; The Book of Jamaica, 1980; The Relation of My Imprisonment, 1984; Continental Drift, 1985; Affliction, 1989; The Sweet Hereafter, 1991; Rule of the Bone, 1995; Cloudsplitter, 1998; The Angel on the Roof, 2000; Collected Short Stories; Searching for Survivors, 1975; The New World, 1978; Trailerpark, 1981; Success Stories, 1986; Short Stories in literary magazines. Honours: Fels Award for Fiction, 1974; John Dos Passos Award; American Academy of Arts and Letters Award, 1985. Address: 1000 Park Avenue, New York, NY 10028, USA.

BANNING Raymond Ernest, b. 16 January 1952, Ramsgate, Kent, England. Pianist. m. Marie-Louise Banning. Education: Royal College of Music, London, England. Appointments: Concert pianist; Professor of Piano, Trinity College of Music; Director, The Oldie Piano Courses; Mentor, CT ABRSM. Publications: Regular contributions, The Oldie magazine. Memberships: Incorporated Society of Musicians; European Piano Teachers' Association. Address: 22 Chestnut Lane, Kingsnorth, Ashford, Kent, TN23 3LR. E-mail: rban1@aol.com

BANNISTER Matthew, b. 16 March 1957. Broadcasting Executive. m. (1) Amanda Gerrard Walker, 1984, deceased 1988, 1 daughter, (2) Shelagh Margaret Mcleod, 1989, 1 son. Education: Nottingham University. Appointments: Presenter, BBC Radio Nottingham, 1978-81; Reporter, Presenter, Capital Radio, London, 1981-83; Deputy Head, News and Talks, 1985-87; Head, 1987-88; Newsbeat, BBC Radio 1, 1983-85; Managing Editor, BBC Greater London Radio, 1988-91; Project Co-ordinator, BBC Charter Renewal, 1991-93; Controller, BBC Radio 1, 1993-96; Director, BBC Radio, 1996-98; Head of Productions, BBC TV, 1999-2000; Director, Marketing and Communications Association, 2000; Chair, Trust the DJ, 2001-; Presenter, BBC Radio 5 Live, 2002-. Membership: Board, Chichester Festival Theatre, 1999-. Address: Trust the DJ, Units 13-14, Barley Shotts Business Park, Acklam Road, London, W10 5YG, England. E-mail: contact@trustthedj.com Website: www.trustthedj.com

BANNISTER Roger G, b. 23 March 1929, London. Athlete; Consultant Physician; Neurologist; University Administrator. m. Moyra Elver Jacobsson, 2 sons, 2 daughters. Education: University College School Exeter; Merton College; Oxford St Mary's Hospital, Medical School, London. Appointments: Winner, Oxford and Cambridge Mile, 1947-50; President, Oxford University, Athletic Club, 1948; British Mile Champion, 1951, 1953, 1954; World Record One Mile, 1954; First Sub Four Minute Mile, 1954; Master Pembroke College, Oxford, 1985-93; Honorary Consultant Neurologist, St Mary's Hospital, Medical School, National Hospital for Neurology and Neurosurgery, London (non-executive director); London and Oxford District and Region; Chair, St Mary's Hospital Development Trust; Chair, Government Working Group on Sport in the Universities, 1995-97; Chair, Clinical Autonomic Research Society, 1982-84. Publications: First Four Minutes, 1955 (republished as Four Minute Mile, 1989); Editor, Brain and Bannister's Clinical Neurology, 1992; Autonomic Faliure (co-editor), 1993; Various Medical Articles on Physiology and Neurology. Honours: Honorary Fellow, Exeter College, Oxford, 1950; Merton College, Oxford, 1986; Honorary Fellow, UMIST, 1974; Honorary LLD, Liverpool, 1972; Honorary DSc, Sheffield, 1978; Grinnell, 1984; Bath, 1984; Rochester, 1986; Williams, 1987; Dr hc, Jvvaskyla, Finland; Honorary MD, Pavia, 1986; Honorary DL, University of Victoria, Canada, 1994; University of Wales, Cardiff, 1995; Loughborough, 1996; University of East Anglia, 1997; Hans-Heinrich Siegbert Prize, 1977. Memberships: Physiological Society; Medical Research Society; Association of British Neurologists; Fellow, Imperial College; Leeds Castle Foundation, 1988-; St Mary's Hospital Medical School Trust, 1994-. Address: 21 Bardwell Road, Oxford, OX2 6SU, England.

BANVILLE John, b. 8 December 1945, Wexford, Ireland. Author. m. Janet Dunham, 2 sons. Education: St Peter's College, Wexford. Appointment: Literary Editor, 1988-2000, Chief Literary Critic and Associate Literary Editor, 2000-, Irish Times, Dublin, 1988;. Publications: Nightspawn, 1971; Birchwood, 1973; Doctor Copernicus, 1976; Kepler, 1983; The Newton Letter: An Interlude, 1985; Mefisto, 1987; The Book of Evidence, 1989; Ghosts, 1993; Athena, 1995; The Untouchable, 1997; Eclipse, 2000; Shroud, 2002; Prague Pictures: Portraits of a City, 2003. Contributions to: New York Review of Books, New Republic, The Nation; Irish Times; The Guardian. Address c/o Gillon Aitken Associates Ltd., 29 Fernshaw Road, London SW10 0TG, England.

BAO Katherine Sung, b. 7 September 1920, Soochou, Kiangsu, China. Paediatric Cardiologist. m. William S Ting, 2 May 1948, 2 sons. Education: MD, National Central University Medical College, Nanking, China, 1944; Intern, Mercer Hospital, Trenton, New Jersey, 1953; Resident, Children's Memorial Hospital, Northwestern University, Chicago, 1954-57. Appointments: Diplomate, American Board of Paediatrics, Fellow, Paediatric Cardiology, Children's Hospital, Los Angeles, 1957-59; Attending Cardiologist, Children's Hospital, Los Angeles, 1960-; Chief of Paediatric Cardiology, City of Hope Medical Center, Duarte; Visiting Paediatric Cardiologist to universities in Taipei National Science Council, Republic of China; President's Appointee, President's Committee on National Medal of Science; Adviser to the Commission on Health and Medical Care Services, Department of Health Services, California; Chief of the Heart Board, Los Angeles Unified School District and PTA Specialty Health Clinics; Attending Paediatrician and Cardiologist, Hollywood Presbyterian Medical Center; Attending Paediatrician and Cardiologist, University of California at Los Angeles. Honours: Physician of the Year, Honorary Service Award, California Congress of PTA Inc; US Representative Senatorial Medal of Freedom. Memberships: Republican Eagle; Life Member, Republican Presidential Task Force; Republican Presidential Round Table: Past President, Chinese Physicians Society of Southern California; President, Hollywood Academy of Medicine, Los Angeles, California; Research Fellow Cardiologist, NIH; Fellow, American Academy of Paediatrics; AMA; AAAS; World Medical Association; California Medical Association; Los Angeles County Medical Association; American Heart Association; International Circuit of Los Angeles; World Affairs Council; New York Academy of Sciences; Scripps Clinic, La Jolla. Address: PO Box 10456, Beverly Hills, CA 90213-3456, USA.

BAR-COHEN Yoseph, b. 3 September 1947, Baghdad, Iraq. Scientist. m. 1 son, 1 daughter. Education: BSc, Physics, 1971, MSc, Materials Science, 1973, PhD, Physics, 1979, The Hebrew University. Appointments: Senior NDE Special, Israeli Aircraft Industry, 1971-79; Postdoctoral studies, Air Force Materials Laboratories, Dayton, Ohio, 1979-80; Senior Physicist, Systems Research Laboratory, Dayton, Ohio at Air Force Materials Laboratory 1980-83; Special Principal, McDonnell Douglas Corporation, Long Beach, California, 1983-91; Adjunct to Full Professor, Mechanical and Aerospace Engineering Department, University of California, Los Angeles, 1989-; NDEAA Group Leader, Senior Research Scientist, JPL, Pasadena, California, 1991-. Publications include: Over 240 publications and 15 patents including: Composite materials stiffness determination and defects

characterization using enhanced leaky Lamb wave dispersion data acquisition method; Ultrasonic drilling and coring; Ultrasonic wave motors; Haptic interfaces mirroring robots operation, artificial muscles using electroactive polymers; Composite materials stiffness determination and defects characterization using leaky Lamb wave (LLW) dispersion data; Scanning aircraft structures using open-architecture robotic crawlers as platforms with NDE boards and sensors. Honours: National Research Council Fellowship Award, 1979; Nova Award of JPL for Outstanding Achievement in Technology Research and Development, 1996, and for Technological Innovation and Leadership, 1998; Fellow, American Society for Nondestructive Testing, 1996; NDE Life Time Achievement Award, International Society for Optical Engineering, 2001; NASA Exceptional Engineering Achievement Award; Fellow, SPIE, 2002. Memberships: American Society for Nondestructive Testing; ASNT; SPIE; American Society of Mechanical Engineers. Address: JPL, 4800 Oak Grove Drive 82-105, Pasadena, CA 91109-8099, USA.

BAR-TAL Daniel, b. 31 January 1946, Russia. Professor of Social Psychology. m. Svetlana, 1 son, 2 daughters. Education: BA, Psychology and Sociology, Tel Aviv University, 1970; MS, Social Psychology, 1973, PhD, Social Psychology, 1974, University of Pittsburgh. Appointments: Lecturer, 1975-79, Senior Lecturer, 1979-83, School of Education, Tel Aviv University; Visiting Associate Professor, Department of Psychology, Vanderbilt University, 1981-82, Brandeis University, 1987-88, Ecole des Hautes Etudes en Sciences Sociales, Paris, 1991-, Department of Psychology, University of Maryland, 1995, Department of Psychology, University of Muenster, Germany, 1997; NIAS, Holland, 2000-2001; Fellow Professor, 1983-89; Professor of Social Psychology, School of Education, Tel Aviv University, 1989-. Publications include: Stereotypes and Prejudice: Changing Conceptions, 1990; Patriotism in the Life of Individuals and Nations, 1997; Security Concerns: Insights From the Israeli Experience, 1998; How Children Understand War and Peace; Shared Beliefs in a Society, 2000. Honours: Otto Klineberg Intercultural and International Relations Prize, SPSSI, 1991; President, International Society of Political Psychology, 1999-2000; Golestan Fellowship, NIAS, 2000-2001. Memberships: American Educational Research Association; American Psychological Association; European Association of Experimental Social Psychology; International Society of Political Psychology; Society for the Advancement of Social Psychology; Society for the Psychological Study of Social Issues; Society for Experimental Psychology; International Association of Applied Psychology. Address: School of Education, Tel Aviv University, Tel Aviv 69978, Israel.

BAR-YISHAY Ephraim, b. 28 June 1948, Israel. Biomedical Engineer. m. Hanna, 3 sons. Education: BSc, Mechanical Engineering, New Jersey Institute of Technology, New Jersey, USA, 1973; PhD, Biomedical Engineering, University of Minnesota, Minnesota, USA, 1978. Appointments: Parker B Francis Fellow, Mayo Clinics, Minnesota, USA, 1982-83; Head, Pulmonary Function Laboratory, Hadassah University Hospital, Mt Scopus, Jerusalem, Israel, 1978-89; Visiting Professor, Children's Hospital, Columbus, Ohio, USA, 1989-91; Head, Pulmonary Function Laboratory, Hadassah University Hospital, Jerusalem, Israel. Publication: Author of over 70 articles and chapters. Honours: New York Academy of Sciences; Listed in Who's Who publications and biographical dictionaries. Memberships: American Physiology Society; American Thoracic Society; European Respiratory Society; Israel Society of Physiology and Pharmacology; Israel Society of Pulmonology. E-mail: ephraimb@cc.huji.ac.il

Dictionary of International Biography

BARAGETTI Sergio, b. 12 February 1968, Monza, Italy. Engineer; Educator. m. Elena Caprile. Education: Degree in Mechanical Engineering, Politecnico di Milano, 1994; PhD, Quality Engineering, Università di Firenze. Appointments: Researcher in Machine Design, 1995, Engineer Educator, 1998, Assistant Professor, 2000-, Università degli Studi di Bergamo, Italy. Publications: Author of more than 60 papers in national and international journals; Author of a machine-design book; 14 papers in international journals. Address: Dipartimento Progettazione e Tecnologie, Università degli Studi di Bergamo, Viale Marconi 5, 24044 Dalmine (BG), Italy. E-mail: sergio.baragetti@unibg.it

BARAKAT Ghaleb Z, b. 20 September 1927, Jaffa, Palestine. Retired Government Minister; Ambassador. m. Jalia Imam, 1 son, 2 daughters. Education: Undergraduate, American University of Beirut, BBA, 1949; Postgraduate, University of Rome, 1956. Appointments: Assistant Director General, International Labour Organisation, Geneva, 1986-90; Travel and Tourism Counsellor, Representative of international institutes, 1991-. Publications: Numerous research papers, reports, articles and lectures. Honours: Honorary Cultural Doctorate, World University, USA, 1997; Jordanian and foreign decorations, medals, certificates of merit. Memberships: IBC Cambridge; American Biographical Institute, USA; Jordan Royal Auto Club; International Association of Golden Helmsmen of Tourism, Berlin; President, Jaffa Society for Social Development, Amman; President, Association of Golden Helmsmen of Tourism, Jordan Chapter; Councillor, Inter Skal Club, Amman; American University of Beirut, Graduates' Club, Amman. Address: PO Box 9064, Amman 11191, Jordan.

BARANOWSKI Tom, b. 3 December 1946, Brooklyn, New York, USA. Professor of Paediatrics (Behavioural Nutrition). m. Janice Carlson Baranowski, 1 son, 1 daughter. Education: AB, Politics, Princeton University, New Jersey, 1964-68; MA, 1969-70, PhD, 1970-74, Social Psychology, University of Kansas, Lawrence. Appointments include: Department of Psychology, University of Kansas, 1970-74; Research Scientist, Battelle Institute, Human Affairs Research Center, Seattle, WA, 1974-76; West Virginia University Medical Center, Charleston Division, 1976-80; Associate Professor, Assistant Professor, Paediatrics and Preventive Medicine and Community Health, University of Texas Medical Branch, Galveston, 1980-90; University of Texas Health Science Center (Houston), School of Public Health, 1985-90; Adjunct Associate Professor, Psychology, University of Houston, 1985-90; Professor, Paediatrics, Medical College of Georgia, 1990-92; Adjunct Professor, Health Promotion and Education, University of Georgia, Athens, 1992-95; Professor and Chair, Behavioural Sciences and Health Education, Rollins School of Public Health, Emory University, 1992-95; Professor, Department of Behavioural Science, University of Texas M D Anderson Cancer Centre, 1995-99; Adjunct Professor, Behavioural Science, University of Texas School of Public Health, 1995-; Professor of Paediatrics (Behavioural Nutrition), Children's Nutrition Research Centre, Department of Paediatrics, Baylor College of Medicine, 1999-; Numerous medical and educational consultancies. Publications: 150 articles in refereed journals; 12 other journal articles; 16 book chapters; 2 textbooks; 35 book reviews, manuals and others; 148 abstracts. Memberships include: American College for Sports Medicine; International Society of Behavioural Nutrition and Physical Activity (Past President); American Psychological Association; American Public Health Association. Address: Children's Nutrition Research Centre, Department of Paediatrics, Baylor College of Medicine, 1100 Bates Street, Houston, TX 77030-2600. E-mail: tbaranow@bcm.tmc.edu

BARBARITO Luigi, b. 19 April 1922, Atripalda, Avellino, Italy. Churchman. Education: Theology, Pontifical Seminary of Benevento, Italy; Doctor in Canon Law, JCD, Pontifical Gregorian University, Rome; Diploma, Pontifical Academy for Diplomatic Service, Rome. Appointments: Ordained priest, 1944; Parochial and social work, diocese of Avellino, 1944-51; Diplomatic Service of the Holy See, Vatican City; Secretary, Apostolic Delegation of Australia and Oceania, 1953-59; Officer of the Council for Extraordinary Affairs of the Holy See at the Secretariat of State of His Holiness, Vatican City, 1959-67; Councillor, Apostolic Nunciature, Paris, France, 1967-69; Titular Archbishop of Fiorentino; Ordained Bishop, 1969; Apostolic Nuncio in Haiti and the Antilles, 1969-75; Apostolic Nuncio in Senegal, Bourkina-Fasso, Niger, Mauritania, Mali, Capo Verde Islands and Guinea Bissau, 1975-78; Apostolic Nuncio in Australia, 1978-86; Apostolic Nuncio to the Court of St James, United Kingdom, 1986-97; Member, Congregation for the Causes of Saints, Vatican City, 1997-2002. Publications: Occasional articles on moral and social matter for local newspapers and magazines. Honours: Knight Commander of the Order of the Republic of Italy, 1966; Knight Commander with Star of the Order of the Infanta of Portugal, 1967; Honorary Member of the Mexican Academy of International Law, 1971; Grand Cross of the Order of Haiti, 1975; Grand Cross of the Order of the Lion of Senegal, 1978; Gold Medallion of the Interfaith International Committee, 1993; Honorary Knight Grand Cross of the Royal Order of Queen Victoria, 1996; Head of Mission Award, 1996. Memberships: Honorary Member, Travellers Club, London; Honorary Member, The Italian Club, London. Address: Via Bravetta 518, 00164-Roma, Italy.

BARBEAU Marcel, b. 18 February 1925, Montreal, Quebec, Canada. Painter; Sculptor. m. Ninon Gauthier, 1 son, 1 daughter. Education: Diploma, Ecole du Meuble, 1942-47; Student, Paul Emile Borduas, 1944-47. Creative Works: Works in many public collections includes: Art Gallery of Greater Victoria, BC; Art Gallery of Ontario, Toronto; British Museum, London; Chrysler Museum, Norfolk, Virginia; Churchill College, Cambridge, England; Musée d'art contemporain de Montreal; Musée des Beaux-Arts, Lyon, France; National Gallery, Ottawa; National Gallery, Washington; Rose Art Museum; Brandeis University, New Jersey; Stedejilck Museum, Amsterdam; Exhibition Iris Cleri Obis Musée d'Art Contemporain de Montreal; The Winnipeg Art Gallery, Musée des Beaux-Arts due Quebec; Public works include: Le saut du tremplin, aluminum tubing and epoxy paint, Montreal Old Harbour Society, Old Harbour Park, Montreal, 1974-76; Fenêtre sur l'avenir, painted stet, McGill University, 1991-92. Publications: Articles, art films and essays. Honours: Zack Prize, Canadian Bienale, 1964; Lynch-Staunton Fellowship, Canada Council, 1973; Sculpture Prize, MacDonald Art Competition, Toronto, 1985; Member, Royal Canadian Academy of Arts, 1993; Painting Gold Medal, Jeux de Francophonie, Paris, 1994; Officer, Canada Order, 1995; 1 of 7 stamps published by Canada Post on Automatists painters signatories of Refus Global, 50th anniversary, 1998; Biennale Internazionale Dell'arte Contemporanea Citte Di Firenze, Prize 5 Premio, Medaille; Commission for official original print for Montreal Jazz Festival, entitled "Django Blue", 2003. Memberships: Signatory, 1998, manifesto Refus Global (Total Refusal), Group Les Automatists, Montreal, 1945-56; Vice President, Conseil de la Peinture de Quebec, 1978-80. Address: 11 rue Sesto Fiorentino, Apt 101, Bagnolet, 93170, France.

BARBER Francis, b. 13 May 1957, Wolverhampton. Actress. Education: Bangor University; Cardiff University. Appointments: Hull Truck Theatre Company; Glasgow Citizens Theatre; Tricycle Theatre; RSC; TV Appearances include: Clem Jack Story; Home Sweet Home; Flame to the Phoenix; Reilly; Ace of Spies; Those Glory Glory Days; Hard Feelings; Behaving Badly; The Nightmare Year; Film Appearances include: The Missionary, 1982; A Zed and Two Noughts; White City Castaway; Prick Up Your Ears; Sammy and Rosie Get Laid; We Think the World of You; The Grasscutter; Separate Bedrooms; Young Soul Rebels; Secret

Friends; The Lake; Soft Top, Hard Shoulder; The Fish Tale; Three Steps to Heaven; Photographing Fairies; Shiner; Still Crazy; Esther Kahn; Mauvaise passe; Stage Appearances include: Night of the Iguana; Pygmalion; Closer; Uncle Vanya.

BARBER Richard William, b. 30 October 1941, Dunmow, Essex, England. Publisher; Author. m. Helen Tolson, 7 May 1970, 1 son, 1 daughter. Education: BA, MA, 1967, PhD, 1982, Corpus Christi College, Cambridge. Publications: Arthur of Albion, 1961; The Knight and Chivalry, 1972; Edward Prince of Wales and Aquitaine, 1976; Companion Guide to South West France, 1977; Tournaments, 1978; The Arthurian Legends, 1979; The Penguin Guide to Medieval Europe, 1984; Fuller's Worthies, 1987; The Worlds of John Aubrey, 1988; Pilgrimages, 1991; British Myths and Legends, 1998; The Holy Grail, 2004; Contributions to: Arthurian Literature. Honours: Somerset Maugham Award, 1972; Times Higher Educational Supplement Book Award, 1978. Memberships: Royal Society of Literature; Royal Historical Society; Society of Antiquaries. Address: Stangrove Hall, Alderton, Nr Woodbridge, Suffolk IP12 3BL, England.

BARDOT Brigitte, b. 28 September 1934, Paris, France. Actress and Animal Rights Campaigner. m. (4) Bernard D'Ormale, 1992. Education: Paris Conservatoire. Career: Films include: Manina: La fille sans voile; Futures vedettes; Le grandes manouveures; En effueillent la marguerite; Une parisienne; En case de malheur; Voulez-vous danser avec moi?; Please not now?; Viva Maria; Les femmes, 1969; Don Juan, 1973. Publications: Initiales BB, 1996; Le Carré de Pluton, 1999. Memberships: President Fondation Brigitte Bardot. Honours: Etoile de Cristal, Academy of Cinema, 1966; Chevalier Légion d'honneur. Address: Fondation Brigitte Bardot, 45 rue Vineuse, 75016 Paris, France. E-mail: fbb@fondationbrigittebardot.fr

BAREHAM Terence, b. 17 October 1937, Clacton-on-Sea, Essex, England. University Professor (retired). Education: Open Scholar and State Scholar, 1959-62, BA (Hons), 1962, MA, 1969, Lincoln College, Oxford; DPhil, Ulster University, Northern Ireland, 1977. Publications: George Crabbe: A Critical Study, 1977; George Crabbe: A Bibliography (joint author), 1978; The Art of Anthony Trollope, 1980; Anthony Trollope (Casebook Series), 1982; Tom Stoppard (Casebook Series), 1989; Malcolm Lowry, 1989; Charles Lever: New Evaluations (editor), 1991; York Notes, Monographs on Robert Bolt, T S Eliot, Shakespeare. Contributions to: Numerous on literature of 17th - 20th Century. Address: 37 Agherton Drive, Portstewart, County Londonderry, Northern Ireland.

BARKER Allen Keith, b. 11 March 1937, Australia. Artist; Painter; Lecturer. m. Marilyn Norton, 1 son. Education: National Art School, Sydney, Australia, 1955-60; Lithography, Central School of Art, London, 1962. Career: Lectured on Colour, Architectural Association, London, 1977-79; Lecturer, The Open College of the Arts, 1987-88; Currently, Personal Tutor and Specialised Lecturer, Central St Martin's School of Art, London; Formed the Structured Theatre Company, ICA, London, Nuffield Theatre, Lancaster University, 1976; Formed Bassett Architectural Constructions and Designs, 1984; Formed the Boreatton Bat Society of Fine Artists and Designers, 1990; Travelling Visually, Master Classes and Performance Workshops, Boreatton Hall, Shrewsbury, 1991; One-man Shows 1967- include: Galerie Junge Generation, Vienna, 1969; Lucy Milton Gallery, London, 1971, 1973; Galerie Van Huisen, Amsterdam, Holland, 1972; Institute of Contemporary Art, London, 1976; Gallerie Morner, Stockholm, Sweden, 1978; All work handled through dealers, 1979-89; Gallery P-INC Studios, London, 1996; Retrospective Exhibition, Bonhams Fine Art, London, 1998; Cambridge University, Sir Norman Foster

Building, Faculty of Law, 1998; Numerous group exhibitions; Works in public collections: Sheffield Museum and City Art Gallery; Leicester Museum and City Art Gallery; Manchester City Art Gallery; Galerie Orez Mobile, Den Haag, Holland; AT and T, New York, USA; Museum Boymans Van Beuningen, Rotterdam, Holland; Cambridge University, Sir Norman Foster Building, Faculty of Law. Publications: Numerous articles about his works in newspapers, magazines and reviews in catalogues, 1967- i.e. Financial Times, London, Sunday Times, London, Studio International, London, Sunday Telegraph, London, The Connoisseur, London, including most recently: 4 page colour article in Living Now Magazine, Tokyo, Japan by Eko Kamibayashi, 1991; 2 page article in TNT Magazine by Tiffany Bakker, London, 1996; The Guardian Guide, Kensington and Chelsea Mail, Evening Standard, Chelsea News, The Pink Paper-London, 1997; The Australian Magazine by Jane Cornwell, 2000. Address: 14 Bassett Road, London W10 6JJ, England.

BARKER Patricia Margaret, b. 8 May 1943, Thornaby on Tees, England. Writer. m. 27 January 1978, 1 son, 1 daughter. Education: BSc, London School of Economics, 1965. Appointment: Patron, New Writing North. Publications: Union Street, 1982; Blow Your House Down, 1984; The Century's Daughter, 1986; The Man Who Wasn't There, 1989; Regeneration, 1991; The Eye in the Door, 1993; The Ghost Road, 1995; The Century's Daughter, retitled Liza's England, 1996; Another World, 1998; Border Crossing, 2001; Double Vision, 2003. Honours: One of Best of Young British Novelists, 1982; Joint Winner, Fawcett Prize, 1982; Honorary M Litt University of Teesside, 1993; Guardian Fiction Prize, 1994; Northern Electric Special Arts Award, 1994; Booker Prize, 1995; Honorary DLitt, Napier University, 1996; Honorary Doctorate, Open University, 1997; Honorary Fellow, London School of Economics, 1997; Honorary DLitt, Durham University, 1998; Honorary DLitt, University of Hertfordshire, 1998; CBE, New Year's Honours List, 2000; Die Welt Literature Prize, 2001; Honorary DLitt, University of London, 2002. Memberships: Society of Authors; PEN; Fellow of the Royal Society of Literature. Address: c/o Gillon Aitken Associates, 18-21 Cavaye Place, London SW10 9PT, England.

BARKIN Ellen, b. 16 April 1955, New York, USA. Actress. m. Gabriel Byrne, 1988, 1 son. Education: City University of New York; Hunter College, Indiana. Appointments: Stage Appearances include: Shout Across the River, 1980; Killings on the Last Line, 1980; Extremities, 1982; Eden Court; TV Appearances include: Search for Tomorrow, Kent State, 1981; We're Fighting Back, 1981; Terrible Joe Moran, 1984; Before Women Has Wings, 1998. Films include: Diner, 1982; Daniel, 1983; Tender Mercies, 1983; Eddie and the Cruisers, 1983; The Adventures of Buckaroo Banzai, 1984; Harry and Son, 1984; Enormous Changes at the Last Minute, 1985; Down by Law, 1986; The Big Easy, 1987; Siesta, 1987; Sea of Love, 1989; Johnny Handsome; Switch; Man Trouble, 1992; Mac, 2993; This Boy's Life, 1993; Into the West, 1993; Bad Company, 1995; Wild Bill, 1995; Mad Dog Times, 1996; The Fan, 1996; Fear and Loathing in Las Vegas; Popcorn; Drop Dead Gorgeous; The White River Kid, 1999; Crime and Punishment in Suburbia, 2000; Mercy, 2000; Someone Like You, 2001. Honour: Emmy Award. Address: c/o CAA, 9830 Wilshire Boulevard, Beverly Hills, CA 90212, USA.

BARLOW Lolete Falck, b. 23 August 1932, Mobile, Alabama, USA. Writer; Poet. m. John Woodman Bryan Barlow, 13 May 1952, 1 son, 2 daughters. Education: Florida State University, 1950-51. Appointment: Poetry Editor, The Pen Woman Magazine, 1992-. Publication: Unheard Melodies, 1996. Contributions to: Books, newspapers and journals. Honours: Della Crowder Miller Memorial Award, 1979; 1st Place, Midwest Poetry Gala, 1987;

Midwest Poetry Honoured Poet Award, 1988; 3rd Place, National Library of Poetry, 1990. Memberships: National League of American Pen Women; Poetry Society of Virginia. Address: 8902 Bay Avenue, Box 754, North Beach, MD 20714, USA.

BARNABY (Charles) Frank, b. 27 September 1927, Andover, Hampshire, England. Physicist; Author. m. 12 December 1972, 1 son, 1 daughter. Education: BSc, 1951, MSc, 1954, PhD, 1960, London University. Appointments: Physicist, UK Atomic Energy Authority, 1950-57; Member, Senior Scientific Staff, Medical Research Council, University College Medical School, 1957-68; Executive Secretary, Pugwash Conferences on Science and World Affairs, 1968-70; Director, Stockholm International Peace Research Institute (SIPRI), 1971-81; Professor of Peace Studies, Frei University, Amsterdam, 1981-85; Director, World Disarmament Campaign (UK), 1982-; Chair, Just Defence, 1982-; Consultant, Oxford Research Group, 1998-; Editor, International Journal of Human Rights. Publications: Man and the Atom, 1971; Disarmament and Arms Control, 1973; Nuclear Energy, 1975; The Nuclear Age, 1976; Prospects for Peace, 1980; Future Warfare, 1983; The Automated Battlefield, 1986; Star Wars Brought Down to Earth, 1986; The Invisible Bomb, 1989; The Gaia Peace Atlas, 1989; The Role and Control of Arms in the 1990's, 1992; How Nuclear Weapons Spread, 1993; Instruments of Terror, 1997. Contributions to: Ambio; New Scientist; Technology Review. Honour: Honorary Doctorates, Frei University, Amsterdam, 1982, University of Southampton, 1996. Address: Brandreth, Station Road, Chilbolton, Stockbridge, Hampshire SO20 6HW, England.

BARNARD Robert, b. 23 November 1936, Burnham on Crouch, Essex, England. Crime Writer. m. Mary Louise Tabor, 7 February 1963. Education: Balliol College, Oxford, 1956-59; Dr Phil, University of Bergen, Norway, 1972. Publications: Death of an Old Goat, 1974; Sheer Torture, 1981; A Corpse in a Gilded Cage, 1984; Out of the Blackout, 1985; Skeleton in the Grass, 1987; At Death's Door, 1988; Death and the Chaste Apprentice, 1989; Masters of the House, 1994. As Bernard Bastable: Dead, Mr Mozart, 1995; Too Many Notes, Mr Mozart, 1995. Honours: Seven Times Nominated for Edgar Awards. Memberships: Crime Writers Association; Chairman, Brontë Society, 1996-99, 2002-; Society of Authors. Address: Hazeldene, Houghley Lane, Leeds LS13 2DT, England.

BARNARD Roger, b. 4 November 1951, London. Artist. Education: West Sussex College of Design, 1970-71; North Staffordshire Polytechnic, 1971-74; BA, Fine Art, 1974. Career: Solo exhibitions include: Tate Gallery, London, 1976, 1978; Air, Scottish Arts Council Gallery, Third Eye Centre, 1977; South Bank London, 1985; Royal Cornwall Museum, 1989; Commissions: mainly photographic include: Travelling Photographic Exhibition for British Refugee Council, 1988; Mixed Media Exhibitions include: Manchester, 1974; Serpentine, 1975; Third Eye Centre, Tate, 1976; Coventry, Air, 1978; ACGB Touring Exhibition including the Hayward Gallery, 1979; Holborn Underground Competition, Whitechapel, 1980; Chichester Festival, 1984; Royal Cornwall Museum, 1990, 1994; Osaka Triennale '90, (painting), Osaka Japan, 1990; Osaka Triennale, '91, (print), Osaka, Japan, 1991; Works in: Royal Institute of Cornwall Collection; Contemporary Art Center, Osaka, Japan; Work held in private collections in England, France, Germany, USA; Founder Member, First Chairman, London Video Arts, 1976-78. Address: 151 Archway Road, London N6 5BL, England.

BARNARD Ross Thomas, b. 27 July 1957, Geelong, Victoria, Australia. Research Scientist. m. Wai-Ping Fang, 1 son. Education: BSc, Melbourne, 1978; BSc, Hons, Monash, 1980; PhD, University of Queensland, 1990; PGDipEd, University of

Queensland, 1995. Appointments: Research Assistant, Department of Surgery, St Vincent's Hospital, University of Melbourne, Victoria, 1980-82; Research Officer, 1982-90, Senior Research Officer, 1990-, University of Queensland, Brisbane; C J Martin Postdoctoral Fellow, University of California, Santa Cruz, 1991-93; R D Wright Awardee, University of Queensland, 1994-96; Senior Research Fellow, Queensland University of Technology, 1996-; Program Leader PanBio Ltd, 1999-2000; Associate Professor and Biotechnology Program Co-ordinator, University of Queensland, 2000-. Publications: Over 60 articles in professional journals. Memberships: New York Academy of Sciences; American Association for Clinical Chemistry; Australian Society for Biochemistry and Molecular Biology. Address: Department of Biochemistry and Molecular Biology, University of Queensland, Brisbane, Queensland, Australia.

BARNER Bruce Monroe, b. 16 January 1951, Delaware, Ohio, USA. Ethicist. Education: BA (Hons) Religion and Philosophy, Muskingum College, 1973; Postgraduate Studies, Electrical Engineering and Journalism, Cleveland State University, 1975-77; Numerous short-term accredited courses on statistical analysis computer programming, 1981-85. Appointments: Technical Writer, Reliance Electric, 1976; Ohio Governor's Highway Safety Representative and Director of Research, Department of Public Safety, State of Ohio, 1980-98; Fatal Crash Analyst, National Highway Traffic Safety Administration, Washington, 1982-83, 1985; Co-founder, Ohio Safety Belt Coalition, 1984-84; Statistician, National Accident Sampling System, 1983; Administrative Researcher, Ohio Governor's Motor Carrier Advisory Committee, 1986-90; Administrative Researcher, Ohio Highway Safety Elderly Driver Taskforce, 1990; Administrative Researcher, DWI Task Force, 1992, 1993; Senior Research Advisor, Safety Management Systems, 1994, 1995; Board Chairman, ALIVE Ministries, Inc., Columbus, Ohio, 1999-. Publications: Numerous publications on aspects of road safety include: Proper versus Improper Use of Child Safety Seats in Ohio, 1989; Repeat DUI Offenders: Their Involvement in Ohio Fatal Crashes, 1993; Emergency Vehicles Involved in Crashes: 1989-1991, 1993; State –wide Shoulder Belt Usage by Type of Roadway/ Posted Speed Limit: A Three-year Comparison, 1994. Honours: Academic Scholarship, Muskingum College, 1969; Editor-in-Chief, Black & Magenta, Muskinhgum College, 1972; Fenn College Engineering Scholarship, 1975. Memberships: Association for the Advancement of Automotive Medicine; Planetary Society; World Future Society; National Space Society; Search for Extra Terrestrial Intelligence Institute; Ohio Governor's Saved by the Belt Club. Address: Post Office Box 510, Galloway, OH 43119-0510, USA

BARNES Clive (Alexander), b. 13 May 1927, London, England. Journalist; Dance and Theatre Critic. m. (2) Patricia Amy Evelyn Winckley, 26 June 1958, 1 son, 1 daughter. Education: King's College, London; BA, St Catherine's College, Oxford, 1951. Appointments: Co-Editor, Arabesque, 1950; Assistant Editor, 1950-58, Associate Editor, 1958-61, Executive Editor, 1961-65, Dance and Dancers; Administrative Officer in Town Planning, London County Council, 1952-61; Chief Dance Critic, 1961-65, New York Correspondent, 1970-, The Times, London; Dance Critic, 1965-78, Drama Critic, 1967-78, New York Times; Associate Editor and Chief Dance and Drama Critic, New York Post, 1978-. Publications: Ballet in Britain Since the War, 1953; Frederick Ashton and His Ballets, 1961; Ballet Here and Now (with A V Coton and Frank Jackson), 1961; Ballett, 1965: Chronik und Bilanz des Ballettjahres (editor with Horst Koegler), 1965; Ballett 1966: Chronik und Bilanz des Ballettjahres (editor with Horst Koegler), 1966; Fifty Best Plays of the American Theatre from 1787 to the Present (editor), 4 volumes, 1969; Best American

Plays: Sixth Series, 1963-1967 (editor with John Gassner), 1971; Best American Plays: Seventh Series (editor), 1975; Inside American Ballet Theatre, 1977; Nureyev, 1982; Best American Plays: Eighth Series, 1974-1982 (editor), 1983; Best American Plays: Ninth Series, 1983-1992 (editor), 1993. Contributions to: Many periodicals. Honours: Knight of the Order of Dannebrog, Denmark, 1972; Commander of the Order of the British Empire, 1975. Address: c/o New York Post, 210 South Street, New York, NY 10002, USA..

BARNES Jim Weaver, b. 22 December 1933, Summerfield, Oklahoma, USA. Writer; Teacher. m. Carolyn, 22 November 1973, 2 sons. Education: BA, Southeastern Oklahoma State University, 1964; MA, 1966, PhD, 1972, University of Arkansas. Publications: Fish on Poteau Mountain, 1980; American Book of the Dead, 1982; Season of Loss, 1985; LA Plata Canata, 1989; Sawdust War, 1992; Paris, 1997; On Native Ground, 1997; Numbered Days, 1999; On A Wing of the Sun, 2001. Contributions to: Nation; American Scholar; Georgia Review; Poetry Northwest; Quarterly West; Prairie Schooner; Mississippi Review; Plus 300. Honours: NEA Fellowship, 1978; Oklahoma Book Award, 1993; Camargo Foundation Fellowships, 1996, 2001; American Book Award, 1998. Memberships: PEN American Center; Associated Writing Programs. Address: 2029 W 1400 S, Spanish Fork, UT 84660, USA.

BARNES Melver Raymond, b. 15 November 1917, Salisbury, North Carolina, USA. Scientific Chemist. Education: Bachelor of Arts, Chemistry, Chapel Hill, North Carolina, 1947; Mathematics and Chemistry courses at McCoy College, Baltimore, MD, University of Utah, Salt Lake City, Brigham Young University, Provo, Utah and University of California, Los Angeles. Appointments: Pittsburgh Testing Laboratories, Greensboro, North Carolina, 1948-49; North Carolina State Highway and Public Works Commission, Raleigh, North Carolina, 1949-51; Edgewood Arsenal, Edgewood, MD, 1951-61; Dugway Proving Ground, Dugway, Utah, 1961-70. Publications: Several Government scientific reports in closed literary papers on natural science. Memberships: American Association for the Advancement of Science; American Chemistry Society; American Physical Society; International Platford Association; Life Patron, International Biographic Association, American Biographical Research Association; United Nations Association of the USA. Listed in: International Register of Profiles; International Who's Who of Intellectuals. Address: 1486 Swicegood Road, Linwood, NC 27299, USA.

BARNES Michael, b. 1934. Author. Education: BA; MEd. Appointments: Former School Principal. Publications: Over 40 books on Northern History and also police work. Contributions to: Periodicals, journals, reviews, magazines, quarterlies and newspapers. Honours: Canada 125 Medal, 1992; Gold Leaf Award for Best Promotion of a Community, 1994; Order of Canada, 1995; Kirkland Lake Celebrity Hall of Fame, 1998; Canadian Honour Roll, 1998. Address: Box 881, Haliburton, Ontario, Canada, K0M 1S0.

BARNETT Anthony (Peter John), b. 10 September 1941, London, England. Author; Publisher. Education: MA, University of Essex. Appointment: Editorial Director, Allardyce, Barnett, Publishers. Publications: Poetry: Blood Flow, 1975; Fear and Misadventure, 1977; The Resting Bell, Collected Poems, 1987. Prose and Poetry: Carp and Rubato, 1995; Anti-Beauty, 1999. Critical and Biographical: The Poetry of Anthony Barnett, 1993. Music Biography: Desert Sands, The Recordings and Performances of Stuff Smith, 1995; Black Gypsy, The Recordings of Eddie South, 1999; Selected Poems, 2004. Contributions to: Anthologies,

journals and periodicals. Address: c/o Allardyce, Barnett, Publishers, 14 Mount Street, Lewes, East Sussex BN7 1HL, England.

BARNIE John Edward, b. 27 March 1941, Abergavenny, Gwent, Wales. Editor; Writer; Poet. m. Helle Michelsen, 28 October 1980, 1 son. Education: BA, Honours, 1963, MA, 1966, PhD, 1971, Birmingham University; Dip Ed, Nottingham University, 1964. Appointments: Lecturer, English Literature, University of Copenhagen, 1969-82; Assistant, then Editor, Planet: The Welsh International, 1985-. Publications: Borderland, 1984; Lightning Country, 1987; Clay, 1989; The Confirmation, 1992; Y Felan a Finnau, 1992; The City, 1993; Heroes, 1996; No Hiding Place, 1996; The Wine Bird, 1998; Ice, 2001; At the Salt Hotel, 2003. Contributions to: American Poetry Review; Critical Quarterly; Poetry Wales; New Welsh Review; Anglo-Welsh Review; Kunapipi; Juke Blues. Honour: Welsh Arts Council Prize for Literature, 1990. Memberships: Yr Academi Gymreig; Harry Martinson-Sällskapet. Address: Greenfields, Comins Coch, Aberystwyth, SY23 3BG, Ceredigion, Wales.

BAROUNIS Aristides, b. 3 July 1930, Andritsena Olympias, Greece. Geotechnical Engineer. m. Betty Lieros, 1 son, 1 daughter. Education: MSc, Mining and Geological Engineering, National Technical University of Athens; Postgraduate Studies in Engineering Geology, NTUA. Appointments: Assistant Professor, Aply Geology NTU, Athens, 1958-62; Chief Engineer and Geologist, Greek Mining Public Work, 1960-68; Professor, Geology and Mining Exploration, Euboea School of Mines, 1965-75; Chief Geotechnical and Geological Engineer, Chief Executive Officer, Geophysics Co Prtn, 1968-. Publications: About 200 publications; 18 papers; 3 books. Honours: Millennium Membership of International Association of Hydrogeologists. Memberships: International Association of Hydrogeologists; International Society of Soil Mechanics and Foundation of Engineering; Greek Geological Society; Greek Engineering Chamber. Address: 10-12 Aristidou str, 105 59 Athens, Greece. E-mail: nbgeoph@otenet.gr

BARR Marylin Lytle, b. 11 August 1920. Poet; Writer. m. Orlando Sydney Barr, 6 November 1942, 1 son, 2 daughters. Education: BA, Beecher College, 1942; MA, Bank Street College of Education, 1967; Graduate courses, Syracuse University, Cambridge University, New York University, 1969-77. Appointments: Teacher, Glen Parkway School, New Haven, Connecticut; The Chelsea School, New York Board of Education. Publications: Drawn from the Shadows, 1991; Concrete Considerations, 1993; Unexpected Light, 1999; The Grahamsville Historic District, 2004. Contributions to: Oxalis; Outloud; Piedmont Literary Review; Catskill Life; Tucumcari Literary Review; Pegasus Review; Poet's Gallery; Zephyr; Poetry Peddler; Confetti; Echoes; Apple Blossom Connection; Poet; S S Calliope; Messages; Implosion; Times Herald Almanac; Glens Falls Review; Mohawk Valley USA; Still Night Writings; Blue Light Review; Wide Open; Anthologies and various collections. Honours: Recognition in poetry contests with publication by Hudson Valley Writers Association, 1988; Stone Ridge Poetry Society, 1990; First Prize, North Shore Poets Forum, 1998. Memberships: Alchemy Club; Poetry Society of America; Poets and Writers; Massachusetts State Poetry Society; Greater Haverhill Poetry Society; North Shore Poets; Catskill Reading Society; International Women's Writing Guild; New Hampshire State Poetry Society. Address: PO Box 75, Grahamsville, NY 12740, USA.

BARR Patricia Miriam, b. 25 April 1934, Norwich, Norfolk, England. Writer. Education: BA, University of Birmingham; MA, University College, London. Publications: The Coming of the Barbarians, 1967; The Deer Cry Pavilion, 1968; A Curious Life

Dictionary of International Biography

for a Lady, 1970; To China with Love, 1972; The Memsahibs, 1976; Taming the Jungle, 1978; Chinese Alice, 1981; Uncut Jade, 1983; Kenjiro, 1985; Coromandel, 1988; The Dust in the Balance, 1989. Honour: Winston Churchill Fellowship for Historical Biography, 1972. Membership: Society of Authors. Address: 6 Mount Pleasant, Norwich NR2 2DG, England.

BARR-KUMAR Raj, b. 5 February 1946, Ceylon. Architect. m. Bernadette. Education: BSc, Built Environment, University of Ceylon, 1971; Graduate Diploma in Architecture, University of London, 1974; Master of Architecture, University of Kansas, 1975; Doctor of Architecture, University of Hawaii, 2002. Appointments: National President, American Institute of Architects, 1997; President, Barr-Kumar Architects Engineer PC; Emens Distinguished Visiting Professor, Ball State University. Publications: Over 50 articles in publications including Architectural Record; The Washington Post; Asia Magazine. Honour: Honorary Fellow, National Architecture Societies of Canada, Japan, Mexico, Philippines, Sri Lanka, Bahamas. Listed in: Biographical Publications. Memberships: American Institute of Architect; Royal Institute of British Architects, others. Address: Barr-Kumar Architects, Engineers, P.C., 1825 Eye Street NW, Suite 400, Washington DC 20006, USA. Website: www.barrarchitects.com

BARRETT Philip, b. 26 May 1925, Donoughmore, Co Cork, Eire. Roman Catholic Priest. Education: Diplomas with Honours in Arts, Philosophy, Theology and Canon Law, St Kieran's College, Kilkenny, Eire, 1950; BA, 1975, BA with Honours, 1993, Open University; MPhil Thesis, Crime and Punishment in a Lancashire Industrial Town: Law and Social Change in the Borough of Wigan 1800-1950, Polytechnic University, Liverpool, 1980; Ordained Priest, Roman Catholic Church, 1950. Appointments: Assistant Priest, St Oswald's, Ashton-in-Makerfield, near Wigan, England, 1950-58; Assistant Priest, St Benet's Netherton, Bootle, 1958-59; Assistant Priest, St Ambrose's, Speke, Liverpool, England, 1959-69; Assistant Priest, St Jude's, Wigan, England, 1969-76; Parish Priest, St Winefred's, Bootle, Liverpool, England, 1977-81; Parish Priest, Holy Family, Platt Bridge, Wigan, England, 1981-2003; Liverpool Archdiocesan Religious Inspector of Schools, 1950's. Publications: Unpublished M Phil Thesis available for reference purposes in Wigan Public Reference Library. Address: Spring View Cottage, 244 Warrington Road, Spring View, Wigan, Lancashire WN3 5NH, England.

BARRINGER Joan Marie, b. 30 September 1955, Washington DC, USA. Counsellor; Teacher; Artist; Writer. Education: BA, Latin American Studies, George Mason University; Graduate degree in Creating and selling Short Stories, Institute of Children's Literature, 1995; MA, Education and Counselling, George Mason University, 1999. Appointments: Librarian, Brazilian Embassy, 1975-83; Directed and created Rainbow City Day Care Army Navy Country Club, Arlington, Virginia, 1983-87; Visitors Services, National Gallery of Art, Washington DC, 1991-94; Workshop Assistant and Receptionist, Women's Center, Vienna, Virginia, 1996-2000; Career Counsellor, Department of Rehabilitation Services, State of Virginia, 1998-99; "Studio of Natural Arts", photography, pastels of animals and oil paintings, 2000-; Art Show, JoAnn Rose Gallery, Reston, Virginia, 2003; Missionary trip to Peru, 2003. Publications: Book of Poems: Metronome, 1979; Poem "Flight of Life" included in anthology, Great Contemporary Poetry, 1981; Colour photograph published in Fairfax and Montgomery Journal, 1992; Designer of CD Cover, 1995; Internet book review, Intuitive Healer, 2002; Editor, Layout Designer, Writer, Photographer, Women's Caucus for Art Newsletter, 2001, 2004. Honours: Sigma Pi Alpha, Spanish Honorary Fraternity, Catawba College, North Carolina, 1974; Honorary Achievement, Co-operative Education, Northern Virginia College, 1984; Teacher with the Happiest Smile, Chantilly Pre-School, 1987; Listed in Who's Who publications and biographical dictionaries, 2003-04. Memberships: Donor and Member, Women's Center; Unity Church Member and Fund Raiser; Association of Research and Enlightenment; Sponsor, Brazilian Children, Childreach and World Vision. Address: 11107 Hampton Road, Fairfax Station, VA 22039, USA.

BARROW Robin St Clair, b. 18 November 1944, Oxford, England. University Professor. m. (1) Hilary Mallinson, 1 son, (2) Lynn Carlier Hansen, 2 daughters. Education: MA, Honours, Christ Church, Oxford, 1967; PGCE, 1968, PhD, 1972, University of London. Appointments: Assistant Master, City of London School for Boys, 1968-72; Lecturer, Philosophy of Education, University of Leicester, 1972-80; Distinguished Visiting Professor, University of Western Ontario, 1977-78; Reader in Philosophy of Education, University of Leicester, 1980-82; Professor of Education, Simon Fraser University, 1982-; Dean of Education, Simon Fraser University, 1992-. Publications: Around 100 articles; Author, 21 books, including: A Critical Dictionary of Educational Concepts, with G Milburn, 1990; Understanding Skills, 1990; Utilitarianism, 1991; Language, Intelligence and Thought, 1993. Honours: Vice Chair, Philosophy of Education Society, Great Britain, 1980-83; President, North Western Philosophy of Education Society, North America, 1988; President, Canadian Philosophy of Education Society, 1992-93; Fellow, Royal Society of Canada, 1996. Address: Faculty of Education, Simon Fraser University, 8888 University Drive, Burnaby, BC V5A 1S6, Canada.

BARROW Willie Taplin, b. 7 December 1924, Burton, Texas, USA. Minister; Human Rights Activist. m. Cly de Barrow, 1 son. Education: Warner Pacific Theological Seminary, Portland, Oregon, USA. Appointments include: Ordained Minister, Church of God; National Youth Director, Church of God; Vice-President, Illinois State Ministerial Assembly; Co-ordinating Committee Member, Chicago March on Washington; First Executive Director, State-wide Coalition Against Hunger; Member of the three-women delegations to visit North Vietnam as a guest of the Southeast Women's Union; National Deputy Campaign Manager and Road Manager, 1984 "Jackson for President Campaign"; Member, Democrat Central Committee; Leader of Delegation to South Africa, 1990; Co-Chairman Board of Trustees, RainbowPush Coalition; First Vice-Chairman National Political Congress of Black Women; Governor's Commission on the Status of Women in Illinois; Board Member, Doctor's Hospital of Hyde Park; Advisory Board Member, Grambling University; AT&T Consumer Board Member; Member, Board of Trustees, Bennett College; Governor's Committee on Nutrition and Human Needs; Hate Crimes Commission; Illinois Commission on African American Males; International Women's Year Commission; Domestic Violence Commission; Chicago Community Health Planning Coalition; Board Member, Malcolm X Community College; Foundation Board Member, CORE; Advisory Board Member, African American Leadership Partnership. Honours include: Special Human Services Award, National Conference of Black Lawyers, 1981; Honorary Doctor of Human Letters, Bennett College, Greensbro, North Carolina, 1991; Honorary Doctor of Divinity, Southern California School of Ministry, Los Angeles, 1992; Witness, Peace Agreement Between Israel and PLO, The White House, 1993; US Senate Outstanding Contribution to Advancement of Women and Social Change Award, 2001; Nelson Mandela Award, Association of African Historians Board of Directors, 2002. Address: 930 East 50th Street, Chicago, IL 60617, USA. E-mail: wbarrow@rainbowpush.org

Dictionary of International Biography

BARRY Kathleen Marie, b. 25 May 1934, Manchester, England. Teacher; Musician. m. Kevin Milton Barry, 2 sons, 1 daughter. Education: Maria Assumpta Training College, London; Trinity College of Music, London. Appointments: Head of Department of Music, St Peter and Paul's Secondary School Lincoln, England, 1955-63; Assistant Music Lecturer, Maria Assumpta Training College, London, England, 1959; Head of Department of Music, Winckley Square Girls' Grammar School, Preston, England, 1963-68; Head of Department of Music, Iona College, Havelock North, New Zealand, 1968-72; Conductor, Hastings Sinfonietta Orchestra, New Zealand, 1978-; Conductor, Hastings Choral Society, New Zealand, 1985-. Honours: Teachers' Certificate, University of London, 1954; AMusTCL, Teaching Paperwork, 1957; ARCM, Singing Teaching, 1958; FTCL, Pianoforte, 1962; Civic Honour for Voluntary Community Service in Music, City of Hastings, New Zealand, 1988. Memberships: Incorporated Society of Musicians; New Zealand Choral Federation. Address: 20/212 Grove Road, Hastings, New Zealand. E-mail: ellinoreb@xtra.co.nz

BARRYMORE Drew, b. 22 February 1975, Los Angeles. Film Actress. m. (1) Jeremy Thomas, 1994, divorced, (2) Tom Green, 2001, divorced 2002. Appointments: Appeared in Dog Food Commercial, 1976; Film debut in TV Movie Suddenly Love, 1978; Films include: Altered States, 1980; ET, The Extra Terrestrial, 1982; Irreconcilable Differences, 1984; Firestarter, 1984; Cat's Eye, 1985; See You in the Morning, 1988; Guncrazy, 992; Poison Ivy, 1992; Beyond Control: The Amy Fisher Story, 1992; Wayne's World 2, 1993; Bad Girls, 1994; Boys in the Side, 1995; Batman Forever, 1995; Mad Love, 1995; Scream, 1996; Everyone Says I Love you, 1996; All She Wanted, 1997; Best Men, 1997; Never Been Kissed, 1998; Home Fries, 1998; The Wedding Singer, 1998; Ever After, 1998; Charlie's Angels (also producer), 2000; Donnie Darko (also producer), 2001; Riding in Cars With Boys, 2001; Confessions of a Dangerous Mind, 2002; Duplex (also producer); So Love Returns (also producer); Charlie's Angels: Full Throttle (also producer), 2003; Duplex, 2003; 50 First Dates, 2004. Address: c/o EMA, 9025 Wilshire Boulevard, Suite 450, Beverly Hills, CA 90211, USA

BARTA Marie L, b. 4 October 1917, Manly, Iowa, USA. Music Educator. Education: Unfinished degree (special piano lessons) Drake University (because of family illnesses). Publications: Book: Only Pianos Stand Alone; The Iowa Music Teacher Magazine. Honours: National Piano Teachers Hall of Fame; Nationally certified adjudicator (20 years). Memberships: Secretary, Music Teachers of North Iowa; Iowa Music Teachers Association. Address: 223, E North St, Manly, IA 50456-5025, USA.

BARTELDS Anne Geert, b. 21 January 1966, Assen, The Netherlands. Composer; Arranger; Conductor; Trumpet Player; Teacher; Publicist; Translator (Dutch, English, German, French). Education: Studied Trumpet, Groningen Conservatory; English Language and Literature and Musicology, Groningen State University. Career includes: Numerous appointments as conductor and composer/arranger; Freelance brass, clarinet and piano player, 1983-; Arranger, Composer and Orchestrator of both serious and light music with 11 music publishers in the Netherlands, The United Kingdom and Germany, 1984-; Private Brass Teacher, 1984-; Private English Teacher, 1989-; Artistic Director, Noordenveld regional wind-band clinics; Conductor, Big Band Noordenveld, Paterswolde, Netherlands, 1992-; Music Critic, Journalist, Dutch regional newspaper, Oostermoer Noordenveld, 1994-; Translator, Editor, Muzika Publishers Tzummarum, 1995-; Conductor, Northern Sym and Swingphonic Brass, Eelde, Netherlands, 1996-; Adjudicator, Schoonebeek Music Festival, 1997; Free-lance Translator, BS Translations, Groningen, 1997-; Correspondent, Winds Magazine, Music en Show, 1998-; Stand-in Brass Teacher,

Delfzijl School of Music, 1999-; Translator, Editor, Gobelin Music Publications Akkrum, 2000-; Brass Teacher, Adorp Musical Society, Adorp, Netherlands; Conductor, Fanfare Adorp Musical Society, Netherlands, 2001; Conductor, Folkloristic Band De Lindelanders, Linde, Netherlands, 2001-; Conductor Linde Youth Ensemble, Netherlands, 2001-; Conductor, DES Musical Society, Linde, Netherlands, 2001-; Conductor, The Eastermoor Singers Annen, Netherlands, 2002-; Conductor, Kunst en Strijd Musical Society, Muntendam, Netherlands, 2002-; Conductor, Christian Musical Society "Amicitia", Musselkanaal, Netherlands, 2003. Publications: Numerous articles in professional journals include most recently: It don't mean a thing if it ain't got that swing: Aspects of the Big Band Era in American Music, 1990; The Use of Transcriptions in wind-music, 1997; 63 Years of Christian Wind Music in Northern Drenthe, 1998; Changes of Identity with Regard to Local Wind Bands in the Northern Part of the Dutch Province of Drenthe, 1998; The reflection of Elements of Afro-American Culture in George Gershwin's Opera "Porgy and Bess", 2002; Published Works for wind-band include: Rhapsodic Essayette for Band; Travesuras Gatunas; The Launching; The Maiden Voyage; Northern Jubilee; The Initial Quest; Impromptu for Brass Band; Little Suite on Highland Folksongs, Festive Intrada; Numerous arrangements. Honours: Invited by the German Foreign Office to a tour of the FGR because of exceptional achievements in the field of the German Language, 1983; 2nd Prize, International Composition Contest, Brilon, Germany; Nominee, Cultural Award, Tynaarlo County Council, 2002; 1st Prize, Longridge Band Composers' Forum 2003; Certificate of Merit for an outstanding contribution in the field of wind-music, IBC; Nominee and finalist, Fodens Richard Award for Brass Band Composition and Arranging 2004 (final results to be announced); Voted International Musician of the Year 2003 for an outstanding contribution to wind and brass band composition, IBC; International Order of Merit for services to music, IBC, 2004; Works used as compulsory contest-pieces in The Netherlands, Belgium and Germany. Memberships include: World Association of Symphonic Bands and Ensembles; British Association of Symphonic Bands and Wind Ensembles; Royal Netherlands Federation of Musical Societies; Netherlands Christian Federation of Musical Societies; Flemish Wind-Music Association; International Military Music Society; International Society for the Investigation and Promotion of Wind-Music; Confédération Musicale de France; Swiss Band-Music Association; Bundesvereinigung deutscher Musikverbände; Australian Band and Orchestra Directors Association; Union Grand-Duc Adolphe, American Bandmasters Association. Address: Tienelsweg 24 NL-9471 PB Zuidlaren, Drenthe, The Netherlands. Website: http://www.hafabra.nl/comp/bartelds.shtml

BARTENEV Georgii M, b. 12 January 1915, Gulkevichi, Russia. Scientist; Professor; Doctor; Researcher. m. Cheslava, 1 daughter. Education: Diploma, Physics Faculty, Moscow State University, 1939; PhD, 1943; Doctor of Science Diploma, 1948; Professor of Physics of Polymers Diploma, 1949. Appointments: Assistant, Physics Department, Moscow State University, 1943-45; Chief, Physics Laboratory, Rubber Research Institute, Moscow, 1946-55; Chief, Department of Solid State and Polymer Physics Laboratory, Moscow Teacher Training University, 1950-72; Chief, Institute of Physics and Chemistry Laboratory, Russian Academy of Science, Moscow, 1972-90; Senior Scientist, Institute of Physics and Chemistry, Russian Academy of Science, Moscow, 1991-. Publications: Contributed to: 1017 articles to professional journals; Author: 21 books and monographs. Honours: Honoured Scientist of Russian Federation; Honoured Inventor in Field; Certificate, All Union Board of Science and Technology Societies of USSR; Silver Medal Gesellschaft Kammer der Technik, Berlin, 1985. Memberships: Mendeleer Chemistry Society. Address: Flat 135 Cherniakhovskogo Str 5, 125319 Moscow, Russia.

Dictionary of International Biography

BARTHEL Günter, b. 17 March 1941, Erfurt, Germany. University Professor. m. Helga, 1 son, 1 daughter. Education: Diploma, 1963; Doctorate, 1966; Dr habil, 1970. Appointments: Deputy Director, Department of African and Near Eastern Sciences, University of Leipzig, 1970-75; Full Professor of Economy of countries in North Africa and the Middle East, 1975-96; Visiting Professor, Austin, Los Angeles and Cambridge, USA, 1982; Chairman, Central Council for Asian, African and Latin American Sciences, 1987-89. Publications: Author and editor of 28 books, including Lexikon Arabische Welt; Over 148 articles; 22 forewords; Over 138 reviews. Honour: National Award, 1983. Memberships: Several national and international societies. Address: Friedensstrasse 7a, 99310 Arnstadt, Germany.

BARTHOLOMEUSZ Hugh, b. 20 July 1953. Doctor. m. Helga, 3 children. Education: Medical Graduate, University of Queensland; Graduate, Princess Alexandra Hospital and Greenslopes Repatriation Hospital. Appointments: Registrar, General Surgeon, Greenslopes Hospital; Advanced Training, Plastic Surgery, Princess Alexandra Hospital, Royal Brisbane Hospital, Queen Elizabeth Hospital; Private Practice, Plastic Surgery, Ipswich; Retired Commanding Officer, Queensland Air Training Corps; Group Captain, RAAF Specialist Reserve; Consultant, Plastic Surgeon to the Director General Defence Health Service; Private Practice, Greenslopes Private Hospital. Honour: Reserve Force Decoration, 1991.Memberships: Chairman, St Paul's National Trust Restoration Committee; Chairman, Medical Executive Committee, Board Member, St Andrews Hospital; Chairman, Council of W Moreton Anglican College, 1993-; World President, International Air Cadet Exchange Association, 1996-98; Secretary, Air Training Corps National Council, 1996-; Vice-President, 1998-2000, Member, 2000-, Australasian Day Surgery Association; Chairman, Friends of University of Queensland, Ipswich, 2000-; RACS Representative, Australian Day Surgery Council; Representative, International Day Surgery Association, 2001-; Secretary, Queensland State Committee, RACS, 2003-. Address: Tri Rhosen House, 1 Court Street, Ipswich 4305, Australia.

BARTKÓ György Jenő, b. 10 May 1947, Budapest, Hungary. Psychiatrist; Director. m. Ilona Herczeg, 1 daughter. Education: MD, Semmelweis University of Medicine, 1967-73; MSc, Health Administration, Haynal Imre University for Health Sciences, Budapest, 1996-98; PhD, Hungarian Academy of Sciences, Budapest, 1996; Professional certifications: Neurologist, 1977, Psychiatrist, 1980, Addictologist, 1995; Clinical Pharmacologist, 2003. Appointments: Clinical Psychiatrist, National Institute for Nervous and Mental Diseases, Budapest, 1979-90; Research Fellow, Mt Sinai School of Medicine, New York, 1990-92; Deputy Medical Director, Jahn Ferenc South Pest Hospital, Budapest, 1992; Managing Director, Medic-CNS Ltd, Budapest, 1997-; President, Pszichoinova Foundation, 2000-. Publications: Editor, Psychiatria Hungarica, journal, 1995; Author, Antipsychotics, book, 2000; Over 80 research publications on schizophrenia, antipsychotics and chronic pain. Honours: DAAD Fellowship, Germany, 1988. Memberships: Member, Hungarian Psychiatric Association, Budapest; Member, Hungarian College of Neuropsychopharmacology, Budapest; Member, European College of Neuropsychopharmacology; Member, Medical Research Council, Ethics Committee for Clinical Pharmacology, 2000-. Address: Gogol u. 26 5/3, Budapest 1133, Hungary.

BARTLETT Neil, b. 15 September 1932, Newcastle upon Tyne, England. Chemist. m. Christina Isabel Cross, 1952, 3 sons, 1 daughter. Education: PhD, University of Durham, 1957. Appointments: University of British Columbia, Canada, 1958-66; Professor of Chemistry, Princeton University, USA, 1966-69; Scientist, Bell Telephone Laboratories, Murray Hill, New Jersey,

1966-69; Professor of Chemistry, University of California at Berkeley, 1969-94; Principal Investigator; Lawrence Berkeley Laboratory, 1969-; Professor Emeritus, 1994-; Carried out research on compounds of rare gases. Publications include: The Oxidation of Oxygen and Related Chemistry, 2001; Over 160 scientific papers and reports. Honours: Honorary doctorates from several universities; Research Corporation Award, 1965; Dannie Heineman Prize, 1971; Robert A Welch Award, 1976; W H Nichols Medal, USA, 1983; Moissan Fluorine Centennial Medal, Paris, 1986; Prix Moissan, 1988; American Chemical Society Award for Distinguished Service to Inorganic Chemistry, 1989; Pauling Medal, American Chemical Society, 1989; Award for Creative Work in Fluorine Chemistry, American Chemical Society, 1992; Bonner Chemiepreis, 1992; Foreign Fellow, Royal Society of Canada, 2001; Honorary FRSC, 2002; Royal Society (London) Davy Medal, 2002. Memberships: Leopoldina Academy, Halle, 1969; Corresponding member, Göttingen Academy, 1977; American Academy of Arts and Sciences, 1977; National Academy of Sciences, 1979; Associé Etranger, Academie des Sciences, France, 1989. Address: Department of Chemistry, University of California, Berkeley, CA 94720, USA.

BARTON Jozsef, b. 31 July 1937, Villany, Hungary. Physician. m. Eva Gerenday, 2 sons. Education: MD, 1961, DD, 1965, Medical University, Pecs; Sports Physician, OTKI, 1979. Appointments: Surgeon, City Hospital, Komlo, 1961-62; Dentist, Stomatology Clinic, Pecs, 1962-65; Sports Doctor, JPU, Pecs, 1965-86; Biomech, University of Physical Education, Budapest, 1986-93; Vice Director, Faculty of Health Sciences, Medical University, Pecs, 1986-93. Publications include: Biomechanics, 1974; Anatomy, Physiology and Hygiene, 1976; Basic Biomechanics, 1994; Biomechanical Gait Analysis, 1995; Handbook of Grafology, 1998. Honours: Excellent Student Award, 1955; Ministry Award, 1976; Excellent Worker, 1983; Nivo Award, 1984. Memberships: Science Society of Physical Education, 1961-96; International Society of Biomechanics, 1975-84; Hungarian Sport Medical Society, 1987-. Address: Siklosi u 80, H-7632 Pecs, Hungary.

BARTON Marie Gaye, b. 23 April 1951, London, England. Music Teacher. Education: Certificate in Education, University of Bristol; BA, The Open University; Licentiate of Trinity College of Music, London, Music Composition Diploma; Licentiate of London College of Music, Piano Teacher's Diploma; Accredited Piano Teacher, British Suzuki Institute; Practitioner Certificate, Neuro-Linguistics Programming. Appointments: Resident Music Mistress, Vinehall School, East Sussex, England, 1974-75; Music Specialist, British School of Brussels, Belgium, 1975-76; Music Teacher, Broomham School, East Sussex, England, 1976-79; Music Teacher and Head of Department, Oxted County School, Surrey, England, 1979-81; Visiting Piano Teacher, Ancaster House School, East Sussex, England, 1981-86; Homewood Comprehensive School, Kent, England, 1985-90; Senior Music Teacher, St Leonard-Mayfield School, The Convent of the Holy Child, East Sussex, England, 1986-96; Piano Teacher in Private Practice, Rye, East Sussex, England, 1976-96; Visiting Piano Teacher, Glenalmond College, Perthshire, Scotland, 1997-2000; Piano Instructor, West Lothian Council, Scotland, 1996-2001; Piano Teacher in Private Practice, Lothian Suzuki Group, Scotland, 1996-. Publications: Short articles in European Piano Teachers' Association Journal, Journal of the British Suzuki Institute, The Edinburgh Herald and Post. Memberships: The Incorporated Society of Musicians, Music in Education and Private Teachers' Sections; The European Piano Teachers' Association; The British Suzuki Institute. Address: 43 Queensferry Street Lane, Edinburgh EH2 4PF, Scotland.

BARUCH Eduard, b. 19 December 1907, Booklyn, New York, New York, USA. Lawyer; Engineer; Consultant. m. Malyn Crusius, 1 son. Education: Engineering, Rhenania Institute, Neuhausen, Switzerland, 1924; Law, Columbia University, New York, 1930; Law, Columbia Law School, 1933. Appointments include: Co-Founder, President, Chief Executive Officer, Heli-Coil, Danbury, Connecticut, 1950-70; Management Consultant, 1970-; Board Member of numerous companies including: Barden Corporation, NBI Mortgage Investment Corporation, Heli-Coil Corporation, Risdon Corporation, Lorlin Industries, Data Control Corporation, Timpete, Denver Colorado, Topp Industries, Los Angeles, Scholler Brothers, Philadelphia, Kappa Industries, Washington DC; Past Board Member, Greater Danbury Chamber of Commerce; Former Vice President and Board Member Danbury Hospital; Industrial Commissioner for the State of Connecticut, 1972-77. Publications: Numerous articles and papers. Honours: Numerous awards include: Cecil J Previdi Award, 2000. Memberships include: Past President Rotary Club; Union Lodge of Masons; Royal Order of Jesters; Psi Upsilon Social Fraternity; Phi Delta Legal Fraternity; Navy League; Society of Automotive Engineers. Address: 936 Intracoastal Drive, Fort Lauderdale, FL 33304, USA.

BARYSHNIKOV Mikhail, b. 28 January 1948, Riga, Ballet Dancer. 1 daughter. Education: Riga Ballet School; Kirov Ballet School, Leningrad. Career: Member, Kirov Ballet Company, 1969-74; Guest Artist with many leading ballet companies, including American Ballet Theatre, National Ballet of Canada; Royal Ballet; Hamburg Ballet; Federal Republic of Germany; Ballet Victoria, Australia; Stuttgart Ballet, Federal Republic of Germany; Alvin Ailey Co, USA, 1974-; Joined New York City Ballet Company, 1978, resigned 1979; Artistic Director, American Ballet Theatre, 1980-90; Co-Founder, White Oak Dance Project, 1990-; Stage debut in Metamorphosis, 1989; Launched perfume Misha, 1989; Ballets (world premieres) Vestris, 1969; Medea, 1975; Push Comes to Shove, 1976; Hamlet Connotations, 1976; Other Dances, 1976; Pas de Duke, 1976; La Dame de Pique, 1978' L'Apres-midi d'un Faune, 1978; Santa Fe Saga, 1978; Opus 19, 1979; Rhapsody, 1980; Films: The Turning Point, 1977; White Nights, 1985; Giselle, 1987; Dancers, 1987; Dinosaurs, 1991; Choreography: Nutcracker, 1976; Don Quixote, 1978; Cinderella, 1984. Publications: Baryshnikov at Work, 1977. Address: c/o Vincent & Farrell Associates, 481 Eighth Avenue, Suite 740, New York, NY 10001, USA.

BASDEO Sahadeo, b. 10 September 1945, Trinidad. m. 3 children. Education: BA, Brandon University, Manitoba, 1970; MA, University of Calgary, Alberta, 1972; Certificate in Elementary French Proficiency, 1974; PhD, Dalhousie University, Nova Scotia, 1975. Appointments: Graduate History and Language Teacher, St Benedict's College, Trinidad, 1964-67; Graduate Teaching Assistant, University of Calgary, 1970-72; Graduate Teaching Assistant, Dalhousie University, 1974-75; Deputy Director, Research and Planning Branch, 1976, Senior Research Analyst, 1976-77; Director of Research, 1977-78; Manitoba Department of Education; Senior Lecturer, University of the West Indies, 1978-88; Senator, Parliament of Trinidad and Tobago, 1981-91; Acted as Minister of Industry, Enterprise and Tourism, 1988-91; Minister of External Affairs and International Trade, Government of Trinidad and Tobago, 1988-91; Senior Lecturer, Associate Professor, Institute of International Relations, University of the West Indies, 1992-94; Professor of History, Okanagan University College, Canada, 1994-. Publications: 3 books; Numerous articles in professional journals. Honours: Silver Medal in History, 1970; Graduate Teaching Fellowship, 1970-72; Isaak Walton Killam Scholarship, Dalhousie University, 1972-75; St Benedict's College, Past Students' Association Award for

Meritorious and Yeoman Service to the Cause of the School, 1986. Address: Department of History, Okanagan University College, 3333 College Way, Kelowna, BC V1V 1V7, Canada.

BASHAR M Abul, b. 26 November 1951, Dhaka, Bangladesh. Educator. m. Selina Bashar, 1 son, 1 daughter. Education: BSc (First Class), Mechanical Engineering, 1972, MSc, Mechanical Engineering, 1979, Bangladesh University of Engineering and Technology; Post Graduate Diploma in Technical Education, 1988, MEd, Management and Administration of Higher Education, 1988, University of Manchester, UK. Appointments include: Lecturer, 1976-78, Assistant Professor, 1978-82, Department of Mechanical Engineering, Technical Teachers Training College, Dhaka, Bangladesh; Associate Professor, Mechanical Engineering Department, Dhaka Engineering College, Gazipur, Bangladesh, 1982-86; Associate Professor and Head of Mechanical Engineering Department, 1986-96, Professor, 1996-2001, Principal, 1998-2001, Technical Teachers Training College, Dhaka, Bangladesh; Dean, Faculty of Education, University of Dhaka, Bangladesh, 1998-2001; Co-ordinator, Tutorial Centre for B Ed and M Ed Courses, Bangladesh Open University, 1998-; Currently, Director General, Directorate of Technical Education, Government of the Peoples' Republic of Bangladesh; Course Organiser for UNESCO, UNDP, 1985-90; Worked for UK Overseas Development Agency Project, 1986-94. Involved with the Colombo Plan Staff Training College, Philippines as local co-ordinator and resource person for In-Country Training Programmes. Publications: Numerous papers presented and books edited which include: 15 books on mechanical engineering related subjects, 1989-90; Papers include: Challenge of Emerging Needs and the Role of TVET Teachers, 1998; Role of Industries and Other Organisations in Curriculum Development, 1999. Memberships include: Premium Member, Association for Supervision and Curriculum Development, USA; Commonwealth Society for Technical and Mathematics Educators; Life Member, Bangladesh Association for the Advancement of Science; Senior Member, American Institute of Industrial Engineers; Life Fellow, Bangladesh Society of Mechanical Engineers; Life Fellow, Institution of Engineers, Bangladesh; Bangladesh Computer Society; Bangladesh National Commission for UNESCO; Bangladesh Technical Education Board; Numerous university boards, councils and committees. Address: Directorate of Technical Education: Shikkha Bhaban, 16 Abdul Gani Road, Dhaka – 1000, Bangladesh. E-mail: tecedu@bdonline.com

BASHFUL Emmett W, b. 12 March 1917, Oscar, Louisiana, USA. m. Juanita, deceased, 1 daughter. Education: BS, Southern University, Baton Rouge, Louisiana, 1940; MA, 1947, PhD, 1955, University of Illinois. Appointments: Teacher, Allen Parish, Louisiana Schools, 1940-41; Assistant Manager, Insurance Keystone Company, 1941-42; First Lieutenant, US Army, Overseas Services, Mediterranean Theatre of Operations, 1942-46; Instructor of Full Professor, Chairman, Department of Political Science, Florida A&M University, 1948-58; Professor, Political Science, Southern University, Baton Rouge, 1958-59; Southern University at New Orleans, 1959-69; Vice President in Charge, 1969-77, Chancellor in Charge, 1977-87, Chancellor Emeritus, 1987-, Dean, Chief Executive Officer, Southern University at New Orleans. Publications: Book: A Study in Judicial Selection, 1958; 3 articles in professional journals. Honours: Ford Foundation Fellowship, 1954-55; Citation, Florida Supreme Court, 1955; Citation, Southern Christian Leadership Conference, 1958; Silver Beaver Award, Boy Scouts of America, 1966; Volunteer Activist Award, 1976; Award, Ten Outstanding Citizens of New Orleans, Institute for Human Understanding, 1978; Weiss Brotherhood Award, National Conference of Christians and Jews, 1987; Living and Giving Award, Juvenile Diabetes Association, 1988; Frederick D Patterson Award for Excellence in the field of Education, 1988; Alumni

Achievement Award, University of Illinois, 1991; Lifetime Achievement Award for Service to Children and Youth, Urban League of Greater New Orleans, 1992; Arthur J Chapital Sr Award, New Orleans Chapter of NAACP for contribution to Public Education, 1994; Award for Contribution to Education, Louisiana Weekly Educational Foundation, 1996; Alpha Award of Merit, 1999. Memberships: Southern University at New Orleans Foundation; Southern University System Foundation; New Orleans Public School Scholarship Foundation; Southern Institute for Education and Research. Address: 5808 Lafaye St, New Orleans, LA 70122, USA.

BASILE Leon Edmund, b. 12 December 1955, Woburn, USA. Writer; Editor. Education: BA, English, History, University of Massachusetts, Boston, 1977; Archives Institute, Emory University; Georgia Department of Archives History, 1978; MA, History, University of Georgia, 1979. Publications: The Civil War Diary of Amos E Stearns, a Prisoner at Andersonville, 1981; Articles contributed to professional journals. Honours: Jefferson Davis Medal in Gold, United Daughters of the Confederacy for Outstanding Research in Southern History, 1976. Membership: New England Historic Genealogical Society. Address: 9 Colonial Road, Woburn, MA 01801-2814, USA.

BASINGER Kim, b. 8 December 1953, Athens, Georgia, USA. Actress. m. (1) Ron Britton, divorced, (2) Alec Baldwin, divorced, 1 daughter. Career: Model, 1971-76; As actress, films include: Never Say Never Again, 1982; The Man Who Loved Women, 1983; 9 1/2 Weeks, 1985; Batman, 1989; Too Hot to Handle, 1991; The Real McCoy, 1993; Wayne's World, 1994; The Getaway, 1994; Prêt-à-Porter, 1994; LA Confidential, 1997; I Dreamed of Africa, 2000; Bless the Child, 2000; 8 Mile, 2002; People I Know, 2002. Honours: Oscar, 1983; Academy Award and Golden Globe for Best Supporting Actress, 1997. Address: 3960 Laurel Canyon Boulevard, #414, Studio City, CA 91604, USA.

BASMAJIAN John V, b. 21 June 1921, Constantinople. Medical Scientist. m. Dora Lucas, 1 son, 2 daughters. Education: MD, Honours, University of Toronto, 1945; Fellowships, honours, Royal College of Physicians of Canada, Glasgow, Edinburgh, Australia, 1977-99; Honorary LLD, Queen's University, 1999; Honorary DSc, McMaster University, 2001; Honorary Diploma, St Lawrence College. Appointments: Hospital residencies, 1946-49; Lecturer to Full Professor of University of Toronto, 1949-56; Professor and Head, Anatomy, Queen's University, Canada, 1956-69; Professor and Director, Emory University Rehabilitation Research and Training Centre, Atlanta, 1969-77; Professor then Professor Emeritus, McMaster University, Canada, 1977-. Publications: Medical books on medical science in several languages; 400 articles, 5 medical movies. Honour: Officer of the Order of Canada, 1995, and Ontario, 1991. Memberships: Honorary Member of many associations and institutions; former President, three scientific bodies, international and North American. Address: 9-210 Fiddlers Green Road, Hamilton, Ontario L9G 1W6, Canada.

BASNET Narayan Bahadur, b. 25 August 1960, Sotang Village, Solukhumbu, Nepal. Paediatrician; Researcher. m. Sangeeta B Basnet, 1 son, 1 daughter. Education: Certificate in General Medicine, 1979; Diploma in Public Administration, 1981; Master degree, Public Administration, 1985; MBBS, 1990; PhD, 2006. Appointments: House Officer, Medical Instructor, 1991-93; Medical Officer, Co-investigator, ARI Project, Kathmandu, Nepal; Medical Co-ordinator, Association of Medical Doctors of Asia, 1994-95; Visiting Researcher, Department of Paediatrics, University of Tokyo, Japan, 2000-2001; Postdoctoral Fellow, Japan Society for the Promotion of Science, 2001-2003. Publications: Articles in medical journals including: Journal of the Nepal Medical Association, 1995; Asian Medical Journal, 1998; International Medical Journal, 1998; Heart Vessels, 2000; Pediatric Cardiology, 2001 Indian Pediatrics, 2001; Several conference abstracts and papers in Nepali; Book: Nepal at the Dawn of the 21st Century: General Health and Medical Information, 2001. Honours: Research Awards, The Graduate School of Medicine University of Tokyo, Japan, 1999, 2001. Memberships: Life Member, Nepal Paediatric Society; Life Member, Nepal Medical Association; Life Member, Nepal Family Planning Association; Life Member, Cardiological Society of India; World Federation for Mental Health; AMDA; Japan Pediatric Society; AAAS. Address: PO Box 1563, Kathmandu, Nepal. E-mail: nbbasnet777@hotmail.com

BASS Aaron C, b. 26 May 1950, Philadelphia, USA. Educator. m. Jade, 3 sons, 2 daughters. Education: MDiv, Lutheran Theological Seminary, Philadelphia, 1998; Associate Degree, Data Processing Community College of Philadelphia; MA, Social Psychology, Temple University; BA, Psychology, Lincoln University. Appointments: Research Assistant, 1974-2000, Pupil Data Analyst, 2000-, Office of Accountability and Assessment, School District of Philadelphia. Publications: Room Provisioning in Title IV – A Day Case in Philadelphia, 1974-75; A Study of Involvement in Early Childhood Programs, 1976-77; Evaluation of Career Education Projects, 1980-81; Evaluation of Special Education Projects in Career Education, 1980-81. Honours: Listed in national and international biographical dictionaries. Memberships: Church of God in Christ International; Omega Psi Phi Fraternity Inc; Phi Delta Kappa Educational Association. Address: 6024 Morton Street, Philadelphia, PA 19144, USA. E-mail: abass@voicenet.com

BASS Evelyn Elizabeth Hughes, b. 28 September 1948, Magnolia, Arkansas, USA. Educator; Writer; Composer; Vocalist. m. John William Bass, deceased, 1 son, 1 daughter. Education: BA, Elementary Education, Arkansas Baptist College, 1971; MSc, Education, Ouachita Baptist University, 1988; Graduate Studies, Grambling State University, 1991; Graduate Studies, Early Childhood, University of Arkansas at Little Rock, 2001. Appointments: Advisor, Instructor, 1999, Head Teacher of Elementary School, 2002-, Grace Holiness Christian Academy; Teacher, Pulaski County Special School District, 1971-96; Instructor, Arkansas Baptist College, 1991; Owner, The Printed Word, 1993; Poetry, Writer, Composer, Vocalist, children's CD, 2003. Honours: Listed in national and international biographical dictionaries. Memberships: Southern Early Childhood Association; Arkansas Retired Teacher Association; Association for Supervision and Curriculum Development. Address: 2918 Dorset Drive, Little Rock, AR 72204, USA. E-mail: evelynbass@sbcglobal.net

BASSANI Guiseppe-Franco, b. 29 October 1929, Milan, Italy. University Professor. m. Serenella Figini, 1 son, 1 daughter. Education: Degree in Physics, University of Pavia, 1952. Appointments: Research Associate, University of Illinois, USA; Research Physicist, Argonne National Laboratory, USA; Professor, Theoretical Physics, University of Messina, Italy; Professor, Solid State Physics, University of Rome, Italy; Professor Solid State Physics, Scuola Normale Superiore, Pisa, Italy. Publications: About 200 scientific articles published in international journals; 1 research book, Electronic States and Optical Transitions in Solids, 1975; 1 book for graduate students, Fisica dello Stato Solido, 2000. Honours: Degree, honoris causa from University of Toulouse, France, 1979; Ecole Politechnique Federale (CH), 1986, Purdue University, USA, 1994; Gold Medal of the President of Italy for Achievements in Science and Culture, 2000. Memberships: American Physical Society; Lincei Academy; Italian Physical Society. Address: Scuola Normale Superiore, Piazza dei Cavalieri, 56126 Pisa, Italy. E-mail: basssani@sns.it

Dictionary of International Biography

BASSEN Ned Henry, b. 8 June 1948, Far Rockaway, New York, USA. Attorney. m. Susan Millington Campbell, 2 daughters. Education: BS, Industrial and Labor Relations, Cornell University, 1970; JD, Cornell Law School, 1973. Appointments: Partner, Kelley Drye & Warren LLP, 1983-92; Chair, Labor and Employment Group, Mudge Rose Guthrie Alexander & Ferdon LLP, 1993-95; Chair, Labor and Employment Group, Hughes Hubbard & Reed LLP, 1995-. Publications: The Effect of Strikes Upon Vacations, 1972; Synopsis of State Laws Regulating Employment of the Handicapped, 1977; What Can an Employer do to Help Protect Against Sexual Harassment Lawsuits?, 1992; EEO Compensation Alert for Government Contractors, 1999. Honours: Cornell Law Review, Note and Comment Editor, 1972-73; Guide to the World's Leading Labour and Employment Lawyers; The Best Lawyers in America; Who's Who in American Law; Who's Who in the World; Who's Who in America; Who's Who in the East. Memberships: American Bar Association; New York Bar Association; CPR Institute for Dispute Resolution; Industrial Relations Research Association; US Council for Industrial Business; Metropolitan Arbitration Group of New York, New Jersey and Connecticut; New York Management Attorneys Conference. Address: Hughes Hubbard & Reed LLP, One Battery Park Plaza, New York, NY 10004-1482, USA.

BASSETT John Walden, b. 21 March 1938, Roswell, New Mexico, USA. Attorney. m. Nolana Knight, 1 son, 1 daughter. Education: AB, Economics, Stanford University, 1960; JD with Honours, University of Texas School of Law, 1964. Appointments: Special Assistant to Attorney General of US, White House Fellow, 1967; New Mexico State Board of Education, 1987-1991. Publications: Associate Editor, University of Texas Law Review. Honours: Order of Coif, University of Texas School of Law, 1964; White House Fellow, 1967; Paul Harris Award, Rotary Club. Address: 5060 Bright Sky Road, Roswell, New Mexico, 88201, USA.

BASSEY Shirley, b. 8 January 1937, Tiger Bay, Cardiff, Wales. Singer; Entertainer. m. (1) Kenneth Hume, divorced 1965, deceased, (2) Sergio Novak, 1971, divorced 1981, 1 daughter, deceased, one adopted son. Appointments: Variety and Revue Singer, 1950s; Concerts and TV appearances world-wide; Semi-Retired, 1981-. Creative Works: I'm In the Mood For Love, 1981; Love Songs, 1982; All By Myself, 1984; I Am What I Am, 1984; Playing Solitaire, 1985; I've Got You Under My Skin, 1985; Sings The Songs From The Shows, 1986; Born To Sing the Blues, 1987; Let Me Sing And I'm Happy, 1988; Her Favourite Songs, 1988; Keep The Music Playing, 1991; Great Shirley Bassey (album), 1999; Various compilations. Honours: CBE; 20 Gold Discs; 14 Silver Discs; TV Times Award, Best Female Singer, 1972; Britannia Award, Best Female Solo Singer in the Last 50 years, 1977; American Guild of Variety Artists Award, Best Female Entertainer, 1976. Address: c/o CSS Stellar Management, Drury House, 34-43 Russell Street, London, WC2B 5HA, England.

BATAVIA Mitchell, b. 8 November 1959, Brooklyn, New York, USA. Assistant Professor of Physical Therapy. m. Evgenia Yakovleva, 1 son. Education: BS, University of Delaware, USA, 1981; MA, Columbia University, 1986; Diploma, Feldenkrais Method, 1987; PhD, New York University, 1997. Appointments: Consultant Physical Therapist, 1989-97; Robert Salant Post-Doctoral Fellow, New York University and New York Medical Center, 1997-98; Assistant Professor of Physical Therapy, New York University, 1998-. Publications: Books: The Wheelchair Evaluation: A Practical Guide, 1998; Clinical Research for Health Professionals: A User-Friendly Guide, 2001; Peer-Reviewed articles as co-author include: An augmented auditory feedback device, 1997; Changing chairs: Anticipating problems in

prescribing wheelchairs, 2001; Karaoke for Quads, 2003; Test-retest Reliability of the Functional Rotation Test in Healthy Adults, 2003. Honours: Dewitt Wallace Reader's Digest Fellow, Rusk Institute of Rehabilitation Medicine, New York University Medical Center, 1978; Cum Laude, University of Delaware, 1981; Traineeship for Physical Therapy Clinical Research Doctoral Studies, NIDRR and New York University, 1993-97; Arch Award, New York University, 1997; Research Challenge Fund, New York University School of Education, 2000; Goddard Award, New York University, 2001. Memberships: American Physical Therapy Association, 1981-, Neurological Section. Department of Physical Therapy, New York University, 380 Second Avenue, 4th Floor, New York, NY 10010, USA. E-mail: mitchell.batavia@nyu.edu Website: www.nyu.edu/education/pt

BATE (Andrew) Jonathan, b. 26 June 1958, Sevenoaks, Kent, England. Professor of English Literature; Critic; Novelist. m. (1) Hilary Gaskin, 1984, divorced 1995, (2) Paula Byrne, 1996, 1 son, 1 daughter. Education: MA, 1980, PhD, 1984, St Catharine's College, Cambridge. Appointments: Harkness Fellow, Harvard University, 1980-81; Research Fellow, St Catharine's College, Cambridge, 1983-85; Fellow, Trinity Hall, and Lecturer, Trinity Hall and Girton College, Cambridge, 1985-90; Visiting Associate Professor, University of California at Los Angeles, 1989; King Alfred Professor of English Literature, 1991-, Leverhulme Personal Research Professor, 1999-, University of Liverpool; Research Reader, British Academy, 1994-96. Publications: Shakespeare and the English Romantic Imagination, 1986; Charles Lamb: Essays of Elia (editor), 1987; Shakespearean Constitutions: Politics, Theatre, Criticism 1730-1830, 1989; Romantic Ecology: Wordsworth and the Environmental Tradition, 1991; The Romantics on Shakespeare (editor), 1992; Shakespeare and Ovid, 1993; The Arden Shakespeare: Titus Andronicus (editor), 1995; Shakespeare: An Illustrated Stage History (editor), 1996; The Genius of Shakespeare, 1997; The Cure for Love, 1998; The Song of the Earth, 2000. Contributions to: Scholarly publications. Honours: Calvin and Rose Hoffman Prize, 1996; FBA, 1999; Honorary Fellow, St Catherine's College, Cambridge, 2000. Literary Agent: David Godwin Associates. Address: c/o Department of English, University of Liverpool, PO Box 147, Liverpool L69 3BX, England.

BATE John Warburton, b. 25 October 1935, Fredericton, New Brunswick, Canada. Civil Engineer. m. (1) divorced, 1 son, 1 daughter, (2) Sharon J Kilmer. Education: BSc, Civil Engineering, University of New Brunswick, 1960. Appointments: Sub-Lieutenant. University Naval Training Division, Royal Canadian Navy, 1957-60; Ove Arup and Partners, London, UK, 1960-63; EGM Cape, MTL, 1963-69; H H Robertson, Hamilton, 1969-78; CON-ENG Contractors, London, Ontario, 1978-81; John Bate and Co Ltd, 1981-; Owner, Manager, Engineer and General Contractor; Director, River Gold Mines (TSE). Honours: President, Association of Professional Engineers, Ontario, 1990-91; Chairman, Canadian Council of Professional Engineers, 1996-97; Companion, Order of Honour, Professional Engineers, Ontario; Fellow, Canadian Society of Civil Engineers. Memberships: Professional Engineers, Ontario; RCMI, London Club; L'Ordre des Ingénieurs du Quebec; International Association of Refrigerated Warehouses. Address: 880 Dundas Street W, No PH5, Mississauga, Ontario, Canada L5C 4H3.

BATELY Janet Margaret (Mrs L J Summers), b. 3 April 1932, Westcliff-on-Sea, Essex, England. University Professor Emeritus. Education: BA, Class 1, 1954, Diploma of Comparative Philology with Distinction, 1956, MA, 1958, Somerville College, Oxford, England. Appointments: Assistant Lecturer, 1955-58, Lecturer in English, 1958-69, Reader in English, 1970-76, Birkbeck College,

Dictionary of International Biography

University of London; Professor of English Language and Medieval Literature, 1977-95, Sir Israel Gollancz Research Professor, 1995-97, Professor Emeritus, 1997-, King's College, London. Publications include: The Old English Orosius, 1980, The Anglo-Saxon Chronicle MS A, 1986; The Tanner Bede, 1992; Articles in many academic publications. Honours: Fellow, King's College, London, 1986; Fellow of the British Academy, 1990; Honorary Fellow of Somerville College, Oxford, 1997; Fellow of the Royal Society of Arts, 2000; CBE (Companion of the British Empire), 2000. Memberships include: Honorary Member, International Society of Anglo-Saxonists; Member, Advisory Committee, Fontes Anglo-Saxonici; International Consultation Board for the Historical Study of Language, University of Glasgow; Member, Honorary Advisory Development Board, Booktrust, 2003-. Address: 86 Cawdor Crescent, London W7 2DD, England. E-mail: janet.bately@kcl.ac.uk

BATEMAN Robert McLellan, b. 1930, Toronto, Canada. Artist. m. (1) Suzanne Bowerman, 1961, 2 sons, 1 daughter, (2) Birgit Freybe, 1975, 2 sons. Education: BA, University of Toronto, 1954; Ontario College of Education, 1955. Appointments: High School Art Teacher, Nelson High School, Burlington, Ontario, 1958-63, 1965-69, Government College, Umuahia, Nigeria, 1963-65, Lord Elgin High School, 1970-76; Lecturer, Resource Person in Art, Photography, Nature and Conservation. Creative Works: Major Exhibitions: Tryon Gallery, London, 1975, 1979; Beckett Gallery, Hamilton, Ontario, 1978, 1987; 1991; Images of the Wild, National Museum of Natural Sciences, Ottawa, 1981-82; Joslyn Art Museum, Omaha, Nebraska, 1987; Leigh Yawkey Woodson Art Museum, Wausau, Wisconsin, 1986-97; Smithsonian Institute, Museum of Natural History, Washington, 1987; Frye Art Museum, Seattle, Washington, 1988; Colorado Springs Fine Arts Museum, 1991; Carnegie Museum of Natural History, 1991; Canadian Embassy, Tokyo, 1992; Suntory Museum, Osaka and Tokyo, 1995-96; National Museum of Wildlife Art, 1997; Everard Read Gallery, Johannesburg, South Africa, 2000; Gerald Peters Gallery, Santa Fe, New Mexico, 2004; Several works in permanent collections. Publications: Books: The Art of Robert Bateman, 1981; The World of Robert Bateman, 1985; Robert Bateman: Artist in Nature, 1990; Robert Bateman: Natural Worlds, 1996; Thinking Like a Mountain, 2000; Birds, 2002. Honours include: Queen Elizabeth Silver Jubilee Medal, 1977; Master Artist, Leigh Yawkey Woodson Art Museum, 1982; Officer of the Order of Canada, 1984; Governor General's Award for Conservation, Quebec City, 1987; Society of Animal Artists Award of Excellence, 1979, 1980, 1986, 1990; Rachel Carson Award, Society of Environmental Toxicology and Chemistry, 1996; Golden Plate Award, American Academy for Achievement, 1998; Order of British Columbia, 2001; Queen's Jubilee Medal, 2002; Awards include 10 honorary doctorates. Memberships include: Royal Canadian Academy of Arts; Elsa Wild Animal Appeal; Sierra Club; Harmony Foundation; Jane Goodall Institute, Canada; Ecotrust; Kenya Wildlife Fund; Audubon Society; Sierra Legal Defense League. Address: PO Box 115, Fulford Harbour, Salt Spring Island, BC V8K 2P2, Canada.

BATES John Raphael, b. 24 October 1940, Wexford, Ireland. Meteorologist. m. Zaira Bates. Education: BSc, Physics, University College, Dublin, Ireland, 1962; PhD, Meteorology, Massachusetts Institute of Technology, USA, 1969. Appointments: Assistant Director, Irish Meteorological Service, Dublin, 1981-87; Head of Global Modelling and Assimilation Branch, Laboratory for Atmospheres, 1987-91, Senior Research Meteorologist, 1991-95, NASA Goddard Space Flight Center, Greenbelt, Maryland, USA; Professor of Meteorology, University of Copenhagen, Denmark, 1995-. Publications: Numerous publications in scientific journals including: Quarterly Journal of the Royal Meteorological Society; Proceedings of the Royal Irish Academy; Journal of the Atmospheric Sciences; Pageoph; Solar Physics; Monthly Weather Review; Journal of the Meteorological Society of Japan; Journal of Climate. Honour: Napier Shaw Memorial Prize, Royal Meteorological Society, 1971. Memberships: Member of the Royal Irish Academy, elected 1986; Member of Academia Europaea, elected, 1998; Fellow of the American Meteorological Society, elected, 2000. Address: Department of Geophysics, University of Copenhagen, Juliane Maries Vej 30, DK-2100 Copenhagen Ø, Denmark. E-mail: jrb@gfy.ku.dk

BATES Kathy, b. 28 June 1948, Memphis, Tennessee, USA. Actress. m. Tony Campisi, 1991, divorced. Education: Southern Methodist University. Career: Various jobs before acting; Theatre includes: Varieties, 1976; Chocolate Cake, 1980; 'night Mother, 1983; Rain of Terror, 1985; Films include: Taking Off, 1971; Arthur 2: On the Rocks, 1988; High Stakes, 1989; Dick Tracy, 1990; Misery, 1990; Prelude to a Kiss, 1991; Fried Green Tomatoes at the Whistle Stop Café, 1991; North, 1994; Diabolique, 1996; The War at Home, 1996; Primary Colors, 1998; Titanic, 1998; A Civil Action, 1999; Dash and Lilly, 1999; My Life as a Dog, 1999; Bruno, 2000; Rat Race, 2001; American Outlaws, 2001; About Schmidt, 2002; Love Liza, 2002; Evelyn, 2003; The Ingrate, 2004; Around the World in 80 Days, 2004; The Bridge of San Luis Rey, 2004. TV Films and Appearances include: No Place Like Home; Murder Ordained; The Love Boat; St Elsewhere; LA Law; Cagney & Lacey; Annie, 1999; My Sister's Keeper, 2002. Honours: Pulitzer Prize (Crimes of the Heart, 1981); Outer Circle Critic's Award ('night Mother, 1983); Obie Award (Frankie and Johnny in the Claire de Lune, 1987); Academy Award for Best Actress and Golden Globe (Misery, 1990). Address: c/o Susan Smith Associates, 121 N San Vincente Boulevard, Beverly Hills, CA 90211-2303, USA.

BATES Scott, b. 13 June 1923, Evanston, Illinois, USA. Professor; Poet. m. 17 April 1948, 4 sons. Education: BA, Carleton College, 1947; PhD, University of Wisconsin, 1954. Appointments: French Professor, Sewanee, Tennessee, 1954-87; Film Professor, University of the South, 1970-. Publications: Guillaume Apollinaire, 1967, 1989; Poems of War Resistance, from 2300 BC to the Present, 1969; Petit Glossaire des mots libres d'Apollinaire, 1975; The ABC of Radical Ecology, 1982, 2nd edition, 1990; Lupo's Fables, 1983; Merry Green Peace, 1991; Songs for the Queen of the Animals, 1992; The ZYX of Political Sex, 1999; The ZYX of Biblical Sex, 2002. Contributions to: New Yorker; Furioso; Sewanee Review; Partisan Review; New Republic; Southern Poetry Review; Tennessee Poetry Journal; Lyric; Quixote; Mountain Summer; Diliman Review; Delos. Honour: American Literary Anthology Prize, 1970. Address: Box 1263, 735 University Avenue, Sewanee, TN 37383, USA.

BATHAEE Soussan, b. 23 January 1953, Tehran, Iran. Engineer. Education: AS degree, Architecture, Riverside Community College, 1992; BSCE, California State University, 2003. Appointments: City Planning, Tehran, Iran, 1972-73; A/E Technician, National Iranian Oil Company, Tehran, Iran, 1973-75; Atomic Energy Organization, Tehran, Iran, 1975-80; Draftsperson, London, England, 1980-83; Draftsperson, Earl Walls Associates, San Diego, USA, 1984-85; Job Captain, Research Facilities Design, 1985-90; Engineering Service Technician, County of San Bernardino, 1991-2002; Freelance Analytical Engineer, LDIC – LSI Design & Integration Corp, 2002-. Honours: Certificate of Recognition, National Republican Party; America's Registry of Outstanding Professionals, 2003-04; Listed in several Who's Who and biographical publications. Memberships: American Society of Civil Engineers; Architectural/Engineering

Institute; The Riverside Greater Chambers of Commerce; The World Affair. Address: 42045 Kaffirboom Court, Temecula, CA 92591, USA. E-mail: soussanbathaee@yahoo.com

BATSTONE Patricia, (Annette Collins), b. 8 July 1941, West Hartlepool, England. Freelance Writer. m. Geoffrey Batstone, 2 sons. Education: BA in Theology; MEd, RE and Literature, PGCE, University of Hull; University of Exeter; PhD, RE and Literature. Career: Proprietor of Cottage Books, which became Patricia Batestone Publications, 2000. Publications: Messages of Devon, 1991; Farewell to Wincolmlee, 1994; Time and the Gospel, 1995; A World of Love, 1996; Memo to God, and Other Lenten Messages, 1998; Still Dancing, Thoughts on Spirituality, 1998; Candles in the Darkness, 1998; In Debt to C. S. Lewis, 1999; Meeting Jesus, 2000; Candles in Draughty Spaces, Meditations for the Millennium, 2000; Penitential Tears; Happy in Hospital? – An Anthology of Experiences by Patients for Patients, editor, 2000; Fifty Days – Reflections for Lent and Beyond, 2001; Lenten Light – A Study of Mark 9:1-29 for Lent and Eastertide, 2001; and prose devotional books; IBRA Notes for 1999 and 2001; Fishcakes and Fantasy: Getting the Message Across Creatively, 1996 (original text of the Winterton Memorial Lecture, UK Alliance); Tolkien's Moral Universe, paper in Canadian, C S Lewis Journal; Contributions to: Springboard; Dial 174; Areopagus; One; Triumph Herald; Poetry Church Anthology; Feather Books; The Dictionary of Methodism; Shafts of Light, the LPMA Millennium Prayer Book, 2000; The Methodist Recorder, articles and correspondence; The Expository Times – sermons; Daughters of Eve – Characterisation, Authenticity and Poetic Licence in Bible-based Narrative Poetry, Feather Books Christianity and Literature Series, No 4, 2001; Retired from publishing 2001. Honour: Areopagus Open, 1996; Highly Commended, Julia Carns Poetry Competition, 1998; Shortlisted, Association of Christian Writers' Annual Anthology Competition; Joint Second, Kestrel Open Competitions, both classes; Shortlisted, Wendy Webb Davidian Competitions, 2002-03; Second prizewinner, Spring Davidian. Memberships: Society of Women Writers and Journalists; Wesley Historical Society; Editor, The Methodist Retreat and Spirituality Network; Administrator, Editor, Association of Teetotallers in Methodism; Former Deputy Editor, Areopagus; Formerly Controlling Editor, Miscellany Postal Workshops, 1990-95; Retired from publishing, 2001. Address: 5 Foxglove Close, Dunkeswell, Devon EX14 4QE, England.

BATTERHAM Robin John, b. 3 April 1941, Brighton, Victoria, Australia. Chief Scientist of Australia; Chief Technologist, Rio Tinto P/L. Education: BE, University of Melbourne; LLD (Hon), PhD, AMusA, Post Nominals, AO, FAA, FTSE, CE, CPE, CSci, FNAE, FAusIMM, FISS, FIChemE; FIEAust; FICD; FAIM. Appointments: Chief, CSIRO Division of Mineral Engineering, 1984-88; Vice President, Resource & Processing Development CRA Ltd, 1988-94; Cr Academy of Technical Science, 1988-93; President, International Mineral Processing Congress, 1989-; Deputy-Chair, Co-op Research Centres, 1992-; G K William Co-op Research Centre, 1993-99; Chair, Australian IMM Proceedings Committee, 1995-99; Deputy Director, Music, Scot's Church, Melbourne; Chairman, International Network for Acid Prevention, 1998-; Chief Scientist of Australia, 1999-; Member, Major National Research Facilities Commission, 2001-; Australia Research Council Member, 1999-; President, Institution of Chemical Engineers, 2004-. Publications: 77 refereed papers in international journals and conferences. Honours: Officer of the Order of Australia; Presidents Medal, Australian Society of Sugar Cane Technologists; Fellow, Academy of Technology and Engineering Sciences; Fellow, Australian Academy of Science; Foreign Fellow, National Academy of Engineering, USA; Foreign Fellow, Swiss Academy of Engineering Sciences; CSIRO Postdoctorate Award;

Esso Award of Excellence in Chemical Engineering, 1992; Distinguished Lecturer, University of British Columbia, University of Waterloo, University of California, Berkeley, University of Utah; Kernot Medal, University of Melbourne, 1996; Chemeca Medal, 2003; Centenary Medal of Australia, 2003. Memberships: Fellow, Iron Steel Society, America; Fellow, Australia Institute of Mining Metallurgy; Fellow, Institution of Chemical Engineers; Fellow, Institute of Australian Engineers; Fellow, Australian Institute of Management; Fellow, Australian Academy of Sciences; Fellow, Australian Academy of Technological Sciences and Engineering. Address: 153 Park Drive, Parkville, Vic 3052, Australia.

BATTERSBY James Lyons, b. 24 August 1936, Pawtucket, Rhode Island, USA. Professor of English. m. Lisa J Kiser, 1 daughter. Education: BS, University of Vermont, 1961; MA, 1962, PhD, 1965, Cornell University. Appointments: Assistant Professor, University of California, Berkeley, 1965-70; Associate Professor, 1970-82, Professor, 1982-, Ohio State University. Publications include: Typical Folly: Evaluating Student Performance in Higher Education; Rational Praise and Natural Lamentation: Johnson, Lycidas and Principles of Criticism; Elder Olson: An Annotated Bibliography; Paradigms Regained: Pluralism and the Practice of Criticism; Reason and the Nature of Texts; Unorthodox Views: Reflections on Reality, Truth, and Meaning in Current Social, Cultural, and Critical Discourse. Honour: Kidder Medal. Memberships: Phi Beta Kappa; Phi Kappa Phi; Kappa Delta Pi; American Society for 18th Century Studies; Modern Language Association; Royal Oak Foundation. Address: Department of English, Ohio State University, 164 W 17th Avenue, Columbus, OH 43210, USA.

BATTIKHI Anwar Munir, b. 10 October 1946, Amman, Jordan. University Professor. m. Sahar M Alaeddin, 2 sons. Education: BSc, 1967, MSc, 1969, Soils and Irrigation, American University of Beirut, Lebanon; PhD, Soil Physics, Iowa State University, USA, 1977. Appointments: Dean of Research, Dean of Postgraduate College, University of Jordan, Amman Jordan, 1993-97; Vice-President, Jordan University of Science and Technology, Irbid, Jordan, 1997-98; President, The Hashemite University, Zarga, Jordan, 1998-2002. Publications: More than 60 books and publications in international and regional journals. Honour: Abdul Hamid Shoman Award for the Best Young Scientist in Agriculture in the Arab World, 1986. Memberships: Soil Science Society of America; Jordan Agricultural Engineering Union; Phi Kappa Phi; Gamma Sigma Delta; Sigma Xi; International Soil Science Society. Address: University of Jordan, PO Box 13900, Amman 11942, Jordan. E-mail: battikhi@ju.edu.jo

BATYRALIEV Talantbek, b. 9 February 1960, Bishtek, Kyrgyzstan. Medical Doctor. m. Jildyz Tazabekova. 2 sons. Education: MD, 1984; PhD, 1988; Doctor of Sciences, 1999; Professor of Cardiology, 2000. Appointments: Head, Department of Pulmonary Hypertension, Kyrgyz Cardiac Research Centre, 1989; Professor of Cardiology, Department of Cardiology, Cukurova University, Turkey, 1993; Director, Department of Cardiology, Orta-Dogu Hospital, Adana, Turkey, 1994; Director, Department of Cardiology, Sani Konukoglu Medical Centre, Turkey, 1997-. Publications: More than 100 publications in peer reviewed journals. Honour: European Cardiologist, 2001. Memberships: Fellow, American College of Angiology; International College of Angiology; Society of Cardiac Angiography and Interventions; European Society of Cardiology; American College of Cardiology. Address: Ali Fuat Cebesoy Blvd, Sani Konukoglu Medical Centre, Cardiology, 27090 Gaziantep, Turkey. E-mail: talantbekb@yahoo.com

Dictionary of International Biography

BAÚ Plínio Carlos, b. 1 January 1953, Carazinho, RS, Brazil. General Surgeon. m. Marilise Kostelnaki Baú, 1 son, 2 daughters. Education: Graduate, Faculty of Medicine, 1976, Postgraduate, General Surgery, 1978, Masters Degree, Education, Faculty of Education, 1991, Doctoral Candidate, Philosophy, 2003-, Pontificia Universidade, Católica RS. Appointments: Adjunct Professor, Department of Surgery, Faculty of Medicine, Pontificia Universidade Católica RS; Doctoral Candidate, Philosophy. Publications: Hernias da parede abdomina, 2002; Various articles on laparoscopic surgery, 1992-2003. Honour: Albert Sabin Prize for Medicine. Membership: Brazilian College of Surgeons. Address: Rua Caraja 46, 91900 370 Porto Alegre RS, Brazil.

BAUMAN Frank Anthony, b. 10 June 1921, Portland, Oregon, USA. Lawyer (Inactive). m. Jane Carter-Bauman, 1 son, 1 stepson, 2 daughters, 1 stepdaughter. Education: US Naval Language, University of Colorado, 1943-44; AB, Stanford University, 1944; JD, Yale University, 1949; Postgraduate, International Law, University of London, 1951-52. Appointments: Member, Oregon US District Court; US Supreme Court; Private Practice, Portland, 1950-71; Wilbur Beckett Oppenheimer Mautz & Souther, Veatch Bauman Lovett, Keane Haessler Bauman & Harper; Lawyers Commission for Civil Rights Under Law, Mississippi, 1969; Representative, UN Australia and New Zealand, 1971-76, Papua New Guinea, 1971-73; Private Practice, Portland, 1978-91; Adjunct Professor of Law, Lewis and Clark Law School, 1978-80; Advocate Lillian Baumann Fund, 1985-; Co-Trustee Mildred P Bauman Trust, 1997-. Publications: The Prospects for International Law, 1973; Can a World Court be Made to Work, 1973; The Promise of the United Nations, 1973. Honours: Recipient, World Peace Award Assembly of the Bahais, Portland, 1985; E B MacNaughton Civil Liberties Award, ACLU, 1998. Memberships include: Past Trustee, President, World Affairs Council of Oregon, 1954-; Past Chairman, Portland Committee of Foreign Relations, 1978-; Past Director and President, Oregon UN Association, 1977-92; Past Director and President, English Speaking Union, Portland, 1992-98; Director, Member, Executive Committee, English Speaking Union, US, New York, 1997-; Salvation Army Advisory Board, Portland, 2003-; ABA; Patron, American Society of International Law; International Law Association, American branch; UN Association, USA; Arlington Club; Yale Club. Address: The Ladd Carriage House, 1331 S W Broadway, Portland, OR 97201, USA. E-mail: FABEsquire@aol.com

BAUMAN Janina, b. 18 August 1926, Warsaw, Poland. Writer. m. Zygmunt Bauman, 18 August 1948, 3 daughters. Education: Academy of Social Sciences, 1951; University of Warsaw, 1959. Appointments: Script Editor, Polish Film, 1948-68. Publications: Winter in the Morning: A Dream of Belonging; Various other books and short stories published in Poland since 1990. Contributions to: Jewish Quarterly; Oral History; Polin; British Journal of Holocaust Education; Thesis Eleven. Honour: Award by Polityka Weekly, Poland, 1991. Address: 1 Lawnswood Gardens, Leeds, Yorkshire LS16 6HF, England.

BAUMAN Robert Patten, b. 27 March 1931. Business Executive. m. Patricia Hughes Jones, 1961, 1 son, 1 daughter. Education: Ohio Wesleyan University; Harvard School of Business. Appointments: Joined Gen Foods Corporation, 1958; Corporation Vice President, 1968; Group Vice President, 1970; Executive Vice President, Corporation Director, 1972-81; Director, Avco Corporation, 1980; Chair, CEO, 1981-85; Vice Chair, Director, Textron Inc, 1985-86; Chair, Chief Executive, Beecham Group, 1986-89; CEO, SmithKline Beecham, 1989-94; Chair, British Aerospace PLC, 1994-98; BTR PLC, London, 1998-99; Non-Executive Director, Bolero.net, 2001-; Director, Cap Cities/ABC Inc; Union Pacific Corporation; Trustee, Ohio Wesleyan University. Publications: Plants as Pets, 1982; From Promise to Performance, 1997. E-mail: RPBauman@aol.com

BAUMAN Zygmunt, b. 19 November 1925, Poznan, Poland. Sociologist. m. Janina Bauman, 18 August 1948, 3 daughters. Education: MA, 1954; PhD, 1956. Appointments: Warsaw University, 1953-68; Tel Aviv University, 1968-75; University of Leeds, 1971-91. Publications: Modernity and the Holocaust; Legislators and Interpreters; Intimations of Postinedermity; Thinking Sociologically; Modernity and Ambivalence; Freedom; Memories of Class; Culture as Praxis; Between Class and Elite; Mortality, Immortality and Other Life Strategies; Postmodernity and its Discontents, 1997; In Search of Politics, 1999; Liquid Modernity, 2000; Individualized Society, 2000; Community: Seeking Safety in an Uncertain World, 2001; Society Under Siege, 2002; Liquid Love: On the Frailty of Human Bonds, 2003; Society Under Siege, 2002l Liquid Love, 2003; Wasted lives, 2004. Contributions to: Times Literary Supplement; New Statesman; Professional Periodicals. Honour: Amalfi European Prize for Sociology; Theodor Adorno Prize, 1998; Dr honoris causa: Oslo, 1997, Lapland, 1999, Uppsala, 2000, West of England, 2001, London, 2002, Sofia, 2002, Charles University, Prague, 2002, Copenhagen, 2002, University of Leeds, 2004. Memberships: British Sociological Association; Polish Sociological Association. Address: 1 Lawnswood Gardens, Leeds LS16 6HF, England.

BAUROV Yuriy Alexeevich, b. 14 March 1947, Russia. Physicist. m. 2 sons. Education: Moscow Aviation Institute, 1972; PhD, 1978. Appointments: Chief of Laboratory, Central Research Institute of Machine Building; Presidency of Council of Directors, Closed Joint-Stock Company, Research Institute of Cosmic Physics. Publications: Book: On the Structure of Physical Vacuum and a New Interaction in Nature (Theory, Experiment, Applications), 2000; Several articles in professional journals. Honour: Diplôme 26 Salon International des Inventions, Genève, 1998. Membership: New York Academy of Sciences, 1994-98. Address: Central Research Institute for Machine Building, 141070, Koroloyov, Moscow Region, Pionerskaya 4, Russia.

BAUSINGER Hermann, b. 17 September 1926. University Professor Emeritus. m. Brigitte Schoepel, 1 son, 3 daughters. Education: Dr Phil, 1952; Dr phil habil, 1959. Appointment: Full Professor, University of Tubingen, 1960-92. Publications: Numerous books, articles and papers contributed to specialist journals and conferences, mainly in the fields of folklore, cultural history and linguistics. Honours: Brüder Grimm-Preis, 1993; Ludwig Uhland-Preis, 1995; Justinus-Kerner-Preis, 1996; Finnish Academy of Science, 1994; Academia Europaea, 1995. Memberships: Ludwig-Uhland-Inst, University of Tuebingen, Director, 1960-92; Deutsche Gesellschaft für Volkskunde, President, 1977-83. Address: Biesingerstr 26, D-72070 Tuebingen, Germany.

BAXTER Alan George, b. 30 January 1963, Melbourne, Australia. Medical Research Scientist. m. Susan Margaret, 1 son. Education: MB BS, 1986, Royal Melbourne Hospital; PhD, Walter and Eliza Hall Institute, 1992. Appointments: Resident Medical Officer, Royal Melbourne Hospital, 1987-88; Postdoctoral Research Officer, Massachusetts General Hospital, 1991-92; C J Martin Postdoctoral Research Officer, Cambridge University, UK, 1992-94; Centenary Institute, Sydney, Australia, 1994-2002; Senior Research Officer, 1996, Group Head, 1998, Centenary Institute; Professor, Molecular Cell Biology, James Cook University, 2003-. Publications: Book: Germ Warfare: Breakthroughs in Immunology, 2000; Articles in medical journals. Honours: C J Martin Fellowship, 1992-95; AZA Three Year Diabetes Fellowship, Diabetes Australia, 1996-98; R Douglas Wright Award, 1997-2000;

NHMRC Fellowship, 2001-; Project Grants NHMRC, 1996-2002. Memberships: Australian Society for Immunology; Australian Diabetes Society; Diabetes Australia. Address: Comparative Genomics Centre, Molecular Sciences Building, James Cook University, Townsville, Queensland 4811, Australia.

BAXTER John, b. 14 December 1939, Sydney, New South Wales, Australia. Writer. Education: Waverly College, Sydney, 1944-54. Appointments: Director of Publicity, Australian Commonwealth Film Unit, Sydney, 1968-70; Lecturer in Film and Theatre, Hollins College, 1974-78; Freelance TV Producer and Screenwriter, 1978-87; Visiting Lecturer, Mitchell College, 1987. Publications: The Off Worlders, 1966, in Australia as The God Killers: Hollywood in the Thirties, 1968; The Pacific Book of Australian Science Fiction, 1970; The Australian Cinema, 1970; Science Fiction in the Cinema, 1970; The Gangster Film, 1970; The Cinema of Josef von Sternburg, 1971; The Cinema of John Ford, 1971; The Second Pacific Book of Australian Science Fiction, 1971; Hollywood in the Sixties, 1972; Sixty Years of Hollywood, 1973; An Appalling Talent: Kent Russell, 1973; Stunt: The Story of the Great Movie Stunt Men, 1974; The Hollywood Exiles, 1976; The Fire Came By (with Thomas R Atkins), 1976; King Vidor, 1976; The Hermes Fall, 1978; The Bidders (in UK as Bidding), 1979; The Kid, 1981; The Video Handbook (with Brian Norris), 1982; The Black Yacht, 1982; Who Burned Australia? The Ash Wednesday Fires, 1984; Filmstruck, 1987; Bondi Blues, 1993; Fellini, 1993; Buñuel, 1994; Steven Spielberg: The Unauthorised Biography, 1996; Woody Allen: A Biography, 1999; Stanley Kubrick, 1999; George Lucas: Mythmaker, 2000; The Making of Dungeons and Dragons: The Movie, 2001; Robert DeNiro: A Pound of Paper, 2002. Feature Film Scripts: The Time Guardian, 1988. TV Series: The Cutting Room, 1986; First Take, 1986; Filmstruck, 1986. Address: c/o Curtis Brown Literary Agents, Haymarket House, 28-29 Haymarket, London SW1Y 4SP, England.

BAY Joann Reeder, b. 29 September 1926, Williamsport, Pennsylvania, USA. Certified Financial Planner. m. John W Bay Sr, 2 sons. Education: BA, English and Psychology, Bucknell University, 1948; Certified Financial Planner; Listed in Registry of Financial Planning Practitioners, CPF Board of Standards; Registered Investment Advisor. Appointments: Personal Financial Planning Consultant, Hay Associates, 1973-78; Founder: J. R. Bay Associates, 1978-; Conducted financial planning seminars for companies including: General Electric; ARCO Chemical Company; Scott Paper Company; Exxon; Sun Company; Public Speaker on personal financial planning for many professional and community groups, most recently for a national planners' conference, Princeton University; Expert Court Witness on trust investments. Honours: One of Best Financial Advisors in the United States, Money Magazine, 1987; National Registry of Who's Who, Library of Congress, Washington DC; Listed in Who's Who publications and biographical dictionaries. Memberships: Chairman of the Investment Committees, Community Y Foundation Board of Trustees and of Community Y of Eastern Delaware County; Member of Boards of Directors of: Delaware Valley Chapter, IAFP, Women in Transition; Philadelphia and Delaware County Estate Planning Associations; National and Local Chapters, Financial Planning Association. Address: 5022 Sylvia Road, Drexel Hill, PA 19026, USA.

BAYLEY Peter (Charles), b. 25 January 1921, Gloucester, England. Professor Emeritus; Writer. Education: MA, Oxford University, 1947. Appointments: Fellow, University College, 1947-72; Praelector in English, 1949-72, University Lecturer, 1952-72, Oxford University; Master, Collingwood College, University of Durham, 1972-78; Berry Professor and Head of English Department, 1978-85, Berry Professor Emeritus, 1985-, University

of St Andrews, Fife. Publications: Edmund Spenser, Prince of Poets, 1971; Poems of Milton, 1982; An ABC of Shakespeare, 1985; Editor: The Faerie Queene, by Spenser, Book II, 1965, Book 1, 1966, 1970; Loves and Deaths, 1972; A Casebook on Spenser's Faerie Queene, 1977. Contributions to: Patterns of Love and Courtesy, 1966; Oxford Bibliographical Guides, 1971; C S Lewis at the Breakfast Table, 1979; The Encyclopedia of Oxford, 1988; Sir William Jones 1746-94, 1998. Address: 63 Oxford Street, Woodstock, Oxford OX20 1TJ, England.

BAYLISS Peter, b. 1 September 1936, Luton, England. Mineralogist. m. Daphne Phyllis Webb. Education: BE, 1959, MSc, 1962, PhD, 1967, University of New South Wales, Australia. Appointments: Professor, University of Calgary, Calgary, Alta, Canada, 1967-92; Professor Emeritus, 1992-. Publications: 101 papers; 15 monographs; Over 31 book reviews; 61 X-ray powder diffraction data. Honours: University Soccer Blue, 1961; Commonwealth Scholarship, 1964; Fellow, Mineralogical Society of America, 1970; Killam Fellowship, 1981; New mineral named peterbaylissite, 1995; Fellow, International Centre Diffraction Data, 2000; Fellow, Mineralogical Society, Great Britain, 2000. Memberships: Mineralogical Association of Canada; Association Internationale pour l'Etude des Argiles. Address: Department of Mineralogy, Australian Museum, 6 College Street, Sydney, NSW 2010, Australia.

BAZELEY Peter James, b. 22 February 1946, Haflong, Assam, India. Civil Servant. m. Matilda Rymbai, 2 sons, 4 daughters. Education: Distinguished Graduate, University of Gauhati, 1972; Indian Administrative Service, 1973; Capsule Courses: Public Administration, Indian Institute of Public Administration, New Delhi, 1983; Management Administration, Institute of Public Administration, Hyderabad, 1985; Management Course, Institute of Management, Kolkata, 1986; Poverty Alleviation, Indian Institute of Administration, Trivandrum, 1989; Public Finance, National Institute of Planning and Public Finance, New Delhi, 1996; Informatics and Information Technology, NIC, New Delhi, 1998; World Bank Management Course, UNDP, Bangkok, 1994. Appointments: Assistant Commissioner, 1973-76, Additional District Magistrate, 1977-79, District Magistrate, 1980-84, Secretary Rural Development, 1985-86, Commissioner and Secretary, Agriculture, 1986-88, Commissioner and Secretary, Education, 1989-92, Principal Secretary, Health and Family Welfare, 1993-98, Principal Secretary, Finance, 1999-2003, Chief Secretary, 2004-, Government of Meghalaya, India; Director, North Eastern Indira Gandhi Regional Institute of Medical Sciences, 1993-98; Chairman, Meghalaya State Electricity Board, 2003-. Publications: Meghalaya: A Pictorial Profile – Land & People; Meghalaya: A Pictorial Profile – Flora & Fauna; Meghalaya: A Pictorial Profile – Places of Interest. Honours: Excellence in Service Award, Friendship Forum of India, 1989; Silver Elephant (India) 2002 Award for Distinguished Service, President of India; Man of the Year 2003, American Biographical Institute, USA. Memberships: Life Member, Red Cross Society of India, 1981-; President, Meghalaya State Bharat Scouts and Guides, 1992-; Life Member, Indian Institute of Public Administration, 1993-; Alumnus of Haggai International, 2001-. Address: Chanchal Raj House, Kench's Trace, Shillong-793004, Meghalaya, India. E-mail: peterbazeley@sancharnet.in

BEACHCROFT Ellinor Nina, b. 10 November 1931, London, England. Writer. m. Richard Gardner, 7 August 1954, 2 daughters. Education: Wimbledon High School, 1942-49; 2nd Class Hons Degree in English Literature, St Hilda's College, Oxford, 1953. Publications: Well Met by Witchlight, 1972; Under the Enchanter, 1974; Cold Christmas, 1974; A Spell of Sleep, 1975; A Visit to Folly Castle, 1976; A Farthing for the Fair, 1977; The Wishing

Dictionary of International Biography

People, 1978; The Genie and Her Bottle, 1983; Beyond World's End, 1985. Memberships: Society of Authors; Children's Writers' Group, twice a Committee Member. Address: 9 Raffin Green Lane, Datchworth, Herts SG3 6RJ, England.

BEALE Geoffrey Herbert, b. 11 June 1913, Wandsworth, London, England. Research Scientist. 3 sons. Education: Imperial College of Science and Technology, 1931-35. Appointments: Research Scientist, John Innes Horticulture Institute, Merton, London, 1935-40; Intelligence Corps, British Army, 1941-46; Scientific Worker, Cold Spring Harbor, New York, USA, 1947; Rockefeller Fellow, Indiana University, USA, 1947-48; Lecturer, Senior Lecturer, 1948-63, Royal Society Research Professor, 1963-78, Edinburgh University. Publications: Numerous articles on genetics of paramecium and malaria parasites and plants; Books: Genetics of Paramecium Aurelia, 1954; Extranuclear Genetics (with J Knowles), 1978; Malaria Parasites (with S Thaithong), 1992. Honours: MBE, 1946, FRS, 1959; FRSE, 1966; Honorary DSc, Chulalongkorn University, Bangkok, Thailand, 1996. Memberships: Royal Society, London; Royal Society, Edinburgh; Genetical Society. Address: 23 Royal Terrace, Edinburgh EH7 5AH, Scotland. E-mail: g.beale@ed.ac.uk

BEAN Sean, b. 17 April 1958, Sheffield, Yorkshire, England. Actor. m. (1) Melanie Hill, 1991, divorced 1997, 2 children, (2) Debra James, 1981, divorced, (3) Abigail Cruttenden, 1997, divorced 2000, 1 child. Education: Royal Academy of Dramatic Art. Creative Works: Appearances include: the Last Days of Mankind & Der Rosenkavalier at Citizen's Theatre, Glasgow, Who Knew Mackenzie? & Gone, Theatre Upstairs, Roy Court, Romeo in Romeo & Juliet, RSC, Stratford-upon-Avon, 1986, Captain Spencer in The Fair Maid of the West, RSC, London; TV Appearances include: Clarissa; Fool's Gold; Role of Mellors in BBC Dramatization of Lady Chatterley's Lover; Inspector Morse; Role Sharpe in TV Series; A Woman's Guide to Adultery; Jacob; Bravo Two Zero; Extremely Dangerous; Films: Caravaggio, Stormy Monday, War Requiem, The Field, Patriot Games, Gone With the Wind, Goldeneye, When Saturday Comes, Anna Karenina, Ronin; The Lord of the Rings: The Fellowship of the Ring; Don't Say a Word; Equilibrium; Tom and Thomas; The Big Empty; Windprints; Essex Boys; Troy, 2004. Address: c/o ICM Ltd, Oxford House, London W1R 1RB, England.

BEAR Carolyn Ann, (Chlöe Rayban), b. 10 April 1944, Exeter, England. Author. m. Peter Julian Bear, 2 daughters. Education: University of Western Australia (1 year); University of Newcastle upon Tyne; BA Hons, Philosophy. Publications: Under Different Stars, 1988; Wild Child, 1991; Virtual Sexual Reality, 1994; Love in Cyberia, 1996; Screen Kiss, 1997; Clash on the Catwalk, 1997; Havana to Hollywood, 1997; Street to Stardom, 1997; Models Move On, 1998; Terminal Chic, 2000. Honours: Shortlisted for Guardian Children's Fiction Prize, 1995; Shortlisted for Guardian Children's Fiction Prize, 1996; Shortlisted for Carnegie Medal Fiction Prize, 1996. Address: 17 Alwyne Villas, London N1 2HG, England.

BEAR Isabel Joy, b. 4 January 1927, Camperdown, Victoria, Australia. Research Scientist. Education: Ass Diploma in Applied Chemistry, MTC, 1950; Ass Diploma in Applied Science, 1950; Fellowship Diploma Applied Chemistry, RMIT 1972; D App Sc, 1978. Appointments: Experimental Scientist, AERE Harwell, 1950-51; Research Assistant, University of Birmingham, UK, 1951-53; Experimental Scientist, CSIRO Division of Industrial Chemistry/Mineral Chemistry, 1953-67; Senior Research Scientist, CSIRO Division of Mineral Chemistry/Products, 1967-72; Principal Research Scientist, 1972-79; Senior Principal Research Scientist, 1979-92; Honorary Fellow, 1992-97. Publications: More

than 70 refereed papers in scientific journals; Co-author: Alumna Ao Zirconia – The History of the CSIRO Division of Mineral Chemistry, 2001. Honours: Appointed, Member of the Order of Australia for services to Science; Leighton Medallist, Royal Australian Chemical Institute. Memberships: Royal Australian Chemical Institute; Australasian Institute of Mining and Metallurgy. Address: 2/750 Waverley Road, Glen Waverley, VIC 3150, Australia.

BEASLEY Clark Wayne, b. 6 June 1942, Pittsburg, Kansas, USA. Professor. m. Barbara Sue Allman, 1 son, 1 daughter. Education: BS, Kansas State College of Pittsburg, 1964; PhD, University of Oklahoma, 1968. Appointments: Instructor, Department of Biology, 1968-69; Assistant Professor, 1969-72, Associate Professor, 1972-77, Chair, 1973-2002, Professor, 1977-99, Distinguished Professor, 1999-, Department of Biology, McMurry University. Publications: 20 papers in refereed journals. Honours: Beta Beta Beta; Phi Sigma; Sigma Xi; Omicron Delta Kappa. Memberships: American Microscopical Society; National Association of Biology Teacher; Southwestern Association of Naturalists; Texas Academy of Science. Address: Department of Biology, McMurry University, Abilene, TX 79697, USA.

BEATRIX Wilhelmina Armgard (Queen of the Netherlands), b. 31 January 1938, Baarn. m. Claus George Willem Otto Frederik Geert von Amsberg, 10 March 1966, 3 sons. Education: Leiden State University. Honour: Hon K.G. Address: c/o Government Information Service, Press & Publicity Department, Binnenhof 19, 2513 AA The Hague, The Netherlands.

BEATTIE Ann, b. 7 September 1947, Washington, District of Columbia, USA. Writer; Poet. m. Lincoln Perry. Education: BA, American University, Washington, DC, 1969; MA, University of Connecticut, 1970. Appointments: Visiting Assistant Professor, 1976-77, Visiting Writer, 1980, University of Virginia, Charlottesville; Briggs Copeland Lecturer in English, Harvard University, 1977; Guggenheim Fellow, 1977. Publications: Secrets and Surprises, 1978; Where You'll Find the Other Stories, 1986; What Was Mine and Other Stories, 1991; With This Ring, 1997; My Life, Starring Dara Falcon, 1998; Park City: New and Selected Stories, 1998; New and Selected Poems, 1999; Perfect Recall, 2000. Contributions to: Various publications. Memberships: American Academy and Institute of Arts and Letters; PEN; Authors' Guild. Honours: Award in literature, 1980; Hon LHD, American University. Address: c/o Janklow and Nesbit, 598 Madison Avenue, New York, NY 10022, USA.

BEATTY Warren, b. 30 March 1937, Richmond, Virginia, USA. Actor. m. Annette Bening, 1992, 4 children. Education: Stella Adler Theatre School. Creative Works: Film Appearances include: Splendor in the Grass, 1961; Roman Spring of Mrs Stone, 1961; All Fall Down, 1962; Lilith, 1965; Mickey One, 1965; Promise Her Anything, 1966; Kaleidoscope, 1966; Bonnie and Clyde, 1967; The Only Game in Town, 1969; McCabe and Mrs Miller, 1971; Dollars, 1972; The Parallax View, 1974; Shampoo, 1975; The Fortune, 1976; Heaven Can Wait, 1978; Reds, 1981; Ishtar, 1987; Dick Tracy, 1989; Bugsy, 1991; Love Affair, Bulworth, 1998; Town and Country, 2001. TV Appearances include: Studio One; Playhouse 90; A Salute to Dustin Hoffman, 1999. Theatre Roles include: A Loss of Roses, 1960. Honours include: Academy Award, Best Director, 1981; Commander, Ordre des Art.s et des Lettres. Address: CAA, 9830 Wilshire Boulevard, Beverly Hills, CA 90212, USA.

BEAUDOIN Gérald-A, b. 15 April 1929, Montreal, Canada. Professor Emeritus. m. Renée Desmarais, 1954, 4 daughters. Education: BA summa cum laude, 1950, LL L magna cum laude and Dean's Prize, 1953, MA in Law, 1954, Université de Montreal; Carnegie Scholar, University of Toronto School of Law, 1954-55; DESD cum laude, Law, University of Ottawa, 1958. Appointments: Practised law with Paul Gérin-Lajoie, QC, Montreal, 1955-56; Legal Adviser, Department of Justice, Ottawa, 1956-65; Assistant Parliamentary Counsel, legal branch of the House of Commons, 1965; Professor of Constitutional Law, 1969-89, Dean of Law, 1969-79, Associate Director, Human Rights Centre, 1981-86, Director, 1986-88, Visiting Professor, 1989-94, Professor Emeritus, 1994-, University of Ottawa's Faculty of Law; Senator, representing Rigaud in Quebec, Senate of Canada, 1988-2004. Publications: Numerous articles and texts on constitutional law. Honours: Queen's Counsel, 1969; Officer of the Order of Canada, 1980; Prix de l'ACFAS in social sciences, 1987; Honorary Doctorate in Law, Université Louvain-La-Neuve, Belgium, 1989; Medal to commemorate 125th anniversary of the Confederation of Canada, 1992; Medal to commemorate 10th anniversary of the International Academy of Constitutional Law, 1994; Ordre du Merite de la Ville de Hull, 1993; Merite du Barreau de Hull, 1996; Medal of The Right Honourable Ramon John Hnatyshyn Award for Law, 1997; Chevalier de l'Ordre de la Pleiade, 1999; Commandeur de l'Ordre de la Couronne du Royaume de Belgique, 2001; Recipient, Walter S Tarnopolsky Human Rights Award, 2002. Memberships: Barreau du Québec, 1954; Canadian Bar Association, 1955; President, Constitutional Law Section, Canadian Bar Association, 1971-73, 1986-87; President, Canadian Law Deans, 1972-73; Chair, Quebec Law Deans, 1975-76; Member, Chair, 1993-96, Deputy Chair, 1996-2004, Legal Affairs Committee; Senate Special Committee on Euthanasia and Assisted Suicide; Special Committee of the Senate on Bill C-110; Special Joint Committee to Amend Section 93 of the Constitution Act 1867; Senate Committee on Palliative Care. Address: 4 de la Guadeloupe Street, Gatineau, Quebec J8Y 1L4, Canada.

BECK Jan Scott, b. 5 May 1955, Newark, New Jersey, USA. Attorney. m. Marla Beck, 2 sons, 1 daughter. Education: BS, Accounting, Rider University, 1977; Juris Doctor, 1980, LLM, Masters in Taxation, 1985, Villanova University School of Law. Appointments: CFO and General Counsel, StarCapital Corp; Managing Director and Chief Executive Officer, The Turbary Group; Vice-President and General Counsel, Tyco International Inc. Memberships: American Bar Association; Florida State Bar Association; New Jersey State Bar Association; American Institute of Certified Public Accountants; New Jersey State Society of Certified Public Accountants; New York State Bar Association; Tax Executives Institute. Address: StarCapital, 3380 Fairlane Farms Road, Suite 12, Wellington, FL 33414, USA. E-mail: jbeck@starcapital.net

BECKER Boris, b. 22 November 1967, Leimen, Germany. Tennis Player. m. Barbara Feltus, divorced, 2001, 1 son. Appointments: Started playing tennis at Blau-Weiss Club, Leimen; Won W German Junior Championship, 1983; Runner-up, US Junior Championship; Coached by Ion Tiriac, 1984-; Quarter Finalist, Australia Championship; Winner, Young Masters Tournament, Birmingham, England, 1985; Grand Prix Tournament, Queen's, 1985; Won Men's Singles Championship, Wimbledon, 1985, 1986, 1989, Finalist, 1988, 1990, 1991, 1995; Finalist, Benson & Hedges Championship, Wembley, London, 1985; Masters Champion, 1988, Finalist, 1989; US Open Champion, 1989; Semi Finalist, French Open, 1989; Winner, Davis Cup, 1989, Australian Open Championship, 1991, 1996, IBM/ATP Tour Championship, 1992, 1995, Grand Slam Cup, 1996. Honours: Sportsman of the Year, 1985; Hon Citizen of Leimen, 1986; Named World Champion, 1991; 64 titles (49 singles). Memberships: Board member, Bayern

Munich Football Club, 2001-; Chair, Laurens Sport for Good Foundation, 2002-. Address: Nusslocher Strasse 51, 69181 Leimen, Baden, Germany.

BECKER Dietrich Walter Pius, b. 3 January 1938, Gleiwitz, Germany. Surgeon; Sub-Command, Navy. m. Karin Elisabeth, 1 son, 2 daughters. Education: Studied Medicine, Justis-Liebig University, Giessen, 1964; State Examination in Medicine and Medical Assistantship, 1964; Approbation as Doctor, Ministry of Science, Wiesbaden, 1966; MD, Justus-Liebig University, 1978. Appointments: Medical Assistant, Divers Hospital, University of Giessen, 1964-66; Medical Trauma Leader, Landesärztekammer Hessen, 1984; Sub-Chief Physician, Academic Training Hospital, Emergency Surgery, Bad Hersfeld, Hessen, Germany, 1971-99; Prof Med Habil Humbold University Berlin, 1998; Specialist in joint surgery; Medical Director, IFBE Medical School, Bad Hersfeld, 1999-; Worked to develop innovative wound dressing for burns using frozen, fresh porcine skin, presented to German Ministry of Defence as dressing for wounds on board ship; Innovative operating methods in reconstructing injured cruciat ligaments of the knee; Determination of the first objective signe for peronaeus tendon luxation by X-ray. Publications: Numerous articles in professional journals including: The Robinson Drainage: A New Principle of Drainage in the Emergency Surgery, video, 1980; The Functional Reconstruction of Previous Ruptures of the Syndesmosis by Stryker-Dacron-Ligament, 1997; Co-author, New Trends in Bone Grafting; Wound Dressing in Burns with Sterile Porcine Skin: Annals of Mediterranean Club for Burns and Fire Disasters, 1999; Großschaden auf See, Chirug Allegmeine, 2001; Tratameinto de quemados a bordo en catastrofes maritimas, Medicina Maritima, 2002. Honours: Medal of Merit of the German Red Cross, Hessen section, 1990; Diploma of Honour, Polish Section, International College of Surgeons, 1991; Cross of Honour in Gold, German Red Cross, 1994; Cross of Honour in Gold, Austrian Association of Veterans, Field Marshall Radetzky, 1994; Great Cross of Honour in Gold with Necktie, 1998; Cross of Honour in Gold, German Bundeswehr, 1999; Medicus and Chirurgus h.c. of the Königlich-Preuss, Infantrie Regiment No 25, Möllendorf. Memberships include: Fellow, Mediterranean Club for Burns and Fire Disasters; Fellow, International Federation of Sports Medicine; International Burns Association; European Burn Association; German Association for Disaster Medicine; German Association of Naval Medicine; German Association for Sports Medicine; Polish-German Association for Medical Co-operation; Member and Board Member, International Maritime Health Association; FIMS. Address: Berberitzenweg 34, 36251 Bad Hersfeld, Germany.

BECKER Heinz Hugo, b. 10 September 1935, Beresina, Romania. Retired Director of Cultural Institute. m. Regula Koenig-Becker, 1 daughter. Education: University studies in History and Political Science in Germany and England; Promotion, Dr Phil., Tübingen, Germany, 1960. Appointments: After entering the service of the Goethe Institute: Director, Jakarta, Indonesia, 1964-67; Director, Salvador-Bahia, Brazil, 1967-69; Director, San Francisco, USA, 1969-71, Director, Tehran, Iran, 1971-74; Director, Montreal, Canada, 1979-81; Director, Tehran, Iran, Regional Director, Middle East, 1974-77; Director, Belgrade, Yugoslavia, Regional Director, Eastern Europe, 1981-88; Director, New York, USA, Regional Director, USA/Canada, 1992-96; Director, Tokyo, Regional Director, East Asia, 1996-2000. Publications: Emigration 1804-1809 from Southern Germany to Russia/Eastern Europe; Frequent articles in quarterlies on German Cultural Foreign Politics. Membership: Lions Club, Schwäbisch Hall, 1990-. Address: Neisseweg 65, D-74523 Schwäbisch Hall, Germany. E-mail: sailor666@gmx.de

Dictionary of International Biography

BECKERT Thomas E (Berhard), b. 22 August 1966, Kempten, Germany. Pharmacist. m. Katrin Buszello, 1 son, 1 daughter. Education: Courses in Pharmacy, 1986-91, Registration as Pharmacist, 1991, Albert-Ludwigs University, Freiburg; Courses in Political Economy, 1992-93, Dr rer nat, Doctor of Natural Sciences, Pharmaceutical technology, 1992-95, Eberhard-Karls University, Tübingen. Appointments include: Scientific Assistant, Department of Pharmaceutical Technology, Eberhard-Karls University, Tübingen, 1992-95; Manager, Apotheke Diezenhalde, Böblingen, 1993-95; Business (marketing), Tübingen and Ulm, 1995-96; Military Service, Military Hospital, Ulm, 1995-96; Head, Technical Customer Service, Pharma Polymers Division, Röhm, GmbH, Darmstadt, Germany, 1996-2001; Member of Board, Dr Rentschler Arzneimittel GmbH, Laupheim, Germany, 2002-. Publications: 2 books and book chapters; Author or co-author, 7 scientific papers in professional journals; 13 poster research presentations at scientific conferences; 8 patents. Honours include: Award for best Abitur in Chemistry, 1986; Scholarship holder Konrad-Adenauer-Stiftung, 1987-90; Member of Town Parliament, 1997; Manuscript Reviewer for scientific journals, 1997-; Adjunct Assistant Professor, University of Rhode Island, USA, 2003. Memberships: Arbeitsgemeinschaft für Pharmazeutische Verfahrenstechnik; Deutsche Pharmazeutischen Gesellschaft; Christian Democratic Union; Controlled Release Society; BPI, Working Group Pharmacy. Address: Anton-Braith-Weg 30, 88447 Warthausen, Germany. E-mail: tombeckert@t-online.de

BECKETT Kenneth Albert, b. 12 January 1929, Brighton, Sussex,England. Horticulturalist; Technical Advisor; Editor. m. Gillian Tuck, 1 Aug 1973, 1 son. Education: Diploma, Horticulture, Royal Horticultural Society. Appointments: Technical Editor, Gardener's Chronicle, Reader's Digest; Retired. Publications: The Love of Trees, 1975; Illustrated Dictionary of Botany, 1977; Concise Encyclopaedia of Garden Plants, 1978; Amateur Greenhouse Gardening, 1979; Growing Under Glass, 1981; CompleteBook of Evergreens, 1981; Growing Hardy Perennials, 1981; Climbing Plants, 1983; The Garden Library, 4 volumes: Flowering House Plants, Annuals and Biennials, Roses, Herbs, 1984; The RHS Encyclopaedia of House Plants, 1987; Evergreens, 1990; Alpine Garden Society Encyclopaedia of Alpines, 2 volumes, 1993-94. Contributions to: The Garden; The Plantsman. Honours: Veitch Memorial Medal, Royal Horticultural Society, 1987; Lyttel Trophy, 1995 and Clarence Elliott Memorial Award, 1995, Alpine Garden Society. Memberships: The Royal Horticultural Society; The Wild Plant Conservation Charity; Friends of the Royal Botanic Gardens, Kew; Botanical Society of the British Isles; Plantsman; International Dendrology Society; Alpine Garden Society. Address: Bramley Cottage, Stanhoe, King's Lynn, Norfolk PE31 8QF, England.

BECKETT Margaret Mary, b. 15 January 1943, Ashton-under-Lyne, Lancashire, England. Politician. m. Leo Beckett, 2 step-sons. Education: Manchester College of Science and Technology, John Dalton Polytechnic. Appointments: Engineering Apprentice, Association of Electrical Industries, Manchester; Experimental Officer, University of Manchester; Researcher, Labour Party Headquarters; Special Adviser at ODA February-October 1997; Parliamentary Private Secretary, Minister for Overseas Development, 1974-75; Assistant Government Whip, 1975-76; Minister, Department of Education, 1976-79; Labour MP Lincoln, 1974-79; Sponsored by TGWU, 1977-; Principal Researcher, Granada TV, 1979-83; Labour Party National Executive Committee, 1980-97; MP, Derby South, 1983-; Opposition Spokesperson, Social Security, 1984-89; Shadow Chief Secretary, 1989-92; Shadow Leader of the House, Campaigns Coordinator, Deputy Leader of the Opposition, 1992-94; Appointed to Privy Council, 1993; Leader of the Opposition, 1994; Shadow Secretary of State for Health, 1994-95; Shadow President, 1995-97,

President, 1997-98, Board of Trade, President of Privy Council, Leader, House of Commons, 1998-2001; Secretary of State, Department of Environment, Food and Rural Affairs, 2001-. Publications: The Need for Consumer Protection, 1972; The National Enterprise Board; The Nationalisation of Shipbuilding, Shiprepair and Marine Engineering; Relevant Sections of Labour's Programme, 1972, 1973; Renewing the NHS, 1995; Vision for Growth - A New Industrial Strategy for Britain, 1996. Memberships: Transport and General Workers' Union, Parliamentary Labour Party Group, National Executive Committee, 1988-98; National Union of Journalists; BECTU; Fabian Society; Anti-Apartheid Movement; Campaign for Nuclear Disarmament; Tribune Group; Socialist Education Committee; Labour Women's Action Committee; Derby Co-op Party; Socialist Environment and Resources Association; Amnesty International; Council of St George's College, Windsor, 1976-1982. Address: House of Commons, London SW1A 0AA, England.

BECKHAM David Robert Joseph, b. 2 May 1975, Leytonstone, London. Footballer. m. Victoria Adams, 4 July 1999, 2 sons. Career: Player with Manchester United, trainee, 1991, team debut, 1992, league debut, 1995, 325 appearances, 78 goals, December 2002; 7 caps for England Under 21s, represented England 1996-, Captain, 2000-, 58 caps, 9 goals December 2002; Joined Real Madrid, 2003-. Publication: David Beckham: My World, 2001. Honours: Bobby Charlton Skills Award, 1987; Manchester United Player of the Year, 1996-97; Young Player of the Year Professional Football Association, 1996-97; Sky Football Personality of the Year, 1997; 5 Premiership Medals; 2 Football Association Medals; European Cup Medal; 2 Charity Shield Winner Medals. Address: SFX Sports Group Europe Ltd, Priest House, 1624 High Street, Knowle, West Midlands, B93 0JU, England. Website: www.manutd.com

BECKHAM Victoria, (Posh Spice), b. 7 April 1975, Cuffley, England. Vocalist. m. David Beckham, 4 July 1999, 2 sons. Career: Member, Spice Girls; Numerous TV and radio appearances, magazine interviews; Film, Spiceworld: The Movie, 1997; World tour including dates in UK, Europe, India and USA. Recordings: Singles: Wannabe, 1996; Say You'll Be There, 1996; 2 Become 1, 1996; Mama/ Who Do You Think You Are, 1997; Step To Me, 1997; Spice Up Your Life, 1997; Too Much, 1997; Stop, 1998; (How Does It Feel To Be) On Top of the World, with England United, 1998; Move Over/Generation Next, 1998; Viva Forever, 1998; Goodbye, 1998; Holler/Let Love Lead the Way, 2000; Out of Your Mind, 2000; Not Such an Innocent Girl, 2001; A Mind of Its Own, 2002; Albums: Spice, 1996; Spiceworld, 1997; Forever, 2001. Honours: Best Video (Say You'll Be There), Best Single (Wannebe), Brit Awards, 1997; 2 Ivor Novello song writing awards, 1997; Best Band, Smash Hits Award, 1997; 3 American Music Awards, 1998; Special Award for International Sales, Brit Awards, 1998. Publications: Learning to Fly, autobiography, 2001. Address: c/o Lee & Thompson, Green Garden House, 15-22 St Christopher's Place, London, W1M 5HE, England. Website: c3.vmg.co.uk/spicegirls

BECKINSALE Kate, b. 26 July 1973, London, England. Actress. 1 daughter with Micheal Sheen. Education: French and Russian Literature, New College, Oxford University, 1991-94. Career: TV includes: One Against the Wind, 1991; Cold Comfort Farm, 1995; Films include: Much Ado About Nothing, 1993; Haunted, 1995; Emma, 1997; Shooting Fish, 1997; The Golden Bowl, 2000; Pearl Harbor, 2001; Serendipity, 2001; Laurel Canyon, 2002; Underworld, 2003; Tiptoes, 2003; Van Helsing, 2004.

BEDA Peter Balazs, b. 10 July 1963, Miskolc, Hungary. Researcher. Education: MSc, Mechanical Engineering, Technical University, Budapest, 1986; PhD, 1990. Appointments: Research

Dictionary of International Biography

Fellow, Hungarian Academy of Sciences, 1986-90; Visiting Researcher, Technical University, Vienna, 1989-90; Senior Research Fellow, Hungarian Academy of Sciences, 1990-. Memberships: Society for Applied Mathematics and Mechanics; American Mathematical Society; European Mechanics Society. Address: Technical University Budapest, Bertalan L 2, H-1111, Budapest, Hungary.

BEDDINGTON John Richard, b. 15 September 1942, Haslemere, Surrey, England. Sports Manager. m. Roseann Madden, 11 July 1972, 2 sons. Education: Eton College, 1956-60; Goethe Institute, 1960-61; College of Law, 1962-65. Appointments: Articled Clerk, Birkbeck, Julius, Coburn and Broad, 1962-65; Marketing Department, BP Chemicals (UK) Ltd, 1966-72; European Director, Grand Prix Tennis Circuit, 1972-77; Vice President, International Management Group, 1977-82; Chairman, Chief Executive Officer, Beddington Sports Management Inc, Toronto, Canada, 1982-; Executive Vice President, Tennis Canada, 1983-95; Tournament Director, Chairman, Canadian Open Tennis Championships, Toronto and Montreal, 1979-95; Chairman, Canadian Open Squash Championships, 1985-95; Group Managing Director, Masters International Ltd, 1995-97; Consultant, Tennis Canada, 1995-98; Chairman, Chief Executive Officer, Beddington Sports Management Ltd, 1997-; Chairman, Canadian Corporate Golf Challenge, 1997-; Tournament Director, Champions Tennis, Royal Albert Hall/Olympia, 1997-; Consultant, Squash Rackets Association, 1997-99; Chairman, British Open Squash Championships, 2003-. Publications include: Play Better Squash, 1974; Several articles in a wide variety of sports publications. Honours: Several organisation awards for sports events; Listed in several Who's Who publications. Memberships: Director, WTA Tour, 1993-98; Duke of Edinburgh Award, Toronto, 1990-95; Professional Squash Association, 1998-2000; Cambridge Club, Toronto; All England Lawn Tennis Club; Fellow, Royal Geographical Society; Lambton Leisure. Address: The Old School House, Hook End, Checkendon, Oxon RG8 0UL, England. E-mail: jrbeddington@btinternet.com

BEDRITSKY Alexander Ivanovich, b. 10 July 1947, Tashkent district, Uzbekistan, USSR. Hydrometeorologist. m. 3 children. Education: Diploma, Tashkent Electro-Technical Institute of Telecommunication, 1966-75; PhD in Geography, 2000. Appointments: Senior Engineer, Computer Center of the WWW Regional Center, Tashkent, 1969-77; Chief Engineer, Middle Asian Regional Scientific Research Hydrometeorological Institute, 1977-80; Deputy Chief of Uzbek Republican Administration for Hydrometeorology, 1980-92, USSR Committee for Hydrometeorology, Tashkent; First Deputy Chairman, Committee for Hydrometeorology and Environmental Monitoring, Russian Federation Ministry for Ecology and Natural Resources, Moscow, 1992-93; Head, Russian Federal Service for Hydrometeorology and Environmental Monitoring, Moscow, 1993-. Honours: Russian Government's Prize, 1999. Memberships: Intergovernmental Council for Hydrometeorology; WMO Executive Council; President, World Meteorological Organization, XIV World Meteorological Congress, 2003. Address: Roshydromet, Novovagan'kovsky Street 12, 123995, Moscow, Russia.

BEEKE Joel Robert, b. 9 December 1952, Kalamazoo, Michigan, USA. Theological Professor; Seminary President; Pastor; Author; Editor. m. Mary Ann Beeke, 1 son, 2 daughters. Education: BA, Thomas Edison College; PhD, Westminster Theological Seminary. Appointments: Minister, Netherlands Reformed Congregation, Sioux Center, Iowa, 1978-81, Netherlands Reformed Congregation, Franklin Lakes, New Jersey, 1981-86; Lecturer, Center for Urban Theological Studies, Philadelphia, Pennsylvania, 1984-86, Westminster Theological Seminary, Philadelphia,

Pennsylvania, 1985-86; Theological Instructor, Netherlands Reformed Theological School, 1986-92; Minister, Heritage Netherlands Reformed Congregation, Grand Rapids, Michigan, 1986-; Adjunct Professor, Westminster Theological Seminary, Philadelphia, Pennsylvania, 1993-; President, Professor, Systematic Theology and Homiletics, Puritan Reformed Theological Seminary, Grand Rapids, Michigan, 1995-. Publications include: Backsliding, 1982; Jehovah Shepherding His Sheep, 1982; Bible Doctrine Student Workbook, 1983; Holiness: God's Call to Sanctification, 1994; Knowing and Living the Christian Life, 1997; Truth that Frees: A Workbook on Reformed Doctrine for Young Adults, 1998; A Reader's Guide to Reformed Literature: An Annotated Bibliography of Reformed Theology, 1999; The Quest for Full Assurance: The Legacy of Calvin and His Successors, 1999; Puritan Evangelism: A Biblical Approach, 1999; Reformed Confessions Harmonized, 1999; Gisbertus Voetius, 1999; The Heidelberg Catechism (5 volumes), 2000; Truth that Frees, 2000; God's Alphabet for Life, 2000; Bringing the Gospel to Covenant Children, 2001; A Loving Encouragement to Flee Worldliness, 2001; The Truths of God's Words, 2001; Family Worship, 2002; An Analysis of Witsius's "Economy of the Covenants", 2002; Building on the Rock (5 volumes), 2003; Puritan Reformed Spirituality, 2004. Memberships: American Society of Church History; Banner of Truth Conference; Calvin Studies Society; Colloquium on Calvin Studies; Conference on Faith and History; Evangelical Theological Society; Sixteenth Century Studies Conference; Society for Reformation Research. Address: 2917 Leonard NE, Grand Rapids, MI 49525, USA.

BEER John Vincent, b. 3 May 1928, Newbury, Berkshire, England. Avian, Wildlife, Pathology, Production Consultant. Education: BSc, 1948, Dip Bact, 1950, Reading University; PhD, Bristol University, 1960. Appointments: Applied Mycologist, Howards of Ilford, 1949-53; Applied Microbiologist, Boots Ltd, Nottingham, 1953-54; Pathologist, Wildfowl Trust, Slimbridge, 1954-69; Director, Oiled Seabird Research Unit, Newcastle, 1969-70; Senior Pathologist, The Game Conservancy Trust, Fordingbridge, 1970-93; Consultant, Gamebird Consultancy, Salisbury, 1993-2002, Chard, 2002-. Publications: Egg Production and Incubation, 1982; Diseases of Gamebirds and Wildfowl, 1988; Various articles on diseases of gamebirds and wildfowl; papers on diseases of waterbirds and gamebirds and incubation of their eggs. Honour: D'Académie Corresponsac Acadèmia de Ciènces Veterinaries, Catalunya. Memberships: Game Conservancy Trust; Fellow, Zoological Society of London; Fellow, Wildfowl and Wetlands Trust; World Pheasant Association; British Society for Medical Mycology; Associate, British Veterinary Poultry Association; Associate, British Veterinary Zoological Society; Woodland Trust; Supporter, The National Gamekeepers Organisation; MIBiol, CBiol, Institute of Biology. Address: Hillside, Combe Hill, Combe St Nicholas, Chard, Somerset, TA20 3NW, England.

BEER BARBULOFF Egon J, b. 11 July 1924, Bela Crkva, Yugoslavia. Retired Electronics Engineer. m. Maria Refugio Padilla, 1 son. Education: Electricity, Electronics Engineer, 1963; PhD, Astronomy, Earth Sciences, 2000. Appointments: Founding Member, Ohio Academy of Science; International Astronomical Society; Charter Member Number One, Lions Club, Guadalajara, Mexico; Director International Relations. Publications: Plate Tectonics and the Gradual Retardation of the Earth's Spin, 1986; Cancer and Hibernation, 1986; The Formation of Planetary Systems, 1989; The Surface Features of Uranus's Moon Miranda, 1989; Acquired Immunodeficiency Syndrome, the Common Cold and Microwave Radiation, 1996, 1998; Suggested Forces Behind Gamma Ray Bursts, 2001, 2002; Suggested Nature of Sunspots, the Evolution of Stars, 2003; Supernovae: Their Origin and Nature; Fusion Versus Fission, 2004. Honours: Great Minds of the 21st

Dictionary of International Biography

Century, American Biographical Institute; The Leaders of International Business Honoured Induction of Life Member; Listed in Who's Who publications and biographical dictionaries. Memberships: American Association for the Advancement of Science; New York Academy of Sciences; Ohio Academy of Science; Astronomical Society of the Pacific; Planetary Society. Address: Ganaderos 5093 A, Jardines de Guadaloupe, Guadalajara, Jalisco 45030, Mexico. E-mail: egon115@hotmail.com

BEERE Susan, b. 26 April 1951, Virginia, USA. Ceramic Tile Artist. m. Hugh L Wilkerson. Education: Palomar Junior College, 1970; Mesa College, 1987. Appointments: Taught children, Del Mar Shores Elementary, 1977-; Private Teacher, 1985-2001. Publications: Many articles in local papers and magazines. Commissions and Creative Works: Numerous commissions including, Nancy Hayward, 1975-2004, Candace Gietzen, 1978-2001; Dr A J Foster, Del Mar Medical Clinic, 1980-83; Richard Reilly, Curator Emeritus of the James S Copley Library, La Jolla, 1991; Del Mar Library, Historic Room, 1984-; Gerhard Design Group, 1998-2000; Georgiana G Rodiger, 1986-2004; Shiela Cameron, 1979-99, Maxine Edwards, 1980-84; Joyce Klein, 1981. Honours: Superior Achievement, Art Competition, 1970; Second Prize, Sculptor, 1971; Competitive Bid Winner, Fine Arts Association, 1979; Award of Merit, San Angelo Museum of Art, 1991; Chosen for cover and in Handmade Tiles by Frank Giorgini, 2nd edition, 1995. Address: PO Box 70, Del Mar, CA 92014, USA. Website: www.susanbeere.com

BEHLEN Charles (William), b. 29 January 1949, Slaton, Texas, USA. Poet. 1 daughter. Education: New Mexico Junior College, 1968-70. Publications: Perdition's Keepsake; Three Texas Poets; Dreaming at the Wheel; Uirsche's First Three Decades; The Voices Under the Floor; Texas Weather. Contributions to: Bloomsbury Review; Cedar Rock; New Mexico Humanities Review; Poetry Now; Puerto del Sol; The Smith; Texas Observer; Borderlands; New Texas '91; New Texas '95. Honours: Pushcart Prize (nominee); Ruth Stephan Reader; Manuscripts Displayed and Placed in Time Capsule by San Antonio Museum of Art; Guest Poet, Tenth Annual Houston Poetry Fest; Dobie-Paisano Fellowship in Poetry (1995-96); The Frank Waters Foundation Fellowship, 1996. Address: 501 West Industrial Drive, Apartment 503-B, Sulphur Springs, TX 75482, USA.

BEILE Werner, b. 5 March 1941, Iserlohn, Germany. Professor of Applied Linguistics. m. Alice Bowes, 1 daughter. Education: Universities of Freiburg, Germany, Edinburgh, Scotland, Bonn and Bochum, Germany, 1960-64, 1966-68; English Language and Literature, Education, Research into the Teaching/Learning of Foreign Languages; Dr Phil, Language Acquisition Research, University of Bochum, 1979. Appointments: Lecturer, Nuffield and Schools Council Modern Languages Project, University of York, England, 1968-70; Lecturer, Ruhr-Universität, Bochum, Germany, 1970-79, 1980-84; Acting Professor of English, Universität Osnabruck, Germany, 1979-80; Professor of Applied Linguistics, 1984-, Dean of the Faculty of Arts, Member of Senate, 1995-99, Bergische Universität Wuppertal, Germany. Publications: Three 6-year courses for the teaching of English in German schools in editions for all types of secondary schools and international editions: Learning English – Modern Course, 1974-79; Green Line, Red Line, Orange Line, 1984-89; Password Green, Password Red, Password Orange, 1994-2000; Teaching materials for German as a foreign language world-wide – 11 projects for Inter Nationes, Bonn since 1974 include: Alltag in Deutschland; Several publications on local history; Many articles on foreign language teaching, especially the use of authentic material, exercise and activity types, interlingual forms, teaching of vocabulary, use of media. Memberships: Association for Language Learning; Deutscher Anglistenverband; Deutsche Gesellschaft für Fremdsprachenforschung; Gesellschaft für Angewandte Linguistik. Address: Leckinger Strasse 208, 58640 Iserlohn, Germany. E-mail: wa.beile@gmx.de

BEK Lise, b. 14 September 1936, Herning, Denmark. Professor of Art History. m. (1) Aksel Bek, deceased 1969, 1 son (2) Johan Vatke. Education: Undergraduate and Postgraduate, Art History, University of Aarhus, Denmark 1956-66; MA, 1960; Doctorate, Faculty of Arts, University of Copenhagen, Denmark, 1980. Appointments: Grammar School Teacher, 1964-68; Post-Graduate Scholar, Lecturer, Assistant Professor, 1967-90, Professor of Art History, 1990-96, Aarhus University, Denmark. Publications: Towards Paradise on Earth, 1980; Elogio umanistico o critica d'arte alla maniera Albertiana, 1995; Historicity of Sight, Consequences and Prognoses for Urban Space and Urban Conservation, 2000; Creating Reality by Sight, 2002; Reality in the Mirror of Art, 2003. Honours: Gold Medal for Prize Paper, Aarhus University, 1962; Post-graduate Scholarship, 1965-66; Aarhus University Research Foundation Anniversary Project Scholarship, 1985-88. Memberships: International Association for Christian Archaeology; Centre de la Renaissance, Tours; Augustine Society, Aarhus, Denmark; International Association for Neolatin Studies; Nordisk Platonselskab; The Scientific Council for the National Encyclopaedia. Address: Parkvej 132, DK-6710 Esbjerg V, Denmark. Website: http://www.hum.au.dk/kunsthis/kunlbe/home.hm

BELAFONTE Harry, b. 1 March 1927, New York, USA. Singer. m. (2) Julie Robinson, 1957, 1 son, 3 daughters. Education: Jamaica, 1935-39. Appointments: US Navy, 1943-45; American Negro Theatre; President, Belafonte Enterprises include: Goodwill Amb for UNICEF, 1987; Host, Nelson Mandela Birthday Concert, Wembley, 1988. Creative Works: European Tours, 1958, 1976, 1981, 1983, 1988; Broadway appearances: Three For Tonight; Almanac; Belafonte At The Palace; Films: Bright Road; Carmen Jones, 1952; Island in the Sun, 1957; The World, the Flesh and the Devil, 1958; Odds Against Tomorrow, 1959; The Angel Levine, 1969; Grambling's White Tiger, 1981; White Man's Burden; Buck and the Preacher, 1971; Uptown Saturday Night, 1974; Concerts in USA, Europe, 1989, Canada, 1990, USA and Canada, 1991, North America, Europe and Far East, 1996. Honours include: Golden Acord Award, Bronx Community College, 1989; Mandela Courage Award, 1990; National Medal of the Arts, 1994; New York Arts and Business Council Award, 1997; Distinguished American Award, John F Kennedy Library, Boston, 2002; Several honorary doctorates. Membership: Board Member, New York State Martin Luther King JR Institute for Non-violence, 1989-.

BELICZA Biserka Tonica, b. 8 February 1942, Zagreb, Croatia. Physician. 1 son, 2 daughters. Education: MD, Medical School, Zagreb, Croatia, 1960-66; Public Health and the Organisation of the Health Service, Zagreb School of Medicine, School of Public Health "Andrija Štampar", 1970-71; PhD, 1975, Postdoctoral Visiting Fellow, Zlatko and Joyce Baloković Scholarship, Harvard University, Department of History of Science, and Harvard Medical School, Department of History Medicine, 1978-79; Assistant Professor, 1977, Associate Professor, 1981, Full Professor, 1986, University of Zagreb School of Medicine; Full Professor, University Josip Juraj Strossmayer in Osijek School of Medicine, 2002. Appointments: Graduate Medical Apprenticeship, Zagreb, 1966-67; Physician, General Practitioner, Peoples Health Centre "Centar", Zagreb, 1967-69; Assistant, 1970, Research Associate, 1975; Senior Research Associate, 1978; Research Advisor, History of Medicine, 1984; Research Advisor, Historical Sciences, 1999-, Croatian Academy of Science and Arts, Institute for the History and Philosophy of Science, Division for the History of Medical Sciences; Chairperson-Director, Division for the History of Medical Sciences, 1975-; Head and Lecturer of Course, History of Medicine, Medical School, University of Zagreb, 1975-, Medical Study in Split, 1976-96; Medical Study in Osijek, 1983-97; Lecturer, Postgraduate Course, Introduction to the Methodology of the Scientific Research, Zagreb School of Medicine, 1985-99; Head of Chair of History of Medicine and Medical Ethics; Courses on History of Medicine, Medical Ethics, Medical Humanities, Faculty of Medicine, University J J Strossmayer, Osijek, Croatia, 1998-; Professor, University of Zagreb Centre for Postgraduate Studies, 2003-. Publications: Research articles on subjects including: Medical humanities, history and philosophy of medicine and health care; Bioethics, human rights, ethics in science and technology, medical law, deontology, patients rights, historical and current development of physician-patients society relationship, historical roots of unconventional/complementary medicine in Europe, Croatian medical heritage, scientific, public health, health care and professional achievements of Croatian physicians, historical epidemiology, ethno-medicine and peoples health culture, the role, status and contribution of women in science, technology, biomedicine, health care and public health. Honours: Associate Research Fellow Member, Division of Medical Sciences, Croatian Academy of Science and Arts; Member, Croatian Commission of UNESCO; Member, Intergovernmental Bioethics Committee of UNESCO, 1990-2001; Croatian National Bioethics Committee for Medicine; Chairperson, Committee of Biomedical Ethics, Division of Medical Sciences, Croatian Academy of Science and Arts; Chairperson, Ethics Committee, Faculty of Medicine, University of J J Strossmayer, Osijek; Croatian-National Delegate, Steering Committee on Bioethics (CDBi). Memberships: Vice-president, International Society for the History of Medicine; Member, European Society for History and Philosophy of Medicine, International Society of History of Science; International Society for Medical Law; Founding member, Croatian Society for History of Medicine, Croatian Medical Association, President, 1996-2001; Founding member, Central and Eastern European Association of Bioethics (CEEAB). Address: Vlaška 70c, 10000 Zagreb, Croatia.

BELJAEV Arnold, b. 15 November 1933, Gorkiy, Russia. Engineer; Mechanic. m. A P Beljaeva, 1 son. Education: Diploma, Engineer-Mechanic, Tomsk Politechnical Institute, 1958; Candidate of Technical Science, 1965; Assistant Professor, 1966; Doctor of Technical Science, 1990; Professor, 1991. Appointments: Assistant Chief Instructor, Assistant Professor, 1958-70, Chief of the Chair of Applied Mechanics, 1971-94, Tomsk Politechnical Institute; Chief of the Chair of Common Engineering Subjects, Novouralsk State Technological Institute, 1994-2002. Publications: More than 300 articles, including 5 monographs, 25 patents, 1958-2002. Honour: Honoured Scientist, Russia. Memberships: Inter-Republican Association of Mechanical Transmission Engineers; Editorial Board, Gearing and Transmission Journal. Address: Novouralsk State Technological Institute, Lenin Str 85, 824130 Novouralsk, Sverdlovsk Region, Russia. E-mail: arnold@npi.novouralsk.ru

BELJAEV Juri Antonovitch, b. 21 December 1944, Voroneg, Russia. Creative Writer; Historian. m. Natalia Listikova, 2 sons. Education: Honours Degree, Moscow State University, 1969; Postgraduate, Moscow Institute of History, 1969-73; PhD, 1980. Appointments: Research Worker, Academy of Sciences of the USSR, 1977-84; Free-lance, 1985-93; President of the Publishing House "Astreya", 1994-96; President, Academy of Russian Letters, 1997-. Publications: Books: Non-Fiction: Dates Above Centuries, 1988; Encyclopaedia: 100 Beasts of the Ancient World, 1997; Beast-like Gods of Ancient Times, 1998; A Temptation by

Armageddon, 2002; Fiction: A Rebus of Genesis, 1999; Living Legends of Ancient Moscow, 1999; The Metaphysics of Love, 2001; Day-Dreams, 2003. Honours include: Poushkin Medal "To zealot of enlightenment"; The Witte Gold Medal; Order of the Labour Banner; Moscow's 850th Anniversary Medal. Memberships: Academy of Russian Letters; Honorary Academician, Poushkin Academy; Academy of Geopolitical Problems; Secretary, Writer's Union of Russia. Address: Velozavodskaya St, House 9, Apt 44, 115280 Moscow, Russia.

BELL David, b. 5 August 1945, Beverly, Massachusetts, USA. Medicine. m. Nancy A Bell, 2 sons, 1 daughter. Education: AB, Harvard University, 1963-67; MD, Boston University, 1967-71; Fellow, American Academy of Paediatrics, 1976. Appointments: Subspecialty in behaviour disorders of children; Clinical Research in Chronic Fatigue Syndrome, 1985-2003. Publications: 15 publications on Chronic Fatigue Syndrome. Memberships: American Academy of Paediatrics; American Association of Chronic Fatigue Syndrome. Address: 77 South Main St, Lyndonville, NY 14098, USA.

BELL Elizabeth, b. 1 December 1928, Cincinnati, Ohio, USA. Composer. m. (1) Frank D Drake, 7 March 1953, 3 sons, (2) Robert E Friou, 16 April 1983. Education: BA, Music, Wellesley College, Wellesley, Massachusetts, 1950; BS, Composition, Juilliard School of Music, New York City, 1953; Studied under Peter Mennin and Vittorio Giannini; Later studied privately with Paul Alan Levi. Career: Performances throughout USA, also Russia, Ukraine, Bulgaria, Armenia, Japan, Australia, Canada, South America; 5 retrospective concerts: Ithaca, New York, Jan 1973, Cincinnati, Apr 1985, New York City, October 1991, May 1998 and October 2003; Radio and television interviews. Major Compositions: Variations and Interludes for piano, 1952; String Quartet, 1957; Songs of Here and Forever, 1970; Fantasy-Sonata for cello and piano, 1971; Symphony No 1, 1971; Second Sonata for piano, 1972; Soliloquy for solo cello or solo violin, 1980; Loss-Songs for soprano and piano, 1983; Perne in a Gyre for clarinet, violin, cello and piano, 1984; Duovarios for 2 pianos, 1987; Millennium for soprano, clarinet and piano, 1988; Spectra for 11 instruments, 1989; Night Music for piano, 1990; River Fantasy for flute and string trio, 1991; Andromeda, Concerto for piano, string orchestra and percussion, 1993; Les Neiges d'Antan, Sonata for violin and piano, 1998. Recordings: 2nd Sonata; Perne in a Gyre; Millennium; Andromeda; Night Music; Variations and Interludes; The Music of Elizabeth Bell, CD, includes Andromeda, String Quartet, Perne in a Gyre, Symphony No 1; Snows of Yesteryear, CD, includes Spectra, Duovarios, Songs of Here and Forever, and Les Neiges d'Antan. Contributions to: Music reviews for Ithaca Journal, 1969-75. Honours: 1st Prize for Perne in a Gyre, 1986, Grand Prize for Spectra, 1996, Utah Composers Competition; Delius Prize for Duovarios, Jacksonville, Florida, 1994; Commissions from New York State Council on the Arts, Inoue Chamber Ensemble, Max Lifchitz, Vienna Modern Masters, others. Memberships include: Broadcast Music Inc; American Music Center; Member of the Board of Governors, American Composers Alliance; Formerly Secretary/Treasurer and Presently Member of the Board, New York Women Composers; Society of Composers Inc; International Alliance of Women in Music. Current Management: American Composers Alliance. Address: 21 Beech Lane, Tarrytown, NY 10591-3001, USA.

BELL Martin, b. 31 August 1938. Broadcaster. m. (1) Nelly Gourdon, 1971, 2 daughters, (2) Rebecca Sobel, 1983, (3) Fiona Goddard, 1998. Education: King's College, Cambridge. Appointments: Joined BBC, 1962; News Assistant, Norwich, 1962-64; General Reporter, London and Overseas, 1964-76; Diplomatic Correspondent, 1976-77; Chief, North American

Correspondent, 1977-89; Berlin Correspondent, BBC TV News, 1989-93; Vienna Correspondent, 1993-94; Foreign Affairs Correspondent, 1994-96; Special Correspondent, Nine O'Clock News, 1997; Reported in over 70 countries, covered wars in Vietnam, Middle East, 1967, 1973, Angola, Rhodesia, Biafra, El Salvadore, Gulf, 1991, Nicaragua, Croatia, Bosnia; Independent Member of Parliament for Tatton, 1997-2001; Humanitarian Ambassador for UNICEF, 2001-. Publication: In Harms Way, 1995; An Accidental MP, 2000. Honours include: Royal TV Society Reporter of the Year, 1995; Institute of Public Relations President's Medal, 1996; Several honorary degrees. Address: 71 Denman Drive, London W11 6RA, England.

BELL Napoleon Arthur, b. 17 June 1927, Dubin, Georgia, USA. Law. m. Dorothy, 1 son, 1 daughter. Education: BA, Mt Union College, Ohio, 1951; LLB, Western Reserve University, 1954. Appointments: Attorney Examiner, Industrial Commission of Ohio, 1955-58; Full-time Practice of Law, 1958-; President, Chairman of the Board, Beneficial Acceptance Corporation; Chairman, Board of Tax Appeals, 1971-74; Counsel to the Governor, 1988-89; Member, Industrial Commission of Ohio, 1989-91; Board of Directors, Columbia Gas of Ohio, 1986-2000. Honours: Award of Merit, Ohio Legal Center; Kappa Alpha Psi, Man of the Year, 1964; Award of Merit, Mahoning County Youth Club, 1964; Award of Merit, United Negro College Fund; Lecturer, Seminar on Workers' Compensation, Ohio Legal Center; Mt Union College, Alumni Chair Award, 1974; Governor's Community Service Award, 1974; National Collegiate Athletic Association, Silver Anniversary Award, 1976; Mt Union College Alumni Award, 1976; Youngstown Coach's Hall of Fame, 1986. Memberships: 5th Ward Committeeman, 1963; Franklin County Democratic Executive Committee, 1965. Address: 2077 Jupiter Hills Ln, Henderson, NV 89012, USA.

BELL BURNELL (Susan) Jocelyn, b. 15 July 1943, Belfast, Northern Ireland. Astronomer. m. Martin Burnell, (dissolved), 1 son. Education: BSc, University of Glasgow, 1965; PhD, Cambridge University, 1968. Appointments: Worked with Gamma-Ray Astronomy, University of Southampton, 1968; X-Ray Astronomy, Mullard Space Science Laboratory, 1974-82; Senior Research Fellow, Royal Observatory, Edinburgh, Scotland, 1982; Head, James Clerk Maxwell Telescope Section; Professor of Physics, Open University, Milton Keynes, England, 1991-99; Visiting Professor for Distinguished Teaching, Princeton University, 1999-2000; President, Royal Astronomical Society, 2002-04; Discovered first four pulsating radio stars (pulsars); Research contributions in the field of X-ray and gamma-ray astronomy; Frequent radio and TV broadcaster on science, on being woman in science and on science and religion. Publications: 2 books; About 70 scientific papers and 35 Quaker publications. Honours: 9 honorary doctorates; Joseph Black Medal and Cowie Book Prize, Glasgow University, 1962; Michelson Medal, Franklin Institute, USA, 1973; J Robert Oppenheimer Memorial Prize, Center for Theoretical Studies, Florida, 1978; Beatrice M Tinsley Prize, American Astronomical Society, 1987; Herschel Medal, Royal Astronomical Society, 1989; Honorary Fellow, New Hall, Cambridge, 1996; Magellanic Premium, American Philosophical Society, 2000. Address: Department of Physics and Astronomy, The Open University, Walton Hall, Milton Keynes, MK7 6AA, England. E-mail: s.j.b.burnell@open.ac.uk

BELLAMY Matthew James, b. 9 June 1978, Cambridge, England. Singer, pianist, songwriter, guitarist with band Muse. Albums (as Muse) include: Showbiz, 1999; Origin of Symmetry, 2001; Hullabaloo, 2002; Absolution, 2003. Hit Singles (as Muse) include: Muscle Museum, 1999; Uno, 1999; Unintended, 2000; Feelin' Good, 2001; New Born, 2001; Plug in Baby, 2001; Dead

Star, 2002; Hysteria, 2003; Time is Running Out, 2003. TV Appearances include: Top of the Pops, 2001; Later With Jools Holland, 2001; Top of the Pops, 2002; CD:UK, 2003.

BELLAMY David James, b. 18 January 1933, England. Botanist; Writer. m. Rosemary Froy, 1959, 2 sons, 3 daughters. Education: Chelsea College of Science and Technology; PhD, Bedford College, London University. Appointments: Lecturer, Botany, 1960-68, Senior Lecturer, Botany, 1968-82, Honorary Professor, Adult Education, 1982-, University of Durham; Television and radio presenter, scriptwriter of series including: Bellamy's New World, 1983; Seaside Safari, 1985; The End of the Rainbow Show, 1986; Bellamy on Top of the World, 1987; Turning the Tide, 1987; Bellamy's Bulge, 1987-88; Bellamy's Birds Eye View, 1988; Moa's Ark, 1989-90; Special Professor of Botany, University of Nottingham, 1987-; Visiting Professor, Natural Heritage Studies, Massey University, New Zealand, 1989-91; Director, Botanical Enterprises, David Bellamy Associates, National Heritage Conservation Fund, New Zealand, Conservation Foundation, London. Publications: The Great Seasons, 1981; Discovering the Countryside with David Bellamy, 4 volumes, 1982-83; The Mouse Book, 1983; The Queen's Hidden Garden, 1984; Bellamy's Ireland, 1986; Bellamy's Changing World, 4 volumes, 1988; England's Last Wilderness, 1989; How Green are You?, 1991; Tomorrow's Earth, 1991; World Medicine, 1992; Poo, You and the Poteroo's Loo, 1997; Bellamy's Changing Countryside, 1998; The Glorious Trees of Great Britain, 2002; Jolly Green Giant, autobiography, 2002; The Bellamy Herbal, 2003; Various books connected with television series. Honours: Officer of the Order of the British Empire; Dutch Order of the Golden Ark; UNEP Global 500 Award; Duke of Edinburgh's Award for Underwater Research; British Academy of Film and Television Arts; BSAC Diver of the Year; Richard Dimbleby Award; Chartered Institute of Water and Environmental Management, fellow. Memberships: Fellow, Linnaean Society; Founder-Director, Conservation Foundation; President, WATCH, 1982-83; President, Youth Hostels Association, 1983; President, Population Concern; President, National Association of Environmental Education. Address: Mill House, Bedburn, Bishop Auckland, County Durham DL13 3NW, England.

BELLE Pamela Dorothy Alice, b. 16 June 1952, Ipswich, England. Author. m. Steve Thomas, 6 August 1990, 2 sons. Education: BA Hons, History, University of Sussex, England, 1972-75; Postgraduate Teaching Certificate, Coventry College of Education, 1975-76. Appointments: Teacher, Northchurch First School, Berkhamsted, Herts, 1978-85; Full time Author, 1985-. Publications: The Moon in the Water, 1983; The Chains of Fate, 1984; Alathea, 1985; The Lodestar, 1987; Wintercombe, 1988; Herald of Joy, 1989; A Falling Star, 1990; Treason's Gift, 1992; The Silver City, 1994; The Wolf Within, 1995; Blood Imperial, 1996; Mermaid's Ground, 1998; No Love Lost, 1999. Contributions to: Occasional articles including Wiltshire Life; Solander (Journal of the Historical Novel Society). Memberships: Society of Authors; Historical Novel Society. Address: 61 New Road, Bromham, Chippenham, Wilts SN15 2JB, England.

BELLEMARE Daniel A, b. 1952, Drummondville, Quebec, Canada. Lawyer; Queen's Counsel. m. Cathy Downes. Education: BA, 1974, LLL Magna Cum Laude, University of Ottawa, 1975; LLM, University of Montreal, 1980. Appointments: Called to the Quebec Bar, 1976; Queen's Counsel, 1990; Assistant Deputy Attorney General of Canada for Criminal Law, 1993-; Head, Federal Prosecution Service; Founding Member, International Association of Prosecutors, 1995-, Member, Executive Committee, 1995-, Vice-President, 1998-2001, re-elected 2001-; President, 2nd IAP Annual Conference, Ottawa, 1997, Vice-President, 7th

Dictionary of International Biography

AIP Annual Conference, London, 2002 ; Member of the Board, St John Ambulance, Quebec Council, 1992-2001, Executive Committee, 1993-94; Member of the Board, Outaouais Region, 2000-2003; Member of the St John's National Restructuring Task Force, 2003. Publications: Books: Electronic Surveillance in Canada, 1981; How to testify in court – The police officer's testimony, 1984; Numerous articles in the area of criminal law. Honours: Canada 125 Commemorative Medal, 1993; Commander of the Order of St John, 1999-; Queen's Jubilee Medal, 2002; Meritorious Service Medal, 2003; St John Ambulance Medal for Long Services, 2003; Chevalier de l'Ordre de la Pléiade, 2004. Memberships: Canadian Bar Association; International Society for the Reform of Criminal Law; 1994-; Editorial Board, Criminal Law Review, 1997-; Judge Advocate General Advisory Panel on Military Justice, 1999-; Canadian Police College Advisory Board, 2002-; Board of Directors, Nathanson Centre for the Study of Organised Crime and Corruption, 2002; Governor Quebec Bar Foundation, 2003-2006; Patron of The Honourable Julius Alexander Isaac Scholarship established at the Windsor University Law School, 2003. Address: Federal Prosecution Service, Department of Justice, 284 Wellington Street, Room 2359, Ottawa, Ontario, Canada K1A 0H8. E-mail: daniel.bellamare@justice.gc.ca

BELOUSOV Yuriy, b. 15 May 1940, Nizhny Novgorod, Vyksa, Russia. University Lecturer. m. Alla Belousova, 1 daughter. Education: Graduated as Mechanical Engineer in Welding Equipment and Welding Technology, Zhdanov Metallurgical Institute, 1962; Candidate of Technical Science, Academy of N E Bauman, Moscow, Russia, 1980; Assistant Professor in Equipment and Technology of Welding Fabrication, Supreme Examination Board of Council of Ministers of the USSR, 1984. Appointments: Worker, Shipbuilding Yards, Kerch, Ukraine, 1962-66; Worker, Shipbuilding Yards, Polarny, Russia, 1966-71; Chief of Research Laboratory, Ministry of Ferrous Metallurgy, Ukraine, 1971-81; Assistant Professor, 1981-88, Department of Welding Equipment and Welding Technology, Dean of Department of Welding, 1988-99, Working for a doctor's degree, 1999-2003, Priazov State Technical University, Ukraine. Publications: Articles in scientific journals and papers presented at conferences include: Theoretical Bases of Mendeleev's Periodical Law, 2000; Pre-requisite of new approach to doctrine of heat, 2003; Theoretical bases of heat calculations for welding and related technologies at high flow density of energy of surface sources, 2003; Evaluation of the concentrations of a surface heat source with normal distribution of thermal power, 2003; Monograph: Quantifying of Space-Time in accordance with one in two Bi-principal of relativity, 2003. Honours: Medals: For Heroic Work; Work Veteran. Memberships: International Welding Association; Associate member, Azov Department of Academy of Economic Science and Business Activity. Address: 80 Nikolaevskaya St, Fl 52, Mariupol 87532, Donetsk Region, Ukraine.

BELOVA Anna, b. 6 January 1961, Alexandrovsk City, Russia. Company Vice-President. m. Mikhail Belov, 2 sons. Education: Master's Degree, Mathematics, System Engineering, 1984; Doctor's Degree, Economics, 2003; Appointments: Engineer, Chief Expert of Foreign Economic Relations, Vympel Corporation, 1984-93; Moscow Office Director, Booz Allen & Hamilton Inc., 1993-98; Deputy Chair of Board, American Chamber of Trading, 1996-98; Vice-President, Consulting Companies, Unicon and SBT, 1998-2001; Deputy Minister, Ministry of Railway Transport, Russian Federation Government, 2001-2003; Vice-President, Deputy Chairperson of Executive Board, Joint Stock Holding Company Russian Railways, 2003-. Honours: Honorary Railway Worker; Medal, One Hundred Years Anniversary of the TransSiberian Main Line; Woman of the Year Award 2001, public acknowledgement of women's achievements in Russia; Trans Business Award, European Marketing Club, Brussels, 2002. Memberships: Co-

Chairperson, National Council of Competitiveness; INTEL European Board of Strategic Advisors; National Register of Corporate Directors. Address: JSCo Russian Railways, 2 Novaya Basmannaya str, Moscow 107174, Russia. Website: www.rzd.ru

BELTZNER Gail Ann, b. 20 July 1950, Palmerton, Pennsylvania, USA. Elementary Vocal Music Specialist. Education: BS summa cum laude, Music Education, West Chester University, 1972; Postgraduate studies, Kean State College, 1972; Temple University, 1980; Westminster Choir College, 1980-83; Lehigh University, 1987; Allentown 2nd Civilian Police Academy. Appointments: Teacher, Music, Drexel Hill Junior High School, 1972-73; Music Specialist, Allentown School District, Pennsylvania, 1973-; Teacher Corps School and Community Development Laboratory, 1978-80; Teacher Corps Community Resource Festival, 1979-81; Teacher Corps Cultural Fair, 1980-81. Honours: 1st Place, Oratorical Contest, Allentown School District, 1964; 1st Place for Musical Composition, West Chester University, 1971; Swope Memorial Scholarship, 1971; Presser Foundation Scholarship, 1971, 1972; Excellence in the Classroom Grant, Rider-Pool Foundation, 1988, 1991-92; Certificate of Appreciation, Lehigh Valley Sertoma Club, 1990; Decorated Dame-Commander, Ordre Souverain et Militaire de la Milice du St Sépulcre; Confederation of Chivalry Grand Council; Maison Internationale des Intellectuels Académie; Order of the White Cross International. Memberships: Allentown Art Museum Auxiliary; Auxiliary of the Allentown Hospital; Women's Committee, Allentown Symphony; American Association of University Women; International Platform Association; Music Educators National Conference; Pennsylvania Music Educators Association; American Orff-Schulwerk Association; Society for General Music; American Association for Music Therapy; Lehigh County Historical Association; Association for Supervision and Curriculum Development; National Association for Female Executives; Lenni Lenape Historical Association; Airedale Terrier Club of Greater Pennsylvania; Museum of Fine Arts, Boston; American String Teachers Association; American Viola Society; International Reading Association; International Platform Association; Organisation of American Kodaly Educators; American Recorder Society; Civil War Roundtable of Eastern Pennsylvania; Choristers Guild; Allentown 2nd and 9th Civilian Police Academies; Board of Directors, Allentown Area, Ecumenical Food Bank; Allentown Arts Commission; Kappa Delta Pi; Phi Delta Kappa; Alpha Lambda. Address: PO Box 4427, Allentown, PA 18015, USA.

BELYAVSKIY Evgeniy Danilovich, b. 26 August 1940, Taganrog, USSR. Radio Physicist. m. Lyudmila, 2 sons. Education: Engineering Degree, USSR, 1964; PhD, Radiophysics, Saratov University, 1970; Dr of Physics, Maths Science, USSR, 1987. Appointments: Worker, Mechanical Plant, Poltava, USSR, 1957-59; Engineer, Orion Research Institute, Kiev, 1965-70; Researcher, 1970-71; Senior Researcher, 1971-89; Head of Laboratory, 1989-96; Professor, Physics, Kiev Politechnical Institute, Ukraine, 1996-. Publications: 92 articles to professional journals. Address: kv 212, Prospect Majokovskogo 79, 02232 Kiev, Ukraine.

BEN-AMOS Dan, b. 3 September 1934, Tel-Aviv, Israel. Professor. m. Batsheva Ben-Amos, 2 sons, 1 daughter. Education: BA, Hebrew University, Jerusalem, 1961; MA, 1964, PhD, 1967, Indiana University, Bloomington, USA. Appointments: Department of Anthropology, UCLA, 1966-67; Folklore and Folklife University of Pennsylvania, 1967-. Honours: Fellowship, American Council of Learned Societies, 1972-73; John Simon Guggenheim Fellowship, 1975-76; National Endowment for the Humanities, 1980-81. Memberships: American Folklore Society; American Anthropological Association; Association of Jewish Studies; World

Union of Jewish Studies; Folklore Fellows International of the Finnish Academy of Science and Letters. Address: 539 E Durham St, Philadelphia, PA 19119, USA.

BEN-RAFAEL Eliezer, b. 3 October 1938, Brussels, Belgium. Professor of Sociology. m. Miriam Neufeld, 3 August 1960, 2 daughters. Education: BA, 1966, MA, 1970, PhD, 1973, Hebrew University, Jerusalem. Appointments: Research Fellow, Harvard University, 1974-75; Professor of Sociology, Tel-Aviv University, 1980-; Directeur d'Études Associé, École des Hautes Études en Sciences Sociales, 1984-85; Visiting Scholar, Oxford Centre for Postgraduate Hebrew Studies, 1989-90; Co-Editor, Israel Social Sciences Review, 1992-; Jima and Zalman Weinberg Chair of Political Sociology, 1997-; President, International Institute of Sociology, 2001-. Publications: The Emergence of Ethnicity: Cultural Groups and Social Conflict in Israel, 1982; Le kibboutz, 1983; Status, Power and Conflict in the Kibbutz, 1988; Ethnicity, Religion and Class in Israeli Society, 1991; Language, Identity and Social Division: The Case of Israel, 1994; Crisis and Transformation: The Kibbutz at Century's End, 1997; Language and Communication in Israel, 2000; Identités juives, 50 sages repondent à Ben-Goring, 2001 (also Hebrew and English, 2002); Identity, Culture and Globalisation, 2001; Editor, Contemporary Sociology, 2/3: Sociology and Ideology, 2003; Co-editor, Contemporary Jewries: Convergence and Divergence, 2003; Identity, Culture and Globalization, 2002; Contributions to: International Sociology; Ethnics Racial Relations; European Journal of Sociology; British Journal of Sociology; International Journal of Comparative Sociology; Journal of Rural Cooperation. Membership: International Institute of Sociology, president, 2001; Israel Society of Sociology, president, 1994-97; Israeli Association for the Study of Language and Society, chair, 2001-. Address: Department of Sociology, Tel-Aviv University, Tel-Aviv 69978, Israel.

BEN-YOHANAN Asher, b. 22 May 1929, Kavala, Greece (Israeli Citizen). Composer; Music Educator. m. Shoshana Zwibel, 1 son, 1 daughter. Education: Studied oboe and piano; Composition studies with Paul Ben-Haim, Israel, Aaron Copland, USA and Luigi Nono in Italy; Studies with Gustave Reese and Jan La Rue, New York University Music Department, New York, USA; MMus, University of Michigan. Career: Compositions performed in Israel, Europe, USA and South America; Head, Music Department, Thelma Yellin Music and Arts School, Tel-Aviv, Israel, 1966-75; Professor of Music, Department of Music, Bar-Ilan University, Israel. Compositions include: Two Movements for orchestra, 1959; String Quartet, 1962-64; Music for orchestra, 1967; Chamber Music for 6, 1968; Quartetto Concertato, 1969; Mosaic, 1971; Concerto for string orchestra, 1973; Four Summer Songs, 1974; Impressions for piano, 1976; Soliloquy for violin, 1977; Desert Winds for flute, 1979; Three Songs without Titles, 1983; Episode for trombone, 1984; Woodwind Quintet, 1985; Divertimento for brass trio, 1988-89; Hidden Feelings for harp, 1990; Meditations for chamber orchestra, 1992. Publications: Music in Israel, A Short Survey, 1975; Music Notation, 1983. Honours: Morse Fellowship in Composition, University of Cincinnati, USA, 1971; Pi Kappa Lambda. Membership: Chairman, Israel Composers' League, 1989-1992. Address: 4 Bloch Street, Tel-Aviv 64161, Israel.

BENARDELLI de LEITENBURG Mainardo Alvise Maria, b. 18 December 1964. Diplomat. Education: Degree in Political Sciences, University of Padova, 1987. Appointments: Diplomat, 1991 Second Secretary, Italian Ministry of Foreign Affairs, Cultural Department; Italian Embassy in Uganda, Rwanda and Burundi in Kampala as First Secretary and Deputy Head of Mission, 1993; First Secretary, Italian Embassy in the Netherlands, The Hague, 1996; First Secretary and Deputy Head of Mission, Italian Embassy in Sri Lanka and the Maldives, Colombo, 1999; Counsellor at

Desk III (Middle East, Balkans) at the Directorate General for Cooperation to Development, Italian Ministry of Foreign Affairs, 2001; Head of Desk II (Cypher and Telecommunications), Service for Informatics and Cypher, Italian Ministry of Foreign Affairs, 2003. Publications: Many articles about culture and social affairs in the Italian Magazines: Diritto allo Studio, Affari Sociali Internazionali; Affari Esteri, Student & C; Book: The Rwandese Civil War in 1994, (under pseudonym Umwantisi), 1997. Honours: Encomienda, of the Spanish Civil Order, 1999; Knight of the Italian Civil Order, 2002; Knight of the Holy Sepulcher Equestrian Order, 2003; Knight of the Constantinian Order of St George, 2003. Memberships: Bottin Mondain France. Address: c/o SICC - Desk II, Ministry of Foreign Affairs, piazzale della Farnesina 1, 00194 Rome, Italy. E-mail mainardo.benardelli@esteri.it

BENAUD Richard, b. 6 October 1930. Cricketer. m. Daphne Elizabeth Surfleet, 1967, 2 sons. Appointments: Right-Hand Middle-Order Batsman and Right-Arm Leg-Break & Googly Bowler, Played for New South Wales, 1948-49 to 1963-64 (Captain, 1958-59, 1963); Played in 63 Tests for Australia, 1951-52 to 1963-64 as Captain, 28 as Captain, scoring 2,201 runs, including 3 hundreds, taking 248 wickets; First to score 2,000 runs and take 200 wickets in tests; Scored 11,719 runs and took 945 wickets in 1st Class Cricket; Toured England, 1953, 1956, 1961; International Sports Consultant; TV Commentator, BBC, 1960-99, Channel Nine, 1977-, Channel 4, 1999-. Publications: Way of Cricket, 1960; Tale of Two Tests, 1962; Spin Me A Spinner, 1963; The New Champions, 1965; Willow Patterns, 1972; Benaud on Reflection, 1984; The Appeal of Cricket, 1995; Anything But...An Autobiography, 1998. Honours: OBE; Wisden Cricketer of the Year, 1962. Address: 19/178 Beach Street, Coogee, New South Wales 2034, Australia.

BENDANG S, b. 12 February 1938, Chungliyimsen, India. Religious Social Worker. m. Imdongla, 2 sons, 1 daughter. Education: B Th, 1966; Bachelor of Religious Education (BRE), Union Theological Seminary, Yavatmal, 1967; BA, Fazl Ali College, Guwahati University, 1972; MA, Religion, Asbury Theological Seminary, USA, 1973. Appointments: Youth Director, 1967-74; Chair of Board of Governors, Founder, Nagaland Bible College (now Clark Theological College, 1975-; Principal, Edith Douglas School, 1977-80; Founder, Principal, Descipleship Bible College, 1980-85; Founder and Principal, Logos Home Academy, 1979-90; Established schools for the Soras, Uraon and Tangsa tribes, 1983-. Publications: Numerous publications in the Ao language, mostly on the subjects of youth affairs and theological studies, titles include Commentary on Ephesians; Baptist Belief; Youth Leaders' Handbook; CYE Cadit Club Youth Handbook; They Met the Master (translator); The Spirit and the Word (translator); The Master Plan of Evangelism; Editor, several AO-language, youth-oriented and theological magazines. Honours: Man of the Year, 2000. Memberships: Honorary Secretary, 1990-99, President, 1999-, AO Literary Society; Executive Trustee, Bethesda Institute National Open School and Indra Gandhi National Open University Study Centres. Address: Tribal Gospel Mission, PO Mokokchung 798601, Nagaland, India.

BENDON Christopher Graham (Chris), b. 27 March 1950, Leeds, Yorkshire, England. Freelance Writer; Critic. m. Sue Moules, 30 August 1979, 1 daughter. Education: BA, English, St David's University College, Lampeter, 1980. Appointments: Editor, Spectrum Magazine, 1983-88. Publications: Books: In Praise of Low Music, 1981; Software, 1984; Matter, 1986; Cork Memory, 1987; Ridings Writings - Scottish Gothic, 1990; Constructions, 1991; Perspective Lessons, Virtual Lines..., 1992; Jewry, 1995; Crossover, 1996; Novella, 1997. Chapbooks: Testaments, 1983; Quanta, 1984; Aetat 23, 1985; The Posthumous Poem, 1988; A

Dyfed Quartet, 1992. Contributions to: Anthologies, magazines and journals. Honours: Hugh MacDiarmid Memorial Trophy, 1st Prize, Scottish Open Poetry Competition, 1988; £1000 Prize, Guardian/WWF Poetry Competition, 1989; several awards, Royal Literary Fund. Membership: The Welsh Academy. Address: 14 Maesyderi, Lampeter, Ceredigion SA48 7EP, Wales.

BENFIELD Derek, b. 11 March 1926, Bradford, Yorkshire, England. Playwright; Actor. m. Susan Elspeth Lyall Grant, 17 July 1953, 1 son, 1 daughter. Education: Bingley Grammar School; Royal Academy of Dramatic Art. Publications: Plays: Wild Goose Chase, 1956; Running Riot, 1958; Post Horn Gallop, 1965; Murder for the Asking, 1967; Off the Hook, 1970; Bird in the Hand, 1973; Panic Stations, 1975; Caught on the Hop, 1979; Beyond a Joke, 1980; In for the Kill, 1981; Look Who's Talking, 1984; Touch & Go, 1985; Fish Out of Water, 1986; Flying Feathers, 1987; Bedside Manners, 1988; A Toe in the Water, 1991; Don't Lose the Place, 1992; Anyone for Breakfast?, 1994; Up and Running, 1995; A Fly in the Ointment, 1996; Two and Two Together, 1998; Second Time Around, 2000; In at the Deep End, 2003; Funny Business, 2004. Membership: Society of Authors.

BENGTSON (John) Erik (Robert), b. 21 July 1938, Degerfors, Sweden. Teacher; Poet; Novelist. m. Peggy Lundberg, 26 July 1963, 2 daughters. Education: MA, Uppsala University, 1964. Appointments: Teacher, Sundstagymnasiet, Karlstad. Publications: I somras, 1963; Orfeus tolv sanger, 1963; Som en a, 1964; Pep Talk, 1977; 10 novels. Honours: Various literary prizes. Address: Hantverkaregatan 12, 654 60 Karlstad, Sweden.

BENICHOU Jacques, b. 30 January 1959, Oran, Algeria. Biostatistician. m. Nathalie Carrel, 1 son. Education: MD, 1985, MA, 1986, PhD, 1989, University of Paris VI, France. Appointments: Guest Researcher, National Cancer Institute, Bethesda, 1986-88; INSERM Researcher, Saint Louis University Hospital, Paris, 1988-90; Fellow, Senior Staff Fellow, National Cancer Institute, Bethesda, 1991-96; Full Professor, University of Rouen Medical School and Rouen University Hospital, France, 1996-. Publications: Co-author, over 100 scientific papers in medical, epidemiological and statistical literatures; Co-editor, Encyclopaedia of Epidemiologic Methods, 2000. Honours: Laurent Catier Award of Haematology, 1986; Clinica et Statistica Award, Biostatics and Clinical Research, 1987; Federal Technology Transfer Award, 1995. Memberships: International Biometric Society. Address: 23 Rue Philibert Caux, 76420 Bihorel, France. E-mail: jacques.benichou@chu-rouen.fr

BENIGNI Roberto, b. 27 October 1952, Misericordia, Tuscany. Actor; Director; Writer. Creative Works: Films include: Beliungua ti voglio bene, 1977; Down By Law, 1986; Tutto Benigni, 1986; Johnny Stecchino, Night on Earth, 1992; Son of the Pink Panther, 1993; Mostro, Life is Beautiful, 1998; Asterisk & Obelisk, 1999; Pinocchio, 2002; Coffee and Cigarettes, 2003. Honours include: Academy Award, Best Actor and Best Foreign Film, 1998.

BENING Annette, b. 29 May 1958, Topeka, USA. Actress. m. (1) Steven White, divorced, (2) Warren Beatty, 1992, 4 children. Creative Works: Stage appearances in works by Ibsen, Chekhov and Shakespeare in San Diego and San Francisco; Other roles in Coastal Disturbances, The Great Outdoors; Films: Valmont; The Grifters; Regarding Henry; Guilty By Suspicion; Bugsy; Love Affair; The American President; Richard III; Blue Vision; Mars Attacks!; Against All Enemies; The Siege; In Dreams; American Beauty; Forever Hollywood; What Planet Are You From?; Open Range, 2003. Address: c/o Kevin Huvane, CAA, 9830 Wilshire Boulevard, Beverly Hills, CA 90212, USA.

BENJUMOVICH Max, b. 23 October 1932, Moscow, Russia. Scientist; Physician. m. Liana Pashinceva, 1 son. Education: MD, PhD, Memorial I M Sechenov 1st Moscow Medical Institute. Appointments: Scientific Worker, Group of Cultivated Tumour Cells Biology, All Union Oncological Scientific Centre, Academy of Medical Sciences of the USSR; Oncology Journal Editor, All-Russian Institute of Scientific and Technical Information, Russian Academy of Sciences, Experimental Morphology of Tumours; Professor, Department of Clinical Pharmacology and Internal Diseases, Moscow State Medical Stomatological University. Publications: English-Russian Medical Dictionary, 1988, 1998, 2001; Comprehensive Russian-English Medical Dictionary, 2000, 2001; Numerous articles in professional journals and presented at conferences include most recently: Computerized database on infarction-like changes of electrocardiogram, 1999; Computerized databases on the cultivation of human tumors: gastric cancer, 1999; Pancreatic cancer, 2000; Oesophagus cancer, Liver cancer, 2001; Proliferative activity of cultured human fat cells, 2001; The application of Poisson units to the determination of median lethal cell culture dose, 2001; Colon cancer, 2002; Use of poisson units in radiology, 2003. Memberships: Corresponding Member, Russian Academy of Natural Sciences; European Tissue Culture Society; European Society of Toxicology in Vitro; Association of Specialists on Cell Cultures, Russia; Memorial A L Mjasnikov Moscow Scientific Cardiologic Society. Address: Moscow State Medical Stomatological University, Staff Hospital No 50, Ulica Vucheticha, d 21, 127206 Moscow, Russia. E-mail: lianamax@mtu-net.ru

BENKA Zlatko, b. 22 July 1951, Lalit, Vojvodina, Yugoslavia. Writer; Journalist. m. Ana Rybar, 2 daughters. Education: Graduate High School, 1974. Career: Author. Publications: Demon But Where, 1973; Water Dust, 1977; Twofold Knife, 1981; Ocean, 1984; Cuirassier, 1986; Linen of Rice, 1988; Goddess on the Throne, 1996; Sliver of the Sandy Wood, 1996; Falling of the Angel, 1996; Loam, 2001. Honours: Award for Poetry, 1973; Golden Stamp, Sremski Karlovci town, 1974; Award of the Year, New Life magazine, 1988; First Prize, newspaper story of radio discussion, Vojvodina, 1992. Memberships: Association of Yugoslavian Journalists; Society of Yugoslavian Writers; Society of Slovakian Writers. Address: 252 34 Lalit, Titova 20, Yugoslavia. E-mail: talas@sombor.com Website: www.ico.co.yu

BENN Christoph, b. 2 March 1960, Lubeck, Germany. Medical Doctor. m. Elisabeth Benn, 1 son, 2 daughters. Education: MD, University of Gottingen, Germany, 1984; MA, Applied Theology, University of Leeds, England, 1985; DTM&H, University of Liverpool, England, 1988; Master of Public Health, Johns Hopkins University, Baltimore, Maryland, USA, 1998. Appointments: Medical Superintendent, Bulongwa Hospital, Tanzania, 1988-92; Moderator, Working Group HIV/AIDS, World Council of Churches, 1994-96; Deputy Director, German Institute for Medical Mission, Tubingen, Germany, 1998-; Member, Board of Directors, Global Fund to Fight AIDS, TB, Malaria, 2002-. Publications: Ethics, Medical Ethics and HIV/AIDS, 1996; Equity and Resource Allocation: Dialogue Between Islam and Christianity. Medicine Health Care and Philosophy, 2002; Influence of Cultural and Religious Frameworks on Future of HIV/AIDS, 2002. Honours: Warrington Yorck Medal, University of Liverpool, 1988; Carl Taylor Award in Bioethics and Internal Health, 1998. Memberships: International AIDS Society; International Association of Physicians in AIDS Care; Deutsche Tropen Medizinische Gesellschaft. Address: Paul-Lechler Strasse 24, D-72076 Tubingen, Germany. E-mail: chrbenn@aol.com

BENNETT Alan, b. 9 May 1934, Leeds, England. Dramatist. Education: BA, Modern History, Oxford, 1957. Career: Junior Lecturer, Modern History, Magdalen College, Oxford, 1960-62;

Co-author and Actor, Beyond the Fringe, Edinburgh, 1960, London, 1961, New York, 1962; Fellow, Royal Academy; Author and Actor, On the Margin, TV series, 1966; Forty Years On, play, 1968. Plays: Getting On, 1971; Habeas Corpus, 1973; The Old Country, 1977; Enjoy, 1980; Kafka's Dick, 1986; Single Spies, 1988; The Wind in the Willows, 1990; The Madness of King George II, 1991, film, 1995; The Lady in the Van, 1999; TV scripts: A Day Out, 1972; Sunset Across the Bay, 1975; A Little Outing, A Visit from Miss Prothero, 1977; Doris and Doreen, The Old Crowd, Me! I'm Afraid of Virginia Woolf, All Day on the Sands, Afternoon Off, One Fine Day, 1978-79; Intensive Care, Our Winnie, A Woman of No Importance, Rolling Home, Marks, Say Something Happened, An Englishman Abroad, 1982; The Insurance Man, 1986; 102 Boulevard Haussmann, 1991; A Question of Attribution, 1991; Talking Heads, 1992; Talking Heads 2, 1998; Films: A Private Function, 1984; Prick Up Your Ears, 1987; The Madness of King George, 1994; TV documentaries: Dinner at Noon, 1988; Poetry in Motion, 1990; Portrait or Bust, 1994; The Abbey, 1995; Telling Tales, 1999; Publications: Beyond the Fringe, 1962; Forty Years On, 1969; Getting On, 1972; Habeas Corpus, 1973; The Old Country, 1978; Enjoy, 1980; Office Suite, 1981; Objects of Affection, 1982; The Writer in Disguise, 1985; Two Kafka Plays, 1987; Talking Heads, 1988; Single Spies, 1989; The Lady in the Van, 1991; The Wind in the Willows, 1991; The Madness of King George III, 1992, screenplay, 1995; Writing Home, 1994; The Clothes They Stood Up In, 1998; Talking Heads 2, 1998; The Complete Talking Heads, 1998; A Box of Alan Bennett, 2000; The Laying on of Hands, 2001; regular contributions to London Review of Books. Screenplays: A Private Function, 1984; Prick Up Your Ears, 1987; The Madness of King George, 1995. Honours: Honorary Fellow, Exeter College, Oxford; Honorary DLitt, Leeds; Evening Standard Award, 1961, 1969; Hawthornden Prize, 1988; 2 Olivier Awards, 1993; Evening Standard Award, 1996; Lifetime Achievement Award, British Book Awards, 2003. Address: Peter, Fraser and Dunlop, The Chambers, Chelsea Harbour, London, SW10 0XF, England.

BENNETT Edward Moore, b. 28 September 1927, Dixon, Illinois, USA. Historian. m. Margery Harder, 1 son. Education: BA, History, Political Science, Butler University, 1952; MA, Russian History, 1956, PhD, American Foreign Relations, 1961, University of Illinois. Appointments: Teaching Assistant, University of Illinois, 1956-60; Instructor, Texas A&M University, 1960-61; Instructor, 1961-62, Assistant Professor, 1962-66, Associate Professor, 1966-70, Professor, 1971-93, Adjunct Professor, 1994-99, Emeritus, 1994-, Washington State University. Publications: Books: Editor: Polycentrism: Growing Dissidence in the Communist Bloc?; Recognition of Russia: An American Foreign Policy Dilemma; Franklin D Roosevelt and the Search for Security; Franklin D Roosevelt and the Search for Victory; Separated by a Common Language: Franklin Delano Roosevelt and Anglo-American Relations, 1933-1939; Co-editor, co-author, Diplomats in Crisis: US-Chinese-Japanese Relations, 1919-1941; Co-author, As the Storm Clouds Gathered: European Perceptions of American Foreign Policy in the 1930s; Chapters: Contributing editor, The Origins of World War II; Contributor: Searching for Allies in a Threatening World; The Challengers to Policy: The Proponents of an Inevitable Soviet-American Conflict; Essays on Joseph Clark Grew and William Christian Bullitt; Articles, essays: Russian Security and American Recognition: The Russian View, 1963; The Russian Orthodox Church and the Soviet State, 1946-1956: A Decade of the New Orthodoxy, 1965; Ethics and Foreign Policy, 1965; American Recognition of the Soviet Union: Imagination and Reality, 1967; The Diplomatic Significance of the Soviet Transpolar Flight to America in 1937, 1988; Colonialism and Neo-Colonialism, 2001; Mandates and Trusteeships, 2001. Honours include: Outstanding Teaching Award, Alpha Gamma Delta, 1965;

Honors Lecturer, Phi Kappa Alpha, 1965; Outstanding Educators of America Award, 1971; Executive Council, American Historical Association, Pacific Coast, 1975-78; Faculty of the Year Award, Washington State University Associated Students, 1979; Member, 1984-90, Chair, 1987-88, Graebner Prize Committee, Society for Historians of American Foreign Relations. Memberships: Phi Alpha Theta, University of Illinois President, 1957; Society for Historians of American Foreign Relations; Organization of American Historians; Tau Kappa Epsilon, Gamma Psi Founder, Butler University. Address: 1240 SE Harvest Drive, Pullman WA 99163-2443, USA. E-mail: embennet@wsunix.wsu.edu

BENNETT John M(ichael), b. 12 October 1942, Chicago, Illinois, USA. Poet; Librarian. m. C Mehrl Bennett, 3 children. Education: BA, cum laude, Spanish and English, 1964, MA, Spanish, 1966, Certificate of Competence in Latin American Studies, 1966, Washington University, St Louis; PhD, Spanish, University of California, Los Angeles, 1970; Certified Poetry Therapist, National Association for Poetry Therapy, 1985. Appointments: Editor, Lost and Found Times, 1974-; Assistant Professor, Department of Romance Languages, 1969-76, Latin American Bibliographic Assistant and Editor, 1976-98, Ohio State University; Curator, Avant Writing Collection, Ohio State University Libraries, 1998-; Volunteer Poetry Therapist, Central Ohio Psychiatric Hospital, 1979-86; Publisher, Editor, Luna Bisonte Productions, 1974-. Publications: White Screen, 1976; Nips Poems, 1980; Jerks, 1980; Blender, 1983; Antpath, 1984; No Boy, 1985; Cascade, 1987; Stones in the Lake, 1987; Twitch, 1988; Swelling, 1988; Milk, 1990; Was Ah, 1991; Fenestration, 1991; Somation, 1992; Blind on the Temple, 1993; Wave, 1993; Blanksmanship, 1994; Just Feet, 1994; Infused, 1994; Eddy, 1995; Spinal Speech, 1995; Fish, Man, Control, Room, 1995; Prime Sway, 1996; Ridged Poeta, 1996; Milky Floor (with Sheila E Murphy), 1996; Door Door, 1997; The Seasons, 1997; Clown Door, 1997; Cul Lit, 1997; Know Other, 1998; Luggage, 1998; Loose Watch: a Lost and Found Times Anthology, 1998; Sendero Luminoso in Context, 1998; Mailer Leaves Ham, 1999; Rolling Combers, 2001; Chac Prostibulario (with Ivan Argüelles), 2001. Contributions to: Poetry, word art, graphics, articles, reviews and translations to numerous publications. Honours: 20 Ohio Arts Council Awards, 1979-2001. Address: 137 Leland Avenue, Columbus, OH 43214, USA.

BENNETT Tony (Anthony Dominick Benedetto), b. 3 August 1926, Astoria, USA. Singer; Entertainer. m. (1) Patricia Beech, 1952, 2 children, (2) Sandra Grant, 1971, 2 daughters. Education: American Theatre Wing, New York; University Berkeley, California. Appointment: Owner, Improv Records. Creative Works: Paintings exhibited at Butler Institute of American Art, Youngstown, Ohio, 1994; Records include: The Art of Excellence, 1986; Bennett/Berlin, 1988; Astoria: Portrait of the Artist, 1990; Perfectly Frank, 1992; Steppin Out, 1993; The Essence of Tony Bennett, 1992; MTV Unplugged, 1994; Here's to the Ladies, 1995; The Playground, 1998; Cool, 1999; The Ultimate Tony, 2000. Publication: The Good Life: The Autobiography of Tony Bennett. Honours include: Several Grammy Awards and Gold Records.

BENNISON Allan Parnell, b. 8 March 1918, Stockton, California, USA. Geologist. m. Deleo Smith, 1 son, 2 daughters. Education: BA, University of California at Berkeley, 1940. Appointments: Geology Fellow, Antioch College, Yellow Springs, Ohio, 1940-42; Photogrammetrist, United States Geological Survey, 1942-45; Assistant Geologist, Tri-Pet Corporation, Cartagena, Colombia, 1946-50; Staff Stratigrapher, Sinclair Oil and Gas, Tulsa, Oklahoma, 1950-68; Geological Consultant, Tulsa, 1968-2000. Publications: Editor, Tulsa Geological Society; Tulsa Physical Environment Geological Map of Tulsa Co; American Association's Highway Geological Maps; and others. Honours:

Distinguished Service Award; Society for Sedimentary Geology, 1990; Distinguished Service Award, American Association of Petroleum Geologists, 1986. Memberships: American Association of Petroleum Geologists; Geological Society of America, Tulsa; Geological Society; and others. Address: 11200 Butler Road, Grass Valley, CA 95945, USA.

BENTLEY Eric, b. 14 September 1916, Bolton, Lancashire, England, US citizen, 1948. Dramatist. m. (1) Maja Tschernjakow, dissolved, (2) Joanne Davis, 1953, twin sons. Education: BA, 1938, BLitt, 1939, Oxford University; PhD, Yale University, 1941. Appointments: Drama Critic, New Republic, 1952-56; Charles Eliot Norton Professor of Poetry, Harvard University, 1960-61; Katharine Cornell Professor of Theatre, SUNY Buffalo, 1975-82; Fulbright Professor, Belgrade, 1980; Professor of Comparative Literature, University of Maryland, College Park, 1982-89. Publications: Larry Park's Day in Court, 1979; Lord Alfred's Lover, 1979; The Kleist Variations, 1982; Monstrous Martyrdoms, 1985; The Pirandello Commentaries, 1985; The Brecht Memoir, 1986; German Requiem, 1990; Round 2, 1991; Bentley on Brecht, 1999. Honours: Honorary Doctorate, University of Wisconsin, 1975; Honorary Doctorate, University of East Anglia, 1979; Festschrift: The Critic and the Play, 1986; Florida Theatre Festival named in his honour, 1992; Honorary Doctorate, New School for Social Research, 1992; Robert Lewis Award for Life Achievement in the Theatre, 1992; Inducted into Theater Hall of Fame, New York, 1998; Honorary Doctorate, Florida International University, 2002. Memberships: American Academy of Arts and Sciences, 1969-; American Academy of Arts and Letters, 1990-. Literary Agent: Jack Tantleff, New York Address: 194 Riverside Drive, New York, NY 10025, USA.

BENTLEY Gerald Eades, b. 23 August 1930, Chicago, Illinois, USA. Teacher; Scholar. m. Elizabeth Budd, 2 daughters. Education: BA, Princeton University, USA, 1952; B Litt, 1954, D Phil, 1956, D Litt, 1985, Oxford University. Appointments: Teacher, University of Chicago, 1956-60; Teacher, University of Toronto, 1960, retired as Professor of English, 1996; Teacher, Université d'Alger, Algeria, 1967-68; Teacher University of Poona, India, 1975-76; Teacher, Fudan University, Shanghai, China, 1982-83; Visiting Professor, Australian Defence Force Academy, Canberra, 1997 Visiting Lecturer, England, Japan, Australia, New Zealand, China, Thailand, Italy, Sri Lanka, India, Wales, Hong Kong, Spain, Singapore, Canada, Italy, Korea, USA. Publications: Editor: William Blake's Vala or the Four Zoas, 1963; Blake Records, 1969, 2004; William Blake: The Critical Heritage, 1975; Blake Books, 1977, reprinted, 2001; Editor, William Blake's Writings 2 volumes, 1978, reprinted, 2001; Blake Books Supplement, 1995; The Stranger from Paradise: A Biography of William Blake, 2001, 2003; Articles in literary journals. Honours: Guggenheim Fellow, 1958-59; D Litt, Oxford, 1985; Fellow, Royal Society of Canada, 1985; Fulbright Professor, 1967-68, 1975-76, 1982-83; Canada Council Fellow, 1963-64, 1970-71, 1977-78; Social Sciences and Humanities Research Council of Canada, 1982-85, 1991-94, 1995-99; Senior Connaught Fellow; Fellow National Library of Australia, 1989; Rockefeller Foundation, Bellagio Fellow, 1991; Visiting Research Fellow, Merton College Oxford, 1993; Visiting Research Fellow, Hatfield College, Durham University, 1996. Memberships: Modern Languages Society; Life Member, Bibliographical Society, London; Oxford Bibliographical Society; Life Member, Friends of National Libraries. Address: 246 MacPherson Avenue, Toronto, Ontario M4V 1A2, Canada.

BENTOIU Annie Maria Alice, b. 1 May 1927, Bucharest, Romania. Writer. m. Pascal Bentoiu, 8 Jan 1949, 1 daughter. Education: Faculty of Law, Bucharest, 1945-48; Institut Francais de hautes Etudes, 1946-47. Publications: Poèmes I; Poèmes II;

Dix méditations sur une rose; Phrases pour la vie quotidienne; Voyage en Moldavie, Vevey, CH, 2001; Translations: Cinquante poèmes en vers et en prose by Tudor Arghezi; A travers la zone interdite by Ileana Malancioiu; L'autre côté by Gellu Naum; Trente poèmes by Mihai Eminescu, 1994; Cinquante poèmes by Mihai Eminescu, 2000; TIMPUL CE NI S-A DAT, Memoirs, 2000. Contributions to: Anthologies, periodicals, journals and magazines. Honours: Prize for Translations, Writers Union of Romania, 1979, 1983, 1991. Memberships: Writers Union of Romania; PEN. Address: Aleea Parva 5 App 60 Bloc D 23B, Scara F 06142 Bucharest, Romania.

BENZING Rosemary Anne, b. 18 September 1945, South India. Teacher; Counsellor; Freelance Journalist; Poet. m. Richard Benzing, 5 April 1969, 1 son, 1 daughter. Education: BA, Honours, English and Philosophy, University College of North Wales, Bangor, 1968; Diploma in Education, 1969; Diploma in Counselling, 1990. Appointments: Teacher, Edward Shelley High School, Walsall, 1968-71; Supply Teacher, Shropshire LEA, 1980-; Counsellor, SRCC, 1988-98. Contributions to: Hybrid; Foolscap; Folded Sheets; Smoke; Borderlines; Envoi; First Time; Purple Patch; Shropshire Magazine; Plowman; White Rose; Poetry Nottingham; Symphony; Psycho Poetica; Third Half; Krax; Bare Wires; Housewife Writers' Forum. Honour: Anglo Welsh Poetry Competition, 1986. Membership: Poetry Society. Address: Roden House, Shawbury, Shrewsbury, Shropshire, England.

BERARDO Felix M, b. 7 February 1934, Waterbury, Connecticut, USA. Sociologist. m. Donna H Berardo, 2 sons. Education: BA, Sociology, University of Connecticut, 1961; PhD (High Honours and Distinction), Sociology and Anthropology, Florida State University, 1965. Appointments: Assistant Professor of Sociology and Rural Sociology, Washington State University, 1965-69; Associate Professor of Sociology, 1969-72, Professor of Sociology, 1972-, Associate Chair, 1972-77, Department Chair, 1985-91, University of Florida; Professor Emeritus, 2003 . Publications: Living is Risky: Staying In Spite of Ourselves; (co-author) The Family: Its Structure and Interaction, 1973; Books (editor, co-editor) include: Privacy and the Family, Special Issue of Journal of Family Issues, 1998; Book chapters, refereed publications, others. Honours include: Phi Beta Kappa; Phi Kappa Phi; Alpha Kappa Delta; Arthur Peterson Award in Death Education, 1986; Certificate of Recognition, National Council on Family Relations, 1988; Awarded Fellow, Gerontological Society, 1992; Awarded fellow, National Council on Family Relations, 1998. Memberships include: American Sociological Association; National Council on Family Relations; Southern Sociological Society; President, Florida Council on Family Relations. Address: Department of Sociology, PO Box 117330, University of Florida, Gainesville, FL 32611-7330, USA.

BERASATEGUI Vicente Ernesto, b. 13 May 1934, Argentina. Ambassador. m. Teresita Mazza. Education: Degree in Law, School of Law, University of Buenos Aires, Argentina; Master in International Relations and Organisation, American University, Washington DC, USA. Appointments: Argentine Foreign Service: Attaché, 1954, Third Secretary, 1959, Second Secretary, 1962, First Secretary, 1966, Second Counsellor, 1967, First Counsellor, 1970, Minister Plenipotentiary, Grade B, 1973, Grade A, 1975; Ambassador Extraordinary and Plenipotentiary, 1985; Head, OAS Division of the Foreign Ministry, 1960; Embassy of the United States of America, 1961-65; Secretary, Policy Making Committee of the Minister for Foreign Affairs, 1967-69; Deputy to the Director General for Political Affairs of the Foreign Ministry, 1970-72; Deputy Permanent Representative to the United Nations, Geneva, 1972-76; Representative to 58 international conferences and meetings, 11 as Head of Delegation, 1959-76; Member of delegations to meetings with Heads of State or Government: Bolivia, 1971, Chile, 1971, Austria, 1994, Spain, 1994, France, 1995, Ireland, 1995, Germany, 1996, Turkey, 1996; Director for Western European Affairs of the Foreign Ministry, 1994-96; Ambassador of the Argentine Republic to the Kingdom of Denmark, 1997-2000; Currently Ambassador of the Argentine Republic to the United Kingdom of Great Britain and Northern Ireland; Numerous positions in the field of disarmament include: Head of the Argentine Delegation to the Conference of the Committee on Disarmament, 1974-76; Observer, First Review Conference of the Treaty on the Non-Proliferation of Nuclear Weapons, 1975; United Nations positions include, Secretary of the First Committee of the General Assembly, Deputy Secretary, Committee on Disarmament, 1980; Representative of the Secretary General, 1992-93; Member of the Advisory Board of the Secretary General on Disarmament Matters, 2001-; Academic activities include: Professor of Foreign Policy, School of Law, University of Buenos Aires, 1971; Professor, Graduate Institute of International Studies, Geneva, 1987-93; Lecturer on International Relations at institutes of advanced studies in Argentina, France and USA. Honours: Grand Cross, Order of the Dannebrod, Denmark; Grand Officer, Order of Distinguished Services, Peru; Commander: Order of Bernardo O'Higgins, Chile, Order of the Condor of the Andes, Bolivia, Order of Civil Merit, Spain, Order of Merit, Italy and France. Memberships: Pi Gamma Mu; Argentine Council for International Relations; Royal Institute for International Affairs, UK; International Institute for Strategic Studies, UK. Address: 65 Brook Street, London, W1K 4AH, England.

BERBARI Adel, b. 26 May 1933, Senegal. Physician. m. Micheline Ghosn, 2 daughters. Education: BSc, 1955; Medical Doctor, 1959. Appointments: Acting Chairman, Department of Physiology, 1968-69; Professor of Medicine and Physiology, 1977-; Chairman, Department of Medicine, Lebanese University, 1987-90; Chairman, Department of Medicine, 1999-2000. Publications: 4 Medical Books; Numerous original articles in professional medical journals. Honour: Listed in several biographical publications. Memberships: American College of Physicians; Council for High Blood Pressure; International and European societies of hypertension. Address: American University of Beirut, Bliss Street, PO Box 113-6044, Beirut, Lebanon. E-mail: ab01@aub.edu.1b

BERECZ Endre, b. 10 January 1925, Csorna, Hungary. Professor Emeritus. m. Maria Illés, 1 son, 1 daughter. Education: Chemist, 1949; Candidate of Chemical Sciences, CSc, 1954; Dr rer nat, 1960; Doctor of Chemical Science, DSc, Eötvös L University, Budapest, 1974; Doctor honoris causa, University of Miskolc, 1995. Appointments: Assistant, First Assistant, Assistant Professor, Eötvös L University, 1949-63; Full Professor, Head of Department of Physical Chemistry, Technical University of Heavy Industries, Miskolc, 1963-92; Dean of the Faculty of Metallurgy, 1965-68; University of Miskolc, 1990-. Publications: 283 science and professional articles; Monographs: 1 Hungarian, 1 English; 8 chapters in monographs; 13 textbooks for university students; 7 patents; 101 reports on research works sponsored by grants and state foundations. Honours: Outstanding Worker of Education, 1968, Metallurgy, 1972; Silver Class Medal of the Order of Labour, 1976; Medals for the Human Environment, 1982, 1989; A Szent-Györgyi Prize, 1995. Memberships: Science and Technology Advisory Committee, 1983-95; Board of Administration, European Federation of Corrosion 1995-2001; National Representative, 1.2 Committee of IUPAC; President, Hungarian Corrosion Association, 1992-. Address: H-1025 Budapest, Zöldmáli lejtő 5, Hungary.

BEREDER Frédéric Laurent, b. 18 May 1960. Architect. m. Jin Wu, 1 son, 1 daughter. Education: Master in Architecture, France, 1986; Diploma, Tokyo Institute of Technology, Japan, 1991; First Class Architect and Building Engineer, Japan, 1997. Appointments: Director, Duct Sarl, 1986-89; Representative, Dumez Japan, 1991-93; Advisor, SE Corporation, 1993-96; President, Nichifutsu Sekkei KK, 1997-2003; Chairman, BEREDER Co Ltd (was Nichifutsu Sekkei KK), 2003-; Adviser, INGEROSEC, 2003-. Honours: 1st Prize Artificial Reefs, 1989; International Order of Merit, IBC; Listed in several biographical publications. Memberships: Ordre des Architects; College Architectural Expert; International College for Architect Experts; The Japan Institute of Architects; Tokyo Society of Architects and Building Engineers. Address: BEREDER Co Ltd, Kannai Keihin Bldg, 2-4-2 Ogi-Cho Naka-Ku, Yokohama 231-0027, Japan. Website: www.bereder.co.jp

BERENTSEN Kurtis George, b. 22 April 1953, North Hollywood, USA. Director of Choral Music. m. Floy Irene Griffiths, 17 March 1984, 1 daughter. Education: BMus, Utah State University, 1975; MA, Music, University of California, Santa Barbara, 1986; Certificate, Religious Studies, Concordia College, 1996. Appointments: Music Director, Hope Lutheran Church, 1975-80; Music Director, First Presbyterian of Santa Barbara, 1982-83; Teaching Assistant, University of California, 1982-84; Minister of Music, Trinity Lutheran Church, Ventura, California, 1984-92; Adjunct Professor, Ventura College, 1986-87; Minister of Music, Christ Lutheran Church, 1992-98; Director of Choral Music, Concordia University, Portland, Oregon. Publications: 45 songs. Honour: 1st Place, ID Federation of Music Clubs State Competition, 1971. Memberships: Association, Lutheran Church Musicians; American Choral Director's Association; Music Educators National Conference. Address: Concordia University, 2811 NE Holman Street, Portland, OR 97211, USA. E-mail: kberentsen@cu-portland.edu

BERESNEVICH Vitaly, b. 14 August 1952, Belarus, Minsk, Latvia. Mechanical Engineer. m. Beresnevich Galina, 2 daughters. Education: Mechanical Engineer, Riga Polytechnical Institute, 1975; Candidate of Technical Science, Riga Polytechnical Institute, 1984; DSc Engineering, Council of Riga Technical University, 1992. Appointments: Assistant, Doctoral Student, Riga Technical University, 1975-80; Researcher, Riga Technical University, 1980-85; Senior Researcher, Riga Technical University, Science Laboratory, 1985-. Publications: 130 publications, books, papers, patents. Honours: Honorary Diploma at the International Exhibition, Plovdiv, Bulgaria, 1985; Silver Medal, Outstanding Scientist of the 20th Century, International Biographical Centre, England, 1999. Memberships: New York Academy of Sciences, USA, 1996-; Member, Research Board of Advisors, American Biographical Institute, USA. Address: Institute of Mechanics, Riga Technical University, 1 Kalku Street, Riga LV 1658, Latvia.

BEREZHNOY Vadim Leonidovich, b. 28 February 1938, Sochy, Krasnodar Region, Russia. Scientist; Metallurgist. m. Svetlana I Naryshkina, 1 son. Education: CMEng Diploma, Technical University, Rostov-on-Don, Russia, 1960; MSc, Institute of Steel and Alloys, Moscow, Russia; DSc, Doctor of Science for Metal Working by Pressure, All-Russia Institute of Light Alloys, Moscow. Appointments: Assistant Professor (Docent) and R&D Group Leader for the Technical University, 1968-77; Contributing Expert for the USSR Committee of Inventions and Discoveries, 1983-91; Head of R&D Sector of Novel Technologies, 1978-93, Chief Scientist, Researcher and Expert, 1993-, All-Russia Institute of Light Alloys; Extrusion Consultant, LG Cable, South Korea, 1997-98. Publications: Author, several books, 195 scientific papers which include: Extrusion with Active Friction Forces, 1988; Friction-Assisted Extrusion as an Alternative to the Indirect and Direct Extrusion of Hard Aluminium Alloys, 1997; Non-Traditional Process Techniques of Extrusion and Pressing, 2000; Technological Principles of Maximizing Strength in the Case of Production of

Press-Quenched Al-Mg-Si Alloy Extrusions, 2000 Innovations: 35 inventions; Discovery of Bulk Friction Effect as a Physical Base for a High Speed Metal Outflow and Mechanical Properties Control; Theory of Friction-Assisted Extrusion and Novel Presses and Technology. Honours: Honorary Award for New Technology, Russian Government, 1995; American Medal of Honor, 2003; Man of the Year 2003, ABI; Listed in Who's Who publications and biographical dictionaries. Memberships: APMI International; 3 science societies and 3 editorial boards of science journals in Russia. Address: Marshal Katukov Street 14-1-142, Moscow 123592, Russia.

BERG Paul, b. 30 June 1926, New York, New York, USA. Molecular Biologist. Education: Graduated, Pennsylvania State University, 1948; Doctorate, Western Reserve University, 1952. Appointments: American Cancer Society Research Fellow, Institute of Cytophysiology, Copenhagen, School of Medicine, Washington University, St Louis, 1952-54; Several positions, Washington University, 1955-74; Assistant Professor, Associate Professor, Microbiology Department, School of Medicine, 1955-59, Professor of Microbiology, 1959-69, Chairman, Microbiology Department, 1969-74; Wilson Professor of Biochemistry, Medical Centre, Stanford University, 1970-94; Director, Beckman Center for Molecular and Genetic Medicine, 1985-2001; Chair, National Advisory Committee, Human Genome Project, 1990-92; Robert W Cahill Professor of Cancer Research, 1994-2000; Director, National Foundation for Biomedical Research, 1994-; Research in genetic engineering, particularly DNA recumbent techniques; Advocated restrictions on genetic engineering research. Publications: Genes and Genomes, 1991; Dealing with Genes: The Language of Heredity, 1992; Exploring Genetic Mechanisms, 1997. Honour: Nobel Prize for Chemistry (with Walter Gilbert and Frederick Sanger), 1980. Address: Stanford University School of Medicine, Beckman Center, B-062, Stanford, CA 94305, USA.

BERGAMINI Eduardo Whitaker, b. 30 April 1944, Riberão Preto, Brazil. Engineer. m. 2 daughters. Education: Engineer, Electrical Engineering, EPUSP, Brazil; MSc, Space Telecommunications, Inst Natl Pesquisas Espacias, (INPE), 1969; MSc, Electrical Engineering, 1973, PhD, Electrical Engineering, Stanford University, USA. Appointments: Research Assistant, INPE, 1968-69, Brazil; Research Assistant, 1971-72, Research Associate, 1972-73, Stanford University, USA; Research Associate, 1974-81, Senior Researcher, 1982-85, Full Researcher, 1985-, Responsible for Application Services in Space Missions, 1994-, INPE, Brazil. Publications: Many publications on incremental computing, parallel computing, space data systems. Honours: NASA International Fellowship, Stanford University, USA, 1969; CNPq (Brazil) Fellowship, Stanford University, 1969-72. Memberships: ISOC Member Interplanetary Internet-IPNSIG and IPNRG; Associate Fellow, AIAA, USA; Senior Member, IEEE; Member, IAF Space Exploration Committee; Member, SpaceOps Executive Committee. Address: INPE/MCT, Avenida dos Astronautas 1758, 12227-010 São José dos Campos, SP, Brazil. E-mail: e.w.bergamini@uol.com.br

BERGE Erling, b. 16 March 1946, Norddal, Norway. Professor. m. Berit Otnes, 3 sons. Education: BA, 1969, MA, 1973, University of Bergen; PhD, Boston University, 1981. Appointments: Research Fellow, Norwegian Research Council and University of Oslo, 1975; Research Associate, Institute of Applied Social Research, and Agricultural University of Norway, 1979-94; Professor of Sociology, Norwegian University of Science and Technology, 1994-. Publications: Law and Governance of Renewable Resources, 1998; Management of Non-Arable Rural Lands, Including Forests, Grasslands and Shrublands, 2002. Memberships:

International Association for the Study of Common Property. Address: Department of Sociology and Political Science, NTNU, No 7491 Trondheim, Norway. E-mail: erling.berge@svt.ntnu.no

BERGER John, b. 5 November 1926, London, England. Author; Art Critic. Education: Central School of Art; Chelsea School of Art, London. Appointments: Painter, Teacher of Drawing; Visiting Fellow, BFI, 1990-; Numerous TV appearances and exhibitions. Publications include: Fiction: A Painter of Our Time, 1958; The Foot of Clive, 1962; Corker's Freedom, 1964; Pig Earth, 1979; Once in Europa, 1989; Lilac and Flag, 1991; To The Wedding, 1995; Photocopies, 1996; King: A Street Story, 1999; Non-fiction includes: About Looking, 1980; Another Way of Telling, 1982; And Our Faces; My Heart; Brief as Photos, 1984; The White Bird, 1985; Keeping a Rendezvous (essays and poems), 1992; Titian: Nymph and Shepherd, 1996; Steps Towards a Small Theory of the Visible, 1996; The Shape of a Pocket, 2001; John Berger Selected Essays, 2001; Radio: Will It Be A Likeness? 1996; Poetry and translations. Honours include: New York Critics Prize, Best Scenario of Year, 1976; George Orwell Memorial Prize, 1977; Prize, Best Reportage, Union of Journalists and Writers, Paris, 1977. Address: Quincy, Mieussy, 74440 Taninges, France.

BERGER Thomas (Louis), b. 20 July 1924, Cincinnati, Ohio, USA. Author. m. Jeanne Redpath, 12 June 1950. Education: BA, University of Cincinnati, 1948; Postgraduate Studies, Columbia University, 1950-51. Appointments: Librarian, Rand School of Social Science, New York City, 1948-51; Staff, New York Times Index, 1951-52; Associate Editor, Popular Science Monthly, 1952-53; Distinguished Visiting Professor, Southampton College, 1975-76; Visiting Lecturer, Yale University, 1981, 1982; Regent's Lecturer, University of California at Davis, 1982. Publications: Crazy in Berlin, 1958; Reinhart in Love, 1962; Little Big Man, 1964; Killing Time, 1967; Vital Parts, 1970; Regiment of Women, 1973; Sneaky People, 1975; Who is Teddy Villanova?, 1977; Arthur Rex, 1978; Neighbors, 1980; Reinhart's Women, 1981; The Feud, 1983; Nowhere, 1985; Being Invisible, 1987; The Houseguest, 1988; Changing the Past, 1989; Orrie's Story, 1990; Meeting Evil, 1992; Robert Crews, 1994; Suspects, 1996; The Return of Little Big Man, 1999; Best Friends, 2003; Adventures of the Artificial Woman. Other: Plays and screenplays: Other People, Stockbridge Theatre festival, 1970. Honours: Dial Fellow, 1962; Rosenthal Award, National Institute of Arts and Letters, 1965; Western Heritage Award, 1965; Ohiona Book Award, 1982; Pulitzer Prize Nomination, The Feud, 1984; LittD, Long Island University, 1986. Address: PO Box 11, Palisades, NY 10964, USA. E-mail: dca@doncongdon.com

BERGEVIN Christiane, Banker. Education: B Commerce (Honours), Finance and Entrepreneurship, McGill University, Montreal, Quebec, Canada. Appointments: Analyst, Real Estate Investment, Standard Life Insurance Company, Montreal (Quebec), Canada, 1984-85; Export Financing Officer, OECD Department, North and West Africa Department, Export Development Corporation, Ottawa, Ontario, Canada, 1985-90; Director, Project Financing and Co-operation, SNC International Inc, Montreal, Quebec, Canada, 1990-96; Vice-President, Project Financing and Co-operation, 1996-97, Senior Vice-President and General Manager, 1997-2001, President, 2001-, SNC-Lavalin Capital Inc, Montreal, Quebec, Canada. Honour: Quebec Ministry of International Relations Bursary, Internship at the Délégation du Québec, London, England, 1984. Membership: Financial Women's Association, Quebec and New York. Address: 455 Rene-Levesque Blvd West, Montreal, Quebec, Canada H2Z 1Z3.

BERGKAMP Dennis, b. 20 May 1969, Amsterdam, Netherlands. Footballer. m. Henrita Ruizendaal, 1 son, 1 daughter. Appointments: Striker, Played for Ajax Amsterdam, 1986-92,

Holland, 1990-2000, Inter Milan, 1992-95, Arsenal, London, England, 1995-; All-time leading scorer for Holland. Honours: Dutch Player of the Year, 1992, 1993; English Player of the Year, 1998; Football Writers' Player of the Year, 1998. Address: c/o Arsenal F C, Arsenal Stadium, Avenell Road, London N5 1BU, England.

BERGMAN Ingmar, b. 14 July 1918, Uppsala, Sweden. Film Director; Theatre Producer. m. (1) Ingrid Karlebovon Rosen, 1971, deceased, 1995, 8 children. Education: Stockholm University. Career: Producer, Royal Theatre, Stockholm, 1940-42; Scriptwriter, Producer, Svensk Filmindustri, 1940-44; Theatre Director, Helsingborg, 1944-46, Gothenburg, 1946-49, Malmo, 1954-63; Leading Director, Royal Dramatic Theatre, Stockholm, 1963; Director, Mme de Sade Theatre, 1989; Chair, European Cinema Society, 1989-; Plays include: A Painting on Wood. The City, The Rite, The Lie, Scenes From a Marriage, To Damascus, 1974; The Merry Widow, Twelfth Night, 1975; Tartuffe, 1980; King Lear, 1985; John Gabriel Borkman, 1985; Miss Julie, 1986; Hamlet, 1986; Maria Stuart, 2000. Films include: Crisis, 1945; It Rains on Our Love, 1946; A Ship Bound for India, 1947; Music in Darkness, 1947; Port of Call, 1948; Prison, 1948; Thirst, 1949; To Joy, 1949; Summer Interlude, 1950; This Can't Happen Here, 1950; Waiting Women, 1952; Summer with Monika, 1952; Sawdust and Tinsel, 1953; A Lesson in Love, 1954; Journey into Autumn, 1955; Smiles of a Summer Night, 1955; The Touch, 1971; Cries and Whispers, 1972; Scenes From A Marriage, 1974; The Serpent's Egg, 1977; Fanny and Alexander, 1981; After the Rehearsal, 1984; Private Confessions, 1998; TV: Making Noise and Acting Up, 1996; Scriptwriter, The Best Intentions, 1991, Faithless, 2000. Publications: Four Stories, 1977; The Magic Lantern (autobiography), 1988; Fanny and Alexander, 1989; Images: My Life in Film, 1993; Sunday's Child, 1994; Private Confessions, 1997. Honours include: Erasmus Prize, 1965; Award, Best Director, National Society of Film Critics, 1970; Order of the Yugoslav Flag, 1971; Luigi Pirandello International Theatre Prize, 1971; Goethe Award, Frankfurt, 1976; Gold Medal, Swedish Academy, 1977; European Film Award, 1988; Le Prix Sonning, 1989; Praemium Imperiale Prize, Japan, 1991; Dorothy & Lilian Gish Prize, 1995. Membership: Swedish Academy of Letters.

BERGNER Heinz, b. 30 April 1936, Berlin, Germany. Professor of English. m. Ilse Bergner, 1 son. Education: PhD, Erlangen University, 1968. Appointments: Assistant Professor, Erlangen University, 1964-68; Associate Professor, Mannheim University, 1968-74; Chair of English Language and Medieval Literature, 1974; Dean, 1976-77, 1987-88, 1993-94; Visiting Professor, Wisconsin-Milwaukee and Madison, 1983, 1989, 1993. Publications: Books on Thackeray, 1967; Short Stories XIX Century, 1969; English Character Writing, 1970; Medieval Lyric, 1983; English Medieval Literature, 1986; Canterbury Tales, 1996;. Memberships: Arthurian Society; International Association of Professors of English; Societas Linguistica Europaea; International Courtly Literature Society; European Society for the Study of English. Address: Justus-Liebig University, Department of English and American Studies, Otto-Behaghel Str, 10 B, D-35394 Giessen, Germany. E-mail: Heinz.Bergner@anglistik.uni-giessen.de

BERGR Veroslav, b. 25 May 1928, Lomnice, Semily, Czech Republic. Painter; Sculptor; Graphic Artist; Illustrator. m. Zdenka Vovsová-Bergrová, 7 May 1952. Education: Student, Ukrainian Academy, Prague, 1950-58; Student, School of Plastic Arts, Prague, 1958-63. Career: Head of Research, Mechanical Workshop, Prague, 1960-89; Co-Author, Czechoslovak patentee #147719; Chief Illustrator, Svetova Literatura periodical, 1975-. Publications: 2 monographs, 1992, 1996. Honours: Medal of Prague Uprising, 1945; Laureate of the Franz Kafka Award, 1998;

State Medal of 55th Anniversary of the End of the Second World War, 2000. Memberships: Association of Painters. Commissions and Creative Works: 25 autonomous expositions, 1959-98; 45 collective expositions; Illustrator of 45 books, mostly poetry; Sculptor, memorial grave #74, Vyšehrad cemetery; Artwork represented in many galleries in Czech Republic and other countries. Address: Marie Cibulkové 30, CZ 14000 Prague 4, Czech Republic.

BERGROVÁ Zdenka, b. 10 March 1923, Prague, Czech Republic. Poet; Author; Translator. m. Veroslav Bergr, 7 May 1952. Education: PhD, Charles University, Prague, 1990. Publications: Author, A Fairy Tale in Verse, 1946; To The Sole Reader, Verses 1968-73, 1990; Fly, Ye Birds' Notes, Verses, 1990; Prague is a Seal, Verses, 1990; Words of a Night, Verses, 1996; Humour Has a Black Bottom, Verses, 1996; Shimmy and other monkey tales, 2002; Vortoj de la nokto, Esperanto verses, 2002; Translated and published 70,000 verses: Pushkin, Lermontov, Chevtchenko, N A Nekrasov, Jesenin, Pasternak, Verlaine and others, 1949-2000. Honours: 1st place, Screenplay Competition, Prague, 1946; Medal of Barricade Fighters for Freedom Association, Prague, 1945; Medal for Translations from Chevtchenko, Kyiv, 1962; Laureate of the Franz Kafka Award, Prague, 1999; State Medal of 55th Anniversary of the End of the Second World War, Prague, 2000; Public acknowledgement from the Capital Prague for attendance at Prague rising in 1945, 2002; Diploma and T G Masaryk Medal (sculpted by Otakar Spaniel) for life-long literary work, Masaryk Academy of Arts, 2002; Josef Jungmann Medal for Literary work, Eastern Nations Friends Society, Czech Republic, 2003. Memberships: Society of Writers; Society of Translators. Address: Marie Cibulkové 30, CZ 14000 Prague 4, Czech Republic.

BERKE Stanley J, b. 14 September 1955, New York, New York, USA. Ophthalmologist. m. Martha, 1 son, 2 daughters. Education: MD, University of Buffalo School of Medicine, 1981; Residency, Nassau University Medical Center, 1985; Fellowship, Cararact and Glaucoma Surgery, Harvard Medical School, 1986. Appointments: Ophthalmic Consultants of Long Island, 1986-; Associate Clinical Professor of Ophthalmology and Visual Sciences, Albert Einstein College of Medicine, New York, New York, USA. Publications: 2 textbook chapters on glaucoma; 30 published articles on glaucoma and cataract surgery. Honours: Principal Investigator, NIH Grant, Collaborative Initial Glaucoma Treatment Study; Best Doctors, New York Magazine. Memberships: American Glaucoma Society; American Academy of Ophthalmology; Association for Research in Vision and Ophthalmology. Address: 360 Merrick Road, Lynbrook, NY 11563, USA. E-mail: sberke@ocli.net Website: www.ocli.net

BERKOFF Steven, b. 3 August 1937, London, England. Writer; Director; Actor. m. (1) Alison Minto, 1970, (2) Shelley Lee, 1976, divorced. Education: Webber-Douglas Academy of Dramatic Art, London, 1958-59; École Jacques Lecoq, Paris, 1965. Appointments: Director of plays and actor in numerous plays, films and TV; Founding Director, London Theatre Group, 1973; Massage, performed at Edinburgh Festival, 1997; Shakespeare's Villains, Theatre Royal, Haymarket, UK and World Tour, 1998, 1999. Plays: In the Penal Colony, 1968; Metamorphosis, 1969; Agamemnon, 1973, 1984; The Fall of the House of Usher, 1974; The Trial, 1976; East, 1978; Hamlet, 1980, 2001; Greek, 1980; Decadence, 1981; West, 1983; Harry's Christmas, 1985; Kvetch and Acapulco, 1986; Sink the Belgrano!, 1986; With Massage, 1987; Lunch, Dog, actor, 1994; Brighton Beach Scumbags, 1994; Dahling You Were Marvellous, 1994; Coriolanus, 1996; Mermaid, 1996; Massage, 1997; Shakespeare's Villains, 1998; Messiah, 2000; Films include: Octopussy; First Blood 2; Beverley Hills Cop; Absolute Beginners; War and Remembrance; The Krays; Decadence. Publications: America, 1988; I am Hamlet, 1989; A

Prisoner in Rio, 1989; The Theatre of Steven Berkoff: Photographic Record, 1992; Coriolanus in Deutschland, 1992; Overview, collected essays, 1994; Free Association, autobiography, 1996; Graft: Tales of an Actor, 1998; Shopping in the Santa Monica Mall, 2000; Ritual in Blood, 2000; Messiah, 2000; Oedipus, 2000; The Secret Love Life of Ophelia, 2001. Honours: Los Angeles Drama Critics Circle Award, 1983; Comedy of the Year Award, Evening Standard, 1991. Address: c/o Joanna Marston, Rosica Colin Ltd, 1 Clareville Grove Mews, London SW7 5AH, England.

BERLIND Bruce, b. 17 July 1926, Brooklyn, New York, USA. Professor of English Emeritus; Writer; Poet. m. (1) 2 sons, 3 daughters, (2) Jo Anne Pagano 17 January 1985. Education: AB, Princeton University, 1947; MA, 1950, PhD, 1958, Johns Hopkins University. Appointments: Instructor to Professor, 1954-88, Charles A Dana Professor of English Emeritus, 1988-, Colgate University. Publications: Bred in the Bone: An Anthology of Verse (co-editor), 1945; Three Larks For a Loony, 1957; Ways of Happenings, 1959; Companion Pieces, 1971; Selected Poems of Agnes Nemes Nagy (translator), 1980; Birds and Other Relations: Selected Poetry of Dezso Tandori (translator), 1987; Through the Smoke: Selected Poetry of Istvan Vas (co-translator), 1989; Imre Oravecz's When You Became She (translator), 1994; Ottó Orbán's The Journey of Barbarus (translator), 1997; Charon's Ferry: Fifty Poems of Gyvla Illyés (translator). Contributions to: Encounter; London Magazine; Stand; New Letters; Poetry; Transatlantic Review; TriQuarterly; Chicago Review; Paris Review; Grand Street; New England Review; Kenyon Review; Translation Review; Honest Ulsterman; Massachusetts Review; American Poetry Review. Honours: Fulbright Award for Translation, 1984; Hungarian PEN Memorial Medal, 1986. Memberships: Poetry Society of America; PEN American Centre; American Literary Translators Association. Address: Box 237, Hamilton, NY 13346, USA.

BERLUSCONI Silvio, b. 1936, Milan, Italy. Politician; Businessman. Education: University of Milan. Appointments: Owner, building and property development company, 1962-; Business interests include: Fininvest; Milan 2 Housing project, 1969; Canale 5 Network, 1980-; Owner, Italia 1 TV network, 1983; Owner, Rete 4 TV network, 1984; Stakeholder, La Cinq commercial TV network, 1985; Stakeholder, Chain, Cinema 5; Owner, Estudios Roma, 1986; Owner, Milan AC Football Club, 1986; Owner, La Standa department store, 1988; Chairman, Arnoldo Mondadori Editore SpA, 1990, half-share, 1991; Founder, President, Forza Italia political movement, 1993-; Full time political career, 1994-; Prime Minister of Italy, 1994, 2001-; MEP, 1999; Minister of Foreign Affairs, 2002; Stood trial on corruption charges. Address: Office of the Prime Minister, Palazzo Chigi Piazza Colonna 370, 00187 Rome, Italy.

BERMAN Isaac b. 1913, Russia, Israeli Citizen 1921. Barrister-at-Law; Politician. Education: Teachers Training College, Jerusalem; University College, London; Inner Temple, London. Appointments: Served with British Army, WWII, 1943-45; Manager, Willis Overland & Kaizer Assembly Plant, Haifa, Israel, 1950-54; Private Law Practice, Tel-Aviv, 1954-; Served with IDF with rank of Major; Speaker of the Knessett, Israel, 1980-81; Minister of Energy and Infrastructure, Israel, 1981-82. Publications: Articles in Jerusalem Post, Haaretz, Maariv, Yediot Ahronot and periodicals. Address: PO Box 32351, Tel-Aviv 61322, Israel.

BERMAN Lev S, b. 18 September 1926, Elensky, Orlovsky Region, Russia. Physicist. Education: Engineer-Researcher, Leningrad Polytechnic Institute, Department of Radiophysics, Leningrad, 1949; Candidate of Science, Institute of Communications, Leningrad, 1959; DSc, Physics and Mathematics,

A F Ioffe Physicotechnical Institute, Leningrad, 1983. Appointments: Engineer in Industry, Electrosyla Factory, Leningrad, 1949-55; Junior Research Worker, Semiconductor Institute, Academy of Science, Leningrad, 1955-59; Senior Research Worker, Head of Research Group, Semiconductor Institute, Academy of Science (after amalgamation A F Ioffe Physicotechnical Institute), 1959-. Publications include: (in Russian) Capacitance Spectroscopy of Deep Level Centers in Semiconductors (Co-author), 1981; (in English) Purity Control of Semiconductors by the Method of Capacitance Transient Spectroscopy, 1995; Over 100 articles on physics of semiconductors. Honours: Prize-winner, Council of Ministers of Soviet Union, 1990; Who's Who in the World, 1997. Membership: New York Academy of Science, 1995. Address: A F Ioffe Physicotechnical Institute, Polytechnicheskaya Str 26, 194021, St Petersburg, Russia.

BERMAN Madeline Carol, b. 10 April 1941, New Brunswick, New Jersey, USA. Educator; Professor. m. Charles Berman, 2 sons. Education: Bachelor's Degree in Education, Cedar Crest College, Pennsylvania, 1963; Master of Arts, Kean University, New Jersey, 1974; Doctor of Education, Rutgers University, New Jersey, 1983. Appointments: Supplemental Instructor for Children with Learning Disabilities, Edison, New Jersey, 1973-77; Learning Disabilities Teacher-Consultant, Bridgewater Schools, New Jersey 1977-84; Director of Student Personnel Services, Clarksburg, New Jersey, 1984-86; Department Chair of Secondary Special Education, East Brunswick Schools, New Jersey, 1986-88; Director of Field and Laboratory Services, Rutgers University, New Jersey, 1988-97; Reading Consultant, Perth Amboy Public Schools, New Jersey, 1997-99; Assistant Professor, Marymount College, Tarrytown, New York, 1999-2002. Publications: The Autistic Child, 1979; Educational and Affective Results of Divorce on Children, 1983; Connections, 1999. Honours: Magna Cum Laude, Kean University 1974; Research Grant, 1983, Merit Award, 1991 and 1994, Rutgers University; Listed in several biographical publications. Memberships: International Reading Association; American Association of Colleges for Teacher Education; Phi Delta Kappa, National Honours Society for Educators; Association for Supervision and Curriculum Development; American Association for University Professors. Address: 5 Calvert Avenue West, Edison, New Jersey 08820, USA.

BERN Murray Morris, b. 26 February 1944, Montgomery, Alabama, USA. Physician. m. Nancy Frazee Bern, 1 son. Education: BA, Vanderbilt University, Nashville, Tennessee, 1966; MD, Tulane University, New Orleans, Louisiana, 1970; Medical Intern, 1970-71, Junior Assistant Resident, Medicine, 1970-72, New England Deaconess Hospital, Boston, Massachusetts; Senior Assistant Resident, Medicine, Boston City Hospital, Harvard Medical Service, Boston, Massachusetts, 1972-73; Fellowship, Haematology and Oncology, New England Deaconess Hospital and Center for Blood Research, 1973-75. Appointments include: Hospital appointments: Senior Staff, Department of Medicine, 1975-96, Section Chief Haematology, 1978-86, New England Deaconess Hospital, 1975-93; Courtesy Staff, St Luke's Hospital, New Bedford, Massachusetts, 1978-2001; Senior Staff, Department of Medicine, 1986-, Section Chief, Haematology/Oncology, 1999-, New England Baptist Hospital, Boston, Massachusetts; Director of Haematology, The Cancer Center of Boston, 1986-; Active Staff, Metro West Hospital, Framingham, Massachusetts, 1994-; Courtesy Staff, Beth Israel Deaconess Medical Center, Boston, Massachusetts, 1993-; Academic appointments: Assistant Clinical Professor of Medicine, Harvard Medical School, Boston, Massachusetts, 1978-82; Assistant Professor of Medicine, New England Deaconess Hospital Harvard Medical School, 1982-94; Clinical Instructor in Medicine, Harvard Medical School, 1999-.

Publications: 66 articles in medical journals as author and co-author include: Role of infusion therapy, 1994; Paclitaxel, cisplatin and etoposide combination chemotherapy: A comparison of dose intensity in two multifractionated dose schemes, 1998; Very Low Dose Warfarin as Prophylaxis Against Ultrasound Detected Deep Vein Thrombosis Following Primary Hip Replacement, 2002; 16 books monographs and textbooks; 62 abstracts. Honours: Clinical Fellow, 1973-, Junior Faculty Fellow, 1975-78, American Cancer Society; James L Tullis Lectureship Award, 1982-. Memberships include: American Cancer Society; Fellow, American College of Physicians; International Society of Haematology; American Society of Hematology; American Society of Clinical Oncology; Massachusetts Society of Clinical Oncologists. Address: 125 Parker Hill Road, Boston, MA 02120, USA.

BERNARD André, b. 23 November 1939, Carleton, Quebec, Canada. Educator. m. Évelyne Tardy, 1 son, 1 daughter. Education: BA, Collège Jean-de-Brébeuf, Montreal, Canada, 1960; MA, McGill University, Montreal, Canada, 1965; PhD, University of Montreal, 1969; DSE, Institut d'Études Politiques, Grenoble, France, 1970; DSR, Fondation Nationale des Sciences Politiques, France, 1970. Appointments: Officer, Canadian Armed Forces including active service from 1961-63, last appointment: Chief Instructor, Corps École des Officiers Canadiens, contingent de l'Université de Montréal; Professor, Department of Political Science, University of Quebec at Montreal, 1969-2001. Publications: Author: La Politique au Canada et au Québec, 1976; Québec: Élections 1976, 1976; What Does Quebec Want? 1978; Systèmes Parlementaires et Modes de Scrutin, 1984; Politique et Gestion des Finances Publiques: Québec et Canada, 1992; Problèmes Politiques, Canada et Québec, 1993; Les Institutions Politiques au Québec et au Canada, 1995; La Vie Politique au Québec et au Canada, 1996; Co-author or co-editor of eight other books and author of numerous other texts. Honours: Member, The Royal Society of Canada, 1995; Doctorat Honoris Causa, Université Pierre-Mendès-France, Grenoble, 1995. Memberships: President, Société Canadienne de Science Politique, 1977-79; President, Association Québec-France, 1985-88; President, Centre d'Études Canadiennes de Grenoble, 1989-91. Address: 3 Clos Saint Germain, 38700 Corenc, France. E-mail: andre.bernard.corenc@wanadoo.fr

BERNE Stanley, b. 8 June 1923, Port Richmond, Staten Island, New York, USA. Research Professor; Writer. m. Arlene Zekowski, July 1952. Education: BS, Rutgers University, 1947; MA, New York University, 1950; Graduate Fellow, Louisiana State University, Baton Rouge, 1954-59; PhD, Marlborough University, 1990. Appointments: Associate Professor, English, 1960-80, Research Professor, English, 1980-, Eastern New Mexico University, Portales; Host, Co-Producer, TV series, Future Writing Today, KENW-TV, PBS, 1984-85. Publications: A First Book of the Neo-Narrative, 1954; Cardinals and Saints: On the aims and purposes of the arts in our time, 1958; The Dialogues, 1962; The Multiple Modern Gods and Other Stories, 1969; The New Rubaiyat of Stanley Berne (poetry), 1973; Future Language, 1976; The Great American Empire, 1981; Every Person's Little Book of P-L-U-T-O-N-I-U-M (with Arlene Zekowski), 1992; Alphabet Soup: A Dictionary of Ideas, 1993; To Hell with Optimism, 1996; Dictionary of the Avant-Gardes, 1998; Gravity Drag, 1998; The Living Underground, 1999; Swimming to Significance, 1999; Extremely Urgent Messages, 2000; Empire Sweets - or How I Learned to Live and Love in the Greatest Empire on Earth!; Legal Tender - or It's All About Money!; You and Me - or How to Survive in the Greatest Empire on Earth! Contributions to: Anthologies and other publications. Honours: Literary research awards, Eastern New Mexico University, 1966-76. Memberships: PEN; New England Small Press Association; Rio Grande Writers Association; Santa

Fe Writers. Literary Agent: Pamela Tree, Rising Tide Press, PO Box 6136, Santa Fe, New Mexico. Address: Box 4595, Santa Fe, NM 87502, USA.

BERNING Jesper, b. 7 February 1944, Copenhagen. Attorney. m. Karin, 2 sons, 1 daughter. Education: Master of Law, 1966, Doctor of Law, 1974, University of Copenhagen. Appointments: Associate Professor, University of CPH, 1972-75; Founder, the law firm of Berning & Schlüter, now merged into Bech Bruun Dragsted. Publications: Financing of Current Assets (doctoral thesis), 1974; The Law of Financing (textbook), 1977; Numerous articles in legal and financial journals. Honour: Fulbright Scholar. Memberships: IBA; IFA; IFMA; Law Association of Denmark. Address: 6 B-C Valleroedgade, DK-2960, Rungsted Kyst, Denmark.

BERNSTEIN Carl, b. 14 February 1944, Washington, District of Columbia, USA. Journalist; Writer. m. Nora Ephron, 14 April 1976, divorced, 2 sons. Education: University of Maryland, 1961-64. Appointments: Copyboy to Reporter, Washington Star, 1960-65; Reporter, Elizabeth Journal, New Jersey, 1965-66, Washington Post, 1966-76; Washington Bureau Chief, 1979-81, Correspondent, 1981-84, ABC-TV; Correspondent, Contributor, Time magazine, 1990-91; Visiting Professor, New York University, 1992-93; Contributing Editor to Vanity Fair, 1997-; Executive Vice President and Executive Director, Voter.com, -2001. Publications: All the President's Men (with Bob Woodward), 1973; The Final Days (with Bob Woodward), 1976; Loyalties: A Son's Memoir, 1989; His Holiness (with Marco Politi), 1996. Honours: Drew Pearson Prize for Investigative Reporting, 1972; Pulitzer Prize Citation, 1972; Honorary LLD, Boston University, 1975. Address: c/o Janklow and Nesbit Associates, 598 Madison Avenue, New York, NY 10022, USA.

BERNSTEIN Louis, b. 10 August 1954, Cumberland, Maryland, USA. Civil Engineer. Education: BSc, Civil Engineering, Massachusetts Institute of Technology, 1977. Appointments: Inspector, O'Brien-Kreitzberg & Associates Inc, San Francisco 1983-84; Manager, L Bernstein Furniture Co Inc, Cumberland, Maryland, 1988-98; Civil Engineer, Westech Engineering, Cumberland, Maryland, 1991-; Project Engineer, Antietam Design, Hagerstown, Maryland, 2002-. Honours: Award of Merit, City of San Francisco. Memberships: Sierra Club Western Maryland Group; Nature Conservancy; ASCE; Society of American Military Engineers; Globetrotters Club; Phi Mu Delta. Address: 731 Washington Street, Cumberland, MD 21502, USA.

BERRY Chuck (Charles Edward Anderson Berry), b. 18 October 1926, St Louis, USA. Singer; Composer. m. Thermetta Suggs, 1948, 4 children. Appointments: TV Appearances, 1955-. Creative Work: Albums: After School Sessions, 1958; One Dozen Berry's, 1958; New Juke Box Hits, 1960; Chuck Berry, 1960; More Chuck Berry, 1960; On Stage, 1960; You Can Never Tell, 1964; Greatest Hits, 1964; Two Great Guitars, 1964; Chuck Berry in London, 1965; Fresh Berrys, 1965; St Louis to Liverpool, 1966; Golden Hist, 1967; At the Fillmore, 1967; Medley, 1967; In Memphis, 1972; Concerto in B Goods, 1969; Home Again, 1971; The London Sessions, 1972; Golden Decade, 1972; St Louis to Frisco to Memphis, 1972; Let the Good Times Roll, 1973; Golden Decade vol II, 1973, vol V, 1974; Bio, 1973; Back in the USA, 1973; I'm a Rocker, 1975; Chuck Berry 75, 1975; Motovatin, 1976; Rockit, 1979; Chess Masters, 1983; The Chess Box, 1989; Missing Berries, 1990; Rarities, 1990; On the Blues Side, 1993. Films: Go, Johnny Go, Rock, Rock, Rock, 1956; Jazz on a Summer's Day, 1960; Let the Good Times Roll, 1973; Hail! Hail! Rock 'n' Roll, 1987. Publication: Chuck Berry: The

Dictionary of International Biography

Autobiography, 1987. Honours include: Grammy Award for Life Achievement, 1984. Address: Berry Park, 691 Buckner Road, Wentzville, MO 63385, USA.

BERRY Ester Lorée, b. 19 September 1945, Licensed Vocational Nurse; Poet. 1 son, 1 daughter. Education: Associate Degree, Nursing and Art, California State University, 1996. Appointments: Poet, Contributor of Poetry to International Library of Poetry; Author: American Poetry. Honours: Honorary Member, Veterans of America Commanders Club; Bronze Leader Award, 2001; Best Poet of the Year, 1999; Editors Choice Award, 1999, 2000, 2001, 2002, 2003; Bronze Commemorative Medallion, 2002-2003; Silver, International Poet of Merit; Red Wagon Award, Children's Hospital of Los Angeles. Memberships: Children's Hospital of Los Angeles; Disabled American Veterans. Address: 31650 Landau Blvd 22, Cathedral City, CA 92234, USA.

BERRY Halle, b. 14 August 1968, Cleveland, Ohio, USA. Actress; Model. m. (1) David Justice, 1993, divorced 1996, 1 daughter, (2) Eric Benet, 2001. Career: Numerous formal beauty contests in 1980s; TV and Film actress, 1989-; Films: Strictly Business, 1991; Jungle Fever, 1991; The Last Boy Scout, 1991; Boomerang, 1992; Father Hood, 1993; Alex Haley's Queen, 1993; The Program, 1993; The Flintstones, 1994; Losing Isaiah, 1995; The Rich Man's Wife, 1996; Executive Decision, 1996; Race the Sun, 1996; Girl 6, 1996; B.A.P.S, 1997; Why Do Fools Fall in Love, 1998; The Wedding, 1998; Bulworth, 1998; Victims of Fashion, 1999; Ringside, 1999; Introducing Dorothy Dandridge (also producer), 1999; X-Men, 2000; Swordfish, 2001; Monster's Ball, 2001; James Bond: Die Another Day, 2002; X-Men 2, 2003; Gothika, 2003; TV appearances: TV debut in sitcom Living Dolls, 1989; Knots Landing, 1991-92. Honours: Harvard Foundation for Intercultural and Race Relations Award; Golden Globe for Best Actress, Screen Actor's Guild Award, 1999; Academy Award, 2002; NAACP Award for Best Supporting Actress, 2003. Membership: National Breast Cancer Coalition. Address: c/o William Morris Agency, 151 South El Camino Drive, Beverly Hills, LA 90212, USA.

BERTOLAMI Orfeu, b. 3 January 1959, São Paulo, Brazil. Physicist. m. M C Bento, October 1992, 1 daughter. Education: Graduate, Physics, São Paulo University, 1981; MSc, Inst Fís Teórica, São Paulo, 1983; Advanced Degree, Mathematics, University of Cambridge, England, 1984; PhD, Physics, University of Oxford, England, 1987. Appointments: Post-doctoral Positions; Institut für Theoretische Physik; University of Heidelberg, Germany, 1987-89; Instituto de Física and Mat, Lisbon, Portugal, 1989-91; Associate Professor, Departmento Física, Instituto Superior Técnico, Lisbon, 1991-; Scientific Associate, Theory Division, CERN, 1993-95; Istituto Nazionale Fisica Nucleare, Turim, 1994-95; Visiting Scholar, Physics Department, New York University, 1999. Publications: Over 100 Publications; 63 of which in specialised international Physics Journals. Honours: Honorary Mentions in the Essay Contest, Gravity Research Foundation, USA, 1995, 1997, 2001, 2003; Third Prize, 1999; Prémio União Latina (Latin America, Portugal), 2001. Memberships: Sociedade Portuguesa de Física; Sociedade Portuguesa de Astronomia. Address: Instituto Superior Técnico, Dept Física, Av Rovisco Pais, 1049-001, Lisboa, Portugal. E-mail: orfeu@cosmos.ist.utl.pt Website: http@///alfa.ist.utl.pt/~orfeu/homeorfeu.html

BERTOLUCCI Bernardo, b. 16 March 1940, Parma. Film Director. m. Clare Peploe, 1978. Creative Works: Director: La Commare Secca, 1962; Prima della Rivoluzione, 1964; Il Fico Infruttuoso in Vangelo 70, 1968; Partner, 1970; La Strategia del Ragno, 1970; Il Conformista, 1970; Last Tango in Paris, 1972; 1900, 1975; La Luna, 1979; Tragedy of a Ridiculous Man, 1981;

The Last Emperor, 1986; The Sheltering Sky, 1989; Little Buddha, 1993; Stealing Beauty, 1995; I Dance Alone, 1996; Besieged, 1998. Publications: In cerca del mistero (poems), 1962; Paradiso e inferno (poems), 1999. Honours: Viareggio Prize, 1962; European Film Award, 1988. Address: c/o Jeff Berg, ICM, 8942 Wilshire Boulevard, Beverly Hills, CA 90211, USA.

BESSON Luc, b. 18 March 1959, Paris, France. Film Director. 1 daughter. Appointments: Assistant, Films in Hollywood and Paris; 1st Assistant for several advertising films. Creative Works: Films directed and produced: Le Dernier Combat, 1982; Subway, 1984; The Big Blue, 1988; Nikita, 1990; Atlantis, 1991; The Professional, 1994; Leon, 1994; The Fifth Element, 1996; Joan of Arc, 1999; The Messenger, 1999; The Dancer, 2000; Exit, 2000; Yamakasi, 2001; Baiser mortel du dragon, 2001; Le Transporteur, 2002; Taxi 3, 2003; Tristan, 2003; Cheeky, 2003; Vice & Versa, 2003; Crimson Rivers 2: Angels of the Apocalypse, 2004. Address: c/o Leeloo Productions, 53 rue Boissée, 91540 Mennecy, France. E-mail: lucbesson@luc-besson.com

BEST George, b. 22 May 1946. Footballer. m. (1) Angela Macdonald Janes, 1978, 1 son, (2) Alexandra Jane Pursey, 1995. Appointments: Joined Manchester United, 1963; 381 League Appearances (137 goals); 46 Football Association Cup Competition appearances (21 goals); 25 League Cup Competition appearances (9 goals); 34 European Competition Appearances (11 goals); Represented Northern Ireland 37 times; Sports Commentator, Sky TV. Honours: Irish Footballer of the Year, 1967; European Footballer of the Year, 1968; British Footballer of the Year, 1969, 1971; Sky TV Greatest Sportsman Award, 1995; Total Sport Magazine Greatest Sportsman of All Time; BBC Lifetime Achievement Award, 2002. Address: c/o British Sky Broadcasting Ltd, Grant Way, Middlesex TW7 5QD, England.

BEST Gerald, b. 1 February 1952, Garrett, Indiana, USA. Consultant. m. Susan S Best, 2 daughters. Education: Associate in Bible Studies, Grace Bible College, 1994; Bachelor of Arts, Christian Counselling, Calvary Theological Seminary, 2001. Appointments: Professional Clinical Member, National Christian Counsellors Association; Licensed Pastoral Counsellor and Minister, 2001; Licensed Investment Consultant, 1978, 2003. Publications: Christian Music Songwriter; Healthcare Quality; Master Your Money; Million Dollar Round Table; Copyrights; Patents; Trademarks; Music; Insurance; Sports; Production. Honours: Corporate Quality Award, 1988; NAHN Award, 1990; Joshua Award, Volunteer Award, 1998; Listed in Who's Who publications and biographical dictionaries. Memberships: YMCA; Business Music Inc; National Christian Counselling Association; Tennis Club; Basketball Club; Music Club. Address: 5667 Creekwood Drive, Sarasota, FL 34233, USA.

BEST Melvyn Edward, b. 8 March 1941, Victoria, British Columbia, Canada. Geophysicist. m. Virginia Marie Best, 1 son, 1 daughter. Education: BSc (Honours), Mathematics and Physics, 1965, MSc, Physics, Nuclear Physics, 1966, University of British Columbia, Vancouver, Canada; PhD, Theoretical Physics, Massachusetts Institute of Technology, Cambridge, USA, 1970; Advanced Structural Geology, Shell Oil Training Center, Houston, 1976; Digital Signal Processing, MIT Continuing Education Course, 1977; Shell Management Course, Ontario, 1981. Appointments include: Geophysicist, Minerals Department, 1972-78, Staff Geophysicist, Special Projects Group, 1977-78, Shell Canada; Royal Dutch Shell Exploration and Production Laboratory, The Hague, the Netherlands, 1978-80; Division Geophysicist, 1980-82; Manager, Petroleum Engineering Research, Shell, Canada, 1982-85; Sub-division Head, Basin Analysis Subdivision, Atlantic Geoscience Centre, 1986-90; Director, Pacific Geoscience Centre, Member, Management Team, Geological Survey of

Canada, 1990-94; Senior Research Scientist, 1994-97; Consulting Geophysicist on resource and environmental problems, Bemex Consulting International, Victoria, British Columbia, Canada, 1997-; Adjunct Professor, University of Calgary, 1998-; Adjunct Professor, University of Victoria, 1998-; Editor, Journal of Environmental and Engineering Geophysics, 1998-2000. Honour: Meritorious Service Award, Canadian Society of Exploration Geophysicists, 1996; Vice President, Environmental and Engineering Geophysics Society, 2003-; Listed in numerous international biographical dictionaries. Memberships: Society of Exploration Geophysicists, 1973-; Canadian Society of Exploration Geophysicists, 1982-; Association of Professional Engineers, Geologists and Geophysicists of Alberta, 1983-; Environmental and Engineering Geophysical Society, 1995; Professional Engineers and GeoScientists of British Columbia, 2000-; Vice President, Environmental and Engineering Geophysical Society, 2003-. Address: 5288 Cordova Bay Road, Victoria BC, V8Y 2L4, Canada.

BETHE Hans Albrecht, b. 2 July 1906, Strasbourg, Germany (now France) (US Citizen). Physicist; Astronomer. Education: University of Frankfurt; PhD, University of Munich, 1928. Appointments: Instructor, Physics, University of Frankfurt, University of Stuttgart, 1928-29; Lecturer, Universities of Munich and Tübingen, 1930-33; Moved to Britain at advent of World War II, 1933; University of Manchester, 1933-34; Assistant Professor, 1935, Professor, 1937-75; John Wendell Anderson Professor of Physics, Cornell University; Chief, Theoretical Physics Division, Los Alamos Science Laboratory, New Mexico, USA; Consultant, Los Alamos, 1947-. Honours: Morrison Prize, New York Academy of Sciences, 1938, 1940; American Medal of Merit, 1946; Draper Medal, National Academy of Sciences, 1948; Planck Medal, 1955, 1961; Nobel Prize for Physics, 1967; Fermi Award; National Medal of Science, 1976. Memberships: Fellow, American Physical Society, President, 1954; Foreign Member, Royal Society, 1957. Address: Newman Laboratory, Cornell University, Ithaca, NY 14853, USA.

BETHELL David Percival, b. 7 December 1923, Bath, England. Designer; Educator. m. Margaret Elizabeth, 1 son, 1 daughter. Education: Gloucester College of Art, 1946-48; West of England College of Art, and University of Bristol, 1948-51. Appointments: Lecturer, Stafford College of Art, 1951-56; Vice-Principal, 1956-65, Principal, 1965-69, Coventry College of Art, 1965-69; Deputy Director, 1969-73, 1973-87, Director, Leicester Polytechnic. Publications: Several books, including A Case of Sorts, 1992, 2001; An Industrious People, 1992; 120 Woodcuts and the Bard, 1994; History of the Royal West of England Academy, 2001; Numerous articles and papers contributed to specialist journals and conferences. Honours: Awarded Freedom of the City of London, 1976; Elected LLD, University of Leicester, 1982; Appointed CBE (Commander of the British Empire), 1983; D Litt, Loughborough University of Technology, 1985; Asst. Worshipful Company of Framework Knitters Livery, 1996; D Ed, University of the West of England, 1999. Memberships: Numerous professional affiliations, including Associate Member, Royal West of England Academy,1954-; Senior Vice-President, 1997; Dr Des University of Bournemouth, 2001; Elected Fellow, Royal Society of Arts, 1967-; Honorary Fellow, Institute of Technical Publications and Publicity, 1966-; Elected Fellow, Chartered Society of Designers, 1967-. Address: 48 Holmfield Road, Stoneygate, Leicester, LE2 1SA.

BETTA Pier Giacomo, b. 24 December 1949, Alessandria, Italy. Medical Doctor. m. Longo Patricia, 1 daughter. Education: Degree, Medicine, 1975; Diploma, Pathology, 1979; Diploma, Oncology, 1982; Diploma, Experimental Pathology, 1986. Appointments:

Chief, Pathology Unit, S Spirito Hospital, Italy, 1989-97; Chief, Pathology Unit, Azienda Ospedaliera Nazionale, Alessandria, 1997-. Honours: Lepetit prize winner, 1975. Memberships: New York Academy of Sciences; American Society of Clinical Oncology; European Society of Mastology; Italian Society of Anatomic Pathology and Cytopathology; Member, Asbestos Commission, established by The Health Ministry, 1996-; President, Alessandria Section, Italian League Against Cancer, 1998-; Co-ordinator, National Commission Environmental Carcinogenesis, 2002-. Address: Pathology Unit Department of Oncology, Azienda Ospedaliera Nazionale, Via Venezia 18,15100 Alessandria, Italy.

BETTINSON Brenda, b. 17 August 1929, King's Lynn, Norfolk, England. Artist; Educator. Education: National Diploma in Design, London, 1950; Eleve Titulaire de L'Ecole Pratique des Hautes Etudes, Sorbonne University, Paris, 1952-. Appointments: Art Editor, WRVR-FM, New York, New York; Professor of Art, Pace University, New York, New York, 1963-90; Chairman, Department of Art and Design, Pace University, 1979-85; Professor Emerita, 1989. Publications: Numerous exhibits in USA and Europe; Work in public collections, USA; Work in private collections in UK, France, Holland, Israel, USA and Canada; One person exhibition, Ogunquit Museum of American Art, 2002. Honour: Gold Medal, National Arts Club, New York, USA, 1966. Membership: Maine Union of Visual Artists; Represented by Mathias Fine Art, Trevett, ME 04571. Address: 10 Mathias Drive, Trevett, ME 04571, USA.

BETTS Barbara Stoke, b. 19 April 1924, Arlington, Massachusetts, USA. Artist; Educator. m. James William Betts, 1 daughter, deceased. Education: BA, Mount Holyoke College, 1946; MA, Columbia University, 1948; Certified Teacher, New York, California, Hawaii; Art Teacher, Walton, New York Union Schools, 1947-48; Presidio Hill School, San Francisco, 1949-51; Free-lance Artist, San Francisco, 1951; Art Teacher, Honolulu, Academy of Arts, summer 1952, 1959, 1963, 1985, spring, 1961, 1964; Librarian, Art Room Aide, Library of Hawaii, Honolulu, 1959; Art Teacher, Hanahauoli School, Honolulu, 1961-62; Hawaii State Department Education, Honolulu , 1958-58, 1964-84; Owner, Ho'olaule'a Designs, Honolulu, 1973-; Art Editor, Scrapbook Press, 2002-; Portfolio Consultants of Hawaii, 1990-; Staff Artist: The Arcadian Newsletter, 2000-; Illustrator: Cathedral Cooks, 1964; In Due Season, 1986; From Nowhere To Somewhere On a Round Trip Ticket, 2003; Exhibited in Hawaii Pavilion Expo '90, Osaka, Japan; State Foundation Culture and Arts; Group Shows since 1964; One Woman Shows, 1991, 1996, 1999; Represented in Arts of Paradise Gallery, Waikiki, 1990-2001; Hale Ku'ai, a Hawaiian Co-operative, 1998-2001; Travelling Exhibitions include: Pacific Prints, 1991; Printmaking East/West, 1993-95; Hawaii Wisconsin Watercolor Show, 1993-94. Memberships: Hawaiian Watercolor Society, Newsletter Editor, 1986-90; National League of American Pen Women, Art Chairman, 1990-92, Secretary, 1992-94, 2000-02, National Miniature Art Shows, 1991, 1992, 1993, 1995; Honolulu Printmakers, Director, 1986, 1987; Association of Hawaiian Artists; Scholarship Aid Programs, Mount Holyoke College. Address: 1434 Punahou St, Apt 1028, Honolulu, HI 96822-4740, USA. E-mail: kimorail@aol.com

BEVEGE David Ian, b. 29 March 1939, Brisbane, Australia. Forester. Divorced. 2 sons, 1 daughter. Education: Diploma Forestry (Australian Forestry School), 1962; BSc Forestry, Queensland, 1962; BSc Forestry (1st Class Honours), Queensland, 1965; PhD, UNE, 1972. Appointments: Research Forester, Queensland Department of Forestry, 1962-82; Post-doctoral Scientist, CSIRO Division of Soils, 1971-72; Chief, Wood Technology Forest Research Division New South Wales Forestry Commission, 1982-86; Assistant Director General, Australian

Dictionary of International Biography

International Development Assistance Bureau, 1986-91; Principal Adviser, Australian Centre for International Agricultural Research, 1991-2002; Retired, 2002. Publications: Over 100 papers and reports between 1963-2002, in the fields of forest research, mining rehabilitation, plant physiology, research management and planning, international development assistance and training; 30 in international refereed journals or publications. Honours: Schlich Memorial Medal AFS, 1961; Hedges Prize, IFA, 1965; Junior Research Fellowship University of New England, 1967-70; Nuffield Foundation, 1971; Rural Credits Development Fund Grant, Reserve Bank, 1978-81, 1987-88; IUFRO Scientific Achievement Award, 1981. Memberships: Institute of Foresters of Australia (MIFA); Associate, Institute of Wood Science (AIWSC); Editorial Committee, Australian Forestry (journal). Address: 2 Carramar Drive, Lillipilli, NSW 2536, Australia.

BEX Brian William Louis, b. 5 February 1943, Chicago, Illinois, USA. Educator. m. Claudia Thorn, 3 sons. Education: Illinois Wesleyan University; Indiana University; LLB, 1965; Juris Doctor, 1967, Blackstone School of Law. Appointments: Founder American Communications Network (International Educational Organization) which incorporates the National Freedom Study Center and the Athenaeum and video tape library for use within the Social Studies curriculum of secondary schools and The Brian Bex Report, 1966-; Founder the Remnant Trust Inc (loans for educational use original works on individual liberty and human dignity), 1998; Publisher, The American Record and then The Remnant Review. Publications: Numerous articles; 12 books include: The Decline and Fall of the American Republic, 1972; The Hidden Hand, 1975; Commonweal, 1977; United States Aborted, 1986; The Vanishing Dinosaur, 1989; Out of Bounds, 1994; Buckwheat & The Giant, 2002; Numerous speaking engagements and seminars each year. Honours: Listed in Who's Who publications and biographical dictionaries. Memberships: American Communications Network; The Remnant Trust. Address: American Communications Network, 100N Woodpecker Road, Hagerstown, IN 47346, USA. Website: www.theremnanttrust.com

BEYER Rolf, b. 27 May 1947, Wiesmoor, Ostfriesland, Germany. Writer. m. Marie-Martine Fillâtre. Education: Johannes Gutenberg University, Mainz, Germany; University of Heidelberg, Germany, 1968-72. Appointments: Teacher, Primary and Secondary Schools for the Handicapped, Mannheim, Germany, 1972-80; Lecturer, Internationales Studienzentrum, University of Heidelberg; Staff Member, Weslyan University, Massachusetts, USA, 1982; Staff Member, Polytechnic of North London, England, 1983; Staff Member, Miami University, Ohio, USA, 1995; Guest Lecturer, International Education Centre, Shah Alam, Malaysia, 2002-. Publications: Author: Ideology and Illusions, 1981; Hegel as political thinker, 1983; The unbound Prometheus, 1985; Germany today. Politics-Economics-Society, 1986; The Queen of Sheba, 1987; Female mystics in Middle Ages, 1989; Visions and Ecstasies, 1993; King Solomon, 1993; Audiobooks: Ruins of Conscience – Hans Henny Jahnn, 1984; King Solomon, 1990; The dream of golden ages, 1990; The Mystery of Beauty, 1991; French Philosophers, 1992; Ancient Mystery Cults, 1993; Poems in World Literature, 1994; Violence, 1995; Marguerite Duras, 1995; Taboos – do we need them? 1996; Abbé Pierre, 1996; Marguerite Yourcenar, 1997; Roland Barthes, 1997; Culture of Native people, 1997; The Goddesses in us, 1998; Myths-stories about our origin, 1999; The Mystery of Religion, 1999; History of Betrayal, 2000; The transcendent Voice, 2000; Philosophy today, 2001; Philosophy of History, 2002; Waiting, 2002; Trust in Reason – Immanuel Kant, 2004. Honours: Included in Kuerschner's Book Calendar, 2003, 2004; Listed in Who's Who publications and biographical dictionaries. Address: Friedrich-Ebert-Strasse 25, D-69207 Sandhausen, Germany. E-mail: rolf.beyer@urz.uni-heidelberg.de

BHARGAVA Krishnakant, b. 29 April 1937, Mumbai, India. Otolaryngologist. m. Usha, 1 son, 1 daughter. Education: MBBS, University of Bombay, 1959; MS (ENT) University of Bombay, 1963; DORL, College of Physicians and Surgeons, Bombay, 1961. Appointments: Head and Honorary Professor Emeritus, Otolaryngology Department; LTM Medical College and LTMG Hospital, Mumbai; Honorary Otolaryngologist, Smt BCJ General Hospital, Mumbai. Publications: More than 80 publications in national and international Journals; Author of "A Short Textbook of ENT Diseases". Honours: Many awards in medical career; Rotary International District 3140; Trophy for Community Service – 3 times; PolioPlus Immunization Trophy – 7 times. Memberships include: President, The Association of Otolaryngologists of India, 1998, Golden Jubilee Year; Rotary Club of Bombay West, 1986; Chairman, Rotary District PolioPlus Committee, 1990-1997; Consultant, Rotary International PolioPlus Committee, USA, 1995-96; Advisor, Rotary District PolioPlus Committee, 1997-2005. Address: Gopal Bhuvan, Tagore Road, Santacruz (W), Mumbai 400 054, India. Website: www.entcure.com

BHARGAVA Pushpa Mittra, b. 22 February 1928, Rajasthan, India. Scientist; Writer; Consultant. m. Edith, 11 August 1958, 1 son, 1 daughter. Education: BSc, 1944; MSc, 1946; PhD, 1949. Appointments: Lecturer, Chemistry, Lucknow University; Research Fellow, National Institute of Sciences; Project Associate, McArdle Memorial Laboratory for Cancer Research, University of Wisconsin, USA; Special Wellcome Research Fellow, National Institute of Medical Research, London, UK, 1949-58; Appointed Scientist B, Regional Research Laboratory, Hyderabad, India, 1958; Promoted to Scientist C, E and F; Scientist in Charge, Director, CCMB, Hyderabad, 1977-1990; CSIR Distinguished Fellow, 1990-93; Director, Anveshna Consultants, Hyderabad, 1993-. Publications: Over 125 major science publications; Nearly 300 articles; 4 books. Honours: Over 70 major national and international honours and awards; Padma Bhushan from the President of India; Chevalier de la Legion d'Honneur; Honorary DSc; National Citizen Award; Visiting Professorship, College de France; Life Fellow, Clare Hall, Cambridge; Wattumal Memorial Prize for Biochemistry; FICCI Award, Medical Sciences; Ranbaxy Award for Medical Sciences; SICO Award for Biotechnology; Goyal Prize; R D Birla Award for Medical Sciences. Memberships: President or Past President: Society of Biological Chemicals of India; Indian Academy of Social Sciences; Association for Promotion of DNA Fingerprinting and Other DNA Technologies; Society for Science Values; 125 major national and international standing committees. Address: H. No. 12-5-27 Vijayapuri, Tarnaka, Hyderabad 500 017, India. E-mail: chanchak@nettlinx.com

BHAT Niranjan Chidanand, b. 12 February 1972, Sangli, MS, India. Accredited Industrial and Management Consultant; Chartered, Consulting and Professional Engineer; Licensed Insurance Surveyor and Loss Assessor; Licensed Electrical Supervisor (PWD); Competent Person (SMPV); Valuer (Plant and Machinery). Education: Diploma in Welding Technology, 1989; Qualified Electrical Engineer, AMIE (I), 1991; BEng, Mechanical, 1993; Qualified Welding Engineer, AMIIW, 1995; Qualified Industrial Engineer, AMIIE, 1997; PhD, Welding Technology, USA, 1998; Other Diplomas in CSSA, Business Management (FM&PM), TQM & ISO-9000, EMS and ISO-14000, Industrial Safety, QA and QS-9000, Computer Software CMM; Certifications as CQE, B and PV Inspector, NDE Level II Examiner in RT/MT/UT/PT/VT/LT/ET, ISNT and WRI-CWI, CWT-BCI, Internationally Registered Welding Technology Specialist (IRTS) Level-6; Specialisation: Contracts, Engg/Maintenance and Marine-Cargo (pre-shipment) Inspections, Environmental, Export, Industrial, Maintenance, Project, Quality & Safety Management, and Insurance Surveys having worked on 101 special projects and completed over 3,000 inspections/surveys; Empanelments: As Consultant/Expert for BESO; (DACON) AFDB; (DACON/DG MARKET) World Bank; (DICON) ADB; (DINCON) EXIM Bank India; ICLCL; IFC; ITS; MCCIA; ROE, (ITC/WTO) UNCTAD/ UNDP/UNEP/UNIDO/UNOPS/UNV; US-TDA. Appointments: Associate Consultant in Industrial and Management Consultancy, R G Joshi and Associates, Pune, 2001-04; Executive Engineer (Insp), Industrial Division, Société Générale de Surveillance (SGS) India Ltd, Pune Branch, 1996-2001; Inspection Engineer, Boilers and Pressure Vessels Inspection Wing, SEA Services (P) Pvt Ltd, Pune, 1995-96; QA Incharge, DD Enterprises (Pressure Vessel Fabrication Shop), Pune, 1994-95; Sandwich Trainee Engineer, Manufacturing Division (Plant 8, RF Boilers), Thermax Ltd, Pune, 1993. Publications: 8 Technical Papers on Welding Technology; Fabrication and Construction of Coded Boilers; Project Report on Tube-Bending Machine; Technical Thesis on Welding Technology; Management Course on TQM and ISO-9000; Introduction to ASME Boiler and Pressure Vessel Codes; Project Report on Boiler Fabrication and Erection; General Inspection, Welding and NDT Questionnaire; Pipes and Conduits; Sampling Inspection Procedure; Plant Standardisation; Introduction, Inspection Procedure and Design Checklist of Boilers and Pressure Vessels; Energy Saving and Conservation Questionnaire; Management Thoughts and Leadership Skills; Specification for Insulation and Cladding; Procedure for Packaging; Millennial Maitreya Project; Non-Life General Insurance; Model Client – Consultant Contract; Techno-Economic Feasibility Studies; Perfect Management System; Distance Education Mode (Self-Directed or Independent Learning); Management Mantras for Service Industry; Progressive Thinking; Law of Twelve Divisions for Personal Financing; Corporate Games and Boardroom Blues. Honours: Certificate of Merit in Welding Technology, 1989; Abhiyantriki Visharad, 1993; Certificate of Proficiency in Business Management, 1994; Best Surveyor, 1997; Outstanding Personalities, 1998; Master of Success; Man of the Year, 1999; Best Citizen of India, 2000; Ivory Eagle, 2001. Memberships: Fellow, Management Studies Promotion Institute; United Writers Association of India; Institute of Chartered Managers; Electrochemical Society of India; Indian Society of Mechanical Engineers; Indian Institute of Plant Engineers; Indian Society of Business Management; Indian Society of Engineers and Technicians; Indian Institute of Welding; Council Member, Indian Welding Society; Regional Ambassador of International Technology Institute; Ordinary member, 12 national and international professional bodies. Address: #4, Akash Apts, Karve Road, Near Maruti Mandir, Kothrud, Pune 411038, MS, India. E-mail: niranjan_bhat@hotmail.com

BHATTACHARYA Prabir Chandra, b. Shillong, India. Economist; Educator. m. Chitra Acharya. Education: MA, University of Allahabad, India; MSc Econ, London School of Economics,1978; PhD, London School of Economics. Appointments: Tutor, Economics, University College London, 1985-87; Lecturer, Economics, University of Keele, 1988-90; Honorary Senior Research Fellow, University College London, 1997; Professor of Economics, Yokohama National University, Japan, 2001; Senior Lecturer in Economics, Herriot-Watt University, Edinburgh, 1990-. Publications: Rural-urban migration in economic development, 1993; A multi-sector model of LDC, 1994; Migration, employment and development: a three-sector analysis, 1998; Socio-economic determinants of early childhood mortality: a study of three Indian states, 1999; Small firms and unemployment in a two-sector model, 1999; Aspects of banking sector reforms in India, 2001; Rural-to-urban migration in LDCs: a test of two rival models, 2002; Urbanisation in developing countries, 2002. Memberships: Royal Economic Society; Scottish Economic Society; Life Member, Indian Economic Association.

Address: Department of Economics, School of Management, Heriot-Watt University, Riccarton, Edinburgh EH14 4AS, Scotland. E-mail: p.c.bhattacharya@hw.ac.uk

BHATTACHARYYA Mukti Nath, b. 22 January 1935, India. Physician. m. Brenda, 2 sons. Education: MBBS, University of Calcutta, India; Diploma in Obstetrics and Gynaecology; MRCOG; FRCOG. Appointments: Various positions in several hospitals; Consultant Physician, Genito-Urinary Medicine, Sheffield Royal Infirmary, England, 1973; Lecturer, Medicine, University of Sheffield, 1973; Consultant Physician, Genito-Urinary Medicine, Manchester Royal Infirmary, 1979-97; Concurrently, Honorary Clinical Lecturer, Genito-Urinary Medicine, University of Manchester; Retired 1997; Governor, William Hulme Grammar School; Member of the Court of the University of Manchester. Publications: Many scientific papers in professional journals. Honours: Elected Fellow, British Medical Association, 2001; Award, Serving Brother of the Order of St John, 2001; Deputy Lieutenant of the County of Greater Manchester, 2003. Memberships: Personnel Committee, University of Manchester; University Honorary and Ex Officio Degrees Committee. Chairman, Manchester Division of the British Medical Association, 1987-90, 1998-2001; Former Member, National Organisation Committee, British Medical Association, Former Chairman, North West Regional Council, British Medical Association; Council Member, Order of St John, Greater Manchester; Former Chairman, St John Ambulance, Oldham Working Group Committee; Manchester Rotary Club, President, 1993-94; Council Member, Manchester Literary and Philosophical Society. Address: 56 Green Pastures, Stockport, Cheshire SK4 3RA, England. E-mail: mukti.n.bhattacharyya@man.ac.uk

BHUMIBOL ADULYADEJ (King of Thailand), b. 5 December 1927, Cambridge, USA. Education: Bangkok, Lausanne, Switzerland. m. Queen Sirikit, 28 April 1950, 1 son, 3 daughters. Address: Chitralada Villa, Bangkok, Thailand.

BIAGI Paolo, b. 30 January 1948. Brescia, Northern Italy. Archaeologist. Education: Dott, Milan University, 1972; PhD, London University, Prehistoric Archaeology, 1981. Appointments: University Researcher, Genoa University, 1980-88; Associate Professor of Palaeoethnology, 1983-2003, Full Professor of Palaeoethnology, 2002-, Ca'Foscari, University of Venice. Publications: Over 270 articles on prehistoric archaeology printed in European, USA and Pakistani journals. Honour: Gold Medal, Shah Abdul Latif University, Khairpur, Pakistan, 1999; Gold Medal, Brescia Municipality, Italy, 2002. Memberships: Prehistoric Society; Lithic Studies Society; Current Anthropology; Society for Arabian Studies; Ateneo di Scienze di Brescia. Address: Via Solferino 11, I-25122 Brescia, Italy.

BIALY Franciszek Jósef, b. 4 September 1931, Chorzów, Upper Silesia. Historian; Researcher. m. Zofia Kulik, 2 daughters. Education: Student, 1951-55, MA, 1955, PhD, 1961, University of Wroclaw, Poland. Appointments: Assistant, 1955-60, Research Associate, 1961-69, Polish Academy of Sciences; Research Associate, 1969-85, Habilitation, 1985, Professor, 1992-, University of Wroclaw, Poland. Publications: German Voluntary Military Units on the Territory of Silesia 1918-23, 1976; A Moeller van den Bruck and the Conservative Revolution, 1980; The National Socialist Movement in Silesian Provinces, 1987; Co-author of 14 monographs of Silesian towns; Contributor of articles to: Encyclopaedia of Wroclaw; Encyclopaedia of Silesian Uprisings; Encyclopaedia of Economic History of Poland up to the year 1845. Honours: Award of the Minister of Science Education and Technology; Medal of Merit for the Lower Silesia,

1975; Golden Cross of Merit, 1990; Listed in Who's Who publications and biographical dictionaries. Address: 36/28 Bobrza Street, 54-220 Wroclaw, Poland. E-mail: f.lub@wp.pl

BIART Philippe Marie Georges Jules Marcel Roger, b. 20 January 1944, Ixelles, Brussels, Belgium. Managing Director. m. Yolande Kelder, 2 sons, 1 daughter. Education: BEcon (Honours); Diploma, Business Management (Honours), 1966. Appointments: Senior Account Executive, Lintas SSC and B, Brussels and Stockholm, 1968-72; Marketing Manager, H J Heinz, Belgium, 1972-74; Henkel Belgium, 1974-76; Director, John Warren SA-NV Wavre, 1975-86; President, Managing Director, Smith and Nephew, SA-NV Belgium, 1977-, President, Managing Director, BSN Medical SA-NV Belgium, 2001-, BV The Netherlands, 1981-86, Utd, Belgium, 1988-91; President and Chief Executive Officer, UNAMEC, Belgium, 1989-; Judge in Commercial Matters, Ministry of Justice, Belgium, 1990-; President and Chief Executive Officer, EDIHealth, Belgium, 1994-; Director, Smith and Nephew, Spain, 1994-2003; Director, VAL-I-PAC, Belgium, 1997-2003; Director, Treasurer and President, Commission, CCIB, Brussels, 1998-; Member Ethical Committee, FarmaPlus (Association of the Pharmaceutical Industry), 1998-; Founding Member of BENSC (Belgian Enterprise Network for Social Cohesion), 1998-; Member, SME Coordination Committee (Federation of Belgium Companies); Director, Tape Services, SA-NV, Belgium, 2000; Director, Union of Brussels Enterprises, 2003-. Publication: Cigarette pack design patent, Sweden, 1971. Honours: Chevalier Order of Crown (Belgium), 1976; Chevalier Order of Leopold, 1981; Officer Order of Crown, 1986; Honorary Commanding Officer, Belgian Air Force, 1999. Memberships: CCIB (Brussels Chamber of Commerce); UNAMEC (Trade Association, Medical and Healthcare Industry, Brussels); ALICHEC; Institute of Enterprises (Brussels); EUCOMED (European Confederation of Medical Associations, Brussels); Technopol, Brussels; UNICE/ SME; Cercle de Lorraine. Address: Avenue Brugmann 128, 1190 Brussels, Belgium.

BICAS Harley Edison Amaral, b. 12 October 1937, Ribeirão Preto, Brazil. Medical Doctor. m. Maria Lemos, 3 sons, 2 daughters. Education: Medicine, Faculty of Medicine, Ribeirão Preto, University of São Paulo, 1962; Masters degree in Chemistry, Secretary of State of Education and Culture, Brazil, 1960. Appointments: Assistant Professor of Ophthalmology, 1964-72; Associate Professor of Ophthalmology, 1972-81; Full Professor of Ophthalmology, 1981-, Department of Ophthalmology, Faculty of Medicine of Ribeirão Preto, University of São Paulo, Brazil; Head of Department, 1980-88, 1996-98, 2000-02; Editor-in-Chief, Arquivos Brasileiros de Oftalmologia, 1999-. Publications: Over 200 articles; 37 chapters of books; 5 books. Honours: William Kettlewell Endowed Chair in Visual Sciences, 1993; Gold Medal, University of Salvador, Buenos Aires, Argentina; Best Presentation Award, Brazilian Congresses of Ophthalmology, 1977, 1981, 1997; Annual Award, Brazilian Society of Ophthalmology, 1967, 1970. Memberships: Latin American Council of Strabismus; Brazilian Center of Strabismus; Pan American Association for Research in Opththalmology; Brazilian Academy of Ophthalmology; Academy of Sciences of Ribeirão Preto. Address: Departmento de Oftalmologia, Faculdade de Medicina de Ribeirão Preto, USP 14089-900, Ribeirão Preto SP, Brazil. E-mail: heabicas@fmrp.usp.br

BIDABAD Bijan, b. 6 September 1959, Tehran, Iran. Consultant; Educator. m. Nedereh Rastin, 1 son, 1 daughter. Education: BA, Political Science, Allameh Tabatabai University, 1978; MS, Economics, Shiraz University, 1983; PhD, Economics, Islamic Azad University, 1989. Appointments: Planning Expert, Plan and Budget Organization, 1982-90; Economic Advisor, Ministry of Finance and Economic Affairs, 1989-95; Economic Advisor, Research Center of Parliament, 1994-99; Economic Advisor, Office of President, Institute for Strategic Studies, 1995; Research Professor of Economics, Monetary and Banking Research Academy, 2002. Publications: 110 publications in Farsi language; 22 in English language; The New International Scholastic Order; Estimation of the Engel's Curves for Iran; Least Absolute Error Estimation; l-norm Estimation; Complex Probability and Markov Stochastic Processes; Macro-ecomometric model of Iran. Honours: PhD, Full Scholarship, 4 years. Memberships: In Sufism (Darvish Nematollahi Gonabadi). Address: No 18, 12th Street, Mahestan Avenue, Shahrak Gharb, Tehran 14658, Iran. E-mail: bijan_bidabad@msn.com

BIDDISS Michael Denis, b. 15 April 1942, Farnborough, Kent, England. Professor of History; Writer. m. Ruth Margaret Cartwright, 8 April 1967, 4 daughters. Education: MA, PhD, Queens' College, Cambridge, 1961-66; Centre des Hautes Etudes Européennes, University of Strasbourg, 1965-66. Appointments: Fellow in History, Downing College, Cambridge, 1966-73; Lecturer/Reader in History, University of Leicester, 1973-79; Professor of History, University of Reading, 1979-. Publications: Father of Racist Ideology, 1970; Gobineau: Selected Political Writings (editor), 1970; Disease and History (co-author), 1972, new edition, 2000; The Age of the Masses, 1977; Images of Race (editor), 1979; Thatchersim: Personality and Politics (co-editor), 1987; The Nuremberg Trial and the Third Reich, 1992; The Uses and Abuses of Antiquity (co-editor), 1999; The Humanities in the New Millennium (co-editor), 2000. Memberships: Historical Association, president, 1991-94; Faculty, History and Philosophy of Medicine, Society of Apothecaries, London, president, 1994-98; Royal Historical Society, joint vice president, 1995-99. Address: School of History, University of Reading, Whiteknights, Reading RG6 6AA, England.

BIELINSKA-WAZ Dorota Joanna, b. 9 June 1968, Bydgoszcz, Poland. Physicist. m. Piotr Waz, 14 September 1991. Education: MSc, 1987-92, European Law, 1994-95, PhD, Theoretical Physics, 1992-97, Nicholas Copenicus University. Appointments: Head, Governing Council of Postgraduate Students, Torun, 1995-97; Teaching, Research Assistant, 1997-98, 2001, Research Associate Adjunct, 2002-, Institute of Physics, University of Torun; Dr of Physics, 1998; Research Associate Adjunct, Biophysics Department, University of Bydgoszcz, 1998-99. Publications: 15 articles in professional journals; 8 publications as abstracts of conference presentations. Honours: NATO Fellowship, Turkey, 1994; NATO Fellowship, Germany, 1996; REHE Grant, Spain, 1997; Alexander von Humboldt Fellowship, Germany, 1999-2000. Address: Krasinskiego 21/23/51, 87-100 Torun, Poland.

BIGGIERO Lucio, b. 21 April 1955, Rome, Italy. Professor. Education: Higher Education in Industrial Organisation, University of Modena (I), 1980. Appointments: Professor of Organisation Science, University of L'Aquila and Luiss University (Rome, I). Publications: Articles in the following journals: Human Systems Management; Journal of Management and Governance; Nonlinear Dynamics; Journal of Tech. Transfer; International Review of Sociology. Memberships: AOM;EGOS; AIRS; ISA; ICA; ISSS. Address: Luiss University, via Tommasini 1, 00167 Rome, Italy. Website: www.luiss.it

BIH Herng-Dar, b. 15 September 1959, Taiwan. Professor. Education: MS, National Taiwan University, 1982; PhD, Environmental Psychology, City University of New York, 1992. Appointment: Director, Graduate Institute of Building and Planning, National Taiwan University. Publication: The Meaning of Objects, 1992. Honours: American Psychology Association Dissertation

Research Award, 1990; 1st Prize, Student Paper, Environmental Design Research Association, 1991. Memberships: American Psychology Association; Environmental Design Research Association. Address: 1, Sec 4, Roosevelt Road, NTU, Taipei, Taiwan.

BIHARI Mihàly, b. 24 February 1943, Budapest, Hungary. Jurist; Sociologist; Political Scientist. m. Zsuzsanna Varga, 2 sons, 1 daughter. Education: MA, Jurist, Faculty of Law, 1971, MA, Sociologist, Faculty of Arts, 1974, ELTE, Budapest, Hungary; DSc, Political Science, 1993. Appointments: Assistant Professor, 1971-84, Reader, 1984-93, Professor, 1993-, Department of Political Science, ELTE, Budapest, Hungary; Deputy of National Assembly of Hungary, 1994-98; Judge of the Constitutional Court of Hungary, 1999-. Publications: Author: Politikai Rendszer ès Demokràcia, 1989; Reform ès Demokràcia, 1990; Demokratikus út a szabadsàghoz, 1990; Magyarország Története 1918-1990, 1995; Magyar Politika 1945-1995, 1996; Co-author: Politològia, 1992. Honour: Bibò Award, 1996; Memberships: Hungarian Political Science Association, Chairman, 1992-94, Member of Presidency, 1994-. Address: ELTE AJK, Politikatudományi Intèzet, Budapest, Egyetem Tèr 103, 1053 Hungary. E-mail: bihari@mkab.hu

BIJL Jacob Pieter, b. 27 March 1953, Klaaswaal, The Netherlands. Minister. m. Helena Johanna Bijl de Bruijne, 3 sons. Education: Doctorandus of Theology, University of Utrecht, Netherlands, 1994. Appointment: Minister of the Dutch reformed Church, Rhoon, Netherlands, 1995-. Publications: Books: Open a Book about a Monument, 1992; Portrait of a Village in the Hoekse Waard, 1993; A New Church in Cromstryen, 1994; Klaaswaal, A Picture of a Lost World, 2002; Stand Still a Moment (articles about true stories of people during World War II), 1997-2003. Address: Singel 1, 3161, BJ Rhoon, The Netherlands.

BIKBULATOV Igor, b. 19 October 1941, Buribye, Bashkortostan, Russia. Scientist. m. Nina Muravyova, 3 daughters. Education: Bachelor of Technical Sciences, 1963, Doctor of Chemical Sciences, 1970, Professor of Faculty of General Chemical Technologies, 1985, Ufa Oil Institute. Appointments: Operator, chemical plant producing chemical rubber, Research Laboratory Engineer, Head of Laboratory, Head of the Sterlitamak Branch, Head of the Faculty of Ecology and Rational Use of Nature, Ufa Oil University, Stelitamak, Bashkorostan, Russia. Publications: Wasteless production of chlorohydrins; Microwave radiation and intensification of chemical processes; Polymeric covering for isolating the surfaces of open reservoirs; Capsule of a pipeline; A building for placing chemical productions; Chrolohydrins I. Obtaining chloric acid in saturated chloride-ion solution. Honours: Inventor of the USSR; Honoured Higher School Worker of the Russian Federation; Honoured Worker of Science of Bashkorostan. Memberships: Academician, International Academy of Science of Pedagogical Education; Scientific Society of Ufa State Oil Technical University. Address: October Avenue 2, Stelitamark, Bashkortostan, Russia. E-mail: infor@sfugntu.bashnet.ru

BILLINGS Stephen Alec, b. 14 August 1951, Staffordshire, England. Professor of Signal Processing and Complex Systems. m. Catherine Grant Billings, 1 son, 1 daughter. Education: First Class Honours Degree, Electrical Engineering, Liverpool University, 1969-72; PhD, Control Systems, Sheffield University, 1972-75. Appointments: Lecturer, 1975-83, Senior Lecturer, 1983-85, Department of Control Engineering, Reader, 1985-90, Professor of Signal Processing and Complex Systems, 1990-, Department of Automatic Control and Systems Engineering, University of Sheffield. Publications: Over 200 journal articles and over 50 conference papers. Honours: Honoured by the Institute of Scientific Information (ISA), USA as one of the worlds most

highly cited researchers in all branches of engineering, 1980-2000; Awarded D. Eng., Liverpool University, 1990. Memberships: Fellow, Institute of Electrical Engineers (UK); Chartered Engineer; Fellow, Institute of Mathematics and its Applications; Chartered Mathematician. Address: Department of Automatic Control and Systems Engineering, University of Sheffield, Mappin Street, Sheffield S1 3JD, England. E-mail: s.billings@sheffield.ac.uk

BILSBOROUGH John, b. 7 October 1941, Bolton-Le-Sands, Lancashire, England. Writer. m. Susan Elizabeth Cox, 1 daughter. Education: Certificate in Education, University of Lancaster. Appointments: Freelance Writer; Broadcaster; Resident Poet, BBC Radio 4 and BBC Radio Wales; Newspaper and Magazine feature writer; Acclaimed Performance Poet; Lyricist for stage musicals, The Razzle-Dazzle Man, Merlin and Once Upon a Spell. Publications: Many poems commissioned by BBC Radio 4 and other Radio and TV networks worldwide; Books: Mister Puniverse; Worst in the World; Radio Rhymes; 57 Poems; Anthologised in Over Milk Wood, The Poet's House and Poetry on Sex. Honours: Pontardawe International Celtic Folk Festival, Worst Song in the World Champion, 1982; Dylan Thomas Centre, Stand and Deliver, Performance Poetry Champion, 1999-. Memberships: The Welsh Academy; Founder Member, Glyn Abbey Trust; Founder Member, Touch and Go, Cael a Chael, Publishing Co-Operative. Address: Chapel House, Glyn Abbey, Llanelli, Carmarthenshire, Wales, SA15 5TL.

BIMBERG ZU LENNINGHAUSEN Guido von, b. 14 March 1954, Halle, Germany (US national, 1997). Musicologist and Entertainment Business Executive. m. Christiane Bimberg, 11 April 1981, 1 son. Education: Studied Musicology, Music Education, Piano, Literature, Art History, Theatre (Halle, Berlin, Munich, Tashkent, Moscow, Harvard and Stanford); Business Administration (Schwyz, Lausanne, Harvard); PhD, 1979; MBA, Schwyz-Lausanne and Harvard, 1979; Research Fellowship, Baltic, Central Asian, Caucasian, Russian, Siberian and Ukrainian Archives, 1979-80; Habilitation, 1981, PhD in Business Administration, Lausanne and Harvard, 1982. Appointments: Founder of several rock bands, 1970-82; Founder, 1973, Chairman, 1979-86, German Society of Music Agencies and Discjockeys; Manager, German, Russian, Caribbean and USA popstars; Creator, TV show formats; Copyright counsellor; Lyricist and Composer, charts and musicals; Associate Professor, Music History, Halle, 1979-83; Chair Professor of Musicology, Dresden; Chair Professor Musicology, Martin Luther University, Halle, 1983-95; Chair Professor Musicology, Music Academy of Dortmund, 1995-; Chair Professor, Music and Interdisciplinary Studies, 1983-86, Havanna University, 1990-; Fellow Chair of Entertainment and Media Business, Washington University, 1992-, German Academy of Humanities, 1992-; Chair Professor, Entertainment and Media Business, Central University of California, Los Angeles, 1995-; Professor, Honorary Senator, Moscow University, 1995-; Chair Professor, Entertainment Business, International School of Business Administration, Academy of Sciences, Berlin, 1997-; Numerous visiting professorships and Permanent University Fellowships in Europe, America, Africa, Asia and Australia; Senior Consultant, 1991-, Supervisory Board, 2001-, MRI Inc; Co-director, 1994-, CCO, 2000-, Music Tourist Agency, Nashville; Vice President, Media Science Inc, 2000-; CEO, Music and Media Business Inc, Los Angeles, 2001-; Board of Directors: Digital Media Corporation, 2000-; Entertainment Network Inc, 2001-; Congress and Festival Director, Werckmeister Festival, Alicante Festival, Singapore Music Festival, Tokyo Classics, Broadway Summit, Los Angeles Hit Factory, Nashville Music Contest and International Musical Congress and Festival ICMF New York; Honorary Consul, Russian Federation, 2002; Director, Co-Director, several music congresses and festivals, including: Fasch Festival, Werckmeister Festival, Alicante Festival, Singapore Music Festival, Tokyo

Classics, Los Angeles Hit Factory, Nashville Music Contest; Senator, German Academy of Sciences and Arts, Westphalian Music Academy; President: German Academy of the Humanities, Bonn, 1998-; International Entertainment Business Society; German Music Research Foundation; German Handel Society; Vice President: German Musicological Society; German Fasch Society; Werckmeister Society; Member, Board of Directors, International Society for Music Education; Member of Council, American Musicological Society; Member, Association Board, College Music Society; Member, International Musicological Society; Royal Music Association, Japanese Musicological Society. Publications: Over 20 scholarly books including: Opera in 18th-century Russia, 1981, 3rd edition, 2003; Dramaturgy of the Handel Operas, 1985, 2nd edition, 2003; Anatolij Lunacharsky: Essays in music, 1985, 2nd edition, 2001; The Wonderful Sound, German, 1985-2002, million copies in many countries; Schütz-Bach-Händel, 1989; Mozarts Entfuhrung aus dem Serail, 1990; Music of Russian and German Composers, 1990; Fasch and Music in 18th Century Europe, 1995; Andreas Werckmeister, Die musicalische Temperatur, co-author, 1996; Denkmäler der Musik in Mitteldeutschland, co-editor, 1996-; General education and thematic catalogue of Fasch works, co-editor, 1996; Music in the 18th Century European Society, 1997, 2nd edition, 2002; Perspectives in Musicology and Music Education for the 21st Century, 1997, 2nd edition, 2002; Music in Canada/La Musique au Canada, 1997, 2nd edition, 2002; Music Sources from the Westphalian Music Archive, 1997; Denkmäler der Musik in Westfalen, 1997; International Studies Women in Music, 1999; Women in Music in Westphalia, 1999; Broadway on the Ruhr: The Musical Comedy in the New Millennium, co-editor, 2000; Music Technology, 2001; Digital Music Business, 2001; Leni Timmermann, 2002; Introducing Music, 2002; Musicology and Entertainment Business, 2002; Baroque Music Recovered by the Telemann Orchestra Tradition, (co-author), 2002; Eitelfriedrich Thom – Great Germans in Theory and Practice of Music, co-author, 2003; La musique en activité, 2004; Music books for children. Contributions: over 200 articles to professional international journals. Honours: Modest Musorgsky Prize, 1990; American Musicology Award, 1992; Canadian Culture Prize, 1992; Guido Adler Prize of German Musicology, 1994; Gold Crown Medal Hong Kong Music Association, 1995; Prize Musica Westphalia, 1997; Bundesverdienstkreuz, 1998; German Handel Prize, 1998; German National Prize for Music and Musicology, 2000; Innovation Prize for music and media technology, 2000; Grosses Bundes-Verdienstkreuz des Verdienstordens, 2002; Knight of the Empire, 2003; Dr hc, Universities of Moscow, 2003, and New York, 2003; Books in commemoration of 50th Birthday: No Limits (edited by Professor Dr Hiroshi Watanabe), 2004; Festschrift Guido Bimberg/RuedigerPfeiffer (edited by Dr Ching-Wah Wang), 2004. Address: German Academy for Humanities, Postfach 550133, D-44209 Dortmund, Germany. E-mail: prof.dr.bimberg@crossoverstudies.com

BINCHY Maeve, b. 28 May 1940, Dublin, Ireland. Writer. m. Gordon Thomas Snell, 29 January 1977. Education: BA, University College, Dublin, 1960. Appointments: Teacher, History and French, Pembroke School, Dublin, 1961-68; Columnist, Irish Times, London, 1968-2000; Writer. Publications: My First Book, 1976; The Central Line: Stories of Big City Life, 1978; Maeve's Diary, 1979; Victoria Line, 1980; Light a Penny Candle, 1982; Maeve Binchy's Dublin Four, 1982; The Lilac Bus, 1984; Echoes, 1985; Firefly Summer, 1987; Silver Wedding, 1988; Circle of Friends, 1991; The Copper Beech, 1992; The Glass Lake, 1995; Evening Class, 1996; Tara Road, 1999; Scarlet Feather, 2000; Aches and Pains, 2000; Quentins, 2002. Honours: International TV Festival Golden Prague Award, Czech TV, 1979; Jacobs Award, 1979; Hon DLit, National University of Ireland, 1990, Queen's Belfast, 1998. Address: Dalkey, Co. Dublin, Ireland.

BING Fu (also named Wang Yun), b. 28 December 1931, Nanjing, China. Writer. m. Xu Mo, 2 daughters. Education: Nanjing Accounting College. Appointments: Freelance Writer; Adviser of New South Wales Chinese Writers Association, Australia; Adviser of Sydney Chinese Writers Association, Australia; Vice Chairman, Barwell Garden Poets Union; Adviser Barwell Garden Poetry Magazine. Publications: Poetry Collections: Waves; Selected Poems of Bing Fu; The Firefly; The Love Songs of Phoenix Tree; Dream and Non Dream; The Man Who Looks at the Sea; Prose Collections: Clouds Gone Hurriedly; The Sea, The Sun and The Dreams – Notes in Australia; Prose and Essays by Bing Fu. Honours: The First Shanghai Literary Award; Excellent Film Award, 1983; Gold Rooster Award, First International Cartoon Movie Festival Award, Japan,1985; Haiuk Award, Fifth National Culture Festival, Japan; 21st Sydney World Poets Congress Committee Award, Australia, 2000. Memberships: China Writers' Association; China Filmmakers' Association; A Director, Shanghai Writers' Association; Head of Shanghai Poetry Commission. Address: 4-45 Caledonian Street, Bexley, NSW 2207, Australia. E-mail: bingfu88@hotmail.com

BINNS Patrick George, b. 8 October 1948, Weyburn, Saskatchewan, Canada. Politician. m. Carol MacMillan, 8 May 1971, 3 sons, 1 daughter. Education: MA, Community Development, University of Alta, Canada, 1971. Appointments: Rural Development Council of Prince Edward Island, 1972; Government of Prince Edward Island, 1974-78; Elected to Prince Edward Island Legislative Assembly, 1978, held cabinet portfolios in industry, municipal affairs, fisheries, environment, labour, housing, 1979-84; Representative, federal riding of Cardigan as MP, House of Commons, 1984-88; President, both Island Bean Ltd and Pat Binns & Associates, 1988-96; Elected Leader, Progressive Conservative Party of Prince Edward Island, 1996; Elected to Prince Edward Island Legislative Assembly as MLA for Murray River-Gaspereaux, 1996; Sworn in as Premier, President of Executive Council and Minister Responsible for Intergovernmental Affairs, 1996; Re-elected, 2000 and 2003. Honour: Queen's Silver Jubilee Medal for Outstanding Public Service, 1978; Queen's Golden Jubilee Medal, 2002. Membership: Founder and Active Organiser, Northumberland Fisheries Festival. Address: PO Box 2000, 95 Rochford Street, 5th Floor, Charlottetown, Prince Edward Island, C1A 7N8, Canada.

BINOCHE Juliette, b. 9 March 1964, Paris, France. Actress. 1 son, 1 daughter. Education: National Conservatory of Drama; Private Theatrical Studies. Creative Works: Films include: Les nanas; La vie de famille; Rouge Baiser; Rendez-Vous; Mon beau-frère a tué ma soeur; Mauvais Sang; Un tour de manège; Les amants du Pont-Neuf; The Unbearable Lightness of Being; Wuthering Heights, 1992; Damage, 1992; Trois Couleurs: Bleu, 1993; Le Hussard sur le Toit, 1995; The English Patient, 1996; Alice et Martin, 1999; Les Enfants du Siècle, 1999; La Veuve de Saint-Pierre, 2000; Chocolat, 2001; Code Unknown, 2001; Décalage horaire, 2002; Country of My Skull, 2004; Play: Naked, 1998. Honours: Academy Award, Best Supporting Actress, 1996; Berlin Film Festival Award, 1996; BAFTA Award, 1997. Address: c/o UTA, 9560 Wilshire Boulevard, Floor 5, Beverly Hills, CA 90212, USA.

BIONDI Giuseppe Gilberto, b. 21 July 1948, Cesena, Italy. Classicist; Educator. Education: Graduate, Classical Philology, University of Bologna, Italy, 1971; Visiting Professor, Department of Classics, University of California, Berkeley, 1992-93. Appointments: Teacher, Greek and Latin Grammar, 1978-79; Teacher, Latin Literature, 1979-84; Assistant, University of Bologna, 1984-86; Professor, 1986-, Director, Department of Classical and Medieval Philology, 1996-2001, Chairman, Degree

Course Humanities, 1995-2001, Principal Faculty, 2001-, University of Parma, Italy. Publications: Semantica di Cupidus, 1979; Il Nefas Argonautico, 1984; Seneca, Medea-Fedra, 1989, 10th edition, 2001; Lutazio Catulo e i Preneoterici, 1998; I Poetae Novi – Catullo, 1998. Address: via Dante 183, 47023 Cesena, Italy. E-mail: giuseppe.biondi@unipr.it

BIRCA-GALATEANU Serban, b. 21 May 1944, Urziceni, Romania. Associate Professor. Education: Graduate Engineer, MSc equivalent, Electronics, 1967, PhD, Electronics, 1976, Polytechnic University, Bucharest; PhD, Electronics, University of Nantes, 1993. Appointments: Assistant, 1967, Assistant Professor, 1976, Associate Professor, 1990, Polytechnic University, Bucharest; Associate Professor, University of Nantes, France, 1990-93; Associate Professor, IUFM, Nantes, 1993-. Publications: 38 technical papers in periodicals and 76 conference papers, about power electrons including dc-dc converters, class E rectifiers, choppers, inverters, and about other topics including electron measuring instruments, optoelectron circuits, control circuits, wide-band RC amplifiers, active RC filters; Technical books: Handbook of Power and Control Electronics, 1976, 2nd ed, 1983; Calculated Examples of Power Electronics, 1979, 1991; Wide-band RC amplifiers, 1981; Optoelectronics - applications, 1983, and Opto circuits, 1986; Practical Training in Power Electronics, 1985; 5 patents on electron measuring instruments, Romania, 1979-83. Honour: Team Award, Research and Development, Romanian Ministry of Educ, 1967. Membership: Member, 1990, Senior Member, 1996, IEEE, Power Electronics Society. Address: 9 pl V Mangin, 44200 Nantes, France.

BIRD Harold Dennis (Dickie), b. 19 April 1933, Barnsley, Yorkshire, England. County Test Cricket Umpire. Education: MCC Advanced Cricket Coach. Appointments: Umpired 159 international matches including 68 Test Matches, World Cup Matches, One Day International matches; Umpired 3 World Cup Finals; Umpired 4 World Cup Tournaments; Umpired Queen's Silver Jubilee Test Match, 1977, Centenary Test Match, 1980-. Women's World Cup, Women's World Cup Final, New Zealand, 1982; Umpired 32 major cup finals at Lord's including: Gillette Cup Finals, Nat West Cup Finals, Benson & Hedges Cup, Rothmans Cup, Sharjah, United Arab Emirates and the Final; Umpire, Asia Cup, Sharjah, 1984; Umpire, Rothmans Cup, Sharjah, 1985; Umpire, Asia Cup, Sri Lanka and Final, 1985; Umpire, Champion's Cup, Sharjah, 1986; Umpire, all major cup quarter-finals, semi-finals, England; Played County Cricket for Yorkshire County Cricket Club, Leicestershire County Cricket Club; Umpire, Bicentenary Test Match, England, 1987; Umpire, 3 test matches, Zimbabwe v India, 1992; Zimbabwe v New Zealand, 2 tests, Zimbabwe, 1992; West Indies v Pakistan test series, 3 matches, 1993; Umpire 60th Diamond Test Match, Pakistan v Australia, Karachi, 1994; West Indies Test Match, Kampur, 1994; 3 test matches in New Zealand, New Zealand v Pakistan, 1994; Umpire, 2 test matches in Australia, Australia v Pakistan, 1995. Publications: Not Out; That's Out; From the Pavilion End; Dickie Bird, My Autobiography, 1997; White Cap and Bails, 1999; Dickie Bird's Britain, 2002. Honours: Voted Yorkshire Personality of Year, 1977; Reception to meet HM Queen Mother, Clarence House, London, 1977; MBE, 1986; World Record, umpiring 67 Test Matches; World Record, Umpire 92 One-Day International Matches; Met numerous celebrities including HM the Queen, 17 times including private lunch, Buckingham Palace, 1991; PM John Major, 1991; Ex-PM Margaret Thatcher, 1981; Radio: Guest on Down Your Way with Brian Johnston, 1975; TV appearances: Parkinson, 1979, Through the Keyhole, 1990, This is Your Life, 1992; Breakfast with Frost, 1996; Clive James, 1996; BBC Documentary of his life, 1996; Guest, Desert Island Discs with Sue Lawley, 1996; Clive Anderson TV Show, 1998; Gloria Hunniford, 1998, Trevor Macdonald Show, 1999; World Panel Test Umpires, 1992; Honorary Life Member, Yorkshire County Cricket Club, 1994; Honorary Life Member, MCC, 1996; Life Long Achievement Award, 1996 Honorary Life Member, Leicestershire County Cricket Club, 1996; Honorary Doctorate, Sheffield Hallam University, 1996, Yorkshire Man of Year, 1996; People of Year Award, 1996; Variety Club of Great Britain Award; Honorary LLD, Leeds University, 1997; Freeman of the Borough of Barnsley, 2000; Barnsley Millennium Award of Merit for outstanding service to the community, 2000; Dinner with Tony Blair at Chequers, 2001; Appeared on John Inverdale Show, On-side, BBC1, 2001; Guest on A Question of Sport, 4 times. Memberships: MCC; Lord's Taverners; World Cup Panel of Umpires, 1987. Address: White Rose Cottage, 40 Paddock Road, Staincross, Barnsley, South Yorkshire S75 6LE, England.

BIRD Kai, b. 2 September 1951, Eugene, Oregon, USA. Author. m. Susan Gloria Goldmark, 7 June 1975, 1 son. Education: MS, Journalism, Northwestern University, 1975; BA, History, Carleton College, 1973. Publications: The Chairman: John J McCloy, The Making of the American Establishment, 1992; Hiroshima's Shadow: Writings on the Denial of History and the Smithsonian Controversy, (editor with Lawrence Lifshultz), 1998; The Color of Truth: McGeorge Bundy and William Bundy, Brothers in Arms. A Biography, 1998. Contributions to: New York Times; Los Angeles Times; Washington Post; Boston Globe; Christian Science Monitor; Foreign Policy; Journal of Diplomatic History; Washington Monthly; Foreign Service Journal. Honours: Woodrow Wilson International Center for Scholars, Fellow; John D and Catherine T MacArthur Foundation Writing Fellowship; German Marshall Fund Fellow; Alicia Patterson Journalism Fellowship; Guggenheim Fellowship. Address: 1914 Biltmore Street, North West, Washington, DC 20009, USA.

BIRLEY Julia (Davies), b. 13 May 1928, London, England. Writer. m. 12 September 1954, 1 son, 3 daughters. Education: BA, Classics, Oxon. Publications: Novels: The Children on the Shore; The Time of the Cuckoo; When You Were There; A Serpent's Egg; Dr Spicer; Short Stories. Contributions to: Guardian. Memberships: PEN; Charlotte Yonge Society. Address: Upper Bryn, Longtown, Hereford HR2 0NA, England.

BIRMINGHAM Stephen, b. 28 May 1931, Hartford, Connecticut, USA. Writer. m. Janet Tillson, 5 January 1951, divorced, 2 sons, 1 daughter. Education: BA (cum laude), Williams College, 1950; Postgraduate Studies, University of Oxford, 1951. Appointment: Advertising Copywriter, Needham, Harper & Steers Inc, 1953-67. Publications: Young Mr Keefe, 1958; Baraba Greer, 1959; The Towers of Love, 1961; Those Harper Women, 1963; Fast Start, Fast Finish, 1966; Our Crowd, 1967; The Right People, 1968; Heart Troubles, 1968; The Grandees, 1971; The Late John Marquand, 1972; The Right Places, 1973; Real Lace, 1973; Certain People, 1977; The Golden Dream: Suburbia in the 1970's, 1978; Jacqueline Bouvier Kennedy Onassis, 1978; Life at the Dakota, 1979; California Rich, 1980; Duchess, 1981; The Grandes Dames, 1982; The Auerbach Will, 1983; The Rest of Us, 1984; The LeBaron Secret, 1986; America's Secret Aristocracy, 1987; Shades of Fortune, 1989; The Rothman Scandal, 1991; Carriage Trade, 1993; The Wrong Kind of Money; Numerous articles for newspapers and magazines. Memberships: New England Society of the City of New York; Phi Beta Kappa. Address: 1247 Ida Street, Cincinnati, OH 45202, USA.

BIRNBAUM Edward L, b. 2 August 1939, Brooklyn, New York, USA. Attorney. m. Madeleine, 1 son, 1 daughter. Education: LLB, New York University School of Law, 1964. Appointments: Head of Litigation Department, Herzfeld & Rubin PC for over 30 years;

Admitted to: New York State Bar, 1964, US District Court, Southern and Eastern Districts of New York, 1967, US Court of Appeals, Second Circuit, 1970, US Supreme Court, 1971, US District Court, Western District of New York, 1983, US District Court for the District of Arizona, 1992; Arbitrator, American Arbitration Association and United States District Court, Eastern District of New York; Small Claims Arbitrator Civil Court, Queens County; Lecturer for: New York State Bar Association; Practising Law Institute; New York State Trial Lawyers Association; The Nassau Academy of Law; Federal Publications; Queens County Bar Association; National Academy of Continuing Education; Adjunct Faculty, New York University School of Continuing Education. Publications: Author: Defendant's Trial Tactics, 1978; Numerous articles in professional journals. Honours: Listed in Who's Who publications and biographical dictionaries. Memberships: New York State Bar Association; Nassau County Bar Association; New York County Lawyers Association; New York State Trial Lawyers Association; The Association of Trial Lawyers of America; New York University School of Law Moor Court Justices Association. Address: 70 Shelley Lane, Great Neck, NY 11023, USA. E-mail: ebirnbaum@herzfeld-rubin.com

BIRT John, Baron of Liverpool, b. 10 December 1944, Liverpool, England. Broadcasting Executive. m. Jane Frances Lake, 1965, 1 son, 1 daughter. Education: St Mary's College, Liverpool; St Catherine's College, Oxford. Appointments: TV Producer, Nice Time, 1968-69; Joint Editor, World in Action, 1969-70; Producer, The Frost Programme, 1971-72; Executive Producer, Weekend World, 1972-74; Head, Current Affairs, London Weekend TV, 1974-77; Co-Producer, The Nixon Interviews, 1977; Controller, Features and Current Affairs, LWT, 1977-81; Director of Programmes, 1982-87; Deputy Director General, 1987-92, Director General, 1992-2000, BBC; Vice President, Royal TV Society, 1994-2000; Adviser to Prime Minister on criminal justice, 2000-01, Strategy Adviser, 2001-; Adviser to McKinsey and Co Inc; Chair, Capital Ventures Fund, 2000. Publications: The Harder Path – The Autobiography. Honours: Visiting Fellow, Nuffield College, Oxford, 1991-99; Honorary Fellow: University of Wales, Cardiff, 1997; St Catherine's College, Oxford, 1992; Hon DLitt, Liverpool John Moores, 1992; City, 1998; Bradford, 1999; Emmy Award, US National Academy of Television, Arts and Sciences; Life Peerage, 2000. Memberships: Media Law Group, 1983-94; Working Party on New Technologies, 1981-83; Broadcasting Research Unit, Executive Committee, 1983-87; International Museum of TV and Radio, New York, 1994-2000; Opportunity 2000 Target Team, Business in the Community, 1991-98. Address: House of Lords, London SW1A 0PW, England.

BISCHOF Marco, b. 24 April 1947, St Gallen, Switzerland. Independent Scholar; Science Writer; Consultant. Education: Diploma, Breathing Therapy, Institute for Breathing Therapy and Breathing Education, West Berlin, Germany, 1974-76; Matura Certificate (BA/BSc equivalent), State College for Adults, Zurich, Switzerland, 1979-81; Cultural and Medical Anthropology, Comparative Religion, Psychology, University of Zurich, Switzerland, 1981-85. Appointments: Free-lance Journalist, Arts and Reviews, Zurich, 1966-68; Self Employed, Breathing, Relaxation and Body Therapist, 1976-; Co-founder and Member of Advisory Board, Research Laboratory for Biophysical Balneology, Zurzach, Switzerland, 1980-91; Lecturer, Switzerland, Germany and Austria, 1981-; Free-lance Writer specialising in frontier sciences, 1981-; Independent Scholar and Author, Consultant to various research projects, companies and institutions, 1985-; Collaborator, 1980-91, Member of Board of Directors, 1992-, Managing Director, 1994-95, International Institute of Biophysics, Kasierlauten (now based in Neuss), Germany; Visiting Scholar, Center for Frontier Sciences, Temple University,

Philadelphia, USA, 1992; Scientific Consultant, Patient Information, Berlin, Germany, 1996-98; Lecturer and Member of Working Group for Agrarian Culture and Social Ecology, Humboldt University, Berlin, Germany, 2000-2001. Publications: Numerous articles in scientific publications and book chapters include most recently: Field concepts and the emergence of a holistic biophysics, 2000; Tachyons, Orgone Energy, Scalar Waves – Subtle Fields Between Myth and Science, 2002; Introduction to Integrative Biophysics, 2003. Honours: 1995 Network Book Prize for the book Biophotonen, Scientific and Medical Network, 1996; 1997 Swiss Award for life achievement and the book Biophotonen, Swiss Parapsychology Foundation, Berne, Switzerland, 1997; Special Award, German Transpersonal Society, 1998. Memberships: Swiss Authors' Society; Swiss Science Writers' Association; Society for Scientific Exploration, USA; International Society for the Study of Subtle Energy and Energy Medicine, USA; Scientific and Medical Network, UK; International Union for Medical and Applied Electrography; Editorial Board, Consciousness and Physical Reality, St Petersburg, Russia. Address: Gotlandstr 7, D-10429 Berlin, Germany. E-mail: mb@marcobischof.com Website: www.marcobischof.com

BISH David, b. 5 March 1952, Virginia, USA. Professor. m. Karen, 1 daughter. Education: BS, (high honours), Geology, Furman University, 1974; PhD, Mineralogy, Pennsylvania State University, 1977. Appointments: Research Fellow, Department of Geological Sciences, Harvard University, 1977-80; Technical Staff Member, Los Alamos National Laboratory, 1980-2003; Murray Professor, Indiana University, 2003-. Publications: Author and co-author, over 100 peer-reviewed articles, book chapters and books. Honours: Xerox Award in Material Science; Jackson Award of the Clay Minerals Society; Brindley Award of the Clay Minerals Society; Fellow of the Mineralogical Society of America; 1999 R&D 100 Award; President of the Clay Minerals Society 1998-99; President, International Natural Zeolite Association, 2002-06. Memberships: The Clay Minerals Society; Mineralogical Society of America; American Geophysical Union; International Association for the Study of Clay Minerals. Address: Department of Geological Sciences, Indiana University, Bloomington, IN 47405, USA E-mail: bish@indiana.edu

BISH Robert Leonard, b. 30 November 1941, Suva, Fiji. Researcher. m. Patricia Field, 1 son, 2 daughters. Education: BSc (Sydney), 1964. Appointments: Technical Assistant 2, Defence Standards Laboratory (Sydney), 1965-69; Experimental Officer 1, 1969-70, Experimental Officer 2, 1970-74, Defence Standards Laboratory (Sydney); Experimental Officer 2, Aeronautical and Maritime Research Laboratory, Melbourne, 1974-2003. Publications: Papers in professional journals. Honour: 20th Century Award for Achievement (IBC), 1995. Address: PO Box 122, Niddrie, Vic 3042, Australia.

BISHOP James Drew, b. 18 June 1929, London, England. Journalist. m. 5 June 1959, 2 sons. Education: BA, History, Corpus Christi College, Cambridge, 1953. Appointments: Foreign Correspondent, 1957-64, Foreign News Editor, 1964-66, Features Editor, 1966-70, The Times; Editor, 1971-87, Editor-in-Chief, 1987-94, The Illustrated London News. Publications: Social History of Edwardian Britain, 1977; Social History of the First World War, 1982; The Story of The Times (with Oliver Woods), 1983; Illustrated Counties of England, editor, 1985; The Sedgwick Story, 1998. Contributions to: Books, newspapers and magazines. Membership: Association of British Editors, chairman, 1987-96; Chairman, National Heritage, 1998-. Address: 67 Parliament Hill, London NW3 2TB, England.

BISSET Jacqueline, b. 13 September 1944, Weybridge, Surrey, England. Education: French Lycée, London. Career: Films include: The Knack, debut, 1965; Casino Royale, 1967; Bullitt, 1968; The Detective, 1968; Airport, 1970; Believe in Me, 1971; Stand Up and Be Counted, 1972; The Thief Who Came to Dinner, 1973; Murder on the Orient Express, 1974; The Deep, 1976; Le Manifique, 1977; Secrets, 1978; When Time Ran Out, 1980; Rich and Famous, 1981; Class, 1982; Forbidden, 1986; High Season, 1988; Wild Orchid, 1989; September, 1994; La Céremonie, 1995; End of Summer, 1995; Once You Meet a Stranger, 1996; Courtesan, 1996; Let the Devil Wear Black, 1998; Dangerous Beauty, 1998; Joan of Arc, 1999; In the Beginning, 2000; Jesus, 2000; Britannic, 2000. Address: William Morris Agency, 151 El Camino Drive, Beverly Hills, CA 90212, USA.

BISTRICEANU Marian, b. 22 September 1941, Negoiu, Dolj, Romania. Endocrinologist. m. Pestrea Ioana, 29 December 1966, 1 daughter. Education: Faculty of Veterinary Medicine, Timisoara, 1965; Faculty of Medicine, Craiova, 1976. Appointments: Preparatory Assistant, Assistant 1966-90, Lecturer 1990-92, Assistant Professor 1992-95, Professor of Endocrinology, 1995. Publications: 162 papers, 13 books: Physiology and Physiopatology of The Endocrine System; Immunopathology of The Endocrine System; Textbook of Clinical Endocrinology; Gynaecologic Endocrinology; Advances in Immunopathology; Clinical Endocrinology, 2000. Honours: Romanian Academy Award, 1983; Romanian Academy of Medical Science Award, 1996. Memberships: Romanian Science Organisation, 1987; International Society of Endocrinology, 1990; Balcanic Medical Union, 1991; International Brain Research Organisation, 1991; Romanian Academy of Medical Science, 1997. Address: Madona Dudu str, bl 4, ap 3, Craiova 1100, Romania.

BITTING Kevin Noel, b. 18 December 1957, Kenmore, New York, USA. Paediatric Craniofacial Orthotist. Education: BA, Psychology, Villanova University, 1980; Degree, Prosthetics, Northwestern University Medical School, 1989; BOC, Board of Orthotic Certification; Appointments: Clinical Orthotist, Clinical Prosthetist, SW Orthotic Prosthetic Laboratory Service, 1988-99; Chief, Paediatric Craniofacial Orthotist, Cranial Therapies Inc, Burbank, California, 1991-. Address: Cranial Therapies Inc, 4444 Lankershim Boulevard, Ste 108, Toluca Lake, CA 91602, USA.

BITZES John G, b. 9 December 1926, Omaha, Nebraska, USA. Teacher. m. Helen L, deceased, 2 sons. Education: BA, University of Nebraska, 1954; MA, University of Nebraska at Omaha, 1964; PhD, University of Nebraska, Lincoln, 1976. Appointments: Teacher, Creston High School, 1959-61; Teacher Omaha Public Schools, 1961-92, Retired 1992; Lecturer, Russian History, University of Nebraska at Omaha, Defutt Air Force Base, Nebraska, 1964-72. Publications: The Anti Greek Riot of 1909, 1971; Greece and World War II to April 1941, 1989; Chapter: Third World at the Crossroads in The West and Third World Region by Dr Shiekh R Ali, 1989; Symposium Paper, The Battle of Crete Revisited, 1991. Honours: Rotary Honor for Improvement, Grade School, 1940; Phi Beta Kappa, 1954; J L Sellers Award for best article, 1971; Human Relations Award, Omaha Education Association, 1992. Memberships: Nebraska Historical Society; Phi Beta Kappa; Order of Aheya, chapter 395, St Louis, Missouri; St Nicholas Greek Orthodox Church, St Louis. Address: 395 Branchport Drive, Chesterfield, MO 23017, USA.

BJONER Ingrid, b. 8 November 1927, Kraakstad, Norway. Opera and Concert Singer (Soprano). Education: Conservatory of Music, Oslo, with Gudrun Boellemose; Hochschule für Musik, Frankfurt, with Paul Lohmann; Further study with Ellen Repp in New York; Graduate Pharmacist, University of Oslo, 1951. Career:

Sang Third Norn and Gutrune in Norwegian radio recording of Götterdämmerung, 1956 with Kirsten Flagstad; Stage Debut, Oslo, 1957, as Donna Anna; Drottningholm Opera, 1957, as Handel's Rodelinda; Member, Wuppertal Opera, Germany, 1957-59; Deutsche Oper am Rhein Dusseldorf, 1959-61; Bayreuth Festival 1960, as Freia, Helmvige and Gutrune; Has sung with Bayerische Staatsoper Munich from 1961, notably as the Empress in Die Frau ohne Schatten 1963 and as Isolde, in the centenary production of Tristan and Isolde, 1965; Metropolitan Opera debut 1961, as Elsa in Lohengrin; Covent Garden from 1967, as Senta, Sieglinde and Leonore (Fidelio); Salzburg Festival, 1969-1970, Leonore; Sang the Duchess of Parma in the US premiere of Doktor Faust by Busoni, Carnegie Hall, 1974; Oslo and Copenhagen, 1985-86, as Elektra; Further appearances at La Scala, Vienna, Hollywood Bowl, Hamburg, Deutsche Oper Berlin, Cologne Opera, Warsaw and Vancouver; Season 1986-87 sang Isolde at Bayreuth and the Kostelnicka in Jenufa at Karlsruhe; Staatsoper Munich 1988, as the Dyer's Wife in Die Frau ohne Schatten; Oslo Opera, 1989, Senta; The Dyer's Wife at Karlsruhe, 1990; Concert appearances worldwide, often in the songs of Grieg; Professor at Royal Academy of Music, Copenhagen, 1991-; Professor at Royal Academy of Music, Oslo, 1992-. Recordings include: Götterdämmerung, Decca; Die Frau ohne Schatten, DGG; Wagner's Wesendonck Lieder; Songs by Sibelius. Honours include: Order of St Olav, Norway, 1964; Bavarian Order of Merit. Address: Gregers Grams vei 33, 0382 Oslo 3, Norway.

BJÖRK (Björk Godmunsdottir), b. 21 November 1965. Reykjavik, Iceland. 1 son, 1 daughter. Career: Solo release, aged 11; Singer, various Icelandic groups include: Exodus; Tappi Tikarras; Kukl; Singer, The Sugarcubes, 1987-92; Solo artiste, 1992-; Recent appearances include Reading Festival, 1995. Recordings: Solo albums: Björk, 1977; Debut, 1993; Post, 1995; Telegram, 1996; Homogenic, 1997; Vespertine, 2001; Hit singles: with The Sugarcubes: Birthday; Solo singles: Venus As A Boy; Violently Happy; Human Behaviour; Big Time Sensuality; Play Dead; Army Of Me; Isobel; It's Oh So Quiet; Possibly Maybe; I Miss You/Cover Me; Hyperballad; Hunter; Bachelorette; All Is Full Of Love; Alarm Call; Selmasongs, 2000; Other recordings: Gling-Go, Trio Gudmundar Ingolfssonar, 1990; Ex-El, Graham Massey, 1991; Tank Girl, 1995; Mission Impossible, 1996; Nearly God, 1996; Archive, 1997; Tibetan Freedom Concert, 1997; Not For Threes, 1998; Great Crossover Potential, 1998; Y2K Beat The Clock Version 1, 1999; Film: Dancer in the Dark, 2000. Honours: BRIT Award, Best International Female Artist, 1996; Platinum and Gold records. Address: One Little Indian, 250 York Road, London SW11 3SJ, England.

BLACK David Macleod, b. 8 November 1941, Cape Town, South Africa (British citizen). Lecturer; Poet. m. Jeanne Magagna, 28 January 1984. Education: MA, University of Edinburgh, 1966; MA in Religious Studies, University of Lancaster, 1971. Appointments: Teacher, Chelsea Art School, London, 1966-70; Lecturer and Supervisor, Westminster Pastoral Foundation, London. Publications: Rocklestrakes, 1960; From the Mountain, 1963; Theory of Diet, 1966; With Decorum, 1967; A Dozen Short Poems, 1968; Penguin Modern Poets 11, 1968; The Educators, 1969; The Old Hag, 1972; The Happy Crow, 1974; Gravitations, 1979; Collected Poems 1964-1987, 1991; A Place for Exploration, 1991. Contributions to: Translations of Goethe published in Modern Poetry in Translation, 1998, 2000 Honours: Scottish Arts Council Prize, 1968 and Publication Award, 1991; Arts Council of Great Britain Bursary, 1968. Address: 30 Cholmley Gardens, Aldred Road, London NW6 1AG, England.

BLACK Rhyll, b. 17 June 1940, Mildura, Victoria, Australia. Occupational Physician. m. Lance Victor Black, deceased, 1 son, 1 daughter. Education: Bachelor of Music, 1960, Bachelor of

Dictionary of International Biography

Medicine and Surgery (MBBS), 1980, University of Melbourne, Australia; Master of Public Health, Monash University, Australia, 1988; Fellow, Australian Faculty of Occupational Medicine, 1988. Appointments: Bassoonist, West Australia Symphony Orchestra, 1960-61; Principal Bassoonist, Australian Elizabethan Trust Orchestra, 1961-65; Bassoonist, Victoria Symphony Orchestra, 1966-75; Resident Medical Officer, 1980-84, Physician, 1987-96, Victoria Police Hospital; Physician, Police Clinic, Freemasons Hospital, 1996-2003; Physician, St Kilda Road Medical Clinic, 2003-. Publication: Occupational Stress Factors in Orchestral Musicians (thesis). Memberships: Victoria Medical Women's Society; Dante Alighieri Society; Honorary Member, Past and Present Police Women's Society; Victoria Artists Society; Humanist Society. Address: 157 Barkly Street, Brunswick, Victoria, Australia 3056.

BLACKBURN Alexander Lambert, b. 6 September 1929, Durham, North Carolina, USA. Novelist; Editor. m. Inés Dölz, 14 October 1975, 2 sons, 1 daughter. Education: BA, Yale University, 1947-51; MA, English, University of North Carolina, 1954-55; PhD, English, Cambridge University, England, 1959-60, 1961-63. Appointments: Instructor, Hampden-Sydney College, 1960-61, University of Pennsylvania, 1963-65; Lecturer, University of Maryland Euro Division, 1967-72; Professor of English, University of Colorado at Colorado Springs, 1973-95; Emeritus Professor English, 1996-. Publications: The Myth of the Picaro, 1979; The Cold War of Kitty Pentecost, novel, 1979; Editor, The Interior Country: Stories of the Modern West, 1987; A Sunrise Brighter Still: The Visionary Novels of Frank Waters, 1991; Editor, Higher Elevations: Stories from the West, 1993; Suddenly a Mortal Splendor, novel, 1995; Creative Spirit: Toward a Better World: Essays, 2001. Contributions to: Founder and Editor-in-Chief; Writers Forum, 1974-95. Honours: Faculty Book Award, Colorado University, 1993; Runnerup, Colorado Book Award, 1996; International Peace-Writing Award, 2003. Memberships: Authors Guild; PEN West; Colorado Authors League. Address: 6030 Twin Rock Court, Colorado Springs, CO 80918, USA.

BLACKBURN Julia Karen Eugenie, b. 12 August 1948, London, England. Writer. m. (1) May 1978, divorced 1995, 1 son, 1 daughter, (2) December 1999. Education: BA Hons, English Literature, York University. Publications: The White Men, 1978; Charles Waterton, 1989; The Emperor's Last Island, 1991; Daisy Bates in the Desert, 1994; The Book of Colour, 1995; The Leper's Companions, 1999; For a Child: A Selection of the Poems of Thomas Blackburn, 1999; Old Man Goya, 2002. Memberships: Society of Authors; PEN; Fellow, Royal Society of Literature, 2003. Address: c/o Toby Eady, Third Floor, 9 Orme Court, London W2 4RL, England.

BLACKFORD Christopher Thomas, b. 20 January 1960, Windsor, Berkshire, England. Journalist. Education: BA, Honours, Philosophy and Literature, Warwick University, England, 1978-81; Postgraduate Certificate in Education, Birmingham University, England, 1982-83. Appointments: English Teacher, Moreton School, Wolverhampton, 1983-86; Lecturer, Media Studies, Solihull College of Technology, Solihull, 1987-89; Editor and Publisher, Rubberneck, 1985-; Freelance Journalist, 1990-. Publications: The Guinness Encyclopedia of Popular Music, 1993; Virgin Encyclopedia of Popular Music, 1997; Joe Harriott: Forgotten Father of European Free Jazz, 1997; AA Best Pubs and Inns, 1998; AA Hotels in France, 1998; The Wedding of All Essential Parts: The Recordings of Edward Vesala, 2004; Magazines/Journals, Contributor to Avant, Double Bassist, Jazz on CD, Jazz the Magazine, Resonance, Variant, The Wire. Address: 21 Denham Drive, Basingstoke, Hampshire RG22 6LT, England.

BLACKMAN Honor, b. 22 August 1926, London. Actress. Creative Works: Films include: Fame is the Spur, 1947; Green Grow the Rushes, 1951; Come Die My Love, 1952; The Rainbow Jacket, 1953; The Glass Cage, 1954; Dead Man's Evidence, 1955; A Matter of Who, 1961; Goldfinger, 1964; Life at the Top, 1965; Twist of Sand, 1967; The Virgin and the Gipsy, 1970; To the Devil a Daughter, 1975; Summer Rain, 1976; The Cat and the Canary, 1977; Talos - The Mummy; To Walk with Lions; Bridget Jones's Diary, 2001; Plays include: Madamoiselle Colombe, 2000; TV appearances include: Four Just Men, 1959; Man of Honour, 1960; Ghost Squad, 1961; Top Secret, 1962; The Avengers, 1962-64; The Explorer, 1968; Visit From a Stranger, 1970; Out Damned Spot, 1972; Wind of Change, 1977; Robin's Nest, 1982; Never the Twain, 1982; The Secret Adversary, 1983; Lace, 1985; The First Modern Olympics, 1986; Minder on the Orient Express, 1986; Dr Who, 1986; William Tell, 1986; The Upper Hand (TV series). Address: c/o Jean Diamond, London Management, 2-4 Noel Street, London W1V 3RB, England.

BLACKWOOD Simon Anthony James, b. 17 May 1948, Chelmsford, Essex. Artist. m. Laura Charlotte Maberley Balston, 1 daughter. Education: Dip AD Foundation, Colchester School of Art, 1965-67; Dip AD, Coventry School of Art, 1967-70; Academy for Continuous Education, Sherbourne, Gloucestershire, under John G Bennett, 1971-72. Career: Founder Member, Beshara Design Centre, the Industrial Buildings preservation Trust and Rotherhithe Workshops Ltd, London, 1972-80; Involved in raising funds and the conversion of a group of Docklands Warehouses for use as artists' and designers' studios and a centre for dance and the performing arts; Opened the Riverside Studio Dance Centre, Rotherhithe, 1976; Attended the Beshara School of Intensive Esoteric Education, Gloucestershire, extensive travels Europe and the Near East, 1976; Set up studio/gallery and picture conservation business, Scotland, 1981; Established new studio, Istanbul, Turkey, 1988; Commissioned to live in Provence to work on a series of 7 paintings for the Chateau du Tourreau, Vaucluse, France, 1989; Painting in Turkey, Scotland, France and USA, restoring paintings on canvas and panel and works on paper in the UK; One-man Exhibitions: Dundas Gallery, Carlisle, 1985; Netherbow Arts Centre, Carlisle, 1986; Anthony Mould Ltd, New Bond Street, London, 1991; William Hardie Gallery, Glasgow, 1992; Brian Sinfield Gallery, Burford, Oxon, 1992, 1994; Kusav Arts, Istanbul, Turkey, 1993; Cynthia Bourne Gallery, London, 1996; Various group shows in Scotland, England and Istanbul, Turkey; Work in Collections: The Fleming Collection; Nomura International; Breakthrough Technologies; The Sabanci Family Corporation, Turkey; Mr & Mrs Dobbs-Higginson, France; Mr & Mrs William Mellon, UK; Mr & Mrs Nicholas Ward, UK; Mr Peter Webster, New York City. Address: 10 & 11 Bourtreet Terrace, Hawick, Roxburgh TD9 9HN, Scotland. E-mail: blackwoodfinearts@mac.com

BLAINEY Geoffrey Norman, b. 11 March 1930, Melbourne, Victoria, Australia. Writer. Education: Wesley College, Melbourne; Queen's College, University of Melbourne. Publications: The Peaks of Lyell, 1954; A Centenary History of the University of Melbourne, 1957; Gold and Paper, 1958; Mines in the Spinifex, 1960; The Rush That Never Ended, 1963; A History of Camberwell, 1965; If I Remember Rightly: The Memoirs of W S Robinson, 1966; Wesley College: The First Hundred Years (co-author and editor), 1967; The Tyranny of Distance, 1966; Across a Red World, 1968; The Rise of Broken Hill, 1968; The Steel Master, 1971; The Causes of War, 1973; Triumph of the Nomads, 1975; A Land Half Won, 1980; The Blainey View, 1982; Our Side of the Country, 1984; All for Australia, 1984; The Great Seesaw, 1988; A Game of our Own: The Origins of Australian Football, 1990; Odd Fellows, 1991; Eye on Australia, 1991; Jumping Over the Wheel, 1993; The

Golden Mile, 1993; A Shorter History of Australia, 1994; White Gold, 1997; A History of the AMP, 1999; In Our Time, 1999; A History of the World, 2000; This Land is All Horizons, 2002; Black Kettle and Full Moon, 2003. Honours: Gold Medal, Australian Literature Society, 1963; Encyclopaedia Britannica Gold Award, New York, 1988. Memberships: Australia Council, chairman, 1977-81; Commonwealth Literary Fund, chairman, 1971-73; Professor of Economic History and History, University of Melbourne, 1968-88; Inaugural Chancellor of University of Ballarat, 1994-98; Chairman, National Council for Centenary of Federation, 2001. Address: PO Box 257, East Melbourne, Victoria 3002, Australia.

BLAIR Anthony Charles Lynton (Tony), b. 6 May 1953, Edinburgh, Scotland. Member of Parliament; Politician. m. Cherie Booth, 1980, 3 sons, 1 daughter. Education: Fettes College, Edinburgh; St Johns College, Oxford. Appointments: Barrister, Trade Union and Employment Law; MP, Sedgefield, 1983-; Shadow Treasury Spokesman, 1984-87, Trade and Industry Spokesman, 1987-88, Energy Spokesman, 1988-89, Employment Spokesman, 1989-92, Home Affairs Spokesman, 1992-94; Leader, Labour Party, 1994-, Prime Minister, First Lord of the Treasury and Minister for the Civil Service, 1997-. Publication: New Britain: My Vision of a Young Country, 1996; The Third Way, 1998. Honours: Honorary Bencher, Lincolns Inn, 1994; Honorary LLD, Northumbria; Charlemagne Prize, 1999. Address: 10 Downing Street, London SW1A 2AA, England.

BLAIR David Chalmers Leslie Jr, b. 8 April 1951, Long Beach, California, USA. Alternative Rock Artist; Composer; Artist; Author. Education: BA, French, ESL certificate, California State University at Long Beach, 1979; Postgraduate Studies, Université de Provence, Aix-en-Provence, France, 1979-80. Publications: Novels: Death of an Artist, 1982; Vive la France, 1993; Death of America, 1994; Mother, 1998; Evening in Wisconsin, 2001; The Girls (and Women) I Have Known, 2001; A Small Snack Shop in Stockholm, Sweden, 2002; Composer, Writer and Recorder of 108 albums including: Her Garden of Earthly Delights; Sir Blair of Rothes; Europe; St Luke Passion. Memberships: Libertarian Party, USA. Address: 19331 105th Avenue, Cadott, WI 54727, USA. Website: www.motorcoat.com/davidblair

BLAKE Quentin Saxby, b. 16 December 1932, Sidcup, Kent, England. Artist; Illustrator; Teacher. Education: Downing College, Cambridge; London Institute of Education; Chelsea School of Art. Appointments: Freelance Illustrator, 1957-; Tutor, Royal College of Art, 1965-86, Head, Illustration Department, 1978-86, Visiting Professor, 1989-, Senior Fellow, 1988; Children's Laureate, 1999. Publications: Illustrations for over 250 works for children and adults, including collaborations with Roald Dahl, Russell Hoban, Joan Aiken, Michael Rosen, John Yeoman; Non-fiction: La Vie de la Page, 1995; Quentine Blake: Words and Pictures, 2000; Tell Me a Picture, 2001; Laureate's Progress, 2002. Honours: Honorary Fellow: Brighton University, 1996; Downing College, Cambridge, 2000; Honorary RA; Chevalier des Arts et des Lettres, 2002; Dr hc: London Institute, 2000, Northumbria, 2001, RCA, 2001. Address: Flat 8, 30 Bramham Gardens, London SW5 0HF, England.

BLAKEMORE Colin, b. 1 June 1944, Stratford-on-Avon, England. Neurophysiologist; Professor of Physiology. m. Andree Elizabeth Washbourne, 1965, 3 daughters. Education: Natural Sciences, Corpus Christi College, Cambridge, 1965; PhD, Physiological Optics, Neurosensory Laboratory, University of California at Berkeley, 1968. Appointments: Demonstrator, Physiological Laboratory, Cambridge University, 1968-72; Lecturer in Physiology, Cambridge, 1972-79; Fellow and Director of Medical Studies, Downing College, 1971-79; Professorial Fellow of Magdalen College, Oxford, 1979-; Wayneflete Professor of Physiology, Oxford University, 1979-; Chief Executive European Dana Alliance for the Brain, 1996-; President, 1997-98, Vice President, 1990-, British Association for the Advancement of Science; President, British Neuroscience Association, 1997-2000; Director, McDonnell-Pew Centre for Cognitive Neuroscience, Oxford, 1990-; Director, MRC Interdisciplinary Research Centre for Cognitive Neuroscience, Oxford, 1996-; Associate Director, MRC Research Centre in Brain and Behaviour, Oxford, 1990-;. Publications: Editor, Handbook of Psychobiology, 1975; Mechanics of the Mind, 1977; Editor, Mindwaves, 1987; The Mind Machine, 1988, Editor, Images and Understanding, 1990; Vision: Coding and Efficiency, 1990; Sex and Society, 1999; Oxford Companion to the Body, 2001; Contributions to: Constraints on Learning, 1973; Illusion in Art and Nature, 1973; The Neurosciences Third Study Program, 1974; and to professional journals. Honours: Robert Bing Prize, 1975; Man of the Year, 1978; Christmas Lectures for Young People, Royal Institute, 1982; John Locke Medal, 1983; Netter Prize, 1984; Bertram Louis Abrahams Lecture, 1986; Cairns Memorial Lecture and Medal, 1986; Norman McAllister Gregg Lecture and Medal, 1988; Royal Society Michael Faraday Medal, 1989; Robert Doyne Medal, 1989; John P McGovern Science and Society Lecture and Medal, 1990; Montgomery Medal, 1991; Sir Douglas Robb Lectures, 1991; Honorary DSc, Aston, 1992; Honorary Osler Medal, 1993; Ellison-Cliffe Medal, 1993; DSc, Salford, 1994; Charles F Prentice Award, 1994; Annual Review Prize Lecture, 1995; Century Lecture, 1996; Alcon Prize, 1996; Newton Lecture, 1997; Cockcroft Lecture, 1997; Memorial Medal, 1998; Alfred Meyer Award, 2001; British Neuroscience Association Outstanding Contribution to Neuroscience, 2001. Memberships: Editorial Board, Perception, 1971; Behavioural and Brain Sciences, 1977; Journal of Developmental Physiology, 1978-86; Experimental Brain Research, 1979-89; Language and Communication, 1979; Reviews in the Neurosciences, 1984-; News in Physiological Sciences, 1985; Clinical Vision Sciences, 1986; Chinese Journal of Physiological Sciences, 1988; Advances in Neuroscience, 1989-; Vision Research, 1993-; Honorary Member, Physiological Society, 1998; Associate Editor, NeuroReport, 1989-; Honorary Associate, Rationalist Press Association, 1986-; Editor-in-Chief, IBRO News, 1986-; Leverhulme Fellowship, 1974-75; BBC Reith Lecturer, 1976; Lethaby Professor, RCA, London, 1978; Storer Lecturer, University of California at Davis, 1980; Regents' Professor, 1995-96; Macallum Lecturer, University of Toronto, 1984; Fellow, World Economic Forum, 1994-98; Honorary Fellow, Corpus Christi College, Cambridge, 1994-; Founder, Fellow, Academy of Medical Sciences, 1998-; Foreign Member, Royal Netherlands Academy of Arts and Sciences, 1993; Member, Worshipful Company of Spectacle Makers and Freemen of the City of London, 1997; Member, Livery, 1998; Patron and Member, Professional Advisory Panel Headway (National Head Injuries Association), 1997-; Patron, Association for Art, Science, Engineering and Technology, 1997- Address: University Laboratory of Physiology, Parks Road, Oxford OX1 3PT, England.

BLAKEMORE John Stewart, b. 24 November 1939, Newcastle, New South Wales, Australia. International Management Consultant. m. Deirdre June Flynn, 10 April 1965, 2 sons. Education: BSc, University of New South Wales, Sydney, 1964; MSc University of Newcastle, New South Wales, 1966; PhD, 1969; Postgraduate, Australian School of Nuclear Technology, 1970. Appointments: Research Scientist, AAEC, Lucas Heights, New South Wales, 1969-70; Chief Metallurgist, John Lysaght, Newcastle, 1970-77; Tubemakers, Newcastle, 1977-79; Engineering Manager, Wormald Machinery Group, 1979-82; General Manager, Pyrotek, Sydney, 1982-84; Marketing Director,

Dictionary of International Biography

John Morris, Sydney, 1983-84; Divisional General Manager, GEC, Sydney 1984-85; Managing Director, Blakemore Consulting, Sydney, 1985-; Director, MASC P/L NSW. Publications: The Quality Solution, 1989; The Quality Solution for the Plastics Industry, 1995; Quality Habits of Best Business Practice, 1995; Strategic Planning for Business, 1998. Honours: Commonwealth Scholarship (Graduate and Post-graduate), 1957; International Nickel Fellow, 1966-69; PhD, 1969. Memberships: Director, Fellow, Australian Institute of Management; Fellow, Institution of Engineers; Member, Institute of Materials; Fellow, Australian Organisation of Quality; Fellow, Quality Society of Australia; Member, Institute of Management Consultants; CMC; CP Eng (UK); CP Eng (Aust); Fellow, Australian Institute of Company Directors; Board Industrial Research and Development, Australia Industry, Member, Engineering and Manufacturing Committee; President, 1970-73, 1978-79, Liberal Party, Newcastle; President, Citizens Group, 1980-81. Listed in: Who's Who in the World. Address: 2/29 Waratah St, Rushcutters Bay, NSW 2011, Australia.

BLANCHETT Cate, b. 1969, Australia. Actress. m. Andrew Upton, 1997, 1 son. Education: Melbourne University, National Institute of Dramatic Art. Appointments: Plays include: Top Girls; Kafka Dances; Oleanna; Hamlet; Sweet Phoebe; The Tempest; The Blind Giant is Dancing; Plenty. Films include: Parkland; Paradise Road, 1997; Thank God He Met Lizzie, 1997; Oscar and Lucinda, 1997; Elizabeth, 1998; Dreamtime Alice, also co-producer; The Talented Mr Ripley; An Ideal Husband; Pushing Tin, 1999; Bandit, 2000; The Man Who Cried, 2000; The Gift, 2000; Bandits, 2000; Heaven, 2001; The Lord of the Rings: The Fellowship of the Ring, 2001; Charlotte Gray, 2001; The Shipping News, 2002; The Lord of the Rings: The Two Towers, 2002; The Lord of the Rings: The Return of the King, 2003; TV includes: Heartland, 1994; GP Police Rescue. Honours: Newcomer Award, 1993; Rosemont Best Actress Award; Golden Globe Award, 1998; BAFTA Award for Best Actress, 1999; Best Actress, National Board of Review, 2001; Golden Camera Award, 2001. Address: c/o Robyn Gardiner, PO Box 128, Surry Hill, 2010 NSW, Australia.

BLANCO Desiderio, b. 11 February 1929, Santa Maria de la Vega, Zamora, Spain. Professor. m. Evelyne Dejardin, 1 son, 2 daughters. Education: Bachelor in Theology, Ecclesiastical School of Theology, Lima, Peru, 1957; Licence in Education, 1962, PhD, Education, 1973, Universidad Nacional Mayor de San Marcos, Peru; Specialised Studies in Semiotics, École Pratique des Hautes Études (now EHSS), Paris, France, 1974-75. Appointments: Dean of Communication School, 1970-84, Vice-Rector, 1984-89, Rector, 1989-94, Director of Graduate School, 1995-, University of Lima, Peru. Publications: Metodología del Análisis Semiótico, 1980; Imagen por Imagen, 1987; Claves Semióticas, 1989; Semiótica del texto filmico, 2003; Vigencia de la Semiótica y otros ensayos, in press. Honour: Great Cross of the Civil Merit Order, S.M. Juan Carlos I, King of Spain, 1993. Memberships: Association Internationale de Sémiotique (AIS); Asociación Peruana de Semiótica. Address: Berlin 675-601, Miraflores, Lima 18, Peru. E-mail: dblanco@correo.ulima.edu.pe

BLANZAT Anne-Marie, b. 24 November 1944, Neuilly, France. Soprano. Education: Studied in Paris. Career: Yniold, Debussy's Pelléas et Mélisande, Aix-en-Provence, 1966, Glyndebourne, 1969; Mélisande, Nantes, France, 1974, Glyndebourne, 1976; Susanna, Juliette, Strasbourg, 1983; La Voix Humaine, Poulenc, Strasbourg, 1991; Sang in modern repertory, Prodromidès, Poulenc and Prey, and in Reameau's Hippolyte et Aricie; Teacher, Conservatoire Municipal Maurice Ravel de Paris, and Ecole Normale de Musique de Paris. Honours: Oscar de l'Art Lyrique, 1974; Officier des Arts et Lettres, 1998. Address: 2 Square Servan, 75011 Paris, France.

BLAS Harold, b. 17 September 1964, Ancash, Peru. Physicist. Education: BA, 1989, Lic (Hon), 1991, National University of Engineering, Lima, Peru; MSc, Institute of Theoretical Physics, São Paulo, Brazil, 1996; PhD, 2000. Appointment: Postdoctorate, Institute of Theoretical Physics, São Paulo, Brazil, 2000-2003. Publications: Articles in professional journals as author and co-author including; Nuclear Physics, 2000, 2001, Annals of Physics, 2000; Journal of Mathematical Physics, 2002; Physical Review, 2001, 2002; JHEP, 2003. Honours: Listed in Who's Who publications and biographical dictionaries. Memberships: Brazilian Society of Physics; American Mathematical Society. Address: Rua Pamplona 145; 01405-900 São Paulo, SP, Brazil. E-mail: blas@ift.unesp.br

BLASCH Robert Edward, b. 1 July 1931, New York, New York, USA. Music Educator; Pianist. m. Betty Lou Russell, 26 August 1966, 1 son, 1 daughter. Education: BA, summa cum laude, Mathematics, Music, Hofstra University, 1952; MA, University of Illinois, 1953; MusB with distinction, 1958, MusM, 1959, University of Michigan; EdD, Columbia University, 1971. Appointments: Chairman, Piano Department, Shenandoah Conservatory, Winchester, Virginia, 1959-62; Professional Accompanist, University of Illinois, Champaign-Urbana, 1962-63; Instructor, Slippery Rock University, Pennsylvania, 1964-65; Professor, Music, Longwood College, Farmville, Virginia, 1965-; Presenter, Piano Recitals, various cultural and educational organisations, 1950-; Group Piano, Keyboard and Multimedia Teacher, Richmond, Virginia, 1996-; Volunteer Piano Teacher, Richmond Public Schools, 2000-. Creative Works: Composer of piano: solo and ensemble pieces, handbell pieces; Compiler, arranger, lesson book: Elementary Piano Compositions, 1985. Publications: Articles in professional journals and magazines and ensemble piano pieces. Honours: Raymond Burrows Scholar at Columbia University, 1969-70; Listed in numerous Who's Who publications. Memberships: College Music Society; Music Teachers National Association; Virginia Music Teachers Association; Richmond Music Teachers Association; Music Educators National Conference, Virginia Music Educators Association; Phi Beta Kappa; Phi Kappa Phi. Address: 10031 Tuxford Road, Richmond, VA 23236-4610, USA.

BLASHFORD-SNELL John Nicholas, b, 22 October 1936, Hereford, England. Colonel; Explorer; Author. m. Judith, 2 daughters. Education: RMA Sandhurst; The Staff College, Dorset. Appointments: Various military postings and commands, and leader of numerous scientific, military and youth development expeditions; Instructor and Adventure Training Officer, RMA Sandhurst, 1963-66; Leader, Great Abbai, Blue Nile Expedition, 1968; Chairman, Scientific Exploration Society, 1969-; Commander, Operation Drake, 1978-81; Director-General, Operation Raleigh, 1984-91; Lecturer, Ministry of Defence, 1991-; Chairman, The Starting Point Appeal, The Merseyside Youth Association, 1993-2001; Chairman, The Liverpool Construction Crafts Guild, 2001-. Publications: Books, including Weapons and Tactics, (co-author), 1972; Where the Trails Run Out, 1974; In the Steps of Stanley, 1975; In the Wake of Drake, (co-author), 1980; Operation Drake, (co-author), 1981; 3 titles co-authored with Ann Tweedy, documenting the story of Operation Raleigh; Mammoth Hunt, (co-author), 1996; Kota Mama, (co-author), 2000; East to the Amazon (with Richard Snailham), 2002. Honours: OBE; Freeman of the City of Hereford, 1984; Honorary DEng, University of Bournemouth, 1997; Honorary DSc, Durham University, 1986; Darien Medal, Colombia, 1972; Livingstone Medal, Royal Scottish Geographical Society, 1975; Patron's Medal, Royal Geographical Society, 1993; Paul Harris Fellow, Rotary International, 1981; Gold Medal, Institute of Royal Engineers, 1994; La Paz Medal, Bolivia, 2001; Chair, Just a Drop Charity, 2002-. Memberships: President, Galley

Hill Gun Club; President, The Centre for Fortean Zoology; The Vole Club; Trustee, Operation New World, 1996-. Address: Scientific Exploration Society, Expedition Base, Motcombe, Dorset, SP7 9PB, England. E-mail: jbs@ses-explore.org

BLASI Paolo, b. 11 February 1940, Florence, Italy. Former Rector. m. Giovanna Stefanelli, 1 son, 2 daughters. Education: Degree in Physics, University of Florence. Appointments: Assistant Professor, Physics, 1963-80; Full Professor, General Physics, 1980-; Director, INFN National Laboratory of Legnaro, 1979-82; Director, Department of Physics, University of Florence, 1983-88; Vice President, National Institute of Optics, 1987-96; Member, Executive Board, INFN, 1988-91; Rector, University of Florence, 1991-2000; Chairman, Conference of Italian Rectors, 1994-98; Vice President, Association of European Universities, 1998-2001; Higher Council of the Bank of Italy, 1999-; Administrative Board, International Association of Universities, 1995-. Publications: Over 80 scientific papers in international reviews of nuclear physics. Honours: Honour Degree, Humanae Litterae, New York University; Sir Harold Acton Award, New York University; Chevalier de l'Ordre National de la Légion d'Honneur, President of the Republic, France. Memberships: Higher Council of the Bank of Italy; Foundation of the Bank "Cassa di Risparmio Di Firenze"; Administrative Board, International Association of Universities; Rotary Club of Florence; British Institute of Florence; European Research Advisory Board, 2001-; Member, Board of Directors, National Council of Research, 1999-2003; Member, European Research Advisory Board (EURAB), 2001-; Member, Conseil National d'Evaluation (CNE), 2003-. Address: Dipartimento di Fisica, Universita degli Studi di Firenze, Via Sansone 1-50019 Sesto F,NO-Firenze, Italy.

BLATNY Pavel, b. 14 September 1931, Brno, Czech Republic. m. Danuse Spirková, 19 June 1982, 1 son, 1 daughter. Education: Musicology, University of Brno, 1958; Berklee School of Music, USA, 1968. Career: Composer; Conductor; Pianist; Chief, Music Department, Czech Television, to 1992; Professor, Janácek's Academy, Brno, to 1990. Compositions include: Concerto for Jazz Orchestra, 1962-64; Roll-call; Willow; Christmas Eve; Noonday Witch; Bells; Twelfth Night, based on Shakespeare's play, 1975; Two Movements for brasses, 1982; Signals for jazz orchestra, 1985; Prologue for mixed choir and jazz orchestra, 1984; Per organo e big band, 1983; Ring a Ring o' Roses, for solo piano, 1984. Honours: Prize of Leos Jánácek, 1984; Antiteatro D'Argento for the whole work, Nepal, Italy, 1988. Membership: President, Club of Moravian Composers. Address: Absolonova 35, 62400 Brno. Czech Republic.

BLAUNSHTEIN Nathan, b. 4 May 1948, Moldova, USSR. Professor of Communication. m. Osnat Blaunshtein, 1 son. Education: MSc, Tomsk University, USSR, 1972; PhD, IZMIR Academy of Science, Moscow, USSR, 1984; DSc, 1991, Professor of Radio Physics and Electronics, 1992, IZMIRAN, Moscow, Russia. Appointments: Teacher, Associate Professor, Professor, Moldovian Pedagogical University Beltsi, Moldova, former USSR, 1976-92; Researcher, Senior Scientist, Associate Professor, Professor, Ben-Gurion University, Beer Sheva, Israel, 1993-. Publications: More than 130 articles on radiophysics, geophysics, communication; 6 manuals; 6 books include: Radio Propagation in Cellular Networks, 1999; Multipath Phenomena in Cellular Networks, 2002; Antennas and Propagation for Wireless Communication, 2004. Honours: Best Paper Award, Journal IEEE Communications and Networks, 2000; US Patent: Method of Earthquake Prediction, 2001. Memberships: IEEE; IEICE; URSI; Optical Society of America; New York Academy of Sciences; American Association for the Advancement of Science. Address: Department of Communication Systems Engineering, Ben-Gurion University, POB 653, Beer Sheva, 84105 Israel. E-mail: natanb@cse.bgu.ac.il

BLEASDALE Alan, b. 23 March 1946. Playwright; Novelist. m. Julia Moses, 1970, 2 sons, 1 daughter. Education: Teachers Certificate, Padgate Teachers Training College. Publications: Scully, 1975; Who's Been Sleeping in My Bed, 1977; No More Sitting on the Old School Bench, 1979; Boys From the Blackstuff (televised), 1982; Are You Lonesome Tonight?, 1985; No Surrender, 1986; Having a Ball, 1986; It's A Madhouse, 1986; The Monocled Mutineer (televised), 1986; GBH (TV series), 1992; On the Ledge, 1993; Jake's Progress (TV), 1995; Oliver Twist, 1999. Honours: BAFTA Writer's Award, 1982; RTS Writer's Award, 1982; Broadcasting Press Guild TV Award for Best Series, 1982; Best Musical, London Stand Drama Awards, 1985; Hon DLitt, Liverpool Polytechnic, 1991; Best Writer, Monte Carlo International TV Festival, 1996; Best Drama Series, TV and Radio Industries Club, 2000. Address: c/o Harvey Unna and Stephen Durbridge Ltd, 24 Pottery Lane, Holland Park, London, W11 4LZ, England.

BLESSED Brian, b. 9 October 1936, Mexborough, South Yorkshire, England. Actor. m. Hildegard Zimmerman, 1978, 1 daughter. Education: Bristol Old Vic. Appointments: Repertory companies in Nottingham and Birmingham; Stage appearances: Hamlet; Richard III; Henry V; State of Revolution; Metropolis; Cats; The Lion in Winter; Hard Times; One man show, An Evening with Brian Blessed; Chitty Chitty Bang Bang, 2002-03; Films include: Flash Gordon; Return to Treasure Island; Trojan Women; Man of La Mancha; Henry V; War and Remembrance; Robin Hood Prince of Thieves; Prisoners of Honour; Much Ado About Nothing; Hamlet; King Lear; Tarzan; Star Wars – The Phantom Menace; Mumbo Jumbo; TV includes: Z Cars; The Three Musketeers; I, Claudius; My Family and Other Animals; Blackadder; Tom Jones. Publications: The Turquoise Mountain; The Dynamite Kid; Nothing's Impossible; Blessed Everest; Quest to the Lost World. Address: c/o Derek Webster, AIM, Nederlander House, 7 Great Russell Street, London WC1B 3NH, England. E-mail: info@aim.demon.co.uk Website: www.a-i-m.net

BLETHYN Brenda Anne, b. 20 February 1946, Ramsgate, Kent, England. Actress. Partner, Michael Mayhew, 1977. Education: Thanet Technical College; Guildford School of Acting. Creative Works: Theatre appearances include: Mysteries, 1979; Steaming, 1981; Double Dealer, 1982; Benefactors, 1984; Dalliance, 1987; A Doll's House, 1987; Born Yesterday, 1988; The Beaux' Stratagem, 1989; An Ideal Husband, 1992; Wildest Dreams, 1993; The Bed Before Yesterday, 1994; Habeas Corpus, 1996; Absent Friends, 1996; Mrs Warren's Profession, 2002-03. Films: The Witches, A River Runs Through It, 1992; Secrets and Lies, 1996; Remember Me, 1996; Music From Another Room, 1997; Girls' Night, 1997; Little Voice, 1999; Night Train, 1999; Daddy and Them, 1999; RKO 281, 1999; Saving Grace, 2000; On the Nose, In the Winter Dark, 1999; The Sleeping Dictionary, 2000; Yellow Bird, Pumpkin, 2000; Anne Frank – The Whole Story, 2001; Lovely and Amazing, 2001; Plots with a View, 2000; Sonny, 2002; Blizzard, 2002. TV includes: Henry VI (Part I), 1981; King Lear, 1983; Chance in a Million, 1983-85; The Labours of Erica, 1987; The Bullion Boys, 1993; The Buddah of Suburbia, 1993; Sleeping with Mickey, 1993; Outside Edge, 1994-96; First Signs of Madness, 1996. Honours include: Best Actress Award, Cannes Film Festival, 1996; Boston Film Critics Award, 1997; LA Film Critics Award, 1997; Golden Globe, 1997; London Film Critics Award, 1997; BAFTA, 1997; Honorary Dr of Letters, 1999. Membership: Poetry Society, 1976-. Address: c/o ICM, 76 Oxford Street, London W1N 0AX, England.

BLICKER Seymour, b. 12 February 1940, Montreal, Quebec, Canada. Writer. m. Susan Wanda Colman, 13 June 1963, 3 sons, 1 daughter. Education: BA, Loyola College, 1962. Appointments: Special Lecturer, Creative Writing, Concordia University, 1978-90. Publications: Novels: Blues Chased a Rabbit, 1969; Shmucks, 1972; The Last Collection, 1976. Stage Plays: Up Your Alley, 1987; Never Judge a Book By Its Cover, 1987; Pals, 1995; Home Free, 1998; Pipe Dreams, 1999. Honours: Canada Council Senior Arts Fellowship, 1974; British Councils International New Playwriting Award for the Americas Region, 1997. Memberships: Writers Union of Canada; Playwrights Union of Canada; Academy of Canadian Cinema and Television; Writers Guild of America West; Writers Guild of Canada. Address: 7460 Kingsley Road #804, Montreal, Quebec H4W 1P3, Canada.

BLIGE Mary J, b. 11 January 1971, New York, USA. Singer. Career: Solo recording artiste; Support to Jodeci, UK tour, 1995. Recordings: Albums: What's The 411, 1992; My Life, 1994; Mary Jane, 1995; Share My World, 1997; The Tour, 1998; Mary, 1999; No More Drama, 2001; Ballads, 2001; Singles: What's The 411, 1992; Sweet Thing, 1993; My Love, 1994; You Bring Me Joy, 1995; All Night Long, 1995; Not Gon' Cry, 1996; Love Is All We Need, 1997; Everything, 1997; Seven Days, 1999; All That I Can Say, 1999; As, with George Michael, 1999; Also appears on: Father's Day, 1990; Changes, 1992; Close To You, 1992; Panther, 1995; Show, 1995; MTV Party To Go, 1995; Waiting To Exhale, 1995; Nutty Professor, 1996; Case, 1996; Ironman, 1996; Love And Consequences, 1998; Miseducation Of Lauryn Hill, 1998; Nu Nation Project, 1998. Address: Steve Lucas Associates, 156 W 56th Street, New York, NY 10019, USA.

BLOCH (Andrew Charles) Danby, b. 19 December 1945, Bognor Regis, England. Publisher. m. Sandra, 1 son, 1 daughter. Education: MA, Oxon, Philosophy, Politics and Economics, 1968, Wadham College, Oxford. Appointments: Researcher, former Oxford Centre for Management Studies (now Templeton College, Oxford), 1968-70; Director, Grosvenor Advisory Services, 1971-74; Financial Services Director, Oxford Fine Arts Ltd (arts and antiques dealers), 1975-85; Director, Raymond Godfrey and Partners, 1974-, (independent financial advisors); Director, Taxbriefs Ltd, 1975- (specialist financial publishers); Chairman, Helm Godfrey Partners Ltd, (independent financial advisors), 2000-; Director, T1Ps.com, 2000- (internet financial newsletter). Publications: Contributed regular weekly columns on tax and financial planning to several national broadsheet newspapers, including The Times, 1979-82; The Sunday Times, 1988-91; The Daily Telegraph, 1982-86; Several books, including: Financial Planning (author); Planning for School and College Fees (co-author); Taxation and Trusts (editor); Personal Financial Planning; Business Financial Planning; Pensions; Portfolio Planning. Memberships: Chair of Governors, Oxford Brookes University, 1998-; Member, Council of Museum of Modern Art, Oxford, 1990-; Institute of Directors; Society of Financial Advisers, LIA; Patron of the Friends of the Pitt Rivers Museum, Oxford. Address: 17 Norham Road, Oxford, OX2 6SF, England.

BLOOM Claire, b. 15 February 1931, London, England. Actress. m. (1) Rod Steiger, 1959, 1 daughter. (2) 1969, (3) Philip Roth, 1990, divorced 1995. Education: London, Bristol and New York. Appointments: Oxford Repertory Theatre, 1946; Stratford-on-Avon, 1948. Creative Works: Performances include: Mary, Queen of Scots in Vivat, Vivat Regina!, New York, 1972; A Streetcare Named Desire, London, 1974; The Innocents, USA, 1976; Rosmersholm, London, 1977; The Cherry Orchard, Chichester Festival, 1981; When We Dead Awaken, 1990; The Cherry Orchard, USA, 1994; Long Day's Journey into Night, USA, 1996; Electra, New York, 1998; Conversations after a Burial, London,

2000; A Little Night Music, 2003. Films include: A Doll's House, 1973; Islands in the Stream, 1975; The Clash of the Titans, 1979; Always, 1984; Sammy and Rosie Get Laid, 1987; Brothers, 1988; Crimes and Misdemeanours, 1989; Mighty Aphrodite, 1994; Daylight, 1995; Shakespeare's Women and Claire Bloom; The Book of Eve, 2001; Imagining Argentina, 2002. TV appreances include: A Shadow in the Sun, 1988; The Camomile Lawn, 1991; The Mirror Crack'd From Side to Side, 1992; Remember, 1993; A Village Affair, 1994; Family Money, 1996; The Lady in Question; Love and Murder; Yesterday's Children; One woman shows: Enter the Actress; These are the Women: A Portrait of Shakespeare's Heroines. Publications: Limelight and After, 1982; Leaving a Doll's House, 1996. Honours include: Evening Standard Drama Award for Best Actress, 1974. Address: c/o Jeremy Conway, 18-21 Jermyn Street, London SW1Y 6HB, England.

BLOOM Orlando, b. 13 January 1977, Canterbury, Kent, England. Actor. Education: National Youth Theatre, London; Scholarship, British American Drama Academy; Guildhall School of Music and Drama, 3 years. Career: Assistant, shooting club. Film appearances include: Wilde, 1997; The Lord of the Rings: The Fellowship of the Ring, 2001; The Lord of the Rings: The Two Towers, 2002; The Lord of the Rings: The Return of the Kings, 2003; Pirates of the Carribean: Curse of the Black Pearl, 2003; Troy, 2004; The Calcium Kid, 2004. TV appearances include: TV series "Casualty"; Midsomer Murders, 2000; Smack The Pony, 2000; The Saturday Show, 2001; So Graham Norton, 2002; The Tonight Show with Jay Leno, 2003; Primetime Live, 2003; V Graham Norton, 2003; V Graham Norton, 2003; The Brendan Leanard Show, 2003; Access Hollywood, 2003; GMTV, 2004; T4, 2004. Honours: Internet Movie Awards, 2002; Empire Award, 2002; MTV Movie Awards, 2002; Hollywood Discovery Awards; MTV Movie Awards, 2004.

BLOOM Walter Russell, b. 2 December 1948. Professor of Mathematics. m. Lynette Myra Butler, 2 daughters. Education: BSc, Hons, University of Tasmania; PhD, ANU; DSc, University of Tasmania. Appointments: Teacher of Mathematics, Hobart Matriculation College, 1967; Lecturer, Mathematics, University of Tasmania, 1974; Lecturer, Mathematics, Murdoch University, 1975; Senior Lecturer, 1982; Associate Professor, 1988; Personal Chair, 1995; Visiting Professor, University of Tübingen, Germany, 1980, 1987, 1991, 1998; Dean, School of Physical Sciences, Engineering and Technology, Murdoch University, 1991-96; Editor, Perth Numismatic Journal, 1992-; Honorary Associate, Numismatics, Western Australian Maritime Museum, 1997-. Publications include: Harmonic Analysis of Probability Measures on Hypergroups; 65 journal articles. Honours: Fulbright Fellowship, 1976; Goethe Institute Language Scholarship, 1979; Alexander von Humboldt Research Fellowship, 1987, 1991, 1998, 1999; Fellow, Honorary Life Member, Australian Mathematical Society; Fellow, Royal Numismatic Society. Memberships: Perth Numismatic Society; Western Australian Delegate to Council, Numismatic Association of Australia; President, WA Branch of the Australian Association of von Humboldt Fellows; President, Deepdale Catchment Group, Toodyay. Address: Murdoch University, Perth, WA 6150, Australia. E-mail: w.bloom@murdoch.edu.au

BLOOMFIELD Louis Aub, b. 11 October 1956, Boston, Massachusetts, USA. Professor of Physics. m. Karen Shatkin, 28 August 1983, 1 son, 1 daughter. Education: BA, Physics, Amherst College, 1979; PhD, Physics, Stanford University, 1983. Appointments: Postdoctoral Member, Technical Staff, AT&T Bell Labs, 1983-85; Assistant Professor of Physics, 1985-91, Associate Professor of Physics, 1991-96, Professor of Physics, 1996-, University of Virginia. Publication: How Things Work: The Physics of Everyday Life, 1997, 2nd edition, 2001. Contributor to: Scientific American. Memberships: American Physics Society, American Association of Physics Teachers. Address: Department of Physics, University of Virginia, 382 McCormick Road, Box 400714, Charlottesville, VA 22904-4714, USA.

BLUM Igor Robert, b. 24 October 1969, Frankfurt am Main, Germany. Dentist; Researcher, Educator. Education: DDS, Dental Surgery, Semmelweis University, Budapest, Hungary, 1990-95; MSc, Oral Surgery, 1995-97, PhD, Restorative Dentistry, 1998-2002, University of Manchester, UK; Dr Med Dent, (Magna cum laude), Dental Medicine, Goethe University of Frankfurt, Germany, 2000-2002. Appointments: Associate Clinician in Dental Implantology, 1998-2001, Associate Clinician in Oral Medicine, 1998-2001, University of Manchester, UK; Founder and Chief Executive Officer, Globaldentistry, 2002; Clinical Teacher in Oral Surgery, 2004-, Clinical Teacher in Prosthodontics, 2004-, University of Manchester, UK; Lecturer at international conferences. Publications: Numerous articles in scientific dental journals as author, first author and co-author include most recently: Contemporary views on dry socket (alveolar osteitis): A clinical appraisal of standardisation, aetiopathogenesis and management: a critical review, 2002; The teaching of the repair of direct composite restorations, 2002; The repair of direct composite restorations: an international survey of the teaching of operative techniques and materials, 2003; Defective direct composite restorations – replace or repair? A Comparison of teaching between Scandinavian dental schools, 2003. Honours: First Class Achievement for Oral Health Sciences Thesis, National Institute of Dentistry, 1995; Achievement in introducing a standardised definition for alveolar osteitis (dry socket) to the dental profession. Listed in Who's Who publications and biographical dictionaries. Memberships: Postgraduate Membership in Oral Surgery; Postgraduate Membership in Prosthodontics; General Dental Council, England; Hessian Dental Chamber of Germany; British Dental Association; Manchester Medical Society; European Association of Osseointegration; Association of Dental Educators in Europe. Address: University Dental Hospital of Manchester, Higher Cambridge Street, Manchester M15 6FH, England. E-mail: i.blum@ntlworld.com

BLUM June, b, 10 December 1929, New York, USA. Artist; Curator. m. Maurice C Blum, deceased. Education: MA, Brooklyn College, 1959; Brooklyn Museum of Art School; Pratt Graphic Art Center; New School of Social Research. Career: Curator, Contemporary Art, Suffolk Museum, Stony Brook, New York, 1971-75; Curator-at-large, Cocoa Beach, Florida, 1975-; Director, Women for Art, Cocoa Beach, 1976-; Director, Individual Museum, Cocoa Beach, 1980-. Solo exhibitions include: Bronx Museum, 1975; National Gallery, Seattle, 1977; Nassau County Museum of Fine Arts, Roslyn, New York, 1980; Brevard C C, Melbourne, and Cocoa, Florida, 1984; King Performing Art Center Gallery, Melbourne, 1990; SOHO 20 Artists, New York, 1998; Museum of Art and Science, Melbourne, 1998. Group shows: include Brooklyn Museum, 1975; Queens Museum, Flushing, New York, 1976; Nassau County Museum Fine Art, Brooklyn, 1980; Brevard Museum, Cocoa, 1995; Museum at Stony Brook, 1996. Publications: Metamorphosis of June Blum, 1976; Betty Friedan Series, 1976; Female Connection, 1978; A Woman's Space, 1980. Honours: Anne Eisner Putnam Memorial Prize, National Academy and National Association of Women Artists, New York, 1968; Honorable Mention, White Mountain Festival of Arts, Jefferson, New Hampshire, 1977. Memberships: Women's Caucus Art; College Art Association; President, East Central Florida Women's Caucus Art, 1980-, Art Chairperson, Vice President, Cocoa Beach Library, 1992-, Member, Time Capsule Committee, 1998;

Chairperson, Holiday Decorating Committee, City of Cocoa Beach, Florida, 2001-. Address: 120 Boca Ciega Road, Cocoa Beach, FL 32931-2602, USA.

BLUM Yehuda Zvi, b. 2 October 1931, Bratislava. Hersch Lauterpacht Professor of International Law. m. Moriah Rabinovitz-Teomim, 30 June 1966, 2 sons, 1 daughter. Education: MJur, Jerusalem, 1955; PhD, International Law, London, 1961. Appointments: Assistant to Judge Advocate-General, Israel Defence Forces, 1956-59; Senior Assistant to Legal Adviser, Israel Ministry of Foreign Affairs, 1962-65; Lecturer, Senior Lecturer, Associate Professor, Professor, Hebrew University, Jerusalem, 1965-; UNESCO Fellow, Sydney, Australia and UN Legal Counsel's Office, New York, 1968; Senior Research Scholar, University of Michigan, 1969; Visiting Professor at law schools in: Texas, 1971; New York, 1976-76; University of Michigan, 1985; University of Southern California, Los Angeles, 1991-92; Tulane University, New Orleans, 1994; University of Miami, 1999; Cardozo School of Law, New York, 2000; University of California, Berkeley, 2002; Ambassador, Permanent Representative of Israel to United Nations, New York, 1978-84; Hersch Lauterpacht Professor of International Law, Hebrew University, Jerusalem, 1991. Publications: Historic Titles in International Law, 1965; Secure Boundaries and Middle East Peace, 1971; For Zion's Sake, 1987; Eroding the United Nations Charter, 1993. Honours: Dr Juris hc, Yeshiva University, New York, 1981; Jabotinsky Prize, 1984. Memberships: American Society of International Law; International Law Association; B'nai B'rith. Address: Faculty of Law, Hebrew University, Mount Scopus, Jerusalem, Israel. E-mail: msblumy@mscc.huji.ac.il

BLUMENFELD Zeev, b. 20 October 1949, Romania. Physician. m. Ruth, 27 December 1972, 3 daughters. Education: MD, Hebrew University, Hadassah Medical School, 1973; Fellowship, UCSF, 1983-85. Appointment: Associate Professor, Faculty of Medicine, Technion – Israel Institute of Technology, Israel, 1994-. Publications: Numerous articles in professional medical journals. Honour: Maurberger Prize, 1969-72. Memberships: Israel Endocrine Society; Israel Fertility Association; Society of Gynaecological Investigation; Endocrine Society; American Society of Reproductive Medicine; Israel Endocrine Society; New York Academy of Sciences. Address: Department of Obstetrics and Gynaecology, Rambam Medical Centre, Technion Faculty of Medicine, Haifa 31096, Israel.

BLUNKETT Rt Hon David, b. 6 June 1947, England. Politician. 3 sons. Education: Sheffield University. Appointments: Worker, East Midlands Gas Board; Teacher, Industrial Relations and Politics, Barnsley College of Technology; Joined Labour Party, 1963; Member, Sheffield City Council, 1970-87, Leader, 1980-87; Member, South Yorkshire County Council, 1973-77; MP for Sheffield Brightside, 1987-; National Executive Committee (NEC) of Labour Party, 1983; Chair, NEC Local Government Committee, 1984; Local Government Front Bench Spokesman in Opposition's Environment Team, 1988-92; Shadow Secretary of State for Health, 1992-94, for Education, 1994-95, for Education and Employment, 1995-97; Secretary of State for Education and Employment, 1997-2001, for the Home Department, 2001-. Publications: Local Enterprise and Workers' Plans, 1981; Building From the Bottom: The Sheffield Experience, 1983; Democracy in Crisis: The Town Halls Respond, 1987; On a Clear Day (autobiography), 1995; Politics and Progress, 2001. Address: House of Commons, London SW1A 0AA, England.

BLUNT Marcus, b. 31 December 1947, Birmingham, England. Composer; Teacher. m. Maureen Ann Marsh, 9 April 1988. Education: BMus, honours, University College of Wales, 1970.

Career: Compositions performed in at least 10 countries and BBC Radio 3, Classic FM; Woodwind Teacher, 1976-. Compositions: Symphony; The Rings of Saturn for Orchestra; Piano Concerto; Once in a Western Island... for violin and orchestra; Concerto Pastorale for oboe d'amore and strings; Aspects of Saturn for strings; Capricorn for 12 wind; Venice Suite for brass ensemble; The Throstle-Nest in Spring for octet; Cerulean for wind quintet; 2 String Quartets; A Celebration of Brahms and Joachim for piano trio; Lorenzo the Much Travel'd Clown for bassoon and piano; The Life Force for piano. Memberships: British Academy of Composers and Songwriters; Performing Right Society; Incorporated Society of Musicians. Address: Craigs Cottage, Lochmaben, Lockerbie, Dumfriesshire DG11 1RW, Scotland.

BNINSKI Kazimierz Andrzej, b. 28 February 1939, Gdynia, Poland. Physician in General Practice. m. Teresa Maria de Gallen Bisping, 2 July 1988, 2 sons, 1 daughter. Education: MD, University of Gdansk, Poland, 1964. Appointments: House Officer, Nelson Hospital, London, England, 1967-68; St Mary Abbots Hospital, London, England, 1969-71; Registrar in Medicine, St Mary's Hospital, 1972-76; Physician VII, US Army, Germany, 1977-80; Junior Partner, General Practice, 1981-87; Director-in-Charge Polish Clinic, London, 1988-. Address: 17 Childs Place, London, SW5 9RX, England.

BOARDMAN Christopher Miles, b. 26 August 1968, England. Cyclist. m. Sally-Anne Edwards, 1988, 3 sons, 1 daughter. Education: Withens College. Appointments: Competed in 9 World Championships; Holder of various national records and 20 national titles; Individual Pursuit, Olympic Games, Barcelona, 1992, Double World Champion, 1997, 1998; World Record for Distance Cycled in 1 hour, 1993, 1996; Won, World 4,000m Cycling Championships, Broke his own world record, 1996; Retired, 2001. Honours include: Bronze Medal, Commonwealth Games, Edinburgh, 1986; 2 Bronze Medals, Commonwealth Games, Auckland, 1990; Gold Medal, Olympic Games, Barcelona, 1992; Winner, Tour de France Prologue and holder, Yellow Jersey, 1994. Address: c/o Beyond Level Four Ltd, Lindfield House, Station Approach, Meols, Wirral L47 8XA, England.

BOATNER Lynn Allen, b. 3 August 1938, Clarksville, Texas, USA. Physicist. m. Martha Alice, 3 sons. Education: BS, 1960, MSc, 1961, Physics, Mathematics, Texas Technological University; PhD, 1966, Physics, Mathematics, Vanderbilt University. Appointments: Section Head, Ceramics and Interfaces at Oak Ridge National Laboratory; Co-leader, Novel Materials Group; ORNL Corporate Fellow, 1993-; Chair, Committee on International Scientific Affairs, American Physical Society; Review editor, Journal of Materials Research; Associate Editor, Optical Materials; Organizer, chair or proceedings editor of numerous international conferences; Officer, executive committee member, committee chair, Materials Research Society, American Physical Society; ASM International. Publications: Author, co-author, over 440 research articles; 13 patents. Honours: Numerous awards for research including Jesse W Beams Prize, American Physical Society; R&D 100 awards, 1982, 1985, 1996; US Department of Energy Research Competition Award, 1984; Science Digest 100 Top Innovators, 1985; Federal Laboratory Consortium Award for Excellence in Technology Transfer, 1997; Elegant Work Prize, Institute of Materials, UK, 1997; Jacquet-Lucas Award of ASM International and International Metallographic Society, 1988; Corresponding Member, Academy of Sciences of Mexico; Frank H Spedding Award for Rare Earth Research. Memberships: Fellow, American Physical Society; Institute of Materials of the UK; American Ceramic Society; American Association for the Advancement of Science; ASM International; Member, National Institute of Ceramic Engineers; American Association for Crystal

Growth; Materials Research Society; Mineralogical Society of America; American Welding Society. Address: Oak Ridge National Laboratory, Condensed Matter Sciences Division, PO Box 2008, Bldg 3150, Oak Ridge, TN 37831-6056, USA.

BOBADILLA Luz Maria, b. Paraguay. Classical Guitarist. Career: Guest Soloist: ISPEA Chamber Orchestra, Resistencia, Argentina; Brasilia Symphony Orchestra, Chamber Orchestra of Tatui, Sao Paulo, Brazil; La Serena Chamber Orchestra, Chile; Quito Symphony Orchestra; String and Flute Quintet, Ecuador; Asuncion Symphony Orchestra; Municipal Chamber Orchestra, Orchestra for Unaccompanied Stringed Instruments, Villarica Chamber Orchestra, Philomusical Chamber Orchestra, American University's Orchestra, Orquesta Juvenil de Asuncion, Paraguay; Radio and Television Performances in Germany, France Brazil, Switzerland; Artistic Director of two Guitar Festivals in Paraguay: Guitarra and Luz, Women and Guitars; Creator and Host of the Paraguayan Radio Talk Show "Guitar and Luz", 1996-; International performances in countries including, Venezuela, Peru, Costa Rica, Uruguay, USA, Belgium, Switzerland, Italy, Spain, France, Germany, Netherlands, Egypt, Israel, Mexico, United Kingdom, Sweden, Russia, Portugal, 1987-; Participant in numerous International Festivals including most recently: Fabrizio Caroso Guitar Festival, Italy, 2002; 5th Annual World Guitar Festival, Russia, 2002; Lausanne Guitar Festival, Switzerland, 2003; XIV International Guitar Festival, Peru, 2003; 5th Annual World Festival of Guitars, Argentina, 2003; Teacher of Master Classes at Universities and Conservatories world-wide. Recordings: Concert in B-Major, Florentin Jiminez Collection, CD, 1990; Classical Guitar Concert, Long Play, 1991; The Best of Agustin Barrios, Cassette, 1992; A Tribute to Mangore, CD, 1994; Luz on the Guitar, CD, 1998; Retrator de America, CD, 2001; Paraguay Con Cuore de Italia, CD, 2002. Honours include: Gold Medal, Paraguayan Classical Guitar Institute, 1987; Top Twelve Performers of the Year Award, Radio Primero de Marzo, 1991; Selected Panamerican Representative, Americal 25th Anniversary founding of the United Nations Women's Roundtable, Geneva, Switzerland, 1995; Distinguished Guest of Honor City of Miami, Florida, USA, 1996; Outstanding Professor and Gold Medallist, Paraguayan National Conservatory of Music, 2000. Membership: Vice-President, International Association of Female Guitarists. Address: Carlos Arguello 1325 c/M Blinder, Asuncion, Paraguay. E-mail: luzmaria@conexion.com.py

BOBAK Joseph A IV, b. 20 December 1971, Windber, Pennsylvania, USA. Professor; Consultant; Counsellor. Education: BA, Criminology, Mount Aloysius College, 1999; MA, Criminology, Indiana University of Pennsylvania, 2001; CFSL, Forensic Science and Law, Duquesne Law School, Cyril H Wecht Institute for Forensic Science and Law, 2002; PhD, Capella University in progress. Appointments: Private Investigator, 1999-2000; Forensic Death Investigator, 2001; Consultant, 2001-; Counsellor, 2002-; Professor of Forensic Science, 2003-; Hostage Negotiator, 2003-. Honours: Certificate of Achievement, Allegheny County Coroner's Office; Listed in biographical publications. Memberships: East Coast Gang Investigators Association; American Academy of Forensic Sciences; American College of Forensic Examiners International; International Association of Hostage Negotiators; American Criminal Justice Society; American Criminology Society. Address: 314 Dobson Street, Windber, PA 15963, USA. E-mail: jbobak@charter.net

BOBEK Stanislaw Emanuel, b. 25 December 1930, Tarnowskie Gory, Poland. Researcher. m. 14 March 1963, 2 sons. Education: MSc, University of Agriculture, Cracow, 1956; Assistant Professor, 1971, Associate Professor, 1978, Professor, 1986. Appointments: Chief, Isotopic Laboratory, 1960-94, Head, Department of Animal

Dictionary of International Biography

Physiology, 1984-94, University of Agriculture, Cracow. Publications: Over 113 in professional journals. Honours: Award, Polish Endocrine Society, 1961; 4 Awards, Ministry of Education and Science, 1971, 1977, 1982, 1985; Award, Science Section, Polish Academy of Sciences, 1985. Memberships: European Society of New Methods in Agriculture, Prague; Polish Endocrine Society; Polish Physiology Society; Polish Biochemistry Society; Biology Commission, Endocrinology Commission and Agricultural Commission, Polish Academy of Sciences. Address: Krowoderskich Zuchow Str 23/43, 31-271 Krakow, Poland.

BOBIC Milos, b. 30 June 1946, Belgrade. Architect. m. Mirjana, 22 December 1993, 3 sons. Education: BArch, 1972, PhD, 1988, University of Belgrade. Appointments: G and B Studio, Belgrade, 1968-78; CEP, Belgrade, 1978-88; University of Belgrade, 1988-94; Bur Urhahn, Amsterdam, 1992-96; Kuiper Compagnons, Rotterdam, 1996-99; DRO, Amsterdam, 1999-. Publications: Several books and articles in professional journals; Architect Critic, Vreme Magazine, Belgrade. Honours: Award, City of Belgrade, 1979; 6th Bio-Ljubljana, 1979; Architectural Award, Belgrade, 1985, 1986, 1987. Memberships: ISOCARP; ISCOGRADA; Open Society Institute, New York; Academie van Bouwkunst, Amsterdam; KU Leuven, Brussels; International School for Landscape, Larenstein. Address: Prinsengracht 689, 1017 Amsterdam, Holland.

BOBIER Claude-Abel, b. 18 March 1934, France. m. Manissier Arlette, 4 September 1959, 3 daughters. Education: BS, 1953; ENS St Cloud, 1956-60; Agreg SN, 1960; Doctor, 1971. Appointments: University of Paris VI, 1960-75; Professor, University of Tunis, 1975-86; MC University of Bordeaux I, 1986-99; Retired as Consultant, 1999. Publications include: Les éléments structuraux recents essentiels de la Tunisie nord-orientale, 1983; Morphologie de la marge Caraibe Colombienne: Relation avec la structure et la sedimentation, 1991; The Post-Triassic Sedimentary Cover of Tunisa: Seismic Sequences and Structure, 1991; Apports de l'analyse morphostructurale dans la connaissance de la physiographie du golfe de Tehuantepec (Mexique est-pacifique), 1993; Sequence stratigraphy, Basin dynamics and Petroleum geology of the Miocene from Eastern Tunisia, 1996; Recent tectonic activity in the South Barbados Prism. Deep towed side scan sonar imagery, 1998; Distribution des sédiments sur la marge du Golfe de Tehuantepec (Pacifique oriental). Example d'interaction tectonique-eustatisme. Honour: International Ambassador's Order, 1998. Memberships: American Association of Petrololeum Geololgists; American Geophysical Union; New York Academy of Sciences. Address: 6 Square du Gue, F-33170 Gradignan, France. 52. 197.

BOBROV Alexander, b. 24 March 1932, Bryansk, Russia. Physician; Psychiatrist. m. Nadezhda Bobrova, 1 son, 1 daughter. Education: Therapeutic Department, 1950-56, Postgraduate Psychiatry Course, 1956-58 The 1st Moscow Medical Institute; Scientific Psychiatry Course, Moscow Scientific Research Institute of Psychiatry, 1958-61. Appointments: Researcher, Moscow Scientific Research Institute of Psychiatry, 1961-65; Researcher, 1965-78, Head of Experts, Methodical Sector, 1978-82, Central Scientific Research Institute of Invalidity, 1965-78; Professor, Head of Psychiatry Department, Irkutsk Institute of Advanced Medical Studies, 1982-. Publications: 135 scientific works including 3 monographs: Protracted non-psychotic hypochondria in the practice of medical-social examination, 1984; Remote period of war skull brain trauma, 1986; Endogenous depression, 2001. Honours: Bronze Medal of the Exhibition of National Economic Achievement, 1975; V M Bechterev Prize, 1987; Medal, Veteran of Labour; Doctor with Excellent Results in Health Service. Memberships: Russian Society of Psychiatrists; Federal Problem

Study – Methodical Psychiatry-Narcology Committee; Scientific Committee in the Presidium of Medical Science Academy. Address: Igoshina Street 5-36, Irkutsk 664074, Russia.

BOCKSERMAN Robert Julian, b. 20 December 1929, St Louis, USA. Consultant. m. Clarice Kreisman, 1957, 1 son, 2 daughters. Education: BS, Agriculture, 1952, MS, Agriculture, 1955, University of Missouri, Columbia; Economics, Marketing, Bradley University, Peoria, Illinois, 1955-56; Pharmacy, St Louis College of Pharmacy, 1958-59; Chemistry, Washington University, St Louis, 1960-65. Appointments: Chemist, Sealtest Corporation, Peoria, Illinois, 1955-56; Production Manager, Allan Drug Co, St Louis, Missouri, 1957-59; Research Chemist, Monsanto Co, St Louis, Missouri, 1960-65; Purchasing Agent, Monsanto Co (Krummerich Plant), Sauget, Illinois, 1966-67; Owner, President, Pharma-Tech Industries, Inc, Union, Missouri, 1967-84; Director, Technical Services, Overlock Howe Consulting Group, St Louis, Missouri, 1984-85; Owner, President, Conatech Consulting Group Inc, St Louis, Missouri, 1985-; Visiting Lecturer: University of Missouri, Columbia, Missouri, University of Missouri, Rolla, Missouri, University of Missouri, Clayton, Missouri. Publications: Contributing author, Packaging Forensics (book); Several articles in professional journals. Honours: Certified Packaging Professional #25771; Speakers Bureau, Institute of Packaging Professionals, Institute of Food Technologists; Packaging Industry Advisory Committee, University of Missouri Engineering School; Listed in several Who's Who publications. Memberships include: Academy of Science, St Louis; Allied Drug and Chemical Association; American Association for the Advancement of Science; American Chemical Society; ASTM; American Technion Society; Industrial Pharmacists Association; International Society of Pharmaceutical Engineers; IOPP; American College of Forensic Examiners; New York Academy of Science; Sigma Xi Scientific Research Society; Missouri Academy of Science. Address: 54 Morwood Lane, Creve Coeur, MO 63141-7621, USA.

BOCKSTAELE Paul Pieter, b. 7 February 1920, Melle, Belgium. Emeritus Professor. Education: Graduated in Theology, 1940; PhD, Mathematics, University of Leuven, 1951. Appointments: Teacher, Mathematics, St Vincentius College, Eeklo, 1947-53; Teachers College Sint-Niklaas, 1953-62; Associate Professor, Mathematics and History of Mathematics, University of Leuven, 1963-67; Professor, 1967-85; Professor Emeritus, 1985-. Publications: Mathematics handbooks; Contributions and articles on history of mathematics and history of science. Honours: Award Koninklijke Vlaamse Academie van België voor Wetenschappen en Kunsten, 1948; Canon Diocese of Ghent, 1967; Officer, Order of Leopold, 1969; Commander, Order of the Crown, 1974; Great Officer, Order of Leopold, 1996. Memberships: International Academy of History of Science, 1971; Deutsche Gesellschaft fur Geschichte der Medizin, Naturwissenschaft und Technik, 1979; Koninklijke Vlaamse Academie van België voor Wetenschappen en Kunsten, 1983. Address: Graetboslaan 9, B-3050 Oud-Heverlee, Belgium.

BODEY Gerald Paul, b. 22 May 1934, Hazleton, Pennsylvania, USA. Physician. m. Nancy Louise Wiegner, 1 son, 2 daughters. Education: Lafayette College, Easton Pennsylvania, 1952-56; AB, magna cum laude, 1956; MD, Johns Hopkins University School of Medicine, Baltimore, Maryland, 1960. Appointments: Emeritus Professor of Medicine, University of Texas MD Anderson Cancer Centre, 1995-; Clinical Professor, University of Texas Health Science Centre, Dental Branch, Houston, Texas, 1977-95; Professor of Internal Medicine and Pharmacology, University of Texas Health Science Centre at Houston, Medical School, Houston, Texas, 1976-2004; Adjunct Professor of Microbiology and Immunology and Medicine, Baylor College of Medicine, Houston, Texas, 1975-1999; Chairman, Department of Medical Specialities,

1987-95 and Chief, Section of Infectious Diseases, 1975-95, Professor of Medicine, 1966-95, The University of Texas M.D. Anderson Cancer Centre. Publications: over 1000 papers in scientific journals, 60 book chapters and 420 abstracts. Honours include: Honorary Member, Sociedade Brasileira de Cancerologia, 1978; Scholar of the Leukemia Society of America, 1984; Honorary Member, Mediterranean Medical Society; Best Doctors in America, 1992-; Editorial Academy, The International Journal of Oncology, 1992-; First Professor Eugene Yourassowsky Award, Universite Libre de Bruxelles, 1995; The University of Texas M.D. Anderson Cancer Centre Faculty Achievement Award in Clinical Research; Honorary Member, Academia Peruana de Cirugia, Peru; La Asociation Costarricense de Oncologia; Listed in 1983 and 1990 by Institute for Scientific Information as one of the 300 most cited authors in all scientific literature. Memberships have included: American Medical Association; Texas Medical Association; American Society of Hematology; Infectious Diseases Society of America; Sigma XI; European Society of Clinical Microbiology and Infectious Diseases; American Society of Microbiology; American Society of Clinical Oncology; American Society of Pharmacology and Clinical Therapeutics; Fellow, American College of Physicians; Fellow, American College of Chest Physicians; Fellow, Royal College of Medicine; Fellow, the Royal Society for Promotion of Health; Member, Lunar Quarantine Operations Team, Apollo 11, 12, 13 and 14, National Aeronautics and Space Administration; Member, Collaborative Cancer Treatment Research Program, Pan American Health Organisation 1976-84; American Scientific Affiliation; International Society for Complexity, Information and Design; Elder, Methodist. Address: University Texas MDACC, 1515 Holcome, Houston, TX 77030, USA.

BODIE (Elizabeth) Idella, b. 2 December 1925, Ridge Spring, South Carolina, USA. Teacher; Author. m. James E Bodie Sr, 15 August 1947, 2 sons, 2 daughters. Education: Associate Degree, Mars Hill Junior College, 1942-44; BA, Columbia College, 1946; Graduate Study, University of South Carolina, 1950-51. Publications: Young readers books: The Secret of Telfair Inn, 1971; Mystery of the Pirates Treasure, 1973; Ghost in the Capitol, 1976; Stranded, 1984, Whopper, 1989; Trouble at Star Fort, 1992; Mystery of Edisto Island, 1994; Ghost Tales for Retelling, 1994. Other: South Carolina Women, 1978; Archibald Rutledge, 1980; The Man Who Loved the Flag, 1997; Carolina Girl: A Writer's Beginning, 1998; The Secret Message, 1998; The Revolutionary Swamp Fox, 1999; Spunky Revolutionary War Heroine, 2000; The Fighting Gamecock, 2000; The Courageous Patriot, 2001; Quaker Commander, 2001; Brave Black Patriots, 2002; The Old Wagoner, 2002; The Wizard Owl, 2003; Heroines of the American Revolution, 2003; Light-Horse Harry, 2004. Contributions to: Guideposts; Mature Living; Sandlapper; Instructor; Christian Home. Honours: Business and Professional Woman of the Year, 1980; Toastmasters International Communication Achievement Award, 1985; Idella Bodie Creative Writing Award, 1985; Willou Gray Educator Award, 1988; Youth Prison Volunteer of Year, 1990; 3 books nominated for South Carolina Children's Book Award. Membership: Society of Children's Book Writers and Illustrators. Address: 1113 Evans Road, Aiken, SC 29803, USA.

BOESLER Pawel Sylwester, b. 30 November 1932, Wielkie Pulkowo, Poland. Psychologist. m. Urszula Janina Szwanke, 1 son, 1 daughter. Education: Master of Psychology, University of Poznan, Poland, 1957; Doctor of Science, Military Academy, Warsaw, Poland 1966; Doctoral Habilitation, University of Poznan, 1977; International Course on Injury Control and Safety Promotion, New Delhi, India, 2000. Appointments: Editor, TV, Poznan, 1957-58; Assistant Professor, Adjunct, Docent, Military Academy, Warsaw, 1958-92; Professor, College of Education, Czestochowa,

Poland, 1992-95; Academy of Special Education, Warsaw, 1995-2003; Academy of Humanities and Economics, Lodz, Poland. Publications: Books: Driver's Safety, 1979; Psychology of Road Accident Prevention, 1981; Articles: Children's Accidental Hazard Recognition, Amsterdam, 1998; Avoidance and Prevention, Album, 2000; Managing Unintentional Injury Risk Situations, 2002. Honours: Service Awards, WHO, New Delhi, India, 2000, WHO Montreal, Canada, 2002; Listed in Who's Who publications and biographical dictionaries. Membership: Polish Psychological Association, 1957-98. Address: ul. Przasnyska 17/16, 01 756 Warsaw, Poland. E-mail: pawelboesler@yahoo.com

BOEV Zlatozar Nikolaev, b. 20 October 1955, Sofia, Bulgaria. Zoologist; Ornithologist. m. Education: Graduate, Department of Zoology of the Vertebrate Animal, Faculty of Biology, University of Sofia, 1975-80; Postgraduate, Zoology Department, National Museum of Natural History, 1984-86. Appointments: Doctor of Philosophy, 1986; Associate Professor, 1992; Doctor of Sciences, 1999; Professor of Zoology, 2001. Publications: Over 170 papers in scientific journals chiefly on fossil and sub-fossil birds; Over 255 articles in popular science journals; 5 textbooks; 12 popular books; 14 countries in Europe, North America and Asia. Memberships include: Society of Avian Palaeontology and Evolution; International Council for Archaeology; Society of European Avian Curators; Association for Environmental Archaeology and others. Address: National Museum of Natural History, Bulgarian Academy of Sciences, 1 Blvd Tsar Osvoboditel, 1000 Sofia, Bulgaria. E-mail: boev@nmnh.bas.bg

BOGDANOFF Stewart R, b. 16 August 1940, London, England. Educator. m. Eileen Dolan, 1 son, 2 daughters. Education: BSc, Kings College, Briarcliff Manor, New York, 1963; MA and Professional Degree, New York University, 1965; Graduate Work NYU, SUNY New Platz, Harvard University, 1972-; Certificate in Administration and Supervision, 1988. Appointments: Coach, intramural director, curriculum writer, fundraiser Thomas Jefferson Elementary School, Lakeland School District, 1965-96; Physical Education Teacher, Lakeland School District, 1965-96; Head Teacher, Thomas Jefferson Elementary School, Lakeland School District, 1984-96; Acting Principal, Thomas Jefferson Elementary School, 1985-86; Educational Consultant, Speaker, Writer, 1996-. Honours include: New York State Teacher of Year, honoured at White House by President Reagan, 1983; Project Inspiration Award, National Association for Sport and Physical Education, 1992; Point of Light Award, President Bush, 1992; International Man of Year Award and Men of Achievement Award, International Biographical Centre, England, 1993; Also listed in numerous Biographical Publications; 1st teacher from NYS inducted into National Teachers Hall of Fame, Emporia, Kansas, honoured by President Clinton at Rose Garden ceremony, Scholarship in name of Stewart Bogdanoff established by Servicemaster, 1993; Founders 2000 Award from American Alliance for Health, Physical Education Recreation and Dance with room dedicated in his honour, National Center in Reston, Virginia, 1995; J C Penny Golden Rule Award, Westchester County United Way Volunteer of Year, 1995; Inducted into Briarcliff High School Hall of Distinguished Alumni, 1995; Golden Years Award, New York State Association for Health, Physical Education, Recreation and Dance; Selected as one of the Fifty Most Influential People in Westchester and Putnam Counties during the 20th Century, Journal News; American Medal of Honor, ABI, 2003; Listed in numerous Who's Who and biographical publications including: Who's Who in American Education; Contemporary Who's Who, ABI, 2003; Great Minds of the 21st Century, ABI, 2003-04. Memberships include: Kappa Delta Pi; New York State Teachers of the Year; Harvard Principals Center, others. Address: 588 Heritage Hills of Westchester, Unit A, Somers, NY 10589, USA.

Dictionary of International Biography

BOGDANOV Bogdan Iliev, b. 7 March 1946, Strangdga, Bourgas, Bulgaria. University Associate Professor. m. Vesselina Christova, 14 December 1969, 2 sons. Education: Diploma Technician, Technical College, Bourgas, 1965; Diploma Engineer, 1970, PhD, 1980, University of Bourgas. Appointments: Chemical Engineer, Oil Co Bourgas, 1970; Research Associate, 1973; Postgraduate Student, 1976, Assistant Professor, 1984, Associate Professor, 1987, Managing Director of Research Centre, 1989-95, Head of Department of Material-Science, 1993-95, Head of Department, Silicate Technology, 1995-2003, University of Bourgas. Publications: 50 publications in scientific journals including Journal of American Cer Society, Crystal Research Technology, Germany; Author, 16 Bulgarian patents. Honours: Postdoctoral grant of Moscow University of Chemistry Technology, Russia, 1984; Guest Lecturer, Loughborough University, England, 1990; Postdoctoral Grant, German Academy Exchange Service, 1990, 1997. Memberships: Bulgarian Chemical Society, 1986-2001; Union of Scientists in Bulgaria, 1988-2001; New York Academy of Sciences, 1997-98. Address: 11, Macedonia Str, entr 2nd, 8000 Bourgas, Bulgaria. 52.

BOGDANOVICH Peter, b. 30 July 1939, Kingston, New York, USA. Film Director; Writer; Producer; Actor. m. (1) Polly Platt, 1962, divorced 1970, 2 daughters, (2) L B Straten, 1988. Appointments: Film Feature-Writer, Esquire, New York Times, Village Voice, Cahiers du Cinema, Los Angeles Times, New York Magazine, Vogue, Variety and others, 1961-.Publications: The Cinema of Orson Welles, 1961; The Cinema of Howard Hawks, 1962; The Cinema of Alfred Hitchcock, 1963; John Ford, 1968; Fritz Lang in America, 1969; Allan Dwan: The Last Pioneer, 1971; Pieces of Time: Peter Bogdanovich on the Movies (in UK as Picture Shows), 1961, enlarged edition, 1985; The Killing of the Unicorn: Dorothy Stratten (1960-1980), 1984; A Year and a Day Calendar (editor), 1991; This is Orson Welles, 1992; Who the Devil Made It, 1997. Films: The Wild Angels, 1966; Targets, 1968; The Last Picture Show, 1971; What's Up Doc?, 1972; Paper Moon, 1973; Daisy Miller, 1974; At Long Last Love, 1975; Nickelodeon, 1976; Saint Jack, 1979; They All Laughed, 1981; Mask, 1985; Illegally Yours, 1988; Texasville, 1990; Noises Off, 1992; The Thing Called Love, 1993; Who The Devil Made It (director), 1997; Mr Jealousy, 1997; Highball, 1997; Coming Soon, 1999; Rated X, 2000; The Independent, 2000 The Cat's Meow (director), 2001. Honours: New York Film Critics' Award for Best Screenplay, British Academy Award for Best Screenplay, 1971; Writer's Guild of America Award for Best Screenplay, 1972; Silver Shell, Mar del Plata, Spain, 1973; Best Director, Brussels Festival, 1974; Pasinetti Award, Critic Prize, Venice Festival, 1979. Memberships: Directors Guild of America; Writer's Guild of America; Academy of Motion Picture Arts and Sciences. Address: c/o William Pfeiffer, 30 Lane of Acres, Haddonfield, NJ 08033, USA.

BOGGS George Robert, b. 4 September 1944, Conneaut, Ohio, USA. Association President. m. Ann, 3 sons. Education: BS, Chemistry, Ohio State University, Columbus, 1966; MA, Chemistry, University of California at Santa Barbara, 1968; Graduate Study in Educational Administration, Natural Sciences and Education, California State University at Chico, 1969-72; PhD, Educational Administration, University of Texas at Austin, 1984. Appointments: Teaching Assistant, Ohio State University, 1965-66, University of California at Santa Barbara, 1966-68; Adjunct Instructor, Austin Community College, 1982; Instructor of Chemistry, Butte College, 1968-85; Chairman, Division of Natural Science and Allied Health, Butte College, 1972-81; Associate Dean of Instruction, 1981-85; Superintendent/President, Palomar Community College District, 1985-2000; President, American Association of Community Colleges, 2000. Publications: Numerous articles in professional journals. Honours: Richardson

Fellowship, 1982-83; Professional of the Year Award, Leadership Alliance, 1994; Harry Buttimer Distinguished Administrators Award, Association of California Community College Administrators, La Jolla, 1994; Proclamation, George R Boggs Day, Mayor and City Council, Vista, California, 1994; Certificate of Achievement in Recognition of Leadership Excellence and Community Service, Congress of United States, 1994; PBS Terry O'Banion Prize for Teaching and Learning, 2000. Memberships: American Chemical Society, 1962-90; Association of California College Administrators, 1980-2000; Southern California Community Colleges Chief Executive Officers' Association, 1985-2000. Address: One Dupont Circle, NW, Suite 410, Washington, DC 20036-1176, USA. E-mail: gboggs@aacc.nche.edu

BOGLE Joanna Margaret, (Julia Blythe), b. 7 September 1952, Carshalton, Surrey, England. Author; Journalist. m. James Stewart Lockhart Bogle, 20 September 1980. Appointments: Local Borough Councillor, London Borough of Sutton, 1974-81; Governor, London Oratory School, 1976-86. Publications: A Book of Feasts and Seasons, 1986; When the Summer Ended (with Cecylia Wolkowinska), 1991; A Heart for Europe (with James Bogle), 1992; Caroline Chisholm, 1993; Come On In - It's Awful!, editor, 1994; We Didn't Mean to Start a School, 1998. Contributions to: local newspapers, 1970-74; South London News, 1984-86; Catholic Times, 1994-; various national newspapers, 1980-. Memberships: Vice Chairman, Catholic Writers Guild, 1992-. Address: Christian Projects, PO Box 44741, London SWIP 2XA, England.

BOGLIUN Loredana, b. 18 January 1955, Pula-Pola, Croatia. Social Psychologist; Professor; Poet. 1 son, 1 daughter. Education: Laurea in Psychology, 1978; Master in Psychology, 1986; PhD, Social Psychology, 1992. Appointments: University Professor, 1991-; Vice President, Istrian Region, Croatia, 1993-2001; International Poetry Festival, Colombia, 1998; International Biennal of Poetry, 1998. Publications: Poesie, 1988; Vorbind Despre Noi, 1989; Mazere, 1993; Istarskite Zidista, 1996; La Peicia, 1996; La Trasparenza, 1996; Soun La Poiana, 2000. Contributions to: La Battana; Istra; Alfabeta; Il Territorio; Diverse Lingue; Balcanica; Republica; Issimo; Razgledi; Erasmus; Vilenica; Sodobnost; Corrispondenze; Approdi; Istria Nobilissima; Voci Nostre; Flowers of Peace; Mundial Fotofestival. Honours: Istria Nobilissima, 1977, 1979, 1983, 1987, 1988, 1989, 1991, 1995; Trofeo Del Buonconsiglio, Trento, 1987; Premio Drago Gervais, Rijeka-Fiume, 1989. Address: Vladimir Nazor 2, 52215 Vodnjan-Dignano, Istria, Croatia.

BOHR Aage Niels, b. 19 June 1922, Copenhagen, Denmark. Physicist. m. (1) Marietta Bettina, deceased, 1978, 2 sons, 1 daughter, (2) Bente Scharff, 1981. Education: Graduated, University of Copenhagen. Appointments: Associate, Department of Science and Industrial Research, London, 1943-45; Research Assistant, Institute of Theoretical Physics, Copenhagen, 1946; Professor of Physics, University of Copenhagen, 1956-; Director, Niels Bohr Institute, 1963-70; Director, Nordita (Nordic Institute of Theoretical Physics), 1975-81. Memberships: Danish, Norwegian, Pontifical, Swedish, Polish, Finnish, Yugoslav Academies of Science; National Academy of Sciences, USA; American Academy of Arts and Sciences; American Philosophical Society; Royal Physiograph Society, Lund, Sweden; Academy of Technical Sciences, Copenhagen; Deutsche Academie der Naturforsche Lepoldina. Publications: Rotational States of Atomic Nuclei, 1954; Co-author, Nuclear Structure, Vol I, 1969, Vol II, 1975. Honours: Honorary PhD, Oslo, Heidelberg, Trondheim, Manchester, Uppsala; Dannie Heineman Prize, 1960; Pius XI Medal, 1963; Atoms for Peace Award, 1969; Ørsted Medal, 1970; Rutherford Medal, 1972; John Price Wetherill Medal, 1974; Nobel

Prize for Physics, 1975; Ole Rømer Medal , 1976. Address: c/o Niels Bohr Institute, Blegdamsvej 15-17, 2100 Copenhagen, Denmark.

BOILLAT Guy Maurice Georges, b. 18 May 1937, Pontarlier, France. Mathematical Physicist. Education: Licence es Sci, University Besancon, 1959; Dr es Sci, Sorbonne, 1964; Study, Institute Henri Poincare, Paris; Theoretical Physics, Copenhagen, Trondheim. Appointments: University of Clermont, 1966-; Research, Italy, 1970-. Publications: 100 publications in professional journals; Co-author, Recent Mathematical Methods in Nonlinear Wave Propagation, 1996; Theme of Research: Nonlinear Fields, Waves and Shocks. Honours: Award, Recipient Commemorative Millennium Memorial award Albert Einstein International Academy Foundation. Memberships: International Parliament for Safety and Peace, Deputy; Academy MIDI, Senator; French Horological Association, Secretary General, 1998-; American Mathematical Society; Unione Matematica Italiana; Corresponding Member Accademia Peloritana dei Pericolanti, 1998-. Address: 16, rue Ronchaux, F-25000, Besancon, France.

BOJKOV Vassil Kroumov, b. 29 July 1956, Velingrad, Bulgaria. Economist. m. Maia Bojkova, 1 son. Education: MSc Mathematics, Sofia University "Kliment Ohridsky, 1981; MSc, Economy, University of National and World Economy, 1998; Management, Marketing and Control in Tourism, Institute for Postgraduate Studies, 2000. Appointments: Chairman, Board of Directors, Nove Holding; President, Bulgarian Shooting Federation; President of the Professional Football Club, CSKA; President, Bulgarian Chess Federation. Honours: Nominee, MR Economics Awards, Bulgaria; Listed in Who's Who publications and biographical dictionaries. Membership: New York Academy of Sciences. Address: 43, Moskovska Str, 1000 Sofia, Bulgaria. E-mail: vb@nove.bg Website: www.nove.bg

BOK Nicolaas Wilhelmus den, b. 21 February 1959, Almkerk, The Netherlands. Minister; Theological Investigator. 1 daughter. Education: Propaedeutic Exam Theology cum laude, University of Utrecht, 1979; Candidates Exam cum laude, Theology, 1983; Church Exam cum laude, Dutch Reformed Church, 1986; Doctorate Exam cum laude, 1988; PhD cum laude, Theology, 1996. Appointments: Student Assistant, History of Philosophy, University of Utrecht, 1985-88; Part time Theological Investigator, Dutch Reformed Church, 1989-95; Vicar, Reformed Church, Zaandam, 1989-93; Part time Minister, Dutch Reformed Church, The Hague, 1997-2003; Part time Theological Investigator. Publications: Various articles on art and literature; Series of articles on Augustine; Contributions to various volumes on theology; Co-author, 2 English studies on Duns Scotus. Honours: Most Promising Article in Student Magazine, 1982; Nominated, Sermon of the Year, 1997. Membership: Research Group, John Duns Scotus. Address: Hovenstraat 1, 3581 RS Utrecht, The Netherlands. E-mail: nicodenbok@hetnet.nl

BOKHARI Syed Monzur H, b. 11 February 1947, Dhaka, Bangladesh. Civil Engineer. m. Syeda Abida Bokhari, 1 son, 1 daughter. Education: BSc, Civil Engineering, 1968; MEng, Water Resources Development, 1976; PEng, Bangladesh Professional Engineers Registration Board, 2003. Appointments include: Senior Planning and Design Engineer, Ministry of Irrigation, Iraq, 1978-83; Saudi Arabian Dames and Moore, Riyadh, 1985-88; Senior Engineer/Deputy Project Director, Local Team Leader, Bangladesh Engineering and Technological Services (BETS), Ltd, 1988-92; Senior Level Local Consultant/SWMC, Danish Hydraulic Institute, 1992-93; Team Leader, 23 Towns Water Supply Project, Department of Public Health Enginering1994; Head, Water Resources Management, BETS Ltd, 1994; Director, Water,

Agriculture and Social Science Division, BETS, Ltd, 1994-; Team Leader, Baral Basin Development Project, BETS, Ltd, 1996-; Team Leader, Preparation of Land Use Plan for the Railway Land of Chittagong, 1998; Deputy Team Leader, Preparation of the Operation and Maintenance Manual of Teesta Barrage and its Head Regulator, BETS Ltd, 1998; Planning Engineer, Feasibility Study for Re-Excavation of Betna River and Branch Khal, BETS Ltd, 2000; Director, BETS Ltd, 1996-; Co-ordinator of more than 25 projects including: National Water Management Plan Project, Gorai River Restoration Project. Publication: Test with Permeable Groyne on a Large Braided River, the Jamuna in Bangladesh, 10th APD-IAHR Congress, Kuala Lumpur, 1996. Honour: Awarded Honour Certificate for research project: Hydrodynamic Model of Chao Phraya River System, Asian Institute of Technology, Bangkok, Thailand. Memberships: Fellow, American Society of Civil Engineers; MIEAust CPEng; MIAHR; Life Fellow Institution of Engineers of Bangladesh; Life Member, National Oceanographic and Maritime Institute, Bangladesh; Life Member AIT Alumni Association, Bangkok. Address: Flat No 8a, Eastern Housing Apartments, 102-104 Bara Maghbazar, Siddeswari, Dhaka 1217, Bangladesh.

BOKSENBERG Alexander, b. 18 March 1936. Astronomer. m. Adella Coren, 1960, 1 son, 1 daughter. Education: BSc, Physics, University of London; PhD, 1961. Appointments: SRC Research Assistant, Department of Physics and Astronomy, University College London, 1960-65; Lecturer in Physics, 1965-75; Head of Optical and Ultraviolet Astronomy Research Group, 1969-81; Reader in Physics, 1975-78; SRC Senior Fellow, 1976-81; Professor of Physics and Astronomy, 1978-81; Sherman Fairchild Distinguished Scholar, California Institute of Technology, 1981-82; Director, Royal Greenwich Observatory, 1981-93; Royal Observatories, 1993-96; Research Professor, University of Cambridge and PPARC Senior Research Fellow, Universities of Cambridge and London, 1996-; Extraordinary Fellow, Churchill College, Cambridge, 1996-. Honours: Chair, New Industrial Concepts Ltd, 1969-81; President, West London Astronomical Society, 1978-; Chair, SRC Astronomy Committee, 1980-81; Numerous other committees on astronomy, 1980-; Visiting Professor, Department of Physics and Astronomy, University College, London, 1981-, Astronomy Center, University of Sussex, 1981-89; Dr h c (l'Observatoire de Paris), 1982; Honorary Doctorate, Paris Observatory, 1982; Asteroid (3205) named Boksenberg, 1988; Honorary Professor of Experimental Astronomy, University of Cambridge, 1991-; Hon DSc (Sussex), 1991; Executive Editor, Experimental Astronomy, 1995-; Honorary President, Astronomical Society of Glasgow; Hannah Jackson Medal, 1998;Membership: Past member of over 30 other councils, boards, committees, etc, 1970-; ESA Hubble Space Telescope Instrument Definition Team, 1973-; Fellow, Royal Society, 1978; SA Astronomical Observatory Advisory Committee, 1978-85; Freeman, Clockmakers Co, 1984; British Council Science Advisory Committee, 1987-91; Liveryman, 1989; Fachbeirat of Max Planck Institut für Astronomie, 1991-95; Fellow, University College, London, 1991-; Member of Court, 1994. Address: University of Cambridge, Institute of Astronomy, The Observatories, Madingley Road, Cambridge, CB3 0HA, England.

BOLAND Michael (John), b. 14 November 1950, Kingston, Surrey, England. Poet. Appointment: Editor, The Arcadian, poetry magazine. Publication: The Midnight Circus; The Trout... Minus One (co-author), 1993; Rainbow Trout (co-author, 2004. Contributions to: Envoi; Purple Patch; Weyfarers; Iota; Candelabrum; First Time; Poetry Now; Firing Squad; Various anthologies. Honours: Patricia Chown Sonnet Award. Memberships: PEN; Society of Civil Service Authors; Keats-

Dictionary of International Biography

Shelley Memorial Association; Wordsworth Trust; Friends of Coleridge. Address: 11 Boxtree Lane, Harrow Weald, Middlesex HA3 6JU, England.

BOLBASOV Vladimir Sergeevich, b. 12 November 1935, Zimovniki, Russia. pa/Chairman of Competitive Commission, Presidium, IAIT. m. Nina Seliverstovna Bolbasova, deceased, 1 son. Education: Taganrog Radiotechical Institute, Engineering-Electronics, 1958; Institute of Electronics, Byelarussian Academy of Sciences, DSc, Electronics, 1973; IA IPT DSc, Law, 1995; Professor, IAIPT, 1995. Appointments: Engineer, Chief Designer, Research Institute, Novosibirsk, 1958-64; Chief Engineer, Leading Researcher, Deputy Chief of Laboratory, Institute of Electronics, Byelarussian Academy of Sciences, 1964-89; USSR Parliament: Chair, Subcommittee for Intellectual Property, Subcommittee for Science, 1989-92; Deputy Director, Department, Commonwealth of Independent States Executive Secretariat (ES CIS), 1992-99. Publications: Over 430 research papers and inventions: Issues of Special Radioelectronics, 1962; Radioelectronics issues, 1965; Summary Proceedings of the Conference in Electronic Technics, 1971; RAS BSSR, 1985; New Legislation of the Industrial Ownership, 1991; Economical problems and perspectives of the CIS development, 1996; Issues of the information technologies creation, 1995, 1996, 1997, 1998, 1999, 2000, 2001, 2002, 2003. Honours: 2 Medals, USSR; Order Russia; Commemorative Medal, 1997 Man of the Year; 20th CAA Diploma and Silver Medal Package; Gold Star Award; Honourable Inventor of Belarus. Memberships: Vice Chair, Byelarussian Society of Inventors and Rationalisers, 1964; Academician, IAS IPT (IA IPT), 1994; IAIT, 1996; Advisor, Research Board of Advisors, ABI, 1998; New York Academy of Sciences, 1998; c/p Honorary Member, IBC Advisory Council, 1999; IAE, 1999; Consular Representative of the United Cultural Convention, ABI, 2001; Outstanding Speaker Award, IBC, 2001. Address: Kulman Str, 15-28, Minsk, 220 100 Belarus.

BOLDON Ato, b. 30 December 1973, Port of Spain, Trinidad (resident of USA, 1988-). Athlete. Education: University of California, Los Angeles. Appointments: Coached by John Smith; Central American and Caribbean Record Holder at 60m indoors (6.49 secs), 100m (9.86 secs) and 200m (19.77 secs). Honours: Gold Medal, World Junior Championships 100m and 200m, 1992; 4th, Commonwealth Games 100m, 1994; Bronze Medal, World Championships 100m, 1995; Gold Medal, NCAA Championships 100m, 1996; Bronze Medals, Olympic Games 100m and 200m, 1996; 100m World Champion, 1997, 1999; Gold Medal, World Championships 200m, 1997; Gold Medal, Goodwill Games, New York, 200m, 1998; Gold Medal, Commonwealth Games 100m, 1998; Silver Medal, 100m, Bronze Medal, 200m, Olympic Games, 2000; Youngest sprinter ever to run under 10 seconds in the 100m and under 20 seconds in the 200m (at end of 2001). Website: www.atoboldon.com

BOLDYREV Alexander Alexandrovitch, b. 5 September 1940, Arkhangelsk City, Russia. Biologist; Professor of Biochemistry. m. Valeria Maltseva, 28 September 1963, 2 daughters. Education: MSc, 1963, PhD, 1967, M V Lomonosov Moscow State University; DSc, Leningrad State University, 1977; Postdoctoral Fellow, University Aarhus, Denmark, 1973-74. Appointments: Senior Science Researcher, Moscow State University, 1975-87; Visiting Professor, King's College London, England, 1982, 1986; Visiting Professor, Waseda University, Tokyo, Japan, 1990, 1993; Head, Laboratory of Clinical Neurochemistry, Institute of Neurology, Moscow, 1993-. Publications: More than 300 science articles and reviews in Russian and international journals; Several textbooks and monographs including: Carnosine and protection of tissues against oxidative stress, 1999. Honours: V S Gulevitch Prize, Russian Academy of Medical Sciences; Honorable

Professor, International Albert Schweizer University; Honorable Professor, King's College, London; Meritorious Science Worker, Russia. Memberships include: International Society for Neurochemistry; Society for Neuroscience; The European Peptide Club; New York Academy of Sciences; London Diplomatic Academy, UK; International Academy of Scientific Discovers and Inventors, Russia; American Association for the Advancement of Sciences, USA. Address: Department of Biochemistry, M V Lomonosov Moscow State University, School of Biology, Room 141, Lenin's Hills 119992, Moscow, Russia. E-mail: aaboldyrev@mail.ru

BOLGER Dermot, b. 6 February 1959, Finglas, Ireland. Novelist; Dramatist; Poet; Editor. m. Bernadette Clifton, 1988, 2 sons. Education: Finglas and Benevin College, Finglas. Appointments: Factory hand, library assistant, professor author; Founder and Editor, Raven Arts Press, 1979-92; Founder and Executive Editor, New Island Books, Dublin, 1992-. Publications: Novels: Night Shift, 1985; The Woman's Daughter, 1987, augmented edition, 1991; The Journey Home, 1990; Emily's Shoes, 1992; A Second Life, 1994; Father's Music, 1997; Finbar's Hotel (collaborative novel), 1997; Ladies Night at Finbar's Hotel (collaborative novel), 1999; Temptation, 2000; The Valparaiso Voyage, 2001. Plays: The Lament for Arthur Cleary, 1989; Blinded by the Light, 1990; In High Germany, 1990; The Holy Ground, 1990; One Last White Horse, 1991; The Dublin Bloom, 1994; April Bright, 1995; The Passion of Jerome, 1999; Consenting Adults, 2000. Poetry: The Habit of Flesh, 1979; Finglas Lilies, 1980; No Waiting America, 1981; Internal Exiles, 1986; Leinster Street Ghosts, 1989; Taking My Letters Back: New and Selected Poems, 1998. Editor: The Dolmen Book of Irish Christmas Stories, 1986; The Bright Wave: Poetry in Irish Now, 1986; 16 on 16: Irish Writers on the Easter Rising, 1988; Invisible Cities: The New Dubliners: A Journey through Unofficial Dublin, 1988; Invisible Dublin: A Journey through Its Writers, 1992; The Picador Book of Contemporary Irish Fiction, 1993; 12 Bar Blues (with Aidan Murphy), 1993; The New Picador Book of Contemporary Irish Fiction, 2000; Druids, Dudes and Beauty Queens: The Changing Face of Irish Theatre, 2001. Contributions to: Anthologies. Honours: A E Memorial Prize, 1986; Macauley Fellowship, 1987; A Z Whitehead Prize, 1987; Samuel Beckett Award, 1991; Edinburgh Fringe First Award, 1991, 1995; Stewart Parker BBC Award, 1991; Playwright in Association, Abbey Theatre, Dublin, 1998. Address: c/o A P Watt, 20 John Street, London WC1N 2DR, England.

BOLITHO Elaine Elizabeth, b. 12 December 1940, Christchurch, New Zealand. Researcher; Writer. m. Ian James Bolitho, 2 sons (1 deceased), 2 daughters. Education: BA, 1988, BA (Hons), PhD, 1993, World Religions, Victoria University, Wellington, New Zealand. Appointments: Government Life Insurance Officer, 1956-63, Full-time Mother, 1964-84; University studies, 1985-92; Researcher and Writer, 1993-. Publications: Books; Meet the Baptists – Postwar Personalities and Perspectives, 1994; Reefton School of Mines – Stories of Jim Bolitho, 1999; Numerous other books, journal and magazine articles and book chapters, relating to religion in New Zealand. Honours: Eileen Duggan Prize for New Zealand Literature, 1986; Sarah Ann Rhodes Research Scholarship; Helen Stewart Royle Scholarship; Epworth Book of the Month, 1993; Omega Award for Excellence in Christian Writing, 1999. Memberships: New Zealand Federation of Graduate Women; Christian Research Association; New Zealand Christian Writers Guild; New Zealand Society of Authors (PEN Inc); Council of Wellington Churches. Address: 33 Kandy Crescent, Ngaio, Wellington 6004, New Zealand.

BOLKIAH HRH Prince Jefri, b. Brunei. Politician. Appointments: Minister of Culture, Youth and Sports; Deputy Minister of Finance; Minister of Finance, 1988-97; Former chair,

Royal Brunei Airlines; Chair, Brunei Investment Agency; Former proprietor, Asprey & Garrad. Address: c/o Ministry of Finance, Bandar Seri Begawan, Brunei. Address: c/o Ministry of Finance, Bandar Seri Begawan, Brunei.

BOLKIAH HRH Prince Mohamed, b. 27 August 1947, Brunei. Politician. Education: Royal Military Academy, Sandhurst, England. Appointment: Ministry of Foreign Affairs, 1984-. Address: Ministry of Foreign Affairs, Jalan Subok, Bandar Seri Begawan, Brunei.

BOLKIAH MU'IZUDDIN WADDAULAH, HM Sultan Sir Muda Hassanal, b. 15 July 1946, Brunei. m. (1) Rajah Isteri Anak Saleha, 1965, 1 sons, 5 daughters, (2) Pengiran Isteri Hajjah Mariam, divorced 2003, 2 sons, 2 daughters. Education: Victoria Institute, Kuala Lumpur, Malaysia; Royal Military Academy, Sandhurst, England. Appointments: Crown Prince and Heir Apparent, 1961; Rurler of State of Brunei, 1967-; Prime Minister of Brunei, 1984-; Minister of Finance and Home Affairs, 1984-86, of Defence, 1986-, also Finance and Law. Honours include: Honorary Captain, Coldstream Guards, 1968; Honorary Marshall, RAF, 1992; Sovereign and Chief of Royal Orders, Sultans of Brunei. Address: Istana Darul Hana, Bandar Seri Begawan, BA 1000, Brunei. E-mail: pro@jpm.gov.bn

BOLSHAKOV Vladimir Ivanovich, b. May 1946, Dniepropetrovsk, Ukraine. Professor. Education: Graduate, Technology Faculty, Dniepropetrovsk Metallurgical Institute, 1969; Postgraduate, Moscow Institute of Civil Engineering. Appointments: Forge and Shop, Dniepropetrovsk Steam Locomotive Repair Plant, 1963; Junior Research Worker, Dniepropetrovsk Institute of Civil Engineering; Professor, Doctor, Technical Sciences, 1985-, Head, Metal Technology Department, 1986-, Rector, Pridneprovskaya State Academy. Publications: Over 690 scientific works including 34 monographs, methodical books and brochures; 56 USSR author certificates and Ukrainian patents. Honours: State Prizewinner, Ukraine, 1999; The Order for Public Service, 2000; Honoured Engineer of Russia, 2000; Listed in international biographical reference works. Memberships: Academy of Higher Education, International Engineering Academy, Moscow; Society of Ferrous Metals, USA; Royal Institute of Materials, London; European Society of Mathematicians & Mechanics, Germany. Address: 5/11 Lazariane Street, Dnepropetrovsk Ukraine, 49010.

BON JOVI Jon (John Bongiovi), b. 2 March 1962, Sayreville, New Jersey, USA. Vocalist; Songwriter; Musician (guitar). m. Dorothea Hurley, May 1989, 1 son, 1 daughter. Career: Singer, local bands: Raze; Atlantic City Expressway; Singer, founder member, US rock group Bon Jovi, 1984-; 40 million albums sold worldwide to date; Numerous worldwide tours, including US, UK, Europe, USSR, South America, Australia, Japan, 1984-; Support tours with Kiss; Scorpions; .38 Special; Headliners, Donington Monsters Of Rock Festival, 1987; Moscow Music Peace Festival, 1989; Numerous television, radio and video appearances worldwide; Own management company, BJM; Own record label Jambco. Recordings: US Number 1 singles include: You Give Love A Bad Name, 1986; Living On A Prayer, 1987; Bad Medicine, 1988; I'll Be There For You, 1989; Solo: Blaze Of Glory, 1990; Destination Anywhere, 1997; Midnight In Chelsea Pt 1, 1997; Real Life Pt 1, 1999; Real Life Pt 2, 1999; Numerous other hits include: Wanted Dead Or Alive; Lay Your Hands On Me; Living In Sin; Born To Be My Baby; Keep The Faith; In These Arms; I'll Sleep When I'm Dead; Bed Of Roses; Always; I Believe; Someday I'll Be Saturday Night; This Ain't A Love Song; Lie To Me; These Days; Hey God; One Road Man; Albums: Bon Jovi, 1984; 7800° Fahrenheit, 1985; Slippery When Wet (13 million copies sold),

1986; New Jersey, 1988; Keep The Faith, 1991; Crossroad (Best Of), 1994; These Days, 1995; Solo album: Blaze Of Glory (film soundtrack, Young Guns II); Contributor, Stairway To Heaven/ Highway To Hell charity record, 1989; Two Rooms (Elton John/ Bernie Taupin tribute album), 1991. Honours: American Music Awards, Favourite Pop/Rock Band, 1988; Favourite Pop/Rock Single, 1991; Bon Jovi Day, Sayreville, 1989; Silver Clef, Nordoff-Robbins Music Therapy, 1990; All albums Gold or Platinum status; Golden Globe, Best Original Song, Blaze Of Glory, 1991; Oscar Nomination, Blaze Of Glory; Best Selling Album Of Year, Crossroad, 1994; BRIT Award, Best International Group, 1996. Current Management: c/o BJM, 809 Elder Circle, Austin, TX 78733, USA.

BONA Jerry Lloyd, b. 5 February 1945, Little Rock, Arkansas, USA. Professor. m. Pamela A Bona, 2 daughters. Education: BS, Applied Mathematics and Computer Science, Washington University, Saint Louis, 1962-66; PhD, Mathematics, Harvard University, 1966-71. Appointments: Research Fellow, Fluid Mechanics Research Institute, University of Essex, 1970-72; L E Dickson Instructor in Mathematics, 1972-73, Assistant Professor, 1973-76, Associate Professor, 1976-79, Professor of Mathematics, 1979-86, University of Chicago; Professor of Mathematics, 1986-95, Acting Chairman, 1990-91, Raymond Shibley Professor of Mathematics, Chairman, 1991-95, Pennsylvania State University; CAM Professor of Mathematics and Physics, Texas Institute for Computational and Applied Mathematics, University of Texas, Austin, 1995-2002; Professor of Mathematics, Chairman, University of Illinois, Chicago, 2002-. Publications: Numerous articles in professional journals and conference proceedings. Honours include: Woodrow Wilson Fellow, 1966-67; W M Keck Award, 1989; Fellow, American Association for the Advancement of Science, 1998. Memberships: American Mathematical Society; American Association for the Advancement of Science; Mathematics Association of America; Mathematics and Education Reform Network; Society for Industrial and Applied Mathematics. Address: Department of Mathematics, Statistics and Computer Science, University of Illinois at Chicago, Chicago, IL 60607, USA.

BOND Alma Halbert, b. 6 February 1923, Philadelphia, Pennsylvania, USA. Author; Psychoanalyst. m. Rudy Bond, deceased, 2 sons, 1 daughter. Education: BA, Temple University, 1944; MA, New York University, 1951; Postdoctoral study of Psychoanalysis, National Psychological Association of Psychoanalysis, 1955; PhD, Columbia University, 1962. Appointments: Psychoanalyst, private practice, 1953-91; Author, 1989-. Publications include: Who Killed Virginia Woolf? A Psychobiography, 1989, 2000; America's First Woman Warrior: The Courage of Deborah Sampson, 1992; Dream Portrait, 1992; Is There Life After Analysis?, 1993; On Becoming a Grandparent, 1994; The Autobiography of Maria Callas: A Novel, 1998, 2000; I Married Dr Jekyll and Woke Up Ms Hyde, 2000; Tales of Psychology: Short Stories to make you Wise, 2002; Numerous articles in popular magazines and journals, and also articles in professional journals. Honour: Runner-up, Hemingway Days First Novel Contest, 1996. Memberships include: Fellow, Institute for Psychoanalytic Training and Research; International Psychoanalytic Association; Dramatists Guild; American Society of Journalists and Authors; Writers Guild; American Psychological Association. Address: Harbour House, 10275 Collins Avenue # 1135S, Bal Harbour, FL 33154, USA. E-mail: almahb@cs.com

BONDI Hermann (Sir), b. 1 November 1919, Vienna, Austria (British Citizen). Mathematician. m. Christine M Stockman, 1947, 2 sons, 3 daughters. Education: BA, Mathematics, Cambridge University, 1940; Research Student, 1941. Appointments: Naval Radar Work, British Admiralty, 1942; Fellowship, Trinity College,

1943; Assistant Lecturer, 1945-48; Visiting Professor, Cornell University, 1951, Harvard University, 1953; Chair of Applied Mathematics, King's College, London; Advisory Posts, Ministry of Defence, National Space Committee, European Space Organization, Department of Energy, National Environment Research Council. Publications: Cosmology, 1960; The University at Large, 1961; Relativity and Common Sense, 1964; Assumption and Myth in Physical Theory, 1967; Science, Churchill and Me (autobiography), 1990; Numerous books on cosmology and related subjects. Honour: Knighted, 1973; Honorary Fellow: Regent's College, 1988, Institute of Physics, 1992, Institute of Mathematics and its Applications, 1993, Indian Academy of Sciences, 1996; Honorary DSc: Sussex, Bath, Surrey, 1974, York, 1980, Southampton, 1981, Salford, 1982, Birmingham, 1984, St Andrews, 1985, Vienna, 1993, Plymouth, 1995; Gold Medal, Institute of Mathematics and its Applications, 1988; GD Birla International Award for Humanism, 1990; Planetary Award, Association of Space Explorers, 1993; President's Decoration for Science and Arts, Austria, 1997; Gold Medal, Royal Astronomical Society, 2001. Membership: Fellow of the Royal Society, 1959. Address: Churchill College, Cambridge, CB3 0DS, England.

BONDS Georgia Anna Arnett, b. 30 December 1917, New York, USA. Writer; Lecturer. m. Alfred Bryan Bonds, 2 sons, 2 daughters. Education: BA, University of North Carolina, 1938; MA, Louisiana State University, 1941; Post Graduate Work, University of North Carolina, 1941-42; Baldwin Wallace College, 1960-. Appointments: Editorial Assistant, The Southern Review; Editorial Assistant Public School Curriculum of Louisiana; Editor of English version of Wheat Growing In Egypt; First Lady of Baldwin Wallace College; Volunteer, World Association of Girl Guides And Girl Scouts; Worked world-wide for peace through international understanding. Publications: The Lake Erie Girl Scout Council, the First Seventy Five Years; First two chapters of A Promise Kept, 1912-2002, ninety years of helping girls succeed; Novel, Who Killed Bob Lawson?, 2003; Numerous articles in popular magazines. Honours: World Friendship and Understanding Through Girl Scouting; Thanks Badges, 1971, 1997. Memberships: Phi Beta Kappa; United Methodist Church; YWCA; AAUW; Eastern Star; AARP. Address: PO Box 768, Berea, OH, USA.

BONEV Boris Ivanov, b. 14 December 1938. Varna, Bulgaria. Aerospace Engineer. m. Nina Boneva, 1 son, 2 daughters. Education: Aircraft and Engine Technician, People's Higher Military Technical School, Gorna Oriakhovitsa, Bulgaria, 1959; Aircraft and Engine Engineer, Bulgarian Airforce Academy, Dolna Mitropolia, Bulgaria, 1968; Candidate of Technical Sciences, "N E Zhukovsky" Air Force Engineering Academy, Moscow, Russia, 1973; Assistant Professor of Aircraft Aerodynamics, 1975, Doctor of Technical Sciences, 1981, Professor of Aircraft Aerodynamics, 1983, Bulgarian Air Force Academy. Appointments: Aircraft Technician Officer, Bulgarian Air Force, 1959-63; Officer Faculty Member in Aerodynamics, 1968-70, Senior Officer Faculty Member, 1973-74, Founder and Head, Aerodynamics Department, 1974-80, Head, Academic Division, 1980-81, Deputy Rector responsible for teaching and scientific activities, Head, Scientific and Research Department, Founder, Scientific Council, 1981-86, Bulgarian Air Force Academy; Director, Central Space Research Laboratory, 1986, Founder and Director, Space Research Institute, 1987-96, Bulgarian Academy of Sciences; Representative of Bulgaria to the Committee on the Peaceful Use of Outer Space of the United Nations (COPUOS-UN), 1987-97, 2002-; Founder and President, Bulgarian Aerospace Agency, 1993-; Founder and General Manager of BASA Aviation Ltd, 1999-. Publications: More than 250 scientific papers in the field of aerodynamics, aircraft and aerospace technologies; Supervisor of 10 graduate students. Address: PO Box 59, BG-1000 Sofia, Bulgaria. Website: http://www.basaaviation.com/bonev_e.shtml

BONGIBAULT Andre, b. 30 March 1945, Paris, France. Artist; Educator. Appointments: Etching Teacher, Art Manager, Fine Art School of Chaville, France, 1977-; Selected exhibitions: National: Chamaliers; Digne les Bains; Strasbourg; Saga Paris; FIAC Paris; Ermont; Bayeux; Versailles; Tours; Salon d'Automne Paris; International: Stavangen; Washington; Belgrade; Bruges; Prague; Cracow; Graz; Liepzig; Nuremberg; Biella; Kuala Lumpur; Osaka; Tokyo; Ljubljana; Kochi; Taipei; Fredrikstad; Bitola; Milan; Frankfurt; Bhopal; Dallas; Los Angeles; Bale; Thessaloniki; Varna; Sungsan; Museum exhibits: Indianapolis; BN Paris; Angers; Kuala Lumpur; Osaka; Bhopal; Auvers sur Oise; Portland; New York; Digne les Bains. Honours: Selected awards: Award, Ecole Estienne, Paris, 1964; Prix Grand Public, Fiest, Paris, 1966; 1st Prize, Print Show, Bayeux, France, 1990; Regulation Award MTG, International Print Triennial, Cracow, Poland, 1994 1st Grand Prix, 4th Bharat Bhavan Print Biennial, Bhopal, India, 1997; Special Award, Exhibition of Mini Prints, Tokyo, Japan, 1999; 2nd Prize, 4th Kochi International Exhibition of Print, Japan, 1999; Etching Prize, 9th International Biennial of Print, Taipei, Taiwan, 1999; Special Award, International Print Biennial, Bitola, Macedonia, 2000. Address: Moulin de la Rochette, route de Meluzien, 89200 Avallon, France. E-mail: simone.gendille@wanadoo.fr

BONHAM CARTER Helena, b. 26 May 1966, Golders Green, London, England. Actress. 1 son. Career: Films include: Lady Jane; A Room with a View; Maurice; Francesco; The Mask; Getting it Right; Hamlet; Where Angels Fear to Tread; Howard's End, 1991; A Dark Adapted Eye (TV), 1994; Mary Shelley's Frankenstein, 1994; The Glace Bay Miners' Museum, 1994; A Little Loving, 1995; Mighty Aphrodite, 1995; Twelfth Night, 1996; Margaret's Museum, 1996; Parti Chinois, 1996; The Theory of Flight, 1997; Keep the Aspidistra Flying, 1997; The Wings of the Dove, 1998; The Revengers' Comedies, 1998; Women Talking Dirty, 1999; Fight Club, 1999; Until Human Voices Wake Us, 2000; Planet of the Apes, 2002; The Heart of Me, 2002; Novocaine, 2002; The Heart of Me, 2003; Till Human Voices Wake Us, 2003; Television appearances include: A Pattern of Roses; Miami Vice; A Hazard of Hearts; The Vision; Arms and the Man; Beatrix Potter. Address: c/o Conway van Gelder Limited, 18/21 Jermyn Street, London, SW1Y 6HP, England.

BONHAM-CARTER Victor, b. 13 December 1913, Bearsted, Kent, England. Author. m. (1) Audrey Stogdon, 22 July 1938, 2 sons, (2) Cynthia Clare Sanford, 9 February, 1979. Education: MA, Magdalene College, 1935. Appointments: Historian, Records Officer, Dartington Hall Estate, 1951-65; Secretary, Royal Literary Fund, 1966-82; Joint Secretary, Society of Authors, London, 1971-78. Publications: The English Village, 1952; Dartington Hall (with W B Curry), 1958; Exploring Parish Churches, 1959; Farming the Land, 1959; In a Liberal Tradition, 1960; Soldier True, US edition as The Strategy of Victory, 1965; Surgeon in the Crimea (editor), 1968; The Survival of the English Countryside, US edition as Land and Environment, 1971; Authors by Profession, 2 volumes, 1978-84; The Essence of Exmoor, 1991; What Countryman, Sir? (autobiography), 1996; A Filthy Barren Ground (editor), 1998. Memberships: Royal Society of Literature, fellow; Exmoor Society, president, 1975-. Address: The Mount House, Milverton, Taunton, Somerset TA4 1QZ, England.

BONINGTON Sir Christian (John Storey), b. 6 August 1934. Mountaineer; Writer; Photographer. m. Muriel Wendy Marchant, 1962, 2 sons. Education: University College School, London. Appointments: RMA Sandhurst, 1955-56; Commissioned, Royal Tank Regiment, 1956-61; Unilever Management Trainee, 1961-62; Writer and Photographer, 1962-; Mountaineer of: Annapurna II, 1960, Central Pillar Freney, Mont Blanc, 1961, Nuptse, 1961, North Wall of Eiger, 1962, Central Tower of Paine, Patagonia,

1963; Member of Team, 1st descent of Blue Nile, 1968; Leader, Annapurna South Face Expedition, 1970; British Everest Expedition, 1972; Brammah Himalayas, 1973; Co-Leader, Changabang, Himalayas, 1974; British Everest Expedition, 1975; Ogre, 1977; Joint Leader, Kongur, North West China, 1981; Panch Chuli II, Kumaon, Himalayas, 1992; Mejslen, Greenland, 1993; Rang Rik Rank, Kinnaur, Himalayas, 1994, Drangnag Ri, Nepal, 1995; Sepu Kangri Expedition, 1998; 1st ascent of Danga II, 2000. Publications: I Chose to Climb (autobiography), 1966; Annapurna South Face, 1971; The Next Horizon (autobiography), 1973; Everest, South West Face, 1973; Everest the Hard Way, 1976; Quest for Adventure, 1981; Kongur: China's Elusive Summit, 1982; Everest: The Unclimbed Ridge (co-author), 1983; The Everest Years, 1986; Mountaineer (autobiography), 1989; The Climbers, 1992; Sea, Ice and Rock (with Robin Knox-Johnston), 1992; Tibet's Secret Mountain, 1999; Quest for Adventure, 2000. Honours include: Founder Medal, Royal Geographical Siety, 1971; Lawrence of Arabia Medal, 1986; Livingstone Medal, 1991; CBE; Honorary DSc, Sheffield; Honorary MA, Salford; Honorary DSc, Lancaster; Honorary DSc, Northumbria; Honorary Doctor of Letters, University of Bradford. Memberships include: Army Mountaineering Association; British Mountaineering Council; Council for National Parks; The Alpine Club. Address: Badger Hill, Nether Row, Hesket Newmarket, Wigton, Cumbria CA7 8LA, England.

BONIRE Josiah Jimoh, b. 10 June 1950, Iluke-Bunu, Nigeria. Lecturer. m. Margaret Olorunyomi, 19 December 1981, 2 sons, 2 daughters. Education: BS, Honours, 1974; MSc, 1977; PhD, Chemistry, 1982. Appointments: Graduate Assistant, 1975, Assistant Lecturer, Lecturer II, Senior Lecturer, Associate Professor, 1993-; Developed, Chemical Process for Preserving Yam (Dioscarea rotundata) from Rot, 1998 and Process for Producing Alum From Kaolin, 1998. Publications: Insights for Living, 1992; Columnist, Nigerian Herald, 1981-90; Towards a Peaceful Living, Vol I, 2002; Contributor of several articles to professional journals. Membership: Royal Society of Chemistry, England. Address: Department of Chemistry, Ahmadu Bello University, Zaria, Nigeria. E-mail: jjbonire@abu.edu.ng

BONO (Paul Hewson), 10 May 1960, Dublin, Ireland. Singer; Lyricist. m. Alison, 2 daughters, 1 son. Career: Founder member, lead singer, rock group U2, 1978-; Regular national, international and worldwide tours; Major concerts include: US Festival, 1983; The Longest Day, Milton Keynes Bowl, 1985; Live Aid, Wembley, 1985; Self Aid, Ireland, 1986; A Conspiracy Of Hope (Amnesty International US tour), 1986; Smile Jamaica (hurricane relief concert), 1988; Very Special Arts Festival, White House, 1988; New Year's Eve Concert, Dublin (televised throughout Europe), 1989; Yankee Stadium, New York (second concert ever), 1992; Group established own record company, Mother Records. Compositions include: Co-writer, Jah Love, Neville Brothers; Lyrics, Misere, Zucchero and Pavarotti; Screenplay, Million Dollar Hotel. Recordings: Albums: with U2: Boy, 1980; October, 1981; War (Number 1, UK), 1983; Under A Blood Red Sky, 1983; The Unforgettable Fire (Number 1, UK), 1984; Wide Awake In America, 1985; The Joshua Tree (Number 1, UK and US), 1987; Rattle And Hum, also film (Number 1, US), 1988; Achtung Baby (Number 1, US), 1991; Zooropa (Number 1, UK and US), 1993; Passengers (film soundtrack), with Brian Eno, 1995; Pop, 1997; All Than You Can't Leave Behind, 2000; Hit singles include: Out Of Control (Number 1, Ireland), 1979; Another Day (Number 1, Ireland), 1980; New Year's Day, 1983; Two Hearts Beat As One, 1983; Pride (In The Name Of Love), 1984; The Unforgettable Fire, 1985; With Or Without You (Number 1, US), 1987; I Still Haven't Found What I'm Looking For (Number 1, US), 1987; Where The Streets Have No Name, 1987; Desire (Number 1, UK),

1988; Angel Of Harlem, 1988; When Love Comes To Town, with B B King, 1989; All I Want Is You, 1989; The Fly (Number 1, UK), 1991; Mysterious Ways, 1992; One, 1992; Even Better Than The Real Thing, 1992; Who's Gonna Ride Your Wild Horses, 1992; Stay, 1993; Hold Me, Thrill Me, Kiss Me (from film soundtrack Batman Forever), 1995; Discotheque, 1997; If God Will Send His Angels, 1998; Sweetest Thing, 1998; Contributor, Do They Know It's Christmas?, Band Aid, 1985; Sun City, Little Steven, 1985; In A Lifetime, Clannad, 1986; Mystery Girl, Roy Orbison, 1988; Special Christmas, charity album, 1987; Folkways - A Vision Shared (Woody Guthrie tribute), 1988; Live For Ireland, 1989; Red Hot + Blue (Cole Porter tribute), 1990; Tower Of Song (Leonard Cohen tribute), 1995; Pavarotti And Friends, 1996; Forces Of Nature, 1999. Honours: Grammy Awards: Album Of The Year, Best Rock Performance, The Joshua Tree, 1987; Best Rock Performance, Desire, 1989; Best Rock Vocal, 1993; BRIT Awards: Best International Group,1988-90; Best Live Act, 1993; World Music Award, Irish Artist Of The Year, 1993; Juno Award, International Entertainer Of The Year, 1993; Q Awards: Best Act In The World, 1990, 1992, 1993; Merit Award, 1994; Best International Group and Award for Outstanding Contribution to the Music Industry, Brit Awards, 2001; Numerous poll wins and awards, Billboard and Rolling Stone magazines; Gold and Platinum discs. Current Management: Principle Management, 30-32 Sir John Rogersons Quay, Dublin 2, Ireland.

BONYTHON Charles Warren, b. 11 September 1916, Adelaide, Australia. Retired Chemical Engineer. m. Cynthia Young, 12 April 1941, 1 son, 2 daughters. Education: St Peters College, Adelaide; BSc, St Marks College, University of Adelaide, 1938. Appointments: Research and Management, ICI Australia Ltd, 1940-66; Director, Dampier Salt Ltd, 1968-79; Active in Heritage and Conservation. Publications: Walking the Flinders Ranges; Walking the Simpson Desert; I'm No Lady: The Reminiscences of Constance Jean, Lady Bonython OBE; The Great Filling of Lake Eyre in 1974. Honours: AO, 1980; Australian Geographic Adventure of the Year, 1990; John Lewis Gold Medal. Memberships: Inaugural Fellow, Royal Geographical Society of South Australia; Nature Foundation of South Australia; Conservation Council of South Australia; Scientific Expedition Group. Address: Romalo House, 24 Romalo Avenue, Magill, SA 5072, Australia.

BOOLAKY Ibrahim, b. 21 July 1937, Mauritius. Social Scientist; Lecturer. m. Jamila Ben Mansour, 1 son. Education: BA, honours, Middlesex University; MSc, Economics, University of London; M Phil, London School of Economics and Political Science. Appointments: Teacher, 1957-62; Journalist, 1962-69; Director General, Islamic Institute, Mauritius, 1969-75; Press Correspondent Researcher, 1976-83; Lecturer, Planning and Development, University of Tunis, 1984-89, Business Studies, London, Dean College, 1981-91, City and Islington College, 1991-97; Business Consultant, 1997-. Publications include: The Impact of Islamic Medicine on the Development of Civilization, 1985; The Melody of Peace, 1988; The Strategy of the 1.5 Million House Programme of Sri Lanka, 1991; Ibn Khaldun's Methods in Traditional Research, 1994; The Systemic Nature of Islamic Medicine, 1997; Old and Modern Pioneers of Islamic Medicine, 1998; A Systems View on the History of Medicine, 1999, ISHM's 36th International Congress, Tunis, 6-11 September 1998; Islamic Medical Manuscripts up to the New Millennium, 2000; A Universal History of Arabic, 2003; The Rise and Fall of Islamic Civilization in Eastern Africa, 2004. Honour: Teachers Certificate. Memberships: Convocation, Senate House, University of London, 1982; Fellow, British Institute of Management, 1983, Institute of Management Specialists, 1984. Address: Le Ranch El-Andalouss, Cite des Juges, Raoued Plage, BP No 29, 2056 Raoued, Tunisia.

Dictionary of International Biography

BOORSTIN Daniel J(oseph), b. 1 October 1914, Atlanta, Georgia, USA. Historian; Librarian of Congress Emeritus. m. Ruth Carolyn Frankel, 9 April 1941, 3 sons. Education: AB, summa cum laude, Harvard University, 1934; BA, 1st class honours, Rhodes Scholar, 1936, BCL, 1st class honours, 1937, Balliol College, Oxford, 1937; Postgraduate Studies, Inner Temple, London, 1934-37; JSD, Sterling Fellow, Yale University, 1940. Appointments: Instructor, Tutor in History and Literature, Harvard University and Radcliffe College, 1938-42; Lecturer in Legal History, Harvard Law School, 1939-42; Assistant Professor of History, Swarthmore College, 1942-44; Assistant Professor, 1944-49, Professor, 1949-56, Professor of American History, 1956-64, Preston and Sterling Morton Distinguished Service Professor, 1964-69, University of Chicago; Fulbright Visiting Lecturer in American History, University of Rome, 1950-51, Kyoto University, 1957; 1st Incumbent of the Chair in American History, University of Paris, 1961-62; Pitt Professor of American History and Institutions, Cambridge University, 1964-65; Director, 1969-73, Senior Historian, 1973-75, National Museum of History and Technology, Smithsonian Institution, Washington, DC; Shelby and Kathryn Cullom Davis Lecturer, Graduate Institute of International Studies, Geneva, 1973-74; Librarian of Congress, 1975-87, Librarian of Congress Emeritus, 1987-, Washington, DC. Publications: The Mysterious Science of the Law, 1941; Delaware Cases, 1792-1830, 1943; The Lost World of Thomas Jefferson, 1948; The Genius of American Politics, 1953; The Americans: The Colonial Experience, 1958; America and the Image of Europe, 1960; The Image or What Happened to the American Dream, 1962; The Americans: The National Experience, 1965; The Landmark History of the American People, 1968, new edition, 1987; The Decline of Radicalism, 1969; The Sociology of the Absurd, 1970; The Americans: The Democratic Experience, 1973; Democracy and Its Discontents, 1974; The Exploring Spirit, 1976; The Republic of Technology, 1978; A History of the United States (with Brooks M Kelley), 1980, new edition, 1991; The Discoverers, 1983; Hidden History, 1987; The Creators, 1992; Cleopatra's Nose: Essays on the Unexpected, 1994; The Daniel J Boorstin Reader, 1995; The Seekers, 1998. Honours: Bancroft Award, 1959; Francis Parkman Prize, 1966; Pulitzer Prize in History, 1974; Dexter Prize, 1974; Watson-Davis Prize, 1986; Charles Frankel Prize, 1989; National Book Award, 1989; Many other honours, including numerous honorary doctorates. Memberships: American Academy of Arts and Sciences; American Antiquarian Society; American Philosophical Society; American Studies Association, president, 1969-71; Organization of American Historians; Royal Historical Society, corresponding member. Address: 3541 Ordway Street North West, Washington, DC 20016, USA.

BOOTH Cherie, b. 23 September 1954, Bury, Lancashire, England. Barrister. m. A C L (Tony) Blair, 1980, 3 sons, 1 daughter. Education: London School of Economics. Appointments: Lincoln's Inn Bar, 1976; In Practice, 1976-77; New Court Chambers, 1977-91; Gray's Inn Square Chambers, 1991-2000; Queens Council, 1995; Assistant Recorder, 1996-99; Governor, London School of Economics, 1998-; Recorder, 1999-; Matrix Chambers, 2000-. Publication: Contributor, Education Law, 1997. Honours: FJMU; FRSA; Fellow, John Moores University, Liverpool, Chancellor, 1998-; Patron, Sargent Cancer Care for Children, 1998-; Patron, Breast Cancer Care, 1997-; SHADO, Liverpool, 1998-; Islington Music Centre, 1999-; Honorary Degree, Open University, 1999; Honorary LLD, Westminster University; Fellow of LSE; Fellow of International Society of Lawyers in Public Service. Memberships: Fellow, Institute of Advisory Legal Studies. Address: 4-5 Gray's Inn Square, Gray's Inn, London WC1R 5AY, England.

BOOTH Martin, b. 7 September 1944, Lancashire, England. Writer. m. 1 son, 1 daughter. Publications: Fiction: Hiroshima Joe, 1985; The Jade Pavilion, 1987; Black Chameleon, 1988; Dreaming of Samarkand, 1989; A Very Private Gentleman, 1991; The Humble Disciple, 1992; The Iron Tree, 1993; Toys of Glass, 1995; Adrift in the Oceans of Mercy, 1996; The Industry of Souls, 1998; Islands of Silence, 2003; Fiction for Children: War Dog, 1996; Music on the Bamboo Radio, 1997; Panther, 1999; POW, 2000; Doctor Illuminatus, 2003; Midnight Saboteur, 2004; Non-fiction: Carpet Sahib: A Life of Jim Corbett, 1986; The Triads, 1990; Rhino Road: the Natural History and Conservation of the African Rhinos, 1992; The Dragon and the Pearl: A Hong Kong Notebook, 1994; Opium: A History, 1996; The Doctor, The Detective and Arthur Conan Doyle: A Biography of Sir Arthur Conan Doyle, 1997; The Dragon Syndicates, 1999; A Magick Life: A Biography of Aleister Crowley, 2000; Cannabis: A History, 2003. Also verse, criticism, screenplays and adult fiction under a pseudonym. Honour: Fellow, Royal Society of Literature, 1980. Address: Gillon Aitken Associates, 18-21 Cavaye Place, London SW10 9PT, England.

BOOTH Rachel Z, b. 10 February 1936, Seneca, South Carolina, USA. Nurse. m. Richard B Booth, 1 son. Education: Furman University, Greenville, 1953-54; Diploma, Greenville General Hospital School of Nursing, 1956; University of Alaska, 1964-66; BSN, University of Maryland School of Nursing, 1968; MS, University of Maryland Graduate School, College Park, 1970; PhD, University of Maryland College of Education, College Park, 1978; DNSc (hon), Chiang Mai University, Thailand, 1999. Appointments: Dean, Professor of Nursing, University of Alabama School of Nursing, 1987-; Director, World Health Organisation Collaborating Centre for International Nursing, University of Alabama at Birmingham, 1992-. Publications include: La enfermeria en la encrucijada del cambio, 1996; Managing an academic program in nursing, 1999; The Nursing Shortage: A Worldwide Problem, 2002. Honours: International Humanitarian Award, Lions International; Centennial Outstanding Achievement Alumni Award, University of Maryland; Distinguished Practitioner, National Academy of Nursing; Honorary Doctor of Science in Nursing, Chiang Mai University, Thailand. Memberships: American Association of Colleges of Nursing; American Nurses Association; Sigma Theta Tau International; National Academy of Practice. Address: 3112 Bradford Place, Birmingham, AL 35242, USA.

BOOTH Rosa-Maria (Rosmar), b. 9 November 1947, Olot, Catalonia, Spain. Artist. m. Peter Charles Booth, deceased. Education: Diploma of Fashion, 1970, Instituto Marti, Barcelona, Spain; Studied Art in Spain under Parejo and J M Agusti, in Paris under Madeleine Scali and in England under K Walch and at Thurrock Technical College under M Martin. Career: Associated with the old group, Crater d'Art, Olot, Spain; Worked as a Fashion Designer; Lived in Paris, 1972-75, then moved to England; Exhibits annually with the Royal Miniature Society; Exhibited at: Mall Gallery; Royal Academy Summer Exhibition several times; Barbican and other venues in the UK, Spain, France, Northern Ireland, Australia, Canada and USA; Work in private collections; Paints large paintings and miniatures in various mediums and specialises in portraits, imaginative subjects and clowns. Publications: The Centenary Book of the Royal Society of Miniature Painters, Sculptors and Gravers; Artistas del Millennium, Enciclopedia Europea. Honours: 17 Awards including: First place under 6 square inches, Montana MAS, 1982; Best in Mixed Media in Allegheny IAE, West Virginia, 1985; 1st Prize, Drawing and Pastel, 1983 and 1st place, Abstract, 1984, 1988, MAS Florida. Memberships: Royal Miniature Society; Founder Member, The Hilliard Society of Minaturists; The Miniature Art Society of Florida; Listed in Who's Who in Art. Address: 36 Windsor Avenue, Grays, Essex RM16 2UB, England.

Dictionary of International Biography

BOOTHROYD Christine, b. 31 March 1934, Batley, Yorkshire, England. Linguist; Poet. m. Don Brinkley, 10 April 1982, 1 stepson, 1 stepdaughter. Education: Leeds College of Commerce, 1951-52; Teachers Certificate, University College of Wales, Aberystwyth, 1966; Diplomas in Italian, Perugia and Florence. Appointments: Teacher of French/Italian, Leeds, 1963-65; Lecturer in charge of Modern Languages, North Oxfordshire Technical College, 1966-77; Part-time Lecturer, French/Italian, Banbury and Harrogate. Publications: The Floating World, 1975; The Snow Island, 1982; The Lost Moon, 1992. Contributions to: Arts Council Anthology 3; Workshop New Poetry; Orbis; Glasgow Magazine; Writers in Concert; Doors; Krax; Moorlands Review; Envoi; Penniless Press; Links; Dalesman; Poetry Nottingham International; Yorkshire Journal. Membership: Harrogate Writers' Circle; Italian Cultural Institute. Address: 35 St George's Road, Harrogate, North Yorkshire HG2 9BP, England.

BORDEI Despina, b. 29 March 1937, Galati, Romania. Professor. m. Gheorghe Bordei, 1 daughter. Education: Graduate, Faculty of Food Science, Aquaculture and Fishing, University of Galati, 1960; Diplomate Engineer, PhD, 1978. Appointments: Assistant Professor, 1960-70, Lecturer, 1971-90, Docent, 1990-91, Professor, 1992-2001, University of Galati. Publications include: The influence of the technological processes on the quality of food product, 1974; Improve use in the food industry, 1985; Biotechnologies in the food industry, 1987; Technical technological and scientific progresses in the food industry, vol I, II, 1992-93; The Engineer's Manual for Food Industry, 1999; Advances in Baking Science and Technology, 2000. Honours: Romanian Academy Award, 1987; Honour Diploma, University Dunârea de jos Galati, 1998; Named in Specialists Dictionary 2000, Romania. Membership: Romanian Wheat Milling and Bakery Specialists Association. Address: Str Traian nr 4 bl W12, ap 15, 6200 Galati, Romania.

BORDIN Ninel, b. 27 December 1930, Moscow, Russia. Physicist. m. Ratner Grigoriy, 1 February 1964, 1 son. Education: MS, Mathematics and Physics, 1952; PhD, 1966. Appointments: Teacher, Physics, Moscow, 1952-58; Engineer, Senior Engineer, 1958-66, Senior Scientist, 1966-92, All Union Science Research Institute, Moscow; Senior Researcher, Jerusalem College of Technology, 1993-. Publications: Over 90 articles in professional journals; Book: Modeling of Solar Cells and Solar Arrays I-V Characteristics, 1986. Honours: Bronze Medal, Exhibition of National Economic Achievement, Moscow, 1980; Medal, USSR Astronaut Federation, Moscow, 1986. Membership: All Union Science Research Institute of Current Sciences, 1967-92. Address: 15/14 Hazanhanim Street, 69270 Tel Aviv, Israel.

BORG Björn Rune, b. 6 June 1956, Sodertalje, Sweden. Tennis Player; Business Executive. m. (1) Mariana Simionescu, 1980, divorced 1984, 1 son by Jannike Bjorling, (2) Loredana Berte, 1989, divorced 1992. Appointments: Professional Player, 1972-; Italian Champion, 1974, 1978; French Champion, 1974, 1975, 1978, 1979, 1980, 1981; Wimbledon Champion, 1976, 1977, 1978, 1979, 1980 (runner-up 1981); WCT Champion, 1976; Grand Prix Masters Champion, 1980, 1981; World Champion, 1979, 1980; Winner, Stockholm Open, 1980; Retired, 1983, returned, 1984, 1992; Founder, Björn Borg Enterprises Ltd. Publication: Björn Borg - My Life and Game (with Eugene Scott), 1980. Honours: Sweden's Sportsperson of the Century; Voted second-best tennis player ever, Sports Illustrated and l'Equipe newspaper. Address: c/o International Management Group, The Pier House, Strand on the Green, Chiswick, London W4 3NN, England.

BORISSOV Alexander Ilyitch, b. 13 October 1939, Moscow. Priest, Theologian, Biologist. Education: Biological Faculty, State Pedagogical Institute in Moscow, 1964; Diploma, Cand Biological Sciences (Genetics), 1969; Theological Seminary, Moscow, 1973; Theological Academy of Moscow, 1978; Candidate of Theological Sciences. Appointments: Researcher, USSR Academy Sciences, 1965-72; Student, Theological Seminary, 1972-73; Deacon Church of the Sign of Our Lady, Moscow, 1973-89; Priest, 1989-91, Head Priest, Prior, Church of St Cosma and St Damian, 1991-; President, The Bible Society for Russia, 1991-; Deputy, Moscow City Council, 1990-93; Member, President Commission for Mercy, 1992-2001; Member, Commission Social Service of the Church, The Moscow Patriarchate, 2001-. Publications: Book: The Fields White for Harvest, 1983, (The Ripen Fields); Translator in R E Davidson's Gene Activity in Easy Development, 1972; S Ohno Evaluation by Gene Duplication, 1973; R Moody, Life After Life. Honours: Candidate Biological Sciences (Genetics), 1969; Candidate, Theological Sciences, 1978; Golden Cross (priest award), 1998; Medal of Saint Prince of Moscow Daniil, Russian Orthodox Church Award, 1999. Membership: Bible Society for Russia. Address: Church of St Cosma and St Damian in Shubino, Stoleshnikov Per 2, Moscow 103009, Russia.

BORKOWSKI Marian, b. 17 August 1934, Pabianice, Poland. Composer; Musicologist; Pianist; Educator. m. Maria Nowak, 2 sons. Education: Master of Music, Academy of Music, Warsaw, 1965; Master of Musicology, Warsaw University, 1966; French Government Scholarship, Composition, Paris Conservatory and Ecole Pratique des Hautes Etudes, 1966-68; Musicology, Paris University, Sorbonne; Philosophy, Sorbonne and Collège de France; Certificates, International Courses of New Music, Darmstadt, Germany, 1972, 1974; Diploma di Merito, Academia Musicale Chigiana, Siena, Italy, 1973, 1975. Appointments: Lecturer, 1968-71, Assistant Professor of Composition, 1971-76, Associate Professor, 1976-89; Full Professor of Composition, 1989-, Chopin Academy of Music, Warsaw; Visiting Professor of Composition and Guest Artist, Canada, France, Italy, USA, Korea, 1989-. Publications: Several scholarly works on contemporary music; Contributions to music magazines. Honours: 2nd prize, Young Composers Competition, Warsaw, 1966; Prize, International Composers Competition, GB Viotti in Vercelli, 1969; 3rd prize, Szymanowski Competition for Composers, Warsaw, 1974; Prize, International New Music Composers Competition, New York, 1990; Awards, Minister of Culture and Art, 1976, 1980, 1982; Silver Cross of Merit, Republic of Poland, 1977; Silver Medal Premio Vittorio Gui, Florence, 1979; Medal, Chopin Academy of Music, Warsaw, 1981; Gold Medal, Merited Worker of the Sea, 1981; Knight's Cross of Order Polonia Restituta, 1984; Medal, 40th Anniversary of People's Poland, 1985; Badge of Merit in Culture, 1985; Medal, Seoul National University, Seoul, Korea, 1988; Bronze Medal, Civil Defence of Poland, 1989; Commander's Cross of Order Polonia Restituta, 2002. Memberships include: Union of Polish Composers; Polish Institute of Music; International Federation of Jeunesses Musicales; Author's Association ZAIKS; Association of Polish Marine Painters; Association of Sacred Music Lovers; Union of Polish Professors; International Society of Contemporary Music; Inamori Foundation, Kyoto, Japan; Laboratory of Contemporary Music Festival (Artistic Director); Society for Electro-Acoustic Music of the United States; Polish-US Fulbright Commission; Adviser, American Biographical Institute; Laboratory of Contemporary Music Association (President); Academy of Phonography (Council). Address: The Chopin Academy of Music, ul Okólnik 2, 00-368 Warszawa, Poland. E-mail: borkowski@chopin.edu.pl

BÖRNER Klaus, b. 22 June 1929, Senftenberg, Germany. Musician; Pianist; University Professor; Conductor; Composer. m. Helga Kibat, 1 son, 1 daughter. Education: Academy of Music Weimar, 1946-50; Piano, Conducting, Musicology; Exam for Piano Teaching, 1949; Conservatoire de Lausanne, 1950-52; Exam de virtuosité, 1952; Master Classes with Alfred Cortot, Edwin Fischer, Wilhelm Kempff. Career: Concerts as Pianist around the world, 70 countries; Solo recitals and soloist with orchestra, chamber music, accompanying singers; Radio, TV in four continents; piano teaching; Conservatory Dusseldorf, 1956-69; Professor, University Mainz 1969-97; Guest Professor: Several times in New Zealand, Hong Kong, Japan, Indonesia; Founder and Director of International Music Summer Camp SYLT, Germany, 1959-89. Publications: Original version of Beethoven Waldstein Sonata; Schumann Papillons: Teaching Experience and Students Reaction; Chance and Dilemma of the Urtext; Fingerings in Piano Sonatas by C. Ph. E. Bach, Henle edition; Piano Duet Repertoire, 2004; Compositions: Trio for horn, violin, piano; Lieder; Fantasy for piano duet; Quartet for 4 bassoons. Honours: Prize of Young Soloists, Weimar 1950; 1st Prize, International Piano Competition, Barcelona 1956 ; Other National Awards. Memberships: Jeunesses Musicales of Germany, 1953-, including a term as Vice-President; Tonkünstlerverband (Association of German Musicians); European Piano Teachers' Association, German Section; Address: Nibelungenstr 38, D-41462 Neuss, Germany.

BOROVIKOV Valeriy Vasiljevich, b. 16 November 1958, Ukraine. Researcher; Teacher. Education: Engineer-Mechanic, AF Mozhayskiy Military Engineering Institute; Candidate of Technical Sciences, 1991; Doctor of Technical Sciences, 1997; Professor 2001; Colonel, 2000. Appointments: Military Cadet, 1983-84; Aeronautical Engineer, 1984-88; Teacher, A F Mozhayskiy Military Engineering Aerospace Academy, 1988-97; Docent, 1997-99; Chair of Cosmodromes, 1999-2002; Chief of Department, Russian Space Agency, 2002-. Publications: Over 150 articles in professional journals. Honours: Medals, 1986, 1988, 1991, 1999. Memberships: New York Academy of Sciences; Member, Scientific Council, A F Mozhayskiy Aerospace University; Member, 2 dissertation councils; Academician, International Academy of Ecology, Man and Nature Protection Sciences, 2001. Address: Bogatyrskiy prospekt 53-3 kv 115, 197372 St Petersburg, Russia.

BOROWSKI Andrzej, b. 11 November 1945, Grybow, Poland. Philologist (History of literature, comparative literature). m. Barbara Kozminska, 2 daughters. Education: MA, Jagiellonian University of Cracow, 1968; PhD, 1976; Habilitation, 1987; Professor, Jagiellonian University. Appointments: Assistant Professor, 1976, Associate Professor, 1987, Professor, 1993, Jagiellonian University; Head of the Department of Estreicher's National Polish Bibliography UJ, 1976; Head, Institute of Polish Philology, Jagiellonian University of Cracow, 1991-2002; Chair, Department of Old Polish Literature, Jagiellonian University of Cracow, 2000; Member, University Senate. Publications: Books: Pojecie i Problem Renesansu Polnocnego (the Problem of the Northern Renaissance), 1987; Renesans (The Renaissance), 1992, 2nd edition, 2002; Powrót Europy (The Home-Coming Europe. The European Studies and Literature), 1999; Słownik sarmatyzmu (Dictionary of Sarmatianism), 2001; Historia literatury polskiej i powszechnej. Starożytność-Oświecenie (History of Polish and European Literature. Antiquity-Enlightenment), 2002; Renesans (The Renaissance) 1992, 2nd enlarged edition, 2002; Translations: E R Curtius Europaeische Literatur und Lateinisches Mittelalter, 1997; Simon de Vries Joodse Riten en Symbolen, 1999. Honours: The Lanckoronski Foundation Scholarship, 1983, 1985; The Scholarship of the Institut für die Wissenschaften vom Menschen, Vienna, 1990. Memberships: International Comparative Literature Association; International Association for Neolatin Studies; Committee for the Literary Sciences of Polish Academy of Sciences. Address: 30611 Krakow, ul Beskidzka 35/27, Poland.

BØRRESEN-DALE Anne-Lise, b. 3 July 1946, Molde, Norway. Professor. 2 daughters. Education: MS, Biochemical Engineering, Technical University of Norway, 1970; PhD, Medical Biochemical Genetics, University of Oslo, Norway, 1978. Appointments: Research Assistant, 1970-72, Research Fellow, 1972-78, Senior Research Fellow, 1978-82, Institute of Medical Genetics, University of Oslo; Senior Biochemist, Department of Medical Genetics, City of Oslo, 1982-86; Senior Scientist, 1987-99, Acting Head, 1999-, Head, 2000-, Department of Genetics, Institute for Cancer Research, Norwegian Radium Hospital; Professor in Tumour Biology, University of Oslo, 1992-; Professor, Molecular Oncology, University of Bergen, Norway, 2000-. Publications: Over 240 scientific papers; 19 chapters in books and invited reviews; 30 article in Nordic journals and books. Honours: Professor Olav Torgersens Prize and Memorial Lecture, 1989; Invited Lecturer, 175th anniversary of the Medical Faculty, University of Oslo, 1989; King Olav V's Cancer Research Prize, 1994; Elected Member, Det Kongelige Norske Videnskabers Selskab, 1998; Honorary Member, Norwegian Biochemical Society, 2001; University of Oslo's Research Prize for Outstanding Research, 2002; SalhusAnsver Medical Prize for Outstanding Research in Tumour Biology, 2002. Memberships: Board Member, MedProbe A/S; Scientific Board, The Norwegian Radium Hospital; Board of Directors, American Association for Cancer Research; Scientific Council; International Agency of Research of Cancer, France; National Committee for Functional Genomics. Address: Department of Genetics, Institute for Cancer Research, The Norwegian Radium Hospital, Montebello, 0310 Oslo, Norway.

BORTOLOTTI Maurizio, b. 7 July 1961, Brescia, Italy. Art Critic. m. Miranda Bresciani, 1 son. Education: Master of Fine Arts, Academy of Fine Arts, Brera, Milan, 1989. Appointments: Contributor to cultural and art magazines: Musica/Realtà, 1990-92; Arte, 1991-93; Tema Celeste, 1992-94; Juliet, 1995-; Domus, 1992-; Teachership, 1999; Visiting Professor, Urbino University, 2003. Publications: Il Critico Come Curatore, 2003. Memberships: International Association of Art, UNESCO, 1999-. Address: 50 Palladio Street, 25124 Brescia, Italy. E-mail: bortolotti9@interfree.it

BOSNAR Alan, b. 25 May 1961, Rijeka, Croatia. Forensic Pathologist. m. Laura, 1 daughter. Education: MD, 1988; MSc, 1994; Specialist in Forensic Medicine, 1994; PhD, 1999. Appointments: Resident, 1988-89; Junior Researcher, 1989-94; Assistant, 1994-99; Senior Assistant, 1999-2002; Assistant Professor, 2003. Publication: Original article as author, Increased Suicide Rate Before and During the War in Southwestern Croatia, 2002. Memberships: American Academy of Forensic Sciences; American College of Forensic Examiners. Address: Laginjina 7, Rijeka 51 000, Croatia. E-mail: alan.bosnar@medri.hr

BOTTOMLEY Virginia Hilda Brunette Maxwell, b. 12 March 1948. Politician. m. Peter Bottomley, 1967, 1 son, 2 daughters. Education: London School Economics. Appointments: Various positions before election as Conservative MP for Surrey South, 1984-; Parliament Private Secretary to Chris Patten, 1985-87; Parliament Private Secretary for Foreign and Commonwealth Affairs, 1987-88; Parliament Under-Secretary, Department of the Environment, 1988-89; Ministry for Health, 1989-92; Secretary of State, Department of Health, 1992-95, with responsibility for family policy, 1994-95; Chairman, Millennium Commission, 1995-97; Secretary of State, Department of National Heritage, 1995-97; Vice Chairman, British Council, 1997-; House of Commons Select Committee on Foreign Affairs, 1997-99. Address: House of Commons, London SW1A 0AA, England.

BOULLATA Issa J, b. 25 February 1929, Jerusalem, Palestine. Professor. m. Marita Seward, 3 sons, 1 daughter. Education: BA, University of London, 1964; PhD, 1969. Appointments: Senior Teacher, Arabic Literature, De La Salle College, Jerusalem, 1949-52; Ahliyyah College, Ramallah, 1952-53; St George's School, Jerusalem, 1953-68; Deputy Headmaster, 1960-68; Professor, Arabic Literature and Language, Hartford Seminary, Hartford, 1968-75; McGill University, Institute of Islamic Studies, Montreal, QC, Canada, 1975-99; Post-retirement appointment, McGill University, Institute of Islamic Studies, Montreal, 1999-. Publications: 19 Books; Over 80 articles in scholarly journals and entries in encyclopaedias; Over 250 book reviews in scholarly journals, edited books and others. Honours: Arberry Memorial Prize, 1972; University of Arkansas Press Award for Translation from Arabic, 1993, 1997. Memberships: Middle East Studies Association of North America; American Association of Teachers of Arabic; International Comparative Literature Association; American Comparative Literature Association; Radius of Arab American Writers, Inc. (RAWI). Address: Institute of Islamic Studies, McGill University, 3485 McTavish Street, Montreal, Quebec, Canada, H3A 1Y1.

BOULTING Noel Edwin, b. 16 December 1940, Rodney Stoke, Nr Cheddar, Somerset, England. Philosopher. m. Patricia Hall 28 March 1964, 1 son, 1 daughter. Education: BA, Philosophy, Birkbeck College; MSc, Philosophy of Science, London School of Economics and Political Science; AcDip; CertEd. Appointments: Philosophy of Education Tutor, Trent Polytechnic; Philosophy of Education Tutor, Mid-Kent College Higher and Further Education; Philosophy Tutor, Extra-Mural Department, University of London; Adjunct Professor, Philosophy, Great Falls University, Montana, USA. Publications: Numerous publications in URAM and SPCW journals; Hobbes and the Problem of Rationality, 1989; Charles S Pierce, 1994; Grounding the Notion of Ecological Responsibility, 1996; The Aesthetics of Nature, 2000; Vico, 2002; To Be or Not to Be Philosophical, 2003. Honour: The URAM Award for Excellence in Creative Scholarly Writing, 1995. Membership: Co-Initiator, 1977, President, NOBOSS: Association for pursuit of philosophy for all-comers with visits by German and American philosophers; Society for the Advancement of American Philosophy. Address: 36 Crosier Court, Upchurch, Nr Sittingbourne, Kent ME9 7AR, England.

BOUMA Arnold Heiko, b. 5 September 1932, Groningen, The Netherlands. Professor. m. Mechelina Helena Kampers, 3 sons. Education: BS, Geology, University of Groningen, Netherlands, 1956; MS, 1959; PhD, University of Utrecht, 1961; Fulbright Post-doctoral Fellowship, Scripps Institute of Oceanography, California, USA, 1962-63. Appointments: Lecturer, University of Utrecht, 1963-66; Associate Professor, Professor, Marine Geology, Texas A&M University, 1966-75; Research Scientist, Geologist in Charge, US Geological Survey, 1975-81; Senior Scientist, Manager, Vice President, Gulf Oil Company, 1981-85; Senior Research Associate, Chevron Oil Company, 1985-88; McCord Endowed Professor, Oil-related Sedimentary Geology, Louisiana State University, 1988-. Publications: 3 books; Co-editor, 9 books; 132 papers in refereed journals; 122 other papers; 58 abstracts; 33 book reviews; 48 reports. Honours: F P Shepard Award for Excellence in Marine Geology, 1982; Best Papers Awards; Teaching Awards; Invited Keynote Speaker; Distinguished Research Master of Engineering, Science and Technology, Louisiana State University, 2004. Memberships: Society for Sedimentary Geology; American Association Petroleum Geologists; International Association Sedimentologists; Dutch Geological and Mining Society; Local Geological Societies. Address: Department of Geology and Geophysics, Louisiana State University, Baton Rouge, Louisiana 70803, USA.

BOUND John Pascoe, b.13 November 1920, Redhill, Surrey, England. Paediatrician, Consultant (Retired). m. Gwendoline, deceased 1998, 2 daughters. Education: MB, BS, DCH, 1943, MD, 1950, University College, London and University College Hospital Medical School; MRCP (Lond), 1950; FRCP, 1971; FRCPCH, 1997. Appointments: House Physician, University College Hospital, 1943; Assistant Medical Officer, Alder Hey Children's Hospital, Liverpool, 1943-44; RAMC, 1944-47; Member, Sprue Research Team, Poona, India for 1 year; House Physician, North Middlesex Hospital, 1947; Paediatric Registrar and Senior Registrar, Hillingdon Hospital, Middlesex, 1948-53; Paediatric Registrar, 1953-54, First Assistant, Department of Paediatrics, 1954-56, University College Hospital, London; Consultant Paediatrician, Victoria Hospital, Blackpool, Lancashire, 1956-83. Publications: Articles on neonatal conditions and perinatal mortality; Articles on congenital malformations including: Incidence of congenital heart disease in the Fylde of Lancashire 1957-71; Seasonal prevalence of major congenital malformations, 1957-81; Neural tube defects, maternal cohorts and age: a pointer to aetiology; Down's Syndrome: prevalence and ionising radiation in an area of North West England, 1957-91; Involvement of deprivation and environmental lead in neural tube defects, 1957-81; Book, Borrowdale Beauty. Honour: International Medal of Honour, International Biographical Centre, Cambridge, 2003. Memberships: British Medical Association, 1943-; Expert Group on Special Care for Babies, Department of Health and Social Security, London, 1969-70; British Paediatric Association, 1960-97, Academic Board, 1972-75. Address: 48, St Annes Road East, Lytham St Annes, Lancs FY8 1UR, England.

BOURG Dominique, b. 11 August 1953, Tavaux, Jura, France. Professor. m. Frédérique Zahnd, 1 son, 2 daughters. Education: PhD, University of Strasbourg II, 1981; Doctorate, Ecole des Hautes Edudes en Sciences Sociale, Paris, 1995; Habilitation, University of Lyon III, 1998. Appointments: Scholar, Alexander von Humboldt Foundation, Heidelberg, Germany, 1990-91; Associate Professor, Institute of Political Sciences, Paris, 1997-; Professor, University of Technology, Troyes, 2000-. Publications include: Transcendance et discours, 1985 L'Homme Artifice, 1996; Le Nouvel Age de l'écologie, 2003; Perspectives on Industrial Ecology (with S Erkman), 2003. Honours: Chevalier of the Legion of Honour, 2001; Prix du Promeneur Solitaire, 2003. Memberships: Commission Coppens (Charte de L'environnement), 2002-2003; Conseil National du Développement Durable, 2003-. Address: 89 avenue Pierre Brossolette, F-10000 Troyes, France. E-mail: dominique.bourg@utt.fr

BOURNE Malcolm Cornelius, b. 18 May 1926, Moonta, Australia. Professor of Food Science; Active Emeritus. m. Elizabeth Schumacher, 3 sons, 2 daughters. Education: BSc, Chemistry, University of Adelaide, 1950; MS, Food Science, 1961, PhD, Agricultural Chemistry, 1962, University of California, Davis, USA. Appointments: Chief Chemist, Brookers (Australia) Ltd, 1949-58; Research Assistant, University California, Davis, 1958-62; Professor, Food Science, 1962-95, Emeritus Professor, Food Science, 1995-, Cornell University. Publications: Many publications in refereed journals; Author, Food Texture and Viscosity, 1982, reprinted, 1994, second edition, 2002; Editor in Chief, Journal of Texture Studies, 1980-. Honours: Fellow, Institute of Food Science and Technology, UK, 1966; Fellow, Institute of Food Technologists and International Award; Inaugural Fellow, 1998, Vice President, 2001-03, President, 2003-2006, International Academy Food Science and Technology; Honorary Fellow, Australian Institute of Food Science and Technology, 1999; Fellow, Royal Australian Chemical Institute, 2003. Address: NYSAES, Cornell University, Geneva, NY 14456, USA.

Dictionary of International Biography

BOUTROS-GHALI Boutros, b. 14 November 1922, Cairo, Egypt. Secretary General, United Nations. m. Maria Leia Nadler. Education: LLB, Cairo University, 1946; PhD, Paris University, 1949. Appointments: Professor, International Law and International Relations, Head, Department of Political Sciences, Cairo University, 1949-77; Founder, Editor, Al Ahram Iktisadi, 1960-75; Ministry of State, Foreign Affairs, Egypt, 1977-91; Member, UN Commission of International Law, 1979-92; Member, Secretariat, National Democratic Party, 1980-92; MP, 1987-92; Deputy PM, Foreign Affairs, 1991-92; Secretary-General, UN, 1992-96; Secretary-General, Organisations Internationales de la Francophonie. Publications: Contribution a l'étude des ententes régionales, 1949; Cours de diplomatie et de droit diplomatique et consulaire, 1951; Le problème du Canal de Suez (jtly), 1957; Egypt and the United Nations (jtly), 1957; Le principe d'égalité des états et les organisations internationales, 1961; Contribution a une théorie générale des Alliances, 1963; Foreign Policies in a World of Change, 1963; L'Organisation de l'unité africaine, 1969; Le mouvement Afro-Asiatique, 1969; Les difficultés institutionelles du panafricanisme, 1971; La ligue des états arabes, 1972; Les Conflits de frontières en Afrique, 1973; Numerous books in Arabic and contributions to periodicals. Address: 2 Av El Nil Giza, Cairo, Egypt.

BOWDEN Charles Lee, b. 29 October 1938, Brownwood, Texas, USA. Physician. m. Virginia Bowden, 2 daughters. Education: University of Texas, Austin, 1957-60; MD, Baylor College of Medicine, Houston, Texas, 1960-64; Intern, Presbyterian-St Luke's Hospital, Chicago, 1964-65; Psychiatry Residency, New York State Psychiatric Institute and Presbyterian Hospital, New York, 1965-68; Candidate of Psychoanalytic Training, Columbia Psychoanalytic Clinic for Training and Research, New York, 1967-68. Appointments: Instructor of Psychiatry, University of Kentucky School of Medicine, Lexington, 1968-70; Assistant Professor of Psychiatry, 1970-73, Associate Professor of Psychiatry, 1973-78, Nancy U Karren Chair of Psychiatry, 1974-, Professor of Psychiatry, 1978-, Chief, Division of Biological Psychiatry, Department of Psychiatry, 1986-98, Chief, Division of Mood and Anxiety Disorders, 1998-2001, Deputy Chair, 1989-97, Interim Chairman, 1996-97, Chairman, 1997-, Professor, Department of Family Practice, 1978-98, Professor of Pharmacology, 1981-, University of Texas Health Science Center, San Antonio. Publications: Numerous articles in professional journals. Honours include: Psychiatric Excellence Award, Texas Society of Psychiatric Physicians, 1997; Gerald L Klerman Senior Investigator Award, 2000, National Depressive and Manic Depressive Association. Memberships include: American Psychiatric Association; American College of Neuropsychopharmacology; American College of Psychiatrists; Society of Biological Psychiatry; European College of Neuropsychopharmacology. Address: Department of Psychiatry (MC 7792), University of Texas Health Science Center, 7703 Floyd Curl Drive, San Antonio, TX 78229-3900, USA.

BOWEN Gwen Lorrayne, b. Denver, Colorado, USA. Dance Educator; Choreographer. Education: BA, University of Denver, 1947-51; Postgraduate, 1951-52. Appointments: Teacher, Lillian Cushing School of Dance; Denver Public Schools; Teacher, Metro State College; Artistic Director, Premiere Dance Arts Co; Founder, Bowen School of Dance Arts, 1953-; Choreographer numerous ballets; Operas; Musicals. Publications: Author of graded systems for ballet, tap dance. Honours: Mortar Board Honour, University of Denver Math; 50 Year Anniversary Award, Dance Magazine, announcement presented in Congress; Listed in many national and international biographical dictionaries. Memberships: Dance Masters of America; Dance Educators of America; Metro Denver Arts Alliance; Kappa Delta Sorority; South Central Improvement Association; Artistic Director, PDAC/Art for All. Address: 714 S Pearl St, Denver, CO 80209, USA.

BOWES Donald Ralph, b. 9 September 1926, Brighton, South Australia. Retired University Teacher. m. Annie Mary Morris, 2 sons, 1 daughter. Education: BSc, Geology and Chemistry, 1945; BSc (Hons 1st class), Mineralogy and Petrology, 1946, MSc, 1948, Adelaide University, Australia; PhD, 1950, DIC, 1950, Imperial College, London University, England; DSc, University of Glasgow, Scotland, 1968. Appointments: Lecturer, Geology, Adelaide University, Australia, 1950-52; Lecturer, Geology, University College of Swansea, Wales, 1953-56; Senior Lecturer, Geology, 1956-72, Reader, Geology, 1972-75, Professor of Geology, 1975-91, Emeritus Professor, 1991-, University of Glasgow, Scotland. Publications: Crystal Evolution in Northwestern Britain and Adjacent Regions, 1978; The Encyclopaedia of Igneous and Metamorphic Petrology, 1989; 250 peer reviewed scientific publications on petrology, geochronology, Precambrian geology and environmental mineralogy; Editor, Transactions of the Royal Society of Edinburgh: Earth Sciences, 1978-85; Consulting Editor, American Journal of Industrial Medicine, 1980-2002. Honours: James Barrans Scholar, University of Adelaide, 1946; 1851 Exhibitioner for Australia, 1947, award held at Imperial College, London, 1948-49; Tate Medal for Geology, University of Adelaide, 1948; Fulbright Scholar, Columbia University, New York, USA 1966; Gold Medal, Charles University, Prague, Czech Republic, 1998; Emanuel Bôrický Medal, Charles University, Prague, 2003. Memberships: Fellow, Royal Society of Edinburgh, Vice-president, 1980-83; Fellow, Geological Society of London; Fellow, Geological Society of America; Fellow, Mineralogical Society. Address: Division of Earth Sciences, University of Glasgow, Glasgow G12 8QQ, Scotland. E-mail: drb@earthsci.gla.ac.uk

BOWIE David (David Jones), b. 8 January 1947, Brixton, London, England. Singer; Actor. (1) Angela Barnet, divorced, 1 son, (2) Iman Abdul Majid, 1992, 1 daughter. Career: Solo recording artist, 1970-; Lead singer, Tin Machine, 1989-91; Actor, films, 1976-; World tours, concerts, television and radio appearances, many as Ziggy Stardust and Aladdin Sane; Performances include: Live Aid, Wembley, 1985; Glass Spider Tour, 1987; ICA ' Intruders at the Palace'; Sound and Vision Tour, 1990; Dodger Stadium, Los Angeles, 1990; Morrissey World Tour, 1991; A Concert For Life (Freddie Mercury Tribute), 1992; Wembley Arena, 1993; USA East Coast Ballroom Tour, 1996; 50th Birthday Benefit Show, 1997; Hammersmith Ballroom, 1998; Docklands Arena, 1999; Placebo US Tour, 1999; 'Hours' Promotional Tour, 1999. Film appearances include: The Man Who Fell To Earth, 1976; Christiane F, 1980; Just A Gigolo, 1981; Cat People, 1982; The Hunger, 1983; Merry Christmas Mr Lawrence, 1983; Ziggy Stardust and The Spiders from Mars, 1983; Labyrinth, 1986; Absolute Beginners, 1986; The Last Temptation Of Christ, 1988; The Linguini Incident, 1990; Basquiat, 1996; Trainspotting, 1996; Il Mio West, 1998; Everybody Loves Sunshine, 1999; Mr Rices Secret, 2000. Theatre includes: The Elephant Man, 1980. Recordings: Numerous solo albums include: The Rise And Fall Of Ziggy Stardust..., 1972; Aladdin Sane, 1973; Diamond Dogs, 1974; David Live, 1974; Young Americans, 1975; Station To Station, 1976; Low, Heroes, 1977; Let's Dance, 1983; Ziggy Stardust - The Motion Picture, 1983; Scary Monsters and Super Creeps, 1980; Black Tie White Noise, 1993; Outside, 1995; Earthling, 1997; David Bowie, 1998; Hours, 1999; Numerous solo hit singles include: Absolute Beginners; Ashes To Ashes; Blue Jean; China Girl; Diamond Dogs; Fashion; Jean Genie; Life On Mars; Rebel Rebel; Space Oddity; Growin' Up; Fame 90; Heart's Filthy Lesson; Hallo Spaceboy; Little Wonder; I Can't Read; with Bing Crosby: Peace On Earth/Little Drummer Boy; with Mick Jagger: Dancing In The Street; with Queen: Under Pressure; Other projects include: Theme for When The Wind Blows, 1986. Honours include: Grammy Awards, 1984; Music Video Awards; Silver Clef Award for Outstanding Achievement, 1987; Ivor Novello Awards include: Outstanding Contribution to British Music, 1990; Q Magazine Inspiration Award (with Brian Eno), 1995; BRIT Award, Outstanding Contribution to Music, 1996; BMI Pop Awards, 1999; MTV Video Music Awards (China Girl), 1984, (Dancing in the Streets), 1986; Rock and Rolls Hall of Fame, 1996; Q Awards, 1995. Address: Isolar Enterprises, 641 5th Avenue, Ste 22Q, New York, NY 10022, USA.

BOWMAN Roberta Pipes, b. 1 July 1915, USA. Writer; Poet; Painter. m. Elton Nuel Bowman, 24 January 1948, 2 sons. Education: Business College, 1941; Texas Christian University, 1942-48. Publications: Make Room for Joy, 1942; In This Our Times, 1977; Writing That Certain Poem, 1988; Poems for Christmas, 1990; Wind, Be Still, 1992; C & W Poems, 1995; Welcome to Today, 1995; Light and Shadows, 1998. Contributions to: Anthologies, newspapers and journals. Honours: 11 Poetry Society of Texas Awards, 1956-96; National Poetry Day, 1966, 1970, 1990, 1995; Chas Hanna Awards, 1985, 1990; Composers, Authors and Artists Mason Sonnet Awards, 1986, 1990, 1996; Lucidity Chapbook Contest, 1995; Hilton Ross Greer Service Award, Poetry Society of Texas, 1998. Memberships: Poetry Society of America; Poetry Society of Texas; Poets of Tarrant County; Composers, Authors and Artists of America; National Composers, Authors and Artists Association. Address: 3521 Eastridge Drive, Fort Worth, TX 76117, USA.

BOYD Brandon, b. 15 February 1976, Van Nuys, California, USA. Composer, singer for band Incubus. Education: Calabasas High School, 1994. Albums (as Incubus); Fungus Amongus, 1996; S.C.I.E.N.C.E., 1997; Enjoy Incubus, 1997; Make Youself, 1999; When Incubus Attacks, Vol 1, 2000; Morning View, 2001; A Crow Left of the Murder; 2004. Singles include: Stellar, Drive, Wish you were here, Are you In, Nice to know you, Talk Shows on Mute, Southern Girl, Here in my Room. Publications: White Fluffy Clouds, 2004. Concerts include: Le Plan Ris-Orangis 1998, House Of Blues, Los Angeles 1998, ATT Acoustic; Hammerstein Ballroom, New York City, NY, 2001, KROQ Mansion Concert, 2002; Lollapalooza, 2003.

BOYD Brian David, b. 30 July 1952, Belfast, Northern Ireland. University Teacher; Writer. m. (1) Janet Bower Eden, 1974, sdivorced 1980, (2) Bronwen Mary Nicholson, 1983, 3 stepdaughters. Education: BA, 1972, MA, Hons, 1974, University of Canterbury, Christchurch, New Zealand; PhD, University of Toronto, Canada, 1979; Postdoctoral Fellow, University of Auckland, 1979-80. Appointments: Lecturer, 1980-85, Senior Lecturer, 1985-92, Associate Professor, 1992-98, Professor 1998-2000, Distinguished Professor, 2001-, University of Auckland, New Zealand; Director, Friends of the Nabokov Museum, St Petersburg; Editorial Board, Nabokov Studies; Visiting Professor, University of Nice-Sophia Antipolis, 1994-95; Nabokov Museum, St Petersburg, 2002; Japan Foundation Visiting Professor, 2003. Publications: Nabokov's Ada: The Place of Consciousness, 1985, (2nd edition 2001); Vladimir Nabokov: The Russian Years, 1990; Vladimir Nabokov: The American Years, 1991; Nabokov's Pale Fire: The Magic of Artistic Discovery, 1999. Editor: Nabokov: Novels and Memoirs 1941-1951, 1996; Nabokov: Novels 1955-1962, 1996; Nabokov: Novels 1969-1974, 1996; Presents of the Past: Literature in English Before 1900, 1998; Words That Count: Early Modern Authorship: Essays in Honor of MacDonald P Jackson, 2004; Co-editor: Nabokov's Butterflies, 2000. Contributions to: Natural History; Atlantic Monthly; Independent on Sunday; Philosophy and Literature. Honours: Claude McCarthy Fellowship, 1982; Goodman Fielder Wattie Prize (Third), 1991; Goodman Fielder Wattie Prize (Second), 1992; James Cook Research Fellowship, 1997-2000; Einhard Prize, 2001. Address: Department of English, University of Auckland, Private Bag 92019, Auckland, New Zealand.

BOYD Liona, b. London, England. Classical Guitarist. m. John Simon. Education: Bachelor of Music in Performance, Honours, University of Toronto, Canada, 1972; Studied with Eli Kassner; Private Classes with Narciso Yepes, Andrés Segovia, Alirio Diaz, Julian Bream; 2 years private study with Alexandre Lagoya, Paris, France. Career: Debut at Carnegie Recital Hall; International concert artist and composer of classical music; Played with symphony orchestras and at international festivals, Rio de Janeiro, Istanbul, New Delhi, Seoul, Havana, Paris, Tokyo; Toured extensively in USA as soloist and with orchestras including Boston Pops under John Williams; Toured with Gordon Lightfoot, Tracy Chapman, recorded with Roger Whittaker and George Zamfir; Played private concerts for world leaders including the British Royal Family, Presidents of the USA, King and Queen of Spain, Prime Ministers of Canada and Great Britain; Played at NATO and Summit Conferences; First Canadian to play at the Kremlin, Moscow. Recordings: 20 including: Baroque Favourites with the English Chamber Orchestra; Two Christmas Albums; Persona with Eric Clapton, David Gilmour and Yoyo Ma; The Spanish Album; Whispers of Love, Camino Latino; In My Own Key – My Life in Love and Music (autobiography), 1999; Numerous music books, videos and TV specials; Composed and arranged many pieces. Honours: Order of Canada; Order of Ontario; 5 Gold records; 3 Platinum Records; 5 Juno Awards; 5 times Winner, Guitarist Magazine Best Classical Guitarist; 5 Honorary Degrees. Memberships: AF of M; AFTRA. E-mail: smmo@lionaboyd.com Website: www.classicalguitar.com

BOYER George William, b. 19 November 1921, Leverton, Boston, Lincolnshire, England. Bishop. m. Leila Mary Christian. Education: Courses and study in art, theology, psychology, comparative religion; Doctor of Divinity, for publication of book The Ancient Patriarchs and Their Teaching, Honorary Doctor of Theology, St Ephrem's Institute, Sweden. Appointments: Bishop for Pre-Nicene Catholic Church, 1958; Missionary Bishop for Western Orthodox Church (Russian Orthodox); Missionary Bishop for The Philippine and Independent Catholic Church; Archbishop for The Apostolic Episcopal Church, United Kingdom; Currently, Primate of Pre-Nicene Ekklesia; Grand Master and Lord Abbot of The Healing, Teaching and Chivalric Order of St Michael and St Raphael. Publications: The Ancient Patriarchs and Their Teachings, 1984; Many lectures and articles on Mystical and Gnostic Christianity, Rose Cross, comparative religion. Honours: Ennobled to Count George Boyer by HIH The Prince August Von Hohenstaufen, 1988; Commander's Cross in the Sovereign Military Order of Swabia and Knights of St Gereon. Address: 53 College Road, Colliers Wood, London SW19 2BP, England. E-mail: george@college53.freeserve.co.uk

BOYKOV Ilya, b. 19 March 1941, Russia. Mathematician. m. S Brusilovskay, 29 March 1968, 1 daughter. Education: Degree, Computer Engineering, 1963; Degree, Mathematics, 1968; Candidate of Science, Kazan State University, 1973; DSc, Siberian Branch, Academy of Sciences, USSR, 1991. Appointments: Engineer, Computer Plant, Penza, 1963-65; Engineer, Research Institute, Penza, 1965-68; Postgraduate, Kazan University, 1968-71; Assistant, Department of Higher Mathematics, Polytechnic Institute, Penza, 1971-72; Associate Professor, Polytechnic Institute, Penza, 1971-74; Head of Department, Higher Mathematics, Polytechnic Institute, Penza, 1974-; Professor, State University, Penza, Russia, 1991-; Professor, Teacher University of Penza, 1991-. Publications: 6 books; 250 papers in professional journals. Honours: Several grants; Soros Professor, 1999; Honorary Professor Albert Schweitzer International University, 2000-; Honorary Worker of High Professional Education of Russia, 2001- Listed in 10 Who's Who publications. Memberships: American Mathematical Society, 1994-; European Mathematical Society,

Dictionary of International Biography

1997-; New York Academy of Sciences, 1995-. Address: Kirov Str 71-58, Penza 440600, Russia. E-mail: boikov@diamond.stup.ac.ru

BOYLE Danny, b. 20 October 1956, Bury, Lancashire, England. Film Director. Appointments: Artistic Director, Royal Court Theatre, 1982-87; Producer, Elephant, TV film, 1989; Director, The Greater Good, TV series, 1991, Mr Wroe's Virgins, TV, 1993, Not Even God is Wise Enough, TV, 1993; Executive Producer, Twin Town, 1996. Creative Works: Films: Shallow Grave, 1994; Trainspotting, 1996; A Life Less Ordinary, 1996; The Beach, 1999; Vacuuming Completely Nude in Paradise, 2001; Strumpet, 2001; Alien Love Triangle, 2002; 28 Days Later, 2002. Honour: Golden Ephebe Award, 1997. Address: c/o ICM, 6th Floor, 76 Oxford Street, London W1N 0AX, England.

BOYLE Gregory John, b. 20 February 1950, Melbourne, Victoria. Psychology Educator; Research Consultant. m. Dolores Mary Bartolo, 2 sons, 2 daughters. Education: BSc, Honours, 1973, MEd, 1978, PhD, 1985, University of Melbourne; MA, 1982, PhD, 1983, University of Delaware. Appointments: Registered Psychologist; Teaching Diplomate (high school); Maths and Science Teacher State Education Department, Victoria, 1974-75; Lecturer in Psychology, Institute of Catholic Education, 1976-85; Part-time private practice in psychology, 1978-; Lecturer in Educational Psychology, University of Melbourne, 1985-89; Research Consultant, Australian Army Psychology Corps, Canberra, ACT, 1987-; Senior Lecturer, Psychology, University of Queensland, 1990-92, Associate Professor, Bond University, Queensland, 1993-95, Full Professor, 1995-; Associate Dean, Research, 2003-. Publications: Numerous articles in international publications; Chapters in books on psychology; 4 volume compendium on individual differences; Book on statistical methods in psychology. Honours: Honorary Fellow, Cattell Research Institute, US, 1987; Teaching Citation CAUT, 1995. Memberships: Australian Psychological Society; American Psychological Society; International Society for Study of Personality and Individual Differences (previously); American Psychological Association (previously); Australian College of Education (previously). Address: Bond University, Gold Coast, Q 4229, Australia.

BOZAYKUT Abdulkadir, b. 12 July 1954. Urfa, Turkey. Paediatrician. m. Ayten Gul, 2 daughters. Education: Atatürk University, 1970-77. Appointments: Doctor, Health Unit, Birecik, Turkey, 1977-80; Assistant, 1980-84, Head Assistant, 1987-89, Assistant Director, 1989-2000, Head of Department, 2000-, Zeynep Kamil Hospital, Istanbul, Turkey. Publications include: Research in measurement of the newborn weight, height and head contour; Causes of prematurity; Importance of Apgar Scor in early diagnosis of Fetal Acidosis; Comparison of cord blood and interleuikin-6 level 5; Plasma cysteine levels in oxygen requiring neonates. Memberships: Associate Member, Turkish Paediatry Society; Director, Mother and Child Health Foundation of Zeynep Kamil; Associate Member, Istanbul Doctors' Chamber. Address: Bilim Street 8/12, Erenköy, Istanbul 34738, Turkey. E-mail: abozaykut@yahoo.com

BRABY Leslie Alan, b. 12 January 1941, Kelso, Washington, USA. Physicist. m. Barbara Shearer, 1 May 1966, 3 sons. Education: BA, Physics, Linfield College, McMinnville, Oregon, 1963; PhD, Radiological Sciences, Oregon State University, 1972. Appointments: Research Scientist, Radiological Physics, Biology and Chemistry Department, Pacific Northwest Laboratory, Richland, Washington, 1963-69; Staff, Oregon State University, General Science Department, 1969-71; Staff Scientist, Radiological Physics Section, 1971-95, Section Manager, Radiation Physics and Chemistry, Biology and Chemistry Department, 1993-95,

Acting Manager, Biology and Chemistry Dept, 1993-95, Pacific Northwest Laboratory, Richland, Washington; Research Professor, Department of Nuclear Engineering, Texas A & M University, 1996-. Publications: Several articles in professional journals. Honour: Director's Award for Excellence, US Department of Energy, Pacific Northwest Laboratory, 1992. Memberships: American Physical Society; Councillor, Physics, Radiation Research Society; Health Physics Society; American Association for the Advancement of Science; National Council on Radiation, Protection and Measurements. Address: 3708 Windridge, Bryan, TX 77802, USA.

BRADFORD Barbara Taylor, b. 10 May 1933, Leeds, Yorkshire, England. Author. m. Robert Bradford, 1963. Appointments: Editor, Columnist, Periodicals in England and USA. Publications: Completed Encyclopedia of Homemaking Ideas, 1968; How To Be The Perfect Wife, 1969-70; Early Steps to Successful Decorating, 1971; Making Space Grow, 1979; A Woman of Substance, 1979; Voice of the Heart, 1983; Hold the Dream, 1985; Act of Will, 1986; To Be the Best, 1988; The Women in His Life, 1990; Remember, 1991; Angel, 1993; Everything to Gain, 1994; Dangerous to Know, 1995; Love in Another Town, 1995; Her Own Rules, 1996; A Secret Affair, 1996; Power of a Woman, 1997. Address: c/o Bradford Enterprises, 450 Park Avenue, Suite 1903, New York, NY 10022, USA.

BRADFORD Karleen, b. 16 December 1936, Toronto, Ontario, Canada. Writer. m. James Creighton Bradford, 22 August 1959, 2 sons, 1 daughter. Education: BA, University of Toronto, 1959. Appointment: Vice-Chair, The Writers' Union of Canada, 1997-98; Chair, Public Lending Right Commission of Canada, 1998-2000. Publications: A Year for Growing, 1977; The Other Elizabeth, 1982; Wrong Again, Robbie, 1983; I Wish There Were Unicorns, 1983; The Stone in the Meadow, 1984; The Haunting at Cliff House, 1985; The Nine Days Queen, 1986; Write Now!, 1988; Windward Island, 1989; There Will be Wolves, 1992; Thirteenth Child, 1994; Animal Heroes, 1995; Shadows on a Sword, 1996; More Animal Heroes, 1996; Dragonfire, 1997; A Different Kind of Champion; Lionhearts Scribe, 1999; Whisperings of Magic, 2001; With Nothing but Our Courage, 2002; You Can't Rush a Cat, 2003; Angeline, 2004. Honour: The Canadian Library Association Young Adult Novel Award, 1993. Memberships: PEN; IBBY; Writers' Union of Canada. Address: RR #2, Owen Sound, Ontario, Canada, N4K 5N4.

BRADFORD Sarah Mary Malet, b. 3 September 1938, Bournemouth, England. Author; Journalist; Critic. m. (1) Anthony John Bradford, 31 April 1959, 1 son, 1 daughter (2) Viscount Bangor, 1 October 1976. Education: Lady Margaret Hall, Oxford, England, 1956-59. Appointment: Manuscript Expert, Christie's, 1975-78. Publications: The Story of Port, 1978, 1983; Portugal and Madeira, 1969; Portugal, 1973; Cesare Borgia, 1976; Disraeli, 1982; Princess Grace, 1984; King George VI, 1989; Elizabeth: A Biography of Her Majesty The Queen, 1996; America's Queen, The Life of Jacqueline Kennedy Onassis, 2000. Contributions to: Reviews in Daily Telegraph, Sunday Telegraph, The Times, Sunday Times, Times Literary Supplement, Literary Review; Mail on Sunday; Daily Mail; Highlife. Address: 29 Fernshaw Road, London SW10 0TG, England.

BRADHURST Jane, 28 October 1926, Sydney, Australia. Playwright; Novelist; Artist. m. Colin Russell-Jones, deceased, 2 sons, 1 daughter. Education: MSc, Sydney University, 1954; DipEd, 1969, BA, 1977, University of Canberra; Associate Diploma in Theatre Practice, Goulburn CAE, 1979. Appointments: Demonstrator, Teacher, Researcher, University of Sydney, 1947-50; Science Teacher, CCEGGS, 1966-72; Full Time Artist and

Writer, 1977-. Publications: The Flowers of the Snowy Mountains, 1972; Document of Our Day: Women of the Pre-Pill Generation, 1986; Three One Act Plays, 1987; Duet String Trio Quartet, 1987; Animalia in Australia, 1992; 100 Poems, 1993; The BD II, 1995; Love in a Hot Climate, 1996; Three Festival Plays, 1998; Summertime (musical), 1998; There is No Mystery (anthology), 1999; Mystery in Manhattan, 2000; The Director and the Doll, 2001; Always on Call – Tales of an Outback Doctor, 2002; Outback Lives and Border Fence Brides, 2004. Honours: Total works purchased by the State Library of New South Wales; Co-Winner, Best Play by Australian Woman Writer, 1975; Co-Winner, Everyman, a Modern Morality Play, 1979; Winner, Best Play, Festival of Australian Drama, 1984. Memberships: Australian Writers Guild; ACT Writers Centre; Gallery Players; Southern Cross Players. Address: PO Box 9009, Deakin, ACT 2600, Australia.

BRADLEY Charlena Wells, b. 2 October 1964, Cleveland, Ohio, USA. Company President and Chief Executive Officer. m. William L Bradley, 1 son. Education: Summer Scholarship, John Carroll University,1982; West Technical High School with honours, 1983; BA, Communication, Cleveland State University, 1988. Appointments: Project Assistant, Jones, Day, Reavis & Pogue, 1988-94; Court House Legal Assistant, 1995-97; Property Assistant, Trammell Crow Co, 1997-98; Certified Fitter, Dillard's South Park, 1998-99; Customer Assistant Account Manager, MBNA, 2001-; Consultant, President, Chief Executive Officer, Executive Producer, Wells Bradley Film Production, 2001-. Publication: Holiness (Christian publication), 1993-2000. Honours: Track and Field Award, 1977; Women's Fencing Award, 1987; Listed in Who's Who publications and biographical dictionaries. Address: 137 Ruth Ellen Drive #401K, Richmond Heights, OH 44142, USA.

BRADLEY Marjorie, b. 22 May 1916, Portsmouth, Hampshire, England. Retired Civil Servant; Poet. m. Reuben Stephen Bradley, 22 June 1938, 3 sons. Education: Municipal College, Portsmouth. Appointments: Junior Clerk, 1933-37; Tax Officer, 1937-38; Secretary, West Riding County Council, 1951-58; Clerical Officer, Department of Health and Social Security, 1958-73. Publication: Coffee Spoons. Contributions to: Envoi; Writer; London Calling; Purple Patch; Civil Service Author; Focus; Weyfarers; Success Magazine. Honours: Civil Service Authors, Herbert Spencer Competition; Open Poetry Competition; Envoi Magazine Open Competition; Salopian Poetry Competition; Success and Springboard Magazine Competitions. Memberships: Society of Civil Service Authors; Patchway Writers Group. Address: 88 Oak Close, Little Stoke, Bristol BS12 6RD, England.

BRADSHAW Jerald, b. 28 November 1932, Cedar City, Utah, USA. Professor Emeritus of Chemistry. m. Karen Lee, 2 daughters. Education: BS, Chemistry, University of Utah, 1955; PhD, Organic Chemistry, University of California, Los Angeles, 1963. Appointments: Chevron Research, 1963-66; Assistant, 1966-69, Associate, 1969-74, Professor, 1974-2000, Professor Emeritus, 2000, Brigham Young University. Publications: 420 scientific papers, 2 books, 34 US patents. Honours: Utah Governor's Medal in Science, 1991; American Chemical Society Utah Award, 1989 and Award in Separations Science, 1996. Membership: American Chemical Society. Address: Brigham Young University, Provo, UT 84602, USA.

BRADY Joan, b. 4 December 1939, San Francisco, California, USA. Writer. m. Dexter Masters, 23 Sept 1963, 1 son. Education: BS, Columbia University, 1965; Open University, 1992-. Publications: The Imposter, novel, 1979; The Unmaking of a Dancer, autobiography, 1982; US Theory of War, novel, 1992,

UK, US, The Netherlands, Germany, France, Spain, Sweden, Denmark, Norway, Korea, Poland. Prologue, autobiography, 1994, UK, The Netherlands, France; Death Comes for Peter Pan, novel, 1996, UK, France, The Netherlands; The Emigré (novel), 1999. Contributions to: Harpers, London Times; Sunday Times, Telegraph, Independent. Honours: NEA Grantee, 1986; Whitbread Novel, 1992; Whitbread Book of the Year, 1993; Prix du Meilleur Livre Étranger, 1995. Address: c/o John Saddler, Curtis Brown Group Ltd; Haymarket House, 28-29 Haymarket, London SW1Y 4SP, England. E-mail; John@curtisbrown.co.uk

BRADY Ross Thomas, b. 20 July 1943, Adelaide, South Australia. Reader and Associate Professor. m. Pompa, 5 January 1973, 1 son, 2 daughters. Education: BSc, 1st class honours and University Medal, University of Sydney, 1966; MA, 1st class honours, University of New England, 1967; PhD, University of St Andrews, 1971. Appointments: Lecturer, Mathematics, University of Western Australia, 1971; Lecturer, Philosophy, 1972-76, Senior Lecturer, 1977-2002, Sub-Dean of Humanities, 1989-93, Reader and Associate Professor, 2003-, LaTrobe University; Visiting Fellow, Australian National University, 1978. Publications: 33 academic papers in professional journals, 3 Chapters in books and 1 Conference Proceeding; Co-Author, Relevant Logics and Their Rivals, volumes 1 and 2. Honours: LaTrobe Central Starter Grant, 1993; ARC Large Grant, 1998-99; Research Enhancement Fund, 2001-03; Australian Centenary Medal, 2003. Memberships: President, 1998-99, Secretary-Treasurer, 2002-, Australasian Association of Logic; Treasurer, 1989-97, Assistant Treasurer, 1998-, Australasian Association for Philosophy; Fellow, Australian Academy of the Humanities, 2001-; Chair of Committee for Australasian Region, Association of Symbolic Logic, 2002-. Address: c/o Philosophy Program, La Trobe University, Melbourne, Victoria 3086, Australia.

BRAGG Melvyn, b. 6 October 1939, Wigton, Cumbria, England. Author; Broadcaster. m. Cate Haste, 1 son, 2 daughters. Education: 2nd Class Honours, Modern History, Wadham College, Oxford, 1961. Appointments: General Trainee, BBC, 1961; Producer on Monitor, 1963; Director, films including portrait of Sir John Barbirolli, 1963; Writer, Debussy film for Ken Russell, 1963; Editor, for BBC2, New Release (Arts Magazine) which became Review, then Arena, 1964; Documentary, Writers World, 1964; Take It or Leave It (Literary Panel Game), 1964; Presenter, for Tyne Tees TV, In the Picture (local arts programme), 1971; Presenter/Producer, for BBC, Second House, 1974-8; Editor/ Presenter, BBC, Read All About It, 1974-78; Interviewer for BBC, Tonight, 1974-78; Editor, Presenter, The South Bank Show, 1978; Head of Arts LWT, 1982-90; Programmes for Channel Four, 1982-90; Controller of Arts, LWT, 1990; Director, LWT Productions, 1992; Deputy Chairman, 1985-90, Chairman, 1990-95, Border TV, 1990-95; Governor LSE, 1997. Publications: Books include: For Want of a Nail, 1965; The Second Inheritance, 1966; Without a City Wall, 1968; The Cumbrian Trilogy, 1984; The Christmas Child, 1984; Love and Glory, 1984; The Nerve, 1971; Josh Lawton, 1972; The Silken Net, 1974; Autumn Manoeuvres, 1978; A Time to Dance (BBC TV adaption 1992), 1991; Crystal Rooms, 1992; CREDO, 1996; The Sword and The Miracle (USA publication), 1997; The Soldier's Return, 1999; A Son of War, 2001; Screenplays: Isadora; The Music Lovers; Jesus Christ Superstar; A Time to Dance, 1992. Musicals: Mardi Gras, 1976; The Hired Man, 1985; Play: King Lear In New York, 1992; Journalist in various newspapers. Honours include: Numerous for the South Bank Show, including 3 Prix Italias; Ivor Novello Award for Best Musical, 1985; Richard Dimbleby Award for Outstanding Contribution to TV, 1987; 2 TRIC Awards, 1990, 1994; Numerous honorary degrees. Address: 12 Hampstead Hill Gardens, London, NW3 2PL, England

Dictionary of International Biography

BRALEY Russell Norton, b. 10 November 1921, Seattle, Washington, USA. Foreign Correspondent; Author; Journalist. m. Madeleine Karacsony Braley, deceased 2002. Education: BA, University of Washington, 1944; French Certificate, Sorbonne, 1950. Appointments: Reporter, Oakland, California Post Enquirer, Copy-boy, 1947-49; Reporter: Stars and Stripes, Darnstadt, Germany, Editor: Sunday Features, 1951-52; Managing Editor, Overseas Weekly, Frankfurt, 1952-55; Foreign Correspondent, New York Daily News, 1955-75; UN Correspondent, 1975-82; Voice of America, 1982-84; Deputy Foreign Editor, The Washington Times, 1985-86. Publications: Bad News: The Foreign Policy of the New York Times, 1982; Regnery-Gateway, Chicago; Articles: The World and I, Chronicles: Human Events, National Review, Cavalier, Bild am Sontag; Accuracy in Media; Listed in several biographical publications. Membership: National Rifle Association. Address: 5200 Crossfield Court # 12, Rockville, MD 20852, USA. Website: www.mountnixon.com

BRAMWELL Fitzgerald, b. 16 May 1945, Brooklyn, New York, USA Chemist. m. Charlott Bramwell, 2 sons, 2 daughters. Education: BA, Chemistry, Columbia University, 1966; MS, 1967, PhD, 1970, Chemistry, University of Michigan. Appointments include: Dean, Graduate Studies and Research, Brooklyn College, CUNY, 1990-95; Executive Director, University of Kentucky Research Foundation, 1995-2001; Vice-President, Research and Graduate Studies, University of Kentucky, 1995-2001; Professor, Chemistry, University of Kentucky, 1995-. Publications include: Instructor's Guide for Investigations in General Chemistry Quantitative Techniques and Basic Principles, 1978; Instructor's Guide for Basic Laboratory Principles in General Chemistry with Quantitative Techniques, 1990; Basic Laboratory Principles in General Chemistry with Quantitative Techniques, 1990. Honours include: Distinguished Service Award, Brooklyn College Graduate Students Organization, 1994, 1995, Brooklyn Subsection of American Chemical Society, 1995; Department of Chemistry Alumni Excellence Award, University of Michigan, 1996; Lyman T Johnson Alumni Association Award, University of Kentucky, 1996; CCNY LSAMP Founders Award, 2000; Kentucky Geological Survey Outstanding Leadership Award, 2000; Claude Feuss Award, Phillips Academy, Andover, 2000; Omicron Delta Kappa, Nu Chapter, 2001. Memberships include: Kentucky Academy of Sciences, 1996-; American Association for the Advancement of Science, 1996-; American Institute of Chemists and Chemical Engineers, 1996-; Sigma Xi, 1971-; American Physical Society, 1967-95; American Chemical Society, 1966-. Address: Chemistry Department, University of Kentucky, Lexington, KY 40506-0055, USA.

BRANAGH Kenneth, b. 10 December 1960, Belfast, Ireland. Actor; Director. m. (1) Emma Thompson, divorced, (2) Lindsay Brunnock. Education: Royal Academy of Dramatic Art. Appointments: Numerous Theatre and Radio Work. Creative Works: Films: High Season; A Month in the Country; Henry V, 1989; Dead Again, 1991; Peter's Friends, 1992; Swing Kids, 1992; Swan Song, 1992; Much Ado About Nothing, 1993; Mary Shelley's Frankenstein; Othello, 1995; In the Bleak Midwinter, 1995; Hamlet, 1996; The Theory of Flight, 1997; The Proposition, 1997; The Gingerbread Man, 1997; Celebrity, 1998; Wild, Wild West, 1998; Love's Labour's Lost, 2000; How to Kill Your Neighbor's Dog, 2002; Rabbit Proof Fence, 2002; Harry Potter and the Chamber of Secrets, 2002; Alien Love Triangle, 2002. Publications: Public Enemy (play), 1988; Beginning (memoirs), 1989; The Making of Mary Shelley's Frankenstein, 1994; In the Bleak Midwinter, 1995; Screenplays for Henry V, Much Ado About Nothing, Hamlet. Honours: Evening Standard Best Film Award; New York Film Critics Circle Best Director Award; Hon DLitt,

Queens University, Belfast, 1990; BAFTA Award, Best Director, 1990. Address: Shepperton Studios, Studio Road, Shepperton, Middlesex TW17 0QD, England.

BRANCH Edgar Marquess, b. 21 March 1913, Chicago, Illinois, USA. University Professor; Educator; Editor; Author. m. Mary Josephine Emerson, 29 April 1939, 1 son, 2 daughters. Education: University College, University of London, England, 1932-33; BA, Beloit College,1934; Brown University, 1934-35; MA, University of Chicago, 1938; PhD, University of Iowa, 1941. Appointments: Instructor, 1941-43, Assistant Professor, 1943-49, Associate Professor, 1949-57, Professor, 1957-64, Chairman, Department of English, 1959-64, Research Professor, 1964-78, Miami University, Oxford, Ohio. Publications: The Literary Apprenticeship of Mark Twain, 1950; James T Farrell, 1963; Clemens of the Call, 1969; James T Farrell, 1971; The Great Landslide Case, 1972; Mark Twain's Early Tales and Sketches, 1851-64, Volume 1, with Robert H Hirst, 1979; Mark Twain's Early Tales and Sketches, 1864-1865, Volume 2, with Robert J Hirst; Men Call Me Lucky, 1985; The Grangerford-Shepherdson Feud, with Robert H Hirst, 1985; Mark Twain's Letters, 1853-1866, Volume 1, with Michael B Frank and Kenneth Sanderson, 1988; Mark Twain and the Starchy Boys, 1992; Roughing It, by Mark Twain, with Harriet Elinor Smith, 1993; Studs Lonigan's Neighborhood and the Making of James T Farrell, 1996; A Paris Year: Dorothy and James T Farrell in Paris 1931-32, 1998. Contributions to: Anthologies, magazines, and journals. Honours: National Endowment for the Humanities Fellowships, 1971-72, 1976-77; Benjamin Harrison Medallion, Miami University, 1978; Guggenheim Fellowship, 1978-79; Distinguished Service Citation, Beloit College, 1979; Mark Twain Circle of America, Lifetime Achievement Award, 1992; Mid American Award for Distinguished Contributions to the Study of Midwestern Literature, Society for the Study of Midwestern Literature, 1994; First Modern Language Association Prize for Distinguished Scholarly Edition, 1995; Pegasus Award, Ohioana Library Association, 1996. Memberships: Phi Beta Kappa; Phi Kappa Psi; Modern Language Association of America; National Council of Teachers of English; Beta Theta Pi; James T Farrell Society. Address: 4810 Bonham Road, Oxford, OH 45056, USA.

BRAND Gregor, b. 7 June 1957, Bettenfeld, Germany. Writer; Publisher. 2 daughters. Education: Assessor Iuris, Faculty of Law, University of Trier, Germany, 1983. Appointments: Research Fellow, University of Trier, Germany, 1983-85; Founder, Gregor Brand Verlag (Publishing House), 1985-. Publications: Books: Ausschaltversuche (poetry), 1985; Der Schwarze Drachen stuerzt ins Meer (poetry), 1987; Spätes Zweites Jahrtausend (poetry), 1998; Gesammelte Gedichte (collected poetry), 2000; Sefer Pralnik, 2001; More than 80 articles. Honours: Listed in more than 12 national and international lexica and encyclopaedias. Memberships include: Czechoslovak Society of Arts and Sciences. Address: Am Denkmal 4, 24793 Bargstedt, Germany. Website: http://www.gregorbrand.de.vu

BRAND Oscar, b. 7 February 1920, Winnipeg, Manitoba, Canada. Folk Singer; Folklorist; Writer. Education: BA, Brooklyn College, 1942. Appointments: President, Harlequin Productions, Gypsy Hill Music; Lecturer on Dramatic Writing, Hofstra University; Coordinator of Folk Music, WNYC; Host, numerous TV folksongs programmes; Curator, Songwriters Hall of Fame, New York City. Publications: Courting Songs, 1952; Folksongs for Fun, 1957; The Ballad Mongers, autobiography, 1957; Bawdy Songs, 1958; The Gold Rush (writer, composer), ballet, 1961; In White America (composer), play 1962; A Joyful Noise (co-writer, composer), musical play, 1966; The Education of Hyman Kaplan (co-writer, composer), musical play, 1968; Celebrate (writer-composer), religious songs, 1968; How to Steal an Election (co-writer, composer), musical play, 1969; Songs of '76, music history, 1973; Thunder Rock (writer, composer), musical play, 1974; Party Songs, 1985. Honours: Laureate, Fairfield University, 1972; Peabody Awards, 1982, 1996; PhD, University of Winnipeg, 1989; Radio Pioneers of America, 1991; Friends of Old Time Radio, 1991. Memberships: American Federation of Television and Radio Artists; Screen Actors Guild; American Federation of Musicians; Dramatists Guild. Address: 141 Baker Hill, Great Neck, NY 11023, USA.

BRANDUS (BRINDUS) Nicolae, b. 16 April 1935, Bucharest, Romania. Composer. m. (1) Maria Ostrowska (2) Ioana Ieronim, 2 sons, 1 daughter. Education: MA, Piano, 1957, MA, Composition, 1964, National University of Music, Bucharest, Romania; PhD, Musicology, Academy of Music, Cluj, Romania, 1981. Appointments: Soloist, Pianist, Philharmonic of Ploiesti, Romania, 1960-69; Professor of Chamber Music, National University of Music, Bucharest, Romania 1969-81 and 1992-; Editor, Revista Musica, Bucharest, 1981-. Publications: About 40 compositions, scores and recordings in Romania and abroad; Book: Interrelation, 1984; Many studies, articles, essays in professional publications on New Music; Lectures as visiting composer in Europe Asia and America. Honours: Cultural Merit, Bucharest, 1969; Prizes, Union of Romanian Composers and Musicologists, 1974, 2002; RTV Prizes, 1975, 1977; George Enescu Prize, Romanian Academy, 1975. Memberships: Union of Composer's and Musicologist's in Romania, 1965-; SACEM, Paris, 1969; ISCM, Romanian Section, 1990-. Address: Str Dr Felix 101, bl 19, Apt 42, 78153, Bucharest, Romania. E-mail: nbrandus@fx.ro Website: www.cimec.ro/musica/pers/branduseng.htm

BRANSON Richard Charles Nicholas, b. 18 July 1950. Founder; Chairman; President. m. (1) 1969, dissolved, (2) Joan Templeman, 1989, 1 son, 1 daughter. Education: Stowe. Appointments: Editor, Student Magazine, 1968-69; Founder, Student Advisory Centre (now Help), 1970; Founder, Virgin Mail-Order Company, 1969, First Virgin record shop, 1971; Recording Company, 1973; Nightclub (The Venue), 1976; Virgin Atlantic Airways, 1984; Founder and Chairman, Virgin Retail Group, Virgin Communications, Virgin Travel Group, Voyager Group; Group also includes publishing, broadcasting, contraction, heating systems, holidays; Chairman, 1986-88; President, 1988-, UK 2000; Director, Intourist Moscow Ltd, 1988-90; Founder, The Healthcare Foundation, 1987; Founder, Virgin Radio, 1993; Founder, Virgin Rail Group Ltd, 1996; Launched Virgin Cola drink, 1994, Babylon Restaurant, 2001; Crossed Pacific in hot air balloon with Per Lindstrand, 1991. Honours: Blue Riband Title for Fastest Atlantic Crossing, 1986; Seagrave Trophy, 1987. Publication: Losing My Virginity, autobiography, 1998. Address: c/o Virgin Group PLC, 120 Campden Hill Road, London W8 7AR, England.

BRASSEAUX Carl Anthony, b. 19 August 1951, Opelousas, Louisiana, USA. Historian. m. Glenda, 21 July 1973, 2 sons, 1 daughter. Education: BA, Political Science, cum laude, University of the South West, Louisiana, 1974; MA, History, 1975; Doctorat de 3e cycle, University of Paris, 1982. Appointments: Assistant Director, Center for Louisiana Studies, 1975-2000; Professor, History and Geography Department, University of Louisiana, Lafayette, 1998-; Director, Center for Cultural and Eco-Tourim, University of Louisiana at Lafayette, 2001-. Publications: 102 scholarly publications in journals in North America and Europe; 32 book length works. Honours: Kemper Williams Prize, 1979; Robert L Brown Prize, 1980; President's Memorial Award, Louisiana Historical Society, 1986; Book Prize, French Colonial Historical Society, 1987; Chevalier, L'Ordre des Palmes Academiques, 1994; University Distinguished Professor, History,

1995; National Daughters of the American Revolution Award, 1995; Fellow, Louisiana Historical Association, 2000-. Membership: Louisiana Historical Association. Address: 201 Parliament Drive, Lafayette, LA 70506, USA.

BRASSEUL Jacques Pierre, b. 23 May 1946, Neuilly sur Seine, France. Professor. m. Claudia Korn. 1 son, 2 daughters. Education: Agregation, University of Paris, 1970; Doctorat d'Etat, University of Lyon, 1980. Appointments: Assistant Professor, University of Paris, France, 1973-80; Professor, University of Lyon, France, 1980-82; Professor, University of Dakar, Senegal, 1982-96; Professor, University of Toamasina, Madagascar, 1986-90; Professor, University of Lyon, France, 1990-93; Professor, University of La Reunion, Reunion Island, 1993-96; Professor, University of Toulon, France, 1996-. Publications: Histoire des faits économiques, 3 volumes, 1997, 1998, 2003; Introduction à l'économie du developpement, 1993; Les Nouveaux Pays Industrialisés, 1993; Amerique latine in Encyclopaedia Universalis, 1995; Petite histoire des faits économiques, 2001. Address: 10 allée Chevalier Paul, 83400 Hyéres, France. E-mail: jacques@brasseul.com

BRATCHER Juanita, b. 23 September 1939, Columbus, Georgia, USA. Journalist; Publisher; Author; Poet; Songwriter. m. Neal Bratcher Sr, deceased, 1 son, 3 daughters. Education: Bachelor of Arts degree, Journalism, Columbia College; Associate of Arts, Liberal Arts, Olive-Harvey College; Matriculation, Alabama State University, Montgomery, Alabama. Appointments: Journalist, 1976-; Investigative Reporter, Chicago Daily Defender; Presenter, TV show, One on One; Guest, panellist or co-host on numerous TV and radio programmes; Member, Regional Auxiliary Council (Atlas Center), 2 years; Press Aide, Cook County Board President, John S Stroger; Member, Editorial Committee of One City magazine publication, Chicago Council on Urban Affairs; Active in community and civic affairs. Publications: Author, 5 books; 13 records released; 2 songs listed in songbook. Honours include: Excellence in Achievement, Zeta Phi Beta Sorority Inc; Outstanding Service in the Media & Telecommunications Award, Delta Sigma Theta Sorority; Service Award, US Department of Education, Region V; Service Award, Boy Scouts of America; Certificates of Merit, Chicago Public Schools; From Whence We Came Award, Allstate Insurance, 2002; Listed in national and international biographical dictionaries. Address: 9026 S Cregier Ave, Chicago, IL 60617, USA. E-mail: juanitabratcher@yahoo.com

BRAUN-FALCO Otto, b. 25 April 1922, Saarbrücken, Germany. University Professor. m. Sissy Golling, 1 son. Education: Study of Medicine, 1940-43, 1946-48; Dr of Medicine, 1949; Professor of Dermatology. Appointments: Professor of Dermatology, 1961; Chairman, Department of Dermatology and Venereology, Philipps University of Marburg/Lahn, Germany, 1961-67; Chairman, Department of Dermatology, Venereology and Allergology, Ludwig-Maximilians-University of Munich, 1967-91; Professor Emeritus, Dermatology, Venereology and Allergology; Member, German Academy of Natural Sciences LEOPOLDINA, Halle and Bavarian Academy of Sciences; President European Society for Dermatological Research, 1972-73; President, International League of Dermatological Societies and International Committee of Dermatology, 1977/1982; President, XVI World Congress of Dermatology, Tokyo, Japan, 1982. Publications: More than 800 scientific papers and about 150 chapters in special dermatological publications and books; Co-author of text book on dermatology; Main areas of research include: Structure and function of normal and diseased skin using histochemical and electron microscopical methods; The origin, diagnosis and treatment of malignant melanoma; Development of dermatoscopy together with W Stolz and M Landthaler for early detection of malignant pigmented skin lesions; Disturbances of hair growth; Early detection of HIV infection of AIDS with dermatological methods; Research on causes and treatment of psoriasis and laser treatment of skin changes. Honours include: Alfred Marchionini Gold Medal, 1982; Stephen Rothman Gold Medal, Society of Investigative Dermatology, Washington DC, USA, 1986; Herxheimer Medal, Deutsche Dermatologische Gesellschaft, 1990; Honorary Doctorates: University of Ghent, Belgium, 1981, Marburg, Germany, 1987, Berlin, Germany, 1991. Liège, Belgium, 1991; Award of Excellence, European Society for Dermatological Research, 1996; Cothenius Gold Medal, German Academy of Natural Sciences LEOPOLDINA, 1997. Memberships: Many dermatological societies world-wide; Honorary member of more than 40 German and foreign societies including: The Royal Society of Medicine, London; The Society of Investigative Dermatology; The American Dermatological Association, Deutsche Dermatologische Gesellschaft. Address: Department of Dermatology, Ludwig-Maximilians-University, Frauenlobstrasse 9-11, 80337, Munich, Germany.

BRAVERMAN Jordan, b. 4 July 1936, Boston, Massachusetts, USA. Author; Columnist. Education: BA, Harvard College, 1958; William Stoughton Scholar, Harvard University Graduate School of Design and Graduate School of Arts and Sciences, 1958-59; MPH, Yale University, 1963; MS of Foreign Service, Georgetown University, Washington DC, 1968. Appointments: Urban Planner, Economist, Quincy City Government, Massachusetts, 1959-61; Administrator, National Blue Cross Association, Chicago, Illinois, 1963-65; Economist, US Department of Health, Education and Welfare, Public Health Service, Washington DC, 1965-67; Management Consultant, EBS Management Consultants, Washington DC, 1967-69; Assistant to Executive Director, American Pharmaceutical Association, Washington DC, 1969-72; Director of Public Policy Research, Pharmaceutical Manufacturers Association, Washington DC, 1972-74; Managing Editor, Topics in Health Care Financing, Rockville, Maryland, 1974-75; Director, Legislative Policy Analysis Division, Health Policy Center, Georgetown University, Washington DC, 1975-77; Columnist, Author, other publishing work, 1978-. Publications: Books including: Crisis in Health Care, 1978, revised, 1980; The Consumer's Book of Health: How to Stretch Your Health Care Dollar, 1982; Health Maintenance Organizations: New Choices for Paying and Receiving Medical Care, 1986; To Hasten the Homecoming: How Americans Fought World War II Through the Media, 1996; Poetry in anthologies, 1994-, including: The Sounds of Poetry, cassettes, 1995-2003; America at the Millennium: The Best Poems and Poets of the 20th Century, 2000; Poetry's Elite: Best Poets of 2000; Best Photos of 2003, photography anthology; Photography in anthologies including: America at the Millennium: The Best Photos of the 20th Century, 2000; Candid Captures, 2001; 19 articles in areas of medical care; Numerous articles and columns in newspapers and magazines including International Medical News Service, Consumer Health Reporter, American Weekly News, The Baltimore Sun, Capital Jester. Honours include: William Stoughton Scholar, Harvard, 1958-59; Nominee, Kulp Book Award, 1978; Editor's Choice, North American Open Poetry Contest, 1994; Editors Choice Award for, Poetry's Elite: The Best Poets of 2000 (poetry anthology), 2001; Poet of the Year, 1996, 1999, Elected, Hall of Fame, 1997, International Poet of Merit, 1997, 1999; Editor's Choice, International Library of Photography, 1998-99; Name Inscribed on National Wall of Tolerance, Montgomery, Alabama, 2001; Editor's Choice Award, 2001. Memberships include: US Holocaust Memorial Museum; International Society of Poets; Harvard, Yale and Georgetown Clubs of Washington; World War II Memorial Society; Smithsonian

Museum; Statue of Liberty and Ellis Island Preservation; American Airmen Museum, England. Address: 2401 H Street NW, Washington, DC 20037, USA.

BRAVINA Svetlana Leonidovna, b. 16 April 1952, Kiev, Ukraine. Physicist. m. 1 August 1975, 1 daughter. Education: Masters Degree, Radioelectronics, 1970; MSc, Kiev National University, 1976; PhD, 1988. Appointments: Engineer, 1976-83, Senior Engineer, 1983-86, Junior Research Scientist 1986-89, Research Scientist, 1989-94, Senior Research Scientist, 1994-, Institute of Physics, National Academy of Sciences, Ukraine. Publications include: Pyroelectricity in some ferroelectric semiconductors, 1991; 4 patents. Honours: Listed in international biographical reference works. Membership: International Society for Optical Engineering. Address: Institute of Physics, National Academy of Sciences, Prospect Nauki 46, 03028 Kiev, Ukraine.

BRAVO Gian Luigi, b. 30 March 1935, Villanova D'Asti, Italy University Professor. m. Pierangela Farris, 1 son. Philosophy Degree, University of Turin, Italy, 1959; Research Graduate, State University "Lomonosov", Moscow, USSR, 1961-63. Appointments: Member of Staff, Personnel Department, Olivetti, Ivrea, Italy, 1960-61; Associate Professor, 1972-90, Professor of Cultural Anthropology, University of Turin, Italy, 1990-. Publications: Books: La Ricera Sociale in URSS tra Parsons e Marx, 1974; Festa Contadina e Societa Complessa, 1984; Italiani Racconto Ethnografico, 2001; Article: Orso e capra a Nuova Vita, 2003; Ethnographic Video: Il Gioco della Tradizione, 1987; Database: Multimedial Catalog of Italian Folk Festivals, 2003. Honours: Premio Internzionale Pitre Award, 1988; Pemio Constantino Nigra Award, 2001. Membership: Chairperson, 2001-2004, National Association of Italian Cultural and Social Anthropologists. Address: Via Roma 30 14040 Mongardino (AT), Italy. E-mail: gianluigi.bravo@unito.it Website: www.saast.unito.it

BRAY Denis Campbell, b. 24 January 1926, Hong Kong. Company Director. m. Marjorie Elizabeth Bottomley, 4 daughters. Education: BA, 1947, MA, 1955, Jesus College, Cambridge; BSc, Economics, London University External Department. Appointments: Royal Navy, 1947-49; Hong Kong Civil Service, 1950-85; District Commissioner, New Territories, 1971; Secretary for Home Affairs, 1973-74, 1980-85; Hong Kong Commissioner, London, 1977-80. Publication: Hong Kong Metamorphosis, 2001. Honours: JP, 1960-65, 1987-; CVO, 1975; CMG, 1977. Address: 8A-7 Borrett Mansions, 8-9 Bowen Road, Hong Kong.

BRAZDA Josef, b. 12 March 1939, Babice u Rosic, Brno, Czechoslovakia. Horn Player. m. Vlasta Brázdová, 8 June 1974, 2 daughters. Education: Private Artistic School, Brno; State Conservatoire, Brno; Janácek Academy of Musical Arts, Brno. Debut: State Philharmonic Orchestra, Brno. Career: Prague Academic Wind Quintet; Prague Chamber Orchestra; Musici d' Praga-Chamber Orchestra; Haydn Sinfonietta Vienna; Solo concertos and sonatas; Horn Instructor. Compositions: Instructive Compositions for 2,3,4 horns. Recordings: Richard Strauss, Horn Concerto No 2; Paul Hindemith, Horn Concerto; Franz Danzi, Horn Concerto E Major; Paul Hindemith, both Sonatas; Joseph Haydn, Horn Concerto D Major, Hob VII; Joseph Haydn, Divertimenti, Baritone Octets, with Haydn Sinfonietta Vienna. Honours: 2nd Prize, IX International Musikwettbewerb, Munich 1960; 1st Prize, XV International Prague Spring Festival, 1962 Address: Roklanska 1095, 25101 Ricany u Prahy, Czech Republic.

BRAZHNIKOV Andrey V, b. 28 October 1959, Kostroma, Russia. Scientist; Educator. m. Elena S Karpenko, 1 daughter. Education: BS, Electrical Engineering, major in Automatics and Telemechanics, Honours Degree, cum laude, 1982; PhD,

Electromechanics 1985. Appointments: Chief of Laboratory, Research Institute, Krasnoyarsk, 1987-88; Deputy Director, Educational Institute, Director of Educational Centre, 1997-2002; Chief of several scientific projects among them 2 international projects, 1991-; Publications: About 50 scientific works include: Additional Resources of Control of Multiphase Inverter Drives, 1993; Prospects for the Use of Multiphase Electric Drives in the Field of Mining Machines, 1995; Improvement of Technical and Economic Characteristics of Drilling Rigs Owing to the Use of Multiphase Electric Drives, 1996; Hydrodynamic Modelling of Force Fields, 1997. Honours: Annual Prizes for Scientific Work, Russian Research and Higher Educational Institutes, 1980-; Prizes for organising scientific work, Academy of Non-Ferrous Metals and Gold, Krasnoyarsk, Russia, 1997-; Listed in Who's Who publications and biographical dictionaries. Memberships: Institute of Electrical And Electronics Engineers; Research Board of Advisors, American Biographical Institute. Address: Academy of Non-Ferrous Metals and Gold, 95 Krasnoyarsky Rabochy Avenue, 660025 Krasnoyarsk, Russia. E-mail: postmaster@color.krasnoyarsk.ru

BREE Peter, b. 23 September 1949, Driebergen-Rijsenburg, The Netherlands. Radio Producer; Presenter. Education: MO-A Degree, University of Groningen, 1972-73; Degrees, Amsterdam Muzieklyceum, 1973-81; Scholarship, London, 1980-81. Appointments: Master of English, various grammar schools, Amsterdam, 1973-77; Principal Oboist, NOS Radio, Hilversum, 1977-79; Freelance Oboist, 1979-94; Producer, AVRO Radio, Hilversum, 1980-83; Producer, Presenter, Veronica Radio, Hilversum, 1982-92; Reviewer, CD-Magazine, Disk, The Netherlands, 1991-92; Producer, Presenter, Concert Radio, Amsterdam, 1994-98; Producer, Presenter, AVRO Radio, Hilversum, 1998-. Publications: Several articles in professional journals. Honours include: Dutch Government Scholarship, London, 1980; Awards, Dutch Cultural Ministry, 1979, 1981; Award, Arts Council of Great Britain, 1980; Silver Vriendenkrans Award, Society of Friends of the Concertgebouw and Royal Concertgebouw Orchestra, 1981. Memberships: ThuisKopie Fonds, 1999-2003; Supervisory Board, Foundation for the Preservation of the Organ of the English Church at Begynhof; Secretary of the Board, International Double Reed Festival Foundation, 1990-95; Chairman, Academy of the Begynhof; Board, Netherlands Bach Society. Address: Middenweg 166, 1097 TZ Amsterdam, The Netherlands.

BREMER Ronald Allan, b. 2 May 1937, Southgate, California, USA. Professional Genealogist. m. Trudy Graham, 4 sons, 9 daughters. Education: Brigham Young University, 1955-56; National Institute of Genealogical Research, 1961; American University, 1961; Cerritos College, Los Angeles Trade Tech, 1963. Appointments: Professor Genealogist, 1958-; Research Specialist, Family History Library, 1969-72; Founder, Federation of Genealogical Societies, USA, 1975; Editor, Roots Digest Magazine, 1983-. Publications: Articles in Roots Digest, Genealogical Helper Magazine, Heritage Quest Magazine and New England Connection Magazine. Honours: Featured Speaker, Special Genealogical Seminar, Mission to the United Nations, New York City. Memberships: Founding Member, Utah Genealogical Association; Founding Member, Southern California Genealogical Society. Address: Post Office Box 345, Paradise, UT 84328, USA. E-mail: ronbremer@juno.com

BREMNER Betty Avice, b. 12 February 1921, Christchurch, New Zealand. Freelance Journalist; Poet. m. William Laohlan Bremner, 26 January 1946, deceased, 1 daughter. Education: Canterbury University, Christchurch; BA, Victoria University of Wellington, 1989. Publication: The Scarlet Runners, 1991-92; In the Dream or out of the Dream, 2003. Contributions to: Sport; Kapiti Poems, III-VI; King's Cross Poets; Dominion; MsCellany. Memberships: Women Writer's Society; PEN International; L'Alliance Française; Poetry Society. Address: 20 Dowse Drive, Maungaraki, Lower Hutt, New Zealand.

BRENDON Piers George Rundle, b. 21 December 1940, Stratton, Cornwall, England. Writer. m. Vyvyen Davis, 1968, 2 sons. Education: MA, PhD, Magdalene College, Cambridge. Publications: Hurrell Froude and the Oxford Movement, 1974; Hawker of Morwenstow, 1975; Eminent Edwardians, 1979; The Life and Death of the Press Barons, 1982; Winston Churchill: A Brief Life, 1984; Our Own Dear Queen, 1985; Ike: The Life and Times of Dwight D Eisenhower, 1986; Thomas Cook: 150 Years of Popular Tourism, 1991; The Windsors (with Phillip Whitehead), 1994; The Motoring Century: The Story of the Royal Automobile Club, 1997; The Dark Valley: A Panorama of the 1930's, 2000. Contributions to: Times; Observer; The Mail on Sunday; New York Times; New Statesman. Honour: The Nicholas-Joseph Cugnot Award for The Motoring Century, 1997. Address: 4B Millington Road, Cambridge CB3 9HP, England.

BRENNER Sydney, b. 13 January 1927, Germiston, South Africa (British Citizen). Molecular Biologist. m. May Woolf Balkind, 3 sons, 1 stepson, 2 daughters. Education: MSc, 1947, MB, BCh, 1951, University of Witwatersrand, Johannesburg; PhD, Oxford University, 1954. Appointments: Virus Laboratory, University of California at Berkeley, 1954; Lecturer in Physiology, University of Witwatersrand, 1955-57; Researcher, 1957-79, Director, Molecular Biology Laboratory, 1979-86, Director, Molecular Genetics Unit, 1986-92, Medical Research Council, Cambridge; Member, Scripps Institute, La Jolla, California, 1992-94; Director, Molecular Sciences Institute, Berkeley, California, 1996-2001; Distinguished Research Professor, Salk Institute, La Jolla, California, 2001-. Honours: Honorary DSc: Dublin, Witwatersrand, Chicago, London, Leicester, Oxford; Honorary LLD, Glasgow, Cambridge; Honorary DLitt, Singapore; Warren Triennial Prize, 1968; William Bate Hardy Prize, Cambridge Philosophical Society, 1969; Gregor Mendel Medal of German Academy of Science Leopoldina, 1970; Albert Lasker Medical Research Award, 1971; Gairdner Foundation Annual Award, Canada, 1978; Royal Medal of Royal Society, 1974; Prix Charles Leopold Mayer, French Academy, 1975; Krebs Medal, Federation of European Biochemical Societies, 1980; Ciba Medal, Biochemical Society, 1981; Feldberg Foundation Prize, 1983; Neil Hamilton Fairley Medal, Royal College of Physicians, 1985; Croonian Lecturer, Royal Society of London, 1986; Rosenstiel Award, Brandeis University, 1986; Prix Louis Jeantet de Médecine, Switzerland, 1987; Genetics Society of America Medal, 1987; Harvey Prize, Israel Institute of Technology, 1987; Hughlings Jackson Medal, Royal Society of Medicine, 1987; Waterford Bio-Medical Science Award, The Research Institute of Scripps Clinic, 1988; Kyoto Prize, Inamori Foundation, 1990; Gairdner Foundation Award, Canada, 1991; Copley Medal, Royal Society, 1991; King Faisal International Prize for Science (King Faisal Foundation), 1992; Bristol-Myers Squibb Award for Distinguished Achievement in Neuroscience Research, 1992; Albert Lasker Award for Special Achievement, 2000; Nobel Prize for Physiology or Medicine, 2002. Memberships: Member, Medical Research Council, 1978-82, 1986-90; Fellow, King's College, Cambridge, 1959-; Honorary Professor of Genetic Medicine, University of Cambridge, Clinical School, 1989-; Foreign Associate, NAS, 1977; Foreign Member, American Philosophical Society, 1979; Foreign Member, Real Academia de Ciencias, 1985; External Scientific Member, Max Planck Society, 1988; Member, Academy Europea, 1989; Corresponding Scientifique Emerite de l'INSERM, Associe Etranger Academie des Sciences, France; Fellow, American

Dictionary of International Biography

Academy of Microbiology; Foreign Honorary Member, American Academy of Arts and Sciences, 1965; Honorary Member, Deutsche Akademie der Natursforsche Leopoldina, 1975; Society for Biological Chemists, 1975; Honorary FRSE; Honorary Fellow, Indian Academy of Sciences, 1989; Honorary Member, Chinese Society of Genetics, 1989; Honorary Fellow, Royal College of Pathologists, 1990; Honorary Member, Associate of Physicians of GB and Ireland, 1991. Address: Kings College, Cambridge, CB2 1ST, England.

BRENTON Howard, b. 13 December 1942, Portsmouth, England. Playwright; Poet. Education: BA, St Catherine's College, Cambridge, 1965. Appointments: Resident Dramatist, Royal Court Theatre, London, 1972-73; Resident Writer, University of Warwick, 1978-79; Granada Artist in Residence, University of California, Davis, 1997; AHRB Research Fellow, Birmingham University, 2000-03. Publications: Plays produced and publications include: Adaptation of Goethe's Faust, 1966; Notes from a Psychotic Journal and Other Poems, 1969; Revenge, 1969; Scott of the Antarctic (or what God didn't see), 1970; Christie in Love and Other Plays, 1970; Lay By (co-author), 1972; Plays for Public Places, 1972; Hitler Diaries, 1972; Brassneck (with David Hare), 1973; Magnificence, 1973; Weapons of Happiness, 1976; The Paradise Run (television play), 1976; Epsom Downs, 1977; Sore Throats, with Sonnets of Love and Opposition, 1979; The Life of Galileo (adaptor), 1980; The Romans in Britain, 1980; Plays for the Poor Theatre, 1980; Thirteenth Night and A Short Sharp Shock, 1981; Danton's Death (adaptor), 1982; The Genius, 1983; Desert of Lies (television play), 1983; Sleeping Policemen (with Tunde Ikoli), 1984; Bloody Poetry, 1984; Pravda (with David Hare),1985; Dead Head (television series), 1987; Greenland, 1988; H.I.D. (Hess is Dead), 1989; Iranian Night (with Tariq Ali), 1989; Diving for Pearls (novel), 1989; Moscow Gold (with Tariq Ali), 1990; Berlin Bertie, 1992; Playing Away (opera libretto), 1994; Hot Irons (essays and diaries), 1995; English version of Goethe's Faust, Parts I and II, 1995; In Extremis, 1997; Ugly Rumours (with Tariq Ali), 1998; Snogging Ken (with Tariq Ali and Andre de la Tour), 1999; Kit's Play, 2000; Democratic Demons, 2000; Episodes of BBC1 drama, Spooks, 2001-03. Honour: Honorary Doctorate University of North London, 1996. Address: c/o Casarotto Ramsay Ltd, National House, 60-66 Wardour Street, London W1V 3HP, England.

BRESENHAM Jack E, b. USA. Professor of Computer Science. Education: BSEE, University of New Mexico, 1959; MSIE, 1960, PhD, 1964, Stanford University. Appointments: Senior Technical Staff Member, Manager, Engineer, Planner, Programmer, Analyst, IBM, 1960-87; Teacher, Professor of Computer Science, Winthrop University, 1987-2003. Publications include: Algorithm for computer control of a digital plotter, 1965, reprinted, 1980, reprinted, 1998; Pixel processing fundamentals, 1996; Teaching the graphics processing pipeline: cosmetic and geometric attribute implications, 2001; The Analysis and Statistics of Line Distribution, 2002; 9 US Patents. Honours include: IBM Outstanding Contribution Award, 1967 and 1984; Distinguished Citizen Award, Wofford College National Alumni Association, 1993; Honorary Director and Invited Lecturer, University of Cantabria, Santander, Spain, July 2000; Jury Member of habilitation a diriger les recherches panel, University of Paris-8 for Jean Jaques Bourdin, 2000; Golden Quill Award in recognition of work to improve writing skills among computer science students, Winthrop University, 2001; Honorary Chair, The 11th International Conference in Central Europe on Computer Graphics, Visualization and Computer Vision, 2003; Named Distinguished Alumnus, School of Engineering, University of New Mexico. Address: Winthrop University, Department of Computer Science, 701 Oakland Avenue, Rock Hill, SC 29733, USA.

BRESLER Lynn Patricia, b. 20 March 1947, Hove, England. Freelance Editor. Education: Business Studies, Brighton Technical College. Appointments: Secretarial work in insurance, retail fashion, Assistant Bursar's Office, University of Sussex, J Walter Thompson Company, New York, 1965-70; Fashion Accessories Buyer, Associated Dry Goods and Woodward Stores. 1970-72; Editor, A & C Black, 1972-78; Temporary Secretary, Covent Garden Bureau, 1978-80; Freelance Editor, 1980-84; Information Book Editor, Usborne Publishing, 1984-86; Freelance Editor, 1986-. Publications: The Usborne Book of Earth Facts; The Young Scientist Book of Evolution (with Barbara Cork); Finchley Remembered (editor). Honours: NVQ Book Editing Level 3, Units 1 and 2; Advanced Member, Society for Editors and Proofreaders. Memberships: Trustee and Membership Secretary, The Finchley Society; Barnet Guild of Artists.

BRESLIN Winifred (Wynn) Boin, b. 6 November 1932, Hackensack, New Jersey, USA. Artist. m. William W Breslin III, 1 son. Education: Scholarship in Fine Arts, Syracuse University, 1950-51; BFA, 1954, MEd, 1961, University of Delaware; Scholarship, Haystack School of Art, 1960. Appointments: Public School Art Teacher, 1954-63; Painting Instructor, Delaware Art Museum, 1956-66; Supervisor, Alexis Idu Pont School District, 1960; Artist-in-Education, Delaware Division of Fine Arts, 1981-95. Publications: From an Artistic Viewpoint, University News, University of Delaware, 1967 Commissions and Creative Works: Teacher and Child (sculpture), Immanuel Episcopal Church, Wilmington, Delaware; Painting, First Federal Savings and Loan, Wilmington, Delaware. Honours: First Prize and Best-in-Show, Chester Co Art Association, Pennsylvania, 1984; 1st prize Painting, University of Delaware Four State Regional Exhibition, 1988. Memberships: Chester Co Art Association, Delaware Association for Art Education, President, 1960-62. Delaware Center for Contemporary Art; Delaware Art Museum, 2001. Address: 470 Terrapin Lane, Newark, DE 19711, USA.

BREWER Derek Stanley, b. 13 July 1923, Cardiff, Wales. Writer; Editor; Emeritus Professor. m. Lucie Elisabeth Hoole, 3 sons, 2 daughters. Education: Magdalen College, Oxford, 1941-42, 1945-48; BA, MA (Oxon), 1948; PhD, Birmingham University, 1956; LittD, Cambridge University, 1980. Appointments: include Professor, International Christian University, Tokyo, 1956-58; Senior Lecturer, Birmingham, 1958-65; Fellow, 1965-90, Master, 1977-90, Professor, 1983-90, Life Fellow, 1990-, Emeritus Professor, 1990-, Emmanuel College, Cambridge; Editor, The Cambridge Review, 1981-86. Publications: Numerous contributions to specialist scholarly journals, and several books, mainly in the fields of medieval and later English literature, especially the works of Geoffrey Chaucer; Titles include, Chaucer, 1953; Proteus, 1958; The Parlement of Foulys, (editor), 1960; Chaucer: The Critical Heritage, 1978; Chaucer and his World, 1978, reprinted, 1992; Symbolic Stories, 1980, reprinted, 1988; English Gothic Literature, 1983; Chaucer: An Introduction, 1984; Medieval Comic Tales (editor), 1996; A Companion to the Gawain-Poet, 1996, (editor); A New Introduction to Chaucer, 1998; Seatonian Exercises and Other Verses, 2000; The World of Chaucer, 2000. Honours: Honorary Doctorates from 7 Universities; Seatonian Prize Poem, 1969, 1972, 1979, 1980, 1983, 1986, 1988, 1992, 1994, 1999. Address: Emmanuel College, Cambridge, CB2 3AP, England. E-mail: dsb27@cam.ac.uk

BRIDGEMAN Victoria Harriet Lucy (Viscountess), b. 30 March 1942, Durham, England. Library Director; Writer. m. Viscount Bridgeman, 1966, 4 sons. Education: MA, Trinity College, Dublin, 1964. Appointment: Executive Editor, The Masters, 1965-69; Editor, Discovering Antiques, 1970-72; Established own company producing books and articles on fine

Dictionary of International Biography

and decorative arts; Founder and Managing Director, Bridgeman Art Library, London and New York. Publications: An Encyclopaedia of Victoriana: An Illustrated History, The British Eccentric, 1975; Society Scandals, 1976; Beside the Seaside, 1976; A Guide to Gardens of Europe, 1979; The Last Word, 1983; 8 titles in Connoisseur's Library series. Honours: European Woman of the Year Award, Arts Section, 1997; FRSA. Address: 19 Chepstow Road, London W2 5BP, England.

BRIDGES Jeff, b. 4 December 1949, Los Angeles, USA. Actor. m. Susan Geston, 3 daughters. Creative Works: Films include: Halls of Anger, 1970; The Last Picture Show, 1971; Fat City, 1971; Bad Company, 1972; The Last American Hero, 1973; The Iceman Cometh, 1973; Thunderbolt and Lightfoot, 1974; Hearts of the West, 1975; Rancho Deluxe, 1975; King Kong, 1976; Stay Hungary, 1976; Somebody Killed Her Husband, 1978; Winter Kills, 1979; The American Success Company, 1980; Heaven's Gate, 1980; Cutter's Way, 1981; Tron, 1982; Kiss Me Goodbye, 1982; The Last Unicorn, 1982; Starman, 1984; Against All Odds, 1984; Jagged Edge, 1985; 8 Million Ways to Die, 1986; The Morning After, 1986; Nadine, 1987; Tucker, the Man and His Dream, 1988; See You in the Morning, 1990; Texasville, 1990; The Fabulous Baker Boys, 1990; The Fisher King, 1991; American Heart, The Vanishing, Blown Away, 1994; Fearless, 1994; Wild Bill, White Squall, 1995; The Mirror Has Two Faces, 1996; The Big Lebowski, 1997; Arlington Road, 1998; Simpatico, 1999; The Muse, 1999; The Contender, 2000; Raising the Hammoth (TV voice), 2000; K-Pax, 2002; Masked and Anonymous, 2003; Seabiscuit, 2003; The Door in the Floor, 2004. Address: c/o Creative Artists Agency, 9830 Wilshire Boulevard, Beverly Hills, CA 90212, USA.

BRIERLEY Peter William, b. 30 October 1938, London. Charity Director. m. Cherry, 3 sons, 1 daughter (adopted). Education: BSc, Hons, Statistics, University College, London, 1961; Diploma in Theology, (London University Board), Honorary Diploma, Bible Training Institute, Glasgow, 1964; Honorary Doctor of Letters, D Litt, Greenwich University. Appointments: Teacher, Mathematics, Statistics, Religious Education, Southampton, 1965-67; Statistician, Civil Service, Ministry of Defence, 1967-70; Statistician, Central Statistical Office, Cabinet Office, 1970-78; Programme Director, British and Foreign Bible Society, 1978-83; European Director, MARC Europe, 1983-93; Executive Director, Christian Research, 1993-; Director of numerous research projects and surveys for various organisations such as Tear Fund, Scripture Union, the Diocese of Rochester; Ansvar Survey of English Social Behaviour; English Church Census. Publications: Author and editor of numerous handbooks, papers, articles and research reports, mainly in the fields of theology, social issues, Christian outreach and Christian research; titles include UK Christian Handbook, 15 issues as editor, from 1973-2004; Religious Trends, Numbers 1-4, 1997-2004; The Tide is Running Out, 2000; Steps to the Future, 2000; Reaching and Keeping Tweenagers, 2003; Turning the Tide, 2002; Scottish Church Census, 2003; Coming Up Trumps! 4 Ways into the Future, 2004; An Introduction to Church Statistics, 2004. Memberships: Numerous professional and denominational affiliations, including Member of the Evangelical Alliance Council, 1994-2000; Council of Reference Member, Deo Gloria Trust, 1990-2000; Member, the General and Executive Councils of the British Councils of the British Church Growth Association, 1984-2003; Social Research Association, 1978-80; Institute of Charity Fundraising Managers 1980-82; Institute of Management, 1985-87, 1991-97; Association and Research Centres in the Social Sciences, 1996-2001. Address: 37 Blyth Wood Park, Bromley, Kent, BR1 3TN, England. E-mail: admin@christian-research.org.uk

BRIERS Richard David, b. 14 January 1934, Merton, England. Actor. m. Ann Davies, 1957, 2 daughters. Education: Royal Academy of Dramatic Art. Creative Works: Stage roles include: Arsenic and Old Lace, 1965; Relatively Speaking, 1966; The Real Inspector Hound, 1968; Cat Among the Pigeons, 1969; The Two of Us, 1970; Butley, 1972; Absurd Person Singular, 1973; Absent Friends, 1975; Middle Age Spread, 1979; The Wild Duck, 1980; Arms and the Man, 1981; Run for Your Wife, 1983; Why Me?, 1985; The Relapse, 1986; Twelfth Night, 1987; King Lear, 1990; Midsummer Night's Dream, 1990; Coriolanus, 1991; Uncle Vanya, 1991; Home, 1994; A Christmas Carol, 1996; The Chairs, 1997; Spike, 1999; Bedroom Farce, 2002. Films: Henry V, 1988; Much Ado About Nothing, 1992; Swan Song, 1993; Mary Shelley's Frankenstein, 1995; In the Bleak Midwinter, 1995; Hamlet, 1996; Love's Labours Lost, 1999; Unconditional Love, 2000; Television series include: Brother-in-Law; Marriage Lines; The Good Life; OneUpManShip; The Other One; Norman Conquests; Ever-Decreasing Circles; All in Good Faith,; Monarch of the Glen. Publications: Natter Natter, 1981; Coward and Company, 1987; A Little Light Weeding, 1993; A Taste of the Good Life, 1995. Address: Hamilton Asper Management, Ground Floor, 24 Hanway Street, London W1P 9DD, England.

BRIGGS Freda, b. 12 December 1930, Huddersfield, UK. Emeritus Professor of Child Development. m. Kenneth, 1 son, 1 daughter, deceased. Appointments: Director, Early Childhood Education, State College, Victoria, 1976-80; Foundation Dean, de Lissa Institute of Early Childhood and Family Studies, University of South Australia, Adelaide, 1980; Senior Lecturer, Child Development; Early Childhood Teacher, Social Worker, (England); Board Member, Children's Education Assistance Department Veterans' Affairs, 1996-2002; Consultant, Department of Education, New South Wales, 1997-; New Zealand Police and Education Ministry, 1985-; Consultant to Education authorities in Spain, Germany, Brazil; Police Consultant, States of Victoria, Queensland and Western Australia, 1985-93; Singapore, 2001; Professor, University of South Australia, 1991-2002. Publications: 13 books and numerous papers and articles published in the fields of educator, child development and child protection, including Themselves, Child Protection: A Guide for Teachers and Childcare Professionals; The Early Years of School – Teaching and Learning (with GK Potter), 1990; Teaching Children to Protect Themselves, 2000. Honours: Citation for Research and Advice, New Zealand Police Authority, the only civilian ever to receive one; Inaugural Australian Humanitarian Award, for services to children in developing countries, and pioneering, non-medical research and education for combating child abuse, 1998; University Chancellor's Community Service Award, 2000, 2001; Senior Australian of the Year Award, 2000; Centenary Medal for outstanding service to the nation in child protection, 2003 . Memberships: Several Government working parties relating to child abuse. Address: 17 Marola Avenue, Rostrevor, SA 5073, Australia. E-mail: freda.briggs@unisa.edu.au

BRIGGS Raymond Redvers, b. 18 January 1934, Wimbledon, London, England. Illustrator; Writer; Cartoonist. m. Jean T Clark, 1963, deceased 1973. Education: Wimbledon School of Art; Slade School of Fine Art, London, NDD; DFA; FSIAD. Appointments: Freelance illustrator, 1957-; Children's author, 1961-. Publications: Midnight Adventure, 1961; Ring-a-Ring o'Roses, 1962; The Strange House, 1963; Sledges to the Rescue, 1963; The White Land, 1963; Fee Fi Fo Fum, 1964; The Mother Goose Treasury, 1966; Jim and the Beanstalk, 1970; The Fairy Tale Treasury, 1975; Fungus the Bogeyman, 1977; The Snowman, 1978; Gentleman Jim, 1980; When the Wind Blows, 1982, stage and radio versions, 1983; The Tinpot Foreign General & the Old Iron Woman, 1984; Unlucky Wally, 1987; Unlucky Wally, Twenty Years On, 1989;

The Man, 1992; The Bear 1994; Ethel and Ernest, 1998. Honours: Kate Greenaway Medals, 1966, 1973; British Academy of Film and Television Arts Award; Francis Williams Illustration Awards, V & A Museum, 1982; Broadcasting Press Guild Radio Award, 1983. Memberships: Royal Society of Literature; Society of Authors. Address: Weston, Underhill Lane, Westmeston, Near Hassocks, Sussex BN6 8XG, England.

BRIGHTMAN Sarah. Singer; Actress. Career: Dancer with Hot Gossip and Pan's People; Stage roles include: Cats; Requiem; the Phantom of the Opera; Aspects of Love (all music by Andrew Lloyd Webber); I and Albert; The Nightingale; The Merry Widow; Trelawney of the Wells; Relative Values; Dangerous Obsession; The Innocents. Concerts include: Barcelona Olympic Games, 1992; Recordings include: 5 Top Ten singles; Eden, album, 1999. Address: c/o JAA, 2 Goodwins Court, London WC2N 4LL, England.

BRINAR Vesna, b. 20 September 1943, Zagreb, Croatia. Professor of Neurology. 1 son, 1 daughter. Education: School of Medicine, 1962-69, Specialist Exam in Neurology and Psychiatry, Zagreb University Hospital Centre, 1974, Postgraduate Study, Experimental Biology, School of Mathematics and Biology, 1972-74, University of Zagreb; Master's Degree, Experimental Biology and Medicine, 1978; Doctoral Thesis, 1980; Habilitation, 1985, School of Medicine, Zagreb; Postdoctoral Clinical and Scientific Training, Charlottenburg Hospital, Medical School of West Berlin, Germany, 1986; Postdoctoral Meeting, St Thomas's Hospital, London, 1988. Appointments include: Professor of Neurology, 1988, Chair of Neurology, 1990-99, 2000-, School of Medicine, University of Zagreb; Clinical Neurologist, 1974-, Head of the Division for Intensive Care and Cerebrovascular Disorders, 1980-92, Head of Division for Autonomic Brain Disorders, 1992-97, Head of Division for Autonomic Nervous Diseases, Vertigo and Ataxia, 1997-, Department of Neurology, University Hospital Centre, Zagreb; President, Organisation Committee, 29th International Danube Symposium, Dubrovnik, Croatia, 1997; Organiser, 2 International Conferences on Multiple Sclerosis, Dubrovnik, 2001, 2003; Invited speaker at many international and domestic conferences; Principal Investigator, Scientific Project: Diagnosis and therapy of the demyelinating diseases, Ministry of Science and Technology, Republic of Croatia, 2001. Publications: 20 articles and 16 abstracts in journals referred in current contents; 43 articles and 55 abstracts in other scientific journals; Books and teaching texts include: Emergencies in Neurology and Brian Death, 1989, 1992; Propeduetical Neurology, 1992; Neurology, 1994; Examination in Neurology, 1999. Honours: Award For Scientific and Practical Work, 1985, Award, Department of Neurology, 1986, University Hospital Centre, Zagreb; Award, Croatian medical Association, 1999. Memberships include: Representative for Croatia, EFNS Scientific panel in Neuroimmunology; Royal Society of Medicine, London; Managing Board, International Danube Symposiums, 1995-; Croatian Neurological Society; Croatian Medical Chamber; Croatian Medical Association; Chairman MS Research Association. Address: Department of Neurology, University Hospital Centre Zagreb, School of Medicine, University of Zagreb, Kišpatićeva 12, 10 000 Zagreb, Croatia. E-mail: vesna.brinar@zg.tel.hr Website: http://salata.mef.hr

BRINK Nils Erik, b. 27 November 1921, Färila, Helsingland, Sweden. Honourable Professor. m. Greta Broborg, divorced, 1 son, 1 daughter, deceased. Education: Student Examination, Hudiksvall, 1943; Cadet School, 1945; Agronomist, 1949, LicAgr, 1954, DrAgr, 1962, Agricultural College of Sweden and Swedish University of Agricultural Science, Upsala; Mathematics, Upsala University, 1950-52. Appointments: Teacher, Agricultural School,

Abra, 1948-49; Teacher in Hydrotechnics, 1949-87, including Mathematics and Hydrology, 1963-69, Docent, Assistant Professor, 1962-87, Agricultural College, Upsala; Conscript Officer, 1951-69 Teacher in Hydrology, Technical High School, Stockholm, 1945-59; Head of the Board of Health, Upsala, 1969-72. Publications: More than 100 articles during 1950-87 in Swedish and international papers including: Streaming to and in plastic drain tubes; Self-purification of sewage water and selage juice in soils, open ditches and streams; Losses waters of nutrients and pesticides from arable land and forests; Measures to minimise losses; Composting of food waste and waste paper. Honours: Honourable Professor, 1985; International Scientist of the Year, IBC 2001; For zealous and upright conduct; Listed in Who's Who publications and biographical dictionaries. Memberships: Free Mansion; Red Cross; Swedish Society for Nature Conservation. Address: N. Parkvägen 5, S-756 45 Upsala, Sweden.

BRITNER Preston Arthur, b. 14 September 1968, Washington, DC, USA. Developmental Psychologist; Professor (Associate). m. Suzanne J La Fleur. Education: BA, Psychology, University of Miami, 1990; MA, Developmental Psychology, University of Virginia, 1993; PhD, Developmental Psychology, University of Virginia, 1996. Appointments: Assistant Professor of Psychology, Smith College, 1996-97; Assistant Professor of Family Studies, 1997-2003, Associate Professor of Family Studies, 2003-, University of Connecticut. Publications: Book: Preventing Child Abuse and Neglect Through Parent Education, 1997; Associate Editor, The Journal of Primary Prevention, 2002-; Numerous journal articles, book chapters and presentations. Honours: Teaching Fellow, University of Connecticut, 2003-04; Raven Society; Iron Arrow; Phi Beta Kappa. Memberships: Sigma Xi; American Psychological Society; Society for Research in Child Development. Address: School of Family Studies, University of Connecticut Unit-2058, Storrs, CT 06269-2058, USA.

BRKANOVIĆ Željko, b. 20 December 1937, Zagreb, Croatia. Composer; Conductor; Professor. m. Ivanka, 27 September 1964, 1 son, 1 daughter. Education: Music School, 10 years; Zagreb Music Academy (piano); Skopje Music Academy (composition); Academia Chigiana, Siena (Italy); High School Stuttgart (Germany). Appointments: Debut: First string quartet in Zagreb, 1974; Conductor, Croatian National Theatre Opera, Split and Zagreb, 1963-69; Musical Editor on radio and television, 1969-80; Professor, Music Academy in Zagreb, 1980-. Compositions: Nomos, Suite for strings, Ricercari, Two Symphonies; Concerto for violin; Concerto for piano and orchestra; Concerto for violin, violoncello and orchestra; Lyrical Concerto for piano and orchestra; Concerto for percussion and 3 clarinets; Concerto Ronda for piano, wind and brass orchestra; Chamber; Piano; Organ music. Recordings: Tonal Sonata, 1977; Divertimento for strings, 1977; Concerto for piano and orchestra, 1981; Concerto for violin, 1983; Antependium, 1989; Second Symphony, 1991; Figures, 1995; Songbook, 1996; Author: CDs, 1996 and 2002. Publications: Professor Dr E Karkoschka, Stuttgart, 1991; Bilten/Croatian Composers' Society, 1992. Contributions to: Schweinfurtische Nachrichten, Vjesnik Zagreb, Vecernji list Zagreb, Slobodna Dalmacija Split, Piano Journal No 49 London, p 46, 1992, Cantus Zagreb 2003, Frankfurter Allgemeine Zeitung, 2003. Honours: Josip Slavenski Award for Concerto for piano and prchestra, 1983; Award by the Ministry of Culture for Concerto for percussion and clarinets, 1997; Vladimir Nazor Award for a concert, 2003. Membership: Croatian Composers' Society. Address: Trg kralja Tomislava 18, 10000 Zagreb, Croatia. E-mail: ivanka.brkanovic@inet.hr

BROADBENT Dennis Elton, b. 6 February 1945, Price, Utah, USA. Psychologist; Director. m. Helen McRae, 1 son, 4 daughters. Education: BS, Psychology, Brigham Young University, 1972; MS,

Education and Developmental Psychology, Florida State University, 1973; PhD, Clinical and Behaviour Therapy, School Psychology, Florida State University, 1979; Diplomate Forensic, Clinical Psychology, American Board of Psychological Specialties, 1999; Diplomate, Mental Health, 2001; Fellow, American Association of Integrative Medicine, 2001. Appointments include: Publisher, Psychological and Family Health Notes, 1983-; Director, Psychological and Family Health Associates, 1980-; Adjunct Professor, Glendale Community College, Glendale, Arizona, 1980-84; Private Clinical, Counselling, Consultant and School Psychologist, Psychological and Family Health Associates, Phoenix, Arizona, 1980-; Executive Director, Family Resource Center, 1980-; Director, Family Resource Center Charities, 1993-96; Director, The Southwest Institute for Behavioral Studies, 1986-; General Partner, The Family Resource Center, 1983-. Publications include: The Great Plan of Happiness, submitted for review; Teaching Values in Arizona Schools, 1990; Behavioral Marriage, Family, and Sexual Counseling: Principles and Techniques, submitted for publication. Honours include: Full University Scholarship, College of Eastern Utah, Brigham Young University; Forensics and Music Awards; Magna Cum Laude, Brigham Young University. Memberships: American Psychological Association; National Council on Family Relations; American College of Forensic Examiners; American Association of Integrative Medicine. Address: 3101 W Peoria Avenue Ste B309, Phoenix, AZ 85029-5210, USA.

BRODKEY Robert, b. 14 September 1928, Los Angeles, California, USA. Professor Emeritus. m. (1) Martha E Mahr, 22 December 1958, (2) Carolyn E Patch, 6 December 1975. Education: Associate of Arts, San Fran City College, 1948; Bachelor of Chemistry, University of California, 1950; MS, ChE, 1950; PhD, ChE, University of Wisconsin, 1952. Appointments: Chemical Engineer, E I Du Pont de Nemours and Co, 1950; Chemical Engineer, Esso Research and Engineering Co, 1952-56; Research Chemical Engineer, Esso Standard Oil Co, 1956-57; Assistant Professor, Department of Chemical Engineering, Ohio State University, 1957-60; Associate Professor, 1960-64; Professor, 1964-92; Emeritus Professor, 1992-. Publications: 45 publications, Fundamental Turbulent Fluid Flow; 27 publications, Mixing; 15 publications, Rheology; 10 publications, Two phase flow; 30 additional publications; Textbooks; reviews; The Phenomena of Fluid Motions; Transport Phenomena, A Unified Approach. Honours: Chemical Engineering Lectureship Award; Senior Research Award, College of Engineering; Senior Research Award, American Society of Engineering Education; Alexander von Humboldt Senior US Scientist Award; Distinguished Senior Research Award, Ohio State University; Visiting Professor Award, Japan Society for the Promotion of Science; Sigma Xi; Phi Lambda Upsilon; Alpha Gamma Sigma; Phi Beta Delta; many others. Memberships: American Physics Society; American Institute of Chemical Engineers; American Association for the Advancement of Science; American Institute of Chemists; Society of Rheology; Society of Engineering Sciences. Address: Department of Chemical Engineering, 121 Koffolt Lab, 140 West 19th Avenue, Columbus, OH 43210-1180, USA.

BROMSEN Maury Austin, b. 25 April 1919, New York, New York, USA. Bibliographer; Historian; Antiquarian Bookseller. Education: BSS Degree, cum laude with honours in History, College of the City of New York, 1939; MA, History, University of California, Berkeley, 1941; MA, Harvard University, 1945; Honorary LHD, Northeastern University, 1987. Appointments: Tutor, History Department, College of City of New York, 1941; Visiting Professor, Catholic University of Chile, 1952; Instructor, History, College of the City of New York, 1943-44; Editor and Director of Office of Bibliography, Pan American Union, (now

OAS), 1950-53; Proprietor and Director, The Maury A Bromsen Company, Dealers in Rare Books, Manuscripts and Fine Arts, 1954-. Publications: Founding Editor, Inter-American Review of Bibliography, 1951-2001; José Toribio Medina: Humanist of the Americas, 1960, translated into Spanish 1968; Simon Bolivar: A Bicentennial Tribute, 1983. Honours: Phi Beta Kappa; Academia Nacional de la Historia, Argentina; Colonial Society of Massachusetts; Sociedad de Bibliofilos Argentinos; Sociedad de Bibliofilos Chilenos; Boston Public Library's Honorary Curator, Latin American Collections; Honorary Curator and Bibliographer of the John Carter Brown Library; The President's Medal, Brown University, 2003. Memberships: Antiquarian Booksellers Association of America; Endowed the Maury A Bromsen – Simon Bolivar Room, John Carter Brown Library, 1999; Bibliographical Society of America; Charter Member, Manuscript Society; Latin American Studies Association; Conference on Latin American History; Life Member, Filson Club; Member, Countway Library of Medicine's Rare Books and Special Collections Subcommittee, Harvard Medical School, 2003. Address: 770 Boylston Street, Suite 23-F, Boston MA 02199, USA.

BRONKAR Eunice Dunalee (Connor), b. 8 August 1934, New Lebanon, Ohio, USA. Visual Artist; Teacher. m. Charles William Bronkar, 1 daughter. Education: BFA, Wright State University, Dayton, Ohio, 1971; M Art Ed, with WSU and teacher certification, 1983; Additional studies, Dayton Art Institute, 1972, Wright State University, 1989; Participation in 12 workshops, 1972-93. Appointments: Part-time Teacher, Springfield Museum of Art, 1967-77; Education Chairman, 1973-74; Lead Teacher, Commercial Art Program, Clark State Community College, Springfield, Ohio, 1984-94; Assistant Professor Rank, 1989; Adjunct Instructor, 1974-84; Adjunct Assistant Professor, 1998-2000; Numerous solo exhibitions; Juried exhibitions: Over 100 national, regional, state and area shows; Cleaned and restored art collections: Seven public and numerous private collections; Advisory Board, Clark County Joint Vocational Commercial Art Program. Publications: Work featured in American Artist Renown, 1981; Catalogues and magazines. Honours: Teacher Excellence Award, Clark State community College, 1992; Over 50 art awards at exhibitions including 3 Best of Shows; 2 commissioned portraits, Continental Hall, Washington DC. Memberships include: Pastel Society of America; Allied Artists of America; National Museum of Women in the Arts; Ohio Watercolor Society; Portrait Society of America. Commissions and Creative Works: Work in public and private collections in Massachusetts, New Mexico, New York, Ohio and others, Athens, Greece, Jerusalem and Jaffa, Israel; Commissioned portraits.

BRØNNUM Jakob, b. 16 April 1959, Copenhagen, Denmark. Author; Editor. m. Anette, 1 son. Education: Master of Theology. Appointments: Chairman, Prose Section of Danish Writer's Association, 1984-2002; Chairman, Baltic Writers Council, 1999-2002; Editor, Praesteforeningens Blad, 1997-; Essays and Lectures on Løgstrup, Kierkegaard and Dostoevky. Publications: 3 novels: Den Lange Søndag, 1984; Mørke, 1986; Kun Sig Selv, 2004; 5 collections of poetry, including: Brød og Bøn, 1993; Europadigte, 1992, 1997; Kulturhistoriske Årstal, 2001, Norwegian translation, 2003; Poetry in magazines and anthologies in Sweden, Russia and Finland. Address: Dråbydalen 30, DK-8400 Ebeltoft, Denmark. Website: www.litteratursiden.dk/sw1942asp

BRONZETTI Giorgio Luigi, b. 15 April 1939, Gavorrano, Italy. Biologist; Professor. m. Carla Bracali, 1 son, 1 daughter. Education: PhD in Biology and Pharmacology; Degree in Biology and Pharmacology. Appointments: Head of Mutagenisis Department; Professor in Toxicology. Publications: 200 publications in international journals; 5 books. Memberships: Various commissions. Address: Research Area Centre, Pisa, Italy. E-mail: g.bronzetti@imd.pi.cnr.it

BROOKE Peter Leonard (Lord Brooke of Sutton Mandeville), b. 3 March 1934, London. Peer; Legislator. m. Lindsay Allinson, 3 sons (by first late wife). Education: MA (Oxon), Balliol College, Oxford, 1953-57; MBA, Harvard Business School. Appointments: Royal Engineers, 1952-53; Research Associate, IMEDE, Lausanne, Switzerland, 1960-61; Spencer Stuart Management Consultants, 1971-79 (Chairman, 1974-79); MP for the Cities of London and Westminster (Westminster South till 1997), 1977-2001; Government Whip and Assistant Government Whip, 1979-83; Parliamentary Secretary, Department of Education and Science, 1983-85, Minister of State, HM Treasury, 1985-87; Paymaster General, 1987-89; Chairman of the Conservative Party, 1987-89; Secretary of State for Northern Ireland, 1989-92; Secretary of State for National Heritage, 1992-94; Chairman, Select Committee on Northern Ireland Affairs, 1997-2001; Appointed to House of Lords in Dissolution Honours, 2001. Honours: Senior Fellow, Royal College of Art, 1987; Member of the Privy Council, 1988; Presentation Fellow, King's College, London, 1989; Companion of Honour, 1992; Honorary Fellow, Queen Mary Westfield, 1996; Hon D Litt, University of Westminster, 1999; Hon D Litt, London Guildhall University, 2001; Trustee, 1974-2001, Fellow, 2002, The Wordsworth Trust. Memberships: Fellow of the Society of Antiquaries; President, British Antique Dealers Association, 1995-; President, British Art Market Federation, 1996-; Pro-Chancellor and Chairman, Council, of the University of London, 2002-. Address: House of Lords, London SW1A 0PW, England.

BROOKNER Anita, b. 16 July 1928, London, England. Novelist; Art Historian. Education: BA, King's College, London; PhD, Courtauld Institute of Art, London. Appointments: Visiting Lecturer in Art History, University of Reading, 1959-64; Lecturer, 1964-77, Reader in Art History, 1977-88, Courtauld Institute of Art; Slade Professor of Art, Cambridge University, 1967-68. Publications: Fiction: A Start in Life, 1981; Providence, 1982; Look at Me, 1983; Hotel du Lac, 1984; Family and Friends, 1985; A Misalliance, 1986; A Friend from England, 1987; Latecomers, 1988; Lewis Percy, 1989; Brief Lives, 1990; A Closed Eye, 1991; Fraud, 1992; A Family Romance, 1993; A Private View, 1994; Incidents in the Rue Laugier, 1995; Visitors, 1998; Undue Influence, 1999; The Bay of Angels, 2000. Non-Fiction: An Iconography of Cecil Rhodes, 1956; J A Dominique Ingres, 1965; Watteau, 1968; The Genius of the Future: Studies in French Art Criticism, 1971; Greuze: The Rise and Fall of an Eighteenth-Century Phenomenon, 1972; Jacques-Louis David, a Personal Interpretation: Lecture on Aspects of Art, 1974; Jacques-Louis David, 1980, revised edition, 1987. Editor: The Stories of Edith Wharton, 2 volumes, 1988, 1989. Contributions to: Books and periodicals. Honours: Fellow, Royal Society of Literature, 1983; Booker McConnell Prize, National Book League, 1984; Commander of the Order of the British Empire, 1990. Address: 68 Elm Park Gardens, London SW10 9PB, England.

BROOKS Andree Nicole Aelion, b. 2 February 1937, London, England. Journalist; Author; Lecturer; Columnist; Educator. m. Ronald J Brooks, 19 August 1959, divorced 1984, 1 son, 1 daughter. Education: Queens College, London, 1952; Journalism Certificate, 1958. Appointments: Adjunct Professor, Fairfield University, 1982-87; Contributing Columnist, New York Times, 1979-95; Associate Fellow, Yale University, 1989-; President, Founder, Womens Campaign School, Yale University; Director, "Out of Spain" a Jewish Sephardic History Curriculum Project, 1998-2000. Publications: Books: Children of Fast Track Parents, 1988; The Woman who Defied Kings, biography, 2002; Russian Dance, 2004.

Contributions to: Over 3000 Articles in Newspapers, Magazines and Journals. Honours: Best Non Fiction Book of Year, National Association of Press Women, USA, 1990; Finalist, National Jewish Book Awards, 2003; Over 30 other Journalism Awards. Address: 15 Hitchcock Road, Westport, CT 06880, USA.

BROOKS (Troyal) Garth, b. 7 February 1962, Tulsa, Oklahoma, USA. Country Music Singer; Songwriter; Musician (guitar). m. Sandra Mahl, 1986, 2 daughters. Education: BS, Journalism and Advertising, Oklahoma State University, 1985. Career: Television specials include: This Is Garth Brooks, 1992; This Is Garth Brooks Too!, 1994; Garth Brooks - The Hits, 1995; Garth Brooks Live in Central Park, 1997; Best selling country album ever, No Fences (over 13 million copies). Recordings: Albums: Garth Brooks, 1989; No Fences, 1990; Ropin' The Wind, 1991; The Chase, 1992; Beyond The Season, 1992; In Pieces, 1993; The Hits, 1994; Fresh Horses, 1995; Sevens, 1997; In The Life Of Chris Gaines, 1999; The Colors Of Christmas, 1999; Scarcrow, 2001; Singles: If Tomorrow Never Comes, 1989; Tour EP, 1994; To Make You Feel My Love, 1998; One Heart At A Time, 1998; Lost In You, 1999. Honours: Grammy Award; CMA Horizon Award, Video of the Year, 1990; CMA Awards: Best Single, Best Album 1991; Music City News/TNN Award, Video of Year, 1991; CMA Entertainer of the Year, 1991-92; Numerous ACM Awards include: Music Entertainer of the Year, 1991-94, Best Single 1991, Best Album 1991; ASCAP Voice of Music Award, 1992; 9 People's Choice Awards; Top-selling solo artist in American music history; RIAA. Memberships: Inducted into Grand Ole Opry; ASCAP; CMA; ACM. Current Management: c/o Scott Stern, GB Management Inc, 1111 17th Avenue South, Nashville, TN 37212, USA.

BROOKS James, b. 11 October 1938, West Cornforth, County Durham, UK. Consultant; Academic. m. Jan, 1 son, 1 daughter. Education: BTech(Hons), Applied Chemistry, 1964; MPhil, Analysis of wool wax and related products, 1966; PhD, chemical constituents of various plant spore walls, 1970; Fellow, Geological Society (FGS), 1974; Fellow, Royal Society of Chemistry, FRSC, 1976; Chartered Chemist (CChem), 1976; DSc, research work in chemistry, geology, petroleum sciences and the origin of life, 2001; Chartered Geologist (CGeol), 2001; Chartered Scientist (CSci), 2004. Appointments: Research Geochemist, BP Research Centre, British Petroleum, 1969-75; Senior Research Fellow, University of Bradford, 1975-77; Visiting Scientist, Norwegian Continental Shelf Institute, 1975-78; Research Associate, Exploration Co-ordinator, Senior Scientist, Section Head of Production Geology, British National Oil Corporation/Britoil, 1977-86; Visiting Lecturer, University of Glasgow, 1978-99; Technical Director, Sutherland Oil and Gas Investments, 1996-98; Brooks Associates, 1986-; Chairman/Director, Petroleum Geology '86 Ltd, 1986-99; Executive Member, Scottish Baptist College, 2001-; Myron Spurgeon Visiting Professor in Geological Sciences, Ohio University, Athens, Ohio, USA, 2003; Collaborative research, teaching, professional and conference activities at numerous universities and research institutes throughout the USA, Canada, Europe, Russia and parts of Asia. Publications include: 15 books as author or editor and over 90 scientific research papers published in peer-refereed journals including: Chemical Structure of the Exine of Pollen Walls and a new function for carotenoids in nature, 1968; Chemistry and Morphology of Precambrian Microorganisms, 1973; Origin and Development of Living Systems, 1973; A Critical Assessment of the Origin of Life, 1978; Biological Relationships of Test Structure and Models for calcification and test formation in the Globigerinacea, 1979; The Chemistry of Fossils: biochemical stratigraphy of fossil plants, 1980; Organic Matter in Meteorites and Precambrian Rocks - clues about the origin of life, 1981; Origin of Life: from the first moments of the universe to the beginning of life on earth, 1985; Tectonic Controls on Oil & Gas occurrences in the Northern North Sea, 1989; Classic Petroleum Source Rocks, 1990; Cosmochemistry and Human Significance, 1999. Honours include: UK Government Exchange Scientist to USSR, 1971; Royal Society Visiting Scientist to India, 1977 and to USSR, 1991; Vice-President, Geological Society, 1984-89; Geological Society Christmas Lecture on Origin of Life, 1983; Golden Medallion and Order of Merit for book Origin of Life, 1985; Secretary, Geological Society, 1988-92; Life Member, American Association of Petroleum Geologists, 1993-; Distinguished Achievement Award, AAPG, 1993; Distinguished Service Award, The Geological Society, 1999; President of the Baptist Union of Scotland, 2002; First holder of Myron Sturgeon Visiting Professor in Geological Sciences, Ohio University, 2003. Memberships: International IPU Committee, 1972-81; NERC Higher Degrees Research Committee, 1981-84; UK Consultative Committee on Geological Sciences, 1987-92; External Examiner, University of London, 1992-97; Series Editor, Geological Special Publications, 1989-93; International Editorial Board of Marine and Petroleum Geology, 1984-96; Council of Geological Society, 1984-92; Chairman, Shawlands Academy School Board, 1991-96; Board of Ministry of the Baptist Union of Scotland, 1998-. Address: 10 Langside Drive, Newlands, Glasgow, G43 2EE, UK. E-mail: jim_brooks@ntlworld.com

BROOKS Mel (Melvin Kaminsky), b. 1926, New York, USA. Actor; Writer; Producer; Director. m. (1) Florence Baum, 2 sons, 1 daughter, (2) Ann Bancroft, 1964, 1 son. Appointments: Script Writer, TV Series, Your Show of Shows, 1950-54, Caesar's Hour, 1954-57, Get Smart, 1965; Founder, Feature Film Production Company, Brooksfilms. Creative Works: Films include: The Critic (cartoon), 1963; The Producers, 1968; The Twelve Chairs, 1970; Blazing Saddles, 1974; Young Frankenstein, 1974; Silent Movie, 1976; High Anxiety, 1977; The Elephant Man (producer), 1980; History of the World Part I, 1981; My Favourite Year (producer), 1982; To Be or Not to Be (actor, producer), 1983; Fly I, 1986; Spaceballs, 1987; 84 Charing Cross Road, 1987; Fly II, 1989; Life Stinks (actor, director, producer), 1991; Robin Hood: Men in Tights, 1993; Dracula: Dead and Loving It, 1995; Svitati, 1999; It's A Very Merry Muppet Christmas Movie (Voice), 2002; Jakers! The Adventures of Piggley Winks (TV Series), 2003. Musical: The Producers: The New Mel Brooks Musical (producer, co-writer, composer), 2001. Honours: Academy Awards, 1964, 1968. Address: c/o The Culver Studios, 9336 West Washington Boulevard, Culver City, CA 90232, USA.

BRORSON Hakan, b. 20 June 1953, Växjö, Sweden. Plastic Surgeon; Orthopaedic Surgeon. m. Karin, 3 sons. Education: Physician, 1971; MB, Lund University, 1974; Swedish Medical Degree, 1979; Specialist, Orthopaedic Surgery, Sweden, 1987, Plastic Surgery, Sweden, 1990; Physician, Norway, 1994; Specialist, Orthopaedic Surgery, Norway, 1995, Plastic Surgery, Norway, 1995. Appointments: Consultant Plastic Surgeon, Department of Plastic and Reconstructive Surgery, Malmö, University Hospital, Hässleholm Hospital, Sweden, Trondheim University Hospital, Norway, 1998; President, XXIV European group of Lymphology Congress, Malmö, Sweden, 2003. Publications: Numerous articles in professional medical journals. Honours include: 1st Prize, Best Paper, Swedish Society of Medicine, Stockholm, 1994; 1st Prize, Best Paper, Nordic Society of Plastic Surgery, Stockholm, 1996; Presidential Prize, 16th International Congress on Lymphology, Madrid, Spain, 1997; 1st Prize, Best Paper, European Association of Plastic Surgeons, Verona, Italy, 1998; Awarded the Tegger's Research Award, 1999; 1st Prize, Best Poster, Swedish Society of Medicine, Stockholm, 2000. Memberships include: Swedish Society of Medicine; Scientific secretary, Swedish Association of Plastic Surgeons;

International Society of Lymphology; International Confederation for Plastic, Reconstructive and Aesthetic Surgery; National Delegate, European Association of Plastic Surgeons; European Group of Lymphology. Address: Malmö University Hospital, Department of Plastic and Reconstructive Surgery, SE-20502 Malmö, Sweden.

BROSNAN Pierce, b. 16 May 1953, Navan, County Meath, Ireland. Actor. m. (1) Cassandra Harris, deceased, 1 son, (2) Keely Shaye Smith, 2001, 2 sons. Education: Drama Centre. Creative Works: Stage appearances include: Wait Until Dark; The Red Devil; Sign; Filumenia. TV appearances include: Detective, Remington Steele (series); Noble House (NBC mini-series); Nancy Astor; Around the World in Eighty Days; The Heist; Murder 101; Victim of Love; Live Wire; Death Train; Robinson Crusoe, 1994; The James Bond Story, 1999. Films: The Mirror Crack'd; The Long Good Friday; Nomads; The Fourth Protocol; Taffin; The Deceivers; Mister Johnson; The Lawnmower Man; Mrs Doubtfire; Love Affair; Robinson Crusoe; Mars Attacks!; The Mirror Has Two Faces; Dante's Peak; The Nephew, 1998; The Thomas Crown Affair, 1999; Grey Owl, 2000; The Tailor of Panama, 2001; Evelyn, 2003; Law of Attraction, 2004; Role of James Bond in Goldeneye 1994, Tomorrow Never Dies 1997, The World is Not Enough 1999; Die Another Day, 2002

BROSS Irwin D, b. 13 November 1921, Halloway, Ohio, USA. Biostatistician. m. Rida S Singer, 7 August 1949, 2 sons, 1 daughter. Education: BA, University of California at Los Angeles, 1942; MA, North Carolina State University, 1949; PhD, University of North Carolina, 1949. Publications: Design for Decision, 1953; Scientific Strategies in Human Affairs: To Tell the Truth Exposition, 1975; Scientific Strategies to Save Your Life, 1981; Crimes of Official Science, 1988; Others: A History of US Science and Medicine in the Cold War, 1996. Contributions to: Author, Co-Author of more than 350 publications; Biostatistics, Cancer Research and Public Health. Address: 109 Maynard Drive, Amherst, NY 14226, USA.

BROUSSINA Larissa, b. 29 September 1939, Moscow, Russia. Immunologist; Homeopath. m. Leonid Broussine, 1 son, 1 daughter. Education: Doctors Diploma, First Medical University named after Sechenov, Moscow, 1967; Postgraduate Course, Immunology Department, Institute of Vaccines and Serums, Moscow, 1976; Certificate in Homeopathy, Medical University named after Semashko, 1990; EAV, Russian Society of Electroacupuncture, 1991. Appointments: Scientist, Allergy Department, Institute of Vaccines and Serum, 1967; Senior Scientific Employee, Institute of Psychiatry, 1981-86; Chief of the Research Department of the Clinical Immunology Laboratory, Medical University of Sechenov, 1986-95; Senior Lecturer in Homeopathy, Institute of Medico-biological and Extreme Problems, 1995-. Publications: Reactivity of Neuralgia subject to experimental allergy encephalomyelitis; Textbooks: Method of breaking of migration of glia, 1976; Method of swelling glia to define the autoimmunologic reactions, 1993; 78 scientific articles in academic journals. Honour: Honorary Medal, Society of Therapeutics, South Korea, 1995. Memberships: International Scientific Board, Academy of International Sciences, San Marino; Russian Society of EAV. Address: fl 7, h 56, Junih Lenincev, Moscow 109443, Russia. E-mail: any_brusina@hotmail.com

BROWN Alexander Claude, b. 19 August 1931, Cape Town, South Africa. Marine Biologist. m. Rosalind Roberts, 5 July 1959, 3 sons. Education: PhD, 1969; DSc, 1979. Appointments: Lecturer; Senior Lecturer, University of Cape Town, 1954-68; Professor, Zoology, 1969-96; Emeritus Professor, 1997, Director, 1997-2000, Center for Marine Studies. Publications: 200 science papers in

Dictionary of International Biography

professional journals, 5 books including: Ecology of Sandy Shores. Honours: Life Fellow, University of Cape Town, 1974; Distinguished Teacher Award, 1981; Gold Medal, Zoological Society of South Africa, 1986; Gilchrist Gold Medal, 1996. Memberships: Fellow, Royal Society of South Africa; Zoological Society of South Africa. Address: Zoology Department, University of Cape Town, Rondebosch 7701, South Africa.

BROWN Bob, b. 27 December 1944, Oberon, New South Wales, Australia. Australian Greens Senator. Education: Medicine, University of Sydney, 1968. Appointments: Medical Practice, Canberra, London, Sydney, Perth, Launceston, -1980; Candidate, United Tasmania Group, 1975; Director, The Wilderness Society, 1979-84; Elected to House of Assembly, 1983; Leader, five Green independents, formed accord with Labor Party, 1989-92; Founding President, Australian Bush Heritage Fund, 1990; Formation of the Australian Greens, 1992; Extensive tours of Australian cities and towns as Australian Greens national spokesperson, 1994-96; Elected to the Senate as first Australian Greens Senator; Re-elected to Australian Senate, 2001. Honours: Australian of the Year, The Australian Newspaper, 1983; UNEP Global 500 Award, 1987; Goldman Environmental Prize, USA, 1990; World's Most Inspiring Politician Award, BBC Wildlife Magazine, 1996; Republican of the Year, Australian Republic Party, 1997; Inaugural Bob Dent, Euthanasia Campaigner of the Year Award from Phillip Nitschke, 1997; Voted Australian Living Treasure, National Trust, 1998. Address: Parliament House, Canberra, ACT 2600, Australia. E-mail: senator.brown@aph.gov.au

BROWN James, b. 3 May 1928, Barnwell, South Carolina, USA. Soul Singer; Broadcasting Executive. m. (1) Deidre Jenkins, (2) Adrienne Brown (deceased 1996). Career: Singer with, then leader of own backing group Famous Flames, 1956-68; Solo performer, recording artist, 1969-; President, JB Broadcasting Ltd, 1968-; James Brown Network, 1968-; Film appearances include: Ski Party, 1964; Come To The Table, 1974; The Blues Brothers, 1980; Concerts include: The Biggest Show Of Stars tour, 1963; The TAMI Show, 1964; Newport Jazz Festival, 1969; Festival Of Hope, Garden City, 1972; Grand Ole Opry, Nashville, 1979; Montreux Jazz Festival, 1981; Coca-Cola Music Festival, Essex, 1992; Pori Jazz, Finland, 1995; Owner, several US radio stations; Co-owner, Brown Stone Records, 1992-. Compositions include: Film scores: Black Caesar, 1972; Slaughter's Big Rip Off, 1972. Recordings: Over 75 albums include: Live At The Apollo, 1963; I Can't Stand Myself, 1968; Hot Pants, 1974; The Payback, 1974; I'm Real, 1988; Universal James, 1992; Hit singles include: Please, Please, Please, 1956; Out Of Sight, 1964; Poppa's Got A Brand New Bag, 1965; It Got You (I Feel Good), 1966; It's A Man's Man's Man's World, 1966; Cold Sweat, 1967; I Got The Feelin', 1968; Say It Loud, 1968; Give It Up Or Turn It Loose, 1969; Get Up, I Feel Like Being A Sex Machine, 1970; Super Bad, 1970; Get On The Good Foot, 1972; Get Up Offa That Thing, 1976; Living In America (used in film Rocky IV), 1986; I'm Real, 1988; Soul Jubilee, 1990; Love Over-Due, 1991; Love Power Peace, 1992; Funky Christmas, 1995; Hookedonbrown, 1996; Say It Live And Loud, 1998; On Stage Live, 1999. Honours: Inducted, Rock'n'Roll Hall of Fame, 1986; Grammy Awards: Best R&B Recording, 1965; Best R&B Performance, 1987; 44 Gold discs; Award Of Merit, American Music Awards, 1992; NARAS Lifetime Achievement Award, 1992; Lifetime Achievement Trophy, Rhythm & Blues Foundation Pioneer Awards, 1993; Lifetime Achievement Award, National Association of Black Owned Broadcasters' Awards, 1993. Current Management: Brothers Management Associates. Address: 141 Dunbar Avenue, Fords, NJ 08863, USA.

BROWN Lawrence Michael, b 18 March 1936, Windsor, Ontario, Canada. Physicist. m. Susan Drucker, 1 son, 2 daughters. Education: BASc, Engineering Physics, University of Toronto;

PhD, Physical Metallurgy, University of Birmingham, England. Appointments: University Demonstrator, Cavendish Laboratory, Cambridge, England, 1964-67; Lecturer, 1967-83, Reader in Microstructural Physics, 1983-89, Professor of Physics, 1989-2001, Emeritus Professor, 2001-, University of Cambridge; Fellow of Robinson College, Cambridge, 1976-. Publications: Many articles in professional scientific journals including: Philosophical Magazine; Acta Materialia, Electron Microscopy and Analysis, Conference Series (Institute of Physics). Honours: Athlone Fellowship, 1957; W M Tapp Research Fellowship, Gonville and Caius College, Cambridge, 1963; Fellow of the Royal Society, 1982; Rosenhain Medal, Institute of Metals, 1980; Rupert Franklin Mehl Award, The Minerals, Metals and Materials Society, USA and the Institute of Metals UK, 1991; DSc (Cantab), 1992; Van Horn Distinguished Lecturer, Case Western Reserve University, 1994; Guthrie Medal and Prize, Institute of Physics, UK, 2000. Memberships: Fellow of the Institute of Physics; Fellow of the Institute of Materials. Address: Cavendish Laboratory, Madingley Road, Cambridge, CB3 0HE, England.

BROWN Lillie McFall, b. 29 February. Elementary School Principal. m. Charles Brown, 1 son. Education: BA, Home Economic Science, Langston University, 1956; MA, Special Education, Chicago Teachers College, 1964; MA, Administration, Seattle University, 1976. Appointments: Home Economics Teacher, Altue Separate Public Schools, 1955-56; First Grade Teacher, 1956-57; Fourth Grade Teacher, 1957-60; Middle School Teacher, Chicago Public Schools, 1960-64; Special Education Primary Teacher, Seattle Public Schools, 1966-67; Special Education Intermediate Teacher, 1967-68; Program Coordinator, 1968-71; Elementary Assistant Principal, 1971-76; Elementary Principal, 1976-. Publications: Articles to professional journals; Treas African American Alliance; Historian Wash Alliance Black School Educators; Others. Honours: Sears Foundation Grantee; Recipient Distinguished Alumni Award, National Association for Equal Opportunity in Higher Education, 1997; Chairperson, Eighteenth College Fair, Seattle, Washington, 2002; Seattle Community College for Puget Sound area, High School Juniors and Seniors; Featuring Langston University, Langston, Oklahoma; Theme, Providing Pathways to Realizing Youths' Potential. Memberships: NAACP; National Association Elementary School Principals; Association of Washington School Principals; Washington State Principals Association; Phi Delta Kappa; Kappa Delta Pi; Delta Sigma Theta. Address: 2736 34th Ave S, Seattle, WA 98144-5561, USA.

BROWN Patricia Ann Fortini, b. 16 November 1936, Oakland, California, USA. University Professor; Art Historian. m. (1) Peter Claus Meyer, May 1957, divorced 1978, 2 sons, (2) Peter Robert Lamont Brown, August 1980, divorced 1989. Education: AB, 1959, MA, 1978, PhD, 1983, University of California at Berkeley. Appointments: Assistant Professor, 1983-89, Associate Professor, 1989-91, Andrew W Mellon Professor, 1991-95, Professor, 1997-, Princeton University; Slade Professor of Fine Arts, University of Cambridge, 2001. Publications: Venetian Narrative Painting in the Age of Carpaccio, 1988; Venice and Antiquity: The Venetian Sense of the Past, 1996; The Renaissance in Venice: A World Apart, 1997; Private Lives in Renaissance Venice, 2004. Contributions to: Art History; Christian Science Monitor; Monitor Book Review; Burlington Magazine; Renaissance Quarterly; New York Times Book Review; Biography. Honours: Premio Salotto Veneto, Italy; Phyllis Goodhart Gordan Book Prize, 1998. Memberships: Renaissance Society of America; American Academy in Rome; College Art Association. Address: Department of Art and Archaeology, Princeton University, Princeton, NJ 08544-1018, USA.

Dictionary of International Biography

BROWN Sheri Lynn, b. 22 November 1968, USA. Artist; Poet; Educator. Education: BA Degree, Commercial Art and Advertising, Concord College, Athens, West Virginia, USA, 1992. Appointments: Owner T J Cool Advertising, 1992-; Writer, Hill Top Records, Hollywood, California, 2001-; Author numerous poems in anthologies. Publications: Poems published with the following: International Library of Poetry; National Library of Poetry; Poetry.com; Hill Top Records; The Poetry Guild. Honours: Bluefield High School, Senior Art Award, Honor Roll, Band, 1987; International Library of Poetry, Editor's Choice Award; National Library of Poetry, Editor's Choice Award, twice; Listed in Who's Who publications and biographical dictionaries. Memberships: Co-Drum Majorette, Bluefield Junior High School; Bluefield High School Art Club, Vice-President, 1987; Scott Street Baptist Church; House of Prayer; International Society of Poets; Concord Advertising Club, 1989-90; Band Member, University of Tennessee Honors Band. Address: 120 Russell Terrace, Bluefield, WV 24701, USA.

BROWNE Jackson, b. 9 October 1948, Heidelberg, Germany. Singer; Songwriter; Musician (guitar, piano). Career: Brief spell with Nitty Gritty Dirt Band, 1966; Solo singer, songwriter, musician, 1967-; Tours and concerts with Joni Mitchell; The Eagles; Bruce Springsteen; Neil Young; Major concerts include: Musicians United For Safe Energy (MUSE), Madison Square Garden (instigated by Browne and Bonnie Raitt), 1979; Glastonbury Festival, 1982; Montreux Jazz Festival, 1982; US Festival, 1982; Benefit concerts for: Amnesty International, Chile, 1990; Christie Institute, Los Angeles, 1990; Victims of Hurricane Inki, Hawaii, 1992; Various concerts for other environmental causes; Nelson Mandela Tributes, Wembley Stadium, 1988, 1990; Sang with Bonnie Raitt and Stevie Wonder, memorial service for Stevie Ray Vaughan, Dallas, Texas, 1990; Compositions: Songs recorded by Tom Rush; Nico; Linda Ronstadt; The Eagles; Co-writer with Glenn Frey, Take It Easy. Recordings: Albums: Jackson Browne, 1972; For Everyman, 1973; Late For The Sky, 1974; The Pretender, 1976; Running On Empty, 1978; Hold Out (Number 1, US), 1980; Lawyers In Love, 1983; Lives In The Balance, 1987; World In Motion, 1989; I'm Alive, 1993; Looking East, 1996; Also featured on No Nukes album, 1980; Sun City, Artists United Against Apartheid, 1985; For Our Children, Disney AIDS benefit album, 1991; The Next Voice You Hear: The Best of Jackson Browne, 1997; Singles include: Doctor My Eyes, 1972; Here Come Those Tears Again, 1977; Running On Empty, 1978; Stay, 1978; That Girl Could Sing, 1980; Somebody's Baby, used in film Fast Times At Ridgemont High, 1982; Tender Is The Night, 1983; You're A Friend Of Mine, with Clarence Clemons, 1986; For America, 1987. Current Management: Donald Miller, 12746 Kling Street, Studio City, CA 91604, USA.

BROWNE John Ernest Douglas de la Valette, b. 17 October 1938, Hampshire, England. Investment Banker. Education: Malvern College, 1957; Graduate, Royal Military Academy, Sandhurst, England, 1959; MSc, Cranfield Institute of Technology, 1967; MBA, Harvard Business School, USA, 1969. Appointments: Grenadier Guards, retired as Major, 1957-66; Associate, Morgan Stanley & Co, 1969-72; Associate, Pember & Boyle, 1972-74; Councillor, Westminster City Council, 1974-78; Director, Middle East Operations, European Banking Company Ltd, 1974-78; Chairman and Chief Executive Officer, Falcon Finance Management Ltd, 1978-95; Member of Parliament (Conservative), Winchester, 1979-92; Vice-President Investments, Smith Barney Inc (Citigroup Global Market Inc), 1995-. Publications: A New European Currency – The Karl Ҟ; Tarantula – An Anglo-American Special Forces Hunt for bin Laden. Honour: Officer, Order of St John. Memberships: Boodles Club; Director, Drug Free America; Fishers Island Club, New York; Fishers Island Yacht Club;

Liveryman, Goldsmiths Company; Honorary Director, Greater Palm Beach Symphony; Grenadier Guards Association; Governor, Malvern College; Governors Club, Florida; Ocean Club, Florida; Program Chairman, Palm Beach County Council on Foreign Relations; President's Country Club, Florida; Special Forces Club; Turf Club. E-mail: johnbrowne@post.harvard.edu

BROWNING (David) Peter (James), b. 29 May 1927, Glastonbury, England. Chief Education Officer. m. Eleanor Berry, 3 sons. Education: English and Modern Languages Tripos, Christ's College, Cambridge; Sorbonne; Universities of Strasbourg and Perugia. Appointments: Personal Assistant to the Vice-Chancellor, Liverpool University, 1952-56; Teacher, Willenhall Comprehensive School, 1956-59; Senior Administrative Assistant, Somerset LEA, 1959-62; Assistant Director of Education, Cumberland LEA, 1962-66; Deputy Chief Education Officer 1966-69, Chief Education Officer, 1969-73, Southampton LEA; Chief Education Officer, Bedfordshire, 1973-89. Publications: Editor: Julius Caesar for German Students, 1957; Macbeth for German Students, 1959; Contributor of articles to professional educational journals. Honours: CBE, 1984; Cavaliere, Order of Merit, Italy, 1985; Médaille d'honneur de l'Oise, 1988; Commandeur, Ordre des Palmes Académique, France, 1989. Memberships include: University Grants Committee, 1974-79; British Educational Administration Society, chairman, 1974-78; European Forum for Educational Administration, chairman, 1977-84; Board of Governors, Cambridge Institute of Education; Library Advisory Council, England, 1978-81; University of Cambridge Faculty Board of Education, 1983-92, vice chairman, 1980-89; Lancaster University Council, 1988-97, University treasurer; Director, National Educational Resources Information Service, 1988-91; Carlisle Diocesan Board of Education, 1989-97, chairman, 1995-97; Cumbria Arts in Education Trust, chairman, 1992-95; FRSA, 1981-93; Director, Wordsworth Rydal Memorial Lectures and Rydal Bach Celebrity Concerts, 1993-; Former Governor numerous schools and colleges. Address: Park Fell, Skelwith Bridge, nr Ambleside LA22 9NP, England.

BROWNLOW Kevin, b. 2 June 1938, Crowborough, Sussex, England. Author; Film Director; Former Film Editor. Publications: The Parade's Gone By, 1968; How It Happened Here, 1968; Adventures with D W Griffith, (editor), 1973; Hollywood: The Pioneers, 1979; The War, the West, and the Wilderness, 1979; Napoleon: Abel Gance's Classic Film, 1983; Behind the Mask of Innocence, 1990; David Lean - A Biography, 1996; Mary Pickford Rediscovered, 1999. Address: c/o Photoplay, 21 Princess Road, London NW1 8JR, England.

BROZOVSKY John A, b. 30 April 1951, Spokane, Washington, USA. Accounting Editor. m. Sue Ellen King, 1 son. Education: BBA, International Business, 1975, MPA, Accounting, 1978, University of Texas; PhD, Accounting, University of Colorado, 1990. Appointments: Computer Programmer, University of Texas, 1974-77; Teaching Assistant, University of Texas, 1977; Texas State Health Department, 1978-80; EDP Auditor, City of Austin, 1980-81; Senior Internal Auditor, Enserch Corporation, 1981-83; Lecturer, California State University-Fresno, 1983-86; Research/ Teaching Assistant, University of Colorado, 1986-89; Assistant Professor, 1989-1996, Associate Professor, 1996-, Virginia Tech. Publications include: Section 530 Worker Classification Relief Provisions After the Small Business Act of 1996, 1997; Some Implications of Homogenizing Restrictions on the Audit Profession: An Experimental Study, 1998; The Effect of Reputation on Audit Firm Profitability: An Experimental Study, 1999. Honours include: Several grants; ANBAR Electronic Intelligence Citation of Excellence, 1997; Lybrand Certificate of Merit, Institute of Management Accountants, 1998. Memberships: American

Dictionary of International Biography

Accounting Association; American Economic Association; American Tax Association; Institute of Management Accountants; National Tax Association. Address: Department of Accounting and Information Systems, Pamplin 3007 (0101), Virginia Tech, Blacksburg, VA 24061, USA.

BRUBAKER William Rogers, b. 8 June 1956, Evanston, Illinois, USA. m. Zsuzsa Berend, 2 sons. Education: BA, Social Studies, Harvard University, 1979; MA, Social and Political Thought, University of Sussex, 1980; PhD, Sociology, Columbia University, 1990. Appointments: Junior Fellow, Society of Fellows, Harvard University, 1988-91; Associate Professor, 1991-94, Professor of Sociology, 1994-, University of California, Los Angeles. Publications: The Limits of Rationality: An Essay on the Social and Moral Thought of Max Weber, 1984; Citizenship and Nationhood in France and Germany, 1992; Nationalism Reframed: Nationhood and the National Question in the New Europe, 1996; Ethnicity without Groups, 2004. Honours: National Science Foundation Young Investigator Award, 1994-99; MacArthur Fellowship, 1994-99; Fellow, Center for Advanced Study in the Behavioral Sciences, 1995-96; Guggenheim Fellowship, 1999-2000. Address: Department of Sociology, UCLA, Box 951551, Los Angeles, CA 90095-1551, USA.

BRÜCK Miroslav, b. 9 July 1964, Skalica, Slovakia. Polygrapher. Divorced, 1 daughter. Education: House of Polygraphy (College), 1983. Publications: Poetry books: Noc, Tráva v Pozadí, 1989; Pokusenie Verit, 1993; Nocné Ostrovy a Iné Záchrany, 1997; Interpretations in Slovak, Polish, Bulgarian, Hungarian and French; Orientacna Mapa NA Zimu, 2001. Honours: Public media awards. Memberships: Klub Nezávislych Spisovatelov (the Club of Independent Writers), 1995-. Address: Peliskova 27, 909 01 Skalica, Slovakia.

BRUEN James Arthur, b. 29 November 1943, Southampton, New York, USA. International Environmental/Products Law Specialist. m. Carol Lynn Heller, 1 son, 1 daughter. Education: Bachelor of Arts, cum laude, Claremont Men's College, 1965; Doctor of Jurisprudence, Stanford Law School, 1968. Appointments: General Attorney, Federal Communications Commission, Washington, DC, 1968-70; Assistant United States Attorney, Criminal Division, 1970-73, Assistant United States Attorney, Civil Division, 1973-75, Chief of the Civil Division, Office of the United States Attorney, 1975-77, Northern District of California, San Francisco; Partner, Landels Ripley & Diamond LLP, 1977-2000; Partner, Farella Braun & Martel LLP, 2000-. Publications: Author, co-author, contributor and editor to numerous professional journals. Honours: Listed in numerous national and international biographical dictionaries. Memberships: International Society for Environmental Epidemiology; Pratising Law Institute; American Bar Association; Chapter of the American Inn of Court; California State Bar Committee on Human Rights. Address: 235 Montgomery Street, San Francisco, CA 94104, USA. E-mail: jbruen@fbm.com

BRUESKE Charlotte I, b. 1 January 1934, Plainview Township, Minnesota, USA. Poet; Composer. Education: AA Degree, Pasadena City College, 1976; BA, California State University, 1984; Studies, Fuller Theological Seminary, Orange County, California. Publications include: Once in a Coon's Age; The Ancestors of Gottlob August Bruss and Bertha Pauline Goede; A Search for the Records of the Orphans of Danaan; Evergreen, 1990; Every New Day, 1991; Lift Up One Another, 1991; Where the Red Ferns Abound, 1995; To Touch this World by Love, 1996; Because of Love, 1997; Consider the Lillies, 1997; co-author; with J'hana Brueske, I Heard a Robin Sing Today, 1997-98; Life Friend, 1998; Where Love Abides, 1998; Anthology: To Every Life, 1998;

Poems of the Seasons, 1998; The Bells in the Steeple, 1999; Anthology of Love: Morning Light, The Hug of Heaven, Break not the Morn at Dawning, 2001; Anthology: Still I See The Dawn, Healing Hands, Sunset, 2002; Seasons of the Heart, 2003. Honour: Certificate of Merit, Virginia Baldwin Talent Associates, 1977. Address: P O Box 134-321, Big Bear Lake, CA 92315, USA.

BRUGADA Pedro, b. 11 August 1952, Girona, Spain. Cardiologist. m. Martine Van Royen, 3 daughters. Education: Medical School, University of Barcelona School of Medicine, 1969-75; Rotating Internship, University of Barcelona, Hospital Clinico, Spain, 1974-75; Residence, Internal Medicine, University of Barcelona School of Medicine, Hospital San Pablo y Santa Tecia Tarragona, Spain, 1975-76; Staff Member, Special Emergency Units, Spanish Social Security, Barcelona, 1976-79; Residence in Cardiology, University of Barcelona School of Medicine, Hospital Clinico, Spain, 1976-79; Specialist in Cardiology: Spain, 1979, Netherlands, 1983, Belgium, 1991; Doctor in Medicine, University of Limburg, Maastricht, Netherlands, 1982. Appointments: Research Fellow, Clinical Cardiac Electrophysiology,1979-80, Assistant Professor, Department of Cardiology, 1980-84, Director, Clinical Electrophysiology Laboratory, Annadal Hospital, 1982-90, Associate Professor, Department of Cardiology, 1984-89, Head, Division of Coronary Disease, Institute for Cardiovascular Diseases, 1988-90, Professor of Cardiology, 1989, University of Limburg, Maastricht, The Netherlands; Professor of Cardiology, Interuniversity Cardiology Institute, 1989; Staff Member, Cardiovascular Centre, OLV Hospital, Aalst, Belgium, 1991. Publications: Over 840 publications, 1979-2003 which include most recently: Book articles: Brugada Syndrome: from cell to bedside, 2001; ECG Phenomenon of Idiopathic and Paradoxical Short QT Intervals, 2002; The Brugada Syndrome in: Non pharmacological treatment of sudden death (ed M Santini), 2003; Journal articles: Prognostic value of electrophysiologic investigations in Brugada syndrome, 2001; Brugada Syndrome: A Decade of Progress, 2002; The ajmaline challenge in Brugada Syndrome. A useful tool or misleading information? 2003; Numerous national and international presentations and invited lectures. Honours include: Numerous research grants; Fritz-Acker Stifftung Award, German Society of Cardiology, 1999; 3rd Mirowski Award, Madrid, Spain, 1999; Cardiologist of the Year 2001, Paris, France; Gulden Spoor for Flemish International Representation, Bruges, Belgium, 2002; Golden Medal of the Catalan Society of Cardiology, Barcelona, Spain. Memberships include: College of Physicians, Barcelona, Spain; European, Spanish, Dutch, Belgian, French, Brazilian Societies of Cardiology; American Heart Association, USA; New York Academy of Sciences. Address: Eikeldreef 10, 9830 Sint-Martens-Latem, Belgium. E-mail: pedro.brugada@pi.be Website: www.brugada.org

BRUK Fridrich, b. 18 September 1937, Kharkov, Ukraine. Composer. m. Nadezhda Bruk, 10 September 1959, 1 son. Education: Silver Medal, Kharkov Music College of the Kharkov Conservatory, 1956; Diploma, Compositions, Conservatory Rimsky-Korsakov, Leningrad, 1961. Debut: Opera The Forty First (based on Boris Lavrenev's story), 1961. Career: Composer, operas, orchestral works, chamber music, music for theatres and films; Popular songs, records; Pedagogue in various Finnish musical institutes. Compositions: String quartet No.1, 1983; Music for children: Spring, 1982, Snowdrop, 1983, Sleigh Bells, 1984, Summer, 1985, Golden Autumn, 1988, Winter, 1988; Sunflecks, suite for orchestra, 1987; Five duets for clarinet (B) and violoncello or bassoon, 1983; Lyrical images, suite for piano, 1985; Variations for piano on the Karelian song Strawberry, 1985; Concert Variations on the old Kalevala song, for violoncello and piano, 1985; The Steppe, suite for woodwind quartet; As Lace Against the Light, 7 songs for 3 voice choir, 1986; Sonata for Cantele,

1986; String quartet No.2, 1987; Concertino for 2 violins and string orchestra or piano, 1987; Sonata for 2 violins, 1988; Sonata for violoncello, 1989; Sonata for 2 trumpets, 1989; Music to TV-films, 1988, 1989; Sonata for viola, 1990; Sonata for clarinet (B), 1991; Sonata for piano, 1994; Seven dialogues for oboe and viola, 1995; Trio for clarinet (B), viola and violoncello, 1996; Symphony Nr 1 for orchestra and trombone solo, 1998; Symphony No 2 for orchestra and piano, 1999; The Wander Singer, oratorio for baritone, soprano, mixed choir and orchestra, poetry: Oiva Paloheimo, 2000; Artist Chagall, Symphony No 3 for orchestra and tenor, 2000; Sounds of Spring, poem for orchestra, 2000; Carelia, symphony No 4 for soprano, bass, drums, piano, harp and string orchestra, poetry: from Kalevala and from Eino Leino, 2001; Musik für Quartett, 2001; The Hand of God, Christmas oratorio for narrator, soloists, children's choir and instrumental ensemble, 2002; Sonata for piano Nr 2, 2002; Symphony Nr 5 for orchestra, 2002; Birds of Passage, Symphony No 6 for baritone and orchestra, poetry: Viljo Kajava, 2001-03; Opera for Children, The Cat's House, libretto: Samuel Marshak, 2003. Recordings: on CD: Compositions by Fridrich Bruk, 1993; Lyrical Images, 1994; From Kalevala, 1994; The Snowdrop, 1996; Dialogues, 1996; Symphony No 3 for orchestra and tenor, Artist Chagall, 2002; Double CD, The Hand of God, 2003; Double CD, The Sunshine, 2004. Honours: Cross of Merit of the Order of the Lion of Finland, 1988; Artists' Supplementary pension of the Finnish State, 1998-; Various Finnish grants and scholarships. Membership: Society of Soviet Composers, 1961-73, 1989-91 (expelled 1973-89); Society of Finnish Composers, 1983; Finnish Composers' Copyright Bureau, 1985; The Guild of Light Music Composers and Authors, 1993; Society of Russian Composers, 1998. Address: Papinkatu 18 A 41, Tampere, 33200 Suomi, Finland.

BRUNDA Daniel Donald, b. 22 October 1930, Lansford, Pennsylvania, USA. Mechanical Engineer; Aerospace Engineer; Electromagnetics Scientist; Electromagnetic Powerline Radiation Engineer and Founder; Inventor; Author. Education: BSME, Lehigh University, 1952; MSME, 1953; Postgraduate, Johns Hopkins University, 1955, Princeton University, 1958-65, Drexel University, 1983. Appointments: Aerodynamicist, Bell Aircraft; Performance Engineer, Glenn L Martin, Baltimore; Aerospace Engineer, US Naval Air Propulsion Centre, Ewing, New Jersey, 1957-72, Local Manager, Independent Research and Development (IRAD), 1972-83; Consultant, Powerline Radiation Energy Engineer, Ewing, New Jersey, 1978-. Publications: Over 20 articles to professional journals; 1 patent; Powerline Radiation, Your Genes, copyrighted report, 2001, book published (by Xlibris) 2004; Control System for Adjusting the Amount of Low Frequency Electromagnetic Radiation of Power Transmission Lines, copyrighted report, 2001; The Design of Safe Electric Transmission and Distribution Lines, copyrighted book, 2001, published (by Xlibris), 2003. Honours: Lifetime Deputy Governor American Biographical Institute; Lifetime Deputy Director General in the Americas, International Biographical Centre; Member of Order of International Fellowship, 2001; Included in International Order of Merit, 2002; Certificate of Commendation for Services Rendered Since 1978, Mayor of Ewing Township, 2001; Work exhibited in IBA Gallery of Excellence, 2001; Scientific Faculty Member of the IBC, 2002; IBC On-Line Hall of Fame, 2002, (http://www.internationalbiographicalcentre.com); Scientific Advisor to the Director General, IBC, 2002; 2000 Outstanding Scientists of the 21st Century; The Lifetime of Achievement 100; IBC Ambassador of Goodwill and 1000 Greats, 2003; Living Science; Living Legends; Great Minds of the 21st Century, ABI, 2003. Memberships: Associate Fellow, Bioelectromagnetic Society; Life Member, ASME; Senior Member, AIAA; Ambassador of Grand Eminence, ABI, 2002; Founding Cabinet Member, World Peace

and Diplomacy Forum, IBC, 2003; Order of Distinction, IBC, 2004; Da Vinci Award, IBC, 2004. Address: 106 West Upper Ferry Road, Ewing, NJ 08628, USA.

BRUNO Alexander Dmitrievich, b. 26 June 1940. Mathematician. 2 sons. Education: MS, Moscow State University, 1962; PhD, 1966, Professor, 1970, Institute of Applied Mathematics. Career: Junior, 1965, Senior, 1971, Leading Researcher, 1987, Head of Mathematical Department, 1995-Keldysh Institute of Applied Mathematics, Moscow. Publications: Analytical form of differential equations, 1971-72; Local Methods in Nonlinear Differential Equations, 1989; The Restricted 3-Body Problem, 1994; Power Geometry in Algebraic and Differential Equations, 2000; and more than 200 papers. Honours: 3rd Prize, 1956, 1st Prize, 1957 Moscow Mathematical Olympiade, 2nd Prize for Students Papers in Moscow St University, 1960, 1961; Listed in numerous biographical publications. Memberships: Institute of Applied Mathematics; Moscow Mathematical Society; American Mathematical Society; Academy of Nonlinear Sciences. Address: Keldysh Institute of Applied Mathematics, Miusskaja Sq 4, Moscow 125047, Russia. E-mail: bruno@keldysh.ru

BRUNO Franklin Roy (Frank), b. 16 November 1961, London, England. Boxer. m. Laura Frances Mooney, 1990, divorced, 2001, 1 son, 2 daughters. Education: Oak Hall School, Sussex. Appointments: Began boxing with Wandsworth Boys' Club, London, 1970; Member, Sir Philip Game Amateur Boxing Club, 1977-80; Won 20 out of 21 contests as amateur; Professional Career, 1982-96; Won 38 out of 42 contests as professional, 1982-89; European Heavyweight Champion, 1985-86 (relinquished title); World heavyweight title challenges against Tim Witherspoon, 1986, Mike Tyson, 1989; Staged comeback, won 1st contest, 1991; Lost 4th World Title Challenge against Lennox Lewis, 1993; World Heavyweight Boxing Champion, 1995-96, lost title to Mike Tyson, 1996; Appearances in Pantomimes, 1990, 1991, 1996, 1997, 1999; Former presenter, BBC TV. Publication: Personality: From Zero to Hero (with Norman Giller), 1996. Honours: SOS Sports Personality of the Year, 1990; TV Times Sports Personality of the Year, 1990; Lifetime Achievement Award, BBC Sports Personality of the Year Awards, 1996. Address: c/o PO Box 2266, Brentwood, Essex CM15 0AQ, England.

BRUSA Elisabetta (Olga Laura), b. 3 April 1954, Milan, Italy. Composer; Professor. m. Gilberto Serembe, 3 May 1997. Education: Diploma, Composition, Conservatorio of Milan with Bruno Bettinelli and Azio Corghi, 1980; Further studies with Hans Keller, London. Debut: First Composition performed, Piccola Scala, 1982. Career: TV Programme on Young Italian Composers, 1983; Various commissions, performances; Radio and TV Broadcasts in Italy, England, USA, Russia, Ukraine, Canada, Australia, Germany, Austria, France, Sweden, Holland, Denmark, Hong Kong, Switzerland, Korea and Albania with Orchestras such as the BBC Philharmonic, BBC Scottish Symphony Orchestra, St Petersburg Symphony Orchestra, National Symphony Orchestra of Ukraine, CBC Vancouver Orchestra, Virtuosi of Toronto; Boris Brott Festival Orchestra, Philhormonisches Orchester Altenburg-Gera, Radio and TV Symphony Orchestra of Tirana, London Chamber Symphony, New England Philharmonic, Tanglewood Music Center Orchestra, Alea III Ensemble, Contemporary Music Forum of Washington DC; Women's Philharmonic of San Francisco; Professor, Composition at: Conservatorio of Vicenza, 1980-82; Conservatorio of Mantova, 1982-84; Conservatorio of Brescia, 1984-85; Conservatorio of Milan, 1985-. Compositions include: Belsize String Quartet, 1981; Fables for chamber orchestra, 1983; Marcia Funebre for piano, 1984; Suite Grotesque for orchestra, 1986; Sonata for piano, 1986; Nittemero Symphony for chamber orchestra, 1988; Symphony No 1 for large orchestra,

1990; Sonata Rapsodica for violin and piano, 1991; La Triade for large orchestra, 1992; Firelights for large orchestra, 1993; Requiescat for large orchestra with solo voice, 1995; Fanfare for large orchestra, 1996; Adagio for string orchestra, 1996; Wedding Song for large orchestra, 1997; Florestan for large orchestra, 1997; Messidor for orchestra, 1998; Merlin for large orchestra, 2004. Recordings: Orchestral Works Vol 1, Naxos; Orchestral Works Vol 2, Naxos. Honours: 1st Prize Washington International Competition, 1982; Fellowship, Tanglewood Music Center, 1983; Fulbright Bursary, 1983; Fellowship, MacDowell Colony, 1988, 1989, 1990. Address: Via Zanella 43/1 20133 Milan, Italy. E-mail: elisabetta.brusa@tiscali.it Website: www.elisabettabrusa.it

BRUSEWITZ Gunnar (Kurt), b. 7 October 1924, Stockholm, Sweden. Author; Artist. m. Ingrid Andersson, 21 October 1946, 2 daughter. Education: Royal Academy of Art. Publications: Hunting - A Cultural History Chronicle of Hunting in Europe, 1967; Bjornjagare och Fjarilsmalare, 1968; Skissbok, 1970; Nature in Gambia, 1971; Skog, 1974; Strandspegling, 1979; Wings and Seasons, 1980; Sveriges Natur, 1984; Memoirs I-III, 1994-98; The Amazing Miss Brooke, 1998. Contributions to: Stockholms Tidningen; Svenska Dagbladet; Various Other Swedish Magazines and Publications. Honours: Stockholm City Presentation Prize, 1970; Dag Hammarskjold Medal, 1975; Honorary PhD, 1982; Die Goldene Blume Von Rheydt Düsseldorf, 1989; Memberships: PEN; World Wildlife Fund; Royal Society of Science in Uppsala. Address: Lisinge, 762 93 Rimbo, Sweden.

BRUTUS Dennis, b. 28 November 1924, Salisbury, Rhodesia. Educationist; Poet; Writer. m. May Jaggers, 14 May 1950, 4 sons, 4 daughters. Education: BA, University of the Witwatersrand, Johannesburg, South Africa, 1947. Appointments: Director, World Campaign for Release of South African Political Prisons; International Defence and Aid Fund, formerly UN Representative; Director, Program on African and African-American Writing in Africa and the Diaspora, 1989-; Visiting Professor at universities in Amherst, Austin, Boston, Dartmouth, Denver, Evanstown, Pittsburgh. Publications: Sirens, Knuckles, Boots, 1963; Letters to Martha and Other Poems from a South African Prison, 1968; Poems from Algiers, 1970; Thoughts Abroad, 1970; A Simple Lust: Selected Poems, 1973; China Poems, 1975; Stubborn Hope, 1978; Strains, 1982; Salutes and Censures, 1984; Airs and Tributes, 1988; Still the Sirens, 1993. Contributions to: Periodicals. Honours: Mbari Prize for Poetry in Africa; Freedom Writers' Award, Kenneth David Kaunda Humanism Award; Academic Excellence Award, National Council for Black Studies, 1982; UN Human Rights Day Ward, 1983; Paul Robeson Award; Langston Hughes Award. Memberships: President, South African Non-Racial Olympic Committee (SAN-ROC); Chair, International Campaign Against Racism in Sport (ICARIS), Africa Network, 1984-; ARENA (Institute for Study of Sport and Social Issues); African Literature Association; American Civil Liberties Union; Amnesty International; PEN; Union of Writers of African Peoples.

BRUZDOWICZ Joanna, b. 17 May 1943, Warsaw, Poland. Composer; Music Critic. Education: Piano with Irena Protasewicz and Wanda Losakiewicz; Composition with Kazimierz Sikorski, MA, Warsaw Conservatory, 1966; Composition with Nadia Boulanger, Olivier Messiaen, Pierre Schaeffer, Paris, 1968-70. Career: Groupe de Recherches Musicales, French Radio and TV, Paris; Groupe International de Musique Electroacoustique de Paris; IPEM; Electronic studios, University of Ghent, Belgian Radio and TV; Founder, Jeunesses Musicales, Poland; Founder President, Frédéric Chopin and Karol Szymanowski Society, Belgium; Vice President, International Federation of Chopin Societies; Music criticism; Advocate of contemporary music. Compositions: Operas: In der Strafkolonie, or La Colonie Pénitentiaire, 1972, revised,

1986, 1995; Les Troyennes, 1973; The Gates of Paradise, 1987; Tides and Waves, opera, musical, 1992; Ballet: Le Petit Prince, 1976; Many film and theatre scores; Orchestral including: Piano Concerto, 1974; Symphony, 1975; Violin Concerto, 1975; Aquae Sextiae for winds, 1978; Double Bass Concerto, 1982; Four Seasons' Greetings, 4 concertos for violins, pianos, flute, marimba, string orchestra, 1989; The Cry of the Phoenix for cello and symphony orchestra, 1994; Chamber including: Trio dei Due Mondi for violin, cello, piano, 1980; Dum Spiro Spero for flute and tape, 1981; Para y contra for double bass and tape, 1981; Trio per Trio for flute, violin, harpsichord, 1982; Dreams and Drums for percussion, 1982; Oracle for bassoon and tape, 1982; Aurora Borealis for harp and organ, 1988; String Quartet No 1, La Vita, 1983, No 2, Cantus Aeterna with speaker, 1988; Spring in America, violin-piano sonata, 1994; Cantata: Urbi et Orbi for tenor, children's choir, 2 trumpets, 2 trombones, organ, 1985; The Cry of the Phoenix, cello concerto, 1994; Piano pieces; Organ music; Electronic and electroacoustic pieces; Film and TV music. Recordings: Several CDs. Address: Mas Terrats, 66400 Taillet, France.

BRYAN Lynne, b. 10 May 1961, Leicester, England. Writer. Education: BA, Humanities, Wolverhampton Polytechnic, 1980-83; MA, Creative Writing, University of East Anglia, 1984-85. Publications: Envy at the Cheese Handout, 1995; Gorgeous, 1999; Like Rabbits, 2002. Contributions to: Anthologies and magazines. Honours: Eastern Arts Grant, 1996; BBC Arts Council Award, 1996; Arts Project Small Award 2000, Author's Foundation Award 2002, East England Arts Grant 2003. Address: c/o Judith Murray, Greene & Heaton, 37 Goldhawk Road, London W12 8QQ

BRYANS Alexander McKelvey, b. 16 September 1921, Toronto. Medicine. m. Elaine, 1 son; 2 daughters. Education: MD, University of Toronto, 1944; FRCP, Canada, 1953; MA, Michigan State University. Appointments: Professor, Paediatrics, Queens University, 1954-88; Professor Emeritus, 1988-. Publications: Several Publications in Medical and Education Literature. Honours: Doctor of Divinity, Queen's University 2001. Memberships: Canadian Medical Association; Canadian Paediatric Society; Royal College of Physicians and Surgeons of Canada; Physicians for Global Survival, Canada. Address: 31 Lakeland Point Drive, Kingston, ON, Canada, K7M 4E8.

BUBANOVIC Ivan, b. 30 January 1965, Gnjilane, Kosovo. Physician; Obstetrics/Gynaecology Specialist. m. Dragana, 1 son, 1 daughter. Education: High Medical School, 1990; Doctoral and Postdoctoral Study, Ultrasound course, 1997-; Cervical, Vulvar and Colposcopic course, 1998; Specialist in Obstetric/Gynaecology, 1998; Master of Medical Science, 2000. Appointments: Head of Obstetrics/Gynaecology Department of Medica Centre, Serbia and Montenegro. Publications: 3 articles in professional medical journals; Books: Immunobiological Basis of Pregnancy; Immunocontraception; Origin of Anti-tumour Immunity Failure in Mammals. Address: Obstetrics/Gynaecology Department of Medica Center, Novosadska 1/c, 18000 Nis, Serbia and Montenegro. Website: www.geocities.com/ibubanovic

BUBKA Sergey Nazarovich, b. 4 December 1963, Voroshilovgrad, Ukraine. Athlete. m. Lilya Tioutiounik, 1983, 2 sons. Appointments: World Champion Pole Vaulter, 1983; 16 World Records from 5-85m 1984 to 6.13m 1992, including world's first 6m jump, Paris, 1985; 18 World Indoor Records, from 5.81 1984 to 6.15 1993; Holder of indoors and outdoors world records, 2002; Now represents OSC Berlin. Honours include: Olympic Gold Medal, 1988. Memberships include: Member, IOC Executive Board, IOC Evaluation Commission for 2008; IOC Athletes' Commission; IAAF Council, 2001-; National Olympic Committee

Board; Chairman, EOC Athletes; Commission; President, S Bubka Sports Club; Elected to Parliament, United Union Faction, 2002- Address: c/o State Committee of Physical Culture & Sport, 42 Esplanadnaya, 252023 Kiev, Ukraine.

BUBLE Nikola, b. 28 January 1950, Split, Croatia. Ethnomusicologist; Conductor. m. Franka Martinoviæ Buble, 2 children. Education: Music Teacher, Teacher Training College, Split, Croatia, 1968-72; Academic Musician and Teacher of Music Subjects, Academy of Music, Sarajevo University, Sarajevo, Bosnia and Herzegovina, 1974; MA, Ethnomusicology, Academy of Music, Zagreb University, Zagreb, Croatia, 1982; Mus D, Musicology, Faculty of Arts and Letters, Ljubljana University, Slovenia, 1988; Scientific Counsellor and University Professor, Ministry of Science and Technology, Croatia, 1988. Appointments include: Lecturer, Conducting, Ethnomusicology and Music Theory, 1976-82, Head, Institute for Music, , 1985-89, Senior Lecturer and Assistant Professor, 1988-94, Associate Professor, 1994-97 Ethnomusicology, Conducting and Music Theory, Faculty of Science, Associate Professor, 1997-2001, Head of the Music Department, 1997-99, Vice-Dean of the Music Department, 1999-2001, Full Professor, Ethnomusicology, Conducting and Music Theory, 2001-, Dean, 2001-, Arts Academy, University of Split, Split, Croatia; Artistic Director of numerous music and arts festivals; Jury member of numerous national and international competitions; Conductor of the Croatian War Navy Orchestra, 1991; Many guest appearances, compositions and recordings . Publications: Author of 17 books including: Music as an Integral Part of Life – Ethnomusicology Themes, 1997; Introduction to Ethnomusicology, 1998; Dalmatian Klapa Songs, 1999; Handbook for the Choir Conductors and Dalmatian Klapa Leaders, 2000; Festival of the Mandolinists, selection of the works of Croatian composers, 2002; Numerous articles in professional journals. Honours include most recently: Red Danice hrvatske s likom Marka Maruliæa for exceptional merits in culture, President of Croatia, 1996; Grants, Lifetime Achievement Award for researching, preserving and promoting music heritage, The Town of Trogir, Croatia, 2002; Medaflia Delta Regione Lazio, for collaboration in the field of music and cultural exchange with Music Conservatory "Santa Cecilie", Rome, Italy, 2003. Memberships include: Associate Memberships: Croatian Folklorists' Guild; Croatian Composers' Guild; Croatian Guild of Music and Dance Pedagogues; International Council for Traditional Music. Address: Arts Academy, University of Split, Vraneiaeva 17, Split 21000, Croatia. E-mail: nikola.buble@umas.hr

BUCHANAN Pat(rick Joseph), b. 2 November 1938, Washington, District of Columbia, USA. American Government Official; Journalist. m. Shelley Ann Scarney, 8 May 1971. Education: AB, English, cum laude, Georgetown University, 1961; MS, Journalism, Columbia University, 1962. Appointments: Editorial Writer, 1962-64, Assistant Editorial Editor, 1964-66, St Louis Globe Democrat; Executive Assistant to Richard M Nixon, 1966-69; Special Assistant to President Richard M Nixon, 1969-73; Consultant to Presidents Richard M Nixon and Gerald R Ford, 1973-74; Syndicated Columnist, 1975-; Various radio and television broadcasts as commentator, panellist, moderator, etc, 1978-; Assistant to President Ronald Reagan and Director of Communications, White House, Washington DC, 1985-87; Candidate for the Republican Party Nomination for President of the US, 1992, 1996; Chairman, The American Cause, 1993-95, 1997-; Chairman, Pat Buchanan & Co, Mutual Broadcasting System, 1993-95. Publications: The New Majority, 1973; Conservative Votes, Liberal Victories, 1975; Right from the Beginning, 1988; Barry Goldwater, The Conscience of A Conservative, 1990; The Great Betrayal, 1998; A Republic, Not an Empire, 2000. Contributions to: Newspapers and periodicals.

Honour: Knight of Malta, 1987. Memberships: Republican Party; Roman Catholic Church. Address: 1017 Savile Lane, McLean, VA 22101, USA.

BUCHWALD Art, b. 20 October 1925, Mt Vernon, New York, USA. Journalist; Author; Playwright. m. Ann McGarry, 11 October 1952, 1 son, 2 daughters. Education: University of Southern California, Los Angeles, 1945-48. Appointments: Syndicated columnist for newspapers around the world. Publications: Paris After Dark, 1950; Art Buchwald's Paris, 1954; The Brave Coward, 1957; More Caviar, 1958; Un Cadeau Pour le Patron, 1958; A Gift From the Boys, 1959; Don't Forget to Write, 1960; How Much is That in Dollars?, 1961; Is it Safe to Drink the Water?, 1962; Art Buchwald's Secret List to Paris, 1963; I Chose Capitol Punishment, 1963; And Then I Told the President, 1965; Son of the Great Society, 1966; Have I Ever Lied to You?, 1968; The Establishment is Alive and Well in Washington, 1969; Counting Sheep, 1970; Getting High in Government Circles, 1971; I Never Danced at the White House, 1973; The Bollo Caper, 1974; I Am Not a Crook, 1974; Irving's Delight, 1975; Washington is Leaking, 1976; Down the Seine and Up the Potomac, 1977; The Buchwald Stops Here, 1978; Laid Back in Washington, 1981; While Reagan Slept, 1983; You CAN Fool All of the People All of the Time, 1985; I Think I Don't Remember, 1987; Whose Rose Garden is it Anyway?, 1989; Lighten Up, George, 1991; Leaving Home: A Memoir, 1994; I'll Always Have Paris, 1996. Honours: Priz de la Bonne Humeur, 1958; Pulitzer Prize in Commentary, 1982. Memberships: American Academy of Arts and Sciences; American Academy of Humor Columnists. Address: Suite 3804, 540 Park Avenue, New York, NY 10021, USA.

BUCK Karen, b. 30 August 1958. Member of Parliament. Partner: Barrie Taylor, 1 son. Education: BSc, MSc, MA, London School of Economics. Appointments: Charity specialising in employment for disabled people; London Borough of Hackney; Policy Officer specialising in health, Labour Party Head Office; Labour Party's Campaigns Unit, 1992-97; Elected, Labour Member of Parliament for Regent's Park and Kensington North; Select Committee on Social Security, 1997-2001; Work and Pensions Select Committee, 2001-. Memberships: Chair, London Group of Labour MPs; Member, Mayor of London's Affordable Housing Commission; Board Member, Constituency SRB projects. Address: House of Commons, London SW1A 0AA, England. E-mail: k.buck@rpkn-labour.co.uk

BUCKERIDGE Anthony Malcolm, b. 20 June 1912, London, England. Writer. m (1) Sylvia Brown, 1936, (2) Eileen Norah Selby, 25 February 1972, 2 sons, 1 daughter. Education: University College, London, 1932-35. Publications: Jennings Series of Children's Books, 25 Titles, 1950-91; Rex Milligan Series, 4 Titles, 1953-56; A Funny Thing Happened, 1953; Jennings Abounding, 1979; Musicals: It Happened in Hamelin, 1980; The Cardboard Conspiracy, 1985. Honour: OBE, for services to literature, 2003. Memberships: Society of Authors; Writers Guild of Great Britain; British Actors Equity. Address: East Crink, Barcombe Mills, Lewes, Sussex BN8 5BL, England.

BUCKINGHAM Amyand David, b. 28 January 1930, Sydney, Australia. Professor Emeritus. m. Jillian Bowles, 1 son, 2 daughters. Education: BSc, Honours, MSc, University of Sydney, 1948-53; PhD, 1956, Sc D, 1985, Corpus Christi College, Cambridge University, England. Appointments: Lecturer, Student, Junior Censor, Christ Church, Oxford, England, 1955-65; University Lecturer, Inorganic Chemistry, Oxford University, 1958-65; Professor of Theoretical Chemistry, Bristol University, 1965-69; Professor of Chemistry, Cambridge University, 1969-97. Publications: Over 320 papers in scientific journals; Author, The

Dictionary of International Biography

Laws and Applications of Thermodynamics, 1964; Editor, Chemical Physics Letters, 1978-99. Honours: University Medal for Chemistry, University of Sydney, 1951; Fellow of the Royal Society, 1975, Hughes Medal, 1996; President of the Faraday Division of the Royal Society of Chemistry, 1987-89, Faraday Medal, 1998; Foreign Associate, US National Academy of Sciences, 1992; Foreign Honorary Member, American Academy of Arts and Sciences, 1992; Foreign Member, Royal Swedish Academy of Sciences, 1995; Fellow of the Institute of Physics, Harrie Massey Medal, 1995; CBE, 1997; Fellow of the Optical Society of America, Townes Medal, 2001. Memberships: Fellow of the Royal Australian Chemical Institute; Fellow of the Royal Society of Chemistry; Fellow of the American Physical Society; Member of the American Chemical Society. Address: Department of Chemistry, University of Cambridge, Lensfield Road, Cambridge, CB2 1EW, England. E-mail: abd1000@cam.ac.uk

BUCUR Romulus Vasile, b. 19 March 1928, Padova, Italy. Chemistry Researcher (Retired). m. Doina Rodica Motiu, 1 daughter. Education: Graduate, Chemistry, University of Cluj, Romania, 1955; PhD, Electrochemistry, University of Bucharest, Romania, 1970. Appointments: Head, Laboratory, Solvay Plant, Ocna Mures, Romania, 1955; Scientific Researcher, Institute of Atomic Physics, Cluj, Romania, 1956-58; Principal Scientific Researcher, 1958-87, Head, Laboratory, 1974-87, Institute of Isotopic and Molecular Technology, Cluj, Romania; Scientific Researcher, Inorganic Chemistry, Uppsala University, Sweden, 1988-93; Scientific Research Associate, Materials Chemistry Department, Ångström Laboratory, Uppsala University, Sweden, 1993-98. Publications: About 120 scientific papers in the field of analysis and separation of heavy water, solid state electrochemistry (metallic hydrides and sulphides), materials for hydrogen storage, and piezoelectric quartz crystal microbalance. Membership: Honorary Member, The International Association for Hydrogen Energy, USA, 1983-. Address: Näktergalsv 5, SE-35242 Växjö, Sweden. E-mail: romulus.bucur@telia.com

BUDAEV Vladimir Michailovich, b. 25 October 1955, Moscow, Russia. Architect. 1 daughter. Education: Diploma in Architecture, Moscow Architectural Institute, 1984. Appointments: Chief-Architect, Park Pobedy, Poklonnaya Gora, Moscow, of the Memorial, Central Museum of the Great Patriotic War, 1941-45, Central Obelisk, Church of Georgiy Pobedonosetz and the Synagogue-Memorial; Architect-constructor, Monument of Tsar Peter the Great, Moskva River; Architect-constructor, Zoo, Moscow, 1997; Architect of several multi-storey municipal buildings, 1998-2001; Head of Architectural and Artistic Planning Institute, Moscow; Deputy Director General and Chief Architect, Central Scientific Kucherenko's Institute of Building Constructions, Moscow, 2003-. Publications: Several papers in professional journals. Honours: Co-winner, International Contest for the best project for Trinity Cathedral, Moscow, 1990; Medal of Holy Sergiy Radonezsky, from Russian Orthodox Church, 1995; Certificate of Honour from President of Russia, 1995; Honoured Architect of Russia, 1996; Medal and Diploma, IBC, 1999; Listed in numerous international directories of biography. Membership: Union of Architects of Russia, FIBA; Corresponding Member of International Academy of Investment and Economy of Building, 2000. Address: Petrovka 26-28, 103051 Moscow, Russia.

BUDENHOLZER Frank Edward, b. 21 August 1945. Catholic Priest; Educator; Chemist. Education: BA, Divine Word College, Epworth, Iowa, 1967; BS, DePaul University, Chicago, Illinois, 1969; MA, Catholic Theological Union, Chicago, Illinois, 1974; PhD, University of Illinois, Chicago, 1977. Appointments: Teaching Assistant, University of Illinois, Chicago, 1972-76; Chinese Language Training, Hsinchu, Taiwan, 1978-80; Associate

Professor, Chemistry, Fu Jen University, 1978-83; Professor, Chemistry, 1983-; Director, Graduate Institute of Chemistry, 1980-84; Dean, College of Science and Engineering, 1984-90; Vice-President, 1990-97; Visiting Scholar, Center for Theology and the Natural Sciences; 1997-98; Visiting Scholar, University of California, 1997-98; Member, Board of Trustees, Fu Jen University, 1999-; Resident Trustee, Fu Jen University, 2001-; Co-ordinator, Center for the Study of Science and Religion, 2001-. Publications: Religion and Science in Taiwan: Rethinking the Connection; Some Comments on the Problem of Reductionism; Classical Trajectory Study of the HFCO-HF+CO Reaction. Memberships: American Chemical Society; American Physical Society; Chinese Chemical Society; Chinese Physical Society; Institute for Religion in an Age of Science; Hastings Center; Institute for Theoretical Encounter with Science and Technology. Address: Department of Chemistry, Fu Jen Catholic University, Hsinchuang 242, Taiwan. E-mail: chem1003@mails.fju.edu.tw

BUDOWSKI Gerardo, b. 10 June 1925, Berlin, Germany. Forester; Ecologist. m. Thelma Palma, 2 daughters. Education: Ingeniero Agrónomo, Universidad Central, Caracas, Venezuela, 1948; MSc, Inter American Institute of Agricultural Sciences, Costa Rica, 1954; PhD, Yale University, Connecticut, USA, 1962. Appointments: Head, Forestry Research, Caracas, Venezuela, 1949-52; Head, Natural Resources, IICA, Costa Rica, 1952-67; Visiting Professor, University of California, Berkeley, USA, 1967; Head, Ecology and Conservation, UNESCO, Paris, 1967-70; Director-General, International Union for the Conservation of Nature, Switzerland, 1970-76; Head, Natural Resources, Tropical Agricultural Center for Research and Training (CATIE), Costa Rica, 1976-86; UN University for Peace, Costa Rica, 1986-; Vice Rector, 1999-2000; Deputy Director, Earth Council, Costa Rica, 1997-99; Professor Emeritus, CATIE and University for Peace. Publications: Book, Conservation as a Tool for Development, 1986; Over 250 book chapters, papers in journals and teaching materials. Honours: Honorary Member, Society of American Foresters; Honorary Member, International Union for the Conservation of Nature; Member of Honour, Worldwide Fund for Nature; Golden Ark, Netherlands; Decorated by the governments of Venezuela, Nicaragua and Peru; Listed in international biographical publications. Memberships: International Society of Tropical Foresters; International Society of Ecotourism, life member; Society of American Foresters, life member. Address: PO Box 198, 2300 Curridabat, Costa Rica. E-mail: gbudowski@upeace.org

BUENKER John David, b. 11 August 1937, Dubuque, Iowa, USA. Historian. m. Beverly J Graves, 3 sons, 3 daughters. Education: BA, Loras College, 1959; MA, 1962, PhD, 1964, Georgetown University. Appointments: Professor of History, Prince Georges Community College, 1962-65; Eastern Illinois University, 1965-70; University of Wisconsin-Parkside, 1970-. Publications: Urban Liberalism and Progressive Reform, 1973; The Income Tax and the Progressive Era, 1985; Wisconsin: The Progressive Era, 1998. Honours: Guggenheim Fellow, 1975; CASE/Carnegie Wisconsin Professor of the Year, 1990-91; National Endowment for the Humanities Fellow, 2001-02; Phi Alpha Theta; Phi Delta Kappa; Alpha Sigma Nu. Memberships: Organization of American Historians; American Historical Association, 1998. Address: 227 William Street, Racine, Wisconsin, 53402, USA.

BÜHNEMANN Gudrun, b. 22 September 1955, Goslar, Germany. Professor of South Asian Studies. Education includes: PhD, Classical Indian and Buddhist Studies, University of Vienna, 1980. Appointments: Postdoctoral Researcher, Centre of Advanced Study in Sanskrit, Pune University, India, 1980-82; Research Assistant, Department of Indology, Hamburg University, Germany, 1982-83; Senior Research Fellow, Bhandarkar Oriental Research

Institute, Pune, 1983-89; Research Fellow, Department of Indian Philosophy, Nagoya University, Japan, 1989-91; Visiting Research Scholar, Institute for Research in Humanities, Kyoto University, 1991-92; Spalding Visiting Fellow, Wolfson College, Oxford, England, 1992; Assistant Professor, Department of South Asian Studies, 1992-94, Associate Professor, Department of Languages and Cultures of Asia, 1994-, Professor, Department of Languages and Cultures of Asia, current, University of Wisconsin-Madison, USA. Publications: 12 books including: Jitari: Kleine Texte beschrieben und ediert, 1982, revised, 1985; Budha-Kausika's Ramaraksastotra. A Contribution to the Study of Sanskrit Devotional Poetry, 1983; Puja. A Study in Smarta Ritual, 1988; Forms of Ganesa. A Study based on the Vidyarnavatantra, 1989; The Iconography of Hindu Tantric Deities. Vol I, The Pantheon of the Mantramahodadhi, 2000, Vol II, The Pantheons of the Prapancasara and the Saradatilaka, 2001; Over 20 articles. Honours: Friedrich Naumann Stiftung, 1976-80; Michael Coulson Junior Fellow in Indology, 1980, Spalding Visiting Fellow in Indian Philosophy and Religion, 1992, Wolfson College; Deutscher Akademischer Austauschdienst, 1980-82; Deutsche Forschungsgemeinschaft, 1983-85; Indian Council of Historical Research, 1987-89; Japan Society for the Promotion of Science, 1989-91; Numata Foundation, 1991-92; Senior Long-term Fellow, American Institute of Indian Studies, 1996; American Council of Learned Societies and National Endowment for the Humanities, 1997-98; Vilas Associate Award, University of Wisconsin-Madison, 2000-02. Memberships include: Japanese Association of Indian and Buddhist Studies, 1989-92; International Association for Buddhist Studies, 1994; Life Member, Bhandarkar Oriental Research Institute, Pune; Currently: American Academy of Religions; American Council for Southern Asian Art; American Oriental Society. Address: Department of Languages and Cultures of Asia, University of Wisconsin-Madison, 1234 Van Hise Hall, 1220 Linden Drive, Madison, WI 53706, USA. E-mail: gbuhnema@facstaff.wisc.edu

BULIGESCU Lucian, b. 17 October 1929, Ploeshti, Romania. Physician; Professor of Internal Medicine. m. 22 August 1952, 1 son. Education: Graduated magna cum laude, School of Medicine, University of Cluj, 1953; DMedScis, 1957; Dr Docent Ès Scis, 1974. Appointments: University Assistant, 1954; Assistant Professor, 1962; Associate Professor, 1977; Professor, Chief, Department of Internal Medicine, Fundeni Clinical Hospital, Bucharest, 1981-2000. Publications: 14 books including 1st treatise in Romanian in field of hepatology - Diseases of the Liver, Biliary System and Pancreas, 2 volumes, 1981; Treatise on Hepatogastroenterology, 2 volumes, 1997-98; 600 articles in magazines and journals. Honours: Award, Journées Franco-Espagnoles de Gastroentérologie, Bilbao, 1967; Honorary Member, Belgian Society for Gastroenterology, 1972. Memberships: European Association for Internal Medicine, 1971-; French Association for the Study of the Liver, 1978-; French Society for Gastroenterology, 1990-; President, Romanian Association for Study of the Liver, 1990-; European and International Associations for the Study of the Liver, 1991-; New York Academy of Sciences, 1994-; Editorial Board, Journal of Hepatology; Editorial Board, Med Chir Dig, Paris. Address: Precupetii Vechi Str No 23, 415700 Bucharest, Romania.

BULLA Clyde Robert, b. 9 January 1914, King City, Missouri, USA. Author. Publications: A Tree is a Plant, 1960; Three-Dollar Mule, 1960; The Sugar Pear Tree, 1961; Benito, 1961; What Makes a Shadow?, 1962; The Ring and the Fire: Stories from Wagner's Niebelung Operas, 1962; Viking Adventure, 1963; Indian Hill, 1963; St Valentine's Day, 1965; More Stories of Favorite Operas, 1965; White Bird, 1966; Lincoln's Birthday, 1967; Washington's Birthday, 1967; Flowerpot Gardens, 1967; Stories of Gilbert and Sullivan Operas, 1968; The Ghost of Windy Hill, 1968; Mika's Apple Tree: A Story of Finland, 1968; The Moon Singer, 1969; New Boy in Dublin: A Story of Ireland, 1969; Jonah and the Great Fish, 1970; Joseph the Dreamer, 1971; Pocahontas and the Strangers, 1971; Open the Door and See All the People, 1972; Dexter, 1973; The Wish at the Top, 1974; Shoeshine Girl, 1975; Marco Moonlight, 1976; The Beast of Lor, 1977; Conquista! (with Michael Syson), 1978; Last Look, 1979; The Stubborn Old Woman, 1980; My Friend the Monster, 1980; Daniel's Duck, 1980; A Lion to Guard Us, 1981; Almost a Hero, 1981; Dandelion Hill, 1982; Poor Boy, Rich Boy, 1982; Charlie's House, 1983; The Cardboard Crown, 1984; A Grain of Wheat, 1985; The Chalk Box Kid, 1987; Singing Sam, 1989; The Christmas Coat, 1989; A Place for Angels, 1995; The Paint Brush Kid, 1999. Memberships: Authors Guild; Society of Children's Book Writers and Illustrators.

BULLOCK Kenneth (Ken), b. 26 July 1929, Liverpool, England (Canadian citizen, 1949-66, Australian citizen, 1966-). Writing Consultant; Writer. m. Shirley, 2003, 2 sons, 2 daughters. Education: Dip Comm, 1961, Royal Canadian Naval College, HMCS, Victoria. Appointments: British Merchant Navy, 1946-49; Service aircrew, RCN, RAN, 1950-72; Papua New Guinea Prime Minister's Department, Office of Information, 1980-83; Writer, Editor, Teacher, Journalist Counsellor/External Tutor, James Cook University, 1984-2003. Publications: Emergency, 1979; Family Guide to Beach and Water Safety, 1980; Silly Billy Learns a Lesson, 1981; Papua New Guinea, 1981; Water Proofing Your Child, 1982; Pelandok, 1986; Port Pirie the Friendly City, 1988; Chopstik, 1993; Beyond Peril, 1996; Swimmers Take Your Marks, 2001; The Fixers, 2003. Contributions to: Papua New Guinea; Post Courier; National Times; Australia; Adelaide Advertiser; Sunshine Coast Daily. Honours: CD, Canadian Military Service Decoration, 1963; Citizen of the Year, 1984, Port Pirie; Canadian Special Service Medal (Contribution to NATO), 1997; Australian Active Service Medal (Vietnam), 1998. Memberships: Formerly Fellowship of Australian Writers; Australian Society of Authors. Address: Apt 37 Leeward Apartments, 1 Grenada Way, Kawana Island, Queensland 4575, Australia. E-mail: shirken2@dodo.com.au

BULLOCK Sandra, b. 22 July 1966, USA. Actress. Education: East Carolina University. Creative Works: Off-Broadway Productions include: No Time Flat (WPA Theatre). TV Roles: The Preppy Murder (film); Lucky Chances (mini series); Working Girl (NBC series). Films: Love Potion 9; The Vanishing; The Thing Called Love; When The Party's Over; Demolition Man; Wrestling Ernest Hemingway; Speed; While You Were Sleeping; Two If By Sea; Moll Flanders; A Time To Kill; In Love and War; Practical Magic; Forces of Nature; Director, Making Sandwiches, 1996; Speed 2, 1997; Hope Floats (also executive producer), 1998; 28 Days, 2000; Famous, 2000; Miss Congeniality, 2000; Murder by Numbers, 2001; Exactly 3:30, 2001; Divine Secrets of the Ya-Ya Sisterhood, 2002; Two Weeks' Notice, 2002; Loverboy, 2004. Address: CAA, 9830 Wilshire Boulevard, Beverly Hills, CA 90212, USA.

BULLOUGH Robert V, b. 12 February 1949, Salt Lake City, Utah. Professor. m. Dawn Ann. Children: 3 sons, 1 daughter. Education: BS, University of Utah, 1971; MED, 1973; PhD, Ohio State University, 1976. Appointments: Assistant, Associate, Full Professor, Educational Studies, University of Utah, 1976-98; Emeritus Professor, 1999; Professor, Teacher Education, Director of Research, Center for the Improvement of Teacher Education and Schooling (CITES); Brigham Young University, 1999. Publications: Democracy in Education; Human Interests in the Curriculum; The Forgotten Dream of American Public Education; First Year Teacher; Becoming a Student of Teaching; Emerging as a Teacher; Teachers and Mentors; First Year Teacher-After Eight Years; Uncertain Lives: Children of Promise, Teachers of Hope. Honours: Phi Kappa Phi; Phi Beta Kappa; Professors of Curriculum; AACTE: Outstanding Writing Award. Memberships: AERA; Phi Delta Kappa. Address: 413 4th Avenue, Salt Lake City, Utah 84103, USA.

BULSON Philip Stanley, b. 21 April 1925, Yeovil, Somerset, England. Structural and Civil Engineer. Education: Plymouth and Devonport Technical College; BSc(Eng), DSc(Eng), University of London; PhD, University of Bristol. Appointments: Engineering Cadet (Army) and Commission in Royal Engineers, 1943-48; Senior and Principal Scientific Officer, Military Engineering, Design and Research, 1953-65, Senior Principal and Deputy Chief Scientific Officer (Individual Merit), 1965-74, Ministry of Defence; Head of Military Engineering Experimental Establishment, Christchurch (MEXE) also known as MVEE(c) and RARDE(c), 1974-85; Visiting Professor, University of Southampton, 1983-; Director, Special Services, Mott, Hay and Anderson, 1986-88; Consultant to Mott MacDonald Group (specialising in the effect of explosions on structures), 1989-2000. Publications: Books as sole author: The Stability of Flat Plates, 1970; Buried Structures, 1985; Explosive Loading of Engineering Structures, 1997; Books as co-author, contributor or editor: Background to Buckling, 1980; Engineering Structures, 1983; Structures Under Shock and Impact, 1989, 1992, 1994; The Future of Structural Testing, 1990; Rapidly Assembled Structures, 1991; Aluminium Structural Analysis, 1992; Research reports for the Ministry of Defence and numerous papers in professional journals. Honour: CBE, 1986. Memberships: Fellow of Royal Academy of Engineering; Fellow of the Institution of Structural Engineers; Fellow of the Institution of Civil Engineers; Fellow of the Institution of Mechanical Engineers; Liveryman, Worshipful Company of Engineers; Member, Athenaeum Club; Chairman, Committee on Structural Use of Aluminium, British Standards Institute. Address: Playford Rise, Sway, Lymington, Hampshire SO41 6DA, England.

BUNCE Pauline Daphne, b. 22 September 1949, England (Australian citizen). Lecturer; Teacher. Education: BA, MEd (UWA); MA (Deakin). Appointments: Secondary school teaching in Western Australia, 1971-81; Overseas teaching and lecturing, India, Sri Lanka, Brunei, Malaysia, Hong Kong, 1982-2004. Publications: Cocos Malay Culture, 1987; The Cocos (Keeling) Islands - Australian Atolls in the Indian Ocean, 1988. Honour: Citizenship Award, Cocos (Keeling) Islands, 1988. Memberships: MACE; FRGS; FRAI. Address: PO Box 267, Claremont, Western Australia 6010, Australia.

BUNCH Richard Alan, b. 1 June 1945, Honolulu, Hawaii. Educator; Poet; Writer. m. Rita Anne Glazar, 11 August 1990, 1 son, 1 daughter. Education: AA, Napa Valley College, 1965; Student, Stanford-in-Britain, Harlaxton Manor, Grantham, Lincolnshire, England, 1966; BA, Communication, Stanford University, 1967; MA, History, University of Arizona, 1969; MDiv, 1970, DD, 1971, Graduate Studies in Philosophy, 1972-75, Vanderbilt University; Graduate Studies in Asian Religions, Temple University, 1975-76; JD, University of Memphis, 1980; Attorney, Horne and Peppel, Memphis, 1981-83; Teaching Credential, Sonoma State University, 1988. Appointments: Teaching Assistant, Philosophy, Vanderbilt University, 1973-74; Instructor, Philosophy, Belmont University, 1973-74; Instructor, Law, University of Memphis, 1982-83; Instructor Humanities, Napa Valley College, 1985-; Instructor, Philosophy, Chapman University, 1986-87; Instructor, Law, Sonoma State University, 1986-87, Instructor, Philosophy, 1990-91; Instructor, Humanities, Diablo Valley College, 1991-94, 1997. Publications: Poetry: Summer Hawk, 1991; Wading the Russian River, 1993; A Foggy Morning, 1996;

Santa Rosa Plums, 1996; South by Southwest, 1997; Rivers of the Sea, 1998; Sacred Space, 1998; Greatest Hits: 1970-2000, 2001; Running for Daybreak, 2004. Prose: Night Blooms, 1992; Play: The Russian River Returns, 1999; Contributions to: Many reviews. Honours: Grand Prize, Ina Coolbrith National Poetry Day Contest, 1989; Jessamyn West Prize, 1990; Pushcart Prize nominations, 1988, 1996, 1997; Poet Laureate of California nomination, 2002. Memberships: Ina Coolbrith Poetry Circle. Address: 248 Sandpiper Drive, Davis, CA 95616, USA.

BUNDITJAROENPUN Somchet, b. 2 January 1962, Bangkok, Thailand. MIS Manager; Consultant. Education: BSc, Chulalongkorn University, Bangkok, Thailand, 1984; Master Degree, MBA Major Information and Computer Science, Greenwich University, USA and Australia, 1998; PhD, International Business Administration, Kennedy-Western University, USA, 2000. Appointments: Programmer, Toyota Motor (Thailand) Co Ltd, 1984-88; Programmer, Triumph (Thailand) International Ltd, 1988-90; Programmer, 1990-94, Assistant MIS Manager, 1995-2000, MIS Manager, 2000-, Cosmo Group of Companies; Consultant, Forward Group of Companies, 1996-; Faculty Member, International University of Professional Studies, USA, 2000-2002; Lead Faculty of Center for Business and Economic Development, Akamai University, USA, 2003-. Honours: Organising Committee Member, Asian Institute of Technology Forum Cum Conference, Bangkok, 2000; Life Fellow, IBA, Cambridge; Bronze Medal, IBA; Listed in national and international biographical dictionaries. Membership: Top Management Committee, Forward Group of Companies. Address: 253/7 Moo 5 Soi Kusolsong 1, Old Railway Road, Samrong, Prapradaeng, Samutprakarn 10130, Thailand. E-mail: somchet@isarankura.com Website: www.forwardinter.com/somchet

BUNDRED Nigel, b. 17 July 1957, England. Professor in Surgical Oncology. m. Sally Bundred, 4 sons. Education: MB.BS, University Medical School, Newcastle, 1980; FRCS (Edinburgh and Glasgow), 1985; FRCS(England), 1986, MD thesis, Newcastle, 1990. Appointments: Surgical Elective, University of Virginia, 1979; House Surgeon, 1980-81, House Physician, 1981, Leicester Royal Infirmary; Demonstrator in Anatomy, University of Newcastle upon Tyne, 1981-82; Concurrently, Senior House Officer, Ingham Infirmary, South Shields, 1982; Lecturer, 1982-83 University Department of Clinical Surgery, Cruden Medical Registrar Scholarship, 1983-84, Surgical Registrar Rotation, 1984-87, Royal Infirmary, Edinburgh; Post Fellowship Career Registrar, East Glamorgan General Hospital, 1987-88; Professorial Surgical Unit, 1989, Lecturer in Surgery, 1989-90, University Hospital of Wales; Lecturer, Selly Oak Hospital, Birmingham, 1990; Senior Lecturer (Consultant Surgeon), 1991-96, Reader in Surgical Oncology, 1991-96, Reader in Surgical Oncology, 1996-2001, University Hospital of South Manchester and Christie Hospital; Professor in Surgical Oncology/Consultant Surgeon, University Hospital of South Manchester, 2001-. Publications: Numerous articles in medical journals including most recently: British Journal of Cancer, 2002, 2003, 2004; Clinical Cancer Research, 2002; Anticancer Research, 2002; British Journal of Surgery, 2003 (x2); European Journal of Surgical Oncology, 2003; Clinical Evidence, 2003; Cancer, 2003. Honours: Patey Prize, SRS, 1991: International Guest Fellowship American College of Surgeons, 1996; Hunterian Professorship, Royal College of Surgeons, 1995. Memberships: NCRN Breast Studies group; European Editor, Journal of Surgical Oncology; BASO; British Breast Group; National Committee, Society of Academic and Research Surgeons; Association of Surgeons of Great Britain and Ireland; European School of Surgical Oncology; British Journal of Surgery Society Ltd; British Journal of Surgery Educational Committee. Address:

South Manchester University Hospital, Education and Research Centre, Southmoor Road, Manchester M23 9LT, England. E-mail: bundredn@man.ac.uk

BUNTON Hope, b. 11 January 1921, Willingham, Cambridgeshire, England. Teacher; Poet. m. John Bunton, 15 July 1961, divorced. Education: University of London, 1939-42; International Language School, London, 1971. Appointments: Our Lady's Convent, Brigg; Edmund Campion Comprehensive School; 6th Form College, Preston. Publications: Until All Is Silence; Beyond Silence; Through My Eyes. Contributions to: Envoi; Writer's Voice; Lancashire Life; Cambridgeshire Life; Lincolnshire Writers; Liverpool Echo; Viewpoint; Breakthru; Bedsitter; Lantern Light; Journal of Indian Writing in English; Anthology of Peace Poems for Lancashire Literature Festival; Haiku magazine; Radio Merseyside; Radio Lancashire; Poetry Now; New Hope International; Parnassus of World Poets; Darius Anthology; Railway Anthology, 1996; Countryside Tales; Acorn Magazine; Imagine Writing Group. Honours: 2nd Prize, Religious Section, 3rd Prize, Topical Section, Chorley Arts Poetry Competition. Address: 10 Clifton Street, Preston, Lancashire PR1 8EE, England.

BUNTS Frank, b. 2 March 1932, Cleveland, Ohio, USA. Artist; Teacher. m. Jean G Bunts. Education: BA, MA, Case Western Reserve University, Ohio, USA, 1964. Appointments: Instructor, Cleveland Art Institute, 1963; Instructor, Kansas State University, 1965-68; Assistant and Full Professor, 1969-80, Director of Graduate Art Studio Programme, 1975-80, University of Maryland; Studio Artist, VIA Art Foundation, 1980-. Publications: Works featured in: Cleveland Museum of Art Bulletin, 1968; University of Maryland Art Catalog, 1972; Catalogue Modern Museum of Art, Rijena, Yugoslavia, 1975; Indianapolis Museum of Art, Painting and Sculpture Today, 1976; The Catalog of American Drawing, Watercolors, Pastels and Collages, 1983; New York Art Review, 1988; Archives of American Art; The Address Book, 1993; ICC Artist Database (CD Rom); Numerous review in newspapers including: Chicago Daily News; Skyline 72; Washington Star; Washington Post; Los Angeles Times. Honours: Works in public collections: Philadelphia Museum of Art; Corcoran Gallery of Art; Library of Congress; Cleveland Museum of Art; San Diego Museum of Art. Address: VIA Art Inc, 15 W 24th Street, New York, NY 10010-3214, USA. E-mail: bunts@earthlink.net

BURACAS Antanas, b. 17 June 1939, Kaunas, Lithuania. Political and Financial Economist. m. Marija Regina Jovaisaite, 2 sons, 1 daughter. Education: Magister of Political Economy, 1962; Dr Political Economy, Institute of World Economy and International Relations, USSR Academy of Sciences, 1967; Dr hab in Political Economy, 1971; Center for Central Banking Studies, Bank of England, 1992. Appointments: Senior Researcher and Head, Departments of Social Infrastructure and Mathematical Modelling, Lithuanian Academy of Sciences 1967-91; Founding Vice Director, Scientific Center, Bank of Lithuania, 1991-92; Professor of Banking and Macroeconomics, Vytauti Magnus University 1991-, Vilnius University, 1996-99; Chairman, State Nostrifcat Commission in Social Sciences, 1994-; Associate Professor and Professor, Kaunas Polytechnic Institute and Vilnius University, 1962-75, 1995-99; Vice-Chairman, Editing Board, Lithuanian Universal Encyclopaedia, 1999-. Publications include: 32 books including: Reference Dictionary of Banking and Commerce in 6 volumes, 1997-2002; Sacred Arts in Lithuania, 1999. Honours: Elected Academician, Lithuanian Academy of Sciences, 1976-; Lithuanian Independence Medal, 2000; Honorary Chairman, Lithuanian Human Rights Association, 2000; Fellow, World Innovation Foundation, 2001; Listed in international and national biographical publications. Memberships: Founding President, Lithuanian

Association for Protection of Human Rights, 1989-94; Co-founding Member, Lithuanian Reform Movement Sajudis, 1988-94; Deputy of its I-II Seimas and Councils; President, Lithuanian Association of History and Philosophy of Science, 1986-92; International Sociological Association, 1982-86. Address: Lūkesciu 15, Vilnius 2043, Lithuania. E-mail: anbura@lrs.lt Website: www.members.xoom.com/buracas

BURAUER Stefan. Scientist. m. 2 sons. Education: Diploma in Chemistry, University of Cologne, 1997; PhD, Physical Chemistry, University of Cologne, 2002. Appointments: Chemist, Modular Institute of Technology, Stockholm, Sweden, 1997-98; Assistant, University of Cologne, Germany, 1998-2002; Project Co-ordinator, EuroTecBroker, Technology Marketing, German Aerospace Centre, Cologne, 2002-. Publications: Numerous articles in professional international journals. Memberships: GDCh; German Society of Chemists; German Society for Physical Chemistry; German Society for Electron Microscopy. Address: German Aerospace Ctr (DLR), Technology Marketing, 51170 Cologne, Germany. E-mail: stefan.burauer@dlr.de

BURBIDGE Geoffrey, b. 24 September 1925. Astrophysicist. m. Margaret Peachey, 1948, 1 daughter. Education: Graduated, Physics, Bristol University, 1946; PhD, University College, London; Agassiz Fellow, Harvard University. Appointments: Research Fellow, University of Chicago, 1952-53; Research Fellow, Cavendish Laboratories, Cambridge; Carnegie Fellow, Mount Wilson and Palomar University, Caltech, 1955-57; Assistant Professor, Department of Astronomy, University of Chicago, 1957; Associate Professor, 1962-63, Professor of Physics, 1963-88, Professor Emeritus, 1988, University of California at San Diego -; Director, Kitt Peak National Observatory, Arizona, 1978-84; Scientific editor, Astrophysics Journal, 1996-. Publications: Quasi-Stellar Objects, with Margaret Burbidge, 1967; A Different Approach to Cosmology, with F Moyle and J Narlikar, 2000; Astrophysics papers in scientific journals. Address: Department of Physics, Center for Astrophysics and Space Sciences, University of California, San Diego, La Jolla, CA 92093, USA.

BURCHFIELD Robert William, b. 27 January 1923, Wanganui, New Zealand. Lexicographer; Grammarian. m. (1) Ethel May Yates, 2 July 1949, 1 son, 2 daughters, divorced, (2) Elizabeth Austen Knight, 5 November, 1976. Education: MA, Victoria University of Wellington, 1948; New Zealand Rhodes Scholar, 1949; BA, 1951, MA, 1955, Magdalen College, Oxford. Appointments: Served in World War II, Royal New Zealand Artillery, New Zealand and Italy, 1941-46; Lecturer, Christ Church, Oxford, 1953-57; Lecturer, Tutorial Fellow, Still Emeritus Fellow, St Peter's College, Oxford, 1955-. Publications: A Supplement to the Oxford English Dictionary, 4 volumes, 1972-86; The Spoken Word, 1981; The English Language, 1985; The New Zealand Pocket Oxford Dictionary, 1986; Studies in Lexicography, 1987; Unlocking the English Language, 1989; Points of View, 1992; The Cambridge History of the English Language, Vol 5, 1994; The New Fowler's Modern English Usage, 1996. Contributions to: Sunday Times; Encounter; Transactions of the Philological Society. Honours: Commander of the Order of the British Empire, 1975; Hon DLitt, Liverpool, 1978, Victoria University of Wellington, 1983; Freedom of City of Wanganui, 1986; Shakespeare Prize, 1994. Memberships: Early English Text Society; American Academy of Arts and Sciences. Address: 14 The Green, Sutton Courtenay, Oxon OX14 4AE, England.

BURDA Renate Margarete, b. 14 January 1960, Munich, Germany. Biologist. Education: Abitur, 1980; Diploma, Biology, Ludwig-Maximilian University, Munich, 1993. Appointments: Science Worker, Fluid Engineering, Technology University,

Dictionary of International Biography

Munich, 1985-2000; Laboratory Worker, Medical Care of Urology, Munich, 1995, 1998, 2000; Chief Assistant, Venomous Spider Working Group, Weissenburg, 1995-; Lector, Journal, Latrodecta, 1995-; Scientist, ABiTec, Munich, 2000-; Medical Information, Smith Kline Beecham, Munich, 1996-97, 2000; Medical Customer Care Center, GlaxoSmith Kline, 2001-; Medical Client Service, Bayer Diagnostics, Munich, 1999-2000. Publications: The Role of Web-Building Spiders; New Results Supporting the Theory that Cribra Orbitalia can be caused by iron deficiency anaemia; Electrophoresis of Scorpion Venoms; Die Rolle Radnetzbauender Spinnen in der Biologischen Schädlingsbekämpfung. Honours: Many exhibitions. Memberships: Judge of Trampoline Sports; Venomous Spider Working Group. Address: Eichenstr 17, 82054 Sauerlach, Germany.

BURDEN Barry Christopher, b. 28 April 1971, Newark, Ohio, USA. Professor. m. Laura Read Hillman, 1 son, 1 daughter. Education: BA, Wittenberg University, 1993; PhD, The Ohio State University, 1998. Appointments: Assistant Professor of Government, 1999-2003, Associate Professor of Government, 2003-, Harvard University. Publications: Why Americans Split Their Tickets, with David C Kimball, 2002; Editor, Uncertainty in American Politics, 2003; Numerous articles in American Political Science Review, American Journal of Political Science and others. Honours: Council of Graduate Schools Distinguished Dissertation Award, Best Social Science Dissertation, completed 1998-2000. Address: Harvard University, Department of Government, Cambridge, MA 02138, USA. Website: http://www.fas.harvard.edu/~burden

BURES Jan Zdenek, b. 1 Jan 1954, Hradec Kralove, Czech Republic. Physician. m. Eva Kosova, 2 sons. Education: MD, 1979, PhD, 1990, Charles University, Prague. Appointments: Physician, Teacher, Researcher, Charles University Teaching Hospital, Hradec Kralove, Czech Republic, 1979-. Publications: Textbook of Internal Medicine; Atlas of Enterscopy; Contributor, articles to professional journals. Honours: Award, Immunology Society, Czechoslovac Academy of Science, 1988. Address: Charles University Teaching Hospital, 500 05 Hradec Kralove, Czech Republic. E-mail: bures@lfhk.cuni.cz

BÜRGEL (Johann) Christoph, b. 16 September 1931, Germany. Professor of Islamic Studies. m. Magdalena Kluike, deceased 7 November 1997, 2 sons. Education: PhD, 1965, Habilitation, 1968, University of Göttingen, Germany. Appointment: Professor of Islamic Studies, Head of the Institute of Islamic Studies, University of Bern, Switzerland. Retired 1995. Publications: The Hofkorrespondenz "Adud ad-Daulas", 1965; Arerroes contra Galenum, 1968; The Feather of Simurgh, 1988; Allmacht und Mächtigkeit, 1991; Translations: 3 epics from Nizami (d. 1209), 1980, 1991, 1997; Anthologies from the Diwan of Rumi, 1974, reprinted 2003, 1992; Hafiz, 1972, reprinted 1977. Honours: Medal, Government of Pakistan; Rückert Prize from the Town of Schweinfust, 1983 and Literature Prize from the Town of Bern, 1993 both for translations of poetry from Arabic, Persian and Urdu. Memberships: UEAI; IASTAM; Humboldt Institute. Address: Eichholzweg 26, CH 3024 Muri/BE, Switzerland. E-mail: johann.buergel@islam.unibe.ch

BURGEN Arnold Stanley Vincent, b. 20 March 1922, London, England. Scientist. m. Olga Kennard, 2 sons, 1 daughter, Education: MB, BS 1945, MD, 1949, London; Member, 1949, Fellow, Royal College of Physicians; Fellow, Royal Society, 1964. Appointments: Demonstrator, Assistant Lecturer, Middlesex Hospital Medical School, 1945-49; Professor, Physiology, McGill University, Montreal, 1949-62; Deputy Director, McGill University Medical Clinic, 1957-62; Professor, Pharmacology, Cambridge University,

1962-71; Director, National Institute for Medical Research, 1971-82; Master, Darwin College, Cambridge, 1982-89; Foreign Secretary, Royal Society, 1981-86. Honours: Honorary DSc, McGill University, Liverpool and Leeds; Honorary MD, Utrecht, Zurich; Honorary Fellow, Downing College, Darwin College, Cambridge, Wolfson College, Oxford. Knight Bachelor, 1976; Wellcome Gold Medal, 1999. Publications: Papers in journals of pharmacology and physiology. Memberships: Academia Europaea; Academy of Finland; American Association of Physicians; Foreign Member, US Academy of Sciences. Address: Keelson, 8A Hills Avenue, Cambridge, CB1 7XA, England.

BURGER Alewyn P, b. 31 January 1927, Middelburg, Transvaal, South Africa. Scientist. m. Erica, 1 son, 4 daughters. Education: MSc, Mathematics, cum laude, University of Pretoria, South Africa, 1952; DScTech, Applied Mathematics, cum laude, Technological University, Delft, Netherlands, 1955; Accredited Professional Translator, South African Translators' Institute, 2001. Appointments: Research Division, Weather Bureau, Pretoria, 1950-57; Head, Applied Mathematics Division, National Physical Research Laboratory, 1957-61; Director, National Research Institute for Mathematical Sciences, 1961-73; Executive Vice President, 1973-76, Council for Scientific and Industrial Research; Chairman, Scientific Advisory Council to the Prime Minister, Scientific Advisor to the Prime Minister, Head of Scientific Planning, Prime Minister's Office, 1977-81; Consultant on atmospheric processes, including to Council for Scientific and Industrial Research, 1982-; Part-time Lecturer, Dynamical Meteorology, University of Pretoria, 1990-. Publications: Articles in scientific journals including: Statistica, The Hague, Netherlands, Proceedings of the Royal Society, London, UK, Tellus, Stockholm, Sweden, Journal of Atmospheric Sciences, Lancaster, Pennsylvania, USA, Contributions to Atmospheric Physics, Wiesbaden, Germany; Editor of conference proceedings volumes. Honours include: Fellow, South African Academy for Science and Arts; Fellow, Royal Society of South Africa; Havenga Prize for Mathematics, South African Academy for Science and Arts, 1973; Honorary Professor of Applied Mathematics, University of Stellenbosch; Fellow, Academy of Science of South Africa; Honorary Member, South African Society for Atmospheric Sciences. Past Presidencies include: Joint Council of Scientific Societies; South African Mathematical Society; South African Society for Atmospheric Sciences. Address: PO Box 17071, Groenkloof 0027, South Africa.

BURGER Henry G, b. 27 June 1923, New York, USA. Vocabulary Scientist and Publisher. m. Barbara G Smith. Education: BA (Honours), Columbia College, 1947; MA, 1965, PhD, Cultural Anthropology, 1967, Columbia University. Appointments: Social Science Consultant, 1956-67; Founding editor and publisher, The Wordtree, 1958- (fulltime, 1994-); Selected for exhibit in 3 institutes; Selected as a topic in Cambridge Encyclopaedia of the English Language, 1995-; 7 time citee in Oxford English Dictionary; Anthropologist, Southwestern Cooperative Educational Laboratory, 1967-69; Adjunct Professor, University of New Mexico, 1969; Professor of Anthropology and Education, University of Missouri, 1969-93; Professor Emeritus, 1993-. Publications: 95 include: 11 books, manuals or monographs; 1 tape-cassette, 1976; 15 journal columns; 31 communications; 37 articles or book chapters; Compiler, editor of The Wordtree, an add-on dictionary (which branches from a mere idea to the precise word for it), 1984. Honours: Phi Beta Kappa; Life Fellow, American Anthropological Association, 1975-; Life Member, Dictionary Society of North America, 1985-; Fellow: World Academy of Art and Science; Vice President, English Speaking Union of Kansas City, 1995-96; Worldwide interview broadcast by Voice of America, 2002. Memberships include: Society for

Conceptual and Content Analysis by Computer; International Association for Semiotic Sciences; Corresponding Member, Académie européenne des sciences, des arts et des lettres. Address: The Wordtree, 10876 Bradshaw, Overland Park, KS 66210-1148, USA.

BURINSKII Alexander, b. 6 October 1939, Moscow, Russia. Physicist. m. Lubov Zhamnova, 29 May 1969, 1 son, 1 daughter. Education: Student, 1957, Postgraduate, 1964, PhD, 1969, Moscow Physics and Technical University; Doctor of Physical and Mathematical Sciences, 2003. Appointments: Engineer Physicist, 1963; Senior Scientific Researcher, 1969; Chief, Laboratory in Computer Centre, 1974; Senior Scientific Researcher in Pedagogical University, 1987; Senior Scientific Researcher, Gravity Group, Nuclear Safety Institute, Russian Academy of Sciences, 1989-. Publications: Publications in numerous journals. Membership: Russian Gravitational Society. Address: Nuclear Safety Institute, Russian Academy of Science, B Tulskaya 52, 115191, Moscow, Russia.

BURKE John Frederick, (Owen Burke, Harriet Esmond, Jonathan George, Joanna Jones, Robert Miall, Sara Morris, Martin Sands), b. 8 March 1922, Rye, England. Author. m. (1) Joan Morris, 13 September 1940, 5 daughters, (2) Jean Williams, 29 June 1963, 2 sons. Appointments: Production Manager, Museum Press; Editorial Manager, Paul Hamlyn Books for Pleasure Group: European Story Editor, 20th Century Fox Productions. Publications: Swift Summer, 1949; An Illustrated History of England, 1974; Dr Caspian Trilogy, 1976-78; Musical Landscapes, 1983; Illustrated Dictionary of Music, 1988; A Travellers History of Scotland, 1990; Bareback, 1998; Death by Marzipan, 1999; We've Been Waiting for You, 2000; Stalking Widow, 2000; The Second Strain, 2002; Wrong Turnings, 2004. Film and TV Novelisations. Contributions to: The Bookseller; Country Life; Denmark. Honour: Atlantic Award in Literature, 1948-49. Memberships: Society of Authors; Danish Club. Address: 5 Castle Gardens, Kirkcudbright, Dumfries & Galloway DG6 4JE, Scotland.

BURKE Kathy, b. London, England. Actress. Education: Anna Scher's Theatre School, London. Creative Works: TV include: Harry Enfield and Chums; Absolutely Fabulous; Common as Muck; Mr Wroes' Virgins; Tom Jones; Gimme Gimme Gimme. Films: Scrubbers; Nil By Mouth; Elizabeth, 1998; This Year's Love, 1999; Love, Honour and Obey, 2000; The Martins, 2001; Once Upon a Time in the Midlands, 2002; Anita and Me, 2002. Theatre includes: Mr Thomas, London; Boom Bang-a-Bang, London (director). Honours: Royal TV Society Award; Best Actress, Cannes Film Festival, 1997.

BURKE Ronald J, b. 22 October 1937, Winnipeg, Manitoba, Canada. Professor. 1 son, 2 daughters. Education: BA, Psychology, English, University of Manitoba, 1960; MA, Psychology, 1962, PhD, Industrial and Organizational Psychology, 1966, University Michigan. Appointments: Teaching Assistant, University of Manitoba, 1959-60; Teaching Fellow, 1960-62, Research Assistant, 1962-66, University of Michigan; Assistant Professor, University of Michigan, 1966-68; Assistant Professor, 1968-69, Associate Professor, 1969-72, Professor, 1972-, York University; Senior Fellow, National Centre for Management Research and Development, School of Business Administration, University of West Ontario, 1988-92; Imperial Life Professor of Organisational Behaviour, National Centre for Management Research and Development, School of Business Administration, University of West Ontario, 1988-92; Associate Dean, Research, FAS, 1992-95; Director of Research, Organizational Studies International, 1995. Publications include: Coping self-efficacy and downsizing in nurses, 1998; Women in Management Research: New Frontiers, 1998; Caution: Women's families may be hazardous to their managerial careers, 1998. Honours include: Institute of Labor and Industrial Relations Fellowship, 1961-62; Several Research Grants. Memberships: Sigma Xi; American Psychology Association; Midwestern Psychology Association; Western Psychology Association; Academy of Management; American Association for the Advancement of Science; Administration Sciences Association of Canada; Society for Personnel Administration; Eastern Psychology Association; Canadian Psychology Association; International Association of Applied Psychology; Society for Industrial and Organizational Psychology; International Congress of Psychology; International Society for Study of Work and Organizational Values. Address: School of Business, York University, 4700 Keele Street, North York, Ontario M3J 1P3, Canada.

BURKERT Andreas Michael, b. 12 May 1959, Gangkofen, Germany. Astronomer. m. Inge C Burkert, 1 son. Education: Diploma in Physics, University of Munich, 1986; PhD, Astrophysics, 1989. Appointments: Research Associate, University of Illinois, 1989-90; Research Associate, University of California, 1990-91; Research Associate, Max Planck Institute for Astrophysics, 1991-94; Head, Theoretical Research Group, Max Planck Institute for Astronomy, 1995-2003; Promotion for a BAT Ib Position to a BAT Ia Position, 1996; Promotion for a BAT Ia Position to a C3 Position, 1997; Full Professor and Director of University Observatory, University Munich, 2003-. Honours: Student Fellowship from the German Government, 1984; Feodor Lynen Postdoctoral Fellowship, Humboldt Foundation; Award for the best PhD in Physics, University of Munich; Feodor Lynen Postdoctoral Fellowship, Humboldt Foundation; Ludwig Biermann Prize, German Astronomical Society. Memberships: German Astronomical Society; American Astronomical Society; German Physical Society; International Astronomical Union. Address: University Observatory Munich, Scheinerstr 1, D-81679 Munich, Germany. E-mail: burkert@usm.uni-muenchen.de

BURKHOLZ Herbert Laurence, b. 9 December 1932, New York, New York, USA. Author. m. Susan Blaine, 1 November 1961, 2 sons. Education: BA, New York University, 1951. Appointment: Writer-in-Residence, College of William and Mary, 1975. Publications: Sister Bear, 1969; Spy, 1969; The Spanish Soldier, 1973; Mulligan's Seed, 1975; The Death Freak, 1978; The Sleeping Spy, 1983; The Snow Gods, 1985; The Sensitives, 1987; Strange Bedfellows, 1988; Brain Damage, 1992; Writer in Residence, 1992; The FDA Follies, 1994. Contributions to: New York Times; Town & Country; Playboy; Penthouse; Longevity. Honour: Distinguished Scholar, 1976. Address: 4 Della Lane, Boonsboro, MD 21713, USA.

BURNO Mark Eugenievich, b. 14 March 1939, Moscow, Russia. Psychotherapist. m. Alla, 1 son. Education: Graduate, Second Medical Institute, Moscow, 1963; Candidate of Medical Science, 1969; Doctor of Medical Science, 1998. Appointments: Psychiatrist, Psychotherapist, Psychiatric Hospital, Kaluga, Russia, 1963-; Psychoneurological Centre, Moscow, 1965-; Lecturer, Russian Medical Academy for Postgraduate Education, Department of Psychotherapy, 1970-; Assistant Professor, docent, currently Professor. Publications: 234 works in English, French, Russian and other Slav languages include: On Psychoprophylaxis of Hard Drinking and Alcoholism by Means of Creative Self-Expression in "Risk Groups", 1987; Creative Self-Expression Therapy, 1989, 1999; Hard Character and Drunkenness, 1990; The Power of Weakness, 1999; Clinical Psychotherapy, 2000; Alcoholism, Creative Self-Expression Therapy, 2002; Creative Self-Expression Therapy is a Direction School in Russian

Dictionary of International Biography

Psychotherapy: The Direction School of Burno. Honours: Vice President, Professional Psychotherapeutic League (Russia); Supervisor of Russian Psychotherapeutic Association; Academician of Moscow Psychotherapeutic Academy; Member of Editorial Board, Independent Psychiatric Journal (Russia); Moscow Psychotherapeutic Journal; International Journal of Art Therapy, The Healing Art. Address: Weshniakovskaja Street 4-1-101 Moscow 111402, Russia.

BURNS Jim, b. 19 February 1936, Preston, Lancashire, England. Writer; Part-time Teacher. Education: BA Honours, Bolton Institute of Technology, 1980. Appointments: Editor, Move, 1964-68; Editor, Palantir, 1976-83; Jazz Editor, Beat Scene, 1990-. Publications: A Single Flower, 1972; The Goldfish Speaks from beyond the Grave, 1976; Fred Engels bei Woolworth, 1977; Internal Memorandum, 1982; Out of the Past: Selected Poems 1961-1986, 1987; Confessions of an Old Believer, 1996; The Five Senses, 1999; As Good a Reason As Any, 1999; Beats, Bohemians and Intellectuals, 2000; Take it Easy, 2003; Bopper, 2003. Contributions to: London Magazine; Stand; Ambit; Jazz Journal; Critical Survey; The Guardian; New Statesman; Tribune; New Society; Penniless Press; Prop; Verse; Others. Address: 11 Gatley Green, Gatley, Cheadle, Cheshire SK8 4NF, England.

BURNS Michael Thornton, b. 30 December 1947, New York, New York, USA. Historian; Farmer. m. Elizabeth Kennan, 1 son. Education: BA, summa cum laude, 1976, MA, 1977, University of California, Los Angeles; MPhil, 1979, PhD, 1981, Yale University. Appointments: Acting Instructor, Yale University, 1978-79; From Assistant Professor to Professor, 1981-2002, Dana Faculty Fellow, 1993-2002, Professor Emeritus, 2002-, Mount Holyoke College, Massachusetts, USA; Visiting Directeur d'Etudes, Ecole des Hautes Etudes, Paris, France, 1991; Affiliated Scholar, 2002-, Centre College, Kentucky, USA. Publications: Books: Rural Society and French Politics, 1991; Main Trends in History (revision of G Barraclough), 1984; Dreyfus: A Family Affair from the French Revolution to the Holocaust, 1992; France and the Dreyfus Affair, 1999. Honours: Fellow, Woodrow Wilson International Center for Scholars, 1992-93; Phi Alpha Theta Best Book Award, 1992; Prix Bernard Lecache, France, 1994. Memberships: Phi Beta Kappa; Phi Alpha Theta; Thoroughbred Club of America; Thoroughbred Owners and Breeders. Address: Cambus-Kenneth Farm, PO Box 1989, Danville, KY 40423, USA.

BURRELL Leroy, b. 21 February 1967, Landsdowne, Philadelphia, USA. Athlete. m. Michelle Finn, 2 sons. Education: University of Houston, Texas. Appointments: Established 'Clean' World Record, Running 100m in 9.9 seconds at US Championships, New York, 1991; Established World Record 100m, 1994; Head Track and Field Coach, University of Houston, 1998-. Honour: Olympic Gold Medal, 4x100m relay, Barcelona, 1992. Address: USA Track & Field Press Information Department, 1 RCA Dome, Suite 140, Indianapolis, IN 46225, USA.

BURRELL Michael Philip, b. 12 May 1937, Harrow, England. Education: BA, MA (Cantab), Peterhouse, Cambridge, 1958-61. Career: Freelance actor since 1961, appearing in major British companies including, the Royal Shakespeare Company, the Chichester Festival Company and Stratford East; Numerous TV appearances; Over 25 feature films; Directing career since 1964, posts include, Associate Director, Royal Lyceum Theatre, Edinburgh 1966-68; Director, Angles Theatre, Wisbech, 1995-2001; Serves on various arts boards, including the Drama Panel of the Eastern Arts Association, 1981-86; King's Lynn Festival and Arts Centre, 1992-95; Theatre Royal, Bury St Edmunds, 1994-2000; Company Secretary, Tiebreak Touring Theatre Ltd, 1987-. Publications: Over 17 plays including the multi-award winning

Hess, 1978, 5 London productions, including one by the RSC at the Almeida; Borrowing Time; My Sister Next Door; The Man Who Lost America; Love Among the Butterflies; Lord of the Fens; Several articles; A current weekly column, In My View, in the Fenland Citizen newspaper. Honours: Oble Award, for Hess, 1980; Best Actor, Best Show, Edmonton Journal Awards, 1984, 1985; Capital Critics Award for Best Actor, Ottawa, 1986; Bronze Award, New York Film Festival, 1988; Edmonton Journal Award for Best Show, for My Sister Next Door, 1989; Honorary President, Peterhouse Heywood Society, 2002-. Memberships: National Liberal Club, London. Address: c/o Richard Stone Partnership, 2 Henrietta Street, London WC2E 8PS, England.

BURROWAY Janet (Gay), b. 21 September 1936, Tucson, Arizona, USA. Professor; Writer; Poet. m. (1) Walter Eysselinck, 1961, divorced 1973, 2 sons, (2) William Dean Humphries, 1978, divorced 1981, (3) Peter Ruppert, 1993, 1 stepdaughter. Education: University of Arizona, 1954-55; AB, Barnard College, 1958; BA, 1960, MA, 1965, Cambridge University; Yale School of Drama, 1960-61. Appointments: Instructor, Harpur College, Binghamton, New York, 1961-62; Lecturer, University of Sussex, 1965-70; Associate Professor, 1972-77, Professor, 1977-, MacKenzie Professor of English, 1989-95, Robert O Lawson Distinguished Professor, 1995-2002, Emerita, 2002-, Florida State University; Fiction Reviewer, Philadelphia Enquirer, 1986-90; Reviewer, New York Times Book Review, 1991-; Essay-Columnist, New Letters: A Magazine of Writing and Art, 1994-. Publications: Fiction: Descend Again, 1960; The Dancer From the Dance, 1965; Eyes, 1966; The Buzzards, 1969; The Truck on the Track, children's book, 1970; The Giant Jam Sandwich, children's book, 1972; Raw Silk, 1977; Opening Nights, 1985; Cutting Stone, 1992. Poetry: But to the Season, 1961; Material Goods, 1980; Essays: Embalming Mom, 2002. Other: Writing Fiction: A Guide to Narrative Craft, 1982, 6th edition, 2002; Imaginative Writing, 2002. Contributions to: Numerous journals and periodicals. Honours: National Endowment for the Arts Fellowship, 1976; Yaddo Residency Fellowships, 1985, 1987; Lila Wallace-Reader's Digest Fellow, 1993-94; Carolyn Benton Cockefaire Distinguished Writer-in-Residence, University of Missouri, 1995; Woodrow Wilson Visiting Fellow, Furman University, Greenville, South Carolina, 1995; Erskine College, Due West, South Carolina, 1997; Drury College, Springfield, Illinois, 1999. Memberships: Associated Writing Programs, vice president, 1988-89; Authors Guild. Literary Agent: Gail Hochman, Brandt & Hochman, 1501 Broadway, New York 10036. Address: 240 De Soto Street, Tallahassee, FL 32303, USA. E-mail: jburroway@english.fsu.edu

BURRY Kenneth A, b. 10 February 1942, Monterey Park, California, USA. Professor. m. Katherine Johnson, 1 son, 1 daughter. Education: BA, Whittier College, California, 1964; MD, University of California, Irvine, 1968. Appointments: Fellow, Reproductive Endocrinology, Department of Obstetrics and Gynaecology, University of Washington School of Medicine, Seattle, 1974-76; Consultant, Veterans Hospital, Portland, Oregon, 1976-99; Assistant Professor, 1976-80, Associate Professor, 1980-89, Professor, 1989-, Director, Oregon Reproductive Research and Fertility Program, 1982-88, Medical Advisor, Infertility Service Laboratory, 1983-, Director, Fellowship Training Program in Reproductive Endocrinology and Infertility, 1984-97, Co-Director, Division of Reproductive Endocrinology and Infertility, Department of Obstetrics and Gynaecology, 1985-88, Assistant Chairman, Department of Obstetrics and Gynaecology, 1989-, Director, Division of Reproductive Endocrinology and Infertility, Department of Obstetrics and Gynaecology, 1992-, Interim Chair, Department of OBE, 2000-01, Vice-Chair, 2001-, Oregon Health Sciences University, Portland. Publications: Numerous articles in professional medical journals. Honours: Lange Book Award, 1966; Medical Honor Society Award, 1968; Multnomah Medical Society

Dictionary of International Biography

Presidential Citation, 1983. Memberships include: American Association for the Advancement of Science; American Federation for Medical Research; American Medical Association; American Society for Reproductive Medicine; Endocrine Society; European Society of Human Reproduction and Embryology; Oregon Medical Association; Pacific Coast Obstetrics and Gynaecology Society; Pacific Coast Reproductive Society, President, 1997; North West Obstetrics and Gynaecology Association; Society of Reproductive Surgeons. Address: OHSU-University Fertility Consultants, 1750 S W Harbor Way, Suite 100, Portland, OR 97201-5133, USA.

BURSHTEIN Sheldon, b. 13 March 1952, Montreal, Quebec, Canada. Lawyer. Education: B(Civ)Eng, 1974, BCL, 1977, LLB, 1978, McGill University. Appointments: Admitted to Law Society of Upper Canada, 1980; Registered Professional Engineer, Ontario, 1980; Registered Trademark Agent, Canada, 1980; Lawyer, Patent Agent and Trademark Agent; Registered Trademark Agent, US (Canadian Applicants), 1982; Partner, Blake Cassels & Graydon, LLP, Toronto, Ontario, 1986-; Registered Patent Agent, Canada, 1987, US (Canadian Applicants), 1987; Certified Specialist, Intellectual Property (Patent, Trademark and Copyright) Law, Law Society of Upper Canada, 1994. Publications: Book, Patent Your Own Invention in Canada, 1991; Co-author, book, The Use of Another's Trademark, 1997; Author, book, Corporate Counsel Guide to Intellectual Property Law, 2000; Co-author other books; Very numerous contributions to journals, conferences on Patents, Trademarks, Copyright and Designs, Confidential Information, Electronic Commerce, Domain Names, Licensing and Franchising, Intellectual Property Aspects of Commercial Transactions, Intellectual Property and Free Trade, Intellectual Property Management, Engineering. Honours: Marie F Morency Memorial Prize, Patent Intellectual Property Institute of Canada, Highest National Standing in Patent Drafting Exam, 1987; Selected as one of the World's Leading Patent Law Experts, Managing Intellectual Property; World's Leading Trademark Law Experts and World's Top 50 Trademark Lawyers, Managing Intellectual Property; Selected, Most Frequently Recommended Intellectual Property Lawyers, and Top 500 Canadian Lawyers Expert; Named The Best of the Best, Trade Marks, Euromoney; Listed in national and international biographical dictionaries. Memberships: Editorial Advisory Board, The Licensing Journal; Advisory Board, Multimedia and Technology Licensing Law Report; Editorial Board, Intellectual Property; Editorial Board, The Trademark Reporter, International Trademark Association; Advisory Board, Chair and Former Chair, Various Committees, Intellectual Property Institute of Canada. Address: c/o Blake Cassels & Graydon, LLP, PO Box 25, Commerce Court West, Toronto, Ontario M5L 1A9, Canada. E-mail: sb@blakes.com

BURTON Gregory Keith, b. 12 February 1956, Sydney, New South Wales, Australia. Barrister-at-Law. m. (1) Suzanne Louise Brandstater, 1994, 1 son, 1 daughter, (2) Penelope Josephine Whitehead, 2004, 1 son, 3 daughters. Education: BCL, Oxon; BA Honours, LLB Honours, University of Sydney; Graded Arbitrator, Accredited Mediator, Conciliator and Evaluator; Associate, Institute Arbitrators and Mediators, Australia; Barrister, New South Wales, High Court and Federal Courts, Queensland, Ireland; Barrister and Solicitor, Victoria, Western Australia, ACT, Northern Territory. Appointments: Solicitor, Freehill Hollingdale and Page, 1980-83; Associate to Sir William Deane, High Court of Australia, 1984-85; Senior Adviser to Federal MP, 1986; Lecturer, Law, Australian National University, 1987-88; Bar, 1989-. Publications: Australian Financial Transactions Law, 1991; Chapters and articles in, and editor of, texts, journals, book and legal encyclopaedias; Directions in Finance Law, 1990; Weaver and Craigie's Banker and Customer in Australia (co-author). Honours: Dux, Trinity Grammar School, Sydney, 1968-73; University Medal, History,

University of Sydney, 1978; Prizes in Equity, Commercial Law, Public Law, English, History, Government; Editorial Committee, Sydney Law Review, 1978-79. Memberships: NSW Bar Association; Business Law Section, Law Council of Australia; Banking and Financial Services Law Association; Commercial Law Association; Australian Institute Administrative Law; Various ADR Organizations; Centre International Legal Studies, Vienna; Centre Independent Studies; Institute of Public Affairs; Sydney Institute; Director, Australian Elizabethan Theatre Trust. Address: 5th Floor, Wentworth Chambers, 180 Phillip Street, Sydney, NSW, Australia 2000.

BURTON Tim, b. 1958, Burbank, California, USA. Film Director. Education: California Arts Institute. Appointments: Animator, Walt Disney Studios, projects include: The Fox and the Hound, The Black Cauldron; Animator, Director, Vincent (short length film). Creative Works: Films director: Frankenweenie, 1984; Aladdin, 1985; Pee-wee's Big Adventure, 1985; Beetlejuice, 1988; Batman, 1989; Edward Scissorhands, 1991; Batman Returns, 1992; Ed Wood, 1994; Batman Forever, 1996; Mars Attacks!, 1996; Sleepy Hollow, 1999; Planet of the Apes, 2001; The Heart of Me, 2002; Big Fish, 2003; Producer, The Nightmare Before Christmas, 1993; Cabin Boy, 1994; James and the Giant Peach, 1996; Lost in Oz (TV), 2000. Publications: My Art and Films, 1993; The Melancholy Death of Oyster Boy and Other Stories, 1997. Honours include: 2 Awards, Chicago Film Festival. Address: Chapman, Bird & Grey, 1990 South Bundy Drive, Suite 200, Los Angeles, CA 90025, USA.

BUSAWON Krishna Kumar, b. 16 September 1963, Highlands, Phoenix, Mauritius. Engineering Educator. m. Jennifer Mary Marshall. Education: Maitrise in Electrical Engineering, 1991, Diplome d'Etude Superieure, Electrical Engineering, 1992, PhD, Control Engineering, 1996, Claude Bernard University Lyon 1, Lyon, France. Appointments: Teaching Assistant, Claude Bernard Lyon 1, Lyon, France, 1992-96; Fellow, Simon Fraser University, Burnaby, Canada, 1996-98; Lecturer, University of Nuevo Leon, Monterrey, Mexico, 1998-2000; Senior Lecturer, Northumbria University, Newcastle upon Tyne, England, 2000-. Publications: Articles in professional journals on non-linear observer and control design. Honours: Higher Education Scholar, Ministere de l'Enseignement Superieur, France, 1991-92; Scholar, Ministere Recherche et de l'Espace, France, 1992-95 Research Grant, Direccion Generale de Investigation of University of Nuevo Leon, 1999. Memberships: Chairman, International Association of Science and Technology for Development, Novosibirsk, Russia, 2002; IEEE. Address: Northumbria University, Ellison Building, Newcastle upon Tyne NE1 8ST, England.

BUSH Barbara Pierce, b. 8 June 1925, Rye, New York, USA. Former First Lady of USA. m. George Bush, 1945, 4 sons, 1 daughter. Education: Smith College. Appointments: Various committees and councils dealing with literature and cancer care; President, Ladies of the Senate, 1981-88; Member, Staff Office of George Bush, 1992-. Honours: Outstanding Mother of the Year, 1984; Numerous honours degrees, Distinguished Leadership, United Negro College Fund, 1986; Distinguished American Woman, Mount St Joseph College, 1987. Publication: Barbara Bush: A Memoir, 1994. Address: 490 E L'Enfant Plaza, SW, Room 6125, Washington, DC 20594, USA.

BUSH George Herbert Walker, b. 12 June 1924, Milton, USA. American Politician. m. Barbara Pierce, 1945, 4 sons, 1 daughter. Education: Phillips Academy, Andover, Massachusetts; Yale University. Appointments: Naval Carrier Pilot, 1942-45; Co-Founder, Director, Zapata Petroleum Corporation, 1953-59; Founder, President, Zapata Offshore Corporation, 1956-64, Chair,

1964-66; Member, House of Representatives, 7th District of Texas, 1967-71; Permanent Representative to UN, 1971-72; Chair, Republican National Committee, 1973-74; Head, US Liaison Office, Peking, 1974-75; Director, CIA, 1976-77; Vice President, USA, 1981-89, President, USA, 1989-93. Publication: Looking Forward: An Autobiography (with Victor Gold), 1988. Publications: Looking Forward: An Autobiography (with Victor Gold), 1988; A World Transformed (with Brent Scowcroft), 1998; All the Best, George Bush, 1999. Honours include: Several honorary degrees; Churchill Award, 1991; Honorary GCB, 1993. Address: Suite 900, 10000 Memorial Drive, Houston, TX 77024-3422, USA.

BUSH George W, b. 6 July 1946, USA. President of the United States of America. m. Laura Welch Bush, twin daughters. Education: Bachelor's Degree, History, Yale University; Master of Business Administration, Harvard University. Appointments: F-102 Pilot, Texas Air National Guard; Founder and Manager, Spectrum 7 Energy Corporation (merged with Harken Energy Corporation, 1986), Midland Texas; Director, Harken Energy Corporation; Professional Baseball Team Executive with Texas Rangers, 1989-94; Elected Governor of Texas, 1994; Re-elected, 1998; Elected President of the United States, 2001-. Address: The White House, Washington, DC 20500, USA.

BUSH Kate (Catherine), b. 30 July 1958, Bexleyheath, Kent, England. Singer; Songwriter. Education: Voice, dance and mime lessons. Career: Limited live performances include: Tour Of Life, Europe, 1979; Secret Policeman's Third Ball, London, 1987; Television appearances include: Bringing It All Back Home documentary, 1991; Writer, director, actress, film The Line, The Cross And The Curve, 1994. Recordings (mostly self-composed): Albums: The Kick Inside, 1978; Lionheart, 1978; Never For Ever (Number 1, UK), 1980; The Dreaming, 1982; Hounds Of Love (Number 1, UK), 1985; The Whole Story (Number 1, UK), 1987; The Sensual World (Number 2, UK), 1989; This Womans Work, 1990; The Red Shoes (Number 2, UK), 1993; Contributor, Games Without Frontiers, Peter Gabriel, 1980; Two Rooms - Celebrating The Songs Of Elton John And Bernie Taupin, 1991; Singles include: Wuthering Heights (Number 1, UK), 1978; The Man With The Child In His Eyes, 1978; Wow, 1979; Breathing, 1980; Babooshka, 1980; Army Dreamers, 1980; Sat In Your Lap, 1981; Running Up That Hill, 1985; Cloudbusting, 1985; Hounds Of Love, 1986; Experiment IV, 1986; Don't Give Up, duet with Peter Gabriel, 1986; This Woman's Work (from film soundtrack She's Having A Baby), 1988; The Sensual World, 1989; Moments Of Pleasure, 1993; Rubberband Girl, 1993; Man I Love, 1994; The Red Shoes, 1994. Honours: Ivor Novello Awards, Outstanding British Lyric, The Man With The Child In His Eyes, 1979; BRIT Award, Best British Female Artist, 1987. Address: PO Box 120, Welling, Kent, DA16 3DA, England.

BUSH Laura Lane, b. 4 November 1986, Midland, Texas, USA. m. George W Bush , 1977, 2 Daughters, 1981.Education: Bachelor's degree, Education, Southern Methodist University, 1968; Masters degree, Library Science, University of Texas, Austin, 1973. Career: School Teacher; Librarian; First Lady, Texas; First Lady, United States, 2001-. TV Appearences: A&E Biography: George W Bush - Son Also Rises, 2000; Express Yourself, 2001; Last Party, 2001; Intimate Portrait, 2003; Larry King Live, 2003; The Tonight Show with Jay Leno, 2004.

BUSSELL Darcy, b. 27 April 1969. Ballerina. m. Angus Forbes, 1997, 1 daughter. Education: Royal Ballet School. Career: Birmingham Royal Ballet, then Sadlers Wells, 1987; Soloist; Royal Ballet, 1988, first solo, 1989; Principal, 1989-. Appearances include: The Spirit of Fugue, created for her by David Bintley;

Swan Lake; The Nutcracker; The Prince of the Pagodas; Cinderella; Sleeping Beauty; Bloodlines; Romeo and Juliet; Giselle; Raymonda; Numerous appearances on TV; Guest with other ballet companies in Paris, St Petersburg and New York. Publications: My Life in Dance, 1998; Favourite Ballet Stories; The Young Dancer. Honours: Prix de Lausanne, 1989; Dancer of the Year, 1990. Address: The Royal Opera House, Covent Garden, London, WC2E 9DD, England.

BUTALA Sharon Annette, b. 24 August 1940, Nipawin, Saskatchewan, Canada. Writer. m. Peter Butala, 21 May 1976, 1 son. Education: BEd, 1962, BA, 1963, Postgraduate Diploma in Special Education, 1973, University of Saskatchewan. Appointment: Writer. Publications: Country of the Heart, novel, 1984; Queen of the Headaches, novel, 1985; The Gates of the Sun, 1986; Luna, novel, 1988; FEVER, fiction, 1990; Upstream, novel, 1991; Harvest, non-fiction, 1992; The Fourth Archangel, novel, 1992; The Perfection of the Morning, non-fiction, 1994; The Garden of Eden, novel, 1998; Coyote's Morning Cry, non-fiction, 1995; Wild Stone Heart, non-fiction, 2000; Old Man on His Back, non-fiction, 2002; Real Life, fiction, 2002. Contributions to: MacLeans; Story; Canadian Fiction Magazine; Saturday Night; Flare; Books in Canada; Prairie Schooner; Great Plains Quarterly; Canadian Forum. Honours: Saskatechewan Book Awards: Non-Fiction and Spirit of Saskatchewan, 1994; Marian Engel Award, 1998; LLD (Hon) University of Regina, 2000; Officer, Order of Canada, 2002. Memberships: The Writer's Union of Canada; PEN Canada; Saskatchewan Writers' Guild. Address: Westwood Creative Artists, 94 Harbord Street, Toronto, Ontario M5S 1G6, Canada.

BUTANI Partab Hassasing, b. 23 December 1928, Karachi (now in Pakistan). Retired. m. Kala. Education: BA, History and Economics, 1949; MA, History and Economics, 1953, BCom, Transport, 1959, Bombay University; Diploma in Dramatic Art, Natya Academy, affiliated to UNESCO, 1960. Appointments: Senior Clerk to the top rung of 'B' Grade Officers' Cadre, Senior Consumers Assistant, Bombay Electric Supply and Transport Undertaking (B.E.S.T), retired, 1984. Publications: Founder, Editor, Contributor, letters, articles and one-act plays, "Pushp" (Flower) magazine, in Sindhi, 1958-60; Founder-Editor, Tourist Guides Association magazine, in English (TOGA), 1967-69. Honours: First Prizes include: Stage Lighting, 1960; Competition in Evening News of India Paper, Why I Love Mulund and Why I Hate Mulund; Further prizes from foreign magazines, Czechoslovak and East German; Appointed Honorary Animal Welfare Officer, Bombay, Animal Welfare Board of India, Ministry of Environment and Forests, Government of India, 1990; Member, Research Board of Advisors, American Biographical Institute Inc, USA, 1997; Distinguished Leadership Award, ABI, USA, 1997; Bharat Jyoti Award (Light of India), India International Friendship Society, 2003; Solo exhibition of 111 colour photographs, Madras, 1982, Calcutta, 1983; Listed in national and international biographical dictionaries. Memberships include: Honorary Secretary, Best Sindhi Sabha, 1958-60; Honorary Secretary, Tourist Guides Association, 1967-69; Trustee, Dhamidevi Charity Trust, Bombay, 1980; Fellow, United Writers' Association, Madras, 1994; Life Member, Indo-Japanese Association, 1995; Life Member, Blue Cross of Hyderabad, Animal Welfare Organization, Hyderabad, 1996; Bombay Natural History Society; Bombay SPCA; Life Member, Beauty Without Cruelty, India Branch, 1997; Life Member, Indian Red Cross Society, 2001; Director, Stray Dog Lovers Association, Vashi, New Bombay, 1990; Committee Member, Litigants' Welfare Forum, Bombay, 1990; Sindhu Bharati, Cultural Organisation, Bombay, 1990; Indian Council of World Affairs, Delhi/Bombay; Speakers' Forum, Bombay, 1990; Asiatic

Society of Bombay, 2001-; Member, People for the Ethical Treatment of Animals, PETA (India), 2002-. Address: 91/1 Mulund Colony, Mulund West, Bombay 400 082, India.

BUTLER (Frederick) Guy, b. 21 January 1918, Cradock, Cape Province, South Africa. Retired Professor of English Literature; Poet; Writer; Dramatist. m. Jean Murray Satchwell, 7 December 1940, 4 children. Education: BA, 1938, MA, 1939, Rhodes University; BA, 1947, MA, 1951, Brasenose College, Oxford. Appointments: Schoolmaster, St John's College, Johannesburg, 1940; Lecturer, University of Witwatersrand, 1948-50; Senior Lecturer, 1951, Professor of English Literature, 1952-86, Rhodes University. Publications: Stranger to Europe 1939-49, 1952, with additional poems, 1960; A Book of South African Verse (editor), 1959; South of the Zambezi: Poems from South Africa, London and New York, 1966; On First Seeing Florence, 1968; Selected Poems, 1975, with additional poems, 1989; Songs and Ballads, 1978; Pilgrimage to Dias Cross, 1987; Out of the African Ark: Animal Poems (editor with David Butler), 1988; A Rackety Colt (novel), 1989; The Magic Tree: South African Stories in Verse (editor with Jeff Opland), 1989; Guy Butler: Essays and Lectures (edited by Stephen Watson), 1994; Collected Poems (edited by Lawrence Wright), 1999. The Prophetic Nun, 2000. Contributions to: Various publications. Honours: 1st Prize, 1949, 2nd Prize, 1953, for Poetry, South African Broadcasting Corporation; Honorary DLitt, University of Natal, 1970, University of Witwatersrand, 1984, Rhodes University, 1994; Central News Agency Award, 1976; Literary Award, Cape Tercentenary Foundation, 1981; Honorary DLitt et Phil, University of South Africa, 1989; Gold Medal, English Academy of South Africa, 1989; Lady Usher Prize for Literature, 1992; Freedom of the City of Grahamstown, 1994. Memberships: English Academy of South Africa, honorary life member; Shakespeare Society of South Africa, national president, 1985. Address: High Corner, 122 High Street, Grahamstown, Cape Province 0461, South Africa.

BUTLER James Walter, b. 25 July 1931, London, England. Sculptor. m. Angela Elizabeth, 5 daughters. Education: St Martin's School of Art; Maidstone School of Art; City and Guilds of London Art School. Career: Major commissions include: Twice life-size portrait statue of President Kenyatta, Nairobi, Kenya; Monument to Freedom Fighters of Zambia, Lusaka, Zambia; Portrait statue of Field Marshall Earl Alexander of Tunis, Wellington Barracks, Birdcage Walk, London; Memorial statue of King Richard III, Castle Gardens, Leicester; The Leicester Seamstress, Hotel Street, Leicester; The Burton Cooper, bronze sculpture, Burton-on-Trent; Portrait statue of Sir John Moore and the attendant figures of Rifleman and Bugler, Sir John Moore Barracks, Winchester; Sculpture for National Guard Sports Stadium, Riyadh, Saudi Arabia; Anniversary Fountain-Dolphin Fountain, Dolphin Square London; Cippico Fountain, Heriot-Watt University, Edinburgh; Portrait statue, John Wilkes, New Fetter Lane, London; Portrait statue of James Greathead, Engineer, Cornhill, London; Memorial statue, Reg Harris, World Cycling Champion, National Cycling Centre, Manchester; Memorial for Royal Electrical and Mechanical Engineers, Arborfield; Bronze portrait bust, Sir Nicholas Bacon, St Alban's School, Hertfordshire; Portrait statue, Thomas Cook, London Road, Leicester; Portrait bronze bust, Sir Frank Whittle, RAF Club, Piccadilly, London; Portrait statue, Billy Wright, Footballer, Molineux Stadium, Wolverhampton; D Day Memorial for the Green Howards, Crepon, Normandy; Seagull Sculpture, Anchorpoint, Singapore; Girl and Teddy bear, KK Women and Children's Hospital, Singapore; Portrait statue, James Brindley, Canal Engineer, Canal Basin, Coventry; Memorial for Fleet Air Arm -"Daedalus", Thames Embankment, London; Royal Seal of the Realm commissioned by the Royal Mint for Queen Elizabeth II; Portrait statue, Jack Walker, Blackburn Rovers FC; Royal

Jubilee Commemorative Medal, The Royal Mint; Portrait statue, Stan Cullis, Wolverhampton Wanderers FC. Memberships: Royal Academy of Art; Royal West of England Academy; Royal Society of British Sculptors. Address: Valley Farm Studios, Radway, Warwick CV 35 0UJ, England.

BUTLER Susan Ruth, b. 20 December 1937. Adjunct Professor; Clinical Psychologist. Education: Master of Arts, Bachelor of Education, McGill University, 1959-63; First Class Teaching Diploma, Province de Quebec, 1961; PhD, Clinical/Educational Psychology, University of London, 1971. Appointments: Adjunct Professor, McGill University, Montreal, Canada; Head, Department of Special Education, University of Sydney, Australia; Postgraduate and Undergraduate, 25 years, University of Sydney, Australia; Head Therapist, Learning Centre of the McGill Montreal Children's Hospital for Children; Consultant: Royal Alexandria Hospital for Children, Sydney, Australia; Great Ormond Street Hospital for Children, London; Memorial Sloan Kettering Cancer Centre (Paediatrics); Neurological Practice of Dr Leonard Rail, Sydney, Australia. Publications include: Early Prediction of Reading Ability; Articles in the Journal of educational Psychology; Series of children's' books, The Rat Pack (RAT), Reading Assistance Tutorial Pack; Series for teenagers, Rat Bags. Honours: Fulbright Scholarship, Memorial Sloan Kettering Cancer Centre; International Scholar, Harvard University; The Art of Teaching Award, McGill University. Memberships: Various national and international organisations; State Registered Clinical Psychologist, New South Wales, Australia. Address: 805A 1212 Pine Ave, Montreal, Quebec, H3G 1A9, Canada. E-mail: susan.butler@mcgill.ca

BUTLIN Ron, b. 17 November 1949, Edinburgh, Scotland; Poet. Writer. m. Regula Staub (the writer Regi Claire), 18 June 1993. Education: MA, Dip CDAE, Edinburgh University. Appointments: Writer-in-Residence, Edinburgh University, 1983, 1985, Midlothian Region, 1990-91, Stirling University, 1993; Writer-in-Residence, The Craigmillar Literacy Trust, 1997-98; Examiner in Creative Writing, Stirling University, 1997-; Writer in Residence, St Andrews University, 1998-. Publications: Creatures Tamed by Cruelty, 1979; The Exquisite Instrument, 1982; The Tilting Room, 1984; Ragtime in Unfamiliar Bars, 1985; The Sound of My Voice, 1987; Histories of Desire, 1995; Night Visits, 1997; When We Jump We Jump High! (editor), 1998; Faber Book of Twentieth Century Scottish Poetry; Our Piece of Good Fortune, 2003; No More Angels, 2004; Vivaldi and the Number 3, 2004. Contributions to: Sunday Herald; Scotsman; Edinburgh Review; Poetry Review; Times Literary Supplement. Honours: Writing Bursaries, 1977, 1987, 1990, 1994, 2003; Scottish Arts Council Book Awards, 1982, 1984, 1985; Scottish Canadian Writing Fellow, 1984; Poetry Book Society Recommendation, 1985. Membership: Scottish Arts Council, literature committee, 1995-96. Address: 7W Newington Place, Edinburgh EH9 1QT, Scotland.

BUTTERFIELD Deborah Kay, b. 7 May 1949, San Diego, California, USA. Artist. m. John E Buck, 2 sons. Education: BA, 1972, MFA, 1973, University of California at Davis, California. Appointments: Visiting Lecturer, Sculpture, 1974-75; Assistant Professor, Sculpture, 1975-77, University of Wisconsin, Madison, USA; Visiting Artist, 1977-79, Assistant Professor, 1979-83, Adjunct Assistant Professor, Graduate Student Consultant, 1984-87, Montana State University, Bozeman, Montana, USA; Numerous municipal and private commissions for sculpture within the USA and Switzerland; Many solo exhibitions in USA, Israel, Germany and England including: Israel Museum, Jerusalem, 1981; Walker Art Center, Minneapolis, 1982; Seattle Art Museum, 1982; Oakland Museum, 1983; San Diego Museum of Art, 1996; The Contemporary Museum, Honolulu, 2004; Numerous group exhibitions within USA including museum collections, also

Dictionary of International Biography

exhibited in Canada, Monaco and Denmark. Honours include: John Simon Guggenheim Memorial Fellowship; National Endowment for the Arts Individual Artist Fellowship; Golden Plate Award, American Academy of Achievement; Honorary Doctor of Fine Arts: Rocky Mountain College, Billings, Montana, Montana State University, Bozeman, Montana, Whitman College, Walla Walda, Washington. Address: 11229 Cottonwood Road, Bozeman, MT 59718, USA. E-mail: buckbutterfield@imt.net

BUZATU Gheorghe, b. 6 June 1939, Sihlea, Vrancea, Romania. University Professor of History. m. Constanta, 1 son. Education: Faculty of History, University of Jassy, Romania, 1956-61; Doctor of History, 1971. Appointments: Scientific Researcher, Romanian Academy, Centre for History and European Civilization, 1961-2001; Professor, History, University of Craiova, Romania, 1995-2001. Publications: The Secret History of WW II; A History of Romanian Oil; History of the Romanians; Editor: The Romanians in World History, 104 volumes, 1986-2003. Honours: Prize of Romanian Academy; The Marshals of Romania, 1999; Romania and the Great Powers, 1939-47, 2003; Listed in several Who's Who publications. Memberships: American Historical Association; Association Pour L'Étude de L'Histoire de Relations Internationales. Address: Centrul de Istorie si Civilizatie Europeana, Str Cuza Voda, 41 Iasi 6600, Romania.

BŮŽEK Jan, b. 16 February 1927, Kutná Hora, Czech Republic. Conductor; Teacher of Music Arts. m. Milada, 1953, 2 daughters. Education: Music Education, Faculty of Pedagogic, 1946-50, Geography, Faculty of Natural Sciences, 1946-50, Doctorate, Faculty of Pedagogic, 1967-72, Charles University, Prague; Academy of Music Arts, Prague, 1963-67. Appointments: Conductor, Philharmonic Orchestra of Kutná Hora, 1946-50; Teacher of Music Arts, Third Secondary School, Teplice, 1950-51; Teacher of Music Arts, Pedagogical Grammar School for Education of Pre-School Teachers, Teplice, 1951-60; Teacher of Music Arts, Higher Pedagogical School, Usti nad Labem, 1960-62; Teacher of Music Arts, Pedagogical Institute, Usti nad Labem, 1962-74; Deputy Director, Teacher of Music History and Music Forms, Academy of Music, Teplice, 1974-78; Teacher of Music History and Harmony, University of Jan Evangelista Purkyne, Faculty of Pedagogic, Usti nad Labem, 1978-87. Publications include: Numerous Vocal Compositions for children's choirs, women's choirs, men's choirs, mixed choirs; Songs; Chamber Music compositions; Melodious Dramas; Illuminative Compositions; Orchestra Compositions; Vocal Instrumental Compositions; Regular musical reviews of concerts. Memberships: Czech Protective Union of Authors, 1950-; Association of Music Artists and Scientists, 1950-. Address: Antala Staska 1970/9, 415 02 Teplice 2, Czech Republic. E-mail: bajax@post.cz

BUZO Alexander John, b. 23 July 1944, Sydney, New South Wales, Australia. Playwright. Author. m. Merelyn Johnson, 21 December 1968. Education: BA, University of New South Wales, 1966. Appointments: Resident Dramatist, Melbourne Theatre Company, 1972-73; Writer-in-Residence, James Cook University, 1985, University of Wollongong, 1989, University of Central Queensland, 1991, University of Indonesia, 1995. Publications: Tautology, 1980; Meet the New Class, 1981; The Search for Harry Allway, 1985; Glancing Blows, 1987; The Young Person's Guide to the Theatre and Almost Everything Else, 1988; The Longest Game, 1990; Prue Flies North, 1991; Kiwese, 1994; A Dictionary of the Almost Obvious, 1998. Plays: Rooted, 1968; The Front Room Boys, 1969; The Roy Murphy Show, 1970; Coralie Landsdowne Says No, 1974; Martello Towers, 1976; Big River, 1980; Shellcove Road, 1989; Pacific Union, 1995. Contributions to: Australian Way; Independent Monthly; Reader's Digest; Playboy; Sydney Morning Herald; Pacific Islands Monthly; New

Straits Times; Australian; Bulletin; Discovery; Heritage; Jakarta Post; Quadrant; Overland. Honours: Gold Medal, Australian Literature Society, 1972; Alumni Award, University of New South Wales, 1998. Memberships: Centre for Australian Language and Literature Studies. Address: 14 Rawson Avenue, Bondi Junction, Sydney, New South Wales 2022, Australia. E-mail: ajbu@ozemail.com.au

BYARS Merlene Hutto, b. 8 November 1931, West Columbia, Lexington County, South Carolina, USA. Accountant; Artist; Writer; Genealogist; Publisher. m. (1) Alvin W Byars (deceased), 4 sons, (2) Friedrich W Klutzow, 12 Oct 1999. Education: Diploma, Long Ridge Writers Group, Connecticut, 1995; Diploma, Journalism/Short Story Writing, 1995; Certificate, The College of Journalism, University of South Carolina, 1988. Publications: A Scrap Book of the State of South Carolina, 1992; South Carolina Scrap Book, 1994; The Plantation Era in South Carolina, 1996; From My Scrap Book, 1997; Visual Art Works, Quilted, a How-to and Scrap Book of Needle Painted Art Pieces; Play: Lintheads and Hard Times, a play (co-author and producer), 1986. Creative Works: Designed and made over 40 quilted pieces and wall hangings now in: The University of South Carolina President's House; Cayce Historical Museum; The State Newspapers Company, South Carolina; Bicentennial quilt, City of Columbia Bicentennial Celebration, 1986. Honours include: 12 Ribbons, South Carolina State Fair for Visual Art Pieces for 1st and 2nd places; 2 sweepstake awards for quilted art pieces, South Carolina State Fair; State of South Carolina Certificate of Service, 1976, 1985; City of Cayce Ambassador Award, 1994; Certificate of Merit, International Biographical Centre (IBC), 1996; International Book of Honour, ABI; Millennium Hall of Fame, ABI, 1999; Honorary Member, Research Board of Advisors, 1999; Marquis Who's Who in the South and Southwest; Who's Who in America; Who's Who in the World; Who's Who of American Women, 1997-98 - 2000-2002; Who's Who in Finance and Industry; Dictionary of International Biography; Fellow, Foundation Magna Cum Laude, University of South Carolina Education Foundation. Memberships include: Lifetime Member, Women's Missionary Society United Lutheran Church of America; Member, Treasurer, Airport High School Booster Club, 1969-76; Saxe Gotha Historical Society, Secretary, Lexington County, 1994-; Life Fellow, IBC; Fellow South Caroliniana Historical Society, 1998-2001; Fellow, University of South Carolina Thomas Cooper Library Society, 1998-2002; Deputy Director General, IBC, 1999; Fellow, South Carolina State Archives and History Centre, 2000; Cayce-West Columbia International Kiwanis, Secretary, 2001. Address: PO Box 3387, Cayce West Columbia, SC 29171-3387, USA.

BYATT Antonia Susan, b. 24 August 1936, England. Author. m. (1) Ian C R Byatt, 1959, 1 son deceased, 1 daughter, (2) Peter J Duffy, 1969, 2 daughters. Education: The Mount School, York; Newnham College, Cambridge; Bryn Mawr College, USA; Somerville College, Oxford. Appointments: Extra-Mural Lecturer, University of London, 1962-71; Lecturer in Literature, Central School of Art and Design, 1965-69; Lecturer in England, University College, London, 1972-81; Senior Lecturer, 1981-83; Associate, Newnham College, Cambridge, 1977-82; Member, Board of Creative and Performing Arts, 1985-87; Board, British Council, 1993-. Publications: Shadow of the Sun, 1964; Degrees of Freedom, 1965; The Game, 1967; Wordsworth and Coleridge in Their Time, 1970; Iris Murdoch, 1976; The Virgin in the Garden, 1978; Still Life, 1985; Sugar and Other Stories, 1987; Possession, 1990; George Eliot: Selected Essays and Other Writings, 1990; Passions of the Mind, 1991; Angels and Insects, 1992; The Matisse Stories, 1994; The Djinn in the Nightingale's Eye, 1995; Imagining Characters, 1995; Babel Tower, 1996; New Writing 6, 1996; Elementals: Stories of Fire and Ice (short stories), 1998; The Oxford

Book of English Short Stories, 1998; The Biographer's Tale, 2000; On Histories and Stories (essays), 2000; Portraits in Fiction, 2001; Bird Hand Book (with V Schrager), 2001; A Whistling Woman, 2002; Radio: Dramatisation of quartet of novels (BBC Radio), 2002. Honours include: Booker Prize for Fiction, 1990; Irish Times-Aer Lingus Literature Prize, 1990. Address: 37 Rusholme Road, London SW15, England.

BYATT Ian Charles Rayner, b. 11 March 1932, Preston, England. Economist. m. Deirdre Kelly, 1 son, deceased, 2 stepsons, 1 daughter. Education: St Edmund Hall, Oxford University, 1952-57; Nuffield College, Oxford University, 1955-57; Harvard University, USA, 1957-58. Appointments: Lecturer in Economics, Durham University, 1958-62; Economic Consultant, H M Treasury, 1962-64; Lecturer in Economics, London School of Economics, 1964-67; Senior Economic Advisor, Department of Education and Science, 1967-79; Undersecretary and Director of Economics and Statistics, Department of Housing and Local Government, 1969-70; Director of Economics, Department of Environment, 1970-72; Undersecretary and Head of Public Sector Economic Unit, H M Treasury, 1972-78; Deputy Chief Economic Adviser, H M Treasury, 1978-89; Director General of Water Services (OFWAT), 1989-2000; Senior Associate, Frontier Economics, 2001-; Honorary Professor, School of Business, Birmingham University, 2001-. Publications: British Electrical Industry, 1875-1914, 1979; Chapters in books on regulation of nationlised industries and privatised utilities (especially water industry); Articles on micro-economic policy in learned journals; Participation in and authorship of government reports. Honours: Knighted, 2000; Hon D Univ, University of Central England; Hon D Univ, Brunell University. Memberships: Council, Royal Economic Society, 1983-90; Board Member, 1987-90, 2000-, International Institute of Public Finance; Governor, Birkbeck College, 1997-, London University; Governor, National Institute of Economic & Social Research, London, 1996-; Member, Productivity Panel, HM Treasury, 2000-, Trustee, Academy of Youth, Birmingham, 2001-; Member, International Advisory Committee, Public Utilities Research Centre, University of Florida, 2001-. Address: 34 Frederick Road, Edgbaston, Birmingham B15 1JN, England. E-mail: ianbyatt@blueyonder.co.uk

BYKOV Anatoly, b. 12 September 1946, Iskitim, Novosibirsk District, Russia. Artist; Painter. m. Irina, 1 son. Education: "I Repin" Institute of Painting, Sculpture and Architecture, Leningrad Department of Art, 1980. Career: Painter, USSR Artistic Fund, 1981-82; Participant in over 50 exhibitions including: Cologne, Germany, 1984; Central Exhibition Hall, Moscow, Russia, 1986; International Exhibition, Hanover, Germany, 1990; Personal Exhibition, Central House of Scientist, Moscow, 1992; Alta Norway, 1992; Several works acquired by Academy of Fine Arts, Artistic Fund of the USSR, Khimsky Art Gallery, Museum of Tobolsk; Many works purchased by galleries and private collectors in Norway, Japan, Austria, Germany. Publications include: Works featured in: Catalogues: 40 Anniversary of Great Victory, 1985; Poesy in Painting, 1994, Academy of Sciences Exhibition, 1996, Khimki Art Gallery, 1996; Newspapers: Moscow Artist, 1990, Altaposten, Norway, 1992, Culture, 1992, Rural Youth, 1993, Vremya, 2002, Vestnik intellektyalnoj sobstvennosti, 2003; Saur Allgemeines Kunstler-lexikon, Reference Book, 1997; Sokolniki Company Calendar, 2002; Book: The Academy of Arts, 1982. Honours: Honorary Diploma, Monuments Protection, 1989; Message of Thanks, President of the Academy of Science of Russia. Membership: Union of Artists, USSR, 1985-; Member, International Confederation of Artists, Moscow Union of Painters, Russia, 1994; Listed in The Contemporary Who's Who, ABI, 2003.

Address: Bulv Donskogo Dom 9 Korp 1, Kv 307 Moscow 117216, Russia. E-mail: pavel-bykov@yandex.ru Website: www.chat.ru/~chamois

BYRNE Gabriel, b. 1950, Dublin, Ireland. Actor. m. Ellen Barken, 1988, divorced, 1 son, 1 daughter. Education: University College, Dublin. Appointments: Archaeologist; Teacher; Actor. Creative Works: Films include: Hanna K Gothic; Julia and Julia; Siesta; Miller's Crossing; Hakon Hakenson; Dark Obsession; Cool World; A Dangerous Woman; Little Women; Usual Suspects; Frankie Starlight; Dead Man; Last of the High Kings; Mad Dog Time; Somebody is Waiting; The End of Violence (director); Tony's Story; Polish Wedding; This is the Dead; The Man in the Iron Mask; Quest for Camelot; An Ideal Husband; Enemy of the State; Stigmata; End of Days; Spider; Ghost Ship; Shade, 2003; Vanity Fair, 2004; Co-Producer, In the Name of the Father. Address: c/o ICM, 8942 Wilshire Boulevard, Beverly Hills, CA 96211, USA.

BYSTROVA Natalia Vladimirovna, b. 27 September 1926, Pskov, Russia. Astronomer. m. Nikolai Bystrov, deceased, 2 sons. Education: BS, Leningrad University, 1950; Dr Ph degree, Main Astronomical Observ. In Pulkovo, 1955; Senior Research Fellow, USSR Academy of Science, 1976. Appointments: Laboratory Assistant, Spectroscopic Laboratory, Leningrad University, 1950-51; Post Graduate Student, 1951-55; Research Fellow, Main Astronomical Observatory, USSR Academy of Science in Pulkovo, 1955-69; Senior Research Fellow, St Petersburg Branch of the Special Astrophysical Observatory. Publications include: The Pulkovo Sky Survey in the Interstellar Neutral Hydrogen Radio Line, 1977; 150 other publications in the study of the ISM. Memberships: International Astronomical Union, Commission 34, 1970-; Founding Member of the European Astronomical Society, 1990-. Address: Pulkovo, St Petersburg Branch of the SAO, 196140, St Petersburg, Russia. E-mail: bnv@fsao.spb.su

BYUN Si Woo, b. 30 August 1966, Andong, Korea. Professor. m. Wonkyoung Kim, 1 son. Education: BA, Yonsei University, Korea, 1989; MA,1991, PhD, 1999, Korea Advanced Institute of Technology (KAIST). Appointments: Programmer, Samsung Co, Seoul, Korea, 1991-92; Senior Programmer, Daewoo Institute of Advanced Engineering, 1992-94; Senior Consultant, Unisys Korea, Seoul, Korea, 1994-98; Senior Consultant, Unisi, Seoul, Korea, 1998-2000; Assistant Professor, Anyang University, Korea, 2000-. Publications: Books: System Analysis and Design, 1999; System Integration – basic design technique, 2000; An Introduction to Computer Game, 2002; Introduction to Relational Database Design; Several articles in scientific journals. Honour: Honour Prize, Microsoftware Windows Program Contest, 1993; Memberships: ACM; IEEE; KISS; IASTED. Address: Anyang University, Department of Digital Media, 908-113 Anyang 5-dong, Kyonggi-do, Anyang.ac.kr.

Dictionary of International Biography

C

CAAN James, b. 26 March 1940, Bronx, New York, USA. Actor; Director. m. (1) DeeJay Mathis, 1961, 1 daughter, (2) Sheila Ryan, 1976, 1 son, (3) Linda O'Gara, 1995, 2 children. Creative Works: Films include: Irma La Douce, 1963; Lady in a Cage, 1964; The Glory Guys, 1965; Countdown, 1967; Games, 1967; Eldorado, 1967; Journey to Shiloh, 1968; Submarine XI, 1968; Man Without Mercy, 1969; The Rain People, 1969; Rabbit Run, 1970; T R Baskin, 1971; The Godfather, 1972; Slither, 1973; Cinderella Liberty, 1975; Freebie and the Bean, 1975; The Gambler, 1975; Funny Lady, 1975; Rollerball, 1975; The Killer Elite, 1975; Harry and Walter Go to New York, 1976; Silent Movie, 1976; A Bridge Too Far, 1977; Another Man, Another Chance, 1977; Comes a Horseman, 1978; Chapter Two, 1980; Thief, 1982; Kiss Me Goodbye, 1983; Bolero, 1983; Gardens of Stone, 1988; Alien Nation, 1989; Dad, 1989; Dick Tracy, 1990; Misery, 1991; For the Boys, 1991; Dark Backward, 1991; Honeymoon in Vegas, 1992; Flesh and Bone, 1993; The Program, 1994; North Star, 1995; Boy Called Hate, 1995; Eraser, 1996; Bulletproof, 1996; Bottle Rocket, 1996; This Is My Father, 1997; Poodle Springs, 1997; Blue Eyes, 1998; The Yards, 1999; The Way of the Gun, 1999; In the Boom Boom Room, 2000; Luckytown, 2000; Viva Las Nowhere, 2000; In the Shadows, 2001; Night at the Golden Eagle, 2002; City of Ghosts, 2002; Dogville, 2003; Dallas 362, 2003; This Thing of Ours, 2003; Jericho Mansions, 2003; Elf, 2003; Director, Actor, Hide in Plain Sight, 1980; Director, Violent Streets, 1981; Starred in television movie, Brian's Song, 1971; The Warden, 2000; Numerous other TV appearances. Address: c/o Fred Specktor, Endeavor, 9701 Wilshire Boulevard, 10th Floor, Beverly Hills, CA 90212, USA.

CABALLE Monserrat, b. 12 April 1933, Barcelona, Spain. Soprano Opera Singer. m. Bernabé Marti, 1 son, 1 daughter. Education: Conservatorio del Liceo; Private studies. Appointments: North American Debut, Manon, Mexico City, 1964; US Debut, Carnegie Hall, 1965; Appearances in several opera houses and at numerous festivals. Creative Works: Lucrezia Borgia; La Traviata; Salome; Aida. Honours: Most Excellent & Illustrious Dobna & Cross of Isabella the Catholic; Commandeur des Arts et des Lettres, 1986; Numerous honorary degrees, awards and medals. Address: c/o Columbia Artists Management Inc, 165 West 57th Street, New York, NY 10019, USA.

CABAÑAS BRAVO Miguel, b. 19 February 1963, Madrid. Art Historian. m. Teresa, 18 December 1993, 2 daughters. Education: Complutense University of Madrid, 1987; Dr History, 1991. Appointments: Postdoctoral Grantee, Universidad Nacional Autónoma de México, México City, 1992-93; Postdoctoral Grantee, New York University, New York, 1993; Associate Professor, Universidad Autónoma de Madrid, Madrid, 1995-96; Professor, Universidad Complutense de Madrid, 1996-98; Científico Titular del Consejo Superior de Investigaciones Científicas, Madrid, 1998-; Head, Department of History of Art, CSIC, 2001-. Publications: Many publications. Memberships: Numerous memberships. Address: CSIC Instituto de Historia, Duque de Medinaceli 6, E-28014 Madrid, Spain.

CABRIJAN Tomislav Viktor, b. 22 October 1934. Physician; Internist. m. Ivanka Tusek, 1 son, 1 daughter. Education: MD, Zagreb, Croatia, 1959; Internal Medicine Specialist, 1968, PhD, 1975, University of Zagreb; Full Professor, Internal Medicine, 1987. Appointments: Ward Internist, Endocrinologist, Sisters of Mercy, University Hospital, Zagreb, 1968-70; Head, Centre for Diabetes, Department of Endocrinology, 1970-90; Head, Department of Endocrinology Diabetes and Metabolic Diseases, 1990; Acting Director, Sisters of Mercy, University Hospital, Zagreb, Croatia, 1990. Publications: Editor (books): Obesity and Apnea Syndrome, 1993; How to Care About Your Diabetes (translation), 1995; Urgent States in Endocrinology, 1996; Rational diagnosis and therapy in Endocrinology, 2000; Contributor of articles to professional journals. Honour: Fellowship, Alexander von Humboldt Foundation, Bonn, Germany, 1972, 1975, 1978, 1982, 1989; Yearly award for science of the Parliament of Croatia, 2000. Memberships: German Diabetes Association, 1989-; Croatian Academy of Medical Sciences, 1990-; European Society for the Study of Diabetes, 1998; American Endocrine Society, 1998; European Federation of Endocrine Societies (EFES) 1999. Address: Petrova Street 110, 10000 Zagreb, Croatia.

CABROL Christian Emile, b. 16 September 1925, Chezy/Marne, France. Honorary Professor of Cardiac Surgery. m. Bérengère, 1 daughter. Appointments: University appointments: MD, 1954; Assistant Professor, 1955; Associate Professor, 1959, Professor, 1961; Hospital positions: Intern, 1948, Resident, 1950, Assistant Surgeon, 1956, Surgeon, 1961, Parisian Hospital (Assistance Publique, Paris); Chief, Surgical Outpatient Clinic, Hopital Tenon, Paris, 1967; Chief, Cardiovascular Department, Hopital de la Pitie, Paris, 1972; Scientific Director, School of Surgery of Assistance Publique, Paris, 1973; Currently: Honorary Professor of Cardiovascular Surgery; Honorary Deputy of the European Parliament; Councillor of the City of Paris. Publications: Articles in scientific medical journals in the field of correction of ascending aorta aneurysm, heart and heart-lung transplants, artificial hearts, thromboendarterectomy of pulmonary arteries. Honours: Faculty of Medicine, Paris, 1954; Academy of Medicine, Paris, 1955; Academy of Surgery, 1955; French Institute, 1956; Claude Bernard Award of the City of Paris, 1986; Gruntzig Award, European Society of Cardiology, 1989; First heart transplantation in Europe, 1968; First heart-lungs transplantation in Europe, 1982; First implantation of a totally artificial heart in France, 1986. Memberships: International Society of Cardiovascular Surgery; European Society for Organ Transplantation; American Association for Thoracic Surgery; Academy of Surgery, France; French Association of Surgery; French Society of Transplantation; Ex-President, International Society for Heart Transplantation; Society of Thoracic Surgeons of French Language; European Society of Cardiovascular Surgery. Address: 36 Rue Vivienne, 75002, Paris, France.

CACKOVIC Hinko, b. Zagreb, Croatia. Resident in Berlin, Germany 1970-. Scientist; Physicist; Artist; Photographer (Art); Painter; Sculptor (mixed media, metalwork). m. Jasna Loboda-Cackovic. Education: Diploma, Physics, University of Zagreb, Croatia, 1962; MSc, Solid State Physics, University of Zagreb, 1964; PhD, Fritz-Haber Institut der Max-Planck-Gesellschaft, Berlin-Dahlem, Germany, and University of Zagreb, 1970. Appointments: Scientist, Institute of Physics, University of Zagreb, 1962-65; Scientist, Atom Institute Ruder Boskovic, Zagreb, 1967-71; Postdoctoral, 1970-72, Scientist, 1965-67, 1970-80, Fritz-Haber Institut der Max-Planck-Gesellschaft, Germany; Scientist, Technical University, Berlin, Germany, 1980-95. Publications: Over 55 scientific articles to professional journals, including: Physics of polymers; Synthetic and biological molecules; Polymer liquid crystals; Self-ordering of the matter; Memory of solid and fluid matter; Order/disorder phenomena in the atomic, molecular and colloidal dimensions; Mutual dependence of order between atomic and colloidal entities; Development of small and wide angle x-rays scattering analysis and of broad line nuclear magnetic resonance analysis; Development of physical instruments; Works of Art in professional journals and books; Photographs cutting out parts of reality to change it; Creative activity in photography/ sculpturing and science (physics, chemistry) is influenced by literature music, astrophysics; New aesthetic spaces are forming, through the fusion of art and science, in sculptures built up by physical instruments and machines; Developing of Universal Art including mentioned multidisciplinary fields; Intention to contribute: to synthesis of science art and harmony, to the ethic and aesthetic part of human living and activity, to freedom in all its facets through culture in the widest sense; Photographs presented at numerous exhibitions in Germany, Austria, France, Switzerland, 1991- and in Internet galleries, 1998-; Innovative works, two-artist group JASHIN, with Jasna Loboda-Cackovic from 1997; Permanent art representations: Gallery Kleiner Prinz, Baden-Baden, Germany, 1991-; Cyber Museum at wwwARTchannel, www.art-channel.net, 1999-; Virtual Gallery of Forschungs-Institut Bildender Künste, Germany, www.fibk.de, 1999-; Permanent representation of art and science biography by Brigitte Schellmann Who's Who in German ® (www.whoswho-german.de). Honours: Two Euro honorary Prizes, Exhibitions, Dresden and Baden-Baden, Germany, 1994, 1995; Prize, for photography, 5th Open Art Prize, Bad Neuheim, Germany, 1995 and prize "Phoenix", First, Second and Third, Photography Prize at Fourth, International Internet Art Competitions, 1998, 2000, 2001, 2003; Distinguished Leadership Award, ABI, 2000; Grants: Technical University Berlin, Germany, 1965-67; Alexander von Humboldt Stiftung, Bad Godesberg, Germany, 1970-72; Max-Planck-Gesellschaft, Fritz-Haber-Institut, Berlin-Dahlem, Germany, 1972-73. Memberships: Deutsche Physikalische Gesellschaft, 1972-95; International Biographical Association, 1998-; Virtual Gallery, Forschungs-Institut Bildender Künste, 1999-; Europäischer Kulturkreis Baden-Baden, 2002-. Address: Im Dol 60, 14195 Berlin, Germany.

CADBURY (Nicholas) Dominic, b. 12 May 1940. Business Executive. m. Cecilia Sarah Symes, 1972, 3 daughters. Education: Eton College; Trinity College, Cambridge; Stanford University, USA. Appointments: Chief Executive, Cadbury Schweppes PLC, 1984-93, Chair, 1993-; Director, Economic Group, 1990-, Chair, 1994-; Joint Deputy Chair, Guinness, 1994-97; Deputy Chair, 1996-; Joint Deputy Chair, EMI Group PLC, 1999-; President, Food and Drink Federation, 1999; Chair, Wellcome Trust, 2000-; Chair, Transense Techs, 2000-; Non-Executive Director, Misys PLC, 2000-. Memberships: Royal Mint Advisory Committee, 1986-94; President, Committee CBI, 1989-94; Food Association, 1989-2000; Stanford Advisory Council, 1989-95. Address: The Wellcome Trust, 183 Euston Road, London, NW1, England.

CAFÉ FILHO Adalberto C, b. 25 May 1960, Rio de Janeiro, Brazil. Professor. 2 daughters. Education: BSc, Agronomy, 1982, MSc, Plant Pathology, 1984, University of Brasilia; PhD, Plant Pathology, University of California at Davis, USA, 1993. Appointments: Research Scientist, Brazilian National Agriculture Research Agency, 1985-87; Assistant Professor, 1987-93, Associate Professor, 1993-, Chairman, Department of Plant Pathology, 1997-2001, University of Brasilia. Publications: Over 50 research articles in professional scientific journals including: Phytopathology; Plant Pathology; Plant Disease; Tropical Pest Management; Revue de Nematologie; Fitopatologia Brasileira; and others. Honours: Visiting Researcher, North Carolina State University, USA, 2001-2002; Fellow, Brazilian National Research Council, 1994-2001 and 2003-05; Jastro Research Award, University of California, 1992. Memberships: Sigma Xi Scientific Research Society, 2002-; American Phytopathological Society, 1988-. Address: SQN 110-G-202, 70753-070 Brasilia, Brazil. E-mail: cafefilh@unb.br

CAFFREY Idris, b. 16 November 1949, Rhayader, Powys. Education: Swansea College of Education, 1968-71. Publications: Pacing Backwards, 1996; Pathways, 1997; Other Places, 1998; Warm Rain, 2000; Departures and Returns, 2002. Address: 5 Lyndale, Wilnecote, Tamworth, B77 5DX, England.

CAGE Nicolas (Nicholas Coppla), b. 7 January 1964, Long Beach, California, USA. Actor. m. (1) Patricia Arquette, 1995, divorced 2000, (2) Lisa Marie Presley, 2002, divorced 2002, 1 son with Kristina Fulton. Creative Works: Films include: Valley Girl, 1983; Rumble Fish; Racing With the Moon; The Cotton Club; Birdy; The Boy in Blue; Raising Arizona; Peggy Sue Got Married; Moonstruck; Vampire's Kiss; Killing Time; The Short Cut; Queens Logic; Wild of Heart; Wings of the Apache; Zandalee; Red Rock West; Guarding Tess; Honeymoon in Vegas; It Could Happen to You; Kiss of Death; Leaving Las Vegas; The Rock, 1996; The Funeral, 1996; Con Air, 1997; Face Off, 1997; Eight Millimeter, 1999; Bringing Out the Dead, 1999; Gone in 60 Seconds, 2000; The Family Man, 2001; Captain Corelli's Mandolin, 2001; Christmas Carol: The Movie (voice), 2001; Windtalkers, 2002; Sonny, 2002; Adaptation, 2002; Matchstick Men, 2003; Producer, The Life of David Gale, 2003. Honours include: Golden Globe Award, Best Actor, 1996; Academy Award, Best Actor, 1996; Lifetime Achievement Award, 1996; P J Owens Award, 1998; Charles A Crain Desert Palm Award, 2001. Address: Saturn Films, 9000 West Sunset Boulevard, Suite 911, West Hollywood, CA 90069, USA.

CAGLAR Mine, b. 14 November 1967, Turkey. Applied Mathematician. m. Mehmet Caglar, 1 son, 1 daughter. Education: BS, Middle East Technical University, 1989; MS, Bilkent University, 1991. Appointments: Assistant in Instruction, Princeton University, USA, 1992-97; Research Scientist, Bellcore, 1997-98; Assistant Professor of Mathematics, Koc University, Istanbul, Turkey, 1999-. Publications: Articles in scientific journals include: A Long Range-Dependent Workload Model for Packet Data Traffic, 2004. Memberships: Sigma Xi; Informs; Bernoulli Society. Address: Koc University, College of Arts and Sciences, Sariyer, Istanbul, Turkey 34450. Website: http://home.ku.edu.tr/~mcaglar

CAI Lily, b. 23 November 1955, Shanghai, China. Choreographer. m. Gang Situ. Career: Principal Dancer, Shanghai Opera House, 1975-83; Artistic Director, Chinese Folk Dance Association, 1983-89; Dance Instructor, Galileo High School, California, 1983-89; Artistic Director, Lily Cai Chinese Dance Company and Chinese Cultural Productions, 1989-. Honours: Numerous awards, citations and fellowships granted in recognition of services to Chinese dance and dance education, including Choreographers' Fellowship, National Endowment for the Arts, 1992-94; Outstanding Achievement Award in Choreography, Isadora Duncan Dance Awards Committee, 1996; Named one of the Top 50 of the Arts, San Francisco LIVE, 1996; Sandra Sakato Memorial Award, Asian American Arts Foundation, 1998; Selected for Artists in Residency Program, California Arts Council, 1987-90, 1992-94, 1996-98; The James Irvine Fellow in Dance Award, 2000. Address: 1286 Pacific Avenue, San Francisco, CA 94109, USA. E-mail: lilycai@aol.com

CAI Xiao-Ding (Kevin), b. 1 July 1957, Chengdu, Sichuan, China. Electrical Engineer. m. Hong Miao, 1 son. Education: BE, 1982; ME, 1987; PhD, 1995. Appointments: Lecturer, University of Electronics Science and Technology of China, China, 1987-90; Senior Hardware Designer, 1994-2000, High Speed Signal Advisor, 2000-2001, Nortel Networks, Canada; Senior Staff Engineer, Sun Microsystems, USA, 2001-. Publications: Articles in scientific journals: Uniform magnetic field generated by two orthogonal sheet current loops, 1989; Analysis of asymmetric TEM cell and its optimum design of electric field distribution, 1989; Generation of uniform magnetic fields with electrically alterable field direction in a geometric plane, 1991; Finite-element analysis of a triple TEM cell, 1994. Honour: Provincial Science and Technology Award, Sichuan, China, 1991. Membership: Institute of Electrical and Electronics Engineers, 1989-2001. Address: 1514 Gilbert Place, Fremont, CA 94536, USA. E-mail: kc2004a@hotmail.com

CAIMBEUL Maoilios MacAonghais, b. 23 March 1944, Isle of Skye, Scotland. Writer; Poet. m. Margaret Hutchison, 2 December 1971, 1 son. Education: BA, Edinburgh University; Teaching Diploma, Jordanhill College, Glasgow, 1978. Appointments: Gaelic Teacher, Tobermory High School, 1978-84; Gaelic Development Officer, Highlands and Islands Development Board, 1984-87; Writer, 1987-. Publications: Eileanan, 1980; Bailtean, 1987; A Càradh an Rathaid, 1988; An Aghaidh na Siorraidheachd, (anthology with 7 other Gaelic poets), 1991; Saoghal Ùr, 2003. Contributions to: Gairm; Lines Review; Chapman; Cencrastus; Orbis; Poetry Ireland Review; Comhar; Gairfish; Baragab; Weekend Scotsman; West Highland Free Press; Anthologies: Air Ghleus 2, 1989; Twenty of the Best, 1990; The Patched Fool, 1991; Somhairle, Dàin is Deilbh, 1991; An Tuil, 1999; An Leabhar Mòr, PNE, 2002. Honours: Award, Gaelic Books Council Poetry Competition, 1978-79; Poetry/Fiction Prize, Gaelic Books Council, 1982-83. Membership: Scottish PEN. Address: 17 Strath, Gairloch, Ross-shire, IV21 2BX, Scotland.

CAIN Joseph Carter III, b. 31 October 1930, Kentucky, USA. Geophysicist. m. Shirley Jane Twigg, 4 sons. Education: BS, Physics, University of Alaska, 1952; PhD, Geophysics, 1957. Appointments: University of Alaska, Geophysical Institute, 1952-59; NASA Goddard Space Flight Center, 1959-74; USGS, 1974-86; University of Colorado, 1986; Florida State University, 1987-. Honour: Fellow, American Geophysical Union. Memberships: Sigma Xi; American Geophysical Union. Address: Florida State University, Fluid Dynamics Institute, Tallahassee, FL 32306-4360, USA.

CAINE Michael (Sir) CBE (Maurice Joseph Micklewhite), b. 14 March 1933, London, England. m. (1) Patricia Haines, divorced, 1 daughter; (2) Shakira Khatoon Baksh, 1 daughter. Career: British Army service in Berlin and Korea, 1951-53; Repertory theatres, Horsham and Lowestoft, 1953-55; Theatre Workshop, London, 1955; Acted in: Over 100 TV plays 1957-63; Films include: A Hill in Korea, 1956; Zulu, 1964; The Ipcress File, 1965; Alfie, 1966; The Wrong Box, 1966; Gambit, 1966; Funeral in Berlin, 1966; Billion Dollar Brain, 1967; Woman Times Seven, 1967; Deadfall, 1967; The Magus, 1968; Battle of Britain, 1969; Play Dirty, 1968; The Italian Job, 1969; Too Late the Hero, 1970; The Last Valley, 1970; Kidnapped, 1971; Pulp, 1971; Get Carter, 1971; Zee and Co, 1972; Sleuth, 1973; The Wilby Conspiracy, 1974; The Eagle Has Landed, The Man Who Would be King, 1975; A Bridge Too Far, The Silver Bears, 1976; The Swarm, California Suite, 1977; Ashanti, 1978; Beyond the Poseidon Adventure, 1979; The Island, 1979; Deathtrap, 1981; The Hand, 1981; Educating Rita, 1982; Jigsaw Man, 1982; The Honorary Consul, 1982; Blame it on Rio, 1983; Water, 1984; The Holcroft Covenant, 1984; Sweet Liberty, 1985; Mona Lisa, 1985; The Whistle Blower, 1985; Half Moon Street, 1986; The Fourth Protocol, 1986; Hannah and her Sisters (Academy Award), 1986; Surrender, 1987; Without a Clue, 1988; Jack the Ripper (TV, Golden Globe Award), 1988; Dirty Rotten Scoundrels, 1988; A Shock to the System, 1989; Bullseye, 1989; Noises Off, 1991; Blue Ice, 1992; The Muppet Christmas Carol, 1992; On Deadly Ground, 1993; World War II Then There Were Giants, 1994; Bullet to Beijing, 1995; Blood and Wine, 1996; Mandela and de Klerk, 1996; 20,000 Leagues Under the Sea, 1997; Shadowrun, 1997; Little Voice, 1998; The Debtors, 1999; The Cider House Rules; Curtain Call, 1999; Quills, 1999; Get Carter, 2000; Shiner, 2000; Last Orders, 2001; Quick Sands, 2001; The Quiet American, 2002; The Actors, 2003; Secondhand Lions, 2003; The Statement. Publications: Michael Caine's File of Facts, 1987; Not Many People Know This, 1988; What's It All About, 1992;

Acting in Film, 1993. Honours: CBE, 1992; Knighted by HM Queen Elizabeth II, 2000; Numerous awards, nominations and citations from film and TV industry institutes, including several Golden Globe and Academy awards. Address: International Creative Management, Oxford House, 76 Oxford Road, London W1R 1RB, England.

CAIRNS David (Adam), b. 8 June 1926, Loughton, Essex, England. Music Critic; Writer. m. Rosemary Goodwin, 19 December 1959, 3 sons. Education: Trinity College, Oxford. Appointments: Music Critic, Evening Standard, and Spectator, 1958-62; Financial Times, 1963-67, New Statesman, 1967-70, Sunday Times, 1973-; Classical Programme Co-ordinator, Philips Records, 1967-73; Distinguished Visiting Scholar, Getty Center for the History of Art and Humanities, 1992; Visiting Resident Fellow, Merton College, Oxford, 1993. Publications: The Memoirs of Hector Berlioz (editor and translator), 1969, 4th edition, 1990; Responses: Musical Essays and Reviews, 1973; The Magic Flute, 1980; Falstaff, 1982; Berlioz, 2 volumes, 1989, 2000; Berlioz Volume II: Servitude and Greatness, 1832-1869, 1999. Honours: Chevalier, 1975, Officier, 1991, de l'Ordre des Arts des Lettres, France; Derek Allen Memorial Prize, British Academy, 1990; Royal Philharmonic Society Award, 1990; Yorkshire Post Prize, 1990; Commander of the Order of the British Empire, 1997; Whitbread Biography Prize, 1999; Royal Philharmonic Society Award, 1999; Samuel Johnson Non-Fiction Prize, 2000. Address: 49 Amerland Road, London SW18 1QA, England.

CAIRNS Hugh John Forster, b. 21 November 1922. Professor of Microbiology. m. Elspeth Mary Forster, 1948, 2 sons, 1 daughter. Education: Medical Degree, Balliol College, Oxford, 1943. Appointments: Surgical Resident, Radcliffe Infirmary, Oxford, 1945; Various appointments in London, Newcastle, Oxford; Virologist, Hall Institute, Melbourne, Australia, 1950-51; Viruses Research Institute, Entebbe, Uganda, 1952-54; Director, Cold Spring Harbor Laboratory of Quantative Biology, New York, 1963-68; Professor, State University of New York, American Cancer Society; Head, Mill Hill Laboratories, Imperial Cancer Research Fund, London, 1973-81; Department of Microbiology, Harvard School of Public Health, Boston, 1982-91; Research work into penicillin-resistant staphylococci, influenza virus, E.coli and DNA replication in mammals. Address: Holly Grove House, Wilcote, Chipping Norton, Exon, OX7 3EA, England.

CALDEIRA Alexandre David, b. 27 October 1958, Rio de Janeiro. Research. m. Leila Maria M B Caldeira, 2 sons. Education: Electronics Engineer, Gama Filho University, 1980; MSc, Nuclear Engineering, Military Institute of Engineering, 1983; PhD, Nuclear Engineering, Energy and Nuclear Researches Institute, 1999. Appointments: Electronics Teacher, Estacio de Sa High Education Society, 1982-84; Researcher, Head Nuclear Data Subdivision, Institute for Advanced Studies, Aerospace Technical Centre, 1984-. Publications include: Nuclear Science and Engineering; Annals of Nuclear Energy; Transport Theory and Statistical Physics. Address: Rua Antares 125, Apto 307, Sao Jose dos Campos, Sao Paulo, 12230-904, Brazil. E-mail: alexdc@ieav.cta.br

CALDER Alexander Charles, b. 30 August 1948, Aberdeen, Scotland. University Lecturer. m. Alexandria M J Robertson. Education: MA, Aberdeen, 1970; MA, Liverpool, 1974; BA, London, 1976, PhD, Aberdeen, 1989. Appointments: Tutor in English, 1990-92, Fellow in English, 1992-93, Lecturer in English, 1993-95, Aberdeen University, Scotland; Visiting Lecturer, Naples, Italy, 1996; Senior Lecturer, University of Zambia, 1997-. Publications: 27 papers on Shakespearean and rhetorical topics including chapters in: The Literature of Place, 1993 and Literature of Region and Nation, 1998. Honours: Visiting Fellow, Centre for

Rhetoric Studies, University of Cape Town, South Africa; Vice-President, Association for Rhetoric and Communication in Southern Africa (ARCSA), 1998-2002. Membership: ARCSA. Department of Literature and Languages, University of Zambia, PO Box 32379, Lusaka, Zambia.

CALDER Nigel (David Ritchie), b. 2 December 1931, London, England. Writer. m. Elisabeth Palmer, 22 May 1954, 2 sons, 3 daughters. Education: BA, 1954, MA, 1957, Sidney Sussex College, Cambridge. Appointments: Research Physicist, Mullard Research Laboratories, Redhill, Surrey, 1954-56; Staff Writer, 1956-60, Science Editor, 1960-62, Editor, 1962-66, New Scientist; Science Correspondent, New Statesman, 1959-62, 1966-71. Publications: The Environment Game, 1967, US edition as Eden Was No Garden: An Inquiry Into the Environment of Man, 1967; Technopolis: Social Control of the Uses of Science, 1969; Violent Universe: An Eyewitness Account of the New Astronomy, 1970; The Mind of Man: An Investigation into Current Research on the Brain and Human Nature, 1970; Restless Earth: A Report on the New Geology, 1972; The Life Game: Evolution and the New Biology, 1974; The Weather Machine: How Our Weather Works and Why It Is Changing, 1975; The Human Conspiracy, 1976; The Key to the Universe: A Report on the New Physics, 1977; Spaceships of the Mind, 1978; Einstein's Universe, 1979; Nuclear Nightmares: An Investigation into Possible Wars, 1980; The Comet is Coming!: The Feverish Legacy of Mr Halley, 1981; Timescale: An Atlas of the Fourth Dimension, 1984; 1984 and Beyond: Nigel Calder Talks to His Computer About the Future, 1984; The English Channel, 1986; The Green Machines, 1986; Future Earth: Exploring the Frontiers of Science (editor with John Newell), 1989; Scientific Europe, 1990; Spaceship Earth, 1991; Giotto to the Comets, 1992; Beyond this World, 1995; The Manic Sun, 1997; Magic Universe: The Oxford Guide to Modern Science, 2003. Contributions to: Television documentaries; Numerous periodicals. Honours: UNESCO Kalinga Prize, 1972; AAAS, honorary fellow, 1986. Memberships: Association of British Science Writers, Chairman, 1960-62; Cruising Association, London, Vice President, 1982-85; Fellow, Royal Astronomical Society, Council, 2001-04; Fellow, Royal Geographical Society; Fellow, American Association for the Advancement of Science. Address: 26 Boundary Road, Crawley, West Sussex RH10 8BT, England. E-mail: nc@windstream.demon.co.uk

CALIZO Cecilia Solidum, b. 25 February 1952, Roxas City, Philippines. Teacher; Engineer. Education: Bachelor of Science, Education, 1972; Bachelor of Science, Chemical Engineering, 1984; Master of Arts, Education, Mathematics, 2000. Appointments: College Registrar, Officer-in-Charge, Teachers College, Principal High School Department, Principal, Elementary Department, Programme Co-ordinator, Information Technology Department, Aklan College. Honours: Magna cum Laude; SEATO Scholarship Award. Memberships: Philippine Institute of Chemical Engineers, Panay Chapter; Philippine Council of Mathematics Teacher Educators Inc; Philippine Society of Information Technology Educators; The Ministry of Teaching Foundation. Address: 113 Magdalena Village, New Buswang, Kalibo, Aklan, Philippines. E-mail: c_calizo@yahoo.com

CALLAHAN Aileen Loughlin, b. Dayton, OH, USA. Artist; College Lecturer. Education: BA, 1968, MFA, 1970, Boston University; Skowhegan School Painting and Sculpture, 1968, 1969; Escuela Nacional de Pintura y Escultura, Mexico City, 1970-72; Studied with David Alfara Siqueiros. Appointments: Lecturer, Art: Boston College, Boston, Massachusetts, 1979-; Regis College, Weston, Massachusetts, 1979- 98; Lesley College, Cambridge, Massachusetts, 1988-91; University of Massachusetts, Boston, 1991-; Solo exhibition, Palacio de Bellas Artes, Mexico City, 1972;

Group exhibitions: Pindar Gallery, New York City, 1989; Amos Eno Gallery, New York City, 1990, 1991; Invitational, American Academy Art, New York City, 1994; Dreitzer Gallery, Brandeis University, 1997; The McMullen Museum of Art, Boston, 1999; Lowenfield Exhibition Hall, Hofstra University, Hempstead, NY, 2001. Honours: Lincoln Fellowship to Mexico, 1970-72; Blanche E Coleman Award, Coleman Trust, 1984; Winner, 1st Place, Pindar Gallery, New York City, 1989; Jurors Award, Small Works, Amos Eno Gallery, New York City, 1990. Membership: Women's Caucus for Art. Address: 69 Harvey Street No 12, Cambridge, MA 02140, USA.

CALLAHAN Lough, b. 18 January 1948, Dayton, Ohio, USA. Investment Management Consultant. m. Mary Reilly Callahan, 5 May 1973, 1 son, 1 daughter, deceased 1996. Education: AB Honours, Holy Cross College, 1969; JD cum laude, Harvard Law School, 1972. Appointments: Lawyer, Davis Polk & Wardell, New York City, 1972-80; Investment Banker, S G Warburg Co Ltd and S G Warburg Securities, 1980-92; Director, 1983-90; Head of International Capital Markets, 1985-88; Joint Head of Fixed Interest Division, 1989-92; Fund Management, Mercury Asset Management Ltd, 1992-99; Director, 1992-99; Managing Director Closed-end Funds Division, 1992-99; Consultant, Ernst & Young, 1999-; Director, Tribune Trust plc, 1999-; Executive Committee, Association of Investment Trust Companies, 2000-; Chairman, The European Technology and Income Company Limited, 2000-02. Memberships: International Primary Markets Association, 1986-91 (Vice-Chairman, 1988-91); Euroclear Clearance System S C Director, 1991-93. Address: 7 Spencer Hill, London SW19 4PA, England.

CALLISON Brian (Richard), b. 13 July 1934, Manchester, England. Writer. m. Phyllis Joyce Jobson, 12 May 1958, 2 sons. Education: Dundee College of Art, 1954-56. Publications: A Flock of Ships, 1970; A Plague of Sailors, 1971; Dawn Attack, 1972; A Web of Salvage, 1973; Trapp's War, 1974; A Ship is Dying, 1976; A Frenzy of Merchantmen, 1977; The Judas Ship, 1978; Trapp's Peace, 1979; The Auriga Madness, 1980; The Sextant, 1981; Spearfish, 1982; Bone Collectors, 1984; Thunder of Crude, 1986; Trapp and World War Three, 1988; The Trojan Hearse, 1990; Crocodile Trapp, 1993; Ferry Down, 1998; The Stollenberg Legacy, 2000. Memberships: Royal Institute of Navigation (M.R.I.N); Society of Authors. Address: c/o Harper Collins Publishers, 77-85 Fulham Palace Road, Hammersmith, London W6 8JB, England.

CALLOW Simon Philip Hugh, b. 15 June 1949, England. Actor; Director; Writer. Education: Queen's University, Belfast; Drama Centre. Creative Works: Stage appearances include: Kiss of the Spider Woman, 1985; Faust, 1988; Single Spies, 1988, 1989; The Destiny of Me, 1993; The Alchemist, 1996; The Importance of Being Oscar, 1997; Chimes at Midnight, 1997; Films include: Four Weddings and A Funeral, 1994; Ace Ventura: When Nature Calls, 1995; James and the Giant Peach (voice), 1996; The Scarlet Tunic, 1996; Woman In White, 1997; Bedrooms and Hallways, 1997; Shakespeare in Love, 1997; Interview with a Dead Man, 1997; No Man's Land, 2000; Thunderpants, 2001; A Christmas Carol, 2001; The Civilization of Maxwell Bright, 2003; Bright Young Things, 2003; George and the Dragon, 2004; TV: Patriot Witness, 1989; Trial of Oz, 1991; Bye Bye Columbus, 1992; Femme Fatale, 1993; Little Napoleons, 1994; An Audience with Charles Dickens, 1996; A Christmas Dickens, 1997; The Woman in White, 1998; Trial-Retribution, 1999, 2000; Galileo's Daughter; The Mystery of Charles Dickens, 2002. Director: Carmen Jones, 1994; Il Trittico, 1995; Les Enfants du Paradis, 1996; Stephen Oliver Trilogy, 1996; La Calisto, 1996; Il Turco in Italia, 1997; HRH, 1997; The Pajama Game, 1998; The Consul, 1999; Tomorrow

Dictionary of International Biography

Week (play for radio), 1999; Several other radio broadcasts. Publications: Being An Actor, 1984; A Difficult Actor: Charles Laughton, 1987; Shooting the Actor, or the Choreography of Confusion, 1990; Acting in Restoration Comedy, 1991; Orson Wells: The Road to Xanadu, 1995; Les Enfants du Paradis, 1996; Snowdon - On Stage, 1996; The National, 1997; Love is Where it Falls, 1999; Shakespeare on Love, 2000; Charles Laughton's the Night of the Hunter, 2000; Oscar Wilde and His Circle, 2000; The Nights of the Hunter, 2001; Dicken's Christmas, 2002; Henry IV Part One, 2002; Several translations; Weekly columns in professional newspapers; Contributions to The Times, The Sunday Times, The Observer, Evening Standard and others. Honours: Laurence Olivier Theatre Award, 1992; Patricia Rothermere Award, 1999; CBE, 1999. Address: c/o BAT, 180 Wardour Street, London, W1V 3AA, England.

CALLWOOD June, b. 2 June 1924, Chatham, Ontario, Canada. Writer. m. Trent Frayne, 13 May 1944, 2 sons, 1 deceased, 2 daughters. Appointments: Reporter, Brantford Expositor, 1941, Toronto Globe and Mail, 1942; Freelance Journalist, 1945-; Columnist, Globe and Mail, 1975-78, 1983-89. Publications: Emma, 1984; Twelve Weeks in Spring, 1986; Emotions, 1986; Jim: A Life with AIDS, 1988; The Sleepwalker, 1990; Trial Without End, 1995; The Man Who Lost Himself, 2000. Honours: City of Toronto Award of Merit, 1974; Order of Canada, 1978, 1986, 2001; Canadian News Hall of Fame, 1984; Windsor Press Club Quill Award, 1987; Order of Ontario, 1989; Udo Award, 1989; Lifetime Achievement Award, 1991; 17 Honorary Degrees; Margaret Lawrence Lecture, 1993. Memberships: Writers Union of Canada, Chair; Canadian Centre PEN, President; Toronto Arts Council; Chair Literary Awards; Book and Periodical Council Chair; Beaver Valley Soaring Club. Address: 21 Hillcroft Drive, Toronto, Ontario M9B 4X4, Canada.

CALNE Roy (Yorke) (Sir), b. 30 December 1930. Professor of Surgery; Consultant Surgeon. m. Patricia Doreen Whelan, 1956, 2 sons, 4 daughters. Education: MB, Guy's Hospital Medical School; BS, Hons, London, 1953. Appointments: Guy's Hospital, 1953-54; RAMC, 1954-56; Departmental Anatomy Demonstrator, Oxford University, 1957-58; Senior House Officer, Nuffield Orthopaedic Centre, Oxford, 1958; Surgeon, Registrar, Royal Free Hospital, 1958-60; Harkness Fellow in Surgery, Peter Bent Brigham Hospital, Harvard Medical School, 1960-61; Lecturer in Surgery, St Mary's Hospital, London, 1961-62; Senior Lecturer and Consultant Surgeon, Westminster Hospital, 1962-65; Professor of Surgery, 1965-98, Emeritus Professor, 1998, University of Cambridge; Ghim Seng Professor of Surgery, National University of Singapore, 1998-. Publications include: Renal Transplantations, co-author, 1963; Lecture Notes in Surgery, 1965; A Gift of Life, 1970; Clinical Organ Transplantation, editor and contributor, 1971; Immunological Aspects of Transplantation Surgery, editor and contributor, 1973; Transplantation Immunology, 1984; Surgical Anatomy of the Abdomen in the Living Subject, 1988; Too Many People, 1994; Art Surgery and Transplantation, 1996; The Ultimate Gift, 1998; Numerous papers and book chapters. Honours include: Hallet Prize, 1957, Jacksonian Prize, 1961, Hunterian Professor, 1962, Cecil Joll Prize, 1966, Hunterian Orator, 1989, Royal College of Surgeons; Honorary MD, Oslo, 1986, Athens, 1990, Hanover, 1991, Thailand, 1993, Belfast, 1994, Edinburgh, 2001; Prix de la Société Internationale de Chirurgie, 1969; Fastin Medal, Finnish Surgical Society, 1977; Lister Medal, 1984; Knighted, 1986; Cameron Prize, Edinburgh University, 1990; Ellison-Cliffe Medal, 1990; Ernst Jung Prize, 1996; Gold Medal of the Catalan Transplantation Society, 1996; Grand Officer of the Republic of Italy, 2000; King Faisal International Prize for Medicine, 2001; Prince Mahidol Prize for Medicine, 2002. Memberships include: Fellow, Royal College of Surgeons; Fellow, Royal Society; Fellow,

Association of Surgeons of Great Britain; European Society for Organ Transplantation, 1983-84; Corresponding Fellow, American Surgical Association. Address: 22 Barrow Road, Cambridge CB2 2AS, England.

CALVERT Peter Anthony Richard, b. 19 November 1936, Islandmagee, County Antrim, Northern Ireland. Emeritus Professor of Politics; Writer. m. Susan Ann Milbank, 1987. Education: Campbell College, Belfast; Queens' College, Cambridge; University of Michigan. Appointments: Lecturer, 1964-71, Senior Lecturer, 1971-74, Reader, 1974-83, Professor, 1984-, University of Southampton. Publications: The Mexican Revolution 1910-1914, 1968; A Study of Revolution, 1970; The Falklands Crisis, 1982; Guatemala, 1985; The Foreign Policy of New States, 1986; Argentina: Political Culture and Instability (with Susan Calvert) 1989; Revolution and Counter Revolution, 1990; Latin America in the 20th Century (with Susan Calvert) 1993; An Introduction to Comparative Politics, 1993; International Politics of Latin America, 1994; Politics and Society in the Third World (with Susan Calvert), 1996, 2001; Revolution and International Politics, 1984, 1996; The South, the North and the Environment (with Susan Calvert), 1999; Comparative Politics: An Introduction, 2002. Editor: The Process of Political Succession, 1987; The Central American Security System, 1988; Political and Economic Encyclopedia of South America and the Caribbean, 1991; Democratization, 1996-; The Resilience of Democracy (with Peter Burnell), 1999. Contributions to: International Affairs; Political Studies; World Today. Membership: Royal Historical Society, fellow; Royal Institute of International Affairs. Address: School of Social Sciences/Politics, University of Southampton, Southampton SO17 1BJ, England.

CAMASSA Michele M, b. 8 May 1959, Latiano, Brindisi, Italy. Biologist. m. Paola Di Turo, 3 sons. Education: Graduate, Biological Science. Appointments: Clinical Analyst, 1987-; Director of Museo del Sottosuolo, Director of Istituto Sperimentale di Biologia del Sotto Suolo – P Parenzan, 1993-; Researcher in Biospeceology. Publications: Many papers in professional journals. Honours: Civilta D'Arneo, 2000. Memberships: Associazione Nazionale dei Musei Scientifici; Societá Speleologica Italiana. Address: Contrada Fieu snc, 72022 Latiano, Brindisi, Italy. E-mail: isbios@libero.it

CAMERON Donald (Allan), (Silver Donald Cameron), b. 21 June 1937, Toronto, Ontario, Canada. Author. m. (1) Catherine Ann Cahoon, 21 August 1959, 3 sons, 1 daughter. (2) Lulu Terrio, 17 May 1980, deceased 6 April 1996, 1 son, (3) Marjorie L Simmins, 14 March 1998. Education: BA, University of British Columbia, 1959; MA, University of California, 1962; PhD, University of London, 1967. Appointments: Associate Professor of English, University of New Brunswick, 1968-71; Writer-in-Residence, 1978-80, Dean, School of Community Studies, 1994-96, Special Assistant to the President, 1997-99, University College of Cape Breton, Nova Scotia; Writer-in-Residence, University of Prince Edward Island, 1985-86, Nova Scotia College of Art and Design, 1987-88. Publications: Faces of Leacock, 1967; Conversations with Canadian Novelists, 1973; The Education of Everett Richardson, 1977; Seasons in the Rain (essays), 1978; Dragon Lady, 1980; The Baitchopper (children's novel), 1982; Schooner: Bluenose and Bluenose II, 1984; Outhouses of the West, 1988; Wind, Whales and Whisky: A Cape Breton Voyage, 1991; Lifetime: A Treasury of Uncommon Wisdoms (co-author), 1992; Once Upon a Schooner: An Offshore Voyage In Bluenose II, 1992; Iceboats to Superferries: An Illustrated History of Marine Atlantic (co-author); Sniffing the Coast: An Acadian Voyage, 1993; Sterling Silver: Rants, Raves and Revelations, 1994; The Living Beach, 1998; Other: Columnist, The Globe and Mail, 1999-2001, Halifax

Sunday Herald, 1998-; Numerous articles, radio dramas, short stories, television scripts and stage plays. Honours: 4 National Magazine Awards; Best Short Film, Canadian Film Celebration; Nominated, Prix Italia for Radio Drama, 1980; City of Dartmouth Book Award, 1992; Atlantic Provinces Booksellers Choice Award, 1992; Honorary Doctor of Civil Law degree (honoris causa), University of King's College, Halifax, Nova Scotia, 2004. Memberships: Writers Guild of Canada, Periodical Writers Association of Canada; Writers Federation, Nova Scotia. Address: D'Escousse, Nova Scotia B0E 1K0, Canada.

CAMERON James, b. 16 August 1954, Kapuskasing, Ontario, Canada. Director; Screenwriter. m. Linda Hamilton, 1966, 1 daughter. Education: Fullerton Junior College. Appointments: Founder, Lightstorm Entertainment, 1990, Head, 1992-; Chief Executive Officer, Digital Domain, 1993-. Creative Works: Films: Piranha II - The Spawning (director); The Terminator (director, and screenplay), 1984; The Abyss (director and screenplay), 1994; Terminator 2: Judgement Day (co-screenwriter, director, producer), 1994; Point Break (executive producer), 1994; True Lies; Strange Days; Titanic, 1996; Solaris (producer), 2002; Terminator 3: Rise of the Machines (writer), 2003. Honours include: Academy Award, Best Director; 11 Academy Awards. Address: Lightstorm Entertainment, 919 Santa Monica Boulevard, Santa Monica, CA 90401, USA.

CAMERON John Clifford, b. 17 September 1946, Philadelphia, Pennsylvania, USA. Attorney. m. Eileen Duffy Cameron, 1 son, 1 daughter. Education: BA, Liberal Arts, University of Pittsburgh, 1969; MBA, Health Administration, Temple University, 1972; JD, Law, Widener University, 1976; LLM, Corporate Law, New York University, 1980. Appointments: Judicial Clerkship, Superior Court of New Jersey, Newark, New Jersey, 1976; Assistant Administrator, St Elizabeth Hospital, Elizabeth, New Jersey, 1977; Vice-President Corporate Legal Affairs, Methodist Hospital Philadelphia, Pennsylvania, 1978-94; Interim Legal Consultant, North Penn Hospital, Lansdale, Pennsylvania, 1994-95; Interim Counsel and Legal Administrator, Hodes, Ulman, Pessin & Katz, Towson, Maryland, 1995-96; Assistant Corporate Secretary, Temple University Health System, Philadelphia, Pennsylvania, 1996-. Publications: Author and lecturer on health-care, business law and corporate law. Honours: Member, Bar of Maryland; Member, New Jersey Bar; Member, Pennsylvania Bar; Fellow, American College of Healthcare Executives. Memberships: American Bar Association; American Hospital Association; American College of Healthcare Executives. Address: 1410 Church Road, Malvern, PA 19355, USA.

CAMERON Ronald Johnston, b. 8 October 1930, Lewisham, England. Sculptor. m. Dorothy, 2 daughters. Education: Camberwell Art College, England, 1951. Career: Independent Sculptor; Commissions include miniatures in gold and silver and very large bronze statues; Commercial commissions include: 60 heads for the film Thunderbirds and the TV series Captain Scarlet and Joe 90; Comic heads of Diddymen for Ken Dodd's children's TV films; Originals of give-away plastic models for Esso, Total and Quaker Oats; Original sculptures for trophies include: Oxford and Cambridge Boat Race, The World Snooker Championship, The Dubai Gold Cup, International Batsman of the Year, medals for the European Games; Currently concentrating on art bronzes of naturalistic female figures shown in many commercial galleries and sold to individual collectors; Private commissions include most recently a large portrait of The Lord Chief Justice, Lord Woolf; Recent collaboration with Professor David March RA led to a combined show in the Gallery of Modern Art, Glasgow, 2002 and the Royal Academy Summer Exhibition 2003. Publications: Decor Magazine; National Newspapers. Honours: NDD; Sculpture Prize

for combined work with Professor David March, Royal Academy Summer Exhibition, 2003. Memberships: London Scottish Regiment; Marie Curie Cancer Charity. Address: 9 Morecambe Street, London SE 17 1 DX, England.

CAMERY John William, b. 5 February 1951, Cincinnati, Ohio, USA. Computer Software Engineer. Education: BA (Honours) Mathematics, University of Cincinnati, 1972; MSc, Carnegie-Mellon University, 1974. Appointments: Mathematician, US Army Material Systems Analysis Agency, Maryland, 1973; Student Assistant Engineering, Spectrum Analysis Task Force, Federal Communications Commission, Park Ridge, Illinois, 1974; Mathematician, US Army Communications Electronics-Engineering Installation Agency, Washington DC, 1975-83; Mathematician, Defense Communications Agency, JDSSC, Washington DC, 1983-86; Programmer Analyst, General Sciences Corp, Laurel, Maryland, 1986-87; Software Engineer, Sygnetron Protection Systems, 1987-88; Consultant, Lockheed-Martin Ocean Systems, Operations, Glen Burnie, Maryland, 1988-89; Computer Software Engineer, RDA Logicon, Leavenworth, Kansas, 1989-2001; Senior Systems Analyst, Anteon Corporation, Wheeler Army Airfield, Hawaii, 2001-. Publications: Simulation Techniques for a Multiple CPU Military Communication System(co-author), 1976; Pentagon Consolidated Telecommunications Centers System (PCTCS), Video Subsystem Reference Manual, 1982; Tying Together New Technologies in Battle Simulation, 2003. Memberships: American Mathematical Society, 1974-; Christian Church; European Math Society; Greater Cincinnati Amateur Radio Association (WA8WNR), 1967; Imperial Hawaii Vacation Club, 1981-; IEEE Computer Society; Republican Party; Société Mathematique de France. Address: 94-647 Kauakapuu Loop, Mililani, HI 96789-1832, USA.

CAMNER Howard, b. 14 January 1957, Miami, Florida, USA. English Teacher; Writer; Poet. Education: BA, English, Florida International University, 1982. Appointments: English Teacher; Screen Writer; Producer and Host of cable TV talk show; New York Performance Poet. Publications: Notes From the Eye of a Hurricane, 1979; Transitions, 1980; Scattered Shadows, 1980; Road Note Elegy, 1980; A Work in Progress, 1981; Poetry From Hell to Breakfast, 1981; Midnight at the Laundromat and Other Poems, 1983; Hard Times on Easy Street, 1987; Madman in the Alley, 1989; Stray Dog Wail, 1991; Banned in Babylon, 1993; Jammed Zipper, 1994; Bed of Nails, 1995; Brutal Delicacies, 1996. Contributions to: Howling Mantra; New York Magazine; Poet's Voice; Without Halos; Poetry Journal; The Diversifier; Amanda Blue; Eleventh MUSE; Louder Than Bombs; Cuthbert's Treasury; Gathering Stars; Poetpourri; Palmetto Review; Perceptions; Florida in Poetry; Poems That Thump In the Dark; Tributary; Security Blanket; Poetry: An American Heritage; After the Meeting on Elbe; American Poets 1990's; The Bristol Banner Anthology Series: Report to Hell, 1996, Graffiti off the Asylum Walls, 1996, Crescendo, 1997, Office Chronicles, Obstacles and Laments, 1997. Honours: Works included in 100 prominent literary collections worldwide; Nominated for Poet Laureate of Florida, 1980; Inducted into the Last Poets, Honorary Member, 1980; Fine Arts Press Poetry Award, 1988; Golden Poet Award, 1988; Silver Poet Award, 1989; Inducted into the Homer Honour Society of International Poets, 1992. Memberships: Poets and Writers; Academy of American Poets; Poetry Society of America; South Florida Poetry Institute; Writers' Exchange; National Writers Association; Authors Guild. Address: 10440 South West 76th Street, Miami, FL 33173, USA.

CAMP Kimberly, b. 11 September 1956, Camden, New Jersey, USA, Artist; Museum Director. Education: BA, Studio arts and Art History, University of Pittsburgh; MSc, Drexel University in

Dictionary of International Biography

Arts Administration. Appointments include: Curator, Exhibition Consultant, 1980-86; Chairman of Board, Creator, Kimkins Inc, 1982-; Program Director, Pennsylvania Council on the Arts, 1986-89; Director, The Experimental Gallery, Smithsonian Institution, 1989-94; President, Museum of African American History, 1994-98; Fellow, Kellogg National Leadership Program, 1997-2000; Executive Director and CEO, The Barnes Foundation, 1998-. Honours include: Chicago Museum of Science and Industry Achievement in Painting, 1985, 1986; Association of Negro Business and Professional Women Community Service Award, 1985; Purchase Award, J B Speed Art Museum, Louisville Chapter Links, 1988; Award of Distinction, Kentucky Art and Craft Foundation, 1994; Sprit of Detroit, Detroit City Council, 1994; Roger L Stevens Award for Contributions to the Arts and Culture, H John Heinz School of Public Policy and Administration, Carnegie Mellon University, 1999. Commissions and Creative Works: Work held in public and private collections throughout the US; Exhibitions of painting and soft sculpture, 1973-2001, include: Gloucester County College, New Jersey; Passaic County Community College, Paterson, New Jersey; Diggs Gallery, Winstom Salem State University, North Carolina; Galerie Francois, Washington DC; 2nd, 3rd, 4th Biennial National Black Arts Festival, Atlanta, Georgia; Junior Black Academy of Arts and Letters, Dallas, Texas. Memberships include: New Jersey State Council on the Arts; Detroit Vis and Convention; American Association of Museums; Empowerment Zone Development Corporation; Junior League; Links. Address: The Barnes Foundation, 300 North Latch's Lane, Merion, PA 19066, USA.

CAMPBELL Alastair John, b. 25 May 1957, England; Civil Servant; Journalist. Partner, Fiona Miller, 2 sons, 1 daughter. Education: Gonville & Caius College, Cambridge. Appointments: Trainee Reporter, Tavistock Times, Sunday Independent, 1980-82; Freelance Reporter, 1982-83; Reporter, Daily Mirror, 1982-86, Political Editor, 1989-93; News Editor, Sunday Today, 1985-86; Political Correspondent, Sunday Mirror, 1986-87, Political Editor, 1987-89; Columnist, 1989-91; Assistant Editor, Columnist, Today, 1993-95; Press Secretary to Leader of the Opposition, 1994-97; Press Secretary to Prime Minister, 1997-2001; Director of Communications, 2001-. Membership: President, Keighley Branch, Burnley Football Supporters' Club. Address: Prime Minister's Office, 10 Downing Street, London SW1A 2AA, England.

CAMPBELL Magda, b. 22 January 1928, Subotica, Yugoslavia. Physician; Child Psychiatrist; Researcher; Educator. m. Francis P Campbell, 1 son, 1 daughter. Education: MD, University of Belgrade, Yugoslavia, 1953; Resident in Psychiatry, Bellevue Hospital, New York University Medical Centre, 1958-59, 1960-62; Fellow in Child Psychiatry, National Institute of Health, Bellevue, 1962-63; Certified, Psychiatry, 1964, Child Psychiatry, 1966, American Board of Psychiatry and Neurology. Appointments: Teaching Assistant, 1963, to Professor of Psychiatry, 1979-95, New York University School of Medicine; Professor Emeritus of Psychiatry, 1995-; Director, Division of Child and Adolescent Psychiatry, Bellevue, 1987-91; Director of Training and Education, 1990-91. Publications: Over 250 articles to refereed journals and chapters in books; Co-author, 2 books. Honours: Grantee, NIMH, 1973-95; Blanche Ittleson Award, 1986; Agnes Purcell McGavin Award, 1990; American Psychiatric Association and Rieger Award, 1989; George Tarjan Award, 1997; American Academy of Child and Adolescent Psychiatry. Memberships: Life Fellow, American Psychiatric Association; American Academy of Child and Adolescent Psychiatry; American College of Neuropsychopharmacology. Address: 333 East 30 Street Apt 7c, New York, NY 10016, USA.

CAMPBELL Neve, b. 3 October 1973, Guelph, Ontario, Canada. Actress. m. Jeff Colt, divorced 1998. Education: National Ballet School, Canada. Career: Dance: The Phantom of the Opera; The Nutcracker; Sleeping Beauty; Films include: Paint Cans, 1994; The Dark, 1994; Love Child, 1995; The Craft, 1996; Scream, 1996; A Time to Kill, 1996; Simba's Pride, 1997; Scream 2, 1997; Wild Things, 1998; Hairshirt, 1998; 54, 1998; Three to Tango, 1999; Scream 3, 2000; Investigating Sex, 2001; Last Call, 2002; The Company, 2003; Blind Horizon, 2004; TV includes: Catwalk, 1992-93; Web of Deceit, 1993; Baree, 1994; The Forget-Me-Not Murders, 1994; Party of Five, 1994-98; The Canterville Ghost, 1996. Honours: Saturn Award for Best Actress, 1996; MTV Movie Award for Best Female Performance, 1996; Blockbuster Entertainment Award for Favourite Actress – Horror, 1997. Address: Creative Artists Agency, 9830 Wilshire Boulevard, Beverly Hills, CA 90212, USA.

CAMPBELL, Ramsey, b. 4 January 1946, Liverpool, England. Writer; Film Reviewer. m. Jenny Chandler, 1 Jan 1971, 1 son, 1 daughter. Appointments: Film Reviewer, BBC Radio Merseyside, 1969-; Full-time Writer, 1973-. Publications: Novels: The Doll Who Ate His Mother, 1976; The Face That Must Die, 1979; The Parasite, 1980; The Nameless, 1981; Incarnate, 1983; The Claw, 1983, US edition as Night of the Claw; Obsession, 1985; The Hungry Moon, 1986; The Influence, 1988; Ancient Images, 1989; Midnight Sun, 1990; The Count of Eleven, 1991; The Long Lost, 1993; The One Safe Place, 1995; The House on Nazareth Hill, 1996; The Last Voice They Hear, 1998; Silent Children, 2000; Pact of the Fathers, 2001; The Darkest Part of the Woods, 2002. Short stories: The Inhabitant of the Lake and Less Welcome Tenants, 1964; Demons by Daylight, 1973; The Height of the Scream, 1976; Dark Companions, 1982; Cold Print, 1985; Black Wine (with Charles L Grant), 1986; Night Visions 3 (with Clive Barker and Lisa Tuttle), 1986; Scared Stiff, 1987; Dark Feasts: The World of Ramsey Campbell, 1987; Waking Nightmares, 1991; Alone With The Horrors, 1993; Strange Things and Stranger Places, 1993; Ghosts and Grisly Things (short stories), 1998; Ramsey Campbell, Probably (non-fiction), 2002; Told by the Dead (short stories), 2003. Novella: Needing Ghosts, 1990. Honours: Liverpool Daily Post and Echo Award for Literature, 1993; World Fantasy Award, Bram Stoker Award, Best Collection, 1994; Best Novel, International Horror Guild, 1998; Grand Master, World Horror Convention, 1999; Lifetime Achievement Award, Horror Writers' Association, 1999. Memberships: British Fantasy Society, president; Society of Fantastic Films. Address: 31 Penkett Road, Wallasey CH45 7QF, Merseyside, England. Website: www.ramseycampbell.com

CAMPBELL Richard James, b. 18 January 1939, Sydney, NSW, Australia. Academic. m. Petronella Bernardina Maria Gilfedder, 2 sons (from previous marriage). Education: BA, 1956-58, BD (Hons 1), 1959-62, MA (Hons 1), 1963-64, University of Sydney; DPhil, University of Oxford, 1965-71. Appointments: Minister, Glebe Presbyterian Church, 1961-65; Graduate Student, 1965-67, College Tutoring, 1966-67, Oxford; Lecturer in Philosophy, 1967-72, Senior Lecturer, 1972-79, Reader, 1980-93, Professor, 1993-, Dean of Arts, 1990-94, Pro Vice-Chancellor and Chair, Board of the Faculties, 1994-98, Head, School of Humanities, 2001-2003, Australian National University; Nuffield Fellow, London, 1974; Visiting Lecturer, University of Cambridge, 1978, 1982; University of Toronto, 1982. Publications: Books: Secondary Education for Canberra, 1973; From Belief to Understanding, 1976; Truth and Historicity, 1992; Editor, Philosophy and the Turn to History, 1993. Numerous articles. Honour: Member, Order of Australia (AM), 1986. Membership: Fellow, Australian College of Education (FACE), 1976. Address: PO Box 16, Braddon, Act 2612, Australia.

Dictionary of International Biography

CAMPESE David Ian, b. 21 October 1962, Queanbeyan, Australia. Rugby Football Player. m. Lara Berkenstein. 2003. Appointments: Partner, Campo's Sports Store; International Debut, Australia v New Zealand, 1982; Captain, Australian Team; Winner, World Cup, 1991; World's Leading Try Scorer with 64; Scored 310 points; Australian Most Capped Player (represented Australia 101 times); Director, David Campese Management Group, 1997-. Publication: On a Wing and a Prayer. Honours: Australian Writers Player of the Year, 1991; English Rugby Writers Player of the Year, 1991; International Rugby Hall of Fame, 2001; Order of Australia Medal, 2002. Address: David Campese Management Group, Suite 4, 870 Pacific Highway, Gordon, NSW 2072, Australia.

CAMPION Jane, b. 30 April 1954, Wellington, New Zealand. Film Director; Writer. Education: BA, Anthropology, Victoria University, Wellington; Diploma of Fine Arts, Chelsea School of Arts, London, completed at Sydney College of the Arts; Diploma in Direction, Australian Film & TV School, 1981-84. Career: Writer/Director, films: Peel, 1981-82; Passionless Moments, 1984; Mishaps of Seduction and Conquest, 1984-85; Girls Own Story, 1983-84; After Hours, 1984; Producer: I episode ABC TV drama series, Dancing Daze, 1986; Director, Two Friends, for ABC TV Drama, 1985-86; An Angel at My Table, 1989-90; Sweetie, 1988; Writer/Director, The Piano, 1993; Director, The Portrait of a Lady, 1997; Holy Smoke, 1999; In the Cut, 2003. Honours: Numerous awards include: for the Piano: Best Picture, 66th Academy Awards Nomination, Best Director, 66th Academy Awards Nomination, LA Film Critics Association, New York Film Critics Circle, Australia Film Critics, Director's Guild of America Nomination, BAFTA Nomination, AFI Awards, Producer, Producer's Guild of America, Best Screenplay, 66th Academy Awards, BAFTA Nomination, AFI Awards; For The Portrait of a Lady: Francesco Pasinetti Award, National Union of Film Journalists, 1996. Address: HLA Management Pty Ltd, 87 Pitt Street, Redfern, NSW 2016, Australia.

CAMPTON David, b. 5 June 1924, Leicester, England. Playwright; Children's Fiction Writer. Publications: On Stage: Containing 17 Sketches and 1 Monologue, 1964; Resting Place, 1964; The Manipulator, 1964; Split Down the Middle, 1965; Little Brother, Little Sister and Out of the Flying Pan, 1966; Two Leaves and a Stalk, 1967; Angel Unwilling, 1967; Ladies Night: 4 Plays for Women, 1967; More Sketches, 1967; Laughter and Fear, 9 One-Act Plays, 1969; The Right Place, 1969; On Stage Again: Containing 14 Sketches and 2 Monologues, 1969; Now and Then, 1970; The Life and Death of Almost Everybody, 1970; Timesneeze, 1970; Gulliver in Lilliput (reader), 1970; Gulliver in The Land of Giants (reader), 1970; The Wooden Horse of Troy (reader), 1970; Jonah, 1971; The Cagebirds, 1971; Us and Them, 1972; Carmilla, 1972; In Committee, 1972; Come Back Tomorrow, 1972; Three Gothic Plays, 1973; Modern Aesop (reader), 1976; One Possessed, 1977; What Are You Doing Here?, 1978; The Do-It-Yourself Frankenstein Outfit, 1978; Zodiac, 1978; After Midnight: Before Dawn, 1978; Pieces of Campton, 1979; Parcel, 1979; Everybody's Friend, 1979; Who Calls?, 1980; Attitudes, 1980; Freedom Log, 1980; Dark Wings, 1981; Look-Sea, 1981; Great Whales, 1981; Who's a Hero, Then?, 1981; Dead and Alive, 1983; But Not Here, 1984; Singing in the Wilderness, 1986; Mrs Meadowsweet, 1986; The Vampyre (children's book), 1986; Our Branch in Brussels, 1986; Cards, Cups and Crystal Ball, 1986; Can You Hear the Music?, 1988; The Winter of 1917, 1989; Smile, 1990; Becoming a Playwright, 1992; The Evergreens, 1994; Permission to Cry, 1996. Contributions to: Amateur Stage; Writers News; Drama; Whispers. Address: 35 Liberty Road, Glenfield, Leicester LE3 8JF, England.

CAMROSE (Viscount), Sir Adrian Michael Berry. b. 15 June 1937, London, England. Writer; Journalist. Education: Christ Church, Oxford, 1959. Appointments: Correspondent, Time Magazine, New York City, 1965-67; Science Correspondent, 1977-96, Consulting Editor (Science), 1996-, Daily Telegraph, London. Publications: The Next Ten Thousand Years: A Vision of Man's Future in the Universe, 1974; The Iron Sun: Crossing the Universe Through Black Holes, 1977; From Apes to Astronauts, 1981; The Super Intelligent Machine, 1983; High Skies and Yellow Rain, 1983; Koyama's Diamond (fiction), 1984; Labyrinth of Lies (fiction), 1985; Ice With Your Evolution, 1986; Computer Software: The Kings and Queens of England, 1985; Harrap's Book of Scientific Anecdotes, 1989; The Next 500 Years, 1995; Galileo and the Dolphins, 1996; The Giant Leap, 1999. Honour: Royal Geographic Society, fellow, 1984-. Memberships: Royal Astronomical Society, London, Fellow, 1973-; British Interplanetary Society, Fellow, 1986-. Address: 11 Cottesmore Gardens, Kensington, London W8, England.

CANAS Jose Atilio, b. 21 September 1956, El Salvador. Physician. m. Carolina Celen-Canas, 1 son, 1 daughter. Education: BS, Biology, George Mason University, Fairfax, Virginia, USA, 1977; MD, Universidad Nacional Pedro Henriquez Ureña, Santo Domingo, Dominican Republic, 1983; Paediatric Residency, 1983-86, Fellowship, Paediatric Endocrinology, 1986, Nassau County Medical Center, New York, USA. Appointments: Director, Paediatric Endocrinology, Nassan County Medical Center, 1989-92; Assistant Professor of Paediatrics, Stonybrook University, SUNY at Stonybrook, 1992-; Director, Juvenile Diabetes Center, Winthrop University Hospital, 2002-. Memberships: Endocrine Society; American Diabetes Association. Address: Winthrop University Hospital, Juvenile Diabetes Center, 120 Mineola Blvd, Suite 210, Mineola, NY 11501, USA. E-mail: acanas@winthrop.org

CAÑAS MURILLO Jesús, b. 25 April 1951, Madrid, Spain. Educator. m. Magdalena Álvarez Franco, 1 daughter. Education: PhD, Hispanic Philology, University Autónoma de Madrid, 1978. Appointments: Professor, Spanish Literature, University Autónoma de Madrid, 1973-79; Professor, Spanish Literature, 1979-2000, Director, Spanish Literature Department, 1986, Director, Department of Spanish Philology, 1986-89, Director, Department of Hispanic Philology, 1991-95, University de Extremadura, Spain. Publications: Author, Editor: Libro de Alexandre, 1988; Blas Nasarre Disertacion, 1992; La comedia Sentimental, 1994; Honor en Lope de Vega, 1995; Editor: La Petimetra, 1989, Cracion apologetica, 1997; Juan Pablo Forner su epoca, 1998; Fuente Ovejuna, 1998. Memberships: Society of Medieval Hispanic Literature; Sociedad Española de Estudios del Siglo XVIII; Asociacion Escritores Extremeños. Address: University de Extremadura Avda de la Universidad S/N, 1071 Cáceres, Spain.

CANFORA Luciano Davide, b. 5 June 1942, Bari, Italy. Professor. m. Renata Roncali, 1 son, 1 daughter. Education: Dr Phi, Dr History, Ancient History. Appointments: University Assistant, Ancient History, 1964, Greek Literature, 1967, Papyrology, 1968, Latin, 1971, Classical Philology, 1975. Publications: Numerous articles in professional journals. Honours: Boston Editorial Committee, Institute for Classical Tradition; Scientific Committee, Enciclopedia Italiana; Director, Quadernidi Storia. Memberships: Fondazione Antonio Gramsci, Rome. Address: via Murat 104, 70123 Bari, Italy. E-mail: l.canfora@lettere.uniba.it

CANNON Jack Philip, b. 21 December 1929, Paris, France. Composer. m. Jane Dyson (Baroness Buijs van Schouwenburg). 1 daughter. Education: Dartington Hall, Devon; Royal College of

Music, London. Appointments: Lecturer, Oxford Extramural Studies, 1950-58; Lecturer in Music, Sydney University, Australia, 1958-60; Deputy Professor of Composition, 1950-58, Professor of Composition, Royal College of Music, London, 1960-95. Publications: Many articles for music journals; 3 operas, chorus/orchestral works, orchestral works, choral works, chamber music, mostly commissioned by national and international bodies; Important historical commissions include: Symphony commissioned by the BBC to mark Britain's entry to the EC, 1972; Symphony commission by Radio France for première at a diplomatic occasion in Paris, 1972; Te Deum commissioned by and dedicated to H M The Queen of England for the Service of Thanksgiving at St George's Chapel, Windsor Castle, 1975. Honours: Grand Prix and Critics' Prize, Paris, 1965; Fellow of the Royal College of Music, 1971; Bard of Gorsedd Kernow, 1997. Memberships: Royal Philharmonic Society; British Academy of Composers and Songwriters; Savile; Chelsea Arts. Address: Elmdale Cottage, March, Aylesbury, Bucks HP17 8SP, England.

CAO Hong-Xing, b. 19 March 1937, Shanghai, China. Meteorologist and System Scientist. m. Pei-Hua Li, 1 son, 1 daughter. Education: Tianjin Railway Engineering School, China, 1952-55; Bachelor, Department of Meteorology, Nanjing University, China, 1957-62. Appointments: Research Assistant, Geophysics, Chinese Academy of Sciences, 1962-63; Chief Forecaster, China Central Meteorological Observatory, 1964-71; Research Associate, 1972-81, Associate Professor, 1985-88, Professor, 1992-, Chinese Academy of Meteorological Sciences; Humboldt Foundation Fellow, Hamburg University, Germany, 1982-84; Member, Working Group I, International Panel of Climate Change, UN, at Hadley Centre for Climate Prediction and Research, UK, 1989-91. Publications: Over 200 articles on atmospheric and systems sciences include: Self-memorization in atmospheric motion, 1993; Modelling of system boundary, 1995; 8 books include: Climate Dynamic Models & Simulations; Fuzzy Sets Theory & Its Application to Meteorology; General Theory of System Boundary (Jieke Theory); Self-memory Principle of Dynamic Systems and Its Applications; Prostrating Meditation. Honours: Awards of Keji Jinbu of China Meteorological Administration, Grade III, 1998. Memberships: China Meteorological Society; Royal Meteorological Society, UK; Royal Society of New Zealand; China Systems Engineering Society; China Life Sciences Society. Address: China Academy of Meteorological Sciences, 46 Zhongguancun-Nandajie 100081, Beijing, China.

CAO Yeshi, b. 20 August 1949, Shanghai, China. Researcher. m. Liu Xinhong, 1 son. Education: BSc, East China University of Science & Technology, 1977; MSc, Nanjing University of Chemical Technology, 1984; Postgraduate Diploma, IHE, Holland, 1986; PhD, Delft University of Technology, Holland, 1994. Appointments: Lecturer, Head of Department, Suzhou Institute of Urban Construction and Environmental Protection, 1984-90; Research Fellow, International Institute for Hydraulic and Environmental Engineering, 1990-94; Senior Scientist, Environmental Technology Institute, 1994-98; Manager, Technical Study Division, Regional Institute of Environ Technology (EC Singapore Initiative), 1998-2002; Senior Scientist, Centre for Advanced Water Technology, Singapore Utilities Institute plc, 2002-. Publications: Several articles in professional journals. Honour: Netherlands Government Fellowship. Membership: International Water Association. Address: Centre for Advanced Water Technology, Innovation Centre (NTU), Block 2, Unit 241, 18 Nanyuang Drive, Singapore 637723. E-mail: yscao@cawt.sui.com.sg

CAO TRONG Thiem, b. 1 April 1942, Thanh Phong, Thanh Liem, Ha Nam, Vietnam. Artist. m. Pham Thi Thinh, 1 son, 2 daughters. Education: Graduate, Porcelain Decoration Faculty, Hanoi Industrial Arts University, 1977; Graduate, Hanoi Fine Arts University, 1984; Graduate, High Ranking Political Theory School, 1985. Career: Composing and studying arts. Publications: Chief Author: Vietnamese Art Museum, 1999; Art Collection of Vietnamese Porcelain, 2000; Art Work – Collection of the Vietnamese Art Museum, 2002; Member of Editorial Council: Author, Vietnamese Industrial Art Works in 2nd half of XXth Century, 1999; Vietnamese National Museums, 2001; Vietnamese Propaganda Pictures 1945-2002, 2002; Selected Vietnamese Art in XXth Century, 2002; Articles include: Vietnamese Art Museum – a glorious stage, 2000; Vietnamese Art in XXth Century from the view of the collection of the art museum, 2001; 35 Years of the Vietnam Art Museum, 2002. Honours: Third Class Resistance War Honour; Third Class Labour Decoration. Memberships: Vietnamese Fine Arts Association; Hanoi Fine Arts Association. Address: No 3 Hoang Cau, Group 90, O Cho Dua, Dong Da District, Hanoi City, Vietnam.

CAPORALINO-DJIAN Caroline, b. 11 March 1963, Oran, France. Biologist. m. Marcel Caporalino, 1 son, 1 daughter. Education: Diplome d'Etudes Universitaires Generales, University of Sciences, Nice, France, 1984; Agronomist ingenior, Ecole Nationale Superieure d'Agronomie, Rennes, France, 1987; Diplome d'Etudes Approfondies, University Sciences & Techniques, Montpellier, France, 1989; PhD, University Claude Bernard, Lyon, France, 1993. Appointments: Engineer, 1993-, Research Engineer, 2002-, National Institute of Agronomic Research, Antibes; Expert on soil nematodes, biotoxins, plant resistance, interactions of plants/pathogens. Publications: Articles in professional journals. Honour: Silver Medal, French Academy of Agriculture, 1994. Membership: International Foundation for Sciences, 1995. Address: INRA, 123 Bd Francis Meilland, F-06606 Antibes, France. E-mail: caporali@antibes.inra.fr

CARABÚS Olga Néllda, b. 23 December 1947, Catamarca, Argentina. Mathematician. m. Franklin Martinez, 1 son, 2 daughters. Education: Professor of Mathematics, National Institute of Teachers Training, Province of Catamarca, Argentina, 1968; Licentiate in Mathematics, 1977, Surveyor Engineer, 1983, Specialist in University Management and Administration, 2002, National University of Catamarca, Argentina; Masters Degree, Mathematical Education, National University of Tucumán, in progress. Appointments: Assistant Professor of Mathematics, 1974, Adjunct Professor, Calculus I and Calculus II, Faculty of Exact Sciences, 1977-89, Secretary General of the Academic Area, 1983-85, 1985-87, Associate Professor, Calculus I, Faculty of Technology, 1989-, Researcher in Teaching and Learning of Mathematics, National University of Catamarca; Consultant, Mathematics, Ministry of Education, Province of Catamarca 1996, 1997, 1998. Publications: What is learnt and what is not learnt in Mathematics, 2001; I want to be a tutor, 2002; Understanding in the learning of calculus, 2002; Didactical engineering in teaching and learning calculus, 2002; Didactic plan for the formation of creative engineers, 2003; Evaluation and Assessment in Mathematics Education, in press; Attended several national and international congresses. Honours: Top Best Grade Average, National Institute of Teachers Training of the Province of Catamarca, Award, Rotary Club of Catamarca, 1968; Flag-Bearer-Professorate, National Institute of Teachers Training of the Province of Catamarca, 1968; Finalist of Thales Prize in Research in Mathematical Education, SAEM Thales, Spain, 2000. Membership: Argentine Mathematical Association. Address: Avda. Virgen del Valle 1071-4700, Catamarca, Argentina. E-mail: olga@arnet.com.ar

Dictionary of International Biography

CARAMAN Petru, b. 20 June 1930, Bucharest. Researcher. m. Fraga-Colombina Caraman, 2 daughters. Education: Degree, Mathematics and Physics, 1953; PhD, Mathematics, 1962; Postdoctoral Thesis, Doctor Docent, 1973. Appointments: Teacher, Liceul Naţional of Iaşi, 1953-55; Research Worker, Mathematical Institute, Octav Mayer, Romanian Academy, Branch of Iaşi, 1955-; Professor, Mathematical Department, University Al I Cuza Iaşi, 1967-71; USA Scholarship, 1971-72; Director, Institute of Mathematics, 1990; Senator, Romanian Parliament, 1996-2000. Publications: 2 mathematical monographs, 1968, 1974; 100 maths works. Honours: Simion Stoilow Prize, Romanian Academy, 1971. Memberships: American Mathematical Society; Amnesty International; Liga Apărării Drepturilor Omului (League of the Defense of Human Rights); Societatea de ştiinţe Matematice din România; Societatea Matematicienilor din România; Alianţa Civică; Partidul Alianţei Civice; Christian Democrat Peasants' National Party; Convenţia Democratică Română. Address: str Palade 12, Iaşi 6600, Romania.

CARANI Dorothy Miriam Meyers, b. 6 April 1927, Pittsburgh, Pennsylvania. Author; Poet; Lyricist. m. Lee Carani, 2 sons, 3 daughters. Education: Self-trained Author. Appointments: Tenant Council President, Senior Apartment Building, College Park, Maryland, USA, 1998; Author. Publications: 15 Anthologies: Poetry Press, Yes Press, American Poetry, December Press, Illiad, Amherst, Sparrowgrass, National Library of Poetry, New Millennium, Famous Poets, Poetic Odyssey; 3 books in progress: Unto Me He Said (biblical); You Might Find it Here (humour); Great Men, Great Minds, Great Words (historical). Honours: American Presidential Eagle Award for contributions to literature, 1990; Silver Jubilee Album Award; England's White Rose Award; Lyndon B Weatherford/Homer Honor Society, International Poets. Memberships: ASCAP; Songwriters Club of America- Tin Pan Alley – Broadway Music; 100 Club; National Author's Registry. Address: 5320 Dorsey Hall Drive, Apt III, Ellicott City, MD 21042-7867, USA.

CARAZO-SALAS Rafael Edgardo, b. 4 September 1972, Costa Rica. Scientist. Partner, Eugenia Piddini. Education: BSc, Honours, Physics with Great Distinction, Concordia University, Canada, 1992-95; Certificate of Advanced Studies in Applied Mathematics and Theoretical Physics, University of Cambridge, Cambridge, England, 1995-96; Postgraduate Diploma DEA, Université Paris 7, Paris, France, 1996-97; PhD, Université Paris 7 and European Molecular Biology Laboratory, Heidelberg, Germany, 1997-2001, 2001-2002; Postdoctoral Fellow, Cancer Research UK, London Research Institute, London, UK, 2002-. Publications: Roles of chromatin in mitotic spindle morphogenesis (doctoral thesis), 2001; Research papers as first author and co-author include most recently: Ran-GTP coordinates regulation of microtubule nucleation and dynamics during mitotic-spindle assembly, 2001; Importin alpha-regulated nucleation of microtubules by TPX2, 2003; Long-range communication between chromatin and microtubules in Xenopus egg extracts, 2003. Honours include: Winner, Walter Raudorf Medal for Physics, Concordia University, Canada, 1995; Costa Rican National Science Award, Clodomiro Picado Twight 2001, 2002. Memberships: American Society for Cell Biology; European Life Sciences Organisation; American Association for the Advancement of Science. Address: CCL Cancer Research UK, 44 Lincoln's Inn Fields, London WC2A 3PX, England. E-mail: rafael.carazo-salas@cancer.org.uk

CARDIN Pierre, b. 2 July 1922, San Biagio di Callatla, Italy. Couturier. Appointments: Worker, Christian Dior; Founder, Own Fashion Houses, 1949; Founder, Espace Pierre Cardin (Theatre Group); Director, Ambassadeurs-Pierre Cardin Theatre (now Espace Pierre Cardin Theatre), 1970-; Manager, Société Pierre Cardin, 1973; Chair, Maxims, 1982-; Honorary UNESCO Ambassador, 1991. Creative Works: Exhibition at Victoria & Albert Museum, 1990. Publications: Fernand Léger, Sa vie, Son oeuvre, Son reve, 1971; Le Conte du Ver a Soie, 1992. Honours include: Grand Officer of Merit, Italy, 1988; Order of the Sacred Treasure (Gold & Silver Star), 1991. Address: 27 Avenue Marigny, 75008 Paris, France.

CARDNELL Valerie Flora, b. 21 April 1928, Kent, England. Singer. Education: 4 year Nursing Course, Middlesex Hospital, London, England; 4 year Music Course, Trinity College of Music, London, England; Music Therapy Course with Juliette Alvin; Qualified Teacher. Appointments: Private Nursing Sister, England; Night Superintendent, St Luke's Hospital for Church of England Clergy, London, England; Professional Singer, oratorios, recitals, concerts, recordings; Member, Vincian Trio; Radio and television programmes; Member Golden Age Singers; Many Educational Music Programmes for BBC including Andy Pandy; Professor of Singing; Music Examiner and Adjudicator. Honours: State Registered Nurse, England; Middlesex Hospital Certificate, London, England; Helen Trust Scholarship to Trinity College of Music; Music Degree FTCL; LTCL Singing; LTCL Piano; LRAM Singing; Winner, Elizabeth Schumann Lieder Competition, Trinity College of Music; Winner, Ricordi Opera Prize, Trinity College of Music; Winner, Silver Medal, Worshipful Company of Musicians; Winner, International Singing Competition, s'Hertogenbosch, Holland; Elected FRSA; Elected Honorary Fellow, Trinity College, London; Apostolic Blessing from His Holiness John Paul II. Memberships: Incorporated Society of Musicians, London, England; Trinity College of Music, London, England. Address: 20 Woodside Close, Surbiton, Surrey, England.

CARDONA Manuel, b. 7 September 1934, Barcelona, Spain. Physicist. m. Inge (Hecht), 2 sons, 1 daughter. Education: Licenciado, Physics, Barcelona University, 1955; DSC, Physics, University of Madrid, 1958; PhD, Applied Physics, 1959, Harvard University. Appointments include: Instructor, Electronics, University of Madrid, 1955-56; Research Assistant, Harvard University, 1956-59; Technical Staff, RCA Laboratories, Zurich, 1959-61; Princeton (New Jersey), 1961-64; Visiting Professor, University of Pennsylvania, Spring, 1964; Associate Professor, Physics, 1964-66; Professor, 1966-71, Brown University; Scientific Member and Director, Max-Planck Institute for Solid State Research, Stuttgart, 1971-2000; Business Managing Director, Max-Planck Institute, 1973-74; Chairman, Scientific Council, Paul Drude Institut, Berlin, 1993-98; Chairman, International Union of Pure Applied Physics (IUPAP) Semiconductor Commission, 1996-2002; Air New Zealand lecturer, 2001. Publications: About 1200 scientific publications in international journals, 11 monographs on solid state physics; Textbook on semiconductors. Honours include: Grants, fellowships, honorary doctorates from universities of Madrid, Barcelona, Sherbrooke (Canada), Rome, Regensburg, Toulouse, Thessaloniki (Greece), Brno (Czechoslovakia); Prizes include: ITALGAS Prize, 1992; Max Planck Prize (with E E Haller, U C Berkeley), 1994; John Wheatley Prize and Frank Isakson Prize, American Physical Society, 1985, 1997; Ernst Mach Medal, Czech Academy of Science, 1999; Nevill Mott Medal, British Institute of Physics, 2001 Miller Visiting Professor, University of California, Berkeley, 3 months, 2000; Fellow, Institute of Physics, 2001; Honorary Member, AF Ioffe Institute, St Petersburg, 2003; Adjunct Professor, Arizona State University, 2003; Honorary Chairman, International Conference of Physics of Semiconductors, Flagstaff, Arizona, 2004. Memberships include: Fellow, American Physical Society; Full Member, National Academy of Sciences of USA; Academia Europaea; Corresponding Member, Royal Academy of Sciences, Spain; Mexican Academy of Sciences; Academy of Sciences, Barcelona; Member, Global Photonics

Dictionary of International Biography

Advisory Board, CUNY, New York, 2004. Address: Max-Planck-Institut für Festkörperforschung, Heisenbergstr. 1, 70569, Stuttgart, Germany.

CAREY John, b. 5 April 1934, London, England. University Professor. m. Gillian Booth, 13 August 1960, 2 sons. Education: Lambe Open Scholar, 1954-57; BA, 1957; D Phil, 1960, St John's College, Oxford. Publications: Milton, 1969; The Violent Effigy: A Study of Dickens' Imagination, 1973; Thackerary, Prodigal Genius, 1977; John Donne: Life, Mind and Art, 1981; Original Copy: Selected Reviews and Journalism, 1987; The Faber Book of Reportage, 1987; Donne, 1990; The Intellectuals and the Masses, 1992; The Faber Book of Science, 1995; The Faber Book of Utopias, 1999; Pure Pleasure, 2000. Contributions to: Principal Book Reviewer, Sunday Times. Honours: Fellow, Royal Society of Literature; Fellow, British Academy; Honorary Fellow, St John's College, 1991, Balliol College, 1992. Address: Merton College, Oxford OX1 4SD, England.

CAREY Peter, b. 7 May 1943, Bacchus March, Victoria, Australia. Author. m. (2) Alison Summers, 1985, 2 sons. Education: Monash University. Appointments: Partner, McSpedden Carey Advertising Consultants, Sydney; Teacher, Columbia University, Princeton University. Publications: The Fat Man in History (short stories), 1974; War Crimes (short stories), 1979; Bliss (novel), 1981; Illywhacker (novel), 1985; Oscar and Lucinda, 1988; The Tax Inspector (novel), 1991; The Unusual Life of Tristan Smith (novel), 1994; Collected Stories, 1995; The Big Bazoohley (children's novel), 1995; Jack Maggs, 1997; The True History of the Kelly Gang, 2000; 30 Days in Sydney: A Wildly Distorted Account, 2001; Screenplays: Bliss; Until the End of the World; Film: Oscar and Lucinda, 1998. Honours include: Miles Franklin Award; National Council Award; Age Book of the Year Award. Address: c/o Amanda Urban, ICM, 40 West 57th Street, New York, NY 10019, USA.

CARL XVI GUSTAF, (King of Sweden), b. 30 April 1946. m. Silvia Sommerlath, 1976, 1 son, 2 daughters. Education: Sigtuna; University of Uppsala; University of Stockholm. Appointments: Created Duke of Jämtland; Became Crown Prince, 1950; Succeeded to the throne on death of his grandfather, King Gustaf VI Adolf, 1973. Honours: Dr hc, Swedish University of Agricultural Sciences, Stockholm Institute of Technology, Abo Academy, Finland. Memberships: Chair, Swedish Branch, World Wide Fund for Nature; Honorary President, World Scout Foundation. Address: Royal Palace, 111 30 Stockholm, Sweden.

CARLETON Elyn, b. Palmyra, Western Australia. Creative Artist; Teacher. m. Laurence E Carleton, 1 son, 2 daughters. Education: Studied privately with Wesley Penberthy, Melbourne, 1968-69; With Paul Olds, Victoria University, Wellington, New Zealand, 1970-74; With Dr Desiderius Orban OBE, Sydney, 1975-79. Career: Teacher and Founder of Creator's Art Group, 1980, and Innovators, 1988; Council and Publicity Officer, Ridley Art Society, 1987-89; Council Member and Executive Officer, New Chertsey Art Club, 1993-97, F.S.C.C.A.G., New South Wales, 1993; Developed unique creative art teaching method, 1980; Exhibitions: New Zealand Academy, Wellington, New Zealand, 1973; Victoria University, 1973; In Mind, Eight Wellington Artists, New Zealand Academy, Wellington, 1974; Other galleries in New Zealand and Australia; Mall Galleries; Royal Institute of Oil Painters; Hampstead Arts Council; Contemporary Portrait Society; United Society of Artists; City of Westminster Arts Council; New Chertsey Arts Club; Creative Images, Bloomsbury Intaglio Crafts, 1987; Two Hemispheres, Richmond Antiquary, 1988; Australian Paintings, Chertsey Hall, 1988-89; Bourne Hall, 1989-97; Queensland House, London, 1990; Loggia, 1991; Edith Grove,

1993; Boxfield, Stevenage, 1994; Work in collections: BHP Headquarters, Sydney; NCR World Headquarters, Dayton, Ohio, USA; Queensland House, London; Stevenage Council; Private collections in UK, Europe, USA, Singapore, New Zealand, Australia; Commissions: BHP Headquarters, Sydney; Other private commissions. Publications: Creative Images; Art Yesterday, Today and Tomorrow; Art Appreciation; Hanging an Exhibition; Constructive Criticism; Abstract Art. Memberships: Runnymede Association of Arts; Ridley Art Society; Fellow, Free Painters and Sculptors. Address: 120 Kangaroo Valley Road, Berry, NSW 2535, Australia.

CARLING William David Charles, b. 12 December 1965, Bradford-on-Avon, England. Rugby Player. m. (1) Julia Carling, 1994, divorced 1996, (2) Lisa Cooke, 1999, 1 son, 1 step-son, 1 step-daughter. Education: Durham University. Appointments: Owner, Inspirational Horizons Co, Insights Ltd; Former Member, Durham University Club; Member, Harlequins Club; International Debut, England v France, 1988; Captain, England Team, 1988-96; Retired, International Rugby, 1997; Played 72 times for England, Captain 59 times (world record); Rugby Football Commentator, ITV, 1997-. Publications: Captain's Diary, 1991; Will Carling (autobiography), 1994; The Way to Win, 1995; My Autobiography, 1998. Address: c/o Mike Burton Management, Bastian House, Brunswick House, Brunswick Road, Gloucester, GL1 1JJ, England. E-mail: will@willcarling.com

CARLS Alice-Catherine, b. 14 June 1950, Mulhouse, France. Professor; Translator. m. Stephen D, 2 sons, 1 daughter. Education: BA, German, University of Paris IV, 1967-70; MA, German, 1970-72; BA Certificate, Polish, University of Paris IV, 1970-73; 2nd Year, Institut Libre d'Etudes des Relations Internationales, Paris, 1972-73; Doctorat de Troisième Cycle, University of Paris I, 1973-76. Appointments: Assistant Professor, Political Science and History, Lambuth College, Jackson, 1985-92; Assistant Professor, History, University of Tennessee, Martin, 1992-96; Associate Professor, History, 1996-2001; Chair, Department of History and Political Science, 1997-2000; Professor of History, 2001-. Publications: Authored, La Ville Libre de Dantzig en crise ouverte, 1982; Jozef Wittlin's Passage Through France, Chapter, 2000; Translation: Le Cavalier polonais, by Wacław Grzędzielski, 1991; La Vie qu'il faut choisir, by Jan Kochanowski,1992; Echapper a ma tombe, by Józef Rostocki, 1995; Une Mouche dans ma soupe, by Józef Rostocki, 1998; La Saga du patient fantassin, by Józef Wittlin, 2000; Louis Loucheur 1872-1931; Ingénieur, homme d'état, modernisateur de la France, 2000 by Stephen D Carls; Le Vent à nouveau me cherche, by Anna Frajlich, 2003; Over seventy articles and one hundred book reviews. Honours: Various Who's Who Publications; French Foreign Affairs Ministry Doctorate Fellowship for Study and Research in Poland, 1973-75; Summer Research Grant, DAAD, 1975; Post Doctorate Research Grant, HHPL, 1981; Summer Doctorate Research Grant, HHIWRP, 1984; International Scholar Award, University of Tennessee at Martin, 1999: Spring Semester Featured Scholar, University of Tennessee at Martin, 1999; Cunningham Teacher Scholar Award, The University of Tennessee at Martin, 2002. Memberships: Southern Conference for Slavic Studies; Southern Historical Association; American Historical Association; American Association for the Advancement of Slavic Studies; Polish Institute of Arts and Sciences; Phi Kappa Phi; United Nations Association of the US; Phi Alpha Theta; Pi Delta Phi; European Union Studies Association; others. Address: Department of History and Philosophy, The University of Tennessee at Martin, Martin, TN 38238, USA.

CARLSON Dan, b. 27 February 1943, Minneapolis, Minnesota, USA. Doctor of Plant Breeding; Inventor of the Sonic Bloom System. Education: University of Minnesota, 1963-65; BS, Plant

Dictionary of International Biography

Breeding, Experimental College, University of Minnesota, 1975; Dr Degree, World University, 1990. Career: United States Armed Forces, 1961-63; Experimental Sheet Metal Technician, Hughes and Douglas Aircraft Companies, Los Angeles, California, 1965-69; Developed titanium boxes used on Explorer and Surveyor missions to the Moon; Developer, Inventor, 1975-80; Chief Executive Officer, Director of Research, Dan Carlson Scientific Enterprises Inc, 1980-; Developed Sonic Bloom a method of organic plant fertiliser helping the world feed itself; Lectures in over 15 countries in Europe, East Asia, South America, USA and Australia, 1986-; Frequently featured on various radio broadcasts. Publications: Acres USA, A Voice for Eco-Agriculture, 1998; Brave New Waves, 2000; Sonic Bloom – Creation Close Up, Creation Illustrated, 2003; Good Vibrations, A Sound Diet for Plants, in The Growing Edge, 1991. Honours: Grower of the largest indoor plant in the world (Purple Passion Plant), Guinness Book of Records; Prestigious awards for great agricultural accomplishments from the Japanese government; Humanitarian of the Year, Institute for Human Potential, 2002; Nominated, Nobel Prize in Economics, 2001, 2002, 2003; Honor of Dignity; Man of the Year 2003; Listed in: Great Minds of the 21st Century, ABI, 2004; Lifetime Achievement Award; 21st Century Award for Achievement; 2000 Outstanding Intellectuals of the 21st Century; Leading Scientists of the 21st Century Order of Excellence Award; International Scientist of the Year, IBC, 2004. Address: W 7964-810th Ave, River Falls, WI 54022, USA. E-mail: inventor@sonicbloom.com Website: www.sonicbloom.com

CARLYLE Robert, b. England. Actor. m. Anastasia Shirley, 1997. Education: Royal Scottish Academy of Music & Drama. Appointments: Director, Rain Dog Theatre Company. Creative Works: Productions include: Wasted; One Flew Over the Cuckoo's Nest; Conquest of the South Pole; Macbeth; Stage appearances include: Twelfth Night; Dead Dad Dog; Nae Problem; City; No Mean City; Cuttin' a Rug; Othello; TV includes: Face; Go on Byrne'; Taggart; The Bill; Looking After Jo Jo, 1998; Hitler: The Rise of Evil, 2003; Gunpowder, Treason and Plot, 2004; Films include: The Full Monty; Carla's Song; Trainspotting; Priest; Marooned; Being Human; Riff Raff; Silent Scream; Apprentices; Plunkett and Macleane, 1999; The World is Not Enough, 1999; Angela's Ashes, 2000; The Beach, 2000; There's Only One Jimmy Grimble, 2000; To End All Wars, 2000; 51st State, 2001; Once Upon a Time in the Midlands, 2002; Black and White, 2002; Dead Fish, 2004. Honours include: Paper Boat Award, 1992; BAFTA Award, Best Actor; Salerno Film Festival Award, 1997; Evening Standard Outstanding British Actor Award, 1998; Bowmore Whiskey/Scottish Screen Award for Best Actor, 2001; David Puttnam Patrons Award. Address: c/o ICM, Oxford House, 76 Oxford Street, London, W1D 1BS, England.

CARMEL Simon J, b. 30 April 1938, Baltimore, Maryland, USA. Retired Associate Professor; Anthropologist; Folklorist. Education: BA, Physics, Gallaudet University, Washington DC, 1961; MA, 1980, PhD, 1987, Anthropology, American University, Washington DC. Appointments: Physicist, National Bureau of Standards, Gaithersburg, Maryland, 1961-81; Adjunct Professor, Assistant Professor, George Washington University, Gallaudet University, 1981-87; Associate Professor, National Technical Institute for the Deaf, Rochester Institute of Technology, 1988-2001; Community Services (Volunteer): Founder, Team Director, first US Deaf Ski Team, 6th Winter Deaflympics, Berchtesgaden, West Germany, 1967; Founder, Leader, US Deaf Ski Association and US Deaf Ski Week Convention, West Park City, Utah, USA, 1968; Ski Alpine Technical Director, Winter Deaflympics, 1971-91; General Chairman, United States Organizing Committee, American Athletic Association of the Deaf, 8th Winter Deaflympics, Lake Placid, New York, USA, 1975; Secretary General, Society of World Deaf

Magicians, 1990-. Publications: Books: International Hand Alphabet Charts, 1982; Deaf-lore: Deaf People, (in press); Article: Deaf Folklore, 1996; Numerous articles on deaf culture and folklore, magic and folk tales; Lectures on "Deaf Holocaust Survivors' Testimonies" at universities, deaf schools and deaf clubs around the USA. Honours: Finalist, National Volunteer Award, National Center for Voluntary Action, 1974; Inductee as Sports Leader, Hall of Fame of the American Athletic Association of the Deaf, 1982; Fulbright Scholarship Award, 1993-94; Edward Miner Gallaudet International Leadership Award, Gallaudet University Alumni Association, 1997. Memberships: American Anthropological Association; American Folklore Society; National Association of the Deaf; International Brotherhood of Magicians; Society of American Magicians; Society of World Deaf Magicians; US Deaf Magicians Society. Address: 9339 Bridgeport Drive, West Palm Beach, FL 33411, USA. E-mail: simoncarmel13@aol.com

CARMEN Ira H, b. 3 December 1934, Boston, Massachusetts, USA. College Professor. m. Lawrence Lowell Putnam, 2 daughters. Education: BA, University of New Hampshire, 1957; MA, 1959, PhD, 1964, University of Michigan. Appointments: Member, Political Science Faculty, University of Illinois, 1968. Publications: Books, Movies, Censorship, and the Law, 1966; Power and Balance, 1978; Cloning and The Constitution, 1986; The Constitution of Human Genomics, 2004. Honours: President George Bush's Educators Advisory Committee, 1989; Recipient of Six Awards for Teaching Excellence, University of Illinois. Memberships: Recombinant DNA Advisory Committee, National Institutes of Health, 1990-1994; Human Genome Organisation, elected 1996. Address: Department of Political Science, 361 Lincoln Hall, University of Illinois, Urbana, IL 61801, USA.

CARNLEY Peter Frederick, b. 17 October 1937, New Lambton, New South Wales, Anglican Archbishop of Perth; Primate of the Anglican Church of Australia. m. Carol Ann Dunstan, 1 son, 1 daughter. Education: BA, 1st class Hons, University of Melbourne, 1962-65; Licentiate, Theology, 1st class Hons, 1962; PhD, St Johns College, Cambridge, 1966-68. Appointments: Deacon, 1962; Priest, 1964; Licentiate of Officiate, Ely, 1966-69; Chaplain, Mitchell College of Advanced Education, Bath, 1970-72; Research Fellow, St John's College, 1971-72; Warden, St John's College, 1972-81; Resident Canon, Brisbane, 1975-81; Examining Chaplain to the Archbishop of Brisbane, 1975-81; Anglican Archbishop of Perth, 1981; Primate of the Anglican Church of Australia, 2000-; Hon Doctor of Letters, University of Newcastle, 2000; Hon Doctor of Letters, University of Western Australia, 2000; Fellow, St John's College, Cambridge, 2000; Fellow, Trinity College, University of Melbourne, 2000; Hon Doctor of the University, Charles Sturt University, 2001; Hon Doctor of Letters, University of Queensland, 2001. Publications: The Structure of Resurrection Belief, 1987; Faithfulness in Fellowship: Reflections on homosexuality and the church, 2001; The Yellow Wallpaper and other sermons, 2001; Reflections in Glass, 2004. Honours: University Prize, Biblical Archaeology, University of Melbourne, 1962, 1963; Lucas Tooth Scholarship, 1966-69; Naden Divinity Student, St John's College, Cambridge, 1968-69; 1998. Memberships: Weld Club; West Australian Club; St John's, Brisbane. Address: Anglican Church Office, GPO Box W2067, Perth, WA 6846, Australia.

CARON H Marcel, b. 16 September 1919, Montreal, Quebec, Canada. Chartered Accountant; Director. m. Madeleine Dussault, 3 sons, 2 daughters. Education: Ecole des Hautes Etudes Commerciales de Montréal; Ls Comm, Ls Comp, University of Montreal. Appointments: Chartered Accounts Clerk, City of Montreal, 1939-43; Junior Audit Clerk, 1943, Manager, 1947, Partner, 1949-84, Retired Executive Partner, 1984-, Clarkson Gordon, Chartered Accountants, Montreal; Partner, Woods

Gordon, Montreal, 1957-84; President, Chambly Industries Inc; Honorary Chairman, Advisory Board of Accountancy, University of Montreal; Governor, Clinical Research Institute Montreal. Honours: Honorary Doctorate, University of Montreal; Officer, Order of Canada, 1980. Memberships: Past President: Canada Tax Foundation; Order Chartered Accounts, Quebec; Chambre de Commerce du Dist de Montréal; Revue Commerce; Canada Committee; Advisory Board, Quebec Ministry of Revenue; Canadian Institute Chartered Accountants; Opéra du Québec; Treasurer Emeritus: La Salle Foundation; Jules and Paul Emile Leger Foundation; Governor, Council for Canadian Unity; Past President, Honorable Member, Advisor, Corporation de l'Ecole des Hautes Etudes Commerciales. Address: 115 Chemin Côte Ste Catherine, Apt 202, Outremont, Quebec H2V 4R3, Canada.

CARPENTER Carol Maureen, b. 9 November 1943, Highland Park, Michigan, USA. Writer; Poet; Instructional Designer. m. Mack L Carpenter, 5 April 1963, 1 son, 1 daughter. Education: BS, 1966, MEd, 1972, EdD, 1984, Wayne State University. Appointments: English Teacher, Detroit Public School, 1966-71; English Instructor, Oakland Community College, 1971-73; Program Co-Ordinator, Instructor, Detroit Institute of Technology, 1974-80; Curriculum Developer, Oakland University, 1980-81; Creative Manager, Planning, Sandy Corporation, 1982-85; Founder, Owner, President, The High Performance Group Inc, 1985-99. Contributions to: Wisconsin Review; Indiana Review; Bellingham Review; Writer's Forum; Cape Rock. Honours: Tompkins Awards, Graduate Division, 1979, 1980; 1st Place, Poetry, Writers Digest Annual Competition, 1992. Address: 10005 Berwick, Livonia, MI 48150, USA.

CARPENTER William, b. 31 October 1940. Writer; Teacher. 2 sons. Education: BA, Dartmouth College, 1962; PhD, University of Minnesota, 1969. Appointments: Assistant Professor, University of Chicago, Illinois, 1967-72; Faculty Member, College of the Atlantic, 1972-. Publications: The Hours of Morning; Rain; Speaking Fire At Stones; A Keeper of Sheep; The Wooden Nickel, 2002. Contributions to: American Poetry Review; Poetry; New England Review. Honours: Associated Writing Programs Award; National Endowment for the Arts Fellowship; Samuel French Morse Prize. Address: 1135 Route One, Stockton Springs, ME 04981, USA.

CARPER Gertrude Esther, b. 13 April 1921, Jamestown, New York, USA. m. J. Dennis, April 1942. Education: Business School, Covington, Virginia; Diploma in Fine Art, Maryland Institute of Art, 1950. Career: Secretary to the Principal, Covington High School; Secretary to the Reverend Joseph Smith, 1940-41. Civic Activities: Volunteer, teaching retarded people; Founder, St Michael's Sanctuary wildlife preserve; Involved in restoration of Lytton Hall, Baltimore. Publications: Expressions for Children, (poetry) 1986; Mentation (poetry). Honours: Citation of Nobless of Humanity, World Parliament of Chivalry, 1990; Deputy Director General, International Biographical Centre; International Order of Merit. Membership: Charter Member, Women in the Arts. Address: Essex Yacht Harbour Marina, 500 Sandalwood Road, Baltimore, MD 21221-5830, USA.

CARPINTERI Alberto, b. 23 December 1952, Bologna, Italy. Structural Engineer. Education: PhD, Nuclear Engineering cum laude, University of Bologna, Bologna, Italy, 1976; PhD, Mathematics cum laude, University of Bologna, 1981. Appointments include: Researcher, Consiglio Nazionale delle Ricerche, Bologna, Italy, 1978-80; Assistant Professor, University of Bologna, 1981-86; Professor of Structural Mechanics, Politecnico di Torino, Italy, 1986-; Founding Member and Director, Graduate School in Structural Engineering, Politecnico di Torino,

Italy, 1990-; Director, Department Structural Engineering, Politecnico di Torino, 1989-95. Publications include: Localized Damage: Computer-Aided Assessment and Control, 1994; Advanced Technology for Design and Fabrication of Composite Materials and Structures, 1995; Structural Mechanics, 1997; Fractals and Fractional Calculus in Continuum Mechanics, 1998; Computational Fracture Mechanics in Concrete Technology, 1999. Honours include: Robert l'Hermite International Prize, 1982; JSME Medal, 1993; Doctor of Physics Honoris Causa, 1994; International Cultural Diploma of Honor, 1995; Honorary Professor, Nanjing Architectural and Civil Engineering Institute, Nanjing, China, 1996; Honorary Professor, Albert Schweitzer University, Geneva, Switzerland, 2000. Memberships: International Congress on Fracture, 1981-, Director, 2001-2005; International Association of Fracture Mechanics for Concrete and Concrete Structures, 1992-, President, 2004-2007; Réunion Internationale des Laboratoires d'Essais et de Recherches sur les Matériaux et les Constructions, 1982-; American Society of Civil Engineers, 1985-; European Structural Integrity Society, 1991-, President, 2002-2006-; European Mechanics Society, 1994-. Address: Chair of Structural Mechanics, Politecnico di Torino, 10129 Torino, Italy.

CARR Willie E E, b. 11 November 1948, Banjul, Gambia. Educational Administrator. m. N'dela Y W Carr, 1 son, 2 daughters. Education: Bachelor of Arts, University of Sierra Leone, 1975; Diploma in Education, 1976; Diploma in Office Management/ Administration, The College of Professional Management, 1997. Appointments: Graduate Teacher, 1976, Senior Master, 1982, Vice-Principal, 1989, Principal 1994, Gambia Secondary Senior School. Memberships include: Gambia Football Association; Athletics Association; National Olympics Committee; National Youth Service Scheme. Address: Gambia Senior Secondary School, PO Box 64, Banjul, The Gambia. E-mail: g.s.s.s1959@hotmail/com

CARRELL Robin Wayne, b. 5 April 1936, Christchurch, New Zealand. Professor of Haematology. m. Susan Wyatt Rogers, 2 sons, 2 daughters. Education: MB ChB, Otago, New Zealand, 1959; BSc Hons, Canterbury, New Zealand, 1965; PhD, 1968, ScD, 2002, Cambridge, England. Appointments: Director, Clinical Biochemistry, Christchurch Hospital, Christchurch, New Zealand, 1968-75; Lecturer, Clinical Biochemistry, University of Cambridge, Cambridge, England, 1976-78; Professor and Director, Molecular Pathology, University of Otago, Christchurch, New Zealand, 1978-85; Professor of Haematology, University of Cambridge, Cambridge, England, 1986-2003. Honour: Hector Medal, Royal Society of New Zealand, 1986. Memberships: FRACP, 1973; FRCPath, 1976; FRCP, 1990; FRSNZ, 1980; FRS London, 2002. Address: Department of Haematology, University of Cambridge, CIMR, Hills Road, Cambridge CB2 2XY, England. E-mail: rwc1000@cam.ac.uk

CARRERAS Jose, b. 5 December 1947, Barcelona, Spain. Singer (Tenor). m. Ana Elisa, 1 son, 1 daughter. Appointments: Debut, Gennaro in Lucrezia Borgia, Liceo Opera House, Barcelona, 1970-71 Season; Appeared in La Boheme, Un Ballo in Maschera, I Lombardi alla Prima Crociata at Teatro Regio, Parm, Italy, 1972; US Debut as Pinkerton in Madame Butterfly with NYC Opera, 1972; Debut, Metro Opera as Cavaradossi, 1974; Debut, La Scala as Riccardo in Un Ballo in Maschera, 1975; Appeared in Film, Don Carlos, 1980, West Side Story (TV), 1985; Appeared at major opera houses and festivals including Teatro Colon, Buenos Aires, Covent Garden, London, Vienna Staatsoper, Easter Festival and Summer Festival, Salzburg, Lyric Opera of Chicago. Creative Works: Recordings include: Un Ballo in Maschera; La Battaglia di Legnano; Il Corsaro; Un Giorno di Regno; I Due Foscari; Simone Boccanegra; Macbeth; Don Carlos; Tosca; Thais; Aida; Cavalleria Rusticana; Pagliacci; Lucia di Lammermoor; Turandot; Elisabetta di Inghilterra; Otello (Rossini). Publication: Singing From the Soul, 1991. Honours: Grammy Award, 1991; Sir Lawrence Olivier Award, 1993; Gold Medal of City of Barcelona; Albert Schweizer Music Award, 1996; Commandeur des Arts et des Lettres; Chevalier Légion d'honneur and numerous other awards. Memberships: President, Jose Carreras International Leukaemia Foundation, 1988-; Honorary Member, Royal Academy of Music, 1990. Address: c/o FIJC, Muntaner 383, 2, 08021 Barcelona, Spain. E-mail: fundacio@fcarreras.es Website: www.fcarreras.es

CARREY Jim, b. 17 January 1962, Newmarket, Canada. Actor. m. (1) Melissa Worner, 1986, divorced, 1 daughter, (2) Lauren Holly, 2001. Appointments: Performed, Comedy Clubs, Toronto. Creative Works: Films include: Peggy Sue Got Married, 1986; The Dead Pool, 1988; Earth Girls Are Easy, 1989; Ace Ventura! Pet Detective; The Mask; Ace Ventura: When Nature Calls, 1995; Dumb and Dumber; Liar Liar, 1996; Batman Forever; The Cable Guy; The Truman Show, 1997; Man on the Moon; How the Grinch Stole Christmas, 2000; Me, Myself and Irene, 2000; The Majestic, 2001; Bruce Almighty, 2003; Pecan Pie, 2003; Eternal Sunshine of the Spotless Mind, 2004; Several TV appearances. Address: UTA, 9560 Wilshire Boulevard, 5th Floor, Beverly Hills, CA 90212, USA.

CARRINGTON Simon Robert, b. 23 October 1942, Salisbury, UK. Conductor; University Professor; Freelance Choral Consultant. m. Hilary Stott, 1 son, 1 daughter. Education: MA, Cantab; Choral Scholar, King's College, Cambridge; Teaching Certificate, New College, Oxford. Appointments: Founder and Co-Director, The King's Singers, 1968-2001; Director, Choral Activities, University of Kansas, Lawrence, 1994-2001; Director, Choral Activities, New England Conservatory, Boston, 2001-; With the King's Singers: 3,000 concerts; 72 recordings, television and radio performances worldwide. Publications: Various choral arrangements. Honours: Grammy Nomination, 1986; Numerous awards and citations at choral festivals worldwide. Memberships: American Choral Directors Association; Association of British Choral Directors; Chorus America. Address: The New England Conservatory, 290 Huntington Avenue, Boston, MA 02115, USA. E-mail: sc@simoncarrington.com

CARROLL John Douglas, b. 3 January 1939, Philadelphia, Pennsylvania, USA. Professor of Marketing, Psychology. m. Sylvia B, 2 sons. Education: BS, University of Florida, 1958; MA, Princeton University, 1960; PhD, 1963. Appointments: Instructor, Research Assistant, Yale University, 1961-63; Member, Technical Staff, Bell Telephone Laboratories, 1963-65; Assistant Professor, New York University, 1965-66; Adjunct Associate Professor, 1968-70; Adjunct Professor, Baruch College of City University, New York, 1971; Acting Professor, University of California, Irvine, 1975-76; Acting Professor, University of California, San Diego, 1975-76; Adjunct Professor, University of Pennsylvania, 1978-79; Procter and Gamble Adjunct Professor, 1987-89; Member of Technical Staff, AT and T Bell Laboratories, 1966-82; Distinguished Member, 1982-90; Visiting Research Professor, University of California, Irvine, 1993; Board of Governors, Professor of Management and Psychology, Rutgers, The State University of New Jersey, 1990-. Publications: Many publications. Honors: Phi Beta Kappa; Sigma Xi; Co-recipient, Alpha Kappa Psi Award; Bell Laboratories Distinguished Technical Staff; Distinguished Scientific Contribution Award; William James Fellow Award; JAMS Best Article Award; Alpha Kappa Psi Award for Most Distinguished Paper in Journal of Marketing; Others. Memberships: Psychometric Society; Classification Society of North America; Society of Multivariate Experimental Psychology; American Psychological Association; American Psychological Society; American Statistical Association; American Marketing Association; INFORMS; Association for Consumer Research; Society for Mathematical Psychology; Society for Consumer Psychology; AAAS; International Federation of Classification Societies. Address: Management Education Center, Rm #125, FOM, Rutgers University, 111 Washington Street, Newark, NJ 07102-3027, USA.

CARRON William John, b. 28 July 1930, Dublin, Ireland. Marine and Landscape Painter. m. Barbara Warren, 1 daughter. Education: Studied Drawing, The National College of Art; Studied Mechanical Engineering, Bolton Street College; Studied, Ceramics and Pottery with Harry Horlock Stringer, Tagg's Yard, London. Career: Teacher, Drawing, Painting, Ceramics/Pottery, Sutton Park School, Dublin; Teacher, Drawing and Painting, St Stephen's Preparatory School, Dundrum, Dublin; One Man Exhibitions: Dublin Painters' Gallery, 1966; Tom Wilson's Studio Gallery, 1978; Kennedy Gallery, 1989; Kilcock Gallery, 1992; Group Shows: RHA Annual Exhibition; Watercolour Society of Ireland; Banquet RHA; Oireachtas; Joint Exhibitions with Barbara Warren: Carroll Gallery, Longford, 1993; Linenhall, Castlebar, 1988; Collections: Artist's Self Portraits, National Collection at Limerick University; Work in Watercolour, Society of Ireland Permanent Collection in Limerick University; Work in Private Collections in Ireland, United Kingdom and USA. Publications: Illustrator, A Painter in the West and Other Poems. Honours: National Crafts Competition, Royal Dublin Society, 1973; Certificate of Merit for Stoneware Pottery, Class 1, Royal Dublin Society; Award for Mechanical (Engineering) Draughtsmanship, Vocational Education Committee of Ireland. Memberships: Elected Member, Watercolour Society of Ireland, 1977; Elected Associate Member, Royal Hibernian Academy, 1996. Address: 'Matakana', Grey's Lane, Howth, Co Dublin, Ireland.

CARTER Jimmy (James Earl Jr), b. 1 October 1924, Plains, Georgia, USA. Politician; Farmer. m. Rosalynn Smith, 1946, 3 sons, 1 daughter. Education: Georgia Southwest College; Georgia Institute of Technology; US Naval Academy. Appointments: US Navy, 1946-53; Peanut Farmer, Warehouseman, 1977; Busman, Carter Farms, Carter Warehouses, Georgia; State Senator, Georgia, 1962-66; Governor of Georgia, 1971-74; President of USA, 1977-81; Distinguished Professor, Emory University, Atlanta, 1982-; Leader, International Observer Teams, Panama, 1989, Nicaragua, 1990, Dominican Republic, 1990, Haiti, 1990; Host, Peace Negotiations, Ethiopia, 1989; Visitor, Korea, 1994; Negotiator, Haitian Crisis, 1994; Visitor, Bosnia, 1994. Publications: Why Not The Best?, 1975; A Government as Good as its People, 1977; Keeping Faith: Memoirs of a President, 1982; The Blood of Abraham: Insights into the Middle East, 1985; Everything to Gain: Making the Most of the Rest of Your Life, 1987; An Outdoor Journal, 1988; Turning Point: A Candidate, a State and a Nation Come of Age, 1992; Always a Reckoning (poems), 1995; Sources of Strength, 1997; The Virtues of Ageing, 1998; An Hour Before Daylight, 2001. Honours include: Onassis Foundation Award, 1991; Notre Dame University Award, 1992; Matsunaga Medal of Peace, 1993; J William Fulbright Prize for International Understanding, 1994. Address: The Carter Center, 453 Freedom Parkway, 1 Copenhill Avenue, North East Atlanta, GA 30307, USA.

CARTER Joan Patricia, b. 11 March 1923, Vancouver, British Columbia, Canada. Artist; Illustrator; Author. m. Alan H Carter, deceased, 2 sons, 1 deceased. Education: Hornchurch College of Further Education; Longbridge College of Further Education; Self taught in calligraphy, illumination of scripts and books, portrait painting, sculpture and silverpoint. Career: Creator of colour silverpoint; Teacher of silverpoint, calligraphy and illuminated calligraphy; Speaker on printing, silverpoint and illuminated calligraphy; Talks on radio, Essex, Suffolk, Norfolk and Yorkshire;

Paints at least 1 commissioned watercolour portrait each year; Exhibitions: RMS; SWA; Royal Academy Summer Exhibition; Paris Salon Summer Exhibition; Library, Schweinfurt, Germany; Many one woman shows in Essex and Norfolk. Publications: Remembrance Books: Hornchurch, Essex, Gidea Park, Essex, Great Yarmouth, Norfolk, Romford, Essex, Norwich Cathedral, Norwich (Normandy Veterans), Lowestoft (Burma Star), Norwich (Norfolk Fire Service); Trystan da Cuna (Church), Normandy, France (Normandy Veterans), Hospital, Romford, Essex; 2 personal illuminated books of verse; Illuminated Calligraphy, 1984; Illuminated Alphabets, 1989; Illuminated Design, 1991; Silverpoint, 1996; An Allergy Cookbook; Solo Cooking on a Shoestring; Vegan-Vegi Cookbook, 2004; Articles in local newspapers and magazines. Honours: Gold Medal, Paris Salon; Silver Medal, Paris Salon; Honorary Mention, Gold Bowl, RMS; Finalist, Hunting Group of Painters. Memberships: Royal Society of Miniature Portraits; Society of Women Artists; Société des Artistes Français; Society of Miniaturists, Florida, USA. Address: 4 Osprey Close, Hoveton, Norwich, Norfolk NR12 8DR, England.

CARTER Lawrence Edward, b. 23 September 1941, Dawson, Georgia, USA. Dean; Professor. m. Marva Griffin, 1 son. Education: BS, Social Sciences, Virginia University of Lynchburg, 1964; MDiv, Theology, 1968, STM, Pastoral Care, 1970, PhD, Pastoral Psychology and Counseling, 1978, Boston University. Appointments: Assistant Minister, Court Street Baptist Church, Lynchburg, Virginia, 1960-64; Minister to Youth, Roxbury United Presbyterian Church, 1965-67; Substitute Teacher, Boston Public Schools, 1966-77; Associate Minister, People's Baptist Church, Roxbury, Massachusetts, 1968-71; Clergy Teaching Advisor, Harvard University Divinity School, Massachusetts, 1976-77; Associate Dean, Marsh Chapel, Boston University, 1978-79; Dean, Martin Luther King Jr International Chapel, Professor of Philosophy and Religion, College Archivist/Curator, Chief of Ceremony, Morehouse College, 1979-. Publications: 3 books; Articles in professional and popular journals. Honours: Over 50 awards, honours, citations and proclamations, 1964-. Memberships: Mercer University School of Theology; Association for Global New Thought; American Academy of Religion; Springfield Foundation for Historic District, Augusta. Address: Morehouse College, 830 Westview Drive SW, Atlanta, GA 30314-3773, USA. E-mail: lcarter@morehouse.edu Website: www.morehouse.edu

CARTER Marion Elizabeth, b. Washington DC, USA. Teacher; Lecturer; Author of Poems, Articles and Books. Education: BA, Wellesley College, Massachusetts; MA, Howard University, DC; MS, Middlebury College, Vermont, MS, Georgetown University, DC; PhD, Catholic University, DC: PhD, Georgetown University, DC. Appointments: Initiated the teaching of French and Spanish on TV for the Public Schools of Washington DC; Fulbright Programme of Spain; Lecturer of English as a Second Language; Visiting Professor, Wellesley College, Massachusetts; Trustee, World University; Given lectures at Washington University, St Louis, University of Kansas, University of Colorado at Boulder, and University of The Andes, Merida, Venezuela and the University of Florida under auspices of Mid-America Conferences on Hispanic Literature; One of two women selected by the National Association for Foreign Student Affairs who visited and evaluated student programmes in Israel and France; Independently visited Jordan and Palestine in conjunction with Howard University Hospitals Child Care Services, she instituted the teaching of French and Spanish to preschoolers at her nearby Foreign Language Centre. Publications: Author, Skyward or E Pluribus Unum, submitted for publication, 2002; it is the story of her family and ancestral ties in poetic-prose styles, tracing life events from 1700's to the brink of the 21st century; Author of A General Linguistics Textbook for

College Students. Honours: Recipient of several academic grants and scholarships; Recipient, Ernest Kay Foundation Award, 1998. At the Church of Epiphany, Washington DC she has served on the Seminarian's Lay Committee, as lector and lay Eucharistic Minister; Attended and addressed IBC-ABI International Congresses, 1975-2002. Address: 402 U Street NW, Washington, DC 20001-2333, USA.

CARTER Mavis, b. 9 March 1939, London, England. Teacher; Poet. m. Edwin Carter, 3 sons, 3 daughters, 2 foster daughters. Education: Digby Stuart Training College, 1957-59. Publications: Seasonal Change, 1986; Turning Up the Volume, 1994. Contributions to: Distaff; Fatchance; Froghore Papers; Orbis; Outposts; Poetry Nottingham; Smiths Knoll; Thursdays; Westwords; Hepworth, A Celebration, anthology; Chayns, a Cornish Anthology. Memberships: Arvon Centres Limited; Taliesin Trust. Address: West Barn, Tarlton, Cirencester, Gloucestershire GL7 6PA, England.

CARTER Rosalynn Smith, b. 18 August 1927, Sumter County, Georgia, USA. Former First Lady of the United States. m. James Earl Carter Jr (39th US President), 3 sons, 1 daughter. Education: Graduate, Georgia Southwestern College, 1946. Appointments: Board of Advisors, Habitat for Humanity, 1984-; Vice Chair, Board of Trustees, The Carter Center Inc, 1986-; President, Board of Directors, Rosalynn Carter Institute of Georgia Southwestern State University, 1988-; Distinguished Fellow, Emory University Department of Women's Studies, 1990-; Co-Founder, Every Child By Two Campaign for Early Immunization, 1991-; Chair, Carter Center Mental Health Task Force, 1991-. Publications: First Lady From Plains (autobiography), 1984; (with Jimmy Carter) Everything to Gain: Making the Most of the Rest of Your Life, 1987; Helping Yourself Help Others: A Book for Caregivers (co-author), 1994; Helping Someone with Mental Illness: A Compassionate Guide for Family, Friends and Caregivers (co-author), 1998. Honours: 7 honorary degrees, 1979-2001; Many awards for humanitarian service especially in the field of mental health including: Volunteer of the Decade, 1980, Into the Light Award, 1997, National Mental Health Association; Award of Merit for Support of the Equal Rights Amendment, National Organization for Women, 1976; Notre Dame Award for International Humanitarian Service, 1992; Eleanor Roosevelt Living World Award, Peace Links, 1992; Kiwanis World Service Medal, 1995; Jefferson Award, American Institute for Public Service, 1996; Presidential Medal of Freedom, 1999; National Women's Hall of Fame, 2001. Address: The Carter Center, One Copenhill, 453 Freedom Parkway, Atlanta, GA 30307, USA.

CARTER Russell Paul Jr, b. 5 June 1927, Trenton, New Jersey. Polymer Chemist; Process Specialist. m. June Marie Watlington, 1 son. Education: BS, Chemistry, LeHigh University, USA, 1947-51; MS, Polymer Chemistry, Akron University, USA, 1958-60. Appointments: Johnson and Fararra Garage, Princeton, 1942-45; Grover and Gulick Lumber Co, Princeton, 1945-46; Redding Plumbing and Heating, Princeton, 1946-50; Heyden Chemical Corp, Princeton, 1950-51; Research Chemist, Compounder, The Goodyear Tire and Rubber Co, 1951-65; Development of Sarin nerve gas, US Army Chemical Corps, 1956-58; Development Chemist, Engineer, The Goodyear Aerospace Corporation, 1965-75; Chemist, Research Specialist in Polyurethane and Polycarbonate Plastics, Mobay/Miles/Bayer Chemical Co, 1975-92; Retired, 1992. Publications: The Mechanism of the Benzidine Rearrangement; Investigation of the Re-Tempering of Over-tempered Chocolate; Some Alkali Metal Complexes as Organic Intermediates; Evaluation of Panel Type Air Cleaners By Means of Atmospheric Dust; Cross-Linked Polyethylene Foam, A Novel New Unbreakable Plastic; A New Type of Unbreakable Golf Tee,

Dictionary of International Biography

Called Riptee; Flame Retardant Polycarbonate; Many others. Honour: The George Gates 'World's Greatest Compounder Award'; Listed in national and international biographical dictionaries. Memberships: Society of Plastics Engineers; American Chemical Society. Address: 12 Orchard Drive, New Martinsville, WV 26155-2818, USA.

CARTWRIGHT Nancy Lynn, b. 24 June 1944, Pennsylvania, USA. Professor. m. Stuart Hampshire, 2 daughters. Education: BS, University of Pittsburgh, 1966; PhD, University of Illinois at Chicago Circle, 1971. Appointments: Professor of Philosophy, University of Maryland, 1971-73; Professor of Philosophy, Stanford University, 1973-91; Professor of Philosophy, London School of Economics, 1991-; Professor of Philosophy, University of California at San Diego, 1998-. Publications: 5 books. Honours: McArthur Fellow; Fellow, British Academy; Member, American Academy of Arts and Sciences; Fellow, Leopoldina Academy of Arts and Sciences, Germany. Address: CPNSS, Lakatos Building, LSE, Houghton Street, London WC2A 2AE, England. E-mail: philcent@lse.ac.uk Website: www.cpnss.lse.ac.uk

CARVALHO Mario Costa Martins de, b. 25 September 1944, Lisbon, Portugal. Lawyer; Writer. m. Maria Helena Taborda Duarte, 3 August 1968, 2 daughters. Education: Graduated Law, School of Lisbon, 1970. Publications: Contos Da Setima Esfera, 1981; A Paixao Do Conde De Frois, 1986; Os Alferes, 1990; Quatrocentos Mil Sestercios... Um Deus Passendo Pela Brisa Da Tarde, 1994 (A God Strolling in the Cool of The Evening); Era Bom Que Trocassemos Umas Ideias Sobre o Assunto, Several staged plays, 1995; Fantasia para dois Coronéis e uma Piscina, 2003. Contributions to: Columnist in jornal de Letras, and Publico; Nouvelle Revue Francaise. Honours: Premio Cidade de Lisboa; Grande Premio APE. Membership: Portuguese Writers Association. Address: R Antonio Pereira Carrilho, 27 R/C 1000/ 046 Lisboa, Portugal.

CARVALHO Paulo de, b. 25 August 1960, Luanda, Angola. Sociologist. m. Anabela Cunha, 2 sons. Education: MA, Sociology, University of Warsaw, Poland, 1990; PhD, Sociology, ISCTE, Lisbon, Portugal, 2004. Appointments: Director of Press Centre, Luanda, Angola, 1991-92; Manager of Consulteste Ltd, 1994-; Lecturer in Sociology and Statistics, 1996-99, Assistant Professor, 1999-, University of Agostinho Neto, Luanda, Angola. Publications: Most important books: Social Structure in Colonial Angola, 1989; Students from Overseas in Poland, 1990; Media Audience in Luanda, Angola, 2002;. How Much Time is Left until Tomorrow? 2002; Numerous newspaper articles about social and economic subjects, Luanda and Lisbon. Honours: Kianda Award on Economic Journalism, Luanda, Angola, 1998; Angolan Cultural Award on Social Research, 2002. Memberships: International Sociological Association; World Association for Public Opinion Research; American Sociological Association; British Sociological Association; American Statistical Association; Angolan Sociological Association. Address: Caixa Postal 420, Luanda, Angola. E-mail: pauldecarvlho@sociologist.com

CARY Alice S, b. 2 June 1920, Gaziantep, Turkey. Physician; Missionary. m. Otis Cary, 1 son, 3 daughters. Education: BA, Wellesley College, 1942; MD, Yale University, School of Medicine, 1945; Intern, 1946, Resident, 1946-47, Internal Medicine and Paediatrics, New Haven Hospital. Appointments: Physician, Doshisha University Health Centre, Kyoto, Japan, 1947-50; Physician, Japan Baptist Hospital, Kyoto, 1955-95; Physician, Louis Pasteur Centre for Medical Research, Kyoto, 1995-96; Director, Aoibashi Family Clinic Counseling Centre, 1981-91; Medical Advisor, United Church Missionaries in Japan; Associate Missionary, United Church Board of World Ministries, 1947-96;

President, Resident Council, Piedmont Gardens, Oakland, 1999-2001. Publications: Chapter, Alive Until Death, in 2 volume The Meaning of Life, 1992 (in Japanese). Honours: Phi Beta Kappa, Wellesley College, 1941; Alpha Omega Alpha, Yale Med, 1943; College Women's Association of Japan, 40th Anniversary Award, 1989; City of Kyoto Award for International Contribution, 1992. Memberships: League of Women Voters, Oakland; Physicians for Social Responsibility; Piedmont Community Church; Oakland Museum of California. Address: 33 Linda Ave, #1601, Oakland, CA 94611, USA.

CARY Phillip Scott, b. 10 June 1958, USA. Professor. m. Nancy Hazle, 3 sons. Education: BA, English Literature and Philosophy, Washington University, St Louis, 1980; MA, Philosophy, 1989, PhD, Philosophy and Religious Studies, 1994, Yale University. Appointments: Teaching Assistant, Philosophy Department, Yale University, 1988-92; Adjunct Faculty, Philosophy Department, University of Connecticut, 1993; Adjunct Faculty, Hillier College, University of Hartford, 1993-94; Arthur J Ennis Postdoctoral Fellow, 1994-97, Rocco A and Gloria C Postdoctoral Fellow, 1997-98, Core Humanities Programme, Villanova University; Assistant Professor of Philosophy, 1998-2001, Associate Professor of Philosophy, 2001-, Scholar in Residence, Templeton Honors College, 1999-, Eastern University, St Davids. Publications: 1 book; 13 articles in professional journals. Honours: University Fellowship, Yale University; Mylonas Scholarship, Freshman History Award, Phi Beta Kappa, Washington University; Listed in national and international biographical dictionaries. Memberships: APA; AAR; SCP. Address: Eastern University, 1300 Eagle Road, St Davids, PA 19087-3696, USA. E-mail: pcary@eastern.edu

CASFORD Michael John, b. 25 April 1940, Hackney, London, England. Artist; Painter. m. Masako Okura. Education: Byamshaw Diploma, London Certificate in Art and Design, Byamshaw School of Art, Kensington, London, 1969-72; Statens Kunstakademi, Oslo, 1972-73. Career: Hospitant and Assistant to Professor Ludwig Eikaas, Statens Kunstakademi, Oslo, 1973-76; Professional Artist, 1976-; Exhibitions include: Galleri I Alana, 1978; Autumn National Exhibition, 1979, 1980, 1983, Oslo; Kunsenerforbund, 1980; Galleri Homansbyen, 1981; Galleri Maxim, 1983; Galleri Teatergaten, 1984; LNM, 1989; Galleri Kongen, Stavanger, 1991; Atelier Gourdon, Oslo, Stavanger, 1992; Geologisk Jubilem Graffik, 1997; Galleri Azur, 2000; Regular exhibitions and sales at Blomquist Auction House, Oslo, including 2 paintings November 2000. Civic Activities: Occasional teaching free of charge. Publications: Work reviewed in magazines and newspapers. Honours: Leverhulme Scholarship, 1969; State Scholarships and Stipends, Oslo, 1972, 1979, 1982, 1989, 1990, 1991. Memberships: Norwegian Art Organisations: NBK, OBK, LNM. Address: Hovsetervn. 94 B, 0768 Oslo, Norway.

CASH Pat, b. 27 May 1965, Australia. Tennis Player. m. Emily, 1 son, 1 daughter. Education: Whitefriars College. Appointments: Coached by Ian Barclay; Trainer, Anne Quinn; Winner, US Open Junior, 1982 Brisbane and in winning Australian Davis Cup team, 1983; Quarter-finals, Wimbledon, 1985, Finalist, Australian Open, 1987, 1988; Wimbledon Champion, 1987; Retired, 1997; Co-Established a tennis training and coaching centre, Queensland; Sports Commentator. Honour: Australian Tennis Hall of Fame. Address: c/o Pat Cash and Associates, PO Box 2238, Footscray, Victoria 3011, Australia.

CASSIAN Nina, b. 27 November 1924, Galati, Romania. Poet; Composer; Film Critic; Translator. Education: University of Bucharest and Conservatory of Music. Appointment: Visiting Professor, New York University, 1985-86. Publications: Verses: 50 books including: (in Romanian) At the Scale 1/1, 1947; Ages of the Year, 1957; The Dialogue of Wind and Sea, 1957; Outdoor Performance, 1961; Everyday Holidays, 1961; Gift Giving, 1963; The Discipline of the Harp, 1965; Blood, 1966; Parallel Destinies, 1967; Ambitus, 1968; Chronophagy 1944-69, 1969; The Big Conjugation, 1971; Requiem, 1971; Lotto Poems, 1974; 100 Poems, 1974; Suave, 1977; Mercy, 1981; Countdown, 1983; Arguing with Chaos, 1994; The Un-Making of the World, 1997; (in English) Lady of Miracles, 1982; Call Yourself Alive?, 1988; Life Sentence: Selected Poems, 1990; Cheer Leader for a Funeral, 1993; Take My Word for It, 1998; Chapbook: Something Old, Something New, 2001. Other: Prose; children's plays and poetry. Honours: Writers Union of Romania Awards, 1967, 1984; Writers Association of Bucharest Award, 1981; Fulbright Grant, 1986; New York Public Library Literary Lion, 1994. Address: 555 Main Street, No 502, Roosevelt Island, New York, NY 10044, USA.

CASTILLO Diana M, b. 22 July 1945, Pontiac, Michigan, USA. Religious Organisation Administrator. Education: AA Humanities, 1992, BA, English, magna cum laude, 1994, University of Cincinnati, Ohio. Appointments: Delayed Birth Certificate Clerk, West Virginia State Health Department, Charleston, 1979-86; Proofreader: Fiecke-Web, 1987, Anderson Publishing Company, 1987-88, Press Community Papers, 1987-88, Dixie News, 1989; Word Processing Specialist, University of Cincinnati, Ohio, 1990-94; Desk Clerk, Grand Canyon National Park Lodges, Arizona, 1996; Focus Juror, Goodwin Raup PC, Arizona, 1998; Intern/student, Denver Rescue Mission, Colorado, Fall 1998. Publications: Short story, A Shrine in the Corner, 1999; Contributions as author, editor, to newsletters. Honours: Presidential Scholarship, West Virginia State College, Institute, West Virginia, 1985; Alpha Sigma Kappa Honor Society, 1992, Golden Key National Honor Society, 1993, University of Cincinnati, Ohio. Memberships: International Union of Gospel Missions, Flagstaff, Arizona, 1996-; International Platform Association, 1997-, Bible Study Fellowship, Port Angeles, Washington, 1998. Address: PO Box 1523, Springfield, MO 65801, USA.

CASTLE Barbara Anne (Baroness Castle of Blackburn), b. 6 October 1910, Chesterfield, England. Journalist; Author. m. Edward Cyril Castle, 1944. Education: St Hugh's College, Oxford. Appointments: Editor, Town and County Councillor, 1936-40; Housing Correspondent and Affairs Advisor, Daily Mirror, 1940-45; Labour Member, Blackburn, 1945-79; Member, National Executive Committee, 1950-79, Vice-Chairman, 1957-58, Chairman, 1958-59, Labour Party; Minister of Overseas Development, 1964-65; Privy Counsellor, 1964; Minister of Transport, 1965-68; First Secretary of State for Employment and Productivity, 1968-70; Secretary of State for Social Services, 1974-76; Member, European Parliament, Greater Manchester North, 1979-84, Greater Manchester West, 1984-89; Leader, British Labour Party, European Parliament, 1979-85; Vice-Chairman, Socialist Group, European Parliament, 1979-86. Publications: Castle Diaries 1964-70, 1984; Sylvia & Christabel Pankhurst, 1987; Castle Diaries 1964-76, 1990; Fighting All the Way, 1993. Honours: Honorary Fellow, St Hugh's College, Oxford, 1966; Bradford & Ilkley Community College, 1985, UMIST, 1991, Humberside Polytechnic, 1991, York University, 1992; Honorary doctorates, Bradford University, 1968, Loughborough, 1969, Lancaster, 1991, Manchester University, 1993, Cambridge University, 1998, De Montfort University, 1998, University of North London, 1998; Cross of Order of Merit, Germany, 1990; Created Life Peer, 1990. Address: House of Lords, London SW1A 0PW, England.

CASTLEMAN Louis Samuel, b. 24 November 1918, St Johnsbury, Vermont, USA. Physical Metallurgist. m. Mildred Blanche Rubin, 4 sons. Education: BSc, Metallurgy, 1939, DSc, Physical Metallurgy, 1950, Massachusetts Institute of Technology, Cambridge, Massachusetts, USA. Appointments: Plant Metallurgist, Sunbeam Electric Manufacturing Company, Evansville, Indiana, 1939-41; Senior Scientist, Acting Section Manager, Westinghouse Manufacturing Corporation, Pittsburgh, Pennsylvania, 1950-54; Metallurgical Specialist, Sylvania Telephone and Electronics Laboratory, Bayside, New York, 1954-64; Professor, Physical Metallurgy, 1969-89, Professor Emeritus, 1989-, Polytechnic University, Brooklyn, New York. Publications: Approximately 15 or more articles on subjects such as: solid state diffusion, retained austenite in steels, damage to metals caused by neutron bombardment, in journals including: Transactions of the Metallurgical Society, AIME, Acta Metallurgica, American Society of Metals, American Nuclear Society. Honours: Recipient, Distinguished Teacher Award, Polytechnic University, Brooklyn, 1975; Fellow AAAS, 1978; Listed in Who's Who publications and biographical dictionaries. Memberships: AIME; ASM; APS; AAAS. Address: 120 Morris Avenue, Apt 6-5, Rockville Center, NY 11570-4240, USA. E-mail: lcastlem@optonline.net

CASTONGUAY ROSATI Diane Claire, b. 27 November 1941, Brooklyn, New York, USA. Artist. m. Vincent S Rosati, 1 son, 1 daughter. Education: BS, cum laude, Wagner College, 1976; MPH, Columbia University School of Public Health, 1980. Appointments: Nurse Epidemiologist, Doctors Hospital of Staten Island, 1977-80; Infection Control Coordinator, Staten Island Hospital, 1980-; Professional Artist. Publications: Several articles in professional journals. Commissions and Creative Works: Numerous exhibitions including: 10 solo shows, 1992-; Pen and Brush Annual Pastel Exhibition, 1992; Mixed Media Shows; Moorings Gallery, Nova Scotia Sign of the Whale Art Gallery, Nova Scotia, Canada, 1992; Silvermine Guild Art Centre, International Print Biennial, 1994, 1996; International Miniprint Exhibition, Conn Graphics Art Centre, 1997; Acadia University Exhibition, invitational 1 person show, Nova Scotia; Curator, Coastline Gallery, Nova Scotia; Works in private collections. Honours include: Gerald Mennin Award for Graphics, National Art Club 97th Annual Exhibiting Members Show, 1995; Honorable Mention, Salmagundi Spring Auction, 1996; Robert Brockman Award, Pen and Brush 15th Pastel Exhibition, 1996; Solo Show Awards in Mixed Media and Pastel, Pen and Brush, 1997; Philip Isenburg Award in Graphics, Pen and Brush, 1997; Dorothy Koatz Myers Award, Salmagundi Non Juried Summer Exhibition, 1997; Silver Medal of Honour, 56th Annual Audubon Artists Show, 1998; Gene Alden Walker Memorial Award, Pen and Brush Graphics Show, 1999. Memberships include: National Art Club; Print Club of Albany; US Printmakers Association; Visual Arts of Nova Scotia; National Association of Woman Artists; The Pen and Brush; Audubon Artists. Address: 1618 McLean Lake Road, RR#2 Sable River, NS B0T 1V0, Canada.

CASTRO Francisco Ferreira de, b. 28 June 1923, Floriano-Piaui, Brazil. Lawyer; Educator. m. Iracema da Costas Silva Castro, 1 son, 2 daughters. Education: BS, Economics, 1941; LLB, Minas Gerais Federal University, Belo-Horizonte, Brazil, 1948; LLD, Brasilia University, 1967. Appointments: State Representative of the Legislative Assembly, 1950-54; Vice Governor and Substitute Governor, State Government of Piaui, 1954-58; State Lawyer, Teresina, 1960-62; Federal Deputy, National Congress, Brasilia, 1958-62; Advisor of Juridical Affairs of Presidency, Federal Government, Brasilia, 1962-64; Professor, Constitutional Law, 1962-70, Professor of Political Science, 1989-93, University of Brasilia; Attorney NOVACAP Co, Brasilia, 1961-64; 1st Class Attorney, Federal District Government, Brasilia, 1964-86; Lawyer, Supreme Tribunal and Superior Federal Appeals Tribunal, Brasilia, 1964-. Publications: Author: The State's Aim – Main Doctrines, 1956; Modernization and Democracy, 1967; Articles in professional journals. Honours: Juridical Medal of the Centenary

Clovis Bevilaqua, Brazilian Government, 1959; Medal, District Federal Government, 1984; Grand Cross Medal, Piaui State Renascenca Merit Order, 1997. Memberships: Past President, Brazil Lawyers Order; Congress Club; Honorary Member, Brazilian Tennis Academy; Planetary Society. Address: SMl MI 09, Conj 05 Casa 16, 7150095 Brasilia Distrito Federal, Brazil. E-mail: ffcastro@nuctecnet.com.br

CASTRO Jorge, b. 17 November 1970, Granada, Spain. Biologist. Education: Degree in Biology, 1993; Doctor in Ecology, 2000. Appointments: Predoctoral Researcher, University of Granada and Spanish Institute of Agronomic Research, 1994-96; Predoctoral Researcher, University of Granada, 1996-2000; Postdoctoral Researcher, Botanical Institute, University of Copenhagen, 2000-; Currently, Assistant Professor of Ecology, Granada University. Publications: Numerous articles in professional scientific journals. Memberships: Spanish Society of Terrestrial Ecology; Botanical Society of America; Spanish Society of Forest Science. Address: Departmento de Biologia Animal y Ecologia, Facultad de Ciencias, Universidad de Granada, E-18071 Granada, Spain. E-mail: jorge@ugr.es

CASTRO Maria Graciela, b. 2 March 1955, Argentina. Scientist. m. P R Lowenstein, 1 son. Education: BSc, Honours, 1979, MSc, 1981, PhD, 1986, Biochemistry, School of Biological Sciences, National University of La Plata, Argentina; Post Doctoral Training, National Institutes of Health, Bethesda, Maryland, USA. Appointments: Senior Research Fellow, Department of Biochemistry and Physiology, University of Reading, England, 1989-91; Lecturer, Department of Molecular and Life Sciences, Abertay University, Dundee, Scotland, 1991-92; Lecturer, Neuroscience, Department of Physiology, University of Wales, College of Cardiff, UK, 1992-95; Senior Lecturer in Medicine and Co-Director, Molecular Medicine and Gene Therapy Unit, 1995-98, Personal Chair in Molecular Medicine, 1998-2001, University of Manchester, England; Member, Neuroscience Panel, The Wellcome Trust, London; Member, European Commission, Expert-Evaluator, Neuroscience Panel, Brussels, Belgium; The Athena Project, mentoring women in science, engineering and technology, Bolton, Lancashire, England; Member of several editorial boards; Member, The National Institute of Neurological Disorders and Stroke Study Section, NIH, Bethesda, Maryland, USA; Director, Molecular Medicine Department, Co-director, Board of Governors, Gene Therapeutics Research Institute, Cedars Sinai Medical Center, 2001-, Full Professor of Medicine, Department of Medicine, 2002-, University of California at Los Angeles, USA. Publications: Numerous articles in medical journals. Honours: Fogarty International Fellowship, 1986-89; Siebens Foundation Fellowship, 1999; Listed in several Who's Who publications; Three National Institutes of Health five-year programme grants to develop gene therapies for neurological disorders. Memberships: British Neuroscience Association; Women in Neuroscience; Society for Neuroscience; Society for Endocrinology; American Gene Therapy Association; Founding Member, International Society of Neuro Virology; Women in Science and Technology in Europe. Address: Gene Therapeutics Research Institute, Department of Molecular Medicine, Cedars-Sinai Medical Center, 8700 Beverly Boulevard, Research Pavilion, Room 5090, Los Angeles, CA 90048-1865, USA.

CASTRO MAGANA Mariano, b. 20 April 1948, San Salvador, El Salvador. Paediatrician. Appointments: Director, Paediatric Endocrinology, Winthrop University Hospital, Mineola, New York, USA; Professor of Paediatrics, State University of New York Health Science Center, New York, USA. Publications: 50 articles in peer reviewed journals; 9 books and book chapters; 100 non-peer reviewed articles and abstracts. Memberships: 26 medical societies including: Society for Paediatric Research; Endocrine Society; European Society for Paediatric Research; LWPES. Address: 120 Mineola Blvd, Suite 210, Mineola, NY 11501, USA.

CATALANO Joseph S, b. 16 October 1928, Brooklyn, New York, USA. Professor. m. Marisa Pagin-Catalano, 1 son, 1 daughter. Education: BA, MA, PhD, St John's University, New York. Appointments: Instructor, Assistant Professor, Associate Professor, St John's University; Professor, Professor Emeritus, Kean University, New Jersey; Adjunct Associate Professor, New School of Social Research. Publications: 5 books; Many articles in professional journals; Major grants, reviews and papers. Address: 1410 York Ave, Apt 3F, New York, NY 10021-3468, USA.

CATANA Aurelia, b. 11 May 1944, Posesti, Prahova, Romania; University Lecturer. m. Gheorge Catana, 2 sons. Education: Honours Degree, University of Bucharest, Faculty of Mathematics, 1961-64; Honours Degree, University of Bucharest, Faculty of Mathematics-Mechanics, 1964-69. Appointments: Mathematics Teacher, 1964-84; School Deputy and General School Inspector, 1984-2004; University Lecturer, Valahia University, Targoviste, Romania, 1997-2004. Publications: Author and joint author of 14 methodic and scientific works including most recently: Problems of Mathematical Analysis, 1993; Arithmetics and the Theory of Numbers (University Course) volumes 1, 2, 2001. Honour: Excellent Teacher Award, Ministry of Education. Membership: National Committee for Educational Alternatives. Address: Strada Gimnaziului Nr 16, Targoviste, Romania 0200. E-mail: dana_catana@yahoo.com

CATON-JONES Michael, b. 15 October 1957, Broxburn, Scotland. Film Director. Education: National Film School. Appointments: Stagehand, London West End Theatres. Creative Works: Films: Liebe Mutter; The Making of Absolute Beginners; Scandal, 1989; Memphis Belle, 1990; Doc Hollywood, 1991; This Boy's Life, 1993; Rob Roy, 1994; The Jackal, 1997; City By The Sea, 2002. Honours: 1st Prize, European Film School Competition.

CAULFIELD Patrick, b. 29 January 1936, London, England. Artist. m. (1) Pauline Jacobs, 1968, divorced, 3 sons, (2) Janet Nathan, 1999. Education: Chelsea School of Art; RCA. Appointments: Teacher, Chelsea College of Art. Creative Works: Exhibitions: FBA Galleries, 1961; Robert Fraser Gallery, London, 1965, 1967; Robert Elkon Gallery, New York, 1966, 1968; Waddington Galleries, 1969, 1971, 1973, 1975, 1979, 1981, 1985, 1997, 1998, 2002; Also in France, Belgium, Italy, Australia, USA, Japan; Retrospective Exhibition, Tate Gallery, London, 1981; Serpentine Gallery, London, 1992; Hayward Gallery, London, 1999; Numerous group exhibitions in England, Europe, New York; Design, for Ballet Party Game, Covent Garden, 1984; Public Collections include: Tate Gallery; Victoria & Albert Museum; Manchester City Art Gallery and other museums and galleries in England, USA, Australia, Germany, Japan. Honours: Senior Fellowship, RCA, 1993; Honorary Fellow, London Institute, 1996. Address: 19 Belsize Square, London NW3 4HT, England.

CAUNA Nikolais, b. 4 April 1914, Riga, Latvia. Scientist; Medical Educator. m. Dzidra Priede. Education: MD, University of Latvia, 1942; MSc, 1964, DSc, 1961, University of Durham, England. Appointments: Lecturer, Anatomy, University of Latvia, Riga, 1942-44; General Practice Medicine, Sarsted and Eschershausen, West Germany, 1944-46; Acting Chairman, Anatomy Department, Baltic University, Hamburg, Germany, 1946-48; Lecturer, Anatomy, Medical School, University of Durham, England, 1948-57; Reader, 1958-61, Professor of Anatomy, School of Medicine, University of Pittsburgh, 1961-75; Professor, Chairman, 1975-83;

Professor Emeritus, 1984-. Publications: Numerous book chapters; Articles for professional journals. Honours: Golden Apple Award, University of Pittsburgh, 1964, 1967, 1973; Research Grant, Royal Society, England, 1958-60; American Cancer Grant, 1961; Camillo Golgi Medal, Italy, 1973; USPHS Grant, 1962-83. Memberships: Anatomy Society of Great Britain and Ireland; American Association of Anatomists; Royal Micros Society; Histochem Society; Member of Editorial Board of several journals. Address: 5850 Meridian Road, Apartment C-311 Gibsonia, Pennsylvania 15044, USA.

CAUSLEY Charles (Stanley), b. 24 August 1917, Launceton, Cornwall, England. Poet; Dramatist; Editor. Education: Launceston College. Appointment: Service in Royal Navy, 1940-46; Teacher, Cornwall, 1947-76. Publications: Survivors Leave, 1953; Union Street, 1957; Johnny Alleluia, 1961; Penguin Modern Poets 3, 1962; Underneath the Water, 1968; Pergamon Poets 10, 1970; Timothy Winters, 1970; Six Women, 1974; Ward 14, 1974; St Martha and the Dragon, 1978; Collected Poems, 1951-75, 1975; Secret Destinations, 1984; 21 Poems, 1986; The Young Man of Cury, 1991; Bring in the Holly, 1992; Collected Poems for Children, 1996; Penguin Modern Poets 6, 1996; Collected Poems, 1951-97, 1997; Collected Poems, 1951-2000, 2000. Other: Several plays: Libretto for William Mathias's opera Jonah, 1990. Contributions to: Various publications. Honours: Queen's Gold Medal for Poetry, 1967; Honorary DLitt, University of Exeter, 1977; Honorary MA, Open University, 1982; Commander of the Order of the British Empire, 1986; T S Eliot Award, Ingersoll Foundation, USA, 1990; Heywood Hill Literary Prize, 2000. Address: 2 Cyprus Well, Launceston, Cornwall, PL15 8BT, England.

CAVACIUTI Peter, b. 13 May 1952, London, England. Artist. Education: Studied 7 years with Professor Fei Cheng Wu, continued with Professor Bao, Central Academy of Art, Beijing. Career: Painter on handmade paper from China, Korea, Japan and Nepal, using Chinese ink and traditional pigments; Developed methods of mixing colours from 17th century; Exhibitions include; The Royal Academy Summer Exhibition, London, 1997; The Royal Watercolour Society, London, 1997; The Royal Institute of Painters in Watercolour, London, 1998; The Suisho Gallery, Cambridge, 1998; The Daiwa Foundation, London (one-man show), 1999, Galerie Leda Fletcher, Geneva, Switzerland, 1999; The Royal Academy Summer Exhibition, 2000; Kettle's Yard, University of Cambridge, 2000; Salon des Artes, London, 2001; The Watercolours and Drawings Fair, London, 2002; The Art on Paper Fair, Royal College of Art, London, 2002; Demonstration at the Victoria and Albert Museum, London, 2002; Christies London – Art 4 Life, 2003; The Daiwa Foundation, London (one-man show), 2004; Works in Public Collections: Clare Hall College, Cambridge; The Urasenke Cultural Foundation, London and Kyoto, Japan. Publications: Series of cards and prints for Art Group Ltd, London; Series of cards and prints and Millennium Calendar for Ikea; Series of cards for Blossoms and Bows Ltd; Illustrations for The Japanese Tea Ceremony, 1999; Illustrations for Taoist Wisdom, 1999; Print for Ikea, 2002; Series of cards for Art Group Ltd, London, 2002; 2002 Calendar for W H Smith; Works reviewed in magazines. Honours: Commission for the Grand Teamaster of Urasenke Zabosai and for the Former Grandmaster Hounsai, Kyoto, Japan; Included in Dictionary of Artists in Britain since 1945, by David Buckman, 1998; Featured in Display, L Llewelyn-Bowen, 2000. Memberships: Far Eastern Painting Society; Kaetsu Chado Society. Address: 2 Oxford Road, Cambridge, CB4 3PW, England.

CAVE Hugh Barnett, b. 11 July 1910, Chester, England. Writer. m. Margaret Long, 2 sons. Education: Boston University. Publications include: Novels and Other Books of Fiction: Fishermen Four, 1942; Drums of Revolt, 1957; The Cross on the Drum, 1959; Black Sun, 1960; The Mission, 1960; The Witching Lands, 1962; Run Shadow Run, 1968; Larks Will Sing, 1969; Murgunstrumm and Others, 1977; Legion of the Dead, 1979; The Nebulon Horror, 1980; A Summer Romance & Other Stories, 1980; The Evil, 1981; Shades of Evil, 1982; The Voyage, 1988; Disciples of Dread, 1988; Hugh Cave's The Corpse-Maker, 1988; Conquering Kilmarnie, 1989; The Lower Deep, 1990; Lucifer's Eye, 1991; Death Stalks the Night, 1995; Bitter/Sweet, 1996; The Dagger of Tsiang, 1997; Escapades of the Eel, 1997; The Door Below, 1997; The Death-Heads' March and Others, 1998; White Star of Egypt, 1999; The Desert Host, 1999; Dark Doors of Doom, 2000; Isle if the Whisperers, 2000; The Dawning, 2000; Bottled in Blonde, 2000; Officer Coffey Stories, 2000; Long Live the Dead, 2000; The Lady Wore Black, 2000; The Evil Returns, 2001; Come Into My Parlor, 2002; The Mountains of Madness, 2003; The Restless Dead, 2003; Non-Fiction Books: Long Were the Nights, 1943; The Fightin'est Ship, 1944; We Build, We Fight, 1944; Wings Across the World, 1945; I Took the Sky Road, with Comdr. Norman M. Miller, 1945; Haiti: Highroad to Adventure, 1952; Four Paths to Paradise: a Book about Jamaica, 1961; Magazines I Remember, 1994; Other: Over 800 stories in 100 pulp fiction magazines in the 1930s and 1940s; 350 fiction pieces in other magazines including 46 in Saturday Evening Post; 41 in Good Housekeeping; Short stories in over 35 countries. Honours: World Fantasy Award, Phoenix Award and Lifetime Achievement Awards: Horror Writers Association, 1991, International Horror Guild, 1997, World Fantasy Association, 1999; Books written about Hugh B. Cave: Pulp Man's Odyssey by Audrey Parente, 1988; Cave of a Thousand Tales by Milt Thomas, 2003. Address: 437 Thomas Street, Sebastian, FL 32958, USA. E-mail: hughbcave@aol.com

CAWS Ian, b. 19 March 1945, Bramshott, Hants, England. Local Government Officer. m. Hilary Walsh, 20 June 1970, 3 sons, 2 daughters. Education: Certificate in Social Work, 1970; Certificate for Social Workers with the Deaf, 1973. Appointments: Senior Social Worker with the Deaf, 1974; County Team Leader of Deaf Services, 1986; Arts Development Officer, 1991. Publications: Looking for Bonfires, 1975; Bruised Madonna, 1979; Boy with a Kite, 1981; The Ragman Totts, 1990; Chamomile, 1994; The Feast of Fools, 1994; The Playing of the Easter Music (with Martin C Caseley and B L Pearce), 1996; Herrick's Women, 1996; Dialogues in Mask, 2000; Taro Fair, 2003. Contributions to: Acumen Magazine; London Magazine; New Welsh Review; Observer; Poetry Review; Scotsman; Spectator; Stand Magazine; Swansea Review. Honours: Eric Gregory Award, 1973; Poetry Book Society Recommendation, 1990. Membership: Poetry Society. Address: 9 Tennyson Avenue, Rustington, West Sussex BN16 2PB, England.

CAZEAUX Isabelle Anne-Marie, b. 24 February 1926, New York, USA. Professor Emeritus of Musicology. Education: BA, magna cum laude, Hunter College, 1945; MA, Smith College, 1946; Ecole normale de musique, Paris, Licence d'enseignement, 1950; Première médaille, Conservatoire National de Musique, Paris, 1950; MS in Library Science, Columbia University, 1959, PhD, 1961, Columbia University. Appointments: Music and phonorecords cataloguer, New York Public Library, 1957-63; Faculty of Musicology, Bryn Mawr College, 1963-92; Faculty of Musicology, Manhattan School of Music, 1969-82; A C Dickerman Professor and Chairman, Music Department, Bryn Mawr College; Visiting Professor, Douglass College, Rutgers University, 1978. Publications: Translations: The Memoirs of Philippe de Commynes, 2 vols, 1969-73; Editor: Claudin de Sermisy, Chansons, 2 vols, 1974; Author: French Music in the Fifteenth and Sixteenth Centuries, 1975; Articles. Honours: Libby van Arsdale Prize for Music, Hunter College, 1945; Fellowships and scholarships from Smith College, Columbia University, Institute of International

Education, 1941-59; Grants from Martha Baird Rockefeller Fund for Music, 1971-72, Herman Goldman Foundation, 1980; Listed in New Grove Dictionary of Music and Musicians, 1980. Memberships: American Musicological Society; International Musicological Society; Société française de musicologie; National Opera Association. Address: 415 East 72nd Street, Apt 5FE, New York, NY 10021, USA.

CELA Camilo José, b. 11 May 1916, Iria Flavia, La Coruña, Spain. Writer; Poet. m. (1) María del Rosario Conde Picavea, 12 March 1944, 1 son, (2) Marina Castano, 1991. Education: University of Madrid, 1933-36, 1939-43. Publications: Fiction: La Familia de Pascual Duarte, 1942, English translation as Pascual Duarte's Family, 1946; Pabellón de reposo, 1943, English translation as Rest Home, 1961; Nuevas andanzas y desventuras de Lazarillo de Tormes, 1944; Caminos inciertos: La colmena, 1951, English translation as The Hive, 1953; Santa Balbina 37: Gas en cada piso, 1952; Timoteo, el incomprendido, 1952; Mrs Caldwell habla con su hijo, 1953, English translation as Mrs Caldwell Speaks to Her Son, 1968; Café de artistas, 1955; Historias de Venezuela: La catira, 1955; Tobogán de hambrientos, 1962; Visperas, festividad y octava de San Camilo del año 1936 en Madrid, 1969; Oficio de tinieblas 5, o, Novela de tesis escrita para ser cantada por un de enfermos, 1973; Mazurca para doe muertos, 1983; Cristo versus Arizona, 1988; Madera de boj, 1999; Also many volumes of stories. Poetry: Pisando la dudosa luz del día, 1945; Reloj de Sangre, 1989. Non-Fiction: Diccionario Secreto, 2 volumes, 1968, 1971; Enciclopedia del Erotismo, 1976-77; Memorias, entendimientos y voluntades (memoirs), 1993. Other: Volumes of essays, travel books. Honours: Premio de la crítica, 1955; Spanish National Prize for Literature, 1984; Nobel Prize for Literature, 1989; Planeta Prize, 1994. Membership: Real Academia Espanola, 1957. Address: c/o Agencia Literaria Carmen Balcells, Diagonal 580, 08021 Barcelona, Spain.

CERWENKA Herwig R, b. 18 June 1964, Leoben, Austria. Surgeon; Researcher. m. Wilma Zinke-Cerwenka, 1 son, 2 daughters. Education: Matura Examination, 1982; Doctor of Medicine, 1988; ECFMG/FMGEMS, 1989; Ius practicandi, 1993; Diploma in Emergency Medicine; Diploma in Surgery. Appointment: Professor of Surgery, Researcher, Department of Visceral Surgery, Karl-Franzens University, Graz, Austria. Publications: Numerous publications in scientific journals and contributions to books. Honours: Performance Grant, Karl-Franzens University; Numerous other grants and awards for congress contributions and publications. Memberships: International Society of Surgery; International Association of Surgeons and Gastroenterologists; Austrian Society of Surgery; Austrian Society of Surgical Research. Address: Department of Visceral Surgery, Karl-Franzens University, Auenbruggerplatz 29, A-8036 Graz, Austria. E-mail: cerwenka@kfunigraz.ac.at

CHADWICK (William) Owen, b. 20 May 1916, Bromley, Kent, England. Historian. m. Ruth Hallward, 28 December 1949, 2 sons, 2 daughters. Education: BA, 1939, St John's College, Cambridge. Appointments: Dean, Trinity Hall, 1949-56, Master, Selwyn College, 1956-83, Dixie Professor of Ecclesiastical History, 1958-68, Regius Professor of Modern History, 1968-83, Cambridge University. Publications: John Cassian, 1950, revised edition, 1968; The Founding of Cuddesdon, 1954; From Bossuet to Newman, 1957, 2nd edition, 1987; Western Asceticism, 1958; Creighton on Luther, 1959; Mackenzie's Grave, 1959; Victorian Miniature, 1960, 2nd edition, 1991; The Mind of the Oxford Movement, 1960; From Uniformity to Unity 1662-1962 (with G Nuttall), 1962; Westcott and the University, 1962; The Reformation, 1964; The Victorian Church, Vol 1, 1966, 3rd edition, 1972; Vol II, 1970, 2nd edition, 1972; Acton and Gladstone, 1976; The Oxford History

of the Christian Church (editor with Henry Chadwick, brother), 1976-; The Secularization of the European Mind, 1977; Catholicism and History, 1978; The Popes and European Revolution, 1981; Newman, 1983; Hensley Henson: A Study in the Friction Between Church and State, 1983; Britain and the Vatican in the Second World War, 1986; Michael Ramsey, 1990, 2nd edition, 1991; The Spirit of the Oxford Movement: Tractarian Essays, 1990; The Christian Church in the Cold War, 1992; A History of Christianity, 1995; A History of the Popes 1830-1914, 1998; Acton and History, 1998. Contributions to: Times (London); New Statesman; Spectator; Guardian; Sunday Times; Observer; History journals. Honours: Wolfson Prize for History, 1981; Knighted, 1982; Order of Merit, 1983. Memberships: Fellow, British Academy; Fellow, Royal Historical Society. Address: 67 Grantchester Street, Cambridge CB3 9HZ, England.

CHAET Eric, b. 25 May 1945, Chicago, USA. Author; Artist; Consultant. m. Brenda Chaet. Education: BA, English, University of Missouri, 1963-66; MA, English, University of Washington, 1966-67; MPhil, American Studies, University of Kansas, 1967-70; Continuous individual study, 1985-. Appointments: Acting Assistant Professor of English, Lincoln University, Pennsylvania, 1970-71; Writing Consultant, Math Instructor, Rough Rock Demonstration School, Navajo Reservation, Arizona, 1975-76; Philosophy Instructor, Bay Community College, Michigan, 1976-78; Independent Consultant: Prioritization, planning and implementation. Publications: How to Change the World Forever for Better, 1990; People I Met Hitchhiking on USA Highways, 2001; Books of Poetry; Song recordings; Posters on cloth, 1986-2000. Address: 1803 County ZZ, De Pere, Wisconsin 54115-9629, USA. E-mail: echaet@gbonline.com

CHAKRABORTY Uday Kumar, b. India. University Professor. m. Mandira, 1989, 1 daughter. Education: BE, Electronic Engineering, 1st class hons, 1985, ME, Computer Engineering, 1st class hons, 1987, PhD, Computer Science, 1994, Jadavpur University. Appointments: Senior Research Associate, Computer Aided Design Centre, Calcutta, 1986-88; Systems Engineer, CMC Ltd, Calcutta, 1988-90; Lecturer, Jadavpur University, 1990-93; Guest Researcher, 1995, 1996, Research Scientist, 1998-99, GMD, St Augustin, Germany; Reader, Department of Computer Science and Engineering, Jadavpur University, 1993-2000; Assistant Professor, University of Missouri, St Louis, USA, 2001-. Publications include: Genetic algorithms - an introduction, 1994; An analysis of schema processing, 1994; An analysis of selection in genetic algorithms, 1995. Honours: S Roy Memorial Scholarship, All Bengal Teachers Association, 1979; J K Mitra Scholarship, Jadavpur University, 1981-84; Fellowship, United Nations Industrial Development Organisation, 1987; Commonwealth Scholarship, 1992; Career Award for Young Teachers, Government of India, 1996; University of Missouri - St Louis Research Award, 2002, 2004. Memberships include: Editorial board, Journal of Computing and Information Technology. Address: Department of Mathematics and Computer Science, University of Missouri – St Louis, 8001 Natural Bridge Road, St Louis, MO 63121, USA. E-mail: uday@cs.umsl.edu

CHAKRAVARTI Aninda K, b. 3 December 1926, Varanasi, India. Emeritus Professor of Geography. m. Maya Chakravarti, 1 daughter. Education: BA, 1949, MA, 1953, MSc, 1961, PhD, 1967, Madison-Wisconsin. Appointments: Lecturer, Assistant Professor, University of Allahabad, 1953-60; Teaching Fellow and Research Assistant, University of Wisconsin, 1960-65; Assistant Professor, 1965-70, Associate Professor, 1965-70, Acting Head, 1977-78, Professor, 1976-94, Emeritus Professor, 1994, Geography, University of Saskatchewan. Publications: Over 50 research papers in national and international journals, monographs and chapters in

Dictionary of International Biography

books dealing mostly with prairie climatology, environment and agricultural geography of South Asia. Honours include: UNESCO/ Pakistan Certificate, Arid Zone, Microclimatology, 1959; Smith-Mundt Fulbright Scholarship, University of Wisconsin, 1960-61; Whitbeck Fellowship, 1961-62, Vilas Fellowship, 1965, University of Wisconsin; Canada Council Leave Fellowship, 1972-73; Distinguished Service Award, 1993, AAG symposium in his honour, 1995, introduction of A K Chakravarti Award for Best Student Paper on South Asia Annual Award, 1996, Association of American Geographers Asian Geography Speciality Group; John Warkentin Award for Scholarly Contributions to the Geography of the Western Interior, Canadian Association of Geographers, Prairie Division, 1997; Prime of Life Achievement, University of Saskatchewan Retirees Association Award, 1997; Listed in the 6th Edition of Five Thousand Personalities of the World, 1997, International Book of Honor, 1999, ABI; Gold Medal, Diploma for 2000 Outstanding Scholars of the 20th Century, 1999, IBC; Dr A K Chakravarti Scholarship in Geography, University of Saskatchewan introduced in 2001. Address: 514 Sturgeon Drive, Saskatoon, SK, S7K 4E1, Canada.

CHAKRAVARTI Balaram, b. 26 January 1935, Bishnupur, India. Author; Educationist. m. Sandhya Chakravarti. Education: BA (Hons), Philosophy, 1954; MA, Philosophy, 1956; PhD, Religion, Philosophy and Culture of Bhutan, 1974. Appointments: Lecturer, Senior Lecturer, Vice Principal, various colleges in West Bengal, India; Served on lien in the National Cadet Corps and the Border Roads Development Board and carried out research on the Himalayas, 1963-75; Principal, Jawaharlal Nehru College, Pasighat, Arunachal Pradesh, India 1975-77; Deputy Advisor, Ministry of Human Resource Development, Government of India, 1977-91. Publications: A Cultural History of Bhutan Vol 1 and II; A Cultural History of North-East India, Vol 1, II, III; The Sens of Himachal & Their Pan Indian Culture Vol I; The Cultural History of Ladakh Vol 1 (in press); South East Asia: India and Thailand; Japan: A Short Cultural History; Cultural History of the Latin America Series: The Indians and the Amerindians Vol I, Peru, Vol II, Mexico, Vol III, Shasta Mountains, Vol IV, The Amazon Valley; Cuba in the Pre-Colombian Times Vol I; Ancient Indian Military Science: 1) Dhanurveda; Ancient Indian Chemistry: 1) The Matrka Bhedatantram; Cultural History of the Pacific Series 1) The Children of the Abotani in India, Fiji & Polynesia Vol I, 2) The Aborigines of India and Australia; Perido Conexion entre Antiguo Indio Ameri-Indio (in Spanish). Honours: Chairman, India and West Session, World Sanskrit Conference, Philadelphia, USA, 1984; Invited to deliver Antonio Binemelis Lecture, Jawaharlal Neru University, New Delhi, 1997; Chairman, Session of Cross Cultural Studies, IV International Conference on Hispanism, New Delhi, 1997; Chairman, Session of Cross-Cultural Studies International Conference on World History, Changchung, China, 1997. Memberships: International Association of Sanskrit Studies, Paris, France; Life Member, The Asiatic Society, Kolkata, India; Charter Member, Smithsonian National Museum of the American Indian, Washington, USA; Indian History Congress, Kolkata, India; President, Bharatiya Itihas Sankalan Samiti, West Bengal Branch, Kolkata, India. Address: 24/2/19 Mandal Para Lane, Kolkata 700 050, India. E-mail: sebpcal@vsnl.net.in

CHALFONT Baron, (Alun Arthur Gwynne Jones), b. 5 December 1919, Llantarnam, Wales. Member, House of Lords; Writer. m. Mona Mitchell, 6 November 1948, 1 daughter, deceased. Education: West Monmouth, Wales. Appointments: Regular Officer, British Army, 1940-61; Broadcaster and Consultant on Foreign Affairs, BBC, 1961-64; Minister of State, Foreign and Commonwealth Office, 1964-70; Minister for Disarmament, 1964-67, 1969-70; Minister in charge of day-to-day negotiations for Britain's entry into Common Market, 1967-69; Permanent Representative, Western European Union, 1969-70; Foreign Editor,

New Statesman, 1970-71; Chairman, Industrial Cleaning Papers, 1979-86, All Party Defence Group of the House of Lords, 1980-96, Peter Hamilton Security Consultants Ltd, 1984-86, VSEL Consortium, later VSEL plc, 1987-95, Radio Authority, 1991-94, Marlborough Stirling Group, 1994-; Director, W S Atkins International, 1979-83, IBM UK Ltd, 1973-90, Lazard Brothers & Company Ltd, 1983-90, Shandwick plc, 1985-95, Triangle Holdings, 1986-90, TV Corporation plc, 1996-; President, Abington Corporation Ltd, 1981-, Nottingham Building Society, 1983-90; All Party Defence Group House of Lords, 1996-. Publications: The Sword and the Spirit, 1963; The Great Commanders (editor), 1973; Montgomery of Alamein, 1976; Waterloo: Battle of Three Armies (editor), 1979; Star Wars: Suicide or Survival, 1985; Defence of the Realm, 1987; By God's Will: A Portrait of the Sultan of Brunei, 1989; The Shadow of My Hand, 2000. Contributions to: Periodicals and journals. Honours: Officer of the Order of the British Empire, 1961; Created a Life Peer, 1964; Honorary Fellow, University College of Wales, 1974; Liveryman, Worshipful Company of Paviors; Freeman of the City of London. Memberships: International Institute for Strategic Studies; Royal Institute of International Affairs; Royal Society of the Arts, fellow; United Nations Association, chairman, 1972-73. Address: House of Lords, London SW1A 0PW, England.

CHALIASOS Evangelos, b. 28 December 1947, Athens, Greece. Educator. Education: Ptychion in Mathematics, 1971, Ptychion in Physics, 1979, University of Athens, Greece; Master of Science in Physical Sciences, Astronomy and Astrophysics, University of Chicago, 1988; Doctorate in Physical Sciences, Relativistic Cosmology, University of Athens, 1990. Career: Freelance; Researcher into cosmology from the point of view of theoretical physics; Post-Newtonian approximation in general relativity; Newman-Penrose formalism; The problem of the direction of time; The problem of the world's dimensionality; Foundations of theoretical plasma physics; Euclidean geometry; Parapsychology; Foundations of theoretical plasma physics. Publications include: The Post-Newtonian Approximation of the General Theory of Relativity and the Chandrasekhar-Contopoulos Transformation in the Two-Body Problem (in Greek); Studies in Relativistic Cosmological Models (in Greek). Honours: Research Assistantship, National Research Foundation of Greece, 1980; Fellowship, University of Chicago, 1980-82; Grant, Greek Ministry of Research and Technology, 1985-87; Referee in various journals. Memberships: Hellenic Astronomical Society; Association of Greek Physicists; Greek Mathematical Society. Address: 365 Thebes Street, GR-12241 Aegaleo (Athens), Greece. E-mail: pirpiricus@mland.gr

CHAMBERLAIN (George Ford) Leo, b. 13 August 1940, Tunbridge, Kent, England. Catholic Priest; Benedictine Monk. Education: Burn Open scholarship, University College, Oxford, England; BA 1861; MA, 1965. Appointments: Entered Noviciate, Ampleforth Abbey, 1961, Solemn Vows, 1965, Ordained Priest, 1968; Housemaster, St Dunstan's House, 1972-92, Senior History Master, 1974-90, Headmaster, 1992-2003, Ampleforth College; Master-elect, St Benet's Hall, Oxford, 2004. Publications: Letters and articles: Ampleforth Journal; Tablet; Daily Telegraph; Times; World Today. Memberships: Council of Management, Kestor Institute, 1985-2003; Headmasters Conference, 1993-2003; Catholic Independent Schools Conference, 1993-2003; East India Club. E-mail: admin@ampleforth.org.uk

CHAMBERLAND Marc André, b. 22 August 1964, Shawmigan, USA. Professor of Mathematics. m. Marion Weber, 2 sons, 1 daughter. Education: BMath, 1988, MMath, 1990, PhD, 1995, University of Waterloo. Appointments: NSERC Post Doctoral Fellow, McMaster University, 1995-1997; Assistant

Professor of Mathematics, 1997-2003, Associate Professor of Mathematics, 2003-, Grinnell College. Publications: Numerous articles in professional journals. Honours: NSERC Post Doctoral Fellowship, 1995-1997; Queen Elizabeth II Scholarship; Harris Fellowship, Grinnell College. Memberships: American Mathematical Society; Mathematical Association of America. Address: Department of Mathematics, Grinnell College, Grinnell, IA 50112, USA. E-mail: chamberl@math.grinnell.edu

CHAMBERS Aidan, b. 27 December 1934, Chester-le-Street, County Durham, England. Author; Publisher. m. Nancy Harris Lockwood, 30 March 1968. Education: Borough Road College, Isleworth, London University. Publications: The Reluctant Reader, 1969; Introducing Books to Children, 1973; Breaktime, 1978; Seal Secret, 1980; The Dream Cage, 1981; Dance on My Grave, 1982; The Present Takers, 1983; Booktalk, 1985; Now I Know, 1987; The Reading Environment, 1991; The Toll Bridge, 1992; Tell Me: Children, Reading and Talk, 1993; Only Once, 1998; Postcards From No Man's Land, 1999; Contributions to: Numerous magazines and journals. Honours: Children's Literature Award for Outstanding Criticism, 1978; Eleanor Farjeon Award, 1982; Silver Pencil Awards, 1985, 1986, 1994; Carnegie Medal, 1999; Stockport School Book Award KS4, 2000; Hans Christian Andersen Award, 2002; Michael L Printz Award, 2002; Honorary Doctorate, University of Umeå, Sweden, 2003; Honorary President, School Library Association, 2003-. Membership: Society of Authors. Address: Lockwood, Station Road, Woodchester, Stroud, Gloucestershire, GL5 5EQ, England.

CHAMBERS Guy, Producer; Writer; Musician. Appointments: Jimmy Nail, Robbie Williams, World Party, The Waterboys, Julian Cope, Lemon Trees. Creative Works: Recordings with Robbie Williams, Cathy Denis, World Party, Holly Johnson, Blast, Julian Cope, Fried, Lemon Trees. Memberships: Musicians Union; PRS. Address: One Management, 43 St Alban's Avenue, London W4 5JS, England.

CHAMBERS Richard Dickinson, b. 16 March 1935, Stanley, County Durham, England. Emeritus Professor of Chemistry. m. Anne Boyd, 1 son, 1 daughter. Education: BSc, Chemistry, 1953-56, PhD, 1956-59, University of Durham, England. Appointments: Postdoctoral Research Fellow, University of British Columbia, Vancouver, Canada, 1959-60; Lecturer, 1960, Reader, 1969, Professor of Chemistry, 1976, Chairman and Head, Department of Chemistry, 1983-86, Emeritus Research Professor, 2000-, University of Durham; Fulbright Scholar and Visiting Lecturer, Case Western Reserve University, Cleveland Ohio, 1966-67; Visiting Professor, University of Paris, 1995; Non-Executive Director, F2 Chemicals Ltd, 1995-2000; Inaugural Recipient, Tarrant Visiting Professor, University of Florida, 1999. Publications: Over 300 research papers, review articles and books in the area of Organofluorine Chemistry. Honours: American Chemical Society Award for Creative Work in Fluorine Chemistry, 1991; Sir Derman Christopherson Research Fellowship, 1988-89; Elected Fellow Royal Society, 1997; Awarded, Prix Moissan, 2003. Memberships: Fellow of the Royal Society; Fellow of the Royal Society of Chemistry; Member of the American Chemical Society. Address: 5 Aykley Green, Whitesmocks, Durham DH1 4LN, England.

CHAMBLISS William J, b. 12 December 1933, Buffalo, New York, USA. Professor. m. Pernille Baadsayer, 2 sons, 1 daughter. Education: BA, UCLA, 1955; MA, Indiana University, 1960; PhD, Indiana University, 1962. Appointments: University of Washington, 1962-66; University of Wisconsin, 1966-67; University of California, Santa Barbara, 1967-74; University of Oslo, Norway, 1974-75; University of Stockholm, Sweden, 1975-76.

Appointments: Assistant Professor, University of Washington, Seattle, 1962-66; Associate Professor, Sociology, University of California, Santa Barbara, 1967-74; Professor, Sociology, University of Delaware, 1976-86; George Washington University, 1986-; Honorary Professorial Fellow, Faculty of Law, University College, Cardiff, Wales, 1976-89. Publications: Books include: On The Take, 1978; Law, Order and Power, co-author, 1984; Criminal Law, Criminology and Criminal Justice: A Case Book (Co-author), 1990; Making Law: The State, Law and Structural Contradictions (co-editor), 1994; Sociology (co-author), 1995; Sociology, 2nd edition, 1997; Power, Politics and Crime, 1999 (revised 2001); Numerous articles. Honours: Honorary Doctorate of Law, University of Guelph, Ontario, Canada; Lifetime Achievement Award, American Sociological Association; Edwin H Sutherland Award, American Society of Criminology. Memberships: Fellow, American Society of Criminology; American Sociological Association. Address: 3121 33RD PL NW, Washington DC, USA.

CHAN Alan, b. 9 January 1960, China. Ergonomics Researcher. m Cindy Ip, 2 sons. Education: BSc, Industrial Engineering, University of Hong Kong, 1982; MPhil, Ergonomics, 1985; DMIB, 1989; PhD, Ergonomics, 1995. Appointments: Manager, Technical Services, YHY Food Products Ltd, 1988-89; Associate Professor, Ergonomics, City University of Hong Kong, 1989-. Publications: More than 70 papers in refereed journals and conference proceedings. Honour: Listed in Who's Who publications. Memberships: Council Member, Pan Pacific Council of Occupational Ergonomics, Japan, 1997-; Council Member, Hong Kong Ergonomics Society, 1999-; Regional Vice-President, Institute of Industrial Engineering, 2001; Director, Institute of Industrial Engineering, Hong Kong; Member of several editorial boards. Address: MEEM Department, City University of Hong Kong, Tat Chee Avenue, Kowloon Tong, Hong Kong, China. E-mail: alan.chan@cityu.edu.hk

CHAN Fo Kwong, b. 6 September 1929, Hong Kong. Managing Director. m. Cheng Kwai Ching, 4 sons, 2 daughters. Education: Graduate, Kwong Chow Leng Hoi Elder University in China, 1998. Appointments: Founder and Curator, Chan Fo Kwong Museum, 1990; Managing Director, Chan Kwong Kee Emporium Co Ltd; Founder and Chairman: Hong Kong International Antique Watch and Clock General Association; Hong Kong International Antique Research Association; Hong Kong International Deserving Genius Association; Hong Kong International Kite Association; Hong Kong International Pot Plant and Gardening General Association; Hong Kong International Lute Chess, Calligraphy and Painting Association. Honours: Certificate of Recognition of Service, Pok Oi Hospital, Yuen Long, Hong Kong, 1979; Certificate of Recognition of Service, Yuen Long Town Hall, Yuen Long, Hong Kong, 1996; Distinguished Service Medal, Scout Association of Hong Kong, 2000. Memberships: Director, Pok Oi Hospital, 1977-79; Yuen Long Public Secondary School Board, 1975-99; Chairman: Hong Kong International Bor-Yea Buddhist Association. Address: Blk B 3/F, 32-34, Tai Tong Road, Yuen Long, Hong Kong.

CHAN Norman Nor, b. 27 May 1967, Hong Kong. Physician. Education: MB ChB, University of Liverpool, 1991; MRCP, London, 1994; Diploma of Child Health, London, 1995; Certificate of Completion of Specialist Training in Diabetes, Endocrinology and General Internal Medicine, UK 2001; MD, UK, 2002. Appointments: Specialist Registrar in Diabetes/Endocrinology: Hemel Hempstead General Hospital, Hertfordshire, 1995-96; Watford General Hospital, Hertfordshire, 1996-97; Chelsea and Westminster Hospital, London, 1997-98; Charing Cross Hospital, London, 1998; University College London, 1998-2000; The

Dictionary of International Biography

Middlesex Hospital, London, 2000-01; Assistant Professor at the Prince of Wales Hospital, The Chinese University of Hong Kong, Hong Kong, 2002-2004; Clinical Director, Analgenics Diabetes Centre, Hong Kong Restart International, 2004-. Publications: Over 70 articles in professional medical journals. Honours: Junior Fellowship, British Heart Foundation, 1998. Memberships: Royal College of Physicians; British Endocrine Society; American Diabetes Association; Honorary Secretary, Hong Kong Atherosclerosis Society. Address: A4 Solemar Villas, 15 Silver Cape Road, Clear Water Bay, Kowloon, Hong Kong.

CHANDLER George F, b. 15 December 1940, Winthrop, Massachusetts, USA. 1 son, 1 daughter. Education: BSME, Naval Architecture, Virginia Tech, 1963; JD, Suffolk University Law School, 1972. Appointments: Professor Engineer, Massachusetts, 1971; Admitted to the Bars of: US Supreme Court; US Court of Appeals for the First, Second, Third, Fourth, Fifth and Eleventh Circuits; States of New York, New Jersey, and Massachusetts; and the US District Courts for Massachusetts, Southern and Eastern Districts of New York, New Jersey and Southern District of Texas. Publications: Numerous articles in professional journals; Contributing author, 3 books. Memberships: Society of Naval Architects and Marine Engineers; Maritime Law Association of the United States; Comite Maritime International; Houston Maritime Arbitrators Association; American Bar Association; Army & Navy Club of Washington DC. Address: Hill Rivkins & Hayden LLP, 712 Main Street, Suite 1515, Houston, TX 77002, USA. E-mail: g.chandler@hillrivkins.co

CHANDLER Rose Wiley, b. 3 October 1921, Kentucky, USA. Teacher; Antique Collector and Dealer; Poet. m. Claude Chandler, 31 May 1942, deceased, 2 daughters. Education: Eastern State Teachers College, 1939-40; Music Course, 1959; University of Kentucky, 1962; Writers Digest Writing School, 1989. Publications: A Gypsy's Delight, 1971; Moonlight Mystique, 1988; Travelling Through Atlanta at Night in the Rain, 1996; Symphony (poetry chapbook), 1997. Contributions to: Anthologies and newspapers. Honours: Golden Poet Award; Prize Kentucky State Poetry Society Contest; Prize, Ocala Chapter, National League of American Pen Women, 1995. Memberships: National Society of Poetry; National Library of Poetry; National League of American Pen Women, Chair, Finance Committee, 1998. Address: 10962 South West 79th Terrace, Ocala, FL 34476, USA.

CHANDRA Naresh, b. 7 August 1946, Meerut Cantonment, India. Teacher; Researcher. m. Dr Lata Rani Bansal, 1 daughter. Education: MSc, Banaras Hindu University, Varanasi, India, 1967; PhD Physics, Queen's University, Belfast, Northern Ireland, 1972. Appointments: Postdoctoral Research Fellow, Instituto di Chimica Fisica, Pisa, Italy, 1973; Resident Research Associate, NASA, Goddard Space Flight Center, Maryland, USA, 1974-76; Visiting Scientist, Fellow, Physics Research Laboratory, Ahmedabad, India, 1977-80; Lecturer, Punjabi University Patiala, India, 1983-85; Assistant Professor, Indian Institute of Technology, Kharagpur, 1985-91; Associate Professor 1991-97, Professor 1997. Publications: Numerous articles contributed to professional journals. Honours: Hari Om Ashram Prerit H C Shah Research Endowment Prize in Theoretical Physics for 1996-97; Fellow of the National Academy of Sciences, India, 2000. Memberships: Indian Society for Atomic and Molecule Physics; American Physical Society. Address: Department of Physics and Meteorology, Indian Institute of Technology, Kharagpur 721 302, India.

CHANEY Edward P(aul) de G(ruyter), b. 11 April 1951, Hayes, Middlesex, England. Professor of Fine and Decorative Arts. m. Lisa Maria Jacka, 15 September 1973, divorced, 2002, 2 daughters.

Education: BA, University of Reading, 1975; MPhil, 1977, PhD, 1982, Warburg Institute, University of London; Researcher, European University Institute, Florence, 1978-81. Appointments: Lecturer, University of Pisa, 1979-85; Adjunct Assistant Professor, Charles A Strong Center, Georgetown University Florence Program, Villa Le Balze, Florence, 1982, 1983; Associate, Harvard University Center for Italian Renaissance Studies, Villa I Tatti, Florence, 1984-85; Shuffrey Research Fellow in Architectural History, Lincoln College, Oxford, 1985-90; Part-time History of Art Lecturer, Oxford Polytechnic, 1991, Oxford Brookes University, 1993-; Historian, London Division, English Heritage, 1991-93; Professor of Fine and Decorative Arts and Chair of History of Collecting Research Centre, Southampton Institute. Publications: Oxford, China and Italy: Writings in Honour of Sir Harold Acton on his Eightieth Birthday (editor with N Ritchie), 1984; The Grand Tour and the Great Rebellion: Richard Lassels and 'The Voyage of Italy' in the Seventeenth Century, 1985; Florence: A Travellers' Companion (with Harold Acton), 1986, 2nd revised edition, 2002; England and the Continental Renaissance: Essays in Honour of J B Trapp (editor with Peter Mack), 1990; English Architecture: Public and Private: Essays for Kerry Downes (editor with John Bold), 1993; The Evolution of the Grand Tour, 1998, 2nd revised edition, 2000; The Evolution of English Collecting, 2003; Inigo Jones's 'Roman Sketchbook', forthcoming. Contributions to: Reference works, books, scholarly journals, periodicals, etc. Honours: Laurea di Dottore in Lingue e Letterature Straniere, University of Pisa, 1983; Honorary Life Member, British Institute of Florence, 1984; Elected Fellow, Society of Antiquaries, 1993; Fellow, Royal Society of Arts, 1999; Commendatore of the Ordine della Stella di Solidarietà Italiana, 2003; Editorial Board of British Art Journal, Rivista: The Journal of the British Italian Society, Wyndham Lewis Annual. Memberships: Beckford Society; Executive Committee Member, British-Italian Society; Catholic Record Society; Georgian Group; Committee Member, ICOMOS; International Berkeley Society; Leonardo da Vinci Society; Renaissance Society; Royal Stuart Society; Society of Architectural Historians; Wyndham Lewis Society; Executive Committee Member, Walpole Society; Honorary Associate, Society of Fine Art Auctioneers. Address: Southampton Institute, East Park Terrace, Southampton, Hampshire SO14 0RY, England.

CHANG Chi-Cheng, b. 7 August 1959, Taipei, Taiwan. Professor of Learning Technology. m. Ting Hsu, 1 daughter. Education: M Ed, Industrial Education, National Taiwan Normal University, 1985; MS, Computer Science, University of Texas, USA, 1992; M Ed, Instructional Systems, 1995, PhD, Workforce Education and Development, 1996, Penn State University, USA. Appointments: Professor in Learning Technology, Institute of Technological and Vocational Education, 2000, Assistant Dean, College of Humanity and Science, 2001-2003, National Taipei University of Technology; Member of Evaluation Committee for Research Project, National Science Council, 2000-; Member of Evaluation Committee for Vocational-Technical High School, Ministry of Education, 2000-; Consultant, Division of Education and Training, Institute of Information Industry, 2000-2001; Member, Editorial Board, Global Chinese Journal on Computers in Education, 2003-; Member of Executive Committee, Global Chinese Society of Computers in Education, 2003-. Publications: Numerous articles in scientific journals and presented at conferences include most recently: An Electronic Performance Support System for performing and learning instructional designing tasks, 2003; A practical case, implications and issues of systematically building a university web-based learning community environment, 2003; The relationship between the usefulness of key components and the implementation benefits for Electronic Performance Support System, 2004. Honours include: Excellent

Software of Information Management System, National Contest of Campus Software Creation, Ministry of Education, 2000; Outstanding Paper, Chinese Association of Video-Audio Education, 2001; Excellent Paper for Distance Education in Global Chinese Society, Open University, Taiwan, 2003; Listed in Who's Who publications and biographical dictionaries. Memberships: Association for the Advancement of Computing in Education; Asia-pacific Society for Computers in Education; Global Chinese Society of Computers in Education; Chinese Association of e-Learning; Chinese Association of Educational and Telecommunication Technology; Chinese Association of Human Research Development; Chinese Association of Curriculum and Instruction. Address: Institute of Technological & Vocational Education, National Taipei University of Technology, No 1, Sec 3 Chung-Hsiao E Rd, Taipei 106, Taiwan. E-mail: fl0980@ntut.edu.tw

CHANG Chih-Jen, b. 31 December 1954, Taipei County, Taiwan. Professor. m. Tzu-chen Chang, 2 daughters. Education: MD, China Medical College, Taichung, Taiwan, 1981. Appointments: Chief, Department of Family Medicine, National Cheng-Kung University, 1987-2001; Director, Diabetes and Obesity Research Centre, National Cheng-Kung University Hospital 1998-2003; Director, Department of Health Promotion, National Cheng-Kung University, 1992-1998; Editorial Board, Taiwan Family Medicine Society, Taiwan, 1998-2003. Publications: Articles in professional medical journals include: Epidemiological evidence of increased bone density in habitual tea drinkers; Discriminating glucose tolerance status by ROIs of DEXA: clinical implication of body fat distribution, 1999; Relationships of age, menopause and central obesity on cardiovascular disease risk factors in Chinese women, 2000. Honours: The Best Doctor of National Cheng-Kung University Hospital, 1987; Paper of the Year, Taiwan Family Medical Society, 1999; Paper of the Year, Taiwan Geriatric Society, 2000, 2001. Memberships: WONCA; American Diabetes Association; Diabetic and Endocrine Society; Geriatric Society, Taiwan; Family Medicine Society, Taiwan. Address: No 138, Sheng-Li Road, Tainan 70428, Taiwan. E-mail: em75210@email.ncku.edu.tw

CHANG Ching-Erh, b. 2 March 1942, Taipei, Taiwan. University Professor. m. Li-kuei Chen Chang, 2 sons. Education: Diploma, Provincial Taipei Normal School, 1960; BA, NTU, 1968; MA, NTU, 1972; PhD, NTU, 1976. Appointments: Municipal Taipei Ta-lung Primary School Teacher, 1960-64; Second Lieutenant in the Army, 1968-69; Research Assistant, Academia Sinica, 1972-76; Instructor, 1976-78, Associate Professor, 1978-84, Full Professor, 1984-, Department of Foreign Languages and Literatures, National Taiwan University. Publications: The Journey to the West: A Critical Study of Its Characters, 1984; Arthur Miller: A Critical Study, 1989; Vitality in Literature, 1994; Reflections and Communications of Literature, 1995; Western Drama and Dramatists, 1999; Christopher Marlowe's Doctor Faustus: Annotations and Commentary, 2001; The Beggar's Opera: Annotations and Commentary, 2003; 47 articles. Honours: Winner, National Science Council Annual Award, 1978-79, 1981-91, 1994-95, 1999; Winner, National Arts and Literature Award, 1987; Outstanding Alumnus of National Taipei Normal College, 1996. Membership: Comparative Literature Association, Republic of China. Address: Department of Foreign Languages and Literatures, National Taiwan University, Taipei, Taiwan 10764.

CHANG Eugene Yu-Sheng, b. 3 October 1940, China. m. Shirley Shi-lan Tsai, 1 son, 1 daughter. Education: BA, Political Science, Tunghai University, Taichung, Taiwan 1963; MA, Political Science, Maxwell School, Syracuse University, New York, 1970. Appointments: Graduate Assistant, 1965-68, Lecturer, 1969-92, Associate Professor, 1972-81, Professor, 1981-95, Associate

Professor, 1995-, Department of Political Science, Tunghai University, Taiwan. Publications include: The American Ocean Policy Since 1945, 1992; Essays on American Politics and United Nations, 1994; Chinese (ROC) Participation in the Creation of the United Nations, 1994; American Ocean Policy: 1932-1958, 1995. Honours: Several fellowships. Memberships: Chinese Political Science Association, Taipei; American Political Science Association; International Political Science Association; YMCA. Address: No 1 Tunghai Road, Tunghai University, Taichung, Taiwan 407, Republic of China.

CHANG Heekyung, b. 28 March 1957, Pusan, Korea. Medical Doctor; Professor. Education: Premedical Course, Liberal Arts and Sciences College, 1975-77, MD, College of Medicine, 1977-81, Master of Medical Science, Pathology, Graduate School, 1982-84, PhD, Pathology, Graduate School, 1987-89, Pusan National University; Postgraduate Training: Rotating Internship, 1981-82, Residency Programme in Anatomical Pathology, 1982-85, Residency Programme in Clinical Pathology, 1985-86, Pusan National University Hospital; Visiting Researcher, Institute of Basic Medical Sciences, University of Tsukuba, Japan, 1993. Appointments: Part-time Instructor, Pathology, Department of Pathology, Medical College, Pusan National University, 1985-86; Chief of Pathology Department, Daewoo Hospital, 1986; Instructor, 1986-90, Assistant Professor of Pathology, 1990-95, Associate Professor of Pathology, 1995-2000, Professor of Pathology, 2000-, Department of Pathology, Medical College, Kosin University; Visiting Associate Professor, Medical School, Harvard University, USA, 1997-99. Publications: Articles in medical journals as first author and co-author include most recently: Potential source of asbestos in non-asbestos textile manufacturing company, 2002; A new strategy for the diagnosis of MAGE-expressing cancers, 2002; Prevalence and prognostic significance of acinar cell differentiation in pancreatic endocrine tumors, 2002; Expression of Melanoma antigen-genes (MAGE) by common primers of MAGEA1 to A6 in colorectal carcinomas among Koreans, 2002. Memberships: Korean Society of Pathology; Korean Society of Cytopathology; Korean Cancer Association; United States and Canadian Academy of Pathology; New England Society of Pathologists; American Association for Cancer Research; International ZONTA Club; Association of Korean Women Professors. Address: Department of Pathology, Medical College of Kosin University, 34 Amnam-Dong, Suh-Ku, Pusan, 602-702, Korea.

CHANG H K, b. 9 July 1940, Shenyang, China. m. Min-Min Chou, 1 son, 1 daughter. Education: BS, Civil Engineering, National Taiwan University, 1962; MSc, Structural Engineering, Stanford University, 1964; PhD, Fluid Mechanics/Biomedical Engineering, Northwestern University, 1969. Appointments include: Assistant Professor, Associate Professor, Civil Engineering, State University of New York, 1969-76; Visiting Professor, Faculté de Médecine, Université Paris, 1981-82, Associate Professor, 1976-80; Professor of Biomedical Engineering and Physiology, Faculty of Medicine, Adjunct Professor of Chemical Engineering, Faculty of Engineering, McGill University, Montreal, Canada, 1980-84; Professor, Biomedical Engineering, Professor of Physiology and Biophysics, University of Southern California, Los Angeles, 1984-90; Chairman, Department of Biomedical Engineering, University of Southern California, 1985-90; Founding Dean, School of Engineering, Professor of Chemical Engineering, Hong Kong University of Science and Technology, 1990-94; Dean of School of Engineering, Director of Pittsburgh Bioengineering Institute, Professor of Chemical Engineering, School of Engineering, Professor of Medicine, School of Medicine, University of Pittsburgh, Pennsylvania, 1994-96; President and University Professor, City University of Hong Kong, 1996-. Publications:

Dictionary of International Biography

Author, 5 books and over 100 scientific articles; 1 Canadian patent; Over 120 formal lectures delivered in Hong Kong and overseas. Honours: Honorary Professor, Peking Union Medical College, Chinese Academy of Medical Sciences, 1987-; Honorary Professor, Northeastern University, China, 1998; Justice of the Peace, HKSAR, 1999; Honorary Professor, China Medical University, China, 2000; Chevalier de la Légion d'Honneur, France, 2000; Foreign Member, Royal Academy of Engineering, England, 2000; Gold Bauhinia Star, Government of HKSAR, 2002. Membership: Numerous professional, learned, charitable and civic associations, including: Fellow, Hong Kong Academy of Engineering Sciences; Fellow, Hong Kong Institution of Engineers; Founding Fellow, American Institute of Medical and Biological Engineering; Founding Member, Hong Kong Institution of Science; Member, Council of Advisors on Innovation and Technology, Government of the Hong Kong Special Administrative Region, 2000-. Address: City University of Hong Kong, Tat Chee Avenue, Kowloon Tong, Hong Kong.

CHANG Horng-jinh, b. 15 March 1949, Taipei, Taiwan. Professor and University President. m. Chuan Ling Lin, 2 daughters. Education: BS, Mathematics, 1971, MS, Mathematics, 1973, PhD, Management Science, 1980, Tamking University, Taipei, Taiwan. Appointments: Associate Professor, 1978-80, Chairman, Department of Statistics, 1981-84, Dean, Evening School, 1984-86, Director, Graduate Institute of Management Science, 1985-89, Dean Graduate School, 1986-89, Vice-President, 1989-98, President, 1998-, Tamking University, Taipei, Taiwan. Publications: Statistics, 1985; Advanced Statistics, 1986; 108 periodical articles; 9 symposium papers, 183 research papers. Honours: Listed in Who's Who publications and biographical dictionaries. Memberships: AAPOR, USA, 1986-; WAPOR, USA, 1990-; Vice-President, Chinese Association of Business Administration, 1996-. Address: Office of the President, 151 Yingchuan Road, Tamsui, Taipei, Taiwan 251, Republic of China. E-mail: chj@mail.tku.edu.tw

CHANG In-Soung, b. 31 March 1964, Seoul, Korea. Associate Professor. m. Ji-Hye Kim, 2 sons. Education: BA, 1990, MSc, 1992, PhD, 1996, School of Chemical Engineering, Seoul National University. Appointments: Research Engineer, Hanwha Chemical Company Inc, Korea, 1996-97; Associate Professor, Department of Environmental Engineering, Hoseo University, Asan, Korea, 1997-; Post Doctoral Fellow, School of Water Sciences, Cranfield University, England, 2000-2001; Visiting Fellow, Department of Engineering Science, Oxford University, England, 2002. Publications: Articles in scientific journals including: Process Biochemistry, 2001, 2002; Water Research, 2001; Desalination, 2001; Transactions of the Institute of Chemical Engineering, 2001; Journal of Environmental Engineering, 2002. Honours: Listed in Who's Who publications and biographical dictionaries. Memberships: International Water Association; Korean Society of Environmental Engineers. Address: Department of Environmental Engineering, Hoseo University, Asan, Chung-nam, 336-795, South Korea. E-mail: cis@office.hoseo.ac.kr Website: www.hoseo.ac.kr/~cis

CHANG Lawrence Hooi-Tuang, b. 26 January 1963, Malaya. Associate Professor. Education: BSc with Ed (Honours), 1987; MSc, 1991; PhD, 1997. Appointments: Research Assistant, University of Malaya, 1987-88; Research Officer, 1991-92, Lecturer, 1997-2003, University of Sciences of Malaysia; Associate Professor, Northern Malaysia University College of Engineering, 2003-. Publications include: Local derivative estimation for scattered data interpolation, 1995. Memberships:

Life Member, Malaysian Mathematical Society; Life Member, YMCA. Address: Northern Malaysia University College of Engineering, 01000 Kangar, Malaysia.

CHANG Michael, b. 22 February 1972, Hoboken, New Jersey, USA. Tennis Player. Appointments: Aged 15 was youngest player since 1918 to compete in men's singles at US Open, 1987; Turned Professional, 1988; Played Wimbledon, 1988; Winner, French Open, 1989; Davis Cup Debut, 1989; Winner, Canadian Open, 1990; Semi-Finalist, US Open, 1992, Finalist, 1996; Finalist, French Open, 1995; Semi-Finalist, Australian Open, 1995, Finalist, 1996; Winner of 34 singles titles by end of 2002. Address: Advantage International, 1751 Pinnacle Drive, Suite 1500, McLean, VA 22102, USA.

CHANG Ming-Hong, b. 9 August 1961, Taiwan. Doctor; Neurologist. m. Shiew-Jue Wei, 2 daughters. Education: MD, Kaosiung Medical College, Taiwan, 1986; Resident, Taipei Veterans General Hospital, 1986-91. Appointments: Attending Physician, Kaohsiung Veterans General Hospital, 1991-2000; Head, Taichung Veterans General Hospital, 2000-. Publications: Many papers published in medical journals including: Neurology; Journal of Neurology; Neurosurgery and Psychiatry; Clinical Neurophysiology; Journal of Clinical Physiology. Honours: Several awards from the National Science Council and Taichung and Kaohsiung Veterans General Hospitals. Memberships: Taiwan Neurological Society. Address: Section of Neurology, Taichung Veterans General Hospital, No 160 Chung-Kang Road, Taichung, Taiwan. E-mail: cmr50@ms10.hinet.net

CHANG Sen-dou, b. 16 August 1928, Shaoxing, Zhejiang, China. Professor of Geography. m. Angela W L Chang, 2 sons. Education: BA, Jinan University, Shanghai, China, 1949; MA, University of Wisconsin, Madison, USA, 1955; PhD, University of Washington, Seattle, USA, 1961. Appointments: Assistant Professor of Geography, San Fernando State University, California, USA, 1962-67; Associate Professor of Geography, 1967-72; Professor of Geography, 1972-, University of Hawaii. Publications: The Morphology of Walled City, 1977; The Floating Population: An Informal Process of Urbanization in China, 1996; Beijing: Perspectives on Preservation, Environmental and Development, 1998. Honour: Fulbright Scholar, Taipei, Taiwan, 1976-77. Memberships: Association of American Geographers; American Geographical Society; Association for Asian Studies. Address: Department of Geography, University of Hawaii, Honolulu, HI 96822. E-mail: sdchang@hawaii.edu

CHANG Shih-Lin, b. 1 May 1946, Anhwei, China. Professor. m. Ling-Mei P Chang, 3 sons. Education: BS, Electrophysics, National Chiao Tung University, 1968; MS, Physics, Clemson University, USA, 1971; PhD, Physics, Polytechnic Institute of Brooklyn, USA, 1975. Appointments: Assistant Professor, 1975-78, Associate Professor, 1979-84, Professor, 1985, Solid State and Material Science, Universidade Estadual de Campinas, Brazil; Professor, Physics, 1985-, National Tsing Hua University, Taiwan; Head, Physics Department, National Tsing Hua University, 1987-90; Director General, Natural Science and Mathematics Department, National Science Council, Republic of China, 1993-94; Deputy Director, Synchrotron Radiation Research Centre, Republic of China, 1995; Dean of Research and Development, National Tsing Hua University, 1998-2004; Director, Joint Research Institute of ITRI/NYHU. Publications: Over 100 scientific papers; 1 book; 1 monograph. Honours: Outstanding Research Award; Dr Sun Yat-Sen Academic Prize; Academic Prize in Natural Science; National Chair Professor in Natural Science (Ministry of Education); Elected member, Asian-Pacific Academy of Materials Science. Memberships: American Crystallographic Association; Asian Crystallographic Association; Physical Society of the Republic of China; American Physical Society. Address: 101, Section 2, Kuang Fu Road, Hsinchu, Taiwan, 300, Republic of China. E-mail: slchang@phys.nthu.edu.tw

CHANG Shuenn-Yih, b. 12 June 1958, Taiwan. Professor. m. Chiu-Li Huang, 2 daughters. Education: BS, 1977-81, MS, 1981-83, National Taiwan University; M Eng, University of California, Berkeley, California, USA, 1988-92; PhD, University of Illinois, Urbana-Champaign, USA, 1992-94. Appointments: Engineer, Eastern International Engineers, 1985-87; Associate Research Fellow, National Center for Research on Earthquake Engineering, 1995-2002; Assistant Professor, National Taipei University of Technology, 2002-. Publications: Application of the Momentum Equations of Motion to Pseudodynamic Testing, 2001; Explicit Pseudodynamic Algorithm with Unconditional Stability, 2002; Accuracy of Time History Analysis of Impulses, 2003; Nonlinear Error Propagation of Explicit Pseudodynamic Algorithm, 2003. Honours: Research Award, National Science Council, Taiwan, Republic of China; Research Award, Chinese Institute of Civil and Hydraulic Engineering. Memberships: Senior Member, Chinese Institute of Civil and Hydraulic Engineering; Chinese Institute of Earthquake Engineering. Address: National Taipei University of Technology, Department of Civil Engineering, #1 Section 3 Jungshiau East Road, Taipei, Taiwan, Republic of China. E-mail: changsy@ntut.edu.tw

CHANG Sungmin, b. 12 June 1967, Busan, Korea. Equity Research Analyst. 1 daughter. Education: BA, Economics, University of California, Berkeley, 1990; MBA, INSEAD, 1996. Appointments: Assistant Manager, International Finance Department, Daewoo Securities Co Ltd, 1991-95; Director, Fixed Income, Daewoo Securities (Europe) Ltd, 1997-98; Management Associate, Structured Finance Unit, ABN Amro, 1998-99; Vice-President, Head of Telcom Team, Research Centre, Samsung Securities Co Ltd, 2000-. Publications: More than 45 in depth reports on Korean telecom operators and Telcom Monthly from July 2000-Aug 2001. Honours: Listed in Who's Who publications and biographical dictionaries. Membership: AIMR. Address: Samsung Securities Co Ltd., 8th Fl, Jongno Tower Bldg, 6 Jogno 2-ga, Jogno-gu, Seoul, Korea 110-789. E-mail: smchang2@hotmail.com

CHANG Walter Tuck Sr, b. 16 February 1920, Honolulu, Hawaii. Machinist; Educator; Administrator; Sunday School Teacher; Realtor. m. Evelyn Show Chiao Haung Chang, 1 son, 1 daughter. Education: Scholastic Honours, Cadet First Lieutenant, The Kamehameha School for Boys, Military Academy, Trade and Religious School, 1934-39; BA, Industrial Arts with Honours and Teachers' Credentials, San Jose State Teachers College, 1939-45; Teachers Credentials, in Driver Education and Training, Vocational Education and Administration, University of California, 1948-55; MA, Education, Administration and Supervision Credentials of High School Teachers, San Francisco State University, 1955-59; Graduate Studies in Elementary School Administration, Supervision of Practice Teachers, University of Hawaii, 1959-64; Doctorate Dissertation, Maurice Kidjel Ratio Concept – Design and Drafting, University of Maryland, 1967-68; Taught Getting Started with the Cali-Pro, University of Maryland, 1967-68. Appointments: Drafting Apprenticeship, Hawaiian Electric Company, Engineering and Estimation Department, 1937-39; Machinist, Leadman, National War Manpower Job Instructor for Joshua Hendy Iron Works, Sunnyvale, California, 1942-45; Journeyman Machinist, Food Machinery Corporation, San Jose, California, 1946; Only Chinese-Hawaiian American Experimental Machinist, Tool Maker, helped to perfect the first guided missile in the world, Ames Aeronautical Laboratory, NASA, Moffett Field, California, 1946-51; Journeyman Machinist,

Oliver United Filters Inc, Oakland, California, 1952-53; Vocational Instructor, San Jose State College, 1942-45; Adult Evening Vocational Instructor, Leland High School, San Jose, 1951; Vocational Instructor, John Swett Union High School, Crockett, California, 1951-59; Vocational Director, Evening High School Principal, 1952-59; Ad-hoc Chairman with 130 State Vocational Directors converted all Technical Schools into City, Community and Junior Colleges, 1956-58; Industrial Arts, English, World History Instructor, McKinley High School, Honolulu, Hawaii, 1959-62; Industrial Arts Instructor, New Industrial Arts Education Department, College of Education, University of Hawaii; Manoa Campus and Supervisor of Practice Teachers, Lab High School, University of Hawaii, 1962-64; Design, Drafting, Architecture, Engineering, Auto Cad, Electronic, Metals Technology, Instructor and Supervisor of Drivers Education and Training, Kamehameha Schools, 1964-90; Introduced Auto-Cad to the State of Hawaii Curriculum, 1985; Implemented Unified Phonics into curriculum making New Keola Elementary School first public school to have homogeneous classes, grades 2-6; Many other positions. Publications: Follow up study of graduates, 1953-58, of the trade and industry program, John Swett UHS, 1959 (thesis in Library of Congress); Getting started with the cali-pro, Maurice Kidjel Ratio Concept, 1965. Honours: National Merit Honor Student; Epsilion Pi Tau; Kappa Delta Pi; Phi Delta Kappa; Most Outstanding Educator; Many others. Memberships: NEA; CTA; AVA; AIAA; HEA; OTA; OIATA; Vice President, President, 94 industrial arts teachers on O'ahu, 1961-62; PTA; Vice President, New Keola Elementary School, Kailua O'ahu, Hawaii, 1961-62. Address: 94-1015 Uke'e Place, Waipahu, HI 96797-4272, USA.

CHANG Yoon-Seok, b. 11 May 1957, Seoul, Korea. Professor. m. Jung-Suk Jang, 1 son, 1 daughter. Education: BS, Chemistry, Yonsei University, Korea, 1983, PhD, Chemistry, Oregon State University, USA, 1990. Director, KBSI, 1993-95, Professor, Hanyang University, Korea, 1995-97; Professor, POSTECH, 1997-. Publications: Over 100 publications. Memberships include: Korean Chemical Society. Address: School of Environmental Science Engineering, POSTECH, 31 Hyojadong, Namku, Pohang, Korea. E-mail: yschang@postech.ac.kr

CHANTOONI Miran K Jr, b. 27 January 1929, Des Moines, USA. Chemist. Education: BS, 1951; MS, 1954; PhD, 1961. Appointment: Research Associate, Department of Chemistry, University of Minnesota, 1962-90. Publications: Several articles contributed to professional scientific journals. Honours: Du Pont Fellow, 1956; Shevlin Fellow, 1956-57; Listed in several international and specialist biographical reference works. Memberships: American Chemical Society; Sigma Xi; American Association for the Advancement of Science. Address: University of Minnesota, Chemistry Department, Institute of Technology, Kolthoff and Smith Halls, 207 Pleasant Street SE, Minneapolis, MN 55455-0431, USA.

CHAPMAN Jean, b. 30 October 1939, England. Writer. m. Lionel Alan Chapman, 1 son, 2 daughters. Education: BA (Hons), Open University, 1989. Appointments: Creative Writing Tutor for East Midlands Arts and Community Colleges. Publications: The Unreasoning Earth, 1981; Tangled Dynasty, 1984; Forbidden Path, 1986; Savage Legacy, 1987; The Bellmakers, 1990; Fortune's Woman, 1992; A World Apart, 1993; The Red Pavilion, 1995; The Soldier's Girl, 1997; This Time Last Year, 1999; A New Beginning, 2001; And a Golden Pear, 2002; Danced Over The Sea, 2004. Other: Many short stories. Honours: Shortlisted, Romantic Novel of Year, 1982, 1996, and Kathleen Fidler Award, 1990. Memberships: Society of Authors; Chairman, Romantic Novelists Association. Address: 3 Arnesby Lane, Peatling Magna, Leicester LE8 5UN, England.

Dictionary of International Biography

CHAPPELL Gregory Stephen, b. 7 August 1948, Adelaide, Australia. Cricketer; Business Executive. m. Judith Elizabeth Donaldson, 1971, 2 sons, 1 daughter. Education: Adelaide College; Prince Alfred College, Adelaide. Appointments: Teams: South Australia, 1966-73, Somerset, 1968-69, Queensland, 1973-84 (Captain 1973-77, 1979-80); Tests for Australia, 1970-84, 48 as Captain, Scoring 7,100 runs (Average 53.8) including 24 Hundreds, and Holding 122 Catches; Scored 108 on Test Debut v England, Perth, 1970; Only Captain to have scored a Century in each innings of 1st Test as Captain (v West Indies, Brisbane 1975); Holds record for most catches in a Test Match (7, v England, Perth 1975); Scored 24,535 1st Class Runs (74 Hundreds); Toured England 1972, 1975, 1977, 1980; Managing Director, AD Sports Technologies, 1993-95, Greg Chappell Sports Marketing, 1995-98; Coach, South Australian Redbacks cricket team, 2002. Publication: Greg Chappell's Health and Fitness Repair Manual, 1998. Honours include: Australian Sportsman of the Year, 1976. Memberships: MCC; South Australian Cricket Association. Address: c/o South Australian Cricket Association, Adelaide Oval, North Adelaide, SA 5006, Australia.

CHARLES Kwame Richard, b. 7 November 1952, Trinidad and Tobago. Management Consultant. m. Marcelline G Mendez, 19 November 1981, 1 son. Education: BA, Psychology, University of Toronto, 1976; MSc, Social Psychology, 1978, PhD, 1980, Howard University. Appointments: Job Analyst, Government of Trinidad and Tobago, 1980-81; Management Consultant, 1981; Human Resource Manager, 1982-88; Professor, University of the West Indies, Bahamas, 1988-92, Trinidad and Tobago, 1992-96; Consultant, Quality Consultants Ltd, 1996-. Publications include: Competing in the Markets of the Americas, 1995; Tourism Education and Human Resource Development for the Decade of the 90's, 1991. Memberships: Caribbean Centre for Excellence; National Quality Council of Trinidad and Tobago. Address: Quality House, 66A Picton Street, Newtown, Trinidad and Tobago.

CHARLIER Roger Henri Liévin Constance Louise, b. 10 November 1924, Antwerp, Belgium. University Professor. m. Patricia Simonet, 1 son, 1 daughter. Education: PhD, Erlangen, 1947; LitD, Paris, 1956; DSc, Paris, 1958; MS, Brussels, 1945; MPolSci, Brussels, 1942; Postgraduate study, McGill University, 1953; Industrial College, Armed Forces, 1956; Education Curriculum Diploma, Parsons College, 1962. Appointments include: Major (Intelligence), World War II; Professor, Finch College, USA, 1954-56; Special Lecturer, Chairman, Department of Geology and Geography, Hofstra University, USA, 1956-59; Visiting Professor, University of Minnesota, USA, 1959-61; Professor of Geology, Parsons College, 1961-62; Professor of Geology, Geography and Oceanography, Northeastern Illinois University, Chicago, 1961-87; Fulbright Scholar, 1974-76; Professor Extraordinary, 1970-86, Professor Emeritus, 1986-, Vrije Universiteit Brussels, Belgium; Professeur associé, 1970-74, hon, 1986-, Université de Bordeaux I, France; Fulbright Fellow, 1974-76; Kellogg Fellow, 1980-82; Scientific Advisor to CEO HAECON, 1984-88, 1989-2000; Scientific Advisor to CEO SOPEX, 1988-89; Professor Emeritus, Northeastern Illinois University, USA, 1988-; Chair, Task Force Environment and Sustainability, EFCA, 1998-2002; Newspaper Correspondent, various US, Belgian, Swiss papers, 1945-60, 1983-99. Publications include: Books: I Was a Male War Bride, 1948; For the Love of Kate, 1958; Pensées, 1962; Economic Oceanography, 1980; Study of Rocks, 1980; Tidal Power, 1982; Ocean Energies, 1993; Coastal Erosion, 1999; Tools for the Black Sea, 2000; Co-editor, Proc 6th Int Congr Hist Oceanog, 2004, Black Sea Seminar, 2002; Articles include: Small Sources of Methane; The Atmospheric Methane Cycle: Sources, Sinks, Distribution and Role in Global Change; Tourism and the Coastal Zone: The Case of Belgium: Ocean and Coastal Management; I was a Male War Bride. Honours include: Belgian Government Awards, 1939, 1975; Chicago Public Schools Award, 1975, 1987, 1992; Outstanding Achievement Presidential Award, 1980; Paul-Henri Spaak Memorial Lecture Award, 1992. Memberships include: Fellow, Geological Society of America; Charter Member, International Association for the History of Oceanography; Fellow, New Jersey Academy of Science, President, 1954-57, Past President, 1957-58; American Association for the Advancement of Science; Royal Belgian Society for Geographical Studies; Education Committee, Marine Technology Society; Association of American University Professors; Académie Nationale des Arts, Sciences et Belles-Lettres, 1970-; Royal Marine Academy of Belgium, 2004-. Address: 2 Ave du Congo, Box 23, Brussels 1050, Belgium.

CHARLTON John (Jack), b. 8 May 1935. Former Football Player; Broadcaster; Football Manager. m. Patricia, 1958, 2 sons, 1 daughter. Appointments: Professional footballer, Leeds Utd FC, 1952-73; Manager, Middlesborough FC, 1973-77, Sheffield Wednesday FC, 1977-83, Newcastle Utd FC, 1984-85, Republic of Ireland Football Team, 1986-95; Played with winning teams in League Championship, 1969, Football Association Cup, 1972, League Cup, 1968, Fairs Cup, 1968, 1971, World Cup (England v Germany), 1966. Publication: Jack Charlton's American World Cup Diary, 1994. Honours: Football Writers Association Footballer of the Year, 1967; OBE. Membership: Sports Council, 1977-82.

CHARLTON Robert (Bobby) (Sir), b. 11 October 1937. Former Footballer. m. Norma, 1961, 2 daughters. Career: Footballer with Manchester Utd, 1954-73; Played 751 games scoring 245 goals; FA Cup Winners' Medal, 1963; First Division Championship Medals, 1956-57, 1964-65, 1966-67; World Cup Winners' Medal (England team), 1966; European Cup Winners' Medal, 1968; 106 appearances for England, scoring 49 goals, 1957-73; Manager, Preston North End, 1973-75; Chairman, NW Council for Sport and Recreation, 1982-; Director, Manchester Utd Football Club, 1984-. Publications: My Soccer Life, 1965; Forward for England, 1967; This Game of Soccer, 1967; Book of European Football, Books 1-4, 1969-72. Honours: Honorary Fellow, Manchester Polytechnic, 1979; Honorary MA, Manchester University; Knighthood; CBE. Address: Garthollerton, Chelford Road, Ollerton, Nr Knutsford, Cheshire WA16 8RY, England.

CHARNEY Lena London, b. 26 January 1919, Symiatycze, Poland. Retired Teacher; Poet. m. Roy L Charney, 10 November 1955, 1 son. Education: BA, cum laude, Hunter College, New York City, 1941; MA, Clark University, Worcester, Massachusetts, 1942; PhD. ABD, Columbia University, 1947-53. Contributions to: various anthologies, reviews, magazines, and journals. Appointments: Millinery designer, Sanjour Studio, 1937, 1939-41; Designer, Co-owner, Lenblac Millinery Store, 1938; Co-owner, Co-manager, Golden Dawn bungalow colony, 1939-46; Secretary to New York City Manager, Insurance Field, 1945; Assistant Editor, Insurance Weekly, 1946; Saleslady, Bonwit-Teller, Arnold Constable and Lane Bryant, 1947-49; Director, Teacher, Workmen's Circle Yiddish School, Shrub Oak, New York; Sunday school teacher, Lakeland Jewish Centre and Temple Beth Am; Teacher, Principal, St Basil's Academy, Garisson, 1968-73; Substitute teacher, various districts, 1974-82; Co-manager, London's Studio Apartments, 1950-59; Owner, Manager, London's Studio Apartments, 1959-; Poet, 1984-. Honours: Finalist, Verve Poetry Competition, 1990; Honourable Mention, Nostalgia Poetry Contest, 1991; Finalist, Greenburgh Poetry Competition, 1993; Diamond Homer Award, Famous Poets Society, 1996, 1998 and 1999; Featured poet at, "An Evening of Poetry", Mount Pleasant Public Library, Pleasantville, New York, 2001. Publications: Historical articles in: Wisconsin History, 1948; The Southwestern Historical Quarterly, 1954; Indiana Magazine of History, 1948; Iowa Journal of History, 1950; Military Affairs, 1951; Michigan

Dictionary of International Biography

History, 1952; Poetry in many publications and anthologies. Honours: Featured poet at An Evening of Poetry, Mount Pleasant Public Library, Pleasantville, New York, 2001. Memberships: Association of American University Women; American Historical Association; Academy of Political Science; National Writers Union; Academy of American Poets; Hudson Valley Writers Centre; Poetry Society of America; Peregrine Poets. Address: PO Box 145, Mohegan Lake, NY 10547, USA.

CHARPENTIER DE CASTRO Eduardo, b. 12 March 1927, Panama. Musician. m. Marcela Del Carmen Herrera, 2 sons, 2 daughters. Education: Diploma in Commerce, Pan American Institute, Panama, 1946; Diploma in Theory and Solfeggio, 1946; Diploma in Harmony, 1947; Diploma in Flute, Summa Cum Laude, Panama Conservatory of Music, 1947; Bachelor of Music, Master of Music, Roosevelt University, Chicago, USA, 1950; Diploma in Chamber Music, Marlboro College, Vermont, 1950; Diploma in Flute, 1951, Diploma in Orchestral Conducting, 1956, National Conservatory of Music, Paris, France; Postgraduate, Eastman School of Music, Rochester, New York, USA, 1957; Doctor of Philosophy in Music and Education, Columbia Pacific University, San Rafael, California, USA 1985. Appointments: Flutist: National Police Band, 1941, National Symphony Orchestra, 1944, Republic Band, 1946, Panama; Birmingham Symphony Orchestra, Alabama, USA, 1960; Music Professor: Professional School, 1946; Theory and Solfeggio, 1946, Flute, 1951, National Conservatory of Music, Richard Newman College, 1958, Bolivar Institute, 1959, Fermin Naudeau Institute, 1965, Panama; Music Professor, Flute and Chamber Music, Birmingham Conservatory of Music, Music Education, Birmingham Southern College, Alabama USA, 1961, University of Panama, 1972; Assessor: Panama National Conservatory of Music, 1971, Panama National Institute of Culture, 1989; Director, Department of Music, University of Panama, 1972; Guest Conductor: Costa Rica; USA (Birmingham, Miami); Colombia, Mexico (Puebla, Guanajuanto, Juarez); Nicaragua; Guatemala; Musical compositions for Symphony Orchestra, Chamber Music, Piano, Voice, Transcriptions, Arrangements; Conductor: Founder of the Southern College Orchestra, Alabama, USA, 1961, Panama National Symphony Orchestra, 1966, University of Panama Chamber Music Orchestra, 1992. Publications: Contributions to newspapers and magazines with music reviews and articles; 2 books: Memory of the Department of Music of the University of Panama; Maestro Eduardo Charpentier De Castro Conductor of Panama Symphony Orchestra from 1966-1988. Honours include: Played flute for General Dwight Eisenhower, 1946; United States Government Research Professor Grant, 1960; Gran Official, Order Vasco Nunez de Balboa, President of the Republic of Panama, 1999; Listed in Who's Who publications, music reference works and biographical dictionaries. Memberships include: National Association for American Composers and Conductors, New York, USA, 1961; American Federation of Musicians, Birmingham, Alabama, 1966; Honorary President National Composers Association, Panama, 1978; United States Copyright Office, Library of Congress, Washington DC, 1982; National Music Council of the International Music Council, Washington DC, 1984; General Association of Composers, Madrid, Spain, 1989. Address: Apartado 9190, Panama 6, Panama.

CHARTERIS Richard, b. 24 June 1948, Chatham Islands, New Zealand. Musicologist; Writer; Editor. Education: BA, Victoria University, Wellington, New Zealand, 1970; MA with 1st Class hons, University of Canterbury, 1972; PhD, 1976, Universities of Canterbury and London. Career: Rothmans Research Fellowship, University of Sydney, 1976-78; Research Fellowship, University of Queensland, 1979-80; Australian Research Council Research Fellow, Music Department, University of Sydney, 1981-90; Australian Research Council Senior Research Fellow (Reader), Music Department, University of Sydney, 1991-94; Professor in

Historical Musicology, Music Department, University of Sydney, 1995-. Publications include: Author of over 130 books and editions devoted to the music of Johann Christian Bach, John Coprario, Alfonso Ferrabosco the Elder, Domenico Maria Ferrabosco, Giovanni Gabrieli, Adam Gumpelzhaimer, Hans Leo Hassler, Thomas Lupo, Claudio Monteverdi and others, and mostly in the series Corpus Mensurabilis Musicae, Musica Britannica, Recent Researches in the Music of the Baroque Era, Boethius Editions, Fretwork Editions, King's Music Editions, Baroque and Classical Music Series; and books on composers, music and early sources in the series Boethius Editions, Thematic Catalogues Series, Musicological Studies and Documents and Altro Polo. Contributions to: Numerous journals and magazines; Music and Letters; Early Music; Royal Musical Association Research Chronicle; Musica Disciplina; Chelys; The Galpin Society Journal; MLA Notes; The Huntington Library Quarterly; Studies in Music. Honours: Fellow, Australian Academy of the Humanities, 1990; Fellow, Royal Historical Society, London, 2002; Australian Centenary Medal, 2003. Address: Music Department, University of Sydney, NSW 2006, Australia.

CHASDI Richard J, b. 21 January 1958. Political Scientist. Education: BA, Politics, Brandeis University, 1981; MA, Political Science, Boston College, 1985; PhD, Political Science, Purdue University, 1995. Appointments: Adjunct Faculty, Centre for Peace and Conflict Studies, Wayne State University, 1996-2001; Adjunct Lecturer, Political Science, Department of Social Sciences, University of Michigan-Dearborn, 1997; Visiting Assistant Professor of International Relations, Department of Political Science, The College of Wooster, 2001-02; Visiting Assistant Professor of History, Department of History, The College of Wooster, 2002; Scholar in Residence, Department of Political Science, Eastern Michigan University, 2003; Adjunct Assistant Professor, Center for Peace and Conflict Studies, Wayne State University, 2003-. Publications include: Terrorism: Stratagems for Remediation from an International Law Perspective, 1994; Middle East Terrorism 1968-1993: An Empirical Analysis of Terrorist Group-Type Behaviour, 1997; Serenade of Suffering: A Portrait of Middle East Terrorism 1968-1993, 1999; Tapestry of Terror: A Portrait of Middle East Terrorism 1994-1999, 2002; Encyclopaedia entries include: Mass Casualty Attacks and Strategic Threats, 2003, Use of Conventional Weapons Technologies and Tactics, 2003. Honours: Outstanding Academic Title in the field of International Relations, Choice magazine, 2000. Memberships: Associate Member, Center for Middle Eastern Studies, University of Chicago; Member, American Political Science Association. Address: Center for Peace and Conflict Studies, Wayne State University, 2320 Faculty Administration Building, Detroit, MI 48202, USA. E-mail: rchasdi@aol.com

CHASE Helen Christina, b. 21 March 1917, New York, New York, USA. Biostatistician. m. Donald F Chase Jr, deceased. Education: AB, Hunter College, New York, 1938; MSc, Biostatistics, College of Physicians and Surgeons, Columbia University, 1951; DrPH, Biostatistics, School of Public Health, University of California at Berkeley, 1961. Appointments: Unemployment Insurance Claims Examiner, New York State Labor Department, 1939-48; Biostatistician, Principal Biostatistician, New York State Health Department, 1948-63; Health Statistician, Chief, Mortality Statistics Branch, National Center for Health Statistics, US Department of Health, Education and Welfare, 1963-69; Director of Research, Association of Schools of Allied Health Professions, 1969-71; Staff Associate, National Academy of Sciences, 1971-72; Medicare Statistician, Social Security Administration, US Department of Health, Education and Welfare, 1973-75; Deputy Chief, Epidemiological Studies Branch, Bureau of Radiological Health, Food and Drug Administration, 1975-80; Adjunct Professor, Graduate School of Nursing, Catholic

Dictionary of International Biography

University, 1966-76. Publications: International Comparison of Infant, Perinatal and Early Childhood Mortality, United States and Six European Countries, 1967; Editor, seven composite reports for United States, Scotland, Norway, Denmark, Netherlands, England and Wales, USDHEW, 1965-68; Editor, Directory of Support Services for Alzheimer's Patients and Their Families, 1986, 1987; Editor, Newsletter of the Conference of Emeritus Members, American Public Health Association, 1987-99; Author or Co-author of over 65 articles in public health in scientific journals. Honours: Lowell J Reed Award, American Public Health Association, 1979; Federation Award, National Association of Retired Federal Employees, 1987. Memberships: Elected Fellow, American Public Health Association, 1954; Fellow, National Heart Institute, National Institutes of Health, 1955-56; Fellow, University of California at Berkeley, 1956-57; Elected Fellow, American Association for the Advancement of Science, 1962; Elected Fellow, Delta Omega Society, 1965; Elected Fellow, American Statistical Association, 1974; Member, American Population Association; Bioeffects Advisory Committee, Bureau of Radiological Health, Food and Drug Administration. Address: 2751 Regency Oaks Blvd #R-106, Clearwater, FL 33759, USA.

CHATFIELD Judith Spencer, b. 20 September 1942, New York City, USA. Garden Historian. m. Fred Schwerin. Education: BA, 1964, MA, 1969, Syracuse University; MPhil, Courtauld Institute of Art, University of London, 1972. Appointments: Art and Garden Tour Director, 1980-; Garden History Lecturer, 1988-; Photographer, Rizzoli, 1988-. Publications: Books: Boboli Gardens, 1972; A Tour of Italian Gardens, 1988; The Classic Italian Garden, 1991; Gardens of The Italian Lakes, 1992, Contributor, The Grove Dictionary of Art, 1996. Honour: Fulbright Fellowship, Fulbright Association, 1967-68. Memberships: Director, Hotchkiss Library Board, 1992-; City Gardens Club, New York City; President, Sharon Garden Club, 1992; Mad Gardeners. Address: 44 Morey Road, Sharon, CT 06069, USA.

CHATTOPADHYAY Rabindranath, b. 1 October 1962, Sreerampore. Teacher. m. Jhuma, 2 daughters. Education: MSc, Physics, Nuclear Physics and Particle Physics as the special and elective papers respectively, BEd, Cal. University, and has submitted thesis for PhD in Upper Atmospheric Research. Appointments: Assistant Teacher, Physics, Haripal G D Institution, Haripal, Hooghly, India, a Governments aided Public High School, 10 +2, about 14 years of teaching experience completed. Publications: 20 research papers; 31 articles of higher academic value; 17 articles of academic interest in regard of science popularisation and two books. Honours: International Man of the Year 2001, IBC; Listed in several Who's Who and biographical publications. Address: Vill & P O – Paschim Gopinathpur, P S Haripal, D T Hooghly, Pin 712403 SD Chandernagore, West Bengal, India.

CHATURVEDI Mahashweta, b. 2 February 1950, Etawah, UP, India. College Reader. m. Uma Kant Chaturvedi, 2 sons, 1 daughter. Education: MA (English), 1966, MA, Sanskrit, 1969, Agra University; MA, Hindi, RU, 1978; Sangeet Prabhakar (Sitar), 1975, Vocal Music, 1976, Tabla, 1977, Sahitya Charya, 1977, Diploma, Journalism, 1980, PhD, RU, 1984, DLitt, RU, 1991; LLB, RU, 1993. Appointments: Lecturer in Hindi, RPPG College, Meerganj, Bly, UP, currently, Reader. Publications: Vedayan; Voice of Agony; Throbbing Lyre; Roaming Aroma; Way of Melody; Eternal Pilgrim; Waves of Joy; Immortal Wings; Stone-God; Back to the Vedas; Mother-Earth; 2 books (English articles), The Streams of Supraconsciousness and On the Sands of Time; 12 books in English; 38 books in Hindi; Founder, Editor, Mandakini (bilingual English/Hindi, International Journal). Honours: Viveka S Award, 1990; Lekhica Award, 1990; Kavya Ratna, 1992; Sahitya Academy

Award, 1994; Sahitya Bharti, 1994; Michael Madhusudan Award, 1995; Gold Medal for poetry, USA, 1996; Medal of Honour, 1997; Gold Record of Achievement, 1998; International Golden Dove Award for poetry, 1999; Subhadrak Chauhan Padak, 1996; Shishu Ballabha Award, 1996; International Shakespeare Award, 2000; Sanskar Bharti Award, 2001; Maha Devi Verma Award, 2002; Dev Vani Ratna Award, 2002; Guru Purnima Award, 2002; Jaisee Award, 2002; Toru Dutta Award 2002 for book, Throbbing Lyre; Laghu Katha Shilpi Award, 2003; Vivekanand Award, 2003; Rashtra Bhasha Ratna Award, 2003; Hindi Ratna, 2003; Decree of Honor, USA, 2003; Kavya Sarita Award, 2004. Memberships: International Writers Association, USA; International Poetry Society; Authors Guild of India, Hindi SSUP; Hindi SS Prayag; Advisor, Indian Institute of Management and Education, Kapurthala; Patron, Photo Today and many others. Address: 24 Aanchal Colony, Shyam Ganj, Bareilly 243005, UP, India.

CHAZANOFF Daniel, b. 1 March 1923, New York City, USA. Musician; Music Educator. m. Nina Trachtenberg, 1 son, 1 daughter. Education: BSc in Education, Ohio State University, 1949; MA, Music and Music Education, 1951, Ed D, 1964, Columbia University. Appointments: Assistant Principal Cellist, Birmingham Alabama Symphony, 1951-52; Director of Music, Teacher, City School District of Rochester, New York, 1964-84; String Instructor, Columbia University, Summers of 1967 and 1968; Music Reviewer, Wolfe Community Newspapers, 1988-95; Lecturer, Music Appreciation, Bronx Community College, City University of New York, 1959-64; Assistant Professor of Music, Northern State College, Aberdeen, South Dakota, 1957-59; Director, Instrumental Music, Chatham Township Public Schools, New Jersey, 1955-57. Publications: 25 music books, 230 articles in specialist journals and periodicals. Compositions: 12 original works. Honours include: Research and Travel Grants; National Honor Music Society; Honorary Graduate, Ohio State University; Orchestra Key, Ohio State University. Memberships: Music Educators' National Conference. Address: 114 Penarrow Road, Rochester, NY 14618-1724, USA.

CHEAL MaryLou, b. 5 November 1926, Michigan, USA. Research Psychologist. m. James Cheal, 2 sons, 1 daughter. Education: BA, Oakland University, Rochester, Michigan, USA, 1969; PhD, Psychology, University of Michigan, 1973. Appointments include: Assistant to Associate Psychologist, McLean Hospital, Harvard Medical School, 1977-83; Faculty Research Associate, Arizona State University, 1983-87; Visiting Professor, Air Force Systems Command University Resident Research Program Appointment, Williams Air Force Base, Arizona, USA, 1986-88; Research Psychologist, University of Dayton Research Institute at Williams Air Force Base, 1986-94; Adjunct Associate Professor, Professor, Department of Psychology, Arizona State University, USA, 1987-; Senior Research Psychologist, University of Dayton Research Institute at the Air Force Armstrong Laboratory, Mesa, Arizona, USA, 1994-95. Publications: 70 publications including: Timing of facilitatory and inhibitory effects of visual attention, 2002; Inappropriate capture by diversionary dynamic elements, 2002; Efficiency of visual selective attention is related to the type of target, 2002. Honours include: Society of Sigma Xi, 1972; Fellow, American Association for Advancement of Science, 1987; Fellow, American Psychological Association, 1987; Charter Fellow, American Psychological Society, 1989; World Intellectual of 1993; Commemorative Medal of Honor, American Biographical Institute, 1993; Professional Women's Advisory Board, 1998; The C T Morgan Distinguished Service to Division 6 Award, American Psychological Association, 1999. Memberships include: American Association for Advancement of Science, 1969-89, Fellow, 1987; Sigma Xi, 1972-; Society for Neuroscience, 1974-; American

Dictionary of International Biography

Psychological Association, member, 1980-86, fellow, 1986-; President, Division 6, 1997-98, Committee on Division/APA Relation, member, 1997-98, chair, 1999, Representative to Council, 2000-2005, division 6; The Psychonomic Society, 1988-; American Psychological Society, charter fellow, 1988-; International Brain Research Organization. Address: 127 Loma Vista Drive, Tempe, AZ 85282-3574, USA.

CHEDID Andrée, b. 20 March 1920, Cairo, Egypt. Poet; Novelist; Dramatist. m. Louis A Chedid, 23 August 1942, 1 son, 1 daughter. Education: Graduated, American University of Cairo, 1942. Publications: Poetry Collections: Textes pour un poème (1949-1970), 1987; Poèmes pour un texte (1970-91), 1991; Par delà les mots, 1995. Novels: Le Sommeil délivré, 1952, English translation as From Sleep Unbound, 1983; Jonathon, 1955; Le Sixième Jour, 1960, English translation as The Sixth Day, 1988; L'Autre, 1969; La Cité fertile, 1972; Nefertiti et le reve d'Akhnaton, 1974; Les Marches de sable, 1981; La Maison sans racines, 1985, English translation as The Return to Beirut, 1989; L'Enfant multiple, 1989. Plays: Bérénice d'Egypte, Les Nombres, Les Montreur, 1981; Echec à la Reine, 1984; Les saisons de passage, 1996. Other: The Prose and Poetry of Andrée Chedid: Selected Poems, Short Stories, and Essays (Renée Linkhorn, translator), 1990; A la Mort, A la Vie, 1992; La Femme de Job, 1993; les Saisons de passage, 1996; Le Jardin perdue, 1997; Territoires du Souffle, 1999; Le Cœur demeure, 1999; Essays; Children's books. Honours: Prix Louise Labe, 1966; Grand Prix des Lettres Francaise, l'Académie Royale de Belgique, 1975; Prix de l'Académie Mallarmé, 1976; Prix Goncourt de la nouvelle, 1979; Prix de Poèsie, Société des Gens de Lettres, 1991; Prix de PEN Club International, 1992; Prix Albert Camus, 1996; Prix Poésie de la SALEH, 1999; Légion d'honneur, Commandeur des Arts et des Lettres. Membership: PEN Club International. Address: c/o Flammarion, 26 rue Racine, Paris 75006, France.

CHEMPIN Beryl Margaret, b. Edgbaston, Birmingham, England. Musician. m. Peter Gilroy Bevan, CBE. Education: Birmingham Conservatoire; FTCL; LRAM; ARCM; LTCL; ABSM; Hon FBC; Studied with Harold Craxton and Kendall Taylor. Career: Member of Keyboard Faculty, Birmingham Conservatoire; Member of Keyboard Faculty, Birmingham University; Private Teacher, Solo Performer and Accompanist; Lecturer and Adjudicator; Writer of CD sleeve notes and programme notes; Conducted Masterclasses in Australia, Hong Kong, South Africa, Finland and UK. Publications: The Physiology of Piano Playing (with Professor Peter Gilroy Bevan), 1995; Book reviews, Many articles on the principles and details of piano teaching. Honours: Midland Woman of the Year, 1977; National Award for Piano Teaching, 1983; Honorary Fellowship of the Birmingham Conservatoire. Memberships: Incorporated Society of Musicians; Royal Society of Musicians (member of Court of Assistants); European Piano Teachers' Association; City of Birmingham Symphony Orchestra Society; King Edward's High School Old Edwardians; Birmingham Conservatoire Association; Beethoven Piano Society of Europe. Address: 10 Russell Road, Moseley, Birmingham B13 8RD, England.

CHEN Bing-Huei, b. 30 January 1954, Taichung, Taiwan. Professor. m. Wen-Huei Wang, 1 son, 1 daughter. Education: BS, Food Science, Fu Jen University, 1977; MS, Agricultural Chemistry, California State University, Fresno, 1983; PhD, Food Science, Texas A and M University, 1988. Appointments: Professor, Department of Nutrition and Food Science, Fu Jen University, Taipei. Publications: More than 70 research articles have been published in internationally renowned journals. Honours: Outstanding Research Awards, National Science Council of Taiwan and Chinese Institute of Food Science and Technology.

Memberships: Institute of Food Technologists; New York Academy of Science; AOAC International. Address: 12F-2, No 162, Sec 5, Ming-Seng E Rd, Taipei, Taiwan 105.

CHEN Chi-Yao, b. 19 November 1930, I-Lan, Taiwan. Insurance Underwriter; Professor. m. Shou-huei, 14 November 1959, 1 son, 2 daughters. Education: BA, National Taiwan University, 1953; Doctoral Program, Wharton School, University of Pennsylvania, 1976. Appointments: Chairman, Fire Insurance Committee, Taipei; Founder, Chairman, Engineering Insurance Association; Advisor, Research, Development and Evaluation Commission Executive Yuan; Member, Examination Board, Special Examination, Ministry of Examinations; Managing Director, Institute of Internal Auditors, Taipei; Chairman, Risk Management Society, Taiwan; Honorary Chairman, Non-Life Insurance Underwriters Society; Executive Vice-President, Fubon Insurance Company; Associate Professor, National Chengchi University; Chairman, Chi-Yun Insurance Education Foundation; Member of Board, The Consumers Association of Taiwan; Member of Board, The Traffic Accident Guarantee Fund; Council Member, Insurance, Ministry of Finance. Publications: Reinsurance - Studies of Current Problems and Trend, 1987; Essence of Reinsurance, 1992; Risk Management and Insurance, 1993; Auto Insurance Claims, 1995; Reinsurance, 1996; Auto Insurance - Principles and Practice, 1999; Reinsurance, Principles and Practice, 2000; Engineering Insurance – Principle and Practice, 2001. Honours: Outstanding Employee Award, Ministry of Finance, 1978; 4th Academy Prize, Society of Risk Management, Japan, 1994; Outstanding Book of the Year, National Council of Science, 1994; Outstanding Director of a Public Organisation, Ministry of Interior Affairs, 1996; Lifetime Contribution to Insurance Award, The Risk Management and Insurance Educational Promotion Foundation, 2003. Memberships: President, Southeast Rotary Club, Taipei, 1993-94; President, Society of Risk Management, Taiwan, 1997-2000; Chairman, 1987-93, President, Non-Life Underwriters Society, Taiwan, 1989-96. Address: 2nd Floor, No 5, Alley 5, Lane 5, Ren-Ai Road, Section 3, Taipei 106, Taiwan.

CHEN Chien-Jen, b. 6 June 1951, Kaohsiung, Taiwan. Professor. m. Fong-Ping Lo, 2 daughters. Education: Doctor of Science, Epidemiology, Johns Hopkins University, USA; Master of Science, Public Health, National Taiwan University; Bachelor of Science, Zoology, National Taiwan University. Appointments: Director, Professor, Graduate Institute of Public Health, National Taiwan University, 1993-94; Director, Graduate Institute of Epidemiology, 1994-97; Director General, Division of Life Sciences, National Science Council, 1997-99; Senior Associate, School of Hygiene and Public Health, Johns Hopkins University, USA, 1994-2004; Adjunct Professor, School of Public Health, Tulane University, USA, 1994-2004; Professor, Graduate Institute of Epidemiology, National Taiwan University, 1994-2004; Dean, College of Public Health, National Taiwan University, 1999-2002; Vice-Chairman, National Science Council, 2002-2003; Minister, Department of Health, 2003-04. Publications: More than 360 original articles published in international refereed journals. Honours: Academician Academia Sinica; National Chair Professor; National Health Medal; Outstanding Research Award. Memberships: Formosan Medical Association; American Association of Cancer Research; International Society of Genetic Epidemiology; International Society of Environmental Epidemiology. Address: College of Public Health, National Taiwan University, 1 Jen-Ai Road, Section 1, Taipei 10018, Taiwan.

CHEN Guodong Baoxing, b. 17 December 1940, Wenzhou, Zhejiang, China. Engineering Technologist. m. Li Daiqi, 2 daughters. Education: Chemical Equipment Department, Hongzhou School of Chemical Technology, 1956-59. Appointments:

Dictionary of International Biography

Instructor of Laboratory, Chemical Mechanical Laboratories, Beijing Institute of Chemical Technology, 1959-65; Visiting Study, Beijing Petroleum Institute, 1960-61; Assistant Engineer, Engineer, Senior Engineer, Tientsin General Paint Factory, 1965-. Publications: Numerous articles in professional journals and conference papers. Memberships: Several. Address: Room 404-405, Building 8, The South of Tao-hua Dike, Qin-jian Bridge, Hong-giao District, Tianjin 300130, PR China.

CHEN Huaitao, b. 10 August 1938, Huayin Shaanxi, China. Teacher. m. Qiuchan Wang, 1 son, 1 daughter. Education: Graduate, Gansu Agricultural University, Lanzhou, China, 1961; Diploma, Veterinary Science, N Balcescu Agricultural Institute, Bucharest, Romania, 1981. Appointments: Assistant, Gansu Agricultural University, 1961-78; Lecturer, 1978-79; Lecturer, N Balcescu Agricultural Institute, 1979-81; Assistant Professor, Gansu Agricultural University, 1987-91, Professor, 1992-. Publications: Veterinary Pathological Anatomy, 2000; Pathological Studies on Pneumoconiosis in Animals, Journal of Gansu Agricultural University, 1992; Studies on the Pathology of Gasping Disease in Equines, Chinese Journal of Veterinary Medicine, 1992; Diagnostic Pathology of Animal Diseases, 1995; Colour Atlas of Rabbit Diseases, 1998. Honours: Award, Government Gansu Province, 1989; Grant State Council, China, 1992; Award, Ministry of Agriculture, China, 1996. Memberships: Chinese Association of Animal Science and Veterinary Medicine; NYAS; AAAS. Address: 1 Yingmencun Anning Dist, 730070 Lanzhou, Gansu, China.

CHEN Jiann-Chu, b. 17 February 1946, Kaohsiung, Taiwan. Professor. m. Su-Ching, 1 son, 1 daughter. Education: Doctor of Agriculture, Faculty of Agriculture, Kyushu University, Fukuoka, Japan, 1976. Publications: 158 scientific journal papers. Honours: Outstanding Research Award, 1992-93, 1994-95, 1997-98; Special Appointed Researcher, 1999, 2002; Academic Award, 2001. Membership: World Aquaculture Society. Address: National Taiwan Ocean University, Department Aquaculture, Keelung 202, Taiwan.

CHEN Naifang, b. November 1940, Nantong, Jiangsu Province, China. Educator; Professor. m. Ding Baohua, 1 son, 1 daughter. Education: Graduate, English Department, Beijing Institute of Foreign Languages (now Beijing Foreign Studies University), 1964. Appointments: Teacher, English Department, Beijing Foreign Studies University, 1964-; Served in Chinese Embassy in Belgium and Chinese Commission to the European Community, 1978-80; Senior Visiting Scholar, University of Massachusetts, USA, 1984-85; Vice-President, Beijing Foreign Studies University, 1988-; Education Counsellor, Chinese Embassy in Belgium and the Chinese Commission to the European Union, 1992-95; President, Beijing Foreign Studies University, 1997-. Publications include: Universe Environment and Life, volume I and II, editor-in-chief; Listening (Elementary, Intermediate and Advanced), Editor; Listening, video tapes, main reviser; On Edgar Snow and his Book Red Star Over China; Build a Bridge of International Exchange; Role of Scientific research in Foreign Languages Universities of the 21st Century; WTO and the Cultivation of Foreign Languages Personnel; Running the University with Characteristics and the Development of Beijing Foreign Studies University. Honours: Honorary Doctor Degree in Education, Rajabhat Institute, Chiang Mai, Thailand; Honorary Doctor Degree to be conferred by Lancaster University, UK. Memberships: Ninth and Tenth National Committee of the Chinese People's Political Consultative Congress and Member of its Foreign Affairs Committee; Delegate to the 16th Communist Party of China National Congress; Deputy Director, Institute of Higher Education Management, China Higher Education Association; China International Educational Exchange Association; Editor-in-Chief, International Forum Magazine.

Address: Beijing Foreign Studies University, 2 North Xisanhuan Avenue, Haidian District, Beijing 100089, PR China. E-mail: cnf@mail.bfsu.edu.cn

CHEN Pang-Chi, b. 8 September 1947, Taichung, Taiwan. Physician; Gastroenterologist. m. Ying-Erl Lin, 2 sons. Education: MD, 1973. Appointments: Chief, Division of Gastroenterology and Clinical Professor, Chang Gung Memorial Hospital; Associate Professor, Medical College, Chang Gung University; Editor-in-Chief, Gastroenterological Journal of Taiwan. Publications: Several in professional journals. Honours: Taiwan Medical Association Award, 1979, 1984; 20th Century Achievement Award, 1995; World Lifetime Achievement Award, 1996; Honorary Taipei Citizen; Dictionary of International Biography; 500 Leaders of Influence; Who's Who in the World; Who's Who in Medicine and Healthcare; 500 Leaders for the New Century; The Barons 500; The Global 500; 500 Founders of the 21st Century. Memberships: ABI; IBC; GEST; DEST; ASGE; IASG; EAGE; AGA. Address: Chang Gung Memorial Hospital, 199 Tun Hwa North Road, Taipei 105, Taiwan.

CHEN Qihong, b. 29 September 1952, Shanghai, China. Professor. m. Xiujuan Luo, 1 daughter. Education: MSc, Inner Mongolia University, Huhehaote, China, 1982; PhD, Fudan University, Shanghai, China, 1999. Appointments: Assistant Professor, Inner Mongolia University, 1982-1987; Associate Professor, Suzhou Institute of Urban Construction and Environmental Protection, 1987-1993; Professor, Shanghai Normal University, 1993-2001; Professor, Shanghai University of Finance and Economics, 2001-. Publications: Several articles in professional publications. Address: Department of Applied Mathematics, Shanghai University of Finance and Economics, 777 Guoding Road, Shanghai 200433, Peoples Republic of China. E-mail: chenqih@online.sh.cn

CHEN Shuxuan, b. 30 March 1936, Fuzhou, Fujian, China. Physicist. m. Chen Shuxia, 1 son, 1 daughter. Education: BSc, Physics, Xiamen University, 1959. Appointments: Graduate school work, 1959-62; Teaching Assistant, Huagiao University, 1962-74; Lecturer, Associate Professor, Xiamen University, 1974-96; Retired, 1996-. Publications: Materiality Theory - Basis of Crossing Theory for Natural Subjects Course, 1994; Thinking Engineering - The Human Brain's Intelligent Activity and Thinking Model, 1994; Announcing Fundamental Problems with Basic Particles, 1998; A New Theory About Wave Motion of Photon, 1999; New Theory of Cell Growth and Disintegration, 2000; Basic Problem About Chemistry, 2000; The Theories of Substance and its Engineering the Technique the Applications, 2002. Honours: 3rd Prize, for Microcomputer System of MM-1000 Friction Tester, National Mechanism-Electron Industrial, 1989; 3rd Prize for Thesis, Fujian Science and Technology Association, 1989; International Excellent Articles Prize for "Thinking Engineering", World Chinese Interchange Association, 2003. Memberships: Chinese Science Institute; Research Fellow, Creative Graduate School. Address: Xiamen University, 19-502 Baicheng, Xiamen, Fujian, China.

CHEN Tien-Shi, b. 13 August 1971, Japan. Associate Professor. Education: PhD, International Political Economy, University of Tsukuba, Japan, 2000. Appointments: The National Museum of Ethnology, Japan, Department of Advanced Studies of Anthropology. Publications: Chinese Diaspora, 2001; The Image and reality of Overseas Ethnic Chinese Entrepreneurs – "Rainbow" Networks and Identities. Essays on Ethnic Chinese Abroad, 2002. Honour: 1st Asia Pacific Research Scholarship Prize, The Asia Pacific Forum, Awaji Conference, Japan. Membership: Association of Asian Studies. Address: 10-1, Senri Expo Park, Suita, Osaka 565-8511, Japan. E-mail: lara@idc.minpaku.ac.jp

Dictionary of International Biography

CHEN Wei-Yin, b. 5 April 1950, Taipei, Taiwan. Education; Research. m. Tsuei-Ju Kao. Education: BS, Chemical Engineering, Tunghai University; MS, Applied Maths and Statistics, State University of New York, Stony Brook; MS, Chemical Engineering, Polytechnic Institute of New York; PhD, Chemical Engineering, City University of New York. Senior Research Engineer, Gulf South Research Institute, 1981-84; Manager, Fuel Research, 1984-87; Research Assistant Professor, Louisiana State University, 1987-90; Assistant Professor, 1990-93, Associate Professor, 1993-2000, Professor, 2000-, University of Mississippi. Publications: Over 100 articles in professional journals. Memberships: American Institute of Chemical Engineers; American Chemical Society; Sigma Xi; Combustion Institute; American Society for Engineering Education; Chinese Institute of Engineers. Address: Department of Chemical Engineering, Anderson Hall, University of Mississippi, MS 38677-1848, USA.

CHEN Willie, b. 15 February 1936, Muar Johore, Malaysia. Journalist; Photo-Journalist. m. Lee Geok Lan, deceased, 1 son, 2 daughters. Education: Diploma, Radio, Electronics, TV, National technical School, Los Angeles, California, USA, 1957; MBA, USA University, 1962; Diploma, Hotel/Motel Operations and Management Course, La Salle University, Chicago, 1987. Appointments: Hearst Metrotone News Inc; CBS News; Head, Hotels Chain Projects, PR China; Television News Provider World-Wide for television news coverage projected for 1000 stations; Regular Writer for American magazines. Publications: More than 2000 news reports written during the period of the Vietnam War. Honours: Award in research for plant mutation under the X-ray; Citation for the Best News Coverage; Award for Best Articles written on food. Memberships: American Society of Magazine Photographers in Communications; Pasir Pelangi Residents Association; Teochoew Association. Address: 120 Jalan Sultanah Aminah, Taman Iskandar, 80050 Johore Bahru, Malaysia.

CHEN Xieyang, b. 4 May 1939, Shanghai, China. Symphony Orchestra Conductor. m. Jian-Ying Wang, 6 April 1973. Education: Piano student, Music Middle School, Shanghai Conservatory, 1953-60; Major in Conducting, Shanghai Conservatory, 1969-65; Musical study with Otto Mueller, Yale University, USA, 1981-82. Debut: Shanghai. Career: Conductor: Shanghai Ballet Orchestra, 1965-81; Aspen Festival, Group for Contemporary Music-New York, Brooklyn Philharmonia, Honolulu Symphony, Philippine State Orchestra, Hong Kong Philharmonic, Shanghai Symphony, Central Philharmonic-Beijing, 1981-83; Vilnius Symphony, Kaunas Symphony, Novosibirsk Symphony-USSR, 1985; Tokyo Symphony, Miyagi Philharmonic, Music Festival-Scotland, 1986-88; Music Director, Principal Conductor, Shanghai Symphony Orchestra; Resident Conductor, Central Philharmonic, Beijing. Recordings: Beethoven symphonies and Chinese composition for French recording company, 1983; Rachmaninov Symphony No 2 and Szymanowski Violin Concerto No 1, 1987; Chen Gang Violin Concerto The Butterfly Lovers and Beethoven's 9 symphonies, 1988. Address: 105 Hunan Lu, Shanghai, China.

CHEN Yi-Jen, b. 9 August 1967, Taipei, Taiwan. Medical Doctor. m. Shu-Fen Lee, 1 son, 1 daughter. Education: MD, Tapei Medical College, 1985-92; PhD, Institute of Clinical Research, National Yang-Ming University, 1998-2000. Appointments: Resident Physician, 1992-95, Fellow in Cardiology, 1995-98, Department of Medicine, Veterans General Hospital-Taipai, Taipei, Taiwan; Attending Physician of Cardiovascular Medicine, Taipei Medical University, Wan-Fang Hospital, 1998-. Publications: Effects of rapid atrial pacing on the arrhythmogenic activity of single cardiomyocytes from pulmonary veins: implication in initiation of atrial fibrillation, 2001; Electrophysiology and arrhythmogenic activity of single cardiomyocytes from canine superior vena cave,

2002. Honours: Award of Dr Du 1992; Outstanding Paper Award of Chinese medical Journal, Taipei, 1997; Research Award, Taipei Medical University, 2000; Research Award, Taipei Medical University, 2002. Memberships: Society of Internal Medicine, ROC, 1995; Society of Cardiology, ROC, 1997; North American Pacing and Electrophysiology, 1999-; Society of Cardiac Ultrasound, ROC, 2001-. Address: Veterans General Hospital Cardiology, 201 Section, 2 Shih-Pah Road, Taipei 11217, Taiwan. E-mail: yjchen@tmu.edu.tw

CHEN Zhongchun, b. 11 March 1963, Hubei, China. Associate Professor. m. Feng Yao, 1 son, 1 daughter. Education: BS, Materials Science and Engineering, Wuhan University of Technology, China, 1983; MS, Materials Science and Engineering, Central South University of Technology, China, 1988; PhD, Materials Science and Engineering, Tohoku University, Japan, 1997. Appointments: Research Associate, Lecturer, Central South University of Technology, China, 1988-93; Assistant Professor, Tohoku University, Japan, 1995-97; Assistant Professor, Yamagata University, Japan, 1997-2002; Research Fellow, University of Alabama at Birmingham, USA, 2001-2002; Associate Professor, Tohoku University, Japan, 2003-. Publications: More than 40 articles in Materials Science and Engineering in academic journals; Co-author of 2 books. Honours: First prize, Science and Technology Progress Award, Ministry of Education of China, 1997; Overseas Researcher, Japanese Ministry of Education, Culture, Sports, Science and Technology, 2001. Memberships: American Ceramic Society; Japan Institute of Metals; Japan Society of Powder and Powder Metallurgy; Japan Society for Technology of Plasticity; Japan Society of Mechanical Engineers. Address: Department of Materials Science and Engineering, School of Engineering, Tohoku University, Aoba-yama 02, Aoba-ku, Sendai 980-8579, Japan. E-mail: czc@material.tohoku.ac.jp

CHENG Fai Chut, b. 15 July 1933, Shanghai, China. Researcher in Electrical Engineering. Education: BSc, Electric Engineering, Tsing Hua University, Beijing, 1957; MPhil, Electric Engineering, University of Hong Kong, 1990. Appointments: Engineer, North East Power Administration, Central Laboratory, Harbin, 1957-73; Technician, Tomoe Electrons Company, Hong Kong, 1973-76; Lecturer, School of Science and Technology, Hong Kong, 1976-80; Part-time Demonstrator, University of Hong Kong, 1980-88; Temporary Teacher, Haking Wong Technical Institute, Hong Kong, 1987-88; Evening Visiting Lecturer, 1988-89, 1990-93, Research Assistant, 1989-92, Teaching Assistant, 1992-93, Honourable Research Associate, 1993-94, Part-time Research Assistant, 1994-95, Hong Kong Polytechnic (now Hong Kong Polytech University); Part-time Research Assistant, 1995-97, Honorary Research Fellow, 1998-99, Honorary Fellow, 2000-2002, Hong Kong Polytech University; Unemployed Researcher, 2003-. Publications: Insulation Thickness Determination of Polymeric Power Cables, 1994; Discussion on Insulation Thickness Determination of Polymeric Power Cables, in journal IEEE Transactions on Dielectrics and Electrical Insulation, 1995. Honours: Decree of Merit Award; Outstanding Achievement Medal, Gold Star Award, Silver Medal, IBC, 1997; Distinguished Leadership Award, 20th Century Achievement Award, Most Admired Man of the Decade, 1997, Man of the Year Commemorative Medal, ABI, 1997; 2000 Millennium Medal of Honour, ABI, 1998; Listed in specialist biographical directories. Memberships: IEEE, US; Hong Kong Institute of Engineers; Institute of Electric Engineers, UK; New York Academy of Sciences. Address: 2-019 Lotus Tower 1, Garden Estate, 297 Ngau Tau Kok Rd, Kowloon, Hong Kong.

CHENG Huai-Rui, b. 10 December 1943, Shaanxi, China. Metallurgist. m. Zhu Yong-Zhen, 1 son, 1 daughter. Education: Bachelor of Engineering, Xian Jiao Tong University, 1964-69;

Dictionary of International Biography

Visiting Scholar, TU Graz, Austria, 1980-81; Visiting Scholar, TU, Wien, Austria, 1981-82. Appointments: Manager, Central Laboratory, Xian Aero-Engine Company, 1983-86; Director, Metallurgic Department, Xian Aero-Engine Company, 1986-99; Professor, Senior Engineer; Honorary Professor, North-West Polytechnical University; Deputy General Manager, Xian Airfoil Technology Co Ltd, 1999-2004. Honours: Outstanding Contribution to Scholar Study Abroad, Ministry of Aviation, 1992; Outstanding Contribution to Development of Science and Technology, State Council, China, 1996; Adviser of Superalloy Committee of China for all life. Memberships: China Aviation Society; China Metal Society. Address: Xujiawan, Beijiao, PO Box 13-197 Xian, China. E-mail: cheng@xat.xa.sn.cn

CHENG Renming, b. 7 June 1955, Beijing, China. Digital Artist. m. Inga Seifert, 1 son, 1 daughter. Education: BA, English Literature, University of Sichuan, China, 1978-82; MA, Mass Communication, University of Oslo, Norway, 1987-93. Appointments: Assistant Manager, Barry F Neal & Associates Pty Ltd, 1982-85; Head of Department, Cables and Optical Fiber Cables, Nokia, China, 1993; Junior Shipbroker, Bassø Offshore A/S, 1995-96; Correspondent, People's Daily, China, 2000; Pioneer of Digital Painting; One of the first artists to start Digitalism. Publications: Digital paintings featured as cover story in Horizon Magazine comparing them with paintings by Andy Warhol, the master of Pop Art; Artist with the largest number of digital paintings, over 1000. Memberships: Royal Photographic Society, UK; American Photographic Museum, USA. Address: Kontrav 7, 1400 Ski, Norway. E-mail: art2001norway@yahoo.no

CHENG Wenyu, b. 28 June 1921, Chengdu, China. Professor of Economics. m. Helen Kuomei Huang, 2 sons, 2 daughters. Education: BA, National Wuhan University, 1943; MA, PhD, University of Chicago, 1950,54; University of Cambridge, England, 1982. Appointments: Professor, Distinguished Professor, Emeritus, Marietta College, 1948-; Professor of Economics, Muskingum College, Ohio, 1987-91; Adjunct Professor, Ohio University, 1992-93; Honorary Professor, Wuhan University, Southwestern University of Finance and Economics. Publications: Author: A Volume of Original Classical Chinese Poems; Translator of poetry and songs from Chinese to English; Economics: A General Survey (in Chinese), 2001. Honours: Award, 50 years of service to Marietta College, 1998; Title: Senior Distinguished Professor of the College. Address: Department of Economics, Marietta College, Marietta, OH 45750, USA.

CHENG Yue, b. 23 August 1958, Wenzhou, Zhejing, China. Molecular Geneticist. m. Yuxing Xiong, 1 daughter. Education: BMed, Anhui Medical College, China, 1982; MMed, Sun Yatsen University of Medical Sciences, China, 1987; PhD, Hong Kong University of Science and Technology, 2002. Appointments: Teaching Assistant, Anhui Medical College, 1982-84; Assistant Professor, Sun Yatsen University of Medical Science, 1989-93; Visiting Assistant Researcher, University of California, Irvine, 1993-95; Visiting Scholar, Hong Kong University of Science and Technology, 1995-2002; Visiting Fellow, Genetics Branch, National Cancer Institute, National Naval Medical Center, USA, 2003-. Publications: Articles in professional scientific journals. Honours: Grant, Sun Yatsen University of Medical Science, 1991; Scholarship, American Chinese Medical Board, 1993; Lifetime Achievement Award, IBC, 2001; Life Fellow, IBA, 2001; Deputy Director General, IBC, 2001; Vice Consul, IBC, 2002; Listed in Who's Who Publications; Fellowship Award, National Institutes of Health, USA, 2003-. Memberships: Chinese Medical Association, 1991-; Hong Kong Professional Teacher's Union, 1998-03; Member, American Association for the Advancement of Science, 2002-; American Association for Cancer Research, 2003-. E-mail: yuecheng@hotmail.com

CHEON Il-Tong, b. 9 February 1936, Seoul, Korea. Professor. m. Yang Ja Lee, 2 sons. Education: BA, Osaka University, Japan, 1961; MS, 1963, PhD, 1966, Kyoto University, Japan. Appointments: Research Fellow, Research Institute for Fundamental Physics, Kyoto University, 1966-67; Professor, Kobe-Gakuin University, 1967-72; IAEA Research Fellow, International Centre for Theoretical Physics, Trieste, 1969; Visiting Professor, Université de Liège, Belgium, 1972-74; Visiting Professor, Technische Universität, Munich, Germany, 1974; Visiting Scientist, McMaster University, Canada, 1974-76; Professor, Yonsei University, Seoul, 1976-2001; Executive Editor, Journal of the Korean Physical Society, 1979-81; Visiting Professor, Rensselaer Polytechnic Institute, Troy, New York, USA, 1980-81; Senior Associate, International Centre for Theoretical Physics, Trieste, Italy, 1981-91; Chairman, Nuclear Physics Division, Korean Physical Society, 1984-86; Advisor, Accelerator Centre, Pohang Institute of Technology, 1991-95; Director, Natural Science Research Institute, Yonsei University, 1991-93; Guest Professor, Institute for Nuclear Study, University of Tokyo, 1994-95; Commissioner, IUPAP, C12, 1999-2001; Executive Vice President, Korean Academy of Science and Technology, 2001-04; Member, Advisory Committee of Democratic Peaceful Unification (Korea), 2003-05. Publications: Over 130 as author or co-author in professional journals; Quantum Mechanics, 1985; Recent Development of Nuclear Study using Electron and Photon Beams, 1995; Short Table of Contents, Coefficients and Mathematical Formulae in Physics, 1998. Honours: Yonsei University Award; Korean Physical Society Award. Memberships: Fellow, Korean Academy of Science and Technology; Korean Physical Society; Physical Society of Japan. Address: Department of Physics, Yonsei University, Seoul 120-749, Korea. E-mail: itcheon@phya.yonsei.ac.kr

CHER (Cherilyn LaPierre Sarkisian), b. 20 May 1946, El Centro, California, USA. Singer; Actress; Entertainer. m. (1) Sonny Bono, 1964, divorced, deceased, 1 daughter, (2) Gregg Allman, 1975, divorced, 1 son. Career: Worked with Sonny Bono in duo Sonny and Cher, 1964-74; Also solo artiste, 1964-; Performances include: Hollywood Bowl, 1966; Newport Pop Festival, 1968; Television includes: Sonny And Cher Comedy Hour, CBS, 1971; Cher, CBS, 1975-76; Sonny And Cher Show, CBS, 1976-77; Vocalist with rock group Black Rose, including US tour supporting Hall & Oates, 1980; Actress, films: Good Times, 1967; Chastity, 1969; Come Back To The Five And Dime, Jimmy Dean Jimmy Dean, 1982; Silkwood, 1984; Mask, 1985; The Witches Of Eastwick, 1987; Moonstruck, 1987; Suspect, 1987; Mermaids, 1989; Love and Understanding; faithful; If these Walls could Talk; Pret-a-Porter; Tea with Mussolini. Recordings include: Singles: with Sonny and Cher: I Got You Babe (Number 1, UK and US), 1975; Baby Don't Go, 1965; Just You, 1965; But You're Mine, 1965; What Now My Love, 1966; Little Man, 1966; The Beat Goes On, 1967; All I Ever Need Is You, 1971; A Cowboy's Work Is Never Done, 1972; Solo hit singles include: All I Really Want To Do, 1965; Bang Bang, 1966; Gypsies Tramps And Thieves (Number 1, US), 1971; The Way Of Love, 1972; Half Breed (Number 1, US), 1973; Dark Lady (Number 1, US), 1974; Take Me Home, 1979; Dead Ringer For Love, duet with Meatloaf, 1982; I Found Someone, 1987; We All Sleep Alone, 1988; After All, duet with Peter Cetera (for film soundtrack Chances Are), 1989; If I Could Turn Back Time, 1989; Jesse James, 1989; Heart Of Stone, 1990; The Shoop Shoop Song (from film soundtrack Mermaids) (Number 1, UK), 1991; Love And Understanding, 1991; Oh No Not My Baby, 1992; Walking In Memphis, 1995; One By One, 1996; Paradise Is Here, 1996; Believe, 1998; Strong Enough, 1999; Albums: with Sonny and Cher: Look At Us, 1965; All I Really Want To Do, 1965; The Wondrous World Of Sonny And Cher, 1966; Sonny And Cher Live, 1972; Solo albums include:

Dictionary of International Biography

All I Really Want To Do, 1965; The Sonny Side Of Cher, 1966; With Love, 1967; Backstage, 1968; Jackson Highway, 1969; Gypsies Tramps And Thieves, 1972; Foxy Lady, 1972; Greatest Hits, 1974; Stars, 1975; I'd Rather Believe In You, 1976; Take Me Home, 1979; I Paralyze, 1984; Cher, 1988; Heart Of Stone, 1989; Love Hurts, 1991; Cher's Greatest Hits 1965-1992, 1992; It's A Man's World, 1995; Believe, 1999; Black Rose, 1999; Living Proof, 2001. Honours include: Oscar, Best Actress, Moonstruck, 1988; Oscar Nomination, Best Supporting Actress, Silkwood, 1984. Address: Reprise Records, 3000 Warner Boulevard, Burbank, CA 19010, USA.

CHERNIGOVSKAYA Tatiana V. Professor. m. 1967, 1 son. Education: Experimental Phonetics, St Petersburg State University, 1970; PhD, Human Physiology, I Sechenov Institute, 1977; DSc. Linguistics and in Human Physiology, I Sechenov Institute, 1993. Appointments: Working for I Sechenov Institute of Russian Academy of Sciences, 1972-; Professor, Department of General Linguistics and Department of Medicine, St Petersburg State University, 1995-; Currently, Professor, Department of General Linguistics and Department of Medicine in St Petersburg State University; Senior Scientist, I Sechenov Institute of Evolutionary Physiology of Russian Academy of Sciences; Lecturer in Psycho and Neurolinguistics, St Petersburg State University, European University, and R Vallenburg Institute of Special Psychology in St Petersburg; Organiser international conferences. Honours: J William Fulbright Foreign Scholarship, 1998; Russian State Scholarship for Outstanding Scientists, 1998-2001; Group leader of several international and national grants. Memberships: Secretary, journal: Sensory Systems; International Neurophysiological Society; International Language Origins Society; International Society of Phonetic Sciences; European Speech Communication Association; International Semiotic Studies Association; Russian National Association of Artificial Intelligence; Russian National Physiological Society; Russian Association of Speech Pathology; Linguistic Society of St Petersburg; Nordic Neurolinguistic Network (NORFA). Address: St Petersburg State University, Philological Faculty, Universitskaya emb, 11, 199034, St Petersburg, Russia.

CHERNYAK Abram Samuilovitch, b. 14 July 1921, Karachev Bryansk Region, Russia. Chemist. m. Bobrova-Chernyak Albina Semenovna. Education: PhD, Chemistry, 1958; DSc, Chemistry, 1972. Appointments: Irkutsk Rare Metals Institute, Russia, 1946-58; Head of Laboratory, Irkutsk Rare Metals Institute, 1959-73; Head of Chair, Irkutsk State University, Russia, 1973-91; Professor, Irkutsk State University, 1991-. Publications: 370 science articles; 5 monographs. Honours: Honoured Science Worker of Russia, 1991. Memberships: Russian Academy of Natural Sciences; New York Academy of Sciences. Address: 63A K Libknekht Street, Apartment 60, 664007 Irkutsk, Russia. E-mail: dekan@chem.isu.ru

CHERNYSHEV Vladimir Konstantinovich, b. 5 June 1927, Serpukhov City, Russia. Scientist. m. Nina Zakharova, 1 son, 1 daughter. Education: Graduate with Honours, Red Diploma, Moscow Engineering Physics Institute, 1949; Candidate of Physical and Mathematical Science, 1970; Doctor of Physical and Mathematical Sciences, 1970; Diploma, Active Member of the International Informatization Academy, 1994. Appointments: Head of Scientific Research Division, 1955, Head of Electro-Physical Department, Deputy Main Designer, 1989, Deputy Scientific Leader, Head of Electro-Physical Department, 1994, Deputy Scientific Leader, Chief Scientist of Electro-Physical Department, 2003-, All-Russian Scientific Research Institute of Experimental Physics (VNIIEF). Publications: Articles in scientific journals as author and co-author include: Magnetic cumulation, 1965; On work of thermonuclear targets with magnetic compression, 1976;

Generation of the Magnetic Flux by Multicascade Capture, 1979; Super power of explosive magnetic energy sources for thermonuclear and physical researches, 1996. Honours: Stalin Prize, 1953; Red Banner Order, 1956; Lenin Order, 1960; Lenin Prize, 1962; USSR State Prize, 1980; Russian Federation Government Prize, 1998; Erwin Marx Award, 2003. Memberships: Council Member, VNIIEF Scientific Technical Council; Council Member, VNIIEF Specialised Dissertation Council; Council Member of one of the sections of VNIIEF Minatom Scientific-Technical Council. Address: Gagarina Street 7-5, 607190 Sarov, Nizhnii Novgorod Region, Russia. E-mail: vcher@elph.vniief.ru

CHEUNG Chiu-Yee, b. 22 April 1954, Hong Kong. Lecturer. m. Tao Li. Education: BA, Jinan University, Peoples Republic of China, 1982; PhD, University of Sydney, 1994. Appointments: Research Assistant, Research Associate, Chinese University of Hong Kong, 1993-95; Lecturer, University of Queensland, Australia, 1995. Publications: Lu Xun: The Chinese 'Gentle' Nietzsche, 2001; Nietzsche in China: An Annotated Bibliography 1904-1992, 1992. Memberships: Chinese Language Society of Hong Kong; Chinese Studies Association of Australia; Oriental Society of Australia. Address: Department of Asian Languages and Studies, University of Queensland, Brisbane, QLD 4072, Australia. E-mail: c.cheung@uq.edu.au Website: www.uq.edu.au/~jaccheun/

CHEUNG James Mo-Oi, b. 25 August 1941, Hong Kong. Pastor; Theological Educator. m. Dorothy, 2 sons. Education: BA, University of Saskatchewan, 1967; MDiv, MA, Trinity Evangelical Divinity School, 1970; THD, Southwestern Baptist Theological Seminary, 1975. Appointments: Assistant Professor, Canadian Theological College, 1973-80; President, The Alliance Bible Seminary, 1980-2001, 2003-; Senior Pastor, Kowloon City Baptist Church, 1984-. Publications: The Modern Charismatic Movement, 1994; Evangelical Movement, 1981; Joshua – Spiritual Wars in the Great Era, 1996; Judges – Salvation in the World of Chaos, 2000; Ecclesiastes, 2002; Co-author, No Crossing Over – Christian Stance on Religious Beliefs, 2004. Honours: Listed in international biographical dictionaries. Address: 206 Argyle St, Kowloon, Hong Kong. E-mail: mocheung@baptist.org.hk

CHEUNG Yiu Ming, b. 19 January 1971, China. Assistant Professor. Education: BSc, 1991-95, M Phil, 1995-97; PhD, 1998-2000. Appointments: Research Associate, 2000; Assistant Professor, The Chinese University of Hong Kong, 2001; Assistant Professor, Hong Kong Baptist University, 2001-. Publications in professional scientific journals include: Dual Multivariate Auto-regressive Modeling in State Space for Temporal Signal Separation (co-author), 2003; An Extended ASLD Trading System to Enhance Portfolio Management (co-author), 2003. Honours: Sir Run Run Shaw Prize, 1992; 2nd Prize, IEEE Undergraduate Paper Contest, Hong Kong Section, 1995; Listed in Who's Who publications and biographical dictionaries. Memberships: IEEE; ACM. ADDRESS: 7/F, Department of Computer Science, Sir Run Run Shaw Building, Hong Kong Baptist University, Kowloon Tong, Kowloon, Hong Kong, China. E-mail: ymc@comp.hkbu.edu.hk Website: http://www.comp.hkbu.edu.hk/~ymc

CHEVRETTON Elfy Brigitte, b. 7 August 1953, Lyon, France. Ear, Nose and Throat Surgeon. Education: BSc, Honours, Pharmacology, King's College, University of London, 1974; MB BS, St George's Hospital Medical School, University of London, 1977; LRCP MRCS, London Conjoint, 1978; FRCS (England) Otolaryngology, 1985. Appointments: General Medical Training, 1978-81; Senior House Officer, St George's Hospital, London, 1981-82; Registrar (Rotating): Bristol Royal Infirmary, Southmead Hospital, Bristol, 1982-85; Temporary Senior Registrar (Rotating),

Royal Bristol Infirmary, Royal United Hospital, Bath, 1985-86; Lecturer and Honorary Registrar, The Royal London Hospital and Research Assistant, Department of Experimental Pathology, St Mary's Hospital Medical School, 1983-90; Senior Registrar (Rotating), The Royal London Hospital, 1990-91, Department of Head and Neck Surgery, The Royal Marsden Hospital, London, 1991, Northwick Park Hospital, 1991-92; Department of Paediatric Otolaryngology, The Hospital for Sick Children, 1992, Northwick Park Hospital, 1992-93; Consultant ENT Surgeon, Guy's and St Thomas' Hospital Trust, 1993-; Honorary Senior Lecturer, Guy's and St Thomas' Medical and Dental School, 1996-. Publications: 19 articles published in medical journals as first author and co-author include most recently: Otological trauma resulting from the Soho Nail Bomb in London, April 1999, 2003; Degloving of the inferior turbinates: a pilot study to assess the effectiveness of a new technique in turbinate reduction, 2003; 3 book chapters, numerous reviews and abstracts; 18 papers presented at conferences and seminars. Honours include: Zimmer Fellowship, 1991; MS, University of London, 1990. Memberships: British Medical Association; Royal Society of Medicine; Hospital Consultants and Specialists Association; British Association of Otolaryngologists – Head and Neck Surgeons; British Association of Head and Neck Oncologists. Address: Department of ENT Surgery, Guy's and St Thomas' Hospitals NHS Trust, St Thomas Street, London SE1 9RT, England.

CHEY William Yoon, b. 21 January 1930, Kijang, Korea. Physician. m. Fan K Tang, 2 sons, 2 daughters. Education: MSc (Med), 1952, DSc (Med), 1966, University of Pennsyvlania, School of Medicine, USA; MD, Seoul National University, College of Medicine, Seoul, 1953. Appointments: Assistant Professor, Associate Professor of Medicine, Temple University Medical Center, 1965-71; Professor of Medicine University of Rochester, School of Medicine and Dentistry, 1991-2000; Director, Isaac Gordon Center for Digestive Disease and Nutrition, 1991-92; Director, Konar Center for Digestive and Liver Diseases, University of Rochester Mecdical Center. Publications: 300 scientific articles in refereed medical journals and chapters in text books. Honours: Board of Governors Award for Best Clinical Research, 2000. Memberships: American Physiological Society; American Gastroenterological Association; American Coll of Gastroenterology; American Pancreatic Association. Address: 133 Crescent Hill Road, Pittsford, NY 14534, USA. E-mail: williamchey@ridds.org

CHEYNE Alexander Campbell, b. 1 June 1924, Errol, Perthshire, Scotland. Church of Scotland Minister; University Professor. Education: MA, 1st class honours, History, 1946, BD, Distinction, Ecclesiastical History, 1956, University of Edinburgh; Oriel College, Oxford, 1948-50; Blitt, Oxon; University of Basel, Switzerland, 1956-57. Appointments: Instructor, Army School of Education, 1948-50; Assistant Lecturer in History, 1950-51, Lecturer in History, 1951-53, University of Glasgow; Lecturer in Ecclesiastical History, University, 1958-64, Professor of Ecclesiastical History, 1964-86, Principal, 1984-86, New College, University of Edinburgh. Publications: The Transforming of the Kirk: Victorian Scotland's Religious Revolution, 1983; Editor, The Practical and the Pious: Essays on Thomas Chalkier 1780-1847, 1985; The Ten Years' Conflict and the Disruption, 1993; Studies in Scottish Christianity, 1999; Contributions to numerous volumes and journals, including Dictionary of Scottish Church History and Theology, 1993 and Oxford Dictionary of the Christian Church, 1997. Honours: Visiting Professor, Wooster College, Ohio, USA, 1973; Chalmers Lecturer, Glasgow and Aberdeen, 1976-80; Visiting Fellow, Wolfson College, Cambridge, 1979; Burns Lecturer, Knox College, Dunedin, New Zealand, 1980; Honorary D Litt, Memorial University, Newfoundland, 1983; President, Scottish Church History Society, 1986-89; Honorary President,

Scottish Church History Society, 1998-; Festschrift: S J Brown and G Newlands (editors), Scottish Christianity in the Modern World: In Honour of A C Cheyne, 2000. Memberships: Scottish Church History Society; Ecclesiastical History Society; Presbytery of Edinburgh, Moderator, 1987-88. Address: 12 Crossland Crescent, Peebles, EH45 8LF, Scotland.

CHI Chi-Hung, b. 7 April 1961, Hong Kong. Professor. m. Yang Hong, 1 son. Education: BSc, University of Wisconsin-Madison, 1984; PhD, Purdue University, 1989. Appointments: Senior Member, Research Staff, Philips Laboratories, USA, 1988-91; Advisory Engineer, IBM Poughkeepsie, USA, 1991-93; Lecturer, Department of Computer Science, Chinese University of Hong Kong, 1993-96; Senior Lecturer, Associate Professor, School of Computing National University of Singapore, 1996-. Publications: Articles in professional journals. Honours: Listed in national and international biographical dictionaries; 7 awards from Phillips Laboratories; 6 US patents. Address: 12 Yew Siang Road, #03-07, Fragrance Court, Singapore 117752. E-mail: chich@comp.nus.edu.sg

CHIA Jean-San, b. 18 July 1956, Taipei, Taiwan. Doctor; Professor. m. Chen Chin-Pei, 2 sons. Education: DDS, Dentistry, 1980; PhD, Microbiology, 1993. Appointments: Attending Physician, Department of Dentistry, National Taiwan University Hospital, 2002; Professor, Department of Microbiology, College of Medicine, National Taiwan University, 1994-. Publications: Numerous in scientific journals published by the American Society for Microbiology. Memberships: International Association for Dental Research; American Society for Microbiology. Address: No 1, Jen-Ai Road, 1st Section, Department of Microbiology, College of Medicine, National Taiwan University, Taipei, Taiwan, ROC. E-mail: chiajs@ha.mc.ntu.edu.tw

CHIANG Chi, b. 3 July 1960, Taipei, Taiwan. Scholar. m. Shi-Fang Yuan, 1 son, 2 daughters. Education: Bachelor, National Taiwan University, 1982; Master, Ohio State University, Columbus Ohio, USA, 1988; PhD, University of Texas at Austin, Texas, USA, 1991. Appointments: Visiting Assistant Professor, Tulane University, New Orleans, Louisiana, USA, 1991-92; Associate Professor, 1992-2000, Professor, 2000-, National Chiao Tung University, Hsinchu, Taiwan. Publications: Papers published in journals including: Naval Research Logistics, 1994, 1998; European Journal of Operational Research, 1996, 1998, 2003; Journal of the Operational Research Society, 1996, 2002; Computers and Operations Research, 2001; International Journal of Production Economics, 2001. Honour: Class A Award, National Science Council, Taiwan, 1994-2000. Memberships: International Society for Inventory Research; Chinese Management Association. Address: 6F-1, 25 Chien-Chung 1 Road, Hsinchu, Taiwan 300, Republic of China. E-mail: cchiang@mail.nctu.edu.tw

CHIBA Masakatsu, b. 28 January 1957, Ishinomaki, Japan. Professor. m. 1 son, 1 daughter. Education: DEng, Graduate School, Tohoku University, 1985. Appointment: Professor, Department of Mechanical Engineering, Iwate University, 1990-. Publications: Several articles to professional journals. Memberships: Japan Society of Mechanical Engineers; Japan Society of Aeronautical and Space Sciences; Japan Society of Microgravity Application. Address: 1-4-1 Kita-Matsuzono, Morioka 020-0105, Japan.

CHIBA Shuji, b. 25 April 1942, Takefu, Japan. Linguist. m. Hisae Hayashi, 2 daughters. Education: BA, 1965, MA, 1968, Tokyo University of Education. Appointments: Lecturer, Otsuma Women's University, Tokyo, 1970-72; Lecturer, Tsuda College, Tokyo, 1972-73, Associate Professor, 1973-84, Professor 1984-; Director of Audio-Visual Center, Tsuda College, 1987-89, 1991-95. Publications: Present Subjunctives in Present-Day English,

1987; Co-editor, A Festschrift for Masatomo Ukaji, 1991; A Festschrift for Toshio Nakao, 1994; A Festschrift for Akira Ota, 1997; A Festschrift for Masaru Kajita, 2003. Honour: Ichikawa Award, 1987. Memberships: English Linguistics Society of Japan; Japan Cognitive Sciences Society; English Literary Society of Japan; Japan Association of College English Teachers; Institute for Research in Language Teaching; Linguistics Society of America; New York Academy of Sciences; Japan Second Language Association. Address: 3-13-19 Minamisawa, Higashi-Kurume-shi, 203-0023 Tokyo, Japan.

CHICHETTO James William, b. 5 June 1941, Boston, Massachusetts, USA. Professor; Priest. Education: BA, Stonehill College, 1964; MA, Holy Cross College, 1968; MA, Wesleyan University, 1978. Appointments: Ordained Priest, Congregation of Holy Cross, 1968; Educator, Missionary, Peru, South America, 1968-72; Associate Editor, Gargoyle Magazine, 1974-80; Editor, 1982-87, Artist, 1990-, The Connecticut Poetry Review; Professor of Writing, Stonehill College, North Easton, Massachusetts, 1982-. Publications: Poems, 1975; Dialogue: Emily Dickinson and Christopher Cauldwell, 1978; Stones: A Litany, 1980; Gilgamesh and Other Poems, 1983; Victims, 1987; Homage to Father Edward Sorin, 1992, 1998; Dream of Norumbega, 2000. Contributions to: Boston Phoenix; Colorado Review; Boston Globe; The Manhattan Review; The Patterson Review; The Connecticut Poetry Review; America; Others. Honours: Book Grant, National Endowment for the Arts, 1980, 1983; Sri Chinmoy Poetry Award, 1984. Membership: Connecticut Literary Forum, 1985-. Address: c/o Stonehill College, North Easton, MA 02357, USA.

CHICHILNISKY Graciela, b. 27 March 1946, Buenos Aires, Argentina. Mathematician; Economist; Writer. 1 son, 1 daughter. Education: Massachusetts Institute of Technology, 1967-68; MA, 1970, PhD, 1971,76, University of California at Berkeley. Appointments: Visiting Professor, Stanford University, 1993-94; Salinbemi Chair, Universita de Siena, Italy, 1994-95; Visiting Professor, University of Paris, 1996; Visiting Professor, Deakin University, 1996; Professor, Columbia University, 1980-; Director, Columbia Center for Risk Management, 1998-; Professor of Mathematics and Economics, UNESCO Chair, Columbia University, 1995-; Director, Program on Information and Resources, 1994-; Lead Author, Intergovernmental Panel on Climate Change, 1999. Publications: Books Include, Catastrophe or New Society? A Latin American World Model; The Evolving International Economy; Sustainability, Dynamics and Uncertainty; Mathematical Economics; Topology and Markets; Markets with Endogenous Uncertainty: Equity and Efficiency; Book reviews; Papers. Honours: Numerous including, Leif Johansen Award, 1995; Siena Fellowship. Memberships: American Mathematical Society; American Economic Association; American Statistical Association. Address: 629 Mathematics, Columbia University, 116th And Broadway, NY 10027, USA. E-mail: gc9@columbia.edu

CHIEN Fredrick Fu, b. 17 February 1935, Peiping, China. President. m. Julie Tien, 1 son, 1 daughter. Education: BA National Taiwan University, 1956; MA, 1959, PhD, 1962, Yale University; Honorary LLD, Sung Kyun Kwan University, Korea, 1972, Caribbean American University, 1988, Boston University, 1997, Idaho State University, 1997; Honorary DLitt, Wilson College, 1993; Honorary Degree in Public Service, Florida International University, 1994. Appointments: Director, North American Affairs, Ministry of Foreign Affairs, 1969-72; Director General, Government Information Office, 1972-75; Administrative Vice Minister, 1975-79, Political Vice Minister, 1979-82, Ministry of Foreign Affairs; US Representative, CCNAA, 1983-88; Minister of State, Chairman, Council for Economic Planning and Development, Executive Yuan, 1988-90; Minister, Ministry of

Foreign Affairs, 1990-96; Speaker, National Assembly, 1996-98; President, Control Yuan, Republic of China, 1999-. Publications: 5 books. Honours: 27 medals from Republic of China, Korea, Vietnam, Paraguay, Dominican Republic, Honduras, El Salvador, Haiti, South Africa, Kingdom of Swaziland and others. Address: Control Yuan, 2 Chung-Hsiao E Road, Sec 1, Taipei, Taiwan, Republic of China.

CHIKUDATE Nobuyuki, b. 10 March 1963, Yamagata, Japan. Professor of Management Studies. Education: MA, Arizona State University, 1987; PhD, State University of New York, Buffalo, New York, 1990; Postdoctoral Fellow, Johns Hopkins University, 1991. Appointments: Adjunct Faculty, Tokyo University of Foreign Studies, Japan, 1992; Assistant Professor, Asia University, Japan, 1993; Associate Professor, Graduate School of Social Sciences, Hiroshima University, Japan, 2003-. Publications: Articles in professional journals including: Management International Review, 1991, 1995, 1997; Journal of Applied Behavioural Science, 1999; Journal of Management Studies, 1999, 2002; Journal of Business Ethics, 2000, 2002. Honours: Outstanding Reviewer Awards, MRD Division Academy of Management, 1998, 2001. Membership: Academy of Management. Address: Graduate School of Social Sciences, Hiroshima University, Higashi senda machi 1-1-89, Naka-ward, Hiroshima City, Hiroshima 730-0053 Japan. E-mail: cikudate@mgt.hiroshima-u.ac.jp

CHILD Mark Sheard, b. 17 August 1937, Stockton-on-Tees, England. University Professor. m. Daphne Hall, 1 son, 2 daughters. Education: BA (Cantab) Chemistry 1st class, 1959, PhD (Cantab), Theoretical Chemistry, 1962, Clare College, Cambridge. Appointments: Research Fellow, Lawrence Radiation Laboratory, University of California, Berkeley, USA, 1962-63; Lecturer, Theoretical Chemistry, University of Glasgow, 1963-66; Lecturer, Theoretical Chemistry, 1966-89, Aldrachian Praelector in Chemistry, 1989-92, Professor, Chemical Dynamics, 1992-94, Coulson Professor of Theoretical Chemistry, 1994-, University of Oxford; Visiting Fellow, University of Wisconsin, Madison, USA, 1963; Visiting Professor, Institute of Advanced Studies, Hebrew University of Jerusalem, 1978-79; Visiting Professor, University of Colorado, USA, 1988-89; Visiting Professor, Université de Paris-Sud, 1989; Visiting Professor, Joseph Fourier University, Grenoble, 1996. Publications: Author and Co-author of over 150 articles in scientific journals; Books: Molecular Collision Theory, 1974, reissued, 1996; Semiclassical mechanisms with molecular applications, 1991. Honour: Fellow of the Royal Society; William Draper Harkins Lecture, University of Chicago, 1985; Tilden Lecture, Royal Society of Chemistry, 1987-87; Condon Lecture, University of Colorado, 1987-88. Memberships: Royal Society; Royal Society of Chemistry

CHIN Takaaki, b. 4 October 1960, Kobe, Japan. Medical Doctor. m. K. Hayashi, 1 daughter. Education: Bachelor of Medicine, Tokushima University, Tokushima, Japan, 1986; Medical Diplomate, 1986; PhD, Kobe University. Appointments: Resident, University Hospital, Kobe, Japan, 1986-87; Doctor Course, Kobe University, Kobe, Japan, 1987-91; Research Fellow, McGill University, Montreal, Canada, 1990-92; Head Physician, Hyogo Rehabilitation Centre, Kobe, Japan, 1992-. Publications: Articles in medical journals including: Developmental Biology, 1996; Prosthetics and Orthotics International, 1997, 1999, 2002; Journal of Rehabilitation Research and Development, 2001; American Journal of Physical Medicine and rehabilitation, 2002, 2003. Honour: Iida Prize, Japanese Society of Prosthetics and Orthotics, 2001. Memberships: Japanese Orthopaedic Association; Japanese Association of Rehabilitation Medicine; Councillor, 1998-, Japanese Society of Prosthetics and Orthotics; Vice-President, 2003-, Japan Branch, International Society for Prosthetics and

Orthotics; International Society of Orthopaedic Surgery and Traumatology. Address: Hyogo Rehabilitation Centre, 1070 Akebono-Cho, Nishi-Ku, Kobe, 651-2181 Japan. E-mail: t-chin@pure.co.jp

CHIRAC Jacques René, b. 29 November 1932, Paris, France. Politician. m. Bernadette Chodron de Courcel, 1956, 2 children. Education: Lycée Carnot; Lycée Louis-le-Grand, Paris; Institute of Political Science, Paris; Harvard University Summer School, USA. Appointments: Military Service, Algeria; Auditor, Cour des Comptes, 1959-62; Special Assistant, Government Secretariat General, 1962 Counsellor, Cour des Comptes, 1965-94; Secretary of State for Employment Problems, 1967-68; Secretary of State for Economy and Finance, 1968-71; Minister for Parliamentary Relations, 1971-72, for Agriculture and Rural Development, 1972-74, of the Interior, 1974; Prime Minister of France, 1974-76, 1986-88; Secretary General, Union des Démocrates pour la République (UDR), 1975, Honorary Secretary General, 1975-76; President, Rassemblement pour la République (formerly UDR), 1976-94, Honorary Secretary General, 1977-80; Mayor of Paris, 1977-95; President of France, 1995-2002; Re-elected President of France, 2002-. Publications: Discours pour la France a l'heure du choix; La lueur de l'espérance: Réflexion du soir pour le matin, 1978; Une Nouvelle France, Reflexion 1, 1994; La France pour tous, 1995. Honours include: Prix Louis Michel, 1986; Grand-Croix de la Légion d'Honneur; Grand Croix de l'Ordre National du Mérite; Chevalier du Mérite. Address: Palais de l'Eysée, 55-57 rue du Faubourg Saint-Honoré, 75008 Paris, France.

CHISHOLM Alison (Fiona Williams), b. 25 July 1952, Liverpool, England. Teacher, Writer, Poet. m. Malcolm Chisholm, 10 July 1971, 2 daughters. Education: ATCL, 1969; FLCM, 1971; LLAM, 1973. Appointments: Teacher, Oxford Academy of Speech and Drama, Middlesbrough; Principal, Richmond Academy of Speech, Southport; Poetry and Creative Writing Tutor, Southport College; Poetry Consultant, BBC Radio Merseyside, 1991-1996. Publications: Alone No More (co-author), 1977; Flying Free, 1985; The Need for Unicorns, 1987; Single Return, 1988; Paper Birds, 1990; The Craft of Writing Poetry, 1992; A Practical Poetry Course, 1994; How to Write 5-Minute Features, 1996; Daring the Slipstream, 1997; How to Write About Yourself (co-author), 1999; Writing Competitions: The way to win (co-author), 2001. Contributions to: Envoi; Outposts; Doors; Orbis; Smoke; Staple; Acumen; Poetry Now; Poetry Nottingham Int; The Formalist. Others; Various anthologies and children's anthologies; BBC Radio Merseyside and Network Northwest; Articles on poetry in numerous writers' magazines. Honours: Prizes, Mary Wilkins Memorial Competition (twice), Success Open, Grey Friars, Rhyme International, Lace, KQBX, Chester, Banstead, Lake Aske, Envoi, Julia Cairns, Ouse Valley, Sefton, New Prospects and Yorkshire Competitions, and US competitions in various categories of World Order of Narrative and Formalist Poets and NFSPS, Ohio Poetry Day Competitions. Memberships: Society of Women Writers and Journalists; Poetry Society; Verse Writers' Guild of Ohio; Association of Christian Writers; Southport Writers' Circle; Society of Authors. Address: 53 Richmond Road, Birkdale, Southport, Merseyside PR8 4SB, England.

CHISSELL Joan Olive, b. 22 May 1919, Cromer, Norfolk, England. Musicologist. Education: ARCM, GRSM, Royal College of Music, 1937-42. Appointments: Piano Teacher, Royal College of Music Junior Department, 1942-53; Lecturer, Extra-Mural Departments, Oxford and London Universities, 1942-48; Broadcaster, BBC, 1943-; Assistant Music Critic, The Times, 1948-79; Reviewer, The Gramophone, 1968-; Jury Member, International Piano Competitions, Milan, Leeds, Zwickau, Budapest, Sydney, Newport and Dublin. Publications: Robert Schumann, 1948; Chopin, 1965; Schumann's Piano Music, 1972; Brahms, 1977; Clara Schumann: A Dedicated Spirit, 1983. Contributions to: A Companion to the Concerto, 1988; Numerous journals and magazines. Honour: City of Zwickau Robert Schumann Prize, 1991. Memberships: Critics Circle; Royal College of Music Society; Royal Life Boat Society. Address: Flat D, 7 Abbey Road, St Johns Wood, London NW8 9AA, England.

CHITESCU Ion, b. 19 July 1947, Bucharest, Romania. Professor of Mathematics. m. Rodica Chitescu, 2 daughters. Education: Licencié, Maths, 1970, PhD, Maths, 1975, University of Bucharest. Appointments: Assistant Professor, 1970-80, Lecturer, 1980-91, Associate Professor, 1991-2000, Professor, 2000-, Faculty of Mathematics, University of Bucharest. Publications: Main books: Monograph: Function Spaces; Mathematical Analysis Dictionary (in collaboration); Measure Theory (in collaboration); 40 papers (research); Fields of interest: Vector measures and integration; Function Spaces; Random Sequences; Probability and Statistics; Optimization; Fractal Theory. Honours: Romanian National Academy Prize, for "Function Spaces", 1985. Memberships: American Mathematical Society; Mathematical Reviews Referee; Mathematical Reports Advisory Board. Address: Str Henri Coanda 44, Sector 1, cod 71119, Bucharest, Romania.

CHIU Dirk M, b. Malaysia. Engineering Educator. m. Lee H Lim, 1 son, 1 daughter. Education: BSc, Engineering, London, 1969; MSc, Edinburgh, 1976; PhD, Manchester, 1978. Appointments: Telecom Engineer, STC; Electronic Design Engineer, Control Systems Ltd; Electronic Senior Engineer, London University; Electronic Lecturer, Singapore Polytechnic; Microelectronic Lecturer, Paisley University; Course Co-ordinator in Electronics, Victoria University of Technology; Visiting Professor, Nankai University, and Dong Hwa University; Associate Professor, UPM. Publications: Electronic Science and Education (book); Over 100 articles on electronic sciences; Semiconductor Electronics; Power Electronics; Microelectronics; Engineering Education. Honours: Taiwan SRC Research Professorship, 2000. Memberships: MIEE; CEng; PEng. Address: 71 Long Valley Way, Doncaster East, Victoria 3109, Australia.

CHO Moon-Boo, b. 13 December 1935, Pukcheju, Republic of Korea. Academic Administrator. m. Hee-Zah Park, 2 sons, 4 daughters. Education: BA, Public Administration, Seoul National University, 1959; PhD, Politics, Seikei University, Japan, 1993. Appointments: Professor, Cheju National University, 1965-97; Visiting Researcher, Law College, Tokyo University, 1980-83; Visiting Scholar, Yale Law School, 1991-92; Dean, College of Social Science, 1985-88; Dean for Academic Affairs, 1998-99; Dean, Graduate School, Public Administration, 1993-95; President, Cheju National University, 1997-2001. Publications: Korean Local Government, 1995; The Structure and Function of Budget Decision Process, 1997. Honours: Presidential Medal, Korea, 1979; Certificate of Meritorious Service, Korean Self-Government, 1995, 1996; Best Decoration in the Decoration of Civil Servants, 2001. Memberships: Cheju Island Education Committee, 1979-80; Vice Chief, Cheju Election Committee, 1984-90; Chief, Regional Consulting Subcommittee, Cheju Provincial Office, 1986-88; Public Welfare Delegate, Cheju Labour Relation Board, 1979-87; Member, Rebuilding Korea, 1998; Member, Director, Korean Association for Public Administration, 1979-; Member, Director, Vice Chief, Korean Association for Public Administrative Law, 1979-; Director, Vice Chief, Korean Association for Local Autonomy, 1989-. Address: 113-7 Il-do-2-dong, Dae-Yoo, Dae-lim Apt 302-501, Cheju-shi, Cheju-do 690-831, Republic of Korea. E-mail: mbc3422@kornet.net

Dictionary of International Biography

CHO Yeol Je, b. 11 December 1952, Kimhae, Kyungnam, Korea. Professor. m. In Suk Kang, 1 son, 1 daughter. Education: BS, 1976, MS, 1979, PhD, 1984, Department of Mathematics, Pusan National University, Korea; Postdoctoral Studies, Department of Mathematics, St Louis University, USA, 1987-88. Appointments: Assistant, Full-Time Instructor, Assistant Professor, Associate Professor, 1979-92, Full Professor, 1992-, Department of Mathematics Education, College of Education: Gyeongsang National University, Korea; Organiser: The International Conference on Nonlinear Functions Analysis Applications, 2000-; Editor of scientific journals including: Journal of Concrete and Applied Mathematics; Nonlinear Analysis Forum; Nonlinear Functions Analysis Applications; PanAmerican Mathematical Journal; Natural and Physical Science. Publications: Books: Theory of 2-Inner Product Spaces, 2001; Geometry of Linear 2-Normed Spaces, 2001; Non-Linear Operator Theory in PM-Spaces, 2001; Iterative Methods for Nonlinear Operator Equations, 2002; 240 papers published in scientific journals. Memberships: The Korean Mathematical Society; The American Mathematical Society; The Japan Mathematical Society; INFA; RGMIA. Address: Department of Mathematics Education, College of Education, Gyeongsang National University, Chinju 660-1701, Korea. E-mail: yjcho@nongae.gsnu.ac.kr

CHO Young-Keol, b. 12 June 1962, Youngyang, Korea. Microbiologist (HIV/AIDS). m. Myunghi Kwon, 2 sons. Education: MD, 1987, MS, 1989, PhD, 1993, Hanyang University, Korea. Appointments: Teaching Assistant, Hanyang University, 1987-90; Public Health Doctor, Korean NIH, 1990-93; Instructor, Associate Professor, 1993-; Visiting Assistant Professor, Harvard Medical School, USA, 1997-98. Publications: Articles as corresponding author in scientific journals including: AIDS Research and Human Retroviruses, 2001, 2003; International Immuno-pharmacology 2001; Journal of Clinical Microbiology, 2002. Honour: Award for "Good Paper in Science", Korean Federation of Science and Technology Societies, 2002. Memberships: International AIDS Society; American Society of Microbiology; Korean Society of Ginseng; Korean Society of Virology; Korean Society for Microbiology; Member, Editorial Board, Journal of Bacteriology and Virology. Address: 1-103 Hyosung Villa, Sangil-dong, Kangdong, Seoul, Korea. E-mail: ykcho2@amc.seoul.kr

CHO Zang-Hee, b. 15 July 1936, Seoul, Korea. Professor of Radiological Sciences (Physics). m. Jung-suk Cho, 3 daughters. Education: MSc, BSc, Seoul University, 1960-62; PhD, Uppsala University, 1966; FilD, Stockholm University, 1972. Appointments: Professor, University of California at Irvine, Columbia University, University of California at Los Angeles, Stockholm University. Publications: 200 scientific peer reviewed publications and books authored. Memberships: US National Academy of Sciences, Institute of Medicine; Korean National Academy of Sciences. Address: 29 Harbour Pointe Drive, Corona Del Mar, CA 92625-1333, USA.

CHODES John Jay, b. 23 February 1939, New York, New York, USA. Writer; Dramatist. Education: BA, Hunter College, City University of New York, 1963; Commercial Photography Certificate, Germain School of Photography, 1965. Appointments: Technical Advisor to Dustin Hoffman, Paramount Pictures Film Marathon Man. Publications: The Myth of America's Military Power, 1972; Corbitt, 1973; Bruce Jenner, 1977; Plays: Avenue A Anthology, 1969; Molineaux, 1979; Frederick Two, 1985; The Longboat, 1987; Molineaux (as Musical), 1995; A Howling Wilderness, 2001; Dante's Cantos Concert, 2002. Contributions to: 110 articles published; 90 photographs published. Honours: Journalistic Excellence Award, 1974; Outstanding Service Award,

1988. Memberships: Dramatists Guild; Professors World Peace Academy; Road Runners Club of New York; Libertarian Party of New York; League of the South. Address: 411 East 10th Street, 22G, New York, NY 10009, USA.

CHOI Byung-Ho, b. 9 January 1957, Taegu, Korea. Professor. m. Hyun-Mi Chong, 1 son. Education: Diploma, 1982, Master, 1985, Yonsei University, Seoul, Korea; PhD, Albert-Ludwig University, Freiburg, Germany, 1991. Appointments: Resident, Yonsei University Hospital, 1982-85; Visiting Professor, Albert-Ludwig University, Freiburg, Germany, 1988-91; Professor, Yonsei University, Seoul, Korea, 1992-. Memberships: Korean Association of Oral and Maxillofacial Surgeons, Editor; International Association of Oral and Maxillofacial Surgeons. Address: Wonju Christian Hospital, Ilsan-Dong, Kangwon-Do, Wonju, Republic of Korea. E-mail: choibh@wonju.yonse.ac.kr

CHOI Dong Ryong, b. 15 February 1945, Tokyo, Japan. Consulting Geologist. m. Chong-Ih Kim, 1 son, 1 daughter. Education: Doctor of Science, Hokkaido University, Japan, 1972. Appointments: Chief Engineer, Kokusai Kogyo Co Ltd, Tokyo, Japan, 1973-77; Postdoctoral Fellow, Assistant Professor, University of Miami, 1977-85; Senior Research Scientist, Australian Geological Survey Organization, 1985-89; Consulting Geologist, Petroleum Exploration, 1989-. Publications: Surge Tectonics and Paleolands in the Pacific; Numerous contributions to professional journals. Honours: Research funds from US National Science Foundation; Listed in 500 Leaders of Influence; Invited Lectures: Japan National Oil Corporation and many others. Memberships: American Association of Petroleum Geology; Geological Society of Australia. Address: 6 Mann Place, Higgins, ACT 2615, Australia.

CHOI Jae Mok, b. 13 May 1961, Gyongbuk, Korea. Professor. m. Soon-Ja Shin, 1 son, 1 daughter. Education: BA, Yeungnam University, Korea, 1985; MA, 1988, PhD, 1991, Tsukuba University, Japan. Appointments: Lecturer, 1991-92, Assistant Professor, 1993-96, Associate Professor, 1997-2001, Professor, 2002-, Department of Philosophy, Yeungnam University. Publications: The Development of Yangming Xue in East Asia, 1996; Writing as Therapy and Discipline, 2003; Writing and Philosophy of 'Nup', 2003; Cross Over Humanities, 2003. Memberships: Korean Philosophical Association; Korean Philosophical Society; The New Korean Philosophical Association. Address: Philosophy Department, College of Liberal Arts, Yeungnam University, 214-1 Daedong, Gyongsan, Gyongbuk 712-749, Korea. E-mail: choijm@yumatl.ac.kr

CHOI Junho, b. 9 June 1969, Seoul, Korea. Researcher. m. Milim Kim. Education: MSc, Metallurgical Engineering, Korea University, Korea, 1996; PhD, Mechanical Engineering, The University of Tokyo, Japan, 2000. Appointments: Researcher, Samsung Motors Inc, Gyeonggi, Korea, 1996-97; Postdoctoral Researcher, National Institute of Advanced Industrial Science and Technology, Tsukuba, Japan, 2000-2003; Researcher, National Institute of Advanced Industrial Science and Technology, Nagoya, Japan. Publications: Articles in scientific journals: Self-assembled monolayers formation on the magnetic harddisk surface and friction measurements, 2002; Nanorheological properties of the PFPE nanomeniscus bridge in the separation range of 10-1000 nm, 2003. Honours: Postdoctoral Fellowship for Foreign Researchers, Japan Society for the Promotion of Science, 2002; Listed in Who's Who publications and biographical dictionaries. Membership: Japanese Society of Tribologists. Address: 702, 18-9 Koroku-cho, Moriyama-ku, Nagoya 463-0054, Japan. E-mail: junho.choi@aist.go.jp

Dictionary of International Biography

CHOI Laisheung, b. 3 May 1961, Shishi City, Quanzhou, Fujian Province, China. Poet; Author. Education: Baptist Institute of Commerce and Careers, 1982; Cambridge Institute of Commerce, 1983; Open University of Hong Kong, 1998. Appointments: Editor-in-Chief, The Chinese Poetry International Quarterly, The Hong Kong Poetry Bimonthly, Chinese Poetry Journal in the World; Vice-Editor-in-Chief, Hong Kong Literary Newspaper; Assistant of the Editor-in-Chief, Chinese Prosaic Poems in Hong Kong; Honorary Head, Chinese Poetry Journal in the World; Honorary Editor-in-Chief, Literature and Art Newspaper, Hong Kong; Honorary President, Contemporary Writers Association; Standing Vice-Head, Council of Hong Kong Literary Promotion; Executive Supervisor, Hong Kong Association of Chinese Culture; Honorary Adviser and Special Contributor to Coconut Literary Society, Philippines. Publications: Author, Emotions in the Starlight, 2001; Poems, prosaic poems, informal essays, prose writings and critical writings published in national and international newspapers and journals and collections of selected works; Contributions to: Poetry; Poetry Monthly; Peoples Daily Newspaper; The Chinese Commercial News; World Newspaper; Sina*Fil Daily; Xiamen Daily; South East Economy & Trade Times; United Daily News; Overseas Chinese News of Fujian. Honours: Literary First Prizes, 1998, 1999, 2000, 2002; Second Prize, 2001; Excellent Poetry Award, China. Membership: Standing Vice-Head, Council for Hong Kong Literary Promotion. Address: PO Box 73464, Kowloon Central Post Office, Kowloon, Hong Kong, China.

CHOI Yong Suk, b. 30 July 1969, Busan, Korea. Professor. m. Seong-min Kim, 1 son. Education: BA, 1993, MS, 1995, PhD, 2000, Computer Science, Seoul National University. Appointments: Researcher, Research Institute of Advanced Computer Technology, Seoul, 1995-2000; Senior Researcher, Samsung Electronics, Seoul, 2000; Professor, Hanyang University, Seoul, 2000-03. Publications: Articles in professional journals. Honours: Korea Research Foundation Grants for New Young Researchers. Memberships: IEEE, ACM, KISS, KACE. Address: Department of Computer Science Education, Hanyang University, Seongdong-ku, Seoul 133-791, Korea. E-mail: cys@hanyang.ac.kr Website: http://comedu.hanyang.ac.kr/~cys

CHOMSKY (Avram) Noam, b. 7 December 1928, Philadelphia, Pennsylvania, USA. Linguist; Philosopher; Professor; Author. m. Carol Doris Schatz, 24 December 1949, 1 son, 2 daughters. Education: BA, 1949, MA, 1951, PhD, 1955, University of Pennsylvania. Appointments: Assistant Professor, 1955-58, Associate Professor, 1958-61, Professor of Modern Languages, 1961-66, Ferrari P Ward Professor of Modern Languages and Linguistics, 1966-76, Institute Professor, 1976-, Massachusetts Institute of Technology; Visiting Professor, Columbia University, 1957-58; National Science Foundation Fellow, Institute for Advanced Study, Princeton, New Jersey, 1958-59; Resident Fellow, Harvard Cognitive Studies Center, 1964-65; Linguistics Society of America Professor, University of California at Los Angeles, 1966; Beckman Professor, University of California at Berkeley, 1966-67; John Locke Lecturer, Oxford University, 1969; Shearman Lecturer, University College, London, 1969; Bertrand Russell Memorial Lecturer, Cambridge University, 1971; Nehru Memorial Lecturer, University of New Delhi, 1972; Whidden Lecturer, McMaster University, 1975; Huizinga Memorial Lecturer, University of Leiden, 1977; Woodbridge Lecturer, Columbia University, 1978; Kant Lecturer, Stanford University, 1979; Jeanette K Watson Distinguished Visiting Professor, Syracuse University, 1982; Pauling Memorial Lecturer, Oregon State University, 1995. Publications: Syntactic Structures, 1957; Current Issues in Linguistic Theory, 1964; Aspects of the Theory of Syntax, 1965; Cartesian Linguistics, 1966; Topics in the Theory of Generative Grammar, 1966; Language and Mind, 1968; Sound Patterns of English (with Morris Halle), 1968; American Power and the New Mandarins, 1969; At War with Asia, 1970; Problems of Knowledge and Freedom, 1971; Studies on Semantics in Generative Grammar, 1972; For Reasons of State, 1973; The Backroom Boys, 1973; Counterrevolutionary Violence (with Edward Herman), 1973; Peace in the Middle East?, 1974; Bains de Sang (with Edward Herman), 1974; Reflections on Language, 1975; The Logical Structure of Linguistic Theory, 1975; Essays on Form and Interpretation, 1977; Human Rights and American Foreign Policy, 1978; Language and Responsibility, 1979; The Political Economy of Human Rights (with Edward Herman), 2 volumes, 1979; Rules and Representations, 1980; Radical Priorities, 1981; Lectures on Government and Binding, 1981; Towards a New Cold War, 1982; Some Concepts and Consequences of the Theory of Government and Binding, 1982; Fateful Triangle: The United States, Israel and the Palestinians, 1983; Modular Approaches to the Study of the Mind, 1984; Turning the Tide, 1985; Barriers, 1986; Pirates and Emperors, 1986; Knowledge of Language: Its Nature, Origin and Use, 1986; Generative Grammar: Its Basis, Development and Prospects, 1987; On Power and Ideology, 1987; Language in a Psychological Setting, 1987; Language and Problems of Knowledge, 1987; The Chomsky Reader, 1987; The Culture of Terrorism, 1988; Manufacturing Consent (with Edward Herman), 1988; Language and Politics, 1988; Necessary Illusions, 1989; Deterring Democracy, 1991; Chronicles of Dissent, 1992; What Uncle Sam Really Wants, 1992; Year 501: The Conquest Continues, 1993; Rethinking Camelot: JFK, the Vietnam War, and US Political Culture, 1993; Letters from Lexington: Reflections on Propaganda, 1993; The Prosperous Few and the Restless Many, 1993; Language and Thought, 1994; World Orders, Old and New, 1994; The Minimalist Program, 1995; Powers and Prospects, 1996; The Common Good, 1998; Profit over People, 1998; The New Military Humanism, 1999; New Horizons in the Study of Language and Mind, 2000; Rogue States: The Rule of Force in World Affairs, 2000; A New Generation Draws the Line, 2000; Architecture of Language, 2000; 9-11, 2001; Understanding Power, 2002; On Nature and Language, 2002; Contributions to: Scholarly journals. Honours: Distinguished Scientific Contribution Award, American Psychological Association, 1984; George Orwell Awards, National Council of Teachers of English, 1987, 1989; Kyoto Prize in Basic Science, Inamori Foundation, 1988; James Killian Faculty Award, Massachusetts Institute of Technology, 1992; Lannan Literary Award, 1992; Joel Selden Peace Award, Psychologists for Social Responsibility, 1993; Homer Smith Award, New York University School of Medicine, 1994; Loyola Mellon Humanities Award, Loyola University, Chicago, 1994; Helmholtz Medal, Akademie der Wissenschaft, Berlin-Brandenburg, 1996; Benjamin Franklin Medal, Franklin Institute, Philadelphia, 1999; Rabinranath Tagore Centenary Award, Asiatic Society, 2000; Peace Award, Turkish Publishers Association, 2002; Many honorary doctorates. Memberships: American Academy of Arts and Sciences; American Association for the Advancement of Science, fellow; American Philosophical Association; Bertrand Russell Peace Foundation; British Academy, corresponding member; Deutsche Akademie der Naturforscher Leopoldina; Linguistics Society of America; National Academy of Sciences; Royal Anthropological Institute; Utrecht Society of Arts and Sciences. Address: 15 Suzanne Road, Lexington, MA 02420, USA.

CHONG Tae Hyong, b. 5 August 1946, Soonchun City, Korea. Professor. m. Young Sook Song, 2 sons, 1 daughter. Education: Bachelor of Engineering, Department of Mechanical Engineering, Hanyang University, Korea, 1970; Master of Engineering, 1977, Dr Eng, 1983, Department of Precision Mechanics, Kyoto University, Japan. Appointments: Lieutenant, Korea Army, 1970-72; Assistant Professor, 1983-87, Associate Professor, 1987-92,

Professor, 1992-, Hangyang University, Korea; Foreign Visiting Professor, Kyoto University, Japan, 1986-87; Foreign Visiting Professor, University of Tokyo, Japan, 1996-97. Publications: Simple Stress Formulae for a Thin-Rimmed Spur Gear; Development of a Computer-Aided Concurrent Design System of Mechanical Design; Multiobjective Optimal Design of Cylindrical Gear Pairs for Reduction of Gear Size and Meshing Vibration; A New and Generalised Methology to Design Multi-Stage Gear Drives by Integrating Dimensional and the Configuration Design Process. Honour: Dr Eng, Kyoto University, Japan, 1983. Memberships: President, KSMTE; KSME; JSME; KSPE; JSPE; AGMA; KGMA. Address: #104-404, Daerim Apt, 501 Daebang-Dong, Dongjak-ku, Seoul, Korea 156-020. E-mail: thchong@hangyang.ac.kr Website: gearlab.hangyang.ac.kr

CHOPIN L Frank, b. 29 April 1942, New Orleans, Louisiana, USA. Attorney. 2 sons, 1 daughter. Education: BBA, Loyola University, New Orleans, 1964; JD, 1966, Diploma in Military Law, 1966, Judge Advocate General's School, University of Virginia School of Law; Postgraduate Studies, National Law Center, George Washington University, 1967-68; LLM Taxation, University of Miami, Florida, 1976; PhD in Law, Cambridge University, England, 1986; Admitted to the Bar: Louisiana, 1966; Florida, 1968; Iowa, 1980; US District Court (Southern District) Florida, 1968; US Court of Appeals, 5th circuit, 1968. Appointments: Partner, Chopin & Chopin, Miami, 1969-77; Partner, Cadwalader, Wickersham & Taft, Palm Beach, Florida, 1980-94; Associate Professor of Law, University of Miami, 1982-96, University of Sherbrooke, Canada, 1982-94; Partner, Chopin, Miller & Yudenfreund, Palm Beach, Florida, 1994-98; Partner, Chopin & Miller, West Palm Beach, Florida, 1999-. Publications: Author: The New Residency Rules for Canadian Tax Considerations, 1985; Numerous articles in legal journals. Memberships: Housing Finance Authority; Trustee, Preservation Foundation, Palm Beach Community Chest Inc; American Bar Association; International Bar Association; Federal Bar Association; Florida Bar Association; St Thomas Moore Law Society; Phi Alhpa Delta. Address: Chopin & Miller, 505 S Flager Drive, Suite 300, West Palm Beach, FL 33401, USA.

CHOU Wanxi, b. 18 July 1930, Dalian Liaoning, China. Professor, Mining Construction. m. Lin Yuyin, 1 son, 1 daughter. Education: Dalian Xieho School of Industry and Commerce, 1944-45; Beijing Private Zhicheng Middle School, 1947-48; Beijing Provincial Senior Middle School, 1948-50; China University of Mining and Technology, 1950-51; Engineer degree, Moscow Mining Institute, 1951-56; Technician, Jiaozhuo Macun Department of Mining Construction, Henan Bureau of Mining Construction, 1956-57; Assistant, Lecturer, Hefei University of Technology, 1957-72; Lecturer, Associate Professor, Professor, Anhui University of Science and Technology, 1972-96. Publications: 1 book, 2 translated books, 110 papers, 15 translated papers. Honours: Advanced Science and Technical Worker, Anhui; Award of Anhui Conference of Science and Technique; Award of Scientifical on Technical Progress, Institutions of higher learning, Anhui. Memberships: Rock Mechanics and Support Committee, China Coal Society; Director, Hong Kong International Education Exchange Centre; Advisor, Research Board of Advisors, American Biographical Institute. Address: Department of Civil Engineering, Anhui University of Science and Technology, Huainan, Anhui 232001, China.

CHOUDHURI Purna Chandra, b. 11 May 1941, Bhanjanagar, Orissa. Academician; Veterinarian. m. Sandhyarani Mishra, 1 son, 1 daughter. Education: BVSc & AH (Hons), 1963; MVSc, Agra, 1968; PhD, CDRI, 1973; FNAVSc, India, 1996; FISVM, 1997. Appointments: Veterinary Assistant Surgeon, 1963-66, ICAR

Junior Fellow, 1966-68; Research Assistant, Biological Products, 1968-70; Senior Fellow, ICAR, 1970-73; Assistant Professor, Medicine, GBP Agricultural University, 1973-78; Associate Professor, PAU, 1978-82; Professor and University Head, ANGRAU, 1982-2001; Member, Board of Management, APA University, 1987-90, President, ISVM, 1990-92; Principal CVSc Tirupati, 1995-97. Publications: 15 in foreign journals; 165 Indian scientific journals; 54 popular articles on veterinary science; 3 books. Honours: Best Clinical Article, Indian Journal Veterinary Medicine, 1992; K S Nair Gold Medal, Indian Vet Journal, 1992; PLN Rao Gold Medal (IVSM), 1993; State Best Teacher Award, 1994-95. Memberships: Indian Society for Veterinary Medicine; Indian Society for Parasitology, superannuated, 2001. Address: 215-Dharma Vihar, Bhubaneswar-30, Orissa, India 751030.

CHOW Chee-Kong, b. 3 October 1923, China. Photographic Artist. m. 2 sons. Education: University of the Philippines, 1965. Appointments: Honorary President, Photographic Society of China; Honorary Vice President, Society of Worldwide Ethnic Chinese Photographers; Life Honorary Advisor, Federation of Asian Photographic Art; Country Representative for Taiwan, Photographic Society of America; Honorary of Millennium Photographic Association; Lecturer on Photography; Judge, National Art Award, National Fine Art Exhibition, International Photo Salon. Publications: Idyllic Photographic Works; On Chinese Photographic Art; On Process of Chinese Photographic Art Development; On Poetic Photography. Honours: Titles: Honorary FPSC, FPSC, FCSPA, AFIAP, Honorary FAPA, Honorary FSCPS, EFAPA, PSNY, FASAA, FPSLA, FHKPC, FCPPA, FCSPA; Award, Education Ministry of China, 1993; Award for Art and Writers, 1965 and 1997. Memberships: Chinese Writers and Artists Association; Chinese Arts Association; Photographic Society of China; Photographic Society of America; Society of Worldwide Ethnic Chinese Photographers. Address: 7F No 1, Lane 13, Li-Shui Street, Taipei, Taiwan.

CHOW Chun Lam James, b. 25 November 1966, Hong Kong. Physicist. Education: BSc, First Class Honour, Applied Physics, City University of Hong Kong, 1989-92; PhD, Physics, University of Hong Kong, 1992-95. Appointments: Demonstrator, University of Hong Kong, 1995; Croucher Research Fellow, University of Cambridge, UK, 1995-97; Research Associate, University of Toronto, Canada, 1997-98; Part-time Research Associate, 1998-; Research Fellow, McMaster University, Canada, 1998-2000; Medical Physics Resident, London Regional Cancer Centre, Canada, 2000-2002; Medical Physicist and Deputy Radiation Safety Officer, Grand River Regional Cancer Centre, Canada, 2002-; Chartered Physicist, Institute of Physics, England, 1996-; European Physicist, European Physical Society, Europe, 1997-; Professional Physicist, Canadian Association of Physicists, Canada, 1999-. Publications: More than 20 presentations and seminars at international conferences; More than 50 publications in cited journals. Honours: Research Board of Advisors, American Biographical Institute; 20th Century Award for Achievement, International Biographical Centre; Croucher Foundation Fellowship; Sir Edward Youde Memorial Scholarship; CMA Donor Scholarship; Li Po Chun Memorial Fellowship; Taufik Ali Memorial Fellowship; Espon Foundation Fellowship; Swire Travel Grant; 20th Century Outstanding Achievement Award, IBC, Cambridge, UK; Medical Physicist, Canadian College of Physicists in Medicine; Listed in several biographical dictionaries. Memberships: American Association of Physicists in Medicine; Institute of Electrical and Electronic Engineers; Institute of Electrical Engineers; Canadian Association of Physicists; American Physical Society; Institute of Physics; New York Academy of Science; IEEE Computer Society; Electrochemical Society; Cambridge Society; Canadian Organization of Medical Physicists;

Dictionary of International Biography

Canadian College of Physicists in Medicine. Address: Clinical Physics Department, Grand River Regional Cancer Centre, PO Box 9056, 835 King Street West, Kitchener, Ontario, Canada N2G 1G3.

CHOW Yung-Teh, b. 28 October 1916, Shih Ching T'ou or Stony Well Village, Wu Yi County, Chejiang Province, China. Retired Professor of Sociology. m. Ying Lu. Education: BA, National Tsing Hua University, 1937; MA, 1951, PhD, 1958, University of Chicago. Appointments: Editor, Doctor James Yang-Chu Yeng's National Association for the Advancement of Mass Education, 1938-39; Research Assistant, Institute for Socio-Economic Research, National Yunnan University, 1939-41; Director, Kunyang Research Station, Institute for Census Research, National Tsing Hua University, Cheng Kung, Yunnan, during World War II, 1941-46; Instructor, National Tsing Hua University, Peking, 1946-48; Assistant Professor, Sociology, Eastern Michigan College, 1958-61; Associate Professor, Sociology, Professor, Moorhead State College, 1962-67; Professor of Sociology, Northern Michigan University, 1967-72; Professor, Sociology, University of Alabama, 1972-74. Publications include: How to Mobilize the Peasants, 1938; China's Gentry (Cooperate with Hsiao-Tung Fei), edited by Mrs Margarette Park Redfield, 1953; Social Mobility in China: Status Careers Among the Gentry in a Chinese Community, 1966; A Comparative Study of Modern Census (A Collection of Articles), 2000. Honours: Receiving grant and several memberships; Grant, offered for revising manuscript for publishing, Wenner-Gren Foundation for Anthropological Research Incorporated, 1961. Memberships: American Sociological Association; Association for Asian Studies. Address: University of Alabama, PO Box 865694, Tuscaloosa, AL 35486-0051, USA.

CHOW YUN-FAT, b. 1956, Lamma Island, China. Film Actor. m. Jasmine Chow. Appointments: Actor, TV Station, TVB, Hong Kong, 1973, appearing in over 1,000 TV series. Creative Works: Films include: The Story of Woo Viet; A Better Tomorrow, 1986; God of Gamblers, 1989; The Killer; Eighth Happiness; Once a Thief, 1991; Full Contact, 1992; Hard Boiled, 1992; Peace Hotel, 1995; Broken Arrow, 1999; Anna and the King, 1999; Crouching Tiger, Hidden Dragon, 2000; King's Ransom, 2001; Bulletproof Monk, 2001. Address: c/o William Morris Agency, 151 El Camino Drive, Beverly Hills, CA 90212, USA.

CHOWDHURY Chitta Ranjan, b. 29 June 1946, Chittagong, India. Consultant Surgeon. m. Devika Chowdhury, 3 daughters. Education: MBBS, Chittagong Medical College, Dhaka University, 1970; FRCS, Royal College of Surgeons Edinburgh, 1979; Lt-Col, RAMC (Retired), 1981; Certificate of Accreditation, Oto-Rhinolaryngology, Royal College of Surgeons, Edinburgh, 1989; FCSHK, College of Surgeons, Hong Kong, 1990; FICS, International College of Surgeons, West German Section, 1990; MBIM. British Institute of Management, 1992; FRCS, Royal College of Surgeons, London, England;. Appointments: Various hospital positions, India and England (mainly Liverpool, London and Newcastle), 1970-83; Consultant (Acting), ENT/Head and Neck Surgeon, British Military Hospital, Hong Kong, Far East Command, H M Forces, 1983-85; Senior Registrar, Royal Marsden Hospital, London, England, 1985-87; Senior Registrar, ENT/Head and Neck Surgery, Newcastle Group of Teaching Hospitals, Freeman Hospital, Newcastle upon Tyne, England, 1987-88; Command Consultant ENT/Head and Neck Surgeon, British Military Hospital, Rinteln, Germany, 1988-91; Consultant ENT/Head and Neck Surgeon, Queen Elizabeth Military Hospital, Woolwich, London, England, 1991-94; Consultant ENT/Head and Neck Surgeon, Barking, Havering and Redbridge NHS Trust, Romford, Essex, England, 1994-. Publications: About 20 articles in various national and international journals. Honours: Fellow,

Foundation Bordeaux, France; Fellow, Surgical Association, Hong Kong. Memberships: British Medical Association; Fellow, Royal Society of Medicine; British Oto-Rhinolaryngology Association; British Association of Paediatric Otolaryngology; British Institute of Management; British Society of Neuro-otology. Address: 18 Elm Grove, Hornchurch, Essex RM11 2QX, England. E-mail: chowdhuryjuni@aol.com

CHOYCE Lesley, b. 21 March 1951, Riverside, New Jersey, USA (Canadian citizen). Professor; Writer; Poet; Editor. m. Terry Paul, 19 August 1974, 2 daughters. Education: BA, Rutgers University, 1972; MA, Montclair State College, 1974; MA, City University of New York, 1983. Appointments: Editor, Pottersfield Press, 1979-; Professor, Dalhousie University, 1986-. Publications: Adult Fiction: Eastern Sure, 1981; Billy Botzweiler's Last Dance, 1984; Downwind, 1984; Conventional Emotions, 1985; The Dream Auditor, 1986; Coming Up for Air, 1988; The Second Season of Jonas MacPherson, 1989; Magnificent Obsessions, 1991; Ectasy Conspiracy, 1992; Margin of Error, 1992; The Republic of Nothing, 1994; The Trap Door to Heaven, 1996; Dance the Rocks Ashore, 1998; World Enough, 1998. Young Adult Fiction: Skateboard Shakedown, 1989; Hungry Lizards, 1990; Wavewatch, 1990; Some Kind of Hero, 1991; Wrong Time, Wrong Place, 1991; Clearcut Danger, 1992; Full Tilt, 1993; Good Idea Gone Bad, 1993; Dark End of Dream Street, 1994; Big Burn, 1995; Falling Through the Cracks, 1996; World Enough, 1998. Poetry: Re-Inventing the Wheel, 1980; Fast Living, 1982; The End of Ice, 1985; The Top of the Heart, 1986; The Man Who Borrowed the Bay of Fundy, 1988; The Coastline of Forgetting, 1995; Beautiful Sadness, 1998. Carrie's Crowd, Childrens Book. Chapter Book: Far Enough Island, 2000. Your Adult Novel: Roid Rage, 1999. Novella: The Summer of Apartment X, 1999. Non-Fiction: An Avalanche of Ocean, 1987; December Six: The Halifax Solution, 1988; Transcendental Anarchy (autobiography), 1993; Nova Scotia: Shaped by the Sea, 1996. Editor: Chezzetcook, 1977; The Pottersfield Portfolio, 7 volumes, 1979-85; Visions from the Edge (with John Bell), 1981; The Cape Breton Collection, 1984; Ark of Ice: Canadian Futurefiction, 1992; The Coasts of Canada, 2002. Honours include: Event Magazine's Creative Nonfiction Competition Winner, 1990; Dartmouth Book Awards, 1990, 1995; Ann Connor Brimer Award for Children's Literature, 1994; Authors Award, Foundation for the Advancement of Canadian Letters; Finalist for The Hackmatack Children's Book Award, 2000; Landmark East Literacy Award, 2000. Address: 83 Leslie Road, East Lawrencetown, Nova Scotia B2Z 1P8, Canada.

CHRISTENSEN Helena, b. 25 December 1968, Copenhagen, Denmark. Model. 1 son. Appointments: Former child model; Adult modelling career, 1988-99; Front cover model, major magazine covers; Major contracts with: Versace; Chanel; Lagerfeld; Revlon; Rykiel; Dior; Prada and others; Magazine Photographer, 1999-. Address: c/o Marilyn's Agency, 4 Rue de la Paix, 75003 Paris, France.

CHRISTENSEN Mogens, b. 7 April 1955, Laesoe, Denmark. Composer; Assistant Professor. m. Helle Kristensen. Education: Diploma in Music History and Music Theory, Royal Academy of Music, Aarhus, 1983; Teaching Certificate, Royal Academy of Music, Aarhus, 1983; Diploma in Composition, Royal Academy of Music, Aarhus, 1988; MMus, University of Aarhus, 1992; Soloist Diploma in Composition, Royal Academy of Music, Copenhagen, 1993. Debut: As a Composer, Denmark, 1982. Career: His music has been performed in almost all European countries, in USA and South America; Being prize-winner at the UNESCO Composers International Rostrum, 1994, his piece Winter Light was broadcast all over the world; Composer-in-Residence, Copenhagen Philharmonic Orchestra; Teacher, Royal Academies of Music, Copenhagen and Aarhus, Academies of

Music in Aalborg and Esbjerg and the Universities of Aarhus and Aalborg; Currently Assistant Professor, Academy of Music, Esbjerg. Compositions include: Orchestral, Zurvan Akarana, 1986; Dreams within Dreams, 1st violin concerto, 1990; Las flores del mar de la muerte, 2nd violin concerto, 1993; Circulus Stellae, 1998; Crystalline Light, 1999; Chamber works, Orphian Fire Mountains, 1988; The Lost Poems of Princess Ateh, 1991; The Khazarian Mirrors, 1993; Vocal works, Hyperions Schicksalslied, 1982; Pessimisticum, 1993. Recordings: CD: Mogens Christensen, Vocal and Chamber Music volume I, 1991, volume II, 1993, volume III, 1995, volume IV, 2004, volume V, 2004; Odriozola and Kristensen play Christensen and Odriozola, including Winter Light, 1995; 1994 Ensemble Nord, including The Lost Poems of Princess Ateh, 1992; Music for Solo Instruments, vol I, 1998; Music for Recorder, 1999. Publications: Winter Light, 1994; 3 Works for Violin Solo, 1995. Contributions to: Betrachtungen über den Tonalitätsbegriff bei Edvard Grieg und Carl Nielsen, from Die Gratulanten kommen, 1993. Honours: Artist Prize of the County of Bergen, 1991; Artist Scholarship of the Danish State, 1993-95; Prize Winner, UNESCO Composers International Rostrum, 1994. Membership: Danish Composers Society. Address: Stavnsholtvej 161, DK-3520 Farum, Denmark.

CHRISTENSEN Paul, b. 18 March 1943, Pennsylvania, USA. Professor; Poet. m. Catherine Anne Tensing, 20 August 1969, 2 sons, 2 daughters. Education: William and Mary College, 1967; University of Cincinnati, 1970; University of Pennsylvania, 1975. Appointments: Instructor, 1974-75, Assistant Professor, 1975-79, Associate Professor, 1979-83, Professor, 1983-, Texas A&M University. Publications: In Seven Poets; Old and Lost Rivers; Signs of the Whelming; Weights and Measures; Where Three Roads Meet, 1996; West of the American Dream: An Encounter with Texas, 2001; Blue Alleys, 2001; The Mottled Air, 2003. Contributions to: Washington Post; LA Times; American Statesman; Sulfur; Parnassus; Southwest Review; Temblor; Madison Review; Quarter After Eight; Antioch Review, Connecticut Review; Sou'west Review. Honours: Writer's Grant, National Endowment for the Arts; Best Short Fiction, 1995, Texas Institute of letters; Distinguished Prose Award, Antioch Review 1999. Membership: Modern Language Association; Texas Institute of Letters. Address: Department of English, Texas A&M University, College Station, TX 77843, USA.

CHRISTIE Julie Frances, b. 14 April 1940, Assam, India. Actress. Education: Brighton Technical College; Central School of Speech & Drama. Creative Works: Films: Crooks Anonymous, 1962; The Fast Lady, 1962; Billy Liar, 1963; Young Cassidy, 1964; Darling, 1964; Doctor Zhivago, 1965; Fahrenheit 451, 1966; Far From the Madding Crowd, 1966; Petulia, 1967; In Search of Gregory, 1969; The Go-Between, 1971; McCabe & Mrs Miller, 1972; Don't Look Now, 1973; Shampoo, 1974; Demon Seed, Heaven Can Wait, 1978; Memoirs of a Survivor, 1980; Gold, 1980; The Return of the Soldier, 1981; Les Quarantiemes rugissants, 1981; Heat and Dust, 1982; The Gold Diggers, 1984; Miss Mary, 1986; The Tattooed Memory, 1986; Power, 1987; Fathers and Sons, 1988; Dadah is Death (tv), 1988; Fools of Fortune, 1989; McCabe and Mrs Miller, 1990; The Railway Station, 1992; Hamlet, 1995; Afterglow, 1998; The Miracle Maker (voice), 2000; Plays: Old Times, 1995; Suzanna Andler, 1997; Afterglow, 1998. Honours include: Motion Picture Laurel Award, Best Dramatic Actress, 1967; Motion Picture Herald Award, 1967. Address: c/o International Creative Management, 76 Oxford Street, London W1D 1BS, England.

CHRISTIE Linford, b. 2 April 1960, St Andrews, Jamaica. Athlete. 1 daughter. Appointments: Cashier, Wandsworth Co-op; Member, Thames Valley Harriers; Winner, UK 100m, 1985, 1987,

200m, 1985 (tie), 1988; Winner, Amateur Athletics Association 100m, 1986, 1988, 200m, 1988; Winner, European 100m Record; Silver Medallist, 100m, Seoul Olympic Games, 1988, Winner 100m Gold Medal, Commonwealth Games, 1990, Olympic Games, 1992; World Athletic Championships, 1993, Weltklasse Grand Prix Games, 1994, European Games, 1994; Winner 100m, Zurich, 1995; Co-Founder (with Colin Jackson), Managing Director, Nuff Respect sports man co, 1992-; Captain, British Athletics Team, 1995-97; Retired, 1997; Successful coach to several prominent UK athletes. Publications: Linford Christie (autobiography), 1989; To Be Honest With You, 1995; A Year in the Life of Linford Christie, 1996. Honours include: Male Athlete of the Year, 1988, 1992; BBC Sports Personality of the Year, 1993. Address: The Coach House, 107 Sherland Road, Twickenham, Middlesex TW9 4HB, England.

CHRISTODOULOU Christodoulos, b. 13 April 1939, Avgorou, Cyprus. Central Bank Governor. m. Maria, 1 daughter. Education: Bachelor's Degree in Political Sciences, Pantios High School of Political Sciences, Athens, Greece, 1968; Bachelor's Degree in Law, Aristotelian University of Salonica, Greece, 1972; PhD, Labour Law, University of Wales, Wales, UK, 1992. Appointments: Director of the Government Printing Office, 1972-85; Permanent Secretary at the Ministry of Labour and Social Insurance, 1985-89; Permanent Secretary at the Ministry of Agriculture and Natural Resources, 1989-94; Minister of Finance, 1994-99; Minister of Interior, 1999-2002; Governor of the Central Bank of Cyprus, 2002-. Publications: Numerous studies and articles on legal, social and economic matters. Address: Central Bank of Cyprus, 80 Kennedy Avenue, 1076 Nicosia, Cyprus. E-mail: chr.c.christodoulou@centralbank.gov.cy Website: www.centralbank.gov.cy

CHRUŚCIEL Tadeusz Lesław, b. 30 January 1926, Lwów, Poland. Physician. 2 sons, 1 daughter. Education: MD, Faculty of Medicine, Medical Academy, Cracow, 1951; Postgraduate Fellow, Oxford, England, 1956; Professorship, State Council, 1986; D.hc (doctor honoris causa) Silesian Medical Academy, Katowice, 1998. Appointments: Academy of Medicine, Cracow, 1948-56; Professor, Chairman, Academy of Medicine, Zabrze, 1956-68; Senior Medical Officer, Drug Dependence, WHO, Geneva, 1968-75; Drug Research Institute, Warsaw, 1976-85; Postgraduate Medical School, Warsaw, 1986-97; retired, 1997. Publications: Over 300 research papers and articles contributed to specialist journals. Honours: Polonia Restituta Commander's Cross, 2001; Numerous research awards. Memberships: International Narcotics Control Board, 1979-83; National Physicians' Council, President, 1989-93; WHO expert advisory panel on drug dependence, 1978-99; Doctor honoris causa, Medical Academy of Katowice, 1998; NPC Member, 2001-; Catholic Association of Polish Physicians, GC Secretary, 2002-; Commission of Social Response to Pharmacotherapy, Polish Academy of Sciences, 2004. Address: 6 Dzika Str, App 284, PL-00-172, Warsaw, Poland.

CHU Chengbin, b. 31 January 1965, Anhui, China. Professor. m. Peng Feng, 2 sons, 1 daughter. Education: Engineering degree, Industrial Automation, 1985; Masters, DEA, Automation, Electronics and Electricity, 1987, PhD, Computer Science and Automation, 1990; Habilitation, Computer Science and Industrial Engineering, 1995. Appointments: Expert Engineer, INRIA, France, 1990-92; Research Officer, INRIA, 1997; Professor, Universite de Technologie de Troyes, 1997-. Publications: Articles in professional journals. Honours: First Prize, Robert Faure Award, 1996; Best Transactions Paper Award, IEEE Robotics and Automation Society, 1998. Memberships: IEEE; ROADEF. Address: UTT-LOSI, 12 rue Marie Curie, BP 2060, 10010 Troyes Cedex, France. E-mail: chu@utt.fr

Dictionary of International Biography

CHU Han-Shu, b. 12 October 1933, Qingtian, Zhejiang, China. Radioastronomer. m. Luo Pei-Fang, 2 daughters. Education: Graduate, Electrical Engineering, National Zhejiang University, 1953; Advanced Study, Institute of Physics, China Academy of Sciences, 1954-56; Advanced Study on Radioastronomy, Academy of Sciences, Russia, 1956-60. Appointments: Research Assistant, 1953, Research Associate, Associate Professor, 1960-, Professor, 1993-, Purple Mountain Observatory, China Academy of Sciences; Worked on Radioastronomy, VLBI Astrophysics: Polarization and high resolution research of Active Galactic nuclei including quasars and BL Lac objects; Design and Construction of advanced sensitive polarization radiotelescopes in cm wave band for studying polarized radiation from sun spots; Pioneered microwave radiometry technology and solar radio astronomy in China; Solution of the problem of the physical nature of spurious polarization in Radioastronomy; Discovery in Active Galactic Nuclei of an unusual 3 jet structure, revealing new unknown non-axial ejection mechanism in AGN; Discovery of CME (Coronal Mass Ejection) and Ejection of Large Scale Magnetic Fields from Active Galactic Nuclei, the CMEs are responsible for Sporadic Ejection of jet components and the drastic variabilities in AGN (including those powerful ejections that produce γ Ray Burst, and those from BL Lac Objects); Discovery of Helical Magnetic Fields and Intrinsically Asymmetric Jets in AGN, the Helical Magnetic Field is responsible for Collimation of the jet and is crucial for Extraction of Black Hole Rotational Energy; Discovery of dramatic variability in jet direction of BL Lac AO 0235+164, and the successful explanation of the puzzle of exceptional violent variabilities by the CME Model. Publications include: The Physical Nature of Spurious Polarization Transformed from the Background Non-Polarized Radiation of Cosmic Extended Radio Sources, 1988; Unusual Features in QSR 3C147 – A Unified Explanation of the Jets and BLR Clouds, 1993; AO 0235+164 – A Heretic BL Lac, 1994; VLBI Observations of the Puzzling BL Lacertae Object 0235+164, 1996; CME and Ejection of Large Scale Magnetic Fields, Helical Magnetic Fields and Intrinsically Asymmetric Jets - New Findings in AGN (Radio Emission from Galactic and Extragalactic Compact Sources, 1998); Discovery of Helical Magnetic Fields and Intrinsically Asymmetric Jets in AGN; Discovery of CME and Ejection of Large Scale Magnetic Fields from AGN (High Energy Processes and Phenomena in Astrophysics, 2003); Author of numerous papers. Honours: Gold Medal, 7th International Nathiagali Summer College on Physics and Contemporary Needs, 1982; Natural Science Award, China Academy of Sciences, 1995; International Man of the Year, 1997-98, IBC; 20th Century Achievement Award, ABI, 1998; 2000 Millennium Medal of Honour, ABI, 1999; 2000 Commemorative Medal of Honour, ABI, 2000; American Order of Excellence, 2001; Presidential Seal of Honour Medal, ABI, 2001; American Medal of Honour, ABI, 2001; 2000 Outstanding Scientists of the 20th Century (and of the 21st Century) Medal, IBC, 2001, 2002; Congressional Medal of Honor, ABI, 2001; Great Minds of the 21st Century Medal, ABI, 2003; ABI World Laureate Medallion, 2002; Lifetime Achievement Award (Gold), IBC, 2002; International Medal for Scientific Achievement, ABI, 2002; World Lifetime Achievement Award, ABI, 2003; The World-Wide Honours List, IBC, 2003; International Register of Profiles, IBC, 2003; International Scientist of the Year 2002, 2003, IBC, 2002, 2003; International Medal of Honour, IBC, 2003; 21st Century Award for Achievement, IBC, 2003; Eminent Scientists of Today Medal, IBC, 2003; Lifetime of Achievement One Hundred, IBC, 2004; Lifetime of Scientific Achievement Award, IBC, 2004; Listed in International Book of Honour, ABI, 2000 and several biographical dictionaries including: The First Five Hundred, IBC, 1998; International Book of Honor, ABI, 1999; Leading Intellectuals of the World, ABI, 2000, 2002-03; 1000 World Leaders of Scientific Influence, ABI, 2002; 500 Founders of the 21st Century, IBC, 2003; 500 Leaders of Science, ABI, 2003; One Thousand Great Scientists, IBC, 2003; American Hall of Fame, ABI, 2003; Dictionary of International Biography, IBC, 2004; Living Legend, Dedication, IBC, 2004; International Register of Profiles, IBC, 2004; Outstanding Scientists of the 21st Century, Dedication, IBC, 2004; Greatest Intellectuals of the 21st Century, 2004; The Cambridge Blue Book, IBC, 2004. Memberships: International Astronomical Union; Astronomical Society of China; Electronics Society of China, Senior Member. Address: Purple Mountain Observatory, China Academy of Sciences, Nanjing 210008, China.

CHUBB Scott Robinson, b. 30 January 1953, New York, USA. Research Physicist. m. Anne Lauren, 1 son, 2 daughters. Education: BA, Princeton University, 1975; MA, State University of New York, 1978; PhD, 1982. Appointments: Research Associate, Northwestern University, 1982-85; Research Associate, National Research Council, 1985-88; Research Physicist, SFA Inc, 1988-89; Research Physicist, Naval Research Laboratory, 1989-2003. Publications: 60 Publications. Honours: National Research Council Fellowship; Sigma Xi. Memberships: American Physical Society; American Geophysical Union. Address: 9822 Pebble Weigh Court, Burke, VA 22015, USA.

CHUDY John Franklin II, b. 24 December 1952, San Bernardino, California, USA. Designer. m. Angela, 2 sons, 4 daughters. Education: Student, Ivy Technical State College. Career: Designer of Interior Architecture, 1984-; Product Designs, 1995-. Honours: Multiple International Patents. Membership: LDS. Address: 35728 Avenue G, Yucaipa, CA 92399, USA.

CHUGANI Mahesh Lakhi, b. 31 October 1964, Bombay, India. Engineer. Education: MS, Electrical Engineering, 1990, PhD, 1996, Rensselaer Polytechnic Institute, USA; BE, Electronics and Telecommunications, College of Engineering, Pune, India, 1987. Appointment: DSP Software Engineer, 1996-2001 Director of Support and Training, 2001-03. Publications: A Mathematical Model of Blood Flow Through Stenotic Arteries, conference presentation, 1994; Labview Signal Processing, 1998; Guide to Practical Signal Filtering, Research and Development, articles, 2000; Digital Signal Processing: A Hands-On Approach, 2005. Honours: Charles M Close Doctoral Research Prize, Rensselaer Polytechnic Institute, 1996; Whitaker Award, 20th Northeast Bioengineering Conference, 1994. Membership: Institute of Electrical and Electronics Engineers. Address: 2017 S Stoneman Ave, Alhambra, CA 91801, USA. E-mail: mchugani@alum.rpi.edu

CHUI Wing-Hung, b. 26 July 1968, Hong Kong. Cardiothoracic Surgeon. m. Bo-Yee Chan, 2 sons. Education: MBBS (HK), FRCS (Edin); FHKAM (Surgery); FCSHK. Appointments: Specialist Cardiothoracic Surgeon; Honorary Clinical Assistant Professor, Grantham Hospital, The University of Hong Kong. Publications: 15 articles in professional journals as co-author and first author include most recently: Surgical management of intracardiac myxomas, 1999; Cognitive dysfunction after cardiopulmonary bypass, 2002; Aortic valve replacement with stentless porcine bioprostheses, 2002; Video-assisted thoracoscopic talc pleurodesis is effective for maintenance of peritoneal dialysis in acute hydrothorax complicating peritoneal dialysis, 2003. Honours: Honorary Clinical Assistant Professor, The University of Hong Kong; Fellow, Hong Kong Heart Foundation. Memberships: Royal College of Surgeons of Edinburgh; Asian Society for Cardiovascular Surgery; British Society for Heart Failure; Hong Kong College of Cardiology. Address: Division of Cardiothoracic Surgery, Department of Surgery, The University of Hong Kong, Grantham Hospital, Hong Kong.

Dictionary of International Biography

CHULUUNDORJ Begziin, b. 24 November 1949, Ulaanbaatar City, Mongolia. Professor of Comparative Linguistics; University President. m. Teyen-Oidov Ts, 1 son, 2 daughters. Education: Bachelor Degree Certificate, Linguistics, University of Mongolia, Ulaanbaatar, Mongolia, 1973; PhD, Mongolia, 1979; Doctor of Science, Russian Federation, 1989; Professor, Mongolia, 1992. Appointments: Head of Department, Foreign Language Institute, Ulaanbaatar, Mongolia, 1979-81; Official, Central Committee of the Party, Ulaanbaatar, Mongolia, 1982-88; Head of Department, The Academy of Management, Ulaanbaatar, Mongolia, 1989-90; Head of Department, 1990, Rector, 1990-91, Foreign Language Institute, Ulaanbaatar, Mongolia; President, State Pedagogical University, Ulaanbaatar, Mongolia, 1992-96; President, University of the Humanities, Ulaanbaatar, Mongolia, 1996-. Publications: 8 monographs on cognitive linguistics, education study, comparative linguistics and knowledge management; 76 articles, 8 published in Czech Republic, Bulgaria, Taiwan, South Korea and Russia. Honours: Leading Official of Public Education, Ulaanbaatar, Mongolia, 1989; 70th Anniversary Medal of People's Revolution, Ulaanbaatar, Mongolia, 1991; University Medal of Highest Honour, Kyung Hee University, Republic of Korea, 1995; Altan Gadas Medal, Government of Mongolia, 1998; Leading Official of Science, Ulaanbaatar, Mongolia, 2000; 80th Anniversary Medal of the People's Revolution, Ulaanbaatar, Mongolia, 2001. Memberships: Social Sciences Sub-Assembly, The Academy of Sciences of Mongolia; Scholars Advising Council under the President of Mongolia; Executive Committee Member, Northeast Asian Forum University Presidents. Address: University of the Humanities, Square Sukhbaatar- 4, Ulaanbaatar –210646/53, Mongolia. E-mail: chukab@hotmail.com

CHUN Byung Suk, b. 1 September 1937, Hongseong, Korea. Publisher. m. 24 March 1963, 3 sons. Education: BA Economics, Korea University, 1960. Appointments: Chief Editor, Jinmyung Publishing Company, 1960-66; President, Moonye Publishing Company, 1966-; Director, 1975-, Vice President, 1985-87, Korean Publishers Association; Director, Korean Publishers Co-operative, 1982-98; Director, Korean Publishing Research Institute, 1991-; Director, Korean Publishing Fund, 1994-; Chief Editor, Korean Publishing Journal, 1994-99. Honours: Order of Cultural Merit, Government of Korea; Commendation, Prime Minister; Commendation, Minister of Culture and Public Information; Award, Korean Publishing Science Society; Publication Ethics Award, Korean Publication Commission; Korea Publishing Culture Award, Hankook Ilbo; Korean Translation Publishing Award, Korean Society of Translator; Chungang Journalism Culture Award, President of Chungang University; Seoul City Culture Award, Seoul Metropolitan Government; Korea Culture Art Prize, Government of Korea. Address: Dohwa-Dong Mapo-Gu, Mapo Samsung Apt 112-1404, Seoul 121-040, Republic of Korea. E-mail: info@moonye.com

CHUN OAKLAND Suzanne. State Senator. m. Michael Sands Chun Oakland, 1 son, 2 daughters. Education: Bachelor of Arts Degrees in Communications and Psychology, University of Hawaii. Appointments: Administrative Assistant, Au's Plumbing and Metal Works, 1979-90; Community Services Specialist, Hawaii State Senate, 1984; Administrative Assistant, Smolenski and Woodell, Attorneys at Law, 1984-86; Research Assistant and Office Manager, City Council Member Gary Gill, 1987-90; State Representative for House District 27, 1990-96; State Senator for Senate District 13, 1996-. Honours include: Healthy Mothers, Healthy Babies, 2001; Hawaii Breastfeeding Advocacy Award, 2001; Hawaii Coalition for Affordable Long Term Care Appreciation Award; Hawaii Association for Marriage and Family Therapy's Friend of the Family Legislative Award, 2001; Hawaii Intergenerational Network, Invaluable Contribution in Connecting

the Generations of Hawaii, 2001; Play It Safe International, plaque for Dedicated Caring to Our Nation's Children, 2003. Memberships include: Chinese Chamber of Commerce; Hawaii Chinese Civic Association; Volunteer Legal Services Hawaii; Hawaii Housing Development Corporation Board of Directors; Children's Trust Fund Advisory Council; Hawaii Women's Legal Foundation. Address: State Capitol, Honolulu, Hawaii 96813, USA. E-mail: senchunoakland@capitol.hawaii.gov

CHUNG Chia Mou (Charles), b. 21 February 1918, Guangdong, China, Came to USA, 1946. Former Jade and Oriental Art Business Owner. Former Reviser with the United Nations. m. (1) Sylvia E E Tuck, 16 January 1955, divorced 1970, 4 children, (2) Betty Lee Sung, 22 July 1972, 4 stepchildren. Education: Central Police College, Chungking, Sichuan, China, 1940; National Cheng-Chi University, Chungking, 1943; BSc, MSc, Washington State University, Pullman, 1948; Postgraduate, New York University, 1948-51. Appointments: Editor, Central Police College, 1941-43; Professional Officer, Exec Yuan, Chungking, 1943-45; Translator, Reviser, Secretariat, United Nations, New York City, 1948-79; President, Jade and Oriental Arts Inc, 1961-99. Publications: The Road for ROC to be Readmitted to UN (in Chinese); 1994; Co-editor, China Anthology (in English), 1996; Chung's Selected Essays (in Chinese), 1998; Articles to Chinese newspapers and professional publications. Honours: 1st prize, National Essay Contest on Police Science and Administration given by Examination Yuan, 1941; Excellent Service Award, President, Executive Yuan, 1945; 2nd Prize Chinese Research Topic Contest, Ta-ti Foundation, 1951; Service Award, Secretary General, UN, 1985; Excellent Service Awards: Central Police University Alumni Association North America, 1993, National Cheng-ta Alumni Association, Eastern US, 1995, Central Police University Alumni Association Eastern US, 1996. Memberships: Central Police University Alumni Association, Eastern US, Chairman, 1991-; National Cheng-ta Alumni Association Eastern US, Executive Director, 1990-94, Honorary Vice President, 1994-99; Adviser, 1999-; World Hakka Federation, Eastern US Chapter, President, 1991-93, Adviser, 1994-; Adviser, World Kwangtung Community Association; Senior Adviser, Chee-Yue Community Association. Address: 165 Park Row, Apt 20F, New York, NY 10038-1138, USA.

CHUNG Moon-Sun, b. 4 October 1968, Seoul, Korea. Research Fellow. m. Min-Joo Lee. Education: BS, 1991, MS, 1994, Mechanical Engineering Department, Sungkyunkwan University; PhD, Mechanical Engineering Department, Korea Advanced Institute of Science and Technology, 2000. Appointments: Engineering Researcher, R&D Centre, Hyundai Aerospace Engineering Co, 1994-95; Research Assistant, Korea Advanced Institute of Science and Technology, 1995-99; Research Assistant, 1999-2000, Postdoctoral, 2000-2002, Korea Atomic Energy Research Institute; Senior Researcher, 2nd R&D Centre, Agency for Defence Development, 2002-; Referee for Journal of Sound and Vibration, 2001-. Publications articles in journals and conference proceedings including: Numerical Heat Transfer, 2000, 2001 (x2), 2002; Journal of Sound and Vibration, 2001, 2003; International Journal of Engineering Science, 2002; Plenary talks of the Fourth Asian Computational Fluid Dynamics Conference, 2000. Honours: Listed in Who's Who publications and biographical dictionaries. Memberships: Korean Society of Mechanical Engineering; Korean Society for Aeronautical and Space Sciences; Korean Society of Computational Fluids Engineering. Address: Hanshin-seorae Apt 4-506, 70-1 Ban Po 4-dong, Seocho-gu, Seoul 137-804, Republic of Korea. E-mail: s_clarinet@hotmail.com

CHURCH Charlotte Maria, b. 21 February, 1986, Llandaff, Cardiff, Wales. Singer. Career: Albums include: Voice of an Angel, 1998; Charlotte Church, 1999; Christmas Offering, 2000; Dream a Dream, 2000; Enchantment, 2001. Performances include: Charlotte Church: Voice of an Angel in Concert, 1999; Dream a Dream: Charlotte Church in the Holy Land, 2000; The Royal Variety Performance 2001, 2001; The 43rd Annual Grammy Awards, 2001. Concerts include: Hollywood Bowl; Hyde Park. Preludes include: Pie Jesu; Panis Anjulicus; Dream a Dream; The Prayer (duet with Josh Groban); It's the Heart that Matters. TV Appearances include: Heartbeat, 1999; Touched by an Angel, 1999; Have I Got News For You, 2002; The Kumars at No. 42, 2002; Parkinson, 2002; Friday Night with Jonathon Ross, 2003.

CHURCHILL Bernardita Reyes, b. 5 March 1938, Manila, Philippines. Professor of History. m. Malcolm Hughes Churchill, 1 son, 1 daughter. Education: BA, magna cum laude, History, University of the Philippines; MA, Southeast Asian History, Cornell University; PhD, Southeast Asian History, Australian National University. Appointments: Chair, Department of History, University of the Philippines, 1984-87; President, Manila Studies Association, 1990-; Governing Council, Philippine Social Science Council, 1994-; President, Philippine National Historical Society, 1994-; Vice Head, National Commission for Culture and the Arts, Committee on Historical Research, Philippines, 2001-2004; President, Philippines Studies Association, 2003-. Publications: Books, monographs and articles on the Philippine Revolution against Spain and the United States; The Independence Movement from the United States; Institutional History, Philippine Historiography; Philippine Local/Regional History. Honours: First Philippines Studies Fellowship, Faculty of Asian Studies, Australian National University, 1981; Centennial Award as Historian, Philippine National Centennial Committee, Women's Sector, 1999; Outstanding Book Award, Philippine National Academy of Science and Technology, 1999. Memberships: Philippine National Historical Society; Philippine National Commission for Culture and the Arts; Philippine Social Science Council; Manila Studies Association; American Studies Association of the Philippines; Philippine Studies Association; Fellow, Philippine Association for the Advancement of Science; Philippine Association for Chinese Studies; Philippine Health Social Science Association; Association for Asian Studies; American Historical Association; Asia Society, WDC; Asian Studies Association of Australia; Asociación Española de Estudios del Pacífico, Madrid Spain. Address: 4715 47th Street NW, Washington, DC 20016, USA.

CHURCHILL Caryl, b. 3 September 1938, London, England. Dramatist. m. David Harter, 1961, 3 sons. Education: BA, Lady Margaret Hall, Oxford, 1960. Publications: Owners, 1973; Light Shining in Buckinghamshire, 1976; Traps, 1977; Vinegar Tom, 1978; Cloud Nine, 1979; Top Girls, 1982; Fen, 1983; Collected Plays, 2 volumes, 1985, 1988; A Mouthful of Birds (with D Lan), 1986; Serious Money, 1987; Ice Cream, 1989; Hot Fudge, 1990; Mad Forest, 1990; Lives of the Great Poisoners (with I Spink and O Gough), 1991; The Skriker, 1994; This is a Chair, 1997; Blue heart, 1997; Faraway, 2000. Other: Various radio and television plays. Address: c/o Casarotto Ramsay Ltd, National House, 60-66 Wardour Street, London W1V 3HP, England.

CHURCHILL Malcolm Hughes, b. 29 September 1937, Cedar Rapids, Iowa, USA. Foreign Service Officer; Writer; Newsletter Editor. m. Bernardita, 1 son, 1 daughter. Education: International Studies, Silliman University, Philippines, 1955-56; BA, International Relations, Dartmouth College, cum laude, Phi Beta Kappa; SE Asian Studies, Cornell University, 1960-61; MA, Economics, George Washington University, 1972. Appointments: Foreign Service Officer, 1961-87; Editor, Owner, The Insiders' Way, Investment Newsletter, 1986-; Lecturer, Lloyd, Thomas and Ball Inc, 1987-; Australian, New Zealand Analyst, BERI Inc, 1992-99. Publications: A Family Odyssey; Louisiana History and Early

Filipino Settlement; Exposing an Exposer; After the U S Withdrawal; Food for Thought, An Unconventional Look at the Philippines; Many other articles. Honours: Meritorious Honour Award, Department of State, 1983. Memberships: Asia Society; Association for Asian Studies; American Foreign Service Association; Forest Landowners Association; Philippine Arts, Letter and Media Council; National Economists Club. Address: The Insiders' Way, 4715 47th Street NW, Washington, DC 20016, USA.

CHURCHMAN David Alan, b. 20 July 1938, New York. Educator; Professor Emeritus. Education: BA, 1960, MA, 1964, The University of Michigan; Doctorate, University of California, Los Angeles, 1972. Appointments: Lieutenant, US Army, 1960-62; Teacher, American International School, Tangier, 1965-66; Teacher, Newtown High School, 1966-68; Research Faculty, University of California, Los Angeles, 1972-76; Professor, California State University, Dominguez Hills, 1976-2003; Sullivan University, 2004-; Southern Oregon University, 2004-. Publications: Articles and papers contributed to professional journals; Several books. Honours: Malone Fell, Saudi Arabia, 1993; Fulbright Scholar Cyprus, 1999-2000. Memberships: Aquarium and Zoo Association; Wednesday Morning Club; California Republican Party; International Association of Conflict Management. Address: BSGP, California State University, Dominguez Hills, CA 90747, USA.

CHVOJ Zdenek, b. 16 March 1948, Prague, Czechoslovakia. Scientist. m. Blanka Svobodova, 1 son, 1 daughter. Education: RNDr, Charles University, Prague, 1976; CSc, Charles University, 1977; DSc, 1990; Doctorate, Technical University, Prague, 1995. Appointments: Lecturer, Technical University Prague, 1969, 1992-; Researcher, Charles University, Prague, 1971-75; Institute of Physics AVCR, Prague, 1975-; Editor-in-Chief, Czechoslovak Journal of Physics. Publications: Co-author, Recent Trends in Crystal Growth, 1988; Kinetic Phase Diagrams, 1991; Co-editor, Collective Diffusion on Surfaces, 2001; More than 100 articles and papers contributed to professional journals. Honours: Honorary Appreciation Award, CSAV, 1982; Recipient, Czech Literature Foundation Award, 1986. Memberships: Czech Union of Mathematicians and Physicists; Czech National Board on Exploration and the Uses of Outer Space. Address: Institute of Physics, AVCR, Cukrovarnicka 10, 16253 Praha 6, Czech Republic.

CHYUAN Shiang-Woei, b. 23 August 1961, Taipei, Taiwan. Scientist; Engineer. m. Hsu Pao-Hui, 16 September 1996, 2 daughters. Education: BS, 1983, MS, 1985, National Cheng Kung University, Tainan, Taiwan. Appointments: Special, 1985-91, Senior Special, 1991-, Chung-Shan Institute of Science and Technology. Publications include: Thermomechanical Response Analysis of Lithographic Mask Structure Using Finite Element Method, 1995; Boundary Element Analysis and Design in Seepage Problems using Dual Integral Formulations; Finite Element Analysis and Engineering Applications Using MSC/NASTRAN. Honours: IDF Achievement Award, Chief of General Staff, Ministry of National Defence, Taiwan, 1988; Listed in several international biographical directories. Address: PO Box 90008-15-3, Lung-Tan, 325 Taiwan.

CICOS Corneliu Crinel, b. 24 March 1952, Craiova, Romania. Research Chemist. m. Lucia Mihaila, 1 son. Education: University Craiova, 1976; Postgraduate, 1983. Appointments: Professor, 1976-78; Researcher 1978-94; PR Researcher, 1994-. Publications: Several articles in professional journals. Memberships: ACS; SRC; SRMM; SRCT. Address: BD 1mai Bl 16A AP3, 1100 Craiova DJ, Romania.

Dictionary of International Biography

CIESZYŃSKI Tomasz Maria Tadeusz, b. 6 November 1920, Poznan, Poland. Professor. m. Maria Elzbieta, 1 son, 1 daughter. Education: Medical Faculty, John Casimir University, Lvov, 1938-44; Diploma, Jagellonian University, Cracow, 1945; Diploma, Faculty of Mathematics, Physics and Chemistry, University of Wroclaw, 1952; MD, 1947; Docent of Surgery, 1968. Appointments: Senior Assistant, Adjunct Chair of Crystallography, University of Wroclaw, 1950-52; Senior Assistant, Orthopaedic Clinic, Medical Academy of Warsaw, 1953; Senior Assistant, Adjunct, Docent, Extraordinary Professor, Second Surgical Clinic, Medical Academy, Wroclaw, 1953-91; Professor of Medical Sciences, 1992-; President and Founder: League of Descendants of Lvov's Professors Murdered by Gestapo in July 1941, 2001-. Publications include: The Natural System of Foods, 1950; Ultrasonic Catheter for Heart Examination, 1956; About the Need to Protect Biological Increment in Poland, in Polish, 1971; Melting Point of Apatites as Bond Energy Property in Relation to Structure, 1974; Equalization of Asymmetric Extremities in Children, 1987; Anabolic and Catabolic Processes in Relation to the Polarity of Electric Fields, 1991; Electric Field inside Bone, in Polish, 1991; The Days Strong by Love, poem in Polish, 1999. Honours include: Golden Cross of Merit, 1975; Cross de Chevalier of the Order of Polonia Restituta, 1990; Medal, University of Tokyo, 1982; Medal, Medical Academy, Wroclaw, 1990. Memberships included: Polish Chemical Society; Society of Polish Surgeons; American Society of Bone Mineral Research. Address: Modrzewiowa 20, Oborniki Slaskie 55-120, Poland.

CILLIERS Andríes Charl, b. 21 November 1933, Stellenbosch, South Africa. Advocate of the High Court; Professor of Law. m. Elizabeth Johanna Liebenberg, 2 sons, 2 daughters. Education: BA, 1953, LLB, 1955, University of Stellenbosch, South Africa; BA Honours, 1958, MA, 1962, University of Oxford; LLD (examination summa cum laude), University of South Africa, 1976. Appointments include: Advocate, Cape Bar, 1959-65; Part-time, Lecturer, University of Stellenbosch, 1961-64; Founder, Department of Law, 1965, First Professor of Law, 1965-93 (retired), First Dean of Law Faculty, 1969, Research Fellow, 1998, new University of Port Elizabeth; Editor, Obiter, University of Port Elizabeth Law Journal, 1988-92; Assessor in High Court, Port Elizabeth and Cape Town, 1966-2003; Consultant, Conference for a Democratic South Africa, 1992-94; Legal Consultant, 1994-; South African Correspondent, JURIST, Legal Education Network, University of Pittsburgh, Pennsylvania, USA, 2000-. Publications: Co-author, The Civil Practice of the Supreme Court of South Africa, 2nd, 3rd, 4th editions, 1966, 1979, 1997; Author, Law of Costs, 3rd edition, 1997; Columnist, SA Attorneys' Journals, 1980-2003; Approximately 30 articles and reviews in South African legal journals. Honours: Rhodes Scholar, 1954; Member, South African Academy for Arts and Science, 1977, 1981; Research Bursaries, Human Sciences Research Council, 1975, UPE Research Committee, 1982, 1991; Fidelity Fund for Attorneys, Notaries and Conveyancers, 1983; Oppenheimer Memorial Trust University Travelling Fellowship, 1993. Memberships include: Law Revision Committee and Law Commission, 1969-73; Editorial Board, SA Yearbook of International Law, 1976-2000; Council of the Teacher's Training College, Port Elizabeth, 1981-84; Council of the University of Port Elizabeth, 1981-84; Correctional Board, Eastern Cape, 1992-93; Selection Committee, Advisory Committee for Universities and Technocons, 1989-93; Co-opted SA member, International Association for Procedural Law, 1987-. Address: 21 Lieberheim, Paradyskloof, Stellenbosch 7600, Western Cape, Republic of South Africa. E-mail: walewska@iafrica.com

CILLIERS-BARNARD Bettie, b. 18 November 1914, Rustenburg, Transvaal. Artist. m. C H Cilliers, 1 son, 1 daughter. Education: BA, Pretoria University, 1937; Hon D Phil,

Potchefstroom University, 1990; Hon DLitt et Phil, Rand Afrikaans University, 1999; Hon D Phil, University of Pretoria, 2002. Appointments: Art Teacher, Innesdale High School, 1938; Lecturer, Pretoria College of Education, 1938-43; Study and working sessions in Paris, 1948, 1956, 1964, 1971, 1981; 71 Solo Exhibitions in South Africa, Paris, London, Taiwan; Graphic Art Exhibitions in Austria, Germany, Spain, Greece, Israel, USA, Australia; Two retrospective exhibitions of her work at Pretoria Art Museum, 1995 and SASOL Art Museum, 1996. Publications: A book on the life and work of Bettie Cilliers-Barnard, by Professor Muller Ballot, launched 1996. Honours: Artistic Award, 1966; Honorary Award for Painting, South African Academy for Science and Art, 1978; State Presidents Decoration for Meritorious Service, 1983; Chancellors Medal, University of Pretoria, 1985; Commemorative Medal of Honour, American Biographical Institute, 1988; Represented South Africa at a number of international exhibitions in Europe. Address: 4 Upper Terrace, Menlo Park, Pretoria 0081, South Africa.

CIMBALA Stephen Joseph, b. 4 November 1943, Pittsburgh, PA, USA. College Professor. m. Elizabeth Ann Harder, 2 sons. Education: BA, Pennsylvania State University, 1965; MA, 1967, PhD, 1969, University of Wisconsin, Madison. Appointments: Assistant Professor of Political Science, State University of New York, Stony Brook, New Brook, 1969-73; Associate Professor, 1973-86, Professor, 1986-, Distinguished Professor, 2000-, Political Science, Pennsylvania State University, Delaware County; Consultant, to various US Government Agencies and Defense Contractors. Publications: Books: The Past and Future of Nuclear Deterrence, 1998; Coercive Military Strategy, 1998; Nuclear Strategy in the Twenty-First Century, 2000; Clausewitz and Chaos, 2001; Many others; Contributing editor, various works; Articles and chapters. Honours: Milton S Eisenhower Award for Distinguished Teaching, Pennsylvania State University, 1995; Distinguished Professor of Political Science, 2000. Address: Department of Political Science, Pennsylvania State University, Delaware County, Media, PA 19063, USA.

CINGOLANI Charles L, b. 18 January 1933, Butler, Pennsylvania, USA. Teacher; Poet. m. Roswitha von Volkmann, 12 July 1969, 1 son, 1 daughter. Education: BA, Stonehill College, 1955; MA, Duquesne University, 1966; PhD, Basel, Switzerland, 1972. Appointment: Point Park College, Pittsburgh, Pennsylvania. Publication: In the Wheat: Songs in Your Presence; The Butler Pennsylvania Poems; Thomas Merton in Auschwitz; Collected Poems. Contributions to: Poetry Quarterly; Coal City Review; New Hope International; Quartos Magazine; Lundian; New Europe; Purple Patch; Foolscap. Website: http://www.cingolani.com. Address: Waldshuterstr 6, 79862 Hoechenschwand, Germany.

CINGOSKI Vlatko, b. 11 June 1962, Ohrid, Macedonia. Assistant Professor; PhD Researcher. m. Vesna Cingoska, 1 daughter. Education: BS, Electrical Engineering, 1986, MS, 1990, University Sts Cyril and Methodious, Macedonia; PhD, Electrical Engineering, Hiroshima University, Graduate School of Engineering, 1996. Appointments: Teaching and Research Assistant, University Sts Cyril and Methodious, 1986-91; Invited Research Assistant, 1991-96, Assistant Professor, 1996-99, Hiroshima University; Assistant General Manager, 1999-2002, Project Coordinator, 2002-, Electric Power Company of Macedonia. Publications: Over 60 articles in professional journals. Honours: Best Paper Award, Japanese Society for Applied Electromagnetics; Editor, Journal of the Japanese Society for Applied Electromagnetic and Mechanics. Memberships: IEEE; International Compumag Society; Japanese Society of Applied Electromagnetics and Mechanics; New York Academy of Sciences.

Dictionary of International Biography

Address: Electric Power Company of Macedonia, Development and Investments Department, 11 October Str, No 9, 1000 Skopje, Macedonia.

CIOCHON Russell Lynn, b. 11 March 1948, Altadena, California, USA. Professor; Chair. m. Noriko Ikeda Ciochon. Education: MA, 1974, PhD, 1986, University of California, Berkeley. Appointments: Lecturer, University of North Carolina, Charlotte, 1978-81; Research Paleontologist, University of California, Berkeley, 1982-83; Research Associate, Institute of Human Origins, Berkeley, 1983-85, SUNY, Stony Brook, 1985-86; Assistant Professor, 1987-90, Associate Professor, 1990-96, Professor, 1996-, University of Iowa. Publications include: Primate Evolution and Human Origins, 1987; The Human Evolution Source Book, 1993; Integrative Paths to the Past, 1994; The Primate Anthology, 1998; Dragon Bone Hill: An Ice Age Saga of Homo erectus, 2004. Memberships: AAAS; American Anthropology Association; Paleoanthropology Society; Phi Beta Kappa. Address: University of Iowa, Department of Anthropology, 114 Macbride Hall, Iowa City, IA 52242-1322, USA.

CIOSEK Jerzy, b. 17 May 1954, Warsaw, Poland. Physicist. m. Magdalena Klecz, 2 daughters. Education: MS, 1979; DS, 1985. Appointments: Assistant, Institute of Quantum Electronics, MUT, 1979; Assistant Lecturer, 1981-85, Lecturer, 1986-95, Head, Thin Film Laboratory, Institute of Optoelectrons, MUT, 1995-; DSc, Material Engineering in Optics, 2001; Reader since 2001. Publications: Several articles in scientific journals. Honours: Gold Medal, Brussels, 1995; Gold Medal, Geneva, 1996; Diploma, Ministry of Industry, 1996; Diploma, Science Research Community, 1996; Prize, MUT's Rector, 1996, 1998. Memberships: SPIE; OSA; Polish Vacuum Society; IEEE Lasers; Electro-Optics Society. Address: Institute of Electron Technology, Al Lotnikow 32/46, 02-668 Warsaw, Poland.

CIPRIANI Settimio, b. 24 April 1919, Pratovecchio, Arezzo, Italy. Professor. Education: Theology Doctor, Gregoriana University of Rome; Holy Scripture Doctor, Pontifical Biblical Institute, Rome. Appointments: New Testament Professor, Pontificia Università Lateranenese, Rome, -1990; Pontificia Facoltà Teologica, Napoli, -1992; Università di Urbino. Publications: Le Lettere Pastorali, 1983; Missione ed Evangelizzazione nel libro degli Atti degli Apostoli, 1994; Primo incontro con la Bibbia, 1996-2000; Le Lettere di Paolo, 1998; La Figura di Pietro nel Nuovo Testamento, 2003. Honours: Prelato Domestico of His Holiness the Pope. Memberships: Studiorum Novi Testamenti Societas, Cambridge; Italian Bible Association, Rome. Address: Via Ponte alle Mosse, 95, 50144 Firenze, Italy.

CIPRO Miroslav, b. 13 December 1918, Pilsen, Czech Republic. Pedagogue. m. Mary Tomáškv?, 1 daughter. Education: Teacher Institute Pilsen, 1937; Doctor of Philosophy, Charles University, Prague, 1951; Doctor of Sciences, Pedagogy, University of Tbilisi, Georgia, 1967. Appointments: Teacher, 1937-; Research Worker, 1953, Director, 1964-; Pedagogical Research Institute, Prague, 1953-; Vice-Minister of Education, Prague, 1971-; Leading Research Worker, UNESO, Paris, France, 1976-; Full Professor, Charles University, Prague, 1980-; President, World Association of Pedagogical Research, 1989-. Publications include: Books: Moral Education of Youth, 1957; Modernisation of the Basic Education, 1968; Idea of the Higher Education, 1981; Development and Problems of the French School, 1985; Principles of Education, 1987; Society and Education, 1996; Dictionary of Pedagogues – Gallery of World Pedagogues, 2002-2003. Honours include: Medal of J A Comenius; Medal of T Masaryk. Memberships: World Association of Pedagogical Research, President, 1989-93;

Founding Member, Movement of T G Masaryk, 1989-. Address: Čechova 21, Prague 7, Czech Republic 17000. E-mail: cipro1918@mbox.vol.cz

ÇIPURI Hasan, b. 10 September 1935, Peshkopia, Albania. Professor; Linguist; Historian; Military Strategist. m. Belquize, 1 son, 1 daughter. Education: Military Academy Skenderberg, 1952-54; Diploma, Faculty of History and Philology, University of Tirana, 1963-67; Doctor of Science Degree, 1987; Professor, 1995. Appointments: Instructor, Chief of Staff, various units of the Albanian Army, 1954-74; Lecturer of Albanian, Croatian and Serbian Languages in Military Academies, 1974-80; Lecturer, Faculty of Foreign Languages and the Albanian Language, Tirana University and Chief of Terminology and Encyclopaedia Department, Defence Academy, 1980-2001. Publications: Translator, 10 military books; Author, 8 books on language and vocabulary; co-author, 20 books; 70 bulletins and military manuals; 130 scientific articles and monographs. Honours: Decoration, President of the Republic; 8 Gold, Silver and Bronze Medals; Universal Award of Accomplishment, American Biographical Institute, 2000; International Personality of the Year, International Biographical Centre, 2001. Memberships: Centre of Albanian Encyclopaedia of Scientific Academy; Scientific Council of Defence Academy, Albanian Republic. Address: Rruga Shyqyri Ishmi, Pall 62 Shkalla 1 Ap 21, Tirana, Albania.

CIVASAQUI Jose, b. 2 January 1916, Satamaken, Japan. Author. m. Setsuko Hirose, 18 September 1940, 2 sons, 1 daughter. Education: Studied Poetry, Edmund Blunden, 1947-50. Appointments: Senior Examiner, Translator, Civilian Employee, US Army, 1946-48; Advisor, Liaison Department, Hakodate Dock Co Ltd, Tokyo, 1948-51; Manager, Liaison Section, Watanabe Confectionery Co Ltd, Tokyo, 1951-54; Literature Staff, Toshiba EMI Ltd, 1955-76; Lecturer, Japan Translation Academy, 1978-84; Sunshine Business College, 1985-94. Publications: Numerous translations from English to Japanese; Poems: In His Bosom; In Thy Grace; Beyond Seeing; Living Water; Doshin Shien; Translation of A Child's Garden of Verses; Invitation to the World of Haiku; Green Pastures; Numerous songs. Honours include: World Poetry Award; Diploma of Merit; Fellow, International Academy of Poets; Runners-Up Prize, Writing Competition, IBC, England, 1987; Premio Internazionale, San Valentino d'Oro, Italia, 1989; Medal for Peace 3rd Class, Albert Einstein International Academic Foundation, 1990; Medallion, Poetry Day, Australia Competition, 1991-92; Michael Madhusudan Academic Award, Calcutta, India, 1992; Congress Medallion for Distinguished Participation, International Biographical Centre and American Biographical Institute, Cambridge and USA, 1993; 4th Order of Merit, Japan, 1993; Man of Year, American Biographical Institute, USA, 1994; Silver Medallion Dove in Peace, Poetry Day, Australia, 1995; Outstanding Speakers of the 21st Century, IBC, England, 2001; International Writer of the Year (Poetry) 2003, IBC, England, 2003. Memberships include: International Shakespeare Association; Japan Song Translation Society; United Poets Laureate International; Shakespeare Globe Center of Japan. Address: Honcho 2-12-11, Ikebukuro, Toshima-ku, Tokyo 170-0011, Japan.

CLACKSON Stephen Gregory, b. 23 April 1961, Taunton, Somerset, England. German Translator. m. Ute Kriesten, 2 sons, 2 daughters. Education: BSc, University London, 1984; PGCE, University of Exeter, 1985; PhD, University of London, 1989; MSc, University of Wales, 1995. Appointments: Fellow, Education, Brunel University, 1988-89; Fellow, Tutor, Natural Philosophy, University of Aberdeen, Scotland, 1990-92; Information Technology, I.V.L, Germany, 1995-98; Founder, Technical Language Bureau, 1998-2000; Founder, Clackson Partners, 2001-.

Publications: Die Traurigen Löwen von Göttingen (book); Numerous articles contributed to professional Journals. Memberships: European Physical Society; British Crystallographic Association; Heraldry Society; Heraldry Society of Scotland; Herold (Berlin). Address: West Manse, Sanday, Orkney KW17 2BN, Scotland. Website: www.clackson.net

CLAPTON Eric (Eric Patrick Clapp), b. 30 March 1945, Ripley, Surrey, England. Musician (guitar); Singer; Songwriter. m. (1) Patti Boyd, 1979, divorced; 1 son, deceased, 1 daughter, (2) Melia McEnery, 2002. Career: Guitarist with groups: The Roosters, 1963; The Yardbirds, 1963-65; John Mayall's Bluebreakers, 1965-66; Cream, 1966-68; Blind Faith, 1969; Derek and the Dominoes, 1970; Delaney And Bonnie, 1970-72; Solo artiste, 1972-; Concerts include: Concert for Bangla Desh, 1971; Last Waltz concert, The Band's farewell concert, 1976; Live Aid, 1985; Record series of 24 concerts, Royal Albert Hall, 1991; Japanese tour with George Harrison, 1991; Film appearance: Tommy, 1974. Compositions include: Presence Of The Lord; Layla; Badge (with George Harrison). Recordings include: Albums: Disraeli Gears, 1967; Wheels Of Fire, 1968; Goodbye Cream, 1969; Layla, 1970; Blind Faith, 1971; Concert For Bangladesh, 1971; Eric Clapton's Rainbow Concert, 1973; 461 Ocean Boulevard, 1974; E C Was Here, 1975; No Reason To Cry, 1976; Slowhand, 1977; Backless, 1978; Just One Night, 1980; Money And Cigarettes, 1983; Behind The Sun, 1985; August, 1986; Journeyman, 1989; 24 Nights, 1992; MTV Unplugged, 1992; From The Cradle, 1994; Rainbow Concert, 1995; Crossroads 2, 1996; Live In Montreux, 1997; Pilgrim, 1998; One More Car One More Rider, 2002; with Jimmy Page and Jeff Beck, 1999; Soundtracks include: Tommy; The Color Of Money; Lethal Weapon; Rush; Hit singles include: I Shot The Sheriff; Layla; Lay Down Sally; Wonderful Tonight; Cocaine; Behind The Mask; Tears In Heaven; Contributed to numerous albums by artists including: Phil Collins; Bob Dylan; Aretha Franklin; Joe Cocker; Roger Daltrey; Dr John; Rick Danko; Ringo Starr; Roger Waters; Christine McVie; Howlin' Wolf; Sonny Boy Williamson; The Beatles: The White Album (listed as L'Angelo Mysterioso). Honours include: 6 Grammy Awards, 1993; Q Magazine Merit Award, 1995; Grammy Award for best pop instrumental performance, 2002. Address: c/o Michael Eaton, 22 Blades Court, Deodar Road, London, SW15 2NU, England.

CLARK Douglas George Duncan, b. 3 October 1942, Darlington, England. Poet. Education: BSc, Honours, Mathematics, Glasgow University, 1966. Appointments: Actuarial Student, Scottish Widows Fund, Edinburgh, 1966-69; Research Investigator, British Steel, Teesside, 1971-73; Computer Officer, Bath University Computing Services, 1973-93. Publications: The Horseman Trilogy in 4 books: Troubador, 1985; Horsemen, 1988; Coatham, 1989; Disbanded, 1991; Dysholm, 1993; Selected Poems, 1995; Cat Poems, 1997; Wounds, 1997; Lynx: Poetry from Bath (editor), 1997-2000; Kitten Poems, 2002. Contributions to: Lines Review; Cencrastus; Avon Literary Intelligencer; Outposts; Acumen; Sand Rivers Journal; Rialto; Completing the Picture: Exiles, Outsiders and Independents; Poet's Voice; Mount Holyoke News; Isibongo; Agnieszka's Dowry; Recursive Angel; Octavo; Perihelion; Autumn Leaves; Fulcrum; Scriberazone. Membership: Bath Writers' Workshop, 1982-1996. Address: 69 Hillcrest Drive, Bath, Avon BA2 1HD, England.

CLARK Eric, b. 29 July 1937, Birmingham, England. Author; Journalist. m. Marcelle Bernstein, 12 April 1972, 1 son, 2 daughters. Appointments: Reporter, The Exchange Telegraph news agency, London, 1958-60; Reporter, The Daily Mail, 1960-62; Staff Writer, The Guardian, 1962-64; Home Affairs Correspondent, Investigations Editor, The Observer, London, 1964-72; Author and journalist, 1972-. Publications: Len Deighton's London Dossier,

Part-author, 1967; Everybody's Guide to Survival, 1969; Corps Diplomatique, 1973, US edition as Diplomat, 1973; Black Gambit, 1978; The Sleeper, 1979; Send in the Lions, 1981; Chinese Burn, 1984, US edition as China Run, 1984; The Want Makers (Inside the Hidden World of Advertising), 1988; Hide and Seek, 1994; The Secret Enemy, in progress; Numerous newspaper articles. Honours: Fellow, English Centre, International PEN. Memberships: Society of Authors; Authors Guild; Crime Writers Association; Mystery Writers of America; National Union of Journalist; American Marketing Association. Address: c/o Child and Company, 1 Fleet Street, London EC4Y 1BD, England.

CLARK Eve Vivienne, b. 26 July 1942, Camberley, Surrey, England. Professor of Linguistics. m. H H Clark, 1 son. Education: MA Honours, 1965, Diploma in General Linguistics, 1966, PhD, Linguistics, 1969, University of Edinburgh. Appointments: Research Associate, Language Universals, 1969-71, Assistant Professor, Associate Professor, 1971-83, Professor of Linguistics, 1983-, Stanford University, Stanford, California, USA. Publications: Books: Co-author, Psychology and Language, 1977; Author: Ontogenesis of Meaning, 1979; Acquisition of Romance, 1985; Lexicon in Acquisition, 1993; First Language Acquisition, 2003. Honours: Fellow, Center for Advanced Study in the Behavioral Sciences, Stanford; Fellow, Guggenheim Foundation; Member, Royal Netherlands Academy of Sciences. Memberships: Linguistic Society of America; SRCD; IASCL; International Pragmatics Association; Fellow, American Association for the Advancement of Science. Address: Department of Linguistics, Stanford University, Stanford, CA 94305-2150, USA.

CLARK Fred, b. 12 December 1930, Limón, Costa Rica. Writer; Barrister-at-Law. m. Dorothy Hyacinth James. 2 sons, 1 daughter. Education: LittB, University of Costa Rica, 1949-51; Postgraduate Studies Stafford College, 1956-57; Barrister-at-Law, Inner Temple, London, England, 1957-60; English Bar, 1960; Certificate in Law, Council of Legal Education, 1960. Appointments: Master of Languages, Merl Grove School, 1951-55; Trust Officer, Government of Jamaica, 1960-61; Private Law Practice, Jamaica, 1961-67; Legal Editor, Corp Trust Co, New York, New York, 1968-69; Senior Legal Editor, Prentice-Hall Inc, Englewood Cliffs, New Jersey, 1969-91; Private Consultant, 1991-98; Special Advisor, US Congressional Advisory Board; National Advisory Board, American Security Council. Publications: Castro; America at War; Springs of Violence; Friends and Enemies. Honours: Distinguished Leadership Award; Presidential Medal of Merit; Honorary PhD; Inscription on Wall of Tolerance, Civil Rights Memorial Center, Montgomery Alabama. Memberships: New York Academy of Science; National Conference for Tolerance; Geographic Society. Address PO Box 291, Bergenfield, NJ 07621-0291, USA.

CLARK Jonathan Charles Douglas, b. 28 February 1951, London, England. Historian. m. Katherine Redwood Penovich, 1996. Education: BA, 1972, PhD, 1981, Cambridge University. Appointments: Research Fellow, Peterhouse, Cambridge, 1977; Leverhulme Trust, 1983; Fellow, All Souls College, Oxford, 1986; Visiting Professor, Committee on Social Thought, University of Chicago, 1993; Senior Research Fellow, All Souls College, Oxford, 1995; Joyce and Elizabeth Hall Distinguished Professor of British History, University of Kansas, 1995-; Distinguished Visiting Lecturer, University of Manitoba, 1999; Visiting Professor, Forschungszentrum Europäische Aufklärung, Potsdam, 2000; Visiting Professor, University of Northumbria, 2001-03. Publications: The Dynamics of Change, 1982; English Society 1688-1832, 1985, 2nd edition as English Society 1660-1832, 2000; Revolution and Rebellion, 1986; Editor, The Memoirs of James 2nd Earl Waldegrave, 1988; Editor, Ideas and Politics in Modern

Dictionary of International Biography

Britain, 1990; The Language of Liberty, 1993; Samuel Johnson, 1994; Editor, Edmund Burke, Reflections on the Revolution in France, 2001; Joint editor, Samuel Johnson in Historical Context, 2002; Our Shadowed Present, 2003. Contributions to: Scholarly books and journals, and to periodicals.memberships: Royal Historical Society, fellow; Ecclesiastical History Society; Church of England Record Society; North American Conference on British Studies; British Society for Eighteenth Century Studies. Address: Department of History, University of Kansas, 1445 Jawhawk Boulevard, Lawrence, KS 66045, USA.

CLARK Joyce Naomi, b. 4 October 1936, Corpus Christi, Texas USA. Retired Registered Nurse; Aeroplane and Instruments Flight Instructor. 1 daughter. Education: Registered Nurse, Baptist Memorial Hospital, Trinity University, San Antonio, Texas, USA, 1958; Coronary Care Nursing, Memorial Medical Center, Corpus Christi Texas; Certified Flight Instructor, 1982, Certified Flight Instructor Aeroplane and Instruments, 1984, Federal Aviation Authority. Appointments: Head Nurse, Paediatrics, Comanche County Memorial Hospital, Lawton, Oklahoma, USA, 1958-59; Staff Nurse, all units, all shifts, USPH Indian Hospital, Fort Sill, Oklahoma, 1961; Staff Nurse, Medical-Surgical, Van Nuys Community Hospital, Van Nuys, California, USA, 1962-63; Head Night Nurse, Labour and Delivery, Memorial Medical Center, Corpus Christi, Texas, 1964; Staff Nurse, Labour and Delivery, Nursery and Post Partum, USNH Corpus Christi, Texas, 1965-68; Night Charge Nurse, Emergency, Trauma Surgery, Operating Room, Christus Spohn Memorial Hospital, 1968-2002; Clinical Instructor, Operating Room Technology, Del Mar College, Corpus Christi, Texas, 1978-79; Flight Instructor, Aeroplane Single Engine Land, 1982-88; Civil Air Patrol; Auxiliary USAF; Air Search and Rescue; Commander, Corpus Christi Composite Squadron Texas Wing; Commander Headquarters, Third Group Texas Wing; Texas Staff Recruiting Pilot; Texas Wing Check Pilot. Honours: Charles A Mella Award for Outstanding Contribution to Surgery, Corpus Christi Surgical Society, 1981; Award of Merit For a Drug Free America, National Association of Chiefs of Police; Charles E "Chuck" Yeager, Aerospace Achievement Award, 1985; Robert L Gilbert Civil Air Patrol Third Group Texas Wing Senior Member of the Year, 1985; Gill Robb Wilson Award Certificate #1021, 1988; Community Leader of America, ABI, 1988; Listed in Who's Who publications and biographical dictionaries. Membership: Aircraft Owners and Pilots Association. Address: 3802 Cimarron Blvd. #221, Corpus Christi, TX 78414-3455, USA. E-mail: jnccfii1@aol.com

CLARK Kathleen Margaret Claire, b. 18 June 1939, Townsville, Queensland, Australia. Political Scientist. m. Nicholas Clark, 1 April 1961, 2 sons, 2 daughters. Education: BA, honours, University of Queensland, 1962; MA, 1964; PhD, University of Melbourne, 1969. Appointments: Lecturer, Tutor, University of Queensland, University of Melbourne, RMIT, 1962-73; Australian Public Service, 1973-89; Australian Capital Territory Public Service, 1989-96; Assistant Secretary, 1983-96; Visiting Fellow, Australian National University, 1991-98; Publications: Australian Foreign Policy Towards a Reassessment, 1973; Creating a Culture to Encourage Students with Disabilities, 1995; Numerous journal articles. Honour: Fellow, Institute of Public Administration, Australia, 1989. Memberships: President, ACT Division, Institute of Public Administration, Australia, 1987-89; International Institute for Strategic Studies; Australian Political Studies Association. Address: 11/2-6 Ourimbah Road, Mosman, Sydney, NSW 2088, Australia.

CLARK (Marie) Catherine (Audrey) Clifton, (Audrey Curling), b. London, England. Writer. m. Clifton Clark, 16 February 1938. Publications: Novels: The Running Tide, 1963;

Sparrow's Yard, 1964. Historical Novels: The Echoing Silence, 1967; Caste for Comedy, 1970; The Sapphire and the Pearl, 1970; Cry of the Heart, 1971; A Quarter of the Moon, 1972; Shadows on the Grass, 1973; Enthusiasts in Love, 1975; The Lamps in the House, 1990; The Saturday Treat, 1993; The Workroom Girls, 1996. Non-fiction: The Young Thackeray, 1966. Contributions to: Periodicals. Honours: Theordora Roscoe Award, 1978; 1st Prize, Wandsworth All London Literary Competition, 1982. Memberships: Society of Authors; Society of Women Writers and Journalists, council member. Address: 35 Hadley Gardens, Chiswick, London W4 4NU, England.

CLARKE Arthur C(harles), b. 16 December 1917, Minehead, Somerset, England. Author. m. Marilyn Mayfield, 1953, divorced 1964. Education: BSc, King's College, London, 1948. Appointments: Assistant Editor, Science Abstracts, 1949-50; Many appearances on UK and US radio and television; Chancellor, Moratuwa University, Sri Lanka, 1979-2002; Vikram Sarabhai Professor, Physical Research Laboratory, Ahmedabad, 1980. Publications: Non-Fiction: Interplanetary Flight, 1950; The Exploration of Space, 1951; The Exploration of the Moon (with R A Smith), 1954; The Challenge of the Spaceship, 1960; The Challenge of the Sea, 1960; Man and Space (with others), 1964; The Coming of the Space Age, 1967; First on the Moon (with the astronauts), 1970; Beyond Jupiter (with Chesley Bonestell), 1973; Arthur C Clarke's Mysterious World (with Simon Welfare and John Fairley), 1980; Arthur C Clarke's World of Strange Powers (with Simon Welfare and John Fairley), 1984; Arthur C Clarke's Chronicles of the Strange and Mysterious (with Simon Welfare and John Fairley), 1987; Astounding Days, 1988; How the World was One, 1992; Arthur C Clarke's A-Z of Mysteries (with Simon Welfare and John Fairley), 1993; The Snows of Olympus, 1994. Fiction: Prelude to Space, 1951; Against the Fall of Night, 1953; Reach for Tomorrow, 1956; The Other Side of the Sky, 1958; Tales of Ten Worlds, 1962; 2001: A Space Odyssey (with Stanley Kubrick), 1968; The Lost World of 2001, 1972; Rendezvous with Rama, 1973; The Fountains of Paradise, 1979; 2010: Space Odyssey II, 1982; The Songs of Distant Earth, 1986; 2061: Odyssey III, 1988; Rama II (with G Lee), 1989; The Garden of Rama (with G Lee), 1991; Beyond the Fall of Night (with Gregory Benford), 1991; The Hammer of God, 1993; Rama Revealed (with G Lee), 1993; 3001: The Final Odyssey, 1997; The Trigger (with Michael Kube-McDowell), 1998; The Light of Other Days (with Stephen Baxter), 2000; Greetings, Carbon-Based Bipeds!, 2000; The Treasure of the Great Reef, 1964; Arthur C Clarke & C S Lewis: A Correspondence; A Time Odyssey (with Stephen Baxter): Time's Eye; Nova; Wolflings; Prelude to 2001 (Roger Caras Interviews). Contributions to: Journals and periodicals. Honours: Kalinga Prize, UNESCO, 1961; Stuart Ballantine Medal, Franklin Institute, 1963; Nebula Awards, Science Fiction Writers of America, 1972, 1974, 1979; John Campbell Award, 1974; Hugo Awards, World Science Fiction Convention, 1974, 1980; Vidya Jyothi Medal, 1986; Grand Master, Science Fiction Writers of America, 1986; Charles Lindbergh Award, 1987; Commander of the Order of the British Empire, 1989; Lord Perry Award, 1992; Knighted, 1998; Many honorary doctorates. Memberships: Association for the Advancement of Science; International Writers Association, fellow; Royal Astronomical Society, Fellow; Society of Authors. Address: 25 Barnes Place, Colombo 7, Sri Lanka.

CLARKE Brenda (Margaret Lilian), (Brenda Honeyman, Kate Sedley), b. 30 July 1926, Bristol, England. Author. m. Ronald John Clarke, 5 March 1955, 1 son, 1 daughter. Publications: The Glass Island, 1978; the Lofty Banners, 1980; The Far Morning, 1982; All Through the Day, 1983; A Rose in May, 1984; Three Women, 1985; Winter Landscape, 1986; Under Heaven, 1988; An Equal Chance, 1989, US edition as Riches of the Heart, 1989;

Sisters and Lovers, 1990; Beyond the World, 1991; A Durable Fire, 1993; Sweet Auburn, 1995; As Brenda Honeyman: Richard by Grace of God, 1968; The Kingmaker, 1969; Richmond and Elizabeth, 1970; Harry the King, 1971; Brother Bedford, 1972; Good Duke Humphrey, 1973; The King's Minions, 1974; The Queen and Mortimer, 1974; Edward the Warrior, 1975; All the King's Sons, 1976; The Golden Griffin, 1976; At the King's Court, 1977; A King's Tale, 1977; Macbeth, King of Scots, 1977; Emma, the Queen, 1978; Harold of the English, 1979. As Kate Sedley: Death and the Chapman, 1991; The Plymouth Cloak, 1992; The Hanged Man, 1993; The Holy Innocents, 1994; The Eve of St Hyacinth, 1995; The Wicked Winter, 1996; The Brothers of Glastonbury, 1997; The Weaver's Inheritance, 1998; The Saint John's Fern, 1999. Address: 25 Torridge Road, Keynsham, Bristol, Avon BS31 1QQ, England.

CLARKE Robert Henry, b. 6 March 1919, London, England. Oceanographer. m. Obla Paliza de Clarke, 2 sons, 1 daughter. Education: Open Scholar in Natural Science, New College Oxford, 1938-40, 1946-47; Bachelor of Arts and Master of Arts with honours in Zoology, Botany and Chemistry, University of Oxford, 1946; Doctor of Philosophy, University of Oslo, Norway, 1957. Appointments: Lieutenant (Sp), RNVR in British Navy, Admiralty Unexploded Bomb Department with operations in various seas, and Directorate of Admiralty Research and Development(India) with special operations in India, Burma and Ceylon, 1940-46; Biologist in the Discovery Investigations, British Colonial Office, 1947-49; Principal Scientific Officer, British National Institute of Oceanography, conducted oceanographical expeditions in all Oceans and in all Seas except the Caspian Sea and the Dead Sea, 1949-71; Lent to FAO of the United Nations in the grade P5 as a whale biologist in Chile, Ecuador and Peru, 1958-61; Fishing off the coast of Peru, 1971-77; Visiting Professor, Universities of Baja California and Yucatan, Mexico, 1977-82; Currently retired but continuing research. Publications: Author of more than 100 research publications, many of book length and mostly on whales (especially the sperm whale), whale conservation, whaling and on squids and deep sea fishes. Honours: Honorary Member, Fundación Ecuatoriana para el Estudio de los Mamíferos Marinos; Honorary Member, Sociedad Geográfica de Lima; Included in the Encyclopaedia of the Azores. Memberships: Scientific Fellow, Zoological Society of London; Institute of Biology of Great Britain; Challenger Society; Marine Biological Association of the United Kingdom; Association of British Zoologists, Member of Council, 1962-65. Address: Apartado 40, Pisco, Peru. E-mail: robertclarke007@hotmail.com

CLARKE Shirley Carl, b. 15 April 1926, Columbiaville, Michigan, USA. Physician; Psychiatrist. Education: BA, Central Michigan University, 1957; DO, Midwest University, Chicago, Illinois, 1962; Internship, Detroit Osteopathic Hospital, 1962-63; Residency, Internal Medicine, Midwestern University, 1963-66; Residency, University of Illinois, Chicago, 1969-73; Board Certified Psychiatry, APA, 1980. Appointments: Psychiatrist, University of Illinois, Chicago Osteopathic College, West Side Veterans Administration Hospital, 1973-96; Solo Pro Bono Psychiatric Practice, 1996-. Publications: The Transference of the Therapist of the Elderly; Evaluation of Bone Marrow Biopsies using 2 Needles and 2 Sites. Honours: Board Certification in Psychiatry, 1980; Listed in Who's Who publications and biographical dictionaries. Memberships: American Psychiatric Association; American Osteopathy Association; Illinois Psychiatric Association; Illinois Osteopathy Association. Address: 400 E Randolph St, Chicago, IL 60601, USA. E-mail:scc100@rcnchicago.com

CLARKE Victor Lindsay (Lindsay Clarke), b. 14 August 1939, Halifax, West Yorkshire, England. Author. m. Phoebe Clare Mackmin, 29 October 1980, 1 daughter. Education: BA, English (II/I), King's College, Cambridge, England, 1958-61. Appointments: Senior Master, Akim-Oda Secondary School, Ghana; Lecturer in English, Great Yarmouth CHE; Coordinator of Liberal Studies, Norwich City College; Co-Director, European Centre, Friends World College; Writer-in-Residence, Associate Lecturer in Creative Writing, University of Wales, Cardiff, Wales. Publications: Sunday Whiteman, 1987; The Chymical Wedding, 1989; Alice's Masque, 1994; Essential Celtic Mythology, 1997; Parzival and the Stone from Heaven, 2001; The Wavat Troy, 2004. Honour: Whitbread Fiction Prize, 1989. Address: c/o Peters, Fraser & Dunlop, Chelsea Harbour, London SW10 0XF, England.

CLARKE William Malpas, b. 5 June 1922, Ashton-under-Lyne, England. Author. m. Faith Elizabeth Dawson, 2 daughters. Education: BA Hons, Econ, University of Manchester, England, 1948; Hon DLitt, London Guildhall University, 1992. Appointments: Financial Editor, The Times, 1956-66; Director-General, British Invisible Exports Council, 1967-87; Chairman, ANZ Merchant Bank, 1987-91; Chairman, Central Banking Publications, 1991-. Publications: City's Invisible Earnings, 1958; City in the World Economy, 1965; Private Enterprise in Developing Countries, 1966; The World's Money, 1970; Inside the City, 1979; How the City of London Works, 1986; Secret Life of Wilkie Collins, 1988; Planning for Europe, 1989; Lost Fortune of the Tsars, 1994; Letters of Wilkie Collins, 1999; The Golden Thread, 2000. Contributions to: The Banker; Central Banking; Euromoney; Wilkie Collins Society Journal. Honour: CBE, 1976. Memberships: Thackeray Society; Wilkie Collins Society; Reform Club. Address: 37 Park Vista, Greenwich, London SE10 9LZ, England.

CLARKSON Ewan, b. 23 January 1929, England. Education: MA, University of Exeter, 1984. Publications: Break for Freedom, 1967; Halic: The Story of a Grey Seal, 1970; The Running of the Deer, 1972; In the Shadow of the Falcon, 1973; Wolf Country: A Wilderness Pilgrimage, 1975; The Badgers of Summercombe, 1977; The Many Forked Branch, 1980; Wolves, 1980; Reindeer, 1981; Eagles, 1981; Beavers, 1981; In the Wake of the Storm, 1984; Ice Trek, 1986; King of the Wild, 1990; The Flight of the Osprey, 1995. Address: Moss Rose Cottage, Preston, Newton Abbot, Devon TQ12 3PP, England.

CLAUDEL Bernard Michel, b. 20 May 1932, Strasbourg, France. Professor (retired). 3 sons. Education: Ecole Normale Superieure, Paris, France, 1952-56; Agregation des Sciences Physiques, 1956; Doctorat es Sciences, 1962. Appointments: Professor, National Institute of Applied Science (INSA), Lyon, France, 1963-97; NSF Senior Foreign Scientist, University Missouri, Columbia, Missouri, USA, 1969-70. Visiting Associate Professor, University Missouri, Columbia, Missouri, USA, 1970-71. Publications: Books: La Catalyse au Laboratoire et Dans l'Industrie, 1967; Elements of Chemical Kinetics, 1970; Bases du Genie Chimique, 1977; Numerous scientific articles in various journals. Honour: Herpin Prize, Academy of Lyon, 1994. Memberships: Member, scientific staff, Research Institute on Catalysis, 1960-79; Board of Administrators, INSA, 1976-82; Head, Department of Energetics, INSA, 1979-82. Address: 154, rue Anatole France, 69100 Villeurbanne, France.

CLAYTON Peter Arthur, b. 27 April 1937, London, England. Publishing Consultant; Archaeological Lecturer. m. Janet Frances Manning, 5 September 1964, 2 sons. Education: School of Librarianship; North West Polytechnic, London, 1958; Institute of Archaeology, London University, 1958-62; University College, London, 1968-72. Appointments: Librarian, 1953-63;

Dictionary of International Biography

Archaeological Editor, Thames & Hudson, 1963-73; Humanities Publisher, Longmans, 1973; Managing Editor, British Museum's Publications, 1974-79; Publications Director, BA Seaby, 1980-87; Writer, Lecturer, 1987-; Consulting Editor, Minerva Magazine, 1990-; Expert Advisor (coins and antiquities), Department for Culture Media and Sport (Treasure Committee). Publications: The Rediscovery of Ancient Egypt; Archaeological Sites of Britain; Seven Wonders of the Ancient World; Treasures of Ancient Rome; Companion to Roman Britain; Great Figures of Mythology; Gods and Symbols of Ancient Egypt; Chronicle of the Pharaohs; Family Life in Ancient Egypt; The Valley of the Kings; Egyptian Mythology. Contributions to: Journal of Egyptian Archaeology; Numismatic Chronicle; Coin & Medal Bulletin; Minerva. Honours: Liveryman of the Honourable Company of Farriers of the City of London, 2000; Freeman of the City of London, 2000. Memberships: Library Association, fellow; Society of Antiquaries of London, fellow; Royal Numismatic Society, fellow. Address: 41 Cardy Road, Boxmoor, Hemel Hempstead, Hertfordshire HP1 1RL, England.

CLEESE John (Marwood), b. 27 October 1939, Weston-Super-Mare, Somerset, England. Author; Actor. m. (1) Connie Booth, 1968, dissolved 1978, 1 daughter, (2) Barbara Trentham, 1981, dissolved 1990, 1 daughter, (3) Alyce Faye Eichelberger, 1993. Education: MA, Downing College, Cambridge. Career: Began writing and making jokes professionally, 1963; Appeared in and co-wrote TV Series: The Frost Report; At Last the 1948 Show; Monty Python's Flying Circus; Fawlty Towers; The Human Face; Founder and Director, Video Arts Ltd, 1972-89; Films include: Interlude; The Magic Christian; And Now For Something Completely Different; Monty Python and the Holy Grail; Life of Brian; Yellowbeard, 1982; The Meaning of Life, 1983; Silverado, 1985; A Fish Called Wanda, 1988; Mary Shelley's Frankenstein, 1993; The Jungle Book, 1994; Fierce Creatures, 1996; The World Is Not Enough, 1999; The Quantum Project, 2000; Rat Race, 2000; Pluto Nash, 2000; Harry Potter and the Philosopher's Stone, 2001; Die Another Day, 2002; Harry Potter and the Chamber of Secrets, 2002; Charlie's Angels: Full Throttle, 2003; Around the World in 80 Days, 2004. Publications: Families and How to Survive Them, (with Robin Skynner), 1983; The Golden Skits of Wing Commander Muriel Volestrangler FRHS and Bar, 1984; The Complete Fawlty Towers (with Connie Booth), 1989; Life and How to Survive It (with Robin Skynner), 1993. Honour: Honorary LLD, St Andrews. Address: c/o David Wilkinson, 115 Hazlebury Road, London SW6 2LX, England.

CLEMENTS Christopher John, b. 21 January 1946, England. Medical Practitioner. m. Vivienne, 2 sons. Education: MB.BS, London Hospital, University of London, 1969; LRCP, MRCS, 1969; DObst, University of Auckland, 1972; DCH, Royal College of Physicians, London, 1973; MSc, University of Manchester, 1980; MCCM, 1980; MFPHM, 1980; FAFPHM, 1994. Appointments include: Registrar, Waikato Hospital, New Zealand, 1971; Medical Director, Hospital de Valle Apurimac, Peru, 1973-74; Chief Medical Officer, Save the Children Fund, Bangladesh Project, 1977, Afghanistan Project, 1977-78; Assistant Director, National Head of Disease Control, Department of Health, Head Office, Wellington, New Zealand, 1983-85; Medical Officer, Expanded Programme on Immunization, World Health Organisation, Geneva, 1985-2002. Publications: Over 100 articles and chapters contributed to books on public health. Memberships: Royal College of Public Health Physicians. Address: 24 Millbank Drive, Mount Eliza, VIC 3930, Australia. E-mail: clementscj@telstra.com

CLEMMOW Caroline Anne, b. 10 February 1959, London, England. Concert Pianist. m. Anthony Goldstone. Education: Royal Academy of Music, London, England, 1977-82. Appointments:

Leading piano duo, with husband, appearing throughout British Isles and abroad, including USA; Chamber music including major tour of Russia, Ukraine; Collaborations with percussionist Evelyn Glennie; Occasional concerto soloist. Publications: 25 piano duo recordings; 7 chamber music recordings. Honours: Associate, Royal College of Music, 1976; Licentiate, 1978, Associate, 1992, Royal Academy of Music. Memberships: Incorporated Society of Musicians. Address: Walcot Old Hall, Alkborough, North Lincolnshire DN15 9JT, England. E-mail: carolineclemmow@aol.com

CLIFFORD Max, b. April 1943, Kingston-upon-Thames, England. Public Relations Executive. m. Elizabeth, 1 daughter. Appointments: Worker, Department Store; Former Junior Reporter, Merton & Morden News; Former Press Officer, EMI Records (promoted the Beatles); Founder, Max Clifford Associates, clients have included Muhammad Ali, Marlon Brando, David Copperfield, O J Simpson, Frank Sinatra, SEAT, Laing Homes. Address: Max Clifford Associates Ltd, 109 New Bond Street, London W1Y 9AA, England.

CLINTON Hilary Rodham, b. 26 October 1947, Chicago, Illinois, USA. Lawyer and Former First Lady of USA. m. Bill Clinton, 1 daughter. Education: Yale University. Career: Rose Law Firm, 1977-, currently Senior Partner; Appointments: Legal Counsel, Nixon Impeachment Staff, 1974; Senator from New York, 2001-; Various teaching positions, committee places, public & private ventures. Publications include: Every Child Needs a Village, 1994; It Takes a Village, 1996; Dear Socks, Dear Buddy, 1998; An Invitation to the White House, 2000; Living History (memoirs), 2003; numerous magazine articles. Honours include: One of Most Influential Lawyers in America, 1988, 1991; AIDS Awareness Award, 1994; Grammy Award, 1997. Address: US Senate, Washington, DC 20510, USA.

CLINTON William Jefferson (Bill), b. 19 August 1946, Hope, Arizona, USA. Former President, USA. m. Hillary Rodham, 1975, 1 daughter. Education: BS, International Affairs, Georgetown University, 1964-68; Rhodes Scholar, University College, Oxford, 1968-70; JD, Yale University Law School, 1970-73. Appointments: Professor, University of Arizona Law School, 1974-76; Democrat Nominee, Arizona, 1974; Attorney-General, Arizona, 1977-79; State Governor of Arizona, 1979-81, 1983-92; Member, Wright, Lindsey & Jennings, law firm, 1981-83; Chairman, Southern Growth Policies Board, 1985-86; Chairman, Education Commissioner of the States, 1986-87; Chairman, National Governor's Association, 1986-87; Vice-Chairman, Democrat Governor's Association, 1987-88; Chairman elect, 1988-89, Chairman, 1989-90; Co-Chairman, Task Force on Education, 1990-91; Chairman, Democrat Leadership Council, 1990-91; President, USA, 1993-2001; Impeached by House of Representatives for perjury and obstruction of justice, 1988; Acquitted in the Senate on both counts, 1999; Suspended from practising law in Supreme Court, 2001-06. Honours: National Council of State Human Service Administrators Association Award; Award, Leadership on Welfare Reform; National Energy Efficiency Advocate Award; Honorary Degree, Northeastern University, Boston, 1993; Honorary Fellow, University College, Oxford, 1993; Honorary DCL, Oxford, 1994; Honorary DLitt, Ulster University, 1995. Address: 55 West 125th Street, New York, NY 10027, USA.

CLITHEROE Frederic, b. 25 September 1941, Bury, Lancashire, England. Librarian; Poet. m. Catherine Eyre, 1 July 1971, 1 son, 1 daughter. Education: BA, Honours, English, University of Exeter, 1966-69; ALA, 1970. Appointments: University of Sussex, 1970-71; Assistant Librarian, University of Keele, 1971-90; Freelance Writer, 1990-. Publications: Ellipsis, 1961; Poems, 1968;

Meerbrook, 1979; Forsbrook, 1981; Countess Torsy, 1989; Harecastle Mint, 1993. Contributions to: Anthologies and periodicals. Honours: Dunn-Wilson Prize, 1966; Award from Beanica Foundation, 1981. Address: Greenfields, Agger Hill, Finney Green, Newcastle, Staffordshire ST5 6AA, England.

CLOONEY George, b. 1962, USA. Actor. m. Talia Blasam, divorced. Creative Works: TV Series: ER, 1984-85; The Facts of Life, 1985-86; Roseanne, 1988-89; Sunset Beat, 1990; Baby Talk, 1991; Sisters, 1992-94; ER, 1994-99; Films: Return of the Killer Tomatoes, 1988; Red Surf, 1990; Unbecoming Age, 1993; From Dusk Till Dawn, 1998; Batman and Robin, 1998; The Peacemaker, 1998; Out of Sight, 1998; The Thin Red Line, 1998; Three Kings, 1999; The Perfect Storm, 1999; Where Art Thou? 2000; Spy Kids, 2001; Ocean's Eleven, 2001; Welcome to Collinwood, 2002; Solaris, 2003; Confessions of a Dangerous Mind (director), 2003; Spy Kids 3-D: Game Over, 2003; Intolerable Cruelty, 2003. Address: Creative Artists, 9830 Wilshire Boulevard, Beverly Hills, CA 90212, USA.

CLOONEY Rosemary, b. 23 May 1928, Maysville, Kentucky, USA. Singer. Appointments: Early appearances with sister, Betty; Joined saxophonist Tony Pastor's band, 1945; Solo Artiste, 1946-. Creative Works: Films include: The Stars Are Singing, 1953; Here Come The Girls, 1954; Red Garters, 1954; Deep In My Heart, 1954; White Christmas, 1954; Albums include: Deep in My Heart, 1954; Hollywood's Best, 1955; Blue Rose, 1956; Clooney Times, 1957; Ring A Round Rosie with the Hi-Lo's, 1957; Swing Around Rosie, 1958; Fancy Meeting You Here with Bing Crosby, 1958; The Ferrers At Home, 1958; Hymns From the Heart, 1959; Rosemary Clooney Swings Softly, 1960; A Touch of Tabasco, 1960; Clap Hands, Here Comes Rosie, 1960; Rosie Solves The Swingin' Riddle, 1961; Country Hits From the Past, 1963; Love, 1963; Thanks For Nothing, 1964; That Travelin' Two Beat, 1965; Look My Way, 1976; Nice to be Around, 1977; Here's To My Lady, 1979; Rosemary Clooney Sings Harold Arien, 1983; My Buddy, 1983; Rosemary Clooney Sings The Lyrics of Johnny Mercer, 1987; Show Tunes, 1989; Girl Singer, 1992; Singles include: You're Just In Love; Beautiful Brown Eyes; Come On - My House; Tenderly; Half As Much; Botcha Me; Too Old to Cut the Mustard (with Marlene Dietrich); The Night Before Christmas; Hey There; This Ole House; Mambo Italiano; Mangos. Publication: This For Remembrance. Address: c/o Production Central, 3500 West Olive, Suite 1420, Burbank, CA 91505, USA.

CLOS Lynne Mobley, b. 2 September 1955, Baton Rouge, Louisiana, USA. Editor; Publisher. m. Christopher J Clos, 2 daughters. Education: BS, Mechanical Engineering, Oakland University, 1978; Master of Basic Science, Museum Studies, Vertebrate Palaeontology, University of Colorado, 1991. Appointments: Corrosion Engineer, GM Proving Ground, 1979-81; Product Engineer, Rockwell International, 1981-87; Freelance Writer, 1991-97; Editor, Publisher, Fossil News, 1998-. Publications: The Value of a Blanket, Parenting New Mexico, 1996; Numerous articles on palaeontology include: A New Species of Varanus from the Miocene of Kenya, 1995; Trilobite Tales and Fossil News, 1995-; Book: Field Adventures in Paleontology, 2003. Honours: Tau Beta Pi; Graduate cum laude with Departmental Honors; Listed in Who's Who publications and biographical dictionaries. Memberships: Society of Vertebrate Paleontology; Western Interior Paleontological Society; The Cycad Society. Address: 1185 Claremont Drive, Boulder, CO 80305, USA. E-mail: lynne@fossilnews.com Website: www.fossilnews.com

CLOSE Glenn, b. 19 March 1947, Greenwich, Connecticut, USA. Actress. m. (1) C Wade, divorced, (2) J Marlas, 1984, divorced, 1 daughter (with J Starke). Education: William and Mary College.

Career: Co-owner, The Leaf and Bean Coffee House, 1991-; Films include: The World According to Garp, 1982; The Big Chill, 1983; The Stone Boy, 1984; Jagged Edge, 1985; Fatal Attraction, 1987; Dangerous Liaisons, 1989; Hamlet, 1989; The House of Spirits, 1990; Hamlet, 1990; 101 Dalmatians, 1996; Mars Attacks! 1996; Air Force One, 1997; Paradise Road, 1997; Tarzan, 1999; Cookie's Fortune, 1999; 102 Dalmatians, 2000; The Safety of Objects, 2001; Pinocchio (voice), 2002. Theatre includes: The Rules of the Game; A Streetcar Named Desire; King Lear; The Rose Tattoo; Death and the Maiden; Sunset Boulevard. Address: Creative Artists Agency, 9830 Wilshire Boulevard, Beverly Hills, CA 90212, USA.

CLOUDSLEY Timothy, b. 18 September 1948, Cambridge, England. University Lecturer. m. Rhona Cleugh, 18 July 1987, 2 sons. Education: BA, Honours, Cantab, 1971; MA, 1974; Postgraduate Research, Durham University, 1972-74. Appointments: Lecturer, Sociology, Newcastle University, 1972-74, Napier University, Edinburgh, 1974-76, Heriot-Watt University, Edinburgh, 1976-77, Glasgow Caledonian University, 1977-. Publications: Poems to Light (Through Love and Blood), 1980; Mair Licht (anthology), 1988; The Construction of Nature (social philosophy), 1994; Coincidence (anthology), 1995; Incantations From Streams of Fire, 1997; Poems, 1998. Contributions to: Northlight Poetry Review; Understanding Magazine; Interactions; Romantic Heir; The People's Poetry; Cadmium Blue Literary Journal; Le Journal des Poètes. Memberships: Open Circle (Arts and Literature Organization), Glasgow, literary secretary, 1990-96. Address: 31 Hamilton Drive, Glasgow G12 8DN, Scotland.

CLOUDSLEY-THOMPSON (Jessie) Anne, (Anne Cloudsley), b. 20 March 1915, Reigate, Surrey, England. Physiotherapist; Artist. m. Professor JL Cloudsley-Thompson, 3 sons. Education: MCSP, ME, LET, University College Hospital, London, England; LCAD, DipBS, Byam Shaw School of Art, London. Appointments: Established Physiotherapy Department, Hatfield Military Hospital, Hertfordshire, England, 1940-42; Superintendent Physiotherapist, Peripheral Nerve Injuries Centre, Wingfield Orthopaedic Hospital, Oxford, England, 1942-44; Superintendent Physiotherapist, Omdurman General Hospital, Sudan, 1960-71; Founder and Honorary Gallery Curator, Africa Centre, London, 1978-82; Visiting Lecturer, Fine Art, University of Nigeria, Nsukka, 1981; Lecturer, Lithography, Working Men's College, London NW1, 1982-91. Publications: Women of Omdurman: life, love and the cult of virginity, 1983, reprinted 1983, 1984, 1987; Articles and reviews; Numerous individual and group exhibitions including: The Royal Academy Summer Exhibition, 1992, 1993; Fresh Art, 2001, 2002, 2003; Cork Street, 2003. Memberships: Chartered Society of Physiotherapy, 1935-; Print Makers Council, 1996-; The London Group, 2002-. Address: 10 Battishill Street, London N1 1TE, England.

CLOUDSLEY-THOMPSON John Leonard, b. 23 May 1921, Murree, India. Professor of Zoology. m. J Anne Cloudsley, 3 sons. Education: BA, 1947, MA, 1949, PhD, 1950, Pembroke College, Cambridge; DSc, University of London, 1960. Appointments: War Service, 1940-44; Lecturer in Zoology, King's College, University of London, 1950-60; Professor of Zoology, University of Khartoum and Keeper, Sudan Natural History Museum, 1960-71; Professor of Zoology, Birkbeck College, University of London, 1972-86; Professor Emeritus, 1986-. Publications: Over 50 books, including: Ecophysiology of Desert Arthropods and Reptiles, 1991; The Nile Quest, novel, 1994; Biotic Interactions in Arid Lands, 1996; Teach Yourself Ecology, 1998; The Diversity of Amphibians and Reptiles, 1999; Monographs, 11 Children's natural history books: Contributions to Encyclopaedia Britannica, Encyclopedia Americana; Articles in professional journals. Honours: Honorary Captain, 1944; Honorary DSc, Khartoum and Silver Jubilee Gold

Medal, 1981; Fellow, Honoris Causa, Linnean Society, 1997; Listed in national and international biographical publications. Memberships: Liveryman, Worshipful Company of Skinners; FI Biol; FWAAS; FRES; FLS; FZS. Address: 10 Battishill Street, Islington, London N1 1TE, England.

CLYNE Henry Horne, b. Wick, Caithness, Scotland. Sculptor; Principal Lecturer. m. Elaine Dunnet, 1 son. Education: DA (Edin), 1953, 1 year, Postgraduate, Highly Commended, Edinburgh College of Art; Travelling Scholarships to Italy and France; Morray House Training College for Teachers, 1954-55; Course in Specialist Ceramics, IWCAT, Tokoname, Aichi, Japan, 1986. Appointments: National Service, Sergeant/Instructor, RAEC, 1955-57; Teacher, Fife County, Scotland, 1957-59; Harkness Fellowship in USA, 1959-61; Lecturer in charge of Sculpture, Norwich School of Art, Norwich, England, 1962-65; Lecturer, Gloucestershire College of Art and Design, 1965-73; Principal Lecturer in charge of Sculpture Department, Winchester School of Art, 1973-86; Retired early to pursue own work and interests, 1986; Set up "Sheepshapes" as small business as a sculptor making ceramic sheep individually handmade, 1990-. Creative works: 15 foot figure for Leonard Rosoman in Richard Buckle's Exhibition "Diaghilev" and a large portrait of Diaghilev, Edinburgh Festival, 1954; Large relief and lettering in stone, St Andrew's School, Kirkaldy, Fife, 1959; 10 foot high sculpture for the University of East Anglia, now in the Sainsbury Collection, 1964; 8 foot long sculpture for Stirling University, Scotland, 1966; Various sculptures for private collections and group exhibitions, UK, USA, Japan and Europe. Honours: Andrew Grant Scholar, Edinburgh College of Art and postgraduate year and travel in Italy and France, 3 years; Harkness Fellowship, USA, 2 years; 2 Bronze Medals, Bicentenaire Cazeres-sur-Garonne, Haute Garonne, France, 1989. Address: Sunnymede, Horsebridge Road, King's Somborne, Stockbridge, Hampshire, SO20 6PT, England.

CLYNE Michael George, b. 12 October 1939, Melbourne, Australia. University Professor. m. Irene Donohoue Clyne, 1 daughter. Education: BA, Hons, 1960, MA, 1962, University of Melbourne; Postgraduate Studies, Bonn, Utrecht, 1961-62; PhD, Monash University, 1965. Appointments: Tutor, Lecturer, Senior Lecturer in German, 1962-72, Associate Professor of German, 1972-88, Professor of Linguistics, 1988-2001, Monash University; Professorial Fellow, Linguistics and Director, Research Unit for Multilingualism and Cross-cultural communication, University of Melbourne, 2001- Visiting Professor, University of Stuttgart, 1972-73, Heidelberg, 1997. Publications: 26 books and numerous articles in the field of linguistics; Books include: Community Languages The Australian Experience, 1991; Inter-Cultural Communication at Work, 1994; German Language in a Changing Europe, 1995; Undoing and Redoing Corpus Planning, 1997; Dynamics of Language Contact, 2003. Honours: Fellow, Academy of Social Sciences, Australia, 1982; Fellow, Australian Academy of Humanities, 1983; Honorary Life Member, Applied Linguistics Association of Australia, 1988; Member, Order of Australia, 1993; Austrian Cross of Honor for Science and the Arts, 1st class, 1996; Honorary PhD, University of Munich, 1997; Jacob and Wilhelm Grimm Prize, 1999; Humboldt Research Prize, 2003; German Cross of Merit, 2003. Address: Department of Linguistics and Applied Linguistics, University of Melbourne, Victoria 3010, Australia.

COCKER Jarvis Branson, b. England. Singer. m. Camille Bidault-Waddington, 1 son. Education: St Martin's College of Art & Design. Appointments: Singer with Pulp (formerly named Arabacus Pulp), 1981-; Made Videos for Pulp, Aphex Twin, Tindersticks; Co-Producer, Do You Remember The First Time? (TV). Creative Works: Singles include: My Legendary Girlfriend,

1991; Razzmatazz, 1992; O U, 1992; Babies, 1992; Common People, 1995; Disco 2000, 1996; Albums include: It; Freaks; Separations; PulpIntro: The Gift Recordings; His 'N' Hers; Different Class, 1995; This is Hardcore, 1998. Address: c/o Savage & Best Ltd, 79 Parkway, London NW1 7PP, England.

COCKER Joe, b. 20 May 1944, Sheffield, South Yorkshire, England. Singer; Songwriter. Appointments: Northern Club circuit, with group, The Grease Band, 1965-69; Solo Artist, 1968-; Regular worldwide tours and major concert appearances. Creative Works: Singles: With a Little Help From My Friends, 1968; Delta Lady, 1969; The Letter, 1970; Cry Me a River, 1970; You Are So Beautiful, 1975; Unchain My Heart, 1987; When the Night Comes, 1990; Up Where We Belong. Honours: Grammy, Best Pop Vocal Performance, 1983; Academy Award, Best Film Song, 1983; Grammy Nomination, 1989. Address: c/o Roger Davies Management, 15030 Ventura Blvd #772, Sherman Oaks, CA 91403, USA.

CODA Andrea Giuseppe, b. 5 June 1949, Torino, Italy. Surgeon. m. Marta Tavano, 1 daughter. Education: MB, BChir, 1973, Postgraduate, Emergency Surgery, 1978, Postgraduate, General Surgery, 1986, University of Turin, Italy. Appointments: Lieutenant, Army Health, Military Hospital, Brescia, Italy, 1975-76; Assistant Surgeon, 1976-78, Vice Director, Department of Surgery, 1978-98, Chief of Day Surgery Unit, Gradenigo Hospital, Turin, Italy. Publications: Articles in professional journals. Memberships: European Hernia Society; Italian Society of Surgery; Italian Association for Hospital Surgeons; Italian Society for Day Surgery and Ambulatory Surgery. Address: 3 C Regina Margherita, 10124, Torino, Italy. E-mail: coda.andrea@tiscali.it

COE Sebastian Newbold, b. 29 September 1956. Member of Parliament. m. Nicola Susan Elliott, 1990, 2 sons, 2 daughters. Education: BSc Hons, Economics, Social History, Loughborough University. Career: Winner, Gold Medal for running 1500m and silver medal for 800m, Moscow Olympics, 1980; Gold Medal for 1500m and silver medal for 800m, Los Angeles Olympics, 1984; European 800m Champion, Stuttgart, 1986; World Record Holder at 800m, 1000m and mile, 1981; Research Assistant, Loughborough University, 1981-84; Member, 1983-89, Vice Chairman, 1986-89, Chairman, Olympic Review Group, 1984-85; Sports Council; Member, HEA, 1987-92; Olympic Committee, Medical Commission, 1987-; Conservative MP for Falmouth and Camborne, 1992-; PPS to Deputy PM, 1995-96; Assistant Government Whip, 1996-97; Private Secretary to Leader of the Opposition, The Rt Hon William Hague, MP, 1997-2001. Publications: Running Free, with David Miller, 1981; Running for Fitness, with Peter Coe, 1983; The Olympians, 1984, 1996; More Than a Game, 1992; Born to Run (autobiography), 1992. Memberships: Associate Member, Academie des Sports, France; Athletes Commission, IOC; IOC Medical Commission, 1988-94; Member, Sport For All Commission, 1998-; IOC Commission 2000, 1999. Address: Conservative Central Office, 32 Smith Square, London SW1P 3HH, England.

COEN Ethan, b. 1958, St Louis Park, Minnesota, USA. Film Producer; Screenwriter. m. Education: Princeton University. Appointments: Screenwriter with Joel Coen, Crime Wave (formerly XYZ Murders); Producer, Screenplay, Editor, Blood Simple, 1984. Creative Works: Films: Raising Arizona, 1987; Miller's Crossing, 1990; Barton Fink, 1991; The Hudsucker Proxy, 1994; Fargo, 1996; The Naked Man; The Big Lebowski, 1998; O Brother, Where Art Thou? 2000; The Man Who Wasn't There, 2001; Fever in the Blood, 2002. Publication: Gates of Eden, 1998. Address: c/o UTA, 9560 Wilshire Boulevard, Beverly Hills, CA 90212, USA.

Dictionary of International Biography

COEN Joel, b. 1955, St Louis Park, Minnesota, USA. Film Director; Screenwriter. Divorced. Education: Simon's Rock College; New York University. Appointments: Assistant Editor, Fear No Evil, Evil Dead; Worked with Rock Video Crews; Screenwriter with Ethan Coen, Crime Wave (formerly XYZ Murders). Creative Works: Films: Blood Simple, 1984; Raising Arizona, 1987; Miller's Crossing, 1990; Barton Fink, 1991; The Hudsucker Proxy, 1994; Fargo, 1996; The Big Lebowski; O Brother, Where Art Thou? 2000; The Man Who Wasn't There, 2001. Honours include: Best Director Award, Cannes International Film Festival, 1996. Address: c/o UTA, 9560 Wilshire Boulevard, Beverly Hills, CA 90212, USA.

COERPER Milo George, b. 8 May 1925, Milwaukee, Wisconsin, USA. Naval Officer; Lawyer; Episcopal Priest. m. Wendy Hicks Coerper, 1 son, 2 daughters. Education: BS, US Naval Academy, 1946; LLB, University of Michigan Law School, 1954; MA, 1957, PhD, 1960, Georgetown University; Certificate, Theology (by extension), University of the South, 1980. Appointments: Ensign, Lieutenant (jg), Lieutenant (sg), US Navy; Aide to Admiral in charge of battleships during the Korean War; Associate Law Firm, 1954-60; Part-time Professor, Catholic University Law School and George Washington University Law School, 1960; Associate, 1961-64, Partner, 1964-95, Retired Partner,1996-, Coudert Brothers International Law Firm; Expert Geographical Indications – World Intellectual Property Organization (WIPO), 1991; Ordained Episcopal Priest in the Diocese of Maryland, 1979; Voluntary Chaplain, Washington National Cathedral, 1986-; Member of Council, The Friends of Canterbury Cathedral in the United States, 1999-. Publications: The Use of Public International Law by Municipal Courts in Cases Arising out of the Taking of Alien Property (PhD dissertation), 1960; A Deeper Dimension, 1995; Certification Marks as a Means of Protecting Wine Appellations in the US, 1998. Honour: Cross of the Order of Merit of the Federal Republic of Germany, 1993. Memberships: American Society of International Law; International Law Association; American Bar Association; Metropolitan Club; Army and Navy Club. Address: Coudert Brothers, 1627 1st NW, 12th Floor, Washington DC 20006, USA.

COHEN Alvin P, b. 12 December 1937, Los Angeles, California, USA. Professor. m. Dade Singapuri, 3 sons. Education: BS, 1960, MA, 1966, PhD, 1971, University of California at Berkeley, USA. Appointments: Assistant Professor of Chinese, 1971-77, Associate Professor of Chinese, 1977-83, Professor of Chinese, 1983-, Department Chairman, 1991-97, University of Massachusetts at Amherst, USA. Publications: Tales of Vengeful Souls: A Sixth Century Collection of Chinese Avenging Ghost Stories, 1982; Introduction to Research in Chinese Resource Materials, 2000; Chinese Religion: Popular Religion, in The Encyclopedia of Religion, 1987; Documentation Relating to the Origins of the Chinese Shadow Puppet Theatre, Asia Major volume 13, 2000. Honours: University of Massachusetts Faculty Research Grant, 1972, 1977, 1980, 1984, 1985; Association for Asian Studies Conference Grant, 1995, 1996, 1997. Memberships: American Oriental Society; Association for Asian Studies; Society for the Study of Chinese Religions; T'ang Studies Society; Warring States Working Group. Address: Department of Asian Languages and Literatures, University of Massachusetts at Amherst, Amherst, MA 01003-9312, USA.

COHEN Andrew David, b. 14 March 1944, Washington DC, USA. University Professor. m. Sabina Rose, 1 son, 1 daughter. Education: BA, French History and Literature, Harvard University, 1965; MA, Linguistics, 1971, PhD, International Development Education, 1973, Stanford University. Appointments: Assistant Professor, English as a Second Language section of English Department, UCLA, 1972-75; Professor, Hebrew University of Jerusalem, Israel, 1975-91; Professor, Applied Linguistics and ESL, University of Minnesota, 1991-. Publications: Assessing Language Ability in the Classroom, 1994; Strategies in Learning and Using a Second Language, 1998; Numerous research articles on language teaching, language learning and bilingual education. Honours: Fulbright Lecturer and Researcher to Brazil, 1986-87; Language Learning Distinguished Scholar in Residence, Georgia State University, February 1996; Scholar of the College, College of Liberal Arts, University of Minnesota, 2002-05. Memberships: American Association for Applied Linguistics; Teachers of English to Speakers of Other Languages; American Council for the Teaching of Foreign Languages; Secretary General, International Association of Applied Linguistics, 1996-2002. Address: 331E Nolte Centre, University of Minnesota, 315 Pillsbury Drive SE, Minneapolis, MN 55455, USA. E-mail: adcohen@umn.edu

COHEN David Walter, b. 15 December 1926, Philadelphia, USA. Periodontist; Educator. m. Betty Axelrod, deceased, 3 daughters. Education: University of Pennsylvania, 1943-45; DDS, University of Pennsylvania, School of Dentistry, 1950; Research Fellow, Pathology and Periodontics, Beth Israel Hospital, Boston, Massachusetts, 1950. Appointments include: Assistant Professor of Periodontology, Vice Chairman of the Department, 1955-59, Associate Professor of Periodontology and Co-Chairman of the Department, 1959-63, Professor of Periodontics, Chairman of the Department, 1963-73, Graduate School of Medicine and Division of Graduate Medicine, Assistant Professor of Oral Medicine and Oral Histopathology, 1956-59, Associate Professor of Oral Histology, Pathology and Oral Medicine and Director of Periodontia, 1959-63, Professor of Periodontics and Chairman of Department, 1963-73, Dean, 1972-83, Dean Emeritus and Professor of Periodontics, 1983-, School of Dentistry, University of Pennsylvania; Clinical Professor of Dental Medicine, 1973-, President, 1986-93, Chancellor, 1993-98, Medical College of Pennsylvania; Chancellor-Emeritus, Medical College of Pennsylvania, Hahnemann University of Health Sciences, 1998-; Numerous visiting professorships and consultant positions. Publications: Co-author or contributor to 25 books including Periodontal Medicine, 1999; Over 120 articles in professional journals as author and co-author include: Periodontal Medicine in the Next Millennium, 2000; Potential Effects of Oral Infections on Systemic Health, 2001. Honours: 42 honours and awards include: Honorary degrees from universities: Boston University, 1975, Hebrew University of Jerusalem, 1976, University of Athens, 1979, Louis Pasteur University, Strasbourg, 1986, University of Detroit, 1989; Gold Medal, American College of Periodontology, 1971; Honorary Member, British Society of Periodontology, 1974; Legion of Merit, French Government, 1982; Betty and D Walter Cohen Endowed Professorship in Periodontal Research, Hebrew University, 1986; D Walter Cohen Endowed Professorship and Chair, University of Pennsylvania School of Dental Medicine, 1991; D Walter Cohen Center for Dental Education in the Middle East, Hebrew University of Jerusalem, 1997. Memberships include: Fellow, American Academy of Oral Pathology; Fellow, American College of Dentists; Fellow, College of Physicians of Philadelphia; Fellow, American Association for the Advancement of Science; American Dental Association; International Association for Dental Research, New York Academy of Sciences. Address: Chancellor's Office, Drexel University College of Medicine, 3300 Henry Avenue, Philadelphia, PA 17129, USA. E-mail: jmm57@drexel.edu.com

COHEN Jack, b. 19 September 1933, Norwich, England. Consultant Reproductive Biologist; Author; Complexity Scientist. m. (1) Carmela Mia Dawidowicz, 2 children, (2) Judith Rosalind, divorced, 4 children. Education: BSc, Zoology, 1954, PhD, 1957,

Dictionary of International Biography

University of Hull; DSc, University of Birmingham, 1974; Fellow, Institute of Biology, 1974; Fellow, Institute for the Study of Coherence and Emergence, 2000; Honorary Professor, Institute of Mathematics, University of Warwick, 2001. Appointments: Postdoctoral Fellow, Medical Research Council Unit, Birmingham, 1957-59; Lecturer in Embryology, University of Birmingham, 1959-68; Research Fellow, Harvard University, USA, 1963-64; Senior Lecturer in Animal Reproduction, University of Birmingham, 1968-87; Honorary Lecturer, 1987-88, Honorary Senior Lecturer, 1988, School of Biological Sciences, University of Birmingham; Senior Embryological Advisor, IVF Clinic, London, 1987-89; Rosi and Max Varon Visiting Professor, Weizman Institute, Israel, 1995-96; Consultant, Mathematics Institute, and Ecosystems Analysis and Epidemiology Unit, Warwick University, 1996-2000; Consultant Reproductive Biologist, Author, Complexity Scientist, Consultant Embryologist, Assisted Conception Unit, Birmingham Women's Hospital. Publications: Author and co-author, 20 books; Numerous contributions to journals; Conference papers and lectures. Memberships: Institute of Biology; Linnean Society; Zoological Society of London; Society for the Study of Fertility; British Society for Developmental Biology. Address: Moat House, Springdale, Gorsley, nr Ross on Wye, Herefordshire, HR9 7SU, England. E-mail: drjackcohen@aol.com

COHEN Leonard, b. 21 September 1934, Montreal, Canada. Singer; Songwriter. 2 children. Education: McGill University. Appointments: Founder, Country & Western Band, The Buckskin Boys, 1951. Creative Works: Recordings include: Songs of Leonard Cohen; Songs From A Room; Various Positions, 1985; I'm Your Man, 1988; The Future, Cohen Live, 1994; Ten New Songs, 2001. Publication: Let Us Compare Mythologies. Honours include: McGill Literature Award. Address: c/o Kelley Lynch, Stranger Management Inc, 419 North Larchmont Boulevard, Suite 91, Los Angeles, CA 90004, USA.

COHEN Samuel M, b. 24 September 1946, Milwaukee, Wisconsin, USA. Physician; Scientist. m. Janet L Olson Cohen, 2 sons, 2 daughters. Education: BS, 1967, PhD, 1972, MD, 1972, University of Wisconsin-Madison, USA; American Board of Pathology, 1976. Appointments: Staff Pathologist, St Vincent Hospital, Worcester, Massachusetts, 1975-81; Associate Professor, University of Massachusetts Medical School, Worcester, Massachusetts, 1977-81; Professor of Pathology and Microbiology, Eppley Institute, University of Nebraska Medical Center, Omaha, Nebraska, 1981-; Vice-Chair, Department of Pathology and Microbiology, 1981-92, Chairman, 1992-. Publications: More than 300 publications and chapters. Honours: Creative Activity Award, University of Nebraska; Alumnus of the Year Citation, University of Wisconsin-Madison Medical School; Memberships include: Society of Toxicology, American Association for Cancer Research; American Medical Association; College of American Pathologists; US-Canadian Academy of Pathology. Address: University of Nebraska Medical Center, Department of Pathology and Microbiology, 983135 Nebraska Medical Center, Omaha, Nebraska 68198-3135, USA. E-mail: scohen@unmc.edu

COHEN-MUSHLIN Aliza, b. 8 April 1937, Tel Aviv, Israel. Professor. Education: BSc, Biology and Chemistry, 1965, MA, Art History, 1974, Hebrew University; BMus, Harpsichord and Organ, Rubin Music Academy, 1972; PhD, Art History, Hebrew University and London University, 1981. Appointments: Senior Lecturer, 1989-2000, Director, Centre for Jewish Art, 1990-, Professor, 2000-, Hebrew University; Editor, Jewish Art, 1986-. Publications: 3 books. Honours: Honorary Professor, Braunschweig University, Germany, 2000. Memberships: Committee, Internationale Palaeographie Latine, 1993-; Steering Committee,

Religious Heritage, Council of Europe, 1998-; Academy of Science, Braunschweig, Germany, 2000-. Address: Centre for Jewish Art, Hebrew University, Mt Scopus, Jerusalem 91905, Israel. E-mail: cja@vms.huji.ac.il Website: www.hum.huji.ac.il/cja

COHN Mildred, b. 12 July 1913, New York, USA. Biochemist. m. Henry Primakoff, 1 son, 2 daughters. Education: BA, Hunter College, 1931; MA, 1932, PhD, 1938, Columbia University. Appointments: Research Associate, Biochemistry, George Washington University, 1937-38; Research Associate, Biochemistry, Cornell Medical College, 1938-46; Research Associate, 1946-58; Associate Professor, 1958-1960, Biochemistry, Washington University, St Louis; Associate Professor of Biochemistry and Biophysics, 1960-61; Full Professor, 1961-1982, Benjamin Rush Professor, 1978-1982, University of Pennsylvania School of Medicine; Career Investigator, American Heart Association, 1964-1978; Senior Member, Fox Chase Cancer Center, 1982-85. Publications: More than 150 articles and chapters in professional journals and books. Honours include: 9 Honorary Degrees and Garvan Medal, American Chemical Society, 1963; Cresson Medal, Franklin Institute, 1975; Chandler Medal, Columbia University; National Medal of Science; Distinguished Service Award, College of Physicians, Philadelphia; PA Governor's Award for Excellence in Science; Stein-Moore Award, Protein Society and many others. Memberships: Phi Beta Kappa; Sigma Xi; American Chemical Society; American Society of Biochemistry and Molecular Biology; American Academy of Arts and Sciences; National Academy of Sciences; American Philosophical Society. Address: University of Pennsylvania School of Medicine, Department of Biochemistry and Biophysics, 242 Anat/Chem, Philadelphia, PA 19104-6059, USA.

COHN Paul Moritz, b. 8 January 1924, Hamburg, Germany. Mathematician. m. Deirdre Sonia Sharon, 2 daughters. Education: BA, 1948, MA, PhD, 1951, Trinity College, Cambridge. Appointments: Chargé de Recherches (CNRS), University of Nancy, France, 1951-52; Lecturer, Mathematics, University of Manchester, England, 1952-62; Reader, Mathematics, Queen Mary College, University of London, 1962-67; Professor and Head, Mathematics Department, Bedford College, University of London, 1967-84; Professor of Mathematics, 1984-86, Astor Professor of Mathematics, 1986-89, Retired, Professor Emeritus, Honorary Research Fellow, 1989-, University College London. Publications: Numerous research papers in abstract algebra and various books including: Universal Algebra, 1965, 2nd edition, 1981; Free rings and their relations, 1971, 2nd edition, 1985; Algebra I, 1974, II, 1977 (a second edition in 3 volumes appeared in the 1980's, and the whole work has been revised and is now being republished as: Classic Algebra, 2000, Basic Algebra, 2002, Further Algebra, 2003); Algebraic Numbers and Algebraic Functions, 1991; Elements of Linear Algebra, 1994; Skew Fields, Theory of General Division Rings, 1995; Introduction to Ring Theory, 2000. Honours: Rouse Ball Prize, 1946; Mathison Prize, 1948; Rayleigh Prize, 1950; Lester R Ford Award, Mathematical Association of America, 1972; Senior Berwick Prize, London Mathematical Society, 1974; Fellow of the Royal Society, 1980. Memberships: London Mathematical Society, 1957, President, 1982-84; American Mathematical Society, 1962; Mathematical Association of America, 1972. Address: Department of Mathematics, University College London, Gower Street, London, WC1E 6BT, England.

COKER Norman Richard, b. 27 January 1927, Grays, Essex. Artist; Lecturer. m. Doreen Annie. Education: Thurrock Technical College, Grays Essex. Career: Tutor, Lecturer, Grays College, 1974-2002; Tutor, Lecturer, The Burren Painting Centre, County Clare, Ireland, 1977-84; Freelance artist; Exhibitions: Nairobi,

Kenya; The McEwan Gallery, Scotland; The Veryan Gallery, Cornwall; Singapore; London; Amsterdam; The Frinton Gallery; One Man Show, Beecroft Gallery, Westcliff-on-Sea, 1991; Numerous works in collections including HRH The Princess Royal, an equestrian portrait with her horse Doublet; Commissions: James Last; The Royal Albert Hall. Publications: Work included in The Encyclopaedia of Flower Painting Techniques; Rosenstiel's Fine Art Publishers; Woodmansterne; Papers Rose Ltd; Jason Products Ltd, New Zealand. Honours: Founder Presidents Honour, Society of Botanical Artists; The East African Wild Life Society Award, 1991. Membership: Founder Member, Society of Botanical Artists. Address: Tensing, Muckingford Road, Linford, Stanford-le-Hope, Essex, SS17 0RF, England.

COLE B J, b. 17 June 1946, North London, England. Musician (pedal steel guitar); Producer. Career: Musician, Country Music circuit, London, 1964-; Pedal steel guitar player, Cochise; Founder member, producer, Hank Wangford Band; Leading exponent of instrument in UK; Currently prolific session musician and solo artiste; Leader, own group Transparent Music Ensemble; Replacement guitarist for the Verve, 1998-. Recordings: Solo albums: New Hovering Dog, 1972; Transparent Music, 1989; The Heart Of The Moment, 1995; As session musician: Tiny Dancer, Elton John, 1970; Wide Eyed And Legless, Andy Fairweather-Low, 1975; No Regrets, Walker Brothers, 1976; City To City, Gerry Rafferty, 1978; Everything Must Change, Paul Young, 1984; Silver Moon, David Sylvian, 1986; Diet Of Strange Places, k d lang, 1987; Montagne D'Or, The Orb, 1995; Possibly Maybe, Björk, 1995; with Hank Wangford: Hank Wangford, 1980; Live, 1982; Other recordings with: Johnny Nash; Deacon Blue; Level 42; Danny Thompson; Alan Parsons Project; Shakin' Stevens; Beautiful South; John Cale; Echobelly.

COLE Natalie Maria, b. 6 February 1950, Los Angeles, California, USA. Singer. m. (1) Marvin J Yancy, 30 July 1976, divorced, (2) Andre Fischer, 17 September 1989, divorced. Education: BA, Child Psychology, University of Massachusetts, 1972. Career: Stage debut, 1962; Solo recording artist, 1975-; Major concerts worldwide include: Tokyo Music Festival, 1979; Nelson Mandela 70th Birthday Concert, Wembley, 1988; Nelson Mandela tribute, Wembley, 1990; John Lennon Tribute Concert, Liverpool, 1990; Homeless benefit concert with Quincy Jones, Pasadena, 1992; Rainforest benefit concert, Carnegie Hall, 1992; Commitment To Life VI, (AIDs benefit concert), Los Angeles, 1992; Television appearances include: Sinatra And Friends, 1977; Host, Big Break, 1990; Motown 30, 1990; Tonight Show, 1991; Entertainers '91, 1991; Recordings: Hit singles: This Will Be, 1975; Sophisticated Lady, 1976; I've Got Love On My Mind, 1977; Our Love (Number 1, US R&B chart), 1977; Gimme Some Time (duet with Peabo Bryson), 1980; What You Won't Do For Love (duet with Peabo Bryson), 1980; Jump Start, 1987; I Live For Your Love, 1988; Pink Cadillac, 1988; Miss You Like Crazy (Number 1, US R&B charts), 1989; Wild Women Do, from film Pretty Woman, 1990; Unforgettable (duet with father Nat "King" Cole), 1991; Smile Like Yours, 1997; Albums: Inseparable, 1975; Natalie, 1976; Unpredictable, 1977; Thankful, 1978; Natalie...Live!, 1978; I Love You So, 1979; Don't Look Back, 1980; Happy Love, 1981; Natalie Cole Collection, 1981; I'm Ready, 1982; Dangerous, 1985; Everlasting, 1987; Good To Be Back, 1989; Unforgettable...With Love (Number 1, US), 1991; The Soul Of Natalie Cole, 1991; Take A Look, 1993; Holly and Ivy, 1994; Stardust, 1996; This Will Be, 1997; Snowfall on the Sahara, 1999; with Peabo Bryson: We're The Best Of Friends, 1980. Honours: Numerous Grammy Awards include: Best New Artist, 1976; Best Female R&B Vocal Performance, 1976, 1977; 5 Grammy Awards for Unforgettable, including Best Song, Best Album, 1992; 5 NAACP Image Awards, 1976, 1988, 1992; American Music Awards: Favourite Female R&B Artist, 1978;

Favourite Artist, Favourite Album, 1992; Soul Train Award, Best Single, 1988; Various Gold discs. Memberships: AFTRA; NARAS. Address: c/o Dan Cleary Management Associates, Suite 1101, 1801 Avenue Of The Stars, Los Angeles, CA 90067, USA.

COLE Susan Stockbridge, b. 26 January 1939, San Francisco, USA. College Professor. m. Willie Robert Cole. Education: AB, 1960, MA, 1961, Speech and Drama, Stanford University; PhD, Speech and Drama, University of Oregon, 1972. Publications: Listed in national and international biographical publications. Honours: President, North Carolina Theatre Conference, 1991-92; Herman Middleton Service Award, 1997; President, Alpha Psi Omega, National Theatre Honour Society, 1997-2002; President, Southeastern Theatre Conference, 1998-99; Suzanne Davis Award, 2002. Memberships: Association for Theatre in Higher Education; American Society for Theatre Research; Southeastern Theatre Conference; North Carolina Theatre Conference; National Association of Schools of Theatre; Lions Clubs International. Address: PO Box 220, Todd, North Carolina 28684-0220, USA. E-mail: coless@appstate.edu

COLL John Charles, b. 24 July 1944, Manly, New South Wales, Australia. University Administrator. m. Frances Maria, 2 sons. Education: BSc, honours, 1966, PhD, 1969, DSc, 1987, University of Sydney. Appointments: Research Associate, University of Illinois, 1969-71; Lecturer, Imperial College, London, 1971-72; Lecturer, Senior Lecturer, 1972-82, Reader in Chemistry, 1983-91, James Cook University; Pro Vice Chancellor, Research, Central Queensland University, Rockhampton, 1991-96; Pro Vice Chancellor, Academic, Professor in Chemistry, Australian Catholic University, 1996-2000; Pro Vice-Chancellor, Research and International, Professor in Chemistry, Australian Catholic University, 2000-. Publications: The Chemistry and Chemical Ecology of Octocorals, 1992; Over 150 articles in professional journals. Honour: Fulbright Travelling Fellow, 1969-71. Membership: Fellow, Royal Australian Chemical Institute. Address: Australian Catholic University, 40 Edward Street, North Sydney, NSW 2060, Australia.

COLLINS Jackie, b. England. Novelist; Short Story Writer; Actress. m. Oscar Lerman. Creative Works: Screenplays: Yesterday's Hero; The World in Full of Married Men; The Stud. Publications: The World is Full of Married Men, 1968; The Stud, 1969; Sunday Simmons and Charlie Brick, 1971; Sinners, 1981; Lovehead, 1974; The Love Killers, 1977; The World is Full of Divorced Women, 1975; Lovers & Gamblers, 1977; The Bitch, 1979; Chances, 1981; Hollywood Wives, 1983; Lucky, 1985; Hollywood Husbands, 1986; Rock Star, 1988; Lady Boss, 1990; American Star, 1993; The World is Full of Married Men, 1993; Hollywood Kids, 1994; Dangerous Kiss, 1999; Hollywood Wives: The New Generation, 2001; Lethal Seduction, 2001. Address: c/o Simon & Schuster, 1230 Avenue of the Americas, New York, NY 10020, USA.

COLLINS Joan, b. 23 May 1933, London, England. Actress. m. (1) Maxwell Reed, 1954, divorced, 1957, (2) Anthony Newley, 1963, divorced, 1970, 1 son, 1 daughter, (3) Ronald Kass, 1972, divorced, 1983, 1 daughter, (4) Peter Holm, 1985, divorced, 1987, (5) Percy Gibson, 2002. Career: Films include: I Believe in You, 1952; Girl in Red Velvet Swing, 1955; Land of the Pharaohs, 1955; The Opposite Sex, 1956; Rally Round Flag Boys, 1957; Sea Wife, 1957; Warning Shot, 1966; The Executioner, 1969; Revenge, 1971; The Big Sleep, Tales of the Unexpected, 1977; Stud, 1979; The Bitch, 1980; Nutcracker, 1982; Decadence, 1994; Hart to Hart, 1995; Annie: A Royal Adventure, 1995; In the Bleak Midwinter, 1995; The Clandestine Marriage, 1998; The Flintstones-Viva Rock Vegas, 1999; Joseph and the Amazing Technicolor Dreamcoat, 1999; These Old Broads, 2000. Numerous TV appearances include: Dynasty, 1981-89; Cartier Affair, 1984; Sins, 1986; Monte Carlo, 1986; Tonight at 8.30, 1991; Pacific Palisades (serial), 1997; Will and Grace (USA), 2000. Publications: J C Beauty Book, 1980; Katy: A Fight for Life, 1981; Past Imperfect, 1984; Prime Time, 1988; Love and Desire and Hate, 1990; My Secrets, 1994; Too Damn Famous, 1995; Second Act, 1996; My Friends' Secrets, 1999. Address: c/o Paul Keylock, 16 Bulbecks Walk, South Woodham Ferrers, Essex, CM3 5ZN, England.

COLLINS Lois, b. 3 February 1929, New Berry, Michigan, USA. Folk Artist. Divorced, 4 sons. Education: Music studies. Career: Numerous art shows and exhibitions of work: Gallerie Bonheur, St Louis, Missouri; Community Art Center, Hancock, Michigan, Marquette County Historical Society Museum, Marquette, Michigan. Publications: Folk Art Finder, 1999; Michigan Art Doors, 2001. Address: 425 N Main, Apt 3, Lanse, MI 49946, USA.

COLLINS Pauline, b. 3 September 1940, Exmouth, Devon, England. Actress. m. John Alderton, 2 sons, 1 daughter. Education: Central School of Speech & Drama. Creative Works: Stage Appearances: A Gazelle in Park Lane (stage debut, Windsor 1962); Passion Flower Hotel; The Erpingham Camp; The Happy Apple; The Importance of Being Ernest; The Night I Chased the Women with an Eel; Come as You Are; Judies; Engaged; Confusions; Romantic Comedy; Woman in Mind; Shirley Valentine; Films: Shirley Valentine, 1989; City of Joy, 1992; My Mother's Courage, 1997; Paradise Road, 1997; Mrs Caldicott's Cabbage War, 2002; TV appearances: Upstairs Downstairs; Thomas and Sarah; Forever Green; No-Honestly; Tales of the Unexpected; Knockback, 1984; Tropical Moon Over Dorking; The Ambassador, 1998; Man and Boy, 2002; Sparkling Cyanide, 2003. Publication: Letter to Louise, 1992. Honours include: Olivier Award, Best Actress, London; Tony, Drama Desk & Outer Critics' Circle Awards, New York.

COLLINS Phil, b. 30 January 1951, Chiswick, London, England. Pop Singer; Drummer; Composer. m. (1) 1976, 1 son, 1 daughter, (2) Jill Tavelman, 1984, divorced, 1 daughter, (3) Orianne Cevey, 1999, 1 son. Education: Barbara Speake Stage School. Appointments: Former Actor, Artful Dodger in London Production of Oliver; Joined Rock Group, Genesis as Drummer, 1970, Lead Singer, 1975-96. Creative Works: Albums with Genesis: Selling England by the Pound, 1973; Invisible Touch, 1986; We Can't Dance, 1991; Solo Albums include: No Jacket Required; But Seriously; Face Value; Hello I Must Be Going; Dance into the Light, 1996; Hits, 1998; Testify, 2002; Films: Buster, 1988; Frauds, 1993. Honours include: 7 Grammy's; 6 Ivor Novello Awards; 4 Brits; 2 Awards, Variety Club of Great Britain; 2 Silver Clef's; 2 Elvis Awards; Academy Award for You'll be in my Heart from Tarzan film, 1999. Membership: Trustee, Prince of Wales Trust, 1983-97.

COLLINS Philip (Arthur William), b. 28 May 1923, London, England. Professor of English (retired); Author. Education: MA, Emmanuel College, Cambridge, 1947. Appointments: Warden, Vaughan College, 1954-62; Senior Lecturer, 1962-64, Professor of English, 1964-82, University of Leicester; Member, Board of Directors, The National Theatre, 1976-82. Publications: James Boswell,1956; English Christmas (editor), 1956; Dickens and Crime, 1962; Dickens and Education, 1963; The Impress of the Moving Age, 1965; Thomas Cooper the Chartist: Byron and the Poets of the Poor, 1969; A Dickens Bibliography, 1970; Dickens: A Christmas Carol: The Public Reading Version, 1971; Bleak House: A Commentary, 1971; Dickens: The Critical Heritage (editor), 1971; Reading Aloud: A Victorian Metier, 1972; Charles Dickens: The Public Readings (editor), 1975; Charles Dickens: David Copperfield, 1977; Charles Dickens: Hard Times (editor), 1978; Dickens: Interviews and Recollections (editor), 1981;

Thackeray: Interviews and Recollections (editor), 1982; Tennyson, Poet of Lincolnshire, 1985; The Annotated Dickens (editor with Edward Giuliano), 1986; Tennyson: Seven Essays (editor), 1992. Contributions to: Encyclopaedia Britannica; Listener; Times Literary Supplement. Address: 26 Knighton Drive, Leicester LE2 3HB, England.

COLLIS Louise Edith, b. 29 January 1925, Arakan, Burma. Writer. Education: BA, History, Reading University, England, 1945. Publications: Without a Voice, 1951; A Year Passed, 1952; After the Holiday, 1954; The Angel's Name, 1955; Seven in the Tower, 1958; The Apprentice Saint, 1964; Solider in Paradise, 1965; The Great Flood, 1966; A Private View of Stanley Spencer, 1972; Maurice Collis Diaries (editor), 1976; Impetuous Heart: The story of Ethel Smyth, 1984. Contributions to: Books and Bookmen; Connoisseur; Art and Artists; Arts Review; Collectors Guide; Art and Antiques. Memberships: Society of Authors; International Association of Art Critics. Address: 65 Cornwall Gardens, London SW7 4BD, England.

COLLISCHAN Judy Kay, b. 19 October 1940, Minnesota, USA. Museum Curator; Director. 1 son. Education: BA, 1962; MFA, 1964; PhD, 1972. Appointments: Associate Professor, SUNY, 1975-82; Director, Public Art Program, 1985-94; Director, Hillwood Art Museum, 1982-94; Administration Director, Printmaking Workshop, 1994-96; Associate Director, Curatorial Affairs, Neuberger Museum of Art, 1996-2001; Private Art Consultant, 2001-. Honours: SUNY University Award; Kress Foundation Grant. Publications: Welded Sculpture of the Twentieth Century; Lines of Vision: Drawings by Contemporary Women; Women Shaping Art: Profiles of Power; Contributed Essays to Master Paintings form the Butler Institute of American Art; Numerous Articles. Memberships: American Association of Museum; College Art Association; International Association of Art Critics. Commissions and Creative Works include: Paintings from the Mind's Eye, 1982; Monumental Drawings by Sculptors, 1983; Reflections: New Conceptions of Nature, 1984; C W Post Public Art Program, 1985-94; American Abstract Artists: The Origins, 1986; Walter Murch, 1986; Why War, 1991; Kay WalkingStick Retrospective, 1991; Printmaking Workshop: Artists of Colour, 1992; Paper Spaces, 1996; Neuberger Museum of Art Biennial of Public Art, 1997; Al Loving, Paintings, 1998; Contemporary Classicism, 1999; Helen Frankenthaler, 1999; Kay Miller, 1999; Mary Frank Paintings, 2000; End Papers: Drawings 1890-1900 and 1990-2000, 2000; Proscenium, Stephen Antonakos, 2001; Marisol, 2001. Address: 248 E 7th Street Apt 11-12, New York, NY 10009, USA.

COLLOMS Brenda, (Brenda Cross, Brenda Hughes), b. 1 January 1919, London, England. Author; Editor. Education: BA, University of London, 1956; MA, University of Liverpool, 1958. Appointment: Editor, The Film Star Diary, Cramp Publishers, London, 1948-63. Publications: Happy Ever After (as Brenda Cross), 1947; The Film Hamlet (as Brenda Cross), 1948; New Guinea Folk Tales (as Brenda Hughes), 1959; Folk Tales from Chile (as Brenda Hughes), 1962; Certificate History, Books 1-4: Britain and Europe, 1966-70; Israel, 1971; The Mayflower Pilgrims, 1973; Charles Kingsley, 1975; Victorian Country Parsons, 1977; Victorian Visionaries, 1982; The Making of Tottie Fox (as Brenda Colloms). Address: 123A Gloucester Avenue, London NW1 8LB, England.

COLOMBO Arrigo, b. 11 September 1921, Busto Arsizio, Italy. Philosopher; University Professor. m. Marie-Josèphe Beauchard. Education: Licence in Scholastic Philosophy, Aloisianum Faculty, Gallarate, 1948; Licence in Theology, S Luigi Faculty, Naples, 1952; Doctor in Philosophy, State University, Milan, 1956;

Research Scholarship, Humboldt Foundation, Germany, 1963-66; Habilitation in Theoretical Philosophy, Rome, 1966. Appointments: Assistant of Philosophy, University of Genoa, 1959-65; Professor of Philosophy, 1966, Associate Professor, 1981, Faculty of Education, University of Lecce; Founder, Director, Centro Interdipartimentale di Ricerca sull'Utopia, 1982; Founder, Director, Laboratorio di Poesia, 1985-99; Founder, Responsible, Movimento per la Società di Giustizia e per la Speranza, 1998. Publications: Il Destino del Filosofo, Manduria, 1971; Le Società del Futuro: Saggio Utopico sulle Società Postindustriali, Bari, 1978; Utopia e Distopia, (editor), Milan, 1987; La Russia e la Democrazia: Il Riemergere della Democrazia Diretta, Bari, 1994; L'Utopia: Rifondazione di un'Idea e di una Storia, Bari, 1997 (his major work); Materiali per l'Utopia: Il Diavolo, Bari, 1999; Materiali per l'Utopia: La Società Amorosa, Bari, 2002; In these works history is revised as a project and then, in modern times, as a construction of a society based on justice: this project and process are the new sense of utopia and of history. Memberships: Cristiani per il Socialismo, 1973-76; Democrazia Proletaria, 1987-91; Rifondazione Comunista, 1991-93; Society for Utopian Studies, USA; Associazione Internazionale per lo Studio delle Utopie, Rome; Moreanum, Angers. Address: Via Monte S Michele 49, 73100 Lecce, Italy. E-mail: arrigo.colombo9@tin.it

COLOME Delfin, b. 14 April 1946, Barcelona, Spain. Diplomat. m. Elena Sanchez, 1 son, 3 daughters. Education: Law Degree, University of Barcelona; Master, International Relations, Diplomatic School, Madrid; PhD, Autonomous University, Madrid. Appointments: Lawyer, 1969-75; Career Diplomat, 1976-, serving in: Oslo, Norway; Sofia, Bulgaria; UNESCO; Mexico; General Director for Cultural Affairs, 1991-96; Ambassador of Spain to the Philippines, 1997-2000; Executive Director, Asia-Europe Foundation, Singapore, 2000-2004. Publications: Books: El Indiscreto Encanto de la Danza; La Caucion mas Fuerte; Numerous articles. Honours: Several Spanish and Foreign Decorations; Doctor, Honoris Causa in Humanities, Ateneo de Manila University, Philippines. Address: Pasaje del Obispo 4-5°A, 28005 Madrid, Spain. E-mail: delfincolome@asef.org.

COLTRANE Robbie, b. 31 March 1950, Glasgow, Scotland. Actor. m. Rhona Irene Gemmel, 2000, 1 son, 1 daughter. Education: Glasgow School. Appointments: Director, Producer, Young Mental Health (documentary), 1973. Creative Works: Stage appearances include: Waiting for God; End Game; The Bug; Mr Joyce is Leaving; The Slab Boys; The Transfiguration of Benno Blimpie; The Loveliest Night of the Year; Snobs and Yobs; Your Obedient Servant (one-man show), 1987; Mistero Buffo; TV: The Comic Strip Presents...; Five Go Mad In Dorset; The Beat Generation; War; Summer School; Five Go Mad in Mescalin; Susie; Gino; Dirty Movie; The Miner's Strike; The Supergrass (feature film); The Ebb-tide; Alice in Wonderland; Guest Roles: The Yong Ones; Kick Up the Eighties; The Tube; Saturday Night Live; Lenny Henry Show; Blackadder; Tutti Frutti; Coltrane in a Cadillac; Cracker; The Plan Man, 2003; TV film: Boswell and Johnson's Tour of the Western Isles; Films include: Mona Lisa; Subway Riders; Britannia Hospital; Defence of the Realm; Caravaggio; Eat The Rich; Absolute Beginners; The Fruit Machine; Slipstream; Nuns on the Run; Huckleberry Finn; Bert Rigby, You're A Fool; Danny Champion of the World; Henry V; Let It Ride; The Adventures of Huckleberry Finn; Goldeneye; Buddy; Montana; Frogs for Snakes; Message in a Bottle; The World is Not Enough, 1999; On the Nose, 2000; From Hell, 2000; Harry Potter and the Philosopher's Stone, 2001; Harry Potter and the Chamber of Secrets, 2002; Van Helsing, 2004; Harry Potter and the Prisoner of Azkaban, 2004. Publications: Coltrane in a Cadillac, 1992; Coltrane's Planes and Automobiles, 1999. Address: c/o CDA, 19 Sydney Mews, London SW3 6HL, England.

COMBRINK Hans Jacob Bernardus, b. 23 October 1940, Lydenburg, Mpumalanga, South Africa. Lecturer. m. (1) Lucia Antonites, deceased, (2) Juliette Lambrechts, 2 sons, 2 daughters. Education: BA cum laude, 1960, BD cum laude, 1963, University of Pretoria; BA Hons, Greek, cum laude, University of Pretoria, 1964; Doctor of Theology, Free University, Amsterdam, 1968. Appointments: Parson Dutch Reformed Church, 1968-70; Head of Biblical Studies Department, Rand Afrikaans University, 1970-73; Senior Lecturer, Department New Testament, 1974-75, University of Pretoria; Senior Lecturer, Department New Testament, 1976-82; Associate Professor, Department of New Testament, 1982-87, Professor and Head, Department of New Testament, 1988-1996; Dean, Faculty of Theology, 1992-94, 1998-2000, University of Stellenbosch; Chair, New Testament Section of Department of Old and New Testament, 1997-2000; Retired, March, 2001; Chair, Stellenbosch University's New Testament Research Association, 2001-; Part-time lecturer and promoter for DTh candidates, 2001. Publications: Die Diens van Jesus, 1968; Structural Analysis of Acts, 1979; Co-author, The Synoptic Gospels and Acts, 1983; The Gospel of John; Hebrews to Revelation: Introduction and Theology, 1993. Honours: Dux Award, University of Pretoria, 1964; South African National Bursary, 1964; Netherlands Stipend, 1965-68; Senior Research Grant Human Sciences Research Council, 1982, 1989; Research Grant Centre for Science Development, 1996. Memberships: Financial Secretary, 1980-85, General Secretary, 1985-90, New Testament Society of South Africa; Executive Committee, Association of South African Theological Institutions, 1992-94; Council of South African Academy of Arts and Sciences, 1991-93; Society of Biblical Literature; Chair, Forum of University Theological Education, 1999-2000; Society of International New Testament Scholars; Tyndale Fellowship for Biblical Research; South African Academy of Religion. Address: Faculty of Theology, University of Stellenbosch, Private Bag XI, Matieland, 7602 South Africa.

COMBS Charles Donald, b. 28 March 1952, Texas, USA. m. Pam Q Combs, 2 sons. Education: AA, South Plains Community College, 1971; BA, 1972, MA, 1974, Political Science, Texas Tech University; PhD, Political Science, University of North Carolina at Chapel Hill, 1980. Appointments: Retail Store Manager, Route Accountant, Bell Dairy Products, Lubbock, Texas, 1972-73; Instructor, Political Science, Elon College, North Carolina, University of North Carolina at Chapel Hill, Texas Tech University, Lubbock, 1973-76; Visiting Instructor of Public Administration, North Carolina Central University, Durham, 1976-77; Senior Program Associate, Rural Practice Project, Robert Wood Johnson Foundation, and Instructor, Department of Social and Administrative Medicine, University of North Carolina, 1977-79; Administrator, Secretary/Treasurer, Surry Family Health Group, Virginia, 1978-81; Director, Health Management Concentration and Master in Urban Studies Degree Program, Department of Urban Studies and Public Administration, Old Dominion University, Director, Peninsula Area Health Education Centre, Eastern Virginia Medical School, Norfolk, 1980-85; Assistant Vice President for Administration and Services, Eastern Virginia Medical School, Norfolk, 1985-87; Associate Vice President, Institutional Advancement, 1987-88, Vice President, 1988-93, Vice President for Planning and Program Development, 1993-, Eastern Virginia Medical School. Publications: Research papers and presentations include: Community Medicine Practicum for Second Year Medical Students, co-author, 1994; The Virginia Generalist Initiative, 1995; The Perhaps Hand: Linking Strategy and Productivity, 1997; Strategies for Survival, 1998; The Virginia Workforce Planning Project, 1999; Medical Modeling and Simulation, 2002. Address: Eastern Virginia Medical School, PO Box 1980, Norfolk, VA 23501, USA. E-mail: combscd@evms.edu

ČOMIĆ Irena, b. 29 March 1938, Subotica, Yugoslavia. Professor of Mathematics. m. Ljubomir, 2 daughters. Education: BSc, 1960; MA, 1966; PhD, 1974. Appointments: Faculty of Technical Sciences, University of Novi Sad, Yugoslavia. Publications include: Various papers on Finsler geometry and its generalisation appearing in mathematical journals and proceedings of conferences. Address: Department of Mathematics, Faculty of Technical Sciences, University of Novi Sad, 21000 Novi Sad, Yugoslavia. E-mail: comirena@uns.ns.ac.yu

CONEY Michael (Greatrex), b. 28 September 1932, Birmingham, England. Writer. m. Daphne Coney, 14 May 1957, 1 son, 1 daughter. Publications: King of the Scepter'd Isle, 1989; A Judge of Men, 1969; Whatever Became of the McGowans?, 1971; The Snow Princess, 1971; Susanna! Susanna!, 1971; Mirror Image, 1972; The Bridge on the Scraw, 1973; Syzygy, 1973; Friends Come in Boxes, 1973; The Hero of Downways, 1973; The Hook, the Eye and the Whip, 1974; Winter's Children, 1974; Monitor Found in Orbit, 1974; The Jaws That Bite, The Claws That Catch, 1975; Charisma, 1975; The Hollow Where, 1975; Trading Post, 1976; Hello Summer, Goodbye, 1976; Brontomek!, 1976; Just an Old-Fashioned War Story, 1977; Penny on a Skyhorse, 1979; The Ultimate Jungle, 1979; Neptune's Children, 1981; Cat Karina, 1982; The Celestial Steam Locomotive, 1983; The Byrds, 1983; Gods of the Greataway, 1984; Fang, the Gnome, 1988; No Place for a Sealion, 1993; A Tomcat Called Sabrina, 1993; Sophie's Spyglass, 1993; Die Lorelie, 1993; The Small Penance of Lady Disdain, 1993; Tea and Hamsters, 1994. Honour: Best British Novel Award, British Science Fiction Association, 1976. Address: 2082 Neptune Road, Sidney, British Columbia V8L 5J5, Canada.

CONLON James, b. 18 March 1950, New York, USA. Conductor. m. Jennifer Ringo, 2 daughters. Education: Bachelor of Music, Juilliard School of Music, New York, 1972. Appointments: Professional conducting debut, Spoleto Festival, 1971; New York debut, La Boheme, Juilliard School of Music, 1972; Member of orchestral conducting faculty, Juilliard School of Music, 1972-75; Debuts: New York Philharmonic, 1974, Metropolitan Opera, 1976, Covent Garden, 1979, Paris Opera, 1982, Maggio Musicale, Florence, 1985, Lyric Opera of Chicago, 1988, La Scala, Milan, 1993, Kirov Opera, 1994; Music Director, Cincinnati May Festival, 1979-; Music Director, Rotterdam Philharmonic, 1983-91; Chief Conductor, Cologne Opera, 1989-96; General Music Director, City of Cologne, Germany and Principal Conductor, Gurzenich Orchestra-Cologne Philharmonic, 1989-2002; Principal Conductor, Paris Opera, 1996-; Frequent guest conductor at leading music festivals; Conducted virtually all leading orchestras in North America; Numerous television appearances. Honours: Grand Prix du Disque, Cannes Classical Award and ECHO Classical Award; Officier de l'Ordre des Arts et des Lettres, 1996; Zemlinsky Prize, 1999; Legion d'Honneur, 2001. Address: c/o Shuman Associates, 120 West 58th Street, 8D, New York, NY 10019, USA. E-mail: shumanpr@cs.com

CONNER Eunice Eileen Crickmore, b. 13 September 1929, Germantown, Ohio. Retired. m. Charles R Conner. Education: Journalism, College, Dayton, Ohio; Writers' Digest Training, Cincinnati, Ohio; American Management School, Dayton, Ohio; Miami-Jacobs Business College, Dayton, Ohio; Federal Emergency Management Courses, Prescott Valley, Arizona; Graduate, FBI Academy. Appointments include: Merica Detective Bureau, Dayton, Ohio, 1 year; Executive Secretary, Permits and Investigations, Ohio Department of Liquor Control, Dayton, Ohio, 9½ years; Numerous offices Prescott Valley Town; Elected to Prescott Valley Town Council, 1989-2002; Veterans of Foreign Wars, Auxiliary, President; Regent, Yarapai Chapter, Daughters of the American Revolution; Ambassador, Prescott Valley, Chamber of Commerce, Arizona, 1998-. Publications: Special Features for Dayton Tribune and Prescott Valley Tribune; Articles in True West Magazine; Ohio Conservation Bulletin; 2 books: Star Buck, 1980; Peaches, Pine and Wine, Family Cookbook, 1st edition, 1971, revised 1998; Newsletters for Experimental Aircraft Association, Ohio Press Club, Flying Shriners. Honours: Numerous awards include: Soroptimist Award, Women of Distinction, 2001; Community Service Award, Yarapai Chapter, Daughters of the American Revolution; 1st Place, Art Award, Prescott Valley Art Guild. Memberships: Past memberships: Charter Member, AARP; Charter Member, Prescott Valley Art Guild; Prescott Valley Garden Club; Prescott Valley Historical Society; Ohio Press Club; Current: Veterans of Foreign Wars Post 10227, Prescott Valley; Yarapai Chapter, Daughters of the American Revolution. Address: 7480 Las Flores, Prescott Valley AZ 86314-5535, USA.

CONNERY Sean (Thomas Connery), b. 25 August 1930. Actor. m. (1) Diane Cilento, 1962, dissolved 1974, 1 son, (2) Micheline Roquebrune, 1975, 2 stepsons, 1 stepdaughter. Creative Works: Appeared in Films: No Road Back, 1956; Action of the Tiger, 1957; Another Time, Another Place, 1957; Hell Drivers, 1958; Tarzan's Greatest Adventure, 1959; Darby O'Gill and the Little People, 1959; On the Fiddle, 1961; The Longest Day, 1962; The Frightened City, 1962; Woman of Straw, 1964; The Hill, 1965; A Fine Madness, 1966; Shalako, 1968; The Molly Maguires, 1968; The Red Tent, 1969; The Anderson Tapes, 1970; The Offence, 1973; Zardoz, 1973; Ransom, 1974; Murder on the Orient Express, 1974; The Wind and the Lion, 1975; The Man Who Would Be King, 1975; Robin and Marian, 1976; The First Great Train robbery, 1978; Cuba, 1978; Meteor, 1979; Outland, 1981; The Man with the Deadly Lens, 1982; Wrong is Right, 1982; Five Days One Summer, 1982; Highlander, 1986; The Name of the Rose, 1987; The Untouchables, 1987; The Presido, 1989; Indiana Jones and the Last Crusade, 1989; Family Business, 1990; the Hunt for Red October, 1990; The Russia House, 1991; Highlander II - The Quickening, 1991; Medicine Man, 1992; Rising Sun, 1993; A Good Man in Africa, 1994; First Knight, 1995; Just Cause, 1995; The Rock, 1996; Dragonheart, 1996; The Avengers, 1998; Entrapment, 1999; Playing By Heart, 1999; Finding Forrester, 2000; The League of Extraordinary Gentlemen, 2003; James Bond in: Dr No, 1963; From Russia with Love, 1964; Goldfinger, 1965; Thunderball, 1965; You Only Live Twice, 1967; Diamonds are Forever, 1971; Never Say Never Again, 1983. Publication: Neither Shaken Nor Stirred, 1994. Honours include: BAFTA Lifetime Achievement Award, 1990; Man of Culture Award, 1990; Rudolph Valentino Award, 1992; Golden Globe Cecil B De Mille Award; 1996 BAFTA Fellowship, 1998. Address: c/o Creative Artists Agency Inc, 9830 Wilshire Boulevard, Beverly Hills, CA 90212, USA.

CONNICK Harry Jr, b. 1968, New Orleans, USA. Jazz Musician; Actor; Singer. m. Jill Goodacre, 1994. Education: New Orleans Centre for the Creative Arts; Hunter College; Manhattan School of Music; Studies with Ellis Marsalis. Creative Works: Albums include: Harry Connick Jr, 1987; 20, 1989; We Are In Love, 1991; Lofty's Roach Soufflé, 1991; Blue Light, Red Light, 1991; Eleven, 1992; 25, 1992; When My Heart Finds Christmas, 1993; She, 1994; Star Turtle, 1996; To See You, 1997; Come By Me, 1999; Contribution to music for film, When Harry Meets Sally; Composed music for Thou Shalt Not (Broadway), 2001; Films as Actor: Memphis Belle; Little Man Tate, 1991; Independence Day; Excess Baggage; Hope Floats; Band Leader Harry Connick's Big Band. Honours include: Grammy Award. Address: Columbia Records, c/o Anita Nanko, 51/12, 550 Madison Avenue, PO Box 4450, New York, NY 10101, USA.

Dictionary of International Biography

CONNOLLY Billy, b. 24 November 1942. Comedian; Actor; Playwright; Presenter. m. (1) Iris Connolly, 1 son, 1 daughter, (2) Pamela Stephenson, 1990, 3 daughters. Appointments: Apprentice Welder; Performed originally with Gerry Rafferty and The Humblebums; 1st Play, The Red Runner, staged at Edinburgh fringe, 1979. Creative Works: Theatre: The Great Northern Welly Boot Show; The Beastly Beatitudes of Balthazar B, 1982; TV include: Androcles and the Lion, 1984; Return to Nose and Beak (Comic Relief); South Bank Show Special (25th Anniversary Commemoration), 1992; Billy; Billy Connolly's World Tour of Scotland (6 part documentary), 1994; The Big Picture, 1995; Billy Connolly's World Tour of Australia, 1996; Erect for 30 Years, 1998; Billy Connolly's World Tour of England, Ireland and Wales, 2002; Gentleman's Relish; Films include: Absolution, 1979; Bullshot, 1984; Water, 1984; The Big Man, 1989; Pocahontas, 1995; Treasure Island (Muppet Movie), 1996; Deacon Brodie (BBC Film), 1996; Mrs Brown, 1997; Ship of Fools, 1997; Still Crazy, 1998; Debt Collector, 1998; Boon Docksaints, 1998; Beautiful Joe, 2000; An Everlasting Piece, 2000; The Man Who Sued God, 2002; White Oleander, 2002; Gabriel and Me, 2002; Numerous video releases of live performances include: Bite Your Bum, 1981; An Audience with Billy Connolly, 1982; Numerous albums include: The Great Northern Welly Boot Show (contains No 1 hit DIVORCE); Pick of Billy Connolly. Publications include: Gullible's Travels, 1982. Honours include: Gold Disc, 1982. Address: c/o Tickety-boo Ltd, The Boathouse, Crabtree Lane, London SW6 5LU, England. E-mail: tickety-boo@tickety-boo.com Website: www.billyconnolly.com

CONNORS James Scott (Jimmy), b. 2 September 1952, Illinois, USA. Tennis Player. m. Patti McGuire, 1978, 1 son, 1 daughter. Education: University of California, Los Angeles. Appointments: Amateur Player, 1970-72; Professional, 1972-; Australian Champion, 1974; Wimbledon Champion, 1974, 1982; USA Champion, 1974, 1976, 1978, 1982, 1983; South Australian Champion, 1973, 1974; WCT Champion, 1977, 1980; Grand Prix Champion, 1978; Commentator, NBC; Played Davis Cup for USA, 1976, 1981. Honour: BBC Overseas Sports Personality, 1982. Address: Tennis Management Inc, 109 Red Fox Road, Belleville, IL 62223, USA.

CONRAN Jasper Alexander Thirlby, b. 12 December 1959, London, England. Fashion Designer. Education: Bryanston School, Dorset; Parsons School of Art & Design, New York. Appointments: Fashion Designer, Managing Director, Jasper Conran Ltd, 1978-. Creative Works: Theatre Costumes: Jean Anouilh's The Rehearsal, Almeida Theatre, 1990; My Fair Lady, 1992; Sleeping Beauty, Scottish Ballet, 1994; The Nutcracker Sweeties, Birmingham Royal Ballet, 1996; Edward II, 1997; Arthur, 2000. Honours include: Fil d'Or (International Linen Award), 1982, 1983; British Fashion Council Designer of the Year Award, 1986-87; Fashion Group of America Award, 1987; Laurence Olivier Award for Costume Designer of the Year, 1991; British Collections Award (in British Fashions Awards), 1991. Address: Jasper Conran Ltd, 6 Burnsall Street, London SW3, England.

CONROY (Donald) Pat(rick), b. 26 October 1945, Atlanta, Georgia, USA. Writer. m. (1) Barbara Bolling, 1969, divorced 1977, 3 daughters, (2) Lenore Guerewitz, 1981, divorced 1995, 1 son, 5 daughters. Education: BA in English, The Citadel, 1967. Publications: The Boo, 1970; The Water is Wide, 1972; The Great Santini, 1976; The Lords of Discipline, 1980; The Prince of Tides, 1986; Beach Music, 1995. Honours: Ford Foundation Leadership Development Grant, 1971; Anisfield-Wolf Award, Cleveland Foundation, 1972; National Endowment for the Arts Award for Achievement in Education, 1974; Governor's Award for the Arts, Georgia, 1978; Lillian Smith Award for Fiction, Southern Regional

Council, 1981; SC Hall of Fame, Academy of Authors, 1988; Golden Plate Award, American Academy of Achievement, 1992; Georgia Commission on the Holocaust Humanitarian Award, 1996; Lotos Medal of Merit for Outstanding Literary Achievement, 1993; Many others. Memberships: Authors Guild of America; PEN; Writers Guild. Address: c/o Houghton Mifflin Co, 222 Berkeley Street, Boston, MA 02116, USA.

CONSTANTINE Margaret (Peggy) L, b. 2 August 1930, Racine, Wisconin, USA. Retired Newspaper Reporter. Education: English, Music, Duke University, North Carolina, USA; Master's Degree, Northwestern University, Illinois, USA; Music Criticism, University of Southern California. Appointments: Journalist, Chicago Sun-Times Newspaper for 27 years; News Reporter; Feature Writer, Music Reviewer and Paper-back Book Reviewer; Writer of short reviews for New York Times since retirement. Publications: Numerous newspaper articles and features. Address: 1225 S Main Street, Racine, WI 53403, USA. E-mail: pegconstan@aol

CONSTANTINESCU Mihai, b. 1 May 1935, Bucharest, Romania. Jurist. m. Domnica Constantinescu, 1 son. Education: Graduate, Faculty of Law, University of Bucharest, 1958; Doctor of Law, University of Bucharest, 1969; Graduate, Strasbourg International University of Comparative Law, 1971. Appointments: Member, Legislative Council, 1972-89; Expert, Constitutional Commission, 1990-91 and 2002-2003; Advisor to the Prime Minister, 1990-92; Judge of the Constitutional Court, 1992-98; Presidential Advisor, 2000-; University Professor and Arbiter at the Commercial Chamber of Romania. Publications: Parliamentary Right, 1994, 1999; The Constitutional Court, 1997; Governmental Ordinance, 2000, 2002; Parliamentary Renaissance in Romania, 2001; Interpretation of the Constitution, 2002; About 500 other commentary articles and publications in Romania and abroad. Honours: Academic Award "Simion Barnutiu", 1980; Order "Andres Bello" First Class, Venezuela; Cavalier, Order "Star of Romania", 2002. Membership: Judicial Association of Romania. Address: 4 Alleea Poiana Cernei str, Sector 6, Bucharest 77321, Romania.

CONTI Tom, b. 22 November 1941, Paisley, Scotland. Actor; Director. m. Kara Wilson, 1967, 1 daughter. Education: Royal Scottish Academy of Music. Creative Works: London Theatre include: Savages (Christopher Hampton), 1973; The Devil's Disciple (Shaw), 1976; Whose Life is it Anyway? (Brian Clarke), 1978; They're Playing Our Song (Neil Simon/Marvin Hamlisch), 1980; Romantic Comedy (Bernard Salde); An Italian Straw Hat, 1986; Two Into One; Treats, 1989; Jeffrey Bernard is Unwell, 1990; The Ride Down Mt Morgan, 1991; Present Laughter (also director), 1993; Chapter Two, 1996; Jesus My Boy, 1998; Films include: Dreamer; Saving Grace; Miracles; Heavenly Pursuits; Beyond Therapy; Roman Holiday; Two Brothers Running; White Roses; Shirley Valentine; Chapter Two; Someone Else's America; Crush Depth; Something to Believe In, 1996; Out of Control, 1997; The Enemy, 2000; TV Works include: Madame Bovary; Treats; The Glittering Prizes; The Norman Conquests; The Beate Klarsfield Story; Fatal Dosage; The Quick and the Dead; Blade on the Feather; The Wright Verdicts; Deadline; Director: Last Licks; Broadway, 1979; Before the Party, 1980; The Housekeeper, 1982; Treats, 1989; Present Laughter, 1993; Last of the Red Hot Lovers, 1999. Honours: West End Theatre Managers Award; Royal TV Society Award; Variety Club of Great Britain Award, 1978; Tony Award, New York, 1979. Address: Artists Independent Network, 32 Tavistock Street, London, WC2E 7PB, England.

CONWAY-SEYMOUR Frances, b. 20 June 1931, Bristol, England. Painter. m. (1) Robert Hurdle, (2) John Seymour, 2 sons, 2 daughters. Education: The West of England College of Art under

Dictionary of International Biography

Tutors: George Sweet, Robert Hurdle, Frances Hoyland; Visitors: Lary Rivers; Peter Lanyon. Career: Art Teacher, Folk House, Bristol and Clifton High School, 1980's; Exhibitions: One-man: Bristol Arts Centre; Biarritz, A La Galerie Vallombreuse; Mixed Exhibitions: Annual Exhibition of Royal West of England Academy (RWA), 1958-; Every 4th year at the Members Exhibition RWA; Bristol City Art Gallery (Bristol 600); Tetbury: Painter of the RWA, 1988; Bruton Gallery; Royal Academy; Arrofine Gallery, Bristol; Other Bristol Galleries; Works in private and public collections. Publications: Works featured in newspaper and journal reviews including Art News review, Western Daily Press, Bristol Evening Post and France West. Honours: Works purchased when a student by WEAC; Courages Award for Bristol 600 Exhibition, City Art Gallery, Bristol; Woman of the Week, Western Daily Press. Membership: Royal West of England Academy. Address: 37 Cornwallis Crescent, Clifton, Bristol BS8 4PH, England.

COOK Petronelle Marguerite Mary, (Margot Arnold), b. 16 May 1925, Plymouth, Devon, England. Writer; Teacher. m. Philip R Cook, 20 July 1949, 2 sons, 1 daughter. Education: BA, 1946, Diploma in Prehistoric Archaeology and Anthropology, 1947, MA, 1950, Oxford University. Publications: The Officers' Woman, 1972; The Villa on the Palatine, 1975; Marie, 1979; Exit Actors, Dying, 1980; The Cape Cod Caper, 1980; Death of a Voodoo Doll, 1981; Zadok's Treasurer, 1981; Affairs of State, 1981; Love Among the Allies, 1982; Lament for a Lady Laird, 1982; Death on the Dragon's Tongue, 1982; Desperate Measures, 1983; Sinister Purposes, 1985; The Menehune Murders, 1989; Toby's Folly, 1990; The Catacomb Conspiracy, 1991; The Cape Cod Conundrum, 1992; Dirge for a Dorset Druid, 1994; The Midas Murders, 1995; The Wellman Chronicles, 2003; The Haunting of Wellman Hall, 2004. As Petronelle Cook: The Queen Consorts of England, 1993; Survivors and Non-Survivors, 2001. Contributions to: Numerous short stories to magazines. Honours: Oxford University Archaeological Society, president, 1945; Fiction Prize, National Writers Club, 1983. Memberships: New England Historic and Genealogical Society. Address: 11 High School Road, Hyannis, MA 02601, USA.

COOK Robert Leslie, b. 2 May 1921, Edinburgh, Scotland. Poet. m. Janet Ritchie, 28 October 1942, deceased 13 December 1997, 2 daughters. Education: Edinburgh University, 1952-57. Publications: Hebrides Overture and Other Poems; Within the Tavern Caught; Sometimes a Word; Time With a Drooping Hand; The Daylight Lingers; World Elsewhere; Voices From Ithaca; Waiting for the End. Contributions to: Antioch Review; Candelabrum; Countryman; Linq; Negative Capability; New English Weekly; Nimrod; Orbis; Outposts; Poetry Review; Prairie Schooner; etc; Several anthologies. Honour: Grierson Verse Prize. Address: 4 Whitecraigs, Kinnesswood, Kinross KY13 9JN, Scotland.

COOLAHAN Catherine Anne, b. 2 November 1929. Artist; Designer. m. Maxwell Dominic Coolahan, 5 March 1951. Education: Associate, Sydney Technical College, 1950. Appointments: Advertising and Publicity Design, Farmer and Co, Sydney, 1950-52; Advertising and Publicity Design, J Inglis Wright, New Zealand Ltd, 1952-53; Advertising and Publicity Design, Carlton Carruthers du Chateau and King, 1954-57; Assistant Education Officer, Dominion Museum, 1957-58; Fashion Illustrator, James Smith Ltd, 1959-60; Publicity Design, Carlton Carruthers, 1960-62; James Smith and Tutor, Wellington Polytechnic School of Design, 1962-64; Self-Employed Graphic Design, Fine Arts, Curriculum Development and Teaching for School of Design, 1964-66; Wellington Polytechnic, 1966-71, 1972-83, 1984, 1985, 1995; Travelling Scholarship, QE II Arts Council, 1971-72. Creative Works include: Flight, Fabric Sculpture,

1984; Predater, Predator, Paper Wood, Flax Ties, Sculpture, 1984; Hunter, Paper Sculpture, 1984; Appropriations, Aquatint, 1986; Lifeguard, 3 Dimensional Etching and Hand Made Paper, 1987; Map of the Sounds, Etching, 1988; Isis and Rangi, Lithograph, 1988; Art Sees, Etching, 1989; New Zealand Portraits, 1990; Winged Victories and Clipped Wings, 1992; Anima, Etching, 1994; Topiary, Multimedia Assemblage, 1998; Foxy, Artists' Book, 1999; Dawn, Artists' Book; 2000; Noah's Ark, Metal and Glass Diorama, 2000; Animus, Etching, 2000. Publications: New Zealand Dictionary of Biography, Vol. 5 (Contributor). Honours include: Represented New Zealand at 36th Venice Bienalle, 1972; Japanese cultural ex as Printmaker to learn papermaking, 1977; QE II Purchase Grant for Retrospective Exhibition at Dowse Art Museum, 1984; QE II Grant to attend National Paper Conference, Tasmanian University Research Co, Hobart, Australia, 1987; Appointed Life Member, New Zealand Crafts Council for work on Education Committee with Craft Design Courses, 1989; Funding Support/Sufferage Centennial Year Trust and QE II Arts Council, Dowse Art Museum, 1992; Doctor of Literature (honoris causa), Massey University, 2003; Listed in: Artists and Galleries of Australia and New Zealand, 1979; Numerous national and international biographical publications; Encyclopaedia of New Zealand, 1986; Concise Dictionary of New Zealand Artists, 2000. Memberships: Board, New Zealand Print Council, 1968-76; Board, New Zealand Design Council, 1977-84; Board, Queen Elizabeth II Arts Council, 1979; Board, Wellington Community Arts Council, 1981; Board, Central Region Arts Council, 1982-85; Design Council Representative, New Zealand Industrial Design Council, 1984; Board, New Zealand Craft Council, 1984-85; Board, Humanz, New Zealand Society of the Humanities, 1995-2002; Chair International Committee, Zonta International Wellington Club, 1998-99; Board, New Pacific Studios, Berkley, California and Masterton, New Zealand, 2000-01. Address: 57 Sefton St, Wadestown, Wellington, New Zealand.

COOMBES Gaz (Gareth). Singer; Musician (guitar). Career: Member, The Jennifers; Lead singer, guitarist, Supergrass, 1994-; Major concerts include: Support to Blur, Alexandra Palace, 1994; UK tour with Shed Seven, 1994; T In The Park Festival, Glasgow, 1995. Recordings: Albums: I Should Coco (Number 1, UK), 1995; In It for the Money, 1997; Supergrass, 1999; Singles: Caught By The Fuzz, 1994; Mansize Rooster, 1995; Lenny, 1995; Alright, 1995; Going Out, 1996; Sun Hits the Sky, 1997; Pumping On Your Stereo, 1999; Mary, 1999. Honours: Q Award, Best New Act, 1995; BRIT Award Nominations: Best British Newcomer, Best Single, Best Video, 1996. Address: c/o Courtyard Management, 22 The Nursery, Sutton Courtenay, Abingdon, Oxon OX14 4UA, England.

COOPER Alice (Vincent Furnier), b. 4 February 1948, Detroit, Michigan, USA. Singer. m Sheryl Goddard, 1 sons, 2 daughters. Career: First to stage theatrical rock concert tours; Among first to film conceptual rock promo videos (pre-MTV); Considered among originators and greatest hard rock artists; Known as King of Shock Rock; Many film, television appearances. Recordings: Singles include: I'm Eighteen; Poison; No More Mr Nice Guy; I Never Cry; Only Women Bleed; You And Me; Under My Wheels; Bed Of Nails; Albums include: School's Out, 1972; Billion Dollar Babies, 1973; Welcome To My Nightmare, 1976; From The Inside, 1978; Constrictor, 1986; Raise Your Fist And Yell, 1987; Trash, 1988; Hey Stoopid, 1991; Last Temptation, 1994; He's Back, 1997. Publications: Wrote foreword to short story book: Shock Rock. Honour: Foundations Forum, Lifetime Achievement Award, 1994. Memberships: BMI; NARAS; SAG; AFTRA; AFofM. Address: PO Box 5542, Beverly Hills, CA 90211, USA.

COOPER Jilly (Sallitt), b. 21 February 1937, Hornchurch, Essex, England. Writer; Journalist. m. Leo Cooper, 1961, 1 son, 1 daughter. Appointments: Reporter, Middlesex Independent Newspaper, Brentford, 1957-59; Columnist, The Sunday Times, 1969-85, The Mail on Sunday, 1985-. Publications: How to Stay Married, 1969; How to Survive from Nine to Five, 1970; Jolly Super, 1971; Men and Super Men, 1972; Jolly Super Too, 1973; Women and Super Women, 1974; Jolly Superlative, 1975; Emily (romance novel), 1975; Super Men and Super Women (omnibus), 1976; Bella (romance novel), 1976; Harriet (romance novel), 1976; Octavia (romance novel), 1977; Work and Wedlock (omnibus), 1977; Superjilly, 1977; Imogen (romance novel), 1978; Prudence (romance novel), 1978; Class: A View from Middle England, 1979; Supercooper, 1980; Little Mabel series, juvenile, 4 volumes, 1980-85; Violets and Vinegar: An Anthology of Women's Writings and Sayings (editor with Tom Hartman), 1980; The British in Love (editor), 1980; Love and Other Heartaches, 1981; Jolly Marsupial, 1982; Animals in War, 1983; The Common Years, 1984; Leo and Jilly Cooper on Rugby, 1984; Riders, 1985; Hotfoot to Zabriskie Point, 1985; Turn Right at The Spotted Dog, 1987; Rivals, 1988; Angels Rush In, 1990; Polo, 1991; The Man Who Made Husbands Jealous, 1993; Araminta's Wedding, 1993; Appassionata, 1996; How to Survive Christmas, 1996; Score! 1999; Pandora, 2002. Address: c/o Vivienne Schuster, Curtis Brown, 4th Floor, Haymarket House, 28-29 Haymarket, London, SW1Y 4SP, England. E-mail: cb@curtisbrown.co.uk

COOPER Leon Niels, b. 28 February 1930, New York, USA. Physicist. m. Kay Anne Allard, 1969, 2 daughters. Education: BA, 1951, MA, 1953, PhD, 1954, Columbia University. Appointments: Institute for Advanced Study, Princeton, 1954-55; Research Associate, University of Illinois, 1955-57; Assistant Professor, Ohio State University, 157-58; Associate Professor, Brown University, Rhode Island, 1958-62; Professor, 1974, Thomas J Watson, Senior Professor of Science , 1974-, Director, Center for Neural Science, 1978-90, Institute for Brain and Neural Systems, 1991-, Brain Science Program, 2000-. Publications: An Introduction to the Meaning and Structure of Physics, 1968; Structure and Meaning, 1992; How We Learn, How We Remember, 1995. Honour: Comstock Prize, NAS, 1968; Joint Winner, Nobel Prize, Physics, 1972; Honorary DSc, Columbia, Sussex, 1973, Illinois, Brown, 1974, Gustavus Adolphus College, 1975, Ohio State University, 1976, Pierre and Marie Curie University, Paris, 1977; Award in Excellence, Columbia University, 1974; Descartes Medal, Academy de Paris, University Rene Descartes, 1977; John Jay Award, Columbia College, 1985. Memberships: National Science Foundation Post-doctoral Fellow, 1954-55; Alfred P Sloan Foundation Research Fellow, 1959-66; John Simon Guggenheim Memorial Foundation Fellow, 1965-66; Fellow, American Physical Society, American Academy of Arts and Sciences; American Federation of Scientists; Member, NAS, American Philosophical Society. Address: Box 1843, Physics Department, Brown University, Providence, RI 02912, USA.

COOPER Richard A (Richard A Austin-Cooper), b. 21 February 1932. Retired Banker. m. (1) Sylvia Anne Shirley Berringer, 1953, dissolved 1963, (2) Valerie Georgina Drage, 1963, dissolved 1974, 1 son, 1 daughter, (3) Mariola Danuta Sikorska, 1979, dissolved 1981, (4) Rosemary Swaisland, 1986, 1 stepson, 1 stepdaughter. Appointments: Royal Artillery, 1950-52; Intelligence Corps, 21 SAS Regt (Artists' Rifles), Essex ACF, 1952-69; 2nd Lt, TAVR, 1968; Hon Artillery Co, 1978-79; Barclays Bank, 1948-60; Head of Cash Department, Bank of Baroda, 1960-63; Securities Officer, Lloyd's Bank, 1963-69; Deputy Head, Stocks & Shares Department, Banque de Paris et des Pays Bas, 1969-74; Assistant Manager, Banking Division, Brook St Bureau of Mayfair Ltd, 1974-75; Chief Custodian and

London registrar, Canadian Imperial Bank of Commerce and Registrar in London for Angostura Bitters Ltd, 1975-78; Personnel Officer, Deutsche Bank AG, London branch, 1978-85; Senior Manager, Head of Human Resources, Deutsche Bank Capital Markets Ltd, 1985-90; Partner, Charsby Associates recruitment consultants, London, 1989-91; Retired, 1991-. Publications: Butterhill and Beyond, 1991; The Beavers of Barnack, 1995; The de Gidlow Family of Ince, 1996; The Peisley Family of Clifton Hampden, Oxon, 1996. Honours: Prizes for athletics, operatic singing and painting; Freeman, City of London, 1964; FHG, 1965; FRSA, 1974; FRSAIre, 1980; FCIB, 1987; Hon LLD (USA); Hon MA; MBIM. Memberships: Member, Board of Management: Barbican YMCA, City of London Central Markets (Leadenhall Market, Billingsgate Market); Member: City of London TAVR Association; Coal Corn and Rates Committee; Management Committee, Barbican School of Music and Drama (and mature student (tenor)); Irish Peers Association, 1964-; Founder Fellow, Institute of Genealogical Studies, Canterbury, 1965-; Life Governor, Sheriff's and Recorders' Fund at the Old Bailey, 1979-; Vice-Chairman, Trustee, The Friends of Eastbourne Hospitals; Governor, American College in Oxford; Chairman, British Cardiac Patients Association, Eastbourne Branch; Member, Special Forces Club; SAS Regimental Association; Intelligence Corps Old Comrades; Artists' Rifles Association; Wellingborough GS Old Boys; Probus, Eastbourne, Sussex. Address: 2 Lea House, 1 Mill Road, Eastbourne, East Sussex BN21 2LY, England.

COPE Malcolm, b. 1 April 1951, Hathersage, England. Academic. Education: BA Honours, History, 1973, LLB Honours, 1975, LLM, 1982, University of Queensland; Admitted as Barrister, Supreme Court of Queensland, 1976. Appointments: Senior Tutor, 1975-77, Lecturer, 1977-88, Senior Lecturer, 1988-91, Associate Dean, 1991-97, Dean, Faculty of Law, 1997-, Queensland University of Technology. Publications: Duress, Undue Influence and Unconscious Bargains, 1985; Constructive Trusts, 1991; Equity Issues and Trends, 1995; Proprietary Claims and Remedies, 1997. Address: 51 Mark Street, New Farm, Brisbane, QLD 4005, Australia. E-mail: m.cope@qut.edu.au

COPEMAN Herbert Arthur, b. 24 September 1923, Brisbane, Queensland, Australia. Medical Practitioner. m. (1) Peggy, deceased, 3 sons, 1 daughter, (2) Noela Marjorie Heyward. Education: MBBS (UQ); FRACP. Appointments: Consultant, Physician and Endocrinologist, Royal Brisbane Hospital, 1957-74; Director, Postgraduate Medical Education, University of Western Australia, Perth, 1975-88. Publications: Research papers on the Endocrinology of Arterial Disease; Meditation, a chapter in Ways of Healing, 1987; Book: Let Us Not Forget to Remember - Memories of a Typhoon Pilot, 1995. Memberships: FRACP; Past President, Fellow, Patron, Australian Postgraduate Federation in Medicine. Address: 2-177 Tranmere Road, Howrah, Tasmania 7018 Australia.

COPISAROW Alcon (Charles) (Sir), b. 25 June 1920. m. Diana, 1953, 2 sons, 2 daughters. Education: University of Manchester; Imperial College of Science and Technology; Sorbonne, Paris; Council of Europe Research Fellow. Appointments: War Service, 1942-47; Lieutenant Royal Navy, 1943-47; British Admiralty Delegation, Washington, 1945; Home Civil Service, 1946-66; Ministry of Defence, 1947-54; Scientific Counsellor, British Embassy, Paris, 1954-60; Director, Forest Products Research Laboratory, Department of Scientific and Industrial Research, 1960-62; Chief Technical Officer, National Economic Development Council, 1962-64; Chief Scientific Officer, Ministry of Technology, 1964-66; Director, McKinsey and Co Inc, 1966-76; Non-Executive Director, British Leyland, 1976-77; Member, BNOC, 1980-83; Chairman, APAX Venture Capital Funds, 1981-94; Director,

Dictionary of International Biography

Touche Remnant Holdings and Portfolio Companies, 1985-96; Special Advisor, Ernst and Young, 1993-99; Chairman of Trustees, Eden Project, 1996-2000; Chairman, ARINSO International, 2000-03. Memberships: Humanitarian Trust, Hebrew University, Jerusalem, 1948-55; Chairman, Commonwealth Forest Products Pre-Conference, Nairobi, 1962; CENTO Conference on Investment in Science, Tehran, 1963; Scientific Manpower Committee, Advisory Council on Scientific Policy, 1963-64; Economic Development Committees for Electronics Industry and Heavy Electrical Industry; Tropical Products Advisory Committee, 1965-66; Press Council, 1975-81; Chairman, General Commissioners for Income Tax, 1975-95; External Member, Council of Lloyds, 1982-90; Deputy Chairman, Board of Governors, English-Speaking Union, 1976-83; Chairman, Youth Business Initiative subsequently The Princes Youth Business Trust, 1982-87; Director, Windsor Festival, 1983-99; Trustee, Duke of Edinburgh's Award, 1978-84, Foundation for Manufacturing Industry, 1995-2001; Royal Jubilee Trusts, 1981-87; Zoological Society, 1990-91; Patron, Conseil National des Ingénieures et des Scientifiques de France, 1992-; Trustee, The Athenaeum. Address: 7 Southwell Gardens, London SW7 4SB, England.

COPLEY Paul, b. 25 November 1944, Denby Dale, Yorkshire, England. Actor; Writer. m. Natasha Pyne, 7 July 1972. Education: Teachers Certificate, Northern Counties College of Education. Appointments: Freelance Actor/Writer. Publications: Staged: Pillion, Bush Theatre, London, 1977; Viaduct, Bush Theatre, London, 1979; Tapster, Stephen Joseph Theatre, Scarborough, 1981; Fire-Eaters, Tricycle Theatre, London, 1984; Calling, Stephen Joseph Theatre, Scarborough, 1986; Broadcast: On May-Day, BBC Radio 4 Sunday Play, 1986, repeated World Service, 1987, Radio 4, 1996; Tipperary Smith, BBC Radio 4, 1994; Words Alive, BBC Education Radio, 1996-2003; Publications: Plays for children: Odysseus and the Cyclops, 1998; The Pardoner's Tale, 1999; Loki the Mischief Maker, 2000; Jennifer Jenks and Her Excellent Day Out, 2000. Membership: Writers Guild. Address: Casarotto Ramsay Ltd, 60 Wardour Street, London W1V 4ND, England.

COPNALL John Bainbridge, b. 16 February 1928, Slinfold, Sussex, England. Artist. 1 son, 2 daughters. Education: Architectural Association, London, 1945-46; Royal Academy Schools, London, 1949-54. Career: Selected solo exhibitions include: Piccadilly Gallery, London, 1955; Sala Vayreda, Barcelona, Piccadilly Gallery, London, 1956; Galerie Wolfgang Gurlitt, Munich, Galerie Boiséree, Cologne, Universa-Haus, Nuremburg, 1957; Institute für Auslandsbezienhungen, Stuttgart, Piccadilly Gallery, London, 1958; Bear Lane Gallery, Oxford, 1969; Institute of Contemporary Arts, London, 1972; Ikon Gallery, Birmingham, Richard Demarco Gallery, Edinburgh, 1973; Prudhoe Gallery, London, Aberdeen Art Gallery and Museum 1974; Galerie Morner, Stockholm, 1979; Oxford Gallery, Oxford, 1983; Austin Desmond Fine Art, London, 1989; Group exhibitions include: Internationale Kunstaustellung Bayreuth, 1957; Wildenstein, London, 1958; Art Spectrum, London, 1971; John Moores 8, Liverpool, 1972; Annely Juda Fine Art, London, 1973; John Moores 9, Liverpool, 1974; British Painting, Hayward Gallery, London; From Britain'75, Helsinki, Finland, 1975; Whitechapel Open, 1980-88; London Group Exhibition, 1980, 1984; Royal Academy Summer Shows, 1980-92; Ten Artists From London, Porin Pori, Finland, 1983; Thirty London Painters, Royal Academy, London, 1985; Modern British Art, Austin Desmond Fine Art, London, 1985-87; British and Irish Modern Art, Christie's London, 1986-89; London Group Exhibition, 1989-94; Surface Tensions, Curwen Gallery, 1994; Work in public collections including: Ateneum Museum, Helsinki, Finland; Aberdeen Art Gallery and Museum; Arts Council of Great Britain; Bristol University; Chelsea

and Westminster Hospital; County Collection of Hertfordshire; Education Committee, Hull; Nuffield Foundation, London, St John's College, Oxford, York University; Work in private collections in Australia, Eire, England, Finland, France, Germany, Scotland, Spain, Sweden, Switzerland, USA. Honours: Turner Gold Medal for Landscape Painting, 1954; EA Abbey Scholarship, 1970; Arts Council Awards, 1972-73; British Council Award, 1979; Elected Member of London Group, 1989. Address: Studio 9, Block B, 1 Fawe Street. London E14, England.

COPPOLA Francis Ford, b. 7 April 1939, Detroit, Michigan, USA. Film writer and director. m. Eleanor Neil, 2 sons (1 deceased), 1 daughter. Education: Hofstra University; University of California. Career: Films include: Dementia 13, 1963; This Property is Condemned, 1965; Is Paris Burning?, 1966; You're A Big Boy Now, 1967; Finian's Rainbow, 1968; The Rain People, 1969; Patton, 1971; The Godfather Part II, 1975; The Great Gatsby, 1974; The Black Stallion (produced), 1977; Apocalypse Now, 1979; One From the Heart, 1982; Hammett (produced), 1982; The Escape Artist, 1982; The Return of the Black Stallion, 1982; Rumble Fish, 1983; The Outsiders, 1983; The Cotton Club, 1984; Peggy Sue Got Married, 1986; Gardens of Stone, 1986; Life Without Zoe, 1988; Tucker: the Man and His Dream, 1988; The Godfather Part III, 1990; Dracula, 1991; My Family/Mia Familia, 1995; Don Huan de Marco, 1995; Jack, 1996; The Rainmaker, 1997; The Florentine, 1999; The Virgin Suicides, 1999; Grapefruit Moon, 2000; Assassination Tango; Supernova; Megalopolis; Executive producer: The Secret Garden, 1993; Mary Shelley's Frankenstein, 1994; Buddy, 1997; The Third Miracle, 1999; Goosed, 1999; Sleepy Hollow, 1999; Monster; Jeepers Creepers; No Such Thing; Pumpkin; Theatre direction includes: Private Lives, The Visit of the Old Lady (San Francisco Opera Co), 1972; Artistic Director, Zoetrope Studios, 1969-; Owner, Niebaum-Coppola Estate, Napa Valley. Honours: Cannes Film Award for The Conversation, 1974; Director's Guild Award for The Godfather; Academy Award for Best Screenplay for Patton, Golden Palm (Cannes), for Apocalypse Now, 1979; Also awarded Best Screenplay, Best Director and Best Picture Oscars for the Godfather Part II; US Army Civilian Service Award; Commandeur, Ordre des Arts et des Lettres. Address: Zoetrope Studios, 916 Kearny Street, San Francisco, CA 94133, USA.

CORBET Philip Steven, b. 21 May 1929, Kuala Lumpur, West Malaysia. University Professor; Consultant Ecologist; Medical Entomologist. 1 daughter. Education: BSc, First Class Honours, Botany, Geology, Zoology, 1949, BSc, First Class Honours, Zoology, 1950, University of Reading; PhD, Entomology, Gonville and Caius College, University of Cambridge, 1953; DSc, Zoology, University of Reading, 1962; ScD, Zoology, Gonville and Caius College, University of Cambridge, 1976; DSc, Zoology, University of Edinburgh, 2003. Appointments: Entomologist, East African Freshwater Fisheries Research Institute, Jinja, Uganda, 1954-57; Entomologist, East African Virus Research Institute, Entebbe, Uganda, 1957-62; Research Scientist (Entomologist), Entomology Research Institute, Canada Department of Agriculture, Ottawa, Ontario, Canada, 1962-67; Director, Research Institute, Canada Department of Agriculture, Belleville, Ontario, Canada, 1967-71; Professor and Chairman, Department of Biology, University of Waterloo, Ontario, Canada, 1971-74; Professor and Director, Centre for Resource Management, University of Canterbury and Lincoln College, Christchurch, New Zealand, 1974-78; Professor, Department of Zoology, University of Canterbury, Christchurch, New Zealand, 1978-80; Professor of Zoology, 1980-86, Head of Department, 1983-86, Department of Biological Sciences, Professor Emeritus of Zoology, 1990-, University of Dundee, Scotland; Honorary Professor, University of Edinburgh, Scotland, 1996-. Publications: Author or co-author of about 200 research reports on freshwater biology, medical entomology and conservation biology; 4 books: co-author, Dragonflies, 1960, reprinted 1985; A Biology of Dragonflies, 1962, reprinted 1983; co-author, The Odonata of Canada and Alaska, volume 3, 1975, revised edition, 1978, reprinted 1998; Dragonflies. Behaviour and Ecology of Odonata, 1999, reprinted 2001, 2004. Honours include: President, 1971-72 and Gold Medal for Outstanding Achievement, 1974, Entomological Society of Canada; Commonwealth Visiting Professor, University of Cambridge, 1979-80; President, British Dragonfly Society, 1983-91; President, Worldwide Dragonfly Association, 2001-2003; Neill Prize, Royal Society of Edinburgh, 2002; Elected Fellowships: Institute of Biology, 1967; Entomological Society of Canada, 1977, Royal Society of Tropical Medicine and Hygiene, 1985; Royal Society of Edinburgh, 1987; Royal Society of Arts, 1991; Honorary Professor, University of Edinburgh, 1996-; Honorary Memberships: British Dragonfly Society 1991; Société française d'odonatologie, 1997; Dragonfly Society of the Americas, 2000. Memberships: The Arctic Club; Entomological Society of New Zealand; Royal Entomological Society; Royal Society of Tropical Medicine and Hygiene; Institute of Ecology and Environmental Management. Address: Crean Mill, Crean, St Buryan, Cornwall TR19 6HA, England. E-mail: pscorbet@creanmill.u-net.com

CORBETT Peter George, b. 13 April 1952, Rossett, North Wales. Artist. Education: BA (Honours), Fine Art, Manchester Regional College of Art and Design, 1974. Career: Artist, oil on canvas; Speaker, Workers Educational Association, Liverpool, 1995; Life Drawing Tutor, Bluecoat Chambers, Liverpool, 1996; Originator "Liverpool European Capital of Culture 2008", 1996/1997; Exhibitions include: Centre Gallery Liverpool, 1979; Liverpool Playhouse, 1982; Acorn Gallery Liverpool, 1985; Major Merseyside Artists Exhibition, Port of Liverpool Building, 1988; Merseyside Contemporary Artists Exhibition, Albert Dock, Liverpool; Surreal Objects Exhibition, Tate Gallery, Liverpool, 1989; Unity Theatre, Liverpool, 1990; Royal Liver Building, Liverpool (two person), 1991; Senate House Gallery, Liverpool University (one man), 1993; Academy of Arts, Liverpool (two man), 1994; Grosvenor Museum Exhibition, Chester (open), 1995; Atkinson Gallery, Southport (one man), 1995; Liverpool Academy of Arts, 1998; Hanover Gallery, Liverpool (two man), 1999; Liverpool Biennial of Contemporary Art, 1999; DFN Gallery, New York (mixed), 2000; Influences and Innovations, Agora Gallery, New York (mixed), 2002; Retrospective Painting Exhibition, Senate House Gallery, University of Liverpool, 2004, included in Liverpool Biennial of Contemporary Art (independent); Works included in Liverpool University Art Collection; Atkinson Gallery, Southport; Private Collections in America, Netherlands, Australia, Germany, Britain. Publications: Numerous poems in poetry anthologies including: A Celebration of Poets, 1999; Parnassus of World Poets, 2001; The Best Poems and Poets of 2002; A Shield of Angels, 2002; The Sound of Poetry (Audio-cassette), 2002; Quantum Leap Magazine, 2003; The Pool of Life (Full anthology of own poems), 2003. Honours include: Honorary Professor of Fine Art, Institute of Co-ordinated Research, Victoria, Australia, 1994 Diploma Winner, Scottish International Open Poetry Competition, 1998; International German Art Prize, 1998; Outstanding Achievement Award, Albert Einstein Academy, USA, 1998; Friedrich Holdrein Award and Gold Medal for Poetry, Germany, 2000; International Peace Prize, United Cultural Convention, USA, 2002; World Lifetime Achievement Award, American Biographical Institute, 2002; Minister of Culture, American Biographical Institute, 2003; Poet of the Year, International Society of Poets, USA, 2003; Short listed for the Lexmark European Art Prize, exhibition of finalists in London, 2004. Memberships: Design and Artists Copyright Society, London; Maison International des Intellectuels, Paris, France;

International Society of Poets, USA; National Poetry Society, London; Founding Member, American Order of Excellence, American Biographical Institute, 2002. Address: Flat 4, 7 Gambier Terrace, Hope Street, Liverpool L1 7BG, England. Website: www.axisartists.org.uk/all/ref7166.htm

CORBETT Robin, (Lord Corbett of Castle Vale), b. 22 December 1933, Fremantle, Australia. Parliamentarian. m. Valerie, 1 son, 2 daughters. Appointments: Trainee, Birmingham Evening Mail; Reporter, Daily Mirror; Deputy Editor, Farmer's Weekly; Editorial Staff Development Executive, IPC Magazines; Labour Relations Executive, IPC; National Executive Committee Member, Honorary Secretary Magazine and Book Branch, National Union of Journalists; Elected Member of Parliament for Hemel Hempstead, 1974-79; Elected Member of Parliament for Birmingham Erdington, 1983-2001; Opposition Front Bench Spokesman on Broadcasting and Media, 1987-94 and Disabled People's Rights, 1994-95; Chairman, House of Commons Home Affairs Select Committee, 1999-2001; Appointed to House of Lords, 2001. Memberships: Vice Chairman Indo-British Parliamentary Group; Chairman, Friends of Cyprus; Vice-Chairman, All Party Motor Group, sustainable development, renewable energy; Member, Wilton Park Academic Council; Vice-President, Lotteries Council; Treasurer, ANZAC Group; Member, Friends of Eden Project; Patron, Hope for Children; Director, Rehab UK. Address: House of Lords, London, SW1A 0PW, England. E-mail: corbettr@parliament.uk

COREY Stephen Dale, b. 30 August 1948, Buffalo, New York, USA. Poet; Literary Editor; Essayist; English Professor. m. Mary Elizabeth Gibson, 28 January 1970, 4 daughters. Education: BA, English, 1971; MA, English, 1974; PhD, English, 1979. Appointments: Instructor of English, University of Florida, 1979-80; Assistant Professor of English, University of South Carolina, 1980-83; Assistant Editor, 1983-86, Associate Editor, 1986-, The Georgia Review. Publications: Synchronized Swimming, 1985, reissued, 1993; The Last Magician, 1981, reissued, 1987; All These Lands You Call One Country, 1992; Greatest Hits: 1980-2000, 2000; There is no Finished World, 2003. Poetry Chapbooks: Fighting Death, 1983; Gentle Iron Lace, 1984; Attacking the Pieta, 1988; Mortal Fathers and Daughters, 1999. Contributions to: Poetry; American Poetry Review; Kenyon Review; New Republic; Kansas Quarterly; Georgia Review; Antioch Review; Yellow Silk; Laurel Review. Honours: Writing Fellowships from the state arts councils of Florida, 1978-79, South Carolina, 1981-82 and Georgia, 1985-86, 1988-89; Water Mark Poets First Book Award, 1981, Swallow's Tale Press Poetry Award, 1984. Address: 357 Parkway Drive, Athens, GA 30606, USA.

CORGIER Monique, b. 10 October 1947, Lyon, France. Researcher. Education: PhD, National Institute of Applied Sciences, University of Lyon, 1974. Appointments: Researcher, Expert Researcher, CNRS, University of Lyon, INSA, Bayer Crop Science (Environmental Chemistry). Publications: Various articles in scientific periodicals. Membership: Advisory Board, Employee Shareholders. Address: 302 Rue Garibaldi, 69007 Lyon, France.

CORKHILL Annette Robyn, (Annette Robyn Vernon), b. 10 September 1955, Brisbane, Australia. Writer; Poet; Translator. m. Alan Corkhill, 18 March 1977, 2 sons, 1 daughter. Education: BA(Hon), 1977; DipEd, 1978; MA, 1985; PhD, 1993. Publications: The Jogger: Anthology of Australian Poetry, 1987; Destination, Outrider, 1987; Mangoes Encounter - Queensland Summer, 1987; Age 1, LINQ, 1987; Two Soldiers of Tiananmen, Earth Against Heaven, 1990; Australian Writing: Ethnic Writers 1945-1991, 1994; The Immigrant Experience in Australian Literature, 1995. Contributions to: Outrider; Australian Literary

Dictionary of International Biography

Studies. Honours: Honorary Mention, The Creativity Centre, Harold Kesteven Poetry Prize, 1987. Address: 5 Wattletree Place, The Gap, Queensland 4061, Australia.

CORNFORTH John Warcup, b. 7 September 1917, Sydney, Australia. Organic Chemist. m. Rita H Harradence, 1 son, 2 daughters. Education: University of Sydney; Doctorate, Oxford University, 1941. Appointments: Worked with Robert Robinson, 1941-46; Scientific Staff, British Medical Research Council, 1946-62; Director, Milstead Laboratory of Chemical Enzymology, Shell Research Ltd, 1962-75; Associate Professor, Warwick University, 1965-71; Visiting Professor, University of Sussex, 1971-75; Royal Society Professor, University of Sussex, 1975-82; Researched stereochemistry of biochemical compounds. Publications: Co-author, The Chemistry of Penicillin, 1949; Numerous papers on chemical and biochemical topics. Honours: Corday-Morgan Medal, Chemical Society, 1953; Flintoff Medal, Chemical Society, 1966; Ciba Medal, Biochemical Society, 1966; Stouffer Prize, 1967; Davy Medal, Royal Society, 1968; Ernest Guenther Award, American Chemical Society, 1969; Prix Roussel, 1972; Honorary DSc, ETH Zurich, 1975, Oxford, Dublin, Liverpool, Warwick universities, 1976, Aberdeen, Hull, Sussex, Sydney universities, 1977; Joint Winner, Nobel Prize for Chemistry, 1975; Royal Medal, Royal Society, 1976; Copley Medal, Royal Society, 1982. Memberships: Corresponding member, Australian Academy of Science, 1977-; Foreign Associate, US National Academy of Sciences, 1978-; Foreign member, Royal Netherlands Academy of Sciences, 1978-; Foreign Honorary member, American Academy, 1973-; Honorary Fellow, 1976-, RSC, 2001, St Catherine's College, Oxford; Honorary Professor, Beijing Medical University, 1986-. Address: Saxon Down, Cuilfail, Lewes, East Sussex, BN7 2BE, England.

CORONA Paolo. Professor. Appointments: Assistant Professor, Electromagnetic Waves, 1968-80; Associate Professor, Measurement Techniques, 1971-74; Associate Professor, Electromagnetic Waves, 1974-80; Visiting Scientist, University of Colorado, Boulder, USA, 1979; Full Professor, Electromagnetic Waves, 1980-; Chairman, Electromagnetic Compatibility EEC COST 243 Cooperative Action, 1993-97; Researcher, Responsible for Electromagnetic Remote Sensing Action, Italian Department of Research, 1995-; Chairman, Engineering Faculty, University of Naples, Parthenope, 1999-. Publications: Over 130 papers, mainly in the fields of antennae (numerical) modelling and experimental evaluation; Radar cross section analysis and experimental evaluation; Characterisation of materials at the microwave frequencies; Electromagnetic compatibility modelling and experimental evaluation. Memberships: Fellow, Institute of Electrical and Electronic Engineers; Italian National Council for Research (CNR); Italian Electrical Association (AEI); International Electrical Commission (IEC); Italian Electrical Commission (CEI). Address: University of Naples Parthenope, Institute of Electromagnetic Waves, Via Acton, 38 - 80133, Naples, Italy.

CORP Lester Desmond, b. 17 April 1946, London, England. Chartered Accountant; Finance Director. m. Mary Ann Robbins. Education: BSc, Economics, London School of Economics and Political Science, London University, 1967; Fellow, Institute of Chartered Accountants in England and Wales (FCA), 1970. Appointments: From Trainee to Manager, Coopers & Lybrand, London, 1967-75; Financial Accountant, Sun Life Assurance, London, 1975-78; Director of Finance and Resources, Conservative Party Central Office, 1978-84; Financial Controller, Leeds Castle Foundation, Maidstone, Kent, England, 1985-88; Director of Finance, Zoological Society of London, London, 1988-94; Finance Director, Grant Leisure Group Ltd, London, 1985-94; Director of Finance, Royal Albert Hall, London, 1994-2001;

Director, Finance and Administration, Parkinson's Disease Society, London, 2002-. Memberships: Vice-Chairman, Conservative Party, Mid Sussex, England, 1975-84; Member, Chartered Management Institute, 1980-; Trustee, Brooke Hospital for Animals, 1994-. Address: 3 Sunte Avenue, Lindfield, West Sussex, RH16 2AB, England.

CORRY Charles Elmo, b. 15 May 1938, Salt Lake City, Utah, USA. Geophysicist; Consultant. 2 sons, 1 daughter. Education: BS, Geology, Utah State University, 1970; MS, Geophysics, 1972, University of Utah; PhD, Geophysics, Texas A&M University, 1976. Appointments: Ground Radio Technician, US Marine Corps, 1956-59; Electronic Missile Checkout, GD/Astronautics, San Diego, 1960-64; Research Associate, Scripps Institution of Oceanography, San Diego, 1965-68, Woods Hole Oceanographic Institution, 1968; Manager, Geophysical Research, AMAX, Golden, 1977-82; Vice President, Nonlinear Analysis Incorporated, Bryan, Texas, 1982-84; Visiting and Adjunct Associate Professor, Geophysics, Texas A&M University, 1983-87; Associate Professor, Geophysics, University of Missouri, Rolla, 1984-89; Coordinator, World Ocean Circulation Experiment, Woods Hole Oceanographic Institution, 1990-95; Consultant, Database Administration, Denver and Colorado Springs, 1995-2001; President, Equal Justice Foundation, 2001-. Publications: 3 books; Numerous articles in professional journals. Memberships: American Geophysical Union; IEEE; Society of Exploration Geophysicists; Fellow, Geological Society of America; American Civil Liberties Union, Marine Corps League. Address: 455 Bear Creek Road, Colorado Springs, CO 80906-5820, USA. E-mail: ccorry@ejfi.org

CORTES Dina, b. 16 March 1959, Aarhus, Denmark. Pediatrician in Specialist Training to Pediatric Endocrinologist and Nephrologist. m. Jorgen Thorup, 2 sons. Education: MD, 1986, Doctor of Medical Science, 1998, University of Copenhagen; Pediatrician, 2002. Appointments: Resident, Department of Paediatric Surgery, Rigshospitalet, 1986, Resident, Department of Pathology, Copenhagen, Herlev, 1990-92, Research Fellow, Department Paediatric Surgery, Rigshospitalet, 1992-96, Resident, Department Paediatrics, Copenhagen, Glostrup, 1997-98, Resident, Department of Paediatrics, Co of Copenhagen, Gentofte, 1998-99, University of Copenhagen; Resident, Department of Orthopaedics, 1987-88, Resident, Department of Surgery, 1988-89, Resident, Department of Medicine, 1989-90, Resident, Department of Paediatrics, 1996-97, Co of Frederiksborg; Senior Lecturer, University of Copenhagen, 2000-; Senior Resident, Department of Pediatrics, Odense University Hospital, University of Odense, 2003-. Publications: Numerous articles in professional scientific and medical journals, titles include, Cryptorchidism - Aspects of pathogenesis, histology and treatment, doctoral thesis, 1998. Memberships: Danish Paediatric Society; Danish Society of Reproduction and Foetal Development; Nordic Association of Andrology; International Children's Continence Society. Address: Bukkeballevej 60, 2960 Rungsted, Denmark.

CORTES Joaquin, b. 1970, Madrid, Spain. Appointments: Joined Spanish National Ballet, 1985; Principal Dancer, 1987-90; Now appears in own shows, blending gypsy dancing, jazz blues and classical ballet; Appeared in Pedro Almodóvar's film The Flower Of My Secret.

CORTES John Emmanuel, b. 11 September 1956, Gibraltar. Botanical Garden Director; Consultant. m. Valerie Diane Pearce, 1 son, 1 daughter. Education: BSc, 1st Class Honours, Botany, Zoology, Royal Holloway College, University of London, 1979; DPhil, Magdalen College, Oxford, 1983. Appointments: General Secretary, Gibraltar Ornithological and Natural History Society, 1976-; Executive Officer, Gibraltar Government, 1983-86; Higher

Dictionary of International Biography

Executive Officer, 1986-88; Hospitals Manager, Gibraltar Health Authority, 1988-90; General Manager, 1990-91; Director, Gibraltar Botanic Gardens, 1991-; Managing Director, Wildlife, Gibraltar Ltd, Environmental Consultants, 1991-. Publications: Numerous magazine and newspaper articles, papers on ecology; Co-author: The Birds of Gibraltar, 1980; The Flowers of Gibraltar, 1996; Editor: Aves Rapaces del Parque Natural Sierra de Grazalema, 1996; Aves de la Bahia de Cadiz, 1998. Honours: Justice of the Peace, 1994-; Gibraltar Heritage Corporate Award, 1997; MBE, for services to Ecology and Conservation, 2003. Memberships: Fellow, Linnean Society of London; Institute of Ecology and Environmental Management; Institute of Biology, Chartered Biologist; Gibraltar Development and Planning Commission; Cemetries Board, Gibraltar Health Authority Board; Board of Parque Natural de Los Alcornocales, Spain; Instituto de Estudios Campo Gibraltarenos; Advisory Member, Species Survival Commission, IUCN; Vice President, Consejo, Iberico para la Defensa de la Naturaleza. Address: 8/8 Buena Vista Road, Gibraltar.

CORY Suzanne, b. 11 March 1942, Melbourne, Australia. Molecular Biologist. m. Jerry Adams, 2 daughters. Education: BSc, 1964, MSc, 1965, University of Melbourne, Australia; PhD, Cambridge University, England, 1968. Appointments: Rothmans Fellow, University of Geneva, Switzerland, 1969-71; Senior Principal Research Fellow, 1988-, Joint Head, Molecular Genetics of Cancer Division, 1988-, Director, 1996-, The Walter and Eliza Hall Institute of Medical Research, Melbourne, Australia; International Research Scholar, Howard Hughes Medical Institute, 1992-97. Publications: Numerous publications, articles and reviews. Honours: Lemberg Medal, Australian Society of Biochemistry and Molecular Biology, 1995; Burnet Medal, Australian Academy of Science, 1997; Australia Prize (Jointly), 1998; Charles S Mott Prize, General Motors Cancer Research Foundation (Jointly), 1998; Companion in the Order of Australia, 1999; L'Oreal-UNESCO Women in Science Award, 2001; Royal Medal, Royal Society, 2002. Memberships: Fellow, Australian Academy of Science, 1986; Fellow, Royal Society, 1992; Foreign Member, US National Academy of Science, 1997; Foreign Honorary Member, American Academy of Arts and Sciences, 2001; Associate Foreign Member, French Academy of Science, 2002. Address: The Walter and Eliza Hall Institute of Medical Research, 1G Royal Parade, Parkville, Victoria 3050, Australia. Website: www.wehi.edu.au

COSBY Bill, b. 12 July 1937, Philadelphia, USA. Actor. m. Camille Hanks, 1964, 5 children (1 son deceased). Education: Temple University; University of Massachusetts. Appointments: Served USNR, 1959-60; President, Rhythm and Blues Hall of Fame, 1968-; TV appearances include: The Bill Cosby Show, 1969, 1972-73, I Spy, The Cosby Show, 1984-92, Cosby Mystery Series, 1994-; Recitals include: Revenge, To Russell, My Brother With Whom I Slept, To Secret, 200 MPH, Why Is There Air, Wonderfulness, It's True, It's True, Bill Cosby is a Very Funny Fellow: Right, I Started Out as a Child, 8:15, 12:15, Hungry, Reunion 1982, Bill Cosby... Himself, 1983, Those of You With or Without Children, You'll Understand; Numerous night club appearances; Executive Producer, A Different Kind of World (TV series), 1987-; Films include: Hickey and Boggs, 1972; Man and Boy, 1972; Uptown Saturday Night, 1974; Let's Do It Again, 1975; Mother, Jugs and Speed, 1976; Aesop's Fables, A Piece of the Action, 1977; California Suite, 1978; Devil and Max Devlin, 1979; Leonard: Part IV, 1987; Ghost Dad, 1990; The Meteor Man, 1993; Jack, 1996; 4 Little Girls. Publications: The Wit and Wisdom of Fat Albert, 1973; Bill Cosby's Personal Guide to Power Tennis, Fatherhood, 1986; Time Flies, 1988; Love and Marriage, 1989; Childhood, 1991; Little Bill Series, 1999; Congratulations! Now

What? 1999. Honours: 4 Emmy Awards and 8 Grammy Awards. Address: c/o The Brokaw Co, 9255 Sunset Boulevard, Los Angeles, CA 90069, USA.

COSTELLO Elvis (Declan McManus), b. 25 August 1955, London, England. Singer; Songwriter; Musician; Record Producer. m. (1) 1 child, (2) Cait O'Riordan, divorced, (3) Diana Krall, 2004. Career: Lead singer, Elvis Costello And The Attractions, 1977-; Appearances include: UK tour, 1977; US tour, 1978; Grand Ole Opry, 1981; Royal Albert Hall, with Royal Philharmonic, 1982; Cambridge Folk Festival, 1995; Television includes: Appearance in Scully, ITV drama, 1985; Also worked with The Specials; Paul McCartney; Aimee Mann; George Jones; Roy Orbison; Wendy James; Robert Wyatt; Jimmy Cliff; Co-organiser, annual Meltdown festival, South Bank Centre, London. Compositions include: Alison, 1977; Watching The Detectives, 1977; (I Don't Want To Go To) Chelsea, 1979; Crawling To The USA, 1978; Radio Radio, 1978; Stranger In The House, 1978; Girls Talk, 1979; Oliver's Army, 1979; Boy With A Problem, 1982; Every Day I Write The Book, 1983; Music for television series (with Richard Harvey): G.B.H., 1991; Jake's Progress, 1995; Other songs for artists including Johnny Cash; June Tabor. Recordings: Albums include: My Aim Is True, 1977; This Years Model, 1978; Armed Forces, 1979; Get Happy, 1980; Trust, 1980; Almost Blue, 1981; Taking Liberties, 1982; Imperial Bedroom, 1982; Goodbye Cruel World, 1984; Punch The Clock, 1984; The Best Of, 1985; Blood And Chocolate, 1986; King Of America, 1986; Spike, 1989; Mighty Like A Rose, 1991; My Aim Is True, 1991; The Juliet Letters, with the Brodksy Quartet, 1993; Brutal Youth, 1994; The Very Best Of Elvis Costello And The Attractions, 1995; Kojak Variety, 1995; Deep Dead Blue, Live At Meltdown (with Bill Frisell), 1995; All The Useless Beauty, 1996; Terror & Magnificence, 1997; Painted From Memory, 1998; The Sweetest Punch: The Songs of Costello, 1999; Best of Elvis Costello, 1999; For the Stars (with Anne Sofie von Otter), 2001; When I Was Cruel, 2002. Honours include: BAFTA Award, Best Original Television Music, G.B.H., 1992; MTV Video, Best Male Video, 1989; Rolling Stone Award, Best Songwriter, 1990. Address: c/o Jill Taylor, By Eleven Management, 12 Tideway Yard, 125 Mortlake High Street, London SW14 8SN, England.

COSTNER Kevin, b. 18 January 1955. Actor. m. Cindy Silva, divorced 1 son, 2 daughter, 1 son by Bridget Rooney. Education: California State University. Appointments: Directing debut in Dances With Wolves, 1990; Films include: Frances, 1982; The Big Chill, 1983; Testament, 1983; Silverado, 1985; The Untouchables, 1987; No Way Out, 1987; Bull Durham, 1988; Field of Dreams, 1989; Revenge, 1989; Robin Hood: Prince of Thieves, 1990; JFK, 1991; The Bodyguard, 1992; A Perfect World, 1993; Wyatt Earp, 1994; Waterworld, 1995; Tin Cup, 1996; Message in a Bottle, 1998; For Love of the Game, 1999; Thirteen Days, 2000; 3000 Miles to Graceland, 2001; Dragonfly, 2002; Open Range, 2003; Co-producer, Rapa Nui; Co-producer, China Moon. Honours include: Academy Award for Best Picture, 1991. Address: TIG Productions, Producers Building 5, 4000 Warner Boulevard, Burbank, CA 91523, USA.

CÔTÉ Yves-Aubert, b. 30 July 1926, Pierreville, Quebec, Canada. Chartered Accountant. m. Marie-Alice Levac, deceased September 2000, 1 son, 3 daughters. Education: Master in Commerce, 1949, Master in Accountancy, 1951, University of Montreal. Appointments: Head Office, The Provincial Bank of Canada, 1949-56; Part-time Lecturer, 1953-56, Full-time Lecturer, 1956, Associate Professor, 1957-61, Head of Department, 1961-84, Full Professor, 1965; Chair of Accountancy, 1985-94, Honorary Professor, 1996-, Department of Accountancy, École des Hautes Études Commerciales, Montreal. Publications: Author and co-

Dictionary of International Biography

author of numerous books, articles in magazines and professional journals, papers and conference proceedings. Honours: Pro Ecclesia and Pontifice medal awarded by Pope Paul VI, 1978; Honorary member, Board of the University of Montreal, 1979; Fellow, Ordre des comptables agréés du Québec, 1984; Mérite HEC on the occasion of the 75th anniversary of the École des Hautes Études Commerciales de Montreal, 1986; Honorary Member of the Board of Directors of the École des Hautes Études Commerciales de Montreal, 1990. Memberships include: Past Member of several committees at the University of Montreal and at the École des Hautes Études Commerciales de Montreal; Governor of the Fondation Cardinal Léger, 1977-; Member of the Board of Director of the Hôpital St-Joseph de la Providence de Montreal, 1993-2002. Address: École des HEC, 3000, chemin de la Côte-Sainte-Catherine, Montreal (Quebec) H3T 2A7, Canada.

ČOTEK Pavel, b. 12 March 1922, Fryšava, Moravia, Czech Republic. Musicologist. m. Zdeňka Tkaná. Education: Graduate, State Music Conservatory, Prague, 1947; Diploma, Composition, Janáčkova Akademie Muzických Umění, Brno, Czech Republic, 1965. Appointments: Director of Music Schools in Slaný, Polička, Litomyšl and Choceň, Czech Republic, 1947-59; University Assistant, 1960-74, Chair of Musicology, 1974-87, Emeritus Docent of Musicology, 1987-, Palacký University, Olomouc, Czech Republic. Publications: About 100 works including orchestral music, chamber music and vocal music; Compositions include: Symphony/Etudes, 1965; Concerto for 2 Percussion and Orchestra, 1967; Glosa for Symphony Orchestra, 1985; Chamber Music, Musica a fiato, 1970. Honours: Numerous honours and prizes for work in music include: Annual Prize, SČSKU (supreme institution for serious music), 1977. Memberships: Association of Musicians, Artists and Scientists; Composers' Society of Prague; Creative Centre Olomouc. Address: Wellnerova 9, Olomouc 770 00, Czech Republic.

COTTON Richard Graham Hay, b. 10 November 1940, Wangaratta, Australia. Molecular Geneticist; Medical Researcher; Farmer. m. Elizabeth Smibert, 2 sons, 1 daughter. Education: B Agrl. Sci., 1963, PhD, 1967, DSc, 1983, University of Melbourne, Parkville, Australia. Appointments: Postdoctoral Scientist, John Curtin School of Medical Research, Australia, 1967, Royal Children's Hospital Research Foundation, Australia, 1968-70; Scripps Clinic, La Jolla, California, 1971, Medical Research Council Laboratory of Molecular Biology, Cambridge, England, 1972; Senior Associate, Department of Paediatrics, University of Melbourne, 1981-; Foundation Deputy Director, Murdoch Institute, Melbourne, 1983-95; Senior Principal Research Fellow, National Health and Medical Research Council, 1993-; Founder, Director, Mutation Research Centre (now named Genomic Disorders Research Centre), 1996-; Honorary Fellow, Murdoch Institute, 1996-; Professorial Associate, University of Melbourne, 1996-; Associate Director (Mutation), Australian Genome Research Facility, 1997-. Publications: Over 200 scientific papers in national and international journals; Initiator and co-editor of the journal, Human Mutation, 1991; Discovered theoretical and practical foundation for monoclonal antibody technique; Patent for chemical cleavage method for mutation detection; Patent for enzyme cleavage method for mutation detection. Honours include: Selwyn Smith Medical Arts Prize, University of Melbourne, 1991; Orator of the Human Genetics Society of Australasia, 1993; Royal Children's Hospital President's Medal, 1995. Memberships: Biochemical Society; American Society for Human Genetics; Human Genome Organisation, Treasurer, 1997-; Australian Society for Biochemistry and Molecular Biology; Honorary Member, Japanese Society for Inherited Metabolic Diseases; Founder, President, Human Genome Variation Society, 2001-. Address: Genomic Disorders Research Centre,

C/- National Neurosciences Facility, 2nd Floor, 161 Barry Street (off Grattan Street), Carlton South 3053, Melbourne, Australia. E-mail: cotton@unimelb.edu.au

COULSON Zoe, b. 22 September 1932, Indiana, USA. Retired Businesswoman. Education: BS, Purdue University, 1954; Advanced Management Program, Harvard Business School, 1983. Appointments: Assistant Home Economics Director, American Meat Institute, 1954-57; Account Executive, J Walter Thompson Company, 1957-60; Consumer Services Director, Leo Burnet and Company, 1960-64; Editor, Business Press Magazine, Donnelley Dunn/Bradstreet, 1964-68; Food Editor, Senior Editor, Director of Goodhousekeeping Seal, Hearst Publishing Company, 1968-81; Corporate Vice-President, Campbell Soup Company, 1981-90; Board of Directors, Rubbermaid Inc. 1982-95; Executive Volunteer, Marketing, Nishney Novgorad and Moscow, Russia, International Executive Service Corporation, 1998, 1999. Publications: Food Editor, Good Housekeeping, monthly articles, 1968-75; Good Housekeeping Cookbook, 1973; Good Housekeeping Illustrated Cookbook, 1980; Article, Case of Mismanaged Ms, Harvard Business Review, 1987. Honour: Distinguished Alumna, Purdue University, 1970. Memberships: Cooper Hospital Board of Trustees, 1982-91; Old Pine Presbyterian Church, Elder, 1994-97, Stewardship Committee, 1998-; Friends of Old Pine, Secretary, 1995-; Harvard Business School Club of Philadelphia, Board of Directors, 2002-, Program Committee, 1997-; Purdue Club of Philadelphia, President, 1999-. Address: 220 Locust St 18B, Philadelphia, PA 19106, USA.

COUPLES Fred, b. 3 October 1959, Seattle, Washington, USA. Professional Golfer. Education: University of Houston. Appointments: Member, Rider Cup Team, 1989, 1991, 1993; Named All-American, 1979, 1980; Winner, numerous tournaments including Kemper Open, 1983; Tournament Players Championship, 1984, Byron Nelson Golf Classic, 1987, French PGA, 1988, Nissan LA Open, 1990, 1992, Tournai Perrier de Paris, 1991, BC Open, 1991, Federal Express St Jude Classic, 1991, Johnnie Walker World Championship, 1991, 1995, Nestle Invitational, 1992, The Masters, 1992, with Jan Stephenson J C Penney Classic, 1983, with Mike Donald, Sazale Classic, 1990, with Raymond Floyd, RMCC Invitational, 1990, Buick Open, 1994, Dubai Desert Classic, 1995, Players Championship, 1996, Skins Game, 1996, Australian Skins Game, 1997; Member, US Team, Presidents Cup, 1997; Champion, Bob Hope Chrysler Classic, 1998; Champion, Memorial Tournament, 1998; Member, President Cup Team, 1998. Honours: Vardon Trophy, 1991, 1992; Named PGA Player of Year, Golf World magazine, 1991, 1992. Address: c/o PGA Tour, 100 Avenue of the Champions, PO Box 109601, Palm Beach Gardens, FL 33410, USA.

COURIER Jim (James Spencer), b. 17 August 1970, Sanford, Florida, USA. Tennis Player. Career: Professional Tennis Player, 1989-; Winner of tournaments including: Orange Bowl, 1986, 1987, Basel, 1989, French Open, 1991, 1992, Indian Wells, 1991, 1993, Key Biscayne, 1991, 1993, Australian Open, 1992-93, Italian Open, 93; Finalist US Open, 1991; Quarterfinalist, Wimbledon, 1991; Runner-up French Open, 1993, Wimbledon, 1993; Semifinalist, Australian Open, 1994, French Open, 1994; Winner of 23 singles titles and six doubles titles and over 16 million dollars in prize money; Retired, 2000. Address: IGM, Suite 300, 1 Erieview Place, Cleveland, OH 44114, USA.

COURTÉS Joseph Jean-Marie, b. 6 February 1936, France. Professor of Semiotics. m. 22 June 1974, 2 sons, 1 daughter. Education: Paris University. Appointments: Professor, University of Toulouse, France. Publications: Le Conte Populaire, Poétique et Mythologie, 1986; Analyse sémiotique du discours, 1991; Du

- 287 -

Signifié au Signifiant, 1992; Sémiotique, Dictionnaire Raisonné de la Théorie du Langage, 1993; Sémiotique narrative et discursive, 1993; Du lisible au visible, 1995; Ethnolittérature, rhétorique et sémiotique, 1995; L'énonciation comme acte sémiotique, 1998; La sémiotique, comprendre l'univers des signes, 2001; La Semiotique du Langage, 2003; Books of semiotics translated in many languages around world. Memberships: Association for the Development of Semiotics; Committee, Semiotics and Linguistics. Address: Toulouse II Université, 31058 Toulouse, France. E-mail: joseph.courtes@wanadoo.fr

COWASJEE Saros, b. 12 July 1931, Secundrabad, India. Professor Emeritus of English; Writer; Editor. Education: BA, St John's College, Agra, 1951; MA, Agra University, 1955; PhD, University of Leeds, 1960. Appointments: Assistant Editor, Times of India Press, Bombay, 1961-63; Teacher, 1963-71, Professor of English, 1971-95, Professor Emeritus, 1995-, University of Regina, Canada; General Editor, Literature of the Raj series, Arnold Publishers, New Delhi, 1984-2000. Publications: Sean O'Casey: The Man Behind the Plays, 1963; Sean O'Casey, 1966; Stories and Sketches, 1970; Goodbye to Elsa (novel), 1974; Coolie: An Assessment (criticism), 1976; So Many Freedoms: A Study of the Major Fiction of Mulk Raj Anand, 1977; Nude Therapy (short stories), 1978; The Last of the Maharajas (screenplay), 1980; Studies in Indian and Anglo-Indian Fiction, 1993; The Assistant Professor (novel), 1996; Strange Meeting and Other Stories, 2004. Editor: Author to Critic: The Letter of Mulk Raj Anand, 1973; Modern Indian Fiction, 1981; Modern Indian Short Stories, 1982; Stories from the Raj, 1982; When the British Left (fiction), 1987; More Stories from the Raj and After, 1986; Women Writers of the Raj, 1990; The Best Short Stories of Flora Annie Steel, 1995; Orphans of the Storm: Stories on the Partition of India, 1995; The Oxford Anthology of Raj Stories, 1998; Four Raj Novels, 2004. Contributions to: Encounter; A Review of English Literature; Journal of Commonwealth Literature; Literary Criterion; World Literature Written in English; Literature East and West; International Fiction Review; Journal of Canadian Fiction. Honours: J N Tata Scholarship, 1957-69; Canada Council and SSHRC Leave Fellowships, 1968-69, 1974-75, 1978-79, 1986-87. Memberships: Cambridge Society; Association of Commonwealth Literature and Language Studies; Regina Humane Society. Address: 308 – 3520 Hillsdale Street, Regina, Saskatchewan, Canada, S4S 5Z5. E-mail: saros.cowasjee@uregina.ca

COWEN Athol Ernest, b. 18 January 1942, Corbridge, Hexham, England. Writer; Poet; Publisher. Publications: Word Pictures (Brain Soup); 1989; Huh!, 1991. Contributions to: Various anthologies. Memberships: Publishers' Association; Poetry Society; Writers' Guild of Great Britain; Musicians' Union; Guild of International Songwriters and Composers; MRI; DG (ABIRA); IOA. Address: 40 Gibson Street, Wrexham LL13 7TS, Wales.

COWLAN Paul Francis, b. 7 June 1950, Farnborough, Kent, England. Songwriter/Performer; Peripatetic Tutor/Lecturer; Poet. Education: BEd, Hons. Contributions to: Stand; Orbis; Tabla; Envoi; Poetry Life; Still; Scintilla; Psychopoetica; Housman Anthology; Helicon; Open University Sonnet Society; Resurgence; South West Arts Review; Trewithen Chapbook; TOPS; A Handful of Care; Vision On; Poetry Digest; Devon Life. Honours: Joint 3rd Place, Envoi Competition 100, 1991; 2nd Place, Poetry Digest Bard of the Year, 1994; 1st Place, Envoi Competition 111, 1995; 1st Place, Poetry Life 8th Competition, 1996; Runner-up, Writers News 1998 Country Poem Competition; 3rd Place, Trewithen Poetry Prize, 1998 (Second Trewithen Chapbook); Runner-up, Stand International Poetry Competition, 1998; Commended, Daily Telegraph/Arvon International Poetry Competition, 1998 (The Ring of Words, 1998); 1st Place, Tabla Poetry Competition, 1998 (The

Tabla Book of New Verse); 2nd Place, Scintilla Open Poetry Competition 2001 (Scintilla 2001). Address: Hainerweg 3, D-60599 Frankfurt am Main, Germany.

COWLEY John M, b. 18 February 1923, South Australia. Professor. m. Roberta J Beckett, 2 daughters. Education: BSc, 1942, MSc, 1945, PhD (MIT), 1949, DSc, 1957, University of Adelaide. Appointments: Research Scientist, Commonwealth Scientific Research Organisation (Australia), 1945-62; Professor of Physics, University of Melbourne, 1962-70; Galvin Professor of Physics, Arizona State University, 1970-94; Regents Professor Emeritus, ASU, 1994-. Publications: Approximately 550 research publications; 1 book; Editor, 5 books. Honours: FRS; FAA; Ewald Prize; Warren Award; Honorary DS, Northwestern University, 1995. Memberships: International Union of Crystallographers; American Physical Society; Microscopy Society of America. Address: Arizona State University, Box 871504, Department of Physics and Astronomy, Tempe, AZ 85287-1504, USA. E-mail: cowleyj@asu.edu

COX Courteney, b. 15 June 1964, Birmingham, Alabama, USA. Actress. m. David Arquette, 1999, 1 daughter. Appointments: Modelling career, New York; Appeared Bruce Springsteen music video, Dancing in the Dark, 1984; Films: Down Twisted, 1986; Masters of the Universe, 1987; Cocoon: The Return, 1988; Mr Destiny, 1990; Blue Desert, 1990; Shaking the Tree, 1992; The Opposite Sex, 1993; Ace Ventura, Pet Detective, 1994; Scream, 1996; Commandments, 1996; Scream 2, 1997; The Runner, 1999; Scream 3, 1999; The Shrink Is In, 2000; 3000 Miles to Graceland, 2001; Get Well Soon, 2001; Alien Love Triangle, 2002; November, 2004; TV series: Misfits of Science, 1985-86; Family Ties, 1987-88; The Trouble With Larry, 1993; Friends, 1994-2004; TV films include: Roxanne: The Prize Pulitzer, 1989; Till We Meet Again, 1989; Curiosity Kills, 1990; Morton and Hays, 1991, Tobber, 1992; Sketch Artist II: Hands That See, 1995. Address: c/o Creative Artists Agency, 9830 Wilshire Boulevard, Beverly Hills, CA 90212, USA.

COX William Martin, b. 26 December 1922, NJ, USA. Attorney at Law. m. Julia Sebastian, 1952, 1 son, 3 daughters. Education: BA, Syracuse University, 1947; JD, Cornell University, 1950. Appointments: Special in Municipal Law, Planning and Zoning; Teacher, Zoning Administration Course, Rutgers University, 1968-98. Publications: Contributor to various professional journals; Author, New Jersey Zoning and Land Use Administration, 22nd edition, 2003. Honours: Man of the Year, Alpha Chi Rho Fraternity, 1976; Certificate of Merit, 1977; Appointed New Jersey Supreme Court to District Ethics Committee, 1977-78; Chairman, District Fee Arbitration Committee, 1978-80; Recipient, Distinguished Service Award, 1980; Resolution of Appreciation adopted by NJ Senate and General Assembly, 1994; William M Cox Award, established in New Jersey by Institute of Municipal Attorneys, 1999. Memberships include: Municipal Land Use Law Drafting Committee, 1969-, chairman, 1993-98; Sussex County History Society; Newton Board of Education; Sussex County Vocational Technical Board of Education; New Jersey State Bar Association; New Jersey Planning Officials; Newton Cemetery Company; The Monarchist League; American Legion; Veterans of Foreign Wars. Address: 1 Legal Lane, PO Box D, Newton, NJ 07860, USA.

CRACKNELL Vernon John, b. 16 January 1933, Oaklands, South Australia. Minister of Religion; Lecturer. m. Raeleen Mary Sundberg, deceased, 2 sons, 2 daughters. Education: AUA, Arts and Education, University of Adelaide; LTh, Melbourne College of Divinity; Grad Dip F Ed, BEd, Grad Dip R Ed, South Australian College of Advanced Education; DMin, Fuller Theological Seminary, Pasadena, California; MEd, Rel Ed, University of South Australia. Appointments: Parish Minister; Executive Officer;

Training Consultant, Scouts Australia; Lecturer in Parish Life and Leadership, Convenor: Distance Education, Parkin-Wesley College; Chaplain, Aldersgate Aged Care, Adelaide Central Mission; Minister of the Word, Uniting Church in Australia, retired; Chair, Gordon Symons Memorial Committee, Education for Ministry with the Aged, Adelaide College of Divinity; Convenor, Master of Ministry Programme, Adelaide College of Divinity; Chaplain, National Servicemen's Association; Academic Supervisor, MTh and MMin Students, Adelaide College of Divinity. Publications: 4 books; Numerous reports, handbooks, etc. Honours: Medal of Merit, 1972, Silver Acorn, 1978, Life Membership, 1984, Bar to the Silver Acorn, 1987, Scout Association of Australia; Awarded Anniversary, National Service in Australia Medal, 2002; Listed in national and international biographical dictionaries. Memberships: Returned Service League, Red Shield Sub Branch; National Serviceman's Association of Australia, South Australian Branch; Scout Service and Social Club; Pilgrim Uniting Church, Adelaide. Address: 11 Denman Terrace, Lower Mitcham, South Australia 5062, Australia.

CRAIG Amanda Pauline, b. 22 September 1959, South Africa. Novelist; Journalist. m. Robin John Cohen, 27 July 1988, 1 son, 1 daughter. Education: Clare College, Cambridge, England, 1979-81. Publications: Foreign Bodies, 1990; A Private Place, 1991; A Vicious Circle, 1996; In a Dark Wood, 2000; Love in Idleness, 2003. Contributions to: The Times; The Telegraph; The Observer; The New Statesman; Literary Review The Independent on Sunday; Columnist, Sunday Times. Honours: Young Journalist of the Year, 1996; Catherine Pakenham Award, 1998. Membership: Society of Authors, Management Committee, 2000. Address: c/o Anthony Harwood, 103 Walton Street, Oxford, OX2 6EB, England.

CRAIG David, b. 17 February 1925, Pittsburgh, Pennsylvania, USA. Retired Judge. m. Ella Van Kirk Craig, 2 daughters. Education: Bachelor of Arts, 1947, Juris Doctor, School of Law, 1950, University of Pittsburgh, USA. Appointments: Practising Attorney-at-Law, 1950-61; City Solicitor, 1961-65, Director of Public Safety, 1965-69, City of Pittsburgh, Pennsylvania, USA; Partner, Baskin Sachs & Craig, 1969-78; Judge, 1978-89, President Judge, 1989-94, Commonwealth Court of Pennsylvania; Visiting Professor: Yale University, University of Pittsburgh, Carnegie-Mellon University. Publications: Author book: Pennsylvania Building and Zoning Laws, 1951; Co-author Vols 22, 23 Summary of Pennsylvania Jurisprudence. Honours: Distinguished Flying Cross (US Bomber Pilot, UK, 1944-45); Listed in Who's Who publications and biographical dictionaries. Memberships: American Society of Planning Officials, President 1963-64; Pennsylvania Bar Institute, President, 1987-88. Address: 1812 Foxcroft Lane Ste 905, Allison Park, PA 15101, USA.

CRAIG Robert Michael, b. 29 May 1944, St Louis, Missouri, USA. Educator. m. Carole Anne Grundy, 1 son. Education: BA, Principia College, 1966; MA, University of Illinois, 1967; PhD, Cornell University, 1973. Appointments: Instructor, Meramec Junior College, 1967-68; Assistant Professor, 1973-78, Associate Professor, 1978-99, Professor, 1999-, Georgia Institute of Technology. Publications include: Articles: Pioneers of Post Modernism, Chapter One: Bernard Maybeck, 1981; Medieval Historicism Amidst Pioneer Modernism: Works by Labrouste and Perret, 1982; The Garden of Ease (Yi Yuan), Suzhou: Designed Diversions, Picture Views, and Objects of Contemplation in a 19th Century Chinese Garden, 1987; Passages to a Different Universe: The Three Gardens of Zhou Zheng Yuan, Suzhou, 1988; Claydon House, Buckinghamshire: A Mirror of Mid-Eighteenth Century Taste, 1992; Modernistic San Gimignano: Recent Atlanta Towers and Neo-Deco, 1993; Art Nouveau and the Rejection of Revivalism, 1994; Is Atlanta Losing Its Early Modern Architectural Heritage?, 1995; Functional Sculpture: The Work of Julian Harris, 1996; Atlanta's Moderne Diner Revival: History, Nostalgia, Youth and Car Culture, 1996; The Archaeology of Atlanta's first Automobile Age, 2000; Beaux-Arts Meets Southern Industry: The Coca-Cola Bottling Plants of Francis Palmer Smith, 2001; Books: From Plantation to Peachtree Street: A Century and a Half of Classic Atlanta Homes, co-author, 1987; Atlanta Architecture: Art Deco to Modern Classic 1929-1959, 1995; John Portman: An Island on an Island, 1997. Honours include: Donaghey Distinguished Lecturer, University of Arkansas, Little Rock, 1993; Centennial Speaker, The Principia, 1998; Award, Excellence, Architectural History, Atlanta Urban Design Commission, 2001; Sustained Service Award (life achievement), Southeast Chapter Society of Architectural Historians (SESAH). Memberships include: Founding Trustee, Past President, Treasurer, Southeast Chapter, Society of Architectural Historians (SESAH); Southeastern College Art Conference (SECAC); Editor, SECAC Review, 1983-87; Society of Architectural Historians (SAH), Secretary, 2000-; Nineteenth Century Studies Association, President, 2000-; Southeastern American Society for 18th Century Studies, President, 1999-2000; Society for Commercial Archaeology; Vernacular Architecture Forum; National Trust for Historic Preservation; Popular Culture Association, Onstage Atlanta. Address: College of Architecture, Georgia Institute of Technology, Atlanta, GA 30332-0155, USA.

CRAPON DE CAPRONA Noël François Marie, (Comte), b. 23 May 1928, Chambéry, Savoie, France. Lawyer; UN Senior Official, retired. m. Barbro Sigrid Wenne, 2 sons. Education: Diploma, Institute of Comparative Law, 1951; LLB, University of Paris, 1952; Postgraduate Studies, School of Political Science, 1952-54. Appointments: Assistant Manager, Sta Catalina Estancias, Argentina, 1947-48; Editor, Food and Agriculture Organization of the United Nations, 1954-57; Liaison Officer, UN and Other Organisations, 1957-65; Chief, Reports and Records, 1966-72; Chief, Conference Operations, 1972-74; Secretary General, 1974-78; Director, FAO Conference, Council and Protocol Affairs, 1974-83. Publication: The Longobards, a tentative explanation, 1995. Honours: FAO Silver Medal, 25 Years of Service; Medal of Honour, City of Salon de Provence, 1992; Who's Who Medal, 2000. Memberships: Society in France of the Sons of the American Revolution; Alumni Association College St Martin de France and Ecole des Sciences Politiques. Address: Lojovägen 73-75, S-18147 Lidingö, Sweden.

CRAVER Charles Henry, b. 6 December 1909, Eldon, Missouri, USA. Illustrator; Educator. m. Nadia Aileen Palmer. Education: St Louis Sch, Fine Art, 1927-30, 1930-36; AB, Washington University, 1993. Appointments: Illustrator, Capper Publications, Topeka, Kansas, 1993-36; Illustrator, So Agriculturist, Nashville, Tennessee, 1936-42; Staff Sargent, US Air Corps, Africa, 1942-45; Christian Board of Publishing, St Louis, 1945-48; Staff Artist, Department of Health, Jefferson City, 1948-79; Bur Chief, 1957; Bur Chief, Missouri Department of Health, Jefferson City, 1959; Instructor, Art Department, Lincoln University, Jefferson City, 1991-94. Awards: Missouri State Seal, 1949; Presidential Citation, Missouri Public Health Association, Jefferson City, 1984. Memberships: Capital City Council on the Arts, Jefferson City; Nichols Centre, Jefferson City; St Louis Artists Guild; Co of Military Historians; Society for Army Historical Research; Military Historical Society. Address: 1305 Moreland Avenue, Jefferson City, MO65101-3734, USA.

CRAWFORD Cindy, b. 1966, USA. Model. m. (1) Richard Gere, 1991, divorced, (2) Rande Gerber, 1998, 1 son, 1 daughter. Career: Major contracts with Revlon & Pepsi Cola; Presenter on own MTV fashion show; Appearances on numerous magazine covers, model for various designers; Face of Kelloggs Special K, 2000; Film: Fair Game, 1995; Released several exercise videos. Publications: Cindy Crawford's Basic Face, 1996; About Face (for children), 2001. Address: c/o Wolf-Kasteler, 231 South Rodeo Drive, Suite 300, Beverly Hills, CA 90212, USA.

CRAWFORD Michael, b. 19 January 1942. Actor; Singer. Appointments: Actor, 1955-; Films for Children's Film Foundation; 100's radio broadcasts; Appeared in original productions of Noyess Fludde and Let's Make an Opera, by Benjamin Britten; Tours, UK, USA, Australia. Stage roles include: Travelling Light, 1965; The Anniversary, 1966; No Sex Please, We're British, 1971; Billy, 1974; Same Time, Next Year, 1976; Flowers for Algernon, 1979; Barnum, 1981-83, 1984-86; Phantom of the Opera, London, 1986-87; Broadway, 1988, Los Angeles, 1989; The Music of Andrew Lloyd Webber (concert tour), USA, Australia, UK, 1992-92; EFX, Las Vegas, 1995-96; Dance of the Vampires, Broadway, 2003; Films include: Soap Box Derby, 1950; Blow Your Own Trumpet, 1954; Two Living One Dead, 1962; The War Lover, 1963; Two Left Feet, 1963; The Knack, 1965; A Funny Thing Happened on the Way to the Forum, 1966; The Jokers, 1966; How I Won the War, 1967; Hello Dolly, 1969; The Games, 1969; Hello Goodbye, 1970; Alice's Adventures in Wonderland, 1972; Condor Man, 1980; TV appearances include: Sir Francis Drake (series), 1962; Some Mothers Do 'Ave 'Em (several series); Chalk and Cheese (series), 1979; Sorry (play), 1979. Publication: Parcel Arrived Safely: Tied with String (autobiography), 2000. Honours: OBE; Tony Award, 1988. Address: c/o ICM Ltd, Oxford House, 76 Oxford Street, London W1D 1BS, England.

CREAGH Dudley Cecil, b. 18 February 1935, Brisbane, Queensland, Australia. Physicist. m. Helen (née Williams), 1 January 1962, 1 son, 1 daughter. Education: BSc (1st Hons); DipEd (Qld); MSc (UNE); MSc (Brist); PhD (NSW); CPhys; CEng; FInstP; FAIP. Appointments: Teacher, Queensland, 1958-59; Lecturer, University of New England, 1959-62; Lecturer, Royal Military College, Duntroon, 1962-65; Senior Lecturer, Royal Military College, Duntroon, 1965-68; Senior Lecturer, Faculty of Military Studies, University of New South Wales, 1968-86; Associate Professor, University College, University of New South Wales, 1986-96; Professor of Physics, University of Canberra, 1996-. Memberships: Fellow and Chartered Physicist, Institute of Physics; Fellow, Australian Institute of Physics; Chartered Engineer, Institute of Electrical Engineers; Chairman, Commission on Crystallographic Apparatus, International Union of Crystallography, 1983-93; Councillor, Asian Crystallographic Association, 1990-; President, Society of Crystallography in Australia, 1991-93; Member, National Committee of Crystallography, Australian Academy of Sciences, 1990-97; Chairman, Technical Committee Australian National Beamline Facility, 1989-96; Vice President, Australian X-Ray Analytical Association, 1991-1993; Councillor, International Radiation Physics Society, 1991-99; Board Member, Australian Synchrotron Research Programme, 1996-; Chairman, Photon Factory Committee, Australian Synchroton Research Programme, 1996-99; Editorial Board, Radiation Physics and Chemistry, 1998-; Vice President, International Radiation Physics Society, 1999-; Member, National Scientific Advisory Board, Australian Synchrotron Project, 2002. Address: 2 Throsby Crescent, Griffith ACT 2603, Australia.

CREEDY Donald Robert Russell, b. 17 October 1929, Adelaide, South Australia. Principal Violinist; Music Lecturer. m. Ruth Elizabeth. Education: Diploma of Teaching, 1984, Bachelor of Education, 1986, South Australia College of Advanced Education; Graduate Diploma, University of New England, Armidale, Australia, 2003. Appointments: Member 1949-94, Principal

Violinist, 1959-77, Adelaide Symphony Orchestra; Director, ABC Credit Union, 1968-72; Music Lecturer, Para Institute, Tafe, 1979-2000; Music Examiner, Australian Music Examination Board, 1980-; President, Adelaide Symphony Orchestra, 1955-58, 1969-70, 1974-75; Committee Member, Musicians Union, South Australia, 1951-53. Honours: Graduate Diploma in Humanities (Musicology); Bachelor of Education; Diploma of Teaching; Listed in Who's Who publications and biographical dictionaries. Membership: Masons, 1953-; Musicians Union, South Australia. Address: 9 King Street, Glenelg, North South Australia, 5045.

CRESSON Edith, b. 27 January 1934, Boulogne-sur-Seine, France. Politician. m. J Cresson, 2 daughters. Education: Hautes Etudes Commerciales, Doctorat de Démographie. Appointments: Economist, Conventions des Institutions Republicanes, 1965; Socialist Party National Secretary, 1974; Mayor of Thure, 1977; Member, Eurpean Assembly, 1979; Ministry of Agriculture, 1981-83; Mayor of Chatellerault, 1983-97; Adjoint au maire, 1997-; Minister, for Foreign Trade and Tourism, 1983-84, Minister, for Industrial Redeployment and Foreign Trade, 1984-86, Minister for European Affairs, 1988-90; PM, 1990-92; President of Schneider International Services Industries et Environnement, 1990-91, 1992-95; Commissaire européen chargé de la recherche et de l'éducation, 1995-99; Presidente de la Fondation pour les Ecoles de la Deuxième Chance. Publications: Avec le Soleil, 1976; Innover ou subir, 1998; Docteur Honoris Causa de l'Open University, UK and l'Institut Weisman, Israel, 1999; Présidente de la Fondation pour les Écoles de la Deuxième Chance, 2002-. Address: 10 Av. George V, Paris, France.

CREYTON Barry, b. 29 December 1939. Actor; Playwright; Composer. Creative Works: Plays: Follow That Husband, 1973; Double Act, 1988; Valentine's Day, 1999; Later Than Spring, 2000; Revues: Secrets, 1998; Screenplays: Fear and Mrs Friend, 1992; Murder is Deadly, 2001; Requiem, 2004. Honour: Norman Kessell Award (Gluggs Award) for Outstanding Contributions to Australian Theatre, 1988. Memberships: Societe Des Auteurs et Compositeurs Dramatiques, France; Writers Guild of America; Australia Writers Guild; British Actors Equity; Australian Actors Equity. Address: Cameron's Management Pty Ltd, 61 Marlborough St, Surry Hills, NSW 2010, Australia.

CRICHTON John Michael, b. 23 October 1942, Chicago, Illinois, USA. Film Director; Author. Education: AB, summa cum laude, 1964, MD, 1969, Harvard University. Appointments: Visiting Lecturer in Anthropology, Cambridge University, 1965; Postdoctoral Fellow, Salk Institute for Biological Sciences, La Jolla, California 1969-70; Visiting Writer, Massachusetts Institute of Technology, 1988; Creator, Co-Executive Producer, ER, NBC, 1994-. Publications: The Andromeda Strain, 1969; Five Patients, 1970; The Terminal Man, 1972; The Great Train Robbery, 1975; Eaters of the Dead, 1976; Jasper Johns, 1977; Congo, 1980; Electronic Life, 1983; Sphere, 1987; Travels, 1988; Jurassic Park, 1990; Rising Sun, 1992; Disclosure, 1994; The Lost World, 1995; The Terminal Man, 1995; Airframe, 1996; Timeline, 1999; Prey, 2002; Non-fiction: Five Patients: The Hospital Explained, 1970; Jasper Johns, 1977, revised edition, 1994; Electronic Life, 1983; Travels, 1988; Screenplays: Westworld, 1975; Twister (with Anne-Marie Martin, 1996; Films include: Westworld, writer, director, 1973; Coma, writer, director, 1978; Jurassic Park, co-writer, 1993; Rising Sun, co-writer, 1993; Disclosure, co-producer, 1994; Twister, co-writer, co-producer, 1996; Sphere, co-producer, 1998; Eaters of the Dead, co-producer, 1998; 13th Warrior, co-producer 1999. Honours include: Edgar Awards, Mystery Writers of America, 1968, 1979; Academy of Motion Pictures Arts and Sciences technical Achievement Award, 1995; Emmy, Best Dramatic Series for "ER", 1996; Ankylosaur named Bienosaurus crichtoni, 2000. Memberships: Authors Guild Council, 1995-; PEN; Phi Beta Kappa; Writers Guild of America; Directors Guild; Academy of Motion Picture Arts and Sciences; Board of Directors, International Design Conference, Aspen, 1985-91; Board of Trustees, West Behavioural Sciences Institute, La Jolla, 1986-91; Board of Overseers, Harvard University, 1990-96. Address: Constant Productions, 2118 Wiltshire Blvd #433, Santa Monica, CA 90403, USA.

CRICK Francis Harry Compton, b. 8 June 1916, Northampton, England. Neuroscientist. m. (1) 1 son, (2) Odile Speed, 1949, 2 daughters. Education: Graduated, Physics, University College, London; PhD, Caius College, Cambridge, 1953. Appointments: British Admiralty, work on development of radar and magnetic mines, 1940-47; Medical Research Council Student, Strangeways Research Laboratory, Cambridge University, 1947-49; MRC Laboratory of Molecular Biology, Cambridge, 1949-76; Keickhefer Distinguished Research Professor, 1977-, President, 1994-95, The Salk Institute, La Jolla, California, USA; Adjunct Professor of Psychology, University of California, San Diego; Research to determine the structure of DNA. Publications include: Of Molecules and Men, 1967; Life Itself, 1981; What Mad Pursuit, 1988; The Astonishing Hypothesis, 1994; Numerous papers on molecular and cell biology. Honours: Joint Winner, Nobel Prize for Physiology in Medicine, 1962; Royal Medal, Royal Society, 1972; Copley Medal, Royal Society, 1975; Michelson-Morley Award, Cleveland, USA, 1981; Numerous memorial lectures and other awards. Memberships: Fellow, 1960-61, Honorary Fellow, 1965, Churchill College, Cambridge; Foreign Honorary Member, American Academy of Arts and Sciences, 1962; Fellow, University College, London, 1962; Honorary Member, American Society of Biological Chemistry, 1963; Honorary, MRIA, 1964; Honorary FRSE, 1966; Fellow, AAAS, 1966; Foreign Associate, NAS, 1969; Member, German Academy of Science, 1969; Foreign Member, American Philosophical Society, Philadelphia, 1972; Hellenic Biochemical and Biophysical Society, 1974; Honorary Fellow, Caius College, Cambridge, 1976; Associate, Académie Française, 1978; Fellow, Indian National Science Academy, 1982; Honorary Fellow, Institute of Biology, 1995; Honorary Fellow, Tata Institute of Fundamental Research, Bombay, 1996. Address: The Salk Institute for Biological Studies, PO Box 85800, San Diego, CA 92186-5800, USA.

CRISTEA Valentin Gabriel, b. 7 June 1968, Targoviste, Romania. Mathematician. Education: Bachelor Degree, Mathematics, University of Bucharest, Romania, 1987-91; Grant Holder, International Congress of Mathematicians, ICM '98, Technische Universität Berlin, Germany, 1998; Arbeitstagung, Max-Planck-Institut fuer Mathematik, Bonn Germany, 1999. Appointments: Assistant Professor of Mathematics "Valahia" University, Targoviste, Romania, 1995-; Assistant Professor of Mathematics, Politechnic University of Bucharest, 1995-96; Mathematician, Instituto de Fisica Aplicada, CSIC, Madrid, Spain, 1994-95 (6 months); Mathematician, CIMAT, Guanajuato, Mexico, 1998 (1 month); Mathematician Max-Planck-Institut fuer Mathematik, Bonn, Germany, 1999 (7 months). Publications: Considerations sur les paires de superconnexions sur des supervarietes, 1991; Remarks about the Supermanifolds, 1992; Totally geodesic graded Riemannian submanifolds of the (4,4)-dimensional graded Riemannian manifold, 1995; Existence and uniqueness theorem for Frenet frames supercurves, 1999; The reduced bundle of the principal superfibre bundle, 2001; Euler's superequations, 2001; Curvilinear Integral I(C) for problems of variations calculus on supermanifolds, 2002. Honours: Distinguished Leadership Award, American Biographical Institute; Listed in biographical dictionaries. Membership: Romanian Society of Mathematical Sciences. Address: Str G-ral Matei Vladescu, BL 30 Sc A, Ap 6 Targoviste, 0200 Jud Dambovita, Romania. E-mail: valentin_cristea@yahoo.com

CRONE David Lloyd, b. 27 May 1941, Hayfield, England. Racing Chemist. m. Caroline Ann Rhodes,1 son, 2 daughters. Education: BSc, 1962, PhD, 1966, University of Bristol. Appointments: Lecturer, University of Hong Kong, 1965-70; Senior Racing Chemist, Hong Kong Jockey Club, 1970-98. Publications: Numerous papers and articles contributed to scientific publications; Editor, Proceedings of the 6th International Conference of Racing Analysts and Vets, 1987; Co-Editor, Testing for Therapeutic Medications, Environmental and Dietary Substances in Racing Horses, 1995. Honours: EurChem; CChem; FRSC; Registered Analytical Chemist. Memberships: Honorary Representative, Royal Society of Chemistry, Hong Kong, 1979-96; Association of Official Racing Chemists. Address: Irish Equine Centre, Johnstown, NAAS, Co Kildare, Ireland.

CRONENBERG David, b. 15 March 1943, Toronto, Canada. Film Director. Education: University of Toronto. Appointments: Directed fillers and short dramas for TV; Films include: Stereo, 1969; Crimes of the Future, 1970; The Parasite Murders/Shivers, 1974; Rabid, 1976; Fast Company, 1979; The Brood, 1979; Scanners, 1980; Videodrome, 1982; The Dead Zone, 1983; The Fly, 1986; Dead Ringers, 1988; The Naked Lunch, 1991; Crash, 1996; Acted in: Nightbreed, 1990; The Naked Lunch (wrote screenplay); Trial by Jury; Henry and Verlin; To Die For, 1995; Extreme Measures, 1996; The Stupids, 1996; Director, writer, producer, actor, Crash, 1996. Publications: Crash 1996; Cronenberg on Cronenberg, 1996. Address: David Cronenberg Productions Ltd, 217 Avenue Road, Toronto, Ontario, M5R 2J3, Canada.

CRONIN James Watson, b. 29 September 1931, Chicago, Illinois, USA. Physicist. m. Annette Martin, 1954, 1 son, 2 daughters. Education: BS, Southern Methodist University, 1951; MS, 1953, PhD, Physics, 1955, University of Chicago. Appointments: National Science Foundation Fellow, 1952-55; Assistant Physicist, Brookhaven National Laboratory, 1955-58; Assistant Professor of Physics, 1958-62, Associate Professor, 1962-64, Professor, 1964-71; Princeton University; Professor of Physics, University of Chicago, 1971-; Loeb Lecturer in Physics, Harvard University, 1976. Honours: Research Corporation Award, 1968; Ernest O Lawrence Award, 1977; John Price Wetherill Medal, Franklin Institute, 1975; Joint Winner, Nobel Prize for Physics, 1980; Honorary DSc, Leeds, 1996; National Medal of Science, 1999. Memberships: NAS; American Academy of Arts and Sciences; American Physical Society. Address: Enrico Fermi Institute, University of Chicago, 5630 South Ellis Avenue, Chicago, IL 60637, USA.

CROPP Glynnis Marjory, b. 23 March 1938, Christchurch, New Zealand. University Professor. Education: MA, 1st class honour in French, University of Canterbury, New Zealand, 1960; L-ès-L, DU, Université de Paris, 1962, 1970. Appointments: Lecturer in French, 1963-70, Senior Lecturer, 1971-78, Reader, 1979-84, Professor and Head, Department of Modern (then European) Languages, 1985-97, Dean, Faculty of Humanities, 1987-97, Professor and Head, School of Language Studies, 1998-2001, Professor Emeritus and Honorary Research Fellow, School of Language Studies, 2001-, Massey University. Publications: 1 book; Several scholarly articles in professional journals. Honour: Chevalier dans l'Ordre des Palmes académiques. Memberships: International Courtly Literature Society; New Zealand Association of Language Teachers; International Boethius Society; AULLA. Address: 8 Moana Street, Palmerston North, New Zealand.

CROSSLAND Bernard, b. 20 October 1923, Sydenham, England. Mechanical Engineer. m. Audrey Elliott Birks, 2 daughters. Education: BSc, 1943, MSc, 1946, Engineering, Nottingham University College; PhD, University of Bristol, 1953; DSc, University of Nottingham, 1960. Appointments: Engineering Apprentice, 1940-44, Technical Assistant, 1943-45, Rolls Royce Ltd, Derby; Lecturer, Luton Regional Technical College, 1945-46; Assistant Lecturer, Lecturer, Senior Lecturer in Mechanical Engineering, University of Bristol, 1946-59; Professor of Mechanical Engineering, Head of Department of Mechanical and Manufacturing Engineering, 1959-84, Dean of the Faculty of Engineering, 1964-67, Senior Pro Vice Chancellor, 1978-82, Queen's University of Belfast; Involved in the investigations of several major disasters including: King's Cross Underground Fire, Bilsthorp Colliery Roof Fall, Southall Train Crash, Ladbroke Grove Rail Crash and numerous others. Publications: Many articles in professional journals and books. Honours: 11 named lectures; 8 prizes; 3 Honorary DEng; 6 Honorary DSc; Honorary Fellowships: FWI, FIEI, Fellow of the University of Luton, FIMechE, FIStructE; CBE, 1980; Kt, 1990. Memberships: Royal Irish Academy; Royal Academy of Engineering; Royal Society; Irish Academy of Engineering. Address: 16 Malone Court, Belfast, BT9 6PA, Northern Ireland.

CROTHERS Derrick Samuel Frederick, b. 24 June 1942, Belfast, Northern Ireland. University Professor. m. Eithne, 2 sons, 1 daughter. Education; MA, Mathematics, Balliol College, Oxford, 1960-63; PhD, Queen's University Belfast, 1963-66. Appointments: Professor, Personal Chair, with tenure, Theoretical Physics, 1985, Reader, Applied Mathematics and Theoretical Physics, 1976-85, Lecturer, Applied Mathematics, 1966-76, Head, Theoretical and Computational Physics Research Division, 1989-2001, Queen's University, Belfast, Northern Ireland. Publications: Over 250 publications in atomic, molecular, optical, nuclear and condensed-matter physics. Honours: Professeur Associe à la Premiere Classe, University of Bordeaux I, 1984; UK-Chair, UK-Japan Collaboration, Theoretical Atomic Collisions, 1988-98; Elected Member, Royal Irish Academy, 1991-; Elected Fellow, American Physical Society, 1994-. Memberships: Fellow, Institute of Mathematics and its Applications; Fellow, Institute of Physics; European Mathematical Society; European Physical Society; American Physical Society. Address: David Bates Building, Queen's University, Belfast, BT7 1NN, Northern Ireland. E-mail: d.crothers@qub.ac.uk

CROUCH Colin, b. 1 March 1944, Isleworth, Middlesex, England. University Professor. m. Joan Ann Freedman, 2 sons. Education: BA, first class, Sociology, London School of Economics, 1969; DPhil, Nuffield College, Oxford, 1975. Appointments: Temporary Lecturer in Sociology, London School of Economics, 1969-70; Research Student, Nuffield College, Oxford, 1970-72; Lecturer in Sociology, University of Bath, 1972-73; Lecturer, 1973-79, Senior Lecturer, 1979-80, Reader, 1980-85, Sociology, London School of Economics and Political Science; Professor of Sociology, Fellow of Trinity College, University of Oxford, 1985-95; Chairman, Department of Social and Political Sciences, Professor of Comparative Social Institutions, European University Institute, Florence, Italy; External Scientific Member, Max-Planck-Institut für Gesellschaftsforschung, Cologne, Germany; Chairman, The Political Quarterly Ltd. Publications: 8 books; Editor, 18 books; 108 other articles and chapters. Honours: Hobhouse Memorial Prize, 1969. Memberships: President of Society for the Advancement of Socio-Economics; Max-Planck-Gesellschaft. Address: Istituto Universitario Europeo, San Domenico Di Fiesole, 50016 FI, Italy. E-mail: colin.crouch@iue.it

CROUCH Helga Ursula, b. 18 January 1941, London, England. Botanical Artist. m. Julian Terence Crouch, 1 daughter. Education: Cardiff College of Art, Wales; Central School of Arts and Crafts, London, England. Career: Graphic Designer, 1964-78; Botanical Illustrator specialising in wild flora, fruits and insects on vellum in watercolour; Tutor of Botanical Art. Publications: Books: Contemporary Botanical Artists; Arte y Botanica; The Art of Botanical Painting; Articles: Country Living Magazine; Kew Magazine; Essex Life. Honours: Certificate of Art and Design (Distinction); Diploma in Art and Design; Certificate of Botanical Merit; Silver Gilt Medal, Royal Horticultural Society. Memberships: Founder Member, Society of Botanical Artists; Fellow, Linnean Society; Cambridge Open Studios; European Boxwood and Topiary Society. Address: The Mill House, Little Sampford, Near Saffron Walden, Essex CB10 2QT, England. E-mail: helgacrouch@netbreeze.co.uk

CROWE Russell, b. 7 April 1964, New Zealand. Actor. m. Danielle Spencer, 2003. Career: Films include: The Crossing, 1993; The Quick and the Dead, 1995; Romper Stomper, 1995; Rough Magic, 1995; Virtuosity, 1995; Under the Gun, 1995; Heaven's Burning, 1997; Breaking Up, 1997; LA Confidential, 1997; Mystery Alaska, 1999; The Insider, 1999; Gladiator, 2000; Proof of Life, 2000; A Beautiful Mind, 2001. Honours: Variety Club Award (Australia), 1993; Film Critics Circle Award, 1993; Best Actor, Seattle International Film Festival, 1993; Management Film and TV Awards, Motion Pictures Exhibitors Association, 1993; LA Film Critics Association, 1999; National Board of Review, 1999; National Society of Film Critics, 1999; Academy Award for Best Actor, 2000; Golden Globe, 2001; BAFTA Award, 2001; Screen Actors' Guild Award for Best Actor, 2001. Address: ICM, 8942 Wilshire Blvd, Beverly Hills, CA, 90211, USA.

CROZIER Brian Rossiter, (John Rossiter), b. 4 August 1918, Kuridala, Queensland, Australia. Journalist; Writer; Consultant. m. Mary Lillian Samuel, 7 September 1940, deceased 1993, 1 son, 3 daughters. Education: Lycée, Montpellier; Peterborough College, Harrow; Trinity College of Music, London. Appointments: Music and Art Critic, London, 1936-39; Reporter, Sub-Editor, Stoke-on-Trent, Stockport, London, 1940-41; Sub-Editor, Reuters, 1943-44, News Chronicle, 1944-48; Sub-Editor and Writer, Sydney Morning Herald, 1948-51; Correspondent, Reuters-AAP, 1951-52; Features Editor, Straits Times, 1952-53; Leader Writer, Correspondent, and Editor, Foreign Report, The Economist, 1954-64; Commentator, BBC English, French, and Spanish Overseas Services, 1954-66; Chairman, Forum World Features, 1965-74; Co-Founder and Director, Institute for the Study of Conflict, 1970-79; Columnist, National Review, New York, 1978-94; Columnist, Now!, 1979-81, The Times, 1982-83, The Free Nation, later Freedom Today, 1982-89; Adjunct Scholar, Heritage Foundation, Washington, DC, 1984-95; Distinguished Visiting Fellow, Hoover Institution, Stanford, California, 1996-2002. Publications: The Rebels, 1960; The Morning After, 1963; Neo-Colonialism, 1964; South-East Asia in Turmoil, 1965, 3rd edition, 1968; The Struggle for the Third World, 1966; Franco, 1967; The Masters of Power, 1969; The Future of Communist Power (US edition as Since Stalin), 1970; De Gaulle, 2 volumes, 1973, 1974; A Theory of Conflict, 1974; The Man Who Lost China (Chiang Kai-shek), 1976; Strategy of Survival, 1978; The Minimum State, 1979; Franco: Crepúsculo de un hombre, 1980; The Price of Peace, 1980, new edition, 1983; Socialism Explained (co-author), 1984; This War Called Peace (co-author), 1984; The Andropov Deception (novel published under the name John Rossiter), 1984 (published in the US under own name), 1986; Socialism: Dream and Reality, 1987; The Grenada Documents (editor), 1987; The Gorbachev Phenomenon, 1990; Communism: Why Prolong its Death-Throes?, 1990; Free Agent, 1993; The KGB Lawsuits, 1995; Le Phénix Rouge (Paris) (co-author), 1995; The Rise and Fall of the Soviet Empire, 1999;

Contributions to numerous journals. Memberships: Traveller's Club, 1955-90; Royal Automobile Club, 1990-. Address: 18 Wickliffe Avenue, Finchley, London N3 3EJ, England.

CRUISE Tom (Thomas Cruise Mapother IV), b. 3 July 1962, Syracuse, New York, USA. Actor. m. (1) Mimi Rogers, 1987, divorced 1990, (2) Nicole Kidman, 1990, divorced 2001, 1 adopted son, 1 adopted daughter. Career: Actor, films include: Endless Love, 1981; Taps, 1981; All The Right Moves, 1983; Losin' It, 1983; The Outsiders, 1983; Risky Business, 1983; Legend, 1984; Top Gun, 1985; The Color of Money, 1986; Rain Man, 1988; Cocktail, 1989; Born on the Fourth of July, 1989; Daytona, 1990; Rush, 1990; Days of Thunder, 1990; Sure as the Moon, 1991; Far and Away, 1992; A Few Good Men, 1992; The Firm, 1993; Interview with the Vampire, 1994; Jerry Maguire, 1996; Mission Impossible, 1996; Eyes Wide Shut, 1997; Mission Impossible 2, 1999; Magnolia, 1999; Vanilla Sky, 2001; Minority Report, 2002; Space Station 3D, voice, 2002; The Last Samurai, 2003; Producer: Without Limits, 1998. Honours: Golden Globe, 2000. Address: C/W Productions, c/o Paramount Studios, 5555 Melrose Avenue, Hollywood, CA 90038, USA.

CRUYFF Johan, b. 25 April 1947, Amsterdam, Netherlands. Footballer. Appointments: Played for Ajax, 1964-73; Top scorer in Dutch league, with 33 goals, 1967; Moved to Barcelona, now Coach of Barcelona; Captained Netherlands, 1974 World Cup Final, 1974; Retired, 1978; Started playing again and signed for Los Angeles Aztecs; Played for Washington Diplomats, 1979-80; Levante, Spain, 1981; Ajax and Feyenoord, 1982; Manager, Ajax, 1987-87, winning European Cup-Winners Cup, 1987; Manager, Barcelona, winning Cup-Winners Cup, 1989, European Cup, 1992, Spanish League, 1991, 1992, 1993, Spanish Super Cup, 1992; Formed Cruyff Foundation for disabled sportspeople and Johan Cruyff University to assist retired sportspeople, 1998. Honour: European Footballer of the Year, 1971, 1973-74..

CRUZ Mauro, b. 8 March 1954, Sto Antonio, Brazil. Dentist; Surgeon; Orthodontist. 1 son, 2 daughters. Education: Degree in Dentistry, UFJF, 1976; Specialist in Oral Surgery, UERJ, 1978; Specialist in Orthodontics, PUC, 1979; Postgraduate in Occlusion, PUC, 1979; Master of Dental Science, Oral Implantology, UCCB, 2002. Appointments: Army 1st Lieutenant, 1977-78; Assistant Professor, Department of Orthodontics, Pontifical Catholic University, Rio de Janeiro, 1978-83; Director, Clinical Centre of Research in Stomatology, 1990-; Scientific Consultant, Bioform Implant and Allumina Membrane, Juiz de Fora, 1990-; President, Brazilian Dental Association, Juiz de Fora, 1997-2000; Director, 2nd International Orthodontic Congress, Juiz de Fora, 1999; Permanent Member, City Civic Council. Publications: 11 interviews; 22 articles to professional journals and magazines; Author: The Little Creek, 2003; Guided Tissue Regeneration, 2004, in press. Honours: Recipient of Awards from: Italian Implant Study Group, 1984, Brazilian Hypnosis Association, 1985, Developing Institute of Personality, 1985, Brazilian Oral Implants Association, 1986, International Order of Journalists, 1990, Dental Syndicate of Juiz de Fora, Brazilian Oral Surgery, 1997, Tiradentes Academy, 1999, Municipal Chamber of Juiz de Fora, 1999, Tribuna de Minas Journal, 2001. Memberships: Brazilian Academy of Dentistry; Mineira Academy of Dentistry; Fellow, Pierre Fauchard Academy; Fellow, International College of Dentists; Fellow, Federation Dental International; Fellow, Brazilian Dental Association; Fellow, Brazilian Oral Surgery Association. Address: Clinest – Av. Rio Branco, 2288/1203 – Centro – Juiz de Fora –MG – 36016-310 Brazil.

CRYSTAL Billy, b. 14 March 1947, Long Beach, NY, USA. Actor; Comedian. m. Janice Goldfinger, 2 daughters. Education: Marshall University. Appointments: Member of group, 3's Company; Solo appearances as stand-up comedian; TV appearances include: Soap, 1977-81; The Billy Crystal Hour, 1982; Saturday Night Live, 1984-85; The Love Boat; The Tonight Show; TV films include: Breaking Up is Hard to Do, 1979; Enola Gay; The Men; The Mission; The Atomic Bomb, 1980; Death Flight; Feature films include: The Rabbit Test, 1978; This is Spinal Tap, 1984; Running Scared, 1986; The Princess Bridge, 1987; Throw Momma From the Train, 1987; When Harry Met Sally..., 1989; City Slickers, 1991; Mr Saturday Night (Director, Producer, co-screenplay writer), 1993; City Slickers II: The Legend of Curly's Gold, 1994; Forget Paris, 1995; Hamlet; Father's Day; Deconstructing Harry; My Grant, 1998; Analyse This, 1998; The Adventures of Rocky and Bullwinkle, 2000; Monsters Inc (voice), 2001; America's Sweethearts, 2001; Mike's New Car (voice), 2002; Analyze That, 2002. Publication: Absolutley Mahvelous, 1986.

CSIKAI Gyula, b. 31 October 1930, Tiszaladány. Professor in Physics. m. Margit Buczkó, 2 sons. Education: University Diploma in Mathematics and Physics, 1953, Candidate, 1957, DSc, 1966, Corresponding, 1973, and Ordinary Member, 1985, Hungarian Academy of Sciences. Appointments: Head, Neutron Physics Department, ATOMKI, Debrecen, Hungary, 1956-57; Head Institute of Experimental Physics, Debrecen, 1967-95; Deputy Minister of Culture and Education of Hungary, 1987; Professor, 1967, Dean, 1972-75, Rector, 1981-86, Kossuth University, Debrecen, Hungary; Professor Emeritus, 2001-. Publications: More than 240 papers in scientific journals; Handbook of Fast Neutron Generators I-II, 1987; Handbook on Nuclear Data, 1987; 2 patents. Honours: First Prize of Hungarian Academy of Sciences, 1967; Eötvös Medal, 1980, Golden Medal of Hungary, 1980; State Award, 1983; Named Honorary Freeman of Tiszaladány, 2000-; Honorary Doctor, Kiev National University, 2001. Memberships: Expert UN-IAEA, Vienna, 1976; The New York Academy of Sciences, 1982; Hungarian Academy of Sciences, 1985; Academia Europea, 1991; Secretary, IUPAP Commission, Nuclear Physics, 1993-96. Address: Institute of Experimental Physics, University of Debrecen, H-4010 Debrecen-10, P O Box 105, Hungary.

CUI Chang Cong, b. 27 March 1937, Xian, China. Cardiologist; Professor. m. Ma Yi, 2 sons, 1 daughter. Education: MD, Xian Medical University, 1959; Fellow of Cardiology, Visiting Professor at LDS Hospital, Utah University Medical School, Salt Lake City, USA, 1985-87. Appointments: Physician, 1st Hospital of Xian Medical University, 1959-65; Attending Doctor, 1965-77, Chief Doctor, Associated Professor, 1977-92, Chief Doctor, Full Professor, 1992-, Xian Medical University. Publications: 137 papers; 10 books. Honours: Award, Chinese Public Health and Technical Science Programme, 1993; Award, Chinese Education and Research, 1999. Memberships: NASPE; AHA; Chinese Medical Association. Address: Department of Cardiology, 1st Hospital, Xian Jiao Tong University, #74 XiaoZi WR, Xian City, Shaanxi, Peoples Republic of China 710061. E-mail: czcui@263.net

CULKIN Macauley, b. 26 August 1980, NY, USA. Actor. m. Rachel Milner, 1998, separated. Education: George Balanchine's School of Ballet, NY. Appointments: Actor, films: Rocket Gibralter, 1988; Uncle Buck, 1989; See You in the Morning, 1989; Jacob's Ladder, 1990; Home Alone, 1990; My Girl, 1991; Only the Lonely, 1991; Home Alone 2: Lost in New York, 1992; The Nutcracker; The Good Son, 1993; The Pagemaster, 1995; Getting Even with Dad, 1995; Body Piercer, 1998; Party Monster, 2003; Saved! 2004; Play: Madame Melville, Vaudeville Theatre, London, 2001. Address: c/o Brian Gersh, William Morris Agency, 151 S El Camino Drive, Beverley Hills, CA 90212, USA.

CURE Susan Carol, b. 18 August, Los Angeles, USA. Biologist. m. Michel Y Cure, 1 son, 2 daughters. Education: BA, Biological Science, Stanford University, 1962; PhD, Medical Microbiology, Stanford University, 1967. Appointments: Postdoctoral Fellow, California Department of Health, 1966-1968; Researcher, Centre d'Études de la Biologie Prénatale, 1970-1974; Lecturer, Associate Professor, American University in Paris, 1971-1976, 1987-; Science Co-ordinator, Association Française Contre les Myopathies, 1989-; Researcher, Genethon, Genoscope, French Genome Centres, 1992-. Publications: Many articles in scientific journals: American Journal of Human Genetics; Nature; Journal of Investigative Dermatology. Memberships: AAAS; American Society of Microbiology; Club du Mt St Leger; Sigma Xi. Address: 3 av Robert Schuman, 75007, Paris, France.

CURRÁS Emilia. Academician; University Professor; Information Scientist. m. José Dueñas. Education: PhD, Chemistry, Sobresaliente cum Laude, Universities of Berlin, Germany and Madrid, Spain; Scientific Documentarian, Institute for Scientific Documentation and Information, Frankfurt/Main, Germany; Diploma in German, German Institute of Culture; Diploma in English, International Institute of Boston. Appointments: Director, Documentation Department of Hanomag-Barreiros, Piritas Españolas, Dynamit Nobel, Germany and Hispanoil; Currently Professor, Universidad Autónoma de Madrid, Spain. Publications: 11 books, 3 of which translated into Portuguese, English and Czech; 2 poetry books; More than 100 papers in national and international journals; Invited lecturer by numerous institutions world-wide; Numerous papers presented at national and international congresses. Honours: Numerous research and travel grants; Dama Comendadora de la Orden de Las Palmas Académicas of Valencia; Honorary Member, ADHI, 2003; Woman of the Year 2004, American Biographical Institute; Kaula Gold Medal; Technological Merit Gold Medal, FEDINE; Fellow, Institute of Information Sciences; Expert Evaluater of the European Union; Honorary President, ISKO España; Distinguished Member, Colegio Oficial de Químicos; Honorary Member, Colegio de Doctores y Licenciados. Memberships include: Academician, Royal Doctor's Academy of Madrid; Academician, Toledo Royal Academy of Fine Arts and Historical Science; Academy of Arts of Brasilia; Vice-President, Science and Technology Section, ATENEO, Madrid; Valencia World Council of Professional Education; ISKO International Society for Knowledge Organisation; Editorial Board, Journal of Information Science; International Awards Committee, Professor Kaula Endowment for Library and Information Science, Tenali, India; Experts International Committee for Evaluation of Scientific Works. Address: Calle O'Donnell 6, c-12, Madrid 28009, Spain. E-mail: emilia.curras@uam.es

CURTIS Jamie Lee, b. 22 November 1958, Los Angeles, California, USA. m. Christopher Guest, 1 child. Education: University of the Pacific, California, USA. Career: Films include: Halloween; The Fog; Halloween 2; Prom Night; Trading Places; The Adventures of Buckaroo Banzai: Across the 8th Dimension; 8 Million Ways to Die; A Fish Called Wanda; Blue Steel; My Girl; Forever Young; My Girl 2; True Lies, 1994; House Arrest, 1996; Fierce Creatures, 1996; Halloween H20, 1998; Virus, 1999; The Tailor of Panama (also director), 2000; Daddy and Them; Halloween H2K: Evil Never Dies. TV includes: Dorothy Stratten: Death of a Centrefold; The Love Boat; Columbo Quincy; Charlie's Angels; Mother's Boys; Drowning Mona (director), 2000. Publications: When I Was Little, 1993; Today I Feel Silly and Other Moods That Make My Day, 1999. Address: c/o Rick Kurtsmann, CAA, 9830 Wilshire Boulevard, Beverly Hills, CA 90212, USA.

CURTIS Sarah, b. 21 May 1936, Preston, England. Journalist; Writer. m. 3 October 1960, 3 sons. Education: BA, 1958, MA, St Hugh's College, Oxford, England. Appointments: Times Educational Supplement, 1958-59; The Times, 1959-61; Editor, Adoption and Fostering, 1976-87; Editor, RSA Journal and Head of Communications RSA, 1989-95. Publications: Thinkstrip, series, 1976-79; It's Your Life, series, 1983; Juvenile Offending, 1989; Children Who Break the Law, 1999 The Journals of Woodrow Wyatt, editor, Vol 1, 1998, Vol 2, 1999, Vol 3, 2000. Contributions to: Times Literary Supplement, novel reviewer, since 1960s; Contributor, New Society, Financial Times, BBC Radio 4. Address: 9 Essex Villas, London W8 7BP, England.

CURTIS Tony (Bernard Schwarz), b. 3 June 1925, New York, USA. Film Actor. m. (1) Janet Leigh, divorced, 2 daughters, (2) Christine Kaufmann, divorced, 2 daughters, (3) Leslie Allen, 2 sons, (4) Lisa Deutsch, 1993. Education: New School of Social Research. Appointments: Served in US Navy; Actor, films include: Houdini; Black Shield of Falworth; So This is Paris?; Six Bridges to Cross; Trapeze; Mister Cory; Sweet Smell of Success; Midnight Story; The Vikings; Defiant Ones; Perfect Furlough; Some Like It Hot, 1959; Spartacus, 1960; The Great Imposter, 1960; Pepe, 1960; The Outsider, 1961; Taras Bulba, 1962; Forty Pounds of Trouble, 1962; The List of Adrian Messenger, 9163; Captain Newman, 1963; Paris When It Sizzles, 1964; Wild and Wonderful, 1964; Sex and the Single Girl, 1964; Goodbye Charlie, 1964; The Great Race, 1965; Boeing, Boeing, 1965; Arriverderci, Baby, 1966; Not With My Wife You Don't, 1966; Don't Make Waves, 1967; Boston Strangler, 1968; Lepke, 1975; Casanova, 1976; The Last Tycoon, 1976; The Manitou, 1978; Sextette, 1978; The Mirror Crack'd, 1980; Venom, 1982; Insignificance, 1985; Club Life, 1986; The Last of Philip Banter, 1988; Balboa, Midnight, Lobster Man from Mars, The High-Flying Mermaid, Prime Target, Center of the Web, Naked in New York, The Reptile Man, The Immortals, 1995; The Celluloid Closet, 1995; Louis and Frank, 1997; Brittle Glory, 1997; TV includes: Third Girl From the Left, 1973; The Persuaders, 1971-72; The Count of Monte Cristo, 1976; Vegas, 1978; Mafia Princess, 1986; Christmas in Connecticut, 1992; A Perry Mason Mystery: The Case of the Grimacing Governor; Elvis Meets Nixon. Publications: Kid Andrew Cody and Julie Sparrow, 1977; The Autobiography, 1993. Honours include: Kt Order of the Republic of Hungary, 1966. Address: c/o William Morris Agency, 151 S El Camino Drive, Beverley Hills, CA 90212, USA.

CUSACK John, b. 28 June 1966, Evanston, Illinois, USA. Actor. Appointments: Piven Theatre Workshop, Evanston, from age 9-19; New Criminals Theatrical Company, Chicago; Films include: Class, 1983; Sixteen Candles, 1984; Grandview USA, 1984; The Sure Thing, 1985; One Crazy Summer, 1986; Broadcast News, 1987; Hot Pursuit, 1987; Eight Men Out, 1988; Tapeheads, 1988; Say Anything, 1989; Fatman and Little Boy, 1989; The Thin Red Line, 1989; The Grifters, 1990; True Colors, 1991; Shadows and Fog, 1992; Roadside Prophets, 1992; The Player, 1992; Map of the Human Heart, 1992; Bob Roberts, 1992; Money for Nothing, 1993; Bullets Over Broadway, 1994; The Road to Wellville, 1994; City Hall, 1995; Anastasia, 1997; Con Air, 1997; Hellcab, 1997; Midnight in the Garden of Good and Evil, 1997; This is My Father, 1998; Pushing Tin, 1998; Being John Malkovich, 1999; America's Sweethearts, 2001; Live of the Party, 2000; Serendipity, 2001; Max, 2002; Adaptation, 2002; Actor, director, writer: Grosse Pointe Blank, 1997; Arigo (producer, actor), 1998; High Fidelity (actor, writer), 1997; The Cradle Will Rock, 1999. Address: 1325 Avenue of the Americas, New York, NY 10019, USA,

CUSACK Sinead Mary, b. 1948. Actress. m. Jeremy Irons, 1977, 2 sons. Appointments: Appearances with RSC include: Lady Amaranth in Wild Oats, Lisa in Children of the Sun, Isabella in Measure for Measure, Celia in As You Like It, Evadne in the Maid's

Tragedy, Lady Anne in Richard III, Portia in the Merchant of Venice, Ingrid in Peer Gynt, Kate in the Taming of the Shrew, Beatrice in Much Ado About Nothing, Lady MacBeth in MacBeth, Roxanne in Cyrano de Bergerac; Other stage appearances at Oxford Fest, Gate Theatre (Dublin), Royal Court; Virago in A Lie of the Mind, 2001, Oxford Festival, Gate Theatre, Dublin, Royal Court and others; numerous appearances in TV drama; Films: Alfred the Great, 1969; Tamlyn, 1969; Hoffman, 1969; David Copperfield, 1970; Revenge, 1971; The Devil's Widow, 1971; Horowitz in Dublin Castle, 1977; The Last Remake of Beau Geste, 1977; Rocket Gibralter, 1993; Venus Peter, 1993; Waterland, 1992; God on the Rocks, 1992; Bad Behaviour, 1993; The Cement Garden, 1993; The Sparrow; Flemish Board; Stealing Beauty. Address: c/o Curtis Brown Group, 4th Floor, Haymarket House, 28-29 Haymarket, London, SW1Y 4SP, England.

CUSSLER Clive (Eric), b. 15 July 1931, Aurora, Illinois, USA. Author; Advertising Executive. m. Barbara Knight, 28 August 1955, 3 children. Education: Pasadena City College, 1949-51; Orange Coast College; California State University. Appointments: Advertising Directorships; Author. Owner, Bestgen and Cussler Advertising, Newport Beach, California, 1961-65; Copy Director, Darcy Advertising, Hollywood, California and Instructor in Advertising Communications, Orange Coast College, 1965-67; Advertising Director, Aquatic Marine Corporation, Newport Beach, California, 1967-79; Vice President and Creative Director of Broadcast, Meffon, Wolff and Weir Advertising, Denver, Colorado, 1970-73; Chair, National Underwater and Marine Agency. Publications: The Mediterranean Caper, 1973; Iceberg, 1975; Raise the Titanic, 1976; Vixen O-Three, 1978; Night Probe, 1981; Pacific Vortex, 1982; Deep Six, 1984; Cyclops, 1986; Treasure, 1988; Dragon, 1990; Sahara, 1992; Inca Gold, 1994; Shock Wave, 1996; Flood Tide, 1997; Serpent, 1999; Atlantis Found, 1999; Blue Gold, 2000; Valhalla Rising, 2001; Fire Ice, 2002; Sea Hunters II, 2002. Honours: Numerous advertising awards; Lowell Thomas Award, New York Explorers Club. Memberships: Fellow, New York Explorers Club; Royal Geographical Society.

CYWIŃSKI Zbigniew, b. 12 February 1929, Toruń, Poland. University Professor, Emeritus. m. Helena Wilczyńska, 11 April 1956, 1 son, 3 daughters. Education: Inż (BSc Eng), 1953; Mgr inż (MSc Eng), 1955; Dr inz (PhD Eng), 1964; Dr hab inż (DSc Eng), 1968; Prof, 1978. Appointments: Consulting Engineer, University of Baghdad, Iraq, 1965-66; Assistant Professor, University of Mosul, Iraq, 1970-73; UNESCO Expert, Ministry of Education, Mogadishu, Somalia, 1979-80; Professor, University of Tokyo, Japan, 1987-88; Vice Dean, 1975-78, Dean, 1984-87, 1993-99, Head, Structural Division, 1994-98, Faculty of Civil Engineering, Technical University of Gdansk. Publications: 3 textbooks, 2 books on structural mechanics; 1 monograph on bridges; 292 published papers; 119 published reviews. Honours: Awards of the Minister of Education, 1964, 1976, 1978; Golden Cross of Merit, 1974; Cavalier Cross, 1980 and Officer's Cross, 1999, Poland's Rebirth Order; Medal, National Commission of Education, 1986; Gdańsk Millennium Medal, 1997. Memberships: Polish Society of Theoretical and Applied Mechanics, Regional Committee Head, 1990-92; International Association of Bridge and Structural Engineering, Alternate Delegate to Permanent Committee, 1994-; Fellow, American Society of Civil Engineers; Polish Society of Bridge Engineers. Address: ul Mściwoja 50/32, 80-357, Gdańsk-Oliwa, Poland.

CZAJKOWSKI Eva Anna, b. 4 September 1961, New Britain, Connecticut, USA. Aerospace Engineering and Technical Manager. Education: BSc, 1983, MEng, 1983, Aeronautical Engineering, Rensselaer Polytechnic Institute; MSc, Aeronautics and Astronautics, Massachusetts Institute of Technology, 1985; PhD, Aerospace Engineering, Virginia Polytechnic Institute and State University, Blacksburg, 1988. Appointments: Intern, New York State Assembly, 1983; Teaching Assistant, Department of Mechanical Engineering, Aeronautical Engineering and Mechanics, Rensselaer Polytechnic Institute, 1983; Research Assistant, US Army Research Office, Rensselaer Polytechnic Institute, 1982-83; Engineering Analyst, Pratt and Whitney Aircraft, Government Products Division, Florida, 1984; Research Assistant, Air Force Research in Aero Propulsion Technology Program, Gas Turbine and Plasma Dynamics Laboratory, Massachusetts Institute of Technology, 1984-85; Teaching Assistant, 1985-88, Research Assistant, 1985-88, Department of Aerospace and Ocean Engineering, Virginia Polytechnic Institute and State University; Aerospace Engineer, Research Staff, 1988-91, Senior Aerospace Engineer, Research Staff, 1991-94, Principal Aerospace Engineer, Research Staff, 1994-2001, Aerospace Engineering and Technical Manager, 2001-. Publications: Several books and articles in professional journals; Encyclopaedias and Technical Conferences. Honours: Numerous. Memberships include: New York Academy of Sciences; World Order, Science-Education-Culture (Dame); World Foundation of Successful Women; Sigma Gamma Tau; Sigma Xi; Tau Beta Pi; Phi Kappa Phi; Gamma Beta Phi; Senior member, American Institute of Aeronautics and Astronautics; American Astronautical Society; American Helicopter Society; Polish Rotorcraft Association; The Planetary Society; National Space Society; London Diplomatic Academy; International Platform Association. Address: 170 Carlton Street, New Britain, CT 06053-3106, USA.

Dictionary of International Biography

D

D' SILVA Regin Domnic, b. 1 June 1942, Bhatghar Wadi, Bassein, India. Retired College Principal. m. Flory Francis Coelo. Education: Inter Arts, 1962, BA, 1965, MA, 1968, University of Bombay; PhD, MS, University of Baroda, 1986; Several Diplomas in Portuguese Language, Archaeology and History. Appointments: Head, Department of History, Ahemdnagar College, 1970-72; Member, Board of Studies in History, University of Poona, 1970-76; Member, Board of Studies in History, University of Bombay, 1974-76, 2000-; Member, Faculty of Arts, University of Bombay, 1990-93, 2000-; Principal, St Gansalo Garcia College of Arts and Commerce, Bassein, India; Participant in several international educational conferences in Portugal, India, Israel, Italy; PhD Guide for MA, M Phil and PhD students, University of Bombay , 1987-; Independent Researcher. Publications: Books: Rise and Development of Christianity in Bassein, 1971; Bassein under the Portuguese (1534-1640). A Socio-Economic Study (PhD thesis), 1986; Life of St Gansalo Garcia, 1987; Simon Cardinal Pimenta, 1990; History of Portuguese Fort at Bassein, 1993; Glory that was Our Lady of Remedy, 1994; Life of Annashaeb Vartak, Minister of Bombay State, 1994; Life and Work of St Francis Xavier, 1994; Glory that was Mother Vailankani, 1996; The First Christian Shrine in Bassein, 1999; Fall of the Portuguese Province of the North (D Litt Dissertation, submitted), 2001. Honours include: Study Grant, Indian Council for Historical Research, 1980; Teacher Fellowship, University Grants Commission, India, 1981-84; Fellowship, 1982-83, Special Scholarship, 2001, Gulbenkian Foundation of Portugal; Scholarship, Board of Scientific Research, Government of Portugal, 1983; Great Indian Achievers Award, Indian Institute of Management Promotion, 1999; Life Time Achievement Award, United Writers Association, Madras, 2000; Rev Fr T A Mattias Award, All India Association of Christian Higher Education, 2001. Memberships: Fellow, United Writers Association; Fellow, Gulbenkian Foundation; President, Bassein Institute of History and Culture; Life Member, Indian History Congress; Life Member, Council of Management Executives; Indian Institute of Historical Research; Church History Association of India. Address: "Lake View", Holi-Rangaon Road, PO Bassein, 401 201 Dist Thane, Maharashtra, India.

DA SILVA Paulo A, b. 29 September 1949, Rio de Janeiro, Brazil. Engineer. 2 sons. Education: BS, Statistics, National School Statistical Sciences, 1978; BS, Telecommunication and Engineering, Military Institute of Engineering, 1979; MSc, Federal University of Rio de Janeiro, 1980; PhD, Florida Institute of Technology, Melbourne, 1989. Appointments: Chairman, O R Graduate Program, 1990-95, Department Head, 1995-97, Professor, 1997-, Military Institute of Engineering. Publications: 2 text books in statistics; Various articles. Honours: Marshall Hermes Medal, Telecommunication and Engineering Graduate Medal, Peacemakers Medal, Brazilian Army. Memberships: New York Academy of Sciences; Sigma Xi. Address: Rua Voluntarios Da Patria 474 Apt 401, Humaita 22270-010, Rio de Janeiro, Brazil. E-mail: estatistica@estatistica.eng.br

DABASY Eva Anna, b. 10 April 1946, Tann, Germany. Educator; Consultant. m. Janos, 1 daughter. Education: Trained Technical Teachers Certificate, Technical Teachers' College, 1968; Diploma of Nutrition and Food Service, Emily McPherson College, Australia, 1968; Bachelor of Education, 1978, Master of Education, 1984, LaTrobe University, Australia. Appointments: Head, Food Science Department, 1972-95; Co-ordinator, Vocational Education and Training Degree Studies, Hospitality, Senior Curriculum Officer and Acting Director for Training, Research and Development Division, 2001, Manager, Teaching and Learning, 2002, William Angliss Institute; Nutritionist, Education and Training Consultant. Publications: Numerous articles in professional journals. Honours: Honorary Professor, Albert Schweitzer International University; Royal Melbourne Institute of Technology University Quality Award, 1997; Listed in biographical dictionaries. Memberships: Australian Institute of Food Science and Technology; Nutrition Society of Australia; Nutrition Australia; International Diplomatic Academy; London Diplomatic Academy; New York Academy of Sciences. Address: 51 Buller Drive, Glen Waverley 3150, Australia. E-mail: evadabasy@optusnet.com.au

DACHEV Miroslav, b. 19 July 1962, Ivailovgrad, Bulgaria. Professor of Semiotics and Literary Criticism. m. Gergana Dacheva, 1 daughter. Education: Master of Philology, University of Sofia, Bulgaria, 1987; Doctor of Sciences, Institute of Literature, Bulgarian Academy of Sciences, 1997. Appointments: Senior Researcher, Bulgarian Academy of Sciences, 1997; Associate Professor, 1999, Vice-Rector of Academic Affairs, 1999-, Professor of Semiotics and Literary Criticism, 2003-, New Bulgarian University, Sofia, Bulgaria. Publications: Books: Dictionary of New Bulgarian Literature (editor), 1994; Semiotics of Colour in Poetic Text, 1997; Beyond the Shadows of the Signs (with summaries in English), 2001; Word and Image (with summaries in English), 2003; Foreign Bulgarian Studies 20th Century (encyclopaedia, editor), in press. Honours: Best Teacher of Academic Year, 2000/2001, New Bulgarian University. Memberships: Bulgarian Association of Semiotics, 1989-; Scientific Council, Institute of Literature, Bulgarian Academy of Sciences, 1999-; National Centre of Distance Education, 2001; Association of Bulgarian Writers, 2003; Association of Bulgarian Private Universities, Vice-President, 2003-. Address: The New Bulgarian University, 21 Montevideo Street, Sofia 1618, Bulgaria. E-mail: mdachev@nbu.bg

DADABAEVA Zarina, b. 17 July 1965, Dushanbe, Tajikistan. Politologist. Widowed, 2 sons. Education: Master's Degree, Teacher Russian Language and Literature, Philology Diploma, 1982-87, Candidate of Historical Science, 1990-94, PhD, Doctor of Political Science, 2002, Tajik State University. Appointments: Teacher of Political History, Institute of Physical Culture, 1987-90; Leading Researcher, International Department, Institute of World Economy and International Relations, 1994-2000; Leading Researcher, 2002-2003, Main Scientific Researcher, 2003-, Institute of Philosophy and Law, Tajik Academy of Science. Publications: 32 articles and 3 books include: Many aspects of the Analysis of Development of the Republic of Tajikistan, in Modern Theory of the Foreign Politologist, 1995; Tajikistan-Russia – Aspects of Co-operation, 1999; Tajikistan, Interethnic Relations in the Period of Society Transformation, 2000; Women in a Political Life of Central Asia (article), 2000. Memberships: Association the Women of Science of Tajikistan; National Association of Tajikistan Politologists. Address: 50/2 Buhoro St, ap N 67, Dushanbe, 734025 Tajikistan. E-mail: darina@ac.tajik.net

DAELMAN Jos (Walter Zone), b. 1 August 1937, Zwijndrecht, Belgium. Librarian; Poet. m. Yolanda Stroobant, 24 November 1959, 1 daughter. Education: Graduate in Library Science, 1970; Graduate in Scientific and Technical Documentation, 1972. Appointments: Branch Librarian, 1958; Teacher, Library School, Antwerp, 1973; Head, Reference Department, 1982, Head, Psycho-Pedagogical Department, Central Public Library, Antwerp, 1987; Professor of Poetry, Academy of Creative Writing, Antwerp, 1995. Publications: Land tussen Zee en Aarde, 1974; Vacuum, (with Cel Overberghe), 1977; De Stilte toewaarts, 1979; De Landschapstuin, 1980; De zwarte Wandelaar (with Cel Overberghe), 1982; Buiten de Roedel, 1983; Het Verlangzamen, 1986; Een Haas in Winterkoren, 1989; Letters from Sark and Other

Places, 1992; Huiswaarts, 1994; Herdersuur, 1996; Beperkte Toegang, 2000; Iedereen Afwezig, 2003. Contributions to: Nieuw Vlaams Tijdschrift; Deus Ex Machina; Gieriek; Journal of Contemporary Anglo-Scandinavian Poetry. Honour: Award for Poetry, Province of Antwerp, 1984. Membership: Vereniging voor Vlaamse Letterkundigen; PEN. Address: Oostvaart 42, 9180 Moerbeke-Waas, Belgium.

DAFOE Willem, b. 22 July 1955, Appleton, Wisconsin, USA. Actor. Education: Wisconsin University. Appointments: Actor, films include: The Loveless, 1981; New York Nights, 1981; The Hunger, 1982; Communists are Comfortable (and 3 other stories), 1984; Roadhouse 66, 1984; Streets of Fire, 1984; To Live and Die in LA, 1985; Platoon, 1986; The Last Temptation of Christ, 1988; Saigon, 1988; Mississippi Burning, 1989; Triumph of the Spirit, 1989; Born on the Fourth of July, 1990; Flight of the Intruder, 1990; Wild at Heart, 1990; The Light Sleeper, 1991; Body of Evidence, 1992; Far Away, So Close, 1994; Tom and Viv, 1994; The Night and the Moment, 1994; Clear and Present Danger, 1994; The English Patient, 1996; Basquiat, 1996; Speed 2: Cruise Control, 1997; Affliction, 1997; Lulu on the Bridge, 1998; Existenz, 1998; American Psycho, 1999; Shadow of the Vampire, 2000; Bullfighter, 2000; The Animal Factory, 2000; Edges of the Lord, 2001; Spider-Man, 2002; Auto Focus, 2002; Once Upon a Time in Mexico, 2003; The Clearing, 2004; The Reckoning, 2004.

DAHL Sophie, b. 1978. Fashion Model. Appointments: Discovered by Isabella Blow; Worked with fashion photographers: Nick Knight, David La Chapelle, Karl Lagerfeld, David Bailey, Enrique Badulescu, Herb Ritts and Ellen Von Unwerth; Appeared in: ID, The Face, Elle, Esquire, Scene magazines; Advertising campaigns for Lainey, Keogh, Bella Freud, Printemps, Nina Ricci, Karl Lagerfeld, Oil of Ulay, Hennes; Music videos for U2, Elton John, Duran Duran; Cameo appearances in films: Mad Cows, Best, 1999; Stage appearance in The Vagina Monologues, Old Vic Theatre, 1999; Judge, Orange Prize for Fiction, 2003. Publication: The Man with the Dancing Eyes, 2003. Address: c/o Storm Model Management, 5 Jubilee Place, London SW3 3TD, England.

DAICHES David, b. 2 September 1912, Sunderland, England. Professor Emeritus; Writer. m. (1) Isobel Janet Mackay, 28 July 1937, deceased 1977, 1 son, 2 daughters, (2) Hazel Neville, 1978, deceased 1986. Education: MA, Edinburgh University, 1934; DPhil, Oxford University, 1939. Appointments: Fellow, Balliol College, Oxford, 1936-37; Assistant Professor, University of Chicago, 1939-43; Professor, Cornell University, 1946-51, Sussex University, 1961-77; University Lecturer, 1951-61, Fellow, Jesus College, 1957-62, Cambridge; Director, Institute for Advanced Studies, Edinburgh University, 1980-86. Publications: 45 books including: The Novel and the Modern World, 1939; Robert Burns, 1950; Two Worlds, 1956; A Critical History of English Literature, 1960; The Paradox of Scottish Culture, 1964; God and the Poets, 1984; Edinburgh: A Traveller's Companion, 1986; A Weekly Scotsman and Other Poems, 1994. Honours: Royal Society of Literature, fellow, 1957; Scottish Arts Council Book Award, 1973; Scottish Book of the Year Award, 1984; Commander of the Order of the British Empire, 1991; Various honorary doctorates. Memberships: Association for Scottish Literary Studies, honorary president; Modern Language Association of America, honorary member; Saltire Society, honorary president. Address: 22 Belgrave Crescent, Edinburgh, EH4 3AL, Scotland.

DAILEY Alice Ann Baker, b. 25 October 1946, Durant, Oklahoma, USA. Exercise Physiologist; Teacher. m. John Arthur, 1 daughter. Education: MS, Exercise Physiology, North Texas State University, 1985; Teacher Certification, Southeastern State University, Durant, 1969; BMus, Piano Performance, University

of Oklahoma, 1968. Appointments: Piano and Music Teacher, Dallas and Houston 1969-75; Liquor License Administrator, Steak and Ale Restaurants Inc, Dallas, 1975-77; Administrative Assistant, Neiman-Marcus, 1977-80; Consultant, Region 10 Education Service Center and Republic Bank, Exercise Physiologist, Health Check, 1985; Library Research, Richard G W Anderson, PhD, Cell Biology Department, University of Texas Health Science Center, 1984-87; Exercise Instructor, Texas Instruments, 1984-87, North Dallas Athletic Club, 1986-87, Verandah Club, 1987-89, Goodbody's, 1988-89; Owner and Instructor, Therapeutic Conditioning, 1980-91; Consultant, Crescent Spa, Landry Center, 1991; Owner, Oasis Mind-Body Conditioning Center, 1991-. Publications: Numerous articles in magazines, periodicals and professional journals; Exercise videos. Honours: Phi Kappa Lambda National Music Honor Society, 1968; Winner, IDEA Make Fitness Happen Educational Opportunity Grant, 1996; Oasis Mind-Body Conditioning Center Winner, Reader's Choice, Best Health Club in Dallas, 1994, 1999, 2000; 2001; IDEA Master Level Personal Fitness Trainer, 2000. Memberships: Advisory Board, Dance for Planet; Board Member, Dallas Dance Council; Founding Member, Institute for the Pilates Method, now Physicalmind Institute; American College of Sports Medicine; International Dance Educators Association; Citizen of the Chickasaw Nation Tribe. Address: 11661 Preston Road, Suite 184, Dallas, TX 75230, USA. E-mail: oasisbody@earthlink.net

DAINTY Sonia Margarita Centeno, b. 4 March 1948, Arecibo, Puerto Rico, USA. Artist; Writer. m. James Albert Dainty, 1 son. Education: Art Academy, Arecibo, Puerto Rico; Cardinal Spelman Center, New York, 1964. Career: Artist painting portraits, still life paintings, cityscapes and landscapes; Made glass for cardinal Spelman Center, New York; Exhibitions: Cardinal Spelman Center, New York, 1964; Bank of New York, 1976; Art Shows on the Lower East Side, New York; The Ten Street Gallery; Produced Portraits and Landscapes for private collectors whilst living in England, 1974-75; Teacher, Boys and Girls Club of New York, 1970's and 1980's; Real Estate Investor; Writer, Newspaper Institute of America; Human Rights Advocator. Publications: Autumn's Morning; The Night Maiden; Human Rights. Honours: Awards, Cardinal Spelman Center; The Bank of New York; World of Poetry, Washington DC. Membership: Smithtown Township Arts Council. Address: 348 Old Dutch Hollow Road, Monroe, NY 10950, USA.

DAL MASO Luigino, b. 13 March 1967, Este, Padua, Italy. Statistican. m. Claudia Braga. Education: Science Doctor, Statistics, Padua University, 1993. Appointments: Researcher, Aviano Cancer Centre, Italy, 1993-2003; Consultant, Pharmacological Institute M Negri, Milan, Italy, 1995-99; Consultant, Pascale Cancer Institute, Naples, Italy, 1996-98; Visiting Scientist, International Agency for Research on Cancer, Lyon, France, 2001-02. Publications: Articles in professional journals. Honours: Fellow, Italian Association Against Cancer, 1993-95; 2 grants, National Minister of Health, Italy, 2000-03. Memberships: Italian Association of Cancer Registries, 1999-2003; Italian Epidemiological Association, 1994-2002. Address: Aviano Cancer Institute, via Pedemontana Occidentale 12, I-33081, Aviano (PN), Italy. E-mail: dalmaso@cro.it

DALAI LAMA The (Tenzin Gyatso), b. 6 July 1935, Taktser, Amdo Province, North East Tibet. Temporal and Spiritual Head of Tibet 14th Incarnation. Appointments: Enthroned at Lhasa, 1940; Rights exercised by regency, 1934-50; Assumed political power, 1950; Fled to Chumbi in South Tibet, 1950; Agreement with China, 1951; Vice-Chair, Standing Committee, Member, National Committee, CPPCC, 1951-59; Honorary Chairman, Chinese Buddhist Association, 1953-59; Delegate to National People's

Dictionary of International Biography

Congress, 1954-59; Chairman, Preparatory Committee for Autonomous Region of Tibet, 1955-59; Fled to India after suppression of Tibetan national uprising, 1959. Publications: My Land and People, 1962; The Opening of the Wisdom Eye, 1963; The Buddhism of Tibet and the Key to The Middle Way, 1975; Kindness, Charity and Insight, 1984; A Human Approach to World Peace, 1984; Freedom in Exile (autobiography), 1990; The Good Heart, 1996; Ethics for the New Millennium, 1998; Art of Happiness, (co-author), 1999; A Simple Path: basic Buddhist Teachings by His Holiness the Dalai Lama, 2000; Stages of Meditation: training the Mind for Wisdom, 2002; The Spirit of Peace, 2002. Honours: Dr Buddhist Philos (Monasteries of Sera, Drepung and Gaden, Lhasa), 1959; Supreme Head of all Buddhist sections in Tibet; Memory Prize, 1989; Congressional Human Rights Award, 1989; Nobel Prize, 1989; The Freedom Award (USA), 1991. Address: Thekchen Choeling, McLeod Ganj 176219, Dharamsala, Himachal Pradesh, India.

DALGLISH Kenneth (Kenny) Mathieson, b. 4 March 1951, Glasgow, Scotland. Football Manager. Appointments: Played for Celtic, Scottish League Champions, 1972-74, 1977; Scottish Cup Winners, 1972, 1974, 1975, 1977; Scottish Cup Winners, 1972, 1974, 1975, 1977; Scottish league Cup winners, 1975; Played for Liverpool, European Cup Winners, 1978, 1981, 1984; FA Cup Winners, 1986, 1989; League Cup winners, 1981-84; Manager, 1986-91; Manager Blackburn Rovers, 1991-97; Newcastle United, 1997-98; Director of Football operations, Celtic, 1999-2000; 102 full caps for Scotland scoring 30 goals. Honours: Footballer of the Year, 1979, 1983; MBE; Freeman of Glasgow. Address: c/o Celtic Football Club, Celtic Park, Glasgow, G40 3RE, Scotland.

DALMAS John, b. 3 September 1926, Chicago, Illinois, USA. Author. m. Gail Hill, 15 September 1954, 1 son, 1 daughter. Education: BSc, Michigan State College, 1954; Master of Forestry, University of Minnesota, 1955; PhD, Colorado State University, 1967. Publications: The Yngling, 1969; The Varkaus Conspiracy, 1983; Touch the Stars: Emergence (with Carl Martin), 1983; Homecoming, 1984; The Scroll of Man, 1985; Fanglith, 1985; The Reality Matrix 1986; The Walkaway Clause, 1986; The Regiment, 1987; The Playmasters (with Rodney Martin), 1987; Return to Fanglith, 1987; The General's President, 1988; The Lantern of God, 1989; The Lizard War, 1989; The White Regiment, 1990; The Kalif's War, 1991; The Yngling and the Circle of Power, 1992; The Orc Wars (collection), 1992; The Regiment's War, 1993; The Yngling in Yamato, 1994; The Lion of Farside, 1995; The Bavarian Gate, 1997; The Three Cornered War, 1999; The Lion Returns, 1999; Soldiers, 2001; The Puppet Master, 2001; Otherwhens, Otherwheres, 2003; The Helverti Invasion, 2003; The Second Coming, 2004; The Regiment: A Trilogy (collection), 2004. Contributions to: Journals, magazines and anthologies. Honours: Xi Sigma Pi Forestry Honorary Society, 1953; Phi Kappa Phi Scholastic Honorary Society, 1954; Sigma Xi Scientific Research Society, 1963. Memberships: Science Fiction Writers of America; Vasa Order of America. Address: 1425 Glass Street, Spokane, WA 99205, USA.

DALTON Timothy, b. 21 March 1946. Actor. Education: Royal Academy of Dramatic Art. Career includes: National Youth Theatre; Theatre includes: Toured with Prospect Theatre Company; Guest Artist, RSC; Co-starred with Vivien Merchant in Noel Coward's The Vortex; Anthony and Cleopatra, 1986; The Taming of the Shrew, 1986; A Touch of the Poet, Young Vic, 1988; Films include: The Lion in Winter, 1968; Cromwell, 1970; Wuthering Heights; Mary, Queen of Scots, 1972; Permission to Kill, 1975; The Man Who Knew Love; Sextette, 1977; Agatha, 1978; Flash Gordon, 1979; James Bond in The Living Daylights, 1987 and Licence to Kill, 1989; The Rocketeer, 1991; The Reef, 1996; The

Beautician and the Beast, 1996; Made Men, 1998; Cleopatra, 1998; Possessed, 1999; Timeshare, 2000; American Outlaws, 2001; Looney Tunes – Back in Action, 2002; TV roles include: Mr Rochester in Jane Eyre, BBC TV, 1983; Master of Ballentrae, HTV, 1983; Mistral's Daughter, TV mini-series, 1984; Florence Nightingale, TV mini-series; Sins, TV mini-series, 1985; Philip von Joel in Framed, mini-series, Anglia TV, 1992; Jack in Red Eagle; Rhett Butler in Scarlett, Sky, 1994; Salt Water Moose, comedy, 1995; The Informant, 1996. Membership: Actors' Equity. Address: c/o ICM, Oxford House, 76 Oxford Street, London W1N 0AX, England.

DALY John Patrick, b. 28 April 1966, Carmichael, CA, USA. Golfer. m. 2 children. Education: University of Arkansas. Appointments: Turned professional, 1987; Won Missouri Open, 1987; Ben Hogan Utah Classic, 1990; PGA Championship, Crooked Stick, 1991; BC Open, 1992; Dunhill Cup, 1993, 1998; BellSouth Classic, 1994; British Open, 1995; BMW International Open, 2001. Recording: My Life (album). Address: c/o PGA America, 100 Avenue of the Champions, Palm Beach Gardens, FL 33418, USA.

DALY Peter Eugene, b. 21 July 1935. Company Director. m. Daphne Lilian, 8 February 1958, 1 son, 1 daughter. Appointments: Chairman, Insurance Enquiries and Complaints Ltd; Chairman, Financial Industry Complaints Service Ltd; Chairman, Aldersgale Finance Pty Ltd; Deputy Chairman, Gerling Australia Insurance Co Pty Ltd; Chairman, Concord Insurance Group. Address: Norwin, 2 Jacov Gardens, Templestowe, VIC 3106, Australia.

DAMIAN Theodor, b. 1951, Botosani, Romania. Priest; Professor. m. Regula-Claudia Damian, 1992, 1 son. Education: BA, 1975, MA, 1978, Faculty of Theology, Bucharest; Diploma, Ecumenical Studies, Bossey, Switzerland, 1979-80; ThM, Princeton Theology Seminary, New Jersey, 1990; PhD, Fordham University, New York, 1993; PhD, Bucharest University, 1999. Appointments: Priest of the Iassy Romanian Orthodox Archdiocese, 1973-78; Archpriest, Dean of Dorohoi Presbytery, Romania, 1978-86; Priest and Founder, Romanian Orthodox Church, Lausanne, Switzerland, 1979-83; Editorial Secretary, Sibiu Archdiocesan Publishing House, 1986-88; Mission to USA Programme in the Presbyterian Church, 1988-89; Home Visiting Therapist, New Hope Guild, New York, 1993; Professor of Philosophy and Ethics, Audrey Cohen College, School for Human Services, New York, 1992-; Editor, Weekly Newsletter with Articles, 1993-96; Parish Priest, St Peter and Paul, Astoria, New York, 1993-; Editorial Board, The Patristic and Byzantine Review, 1994-; Board of Advisors, Faculty, Justinianum Oikomenikon Research Center, Rhode Island, 1995-; Professor, Church History, St Vladimir's Theological Seminary, New York, 1995; Editor, Lumina Lina: Gracious Light, 1996-; Co-ordinator, Staten Island Center of Audrey Cohen College, 1996-. Publications: 7 books of theology, poetry and literary criticism; Numerous articles in professional journals and magazines. Honours: Neamtz Theological Seminary Award, Romania; EPER Grants, Switzerland; Presbyterian Church USA Grant; Stelian Stanicel Award, American Romanian Heritage Centre, USA; Convorbiri Literare Award, Iasi, Romania; Award for Religious Poetry, Deva International Poetry Contest, Deva, Romania. Address: 30-18 50th Street, Woodside, NY 11377, USA.

DANA Léo-Paul, b. 17 February 1958, Montreal, Canada. University Professor. m. Teresa Elizabeth. Education: BA with honours, 1980, MBA, 1983, McGill University; Ecole des Hautes Etudes Commerciales. Appointments: Concordia University, 1984-93; Department of Chartered Accountancy and Graduate Administrative Studies, Faculty of Management, McGill

Dictionary of International Biography

University; Deputy Director, International Business MBA Programme, Nanyang Business School, Singapore, 1998-2000; Founding Editor, Journal of International Entrepreneurship, 2001-. Publications: Author, several books including, Entrepreneurship in Pacific Asia: Past, Present and Future; 115 articles in refereed journals. Address: University of Canterbury Department of Management, Private Bag 4800, Christchurch, New Zealand.

DANA Robert (Patrick), b. 2 June 1929, Allston, Massachusetts, USA. Emeritus Professor of English; Poet. m. (1) Mary Kowalke, 2 June 1951, divorced 1973, 3 children, (2) Margaret Sellen, 14 September 1974. Education: AB, Drake University, 1951; MA, University of Iowa, 1954. Appointments: Assistant Professor, Associate Professor, Professor of English, Cornell College, Mount Vernon, Iowa, 1953-94; Editor, Hillside Press, Mount Vernon, 1957-67; Editor, 1964-68, Contributing Editor, 1991-, North American Review; Contributing Editor, American Poetry Review, 1973-88, New Letters, 1980-83. Publications: My Glass Brother and Other Poems, 1957; The Dark Flags of Waking, 1964; Journeys from the Skin: A Poem in Two Parts, 1966; Some Versions of Silence: Poems, 1967; The Power of the Visible, 1971; In a Fugitive Season, 1980; What the Stones Know, 1984; Blood Harvest, 1986; Against the Grain: Interviews with Maverick American Publishers, 1986; Starting Out for the Difficult World, 1987; What I Think I Know: New and Selected Poems, 1990; Wildebeest, 1993; Yes, Everything, 1994; Hello, Stranger: Beach Poems, 1996; A Community of Writers: Paul Engle and The Iowa Writers' Workshop, 1999; Summer, 2001; The Morning of the Red Admirals, 2004. Contributions to: New Yorker; New York Times; Poetry; Georgia Review; Manoa. Honours: Rainer Maria Rilke Prize, 1984; National Endowment for the Arts Fellowships, 1985, 1993; Delmore Schwartz Memorial Poetry Award, 1989; Carl Sandburg Medal for Poetry, 1994; Pushcart Prize, 1996. Memberships: Academy of American Poets; PEN; Associated Writing Programs; Poetry Society of America. Address: 1466 Westview Drive, Coralville, IA 52241, USA.

DANAILA Leon, b. 1 July 1933, Darabani, Botosani. Neurosurgeon. m. Alexandrina Ionescu. Education: Graduate, Faculty of General Medicine of Jassy, Faculty of Psychology and Philosophy, Bucharest, 1958; Fulbright Scholarship, Neurosurgery Clinic, University Hospital of New York, 1980; PhD, Medicine, 1973; Senior Physician 2nd Degree, 1981. Studies in the Netherlands, Moscow, Budapest, Dusseldorf, Brussels, Glasgow, Edinburgh, Paris. Appointments: General Practitioner, Sanitary District of Comanesti and Darmanesti in Bacau County, 1958-61; Resident Neurosurgeon, Neurosurgery Clinic of Bucharest, 1961-; Head of the Vascular Neurosurgery Department VII, 1981; Professor of Neurosurgery, Bucharest Faculty of Medicine, Professor, Psychoneurology, 1992, Head of Neurosurgery Department, 1996-; Titu Maiorescu University of Bucharest; President, Romanian Neurosurgery, 1997-. Publications: 301 scientific works, 59 in foreign journals; 19 books include: Spinal Neurinoma, 1972; Psychoneurology, 1983; Volumes 2 and 3, Vascular Diseases of the Brain and Spinal Cord, 1985; Romanian Neurosurgery, volumes I and II, 1986, 1987; Cardiovascular Thromboembolism, 1987; Psychiatric Surgery, 1988; Cerebral Atherosclerosis, 1988; The Treatment of Brain Tumors, 1993; Alzheimer Disease, 1996; Sculpture in the Brain, 1998; Apoptosis, 1999, 2002; Handbook of Neuropsychology, 2000; Lasers in Neurosurgery, 2001; Atlas of Surgical Pathology of the Brain, 2000, 2001; Neurological Synthesis, 2002. Honours: 10 Certificates of Innovator; 18 Certificates of Inventor; Award, Romanian Academy, 1995, 2001, 2002, 2003; RE del Vivo International Award, 1996; Honorary Citizenship of Darabani, 1999 and Dorohoi, 1999; ABI World Laureate, 1999. Memberships include: Romanian Medical Academy; Romanian Academy of Scientists; New York Academy

of Scientists; L'Union Medical Balakanique; Balkan Society of Angiology and Vascular Surgery; American Association for the Advancement of Science; European Society for Stereotactic and Functional Neurosurgery. Address: Traian St, No 2, Bl F1, Sc III, Et 2, Ap 4, Sector 3, Bucharest, Romania.

DANCE Charles, b. 10 October 1946, Rednal, Worcestershire, England. Actor. m. Joanna Haythorn, 1970, 1 son, 1 daughter. Appointments: Formerly employed in industry; with RSC, 1975-80, 1980-85; TV appearances include: The Fatal Spring; Nancy Astor; Frost in May; Saigon - The Last Day; Thunder Rock (drama); Rainy Day Women; The Jewel in the Crown (nom for Best Actor BAFTA Award); The Secret Servant; The McGuffin; The Phantom of the Opera, 1989; Rebecca, 1996; In the Presence of Mine Enemies; Hilary and Jackie, 1998; Films include: For Your Eyes Only; Plenty; The Golden Child; White Mischief; Good Morning Babylon; Hidden City; Pascali's Island, 1988; China Moon, 1990; Alien III, 1991; Limestone, 1991; Kabloonak; Century; Last Action Hero; Exquisite Tenderness, 1993; Short Cut to Paradise, 1993; Undertow; Michael Collins; Space Trucker, 1996; Goldeneye; The Blood Oranges; What Rats Won't Do; Hilary and Jackie, 1998; Don't go Breaking my Heart, 1999; Jurij, 1999; Dark Blue World, 2000; Gosford Park, 2001; Ali G in da House, 2001; Black and White; Swimming Pool, 2002; Theatre: Coriolanus (title role), RSC, 1989; Irma La Douce; Turning Over; Henry V; Three Sisters, 1998; Good, 1999; Long Day's Journey Into Night, 2001; The Play What I Wrote, 2002; Radio: The Heart of the Matter, 2001; The Charge of the Light Brigade, 2001. Address: c/o ICM, Oxford House, 76 Oxford Street, London, W1D 1BS, England.

DANCUO-PEHARDA Mirjana, b. 16 January 1929, Karlovac, Croatia. Singer (Soprano). m. Zdenko Peharda. Education: Studied in Zagreb. Debut: National Opera, Zagreb 1945, as Giannetta in L'Elisir d'Amore. Career: Sang Belgrade, Sofia, Brno and elsewhere in Eastern Europe; Guest appearances at Teatro Liceo Barcelona, The Vienna Volksoper, Den Norske Opera, Oslo, Stockholm and Gothenburg in Sweden; Herodia in Salome (Strauss); Other roles have included Mozart's Countess and Donna Anna, Verdi's Amneris, Amelia, Ballo in Maschera and Trovatore Leonora, La Gioconda, Margherita in Mefistofele, Yaroslavna in Prince Igor, Leonore in Fidelio, Marina in Boris Godunov, Wagner's Sieglinde and Elisabeth, the Marschallin in Der Rosenkavalier, Tosca and Desdemona; Kostelnicka in Jenufa, Lady Billows in Albert Herring; Teacher at the Operatic High School in Olslo, 1994-. Honour: Oslo City Culture Prize, 1978. Membership: Norwegian Opera Singers Association. Address: Jerikoveien 89B, 1052 Oslo, Norway.

DANGOGGO Sani Mohammed, b. 26 January 1961, Dogondaji, Nigeria. Lecturer. m. Hauwa'u, 1 son, 5 daughters. Education: BSc honours, Applied Chemistry, University of Sokoto, 1984; MSc, Organic Chemistry, University of Ibadan, 1987; PhD, Applied Chemistry, Usmanu Danfodiyo University, Sokoto, 2000. Appointments: Graduate Assistant, 1985, Assistant Lecturer, 1986, Lecturer II, 1988, Lecturer I, 1990, Senior Lecturer, 1994-, Director of Academic Planning, Usmanu Danfodiyo University. Publications: 14 publications. Memberships: Royal Society of Chemistry, UK; Chemical Society of Nigeria. Address: Usmanu Danfodiyo University, PMB 2346, Department of Pure & Applied Chemistry, Sokoto, Nigeria. E-mail: smdd767@yahoo.com

DANIEL Geoffrey Peter, (Peter Thorne), b. 5 March 1955, Bedford, England. Teacher; Poet. m. Iseabal Flora MacDonald, 12 July 1980, 1 son, 1 daughter. Education: Kings Canterbury, 1968-72; St Andrews University, 1973-77; Durham University, 1977-78; Hamilton College of Education, 1980. Appointments:

Dictionary of International Biography

Head of Drama, Kamuzu Academy, Malawi; Glenalmond College, Perthshire; Head of English, later Sixth Form, Reeds School, Surrey; Deputy Rector, Dollar Academy; Poetry Advisor, Association of Christian Writers. Publication: Gripping the Perch, 1999. Contributions to: Books, magazines and journals. Honour: International Haiku. Memberships: British Haiku Society; Association of Christian Writers; Fellow, Society of Antiquaries, Scotland. Address: Dollar Academy, Dollar, Clackmannanshire, FK14 7DU, Scotland.

DANIELS Jeff, b. 19 February 1955, Athens, Georgia, USA. Actor. Education: Central Michigan University. Appointments: Apprentice Circle Repertory Theatre, New York; Founder, Purple Rose Theatre Company, Chelsea, Michigan; Theatre: The Farm, 1976; Brontosaurus, 1977; My Life, 1977; Feedlot, 1977; Lulu, 1978; Slugger, 1978; The Fifth of July, 1978; Johnny Got His Gun (Obie Award), 1982; The Three Sisters, 1982-83; The Golden Age, 1984; Redwood Curtain, 1993; Short-Changed Review, 1993; Lemon Sky; Films: Ragtime, 1981; Terms of Endearment, 1983; The Purple Rose of Cairo, 1985; Marie, 1985; Heartburn, 1986; Something Wild, 1986; Radio Days, 1987; The House on Carroll Street, 1988; Sweet Hearts Dance, 1988; Grand Tour, 1989; Checking Out, 1989; Arachnophobia, 1990; Welcome Home, Roxy Carmichael, 1990; Love Hurts, 1990; The Butcher's Wife, 1992; Gettysburg, 1993; Speed, 1994; Dumb and Dumber, 1994; Fly Away Home, 1996; Two Days in the Valley, 1996; 101 Dalmatians, 1996; Trial and Error, 1997; Pleasantville, 1998; All the Rage, 1999; My Favourite Martian, 1999; Chasing Sleep, 2000; Escanaba in da Moonlight, 2000; Super Sucker, 2002; Blood Work, 2002; The Hours, 2002; Gods and Generals, 2002; TV films: A Rumor of War, 1980; Invasion of Privacy, 1983; The Caine Mutiny Court Martial, 1988; No Place Like Home, 1989; Disaster in Time, 1992; Redwood Curtain, 1995; Teamster Boss: The Jackie Presser Story; (specials) Fifth of July; The Visit (Trying Times). Publications: Author, Plays: Shoeman, 1991; The Tropical Pickle, 1992; The Vast Difference, 1993; Thy Kingdom's Coming, 1994; Escanaba in da Moonlight, 1995.

DANN Colin Michael, b. 10 March 1943, Richmond, Surrey, England. Author. m. Janet Elizabeth Stratton, 4 June 1977. Publications: The Animals of Farthing Wood, 1979; In the Grip of Winter, 1981; Fox's Feud, 1982; The Fox Cub Bold, 1983; The Siege of White Deer Park, 1985; The Ram of Sweetriver, 1986; King of the Vagabonds, 1987; The Beach Dogs, 1988; The Flight from Farthing Wood, 1988; Just Nuffin, 1989; In the Path of the Storm, 1989; A Great Escape, 1990; A Legacy of Ghosts, 1991; The City Cats, 1991; Battle for the Park, 1992; The Adventure Begins, 1994; Copycat, 1998; Nobody's Dog, 1999; Journey to Freedom, 1999; Lion Country, 2000; Bridge of The Plains 2002. Honour: Arts Council National Award for Children's Literature, 1980. Membership: Society of Authors. Address: Castle Oast, Ewhurst Green, East Sussex, England.

DANNER Karl Heinz, b. 25 February 1940, Rodalben, Rhineland-Palatinate, Germany. Educator. m. Ingrid Karola Danner-Jekel. Education: BA, Laurentian University, Canada, 1964-65, 1981-82; Diplomas, Universities of Madrid and Salamanca, 1978 and 1981; Master of Arts, University of the Saarland, Germany, 1976; Licence/Maîtrise ès Lettres, University of Toulouse-Le Mirail, France, 1984-86; Master and Doctor of Education, Pacific Western University, Los Angeles, California, 1986, 1988; Doctor of Philosophy, Doctor of Literature, American University, 1990, 1994; Professor h.c. Appointments include: Teacher, Modern Languages and Literature, Canada and West Germany; Research Assistant, Associate and Lecturer, University of the Saarland, Germany, 1965-76; Lecturer and Senior Lecturer, Modern Languages, Education Authority, Regional Government

of the Palatinate, Germany, 1980-; Student Exchange Organiser and Liaison Teacher, Exchanges in France and England; Adviser Partner for Cultural Exchange/Relations, 1989-; Founding Member, Member of the Board, General Secretary, International Robert Musil Society, Austria; Founder, President of German-Latin American Friendship Associations, 1989-; Member, Accademia Culturale d'Europa, Italy, 1989; Counsellor on German Culture in Europe and Overseas, 1991-; Honorary Member, Societé de Philosophie, France, 1994; Member of Pontificia Academia, Vatican, Rome, 1996-; Member, Jury of National Foreign Language Competition. Publications: Poetry in English, French, German and German translations from Catalan, English, French, Portuguese, Spanish; Essays, reviews and studies on modern German, English, French, Portuguese/ Brazilian and Spanish literature; Research Publications; Didactics of Modern Languages. Honours include: Scholarship, University of Sudbury, Ontario, Canada, 1964; Poetry Prize, Laurentian University, Canada, 1965; Scholarship, Universidad de Salamanca, Spain, 1981; Medal of Merit of the Capital of Carinthia, Austria, 1984; Order of Carinthia, Austria, 1989; Medaglia d'Oro, Instituto Europeo di Cultura, Italy, 1989; Honorary President, German Federation of Folklore, 1993; Commander of the Order of National Merit, 1995; Doctor of Philosophy, honoris causa, International Christian University, 1999. Memberships: German Schiller Society; German-Indian Children's Fund; Modern Language Association. Address: Casa Carola, Burg 107, D 66955 Pirmasens, Germany.

DANSON Ted, b. 29 December 1947, San Diego, California, USA. Actor. m. (1) Randell L Gosch, divorced, (2) Cassandra Coates, 1977, divorced, 2 daughters, (3) Mary Steenburgen, 1995. Education: Stanford University; Carnegie-Mellon University. Appointments: Teacher, The Actor's Institute, Los Angeles, 1978; Star, NBC-TV series Cheers, 1982-93; CEO Anasazi Productions (Formerly Danson/Fauci Productions); Off-Broadway plays include: The Real Inspector Hound, 1972; Comedy of Errors; Actor, producer TV films including: When the Bough Breaks, 1986; We Are The Children, 1987; Executive Producer TV films: Walk Me to the Distance, 1989; Down Home, 1989; Mercy Mission: The Rescue of Flight 771, 1993; On Promised Land, 1994; Other appearances in TV drama; Films include: The Onion Field, 1979; Body Heat, 1981; Creepshow, 1983; A Little Treasure, 1985; A Fine Mess, 1986; Just Between Friends, 1986; Three Men and a Little Lady, 1990; Made in America, 1992; Getting Even With Dad, 1993; Pontiac Moon, 1993; Gulliver's Travels (TV), 1995; Loch Ness, 1996; Homegrown, 1998; Thanks of a Grateful Nation, 1998; Saving Private Ryan, 1998; Becker, 1998; Mumford, 1999. Address: c/o Josh Liberman, Creative Artists Agency, 9830 Wilshire Boulevard, Beverly Hills, CA 90212, USA.

DANTZIG George Bernard, b. 8 November 1914, Portland, Oregon, USA. Mathematician; Expert in Linear Programming and Operations Research. m. Anne Shmuner, 1936, 2 sons, 1 daughter. Education: BA, University of Maryland, 1936; Horace Rackham Scholar, MA, University of Michigan. Appointments: Statistical Control Headquarters, US Air Force, Chief of Combat Analysis Branch, Mathematical Adviser, 1946-52; Research Mathematician, Rand Corporation, Santa Monica, California, 1952-60; Professor, Chairman of Operations Research Centre, 1960-66; C A Criley Professor of Operations Research and Computer Science, 1966-97, Emeritus Professor, 1997-, Stanford University, Palo Alto, California; Head of Methodology Project, International Institute for Applied Systems Analysis, 1973-74. Publications: Linear Programming and Extensions, 1963; Compact City, with Thomas L Saaty, 1973; Over 150 technical papers. Honours include: National Medal of Science, 1975; National Academy of Sciences Award in Applied Mathematics and Numerical Analysis, 1977; Harvey Prize, 1985; Silver Medal Operational Research Society,

1986; COORS American Ingenuity Award, 1989; Pender Award, University of Pennsylvania, 1995. Memberships: NAS; National Academy of Engineering; Fellow, American Academy of Arts and Sciences; Honorary member, Institute of Electrical and Electronics Engineers. Address: 821 Tolman Drive, Stanford, CA 94305, USA.

DANYLAK Joan Kikel, b. 3 February 1943, Brooklyn, New York, USA. Poet; Author. Education: BA, High Distinction, University of Arizona, 1969. Career: Poet; Publisher; Editor. Publications: Over 15 books include: Honoring Poets and Professional and Creative People. Honours: Elected to 3 Honor Societies in College; Grant, American Poetry Association; President's Award, National Authors Registry, 1996; Medallion and Trophy, Famous Poets Society; Poet of the Year, 2002; Listed in Great Minds of the 21st Century, ABI. Membership: Mensa. Address: 111-20, 73 Avenue, #7A Forest Hills, NY 11375, USA.

DAO Hoang-Trung, b. 2 April 1949, Hanoi, Vietnam. Professor; Administrator; Lexicographer. 1 daughter. Education: BA, Public Administration, 1972, BA, Sociology, 1973. Appointments: Administrator, 1973-75; Table Tennis Coach, 1976-84; Expert on Institution and Organisation for Van Lang Cultural and Welfare Association, Inc, Queensland, Australia, 1985-; Professor, Van Lang University, Ho Chi Minh City, 1998-; Assistant to Dean, Faculty of Physical Education and Sports, Hong Bang University. Publication: English in Verses, 1990. Honours: Gold Medal, Table Tennis Champion for Students of Vietnam, 1963-69; Award for Outstanding Service to Van Lang Cultural and Welfare Association, Inc, Australia and to Van Lang University, Vietnam; Winner, 30 Table Tennis tournaments; Man of the Year 2003 Award, ABI; 2000 Outstanding Intellectuals of the 21st Century Diploma, IBC; Nominated, Man of the Year 2004 Award, ABI; Invited for membership and title of Deputy Governor, ABI Research Association's Board of Governors. Membership: Van Lang Cultural and Welfare Association, Inc, Queensland, Australia. Address: 45/43 Tran Hung Dao Street, District I, Ho Chi Minh City, Vietnam. E-mail: hoangtrungdao1949@yahoo.com

ĐÀO Marie Hoàng-Nga, b. 1 July 1947, Bac-Ninh, Vietnam. Teacher; Medical Director. m. Ngoc-Thuan Ha, 1 son, 3 daughters. Education: Licence-ès-Lettres, English and Vietnamese Linguistics, University of Saigon, Vietnam, 1969; Award Certificate, South East Asia Ministers of Education Organisation, Regional English Language Centre, Singapore, 1974; MA Qual, 1976, BA, English and French Linguistics, University of Queensland, Australia, 1983; Diploma, Practice Management, 1985; JP, 1987, JP Qualified, 1997, Department of Justice, Queensland. Appointments: Lobbyist and Marital Counsellor; Teacher; Community Advocate; Poetess; Social Worker; Soprano Singer and Poetry Reciter in any language (ready to perform when required); Writer; Accountant; Guest Speaker on many subjects including culture, education, human rights, etc; Medical Director, 1983-; Tax Help Volunteer for Australian Taxation Office, 1989-; President, Van-Lang Cultural and Welfare Association, 1997-; President, World and Asian Pacific League for Freedom and Democracy, Queensland Chapter, 1999-; Chairman, Patronage Committee for Trung-Vuong Vietnamese Language School, 1999-. Publications: Author: G??m Th? Thi-Phâ'm (Sword and Poetry poem collection); Collections of many other articles, musical cassettes and CD publications. Honours: Gold Medal, High Jump Champion of Vietnam, 1963; Champion of Table Tennis: Double Prize Gold Cup, Gold Medal, Vietnam, 1969; Gold Medal, Single, Singapore, 1974; 15 Award Certificates, Australian Taxation Office, 1989-; Queensland Multicultural Service Award Certificate Silver Medal by Premier Beattie, Parliament House, 2003; Selected Woman of the Year 2003 and 2004, Contemporary Who's Who, 2003-; Deputy Director General for Oceania, IBC, 2003; World Laureate, 2003; Order of

International Ambassador, 2003. Numerous Memberships include: Ethnic Community Council of Queensland, 1978-; Alumni, Queensland University, 1983-; Reference Group for Brisbane City Council, 2000-; Vietnamese Co-ordinator, Rotary Overseas Medical Aid for Children, Brisbane, 2001-; Deputy Governor for the International Research Board of Advisors, ABI; Secretary General, United Cultural Convention; Professional Women's Advisory Board Member, ABI, 2004-. Address: 1 Scotts Road, Darra, Queensland 4076, Australia. E-mail: ha_dao@hotmail.com

DAR Shimon, b. 15 September 1935, Poland. Archaeologist. m. Lina, 1 son, 2 daughters. Education: Avshalom Institute Land of Israel Diploma, 1957-60; BA distinction, Ancient Near East Studies, 1969-72, MA, distinction, Archaeology and Ancient Near East Cultures, 1974-77, PhD, Archaeology and History of the Jewish People, 1978-82, Tel-Aviv University. Appointments: Teaching Associate, 1980-81, Instructor, 1981-82, Senior Instructor, 1982-83, Lecturer, 1983-86, Classical Archaeology, Senior Lecturer, 1986-90, Associate Professor, 1990, Professor, 1998, Head of Department, 1999, Land of Israel Studies, Bar Ilan University. Publications: 10 books; 60 articles in professional journals; Numerous professional and academic conferences. Honours: Yeshiva Broide Study Prize, Tel-Aviv University, 1971; Havazelet Fund Prize, 1975; Numerous research grants, 1978-2000. Memberships: Israel Exploration Society; Archaeology Survey of Israel; Society for Byzantine Studies in Israel; Golan Research Centre, Hermon Team; Roman Society, England; Inter-University Classical Society, England; Société d'Etudes Samaritaines. Address: Bar-Ilan University, Land of Israel Studies and Archaeology, Ramat-Gan, 52900, Israel. E-mail: dar_ls@maabarot.org.il

DARDE Jean, b. 8 March 1920. Industrialist. m. Michele de Demandolx, 15 November 1947, 3 sons, 2 daughters. Education: Diplome de L'Ecole des Hautes Etudes Commercials (HEC) de Paris, Licencié en Droit, 1941. Appointments: President, SA Soplaril, Vice-President, Soplaril International; Vice-President, Lab SPS; President, Deforges SA. Honours: Legion d'Honneur; Médaille Militaire; Military Cross. Membership: Automobile Club de France. Address: 9 rue Adolphe Yvon, 75116 Paris, France.

DARKE Marjorie Sheila, b. 25 January 1929, Birmingham, England. Writer. m. 1952, 2 sons, 1 daughter. Education: Leicester College of Art, 1947-50; Central School of Art, London, 1950-51. Publications: For Young Adults: Ride the Iron Horse, 1973; The Star Trap, 1974; A Question of Courage, 1975; The First of Midnight, 1977; A Long Way to Go, 1978; Comeback, 1981; Tom Post's Private Eye, 1982; Messages and Other Shivery Tales, 1984; A Rose From Blighty, 1990. For Beginner Readers: Mike's Bike, 1974; What Can I Do, 1975; The Big Brass Band, 1976; My Uncle Charlie, 1977; Carnival Day, 1979. For Young Children: Kipper's Turn, 1976; Kipper Skips, 1979; Imp, 1985; The Rainbow Sandwich, 1989; Night Windows, 1990; Emma's Monster, 1992; Just Bear and Friends, 1996. Memberships: Society of Authors; International PEN. Address: c/o Rogers, Coleridge & White, 20 Powis Mews, London W11 1JN, England.

DARMON Rene-Yves, b. 10 September 1938, Algeria. Professor. m. Nicole, 1 son, 1 daughter. Education: ESSEC, 1961; MBA, Columbia University, 1963; PhD, Wharton School, University of Pennsylvania, 1973. Appointments: Product Manager, 1964-65; Sales Administration Manager, 1966-68; Consultant, 1973-; Assistant Professor, Universite Laval, 1968-73; Associate Professor, 1973-79; Visiting Associate Professor, McGill University, 1976-78; Associate Professor, 1979-83; Professor, 1983-90; Professor of Marketing, ESSEC, 1990-; Head of Marketing Department, 1991-92, 1998-2001; Elected Dean for

Faculty Affairs, 2001-04; Dean of Research, 1992-2001. Publications: 50 Articles in Professional Journals; 17 Books; 4 Book Chapters. Honours: Outstanding Paper Award; Excellence in Reviewing Award; Award for Best Applied Paper in Marketing; Best Paper Award; Mu Kappa Tau Top Paper Award; Best Stidsen Award of Excellence; Honorable Mention Award; Mu Kappa Tau Award for the Best Article; Chevalier dans l'Ordre National du Mérite, France. Memberships: President, Association Francaise de Marketing, 2000-02; European Marketing Academy; Academy of Marketing Science; Administrative Sciences Association of Canada; INFORMS; American Marketing Association. Address: Ecole Sup Scis Econ Commls, Av Bernard Hirsch BP 105, 95021 Cergy-Pontoise, France.

DARNEL Allen G, b. 14 April 1927, Norton, Kansas, USA. Social Dance Teacher. 1 daughter. Education: University of Arizona, Tucson, USA. Career: Owner, Dance City USA and Beginners Only USA Dance Studios, Houston, Texas; National Promotional Director, USA Feather Awards, Beverly Hills, California. Publications: Book, Beginners Only. Honours: Lifetime Achievement Award, USA Ballroom Dancing Association. Address: 5959 Westheimer Road, # 100, Houston, TX 77057-7616, USA. Website: www.beginnersonly.com

DAS Santanu, b. 3 October 1965, Serampore, West Bengal, India. Engineering College Teacher. m. Manimala Das, 2 daughters. Education: Bachelor of Mechanical Engineering, 1988; Master of Mechanical Engineering, 1990, Doctor of Philosophy (Eng.) 1996. Appointments: Management Trainee, PDIL, New Dehli, India; Lecturer and Assistant Professor – Dr BA Technological University, Lonere, India; Assistant Professor and Former Head, Mechanical Engineering Department, Kalyani Government Engineering College, Kalyani, India, continuing. Publications include: Several articles in scientific journals including: History of Metal Cutting in Prakriti, 2000; Application of the Analytic Hierarchy Process for Estimating the State of Tool Wear in the International Journal of Machine Tools and Manufacture, 2003. Honour: Listed in several biographical publications. Address: B1 - 195, Kalyani, West Bengal – 741 235, India. E-mail: sdas@kucse.wb.nic.in

DAŠIĆ Pedrag, b. 16 September 1958, Peć, Serbia and Montenegro. Professor of Information Scientific and Technical Systems. 1 son. Education: Graduate, Faculty of mechanical Engineering, Priština, 1982; Master of Science, Faculty of Mechanical Engineering, Belgrade. Appointments: Technological Designer of CNC Machines, 1982-1985, Research Assistant, 1985-88, Institute Industry "14 October", Kruševac, Serbia and Montenegro; Professor of Information Science and Technological Systems, High Mechanical School, Trstenik and High Technological School, Kruševac, Serbia and Montenegro 1988-; President of Organising Committee of the International Conference of RaDMI, 2001-2003. Publications: 200 scientific papers, 80 of them published abroad; 1 monograph; 5 books; 2 scripts; Editor of 8 books; Over 10 scientific and research projects; 10 scientific software and Web presentations. Honours: 2 innovations for improving production, Industry "14 October", Kruševac; 2nd Award, for scientific and technical creative work and innovations in Kruševac community, 1987. Memberships include: Yugoslav Association for Operational Research; Yugoslav Association for Tribology; Yugoslav Association for Standardisation and Quality; Yugoslav Association for Diagnostics. Address: Ratka Pešića No 59, 37208 Čitluk-Kruševac, Serbia and Montenegro. E-mail: dasicp@ptt.yu Website: www.radi.co.yu

DAVIDSON Donald (Herbert), b. 6 March 1917, Springfield, Massachusetts, USA. Philosopher; Professor; Writer. m. (1) 1 daughter, (2) Nancy Hirshberg, 4 April 1975, deceased 1979, (3)

Marcia Cavell, 3 July 1984. Education: BA, 1939, MA, 1941, PhD, 1949, Harvard University. Appointments: Instructor, Queen's College, New York City, 1947-50; Assistant Professor to Professor, Stanford University, 1951-67; Visiting Professor, University of Tokyo, 1955; Professor, 1967-70, Chairman, Department of Philosophy, 1968-70, Lecturer with rank of Professor, 1970-76, Princeton University; Gavin David Young Lecturer, University of Adelaide, 1968; John Locke Lecturer, Oxford University, 1970; Professor, Rockefeller University, New York City, 1970-76, University of Chicago, 1976-81; Willis S and Marion Slusser Professor University of California at Berkeley, 1981-; John Dewey Lecturer, University of Michigan, 1973; George Eastman Visiting Professor, Balliol College, Oxford, 1984-85; Fulbright Distinguished Lecturer, India, 1985-86; S J Keeling Memorial Lecturer in Greek Philosophy, University College, London, 1986; Thalheimer Lecturer, Johns Hopkins University, 1987; John Dewey Lecturer, Columbia University, 1989; Alfred North Whitehead Lecturer, Harvard University, 1990; Kant Lecturer, University of Munich, 1993; Various other lectureships. Publications: Decision Making: An Experimental Approach (with Patrick Suppes), 1957; Words and Objections (editor with J Hintikka), 1969; Semantics for Natural Language (editor with Gilbert Harman), 1970; The Logic of Grammar (co-editor), 1975; Essays on Actions and Events, 1980; Inquiries into Truth and Interpretation, 1983; Plato's Philebus, 1990; Structure and Content of Truth, 1990; Subjective, Intersubjective, Objective, 2001; numerous essays and articles in philosophical journals. Honours: Teschemacher Fellow in Classics and Philosophy, 1939-41; Rockefeller Fellowship in the Humanities, 1945-46; American Council of Learned Societies Fellowship, 1958-59; National Science Foundation Research Grants, 1964-65; 1968; Fellow, Center for Advanced Study in the Behavioral Sciences, 1969-70; Guggenheim Fellowship, 1973-74; Fellow, All Souls College, Oxford, 1973-74; Honorary Research Fellow, University College, London, 1978; Sherman Fairchild Distinguished Scholar, California Institute of Technology, 1989; Hegel Prize, City Stuttgart, 1991; DDL Honoris causa, Oxford University, 1995; Doctorate of Philosophy, honoris causa, Stockholm University, 1999. Memberships: American Academy of Arts and Sciences; American Association of University Professors; American Philosophical Association; American Philosophical Society; British Academy, corresponding member; Norwegian Academy of Science and Letters, 1987. Address: c/o Department of Philosophy, University of California at Berkeley, Berkeley, CA 94720-2390, USA.

DAVIES Gillian, b. 5 April 1940, Abersoch, North Wales. Judge. Education: Grenoble University; Barrister, Lincoln's Inn, London, 1961; PhD, University of Wales, Aberystwyth, 1997. Appointments: Legal Adviser, 1970-73, Assistant Director General, 1973-80, Associate Director General and Chief Legal Adviser, 1980-91, IFPI (International Federation of the Phonographic Industry); Legal member, Boards of Appeal, 1991-97; Chairman, Board of Appeal and Member, Enlarged Board of Appeal, European Patent Office, 1997-. Publications: Piracy of Phonograms, 1981, 1986; Challenges to Copyright and Related Rights in the European Community (co-author), 1983; Private Copying of Sound and Audio-visual Recordings, 1983; Music and Video Private Copying (co-author), 1993; Copyright and the Public Interest, 1994, 2002; Copinger and Skone James on Copyright (co-author), 14th edition, 1999, supplement, 2002; Many articles on intellectual property law topics. Honours: Deputy Lieutenant, County of Gwynedd, 2001-; Honorary Professor, University of Wales, 1994-. Membership: Association Littéraire Artistique Internationale (ALAI). Address: European Patent Office, Erhardstrasse 27, D-80298, Munich, Germany.

DAVIES Jonathan, b. 24 October 1962. Rugby Player. m. (1) Karen Marie, 1984, deceased 1997, 2 sons, 1 daughter, (2) Helen Jones, 2002. Appointments: Rugby Union outside-half; Played for following rugby clubs: Trimsaran, Neath, Llanelli; Turned professional, 1989; with Cardiff, 1995-97; Played for Welsh national team (v England), 1985; World cup Squad (6 appearances), 1987; Triple Crown winning team, 1988; Tour New Zealand (2 test appearances), 1988; 29 caps, sometimes Captain; Also played for Barbarians Rugby Football Club; Rugby League career; Played at three-quarters; Widnes (world record transfer fee), 1989; Warrington (free transfer), 1993-95; Reverted to rugby union, 1995; Welsh national team; British national team; Tour New Zealand, 1990; 6 caps, former Captain. Publication: Jonathan, 1989. Address: C/o Cardiff Rugby Football Club, Cardiff Arms Park, Westgate Street, Cardiff, Wales.

DAVIES Laura, b. 5 October 1963, Coventry, England. Golfer. Appointments: Turned professional, 1985; Won Belgian Open, 1985; British Women's Open, 1986; US Women's Open, 1987; AGF Biarritz Open, 1990; Wilkinson Sword English Open, 1995; Irish Open, 1994, 1995; French Masters, 1995; LPGA Championship, 1996; Danish Open, 1997; Chrysler Open, 1998, 1999; WPGA Championship, 1999; Compaq Open, 1999; TSN Ladies World Cup of Golf (Individual), 2000; WPGA International Matchplay, 2001; Norwegian Masters, 2002; Represented, England, World Team Championship, Taiwan, 1992; Europe in Solheim Cup, 1990, 1992, 1994. Publication: Carefree Golf, 1991. Honours: Rookie of the Year, 1985; Order of Merit Winner, 1985, 1986, 1992; Rolex Player of the Year, 1996. Address: c/o Women's Professional Golf European Tour, The Tytherington Club, Dorchester Way, Tytherington, Macclesfield, SK10 2JP, England.

DAVIES Mark William, b. 5 September 1962, Brisbane, Australia. Neonatologist. m. Judith Lois Morrison, 1 son, 1 daughter. Education: MBBS, University of Queensland, 1979; DCH, Royal College of Physicians, UK, 1989; Fellow, Royal Australasian College of Physicians, 1997. Appointments: Intern, Royal Brisbane Hospital, Royal Children's Hospital, 1986-87; Junior House Officer, Royal Brisbane Hospital, Royal Women's Hospital, Royal Children's Hospital, 1987-88; Senior House Officer, Worcester Royal Infirmary, England, 1988-89; Registrar, Royal Women's Hospital, Royal Children's Hospital, Brisbane, 1989-90; Senior House Officer, Rosie Maternity Hospital, Cambridge, England, 1990, Doncaster Royal Infirmary, Doncaster, England, 1990-91; Registrar, Royal Hospital for Sick Children, Glasgow, Scotland, 1991-92; Registrar, Glasgow Royal Maternity Hospital, Scotland, 1992; Senior Registrar, Royal Women's Hospital, Brisbane, 1995-97; Senior Neonatal Fellow, Royal Women's Hospital, Melbourne, 1997-99; Royal Children's Hospital Foundation Clinical Research Fellow, Royal Children's Hospital, Royal Women's Hospital, Brisbane, 1999-2000; Staff Consultant Neonatologist, Senior Lecturer in Neonatology, Royal Women's Hospital, University of Queensland, 2000-. Publications: 24 original journal articles; 2 reviews; 15 systematic reviews; 6 letters; 9 abstracts; many others. Honours: Several grants, prizes and awards. Memberships: Australasian Academy of Critical Care Medicine; Paediatric Research Society of Australia and New Zealand; Paediatric Society of Queensland; Perinatal Society of Australia and New Zealand; Royal Women's Hospital Specialist Staff Association; Society of Critical Care Medicine. Address: PO Box 5285, West End, Brisbane, QLD 4101, Australia. E-mail: mwdavies@zemail.com.au

DAVIES (Nicholas) Peter (Gavin), b. 3 January 1965, Liverpool, England. Physician. m. Michelle. Education: BSc (Hons), Physiology, 1986, MBChB, 1989, Leeds University, Leeds, England. Appointments: General Practitioner Registrar, Avondale

Medical Practice, Strathaven, Lanarkshire, Scotland, 1994-94; General Practitioner Principal, Alison Lea Medical Centre, East Kilbride, Scotland, 1996-2001; General Practitioner, Mixenden Stones Surgery, Halifax, Yorkshire, England, 2001-. Publications: Co-author: Patients and the New Contract, 2003; Co-author, End Stage Social Pathology, 2003; Many other articles on medical topics. Honours: Vice-Chairman, Yorkshire Faculty of the Royal College of General Practitioners; Master Practitioner of Neuro-Linguistic Programming, 2002. Memberships: Royal College of General Practitioners; Institute of Neurosemantics. Address: Mixenden Stones Surgery, Halifax HX2 8RQ, England. E-mail: npgdavies@doctors.net.uk

DAVIES Ryland, b. 9 February 1943, Cwym, Ebbw Vale, Wales. Opera and Concert Singer (Tenor). m. (1) Anne Howells (divorced 1981); (2) Deborah Rees, 1983, 1 daughter. Education: FRMCM, Royal Manchester College of Music, 1971. Debut: Almaviva, Barber of Seville, Welsh National Opera, 1964. Career: Glyndebourne Chorus, 1964-66; Soloist and Freelance, Glyndebourne and Sadler's Wells, Royal Opera House, Covent Garden, Welsh National Opera, Scottish Opera, Opera North; Performances in Salzburg, San Francisco, Chicago, New York, Hollywood Bowl, Paris, Geneva, Brussels, Vienna, Lyon, Amsterdam, Mannheim, Rome, Israel, Buenos Aires, Stuttgart, Berlin, Hamburg, Nice, Nancy, Philadelphia; Sang Lysander in A Midsummer Night's Dream at Glyndebourne, 1989, Tichon in Katya Kabanova at the 1990 Festival; Other roles have included Mozart's Ferrando and Don Ottavio, Ernesto, Fenton, Nemorino, Pelléas, (Berlin 1984), Oberon, (Montpellier, 1987); Tamino, Lensky, Belmonte and Enéas in Esclarmonde; Sang Podestà in Mozart's Finta Giardiniera for Welsh National Opera, 1994; Arbace in Idomeneo at Garsington, 1996; Season 1998 with Mozart's Basilio at Chicago; Concert Appearances at home and abroad; Radio and TV Broadcasts; Appeared in films including: Capriccio, Entführung, A Midsummer Night's Dream; Trial by Jury, Don Pasquale. Recordings: include, Die Entführung; Les Troyens; Saul; Così fan tutte; Monteverdi Madrigals; Messiah, Idomeneo, Il Matrimonio Segreto, L'Oracolo (Leoni), Lucia di Lammermoor, Thérèse, Judas Maccabeus, Mozart Requiem, Credo Mass, Mozart Coronation Mass and Vêspres Solenelle. Honours: Boise and Mendelssohn Foundation Scholarship, 1964; Ricordi Prize, 1964; Imperial League of Opera Prize, 1964; John Christie Award, 1965. Address: 71 Fairmile Lane, Cobham, Surrey KT11 2WG, England.

DAVIS Andrew (Frank) (Sir), b. 2 February 1944, Ashridge, Hertfordshire, England. Conductor. m. Gianna, 1 son. Education: DMusB (Organ Scholar), King's College, Cambridge; MA (Cantab), 1967; With Franco Ferrara, Rome, 1967-68; DLitt (Hons), York University, Toronto, 1984. Debut: BBC Symphony Orchestra, 1970. Career: Pianist, Harpsichordist, Organist, St Martin-in-the-Fields Academy, London, 1966-70; Assistant Conductor, BBC Scottish Symphony Orchestra, Glasgow, 1970-72; Appearances, major orchestras and festivals internationally including Berlin, Edinburgh, Flanders; Conductor, Glyndebourne Opera Festival, 1973-; Music Director, 1975-88, Conductor Laureate, 1988-, Toronto Symphony; Conductor, China, USA, Japan and Europe tours, 1983, 1986; Principal Guest Conductor, Royal Liverpool Philharmonic Orchestra, 1974-77; Associate Conductor, New Philharmonic Orchestra, London, 1973-77; Conducted: La Scala Milan, Metropolitan Opera, Covent Garden, Paris Opera; Music Director, Glyndebourne, 1988-; Chief Conductor, 1989-2000, Conductor Laureate, 2000-, BBC Symphony Orchestra; Musical Director, Chicago Lyric Opera, 2000-; Conducted La Clemenza di Tito, Chicago, Oct 1989; Szymanowski King Roger, Festival Hall, London, 1990; Katya Kabanova and Tippett's New Year, (1990) Glyndebourne Festival; Opened 1991 Promenade Concerts, London, with Dream of

Gerontius; Glyndebourne, 1992, Gala and The Queen of Spades; Conducted Elektra, at First Night, 1993 London Proms; Berg's Lulu, Festival Hall, 1994, returned 1997, for Stravinsky's Oedipus Rex, Persephone and The Rakes's Progress; Hansel and Gretel, 1996-97, and Capriccio, 1997-98, for the Met; Philadelphia, Chicago and Boston Orchestras, New York Philharmonic, and other leading American and European orchestras; Contracted to become Music Director and Principal Conductor of the Chicago Lyric Opera, 2000; Season 1999 with a new production of Pelléas et Mélisande at Glyndebourne and Tippett's The Mask of Time at the London Prom concerts. Compositions: La Serenissima (Inventions on a Theme by Claudio Monteverdi); Chansons Innocentes. Recordings include: All Dvorák Symphonies, Mendelssohn Symphonies, Borodin Cycle; Enigma Variations, Falstaff, Elgar; Overtures: Coriolan, Leonore No 3, Egmont, Fidelio Beethoven; Symphony No 10, Shostakovich, and violin concertos; Canon and other digital delights, Pachelbel; Cinderella excerpts; The Young Person's Guide to the Orchestra; Concerto No 2, Rachmaninov; The Planets, Gustav Holst; Symphony No 5, Horn Concerto, Piano Concerto No 2, Hoddinott; Brahms piano concertos; Nielsen Symphonies nos 4 and 5; Currently working on The British Line series with the BBC SO including the Elgar Symphonies and Enigma Variations, Vaughan Williams, Delius, Britten and Tippett; Operatic releases including Glyndebourne productions of Katya Kabanova, Jenufa, Queen of Spades, Lulu and Le Comte Ory. Honours: 2 Grand Prix du Disque Awards, Duruflé's Requiem recording with Philharmonic Orchestra; Gramophone of Year Award, 1987, Grand Prix du Disque, 1988, Tippett's Mask of Time; Royal Philharmonic Society/Charles Heidsieck Award, 1991; CBE, 1992; Royal Phiharmonic Society Award, Best musical opera performance of 1994, Eugene Onegin, on behalf of Glyndebourne Festival Opera, 1995; Gramophone Award for Best Video for Lulu; 1998 Award for Best Contemporary recording of Birtwistle's Mask of Orpheus; Critics Choice Award for Elgar/Payne Symphony No 3; Knight Bachelor, New Years Honours List, 1999. Address: c/o Askonas Holt Ltd, Lonsdale Chambers, 27 Chancery Lane, London WC2A 1PF, England.

DAVIS Carl, b. 1936, New York. Composer; Conductor. m. Jean Boht, 1971, 2 daughters. Education: Studied composition with Hugo Kauder and with Per Norgaard in Copenhagen. Career: Assistant Conductor, New York City Opera, 1958; Associate Conductor, Londo Philharmonic Orchestra, 1987-88; Principal Conductor, Bournemouth Pops, 1984-87; Principal Guest Conductor, Munich Symphony Orchestra, 1990-; Artistic Director and Conductor, Royal Liverpool Philharmonic Orchestra, Summer Pops, 1993-; Musical theatre: Diversions, 1958; Twists, 1962; The Projector and Cranford; Pilgrim; The Wind in the Willows, 1985; Alice in Wonderland, 1987; The Vackees, 1987. Incidental music for theatre includes: Prospect Theatre Co; The National Theatre; RSC. Ballet: A Simple Man, 1987; Lipizzaner, 1988; Liaisons Amoureuses, 1988; Madly, Badly, Sadly, Gladly; David and Goliath; Dances of Love and Death; The Picture of Dorian Grey; A Christmas Carol, 1992; The Savoy Suite, 1993; Alice in Wonderland, 1995; Aladdin, 2000. Music for TV includes: The Snow Goose, 1971; The World at War, 1972; The Naked Civil Servant, 1975; Our Mutual Friend, 1978; Hollywood, 1980; Churchill: The Wilderness Years, 1981; Silas Marner, 1985; Hotel du Lac, 1986; The Accountant, 1989; The Secret Life of Ian Fleming, 1989; Separate But Equal, 1991; The Royal Collection, 1991; A Year in Provence, 1992; Ghengis Cohn, 1993; Thatcher: The Downing Street Years, 1993; Pride and Prejudice, 1995; Oliver's Travels, 1995; Eurocinema: The Other Hollywood, 1995; Cold War, 1998-99; Goodnight, Mr Tom, 1998; The Great Gatsby, 2000; The Queen's Nose; An Angel for May. Operas for TV: The Arrangement; Who Takes You to the Party?; Orpheus in the Underground; Peace. Film

music: The Bofors Gun, 1969; The French Lieutenant's Woman, 1981; Champions, 1984; The Girl on a Swing, 1988; Rainbow, 1988; Scandal, 1988; Frankenstein Unbound, 1989; The Raft of the Medusa, 1991; The Trial, 1992; Voyage, 1993; Widow's Peak, 1994; Topsy Turvy, 2000; series of Thames Silents including Napoleon, 1980, 2000; The Wind; The Big Parade; Greed; The General; Ben Hur; Intolerance; Safety Last; The Four Horsemen of the Apocalypse, 1992; Wings, 1993; Waterloo, 1995; Phantom of the Opera, 1996. Concert works: Music for the Royal Wedding; Variations on a Bus Route; Overture on Australian Themes, Clarinet Concerto, 1984; Lines on London Symphony, 1984; Fantasy for Flute and Harpsichord, 1985; The Searle Suite for Wind Ensemble; Fanfare for Jerusalem, 1987; The Glenlivet Fireworks Music, 1988; Norwegian Brass Music, 1988; Variations for a Polish Beggar's Theme, 1988; Pigeons Progress, 1988; Jazz Age Fanfare, 1989; Everest, 1989; Landscapes, 1990; The Town Fox, 1990; A Duck's Diary, 1990; Paul McCartney's Liverpool Oratorio, 1991. Recordings: Christmas with Kiri, 1986; Beautiful Dreamer, 1986; The Silents, 1987; Ben Hur, 1989; A Simple Man, 1989; The Town Fox and Other Musical Tales, 1990; Leeds Castle Classics, Liverpool Pops at Home, 1995. Honours: Obie Prize Best Review, 1958; Emmy Award, 1972; BAFTA Awards, 1981, 1989; Chevalier des Arts et des Lettres, 1983; Honorary Fellowship, Liverpool University, 1992; Honorary DA, Bard, New York, 1994; Honorary DMus, Liverpool, 2002; Special Achievement Award for Music for Television and Film, 2003. Address: c/o Paul Wing, 16 Highland Road, Amersham, Buckinghamshire, HP7 9AW, England.

DAVIS Colin (Rex) (Sir), b. 25 September 1927, Weybridge, Surrey, England. Conductor. m. (1) April Cantelo, 1949, 1 son, 1 daughter, (2) Ashraf Naini, 1964, 3 sons, 2 daughters. Education: Royal College of Music. Career: Conductor Associate, Kalmar Orchestra and Chelsea Opera Group; Assistant Conductor, BBC Scottish Orchestra, 1957-59; Conductor, Sadler's Wells Opera House (ENO), 1959, Principal Conductor, 1960-65, Musical Director, 1961-65; Artistic Director, Bath Festival, 1969; Chief Conductor, BBC Symphony Orchestra, 1967-71, Chief Guest Conductor, 1971-75; Musical Director, Royal Opera House, Covent Garden, 1971-86; Guest Conductor, Metropolitan Opera, New York, 1969 (Peter Grimes), 1970, 1972; Principal Guest Conductor, Boston Symphony Orchestra, 1972-84; Principal Guest Conductor, London Symphony Orchestra, 1975-95; Bayreuth Festival, first British conductor, 1977 (Tannhäuser); Vienna State Opera, debut, 1986; Music Director and Principal Conductor, Bavarian State Radio Orchestra, 1983-92; Honorary Conductor, Dresden Staatskapelle, 1990-; Principal Conductor, London Symphony Orchestra, 1995; Principal Guest Conductor, New York Philharmonic Orchestra, 1998-; Has worked regularly with many orchestras in Europe and America; Season 1999 with the Choral Symphony at the London Prom concerts and Benvenuto Cellini and Les Troyens at the Barbican Hall, both with the London Symphony Orchestra. Recordings: Extensive recording with Boston Symphony Orchestra, London Symphony Orchestra, Dresden Staatskapelle, Bavarian Radio Symphony Orchestra. Honours: Officier dans L'Ordre National de Legion d'Honneur, 1999; Maximiliansorden, Bavaria, 2000; Best Classical Album and Best Opera Recording (for Les Troyens), Grammy Awards, 2002; Honorary DMus, Keele, 2002, RAM, 2002. Address: c/o Alison Glaister, 39 Huntingdon Street, London N1 1BP, England.

DAVIS Dorothy Salisbury, b. 26 April 1916, Chicago, Illinois, USA. Writer. m. Harry Davis, 25 April 1946. Education: AB, Barat College, Lake Forest, Illinois, 1938. Publications: A Gentle Murderer, 1951; Men of No Property, 1956; The Evening of the Good Samaritan, 1961; Enemy and Brother, 1967; Where the Dark Streets Go, 1969; The Little Brothers, 1974; A Death in the Life, 1976; Scarlet Night, 1980; Lullaby of Murder, 1984; Tales for a

Stormy Night, 1985; The Habit of Fear, 1987; A Gentleman Called, 1989; Old Sinners Never Die, 1991; Black Sheep, White Lambs, 1993. Contributions to: New Republic. Honours: Grand Master's Award, Mystery Writers of America, 1985; Lifetime Achievement Award, Bouchereon XX, 1989. Memberships: Mystery Writers of America; Crime Writers Association, England; Authors Guild. Address: Palisades, New York, NY 10964, USA.

DAVIS Evelyn Marguierite B. Musician; Teacher. Education: Piano and Organ study, various workshop courses, 1956-68. Appointments: Bible Baptist Church, Maplewood, Missouri, 1956-69; Pianist, Vocal Soloist, Bible Instructor, Temple Baptist Church, 1969-71; Organist; Pianist, Vocal Soloist, Bible Instructor, Youth Orchestra Arranger, Bible Baptist Church, Charles, Missouri and Music Instructor, Christian School, ibid, 1971; Composer, Hymns, Cantata; The Eyes of God; Bleed His Love. Honours: Chosen from the St Louis, Missouri Area as organist for Evangelist Doctor Jack Van Impe's Crusade March, 1976; Organist, two Evangelistic crusades for Doctor Oliver B Green. Membership: Life Fellow, International Biographical Association. Listed in: Dictionary of International Biography; International Register of Profiles; World's Who's Who of Women; International Who's Who in Music. Address: Route 2, Box 405, Rogersville, MO 65742, USA.

DAVIS Geena, b. 21 January 1957, Wareham, Massachusetts, USA. Actress. m. (1)Richard Emmolo, 1981, divorced 1983, (2) Jeff Goldblum, divorced 1990, (3) Renny Harlin, 1993, divorced, (4) Reza Jarrahy, 2001, 1 daughter, 2 sons. Education: Boston University. Appointments: Member, Mt Washington Repertory Theatre Company; Worked as model; TV appearances incude: Buffalo Bill, 1983; Sara, 1985; The Hit List; Family Ties; Remington Steele; Secret Weapons, TV film; The Geena Davis Show, 2000. Films include: Tootsie, 1982; Fletch, 1984; Transylvania 6-5000, 1985; The Fly, 1986; The Accidental Tourist; Earth Girls Are Easy, 1989; Quick Change; The Grifters; Thelma and Louise; A League of Their Own; Hero; Angie; Speechless (also producer); Cutthroat Island; The Long Kiss Goodnight, 1996; Stuart Little, 1999; Stuart Little 2, 2002. Honours: Academy Award, Best Supporting Actress, 1989. Address: C/o ICM, 8942 Wilshire Boulevard, Beverly Hills, CA 90211, USA.

DAVIS Muller, b. 23 April 1935, Chicago, Illinois, USA. Attorney. m. (1) Jane Stauss, 28 December 1963, divorced 16 July 1998, 2 sons, 1 daughter, (2) Lynn Straus, 23 January 1999. Education: Honours, Phillips Exeter Academy, 1953; BA, magna cum laude, Yale University, 1957; JD, Harvard Law School, 1960. Appointments: Associate, Jenner & Block, 1960-67; Partner, Davis, Friedman, Zavett, Kane, MacRae, Marcus & Rubens 1967-. Publications: Author, The Illinois Practice Of Family Law, 1995, 1996-97, 1998-1999, with Jody Meyer Yazici, 2000-2001, 2003-2004; Law Review Articles; Co-author: The Parental Couple In A Successful Divorce In Parenthood, Psychodynamic Perspective, 1984; Contributor, Marriage, Health and Professions, 2002; Editorial Board, Equitable Distribution Journal; Co-Chair Committee to Study and Recommend a Comprehensive Rules Design, Domestic Relations Division, Circuit Court of Cook County, Illinois, 2003-. Memberships: American Bar Foundation; American Academy of Matrimonial Lawyers; American Illinois Chicago Federal Bar Association; Past President, Infant Welfare Society; Chairman, Legal Aid Society, 1997-99; Lawyers Club of Chicago; Chicago Club; Tavern Club; Lake Shore Country Club. Address: 140 S Dearborn St, Suite 1600, Chicago, IL 60603, USA.

DAVIS Steve, b. 22 August 1957, Plumstead, London, England. Snooker Player. m. Judith Lyn Greig, 1990, 2 sons. Appointments: Professional snooker player, 1978; Has won 73 titles; In 99 tournament finals, as at 2002; Major titles include: UK Professional

Champion, 1980, 1981, 1984, 1985, 1986, 1987; Masters Champion, 1981, 1982, 1988, 1997; International Champion, 1981, 1983, 1984; World Professional Champion, 1981, 1983, 1984, 1987, 1988, 1989; Winner, Asian Open, 1992, European Open, 1993; Welsh Open, 1994; Member, Board World Professional Billiards and Snooker Association, 1993-. Honours: BBC Sports Personality of Year, 1989; BBC TV Snooker Personality of Year, 1997. Publications: Steve Davis, World Champion, 1981; Frame and Fortune, 1982; Successful, 1982; How to Be Really Interesting, 1988; Steve Davis Plays Chess, 1996. Address: 10 Western Road, Romford, Essex, England.

DAVISON Geoffrey Joseph, b. 10 August 1927, Newcastle-upon-Tyne, England. Writer. m. Marlene Margaret Wilson, 15 September 1956, 2 sons. Education: TD; FRICS. Publications: The Spy Who Swapped Shoes, 1967; Nest of Spies, 1968; The Chessboard Spies, 1969; The Fallen Eagles, 1970; The Honorable Assassins, 1971; Spy Puppets, 1973; The Berlin Spy Trap, 1974; No Names on Their Graves, 1978; The Bloody Legionnaires, 1981; The Last Waltz (Vienna May 1945), 2001; The Colombian Contract, 2001. Membership: Pen and Palette Club. Address: 95 Cheviot View, Ponteland, Newcastle-upon-Tyne NE20 9BH, England.

DAVYDOV Ariel, b. 6 July 1960, Kazakhstan. Composer; Musicologist. m. Elena Leis, 2 daughters. Education: MA in Musicology, Tadjik State Institute of Arts, 1979-84; MA in Composition, 1988-92, Diploma in Composition, Assistanture, 1992-94, St Petersburg State Conservatory. Appointments: Teacher, Dushanbe Musical College, Tadjikistan, 1986-88; Lecturer, St Petersburg State Conservatory, 1992-96; Self-employed Composer, Tel Aviv, Israel, 1996-99; Editor, Israel Publishing House of ICL, Israel, 1999-. Publications: Works published by Israeli Music Center; Symphony No 1, IMC-1185; Raghari, poem for strings, percussion and cembalo, IMC-700; Concerto for double bass and orchestra, IMC-795. Honours: Prime Minister's Prize of Israel, 2003. Memberships: Russian Composers' League, 1994-; Israeli Composers' League, 1997-. Address: PO Box 4795, Beer-Sheva, 84144 Israel. E-mail: adavydov@pochtamt.ru

DAWE (Donald) Bruce, b. 15 February 1930, Fitzroy, Victoria, Australia. Associate Professor; Poet; Writer. m. (1) Gloria Desley Blain, 27 January 1964, deceased 30 December 1997, 2 sons, 2 daughters, (2) Ann Elizabeth Qualtiough, 9 October 1999. Education: BA, 1969, MLitt, 1973, MA, 1975, PhD, 1980, University of Queensland; Hon. DLitt (USQ), 1995; Hon.DLitt (UNSW), 1997. Appointments: Lecturer, 1971-78, Senior Lecturer, 1978-83, DDIAE; Writer-in-Residence, University of Queensland, 1984; Senior Lecturer, 1985-90, Associate Professor, 1990-93, School of Arts, Darling Heights, Toowoomba. Publications: No Fixed Address, 1962; A Need of Similar Name, 1964; Beyond the Subdivisions, 1968; An Eye for a Tooth, 1969; Heat-Wave, 1970; Condolences of the Season: Selected Poems, 1971; Just a Dugong at Twilight, 1974; Sometimes Gladness: Collected Poems, 1978, 5th edition, 1993; Over Here Harv! and Other Stories, 1983; Towards Sunrise, 1986; This Side of Silence, 1990; Bruce Dawe: Essays and Opinions, 1990; Mortal Instruments: Poems 1990-1995, 1995; A Poets' People, 1999. Contributions to: Various periodicals. Honours: Myer Poetry Prizes, 1966, 1969; Ampol Arts Award for Creative Literature, 1967; Dame Mary Gilmore Medal, Australian Literary Society, 1973; Braille Book of the Year, 1978; Grace Leven Prize for Poetry, 1978; Patrick White Literary Award, 1980; Christopher Brennan Award, 1984; Philip Hodgins Medal for Literary Excellence, 1997; Order of Australia, 1992; Distinguished Alumni Award, UNE, 1996; Australian Arts Council Emeritus Writers Award, 2000. Memberships: Australian Association for Teaching English, honorary life member; Centre

Dictionary of International Biography

for Australian Studies in Literature; Victorian Association for Teaching of English, honorary life member. Address: c/o Pearson Education, 95 Coventry St, South Melbourne, Australia, 3205.

DAWIDEK Gervase Milne, b. 26 December 1955. Ophthalmic Surgeon. m. Sarah Sweetnam, 1 son, 1 daughter. Education: BA, Clare College, Cambridge, 1974-77; St Thomas's Hospital, 1977-80; MB, 1981. Appointments: Senior Registrar in Ophthalmology, Birmingham and Midland Eye Hospital, 1994-95; Consultant Ophthalmic Surgeon, Wolverhampton and Midland Counties Eye Infirmary, 1995-98; Consultant Ophthalmic Surgeon, Harold Wood Hospital, Essex, 1998-. Honours: Fellow, Royal College of Surgeons of England, 1998; Fellow Royal College of Physicians of London, 2003. Memberships: Fellow, Royal College of Ophthalmologists, 1989; Fellow, Royal Society of Medicine. Address: 2 Hill Road, Theydon Bois, Epping, Essex CM16 7LX, England.

DAWIDS Richard Greene, b. 5 January 1941, Copenhagen, Denmark. Business Executive. Education: Davidson College, 1960-61; University of Grenoble, France, 1966-67; University of Copenhagen, 1968. Appointments: W Copenhagen Handelbank, 1968-85; Tokyo, 1985-89; Vice-President, Surongo SA, Brussels, 1987-90; President, 1991-2003; Board of Directors: Cie Bois Sauvage, Brussels; Enterprises et Chemins de Fer en Chine, Brussels; Berenberg Bank, Hamburg, Germany. Address: Groupe Surongo SA, 16-17 Rue du Bois Sauvage, 1000 Brussels, Belgium.

DAWKINS (Clinton) Richard, b. 26 March 1941, Nairobi, Kenya. Zoologist; Professor of the Public Understanding of Science. m. (1) Marian Stamp, 19 August 1967, divorced 1984, (2) Eve Barham, 1 June 1984, 1 daughter. Education: BA, 1962, MA, 1966, DPhil, 1966, Balliol College, Oxford. Appointments: Assistant Professor of Zoology, University of California at Berkeley, 1967-69; Fellow, New College, Oxford, 1970-; Lecturer, 1970-89, Reader in Zoology, 1989-95, Charles Simonyi Reader in the Public Understanding of Science, 1995-96, Professor of the Public Understanding of Science, 1996-, Oxford University; Editor, Animal Behaviour, 1974-78, Oxford Surveys in Evolutionary Biology, 1983-86; Gifford Lecturer, University of Glasgow, 1988; Sidgwick Memorial Lecturer, Newnham College, Cambridge, 1988; Kovler Visiting Fellow, University of Chicago, 1990; Nelson Lecturer, University of California at Davis, 1990. Publications: The Selfish Gene, 1976, 2nd edition, 1989; The Extended Phenotype, 1982; The Blind Watchmaker, 1986; River Out of Eden, 1995; Climbing Mount Improbable, 1996; Unweaving the Rainbow, 1998; A Devil's Chaplain, essays, 2003. Contributions to: Scholarly journals. Honours: Royal Society of Literature Prize, 1987; Los Angeles Times Literature Prize, 1987; Honorary Fellow, Regent's College, London, 1988; Silver Medal, Zoological Society, 1989; Michael Faraday Award, Royal Society, 1990; Nakayama Prize, Nakayama Foundation for Human Sciences, 1994; Honorary DLitt, St Andrews University, 1995; Honorary DLitt, Canberra, 1996; International Cosmos Prize, 1997; Kistler Prize, 2001. Address: c/o Oxford University Museum, Parks Road, Oxford, OX1 3PW, England.

DAWSON Ted Murray, b. 19 April 1959, Idaho Falls, Idaho, USA. Neuroscientist; Neurologist. m. Valina Lynn. Education: BS, Montana State University, 1977-81; MD, PhD, University of Utah School of Medicine, 1981-86; Medicine Internship, University of Utah Affiliated Hospitals, 1986-87; Neurology Residency, Hospital of the University of Pennsylvania, 1987-90; Neuroscience, Postdoctoral Fellowship, 1990-92, Movement Disorder Fellowship, 1991-92, The Johns Hopkins School of Medicine. Appointments: Teaching and Research Assistant, Department of Pharmacology, University of Utah School of Medicine, 1984-86;

Assistant Instructor, 1989, Instructor, 1989-90, Department of Neurology, Hospital of the University of Pennsylvania; Postdoctoral Fellow, 1990-92, Assistant Professor, 1993-94, Department of Neuroscience, Senior Clinical Fellow, Department of Neurology, 1991-92, Instructor, 1992-93, Departments of Neuroscience and Neurology, Assistant Professor, 1994-96, Associate Professor, 1996-2000, Professor, 2000-, Departments of Neuroscience and Neurology and Graduate Program in Cellular and Molecular Medicine, Co-Director, Parkinson's Disease Center, Department of Neurology, 1996-2002, Director, Morris K Udall Parkinson's Disease Research Center of Excellence, 1998-, Director, Neuroregeneration and Repair Program, Institute for Cell Engineering, 2000-, Director, Parkinson's Disease and Movement Disorder Center, Department of Neurology, 2002-, The Johns Hopkins University School of Medicine, Baltimore. Publications: Over 250 manuscripts, reviews and book chapters in prestigious scientific journals. Honours: Numerous awards including: International Life Sciences Institute Award, 1994-97; The Ralph Rossen Memorial Lecture, 1997; The Paul Stark Lecture, University of Rochester, 1998; The Klayman Memorial Lecture, Washington University at St Louis, 1999; ISI Highly Cited Researcher Award, 2000; Santiago Grisolla Chair and Medal, 2001. Memberships: American Academy of Neurology; American Federation for Medical Research; American Medical Association; American Neurological Association; American Society for the Advancement of Science; American Society for Microbiology; American Society for Neurochemistry; Molecular Medicine Society; Movement Disorder Society; New York Academy of Sciences; Nitric Oxide Society; Sigma Alpha Epsilon; Society for Neuroscience. Address: Department of Neurology, The Johns Hopkins University School of Medicine, 600 North Wolfe Street, Carnegie 214, Baltimore, MD 21287, USA. E-mail: tdawson@jhmi.edu

DAY Doris, b. 3 April 1924, Cincinnati, Ohio, USA. Singer; Actress. m. (1) Al Jorden, March 1941, divorced 1943, 1 son, (2) George Weilder divorced 1949, (3) Marty Melcher, 3 April 1951, deceased 1968. Career: Former dancer, Cincinnati; Singer, shows including: Karlin's Karnival, WCPO-Radio; Bob Hope NBC Radio Show, 1948-50; Doris Day CBS Show, 1952-53; Solo recording artist, 1950-; Actress, numerous films including: Tea For Two, 1950; Lullaby Of Broadway, 1951; April In Paris, 1952; Pajama Game, 1957; Teacher's Pet, 1958; Pillow Talk, 1959; Midnight Lace, 1960; Jumbo, 1962; That Touch Of Mink, 1962; The Thrill Of It All, 1963; Send Me No Flowers, 1964; Do Not Disturb, 1965; The Glass Bottom Boat, 1966; Caprice, 1967; The Ballad Of Josie, 1968; Where Were You When The Lights Went Out, 1968; Own television series, The Doris Day Show, 1970-73; Doris Day And Friends, 1985-86; Doris Day's Best, 1985-86; TV special, The Pet Set, 1972. Honours: Winner (with Jerry Doherty), Best Dance Team, Cincinnati; Laurel Award, Leading New Female Personality In Motion Picture Industry, 1950; Top audience attractor, 1962; American Comedy Lifetime Achievement Award, 1991. Address: c/o Doris Day Animal League, 227 Massachusetts Avenue NE, Washington, DC 20002, USA.

DAY Marian Theresa, b. 15 February 1947, Bowman, South Carolina, USA. Communications Executive. m. Bobby B Nichols, 1 daughter. Education: BA, summa cum laude, South Carolina State College, 1968; Visiting Undergraduate Scholar, Morgan State University, 1966-67; MA, Atlanta University, 1971; PhD, University of South Carolina, 1977; Southeastern Minority Newspaper Workshop, University of South Carolina, 1988. Appointments: Associate Professor of English, South Carolina State College, 1969-88; Copy Editor, Assistant Slot Editor, The State Newspaper, Columbia, 1988-90; Education Programme Consultant, Education Project Director, State Department of

Dictionary of International Biography

Education, Columbia, Served on Committees and Task Forces including: University of South Carolina's Multicultural Forum, The State Department of Education's Multicultural/Gender Equity Task Force, The US Department of Education's Civil Rights Compliance MOA Task Force, 1990-97; Certified Mediator and Assessor, Workshop Presenter, Motivational Speaker, 1991-; Special Assistant to the Chief Executive Officer, Nicwild Communications Inc, Barnwell, South Carolina, 1997-. Publications: A Tribute to the Rev. Dr. Martin Luther King, Jr: I've Been to the Mountaintop, 1968; A study of spelling abilities and vocabulary comprehension of freshman English students and the improving of these abilities and this comprehension by means of incidental reading of passages as compared to memorizing words and word meanings, 1977; On the Outside Looking In, 1991; Sentencing Black Males under 35 to Death, 1991. Honours include: Governor Russell Award for Excellence in English; Award for Highest Initiation Average in the South Atlantic Region; Recipient, Woodrow Wilson National Fellowship Honourable Mention; National Foundation for Black Americans Fellowship; Listed in Who's Who publications and biographical dictionaries. Memberships: National Association of Female Executives; Georgia Association of Broadcasters; Alpha Kappa Mu; Phi Delta Kappa; Alpha Kappa Alpha; Kappa Delta Pi; Sigma Tau Delta. Address: 375 Woodlawn Drive, Orangeburg, SC 29115, USA. E-mail: wiizard@sc.rr.com

DAY-LEWIS Daniel, b. 20 April, London, England. Actor. m. Rebecca Miller, 1996; 2 sons (1 by Isabelle Adjani). Education: Bristol Old Vic Theatre School. Career: Plays: Class Enemy, Funny Peculiar, Bristol Old Vic; Look Back in Anger, Dracula, Little Theatre, Bristol and Half Moon Theatre, London; Another Country, Queen's Theatre; Futurists, National Theatre; Romeo, Thisbe, Royal Shakespeare Company Hamlet, 1989; TV: A Frost in May; How Many Miles to Babylon?; My Brother Jonathan; Insurance Man; Films: My Beautiful Launderette; A Room with a View; Stars and Bars; The Unbearable Lightness of Being; My Left Foot, 1989; The Last of the Mohicans, 1991; In the Name of the Father, 1993; The Age of Innocence, 1992; The Crucible, 1995; The Boxer, 1997; Gangs of New York, 2002. Honours: Academy Award for Best Actor, BAFTA Award, Best Actor, (for My Left Foot) 1989; Screen Actors' Guild Award for Best Actor, 2003; BAFTA Award for Best Actor in a Leading Role, 2003. Address: c/o Julian Belfrage Associates, 46 Albemarle Street, London W1X 4PP, England.

DAYES Lloyd A, Neurosurgeon. Education: BA, Biology, Pacific Union College, Napa, California, 1955; MD, Loma Linda University School of Medicine, Los Angeles, California, 1955; Jessie Noyes Foundation Scholarship, New York, 1955-59; Rotating Internship, 1959-60, Residency General Surgery, 1960-61, Montreal General Hospital, Montreal, Canada; Neuropathology Fellow, Montreal Neurological Institute, 1961-65; Certified, American Board of Neurological Surgery, 1967; Postgraduate Education, Microneurosurgery, Mt Sinai Medical Center, New York, 1985; Postgraduate Education, Oxford University, Oxford England, 1993. Appointments: Instructor, 1965-66, Assistant Professor, 1966-78, Associate Professor, 1978-88, Professor of Neurosurgery, 1988-, Loma Linda University, Loma Linda, California, USA; Attending Neurosurgeon: Loma Linda University Medical Center, 1965-, Riverside General Hospital, Riverside, California, 1965-, Redlands Community Hospital, Redlands, California, 1972-, Loma Linda Community Hospital, Loma Linda, California, 1978-. Publications: 61 articles in medical journals and book chapters as co-author include most recently: Surgical Techniques for Arteriovenous Malformations in Functional Areas, Focused on Superior Temporal Gyrus, 1998; Total Blood Flow to Arteriovenous Malformations, 1999; Early Antiepileptic Drug Reduction following Anterior Temporal Lobectomy; Numerous

papers presented at conferences and symposia. Memberships include: Alpha Omega Alpha Honor Medical Society; Sigma Xi; California Medical Association; American Association of Neurological Surgeons; Society of Critical Care Medicine; American Chemical Society; American Association for the Advancement of Science; American Society of Law and Medicine; North American Skull Base Society; Fellow: International College of Angiology, International College of Surgeons, American College of Angiology, American College of Surgeons, American Academy of Neurological and Orthopedic Surgeons, Royal Society of Medicine. Address: Division of Neurosurgery, Loma Linda University, School of Medicine, Loma Linda, CA 92354, USA.

DE ARAUGO Sarah Therese, (Tess De Araugo), b. 26 May 1930, Lismore, Victoria, Australia. Writer. m. Maurice De Araugo, 11 April 1950, 2 sons, 2 daughters. Education: Notre Dame de Sion College, Warragal, Victoria. Publications: You Are What You Make Yourself To Be, 1980, revised edition, 1989; The Kurnai of Gippsland, 1985; Boonorong on the Mornington Peninsula, 1993; Dear Fethers – An Historical Saga 1066-1990s, 2000. Contributions to: Encyclopaedias and periodicals. Honours: New South Wales Premier's Award for Australian Literature, 1985; Banjo Award, Australian Literature, National Book Council, 1985; Fellowship, 1987, Writer's Grant, 1989, Australian Literature Board; Short Story Award, PEN International, Australia, 1991. Memberships: Australian Society of Authors; Fellowship of Australian Writers; Royal Historical Society of Victoria; Women Writers of Australia; Nepean Historical Society. Address: 19 Grenville Grove, Rosebud West, Victoria 3940, Australia.

DE BONO Edward (Francis Publius Charles), b. 19 May 1933, Malta. Author; Physician; Inventor; Lecturer. m. Josephine Hall-White, 1971, 2 sons. Education: St Edward's College, Malta; BSc, 1953, MD, 1955, Royal University of Malta; MA, 1957, DPhil, 1961, Oxford University; PhD, Cambridge University, 1963. Appointments: Research Assistant, 1957-60, Lecturer, 1960-61, Oxford University; Assistant Director of Research, 1963-76, Lecturer in Medicine, 1976-83, Cambridge University; Honorary Director and Founding Member, Cognitive Research Trust, 1971-; Secretary-General, Supranational Independent Thinking Organisation, 1983-; Lecturer. Publications: The Use of Lateral Thinking, 1967; The Five-Day Course in Thinking, 1967; The Mechanism of Mind, 1969; Lateral Thinking: A Textbook of Creativity, 1970; The Dog Exercising Machine, 1970; Lateral Thinking for Management: A Handbook of Creativity, 1971; Practical Thinking: Four Ways to Be Right, Five Ways to Be Wrong, 1971; Children Solve Problems, 1972; PO: A Device for Successful Thinking, 1972; Think Tank, 1973; Eureka: A History of Inventions (editor), 1974; Teaching Thinking, 1976; The Greatest Thinkers, 1976; Wordpower: An Illustrated Dictionary of Vital Words, 1977; Opportunities: A Handbook of Business Opportunity Search, 1978; The Happiness Purpose, 1978; Future Positive, 1979; Atlas of Management Thinking, 1981; De Bono's Thinking Course, 1982; Learn to Think, 1982; Tactics: The Art and Science of Success, 1984; Conflicts: A Better Way to Resolve Them, 1985; Six Thinking Hats: An Essential Approach to Business Management from the Creator of Lateral Thinking, 1985; CoRT Thinking Program: CoRT 1-Breadth, 1987; Letters to Thinkers: Further Thoughts on Lateral Thinking, 1987; Masterthinker II: Six Thinking Hats, 1988; Masterthinker, 1990; Masterthinker's Handbook, 1990; Thinking Skills for Success, 1990; I Am Right, You Are Wrong: From This to the New Renaissance: From Rock Logic to Water Logic, 1990; Handbook for the Positive Revolution, 1991; Six Action Shoes, 1991; Serious Creativity: Using the Power of Lateral Thinking to Create New Ideas, 1992; Surpetition: Creating Value Monopolies When Everyone Else is Merely Competing, 1992; Teach Your Child How to Think, 1993; Water Logic, 1993;

Dictionary of International Biography

Parallel Thinking, 1994; Teach Yourself to Think, 1995; Mind Pack, 1995; Edward do Bono's Textbook of Wisdom, 1996; How to be More Interesting, 1997; Simplicity, 1998; New Thinking for the New Millennium, 1999; Why I Want to be King of Australia, 1999; The Book of Wisdom, 2000; The de Bono Code, 2000; Contributions to: Television series, professional journals, and periodicals. Honour: Rhodes Scholar; Honorary Registrar, St Thomas' Hospital Medical School, Harvard Medical School. Membership: Medical Research Society. Address: 12 Albany, Piccadilly, London W1V 9RR, England.

DE BONT Jan, b. 22 October 1943, Netherlands. Cinematographer and Director. Education: Amsterdam Film Academy. Appointments: Cinematographer: Turkish Delight; Keetje Tippel; Max Heulaar; Soldier of Orange; Private Lessons (American debut), 1981; Roar; I'm Dancing as Fast As I Can; Cujo; All The Right Moves; Bad Manners; The Fourth Man; Mischief; The Jewel of the Nile; Flesh and Blood; The Clan of the Cave Bear; Ruthless People; Who's That Girl; Leonard Part 6; Die Hard, Bert Rigby - You're A Fool; Black Rain; The Hunt for Red October; Flatliners; Shining Through; Basic Instinct; Lethal Weapon 3, 1992; TV Photography: The Ray Mancini Story; Split Personality (episode of Tales From the Crypt); Director, films: Speed (debut), 1994; Twister; Speed 2: Cruise Control (also screenplay and story); The Haunting. Address: C/o David Gersh, The Gersh Agency, 232 North Canon Drive, Beverly Hills, CA 90210, USA.

DE BROMHEAD Jerome, b. 2 December 1945, Waterford, Ireland. Composer. m. 3 sons. Education: MA, Trinity College, Dublin; Studied with A J Potter and James Wilson, RIAM Dublin; Further studies under Seoirse Bodley and Franco Donatoni. Career: Music Producer, radio, 1980-94. Compositions: Symphony No 1, 1985; Symphony No 2, 1994; Concerto for guitar and strings, 1991; Harpsichord work Flux, performed ISCM, 1987. Recording: Gemini for solo guitar, CD; Publication: Flux pub Tonos of Darmstadt. Honours: Elected to Aosdana, 1986; Represented Ireland at UNESCO International Rostrum several times; Featured composer mostly modern festival, 1993. Memberships: Aosdana, Irish Academy of Creative Artists; Association of Irish Composers. Address: Martello Cottage, Strand Road, Killiney, Co Dublin, Ireland.

DE BURGH Chris (Christopher Davison), b. 15 October 1948, Argentina. Singer; Songwriter. m. Diane Patricia Morley, 2 sons, 1 daughter. Education: Trinity College, Dublin. Career: Irish tour with Horslips, 1973; Solo artiste, 1974-; Album sales, 40 million to date; Sell-out concerts world-wide; Performances include: Carol Aid, London, 1985; The Simple Truth, benefit concert for Kurdish refugees, Wembley, 1991; Royal Albert Hall, London. Recordings: Singles include: Flying, 1975; Patricia The Stripper, 1976; A Spaceman Came Travelling, 1976; Don't Pay The Ferryman, 1982; High On Emotion, 1984; Lady In Red (Number 1, UK), 1984; Love Is My Decision, theme from film Arthur 2, 1988; Missing You, 1988; Albums: Far Beyond These Castle Walls, 1975; Spanish Train And Other Stories, 1975; At The End Of A Perfect Day, 1977; Crusader, 1979; Eastern Wind, 1980; Best Moves, 1981; The Getaway, 1982; Man On The Line, 1984; The Very Best Of Chris De Burgh, 1985; Into The Light, 1986; Flying Colours, 1988; From A Spark To A Flame - The Very Best Of Chris De Burgh, 1989; High On Emotion - Live From Dublin, 1990; Power Of Ten, 1992; This Way Up, 1994; Beautiful Dreams, 1995; The Love Songs, 1997; Quiet Revolution, 1999; Notes from Planet Earth – The Ultimate Collection, 2001; Timing is Everything, 2002. Honours: ASCAP Award, The Lady In Red, 1985, 1987, 1988, 1990, 1991, 1997; IRMA Awards, Ireland, 1985-90; Beroliner

Award, Germany; BAMBI Award, Germany; Midem Trophy, France. Current Management: Kenny Thomson, 754 Fulham Road, London SW6 5SH, England.

DE CRESPIGNY (Richard) Rafe (Champion), b. 16 March 1936, Adelaide, South Australia, Australia. m. Christa Charlotte Boltz, 1 son, 1 daughter. Education: BA, 1957, MA, 1961, Cambridge University; BA, University of Melbourne, 1961; BA, 1962, MA, 1964, PhD, 1968, Australian National University. Appointments: Lecturer, 1965-70, Senior Lecturer, 1970-73, Secretary-General, 28th International Congress of Orientalists, 1971, Reader in Chinese, 1973-2001, Dean of Asian Studies, 1979-1982, Australian National University, Canberra; Master, University House, 1991-2001; Adjunct Professor of Asian Studies, 1999-. Publications: The Biography of Sun Chien, 1966; Official Titles of the Former Han Dynasty (with H H Dubs), 1967; The Last of the Han, 1969; The Records of the Three Kingdoms, 1970; China: The Land and Its People, 1971; China This Century: A History of Modern China, 1975, 2nd edition, 1992; Portents of Protest, 1976; Northern Frontier, 1984; Emperor Huan and Emperor Ling, 1989; Generals of the South, 1990; To Establish Peace, 1996. Membership: Australian Academy of the Humanities, fellow; Chinese Studies, Association of Australia, President, 1999-2001. Address: Faculty of Asian Studies, Australian National University, Canberra 0200, Australia.

DE DUVE Christian René, b. 2 October 1917, Thames Ditton, Surrey, England (Belgian Citizen). Biochemist. m. Janine Herman, 1943, 1 son. Education: Graduated in Medicine, University of Louvain, Belgium, 1941. Appointments: Professor of Physiological Chemistry, 1947-85, Emeritus Professor, 1985-, University of Louvain Medical School, Belgium; Professor of Biochemical Cytology, 1962-88, Emeritus Professor, 1988-, Rockefeller University, New York City. Honours: Prix des Alumni, 1949; Prix Pfizer, 1957; Prix Francqui, 1960; Prix Quinquennal Belge des Sciences Médicales, 1967; Gairdner Foundation International Award of Merit, Canada, 1967; Dr H P Heineken Prijs, Netherlands, 1973; Nobel Prize for Medicine, 1974; Honorary DSc, Keele University, 1981; Doctor honoris causa, Rockefeller University, 1997; Numerous other honorary degrees. Memberships: Royal Academy of Medicine, Belgium; Royal Academy of Belgium; American Chemical Society, Biochemical Society; American Society of Biological Chemistry; Pontifical Academy of Sciences; American Society of Cell Biology; Deutsche Akademie der Naturforschung, Leopoldina; Koninklijke Akademie voor Geneeskunde van België; American Academy of Arts and Sciences; Royal Society, London; Royal Society of Canada. Address: c/o Rockefeller University, 1230 York Avenue, New York, NY 10021, USA.

DE FEO Lucio, b. 12 November 1934, Avellino, Italy. Consultant. m. Colarusso Giovanna, 2 daughters. Education: Degree in Pharmachemistry. Appointments: Chemistry Assistant; Marketing Manager, CERBA Pharmaceuticals SpA; President, Technical Manager, Med-I-Trade and General Medical Supply. Publications: Author of monographs on biological and microbiological aspects in medicine. Memberships: Italian Microbiologists Association. Address: Rampa S Maria Delle Grazie 16, 83100 Avellino, Italy.

DE FINIS Lia (Rosalia Carmela), Head Teacher. Education: Degree in Classic Arts, University of Padua, 1950. Appointments: Full Teacher of Classic Arts in secondary schools, 1960-; Head-Mistress, Secondary School "G Prati", Trento, Italy, 1972-98; Director of the Review, Trentino's Studies of Historical Sciences, 1989-. Publications: Editor, 12 volumes concerning Acts of Cultural Conventions; 12 books and articles and some notes about historical-didactic-pedagogical subjects. Honours: Commendatore of the

Italian Republic, 1996; Grand' Ufficiale of the Italian Republic, 1998; Decorated with the Trento Town Seal – S Venceslao's Eagle, 1998. Memberships: Chairwoman, Classic Culture Italian Association, Trento's Delegation, 1975; Agiati's Academy of Sciences, Literature and Arts, 1975-; Chairwoman, Cultural Association A Rosmini, 1989-; Correspondent Member, Veneto's Archives – Deputation of Venetian Land's History; Accesi's Academy, Trento; Co-ordinator, Head Masters of the Superior Secondary Schools, -1988; Government Representative, Trento's University Board, 1985; Representative of the Province of Trento, S Chiara's Cultural Centre Board; Representative of the Province of Trento, Provincial Committee on Equal Opportunities, 1996-99; Chairwoman, Soroptimist International Club, 1989-91. Address: Via G A Prato, 24, 1-38100 Trento, Italy.

DE HAVILLAND Olivia Mary, b. 1 July 1916, Tokyo, Japan. Actress. m. (1) Marcus Aurelius Goodrich, 1 sons, (2) Pierre Paul Galante, 1955, divorced 1979, 1 daughter. Appointments: Actress, films including: Captain Blood, 1935; Anthony Adverse, 1936; The Adventures of Robin Hood, 1938; Gone With The Wind, 1939; Hold Back the Dawn, 1941; Princess O'Rourke, 1942; To Each His Own (Academy Award), 1946; The Dark Mirror, 1946; The Snake Pit, 1947; The Heiress (Academy Award), 1949; My Cousin Rachel, 1952; Not as a Stranger, 1954; The Proud Rebel, 1957; The Light in the Piazza, 1961; Lady in a Cage, 1963; Hush Hush Sweet Charlotte, 1964; The Adventurers, 1968; Airport '77, 1976; The Swarm, 1978; The Fifth Musketeer; Plays: Romeo and Juliet, 1951; Candida, 1951-52; A Gift of Time, 1962; TV: Noon Wine, 1966; Screaming Women, 1972; Roots, The Next Generations, 1979; Murder is Easy, 1981; Charles and Diana: A Royal Romance, 1982; North and South II, 1986; Anastasia (Golden Globe award), 1986; The Woman He Loved, 1987. Publications: Every Frenchman Has One, 1962; Contributor, Mother and Child, 1975. Honours: Numerous awards include: Academy awards, 1946, 1949; New York Critics Award, 1948, 1949; Look Magazine Award, 1941, 1946, 1949; Venice Film Festival Award, 1948; Filmex Tribute, 1978; American Academy of Achievement Award, 1978; American Exemplar Medal, 1980; Golden Globe, 1988; DRhc, American University of Paris, 1994. Address: BP 156-16, 75764 Paris, Cedex 16 France.

DE KLERK Frederik Willem, b. 18 March 1936, Johannesburg, South Africa. Politician. m. (1) Marike Willemse, 1959, 2 sons, 1 daughter, (2) Elita Georgiadis, 1998. Education: Potchefstrom University. Appointments: In law practice, 1961-72; Member, House of Assembly, 1972; Information Officer, National Party, Transvaal, 1975; Minister, Posts, Telecommunications and Social Welfare and Pensions, 1978; Minister, Posts, Telecommunications and Sport and Recreation, 1978-79; Minister, Mines, Energy and Environmental Planning, 1979-80; Mineral and Energy Affairs, 1980-82; Internal Affairs, 1982-85; National Education and Planning, 1984-89; Acting State President South Africa, August-September, 1989; State President, South Africa, 1989-94; Executive Deputy President, Government of National Party, 1994-96; Leader of Official Opposition, 1996-97; Former, Chairman, Cabinet and Commander-in-Chief of the Armed Forces; Former, Chairman, Council of Ministers. Publications: The Last Trek: A New Beginning (autobiography), 1999; Various articles and brochures for the National Party Information Service. Honours: Joint winner, Houphouet Boigny Prize (UNESCO), 1991; Asturias Prize, 1992; Liberty Medal (SA), 1993; Shared Nobel Prize for Peace with Nelson Mandela, 1993. Address: 7 Eaton Square, London, SW1, England.

DE LA BILLIÈRE Peter (Sir), b. 29 April 1934, Plymouth, Devon. Retired Army Officer. m. Bridget Constance Muriel Goode, 1965, 1 son, 2 daughters. Education: Royal College of Defence Studies, Staff College. Appointments: Joined King's Shropshire Light Infantry, 1952; Commissioned Durham Light Infantry; Served Japan, Korea, Malaya, Jordan, Borneo, Egypt, Aden, Gulf States, Sudan, Oman, Falklands; Commanding Officer 22 Special Air Service Regiment (SAS), 1972-74; General Staff Officer 1 (Directing Staff) Staff College, 1974-77; Commander, British Army Training Team, Sudan, 1977-78; Director, SAS, Commander, SAS Group, 1978-83; Commander, British Forces, Falklands and Military Commissioner, 1984-85; General Officer Commanding, Wales, 1985-87; General Officer Commanding South East District and Permanent Peace Time Commander, Joint Forces Operations Staff, 1987-90; Commander, British Forces, Middle East, 1990-91; Adviser to HM Government on Middle East Affairs; Current appointments: Director, Robert Fleming Holdings Ltd, 1977-99; Chairman, FARM Africa; Chairman, Meadowland Meats Ltd, 1994-2002; President, Army Cadet Force, 1992-99. Publications: Storm Command: A Personal Story, 1992; Looking For Trouble (autobiography), 1994. Honours include: Several honorary doctorates; Order of Bahrain, 1st class, 1991; Chief Commander, Legion of Merit, USA, 1992; Meritorious Service Cross, Canada, 1992; Order of Abdul Aziz, 2nd class, Saudi Arabia, 1992; Kuwait Decoration, 1st class, 1992; Qatar Sash of Merit, 1992; KCB; KBE; DSO; MC and Bar; MSC DL. Address: c/o Naval and Military Club, 4 St James's Square, London SW1Y 4JU, England.

DE LA HOUSSAYE Brette Angelo Pepe, b. 20 August 1960, Los Angeles, California, USA. Researcher; Engineer. Education: BSEET, DeVry Institute, City of Industry, California, 1989. Appointments: Engineer Researcher, private practice, 1990-to present; Discovered alternate method for calculating energy using Newton's Second Law of Motion and Work Energy Theorem, applications also include integral calculus. Memberships: IEEE; American Physical Society; National Trust for Historic Preservation; American Museum of Natural History. Address: 7719 Goodland Ave, North Hollywood, CA 91605, USA.

DE LA MAZA Luis M, b. 12 August 1943, Ribadesella, Spain. Professor. m. Maria, 1 son, 1 daughter. Education: MD, Facultad de Medicina, Madrid, Spain, 1966; PhD, University of Minnesota, USA, 1974. Appointments: Assistant Professor, University of Minnesota, USA, 1974-75; Visiting Associate, National Institutes of Health, USA, 1975-79; Professor, Department of Pathology, University of California, Irvine, USA, 1979-. Publications include: Numerous articles in scientific and medical journals; Books: Medical Virology, Volumes 1-10; Color Atlas of Diagnostic Microbiology. Honours: Excm Diputacion Provincial de Asturias, Spain, 1961; Wasserman Award, Spain. 1964. Memberships: American Society for Microbiology; American Association for the Advancement of Sciences; American Society of Clinical Pathologists. Address: Department of Pathology, Medical Sciences, Room D440, University of California, Irvine, CA 92697, USA.

DE LA RENTA Oscar, b. 22 July 1932, Santo Domingo. Fashion Designer. (1) Françoise de Langlade, 1967, deceased 1983, (2) Anne de la Renta, 1989. Education: Santo Domingo University; Academia de San Fernando, Madrid. Appointments: Staff designer, under Cristobel Balenciaga, AISA couture house, Madrid; Assistant to Antonio Castillo, Lanvin-Castillo, Paris, 1961-63; Designer, Elizabeth Arden couture and ready-to-wear collection, New York, 1963-65; Designer and partner, Jane Deby Inc, New York, 1965; After her retirement, firm became Oscar de la Renta Inc, purchased by Richton International, 1969; Chief Executive, Richton's Oscar de la Renta Couture, Oscar de la Renta II, Oscar de la Renta Furs, Oscar de la Renta Jewelry, Member of Board of Directors, Richton Inc, 1969-73; Oscar de la Renta Ltd, 1973; Chief Executive Officer, 1973—; Couturier for Balmain, Paris, Nov, 1992-; Producer, 80 different lines including high-fashion clothing, household linens, accessories and perfumes for shops in USA, Canada, Mexico and Japan; Owner, Oscar de la Renta Shop, Santo Domingo, 1968-. Honours: Recipient, numerous fashion awards; Caballero, Order of San Pablo Duarte, Order of Cristobal Colon. Address: Oscar de la Renta Ltd, 550 7th Avenue, 8th Floor, New York, NY 10018, USA.

DE LA TOUR Frances, b. 30 July 1944, Bovingdon, Hertfordshire, England. Actress. m. Tom Kempinski, 1972, divorced 1982, 1 son, 1 daughter. Education: Lycée français de Londres, Drama Centre, London; With the Royal Shakespeare Company, 1965-71. Appointments: Stage appearances include: As You Like It, 1967; The Relapse, 1969; A Midsummer Night's Dream, 1971; The Man of Mode, 1971; Small Craft Warnings, 1973; The Banana Box, 1973; The White Devil, 1976; Hamlet (title role), 1979; Duet for One, 1980; Skirmishes, 1981; Uncle Vanya, 1982; Moon for the Misbegotten , 1983; St Joan, 1984; Dance of Death, 1985; Brighton Beach Memoirs, 1986; Lillian, 1986; Facades, 1988; King Lear, 1989; When She Danced (Olivier Award), 1991; The Pope and the Witch, 1992; Greasepaint, 1993; Les Parents Terrible (Royal National Theatre), 1994; Three Tall Women, 1994-95; Blinded by the Sun (Royal National Theatre), 1996; The Play About the Baby (Almedia Theatre), 1998; The Forest (Royal National Theatre), 1998-99; Antony and Cleopatra (RSC), 1999; Fallen Angels (Apollo), 2000-01; The Good Hope and Sketches by Harold Pinter, (Royal National Theatre), 2001-02; Dance of Death (Lyric), 2003; Films include: Our Miss Fred, 1972; To The Devil a Daughter, 1976; Rising Damp, 1980; The Cherry Orchard, 1998; Love Actually, 2003; TV appearances include: Crimes of Passion, 1973; Rising Damp, 1974, 1976; Cottage to Let, 1976; Flickers, 1980; Skirmishes, 1982; Duet for One, 1985; Partners, 1986; Clem, 1986; A Kind of Living (series), 1987, 1988; Downwardly Mobile (series), 1994; Cold Lazarus, 1996; Tom Jones, 1997. Honours: Best Supporting Actress Plays and Players Award, 1973; 3 Best Actress Awards, 1980; Best Actress Standard Film Award, 1980; Best Actress SWET Award, 1983; Honorary Fellow, Goldsmiths College, University of London, 1999; Best Actress, Royal Variety Club, 2000. Address: c/o Kate Feast Management, 10 Primrose Hill Studios, Fitzroy Road, London, NW1 8TR, England.

DE NIRO Robert, b. 1943, New York, USA. Actor. m. Diahnne Abbott, 1976, 1 son, 1 daughter, 2 children by Toukie Smith. Appointments: Actor, films include: The Wedding Party, 1969; Jennifer On My Mind, 1971; Bloody Mama, 1971, Born To Win, 1971; The Gang That Couldn't Shoot Straight, 1971; Bang the Drum Slowly, 1973; Mean Streets, 1973; The Godfather Part II, 1974 The Last Tycoon, 1976, Taxi Driver, 1976; New York, New York 1900, 1977; The Deer Hunter, 1978; Raging Bull, 1980; True Confessions, 1981; The King of Comedy, 1982; Once Upon a Time in America, 1984; Falling in Love, 1984; Brazil, 1984; The Mission, 1985; Angel Heart, 1986; The Untouchables, 1987; Letters Home From Vietnam, 1988; Midnight Run, 1988; We're No Angels, 1989; Stanley and Iris, 1989; Good Fellas, 1989; Jacknife, 1989; Awakenings, 1990; Fear No Evil, 1990; Backdraft, 1990; Cape Fear, 1990; Guilty of Suspicion, 1991; Mistress, 1992; Night and the City, 1992; Mad Dog and Glory, 1992; This Boy's Life, 1993; Mary Shelley's Frankenstein, 1993; The Fan, 1996; Marvin's Room, 1996; Sleepers, 1996; Great Expectations, 1997; Jackie Brown, 1998; Ronin, 1998; Analyse This, 1999; Flawless (also producer), 1999; Men of Honor, 2000; 15 Minutes, 2001; The Score, 2001; Showtime, 2002; City by the Sea, 2002; Analyze That, 2002; President, Tri Beca Productions, 1989-; Producer, Thunderheart, 1992; Entrophy, 1999; Meet the Parents, 2000; Conjugating Niki, 2000; Prison Song, 2001; About a Boy, 2002. Honours include: Commander, Ordre des Arts et des Lettres;

Academy Award, Best Supporting Actor, 1974; Academy Award, Best Actor, 1980. Address: CAA, 9830 Wilshire Boulevard, Beverly Hills, CA 90212, USA.

DE OLIVEIRA Mariana, b. 29 August 1939, Portugal. Cosmetologist. Divorced, 2 sons, 1 daughter. Appointments: Professional Cosmetologist and salon owner, 1974-; Founder and Chief Executive Officer, De Oliveira Hair Care Systems Inc; Has personally developed and patented products for the treatment of hair loss and skin disorders. Publications: Numerous articles in popular and professional journals. Honours: 2001 International Gold Award for Excellence and Business Prestige, Business Initiative Directions, New York, USA; 2002 World Quality Commitment Star Award, Business Initiative Directions, Paris, France; 2002 Euro Market Award, European Market Research Centre, Brussels, Belgium. Address: 788 Adelaide St W, Toronto, Ontario, Canada. E-mail: info@deoliveirasystems.com Website: www.deoliveirasystems.com

DE PALMA Brian, b. 11 September 1940, Newark, New Jersey, USA. Film Director. m. Gale Ann Hurd, 1991, 1 daughter. Education: Sarah Lawrence College, Bronxville; Columbia University. Appointments: Director: (short films) Icarus, 1960; 660124: The Story of an IBM Card, 1961; Wotan's Wake, 1962; (feature length) The Wedding Party, 1964; The Responsive Eye (documentary), 1966; Murder à la Mod, 1967; Greetings, 1968; Dionysus in '69 (co-director), 1969; Hi Mom!, 1970; Get to Know Your Rabbit, 1970; Sisters, 1972; Phantom of the Paradise, 1974; Obsession, 1975; Carrie, 1976; The Fury, 1978; Home Movies, 1979; Dressed to Kill, 1980; Blow Out, 1981; Scarface, 1983; Body Double, 1984; Wise Guys, 1985; The Untouchables, 1987; Casualties of War, 1989; Bonfire of the Vanities, 1990; Raising Cain, 1992; Carlito's Way, 1993; Mission Impossible, 1996; Snake Eyes, 1998; Mission to Mars, 2000; Femme Fatale, 2002. Address: Paramount Pictures, Lubitsch Annex #119, 555 Melrose Avenue #119, W Hollywood, CA 90038, USA.

DE ROSA Gabriele, b. 24 June 1917, Castellammare di Stabia, Italy. University Professor. m. (1) Gabriella Torrese, 4 September 1944, december 1977, 2 sons, 1 daughter, (2) Carla Sabine Kowohl, 8 December 1978. Education: Doctor in Law, 1941. Appointments: Tenured University Lecturer, 1958; Full Professor of Contemporary History; Chancellor, University of Salerno, 1968-75; President, Istituto Luigi Sturzo, Rome; Senator, 1987-94; Deputy, 1994-96; Director, review Ricerche di storia sociale e religiosa, Rome. Publications: Storia politica dell'Azione Cattolica, 1953; Giolitti e il fascismo, 1957; Storia del Partito Popolare Italiano, 1958; Filippo Meda e l'età liberale, 1959; I gesuiti in Sicilia e la rivoluzione del 1848, 1963; Vescovi popolo e magia nel Sud, 1971; Luigi Sturzo, 1977; Tempo religioso e tempo storico, vol I, 1987, vol II, 1994, vol III, 1998; Chiesa e religione popolare nel Mezzogiorno, 1991. Contributions to: Il Tempo; Avvenire; Il Giornale. Honour: Commenda, S Gregorio Magno, Papal Award. Address: Istituto Sturzo, via delle Coppelle 35, 00186 Rome, Italy.

DE ROULET Daniel, b. 1944, Geneva, Switzerland. Writer. m. Chiara Banchini, 1995, 1 son. Education: Architect, University of Geneva, 1971. Publications: A Nous Deux, Ferdinand, 1991; Virtuellement Vôtre, 1993; La Vie, Il y a des Enfants Pour ça, 1994; La Ligne Bleue, 1995; Bleu Siecle, 1996; Gris-bleu, 1999; Nationalite Frontaliere, 2003. Honours: Prix Dentan, 1994; Prix Alpes-Jura, 1996; Prix de littérature du Canton de Berne, 1999; Spycherpreis, 2003. Membership: Auteurs de Suisse. Address: Editions du Seuil, 27 rue Jacob, 75006 Paris, France.

DE SILVA Handunnetti S V, b. 11 October 1960, Colombo, Sri Lanka. Education: BSc in Physics, University of Colombo, Sri Lanka, 1986; MS in Physics, University of Missouri-Rolla, USA,

1995. Appointments: Teaching Assistant, University of Nebraska at Lincoln, 1996; Assistant Lecturer, University of Colombo. Honours: National Dean's List of 1995/96; American Medal of Honor, IBC, 2002, 2003; Lifetime Achievement Award, IBC; Listed in national and international biographical dictionaries; ABI Hall of Fame; World Lifetime Achievement Award; The 100 Most Intriguing People of 2002; International Medal of Honour; World Freedom Medal; The Presidential Seal of Honor, 2003; Universal Award of Accomplishment, 2003; Congressional Medal of Excellence. Address: 1429 N 34th Street, Apt 2, Lincoln, NE 68503, USA.

DE SOUSA Alice, b. 11 January 1966, Portugal. Actress; Producer; Artistic Director. Education: BA, Honours, EEC Law, 1st Class, 1995; MA, Portuguese Studies, 1997. Career: Numerous roles in television, radio and film productions; Lead roles in over 30 productions, including Hermione, The Winter's Tale; Millamant, The Way of the World; Elvira, Blithe Spirit; Producer of more than 60 theatre productions, since 1988. Producer of an acclaimed open-air Shakespeare Festival, at Well Hall Pleasaunce, 1999; Producer of the UK première of Never Nothing From No One, at the Cockpit Theatre, 2000; Produced sell-out productions of Hamlet, Company, Pymaglion, Richard III, You're Gonna Love Tomorrow, Hedda Gabler, Peep Show, The Crime of Father Amaro and Cousin Basillio; Shadows on the Sun; The Importance of Being Earnest, at the Greenwich Playhouse. Address: 189 Greenwich High Street, London, SE10 8JA, England.

DE VEER Edward, b. 28 September 1942, Venezuela (Dutch Citizen). President; Chief Executive Officer. m. Ellen Roos, 2 sons, 1 daughter. Education: University of Miami, 1964; Business Administration with speciality in Finance. Appointments: President and Chief Executive Officer: MetaCorp N V; Aruba Renaissance Beach Resort; Crystal and Seaport Casino; Brouwerij Nacional Balashi; Tropical Bottling Co; Associated Transport Co. Honours: Order of Knighthood of Oranje Nassau, Holland; Order of Knighthood of the Dannebrog, Denmark; Paul Harris Fellow, Rotary International; Man of the Year, Diario of Aruba newspaper, 1986; Premio Oro Aruba, 1987; Listed in Who's Who and biographical publications. Memberships: Board of Directors, Maduro and Curiel's Bank, Aruba Hotel and Tourism Association; President's Council, University of Miami; Board of Trustees, New York Military Academy; Vice-Consul of Denmark; Director, Chamber of Commerce, Aruba, 1972-81, President, 1979; Member, Aruba Little League Foundation; Board member, ALM, 1980-83. E-mail: edeveer@metacorp.aw

DE VETTA-VAN REENEN Helena Maria, b. 20 May 1928, Gouda, Netherlands. Psychologist; Theologian. m. William De Vetta, deceased, 1 son, 1 daughter. Education: Matriculation Diploma, 1967; BA, 1967, BA honours, 1969, MA, Psychology, 1971, DLitt, Phil, Psychology, 1977, Diploma Datametrics, Statistics, 1998, University of South Africa; MPhil, Theology, University of St Augustine, 2001. Appointments: Counselling Psychologist, Family Advice Centre, Bulawayo, Zimbabwe, 1967-69; Clinical Psychologist, St Giles Medical Rehabilitation Centre, Harare, Zimbabwe, 1970-74; Lecturer, Abnormal Psychology, University of Zimbabwe, Harare, Zimbabwe, 1975-77; Head, Department Psychology, University of Zululand, Kwa-Dlangezwa, South Africa, 1979-82; Head Student Counselling and Research, Medical University of South Africa, Ga-Rankuwa, 1983-93; Private Practice, 1993-. Publications: Books: 1971, 1976, 2002; Articles in numerous medical and scientific journals; Numerous presentations at international psychology conferences. Memberships: Psychological Association of South Africa; South African Association for Research and Development in Higher

Education; APA; International Association for Cross-Cultural Psychology; International Association of Applied Psychology. Address: PO Box 42193, Boordfontein, 0201 South Africa.

DE VILLIERS François Pierre Rousseau, b. 10 May 1950, Namibia. Professor of Paediatrics. m. J Gai, deceased 2001, 1 son, 1 daughter. Education: MBChB, 1974; BA, 1983; MMed, 1987; PhD, 1990; FACP, 2000; FCPaed (SA), 2001. Appointments: Professor and Chair, Paediatrics, 1994, Deputy Dean, 1997-2001, Medical University of South Africa. Publications: Book: Practical Management of Paediatric Emergencies, 3rd Edition; Numerous articles in professional journals. Honour: Research Excellence Award, Medunsa, 1998; Research Excellence Award for Senior Researcher, Medunsa, 2001. Memberships: New York Academy of Sciences; International Society for the Study of Paediatric and Adolescent Diabetes; American College of Physicians. Address: PO Box 1062, Buccleuch 2066, South Africa.

DE VRIES Susanna Mary, (Susanna Devries-Evans), b. 6 October 1935. Author; Lecturer in Art History. m. Jake de Vries, 25 July 1982. Education: Cours de Civilisation Francaise, Sorbonne, University of Paris, 1953; Universidad Menendez Pelayo, Santander, Spain, 1954; Complutense University, Madrid. Appointments: Lecturer, Continuing Education Department, University of Queensland, 1991. Publications: Historic Sydney: Its Early Artists, 1982, 2nd edition, 1987; The Impressionists Revealed: Masterpieces and Collectors, 1982, 2nd edition 1994; Pioneering Women, Pioneer Land, 1988; Conrad Martens on the Beagle; Strength of Spirit: Pioneering Women of Achievement from the First Fleet to Federation, 1992; Blue Ribbons, Bitter Bread: the Life of Joice Loch, 2000, 2nd edition, 2002; Complete Book of Great Australian Women, various editions from 2001; Heroic Australian Women in War, 2004; Great Pioneer Women of the Outback, 2005. Contributions to: Periodicals. Honours: Fellowship, Literary Board, Australia Council, 1990; Winston Churchill Fellowship, Arts History, 1994; Tyrone Guthrie Fellowship, Ireland, 2000. Memberships: Lyceum Club, Brisbane; Australian Society of Authors. Address: 10 Matingara Street, Chapel Hill, Brisbane 4069, Australia.

DE'AMBROSIS Elena Anne, b. 13 December 1968, Ipswich, Queensland, Australia. Speech pathologist; Audiologist; Teacher. m. Andrew Finlay. Education: Bachelor of Speech Therapy, 1990; Postgraduate Diploma of Audiology, 1991; Master of Audiology, 2000; Bachelor of Education, 2003. Appointments: Audiologist, Speech Pathologist, Neurosensory Unit, 1993-96; Clinic Manager, Ipswich Branch, Queensland Hearing, 1996-2000; Speech Pathologist, Queensland Hearing, whilst completing university studies, 2001-; Teacher, Raceview State School, 2003-. Publications: Abstracts published in the proceedings of the 14th National ASA Conference, 2000 and XXVI International Congress of Audiology, 2002. Honours: Elizabeth Usher Speech Therapy Prize, 1990; Listed in Who's Who publications and biographical dictionaries. Memberships: Speech Pathology Association of Australia; Private Speech Pathology Association; Full Member, Audiological Society of Australia. Address: Queensland Hearing, Flinders Place, 14 Brisbane Street, Ipswich, Queensland 4305, Australia. E-mail: eafinlay@optusnet.com.au

DEAN Christopher, b. 27 July 1958, Nottingham, England. Ice Skater. m. (1) Isabelle Duchesnay, 1991, divorced, 1993, (2) Jill Ann Trenary, 1994, 2 sons. Appointments: Police Constable, 1974-80; British Ice Dance Champion (with Jayne Torvill), 1978-83, 1993; European Ice Dance Champion (with Jayne Torvill), 1981, 1982, 1984, 1994; World Ice Dance Champion (with Jayne Torvill), 1981-84; World professional Champions, 1984-85, 1990, 1995-96; Choreographed Encounters for English National Ballet, 1996;

Stars on Ice, USA, 1998-99, 1999-2000; Ice Dance: World tours with own and international companies of skaters, 1985, 1988, 1994, 1997, tours of Australia and New Zealand, 1984, 1991, UK, 1992, Japan, 1996, USA and Canada, 1997-98. Publications: Torvill and Dean's Face the Music and Dance (with Jayne Torvill), 1993; Torvill and Dean: An Autobiography (with Jayne Torvill), 1994; Facing the Music (with Jayne Torvill), 1996. Honours: BBC Sportsview Personality of the Year (with Jayne Torvill), 1983-84; Honorary MA, 1994. Address: c/o Sue Young, PO Box 32, Heathfield, East Sussex, TN21 0BW, England.

DEAN Colin Leslie, b. 3 September 1953, Australia. Poet; Philosopher. Education: BSc, 1984; BA, 1988; BLitt (Hon), 1991; MA, 1994; BLitt (Hon), 1999; MA, 2002. Appointments: Resident Poet for ASP; Chief Executive Officer, Gamahucher Press; Working for a PhD. Publications include: Evil Flowers, Poems by C Dean; Poisonous Flowers, Poems by C Dean; Vespiary Femme Fatales, Poems by: C Dean; Xanadu: Poems by C Dean; Wet Flowers, Poems by C Dean; Amore la Mal Incantare, Poems by C Dean; Hungers Unholy: Poems by C Dean; La Belle Dames sans Merci; Arachnids: Homme Fatales, Poems by C Dean; Erotic Fairy Tales, Poems by C Dean; Contentless Thought; The Nature of Philosophy; Epistemology; A Moral Philosophy; The Australian Aboriginal Dreamtime; The Absurdity of Understanding Metaphor; The Aesthetics of Incorrectness; Absurdities of Metapsychology; The Religions of the Pre-contact Victorian Aborigines; A Consequence of the Epistemological Holism of Quine; Altering Consciousness, Essence; The Absurdities or Meaninglessness of Mathematics and Science; Essence the Metaphysical Ground of Logic; The Relationship between Analysis and Insight in Madhyamika Buddhism; Absurdities or Meaninglessness of Irrationality is No Hindrance to Truth; Aristotelian Logic as an Epistemic Condition of Truth; The Aesthetics of Anti-Poetry Manifesto; The Absurdities of Psychoanalysis and Science; The Dialectic Reductio ad Absurdum Argument. Membership: Australian Institute of Physics, 1984. Address: 72 Plume Street, Norlane, Geelong 3214, Australia.

DEANE Seamus (Francis), b. 9 February 1940, Derry City, Northern Ireland. Professor of Irish Studies; Writer; Poet. m. Marion Treacy, 19 August 1963, 3 sons, 1 daughter. Education: BA, Honours, 1st Class, 1961, MA, 1st Class, 1963, Queen's University, Belfast; PhD, Cambridge University, 1968. Appointments: Visiting Fulbright and Woodrow Wilson Scholar, Reed College, Oregon, 1966-67; Visiting Lecturer, 1967-68; Visiting Professor, 1978, University of California at Berkeley; Professor of Modern English and American Literature, University College, Dublin, 1980-93; Walker Ames Professor, University of Washington, Seattle, 1987; Julius Benedict Distinguished Visiting Professor, Carleton College, Minnesota, 1988; Keough Professor of Irish Studies, University of Notre Dame, Indiana, 1993-. Publications: Fiction: Reading in the Dark, 1996. Poetry: Gradual Wars, 1972; Rumours, 1977; History Lessons, 1983; Selected, 1988. Non-Fiction: Celtic Revivals: Essays in Modern Irish Literature, 1880-1980, 1985; A Short History of Irish Literature, 1986, reissued, 1994; The French Revolution and Enlightenment in England, 1789-1832, 1988; Strange Country: Ireland, Modernity and Nationhood, 1790-1970, 1997. Editor: The Adventures of Hugh Trevor by Thomas Holcroft, 1972; The Sale Catalogues of the Libraries of Eminent Persons, Vol IX, 1973; Nationalism, Colonialism and Literature, 1990; The Field Day Anthology of Irish Writing, 3 volumes, 1991; Penguin Twentieth Century Classics: James Joyce, 5 volumes, 1993. Honours: AE Memorial for Literature, 1973; American-Irish Fund, Literature, 1989; Guardian Fiction Prize, 1997; Irish Times International Fiction Award, 1997; Irish Times Fiction Award, 1997; London Weekend Television South Bank Award for Literature, 1997; Ruffino Antico-

Fattore International Literature Award, Florence, 1998; Honorary DLitt, Ulster, 1999. Memberships: Aosdana (Irish Artists' Council); Field Day Theatre and Publishing Company, director; Royal Irish Academy. Address: Institute of Irish Studies, 1145 Flanner Hall, University of Notre Dame, IN 46556, USA.

DEBAKEY Selma, b. Lake Charles, Louisiana, USA. Professor of Scientific Communication. Education: BA, Languages, Newcomb College; Postgraduate studies, French and Philosophy, Tulane University. Appointments: Director, Department of Medical Communications, Ochsner Clinic and Alton Ochsner Medical Foundation, New Orleans, 1942-68; Medical Writer and Editor; Consultant Editor; Internationally renowned course developer. Main professional interests: Internationally recognised authority in the field of medical writing and editing, most especially in the use of humour in the form of cartoons to depict faulty reasoning and language use; Ethics; Literacy; Publishing. Publications: A huge body of work, as writer, editor, consultant, course developer; Co-author, Current Concepts in Breast Cancer, 1967; Numerous articles and papers contributed to specialist peer-reviewed journals; Over 1000 articles as Editor; Judge for several prestigious medical writing awards, including Modern Medical Monographs Awards, AORN DuPuy Writer's Awards. Honours: Named in Texas Hall of Fame; Listed in numerous international and specialist biographical directories, including: Dictionary of International Biography; Outstanding People of the 21st Century; 2000 Outstanding Intellectuals of the 21st Century; 2000 Outstanding Scientists of the 21st Century; 2000 Outstanding Scholars of the 21st Century; 2000 Outstanding Women of the 20th Century; Who's Who in America; Who's Who in the World; Profiled in numerous newspapers and magazines. Memberships: American Association for the Advancement of Science; American Medical Writers' Association; Association of Teachers of Technical Writing; Council of Biology Editors; Society for Health and Human Values; Society for Technical Communication. Address: Baylor College of Medicine, 1 Baylor Plaza, Houston, TX 77030 3411, USA.

DECHEN Tenzin Sangmo (Rinpoche, Lama), b. 21 June 1953, Finowfurt, Eberswalde, Germany. Teacher. Education: Extensive studies of Buddhist Philosophy and Religion. Appointments: Buddhist Nun; Author; Teacher; Counsellor of Educators for peace, UN, UNICEF, UNESCO. Publications: Meditationshandbuch Lamrim; Medizinbuddhismus; Die Weisheit des Buddhismus; Guruhingabe; Many commentaries on Buddhist Sutra and Tantra. Honour: Recognition Certificate, International Educators for World Peace, World Peace Academy, 2000. Memberships: National Chancellor for Germany. International Association of Educators for World Peace, 2000; Ganden Tashi Choeling E.V. Address: Buddhist Monastery, Ganden Tashi Choeling; Mehringdamm 53, 10961 Berlin, Germany. E-mail: info@tashi-choeling.de Website: www.tashi-choeling.de

DEDE Fate-Vassilis, b. 6 January 1939, Nivitsa-Ipiro, Greece. Physician; Author. m. Drita, 2 sons, 2 daughters. Education: Nurse, Orderly, 1960-62; University Student, 1962-68; Diploma, Politics, 1968-80; Diploma, Philology, 1984-88; Diploma, Doctor, 1996. Appointments: Physician, Greece, 1990-; Author, Poet. Publications: Non-Greek: The Dawn Star (poems), 1966; The Country and him (verse), 1968; Flowing lands (poems), 1978; I'll be a sailor (children's verse), 1980; The Sound of the earth (poems), 1985; Words the sea hid from us (poems), 1991; Birth of Birds of Love; Where you are, my Mother the Sea (verse); My eyes ask for you; An interminable yearning; Yesterday I saw you in a dream; Dawn of Peace (poems); Greek, English, French, German: When the heart sings (poems); I am coming to you (poems); The Rock of Faith (drama in verse); Broken stones (poems); The beauty of the sea (short stories); The beauty of life (fiction); And this day has gone (poems); When will I go? (verse); We are all beggars (verse). Honours: 6 gold medals; 11 silver medals (2 from Academia International de Lutèce, Paris , France); 13 silver crowns and statuettes; 42 diplomas, prizes and distinctions; Chevalier Grand Officer, The Golden Sword of St George in Locrida; Honorary Doctor in Literature, USA. Memberships: International Writers and Artists Association, New York, USA; Life Member, World Academy of Arts and Culture, USA; Life Member, Academia Internationale de Lutèce, Paris, France; Honorary Academician, Accademia del Fiorino, Italy; Meritorious Academician, Accademia Ferdinandea, Italy; National Greek Authors Society; Honorary Member, Societa Storica Cataneze; Magistero Siciliano di Servizio Sociale. Address: PO Box 80721, Piraeus 18510, Greece. Website: http:// literature.ncsr.gr

DEEKEN Alfons Theodor, b. 3 August 1932, Emstek, Niedersachsen, Germany. Philosopher; Educator; Writer. Education: MA, Berchmanskolleg, Munich, Germany, 1958; MA, Sophia University, Tokyo, 1966; PhD, Fordham University, New York, 1973. Appointments: Assistant Professor to Professor, 1973-82, Professor of Philosophy, 1982-2003, Professor Emeritus, 2003-, Sophia University, Tokyo, Japan. Publications: Growing Old and How to Cope With It, 1972; Process and Permanence in Ethics: Max Scheler's Moral Philosophy, 1974; Confronting Death, 1996; Kirisutokyoo to Watakushi, 1995; Humor wa Oi to Shi no Myooyaku, 1995; Death Education, 2001; Hikari no dialogue, 2002; Yoku Iki, Yoku Warai, Yoki Shi to Deau, 2003. Honours: Best Ethics Book of 1974, Catholic Press Association, America, 1975; Kikuchi Kan Literary Award, Literary Association of Japan, 1991; Cross of the Order of Merit of the German Federal Republic, President of Germany, 1998; Cultural Award, City of Tokyo, 1999;. Memberships: Japanese Society of Clinical Thanatology, President, 2001-; Japanese Association of Death Education and Grief Counselling, President 1974-2003; Japanese Association for Clinical Research on Death and Dying; International Work Group Death, Dying and Bereavement. Sophia University, S J House, Kioicho 7-1, Chiyoda-ku, 102-8571 Tokyo, Japan.

DEERING Anne-Lise, b. Norway. Clay Artist; Potter. Education: Science Degree, Norway, 1954; Oil Painting, Southern Illinois University, Carbondale, Illinois, 1958; Ceramics, Foothill College, Los Altos, California, 1975; BA, Art, Penn State University, University Park, Pennsylvania, 1977; Computer Graphic Design and Medallic Art, Penn State University, 1990-91; Residential Real Estate Appraisal Courses, Marketing Strategy, Sales and Promotion Courses, PA Realtors Institute, 1994-96. Career: Middle Eastern Dance Teacher, 1975-80; Self-employed Clay Artist and Potter, 1977-98; Member, 1977-2000, Juried Member, 1981-2000, Board of Directors, 1984-97, Pennsylvania Guild of Craftsmen (PGC); Participant in PGC Craft Fairs for 10 years; Artist Member, Art Alliance of Central Pennsylvania, 1978-99; Participant in Art Alliance Gallery Shop, 1989-99; Licensed Real Estate Sales Person, 1991-99; Exhibits include: American Medallic Sculpture Association juried exhibit, Newark Museum, New Jersey, 1990; Invitational, Mountain Top Gallery, Cresson, Pennsylvania, 1998; The Pen and Brush Gallery juried exhibit, New York City, 1998, 1999, 2000, 2001; American Numismatic Association, Colorado Springs, 2001; Penn State University, 2002, Wroclav, Poland, 2002; ASMA juried exhibit, Ornamental Metal Museum, Memphis, Tennessee, 2003; Co-ordinator and chair of ASMA members juried exhibit, Nordic Heritage Museum, Seattle, Washington, 2004; In charge of ASMA medals displays at numerous libraries throughout the greater Seattle area, 2004; Medal in private collections and the permanent collection of the Museum of Medallic Art, Wroclav, Poland. Memberships: Pennsylvania Guild of Craftsmen and Central Pennsylvania Chapter, 1977-2000; Member of American Medallic Sculpture Association (AMSA), 1990-, Newsletter Editor, 2000-, Secretary, 2001-.

DEFORD Frank, b. 16 December 1938, Baltimore, Maryland, USA. Writer; Editor. m. Carol Penner, 28 August 1965, 1 son, 2 daughters. Education: BA, Princeton University, 1962. Appointments: Writer, Commentator, Cable News Network, 1980-86, National Public Radio, 1980-89, 1991-, NBC, 1986-89, ESPN, 1992-1996; HBO, 1996-; Editor-in-Chief, The National, 1989-91; Writer, Newsweek Magazine, 1991-93, 1996-98; Contributing Editor, Vanity Fair, 1993-96; Sports Illustrated, 1962-89, 1998-. Publications: Five Strides on the Banked Track, 1969; Cut'N'Run, 1971; There She Is, 1972; The Owner, 1974; Big Bill Tilden: The Triumphs and the Tragedy, 1977; Everybody's All-American, 1981; Alex: The Life of a Child, 1982; Spy in the Deuce Court, 1987; World's Tallest Midget, 1988; Casey on the Loose, 1989; Love and Infamy, 1993; The Best of Frank Deford, 1999; The Other Adonis, 2001; An American Summer, 2002. Contributions to: Numerous magazines. Honours: Sportswriter of the Year, National Association of Sportswriters and Sportscasters, 1982-88; Emmy, 1988; Cable Ace, 1996; Peabody Award, 1999; National Association of Sportwriters and Sportscasters, Hall of Fame, 1998. Address: Box 1109, Greens Farms, CT 06838, USA.

DEGEN Rolf, b. 25 July 1926, Germany. Child Neurologist. m. H E Schulz, 18 June 1955, 2 daughters. Appointments: Head, Department of Child Neurology, University Children's Hospital, Leipzig, 1966-73; Head, EEG Department and Department of Outpatient Epileptic Children, Epilepsy Centre, Bethel, Germany, 1973-91; Head, Practice for Epileptic Outpatients, 1991-. Publications: 5 books, 2 paperbacks and over 140 articles in medical journals. Honour: Honorary Member, German Section of the International League Against Epilepsy. Memberships include: German Association of Clinical Neurophysiology; German Pediatric Association. Address: Telgter Str 42, 33619 Bielefeld, Germany.

DEGENHARD Andreas, b. 23 May 1970, Osnabrück, Germany. Physicist. Education: Diploma in Theoretical Physics, 1995; PhD summa cum laude, Mathematical Physics, 1999. Appointments: Postdoctoral, Department of Theoretical Physics, University of Bielefeld, 1999; Postdoctoral Studies, Institute of Cancer Research, King's College, 1999-2002; Lecturer, University of Bielefeld, 2002-. Publications: Articles in professional journals. Honours: Exceptional grade assessment, Institute of Cancer Research, London; Listed in national and international biographical dictionaries. Memberships: German Physical Society; European Society of Magnetic Resonance in Medicine and Biology. Address: Faculty of Physics, University of Bielefeld, Universitätsstrasse 25, D-33615 Bielefeld, Germany. E-mail: adegenha@physik.uni-bielefeld.de Website: www.degenhard.org

DEGHETT Stephanie Coyne, b. 31 August 1951, Saranac Lake, New York, USA. Creative Writing Professor; Poet. m. Victor J DeGhett, 1980, 1 daughter. Education: BA, English, State University College, Potsdam, 1976; MA, English, University of Vermont, Burlington, 1982. Appointments: Graduate Teaching Fellow, University of Vermont; Instructor, English Department, State University of New York at Canton; Instructor, Creative Writing Program, State University College at Potsdam; Poetry Editor, Blueline magazine, 1988-. Publications: Poem: The Physics of Sensation, 1996. Contributions to: River of Dreams: American Poems from the St Lawrence Valley, a poetry anthology, 1990; Fringillirosadae, a poem, New England Review, 1994; Some Old Extravagance of Being, a poem, American Poets, 1999; With Child, a poem, Potpourri, 2000; Field Notes; North Country; Old Roses; Wordsmith; Airfoil; Wordsmith. Memberships: SUNY Writers Council, Poets and Writers. Address: English Department, State University College, Potsdam, NY 13676, USA.

Dictionary of International Biography

DEGUN-MATHER Marcia Diana, b. 27 April 1935, Hampstead, London, England. Clinical Psychologist. Divorced. Education: BA honours degree, Psychology, Reading University, 1957; Postgraduate In-service Training, Clinical Psychology, Liverpool Regional Health Authority and Liverpool University, 1957-60. Appointments: Field Supervisor, Lecturer and Examiner, Clinical Psychology Doctorate, University of East London, 1973-97; Specialist Lecturer, Hypnosis on Clinical Psychology Course, University of East London, 1981-; Head, Clinical Psychology Department, Warley Psychiatric Teaching Hospital, Brentwood, 1969-88; Principal Clinical Psychologist, 1988-91, Consultant Clinical Psychologist, Head of Adult Mental Health Speciality, 1991-97, NHS Trust; Specialist Lecturer, Diploma Course in Clinical Hypnosis, University College, London, 1993-; Consultant Clinical Psychologist, Lead Psychologist in Eating Disorder Service, NHS Trust, 1998-. Publications: Contributor to textbooks: Symptoms of Psychopathology, 1970; Hypnosis: Current Clinical, Experimental and Forensic Practices, 1988; Hypnotherapy: A Handbook, 1991. Memberships: Associate Fellow, British Psychological Society; Member, British Society of Experimental and Clinical Hypnosis; Member, British Association of Behavioural and Cognitive Psychotherapy; Member, International Society for Traumatic Stress Studies; Fellow, Royal Society of Medicine, London. Address: Peacehaven, 47 Peartree Lane, Doddinghurst, Brentwood, Essex CM15 0RJ, England.

DEIGHTON Len, b. 18 February 1929, London, England. Writer. m. Publications: The Ipcress File, 1962; Horse Under Water, 1963; Funeral in Berlin, 1964; Ou Est Le Garlic/Basic French Cooking, 1965, 1979; Action Cook Book, 1965; Cookstrip Cook Book, 1966; Billion Dollar Brain, 1966; An Expensive Place to Die, 1967; Len Leighton's London Dossier, 1967; The Assassination of President Kennedy, co-author, 1967; Only When I Larf, 1968; Bomber, 1970; Declarations of War, 1971; Close-up, 1972; Spy Story, 1974; Eleven Declarations of War, 1975; Yesterday's Spy, 1975; Twinkle, Twinkle, Little Spy, 1976; Catch a Falling Spy, 1976; Fighter, 1977; SS-GB, 1978; Airshipwreck, co-author, 1978; Blitzkreig, 1979; Battle of Britain, co-author, 1980, 1990; XPD, 1981; Goodbye Mickey Mouse, 1982; Berlin Game, 1983; Mexico Set, 1984; London Match, 1985; Game, Set and Match, 13 part TV series; Winter: A Berlin Family 1899-1945, 1987; Spy Hook, 1988; Spy line, 1989; Spy Sinker, 1990; Basic French Cookery Course, 1990; ABC of French Food, 1989; Mamista, 1991; City of Gold, 1992; Violent Ward, 1993; Blood, Tears and Folly, 1993; Faith, 1994; Hope, 1995; Charity, 1996. Address: c/o Jonathan Clowes Ltd, 10 Iron Bridge House, Bridge House, Bridge Approach, London NW1 8BD, England.

DELACOTE Jacques, b. France. Maestro. m. Maria-Lucia Alvares-Machado. Education: Paris Conservatory; Vienna Academy of Music, with Professor Hans Swarowsky. Career: Assistant to Leonard Bernstein and Darius Milhaud; Performed with New York Philharmonic Orchestra, 1972; Guest conductor, numerous orchestras in USA and Europe; Opera conductor, many European state opera houses. Publications: Many appearances with rado orchestras; Recordings include: La Traviata; Turandot; Carmen; Romeo and Juliet, and others. Honours: First Prize, Gold Medal, Dimitri-Mitropoulos Competition, New York, 1971. Address: c/o Agency Dr Germinal Hilbert, Maximilianstr 22, 80539, Munich, Germany.

DELANEY Shelagh, b. 25 November 1939, Salford, Lancashire, England. Playwright. 1 daughter. Education: Broughton Secondary School. Publications: Plays: A Taste of Honey, 1958; The Lion in Love, 1960. Films: A Taste of Honey; The White Bus, 1966; Charlie Bubbles, 1968; Dance with a Stranger, 1985. Television Plays: St Martin's Summer, 1974; Find Me First, 1979. Television

Series: The House That Jack Built, 1977 (stage adaptation, New York, 1979). Radio Plays: So Does The Nightingale, 1980; Don't Worry About Matilda, 1983. Honours: Charles Henry Foyle New Play Award; Arts Council Bursary, 1961; New York Drama Critics Award, 1961; British Film Academy Award, Robert Flaherty Award, 1961; Prix Film Jeunesse Etranger, Cannes, 1985. Address: c/o Sayle Screen Ltd, 11 Jubilee Place, London SW3 3TD, England.

DELBANCO Nicholas Franklin, b. 27 August 1942, London, England. Writer. m. Elena Carter Greenhouse, 12 September 1970, 2 daughters. Education: BA, History and Literature, Harvard College, 1963; MA, English Comparative Literature, Columbia University, 1966. Appointments: Member, Language and Literature Division, Bennington College, 1966-85; Director, Bennington Writing Workshops, 1977-85; Visiting Professor, Iowa Writers Program, University of Iowa, 1979; Adjunct Professor, School of the Arts, Columbia University, 1979-96; Visiting Artist-in-Residence, Trinity College, 1980; Visiting Professor, Williams College, 1982; Professor of English, Skidmore College, 1984-85; Professor of English, Director, MFA Program, University of Michigan, 1985-; Director, Hopwood Awards Programme, 1988-. Publications: The Martlet's Tale, 1966; Grasse 3/23/66, 1968; Consider Sappho Burning, 1969; News, 1970; In the Middle Distance, 1971; Fathering, 1973; Small Rain, 1975; Possession, 1977; Sherbrookes, 1978; Stillness, 1980; Group Portrait: Conrad, Crane, Ford, James, and Wells, 1982; About My Table and Other Stories, 1983; The Beaux Arts Trio: A Portrait, 1985; Running in Place: Scenes from the South of France, 1989; The Writers' Trade, and Other Stories, 1990; In the Name of Mercy, 1995; Old Scores, 1997; The Lost Suitcase: Reflections on the Literary Life, 2000; What Remains, 2000; The Countess of Stanlein Restored, 2001. Contributions to: Periodicals. Honours: National Endowment for the Arts Creative Writing Fellowships, 1973, 1982; Guggenheim Fellowship, 1979. Memberships: Authors League; Authors Guild; Signet Society; Phi Beta Kappa; New York State Writers Institute; PEN. Address: c/o Department of English, University of Michigan, 7601 Angell Hall, Ann Arbor, MI 48109, USA.

DELILLO Don, b. 20 November 1936, New York, New York, USA. Author. Education: BA in Communication Arts, Fordham University, 1958. Publications: Americana, 1971; End Zone, 1972; Great Jones Street, 1973; Ratner's Star, 1976; Players, 1977; Running Dog, 1978; Amazons, 1980; The Names, 1982; White Noise, 1985; The Day Room, 1987; Libra, 1988; Mao II, 1991; Underworld, 1997; Valparaiso, 1999; The Body Artist, 2001. Contributions to: Periodicals. Honours: National Book Award, 1985; Irish Times-Aer Lingus International Fiction Prize, 1989; PEN/Faulkner Award, 1992; Jerusalem Prize, 1999; Howells Medal, 2000. Literary Agent: Wallace Literary Agents Inc. Address: c/o Wallace & Sheil, 177 East 70th Street, New York, NY 10021, USA.

DELLON A Lee, b. 18 April 1944, Bronx, New York, USA. Plastic Surgeon. m. (1) 3 sons, (2) Luiann O Greer, 2004. Education: BA, 1966, MD, 1977, Johns Hopkins University; National Cancer Institute, National Institutes of Health, 1972-74; Columbia Presbyterian Hospital, 1970-72; General Surgery, Johns Hopkins Hospital, 1974-78; General and Plastic Surgery Residency, Union Memorial Hospital, 1977, Appointments: Raymond Curtis Hand Surgery Fellowship, Baltimore; Professor of Plastic Surgery and Neurosurgery, Johns Hopkins University, Baltimore, Maryland 1978-; Clinical Professor of Plastic Surgery and Neurosurgery, Professor of Anatomy, University of Arizona, Tucson, Arizona, 2000-. Publications: 4 books including: Surgery of the Peripheral Nerve (Chinese and Japanese translations), 1988; Somatosensory Testing and Rehabilitation, 1997; Evaluation of

Sensibility and Re-Education of Sensations in the Hand, 1981; 340 peer reviewed scientific articles; patent Holder: Disk-criminator™; Pressure-specified sensory device™; Neurotube™. Honours: Eagle scout with 2 palms; Boy Scouts of America; Phi Beta Kappa; Alpha Omega Alpha; President, American Society of Peripheral Nerve Surgery, 1993; President Elect, American Society of Reconstructive Microsurgery, 2004. Memberships: Editorial Boards of 7 journals including: Plastic and Reconstructive Surgery; Journal of Reconstructive Microsurgery; Annals of Plastic Surgery; Journal of Hand Therapy. Address: Institute for Peripheral Nerve Surgery, Suite 370, 3333 N Calvert Street, Baltimore, MD 21218. E-mail: aldellon@erols.com

DELLOW Ronald Graeme, b. 29 September 1924, Auckland, New Zealand. Retired University Lecturer; Choral Conductor; Organist; Harpsichordist. m. Jane Brown Currie Cowan, 1 son, 3 daughters. Education: MusB, Auckland University College; Associate, RSCM; FRCO; LTCL. Appointments: Lecturer, Department of Music, Auckland University College, 1949; Adult Education Tutor, 1950-64; Extension Lecturer, Music, University of Auckland, 1964-89; Organist and Choirmaster, Pitt Street Methodist Church, Auckland, 1964-78; Director of Music, All Saints Church, Ponsonby, Auckland, 1986-2002. Compositions include: 6 recorder trios, 1971; Anthem, Let the Children Come to Me, 1972; Missa Brevis, boys' choir and organ, 1974; Jubilate, chorus and organ, 1977; Magnificat, 1978; Suite, 4 recorders, 1978. Honours: Auckland Centennial Music Scholar, 1943; Prize for Fantasia for Viols, Viola de Gamba Society, England, 1958; MBE, 1980; Fellow, New Zealand Association of Organists, 1996. Memberships: Special Commissioner, 1962-, RSCM; Various offices, Auckland Festival Society; Past President, Auckland Dorian Singers, Auckland Organists Association; Musical Director, 1954-89, New Zealand Society of Recorder Players; Governor, 1963-, Dolmetsch Foundation; Auckland Bach Cantata Society, Music Director, 1978-91. Address: 8 Lynch Street, Point Chevalier, Auckland 2, New Zealand.

DELPY Julie, b. 8 November 1969, France. Film Actress. Education: New York University Film School. Appointments: Actress, films include: Detective, 1985; Mauvais Sang, 1986; La Passion Béatrice, 1987; L'Autre Nuit, 1988; La Noche Oscura, 1989; Europa Europa, 1991; Voyager, 1991; Warszawa, 1922; Young and Younger, 1993; The Three Musketeers, 1993; When Pigs Fly, 1993; The Myth of the White Wolf, 1994; Killing Zoe, 1994; Mesmer, 1994; Trois Couleurs Blanc, 1994; Trois Couleurs Rouge, 1994; Before Sunrise, 1995; An American Werewolf in Paris, 1997; The Treat; LA without a Map; Blah, Blah, Blah (director); The Passion of Ayn Rand, 1999; TV: ER. Address: c/o William Morris Agency, 151 El Camino Drive, Beverley Hills, CA 90212, USA.

DEMIDCHIK Yevgenii Pavlovich, b. 2 January 1925, Borisov, Belarus. Surgeon; Oncologist. m. Raisa, 1 son. Education: Graduate, Minsk State Medical Institute, 1957; Doctor of Medical Science, 1987; Professor, 1988; Honored Doctor, Republic of Belarus, 1996; Academician, National Academy of Sciences of the Republik of Belarus, 1996. Appointments: Head, Tyroid Cancer Center, Republic of Belarus. Publications: 310 publications including 13 monographs. Honours: Diploma, Honoured Medal, Author of the Scientific Discovery, Occurrence of the Synapsis Transformation Block under the effect of the impulse magnetic field. Memberships: Association of Oncologists. Address: Thyroid Cancer Centre, 64 Fr, Skorina av, Minsk, BY 220013, Belarus.

DEMIN Andrey Konstantinovich, b. 17 September 1956, Moscow, USSR. Physician. m. Irina Anatolyevna Zhidkova, 2 sons, 1 daughter. Education: MD, O W Kuusinen State University, Petrozavodsk, USSR, 1980; PhD, Medical Sciences, N A

Semashko Research Institute, Moscow, 1988; Manager in State and Municipal Management, Russian Academy State Sve, Moscow, 1999; D in Political Science, Highest Attestation Commission of Russia, Moscow 2001; Professor in Social Medicine, Health Care Economics and Administration, Ministry of Education, Russian Federation, 2002. Appointments: Assistant Professor, O W Kuusinen State University, Petrozavodsk, 1980-84; Junior to Senior Researcher, N A Semashko Research Institute, Moscow, 1987-90; Associate Professor to Professor, I M Sechenov Moscow Medical Academy, 1990-; Deputy Head of Department, Staff Consultant, Administration of President of Russian Federation, Moscow 1992-2001; President, Chairman of the Board, Russian Public Health Association, Moscow, 1996-. Publications: Author, First State report on Population Health in the Russian Federation, 1992; Co-author, editor, Health Education Promotion among Children, Adolescents and Youth in Russia, 1998; Co-author, editor, Alcohol and Population Health in Russia 1900-2000, 1999; Author, Political Problems of Social Security of Population in G7 Countries, 2000; Contributor of articles to professional journals. Honours: Listed in Who's Who publications and biographical dictionaries. Memberships: Canadian Public Health Association, 1993-; Centre for Russian Environmental Policy, 1993-; Member, Scientific Council, 1997-, European Public Health Association; Member, Governing Board, 2001-, World Federation of Public Health Associations. Address: Angelov Pereulok, Dom 7, Korpus 4, Kvartira 363, Moscow 125367, Russian Federation. E-mail: hefrus@online.ru Website: www.rpha.newmail.ru

DEMONTE Claudia A, b. 25 August 1947, Astoria, New York, USA. Artist. m. Ed McGowin. Education: BA, College of Notre Dame, 1969; MFA, Catholic University of America, 1971. Appointments: Professor, Art Department, University of Maryland, 1972-; Chairman, Art Program, New School for Social Research, New York, USA, 1980-1990. Publications: Woman of the World, a global collection of Art. Honours: Agnes Gund Foundation; New York Foundation on the Arts; Anchorage Foundation of Texas; Listed in several biographical publications. Membership: Euro American Women Council. Address: 96 Grand Street, New York, NY 10013, USA.

DENCH Dame Judith (Judi), b. 9 December 1934, York, Yorkshire, England. Actress. m. Michael Williams, 1971, deceased, 1 daughter. Education: Central School of Speech Training and Dramatic Art. Career: Appeared Old Vic, leading roles, 1957-61; Royal Shakespeare Company, 1961-62; Leading roles include: Anya (The Cherry Tree); Titania (A Midsummer Dream); Isabella (Measure for Measure); West African Tour with Nottingham Playhouse, 1963; Subsequent roles include: Irina (The Three Sisters, Oxford Playhouse, 1964); Title role, St Joan and Barbara (Nottingham Playhouse, 1965); Lika (The Promise, 1967); Sally Bowles (Cabaret, 1968); Numerous appearances in lead roles and tours to Japan, 1970, 1972, and Australia, 1970 as Associate Member Royal Shakespeare Company, 1969-, these include: Viola (Twelfth Night); Beatrice (Much Ado About Nothing); Duchess (Duchess of Malfi); Other Performances include: Miss Trant (The Good Companions, 1974); Nurse (Too Good to Be True, 1975, 1976); Cymbeline, 1979; Lady Bracknell (The Importance of Being Ernest, 1982); Pack of Lies, 1983; Waste, 1985; Antony and Cleopatra, 1987; Hamlet, 1989; The Seagull (Royal National Theatre, 1994); Plays Directed: Much Ado About Nothing, 1988; Look Back in Anger, 1989; The Boys from Syracuse, 1991; Absolute Hell (Royal National Theatre, 1995); A Little Night Music, 1995; Amy's View, 1997; Filumena, 1998. Films include: A Study in Terror, 1965; Four in the Morning, 1966; A Midsummer Night's Dream (RSC, 1968); Dead Cert, Wetherby, 1985; A Room with a View, 1986; 84 Charing Cross Road, 1987; Henry V, 1989; Goldeneye, 1995; Tomorrow Never Dies, 1996; Mrs Brown, 1997,

Shakespeare in Love, 1998; Tea with Mussolini, 1998; The World is Not Enough, 1999; Chocolat, 2000; Iris, 2001; The Shipping News, 2001; The Importance of Being Earnest, 2002; Die Another Day, 2002. TV includes: Major Barbara; Talking to a Stranger; The Funambulists; Age of Kings; Jackanory; Neighbours; Marching Song; On Approval; Langrishe Go Down; Love in a Cold Climate; A Fine Romance; Going Gently; Saigon-Year of the Cat, 1982; Ghosts, 1986; Behaving Badly, 1989; Absolute Hell; Can You Hear Me Thinking?; As Time Goes By; Last of the Blonde Bombshells. Publications: Judi Dench: A Great Deal of Laughter (biography); Judi Dench - With a Crack in Her Voice (biography), 1998. Honours include: Numerous Honorary degrees and Honorary Fellowship (Royal Holloway College); Best Actress: Variety London Critic's (Lika, The Promise, 1967); Guild of Directors (Talking to a Stranger, 1967); Society West End Theatre (Lady MacBeth, 1977); New Standard Drama Awards: Juno and the Paycock, 1980; Lady Bracknell (The Importance of Being Ernest, 1983); Deborah (A Kind of Alaska, 1983); Variety Club Award for Best Actress, Filumena, 1998; Academy Award, Best Supporting Actress (Shakespeare in Love), 1999; BAFTA Award for Best Actress (Last of the Blonde Bombshells); BAFTA Award for Best Actress (Iris), 2002. Address: c/o Julian Belfrage Associates, 46 Albermarle Street, London, W1X 4PP, England.

DENEUVE Catherine (Catherine Dorléac), b. 22 October 1943, Paris, France. Actress. m. David Bailey (divorced), 1 son (by Roger Vadim), 1 daughter (by Marcello Mastroianni). Appointments: Film debut in: Les petitis chats, 1959; President, Director-General, Films de la Citrouille, 1971-79; Films include: Les portes claquent, 1960; L'homme à femmes, 1960; le Vice et la Vertu, 1962; Et Satan conduit le bal, 1962; Vacances portugaises, 1963; Les parapluies de Cherbourg (Palme D'Or, Cannes Festival), 1963; Les plus belles escroqueries du monde, 1963; La chasses à l'homme, 1964; Un monsieur de compagnie, 1964; La Costanza della Ragione, 1964; Repulsion, 1964; Le chant du monde, 1965; La Vie de chateau, 1965; Liebes Karusell, 1965; Les créatures, 1965; Les demoiselles de Rochfort, 1966; Belle de jour (Golden Lion, Venice Festival), 1967; Benjamin, 1967; Manon 70, 1967; Mayerling, 1968; La chamade, 1966; Folies d'avril, 1969; Belles d'un soir, 1969; La sirène du Mississippi, 1969; Tristana, 1970; Peau d'âne, 1971; Ça n'arrive qu'aux autres, 1971; Liza, 1971; Un flic, 1972; Touche pas la femme blanche, 1974; Hustle, 1976; March or Die, 1977; Coup de foudre, 1977; Ecoute voir...1978; L'argent des autres, 1978; A nous deux, 1979; Ils sont grandes ces petits, 1979; Le dernier métro, 1980; Je vous aime, 1980; Hotel des Americaines, 1981; L'africain, 1983; The Hunger, 1983; Le bon plaisir, 1984; Paroles et musiques, 1984; Le lieu du crime, 1986; La reine blanche, 1991; Indochine (César Award), 1992; Ma saison préférée, 1993; La Partie d'Echecs, 1994; The Convent, 1995; Les cent et une nuits, 1995; Les Voleurs, 1995; Genéalogie d'un crime, 1997; Le Vent de la nuit, 1999; Belle-Maman, 1999; Pola x, 1999; Time Regained, 1999; Dancer in the Dark, 2000; Je centre a la maison, 2001; Absolument fabuleux, 2001; 8 Femmes, 2002. Honours: Honorary Golden Bear, Berlin Film Festival, Arts de l'Alliance française de New York Trophy, 1998. Memberships include: Co-Chairman, UNESCO Campaign to protect World's Film Heritage, 1994-. Address: c/o Artmedia, 20 avenue Rapp, 75007 Paris, France.

DENG Wei, b. 13 April 1959, Beijing, China. Photographer; Visiting Professor; Researcher. Education: Graduate, Photography Department, Beijing Film Academy, 1982. Appointments: Took portrait photographs of eminent Chinese cultural figures, 1980-85; Took portrait photographs of eminent world figures, 1991-97. Publications: Great Names in Chinese Culture, first portrait photo album of eminent figures in China,, 1986; Deng Wei' Diary, 1999; A Photographic Record of Eminent World Figures, picture album,

2000; Deng Wei, A Look at the World, 2001; Top-Notch Photographic Works by Deng Wei, picture album, 2003; Selection of Photographic Works by Deng Wei, picture album, 2003. Exhibitions: Photographic Exhibition of Deng Wei, held in several large cities in China, 2001-. Honours: Invited to lecture in Great Britain, 1990. Address: Xinjiekou Houmao Hu Tong #5, Beijing 100035, China.

DENISOV Evgenii, b. 19 June 1930, Kaluga, Russia. Researcher. m. Taissa, 2 sons. Education: Graduate, Moscow State University, 1953; PhD, Chemistry, 1957; Doctor of Science, Chemistry, 1965. Appointments: Postgraduate Student, Moscow State University, 1953-56; Junior Senior Researcher, 1956-67, Head of Laboratory, 1967-2000, Principal Researcher, 2001-, Institute of Problems of Chemical Physics. Publications: 18 monographs, Kinetics, Physical Chemistry; 485 Papers, Oxidation, Free Radical Kinetics. Honours: Award from Printing House Nauka for papers published, 1997; S Arrhenius Medal, Academy of Endeavors; Honoured Scientist of Russia, 2001. Memberships: Academy of Endeavors; International Academy of Sciences. Address: Chernogolovka Central St 4A/39, Moscow Region 142432, Russia.

DENTON Kenneth Raymond, b. 20 August 1932, Chatham, Kent, England. Artist; Landscape and Marine Painter. m. Margaret, 3 sons. Education: Rochester Technical and School of Art; Medway College of Design; David Mead, Painting and Music (Piano). Career: 45 one-man exhibitions internationally; Former Lecturer, Medway College of Design, Maidstone College of Art, Erith College. Publications: Over 200 prints, calendars and greetings cards; Co-producer and part writer: Celebration of 50 years of the Royal Society of Marine Artists; Numerous articles in art magazines and books; Featured in art dictionaries and reference works; Appearances on radio and television. Honours: Prize Winner, Hunting Group Art Awards; Fairbairn Memorial Prize. Memberships: Royal Society of Marine Artists; International Society of Marine Artists; East Anglian Group of Marine Artists; Fellow, Royal Society of Arts; Fellow, British Institute of Design; Retired Member, Chartered Society of Designers. Address: Priory Farm Lodge, Sporle, Kings Lynn, Norfolk PE32 2DS, England. Website: www.denton.uk.net

DEOSARAN Ramesh, b. 28 March 1944, Trinidad and Tobago, West Indies. Professor of Criminology and Social Psychology. m. Nirmala Deosaran. Education: BSc, First Class Hons, 1972, MA, 1974, PhD, 1976, University of Toronto, Canada. Appointments: Visiting Professor at the universities of: Stanford, California at Los Angeles, California at Berkeley, John Jay College of Criminal Justice, Hawaii, Madras, Florida State, City of New York, Bonn, Berlin, Munich, Frankfurt and Hamburg and Frankfurt School of Social Research, Germany, 1980-99; Head, Department of Behavioural Sciences, The University of the West Indies, 1989-99; Director, The Ansa McAl Psychological Research Centre, The University of the West Indies, 1989-99; Deputy Dean (Graduate Studies and Research), Faculty of Social Sciences, 1995-97; Director, Centre for Criminology and Criminal Justice, The University of the West Indies, 1997-; Chairman, Advisory Committee, School of Continuing Studies, 1998-2001. Publications: 13 books; over 71 papers, chapters in books and policy reports. Honours: Tunapuna Regional Corporation Award of Recognition for Public and Community Service, 2001; Editorial board, Journal of Ethnicity and Criminal Justice, 2001-; Editorial Board, A Critical Journal of Crime, Law and Society, 2003-; Fellow, Society for the Psychological Study of Social Issues, 2000; Editorial consultant, Police Practice and Research: An International Journal 1999-; Certificate of Honour and Keys to the City of San Francisco, 1999; Editor, Caribbean Journal of Criminology and Social Psychology, 1996-; Senior Fulbright Research Award, 1987-

88. Memberships: Academy of Criminal Justice Sciences; American Psychological Association; American Society of Criminology; British Psychological Society; British Society of Criminology; Canadian Law and Society Association; Canadian Psychological Association; Caribbean Studies Association; International Association for Applied Psychology; International Communication Association, International Society for Humour Studies; International Society for Political Psychology; Society for the Psychological Study of Social Issues. Address: Centre for Criminology and Criminal Justice, The University of the West Indies, St Augustine Campus, Trinidad and Tobago, West Indies. E-mail: crimrd@trinidad.net

DEPARDIEU Gerard, b. 27 December 1948, Chateauroux, France. Actor; Vineyard Owner. m. Elisabeth Guignot, 1970, 1 son, 1 daughter. Education: Cours d'art dramatique de Charles Dullin and Ecole d'art dramatique de Jean Laurent Cochet. Appointments: President, Jury, 45th Cannes International Film Festival, 1992; Appeared in several short films. Creative Works: Feature Films include: Les gaspards, 1973; Les valseuses, 1973; Pas si mechant que ca, 1974; 1900, 1975; La derniere femme, 1975; Sept morts sur ordonnance, 1975; Maîtresse, 1975; Barocco, 1976; René la Canne, 1976; Les plages de l'Atlantique, 1976; Baxter vera Baxter, 1976; Dites-lui que je l'aime, 1977; Le camion, 1977; Reve de singe, 1977; Le sucre, 1978; Buffet froid, 1979; Loulou, 1979; Le dernier metro, 1980 (César award Best Actor, France); Le choix des armes, 1981; La femme d'à côté, 1981; La chèvre, 1981; Le retour de Martin Guerre, 1981 (Best Actor Award, American Society of Film Critics); Danton, 1981; Le grand frère, 1982 La lune dans le carniveau, 1983; Les compères, 1983; Fort Saganne, 1983; Tartuffe (also Director), 1984; Rive Droit, Rive Gauche, 1984; Police, 1984; One Woman or Two, 1985; Jean de Florette, 1985; Tenue de soirée, 1985; Rue de départ, 1986; Les fugitifs, 1986; Cyrano de Bergerac, 1989 (César award Best Actor); Uranus, 1990; Green Card (Golden Globe for Best Comedy Actor), 1991; Mon Pere Ce Heros, 1991; 1492: Conquest of Paradise, 1991; Tous les matins due monde, 1991; Germinal, 1992 A Pure Formality, 1993; Le Colonel Chabert, 1993; La Machine, Elisa, Les Cents et Une Nuits, Les Anges Gardiens, Le Garçu, all 1994; Bogus, 1995; Unhook the Stars, 1995; Secret Agent, 1995; Vatel, 1997; The Man in the Iron Mask, 1997; Les Portes du Ciel, 1999; Astérix et Obélix, 1999; Un pont entre deux rives (also Director), 1999; Vatel, 1999; Les Acteurs, 2000; Chicken Run, 2000; Le Placard, 2001; 102 Dalmatians, 2001; Astérix et Obélix: Mission Cleopatra, 2002; Bon Voyage, 2004. Several plays and television productions. Publication: Lettres volées, 1988. Honours: Numerous national and international awards. Address: Art Media, 10 Avenue George V, 75008 Paris, France.

DEPP Johnny, b. 9 June 1963, Owensboro, Kentucky, USA. Actor. m. (1) Lori Anne Allison (divorced), (2) Vanessa Paradis, 1 son, 1 daughter. Appointments: Former rock musician; TV appearances include 21 Jump Street; Films include: A Nightmare on Elm Street; Platoon; Slow Burn; Cry Baby; Edward Scissorhands, 1990; Benny and Joon, 1993; What's Eating Gilbert Grape, 1991; Arizona Dream; Ed Wood; Don Juan de Marco, 1994; Dead Man; Nick of Time; Divine Rapture; The Brave (also writer and director), 1997; Donnie Brasco, 1997; Fear and Loathing in Las Vegas, 1998; The Astronaut's Wife, 1998; The Source, 1999; The Ninth Gate, 1999; The Libertine, 1999; Just to Be Together, 1999; Sleepy Hollow, 1999; Before Night Falls, 2000; The Man Who Cried, 2000; Chocolat, 2000; Blow, 2001; From Hell, 2001; Lost in La Mancha, 2002; Once Upon a Time in Mexico, 2002; Pirates of the Caribbean: The Curse of the Black Pearl, 2003. Address: 500 S Sepulveda Boulevard, Suite 500, Los Angeles, CA 90049, USA.

DERKOWSKI Wojciech, b. 30 June 1966, Kutno, Poland. Neurologist; Physician. m. Jagoda Maria Cieszynska, 2 sons, 2 daughters. Education: BM, 1991; Specialisation, Neurologist, 1994; Specialist Neurologist, 1998. Appointments: Assistant, Internal Ward, Kluczbork, Poland, 1991-92; Neurology Ward, Opole, Poland, 1992-99; Physician, House of Social Welfare for Children, 1993-95; Senior Assistant, 1998, Vice Head, 1999, Neurological Ward. Opole; Senior Assistant, Neurological Outpatient Department, Public Health Service, Kluczbork, 1999-. Honours: Delegate, 15th International Physics Olympiad, Sigtuna, Sweden, 1984; 3rd place, 33rd Physics Olympiad, Warsaw, 1984; 2nd place 27th Astronomy Olympiad, Chorzow, Poland, 1984; 3rd Prize, 26th International Mathematics Olympiad, Helsinki, 1985; Polish Children's Fund Fellow, 1983-85, 1991. Memberships: Polish Neurological Society; Polish Society of Clinical Neurophysiology; Polish Stroke Society. Address: Neurological Outpatient Department, Poradnia Neurologiczna, Kluczbork, Grunwaldzka 26, 46-203 Kluczbork, Poland.

DERN Laura, b. 10 February 1967, Los Angeles, USA. Appointments: Film debut aged 11 in Foxes, 1980; TV appearances include: Happy Endings; Three Wishes of Billy Greer; Afterburn; Down Came a Blackbird; Director, The Gift, 1999; Films: Teachers; Mask; Smooth Talk; Blue Velvet; Haunted Summer; Wild of Heart; Rambling Rose; Jurassic Park; A Perfect World; Devil Inside; Citizen Ruth, 1996; Bastard Out of Carolina, 1996; Ruby Ridge, 1996; October Sky, 1999; Dr T and the Women, 2000; Daddy and Them, 2001; Focus, 2001; Novocaine, 2001; Jurassic Park III, 2001; I Am Sam, 2001.

DERSHOWITZ Alan (Morton), b. 1 September 1938, New York, New York, USA. Lawyer; Professor of Law; Writer. m. Carolyn Cohen, 2 sons, 1 daughter. Education: BA, Brooklyn College, 1959; LLB, Yale University, 1962. Appointments: Called to the Bar, Washington, DC, 1963, Massachusetts, 1968, US Supreme Court, 1968; Law Clerk to Chief Judge David L Bazelon, US Court of Appeals, 1962-63, to Justice Arthur J Goldberg, US Supreme Court; Faculty, 1964-, Professor of Law, 1967-, Fellow, Center for Advanced Study of Behavioral Sciences, 1971-72, Felix Frankfurter Professor of Law, 1993-, Harvard University. Publications: Psychoanalysis, Psychiatry and the Law (with others), 1967; Criminal Law: Theory and Process, 1974; The Best Defense, 1982; Reversal of Fortune: Inside the von Bulow Case, 1986; Taking Liberties: A Decade of Hard Cases, Bad Laws and Bum Raps, 1988; Chutzpah, 1991; Contrary to Popular Opinion, 1992; The Abuse Excuse, 1994; The Advocate's Devil, 1994; Reasonable Doubt, 1996; The Vanishing American Jew, 1997; Sexual McCarthyism, 1998; Just Revenge, 1999; The Genesis of Justice, 2000; Supreme Injustice, 2001; Letters to a Young Lawyer, 2001; Shouting Fire, 2002. Contributions to: Periodicals. Honours: Guggenheim Fellowship, 1978-79; Honorary doctorates. Memberships: Order of the Coif; Phi Beta Kappa. Address: c/o Harvard University Law School, Cambridge, MA 02138, USA.

DESAI Anita, b. 24 June 1937, Mussoorie, India. Writer. m. Ashvin Desai, 13 December 1958, 2 sons, 2 daughters. Education: BA, Honours, Miranda House, University of Delhi. Publications: Cry, The Peacock; Voices in the City; Fire on the Mountain; Clear Light of Day; In Custody, (also filmed, 1994); Baumgartner's Bombay; Where Shall We Go This Summer?; Bye Bye Blackbird; The Peacock Garden; Cat on a Houseboat; The Village by the Sea, (also BBC TV Serial, 1992); Games at Twilight; Journey to Ithaca, 1995; Fasting, Feasting, 1999; Diamond Dust and Other Stories, 2000. Honours: Winifred Holtby Award, Royal Society of Literature, 1978; Sahitya Akademi Award for English, 1978; Federation of Indian Publishers Award, 1978; Padma Shri Award, India, 1989; Hadassah Magazine Award, 1989; Guardian Prize for Children's Fiction, 1993; Literary Lion, New York Public

Library, 1993; Neil Gunn International Writers Fellowship, Scotland, 1994. Memberships: Royal Society of Literature; Sahitya Akademi of India; PEN; Fellow, American Academy of Arts and Letters, 1992; Fellow, Girton College and Clare Hall, Cambridge. Address: c/o Rogers, Coleridge and White Ltd, 20 Powis Mews, London W11 1JN, England.

DESHPANDE Shashi, b. 19 August 1938, Dharwad, India. Novelist. m. D H Deshpande, 1962, 2 sons. Education: BA Honours, Economics, 1956, Diploma, Journalism, 1970, MA, English, 1984, University of Mysore; BL, University of Mysore, Karnataka, 1959. Publications: The Dark Holds no Terrors, 1980; If I Die Today, 1982; Roots and Shadows, 1983; Come Up and Be Dead, 1985; That Long Silence, 1988; The Binding Vine, 1993; A Matter of Time, 1996; Small Remedies, 2000. Short stories: The Legacy and Other Stories, 1978; It Was Dark, 1986; The Miracle and Other Stories, 1986; It Was the Nightingale, 1986; The Intrusion and Other Stories, 1994; The Stone Women, 2000; Collected Short Stories, Vol I, 2003; Writing from the Margin and other essays, 2003. Honours: Rangammal Prize, 1984; Sahitya Academy Award, 1990; Nanjangud Thirumalamba Award, 1991. Address: 409 41st Cross, Jayanagar V Block, Bangalore 560041, India.

DESSI Gigi, b. 21 June 1938, Serdiana (CA), Italy. Retired Accountant; Poet. m. Orsola, 2 sons, 1 daughter. Education: Diploma in Accountancy. Appointments: Started working at a very young age for a publishing company; Worked as an Accountant until retirement. Publications: Vetri frantumati, 1974; L'incomprensibile uomo, 1976; Dioniso e l'uomo, 1978; La Pressione del tempo, 1982 (published in English as "Pressures" in USA and English speaking countries); Finestra dei trapassi, 1984; Tanche di memoria, 1987; Il disegno, 1998. Honours include: Premio critica letteraria "Renato Serra", 1986; Premio "Calliope", 1992. Address: via Sallustio no 39, 09042 Monserrato (CA), Italy. E-mail: pierluigi@dessiemonari.it

DETTLAFF Tatjana, b. 8 October 1912, Moscow region, Russia. Biologist. m. Nikolay Ivanovich Lazarev, 1 son, 1 daughter. Education: Postgraduate studies, 1934-37, Doctoral, 1949, Professor, 1970, Moscow University. Appointments: Institute of Experimental Medicine, Moscow, 1937; Institute of Evolutionary Morphology, Moscow, 1940-41; Assistant head of laboratory, Kazakhstan Filial Academy of Science, Alma-Ala, 1942-43; Doctorant Institute of Evolutionary Morphology, Moscow, 1944-49; Assistant, Institute of Evolutionary Morphology, Moscow, 1949-67; Head of laboratory, Institute of Animal Morphology, Moscow, 1967-87; Cons, Institute of Developmental Biology, Moscow, 1987-91. Publications: Author, co-author and editor of several books; 160 articles; Co-author of book, On the Way of Understanding the Time Phenomenon, 1995. Honours: Kowalevskij's Award. Memberships: International Institute of Embryology; RAN, Moscow, Russia. Address: Institution of Developmental Biology, Vavilov Str 26, 117334 Moscow, Russia.

DETTORI Lanfranco, b. 15 December 1970, Milan, Italy. Flat Race Jockey. m. Catherine Allen, 1997, 1 son, 3 daughters. Appointments: Ridden races in England, France, Germany, Italy, USA, Dubai, Australia, Hong Kong and other countries in Far East, 1992-; 1000 rides and 215 wins in UK, 1995; Horses ridden include Lamtarra, Barathea, Vettori, Mark of Distinction, Balanchine, Moonshell, Lochsong, Classic Cliché, Dubai Millennium, Daylami; Sakhee; major race victories include: St Leger (twice), The Oaks (twice); The Breeders Cup Mile; Arc de Triomphe (twice); French 2000 Guineas (twice); English 1000 Guineas; Queen Elizabeth II Stakes; Prix L'Abbaye; The Japan Cup (twice); The Dubai World Cup; Rode winner of all 7 races at

Ascot, 28 October 1996. Publication: A Year in the Life of Frankie Dettori, 1996. Honours: Jockey of the Year, 1994, 1995; BBC Sports Personality of the Year, 1996; International Sports Personality of the Year, Variety Club, 2000. Address: c/o Peter Burrell Classic Management, 53 Stewarts Grove, London, SW3 6PH, England. E-mail: pburrell@classicmanagement.com

DEVAPOOJITHAYA Arikkady Srisha, b. 11 December 1944, Kasaragod, India. Professor of English, retired; Poet. m. B V Usharani, 26 April 1969, 1 son, 1 daughter. Education: MA, English Language, 1966; MA, Kannada, 1971; MA, Sanskrit, 1973; MA, Hindi, 1975. Appointments: Professor of English, 1966-, Head Department of English, 1988-, Head, Postgraduate Department of English, 1998-99, Government College, Kasaragod, Kerala; Attending poets' conferences for many years as a Kannada poet in Indian States of Kerala and Karnataka; Regular Broadcast of Poems, All India Radio. Publications: Kasaragodina Kavithegalu, 1978; Idu Varthamana, 1979; Thappenu, 1987; Kavi Goshthi, 1994; Banjaru Bhoomi, 1996. Contributions to: Udayavani; Thushara; Mallige; Navabharatha; Tainudi; Hosa Digantha; Suguna Digest. Honour: Muddana Kavya Rajya Prashasthi. Memberships: Navya Sahithya Sangha; Kasaragodu Jilla Lekhakara Sangha, executive committee; Kasaragod; Kerala Government College Teachers' Association, 1966-. Address: Srinivas Compound, Navakana, Badiadka, Post Perdala, PIN 671551, Kerala, India.

DEVERALL Brian James. Education: BSc, Botany, Hons 1, Edinburgh, 1957; DIC, 1960, PhD, 1960, Plant Pathology, London. Appointments include: Harkess Fellow, Commonwealth Fund, New York, 1960-62; PostDoctoral Fellow, University of Wisconsin, 1960-61, University of Nebraska, 1961-62; Lecturer, Imperial College University of London, England, 1962-70; Principal Scientific Officer, Wye College, University of London, England, 1970-72; Professor of Plant Pathology, University of Sydney, Australia, 1973-2001; Emeritus Professor, University of Sydney, 2001-. Publications: 6 Monographs and edited books; Numerous research and review papers in leading international journals; 20 Review Chapters. Memberships: British Mycological Society, 1962-97; British Plant Pathology Society, since foundation in 1982-; Australasian Plant Pathology Society, 1972-, President, 1987-89; American Phytopathological Society, 1993-2002; International Society for Plant Pathology, Vice President, 1993-98. Address: Faculty of Agriculture, Food and Natural Resources, University of Sydney, NSW 2006, Australia.

DEVITO Danny, b. 1944, New Jersey, USA. Actor; Director. m. Rhea Perlman, 1982, 2 sons, 2 daughters. Education: American Academy of Dramatic Arts; Wilfred Academy of Hair and Beauty Culture. Appointments: Hairdresser for 1 year; Stage appearances include: The Man With a Flower in His Mouth; Down the Morning Line; The Line of Least Existence; The Shrinking Bride; Call Me Charlie; Comedy of Errors; Merry Wives of Windsor; Three by Pirandello; One Flew Over the Cuckoo's Nest; Film appearances include: Lady Liberty; Scalawag; Hurry Up or I'll be 30; One Flew Over the Cuckoo's Nest; Deadly Hero; Car Wash; The Van; World's Greatest Lover; Goin' South; Going Ape; Terms of Endearment; Romancing the Stone; Johnny Dangerously; Head Office; Jewel of the Nile; Wiseguys; Ruthless People; My Little Pony (voice); Tin Men; Throw Momma From the Train (also director); Other People's Money, 1991; Batman Returns, 1992; Hoffa (also producer, director), Other People's Money, 1991; Batman Returns, 1992; Renaissance Man, 1994; Junior, 1994; Matilda (also director, co-producer); Mars Attacks, 1997; The Rainmaker, 1997; LA Confidential, 1997; Man on the Moon, 1999; Drowning Mona, 2000; Screwed, 2000; Heist, 2001; What's the Worst That Could Happen? 2001; Death to Smoochy, 2002; Austin Powers in Goldmember, 2002; Television appearances include:

Taxi (also director), Feeling Mary (director only); Valentine; The Rating Game (director); All the Kids Do It, A Very Special Christmas Party; Two Daddies? (voice); The Selling of Vince DeAngelo (director); Amazing Stories (also director); The Simpsons (voice). Address: c/o Fred Specktor, Creative Artists Agency, 9830 Wilshire Boulevard, Beverly Hills, CA 90212, USA.

DEVLIN Dean, b. 27 August 1962. Actor; Screenplay Writer; Producer. Creative Works: Film produced: The Patriot, 2000; Films written and produced; Stargate, 1994; Independence Day, 1996; Godzilla, 1998; Film screenplay: Universal Solider, 1992; Actor: My Bodyguard, 1980; The Wild Life, 1984; Real Genius, 1985; City Limits, 1985; Martians Go Home, 1990; Moon 44, 1990; Total Exposure, 1991; TV series: The Visitor (creator, executive producer), 1997; TV appearances in: North Beach, 1985; Rawhide, 1985; Hard Copy, 1987; Generations, 1989; Guest appearances in: LA Law; Happy Days; Misfits of Science. Address: c/o Creative Artists Agency, 9830 Wilshire Boulevard, Beverly Hills, CA 90212, USA.

DEWHIRST Ian, b. 17 October 1936, Keighley, Yorkshire, England. Retired Librarian; Writer; Poet. Education: BA Honours, Victoria University of Manchester, 1958. Appointment: Staff, Keighley Public Library, 1960-91. Publications: The Handloom Weaver and Other Poems, 1965; Scar Top and Other Poems, 1968; Gleanings From Victorian Yorkshire, 1972; A History of Keighley, 1974; Yorkshire Through the Years, 1975; Gleanings from Edwardian Yorkshire, 1975; The Story of a Nobody, 1980; You Don't Remember Bananas, 1985; Keighley in Old Picture Postcards, 1987; In the Reign of the Peacemaker, 1993; Down Memory Lane, 1993; Images of Keighley, 1996; Co-editor, A Century of Yorkshire Dialect, 1997. Contributions to: Yorkshire Ridings Magazine; Lancashire Magazine; Dalesman; Cumbria; Pennine Magazine; Transactions of the Yorkshire Dialect Society; Yorkshire Journal. Honour: Honorary Doctor of Letters, University of Bradford, 1996; MBE, 1999. Memberships: Yorkshire Dialect Society; Brontë Society; Edward Thomas Fellowship; Associate of the Library Association; Fellow, Royal Society of Arts, 2000. Address: 14 Raglan Avenue, Fell Lane, Keighley, West Yorkshire BD22 6BJ, England.

DEWHURST Eileen Mary, b. 27 May 1929, Liverpool, England. Author. Divorced. Education: BA (Hons) English Language and Literature, St Anne's College, Oxford, 1951. Publications: Crime novels: Death Came Smiling, 1975; After the Ball, 1976; Curtain Fall, 1977; Drink This, 1980; Trio in Three Flats, 1981; Whoever I Am, 1982; The House That Jack Built, 1983; There Was a Little Girl, 1984; Playing Safe, 1985; A Private Prosecution, 1986; A Nice Little Business, 1987; The Sleeper, 1988; Dear Mr Right, 1990; The Innocence of Guilt, 1991; Death in Candie Gardens, 1992; Now You See Her, 1995; The Verdict on Winter; 1996; Alias the Enemy, 1997; Roundabout, 1998; Death of a Stranger, 1999; Double Act, 2000; Closing Stages, 2001; No Love Lost, 2002; Easeful Death, 2003; Naked Witness, 2003. Contributions to: Ellery Queen's Mystery Magazine; Crime Writer's Association Annual Anthologies. Memberships: Crime Writers Association; Society of Authors. Address: c/o Gregory and Company, 3 Barb Mews, London W6 7PA, England.

DEXTER Colin, b. 29 September 1930, Stamford, Lincolnshire, England. Writer. Education: Christ's College, Cambridge; MA (Cantab): MA (Oxon). Publications: Last Bus to Woodstock, 1975; Last Seen Wearing, 1976; The Silent World of Nicholas Quinn, 1977; Service of All the Dead, 1979; The Dead of Jericho, 1981; The Riddle of the Third Mile, 1983; The Secret of Annexe 3, 1983; The Wench is Dead, 1989; The Jewel That Was Ours, 1991; The Way Through the Woods, 1992; Morse's Greatest Mystery,

1993; The Daughters of Cain, 1994; Death is Now My Neighbour, 1996; The Remorseful Day, 1999. Honours: Silver Dagger, 1979, 1981, Gold Dagger, 1989, 1992, Diamond Dagger, 1997, Crime Writers' Association; Macavity Award, Best Short Story, 1995; Lotos Club Medal of Merit, New York, 1996; Sherlock Holmes Award, 1999; Officer of the Order of the British Empire, 2000; Freedom, City of Oxford, 2001. Memberships: Crime Writers' Association; Detection Club. Address: 456 Banbury Road, Oxford OX2 7RG, England.

DHALL Dharam Pal, b. 8 December 1937, Kenya. Vascular Surgeon. m. Tehseen, 1 son, 1 daughter. Education: MBChB, 1961; FRCS, 1965; PhD, 1967; MD, 1968; FRACS, 1994, MACE, 2002. Appointments: Senior Registrar, Lecturer, Surgery, Aberdeen University; Professor of Surgery, University of Nairobi; Senior Consultant Surgeon, Canberra Hospital; Visiting Fellow, John Curtin School of Medical Research, Canberra; Director, Institute of Sathya Sai Education, Canberra, Director, Educare Community Services Pty Ltd; Academic Adviser, University of Central Queensland for Master of Learning Management in Human Values, University of Queensland; Adjunct Professor of Bioethics, University of Canberra. Publications: Approximately 200 articles in Scientific Medical Journals; 15 books on the teachings of Sri Sathya Sai Baba Sai Education including Human Values, The Heart of Dynamic Parenting; Workshops on Dynamic Parenting; Stepping Stones to Peace; Dynamic Dharma; Over one hundred articles in professional journals. Honours include: Hallett Award, 1963; National Heart Foundation; NH and MRC, Australia; Pharmacia Uppsala, Sweden. Memberships: World Education Federation; Associate Member, Australian Counselling Association; Member, Australian College of Educators. Address: PO Box 697, Queanbeyan, NSW 2620, Australia. E-mail: paldhall@aol.com

DI MELCHIORRE Silvio, b. 23 May 1972, Buenos Aires, Argentina. Airline Consultant; Political Scientist; Private Investor. Education: Participant, Jornadas Nietzsche, 1994, 1998; Political Scientist with speciality, International Relations, University of Buenos Aires, 1997; Graduate, IATA-UFTAA Basic Course, IATA Learning Centre, 1998; Participant, Quinto Programa de Simulación Búrsatil, University of Buenos Aires, 1999. Appointments: Managing Director, BII Worldwide, Buenos Aires, 1991-92; President, SDM Internacional, Buenos Aires, 1993-95; Consulting in field, Buenos Aires, 1993-95; Banking Mediator, Buenos Aires, 1995-96; Founder Director, Biblioteca Silvio Di Melchiorre, Buenos Aires, 1996-97; Airline Consultant, Buenos Aires, 1996; Airways Policy Adviser, Buenos Aires, 1997-2000; Private Investor, Buenos Aires, 2000-. Publications: Editor, Director, TAIN Magazine, Buenos Aires, 1987-88; Boletín Informativo Internacional, Buenos Aires, 1989-90; Author: Information Service, IO Club, 1992; TV Novel, Ramsés II, 1995; Political Expression, Airways Policy, 1998; Banking Publication, La Banque, 1998. Memberships: Donor countries information service to Fundación Poder Ciudadano, Buenos Aires, 1994; Donor publications to Library of University Del Salvador, Buenos Aires, 1996-97; Instituto del Servicio Exterior de la Nación, Buenos Aires, 1997-98; Bolsa de Comercio de Buenos Aires, 1997-2001. Address: Bartolomé Mitre 1676 Piso 3 Dpto 11 Cuerpo 2 C1037ABF, Buenos Aires, Republic of Argentina. E-mail: sdimelchiorre@hotmail.com

DIAMESSIS Spyros (Spyridon), b. 6 August 1940, Athens, Greece. Ministers' Counsellor. m. Olga Christidau-Diamessis, 1 son, 1 daughter. Education: BSEE, 1961, BA, Philosophy, 1963, MS, Electrical Engineering, 1964, MS, Education, 1970, University of Penna; Doctorate in Electrical Engineering, National Technical University of Athens, Greece, 1972. Appointments: Assistant

Dictionary of International Biography

Instructor, Instructor, Lecturer, Researcher, University of Penna, Communication Research Laboratory, National Technical University, Air Force Academy, National Research, USA and Greece, 1961-75; Member, Board of Education of Greece, 1976-2002; Board Member, Institute of Crosscultural Education and Education for the Diaspora, 1998-2003. Publications: 260 articles and publications on technology and energy, education and pedagogy, philosophy, language and terminology, computers, philosophy of education, sociology of education, information and documentation, Greek culture, and others. Honours: Gold Medal Prize, University of Penna; Athens Cup, Engineering Honor Society; Society of Athenians. Memberships: IEEE; Greek Technical Chamber; Association of Greek Electronic Mechanical Engineers; AEDE; DRG; DSNA; CETIL; CDCC; Olympic Idea Society. Address: 26 Narkisson St, Paleo Psychico, Athens 15482, Greece. E-mail: sdiame@pi-schools.gr

DIAMOND Neil Lesley, b. 24 January 1941, Brooklyn, New York, USA. Pop Singer; Composer. m. (1) 2 children, (2) Marcia Murphey, 1975, 2 children. Education: New York University. Appointments: Formerly with Bang Records, Uni, MCA Records, Los Angeles; Now recording artist with Columbia Records; Guest Artist, TV network shows. Publications: Songs include: Solitary Man; Cherry, Cherry; Kentucky Woman; I'm A Believer; September Morn; Sweet Caroline; Holly, Holy; A Little Bit Me, A Little Bit You; Longfellow Serenade; Song Sung Blue; America; I am I Said; Recordings: Numerous albums, 1966-; 19 Platinum albums; 28 Gold albums; Composer, film scores; Jonathan Livingston Seagull, 1973; Ebery Which Way But Loose, 1978; The Jazz Singer (also actor), 1980. Honours include: Grammy Award, Jonathan Livingston Seagull, 1973. Address: c/o Columbia Records, 2100 Colorado Avenue, Santa Monica, CA 90404, USA.

DIARRA DEMBELE Fatoumata, b. 15 February 1949, Koulikoro, Mali. Judge. m. Korotogoma Diarra, 4 sons, 2 daughters. Education: LLB, Dakar University, 1971; Graduate, National School Administration, Bamako, Mali, 1974; Graduate, National Judges School of Paris, 1977. Appointments: Investigative Judge, Investigation Office of First Instance Tribunal of Bamako, 1977-80; Trial Attorney, Office of the Prosecutor, Tribunal of Bamako, 1980-81; Vice-President, Labour Court of Bamako, 1981-82; Investigative Judge, Investigation Office of the First Instance Tribunal of Koulikoro, 1982-84; Senior Investigation Office of Bamako, 1984-86; Legal Advisor, National Assembly of Malawi, 1986-91; Legal Advisor, Transition Commission for Reinstallation of Republic Institutions, Office of Head of State, 1991; General Director, Malian Office for Intellectual Property and Copyright, 1991-93; Official, Republic Office of the Commissioner for Promotion of Women, 1993-94; Appeals Court Advisor, Criminal Chamber, 1994-96; President, Criminal Chamber of Bamako Appeals Court, 1996-99; National Director, Justice Administration, 1999-2001; Judge, Trial Chamber of International Criminal Tribunal for Former Yugoslavia, 2001-2003; Judge, International Criminal Court, The Hague, 2003-. Publications: Le role des femmes dans la question des conflits armés; Droits des femmes en jeux et d'efes; Les violences faites aux femmes; Droit et Exclusion; L'aide Juridique; L'Excision et le Droit; Positif Malien; Obstacles à l'exercice des Droits des Femmes au Mali. Honours: Officier de l'Ordre National du Mali; Prix Special de Participation à la Promotion des Droits. Memberships: President, Malian Electoral Support Network, 1997-; National Committee for Review of Code of Family Law, 1997-; Working Group for orientation and integration Malian Presidency of the CEDEAO, UEMOA and CILSS, 1999-; Association of Malian Women Lawyers; International Federation of Women with Legal Careers; Federation of African Women Lawyers; International Council for French Speaking Women; Lions' Club. Address: Haagweg 133, Rijswijk 2281 AE, Netherlands. E-mail: fatoumata.diarra@icc-cpi.inf

DIAZ Cameron, b. 30 August 1972, Long Beach, California, USA. Actress. Appointments: Films include: The Mask, 1994; The Last Supper, 1995; Feeling Minnesota, 1996; She's the One, 1996; A Life Less Ordinary, 1997; There's Something About Mary, 1998; Very Bad Things, 1998; Being John Malkovich, 1999; Invisible Circus, 1999; Any Given Sunday, 1999; Charlie's Angels, 2000; Things You Can Tell Just by Looking at Her, 2000; Shrek (voice), 2001; Vanilla Sky, 2001; The Sweetest Thing, 2002; Gangs of New York, 2002; Minority Report, 2002; Charlie's Angels: Full Throttle, 2003; Shrek 2 (voice), 2004. Address: c/o International Creative Management, 8942 Wilshire Boulevard, Beverly Hills, CA 90211, USA.

DICKINSON Angie (pseudonym of Angeline Brown), b. 30 September 1931, Kulm, North Dakota, USA. Actress. Education: Glendale College. Appointments: Actress in films: Lucky Me, 1954; Man With the Gun; The Return of Jack Slade; Tennessee's Partner; The Black Whip; Hidden Guns; Tension at Table Rock; Gun the Man Down; Calypso Joe; China Gate; Shoot Out at Medicine Bend; Cry Terror; I Married a Woman; Rio Bravo; The Bramble Bush; Ocean's 11; A Fever in the Blood; The Sins of Rachel Cade; Jessica; Rome Adventure; Captain Newman MD; The Killers; The Art of Love; Cast a Giant Shadow; The Chase; Poppy is Also a Flower; The Last Challenge; Point Blank; Sam Whiskey; Some Kind of Nut; Young Billy Young; Pretty Maids All in A Row; The Resurrection of Zachery Wheeler; The Outside Man; Big Bad Mama; Klondike Fever; Dressed to Kill; Charlie Chan and the Curse of the Dragon Queen; Death Hunt; Big Bad Mama II; Even Cowgirls Get The Blues; The Maddening; Sabrina; The Sun - The Moon and the Stars; Pay it Forward; Sealed with a Kiss, 1999; The Last Producer, 2000; Duets, 2000; Pay It Forward, 2000; Big Bad Love, 2001; Ocean's Eleven, 2001; TV series: Police Woman; Cassie & Co; TV films: The Love War; Thief; See the Man Run; The Norliss Tapes; Pray for the Wildcats; A Sensitive Passionate Man; Overboard; The Suicide's Wife; Dial M for Murder; One Shoe Makes it Murder; Jealousy; A Touch of Scandal; Still Watch; Police Story: The Freeway Killings; Once Upon a Texas Train; Prime Target; Treacherous Crossing; Danielle Steel's Remembrance; Mini-series: Pearl; Hollywood Wives; Wild Palms.

DIERINGER Gregg, b. 18 October 1956, Athens, Ohio, USA. Plant Ecologist. m. Leticia Cabrera, 2 sons. Education: BS cum laude, 1979, MS, 1981, University of Akron; PhD, University of Texas at Austin, 1988. Appointments: Teaching Assistant, University of Akron, 1979-81; Teaching Assistant, 1983, Research Assistant, 1983-84, Teaching Assistant, 1984-88, Instructor, 1990-92, University of Texas at Austin; Instructor, Austin Community College, 1988, 1989-92; Assistant Professor, Southwest Texas State University, 1989; Visiting Professor, Instituto de Ecologia, Veracruz, Mexico, 1992-93; Assistant Professor, 1993-97, Associate Professor, 1997-99, Western Illinois University; Lecturer, University of Texas at Brownsville, 1999-2002; Associate Professor, Chair, Department of Biological Sciences, Northwest Missouri State University, 2003-. Publications: Numerous articles in professional journals; Presentations at scientific meetings; General reports and book reviews. Honours: Eagle Scout, 1973; Phi Sigma Alpha, University of Akron, 1978; Scholarship to attend Rocky Mountain Biological Station, 1983; Several research grants. Memberships: Botanical Society of America; Torrey Botanical Society. Address: Department of Biological Sciences, Northwest Missouri State University, 800 University Dr, Maryville, MO 64468, USA. E-mail: greggd@mail.nwmissouri.edu

DIESING Paul Robert, b. 3 September 1922, Elgin, Illinois, USA. University Professor. m. Eleanor Zuckman, 2 sons, 2 daughters. Education: Concordia Teachers College, River Forest, Illinois, 1940-43; MA, 1948, PhD, 1952, Department of Philosophy,

University of Chicago. Appointments: Instructor, Philosophy, University of Illinois, Urbana, 1952-62; Visiting Professor, University of Colorado, Boulder, 1962-63; Professor of Philosophy, 1963-74, Political Science, 1968-92, Sociology, 1992-93, State University of New York, Buffalo. Publications: Reason in Society, 1962; Patterns of Discovery in the Social Sciences, 1971; Conflict Among Nations, 1977; Science and Ideology in the Policy Sciences, 1982; How Does Social Science Work? 1991; Hegel's Dialectical Political Economy, 1999. Memberships: American Philosophical Association; Society for Social Studies of Social Science; Association for Evolutionary Economics; Union of Radical Political Economists. Address: 380 Springdale Dr, Bradenton, FL 34210, USA.

DILLINGHAM William Byron, b. 7 March 1930, Atlanta, Georgia, USA; Emeritus Professor of American Literature; Writer. m. Elizabeth Joiner, 3 July 1952, 1 son, 2 daughters. Education: BA, 1955, MA, 1956, Emory University; PhD, University of Pennsylvania, 1961. Appointments: Instructor, 1956-58, Assistant Professor, Associate Professor, Professor, Charles Howard Candler Professor of American Literature, 1959-96, Emeritus Professor 1996-; Emory University; Editorial Boards, Nineteenth-Century Literature, South Atlantic Bulletin. Publications: Humor of the Old Southwest, 1965, 3rd edition, 1994; Frank Norris: Instinct and Art, 1969; An Artist in the Rigging: The Early Work of Herman Melville, 1972; Melville's Short Fiction, 1853-1856, 1977; Melville's Later Novels, 1986; Practical English Handbook, 9th edition, 1992, 10th edition, 1996; Melville and His Circle: The Last Years, 1996. Contributions to: Many articles and reviews to scholarly journals. Address: 1416 Vistaleaf Drive, Decatur, GA 30033, USA.

DILLON Doris, b. 1 December 1929, Kansas City, Missouri, USA. Artist; Lecturer; Professor. m. Louis Kenofer, 1 son, 1 daughter. Education: BA, Art and Interior Design, MA, Art History, University of Denver. Appointments: Deputy District General (IBC); Continental Governor of the ABI; Advisory Panel, Colorado Council of the Arts and Humanities; Member of the Board, Asian Art Association, Denver Art Museum; Life Fellow, IBC; Consular Representative of the United Cultural Council. Publications: Art Exhibits: By invitation: Dublin, Ireland; St John's College, Cambridge, England; 26th Congress on the Arts and Communications, Lisbon, Portugal; Aerospace: Century XXI, University of Colorado, Boulder, Colorado, USA; One Person Show, Colburn Earth/Science Museum, Asheville, North Carolina, USA; International Platform Association, Washington DC; Nelson Rockefeller Collection Gallery, New York; St John's College, Cambridge University, England; Denver Art Museum Group Show; Colorado State Centennial; Denver Museum of Natural History. Honours: Art 1st place, Western States Rocky Mountain Conference Center, USA; Best of Show by Vote, International Platform Association, Washington, DC; International Woman of the Year, IBC; Excellence in the Arts, Key Award, ABI; AAUW Salute to Women Award. Memberships: International Governors' Club (ABI); National League of Pen Arts Women; International Platform Association; Mensa International Scholarship Juror. Address: 135 Delphia Drive, Brevard, NC 28712, USA.

DILLON Matt, b. 18 February 1964, New Rochelle, New York, USA. Actor. Appointments: Films include: Over the Edge, 1979; Little Darlings, 1980; My Bodyguard, 1980; Liar's Moon, 1982; Tex, 1982; The Outsiders, 1983; Rumble Fish, 1983; The Flamingo Kid, 1984; Target, 1985; Rebel, 1985; Native Son, 1986; The Big Town (The Arm), 1987; Kansas, 1988; Drugstore Cowboy, 1989; A Kiss Before Dying, 1991; Singles, 1992; The Saint of Fort Washington, 1993; Mr Wonderful, 1993; Golden Gate, 1994; To Die For; Frankie Starlight; Beautiful Girls; Grace of My Heart;

Albino Alligator; In and Out, 1997; There's Something About Mary, 1998; One Night at McCool's, 2000; Deuces Wild, 2000; City of Ghosts, 2002; Employee of the Month, 2004; Loverboy, 2004. Address: c/o William Morris Agency, ICM, 151 S El Camino Drive, Beverly Hills, CA 90212, USA.

DIMBLEBY David, b. 28 October 1938, London, England. Broadcaster; Newspaper Proprietor. m. (1) Joceline Gaskell, 1967, dissolved, 1 son, 2 daughters, (2) Belinda Giles, 2000, 1 son. Education: Christ Church, Oxford; University of Paris; University of Perugia. Appointments: Presenter and interviewer, BBC Bristol, 1960-61; Broadcasts include: Quest; What's New?; People and Power, 1982-83; General Election Results Programmes, 1979, 1983, 1987; various programmes for the Budget, by-elections, local elections; Presenter, Question Time BBC, 1993-; Documentary films include: Ku-Klux-Klan; The Forgotten Million; Cyprus: The Thin Blue Line, 1964-65; South Africa: The White Tribe, 1979; The Struggle for South Africa, 1990; US-UK Relations: An Ocean Apart, 1988; David Dimbleby's India, 1997; Live commentary on many public occasions including: State Opening of Parliament; Trooping the Colour; Wedding of HRH Prince Andrew and Sarah Ferguson; H M The Queen Mother's 90th Birthday Parade; Funeral of Diana, Princess of Wales, 1997; Memorial Services including Lord Olivier. Publication: An Ocean Apart (with David Reynolds), 1988. Honours: Supreme Documentary Award, Royal TV Society; US Emmy Award, Monte Carlo Golden Nymph; Royal TV Society, Outstanding Documentary Award, 1990, 1997. Address: 14 King Street, Richmond, Surrey, TW9 1NF, England.

DIMBLEBY Jonathan, b. 31 July 1944. Broadcaster; Journalist; Author. m. Bel Mooney, 1968, 1 son, 1 daughter. Education: University College, London. Appointments: Reporter, BBC Bristol, 1969-70; BBC Radio, World at One, 1970-71; Reporter, This Week, Thames TV, 1972-78, 1986-88, TV Eye, 1979; Reporter, Yorkshire TV, Jonathan Dimbleby in Evidence: The Police (series); The Bomb, 1980; The Eagle and the Bear, 1981; The Cold War Game, 1982; The American Dream, 1984; Four Years On - The Bomb, 1984; Associate Ed/Presenter, First Tuesday, 1982-86; Presenter/Ed, Jonathan Dimbleby on Sunday, TV AM, 1985-86; On the Record, BBC TV, 1988-93; Charles: The Private Man, The Public Role, Central TV, 1994; Jonathan Dimbleby, London Weekend TV, 1995-; Presenter, Any Questions?, BBC Radio 4, 1987-; Any Answers?, 1989-; Writer/Presenter, The Last Governor, Central TV, 1997; An Ethiopian Journey, LWT, 1998; A Kosovo Journey, LWT, 2000; Michael Heseltine – A Life in the Political Jungle, LWT, 2000. Publications: Richard Dimbleby, 1975; The Palestinians, 1979; The Prince of Wales: A Biography, 1994; The Last Governor, 1997. Honours: Richard Dimbleby Award, 1974. Memberships: VP, Council for Protection of Rural England, 1997-; Soil Association, 1997-; President, Voluntary Service Overseas, 1999-; Bath Festivals Trust, 2003. Address: c/o David Higham Associates Ltd, 5 Lower John Street, W1R 4HA, England.

DIMITRIJEVIC Miroslav, b. 27 January 1950, Rasevica, Serbia. Writer; Publicist; Journalist. m. Zorica Tomic-Dimitrijevic, 2 daughters. Education: Serbian Language and Literature, Faculty of Philology, Belgrade; Journalist School, Association of Journalists of Serbia. Appointments: Chief Editor, Paracin's 14 Days, fortnightly newspaper; Chief Editor, Days, literature magazine; Founder and Owner: In the Naked, first private satirical magazine; Agape, first Serbian oratory magazine; Founder and first Editor of the series, The First Book, Paracin; Chief Editor, Publishing House, Vuk Karadzic, Paracin; Chief Editor, Publishing House, Zaharije Orfelin, Paracin; Owner and Chief Editor, Publishing House, The Literary Cell Sveti Sava, Paracin; President, Literary Club, Ikad, Paracin; President, Literary Club, Mirko Banjevic, Paracin. Publications: 53 books in the fields of literature, historiography, ethnology and journalism; Literary works include: Hreb – poems; Growing up of Angels, poems; Orations; Seven-Headed, poems; The Pointing Day of Death, novel; Honours to Everybody – Democracy to Nobody, aphorisms; Historiographic works include: Davidovac; Donje Vidovo; Ratari; Mirilovac; Plana; Potocac; Cicevac; Ethnographical work: Windy Waters, folk literature; Numerous newspaper and magazine articles. Honours: Award, Association of Journalists of Serbia, 1975; Award, Mirko Jovic Fund, 1982; Svetolik Rankovic Award, 1983; Award of the Municipality of Paracin for Literature, 1987; Our Voice Award, 1990; Orpheus of Pomoravlje Award for the Book of the Year, 1997; A Satirical Quill Award, for the Book of the Year, 2002. Memberships: Association of Writers of Serbia, Member of the Board for International Co-operation, First President, Pomoravlje District Branch; Association of Journalists of Serbia; Founder and Member, Democratic Party in Paracin, 1990; Founder, Serbian Democratic Party and Member of the headquarters of the Serbian Democratic Party in Belgrade, 1992; Candidate for MP for the Democratic Party in the elections of 1990, 1992. Address: Milovana Glisica Street 26/1, 35250 Paracin, Serbia. E-mail: dim.kata@eunet.yu

DIMOV Maxim Jekov, Executive. Education: MA, International Economic Relations, University for National and Work Economy, 1986; Attended German Language School. Appointments: Chairman of the Board, Albena Style Holding, 1997-99; Chairman of the Board, McCup Holding, 1999-2000; Chairman of the Board, Hom Ludens Consortium, 2002-; Deputy Chairman of the Supervisory Board, Roseximbank, 2001-2002; Board Member, IF Framlington Bulgaria Fund, 1997-2001. Publications: Financial Engineering, 1988; Problems of International Co-ordination Against Money Laundering, 1989; Harmonization of the Bulgarian and European Financial Systems, 1993. Honours: Specialist, National Audit Office, Paris, 1994; Honorary, Corresponding Member, International Informatization Academy, Moscow. Memberships: Bulgarian Antarctic Institute; Bulgarian-German Forum; Bulgarian Russian Business Association. Address: 42-B Rodopski Izvor, Sofia 1680, Bulgaria.

DINEFF Peter Doncheff, b. 2 July 1947, Sofia, Bulgaria. Educator, Electromechanics. m. Valia Velkowa Dinewa, 2 daughters. Education: MS, 1971, PhD, 1978, Technical University of Sofia. Appointments: Design Engineer, Computer Institute of Sofia, 1971-74; Doctor's degree, 1974-77; Researcher, 1978-88, Senior Researcher, 1988-91, Associate Professor, 1991-, Technical University of Sofia; Director of Innovation and Research Department, International Consulting and Training Center on Aviation Security, Sofia, Bulgaria, 2001-. Publications: Electrophysical and Mechanical Technology, 1991; Electrotechnology Part 1: Introduction to Electrotechnology, 1998; Practical Technology of Materials, 2001; Articles in professional journals in fields of electrotechnology and electromachining, polymer science and electrochemistry. Honours: Gold Medal, Expo '85, Plovdiv, Bulgaria, 1985; Honours Patents Office of Bulgaria, 1985; Gold Medal for Invention, 2001, 2002, Gold Medal with Mention for Invention, 2002, Bronze Medal for Invention, 2001, Brussels EUREKA World Exhibition on Invention, Research and New Technology; Gold Medal in Recognition of Innovative Excellence in the Category of Industrial Equipment, 2002, Bronze Medal in Recognition of Innovative Excellence in the Category of Safety and Security, 2002, INPEX, World Exhibition of Innovation, Research and New Technology, Pittsburgh, USA; Gold Medal for Invention, Moscow International Saloon of Invention and Investment, 2002. Memberships: IFIA (Corresponding), 1995; New York Academy of Sciences, 1995-96; Union of Inventors, Bulgaria; Union of Scientists, Bulgaria. Address: Technical University of Sofia, Department of Electrical Apparatus, 1797 Sofia, Bulgaria.

DING Zhaokun, b. 4 October 1955, Guangdong, China. Professor. m. Youqing Xu, 1 daughter. Education: PhD Studies, University of New England, Australia, 1994-97; Postdoctoral, National Research Council of Canada, 1998-2000. Appointments: Senior Research Scientist, University of Toronto, Canada, 2000-02; Specially Appointed Professor, Institute for Marine Biology, Shantou University, China, 2002-. Publications: Articles as co-author include most recently: Purification and characterization of biliverdin Ixa from salmon (Salmo salar), 2002; Lactic acid is absorbed from the small intestine of sheep, 2003; Characterization and isolation of biliverdin reductase from Salmon (Salmo Salar) Liver, 2003. Honours: Prize for excellent teaching, Zhongshan University, China, 1991; 6 Prizes for excellent papers, Zhongshan University, China, 1992-95; Visiting Fellowship, Griffith University, Australia, 1993; PhD Scholarships: Australian Overseas Postgraduate Research Scholarship and University of New England Research Scholarship, 1994-97; Postdoctoral Fellowship, National Research Council of Canada, 1998-99. Memberships: World Aquaculture Society; The Scientist, USA; Science Advisory Board, USA; China Society of Fisheries. Address: Institute for Marine Biology, Shantou University, 243 University Road, Shantou City, Guangdong, China 515063. E-mail: zhaokund@hotmail.com

DINI Luciana, b. 19 January 1955, Rome, Italy. Full Professor. Education: MD, Biology, University of Rome "La Sapienza", 1977. Appointments: Researcher, University of Rome "Tor Vergata", Department of Biology, 1982-92; Associate Professor of Comparative Anatomy and Cytology, Department of Biology, 1992-2000, Full Professor of Comparative Anatomy and Cytology, Department of Biological and Environmental Science Technology, 2000-, University of Lecce, Lecce, Italy. Publications: Articles in scientific journals including: Journal of Clinical Investigation, 1994; Blood, 1994; Hepatology, 1995; Microscopy Research Technology, 2002; Cell and Tissue Research, 2003. Honour: Award Winner for best work in the field of cellular biology, Societa Nazionale di Scienza, Lettere ed Arti, 1987. Memberships: European Microscopy Society; European Cell Death Organisation. Address: Department of Biological and Environmental Science Technology, University of Lecce, Via Per Monteroni, Lecce 73100, Italy. E-mail: luciana.dini@unile.it

DINNERSTEIN Leonard, b. 5 May 1934, New York, New York, USA. Professor Emeritus of History; Writer. m. Myra Anne Rosenberg, 20 August 1961, 1 son, 1 daughter. Education: BA, City College of New York, 1955; MA, 1960, PhD, 1966, Columbia University. Appointments: Instructor, New York Institute of Technology, 1960-65; Assistant Professor, Fairleigh Dickinson University, 1967-70; Associate Professor, 1970-72, Professor of American History, 1972-, University of Arizona, Tucson. Publications: The Leo Frank Case, 1968; The Aliens (with F C Jaher), 1970, as Uncertain Americans, 1977; American Vistas (with K T Jackson), 1971, 7th edition, 1995; Antisemitism in the United States, 1971; Jews in the South (with M D Palsson), 1973; Decisions and Revisions (with J Christie), 1975; Ethnic Americans: A History of Immigration and Assimilation (with D M Reimers), 1975, 3rd edition, 1988; Natives and Strangers (with R L Nichols and D M Reimers), 1979, 4th edition, 2003; America and the Survivors of the Holocaust, 1982; Uneasy at Home, 1987; Antisemitism in America, 1994. Address: 1981 Miraval Cuarto, Tusson, AZ 85718, USA

DION Celine, b. 30 March 1968, Charlemagne, Quebec, Canada. Singer. m. Rene Angelil, 17 December 1994, 1 son. Career: Recording Artiste, 1979-; Winner Eurovision Song Contest for Switzerland, 1988; Recorded in French, until, 1990; 35 million albums sold. Creative Works: Albums: Unison, 1990; Dion chante Plamondon, 1991; Sleepless in Seattle, 1993; The Colour of My

Love, 1993; D'eux, 1995; Falling Into You, 1996; Let's Talk About Love, 1998; These are Special Times, 1998; All the Way, 1999; A New Day Has Come, 2002. Singles include: Beauty and the Beast, 1992; If You Asked Me To; Nothing Broken But My Heart; Love Can Move Mountains; When I Fall In Love; The Power of Love; Misled; Think Twice; Because You Loved Me; My Heart Will Go On; Immortality, 1998; Treat Her Like a Lady, 1998; That's the Way, It Is, 1999; The First time I Ever Saw your Face, 2000. Publications: All the Way, 2000; My Story, My Dreams, 2001; Honours: Pop Album of Year, 1983; Female Artist of Year, 1983-85, 1988; Discovery of the Year, 1983; Best Quebec Artist Outside Quebec, 1983, 1988; Best Selling Record, 1984, 1985; Best Selling Single, 1985; Pop Song of the Year, 1985, 1988; Journal de Quebec Trophy, 1985; Spectrel Video Award, Best Stage Performance, 1988; Album of the Year, 1991; Female Vocalist of the Year, 1991-93; Academy Award for Best Song written for a motion picture or TV, 1992; Grammy Award, 1993, 1999. Address: Les Productions Feeling, 2540 boulevard Daniel-Johnson, Porte 755, Laval, Quebec H7T 2S3, Canada.

DIPPEL Horst, b. 30 April 1942, Düren, Germany. University Professor. m. Gudrun Lückert, 3 daughters. Education: Study of History, Political Science and Philosophy at the Universities of Cologne, Heidelberg and Göttingen, 1962-70; PhD, University of Cologne, 1970; Habilitation, University of Hamburg, 1980. Appointments: Heisenberg Scholar, Deutsche Forschungsgemeinschaft, 1981-86; Professor of British and American Studies, University of Kassel, Germany, 1992-. Publications: Numerous books and articles in particular on Western constitutional history; Editor, Georg Forster Studien, 1997-; Editor, Constitutions of the World 1850 to the present, 2002-; Editor, Constitutions of the World from the late 18th Century to the Middle of the 19th Century, 2004-; www.modern-constitutions.de. Address: Department of Social Sciences, University of Kassel, D-34109 Kassel, Germany. E-mail: hdippel@uni-kassel.de; Website: www.uni-kassel.de/~dippel/

DIRNBACH Zora, b. 22 August 1929, Osijek, Croatia. Writer; Dramaturgist. Education: Absolved studies, History of Art, University of Zagreb, Croatia. Career: Freelance Journalist, 1949-55; Dramaturgist and Producer of radio plays, Radio Drama Department of Radio Zagreb, 1955-63; Dramaturgist, Writer, Producer, Television Drama Department of Radio-televizija Zagreb, 1963-91. Publications: Numerous articles in Croatian newspapers and broadcast on Radio Zagreb; Author of screenplays: The Ninth Circle, Games on Scaffolds; 9 radio plays including: Alchimon's Apple, The Chess Party, The Barsalli Sisters; 7 produced TV plays including: The Long, Long Journey, Our Dear Benefactors, Nocturno; TV series: Dossier, Discovering My Identity, Satan's Seed; 4 theatre plays: Nocturnal Soliloquies of Madame Henirette Von S, Alchimon's Apple, The Night When the Rats Came, Come-Back; Books: Kain's Heritage, 1997; The Diary of an Enfant Terrible, 2000; Like Wind, Like Frost, 2001. Honours: Award for Best Screenplay, Yugoslav Contest, 1956; Awards for Best Radio Plays broadcast on Radio Zagreb, 1957, 1968; Golden Arena for the Best Screenplay, Pula Film Festival. Memberships: Association of Croatian Journalists; Pen Club of Croatia. Address: Zagreb, Croatia. E-mail: zora-dirnbach@zg.htnet.hr

DIVINSKY Nathan J(oseph), b. 29 October 1925, Winnipeg, Manitoba, Canada. Mathematician. 3 daughters. Education: BSc, University of Manitoba, 1946; SM, 1947, PhD, 1950, University of Chicago, USA. Appointment: Editor, Canadian Chess Chat, 1959-74. Publications: Around the Chess World in 80 Years, 1963; Rings and Radicals, 1965; Linear Algebra, 1970; Warriors of the Mind (with R Keene), 1988; Chess Encyclopedia, 1990; Life Maps

of the Great Chessmasters, 1994. Memberships: Life Master, ACBL (Bridge League); Commonwealth Chess Association, president, 1988-94; Canada's Representative to FIDE (World Chess Federation), 1987-94. Address: 5689 McMaster Road, Vancouver, British Columbia V6T 1K1, Canada.

DIXON Alan (Michael), b. 15 July 1936, Waterloo, Lancashire, England. Josephine Stapleton, 13 August 1960. Education: Studied Art, Goldsmiths College, University of London, 1956-63; University of London Diploma in Visual Arts. Appointment: Teacher of Art, Schools in London and Peterborough, England, 1959-87. Publications: Snails and Reliquaries, 1964; The Upright Position, 1970; The Egotistical Decline, 1978; The Immaculate Magpies, 1982; The Hogweed Lass, 1991; A Far-Off Sound, 1994; Transports, 1996. Contributions to: Poetry; Partisan Review; The Observer; The Times Literary Supplement; The Listener; New Statesman; London Review of Books; The Nation; London Magazine; Encounter; The Spectator; Prairie Schooner; The Scotsman. Address: 51 Cherry Garden Road, Eastbourne, BN20 8HG, England.

DIXON Peter, b. 6 April 1937, London, England. Senior Lecturer in Art and Education; Poet. m. Marion Blades, 8 August 1964, 1 son, 1 daughter. Education: Qualified as a Teacher, 1960. Appointments: Teacher, primary and secondary schools, 1960-70; Lecturer in Art and Education, Saffron Walden, 1970-75; Senior Lecturer in Art and Education, King Alfred College, Winchester, 1975-. Publications: Grow Your Own Poems, 1988, 3rd reprint, 1992; I Heard a Spider Sobbing, 1989; Big Billy, 1990; Matt, Wes, Pete, 1996; Lost Property Box; Peter Dixon's Grand Prix of Poetry, 1999; Juggler, 2000; Penguin in the Fridge, 2001; The Colour of my Dreams, 2002. Contributions to: Times Newspapers; Learning magazine, USA; Parents magazine, UK. Membership: National Poetry Society, London. Address: 30 Cheriton Road, Winchester, Hampshire S022 5AX, England.

DIXON Shirley Lee, b. 10 December 1947, New York City, New York, USA. Physician; Administrator. Education: BS, Biology, Education, City College of New York, 1969; MD, Howard University Medical School, 1976; Visiting Fellow, Internship, 1976-77, Visiting Fellow, Residency, 1979-81, Harlem Hospital Center, Columbia University; MPH, Columbia University School of Public Health, 1983; Life Fellow, American Board of Forensic Examiners, 2001. Appointments: Research Technician, Department of Immunology, Albert Einstein College of Medicine, 1970-72; Commissioned Officer, National Health Service Corps, US Public Health Service, Staten Island, 1977-78, Hospital for Joint Diseases, 1978-79; Attending Physician, Sydenham Neighborhood Family Care Center, Department of Ambulatory Care, Harlem Hospital, 1981-83; Attending Physician, in charge of Adult Medical Screening, Sheltering Arms Children's Service, 1982-84; Family Internist, Rochdale Medical Center, Associate Attending, La Guardia Hospital, La Guardia Medical Group PC, 1983-85; Community Health Educator and Speaker, Pfizer Corporation, 1984; Emergency Room Attending, Interfaith Medical Center, Downstate University Hospital, 1985-87; Attending Physician, Night Screening Clinic, Lincoln Medical and Mental Health Center, New York Medical College, 1989-91; Member, Citizen Ambassador Program Anniversary Caravan to the Soviet Union, 1991; Medical Director, Brooklyn-Queens Division, 1986-93, Medical Officer, Triborough District, 1993-96, US Postal Service; Emergency Room Attending, Veterans Administration Hospital, Bronx, Mount Sinai School of Medicine, 1993-96; Life Diplomate, American Board of Disability Analysts, 2001. Honours: Health Professions Scholarship; National Medical Fellowship; US Public Health Service Scholarship. Memberships: New York Academy of Sciences, 1982; Lifetime Member, American Professional

Dictionary of International Biography

Practice Association; Member, Citizen Ambassador Program; American College of Occupational and Environmental Medicine, 1994; Life Fellow, American Board of Forensic Examiners, 2001; Certified in Illness Trauma, Disability Trauma and Stress Management, 2001, Diplomate, 2002, Fellow, 2004, American Academy of Experts in Traumatic Stress; Charter Member, American Lawyer, Media, Expert Witnesses and Consultants Network; Fellow, Foreign Policy Research Institute, 2001; Life Fellow, ABI; Deputy General, Vice Consul, Medical Adviser, Companion of Honour, IBC. Address: 752 West End Ave, Apt 6E, New York, NY 10025-6230, USA.

DIXON Stephen, b. 6 June 1936, New York, New York, USA. Writer; University Teacher. m. Anne Frydman, 17 January 1982, 2 daughters. Education: BA, City College of New York, 1958. Publications: No Relief, 1976; Work, 1977; Too Late, 1978; Quite Contrary, 1979; 14 Stories, 1980; Movies, 1983; Time to Go, 1984; Fall and Rise, 1985; Garbage, 1988; Love and Will, 1989; The Play and Other Stories, 1989; All Gone, 1990; Friends, 1990; Frog, 1991; Long Made Short, 1993; The Stories of Stephen Dixon, 1994; Interstate, 1995; Man on Stage, 1996; Gould, 1997; Sleep, 1999; 30, 1999; Tisch, 2000; I, 2002; Old Friends, 2004. Contributions to: 400 short stories to magazines and journals including Atlantic; Harper's; Esquire; Playboy; Paris Review; Triquarterly; Western Humanities Review; Ambit; Bananas; Boulevard; Glimmer Train; Partisan Review; O. Henry Prize Stories, 1977, 1982, 1993; Best American Stories, 1993, 1996. Honours: Stegner Fiction Fellowship, Stanford University, 1964-65; National Endowment of the Arts Grants, 1974-75, 1990-91; American Academy and Institute of Arts and Letters Award, 1983; John Train Prize, Paris Review, 1984; Guggenheim Fellowship, 1985-86; National Book Award Finalist, 1990, 1995; PEN Faulkner Fiction Prize Finalist, 1991. Address: 1315 Boyce Avenue, Baltimore, MD 21204, USA.

DJEBAR Assia (Fatima-Zohra Imalayen), b. 4 August 1936, Cherchell, Algeria. Novelist; Essayist; Playwrite; Filmmaker. m. (1) Ahmed Ould Rouis, 1958, divorced, (2) Malek Alloula, 1980. Education: Lycée Blida-Alger, Algeria, Lycée Fénélon, Paris, France, 1954; École Normale Supérieure, France, 1955-58; Licence es lettres in History, Sorbonne-Paris, 1958-59; Doctorat es Lettres, French Literature and Civilization, Montpelier III. Appointments: Author, 1957-; Teacher of History, University of Rabat, Morocco, 1959-62, University of Algers, 1962-; Transfer to Algerian Cultural Centre, Paris, 1985; Distinguished Foundation Professor and Director, Centre for French and Francophone Studies, Louisiana State University, 1997-2001; Silver Chair Professor of French and Francophone studies, New York University, 2001-. Publications: Novels: La Soif, 1957; Les Impatients. 1958; Les Enfants du Nouveau Monde. 1962; Les Alouettes Naives. 1967; L'Amour, la fantasia, first novel of projected quartet, 1985; Ombre sultane, second novel of projected quartet, 1987; Vaste est la prison, third novel of projected quartet, 1995; Loin de Medine, 1991; Les nuits de Strasbourg, 1997; La femme sans Sepulture, 2002; La disparition de la langue francaise-roman, 2003; Plays: Rouge l'Aube, written in 1959, performed at the third Panafrican Cultural Festival held in Algiers, 1969; Filles d'Ismaël dans le vent et la tempête, musical drama in 5 acts, 1999, performed in Italian in Teatro di Roma, 2000; Aicha et les femmes de Médine, musical drama in 3 acts, 2000, performed in Dutch and Arabic at the Rotterdam theatre (project cancelled), 2001. Poetry: Poems pour l'Algerie heureuse, 1969; Films written and directed: La Nouba des femmes du Mont Chenoua, 1977; La Zerda ou les chants de l'oubli, 1982; Short story collections: Femmes d'Alger dans leur appartement, 1980, 2002; Oran, langue morte, 1997; Essays and Non-fiction: Le Blanc de l'Algerie, récit, 1996; Ces voix qui m'assiegent ... en marge de ma francophonie, literary essay, 1999; Books translated into 17

languages. Honours: Venice International Critics Prize, for first film, 1979; Maurice Maeterlink Prize, Brussels, 1995; Winner, International Literary Neustadt Prize for her contribution to World Literature, USA, 1996; Winner, Yourcenar Prize, USA, 1997; Fonlon-Nichols Prize, African Literature Association, USA, 1997; Winner, International Prize of Palma, Italy, 1998; Winner, Friedenspreis des Deutschen Buchhandels, Germany, 2000. Memberships: Académie Royale de Langue Française de Belgique. Address: Department of French, 6th Floor, 19 University Place, New York, NY 10003, USA. E-mail: assia.djebar@nyu.edu

DJODEYRE Mohammad Reza, b. 18 September 1966, Mashhad, Iran. Ophthalmologist. m. Ana Isabel Ruiz Rizaldos, 1 son, 1 daughter. Education: Medical Doctor Degree, Mashhad University of Medical Science, Iran, 1992; Resident of Family Physician, Hospital Punta Europa Algeciras, Spain and Hospital General, Albacete, Spain, 1994-96; Speciality of Ophthalmology, Hospital La Paz, Madrid, Spain, 2000; Subspecialty of Cataract and Refractive Surgery, Clinica Baviera. PhD, Universidad Autonoma de Madrid, 2004. Appointments: Investigator in Pain and Spasm, Spinal Cord Injury Investigation Centre of Khorasan, Iran, 1990-92; Ophthalmologist, Cataract and Refractive Surgeon, Clinica Baviera of Zaragoza and Pamplona, Spain, 2001-. Publications: Resultados de Tratamiento con cirugía y radiaciones ionizantes (90Sr38) en el pterigium, 1997; Actualización en cirugía oftálmica pediátrica, 2000; Clinical Evaluation and Risk Factors of Time to Failure of Ahmed Glaucoma Valve Implant in Pediatric Patients, 2001. Honours: Scholarship for education in Paris, Ministry of Education of France, 1977; Scholarship for speciality in ophthalmology, Ministry of Health Medical Education of Iran, 1992; Listed in Who's Who publications and biographical dictionaries. Memberships: Medical College of Iran; Medical College of Madrid; Spanish Society of Ophthalmology; Iranian Society of Calligraphy; Editorial Board of Avicena. Address: C/ Echegaray y Caballero 120, 50001 Zaragoza, Spain. E-mail: rezaoft@yahoo.es

DJUGUM Mirsad, b. 30 July 1957, Tomislavgrad, Bosnia and Herzegovina. Doctor of Medicine. m. Hikmeta Pehlivanovich, 2 sons. Education: Medical Faculty, Tuzla, Bosnia and Herzegovina; Residency in Internal Medicine, Clinical Centre of the University of Sarajevo, Bosnia and Herzegovina. Appointments: Office of Public Health, Tomislavgrad, Bosnia and Herzegovina; Institute of Acupuncture of Bosnia and Herzegovina; Docent, Courses for Chinese Traditional Medicine, KreisKlinik, Marktoberdorf, Germany; Leading Physician, Practice of Internal Medicine "Dugum", Sarajevo, Bosnia and Herzegovina; Director, Poliklinka Atrijum, Sarajevo, Bosnia and Herzegovina. Publications: Co-author, Akupunktura, 1997-98; Papers in scientific journals and presented at conferences include: Incidence of increased values of CRP in patients with unstable angina, 2002; Control of hypertension in Sarajevo Canton at randomly selected patient sample with treated hypertension, 2003; Comparative analysis of Carvedilol, Metoprolol and Atenolol in treatment of patients with congestive heart failure, 2003; Comparison of EDV and ESV as prognostic indicators in patients after AMI, 2003. Honour: Professor of Chinese Traditional Medicine, Open University, Colombo, Sri Lanka. Address: Atrium, TRG ZavnoBiH-a 18, 7000, Sarajevo, Bosnia and Herzegovina. E-mail: mdjugum@hotmail.com

DOBBS Michael John, b. 14 November 1948. Author. m. Amanda L Collingridge, 1981, 2 sons. Education: Christ Church, Oxford; Fletcher School of Law & Diplomacy, USA. Appointments: UK Special Adviser, 1981-87; Chief of Staff, UK Conservative Party, 1986-87; Joint Deputy Chairman, 1994-95; Deputy Chairman, Saatchi & Saatchi, 1983-91; Deputy Chairman, Conservative Party,

1994-95; Chairman, Spirit Advertising, 1998-. Publications: House of Cards, 1989; Wall Ganes, 1990; Last Man to Die, 1991; To Play the King, 1993; The Touch of Innocents, 1994; The Final Cut, 1995; Goodfellowe MP, 1997; The Buddha of Brewer Street, 1998; Whispers of Betrayal, 2000; Winston's War, 2002. Address: 12 Onslow Court, Drayton Gardens, London, SW10 9RL, England. E-mail: michldobbs@aol.com

DOBER Hans Martin, 11 March 1959, Neuwied/Rhein, Germany. Clergyman. m. Susanne Dober. 2 sons, 1 daughter. Education: Dr phil, 1990; Privat Dozent, Dr. phil. theol. habil., 2001. Clergyman of the Protestant Church, 1992-; Assistant of Practical Theology, University of Tübingen, Germany, 1994-2002. Publications: Die Zeit Ernst Nehmen, 1990; Flanerie Sammlung Spiel, 2000; Die Moderne Wahrnehmen, 2002; Articles: Schleiermacher und Levinas, 2002; Ich und mich sind immer zu eifrig im Gespräche, 2002. Address: Eichhoernchenweg 5, 78532 Tuttlingen, Germany.

DÖBEREINER Jürgen, b. 1 November 1923, Königsberg Pr, Germany. Veterinarian. m. Johanna Kubelka, deceased 2000, 2 sons, 1 deceased 1996, 1 daughter. Education: DMV, Rio de Janeiro, 1954; MSc, University Wisconsin-Madison, USA, 1963; Dr med vet hc, Justus-Liebig-University Giessen, Germany, 1977. Appointment: Research Worker in Animal Pathology, Ministry Agriculture-Embrapa, Rio de Janeiro, Brazil, 1955-. Publications: More than 170 scientific papers; Co-author, Plantas Tóxicas do Brasil, 2000; Editor-in-Chief, Pesquisa Agropecuaria Brasileira (Brazilian Journal of Agricultural Research), 1965-76; Editor, Pesquisa Veterinaria Brasileira (Brazilian Journal of Veterinary Research), 1981-. Membership: President, Brazilian College of Animal Pathology, 1978-2008; President, Brazilian Association of Science Editors, 2000-2004; President, The Johanna Döbereiner Research Society, 2002-2006. Address: Embrapa-CNPAB/Sanidade Animal, Km 47, Seropédica, Rio de Janeiro 23851-970, Brazil.

DOBROLYUBOVA Tamara Ivanovna, b. 11 December 1946, Station Dauria, Borzinskiy Region, Chitinskaja Area, Russia. Designer; Master of Embroidery. m. Vladimir Nikolayevich Dobrolyubov, 1 son, 1 daughter. Education: Geophysics and Hydrology, Geological Department, Byelorussian State University, 1970. Career: Geophysicist and Hydrologist, 1970-92; Embroidress and Designer, 1992-; Specialist in creating with cloth, hand-made techniques, knits with needles and hooks, folk and ethnologically inspired designs; Wall panels: "Chocloma"; "Gzhel"; "Gzhel's Majolica"; "Shawls"; Numerous Exhibitions include 6 personal exhibitions: Central Artist's House in Moscow, 1995, 1998; Savitskiy Fine Art Gallery, Penza, 1997; Culture centre of Slovenia, 1999; Metropolis (Club Luxor), 2001, 2002; 2 Collections of dress "Samozvety" and "My Russia", 2000-2002. Publications: Illustrations of work included in magazines, catalogues, albums and leaflets; Catalogue, Moscow Luxe, 1997; Magazine, Planet of Beauty, 1996, 2000; Magazine, La Coiffures de Paris, 2001. Honours: Prize-winner, All Russian Exhibition Centre; Prize-winner, Spring '96 Exhibition; Prize-winner, All Russian Exhibition "Embroidered Painting" for collection of wall panels, 1996; Prize-winner, Festival of Amateur Art " A S Pushkin and Russian Culture", 1999. Numerous diplomas from exhibitions. Membership: Russian Creative Unity of Artists. Address: ul Sadovaja 12 kv 27, Odintsovo 143000, Moscow Region, Russia. E-mail: c.t.a.r.@vimcom.ru

DODERER Gerhard, b. 25 March 1944, Kitzingen, Germany. Musicologist; Organist. m. C Rosado Fernandes, 11 September 1970. Education: PhD, University of Wüzburg; Bay. Staatskonservatorium of Würzburg. Career: Organ recitals, since

1970 in many European and Non-European countries; Professor of Musicology, Universidade Nova de Lisboa, 1981-. Recordings: Longplays and CDs on historical Portuguese organs. Publications: Portuguese Clavichords of 18th Century, 1971; Organa Hispanica, 1971-84, 9 vols; Orgelmusik und Orgelbau in Portugal, 1976; Domenico Scarlatti: Libro di Tocate, 1991; The Organs at Braga Cathedral, 1992; J de la Té y Sagau: Cantatas Humanas a Solo (1723), 1999. Memberships: American, Spanish, Portuguese and German Musicological Societies. Address: Rua do Borja 131-B, 3A Lisboa, Portugal.

DOLE Elizabeth Hanford, b. 29 July 1936, Salisbury, North Carolina, USA. Administrator. m. Robert J Dole, 1975. Education: Duke University; Harvard University; University of Oxford. Appointments: Called to Bar, District of Columbia, 1966; Staff Assistant to Assistant Secretary for Education, Department of Health, Education & Welfare, 1966-67; Practising lawyer, Washington DC, 1967-68; Associate Director Legislative Affairs, then Executive Director Presidents Commission for Consumer Interests, 1968-71; Deputy Assistant, Office of Consumer Affairs, The White House, Washington DC, 1971-73; Commissioner, Federal Trade Commission, 1973-79; Assistant to President for Public Liaison, 1981-83; Secretary of Transport, 1983-87; Candidate for Republican presidential nomination, 1999; Senator from North Carolina, 2003-. Memberships: Trustee, Duke University, 1974-88; Member, Visiting Committee, John F Kennedy School of Government, 1988-; Secretary of Labour, 1989-90; President, American Red Cross, 1991-98; Member, Commission, Harvard School of Public Health, 1992-; Board of Overseers, Harvard University, 1989-95. Address: Office of the Senator from North Carolina, Suite B34, Dirksen Building, US Senate, Washington, DC 20510, USA.

DOLE Robert J, b. 22 July 1923, Russell, Kansas, USA. Politician. m. (2) Elizabeth Hanford Dole, 1975, 1 daughter. Education: University of Kansas; Washburn Municipal University. Appointments: Member, Kansas Legislature, 1951-53; Russell County Attorney, 1953-61; Member, House of Representatives, 1960-68; US Senator from Kansas, 1969-96, Senate Majority Leader, 1995-96; Senate Republic Leader, 1987-96; House Majority Leader, 1985-87; Minority Leader, 1987; Chairman, Republican National Committee, 1971-72; Vice-Presidential Candidate, 1976; Presidential Candidate, 1996; Member of Counsel, Verner, Liipfert, Bernhard, McPherson and Hand, Alston and Bird, 2003-. Publications: Great Political Wit (co-ed), 1999; Great Presidential Wits, 2001. Memberships: Chairman, Senate Finance Committee, Dole Foundation, 1981-84; Director, Mainstream Inc; Advisor, US Delegate to FAO Conference, Rome, 1965, 1974, 1977; Member, Congressional delegate to India, 1966, Mid E, 1967; Member, US Helsinki Commission; Delegate to Belgrade Conference, 1977; Trustee, William Allen White Foundation, University of Kansas; Member, National Advisory Committee, The John Wesley Colleges; American Bar Association; National Advisory Committee, on Scouting for the Handicapped; Kansas Association for Retarded Children; Advisory Board of Utd Cerebral Plasy, Kansas; Honorary Member, Advisory Board of Kidney Patients Inc; Presidential Medal of Freedom, 1997; Distinguished Service Award, 1997. Address: Suite 410, 901 15th Street, NW Washington DC 20005, USA.

DOLL Mary Aswell, b. 4 June 1940, New York, New York, USA. Professor of English. m. William Elder Doll Jr, 25 June 1966, divorced 1994, 1 son. Education: BA, Connecticut College, New London, 1962; MA, Johns Hopkins University, 1970; PhD, Syracuse University, 1980. Appointments: Assistant Professor, State University of New York, Oswego, 1978-84; Lecturer, University of Redlands, California, 1985-88; Assistant Professor,

Loyola University, 1988; Visiting Assistant Professor, Tulane University, 1988; Associate Professor, 1989-93, Professor, 1993-, Our Lady of Holy Cross College; Professor, Savannah College of Art and Design. Publications: Rites of Story: The Old Man at Play, 1987; Beckett and Myth: An Archetypal Approach, 1988; In the Shadow of the Giant: Thomas Wolfe, 1988; Walking and Rocking, 1989; Joseph Campbell and the Power of the Wilderness, 1992; Stoppard's Theatre of Unknowing, 1993; To the Lighthouse and Back, 1996; Like Letters in Running Water: A Mythopoetics of Curriculum, 2000. Contributions to: Periodicals. Honours: Outstanding Book Citation Choice, 1989; Sears-Roebuck Teaching Excellence Award. Memberships: Modern Language Association; President, Thomas Wolfe Society, 1999-2001; American Academy of Religion. Address: 527 E 56 Street, Savannah, Georgia 31405, USA.

DOLL Michael William, b. 29 August 1949, Monett, Missouri, USA. Investment Banker; Business and Investment Consultant. m. Sharon Lee, 2 sons, 1 daughter. Assigned as a Chaplain, 1967-. Education: BA Ed, Wichita State University, 1972; Charter Ecumenical Ministries, Doctor of Divinity, 1994; World Christianship Ministries, Doctor of Divinity, 1998; Ordained Minister, 1998. Appointments: Photographer, 1962-; Farmer, Rancher, Foreman, Supervisor of hired hands; Publishing Company Executive, 1973-86; Stockbroker, Investment Banker, 1987-92; Business and Investment Consultant, 1992-. Honours: Presidential Achievement Awards, President Ronald Reagan, 1981-88; Commissioned Captain, Royal Medallion Garde-St George Division; Colonel, Honorable Order of Kentucky Colonels, 1995; Man of the Year 2002; American Medal of Honor, ABI, 2002; Lifetime Achievement Award, International Freelance Photographers Association; Inducted into Leading Intellectuals Hall of Fame, ABI; Lifetime Achievement Award, IBC; Listed in national and international biographical dictionaries. Memberships: Phi Delta Kappa; Sigma Chi Sigma Fraternity; Gideons International; International Free Lance Photographers; Scabbard and Blade Military Fraternity; Member, Research Board of Advisors, American Biographical Institute (ABI); Fellow, ABI; Secretary General United Cultural Convention. Address: 4262 Cumberland, Wichta, KS 67216-2963, USA. E-mail: coldoll@prodigy.net Website: www.10ebooks.com/sample/michaeldoll

DOLLFUS Audouin Charles, b. 12 November 1924, Paris, France. Physicist; Astronomer. m. Catherine Browne, 1959, 4 children. Education: Doctor of Mathematics, Faculty of Sciences, University of Paris. Appointments: Astronomer, Astrophysical Section, Meudon Observatory, Paris, 1946-; Head of Laboratory for Physics of the Solar System; Astronomer, Observatoire de Paris, 1965; Discovered Janus, innermost moon of Saturn, 1966;Emeritus President, Observatoire de Triel, 1994-; Research into polarisation of light. Publications: 350 scientific publications on astrophysics. Honours: Grand Prix of Academie des Sciences; International Award Galabert for Astronautics; Diploma Tissandier, International Federation of Astronautics. Memberships: International Academy of Astronautics; Société Astronomique de France; Aéro-club de France; French Association for the Advancement of Science; Royal Astronomical Society, London; Society of French Explorers; Explorers Club, USA; Société Philomatique de Paris; Honorary member, Royal Astronomical Society of Canada. Address: 77 rue Albert Perdreaux, 92370 Chaville, France.

DOLPHIN David, b. 15 January 1940, London. Professor of Chemistry. m. Diane Kent, 3 sons. Education: BSc, 1962, PhD, 1965, DSc, 1982, University of Nottingham. Appointments: Associate Professor, Harvard University, 1966-73; Professor, University of British Columbia, 1974-. Publications: 18 books on chemistry, biochemistry, spectroscopy, 400 research publications; Numerous patents. Honours: Fellow, Royal Society; Fellow, Royal Society of Canada; Prix Gallien, 2002; Guggenheim Fellow. Memberships: Fellow, Chemical Institute of Canada; Fellow, Royal Society of Chemistry. Address: Department of Chemistry, University of British Columbia, 2036 Main Mall, Vancouver, BC, V6T 1Z1, Canada. Email: ddolphin@qltinc.com

DOMINGO Placido, b. 21 January 1941, Madrid, Spain. Opera Singer. m. Marta Ornelas, 3 sons. Education: National Conservatory of Music, Mexico City. Appointments: Operatic debut, Monterrey, Mexico, 1961; Debut, Metropolitan Opera, NY, 1968; British debut, Verdi's requiem, Festival Hall, 1969; Covent Garden debut in Tosca, 1971; Returned to sing in Aida, Carmen, 1973; La Boheme, 1974; Un ballo in maschera, 1975; La Fanciulla del West; Has taken leading roles in about 50 operas; West NY City Opera, 1965-; Artistic Director, Washington Opera, 1994-, LA Opera, 2000-; Artistic Advisor and Principal Guest Conductor, Los Angeles Opera; Recent engagements include: Tosca (conducting), Romeo & Juliet, Metropolitan Opera, NY; Aida, Il Trovatore, Hamburg; Don Carlos in Salzburg; I vespri siciliani and La forza del destino in Paris; Turandot in Barcelona; Otello in Paris, London, Hamburg; Carmen in Edinburgh; Turandot, Metrop, NY; Film: Madame Butterfly w Von Karajan, La Traviata, 1982; Carmen, 1984; Otello, 1986; Stage debut in My Fair Lady, 1988; Recent recordings include: Aida, Un ballo in maschera, Tosca. Publication: My First Forty Years (autobiography), 1983. Honours: Fellow, N College of Music; Dr hc, Royal College of Music, 1982, Univ Computense de Madrid, 1989; Commandeur, Legion d'Honneur; KBE, 2002. Address: c/o Vincent and Farrell Associates, Suite 740, 8th Avenue, New York, NY 10001, USA.

DOMOKOS Ernö, b. 20 July 1945. Leliceni, Romania. Economist; University Professor. m. Susana Domokos, 1 son, 1 daughter. Education: Economist, ASE University, Bucharest, 1968; Postgraduate Management Studies, 1976; PhD, Management, 1986. Appointments: Various positions in lower, middle and top management; Currently University Professor. Publications: More than 500 articles and studies and 25 books of Management and Marketing include most recently as author and co-author: Introduction to Management Practice, 1995; Management and Computer Science, 1997; Theoretical and Practical Basis of Management, 2000, 2002, 2003; Towards European Integration, Hungarian and Romanian versions, 2002; Ways of Waste – Recycling in Terra Siculorum, Pallas, 2002; Marketing, University Manual, 2003. Honour: Oskar-Capital Prize for the Best Economic Book of the Year 1995. Memberships: World Council of Hungarian Professors; International Union of Hungarian Writers. Address: No 6 Spitalului Str, SF Gheorghe 520 050, Romania. E-mail: domokos@planet.ro

DONALDSON David, b. 13 February 1936, Birmingham, England. Physician. Education: MB, ChB, University of Birmingham Medical School, 1959; MRCP, London, 1963; MRCPath, London, 1969; FRCPath, London, 1981; FRCP, London, 1999; FI Biol, London 2002; FRSC, London, 2001. Appointments: House Physician, Selly Oak Hospital, Birmingham, 1959-60; House Surgeon, Children's Hospital, Birmingham, 1960; Senior House Officer, Clinical Pathology, Queen Elizabeth Hospital, Birmingham, 1960-61; Assistant Resident Medical Officer, Registrar in General Medicine, General Infirmary, Leeds, 1961-62; Registrar, General Medicine, Victoria Hospital, Keighley, 1963-64; Lecturer, Honorary Senior Registrar, Chemical Pathology, Institute of Neurology, National Hospitals for Nervous Diseases, London, 1964-70; Consultant, Chemical Pathology, East Surrey Hospital, Redhill, 1970-2001, Crawley Hospital, Crawley, 1970-2001; Gatwick Park Hospital, Horley, 1984-; Vice Chairman,

Dictionary of International Biography

Medical Sub-Committee, Marie Curie Memorial Foundation, 1978-83; Clinical Director, Pathology Department, East Surrey Hospital, 1991-94; Chairman, East Surrey Division, British Medical Association, 1992-93; Chairman, South West Thames Chemical Pathology Advisory Group, South Thames Regional Health Authority, 1995-2000; Deputy Honorary Editor, Editorial Board, Journal of The Royal Society for the Promotion of Health, 1997-. Publications: Over 100 publications in professional journals and chapters in books; Books: Essential Diagnostic Tests in Biochemistry and Haematology (co-author), 1971; Diagnostic Function Tests in Chemical Pathology (co-author), 1989; Psychiatric Disorders with a Biochemical Basis, 1998. Honour: Recipient, Mori Felicitation Award, International College of Nutrition, 2002. Memberships include: Fellow, International College of Nutrition, Royal Society of Medicine, Royal Society for the Promotion of Health, Royal Geographical Society, Medical Society of London, Hunterian Society; Member, American Association for the Advancement of Science, Association of Clinical Biochemists, Association of Clinical Pathologists, European Atherosclerosis Society, British Atherosclerosis Society, British Association for the Advancement of Science, New York Academy of Sciences, Faculty of History and Philosophy of Medicine and Pharmacy (Worshipful Society of Apothecaries of London), Harveian Society of London. Address: 5 Woodfield Way, Redhill, Surrey RH1 2DP, England.

DONALDSON Robert Euan, b. 27 January 1928, Ivanhoe, Victoria, Australia. Minister; Author; Teacher; Lecturer; Publisher. m. Margaret Florence, 1 son, 1 daughter. Education: BA, Melbourne University, 1957; BD, Westminster Theological Seminary, 1957; MA, Honours, Melbourne University, 1964; DipEd, All honours, Melbourne University, 1977; Doctor of Theology, Berean Graduate School of Divinity, 1978. Appointments: Teacher, Editor, All Saints College, New South Wales, 1960; Teacher, Editor, Scotch College, Tasmania, 1961-62; Pastoral Calls, Maritime Provinces, Presbyterian Church, Canada, 1963; Pastoral Appointment, Presbyterian Church of Victoria, 1965; Pastoral Work, Auckland, Minister, St Ninian's PC, Blenheim, Presbyterian Church of New Zealand, 1966-67; Pastoral Appointments, Reformed Presbyterian Church Evangelical Synod, Pastor, Church on the County Line, Illinois, USA, 1967-70; Teacher, Victoria, Australia, 1970, 1974-77; Minister, Gospel Presbyterian Church, Victoria, 1971-77; Doctor of Theology and later studies, 1978-80; Principal, Craigmore Christian School, Adelaide, 1981; Teacher, South Australia, 1982; Headmaster, Independent Baptist Grammar School, Victoria, 1983-84; Teacher, Adelaide, 1985-87; Minister, The Australian Presbyterian Bible Church Inc, (Australian Bible Church), 1988-, VP from inception World Wide Web Witness Inc, 1996-; Founding Member, Evangelical Presbyterian Alliance. Publications: 76 books (see website for full text) of wide-ranging topics to demonstrate infallibility and unique validity of the Bible and the cogent claims of Christ, constituting a heavily indexed and integrated set of some 7.3 million words, "In Praise of Christ Jesus", and varied articles, 1992-2004; Multi-Media CD-ROM all published works with oral lectures added, 38th edition. Honours: Council Scholarship, Dux, Scotch College, Melbourne, with State General and Economics Exhibitions; Major Resident Scholarship, Ormond College, University of Melbourne; Included in several international directories of biography; Man of the Year 2001, 2003, 2004, IBC; Nominated Man of the Year 2003, ABI, USA. Address: World Wide Web Witness Inc, 23 Wendy Ave, Valley View, SA 5093, Australia. E-mail: team@webwitness.org.au Website: URL – http://webwitness.org.au

DONATI-COLAGE Liliana, b. 8 November 1922, Rome, Italy. Retired Teacher. m. Gino Colage, 1 daughter. Education: Doctorate in Foreign Languages, University of Rome, Rome, Italy, 1949;

Summer Study Programme, Sorbonne University, Paris, France, 1951; Certificate of French Mastery, Alliance Française, Paris, France, 1951; Master of Science, Case Western Reserve University, Cleveland, Ohio, USA, 1967. Appointments: French Teacher, Scuola di Aviamento, Ceprano, Italy, 1949-51, Scuola Cola di Rienzo, Rome, Italy, 1951-57, Cleveland Public Schools, Cleveland, Ohio, 1962-85; Italian Teacher, Adult Education, Cleveland, Ohio: Chagrin Falls/Kenston Public Schools; Orange City Public Schools; Mayfield City Public Schools; Cleveland heights Public Schools; Translator, Interpreter, Nationality Services, Cleveland, Ohio, Corporate, Commercial Services, Private, Individual Services. Publications: Published author of poetry in Italian; Writer for Italian Cultural Magazine, Alma Nova; Lecturer in Italian and English. Honours: Silver Medal, Religious Competition, Rome, Italy, 1932; Diploma, XXVI Concorso Internazionale (Concorso di Poesia Stramiera), Locri, Italy, 1971; Awards, George Gund Foundation, Martha Holden Jennings Foundation, Cleveland Public Schools. Memberships: American Translators Association; State Teachers Retirement System; National Education Association; Ohio Education Association; Maison Française; President, Board of Directors, Chair of Fournier Fund, Il Cenacolo Italiano di Clevelend; Italian Cultural Garden Federation; Archaeological Institute of America; Cleveland Public Library; Cleveland Museum of Art. Address: 6009 Catalano Drive, Mayfield Heights, OH 44124, USA.

DONEV Doncho, b. 25 November 1949. Shtip, Macedonia. Physician; University Professor. m. Liljana Doneva, 1 son, 2 daughters. Education: MD, 1973, Specialist in Social Medicine, 1981, PhD, 1993, Skopje University School of Medicine; Postgraduate Studies, Sarajevo University School of Medicine, 1984-86; Postdoctoral Studies, Hubert Humphrey Fellowship Program, Emory University School of Public Health, Atlanta, Georgia, USA, 1993-94. Appointments: General Practitioner, Medical Centre, Shtip, 1973-77; Doctor on Specialization, 1977-81, Specialist, Social Medicine, 1981-89, Chief of the Department of Social Medicine, Republic Institute for Health Protection, Skopje, 1989-96; Director, Institute for Social Medicine, Joint Institutes at the Faculty of Medicine, Skopje, 1997-; Chief of the Chair of Social Medicine, Faculty of Medicine, Skopje, 1994-99; Assistant Professor, 1993, Associate Professor, 1998, Regular, Full-Time Professor, 2003-, Faculty of Medicine and Faculty of Dentistry, Skopje; Participant in numerous congresses, training courses and conferences. Publications: Over 100 professional and scientific articles; Long-term Plan for the Health Care Development in Macedonia by the Year 2000, 1985; Status and Perspectives of Emergency Medical Service in Macedonia, 1991; PHARE Consensus Programme Project Publications: Over 100 professional and scientific articles including Dictionary and Glossary of Social Protection Terms, 2000; Book chapter, General Principles for Prevention of Diseases, 2000; 3 poems. Honours include: Ministry of Health of Republic of Macedonia Award – Primarius, 1994; Award Macedonian Medical Association, 1997; Award, Faculty of Medicine, Skopje, 1997; Stability Pact for South East Europe Public Health Co-operation, 2001; Recognition, Andrija Stampar School of Public Health, Zagreb University, 2002; International Poet of Merit Silver Bowl Award, International Society of Poets, 2002; Editors Choice Award, International Library of Poetry, 2002; Croatian Medical Journal Recognition, 2002; A number of ABI and IBC Awards. Memberships include: Macedonian Medical Association; Macedonian Chamber of Medicine; World Federation of Public Health Associations; Macedonian Red Cross; Macedonian Association for Management; Macedonian American Alumni Association, President; The World Society of Poets, Distinguished Member; ABI Research Board of Advisors; IBC Research Council Member. Address: Ivan Agovski 11/2-18, 1000 Skopje, Republic of Macedonia. E-mail: donev@freemail.org.mk

Dictionary of International Biography

DONG Mingmin, b. 5 April 1944, Gui Yang, China. Physician. m. Wei Min Xie, 1 son, 1 daughter. Education: BS, 1961-66, MS, 1978-82, MD, 1982-86, Henan Medical University, China. Appointments: Junior Otolaryngologist, 1967-72; Resident of Otolaryngology, 1973-76; Senior Resident, 1977-78; Visiting Surgeon and Lecturer, Otolaryngology, 1983-86; Associate Professor and Associate Chief of Surgery, 1986-92; Professor, Chief Surgeon and Director ENT Department, The First Clinical Medical College, Zhengzhou University, Henan, China, 1992-. Publications: Quantitative assay of telonoras activity in head and squamous cells, carcinomas and other tissues; Expression of BPNF and FGF-2 following axotomy in fat facial motoneuous. Memberships: ARO; Director, Henan Province, ENT Academy; Editorial Board, Chinese Journal of Otolanryngology. Address: The ENT Department, The First Clinical Medical College of Zhengzhou University, Zhengzhou, Henan Province 450052, China. E-mail: dmmentent@yahoo.com

DONG Qizhong, b. 25 May 1935, Taihe Co, Jiangxi Province, China. Artist. m. Yingmei Lei, February 1964, 2 sons. Education: Graduate, Art Department of Beijing Art Teachers College, 1958. Appointments: Teacher, Shanxi Art College and Art Department, Shanxi University, 1958-65; Artist, Shanxi Artists' Association, 1965-95. Creative Works: Woodcuts exhibited in National Art Exhibition, more than 30 occasions, over 30 works selected for UN and exhibited in more than 30 countries and regions, more than 150 articles published; Book: The Selected Woodcuts of Dong Qizhong. Memberships: Member, Director, National Artists' Association of China; Director, Graphic Society of China; Vice-Chairman, Shanxi Federation of Literary and Art Circles; Honorary Chairman, Shanxi Artists' Association; Director, Ex-libris Research Association of China. Honours: The Autumnal Evening (woodcut), Excellent Creative Prize, National 9th Art Exhibition; The Morning Song of a Mountain Village (woodcut), Silver Medal of Shanxi Provincial Literary and Arts Awards; Luxun Prize, 1996. Address: Shanxi Artists' Association, No 378 Yingze Street, Taiyuan, Shanxi, China.

DONMA Hatice, b. 1931, Turkey. Painter of Environment. m. Mustafa Sadik Donma, 1 son, 1 daughter. Education: Painting Diploma, 1978. Appointments: Artist opened fiftyone personal expositions all in official foundations; joined fifty mixed expositions organized by governmental and formal institutions. Publications: include, Art in our Region; Art and Cinema; Green Corner; This is Mediterranean; Photographs of paintings have been published in the book, Istanbul and the Celebrations for the 75th Anniversary of the Republic; Cover page of, Poetry Composition, Painting, Information Competitions. Honours: include, Achievement Award, Monopoly Third Traditional Paintings Contest (on the topic of landscapes); Certificate of Acknowledgement, Environmental Research and Protection Foundation; Plaquette, Habitat II City Summit; Plaquette and Certificate of Acknowledgement, Antalya Chamber of Commerce and Industry; Sculpture of Golden Cotton and Plaquette; Sculpture of Golden Orange and Plaquette; Certificate of High Honour, Istanbul-Bakirkoy Municipality; Plaquette and certificate of Acknowledgement, Ministry of National Education; Plaquette, Istanbul Beyoglu Municipality, 2003; Certificate of Commendation, Istanbul Governorship, City National Education Department, City Environment and Forestry Department, 2003. Memberships: Painting and Sculpture Museums Association; Turkish Professional Union of the Fine Artistic Work Owners; Societe Europeene de Culture. Address: 11 Kisim, Mesa Villa No. 22, 34158 Atakoy Istanbul, Turkey. E-mail: hdonna@hotmail.com

DONNER Richard, b. 1939, New York, USA. Director; Producer. Appointments: Actor off-Broadway; Collaborated with director Martin Ritt on TV adaption of Somerset Maugham's Of Human Bondage; Moved to California and began commercials, industrial films and documentaries; Films: X 15, 1961; Salt and Pepper, 1968; Twinky, 1969; The Omen, 1976; Superman, 1978; Inside Moves, 1981; The Toy, 1982 Ladyhawke, 1985; The Goonies, 1985; Lethal Weapon, 1987; Scrooged, 1988; Lethal Weapon 2, 1989; Radio Flyer, 1991; The Final Conflict (executive producer), 1991; Lethal Weapon 3, 1992; Free Willy (co-executive producer), 1993; Maverick, 1994; Assassins, 1995; Free Willy 3: The Rescue; Lethal Weapon 4, 1998; Blackheart (producer), 1999; Conspiracy Theory; TV films: Portrait of a Teenage Alcoholic; Senior Year; A Shadow in the Streets; Tales From the Crypt presents Demon Knight (co-executive producer); Any Given Sunday, 1999; X-Men (executive producer), 2000; Series episodes of: Have Gun Will Travel; Perry Mason; Cannon; Get Smart; The Fugitive; Kojak; Bronk; Twilight Zone; The Banana Splits; Combat; Two Fisted Tales; Conspiracy Theory. Address: The Donners Company, 9465 Wilshire Boulevard, #420, Beverly Hills, CA 90212, USA.

DONOVAN Paul James Kingsley, b. 8 April 1949, Sheffield, Yorkshire, England. Author; Journalist. m. Hazel Case, 27 October 1979, 1 son, 2 daughters. Education: MA, Oriel College, Oxford. Appointments: Reporter and TV Critic, Daily Mail, 1978-85; Showbusiness Editor and Critic, Today, 1986-88; Radio Columnist, Sunday Times, 1988-. Publications: Roger Moore, 1983; Dudley, 1988; The Radio Companion, 1991; All Our Todays, 1997. Contributions to: Newspapers including The Times, Sunday Times, Observer, Guardian; New Dictionary of National Biography. Address: 11 Stile Hall Gardens, London W4 3BS, England.

DOOSE Chris A Sr, b. 2 June 1951, San Angelo, Texas, USA. US Treasury Agent; Pilot (Retired). m. Cindy Lane, 1 son, 1 daughter. Education: BS, University of State of New York, 1987; MA, Austin Presbyterian Theological Seminary, 2000; Postgraduate studies, History and Government, Angelo State University, Texas. Appointments: CW3 US Army Attack Helicopter Pilot, Retired; GS-13 Treasury Agent, Pilot Retired; Airline Transport Pilot; MEL, Helicopter Instructor; MEL, Helicopter CFII Advanced Ground Instructor; Retired Federal Law Enforcement Officer, 32 years. Honours: US Customs Service Awards for Service and Duty in South America for Meritorious Duty in War on Drugs. Publications: All classified by Treasury Department. Memberships: FLEOA; Phi Kappa Psi Fraternity; Vietnam Veterans Association; VFW; DAV Association; Life Member MAFA. Address: 606 Ashford Drive, San Angelo, TX 76901, USA. E-mail: ccdoose@aol.com

DOOSE Cindy Lane, b. 16 October 1970, San Angelo, Texas, USA. Director. m. Chris A Doose, Sr. Education: AA, Harris County Community College; BA, Art History, USNY at Albany, Regents College. Appointments: Director Munn Asset Management Trust, 1996-; Currently, Artist in oils successfully selling paintings in Texas. Publications: Numerous oil paintings. Honours: Phi Beta Kappa Honor Society; Delta Delta Delta Sorority; Junior League of San Angelo; Officer, San Angelo Symphony Guild; Delegate National Republican Women. Memberships: Junior League of San Angelo; San Angelo Symphony Guild; NRC. Address: 606 Ashford Drive, San Angelo, TX 76901, USA.

DORF Stephen, b. 29 July 1973, Atlanta, Georgia. Actor. Appointments: Started acting aged 9; Films: The Gate; The Power of One; An Ambush of Ghosts; Judgement Night; Rescue Me; Backbeat; SFW; Reckless; Innocent Lies; I Shot Andy Warhol; City of Industry, 1997; Blood and Wine, 1997; Blade, 1998; Entropy, 1999; Quantum Project, 2000; Cecil B Demented, 2000; The Last Minute, 2001; Zoolander, 2001; All For Nothin', 2002; Deuces Wild, 2002; Riders, 2002; FearDotCom, 2002; Den of Lions, 2002; TV films: I Know My First Name is Steven, 1989;

Always Remember I Love You, 1989; Do You Know the Muffin Man? 1989; A Son's Promise, 1990; Earthly Possessions, 1999; TV series: What a Dummy, 1990. Address: 9350 Wilshire Boulevard, Suite 4, Beverly Hills, CA 90212, USA.

DORFMAN Ariel, b. 6 May 1942, Buenos Aires, Argentina (Chilean citizen). Research Professor of Literature and Latin; Author; Dramatist; Poet. Education: Graduated, University of Chile, Santiago, 1967. Appointment: Walter Hines Page Research Professor of Literature and Latin, Centre for International Studies, Duke University, Durham, North Carolina, 1984-. Publications: Fiction: Hard Rain, 1973; My House is On Fire, 1979; Widows, 1983; Dorando la pildora, 1985; Travesia, 1986; The Last Song of Manuel Sendero, 1986; Mascara, 1988; Konfidenz, 1996. Poetry: Last Waltz in Santiago and Other Poems of Exile and Disappearance, 1988. Plays: Widows, 1988; Death and the Maiden, 1991; Reader, 1992; Who's Who (with Rodrigo Dorfman), 1997. Films: Death and the Maiden, 1994; Prisoners in Time, 1995; My House is on Fire, 1997. Non-Fiction: How to Read Donald Duck (with Armand Mattelart), 1971; The Empire's Old Clothes, 1983; Some Write to the Future, 1991; Heading South, Looking North: A Bilingual Journey, 1998. Honours: Olivier Award, London 1991; Time Out Award, 1991; Literary Lion, New York Public Library, 1992; Dora Award, 1994; Charity Randall Citation, International Poetry Forum, 1994; Best Film for Television, Writers Guild of Great Britain, 1996. Address: c/o Centre for International Studies, Duke University, Durham, NC 27708, USA.

DORR James Suhrer, b. 12 August 1941, Pensacola, Florida, USA. Writer; Poet. m. Ruth Michelle Clark, 1975, divorced 1982. Education: BS, Massachusetts Institute of Technology, 1964; MA, Indiana University, 1968. Appointments: Technical Writer, Editor, Wrubel Computing Center, Bloomington, Indiana, 1969-81; Writer, Marketing Consultant, The Stackworks, 1982; Associate Editor, Bloomington Area Magazine, 1983-86; Freelance Writer, 1982-. Publications: Towers of Darkness (poetry), 1990; Strange Mistresses (short fiction), 2001. Contributions to: Borderlands II, 1991; Grails, 1992; Dark Destiny I and II, 1994-95; Dante's Disciples, 1996; Darkside: Horror for the Next Millennium, 1996; Dark Tyrants, 1997; Gothic Ghosts, 1997; Asylums and Labyrinths, 1997; The Best of Cemetery Dance, 1998; New Mythos Legends, 1999; Other anthologies, periodicals, journals, reviews, magazines, quarterlies, and newspapers. Honours include: Rhysling Honorary Mention, 1993, 1995, 1996, 1997, 2000, 2001; Darrell Nominee, 1998, 2nd Place, 2003; Anthony Nominee, 1998. Memberships: Science Fiction and Fantasy Writers of America; Horror Writers Association; Science Fiction Poetry Association; Short Mystery Fiction society. Address: 1404 East Atwater, Bloomington, IN 47401, USA.

DOSTALER Gilles, b. 26 November 1946, Montréal, Canada. Professor. Education: MA, Economics, McGill University, Montréal, 1972; PhD, Economics, Université de Paris 8, France, 1975. Appointments: Assistant Professor, Sociology, 1975-79, Assistant Professor, Economics, 1979-82, Associate Professor, Economics, 1982-91, Full Professor, Economics, 1991-, Université du Québec à Montréal. Publications: Many books, journal articles and other papers. Honours: Doctorate Fellowships; Many research grants. Memberships: Association Charles Gide pour l'Étude de la Pensée Économique; History of Economics Society; European Society for the History of Economic Thought. Address: Département des sciences économiques, Université du Québec à Montréal, CP 8888, Succursale Centre-ville, Montréal H3C 3P8, Québec, Canada. E-mail: dostaler.gilles@uqam.ca

DOU Hua-Shu, b. 24 August 1958, Shandong, China. Research Scientist. m. Ying Ying Chen, 1 son. Education: BSc, 1982, MSc, 1984, Northeast University; PhD, Beijing University of Aeronautics

and Astronautics, 1991. Appointments: Lecturer, Northeast University, 1984; Postdoctoral, 1991, Associate Professor, 1993, Tsinghua University; Visiting Researcher, Tohoku University, 1994; Visiting Professor, Hosei University, 1995; Research Scientist, University of Sydney, 1996; Research Fellow, National University of Singapore, 2002. Publications: include, AIAA Journal, Transaction of ASME, Computational Mechanics; Journal of Non-Newtonian Fluid Mechanics; Computer Method in Applied Mechanics and Engineering; Acta Mechanica Sinica; Acta Aerodynamica Sinica; Journal of Engineering Thermophysics; International Journal of Computational Engineering Science; Rheologica Acta. Honours: Outstanding Achievement Award for Teaching and Research, 1994; Second Prize of Science and Technology Progress, 1994, 1995; Guest Professorship, Hosei University, Japan, 1995; Third Prize, National Natural Science of China, 1997. Memberships: ASME; AIAA; CSET. Address: Department of Mechanical Engineering, Fluid Mechanics Laboratory, National University of Singapore, Singapore 119260.

DOUGLAS Charles, b. 4 July 1941, Milan, Tennessee, USA. Specialist Graphic Artist. 2 sons. Education: Photo Colour School, 1958; Graduated high school, Polk Clark High, Milan, 1959; Basic Art Certificate, 1962: Illustrating and Specialized Studies, 1964. Appointments: Facilities Management, UCLA; Researching for Art Workshops; Book Illustrating; Graphic design work and Fine Art. Honours: International Citizen of the Year Award, 1995; Who's Who International Entrepreneurs, 1997; Who's Who of Business Professionals, UCLA Management, 1997; UCLA Management Award, 2000. Address: 3206 W 113th Street, Apt 9, Inglewood, CA 90303, USA.

DOUGLAS Frances Sonia, b. 12 May 1931, Stanaford, West Virginia, USA. Pastor of True Deliverance Temple. m. Paul A Douglas Sr, deceased, 3 sons, 5 daughters. Appointments: Housekeeper, 1955-70; Sales Representative for Amway Products, Niagara Falls, New York, 1970, Stuart McGuire Shoes, Niagara Falls, New York, 1970, Lady Finelle Products, Niagara Falls, New York, 1980; Founder Pastor of True Deliverance Temple, Niagara Falls, 1974-; Chairman, Cleveland Avenue School Parent Group, Niagara Falls; Chairman, Harriet F Abate School Parent Group, Niagara Falls; Vice Chairman, 2000-2001, Board of Directors, 2001-, Niagara Falls Faith Based Collaborative; Former Treasurer, Niagara Falls Ministerial Council; Founder Emmanuel Temple No 2 Church. Honours: Honorary Doctorate, Christian Fellowship Educational Bible College; Certificate of Appreciation for Outstanding Community Service, Rainbow Senior Citizens Inc, 1986. Address: 4004 Cliff Street, Niagara Falls, NY 14305, USA.

DOUGLAS Kirk, b. 9 December 1916, Amsterdam, New York, USA. Actor. m. (1) Diana Dill, 2 sons, (2) Anne Buydens, 2 sons. Education: St Lawrence University; American Academy of Dramatic Arts. Appointments: President, Bryna Productions, 1955-; Director, Los Angeles Chapt, UN Association. Stage appearances: Spring Again; Three Sisters; Kiss and Tell; The Wind is Ninety; Alice in Arms; Man Bites Dog; The Boys of Autumn; Films include: The Strange Love of Martha Ivers; Letters to Three Wives; Ace in the Hole; The Bad and the Beautiful; 20,000 Leagues under the Sea; Ulysses; Lust for Life; Gunfight at Ok Corral; Paths of Glory; the Vikings; Last Train from Gun Hill; The Devil's Disciple; Spartacus; Strangers When We meet; Seven Days in May; Town Without Pity; The List of Adran Messenger; In Harms Way; Cats a Giant Shadow; The Way West; War Waggon; The Brotherhood; The Arrangement; There Was a Crooked Man; Gunfight, 1971; Light at the Edge of the World; Catch Me a Spy; A Man to Respect, 1972; Cat and Mouse; Scalawag (director), 1973; Once is Not Enough, 1975; Posse (producer, actor), 1975; The Moneychangers (TV), 1976; Holocaust 2000, 1977; The Fury, 1977; Villain, 1978;

Dictionary of International Biography

Saturn 3, 1979; The Final Countdown, 1980; The Man From Snowy River, 1986; Tough Guys, 1986; Queenie (TV mini series), 1987; Oscar, Welcome to Veraz, Greedy, 1994; Diamonds, 1999; Family Jewels, 2002. Publications: The Ragman's Son: an Autobiography, 1988; Novels: Dance With The Devil, 1990; The Secret, 1992; The Gift, 1992; Last Tango in Brooklyn, 1994; Climbing the Mountain: My Search for Meaning, 1997; The Broken Mirror (novel), 1997; My Stroke of Luck, 2002. Honours: Academy awards, critics awards; Commandeur, Ordre des Arts et Lettres, 1979; Légion d'honneur, 1985; Presidential Medal of Freedom, 1981; American Film Industries Lifetime Achievement, 1991; Kennedy Center Honors, 1994; Lifetime Achievement Award, Screen Actors' Guild, 1999; Golden Bear, Berlin Film Festival, 2000; National Medal of Arts, 2002. Address: The Bryna Company, 141 S El Camino Drive, Beverly Hills, CA 90212, USA.

DOUGLAS Marilyn Ann, b. 4 September 1943, Cleveland, Ohio, USA. Nurse Researcher. m. John Henry Douglas, 1 son, 1 daughter. Education: BSN, Ohio State University, Columbus, Ohio, 1968; MSN, Cardiovascular Nursing, Catholic University of America, Washington, DC, 1975; DNSc, University of California, San Francisco, 1989. Appointments: Head Nurse ICU, US Peace Corps, Colombia, 1970-72; Cardiovascular Clinical Nurse Specialist, Stanford University Hospital, 1979-88; Associate Chief, Nursing Service for Research at Veteran's Affairs, Palo Alto Health Care System, California, 1997-. Publications: Numerous articles; Founding Co-Editor, Progress in Cardiovascular Nursing, 1985-90; Editor, Journal of Transcultural Nursing, 1997-. Honours: Leininger Award, 1996; Fellow, American Academy of Nursing, 1998. Memberships: American Heart Association; American Association of Critical Care Nurses; Transcultural Nursing Society. Address: 360 Maclane Street, Palo Alto, CA 94306, USA. E-mail: martydoug@comcast.net

DOUGLAS Michael Kirk, b. 25 September 1944, New Brunswick, NJ, USA. m. (1) Diandra Mornell Luker (divorced), 1 son, (2) Catherine Zeta Jones, 2000, 1 son, 1 daughter. Appointments: Actor in films: It's My Turn; Hail Heroll, 1969; Summertime, 1971; Napoleon and Samantha, 1972; Coma, 1978; Running, 1979; Star Chamber, 1983; Romancing the Stone, 1984; A Chorus Line, 1985; Jewel of the Nile, 1985; Fatal Attraction, 1987; Wall Street, 1987; Heidi, 1989; Black Rain, 1989; The War of the Roses, 1990; Shining Through, 1990; Basic Instinct, 1992; Falling Down, 1993; The American President, 1995; The Ghost and the Darkness, 1996; The Game, 1997; A Perfect Murder, 1998; Traffic, 2000; Wonder Boys, 2000; One Night at McCool's, 2000; Don't Say a Word, 2001; A Few Good Years, 2002; It Runs in the Family, 2003; Monkeyface, 2003; Producer, films including: One Flew Over the Cuckoo's Nest, 1975; The China Syndrome; Sarman (executive producer); Romancing the Stone; Jewel of the Nile, Flatliners, 1990; Made in America (co-executive, producer); Disclosure, 1994; A Perfect Murder, 1998; One Night at McCool's, 2000; Godspeed; Lawrence Mann, 2002; Actor in TV series: Streets of San Francisco. Honours include: Academy Award for Best Actor for Wall Street, 1988; Spencer Tracey Award, 1999; UN Messenger of Peace, 2000. Address: C/o Creative Artists Agency Inc, 9830 Wilshire Boulevard, Beverly Hills, CA 90212, USA. Website: www.michaeldouglas.com

DOUGLAS-DOMMEN Marguerite France, b. 12 July 1918, England. Painter. m. John Haig Douglas, 1 son, 3 daughters. Education: École des Beaux Arts, Lausanne, Switzerland; Studied painting under Walter Russell, Tom Monnington and Earnest Jackson, Royal Academy Schools, Royal Academy, London, 1936-39. Career: Timber Measurer, Women's Land Army, 1939-45; Artist working on drawings, monoprints and painting in all media; Exhibitions: Landscapes and portraits with Society of Scottish

Artists and the Society of Scottish Watercolour Painters under the name Douglas; Exhibition in Ancona, Italy, 1968; Paintings in oils and watercolours in many private collections. Publication: Illustrated an edition of poems by James Hogg 1770-1835 (The Ettrick Shepherd) for a bicentenary celebration, 1970-. Honour: Diploma of Merit, Ancona Exhibition, Italy, 1968. Memberships: Corresponding Member, International Institute of Arts, 1959; Reynolds Club (Ex Royal Academy Schools Students). Address: Craigsford, Earlston, Berwickshire, TD4 6DJ, Scotland.

DOVE Rita (Frances), b. 28 Aug 1952, Akron, Ohio, USA. Poet; Writer; Professor. m. Fred Viebahn, 23 Mar 1979, 1 daughter. Education: BA, summa cum laude, Miami University, Oxford, Ohio, 1973; Postgraduate studies, University of Tübingen, 1974-75; MFA, University of Iowa, 1977. Appointments: Assistant Professor 1981-84, Associate Professor 1984-87, Professor of English, 1987-89, Arizona State University, Tempe; Writer-in-Residence, Tuskegee Institute, 1982; Associate Editor, Callaloo, 1986-; Advisor and Contributing Editor, Gettysburg Review, 1987-, TriQuarterly, 1988-, Georgia Review, 1994, Bellingham Review, 1996-; Professor of English, 1989-93, Commonwealth Professor, 1993-, University of Virginia; Poet Laureate of the USA, 1993-95. Publications: Poetry: Ten Poems, 1977; The Only Dark Spot in the Sky, 1980; The Yellow House on the Corner, 1980; Mandolin, 1982; Museum, 1983; Thomas and Beulah, 1986; The Other Side of the House, 1988; Grace Notes, 1989; Selected Poems, 1993; Lady Freedom Among Us, 1994; Mother Love, 1995; Evening Primrose, 1998; On the Bus with Rosa Parks, 1999; American Smooth, 2004. Other: Fifth Sunday (short stories), 1985; Through the Ivory Gate (novel), 1992; The Darker Face of the Earth (verse play), 1994; The Poet's World (essays), 1995. Contributions to: Magazines and journals. Honours: Many honorary doctorates; Fulbright Fellow, 1974-75; National Endowment for the Arts Grants, 1978, 1989; Portia Pittman Fellow, Tuskegee Institute, 1982; Guggenheim Fellowship, 1983-84; Peter I.B. Lavan Younger Poets Award, Academy of American Poets, 1986; Pulitzer Prize in Poetry, 1987; General Electric Foundation Award for Younger Writers, 1987; Rockefeller Foundation Residency, Bellagio, Italy, 1988; Ohio Governor's Award, 1988; Mellon Fellow, National Humanities Center, 1988-89; Fellow, Center for Advanced Studies, University of Virginia, 1989-92; NAACP Great American Artist Award, 1993; Renaissance Forum Award, Folger Shakespeare Library, 1994; Charles Frankel Prize, 1996; Levinson Prize, 1998; Duke Ellington Lifetime Achievement Award, 2001; Emily Courie Leadership Award, 2003. Memberships: PEN Club; American Society of Composers, Authors and Publishers; American Philosophical Society; Academy of American Poets; Associated Writing Programs; Phi Beta Kappa, Senator, 1994-; Phi Kappa Phi; Poetry Society of America; Poets and Writers. Address: Department of English, 219 Bryan Hall, University of Virginia, Charlottesville, VA 22903, USA.

DOWD Timothy Clay, b. 17 May 1954, Scarborough, England. Ophthalmic Surgeon. m. Dreda, 1 son. Education: Guy's Hospital Medical School, University of London, 1973-79. Appointments: House Officer, Clatterbridge Hospital, 1979-80; Senior House Officer, St Bartholomew's Hospital, London, 1980-81; Senior House Officer, Neurosurgery, Walton Hospital, 1981; Senior House Officer, St Pauls Eye Hospital, Liverpool, 1981-83; Research Registrar, Nuffield Laboratory of Ophthalmology, University of Oxford, 1983-84; Registrar, St Paul's Eye Hospital, 1984-87; Research Registrar, University of Liverpool, 1987-88; Senior Registrar, Northern Region, 1988-92; Consultant Ophthalmic Surgeon, North Riding Infirmary, 1992-2003; Consultant Ophthalmic Surgeon, James Cook University Hospital, Middlesbrough, 2003-. Publications: Various chapters and papers on ophthalmic subjects. Honours: BSc, Honours, University of

London, 1976; MB BS, University of London, 1979; MRSC LRCP, 1979; FRCS Glasgow, 1985, FRCS (Glasgow), 1985; FRC Ophth (UK), 1989. Memberships: Royal College of Ophthalmologists; North of England Ophthalmological Society; American Academy of Ophthalmology; British Ophthalmic Anaesthesia Society (Treasurer). Address: James Cook University Hospital, Department of Ophthalmology, Middlesbrough TS4 3BW, England.

DOWNES David Anthony, b. 17 August 1927, Victor, Colorado, USA. Professor of English Emeritus; Writer. m. Audrey Romaine Ernst, 7 September 1949, 1 son, 3 daughters. Education: BA, cum laude, Regis University, 1949; MA, Marquette University, 1950; PhD, University of Washington, 1956. Appointments: Assistant Professor, Professor, Chairman of Department, University of Seattle, 1953-68; Professor of English, Dean of Humanities and Fine Arts, 1968-72, Director of Educational Development Projects, 1972-73, Director of Humanities Programme, 1973-74, Director of Graduate English Studies, 1975-78, Chairman of Department, 1978-84, Professor Emeritus, 1991, California State University, Chico; Consultant Cowles Rare Book Library, Gonzaga University, 1997. Publications: Gerard Manley Hopkins: A Study of His Ignatian Spirit, 1959; Victorian Portraits: Hopkins and Pater, 1965; Pater, Kingsley and Newman, 1972; The Great Sacrifice: Studies in Hopkins, 1983; Ruskin's Landscape of Beatitude, 1984; Hopkins' Sanctifying Imagination, 1985; The Ignatian Personality of Gerard Manley Hopkins, 1990; Hopkins' Achieved Self, 1996; The Belle of Cripple Creek Gold, 2001. Contributions to: Scholarly books and journals. Honours: Exceptional Merit Awards for Scholarship, 1984, 1988, 1990, 1992; Honorary Doctor of laws, Gonzaga University, 1997. Address: 1076 San Ramon Drive, Chico, CA 95973, USA.

DOWNEY Robert Jr, b. 4 April 1965, New York, USA. Actor. m. Deborah Falconer, 1 child. Sentenced to probation for possession of cocaine; imprisoned for further drugs offence breaching terms of probation, 1997; released for rehabilitation, 1998; imprisoned again, 1999, freed, 2000, charged with drugs possession, 2000. Appointments: Actor in films including: Pound, 1970; Firstborn; Weird Science; To Live and Die in L.A.; Back to School; The Pick-Up Artist; Johnny B Good; True Believer; Chances Are; Air America; Soapdish; Chaplin (BAFTA Award); Heart and Souls; Short Cuts; The Last Party; Natural Born Killers; Only You; Restoration; Mussolini; The Untold Story (TV mini-series); Restoration; Danger Zone; Home for the Holidays; Richard III; Bliss Vision, 1997; The Gingerbread Man, 1997; Two Girls and a Guy, 1998; In Dreams, 1999; Friends and Lovers, 1999; Wonder Boys, 2000; Television includes: Ally McBeal, 2000; Black and White, 2000.

DOYLE Brian B, b. 20 May 1941, Boston Massachusetts, USA. Psychiatrist. m. Margaret M Ready, 1 son, 2 daughters. Education: BA, Harvard College, USA, 1962; MD, CM, McGill University, USA, 1966. Appointments: Clinical Professor of Psychiatry and of Family Medicine, Georgetown University School of Medicine, USA, 1983-; Host, Medical Answers, USA Public Broadcasting System (television), 1996-. Publications: 4 monographs; 28 articles on anxiety and depression. Honours: Alpha Omega Alpha; Distinguished Life Fellow, American Psychiatric Association; Member, American College of Psychiatrists; Academy of Medicine, District of Columbia, USA. Memberships: American Medical Association; APA. Address: 1325 18th Street NW, App 209, Washington DC 20036, USA. E-mail: doc@bbdoylemd.org

DOYLE Roddy, b. 1958, Dublin Ireland. Writer. m. Bellinda, 2 sons. Publications: The Commitments, 1987, filmed 1991; The Snapper, 1990, filmed, 1992; The Van, 1991; Paddy Clarke Ha Ha Ha, 1993; The Women Who Walked Into Doors, 1996; A Star Called Henry, 1999; The Giggler Treatment, 2000; Rory and Ita,

2002. Honour: Booker Prize for Paddy Clarke Ha Ha Ha, 1993. Address: c/o Patti Kelly, Viking Books, 375 Hudson Street, New York, NY 10014, USA.

DRABBLE Margaret, b. 5 June 1939, Sheffield, England. Author. m. (1) Clive Swift, 2 sons, 1 daughter, (2) Michael Holroyd, 1982. Education; Newnham College, Cambridge. Appointments: Editor, The Oxford Companion to England Literature, 1979-84; Chairman, National Book League, 1980-82; Vice-Patron, Child Psychotherapy Trust, 1987-. Publications: A Summer Bird-Cage, 1963; The Garrick Year, 1964; The Millstone, 1965 Jerusalem the Golden, 1967; The Waterfall, 1969; The Needle's Eye, 1972; Arnold Bennett: A Biography, 1974; The Realms of Gold, 1975; The Genius of Thomas Hardy (editor), 1976; The Ice Age, 1977; For Queen and Country: Britain in the Victorian Age, 1978; A Writer's Britain, 1979; The Middle Ground (novel), 1980; The Oxford Companion to English Literature (editor), 1985; The Radiant Way (novel), 1987; A Natural Curiosity, 1989; Safe as Houses, 1990; The Gates of Ivory, 1991; Angus Wilson: A Biography, 1995; The Witch of Exmoor (novel), 1996; The Peppered Moth (novel), 2001; The Seven Sisters (novel), 2002. Honours include: John Llewelyn Rhys Memorial Prize, 1966; E M Forster Award, American Academy of Arts and Letters, 1973; Hon D Litt, Sheffield, 1976, Bradford, 1988, Hull, 1992; Honorary Fellow, Sheffield City Polytechnic, 1989; Honorary member, American Academy of Arts and Letters, 2002. Address: c/o PFD, Drury House, 34-43 Russell Street, London, WC2B 5HA, England.

DRAGOUN Otokar, b. 15 March 1937, Sedlec, Czech Republic. Physicist. m. Nadezda Novotná, 5 July 1961, 2 daughters. Education: Diploma in Engineering, Czech Technical University, Prague, 1962; PhD, Physics, 1967, DSc, Physics, 1985, Charles University, Prague. Appointments: Researcher, Nuclear Physics Institute, Czech Academy of Science; Head of Research Group, 1971-; Postdoctoral Fellow, Max-Planck Institute for Nuclear Physics, Heidelberg, Germany, 1966-69; Visiting Professor, Faculty of Physics Technical University, Munich, Spring 1992, Summer 1994; External Lecturer, Charles University, Prague, 1986-; External Lecturer, Czech Technical University, Prague, 1999-; Member of the Karlsruhe Tritium Neutrino Experiment, 2001-. Publications: Contributor of reviews and science papers on nuclear, nuclear atomic and neutrino experimental physics in international journals; Patentee in field. Honours: Medal Science Achievement, Union Czech Mathematicians and Physicists, 1988. Membership: Union Czech Mathematicians and Physicists. Address: Nuclear Physics Institute of the Academy of Sciences of Czech Republic, CZ-25068, Rez near Prague, Czech Republic.

DRĂGUȘIN Constantin, b. 16 July 1935, N Titulescu, Jud Olt, Romania. University Professor. m. Lucia Drăgu in, deceased, 1 son. Education: University Diplomate, 1964, Doctor in Mathematical Sciences, 1977, Mathematical Faculty, Bucharest University. Appointments: Assistant Professor, 1964-75; Lecturer, 1975-90; Senior Lecturer, 1990-92; Full Professor, 1992-. Publications: 22 papers in speciality reviews and 18 books concerning mathematical analysis and probability theory. Honour: Distinguished Lecturer, 1982. Membership: Scientific Secretary, Transportation Faculty, Polytechnic University of Bucharest. Address: Timișoara Boulevard, nr 39, Bl P15, Ap 118, 061312 Bucharest, Romania. E-mail: dragusin@mathem.pub.ro

DRAKE Albert Dee, b. 26 March 1935, Portland, Oregon, USA. Professor Emeritus of English; Writer; Poet. m. 28 December 1960, divorced 1985, 1 son, 2 daughters. Education: Portland State College, 1956-59; BA, English, 1962, MFA, English, 1966, University of Oregon. Appointments: Research Assistant, 1965; Teaching Assistant, 1965-66, English Department, University of

Dictionary of International Biography

Oregon; Assistant Professor, English, 1966-70, Associate Professor, English, 1970-79, Professor, English, 1979-91, Professor Emeritus, English, 1995, Michigan State University; Director Clarion Science Fiction and Fantasy Workshop, 1983, 1988-90. Publications: Michigan Signatures (editor), 1969; 3 Northwest Poets, 1970; Poems, 1972; Assuming the Position, 1972; Riding Bike, 1972; By Breathing In and Out, 1974; Cheap Thrills, 1975; Returning to Oregon, 1975; Roadsalt, 1976; Reaching for the Sun, 1979; Garage, 1980; Homesick, 1988; Hot Rodder, 1993; Flat Out, 1994; Fifties Flashback, 1998. Contributions to: Poetry Northwest; Poetry Now; Northwest Review; Shenandoah; South Dakota Review; Arts in Society; Wormwood Review; West Coast Poetry Review; Windsor Review; Midwest Quarterly; Assembling; TransPacific; December. Honours: Poetry Prize, St Andrews Review, 1974; National Endowment for the Arts Grants, 1975, 1984; Michigan Council for the Arts Grant, 1981. Address: 9727 South East Reedway, Portland, OR 97266, USA.

DRAPALIK Betty R, b. 4 July 1932, Cook County, Illinois, USA. Artist. m. Joseph J Drapalik, 30 October 1951, 1 son, 1 daughter. Education: College Night School, College of Lake County, 1982; Numerous Art Workshops with: Phil Austin, Bridget Austin, Catherine Wilson Smith, Tom Francesconi, Tony van Hasselt, Rose Edin, Diane Maxey, Tom Trausch, Tom Lynch, John Dioszegi, Ratinda Das, Ingrid Albrecht, Sharon Crosbie. Appointments: Secretary Clerk, Service School Command, Great Lakes Naval Base; Secretary to the Assistant Director, Arden Shore Boys' Home, Lake Bluff, Illinois, prior to 1987; Artist, Homemaker, 1987-. Publications: Works featured in publications including: The Artists Magazine, Art Clinic, 1997; Celebrating Door County's Wild Places, 2001; Lake County and Its Arts, Volumes III, IV, 1999 and Volume VI, 2003; Watercolor Secrets by Tom Lynch. Honours: Numerous art awards include most recently: Hardy Gallery Purchase Award, 1998; Lake County Art League Fine Arts Festival 1st Place Watercolor, 1999; Kenosha Art Association Art Event Best of Show, 2001; Lakes Region Watercolor Guild Artist of the Month, 2004; First Lady of Zion Awards Best of Show, 2004. Memberships: Life Member, Midwest Watercolor Society (now Transparent Watercolor Society of America); Red River Watercolor Society; Lake County Art League (Past President); Lake Region Watercolor Guild (Exhibit Chair); National Museum of Women in the Arts; Art Institute of Chicago; Kenosha Art Association; Deer Path Art League. Address: 2018 West Grove Avenue, Waukegan, IL 60085-1607, USA.

DRAYTON Mary Josephine, b. 13 January 1916, Dunedin, New Zealand. Retired Teacher and Principal; Local and Regional Councillor. m. Ronald Wilfred Drayton, deceased. Education: MA Honours, History, 1937; Diploma in Education, 1940. Appointments: Head of Department, 1947-57, First Assistant, 1955-57, Acting Principal, 1957-59, Whangarei Girls High School; Principal, Tauranga Girls College, 1959-1981; Elected to University of Waikato Council, 1979, Court of Convocation, 1987-94; Acting Principal, Hamilton Girls' High School, 1981-82; Pro-Chancellor, 1986-87, Chancellor, 1988-91, Waikato University; Tauranga City Council Member, 1985-92, Deputy Mayor, 1986-89, Chairperson, Town Planning Committee, 1986-89; Director, Trust Bank, Bay of Plenty, 1988-91; Member, Tauranga District Council, 1989-92; Regional Councillor, Bay of Plenty, 1989-92, re-elected, 1992-95, 1995-98, Deputy Chairperson, Resource Planning Committee, 1992-95, Chairman, Resource Planning Committee, 1995-98, Bay of Plenty Regional Council; Chairperson, Tauranga Sub-Region Landfill Working Party, 1991-92; Director, Quayside Holdings and Quayside Securities, 1993-99; Tepapa National Services TePaerangi: Sector Reference Group-Training & Skill Development, 2003-06. Honours: Woolf Fisher Travelling Fellowship to Hawaii and California, 1971; MBE, 1980;

Paul Harris Fellow, 1987; Commemoration Medal, 1990; Honorary Doctorate, University of Waikato, 1993; Companion, New Zealand Order of Merit, 2000. Address: 197 Ngatai Road, Tauranga, New Zealand.

DRESSLER John C, b. 7 August 1949, Akron, Ohio, USA. Professor of Horn, Musicology and Music Theory. Education: Bachelor of Music Education, Baldwin-Wallace College. 1071; Master of Music with Distinction, 1974, Doctor of Music with Distinction, 1987, Indiana University. Appointments: Teaching: Instructor, Jacksonville University, Florida, 1974-76; Instructor (Sabbatical leave replacement), University of the Pacific, Stockton, California, 1976-77; Instructor (Sabbatical leave replacement, Tennessee Technological University, Cookeville, Tennessee, 1977-78; Assistant Professor, University of Georgia, Athens, Georgia, 1980-86; Associate Professor, Baylor University, Waco, Texas, 1986-89; Professor of Horn, Musicology and Music Theory, Murray State University, 1989-; Orchestral positions include: Extra/Substitute Horn, Indianapolis Symphony and Opera Orchestras, 1996-; Principal Horn, Jackson (Tennessee) Symphony Orchestra, 1999-. Publications: Gerald Finzi: A Bio-bibliography, 1997; Alan Rawsthorne: A Bio-bibliography, forthcoming, 2004; Reviews of new recordings in The Horn Call (quarterly journal of the International Horn Society), column appears in each issue; Numerous articles in professional journals; Recording: Kentuckiana Brass and Percussion Ensemble (CD), 2000. Honours: M Mus and D Mus awarded with Distinction; Recipient of: Summer Faculty Development Research Awards, Murray State University; Sarah Moss Fellowship Award, University of Georgia. Memberships: American Musicological Society; International Horn Society; Omicron Delta Kappa. Address: Department of Music, Murray State University, Murray, KY 42071, USA. E-mail: john.dressler@murraystate.edu

DRETAR Tomislav, b. 2 March 1945, Nova Gradiska, Croatia. Poet; Translator. m. Emira Rakanovic, 2 daughters. Education: Pedagogy Faculty, Rijeka, Croatia; Postgraduate Studies, University of Sarajevo, Bosnia and Herzegovina. Publications: 9 books of poetry; 300 articles, essays and critiques. Membership: Hrvatsko Drustvo Knjizevnika, Herzeg-Bosnia. Address: 125 Rue Elise, 1050 Brussels, Belgium. E-mail: tomisdret@msn.com

DREYFUSS Richard Stephen, b. 29 October 1947, New York, USA. Actor. m. Jeramie, 1983, 2 sons, 1 daughter. Education: San Fernando Valley State College. Appointments: Alternative military service, Los Angeles County General Hospital, 1969-71; Actor, stage appearances include: Julius Caesar, 1978; The Big Fix (also producer), 1978; Othello, 1979; Death and the Maiden, 1992; The Prison of Second Avenue, 1999; Films include: American Graffiti, 1972; Dillinger, 1973; The Apprenticeship of Duddy Kravitz, 1974; Jaws, 1975; Inserts, 1975; Close Encounters of the Third Kind, 1976; The Goodbye Girl, 1977; The Competition, 1980; Whose Life Is It Anyway?, 1981; Down and Out in Beverly Hills, 1986; Stakeout, 1988; Moon over Parador, 1989; Let It Ride, 1989; Always, 1989; Rosencrantz and Guildenstern are Dead, 1990; Postcards from the Edge, 1990; Once Around, 1990; Randall and Juliet, 1990; Prisoners of Honor, 1991; What About Bob?, 1991; Lost in Yonkers, 1993; Another Stakeout, 1993; The American President, 1995; Mr Holland's Opus, 1995; Mad Dog Time, 1996; James and the Giant Peach, 1996; Night Falls on Manhattan, 1997; The Call of the Wild, 1997; Krippendorf's Tribe, 1998; A Fine and Private Place, 1998; The Crew, 2000; The Old Man Who Read Love Stories, 2000; Who is Cletis Tout? 2001; (TV movie) Oliver Twist, 1997; Director, producer, Nuts, 1987; Hamlet (Birmingham), 1994. Publication: The Two Georges (with Harry Turtledove), 1996. Honours: Golden Globe Award, 1978; Academy Award for Best Actor in the Goodbye Girl, 1978. Memberships:

American Civil Liberties Union Screen Actors Guild; Equity Association; American Federation of TV and Radio Artists; Motion Picture Academy of Arts and Sciences. Address: William Morris Agency, 151 S El Camino Drive, Beverly Hills, CA 90212, USA.

DRIVER Minnie (Amelia), b. 21 January 1970. Actress. Appointments: Actress, TV appearances include: God on the Rocks; Mr Wroe's Virgins; The Politician's Wife; Film appearances include: Circle of Friends; Goldeneye; Baggage; Big Night; Sleepers; Grosse Point Blank; Good Will Hunting; The Governess; Hard Rain; An Ideal Husband, 1999; South Park: Bigger, Longer and Uncut, 1999; Slow Burn, 2000; Beautiful, 2000; Return to Me, 2000; The Upgrade, 2000; High Heels and Lowlifes, 2001; D.C. Smalls, 2001; Play: Sexual Perversity in Chicago, Comedy Theatre, London, 2003. Honours: Best Newcomer, 1997, Best Actress, 1988, London Circle of Film Critics. Address: c/o Lou Coulson, 1st Floor, 37 Berwick Street, London, W1V 3LF, England.

DROBYSHEVSKI Edward, b. 18 April 1936, St Petersburg, Russia. Astro- and Plasma Physicist, Researcher. m. Natalya Kotyurgina, 2 sons, 1 daughter. Education: Engineer Researcher, Leningrad Polytechnic. Institute, 1959; Russian Degree of Candidate of Physics – Mathematical Sciences, 1965, Russian Degree of Doctor of Physics – Mathematical Sciences, 1982, Ioffe Physics-Technical Institute. Appointments: Senior Laboratory Assistant, 1959; Junior Scientist, 1960; Senior Scientist, 1979; Leading Scientist, 1986; Major Scientist, 1992, Head of Dense Plasma Dynamics Laboratory, 1991, Ioffe Physico-Technical Institute of Russian Academy of Sciences, 1959-. Publications: Author: Was Jupiter the Protosun's Core, 1974; Callisto Project, 1989; Daemon Detection Experiment, 2000. Honours: Name "Drobyshevski" is given to Minor Planet No 4009 by International Astronomical Union, 1992; Russia President Stipend for Eminent Scientist of Russia, 1992. Memberships: COSPAR, European Astronomical Society; Hypervelocity Impact Society. Address: Ioffe Physico-Technical Institute, Russian Academy of Sciences, 194021 St Petersburg, Russia. E-mail: emdrob@mail.ioffe.ru

DRUMMOND Richard Henry, b. 14 December 1916, San Francisco, California, USA. Theological Professor. m. Pearl Estella Oppegaard, 2 sons, 1 daughter. Education: BA, 1938, MA, 1939, Classics (Highest Honours in Latin), University of California, Los Angeles. PhD, Classics, University of Wisconsin, 1941; Postgraduate Studies, Gettysburg Theological Seminary, 1941-44; Naganuma School of Japanese Language, Tokyo, Japan, Kobe, Japan. Appointments: Fraternal Worker, Japan, Presbyterian Church, USA, 1949-62; Professor of Ecumenical Mission and History of Religions, University of Dubuque Theological Seminary, 1962-93; First Incumbent, Florence Livergood Warren Chair of Comparative Religions UDTS, 1984-87. Publications: Books: A History of Christianity in Japan, 1971; Gautama the Buddha, an Essay in Religious Understanding, 1974; Unto the Churches, 1978; Toward a New Age in Christian Theology, 1985; A Life of Jesus the Christ, 1989; A Broader Vision: Perspectives on the Buddha and the Christ, 1995; Numerous articles. Honours: Phi Beta Kappa, Research Fellowship in Classics, 1940-41; Teaching Fellowship, 1941-44; Faculty Fellowship, Sealantic Fund 1968-69, Japan; Outstanding Educators of America, 1972, 1974; University Fellow, University of Dubuque, 1991; Outstanding Scholars of the 20th Century, IBC; Listed in Who's Who publications. Memberships: American Academy of Religion; American Society of Missology; Midwest Association of Professors of Mission; North American Academy of Ecumenists. Address: 801 Davis Street, Apt 204, Dubuque, IA 52001, USA.

DRYSDALE Helena Claire, b. 6 May 1960, London, England. Writer. m. Richard Pomeroy, 21 May 1987, 2 daughters. Education: Trinity College, Cambridge, 1978-82; MA, Honours, History, Art History, Cambridge. Publications: Alone Through China and Tibet, 1986; Dancing With the Dead, 1991; Looking for Gheorghe: Love and Death in Romania, 1995; Mother Tongues, 2001. Contributions to: Vogue; Marie Claire; Independent; Independent on Sunday; Harpers and Queen; Cosmopolitan; World. Honours: Exhibitioner, Trinity College; Shortlisted, Esquire/Waterstones Non-Fiction Award, 1995; PEN/J R Ackerley Award for Autobiograhy, 1995. Membership: Royal Geographical Society, Society of Authors.

DRYZEK John Stanley, b. 23 June 1953, Maids Moreton, England. Professor. m. Margaret Clark, 1 son, 1 daughter. Education: BA honours, Economics and Politics, University of Lancaster, England, 1974; MS, Politics, University of Strathclyde, Scotland, 1976; PhD, Government and Politics, University of Maryland, USA, 1980. Appointments: Assistant Professor, Political Science, Ohio State University, USA, 1980-86; Professor and Head, Department of Political Science, University of Oregon, USA, 1986-95; Professor and Head, Department of Political Science, University of Melbourne, Australia, 1995-2000; Professor and Head, Social and Political Theory Programme, Australian National University, 2001-02. Publications: Books and articles in international journals. Honours: Spitz Prize for best book in liberal or democratic theory, Conference for the Study of Political Thought, 1998; Fellow, Academy of the Social Sciences in Australia. Memberships: American Political Science Association; The Wilderness Society. Address: 9 Jagara Street, Aranda, ACT 2614, Australia. E-mail: jdryzek@coombs.anu.edu.au Website: http://socpol.anu.edu.au/people/

DU TOIT Anna Sophia Adeline, b. 14 October 1952, Edenburg, South Africa. Lecturer. Education: BA, 1973; BA (Hons), 1979; MA, Information Science, 1990; Postgraduate, Diploma, Marketing Management, 1990; D Litt et Phil Degree, 1996. Appointments: Information Manager, Meat Board; Techno-Economist, CSIR; Lecturer, University of South Africa; Senior Lecturer, Professor, Rand Afrikaans University Johannesburg, South Africa. Publications: Establishing a knowledge management program for competitive advantage in an enterprise, 2001; Competitive intelligence in the knowledge economy, 2003; 40 other articles. Memberships: European Operations Management Association; Society for Competitive Intelligence Professionals; South African Institute for Management Scientists. Address: Department of Information Studies, RAU University, PO Box 524, Auckland park 2006, South Africa.

DUBERSTEIN Larry, b. 18 May 1944, New York, New York, USA. Writer; Cabinetmaker. 3 daughters. Education: BA, Wesleyan University, 1966; MA, Harvard University, 1971. Publications: Nobody's Jaw, 1979; The Marriage Hearse, 1983; Carnovsky's Retreat, 1988; Postcards From Pinsk, 1991; Eccentric Circles, 1992; The Alibi Breakfast, 1995; The Handsome Sailor, 1998; The Mount Monadnock Blues, 2003. Contributions to: Articles, essays, reviews to: Saturday Review: Boston Review; The National; The Phoenix; New York Times Book Review; Boston Globe; others. Honours: New American Writing Award, 1987, 1991; New York Times Notable Book of 1998. Address: Box 390609, Cambridge, MA 02139, USA.

DUBOIS Jean, b. 4 January 1926, Denver, Colorado, USA. Writer; Poet. m. Edward N Dubois, 21 August 1947, 1 son, 2 daughters. Education: BA, University of Wyoming, 1947; MA, The Pennsylvania State University, 1963. Publications: Silent Stones, Empty Passageways, 1992; The Same Sweet Yellow, 1994.

Contributions to: Poets On; Thema; Modern Haiku; Brussels Sprout; Wall Street Journal; Mayfly. Membership: Haiku Society of America, Address: P O Box 1430, Golden, CO 80402, USA.

DUBURS Gunars, b. 12 June 1934, Riga, Latvia. Chemist. m. Renate Duburs, 1 daughter. Education: Chemist, Latvian University, 1957; PhD, 1961; Dr.chem.habil, 1979; Professor, 1988. Appointments: Research Scientist, 1957-64, Head of Laboratory, 1964-, Scientific Director, 1987-2004, Institute of Organic Synthesis. Publications: 465 science papers, 169 patents. Honours include: D Grindel's Award, 1996; Award of the Latvian Cabinet of Ministers, 1999; Award of the Latvian Academy of Science and Patent Office, 2000; O Schmiedeberg's Medal, 2001; Listed in numerous biographical publications. Memberships: Latvian Academy of Science; International Society of Heterocyclic Chemistry; Albert Schweitzer International University; UNESCO Molecular and Cell Biology Network. Address: 21 Aizkraukles Street, Latvian Institute of Organic Synthesis, Riga, LV 1006, Latvia.

DUC Ha Minh, b. 3 May 1935, Thanh Hoa Province, Vietnam. Professor; Writer. m. Pham Bich Ngoc. Education: Graduate, Literature Department, Ha Noi Teaching College, 1957; Doctor of Literature, 1984. Appointments: Deputy Professor, 1984; Professor, 1990; Dean, Press Faculty of Hanoi University, 1990-2000; Director, Literature Institute, 1995; Editor in Chief, Literature Review, 1995; Chairman, Academic Title, Nomination Council on Literature, 1995-; Member, Central Literary & Arts Criticism Theory Council, 2004. Publications: Writers and Works; Poem and Some Problems on Vietnamese Modern Poetry; Ho Chi Minh; Marx Anghen Lenin and Problems on Literatural Theory; Time and Pages; Time and Witness; Press Problems on Theory and Fact; A Period of Poetry; Professor and His Working Place; Essay, Time and Witness; Nam Cao Writer Career and Works; Treatise in Literature. 1999: Going through the Autumn, poem; Ho Chi Minh – Literary and Journalism knowledge; Ho Chi Minh – A Journalist, monograph and selection; 2000; In the Middle of Winter, poem, 2001; Some Problems on Theory and Fact of Literature, 2001; Journalistic Theory basic, general feature and style; Three times to America; Writers and Works, 2001; Literature Field: Talent and Style, 2001; Midnight's Thought, poem, 2002; The spot of sky with the wind and sand blowing, poem, 2003; The national identity culture, literature and art with varied artistic types, in progress, 2003; Literary Criticism & Theory Collection of Professor Ha Minh Duc, 3 volumes, 8 = 2400 pages, 2004. Honours: The First Prize, Literature; The Excellent Teacher; The First Labour Decoration, 2000; The National Award on Literatural Criticism and Theory; The People Teacher; The National Award on Science Researching; The National Award on Literature and Arts, 2001. Memberships: National Council on Education; Vietnamese Writers Association; Criticism and Theory Council; Vietnamese Journalists Association; National Council on Education. Address: 20 Ly Thai To Street, Hanoi, Vietnam.

DUCHOVNY David, b. 7 August 1960, New York, USA. Actor. m. Tea Leoni, 1997, 1 son, 1 daughter. Education: Yale University; Princeton University. Appointments: Stage appearances include: Off-Broadway plays, The Copulating Machine of Venice, California and Green Cuckatoo; TV series: The X Files; Films include: New Year's Day, 1989; Julia Has Two Lovers, 1990; The Rapture, 1991; Don't Tell Mom The Babysitter's Dead, 1991; Chaplin, 1992; Red Shoe Diaries, 1992; Ruby, 1992; Kalifornia, 1993; Venice, Venice, Apartment Zero; Close Enemy; Loan; Independence Day; Playing God; The X Files, 1998; Return To Me, 2000; Evolution, 2001; Zoolander, 2001; Full Frontal, 2002; XIII, 2003; Connie and Carla, 2004; House of D, 2004; Television

includes: Twin Peaks, 1990; The X-Files, 1993-; Life With Bonnie, 2002. Address: 20th Century Fox Film Corporation, PO Box 900, Beverly Hills, CA 90213, USA.

DUCHROW Ulrich H H, b. 13 June 1935, Hanover, Germany. Theologian. m. Ulrike, 2 sons, 1 daughter. Education: Studies of Theology, Philosophy, 1955-63; Dr Theol, 1963; Assistant Professor, 1968; Professor, Theology Faculty, University of Heidelberg, 1984. Appointments: Protestant Institute for Interdisciplinary Research, Heidelberg, 1963-70; Director, Department of Studies, Lutheran World Federation, 1970-77; Professor Ecumenical Institute, Bossey, 1977-78; Ecumenical Officer, Protestant Church in Baden, 1979-2000, Professor of Theology, University of Heidelberg, 1979-; Co-Founder, Co-President, ecumenical grassroots movement Kairos Europa - Towards a Europe for Justice. Publications: 350 include (in various languages) Alternatives to Global Capitalism: Drawn from Biblical History, Designed for Political Action, 1995, 2nd edition 1998; God or Mammon: Economies in Conflict, 1996; Christianity in the Context of Globalized Capitalistic Markets, 1997; People's and Social Movements in Western Europe, 1997; Property for People, Not for Profit, 2004. Memberships: International Bonhoeffer Society; International Association of Mission Studies. Address: Alfred Jost Str 7, D-69124 Heidelberg, Germany.

DUCKWORTH Marilyn, b. 10 November 1935, Auckland, New Zealand. Writer. m. (1) Harry Duckworth, 28 May 1955, (2) Ian Macfarlane, 2 October 1964, (3) Dan Donovan, 9 December 1974, (4) John Batstone, 8 June 1985, 4 daughters. Publications: A Gap in the Spectrum, 1959; The Matchbox House, 1960; A Barbarous Tongue, 1963; Over the Fence is Out, 1969; Disorderly Conduct, 1984; Married Alive, 1985; Rest for the Wicked, 1986; Pulling Faces, 1987; A Message From Harpo, 1989; Explosions on the Sun, 1989; Unlawful Entry, 1992; Seeing Red, 1993; Leather Wings, 1995; Cherries on a Plate, editor, 1996; Studmuffin, 1997; Camping on the Faultline, 2000; Swallowing Diamonds, 2003. Contributions to: Landfall; New Zealand Listener; Critical Quarterly; Islands; others. Honours: New Zealand Literary Fund Scholarship in Letters, 1961, 1994; Katherine Mansfield Fellowship, 1980; New Zealand Book Award for Fiction, 1985; Shortlisted, Wattie Book of the Year Award, 1985; Officer of the Order of the British Empire, 1987; Fulbright Visiting Writers Fellowship, 1987; Australia-New Zealand Writers Exchange Fellowship, 1989; Victoria University of Wellington Writers Fellowship, 1990; Auckland University Literary Fellowship, 1996; Shortlisted, Commonwealth Writers Prize, 1996. Membership: NZSA/PEN, New Zealand. Address: 41 Queen Street, Wellington, New Zealand.

DUCORNET Erica Lynn, (Rikki Ducornet), b. 19 April 1943, New York, New York, USA. Writer; Artist; Teacher. 1 son. Education: Bard College, 1964. Appointments: Novelist-in-Residence, University of Denver, 1988-; Visiting Professor, University of Trento, Italy, 1994. Publications: The Stain, 1984; Entering Fire, 1986; The Fountains of Neptune, 1989; Eben Demarst, 1990; The Jade Cabinet, 1993; The Butcher's Tales, 1994; Phosphor in Dreamland, 1995; The Word "Desire", 1997; The Fan-Maker's Inquisition, 1999. Contributions to: Periodicals. Honours: National Book Critics Circle Award Finalist, 1987, 1990, 1993; Critics Choice Award, 1995; Charles Flint Kellogg Award in Arts and Letters, 1998. Membership: PEN. Address: c/o Department of English, University of Denver, Denver, CO 80208, USA.

DUCULESCU Victor, b. 2 June 1931, Bucharest, Romania. University Professor. m. Georgeta Duculescu. Education: BL, University of Bucharest, 1952; Doctor, International Law, Institute of Law, Bucharest, 1970; Diploma, Faculty of Comparative Law, Strasbourg, 1970; Certificate, The Hague Academy of International Law, 1973; Certificate, Institute of Public Administration, Paris, 1995; Certificate, Research Centre of the Library of Congress, Washington DC, 1996. Appointments: From Assistant to Professor, 1951-; Scientific Researcher, 1967-78; Parliamentary Counsellor, Legal Adviser, Legislative Department, Romanian Senate, 1990-99. Publications: Author or Joint-Author of 16 books including: State Succession to International Treaties, 1972; Continuity and Discontinuity in International Law, 1982; The Secret Diplomacy, 1992; The Legal Protection of Human Rights, 1st edition, 1994, 2nd edition, 1997; The Constitutional Comparative Law (2 volumes), 1st edition,1996, 2nd edition, 1999; On the Eve of the Third Millennium, 1997; Treaty of Parliamentarian Law, 2 volumes, 2001; Institutions of Public Law and International Relations in their Dynamics, 2002; The European Justice, 2002; A Treatise of Constitutional Comparative Law, 2 volumes, 2003; The Law of European Integration: An Elementary Treatise, 2003. Honours: Scientific Merit, Romanian Academy, 1979; The Scientific Merit Coriolan Brediceanu, 1998; Prize, Mircea Manolescu, 1999; Distinguished Leadership Award, ABI, 2000; Man of the Year, 2001, 2003, ABI; American Medal of Honor, 2001; Diploma and Merit Medal, Union of Lawyers of Romania, 2001. Memberships: Association of Lawyers of Romania, 1957; Romanian Association for Law and International Relations, 1967; American Society for International Law, 1972; Centre for European Constitutional Law (Rigas Network, Athenes), 1999; European Association of Lawyers for Democracy and World Human Rights, 2001; Romanian Association of Lawyers, 2001; Association of European Recognised Experts (AEXEA), 2003. Address: Str Motoc 6 Bloc P55, Sec 5, Ap 88, Bucharest 051.774, Romania. E-mail: duculescu@pcnet.ro Website: http://www.duculescu.go.ro

DUDOLE Claude, b. 22 June 1945, France. Sculptor; Conceptor. 2 sons. Education: Academy Julian, Paris; Art School, Gr. Appointments: French Air Army, 1966; Sculptor; Conceptor. Publications: The Dialectic Of The Uncertitudes; The Strategy Of The Missing; Virtuals Installations. Memberships: Taylor Foundation; SAIF; Foundation Of Future Art; Greci Marino Academy. Address: Atalier 04 H22, 55 Av de Flandre, 75019 Paris, France. Website: www.ifrance.com/dudole

DUFFEY Joseph D, b. 1 July 1932, Huntington, West Virginia, USA. Educator. m. Anne Wexler, 2 sons. Education: Bachelor of Arts, Marshall University, Huntington, West Virginia, 1954; Bachelor of Divinity, Andover Newton Theological School, 1958; Master of Sacred Theology, Yale University, 1963; Doctor of Philosophy, Hartford Seminary Foundation, 1969. Appointments: Assistant Professor, Associate Professor, Acting Dean, Hartford Seminary Foundation, 1960-66; Rockefeller Doctoral Fellowship, 1966-70; Fellow, JFK School of Government, Harvard University, 1971-72; Adjunct Professor, Yale University, 1972-74; Assistant Secretary of State for Education and Cultural Affairs, United State Department of State, 1977; Chairman, National Endowment for the Humanities, 1977-82; Chancellor, University of Massachusetts at Amherst, 1982-91; President, American University, Washington DC, 1991-93; Director, United State Information Agency, 1993-99; Senior Vice President, Sylvan International Universities, 1999-2001. Publications: Numerous articles on higher education, social and economic issues in professional journals, conference proceedings and chapters in books include: Global Competitiveness: Getting the US Back on Track, 1990; Toward the Third Millennium: The Role of the United States in the New North America, 1995; Hollywood and American Culture, 1998; Europe and the United States: A Growing Cultural Gap? 1999; The American Century and Its Discontents, 1999. Honours: 14 Honorary Degrees from American colleges and universities;

Honorary Doctor of Letters, Ritsemaken University, Japan; Commander of the Order of the Crown, King of Belgium, 1980; Stern Lecturer, Syracuse University; Lind Lecturer, Northwestern University; Sparkman Lecturer, University of Alabama; Lesser Lecturer, University of Southern California. Address: 2801 New Mexico Avenue NW, Washington DC 20007, USA. E-mail: jduffey@earthlink.net

DUFFY Lawrence Kevin, b. 1 February 1948, Brooklyn, New York. Biochemist; Educator. m. Geraldine, 2 sons, 1 daughter. Education: BS, Chemistry, Fordham University, 1969; MS, Chemistry, University of Alaska, 1972; PhD, Biochemistry, 1977. Laboratory Instructor, University of Alaska, 1969-71; Research Assistant, University of Alaska Fairbanks, 1974-76; Post-doctoral Fellow, Boston University, 1977-78; Post-doctoral Fellow, Roche Institute of Molecular Biology, 1978-80; James W McLaughlin Fellow, University of Texas, 1980-81; Research Assistant Professor, University of Texas Medical Branch, 1982-83; Instructor, Middlesex Community College, 1983-84; Assistant Biochemist, McLean Hospital, Belmont, 1983-85; Assistant Professor, Biochemistry, Harvard Medical School, 1983-87; Science and Organic Chemistry Instructor, Roxbury Community College, 1984-87; Associate Biochemist, Brigham and Women's Hospital, 1985-87; Research Associate, Duke University Centre, 1986-87; Professor, Chemistry and Biochemistry, University of Alaska Fairbanks, 1987-; Co-ordinator, Program in Biochemistry and Molecular Biology, 1987-90, 1992-93; Adjunct Researcher, Brigham and Women's Hospital, 1987-90; Affiliate Professor, Centre for Alcohol Addiction Studies, 1995-98; Head, Department of Chemistry and Biochemistry, 1994-99; Co-ordinator, RSI Scientist in Residence Programme, 1996-2003; President, UAF Faculty Senate, 2000; Associate Dean for Graduate Studies and Outreach, 2001; Member, Metals Working Groups. Arctic Monitoring and Assessment Program. Publications: 228 scientific papers and abstracts. Honours: Fiest Outstanding Advisor Award; ACS Analytical Chemistry Award; Phi Lambda Upsilon; NIDCD Minority Research Mentoring Award, 1996; University of Alaska Alumni Award for Professional Achievement, 1999; others. Memberships: American Chemical Society; New York Academy of Sciences; Member of Editorial Board, The Science of the Total Environment, 1999; Usibelli Award for Research, 2002. Address: 2712 Tall Spruce, Fairbanks, Alaska 99708-0986, USA.

DUGAR Chand Ratan, b. 11 April 1953, Sardarshar, Rajasthan, India. President Director. m. Kamala 6 February 1975. Education: BCom (Hons), Calcutta University, 1969-72; ICA, Chartered Accountants Examination, 1970-74. Appointments: Audit Article Clerkship for Chartered Accountant from M/S Singhi Co, Calcutta, India, 1971-75; Senior Assistant, M/S Singhi & Co, 1975-76; Chief Accountant, Commercial Manager, VP Finance & Marketing, Joint President, M/S Spinning Mills, 1976-91; Advisor, Indophil Textile Mills Philippines & Indothai Synthetic Thailand, 1992; General Manager, 1992-97, President Director, Pt Elegant Textile Industry, 1996-. Honours: Indonesia Development, Citra Award, 1990-99; Best Executive Award conferred by ASEAN Programme Consultant Indonesian Consortium, Indonesian Environmental Management & Information Center; Sahwali Award as Environmentally Friendly Businessman, 1996; Grid Award, Grid Organisation Development Group, Malaysia, 1996. Membership: Fellow Institute of Chartered Accountants of India. Address: Pt Elegant Textile Industry, Menara Batavia Level 16, Kaveling 126 Jakarta 10220, Indonesia.

DUHOVNIK Jože, b. 23 March 1948, Količevo, Slovenia. Designer; Professor. m. Majda, 3 sons. Education: Degree, Mechanical Engineering, 1971, Master of Science, 1974, Doctor of Science, 1980, Faculty of Mechanical Engineering, University of Ljubljana; Postdoctoral Specialisation, University of Tokyo, Japan, 1982-83. Appointments include: Assistant, Faculty of Mechanical Engineering, University of Ljubljana, 1972-78; Director, Design Bureau, Mechanical Workshops STC (Slovenian Road Construction Company), 1978-80; Assistant Professor of Machine Design, 1980-91, Associate Professor of Machine Design, 1991-96; Professor, Department of Mechanical Engineering, 1996-, Chair of Department of Design and Development, Faculty of Mechanical Engineering, 2001-, University of Ljubljana; Chief Executive, Litostroj Corporation, 1991-96; Senior Director, Dr Duhovnik d.o.o., 1994; Visiting Professor, Sarajevo University – Zenica, 1998; Professor, EGPR Course in virtual classroom Delft-Ljubljana-Laussanne, 2001. Publications: More than 65 papers in refereed scientific journals and conference proceedings; Research works include most recently: Research of PDM systems for a tool-maker's shop, 1999; Analysis of tomographic images using image processing, 1999; Concurrent engineering in design process, 2000; Virtual enterprises by tool makers, 2000; Hydraulics flow through hydro turbine, 2001; Patents include: 3 patents for manure spreading machine, 2002. Honours: Invited Lecturer, University of Tokyo, Japan, 1982, Tsukuba, Department of Mechanical Engineering and Robotics, Japan, 1983, University of Illinois, USA, 1995, Faculty of Mechanical Engineering, Boston, USA, 1997, E-GPR Course, Delft, Ljubljana, Lausanne, 2001 (for 3 years). Memberships: VDI; Europgraphics; WDK; New York Academy of Sciences; Design Society; Member of Council of Science, Slovenian Government. Address: University of Ljubljana, Mechanical Engineering, Askerčeva 6, 1000 Ljubljana, Slovenia. E-mail: jozeduhovnik@lecad.uni.lj.si

DUKAKIS Olympia, b. 20 June 1931. Actress. m. Louis Zorich, 3 sons. Education: Boston Univ. Appointments: Teacher of Drama, New York University graduate programme for 15 years; Founding member, The Charles Playhouse, Boston, Whole Theatre, Montclair, New Jersey; Appeared in over 100 regional theatre productions; Off-Broadway shows including: Mann Ish Mann; The Marriage of Bette and Boo; Titus Andronicus; Peer Gynt; The Memorandum; The Curse of the Starving Class; Electra; Appearances in Broadway productions of Abraham Cochrane; The Aspern Papers; The Night of the Iguana; Who's Who in Hell; Mike Nichol's Social Security; Numerous TV appearances, TV include: Tales of the City (series); Films include: The Idolmaker; John Loves Mary; Death Wish; Rich Kids; Made for Each Other; Working Girl; Moonstruck; Dad; Look Who's Talking; Steel Magnolias; In the Spirit; Look Who's Talking Too; The Cemetery Club; Digger; Over the Hill; Look Who's Talking Now; Naked Gun 331/3; The Final Insult (Cameo); I Love Trouble; Jeffrey; Mighty Aphrodite; Mr Holland's Opus; Picture Perfect; My Beautiful Son, 2001; Ladies and The Champ, 2001; And Never Let Her Go, 2001; The Intended, 2002. Honours: Academy Award for Best Supporting Actress for Moonstruck, 1988; 2 Obie awards. Membership: Board, National Museum of Women in the Arts, Washington DC. Address: William Morris Agency, 151 S El Camino Drive, Beverly Hills, CA 90212, USA.

DUKE Chris, b. 4 October 1938. London. England. Professor; Scholar. m. Elizabeth Sommerlad, 3 sons, 2 daughters. Education: BA, 1st Class Honours, 1960, PGCE, 1961, MA, 1963, Jesus College, Cambridge, England; PhD, King's College, London, England, 1966. Appointments: Woolwich Polytechnic, England, 1961-66; University of Leeds, 1966-69; Director (Founding), Continuing Education, Australian National University, 1969-85; Professor, Continuing Education, 1985-96, Pro-Vice-Chancellor, 1991-95, University of Warwick, England; President, UWS Nepean, Sydney, Australia and Professor of Lifelong Learning, 1996-2000; Director and Professor of Continuing Education, University of Auckland, New Zealand, 2000-2002; Professor and

Director of Community and Regional Partnerships, RMIT University, Melbourne, Australia, 2002-. Publications: Many books, edited volumes, chapters and journal articles in the fields of higher education, adult, continuing and non-formal education and lifelong learning and in policy and management of higher education; Recent books include: The Learning University, 1992, reprinted 1996; The Adult University, 1999; Managing the Learning University, 2002. Honours: Hon. DLitt. Keimyung University, Republic of Korea; Fellow, Australian College of Education. Memberships: Leadership and membership of international and national professional bodies in the fields of adult and continuing education. Address: 26 Nepean Street, Emu Plains, NSW 2750, Australia. E-mail: chris.duke@rmit.edu.au

DUKES Rebecca W, (Becky) b. 21 November 1934, Durham, North Carolina, USA. Vocalist; Musician (Piano); Songwriter. m. Charles A Dukes Jr, 20 December 1955, 2 sons, 1 daughter. Education: BA, Duke University; Vocal student with Todd Duncan. Career: Numerous stage performances including The Kennedy Center, Duke University, The University of Maryland, Chateau de la Gesse, France, Capitol Hill Club and numerous hotels and special events; Most recent stage show as feature artist for Philharmonic sponsored concert; Performed with US Navy Band commemorating 200 years of balloon flight in America; 3 cable specials. Compositions: Over 100 with 60 individual compositions recorded. Recordings include: Alive, 1992; Rainbow, 1994; Borrow the Sun, 1995; Almost Country, 1999; Rhapsody of Moods, 2001. Publications: Poetry published in several editions, 1992-94. Honours: 7 ASCAP Awards for Pop Writing, 1994-2001; Numerous Awards, Mid-Atlantic Song Contest, 1984-92; American Women Composers' Song Contest Award; 2 Billboard Awards, For the Children of the World, 1996, Its Own Time, 2000. Memberships: ASCAP; NARAS; SAI; SAW; NSAI; FMMC. Address: 7111 Pony Trail, Hyattsville, MD 20782, USA.

DUMITRESCU-IONESCU Doina, b. 17 July 1949, Sibiu, Romania. Plastic Surgeon; Reconstructive Microsurgeon. m. Emil Dumitrescu. Education: MD, Institute of Medicine and Pharmacy "Iului Hateganu", Cluj, Romania, 1974; PhD, Institute of Medicine and Pharmacy "Carol Davila", Bucharest, 1987. Appointments: Internship in Surgery, 1973-76; Specialisation in Plastic Surgery, 1976-79; University Assistant Lecturer, 1980-93; Senior Lecturer, 1993-96; Head of the Plastic and Reconstructive Microsurgery Department and Clinic, 1984-, Assistant Professor, 1996-2000; Professor, 2000-; Initiated, organised and developed the speciality of reconstructive microsurgery in Romania in all 5 branches: experimental, peripheral nerves, brachial plexus replantation, free flap transfer, 1979-87; 2,800 microsurgery patients, 52 specialists. Publications: Hepatic regeneration in alcoholic intoxication demonstrated on a 80-85% extended subtotal hepatectomy, 1974; 200 peripheral nerves sutured by one microsurgeon, 1983; Microsurgery a guarantee of success in replanted limbs, 1984; Conclusions on peripheral nerves microsurgery and grafting, 1983-88; Microsurgery in post traumatic lesions of peripheral nerves, 1987; Neurotized free flap transfer, 1987; Microsurgery in brachial plexus post traumatic lesions, 1988, 1994, 1997. Honours: 6 patents: Reconstruction of the upper mobile eyelid; Anastomosis of median nerve artery; Contribution to peripheral nerves grafting; Reconstruction of a large cheek defect; Forceps for intraoperatory modelling of the breast; Microsurgery table. Memberships: Vice President, Romanian Academic Society of Plastic and Reconstructive Microsurgery. Address: Str Erou Iancu Nicolae 11-19, Sat Pipera, Com. Voluntari, Ilfov, Romania. E-mail: ddoina@ejj.ro

DUMONT André, b. 12 April 1929, Campbellton, New Brunswick, Canada. Writer. 2 sons, 2 daughters. Education: BA, 1961; BEd, 1964. Publications: Francais Renouvele I, 1964, II,

1966; Le Parti Acadien (co-author), 1972; Jeunesse Mouvementée, 1979; Quand Je Serai Grand, 1989; Pour un Francais Moderne, 1990; Avancez en Arrière, 1996. Contributions to: Over 100 articles on different topics, mostly political. Address: 830 Av Ernest-Gagnon, App 505, Québec, QC G1S 3R3, Canada.

DUNAWAY (Dorothy) Faye, b. 14 January 1941, Bascom, Florida, USA. Actress. m. (1) Peter Wolf, 1974, (2) Terry O'Neill, 1981, 1 son. Education: Florida University; Boston University. Appointments: Lincoln Center Repertory Company, New York, 3 years, appearances in: A Man For All Seasons; After the Fall; Tartuffe; Off-Broadway in Hogan's Goat, 1965; Old Times, Los Angeles; Blanche du Bois in A Streetcar Named Desire, 1973; The Curse of an Aching Heart, 1982; Films include: Hurry Sundown; The Happening; Bonnie and Clyde, 1967; The Thomas Crown Affair, 1968; A Place For Lovers, 1969; The Arrangement, 1969; Little Big Man, 1970, Doc, 1971; The Getaway, 1972; Oklahoma Crude, 1973; The Three Musketeers, 1973; Chinatown, 1974; Damned, 1976; Network, 1976; The Eyes of Laura Mars, 1978; The Camp, 1979; The First Deadly Sin, 1981; Mommie Dearest, 1981; The Wicked Lady, 1982; Supergirl, 1984; Barfly, 1987; Burning Secret, 1988; The Handmaid's Tale, 1989; On A Moonlit Night; Up to Date, 1989; Scorchers; Faithful; Three Weeks in Jerusalem; The Arrowtooth Waltz, 1991; Double Edge; Arizona Dream; The Temp; Dun Juan DeMarco, 1995; Drunks; Dunston Checks In; Albino Alligator; The Chamber; Fanny Hill, 1998; Love Lies Bleeding, 1999; The Yards, 1999; Joan of Arc, 1999; The Thomas Crown Affair, 1999; The Yards, 2000; Stanley's Gig, 2000; Yellow Bird, 2001; Changing Hearts, 2002; Rules of Attraction, 2002; Mid-Century, 2002; The Calling, 2002; TV include: After the Fall, 1974; The Disappearance of Aimee, 1976; Hogan's Goat; Mommie Dearest, 1981; Evita! - First Lady, 1981; 13 at Dinner, 1985; Beverly Hills Madame, 1986; The Country Girl; Casanova; The Raspberry Ripple; Cold Sassy Tree; Silhouette; Rebecca; Gia, 1998; Running Mates, 2000; The Biographer, 2002. Publications: Looking for Gatsby (Autobiography with Betsy Sharkey), 1995. Honours include: Academy Award for Best Actress for Network. Address: c/o Ed Limato, ICM, 8942 Wilshire Boulevard, Beverly Hills, CA 90211, USA.

DUNBAR Adrian, b. Enniskillen, Northern Ireland. Actor. m. Anna Nygh, 1 stepson, 1 daughter. Education: Guildhall School of Music and Drama, London, UK. Career: Films include: The Fear; A World Apart; Dealers; My Left Foot; Hear My Song, 1992; The Crying Game, 1993; Widow's Peak, 1994; Richard III, 1995; The Near Room, 1996; The General, 1998; Wild About Harry, 2000; Shooters, 2000; The Wedding Tackle, 2000; How Harry Became a Tree, 2001; Triggerman, 2002; Darkness, 2002; Stage appearances include: Ourselves Alone, Royal Court Theatre, 1985; King Lear, Royal Court; TV appearances include: Reasonable Force; Cracker.

DUNHAM William Wade, b. 8 December 1947, Pittsburgh, Pennsylvania, USA. Professor of Mathematics. m. Penelope Higgins, 26 September 1970, 2 sons. Education: BS, University of Pittsburgh, 1969; MS, 1970, PhD, 1974, Ohio State University. Appointment: Truman Koehler Professor of Mathematics, Muhlenberg College, 1992-. Publications: Journey Through Genius: The Great Theorems of Mathematics, 1990; The Mathematical Universe, 1994; Euler: The Master of Us All, 1999. Contributions to: American Mathematical Monthly; Mathematics Magazine; College Mathematics Journal; Mathematics Teacher. Honours: Phi Beta Kappa, 1968; M M Culver Award, University of Pittsburgh, 1969; Master Teacher Award, Hanover College, 1981; National Endowment for the Humanities Summer Seminars on Great Theorems, 1988-96; Humanities Achievement Award for Scholarship, Indiana Humanities Council, 1991; George Pólya

Award, Mathematical Association of America, 1993; Trevor Evans Award, Mathematical Association of America, 1997. Memberships: Mathematical Association of America; National Council of Teachers of Mathematics. Address: Department of Mathematics, Muhlenberg College, Allentown, PA 18104, USA.

DUNN Charleta J, b. 18 January 1927, Clarendon, Texas, USA. Clinical Psychologist. m. Roy E Dunn Jr, 2 sons, 1 daughter. Education: BS, 1951, MEd, 1954, West Texas University at Canyon; DEd, University of Houston, Houston, Texas, 1966; Postdoctorate in Clinical Psychology, University of Texas Medical Branch, Galveston, Texas, 1971. Appointments: Teacher, Amarillo Public Schools, 1951-62; Assistant Professor, University of Houston, 1966-70; Director Pupil Appraisal, Goose Creek, ISD, Baytown, Texas, 1971-73 Full Professor, Texas Women's University, 1974-90. Publications: 6 research-based monographs (Funded Research Grants); 3 books: World of Work, 1971; Sisk: Book of Ages, 1998; Burcham and Allied Families, 2000. Memberships: National Registrar of Mental Health; American Psycho-Therapy Association.

DUNN Douglas (Eaglesham), b. 23 October 1942, Inchinnan, Scotland. Professor of English; Writer; Poet. m. Lesley Jane Bathgate, 10 August 1985, 1 son, 1 daughter. Education: BA, University of Hull, 1969. Appointments: Writer-in-Residence, University of Hull, 1974-75, Duncan of Jordanstone College of Art, Dundee District Library, 1986-88; Writer-in-Residence, 1981-82, Honorary Visiting Professor, 1987-88, University of Dundee; Fellow in Creative Writing, 1989-91, Professor of English, 1991-, Head, School of English, 1994-99, University of St Andrews; Director, St Andrews Scottish Studies Institute, 1993-. Publications: Terry Street, 1969; The Happier Life, 1972; Love or Nothing, 1974; Barbarians, 1979; St Kilda's Parliament, 1981; Europea's Lover, 1982; Elegies, 1985; Secret Villages, 1985; Selected Poems, 1986; Northlight, 1988; New and Selected Poems, 1989; Poll Tax: The Fiscal Fake, 1990; Andromache, 1990; Scotland: An Anthology (editor), 1991; The Faber Book of 20th Century Scottish Poetry (editor), 1992; Dante's Drum-Kit, 1993; Boyfriends and Girlfriends, 1994; The Oxford Book of Scottish Short Stories (editor), 1995; Norman MacCaig: Selected Poems (editor), 1997; The Donkey's Ears, 2000; 20th Century Scottish Poems (editor), 2000; The Year's Afternoon, 2000. Contributions to: Newspapers, reviews, and journals. Honours: Somerset Maugham Award, 1972; Geoffrey Faber Memorial Prize, 1975; Hawthornden Prize, 1982; Whitbread Poetry Award, 1985; Whitbread Book of the Year Award, 1985; Honorary LLD, University of Dundee, 1987; Cholmondeley Award, 1989; Honorary DLitt, University of Hull, 1995. Membership: Scottish PEN. Address: c/o School of English, University of St Andrews, St Andrews, Fife KY16 9AL, Scotland.

DUNN Kelvyn Lawrence, b. 17 August 1963, Dandenong, Melbourne, Australia. Contract Entomologist; Secondary Teacher. 1 daughter. Education: Bachelor of Science, Australian National University, 1983-85; Graduate Diploma of Education, Victoria College, now Deakin University, 1987; CELTA, University of Cambridge/RSA, 2000. Appointments: Research Assistant, Agricultural Entomology, Department of Natural Resources and Environment, Agvic, Melbourne, Victoria, 1989-92, 1996-99; Research Assistant, Endangered Species, Griffith University, Faculty of Environmental Sciences, Brisbane, Queensland, 1992-94; Currently Secondary School Teacher of Biology, Mathematics, Science. Publications include: Review of Australian Butterflies: Distribution, Life History and Taxonomy, parts 1-4, with L E Dunn, 1991; The Conservation Status of Australian Butterflies, co-author, 1994; An illustrated guide to the parasitic wasps associated with citrus scale insects and mealybugs in Australia, co-author, 2000;

Over 120 articles and reports in entomological journals and bulletins. Honour: Golden Key International Honour Society, Monash University, 2004. Membership: Entomological Society of Victoria. Address: 15 Yackatoon Road, Upper Beaconsfield 3808, Victoria, Australia. E-mail: kelvyn_dunn@yahoo.com

DUNNETT Denzil Inglis, b. 21 October 1917, Sirsa, India. Retired Diplomat; Poet. m. Ruth Rawcliffe, 20 March 1946, 2 sons, 1 daughter. Education: Edinburgh Academy, 1922-35; MA Lit Hum, Corpus Christi College, Oxford, 1939. Appointments: Editorial Staff, The Scotsman, 1946-47; Diplomatic posts: Bulgaria, Paris, Buenos Aires, Congo, Madrid, Mexico, Senegal, 1946-77. Publication: Bird Poems, 1989; The Weight of Shadows, poems descriptive and religious, 2001. Contributions to: Scottish Review; Scottish Bookman; Satire Review; Anthology of the Anarhyme. Address: 11 Victoria Grove, London W8 5RW, England.

DUNPHY Joseph F, b. 15 November 1948, New York City, New York, USA. Financial Planner. m. Arlene, 2 sons, 1 daughter. Education: BA, English, Drew University, Madison, New Jersey, 1970-72; Certificate in Publishing and Graphic Design, 1875-76, Certificate in Financial Management, 1977-80, Certificate in Paralegal Studies (Litigation), 1982-83, New York University; Master of Business Administration, Corporate Finance, Fairleigh Dickinson University, Rutherford, New Jersey, 1985-90. Appointments: US Army, Radioteletype Operator, 304th Signal Battalion, Seoul and Wonju, Korea, 1968-70; News Editor, Discount Merchandiser Magazine, 1972-74; Editor, 1974-79, News Editor, 1979-88, Chemical Week Magazine, McGraw-Hill Publications Co; News Editor, Plastics Today, JSD Publishing Co, Falls Church, Virginia, 1988-89; Broker, First Interregional Equity Corporation, Short Hills, New Jersey, 1990-93; Financial Planner, CJM Planning, 1993-96, Full Service Financial Planner, Prime Capital Securities Inc, 1996-; Active, Reserve and National Guard Duty, US Army National Guard, 31 years; Volunteer Medic, New Jersey Naval Militia Joint Command, Fort Dix, New Jersey. Publications: Special report on illegal dumping of hazardous chemical wastes, nation-wide, 1978; Author: Financial Planning for Senior Executives: Executive MBA Seminar. Honours: Army Achievement Medal, 1983; State Active Duty Medal for response to Hurricane Floyd, 2000 and September 11, 2001; Certified in Homeland Security, American College of Forensic Examiners International Inc, 2003; Listed in Who's Who publications and biographical dictionaries. Memberships: Board of Governors, Fairleigh Dickinson University; Life Member: Veterans of Foreign Wars, American Legion; Signal Corps Regimental Association; Adult Leader, Boy Scouts, Troop 12, Montclair, New Jersey and Troop 28 Bloomfield, New Jersey. Address: 15 Haussler Terrace, Clifton, NJ 07013-4107, USA. E-mail: jfdunphy@verizon.net

DUNWOODY Richard, b. 18 January 1964, Belfast, North Ireland. Jockey. Appointments: Rode winner of: Grand National (West Tip), 1986, (Minnehoma), 1994; Cheltenham Gold Cup (Charter Party), 1988; Champion Hurdle (Kribensis), 1990; Champion National Hunt Jockey, 1992-93, 1993-94, 1994-95; Held record for most wins at retirement in 1999; Group Manager, Partner, Dunwoody Sports Marketing, 2002. Publications: Hell For Leather (with Marcus Armytage); Dual (with Sean Magee); Hands and Heels (with Marcus Armytage); Obsessed. Honours: National Hunt Jockey of the Year 1990, 1992-95; Champion of Champions, 2001. Address: c/o Dunwoody Sports Marketing, The Litten, Newtown Road, Newbury, Berkshire, RG14 7BB, England. E-mail: richard.d@du-mc.co.uk

DUPUY-ENGELHARDT Hiltraud, b. 21 December 1940, Mannheim, Germany. Professor. m. Jean-Marie Dupuy. Education: Staatsexamen, 1966, 1968; Dr phil, 1968; Doctorat d'Etat, PhD,

1987. Appointments: Studienrätin zA, 1970; Lectrice d'Allemand, 1971; Assistante Associée, 1971-75; Assistante Non-Agrégée, 1976-81; Maître Assistante, 2nd class, 1981, 1st class, 1987; Maître de Conférences, 1988; University Professor, 2nd class, 1989, 1st class, 2000; Professor Emeritus, 2001. Publications: Numerous articles in national and international journals. Memberships: AGES; ANCA; ASL; GAL; IDS. Address: 17 La Hingrie, F-68660 Rombach-le-Franc, France. E-mail: hiltraud@libertysurf.fr

DURAN Marco A, b. 15 February 1963, Mexico City, Mexico. Medical Doctor; Pathologist. m. Macias Berenice, 1 son, 1 daughter. Education: MD, National Autonomous University of Mexico; Speciality of Pathology, certified by the Mexican Board of Pathology. Appointments: Pathologist and Researcher, General Hospital of Mexico; Professor of Pathology, National Autonomous University of Mexico. Publications: About 40 publications. Honour: Diploma and Medal, National Autonomous University of Mexico. Membership: Mexican Association of Pathologists. Address: 2a Cerrada de Puente Titla No 10, Col Ricardo Flores, Magon C P 09820 Mexico City, Mexico. E-mail: marcoaduranpa@starmedia.com

DURANY Nuria, b. 3 August 1961, Barcelona, Spain. Professor. Education: BSc, 1985, MEd, 1989, PhD, Biochemistry, 1996. Appointments: Professor, Faculty of Medicine Board, 1994-96, Department of Biochemistry Council, 1995-96, University of Barcelona; Secretary, Health Science Faculty, International University of Catalonia, 2000-; Member, International Advisory Board, European Society for Clinical Neuropharmacology, 2000-. Publications: 30 articles in professional journals. Honours: Alexander von Humboldt Scholarship. Memberships: Australian Biochemistry Society; Federation of European Biochemical Societies; Spanish Bioethics Society; Spanish Alexander von Humboldt Club; Spanish Association of Biochemistry and Molecular Biology; Catalonian Association of Biology. Address: Health Science Faculty, International University of Catalonia, Gomera s/n, 08190 Sant Cugat del Valles, Barcelona, Spain. E-mail: ndurany@csc.unica.edu

DURLIK Ireneusz G, b. 20 January 1931, Skarzysko, Kamienna, Poland. Full Professor of Engineering Management. m. 2 sons. Education: MSc, Industrial Engineering, Technical University of Warsaw, 1962; PhD, Manufacturing Engineering, Technical University of Cracow, 1966; DSc, Design Production Systems, Technical University of Warsaw, 1974; Professor, 1989; Full Professor, 1993. Appointments: Industry Engineer, Military Industry, 1957-62; Director of Consulting Office and Project Manager, Electronic Industry Union, 1962-78; Director of Research and Development, Union of Telecommunications Industry, 1978-80; Associate Professor and Director of Institute, Technical University of Gdansk, 1980-88; Professor and Head of Department of Production and Operational Management, 1988-95; Vice-Rector, Technical University of Czestochowa, 1995-99; Head of Department of Strategic Studies and Technology Management, 1996-2001; Director of European Centre for Postgraduate Studies, 1999-. Publications include most recently: Engineering Management – Strategies and Designing Production Systems, 2 volumes, 1996, 1998; Restructurization of Business Processes. Theory and Practice, 1998; Reengineering and Information Technology in Restructurization Business Processes, 2002; 10 other books (Technical and Management); 262 articles and scientific papers; Promoter of 12 PhD Students. Honours: Awards of Ministry of Education, 1967, 1974, 1988, 1998; Polish Organiser of the Year, Association of Polish Engineers, 1990; Rector Awards, Technical University of Gdansk, 1982, 1985, 1987, 1990, 1991, 1992, 1994, 1995; Polish Republic President,

Honorary Order 3rd Class-Cavalier Cross, 1989; Polish President Honorary Order 2nd Class-Officer Cross, 2001. Memberships: Polish Academy of Science, Committee of Organisation and Management; American Association for the Advancement of Science; European Academy for Industrial Management; Honorary Title of First Side Director of Loyola Marymount University (Los Angeles) in Poland; Polish Association of Engineers; Science Association of Organisation and Leadership, Poland. Address: European Centre for Postgraduate Studies, 98/34 KEN Str., 02-722 Warsaw, Poland. E-mail: durlik@europcent.edu.pl

DUROV Vladimir Alekseevich, b. 29 January 1950, Arkhangelsk, Russia. Chemist. m. Ol'ga Nikolaevna Durova, 1 daughter. Education: MSc, 1973, PhD, 1978, DSc, 1989, Lomonosov Moscow State University; Professor of Physical Chemistry, Academic Rank, Ministry of Higher Education of Russia, 1993. Appointments: Junior Researcher, 1977-82, Senior Researcher, 1982-90, Leading Researcher, 1991-93, Research Professor, 1994-1995, Professor of Chemistry (Full Professor), 1995-, Department of Physical Chemistry, Lomonosov Moscow State University. Publications: Over 160 articles in refereed journals; 5 monographs; 10 textbooks. Honours: Grantee, Russian Foundation of Basic Research; Grantee, Russian University Foundation; Distinguished Professor of Chemistry Award, International Soros Science Education Program. Memberships include: Bureau of Scientific Council on Chemical Thermodynamics and Thermochemistry, 1987-; Bureau of the Scientific and Methodical Council on Chemistry, 1992-; Joint Task Group of IUPAC and CODATA on Standardisation of Physico-Chemical Properties Electronic Datafile, 1998-; International Advisory Board of the International Conferences on Chemical Thermodynamics, 1999-; International Advisory Committee of the European Molecular Liquids Group, 1999-; Editorial Board of the Journal of Molecular Liquids, 1999-; Academician, International Academy of Creative Endeavours, 2000-; Active member, Academician, International Academy of Sciences. Address: Department of Physical Chemistry, Faculty of Chemistry, Lomonosov Moscow State University, W-234, Moscow 119899, Russia. E-mail: durov@phys.chem.msu.ru

DURR Afifi, b. 27 September 1935. Translator. 3 sons. Education: BA, Mass Communications. Appointments: Middle East Cultural Awareness Courses and Arabic Language Courses; Video Production/Translation, Arabic and Audio; Arabic Translator and Interpreter. Honours: MBA. Memberships: American Translator Association; Ethnic Heritage Council, Seattle Branch; Chair, Arab Center of Washington, Seattle; Children Around the World; Red Cross International. Address: 1535 NE 148th St, Shoreline, WA 98155-7217, USA. E-mail: afifi@nwlimb.com

DURST Robert J II, b. 23 January 1943, Pittsburgh, Pennsylvania, USA. Attorney. m. Sandra C Durst, 2 sons. Education: BA, Gettysburg College, 1964, JD, Villanova University, School of Law, 1967; Attorney, Stark & Stark, Princeton, New Jersey; Certified Civil Trial Attorney, 1988-; Certified Matrimonial Mediator, 1996-; Certified Matrimonial Law Attorney, 1998-. Appointments include: Admitted to the Bar: Pennsylvania, 1967, New Jersey, 1969, United States District Court, District of New Jersey, 1968; United States Supreme Court, 1973; Executive Committee, New Jersey State Bar Association, Family Law Section, 1980-87, 1995-96, 1998-; Chairman, National Marital Torts Association, American Bar Association, Family Law Section, 1996-98; Co-chair, National Marriage and Cohabitation Committee, American Bar Association, 1992-98; Editorial Boards: National Journal of the American Academy of Matrimonial Lawyers, 1999-2000; The Matrimonial Strategist, 2000-03; New Jersey State Bar Association, Family Law Section, Family Lawyer,

2002; Co-Director, New Jersey Family Law Summer Institute, 1996-. Publications include: Emerging Tort Theories Affecting Married and Domestic Partners, 1994; Life Insurance as a Security Vehicle in Dissolution Cases (co-author), 1994; Maximizing the Impact of a Vocational Expert, 1999; Numerous lectures and seminars. Honours: National Association of Displaced Homemaker's Annual Award for Service to Divorced Women, 1989; Top Divorce Lawyers in New Jersey, NJ Monthly Magazine, 1997-98, 1999-2000, 2002-03; New Jersey State Legislature Award for Service to Women and Families, New Jersey Displaced Homemakers, 1998; Martindale-Hubbel, Pre-Eminent Attorneys; Listed in Who's Who publications and biographical dictionaries. Memberships: American Bar Association; New Jersey Bar Association; New Jersey State Bar Foundation; Hunterdon County Bar Association; Mercer County Bar Association; Pennsylvania Bar Association; Bucks County, Pennsylvania Bar Association, 2002; Fellow National Academy of American Lawyers; Diplomate, American College of Family Trial Lawyers. Address: Stark & Stark, 993 Lenox Drive, PO Box 5315, Princeton, NJ 08543-5315, USA. E-mail: rdurst@stark-stark.com

DUŠEK Pavel, b.1 June 1961, Pardubice, Czech Republic. President of the Czech Council of Humanitarian Organisations. m. Marta, 1 daughter. Education: Graduate Engineer, Faculty of Management, College of Economics, 1984. Appointments: Member of Czech Parliament, 1990-92; Vice President, Government Board for People with Disabilities, 1991-2002; President, Board of Representatives from Organisations of Disabled People, 1991-2002; President, Czech Council of Humanitarian Organisations, 1999-; Member, Government Council for Human Rights, 1999-2002. Publication: Disability Movement in Czech Republic. Honour: American Medal of Honor. Membership: Journalist Syndicate. Address: Milánská 471, 10900 Prague 10, Czech Republic. E-mail: pavel.dusek@seznam.cz

DUTHOY Robert Michel, b. 11 January 1942, Ieper, Belgium. Professor. m. Mia Maes. Education: Candidate in History, 1963, Licentiate in Classical Philology, 1964, Doctor of Philosophy and Letters, 1970, University of Ghent. Appointments: Assistant, 1964-70, Senior Assistant, 1971-76, Lecturer, 1977-91, Professor of Ancient History, 1991-, University of Ghent. Publications: The Taurobolium, 1970; Les Augustales, 1976; Contributions on ancient Roman society in professional scientific journals of Ancient History. Memberships: Association Internationale d'Epigraphie grecque et latine. Address: Zwaanaardestraat 1, B-9112 Sint-Niklaas, Belgium.

DUVAL Cynthia, b. 6 October 1932, Port Talbot, South Wales (American citizen since 1996). Fine Arts Appraiser; Museum Curator; Art History Professor. m. Marcel, 1 son. Education: Matriculation, University of London; Chelsea College of Art and Design affiliated, London University. Appointments: Specialist Appraiser, Sotheby's, New York, 1973-77; Administrator, Curator of Decorative and Fine Arts Programs, John and Mable Ringling Museum of Art, Sarasota, 1978-86; Administrator, Manager, Curator, John and Mable Ringling House, Sarasota, 1979-86; Assistant Director, Curator of Decorative Arts, Museum of Fine Arts, St Petersburg, 1988-93; Consultant to Jon Thompson, Director of Wonders, the Cultural Series, Memphis, 1993-98; Historic interior, Decorative Arts Curatorial Consultant, Vanderbilt Mansion, North Carolina, 1994-; Adjunct Art History Professor, St Petersburg College, 1994-; Adjunct Decorative Arts Curator, Museum of Arts and Sciences, Daytona Beach, 1994-; Associate Director, Art Reach International, 2000-; Coordinator, Museum Studies Programme, St Petersburg College, 2003-; Curator, Florida International Museum, 2003-. Honours: Designer's Image Award, 1984; International Representative for Florida's Visual Arts, 1985; Advisor for the historic interior of the Governor's Mansion, 1984-

Dictionary of International Biography

86; Listed in national and international biographical dictionaries. Memberships: American Association of Museums; National Trust; Florida Art Museums Association; Appraiser's Association of America. Address: 1109 Pinellas Bayway (303), Tierra Verde, FL 33715, USA. E-mail: marceld@ij.net

DUVALL Robert, b. 5 January 1931, San Diego, USA. Actor. m. (1) Gail Youngs, divorced, (2) Sharon Brophy, 1991. Education: Principia College, Illinois, USA; Student, Neighbourhood Playhouse, New York. Appointments: Actor, stage appearances include: A View From the Bridge (Obie Award), 1965; Wait Until Dark, 1966; American Buffalo; Films include: To Kill a Mockingbird, 1963; Captain Newman, MD, 1964; The Chase, 1965; Countdown, 1968; The Detective, 1968; Bullitt, 1968; True Grit, 1969; The Rain People, 1969; M*A*S*H, 1970; The Revolutionary, 1970; The Godfather, 1972; Tomorrow, 1972; The Great Northfield; Minnesota Raid, 1972; Joe Kidd, 1972; Lady Ice, 1973; The Outfit, 1974; The Conversation, 1974; The Godfather Part II, 1974; Breakout, 1975; The Killer Elite, 1975; Network, 1976; The Eagle Has Landed, 1977; The Greatest, 1977; The Betsy, 1978; Apocalypse Now, 1979; The Great Santini, 1980; True Confessions, 1981; Angelo My Love (actor and director), 1983; Tender Mercies, 1983; The Stone Boy, 1984; The Natural, 1984; The Lightship, 1986; Let's Get Harry, 1986; Belizaire the Cajun, 1986; Colors, 1988; Convicts; Roots in Parched Ground; The Handmaid's Tale, 1990; A Show of Force, 1990; Days of Thunder, 1990; Rambling Rose, 1991; Newsies, 1992; The New Boys, 1992; Stalin, 1992; The Plague; Geronimo; Falling Down, 1993; The Paper, 1994; Wrestling Ernest Hemingway, 1994; Something to Talk About: The Stars Fell On Henrietta; The Scarlet Letter; A Family Thing (also co-producer); Phenomenon, 1996; The Apostle, 1997; Gingerbread Man, 1997; A Civil Action, 1999; Gone In Sixty Seconds, 2000; A Shot at Glory (also producer), 2000; The 6th Day, 2000; Apocalypse Now: Redux, 2001; John Q, 2002; Assassination Tango (also producer), 2002 ;Director, We're Not the Jet Set; Assassination Tango, 2002; Several TV films and appearances. Address: c/o William Morris Agency, 151 S El Camino Drive, Beverly Hills, CA 90212, USA.

DUVALL Shelley, b. 7 July 1949, Houston, Texas, USA. Actress; Producer. Appointments: Founder, TV production company, Think Entertainment; Actress in TV films: Brewster McCloud; Mccabe and Mrs Miller; Thieves Like Us; Nashville; Buffalo Bill and the Indians; Three Women (Cannes Festival Prize, 1977); Annie Hall; The Shining; Popeye; Time Bandits; Roxanne; Suburban Commando; The Underneath; Portrait of a Lady; Changing Habits; Alone, 1997; Home Fries, 1998; Space Cadet; Big Monster on Campus; The 4th Floor; Dreams in the Attic; Manna From Heaven, 2001; Television includes: Bernice Bobs Her Hair; Lily; Twilight Zone; Mother Goose Rock'n'Rhyme; Faerie Tale Theatre (Rumpelstiltskin, Rapunzel); Tall Tales and Legends (Darlin' Clementine); Executive producer: Faerie Tale Theatre; Tall Tales and Legends; Nightmare Classics; Dinner at Eight (film); Mother Goose Rock'n'Rhyme; Stories from Growing Up; Backfield in Motion (film); Bedtime Stories; Mrs Piggle-Wiggle.

DUYKER Edward Adrian Joseph, b. 21 March 1955, Melbourne, Australia. Historian. m. Susan Wade, 2 sons. Education: BA, Honours, La Trobe University, Australia, 1977; PhD, University of Melbourne, Australia, 1981. Appointments: Research Officer, Department of Defence, Canberra, Australia, 1981-83; Teaching Fellow, Griffith University, Brisbane, Australia, 1983; Independent Historian and Author, 1984-; Honorary Consul, Republic of Mauritius, 1996-2002; Honorary Associate, Department of French Studies, University of Sydney, Australia, 2002-. Publications: Numerous books and monographs include: The Dutch in Australia, 1987; An Officer of the Blue: Marc-Joseph

Marion Dufresne 1724-1772, South Sea Explorer, 1994; Nature's Argonaut: Daniel Solander 1733-1782, Naturalist and Voyager with Cook and Banks, 1998 (reprinted 1999); Citizen Labillardière: A Naturalist's Life in Revolution and Exploration (1755-1834), 2003. Honours: Chevalier de l'Ordre des Palmes Académiques, France, 2000; Centenary Medal, Australia, 2003; Order of Australia Medal, 2004. Memberships: Fellow, Linnean Society of London; Fellow, Royal Geographical Society; Fellow, Royal Historical Society. Address: PO Box 20, Sylvania-Southgate, NSW 2224, Australia.

DWYER John M, b. 8 June 1937, Ann Arbor, Michigan, USA. Associate Professor. 2 daughters. Education: BA, MS, University of Michigan, Ann Arbor; PhD, Texas A&M University, 1972. Appointments: Assistant Professor, Statistics, University of Wyoming, 1962-66; University of Detroit Mercy, 1969-; Visiting Associate Professor, Northern Michigan University, 1983-84. Publications: Several articles in professional journals. Memberships: AAAS; Association of Computing Machinery; Mathematical Association of America; American Association of University Professors; Computer Professionals for Social Responsibility, Member, Board of Directors and Treasurer, (CPSR); Union of Concerned Scientists; MichEA/NEA. Address: University of Detroit Mercy, Department of Mathematics and Computer Science, PO Box 19900, Detroit, MI 48219-0900, USA.

DYAULI David Philipo, b. 11 October 1930, Iambi, Singida, Tanzania. Medical Doctor; Paediatrician. m. Eliwaza Dyauli, 4 sons, 3 daughters. Education: Bumbuli Medical Assistants Training School, 1950-53; BSc, Gustavus College, USA, 1964; MB, CHB, 1969 (UEA); DCH, Glasgow, Scotland, 1975. Appointments: Registrar, Kiomboi District Hospital, Tanzania; Medical Officer in Charge, Iambi Leprosy Hospital, Iambi Integrated Lutheran General Hospital, Tanzania; Paediatrician and Medical Secretary, Evangelical Lutheran Church, Central Diocese, Tanzania; Chairman, ELCT Medical Board, Tanzania. Publication: Participatory Action Research on AIDS and the Community as a Source of Care and Healing, 1993. Honour: Medical Association of Tanzania's Ngirwamungu Memorial Lecture, 1988. Memberships: Medical Association of Tanzania; Paediatric Association of Tanzania; Christian Medical Board of Tanzania; Tanzania Christian Medical Association. Address: Huduma Clinic, PO Box 752, Singida, Tanzania.

DYBKAER René, b. 7 February 1926, Copenhagen. Physician. m. Nanna Gjoel. Education: MD, 1951, University of Copenhagen; Specialist Clinical Chemistry, 1957. Appointments: Various medical residencies, 1951-55; Reader, Copenhagen University Institute of Medical Microbiology, 1956-70; Head, Department of Medical Microbiology, Royal Dental School of Copenhagen, 1959-70; Head, Department of Clinical Chemistry at De Gamles By, 1970-77, at Frederiksberg Hospital, 1977-96, at Department of Standardization in Laboratory Medicine, H:S Kommunehositalet, 1997-99, H:S Frederiksberg Hospital, 2000. Publications: Books: Quantities and units in clinical chemistry, 1967; Good practice in decentralised analytical clinical measurement, 1992; Continuous quality improvement in clinical laboratories, 1994; Compendium on terminology and nomenclature in clinical laboratory sciences, 1995; numerous articles to professional journals. Honours: Commemorative Lecture Enrique Concustell Bas, 1988; Henry Wishinsky Distinguished International Services Award, 1993; Honorary member of various national clinical laboratory societies; Professor James D Westgard Quality Award, 1998. Memberships: Vice President, 1973-78, President, 1979-84, Past President, 1985-90, International Federation of Clinical Chemistry; President, European Confederation of Laboratory Medicine, 1994-97; Chairman, Danish Society of

Clinical Chemistry, 1991-93. Address: H:S Frederiksberg Hospital, Department of Standardization in Laboratory Medicine, Nordre Fasanvej 57, DK-2000 Frederiksberg, Denmark.

DYER Charles, b. 17 July 1928, Shrewsbury, England. Playwright. m. Fiona, 20 February 1960, 3 sons. Publications: Turtle in the Soup, 1948; Who On Earth, 1950; Poison in Jest, 1952; Jovial Parasite, 1955; Red Cabbage and Kings, 1958; Rattle of a Simple Man, novel, play, film, 1962; Staircase, novel, play, film, 1966; Mother Adam, 1970; Lovers Dancing, 1982; various screenplays. Address: Old Wob, Gerrards Cross, Buckinghamshire SL9 8SF, England.

DYKE Greg, b. 20 May 1947. Television Executive. 1 son, 1 stepson, 1 daughter, 1 stepdaughter. Education: York University; Harvard Business School. Appointments: Management Trainee, Marks & Spencer; Reporter, local paper; Campaigner for Community Relations Council, Wandsworth; Researcher, The London Programme; London Weekend TV (LWT); Later, Founding Producer, The Six O'Clock Show; Joined TV-AM, 1983; Director of Programmes, LWT, 1987-91; Group Chief Executive, LWT (Holdings) PLC, 1991-94; Chairman, GMTV, 1993-94; Chairman, Chief Executive Officer, Pearson TV, 1995-99; Chairman, Channel 5 Broadcasting, 1997-99; Former TVB Hong Kong; Director, BSkyB, 1995; Phoenix Pictures Inc, New York, Pearson PLC, 1996-99 and others; Director (non-executive) Manchester Utd, 1997-99; Director General, BBC, 2000-04. Memberships: Trustee Science Museum, 1996-; English National Stadium Trust, 1997-99.

DYLAN Bob (Robert Allen Zimmerman), b. 24 May 1941, Duluth, Minnesota, USA. Singer; Musician (guitar, piano, harmonica, autoharp); Poet; Composer. Musical Education: Self-taught. Career: Solo folk/rock artist, also performed with The Band; The Travelling Wilburys; Grateful Dead; Songs recorded by estimated 3000 artists, including U2, Bruce Springsteen, Rod Stewart, Jimi Hendrix, Eric Clapton, Neil Young; Numerous tours: USA, Europe, Australia, 1961-; Film appearances include: Pat Garrett and Billy The Kid; Concert For Bangladesh; Hearts Of Fire. Compositions include: Blowin' In The Wind; Like A Rolling Stone; Mr Tambourine Man; Lay Lady Lay; Forever Young; Tangled Up In Blue; Gotta Serve Somebody; Don't Think Twice; It's Alright; A Hard Rain's Gonna Fall; The Times They Are A-Changin'; Just Like A Woman; I'll Be Your Baby Tonight; I Shall Be Released; Simple Twist Of Fate; Paths Of Victory; Dignity. Recordings: Over 40 albums include: The Freewheelin' Bob Dylan, 1964; Bringing It All Back Home, 1965; Highway 61 Revisited, 1965; Blonde On Blonde, 1966; John Wesley Harding, 1968; Nashville Skyline, 1969; Self Portrait, 1970; New Morning, 1970; Before The Flood, 1974; Hard Rain, 1976; Desire, 1976; Street Legal, 1978; Slow Train Coming, 1979; Infidels, 1983; Empire Burlesque, 1985; Knocked Out Loaded, 1986; Down In The Groove, 1988; Biograph (5 record set), 1988; Oh Mercy, 1989; Under The Red Sky, 1990; MTV Unplugged, 1995; Time Out of Mind, 1998; Love and Theft, 2001; with The Band: Planet Waves, 1974; Blood On The Tracks, 1975; with Travelling Wilburys: Travelling Wilburys, 1988; Vol 3, 1990; with Grateful Dead, Dylan And The Dead, 1989; Singles include: One Too Many Mornings, 1965; Mr Tambourine Man, 1966; Love Sick, 1997. Publications: Tarantula, 1966; Writings And Drawings, 1973; The Songs Of Bob Dylan 1966-75, 1976; Lyrics 1962-85, 1986; Drawn Blank, 1994; Highway 61 Revisited (interactive CD-ROM). Honours include: Honorary D Mus, Princeton University, 1970; Inducted, Rock and Roll Hall of Fame, 1988; Grammy, 1990. Address: c/o Columbia Records, 550 Madison Avenue, New York, NY 10022, USA.

DYSON Freeman J(ohn), b. 15 December 1923, Crowthorne, England (US citizen, 1957). Professor of Physics Emeritus. m. (1) Verena Haefeli-Huber, 11 August 1950, divorced 1958, 1 son, 1 daughter, (2) Imme Jung, 21 November 1958, 4 daughters. Education: BA, Cambridge University, 1945; Graduate Studies, Cornell University, 1947-48, Institute for Advanced Study, Princeton, New Jersey, 1948-49. Appointments: Research Fellow, Trinity College, Cambridge, 1946-49; Warren Research Fellow, University of Birmingham, England, 1949-51; Professor of Physics, Cornell University, 1951-53; Professor of Physics, 1953-94, Professor Emeritus, 1994-, Institute for Advanced Study. Publications: Symmetry Groups in Nuclear and Particle Physics, 1966; Neutron Stars and Pulsars, 1971; Disturbing the Universe, 1979; Values at War, 1983; Weapons and Hope, 1984; Origins of Life, 1986; Infinite in All Directions, 1988; From Eros to Gaia, 1992; Imagined Worlds, 1997; The Sun The Genome and the Internet, 1999. Honours: Heineman Prize, American Institute of Physics, 1966; Lorentz Medal, Royal Netherlands Academy of Sciences, 1966; Hughes Medal, Royal Society, 1968; Max Planck Medal, German Physical Society, 1969; J Robert Oppenheimer Memorial Prize, Center for Theoretical Studies, 1970; Harvey Prize, Israel Institute of Technology, 1977; Wolf Prize, Wolf Foundation, 1981; National Book Critics Circle Award, 1984; Templeton Prize for Progress in Religion, 2000. Honorary doctorates. Memberships: American Physical Society; National Academy of Sciences; Royal Society, fellow. Address: 105 Battle Road Circle, Princeton, NJ 08540, USA.

DYSON James, b. 2 May 1947, Designer. m. Deidre Hindmarsh, 1967, 2 sons, 1 daughter. Education: Royal College of Art. Appointments: Director, Rotork Marine, 1970-74; Managing Director, Kirk Dyson, 1974-79; Developed and designed, Dyson Dual Cyclone vacuum cleaner, 1979-93; Founder, Chairman Prototypes Ltd, 1979-; Dyson Appliances Ltd, 1992-; Hon DLitt (Staffordshire), 1996; Hon DSc, Oxford Brookes, 1997, Huddeersfield, 1997, Bradford, 1998. Publications include: Doing a Dyson, 1996; Against the Odds (autobiography), 1997. Honours: Numerous design awards and trophies. Address: Kingsmead Hill, Little Somerford, Wiltshire, SN15 5JN, England.

DYSON Robert Harris Jr, b. 2 August 1927, York, Pennsylvania, USA. Archaeologist; Professor; Administrator. Education: AB, magna cum laude, Harvard College, 1950; PhD, Harvard University, 1966; AM (Hon), University of Pennsylvania, 1971. Appointments: Curator, Near Eastern Archaeology, 1967-95; Professor of Anthropology, 1967-95; Dean, Faculty of Arts and Sciences, University of Pennsylvania, 1979-1982; Director, 1982-94, Director Emeritus, 1995-, University of Pennsylvania Museum; Professor Emeritus, 1995-. Publications: Several articles in professional journals; Tappeh Hesar, Reports of the Restudy Project, Firenze, 1976, 1989. Honours: Chevalier de l'Ordre des Artes et des Lettres, France; Order Houmouyan 4th Rank, Iran. Memberships include: American Philosophical Society; British School of Archaeology in Iraq; British Institute of Persian Studies. Address: University of Pennsylvania Museum, Philadelphia, PA 19104, USA.

DZEMJANOVA Emilia, b. 20 May 1959, Snina, Slovakia. Professor; Concert Organist. Education: Conservatory Kosice, Slovakia; Academy of Music, Bratislava, Slovakia; ArtD (Doctor of the Arts), 1999, Masterclass Flor Peeters at Mechelen, Belgium. Career: Recitals, Concerts with Orchestra, Recordings for Radio and TV; Appearances in major European Cities, including Music Festivals, Organ Festivals; Professor at the Conservatory in Kosice, 1982-. Recordings: Contemporary Czechoslovak Composers, including Eben, Suchon and Burlas. Publications: Organ Works of Eugen Suchon (revised edition) HF Bratislava, 1989; Organ School,

1991; Collection of organ compositions, 1997; Method of The Organ Playing, 2002. Honours: Prizes in National Competitions, 1983. Memberships: Neue Bachgesellschaft. Current Management: Slovkoncert, Bratislava, Slovakia. Address: Huskova 31, 040 11 Kosice, Slovakia.

Dictionary of International Biography

E

EARLAND-BENNETT Peter Michael, b. 18 November 1945, Hastings, England. Free-Lance Natural Historian; Consultant Lichenologist. m. Doreen Elsie Dixon, divorced, 2 sons. Education: BSc (Hons), Geology, Leicester University, 1964-68; Certificate of Museum Studies; Diploma, Museums Association, 1971. Appointments: Scientific Assistant, Geological Survey Museum, London, 1964-64; Natural Sciences Assistant, Peterborough Museums Service, 1968-69; Keeper of Natural History, Calderdale Museum Service, 1969-79; Antiques Dealer, 1981-; Consultant Lichenologist, 1981-; Freelance Natural Historian, 1981-. Publications: Assisting author: Snakes an Illustrated Guide, 1991; Contributing author: The Atlas of Endangered Species, 1991; Many scientific articles on lichens especially in Huntingdonshire and Isle of Man; Finder of new lichenicolous fungi and author on them: Observations on the genus Psammina including the description of two new algicolous and lichenicolous species (co-author), 1999; Lichenopeltella coppinsii, a new species on Verrucaria muralis from the British Isles (co-author), 1999. Memberships: British Lichen Society, council member 1972-74, 1995-97; British Button Society; British Numismatic Society; Fellow, Royal Numismatic Society. Address: 160 High Street, Wickham Market, Woodbridge, Suffolk, IP13 0QY, England.

EASTHAM Anthony Richard, b. 21 April 1944, Lingfield, England. Engineer; Professor; University Administrator. m. Judith Anna, 1 son, 1 daughter. Education: BSc, Physics, London, England, 1965; PhD, Applied Physics, Surrey, England, 1969. Appointments: Director of Research Sciences and International Programmes, Professor of Electrical and Computer Engineering, Queen's University, Ontario, Canada, 1985-95; Visiting Professor, University of Tokyo, Japan, 1996; Associate Vice-President for R&D, Professor of Civil Engineering and Electrical Engineering, Hong Kong University of Science and Technology, Hong Kong, 1998-; President, Chief Executive Officer, Hkust RandD Corporation Ltd, 2000-. Publications: 5 chapters and monographs; 65 journal papers; 81 conference proceeding papers; 35 research reports. Honours: Joint Holder, Ross Medal, Engineering Institute of Canada, 1978; Award for Excellence in Teaching, Queen's University, 1980; Queen's University Prize for Excellence in Research, 1982; Commemorative Medal, 125th Anniversary of Confederation of Canada, 1992; Outstanding Service Award, High Speed Rail Association, 1993. Memberships: Professional Engineer, Ontario, Canada; IEEE; Chartered Institute of Logistics and Transport; High Speed Rail Association; Canadian Chamber of Commerce in Hong Kong. Address: 8 Uk Tau Village, Pak Tam Road, Sai Kung Country Park, Sai Kung, NT, Hong Kong. E-mail: rdtony@ust.hk

EASTWOOD Clint, b. 31 May 1930, San Francisco, USA. Actor; Film Director. m. (1) Maggie Johnson, 1 son, 1 daughter; 1 daughter by Frances Fisher; m. (2) Dina Ruiz, 1996, 1 daughter. Education: Los Angeles City College. Appointments: Lumberjack, Oregon; Army service; Actor, TV series, Rawhide, 1959-65; Owner, Malpaso Productions, 1969-; Mayor, Carmel, 1986-88. Films include: The First Travelling Saleslady; Star in the Dust; Escapade in Japan; Ambush at Cimarron Pass; Lafayette Escadrille; A Fistful of Dollars, 1964; For a Few Dollars More, 1965; The Good, the Bad and the Ugly, 1966; The Witches, 1967; Hang 'Em High, 1968; Coogan's Bluff, 1968; Where Eagles Dare, 1969; Paint Your Wagon, 1968; Kelly's Heroes, 1970; Two Mules for Sister Sara, 1970; Dirty Harry, 1971; Joe Kidd, 1972; High Plains Drifter (also director), 1973; Magnum Force, 1973; Thunderbolt and Lightfoot, 1974; The Eiger Sanction (also director), 1975; The Outlaw Josey Wales (also director), 1976; The Enforcer, 1976; The Gauntlet (also director), 1978; Every Which Way But Loose, 1978; Escape

From Alcatraz, 1979; Bronco Billy (also director), 1980; Any Which Way We Can, 1980; Firefox (also director), 1982; Honky Tonk Man (also director), 1982; Sudden Impact (also director), 1983; Tightrope, 1984; City Heat, 1984; Pale Rider (also director), 1985; Heartbreak Ridge (also director); Director, Breezy, 1973; Bird, 1988; The Dead Pool, 1988; Pink Cadillac, 1989; White Hunter, Black Heart (also director), 1989; The Rookie (also director), 1990; Unforgiven (also director), 1992; In the Line of Fire, 1993; A Perfect World (also director), 1993; The Bridges of Madison County (also director, producer), 1995; The Stars Fell on Henrietta (co-producer); Absolute Power (also director), 1997; True Crime, 1998; Director, Midnight in the Garden of Good and Evil, 1997; Space Cowboys (also director), 2000; Blood Work (also director, producer), 2002. Honours: Academy Awards, 1993; Fellow, BFI, 1993; Irving G Thalberg Award, 1995; Legion d'honneur, Commander, Ordre des Arts et Lettres, American Film Institute's Life Achievement Award, 1996; Screen Actors Guild, 2003. Address: c/o Leonard Hirshan, William Morris Agency, 151 S El Camino Drive, Beverly Hills, CA 90212, USA.

EBEL Suzanne, (Suzanne Goodwin, Cecily Shelbourne), Writer. Publications: Love, The Magician, 1956; Journey from Yesterday, 1963; The Half-Enchanted, 1964; The Love Campaign, 1965; The Dangerous Winter, 1965; A Perfect Stranger, 1966; A Name in Lights, 1968; A Most Auspicious Star, 1968; Somersault, 1971; Portrait of Jill, 1972; Dear Kate, 1972; To Seek a Star, 1973; The Family Feeling, 1973; Girl by the Sea, 1974; Music in Winter, 1975; A Grove of Olives, 1976; River Voices, 1976; The Double Rainbow, 1977; A Rose in Heather, 1978; Julia's Sister, 1982; The Provencal Summer, 1982; House of Nightingales, 1986; The Clover Field, 1987. As Suzanne Goodwin: The Winter Spring, 1978 (USA - Stage of Love, as Cecily Shelbourne, 1978); The Winter Sisters, 1980; Emerald, 1980; Floodtide, 1983; Sisters, 1985; Cousins, 1986; Daughters, 1987; Lovers, 1988; To Love a Hero, 1989; A Change of Season, 1990; The Rising Storm, 1992; While the Music Lasts, 1993; The Difference, 1995; Sheer Chance, 1997; French Leave, 2001. Non-fiction: Explore the Cotswolds by Bicycle (with Doreen Impey), 1973; London's Riverside: From Hampton Court in the West to Greenwich Palace in the East (with Doreen Impey), 1975. Address: 52A Digby Mansions, Hammersmith Bridge Road, London W6 9DF, England.

EBERTS John Jacob, b. 3 July 1949, Philadelphia, Pennsylvania, USA. Teacher. m. Joellen, 1 son, 1 daughter. Education: BS, 1972, M.ED, 1974, Pennsylvania State University; MS, 1990, MA, 2001, St John's University; PhD, International University of Metaphysics, 1998. Appointments: Teacher, Social Studies, Glendale, Pennsylvania; Teacher, Social Science, Pinellas County, Florida; Adjunct Professor, Social Science, St Petersburg College, Pinellas County; Adjunct Professor, Social Science, Pasco Hernado Community College, Florida; Department Chair, Social Science, Dunedin High School, Florida. Honours: Outstanding Educator, Pinellas County, 1990-91, 1994-95, 1995-96, 1997-98; Pennsylvania State Outstanding Teacher Alumni, 1994; Social Studies Teacher of the Year, Pinellas County, Florida, 1999; International Man of the Year for Education, 2001. Memberships: American Sociological Association; International Association of Counsellors and Therapists; Royal Institute of Philosophy, England; Philosophical Society of England; American Association for Sociology of Religion; London Diplomatic Academy; Fellow, Royal Anthropological Institute of Great Britain and Ireland; Appointed Cavalier, The World Order of Science, Education, Culture. Address: 2746 Kavalier Drive, Palm Harbor, FL34684, USA. E-mail: jeberts3@tampabay.rr.com

Dictionary of International Biography

EBRAHIMI Seyed Nasrollah, b. 2 January 1966, Iran. Assistant Professor of International Law. m. Soghra Ahmadi, 4 sons. Education: Diploma, Social Economy, Iran, 1986; LLB, Judiciary Law, Tehran University, Iran, 1990; LLM, International and Commercial Law, 1994, PhD, Private International Law, 1998, Sheffield University, England; Attended numerous short courses and seminars. Appointments: International Legal Advisor, Bureau of International Legal Services of the Iranian Presidency Institution, Tehran, Iran, 1992-; International Legal Advisor, National Iranian Oil Company, Ministry of Oil, Tehran, Iran, 1998-; Associate Professor of International Law, Research and Science Unit, Islamic Azad University, Tehran, 1998-; Director, Legal and Contractual Affairs, Petroleum Engineering and Development Company (subsidiary to National Iranian Oil Company), 2000-. Publications: Numerous articles published in professional journals and presented and conferences and seminars include most recently: Iranian Child Protection Law – Towards a Concept of Adoption, 2002; Islamic Utopia: A Reality, 2002; Legal Institutions protecting children under Iranian law, 2003; Legitimacy of USA War against Iraq under public international law prospectus, 2003. Honours: Chancellor of the Highest Council of the Cultural Revolution; First Class Honours, scoring the highest marks at the Special Board Examination , Iranian Ministry of Culture and Education. Memberships: Centre of International, Comparative and European Law, Faculty of Law, University of Sheffield, England; British Institution on International Law, London, England; International Family Law Institution, The Hague, Netherlands; Chartered Institute of Arbitrators, UK. Address: 3rd Floor, No 600, 9th Street, Hormozan Street, Shahrak-e-Gharb, Tehran, Iran.

ECCLESTON Christopher, b. 16 February 1964, Salford, England. Actor. Appointments: Actor, films: Let Him Have It, 1991; Shallow Grave, 1995; Jude, 1996; Elizabeth, 1998; A Price Above Rubies, 1998; Heart, 1999; Old New Borrowed Blue, 1999; Existenz, 1999; Gone in 60 Seconds, 2000; The Invisible Circus, 2001; The Others, 2001; I am Dina, 2002; 28 Days Later, 2002; TV appearances: Cracker, 1993-94; Hearts and Minds, 1995; Our Friends in the North, 1996; Hillsborough, 1996; Strumpet, 2001; Flesh and Blood, 2002; Theatre includes: Miss June, 2000. Address: Hamilton Asper Management, Ground Floor, 24 Hanway Street, London W1P 9DD, England.

ECCLESTONE Bernie, b. October 1930. Business Executive. m. (1) 1 daughter, (2) Slavica, 2 daughters. Education: Woolwich Polytechnic, London. Appointments: Established car and motorcycle dealership, Bexley, Kent; Racing-car driver for short period; Set up Brabham racing team, 1970; Owner, Formula One Holdings, now controls Formula One Constructors Association, representing all top racing-car teams; Vice-President in charge of Promotional Affairs, Federal Institute de l'Automobile (FIA), racing's international governing body. Address: Formula One Administration Limited, 6 Prince's Gate, London SW7 1QJ, England. Website: www.formula1.com

ECONOMIDES Anastasios, b. 29 November 1961, Thessaloniki, Greece. Professor. Education: Diploma, Electrical Engineering, Aristotelean University of Thessaloniki, 1984; MSc, Computer Engineering, 1987, PhD, Computer Engineering, 1990, University of Southern California, USA. Appointments: Lecturer, Informatics, 1993-96, Assistant Professor, Computer Networks, 1996-, University of Macedonia, Thessaloniki, Greece. Publications: More than 50 papers on computer networks, tele-education and educational technology in scientific journals and conference proceedings. Honours: Fulbright Fellowship, 1985-86; Postgraduate Greek State Fellowship, 1985-89; Research Assistantship, University of Southern California, 1986-90;

Outstanding Academic Achievement, University of Southern California, 1990. Memberships: IEEE; ACM. Address: University of Macedonia, Egnatia 156, Thessaloniki 54006, Greece.

EDBERG Stefan, b. 19 January 1966, Vastervik, Sweden. Tennis Player. m. Annette, 1 daughter. Appointments: Tennis player, winner of: Junior Grand Slam, 1983; Milan Open, 1984; San Francisco, Basle and Memphis Opens, 1985; Gstaad, Basle and Stockholm Opens, 1986; Australian Open, 1986, 1987; Wimbledon, 1988, 1990, finalist, 1989; US Open, 1991; Masters, 1989; German Open, 1992; US Open, 1992; Winner (with Anders Jarryd) Masters and French Open, 1986, Australian and US Opens, 1987; Member, Swedish Davis Cup Team, 1984, 1987; Semi-finalist, numerous tournaments; Retired in 1996 having won 60 professional titles and more than 20 million dollars in prize money; Founded the Stefan Edberg Foundation to assist young Swedish tennis players. Honour: Adidas Sportsmanship Award (four times). Address: c/o ATP Tour 200, ATP Tour Boulevard, Ponte Vedra Beach, FL 32082, USA.

EDEH Emmanuel Matthew Paul, b. 20 May 1947, Akpugo, Nigeria. Clergyman. Education: BD, Theology, 1976; BA, Philosophy, 1980; MA, Philosophy, 1981; PhD, Metaphysics, 1984; Clinical Pastoral Education, 1984. Appointments: Teacher, Nigeria, 1976-78; Teacher, USA, 1982-84; Rector, Our Saviour Polytechnic, Emene, 1989-93; Vice Chancellor, Madonna University College, Okija, Onitsha, 1993-99; Professorship of Philosophy of Education, Enugu State University of Science and Technology, Enugu, 1999; Founder, Chancellor, Madonna University, Okija, Onitsha, 1999-; Founder, Chancellor, Caritas University, Amorji Nike, Emene, 2004; Founded numerous establishments: Catholic Prayer Ministry, 1984; Congregation of the Sisters of Jesus the Saviour, 1985; Our Saviour Polytechnic, OSISATECH, 1989; Our Saviour College of Education, 1989; The Pilgrimage Centre of Eucharistic Adoration, 1990; Congregation of the Fathers and Brothers of Jesus the Saviour, 1991; OSISATECH Boys Secondary School, 1992; OSISATECH Girls Secondary School, 1992; Congregation of the Contemplatives of Jesus the Saviour, 1993; Elizabeth Primary School, 1997; Madonna Nursery and Primary School, Abuja, 1999; Madonna University, Okija, Nigeria (the first Catholic University of West Africa), 1999; Caritas University, Amorji, Nike Emene (the 2nd Catholic University in West Africa), 2004; Established Printing Press, Enugu; Founder numerous medical institutions including: Our Saviour Hospital/Maternity, Elele, 1986; Our Saviour Rehabilitation Centre, Elele, 1992; our Saviour Motherless Babies Home, Elele, 2992; Modonna University Medical Centre, Okija, 2000; Madonna University Teaching Hospital, Elele, 2002. Publications: Published numerous learned articles and book including: Legal Positivism: A Violation of Nautral Law Doctorine, 1981; Towards an Igbo Metaphysics, 1985; The Pilgrimage Centre of Eucharistic Adoration, 1997; Jesus the Saviour in our Midst, 1998; The Holy Spirit Acting in our Midst, 2000. Memberships: Congregation of the Holy Ghost Fathers. Address: Pilgrimage Centre of Eucharistic Adoration, Box 22, Elele, Rivers State, Nigeria.

EDGE (THE) (David Evans), b. 8 August 1961, Ireland. Musician. Appointments: Guitarist, Founder Member, U2, 1978-; Toured Australasia, Europe, USA, 1980-84; Live Aid Wembley, 1985; Self Aid Dublin, A Conspiracy of Hope (Amnesty International Tour), 1986; World tour, 100 performances, Europe and USA, 1987; Tour, Australia, 1989; New Year's Eve Concert Point Depot Dublin (Broadcast live to Europe and USSR, 1989; World tour, 1992-93; Dublin Concert, 1993. Recordings: Albums with U2: Boy, 1980; October, 1981; War, 1983; Under A Blood Red Sky, 1983; The Unforgettable Fire, 1984; The Joshua Tree,

1987; Rattle and Hum, 1988; Achtung Baby, 1991; Zooropa, 1993; Pop, 1997; All That You Can't Leave Behind, 2000; Singles with U2 include: With Or Without You; I Still Haven't Found What I'm Looking For; Where the Streets Have No Name, 1988 (all 3 no 1 in US charts); Desire, 1988; Stay, 1993; Discotheque, 1997 (all 3 UK no 1); Sweetest Thing, 1998; Beautiful Day, 2000; Stuck in a Moment You Can's Get Out Of, 2001. Honours: Gold Disc for War, USA; Platinum Disc for Under a Blood Red Sky, UK; Band of Year (Rolling Stone Writers Poll), 1984; Grammy Awards: Album of Year, Best Rock Performance, Best Video; Best Live Act, BPI Awards, 1993. Address: c/o Regine Moylet Publicity, 9 Ivebury Court, 325 Latimer Road, London, W10 6RA, England.

EDGECOMBE Jean Marjorie, b. 28 February 1914, Bathurst, New South Wales, Australia. Author. m. Gordon Henry Edgecombe, 2 February 1945, 2 daughters, 2 sons. Education: BA, Honours, Sydney University, 1935. Publications: Discovering Lord Howe Island, (with Isobel Bennett), 1978; Discovering Norfolk Island, (with Isobel Bennett), 1983; Flinders Island, the Furneaux Group, 1985; Flinders Island and Eastern Bass Strait, 1986, 2nd edition, 1994; Lord Howe Island, World Heritage Area, 1987; Phillip Island and Western Port, 1989; Norfolk Island, South Pacific: Island of History and Many Delights, 1991, revised 2nd edition, 1999; Discovering Flinders Island, 1992, revised 2nd edition, 1999; Discovering King Island, Western Bass Strait, 1993, revised 2nd edition, 2004. Contributions to: Articles and poems to various publications. Honour: Medal of the Order of Australia, 1995. Membership: Australian Society of Authors; Hornsby Shire Historical Society. Address: 7 Oakleigh Avenue, Thornleigh, 2120 New South Wales, Australia.

EDHEBRU Okiogbero Jonathan, b. 15 January 1958, Emede, Nigeria. Accountant; Management Consultant. Education: BA, Business Administration, Kensington University, Glendale, USA, 1986; Diploma, Criminal Justice Administration, University of Lagos, Nigeria, 1991; LLB, University of Abuja, Nigeria, 2000. Appointments: Teacher, Sarawa, Hadeja Kano State, Nigeria, 1975-77; Head of Accounts Department, BeeBee Enterprises Nigeria Limited (Chalk and Candle Manufacturers), 1982-84; General Manager, Commerce and Marketing Research Limited, 1987-2000; Management Consultant to Jebba Toll Gate, Jebba, Kwara State, Nigeria, 1996-99; Tax Monitoring Agent to Lagos State Government, 1995-96.; Federal Government Accredited Management Trainer, 1999; Contested as Delta State Governor, National Conscience Party, Nigeria, 2003. Publications: Co-author, 600 Questions and Answers, Commerce Book, 1985; Accounting Book, in progress; Publisher, Export-Import Trade News, 1993-94. Memberships: Associate Member, Chartered Institute of Taxation of Nigeria; Associate Member, Institute of Company and Commercial Accountants. Address: PO Box 1462, Surulere, Lagos, Nigeria.

EDWARDS Anthony, b. 19 July 1962, Santa Barbara, California, USA. Education: RADA, London. Appointments: Member, Santa Barbara Youth Theatre in 30 productions, aged 12-17; Commercials aged 16; Stage appearances: Ten Below, New York, 1993. Actor, films: Fast Times at Ridgemont High, 1982; Heart Like a Wheel, 1982; Revenge of the Nerds, 1984; The Sure Thing, 1985; Gotcha!, 1985; Top Gun, 1985; Summer Heat, 1987; Revenge of the Nerds II, 1987; Mr North, 1988; Miracle Mile, 1989; How I Got Into College, 1989; Hawks, 1989; Downtown, 1990; Delta Heat, 1994; The Client, 1994; Us Begins with You, 1998; Don't Go Breaking My Heart, 1999; Jackpot, 2001; TV series: It Takes Two, 1982-83; Northern Exposure, 1992-93; ER, 1994-; Soul Man; TV films: The Killing of Randy Webster, 1981; High School USA, 1983; Going for Gold: The Bill Johnson Story, 1985; El Diablo, 1990; Hometown Boy Makes Good, 1990; In Cold Blood, 1996; TV

specials: Unpublished Letters; Sexual Healing. Address: C/o United Talent Agency, 9560 Wilshire Boulevard, Suite 500, Beverly Hills, CA 90212, USA.

EDWARDS Blake, b. 26 July 1922, Tulsa, OK, USA. Film Director; Screen Writer. m. Julie Andrews, 1969. Appointments: US Coast Guard Reserve WWII; Writer for radio shows: Johnny Dollar; Line-Up; Writer, Creator: Richard Diamond; Creator TV shows: Dante's Inferno; Peter Gunn; Mr Lucky; Co-producer and writer: Panhandle, 1947; Stampede, 1948; Writer on films: All Ashore, 1952; Sound Off, 1952; Cruisin' Down the River, 1953; Drive a Crooked Road, 1954; My Sister Eileen (musical version), 1955; Operation Mad Ball, 1957; Notorious Landlady, 1962; Director, writer, films include: Bring Your Smile Along, 1955; He Laughed Last, 1955; Mr Cory, 1956; This Happy Feeling, 1958; Director, films: Operation Petticoat, 1959; High Time, 1960; Breakfast at Tiffany's, 1961; Days of Wine and Roses, 1962; The Carey Treatment, 1972; Producer, co-writer, director: The Soldier in the Rain, 1963; The Pink Panther, 1964; A Shot in the Dark, 1964; What Did You Do in the War, Daddy, 1966; Peter Gunn, 1967; The Party, 1968; Darling Lili, 1969; Wild Rovers, 1971; The Tamarind Seed, 1974; The Return of the Pink Panther, 1975; The Pink Panther Strikes Again, 1976; Revenge of the Pink Panther, 1978; 10, 1979; SOB, 1980; Victor/Victoria, 1981; Trail of the Pink Panther, 1982; Curse of the Pink Panther, 1983; Blind Date, 1986; Sunset, 1988; Skin Deep, 1989; Switch, 1991; Son of the Pink Panther, 1993; Producer, writer: Experiment in Terror, 1962; Co-writer, director: The Great Race, 1964; Writer, director, co-producer: Victor/Victoria (stage musical), Broadway, 1995. Address: c/o Blake Edwards Company, Suite 501, 10520 Wilshire Boulevard, Apt 1002, Los Angeles, CA 90024, USA.

EDWARDS Elizabeth, b. 13 October 1915, Holmfirth, Yorkshire, England. Retired Lecturer. m. Harry Lampen Edwards, 28 December 1968. Education: BA, Admin, Teachers Diploma, Manchester University, 1945-49. Appointments: Broadway Secondary Modern School, Cheadle; Leamington Spa Milverton College of Further Education; Buxton College of Further Education; Bournemouth College of Technology. Publications: A History of Bournemouth, 1981; Co-author, Tails of the Famous, 1987, with Margaret Brown; Famous Women in Dorset, 1992; Margaret Brown - Shelley Was Her Life, 1994; Bournemouth Past, 1998. Contributions to: Dorset Life; Hampshire Life; Choice; Yours; Gentlemen's Magazine. Friends Literary Society; Tutor, French Conversation, University of the Third Age. Address: 24 St Mary's Court, 59 Belle Vue Road, Bournemouth BH6 3DF, England.

EDWARDS Gareth Owen, b. 12 July 1947. Rugby Union Player (retired); Businessman. m. Maureen Edwards, 1972, 2 sons. Education: Cardiff College of Education. Appointments: Welsh Secondary Schools Rugby international, 1965-66; English Schools 200 yards Champion (UK under 19 record holder), 1966; Welsh national team: 53 caps, 1967-78; Captain 13 times, youngest captain (aged 20), 1968; Played with clubs: Cardiff, 1966-78; Barbarians, 1967-78; British Lions, 1968, 1971, 1974; Joint Director, Euro-Commercials (South Wales) Ltd, 1982-; Players (UK) Ltd, 1983-889 Chairman, Hamdden Ltd, 1991-; Chairman, Regional Fisheries Advisory Committee, Welsh Water Authority, 1983-89. Publications: Gareth - An Autobiography, 1978; Rugby Skills, 1979; Gareth Edwards on Rugby, 1986; Gareth Edwards' 100 Great Rugby Players, 1987. Address: Hamdden Ltd, Plas y Ffynnon, Cambrian Way, Brecon, Powys, LD3 7HP, Wales.

EDWARDS Harold (Harry) Raymond, b. 10 January 1927, Sydney, Australia. Economist. m. Elaine Lance, 18 August 1951, 1 son, 4 daughters. Education: BA, Honours, Sydney, 1948; DPhil, Oxford, 1957; Hon DLitt, Macquarie University, 1992.

Appointments: Professor, University of Sydney, 1962-; Foundation Professor, Economics, Founder, Graduate School of Management, Macquarie University, 1966-72; MP, Shadow Minister for Industry, Science, Finance, Leader of Australian Parliament Delegation and Member of International Executive, Inter-Parliamentary Union, Geneva, 1978-82, inaugurated National Prayer Breakfast, 1986, House of Representatives, Canberra, Parliament of Australia, 1972-93; Microfinance Consultant, Development Economics, Adviser 1985- and First Chairman of the Board, Opportunity International Australia Ltd, Overseas Aid Organisation; Visiting Professor, Macquarie University, 1993-. Publications: Competition and Monopoly in the British Soap Industry, OUP, 1962; Articles in various journals. Honours: Queen Elizabeth Silver Jubilee Medal, 1977; Australia Centenary Medal, 2003. Memberships: Fellow, Academy of the Social Sciences in Australia; Fellow, Australian Institute of Management; Layman, Uniting Church in Australia. Address: 12 John Savage Crescent, West Pennant Hills, NSW 2125, Australia.

EDWARDS Hiromi, b. 20 December 1954, Yamaguchi, Japan. Instructor; Translator. m. Tim L Edwards, 3 daughters. Education: AA, University of South Carolina, USA, 1989; MA, 1992, M Ed, 1995, University of Maryland, USA. Appointments: Instructor, University of Maryland; Journalism, Japan Editorial Review; Translator for Shinsei Bukkyo (Newly Originated Buddhism). Publications include: Importance of Co-Ed Education, 2002; Questions of Liberalized Value, 2002 Fallacies of Feminist Movement in Japan, 2003. Honours: Scott Sander Scholarship, 1989; National Dean's List, 1988-90; Magna Cum Laude, 1992. Memberships: Okinawa Psychological Association; American Psychological Association; National Council on Family Relations. Address: 784 Shukui, Tabuse-cho, Kumage-gun, Yamaguchi, Japan. E-mail: tedwards@mx5.tiki.ne.jp

EDWARDS Jonathan, b. 10 May 1966, London, England. Athlete. m. Alison Joy Briggs, 2 sons. Career: Athlete, Bronze Medal, World Championships, 1993; Gold Medal, Fifth Athletics World Championships, Gothenburg, twice breaking own record for triple jump, clearing 18.29m, 1995, Edmonton, 2001; Silver Medal, Olympic Games, Atlanta, 1996; World Championships, 1997, 1999; Gold Medal, European Championships, 1998; European Indoor Championships, 1998; Goodwill Games, 1998; Sports Fellowship, University of Durham, 1999; Olympic Games, 2000; World Championships, 2001; Commonwealth Games, 2002;. Publication: A Time to Jump, 2000. Honours: BBC Sportsman of the Year, 1995; IAAF Athlete of the Year, 1995; BBC Sports Personality of the Year, 1995; British Male Athlete of the Year, 1995, 2000, 2001; CBE. Address: c/o Jonathan Marks, MTC, 20 York Street, London W1U 6PU, England. E-mail: info@mtc-uk.com Website: www.mtc-uk.com

EDWARDS Linda Mary Teressa, (Lloyd), b. 3 July 1951, Southport, England. Assistant Verger. 3 sons, 1 daughter. Publications: Poetry: Words of Wisdom; The Cracked Mirror; Valley of Thought; Light of the World. Contributions to: Christian Viewpoint. Address: Church Institute House, Church Lane, Bromborough, Wirral L62 7AB, England.

EDWARDS Philip Walter, b. 7 February 1923, Cumbria, England. Retired Professor of English; Writer. m. Sheila Mary Wilkes, 8 May 1952, 3 sons, 1 daughter. Education: BA, 1942, MA, 1946, PhD, 1960, University of Birmingham. Appointments: Lecturer, University of Birmingham, 1946-60; Professor, Trinity College, Dublin, 1960-66; University of Essex, 1966-74, University of Liverpool, 1974-90. Publications: Sir Walter Ralegh, 1953; Kyd, The Spanish Tragedy, 1959; Shakespeare and the Confines of Art, 1968; Massinger: Plays and Poems, 1976; Shakespeare's Pericles, 1976; Threshold of a Nation, 1979;

Hamlet, 1985; Shakespeare: A Writers Progress, 1986; Last Voyages, 1988; The Story of the Voyage, 1994; Sea-Mark, 1997; The Journals of Captain Cook, 1999. Membership: British Academy, fellow, 1986-. Address: High Gillinggrove, Gillinggate, Kendal, Cumbria LA9 4JB, England.

EDWARDS Robert, b. 27 September 1925. Physiologist. m. Ruth E Fowler, 1956, 5 daughters. Education: University of Wales; University of Edinburgh. Appointments: Research Fellow, California Institute of Technology, 1957-58; Scientist, National Institute of Medical Research, Mill Hill, 1958-62; Glasgow University, 1962-63; Department of Physiology, University of Cambridge, 1963-89; Ford Foundation Reader in Physiology, 1969-85; Professor of Human Reproduction, 1985-89, Professor Emeritus, 1989-, University of Cambridge. Publications: A Matter of Life, with P C Steptoe, 1980; Conception in the Human Female, 1980; Mechanisms of Sex Differentiation in Animals and Man, with C R Austin, 1982; Human Conception in Vitro, with J M Purdy, 1982; Implantation of the Human Embryo, with J M Purdy and P C Steptoe, 1985; In Vitro Fertilisation and Embryo Transfer, with M Seppala, 1985; Life Before Birth, 1989; Numerous articles in scientific and medical journals. Honours: Honorary Member, French Society for Infertility; Honorary Citizen of Bordeaux; Hon FRCOG; Hon MRCP; Hon DSc (Hull, York, Free University Brussels); Gold Medal, Spanish Fertility Society, 1985; King Faisal Award, 1989. Memberships: Fellow, Churchill College, Cambridge, now Extraordinary Fellow; Scientific Director, Bourn Hall Clinics, Cambridge and London; Chair, European Society of Human Reproduction and Embryology, 1984-86; Visiting Scientist, Johns Hopkins University, 1965, University of North Carolina, 1966, Free University of Brussels, 1984; Honorary President, British Fertility Society, 1988-; Life Fellow, Australian Fertility Society; Chief Editor, Human Reproduction, 1986-. Address: Duck End Farm, Dry Drayton, Cambridge, CB3 8DB, England.

EFROS Victor, b. 11 June 1942, Ekaterinburg Province of Russia. Physicist. m. N Pushkina, 1 son. Education: MSc, Moscow State University, 1966; PhD, 1974, DSc, 1987, Kurchatov Institute, Moscow. Appointments: Senior Scientist, 1974-89, Head Scientist, 1989-, Russian Research Centre, Kurchatov Institute; Foreign Professor, Department of Physics, University of Trento, Italy, 2000-2002; Research Work: Nills Bohr Institute, University of Surrey, University of Trento, Technical University of Vienna, Chalmers University of Gothenburg, European Centre for Theoretical Nuclear Physics, University of Saskatchewan. Publications: About 100 articles in professional journals. Honours: Kurchatov Prizes, 1973, 1990, 2001. Address: Russian Research Centre, Kurchatov Institute, 123182 Moscow, Russia.

EGGEHORN Ylva Elisabet, b. 6 March 1950, Stockholm, Sweden. Author; Poet. m. Georg Eggehorn, 1 son, 1 daughter. Education: Student Exam, Adolf Fredrik High School of Music, Stockholm, 1968; Literature and Theology, Stockholm and Uppsala Universities, 1968-72; Courses in Scandinavian Languages and Literature Theory, Stockholm University, 1970, 1993. Career: First collection of poetry published at the age of 13; Subsequently 15 volumes of poetry published and 3 novels; Hymnwriter represented with 10 Hymns in the New Swedish Book of Hymns; Columnist in several newspapers; Editor, Vir Lösen, cultural magazine, 1998-2001; Lecturing 70-100 times a year; Translator, Dietrich Bonhoeffer, Sapho and others; Radio and TV appearances every year since 1970; Guest Professor, Pearson Professorship, Bethany College, Kansas, USA, 2003. Publications include: Child of the Sea, 1963; Shall We Share, 1970; Jesus Loves You, 1972; On the Ground, 1974; For a New Earth, 1977; He Comes, 1975; Heartbeat, 1980; Breakthrough, 1983; Grandchild of Europe, 1985; A Letter for My Beloved, 1986; Mary went through the thorn wood, 1987;

Lydia by the Lamplight, 1990; Radio Time, 1994; One of these Hours, 1996; A Secret Sign, 1998; King of the Lilies of the Valley, 2000; A Carousel with Madonnas, 2002; Love boldly, 2003. Honours: Awards from the Swedish Academy, 1983, 2002; The Litteris and Artibus Medal from the King of Sweden, 1999; The Wallin Medal, The Stefans Medal, 2000; The The Tzube Prize, 2001. Memberships: The Pen Club; Writers Union of Sweden, second vice-president, 1998-2000. Address: Fagerlundsvägen 15, 14871 Sorunda, Sweden. E-mail: yeggehorn@hotmail.com

EGLINTON Edna Mary, b. 26 October 1924, London, England. Poet. m. George Arthur Eglinton, 12 January 1946, 1 son, 1 daughter. Publications: Pisgah, 1977; Holiday Viewing, 1982; Listen to Us (1 of 6 poets), 1983; Hands Together (with David Santer), 1994; How Are Your Spirits, 2001; Forever Panto, 2001. Contributions to: Magazines and anthologies for children and adults. Honours: Prizes in competitions. Memberships: Friends of the Arvon Foundation; Association of Christian Writers. Address: 9 North Street, North Tawton, Devon EX20 2DE, England.

EHRENBERG Miriam, b. 1930, New York, USA. Psychologist. m. Otto Ehrenberg, 2 daughters. Education: PhD, New School University, 1970. Appointments: Director, Psychotherapy, Spence Chapin Services, 1970-80; Private practice of psychotherapy, 1970-; Clinical Professor of Psychology, J Jay College, CUNY, 1990-; Executive Director, Institute for Human Identity, 1995-. Publications: The Psychotherapy Maze; The Intimate Circle; Optimum Brain Power. Membership: American Psychological Association. Address: 118 Riverside Drive, New York, NY 10024, USA.

EICHLER Margrit, b. 28 September 1942, Berlin, Germany. Professor of Sociology. m. Donald Payne, 1 son. Education: University of Goettingen, Germany, 1962-65; Free University of Berlin, 1965-66; Graduate Student, Duke University, USA, 1966-70; MA, Duke University, USA, 1968; PhD, Duke University, 1972. Appointments: Lecturer, 1971, Assistant Professor, Sociology, 1972-75, Adjunct Professor, 1975-77, University of Waterloo; Associate Professor, Sociology, 1975-80, Professor, 1980-, Ontario Institute for Studies in Education; Cross-appointment, Department of Sociology, 1981-, University College, 1997-, New College, 1999-, University of Toronto, Visiting Scholar, University of Calgary, 1990-91; Nancy Rowell Jackman Chair in Women's Studies, Mount Saint Vincent University, 1992-93; Director, Institute for Women's Studies and Gender Studies, University 50%, continuing at OISE/UT at 50%, 1999-2003. Publications: Children's book: Martin's Father, 1971; Books include: The Double Standard: A Feminist Critique of Feminist Social Science, 1980; Canadian Families Today: Recent Changes and their Policy Consequences, 1983, 1988; Family Shifts, Families, Policies and Gender Equality, 1997; Monographs, book chapters, reviews, articles in refereed journals, conference proceedings. Honours include: Elected Fellow, Royal Society of Canada, 1994; European Academy of Sciences, 2002; Outstanding Contribution Award, Canadian Sociology and Anthropology Association, 1996. Memberships include: Canadian Research Institute for the Advancement of Women, President, 1981-82; Canadian Sociology and Anthropology Association, President, 1990-91. Address: Ontario Institute for Studies in Education, University of Toronto, 252 Bloor St W, Toronto ON, Canada M56 1V6.

EIDE Finn Egil, b. 30 July 1940, Sadnes, Norway. Artist. m. Reidun Kårevik, 2 sons. Education: Master of Philosophy; Stord/Haugesund University College; University of Bergen; University of Trondheim; The Ministry of Education. Appointments: Artist: About 150 solo and group exhibitions in Mexico, Norway, Iceland and Faroe Islands; Work represented in banks, galleries, European Cities of Culture, 2000, Bergen, schools, businesses, museums and government buildings; Represented in many private collections. Publications: Streif, drawings and poems; To, short stories, poems and paintings; Spor, poems and paintings; Illusjonen, poems; Songen om dei store slettene, poems and paintings; På søk I et rasskadd hjernelandskap, poems and paintings; Så møtte han huldra, illustration of fairytales from Western Norway; Under breen; Article, On Creating for College of Further Education magazine. Honours: Guaranteed Income for Artist, Ministry of Culture, 1987-; The Norwegian Illustration Fund Prize, 1983, 1987; Sogn og Fjordane County, Cultural Stipend, 1981, 2000. Memberships: Young Artists' Society; The Association of Norwegian Visual Artists; Sogn og Fjordane Artists' Association; The Norwegian Art Information Center; Annual Online Database; Dictionary/Encyclopaedia; The Norwegian Art Information Center; The Norwegian Artists Encyclopaedia (82). Address: Korsveien 11, N-6770 Nordfjordeid, Norway.

EIGEN Manfred, b. 9 May 1927, Ruhr, Germany. Physical Chemist. m. Elfriede Müller, 1 son, 1 daughter. Education: Doctorate, Göttingen University, 1951. Appointments: Assistant, Professor, Head of Department, 1953-, Director, 1964, Max-Planck Institute of Physical Chemistry, Göttingen; Honorary Professor, Technical University, Göttingen, 1971-; President, Studienstiftung des Deutschen Volkes, 1983-. Honours: Hon Dr, University of Washington, St Louis University, Harvard University, Cambridge University; Numerous other honorary degrees; Foreign honorary member, American Academy of Arts and Sciences; Otto Hahn Prize, 1967; Joint Winner, Nobel Prize for Chemistry, 1967. Memberships: Akademie der Wissenschaften, Göttingen; Foreign Associate Member, National Academy of Sciences, USA; Foreign Member, Royal Society, UK; Academie Française, 1978. Address: Georg-Dehio-Weg 14, 37075, Germany.

EISEN Timothy George Quentin, b. 13 December 1963. Physician. Education: BSc, First Class Honours in Cell Pathology, Middlesex Hospital Medical School, University of London, 1984; MB B.Chir, University of Cambridge, School of Clinical Medicine, 1986; MRCP (UK), 1990; PhD, Marie Curie Research Institute and Institute of Cancer Research, University of London, 1996; Certificate of Completion of Specialist Training in Medical Oncology, General Medical Council, 1997; FRCP (UK), 2002. Appointments include: Clinical Research Fellow, Marie Curie Research Institute, Oxted, Surrey, 1991-95; Honorary Senior Registrar, Royal Marsden Hospital, Surrey, 1993-95, Senior Registrar Rotation, Royal Marsden Hospital, 1995-98; Senior Lecturer and Honorary Consultant in Medical Oncology, University College London Hospitals and North Middlesex Hospital, 1998-2000; Senior Lecturer and Honorary Consultant in Medical Oncology, Institute of Cancer Research and Royal Marsden National Health Trust, 2001-. Publications: Numerous articles in medical journals as author and co-author. Honours: MRC Intercalated Award, University of London, 1983; Medical Defence Union, Elective Bursary, 1985; Honours, Clinical Immunology Course, Harvard Medical School, Boston, USA, 1985; Fison's Prize in Paediatrics, 1986. Address: The Royal Marsden Hospital, Fulham Road, London SW3 6JJ, England.

EISENBERG Adi, b. 18 February 1935, Breslau, Germany (now Wroclaw, Poland). Professor of Chemistry. m. (1) Divorced, 1 son, (2) Katia C. Zimmerman, 1 September 2002, 3 step-children. Education: BS. Chemistry, Worcester Polytechnic, 1957; MA, 1959, PhD, 1960, Princeton University. Appointments: Chemist, DuPont Chambers Works, 1957; Research Assistant, 1957-58, Thiokol Fellow, 1958-59, Proctor and Gamble Fellow, 1959-60, Research Associate, 1960-61, Princeton University; NATO Fellow,

Dictionary of International Biography

Basel, Switzerland, 1961-62; Assistant Professor, University of California at Los Angeles, 1962-67; Associate Professor, McGill University, Canada, 1967-74; Professor, 1975-; Director, Polymer McGill, 1991-98; Otto Maass Professor, McGill University, 1992-. Publications: 8 books; 4 contributions to encyclopaedias; 80 abstracts and conference presentations; 1 patent; Numerous articles in refereed journals. Honours: APS Fellow, 1972-; CIC Fellow, 1984-; Killiam Research Fellowship, 1987-89; CIC (Macromol Science and Engineering Division) Dunlop Lecture Award, 1988; Dow Distinguished Lecturer, University of Massachusetts at Amherst, 1996; EWR Steacle Award, 1998. Memberships include: CIC, Macromol Science and Engineering Division, Fellow, 1984-; ACS, Poly Divisional Program Committee, 1975-83; APS, 1964-, Fellow, 1972-, Chairman, DHPP,1976-77; Rheology Society, 1963-, Executive Committee, 1983-85; Sigma Xi, 1957-70. Address: McGill University, Department of Chemistry, 801 Sherbrooke Street West, Montreal, Quebec, H3A 2K6, Canada. Website: http://bravo436.chem.mcgill.ca

EISHINSKII Alexandr Moiseevich, b. 1 October 1936, Dnepropetrovsk, Ukraine. Mathematician. Divorced. Education: Degrees, 1954, 1965. Appointments: Teacher of Mathematics; Science Research Worker. Publications: Co-author of 9 patents; Author and co-author of 8 books: Etudes of the analytical geotechnology, 1989; Mathematical algorithms of thermochemical geotechnology, 1992; Some questions of destruction of mining rocks, 1995; Mathematical algorithms of chemical cinetics, 1998; Torsion of the anisotrops and nonhomogeneous bodies, 1999; Exact Solutions of some problems of mechanics, 2000; The theory and practice of thermochemical technology of extracting and processing coal, 2000; Exact Solutions of some problems of analytical mechanics, 2003. Honours: Research Board of Advisors, ABI; Order of International Ambassadors, ABI; Silver and Gold Medals, IBC, England. Memberships: New York Academy of Sciences; Member, International Academy of Ecology and Life Protection Sciences, St Petersburg. Address: Ioseftal 24 Apt 9, Kiryat-Ata, 28014 Israel.

EISNER Michael Dammann, b. 7 March 1942, Mt Kisco, New York, USA. Entertainment Executive. m. Jane Breckenridge, 1967, 3 sons. Education: Denison University. Appointments: Senior Vice President, prime-time production and development, ABC Entertainment Corporation, 1973-76; President, COO, Paramount Pictures Corporation, 1976-84; Chairman, Chief Executive Officer, The Walt Disney Company, 1984-. Honour: Légion d'honneur. Address: Walt Disney Company, 500 South Buena Vista Street, Burbank, CA 91521, USA.

EKANEM Patrick Udofe, b. 15 July 1952, Akwa Ibom State, Nigeria. Teacher. m. Mfon Patrick Ekanem, 3 sons, 1 daughter. Education: Teachers' Grade II Certificate, 1975; Bachelor of Arts Degree, Theatre Arts, 1981; Postgraduate Diploma in Education, 1988. Appointments: Artist in Residence, Cultural Officer, Sokoto State Council for Arts and Culture; Principal, Secondary School, Ibiaku Uruan, Akwa Ibom State; Principal of many schools across the State, 1985-; Currently, Senior Principal, West Itam Secondary School, the largest co-educational school in Akwa Ibom State. Publications: Initiation into Ekpe Society (Degree Thesis, 1981); Effective Teaching/Learning in Our Schools (The Case of Secondary Schools in Itu); Moral Decadence in Our Schools – The New Millennium Experience; Poetry: Grandson of Helotry; The Yokes of Poverty. Honours: Chieftancy Title of Obong Ifiok, Obong Itams Traditional Ruling Council; Many merit and excellence awards from various diverse organisations. Memberships: All Nigerian Conference of Principals of Secondary Schools; State Executive Member, Nigerian Union of Teachers. Address: West Itam Secondary School, Ekit Itam II-Itu, PMB 1158, Uyo, Akwa Ibom State, Nigeria. E-mail: pat-ekanem@yahoo.com

EKPO Michael Efiong Akpan, b. 10 August 1952, Mbiaya Uruan, AKS, Nigeria. m. Dora Michael Ekpo, 1 son, 2 daughters. Education: WASC, 1971; Nigeria Certificate in Education, 1975; BSc (Hons), Education and Zoology, 1979; M Ed, Science Education and Curriculum, 1988; Senior Administration Exam, 1992. Appointments: Senior Lecturer, Science Education, 1991; Chief Education Officer, 1993; Apostle, Ordained Senior Minister of the Gospel of Jesus Christ, 2000. Director of Education, 2002; Publications: The Nature of Science and Traditional Cosmological Ideas Among Science Teachers in AKS (M Ed Thesis), 1988; Human Learning in Nigeria Cultural Setting, 1988; Science Education and the Quality of Life in Nigeria, 1988; Problems Militating Against Development of Sc/Tech in AKS, 1991. Honours: Award of Excellence for outstanding contributions to the general development of AKS, Niger Delta and Nigeria. Niger Delta Youth Forum, 2001. Memberships: Science Teachers Association of Nigeria; National Steering Committee on Education for All. Address: Director, Directorate of Secondary/Higher Education, Ministry of Education, Uyo, Akwa Ibom State, Nigeria

EL ZAYAT Ahmed, b. 2 September 1965, Egypt. Lead Environmental Engineer. m. Ghada Al Agamawy, 1 son. Education: BSc, Civil Engineering, 1987, Diploma of Higher Studies in Sanitary Engineering, 1998, MSc, Environmental Engineering, 2003, Cairo University, Giza, Egypt. Appointments: US Aid, Provincial Cities Development Program; WHO, Health Cities Program "Technical Focal"; Sanitary Engineer, Dutch Aid, IWACO, DHV, FaDWSP, Egypt; Saudconsult, Senior Environmental Engineer, KSA, Saudi Arabia. Publication: Biological Nutrient Removal for Wastewater Treatment $A^2/0$ System, Water Middle East Conference, 2003. Memberships: ATV-DVWK; ASCE; AWWA; EWRI. Address: KSA, PO Box 2341, Riyadh 11451, Saudi Arabia. E-mail: ahmed_el_zayat@yahoo.com

EL-BIALY Tarek Hessin Ahmed, b. 28 April 1965, Egypt. Orthodontist; Bioengineer. m. Taghreed Ghodaya, 3 sons, 1 daughter. Education: BDS, 1987, MS, Orthodontics, 1993, Faculty of Dentistry, License of Law Degree, Faculty of Law, 1994 Tanta University, Egypt; MS, Oral Sciences, College of Dentistry, 2000, PhD, Bioengineering, College of Engineering, Certificate of Speciality in Orthodontics, 2001, University of Illinois at Chicago, USA. Appointments: Undergraduate Laboratory Instructor, 1989-93, Assistant Lecturer, 1993-97, Department of Orthodontics, Faculty of Dentistry, Tanta University, Egypt; Teaching Assistant, Department of Orthodontics, University of Illinois at Chicago, USA, 1999-2001; Lecturer, 2001-, Department of Orthodontics, Post Doctoral Research Associate, Department of Mechanical Engineering/Bioengineering, 2001-2002, Tanta University, Egypt; Visiting Assistant Professor, University of Illinois at Chicago, 2001-; Assistant Professor of Orthodontics and Bioengineering, Consultant of Orthodontics, Consultant Clinics, Faculty of Dentistry, King Abdul Aziz University, Jeddah, Saudi Arabia, 2002-. Publications: 13 articles in scientific journals as co-author include most recently: Vibratory coherence as an alternative to radiography in assessing bone healing after osteo-distraction, 2002; The effect of pulsed ultrasound on mandibular distraction, 2002; Growth Modification of the Rabbit Mandible Using Therapeutic Ultrasound: Is It Possible to Enhance Functional Appliance Results, 2004 (in press); 10 Abstracts; 4 local and international presentations. Honours: Postdoctoral Poster Clinical Award, Clinic and Research Day, College of Dentistry, University of Illinois at Chicago, 1999; Reviewer, Am. J. Orthod. Dentofac.Orthop., 1999; Education Research Group, Award Assessor, International Association for Dental Research, 2002. Memberships: Egyptian Orthodontic Society; Illinois Society of Orthodontists; American Association of Orthodontists; World Federation of Orthodontists; American Association for Dental Research; International Association for

Dictionary of International Biography

Dental Research. Address: Faculty of Dentistry, Division of Orthodontics, Department of Preventive Dental Sciences, King Abdul Aziz University, PO Box 80209, Jeddah 21589, Saudi Arabia. E-mail: telbialy@hotmail.com

EL-HOFY Mohammed Ibrahem, b. 8 November 1956, Basiuun, Garbia, Egypt. Associate Professor. m. Hoda Abdel Hafiz Mahram, 2 sons. Education: BS, Tanta University, Egypt, 1978; MS, Cairo University, Egypt, 1985; PhD, Physics and Mathematics, Moscow State University, Russia, 1993. Appointments: Demonstrator, 1982-93, Lecturer, 1993-2000, Associate Professor, 2000-, Faculty of Science, Menoufia University, Shebin El Koom, Egypt. Publications: Research in instability of Y_{123} HTC at zero oxygen deficiency; Prediction of the optimum grain size to attain maximum Jc and Tc in Y_{123} system; Calculation of the jump distance of the migrating ion in ionic conducting glasses. Honours: Listed in Who's Who publications and biographical dictionaries. Address: Menoufia University, Faculty of Science, Shebin El Koom, Egypt.

EL-TURK Said, b. 16 May 1947, Amman, Jordan. Chairman; Director General. m. Abir Al-Taher, 2 sons, 2 daughters. Education: BS, Hammersmith College, London, 1970; MS, University of Nebraska, 1975; PhD, Kennedy Western University, 1991. Appointments: Design Engineer, Sir Frederick Snow and Partners, London, 1970-72; President, Leo Daly Omaha, 1972-74; Chairman, El-Turk Trading Establishment, Amman, 1974; New English School, Amman, 1988; Representative, Gate Avionics Ltd. Publication: A Page of The Red Days, in Arabic. Memberships: Society of Engineers; Fellow, Institution of Structural Engineers; Amman Society of Engineers; US Institute of Structural Engineers; US/Arab Chamber of Commerce. Address: El-Turk Contracting Trading Est, PO Box 5476, Amman, Jordan. E-mail: ctc@nets.com.jo

ELDAR Reuben, b. 27 November 1926, Ossiek, Croatia. Physician. Widower, 2 daughters. Education: MD, Hebrew University Hadassah Medical School, Jerusalem, Israel, 1955; DPH, London School of Hygiene and Tropical Medicine, London University, England, 1965. Appointments: Director General, Medical Corps Israel Defence Forces; Medical Officer and Consultant, World Health Organisation; Director, Rambam Medical Centre, Haifa, Israel; Director of Loewenstein Hospitar-Rehabilitation Centre, Head, Fleischman Unit for the Study of Disability, Loewenstein Hospital Rehabilitation Centre, Raanana, Israel; Visiting Professor, University of Split and Ossiek, Croatia. Publications: Over 90 publications in scientific journals; Book: Quality of Medical Care in Croatia, 2003; 8 chapters in 7 books. Honours: Golden Medal, Phi Lambda Kappa Society, USA, 1955; Prize for the year's outstanding MD thesis, Hebrew University, Jerusalem, 1955; McGow Medal for excellence in health administration education, 1983. Membership: International Society for Quality in Health Care. Address: 12 Fischman-Maimon Street, Tel Aviv 64236, Israel. E-mail: eldrub@netvision.net.il

ELDERGILL Anselm, b. 21 March 1959, London, England. Specialist in Mental Health Law. Partner, Helen Landsell. 2 sons. Education: London School of Economics; University of Oxford; The College of Law. Appointments include: Mental Health Act Commissioner, 1992-2002; Chairman Mental Health Act Commission Legal and Ethical Committee, 1997-98; Consultant Department of Health – Legislation Branch, Reform of the Mental Health Act 1983, 2001; Visiting Professor in Mental Health Law, University of Northumbria, 2001; Legal Chairman of 10 independent NHS and social services inquiries into homicides committed by psychiatric patients, 1999-2001, 2002-2003; Adviser to foreign states on the reform of their mental health legislation, 1999-2001; Adviser, Mental Health Bill, Department of Health,

2001-2002; Speaker at numerous conferences and congresses including most recently: Law Society Royal College of Psychiatrists Conference on Mental Health Law Reform, London, 2002; Institute of Mental Health Act Practitioner's Annual Conference, London, 2002, 2003; North of England Law Conference, Newcastle, 2003. Publications include: Textbook, Mental Health Review Tribunals – Law & Practice, 1998, reprinted, 2001; Book chapter: The law and individual rights in The treatment of the personality disordered offender (ed R Blackburn et al), 2000; Articles in professional journals include: Psychopathy, the law and individual rights, 1999; White Paper: Reform of the Mental Health Act , 2001; Is Anyone Safe? Civil Compulsion under the Draft Mental Health Bill, 2002; The Principles of Mental Health Legislation, 2003; Numerous reports and discussion papers. Honours include: Alexander Maxwell Law Trust Scholar; David Hallett Prize for Government; Honorary Legal Adviser in The treatment of the African Regional Council for Mental Health; Ranked 1 in the Healthcare Law section of Chambers (UK); Listed in Who's Who publications and biographical dictionaries. Memberships: President, Mental Health Lawyers Association; International Scientific Committee, International Academy of Mental Health Law. Address: 1 Larches Avenue, London SW14 8LX, England, E-mail: medicolegal@email.com

ELENAS Anaxagoras, b. 8 January 1960, Hrisoupolis, Greece. Assistant Professor in Civil Engineering. m. Areti Charissi, 1 son, 1 daughter. Education: Dipl-ing, University of Stuttgart, Germany, 1984; Dr-Ing, Ruhr-University of Bochum, Germany, 1990. Appointments: Researcher, Ruhr-University, Bochum, Germany, 1985-90; Greek Army, 1991; Lecturer, 1992-97, Assistant Professor, 1997-, Democritus University, Thrace, Greece. Publications: Over 60 in refereed international journals and conferences. Memberships: Technical Chamber of Greece; Seismological Society of America; Earthquake Engineering Research Institute. Address: Democritus University of Thrace, Institute of Structural Mechanics and Earthquake Engineering, vas Sofias 1, GR-67100 Xanthi, Greece.

ELEY Daniel Douglas, b. 1 October 1914, Wallasey, Cheshire, England. Physical Chemist. m. Brenda M Eley, deceased 1992, 1 son. Education: BSc (Hons), Chemistry, 1934, MSc, 1935, PhD, 1937, Manchester University; PhD, 1940, ScD, 1956, St John's College and Colloid Science Department, Cambridge University. Appointments: Researcher for Ministry of Supply and Teacher, Natural Science Tripos, Colloid Science Department, Cambridge University, 1940-45; Lecturer in Colloid Chemistry, 1945-51, Reader in Biophysical Chemistry, 1951-54, Bristol University; Professor of Physical Chemistry, 1954-80, Dean, Faculty of Pure Science, 1959-62, Professor Emeritus, 1980-, Nottingham University. Publications: Numerous papers in scientific journals on solutions, surface chemistry and catalysis, organic semiconductors and related topics; Catalysis and the Chemical Bond, Reilly Lectures, University of Notre Dame, Indiana, 1954; Editor, Adhesion, 1961; A Co-editor, Advances in Catalysis, 1956-98. Honours: Woodiwiss Scholar, 1933, Mercer Scholar, 1934, Darbishire Fellow, 1936, Manchester University; Senior Award, Department of Scientific and Industrial Research, 1937; OBE, 1961; FRS, 1964; Corresponding Member, Bavarian Academy of Science, 1971; Leverhulme Emeritus Fellow, 1981. Memberships: Council, 1951-54, 1960-63, Vice-President, 1963-66, Faraday Society; CCHEM, FRSC, Royal Society of Chemistry; Emeritus Member, Biochemical Society; Meetings Secretary, 1961-63, Honorary Secretary, 1963-65, Honorary Member, 1983-, British Biophysical Society. Address: Brooklands, 35 Brookland Drive, Chilwell, Beeston, Nottingham, NG9 4BD, England.

ELFMAN Danny, b. 29 May 1954, USA. Composer; Musician (guitar); Vocalist. Career: Lead singer, songwriter, guitarist, band Oingo Boingo; Compositions: Film scores: Pee-Wee's Big

Adventure; Beetlejuice; Batman; Batman Returns; Dick Tracy; Darkman; Edward Scissorhands; Sommersby; Other music for films includes: Weird Science; Ghostbusters II; Something Wild; Television series score: The Simpsons. Recordings: Albums: with Oingo Boingo: Only A Lad, 1981; Nothing To Fear, 1982; Good For Your Soul, 1983; Dead Man's Party, 1985; Boingo, 1986; Skeletons In The Closet, 1989; Dark At The End Of The Tunnel, 1990; Article 99, 1992; Batman Returns, 1992; Dolores Claiborne, 1995; Mission Impossible, 1996; The Frighteners, 1996; Mars Attacks! 1996; Men In Black, 1997; Good Will Hunting; Scream 2; My Favorite Martian; Psycho; Sleepy Hollow. Honour: Emmy Nomination, The Simpsons. Current Management: L A Personal Development, 950 N. Kings Road, Suite 266, West Hollywood, CA 90069, USA.

ELIAS Taiseer, b. 16 June 1960, Israel. Musician. m. Miranda, 1 son, 1 daughter. Education: Graduate, Classical Violin Performance, Rubin Conservatory, Haifa, Israel, 1980; B Mus, Music Academy in Jerusalem, Jerusalem, 1984; MA (cum laude), Musicology, 1992, Postgraduate, 2000-2003, Hebrew University, Jerusalem. Appointments: Music Teacher, Teachers' Seminar of David Yalin, Jerusalem, 1983-83; Musical Consultant and performer, Israel Educational television, 1986-88; Musical Director and Conductor of the Classical Arabic Orchestra of the Ministry of Education, 1989-90; Musical Director, various Israeli TV Programs, 1990-2002; Director of the Music Department of the Voice of Israel in Arabic, 1995-2003; Associate Professor, Music Department, Bar Ilan University; Head of the Eastern Music Department, Jerusalem Academy of Music and Dance, 1996-; Founding Member, Bustan Abraham Ensemble, 1990-2003; Member of White Bird, 1990-2004; Musical Director of Zyriab Trio, 1990-2004; Numerous national and international performances include: Concert tour in Europe, USA and Canada, 1994; The Royal Albert Hall, London, 1995; World-wide concert tour with Bustan Abraham Ensemble, 1997-2000; Concert Series with the Haifa Symphony Orchestra, 1999; Concert tour, Munich, London and Amsterdam, 2001; Concert in the Olympic Stadium, Barcelona, Spain, 2002; Concerto for Oud and Symphonic Orchestra, French Senate (and other concert halls in France), 2003. Compositions include: Instrumental music: Metamorphosis, Jazz Kar Kurd, Fanar, Sereen, Mabrouk, Khamsa; Cactus Flower, duo for oud and guitar; White Bird, duo for oud and guitar; The Village, duo for violin and banjo; A Deer in the Forest, solo for oud; Abrandi, duo for oud and Indian sarod; Peace, duo for oud and flamenco guitar; Music for films and theatre: Mafatih , Bint al-sultan, Majnoun Layla; Numerous music pieces for TV and radio. Publications include: Musical Heritage in Jerusalem, 1997; Problems Facing the Arab Musician or Student of Western Classical Music, 1999; Improvisation in Instrumental Arab Music, 2000. Honours include: First Prize in Violin Competition, IBA, 1978; DAAD, German Academic Exchange Service Scholarship, 1992; Excellence Prize for Outstanding Doctoral Student, Council for Higher Education and the Hebrew University, 2003. Memberships include: Committee for Music Education Programmes, Ministry of Education; Repertory Committee "Sal Tarbut"; Numerous other artistic committees and council for the arts. Address: El-Fawar, PO Box 686, Shfar-'Am 20200, Israel. E-mail: taiseerelias@hotmail.com

ELIASON Phyllis Marie, b. 21 December 1925, Greenacres City, Florida, USA. Missionary Teacher. m. Albert Augustus Eliason, 2 sons, 2 daughters. Education: Diploma from Leadership Training Institute, Warrenton, Missouri, 1961, 1989; BA, University of Guam, 1971; Masters of Education in Guidance and Counselling, 1974. Publications: Monthly newsletters to mailing list of over 1000; Articles in Underhill Bulletin, Underhill Society of America.

Honours: Ancient Order of the Chamorii, from Governor Joseph Ada, 1993; Honorary Citizen of Huntsville, Alabama, 1966. Address: 1604 East Martha Lane, Pasadena, TX 77502, USA.

ELJRUSHI Gibril Suliman, b. 1 June 1948, Misurata, Libya. University Professor; Researcher. m. Bathaina, 1 daughter. Education: BSc, Mechanical Engineering, University of Tripoli, Libya, 1974; Master of Engineering, Steven's Institute of Technology, New Jersey, USA, 1982; PhD, Mechanical Engineering, University of Miami, Florida, USA, 1987. Appointments: Chairman, Department of Thermal Energy Conversion, Solar Energy Study, 1988-90; General Director, Technical Affairs, Iron and Steel Complex, 1990-91; Director, Student Affairs, Office of Research, Scientific Committee, Higher Institute for Industry, 1992-99; Dean, College of Engineering, University of Misurata, 2000-. Publications: More than 50 papers in conferences and/or journals locally and internationally in the field of renewable energy, industry, environment and engineering education. Honour: Al Fatah Medal for Engineering Works, Libyan Government, 1990. Memberships: American Society for Mechanical Engineering; ASME; New York, USA; International Association for Hydrogen Energy; IAHE, USA; Society for Science and Technology, Libya. Address: PO Box 3035, Misurata, Libya. E-mail: gibril.s@yahoo.com

ELKAMCHOUCHI Hassan Mohamed, b. 29 May 1943, Alexandria, Egypt. Professor. m. Neema M Abdel-Aziz, 2 sons, 2 daughters. Education: BSc, Electronic Communications, 1966; MSc, 1970, PhD, 1973, Alexandria University, Egypt; BSc, Special Mathematics, Faculty of Science, London University, 1969. Appointments: Head, Communication Section, Faculty of Engineering, Alexandria University; Member, National Radio Science Committee, Egypt; Professor of Communications, Faculty of Engineering, Alexandria University. Publications: Over 78 papers in professional journals. Honours: Egyptian National Award for Engineering Sciences, 2002. Memberships: Senior Member, IEEE; National Radio Science Committee; Egyptian Engineering Society; Scientific Committee for Promotion of University Staff in Egypt. Address: 719 Elhoriya Avenue, Loran, Alexandria, Egypt. E-mail: helkamchouchi@ieee.org

ELLEN Jane, b. 11 May 1956, San Pedro, California, USA. Composer; Music Educator; Researcher. Education: BA summa cum laude with distinction, Music Performance and Religious Studies, University of New Mexico, 1992; Post graduate studies, 1992-93. Appointments: Freelance composer, lecturer and music instructor, 1986-; Parish organist, Our Lady of the Annunciation, Albuquerque, 1994-98; Resident instructor, Older Adult Service and Information System, 1996-; Contract instructor, ElderHostel, University of New Mexico, 1997-2002; Private music studio, 1998-2002; National Director, Sigma Alpha Iota American Composers Bureau, 2003-. Publications: 46 choir, chamber and piano compositions; Contributor, Performa Magazine, 1998. Honours include: ASCAP Standard Work Grants, 1990-; First place award, National League of American Pen Women Biennial Competition, 1996; First, second and third place awards, NLAPW Biennial Competition, 1998; many others. Memberships: American Society of Composers, Authors and Publishers; International Alliance of Women in Music; Music Teachers National Association; Professional Music Teachers of New Mexico; New Mexico Women Composers' Guild; Albuquerque Music Teachers Association. Address: 2226-B Wyoming Blvd NE #182, Albuquerque, NM 87112-2620, USA. E-mail: jane@janeellen.com Website: www.janeellen.com

ELLINGSEN Mark, b. 18 June 1949, Brooklyn, New York, USA. Seminary Professor. m. Betsey Shaw Ellingsen, 2 sons, 1 daughter. Education: BA magna cum laude, Gettysburg College,

1971; MDiv magna cum laude, 1974, MA, 1975, MPhil, 1976, PhD, 1980, Yale University. Appointments: Pastor, Evangelical Lutheran Church in America, 1976-; Assistant Professor, Luther-Northwestern Lutheran Seminaries, St Paul, Minnesota, 1979-82; Associate Professor, Institute for Ecumenical Research, Strasbourg, France, 1982-88; Part-time Instructor, Randolph Community College, Asheboro, North Carolina, 1992-93; Associate Professor, Interdenominational Theological Center, Atlanta, Georgia, 1993-; Part-time Instructor, Emory University, Atlanta, Georgia, 2003-04. Publications: 11 books; Over 200 articles; Over 40 book reviews; Presented many other lectures and papers. Honours: Phi Beta Kappa, 1971; Undergraduate Departmental Honors in Religion and Philosophy, 1971; Yale University Day Fellowship, 1974; AAL Fellowship, 1981; Christianity Today's Readers Choice Award, 1992; Biography included in national and international publications. Memberships: American Academy of Religion; American Society of Church History. Address: Interdenominational Theological Center, 700 Martin Luther King Jr Drive, S W Atlanta, Georgia 30314, USA.

ELLIOT Ligia Gomes, b. 30 March 1944, Rio de Janeiro, Brazil. Researcher; Evaluator. Education: Primary Schoolteacher, 1962; High School Teacher, State University of Rio de Janeiro, 1969; MA Education, Federal University of Rio de Janeiro, 1976; MA, Latin American Studies, University of California, Los Angeles, 1979; PhD, Education, UCLA, 1980. Appointments: Primary Schoolteacher, Secretary of Education, Rio de Janeiro, 1962-70; Normal School Teacher, Secretary of Education, Rio de Janeiro, 1970-76; Professor of Graduate Course in Education/Evaluation, Federal University of Rio de Janeiro, 1981-95; Director of Evaluation Center at Cesgranrio Foundation, 1998-. Publications: Projeto Semear: Equalizing Opportunities for Adolescents at Risk in Rio de Janeiro (Co-author), in Roslyn A Mickelson (editor): Children on the Streets of the Americas: Globalization, Homelessness and Education in the United States, Brazil and Cuba, 2000; Articles in professional journals; Avaliacao Educacional: Conversa de Professores (author), Vitoria, ES: SEE- PROCAP, 2003. Memberships: UCLA Doctoral Alumni Association, Graduate School of Education, 1981. Address: Rua Gal Ribeiro da Costa 114/803, Rio de Janeiro, RJ 22 010-050, Brazil.

ELLIOTT Walter Albert, b. 24 October 1926, Wembley, England. Artist; Author. m. Beryl Jean, deceased, 1 son, 1 daughter. Education: DeHaviland Engineering College; Harrow College of Art; Hammersmith Polytechnic. Appointments: Engineering Apprentice, DeHaviland Engineering College, Edgeware, Middlesex and Hatfield, England; Design Development Engineer, Aero Gas Turbines and Rocket Motors; Self-employed Artist and Writer; Exhibitions throughout Great Britain, France, Italy; Paintings exhibited at Salon de National, Paris France, Royal Institute Gallery, London, Mall Gallery, London; Paintings in collections in America, Canada, Australia and Europe; Triptych (pastel), The Ascent of Man, exhibited in the North Devon Athenaeum, now on display at the Elliott Gallery, Braunton, Devon, England. Publications: Contributor of articles to professional journals; Author, illustrator, The Dream of Gotama (320 page book, 21 illustrations), 2003; Art works included in: Artists and Masters of the 20th Century; An Encounter with Great and New Artists from 1700 to the present. Honours: 1st Prize, 1948, 2nd Prize, 1950 DeHaviland Aircraft Industry Art Exhibition; 1st Prize, Devon County Art Exhibition; Gold Medal, Academy of Italy, 1981; Gold Medal for artistic merit, International Parliament for safety and Peace, USA; Pastel painting, Refugees, chosen for millennium 2000 book, Pastel Painting and Drawing 1989-2000, Pastel Society of London, 2003; Listed in Who's Who publications and biographical dictionaries. Memberships: Fellow, British Interplanetary Society, London; Life Fellow International Biographical Association;

Fellow, American Institute of Biographical Research; International Association of Art; Federation of British Artists; Academy of Italy; Elected Member: Pastel Society, London, United Society for Artists, London, Society of Graphic Fine Art, London; President, Ilfracombe Art Society. Address: Sollake, 2 Warfield Villas, Ilfracombe, North Devon, EX34 9NZ, England. E-mail: artform222@aol.com

ELLIS Ella Thorp, b. 14 July 1928, Los Angeles, California, USA. Writer. m. Leo H Ellis, 3 sons. Education: Sculpture, University of Cordoba, Argentina, 1961-62; BA, English and History, University of California, Los Angeles, California, USA, 1966; MA, English, San Francisco State University, California, USA, 1975. Appointments: Author; Extension Instructor, Creative Writing, University of California, Berkeley, 1972-77; Lecturer, Creative Writing, San Francisco State University, 1974-80; Lecturer, Novel, University Women's Studies, Buenos Aires, Argentina, 1981-85; Extension Lecturer in Longer Fiction, 1987-95. Publications: Roam the Wild Country (also Danish edition and paperback), 1967; Riptide, 1969; Celebrate the Morning, 1972; Where the Road Ends, 1974; Hallelujah, 1976; Sleepwalker's Moon, 1980; Hugo and the Princess Nena (also Danish edition), 1983; Swimming with Whales, 1995; The Year of My Indian Prince (also Danish edition and paperback) 2001. Honours: Roam the Wild Country, Time Magazine's Ten Best Juvenile List, ALA Notable Honors List; Celebrate the Morning, Junior Literary Guild Book of the Month Selection; The Year of My Indian Prince nominated for the William Allan White Award. Memberships: Authors' Guild; Society of Children's Book Writers; Society of Women Geographers; Amnesty International; San Francisco Opera Guild. Address: 1438 Grizzly Peak Blvd, Berkeley, CA 94708, USA. E-mail: ellathorpellis@hotmail.com

ELLIS-JONES Ian David, b. 3 March 1955, Sydney, New South Wales, Australia. Lawyer; Educator. m. Elspeth Heather Leggett, 2 sons, 1 daughter. Education: BA (Syd), 1976; LLB (Syd), 1978; LLM (UTS), 1997; DD (ULC), 2002. Appointments: Admitted as a Solicitor of the Supreme Court of New South Wales, 1978; Legal Officer, 1978-85, Senior Legal Officer, 1985-87, New South Wales Public Service; Commissioner of Inquiry under the Local Government Act (New South Wales), 1982-87, 1992-93; Manager, Legal Branch, New South Wales Department of Local Government, 1987-89; Senior Solicitor, Sly & Weigall, Lawyers, Sydney, 1989-92; Partner, 1992-95, Consultant, 1995-2000, Henningham & Ellis-Jones, Solicitors and Mediators, Riverview and Turramurra, New South Wales; Part-time Lecturer, 1993, Full-time Associate Lecturer, 1994-96, Lecturer, 1996-98, Senior Lecturer, 1998-, Faculty of Law and Legal Practice, University of Technology, Sydney; Consultant, Dunhill Madden Butler, Lawyers, Sydney, 1996-99; Director, University of Technology, Sydney, Community Law and Legal Research Centre, 1997-2002; Principal, Ian Ellis-Jones, Lawyer, Turramurra, New South Wales, 1999-; President, Humanist Society of NSW Inc and the Council of Australian Humanist Societies Inc, 2000-2002; Visiting Lecturer and External Examiner, New South Wales Institute of Psychiatry, 2003. Publications: Books: Essential Administrative Law (1st edition 1997, 2nd edition, 2001, 3rd edition 2003; The Anisminic Revolution in Australian Administrative law, 1998; Numerous journal articles in Australian Humanist; Humanist in Canada; Law Society Journal and others. Honour: Equity and Diversity Award, University of Technology, Sydney, 1999. Memberships: Australian Society of Authors; Australian law teachers Association; Law Society of New South Wales; Humanist Society of New South Wales. Address: University of Technology, Sydney, PO Box 123, Broadway, NSW 2007, Australia. E-mail: ian@law.uts.edu.au

ELLSON Peter Kenneth, b. 22 July 1937, Surrey, England. Poet; Painter; Publisher. m. (1) Barbara Norman, 1966, deceased 1972, (2) Anke Kornmuller, 1978, divorced 1993. Publications: Poems, 1978; Halde, 1983. Contributions to: Tuba Magazine; New Leaf. Address: Route des Vans, La Republique, 30160 Bordezac-Gard, France.

ELLUL Max Joseph, b. 20 December 1970, Attard, Malta. President; Chief Executive Officer. m. Christabel Ellul Saliba, 1 son. Education: BEduc, University of Malta, 1988-89; Marketing Diploma, distinction, Cambridge, 1990-91; MBA, Marketing, 1992-96, Doctorate in Business Administration, Marketing, 1996-98, Columbia State University; DLitt, Medieval History, Calamus University, 2002. Appointments include: Marketing Manager, Grands Group of Companies, Malta, 1990-91; Marketing and Entertainment Consultant, Tarxien, Malta, 1991-; Chief Executive Officer, 1994-, President, 1998-, M and E Management Group; Director, Debil Entertainment Consultants, London, England, 1994-; Vice-President, Watermelon Publishing, London, England, 1995-; Government Consultant, National Parks, Ministry for Public Works and Construction, Malta, 1996-1998; Chief Executive Officer, Transworld Management Group, Dublin, Ireland, 1997-2000; Marketing Consultant, Friends of Rosslyn, Edinburgh, Scotland, 1998-2002; Director, Leisure Support Services Ltd, Valletta, Malta, 1998-; Director, Mediterranean Tourism Marketing Ltd, Valletta, Malta, 1997-2000; Director, MCJ Retailers Ltd, Msida, Malta, 1999-; Government Consultant, United Arab Emirates, 2001-; Director, M and E, Electro Mechanical, Services LLC, Dubai, UAE, 2003-. Publications: Patterns of Life, 2003; Theatre of the Mind, 2003; Various articles in local and international newspapers, journals, magazines and specialised publications. Honours: Companionate of Merit of the Order of Saint Lazarus of Jerusalem; Knight Commander of the Order of Saint Lazarus of Jerusalem; Knight Grand Cross of the Order of Saint Andrew; Knight Grand Cross of the Guard of St Germain; Commander's Cross of the Order Saint Stanislas; Knight of the Order of Saint Joachim. Memberships include: Malta Institute of Management, 1992; Institute of Training and Development, UK, 1994; Institute of Commercial Management, UK, 1994; Malta Marketing Institute, 1991; Malta Chamber of Commerce, 1992; Malta Export Trading Corporation, 1992; Fellow, Institute of Sales and Marketing Management, UK, 1998; Fellow, The Marketing Society, UK, 2002. Address: M and E House, Block H, First Floor, Sundown Court, Triq ir-Russett, Kappara, SGN 08, Malta. E-mail: maxjellul@yahoo.co.uk

ELMAS Melek Bar, b. 30 January 1960, Izmir, Turkey. Computer Sciences Engineer. m. Ali Elmas 1 son, 1 daughter. Education: Computer Sciences Department, Faculty of Engineering, Hacettepe University, 1977-82. Appointments: Project Manager, Finance Sector, KOC-System AS, 1982-85; Regional Manager, Marmara Region, Biltek Company, 1985-87; Vice-President responsible for software development, Biltim AS, 1987-90; Freelance Consultant in Information Technology, 1990-92; Executive Vice-President responsible for marketing, Mardata AS, 1992-94; Main Shareholder, Founder and Chief Executive Officer, Merlin AS, 1994-. Publications include: New Generation Technologies in Finance, 1996; Future of IT/IS, 1998; Life is Beautiful: A series of articles published in Netyorum, 2000; Lost Money in Typing, 2003. Honours: United Nations Portrait Gallery of Excellent Women Entrepreneurs, 2000; Best Entrepreneur Woman of the year, Ekonomist Magazine, 2001; Best Entrepreneur Woman of IT Sector, Dunya Daily, 2001; Best Software Project of the Year, Interpro Research, 2002. Memberships: Informatics Association of Turkey; Turkish Information Technology Services Association; Association of Software Industrialists; Woman Entrepreneurs Association. Address: Badem 11 Villa 8, Bahcesehir, 34538 Istanbul, Turkey. E-mail: melek.bar.elmas@merlin.com.tr

ELS Ernie, b. 17 October 1969, Johannesburg, South Africa. Professional Golfer. m. Leizl Els, 1 son, 1 daughter. Career: Professional, 1989-; Winner, US Open, 1994, 1997; Toyota World Matchplay Championships, 1994, 1995, 1996; South Africa PGA Championship, 1995; Byron Nelson Classic, 1995; Buick Classic, 1996, 1997; Johnny Walker Classic, 1997; Bay Hill Invitational, 1998; Nissan Open, 1999; Int presented by Quest 2000; Standard Life Loch Lomond, 2000; Open Championship, 2002; Genuity Championship, 2002; British Open, 2002; Fourth World Match Play title, 2002; Member, Dunhill Cup Team, 1992-2000; World Cup Team, 1992, 1993, 1996, 1997, 2001; Member, President's Cup, 1996, 1998, 2000; Founder, Ernie Els Foundation to help disadvantaged children, 1999. Honour: South African Sportsman of Year, 1995. Address: 46 Chapman Road, Klippoortjie 1401, South Africa.

ELSBERG John William, b. 4 August 1945, New York, New York, USA. Publications Manager. Poet. m. Constance Waeber, 17 June 1967, 1 son. Education: BA, Columbia College, 1967; MA, University of Cambridge, England, 1973. Appointments: Editor in Chief, US Army Centre of Military History; Adjunct Professor, University of Maryland; Lecturer, Northern Virginia Community College; Editor, Bogg Magazine, 1980-; Fiction Editor, Gargoyle Magazine, 1977-80. Publications: Cornwall and Other Poems, 1972; Poems by Lyn Lifshin and John Elsberg, 1979; The Price of Reindeer, 1979; Walking as a Controlled Fall, 1980; Home-style Cooking on Third Avenue, 1982; Limey and the Yank, 1982; Torn Nylon Comes with the Night, 1987; 10 or Less, 1989; The Affair, 1991; Father Poems, 1993; 2nd edition, 1994; Offsets, 1994; 2nd edition, 1998; The Randomness of E, 1995; Family Values, 1996; Broken Poems for Evita, 1997; A Week in the Lake District, 1998; Small Exchange, 1999; Sailor, 1999, 2nd edition, 2002; South Jersey Shore, 2004. Contributions to: Poetry Now; Gargoyle; Tribune; Orbis; Cambridge Review; Maryland Poetry Review; Amelia; Real Poetry; New Hope International; Outposts; Hanging Loose; Lost and Found Times; Printed Matter; Wind; Tight; Atom Mind; Beltway; Modern Haiku; American Tanka; New Orleans Review; Score; Artemis; RawNervz; Membrane; Blue Unicorn. Memberships: Fellow, Virginia Centre for the Creative Arts; Writers' Centre, Bethesda, Maryland; Poets and Writers; Washington Poetry Committee; Poetry Society of America. Address: 422 North Cleveland Street, Arlington, VA 22201, USA.

ELSTON Wolfgang E, b. 13 August 1928, Berlin, Germany. Geologist; Professor. m. Lorraine, deceased, 27 July 2000, 2 sons. Education: BS, cum laude, City College of New York, 1949; MA, Columbia University, 1953; PhD, 1953. Appointments: Assistant Professor, Texas Technological University, 1955-57; Assistant Professor, Professor, University of New Mexico, 1957-92; Senior Research Professor, 1992-, Co-ordinator, University of New Mexico-Los Alamos National Laboratory Volcanology Programme, 1992-2000. Publications: Hundreds of titles on volcanology, planetology, economic geology. Honours: Visiting Research Fellow, Royal Society, UK; Foundation Visitor, University of Auckland, New Zealand; Fellow, Geological Society of America; Exchange Scientist, National Science Foundation, University of Queensland; Honorary Life Member, New Mexico Geological Society. Memberships: American Geophysical Union; Geological Society of America; Society of Economic Geologists; American Association of Petroleum Geologists; Meteoritical Society. Address: Department of Earth and Planetary Sciences, University of New Mexico, Albuquerque, NM 87131-1116, USA.

ELSUNNI Mohamed Eltayeb, b. 15 April 1950, Wadmedani, Sudan. Electrical Engineer. m. Hanan Alfadil Alnour Shamseldin. Education: MSc, Belyorussian University, Minsk, 1978; MSc, Strathclyde University, Glasgow, Scotland, 1982. Appointments:

Dictionary of International Biography

Chartered Engineer, Assistant Engineer, Ministry of Irrigation, Wadmedani, 1978-80; Engineer, 1980-83, Chief Engineer, 1983-85, Research Engineer, 1985-89, Section Engineer, 1989-99, Senior Engineer, 1999- Central Region, Saudi Consol Electric Co, Alkarj, Saudi Arabia. Honours: Listed in Who's Who publications and biographical dictionaries. Memberships: Secretary General, Engineering Syndicate, Wadmedany, 1982-86, President, 1987-89; Secretary General, Dem Allica, Wadmedani, 1985-89; IEE; Institute of Engineering, Australia; Institute of Electrical Engineers, UK; New York Academy of Sciences. Address: PO Box 75, Alkharj 11942, Saudi Arabia.

ELTIS Walter (Alfred), b. 23 May 1933, Warnsdorf, Czechoslovakia. Economist. m. Shelagh Mary Owen, 5 September 1959, 1 son, 2 daughters. Education: Emmanuel College, Cambridge; BA, Cambridge University; MA, Nuffield College, 1960; DLitt, Oxford University, 1990. Appointments: Fellow, Tutor, Economics, 1963-88, Emeritus Fellow, 1988-, Exeter College, Oxford; Director General, National Economic Development Office, London, 1988-92; Chief Economic Adviser to the President of the Board of Trade, 1992-95; Visiting Professor, 1992-, University of Reading. Publications: Growth and Distribution, 1973; Britain's Economic Problem: Too Few Producers (with Robert Bacon), 1976; The Classical Theory of Economic Growth, 1984 (2nd Edition, Palgrave 2000); Keynes and Economic Policy (with Peter Sinclair), 1988; Classical Economics, Public Expenditure and Growth, 1993; Britain's Economic Problem Revisited, 1996; Condillac, Commerce and Government (editor, with Shelagh M Eltis); Britain, Europe and EMU, 2000. Contributions to: Economic journals and bank reviews. Memberships: Reform Club, chairman, 1994-95; Royal Automobile Club; Political Economy Club; Vice President, European Society for the History of Economic Thought, 2000-04. Address: Danesway, Jarn Way, Boars Hill, Oxford OX1 5JF, England.

ELTON Ben(jamin Charles), b. 3 May 1959, England. Writer; Comedian. m. Sophie Gare, 1 son, 1 daughter. Education: BA, Drama, University of Manchester. Appointments: Writer, TV series and for British Comedians; Stand-up Comedian: Tours, 1986, 1987, 1989, 1993, 1996, 1997; Host, Friday Night Live, TV Comedy Showcase, 1986-88; Co-writer, Presenter, South of Watford (documentary tv series), 1982; Writer/Director, Inconceivable, film, 2000. Publications: Bachelor Boys, 1984; Stark, 1989; Gridlock, 1991; This Other Eden, 1993; Popcorn, 1996; Blast from the Past, 1998; Inconceivable, 1999; Dead Famous, 2001; Plays: Gasping, 1990; Silly Cow, 1991; Popcorn, 1996; Blast from the Past, 1998; The Beautiful Game, musical, book and lyrics, 2000; Maybe Baby, writer/director, feature film, 2000; High Society, 2002; We Will Rock You, musical, 2002; Other: Recordings, The Young Ones, 1982; Happy Families, 1985; Blackadder, 1985, 1987, 1989; Filthy Rich and Catflap, 1986; Motormouth, 1987; Motovation (album), 1988; The Man From Auntie, 1990, 1994; The Very Best of Ben Elton Live, 1990; A Farties Guide to the Man From Auntie, 1990; Ben Elton Live, 1993; Stark, 1993; The Thin Blue Line (sitcom); 1995, 1996; Ben Elton Live, 1997; The Ben Elton Show, 1999. Honours: Best Comedy Show Awards, Brit Academy, 1984, 1987; Gold Dagger Award, 1996; TMA Award, 1997; Lawrence Olivier Award, 1998. Address: c/o Phil McIntyre, 2nd Floor, 35 Soho Square, London, W1D 3QX, England.

EMADI Mohammad Hossein, b. 22 May 1960, Shiraz, Iran. Agriculturist; System Analyst; Rural Development Strategist. m. Fatima, 2 sons, 1 daughter. Education: Diploma, 1978; BSc, Animal Sciences, Shiraz University, 1986; MSc, Agricultural Education, Tehran University, 1990; PhD, Systems Agricultural and Rural Development, UWS, Australia, 1995. Appointments: Executive Manager, Seed Company, 1988-90; Research Deputy, Rural Research Center, RRC, 1995-; Vice Minister, Ministry of Agriculture, 1997-. Publications: 5 books have been published; 32 articles. Honours: Best Selected PhD Thesis awards and Best Selected Research in Nomadic issues, 2004, Ministry of Culture, Iran. Memberships: IK, Representative of Iran; Member, of ODI; AGRECOL; Resource person for APO; FAO; AAEE; APEAN; Representative of CIRAN in Middle East. Address: P O Box 14155-6371, Tehran, Iran.

EMANUEL Elizabeth Florence, b. 5 July 1953, London, England. Fashion Designer. m. David Leslie Emanuel, 1975, separated 1990, 1 son, 1 daughter. Education: Harrow College of Art. Appointments: Opened London salon, 1978; Designer, wedding gown for HRH Princess of Wales, 1981; Costumes for Andrew Lloyd Webber's Song and dance, 1982; Sets and costumes for ballet, Frankenstein, The Modern Prometheus, Roy Opera House, London, La Scala Milan, 1985; Costumes for Stoll Moss production of Cinderella, 1985; Costumes for films: Diamond Skulls, 1990; The Changeling, 1995; Uniforms for Virgin Atlantic Airways, 1990; Britannia Airways, 1995; Launched international fashion label Elizabeth Emanuel, 1991; Launched Bridal Collection for Berkertex Brides UK Ltd, 1994; Launched bridal collection in Japan, 1994; Opened new shop and design studio, 1996; Launched own brand label (with Richard Thompson), 1999. Publications: Style for All Seasons (with David Emanuel), 1982. Address: 49 Dorset Street, London, W1H 3FH, England.

EMEL'YANOV Vladimir, b. 1 June 1943, Moscow, Russia. Physicist. Divorced, 2 daughters. Education: Graduate, Faculty of Physics, 1966, Diploma of Physicist, postgraduate study, Diploma of Candidate of Science (PhD), 1973, Diploma of Doctor of Science, 1988, Moscow State University. Appointments: Research Fellow, 1973-75, Assistant Professor, 1975-89, Full Professor, 1989-, Physics Faculty, Moscow State University. Publications: 300 articles; 3 monographs: Co-operative effects in Optics, 1988; Interaction of strong laser radiation with solids, 1990; Co-operative effects in Optics, Superradicurd and Phase Transitions, 1993. Honours: Prize Winner, International Publishing Company "Nauka", 1995; Lomonosov Prize Winner, highest award of Moscow State University, 1999; Listed in international biographical dictionary. Memberships: SPIE. Address: Physics Faculty, Moscow State University, 119899 Moscow, Russia. E-mail: emel@em.msk.ru

EMERY Alan E H, b. 21 August 1928, Manchester, England. Physician. m. Marcia Lynn Maler, 3 sons, 3 daughters. Education: University of Manchester, England; PhD, Johns Hopkins University, USA. Appointments: Reader, Medicine, Manchester University, 1964-68; Foundation Professor, Human Genetics, Edinburgh University, 1968-83; Research Professor and Fellow, Edinburgh University, 1983-90; Research Director, 1990-2000, Chief Scientific Adviser, 2000-, European Neuro-Muscular Centre; Visiting Professor, Peninsula Medical School, Exeter, 2002-. Publications: Around 300 medical science papers; 21 books. Honours: Various visiting professorships and named lectures; Honorary MD, University of Naples and University of Wurzburg; National Foundation USA, International Award; Gaetano Gold Medal; Honorary Membership or Fellowship: Dutch Society of Human Genetics; Association of British Neurologists; Royal Society of South Africa; Hon MD, Naples, Wurzburg; International Award for Genetic Research, USA; Gaetano Conte Prize for Clinical Research, 2000; Pro Finlandiae Gold Medal for contributions to Neuroscience, 2000; Lifetime Achievement Award, WFN, 2002. Memberships: FRCP; FRCPE; FLS; FRSE. Address: Peninsula Medical School, Department of Neurology, Royal Devon and Exeter Hospital, Exeter EX2 5DW, England.

Dictionary of International Biography

EMERY Robert Firestone, b. 18 January 1927, Kenton, Ohio, USA. Economist. m. Phyllis Eileen Swanson, 1 son, 2 daughters. Education: BA, Oberlin (Ohio) College, 1951; MA University of Michigan, 1952; PhD, University of Michigan, 1956. Appointments: Teaching Fellow, University of Michigan, 1954-55; Economist, Federal Reserve Board, Washington, 1955-92; Adjunct Professor of Economics, Southeastern University, 1960-88; Chairman, Department of Financial Administration, 1963-65; Dean, Senior Division, 1965-68; International Economic Consultant, 1992-. Publications: 5 books including: The Bond Markets of Developing East Asia, 1997; Korean Economic Reform, 2001. Honours: Horace H Rackham Graduate Fellow, University of Michigan, 1952-53; Fulbright Graduate Research Student, 1953-54; Listed in several biographical publications. Memberships: Society of Government Economists, 1976-; International Economists' Club, 1973-1992. Address: 3421 Shepherd Street, Chevy Chase, MD 20815, USA.

EMMERICH Roland, b. 10 November 1955, Stuttgart, Germany. Director; Screenplay Writer; Executive Producer. Education: Film School in Munich. Appointments: Producer (as student) The Noah's Ark Principle, shown at Berlin Film Festival (sold to over 20 countries), 1984; Founder, Centropolis Film Productions; Films: Making Moon 44; Universal Soldier; Stargate; Independence Day; The Thirteenth Floor (producer); The Patriot; TV series: The Visitor (producer), 1997. Address: c/o Creative Artists Agency, 9830 Wilshire Boulevard, Beverly Hills, CA 90212, USA.

EMMETT Nicholas, b. 22 July 1935, Dublin, Ireland. Writer; Translator. m. Anne Brit Emmett, 20 May 1965. Education: Philosophy course, Oslo University; Literature course, Galway University. Appointments: Taxi-Owner and Driver, 6 years; Interpreter-Translator, Indian Embassy, Oslo, Norway, 1973; Founding Co-Editor, Ragtime, English cultural magazine, Norway. Publications: The Cave, novel, 1987; The Red Mist and Other Stories, 1988; Brains on the Dump, short story, 1991. Contributions to: 84 short stories and articles in newspapers, anthologies and magazines, England, USA, Ireland, Norway; 23 stories broadcast on BBC and Irish National Radio. Honour: Writing Grant, Irish Arts Council. Memberships: Society of Authors; The Irish Writers Union. Address: Rathcoffey North, Donadea, Co Kildare, Ireland.

EMSBACH Michael, b. 26 March 1949, Braunschweig, Germany. Psychologist. m. Viola Emsbach. Education: PhD, 1979, Diploma, Psychologist, 1982, University of Hamburg; Graduate, Insurance Business Economist, Chamber of Commerce, Hanover, Germany, 1988. Appointments: Trainer, Allianz Insurance Co, Hamburg, 1983-86; Psychologist, Unternehmensgruppe Gauselmann, Espelkamp, Germany, 1986-88; Christliches Jugenddorfwerk, Hanover, Germany, 1989-92; Federal Traffic Authority, Flensburg, 1993-95; Lecturer, University of Flensburg, 1995-97; Psychologist, Federal Traffic Research Institute, Berg Gladbach, 1997-2001; University of Flensburg, 2001-. Publications: The Sophists' Enlightenment, 1980; Evaluation of a traffic safety campaign, 1998; Contribution of articles to professional journals including: Sozialpaedagogik; Journal for Gerontology and Geriatrics; Perspectives of Traffic Safety Training for Senior Citizens, 2001. Address: Rheinpromenade 42, 46446 Emmerich, Germany. E-mail: emsbach@uni-flensburg.de

EMSHOFF Rüdiger, b. 5 April 1960, Mühlheim/Ruhr, Germany. Surgeon. m. Iris Emshoff, 1 daughter. Education: MD, University of Düsseldorf, Germany, 1987; DMD, Medical School, Budapest, Hungary, 1990. Appointments: Resident, Department of Oral and Maxillofacial Surgery, 1991, Consultant, Department of Oral and Maxillofacial Surgery, 1998, Associate Professor of Surgery, 2001, University of Innsbruck, Austria. Publications: 69 international scientific papers. Honours: Listed in Who's Who publications and biographical dictionaries. Membership: American Academy of Oral and Maxillofacial Radiology. Address: Höhenstr 5, 6020 Innsbruck, Austria. E-mail: ruediger_emshoff@hotmail.com

ENACHESCU Constantin, b. 28 November 1938, Bucharest, Romania. University Professor. Education: Doctor of Medicine, Faculty of General Medicine, Bucharest, 1955-61; PhD, Philosophy and Psychology, Psychology Department, Faculty of Philosophy, University of Bucharest, 1967-71; Doctor in Medicine, specialisation on Psychiatry, Faculty of General Medicine, IMF, Bucharest, 1974; Doctor in Psychology, Faculty of Sociology, Psychology and Pedagogy, University of Bucharest, 1995. Appointments: Psychiatric Resident, 1961-66, Psychiatric Specialist, 1966-72, Primary Psychiatrist, 1972, Clinical Hospital Al. Obregia, Bucharest. Principal Research Fellow, Institute of Neurology and Psychiatry, Medical Academy of Bucharest, 1973-75; Senior Lecturer, 1995-, University Conferencer, 1999-, Professor, 2004, Special Psycho Pedagogy Department, Faculty of Psychology and Sciences of Education, University of Bucharest. Publications: Books: Elements of Projective Psychology, 1973; The plastic expression of the personality, 1975; Psychology of the patoplastic activity, 1977; Neuropsychology, 1996, Socrates, 1994, Interior life experience and self knowledge. From Socrates to Freud, 1997; Treatise of Mental Hygiene, 1996; Treatise of Psychopathology, 2001; Treatise of Moral Psychology, 2002; Madness Phenomenology, 2003; Treatise of Psychoanalysis and Psychotherapy, 2003; Treatise of Psychosexology, 2003; Numerous articles in scientific journals. Memberships include: World Psychiatric Association; International Association for Suicide Prevention; British Association for Art Therapist, London; Union Medicale Balcanique; Societatii de Psihiatrie, Romania; Acosiatei Psihologilor, Romania. Address: University of Bucharest, Ap 29, etaj 5, Traian Street Nr 77-79, Sector 3, 742791 Bucharest, Romania. E-mail: vlade@fx.ro

ENDELEY Samuel Moka Liffafa, b. June 1923, Buea, S W Province, Cameroon. Jurist; Traditional Ruler. m. Gladys Silo Steane, 5 sons, 1 daughter. Education: Government Scholarship, Government College, Umuahia, Eastern Nigeria, 1940; First Grade pass, Cambridge School Certificate Examination, Presbyterian Church of Scotland's Hope Waddell Training Institute, 1940-45; Pharmaceutical Chemist and Druggist Diploma, Nigeria School of Pharmacy, Yaba, Lagos, 1946-50; Barrister-at-law Degree, Inns of Court School of Law, London, 1957-59. Appointments: Government Pharmacist, Colonial Nigerian Government, Lagos, Port Harcourt (Nigeria), Tiko, Bota, Victoria, Kumba (Cameroon), 1950-57; Called to the English Bar, 1960; Called to Nigerian Bar, 1960; Set up practice, Buea, Cameroon, 1960-; Judge, High Court of West Cameroon, President, Buea West Cameroon Bench of Federal Court of Justice, 1966; Appeals Judge of West Cameroons Supreme Court of Appeal, 1966-68; Judge of Full Bench of Federal Court of Justice, Yaounde, 1968; Appointed Member, Higher Judicial Council, 1969; Appointed Chief of Justice, Supreme Court of West Cameroon, 1970-72; Vice President, Supreme Court of the United Republic of Cameroon, 1972; President, Administrative Bench, Supreme Court of the United Republic of Cameroon, Member, Nigerian-Cameroon Joint Frontier Commissioner and Leader of the Cameroon's Technical Team in that Commission, 1973; Chairman, Cameroon Development Corporation, 1982. Honours: Knight, 1970, Officer, 1975, Knight Commander, 1983, Knight Grand Commander, 1991, Cameroon Grand Order of Valour. Memberships: Every Cameroons Law Harmonisation and Law Revision Commission, 1961-; International Commission of Juriste, World Association of Judges; Charter Member, World Peace through Law Centre; International Advisory Board, African Law Reports Editorial Committee, Oxford, England. Address: PO Box 3, Buea, S W Province, Cameroon Republic.

ENGDAHL Sylvia, b. 1933, Los Angeles, California, USA. Science Fiction Author. Education: BA, University of California at Santa Barbara, 1955; Graduate work, Portland State University, 1956-57 and 1978-80. Appointments: Teacher, elementary school, 1955-56; Computer Programmer, 1957-67; Freelance Writer, 1968-81; Part-time online teacher, 1985-97. Publications: Young Adult science fiction novels: Enchantress from the Stars, 1970, new edition 2001; Journey Between Worlds, 1970; The Far Side of Evil, 1971, new edition 2003; This Star Shall Abide, 1972 (published in UK as Heritage of the Star); Beyond the Tomorrow Mountains, 1973; Universe Ahead: Stories of the Future (anthology), 1975; Anywhere, Anywhen: Stories of Tomorrow (anthology), 1976; The Doors of the Universe, 1981; Young Adult non-fiction: The Planet-Girded Suns: Man's View of Other Solar Systems, 1974; The Subnuclear Zoo: New Discoveries in High Energy Physics, (with Rick Roberson) 1977; Tool for Tomorrow: New Knowledge About Genes, (with Rick Roberson) 1979; Picture Book, for young children: Our World is Earth, 1979; Adult science fiction trilogy: Children of the Star (reprint of This Star Shall Abide, Beyond the Tomorrow Mountains and The Doors of the Universe), 2000. Honours: Newbery Honour Award, for Enchantress from the Stars, 1971; Christopher Award, for This Star Shall Abide, 1973; Phoenix Award of the Children's Literature Association, for Enchantress from the Stars, 1990. Address: Eugene, Oregon, USA. E-mail: sle@sylviaengdahl.com Website: www.sylviaengdahl.com

ENGEL Juergen Kurt, b. 31 August 1945, Gerbitz, Germany. Chemist; Researcher. m. Rita Busset, 1 son, 1 daughter. Education: Diploma, Engineering, Naturwissenschaft-Technishe Akademie, Isny, Germany, 1969; Diploma, Chemistry, Technische Universität, Braunschweig, Germany, 1972; Diploma, Natural Sciences, 1975; Habilitation, Pharmacy, Universität Regensburg, Regensburg, Germany, 1985. Appointments: Laboratory Leader, Pharmaceutical Division, 1976-1980, Head Research Co-ordination, 1980-87, Head Medicinal Chemistry Synthesis, 1982-87, Degussa AG, Frankfurt, Germany; Head Chemical and Pharmaceutical Research and Development, 1987-93, Head, Research and Development, 1993-2000, ASTA Medica AG, Frankfurt, Germany; Chief Executive Officer, Zentaris AG, Frankfurt, Germany, 2001-; COO Aeterna, 2003-; Professor, School of Pharmacy Universität Regensburg, 1990-; Professor, Technical University, Dresden, 1993-. Publications: Memofix Pharmazie, 1995; Pharmaceutical Substances, 2000; Editor: Arzneimittel, 1987; Memofax, 2001; Contributor of numerous articles to professional journals; Chapters to books; Patentee in field. Honours: Recipient Galileo Galilei Silver Medal, 5th International Symposium on Platinum and Other Substances, Padua, Italy; Galenus-von-Pergamon Award, 1995. Memberships: German Chemical Society, Chairman Board of Directors, Medicinal Chemistry Section; German Pharmaceutical Society; International Society for Heterocyclic Chemistry; German Society for Biochemistry and Molecular Biology, Advisory Board. Address: Zentaris GmbH, Weismuellerstrasse 45, 60314 Frankfurt, Germany. E-mail: juergen.engel@zentaris.de

ENGELS Deen, (Bert Fermin), b. 7 December 1926, Indonesia. Retired Teacher; Poet. m. Cili van Neer, 1 March 1958, 1 son, 4 daughters. Education: Diploma Teachers Training, Heerlen, 1957; Diploma Teachers Training Special Education, Tilburg, 1961. Appointments: Schools for Retarded Children, 1958-64; Gipsy Children's School, 1964-66; School for Children with Difficulties in Learning and Education, Maastricht, 1966-68; School for Children with Difficulties in Hearing and Speech, Hoensbroek, 1968-90. Publications: Poems by Ulrich Bouchard and Deen Engels, 1980; Don't Blow, 1981; Kicking Occiput, 1983; Together in the Holes, 1986; Menu for Surviving, 1987; The Tricks of the Death, 1988; The Snares of Existence, 1989; Abiding in the Fridge,

1991; The Flowers Shark, 1992; Whitehaven, 1994; Vehicles, 2000; Cosmetics, 2000; Steel Bridge, 2004. Contributions to: Appel; Gist; Concept; Vlam; WeL; In zekere zin; Horizon; Schreef; Vlaanderen; Nieuw Vlaams Tijdschrift-Gierik; International Poetry. Honours: Poetry Prize, Sint-Truiden, 1979; Secundo Precio en la Categoria Prosa y Poesia, Consulado de Costa Rica, The Hague, 1990. Membership: Vereniging van Limburgse Auteurs. Address: Mauritslaan 1, 6371 ED Landgraaf, Netherlands.

ENGLAND Gerald, b. 21 December 1946, Ackworth, England. Retired Financial Advisor; Poet; Editor; Webmaster. m. Christine Ann Smedley, 22 June 1974, 2 sons. Education: Strathclyde University, 1964-66; Leeds College of Technology, 1967-68; HNC Chemistry, Sheffield Polytechnic, 1969-71; Open University, 1973-74. Appointments: Technician, Sheffield University, 1969-74; Editor, Headland, 1969-79, New Hope International, 1980-; Aabye, 1998-2002; Agent, Britannic Assurance, 1974-98. Publications: Poetic Sequence for Five Voices, 1966; Mousings, 1970; The Wine, the Women and the Song, 1972; For Her Volume One, 1972; Meetings at the Moors Edge, 1976; The Rainbow, 1980; Daddycation, 1982; Futures, (with Christine England), 1986; Stealing Kisses, 1992; Limbo Time, 1998. Contributions to: Bogg; Brussel Sprout; Candelabrum; Crooked Roads; Envoi; Folio; Green's Magazine; Haiku Quarterly; Hybrid; Inkshed; International Journal on World Peace; Krax; Legend; Lo Straniero; Moorlands Review; New Wave; Owen Wister Review; Pennine Ink; Periaktos; Pididdle; Prophetic Voices; Radio Void; Verve; Waterways; Wormwood Review; Z Miscellaneous. Memberships: Yorkshire Dialect Society, Council Member; Pennine Poets; Wordwizards; Ukku; Paradoxist Movement; International Writers and Authors Association. Address: 20 Werneth Avenue, Gee Cross, Hyde, Cheshire SK14 5NL, England.

ENGLISH Robert G, b. 12 August 1945, Portland, Oregon, USA. Poet. Education: Adams State College, Alamosa, Colorado, 1964-65; Lake Region Jr College, Devils Lake, North Dakota, 1965-66; New Mexico State Community College, Alamogordo, 1966-68. Appointments: Army, rank E5, 1968-71; Material Clerk, US West Communications; Gallery Co-ordinator, Sam English Studio Gallery, 1981-97; Writer; Owner and Director, national poetry contest, Poetry in Print. Publications: Poetry appears in numerous anthologies in National Library of Poets including: Great Poems of Our Time; The Space Between; Whispers in the Wind; Treasured Poems of America, 1995; Best Poems of 1995; A Moment in Time; Between the Raindrops; Treasured Poems of America, 1996; Beyond the Stars; Best Poems of 1996; A Voyage to Remember; The Best Poems of the '90s; Author: Only Yours!; Susanna My Rose; Poetical Jest – My Gestful World; The Dream Catcher; Cytherea; Poetry in Print; Portraits in Poetry. Honours: World of Poetry Recipient, Editor's Choice Award, 1991; Editor's Choice Award, National Library of Poets, 1993-96; International Poetry Hall of Fame; Semi-Finalist, International Society of Poets, 1995, 1996; Wall of Tolerance, National Campaign for Tolerance; Listed in national and international biographical dictionaries; Honor of Dignity, ABI, 2002; American Hall of Fame, ABI; World Lifetime Achievement Award, ABI. Memberships: World of Poetry; International Society of Poets. Address: Poetry in Print, PO Box 30981, Albuquerque, NM 87190, USA.

ENIKEYEV Damir, b. 1 January 1939, Ufa, Russia. Physician. 1 daughter. Education: Undergraduate, MD, 1957-63; Postgraduate, PhD, 1963-66, Doctor of Medical Sciences Bashkir State Medical University, Ufa, Russia. Appointments: Assistant Professor, 1966, Professor of Pathophysiology, 1988-, currently Head of Chair of Pathophysiology, Bashkir State Medical University. Publications: More than 400 publications on various aspects of pathophysiology include: 12 monographs, 2 textbooks for medical students, 22 educational supplies; Major publications include: Iridoplasty, 1996; Interaction of immunisation and reanimation, 1997; Local allergic conditions and reanimation, 1999; Helicobacterial gastritis in children, 2001. Honours: Honorary Degrees: USSR Inventor, 1985; Honorary Scientist of Bashkiria, 1993; Knight of Science and Arts, 2000; Professor, Honorary Scientist, Republic of Bashkortostan; Scientific awards: Diploma of Vereinigung; Diploma, Europaische Akademie der Naturwissenschaften; Pavlov Silver Medal, 1998; Popov Silver Medal, 1999; Medal for contribution to the development of science and economics, Russian Academy of Natural Sciences, 1999; Tretyakov Silver Medal, 1999; Russian Academy of Natural Sciences Silver Memorial Medal, 2003; Mechnikov Silver Medal, 2003; Kapitsa Silver Medal, 2003; Listed in Who's Who publications and biographical dictionaries. Memberships: International Pathophysiology Society; All-Russian Society of Pathophysiologists; Chairman, Bashkir Republican Regional Society of Pathophysiologists; Ecopathology Society; Committees, Extreme and Therminal States, Scientific Bases of Reanimatology; Member of the Editorial Boards: Pathological Physiology and Experimental Therapy; Clinical Medicine and Pathophysiology; Academician: International Higher Education Academy of Sciences; Russian Academy of Natural Sciences; International Academy of Authors of Scientific Discoveries and Inventions. Address: 9a K. Marks str, Flat 5, Ufa, Russia.

ENKHSAIKHAN Mendsaikhan, b. 4 June 1955, Ulaanbaatar, Mongolia. Economist. m. Shurentsetseg, 1 son, 1 daughter. Education: Bachelor's Degree, Master's Degree, Economics, Kiev State University, Ukraine, USSR, 1973-78; PhD, Economics, Academy of Science, Moscow, USSR, 1984-87. Appointments: Economist, Researcher, Deputy Chief of the Department, Ministry of Foreign Affairs, 1978-88; Specialist, Ministry of Economic Foreign Relations and Supply, 1988-89; Director, Market Research Institute, 1989-90; Member of Peoples Great Khural and Chairman, Standing Committee of the Parliament (State Small Khural), 1990-92; Member of Parliament (State Great Khural), 1992-93; Chairman of the Presidential Office, 1993-96; Prime Minister of Mongolia, 1996-98; Chief Executive Officer of Premier International, LLC, Chief Editor, Mongol Times Newspaper, Member National Consultative Committee and Advisory Council of Democratic Party, 1998-2003; Leader, Democratic Party, 2003-. Publications include: Philosophy of Freedom; Modern Political Parties. Honours: Order of Freedom, Democratic Union, Mongolia. Membership: Democratic Party, Mongolia. Address: Democratic Central Office, Sukhbaatar Square 9-8, Ulaanbaatar 13, Mongolia (Central Post Office, Box #1085, Ulaanbaatar, Mongolia). E-mail: enkhsaikhan@magicnet.mn Website: www.demparty.mn

ENRIGHT D(ennis) J(oseph), b. 11 March 1920, Leamington, Warwickshire, England. Writer; Poet; Editor. m. Madeleine Harders, 3 November 1949, 1 daughter. Education: BA, Honours, 1944, MA, 1946, Downing College, Cambridge; DLitt, University of Alexandria, Egypt, 1949. Appointments: Professor of English, Far East, 1947-70; Co-Editor, Encounter, 1970-72; Director, Chatto and Windus Publishers, 1974-82. Publications: The Laughing Hyena and Other Poems, 1953; Academic Year, 1955; Bread Rather Than Blossoms, 1956; Some Men are Brothers, 1960; Selected Poems, 1969; Memoirs of a Mendicant Professor, 1969; Daughters of Earth, 1972; The Terrible Shears: Scenes From a Twenties Childhood, 1974; Sad Ires and Others, 1975; Paradise Illustrated, 1978; A Faust Book, 1979; The Oxford Book of Death (editor), 1983; A Mania for Sentences, 1983; The Alluring Problem, 1986; Collected Poems, 1987; Fields of Vision, 1988; The Faber Book of Fevers and Frets (editor), 1989; Selected Poems, 1990; Under the Circumstances, 1991; The Oxford Book of Friendship (editor with David Rawlinson), 1991; The Way of

the Cat, 1992; Old Men and Comets, 1993; The Oxford Book of the Supernatural (editor), 1994; Interplay: A Kind of Commonplace Book, 1995; The Sayings of Goethe (editor), 1996; Collected Poems 1948-1998, 1998; Play Resumed: A Journal, 1999; Signs and Wonders: Selected essays, 2001. Contributions to: Journals, reviews, and magazines. Honours: Cholmondeley Award, 1974; Queen's Gold Medal for Poetry, 1981; Honorary Doctorates, University of Warwick, 1982, University of Surrey, 1985; Officer of the Order of the British Empire, 1991; Companion of Literature, 1998. Membership: Royal Society of Literature, Fellow. Literary Agent: Watson Little Limited, Capo di Monte, Windmill Hill, London NW3 6RJ, England. Address: 35A Viewfield Road, London SW18 5JD, England.

ENYA (Eithne Ni Bhraonain), b. 17 May 1961, Gweedore, County Donegal, Ireland. Singer; Musician (piano, keyboards); Composer. Musical Education: Classical piano; Career: Member, folk group Clannad, 1980-82; Solo artiste, 1988-; 25 million albums sold to date. Compositions: Music for film and television scores: The Frog Prince, 1985; The Celts, BBC, 1987; LA Story, 1990; Green Card, 1990. Recordings: Albums: with Clannad: Crann Ull, 1980; Fuaim, 1982; Solo albums: Watermark, 1988; Shepherd's Moon, 1991; Enya, 1992; The Celts (reissued), 1992; The Book Of Trees, 1996; On My Way Home, 1998; Storms in Africa, 1998; A Day Without Rain, 2000; Singles include: Orinoco Flow (Number 1, UK), 1988; Evening Falls, 1988; Oiche Chiun, 1988; Orinoco Flow, 1988; Storms In Africa (Part II), 1989; Caribbean Blue, 1991; How Can I Keep From Singing, 1991; Book Of Days, 1992; Anywhere Is, 1995; Only If, 1997; May It Be, 2001; Only Time, 2001; Wild Child, 2001. Honours: 3 Grammy Awards; 6 World Music Awards including Best Selling Artist in the World, 2001. Address: 'Manderley', Victoria Road, Killiney, County Dublin, Ireland.

EPHRON Nora, b. 19 May 1941, New York, USA. Author; Scriptwriter. Education: BA, Wellesley College. m. (1) Dan Greenberg, (2) Carl Bernstein, 2 sons, (3) Nicholas Pileggi. Appointments: Reporter, New York Post, 1963-68; Freelance Writer, 1968-; Contributing Editor, New York Magazine, 1973-74; Film appearances: Crimes and Misdemeanours; Husband and Wives. Publications: Wallflower at the Orgy, 1970; Crazy Salad, 1975; Scribble, Scribble, 1978; Heartburn, 1983; Nora Ephron Collected, 1991; Screenplays: Silkwood (with Alice Arlen), 1983; Heartburn, 1986; When Harry Met Sally..., 1989; Cookie (co-executive producer, co-screenwriter with Delia Ephron); Sleepless in Seattle (also director), 1993; Mixed Nuts (also director); Michael (also director), 1996; You've Got Mail (also director), 1998; Red tails in Love: a Wildlife Drama in Central park (also producer and director), 2000; Hanging Up (also producer), 2000. Address: c/o Sam Cohm International Creative Management, 40 West 57th Street, New York, NY 10019, USA.

EPPSTEIN Ury, b. 3 February 1925, Saarbrücken, Germany. Musicologist. m. Kikue Iguchi, 2 sons. Education: MA, Hebrew University of Jerusalem, 1949; Diploma in Japanese Language, Tokyo University of Foreign Studies, 1959; Diploma in Japanese Music, Tokyo University of Fine Arts and Music, 1963; PhD, Tel Aviv University, 1984. Appointments: Academic Assistant, Music Research Centre, Hebrew University, 1966-1972; Lecturer, Musicology and Theatre Departments, Tel Aviv University, 1972-1977; Lecturer, Departments of Musicology, Theatre, East Asian St, Hebrew University, 1972-; Guest Lecturer, Copenhagen University; East Asian Institute and Musicology Department, Lund University, 1986; Guest Lecturer, Dokkyō University, Japan; Tokyo University of Fine Arts and Music, 1997. Publications: Kanjinchō, translation of Kabuki play from Japanese, 1993; The Beginnings of Western Music in Meiji Era Japan, 1994; Musical Means to

Dictionary of International Biography

Political Ends - Japanese School Songs in Manchuria, 1996; Governmental Policy and Controversy - The Beginnings of Western Music in Japan, 1998. Honours: Order of the Rising Sun conferred by the Emperor of Japan, 1989; Israel Ministry of Education and Culture Prize for translation of Kabuki drama from Japanese. Memberships: European Association for Japanese Studies, Israel Musicological Society. Address: 80 Tchernihovsky St, Jerusalem, Israel.

EPSTEIN (Michael) Anthony (Sir), b. 18 May 1921, London, England. Medical Scientist; University Teacher. 2 sons, 1 daughter. Education: Trinity College, Cambridge; Middlesex Hospital Medical School, London. Appointments: House Surgeon, Middlesex Hospital, London and Addenbrooke's Hospital, Cambridge, 1944; Lieutenant and Captain, Royal Army Medical Corps, 1945-47; Assistant Pathologist, Middlesex Hospital Medical School, 1948-65; Berkeley Travelling Fellow, 1952-53; French Government Scholar, Institut Pasteur, Paris, 1952-53; Visiting Investigator, Rockefeller Institute, New York, 1956; Honorary Consultant Virologist, Middlesex Hospital, 1965-68; Reader in Experimental Pathology, Middlesex Hospital Medical School, 1965-68; Honorary Consultant Pathologist, Bristol Hospitals, 1968-82; Professor of Pathology, 1968-85, Head of Department, 1968-82, University of Bristol; Emeritus Professor of Pathology, University of Bristol and Fellow, Wolfson College, Oxford, 1986-. Publications: Over 240 original contributions to major scientific journals; Joint Founder Editor, International Review of Experimental Pathology, volumes 1-28, 1962-86; Joint Editor, 5 scientific books including The Epstein-Barr Virus 1979; The Epstein-Barr Virus: Recent Advances, 1986; Oncogenic γ-herpesviruses: An Expanding Family, 2001. Honours include: Paul Ehrlich and Ludwig Darmstaedter Prize and Medal, West Germany, 1973; Fellow, Royal Society, 1979; Honorary Professor, Sun Yat Sen University, China, 1981; Bristol Myers Award for Cancer Research, USA, 1982; Honorary Fellow, Queensland Institute of Medical Research, 1983; CBE, 1985; Prix Grifuel, France, 1986; Honorary Fellow, Royal College of Physicians of London, 1986; Extraordinary Governing Body Fellow, Wolfson College, Oxford, 1986-2001; Honorary MD, University of Edinburgh, 1986; Honorary Professor, Chinese Academy of Preventive Medicine, 1988; Gairdner International Award, Canada, 1988; Honorary Fellow, Royal Medical Society of Edinburgh, 1988; Member, Academia Europea, 1988; Honorary Fellow, Royal Society of Edinburgh, 1991; Knight Bachelor, 1991; Royal Medal, The Royal Society of London, 1992; Fellow, University College London, 1992; Honorary Fellow, Royal College of Pathologists of Australasia, 1995; Honorary DSc, University of Birmingham, 1996; Honorary MD, Charles University of Prague, 1998; Founder Fellow, Academy of Medical Sciences, 1998; Honorary Fellow, Wolfson College Oxford, 2001. Address: Nuffield Department of Clinical Medicine, University of Oxford, John Radcliffe Hospital, Oxford, OX3 9DU, England.

ERBOVA Karla, b. 30 April 1933, Plzen, Czech Republic. Assistant to Manager. m. Milos Halouska, 1 son, 1 daughter. Education: Studies for Graduate Assistant of Manager, State Institute for Stenography, 1974-76. Publications: Books - Poem Collections: Neklid (The Discomposure), 1966; Komu mé kosti (For Whom My Bones), 1991; Via Dolorosa, 1992; Vzdyt milujes svou lásku ke mne (But You Do Love Your Love to Me), 1993; Iokasty, Glauké, Klytaimestry, 1994; Obrazy obrazu (Pictures of Pictures), 1995; Armor, 1995; Námesti zázraku (Square of Miracles), 1996; Mukán, 1997; Terra cota, 1998; Krajina s osamelym jezdcem, 1999; Osloveni (Apostrophe, with Jiri Posledni, graphic artist), 1999; Zivly (Elements, with Jiri Posledni, graphic artist), 1999; Plzni (Plzen, with Miroslav Triska, graphic artist), 2001; Liánový most (The Slide Bridge), 2002; Již nikdy

nedovolím požáru (I Will Never Allow the Fire, in Czech and Polish), 2003; V básni se rozední (Sunrise in the Poem, in Czech and French), 2003. Honours: Zvlástní cena Rozhlasové zatvy za básnickou skladbu Jakub zápasi s andelem, (Prize of Czechoslovak Broadcasting Corporation for Poetry James Fights with Angel), 1987; Cena Mesta Plzne za Celozivotní Dílo, 1995; Prize of Town of Plzen for Lifetime's Work, 1995; Jan Zahradnícek Prize, Fund for Czech Poetry, Czechoslovak Culture Club, Los Angeles, USA; Bohumil Polan Prize for The Slide Bridge, 2003. Memberships: Commission of Writers, 1989-; Czech Centre on International PEN Club, 1996-; National Library Society, 1995, Chairwoman, 1995-97. Address: Jasmímová 49, 106 00 Praha 10, Czech Republik.

ERIOMENKO Victor I, b. 17 January 1956, Kursk Region, Russia. Physiologist. m. Lyudmilla Eriomenko, 1 daughter. Education: Doctor of Science, Professor, Endocrinologist, Kursk Agricultural Institute, 1973-78. Appointments: Assistant, Associate Professor, Professor, Department of Biochemistry and Biological Technologies. Publications: More than 100 publications on biochemistry and physiology. Memberships: Council of Scholars, Kursk Agricultural Academy. Address: Dubrovinsky Str 1A, Apt 78, Kursk, Russia.

ERKINER Engin, b. 22 July 1950, Adana, Turkey. Writer. m. Yildiz Koremezli, 2 children, previous marriages. Education: BS, Chemistry, 1972, MS, Chemistry, 1974, Middle East Technical University, Ankara. Appointments: Chemist, Hacettepe Hospital, Ankara. Currently, Writer and Publisher. Publications: Books: Return of a Worker, short stories, 1985; Unbearable Freedom, short stories, 1986; End of the Road, novel, 1989; A Beautiful Death, novel, 1991; A Journey to Today, collection of articles, 1997; European Community and Turkey, 1998; Sub-Imperialism and Turkey, 2000; Home Occupations in Paris, 2001; Numerous articles in magazines and newspapers; Publisher and Editor, bimonthly magazine Yazin, 1985-. Memberships: German Writers Union; German Journalists Union. Address: Kasseler str 1a, 60486 Frankfurt, Germany. E-mail: erkiner@aol.com

ERMAKOV Voldemar, b. 9 November 1936, Magnitogorsk, Russia. Medical Doctor. m. Tatiana Ermakova, 1 son, 1 daughter. Education: MD, Medical School, Moscow; Candidate Medical Sciences, Gamaleia Institute of Epidemiology, Moscow, 1969; Medical Diplomate, Diplomat in Internal Medicine. Appointments: Research Officer, Institute Tropical Medicine, Moscow, 1960-62; Malariologist WHO, Dacca, East Pakistan, 1963-65; Director, The WHO International Training Course on epidemiology, WHO, Geneva, Moscow, Prague, Alexandria, 1969-81; Dean, Faculty of International Health, Central Institute of Advanced Medical Studies, Moscow, 1980-86; Director, The WHO Collaborating Center on Health Manpower Development, Moscow, 1980-86; Director, The WHO International Training Course for Public Health Administrators, Moscow, Geneva, 1980-86; Consultant, Primary Health Care, WHO, Kabul, Afghanistan, 1985; Regional Advisor in Health Manpower Development, WHO, Manila, 1986-92; Associate Professor, Chair of International Health, Russian Medical Academy of Postgraduate Studies, Moscow, 1993-99. Publications: International Quarantine, Moscow, 1982; Articles to professional journals and newspapers on the WHO and health care management. Membership: New York Academy of Sciences. Address: 31 Leningradskoe Shosse, Apt 26, 125212 Moscow, Russia.

ERSKINE Barbara, b. 10 August 1944, Nottingham, England. Writer. m. 2 sons. Education: MA Honours, Edinburgh University, 1967. Publications: Lady of Hay, 1986; Kingdom of Shadows, 1988; Encounters, 1990; Child of the Phoenix, 1992; Midnight is a Lonely Place, 1994; House of Echoes, 1996; Distant Voices, 1996; On the Edge of Darkness, 1998; Whispers in the Sand, 2000;

Dictionary of International Biography

Hiding from the Light, 2002; Sands of Time 2003. Contributions to: Numerous short stories to magazines and journals. Membership: Society of Authors; Scientific and Medical Network. Address: c/o Blake Friedmann, 122 Arlington Road, London, NW1 7HP.

ERTLER Klaus-Dieter, b. 20 November 1954, Feldbach, Austria. Professor. Education: MA, 1982; PhD, 1985; Habilitation, 1999. Appointments: Lecturer, University of Graz, Austria, 1982-2000; Visiting Professor, University of Heidelberg, Germany, 2000-02; Visiting Professor, University of Aachen, Germany, 2002-03; Visiting Professor, University of Kassel, Germany, 2003-04. Publications: Author, 6 books; Editor, 2 books; Articles in professional journals. Address: Institut fuer Romanistik, Universität Graz, Merangasse 70, A-8010 Graz, Austria.

ERZEN Jale Nejdet A, b. 12 January 1943, Ankara, Turkey. Painter; Art Historian; Critic. Education: BFA, MFA, Art Center College of Design, Los Angeles, 1974; PhD, Istanbul Technical University, 1980. Appointments: Professor Dr, Middle East Technical University, Ankara, Turkey, 1974-; Visiting Artist, Fulbright Fellow, Lawrence University, Wisconsin, USA, 1985-86; Part-time Instructor, Bilkent University, 1987-92; Visiting Professor, Bologna University, Italy, 1999. Publications: Sinan – An Aesthetic Analysis, 1997; Books on Turkish modern artists; Articles on Ottoman architecture, aesthetics, environmental aesthetics. Honours: Fulbright Fellowship, 1985; Chevalier dans les Arts et Lettres, French Ministry of Culture, 1990; American Research Institute in Turkey, 1976; Best Critic of the Year, Istanbul Art Fair, 2000. Memberships: International Association of Aesthetics; President, Turkish Association of Aesthetics; American Association of Aesthetics; Turkish Society of Philosophy; International Association of Artists; Paintings in private and national collections, Turkey, USA and Europe. Address: Faculty of Architecture, Middle East Technical University, Inönü Blvd, 06531 Ankara, Turkey. E-mail: erzen@arch.metu.edu.tr

ESAKI Leo, b. 12 March 1925, Osaka, Japan. Physicist. m. (1) Masako Araki, 1959, 1 son, 2 daughters, (2) Masako Kondo, 1986. Education: Graduated, University of Tokyo, 1947, PhD. Appointments: With Sony Corporation, 1956-60; IBM Fellow, 1967-92, IBM T J Watson Research Center, New York, 1960-92, Manager, Device Research, 1962-92, IBM Corporation, USA; Director, IBM Japan, 1976-92, Yamada Science Foundation, 1976-; President, University of Tsukuba, Ibaraki, Japan, 1992-98; Chair, Science and Technology Promotion Foundation of Ibaraki, 1998-; Director General, Tsukuba International Congress Center, 1999-; President, Shibaura Institute of Technology, 2000-. Publications: Numerous articles in professional journals. Honours: Nishina Memorial Award, 1959; Asahi Press Award, 1960; Toyo Rayon Foundation Award, 1961; Morris N Liebmann Memorial Prize, 1961; Stuart Ballantine Medal, Franklin Institute, 1961; Japan Academy Award, 1965; IBM Fellow, 1967; Joint Winner, Nobel Prize for Physics, 1973; Order of Culture, Japanese Government, 1974; Sir John Cass Senior Visiting Research Fellow, London Polytechnic, 1981; US-Asia Institute, Science Achievement Award, 1983; American Physical Society, Institute Prize for New Materials, 1985; IEEE Medal of Honour, 1991; Japan Prize, 1998; Grand Cordon Order of Rising Sun, First Class, 1998. Memberships: Japan Academy; American Philosophical Society; Max-Planck Gesellschaft; Foreign Associate, NAS; American National Academy of Engineering. Address: Shibaura Institute of Technology, 3-9-14 Shibaura, Minato-ku, Tokyo 108, Japan.

ESCOBAR Roberto B, b. 11 May 1926, Santiago, Chile. University Professor; Musician. m. Marta Cruchaga, 19 Mar 1950, 2 sons. Education: MA, Philosophy, Catholic University, Valparaiso; Conservatorio Nacional and Escuela Moderna de Musica, Santiago; Manhattan School of Music, New York. Career: Composer; Conductor, Chilean Modern Music Ensemble, 1973-78; Musicologist. Compositions: Over 60 works performed publicly, including: Laberinto, 1971, first performed in USA, 1976; Symphonia de Fluminis, 1987, 1st performance, USA, 1992; Sinfonia Andres Bello, 1992, 1st performance, Chile, 1993. Recordings: Preludios Franceses; Homenaje a Amengual; Talagante; Cuarteto Estructural, Cuarteto Funcional, Macul, La Granja, Elegia, Quinteto La Paloma. Publications: Catalogue of Chilean Music, 1969; Chilean Musicians and Their Music, 1971; Study in Black and White, 1973; Chilean Composers, 1997. Contributions to: Various journals. Honours: Goethe Prize for Composition, 1982; Honorary Professor, University of Missouri, 1989; Claudio Arrau Prize, Chile, 1993, Distinguished Professor (Life Appointment) U de Chile 1997. Memberships: President, Chilean Composers' Association, 1974-78; President, Sociedad Chilena de Filosofia, 1985-88. Address: PO Box 16360, Santiago 9, Chile.

ESCOBEDO Helen, b. 28 July 1934, Mexico City. Environmental Sculptor. m. Hans-Jürgen Rabe, 1 son, 1 daughter. Education: Diploma in Humanities, Universidad Motolinia, Mexico City, 1951; Three Year , Scholarship, Royal College of Art, Sculpture School, London, 1952; Diploma, ARCA, 1954. Appointments: Head, Fine Arts Department, 1961-74, Director, Museums and Galleries, 1974-78, Research Fellow, Department of Humanities, 1978-81, National University of Mexico, Mexico City; Technical Director, Museo Nacional (MUNAL), Mexico City, 1981-82; Director: Museo de Arte Moderno, Mexico City, 1982-84. Publications: Editor, Mexican Monuments: Strange Encounters, 1987; Only a Tree, illustrated poems, 1991; Co-author, Monumentos Mexicanos, 1993; Helen Escobedo Pasos en la Arena, by Graciela Schmilchuk, 2001. Honours: Competition Award for Sculpture, Nacional University of Mexico, 1976; Finalist, International Water Sculpture Competition, New Orleans World Fair, USA, 1980; Elected Associate Member, Academie Royal de Sciences, Lettres at Beaux Arts de Belgique, 1986; Guggenheim Fellowship, 1991; FONCA Fellowship, 1999; Elected Member of Board of Directors of ISC. Address: 1a Cda de San Jerónimo 19, San Jerónimo Lídice, Mexico, DF c.p. 10200, Mexico. E-mail: helenescobedo@yahoo.com Website: www.helen-escobedo.com

ESIK Olga, b. 7 April 1950, Szeged, Hungary. Physician. m. Lajos Trón, 1 daughter. Education: MD, Szent-Györgyi Albert Medical University, Szeged, 1974; PhD, 1989, DSc, 2000, Hungarian Academy of Sciences, Budapest, 2000. Appointments: Assistant, Kaposi Mór County Hospital, Department of Medicine, Kaposvár, 1975-79; Assistant, Department of Radiology, Szent-Györgyi Albert Medical University, 1979-90; Principal Assistant, Municipal Department of Oncoradiology, Uzsoki Hospital, Budapest, 1990-92; Deputy Department Head, National Institute of Oncology, Budapest, 1992-98; Associate Professor, Professor, Chair, Haynal Imre University of Health Sciences, Budapest, 1999-2001; Head of Section of Radiotherapy, Faculty of Medicine, Semmelweis University, 2001-2003; Professor and Chair, Department of Oncotherapy, University of Pécs. Publications: 134 Peer-reviewed scientific publications; 5 edited books/periodicals; 37 book chapters; 6 grants as project leader. Honours: Markusovszky Lajos Award, 1998 and 2002; Honorary Doctor, University of Kaposvár, 2002. Memberships: Curatorium of Hungarian PET Foundation, 1994-; Secretary, President, Hungarian Society for Radiation Oncology, 1992-2000; Board Member, Hungarian Society for Oncologists, 1995-; Board Member, European Society for Therapeutic Radiology and Oncology, 1998-2001; Hungarian College of Radiotherapy and Oncology, 2000-; President, National Board of Certification in Radiotherapy, 2000-. Address: Department of Oncotherapy, University of Pécs, Édesanyak Utja 17, H-7624, Budapest. E-mail: olga.esik@aok.pte.hu

Dictionary of International Biography

ESLER Gavin William James, b. 27 February 1953, Glasgow, Scotland. Broadcaster; Author. m. Patricia Warner, 1 son, 1 daughter. Education: BA, Honours, Kent; MA, Leeds; MA, Honoris Causa, Kent; Elected Fellow of Royal Society for the Arts, 2000. Appointments: BBC Television News and Radio Presenter; Columnist The Scotsman Newspaper. Publications: Novels: Loyalties, 1990; Deep Blue, 1992; The Blood Brother, 1995. Non-Fiction: The United States of Anger, 1997. Contributions to: Anthologies, journals, periodicals, quarterlies, newspapers and magazines. Address: c/o Curtis Brown, Haymarket House, London, England.

ESTEFAN Gloria (Fajado), b. 1 September 1957, Havana, Cuba. Singer; Songwriter. m. Emilio Estefan, 1 September 1978. Education: BA, Psychology, University of Miami, 1978. Career: Singer, backed by Miami Sound Machine, 1974-; Billed as Gloria Estefan, 1989-; Appearances include: Tokyo Music Festival, Japan, 1985; World tour, 1991; The Simple Truth, benefit concert for Kurdish refugees, Wembley, 1991; White House State Dinner, for President of Brazil, 1991; South American tour, 1992; Royal Variety Performance, London, before Prince and Princess of Wales, 1992; Co-organiser, benefit concert for victims of Hurricane Andrew, Florida, 1992; 45 million albums sold to date. Compositions include: Anything For You; Don't Wanna Lose You; Oye Mi Canto (co-written with Jorge Casas and Clay Ostwald); Cuts Both Ways; Coming Out Of The Dark (co-written with Emilio Estefan and Jon Secada); Always Tomorrow; Christmas Through Their Eyes (co-written with Dianne Warren). Recordings: Albums: Renacer, 1976; Eyes Of Innocence, 1984; Primitive Love, 1986; Let It Loose, 1988; Anything For You (Number 1, UK), 1989; Cuts Both Ways, 1989; Exitos De Gloria Estefan, 1990; Into The Light, 1991; Greatest Hits, 1992; Mi Tierra, 1993; Christmas Through Your Eyes, 1993; Hold Me, Thrill Me, Kiss Me, 1994; Abriendo Puertas, 1995; Destiny, 1996; Gloria!; Santo Santo, 1999; Alma Caribeño: Caribbean Soul, 2000; Also featured on: Jon Secada, Jon Secada (also co-producer), 1991; Til Their Eyes Shine (The Lullaby Album), 1992; Hit singles include: Dr Beat, 1984; Conga, 1986; Hot Summer Nights, used in film soundtrack Top Gun, 1986; Bad Boy, 1986; Words Get In The Way, 1986; Rhythm Is Gonna Get You, 1987; Can't Stay Away From You, 1988; Anything For You (Number 1, US), 1988; 1-2-3, 1988; Oye Mi Canto (Hear My Voice), 1989; Here We Are, 1989; Don't Wanna Lose You, 1989; Get On Your Feet, 1989; Coming Out Of The Dark (Number 1, US), 1991; Remember Me With Love, 1991; Always Tomorrow, 1992; Cuts Both Ways, 1993; Go Away, 1993; Mi Tierra, 1993; Turn the Beat Around, 1994; Abrienda Puertos; Tres Deseos; Mas Alla. Honours: Grand Prize, Tokyo Music Festival, 1985; Numerous Billboard awards, 1986-; American Music Award, Favourite Pop/Rock Duo or Group, 1989; Crystal Globe Award, 21 Club, New York, 1990; Latin Music Award, Crossover Artist Of Year, 1990; Humanitarian Award, B'Nai B'rith, 1992; Desi Entertainment Awards, Performer Of Year, Song Of Year, 1992; Humanitarian Award, National Music Foundation (for helping victims of Hurricane Andrew), 1993. Address: c/o Estefan Enterprises, 6205 Bird Road, Miami Beach, FL 33155, USA.

ESTEVEZ Emilio, b. 12 May 1962, New York, USA. Actor. m. Paula Abdul, 1992, divorced 1994, 1 son, 1 daughter. Appointments: Actor, films include: Tex, 1982; Nightmares, 1983; The Outsiders, 1983; The Breakfast Club, 1984; Repo Man, 1984; St Elmo's Fire, 1984; That Was Then...This is Now, 1985; Maximum Overdrive, 1986; Wisdom (also writer and director), 1986; Stakeout, 1987; Men at Work, 1989; Freejack, 1992; Loaded Weapon, 1993; Another Stakeout, 1993; Champions II, 1993; Judgement Night, 1993; D2: The Mighty Ducks, 1994; The Jerky Boys (co-executive, producer); Mighty Ducks 3; Mission Impossible, 1996; The War at Home, 1996; The Bang Bang Club,

1998; Killer's Head, 1999; Sand, 2000; Rated X, 2000; The LA Riot Spectacular, 2004. Address: c/o UTA, 5th Floor, 9560 Wilshire Boulevard, Beverly Hills, CA 90212, USA.

ETHERIDGE Melissa Lou, b. Leavenworth, Kansas, USA. Singer; Songwriter; Musician (guitar). Musical Education: Berklee College of Music, Boston. Career: Musician, Los Angeles bars, 5 years; Recording artiste, 1988-. Recordings: Albums: Melissa Etheridge, 1988; Brave And Crazy, 1989; Never Enough, 1992; Yes I Am, 1993; Your Little Secret, 1995; Breakdown, 1999; Singles: I'm the Only One, 1994; Come to My Window, 1994; If I Wanted To, 1995; Nowhere to Go, 1996; Angels Would Fall, 1999. Honours: Grammy Nomination, Bring Me Some Water, 1988. Current Management: Bill Leopold, W F Leopold Management, 4425 Riverside Drive, Ste 102, Burbank, CA 91505, USA.

ETLIN Richard Allan, b. 28 February 1947, New York City, New York, USA. Architectural Historian. m. Beatrice C Rehl, 2 sons. Education: BA cum laude, Certificate for Special Programme in European Civilization, 1969, MArch, 1972, PhD, 1978, Princeton University. Appointments: Assistant Professor, 1975-81, Co-Director, European Summer Program, College of Architecture, 1979, University of Kentucky; Guest Critic, Advisor, European Honors Programme in Rome, Rhode Island School of Design, 1980-81; Assistant Professor, 1975-81, Associate Professor, 1983-89, Professor, School of Architecture, 1989-, Distinguished University Professor, 2000-, Affiliate Professor, Department of Art History and Archaeology, 1996-, University of Maryland; Visiting Associate Professor, Department of Art History, Johns Hopkins University, 1987; Visiting Professor, Graduate School of Architecture, Columbia University, 1991; Director, Restoring Ancient Stabiae, School of Architecture, University of Maryland, 1998-2001; Director, Castellammare di Stabia Urban Revitalisation Project, School of Architecture, University of Maryland, 2001-2003; Vice President, Restoring Ancient Stabiae fondazione-onlus, 2002-03. Publications: Books: The Architecture of Death: The Transformation of the Cemetery in Eighteenth-Century Paris, 1984; Modernism in Italian Architecture, 1890-1940, 1991; Nationalism in the Visual Arts (editor), 1991; Frank Lloyd Wright and Le Corbusier: The Romantic Legacy, 1994; Symbolic Space: French Enlightenment Architecture and its Legacy, 1994; In Defense of Humanism: Value in the Arts and Letters, 1996; Art, Culture, and Media under the Third Reich (editor), 2002. Honours: Fulbright-Hays Predoctoral Fellowship, 1973-74, Postdoctoral Fellowship, 1980-81; National Endowment for the Arts Project Fellowship, 1979-80; Fellowship, American Academy in Rome, 1980-81; Guggenheim Fellowship, 1985-86; Most Outstanding Book in Architecture and Urban Planning in 1991, Association of American Publishers; Alice Davis Hitchcock Award, Society of Architectural Historians, 1993; International Book Award, American Institute of Architects, 1992, 1995; Paul Mellon Senior Fellow, Center for Advanced Study in the Visual Arts, National Gallery of Art, 1992-93; Wilson H Elkins Professor, University of Maryland Statewide System, 1997-98; National Endowment for the Humanities Fellowship, 1998-99; Member, Board of Senior Fellows in Landscape Architecture, Dumbarton Oaks-Harvard University, 1999-2005. Memberships: College Art Association; Society of Fellows of American Academy in Rome. Address: School of Architecture, University of Maryland, College Park, MD 20742-1411, USA. E-mail: retlin@umd.edu

ETO Shinkichi, b. 16 November 1923, Mukden, China. Educationist. m. Kazuko Ono, 1 son, 2 daughters. Education: BL, Law Faculty, University of Tokyo, Japan, 1948. Appointments: Associate Professor of International Relations, 1958, Professor, 1972, Professor Emeritus, 1987, University of Tokyo, Japan;

President, Asia University, 1987-95; Chancellor, Tokyo Eiwa Educational Institution, 1998-2002. Publications: My Thirty Three Years Dream: The Autobiography of Miyazaki Toten (translated from the Japanese with M B Jansen), 1982; China's Republican Revolution (editor with H Z Schiffrin), 1994. Honours; Purple Ribbon Medal, Japanese Government, 1991; Second Order of the Sacred Treasure, Emperor of Japan, 2001. Memberships: Director Emeritus, Japan Association of International Law; Director Emeritus, Japan Association of International Relations. Address: 4-46-9 Kugayama, Suginami-ku, Tokyo 168-0082, Japan.

ETTY Robert, b. 6 November 1949, Waltham, Lincolnshire, England. Schoolteacher; Poet. m. Anne Levison, 3 April 1975, 1 son, 1 daughter. Education: BA. Publications: Hovendens Violets, 1989; New Pastorals, 1992; Marking Places, 1994; A Selection, 1997; Small Affairs on the Estate, 2000; The Blue Box, 2001. Contributions to: Poetry Review; The North; Spectator; Outposts; Rialto; Staple; Stand; Verse; The Independent. Honours: Lake Aske Award, Nottingham Poetry Society, 1990; 1st Prize, Wykeham Poetry Competition, 1991; 1st Prize, Kent and Sussex Open Poetry Competition, 1992; Other awards, 1989-01. Address: Evenlode, Church Lane, Keddington, Louth, Lincolnshire LN11 7HG, England.

EUBANK Chris, b. 8 August 1966, Dulwich, England. Middleweight Boxer. m. 4 children. Career: WBC International Middleweight Boxing Champion, 2 defences, March-November, 1990; WBO Middleweight Boxing Champion, 3 defences, November 1990-August 1991; WBO World Super-Middleweight Boxing Champion, 14 defences, September 1991-March 1995; Lost title to Steve Collins, Cork, Sept 1995; Failed to regain title against Joe Calzaghe, Sheffield, October 1997; Unsuccessful fights for WBO Cruiserweight title against Carl Thompson, Manchester, April 1998, Sheffield, July 1998; Patron Breakthrough; Ambassador, International Fund for Animal Welfare; Spokesperson, National Society for the Prevention of Cruelty to Children. Address: 9 The Upper Drive, Hove, East Sussex, BN3 6GR, England.

EVANGELISTA Linda, b. St Catherine, Toronto, Ontario, Canada. Model. m. Gerald Marie (divorced 1993). Career: Face of Yardley Cosmetics; Numerous catwalk appearances. Address: c/o Elite Model Management, 40 Parker Street, London WC2B 5PH, England.

EVANS Brian David, b. 29 May 1937, London. Writer; Library and Information Professional. m. Gill Chambers, 1958, deceased, 1979, 2 sons, 1 daughter. Education: North-Western Polytechnic, London; BA, Open University, University of Westminster. Appointments: Freelance Writer; Lecturer; Researcher on local history; Former Reference and Information Librarian, Havering Libraries; Librarian-in-Charge, Earlsfield Library, Wandsworth; Branch Librarian, Corringham Library, Thurrock, Essex. Publications: Books: Bygone Romford; Century of Ilford; Thurrock Past and Present; Islington: A Second Selection; Hackney from Stamford Hill to Shoreditch; 22 others; Contributions to Encyclopaedias of London; Series of articles on Havering History. Honours: BA, Open University; ALA; MCLIP; Honorary Life Member, Romford Historical Society; Historical Advisor, Romford Recorder; President, Rotary Club of Romford, 1996-97, Public Relations Officer, 1988, Secretary, 2002-; Public Relations Officer, Rotary District 1240, 2003. Memberships: Great Eastern Railway Society; Life member, National Trust; Founder member, Havering Heritage Forum; Vice Chairman, Friends of Havering Museum. Address: 13 The Terlings, Brentwood, Essex. E-mail: subriety@onetel.net.uk

EVANS Chris, b. 1966, Warrington, England. Broadcaster. m. (1) Carol McGiffin, 1991, divorced, (2) Billie Piper. Career: Numerous sundry jobs; Joined Piccadilly Radio, Manchester; Producer, GLR Radio, London; Presenter of numerous television programmes including Don't Forget Your Toothbrush, co-presenter, The Big Breakfast; Presenter, Radio 1 Breakfast Show, 1995-97; Virgin Radio Breakfast Show, 1997-; Established Ginger Productions, media production company; Presenter and Executive Producer, TFI Friday, Channel 4. Honours: British Comedy Award Prizes, Best Entertainment Series, Top Channel 4 Entertainment Presenter, 1995. Address: Ginger Productions, 131-151 Great Titchfield Street, London W1P 8DP, England.

EVANS Janet M, b. 16 September 1956, Raleigh, North Carolina, USA. Publisher. 2 sons. Education: Technical and Administrative Training. Appointments: Marketing assistant, Evans and Wade Advertising Ltd, 1977-78; Chief Executive Officer, American Biographical Institute: Chairman, ABI Research Association, 1979-97; Magazine and Newsletter Editor, 1979-; Director, Conference on Culture and Education, 1984; Executive Director, World Institute of Achievement, 1985-; President, American Biographical Institute, 1997-; General-in-Residence, United Cultural Convention, 2001-. Publications: Editor, Publisher, Biographical Reference. Honours: Honorary Life Fellow, International Biographical Association. Memberships: Foundation for International Meetings, Board Member 1992; Publishers' Association of the South; Raleigh Chamber of Commerce; American Society of Professional and Executive Women; National Association of Independent Publishers; Publishers Marketing Association. Address: American Biographical Institute, PO Box 31226, 5126 Bur Oak Circle, Raleigh, NC 27622, USA.

EVANS Julian Richard Guy, b. 3 October 1952, Haverfordwest, Pembrokeshire, Wales. Materials Engineer. m. Joanna Pascoe, 1 son, 1 daughter. Education: BSc, Industrial Metallurgy, University of Birmingham, 1970-73; PhD, School of Materials Science, University of Bath, 1973-76. Appointments: Research Officer, School of Materials Science, University of Bath, 1976-78; Volunteer, Christian Study Centre, Peter Selwood Charitable Trust, Hampshire, 1978-79; Research Scientist, Research Centre, Thomas De La Rue & Co Ltd, Maidenhead, 1979-80; Research Fellow, Department of Ceramics, University of Leeds, 1980-84; Lecturer, 1984-92, Reader in Ceramics Processing, 1992-98, Department of Materials Technology, Brunel University; Professor of Materials, Queen Mary, University of London, 1998-. Publications: Author of over 220 publications, 170 in refereed journals, 7 in collective works mainly on: powder processing, notably ceramic injection moulding, novel ceramic forming processes, solid freeforming, direct ink-jet printing of ceramics and more recently combinatorial methods for oxides. Honour: Ivor Jenkins Award, Institute of Materials, 2002. Memberships: Fellow Institute of Materials, 1996; Chartered Engineer. Address: Department of Materials, Queen Mary, University of London, Mile End Road, London E1 4NS, England. E-mail: j.r.g.evans@qmul.ac.uk

EVE Trevor, b. 1 July 1951. Actor. m. Sharon Patricia Maughn, 1980, 2 sons, 1 daughter. Education: Kingston Art College; RADA. Career: Actor, Theatre includes: Children of a Lesser God, 1981; The Genius, 1983; High Society, 1986; Man Beast and Virtue, 1989; The Winter's Tale, 1991; Inadmissible Evidence, 1993; Uncle Vanya, 1996; TV includes: Shoestring, 1980; Jamaica Inn, 1990; A Sense of Guilt, 1990; Parnell and the Englishwoman, 1991; A Doll's House, 1991; The Politician's Wife, 1995; Black Easter, 1995; Under the Sun, 1997; Evilstreak, 1999; David Copperfield, 1999; Waking The Dead, 2000, 2001, 2002; Films include: Hindle Wakes; Dracula; A Wreath of Roses; The Corsican

Brothers; Aspen Extreme; Psychotherapy; The Knight's Tale; The Tribe; Appetite; Possession; Producer for Projector Productions: Alice Through the Looking Glass, 1998; Cinderella; Twelfth Night, 2002. Honours include: Olivier Award for Best Supporting Actor, 1997. Address: c/o ICM Ltd, Oxford House, 76 Oxford Street, London, W1N 0AX, England.

EVERETT Oliver, b. 28 February 1943, Brentwood, Essex, England. Librarian Emeritus. 2 sons, 2 daughters. Education: English Speaking Union Exchange Scholar, Western Reserve Academy, Ohio, USA, 1961-62; MA, Christ's College, Cambridge, England, 1962-65; MA, Fletcher School of Law and Diplomacy, Tufts University, Massachusetts, USA, 1965-66; London School of Economics, 1966-67. Appointments: British Diplomatic Service, 1967-78, including 1st Secretary, British High Commission, New Delhi, India, 1969-73; Assistant Private Secretary to the Prince of Wales, 1978-80; 1st Secretary, British Embassy, Madrid, 1980-81; Private Secretary to the Princess of Wales, 1981-83; Librarian, Royal Library, Windsor Castle, and Assistant Keeper of the Royal Archives, 1984-2002; Librarian Emeritus, Royal Library, Windsor Castle, 2002-. Publications: Windsor Castle Official Guide Book, 1990; Article: Prince Albert and the Royal Library, Windsor Castle, 2001; Introductions to numerous Royal Library exhibition catalogues; Entries in the new DNB. Honour: Commander of the Victorian Order, 1991. Memberships: Roxburghe Club (bibliophiles); English Speaking Union Lecturer. Address: 48 Egerton Gardens, London, SW3 2BZ, England. E-mail: olivereverett@royalcollection.org.uk

EVERETT Rupert, b. 29 May 1960, Norfolk, England. Actor. Education: Central School for Speech and Drama, London. Appointments: Apprentice, Glasgow Citizen's Theatre, 1979-82; Model, Versace, Milan; Image of Opium perfume for Yves Saint Laurent; Stage appearances include: Another Country, 1982; The Vortex, 1989; Private Lives; The Milk Train Doesn't Stop Here Anymore; The Picture of Dorian Gray; The Importance of Being Earnest; Films include: Another Country, 1984; Dance With a Stranger, 1985; The Right Hand Man, 1985; Duet for One; Chronicle of Death Foretold, 1987; Hearts of Fire, 1987; Haunted Summer, 1988; The Comfort of Strangers, 1989; Inside Monkey Zetterland; Pret à Porter, 1995; The Madness of King George, 1995; Dunstan Checks In; My Best Friend's Wedding, 1997; A Midsummer's Night's Dream, 1998; B Monkey, 1998; An Ideal Husband, 1999; Inspector Gadget, 1999; The Next Best thing, 2000; Unconditional Love, 2002; The Importance of Being Earnest, 2002; TV includes: Arthur the King; The Far Pavilions, 1982; Princess Daisy, 1983. Publications: Hello Darling, Are You Working?, 1992; The Hairdressers of San Tropez, 1995. Address: c/o ICM, 8942 Wilshire Boulevard, Beverly Hills, CA 90211, USA.

EVERS Gene, b. 26 March 1951, New York, New York, USA. Independent Writer. Education: AA, Humanities, Nassau Community College, 1973; BA, Humanities, State University of New York, Old Westbury; Philosophy, Stony Brook University, 1973. Publications: Over 15 published poems, 1995-: The Poems Rainbow, Man in the Moon, Angel at Noon, Heavens Dawn, Big Red Mountain, She Sat upon the Cloud; Songs: Cindy Girl, 1996; Ohio, 1997; Northern Wind, 1998; Where my Heart lies, 1998; A Christmas Journey, movie, to be published; Collection of short stories. Contributions to: National Library of Poetry; Poetry Guild. Honours: Editor's Choice Poems, 1995, 1996, Outstanding Achievement Award, 1995, 1996, 1997, National Library of Poetry; Poet of the Year 1996, International Society of Poets; International Society of Poets Hall of Fame, 1996; Distinguished Member, International Society of Poets, 1996, 1997; Invited to join International Platform Association, 1998; Listed in several Biographical Publications. Membership: New York Writer's Guild. Address: 2296 Lincoln Street, Bellmore, NY 11710, USA.

EVERT Chris(tine) Marie, b. 21 December 1954, Fort Lauderdale, Florida, USA. Former Lawn Tennis Player. m. (1) J Lloyd, 1979, divorced 1987, (2) A Mill, 1988, 3 sons. Education: High School, Ft Lauderdale. Career: Amateur, 1970-72; Professional, 1972-. Winner of: French Championship, 1974, 1975, 1979, 1980, 1982, 1985, 1986; Wimbledon Singles: 1974, 1976, 1981; Italian Championship: 1974, 1975, 1980; South African Championship: 1973; US Open: 1975, 1976, 1977, 1979, 1980, 1982 (record 100 victories); Colgate Series, 1977, 1978; World Championship, 1979; Played Wightman Cup, 1971-73, 1975-82; Federation Cup, 1977-82; Ranked No 1 in the world for seven years; Won 1309 matches in her career; Holds 157 singles titles and 18 Grand Slam titles. Appointments: President, Women's Tennis Association, 1975-76, 1983-91; Director, President's Council on Physical Fitness & Sports, 1991-; NBC TV sports commentator and host for numerous TV shows; Other: Established Chris Evert Charities, 1989; Owner, Evert Enterprises/IMG, 1989-; Chris Evert Pro-celebrity Tennis Classic, 1989-. Publications: Chrissie (autobiography), 1982; Lloyd on Lloyd (with J Lloyd) 1985. Honours include: International Tennis Hall of Fame, 1995; International Tennis Federation Chartrier Award, 1997; Named by ESPN as One of Top 50 Athletes of the 20th Century, 1999. Address: Evert Enterprises, 7200 W Camino Real, Suite 310 Boca Raton, FL 33433, USA.

EZIN Jean-Pierre Onvêhoun, b. 7 December 1944, Guezin, Benin. University Professor. m. Victoire Akele, 3 sons, 1 daughter. Education: Doctorat de 3e cycle, 1972, Doctorat d'Etat, 1981, University of Lille I, France. Appointments: Lecturer, Catholic University of Lille, France, 1972-73; Lecturer, National University of Benin, 1973-77; Associate Professor, University of Lille I, France, 1978-81; Professor, National University of Benin, 1981-. Publications: At least 20 books, papers and articles on mathematics, mathematical physics and Riemannian geometry. Honours: Officier des Palmes Academiques Françaises; Vice-Chancellor of National University of Benin, 1990-92. Memberships: American Mathematical Society; Societé Mathématique de France; African Mathematical Union; Senior Associate, Abus Salome International Centre for Theoretical Physics; Lions Clubs International. Address: Institut de Mathématiques et des Sciences Physiques, IMSP, BP 613, Porto Novo, Benin. E-mail: jp.ezin@imsp-mac.org

ÉZSIÁS András (Andrew), b. 1 November 1953, Budapest, Hungary. Consultant Maxillofacial Surgeon. m. (1) Zsuzsanna Bártfai, divorced 1986, 1 son, (2) Edina Érsek, 1 son, 2 daughters. Education: Temesvári Pelbárt Franciscan College and Gymnasium, Esztergom, Hungary; DMD, Semmelweis University, Budapest, 1977; MD, 1981; Specialist Certificate in General Surgery, Postgraduate Institute of Budapest, 1986; Specialist Board Certificate in Oral and Maxillofacial Surgery, Royal College of Surgeons, England, Specialist Training Authority, UK, 1996; Diplomate, European Board of Oro-Maxillofacial Surgery, 2000. Appointments: Postgraduate Trainee Surgeon, Janos Hospital, Budapest, Hungary, 1981-86; Sub-lieutenant, Hungarian Army Medical Corps, 1981-82; Senior House Officer, Liverpool Dental Hospital, England, 1988-90; St Lawrence Hospital, Chepstow, Wales, 1990-91; Registrar, Queen Alexandra Hospital, Portsmouth, England, 1991-92; St Lawrence Hospital and University Hospital of Wales, Cardiff, 1992-94; Senior Registrar, Cheltenham and Gloucester Hospitals, England, 1994-95; John Radcliffe Hospital, Oxford, England, 1995-98; Consultant, Prince Charles, Princess of Wales and Royal Glamorgan Hospitals, Wales, 1998-; Honorary Consultant, Welsh Regional Burns and Plastic Surgery Unit, Morriston Hospital, Wales, 2000-. Publications: Contributor, articles to professional journals. Memberships: Fellow, Royal College of Surgeons, England; Fellow and Examiner, Royal College of Surgeons, Edinburgh; Fellow and Examiner, European Board of Oro-Maxillofacial Surgery; Fellow, International Association of Oral and Maxillofacial Surgeons; Fellow, British Association of Oral and Maxillofacial Surgeons; Member, European Association for Cranio-Maxillofacial Surgery; Member, British Association of Head and Neck Oncologists; Member, European Academy of Facial Plastic Surgery; Elected member, European Academy of Sciences and Arts. Address: 9 Gateside Close, Cardiff CF23 8PB, Wales. E-mail: ezsias@ntlworld.com

Dictionary of International Biography

F

FABEND Firth Haring, (Firth Haring), b. 12 August 1937, Tappan, New York, USA. Writer; Historian. m. Carl Fabend, 12 February 1966, 2 daughters. Education: BA, Barnard College, 1959; PhD, New York University, 1988. Publications: As Firth Haring: The Best of Intentions, 1968; Three Women, 1972; A Perfect Stranger, 1973; The Woman Who Went Away, 1981; Greek Revival, 1985; As Firth Haring Fabend: A Dutch Family in the Middle Colonies, 1660-1800; Zion on the Hudson: Dutch New York and New Jersey in the Age of Revivals. Contributions to: de Halve Maen; New York History. Honours: Ms Award, New York State Historical Association, 1989; Hendricks Prize, 1989; Fellow, Holland Society of New York, 1993; Fellow, New Netherland Project, 1996. Address: Upper Montclair, NJ 07043, USA.

FABRE Alain, b. 23 June 1947, Perpignan, France. Professor of Electronics. Education: MS, Electronics, 1972, PhD, Physics, 1974, University of Bordeaux, France; Post Doctoral Thesis, University of Perpignan, 1987. Appointments: Assistant Professor, Electronics, University of Oran, Algeria, 1974-87; Assistant Professor, Electronics, Ecole Centrale Paris, France, 1987-95; Head of analogue IC design group (COCAR) laboratoire d'Electronique et de Physique Appliquée, Ecole Centrale, Paris, France, 1988-95; Full Professor, Electronics, Ecole Nationale Supérieure d'Electronique, Informatique et Radiocommunications de Bordeaux (ENSEIRB); Head, High Speed Analogue IC Design team, Telecommunication Circuits and Systems (TCS) group, laboratoire IXL, Université Bordeaux I, France; Responsible for the 3rd Year option in telecommunications, ENSEIRB. Publications: 2 volumes on practical aspects of electrical and electronic measures, 1983, 1984; Author, co-author, more than 90 research papers in international scientific reviews or conference proceedings; co-author of one article in the encyclopaedia of Electrical and Electronics Engineering, Wiley, USA, 1999; 1 international patent; Research in fields of High speed analogue circuits, low noise amplifiers (LNA), UWB amplifiers, analogue RF controlled filters, ASICS, current mode circuits, theoretical tasks of translinear circuits. Membership: Senior Member, Institute of Electrical and Electronic Engineers, USA. Address: Microelectronics Lab IXL, University of Bordeaux I, 351 Cours de la Liberation, 33405 Talence, France.

FABRE DE LA RIPELLE Michel, b. 21 December 1924, Paris, France. Director of Research. m. Marie-Pierre de Bon, 1 son, 1 daughter. Education: Physics and Mathematics, La Sorbonne, 1946; Diploma for Higher Studies, Nuclear Physics and Electronics, Probability and Quantum Mechanics, 1947; PhD, Science, Professor Louis de Broglie, 1956. Appointments: Researcher, National Centre for Scientific Research, 1947-; Postdoctoral studies, Kioto University, Japan, 1961-62; Scientific Attaché, French Embassy, Japan, 1964-68; Director of Research, Institute of Nuclear Physics, University Paris-Sud Orsay, France, 1968-. Publications: Over 70 papers in international scientific journals on few and many body problems. Address: Institute of Nuclear Physics, University Paris-Sud, 91406 Orsay, France.

FAES Urs, b. 13 February 1947, Aarau, Switzerland. Writer. Education: MA, Dr Phil I, Studies in History, German Literature, Philosophy, University of Zurich, Switzerland. Appointments: Journalist, 1979-81; Dramatist, 1982-86; Writer and Free-lance Journalist, 1982-. Publications: Eine Kerbe im Mittag (poems), 1975; Heidentum und Aberglaube (essay), 1979; Regenspur (poems), 1979; Webfehler (novel), 1983; Zugluft (play), 1983; Der Traum vom Leben (short stories), 1984; Kreuz im Feld (play), 1984; Bis ans Ende der Erinnerung (novel), 1986; Wartzimmer (play), 1986; Partenza (radio play), 1986; Sommerwende (novel),

1989; Alphabet des Abschieds, 1991; Eine andere Geschichte (radio play), 1993; Augenblicke im Paradies (novel), 1994; Ombra (novel), 1997; Und Ruth (novel), 2001. Honours: Prize, City of Zurich, 1986; Prize for Literature, 1991; Prize for Literature Solothurn, 1999; Schiller-Prize, 2001. Memberships: PEN of Switzerland; Authors of Switzerland (AdS). Address: Siriusstrasse 4, CH-8044 Zurich, Switzerland. E-mail: urs.faes@bluewin.ch

FAGNEN Claude, b. 28 November 1945, Asnieres, France. Archivist. m. Sylvaine Menez, 1 daughter. Education: Archiviste paléographe, Ecole des Chartes, Paris, 1967-71; Licence Histoire, Sorbonne, Paris, 1964-67; Ecole Pratique des Hautes Etudes, IVeme Section, Paris, 1967-71. Appointments: Director, Finistere departmental Archives, 1973-. Publications: Around 40 articles in professional journals; 3 books. Honours: Chevalier de l'Ordre des Arts et Lettres, 1985. Memberships: Friends of Old Quimper Association; Finistere Society of History and Archaeology. Address: 7 allee Henri Bourde de la Rogerie, 29000 Quimper, France. E-mail: claude.fagnen@cg29.fr

FAHD IBN ABDUL AZIZ, b. 1923, Riyadh. King of Saudi Arabia. Appointments: Minister of Education, 1953; Minister of Interior, 1962-75; Second Deputy Prime Minister, 1967-75; First Deputy Prime Minister, 1975-82; Prime Minister, 1967-75; Crown Prince, 1975; Succeeded to throne on death of brother, 13 June 1982; Assumed title: Servant of the Two Shrines, 1986. Address: Royal Diwan, Riyadh, Saudi Arabia.

FAHEEM Mohammad, b. 2 June 1961, Karachi, Pakistan. Physician; Anaesthetist. m. Nazia, 2 sons, 1 daughter. Education: BSc; MBBS, 1986; FFARCSI, 1994; DEAA, 1996; Diploma in Management, Royal College of Surgeons in Ireland and Institute of Public Administration, 2001; MA, Healthcare Management, Institute of Public Administration. Appointments include: Anaesthetic Registrar: Meath, Adelaide, National Children's Hospital, Dublin, Eire, 1992-93; Beaumont Hospital, Dublin, Eire, 1993-94; The Children's Hospital, Temple Street and Rotunda Hospital, 1994-95; Mater Misericordiae Hospital, 1995; Our Lady's Hospital for Sick Children, Crumlin, Dublin, 1996; Consultant Anaesthetist, Portlaoise General Hospital, Eire, 1997-97, Sligo General Hospital, Eire, 1997, Cavan General Hospital, Eire, 1997-2001, Roscommon General Hospital and Portiuncula Hospital, Eire, 2001-2003, Midland Regional Hospital at Mullingar, Eire, 2003-. Publications: Journal articles: Diaphragmatic rupture after epidural anaesthesia in a patient with diaphragmatic eventration, 1999; Sliding of skin over subcutaneous tissue as a cause of epidural catheter migration, 2002; Poster Presentations: Postepidural rupture of Diaphragm in a case with Diaphragmatic Eventration, 1998; Wallenberg's Syndrome as a cause of Ondine Curse, 1999. Honours: Fellow, College of Anaesthetists, Royal College of Surgeons, Ireland; Diplomate, European Academy of Anaesthesiology. Memberships: Association of Anaesthetists of Great Britain and Ireland; International Anaesthesia Research Society; Obstetric Anaesthetists Association; Association of Pediatric Anaesthetists; European Society of Regional Anaesthetic; Irish Medical Organisation; Irish Hospital Consultant's Association; Clinicians in Management Group, Ireland. Address: 7 Belvedere Hills, Ballinderry, Mullinger, Co Westmeath, Ireland. E-mail: faheem@esatclear.ie

FAINLIGHT Ruth (Esther), b. 2 May 1931, New York, New York, USA. Writer; Poet; Translator; Librettist. m. Alan Sillitoe, 19 November 1959, 1 son, 1 daughter. Education: Colleges of Arts and Crafts, Birmingham, Brighton, UK. Appointment: Poet-in-Residence, Vanderbilt University, USA, 1985, 1990. Publications: Poetry: Cages, 1966; To See the Matter Clearly, 1968;

The Region's Violence, 1973; Another Full Moon, 1976; Sibyls and Others, 1980; Climates, 1983; Fifteen to Infinity, 1983; Selected Poems, 1987, 2nd edition, revised, 1995; The Knot, 1990; Sibyls, 1991; This Time of Year, 1994; Sugar-Paper Blue, 1997; Burning Wire, 2002; Visitação: Selected Poems in Portuguese translation, 1995; Encore La Pleine Lune, Selected Poems in French translation, 1997; Poemas, translation of selected poems in Spanish, 2000; Bleue Papier-Sucre, 2000; La Verita Sulla Sibilla, selected poems in Italian translation, 2003. Translations: All Citizens Are Soldiers, from Lope de Vega, 1969; Navigations, 1983; Marine Rose: Selected Poems of Sophia de Mello Breyner, 1988. Short Stories: Daylife and Nightlife, 1971; Dr Clock's Last Case, 1994. Libretti: The Dancer Hotoke, 1991; The European Story, 1993; Bedlam Britannica, 1995. Contributions to: Atlantic Monthly; Critical Quarterly; English; Hudson Review; Lettre Internationale; London Magazine; London Review of Books; New Yorker; Poetry Review; Threepenny Review; Times Literary Supplement. Honours: Cholmondeley Award for Poetry, 1994; Hawthornden Award for Poetry, 1994. Memberships: Society of Authors; PEN; Writers in Prison Committee. Address: 14 Ladbroke Terrace, London W11 3PG, England.

FAIRBRASS Graham John, b. 14 January 1953, Meopham, Kent, England. Traveller; Writer; Poet; Painter. Education: BA, Arts, Open University, 1991; Coleg Harlech, 1995-96; Diploma, University of Wales, 1996; Norwich School of Art and Design, 1996-99. Publication: Conquistadors Shuffle Moon, 1989. Contributions to: Poetry Now, 1994; Anthology South East; Parnassus of World Poets, 1994, 1995, 1997; Poetry Club Anthology, vol l, 1995; Birdsuit, 1997-99. Address: 6 Hornfield Cottages, Harvel, Gravesend, Kent DA13 0BU, England.

FAIRFAX John, b. 9 November 1930, London, England. Writer, Poet. 2 sons. Appointments: Co-Founder and Member of Council of Management, Arvon Foundation; Director, Phoenix Press, Arts Workshop, Newbury; Poetry Editor, Resurgence. Publications: The Fifth Horseman of the Apocalypse, 1969; Double Image, 1971; Adrift on the Star Brow of Taliesin, 1974; Bone Harvest Done, 1980; Wild Children, 1985; The Way to Write, 1981; Creative Writing, 1989; Spindrift Lp, 1981; 100 Poems, 1992; Zuihitsu, 1996; Poem Sent to Satellite E2F3, 1997; Poem on Sculpture, 1998; Poem in Hologram, 1998; Commissioned poems: Boots Herbal Garden, engraved on glass for several institutes, 1999, 2000; Poems in Virtual Reality, 2003, 2004. Contributions to: Most major literary magazines. Membership: The Arvon Foundation, co-founder, 1968. Address: The Thatched Cottage, Eling, Hermitage, Newbury, Berkshire RG16 9XR, England.

FAITHFULL Marianne, b. 29 December 1947, Hampstead, London, England. Singer. 1 son. Career: Recording artist, 1964-; Tours, appearances include: UK tour with Roy Orbison, 1965; US tour with Gene Pitney, 1965; Uxbridge Blues and Folk Festival, 1965; Montreux, Golden Rose Festival, 1966; Roger Water's The Wall, Berlin, 1990; Chieftains Music Festival, London, 1991; Acting roles include: I'll Never Forget Whatisname, 1967; Three Sisters, Chekkov, London, 1967; Hamlet, 1970; Kurt Weill's Seven Deadly Sins, St Ann's Cathedral, New York, 1990; Film appearance, Girl On A Motorcycle, 1968. Recordings: Singles include: As Tears Go By; Come And Stay With Me; This Little Bird; Summer Nights; Something Better/Sister Morphine; The Ballad Of Lucy Jordan; Dreaming My Dreams; Electra, 1999; Albums: Come My Way, 1965; Marianne Faithfull, 1965; Go Away From My World, 1966; Faithfull Forever, 1966; Marianne Faithfull's Greatest Hits, 1969; Faithless, with the Grease Band, 1978; Broken English, 1979; Dangerous Acquaintances, 1981; A Child's Adventure, 1983; Strange Weather, 1987; Blazing Away, 1990; A Secret Life, 1995; 20th Century Blues, 1997; The Seven

Deadly Sins, 1998; Vagabond Ways, 1999; Contributor, Lost In The Stars - The Music Of Kurt Weill, 1984; The Bells Of Dublin, The Chieftains, 1992. Publications: Faithfull (autobiography), 1994; Marian Faithfull Diaries, 2002. Honours include: Grammy Nomination, Broken English, 1979. Address: c/o The Coalition Group Ltd, 12 Barley Mow Passage, London, W4 4PH, England. Website: pithuit.free.fr/FAITHFULL

FAKIOLAS Efstathios Tassos, b. 26 November 1971, Moscow, Russian Federation (Greek Citizen). Strategy Analyst. m. Eirini Tsoucala, 1 son. Education: BA, International Studies, 1989-93, Master of Arts, International Politics and Security, 1993-96, Athens Panteion University; Master of Arts, International Relations and Strategic Studies, Lancaster University, England, 1994-95; Currently PhD Student, Department of War Studies, King's College, London, England. Appointments: Civil Servant, Finance Department, Social Insurance Fund Organisation for the Employees of the Hellenic Broadcasting Corporation and Tourism, September-November 2002; Strategy Analyst, Strategic Planning Department, Group Strategy Division, Agricultural Bank of Greece, 2002-. Publications: 12 peer-reviewed journal articles include most recently: Security, Strategy and Dialectic Realism: Ontological and Epistemological Issues in Constructing a New Approach to International Politics, 1999; Reflecting on the Relationship Between Security and Military Strategy, 2001; Theories of European Integration: A Neglected Dimension, 2002; Co-author, 1 book chapter; Numerous other articles in journals, periodicals and newspapers. Honours include: NATO Science Fellowships, 1994-95, 1996-99; Several scholarships and grants; 4 Distinctions, Athens Panteion University of Political and Social Sciences, 1989-93; Memorial Diploma, Public Benefit Foundation "Alexander S Onasis", 1995; British International Studies Association Research Award, 1998. Memberships include: International Institute for Strategic Studies; Royal United Services Institute for Defence Studies; International Studies Association; International Political Sciences Association; Academy of Political Science, USA; Hellenic Association of International Law and International Relations. Address: 86 Xanthipou Street, Papagou/Holargos, 155 61, Athens, Greece. E-mail: efakiolas@hotmail.com

FALADE Funso Alphonsus, b. 5 February 1954, Nigeria. Civil Engineer. m. T C Falade, 5 daughters. Education: Diploma, Quantity Surveying, Yaba College of Technology, Nigeria, 1976-78; MSc, Moscow Institute of Civil Engineering, USSR. 1979-84; PhD, Civil Engineering, University of Lagos, Nigeria, 1993-98. Appointments: Assistant Lecturer, 1986-89, Lecturer II, 1989-91, Lecturer I, 1991-95, Senior Lecturer, 1995-98, Associate Professor, 1998-, Department of Civil Engineering, University of Lagos, Nigeria. Publications: 35 articles on innovative construction materials and engineering education published in local and international reputable journals. Honours: Listed in Who's Who publications and biographical dictionaries. Memberships: Nigerian Society of Engineers; Council for Regulation of Engineering in Nigeria; American Society of Civil Engineers; UNESCO International Centre for Engineering Education. Address: Department of Civil Engineering, University of Lagos, Akoka, Lagos, Nigeria. E-mail: ffalade@hotmail.com

FALDO Nick, b. 18 July 1957, Welwyn Garden City, England. Professional Golfer. m. (1) Melanie, divorced, (2) Gill, divorced, 1 son, 2 daughters, (3) Valerie Bercher. Career: Professional, 1976-; Winner numerous tournaments including: Colgate PGA Championship, 1978, 1980, 1991; 5 titles on PGA European Tour; Open Championship, Muirfield, 1987; French Open and Volvo Masters, Valderrama, 1988; Masters, Augusta, Georgia, 1989; French Open, 1989; US Masters, 1990, 1996; Open Championship, St Andrews, 1990; Irish Open, 1991, 1992, 1993; Open

Championship, Muirfield, 1992; Toyota World Match-Play Championship, 1992; Scandinavian Masters, 1992; European Open, 1992; Johnnie Walker World Championship, 1992; Alfred Dunhill Belgian Open, 1994; Doral Ryder Open, USA, 1995; World No 1, Sony Ranking, 1992-94; Johnnie Walker Asian Classic, 1993. Publications: In Search of Perfection, (with Bruce Critchley), 1995; Faldo - A Swing for Life, 1995. E-mail: nfdo@faldodesign.com

FALK Heinz, b. 29 April 1939, St Pölten. Professor Organic Chemistry. m. Rotraud, 1 son. Education: Dr Phil, University of Vienna. Appointments: Assistant, University Vienna, 1966; Post-Doctoral ETH, Zurich, 1971; Habilitation, University of Vienna, 1972; Assistant Professor, Physical Organic Chemistry, 1975; University Professor, Organic Chemistry, University Linz, 1979; Guest Professor, University of Barcelona, 1982; Dean, Science Technical Faculty, University of Linz, 1989-91. Publications: 280 papers in refereed journals; Several patents. Honours include: Loschmidt Medal, 1998, and others. Memberships include: Austrian Academy of Science; Austrian Chemical Society; German Chemical Society; European Society of Photochemistry; American Society of Photochemistry Photobiology; New York Academy of Science; European Academy of Sciences. Address: Institute for Organic Chemistry, Johannes Kepler University Linz, Altenbergerstr 14, A 4040 Linz, Austria. Website: Heinz@falk.net

FALLOWELL Duncan Richard, b. 26 September 1948, London, England. Writer. Education: Magdalen College, Oxford. Publications: Drug Tales, 1979; April Ashley's Odyssey, 1982; Satyrday, 1986; The Underbelly, 1987; To Noto, 1989; Twentieth Century Characters, 1994; One Hot Summer in St Petersburg, 1994; Gormenghast, 1998; A History of Facelifting, 2003. Address: 44 Leamington Road Villas, London W11 1HT, England.

FALOUGHI Ephraim Fagha, b. 17 November 1943, Port Harcourt, Rivers State, Nigeria. Industrialist. m. 1 son, 5 daughters. Education: Honorary Doctorate, Science and Technology, All Saints University, New York, USA; Honorary Doctorate of Philosophy, Malborough University, USA. Appointments: President and Chief Executive, NTCN Limited, interior decorators, 1973-; President, NTCN Industries, carpet manufacturers; President, Chief Executive, Telecommunications World Service Limited; Chief Executive, Sincerely Yours Nigeria Limited, licensed customs agent; Chairman, Sovereign Trust Insurance Co Ltd; Chairman, TEEOF Holding Limited, property developers and management; Special Senior Apostle and Elder-in-Charge, Oke Iye House of Prayer of the Eternal Sacred Order of the Cherubim and Seraphim. Honours: Nigerian Industrial Development Award, 1996; ECOWAS International Gold Award, 1998; Development in Nigeria Merit Award, 2001; Distinguished Leadership Role Award, 2002; Patriotic Men of Integrity International Award, Royal Achievers International Media Network, 2002; Niger Delta Development Merit Award, 2003; Prime International Achievers Gold Award, 2003; Great African Merit Award, 2003; Paul Harris Fellow, Rotary International. Memberships: Senior Fellow, Institute of Internal Auditors of Nigeria; Fellow Member, FMUGA, Marlborough University, USA, 2003. Address: 39 Itire Road, Surulere, Lagos, Nigeria. E-mail: ntcnltd@multilink.com

FALZEDER Ernst M, b. 17 February 1955, Linz, Austria. Psychologist. 1 son, 1 daughter. Education: Maturity Certificate, 1973; Graduate university training in Psychology, Psychopathology and Psychiatry, Faculties of Philosophy and Natural Sciences, University of Salzburg, Austria, 1973-85; PhD, University of Salzburg, 1985; Training as Group Therapist, IPG Salzburg, 1974-76; Psychoanalytic training at the Salzburg Study Group for Psychoanalysis, 1985-. Appointments: Assistant, Psychological

Institute, University of Salzburg, 1979-85; Lecturer, Universities of Salzburg and Innsbruck, 1985-; Assistant Professor, Psychological Institute, University of Salzburg, 1986-87; Research Fellowships in Switzerland, USA, include: The Foundation Louis Jeantet for the History of Medicine, Geneva, Switzerland, 1992-97; Woodrow Wilson Center, Washington, DC, 1997-98; Department of History of Science, Harvard University, Cambridge, Massachusetts, 1998-99. Publications: More than 100 including main editor of the correspondence of Sigmund Freud and Sándor Ferenczi, 3 vols, 1993-2000; Editor, Freud/Abraham Correspondence, 2002. Honours include: Gustav Hans Graber-Prize of the International Society for Pre and Perinatal Psychology, 1986; Nomination for Gradiva Award, National Association for the Advancement of Psychoanalysis, 1997. Memberships: Founding and Board member, Austrian Society for Sexological Research, 1979; Member, editorial board, journal Psychoanalyse, 1985-86. Address: Spital am Pyhrn Nr 290, A-4582, Austria.

FAN Charles Chwei-Lin, b. China. Economic and Statistical Methodologist. Education: BS, National Kwangsi University, Kwei-Lin, China, 1947; MS, Montana State University, Bozeman, 1961; PhD, University of Hawaii, Honolulu, USA, 1967. Appointments: Assistant Professor, National Kwangsi University, Kwei-Lin, 1947-49; Sugarcane Farm Economist, Taiwan Sugar Company, 1950-58; Editorial Member, Taiwan Sugar Industry Handbook Compilation Committee, 1951; Associate Professor of Statistics and Mathematics, Southern University, Baton Rouge, Louisiana, USA, 1967-69; Statistician, Economist and Methodologist, Ministry of Treasury and Economics, Government of Ontario, 1970-89; Retired, 1990. Publication: The Collected Essays of Cheng Ying, Taipei, 1985 (Cheng Ying is a pen name of Charles C L Fan). Honours: Distinguished Service Award, Ministry of Economic Affairs, Taiwan, 1956; Exchange Visitor, Institute of International Education, New York, 1959-61; Fellow, Council on Economic and Cultural Affairs, New York, 1959-61; Consultant, Chinese/English Dictionary of Agricultural Economics, England, 1973; World Citizen of the Year, ABI, 2002. Memberships: AAUP, 1969-98; Life Member, AAEA; IAAE, 1970-2004; CAES, 1970-2004. Address: Box 38058, Dixie Mall Post Office, 1250 South Service Road, Mississauga, Ontario L5E 3G3, Canada.

FANG Rong Rémi, b. 10 August 1958, Ping-Jiang, Hunan, China. Physicist. Education: Graduate, Tsinghua University, 1982; Postgraduate, Institute of High Energy Physics, China, 1985; PhD, Louis Pasteur University, France, 1997. Appointments: Lecturer, University of Science and Technology of China, 1958-88; Visiting Associate Professor, Paris University IV, 1989-91; Visiting Scholar, Centre of Research of Nuclear Physics, Strasbourg, France, 1991-92; Engineer, Computer Software, Aerial Nuclear Irradiation Centre, Strasbourg, France, 1993-. Publications: Several articles in professional journals concerning Rule of Charge Accumulation, and Stability Conditions. Honour: Lifetime Achievement Award, ABI. Memberships: AAAS; New York Academy of Sciences; Fellow, ABI. Address: 8 rue Louis Pasteur, 67450 Mundolsheim, France. E-mail: r.fang@aerial-crt.com

FANNING Elizabeth Ann, b. 14 April 1918, Wellington, New Zealand. Retired Academic. m. Thomas Benjamin Westerman. Education: BDS, Otago University, 1949; DDS, University of New Zealand, 1960; DDSc, University of Adelaide, 1962; FRACDS, FICD, 1968. Appointments: Private Dental Practice; Instructor in Pedodontics, Harvard School of Dental Medicine, 1960; Reader in Preventive Dentistry, University of Adelaide, 1962-82; Volunteer Dentist, Grenfell Association, Labrador and Arctic region; Radio Dentist, South Australia, 1963-82. Publications: Books: Your Teeth and How To Keep Them; Ideas for Children's Parties; Party Fun; Diet Counselling Manual in Normal Nutrition for Members of the

Dental Team, co-editor and contributor; 60 papers in scientific journals, Australia and overseas. Honours: Milton Research Fellowship, Maternal and Child Health, Harvard University, 1958; Rotary Award, Vocational Excellence, 1984. Memberships: Life Member, South Australian and Queensland Branches, Australian Dental Association, 1982; Dental Standing Committee, National Health and Medical Research Council of Australia; Federal Government Committee on Overseas Professional Qualifications; Australian Nutrition Foundation; National Patron, Home Economics Association. Address: 3 Banksia Close, The Domain, 74 Wardoo Street, Ashmore, Qld 4214, Australia.

FARAG Radwan Sedky, b. 27 November 1941, Cairo, Egypt. Professor of Biochemistry. m. Fatma Mahmoud El-Shishi, 1 son. Education: BSc, 1963, MSc, 1967, Faculty of Agriculture, Cairo University, Egypt; PhD, St Bartholomew's Hospital Medical College, London University, 1974. Appointments: Demonstrator, 1963-67, Associate Lecturer, 1967-74, Lecturer, 1974-79, Director of Central Laboratory, 1975-95, Associate Professor, 1979-84, Professor of Biochemistry, 1984-, Head of Biochemistry Department, 1988-94, Faculty of Agriculture, Cairo University; Over 40 MSC and 45 PhD students obtained their degrees under his direct supervision. Publications: Author; Chromatographic Analysis, 1990; Lipids, 1991; Physical and Chemical Analysis of Fats and Oils, 1995; Principles of Biochemistry, 1999. Over 120 papers in prominent journals. Honours: Egyptian State Award, Egyptian Academy of Scientific Research and Technology, 1978, 1984; 20th Century Award Achievement, IBC, 1997. Memberships: National Encyclopedia, Egypt; American Oil Chemists Society; International Association for Cereal Science and Technology; New York Academy of Sciences; American Association for the Advancement of Science; National Committee of Biochemistry and Molecular Biology. Address: Biochemistry Department, Faculty of Agriculture, Cairo University, PO 12613, El-Gamma St, Giza, Egypt.

FARHI Nicole, b. 25 July 1946. Fashion Designer. m. David Hare, 1992; 1 daughter with Stephen Marks. Education: Cours Berçot Art School, Paris. Appointments: Designer, Pierre d'Albi, 1968; Founder, French Connection with Stephen Marks, 1973; Former designer, Stephen Marks; Founder and designer, Nicole Farhi, 1983-; Nicole Farhi For Men, 1989-; Opened Nicole's Restaurant, 1994. Honours: British Fashion Award for Best Contemporary Design, 1995, 1996, 1997; FHM Awards Menswear Designer of the Year, 2000; Maxim Awards, British Designer of the Year, 2001. Address: 16 Foubert's Place, London W1F 7PJ, England.

FARIA Gentil Luiz de, b. 10 March 1946, Lucélia, Brazil. Educator; Lawyer. m. Carlota Rodrigues, 1 daughter. Education: BA, 1970, MA, 1976, PhD, 1980, BLaw, 1980, University of Sao Paulo; Postgraduate, Indiana University, 1977-78; Postdoctoral Research, Konstanz University, 1981. Appointments: Visiting Professor of Comparative Literature, Federal University of Paraiba, 1985-86; Professor of Comparative Literature, Unesp-University Estadual Paulista, 1987-99; Secretary of Education, Rio Preto, Brazil, 1997-2000. Publications include: A presenca de Oscar Wilde na belle epoque literaria brasileira, 1988; Preface to Teatro de Oscar Wilde, 1995; Literatura Comparada e Traducao, 1996; The Intellectual's Role in the Postmodern Third World, 1996; Comparative Literature below the Equator: The Cultural Dilemma of Choosing the Best Colonizer, 2000; Jorge Amado, 2004. Honours: Fulbright Fellowship; British Council Fellow; French Government Scholar; Fellowship for Distinguished Scholar, Brazilian Ministry of Education, 1991-93; School of Criticism and Theory Fellowship. Memberships: Modern Language Association of America; British Comparative Literature Association;

International Comparative Literature Association; Brazilian Comparative Literature Association. Address: 730 Cap Justino do Espirito Santo, Rio Preto SP 15090-400, Brazil.

FARMAN Allan George, b. 26 July 1949, Birmingham, England. Professor of Radiology and Imaging Sciences. m. Taeko Takemori. Education: BDS, 1971; LDSRCS, 1972; PhD, 1977; Dip ABOMR, 1982; EdS, 1983; MBA, 1987; DSc, 1996; Dip JBOMR, 1997. Appointments: Professor, Radiology and Imaging Sciences, School of Dentistry, University Louisville; Clinical Professor, Diagnostic Radiology, University Louisville School of Medicine, 1980-. Publications: 300 science articles, numerous texts and contributions to textbooks; Oral and Maxillofacial Diagnostic Imaging; Editor: Panoramic Imaging News, 2001-. Honours: President of Honour, First Latin-American Regional Meeting on Dentomaxillofacial Radiology, 1996. Memberships: International Association of Dentomaxillofacial Radiology, President, 1994-97; American Academy of Oral and Maxillofacial Radiology, Editor, 1988-95; American Dental Association, Representative to International DICOM Committee, 2001-; Founder, Organiser, International Congress Computed Maxillofacial Imaging, 1995-. Address: c/o School of Dentistry, University of Louisville, Louisville, KY 40292, USA.

FARMAN FARMA Hassan Kalan, b. 23 August 1969, Hamedan, Iran. Medical Doctor; Researcher. m. Leila Mohammady Sadeh Knoo, 1 son. Education: MD, Hamadan Medical College, 1986; PhD, English and Persian Literature, Tehran University, 1989; MSc, Immunology, Kerman Medical College, Iran, 1996. Appointments: Dean of Central Library of Kerman Medical University, 1994-98; Dean of Health Department, Hamadan College, 1996-98. Publications: Articles in professional journals. Honours: Great Board Certification, Ministry of Ershad, Islamic Republic of Iran, 2002; World Researcher, 1998, 2003, Who's Who in the World; Listed in Who's Who publications and biographical dictionaries. Memberships: Japanese Society of Gastroenterology; New York Academy of Science; American Pediatric Society. Address: No 16 Gelayol Alley, Mahmoodeh Town, Karaj, Iran.

FARMER Beverley, b. 1941, Australia. Novelist. Publications: Alone, 1980; Short stories: Milk, 1983; Home Time, 1985; A Body of Water: A Year's Notebook, 1990; Place of Birth, 1990; The Seal Woman, 1992; The House in the Light, 1995; Collected Stories, 1996.

FARR Dennis Larry Ashwell, b. 3 April 1929, Luton, Bedfordshire, England. Art Historian. m. Diana Pullein-Thompson, 1 son, 1 daughter. Education: BA Hons, 1950, MA, 1956, Courtauld Institute of Art, London University. Appointments: Assistant Witt Librarian, Courtauld, 1952-54; Assistant Keeper, Tate Gallery, 1954-64, Curator, Paul Mellon Collection, Washington DC, 1965-66; Deputy Keeper/Senior Lecturer, Glasgow University Art Collection, 1967-69; Director, Birmingham Museums and Art Gallery, 1969-80; Director, Courtauld Institute Galleries, 1980-93. Publications: William Etty, 1958; Tate Gallery Modern British School Catalogue (2 volumes with M Chamot and M Butlin), 1964; English Art 1870-1940, 1978; Lynn Chadwick, Sculptor (with Eva Chadwick), 1990, second edition, 1998; Francis Bacon, A Retrospective Exhibition, Yale Centre for British Art (with M Peppiatt and S Yard), 1999; Lynn Chadwick Retrospective, Tate Britain, 2003; and many exhibition catalogues and publications for the Courtauld Collections; General Editor, Clarendon Studies in History of Art, 1985-2001. Contributions: Burlington Magazine; Museums Journal; TLS; Apollo; DNB, Oxford DNB. Honours: FRSA, 1971; FMA, 1973; Hon DLitt, Birmingham University, 1981; CBE, 1991.

Dictionary of International Biography

Memberships: Athenaeum, 1971; President, Museums Association, 1980; Chairman, Association of Art Historians, 1983-86; Member, Comité Internationale d'Histoire de l'Art, 1983. Address: Orchard Hill, Swan Barn Road, Haslemere, Surrey GU27 2HY, England.

FARROW Mia Villiers, b. 9 February 1945, California, USA. Actress. m. (1) Frank Sinatra, 1966, divorced 1968, (2) André Previn, 1970, divorced 1979, 14 children including 1 son with Woody Allen. Career: Stage debut in The Importance of Being Ernest, New York, 1963; other stage appearances include: The Three Sisters, House of Bernard Alba, 1972-73; The Marrying of Ann Leete, Ivanov, RSC, London, 1976; Romantic Comedy, Broadway, 1979; Films include: Guns at Batasi, 1964; Rosemary's Baby, 1968; John and Mary, Secret Ceremony, 1969; The Great Gatsby, 1973; Full Circle, A Wedding, Death on the Nile, 1978; A Midsummer Night's Sex Comedy, 1982; Broadway Danny Rose, 1984; Hannah and Her Sisters, 1986; Radio Days, 1987; Another Woman, 1988; Oedipus Wrecks, 1989; Alice, Crimes and Misdemeanours, 1990; Husband and Wives, Shadows and Fog, 1992; Widow's Peak, 1994; Miami Rhapsody, 1995; Private Parts, 1997; Reckless, 1995; Coming Soon, 2000; TV appearances include: Peyton Place, 1964-66; Peter Pan, 1975. Publication: What Falls Away (autobiography), 1996. Honours: Academy Award; Best Actress, 1969; David Donatello, 1969; Film Festival Award, 1969; San Sebastian Award. Address: International Creative Management, c/o Sam Cohn, 40 West 57th Street, New York, NY 10019, USA. Website: www.mia-farrow.com

FATIHI Mohamed, b. 1 January 1951, Zaouiat Sidi Hamza, Morocco. Professor. m. Zhor Abedelouafi, 1 son. Education: Bachelors degree, History and Geography, 1976; Diploma of Advanced Studies in History, 1978; Masters degree, 1983, PhD, 1989, Measurement and Evaluation. Appointments: Chief, In-Service Training, 1985-86; Chief, Division of Evaluation, 1996-98; Director, Evaluation of Educational System, 1998. Publications: Articles in professional journals. Honours: Representative of Morocco at le IEA. Memberships: Board of Editors, two reviews; Various educational and cultural associations. Address: 33 Avenue Ogbo, #8 Agdal, Rabat, Morocco. E-mail: fahiti@men.gov.ma

FATOKUN Jeremiah Olujide, b. 4 September 1943, Ibadan, Nigeria. Agricultural Engineer. m. Olabisi Olufunmilayo, 4 sons, 2 daughters. Education: BSc honours, Agriculture, 1971; MSc Water Management, 1975. Appointments: Principal, Bakura College of Agriculture, Ahmadu Bello University, 1971-77; Head, Engineering Department, 1977-84, General Manager, 1985-91, Managing Director, 1991-93, Ogun-Oshun River Basin Development Authority, Abeokuta, Nigeria; Private Water Resources Development Consultant, 1993-. Publications: 7 significant articles in professional journals. Memberships: Nigerian Society of Agricultural Engineers; Hydrological Sciences Association of Nigeria. Address: Iyaniwura House, PO Box 28303, Ibadan, Nigeria.

FATOKUN Olaposi Samuel, b. 16 January 1965, Owo, Ondo State, Nigeria. Civil Engineer. m. Adenike Apinke Coker, 1 son, 1 daughter. Education: BSc (Honours), Civil Engineering, University of Ife (now Obafemi Awolowo University), 1981-86; MSc, Foundation and Geotechnical Engineering, University of Lagos, Nigeria, 1994-95. Appointments: Padif Partnership Ltd (Architects, Engineers and Planners), Jos, Nigeria, 1988-93, last position: Resident Project Engineer (Yola); Federal Ministry of Works and Housing, Lagos, Nigeria, 1993-97, last position: Senior Civil Engineer and Head Civil Section, Lagos State Field Headquarters, Alausa; Principal Research Officer and Head Geotechnics Section, Nigeria Building and Road Research Institute, 1997; Civil-Geotechnical Engineer, Technical/Design Department, 1997-2003,

Manager, Technical/Design Department, 2003-, Trevi Foundations Nigeria Ltd, Lagos, Nigeria. Publications: Papers presented at conferences: Marina shore protection: Application of T-1 single jet fluid grouting technique to form an impervious retaining wall, 1999; Earth dam foundation remediation: Using the T-1S double fluid jet grouting technique to form an impervious curtain wall, 2001. Honour: Award for outstanding lecture delivered at the 1st ISSMGE international lecture tour for African Region on in-situ site characterisation. Memberships: International Society for Soil Mechanics and Geotechnical Engineering; Chartered Engineer, Council for the Regulation of Engineering in Nigeria; Member, Deep Foundations Institute and member of micropile committee, New Jersey, USA; Corporate Member, Nigerian Society of Engineers; Nigerian Geotechnical Association; Canadian Geotechnical Society. Address: TREVI Foundations Nig. Ltd, Plot 4 Block B, Gbagada Industrial Scheme II, PO Box 70621, VI Lagos, Nigeria. E-mail: posifatokun@yahoo.com

FATUŠIĆ Zlatan, b. 5 July 1955, Lukavac, Bosnia and Herzegovina. Gynaecologist. m. Dusanica, 2 sons. Education: International Highschool of Ultrasound in Gynaecology and Obstetrics (Ian Donald School, Dubrovnik), 1997. Appointments: Specialist, Gynaecology and Obstetrics, 1988; Professor, Medical Faculty, University of Tuzla, 1997-; Head, Obstetrics and Gynaecology Clinic, University Clinical Centre, 1998-; President Perinatal Association of Bosnia and Herzegovina, 2000-. Publications: Books: History of Gynaecology; Ultrasound in Gynaecology; Atlas of Ultrasound; Articles in medical journals include: Perinatal Mortality in the Federation of Bitt, 2001 and many articles in books of abstracts. Honour: Man of the Year 2003, American Biographical Institute. Memberships: Member of Presidency of World Association of Perinatal Medicine; Member of Presidency of Association of Perinatal Medicine of South/East Europe. Address: Slatina 3/28, 75000 Tuzla, Bosnia and Herzogovina.

FAULKS Sebastian, b. 20 April 1953, Newbury, Berkshire, England. Author; Journalist. m. Veronica Youlten, 1989, 2 sons, 1 daughter. Education: Wellington College; Emmanuel College, Cambridge. Appointments: Reporter, Daily Telegraph newspaper, 1979-83; Feature Writer, Sunday Telegraph, 1983-86; Literary Editor, The Independent, 1986-89; Deputy Editor, The Independent on Sunday, 1989-90; Associate Editor, 1990-91; Columnist, The Guardian, 1992-, Evening Standard, 1997-99; Mail on Sunday, 1999-2000. Television: Churchill's Secret Army, 2000. Publications: The Girl at the Lion d'Or, 1989; A Fool's Alphabet, 1992; Birdsong, 1993; The Fatal Englishman, 1996; Charlotte Gray, 1998; On Green Dolphin Street, 2001. Address: c/o Aitken and Stone, 29 Fernshaw Road, London, SW10 0TG, England.

FAVRE Pascal, b. 19 June 1949, Billens, Fribourg, Switzerland. Musician; Teacher; Conductor; Composer. m. Maria, 1 son, 1 daughter. Education: Psychology, University of Paris VIII, Centre Romand D'Enseignement à distance, (Open University, Switzerland); Trumpet with Jean-Pierre Mathey, Theory with Louis-Marc Sutter, Composition, Instrumentation with Jean Balissat, Conducting with Michel Rochat, Music Academy of Lausanne; Special courses on Gregorian song in Solesmes, trumpet with James Stamp and Thomas Steven. Career: Former Conductor, The Military Band of the 7th Regiment, Ensemble de Cuivres Valaisan, Wind-Orchestra of the City of Bern, The Swiss Youth Band, 1990, 2001; Conductor, Brass Band of Crissier, 1976-; Conductor, Wind Orchestra, Music Academy of Lausanne; Musical Director of the Aventicum Musical Parade (Tattoo); Professor for Saxhorns, Music School of Crissier; Professor for Conducting Wind and Brass Instruments and Instrumentation, Music Academy of Lausanne, 1980- and Music Academy of Sion, 1990-; Formerly

Expert at the European Brass-Band Contest, Munich, Germany and at the International Wind Band Contest, Bourbon-Lancy, France. Compositions: Over 50 compositions include most recently: The Trip of the Mystery Ship for wind band; Fanfare for Youth; Introduction, Romances and Dances for brass band, wind band and fanfare; Wounded Knee for brass band, 2001; Le Kiosque à Musiques, radio signature tune; El Camino de Santiago, for wind band; Toccata, Arias and Dances for accordions orchestra; Jambo, an African Safari. Publications: Memento, Warm-up method for ensemble, with the rules of James stamp simplified; Articles in Unisono, Journal of the Swiss band Association. Honours: Special Prize for the best examination by brass players, 1976; Special Education prize for excellent education method, 1978; Conductor Diploma, 1982; 2nd Prize, International Composition Contest for Wind Orchestra, Fédération Musicale de Poitou-Charentes, France; Stephan Jaeggi Prize for Swiss Musicians, 2001. Memberships: Former Vice-Chairman, Musical Board, Swiss Wind Band Association; Chairman of Musical Board, Canton de Vaud Wind Band Association, Lausanne; Music Committee, WASBE-Switzerland. Address: Bois-Girard, CH-1774 Montagny-les-Monts, Switzerland. E-mail: favpmmf@vtx.ch

FAWAZ George A Y, b. 22 November 1913, Deirmimas, Lebanon. Emeritus Professor of Pharmacology and Therapeutics. m. Eva Niemiec, 2 daughters. Education: BA, High Distinction, American University of Beirut, 1930; PhD, Pregl's Institute of Microchemistry, University of Qraz, Austria, 1936; MD, University of Heidelberg, Germany, 1954. Appointments: Instructor in Biochemistry, Adjunct Professor, Biochemistry, Associate Professor of Biochemistry, American University of Beirut, Lebanon, 1938-46; Rockefeller Fellow in Chemistry, Harvard University, USA, 1946-48; Professor of Pharmacology and Therapeutics and Head of Department, American University of Beirut, 1949-64; Visiting Professor of Chemistry, University of California, Berkeley, USA, 1964-65; Professor and Chairman, Department of Pharmacology and Therapeutics, 1966; Emeritus Professor, Department of Pharmacology and Therapeutics, 1973-. Publications: 86 publications; 65 scientific papers in international medical journals as first author; 22 non-scientific articles. Honours: First Class Order of Merit, Government of Germany, 1964; The Great Order of Merit, Government of Germany, 1974; Gold Medal, Lebanese Chamber of Medicine, Lebanon, 1990; Cedar Cross, Commander Class, Government of Lebanon, 1992. Address: American University of Beirut, PO Box 11-0236, Beirut, Lebanon.

FEAST Michael William, b. 29 December 1926, Deal, Kent, England. Astronomer. m. Constance Elizabeth Maskew, 1 son, 2 daughters. Education: PhD, Physics, Imperial College, London, 1949. Appointments: NRC Postdoctoral Fellow, Ottawa, Canada, 1949-52; Astronomer, Radcliffe Observatory, Pretoria, 1952-74; South African Astronomical Observatory, 1974-92, Director, 1976-92; Royal Society Visiting Fellow, Cambridge University, 1992-93; Honorary Professor, University of Cape Town, 1983-. Publications: About 350 scientific publications. Honours: Vice-President International Astronomical Union, 1979-85; Associate (Honorary Fellow), Royal Astronomical Society, London, 1980; Gill Medal, Astronomical Association of South Africa, 1983; De Beer Gold Medal, South African Institute of Physics, 1992; DSc, honoris causa, University of Cape Town, 1993. Memberships: South African Academy; Fellow, Royal Society of South Africa; Royal Astronomical Society; Astronomical Society of South Africa. Address: Astronomy Department, University of Cape Town, Rondebosch 7701, South Africa. E-mail: mwf@artemisia.ast.uct.ac.za

FEATHERSTONE Gary, b. 2 September 1949, Sydney, Australia. Composer; Performer. Education: Sydney Conservatorium, four years, studying piano and music education.

Debut: Radio 2CH, Sydney, aged 15. Career: Performances in England, France, Poland, Germany and Australia; Recordings for ABC Radio and 2MBS, FM Radio, Sydney; Examiner in Piano, Australian Music Examinations Board, 1987-2002; Director of Music, Pittwater House Schools, 1980-90. Compositions: 2 Concertos for Piano and Orchestra; Rhapsody on Original Theme for Piano and Orchestra; Serenade for Strings, 2000; Symphonic Fantasia – Peter Ibbetson, full orchestra, 2001. Recording: Barcarolle, for ABC-FM, Australian Composers Piano Concert, 1995; CD of Serenade for Strings by Nevsky Quartet, St Petersburg, Russia, 2002; CD of Symphonic Fantasia – Peter Ibbetson by Slovak Radio Orchestra, 2002; 3 compositions on 2 CD set of Australian Piano Music, 2002. Publications: Piano Pieces for Children, 1989; Idyll, for flute and piano, 1990; Prelude in E Flat major, for piano, 1990; Improvisation, for piano, 1993; Pieces for Musical Children, 1993; I Need Love, for voice and piano, 1995; Four Nocturnes, 1995; The Waltzes, for piano, 1995; Barcarolle, for piano, 1995; Berceuse, for piano, 1996; Scherzo, for piano, 1996; Two Dance Songs, piano, 1997; 24 Preludes, piano, 1999; Romance for Violin and Piano, 2001. Honours: Margaret Price Music Achievement, 1967; Associate in Music, Australia, 1970; Accredited Composer, Australian Music Centre, 1990; Large number of music compositions in the examination syllabus of Australian Music Examinations Board; Listed in National and International Biographical Dictionaries. Memberships: Australian College of Education; Australian Society for Keyboard Music; Fellow, Australian Composers; Accredited Composer, Australian Music Centre. Address: 29 Balmain Road, McGraths Hill, NSW 2756, Australia. Website: www.amcoz.com.au

FEDORTSEVA Regina, b. 26 March 1940, Leningrad, Russia. Biologist. m. Oleg Fedortsev. Education: MSc, University of Leningrad, 1966; Biology Degree, Leningrad, 1974; Science Candidate, PhD, Institute of Cytology Academy of Science. Appointments: Laboratory Assistant, 1966-72, Junior Researcher, 1972-82, Institute of Cytology, Leningrad; Senior Researcher, Institute of Cytology, St Petersburg, 1982-93; Head of Laboratory, Senior Scientific Researcher, All Russian Centre of Ecological Medicine, St Petersburg, 1993-97; Head of Laboratory, Senior Scientific Researcher, All Russian Centre of Emergency and Radiation Medicine, Emercom of Russia, St Petersburg, 1997-. Publications: Over 90 articles in professional journals. Honours: Several. Memberships: International Society of Haematology; European Cytogenetics Association; European Society of Human Genetics; Russian Society of Clinical Cytology; Russian Society of Medical Genetics; European Haematology Association. Address: All Russian Centre of Emergency and Radiation Medicine Emercom of Russia, 4/2 Lebedeva Str, 194044 St Petersburg, Russia. E-mail: fedorts@arcezm.spb.ru

FEDULOV Alexander Mikhailovich, b. 8 November 1958, Shchigry, Kursk region, Russia. Lawyer. Divorced, 1 son. Education: Doctor of Jurisprudence, 1991; Academician, Academy of Problems of Security, Defence, Law and Order, 2001. Appointments: Deputy, State Duma of the Federal Assembly of RJ, 3rd convocation; Counsellor of the State Secretary, Union State of Belarus and Russia. Publications: Over 75 articles including: For Globalization of World Community, 2001; Monograph of Investigation. Honours: Medal of the Baltic Humanities School, Poland; Anatoly Koni Medal, 2000; Badge, 200th Anniversary of the Ministry of Internal Affairs. Memberships: Honourable Professor of the Baltic Humanities School, Poland. Address: Flat 142, 19 Kutuzovsky Prospekt, Moscow.

FEHM Tanja, b. 23 April 1971, Nuremberg, Germany. Medical Doctor. Education: MD, Medical School, Erlangen, Germany, 1990-97; Postdoctoral Fellow, Adjunct Assistant Professor,

University of Texas, Southwestern Medical School, Dallas, Texas, USA, 1999-2001 Appointments: Clinical Researcher, University of Tuebingen, Germany, 2001-; Adjunct Assistant Professor, Cancer Immunobiology Center, University of Texas, Southwestern Medical School, Dallas, Texas, USA, 2001-. Publications: Original papers in medical journals: Breast Cancer Research and Treatment; Clinical Cancer Research; Oncology; Tumor Biology; Journal of Clinical Oncology. Honours: Poster Prize, German Cancer Society, 2002; Grantee, German Research Society. Memberships: AACR; GMSD. Address: Braunsbacher Str 20, 80765 Fuerth, Germany. E-mail: tanja.fehm@t-online.de

FEHR Manfred, b. 25 March 1936, Jena, Germany. Chemical Engineer. m. Giomar Yemaíl, 1 son, 1 daughter. Education: BS, Université Laval, Quebec, 1967; MS, University of Alberta, Edmonton, 1969; PhD, Université Laval, Canada, 1978; Postdoctoral Fellow, Kungliga Tekniska Högskolan, Sweden, 1990; fluent in 5 languages. Appointments: Professional handball player, 2 clubs; International consultant, 32 clients; Marketing administrator 3 companies; Research and process engineer 4 companies; Lecturer and professor, 6 universities; International professional activities; Registered engineer, 2 countries; Citizen of 3 countries. Publications: 108 journal and newspaper articles; 86 research reports; 78 conference and symposium presentations; 40 invited speaking engagements; 1 book. Honours: 4 scholarships in Canada, 1963-75; 20 newspaper and radio interviews in Argentina and Brazil, 1992-2004; Consular Warden in Brazil, 1991-2001; More than 50 citations in international biographical dictionaries, 1981-2004, 92 awards, 1963-2004; 193 honourable mentions. Memberships: 34 professional associations in various countries; President of Environmental Foundation; former local chapter president of engineering association. Address: PO Box 811, 38400974 Uberlândia, Brazil. E-mail: josemanf@yahoo.com

FEILDEN Geoffrey Bertram Robert, b. 20 February 1917, London, England. Chartered Engineer. m. (1) Elizabeth Ann Gorton, 1 son, 2 daughters, (2) Elizabeth Diana Angier, 1 stepson, 2 stepdaughters. Education: Major scholar, King's College, Cambridge, England, 1936-39. Appointments: Technical Trainee, Lever Brothers and Unilever Ltd, 1939-40; Power Jets Ltd, 1940-46; Chief Engineer, Turbine Department, 1946, Engineering Director, 1954-59, Ruston and Hornsby Ltd; Managing Director, Hawker-Siddeley Brush Turbines Ltd, 1959-61; Group Technical Director, Davy-Ashmore Ltd, 1961-68; Deputy Director General, 1968-70, Director General, 1970-81, British Standards Institution; Non-Executive Director, Averys Ltd, 1974-79; Senior Partner, Feilden Associates, 1981-; Non-Executive Director, Plint and Partners Ltd, 1982-2001. Publications: Contributor, Gas Turbine Principles and Practice, 1955; A Standard Gas Turbine to Burn a Variety of Fuels, IMechE, 1956; First Bulleid Memorial Lecture, Nottingham University, 1959; Chairman of Committee, Engineering Design Report, 1963; The Contributions of Power Jets Ltd to Jet Propulsion, Royal Aeronautical Society, 1993. Honours: FRS, 1959; Hon DTech, Loughborough, 1970; Hon DSc, Queens University, Belfast, 1971; Joint Winner, MacRobert Award for Innovation, 1983; Senior Fellow, Royal College of Art, 1986; Hodgson Prize, Royal Aeronautical Society, 1994; Hon Dtech, Lincoln University, 2003; Hon Freedom of the City of Lincoln, 2003. Memberships: Committees and Sub-Committees of Aeronautical Research Council, 1947-62; British Transport Commission Research Advisory Council, 1956-61; Council for Scientific and Industrial Research (DSIR), 1961-665; Design Council, 1966-78; Visiting Committee to Royal College of Art, 1968-84, Chairman, 1977-84; Central Advisory Council for Science and Technology, 1970-71; Research, Development and Engineering for Northern Ireland, 1983-86; Chairman, UK Committee for CODATA, 1989-97. Address: 1 Hambutts Mead, Painswick, Gloucester GL6 6RP, England.

FEINBERG Elen A, b. 22 January 1955, New York City, USA. Artist; Professor. Education: Tyler School of Art, Rome, Italy, 1974-75; BFA, Cornell University, Ithaca, New York, 1976; MFA, Indiana University, Bloomington, Indiana, 1978. Appointments: Regent's Professor of Art, 1994-97; Currently, Regent's Professor of Art, University of New Mexico, Albuquerque, New Mexico. Honours include: Several grants and fellowships; National Endowment for the Arts Fellowship in Painting, 1988; Ingram Merrill Foundation Award in Painting, 1989; Ruth Chenven Foundation Award in Painting, 1991; Roswell Museum and Art Centre, AIR Fellowship, 1984-85; MacDowell Colony Fellowship, 1986; Basil H Alkazzi Award (USA) in Painting, 1997; Virginia Center for the Creative Arts Fellowship, Sweet Briar, Virginia, 1998; Federal Chancellery of Vienna, Fellowship in Painting, Austria, 1999. Commissions and Creative Works: Public collections include: Israel Museum, Jerusalem; Los Angeles County Museum of Art; Bundeskanzleramt, Vienna, Austria; Milwaukee Museum, Wisconsin; Fresno Art Center, California; Santa Cruz Museum of Art; Albuquerque Museum, New Mexico; Arizona State University Art Museum, Tempe; Washington & Jefferson College Art Museum, Washington, Pennsylvania; Museum of Fine Arts, Santa Fe, New Mexico; Roswell Museum, New Mexico; Morgan Guarantee Trust, New York; IBM, Atlanta; Northern Trust Bank, Chicago, Illinois; Tamarind Institute, Albuquerque, New Mexico; National Economic Research Associates, New York; Numerous private collections, galleries; Solo exhibitions include: Sarah Morthland Gallery, New York, 1999; Galerie Rauminhalt, Vienna, Austria Ruth Bachofner Gallery, Santa Monica, California, 1999; District Fine Arts, Washington DC (solo), 2000, 2003. Address: 613 Ridge Place, NE, Albuquerque, New Mexico 87106, USA.

FEINSTEIN Robert N, b. 10 August 1915, Milwaukee, Wisconsin, USA. Biochemist; Poet. m. Betty J Greenbaum, 5 May 1941, 2 daughters. Education: BS, Chemistry, 1937, MS, Biochemistry, 1938, PhD, Physiological Chemistry, 1940, University of Wisconsin. Appointments: Research Assistant, Michael Reese Hospital, Chicago; Research Associate, May Institute for Medical Research, Cincinnati, Ohio; Associate Professor, University of Chicago; Senior Biochemist, Argonne National Laboratory. Publications: Oysters in Love, 1984; Son of an Oyster, 1989; Oyster's Last Stand, 1994. Contributions to: Lyric; Light year; Light; Plains Poetry Journal; Saturday Evening Post; Wall Street Journal; Christian Science Monitor. Honours: Prize, Individual Magazines, Erew, 1981, Lyric, 1987, Archer, 1987, 1988, Heartland Journal, 1989, Amelia, 1991, Parnassur, 1995. Address: 250 Village Drive, Apt 334, Downers Grove, IL 60516, USA.

FEKETE John, b. 7 August 1946, Budapest, Hungary. Professor of English and Cultural Studies; Writer. Education: BA, Honours, English Literature, 1968, MA, English Literature, 1969, McGill University; PhD, Cambridge University, 1973. Appointments: Visiting Assistant Professor, English, McGill University, Montreal, Quebec, 1973-74; Associate Editor, Telos, 1974-84; Visiting Assistant Professor, Humanities, York University, Toronto, Ontario, 1975-76; Assistant Professor, 1976-78, Associate Professor, 1978-84, Professor, English, Cultural Studies, 1984-, Trent University, Peterborough, Ontario. Publications: The Critical Twilight: Explorations in the Ideology of Anglo-American Literary Theory from Eliot to McLuhan, 1978; The Structural Allegory: Reconstructive Encounters With the New French Thought, 1984; Life After Postmodernism: Essays on Culture and Value, 1987; Moral Panic: Biopolitics Rising, 1994. Contributions to: Canadian Journal of Political and Social Theory; Canadian Journal of Communications; Science-Fiction Studies. Address: 1818 Cherryhill Road, Peterborough, Ontario K9K 1S6, Canada.

FELBER Ewald, b. 24 March 1947, Vienna, Austria. Professor, Musician, Composer. m. Elfriede Halmschlager, 1 son. Education: Music Teacher, University of Music, Vienna, 1976; Primary School Teacher, State College, Vienna, 1983; Doctor Phil, Musicology, University of Vienna, 1993; Diploma, Summer Course, University of Santiago de Compostela, Spain, 1980. Appointments: Guitar Teacher, High School, Vienna, 1973-81; Professor, State College of Teacher Education, Vienna, 1981-; Concert Activities, 1970-; Visiting Professor at various foreign universities. Publications: Book: Klangfarben zur Musik von Ewald Felber, 1998; Musical Notes (own compositions), 2004; Records and CDs. Honours: Professor, 1983; Oberstudienrat, 1998; Winner, Composing Competition, 2003. Memberships: Board Member, Vienna International Summer Course for New Music; AKM (Authors, Composers and Music Editors). Address: Rosentalgasse 5-7/2/6, A-1140 Vienna, Austria. E-mail: fee@pabw.at

FELBER Sonja Veronika, b. 21 March 1965, St Pölten. Mechanical Engineer. Education: E Grad, University Technology, Vienna, 1992; DSc, 1996. Appointments: Research Scientist, OMV Vienna, Austria, 1991-92; Assistant, 1993-2001, Professor, 2002-, University of Technology, Vienna. Publications: New Findings in Crack-Arrest, Test of Heat Affected Zones, Test Methods, CTOD Tests, Pipeline Steels, Pressure Vessel Steels, TM Steels; Simulation of Heat Affected Zones, Building of Pipelines. Memberships: Austrian Welding Foundation; Austrian Iron and Steel Institute; IIW. Address: TVFA, E 030, Institute for Materials Research and Testing, Vienna University of Technology, A-1040 Vienna, Karlspl 13, Austria.

FELDMAN Paula R, b. 4 July 1948, Washington, District of Columbia, USA. Professor of English; Writer. Education: BA, Bucknell University, 1970; MA, 1971, PhD, 1974, Northwestern University. Appointments: Assistant Professor, English, 1974-79, Associate Professor, English, 1979-89, Professor, English, 1989-, Director, Graduate Studies in English, 1991-93; C Wallace Martin Professor of English, 1999-, Louise Frye Scudder, Professor of Liberal Arts, 2000-, University of South Carolina, Columbia. Publications: The Microcomputer and Business Writing (with David Byrd and Phyllis Fleishel), 1986; The Journals of Mary Shelley (editor with Diana Scott-Kilvert), 2 volumes, 1987; The Wordworthy Computer: Classroom and Research Applications in Language and Literature (with Buford Norman), 1987; Romantic Women Writers: Voices and Countervoices (editor with Theresa Kelley), 1995; British Women Poets of the Romantic Era: An Anthology, 1997; A Century of Sonnets: The Romantic Era Revival 1750-1850 (Editor with Daniel Robinson), 1999; Records of Woman, (Editor), 1999. Contributions to: Papers of the Bibliographical Society of America, 1978; Studies in English Literature, 1980; Approaches to Teaching Shelley's Frankenstein, 1990; Blake: An Illustrated Quarterly, 1993; Keats-Shelley Journal, 1997; New Literary History, 2002. Address: Department of English, University of South Carolina, Columbia, SC 29208, USA.

FERGUSON Alexander Chapman (Sir), b. 31 December 1941, Glasgow, Scotland. Football Club Manager. m. Catherine Holding, 1966, 3 sons. Appointments: Footballer, Queen's Park, 1958-60, St Johnstone, 1960-64, Dunfermline Athletic, 1964-67, Glasgow Rangers, 1967-69, Falkirk, 1969-73, Ayr Utd, 1973-74; Manager, East Stirling, 1974, St Mirren, 1974-78, Aberdeen, 1978-86, Scottish National Team (assistant manager), 1985-86, Manchester Utd, 1986- (winners FA Cup 1990, 1994, 1996, 1999, 2004; European Cup Winners' Cup, Super Cup, 1991; FA Premier League Championship 1992/93, 1993/94, 1995/94, 1996/97, 1998/99, 1999/2000, 2000/01, 2002/03; League and FA Cup double 1994 and 1996 (new record); Champions League European Cup, 1999. Publications: A Light in the North, 1984; Six Years at United,

1992; Just Champion, 1993; A Year in the Life, 1995; A Will to Win, 1997; Managing My Life: My Autobiography, 1999; The Unique Treble, 2000. Honours include: KBE, 1999; CBE; Voted Best Coach in Europe, UEFA Football Gala, 1999; Freeman, Cities of Aberdeen, Glasgow and Manchester. Address: c/o Manchester United Football Club, Old Trafford, Manchester M16 0RA, England.

FERGUSON James Edward, II, b. 25 October 1951, Los Angeles, California, USA. Professor. m. Lynn, 3 sons. Education: MD, Bowman Gray School of Medicine, 1973-77; Internship, San Francisco, 1977-78; Residency, Stanford University School of Medicine, 1978-80; Chief Resident, Bowman Gray School of Medicine, 1980-81; Postdoctoral Fellowship, Stanford University School of Medicine, 1982-84. Appointments: Clinical Faculty, Bowman Gray School of Medicine, 1981-82; Assistant Professor, Stanford University School of Medicine, 1984-87; Assistant Professor, University of Virginia School of Medicine, 1987-90; Associate Professor, University of Virginia School of Medicine, 1990-96; Professor, University of Virginia School of Medicine, 1996-2002; The John W Greene, Jr. Professor and Chair, Department of Obstetrics and Gynecology, University of Kentucky, 2002- . Publications: Numerous articles, books, reports. Honours: Elected fellow, American College of Obstetrician and Gynecologists; Listed in several who's who publications; Senior Member, American Institute of Ultrasound Medicine. Memberships include: American Medical Association; Society for Maternal-Fetal Medicine; American Association for the Advancement of Science; American Physiological Society; Society for Gynecological Investigation. Address: Department of Obstetrics and Gynecology, 800 Rose Street, University of Kentucky College of Medicine, Lexington, KY 40536, USA.

FERGUSON Robert Thomas, b. 2 June 1948, Stoke on Trent, England. Writer. m. 3 April 1987. Education: BA, University College, London, 1980. Publications: Enigma: The Life of Knut Hamsun, 1987; Henry Miller: A Life, 1991; Henrik Ibsen: A New Biography, 1996; The Short Sharp Life of T E Hulme, 2002. Contributions to: Best Radio Drama, 1984; Best Radio Drama, 1986. Honours: BBC Methuen Giles Cooper Awards, 1984, 1986; J G Robertson Prize, 1985-87. Address: Trudvangvn 25, 0363 Oslo, Norway.

FERGUSON William (Rotch), b. 14 February 1943, Fall River, Massachusetts, USA. Associate Professor of Spanish; Writer; Poet. m. Nancy King, 26 November 1983. Education: BA, 1965, MA, 1970, PhD, 1975, Harvard University. Appointments: Instructor, 1971-75, Assistant Professor, 1975-77, Boston University; Visiting Professor, 1977-79, Assistant Professor, 1979-83, Associate Professor of Spanish, 1983-, Adjunct Professor of English, 1989-, Chairman, Foreign Languages, 1990-98, Clark University, Worcester, Massachusetts; Visiting Lecturer in Spanish Renaissance Literature, University of Pennsylvania, 1986-87; Associate Editor, Hispanic Review, 1986-87. Publications: Dream Reader (poems), 1973; Light of Paradise (poems), 1973; La versificación imitativa en Fernando de Herrera, 1981; Freedom and Other Fictions (stories), 1984. Contributions to: Scholarly journals, anthologies, periodicals and magazines. Memberships: American Association of University Professors; International Institute in Spain; Modern Language Association; Phi Beta Kappa; Sigma Delta Pi. Address: 1 Tahanto Road, Worcester, MA 01602, USA.

FERLITA Ernest Charles, b. 1 December 1927, Tampa, Florida, USA. Jesuit Priest. Education: BS, Spring Hill College, 1950; STL, St Louis University, 1964; DFA, Yale University, 1969. Publications: The Theatre of Pilgrimage, 1971; Film Odyssey (co-author), 1976; The Way of the River, 1977; The Parables of Lina Wertmuller (co-author), 1977; Religion in Film (contributor), 1982; Gospel Journey, 1983; The Mask of Hiroshima in Best Short Plays, 1989; The Uttermost Mark, 1990; The Paths of Life, 1992, 1993, 1994; The Road to Bethlehem, 1997; Two Cities, 1999; In the Light of the Lord, 2003. Honours: 1st Prize, Christian Theatre Artists Guild, 1971; American Radio Scriptwriting Contest, 1985; Miller Award, 1986; 2nd Prize, International Competition of Religious Drama, 1999; International Writer of the Year, 2003. Memberships: Dramatists Guild; International Hopkins Society. Address: Loyola University, 6363 St Charles Avenue, New Orleans, LA 70118, USA. E-mail: ferlita@loyno.edu

FERNANDEZ Mary Joe, b. 19 August 1971, Dominican Republic. Tennis Player. m. Tony Godsick, 2000. Career: Ranked No 1 USA, 1984; Turned professional, 1986; Reached quarter-finals of French open, 1986, quarter-finals, Geneva, 1987, semi-finals Eastbourne, 1988, semi-finals, French Open, 1989, runner up to Graf in singles and runner up with Fendick in doubles, Australian Open, 1990; Reached semi-finals at Wimbledon and Australian Open, Italian Open, 1991; Runner-up Australian open, 1992; Won Bronze Medal in singles and Gold in doubles with G Fernandez, Olympic Games, 1992; Reached semi-finals US Open, 1992; Reached semi-finals Italian Open, quarter-finals Australian Open, 1993; Won singles title, Strasbourg, 1994; Winner, (with Davenport) French Open Doubles, 1996; Winner doubles, Hilton Head, Carolina, 1997, Madrid, 1997, won singles title German Open, 1997; Member, US Federal Cup Team, Atlantic City, 1991, 1994-99; Spokesperson for Will to Win Scholarship Programme, 1998; Retired, 2000. Publication: Mary Joe Fernandez (with Melanie Cole).

FERNANDO Antony, b. 30 May 1932, Sri Lanka. University Lecturer. m. Sumana Vivian, 25 March 1979. Education: Higher Diploma in Religious Education, Institute Catholic Paris, 1959; ThD, Greg, Rome, 1961; PhD, Lanka, 1978. Appointments: Lecturer, Buddhism, National Seminary, Sri Lanka, 1961-76; Lecturer in Christianity and World Religions, Kelaniya University, Sri Lanka, 1978-97; Co-Director, Founder, Inter-Cultural Research Centre, Sri Lanka, 1985-; Founder-Director, Inter-Cultural School of English for Adults, 1990-. Publications include: Books in English: Buddhism Made Plain, 1985; Christianity Made Intelligible, as One of the World's Religions, 1990; Christian Path to Mental Maturity, 1996; Foundation to English, 1990; We Sri Lankans, Student Reader 2002; Books in Sinhala: Diverse Forms of Contemporary Christianity, 1994; History, Literature and Art of Christianity, 1995; An Anthology of Western Christian Literature, editor, 1997. Honour: International Man of the Year, 1997-98, IBC; 20th Century Award for achievement in field of education, IBC; Academic Counsellor of the London Diplomatic Academy, Wakefield, West Yorkshire, England, 2002-. Memberships: Chairperson, Department of West Classics, Kelaniya University, Sri Lanka, 1978-97; Managerial Board, Ecumenical Institute, 1980-. Address: Inter-cultural House, 21G4 Paramuna Mawata Eldeniya, Kadawata, Sri Lanka.

FERREIRA Hendrik, b. 17 July 1954, Germiston, South Africa. Professor. m. Hester Susanna Potgieter. Education: BSc, Electrical Engineering, 1976, MSc, Electronic Engineering, 1978, DSc, Engineering, 1980, University of Pretoria; Professional Engineer Registration, Engineering Council of South Africa, 1982. Appointments: Postdoctoral Study, Linkabit Corporation, San Diego, USA, 1980-81; Consulting Engineer, GH Marais & Partners, Pretoria, South Africa, 1981-83; Senior Lecturer, 1983-84, Associate Professor, 1985-89, Professor, 1989-, Rand Afrikaans University, South Africa. Publications: Numerous papers and articles in professional journals; Contributions in books; Book

reviews. Honours: Presidential Award for Young Investigators, Foundation for Research Development, 1990-93. Memberships: IEEE; SAIEE; AMS; PSA; Fellow, PSSA. Address: Box 984, Melville 2109, South Africa. E-mail: hcf@ing.rau.ac.za

FERREIRA DA SILVA Antonio, b. 1 April 1947, Conceicão do Jacuípe, Berimbau, Bahia, Brazil. Physicist; Researcher. m. Vera Conceicão da Silva. 1 son, 1 daughter. Education: BSc, Federal University of Bahia, 1970; MSc, University of Campinas, 1975; PhD, 1979, Docent in Physics, 1985, Linköping University, Sweden; Full Professor, Federal University of Bahia, 2000. Appointments: Visiting Researcher, University of Kyoto, Japan, 1979; Head, Division of Science and Technology, 1981-82, Senior Researcher, 1986-, Instituto Nacional Pesquisas Espaciais, Sao José dos Campos, Brazil; Visiting Researcher, Brown University, USA, 1982; Consultant, Brazilian National Research Council, 1986-; Visiting Scientist, Linköping University, 1996; Consultant, Condensed Matter Physics. Publications: More than 120 international publications. Honour: One of Brazilian Scientists most cited internationally, Science Ranking (Brazilian), 1999. Memberships: American Physical Society; Brazilian Physical Society. Address: Instituto de Fisica, Universidade Federal da Bahia, 40210-340 Salvador, Bahia, Brazil.

FERREYRA Beatriz (Mercedes), b. 21 June 1937, Cordoba, Argentina. Composer. Education: Piano study with C Bronstein, Buenos Aires, 1950-56; Harmony with Nadia Boulanger, 1962-63; Composition with György Ligeti and Earle Brown, Darmstadt, 1967; Electronic Techniques with Pierre Schaeffer, GRM Paris, 1963-64. Debut: GRM, Paris, 1964. Career: Professor Assistant: GRM, 1965-70, GMEB, 1973; B Baschet Musical Instrument Development, 1971; Music Therapy, 1973-76, 1989; Dartmouth College Computer System, 1975; Jury at International Music Competitions between 1976 and 2004; Films: Antartide, 1971, Mutations, 1972; Homo Sapiens, TV, 1975. Compositions: Demeures Aquatiques, 1967; Médisances, 1968; L'Orvietan, 1970; Siesta Blanca, 1972; Canto del Loco, 1976; Cercles des Rondes, 1982; Echo, 1978; Jeux des Rondes, 1980-84; Cercles des Rondes, 1982; La Calesita, 1982; Boucles, rosettes et serpentines, 1982; Bruissements, 1983; Arabesque autour d'une corde raide, 1984; Passacaille deboitée pour un lutin, 1984; Petit Poucet Magazine, 1985; The UFO Forest, 1986; L'Autre...ou le chant des marécages, 1987; Souffle d'un petite Dieu distrait, 1988, definitive version, 1997; Brise sur une fourmillÈre, 1988; Tata, tocame la toccata, 1990; Remolinos, 1990; Mirage Contemplatif?, 1991; Río de los pájaros, 1993-98; Río de los pájaros econdidos, G R M 1999-2000; Río de los pájaros azules, 1999; Jazz't for Miles, 2001; La Ba-balle du chien-chien à la mé-mère, 2001; Tangatita para el Maestro, 2001; Vivencias, 2001; Cantos de antes, 2002; Les chemins du vent des glaces, 2002; Murmureln, 2003; Le Solfegiste solfegé, 2003. Recordings include: Souffle d'un petit Dieu distrait, American Composers Forum, USA, 1997; Petit Poucet Magazine, Siesta Blanca, Canto del Loco, The UFO Forest, Souffle d'un petit Dieu distrait: Chrysopée Electronique, Bourges, France, 2000; Rio de los pajaros. Echos: IMEB/UNESCO/CIME, Cultures électroniques no 14, Prix Magesterium, Bourges, France, 2000; Jazz't for Miles: MIT Computer Music Journals, 2001, USA; La Ba-balle du chien-chien à ma mé-mère: Compendium International, Brourges, France, 2000; Rios del Sueño, Medisances, l'Orvietan, Cantos de antes and Vivencias: Motus-Aousma, France, 2003. Publications: Works featured in: Le Groupe Solfège du GRM et le Traité des Objets Musicaux, 2001; Le solfège sonore de Pierre Schaeffer et la composition musicale, 1999; A conversation with Beatriz Ferrerya, 2001; Honours: Diplome de meilleur disque, Medisances, 1971; Prix du Centre National du Cinéma Français, 1972; 3rd Prix de L'Electronic Music Competition, Sweden, 1975; Prix Rissolli Della Prima Opera, Italy, 1978; Prix Fance Culture (radio) de l'Innovation, Concours International de Création Radiophonique, France, 1986; Prize from Journées d'Informatique Musicale, Paris, 1999. Rio de los pájaros, Magisterium Prize at the 27th International Competition of electroacoustic music and sonic art; 2nd Prize, Hungarian Radio for Cantos de antes, 2003. Management: National and International – Seminaries and conferences from 1998. Address: Bethleem, Nesle Hodeng, 76270 Neufchâtel-en-Bray, France.

FERRIS Paul (Frederick), b. 15 February 1929, Swansea, Wales. Writer. Publications: A Changed Man, 1958; The City, 1960; Then We Fall, 1960; The Church of England, 1962; A Family Affair, 1963; The Doctors, 1965; The Destroyer, 1965; The Nameless: Abortion in Britain Today, 1966; The Dam, 1967; Men and Money: Financial Europe Today, 1968; The House of Northcliffe, 1971; The New Militants, 1972; The Detective, 1976; Talk to Me about England, 1979; Richard Burton, 1981; A Distant Country, 1983; Gentlemen of Fortune, 1984; Children of Dust, 1988; Sex and the British, 1993; Caitlin, 1993; The Divining Heart, 1995; Dr Freud: A Life, 1997; Dylan Thomas: The Biography, 1999; Infidelity, 1999; New Collected Letters of Dylan Thomas, 2000; Cora Crane, 2003; Television Plays: The Revivalist, 1975; Dylan, 1978; Nye, 1982; The Extremist, 1983; The Fasting Girl, 1984. Address: c/o Curtis Brown Ltd, Haymarket House, 28/29 Haymarket, London SW1 4SP, England.

FERRY Bryan, b. 26 September 1945, Washington, County Durham, England. Singer; Songwriter; Musician. 4 sons. Education: Fine Art, Newcastle University. Career: Formed Roxy Music, 1971; Solo artiste, 1973-; Worked with: Brian Eno; Phil Manzanera; Andy Mackay; Steve Ferrone; David Williams; Robin Trower; Pino Palladino; Nile Rodgers; Carleen Anderson; Shara Nelson; Jhelisa; Numerous worldwide tours; Major concerts include: Crystal Palace, 1972; Live Aid, Wembley, 1985; Radio City, New York, 1988; Wembley, 1989; Support tours, Alice Cooper, David Bowie; Television appearances include: Subject of Without Walls documentary, 1992; Videos: New Town (live), 1990; Total Recall (documentary), 1990. Recordings: Singles include: Love Is The Drug, 1975; Dance Away, 1979; Angel Eyes, 1979; Over You, 1980; Jealous Guy, 1981; Slave To Love, 1985; The Right Stuff, 1987; I Put A Spell On You, 1993; Albums: Solo: These Foolish Things, 1973; Another Time Another Place, 1974; Let's Stick Together, 1976; In Your Mind, 1977; The Bride Stripped Bare, 1978; Boys And Girls, 1985; Bete Noire, 1987; The Ultimate Collection, 1988; Taxi, 1993; Mamounia, 1994; As Time Goes By, 1999; Frantic, 2002; with Roxy Music: Roxy Music, 1972; For Your Pleasure, 1973; Stranded, 1973; Country Life, 1974; Siren, 1975; Viva Roxy Music, 1976; Manifesto, 1979; Flesh And Blood (Number 1, UK), 1980; Avalon, (Number 1, UK), 1982; The High Road (live mini-album), 1983; The Atlantic Years, 1983; Street Life, 1987; Recent compilations include: The Thrill Of It All, 1995; More Than This - The Best Of Roxy Music and Bryan Ferry, 1995. Honours include: Grand Prix Du Disque, Best Album, Montreux Golden Rose Festival, 1973. Address: c/o Barry Dickins, ITB, 3rd Floor, 27A Floral Street, London, WC2E 9DQ, England.

FERZAK Franz Xaver, b. 27 October 1958, Neuenhinzenhausen, Germany. Publisher; Writer; Engineer. Education: Diploma of Mechanical Engineering, 1982. Appointments: Author, Publisher, 1986-; Translator, MVV Peiting, 1996-97, 2002. Publications: Nikola Tesla, 1986, Karl Freiherr von Reichenbach, 1987; Giordano Bruno, 1996; Wilhelm Reich, 1991; Jesus of Qumran, 1997; Viktor Schauberger, 2001. Honours: Listed in Who's Who publications and biographical dictionaries. Address: Am Bachl 1, 93336 Altmannstein, Germany.

FESSEL W Jeffrey, b. 20 June 1932, London, England. Physician; Medical Researcher. m. Nicole, 1 son. Education: MBBS, University of London, 1955; MRCP, London, 1956; FACP, 1966; FRCP, Edinburgh, 1971; FACR, 1987. Appointments: Clinical Professor of Medicine, 1983-96, Emeritus Clinical Professor of Medicine, 1996-, University of California at San Francisco; Chief of Medicine, 1979-89, Director, 1989-, Clinical Trials Unit, Kaiser Permanente, San Francisco. Publications: Over 100 papers and book chapters in peer-reviewed journals. Honours: Liston Gold Medal, University College Hospital, London. Memberships: Royal College of Physicians; American College of Rheumatology; American College of Physicians; HIV Academy. Address: 2238 Geary Blvd, San Francisco, CA 94115, USA. E-mail: jeffrey.fessel@kp.org

FEY Carl, b. 28 May 1969, Dallas, Texas, USA. Professor. m. Natalia. Education: BS, Bates College, USA; PhD, Ivey School of Business, USA. Appointments: Assistant Professor, Associate Dean of Research, Stockholm School of Economics, St Petersburg, 1997-. Publications: Articles in professional journals. Honours: Runner-up, Best Paper Award, International Management, Academy of Management; $250,000 grant, National Research Foundation. Memberships: AIB; AUM. Address: Stockholm School of Economics, PO Box 6501, 11383 Stockholm, Sweden. Website: www.hhs.se/iib

FIECHTER Jean Jacques, b. 25 May 1927, Alexandria, Egypt. Historian; Novelist. 2 sons. Education: MA, History, 1950; PhD, History, Cum Laude, 1965. Appointments: CEO President, Blancpain Watches, 1950-80; General Manager, Swiss Watch Industrial Corporation, 1960-80; Independent Historian, 1981-. Publications: More than 10 biographies and historical works including: Gouvernor Morris; Baron de Besenval; The Harvest of Gods; Mykerinos, le dieu englouti; 2 novels: Death by Publication; A Masterpiece of Revenge. Honours: Grand Prize, Literature, Bern State; General History Prize, French Academy; French Grand Prize for detective novel. Memberships: PEN International (Swiss French Section). Address: 80 Rte Geneve, 1028 Preverenges, Switzerland.

FIENNES Ranulph (Twisleton-Wykeham), b. 7 March 1944, Windsor, England. Explorer; Writer. m. Virginia Pepper. Education: Eton College. Appointments: British Army, 1965-70; Special Air Service, 1966; Sultan of Muscat's Armed Forces, 1968-70; Led British Expeditions to White Nile, 1969, Jostedalsbre Glacier, 1970, Headless Valley, British Columbia, 1970; Transglobal expedition, first circumpolar journey round the world, 1979-82, North Pole (5 expeditions), 1985-90, Ubar Expedition (discovered the lost city of Ubar, Oman), 1992, First unsupported crossing of Antarctic continent, 1993; Lectures; Television and film documentary appearances. Publications: A Talent for Trouble, 1970; Ice Fall on Norway, 1972; The Headless Valley, 1973; Where Soldiers Fear to Tread, 1975; Hell on Ice, 1979; To the Ends of the Earth: The Transglobe Expedition - The First Pole-to-Pole Circumnavigation of the Globe, 1983; Bothie the Polar Dog (with Virginia Fiennes), 1984; Living Dangerously (autobiography), 1988; The Feather Men, 1991; Atlantis of the Sands, 1992; Mind Over Matter: The Epic Crossing of the Antarctic Continent, 1994; The Sett, 1996; Ranulph Fiennes: Fit For Life, 1998; Beyond the Limits, 2000; The Secret Hunters, 2001; Captain Scott, 2003. Honours: Dhofar Campaign Medal, 1969; Sultan of Muscat Bravery Medal, 1970; Krug Award for Excellence, 1980; Gold Medal and Honorary Life Membership, Explorer's Club of New York, 1983; Livingstone's Gold Medal, Royal Scottish Geographic Society, 1983; Founder's Medal, Royal Geographic Society, 1984; Guiness Hall of Fame, 1987; Polar Medal and Bar, 1987, 1994; ITN Award, 1990; Officer of the Order of the British Empire, 1993; British Chapter, The Explorers' Club Millennium Award For Polar

Exploration, 2000; Honorary DSc, Portsmouth University, 2000. Membership: Honorary Membership, Royal Institute of Navigation, 1997. Address: Greenlands, Exford, Somerset TA24 7NU, England.

FIGES Eva, b. 15 April 1932, Berlin, Germany. Writer. 1 son, 1 daughter. Education: BA, Honours, English Language and Literature, University of London, 1953. Publications: Winter Journey, 1967; Patriarchal Attitudes, 1970; B, 1972; Nelly's Version, 1977; Little Eden, 1978; Waking, 1981; Sex and Subterfuge, 1982; Light, 1983; The Seven Ages, 1986; Ghosts, 1988; The Tree of Knowledge, 1990; The Tenancy, 1993; The Knot, 1996. Honour: Guardian Fiction Prize, 1967. Membership: Society of Authors. Address: 24 Fitzjohns Avenue, London NW3 5NB, England.

FIGGIS Mike, b. 28 February 1949, Kenya. Film Director; Writer; Musician. Career: Came to England, 1957; Studied music, performing in band, Gas Board; Musician, experimental theatre group, The People Show, early 1970s; Maker of independent films including: Redheugh; Slow Fade; Animals of the City; TV film, The House, Channel 4; Films include: Stormy Monday (also screenplay and music), 1988; Internal Affairs (also music), 1990; Liebestraum (also screenplay and music), 1991; Mr Jones, 1993; The Browning Version, 1994; Leaving Los Vegas (also screenplay and music), 1995; One Night Stand, 1997; Flamenco Women, 1997; Miss Julie, 1999; The Loss of Sexual Innocence, 1999; Time Code, 1999. Honours: IFP Independent Spirit Award, 1996; National Society of Film Critics Award. Address: c/o ICM, 8942 Wilshire Boulevard, Beverly Hills, CA 90211, USA.

FIJAŁKOWSKI Dariusz, b. 31 May 1962, Kraków, Poland. Teacher. m. Ewa Fijałkowska, 3 sons. Education: Graduate in History, Jagellonian University. Appointments: History teacher, 19 years; Author of poetry and essays; Over 20 poetry and prose readings. Publications: 7 poems; 1 piece of prose; 4 prefaces and introductions to other peoples work. Memberships: Vice President, Kraków branch, Union des Gens de Lettres Polonais. Address: Wrocławska Str 66, Flat 129, 30-017 Kraków, Poland.

FILIACI Franco, b. 4 August 1944, Arquata del Tronto (AP), Italy. Medical Doctor. m. Piera Enza Settembrini, 1 son, 2 daughters. Education: Resident, ENT, University "La Sapienza", Rome, Italy, 1973; Resident, Allergology and Immunology, University of Florence, 1976. Appointments: ENT Assistant, 1975-79; Audiology Assistant, 1979-80; Associate Professor, Practice ENT, 1982-86; Associate Professor, Otolaryngology, 1986-. Publications: Editor, ENT Section, Italian Journal of Allergy and Clinical Immunology, 1991; Author: ENT Allergo-Immunology Problems, 1983; Contributor of articles to international journals. Honours: Director, National Research Institute, Rome, 1975-83; G Ferreri Award, Italian Society of ENT, 1972; Member, Scientific Council Cardiorespiratory, National Institute of Research, Rome, 1983-86. Memberships: European Rhinologic Society; Italian Society of Allergology and Clinical Immunology, Director Research group on Rhinitis, 1998. Address: University of Rome "La Sapienza", Policlinics 179, 00161 Rome, Italy. E-mail: franco.filiaci@uniroma1.it

FILIPOVIC Damir, b. 28 July 1965, Zagreb, Croatia. Systems Engineer. Education: BSc, 1990, MSc, 1994, Electrical Engineering, University of Zagreb; PhD, Electrical Engineering, Technical University, Munich, Germany, 1998. Appointments: System Engineer, Koncar Institute, Zagreb, 1989-90; Assistant Researcher, Faculty of Electrical Engineering, University of Zagreb, 1990-94; Assistant Researcher, Technical University, Munich, 1994-98; MTU AeroEngines, Daimler Chrysler. Publications: Co-author, Intelligent Observer and Control Design for Nonlinear Systems; Articles in professional journals; Patentee in field. Memberships: Mensa. Address: Triebstr 10a, D-80993 Munich, Germany. E-mail: damir.filipovic@muc.mtu.de

FILIPYEV Alexander, b. 2 February 1955, Moscow, Russia. Banker. m. Danilina Natalia, 1 son, 1 daughter. Education: Economist, Moscow Financial Institute, 1977; Doctor of Economics, Moscow Financial Institute, 1987; Corresponding Member, International Academy of Engineering, 1999. Appointments: Economist, State Bank of USSR, 1977; Director, International Bank for Economic Co-operation, 1988; Deputy Chairman, UNEXIM Bank, 1993; First Deputy Chairman, Bank for Foreign Trade, 1996; First Deputy Chairman, Rosbank, 1998; Chairman, MFK Bank, 2002. Publications: Over 50 articles in different Russian periodicals. Memberships: Central and Eastern Europe Banking Association; Italian-Russian Chamber of Commerce. Address: 11 Masha Poryvaeva St, PO Box 208, Moscow 107078, Russia. E-mail: filipiev@rosbank.ru

FINE Rana, b. 17 April 1944, New York, USA. Professor of Oceanography. m. James S Mattson. Education: BA, Mathematics, New York University, 1965; MA, Mathematics, University of Miami, 1973; PhD, Marine Science, 1975. Appointments: Systems Analyst, Service Bureau Corporation, Miami, 1965-69; Postdoctoral Research Associate, Rosentiel School of Marine and Atmospheric Science, University of Miami, 1976-77; Research Assistant Professor, 1977-80; Research Associate Professor, 1980-84; Associate Program Director, Ocean Dynamics, National Science Foundation, 1981-83; Associate Professor, Rosenstiel School of Marine and Atmospheric Science, University of Miami, 1984-90; Chairperson, Division of Marine and Atmospheric Chemistry, 1990-94; Professor, 1990-. Publications include: Co-author: Pathways of waters between the Pacific and Indian Oceans, 1996; The impact of major oceanographic research programs, 1997; Rates of North Atlantic Deep Water Formation, 2001. Honours: Orange Key Leadership; Editor's Citation for Excellence in Refereeing; Elected Secretary and President, Ocean Sciences Section, AGU; Fellow in America Geophysical Union; Elected to the nominating Committee and elected Chair of Atmospheric and Hydrospheric Sciences of the American Association for the Advancement of Science; Fellow, American Association for the Advancement of Science; Fellow, American Meteorological Society. Memberships: American Association for the Advancement of Science; American Geophysical Union; Fellow, American Meteorological Society; The Oceanography Society. Address: RSMAS/MAC/U Miami, 4600 Rickenbacker Cswy, Miami, FL 33149-1031, USA.

FINER Stephen Alan, b. 27 January 1949, London, England. Artist. Career: Solo Exhibitions: Four Vine Lane, London, 1981, 1982, 1985; Anthony Reynolds Gallery, London, 1986, 1988; Berkeley Square Gallery, London, 1989; Bernard Jacobson Gallery, London, 1992, 1995; Woodlands Art Gallery, 1994; Agnew's, London, 1998; Pallant House Gallery, Chichester, Sussex, 2001, Charleston, Sussex, 2002; Art Space Gallery, London, 2004; Selected Mixed Exhibitions: British Art, 1940-80, from the Arts Council Collection, Hayward Gallery, London, 1980; Collazione Inglese II, Venice Biennale, Italy, 1984; Academicians' Choice, Stephen Finer invited by Kitaj, Mall Galleries, London; The Portrait Now, National Portrait Gallery, London, 1993-94, 1990; The Discerning Eye, Stephen Finer invited by Martin Gayford, Mall Gallery, London, 1996; Men on Women, Touring Exhibition Stephen Finer invited by Peter Edwards, Wales, 1997-98; 50 Contemporary Self-Portraits, Six Chapel Row, Bath, 1998; British Art, 1900-98, Agnew's, London, 1998; About the Figure, Six Chapel Row, Bath, 1999; Painting the Century, 101 Portrait

Masterpieces, 1900-2000, National Portrait Gallery, London, 2000-01; The National Portrait Gallery Collects, Bodelwyddan Castle, Wales, 2003; Public Collections: Arts Council; The British Council; Contemporary Art Society; Los Angeles County Museum of Art; National Portrait Gallery, "David Bowie", London; Pallant House Gallery, "Sir Morris Finer", Chichester, Sussex, Southport Art Gallery. Selected publications: Allgemeines Kunstlerlexikon; Dictionary of British Artists Since 1945; Handbook of Modern British Painting and Printmaking, 1900-2000; The Portrait Now, Robin Gibson, National Portrait Gallery, 1993; Painting the Century 101 Portrait Masterpieces, 1900-2000, Robin Gibson, National Portrait Gallery, London, 2000; Stephen Finer: Presence and Identity, Martin Golding, Modern Painters, Spring, 2000; Intimacy and Mortality, Finer's People, Robin Gibson, Charleston Trust, 2002. Address: 20 Kipling Street, London SE1 3RU, England. Websites: www.stephenfiner.com and www.artspacegallery.co.uk

FINK Merton, (Matthew Finch, Merton Finch), b. 17 November 1921, Liverpool, England. Author. m. (1) 15 March 1953, 1 son, 1 daughter, (2) 24 November 1981. Education: School of Military Engineers, 1942; School of Military Intelligence, 1943; LDS, Liverpool University, 1952. Publications: Dentist in the Chair, 1953; Teething Troubles, 1954; The Third Set, 1955; Hang Your Hat on a Pension, 1956; The Empire Builder, 1957; Solo Fiddle, 1959; Matchbreakers, 1961; Five Are the Symbols, 1962; Chew this Over, 1965; Eye with Mascara, 1966; Eye Spy, 1967; Simon Bar Cochba, 1971; A Fox Called Flavius, 1973; Open Wide, 1976. Contributions to: Dental Practice, 1956-; Bath Chronicle, 1995. Honour: Richard Edwards Scholar, 1950. Memberships: Civil Service Writers; Deputy Chairman, Bath Literary Society; British Dental Association; Chairman, Service Committee, Bath British Legion. Address: 27 Harbutts, Bathampton, Bath BA2 6TA, England.

FINK-JENSEN Jens, b. 19 December 1956, Copenhagen, Denmark. Author; Poet; Photographer; Composer; Architect MAA. 1 daughter. Education: Architect MAA, Royal Academy of Fine Arts, Copenhagen, 1986; Multimedia Designer, 1997. Publications: The World in An Eye, poetry, 1981; Travels in Sorrow, poetry, 1982; Dancing Under the Gallows, poetry, 1983; The Beasts, short stories, 1986; Near the Distance, poetry, 1988; Jonas and the Conch Shell, childrens book, 1994; The Sea of Change, poetry, 1995; Jonas and the Sky Tent, childrens book, 1998; Everything is an Opening, poetry, 2002; The Jonas books illustrated by Mads Stage. Contributions to: Poems, short stories and articles in Danish and international anthologies, magazines and journals. Honours: Danish Arts Foundation, 1982; The Ministry of Culture's Commission for the Illustrated Danish Book, 1992; The Danish Literature Council, 1997 and 1998. Memberships: Danish PEN; The Danish Writer's Association; The Danish Union of Journalists. Address: Holger Danskes Vej 56 2tv, DK-2000 Frederiksberg, Denmark. E-mail: jensfink@adr.dk Website: www.jensfink.dk

FINKELSHTAIN Gennadi, 16 June 1959, Leningrad, USSR. Power Engineering General Manager. m. Ala, 1 son, 1 daughter. Education: BSc, Power Management, Leningrad Institute for Technology, USSR, 1981. Appointments: Chief Engineer, Leningrad Technology Institute, USSR, 1984-88; General Manager, 2000-, Chief Technical Officer, 2002-, More Energy, Israel. Publications: Numerous scientific publications in scientific journals and papers presented at conferences. Honours: Many patents related to fuel cells technology. Memberships include: Small Fuel Cells. Address: 14, Shabazi, Yehud 56101, Israel.

FINN Neil, b. 27 May 1958, Te Awamutu, New Zealand. Singer; Musician (guitar); Songwriter. Career: Member, Split Enz, 1977-85; Founder member, Crowded House, 1985-; Duo with brother

Tim, 1995; International concerts include: A Concert For Life, Centennial Park, Sydney, 1992; WOMAD Festival, 1993; Television appearances include: Late Night With David Letterman, NBC; The Tonight Show, NBC; In Concert '91, ABC; Return To The Dome, Ch4; MTV Unplugged; Top Of The Pops, BBC1. Recordings: Albums: with Split Enz: Frenzy, 1978; True Colours, 1979; Beginning Of The Enz, 1980; Waita, 1981; Time And Tide, 1982; Conflicting Emotions, 1984; See Ya Round, 1985; History Never Repeats Itself - The Best Of Split Enz, 1993; Oddz & Endz, 1993; Rear Enz, 1993; with Crowded House: Crowded House, 1986; Temple Of Low Men, 1988; Woodface, 1991; Together Alone, 1993; Seductive & Emotional, 1994; Unplugged in the Byrdhouse, 1995; Recurring Dream, 1996; Originals, 1998; with Tim Finn: Finn, 1995; Solo Albums: Try Whistling This, 1998; Encore!, 1999; Singles: with Split Enz include: I See Red; I Got You; History Never Repeats; Six Months In A Leaky Boat; with Crowded House include: Don't Dream It's Over; Something So Strong; Better Be Home Soon; Chocolate Cake; Fall At Your Feet; Four Seasons In One Day; Distant Sun; Nails In My Feet; Solo Singles: Sinner, 1998; She Will Have Her Way, 1998; Last One Standing, 1999; Can You Hear Us, 1999. Honours: Q Awards: Best Live Act (with Crowded House), 1992; Best Songwriter, 1993; OBE, for services to New Zealand, 1993. Current Management: Grant Thomas Management, 3 Mitchell Road, Rose Bay, NSW 2029, Australia.

FINNEY Albert, b. 9 May 1936. Actor. m. (1) Jane Wenham, divorced, 1 son; (2) Anouk Aimée, 1970, divorced, 1978. Education: Royal Academy of Dramatic Art. Appointments: Appointments: Birmingham Repertory Company, 1956-58; Shakespeare Memorial Theatre Company, 1959; National Theatre, 1965, 1975; Formed Memorial Enterprises, 1966; Associate Artistic Director, English Stage Company, 1972-75; Director, United British Artists; Plays include: Julius Caesar; Macbeth; Henry V; The Beaux Strategem; The Alchemist; The Lizard on the Rock; The Party, 1958; King Lear; Othello, 1959; A Midsummer Night's Dream; The Lily-White Boys, 1960; Billy Liar, 1960; Luther, 1961, 1963; Much Ado About About Nothing; Armstrong's Last Goodnight, 1965; Miss Julie, 1965; Black Comedy, 1965; Love for Love, 1965; A Flea in Her Ear, 1966; A Day in the Death of Joe Egg, 1968; Alpha Beta, 1972; Krapp's Last Tape, 1973; Cromwell, 1973; Chez Nous, 1974; Loot (Director), 1975; Hamlet, 1976; Tamburlaine the Great, 1976; Uncle Vanya, 1977; Present Laughter, 1977; The Country Wife, 1977-78; The Cherry Orchard, 1978; Macbeth, 1978; Has 'Washington' Legs?; The Biko Inquest (director), 1984; Sergeant Musgrave's Dance (director), 1984; Orphans, 1986; J J Farr, 1987; Another Time, 1989; Reflected Glory, 1992; Art, 1996; Films include: The Entertainer; Saturday Night and Sunday Morning, 1960; Tom Jones, 1963; Night Must Fall, 1963; Two For the Road, 1967; Scrooge, 1970; Gumshoe, 1971; Murder on the Orient Express, 1974; Wolfen, 1979; Looker, 1980; Shoot the Moon, 1981; Annie, 1982; Life of John Paul II, 1983; The Dresser, 1983; Under the Volcano, 1983; Miller's Crossing, 1989; The Image, 1989; The Run of the Country (also director), 1995; Washington Square, Breakfast of Champions (also director), 1999; Simpatico (also director), 1999; Delivering Milo (also director), 1999; Erin Brokovich (also director), 2000; TV appearances include: My Uncle Silas, 2001, 2003; The Lonely War, 2002; The Gathering Storm, 2002. Honours: Hon DLitt (Sussex), 1966; Lawrence Olivier Award, 1986; London Standard Drama Award for Best Actor, 1986; Dilys Powell Award, London Film Critics Circle, 1999; BAFTA Fellowship, 2001; Emmy Award, 2002; BAFTA Award for Best Actor, 2003; Golden Globe, 2003. Address: c/o Michael Simkins, 45/51 Whitfield Street, London W1P 6AA, England.

FIORENTINO Linda, b. 9 March 1960, Philadelphia, Pennsylvania, USA. Actress. Education: Rosemont College; Circle in the Square Theatre School. Career: Member, Circle in the Square Performing Workshops; Films: Vision Quest, 1985; Gotcha, 1985; After Hours, 1985; The Moderns, 1988; Queens Logic, 1991; Shout, 1991; Wildfire, 1992; Chain of Desire, 1993; The Desperate Trail, 1994; The Last Seduction, 1994; Bodily Harm, 1995; Jade, 1995; Unforgettable, 1997; The Split, 1997; Men in Black, 1997; Kicked in the Head, 1997; Dogma, 1998; Ordinary Decent Criminal, 1999; Where the Money Is, 1999; What Planet Are You From? 2000; Liberty Stands Still, 2002; Films for TV include: The Neon Empire, 1989; The Last Game, 1992; Acting on Impulse, 1993; Beyond the Law, 1994; The Desperate Trail. Address: c/o United Talent Agency, 9560 Wilshire Boulevard, Floor 5, Beverly Hills, CA 90212, USA.

FIRTH Colin, b. 10 September 1960. Actor. Education: Drama Center, London. Career: Theatre includes: Another Country, 1983; Doctor's Dilemma, 1984; The Lonely Road, 1985; Desire Under the Elms, 1987; The Caretaker, 1991; Chatsky, 1993; Three Days of Rain, 1999; TV appearances: Dutch Girls, 1984; Lost Empires (series), 1985-86; Robert Lawrence in Tumbledown, 1987; Out of the Blue, 1990; Hostages, 1992; Master of the Moor, 1993; The Deep Blue Sea, 1994; Pride and Prejudice (Mr Darcy), 1994; Nostromo, 1997; The Turn of the Screw, 1999; Donovan Quick, 1999; Radio: Richard II in Two Planks and a Passion, 1986; The One Before the Last (Rupert Brooke), 1987; Films: Another Country, 1983; Camille, 1984; A Month in the Country, 1986; Femme Fatale, 1990; The Hour of the Pig, 1992; Good Girls, 1994; Circle of Friends, 1995; The English Patient, 1996; Fever Pitch, 1996; Shakespeare in Love, 1998; The Secret Laughter of Women, 1999; My Life So Far, 1999; Relative Values, 1999; Londinium, 2000; Bridget Jones's Diary, 2000; The Importance of Being Earnest, 2002; Hope Springs, 2003; Love Actually, 2003. Honours: Radio Times Actor Award for Tumbledown, 1996; Best Actor Award, Broadcasting Press Guild for Pride and Prejudice. Address: c/o ICM Ltd, Oxford House, 76 Oxford Street, London, W1N 0AX, England.

FISCHER Ernst Otto, b. 10 November 1918, Munich, Germany. Inorganic Chemist. Education: Diploma in Chemistry, 1949, Doctorate, 1952, Munich Technical University. Appointments: Associate Professor, 1957, Professor, 1959, Professor and Director, Inorganic Chemistry, 1964, Munich Technical University; Research on Organometallic Compounds of Transition Metals. Publications: 500 scientific publications; $Fe(C_5H_5)_2$ Structure, 1952; $Cr(C_6H_6)_2$, 1955; Ubergansmetall-Carben-Komplexe, 1964; Metal-Complexes Vol I, with H Werner, 1966; Ubergansmetall-Carben-Komplexe, 1973. Honour: Gottinger Academy Prize for Chemistry, 1957; Alfred-Stock-Gedachtnis Prize, 1959; Hon Dr rer nat, Munich, 1972, Erlangen, 1977, Veszprem, 1983; Joint Winner, Nobel Prize for Chemistry, 1973; Hon DSc, Strathclyde, 1975; American Chemical Society Centennial Fellow, 1976. Memberships: Bayerische Akademie der Wissenschaften, 1964; Deutsche Akademie der Naturforscher Leopoldina, 1969; Corresponding Member, Austrian Academy of Sciences, 1976; Academy of Sciences, Gottingen, 1977; Foreign Member, Accademi Nazionale dei Lincei, 1976; Foreign Honorary Member, American Academy of Arts and Sciences, 1977. Address: Sohnckestrasse 16, 81479 Munich 71, Germany.

FISCHER Philip R, b. 19 June 1955, Indiana, USA. Pediatrician; Teacher. m. Juli A Peterson Fischer, 3 sons, 2 daughters. Education: BSc, Biology, 1976, MD, 1981, University of California; DTM&H, Liverpool School of Tropical Medicine, England. Appointments: Medical Missionary, Evangelical Medical Centre, Nyankunde, Zaire, 1985-91; Assistant Professor, Pediatrics, University of Utah, 1991-98; Associate Professor Pediatrics, 1999-2000, Professor of Pediatrics, Chief of Inpatient Pediatrics, 2000-, Mayo Clinic College of Medicine, Minnesota, USA. Publications: Over 100 in medical journals. Honours: Percival Award for Pediatrics, University of California, Irvine, 1981; Warrington Yorke Medal in International Community Health, Liverpool School of Tropical Medicine, 1985; Teaching Awards, 1995, 1998, 2000, 2001. Memberships: Christian Medical Association; American Academy of Pediatrics; American Society of Tropical Medicine and Hygiene; Royal Society of Tropical Medicine; International Society of Tropical Medicine; International Society of Travel Medicine. Address: Mayo Clinic, 200 First St SW, Rochester, MN 55905, USA. E-mail: fischer.phil@mayo.edu

FISCHER Thomas Covell, b. 2 May 1938, Cincinnati, Ohio, USA. Legal Educator; Consultant; Writer. m. K Brenda Andrew. Education: AB, University of Cincinnati, 1960; University of Washington, 1960-62; JD, Georgetown University Law Center, 1965; Loyola University, Chicago, 1964-66. Appointments: Assistant Executive Director, Chicago, 1964-66; Assistant Dean, Georgetown University Law Center, Washington, 1966-72; Administrative Dean, Antioch School of Law, Washington, 1972-73; President, Thomas C Fischer Associates, Washington, 1973-74; Assistant Executive Director, American Bar Foundation, Chicago, 1974-76; Associate Dean and Professor of Law, University of Dayton School of Law, Dayton, 1976-78; Dean, Professor of Law, Emeritus, Chairman for International Law and Policy, New England School of Law, Boston, 1978-2003; Distinguished Academic in Residence, Seattle University School of Law, 2003-; Sabbaticals and Visiting Scholarships in: Europe; Germany; Southeast Asia; England. Publications: Numerous articles in professional journals. Honours: Maham Award; Memorial Scholarship; Visiting Fellow, Wolfson College, Cambridge; Fellow, Inns of Court. Memberships: Cincinnatus Society. Address: Seattle University School of Law, 900 Broadway, Seattle, WA 98122, USA.

FISCHER-MÜNSTER Gerhard, b. 17 November 1952, Münster- Sarmsheim, Germany. Composer, Soloist, Lecturer, Conductor. m. Bettina, 1 son, 1 daughter. Education: Peter Cornelius Konservatorium Mainz, Staatliche Musikhochschule und Johannes-Gutenberg- Universität Mainz, Staatsexamen, 1974; Seminar for conducting, Bingen, Exam. Career: First Compositions in 1965. Concerts as Soloist, Piano and Clarinet; Concerts as Conductor of different orchestras and ensembles. TV records, Radio records/performances in Germany, Italy, Austria, Switzerland, France, Belgium, USA, Japan; Guest Conductor European Symphony Orchestra, Luxembourg 1993; Performances at International Festivals. Guest Lecturer at various Institutes; Founder of Symphonic Wind Orchestra of Conservatory Mainz 1991; Founder of Wind Chamber Ensemble1981; Lecturer Peter-Cornelius Konservatorium, 1975-. Publications: Over 400 compositions (main: 4 Symphonies, Psalm 99, Schizophonie, Sonatas, Haiku-Lieder words by Sigrid Genzken-Dragendorff, Sonett words by Shakespeare, Symphonic Lieder words by Brigitte Pulley-Grein, Piano Concertino, Daliphonie); Harmonie aus dem Einklang (historical/physical work)' Lehrplan Klarinette; Publications in Music Journals; Publications about Fischer-Münster at different Universities; Jury member at numerous music contests; Guest Lecturer, University Mainz. Honours: Medal, Adv. Ministry of Culture 1984, 1989, 1992, 2000; Award, Adv. Management of International Music Festival of Switzerland, 1985; Honorary Member, IBC Advisory Council; St. Rochus Cup (Bingen) for cultural achievement; Honorary Member, ABI Research Board of Advisers. Memberships: Deutscher Komponisten-Interessenverband; World Association for Symphonic Bands and Ensemble (WASBE), GEMA, Association

Dictionary of International Biography

for German Lecturers and Artists; Fördergesellschaft Peter-Cornelius-Konservatorium. Address: Auf den Zeilen 11, D-55424 Münster-Sarmsheim, Germany. E-mail: Fischer-Muenster@gmx.de

FISHBURNE Laurence, b. 30 July 1961, Augusta, Georgia, USA. Actor. m. Hanja Moss, 1985, divorced 1 son, 1 daughter. Career: Stage appearances include: Short Eyes; Two Trains Running; Riff Raff (also writer and director); TV appearances include: One Life to Live (series, debut age 11); Pee-wee's Playhouse; Tribeca; A Rumour of War; I Take These Men; Father Clements Story; Decoration Day; The Tuskegee Airmen; Miss Ever's Boys; Always Outnumbered; Films include: Cornbread Earl and Me, 1975; Fast Break; Apocalypse Now; Willie and Phil; Death Wish II; Rumble Fish; The Cotton Club; The Colour Purple; Quicksilver; Band of the Hand; A Nightmare on Elm Street 3; Dream Warriors; Gardens of Stone; School Daze; Red Heat; King of New York; Cadence; Class Action; Boyz N the Hood; Deep Cover; What's Love Got to Do With It?; Searching for Bobby Fischer; Higher Learning; Bad Company; Just Cause; Othello; Fled; Hoodlums (also exec producer); Event Horizon; Welcome to Hollywood; Once in the Life (also writer); The Matrix, 1999; Michael Jordan to the Max, 2000; Once in the Life, 2000; Osmosis Jones, 2001; The Matrix Reloaded, 2003; The Matrix Revolutions, 2003 Address: c/o Paradigm, 10100 Santa Monica Boulevard, 25th Floor, Los Angeles, CA 90067, USA.

FISHER Allen, b. 1 November 1944, Norbury, Surrey, England. Painter; Poet; Art Historian. Education: BA, University of London; MA, University of Essex. Appointment: Head of Art, Professor of Poetry and Art, University of Surrey Roehampton. Publications: Over 100 books including: Place Book One, 1974; Brixton Fractals, 1985; Unpolished Mirrors, 1985; Stepping Out, 1989; Future Exiles, 1991; Fizz, 1994; Civic Crime, 1994; Breadboard, 1994; Now's the Time, 1995; The Topological Shovel (essays), Canada, 1999. Contributions to: Various magazines and journals. Honour: Co-Winner, Alice Hunt Bartlett Award, 1975. Address: 14 Hopton Road, Hereford HR1 1BE, England.

FISHER Carrie, b. USA. Actress and Author. m. Paul Simon, 1983, divorced, 1984. Education: Central School of Speech & Drama, London. Career: First appearances: at a nightclub, with mother, aged 13, Broadway chorus in Irene, aged 15; Stage appearances: Censored Scenes from Hong Kong, Agnes of God, both Broadway; Films include: Star Wars; The Empire Strikes Back; Return of the Jedi; The Blues Brothers; Garbo Talks; The Man With One Red Shoe; When Harry Met Sally; Hannah and Her Sisters; The 'Burbs; Sibling Rivalry; Drop Dead Fred; Soapdish; This is My Life; Austin Powers: International Man of Mystery; Scream 3; Famous; Heartbreakers, 2001; Jay and Silent Bob Strike Back, 2001; A Midsummer Night's Rave, 2002; Several TV appearances. Publications: Postcards from the Edge, also screenplay, 1987; Surrender the Pink, 1990; Delusions of Grandma, 1994; Several short stories. Honours: Photoplay Best Newcomer of the Year, 1974; PEN for first novel (Postcards from the Edge, 1987). Address: Creative Artists Agency, 9830 Wilshire Boulevard, Beverly Hills, CA 90212, USA.

FISHER Charles Harold, b. 20 November 1906, Hiawatha, West Virginia, USA. Chemistry Researcher and Teacher. m. Elizabeth Snyder. Education: BS, Roanoke College, 1928; MS, 1929, PhD, 1932, University of Illinois, Urbana. Appointments: Instructor, Chemistry, Harvard University, 1932-35; Research Group Leader, US Bureau of Mines, Pittsburgh, Pennsylvania, 1935-40; Research Group Leader, USDA East Regional Research Center, Philadelphia, 1940-50; Director, USDA Southern Regional Research Center, New Orleans, Louisiana, 1950-72; Consultant,

Textile Research, Republic of South Africa, 1967, Food Technology, Pan American Union, 1968; Research Associate, Roanoke College, Salem, Virginia, 1972-; Consultant, Paper Technology, Library of Congress, 1973-76; Established Lawrence D and Mary A Fisher Scholarship, Roanoke College, 1978. Publications: Over 200 including (co-author) book: Eminent American Chemists, 1992; 72 patents include (co-inventor) Acrylic Rubber, 1992. Honours include: Honorary DSc, Tulane University, 1953, Roanoke College, 1963; Southern Chemists Award, 1956; Herty Medal, 1959; Chemical Pioneer Award, 1966; Polymer Science Pioneer, Polymer News, 1981; Distinguished Alumnus, Roanoke College, 1992; Hall of Fame, Salem Educational Foundation, 1996. Memberships include: American Chemical Society, Board, 1969-71; American Institute of Chemists, President, 1962-63, Board Chairman, 1963, 1973-75; Roanoke College Alumni Association, President, 1978-79; Board Member, Salem Educational Foundation, 1990-99; Board Member, Salem Historical Society, 1991-93; American Institute of Chemical Engineers. Address: Roanoke College, 221 College Lane, Salem, VA 24153, USA.

FISHER John William, b. 15 February 1931, Ancell, Missouri, USA. Professor Emeritus; Structural Engineer. m. Nelda Rae Adams, 3 sons, 1 daughter. Education: BScE, Washington University, St Louis, Missouri, USA, 1956; MS,1958, PhD, 1964, Lehigh University, Bethlehem, Pennsylvania, USA. Appointments: US Army, 1951-53; Assistant Bridge Research Engineer, National Academy of Sciences, AASHO Road Test, Ottawa, Illinois, 1958-1961; Research Instructor, 1961-1964; Assistant and Associate Professor of Civil Engineering, 1966-1969; Professor of Civil and Environmental Engineering, 1969-2002; Associate Director, Fritz Engineering Laboratory, 1971-1985; Director, ATLSS, 1986-1999; Joseph T Stuart Chair in Civil Engineering, 1988-2002; Co-Director, ATLSS Engineering Research Center (Center for Advanced Technology for Large Structural Systems), 1999-2001; Professor Emeritus, 2002. Publications: Co-author: 250 articles in professional journals; 4 books. Honours: Named Engineer of the Year in Research, Institute of Bridge Integrity and Safety, 1992; Honorary Member, American Society of Civil Engineers; John A Roebling Medal for Lifetime Achievement in Bridge Engineering, 1995; Transportation Board Distinguished Lecturer, 1997; International Institute of Welding Portevin Lecturer, 1997; Named the Richard J Carrol Memorial Lecture in Civil Engineering, John Hopkins University, 1999; The John Fritz Medal awarded by the five engineering societies of the United Engineering Foundation, 2000; Roy W Crum Distinguished Service in 2000 Award by the Transportation Research Board, 2001; Achievement Educator Award, American Institute of Steel Construction, 2001; Laureate of the International Award of Merit in Structural Engineering, International Association for Bridge and Structural Engineering, 2001. Memberships: National Academy of Engineers; Corresponding Member, Swiss Academy of Engineering Sciences; Transportation Research Board Executive Committee, 1997-2000; Committee A2CO2 Steel Bridge Committee; Specification Committee, American Institute of Steel Construction; Honorary Member of American Society of Civil Engineers; Specifications Committee, American Railroad Engineering and Maintenance-of-Way Association; American Welding Society; American Society for Engineering Education. Address: ATLSS Center, Lehigh University, 117 ATLSS Drive, Bethlehem, PA 18015, USA. E-mail: jwf2@lehigh.edu

FITCH Val Lodgson, b. 10 March 1923, Nebraska, USA. Physicist. m. (1) Elise Cunningham, 1949, died 1972, 2 sons, 1 deceased, (2) Daisy Harper Sharp, 1976. Education: BEng, McGill University, 1948; PhD, Physics, Columbia University, 1954. Appointments: US Army, 1943-46; Instructor, Columbia

University, 1953-54; Instructor, 1954-60, Professor of Physics, 1960-, Chair, Department of Physics, 1976, Cyrus Fogg Bracket Professor of Physics, 1976-84, Princeton University; James S McDonald Distinguished University Professor of Physics, 1984-. Honour: Research Corporation Award, 1968; Ernest Orlando Laurence Award, 1968; John Witherill Medal, Franklin Institute, 1976; Joint Winner, Nobel Prize for Physics, 1980. Membership: Sloan Fellow, 1960-64; Member, NAS, American Academy of Arts and Sciences, President's Science Advisory Committee, 1970-73; American Philosophical Society. Address: PO Box 708, Princeton University, Department of Physics, Princeton, NJ 08544, USA.

FITZGERALD Tara, b. 18 September 1969. Actress. Career: Stage debut in Our Song, London; Ophelia in Hamlet, London, 1995; Antigone, 1999; TV appearances include: The Black Candle; The Camomile Lawn; Anglo-Saxon Attitudes; Six Characters in Search of An Author; Fall From Grace; The Tenant of Wildfell Hall; The Student Prince; Women in White; Frenchman's Creek; In the Name of Love; Theatre includes: Our Song (London); Hamlet (New York); Films: Sirens, 1994; The Englishman Who Went up a Hill but Came Down a Mountain, 1995; Brassed Off, 1996; Childhood, 1997; Conquest, 1998; New World Disorder, 1998; The Cherry Orchard, 1999; Rancid Aluminium, 1999; Dark Blue World, 2000. Address: c/o Caroline Dawson Associates, 19 Sydney Mews, London, SW3 6HL, England.

FITZPATRICK Horace, Earl of Upper Ossory and Castletown, b. 1934 Louisville, Kentucky, USA (British National). University Research Professor; Musician. Education: BA, 1956, MMus, 1958, Yale University; Diploma (1st Honours); State Academy of Music and Drama, Vienna, 1959; Studied horn with Reginald Morley-Pegge, London, Philip Farkas, Chicago, John Barrows, Yale, Gottfried v. Freiberg, Vienna; Teenage conducting studies with uncle, Glenn Welty, leading free-lance conductor, Chicago Radio; Later with Paul Hindemith (Yale), Hans Swarowsky (Vienna), and Robert Heger (Munich); Doctor of Philosophy, Oxford University, 1965. Career includes: Various orchestral posts as principal horn, 1958-66, including: Metropolitan Opera, Radio Symphony of the Air (New York under Leonard Bernstein), Vienna Philharmonic and State Opera (deputy); Orchestra da Camera di Palazzo Pitti, Florence; Cairo State Opera; Hamburg Kammerorchester; Royal Opera House Covent Garden; London Mozart Players; Deputy Curator, Yale Collection of Musical Instruments, 1956-58; First ever Lecturer in European Music, American University, Cairo, 1959-60; First ever solo recording on 18th century horn, Golden Crest Records, 1959; Solo Debut on Natural Horn, Wigmore Hall, London, 1964; International appearances as Soloist on Natural Horn including, Salzburg, City of London, Flanders (Bruges), Edinburgh and Vienna Festivals, 1964-88; Tutoring in Music History, Wadham College, Oxford University, 1961-64; Stipendiary Lecturer, St Catherine's College, Oxford University, Member of Faculty of Music, History of Instruments, 1963-71; Pioneering research into use of music (mainly Classical period 1740-1830), according to Greek philosophical principles, as a form of healing support, 1996-; Director, International Summer Academy for Historic Performance, Austria, 1971-80; Secured Philip Bate Collection for Oxford University, set up Oxford Foundation for Historic Musical Instruments, 1964-71; Established Atelier for Historic Wind Instruments, Oxford, 1971; Professor of Natural Horn, Guildhall School of Music and Drama, 1972-79; Founded Hanover Band, 1974 and the Florilegium, 1975; Leverhulme Visiting Professor, Johannes Gutenberg-Universität, Mainz, 1981-86; Leverhulme Visiting Research Professor, Music University "Mozarteum", Salzburg, 1985-; Research Unit and Laboratory Orchestra (historic instruments) at Salzburg in dialogue with the Royal Swedish Academy of Music and the Royal Technical Institute, Stockholm, 1985-; Chairman, Aula Classica, a research, education and performance network to study the music of the Mozartean Era through its related disciplines, 1988-; Patronage of the Secretary General of the Council of Europe, 1989; Professorial Research Fellow, Institute of Musicology, University of Vienna, 1994-2000. Publications include: The Horn and Horn-Playing and the Austro-Bohemian Tradition 1680-1830, 1970; Telemann, 1973; 17 articles in The New Grove; Articles in German, French and Spanish music encyclopaedias; Concert and book reviews For The Times, Times Literary Supplement and Oxford Mail. Honours: Numerous research grants and scholarships; Medaglia d'Oro per la Cultura, Italy, 1959; Order of St Martin, Austria, 1977; Listed in biographical dictionaries. Memberships: Athenaeum, 1981-97; Country Club UK. Address: 16 Sutherland Street, London, SW1V 4LA, England.

FJERDINGSTAD Erik, b. 4 October 1940. Physical Chemist. Education: Student, 1959, Filosoficum, 1960, BSc, 1962, Magister Scientiarum, 1966, BEd, 1967, Diploma of Public Health, 1972. Appointments: Instructor, University of Copenhagen, 1962-66; Adjunct Virum Gymnasium, 1966-72; Assistant Professor, University of Copenhagen, 1972-76; Associate Professor, 1976-80; Now retired. Publications: Articles in international journals about the environment, heavy metals; Compendia for university students in biology and hygiene, seminar reports. Honours: Scholarship to Nordic School of Public Health, Affiliation Gothenburg University. Memberships: AAS; NYAS; LFIBA; Dan-Soc Mater Res; Dan. magister organizations. Address: Bredebovej 23 mf, DK-2800 Kgs Lyngby, Denmark.

FLAHAULT Francois, b. 26 September 1943, Janze, France. Director of Research. 2 sons. Education: Master in Philosophy, 1964; MPhil, Philosophy, 1970; MPhil, Semantico, Ecole des Hautes Etudes en Sciences Sociale, Paris, 1976; PhD, Paris VII University, La Persee des Coutes, 1985. Appointments: Professor of Philosophy, 1967-71; Professor at the National Association for Adults Education, 1971-80; Researcher, CNRS, 1980-; Visiting Faculty Member, Departments of Philosophy, Psychology and Psychoanalysis, different universities in Paris. Publications: La Parole intomediaire, 1978; La Pensee des Coutes, 2001; Le Sentiment d'exister, 2002; Pourquoi limiter l'expansion du captialisme? 2003; Malice, 2003. Honours: Bronze Medal, CNRS, 1981; Director, Centre de Recherches sur les Arts et le Language, 1995-2001. Address: 7 rue de Nicolas Houel, 75005 Paris, France. E-mail: flahault@club-internet.fr

FLAKE Floyd Harold, b. 30 January 1945, Los Angeles, California. Clergy; Corporate Executive. m. Margarett Elaine McCollins, 2 sons, 2 daughters. Education: BA, Wilberforce University, 1967; DMin, United Theological Seminary, 1994. Appointments: Sales Representative, J Reynolds, 1967-68; Marketing Analyst, Xerox Corporation, 1968-70; Associate Dean of Students, Lincoln University, 1970-73; Dean of Students, Interim Dean of the Chapel, Director of MLK Centre, Boston University, 1973-76; US Congressman, 1986-97; SR Pastor, Chief Executive Officer, The Greater Allen Cathedral AME of New York, 1976-; President, Edison Charter Schools, 1998-2002; President, Wilbeyonce University, 2002-. Publications: Author, The Way of the Bootstrapper; Numerous articles on education and faith-based initiative in various publications; Co-author, Practical Virtues, 2002. Honours: Honorary Doctorates: Boston University, Wilberforce, Cheney and Lincoln; Achievement in Religion, Ebony Magazine. Memberships: Board of Directors, Fannie Mae Foundation; Board of Directors, Edison Schools; Senior Fellow, Manhattan Institute; Brookin Institute for Custom and Metropolitan Policy. Address: 110-31 Merrick Blvd, Jamaica, NY 11433, USA.

Dictionary of International Biography

FLEISCHMANN Ernest (Martin), b. 7 December 1924, Frankfurt, Germany. Music Administrator. Divorced, 1 son, 2 daughters. Education: Bachelor of Commerce, Chartered Accountant, University of the Witwatersrand, South Africa, 1950; Bachelor of Music, University of Cape Town, 1954; Postgraduate work, South African College of Music, 1954-56. Debut: Conductor with Johannesburg Symphony Orchestra, 1942. Career: Conductor of various symphony orchestras and operas, 1942-55; Music Organiser, Van Riebeeck Festival, Cape Town, 1952; Director of Music and Drama, Johannesburg Festival, 1956; General Manager, London Symphony Orchestra, 1959-67; Director for Europe, CBS Records, 1967-69; Managing Director, Los Angeles Philharmonic and General Director, Hollywood Bowl, 1969-98; Artistic Director, Ojai Festival, 1998-2003; President, Fleischmann Arts, International Arts Management and Consulting Services, (consultant to orchestras, festivals and government bodies in USA and Europe), 1998-. Publications: Commencement address, The Orchestra is Dead, Long Live the Community of Musicians, Cleveland Institute of Music, 1987; The Recession, Cultural Change, and a Glut of Orchestras, paper for Economics of The Arts, Salzburg Seminar, 1993. Honours include: Doctor of Music (honoris causa), Cleveland Institute of Music, 1987; Grand Cross of the Order of Merit, Germany, 1996; First Living Cultural Treasure of the City of Los Angeles, 1998; Officer, Ordre des Arts et Lettres, France, 1998; Knight First Class, Order of the White Rose, Finland, 1999; Gold Baton Award, American Symphony Orchestra League, 1999. Memberships: Board of Councillors, USC Thornton School of Music; Board of Directors, Los Angeles Philharmonic Association. Address: 2225 Maravilla Drive, Los Angeles, CA 90068, USA.

FLEMING Blanche Miles, b. 4 November 1918, Salem, New Jersey, USA. Education Administrator. m. Daniel E Fleming II, 1 son. Education: BS, Delaware University, 1939; MA, Columbia University, 1947; PhD, Union Graduate School, 1976; Certified Professor of Education.. Appointments: Director, National Teaching Corps, University of Delaware, Newark, Delaware, 1970-72; Co-ordinator, Undergraduates, Delaware State College, Dover, 1971; Director, Secondary Education, Delaware Board of Education, Wilmington, Delaware, Principal Bayard Junior High School, 1980-83; Supervisor of Social Studies, Intern to the Superintendent of Schools, 1994-95; Helping Hands Community Service Inc, 1997. Publications: Article: The Bancroft Story, 1956; History of NAUW Wilmington, 1996; Revised Bylaws for the National Coalition of 100 Women, 2002. Honours include: Woman of the Year, National Association of University Women, Wilmington Branch, 1976; NAUW Sectional, Woman of the Year, 1977; Outstanding Educator Award, Director of Secondary Schools, Wilmington, 1978; Legacy of Delaware – The Book of Delaware Women, 1987; Family Award, Miles Family for outstanding support and caring, 1992; City of Wilmington Certificate of Appreciation, Mayor's Award, 1997; Award for 20 years leadership on Board of Directors, Housing Opportunities of North Delaware, 2001; Certificate, 25 years of active membership of Phi Delta Kappa, 2002; Elected to St Labre Indian School Education Century Society, 2003. Memberships: National Coalition of 100 Women; National Association of University Women; League of Women Voters; Common Cause; Delta Kappa Gamma Society International; Phi Delta Kappa, Pi Beta Lambda, Columbia University; Wilmington Friends School-Parent; Academy of Lifelong Learning, University of Delaware. Address: 2806 West 5th Street, Wilmington, DE 19805, USA. E-mail: 36345@udel.edu

FLETCHER Sarah C Lee, b. 7 May 1925, Webb, USA. School Teacher. m. G Maurice Fletcher, 2 sons, 1 daughter. Education: Business Associate Degree, Bob Jones College, 1946; Student, Calhoun College, 1968-70, Troy State University, 1970-72;

Bachelor of Religious Education, 1995; Master of Religious Education, 1996. Appointments: Atlanta and Saint Andrews Rwy Co, 1944-46; Secretary to Publisher Dothan Eagle, 1947-48; Teacher, Morgan County Schools, 1967-69, Newton, 1969-72, Trinity Christian School, 1972-73, Berachah Chrisitan School, 1973-75; Secretary, Dominion Textile, Yarmouth, Nova Scotia, Canada, 1975-76; Teacher, Mueller Christian School, Miami, Florida, 1976-79; Teacher, Berean Christian, Dothan, 1979-86; Teacher, Grace Bible AC, Dothan, 1987-1990, Clinton Christian Academy, Upper Malboro, Maryland, 1990-91. Publications include: To Love Again, 1996; The Set of the Sales, 1997; Love in Bloom, 2001. Honours: Numerous. Memberships: AEA; UBWMU; Kappa Rho Literary Society; Young Peoples Fellowship Club. Address: 1119 Garden Lane, Dothan, AL 36301, USA.

FLIN Piotr, b. 11 March 1945, Krakow, Poland. Astronomer. m. Zofia Pstrucha, 1 daughter. Education: MSc, Astronomy, 1968, MSc, Physics, 1972, PhD, 1976, Jagiellonian University, Cracow; DSc, Habilitation, Nicolaus Copernicus University, Torun, 1991. Appointments: Assistant, 1968-70, Senior Assistant, 1970-76, Research Fellow, 1976-82, Senior Research Fellow, 1982-88, Jagiellonian University Observatory; Senior Lecturer, Center for Interdisciplinary Studies, Pontifical Academy of Theology, Cracow, 1988-91, 1997-2000; Extraordinary Professor, Cracow Pedagogical, 1992-95; Extraordinary Professor, Pedagogical University, Kielce, 1993-; Head of the Astrophysics Department, 1993-; Distinguished Scientist, Bogolubov Laboratory of Theoretical Physics, Joint Institute for Nuclear Research, Dubna, Russia, 2001-03. Publications include: Global or Local Anisotropy in Galaxy Orientation?, 1995; The Orientation of Galaxies in Poor Clusters, 1997; Properties of Nearby Clusters of Galaxies, 2000; The anisotropy of galaxy orientation in Coma/A1367 Supercluster, 2001. Honours: Silver and Gold Honorary Award, Polish Amateurs Astronomical Society, 1971, 1975; Nicolaus Copernicus Medal, 1974; Bronze Cross of Merit, 1976. Memberships include: International Astronomical Union, 1985; American Astronomical Society, 1992; Euro-Asiatic Astronomical Society, 1994; Ukrainian Astronomical Association, 2000. Address: Institute of Physics, Pedagogical University, ul Swietokrzyska 15, 25-406 Kielce, Poland.

FLITSANOV Uri, b. 27 July 1959, Tashkent, Soviet Union. Mechanical Engineer; Scientist; Consultant. m. Olga Rovner, 2 sons, 1 daughter. Education: Diploma with honours, Mechanical Engineering, University of Engineers for Industry and Agriculture, 1976-81; Doctor of Philosophy in Engineering, Moscow State University of Engineering for Industry and Agriculture, USSR, 1982-86. Appointments: Senior Engineer, Regional Production Amalgamation for Production Technical Supply of Agriculture, Tashkent, 1981-82; Scientist, Moscow State University of Engineering for Industry and Agriculture, 1982-86; Lecturer, Associate Professor, Head of Science Research Department, University of Engineers for Industry and Agriculture, 1986-91; Project Leader, School of Technicians and Officers, Michmoret, Israel, 1992-93; Scientist, The Volcani Center, Institute of Agricultural Engineering, Israel, 1993-98; Senior Scientist, Technion, Israel Institute of Technology, 1998-2002; Research Associate, Tel-Aviv University, Israel, 2002-. Publications: Over 65 articles in professional journals. Honours: Yehoshua Menis Prize for research activity, Institute of Agricultural Engineering. Address: Hertzog 12/4 st, Hadera, 38370, Israel. E-mail: yuriflt@eng.tau.ac.il

FLOROS Constantin, b. 4 January 1930, Salonica, Greece. Professor of Musicology. Education: Composition and Conducting, Vienna Music Academy, 1953; Doctorate, Musicology, Art History, Philosophy and Psychology, Vienna University, 1955.

Dictionary of International Biography

Appointments: Habilitation, Musicology, Hamburg University, 1961; Supernumerary Professor, 1967, Professor of Musicology, 1972, Professor Emeritus, 1995, University of Hamburg. Publications: 22 books; Numerous papers; Monographs on Mozart, Beethoven, Joh Brahms, Bruckner, Mahler (4 volumes), Alban Berg and G Ligeti; Translated oldest Byzantine and Slavic notations and developed new method of semantic analysis. Honours: President, Gustav Mahler Vereinigung, Hamburg, 1988; Honorary Doctorate, University of Athens, 1999; Member, European Academy of Sciences and Arts, 2002. Address: Schlangenkoppel 18, 22117 Hamburg, Germany.

FLYNN Margaret Alberi, b. 22 November 1915, Hurley, Wisconsin, USA. Nutritionist; Dietician. Widowed, 1 son, 1 daughter. Education: BS, St Catherine College, St Paul, 1937; MS, University of Iowa, 1938; PhD, University of Missouri, 1960; Registered Dietician; Diplomate, American Board of Nutrition. Appointments: Instructor, St Catherine College, St Paul, 1937-38; Research Assistant, Paediatrics, University of Iowa, Iowa City, 1939-40; Instructor, Dietetics, Levi Memorial Hospital, Hot Springs, Arkansas, 1942-46; Teaching Dietician, Holy Name Hospital, Teaneck, New Jersey, 1950-54; Research Assistant, Paediatrics, 1961-63, Assistant Professor, Nutrition and Dietetics, 1966-69, Associate Professor, Medicine, 1969-75, Professor of Medicine, 1975-86, Professor Emeritus of Medicine, 1986-, University of Missouri, Columbia. Publications: 60 research articles on different research projects published in medical journals. Honours: Faculty Alumni Award, 1976; National Cancer Institute Grantee, 1977; National Meat Board/Wallace Genetic Foundation Grantee, 1978-; Distinguished Faculty Awardee, 1988; Named Sesquicentennial Professor, University of Missouri, 1989. Memberships: Fellow, American College of Nutrition; American Society of Clinical Nutrition; American Institute of Nutrition. Address: 300 Kildaire Woods Drive, Apt 233, Cary, NC 27511, USA.

FO Dario, b. 24 March 1926, Leggiuno-Sangiamo, Italy. Dramatist; Actor. m. Franca Rame, 1954, 1 child. Education: Academy of Fine Arts, Milan. Appointments: Dramatist and Actor in agitprog theatre and television; Co-Founder (with Franca Rame), Dramatist, Actor, Nuova Scena acting groupe, 1968; Collettivo Teatrale la Comune, 1970. Publications: Numerous plays, including: Le commedie, I-IX, 1966-91, 1992; Morte accidentale di un anarchico (Accidental Death of an Anarchist), 1974; Non si paga, non si paga! (We Can't Pay? We Won't Pay!), 1974; Tutta casa, letto e chiesa (Adult Orgasm Escapes From the Zoo), 1978; Female Parts (with Franca Rame), 1981; Manuale et minimo dell attore, 1987; Mistero Buffo, 1977; Coming Home; History of Masks; Archangels Don't Play Pinball; Hooters, Trumpets and Raspberries; The Tricks of the Trade, 1991; Il papa e la stega (The Pope and the Witch), 1989; L'Eroina-Grassa e'Bello, 1991; Johan Padan a la Descoverta de le Americhe, 1991; Dario Fo Recita Ruzzante, 1993; Il diavolo con le zinne, 1997. Honour: Hon DLitt, Westminster, 1997; Nobel Prize for Literature, 1997. Address: c/o CTFR, Viale Piave 11, 20129 Milan, Italy.

FONDA Bridget, b. 27 January 1964, Los Angeles, CA, USA. Actress. Education: NY University theatre programme; Studied acting at Lee Strasburg Institute and with Harold Guskin. Career: Workshop stage performances include Confession and Pastels; Films: Aria (Tristan and Isolde sequence), 1987; You Can't Hurry Love, 1988; Shag, 1988; Scandal, 1989; Strapless, 1989; Frankenstein Unbound, 1990; The Godfather: Part III, 1990; Doc Hollywood, 1991; Out of the Rain, 1991; Single White Female, 1992; Singles, 1992; Bodies Rest and Motion, 1993; Point of No Return, 1993; Little Buddha, 1994; It Could Happen To You, 1994; Camilla, 1994; The Road to Welville, 1994; Rough Magic, 1995;

Balto (voice), 1995; Grace of My Heart, 1996; City Hall, 1996; Drop Dead Fred; Light Years (voice); Iron Maze; Army of Darkness; Little Buddha; Touch; Jackie Brown; Finding Graceland; The Break Up; South of Heaven West of Hell; Monkey Bone; Lake Placid; Delivering Milo; TV series: 21 Jump Street; Jacob Have I Loved; WonderWorks (episode), 1989; The Edge (The Professional Man); TV film: Leather Jackets, 1991; In the Gloaming, 1997. Address: c/o IFA, 8730 West Sunset Boulevard, Suite 490, Los Angeles, CA 90069, USA.

FONDA Jane, b. 21 December 1937. Actress. m. (1) Roger Vadim, 1967, divorced 1973, deceased 2000, 1 daughter, (2) Tom Hayden, 1973, divorced 1989, 1 son, (3) Ted Turner, 1991, separated. Education: Vassar College. Films include: Tall Story, 1960; A Walk on the Wild Side, 1962; Sunday in New York, 1963; La Ronde, 1964; Barbarella, 1968; They Shoot Horses Don't They? 1969; Steelyard Blues, Tout va Bien, 1972; The Blue Bird, 1975; Fun with Dick and Jane, 1976; Coming Home, California Suite, 1978; The China Syndrome, 1979; Nine to Five, 1980; On Golden Pond, 1981; Agnes of God, 1985; Stanley and Iris, 1990; Lakota Woman, Producer, 1994; Stage Work includes: Invitation to a March; The Fun Couple; Strange Interlude; TV: The Dollmaker, 1984. Publications: Jane Fonda's Workout Book, 1982; Women Coming of Age, 1984; Jane Fonda's Workout and Weightloss Program, 1986; Jane Fonda's New Pregnancy Workout and Total Birth Program, 1989; Jane Fonda Workout Video; Jane Fonda Cooking for Healthy Living, 1996. Honours: Academy Award Best Actress, 1972, 1979; Emmy Award, The Dollmaker, 1984. Address: c/o Kim Hodgert, CAA, 9830 Wilshire Boulevard, Beverly Hills, CA 90212, USA.

FONDA Peter, b. 23 February 1940, NY, USA. Film Actor, Director and Producer. m. Susan Brewer, divorced 1974, 2 children. Education: University of Omaha. Career: Tammy and the Doctor, 1963; The Victors, 1963; Lilith, 1964; The Young Lovers, 1964; The Wild Angels, 1966; The Trip, 1967; Easy Rider (also co-screenplay writer, co-producer), 1969; The Last Movie, 1971; The Hired Hand (also director), 1971; Two People (also director), 1973; Dirty Mary, Crazy Harry, 1974; Race With the Devil, 1975; 92 in the Shade, 1975; Killer Force, 1975; Fighting Mad, 1976; Future World, 1976; Outlaw Blues, 1977; High Ballin', 1978; Wanda Nevada (also director), 1979; Open Season; Smokey and the Bandit II, 1980; Split Image, 1982; Certain Fury, 1985; Dead Fall, 1993; Nadja, 1994; Love and a 45, 1994; Painted Hero, 1996; Escape From LA, 1996; Idaho Transfer (also director); Ulee's Gold, 1997; Spasm; Fatal Mission; Reckless; Cannonball Run (cameo); Dance of the Dwarfs; Mercenary Fighters; Jungle Heat; Diajobu My Friend; Peppermint Frieden; The Rose Garden; Family Spirit; South Beach; Bodies Rest and Motion; Deadfall; Molly and Gina; South of Heaven West of Hell; The Limey; Keeping Time; TV films: The Hostage Tower, 1980; Don't Look Back, 1996; A Reason to Live; A Time of Indifference; Sound; Certain Honorable Men; Montana. Address: IFA Talent Agency, 8730 West Sunset Boulevard, Suite 490, Los Angeles, CA 90069, USA.

FONF Vladimir, b. 13 August 1949, Michurinsk, Russia. Mathematician. Divorced, 1 daughter. Education: MSc, Mathematics, 1971; PhD, Mathematics, 1979; DSc, Mathematics, 1991. Appointments: Docent, Professor, Kharkov Railroad Institute, Ukraine, 1983-93; Associate Professor, Ben-Gurion University, Israel, 1993-97, Professor, Ben-Gurion University of the Negev, 1997-. Publications: More than 60 articles in mathematical journals in: Bulgaria, Canada, England, Germany, Israel, Poland, Spain, USA, USSR; Co-author, Handbook of Banach Spaces, 2001. Honour: Guastella Fellowship, 1993-96. Membership: Israel Mathematical Union. Address: Department of Mathematics, Ben-Gurion University of the Negev, PO Box 653, Beer-Sheeva 84105, Israel. E-mail: fonf@math.bgu.ac.il

Dictionary of International Biography

FONTAINE Guy, b. 24 December 1936, Corbeil, France. Physician; Cardiologist. m. Ilfat Masri, 1 son, 3 daughters. Education: MD, 1966; Cardiologist, 1969; PhD, 1991; HDR, 1993. Appointments include: Member of Cardiology Staff, 1968-, Director of Coronary Care Unit, Hopital de la Salpetrière, Paris; Researcher into numerous aspects of cardiology including pacemaker science, epicardial mapping, ablation using direct current energy; Identification of Arrhythmogenic Right Ventricular Dysplasia (ARVD), 1977; Registry of ARVD patients, France; European Community Registry on ARVC/D Partner for France; Visiting Professor of Internal Medicine, Arizona, USA, 1986; Visiting Professor, University of Shanghai, China, 1990. Publications: More than 820 scientific articles including 214 book chapters; 5 books include: The Essentials of Cardiac Pacing, 1976; Numerous invited international lectures. Honours: Master Teacher Award, Cardiovascular Reviews and Reports, 1990; Prix, Electricité-Santé, 1992; Prix, Medtronic, 1994; Prix, Fondation Pierre Rijlant, 1995. Memberships: French Society of Cardiology, 1969; FAHA, 1982; FACC, 1983; NASPE, 1986; WHF, Scientific Council on Cardiomyopathies, 1988; Corresponding Member, Académie Nationale de Médicine, 1993; FESC, 1994; Golden caduceus of Assistance Publique des Hopitaux de Paris, 1997. Address: 67 Av du Général de Gaulle, St Mandé 94160, France. E-mail: guy.fontaine@bct.ap-hop-paris.fr

FONTENLA-ROMERO Oscar, b. 5 September 1974, Ferrol, Spain. Computer Science. Education: Bachelor degree, 1997, Master Degree, 1998, PhD, 2002, Computer Science, University of A Coruña, Spain. Appointments: Programmer, Softgal company, 1998; Pre-doctoral Researcher, 1999-2002; Post-doctoral Research Associate, 2002-. Publications: Articles in international journals and at 15 international conferences and congresses. Honours: Listed in national and international biographical dictionaries; Isidro Parga Pondal Technological Innovation Award, Spain. Address: Faculty of Information, Campus de Elviña s/n, 15071 A Coruña, Spain. E-mail: oscarfon@udc.es Website: www.dc.fi.udc.es/lidia

FONTINOY Charles-Marie, b. 12 March 1920, Stavelot, Belgium. Retired University Professor. Education: Licencié en philosophie et lettres, 1941; Agrégé de l'Enseignement Secondaire Supérieur, 1941; Docteur en langues orientales, 1963. Appointments: Secondary School Teacher, Athénée Royal l'Aywaille, Belgium, 1945-66; Professor, Hebrew Bible and Semitic Languages, State University of Liège, Belgium, 1966-85; Chairman, Department of Oriental Studies, 1980-85. Publications: Articles in professional journals. Honours: Recipient, various grants, 1954-66; Various awards including: Grand Officier de l'ordre de Léopold II, Brussels, 1981. Memberships: Belgian Society of Oriental Studies. Address: La Bovière 3, B-4920 Aywaille, Belgium.

FORAN Charles William, b. 2 August 1960, North York, Ontario, Canada. Writer. m. Mary Ladky, 2 daughters. Education: BA, University of Toronto, 1983; MA, University College, Dublin, 1984. Appointments: Librarian and Freelance Journalist, New York State, 1985-88; Teacher, Beijing College, 1988-90; Freelance Writer and Journalist, 1990-. Publications: Coming Attractions (5 short stories), 1987; Sketches in Winter (non-fiction), 1992; Kitchen Music (novel), 1994; The Last House of Ulster (non-fiction), 1995; Butterfly Lovers (novel), 1996; The Story of My Life (So Far) (non-fiction), 1998; House on Fire (novel), 2001. Contributions to: Globe and Mail; The Walrus, GQ. Honours: Finalist, QSpell Award and National Magazine Award, 1992, 1994, 1996; Winner, QSpell Award, Non-Fiction, 1995; Finalist, Governor General's Literary Award, Non-Fiction, 1995; Winner, QSpell Award, Fiction, 1997, Winner National Magazine Awards,

2000. Memberships: PEN Canada; Writers Union of Canada. Address: 298 Boswell Avenue, Peterborough, Ontario K9J 5G3, Canada.

FORBES Bryan, b. 22 July 1926, Stratford, London, England. Film Executive; Director; Screenwriter. m. Nanette Newman, 1955, 2 daughters. Education: Royal Academy of Dramatic Art. Appointments: Writer, Producer, Director of numerous TV programmes. Publications: Truth Lies Sleeping, 1951; The Distant Laughter, 1972; Notes for a Life, 1974; The Slipper and the Rose, 1976; Ned's Girl, 1977; International Velvet, 1978; Familiar Strangers, 1979; That Despicable Race, 1980; The Rewrite Man, 1983; The Endless Game, 1986; A Song at Twilight, 1989; A Divided Life, 1992; The Twisted Playground, 1993; Partly Cloudy, 1995; Quicksand, 1996; The Memory of all That, 1999. Honours: Best Screenplay Awards; UN Award; Many Film Festival Prizes; Honorary DL, London, 1987; Honorary Doctor of Literature, Sussex University, 1999. Memberships: Ex-President, Beatrix Potter Society; President, National Youth Theatre of Great Britain. Address: c/o The Gallery, Virginia Water, Surrey, GU25 4RN, England.

FORD Anna, b. 2 October 1943. Broadcaster. m. (1) Alan Holland Bittles, (2) Charles Mark Edward Boxer, deceased 1988, 2 daughters. Education: Manchester University. Appointments: Work for student interests, Manchester University, 1966-69; Lecturer, Rupert Stanley College of Further Education, Belfast, 1970-72; Staff Tutor, Social sciences, North Ireland Region, Open University, 1972-74; Presenter and Reporter, Granada TV, 1974-76, Man Alive, BBC, 1976-77, Tomorrow's World, BBC, 1977-78; Newscaster, ITN, 1978-80; W TV am, 1980-82; Freelance broadcasting and writing, 1982-86; BBC news and current affairs, 1989-. Publication: Men: A Documentary, 1985. Honour: Hon LLD (Manchester), 1998; Honourable Bencher Middle Temple, 2002. Membership: Trustee, Royal Botanic Gardens, Kew. Address: BBC Television Centre, Wood Lane, London, W12 7RJ, England.

FORD Harrison, b. 13 July 1942, Chicago, USA. Actor. m. (1) Mary Ford, 2 sons, (2) Melissa Ford, divorced 2004, 1 son, 1 daughter. Education: Ripon College. Career: Numerous TV appearances; Films include: Dead Heat on a Merry-Go-Round, 1966; Luv, 1967; The Long Ride Home, 1967; Getting Straight, 1970; Zabriskie Point, 1970; The Conversation, 1974; American Graffiti, 1974; Star Wars, 1977; Heroes, 1977; Force 10 from Navarone, 1978; Hanover Street, 1979; Frisco Kid, 1979; The Empire Strikes Back, 1980; Raiders of the Lost Ark, 1981; Blade Runner; Return of the Jedi, 1983; Indiana Jones and the Temple of Doom; Witness; The Mosquito Coast, 1986; Working Girl, 1988; Frantic, 1988; Indiana Jones and the Last Crusade, 1989; Presumed Innocent, 1990; Regarding Henry, 1991; The Fugitive, 1992; Patriot Games, 1992; Clear and Present Danger, 1994; Sabrina, 1995; Air Force One, 1996; Six Days and Seven Nights, 1998; Random Hearts, 1999; What Lies Beneath, 2000; K-19: The Widowmaker (also executive producer), 2002; Hollywood Homocide, 2003. Address: 10279 Century Woods Drive, Los Angeles, CA 90067, USA.

FORD-CHOYKE Phyllis May, b. 25 October 1921, Buffalo, New York, USA. Editor; Poet. m. Arthur Davis Choyke Jr, 18 August 1945, 2 sons. Education: BS, summa cum laude, Northwestern University, 1942. Appointments: Corporate Section, Artcrest Products Co Inc, Chicago, 1958-88; Vice President, 1964-88, President, 1988-90, Partford Corporation, Chicago; Founder-Director, Harper Square Press, 1966-. Publications: Apertures to Anywhere, 1979; Editor: Gallery Series One: Poets, 1967; Gallery Series Two: Poets-Poems of the Real World, 1968; Gallery Series Three: Poets: Levitations and Observations, 1970; Gallery Series

Four: Poets, I Am Talking About Revolution, 1973; Gallery Series Five: Poets, To An Aging Nation, 1977. Honour: Bonbright Scholar, 1942. Memberships: Daughters of the American Revolution; Society of Midland Authors, board of directors, 1988-96, treasurer, 1987-93, president, 1994-95; Mystery Writers of America; Chicago Press Veterans Association; Arts Club, Chicago; John Evans Club of Northwestern University; Phi Beta Kappa. Address: 23 Windsor Drive, Elmhurst, IL 60126, USA.

FORMAN Milos, b. 18 February 1932, Caslav. Education: Film Faculty, Academy of Music and Dramatic Art, Prague. Appointments: Director, Film presentations, Czech TV, 1954-56; of Laterna Magika, Prague, 1958-62; Member, artistic committee, Sebor-Bor Film Producing Group; Director, films including: Talent Competition; Peter and Pavla, 1964; The Knave of Spades; A Blonde in Love, 1965; Episode in Zruc; Like a House on Fire (A Fireman's Ball), 1968; Taking Off, 1971; Co-Director, Visions of Eight, 1973; One Flew Over the Cuckoo's Nest, 1975; Hair, 1979; Ragtime, 1980; Amadeus, 1983; Valmont, 1988; The People Vs Larry Flint, 1995; Appeared in New Year's Day, 1989; Keeping the Faith, 2000. Publications: Turnaround: A Memoir (with Jan Novak), 1993. Honours: Czech Film Critics' award for Peter and Pavla, 1963, Grand Prix 17th International Film Festival, Locarno, for Peter and Pavla, 1964; Prize Venice Festival, 1965; Grand Prix, French Film Academy for a Blonde in Love, 1966; Klement Gottwald State Prize, 1967; Academy Award (Best Director) for One Flew Over the Cuckoo's Nest, 1976; Academy Award, César Award, 1985; Golden Globe for Best Director, 1996; Silver Bear for Best Director, Berlin Film Festival, 2000. Address: C/o Robert Lantz, 888 7th Avenue, New York, NY 10106, USA.

FORMAN Richard T T, b. USA. PAES Professor of Landscape Ecology. Education: BS, Haverford College, 1957; PhD, University of Pennsylvania, 1961. Appointments: Volunteer, American Friends Service Committee, Guatemala and Honduras, 1961-63; Assistant Professor, University of Wisconsin, 1963-66; Faculty Member, 1966-84, Professor of Botany, 1976-84, Director, Graduate Programme, 1979-83, Rutgers University, New Jersey; Professor of Landscape Ecology, Harvard University, Massachusetts, 1984-; Director, Hutcheson Memorial Forest Center, New Jersey, 1972-84; Instructor, Field Stations, Wisconsin, Costa Rica, St Croix, New Mexico, 1964-76; Fellow, Clare Hall, University of Cambridge, England, 1985-. Publications: Books include: Pine Barrens: Ecosystem and Landscape, 1979, 1998; Landscape Ecology, 1986; Changing Landscapes: An Ecological Perspective, 1990; Land Mosaics: The Ecology of Landscapes and Regions, 1995; Landscape Ecology Principles in Landscape Architecture and Land-Use Planning, 1996; Road Ecology: Science and Solutions, 2003; Numerous articles in scientific journals. Honours: Fulbright Scholar, Bogota, Colombia, 1970-71; Chercheur, CNRS Montpellier, France, 1977-78; Award for Excellence in Teaching, Lindback Foundation, 1984; Honorary MA, Harvard University, 1985; Honorary LHD, Miami University, 1987; Honorary DSc, Florida International University, 2001; Honorary Professor, Academia Sinica, China, 1995; Medal, University of Florence, Italy, 1997; Medal, Charles University, Prague, Czech Republic, 1998; Miegunyah Fellow, University of Melbourne, Australia, 1999; Distinguished Landscape Ecologist Award, 1992, Distinguished Scholarship Award, 1999, International Association of Landscape Ecology. Memberships: Fellow, American Association for the Advancement of Science; Ecological Society of America, Vice-President, 1982-83; Torrey Botanical Club, President, 1980-81, Bulletin Editorial Board, 1967-70; Member, National Research Council committees, 1994-97, 1999-2002, 2003-; Honorary Member, Societa Italiana di Ecologia del Paesaggio, 2000-; The Nature Conservancy, Board of Trustees,

Massachusetts Chapter, 2001-; International Association of Landscape Ecology, Vice-President, 1982-88. Address: Harvard University, Harvard Design School, Cambridge, MA 02138, USA.

FORSYTH Frederick, b. 25 August 1938, Ashford, Kent, England. Writer. m. (1) Carole Cunningham, 1973, 2 sons, (2) Sandy Molloy. Education: University of Granada. Appointments: Reporter, Eastern Daily Press, 1958-61, Reuters News Agency, 1961-65; Reporter, 1965-67, Assistant Diplomatic Correspondent, BBC, 1967-68; Freelance journalist, Nigeria and Biafra, 1968-69; Narrated Soldiers (TV), 1985; Several TV appearances. Publications: Novels: The Day of the Jackal, 1971; The Odessa File, 1972; The Dogs of War, 1974; The Shepherd, 1975; The Devil's Alternative, 1979; The Fourth Protocol, 1984; The Negotiator, 1989; The Deceiver, 1991; Great Flying Stories, 1991; The Fist of God, 1993; Icon, 1996; The Phantom of Manhattan, 1999; Quintet, 2000; The Veteran and Other Stories, 2001; Other: The Biafra Story, 1969, revised edition as The Making of an African Legend: The Biafra Story, 1977; Emeka, 1982; No Comebacks: Collected Short Stories, 1982; The Fourth Protocol (screenplay), 1987. Honour: Edgar Allan Poetry Award, Mystery Writers of America, 1971; CBE. Address: c/o Bantam Books, 62-63 Uxbridge Road, London, W5 5SA, England.

FORTE James Peter, b. 19 September 1936, Boston, Massachusetts, USA. Composer; Poet; Author. m. Nancy Mosehauer Forte. Education: BA, Music, State University of New York, Albany, 1979; Brandeis University, Lowell State University, Longy School of Music, Boston University. Appointments: Independent poet, 1950-, composer, 1952-, music teacher, 1966-92, concert manager, 1974-, author, 1976-; Music Director, Robbins Library Concert Series, Arlington, Massachusetts, 1973-78; Manager, Northeastern University Symphony Orchestra, 1978-81; Founder, Chairman, Arlington Alive (Arlington Arts Council), 1979-86; Concert series director, Northeastern University Department of Music, 1979-81; Founding member and Chairman, Massachusetts Arts Lottery Advisory Committee, 1981-84; Founder, Director, Electric Symphony, 1988-; Director, Electric Symphony Festival, New England, 1990-. Civic Activities include: Member, Arlington Historical Commission, 1972-82; Arlington Citizens' Involvement Committee, 1974-83; Member, Robbins Library Cultural Enrichment Series Committee, 1978-81; Master of Ceremonies, Member, Guidebook Editor, Arlington Town Day Committee, 1978-82; Member, Town Meeting, Town of Arlington, 1980-83; Member, Arlington Cable Access Steering Committee, 1981; Member, Arlington Selectmen's Committee on Service Priorities, 1981. Publications: Books of poetry: Arrowshaft, 1983; Foam Upon the Shore, 1988; Chaconne, 1990; Alone, 1990; Man of Stone, 1992; The Transparent Hero, 1993; The White Eagle, 1995; New Water, 1995; When the Rope is Untied, 1996; White Tiger White Stripes, 2002; Books: Fragments of the Whole, 1990, 1992; The Urban Vegetarian (co-author, cookbook), 1992; Music: Numerous orchestral, choral, chamber works including The Holy Child, 1968; Homeland, 1970; Angel Bells, 1975; Sinfonia for Strings: For Those Who Must Journey Into Eternity, Symphony No. 1, 1971-72; Piano Sonatas, Nos 1-5, 1969, 1971, 1973, 1982, 1983; String Quartets, Nos 3 and 4, 1967, 2002; Electronic music and music for synthesisers, acoustic instruments and voice, including Hidden Mountain, 1990; The Sacred Meadow, 1991; Deep Winter, 1993; CDs: Golden Light, 1997; At the Edge of Dawn, 1998; Rokka's Return, 2000; Through the Mist, 2001; Music of James Forte, 2002; Suite for Strings, 2003; And the Day After I Die, Choral Music, 2003; 6 cassettes. Honours include: Citizen of the Year, Arlington Chamber of Commerce, 1976; Arlington Town Day Committee Award, 1983; Muse Award, Public Action for the Arts, Boston, 1983; Proclamation, Town of Arlington, 1984; International Man of the Year, IBC, 1998-99;

Dictionary of International Biography

20th Century Award of Achievement, IBC, 1999; Listed in several international and specialist biographical reference works. Memberships include: Massachusetts Music Teachers Association; Music Teachers National Association; American Federation of Musicians; American Legion; Fellow, International Biographical Association; American Society of Composers, Authors and Publishers. Address: Box 1316, Arlington, MA 02474, USA. E-mail: mail@wildflowerpublishers.com Website: www.wildflowerpublishers.com

FOSTER Brendan, b. 12 January 1948, Hebburn, County Durham, England. Athlete. m. Susan Margaret Foster, 1972, 1 son, 1 daughter. Education: Sussex University; Carnegie College, Leeds. Career: Competed: Olympic Games, Munich, 5th in 1500 m, 1972; Montreal, bronze medal in 10,000m, 5th in 5000m, 1976; Moscow, 11th in 10, 000m, 1980; Commonwealth Games, Edinburgh, bronze medal at 1500m, 1970; Christchurch, silver medal at 5,000m, 1974; Edmonton, gold medal at 10,000m, bronze medal at 5000m, 1978; European champion at 5000m, 1974 and bronze medallist at 1500m, 1974; World record holder at 3000m and 2 miles; European record holder at 10,000m Olympic record holder at 5000m; Director, Recreation, Gateshead, March, 1982; Managing Director, Nike International, 1982-86; Vice President, Marketing (Worldwide), Vice President (Europe), 1986-87; Chairman and Managing Director, Nova International; BBC TV Commentator, 1980-. Publications: Brendan Foster with Cliff Temple, 1978; Olympic Heroes 1896-1984, 1984. Honours: Hon MEd, Newcastle University; Hon DLitt, Sussex University, 1982; BBC Sports Personality of the Year, 1974. Address: Nova International, Newcastle House, Albany Court, Monarch Road, Newcastle upon Tyne, NE4 7YB, England.

FOSTER Charles Allen, b. 26 August 1941, Monroe, Louisiana, USA. Lawyer. m. Susan Brown Coomes, 2 sons, 1 daughter. Education: AB, History, Princeton University, USA, 1963; BA, First Class Honours, 1965, MA, 1971, Oxford University, England; JD, magna cum laude, Harvard Law School, 1967. Appointments: Teaching Fellow, English Composition, Harvard College; Associate, 1967-72, Partner, 1972-73, McLendon, Brim, Brooks, Pierce & Daniels, Greensboro, North Carolina; Secretary, Director, General Counsel, Spanco Industries Inc, Greensboro and Sanford, North Carolina and Conestee, South Carolina, 1973-75; Partner 1975-80, Of Counsel 1980-81, Turner, Enochs, Foster, Sparrow & Burnley PA, Greensboro, North Carolina, 1975-81; Partner, Foster, Conner, Robson & Gumbiner, PA, 1983-88; Partner, Patton Boggs LLP (formed when Foster, Conner, Robson & Gumbiner merged with Patton, Boggs & Blow), 1988-99; Shareholder, Greenberg Traurig, 1999-; Senior Lecturer in Law, Duke University Law School, 1980-89; United States Government Representative, International Energy Agency Dispute Resolution Centre, Paris France, 1983- Publications: Construction and Design Law in the United States (5 volumes), 1984; The Construction Law Advisor, monthly newsletter, 1983-; The Law and Commercial Practice of Commercial Arbitration, 1986. Honours: National Merit Scholar, General Motors Scholar, Princeton University, 1959-63; Fulbright Scholar, Williams Fund Award for Best Law Examinations, President, The Ellesmere Society (University Law Society), Oxford University, England, 1963-65; Judge Bryce Bromely Prize Scholar, Harvard Law School, 1965-67. Memberships: American Bar Association; North Carolina Bar Association; American Law Institute; National Panels of Labor, Construction and International Commercial Arbitrators of the American Arbitration Association; Admitted to: United States Supreme Court; Fourth, Fifth, Ninth, Tenth, Eleventh, Circuit Court of Appeals; Federal Circuit Court of Appeals; United States District Courts: Middle, Western, Eastern Districts of North Carolina; Northern and Southern Districts of

Texas, District of Columbia; United States Tax Court; District of Columbia. Address: 3846 Cathedral Avenue, NW, Washington DC 20016, USA.

FOSTER David (Manning), b. 15 May 1944, Sydney, New South Wales, Australia. Novelist. Education: BSc, Chemistry, University of Sydney, 1967; PhD, Australian National University, Canberra, 1970. Publications: The Pure Land, 1974; The Empathy Experiment, 1977; Moonlite, 1981; Plumbum, 1983; Dog Rock: A Postal Pastoral, 1985; The Adventures of Christian Rosy Cross, 1986; Testostero, 1987; The Pale Blue Crochet Coathanger Cover, 1988; Mates of Mars, 1991; Self Portraits (editor), 1991; A Slab of Fosters, 1994; The Glade Within the Grove, 1996; The Ballad of Erinungarah, 1997; Crossing the Blue Montain (contributor), 1997; In the New Country, 1999; The Land Where Stories End, 2001. Short Stories: North South West: Three Novellas, 1973; Escape to Reality, 1977; Hitting the Wall: Two Novellas, 1989. Honours: The Age Award, 1974; Australian National Book Council Award, 1981; New South Wales Premier's Fellowship, 1986; Keating Fellowship, 1991-94; James Joyce Foundation Award, 1996; Miles Franklin Award, 1997; Courier Mail Award, 1999; Shortlisted, International Dublin IMPAC Award, 1998. Address: PO Box 57, Bundanoon, New South Wales 2578, Australia.

FOSTER David Ramsey, b. 24 May 1920, London, England. Business Executive. m. Alexandra Chang, 2 daughters. Education: Economic Tripos, Gonville and Caius College, Cambridge, England, 1938-40. Appointments: Lieutenant Commander, Royal Naval Volunteer Reserve, 1941-46; Colgate-Palmolive Company, 1946-79, General Manager, Europe, 1956-60, Vice-President, Household Products Division, 1961-65, Executive Vice-President, Chief Executive Officer, Chairman, 1968-79. Publications: Book: Wings Over the Sea; Articles in Executive Golfer. Honours: Distinguished Service Order; Distinguished Service Cross and Bar; Twice Mentioned in Dispatches. Memberships: Royal Ancient Golf Club St Andrews; Hawks Club, Cambridge; Fleet Air Arm Officers Club; Sunningdale Golf Club, UK; Life Member, Royal Cinque Ports Golf Club; Racquet Tennis Club, New York City. Address: 540 Desert West Drive, Rancho Mirage, CA 92270, USA.

FOSTER Edward (Halsey), b. 17 December 1942, Northampton, Massachusetts, USA. Poet; Publisher; Editor; Teacher. Divorced, 1 son, 1 daughter. Education: AB, Columbia College, 1965; MA, 1966, PhD, 1970, Columbia University. Appointments: Assistant Professor, Associate Professor, Professor, Director, Division of Humanities and Social Sciences, 2002-, Stevens Institute of Technology, 1985-; Visiting Professor, Ankara University, 1978-79, University of Istanbul, 1985-86, Drew University, 1990, 1992, 1994, 1996; Poetry Editor, MultiCultural Review, 1991-95; Editor, Talisman: A Journal of Contemporary Poetry and Poetics, 1988-; President, Talisman House Publishers, 1993-. Publications: The Space Between Her Bed and Clock, 1993; The Understanding, 1994; All Acts Are Simple Acts, 1995; Adrian as Song, 1996; Boy in the Key of E, 1998; Answerable to None, 2000; The Angelus Bell, 2001; Mahren, 2002; The World in Time and Space, editor, 2002. Contributions to: Five Fingers Review; Bombay Gin; American Letters and Commentary; MultiCultural Review; New Jersey History; Rendezvous; Hudson Valley Review; Ararat: A Quarterly Small Press, Western American Literature; Journal of The West; The Greenfield Review; Sagetrieb; American Book Review; Double Eye; Exact Change; First Intent; Poetry New York; Poetry USA. Membership: Modern Language Association; PEN. Address: Talisman House Publishers, PO Box 3157, Jersey City, NJ 07303-3157, USA.

FOSTER Jodie (Alicia Christian), b. 19 November 1962, Los Angeles, USA. Actress; Film Director and Producer. 2 sons. Education: Yale University. Career: Acting debut in TV programme, Mayberry, 1969; Films include: Napoleon and Samantha, 1972; Kansas City Bomber, 1972; Menace of the Mountain; One Little Indian, 1973; Tom Sawyer, 1973; Alice Doesn't Live Here Any More, 1975; Taxi Driver, 1976; Echoes of a Summer, 1976; Bugsy Malone, 1976; Freaky Friday, 1976; The Girl Who Lives the Lane, 1977; Candleshoe, 1977; Foxes, 1980; Carny, 1980; Hotel New Hampshire, 1984; The Blood of Others, 1984; Siesta, 1986; Five Corners, 1986; The Accused, 1988; Stealing Home, 1988; Catchfire, 1990; The Silence of the Lambs, 1990; Little Man Tate (also director), 1991; Shadows and Fog, 1992; Sommersby, 1993; Maverick, 1994; Nell, 1994; Home for the Holidays (director, co-producer only), 1996; Contact, 1997; The Baby Dance (executive producer only), 1997; Waking the Dead (executive producer only), 1998; Contact, 1998; Anna and the King, 1999; Panic Room, 2002; The Dangerous Lives of Altar Boys (also producer), 2002. Honours: Academy Award for Best Actress, 1989, 1992; Hon DFA, Yale, 1997. Address: E G G Pictures Production Co, 7920 Sunset Boulevard, Suite 200, Los Angeles, CA 90046, USA.

FOSUDO Anthony Olusola, b. 18 March 1958, Ejinrin, Nigeria. Lecturer; Theatre Artiste. m. Yetunde Aiyegbusi, 3 sons, 1 daughter. Education: Certificate in Dramatic Arts, 1981; Diploma in Modern Salesmanship, 1980; Diploma in Theatre Arts, 1985; BA, Theatre Arts, 1988; MA, Theatre Arts, 1989; MPhil, Theatre Arts, 2004; PhD, in progress. Appointments: Performing Artiste, UNIFE Theatre Company; Artiste-in-Residence, Lagos State Arts Council; Lecturer, Lagos State University; Managing Consultant, Satellite Town Theatre, Lagos; Artistic Director, Centre State Productions, Lagos. Publications: A Manual for Creative Writers, 2004; Gender Issues in Bode Osanyin's Woman in Arts and The Man – Bode Osanyin. Honours: Best Producer, Feature Film, National Merit Award for Arts and Culture, 1997; Award for Acting, New Generation Foundation. Memberships: Society of Nigerian Theatre Artists; British Film Institute; Knight of Saint John. Address: Department of Theatre Arts and Music, Lagos State University, Ojo, Lagos, Nigeria. E-mail: solafosudo@yahoo.com

FOWLER Murray Elwood, b. 17 July 1928, Glendale, Whidbey Island, Washington, USA. Veterinarian; University Professor. m. Audrey Cooley, 2 sons, 3 daughters. Education: BS, Animal Science, Utah State Agricultural College (now State University) 1952; DVM, Iowa State College (now State University), 1955; Foreign Animal Disease Course, USDA, Plum Island, New York, 1975. Appointments: Veterinarian, private practice, 1955-58; Instructor, 1958-60, Assistant Professor, 1960-66, Associate Professor, 1966-72, Professor, 1972-73, Department of Clinical Sciences, Large Animal Medicine and Surgery, Professor and Chairman of Department of Medicine, 1973-83, Professor, 1983-91, School of Veterinary Medicine, Professor Emeritus, Department of Medicine and Epidemiology, School of Veterinary Medicine, 1991-, University of California, Davis; Research Fellow, Toxicology Medical Research Council Labs, Carshalton, 1964-65; Chief of Service for Zoological Medicine, VMTH, UCD, 1968-91; Research Fellow, San Diego Zoological Garden, California, 1972-73; Professor of Veterinary Medicine, Makerere University, Kampala, 1973. Publications: Numerous papers; 16 books include: (author) Medicine and Surgery of South American Camelids, 1998; (co-editor) Zoo and Wild Animal Medicine, 5th ed, 2003; (co-author) Color Atlas of Camelid Hematology, 1998; (author) Poisonous Plants - A Veterinary Guide to Toxic Syndromes (CD ROM), 1998. Honours: Awards include: Murray E Fowler Achievement Award, presented by California Llama Association, 1995; Emil P Dolensek Memorial Award, American Association of Zoo Veterinarians, 1995; Tribute to Murray Fowler, International Llama Association; R Marlin Perkins Award, American Zoo & Aquarium Association's highest honour, 2001; Animal Welfare

Award for lifelong devotion to zoo & wild animals, American Veterinary Medical Association, 2002. Address: Dr Murray E Fowler, 427 Cabrillo Ave, Davis, CA 95616, USA.

FOX Edward, b. 13 April 1937. Actor. m. (1) Tracy Pelissier, 1958, divorced 1961, 1 daughter. 1 daughter by Joanna David. Education: Royal Academy of Dramatic Art. Career: Actor, 1957-; Provincial repertory theatre, 1958; Worked widely in films, stage plays and TV; Stage appearances include: Knuckle, 1973; The Family Reunion, 1979; Anyone for Denis, 1981; Quartermaine's Terms, 1981; Hamlet, 1982; The Dance of Death, 1983; Interpreters, 1986; The Admirable Crichton, 1988; Another Love Story, 1990; The Philanthropist, 1991; My Fair Lady; Father, 1995; A Letter of Resignation, 1997; The Chiltern Hundreds, 1999; The Browning Version, 2000; The Twelve Pound Look, 2000; Films include: The Go-Between, 1971; The Day of the Jackal; A Doll's House, 1973; Galileo, 1976; A Bridge Too far; The Duellists; The Cat and the Canary, 1977; Force Ten from Navarone, 1978; The Mirror Crack'd, 1980; Gandhi, 1982; Never Say Never Again, 1983; Wild Geese; The Bounty, 1984; The Shooting Party; Return from the River Kwai, 1989; Circles of Deceit (TV), 1989; Prince of Thieves, 1990; They Never Slept, 1991; A Month by the Lake, 1996; Prince Valiant, 1997; Television includes: Daniel Deronda, 2002. Honours: Several awards for TV performance as Edward VIII in Edward and Mrs Simpson.

FOX James, b. 19 May 1939, London, England. Actor. m. Mary Elizabeth Fox, 1973, 4 sons, 1 daughter. Career: Actor, films include: Mrs Miniver, 1952; The Servant, 1963; King Rat, 1965; Those Magnificent Man in Their Flying Machines, 1965; Thoroughly Modern Millie, 1966; Isadora, 1967; Performance, 1969; Passage to India, 1984; Runners, 1984; Farewell to the King, 1987; Finding Mawbee (video film as the Mighty Quinn), 1988; She's Been Away, 1989; The Russia House, 1990; Afraid of the Dark, 1991; Patriot Games, 1991; As You Like It, 1992; The Remains of the Day, 1993; The Old Curiosity Shop, 1994; Gulliver's Travels, 1995; Elgar's Tenth Muse, 1995; Uncle Vanya, 1995; Anna Karenina, 1997; Mickey Blue Eyes, 1998; Jinnah, 1998; Up at the Villa, 1998; The Golden Bowl, 1999; Sexy Beast, 2000; The Lost World, 2001. Publication: Comeback: An Actor's Direction, 1983. Address: c/o ICM Oxford House, 76 Oxford Street, London, W1D 1BS, England.

FOX Michael J, b. 9 June 1961, Edmonton, Alberta, Canada. Actor. m. Tracy Pollan, 1988, 1 son, 2 daughters. Career: TV appearances include: Leo and Me, 1976; Palmerstown USA, 1980; Family Ties, 1982-89; Spin City, 1996-2000; TV films include: Letters from Frank, 1979; Poison Ivy, 1985; High School USA, 1985; Films include: Midnight Madness, 1980; Class of '84, 1981; Back to the Future, 1985; Teen Wolf, 1985; Light of Day, 1986; The Secret of My Success, 1987; Bright Lights, Big City, 1988; Back to the Future II, 1989; Back to the Future III, 1989; The Hard Way, 1991; Doc Hollywood, 1991; The Concierge, 1993; Give Me a Break, 1994; Greedy, 1994; The American President, 1995; Mars Attacks!, 1996; The Frighteners, 1996; Stuart Little (voice), 1999; Atlantis: The Lost Empire (voice), 2001; Interstate 60, 2002; Stuart Little 2 (voice), 2002. Address: c/o Kevin Huvane, CAA, 9830 Wilshire Blvd, Beverly Hills, CA 90212, USA.

FRANCHI Giuseppe, b. 16 November 1924, Siena, Italy. University Professor. m. Rampazzo Rosana, 1 son. Education: Laurea Pharmacy, University of Siena, 1948; Libera Docenza, Pharmaceutical Technology and Legislation, 1958; Libera Docenza, Pharmaceutical Chemistry, 1962. Appointments: Lecturer and Professor, Pharmaceutical Technology and Legislation, 1958-75; Dean Faculty of Pharmacy, University of Siena, Italy, 1976-88; Pharmaceutical Chemistry Department,

University of Siena, Director, 1976-81, 1995-97; Retired, 1997. Publications: 92 papers on pharmaceutical chemistry and pharmaceutical techniques, 1951-97; 1 book on analytical chemistry; 2 patents on pharmaceutical technological equipment. Honours: Gold Medal for services to school, culture and art, 1984; Commendatore al merito della Repubblica Italiana, 1997. Memberships: Accademia delle Scienze di Siena, detta dei Fisiocritici, 1954, President, 1990-98; Association of Italian Teachers and Researchers in Pharmaceutical Technology and Legislation, 1971, President, 1981-97; Italian Society of Pharmaceutical Sciences, 1966; Pharmaceutical Society of Latin Mediterranean Countries, 1963; Rotary Club 2070 District, 1980. Address: Via della Sapienza 39, 53100 Siena, Italy.

FRANCIS Clare, b. 17 April 1946, Surrey, England. Writer. 1 son. Education: Economics Degree, University College, London. Appointment: Chair, Advisory Committee on Public Lending Right, 2000-2003. Publications: Come Hell or High Water, 1977; Come Wind or Weather, 1978; The Commanding Sea, 1981; Night Sky, 1983; Red Crystal, 1985; Wolf Winter, 1987; Requiem, 1991; Deceit, 1993; Betrayal, 1995; A Dark Devotion, 1997; Keep Me Close, 1999; A Death Divided, 2001; Homeland, 2004. Honours: Member, Order of British Empire; Fellow, University College, London; University of Manchester Institute of Technology, honorary fellow. Membership: Society of Authors, chairman, 1997-99. Address: c/o John Johnson Agency, Clerkenwell House, 45-47 Clerkenwell Green, London EC1R 0HT, England.

FRANCIS Marion David, b. 9 May 1923, Campbell River, British Columbia, Canada. Research Chemist. m. (1) Emily Liane Williams, deceased, (2) Jacqueline S Lohman, 1 son, 1 daughter. Education: BA, 1946, MA, 1949, University of British Columbia; PhD, University of Iowa, 1953. Appointments: Laboratory Instructor, University of British Columbia, 1946-49; Chemist, Canadian Fishing Co, 1946; Research Assistant, University of Iowa, 1949-51; Research Chemist, 1952-76, Senior Scientist, 1976-85, Procter and Gamble; Senior Scientist, Norwich Eaton Pharmaceuticals Inc, 1985-89; Research Fellow, Victor Mills Society, 1990-93; Consultant, 1993-. Publications: 140 abstracts, reviewed articles and chapters in books. Honours: US Public Health Predoctoral Fellowship, 1951-52; Cincinnati Chemist of the Year, 1977, National Industrial Chemists Award, 1994, Morley Medal, 1996, Hero of Chemistry, 2000, American Chemical Society; Professional Accomplishment Award, Professional and Scientific Societies Council, 1979; Technical Innovation Award, Victor Mills Society, 1990; Perkin Medal, Society of Chemical Industry, 1996. Memberships: American Chemical Society; American Society for Bone and Mineral Research; Fellow, AAAS; Fellow, American Institute of Chemists. Address: 23 Diplomat Drive, Cincinnati, OH 45215, USA. E-mail: dinbug5me@cs.com

FRANIN Dina, b. 29 March 1959, Zagreb, Croatia. Author; Poet. Education: Graduate, Law Faculty, Zagreb University, 1987. Publications: Poetry: Primal Scream (collection of poems), 1995; Woman's Pride is a Hard Stone (collection of poems), 1996; The Last Juices of Summer (collection of poems), 1999; The Sheltered Moon (collection of haiku), 1999; Blue Nature (collection of poems), 2002; Short stories: Here Beside Me, 1996; The Pair of Scales, 1999; Numerous poems published in anthologies and magazines nationally and internationally. Honours: Honourable Mention, 6th Annual Haiku Competition, Croatian Haiku Association, 1998; 3rd Prize, International Kumamoto Kusamakura Haiku Competition, Japan, 1999; 3rd Honourable Mention, International Competition, Hawaii Education Association, 1999; Editor's Award, International Library of Poetry, Owing Mills, USA, 1999; 1st Prize, 8th Annual Haiku Competition, Croatian Haiku Association, 2000; Commended Haiku, International Yellow Moon Literary Competition, Australia, 2000; Highly Commended Poem, International Yellow Moon Literary Competition, Australia, 2000. Memberships: Matica Hrvatska; The Association of Croatian Haiku Poets; The Association of Artists August Šenoa; The Association of Artists Vjekoslav Majer; The Association of Artists Tin Ujević; Editor's Board of miscellany Naša riječ; Distinguished Member of the International Society of Poets. Address: Republike Austrije 21, 10000 Zagreb, Croatia. E-mail: dinafranin@yahoo.com

FRANJEVIC Vlado, b. 4 August 1963, Martinac, Croatia. Art Technician. m. Yvonne Heeb, 2 children. Education; Graduated, School of Applied Art, Zagreb, Croatia. Signwriter, Restorer and Ceramic Jewellery Maker, Croatia; Moved to Switzerland, 1989, Liechtenstein, 1993; Art works exhibited Liechtenstein, Switzerland, Germany, Croatia, France, Monaco, Indonesia, Bulgaria, Serbia; Leading Art-Workshop in Jogjakarta, Indonesia, 2002. Publications: Uraufführung, 2001. Honours: Support Grant, Society of German Authors, 2000; One year Scholarship, Culture Adviser of the Parlament of the principality of Liechtenstein, 2002-03. Memberships: Society of Interest of German Authors; Society of Fine Artists in Zagreb, Croatia. Address: Dorfstrasse 70, 9495 Triessen, Principality of Liechtenstein. E-mail: vlado@adon.li

FRANKLAND (Anthony) Noble, b. 4 July 1922, Ravenstonedale, England. Historian; Biographer. m. (1) Diana Madeline Fovargue Tavernor, 28 February 1944, deceased 1981, 1 son, 1 daughter, (2) Sarah Katharine Davies, 7 May 1982. Education: Open Scholar, MA, 1948, DPhil, 1951, Trinity College, Oxford. Appointments: Official British Military Historian, 1951-60; Deputy Director of Studies, Royal Institute of International Affairs, 1956-60; Director, Imperial War Museum, 1960-82. Publications: Crown of Tragedy: Nicholas II, 1960; The Strategic Air Offensive Against Germany (co-author), 4 volumes, 1961; The Bombing Offensive Against Germany: Outlines and Perspectives, 1965; Bomber Offensive: The Devastation of Europe, 1970; Prince Henry, Duke of Gloucester, 1980; Witness of a Century: Prince Arthur, Duke of Connaught, 1850-1942, 1993; History at War: The Campaigns of an Historian, 1998; Encyclopaedia of Twentieth Century Warfare (general editor and contributor), 1989; The Politics and Strategy of the Second World War (joint editor), 9 volumes. Contributions to: Encyclopaedia Britannica; Times Literary Supplement; The Times; Daily Telegraph; Observer; Military journals. Honours: Companion of the Order of the Bath; Commander of the Order of the British Empire; Holder of the Distinguished Flying Cross. Address: 26/27 River View Terrace, Abingdon, Oxon, OX14 5AE, England.

FRANKLIN Aretha, b. 25 March 1942, Memphis, TN, USA. Singer. m. (1) Ted White, divorced, (2) Glynn Turman, 1978. Career: First recordings, father's Baptist church, Detroit; Tours as gospel singer; Moved to New York, signed with Columbia Records, 1960, Atlantic, 1966, Arista, 1980. Publications: Recordings include: Aretha, 1961; The Electrifying Aretha Franklin, 1962; Laughing on the Outside, The Tender, the Moving, the Swinging Aretha Franklin, 1963; Running Out of Fools, The Gospel Sound of Aretha Franklin, 1964; Soul Sister, 1966; I Never Loved a Man the Way I Love You, 1967; Lady Soul, Aretha Now, Aretha in Paris, 1968; Aretha's Gold, 1969; This Girl's in Love With You, Spirit in the Dark, 1970; Live at Fillmore West, 1971; Young Gifted and Black, Amazing Grace, 1972; Hey Now Hey, The Best of Aretha Franklin, The First Twelve Sides, 1973; Let Me in Your Life, With Everything I Feel in Me, 1974; You, 1975; Sparkle, Ten Years of Gold, 1976; Sweet Passion, 1977; Almighty Fire, 1978; La Diva, 1979; Aretha, 1980; Love All the Hurt Away, 1981; Jump to It, 1982; Get It Right, 1983; One Lord, One Faith, 1988; Through the Storm, 1989; What You Can See is What You Sweat,

1991; Jazz to Soul, 1992; Aretha After Hours, Chain of Fools, 1993; Unforgettable: A Tribute to Dinah Washington, 1995; Love Songs, 1997; The Delta Meets Detroit, 1998; A Rose is Still a Rose, 1998; Amazing Grace, 1999. Publications: Aretha: From these Roots (with David Rib). Honours: Numerous Grammy Awards, 1967-87; American Music Award, 1984; John F Kennedy Centre Award, 1994; Rock and Roll Hall of Fame, 1987. Address: 8450 Linwood Street, Detroit, MI 48206, USA.

FRANKLIN H Bruce, b. 28 February 1934, Brooklyn, NY, USA. Professor. m. 3 children. Education: BA, Amherst College, Massachusetts, 1955; Doctor of Philosophy, English and American Literature, Stanford University, 1961; Certificate of Environmental Horticulture, College of San Mateo, California, 1974. Appointments: Batch Worker, Mayfair Photofinishing Company, NY, 1951, 1952; Upholster, Carb Manufacturing Company, 1953; Foreman, Shipping Department, 1954; Tugboat Deckhand; Mate; Pennsylvania RR Marine Department, Pier H, Jersey City, NJ, 1955-56; Navigator; Intelligence Officer, Strategic Air Command, United States Air Force, 1956-59; Lecturer, Department of Adult Education, San Jose, California, 1963-64; Assistant Professor, English and American Literature, Stanford University, 1961-64; Assistant Professor, English and American Literature, The Johns Hopkins University, 1964-65; Lecturer, Free University of Paris, France, 1967; Lecturer, Venceremos College, Redwood City, California, 1971; Associate Professor, English and American Literature, Stanford University, 1965-72; Visiting Lecturer, American Studies, Yale University, 1974-75; Professor, English, Rutgers University, 1975-80; Professor II, English, 1980-87; John Cotton Dana Professor, English and American Studies, Rutgers, The State University, 1987-. Publications: The Wake of the Gods; Future Perfect; War Stars; Prison Literature in America; Vietnam and other American Fantasies; Many others. Honours: Stanford Willson Fellow; The Alexander Cappon Prize; Many others. Address: English Department, Rutgers University, Newark, NJ 07102, USA. E-mail: hbf@andromeda.rutgers.edu

FRANKLIN Walt, b. 19 June 1950, Schwabach, Germany. Poet; Writer. m. Leighanne Parkins, 4 September 1982, 1 son, 1 daughter. Education: BS, Psychology, 1973, Elementary Education Teaching Certificate, 1975, Alfred University; Self-taught in ecology, homesteading, bioregionalism. Appointments: Counselor, Grafton School, 1976-80; Advisor, Human Services, ARC, Alfred, New York 1981-90; Publisher and Editor, Great Elm Press, Greenwood, New York, 1984-92. Publications: Talking to the Owls, 1984; Topographies, 1984; The Glass Also Rises, 1985; Little Water Company, 1986; Ekos: A Journal Poem, 1986; The Ice Harvest, 1988; Instrument, 1988; Rootwork and Other Poems, 1988; The Wild Trout, 1989; Uplands Haunted by the Sea, 1992; The Flutes of Power, 1995; Letters from Susquehannock, 1995. Contributions to: About 350 publications. Honours: Numerous small press awards, including Abacus and Rose, 1988. Memberships: Poets Theatre, Hornell, New York; Appalachian Writers Association; Poets and Writers. Address: 1205 Co Rt 60, Rexville, NY 14877, USA.

FRASER Lady Antonia, (Lady Antonia Pinter), b. 27 August 1932, London, England. Author. m. (1) Sir Hugh Fraser, 1956, dissolved 1977, 3 sons, 3 daughters, (2) Harold Pinter, 1980. Education: MA, Lady Margaret Hall, Oxford. Appointment: General Editor, Kings and Queens of England series. Publications: King Arthur and the Knights of the Round Table, 1954; Robin Hood, 1955; Dolls, 1963; A History of Toys, 1966; Mary Queen of Scots, 1969; Cromwell, Our Chief of Men, 1973; King James: VI of Scotland, I of England, 1974; Kings and Queens of England (editor), 1975; Scottish Love Poems: A Personal Anthology (editor), 1975; Love Letters: An Anthology (editor), 1976, revised

edition, 1989; Quiet as a Nun, 1977; The Wild Island, 1978; King Charles II, 1979; Heroes and Heroines (editor), 1980; A Splash of Red, 1981; Mary Queen of Scots: Poetry Anthology (editor), 1981; Oxford and Oxfordshire in Verse: An Anthology (editor), 1982; Cool Repentance, 1982; The Weaker Vessel: Woman's Lot in Seventeenth Century England, 1984; Oxford Blood, 1985; Jemima Shore's First Case, 1986; Your Royal Hostage, 1987; Boadicea's Chariot: The Warrior Queens, 1988; The Cavalier Case, 1990; Jemima Shore at the Sunny Grave, 1991; The Six Wives of Henry VIII, 1992; The Pleasure of Reading (editor), 1992; Political Death, 1994; The Gunpowder Plot, 1996; The Lives of the Kings and Queens of England, 1998; Marie Antoinette: the Journey, 2001. Other: Several books adapted for television. Contributions to: Anthologies. Honours: James Tait Black Memorial Prize, 1969; Wolfson History Award, 1984; Prix Caumont-La Force, 1985; Honorary DLitt, Universities of Hull, 1986, Sussex, 1990, Nottingham, 1993 and St Andrews, 1994; St Louis Literary Award, 1996; CWA Non Fiction Gold Dagger, 1996; Shortlisted for NCR Award, 1997; Norten Medlicott Medal, Historical Association, 2000. Memberships: Society of Authors, chairman, 1974-75; Crimewriters' Association, chairman, 1985-86; Writers in Prison Committee, chairman, 1985-88, 1990; English PEN, vice president, 1990-. Address: c/o Curtis Brown Ltd, 162-168 Regent Street, London W1R 5TB, England.

FRASER Conon, b. 8 March 1930, Cambridge, England. Retired Documentary Film Producer and Director; Writer. m. Jacqueline Stearns, 17 March 1955, 5 sons. Education: Marlborough College, 1943-47; Royal Military Academy, Sandhurst, 1948-50. Publications include: The Underground Explorers, 1957; Oystercatcher Bay, 1962; Looking at New Zealand, 1969; Beyond the Roaring Forties, 1986; Contributing Editor, Enderby Settlement Diaries, 1999. Contributions to: New Zealand's Heritage; Argosy (UK); New Zealand Listener. Honours: Silver Medal for Documentary Film, Coal Valley, Festival of the Americas, 1979; Silver Screen Award, United States Industrial Film Festival, 1980; Mitra Award of Honour, 26th Asian Film Festival, 1980. Address: 39a Henry Hill Road, Taupo, New Zealand.

FRASER George MacDonald, b. 2 April 1925, Carlisle, England. Author; Journalist. m. Kathleen Margarette Hetherington, 1949, 2 sons, 1 daughter. Education: Glasgow Academy. Appointment: Deputy Editor, Glasgow Herald newspaper, 1964-69. Publications: Flashman, 1969; Royal Flash, 1970, screenplay, 1975; The General Danced at Dawn, 1970; Flash for Freedom, 1971; Steel Bonnets, 1971; Flashman at the Charge, 1973; The Three Musketeers, screenplay, 1973; The Four Musketeers, screenplay, 1974; McAuslan in the Rough, 1974; Flashman in the Great Game, 1975; The Prince and the Pauper, screenplay, 1976; Flashman's Lady, 1977; Mr American, 1980; Flashman and the Redskins, 1982; Octopussy, screenplay, 1983; The Pyrates, 1983; Flashman and the Dragon, 1985; Casanova, television screenplay, 1987; The Hollywood History of the World, 1988; The Sheikh and the Dustbin, 1988; The Return of the Musketeers, screenplay, 1989; Flashman and the Mountain of Light, 1990; Quartered Safe Out Here, 1992; The Candlemass Road, 1993; Flashman and the Angel of the Lord, 1994; Black Ajax, 1997; Flashman and the Tiger, 1999. Honour: OBE, 1999; The Light's on at Signpost, 2002. Address: Baldrine, Isle of Man, Britain.

FRASER Ian Masson, b. 15 December 1917, Forres, Moray, Scotland. Ordained Minister. m. Margaret D D Stewart, 2 sons, 1 daughter. Education: MA, BD (New College for Theology), with distinction in Systematic Theology, 1936-42; PhD, 1955, Edinburgh University, Scotland. Appointments: Manual Working Industrial Chaplain, Fife, Scotland, 1942-44; Interim appointment, Hopemouth Church, Arbroath, Scotland, 1944-45; Scottish

Secretary, Student Christian Movement, 1945-48; Parish Minister, Rosyth, Fife, Scotland, 1948-60; Warden of Scottish Churches House, Dunblane, Scotland, 1960-69; Executive Secretary, 1969-73, Consultant and Programme Co-ordinator, 1973-75, World Council of Churches; Dean and Head of the Department of Mission, Selly Oak Colleges, Birmingham, England, 1973-82; Voluntary Research Consultant, Scottish Churches' Council, 1982-90, Action of Churches Together in Scotland, 1990-. Publications: Numerous articles and books including most recently: Strange Fire, a book of life stories and prayers, 1994; A Celebration of Saints, 1997; Signs of Fire (audio cassette), 1998; Salted with Fire, more stories, reflections, prayers, 1999; Caring for Planet Earth, children's stories and prayers, 2002; R B Cunningham Graham – Fighter for Justice, 2002; Action of Churches Together in Scotland, Ecumenical Adventure, beginnings in the 1860's, of the work of Scottish Churches House and Council, 2002; Many Cells One Body, 2003. Honours: Cobb Scholarship, Cunningham Fellowship, Gunning Prize, New College, Edinburgh. Address: Ferndale, Gargunnock, by Stirling FK8 3BW, Scotland.

FRASHERI Sotiraq Thoma, b. 6 August 1951, Korce, Albania. Zoological Technician and Extensionist. m. Elenica, 2 daughters. Education: Student, 1969-73, Graduate, 1974, Veterinary Faculty, Zoological Technique Branch, High Agricultural University, Kamez, Tirana, Albania; Studies into the Simental breed of cows imported from Austria and bred in the ex-Agricultural Enterprise of Maliq, District of Korce. Appointments: Zoological Technician, District of Skrapar, 1973-75; Zoological Technician, Rembec Sector, 1975-80; Zoological Technician, Plase Sector, ex-Agricultural Economy of Plase, District of Korce, 1980-84; Researches into the herd of Ostfriz cows imported from Germany and crossbreeding in the Sectors of Rembec and Plase; Researches into the effectiveness of extension and the zoological technique service in association with local farmers in the Commune of Pirg, Korce District, 1994-2000; Created 12 Associations of Agricultural Marketing in the villages of the Commune of Pirg. Publication: Studies in the Field of Zoo-technique and Extension Service. Honour: Certificate of Excellence for Outstanding Performance and Lasting Contribution, Project Tarentaise, 2001. Address: Toena Publishings, Rr "Muhamet Gjollesha", K Postare 1420, Tirana, Albania.

FRATTI Mario, b. 5 July 1927, L'Aquila, Italy. (US citizen, 1974). Playwright; Educator. 3 children. Education: PhD, Ca Foscari University, 1951. Appointments: Drama Critic, 1963-, Paese, 1963-, Progresso, 1963-, Ridotto, 1963; Adelphi College, teacher, 1964-65; Faculty, Columbia University, 1965-66; Professor of Literature, New School, Hunter College, 1967-; Faculty, Hofstra University, 1973-74. Publications: Plays: Cage-Suicide, 1964; Academy-Return, 1967; Mafia, 1971; Bridge, 1971; Races, 1972; Eleven Plays in Spanish, 1977; Refrigerators, 1977; Eleonora Duse-Victim, 1981; Nine, 1982; Biography of Fratti, 1982; AIDS, 1987; Porno, 1988, Encounter, musical, 1989; Family, 1990; Friends, 1991; Lovers, 1992; Leningrad Euthanasia, 1993; Holy Father, 1994; Sacrifices, 1995; Jurors, 1996; 8 Plays in Russian, 1997; 4 Plays in Japanese, 7 Mini Dramas in Spanish, 1997; 4 Dramas in Spanish, 1998; Candida and her Friends, 1999; Erotic Adventures in Venice, 2000; Puccini – A Musical, 2000; Terrorist, 2002; Blindness, 2003. Honours: Tony Award, 1982; Other awards for plays and musicals. Memberships: Drama Desk; American Theatre Critics; Outer Critics Circle, Vice-President. Address: 145 West 55th Street, Apt 15D, New York, NY 10019, USA.

FREASIER Aileen W, b. 12 November 1924, Edcouch, Texas, USA. Educator. m. Ben C Freasier, deceased, 3 sons, 2 daughters. Education: BS, Home Economics, Texas A&I University, 1944;

M Ed, Special Education, 1966, 90 hours above the Master's level, Louisiana Tech University. Appointments: Fourth Grade Teacher, Robstown Elementary School, Robstown, Texas, 1948-49; EMR Class teacher, San Antonio Independent School District, San Antonio, Texas, 1961-62; TMR Day Care Program Teacher, Lincoln Parish Association for Retarded Children, Ruston, Louisiana, 1965-71; Teacher, Lincoln Parish Association for Retarded Children's Summer Program, Ruston, Louisiana, 1969; EMR, TMR Class Teacher, Lincoln Parish Schools, I A Lewis, Lincoln Center, Ruston, Louisiana, 1971-77; EMR Resource Room Teacher, Hico Elementary, Lincoln Parish Schools, Hico Louisiana, 1977-80; Coordinating Teacher, Early Childhood Program, Lincoln Parish Schools, Ruston, Louisiana, 1980-81; IEP Facilitator/Educational Diagnostician, Special Schools District #1, Louisiana Training Institute, Monroe, Louisiana, 1981-95; Retired Senior Program Volunteer PreGED Class Tutor, Lincoln Parish Detention Center, Ruston, Louisiana, 1995-. Publications: 20 publications in professional special education, correctional education, and technology education journals; 11 commercial workbooks/duplicating masters books for special education students; 3 international, 45 national, 24 state presentations to special education, correctional and technology-using educators. Honours include: Mary C Wilson Award, Lincoln Parish Schools, 1978; State Named Bolivar L Hait Research and Projects Endowment Honoree, American Association of University Women, Louisiana Division, 1982; Special Schools District # 1, Teacher of the Year, 1988; Phi Delta Kappa Service Award, 1991; J E Wallace Wallin Education of the Handicapped Children Award, Louisiana Federation of the Council for Exceptional Children, 1994; President's Award for Outstanding Service, Louisiana Council for Exceptional Children, Technology and Media, 1997. Memberships include: American Association of University Women; Council for Exceptional Children, Correctional Education Association; Daughters of the American Revolution; Delta Kappa Gamma; Kappa Kappa Iota; Lincoln Parish Retired Teachers; Louisiana Reading Association; Phi Delta Kappa; Ruston Mayor's Commission for Women. Address: PO Box 1595, Ruston, LA 71273-1595. E-mail: aileenwf@bayou.com

FREEMAN Cathy, b. 16 February 1973, Mackay, Australia. Athlete. m. Alexander Bodecker. Career: Public Relations Adviser; Winner, Australian 200m, 1990-91, 1994, 1996; Australian 100m, 1996; Amateur Athletics Federation 400m, 1992, 200m, 1993; Gold Medallist 4x100m, Commonwealth Games, 1990; Gold Medallist 200m, 400m, Silver Medallist 4x100m, Commonwealth Games, 1994; Silver Medallist 400m, Olympic Games, Atlanta, 1996; Winner, World Championships 400m, Athens (first Aboriginal winner at World Championships), 1997; Set 2 Australian 200m records, 5 Australian 400m records, 1994-96; 1st, World Championships, Seville, 400m, 1999; Gold Medallist, Sydney Olympic Games 400m, 2000; took break from atheletics in 2001; returned to international competition, Gold Medal 4x400m relay, Commonwealth Games, Manchester, 2002; Media and Communications Officer, Australia Post. Honours: Numerous national awards include: Australian of the Year, 1998; OAM, 2001. Address: c/o Melbourne International Track Club, 43 Fletcher Street, Essendon, Vic 3040, Australia.

FREEMAN David Franklin, b. 13 April 1925, Raleigh, North Carolina, USA. Adult and Child Psychiatrist and Psychoanalyst. m. Constance Covell Freeman, 1 son, 2 daughters. Education: BS, Wake Forest College, North Carolina, 1948; MD, Bowman Gray School of Medicine, Winston-Salem, 1951; Internship, Philadelphia General Hospital, 1951-52; Resident, Adult and Child Psychiatry, Boston Psychopathic Hospital, Massachusetts, 1952-55; Research Fellow, Psychiatry, Harvard University, 1952-55; 2nd Year Child Psychiatry, Worcester Youth Guidance Center, Massachusetts,

1955-56; Candidate, Adult and Child Psychoanalysis, Boston, Washington, UNC-Duke University Psychoanalytic Institutes, 1955-66. Appointments: Private Practice, Adult and Child Psychiatry, Lincoln, Massachusetts, 1956-61; Director, North Central Mental Health Consultation Service, Fitchburg, Massachusetts, 1956-57; Staff Psychiatrist, Douglas A Thom Clinic for Children, Boston, Massachusetts, 1957-61; Assistant in Child Psychiatry, Boston University School of Medicine, 1960-61; Consultant, several child psychiatry clinics, 1956-66; Clinical Faculty, Assistant Professor to Clinical Professor, University of North Carolina, 1961-95; Adjunct Professor, University of North Carolina at Chapel Hill, 1995-; Training and Supervising Psychoanalyst, UNC-Duke University Psychoanalytic Education Program, 1972-; Psychiatric Consultant, NE Home for Little Wanderers, Boston, Massachusetts, 1959-61; Director, Child Psychiatry Outpatient Clinic, North Carolina Memorial Hospital, Chapel Hill, 1961-63; Private Practice, Adult and Child Psychiatry and Psychoanalysis, Chapel Hill, North Carolina, 1963-. Publications: Several articles in professional medical journals. Honours include: Alpha Omega Alpha, 1950; Herman Lineberger Award, 1997; NC Psychoanalytic Foundation, 2003. Memberships include: Life member: American Psychiatric Association; International Psychoanalytical Association; North Carolina Psychiatric Association; American Academy of Child and Adolescent Psychiatry; North Carolina Medical Society; American Psychoanalytic Association; Association for Child Psychoanalysis Life Member and Past President/Director: North Carolina Psychoanalytic Society; North Carolina Council of Child Psychiatry; Founder and Chair: North Carolina Psychoanalytic Foundation, 1995-2000. Address: 101 Ashe Place, Chapel Hill, NC 27517, USA.

FREIBERG Irmtraut, b. 18 November 1962, Freiburg/Brg, Germany. Professor of Music Theory. Education: Teaching Diploma, Recorder, 1987, Elementary Music Education, 1988, Music Theory, 1988, University of Music, Heidelberg, Germany; Soloist Diploma Recorder, 1993, Harpsichord, 2001, Mag art, 1991, 1993, 2001, University of Music, Vienna; Pedagogic Musicology, 1994, Dr Phil, 1996, University of Vienna. Appointments: Teacher, Recorder, Harpsichord, Ensemble, Music School of Vienna, 1994-2004; Professor of Music Theory, Privatuniversität Konservatorium, Vienna, 1996-. Publications: F Geminiani: 4 Sonates; J Pachelbel: 2 Fugues; A Poglietti: Canzona; G F Händel: Duets; N à Kempis: 10 Symphonies; J Strauss: Contradances; F M Techelmann: Suite; Several articles about thoroughbass and accompaniments; Books: Die Entwicklung des Generalbasses, 2001; Der frühe italienische Generalbass, 2004. Honours: Awards for the Ministry of Science and Research, 1991, 1994. Membership: Club der Wiener Musikerinnen; AGMÖ, Gesellschaft für Musikwissenschaft. Address: Favoritenstr 137/8, A-1100 Vienna, Austria. E-mail: irmtraut.freiberg@chello.at

FREIBERT Lucy M, b. 19 October 1922, Louisville, Kentucky, USA. Educator. Education: BA, English, Spalding College, 1957; MA, English, St Louis University, 1962; PhD, English, University of Wisconsin, 1970; Appointments: Secondary Presentation Academy, 1957-60; Spalding College, 1960-71; University of Louisville, 1971-93; Professor Emerita of English, 1993-. Publications: Hidden Hands: An Anthology of American Women Writers (with Barbara White), 1985; Creative Women of Brook Farm, in Women in Spiritual and Communitarian Societies in the US, 1993; Articles in various journals. Honours: Woman of Distinction, Center for Women and Families, 1993; Trustees Award, University of Louisville, 1991; Distinguished Teaching Professor, 1987; Susan Koppleman Award, American Culture and Popular Culture Associations for Hidden Hands, 1986. Memberships: National Women's Studies Association, Journal

Board member, 1993-2001; Modern Language Association, Life Member; Melville Society; National Organization for Women. Address: 1507 Hepburn Avenue #2, Louisville, Kentucky 40204, USA.

FREITAG Erik, b. 1 February 1940, Vienna, Austria. Composer; Violin Teacher. Education: Studied at the Vienna Hochschule für Musik and with Karl-Birger Blomdahl, Stockholm. Career: Violinist Swedish Radio, 1964-66; Philharmonic Orchestra, Stockholm, 1967-1970; Section Leader, Conservatory of Vienna; Composer-in-Residence at the University of North Western Michigan in association with the International Festival Earth/Arts Traverse, Michigan, 1996. Compositions: Quintet for clarinet, horn, violin, cello and piano; Circuits magiques for string quartet; Limericks - 5 songs for medium voice and 6 instruments; Immagini for violin solo, flute, oboe, violin, viola, cello, double bass and piano. Recordings: CDs: Helle Nacht for strings, 1990; Sonata for cello and piano, 1990; Triaphonie I for horn, violin and piano, 1995; Soul-Sky for violin solo, 1995; El retablo de la catedral de Tarragona for chamber ensemble, 1992; Quintet for clarinet, horn, violin, cello and piano; Triaphonie II, III, IV in der tidesstunde von altons alfred schmidt, Limericks; Radio: Yoziguanatzi for Orchestra, 1994; Triaphonie II for saxophone, violin and piano; Passages in the Wind, Poems by John Gracen Brown for baritone and 7 instruments; Reflections in Air for string trio; 3 pieces for string quartet; Strindberg-ljus och skugga for chamber orchestra; Idun for violin and piano; Chamber concerto for small orchestra; Sonata Nachtstücke for violin and viola. Honours: Competition Prize Nordelbische Tage, Hamburg, 1975; Prize, Austrian Ministry of Education. 1975; Prize, City of Vienna, 1979; Theodor Körner Prize, 1981. Memberships: Austrian Society of Composers; ISCM Austrian Section; Ensemble Wiener Collage (administration). Address: Schippergasse 20, A-1210 Vienna, Austria.

FRENKEL David-Arie, b. 2 February 1940, Tel-Aviv, Israel. Associate Professor of Law; Member of the Israel Bar. m. Naomi Davis, 2 sons, 3 daughters. Education: Master of Jurisprudence, 1961, Doctor of Laws, 1975, Hebrew University of Jerusalem. Appointments: Lawyer in Private Practice, 1963-69; Researcher and Instructor, Faculty of Law, Hebrew University of Jerusalem, 1969-75; Deputy Legal Adviser, Ministry of Education, 1974-76; Legal Adviser, Ministry of Health, 1976-81; Private Practice, 1981-89; Legal Adviser, Municipality of Beer Sheva, 1990-97; Adjunct Senior Lecturer in Law, Faculty of Health Sciences, 1994-97; Senior Lecturer in Law, Department of Business Administration, School of Management, 1997-99; Associate Professor of Law, 1999-, Department of Business Administration, School of Management, Ben-Gurion University, Beer-Sheva, Israel; Chairman, Ethics Committee, Southern District, Ministry of Health, Israel. Publications: 9 books, including: Associations Law in Israel, 2000; Partnership Law in Israel, 2002; 18 chapters in collective volumes; Over 35 articles in scientific journals; 12 articles in professional journals; 6 published scientific reports and researches. Honours: Fellow, Royal Society of Health, UK,1979; Fellow, Royal Institute of Public Health and Hygiene, UK, 1979; Award of Excellence for a research work, Academy of Business and Administrative Sciences, New York, 2001. Memberships: Academy of Legal Studies in Business; European Business Ethics Network; International Dental Ethics and Law society; Society of Medicine and Law; International Society of Business Economics and Ethics. Address: Department of Business Administration, School of Management, Ben-Gurion University, PO Box 653, 84105 Beer-Sheva, Israel. E-mail: dfrenkel@bgumail.bgu.ac.il

FREUD Bella, b. 17 April 1961, London, England. Fashion Designer. Education: Accademia di Costuma e di Moda, Rome; Institutto Mariotti, Rome. Appointments: Assistant to Vivienne

Dictionary of International Biography

Westwood on her designer collections, 1986-89; Launched own label presenting autumn/winter collection of tailored knitwear and accessories, 1990; Exhibited, London Designer Show, 1991, London Fashion Week, 1993. Honours: Winner, Innovative Design - the New Generation Category (British Fashion Awards), 1991. Address: 21 St Charles Square, London, W10 6EF, England.

FREUD Esther Lea, b. 2 May 1963, London, England. Writer. 1 son, 1 daughter. Education: Trained as an actress, Drama Centre, London, 1981-83. Publications: Hideous Kinky, 1992; Peerless Flats, 1993; Gaglow, 1997; The Wild, 2000; The Sea House, 2003. Address: c/o Georgia Garrett & A P Watt, 20 John Street, London, WC1N 2DR, England.

FREUD Lucian, b. 8 December 1922. Painter. m. (1) Kathleen Epstein, 1948, divorced 1952, 2 daughters, (2) Lady Caroline Maureen Blackwood, 1953, divorced 1957, deceased 1996. Education: Central School of Art, East Anglian School of Painting and Drawing. Appointments: Teacher, Slade School of Art, London, 1948-58; First one-man exhibition, 1944; Exhibitions, 1946, 1950, 1952, 1958, 1963, 1972, 1978, 1979, 1982, 1983, 1988, 1990-96; Retrospectives: Hayward Gallery, 1974, 1988, 1989; Tate Gallery, Liverpool, 1992; Works included in public collections: Tate Gallery, National Portrait Gallery, Victoria and Albert Museum, Arts Council of Great Britain, British Council, British Museum, Fitzwilliam Museum (Cambridge), National Museum of Wales (Cardiff), Scottish National Gallery of Modern Art (Edinburgh), Walker Art Gallery (Liverpool), Ashmolean Museum of Art, Oxford, in Brisbane, Adelaide, Perth (Australia), Musée National d'Art Moderne (Paris, France), Art Institute of Chicago, Museum of Modern Art (NY), Cleveland Museum of Art (OH), Museum of Art Carnegie Institute (Pittsburgh), Achenbaach Foundation for Graphic Arts and Fine Arts (San Fran), The St Louis Art Museum, Hirshborn Museum and Sculpture Garden, Smithsonian Institute (Wash), Rubenspeis, City of Siegen, 1997. Address: c/o Diana Rawstron, Goodman-Derrick, 90 Fetter Lane, London, EC4A 1EQ, England.

FREWER Glyn Mervyn Louis, (Mervyn Lewis), b. 4 September 1931, Oxford, England. Author; Scriptwriter. m. Lorna Townsend, 11 August 1956, 2 sons, 1 daughter. Education: MA, English Language and Literature, St Catherine's College, Oxford, 1952-1955. Appointments: Student Officer, British Council, Oxford, 1955; Copywriter, various agencies, 1955-64; Advertising Agency Associate Director, 1974-85; Retired; Proprietor antiquarian/ secondhand bookshop, 1985-2001. Publications: The Hitch-Hikers (BBC Radio Play), 1957; Adventure in Forgotten Valley, 1962; Adventure in the Barren Lands, 1964; The Last of the Wispies, 1965; Death of Gold (as Mervyn Lewis), 1970; The Token of Elkin, 1970; Crossroad, 1970; The Square Peg, 1972; The Raid, 1976; The Trackers, 1976; Tyto: The Odyssey of an Owl, 1978; Bryn of Brockle Hanger, 1980; Fox, 1984; The Call of the Raven, 1987; also scripts for children's television series, industrial films, etc. Contributions to: Birds; Imagery; The Countryman. Honours: Junior Literary Guild of America Choice, for Adventure in Forgotten Valley, 1964; Freeman of the City of Oxford, 1967. Address: Cottage Farm, Taston, Oxford OX7 3JN, England.

FREZZA Fabrizio, b. 31 October 1960, Rome, Italy. Researcher. Education: Laureate, Electronic Engineering, 1986, La Sapienza University of Rome; Doctorate, Applied Electromagnetics, 1991. Appointments: Academy Association, 1986-90, Assistant Professor, 1990-98, Temporary Professor, Electromagnetics, 1994-98, Associate Professor of Electromagnetics, 1998-, La Sapienza University of Rome. Publications: Over 200 articles and papers contributed to books, specialist journals, and conference proceedings; 1 patent. Honours: Gi Carosio Prize, La Sapienza

University of Rome, and Italcable Co, 1986; Gi Barzilai Prize, 10th Italian Conference on Electromagnetics, 1994. Memberships: Institute of Electrical and Electronic Engineering, Senior Member, 1995-; Sigma Xi; AEI; AIDAA. Address: Via dei Savorelli 120, 00165 Rome Lazio, Italy.

FRIEDAN Betty (Naomi), b. 4 February 1921, Peoria, Illinois, USA. Feminist Activist; Writer. m. Carl Friedan, June 1947, divorced May 1969, 2 sons, 1 daughter. Education: AB, Smith College, 1942. Appointments: Research Fellow, University of California at Berkeley, 1943; Founder-1st President, National Organization for Women, 1966-70; Contributing Editor, McCall's magazine, 1971-74; Senior Research Associate, Columbia University, 1979-81; Research Fellow, Harvard University, 1982-83; Chubb Fellow, Yale University, 1985; Guest Scholar, Woodrow Wilson Center for International Scholars, 1995-96; Many other lectureships. Publications: The Feminine Mystique, 1963; It Changed My Life: Writings on the Women's Movement, 1976; The Second Stage, 1981; The Fountain of Age, 1993; Life So Far: A Memoir, 2000. Contributions to: Periodicals. Honours: Humanist of the Year Award, 1974; Mort Weisinger Award for Outstanding Magazine Journalism, 1979; Author of the Year, 1982, American Society of Journalists and Authors; Eleanor Roosevelt Leadership Award, 1989; Various honorary doctorates. Memberships: American Society of Journalists and Authors; American Sociology Association; Association of Humanistic Psychology; Authors Guild; National Organizatioin for Women; National Press Club; PEN; Phi Beta Kappa. Address: 420 7th Street North West, Apt 1010, Washington, DC 20004, USA.

FRIEDLAND Klaus Dietrich Eberhard, b. 28 June 1920, Erfurt. Historian. m. Eva, 1 son, 1 daughter. Education: Naval Officers First Exam, 1940; Dr Philosophy, Kiel, 1952; Hon Professor, 1971. Appointments: Secondary School Teacher, 1903; Archivist, 1962; University Lecturer, 1965; Chief Librarian, 1970; Editor, Hansische Geschichtsblatter, 1975; President, International Commission for Maritime History, 1985. Publications: Die Hanse; Emergence of English German Trade Partnership; Man and Sea in Hanseatic Time. Honours: International Order of Merit; Honorary Medal, Town of Tallinn; Honorary Award, History and Naval Culture, Spanish Armada; Honorary Member German Naval Commission. Memberships: Association of Baltic and Northern Seas; History Commission of Niedersachsen; Rotary International. Address: Kreienholt 1, D 24226, Heikendorf, Germany.

FRIEDMAN Norman, b. 10 April 1925, Boston, Massachusetts, USA. Writer; Psychotherapist. m. Zelda Nathanson, 7 June 1945, 1 son, 1 daughter. Education: AB, 1948, AM, 1949, PhD, 1952, Harvard University; MSW, Adelphi, 1978. Appointments: Teaching Fellow, Harvard University, 1950-52; Instructor, Associate Professor, University of Conneticut, 1952-63; Associate Professor, Professor, Queens College, CUNY, 1963-88; Fulbright Lecturer, Universities of Nantes and Nice, France, 1966-67; New School, New York City, 1964-66, 1993. Publications: The Intrusions of Love: Poems, 1992; The Magic Badge: Poems 1953-84, 1984. Contributions to: New Mexico Quarterly; Georgia Review; Northwest Review; Nation; Texas Quarterly. Honours: NWR Annual Poetry Prize, 1963; Borestone Mt Poetry Awards, 1964, 1967; 4th, All Nations Poetry Contest. Memberships: MLA; PSA. Address: 33-54 164th Street, Flushing, NY 11358, USA.

FRITH Roger Crispian, b. 4 April 1936, Wanstead, Essex, England. Poet; Freelance Writer. Appointments: Poet-in-Residence, Keele University Summer School, 1969, Ohio State University Summer School, New College, Oxford, 1979-89. Publications: The Serving Boy, 1969; Immortality Farm, 1978; Dreams and Realities, 1980; No Man's Land and Other Poems, 1984; Black

Tern, 1984; Waiting for Nightingales, 1996; Darkness, 2001. Contributions to: Tribune; Ecologist; Poetry Now; BBC Radio 3; John Clare Society Journal; Richard Jefferies' Society Review. Address: 84 St Andrews Road, Hatfield Peverel, Chelmsford, Essex CM3 2EP, England.

FRITZE Lothar, b. 5 April 1954, Karl-Marx-Stadt. Researcher; Political analyst. m. Ulrike Fritze Otto, 2 sons. Education: Dipl-Ing oec, Betriebswirtschaft, 1978; Dr phil, Promotion in Philosophie, 1988; Dr phil habil, Habilitation in Politikwissenschaft, 1998. Appointments: Scientific collaborator, Forschungsinstitut fuer Textiltechnologie, Karl-Marx-Stadt, 1972-90; Institut fuer Wirtschafts u Sozialforschung, Chemnitz, 1992-93; Hannah-Arendt-Institut fuer Totalitarismusforschung, Dresden, 1993-. Publications: Books: Innenansicht eines Ruins: Gedanken zum Untergang der DDR, 1993; Panoptikum DDR-Wirtschaft: Machtverhaeltnisse, Organisationsstrukturen, Funktionsmechanismen, 1993; Die Gegenwart des Vergangenen: Ueber das Weiterleben der DDR nach ihrem Ende, 1997; Taeter mit gutem Gewissen: Ueber menschliches Versagen im diktatorischen Sozialismus, 1998; Die Toetung Unschuldiger. Ein Dogma auf dem Pruefstand, 2004; Numerous articles to professional journals. Honours: Privatdozent, Technical University, Chemnitz; Award, Gesellschaft fuer Deutschlandforschung, 1998. Address: Georgistrasse 2, D-09127 Chemnitz, Germany.

FROST David (Paradine) (Sir), b. 7 April 1939, Tenterden, Kent, England. Television Personality; Author. m. (1) Lynn Frederick, 1981, divorced 1982, (2) Lady Carina Fitzalan-Howard, 1983, 3 sons. Education: MA, Gonville and Caius College, Cambridge. Appointments: Various BBC TV series, 1962-; Many ITV series, 1966-; Chairman and Chief Executive, David Paradine Ltd, 1966-; Joint Founder and Director, TV-am, 1981-93; Regular appearances on US television. Publications: That Was the Week That Was, 1963; How to Live Under Labour, 1964; Talking with Frost, 1967; To England With Love, 1967; The Presidential Debate 1968, 1968; The Americans, 1970; Whitlam and Frost, 1974; I Gave Them a Sword, 1978; I Could Have Kicked Myself, 1982; Who Wants to be a Millionaire?, 1986; The Mid-Atlantic Companion (jointly), 1986; The Rich Tide (jointly), 1986; The World's Shortest Books, 1987; David Frost: An Autobiography, Part I: From Congregations to Audiences, 1993. Honours: Golden Rose Award, Montreux, 1967; Richard Dimbleby Award, 1967; Silver Medal, Royal Television Society, 1967; Officer of the Order of the British Empire, 1970; Religious Heritage of America Award, 1970; Emmy Awards, 1970, 1971; Albert Einstein Award, 1971; Knighted, 1993. Address: c/o David Paradine Ltd, 5 St Mary Abbots Place, London W8 6LS, England.

FRY Gerald Walton, b. 15 June 1942, Wichita, Kansas, USA. Professor. m. Tasanee Pongpanich, 1 son. Education: BA with distinction, Stanford University, 1964; MPA, Woodrow Wilson School, Princeton University, 1966; PhD, Stanford University, 1977. Appointments: Program Officer, The Ford Foundation, 1976-1980; Professor of International Studies/Political Science, University of Oregon, 1981-200; Director, International Studies, University of Oregon, 1987-92; Director, Centre for Asian and Pacific Studies, University of Oregon, 1992-94; Professor of International/Intercultural Education, 1998-2000; Director of Graduate Studies, Department of Education Policy and Administration, University of Minnesota, 2000-. Publications: Author and Co-author, 7 books. Honours: Foreign Area Fellow, Social Science Research Council and the American Council of Learned Societies; Pew Faculty Fellow, Kennedy School, Harvard University. Memberships: Fellow, International Academy for Intercultural Research; Comparative and International Education Society; Association of Asian Studies. Address: Department of Educational Policy and Administration, University of Minnesota, 330 Wulling Hall, 86 Pleasant St SE, Minneapolis, MN 55455-0221, USA. E-mail: gwf@umn.edu

FRY Stephen John, b. 24 August 1957. Actor; Writer. Education: Queen's College, Cambridge, England. Appointments: Columnist, The Listener, 1988-89, Daily Telegraph, 1990-; Appeared with Cambridge Footlights in revue, The Cellar Tapes, Edinburgh Festival, 1981; Re-wrote script: Me and My Girl, London, Broadway, Sydney, 1984; Plays: Forty Years On, Chichester Festival and London, 1984; The Common Pursuit, London, 1988 (TV, 1992); TV series: Alfresco, 1982-84; The Young Ones, 1983; Happy Families, 1984; Saturday Night Live, 1986-87; A Bit of Fry and Laurie, 1989-95; Blackadder's Christmas Carol, 1988; Blackadder Goes Forth, 1989; Jeeves and Wooster, 1990-92; Stalag Luft, 1993; Laughter and Loathing, 1995; Gormenghast, 2000; Radio: Loose Ends, 1986-87; Whose Line Is It Anyway?, 1987; Saturday Night Fry, 1987; Harry Potter and the Chamber of Secrets (Narrator, CD), 2002; Harry Potter and the Prisoner of Azkaban (Narrator, CD), 2004; Films: The Good Father; A Fish Called Wanda; A Handful of Dust; Peter's Friends, 1992; IQ, 1995; Wind in the Willows, 1997; Wilde, 1997; A Civil Action, 1997; Whatever Happened to Harold Smith? 2000; Relatives Values, 2000; Discovery of Heaven, 2001; Gosford Park, 2001; Thunderpants, 2002; Bright Young Things, 2003; Tooth, 2004; The Life and Death of Peter Sellers, 2004. Publications: Paperweight (collected essays), 1992; The Liar (novel); The Hippopotamus, 1994; Fry and Laurie 4 (with Hugh Laurie), 1994; Paperweight, 1995; Making History, 1996; Moab is My Washpot (autobiography), 1997; The Star's Tennis Balls (novel), 2000. Honour: Hon LLD (Dundee), 1995. Memberships: Patron, Studio 3 (arts for young people); Freeze (nuclear disarmament charity); Amnesty International; Comic Relief. Address: c/o Hamilton Asper Management, Ground Floor, 24 Hanway Street, London, W1P 9DD, England.

FRYBA Ladislav, b. 30 May 1929, Studenec. Professor. m. Dagmar Frybova. Education: Ing, 1953, DSc, 1959, Docent, 1966, Professor, 1993, Czech Technical University; Doctor honoris causa, University of Pardubice, 2004. Appointments: Head, Bridge Department, Railway Research Institute, 1972-84; Professor, Institute of Theoretical and Applied Mechanics, Academy of Sciences of the Czech Republic, 1984-. Publications: 6 books, co-author 6 books, 189 papers in 8 world languages; Best known world-wide: Dynamics of Railway Bridges, 2nd edition, 1996; Vibration of Solids and Structures Under Moving Loads, 3rd edition, 1999. Honours: Medals, Czechoslovak Academy of Sciences, Czech Society for Mechanics; 4 medals from Japanese Universities and Society of Japanese Association of Mechanical Engineering; Diploma, European Association for Structural Dynamics. Memberships: Chairman, Committees of Experts of the European Rail Research Institute, Utrecht, 1967-2001; President, Czech Society for Mechanics, 1991-; President, European Association for Structural Dynamics, 1996-99; Member, Engineering Academy of the Czech Republic, 1996-; Research Board of Advisors, American Biographical Institute, 1999; Member, Editorial Board of the Journal of Sound and Vibration, 2001-.

FUCHS Michael, b. 9 December 1964, Ulm, Baden-Württemberg, Germany. Education: Drittes Staatsexamen der Humanmedizin, Albert-Einstein Universitat, Ulm, 1991; Arzt im Praktikum (AiP) Klinik für Innere Medizin, Medizinische Universität zu Lübeck, Schleswig-Holstein, 1992-93; Instructor in Medicine, Division of Gastroenterology, Brigham and Women's Hospital, Harvard Medical School and Harvard Digestive Diseases Center, Boston, Massachusetts, 1993-96; Staff member, Division of Gastroenterology, University of Lubeck, Germany, 1996-2001;

Assistant Professor of Medicine, University of Ulm, Germany, 2002-. Publications: 5 chapters in books; 20 in professional journals. Honours: German Research Council Award, 1993-2004; Young Investigator Award, European Association for the Study of Liver, 1995, 1999; Scholarships/fellowships include: Research Grant, Medical University of Lubeck, 1998-2000. Memberships: German Society for Gastrointestinal Diseases and Metabolism; Gastroenterological Research Group; American Association for the Advancement of Science; American Association for Study of Liver Disease; German Association for the Study of Liver; European Association for the Study of Liver; American Society for Cell Biology; American Physiological Society. Address: Selbert str 79, D-89075 Ulm, Germany.

FUENTES Carlos, b. 11 November 1928, Panama City, Panama. Professor of Latin American Studies; Writer. m. (1) Rita Macedo, 1957, 1 daughter, (2) Sylvia Lemus, 24 Jan 1973, 1 son, 1 daughter. Education: Law School, National University of Mexico; Institute de Hautes Études Internationales, Geneva. Appointments: Head, Cultural Relations Department, Ministry of Foreign Affairs, Mexico, 1955-58; Mexican Ambassador to France, 1975-77; Professor of English and Romance Languages, University of Pennsylvania, 1978-83; Professor of Comparative Literature, 1984-86, Robert F Kennedy Professor of Latin American Studies, 1987-, Harvard University; Simon Bolivar Professor, Cambridge University, 1986-87; Professor-at-Large, Brown University, 1995-. Publications: La Region Mas Transparente, 1958; Las Buenas Conciencias, 1959; Aura, 1962; La Muerte de Artemio Cruz, 1962; Cantar de Ciegos, 1964; Cambio de Piel, 1967; Zona Sagrada, 1967; Terra Nostra, 1975; Una Familia Lejana, 1980; Agua Quemada, 1983; Gringo Viejo, 1985; Cristóbal Nonato, 1987; Myself with Others (essays), 1987; Orchids in the Moonlight (play), 1987; The Campaign, 1991; The Buried Mirror, 1992; El Naranjo, 1993; Geography of the Novel: Essays, 1993; La frontera de cristal (stories), 1995; Los Años con Laura Diaz (novel), 1999; Los Cincosoles de Mexico (anthology), 2000; Inez, 2000; Ce que je crois, 2002; La Silla de Aguila, 2003. Contributions to: Periodicals. Honours: Biblioteca Breva Prize, Barcelona, 1967; Rómulo Gallegos Prize, Caracas, 1975; National Prize for Literature, Mexico, 1984; Miguel de Cervantes Prize for Literature, Madrid, 1988; Légion d'Honneur, France, 1992; Principe de Asturias Prize, 1992; Latin Civilisation Prize, French and Brazilian Academies, 1999; DLL, Ghent, 2000, Madrid, 2000; Mexican Senate Medal, 2000; Los Angeles Public Library Award, 2001; Commonwealth Award Delaware, 2002. Memberships: American Academy and Institute of Arts and Letters; El Colegio Nacional, Mexico; Mexican National Commission on Human Rights. Literary Agent: Brandt & Brandt. Address: c/o Brandt & Brandt, 1501 Park Avenue, New York, NY 10036, USA.

FUENTES Martha Ayers, b. 21 December 1923, Ashland, Alabama, USA. m. Manuel Solomon Fuentes, 11 April 1943. Education: BA, Education University of South Florida, USA, 1969. Appointments: Playwright/Author, at present; Jewellery Sales, Tampa, Florida, 1940; Later served in various business positions; Author, 1953. Publications: Pleasure Button, full length play, 1995-96; Jordan's End, 1998. Honours: Iona Lester Scholarship, Creative Writing, University Southern Florida, George Sergel Drama Award, University of Chicago, Southeastern Writers Conference; Instructor, Playwriting and TV; Feature Writer for national magazines. Memberships: Dramatist Guild; Authors Guild; Florida Theatre Conference; North Carolina Writers' Network; Florida Studio Theatre, Sarasota, Florida; United Daughters of the Confederacy; Southern Heritage Society. Address: 102 Third Street, Belleair Beach, FL 33786-2311, USA.

FUJIMAKI Norio, b. 15 February 1953, Niigata, Japan. Researcher. m. 10 July 1988, 2 daughters. Education: BSc, 1975, MSc, 1977, PhD, 1980, Electronic Engineering, University of Tokyo. Appointments: Fujitsu Laboratories Ltd, 1980-99; National Institute of Information and Communication Technology (previous name, Communications Research Laboratories), 1999-. Publications: Neuromagnetism (co-author), 1997; Handbook of Quantum Engineering (co-author), 1999; Several articles in professional journals including: IEEE Transactions; Journal of Applied Physics; Neuroscience Research; Human Brain Mapping; Neuro Image. Memberships: Institute of Electrical and Electronics Engineers; Institute of Electronics, Information and Communications Engineers; Japan Society of Applied Physics; Japan Biomagnetism and Biomagnetics Society; Japan Society of Medical Electronics and Biological Engineering; Society for Neuroscience; Japan Neuroscience Society. Address: Brain Information Group, National Institute of Information and Communications Technology, 588-2, Iwaoka, Iwaoka-cho, Nishi-ku, Kobe 651-2492, Japan. E-mail: fujimaki@po.nict.go.jp

FUJIOKA Masaki, b. 5 January 1961, Shimonoseki City, Japan. Medical Doctor; Plastic Surgeon. m. Ruriko. Education: Graduate, Jichi Medical School, 1985; Medical Course Diploma, 1997. Appointments: Associate Professor, Medical Department, Nagasaki University, Japan, 1997; Chairman, Department of Plastic and Reconstructive Surgery, Miyazak Social Insurance Hospital, 1998; Chairman, Department of Plastic and Reconstructive Surgery, National Nagasaki Medical Center, 2003. Publication: Primary care Manual of Plastic and Reconstructive Surgery, 2003. Membership: American Association for the Advancement of Science. Address: National Nagasaki Medical Center, 1001-1 kubara-2, Ohmura City, Japan 856-8562. E-mail: mfujioka@nmc.go.jp

FUJISAKI Haruo, b. 19 January 1941, Kochi, Japan. Physicist. Education: BS, Physics, University of Tokyo, 1965; MS, Physics, 1967; DSc, Physics, 1970. Appointments: Lecturer in Physics, 1970-72, Associate Professor, 1973-82, Professor, 1983-, Chairman, Department of Physics, 1979, Chairman, Graduate School, 1993, 1995, 2001, Rikkyo University, Tokyo. Publications: Many articles in professional journals. Honour: Matsunaga Science Foundation Fellowship, 1975. Memberships: Physical Society of Japan; University Alumni Association, Japan; Nature Conservation Society, Japan. Address: Department of Physics, Rikkyo University, 3-34-1 Nishi-Ikebukuro, Toshima-ku, Tokyo 171-8501, Japan.

FUJITA Fukashi, b. 9 August 1926, Kobe City, Japan. Businessman (Retired). m. Yuriko Matsushita, 1 son, 1 daughter. Education: Bachelor of Economics, Kobe University, 1950. Appointments: Marubeni Corporation (International Trade Businesses), 1950-62; Company Representative, Marubeni Corporation, Los Angeles, 1957-61; Japan Management Association (Business Consultant Group), 1962-65; Head Office, Nestlé Japan, Ltd, Kobe, 1965-85; Retired, 1985. Honours: Award for co-ordinating donors, Japan Red Cross; Award for volunteer help, Committee, FESPIC KOBE 89. Membership: Tea Ceremony Masters Association Club. Address: 764-2 Nishiwaki, Ohkubo-cho, Akashi-city, Hygo Pref, 674-0054 Japan.

FUKASAWA Yoshihiro, b. 2 July 1957, Iwate, Japan. Professor of Art; Graphic Designer. m. Akemi, 2 sons. Education: Bachelor of Pedagogy. Appointment: Associate Professor, Morioka College, Iwate, Japan, 1989-. Publications: Articles in academic publications including, Art Journal, 1999, 2000; Artex, 2002; Contemporary Illustration in Japan, 2003. Honours include: Grand Prix au Carrousel du Louvre; Prix Tricolore de la Paix de l'Art; L'art japonaise fait sa révolution á Paris, 2003. Memberships: Iwate Designers Association; Chiba Designers Association; Japan Design Association. Address: 399-16 Hanokisawayama, Takizawa 020-0173, Iwate, Japan.

FUKUDA Masafumi, b. 29 May 1962, Sukagawa-City, Fukushima Prefecture, Japan. Functional Neurosurgeon. m. Masako, 2 sons. Education: Graduate, Faculty of Medicine, 1987, University Diploma, 2002, Niigata University, Japan. Appointments: Department of Neurosurgery, National Nishi-Niigata Central Hospital, Niigata-City, Japan, 1995-99; Postdoctoral research Fellow, Center for Neuroscience, North Shore University Hospital, Manhasset, New York, 1999-2001; Department of Neurosurgery, Shibata Prefecture Hospital, 2001-2003; Department of Neurosurgery, Brain Research Institute, Niigata University, Japan. Publications: 25 articles in medical journals as first author and co-author include: Functional correlates of pallidal stimulation for Parkinson's disease, 2001; Networks mediating the clinical effects of pallidal brain stimulation for Parkinson's disease. A PET study of resting-state glucose metabolism, 2001; Functional brain networks in Parkinson's disease, 2001; Pallidal stimulation for Parkinsonism: Improved brain activation during sequence learning, 2002. Honours: Listed in Who's Who publications and biographical dictionaries. Memberships: Japan Neurosurgical Society; Japan Epilepsy Society; Japanese Society of Clinical Neurophysiology; Japanese Society of Stereotactic and Functional Neurosurgery; Japan Epilepsy Surgery Society. Address: Department of Neurosurgery, Brain Research Institute, Niigata University, 1-757 Asahimachi-dori, Niigata-City, 951-8585 Japan. E-mail: mfuku529@bri.niigata-u.ac.jp.

FULLER Cynthia Dorothy, b. 13 February 1948, Isle of Sheppey, England. Poet; Adult Education Tutor. divorced, 2 sons. Education: BA Honours, English, Sheffield University, 1969; Postgraduate Certificate of Education, Oxford University, 1970; MLitt, Aberdeen University, 1979. Appointments: Teacher of English, Redborne School, 1970-72; Freelance in Adult Education, University Departments at Durham and Newcastle Universities, also Open University and Workers Education Association. Publications: Moving towards Light, 1992; Instructions for the Desert, 1996; Only a Small Boat, 2001. Contributions to: Poems in various magazines including: Other Poetry; Iron; Poetry Durham; Literary Review. Honour: Northern Arts Financial Assistance. Address: 28 South Terrace, Esh Winning, Co Durham DH7 9PR, England.

FULLER Jean Violet Overton, b. 7 March 1915, Iver Heath, Bucks, England. Author. Education: Brighton High School, 1927-31; Royal Academy of Dramatic Art, 1931-32; BA, University of London, 1945; University College of London, 1948-50. Publications: The Comte de Saint Germain, 1988; Blavatsky and Her Teachers, 1988; Dericourt: The Chequered Spy, 1989; Sickert and the Ripper Crimes, 1990; Cats and other Immortals, 1992; Krishnamurti and the Wind, 2003. Honour: Writers Manifold Poems of the Decade, 1968. Membership: Society of Authors. Address: Fuller D'Arch Smith Ltd, 37B New Cavendish Street, London, England.

FULLERTON Alexander Fergus, b. 20 September 1924, Saxmundham, Suffolk, England. Writer. m. Priscilla Mary Edelston, 10 May 1956, 3 sons. Education: Royal Naval College, Dartmouth, 1938-41; School of Slavonic Studies, Cambridge University, 1947. Appointments: Editorial Director, Peter Davies Ltd, 1961-64; General Manager, Arrow Books, 1964-67. Publications: Surface!, 1953; A Wren Called Smith, 1957; The White Men Sang, 1958; The Everard Series of naval novels: The Blooding of the Guns, 1976; Sixty Minutes for St George, 1977; Patrol to the Golden

Horn, 1978; Storm Force to Narvik, 1979; Last Lift from Crete, 1980; All the Drowning Seas, 1981; A Share of Honour, 1982; The Torch Bearers, 1983; The Gatecrashers, 1984. Special Deliverance, 1986; Special Dynamic, 1987; Special Deception, 1988; Bloody Sunset, 1991; Look to the Wolves, 1992; Love for an Enemy, 1993; Not Thinking of Death, 1994; Into the Fire, 1995; Band of Brothers, 1996; Return to the Field, 1997; Final Dive, 1998; In at the Kill, 1999; Wave Cry, 1999; The Floating Madhouse, 2000; Single to Paris, 2001; Flight to Mons, 2003; Westbound, Warbound, 2003; Stark Realities, 2004. Address: c/o John Johnson Ltd, 45 Clerkenwell Green, London EC1R 0HT, England.

FUNKHOUSER Erica, b. 17 September 1949, Cambridge, Massachusetts, USA; Poet. m. Thaddeus Beal, 1 September 1973, divorced, 1 son, 1 daughter. Education: BA, English, Vassar College, 1971; MA, English, Stanford University, 1973. Appointments: Lecturer in English, Lesley College, Massachusetts; Dramaturg, Revels Inc, Cambridge, Massachusetts; Lecturer in Poetry, Massachusetts Institute of Technology, 1998-. Publications: Natural Affinities, 1983; Sure Shot, 1992; The Actual World, 1997; Pursuit, 2002. Contributions to: Anthologies, reviews and magazines. Honours: Sylvia Plath Poetry Contest Winner, 1979; Fellowship, The Artists Foundation, Massachusetts Council on the Arts and Humanities, 1982; Consuelo Ford Award, Poetry Society of America, 1989. Memberships: Poetry Society of America; Academy of American Poets. Address: 179 Southern Avenue, Essex, MA 01929, USA.

FURNADZIEVA Nadya, b. 26 September 1954, Plovdiv, Bulgaria. Publisher. Divorced, 1 daughter. Education: MA, German Language and Literature, Sofia University, 1977. Appointments: Editor and Translator, Hristo G Danov Publishers; Translator, German Literature: The Tin Drum, Günter Grass; Publisher, Owner, Manager, Lettera Publishers, 1990-. Publications: Translations: Die Verwirrungen des Zöglings Törless, R Musil; Die Blechtrommel, Günter Grass. Honours: National and international awards for translation; State Award from the Republic of Austria for translation, 1997; National Award from the Bulgarian Ministry of Culture, 1999. Memberships: National Council for Books; Board of the Association of Bulgarian Publishers. Address: 69 Shesti Septemvri Blvd, Plovdiv 4002, Bulgaria.

FURTWÄNGLER Virginia Walsh, (Ann Copeland), b. 16 December 1932, Hartford, Connecticut, USA. Writer; Teacher. m. Albert Furtwangler, 17 August 1968, 2 sons. Education: BA, College of New Rochelle, 1954; MA, Catholic University of America, 1959; PhD, Cornell University, Kent, 1970. Appointments: Writer-in-Residence, College of Idaho, 1980, Linfield College, 1980-81, University of Idaho, 1982, 1986, Wichita State University, 1988, Mt Allison University, 1990, St Mary's University, 1993; Hallie Brown Ford Chair of English, Willamette University, 1996. Publications: At Peace, 1978; The Back Room, 1979; Earthen Vessels, 1984; The Golden Thread, 1989; Strange Bodies on a Stranger Shore, 1994; The ABC's of Writing Fiction, 1996. Contributions to: Anthologies and magazines. Honours: Kent Fellowship; Canada Council Grant; National Endowment for the Arts Writing Fellowship, 1994; Ingram Merrill Award. Memberships: Authors Guild; Writers Union of Canada; International Womens Writing Guild. Address: 235 Oak Way North East, Salem, OR 97301, USA.

FUZAYLOV Kosimdzhon, b. 20 November 1945, Undzhi Village, Khujand District, Sughd Region, Republic of Tajikistan. Teacher. m. Bobojonova Biuluk, 1 son, 4 daughters. Education: Graduate, Faculty of Foreign Languages, 1967; Qualification, Institute of Foreign Languages, Tashkent, Uzbekistan, 1970; Rank of Senior Teacher, Governing Body of English Department, 1970; Qualification, Institute of Foreign Languages, Pyatigorsk, Russia, 1976; Associate Professor, Khujand Branch Technological University of Tajikistan, 1996; Doctor of Philosophy, 2002. Appointments: Head of English Section, 1967; Chairman, Trade Union Committee of the Faculty, 1972; Chairman of the Quarterly Council, 1975-92; Chairman of the English Department, 1993, Deputy Director, 1996-98, Dean of the Faculty of Economy and Finance, 1998; Chairman of the English Chair, 2000; Professor of the English Chair, 2003-, Khujand Branch Technological University of Tajikistan; Faculty Member and Visiting Professor, Zoroastrian College Avesta and Scriptural Studies Department of India. Publications: Methodical articles: Games at the English classes; Field of Wonders; How to organise a week of English; How to organise a month of English; Analysis of English lessons and how to do that; Teaching of Participles of English in the Tajik Lecture-halls; The functions of participles in the sentence; Books: Topics of everyday life through exercises; Collected exercises in English; Khordeh Avesta; Avesta Avesta Yashts vol 1; Avesta Yashts vol 25. Honours: Excellent Teacher of the Republic of Tajikistan, Ministry of Education, 1996; Honour Certificates, Leninabad Region and Khujand Branch Technological University, 1996; Award Certificate, Organising Committee, 21st Congress of Natural Medicine, 2002; Honour Certificate, Ministry of Light and Textile Industry, 2002; Professor Emeritus, Governing Body, All India Shah Behram Baug Society, 2003. Memberships: Governing Body, All India Shah Behran Baug Society for Scientific and Educational Research; Scientific Council, Khujand Branch Technological University. Address: M Avezova str 140, Undzi Village, Khujand District, Sughd Region, Republic of Tajikistan. E-mail: rustomeher@hotmail.com

FYODOROV Nikolai Vasilyevich, b. 9 May 1958, Chuvash Republic. Politician. m. Svetlana Yuryevna Fyodorova, 1 son, 1 daughter. Education: Graduate, Law Faculty, Kazan State University, 1980; Cand. Sc. (Law), Moscow Institute of State and Law, 1985; Appointments: Teacher, Chuvash State University, 1980-82, 1986-89; Member, USSR Supreme Soviet, 1989-91; Minister of Justice of Russia, 1990-93; President of Chuvash Republic, 1994-, re-elected, 1997 and 2001; Member, Council of Federation, 1996-2002; Representative of Russia in the Parliamentary Assembly of Council of Europe. Publications: More than 100 books and articles in economy, law and national relations. Honours: State Counsellor of Justice of Russia; The Russian Federation State Prize in the field of science and technology for restoration of the historical part of Cheboxary, 1999; Order, For Merits in Fatherland IV class; The highest All-Russian Femida Prize, 1997; Peter the Great National Prize; Honorary Construction Worker of Russia; Order of the Saint Duke Daniil Moskovskii 1 class and Order of Reverend Sergii Radonezhskii, Russian Orthodox Church. Address: 1 Republic Square, House of Government, 428004 Cheboxary, Chuvash Republic, Russia. E-mail: president@cap.ru

Dictionary of International Biography

G

GABITOV Azat Ismailovitsh, b. Starosubkhangulovo, Bashkortostan, Russia. Civil Engineer. m. Dilbar Marselyenva Gabitova, 1 son, 1 daughter. Education: Engineer in Civil Engineering, 1984, Candidate of Technical Sciences, 1988, Ufa Petroleum Institute, Ufa, Russia; Doctor of Technical Sciences, State Supreme Attestation Committee of the Russian Federation, Moscow, Russia, 1999. Appointments: Junior Researcher, 1984-85, Postgraduate, 1985-88, Ufa Petroleum Institute; Senior Lecturer, Ufa Petroleum Institute (renamed to Ufa State Petroleum Technological University in 1993), 1989-96; Dean, 1996-2000, Professor, 2000-, Ufa State Petroleum Technological University. Publications: More than 130 research publications including monographs: Corrosion Inhibitors Volume 1: Principles of the Theory and Practice of Usage (co-author), 1997; The Theory and Practice of Corrosion Control: Results and Prospects, 1998; Advanced Systems to Protect Underground Communications from Electrochemical Corrosion. Volume 1: Cathodic Protection of Highly Branched Pipeline Networks (co-author), 1999; Corrosion Inhibitors. Volume 2: Stress-Corrosion Diagnostics and Protection (co-author), 2002; 11 USSR and Russian Federation patents. Address: Ufa State Petroleum Technological University, 1 Kosmonavtov Street, Ufa, Bashkortostan, 450062 Russia. E-mail: azat7@ufanet.ru

GABRIEL (formerly Rezkallah) Kamiel S, b. 14 May 1954, Egypt. Professor, Director, Microgravity Research Group. m. Linda Miller, 2 sons, 2 daughters. Education: BSc, 1977, MSc, 1982, University of Alexandria, Egypt; PhD, University of Manitoba, 1987; Space Science Diploma, International Space University, 1990; MBA, University of Saskatchewan, 2001. Appointments: Associate Dean, Graduate Studies, Research and Extension, 2001-04; Professor, Director, Microgravity Research Group, 1994-; Associate Provost, research and Graduate programs, 2004-. Publications: Book: Microgravity Two-Phase Flow and Heat Transfer, forthcoming. Honours: Ralph Teetor Educational Award, Aerospace, 1991; SAE Outstanding Faculty Award, 1994; University of Saskatchewan Distinguished Faculty Supervisor Award, 2003. Memberships: Executive, Astronautics Section, Canadian Astronautics and Space Institute; American Society of Mechanical Engineers; Society of Automotive Engineers. Address: University of Ontario, Institute of Technology, 2000 Simcoe Street North, Oshawa, Ontario, L1H 7K4, Canada.

GABRIEL Peter, b. 13 February 1950, Cobham, Surrey, England. Singer; Composer. Appointments: Co-Founder, Genesis, 1966; Solo Artiste, 1975-; Appearances worldwide in concerts; Founder, World of Music, Arts and Dance (WOMAD), music from around the world, 1982; Founder, Real World Group, 1985; Real World Studios, 1986; Real World Records, 1989; Real World Multimedia, 1994; Launched Witness Human Rights Programme, 1992. Creative Works: Singles: Solsbury Hill; Games Without Frontiers; Shock The Monkey; Sledgehammer; In Your Eyes; Don't Give Up; Biko; Big Time; Red Rain; Digging in the Dirt; Steam; Blood of Eden; Kiss That Frog; Solo albums: PG I-IV, PG Plays Live, 1983; So, 1986; Shaking the Tree (compilation), 1990; Us, 2992; Ovo, 2000; Up, 2002; Soundtrack albums: Birdy; Passion (Last Temptation of Christ). Honours: Ivor Novello Awards, 1983, 1987; Brit Awards, 1987, 1993; 9 Music Video Awards; Video Vanguard Trophy, 1987; Grammy Awards, 1990, 1993. Address: c/o Real World, Box Mill, Box, Wiltshire, SN14 9PL, England.

GADDAFI Col. Mu'ammar Muhammad al, b. 1942, Serte, Libya. Libyan Army Officer; Political Leader. m. 1970, 8 children. Education: University of Libya, Benghazi. Appointments: Served, Libyan Army, 1965-; Chair, Revolutionary Command Council, 1969-; Commander-in-Chief of Armed Forces, 1969; Prime Minister, 1970-72; Minister of Defence, 1970-72; Secretary General of General Secretariat of General Peoples Congress, 1977-79; Chair, OAU, 1982-83. Publications: The Green Book, 3 vols; Military Strategy and Mobilization; The Story of the Revolution. Honours: Title, Colonel; Rank of Major-General, 1976. Membership: President, Council, Federation of Arab Republics, 1972. Address: Office of the President, Tripoli, Libya. 395395

GADDIS ROSE Marilyn, b. 2 April 1930, Fayette, Missouri, USA. University Professor; Translator. m. Stephen David Ross, 1 son. Education: BA, Central Methodist College, 1952; MA, University of South Carolina, 1955; PhD, University of Missouri, 1958; DHum Letters, Central Methodist College, 1987. Appointments: Binghamton University, 1968-91, Distinguished Service Professor, 1991-. Publications: Booklength translations (Villiers de l'Isle Adam, Louise Colet, Sainte Beuve, Julien Green), Translation and Literary Criticism, 1997. Honours: Alexander Gode Medal, American Translators Association; Fulbright Scholarship, 1952-53; Australian National University Fellow; ATA Annual named lecture established 1998. Memberships: Modern Language Association; American Translators Association; American Literary Translators Association; Canadian Association of Translation Studies.

GAFITANU Mihai, b. 16 September 1934, Iasi, Romania. Professor, Engineering. m. Eliza, 2 sons. Education: Mechanical Engineering, Technical University of Iasi, 1957; DSc, Technical University, Polytechnica, Bucharest, Romania, 1968. Appointments: Assistant, 1957-62, Lecturer, 1962-69, Assistant Professor, 1969-72, Professor, 1972-, Vice Dean, 1964-72, Vice Rector, 1972-76, Rector, 1976-84, 1996-2000, Head of Department, 1985-96, Technical University of Iasi. Publications: 9 monographs; 14 texts and handbooks; 275 papers in scientific journals, proceedings; 13 international patents. Honours: Romanian Academy Prize, 1985; Gold Medals, Inventions Expo, Geneva, 1994, Brussels, 1997; Listed in several biographical publications. Memberships: Vice President, Society of Tribology, 1981; Romanian Academy of Technical Sciences, 1998-; National Council, Academy Accred, 1994-; National Council Academic Titles Attest, 1991-98; National Council Scientific Research, 1998-; Doctor Honoris Causa – Technical University of Moldavia, Chisinau, 1999; Northern University of Baia Mare, Romania, 2002. Address: 24A, Titu Maidrescu St, Iasi 6600, Romania.

GAGRAT Rustam Jehangir, b. 5 November 1959, Bombay, India. Lawyer. m. Lia Gagrat, 1 son. Education: BA (Hons) Politics, Elphinstone College, Bombay, 1979; BA (Hons) Law, 1981, MA, 1985, Downing College, Cambridge University; Solicitor, Bombay, 1984; Solicitor, England and Wales, 1987; PIL, Harvard University Law School, 1993. Appointments: Advocate Supreme, Court of India; Solicitor, Supreme Court of England; Senior Partner, Gagrat and Co, Advocates and Solicitors, Bombay; Partner, Gagrat and Co, Supreme Court Advocates, Delhi; Company Director of Public and Private Companies; Trustee of Public and Private Trusts; Member, Committees of Chambers of Commerce. Publications: Presented and published papers at international and domestic law conferences. Honours: Tata Scholar, Cambridge University; Rustomji Mulla Prize, Bombay Law Society. Memberships: Supreme Court of India Bar Association; Bombay Bar Association; Bombay Law Society; Law Society of England; International Law Association; International Bar Association; Oxford and Cambridge Society. Address: 9 Om Ratan, Pochhanavala Road, New Worli, Bombay 400 025, India.

GAINSFORD Ian Derek (Sir), b. 24 June 1930. Consultant Dental Surgeon. m. Carmel Liebster, 1 son, 2 daughters. Education: BDS, King's College and Kings's College Hospital Medical

Dictionary of International Biography

School, 1955; DDS Honours, Toronto University, Canada; FDSRCS Eng 1967; FDSRCSE, 1998. Appointments: Junior Staff, King's College Hospital, 1955-57; Staff Member, Department of Conservative Dentistry, London Hospital Medical School, 1957-70; Senior Lecturer/Consultant, Department of Conservative Dentistry, King's College Hospital, 1970-95; Deputy Dean of Dental Studies, 1973-77; Director of Clinical Dental Services, King's College Hospital, 1977-87; Dean of Dental Studies, 1977-83, Dean, Faculty of Clinical Dentistry, 1982-87, Dean, 1988-97, King's College School of Medicine and Dentistry, King's College London; Vice-Principal, King's College London, 1994-97. Publication: Silver Amalgam in Clinical Practice, 1965, 3rd edition, 1992. Honours: FICD, 1975; MGDS RCS, 1979; FKC, 1984; Honorary Scientific Advisor, British Dental Journal, 1982; Honorary Member, American Dental Association, 1983; Honorary President, British Friends of Magen David Adom, 1995-; Kt, 1995; Honorary President, The Maccabaeans, 2000-; Regent Royal College of Surgeons of Edinburgh, 2002-. Memberships: President, British Society for Restorative Dentistry, 1973-74; British Dental Association, 1956-, President Metropolitan Branch, 1981-82; International Dental Federation, 1966-; American Dental Society of London, 1960, President, 1982; American Dental Society of Europe, 1965-, Honorary Treasurer, 1971-77, President, 1982; GDC, 1986-94, Chairman, Education Committee, 1990-94, Chairman, Specialist Training Advisory Committee, 1996-99; Examiner for Membership in General Dental Surgery, RCS, 1979-84, Chairman, 1988-90; Fellow RSM, 1967-; President, Western Marble Arch Synagogue, 1998-2000. Chairman, UK Friends for Emergency Medical Centre in Arad. Address: 31 York Terrace East, London NW1 4PT, England.

GAJDUSEK Daniel Carleton, b. 9 September 1923, Yonkers, New York, USA. Paediatrician; Virologist. Education: Graduated, Medicine, Harvard University, 1941; Internships and Residencies in several children's hospitals; Physical Chemistry, California Institute of Technology; Research Fellowship, Virology Department, Harvard University. Appointments: Walter Reed Army Medical Center, 1952-53; Institut Pasteur, Tehran, Iran and University of Medicine, 1954-55; Visiting Investigator at Walter and Eliza Hall, Institute, Australia, 1955-57; Laboratory Chief, National Institute of Neurological Disorders and Stroke, NIH, Bethesda, Maryland, USA, 1958-97; Chief of Study of Child Growth and Development and Disease Patterns in Primitive Cultures, and of Laboratory of Slow, Latent and Temperate Virus Infections, 1958-97; Chief of Central Nervous System Studies Laboratory, 1970-97; Professor, Institute of Human Virology, University of Maryland, 1996-. Publications: Hemorrhagic Fevers and Mycotoxicoses, 1959; Slow, Latent and Temperate Virus Infections, 1965; Correspondence on the Discovery of Kuru, 1976; Kuru (with Judith Farquhar), 1980; Research, Travel and Field Expedition Journals (55 vols), 1940-99; Vilinisk Encephalomyelitis, 1996; over 1,000 papers on microbiology, immunology, paediatrics, neurology, cognitive and psychosexual development and genetics. Honours: Several honorary degrees; Meade Johnson Award, American Academy of Pediatrics, 961; Dautrebande Prize, 1976; Shared Nobel Prize for Physiology or Medicine, 1976; Cotzias Prize, 1978; Huxley Medal, Royal Anthropological Institute of Great Britain and Ireland, 1988; Stuart Mudd Prize, 1989; Award of 3rd International Congress on Alzheimer's Disease, 1992; Award of 3rd Pacific Rim Biotechnology Conference, 1992; Gold Medal, Slovak Academy of Science, 1996; Honorary Professor, 10 Chinese universities, 1993-2002; Honorary Adviser, 3 Chinese academies, 1999-2002. Memberships: Society for Paediatric Research; American Pediatric Society; National Academy of Sciences; American Academy of Arts and Sciences; American Philosophica Society; Deutsche Akademie der Naturforscher Leopoldina; Third World Academy

of Science; American Academy of Neurology; Russian Academy of Medicine; Sakha (Iakut) Siberian Academy of Science (branch of Russian Academy of Science). Address: Institut Alfred Fessard, CNRS, Avenue de la Terrasse, 91198 Gif-sur-Yvette, Cedex, France.

GALE (Gwendoline) Fay, b. 13 June 1932, Balaklava, South Australia. Social Scientist. 1 son, 1 daughter. Education: BA (Honours), 1954, PhD, 1962, DUniv, 1994, University of Adelaide; Hon DLitt, UWA, 1998. Appointments: Lecturer, 1966-70, Senior Lecturer, 1971-74, Reader, 1975-77, Professor of Geography, 1978-89, University of Adelaide; Pro Vice Chancellor, University of Adelaide, 1988-89; Vice Chancellor, University of Western Australia, 1990-97; President, Australian Vice Chancellors Committee (AVCC), 1996-97; President, Academy of Social Sciences in Australia, 1998-2000; President, Association of Asian Social Science Research Councils, 2001-03. Publications include: Urban Aborigines, 1970; Race Relations in Australia: The Aboriginal Situation, 1975; Adelaide Aborigines: A Case Study of Urban Life 1966-81, 1982; Tourists and the National Estate: Procedures to Protect Australia's Heritage, 1987; Aboriginal Youth and the Criminal Justice System: The Injustice of Justice, 1990; Juvenile Justice: Debating the Issues, 1993; Tourism and the Protection of Aboriginal Cultural Sites, 1994; Strategies to Redress Gender Imbalance in the Numbers of Senior Academic Women, 1996; Cultural Geographies (editor) 1998. Honours include: Fellow, Academy of Social Sciences, 1978; Emeritus Professor, University of Adelaide, 1989; Officer, Order of Australia, 1989; Honorary Life Member, Institute of Australian Geographers, 1994; Fellow, Australian Institute of Management, 1994; Emeritus Professor, University of Western Australia, 1997; John Lewis Gold Medal, 2000; Honorary Life Fellow, Academy of The Social Sciences, 2001; Griffith Taylor Medal, 2002; Honorary Fellow, Association for Tertiary Education Management, 2003. Address: Academy of the Social Sciences, Box 1956, Canberra, ACT 2600, Australia.

GALL Sally Moore, b. 28 July 1941, New York, New York, USA. Librettist. m. William Einar Gall, 8 December 1967. Education: BA cum laude, Harvard University, 1963; MA, 1971, PhD, 1976, New York University. Appointments: Poetry Editor, Free Inquiry, 1981-84; Founding Editor, Eidos, The International Prosody Bulletin, 1984-88. Publications: The Modern Poetic Sequence: The Genius of Modern Poetry (co-author), 1983; Maximum Security Ward and Other Poems (editor), 1984; Poetry in English: An Anthology (versification editor), 1987; Eleanor Roosevelt (cantata libretto), 2000; The Ballerina and the Clown (song cycle), 2004; Operas performed (libretti): The Singing Violin, 1995; Kill Bear Comes Home, 1996; The Little Thieves of Bethlehem, 1997; Paris and Oenone, 1999; Daphne at Sea, 2000; Musical Theatre: The Lysistrata Affair, 1995. Contributions to: Reference books, professional journals and literary magazines. Honours: Penfield Fellow, New York University, 1973-74; Academy of American Poets Award, New York University, 1975; Key Pin and Scroll Award, New York University, 1976; Co-Winner, Explicator Literary Foundation Award, 1984. Co-winner, National Opera Association Chamber Opera Competition, 1998; ASCAP Awards, 1996-. Memberships: American Music Center; ASCAP; Dramatists Guild; National League of American Pen Women; National Opera Association; San Diego Opera, Advisory Director; Opera America; Poets and Writers. Address: 5820 Folsom Drive, La Jolla, CA 92037, USA.

GALLAGHER Liam, b. 21 September 1972, Burnage, Manchester. Singer; Musician; Producer. m. Patsy Kensit, 1997, divorced 2000, 1 son; 1 son with partner Nicole Appleton . Career: Singer with Oasis, 1991-; Tours in USA and Britain; Founder and

Dictionary of International Biography

recorded for Big Brother records, 2000-. Publications: Singles include: Supersonic, 1994; Shakermaker; Live Forever; Cigarettes and Alcohol; Some Might Say; Wonderwall; Cast No Shadow; Don't Look Back in Anger; D'You Know What I Mean; All Around the World; Go Let It out; The Hindu Times; Albums: Definitely Maybe, 1994; What's the Story Morning Glory?, 1995; Be Here Be Now, 1997; The Masterplan, 1998; Standing on the Shoulder of Giants, 2000; Familiar to Millions (live), 2001; Heathen Chemistry, 2002. Honours: 4 platinum discs for Definitely Maybe, 8 platinum discs for (What's the Story) Morning Glory, 1996; 3 Brit Awards, 1996. Address: C/o Ignition Management, 54 Linhope Street, London, NW1 6HL, England. Website: www.oasisnet.com

GALLAGHER Noel. b. 29 May 1967, Manchester. Songwriter; Musician; Singer. m. Meg Matthews, 1997, divorced, 1 daughter. Career: Formerly worked with Inspiral Carpets; Songwriter, Guitarist and Singer with Oasis, 1991-; Tours in USA and Britain. Publications: Recordings with Oasis, singles include: Supersonic, 1994; Shakermaker; Live Forever; Cigarettes and Alcohol; Some Might Say; Wonderwall; Cast No Shadow; Don't Look Back in Anger; D'You Know What I Mean; All Around the World; Go Let It Out; The Hindu Times; Albums: Definitely Maybe, 1994; (What's the Story) Morning Glory?, 1995; Be Here Now, 1997; The Masterplan, 1998; Standing on the Shoulder of Giants, 2000; Familiar to Millions (live), 2001; Heathen Chemistry, 2002. Honours: 4 platinum discs for Definitely Maybe, 8 platinum discs for (What's the Story) Morning Glory, 1995; Be Here Now, 1997; 3 Brit Awards, 1996; Best song, Grammy Awards (Wonderwall), 1997. Address: c/o Ignition Management, 54 Linhope Street, London, NW1 6HL, England. Website: www.oasisnet.com

GALLANT Roy Arthur, b. 17 April 1924, Portland, Maine, USA. Author; Teacher. m. Kathryn Dale, 1952, 2 sons. Education: BA, 1948, Bowdoin College; MS, 1949, Columbia University; Doctoral work, Columbia University, 1953-59. Appointments: Managing Editor, Scholastic Teachers Magazine, 1954-57; Author-in-Residence, Doubleday, 1957-59; Editorial Director, Aldus Books, London, 1959-62; Editor-in-Chief, The Natural History Press, 1962-65; Director, Southworth Planetarium, University of Southern Maine, 1980-2000; Consultant, The Edison Project, Israel Arts and Sciences Academy. Publications: Approximately 100 books, including: Our Universe, 1986, 1994; Private Lives of the Stars, 1986; Rainbows, Mirages and Sundogs, 1987; Before the Sun Dies, 1989; Ancient Indians, 1989; The Peopling of Planet Earth, 1990; Earth's Vanishing Forests, 1991; A Young Person's Guide to Science, 1993; The Day the Sky Split Apart, 1995; Geysers, 1997; Sand Dunes, 1997; Limestone Caves, 1998; Planet Earth, 1998; When the Sun Dies, 1998; Glaciers, 1999; The Ever-Changing Atom, 1999; Earth's Place in Space, 1999; Early Humans, 1999; Dance of the Continents, 1999; The Origins of Life, 2000; The Life Stories of Stars, 2000; Stars, 2000; Rocks, 2000; Minerals, 2000; Fossils, 2000; Comets and Asteroids, 2000; The Planets, 2000; Water, 2000; Space Station, 2000; Meteorite Hunter, 2002; Earth's History, 2002; Earth's Structure and Composition, 2002; Earth's Atmosphere, 2002; Earth's Water, 2002; Earth's Natural Resources, 2002; Earth's Restless Crust, 2002; Biodiversity, 2002; Inheritance, 2002. Honours: Thomas Alva Edison Foundation Mass Media Award, 1955; Distinguished Achievement Award, University of Southern Maine, 1981; Geographic Society of Chicago Publication Award, 1980; Awarded Professor emeritus status by USM, 2001; Distinguished Professional Staff Award, USM, 2001; Lifetime Achievement Katahdin Award from Maine Library Association, 2001; John Burroughs Award for Nature Writing, 1995. Address: PO Box 228, Beaver Mountain Lake, Rangeley, ME 04970, USA.

GALLINER Peter, b. 19 September 1920, Berlin, Germany. Publisher. m. (1) Edith Marguerite Goldsmidt, 1 daughter, (2) Helga Stenschke. Education: Berlin and London. Appointments: Reuters, London, England, 1944-47; Foreign Manager, Financial Times, London, 1947-60; Chairman of Board, Managing Director, Ullstein Publishing Group, Berlin, Germany, 1961-64; Vice-Chairman, Managing Director, British Printing Corporation, 1965-70; International Publishing Consultant, 1965-67, 1970-75; Chairman, Peter Galliner Associates, 1970-; Director, International Press Institute, 1975-93; Chairman, International Encounters, 1995-. Honours: Order of Merit, 1st Class, Germany, 1965; Ecomienda, Orden de Isabel la Catolica, Spain, 1982; Commander's Cross, Order of Merit, Germany, 1990; Turkish Press Freedom Award, Turkey, 1995; Media and Communication Award, Krakow, Poland, 1998. Address: Bregenzer Str 3, D-10707 Berlin, Germany; Untere Zaeune 9, CH-8001 Zurich, Switzerland.

GALOVICOVA Anna, b. 1 October 1950, Bratislava, Slovakia. Psychologist. m. Peter Galovic, 2 sons. Education: Graduated with Honours, Psychology, Charles University, Prague, 1975; Diploma work, psychological analysis of yoga, 1990. Appointments: Psychologist, reeducation centre, 1977-80; Czechoslovak Embassy, Algeria, 1980-85; Directrice, town cultural centre, 1985-92; Guru, Deep Centre for Spiritual Development, Spa Piest'any, 1992-99; Directrice, Harmony Clinic, Spa Trenc, Teplice, 1999-. Publications: Analysis of the Psychological Aspects of Yoga; Application of Yoga in the Healing of the Patients with Bechterev Disease; Yoga as the Innovation of the Rehabilitation in Slovak Spas, 1988; Yoga as Prevention of the Diseases of Civilization, 1990; Application of the Complex System Yoga in Daily Life in Education, 1992; Vegetarianism and Health, 2000; Influence of Yoga on Psychic Development, 2000; Mental Training for Top Sportsmen. Honours: Fellow, College of Human Sciences, Montreal, Canada, 1990; Appreciation of Sociography in Reeducation. Memberships: International Sri Deep Madhavananda Ashram Fellowship, Vienna, 1987; Civil Association of Slovak-Indian Friendship, Chairman, 1990-. Address: Gastanova 16, Piest'any, Slovakia.

GALTON Raymond Percy, b. 17 July 1930, England. Author; Scriptwriter. m. Tonia Phillips, 1956, 1 son, 2 daughters. Contributions to: Television with Alan Simpson: Hancock's Half House, 1954-61; Comedy Playhouse, 1962-63; Steptoe and Son, 1962-74; Galton-Simpson Comedy, 1969; Clochermerle, 1971; Casanova, '74, 1974; Dawson's Weekly, 1975; The Galton and Simpson Playhouse, 1976-77. With Johnny Speight: Tea Ladies, 1979; Spooner's Patch, 1979-80. With John Antrobus: Room at the Bottom, 1986. Films with Alan Simpson: The Rebel, 1960; The Bargee, 1963; The Wrong Arm of the Law, 1963; The Spy with a Cold Nose, 1966; Loot, 1969; Steptoe and Son, 1971; Steptoe and Son Ride Again, 1973; Den Siste Fleksnes, 1974; Die Skraphandlerne, 1975. Theatre with Alan Simpson: Way Out in Piccadilly, 1969; The Wind in the Sassfras Trees, 1968; Albert och Herbert, 1981; Fleksnes, 1983; Mordet pa Skolgatan 15, 1984. With John Antrobus: When Did You Last See Your Trousers?, 1986. Address: The Ivy House, Hampton Court, Middlesex, England.

GALTUNG Johan, b. 24 October 1930, Oslo, Norway. Director; Professor of Peace Studies. m. Fumiko Nishimura, 3 sons, 1 daughter. Education: PhD, Mathematics, 1956, PhD, Sociology, 1957, University of Oslo. Appointments: Assistant Professor, Columbia University, 1957-60; Director, Founder, International Peace Research Institute, Oslo, 1959-69; Professor, Peace Research, University of Oslo, 1969-77; Visiting Professor, Peace studies around the world, 1977-99; Director, Founder, TRANSCEND: A Conflict Reduction Network, 1993-.

Publications: Essays in Peace Research, vols I-VI, 1975-88; Essays in Methodology, vols I-IV, 1977-88; Human Rights in Another Key, 1994; Peace by Peaceful Means, 1996; Searching for Peace, 2002. Honours: 8 Dr hon causa, and 4 Honorary Professorships. Memberships: Founder, International Peace Research Association; First President, World Futures Studies Federation. Address: 51 Bois Chatton, F-01210 Versonnex, France.

GALVÃO Roberto Diéguez, b. 26 February 1943, Recife, Pe, Brazil. Professor. Education: BSc Mechanical and Industrial Engineering, Catholic University of Rio de Janeiro, 1965; MSc, Industrial Engineering, University of Alabama, USA, 1967; PhD, Management Science, Imperial College of Science and Technology, University of London, England, 1977. Appointments: Assistant to Plants and Terminals Manager, Marketing Department, Esso, Brazil, 1968-73; Professor, Post Graduate Department of Production Engineering, Federal University of Rio de Janeiro, Brazil, 1977-. Publications: Over 35 articles in scientific journals and contributions to books as author and co-author include most recently: A note on solutions to the maximal expected covering location problem, 2002; A hierarchical model for the location of perinatal facilities in the municipality of Rio de Janeiro, 2002; Dual-based heuristics for a hierarchical covering location problem, 2003; An algorithm to locate perinatal facilities in the municipality of Rio de Janeiro, 2003. Honour: Award for Outstanding Contributions, Brazilian Operational Research Society. Memberships: INFORMS, USA; Brazilian Operational Research Society, Brazil. Address: Rua Igarapava 103, Apt 201, 22450-200 Rio de Janeiro, RJ, Brazil. E-mail: galvao@pep.ufrj.br

GAMBLE Tom, b. 6 February 1924, Stockton-on-Tees, England. Artist. 1 son. Education: Constantine College, Middlesbrough, Cleveland. Career: Royal Navy, 1942-46; Senior Lecturer, Loughborough College of Art and Design, -1984; Course Tutor, Royal Watercolour Society. Exhibitions: Royal Academy; Royal Watercolour Society's Bankside Gallery; Singer & Friedlander/ Sunday Times Exhibitions; The Mall Gallery; Royal Festival Hall; The Arts Club; Painter/Stainers Hall; Cleveland Art Gallery; American and Canadian Watercolour Societies; Exposicion Internacional de Acuarela, Barcelona; Paterson's Gallery, London; Brian Sinfield, Oxford; The Century Gallery, Darchet; Woodgates Gallery, East Bergholt, Suffolk; Milne & Moller and other private galleries; Art in Action, Oxford for 10 years; Works in public and private collections including: H M the Queen; Lloyds of London; University of Loughborough; Leicester and Nottingham County Councils; Cleveland Art Gallery Middlesbrough and private collections in the UK, USA, Canada, Germany and New Zealand; Invited artist by John Ward RA for "Discerning Eye" exhibition, Mall Galleries. Publications: Works featured in various publications including: Visions of Venice by Michael Spender; The Old Water Colour Society's Volume No 63, article by Judy Egerton; International Waters, Exhibition Catalogue, American and British Watercolour Societies; Exposicion Internacional de Acuarela, Barcelona, 1992 and 1995; Antique Collecting Magazine; Saga Magazine, The Artist Magazine; Watercolours, Drawings and Prints, article by Sandy Fillingham; Gardens of England and Wales 1997. Honours: Gold Medal, Worshipful Company of Painter/ Stainers; Freeman of the City of London. Memberships: Liveryman, Worshipful Company of Painter/Stainers; Fellow, Royal Watercolour Society; Art Workers Guild; Arts Club. Address: 10 Blythe Green, East Perry, Huntingdon, Cambridgeshire PE28 0BJ, England.

GAMBON Sir Michael John, b. 19 October 1940, Dublin, Ireland. Actor. m. Anne Miller, 1962, 1 son. Appointments: Former, Mechanical Engineer; Actor with Edwards/Macliammoir Co, Dublin, 1962, National Theatre, Old Vic, 1963-67; Birmingham Repertory and other provincial theatres, 1967-69; Title roles include: Othello; Macbeth, Coriolanus, King Lear, Anthony and Cleopatra, Old Times; RSC, Aldwych, 1970-71; The Norman Conquests, 1974; Otherwise Engaged, 1976; Just Between Ourselves, 1977; Alice's Boys, 1978; with National Theatre, 1980; with RSC, Stratford and London, 1982-83; TV appearances include: Ghosts; Oscar Wilde; The Holy Experiment; Absurd Person Singular; The Borderers; The Singing Detective; The Heat of the Day; Maigret, 1992; The Entertainer, Truth; Films: The Beast Must Die, 1975; Turtle Diary, 1985; Paris by Night, 1988; The Cook, the thief, his wife and her lover; A Dry White Season, 1989; The Rachel Papers, 1989; State of Grace, 1989; The Heat of the Day, 1989; Mobsters, 1992; Toys, 1992; Clean Slate, 1993; Indian Warrior, 1993; The Browning Version, 1993; Mary Reilly, 1994; Two Deaths, 1994; Midnight in Moscow, 1994; A Man of No Importance, 1995; The Innocent Sleep, 1995; All Our Fault, 1995; Two Deaths, 1996; Nothing Personal, 1996; The Gambler, 1996; Dancing at Lughnasa, 1997; Plunket and McClean, 1997; The Last September, 1998; Sleepy Hollow, 1998; The Insider, End Game, 1999; Charlotte Gray, 2001; Gosford Park, 2001; Ali G Indahouse, 2001; Path to War, 2001; The Actors, 2002; Open Range, 2002; Harry Potter, The Prisoner of Azkaban, 2004; Honours include: London Theatre Critics Award for Best Actor; Olivier Award for Best Comedy Performance; Evening Stand Drama Award. Membership: Trustee, Roy Armouries, 1995-. Address: c/o ICM, Oxford House, 76 Oxford Street, London, W1N 0AX, England.

GANDHI Bipin Ramanlal, b. 7 February 1949, Amreli, India. Agrochemical Engineer; Poet. m. Veena, 26 November 1973, 1 son, 1 daughter. Education: BEC, Mechanical Engineering, 1971. Publication: Udbhav (collection of English poems), 1986. Contributions to: Poet; Premier Poets; Skylark; Mudrankan; Eureka. Honour: International Eminent Poet Award, 1988. Memberships: International Poets Academy, Madras, India, fellow; Mudra Amreli, Gujarat, India, fellow. Address: Mangal Mandir, Manekpara, Amreli, Gujarat 365601, India.

GANTI Prasada Rao, b. 25 August 1942, Seethanagaram (AP), India. Educator. m. Meenakshi Vedula, 1 son, 2 daughters. Education: BE, (Hons), Electrical Engineering, Andhra University, Waltair, India, 1963; M Tech, Control Systems Engineering, 1965, PhD, Electrical Engineering, 1970, Indian Institute of Technology, Kharagpur, India. Appointments: Assistant Professor, Department of Electrical Engineering, PSG College of Technology, Coimbatore, India, 1969-71; Assistant Professor, 1971-78, Professor, 1978-97, Chairman, Curriculum Development Cell, Electrical Engineering, 1978-80, Indian Institute of Technology, Kharagpur, India; Commonwealth Postdoctoral Research Fellow, Control Systems Centre, University of Manchester Institute of Science and Technology, Manchester, England, 1975-76; Alexander von Humboldt Foundation Research Fellow, Ruhr University, Bochum, Germany, 1981-83; 1985, 1991; Scientific Advisor, Directorate of Power and Desalination Plants, Water and Electricity Department, Government of Abu Dhabi, 1992-; Visiting Professor, Henri Poincare University, Nancy, France, 2003; Advisor to UNESCO-EOLSS Joint Committee. Publications: Author and Co-author of 4 books and over 150 research papers; Co-editor of 1 book. Honours include: IIT Kharagpur Silver Jubilee research Award, 1985; The Systems Society of India Award, 1989; International Desalination Association Best Paper award, 1995; Honorary Professor, East China University for Science and Technology. Memberships: Life Fellow, Institution of Engineers, India; Fellow, Institution of Electronic and Telecommunications Engineers, India; Fellow, IEEE, USA; Fellow Indian National Academy of Engineering; Member of numerous editorial boards. Address: PO Box 2623, Abu Dhabi, United Arab Emirates. E-mail: gantirao@emirates.net.ae

Dictionary of International Biography

GARCÍA ALVAREZ Jaime, b. 16 November 1932, Santa Maria de Ordás, Leon, Spain. Professor. Education: Graduate in Philosophy, Pontifical University, Salamanca; Doctor of Philosophy, Catholic Institute of Paris, France. Appointments: Director of Publications, Theology Faculty; Director of Department of Philosophy; Professor of Philosophy and Tutor of UNED. Publications: Experience of God in the Community, 1996; Saint Augustin or the Voice of the Heart, 1997. Honours: Guest Professor, University of Strasbourg, France; Guest Professor, University of Laval-Quebec, Canada. Memberships: International Society for the Study of Medieval Philosophy; International Association of Patristic Studies. Address: Faculty of Theology, Martínez del Campo, 10, E 09003 Burgos, Spain.

GARCÍA DE ALBA GARCÍA Javier Eduardo, b. 9 October 1946, Guadalajara, Jalisco, Mexico. Medical Doctor. m. Ana Leticia Salcedo Rocha, 1 son, 3 daughters. Education: Medical Doctor, University of Guadalajara, Guadalajara, Mexico, 1970; Master in Public Health, Public Health School of Mexico, Mexico City, 1971; Doctor in Anthropology, National Autonomous University of Mexico, Mexico City, 1997. Appointments: Public Health Secretary, State Epidemiologist, 1975; Head of University Research Department, 1993, Co-ordinator of Public Health Postgraduate Studies, 1997, University of Guadalajara, Mexico; Head of Social and Epidemiological Research Unit, Mexican Institute of Security, 2003. Publications: 11 books; 15 book chapters; 74 articles. Honours: National Public Health Research Award, 1994; Jalisco State Public Health Award, 2001. Memberships: Academia Mexicana de Cirugía; Society for Applied Anthropology; American Anthopological Association; American Diabetes Association. Address: 12 de Diciembre No 616, Col Chapalita, Zapopan, Jalisco, Mexico CP 45040. E-mail: javier_91046@yahoo.com

GARCIA Y GARCIA Ernesto Luis, b. 23 August 1946, Cogolludo, Spain. Medical Physician. m. Maria Soledad Vicente López, 5 October 1971, 2 sons, 1 daughter. Education: Degree in Licenciate, Medicine and Surgery, Medical Faculty Zaragoza, Spain; Certified in Pureiculture, 1975; Certified in Company Medicine, 1976; Resident in Rehabilitation and Physical Medicine Specialist, Miguel Servet Hospital, 1974-77; Doctor in Medicine and Surgery, 1991. Appointments: General Physician, General Health Management in cities of Guadalajara, Aragon and Catalonia, Spain, 1970-73; Emergency Medicine Officer, Royal and Provincial Hospital, Zaragoza, Spain, 1973-88; Specialist, Rehabilitation Department, Chief, Unit of Phoniatry and Logotherapy, Miguel Servet Hospital, Zaragoza, 1977-; Director, Centre of Phoniatric and Logotherapy Aragon, Zaragoza, 1980-; Specialist, Rehabilitation, Cerebral Palsy Centre, ASPACE, Aragon 1980-92; Chief of the Rehabilitation Service of the Assistance Centre Palmerola; Lecturer on rehabilitation, phoniatry and the handicapped at scientific sessions and congresses. Publications: Articles in professional journals on human communication disorders; Editor of book chapters and magazines. Honours include: Premium FAMI Aragon, 1995; Aragon Man of 2002; Recognition as team member for Choclear Implant, School of Doctors of Zaragoza, 2002. Memberships: President, Founding Manager, Spanish Phoniatry Magazine; Chairman, Spanish Medical Society of Phoniatry, 1992-97; Aragon Society of Rehabilitation and Physical Medicine; Spanish Society of Medical Physicians and rehabilitation; Aragon Society of Otorinolaryngology; Member numerous investigative commissions; Collaborative Associate, NGO's and humanitarian associations. Address: Hospital Miguel Servet, Department of Rehabilitation, c/ Isabel la Catolica 1-3, 50007 Zaragoza, Spain. E-mail: egarciag@hmservet.insalud.es

GARDNER Mariana Carmen Zavati, b. 20 January 1952, Bacau, Romania. Poet. m. John Edward Gardner, 8 August 1980, 1 son, 1 daughter. Education: Baccalauréat with distinction, Vasile Alecsandri Boarding College for Girls, 1971; MSc, Philology, 1st class hons, Alexandru Ioan Cuza University of Iasi, 1975; PGCE, University of Leeds, 1987; Postgraduate Courses: Goethe Institut Rosenheim, Germany, 1991; L'Ecole Normale Supérieure, Auxerre, France, 1991. Appointments: Teacher, Modern Languages (English, French, German, Latin, Spanish, Italian), various high schools in Romania and England, 1975-99; Part-time Assistant Lecturer, University of Iasi, 1975, 1976; Full-time Assistant Lecturer, University of Bacau, 1979. Publications include: Volumes of verse: Whispers; The Journey; Watermarks; Travellers/Calatori; The Spinning Top; Pilgrims/Pelerini; The Remains of the Dream Catcher; Bequests/Mosteniri; Poems included in anthologies: Between a Laugh and a Tear; Light of the World; The Sounds of Silence; The Secret of Twilight; A Blossom of Dreams; The Lyre's Song; Honoured Poets of 1988; Last Good-Byes; A Celebration of Poets; The Definitive Version; A Celebration of Poets; Sunrise and Soft Mist; Memories of the Millennium; Nature's Orchard; Lifelines; Antologia Padurii V; International Notebook of Poetry 2000, 2001, 2002; Journal of the American Academy of Arts and Sciences; Eastern Voices; Family Ties; Sunkissed; Reflections of Time; Translations: Cerul Meu de Hirtie/My Paper Sky – Poems by Al Florin Tene. Honours: Editor's Choice Award, International Society of Poets, UK, 1996; Editor's Choice Award, International Library of Poetry, UK, 1997; Editor's Choice Award, National Library of Poetry, UK, 1998; 3rd Prize, Bronze Medal, North American Poetry Competition, USA, 1998; The American Romanian Academy Award, The Ionel Jianu Award for Arts, American Romanian Academy of Arts and Sciences, Canada, 2001; Listed in national and international biographical dictionaries. Memberships: American Romanian Academy of Arts and Sciences; LiterArt XXI, International Association of Romanian Writers and Artists. Address: 14 Andrew Goodall Close, East Dereham, Norfolk NR19 1SR, England.

GARDOM Garde Basil (Hon), b. 17 July 1924, Banff, Alberta, Canada. Former British Columbia Lieutenant Governor. m. Theresa Helen Eileen Mackenzie, 1 son, 4 daughters. Education: BA, LLB, LLD (Hon) University of British Columbia and University of Victoria. Appointments: Called to Bar, British Columbia, 1949; Elected MLA for Vancouver-Point Grey Province, 1966; Re-elected, 1969, 1972, 1975, 1979, 1983; Government House Leader, 1977-86; Attorney General for British Columbia, 1975-79; Minister of Intergovernmental Relations, British Columbia, 1979-86; Chairman, Constitution Committee and Legislation Committee, 1975-86; Member, Treasury Board and Planning and Priorities Committee, 1983-86; Minister Responsible for Official Visits to Expo '86; Policy Consultant, Office of the Premier, 1986-87; Agent General for British Columbia in the UK and Europe, 1987-92; Director, Crown Life Insurance Co, 1992-95; Director Brouwer Claims Canada Ltd; Lieutenant Governor for BC, 1995-2001. Honours: Queen's Council; Freeman of the City of London, 1992; Lifetime Achievement Award, University of British Columbia; Knight of Justice, The Order of St John; Honorary Colonel, The British Columbia Regiment (DCO); Honorary Vice Patron, St John Ambulance; Director and Life Member, The Canadian Club of Vancouver; Honorary Patron: Royal British Columbia Museum; (BC) Alcohol-Drug Education Service; Honorary Life Member: The Heraldry Society of Canada; The Royal United Services Institute of Vancouver Island; The Friends of the Government House Gardens Society; The Vancouver Club and The Union Club of BC; Vancouver Lawn Tennis and Badminton Club; Brock House Society; Honorary Director, Boys' and Girls' Clubs of Greater Vancouver; Member, BC Sports Hall of Fame; Patron, Nature Conservancy Canada; Honorary BC Chairman, CNIB Campaign

Dictionary of International Biography

for Digital Library Services; Honorary Chairman, The Biblical Museum of Canada; Member, Campaign for the Construction of UBC Rowing Facilities at Richmond, BC. Memberships: Canadian Bar Association, 1949-; British Columbia Sports Hall of Fame; Phi Delta Theta; Union Club of British Columbia; The Vancouver Club; Vancouver Lawn Tennis and Badminton Club; Royal Overseas Club. Address: 2122 S W Marine Drive, Vancouver, BC V6P 6B5, Canada.

GARECKI Janusz, b. 26 October 1942, Tomaszow Mazowiecki, Poland. Research Worker. m. Matgrzata Wrótna, 12 January 1980, 2 sons, 1 daughter. Education: MSc, Astrophysics, 1965, MSc, Mathematics and Theoretical Physics, 1969, PhD in Physical Science, 1974, Jagellonian University. Appointments: Researcher, Jagellonian University, 1965-73; Lecturer, Pedagogical University, Szczecin, 1974-84; Lecturer, Maths and Theoretical Physics, 1985-, Leader, General Relativity and Cosmology Group, 1990-, University of Szczecin. Publications: Articles to scientific journals. Honours: Award of Ministry of Science and Technology, 1975, 1979; Honourable Mention, Gravity Research Foundation, 1995, 1999. Memberships: General Relativity and Gravitation Society; Polish Physics Society; Einstein Foundation International; American Mathematical Society; National Geographic Society. Address: Institute of Physics, University of Szczecin, Wielkopolska 15, 70-451 Szczecin, Poland. E-mail: garecki@wmf.univ.szczecin.pl

GARMANOV Maksim E, b. 29 May 1961, Moscow, Russia. Chemist; Electrochemist; Researcher; Scientist. Education: Highest Degree with honours, Chemical Faculty, Moscow State University, Russia, 1983; Postgraduate Course, The Karpov's Physico-Chemical Research Institute, Moscow, Russia, 1990. Appointments: Special Researcher, Institute of Physical Chemistry, Academy of Sciences, Moscow, 1983-86; Junior Scientist, 1986-87, Postgraduate Student, 1987-90, The Karpov's Physico-Chemical Research Institute, Moscow; Junior Scientist, 1990-92, Scientist, 1992-, Institute of Physical Chemistry, Academy of Sciences, Moscow; Supernumerary Manager on marketing and production of organic corrosion inhibitors, IPHCAN Ltd, Moscow, 1992-. Publications: Numerous articles in professional scientific journals. Honours: Highest degree with Honours, Moscow State University, 1983; Listed in national and international biographical honours and grand editions. Memberships: Trade Union of Scientific Workers; New York Academy of Sciences. Address: The Institute of Physical Chemistry of RAS, Leninsky Prospect 31, Moscow 119991, Russia. Website: http:// maxsuper.boom.ru/ index.html

GARNER James (James Baumgardner), b. 7 April 1928, Norman, Oklahoma, USA. Actor. m. Lois Clarke, 1995, 1 son, 2 daughters. Appointments: Former travelling salesman, oil field worker, carpet layer, bathing suit model; Toured with road companies; Actor, TV appearances include: Cheyenne, Maverick, 1957-62; Nichols, 1971-72; The Rockford Files, 1974-79; Space, 1985; The New Maverick; The Long Summer of George Adams; The Glitter Dome; Heartsounds; Promise (also executive producer); Obsessive Love; My Name is Bill (also executive producer); Decoration Day; Barbarians at the Gate; The Rockford Files; A Blessing in Disguise; Dead Silence; First Monday (series), 2002; Films include: Toward the Unknown; Shoot-Out at Medicine Bend, 1957; Darby's Rangers, 1958; Sayonara; Up Periscope, 1959; The Americanization of Emily, 1964; 36 Hours; The Art Of Love, 1965; A Man Could Get Killed, 1966; Duel at Diablo, 1966; Master Buddwing, 1966; Grand Prix, 1966; Hour of the Gun, 1967; Marlowe, 1969; Support Your Local Sheriff, 1971; Support Your Local Gunfighter, 1971; Skin Game, 1971; They Only Kill Their Masters, 1972; One Little Indian, 1973; Health, 1979; The Fan,

1980; Victor/Victoria, 1982; Murphy's Romance, 1985; Promise (made for TV), 1986; Sunset, 1987; Decoration Day (TV film), 1990; Fire in the Sky, 1993; Maverick (TV), 1994; My Fellow Americans, 1996; Twilight, 1998; Space Cowboys, 2000; Atlantis: The Lost Empire, 2001; Roughing It (TV), 2002; Divine Secrets of the Ya-Ya Sisterhood, 2002. Honours: Emmy Award; Purple Heart.

GARNETT Michael Pearson, b. 24 November 1938. m. 1975, 2 sons. Education: Framlingham College, Suffolk; Diploma in Business and Company Law, British Institute of Careers, New South Wales. Appointments: Military Service, RAF (Malaya) and RAAF (Australia) Flight Lieutenant; Tea Plantation Manager, North East India, 1960-67; Government and Public Affairs, BP Australia Ltd, 1967-94; Chief Executive, Australian Royal Tennis Association, 1994-99. Publications: A History of Royal Tennis in Australia, 1983; Tennis, Rackets and Other Ball Games, 1986; Royal Tennis for the Record, 1991; A Chase Down-Under, 1999. Honours: General Service Medal w/c Malaya, 1958; Australian Sports Medal, 2001. Memberships: Royal Melbourne Tennis; Naval and Military, Melbourne. Address: The Chase, Romsey Vic 3434, Australia.

GARNETT Richard (Duncan Carey), b. 8 January 1923, London, England. Writer; Publisher; Translator. Education: BA, King's College, Cambridge, 1948; MA, 1987. Appointments: Production Manager, 1955-59, Director, 1957-66, Rupert Hart-Davis Ltd; Director, Adlard Coles Ltd, 1963-66; Editor, 1966-82, Director, 1972-82, Macmillan London; Director, Macmillan Publishers, 1982-87. Publications: Goldsmith: Selected Works (editor), 1950; Robert Gruss: The Art of the Aqualung (translator), 1955; The Silver Kingdom (in US as The Undersea Treasure), 1956; Bernard Heuvelmans: On the Track of Unknown Animals (translator), 1958; The White Dragon, 1963; Jack of Dover, 1966; Bernard Heuvelmans: In the Wake of the Sea-Serpents (translator), 1968; Joyce (editor with Reggie Grenfell), 1980; Constance Garnett: A Heroic Life, 1991; Sylvia and David, The Townsend Warner/Garnett Letters (editor), 1994. Address: Hilton Hall, Hilton, Huntingdon, Cambridgeshire PE28 9NE, England.

GARRETT Lesley, b. 10 April 1955. Opera Singer. m. 1991, 1 son, 1 daughter. Education: Royal Academy of Music; National Opera Studio. Career: Winner, Kathleen Ferrier Memorial Competition, 1979; Performed with Welsh National Opera; Opera North; At Wexford and Buxton Festivals and at Glyndebourne; Joined ENO (Principal Soprano), 1984; Major roles includes: Susanna, Marriage of Figaro; Despina, Cosi Fan Tutte; Musetta, La Bohème; Jenny, Rise and Fall of the City of Mahaggony; Atalanta, Xerxes; Zerlinda, Don Giovanni; Yum-Yum, The Mikado; Adèle, Die Fledermaus; Oscar, A Masked Ball; Dalinda, Ariodante; Rose, Street Scene; Bella, A Midsummer Marriage; Eurydice, Orpheus and Eurydice; Title roles in the The Cunning Little Vixen and La Belle Vivette; Numerous concert hall performances in UK and abroad (including Last Night of the Proms); TV and radio appearances. Honours: Hon DArts (Plymouth), 1995; Best selling Classical Artist, Gramophone Award, 1996. Address: The Music Partnership Ltd, 41 Aldebert Terrace, London, SW8 1BH, England.

GASCH Bernd Carl, b. 5 February 1941, Karlsbad, Germany. Professor. m. Angela, 1991, 1 son, 1 daughter. Education: Diploma in Psychology, 1965; Doctors Degree, 1970. Appointments: Research Assistant, University of Erlangen-Nuremberg, 1965-66; Founder and Head, Team for Psychological Management, 1972; Head, Centre for the Advancement of Tertiary Learning and Teaching, University of Augsburg, Germany, 1973-77; Head, Central Research Group for the Evaluation of Models of Legal Education, Mannheim, 1977-78; Visiting Fellow, Australian

Dictionary of International Biography

National University, Australia, 1978; Professor of Psychology, University of Dortmund, Germany, 1979; Special Commissioner, Organizational Psychology, University of Dortmund, 1980-90; Visiting Professor, University of Wollongong, Australia, 1984-85; Dean, Faculty of Social Sciences, University of Dortmund, 1987-90 and at present second term as Dean; Vice Rector, University of Dortmund, 1990-94; Visiting Professor, Universita Luigi Bocconi, Milano, 1992; Visiting Scholar, Obermann Centre for Advanced Studies, University of Iowa, USA, 1999. Publications: 7 books; Numerous articles; Several television productions. Memberships: German Association for Psychology; International Association of Applied Psychology; Association for Tertiary Education. Address: University of Dortmund, Fakultaet 14, Postfach 500500, D-44221 Dortmund, Germany. E-mail: bernd.gasch@t-online.de

GASCOIGNE Paul John, b. 26 May 1967, Gateshead, England. Footballer. m. Sheryl Failes, divorced, 1 son. Career: Played for Newcastle United, 1985-88; Tottenham Hotspur, 1988-92, Lazio, Italy, 1992-95, Glasgow Rangers, 1995-98; Middlesbrough, 1998-2000; Everton, 2000-02; Burnley, 2002; Signed as player/coach, Gansu Tianma (Gansu Sky Horses), Chinese B-League, 2003; Played for England, 13 under 21 caps, 57 full caps, World Cup Italy, 1990. Publication: Paul Gascoigne, autobiography with Paul Simpson, 2001. Honours: BBC Sports Personality of the Year, 1990; FA Cup Winners Medal, 1991. Address: c/o Robertson Craig & Co, Clairmont Gardens, Glasgow, G3 7LW, Scotland.

GASKIN Catherine Marjella, b. 2 April 1929, County Louth, Dundalk, Ireland. Novelist. m. Sol Cornberg, 1 December 1955, deceased, 1999. Education: Holy Cross College, Sydney, Australia; Conservatorium of Music, Sydney. Publications: This Other Eden, 1946; With Every Year, 1947; Dust in Sunlight, 1950; All Else is Folly, 1951; Daughter of the House, 1952; Sara Dane, 1955; Blake's Reach, 1958; Corporation Wife, 1960; I Know My Love, 1962; The Tilsit Inheritance, 1963; The File on Devlin, 1965; Edge of Glass, 1967; Fiona, 1970; A Falcon for a Queen, 1972; The Property of a Gentleman, 1974; The Lynmara Legacy, 1975; The Summer of the Spanish Woman, 1977; Family Affairs, 1980; Promises, 1982; The Ambassador's Women, 1985; The Charmed Circle, 1988. Memberships: Society of Authors; Author's Guild of America. Address: Villa 139, The Manors, 15 Hale Road, Mosman, NSW 2088, Australia.

GASPARYAN Vahe Chris, b. 5 April 1971, Yerevan, Armenia. Cardiac Surgeon. m. Lusine Grigoryan, 2 daughters. Education: MD Degree, Diploma with Excellence, Yerevan State Medical University, Yerevan, Armenia, 1987-93; Residency in Cardiovascular Surgery, 1993-95; Research Scholarship, Assistant Professor Degree, 2000. Appointments: Cardiac Surgeon, Mikaelian Surgical Institute, Yervan, Armenia, 1995-96; Training in Cardiac Surgery, New York, USA, 1995, Paris, France, 1998; Fellowship in Cardiac Surgery, Glasgow, 2002-2003; Chief of Cardiac Surgery Department, Erebouni Medical Centre, Yerevan, 2003-. Publications: Articles in professional medical journals including, Journal of Thoracic and Cardiovascular Surgery, 1999, 2000; Asian Cardiovascular and Thoracic Annals, 2002. Honours: Alexis Carrel Award, Rome, Italy, 1995; Merit Award, Singapore, 2000. Membership: Asian Society for Cardiovascular Surgery, 2001-. Address: 26 Papazian St, Apt 24, 375012, Yerevan, Armenia. E-mail: vahegasparyan@yahoo.com

GATES William Henry (Bill), b. 8 October 1955, Seattle, USA. Computer Software Executive. m. Melinda French, 1994, 1 son, 2 daughters. Education: Harvard University. Appointments: Joined MITS, 1975; Programmer, Honeywell, 1975; Founder, Chairman, Board, Microsoft Corporation, 1976-, CEO, 1976-99; Software Architect, 1999-. Publications: The Future, 1994; The Road Ahead,

1996; Business at the Speed of Thought, 1999. Honours: Howard Vollum Award, Reed College, Portland, Oregon, 1984; Named CEO of Year, Chief Executive Magazine. Address: Microsoft Corporation, 1 Microsoft Way, Redmond, WA 98052, USA.

GATHORNE-HARDY Jonathan, b. 15 May 1933, Edinburgh, Scotland. Author. m. (1) Sabrina Tennant, 1962, 1 son, 1 daughter, (2) Nicolette Sinclair Loutit, 12 September 1985. Education: BA, Arts, Trinity College, Cambridge, 1957. Publications: One Foot in the Clouds (novel), 1961; Chameleon (novel), 1967; The Office (novel), 1970; The Rise and Fall of the British Nanny, 1972; The Public School Phenomenon, 1977; Love, Sex, Marriage and Divorce, 1981; Doctors, 1983; The Centre of the Universe is 18 Baedeker Strasse (short stories), 1985; The City Beneath the Skin (novel), 1986; The Interior Castle: A Life of Gerald Brenan (biography), 1992; Particle Theory (novel), 1996; Alfred C. Kinsey - Sex The Measure of All Things, A Biography, 1998. Other: 11 novels for children. Contributions to: Numerous magazines and journals. Address: 31 Blacksmith's Yard, Binham, Fakenham, Norfolk NR21 0AL, England.

GATTI Armand, b. 26 January 1924, Monaco (French citizen). Playwright. Career: Parachutist with the SAS in London, 1943. Publications include: Le Poisson noir, 1958; Le Crapaud-Buffle, 1959; Le Voyage de Grand Chou, 1960; Chant public devant deux chaises électriques, 1966; V comme Vietnam, 1967; La Passion du général Franco, 1968; Un homme seul, 1969; Petit manuel de guérilla urbaine, 1971; La colonne Durutti, 1974; Die Hälfte des Himmels un wir, 1975; Le labyrinthe, 1982; Opéra avec titre long, 1987; Oeuvres théâtrales, 3 tomes regroupant 44 pièces de 1958 à 1990, 1991; Le chant d'amour des alphabets d'Auschwitz, 1992; Gatti à Marseilles, 1995; La journée d'une infirmière, 1995; Notre tranchée de chaque jour, 1996; L'enfant-rat, 1997; La part en trop, 1997 Les personnages de théâtre meurent dans la rue, 1998; La parole errante, 1999; L'anarchie comme un battement d'ailes, 2000. Honours: Prix Fénéon, 1959; Grand prix national du théâtre, 1988; Officier des Arts et des Lettres, 1989; Médaille de vermeil Picasso, UNESCO, 1999; Chevalier de la Légion d'honneur, 2000; Commandeur des Arts et des Lettres, 2003. Address: La parole errante, 9 rue François Debergue, 931000 Montreuil, France.

GATTING Michael William, b. 6 June 1957, Kingsbury, Middlesex, England. Cricketer. m. Elaine Mabbott, 1980, 2 sons. Career: Right-hand batsman and right-arm medium bowler, played for Middlesex, 1975-98, Captain, 1983-97; 79 Tests for England, 1977-95, 23 as Captain; Scoring 4,409 runs (average 35.5) including 10 hundreds; Scored 36,549 first-class runs (94 hundreds); Toured Australia (Captain), 1986-87; Captain, rebel cricket tour to South Africa, 1989-90; 92 limited-overs internationals, 37 as Captain; Member, England Selection Committee, 1997-; Director of Coaching, Middlesex Cricket Club, 1999-2000; Director, Ashwell Leisure, 2001-. Publications: Limited Overs, 1986; Triumph in Australia, 1987; Leading From the Front (autobiography), 1988. Honour: OBE; Wisden Cricketer of The Year, 1984. Address: c/o Middlesex County Cricket Club, Lord's Cricket Ground, St John's Wood Road, London, NW8 8QN, England.

GAULTIER Jean-Paul, b. 24 April 1952, Arcueil, Paris. Fashion Designer. Career: Launched first collection with his Japanese partner, 1978; Since then known on international scale for his men's and women's collections; First junior collection, 1988; Costume designs for film The Cook, The Thief, His Wife and Her Lover, 1989, for ballet le Défilé de Régine Chopinot, 1985; Madonna's World Tour, 1990; Released record, How to Do That (in collaboration with Tony Mansfield), 1989; Launched own perfume, 1993; Designer of costume for Victoria Abril in Pedro Almodóvar's film Koka, 1994; film, La Cité des Enfants Perdus, 1995; The Fifth Element, 1996; Absolutely Fabulous, 2001; Launched perfume brands Jean-Paul Gaultier, 1993, La Mâle, 1995, Fragile, 1999. Honours: Fashion Oscar, 1987; Progetto Leonardo Award for How to Do That, 1989; Chevalier des Arts et des Lettres. Address: Jean-Paul Gaultier SA, 30 rue du Faubourg-Saint-Antoine, 75012 Paris, France.

GAVAYEVA Nadezhda N, b. 7 February 1951, Saransk, Russia. Professor of English. Education: Diploma, Mordovian State University, 1973; Candidate of Philological Sciences, 1985; Associate Professor, 1991. Appointments: Postgraduate, Leningrade State University, 1973-77; Assistant, English Language Department, 1978-86, Teacher of English, 1978-86, Senior Teacher, 1986-89, Associate Professor, 1989-, Mordovian State University. Publications: 43 publications on text linguistics, ways of teaching English as a foreign language, cultural aspects of teaching English. Honours: Gold Medal, high school, 1968; Honoured Doctor, Udmurt State University, Russia, 1995. Address: 52-15 Demokraticheskaya Street, Saransk, Mordovia 430000, Russia.

GAVRILOVA Maria K, b. 7 December 1928, Yakutsk, USSR. Scientific Worker; Geographer. m. Bosikov Vasili, 1 daughter. Education: Geographer-Climatologist, Lomonosov Moscow State University, 1949-1954; DSc, Geography, Voyeikov Main Geophysics Observatory, Leningrad, 1954-1958. Appointments: Junior Research Associate, Scholar Secretary, Senior Research Associate, Head of Laboratory, Principal Research Associate, Permafrost Institute of SB of RAS, Yakutsk, 1958-; Principal Scholar Secretary, Adviser, Academy of Sciences of the RS, Yakutsk, 1994-; Professor, Ammosov Vakut State University, 1994-. Publications: Monographs: Climate of the Central Yakutia,1962, 1973; Radiation Climate of the Arctic, 1963, 1966; Climate and Perennially Frozen Ground, 1978; Modern Climate and Permafrost on Continents, 1981; Climates of Cold Regions of the Earth, 1998, 2003. Honours: Merited Scientist of the Russian Federation; Merited Scientist of the Republic of Sakha, Yakutia; Honoured Member, Russian Geographic Society; Honoured Worker of the Hydrometeorological Service of the Russian Federation; Prize winner of 7 scientific medals. Memberships: Academician of the Academy of Sciences of the Republic of Sakha, Yakutia; Academician of the Russian Academy of Natural Sciences; Full Member, North Forum Academy; New York Academy of Sciences. Address: Academy of Sciences of the Republic of Sakha, Yakutia, Lenina Ave 33, Yakutsk, 677007, Republic of Sakha, Yakutia, Russia. E-mail:gavrilova@mpi.ysn.ru

GAYVORONSKY Ludmila (Nikitina), b. 4 December 1939, Kharkov, Ukraine. Artist. m. Alexander Eremenko, 1 son. Education: Diploma of Excellence, Hydrometeorological Institute, 1956-61; PhD, Geography, World Meteorological Center, Moscow, 1961-65; Diploma, Academy of Art, Moscow, 1964-68. Appointments: Engineer, Chief Engineer, World Meteorological Center, Moscow, 1965-66; Editor, Chief Editor, Science Magazine, Moscow, 1966-79; Art Instructor, Staten Island, New York, 1983-93; Librarian, New York, 1986-93; Art Instructor, Assistant to Director, Library Arts Center, Newport, New Hampshire, 1993-; Professor of Fine Art, Lebanon College, Lebanon, New Hampshire, 1997-. Publications: Several articles in professional journals and encyclopedias. Honours: Gold Medal, Moscow Festival of Arts; Juror's Prize of Distinction, Moscow; Medal of Honour, Ukrainian Institute of America, New York City; Certificate of Appreciation, US Coast Guard; American Medal of Honor, ABI. Memberships include: Academical Knight, Accademia del Verbano, Vercelli, Italy; World Phenomenological Institute, Boston, Massachusetts; New Hampshire Art Association. Commissions and Creative

Works: Backdrop Panel for the Dicken's Fair, Newport, New Hampshire; Participating Artist in the wall mural for the town of Newport; Wall murals for Sinergia, Inc, New York City; Stage art construction for New York City Children's Week, Lincoln Center, New York City. Address: 26 Church Street, Apt 5, Newport, NH 03773, USA.

GEBAUER Phyllis, b. 17 October 1928, Chicago, Illinois, USA. Novelist; Writer; Teacher. m. Frederick A Gebauer, 2 December 1950, deceased. Education: BS, Northwestern University, 1950; MA, University of Houston, 1966; Postgraduate, several universities. Appointments: Workshop Leader, Santa Barbara Writers' Conference, 1980-; Instructor, University of California at Los Angeles Extension Writers' Program, 1989-; Lecturer, San Diego State University Writers Conference, 1995-. Publications: The Pagan Blessing, 1979; The Cottage, 1985; The Final Murder of Monica Marlowe, 1986; Criticism, The Art of Give and Take, 1987. Honours: 1st Prize for Fiction, Santa Barbara City College, 1972; 1st and 2nd Prizes for Fiction, Santa Barbara City College, 1973. Memberships: PEN Center, USA, West; Dorothy L Sayers Society; Mystery Writers of America. Address: 515 West Scenic Drive, Monrovia, CA 91016-1511, USA.

GÉBLER Carlo, b. 21 August 1954, Dublin, Ireland. Writer; Film-Maker. m. Tyga Thomason, 23 August 1990, 3 sons, 2 daughters. Education: BA, English and Related Literature, University of York, 1976; Graduate, National Film and Television School, 1979. Appointments: Part-time Teacher, Creative Writing, HMP Maze, Co Antrim, 1993-95; Appointed Writer-in-Residence, HMP Maghaberry, Co Antrim, 1997. Publications: The Eleventh Summer, 1985; August in July, 1986; Work & Play, 1987; Driving through Cuba, 1988; Malachy and His Family, 1990; The Glass Curtain: Inside an Ulster Community, 1991; Life of a Drum, 1991; The Cure, 1994; W9 and Other Lives, 1998; How to Murder a Man, 1998; Frozen Out, 1998; The Base, 1999; Father & I, 2000; Dance of Death, 2000; Caught on a Train, 2001; 10 Rounds, 2002; August' 44, 2003. Membership: Elected to Aosdána, Ireland, 1990. Address: c/o Antony Harwood, 103 Walton Street, Oxford, OX2 6EB, England.

GEDALECIA David, b. 8 June 1942, New York, USA. Professor of History. m. Pei-hsin Chia, 1 son, 1 daughter. Education: BA, Queens College, City University New York, 1965; AM, 1967, PhD, 1971, Harvard University. Appointments: Professor of History, 1971-, Chairman, Department of History, 1985-87, Michael O. Fisher Chair in History, 1999-, College of Wooster, Ohio. Publications: The Philosophy of Wu Ch'eng: A Neo-Confucian of the Yüan Dynasty, 1999; Solitary Crane in a Spring Grove, 2000. Honours: NDEA Title VI Fellowships (Chinese), 1965-71; Teaching Fellowship, Harvard University, 1969-70; ACLS Fellowship, 1982; Phi Beta Kappa. Membership: Association for Asian Studies. Address: Department of History, College of Wooster, OH 44691, USA.

GEDDES Gary, b. 9 June 1940, Vancouver, British Columbia, Canada. Professor of English; Writer; Poet. m. (1) Norma Joan Fugler, 1963, divorced 1969, 1 daughter, (2) Jan Macht, 2 May 1973, 2 daughters. Education: BA, University of British Columbia, 1962; Diploma in Education, University of Reading, 1964; MA, 1966, PhD, 1975, University of Toronto. Appointments: Lecturer, Carleton University, Ottawa, Ontario, 1971-72; University of Victoria, British Columbia, 1972-74; Writer-in-Residence, 1976-77, Visiting Associate Professor, 1977-78, University of Alberta, Edmonton; Visiting Associate Professor, 1978-79, Professor of English, 1979-98, Concordia University, Montreal, Quebec; Distinguished Professor of Canadian Culture, Western Washington University, 1999-. Publications: 20th Century Poetry and Poets,

1969, 4th edition, 1996; 15 Canadian Poets (editor with Phyllis Bruce), 1970, 3rd edition, 1988, 4th edition as Poems for a New Millennium, forthcoming; Poems, 1970; Rivers Inlet (verse), 1972; Snakeroot (verse), 1973; Letter of the Master of Horse (verse), 1973; The Acid Test, 1981; The Inner Ear: An Anthology of New Canadian Poets (editor), 1983; The Terracotta Army (verse), 1984; Changes of State (verse), 1986; The Unsettling of the West (stories), 1986; Hong Kong (verse), 1987; Letters from Managua, 1990; Light of Burning Towers (verse), 1990; Letters from Managua: Meditations on Politics (essays), 1990; The Art of Short Fiction: An International Anthology, 1992; Girl By the Water, 1994; The Perfect Cold Warrior, 1995; Active Trading: Selected Poems, 1970-96; Flying Blind (verse), 1998; Sailing Home: A Journey Through Time, Place and Memory (non-fiction), 2001; Skaldance (verse), 2004. Honours: E J Pratt Medal; National Poetry Prize, Canadian Authors Association; America's Best Book Award; Writers Choice Award; National Magazine Gold Award; Archibald Lampman Prize; Milton Acorn Competition; Gabriela Mistral Prize, 1996. Memberships: League of Canadian Poets; Writers' Guild of Canada; Playwright's Guild of Canada. Address: 975 Seaside Drive, RR 2, Sooke, British Columbia, V0S 1N0, Canada.

GEE Maurice Gough, b. 22 August 1931, Whakatane, New Zealand. Writer. Education: MA, University of Auckland, 1954. Appointments: Robert Burns Fellow, University of Otago, 1964; Writing Fellow, Victoria University of Wellington, 1989; Katherine Mansfield Fellow, Menton, France, 1992. Publications: Plumb, 1978; Meg, 1981; Sole Survivor, 1983; Collected Stories, 1986; Prowlers, 1987; The Burning Boy, 1990; Going West, 1993; Crime Story, 1994; Loving Ways, 1996; Live Bodies, 1998; Ellie and the Shadow Man, 2001. Other 10 novels for children. Honours: New Zealand Book Awards, 1976, 1979, 1981, 1991, 1993; James Tait Black Memorial Prize, 1979; Honorary DLitt, Victoria University of Wellington, 1987. Membership: PEN New Zealand Centre, national vice president, 1990-91. Address: 41 Chelmsford Street, Ngaio, Wellington, New Zealand.

GEENEN Vincent G, b. 6 February 1958, Belgium. Professor. 2 sons. Education: MD, 1982; PhD, 1987, University of Liege. Appointments: Professor, ULG, 1996-; Clinic Head in Internal Medicine, CHU, Liege, 1998-; Research Professor, NFSR, 1999-; Director, Liege Center of Immunology, 2001-04; Co-ordinator, FP6 Euro-Thymaide Project, 2004-08; Contribution to thymus physiology, the role of a thymus defect in the development of autoimmunity and thymus-based tolerogenic therapy. Publications: More than 100 in professional journals, 19 chapters, 5 books. Honours: 7 Awards. Memberships: 25 scientific societies. Address: Institute of Pathology, CHU-B23 University of Liege, B-4000 Liege-Sart Tilman, Belgium.

GEERTZ Clifford (James), b. 23 August 1926, San Francisco, California, USA. Professor of Social Science; Writer. m. (1) Hildred Storey, 30 October 1948, divorced 1982, 1 son, 1 daughter, (2) Karen Blu, 1987. Education: AB, Antioch College, 1950; PhD, Harvard University, 1956. Appointments: Research Assistant, 1952-56, Research Associate, 1957-58, Massachusetts Institute of Technology; Instructor and Research Associate, Harvard University, 1956-57; Fellow, Center for Advanced Study in the Behavioral Sciences, Stanford, 1958-59; Assistant Professor of Anthropology, University of California at Berkeley, 1958-60; Assistant Professor, 1960-61, Associate Professor, 1962-64, Professor, 1964-68, Divisional Professor, 1968-70, University of Chicago; Senior Research Career Fellow, National Institute for Mental Health, 1964-70; Professor of Social Science, 1970-, Harold F Linder Professor of Social Science, 1982-, Professor Emeritus, 2000-, Institute for Advanced Study, Princeton, New Jersey; Visiting Lecturer with Rank of Professor, Princeton

University, 1975-2000; Various guest lectureships. Publications: The Religion of Java, 1960; Old Societies and New States (editor), 1963; Agricultural Involution: The Processes of Ecological Change in Indonesia, 1963; Peddlers and Princes, 1963; The Social History of an Indonesian Town, 1965; Person, Time and Conduct in Bali: An Essay in Cultural Analysis, 1966; Islam Observed: Religious Development in Morocco and Indonesia, 1968; The Interpretation of Cultures: Selected Essays, 1973; Myth, Symbol and Culture (editor), 1974; Kinship in Bali (with Hildred Geertz), 1973; Meaning and Order in Moroccan Society (with Hildred Geertz and Lawrence Rosen), 1979; Negara: The Theatre State in Nineteenth Century Bali, 1980; Local Knowledge: Further Essays in Interpretive Anthropology, 1983; Bali, interprétation d'une culture, 1983; Works and Lives: The Anthropologist as Author, 1988; After the Fact: Two Countries, Four Decades, One Anthropologist, 1995; Available Light: Anthropological Reflections on Philosophical Topics, 2000. Contributions to: Scholarly books and journals. Honours: Talcott Parsons Prize, American Academy of Arts and Sciences, 1974; Sorokin Prize, American Sociological Association, 1974; Distinguished Lecturer, American Anthropological Association, 1983; Huxley Memorial Lecturer and Medallist, Royal Anthropological Institute, 1983; Distinguished Scholar Award, Association for Asian Studies, 1987; National Book Critics Circle Prize in Criticism, 1988; Horace Mann Distinguished Alumnus Award, Antioch College, 1992; Fukuoka Asian Cultural Prize, 1992. Memberships: American Academy of Arts and Sciences, fellow; American Association for the Advancement of Science, fellow; American Philosophical Society, fellow; British Academy, corresponding fellow; Council on Foreign Relations, fellow; National Academy of Sciences, fellow; Royal Anthropological Institute, honorary fellow. Address: c/o School of Social Science, Institute for Advanced Study, Princeton, NJ 08540, USA.

GEFFEN David, b. 21 February 1943, Brooklyn, New York, USA. Film, Recording and Theatre Executive. Appointments: William Morris Talent Agency, 1964; Launched new film studio with Steven Spielberg and Jeffrey Katzenberg; Founder, Music Publishing Company Tunafish Music with Laura Nyro; Joined Ashley Famous Agency; Appointed Vice President, Creative Man (now International Creative Man), 1968; Founder, Asylum Records and Geffen-Roberts Management Company with Elliot Roberts, 1970; Sold Asylum to Warner Communications, but remained President, 1971, merged it with Elektra, signed up Bob Dylan and Joni Mitchell; Vice-Chairman, Warner Bros Pictures, 1975-76; Founder, Geffen Records, President, 1980-, signed up Elton John, John Lennon and Yoko Ono and many others, sold label to Music Corporation of America Inc, 1990; Founder, Geffen Film Company, Producer: Little Shop of Horrors; Beetlejuice, 1988; Men Don't Leave; Defending Your Life; Co-producer, musical, Dreamgirls, 1981-85; Little Shop of Horrors; Cats, 1982; Madame Butterfly, 1986; Social Security; Chess, 1990; Miss Saigon; Founder, DGC record label; Co-founder, Dreamworks, SKG, 1995-. Address: Dreamworks SKG, 100 Universal Plaza, Building 477, Universal City, CA 91608, USA.

GEISELMAN Paula Jeanne, b. 30 June 1944, Ohio, USA. Physiological Psychologist. Education: AB, High Honor, Psychology, Cutler Honors Program, Ohio University, 1971; MSc, Experimental Psychology, Ohio University, 1976; PhD, Physiological Psychology, University of California, Los Angeles, USA, 1983. Appointments include: Teaching Assistant, 1981, Teaching Fellow, 1982, Department of Psychology, University of California; Assistant Professor, Assistant Research Psychologist, Department of Psychology, University of California, Los Angeles (visiting 1983-86), 1986-91; Member, Graduate College Faculty, 1991-, Associate Professor, 1991-, Department of Psychology,

Louisiana State University, Baton Rouge; Adjunct Associate Professor, Pennington Biomedical Research Center, Louisiana State University, 1991-; Adjunct Associate Professor, Stanley S Scott Cancer Center, Louisiana State University Medical Center, New Orleans, 1998; Chief, Women's Health Eating Behavior and Smoking Cessation Program, Pennington Biomedical Research Center, Louisiana State University, 2000-. Publications: 35 papers in professional journals; 5 book chapters; 112 abstracts; Developed the following assessment instruments: Geiselman Macronutrient Self-selection Paradigm (c); Geiselman Food preference Questionnaire (c). Honours: Psi Chi, 1969; Sigma Xi, 1983; Awards, fellowships include: State of Louisiana Governor's award for Commitment to Excellence in Education, 1994; Fellow, International Behavioral Neuroscience Society, 1995. Memberships include: American Association for the Advancement of Science; Society for Neuroscience; Charter Member, Women in Neuroscience; New York Academy of Sciences; Head of Physiological Psychology; American Psychological Association; Eastern Psychological Association; Charter Member: Society for Study of Ingestive Behavior; American Psychological Society; Founding Member, International Behavioral Neuroscience Society; Fellow, North American Association for the Study of Obesity, 1998-. Address: Women's Health Eating Behavior and Smoking Cessation Program, Pennington Biomedical Research Center, 6400 Perkins Road, Baton Rouge, LA 70808-4124, USA.

GENEST Christian, b. 11 January 1957, Chicoutimi, Québec, Canada. Statistician. m. Christine Simard, 2 sons, 1 daughter. Education: BSpSc, Université du Québec à Chicoutimi, 1977; MSc, Université de Montréal, 1978; PhD, University of British Columbia, 1983. Appointments: Assistant Professor, University of Waterloo, Ontario, 1984-87; Assistant Professor, 1987-89, Associate Professor, 1989-93, Full Professor, 1993-, Université Laval, Québec; Visiting Professor, numerous universities worldwide. Publications: Numerous scientific and professional articles; Editor, The Canadian Journal of Statistics, 1998-2000. Honours: Pierre-Robillard Award, 1984; Distinguished Services Award, Statistical Society of Canada, 1997; Laval University Summa Research Award, 1999; Academic Achievement Award, CRM-SSC, 1999; Fellowship, American Statistical Association, 1996; Fellowship, Institute of Mathematical Statistics, 1997. Memberships: ASA; IMS; SSC; SFdS; ASSQ; ISI; and others. Address: Département de Mathématiques et de Statistique, Université Laval, Québec, Canada G1K 7P4.

GENSLER Kinereth Dushkin, b. 17 September 1922, New York, New York, USA. Poet. Widow, 2 sons, 1 daughter. Education: BA, University of Chicago, 1943; MA, Columbia University, 1946. Appointment: Editor, Alice James Books, 1976-2001. Publications: Threesome Poems, 1976; The Poetry Connection (co-author), 1978; Without Roof, 1981; Journey Fruit, 1997. Contributions to: Anthologies, books, journals, and periodicals. Honours: Members Award, Poetry Society of America, 1969; Power Dalton Award, New England Poetry Club, 1971; Borestone Mountain Award, 1973; Residency, Ragdale, 1981; Residency, MacDowell Colony, 1982, 1983. Memberships: Academy of American Poets; Alice James Poetry Cooperative Society; Poetry Society of America. Address: 221 Mt Auburn Street, Cambridge, MA 02138, USA.

GENTSLER Gennadi Leonidovich, b. 9 April 1955, Tylinsky Uchkhoz, Novosibirsk Oblast, Russia. Civil and Environmental Engineer. 1 daughter. Education: 3 Diplomas, Sanitation Training, Novosibirsk, Russia, 1968-70; Lecturer Mastership, University, All Union "Znaniye" Society, Novosibirsk, Russia, 1970-72; Qualified Engineer, Civil Engineering Institute, Novosibirsk, 1972-77; Patent Science Engineer, Advanced Training Institute, Novosibirsk, 1977-79; Ph Dr, Postgraduate School, Civil

Engineering Institute, Novosibirsk, 1982-85. Appointments: Engineer and Senior Adjustment Engineer, Start-and-Adjustment Office for Water Supply and Sewage, Novosibirsk, 1977-80; Senior Research Engineer, Civil Engineering Institute, Novosibirsk, 1980-85; Senior Researcher, Institute of Mining, Academy of Sciences of the USSR, Novosibirsk, 1985-91; Associate Professor, Institute of Light Industry, Novosibirsk, 1988-90; Assistant General Director for Research, Research and Industrial Enterprise "MEDESO", Novosibirsk, 1991-92; General Director, 1992-98, Assistant General Director for Research, 1998- Design and Research Enterprise "SIBPROJECT", Novosibirsk; Visiting Professor, Lennox Institute of Water Technology, Massachusetts, USA, 1998-; Professor, Harbin Polytechnic Institute, China, 2001-. Publications: 159 patents, articles and brochures on water and sewage treatment; Scientific editor of 3 books; Author of the scientific theories: Flotation Purification of Natural and Sewage water, Design of the Flotation equipment and technologies, Multi-circuit protection of sewerage treatment facilities. Honours include: Exemplary Young Worker of Sanitary Defence of the USSR, 1969; Inventor of the USSR, 1981; Best Inventor of Novosibirsk Oblast, 1989; Social Project Contest Winner, Presidium of the USSR Academy of Sciences, Siberian Branch, 1990; Honorary Inventor of the Russian Federation, President of Russia, 1998; A S Popov Medal, 1998; P L Kapitsa Medal, 2000; Knight of Science and Arts, 2000; Peter the Great Medal for Achievements in Resurrecting Science and Economy of Russia, 2002; E Dashkova Medal, 2002; Archimedes Gold Medal, 2002; Honorable Medal for Virtues in Labor to the Advantage of the City of Novosibirsk commemorating its 110th Anniversary, 2003. Memberships include: All-Union Society of Inventors and Innovators; International Academy of Ecology and Nature Management; Chairman, Novosibirsk Branch, International Academy of Authors of Scientific discoveries and Inventions, 1998-; Water Online Community; New York Academy of Science; AAAS; European Academy of Natural Science. Address: Sibirskaya Street 51, kv 52, Novosibirsk 630132, Russia. E-mail: sibGN@online.nsk.su

GENZELIS Bronius, b. 16 February 1934, Trakai, Lithuania. Professor. m. Apolonija. Education: Moscow University, 1959; PhD, 1965; Docent of Vilnius University, 1969; Habil Doctor of Philosophy, 1974; Professor, 1976; Habil Doctor of Humanities Science, 1993. Appointments: Lecturer, Docent, Professor, Vilnius University, 1964-92; Member, Supreme Council of USSR, 1989-90; MP of Lithuania, 1990-96; Chairman of the Committee of Education, Science and Culture of the Parliament of Lithuania, 1992-96; Professor of Vytautas Manus University, 1997. Publications: Books: History and We, 1998; Movement of Independent of Lithuania (Sajudis): Prehistory and History, 1999; Outline of the History of Lithuanian Culture, 2001, 2002; Articles: Charges in Stereotypes, Poles Our Enemies, Poles Our Friends, 1998; The Originator of the Lithuanian National Renaissance, 1999. Address: Smelio - 10, Vilnius 2055, Lithuania.

GEORGAKOPOULOS Eleftherios, b. 13 August 1967, Mannheim, Germany. Research and Development Company Executive. Education: Molecular Biology and Genetics Diploma, University of Heidelberg, Germany, 1991; PhD, Neurosciences, Medical School, University of Heidelberg, Germany, 1995. Appointments: Lecturer, Department of Biochemistry, University of Athens, Greece, 1995-96; Director, Molecular Biology and Genetic Department, Athens Medical Centre, Greece, 1997-2001; Director, Biotechnology Department, Iatriki Techniki, Athens Greece, 2001-2003; Senior Research Scientist, Forth-Photonics, SA, Athens, Greece, 2003; Biotechnology Consultant, Gsk SA, Greece, 1999-, P N Gerolymatos S A, Athens Greece, 2000-2002, Regulon Inc, Palo Alto, California, 2001, Medican Hellas SA, Athens, Greece, 2002-; Head of Research Activities, Pegasus

Genomics SA, Athens, Greece, 2003; Founder, President, Acrongenomics Inc, Nevada, USA and Acrongenomics Hellas, Athens, Greece, 2004. Publications: Articles in scientific journals as first author and co-author include: Hepatocyte growth factor induced proliferation of primary hepatocytes is mediated by activation of phosphatidylinositol 3-kinase, 1996; A highly efficient and rapid RNA isolation procedure from formalin fixed paraffin embedded tissue for reverse transcription PCR (RT-PCR), 2003; Over 30 papers presented at congresses; 8 patents include: New method for the detection of 17-1A cancer antigen (GA 722-1 and GA 733-2) in peripheral blood and tissues and identification of metastatic cancer cells in patients with various types of cancer; New method for total ribonucleic acid isolation (total RNA) using parafinized tissues. Honours include: Grantee: GlaxoSmithKline, Novartis, P N Gorolymatos SA, Athens Medical Centre SA, Hellenic Co-operative Oncology Group; Awards from: 9th and 10th Hellenic Congresses of Clinical Oncology, 2000, 2001, European Association of Medical Oncology, 2000; Minister of Development and the Organisation of Industrial Property, 2002. Memberships: Hellenic Association for HIV Research; Hellenic Medical Association for Neuroscience; Hellenic Association of Molecular Biology; New York Academy of Sciences; American Association for Advancement Research. Address: Acrongenomics Hellas SA, 38A Posidonos Avenue, Alimos, Athens 17544, Greece. E-mail: egeorgeak@acn.gr

GEORGE John Caleekal, b. 16 June 1921, Peermade, India. University Professor. m. Molly Achamma, 2 sons, 1 daughter. Education: BSc, 1942, PhD, 1948, University of Bombay. Appointments: Demonstrator, Ismail Yusuf College, 1945-48; Lecturer, Institute of Science, Bombay, 1948; Zoologist, Department of Anthropology, Government of India Ministry of Education, 1948-50; Reader, Founding Head, M.S. University, Baroda, 1950-56; Professor, Head, 1957-67; Professor, University of Guelph, Canada, 1967-86; Acting Chairman, Department of Zoology, 1974; University Professor Emeritus, University of Guelph, 1986-. Publications: Avian Myology; 12 Book Chapters; 400 Research Papers. Honours: Sohoni Prize for Biology, 1942; Fulbright And Smith-Mundt Fellowship, 1953-54; Dutch Government Research Scholarship, 1958; Dorabji Tata Travel Grant, 1958; Fulbright Senior Scholarship, 1961-62; Guelph Sigma Xi; Award for Excellence in Research, 1979; Award For Outstanding Academic Achievement, (FOKANA) 1990; Award for Lifetime Contributions to Comparative Endocrinology, Society for Reproductive Biology and Comparative Endocrinology, 2001. Memberships: Fellow, New York Academy of Sciences; Sigma Xi, The Research Society. Address: 87 Harvard Road, Guelph ONT N1G 2X9, Canada.

GEORGE John Valiyaveetil, b. 6 March 1934, Mayvelloor, Kerala, India. Senior Physician in Medicine. m. Ammu George. 1 son, 2 daughters. Education: Bachelor of Medicine and Surgery, 1957, MD in General Medicine, 1967, Medical College Trivandrum, Kerala, India. Appointments: Medical Officer of Health Services of Kerala, 1960-75; Civil Surgeon 1975-81; Deputed as Physician, Department of Health, Republic of Zambia, 1981-84; District Medical Officer and Deputy Director of Health Services, Kerala State, 1984-85; Since 1985, Consultant Physician in Private Hospitals. Publications: Novel, Mary Magdalene Orphanage, in which Life, Evolution and Big Bang discussed, under consideration for publication; Published Malayalam Novel, Hindustan Robot, the International Leader. Honours: PNAM Prize for Ophthalmology for getting the highest marks in the University; Doctor of the Millennium Award, 2000; Bharat Jyoti Award from India International Friendship Society, New Delhi. Membership: Life Member of Indian Medical Association. Address: 373/VIII Valiyaveetil House, Pathanamthitta, 689645 Kerala, India.

GEORGE Patricia, b. 21 February 1947, USA. Professional Artist. m. Edward P George Jr, 2 daughters. Education: BA, University of California, Los Angeles. Career: Professional Performer and Oil Painter, major Motion Picture Studios and TV Studios; Teacher, Los Angeles City School District; Chair, Dance Department; Directed Educational Program CBS-TV; Paintings in private collections in USA, France, Greece, Japan, Panama, United Arab Republic, Canada, Cayman Islands; Works in corporate collections include: Hilton Hotels, Long Beach, California; J C Penny Business Systems, Dallas, Texas; Instar Corporation, Montgomery, Alabama; Faulding Inc, Australia Numerous solo and group exhibitions include most recently: International Art Exhibition in conjunction with the Festival of Paris, Paris, France, 1999; Chosen as one of the artists to create paintings for the 20th Anniversary of the White House. Honours: Prize of Honor, Museum Paul Dumail, Tonniens, France, 1989; Laureate Award, Vieux de la Colombier, Paris, France, 1990; Cover Winner, Manhattan Arts Magazine, New York, 1993; Award of Excellence, Sixth Annual Manhattan Arts International Competition, 1997; Grand Cordon of the Templars, International Exhibition, Museum of Sapporo, Japan, 1997; Grand Award, International Art Exhibition, Paris, France, 1999. Address: 4141 Ball Road Studio 221, Cypress, CA 90630, USA.

GEORGE Victor André Gilles Joseph, b. 27 October 1937, Bois-et-Borsu, Belgium. Teacher; Poet. Publications: Adju K'pagnon, 1963; Gris Pwin, 1965; In Paradisum, 1978; Rècinèyes, 1979; Totes lès-Ameûrs dè Monde, 1983; Tchonson d'â ci qu'a passé l'Baye. Contributions to: Les Cahiers Wallons; La Vie Wallonne; Dialectes de Wallonie. Honours: Prix des Critiques Wallons, 1963; Prix Biennal de la Ville de Liège, 1965; Prix Durbuy, Huy, 1966; Prix Michaux, Namur, 1978; Prix du Ministere de la Communauté Française, 1982. Memberships: Secretary, Société de Langue et de Litterature Wallonnes, Liège; Vice Président, Rèlis Namurwès, Namur. Address: Tièr Laurent 6, B-4560 Bois-et-Borsu, Belgium.

GEORGESCU Adelina, b. 24 April 1942, Turnu Severin, Romania. Mathematician; Professor. 2 sons. Education: MSc, Faculty of Mathematics and Mechanics, Department of Fluid Mechanics, 1965; PhD, Institute of Mathematics, Bucharest, 1970. Appointments: Researcher, Institute of Fluid Mechanics and Aerospace Constructions, Bucharest, Romania, 1965-70; Researcher, Institute of Mathematics, Bucharest, 1970-75; Main Research Worker, Institute of Fluid Mechanics and Aerospace Constructions, 1975-90, Main Researcher, Institute of Mathematics, 1990-91; Senior Researcher, 1991-97, Director, 1991-95, Institute of Applied Mathematics of the Romanian Academy, Bucharest; Professor, 1997-, Chair of Applied Mathematics, 2000-, University of Pitezti, Romania. Publications: 15 research books include: Hydrodynamic stability theory, 1985; Asymptotic treatment of differential equations, 1995; FitzHugh-Nagumo model: bifurcation and dynamics, 2000; Other books concern: bifurcation theory, synergetics, fluid dynamics, asymptotics; 181 scientific papers published in mathematical journals; 37 articles published in proceedings of scientific meetings (congresses, conferences, workshops). Honours: Romanian Academy Prize, 1976; Listed in Who's Who publications and biographical dictionaries. Memberships: American Mathematical Society; Gesellschaft für Angewandte Mathematik und Mechanik; EUROMECH; Society for Mathematician Sciences from Romania; Founder, President, 1993, Romanian Society of Applied and Industrial Mathematics. Address: Str Baneasa 2-6, bl 7/1, sc 3, et 1, ap 33, 012953 Bucharest, Romania. E-mail: adelinageorgescu@yahoo.com

Dictionary of International Biography

GEORGIEV Evgenii Velinov, b. 5 February 1929, Sofia, Bulgaria. Lecturer. Education: Higher Agricultural Institute, 1946-51; PhD, Agronomy, 1956; DSci, Technics, 1989. Appointments: Assistant, 1957-58, Senior Assistant, 1958-60 Higher Agricultural Institute, Plovdiv, Bulgaria; Senior Assistant, 1960-71, Associate Professor, 1971-90, Professor, 1990-94; Retired, 1994, Department of Fatty and Essential Oils Technology, Higher Institute of Food and Flavour Industries, Plovdiv, Bulgaria. Publications: 156 science articles; 4 text books; 3 manuals; Handbook for specialists in the aromatic and cosmetics industries; Bibliography on Bulgarian Essential Oils. Honours: Honorary Diploma for important contributions to the Bulgarian aromatic products industry, 1985; Honourable Inventor, 1986. Memberships: Union of Bulgarian Scientists; Bulgarian Federation of Scientific and Technical Unions: Union of Inventors, Union of Chemists in Bulgaria; Science Council on Food and Flavour Products Technology. Address: Str Vassil Drumev No 1, 4000 Plovdiv, Bulgaria.

GEORGIEV Tchavdar, b. 19 December 1945, Sofia, Bulgaria. Physician; Pathologist. m. Lylia Dimitrova (Arnaudova) Georgieva. Education: MD, 1971, PhD, 1971-77, MSci, 1977-78, DSc, 1978-88, Medical Faculty, Sofia, Bulgaria; MSc; Diploma for Medical Speciality. Appointments: Assistant Professor, 1971-74, 1977-79, Research Assistant, 1979-81, Senior Assistant Professor, Head Assistant Professor, 1981-97, Associate Professor, 1997-2003, Department of Pathology, Sofia, Bulgaria. Publications: Books: Annales d'Endocrinologie, 1978; Prolactinomas, 1985; Pituitary Adenomas, 1987; Akush i Genekol, 1991; Citologia, 1992; Textbook, Textbook of Clinical Endocrinology, 1981; Numerous articles in professional medical journals. Honour: National Book Prize, 1988. Memberships: New York Academy of Science; European Society of Pathology; Bulgarian Society of Pathology; Bulgarian Scientific Society; Bulgarian Academy of Sciences. Address: Department of Pathology, Medical Faculty, Blv 6 Sofiiski No 1, Sofia 1431, Bulgaria. E-mail: chavdar_georgiev@hotmail.com

GEORGIEV Viden, b. 1 February 1925, Gintsi, Sofia Region, Bulgaria. Physician. m. Elena Kisselkova, 1 son, 1 daughter. Education: Doctor of Medicine, Medical University, Sofia, Bulgaria, 1954; Doctor of Philosophy, Institute of Experimental Medicine, Saint Petersburg, Russia, 1962. Appointments: Assistant, 1955-58, Senior Assistant, 1959-63, Associate Professor, 1967-75, Professor of Physiology, 1975-, National Sports Academy, Sofia, Bulgaria; Researcher, Sorbonne, Paris, France, 1964-66. Publications: Author: Proprioceptors and Circulation, (monograph), 1965; Vascular Reactions in Sportsmen after Physical Efforts (monograph), 1973; Nervous System and Sport (book), 1975; Peripheral and Brain Circulation at Physical Efforts (monograph), 1991. Memberships: Bulgarian Society of Physiological Sciences; Bulgarian Society of Sports Medicine; New York Academy of Sciences. Address: 14 Tsar Peter Street, Sofia 1463, Bulgaria.

GER Yeong-Kuang, b. 27 November 1954, Taiwan, Republic of China. Professor. m. Doris Che, 2 sons. Education: BA, 1978, MA, Department of Political Science, 1980, National Taiwan University; MA, 1981, PhD, 1985, Department of Political Science, University of Wisconsin-Madison, USA. Appointments: Member, Supervisory Board, China Youth Corps; Honorary President, Hong Kong Research Centre of Relations Across Taiwan Straight; Vice-Chairman, International Young Democrat Union; Secretary General, World League for Freedom and Democracy, Republic of China Chapter; Professor, Department of Political Science National Taiwan University. Publications: Cultural Pluralism and National Integration, 1991; Party Politics and Democratic Development, 1996; The Story of Taiwan: Politics, 1998; Chinese Democracy: The Taiwan Model; Political Change and Political Development:

The Taiwan Experience; Over 50 published or conference papers and articles. Honours: Dr Sun Yat-Sen Scholarship Award, 1980-82; Ten Outstanding Young Persons Award, 1993; Research Award, National Science Commission, 1992, 1995, 1996, 1997; Listed in Who's Who publications and biographical dictionaries. Memberships: Phi Tau Phi Scholastic Honour Society; Chinese Political Science Association; National Professors Association; President, The Mirror Society. Address: World League for Freedom and Democracy, ROC Chapter, 10th Fl. No 7 Roosevelt Road, Sec 1, Taipei, Taiwan, China. yger@ms34.hinet.net

GERASSIMOVA Ludmila Efimovna, b. 11 January 1938, Voronezh, Russia. Philologist. m. Vsevolod Borisovich Gerassimov, 1 daughter. Education: Philologist, 1960, PhD, Associate Professor, 1965, Saratov State University; Full Professor, 1998. Appointments: Senior Lecturer, 1965, Associate Professor, 1979, Full Professor, 1998, Saratov State University. Publications: Books: Ideological Novel: Conflicts and Characters, 1970; Our Contemporary in the Prose of 1970's, 1977; Russian Literature of 20th Century 1960-1990, 1998; Articles include: Polydiscourse in the novel Doctor Zhivago, 2000. Honour: Certificate of Honour on creative activity on the theory of literary criticism, Russian Academy of Science and Humanities. Address: Sobornaya 15, Kv 35, Saratov 410028, Russia.

GERDNER Linda A, b. 17 September 1955, Burlington, Iowa, USA. Nurse Researcher; Educator. Education: BSN, Iowa Wesleyan College, Mount Pleasant, Iowa, 1980; MA, Nursing, 1992, PhD, Nursing and Aging, 1998, University of Iowa College of Nursing, Iowa City, Iowa. Appointments: Clinical Nursing Instructor, Iowa Wesleyan College, 1981-83; Clinical Nursing Instructor, Southeastern Community College, Keokuk, Iowa, 1983-85; Staff Development Co-ordinator, Elm View Care Centre, Burlington, Iowa, 1985-89; Teaching Assistant, 1989-92, Research Assistant, 1991-93 The University of Iowa College of Nursing; Nursing Instructor, Grand View College, Division of Nursing, Des Moines, Iowa, 1992-93; Instructor, Department of Psychiatry and Behavioral Sciences, University of Arkansas for Medical Sciences, Little Rock, Arkansas, 1998-2000; Postdoctoral Fellow, Veteran's Affairs Medical Center, Division of Health Services Research and Development, Little Rock, Arkansas, 1998-2000; Assistant Professor, University of Minnesota School of Nursing, Minneapolis, Minnesota, 2001-. Publications: More than 40 publications with a research and scholarly focus on the management of problematic behaviours in persons with Alzheimer's Disease and related disorders and family care giving issues; Numerous conference and seminar presentations. Honours: Best Graduate Student Paper Award, 1993, 1994; Sigma Theta Tau Best of Image Award in the area of Clinical Excellence, 1997; Dissertation Research Award, American Society on Aging 45th Annual Meeting, 1999; International Psychogeriatric Association, Bayer Research Award, 1999. Memberships: Sigma Theta Tau International 1992-; American Nurses' Association/Iowa Nurses' Association, 1992-98; Midwest Nursing Research Society, 1993- Mid-American Congress on Aging, 1994-95; Gerontological Society of America, 1998- International Psychogeriatric Association, 1999-; Council on Nursing and Anthropology, 2000-; Affiliate member, American Association for Geriatric Psychiatry, 2001-. Address: University of Minnesota School of Nursing, 6-101 Weaver-Densford Hall, 308 Harvard Street, SE, Minneapolis, MN 55455-0342, USA. E-mail: gerdn001@umn.edu

GERE Richard, b. 31 August 1949. Actor. m. Cindy Crawford, 1991, divorced. Education: University of Massachusetts. Career: Formerly played trumpet, piano, guitar and bass and composed music with various groups; Stage performances with Provincetown Playhouse and Off-Broadway; Appeared in London and Broadway productions of The Taming of the Shrew, A Midsummer Night's Dream and Broadway productions of Habeas Corpus and Bent; Founding Chairman and President, Tibet House, New York; Actor, films include: Report to the Commissioner, 1975; Baby Blue Marine, 1976; Looking for Mr Goodbar, 1977; Days of Heaven, 1978; Blood Brothers, 1978; Yanks, 1979; American Gigolo, 1980; An Officer and a Gentleman, 1982; Breathless, 1983; Beyond the Limit, 1983; The Cotton Club, 1984; King David, 1985; Power, 1986; No Mercy, 1986; Miles From Home, 1989; 3000, 1989; Internal Affairs, 1990; Pretty Woman, 1990; Rhapsody in August, 1991; Sommersby (co-executive, producer), 1993; Mr Jones (co-exec producer), 1994; Intersection, 1994; First Knight, 1995; Primal Fear, 1996; Red Coirner, 1997; Burn Hollywood Burn, 1998; Runaway Bride, 1999; Dr T and the Women, 2000; Autumn in New York, 2000; The Mothman Prophecies, 2002; Unfaithful, 2002; Chicago, 2002. Publication: Pilgrim Photo Collection, 1998.

GERGELY Aniko Eva, b. 31 January 1938, Budapest, Hungary. Editor; Translator, m. Illes Desi, 5 August 1962, 2 sons. Education: MA, University of Eötvös Lorand, Budapest, 1963. Appointments: Editor, Kossuth Publishing House, 1963-80; Editor-in-Chief, Nök Magazinja, 1980-89; Publisher, Editor-in-Chief, 1989-92; Editor, Vince Books, 1993-. Publications: Ungarische Spezialitäten; Several translations. Membership: Association of Hungarian Journalists. Address: Lagymanyosi U 13, Budapest, Hungary.

GERKE MENDIETA Carlos, b. 15 April 1942, Sucre, Bolivia. Lawyer. m. Marcia Siles, 1 son, 2 daughters. Education: Licenciado en Derecho, Political and Social Sciences, 1967; Lawyer, 1967. Appointments: Private Practice; University Professor, Commercial Law, Civil Law. President, La Paz Bar; Member, Andean Judiciary Committee; Member, Advisory Committee of the Bolivian Foreign Office; National President, Bolivian Catholic University. Publications: New Law of Administrative Procedure in Bolivia, 2002; Intellectual Property Law under Bolivian Law; Domicile in the Bolivian Civil Code. Honours: Diploma and Gold Medal, Best Student of Law School; Knight of the Order of Saint Gregorius Magnus, awarded by Pope John Paul II. Memberships: Member of the Honour Council, Andean Judiciary Committee; Order of Saint Gregorius Magnus; Bolivian Genealogy Society; Bolivian Philately Society. Address: PO Box 14606, La Paz, Bolivia.

GERMAIN Alain, b. 16 February 1948, Carentan, France. Stage Director; Choreographer. Education, CAFAS, 1968; Diplôme d'état de l'École nationale superieure des Arts décoratifs de Paris, 1970; Diplôme d'état de l'École nationale superieure des Beaux Arts de Paris, 1973; Diplôme de danse contemporaine. Appointments: Creation de la compagnie Alain Germain, Paris, 1972. Honours: Fondation de la Vocation, 1978. Publications: Le Tour du monde en 80 langues, 1995; Les origines de l'Homme, 1997; La Ville Invisible, 1999; Les Grenouilles de Saint-Pierre, 2001; L'Affaire Callas, 2002; Alain Germain: mémoires de seine, 2003; Meurtre à la française, 2004; Various articles on art, theatre, dance and costumes. Membership: Societe authors compositeurs. Address: 29 Rue de Paradis, 75010 Paris, France. E-mail: compagnie@alaingermain.com Website: www.alaingermain.com

GERRISH Brian Albert, b. 14 August 1931, London, England. Theologian; Writer. m. (1) 1 son, 1 daughter, (2) Dawn Ann De Vries, 3 August 1990, 1 daughter. Education: BA, 1952, MA, 1956, Queens' College, Cambridge; STM, Union Theological Seminary, New York City, 1956; PhD, Columbia University, 1958. Appointments: Associate Professor, 1965-68, Professor, 1968-85, John Nuveen Professor, 1985-96, John Nureen Professor Emeritus, 1996-, Divinity School, University of Chicago; Co-Editor, Journal of Religion, 1972-85; Distinguished Service Professor of Theology, Union Theological Seminary, Virginia, 1996-2002. Publications:

Grace and Reason: A Study in the Theology of Luther, 1962, Japanese translation, 1974, reprint, 1979; Tradition and the Modern World: Reformed Theology in the Nineteenth Century, 1978; The Old Protestantism and the New: Essays on the Reformation Heritage, 1982; A Prince of the Church: Schleiermacher and the Beginnings of Modern Theology, 1984, Korean translation, 1988, reprint, 2001; Grace and Gratitude: The Eucharistic Theology of John Calvin, 1993, reprint, 2002; Continuing the Reformation: Essays on Modern Religious Thought, 1993; Saving and Secular Faith: An Invitation to Systematic Theology, 1999; The Pilgrim Road: Sermons on Christian Life, 2000. Editor: The Faith of Christendom: A Source Book of Creeds and Confessions, 1963; Reformers in Profile, 1967; Reformatio Perennis: Essays on Calvin and the Reformation in Honor of Ford Lewis Battles, 1981; Reformed Theology for the Third Christian Millennium: The 2001 Sprunt Lectures, 2003. Honours: Guggenheim Foundation Fellowship, 1970; Honorary Doctorate, University of St Andrew's, Scotland, 1984. Memberships include: Fellow, American Academy of Arts and Sciences. Address: 9142 Sycamore Hill Place, Mechanicsville, VA 23116, USA.

GERSTER Richard, b. 29 May 1946, Winterthur, Switzerland. Economist. m. Doris Gerster, 1 son, 2 daughters. Education: PhD Econ, University of St Gall, Switzerland, 1973. Appointments: Programme Co-ordinator, Helvetas, 1972-81; Director, Swiss Coalition of Development Organisations, 1981-98; Director, Gerster Consulting (www.gersterconsulting.ch), for public policy and international development, 1998-. Publications: Switzerland as a Developing Country, 1998; Alternative Approaches to Poverty Reduction Strategies (SDC working paper), 2000; Patents and Development, Third World Network, 2001; Globalisation and Justice, 2001. Honour: Christoph Eckenstein Award for the Relations Switzerland-Third World, 1987; Blue Planet Award, 2002. Memberships: Member of Parliament in the Canton of Zürich, 1987-92; Member, Governing Board of State Bank of Zürich, 1988-2003; Member, Development Advisory Council to the Government of Austria, 2000-. Address: Goeldistr 1, CH-8805 Richterswil, Switzerland.

GEVE Thomas, b. 1929, Germany. Engineer; Writer. m. 1963, 1 son, 2 daughters. Education: National Diploma of Building, 1950; BSc, 1957. Publications: Youth in Chains, 1958, enlarged edition, 1981; Guns and Barbed Wire, 1987; There Are No Children Here, 1997; Nichts als das Leben, film, 1997; Aufbrüche, 2000. USA. Address: PO Box 4727, Haifa, Israel.

GEVORKYAN Elmira, b. 1 February 1932, Yerevan, Armenia. Neurologist; Professor. m. Pavel Ananikyan, 1 son, 1 daughter. Education: General Practitioner, Diploma, Yerevan Medical State University, 1949-55; Neurology residentship, Moscow Burdensko Neurosurgical Institute, 1959-63; Candidate of Medical Science, 1963; Doctor of Medical Science, 1972; Professor of Neurology, 1976. Appointments: Practical work of medical doctor in Armenia, 1955-59; Assistant Professor, 1963-69, Associated professor, 1969-76, Professor of Neurology, 1976, Head of the Neurology Chair of Yerevan State Medical University, 1976-96; Head of Armenian Neurological Association, 1986-; Head Neurologist of Armenia, 1974-2003. Publications: Over 200 articles in medical journals, monographs and books. Memberships: New York Academy, 1995-; Deputy Director, IBRO, Armenian Branch, 1996-; International Biological Academy, 1997-; International Ecology Academy, 1998-; Russian Academy of Medical-Technical Science, 2001-; Armenian Surgical Academy, 2001-. Address: 375002, Mashtots Str, 21, Apt 16, Yerevan, Armenia. E-mail: agevorkyan@yahoo.com

Dictionary of International Biography

GEYSEN Willy Josef, b. 19 March 1939, Overpelt, Belgium. Electrical and Mechanical Engineer. m. Maria V Thijs, 17 July 1968. Education: MS, Electro-Mechanical Engineering, 1967, PhD, 1970, Electro-Mechanical Engineering, Katholieke Universiteit Leuven, Belgium; LLM, State Jury, Belgium, 1980. Appointments: Teacher, Technical High School, Belgium; Associate Professor, 1969-75, Professor, 1975-2001, Professor Emeritus, 2001-, Katholieke Universiteit Leuven, Belgium; Spokesperson, Director External Relations, 1990-95; Senior Advisor to the Rector on External Affairs, 1995-; Advisor to labour and insurance industries, Belgium, 1975-; Forensic expert (fire and explosions), Belgium, 1975-. Publications: Numerous books (in Dutch) and international papers. Address: Jachtlaan 26, B-3001 Leuven, Belgium. E-mail: willy.geysen@rec.kuleuven.ac.be

GHAFOOR Abdul, b. 10 February 1928, Mansehra, Pakistan. m. Tahera, 1 son, 1 daughter, deceased. Education: BA, Honours, Urdu Language and Literature, 1955; PhD, Honours, Engineering, USA, 1995. Appointments: Lt Colonel and Acting Brigadier, Engineer Corps, Pakistan Army, 1952-77; Chief Engineer, Government of Punjab, Provincial Government of Pakistan, 1977-79; Director of Works and Chief Engineer, Private Limited Construction Company, 1979-81; General Manager and Chief Engineer, Saudi Development Company, Jeddah, 1981-82; Chief Resident Engineer, private Consulting Engineers firm, Pakistan, 1982-85; Project Director, Riyadh, Saudi Arabia consultant engineers company, 1985-86; Chief Engineer, consulting engineers firm, Pakistan, 1987; Chief Engineer, construction company, Pakistan, 1988-90; Director of Works in Pakistan, private trading and finance company, 1990; Chairman, Chief Executive, Private Ltd Consulting Engineers, 1990-98; Director General Al-Beruni Group for Education, 1998-. Publications: Anne Frank – Diary of a Young Girl, Urdu Edition; Silver Spoon Guide for Quality English Writing; Numerous articles in professional magazines and newspapers. Honours: Several medals and letters of appreciation. Memberships: Life Fellow, American Society of Civil Engineers, USA; Fellow, Institution of Engineers, Pakistan, Structure Institute of Engineers, USA; PE of Pakistan Engineering Council; Member, Advisory Council, IBC; Deputy Governor, ABIRA, USA. Address: House no 36, Street 5, F-8/3, Islamabad, Pakistan.

GHANEM Shihab Muhammad Abduh, b. 16 October 1940, Aden. Engineer; Economist; Poet; Translator. m. Jihad Ali Luqman, 2 sons, 1 daughter. Education: BSc, Mechanical Engineering, 1963, BSc, Electrical Engineering, 1964, Aberdeen; PG Diploma, Water Resources Engineering, 1970, ME, Water Resources Development, 1975, Roorkee University; PhD, Economics, Industrialization, 1989, University of Wales, Cardiff. Appointments: Deputy Permanent Secretary and Director of Planning, Ministry of Public Works and Communications, Aden, 1966-72; Chief Engineer, Eterno Supplies, Lebanon, 1972-74; Plant Manager, Gulf Eternit, Dubai, 1974-85; Director of Engineering of Dubai Ports Authority and Jebel Ali Freezone, 1988-2000; Adviser and Director, Research and Development of Ports, Customs and Free Zone Corporation, Dubai, 2000-02; Managing Director, Mohammed Bin Rashid Technology Park, 2002-. Publications: 8 books of Arabic Verse; 5 books of English translations of Arabic Verse; 1 book on Industrialization in United Arab Emirates; 9 other books; Various articles in journals. Honours: Ministry of Education Prize for Arabic Essay, Aden, 1958; Lake Prize for English Essay, Aden, 1960; 1st Prize for Poetry, United Arab Emirates, 1993; Rashed Prize for Excellence, Dubai, 1989; IBHA Club Prize for Poetry, Saudi Arabia, 1996; Kirali Kala Kendram Honour for Literature, 1996; Alowais Prize for Research, 1999; Various scholarships. Memberships: F.I. Mech.E. (UK); M.I.E.E. (UK); C.Eng (UK); F.C.M.I; Society of Engineers (UAE), IAIA (USA). Address: PO Box 11613, Dubai, United Arab Emirates. E-mail: smaghanem@yahoo.com

GHATAK Kamakhya Prasad, b. 13 October 1953, Calcutta, India. Teacher. m. Sukla Ghatak, 1 daughter. Education: BE, Electronics and Telecommunication Engineering, Calcutta University, 1974; MTech, Radio Physics and Electronics, 1976; PhD, Technology, 1988; Doctor of Engineering, Jadavpur University, 1991 (first recipient since inception of University in 1955). Appointments: Lecturer, Radio Physics and Electronics, 1983-87; Reader, ETCE Department, Jadavpur University, 1988-93; Full Professor, Department of Electronic Science, Calcutta University, 1994-; Dictionary of International Biography; Man of the Year, ABI, 1998-. Publications: Principal co-author of more than 400 research papers on semiconductor science in international journals; More than 100 papers at conferences world-wide; Supervised 15 PhD candidates and 25 BE, MTech, MSc Theses. Honours: Indian National Science Academy Award; Invited Speaker, SPIE, USA. Memberships: FIE; FIETE; FNAS. Address: 91 Amherst Street, Calcutta 700009, India.

GHEORGHE Calcan, b. 16 April 1956, Săgeata, Buzău, Romania. Professor. m. Grațiela Georgeta Calcan, 1 son. Education: History-Philosophy Faculty, Al.I.Cuza, University, Iași, 1976-80; Doctorate, Al.I.Cuza University, Iași, 1990-95. Appointments: Professor of History, Philosophy, History of Art, History of Religions, Practical Technology High School No 6, Ploiești, 1980-90; National College, Mihai Viteazul, Ploiești, 1991-2002; Professor, History, Oil and Gas University, Ploiești. Publications: 4 books; Over 80 studies, articles, reviews about the history of Romanian oil and international recognition of the Alliance achieved by the Romanian people in 1918. Honours: Doctor of Historical Sciences; Headmaster National College, Mihai Viteazul, Ploiești; Chevalier des Palmes Academiques; 1st prize, Session of Scientific Communications, Iași, 1979; 1st prize country, Session of pupils scientific communication (co-ordinator), 1987, 1996. Memberships: Vice President, Scientific Foundation (FOSP); Historical Studies Society Prahova; Vice President, Association Cult of the Heroes; Archivist Society; Friends of the Archivists, Prahova, Address: 2C Bulevardul, București, Bl 15C, ap 42, Ploiești 2000, Romania. E-mail: calcan@xnet.ro

GHORASHI Mehrdaad, b. 2 February 1964, Tehran, Iran. Mechanical Engineer; Researcher; Consultant; Educator. m. Marjaneh Nikpour Rahmatabadi, 1 son, 1 daughter. Education: BSc, Mechanical Engineering (ME), 1987; MSc, ME, 1989; PhD, ME, 1994; MSc, Economic and Social Systems Engineering, 1998. Appointments: Consultant, Indamine Co, Tehran, 1999-2000; Manager, Quality Control Department, Indamine Co, Tehran, 1989-90; Manager, Research and Development Department, Mazda Co, Tehran, 1990-94; Assistant Professor of ME, 1995-2001, Associate Professor, 2001-, Chairman of the Naval Engineering Division, 1996-98, Vice-President of Research, Mechanical Engineering Department, 2000-2001, Vice President of Education, 2001-2002, Mechanical Engineering Department, Sharif University of Technology; Member, Higher Education Planning Council, Tehran, 1996-1998; Visiting Professor, Mechanical Engineering Department, Virginia Tech, USA, 2002-2003. Publications: 19 papers in professional journals and 19 papers in international conferences. Honours: Awards, Minister of Road and Transport, Minister of Education and Training and President of Sharif University, all for graduation as the first PhD in Mechanical Engineering in Iran, 1994; University Distinguished Professor, 1998. Membership: American Society of Mechanical Engineers (ASME), 1997-. Address: Mechanical Engineering Department, Sharif University of Technology, Tehran, PO Box 11365-9567, Iran. E-mail:ghorashi@sharif.edu Website: http://sina.sharif.edu/~ghorashi

Dictionary of International Biography

GHOSH Supriya Ranjan, b. 4 August 1947, Kolkata, Bengal, India. Government Executive. m. Juthika Ghosh, 1 daughter. Education: Bachelor of Arts; Diploma in Mass Communication. Appointment: Assistant Director, Food and Supplies Department, Government of Bengal, Khadya Bhavan Kolkata, India. Publications: Published poems in literary magazines and poetry journals in English; Film journalism in reputed cine club magazines. Membership: Cine Central, Kolkata. Address: 3/C Sanatan Seal Lane, Bowbazar, Kolkata-700012, Bengal, India.

GHUBASH Rafia Obaid, b. 13 November 1956, Dubai. University President. Education: MB, BCh, Cairo University, Cairo, Egypt, 1983; Diploma in Child and Adolescent Psychiatry, 1988, Diploma in Psychiatry, 1988, Board Certification in Psychiatry, 1990, Institute of Psychiatry, University of London, England; Certification in Epidemiology and Medical Statistics, London School of Hygiene and Tropical Medicine, London, England, 1990; PhD, Community and Epidemiological Psychiatry, University of London, England, 1992; Arab Board Certificate in Psychiatry, 1997. Appointments: Internship, Rashid Hospital, Dubai, 1983-85; Teaching Assistant, Faculty of Medicine and Health Sciences, United Arab Emirates University, 1985; Clinical Associate, Maudsley and Bethlem Hospitals, Institute of Psychiatry, University of London, 1985-88; PhD Fieldwork in Dubai, 1988-91; Clinical Assistant, Maudsley Hospital, London, 1992; Assistant Professor of Psychiatry, 1992-2000, Assistant Dean for Female Student Affairs, 1993, Vice Dean 1999, Dean, 2000, Faculty of Medicine and Health Sciences, 1999; Associate Professor of Psychiatry, 2000, Faculty of Medicine and Health Sciences, United Arab Emirates University; President, Arabian Gulf University, Bahrain, 2001-. Publications: Books: Medicine in the United Arab Emirates, Origin and Development, 1997; Sad Letters, A study of depression among the Arab population, 1998; 25 articles as first author and co-author in scientific medical journals. Honours include: Scholarship to Cairo University, Government of United Arab Emirates, 1976-82; Rashid Award for Scientific Excellence, 1988, 1992; Al Awis 1st Prize for Research, 1994, 1995; Award of Education for Research, Datamatix, United Arab Emirates, 2002; Memberships include: Emirates Medical Association, 1983-; Fellow, Royal College of Medicine, 1989-91; General Medical Council, UK, 1997-; Bahrain Centre for Studies and Research Trustees Council. Address: Arabian Gulf University, PO Box 26671, Adlya, Kingdom of Bahrain. E-mail: rafia@agu.edu.bh

GIACCONI Riccardo, b. 6 October 1931, Genoa, Italy (US Citizen). Astrophysicist. m. Mirella Manaira, 1957, 1 son, 2 daughters. Education: Doctorate, University of Milan, 1954. Appointments: Assistant Professor of Physics, University of Milan, 1954-56; Research Associate, Indiana University, 1956-58; Research Associate, Princeton University, 1958-59; American Science and Engineering Inc, 1958-73; Associate, Harvard College Observatory, 1970-72; Associate Director, Center for Astrophysics, 1973-81; Professor of Astrophysics, Harvard University, 1973-81; Professor of Astrophysics, 1981-99, Research Professor, 1999-, Johns Hopkins University; Director, Space Telescope Science Institute, Baltimore, 1981-92; Professor of Astrophysics, Milan University, Italy, 1991-99; Director General, European Southern Observatory, Garching, Germany, 1993-99; President, Associated Universities Inc, 1999-; Carried out fundamental investigations in the development of x-ray astronomy. Publications X-Ray Astronomy (co-editor), 1974; Physics and Astrophysics of Neutron Stars and Black Holes (co-editor), 1978; A Face of Extremes; The X-ray Universe (co-editor), 1985; Numerous articles in professional journals. Honours: Space Science Award, AIAA, 1976; NASA Medal for Exceptional Scientific Achievement, 1980; Gold Medal, Royal Astronomical Society, 1982; A Cressy Morrison Award in Natural Sciences, New York Academy of

Sciences, 1982; Wolf Prize, 1987; Laurea hc in Physics, Rome, 1998; Nobel Prize in Physics, 2002; Numerous other awards. Memberships: American Academy of Arts and Sciences; American Astronomical Society; American Physical Society; Italian Physical Society; International Astronomical Union; Max Planck Society; Foreign member, Accademia Nazionale dei Lincei. Address: Associated Universities Inc, 1400 16th Street, NW, Suite 730, Washington, DC 20036, USA.

GIACOMARRA Mario Gandolfo, b. 1 November 1949, Castellana Sicula, Italy. University Professor. m. Maria Nicoletta Cappello, 2 daughters. Education: BA, Foreign Languages and Literatures, 1972. Appointments: Assistant, Cultural Anthropology, 1975-86, Associate Professor, 1986-2001, Chief Professor, 2001-, Sociology of Communication, University of Palermo, Faculty of Letters. Publications: 4 articles in professional journals. Honours: Director, Socioanthropological Institute, 1998-2000; Director, Social Services Course, 1999-2002. Memberships: Counsellor, Italian Association of Sociology; Counsellor, Sicilian Association of Semiotics. Address: Faculty of Letters and Philosophy, Viale Delle Scienze, 90218 Palermo, Italy. E-mail: giacomarra@unipa.it

GIANNINI David, b. 19 March 1948, USA. Poet. Publications: Opens, 1970; Stories, poems, 1974; Fourfield, 1976; Close Packet, 1978; Three, 1978; Stem, 1982; Antonio and Clara, 1992; Keys, 1992; Fist, 1997; Others; Lines, 1997; Arizona Notes, 1998; RIM, 1998. Contributions to: Sonora Review; Longhouse; Shadowplay; Tel-Let; Talisman; Room; George Mason Review; Shearsman, Malaysia; MJP, Canada. Honours: Osa and Lee Mays Award for Poetry, 1970; Massachusetts Artists Foundation Fellowship Award, 1990; University of Florida Award, 1991. Address: PO Box 630, Otis, MA 01253, USA.

GIBB Barry, b. 1 September 1947, Isle of Man, emigrated to Australia, 1958, returned to UK, 1967. Singer and Songwriter. m. Linda Gray, 4 children. Career: Formed Bee Gees with brothers Robin and the late Maurice and Andy. Publications: Albums with BeeGees include: Bee Gees 1st; Odessa; Main Course; Children of the World; Saturday Night Fever; Spirits Having Flown; High Civilisation; Size Isn't Everything; Still Waters; One Night Only; This Is Where I Came In; Their Greatest Hits – The Record; Singles include; NY Mining Disaster 1941; Massachusetts; To Love Somebody; Holiday; I've Gotta Get a Message to You; I Started a Joke; Lonely Days; How Can You Mend a Broken Heart; Jive Talkin'; Staying Alive; Night Fever; How Deep Is Your Love; Too Much Heaven; Tragedy; Love You Inside Out; One; You Win Again; First of May; Writer of songs for other artists including: Elvis Presley (Words); Sarah Vaughn (Run To Me); Al Green, Janis Joplin, Barbara Streisand (Guilty album); Diana Ross (Chain Reaction); Dionne Warwick (Heartbreaker); Dolly Parton and Kenny Rogers (Island in the Stream); Ntrance (staying Alive)Take That (How Deep is Your Love); Boyzone (Words); Yvonne Elliman (If I Can't Have You). Honours: 7 Grammy Awards; elected to Rock and Roll Hall of Fame, 1996; International Achievement, 1997; 5th most successful recording artists ever, have sold over 100 million records worldwide. Address: c/o Middle Ear, Studio, 1801 Bay Road, Miami Beach, FL 33139, USA.

GIBB Robin, b. 22 December 1949, Isle of Man, emigrated to Australia, 1958, returned to UK 1967. Singer and Songwriter. m. Divina Murphy, 1 son. Career: Formed Bee Gees with brothers Barry, and the late Maurice and Andy. Publications: Albums with the Bee Gees include: Bee Gees 1st; Odessa; Main Course; Children of the World; Saturday Night Fever; Spirits Having Flown; High Civilisation; Size Isn't Everything; Still Waters; One Night Only; Their Greatest Hits – The Record; Solo album: Magnet, 2003; Singles include: NY Mining Disaster 1941; Massachusetts;

To Love Somebody; Holiday; I've Gotta Get a Message to You; I Started a Joke; Lonely Days; How Can You Mend a Broken Heart; Jive Talkin'; Stayin' Alive; Night Fever; How Deep Is Your Love; Too Much Heaven; Tragedy; Love You Inside Out; One; You Win Again; First of May; Writer, songs for other artists including: Elvis Presley (Words); Sarah Vaughn (Run to Me); Al Green, Janis Joplin, Ntrance (Stayin' Alive); Take That (How Deep is Your Love); Boyzone (Words); Yvonne Elliman (If I Can't Have You). Honours: 7 Grammy awards; Elected to Rock and Roll Hall of Fame, 1996; International Achievement Award, American Music Awards, 1997; Brit Award for Outstanding Contribution to Music, 1997; World Music Award for Lifetime Achievement, 1997; 5th most successful recording artists ever, have sold 100 million records worldwide. Address: Middle Ear, 1801 Bay Road, Miami, FL 33139, USA.

GIBB Thomas R P, b. 10 February 1916, Belmont, MA, USA. Retired Professor. m. (1) 1 son, 1 daughter, (2) Reen Meergans. Education: BS, Bowdoin College, 1936; PhD, Chemistry, MIT, 1940. Appointments: Instructor, Assistant Professor, MIT; Professor, Tufts University; Emeritus Professor, 1980. Publications: 2 books; Several papers. Honours: Phi Beta Kappa; Alpha Chi Sigma; Fellow, Sigma Xi and AAAS. Memberships: American Chemical Society; American Association for the Advancement of Science. Address: 55 Main St, Dover, MA 02030, USA.

GIBSON Mel, b. 3 January 1956, Peekshill, New York, USA. Actor; Producer. m. Robyn Moore, 5 sons, 1 daughter. Education: National Institute for Dramatic Art, Sydney. Career: Founder, ICONS Productions; Actor, films include: Summer City; Mad Max, 1979; Tim, 1979; Attack Force Z; Gallipoli, 1981; The Road Warrior (Mad Max II), 1982; The Year of Living Dangerously, 1983; The Bounty, 1984; The River, 1984; Mrs Soffel, 1984; Mad Max Beyond the Thunderdome, 1985; Lethal Weapon; Tequila Sunrise; Lethal Weapon II; Bird on a Wire, 1989; Hamlet, 1990; Air America, 1990; Lethal Weapon III, 1991; Man Without a Face (also director), 1992; Maverick, 1994; Braveheart (also director, co-producer), 1995; Ransom, 1996; Conspiracy Theory, 1997; Lethal Weapon 4, 1998; Playback, 1997; The Million Dollar Hotel, 1999; The Patriot, 2000; What Women Want, 2000; We Were Soldiers, 2002; Signs, 2002; The Singing Detective, 2003; Plays include: Romeo and Juliet; Waiting for Godot; No Names No Pack Drill; Death of a Salesman. Honours include: Commandeur, Ordre des Arts et des Lettres. Address: c/o ICONS Productions, 4000 Warner Boulevard, Room 17, Burbank, CA 91522, USA.

GIDDENS Anthony, b. 18 January 1938. University Administrator; Sociologist. m. Jane M Ellwood, 1963. Education: Hull University; London School of Economics; Cambridge University. Appointments: Lecturer, late Reader, Sociology, University of Cambridge, 1969-85; Professor of Sociology, 1985-97; Fellow, King's College, 1969-96; Director, London School of Education, 1997-2003. Publications: Capitalism and Modern Social Theory, 1971; Ed, Sociology of Suicide, 1972; Politics and Sociology in the Thought of Max Weber, 1972; Editor and translator, Emile Durkheim: Selected Writings, 1972; Ed, Positivism and Sociology, 1974; New Rules of Sociological Method, 1976; Studies in Social and Political Theory, 1976; Central Problems in Social Theory, 1979; Class Structure of the Advanced Societies (2nd editor), 1981; Contemporary Critique of Historical Materialism (vol 1), Power, Property and State, 1981, (vol 2), Nation, State and Violence, 1985; Jointly, Classes, Power and Conflict, 1982; Profiles and Critiques in Social Theory, 1983; Joint editor, Social Class and the Division of Labour, 1983; Constitution of Society, 1984; Social Theory and Modern Sociology, 1987; Joint editor, Social Theory Today, 1987; Sociology, 1989; The Consequences of Modernity, 1990; Modernity and Self-Identity,

1991; The Transformation of Intimacy, 1992; Beyond Right and Left, 1994; In Defence of Sociology, 1996; Third Way, 1998. Honours include: Prince of Asturias Award, Spain, 2002. Address: London School of Economics, Houghton Street, London, WC2A 2AE, England.

GIELEN Uwe Peter, b. 15 August 1940, Berlin, Germany. Professor of Psychology. Education: MA, Psychology, Wake Forest University, 1968; PhD, Social Psychology, Harvard University, USA, 1976. Appointments: Assistant Professor of Psychology, City University of New York, 1977-80; Associate Professor, 1980-87; Professor, 1987-, Chairman, 1980-90; Director, Institute for International and Cross-Cultural Psychology, 1998-, St Francis College, New York, USA. Publications: 11 books; 100 other publications; Editor-in-Chief, World Psychology, 1995-97; International Journal of Group Tensions, 1997-2002; Co-editor, Psychology in the Arab Countries; International Perspectives on Human Development; The Family and Family Therapy in International Perspective; Cross-Cultural Topics in Psychology; Handbook of Culture, Therapy and Healing. Honours: Kurt Lewin Award, 1993; Wilhelm Wundt Award, 1999, New York State Psychological Association. Memberships: Fellow, American Psychological Association; Fellow, American Psychological Society; President, International Council of Psychologists, 1994-95; President, Society for Cross-Cultural Research, 1998-99. Address: Department of Psychology, St Francis College, Brooklyn, NY 11201, USA. E-mail: ugielen@hotmail.com

GIFF John Jeremiah, b. 1967, Palermo, Sicily. Reader in Literature. Education: BA, Honours, English, Cambridge University, 1988; MPhil, Publishing and Book Production, Stirling University, Scotland, 1990. Appointments: Trainee Pilot, Anglia Communications, 1991; Meteorological Presenter, Anglia Environmental Services, 1992-94; Freelance Editor, 1994-96; Tutor, 1996-98, Reader, Literature, 1998- West Norfolk Community College. Honours: Best Postgraduate in Year, Stirling University Publishing Faculty. Memberships: MCC; Rotoract; CAMRA. Address: 4 Orchard Court, Orchard Street, Cambridge CB1 1PR, England.

GIGGAL Kenneth, (Henry Marlin, Angus Ross), b. 19 March 1927, Dewsbury, Yorkshire, England. Writer. Publications: The Manchester Thing, 1970; The Huddersfield Job, 1971; The London Assignment, 1972; The Dunfermline Affair, 1973; The Bradford Business, 1974; The Amsterdam Diversion, 1974; The Leeds Fiasco, 1975; The Edinburgh Exercise, 1975; The Ampurias Exchange, 1976; The Aberdeen Conundrum, 1977; The Congleton Lark, 1979; The Hamburg Switch, 1980; A Bad April, 1980; The Menwith Tangle, 1982; The Darlington Jaunt, 1983; The Luxembourg Run, 1985; Doom Indigo, 1986; The Tyneside Ultimatum, 1988; Classic Sailing Ships, 1988; The Greenham Plot, 1989; The Leipzig Manuscript, 1990; The Last One, 1992; John Worsley's War, 1992. Other: Television scripts and films. Contributions to: Many magazines, national and international. Honour: Truth Prize for Fiction, 1954. Memberships: Savage Club; Arms and Armour Society. Address: The Old Granary, Bishop Monkton, Near Harrogate, North Yorkshire, England.

GIHWALA Dines Chandra Manilal, b. 17 March 1953, Cape Town, South Africa. Attorney. m. Shanti, 2 sons, 1 daughter. Education: B Proc., University of Western Cape, 1977; Higher Diploma in Tax Practice, Rand Afrikaans University, 1997. Appointments: Senior Partner, Wilkinson, Joshua & Gihwala, 1978; Chairman and Senior Partner, Wilkinson, Joshua, Gihwala and Abercrombie Inc, 1988; Acting Appointment, Judge, Supreme Court of South Africa, 1997; Chairman, Hofmeyr, Herbstein & Gihwala Inc, 1999. Publications: Several reported judgements in

Dictionary of International Biography

the South African Law Reports. Honours: Gold Merit Award for the outstanding contribution made during South Africa's first democratic election, Electoral Commission of South Africa, 1994; Member, Standing Advisory Committee on Company Law, 1996; Proclamation by the Governor of Arizona, USA for contribution to a new Democratic South Africa, 1997; Director of the Perishable Goods Export Control Board as the Ministerial Representative of the Government Agency, 1998; The only attorney to be appointed as an independent chairman of the Disciplinary Committees of the Public Accountants' and Auditor's Board. Memberships: Cape Law Society; Erinvale Golf Club. Address: 112 Erinvale Drive, Erinvale Estate, Somerset West 7130, South Africa. E-mail: dinesg@hofmeyr.com

GIL David Georg, b. 16 March 1924, Vienna, Austria. Professor of Social Policy; Author. m. Eva Breslauer, 2 August 1947, 2 sons. Education: Certificate in Psychotherapy with Children, Israeli Society for Child Psychiatry, 1952; Diploma in Social Work, School of Social Work, 1953, BA, 1957, Hebrew University, Jerusalem, Israel; MSW, 1958, DSW, 1963, University of Pennsylvania. Appointment: Professor of Social Policy, Brandeis University. Publications: Violence Against Children, 1970; Unravelling Social Policy, 1973, 5th edition, 1992; The Challenge of Social Equality, 1976; Beyond the Jungle, 1979; Child Abuse and Violence (editor), 1979; Toward Social and Economic Justice (editor with Eva Gil), 1985; The Future of Work (editor with Eva Gil), 1987; Confronting Injustice and Oppression, 1998. Contributions to: Over 50 articles to professional journals, book chapters, book reviews. Honours: Leadership in Human Services, Brandeis University, Heller School, 1999; Social Worker of the Year, National Association of Social Workers, Massachusetts, 2000. Memberships: National Association of Social Workers; American Orthopsychiatric Association; Association of Humanist Sociology. Address: Heller Graduate School, Brandeis University, Waltham, MA 02454-9110, USA.

GILBERT John Andrew, b. 3 September 1948, Frankfurt, Germany. Professor. 1 son, 1 daughter. Education: BS, Aerospace, 1971, MSc, Applied Mechanics, 1973, Polytechnic Institute of Brooklyn; PhD, Mechanics, Illinois Institute of Technology, Chicago, Illinois, 1975. Appointments include: Assistant, Associate, Professor, University of Wisconsin-Milwaukee, 1976-85; Director of Civil Engineering Program, 1985-90, Department of Mechanical Engineering, Huntsville, 1985-90, Professor of Mechanical Engineering, Department of Mechanical and Aerospace Engineering, Huntsville, 1985-, Adjunct Professor of Materials Science, Tuscaloosa, 1988-, Adjunct Professor of Materials Science, Birmingham, 1989-, Centre for Applied Optics, Huntsville, 1995-, University of Alabama; President and Chief Executive Officer, Optechnology Inc, 1989-; Director, Consortium for Holography, Applied Mechanics and Photonics (CHAMP), 1993-. Publications: 2 patents, 2 peer-reviewed chapters, numerous articles in refereed journals. Honours: Numerous include: Distinguished Teaching Award, University of Alabama Huntsville Foundation, 1998; Nominated for CASE US Professor of the Year Award, Dr Frank Franz, president, University of Alabama Huntsville, 1998; President's Award for Outstanding Performance, Alabama Section, American Society of Civil Engineers, 1998; Outstanding Faculty Member, College of Engineering, University of Alabama Huntsville, 1999; Master of Ceremonies, 15th Annual Service Awards program, University of Alabama Huntsville, 1999; Sigma Xi. Memberships include: Society for Experimental Mechanics; American Academy of Mechanics; Mechanics Fellowship; British Society for Strain Measurement; American Society for Engineering Education. Address: Department of Mechanical and Aerospace Engineering, University of Alabama, Huntsville, AL 35899, USA.

GILBERT Robert Andrew, b. 6 October 1942, Bristol, England. Antiquarian Bookseller; Editor; Writer. m. Patricia Kathleen Linnell, 20 July 1970, 3 sons, 2 daughters. Education: BA, Honours, Philosophy, Psychology, University of Bristol, 1964. Appointment: Editor, Ars Quatuor Coronatorum, 1994-2002. Publications: The Golden Dawn: Twilight of the Magicians, 1983; A E Waite: A Bibliography, 1983; The Golden Dawn Companion, 1986; A E Waite: Magician of Many Parts, 1987; The Treasure of Montsegur (with W N Birks), 1987; Elements of Mysticism, 1991; World Freemasonry: An Illustrated History, 1992; Freemasonry: A Celebration of the Craft (J M Hamil), 1992; Casting the First Stone, 1993. Editor with M A Cox: The Oxford Book of English Ghost Stories, 1986; Victorian Ghost Stories: An Oxford Anthology, 1991; The Golden Dawn Scrapbook, 1997; Editor, The House of the Hidden Light, 2003. Contributions to: Ars Quatuor Coronatorum; Avallaunius; Christian Parapsychologist; Gnosis; Hermetic Journal; Cauda Pavonis; Yeats Annual. Memberships: Society of Authors; librarian, Societas Rosicruciana in Anglia. Address: 4 Julius Road, Bishopston, Bristol BS7 8EU, England.

GILBERT Walter, b. 21 March 1932, Boston, Massachusetts, USA. Molecular Biologist. m. Celia Stone, 1953, 1 son, 1 daughter. Education: Graduated, Physics, Harvard University, 1954; Doctorate in Mathematics, Cambridge University, 1957. Appointments: National Science Foundation Fellow, 1957-58; Lecturer, Research Fellow, 1958-59, Professor of Biophysics, 1964-68, Professor of Molecular Biology, 1969-72, American Cancer Society Professor of Molecular Biology, 1972, Harvard University; Devised techniques for determining the sequence of bases in DNA. Honours: US Steel Foundation Award in Molecular Biology (NAS), 1968; Joint Winner, Ledlie Prize, Harvard University, 1969; Joint winner, Warren Triennial Prize, Massachusetts General Hospital, 1977; Louis and Bert Freedman Award, New York Academy of Sciences, 1977; Joint winner, Prix Charles-Léopold Mayer, Académie des Sciences, Institute de France, 1977; Harrison Howe Award of the Rochester branch of the American Chemical Society, 1978; Joint winner, Louisa Gross Horowitz Prize, Columbia University, 1979; Gairdner Foundation Annual Award 1979; Joint winner, Albert Lasker Basic Medical Research Award, 1979; Joint winner, Prize for Biochemical Analysis, German Society for Clinical Chemistry, 1980; Sober Award, American Society of Biological Chemists, 1980; Joint Winner, Nobel Prize for Chemistry, 1980; New England Entrepreneur of the Year Award, 1991; Ninth National Biotechnology Ventures Award, 1997. Memberships: Foreign member, Royal Society; NAS; American Physical Society; American Society of Biological Chemists; American Academy of Arts and Sciences. Address: Biological Laboratories, 16 Divinity Avenue, Cambridge, MA 02138, USA.

GILES Richard Lawrence, b. 24 May 1937, Petersham, New South Wales, Australia. Teacher; Writer. m. Faye Laurel, 3 May 1969. Education: BA, 1957; DipEd, 1969; ATCL, 1971; AMusA, 1973. Publications: Technology, Employment and the Industrial Revolution, 1984; For and Against, 1989, 2nd edition, 1993; Debating, 1992; Understanding Our Economy, 1995. Contributions to: Good Government; Progress; The Individual; Australian Land Economics Review. Membership: Association for Good Government. Literary Agent: John Wiley and Sons. Address: PO Box 251, Ulladulla, New South Wales 2539, Australia.

GILFANOV Marat, b. 18 July 1962, Kazan, USSR. Astrophysicist. m. Marina Gilfanova, 1 daughter. Education: Diploma Physics, Moscow Physical-Technical Institute, 1985; PhD, Physics, Space Research Institute, Moscow, 1989; Doctor of Physics and Mathematics, Space Research Institute, Moscow,

1996. Appointments: Junior Scientist, Space Research Institute, Moscow, 1985-88; Scientist, 1988-91; Senior Scientist, 1991-96; Leading Scientist, 1996-; Max-Planck-Institut für Astrophysik, Garching, Germany, 1996-. Publications: Over 200 in international scientific journals. Honours: COSPAR, Commission E Zeldovich medal, 1992. Memberships: COSPAR, Commission E; International Astronomical Union, 1994-; Scientific Council of Space Research Institute, 1997-; Wissenschaftlicher Institutsrat, Max-Planck-Institut für Astrophysik. Address: Max-Planck-Institut für Astrophysik, Karl-Schwarzschild-Str 1, 85741 Garching, Germany.

GILLARD S Craig, b. 4 April 1961, Glace Bay, Nova Scotia, Canada. Urologist. m. Marielle L Gillard. Education: BA, BS, St Anselm College, 1983; Georgetown University School of Medicine, 1990. Appointment: Urologist, Jordan Hospital, Plymouth, Massachusetts, USA, 1998-. Memberships: American Urology Association; Massachusetts Medical Society; American Medical Association. Address: 110 Long Pond Road, Plymouth, MA 02360, USA.

GILLHAM Peter Francis, b. 13 November, Cleveland, Australia. Nutritional Researcher; Educator. 2 sons, 2 daughters. Education: Self-taught in the field of nutrition and nutritional research. Appointments: Owner and Chief Executive Officer, Peter Gillham's Nutritional Enterprises, Wholesale, Retail and Export of Nutritional Products; Researcher and Educator of nutritional information that works; Major nutritional discoveries. Publications: The Miracle Nutrient; Many articles and lectures; Magnesium – Miracles in Minutes; Oxygen – Gillham Germ Theory; Look, Act and Feel Younger, Beverley Hills Weekly. Honours: Man of the Year, 2001; American Medal of Honor; Listed in national and international biographical dictionaries. Address: PO Box 27102, Los Angeles, CA 90027, USA. E-mail: petergllhm@aol.com Website: naturalcalm.net

GILLIAM Terry Vance, b. 22 November 1940, Minnesota, USA. Animator; Film Director; Actor; Illustrator; Writer. m. Margaret Weston, 1 son, 2 daughter. Education: Occidental College. Appointments: Associate Editor, HELP! magazine, 1962-64; Freelance illustrator, 1964-65; Advertising copywriter/art director, 1966-67; with Monty Python's Flying Circus (UK), 1969-76; Animator: And Now For Something Completely Different (film); Co-director, actor, Monty Python and the Holy Grail; Director, Jabberwocky; Designer, actor, animator, Monty Python's Meaning of Life (film), 1983; Co-writer, director, Brazil, 1985; The Adventures of Baron Munchausen, 1988; Director, The Fisher King (film), 1991; Twelve Monkeys, 1996; Presenter, TV series: The Last Machine, 1995; Executive Producer, Monty Python's Complete Waste of Time, 1995; Director and co-writer, Fear and Loathing in Las Vegas, 1998; Executive Producer, Monty Python's Complete Waste of time (CD-Rom), 1995; Appeared in Lost in La Mancha, documentary, 2002; Director, Good Omens, 2003. Publications: Monty Python's Big Red Book; Monty Python's Paperback, 1977; Monty Python's Scrapbook, 1979; Animations of Mortality, 1979; Monty Python's The Meaning of Life; Monty Python's Flying Circus - Just the Words (co-ed), 1989; The Adventures of Baron Munchausen, 1989; Not the Screenplay or Fear and Loathing in Las Vegas, 1998; Gilliam on Gilliam, 1999; Dark Knights and Holy Fools, 1999. Honour: Hon DFA, Royal College of Art, London, 1989. Address: c/o Jenne Casarotto, National House, 60-66 Wardour Street, London, W1V 4ND, England.

GILLIS Richard, b. 22 April 1950, Dundee, Scotland. Solicitor; Managing Director. Education: Admitted as a Solicitor, 1975; Kenya Advocate, 1978. Appointments: Solicitor, Greater London

Council, 1975-77; Solicitor, Archer & Wilcock, Nairobi, Kenya, 1977-80; Shoosmiths, 1980-81; Assistant to the Secretary, TI Group plc, 1981-85; Secretary, ABB Transportation Holdings Ltd (British Rail Engineering Ltd until privatisation), Trustee, Company Pension Scheme, 1985-95; Clerk to the Council and Company Secretary, University of Derby, 1995-2002; Managing Director, family investment companies, 2001-; Secretary, Justice report on perjury; Director then Vice-Chairman, Crewe Development Agency, 1992-95; The Order of St John: Chairman, Property Committee, Derbyshire Council of the Order of St John, 1994-2003; Trustee, Priory of England and the Islands of the Order of St John and Trustee, St John Ambulance, 1999-2003; Chairman, Audit Committee and Priory Regulations Committee, Regional Member of Priory Chapter, 1999-; Court of Assistants, Worshipful Company of Basketmakers, 2004-. Honours: O.St.J, 1999; Honorary Life Member, Court of the University of Derby, 2003. Memberships: CBI East Midlands Regional Council, 1993-95; Stakeholders' Forum, Derby City Challenge, 1993-98; Guild of Freemen of the City of London; Provincial Grand Lodge of Warwickshire; Bonnetmaker Craft of Dundee; Maccabæans; FRSA; Clubs: Athenæum; City Livery; New (Edinburgh). Address: 317 Clepington Road, Dundee, DD3 8BD, Scotland.

GILLMAN Gavin Patrick, b. 15 May 1941, Townsville, Australia. Soil Scientist. m. Kay Thelma, 2 sons, 1 daughter. Education: BSc, 1963, BSc Honours, 1964, PhD, 1978, University of Queensland; MSc, James Cook University, 1970. Appointments: Senior Principal Research Scientist, CSIRO, Australia, 1968-90; Honorary Fellow, CSIRO, Australia, 1989-; Officer in Charge, Leader, Humid Forest Program, International Institute of Tropical Agriculture, Cameroon, 1990-94. Publications: Book, The Mineralogy, Chemistry and Physics of Tropical Soils with Variable Charge Clays; 60 papers in international journals. Honours: Visiting Professor, Yale University and University of Georgia. Address: 14 Lupin Court, Annandale, QLD 4814, Australia. E-mail: gavin.gillman@csiro.au

GILLY François-Noel, b. 1 May 1955, Lyon, France. University Surgeon. 2 daughters. Education: Medical Doctor, 1984; Digestive Surgeon, 1986. Appointments: Surgeon, civil hospitals in Lyon, 1986-; University Professor, 1995; Dean of Medical Faculty, Lyon University, 1999-. Publications: Articles in professional medical journals. Honours: Chevalier des Palmes Academiques; Prix Patey Mathieu; Prix A Ponet. Memberships: Academie Nationale de Chirugie; ICHS; ISIORT; IAGS; AFC. Address: Department of Surgery, Lyon University CHLS, 69495 Pierre Benite Cedex, France. E-mail: francogi@lyon-sud.univ-lyon1.fr

GILMORE Gordon Ray, b. 7 September 1935, Mesa, Arizona, USA. Retired Naval Officer; Corporate Manager. m. Donna K Miller, 4 sons. Education: BS, Petroleum Engineering, 1958; MSc, Management, 1968. Appointments: Naval Officer, 1958-83, retiring as Captain; Served Vietnam, 1965-67; Joined private industry, 1983; Retired as President, John Brown US Services, 1995. Publications: Articles about war in Vietnam and Cambodia, published in various military magazines and journals. Honours: Navy-Marine Corps Medal for Heroism, 1964; Bronze Star with Combat V, 1967; 3 Meritorious Service Medals; 9 other awards; Legion of Merit, 1983. Memberships: Military Officers Association of America; Association of Naval Civil Engineer Corps Officers; Navy League; National Rifle Association. Address: 1405 Corte Canalete, Bakersfield, CA 93309, USA.

GILMOUR D James, b. 10 July 1947, Philadelphia, Pennsylvania, USA. Consulting Information Technologist. m. Deborah Ann Kaufold. Education: BSc, Muhlenberg College, 1969; MSA, George Washington University, 1974; MBA, Temple

Dictionary of International Biography

University, 1981; MS, University of Pennsylvania, 1994; MPhil, University of Pennsylvania, 1998; MEd Candidate, Temple University. Appointments: Consultant and Principal, D James Gilmour Inc; AVP, Core States Financial Corporation; Staff Economist, Sun Oil Corporation; National Security Agency (active duty, US Navy). Publications: An Econometric Model of Core States Financial Corporation, 1994; The Core States, University of Pennsylvania Strategic Planning Model, 1996; The Philadelphia Ethos, 1998; 1776 And All That: A Memorable History of Philadelphia, 1992; Patents: 451 H&G Autoloder. Honours: Beta Gamma Sigma (honorary business fraternity); Lead Cohort: MPhil, University of Pennsylvania; Founding Member, Center for Organisational Dynamics, University of Pennsylvania; Honorary Ambassador, Organisational Dynamics, University of Pennsylvania; Alpha Tau Omega. Membership: Mensa; 999; Clan Morrison; IAEE. Address: 15 Keats Road, Yardley, Pennsylvania 19067-3219, USA.

GILMOUR Pat, b. 19 March 1932, Woodford, Essex, England. Art Historian; Curator. m. Alexander Tate Gilmour, 2 daughters. Education: Sculpture, Glasgow School of Art, 1956-58; Distinction in Art, Distinction in Theory of Education, Sidney Webb College, London Institute of Education, 1962-65; Diploma in Design Education, Hornsey College of Art, 1968-70; BA (Hons), History of Art and English Literature, London University, 1971-73. Appointments: Journalist, West Sussex Gazette, 1949-55; Assistant to Editor, Percival Marshall Publishers, London, 1959-62; Lecturer II, in charge of Art and Design, Southwark College for Further Education, 1959-62; Founding Curator of Prints, Modern Collection, Tate Gallery, London, 1974-77; Senior Lecturer in charge of Contextual Studies, North East London Polytechnic (now University of East London), 1977-79; Head, Department of Art History and Liberal Studies, Central School of Art and Design, London, 1979-81; Senior Curator, Founding and Managing the Department of International Prints and Illustrated Books, National Gallery of Australia, Canberra, 1981-89; Study Scholarship, Rifkind Center for German Expressionist Art, Los Angeles County Museum, USA, 1990; Free-lance Art Historian and Curator, 1990-; Visiting Professor, University of East London, 1991-99; Expert Witness on Picasso: Kornfeld v. Tunick, 1993; Editorial Board, Print Quarterly, 1996-; Selector, Cataloguer and Supervisor of numerous exhibitions in Great Britain and Australia, 1972-99; Member of Prize Juries including: President of the Jury, Ljubljena International Print Biennale, 1993; Art Foundation Prize, Great Britain, 1997; Lecturer in field. Publications include: Books include: Modern Prints, 1970; Henry Moore, Graphic in the Making, 1975; Artists at Curwen, 1977; Artists in Print, (BBC), 1981; Innovation in Collaborative Printmaking: Kenneth Tyler 1963-1993, 1992; Over 20 exhibition catalogues; Entries in Macmillan Dictionary of Art; Numerous articles in professional journals. Honours: National Book League Prize, 1975, 1977; Collection of Kenneth Tyler's work presented to the Tate Gallery in her honour, 2004. Memberships include: Council Member, Institute of Contemporary Arts, London, 1979-81; Committee, Print Council of Australia, 1983-89; Corresponding Editor, 1986-89, Guest Editor, 1990-91, The Tamarind Papers. Address: 25 Christchurch Square, Victoria Park, London E9 7HU, England.

GINGER Andrew John, b. 12 April 1970, Leeds, England. Lecturer. Education: 1st Class Honours Degree, Modern Languages, French/Spanish, Trinity College, University of Oxford, England, 1992; DPhil, Trinity College, then Exeter College, University of Oxford, 1996. Appointments: Queen Sofia Junior Research Fellow, Exeter College, University of Oxford, England, 1994-95; Lecturer in Hispanic Studies, University of Edinburgh, Scotland, 1996-. Publications include: Political Revolution and Literary Experiment in the Spanish Romantic Period (1830-1850),

1999; Antonio Ros de Olano's Experiments in Post Romantic Prose (1857-1884): Between Romanticism and Modernism, 2000; Identity and Dissociation in the Mid-Nineteenth-Century Paintings of Eugenio Lucas and Contemporaneous Fiction, in ed. Bonnadio/ de Ros, Crossing Fields, 2003; Spain: Cultural Survey in ed. Murray, Encyclopaedia of the Romantic Era, 2003. Memberships: Association of Hispanists of Great Britain and Ireland; British Comparative Literature Association. Address: DELC (Hispanic Studies), School of Literatures, Languages and Cultures, College of Humanities and Social Sciences, University of Edinburgh, David Hulme Tower, George Square, Edinburgh, Scotland.

GINGRICH Newt (Newton Leroy), b. 17 June 1943, Harrisburg, USA. American Politician. m. (2) Marianne Ginther, 1981, 2 daughters by previous marriage. Education: Emory & Tulane Universities. Appointments: Member, Faculty, WA GA College, Carrollton, 1970-78, Professor of History, 1978; Member, 96-103rd Congresses from 6th District of Georgia, 1979-92; Chair, GOPAC, now Chair Emeritus; House Republican Whip, 1989; Speaker, House of Representatives, 1994-; Adjunct Professor, Reinhardt College, Waleska, Georgia, 1994-95; Co-founder, Congressional Mil Reform Caucus, Congressional Space Caucus. Publications: Window of Opportunity, 1945, 1995; To Renew America, 1995. Membership: AAAS. Address: The Committee for New American Leadership, 1800 K Street #714, Washington, DC 20006, USA.

GINOLA David, b. 25 January 1967, Gassin, Var, France. Professional Footballer; Sportsman. m. Coraline Delphin, 1990, 2 daughters. Career: Football clubs: 1st division Toulon clubs, 1986-87; Matraracing, Paris, 1987-88; Racing Paris 1, 1988-89; Brest-Armorique, 1989-90; Paris-Saint-Germain (French national champions, 1993-94, winners Coupe de France, 1993, 1995, winners coupe de la ligue, 1995) 1991-95; Newcastle Utd, England, 1995-97; Tottenham Hotspur, 1997-2000; Aston Villa, 2000-02; 17 international caps; Anti-landmine campaigner for Red Cross, 1998-. Honours: Football Writers' Association, Player of the Year, 1999; Professional Football Association Player of the Year, 1999. Publication: David Ginola: The Autobiography (with Niel Silver), 2000. Website: www.ginola14.com

GINOS James, b. 1 February 1923, Hillsboro, Illinois, USA. Retired Research Chemist; Medical Scientist. m. Chrisilla Katsas, 2 sons. Education: BA, Columbia University, 1954; MS, Chemical Engineering, Stevens Institute Technology, 1962; PhD, Organic Chemistry, Stevens Institute Technology, 1964. Appointments: Chemist, Colgate Palmolive Co, Jersey City, 1953-57; Chief Chemist, Diamond Shamrock Corp, Newark, New Jersey, 1957-58; Project Co-ordinator, Nopco Chem Co, Harrison, New Jersey, 1959-64; Assistant Scientist, Brookhaven National Laboratories, Upton, New York, 1964-68; Research Assistant Professor, Mount Sinai School Medicine, New York City, 1968-70; Associate Scientist, 1970-74, Scientist, 1974-75, Brookhaven National Laboratory; Research Associate Professor, Cornell University Medical College, 1975-92; SN, Research Associate, Neurooncology Laboratory, Memorial Sloan-Kettering Cancer Center, New York City, 1980-84; Associate Laboratory Member, 1984-89, Associate Laboratory Member, Nuclear Medicine Cyclotron Core, 1989-93, retired 1993. Publications: Numerous articles in professional journals. Memberships: American Chemical Society; AAAS; Harvey Society; American Society of Pharmacology and Experimental. Address: 200 Winston Dr, Apt 3016 Cliffside Park, NJ 07010, USA.

GINZBURG Vitaly, b. 4 October 1916, Moscow, Russia. Physicist. m. Nina Ginzburg, 1946, 1 daughter. Education: Graduated, Physics, Moscow University, 1938, Postgraduate,

Physics Institute, Academy of Sciences. Appointments: P N Lebedev Physical Institute, USSR (now Russian) Academy of Sciences, 1940-; Professor, Gorky University, 1945-68; Moscow Institute of Physics, 1968-. Publications: The Physics of a Lifetime, 2001. Honours include: Honorary DSc, Sussex, 1970; Mandelstam Prize, 1947; Lomonosov Prize, 1962; USSR State Prize, 1953; Order of Lenin, 1966; Gold Medal, Royal Astronomical Society; 1991; Bardeen Prize, 1991; Wolf Prize, 1994, 1995; Varilov Gold Medal, Russian Academy of Sciences, 1995; Lomonsov Gold Medal, Russian Academy of Sciences, 1995; UNESCO Nils Bohr Gold Medal, 1998; APS Nicholson Medal, 1998; IUPAP O'Ceallaigh Medal, 2001; Order of Lenin; many others. Memberships: Foreign member, Royal Danish Academy of Sciences and Letters; Foreign honorary member, American Academy of Arts and Science; Honorary Fellow, Indian Academy of Science; Foreign fellow, Indian National Science Academy; Foreign associate, NAS, USA; Foreign member, Royal Society, London; Academia Europaea. Address: P N Lebedev Physical Institute, Russian Academy of Sciences, Leninsky Prospect 53, 117924 GSP, Moscow B-333, Russia.

GIRARDI Federico Pablo, b. 20 December 1967, Rosario, Argentina. Physician; Spine Surgeon. m. Florencia Ferrero, 1 son, 1 daughter. Education: MD, Faculdad de Ciencias Medicas, Universidad Nacional de Rosario, Rosario, Argentina, 1999. Appointments: Orthopaedic Surgery Residency, Buenos Aires University, Argentina; Spine Fellowship, Staff Physician, Spinal Surgeon, Hospital for Special Surgery, Weill Medical College of Cornell University, USA. Publications: More than 40 in many peer reviewed journals including: Spine; Journal of Spinal Disorders; Orthopedic Clinic of North America; Orthopedics; Journal of Bone and Joint Surgery. Memberships: American Medical Association; North American Spine Society; European Spine Society; Scoliosis Research Society, Spine Arthroplasty Society; International Lumbar Spine Society. Address: 535, 70th Street, New York, NY 10029, USA. E-mail: girardif@hss.edu Website: www.hss.edu

GIVENCHY Hubert de, b. 21 February 1927, Beauvais, France. Fashion Designer. Education: Ecole Nat Supérieure des Beaux-Arts, Paris; Faculté de Droit, Univ de Paris. Appointments: Apprentice, Paris fashion houses of Lucien Lelong, 1945-46, Robert Piguet, 1946-48, Jacques Fath, 1948-49, Elsa Shiaparelli, 1949-51; Established own fashion house in Parc Morceau, Paris, 1952-56, Avenue George V, 1956; President, Director-General Society Givenchy-Couture and Society des Parfums Givenchy, Paris, 1954; Honorary President, Administrative Council Givenchy SA, 1988-; President, Christie's France, 1997-; Work included in Fashion: An Anthology, Victoria & Albert Museum, London, 1971; Costume designer for films: Breakfast at Tiffany's, 1961; Charade, 1963; The VIPs, 1963; Paris When It Sizzles, 1964; How to Steal a Million, 1966. Honour: Chevalier, Légion d'honneur. Address: 3 Avenue George V, 75008 Paris, France.

GJESSING Ketil, b. 18 February 1934, Oslo, Norway. Education: Magister Artium and Candidatus Philologae, majoring in Literature, University of Oslo, 1965. Appointments: Teacher, Atlantic College, now United World College of the Atlantic, 1965-66; Dramaturge, Radio Drama Department of Norwegian Broadcasting Corporation, 1965-99, Retired, 2000-. Publications: Collections of poetry: Kransen om et møte, 1962; Frostjern, 1968; Private steiner bl a, 1970; Utgående post, 1975; Snøen som faller i fjor, 1977; Bjelle, malm, 1979; Vinger, røtter, 1982; Slik pila synger i lufta, 1985; Nådefrist, 1988; Dans på roser og glass, 1996; Represented in a Slovak language anthology of Norwegian poetry, German language selection of 60 poems was published in 2000; Short story published in Danish, Japanese and Swedish translation. Honours: Gyldendals legat, 1978; Språklig Samlings Literary Prize, 1995. Memberships:

Norwegian Association of Writers; Norwegian Writers' Centre; Norwegian Association of Translators. Address: Dannevigsvn 12, 0463 Oslo, Norway.

GJORCEV Angelko, b. 19 September 1948, Trstenik, Saint Nicole, Republic of Macedonia. Pneumologist; Allergologist. m. Lujza Grueve Gjorceva, 1 daughter. Education: Graduate, Faculty of Medicine, Skopje, 1972; Specialisation in Internal Medicine, 1976-80; PhD, Medicine, 1990; Numerous specialisation and study tours abroad. Appointments: Clinic for Infective Diseases, 1975-76; Assistant, Internal Medicine, 1977, Lecturer, 1990, Professor, Internal Medicine and pneumoallergy, 1995, Chief of Asthma Centre, 1997-, Clinic for Pneumology and Allergology, Faculty of Medicine, Skopje; President, National Asthma Campaign. Publications: Over 250 in Macedonian, Yugoslavian and international journals; 3 books: Asthma bronchial-enigma and challenge; Macedonian national plan and program for diagnosis and management of bronchial asthma – reality or vision; Macedonian consensus for diagnosis and management of asthma and chronic obstructive pulmonary disease. Honours: Recipient of all the highest awards of the Macedonian Doctor's Chamber and the Macedonian Doctor's Association. Memberships: American Thoracic Society; European Thoracic Society; British Thoracic Society; Société française de maladie respiratoire; Macedonian Respiratory Society; European Respiratory Society European Academy for Allergology and Clinical Immunology; American Academy for Allergology and Clinical Immunology; Medical Doctor Chamber of Macedonia; Doctor's Club of Macedonia; International Academy of Science "Knez Scerbatov". Address: Nju Delhiska 2-II/18, 1000 Skopje, Republic of Macedonia.

GLADKOVSKY Victor Andreevich, b. 29 May 1925, Yekaterinburg, Russia. Science Worker. m. Inna Gubasheva, 1 son. Education: Graduate, Mechanical Department, Ural State Technical University, 1948; Doctor Technician, Leningrad State Technical University, 1970. Appointments: Science worker, Institute of Physics and Metals, Yekaterinburg and Institute of Metallurgy, Tceljabinsk, 1948-; Head, Chairman of Strength of Materials, Perm State Technical University, 1962-93; Professor, 1993-. Publications: Over 200 research papers, 15 inventions. Memberships: Several. Address: 29a Komsomol Ave, Perm Technical University, Perm 614600, Russia. E-mail: sopromat@pstu.ac.ru

GLADYSHEV Georgi, b. 19 September 1936, Alma-Ata, Kazakhstan. Chemist. 1 son, 1 daughter. Education: Department of Chemistry, State University, Alma-Ata, 1954-59; Candidate of Science, 1962; DSc, 1966, Professor, 1969. Appointments: Science Worker, Visiting Professor, State University, Alma-Ata, 1963-66; Visiting Science Consultant, 1966-80; Head of Laboratory, Visiting Professor, 1970-; President, International Academy of Creative Endeavours, 1989-; Director of Institute, 1990-. Publications: Over 450 scientific works including monograph: Thermodynamics Theory of the Evolution of Living Beings, 1999. Honours: President, Founder, International Academy of Creative Endeavours, Gold Medal, W Gibbs, 1991; 20th Century Award for Achievement, 1992; World Intellectual, 1993; International Order of Merit, 1994; Gold Pavlov's pin, 1999. Memberships: International Higher Education Academy of Science; International Academy of Science; International Academy of Creative Endeavours; World Literature Academy; Russian Academy of Natural Science; New York Academy of Sciences. Address: Institute of Chemical Physics, 4 Kosygina, 117977 Moscow, Russia.

Dictionary of International Biography

GLANVILLE Brian Lester, b. 24 September 1931, London, England. Author; Journalist. m. Elizabeth Pamela De Boer, 19 March 1959, 2 sons, 2 daughters. Appointments: Literary Adviser, Bodley Head, 1958-62; Football Correspondent and Sports Columnist, Sunday Times, 1958-92; Sports Columnist, The People, 1992-96, The Times 1996-98; Sunday Times, 1998-. Publications: The Reluctant Dictator, 1952; Henry Sows the Wind, 1954; Along the Arno, 1956; The Bankrupts, 1958; After Rome Africa, 1959; A Bad Streak, short stories, 1961; Diamond, 1962; The Director's Wife, short stories, 1963; The King of Hackney Marshes, short stories, 1965; A Second Home, 1965; The Olympian, 1969; A Cry of Crickets, 1970; Goalkeepers are Different, children's novel, 1971; The Thing He Loves, short stories, 1973; The Comic, 1974; Never Look Back, 1980; Kissing America, 1985; Love Is Not Love, 1985; Short Stories: The Catacomb, 1988; Dictators, 2001. Sporting Books: Soccer Nemesis, 1955; Footballer's Companion, editor, 1962; The Joy of Football, editor, 1986; Champions of Europe, 1991; Story of the World Cup, 1993; Football Memories, 1999. Plays: A Visit To The Villa; The Diary; I Could Have Been King. Musical: Underneath The Arches (Chichester and Prince of Wales Theatres). Contributions to: New Statesman; Spectator. Honours: Silver Bear Award, Berlin Film Festival, 1963; Thomas Y Coward Award, New York, 1969. Address: 160 Holland Park Avenue, London W11 4UH, England.

GLASER Donald Arthur, b. 21 September 1926, Cleveland, Ohio, USA. Physicist. 1 son, 1 daughter. Education: Graduated, Case Institute of Technology, 1946; PhD, California Institute of Technology, 1949. Appointments: Physics Department, 1949, Professor of Physics, 1957, University of Michigan; Professor of Physics, 1959, Professor of Physics and Biology, 1964, University of California at Berkeley; Inventor of the bubble chamber, used to study short-lived subatomic particles. Publications include: Influence of Remote Objects on Local Depth Perception, 1991; Shape Analysis and Stereopsis for Human Depth Perception, 1992; Depth, Discrimination of a Line is Improved by Adding Other Nearby Lines, 1992; Temporal Aspects of Depth Contrast, 1993; Comparison of Human Performance with Algorithms for Estimating Fractal Dimension of Fractional Brownian Statistics, 1993; Depth Discrimination of a Crowded Line Is Better When It Is More Luminant than the Lines Crowding It, 1995; Stereopsis Due to Luminance Difference in the Two Eyes, 1995; Multiple Matching of Features in Simple Stereograms, 1996; Many papers written jointly with other physicists. Honour: Henry Russell Award, 1955; Charles Vernon Boys Prize, The Physical Society, 1958; Nobel Prize for Physics, 1960; Several other awards. Membership: NAS. Address: Department of Molecular and Cell Biology, 337 Stanley Hall, University of California at Berkeley, CA 94720, USA.

GLASER Peter Edward, b. 5 September 1923, Zatec, Czech Republic. Mechanical Engineer. m. Eva, 2 sons, 1 daughter. Education: Diploma, Leeds College of Technology, 1943; 1st State Exam, Technical University, Prague, 1948; PhD, Columbia University, 1955. Appointments: Section Manager, Vice President, Arthur D Little Inc, Cambridge, MA, 1955-94; Project Manager, Apollo 11 Laser Ranging Retroflector Array, 1969; NASA Advisory Council, 1984-89; President, 1988-, Chairman, 1990-96, SUNSAT Energy Council; Chair, Space Power Committee, International Astronautical Federation, 1984-88; Committee of the National Academy of Sciences; Office of Technology Assessment; United States Congress; President, Power from Space Consulting, Inc, Lexington, Massachusetts, 1995-. Publications: More than 900 technical papers and books on space technology, solar power satellites, terrestrial solar energy applications, lunar surface characteristics, including: The Lunar Surface Layer, 1964; Solar Power Satellites, 1997; Guest Editor, Space Policy, 2000. Memberships: American Society of Mechanical Engineers; Board

Member, National Space Society; American Association for the Advancement of Science; Fellow, American Institute for Aeronautics and Astronautics; International Academy of Astronautics; American Society for Macroengineering; International Aeronautical Federation; Many others. Address: Power From Space Consulting Inc, 62 Turning Mill Road, Lexington, MA 02420-1010, USA.

GLATTRE Eystein Junker, b. 16 April 1934, Kristiansand, Norway. Epidemiologist. m. Ruth Lillian Jordal, 3 daughters. Education: MD, University of Oslo, 1962; Fellowship in Medical Statistics, Med Stat Institute, Oslo, 1965-67, Mayo Graduate School of Medicine, Rochester, USA, 1967-68; PhD, History of Ideas (Bio-temporal Structures), University of Aarhus, Denmark, 1980. Appointments: Assistant Professor, Nordic School of Public Health, Sweden, 1968-69; Consultant, Statistics Norway, 1969-70, Amanuensis, Institute of Preventive Medicine, University of Oslo, 1970-79; Senior Epidemiologist, 1980-91, Head of Department, 1992-2002, Cancer Registry of Norway; Leader of Norwegian Thyroid Cancer Project, 1985-; Board Member, Norwegian Canine Cancer Registry, 1990-2000; Professor in Epidemiology, Norwegian Veterinary College, 1992-2002; Main project since 1997 has been the development of fractal epidemiology. Publications: Around 160 papers and books on cancer research, trace element research, disease classification, cartography, vital statistics, theory of science and mathematics including: A Temporal Quantum Model, 1972; (co-author) Atlas of Cancer Incidence in Norway 1970-79, 1985; Prediagnostic s-Selenium in a Case-Control Study of Thyroid Cancer, 1989; Case-control study testing the hypothesis that seafood increases the risk of thyroid cancer, 1993; Human papillomavirus infection as a risk factor for squamous cell carcinoma of the head and neck, 2001; Fractal Analysis of a case-control study, 2002; The Norwegian Thyroid Cancer Project: History, achievements and present view on carcinogenesis, 2003; Fractal meta-analysis and causality embedded in complexity: Advanced understanding of disease aetiology, 2004. Honour: H M King Olav's Award for young mathematicians, 1953. Memberships: Norwegian Medical Association; Norwegian Epidemiological Association; European Thyroid Association; Czech Society for Experimental and Clinical Pharmacology and Toxicology. Address: Dron Ingeborgs v 14 N-3530 Royse, Norway.

GLENDINNING Victoria, b. 23 April 1937, Sheffield, England. Author; Journalist. m. (1) O N V Glendinning, 1958, 4 sons, (2) Terence de Vere White, 1981, (3) K P O'Sullivan, 1996. Education: BA, Honours, Modern Languages, Somerville College, Oxford, 1959; Diploma, Social Administration, 1969. Appointment: Editorial Assistant, Times Literary Supplement, 1970-74. Publications: A Suppressed Cry: Life and Death of a Quaker Daughter, 1969; Elizabeth Bowen: Portrait of a Writer, 1977; Edith Sitwell: A Unicorn Among Lions, 1981; Vita: The Life of Victoria Sackville-West, 1983; Rebecca West: A Life, 1987; The Grown-ups (novel), 1989; Hertfordshire, 1989; Trollope, 1992; Electricity (novel), 1995; Sons and Mothers (co-editor), 1996; Jonathan Swift, 1998; Flight (novel), 2002. Contributions to: Various journals, newspapers and magazines. Honours: Duff Cooper Memorial Award, 1981; James Tait Black Prize, 1981; Whitbread Awards, 1983, 1992; Whitbread Award, Trollope, 1992; Honorary DLitt, Southampton University, 1994, University of Ulster, 1995, Trinity College, Dublin, 1995, University of York, 2000; Commander of the Order of the British Empire, 1998. Memberships: Royal Society of Literature, Vice-President; English PEN, President, 2001-03; Vice-President, English PEN, 2004. Address: David Higham Associates, 5/8 Lower John Street, Golden Square, London W1, England.

Dictionary of International Biography

GLENN John Herschel, b. 18 July 1921, Cambridge, Ohio, USA. US Senator. m. Anna Margaret Castor, 1943, 1 son, 1 daughter. Education: Muskingum College; Naval Aviation Cadet program. Appointments: Marine Corps, 1943; Test Pilot, USN and Marine Corps; 1 of 1st 7 Astronauts in US Space Program, 1959; 1st American to orbit Earth, 1962; Resigned, US Marine Corps, 1965; Director, Roy Crown Cola Company, 1965-74; Consultant, NASA; US Senator, Ohio, 1975-99; Announced return as astronaut, 1997, on board Discovery shuttle, 1998. Publications: We Seven, co-author, 1962; P.S., I Listened to Your Heart Beat. Honours include: DFC 6 times; Air Medal with 18 Clusters; Set environmental speed record for 1st flight to average supersonic speeds from Los Angeles to New York, 1957; Space Congressional Medal of Honour; 1st Senator to win 4 consecutive terms in office. Address: Ohio State University, John Glenn Institute, 100 Bricker Hall, 190 North Oval Mall, Columbus, OH 43210, USA.

GLENNIE Evelyn, b. 19 July 1965, Aberdeen, Scotland. Musician. m. Gregorio Malcangi, 1993. Education: Ellon Academy, Aberdeenshire; Royal Academy of Music; Furthered studies in Japan on a Munster Trust Scholarship, 1986. Appointments: Solo debut Wigmore Hall, 1986; Concerts with major orchestras worldwide; Tours UK, Europe, USA, Canada, Australia, New Zealand, Far East, Japan, Middle East, South America, China; Performs many works written for her including Bennett, Bourgeois, Heath, Macmillan, McLeod, Muldowney and Musgrave; First solo percussionist to perform at the Proms, London, 1989, subsequent appearances, 1992, 1994, 1996, 1997. Creative work: Recordings include: Rebounds; Light in Darkness; Dancin'; Rhythm Song; Veni, Veni, Emmanuel; Wind in the Bamboo Grove; Drumming; Sonata for two pianos and percussion – Bela Bartok; Last Night of the Proms – 100th Season; Her Greatest Hits; The Music of Joseph Schwantner; Street Songs, Reflected in Brass; Shadow Behind the Iron Sun. Publications: Good Vibrations (autobiography), 1990; Great Journeys of the World, Beat It! Honours: Honorary Doctorates include: Honorary DMus from the Universities of Aberdeen, 1991, Bristol, 1995, Portsmouth, 1995, Surrey, 1997; Queens University, Belfast, 1998, Exeter, Southampton, 2000; Hon DLitt from Universities of Warwick, 1993, Loughborough, 1995; Numerous prizes include Queen's Commendation Prize (RAM); Gold Medal Shell/LSO Music Scholarship, 1984; Charles Heidsieck Soloist of the Year Award, Royal Philharmonic Society, 1991; OBE, 1993; Personality of the Year, International Classical Music Awards, 1993; Young Deaf Achievers Special Award, 1993; Best studio percussionist, Rhythm Magazine, 1998, 2000; Best Live Percussionist, Rhythm Magazine, 2000; Classic FM Outstanding Contribution to Classical Music, 2002; Walpole Medal of Excellence, 2002; Musical America, 2003; 2 Grammy Awards. Address: PO Box 6, Sawtry, Huntingdon, Cambs, PE17 5YF, England. E-mail: derren@evelyn.co.uk

GLOAG Julian, b. 2 July 1930, London, England. Novelist. 1 son, 1 daughter. Education: Exhibitioner, BA, 1953, MA, 1957, Magdalene College, Cambridge. Publications: Our Mother's House, 1963; A Sentence of Life, 1966; Maundy, 1969; A Woman of Character, 1973; Sleeping Dogs Lie, 1980; Lost and Found, 1981; Blood for Blood, 1985; Only Yesterday, 1986; Love as a Foreign Language, 1991; Le passeur de la nuit, 1996; Chambre d'ombre, 1996. Teleplays: Only Yesterday, 1986; The Dark Room, 1988. Memberships: Royal Society of Literature, fellow; Authors Guild. Address: 36 rue Gabrielle, 75018 Paris, France

GLOVER Danny, b. 22 July 1946, Georgia, USA. Actor. m. Asake Bomani, 1 daughter. Education: San Francisco State University. Appointments: Researcher, Office of Mayor, San Francisco, 1971-75; Member, American Conservatory Theatre's Black Actor Workshop; Broadway debut, Master Harold...and the Boys, 1982; Other stage appearances include: The Blood Knot, 1982; The Island; Sizwe Banzi is Dead; Macbeth; Suicide in B Flat; Nevis Mountain Dew; Jukebox; Appearances in TV films and series; Founder, with wife, Bomani Gallery, San Francisco; Actor films: Escape From Alacatraz, 1979; Chu Chu and the Philly Flash, 1981; Out, 1982; Iceman, 1984; Places in the Heart, 1984; Birdy, 1984; The Color Purple, 1984; Silverado, 1985; Witness, 1985; Lethal Weapon, 1987; Bat 21, 1988; Lethal Weapon II, 1989; To Sleep With Anger, 1990; Predator 2, 1990; Flight of the Intruder, 1991; A Rage in Harlem, 1991; Pure Luck, 1991; Grand Canyon, 1992; Lethal Weapon II, 1992; The Saint of Fort Washington, 1993; Bopha, 1993; Angles in the Outfield, 1994; Operation Dumbo Drop, 1995; America's Dream, 1996; The Rainmaker, 1997; Wings Against the Wind, 1998; Beloved, 1998; Lethal Weapon IV, 1998; Prince of Egypt (voice), 1998; Antz (voice), 1998; The Monster, 1999; Bàttu, 2000; Boseman and Lena, 2000; Wings Against the Wind, 2000; Freedom Song, 2000; 3 A M, 2001; The Royal Tenebaums, 2001; The Real Eve (TV series), 2002; Good Fences (TV), 2003; Saw, 2004; The Cookout, 2004. Address: c/o Cary Productions Inc, PMB 352, 6114 LaSalle Avenue, Oakland, CA 9461, USA.

GLOVER Judith, b. 31 March 1943, Wolverhampton, England. Author. 2 daughters. Education: Wolverhampton High School for Girls, 1954-59; Aston Polytechnic, 1960. Publications: Drink Your Own Garden (non-fiction), 1979; The Sussex Quartet: The Stallion Man, 1982, Sisters and Brothers, 1984, To Everything a Season, 1986; Birds in a Gilded Cage, 1987; The Imagination of the Heart, 1989; Tiger Lilies, 1991; Mirabelle, 1992; Minerva Lane, 1994; Pride of Place, 1995; Sussex Place-Names (non-fiction), 1997. Address: c/o Artellus Ltd, 30 Dorset House, Gloucester Place, London NW1 5AD, England.

GLYN Susan, b. 17 May 1923, London, England. Poet; Sculptor; Stained Glass Designer. m. Anthony Glyn, 2 daughters, 1 deceased. Education: Studied Philosophy, London University, 1962-64. Appointments: Called to Bar, 1950; Barrister, Wales and Chester Circuit, 1950-64; Paris Art Correspondent, The Tablet, 1967-87; Hanging Committee, Art Sacré Salon, Paris, 1965-88; Hanging Committee, Union des Femmes Peintres, 1983-86; International Editor, Studia Mystica Quarterly, California State University, 1969-84. Publications: The State of British Industry: National News Letter, 1948; Green Blood and other poems, 1960; A New Look at Britain's Economic Policy by Dame Juliet Rhys-Williams (editor), 1965; Next Stop Eternity (poems), 1999; The Word and the Image (illustrator), 1999; Phoenix Time (poems), 2000; Companion Guide to Paris (editor revised edition), 2000; New Christian Poems, 2001; Earth and Heaven (poems), 2003. Contributions to: Numerous poems in poetry magazines and reviews including English, The Poetry Review and The Glass; Articles and reviews in literary and art magazines; Seven poetry prizes; Radio and television interviews in New York, Chicago, London, Paris, Birmingham, Bristol and Portsmouth and eight poems broadcast. Membership: Arts Centre Group, London. Address: Marina Baie des Anges, Ducal, Appt U-03, Villeneuve-Loubet, F-06270, France.

GMEINER Antoinette Christine, b. 19 November 1961, Johannesburg, South Africa. Director, Organisational Behaviour. m. Franz Gmeiner, 1 son, 2 daughters. Education: B. Cur., 1984; B. Cur., Education and Administration, 1986; M. Cur., Psychiatric Nursing, 1987; D. Cur., Psychiatric Nursing, 1993; Currently studying for MBA, De Montford, South Africa. Appointments: Lecturer, Senior Lecturer, Associate Professor, Rand Afrikaans University, -1993; Director, Orion Group, 1993-. Publications: Editor, 1 book; 1 book chapter; Many articles in national and international academic journals. Honours: Academic Awards; NRF

Rated (only 10 researchers in South Africa are rated). memberships: Institute of Directors, Southern Africa; South African Excellence Foundation; South African Council of Coaches and Mentors; Victor Franki Foundation. Address: PO Box 2011, Johannesburg, South Africa 2000. E-mail: agmeiner@oriongroup.co.za

GMEINER Franz, b. 10 March 1958, Austria. Chartered Accountant. m. Antoinette Gmeiner. 1 son, 2 daughters. Education: B Com, South Africa, 1982; B Com Honours, South Africa, 1983; Chartered Accountant, South Africa, 1983. Appointments: Business Analyst, Sentrachem, 1983-85; Partner, Cohen & Gmeiner Accountants, 1985-98; Chief Executive Officer, Orion Group, 1999-. Honours: Top Ten, Board Exam Accountants and Auditors, 1983; Academic Colours, Rand Afrikaans University, 1983. Memberships: South African Institute of Chartered Accountants; Rand Club; Country Club, Johannesburg. Address: 16th Floor, Devonshire House, 49 Jorissen Street, Braamfontein, Johannesburg, South Africa. E-mail: fgmeiner@oriongroup.co.za

GO Shuken, b. 28 July 1953, Ikeda City, Osaka, Japan. Language Educator. m. Takami Okuda, 2 daughters. Education: Bachelor of Arts, English, Whittier College, USA, 1972-76; Certificate in Teaching English as a Foreign Language, English Language Centre, UK, 1995; Diploma in General Counselling, Institute of Counselling, UK, 2002-2003. Appointments: Drafter and Surveyor, Swiss SGS, Kobe, Japan, 1977-82; Market Analyst, Far East Trade Service Centre, Osaka, Japan, 1983-88; Director, SKG Language Services, Nishinomiya, Japan, 1988-95; Director, Go Communications LLC, Kobe, Japan, 1995-. Publications: Articles in the ISU Review, Whittier College, USA, 1973-76; Articles in the Courier Mail, Australia, 1995. Honours: Excellence in French, French Government Award, 1972; Special International Scholarship, Whittier College, 1972. Memberships: Phi Sigma Tau, National Honor Society, USA, 1972- National Geographic Society, USA, 1996-. Address: 4-8-35 Kanokodai-Kitamachi, Kita-ku, Kobe, Japan 651-1513. E-mail: going5@nifty.com

GOAMAN Michael, b. 14 February 1921, East Grinstead, England. Stamp and Banknote Designer. m. Sylvia Goaman, 3 daughters. Education: RU School of Art; Central School of Arts and Crafts. Career: Designer; Stamps and bank notes; Stained glass private commissions; Millennium Window, St Peters Church, Bramshaw. Publications: European Stamp Design, D Scott Academy Ed.; Articles in various magazines. Membership: WWF. Address: Pilgrims Furzley, Bramshaw, Lyndhurst, Hants SO 43 7JL, England.

GOAMAN Sylvia, b. 30 April 1924, London, England. Textile Designer. m. Michael Goaman, 3 daughters. Education: Academy Julian; Slade School of Art; Central School of Arts and Crafts. Career: Textile Designer; Millennium Tapestry; Millennium Window, St Peters Church, Bramshaw; Various private commissions in stained glass. Membership: Women's Institute. Address: Pilgrims Furzley, Bramshaw, Lyndhurst, Hants SO43 7JL, England.

GODARD Philippe Henri Jean, b. 6 February 1937, Versailles, France. Civil Engineer. m. (1) Danièle Calliet (2) Danièle Caro, 2 sons, 3 daughters. Education: Licencié ès Sciences Physics; Civil Engineer, Ecole Centrale du Nord (IDN). Appointments: Director, "Société Générale d'Entreprise", New Caledonia, 1968-71; Director, BET "OTEC", New Caledonia, 1972-75; Expert at the Court of Appeal and the Tribunal, New Caledonia, 1976-88; President of the Company of Judicial Experts, New Caledonia. Publications: Books include: Wallis et Futuna; Reflets de la Nouvelle-Calédonie; le Memorial Calédonien (9 volumes); Fleurs en Nouvelle Caledonie; Futuna, Perle du Pacifique; La Nouvelle-

Calédonie que J'aime; The First and Last Voyage of the Batavia; The Tasmanian Tiger: A Lesson to be learnt; Lattes, the Mysterious Megaliths of the Marianas; Louis de Saint-Alouarn, Lieutenant des Vaisseaux du Roy; Several articles in French and Swiss magazines. Honour: Chevalier de la Légion d'Honneur. Address: 4 Lumeah Court, Darlington, 6070 WA, Australia.

GODBERT Geoffrey Harold, b. 11 June 1937, Manchester, England. Poet. 1 son, 1 daughter. Education: Royal Manchester College of Music, Performance. Publications: Ides of March, 1975; The Lover Will Dance Incredibly, 1981; Still Lifes (co-author), 1983; Journey to the Edge of Light, 1985; The Brooklyn Bridge, 1985; The Theatre of Decision, 1985; For Now (co-author), 1991; Are You Interested in Tattooing?, 1996; I Was Not, Was Not, Mad Today, 1997. Contributions to: Anthologies and magazines. Address: 12 High Street, Milverton, Somerset TA4 1LL England.

GODFREY Paul, b. 16 September 1960, Exeter, Devon, England. Playwright; Director; Screenwriter. Publications: Inventing a New Colour, 1988; A Bucket of Eels, 1989; Once in a While the Odd Thing Happens, 1990; The Panic, 1991; The Blue Ball, 1993; The Modern Husband, 1994; The Candidate, 1995; The Invisible Woman, 1996; Catalogue of Misunderstanding, 1997; Collected Plays, Volume One, 1998; Tiananmen Square, 1999; The Oldest Play, 2000; Linda, 2000. Address: c/o A P Watt Ltd, 20 John Street, London, WC1, England. E-mail: rkraitt@apwatt.co.uk

GOH Robbie Boon Hua, b. 31 October 1964, Singapore. Academic. m. Mervyln, 2 sons. Education: BA direct honours, first class, 1988; MA, National University of Singapore, 1989; PhD, The University of Chicago, 1993. Appointments: Associate Professor, Deputy Head, Department of English, National University of Singapore. Publications: Over 50 books and scholarly articles in books and journals. Honours: Fulbright Fellowship, 1996; Listed in national and international biographical dictionaries. Memberships: Fulbright Association of Singapore. Address: Department of English Language and Literature, National University of Singapore, 7 Arts Link, Singapore 117570. E-mail: ellgohbh@nus.edu.sg

GOINO Tadashi, b. 27 June 1950, Niigata, Japan. Artist; Writer. Appointments: Painter, novelist, writer, photographer, musician, composer; Founder, WIPPII General Research Institute, active campaigner on environment, 1974-; Involved with organic farming and renewing forests; Donated over nine thousand original Japanese prints to schools, museums, libraries both nationally and abroad; Established Goino Procedure using natural materials to treat cancer, in Ukraine, Russia, Malta and Latvia, he announced The Theoretical Medical Science of Cancer Control by the Goino Procedure in 1996, this was put forward at an international medical conference in New York, 2001, where it attracted a great deal of attention and at an international medical symposium related to heart disease and strokes in Florence, Italy, 2002; Co-founder, co-president, 911 (non-profit rescue organisation) St Petersburg, Russia, 1995-; Exhibitions and lectures on Ukiyo-e art include: The Ukiyo-e Prints That Van Gogh Loved and Tadashi Goino Exhibition, The Hermitage, Russia; Organised Utagawaha Monjinkai. Publications include: (book) Hokke Sanbukyo Taikei (The Outline of Triple Sutras of Hokke); (novel) Shichijigen yorino Shisha (Messenger from the seventh dimension). Honours: Numerous honorary doctorates, professorships, academicianships include Honorary Professor, European University (in medicine); Academician, Armenian National Academy of Sciences, 1998; Honorary Academician, Russian Academy of Art; Professor, Social Hygiene and Organising of Health (elected by the highest Judging Committee among academies in the Russian Federation); Honorary Academician, Ukrainian Medical Stomatological Academy; The

Malta Knight Order; Other honours include: St Stanislav Order, 1998; Pavel Tretyakov Medal (Art), 1998; Pavlov Medal (Physiology), 1998; Jukov Medal (Culture), 1998; Popov Medal (Invention, Discovery), 1998; Kapitsa Prize (Physics), 1999; Peter Gold Medal Prize (Economics), 1999; Tretyakov Gold Medal in Culture and Art, 2000; Vernadsky Star Medal, 2000; Medal, Pushkin's 200 Year Anniversary, 2000. Memberships include: President, International Academy of Sciences of Nature and Society (Japanese Branch). Address: WIPPII General Research Institute, 2082 Taira, Omachi, Nagano, Japan.

GOLAN Shammai, b. 5 April 1933, Poland. Emigrated to Israel, 1947. Holocaust Survivor; Hebrew Writer; Diplomat. m. Arna Ben-Dror, 2 sons, 2 daughters. Education: BA, Literature and History, Hebrew University of Jerusalem, 1961. Appointments: Director, Writers' House, Jerusalem, 1971-78; Head, Department of Jewish Education and Culture for the Diaspora, Buenos Aires, Argentina, 1978-81; Chairman, Hebrew Writers' Association, 1981-84, 1989-91; Counsellor, Cultural Affairs, Embassy of Israel, Mexico, 1984-87, Moscow, 1994-99; Director and Secretary, Board of Directors, Society of Authors, Composers and Music Publishers in Israel, 2000-. Publications: Novels and short stories: The Last Watch; Guilt Offerings; The Death of Uri Peled; Escape for Short Distances; Canopy: The Ambush; Holocaust: Anthology; Scenarios; Radio plays; Numerous articles. Honours: Literary Awards: Barash, 1962; Acum, 1965; Ramat-Gan, 1973; The Agnon Jerusalem, 1976; Prime Minister's Prize, 1992. Memberships: Hebrew Writers' Association; PEN Centre; ACUM; Cultural Academy of Mexico; Council, Yad Vashem Museum Memorial. Address: 1 Haamoraim Str, Tel Aviv 69207, Israel.

GOLDBERG Abraham (Sir), b. 7 December 1923, Edinburgh, Scotland. Professor of Medicine. m. Clarice Cussin, 2 sons, 1 daughter. Education: MBChB, University of Edinburgh, 1941-46; MD (Gold Medal), Edinburgh, 1956; FRCP, Glasgow, 1964; FRCP, Edinburgh, 1965; DSc, University of Glasgow, 1966; FRCP, London, 1967; FRSE, 1971; FFPM, 1989. Appointments include: Nuffield Research Fellow, University College Hospital Medical School, 1952-54; Medical Research Council Travelling Fellow in Medicine, University of Utah, USA, 1954-56; Regius Professor of Materia Medica, University of Glasgow, 1970-78; Chairman, Medical Research Council Grants Committee, 1973-77; Regius Professor of the Practice of Medicine, now Emeritus, University of Glasgow, 1978-89; Chairman, Committee on the Safety of Medicines, 1980-86; Honorary Professorial Research Fellow, Department of Modern History, University of Glasgow, 1996-. Publications: Diseases of Porphyrin Metabolism (co-author), 1962; Recent Advances in Haematology (co-editor), 1971; Disorders of Porphyrin Metabolism (co-author), 1987; Pharmaceutical Medicine and the Law (co-editor), 1991; Papers on clinical and investigative medicine, 1951-. Honours: Editor, Scottish Medical Journal, 1962-63; Sydney Watson Smith Lecturer, Royal College of Physicians, Edinburgh, 1964; Henry Cohen Lecturer, University of Jerusalem, 1973; Knighted (KB), 1983; Fitzpatrick Lecturer, Royal College of Physicians, London, 1988; Goodall Memorial Lecturer, Royal College of Physicians and Surgeons of Glasgow, 1989; Lord Provost Award for Public Service, City of Glasgow, 1988; Foundation President, Faculty of Pharmaceutical Medicine of the Royal Colleges of Physicians, 1989. Membership: Association of Physicians of Great Britain and Ireland. Address: 16 Birnam Crescent, Bearsden, Glasgow, G61 2AU, Scotland.

GOLDBERG Vladislav, b. 4 January 1936, Moscow, USSR. Mathematician; Educator. m. Ludmila Goldberg Pikuleva, 2 sons. Education: MSc, 1953-58, PhD, 1958-61, Moscow St University, USSR. Appointments: Senior Scientific Editor, Publishing House, MIR, Moscow, 1961; Associate Professor, Mathematics

Department, Yaroslavl Pedagogical Institute, 1961-64; Professor, Mathematics Department, 1964-78, Senior Research Scientist, 1968-78, Moscow Institute of Steel and Alloys; Visiting Professor, Mathematics Department, Lehigh University, Bethlehem, Pennsylvania, USA, 1979-81; Professor, 1981-85, Distinguished Professor, 1985-, Mathematics Department, New Jersey Institute of Technology, Newark, New Jersey, USA. Publications: 15 books and over 100 papers in Mathematics. Honours: MSc, Honours, 1958; National Science Foundation Grant, 1980-82; Elected Corresponding Member of Academy Peloritana Pericolanti, Italy, 1981; J Perlis Award for Excellence in Research, 1985; Excellence in Teaching Awards, 1991, 1998; Visiting Member, Math Forschungsinstitut Oberwolfach, Germany, 1991, 1992, 1994, 1995, 1998, 2002, 2003, 2004. Memberships: Moscow Mathematical Society, 1960-79; American Mathematical Society, 1979-; Tensor Society, Japan, 1981-. Address: Department of Mathematical Sciences, New Jersey Institute of Technology, University Heights, Newark, NJ 07102, USA.

GOLDBERG Whoopi, b. 13 November 1949, New York, USA. Actress. m. (2) D Claessen, 1986, divorced 1988, 1 daughter, (3) L Trachtenberg, 1994, divorced, 1995. Career: First appearance aged 8, Hudson Guild Theatre, New York; Helen Rubenstein Children's Theatre, San Diego, moved 1974; Co-founder, San Diego Repertory Theatre, appeared in 2 productions, Brecht's Mother Courage and Marsha Norman's Getting Out; Moved to San Francisco, Jointed Blake Street Hawkeyes Theatre, appeared in The Spook Show and Moms, co-wrote, a one-woman show in US Tours, debut, The Lyceum Theatre, Broadway, 1984; Films include: The Color Purple, 1985; Jumpin' Jack Flash, Ghost, 1990; Sister Act; Made in America, 1992; Sister Act II; Corrina Corrina, 1993; Star Trek Generation 5; Moonlight and Valentino; Bogus; Eddie; The Associate, 1996; The Ghost of Mississippi, 1996; How Stella Got Her Groove Back, 1998; Deep End of the Ocean, 1999; Jackie's Back! 1999; Girl Interrupted, 1999; Rat Race, 2001; Call Me Claus, 2001; Kingdom Come, 2001; Monkeybone, 2001; Golden Dreams, 2001; Star Trek: Nemesis, 2002; Blizzard (voice), 2002; TV Appearances in Moonlighting, 1985-86; own TV show, 1992-93. Honours: Several nominations as best actress for The Color Purple including Academy Award, Golden Globe; Emmy Nomination for Moonlighting; Grammy for Best Comedy Album, 1985.

GOLDBLUM Jeff, b. 22 October 1952, Pittsburgh, USA. Actor. m. (2) Geena Davis, divorced. Education: Studied at New York Neighbourhood Playhouse. Career: Actor, films include: California Split, 1974; Death Wish, 1974; Nashville, 1975; Next Stop Greenwich Village, 1976; Annie Hall, 1977; Between the Lines, 19777; The Sentinel, 1977; Invasion of the Body Snatchers, 1978; Remember My Name, 1978; Thank God it's Friday, 1978; Escape From Athena, 1979; The Big Chill, 1983; The Right Stuff, 1983; Threshold, 1983; The Adventures of Buckaroo Banzai, 1984; Silverado, 1985; Into the Night, 1985; Transylvania 6-5000, 1985; the Fly, 1986; Beyond Therapy, 1987; The Tall Guy, 1989; Earth Girls Are Easy, 1989; First Born (TV), 1989; The Mad Monkey, 1990; Mister Frost, 1991; Deep Cover, 1992; The Favour, The Watch and the Very Big Fish, 1992; Father and Sons, 1993; Jurassic Park, 1993; Lushlife (TV), 1994; Future Quest (TV), 1994; Hideaway, 1995; Nine Months, 1995; Independence Day, 1996; The Lost World, 1997; Holy Man, 1998; Popcorn, 1999; Chain of Fools, 2000; Angie Rose, 2000; Cats and Dogs, 2001; Producer: Little Surprises, 1995; Holy Man, 1999. Address: c/o Peter Lemie, William Morris Agency, 151 El Camino Drive, Beverly Hills, CA 90212, USA.

GOLDENBERG Iosif Sukharovich, b. 1 May 1927, Ukraine. School Teacher. Education: PhD, Philology Department, Kharkov State University, 1949. Publications: Tavolga, English translation as Meadow-sweet; Nad Propast'yu v Tishi, English translation as On the Verge of Abyss in the Silence; Zalozhniki Zaveta, English translation as Hostages of Behest; Izbrannoe, English translation as Selected Rhymes. Contributions to: Periodicals. Address: Building AB-1, Apt 43, 142292 Pushchino, Moscow Region, Russia.

GOLDER Herbert Alan, b. 29 October 1952, Philadelphia, Pennsylvania, USA. Professor; Writer; Film Maker. Education: BA, Boston University, 1975; MA, 1977, M Phil, 1979, Yale University; Oxford University, 1982; PhD, Yale University, 1984. Appointments: Instructor, Lecturer, Classics, Yale University, 1977-80; Assistant Professor of Classics, Syracuse University, 1982-85; Visiting Assistant Professor of Classics, 1984-85, Assistant Professor of Classics, 1985-87, Emory University; Assistant Professor of Classics, 1988-93, Associate Professor of Classics, 1993-, Boston University; Editor-in-Chief, Arion, A Journal of Humanities and the Classics at Boston University, 1990-. Publications include: The Greek Tragedy in New Translations, general editor with William Arrowsmith, 23 volumes, 1985-96; Sophocles Aias, 1999; Euripides, The Bacchae, 2001; Films include: Invincible, co-writer (English adaptation) and assistant director (to Werner Herzog). Honours: Phoenix Award for Significant Editorial Achievement, 1992; Emmy Award, nomination, 1999; PEN/Book of the Month Club Translation Prize, nomination, 2000. Address: c/o Arion, 621 Commonwealth Avenue, Boston, MA02215, USA. E-mail: redlog@bu.edu

GOLDING Allan Peter, b. 26 March 1960, Jamestown, South Australia. Physician. m. Dymphna, 2 sons, 1 daughter. Education: MBBS, University of Adelaide, Australia, 1984; Diploma in Obstetrics, Gynaecology and Neonatal Care, Royal Australian and New Zealand College of Obstetrics and Gynaecology, 1987; Registered Medical Board of South Australia; Certificate, Civil Aviation Medicine, Australia, 2001. Appointments include: Intern, Royal Adelaide Hospital, Adelaide, 1984; Resident Medical Officer, Lyell McEwin Health Service, Elizabeth Vale, 1985-86; Resident Medical Officer, Modbury Hospital, Modbury, South Australia, 1987; Rural General Practice, Medicine, Surgery and Obstetrics, Port Pirie, South Australia, 1988-; Clinical Lecturer, University of Adelaide, Department of General Practice, 1993-; Designated Aviation Medical Examiner, 2000-; Steering Committee, Mid-North Rural South Australia Division General Practice, 1994-; Chairman, Drug and Therapeutics Committee, Port Pirie Regional Health Service Inc, 1994-2000; Mental Health Advisory Committee, Mid-North Regional Health Service Inc, 1996-2000; Medical Officer, Port Pirie Abattoir, 1991-; Club Surgeon, Port Pirie Racing and Harness Club, 1993-95; Club Doctor, Port Pirie Power Boat Club, 1990-2003. Publications: Articles in medical journals as co-author: South Australian Hypertension Survey. General Practitioner Knowledge and Reported Management Practices – A Cause for Concern? 1992; A Comparison of Outcomes with Angiotensin-Converting Enzyme Inhibitors and Diuretics for Hypertension in the Elderly. Memberships include: Fellow, Royal Australian College of General Practitioners; Fellow, Australian College of Rural and Remote Medicine; Port Pirie Medical Practitioners Society; Australian Medical Association; Sports Medicine Australia; International Federation of Sports Medicine; Arthritis Foundation of Australia; Rural Doctors Association of Australia; Australasian Society of Aerospace Medicine; Port Pirie Asthma Support Group; Life Member, Asthma Foundation; Leader Member, Lord Baden-Powell Society. Address: Central Clinic, 101 Florence Street, Port Pirie, SA 5540, Australia. E-mail: supadocs@westnet.com.au

GOLDMAN William, b. 12 August 1931, Chicago, Illinois, USA. Author. m. Ilene Jones, 1961, 2 daughters. Education: Columbia University. Publications: Novels: The Temple of Gold, 1957; Your

Turn to Curtsey, My Turn to Bow, 1958; Soldier in the Rain, 1960; Boys and Girls Together, 1964; The Thing of It Is, 1964; No Way to Treat a Lady (as Harry Longbaugh); Father's Day, 1971; Marathon Man, 1974; Wigger, 1974; Magic, 1976; Tinsel, 1979; Control, 1982; The Silent Gondoliers, 1983; The Color of Light, 1984; Play: Blood Sweat and Stanley Poole (with James Goldman), 1961; Musical comedy: A Family Affair (with James Goldman and John Kander), 1962; Non-fiction: Adventures in the Screen Trade, 1983; Hype and Glory, 1990; Four Screenplays, 1995; Five Screenplays, 1997; Screenplays: Harper, 1966; Butch Cassidy and the Sundance Kid, 1969; The Princess Bride, 1973; Marathon Man, 1976; All the President's Men, 1976; A Bridge Too Far, 1977; Magic, 1978; Heat, 1985; Brothers, 1987; Year of the Comet, 1992; Memoirs of an Invisible Man, 1992; Chaplin, 1992; Indecent Proposal, 1993; Maverick, 1994; Ghost and the Darkness, 1996; Absolute Power, 1997; Hearts in Atlantis, 2001. Honours: Academy Awards, 1970, 1977. Address: c/o William Morris, 151 El Camino Drive, Beverly Hills, CA 90212, USA.

GOLDSMITH Harvey, b. 4 March 1946, London, England. Chief Executive; Impresario. m. Diana Gorman, 1971, 1 son. Education: Christ's College; Brighton College of Technology. Appointments: Partner, Big O Posters, 1966-67; Organised first free open-air concert, Parliament Hill Fields, with Michael Alfandary, 1968; Opened Round House, Camden Town, 1968, Crystal Palace Garden Party series concerts, 1969-72; Merged with John Smith Entertainment, 1970; Formed Harvey Goldsmith Entertainment (rock tours promotion co), 1976; Acquired Allied Entertainment Group (rock concert promotions co), 1984; Formed Classical Productions with Mark McCormack, 1986; Promoter and Producer, pop rock, classical musical events including: Concerts: Bruce Springsteen; The Rolling Stones; Elton John; The Who; Pink Floyd; Opera: Aïda, 1988, Carmen, 1989, Tosca, 1991, Earls Court; Pavarotti at Wembley, 1986; Pavarotti in the Park, 1991; The Three Tenors, 1996; Mastercard Masters of Music, 1996; The Eagles, 1996; Music for Monserrat, 1997; The Bee Gees, 1998; Ozzfest, 1998; Paul Weller, 1998. Honour: CBE, 1996. Memberships include: Chairman, Concert Promoters Association, 1986; Chairman, National Music Festival, 1991; Co-Chairman, President's Club, 1994; Vice Chairman, Prince's Trust Action Management Board, 1993; VP, REACT, 1989; VP, Music Users Council, 1994; Trustee, Band Aid, 1985; Trustee, Live Aid Foundation, 1985; Trustee, Royal Opera House, 1995; Trustee, CST, 1995; British Red Cross Coms Panel, 1992; Prague Heritage Fund, 1994; London Tourist Board, 1994. Address: Harvey Goldsmith Entertainment Ltd., Greenland Place, 115-123 Bayham Street, London NW1 0AG, England.

GOLDSMITH Howard, (Ward Smith, Dayle Courtney), b. 24 August 1945, New York, New York, USA. Author; Editor. Education: BA, Honours, City University of New York, 1965; MA, Honours, University of Michigan, 1966. Appointments: Editorial Consultant, Mountain View Center for Environmental Education, University of Colorado, 1970-85; Senior Editor, Santillana Publishing Company, 1980-85; Contributing Editor, Children's Magic Window, 1987-90. Publications: The Whispering Sea, 1976; What Makes a Grumble Smile?, 1977; The Shadow and Other Strange Tales, 1977; Terror by Night, 1977; Spine-Chillers, 1978; Sooner Round the Corner, 1979; Invasion: 2200 A.D., 1979; Toto the Timid Turtle, 1980; The Ivy Plot, 1981; Three-Ring Inferno, 1982; Plaf Le Paresseux, 1982; Ninon, Miss Vison, 1982; Toufou Le Hibou, 1982; Fourtou Le Kangourou, 1982; The Tooth Chicken, 1982; Mireille l'Abeille, 1982; Little Dog Lost, 1983; Stormy Day Together, 1983; The Sinister Circle, 1983; Shadow of Fear, 1983; Treasure Hunt, 1983; The Square, 1983; The Circle, 1983; The Contest, 1983; Welcome, Makoto!, 1983; Helpful Julio, 1984; The Secret of Success, 1984; Pedro's Puzzling

Birthday, 1984; Rosa's Prank, 1984; A Day of Fun, 1984; The Rectangle, 1984; Kirby the Kangaroo, 1985; Ollie the Owl, 1985; The Twiddle Twins' Haunted House, 1985; Young Ghosts, 1985; Von Geistern Besessen, 1987; The Further Adventures of Batman, 1989; Visions of Fantasy, 1989; The Pig and the Witch, 1990; The Mind-Stalkers, 1990; Spooky Stories, 1990; Little Quack and Baby Duckling, 1991; The Proust Syndrome, 1992; The President's Train, 1991; Thomas Edison Had a Bright Idea, 1993; Evil Tales of Evil Things, 1993; The Twiddle Twins' Music Box Mystery, 1996; The Gooey Chewy Contest, 1996; The Twiddle Twins' Amusement Park Mystery, 1997; McGraw-Hill Science Through Stories Series, 1998; The Twiddle Twins' Single Footprint Mystery, 1999; The Tooth Fairy Mystery, 1999; Danger Zone, 2000; Strike up the Band, 2000; See It Fly, 2000; Thomas Edison to the Rescue!, 2003; Mark Twain at Work, 2003. Contributions to: Periodicals, journals, magazines, reviews and newspapers. Honours: Several. Memberships: Poets and Writers; Science Fiction Writers of America; Society of Children's Book Writers and Illustrators; Phi Beta Kappa; Sigma Xi; Phi Kappa Phi; Psi Chi. Address: 41-07 Bowne Street #6B, Flushing, NY 11355-5629, USA.

GOLDSMITH Jerry, b. 10 February 1929, Los Angeles, USA. Film Music Composer. m. Carol Sheinkopf. Education: Los Angeles City College; Berklee College of Music. Career: Composer, TV scores: Twilight Zone; General Electric Theatre; Doctor Kildare; Gunsmoke; Climax Playhouse 90; Studio One; Star Trek: Voyager; Film scores include: The Stripper, 1962; The Prize, Seven Days in May, 1963; In Harm's Way, The Man From UNCLE, Von Ryan's Express, A Patch of Blue, The Blue Max, Our Man Flint, Seconds, Stagecoach, 1965; The Sand Pebbles, 1966; In Like Flint, 1967; Planet of the Apes, 1968; Tora! Tora! Tora!, Patton, 1970; Wild Rovers, 1971; The Other, The Red Pony, 1972; Papillon, 1973; QB VII, Chinatown, 1974; Logan's Run, 1975; The Omen, Islands in the Stream, 1976; MacArthur, Coma, 1977; The Boys From Brazil, Damien - Omen II, 1978; Alien, 1979; Masada, Star Trek: The Motion Picture, 1979; The Final Conflict, 1981; Outland, Raggedy Man, 1981; Poltergeist, First Blood, Twilight Zone: The Movie, Psycho II, Under Fire, 1983; Gremlins, 1984; Legend, Explorers, Rambo: First Blood II, 1985; Poltergeist II: the Other Side, Hoosiers, 1986; Innerspace, Extreme Prejudice, 1987; Rambo II, 1988; Criminal Law, The 'Burbs', Leviathan, Star Trek V: The Final Frontier, Total Recall, Gremlins, The Russia House, 1990; Sleeping With the Enemy, Medicine Man, 1991; Basic Instinct, Forever Young, 1992; The Vanishing, Dennis the Menace, Malice, 1993; City Hall, 1995; Star Trek: First Contact, 1996; LA Confidential, 1997; Air Force One, 1997; The Edge, 1997; Deep Rising, 1997; US Marshals, 1998; Small Soldiers, 1998; Mulan, 1998; Star Trek: Insurrection, 1998; The Mummy, 1999; The 13th Warrior, 1999; The Haunting, 1999; Hollow Man, 2000; Along Came a Spider, 2001; The Last Castle, 2001; The Sum of All Dears, 2002; Star Trek: Nemesis, 2002; Ballet scores include: A patch of Blue, 1970; Othello, 1971; Capricorn One, 1989. Honours: Max Steiner Award, National Film Society, 1982; Richard Kirk Award, BMI, 1987; Golden Score Award, American Society of Music Arrangers, 1990; Career Achievement Award, Society for Preservation of Film Music, 1993; 1st American Music Legend Award, Variety, 1995. Address: c/o Savitsky & Co, Suite 1450, 1901 Avenue of Stars, Los Angeles, CA 90067, USA.

GOLDSMITH Zac, b. 20 January 1975, Westminster, London. Editor. m. Sheherazada Ventura-Bentley, 2 daughters. Appointments: Member, International Honours Programme, Global Ecology Course, visiting Eastern Europe, India, Thailand, New Zealand, Mexico, United States, 1993-94; Worked with Redefining Progress, Non-Governmental Organisation, San Francisco, USA, 1994-95; Member, currently Associate Director, International

Society for Ecology and Culture based in California, USA, Bristol, UK, Ladakh, India; 1995-97; Ran tourist education programme, Ladakh, India; Editor, The Ecologist Magazine, 1997-; Board Member, JMG Foundation; The Fondation de Sauve; L'Association Goldsmith pour L'Environment, L'Artisanat et le Mond Rural. Founder, FARM, campaigning membership organisation for British farmers; Delivered speeches at venues including: The Schumacher Memorial Lectures; The Oxford Union; Numerous schools colleges and think-tanks in the UK. Publications: Newspaper articles for: The Times, The Sunday Times, The Daily Mail, The Mail on Sunday, The Independent, The Guardian, The Observer, The Standard, The Express, The Telegraph, Tribune, many regional British newspapers; Magazine articles in: The Ecologist Magazine (over 30), Country Life, The Big Issue, The New Statesman, The Week, Global Agenda 2003, Geographical, Tatler, Vanity Fair. Memberships: Aspinalls; Travellers; Mark's. Address: Unit 18 Chelsea Wharf, 15 Lots Road, London SW10 0QJ, England. E-mail: zeco@compuserve.con

GOLDSTEIN Robert Justin, b. 28 March 1947, Albany, New York, USA. College Professor. Education: BA, University of Illinois, 1969; MA, 1971, PhD, 1976, University of Chicago. Appointments: Research and Administrative Assistant, University of Illinois, 1972-73; Lecturer, San Diego State University, 1974-76; Assistant Professor, Associate Professor, Full Professor, Oakland University, Rochester, Michigan, 1976-. Publications: Political Repression in Modern America, 1978, revised edition, 2001; Political Repression in Nineteenth Century Europe, 1983; Political Censorship of the Press and the Arts in Nineteenth Century Europe, 1989; Censorship of Political Caricature in Nineteenth Century France, 1989; Saving "Old Glory": The History of the American Flag Desecration Controversy, 1995; Burning the Flag: The Great 1989-90 American Flag Desecration Controversy, 1996; Desecrating the American Flag: Key Documents from the Controversy from the Civil War to 1995, 1996; The War for the Public Mind: Political Censorship in Nineteenth Century Europe, 2001; Flag Burning and Free Speech: The Case of Texas V Johnson, 2000; Political Censorship: The New York Times Twentieth Century in Review, 2001. Address: Department of Political Science, Oakland University, Rochester, MI 48309, USA. E-mail: goldstei@oakland.edu

GOLMAN Klaes, b. 9 February 1945, Malmö, Sweden. Professor; General Manager. m. Margit, 1 son, 1 daughter. Education: Cand Scient, Biochemistry, 1970; PhD, Pharmacology, 1979. Appointments: Dr Philos, 1979; Professor, Experimental Diagnostic Radiology, 1982; General Manager, 1988. Publications: Over 100 within X-ray and MRI Contrast media. Honours: Silvaneous Thomson Lecture. Memberships: SUR; AUR; ESUR; Danish Society of Pharmacology; Swedish Society of Radiology. Address: Mellemvane 3B, 2970 Hoersholm, Denmark. E-mail: klaes.golman@amersham.com

GOMES DE MATOS Francisco Cardoso, b. 3 September 1933, Crato, Brazil. University Professor. m. Helen Herta Bruning, 1 son, 2 daughters. Education: Bachelor in Law and Languages, Federal University, Pernambuco, 1958; Master's in Linguistics, University of Michigan, 1960; PhD in Applied Linguistics, Catholic University of Sao Paulo, 1973. Appointments: Visiting Professor, Catholic University of Sao Paulo, 1966-79; Fulbright Visiting Professor, University of Georgia, Athens Georgia, USA, 1985-1986; Professor, Federal University of Pernambuco, 1980-; Co-founder, Brazil-America Association. Publications: Plea for Universal Declaration of Linguistic Rights, 1984; Plea for Communicative Peace, 1993. Honours: Benefactor Member, International Society for the Teaching of Portuguese as a Foreign Language; Listed in biographical publications. Memberships:

Dictionary of International Biography

Brazilian Linguistics Association; Brazilian Academy of Philology. Address: Rua Setubal 860-B, Apto 604, 51030-010 Recife, Brazil. E-mail: fcgm@hotlink.com.br

GOMEZ Ricardo Juan, b. 23 January 1935, Buenos Aires, Argentina. Professor of Philosophy. m. Lola Proano, 2 sons, 1 daughter. Education: Professor of Mathematics, Physics, Buenos Aires, 1959; Professor of Philosophy, 1966; Masters of Arts, History, Philosophy of Science, Indiana University, 1978; Philosophical Doctor, 1982. Appointments: Professor, Philosophy of Science, University of La Plata, Argentina, 1967-76; Professor, Scientific Methodology, University of Buenos Aires, 1971-76; Visiting Lecturer, Indiana University, 1983; Currently, Tenured Professor, Philosophy Department, California State University, Los Angeles. Publications: 4 books; 45 articles, national and international journals. Honours: Honour Diploma, University of Buenos Aires; Outstanding Professor, California State University; Distinguished Scholar Award; Honours Professor of the Year. Memberships: American Philosophical Association; Philosophy of Science Association; North American Kaut Society; Society for Philosophy and Technology; others. Address: Department of Philosophy, California State University, Los Angeles, CA 90032, USA.

GÖNCZ Árpád, b. 10 February 1922, Budapest, Hungary. Politician; Writer; Dramatist; Translator. m. Maria Zsuzsanna Göntér, 1947, 2 sons, 2 daughters. Education: DJ, Pázmány Péter University, 1944; University of Agricultural Sciences. Appointments: Active with Independent Smallholders' Party, 1947-48; Imprisoned for political activities, 1957-63; Founding Member, Free Initiative Network, Free Democratic Federation, Historic Justice Committee; Member and Speaker of Parliament, 1990; Acting President, 1990, President, 1990-2000, Republic of Hungary. Publications: Men of God (novel), 1974; Hungarian Medea (play), 1979; Iron Bars (play), 1979; Encounters (short stories), 1980; 6 plays, 1990; Homecoming (short stories), 1991; Shavings (essays), 1991. Honours: Honorary Knight Commander of the Order of St Michael and St George, England, 1991; Dr hc, Butler, 1990, Connecticut, 1991, Oxford, 1995, Sorbonne, 1996, Bologna, 1997; George Washington Prize, 2000; Pro Humanitate Award, 2001; Polish Business Oscar Award, 2002. Membership: Hungarian Writers' Union, President, 1989-90. Address: Office of the President, Kossuth tér 1-3, 1357 Budapest, Hungary.

GONZALEZ Luis Alberto, b. 2 June 1943, Santa Fe, Argentina. Teacher of English; Translator. Education: Public Translator and Teacher of English, National University of Córdoba, 1973; Grade Twelve with distinction, Trinity College, London, England, 1997; MA TEFL, University of Reading, England, 2003. Appointments: English Teacher, Córazon de Maria Secondary School, Córdoba, 1964-96; English Teacher, Liceo Militar Gral Paz, 1977-87; Teacher, British Culture Association, 1974-; Lecturer, National Technological University, Córdoba, 1977-79; Co-ordinator of International Examinations, Oral Examiner, International Cambridge Examinations; Lecturer, Villa Maria, 1998-99; Lecturer, Catholic University of Salta, 1999-2001; Member, Executive Board, Faculty of Languages, National University of Córdoba, 2002-03; Currently, Senior Lecturer, Language and Grammar, Faculty of Languages, National University of Córdoba. Publications: Numerous short stories, proceedings, journal articles and contributions to anthologies. Honours: Scholarship, Gonzaga University, Washington, 1965; Grantee, Experiment in International Living, 1974; Grantee, British Council; Certificate, New Latin American Writer, 2003; Listed in national and international biographical dictionaries; Lectured in many countries around the world. Memberships: Argentine Linguistics Association;

Linguistics Research Centre of Córdoba. Address: La Habana 1686, Barrio América Residencial 5012, Córdoba, Argentina. E-mail: clpgonzl@onenet.com.ar

GONZÁLEZ APAOLAZA Raúl, b. 20 October 1944, Pachuca, Hidalgo, Mexico. Electrical Engineer. m. Margarita Cruz Navarro, 3 sons. Education: Master's Degree, Hydraulic Engineering; Master's Degree, Electric Engineering. Publications: Power Stations, 1972; Electrical Substations, 1975; The Education of Engineering in Mexico, 1977; The National Polytechnic Institute, 1986-87; The Mexican Engineers, 1993; The Employment in Mexico, 1998. Honours: Recognition for his invaluable and permanent support for the sake of the Technological Education and for his designation like Secretary of Education. Memberships: Mexican Association of Mechanical Engineers and Electricians; Mexican Union of Engineers Association. Address: Mollendo St 1046, Res. Zacatenco o7369 Del. Gustavo A Madero, Mexico City, Mexico. E-mail: seprga@hgo.sep.gob.mx

GONZÁLEZ GORTÁZAR Fernando, b. 19 October 1942, Mexico City, Mexico. Architect. 2 daughters. Education: Architecture Degree, Escuela de Arquitectura del Instituto Tecnológico de la Universidad de Guadalajara, 1966. Career: Centro de Seguridad Pública building in Guagalajara, Mexico, The Mayan People Museum, Dzibilchaltún, Yucatán, Mexico, Centro Universitario de los Altos, Tepatilán, Jalisco, Mexico, 1993; Sculpture, El árbol de El Escorial, El Escorial, Madrid, Spain and Homenaje a la Amistad, Universidad de Colima, Mexico, 1995; Plazuela Palmas, Mexico City, 1996; Project for the Embassy of Mexico in Germany and collection of sculptures, Homenajes, 1997; Project for the San Juán de Aragón Zoo, Mexico City; Extraordinary Professorship, Federico Mariscal, Faculty of Architecture, Universidad Nacional Autonoma de Mexico, 2000; Exhibitions, Años de Sueños, Rufino Tamayo Museum, Mexico City, 1999, Fernando González Gortázar: Arquitectura y escultura 1965-2001, Foundation Colegio Oficial de Arquitectos de Madrid, Madrid, Spain and Kévéz Studio Gallery, Budapest, Hungary, 2001; Project of the Main Auditorium, Centro Universitario de los Altos, 2002; Remodelling of the Fatima Plaza and Sculpture, El Viento Blanco, Monterrey, SPGG Mexico, Projecto de Landscape of the Main Building Gardens, Universidad de Monterrey, Main project for the Universidad de Monterrey, 2003. Publications: Books as author or co-author: Mathías Goeritz in Guadalajara, 1991; Arquitectura Mexicana del siglo XX, 1994; La fundación de un sueño: la Escuela de Arquitectura de Guadalajara, 1995; Books about or including his works: Mexico: Nueva Arquitectura by Antonio Toca y Anibal Figueroa, 1991; Fernando González Gortázar by Manuel Larrosa, 1999; Fernando González Gortázar: Sí aún, by Carlos Ashida, 2000; Fernando González Gortázar Arquitectura y Escultura 1965-2001, 2001. Honours: 1st Prize for Sculpture, Primera Exposicioin-Concurso, City of Guadalajara, 1965; Medal, Clemente Orozco, Government of Jalisco, 1984; Henry Moore Grand Prize, Hakone Open Air Museum and Utsukushi-ga-hara Open Air Museum, Japan, 1989; Premio Jalisco in Plastic Arts, 1989. Memberships include: Co-founder, Sociedad de Amigos del Museo Regional de Guadalajara; Charter Member and Correspondent, La Jornada Newspaper, Mexico City; National System of Creators of Art in Mexico; Elected Member, Academia de Arte, Mexico. Address: Camino a Toluca 415, Lomas Virreyes, 11000 Mexico DF, Mexico. E-mail: gortazarazar@yahoo.com.mx

GONZALEZ-MARINA Jacqueline, b. 19 February 1935, Madrid, Spain. Lecturer; Translator and Official Interpreter in 7 Languages; Poet; Writer; Publisher; Journalist; Editor; Artist. m. (1) 2 sons, 1 daughter, (2) Desmond Savage, 22 December 1982. Education: BA, Modern Philology, 1959, MA, Modern Philology,

1962, University of Barcelona. Appointments: Lecturer, University of Barcelona, 1960-68, St Godrics College, London, 1970-91; Founder, Editor, Dandelion Magazine, 1979-; Editor, Fern Publications, 1979-; Editor, The Student Magazine (International), 2000- Lecturer in Modern Languages, American Intercontinental University, London, 1994-2000; More than 60 art exhibitions, one person and collective in England and Spain. Publications: Dieciocho Segundos, 1953; Tijeras Sin Filo, 1955; Antología de Temas, 1961; Short Stories, 1972; Brian Patten, 1975; A Survival Course, 1975; Once Poemas a Malaga, 1977; Poesía Andaluza, 1977; Adrian Henri, 1980; Historias y Conversaciones, 1995; Mediterranean Poetry, bilingual anthology, 1997; Conversaciones en Español, 1998; Drawing and Painting for Fun, 1998; The Millennium Anthology, poetry and prose, Vol 1, 1999, Vol II, 2000; The International Book of Short Stories, 2002; Cats in the Palm Tree and Other Stories (co-writer), 2002; Dali & I, poems, 2003; Contributions to: Countless anthologies and international magazines; Writer and broadcaster for the BBC, London, 1975-78. Honours: Royal Academician, Royal Academy of St Telmo, Malaga, Spain, 1975; Honorary Member of the Atheneum in Alicante, Spain, 1999. Memberships: Society of Women Writers and Journalists, London, 1980-; The Historical Association Saxoferreo, Cordoba, Spain, 1997-. Address: "Casa Alba", 24 Frosty Hollow, East Hunsbury, Northants NN4 0SY, England.

GONZALEZ-GONZALEZ Jesus Maria, b. 25 January 1961, Herreros de Suso, Avila, Spain. Stomatologist. m. Maria Teresa Rubio Hortells, separated 2003, 2 children. Education: BMed, University of Salamanca, 1985; Programmer Basic, Pontificia University of Salamanca, 1988; Specialist in Stomatology, University of Murcia, 1992; DMed, University of Alicante, 1992. Appointments: Medical Practitioner, State Health Service, Salamanca and Provence, 1987-88, La Manga, Murcia, 1990; Dentist, State Health Service, Cartagena, Murcia, 1990, 1991, Bejar and Ciudad Rodrigo, Salamanca, 1992; Private Practice in Stomatology, Murcia, 1991, Salamanca, 1991-; Speaker in field, 13 reports in congress. Publications: Several books in Spanish; Articles in professional journals and magazines; 2 patents. Honours: Honorable Mention, Children's Meeting of Painting, Town House of Salamanca, 1974 and Military Service, Lerida, 1986; Listed in numerous Who's Who publications and biographical dictionaries. Memberships: Professional Association of Dentists, Spain; Ski Club of Salamanca; New York Academy of Sciences; Founder President, Asociacion de Padres de Familia Separados de Salamanca y Pro-Derechos de Nuestros Hijos. Address: c/ Avila, No 4, lo A, 37004 Salamanca, Spain.

GOOCH Graham Alan, b. 23 July 1953, Leytonstone, England. Cricketer. m. Brenda Daniels, 3 daughters. Career: Right-hand opening batsman, right-arm medium bowler; Played for Essex 1973-97, (captain, 1986-87, 1989-94), West Prov, 1982-83,1983-84; Played in 118 tests for England, 1975 to 1994-95, 34 as captain, scoring 8900 runs (England record, average 42.5) including 20 hundreds (highest score 333 and Test match aggregate of 456 v India, Lord's 1990, becoming only batsman to score triple century and century in a first-class match and holding 103 catches; scored 44,841 runs (128 hundreds) and held 555 catches in first-class cricket; Toured Australia 1978-79, 1979-80, 1990-91 (captain) and 1994-95; 125 limited-overs internationals, including 50 as captain (both England records); Member, England Selection Committee, 1996-; Manager, England Tour to Australia, 1998-99; Head Coach, Essex, 2001-. Publications: Testing Times, 1991; Gooch: My Autobiography, 1995. Honours include: OBE; Wisden Cricketer of the Year, 1980. Address: c/o Essex County Cricket Club, The County Ground, New Writtle Street, Chelmsford, Essex, CM2 0PG, England.

GOOD-BLACK Edith Elissa, b. 10 January 1945, Hollywood, California, USA. Writer. m. Michael Lawrence Black, deceased. Education: BA, English, California State University, Northridge, 1974; Student, University of California, Los Angeles and University of California, Berkeley, 1962-92; Explorer, Mayan ruins, Mexico, 1963. Appointments: Participant, numerous dance, art, music, literature, mathematics and science classes; Dancer, Hajde Dance Troop, Berkeley, California, 1962-66; One-woman shows, Los Angeles, 1962-95; Singer, coffee houses, cafés, nightclubs, half-way houses, libraries, and others, Los Angeles, 1986-. Publications include: (pseudonym, Pearl Williams) The Trickster of Tarzana, 1992; Short Stories, 1995; Mad in Craft, 1995; Missives, 1995; Contributed poetry to CDs, radio broadcasts, internet broadcasts, publications. Honours: Summa Cum Laude, California State University; Writing chosen by a jury of experts for permanent collection in the Library of Congress; Achievement Prize, International Biographical Centre, 2000; Listed in numerous Who's Who and biographical publications. Memberships: MENSA, American Society of Composers, Authors and Publishers; Plummer Park Writers; Westside Writers; Democratic clubs, California and Mexico, 1962-; Supporter, mental health organisations, 1962-; Delegate to local conventions, fundraiser, canvasser, office worker, driver and participant in consciousness raising groups in support of civil rights; CORE, San Francisco, Berkeley, Los Angeles, and Oakland, 1965; Peace in Alliance for Survival, Berkeley, Oakland, Los Angeles, 1964-80; Women's rights, Westside Women's Center, Woman's Building, Los Angeles, 1974-80; Environment in Earth Day, Los Angeles, 1977; Physical and Mental Health; Consultant, tutor and book reviewer, Mental Health Association, Los Angeles, 1962-. Address: 1470 South Robertson Blvd, B, Los Angeles, CA 90035-3402, USA.

GOODING Cuba Jr, b. 2 September 1968, Bronx, New York, USA. Actor. m. Sara, 1994, 2 children. Career: TV appearances include: Kill or Be Killed, 1990; Murder with Motive: The Edmund Perry Story, 1992; Daybreak, 1993; The Tuskagee Airmen; Film appearances include: Coming to America, 1988; Sing, 1989; Boyz N the Hood, 1991; Gladiator, 1992; A Few Good Men, 1992; Hitz, 1992; Judgement Night, 1993; Lightning Jack, 1994; Losing Isiah, 1995; Outbreak, 1995; Jerry Maguire, 1996; The Audition, 1996; Old Friends, 1997; As Good As It Gets, 1997; What Dreams May Come, 1998; A Murder of Crows, 1999; Instinct, 1999; Chill Factor, 1999; Men of Honor, 2000; Pearl Harbor, 2001; Rat Race, 2001; In the Shadows, 2001; Snow Dogs, 2002; Boat Trip, 2002; Psychic, 2003; The Fighting Temptations, 2003; Radio, 2003; Honours: 2 NAACP Awards; acady Award; Best Supporting Actor (for Jerry Maguire), 1997; Chicago Film Critics Award; Screen Actor Guild Award. Address: c/o Rogers and Cowan, 1888 Century Park East, Suite 500, Los Angeles, CA 90067, USA.

GOODMAN John, b. 20 June 1952, St Louis, USA. Film Actor. m. Annabeth Hartzog, 1989, 1 daughter. Education: South West Missouri State University. Career: Broadway appearances in: Loose Ends, 1979; Big River, 1985; TV appearances include: The Mystery of Moro Castle; The Face of Rage; Heart of Steel; Moonlighting, Chiefs (min-series); The Paper Chase; Murder Ordained; The Equalizer; Roseanne (series); Normal, Ohio, 2000; Pigs Next Door, 2000; Films include: The Survivors, 1983; Eddie Macon's Run, 1983; Revenge of the Nerds, 1984; CHUD, 1984; Maria's Lovers, 1985; Sweet Dreams, 1985; True Stories, 1986; The Big Easy, 1987; Burglar, 1987; Raising Arizona, 1987; The Wrong Guys, 1988; Everybody's All-American, 1988; Punchline, 1988; Sea of Love, 1989; Always, 1989; Stella, 1990; Arachnophobia, 1990; King Ralph, 1990; Barton Fink, 1991; The Babe, 1992; Born Yesterday, 1993; The Flintstones, 1994; Kingfish: A Story of Huey P Long, 1995; Pie in the Sky, Mother Night, 1996; Fallen, 1997; Combat!, 1997; The Borrowers, 1997;

Dictionary of International Biography

The Big Lebowski, 1998; Blues Brothers 2000, 1998; Dirty Work, 1998; The Runner, 1999; Coyote Ugly, 2000; One Night at McCool's, 2000; Happy Birthday, 2001; My First Mister, 2001; Storytelling, 2001; Monsters Inc (voice), 2001; Dirty Deeds, 2002. Address: c/o Fred Spektor, CAA 9830 Wilshire Boulevard, Beverly Hills, CA 90212, USA.

GOODWIN (Trevor) Noël, b. 25 December 1927, Fowey, Cornwall, England. Writer and Critic (Music, Dance). m. Anne Mason Myers, 23 November 1963, 1 stepson. Education: BA (London). Career: Assistant Music Critic: News Chronicle, 1952-54; Manchester Guardian, 1954-55; Music and Dance Critic, Daily Express, 1956-78; Associate Editor, Dance and Dancers, 1958-; Executive Editor, Music and Musicians, 1963-71; London Dance Critic, International Herald Tribune, Paris, 1978-83; London Correspondent, Opera News, New York, 1980-91; Overseas News Editor, 1985-91, Editorial Board, 1991-, Opera; Planned and presented numerous radio programmes of music and records for BBC Home and World Services since 1954; Frequent contributor to music and arts programmes on Radios 3 and 4. Publications: London Symphony, portrait of an orchestra, 1954; A Ballet for Scotland, 1979; A Knight at the Opera (with Geraint Evans), 1984; Royal Opera and Royal Ballet Yearbooks (editor), 1978, 1979, 1980; New Grove Dictionary of Music and Musicians (area editor, writer), 1980; A Portrait of the Royal Ballet (editor), 1988. Contributions to: Numerous journals and magazines; Encyclopaedica Britannica, 15th edition, 1974; New Grove Dictionary of Music, 1980, 2000; Encyclopaedia of Opera, 1976; Britannica Books of the Year, annually, 1980-93; Cambridge Encyclopaedia of Russia and the Soviet Union, 1982, and revised edition, Cambridge Encyclopaedia of Russia and the former Soviet Union, 1994; New Oxford Companion to Music, 1983; Pipers Enzyklopädie des Musiktheaters, 1986-91; New Grove Dictionary of Opera, 1992; Viking Opera Guide, 1993; International Dictionary of Ballet, 1993; Metropolitan Opera Guide to Recorded Opera, 1993; International Encyclopaedia of Dance, 1998; Larousse Dictionaire de la Danse, 2000; New Dictionary of National Biography, forthcoming. Memberships include: Trustee-Director, International Dance Course for Professional Choreographers and Composers; Formerly: Arts Council of Great Britain, Dance and Music Advisory Panels; HRH The Duke of Kent's UK Committee for European Music Year. Address: 76 Skeena Hill, London SW18 5PN, England.

GOONEWARDENA Lakshman Gamani, b. 8 May 1929, Colombo, Sri Lanka. Tax Administrator; Expert. Education: BA Honours, Ceylon; BD London; ITP, Harvard Law; PhD, California; Dip in Th, Geneva; FTII, Sri Lanka. Appointments: Deputy Commissioner of Inland Revenue, Sri Lanka; Tax Expert, Commonwealth Assignment, Botswana; Deputy Commissioner of Taxes, Botswana. Publications: Paper on Tax Treaties, Harvard Law School; Book on Tax Management and Administration. Honours: University Exhibition, Sri Lanka; Mervyn Kalatileka Prize for Greek; Scholarship to Bossey Ecumenical Institute, Celigny, Switzerland. Address: 43 Edmonton Road, Colombo 6, Sri Lanka.

GOORHIGIAN Martin, b. 1 July 1932, New York, New York, USA. Teacher; Poet. m. Louise Zarifian, 23 June 1963, 1 son, 1 daughter. Education: BA, University of Connecticut, 1954; MS, University of Bridgeport, 1966. Publications: Ani, 1989; Between Ice Floes, 1990; The Road Narrows, 1991. Contributions to: Meriden Record Journal; High Tide; Sound and Waves of West Haven; Laurels; Hob Nob; Prophetic Voices; Parnassus; Night Roses; Wide Open; Plowman; Tucumcari. Honour: 4th Prize for Poetry, Sparrowgrass Poetry Forum, 1991. Memberships: Letters Committee, Milford Fine Arts, chairman, 1986-88. Address: 12 Cardinal Drive, Milford, CT 06460, USA.

GOPE Surya Nath, b. 10 February 1945, Hakpara village, District of Siraha, Nepal. Professor. m. Sumitra Devi Yadav, 2 sons. Education: BA, Bihar University, Muzaffarpur, India, 1966; MA, Hindi, Tribhuvan University, Kathmandu, Nepal, 1968; DPhil, University of Allahabad, India, 1984. Appointments: Lecturer, Padma Kanya College for Women, KTM, 1970-72; Lecturer, Central Department of Hindi, TU, 1971-87; Associate Professor, Reader, Central Department of Hindi, TU, Kathmandu, Nepal, 1987-98; Professor of Hindi, Tribhuvan University, Kathmandu, Nepal, 1998-. Publications: 5 articles in professional journals. Honours: Vidya Sagar (DLitt), Vikramshila Hindi Vidyapeeth, Bhagalpur, India, 1999; International Tulsi Award, USA; World Hindi Award, UK. Memberships: PhD (Hindi) evaluation, Calcutta University and Aligarh Muslim University, India, 2001-; Academic Council of Mahendra Sanskrit University, Nepal, 2002-; WAVES, USA, 2002-. Address: Central Department of Hindi, Tribhuvan University, Kirtipur, Kathmandu, Nepal. E-mail: sngope@enet.com.np

GORBACHEV Mikhail Sergeyevich, b. 2 March 1931, Privolnoye, Krasnogvardeisky, Stavropol, Russia. Politician. m. Raisa Titarenko, 25 September 1953, 1 daughter. Education: Faculty of Law, Moscow State University, 1955; Stavropol Agricultural Institute, 1967. Appointments: Machine Operator, 1946; Joined CPSU, 1952; Deputy Head, Department of Propaganda Stavropol Komsomol Territorial Committee, 1955-56; First Secretary, Stavropol Komsomol City Committee, 1956-58; Second, then First Secretary Komsomol Territorial Committee, 1958-62; Party Organizer, Stavropol Territorial Production Board of Collective and State Farms, 1962; Head Department of Party Bodies of CPSU Territorial Committee, 1963-66; First Secretary, Stavropol City Party Committee, 1966-68; Second Secretary, Stavropool Territorial CPSU Committee, 1968-70, First Secretary, 1970-78; CPSU Central Secretary for Agricultural, 1978-85; General Secretary, CPSU Central Committee, 1985-91; Chairman, Supreme Soviet, 1989-90; President, USSR, 1990-91; Head, International Foundation for Socio-Econ and Political Studies, 1992-; Head, International Green Cross, 1993-; Co-founder, Social Democratic Party of Russia, 2000. Publications: A Time for Peace, 1985; The Coming Century of Peace, 1986; Speeches and Writings, 1986-90; Peace Has No Alternative, 1986; Moratorium, 1986; Perestroika: New Thinking for Our Country and the World, 1987; The August Coup (Its Cause and Results), 1991; December-91, My Stand, 1992; The Years of Hard Decisions, 1993; Life and Reforms, 1995. Honours: Indira Gandhi Award, 1987; Nobel Peace Prize, 1990; Peace Award World Methodist Council, 1990; Albert Schweitzer Leadership Award, Ronald Reagan Freedom Award, 1992; Honorary Citizen, Berlin, 1992; Freeman of Aberdeen, 1993; Urania-Medaille, Berlin, 1996; Honorary Degrees: University of Alaska, 1990; University of Bristol, 1993; University of Durnham, 1995; Order of Lenin, 3 times; Orders of Red Banner of Labour, Badge of Honour and other medals. Address: International Foundation for Socio-Economic and Political Studies, Leningradsky Prosp 49, 125468 Moscow, Russia.

GORDON Dotsie M, b. 12 April 1943, Ridge District, St Elizabeth, Jamaica. Human Resource Professional. m. Aston M Gordon, 2 sons. Education: Certified Administrative Manager, 1986; Certificate in Personnel Management, College of Arts Science and Technology, Now University of Technology, 1990; Certified Human Resource Professional, 1996; MA, Law and Employment Relations, University of Leicester, UK, 2002. Appointments: Agricultural Workers' Centre, Department of the Treasury, 1962-64; Building and Loan Trust Company, 1964-66; Citibank, 1966-70; Founder, Managing Director, Dot Personnel Services JA Ltd, 1971-. Honours: Honorary Member, Jamaica Professional Secretaries' Association; CAM Board of Regents;

CVSS; Meritorious Award, 1994; Jamaican Employers Federation, Meritorious Award, 1999. Memberships: Institute of Personnel and Development; Human Resource Professionals Association of Ontario; Society for Human Resource Management; Association for the Advancement of Management; Jamaica Association for Training and Development; Jamaica Computer Society; Jamaica Professional Secretaries Association; University of Technology Alumni Association. Address: 1 Oakdale, Kingston 8, Jamaica, West Indies. E-mail: Dotpersonnel@colis.com

GORDON John William, b. 19 November 1925, Jarrow-on-Tyne, England. Writer. m. Sylvia Young, 9 January 1954, 1 son, 1 daughter. Publications: The Giant Under the Snow, 1968, sequel, Ride the Wind, 1989; The House on the Brink, 1970; The Ghost on the Hill, 1976; The Waterfall Box, 1978; The Spitfire Grave, 1979; The Edge of the World, 1983; Catch Your Death, 1984; The Quelling Eye, 1986; The Grasshopper, 1987; Secret Corridor, 1990; Blood Brothers, 1991; Ordinary Seaman (autobiography), 1992; The Burning Baby, 1992; Gilray's Ghost, 1995; The Flesh Eater, 1998; The Midwinter Watch, 1998; Skinners, 1999; The Ghosts of Blacklode, 2002. Contributions to: Beginnings (Signal 1989); Ghosts & Scholars 21. Membership: Society of Authors. Address: 99 George Borrow Road, Norwich, NR4 7HU, England.

GORDON Philip H, b. 13 September 1942, Saskatoon, Saskatchewan, Canada. Physician. m. Rosalie, 1 son, 1 daughter. Education: MD, University of Saskatchewan, 1966; LMCC, 1966; Diplomate, National Board of Medical Examiners, 1968; Certifications: Royal College of Surgeons of Canada, 1972, General Surgery, Province of Quebec, 1972; Diplomate, American Board of Surgery, 1973: Diplomate, American Board of Colon and Rectal Surgery, 1974, Recertification, 1994; Training in medicine and surgery, 1966-74 at Irish General Hospital, Montreal, Canada, McGill University, Montreal, Montefiore Hospital Pittsburgh, USA, University of Minnesota, USA, St Mark's Hospital, London, England. Appointments: Clinical Assistant, 1974-77, Assistant Surgeon, 1977-79, Associate Surgeon, 1979-87, Senior Surgeon, Director, Division of Colon and Rectal Surgery, 1987-, Director Clinical Teaching Unit II, 1989-, Vice-Chairman, Department of Surgery, 1993-, Department of Surgery, Sir Mortimer B. Davis, Jewish General Hospital, Montreal, Canada; Lecturer, 1978-79, Assistant Professor of Surgery, 1979-84, Associate Professor of Surgery, 1984-89, Professor of Surgery, 1989-, Director, Section of Colorectal Surgery, 1996-, Department of Surgery, Professor of Oncology, Department of Oncology, 1992-, McGill University, Montreal, Canada; Advisory Council, American Board of Colon and Rectal Surgery, 2001-. Publications: Author and co-author of over 125 articles in medical journals; 5 textbooks; 28 textbook chapters; numerous abstracts, editorials, book reviews and papers presented at national and international conferences and symposia. Honours include: William & Mary Diefenbaker Fellowship, 1962; Agora Award "Ambassador by Appointment", Palais de Congress, City of Montreal, 1988; American Medical Illustrators Best Illustrated Medical Textbook of the Year 1992; Award of Appreciation, American Society of Colon and Rectal Surgeons, 1999; Dr Carl Arthur Goresky Memorial Award, McGill Inflammatory Bowel Disease Research Group, 2002; Listed in numerous Who's Who publications and biographical dictionaries. Memberships include: Fellow, Royal College of Surgeons of Canada, Royal Society of Medicine, American College of Surgeons, American and Canadian Society of Colon and Rectal Surgeons; Founding President, Canadian Society of Colon and Rectal Surgeons; Past President, American Society of Colon and Rectal Surgeons; Past President, American Board of Colon and Rectal Surgery. Address: Sir Mortimer B Davis, Jewish General Hospital, 3755 Cote Ste, Catherine Road, Suite G-314, Montreal, Quebec, Canada H3T 1E2. E-mail: philip.gordon@mcgill.ca

GORE Albert Jr, b. 31 March 1948. Politician. m. Mary E Aitcheson, 1970, 1 son, 3 daughters. Education: Harvard University; Vanderbilt University. Appointments: Investigative reporter, editorial writer, The Tennessean, 1971-76; Home-builder and land developer, Tanglewood Home Builders Co, 1971-76; Livestock and tobacco farmer, 1973-; Head, Community Enterprise Board, 1993-; Member, House of Representatives, 1977-79; Senator, from Tennessee, 1985-93; Vice President, USA, 1993-2001; Democrat candidate in Presidential Elections, 2000; Lecturer, Middle Tennessee State, Fisk, Columbia Universities, 2001-; Vice-Chairman, Metropolitan West Financial, 2001-. Publication: Earth in the Balance, 1992. Honours include: Dr hc (Harvard) 1994, (NY), 1998. Address: Metwest Financial, 11440 San Vicente Boulevard, 3rd Floor, Los Angeles, CA 90049, USA.

GORES Joseph (Nicholas), b. 25 December 1931, Rochester, Minnesota, USA. Writer; Novelist; Screenwriter. m. Dori Corfitzen, 16 May 1976, 1 son, 1 daughter. Education: BA, University of Notre Dame, 1953; MA, Stanford University, 1961. Appointment: Story Editor, B L Stryker Mystery Movie Series, ABC-TV, 1988-89. Publications: A Time of Predators, 1969; Marine Salvage (non-fiction), 1971; Dead Skip, 1972; Final Notice, 1973; Interface, 1974; Hammett, 1975; Gone, No Forwarding, 1978; Come Morning, 1986; Wolf Time, 1989; Mostly Murder (short story collection), 1992; 32 Cadillacs, 1992; Dead Man, 1993; Menaced Assassin, 1994; Contract Null and Void, 1996; Cases, 1998; Speak of the Devil, short story collection, 1999; Statkeout on page Street, short story collection, 2000; Cons, Scams and Grifts, 2001. Contributions to: Numerous magazines and anthologies; 8 film scripts; 25 hours of television drama. Honours: Edgar, Best First Novel, 1969, Best Short Story, 1969, Edgar, Best Episodic TV Drama, 1975, Mystery Writers of America; Falcon, Maltese Falcon Society of Japan, 1986. Memberships: Mystery Writers of America, president, 1986; International Association of Crime Writers; Crime Writers Association; Private Eye Writers of America. Address: PO Box 446, Fairfax, CA 94978, USA.

GORI Fabio, b. 5 August 1947, Montale (Pistoia), Italy. Professor. Education: Laurea Degree with Honours, Chemical Engineering, 1971, Research Scholarship, Engineering, 1971-72, University of Bologna. Appointments: Professor, University of Reggio Calab, 1986-90; Professor, SUNY at Stony Brook, USA, 1988; Professor, Technical University of Milano, 1990-92; Professor, Heat Transfer, University of Rome "Tor Vergata", 1992-. Publications: 2 books on Thermodynamics, in Italian; Chapter on Heat Transfer in the Encyclopedia of Energy; 34 papers in international journals and 62 papers on proceedings of international conferences with referees; 3 patents. Memberships: American Society of Mechanical Engineering; Italian Union of Thermal Fluid-Dynamics. Address: Department of Mechanical Engineering, University of Rome "Tor Vergata", Via Del Politecnico 1, 00 133 Rome, Italy. Website: www.termofluidodinamica.it

GORJI Ali, b. 14 November 1966, Mashhad, Iran. Physician. m. Maryann Khaligli Ghadiri, 1 daughter. Education: Medicine, 1984-90, Toxicology, 1990-94, Mashhad University, Iran; Neurophysiology, Muenster University, Germany, 1998-2003. Appointments: Chairman, Chemical Warfare Victims Centre, Mashhad, 1988-91; Assistant Professor, Toxicology Department, Mashhad University, 1990-94; Senior Assistant, Neurophysiology Department, Muenster University, 2002; Assistant Editor, Avicenna Journal of Science and Culture, 2002. Publications: Book, Progress in Depression, in press; Numerous papers and articles in professional journals. Honours: Special Award of Physiology Congress, 2003. Memberships: Iranian Physician Consul. Address: Institute of Physiology, Muenster University, Robert-Koch-Str 27a, 48149 Muenster, Germany. E-mail: gorjial@uni-muenster.de

Dictionary of International Biography

GOROKHOV Igor M, b. 6 April 1932, Leningrad, Russia. Professor of Geochemistry. m. Irina A Ostrovskaya, 1 daughter. Education: Certificate of research chemist (honours), Leningrad State University, 1954; PhD, Chemical Sciences, Leningrad Technology Institute, 1965; Senior Research Officer, Geochemistry, Higher Education Board of the USSR, Moscow, 1979; DSc, Geology and Mineralogical Sciences, Institute of Geochemistry, Kiev, Ukraine, 1981. Appointments: Junior Research Fellow, USSR Academy of Science, V G Khlopin Radium Institute, Leningrad, 1954-61; Junior Research Fellow, USSR Academy of Science, Laboratory of Precambrian Geology, Leningrad, 1961-67; Junior Research Fellow to Head of Laboratory, Russian Academy of Science, Institute of Precambrian Geology and Geochronology, St Petersburg, 1967-. Publications: 2 books; Over 100 articles in scientific journals. Honours: Medal for scientific service, Geological Survey, Prague, 1986; Medal for scientific service, Geological Survey, Bratislava, 1986; State Scientific Grants, 1994, 1997, 2000; Award, INTERPERIODICA Publishing House, 1996. Memberships: Board of Directors, Council on Isotope Geology and Geochronology, 1973-91; Council on Geochemistry, 1992-93, 1999-; Committee on the Upper Precambrian, Moscow, 1988-; Editorial Board, Chemical Geology, 1987-99; New York Academy of Sciences, 1995. Address: Institute of Precambrian Geology and Geochronology, Russian Academy of Sciences, nab Makarova 2, 199034 St Petersburg, Russia. E-mail: gorokhov@igl405.spb.edu

GORRELL Dena Ruth, b. 8 June 1932, Loyal, Oklahoma, USA. Writer; Poet. m. John S Gorrell, 14 November 1953, 1 son, 1 daughter. Education: Associate in Commerce, Oklahoma State University, 1952; Diploma, Institute of Children's Literature, 1989. Publications: Truths, Tenderness and Trifles, 1986; Sunshine and Shadow, 1989. Contributions to: Edmond Sun; Living Streams; Poets at Work; Muse; Wide Open Magazine; Odessa Poetry Review; Independent Review. Honours: Grand Prize, 1989, 2nd Prize, 1989, International Society for The Advancement of Poetry; 1st Prize, Creative Endeavors Spring Contest, 1990, Cimarron Valley Writers, 1990, Poets at Work, 1990, Tulsa Tuesday Writers, 1990; 2nd Prize, Poetry Press, 1990. Memberships: Poetry Society of Oklahoma; Academy of American Poets; International Society for the Advancement of Poetry; National Federation of State Poetry Societies; National League of American Pen Women. Address: 14024 Gateway Drive, Edmond, OK 73013, USA.

GOSLIN Gerald, b. 7 January 1947, Detroit, Michigan, USA. Concert Pianist. Education: Majored in Music, Cass Technical High School; Wayne State University. Career: Professor of Music; Performed in numerous concerts, lectures and workshops; Appearances of television and radio; Television appearances include, Kelly & Co, Channel 7 Action News, Metrovision Cable, Channel 62 and WQRS FM; Teacher of music for over 45years; Adjunct Professor of Piano; Voice at Oakland Community College; Choirmaster and Organist, Bushnell Congregational Church. Recordings: 2 recordings; Currently working on a CD and video. Honours: Judge, Leontyne Price vocal Arts Competition, 1986-; Judge, Verdi Opera Association Vocal Competition, 1997-98; Host, Piano Hour, WHND; Who's Who In The Midwest; Who's Who In America; Who's Who In Entertainment; Who's Who In The World; Dictionary of Biographical Information; Order of International Fellowship; 2000 Outstanding People of the 20th Century; International Man of Honour; Man Of The Year; Annual Associate; The 2000 Millennium Medal of Honour. Memberships: Mischa Kottler Memorial committee; Professional Concerns Committee, Detroit Chapter of The American Guild of Organists; American Choral Directors Association; American Guild of Organists; Detroit Federation of Musicians. Address: 22600 Middlebelt Road, C10, Farmington Hills, MI 48336-3672, USA.

GOSLING-HARE Paula Louise, (Ainslie Skinner), b. 12 October 1939, Michigan, USA. Author; Crime and Suspense Fiction. m. (1) Christopher Gosling, September 1968, divorced 1978, 2 daughters, (2) John Hare, 1982. Education: BA, Wayne State University. Appointments: Copywriter, Campbell Ewald, USA; Copywriter, Mitchell & Co, London; Copywriter, Pritchard Wood, London: Freelance Copywriter, 1974-. Publications: A Running Duck, 1976; Zero Trap, 1978; The Woman in Red, 1979; Losers Blues, 1980; Minds Eye (as Ainslie Skinner), 1980; Monkey Puzzle, 1982; The Wychford Murders, 1983; Hoodwink, 1985; Backlash, 1987; Death Penalties, 1990; The Body in Blackwater Bay, 1992; A Few Dying Words, 1994; The Dead of Winter, 1995; Death and Shadows, 1999; Underneath Every Stone, 2000; Ricochet, 2002; Tears of the Dragon, 2004. Honours: Gold Dagger, Crime Writers' Association; Arts Achievement Award, Wayne State University. Memberships: Crimewriters' Association, chairman, 1982; Society of Authors. Address: c/o Greene & Heaton Ltd, 37 Goldhawk Road, London W12 8QQ, England.

GOTTRUP Finn, b. 2 April 1944, Billund, Denmark. Doctor of Medicine; Professor. m. Eva Stubkjaer, 1 son, 1 daughter. Education: MD, 1971, Specialist in Anatomy, 1980, Doctoral Thesis (MDSci), 1981, Aarhus University; Specialist in General Surgery, 1985, Specialist in Surgical Gastroenterology, 1990, Copenhagen. Appointments: Associate Professor in Anatomy, Assistant Professor of Surgery, 1986, Professor, 1991, Head (Director), 1996, Copenhagen Wound Healing Centre, 1996; Professor of Surgery, University of Southern Denmark, 2003. Publications: Chapters in several books; Articles in medical journals, newspapers and magazines on surgery and wound healing. Honours: N C Nielsen Award to a Danish Surgeon, 1992; President of Danish Wound Healing Society, 1993; President, European Wound Management Association (EWMA), 1997; President of European Tissue Repair Society (ETRS), 1998. Memberships: Several societies in the field of surgery and wound healing; Co-editor, 2 journals and on several editorial boards. Address: University Centre of Wound Healing, Odense University Hospital, DK-5000 Odense C, Denmark.

GOUHER Ahmed, b. 5 July 1967, Hyderabad, India. Management Consultant. m. Saria Gouher. Education: PGDBM, Business Management, 1993, LLB, Corporate Law, 1997, PhD, Foreign Trade, 1998, Marathwada University, India; MMS, International Marketing, Pune University, India, 1995; MAPPM, Public Personal Management, Osmania University, India, 1996; Certificate, International Relations, American Studies Research Centre, India, 1996; PGDPM, Project Management, Hyderabad Central University, 1998; MAIR, International Industrial Relations, Wayne State University, Detroit, Michigan, USA, 2002. Appointments: Chief Executive Officer, Gouher International Consulting Inc. North America; Visiting Professor of International Trade and Industrial relations, Osmania University, Hyderabad, India; Consultant for Business and Industry. Publications: Numerous articles in professional journals and papers presented at seminars include: Foreign Direct Investment in Indian Economy with special reference to Andhra Pradesh, 1996; The Economics of Urban Housing in India, 1997; Foreign Trade Development in India, 1998; Government and Business Stakeholding in the New Millennium. Honours: Recipient of several leadership awards; Listed in Who's Who publications and biographical dictionaries. Memberships: Industrial Relations Research Association, USA; Society for Human Resource Management, USA; Indian Institute of Economics, India; Alumni Member, Wayne State University, Detroit, USA. Address: 500 Shana Street, Canton, MI 48187, USA. E-mail: gouher@usa.net

Dictionary of International Biography

GOULD Elliott, b. 29 August 1938, Brooklyn, New York, USA. Actor. m. (1) Barbra Streisand, 1963, divorced 1971, 1 son, (2) Jenny Bogart, 1 son, 1 daughter. Career: Actor, theatre appearances include: Say Darling, 1958; Irma La Douce, 1960; I Can Get It For You Wholesale, 1962; Drat! The Cat, 1965; Alfred in Little Murders, 1967; Toured in the Fantastiks with Liza Minelli; National tour with Deathtrap; Films include: The Confession, 1966; The Night They Raided Minsky's, 1968; Bob and Carol and Ted and Alice, 1969; Getting Straight, 1970; M*A*S*H, 1970; The Touch, 1971; Little Murders, 1971; The Long Good-Bye, 1972; Nashville, 1974; I Will...I Will...For Now, 1976; Harry and Walter Go to New York, 1976; A Bridge Too Far, 1977; The Silent Partner, 1979; The Lady Vanishes, 1979; Escape to Athens, 1979; The Muppet Movie, 1979; Falling in Love Again, 1980; The Devil and Max Devlin, 1981; Over the Brooklyn Bridge, 1984; The Naked Face, 1984; Act of Betrayal, 1988; Dead Men Don't Die, 1989; Secret Scandal, 1990; Strawanser, The Player, Exchange Lifeguards, Wet and Wild Summer, Naked Gun 331/3, the Final Insult (cameo), White Man's Burden, The Glass Shield, Kicking and Screaming, A Boy Called Hate, Johns, The Big Hit, American History, X, Bugsy, Hoffman's Hunger, Capricorn One; Boys Life 3, 2000; Ocean's Eleven, 2001; Numerous TV appearances including Doggin' Around (BBC TV); Once Upon a Mattress (CBC). Website: www.elliottgould.net

GOULD Stephen Jay, b. 10 September 1941, New York, New York, USA. Professor of Geology and Zoology; Curator; Writer. m. Deborah Ann Lee, 3 October 1965, 2 sons. Education: AB, Antioch College, 1963; PhD, Columbia University, 1967. Appointments: Assistant Professor, 1967-71, Associate Professor, 1971-73, Professor of Geology, 1973-, Alexander Agassiz Professor of Zoology, 1982-, Assistant Curator, 1967-71, Associate Curator, 1971-73, Curator, 1973-, Invertebrate Paleontology, Museum of Comparative Zoology, Harvard University; Lecturer, Cambridge University, 1984, Yale University, 1986, Stanford University, 1989. Publications: Ontogeny and Phylogemy, 1977; Ever Since Darwin, 1977; The Panda's Thumb, 1980; The Mismeasure of Man, 1981; Hen's Teeth and Horse's Toes, 1983; The Flamingo's Smile, 1985; Time's Arrow, Time's Cycle, 1987; An Urchin in the Storm, 1987; Wonderful Life, 1989; Bully for Brontosaurus, 1991; Finders, Keepers (with R W Purcell), 1992; Eight Little Piggies, 1993; Questioning the Millennium: A rationalist's Guide to a Precisely Arbitrary Countdown, 1997; Leonardo's Mountain of Clams and the Diet of Worms, 1998; The Living Stones of Marrakech, 2000. Contributions to: Journals. Honours: American Book Award, 1981; National Book Award, 1981; John D and Catharine T MacArthur Foundation Fellowship, 1981-86; National Book Critics Circle Award, 1982; Outstanding Book Award, American Educational Research Association, 1983; Phi Beta Kappa Book Awards, 1983, 1990; Brandeis University Creative Arts Award, 1986; Medal, City of Edinburgh, 1990; Forkosch Award, 1990; Rhone-Poulenc Prize, 1991; Silver Medal, Linnean Society, 1992; Over 35 honorary doctorates; Numerous other awards, medals, etc. Memberships: American Academy of Arts and Sciences, fellow; American Society of Naturalists, president, 1977-80; History of Science Association; National Academy of Sciences; Paleontological Society, president, 1985-; Sigma Xi; Society for the Study of Evolution, president, 1990; Society for the Systematic Study of Zoology. Address: c/o Museum of Comparative Zoology, Department of Earth Sciences, Harvard University, Cambridge, MA 02138, USA.

GOURA George Stepanovich, b. 15 May 1929, Armenia, Leninacan, USSR. Mechanical Engineer. m. Kluyeva Victoriya Alexandrovna, 2 daughters. Education: Higher School: Railway Institute at Rostov at River Don, USSR, 1946-51; Candidate of Technical Science, USSR Academy of Science, Moscow, 1962;

Doctor's degree of Technical Science, Kiev Civil Aviation Institute, USSR, 1974. Appointments: Chief, Service and Supply of Locomotive Maintenance, South-Donetsk and Donetsk Railways Department, USSR Railway Ministry, 1952-; Teacher, Railway Technical Secondary School, Tikhoretsk, Kuban, 1954-55; Teacher, 1955-58, Dean of Mechanical Faculty, 1957-58, Railway Institute, Byelorussia; Post-graduate course, 1958-61, Higher engineer-researcher, 1961-62, Institute of engineering science, Academy of Sciences USSR, Moscow; Head, Power Transmissions Constructions Department, Lugansk Diesel Locomotive Institute, 1962-65; Senior Lecturer, 1965-76, Professor, 1976, Head of Chair, 1971-99, Dean of General Technical Faculty, 1974-77, Krasnodar Polytechnic Institute, Kuban; Rector, Irkutsk Railway Engineers Institute, 1980-82; Head of Chair, Professor, Sochi State University of Tourism and Resort Business; Involved in the creation of Health Resort of Professional Higher Education, Sochi, 1966-. Publications: Over 160 publications and inventions in professional scientific and engineering journals and bulletins; Author of the modern theory of non-free motion of body with due regard for non-stationary processes and deformations in friction contact zone; Creator of original landing gears of aircrafts; Creator of the testing method of materials on abrasive wearing at high speeds of sliding with applying of a composition elastic-abrasive cloth; Creator of precise processing and assembly technology of fiber connections; Creator of schematic plans of Kursk submarine lift. Honours: Honorary Diploma, International Scientific Congress on Tribology, 1985; Title of Honoured Worker of the Science and Engineering of Russian Federation, President of Russia, 1996; Title of Honorary Worker of Higher Education in Russia, Minister of Education, 1999; Silver Medal of distinguished contribution to development of Kuban, 1999; Laureate Professor of Zhukovsky Prize, Russian Transport Academy of Science in Aeronautical field of research, 1999; Honourable Citizen of the City of Sochi. Memberships: Society of Researchers, New York Museum of Natural History; Russian Transport Academy of Science; Scientific-Methodical Council on Tribology, Ministry of Education of Russia; Interdepartmental Scientific Council on Tribology of Russia; Russian Association of Tribology Engineers. Address: Abrikosovaya Str 17 A, Room 22, Sochi, Russia 354003. E-mail: goura@mail.ru Website: goura.narod.ru

GOVAERTS Marc Maria Carolus Justinus, b. 1 December 1960, Duffel, Belgium. Veterinarian. m. Aissatou Hamadou. Education: BSc, Catholic University of Louvain, Belgium, 1978-79; BSc Veterinary Sciences, 1979-81, DVM, 1981-84, University of Liège, Belgium; Doctor in Tropical Veterinary Medicine, Institute of Tropical Medicine, Antwerp, Belgium, 1984-85; PhD, Agricultural and Applied Biological Sciences, Catholic University of Leuven, Belgium, in progress, 1998-. Appointments: Associate Expert, Vétérinaires Sans Frontières, Lyon, France and Office National des Aménagements HydroAgricoles du Niger, Niger, 1986-87; Consultant, European Community Commission, European Development Fund, Niger, 1987; Associate Expert, Vétérinaires Sans Frontières, France and Niger, 1987-89; Veterinary Practitioner, Clinique Vétérinaire du Dr Peuchot, Bourbourg, France, 1990-91; Scientific Collaborator, Bogor Agricultural University, Bogor, Indonesia and Catholic University of Leuven, Belgium, 1991-95; Scientific Collaborator, Catholic University of Leuven, Belgium, 1995-96; Scientific Collaborator, Catholic University of Leuven and Solvay Duphar b.v. The Netherlands, 1996; Freelance Scientist, Catholic University of Leuven, 1996-97; Scientific Collaborator, Catholic University of Leuven, 1997-2001; Research Associate, Queen's University, Belfast, 2001-03. Publications: Articles in scientific journals as first author and co-author include: Positioning of an Indonesian Theileria sp. isolate within the T. orientalis/sergenti/buffeli phylogenic tree, 1998; Homologues of natural killer cell receptors NKG2-D and NKR-P1 expressed in cattle, 2001; Characterisation of the 33kDa piroplasm surface antigen of Theileria orientalis/sergenti/buffeli isolates from West Java, 2002; Genomic approach to the identification of Mycobacterium bovis diagnostic antigens in cattle, 2003. memberships: Belgian Society of Parasitology, Past Secretary, 1997-99; Belgian Society of Protozoology; Society of Tropical Veterinary Medicine; Belgian Immunological Society; New York Academy of Sciences; Irish Society of Immunology. Address: 26 Dunraven Parade, Belfast, BT5 6BT, Northern Ireland. E-mail: m.govaerts@qub.ac.uk

GOVINDAN Trivellore E, b. 17 June 1962, Madras, India. Professor. Education: BSc, Statistics, Madras University; MSc, Statistics, Indian Institute of Technology, Kanpur, 1984; PhD, Mathematics, Indian Institute of Technology, Bombay, 1992. Appointments: Lecturer, 1991-97, Reader, 1997-99, UICT, Bombay University; Visiting Professor, CINVESTAV, Mexico, 1999-2001; Professor, UAEM, Mexico, 2001-2003; Professor, CIMAT, Mexico, 2003-. Publications: Articles in scientific journals as author and co-author include most recently: Non-stationary continuous time Markov control processes with discounted costs on infinite horizon, 2001; An existence result for the Cauchy problem for stochastic systems with heredity, 2002; Existence and stability of solutions of stochastic semilinear functional differential equations, 2002; Existence and stability of solutions of stochastic semilinear evolution equations, 2003; Stability of mild solutions of stochastic evolution equations with variable delay, 2003. Honours: Man of the Year 2003, American Biographical Institute; Great Minds of the 21st Century, American Biographical Institute. Membership: Indian Society for Probability and Statistics. Address: Departamento de Probabilidad y Estadistica, CIMAT, Guanajuato 36000, Mexico. E-mail: govindan@cimat.mx

GOVRIN Nurit, b. 6 November 1935, Israel. Educationist; Researcher; Writer. m. Shlomo Govrin, 3 sons. Education: BA, Hebrew Literature, Bible Studies; MA, Hebrew Literature; PhD, Hebrew Literature; Tel-Aviv University; Harvard University, USA; University of Oxford, England. Appointments: Administrative positions, Tel-Aviv University; Teaching, University of California at Los Angeles, Columbia University, New York, Hebrew Union College; Assistant, 1965-68, Teacher, 1968-72, Lecturer, 1972-74, Senior Lecturer, 1974-78, Associate Professor 1978-90, Full Professor, 1990-, Tel-Aviv University; Held various administrative positions at Tel-Aviv University; Public Council for Culture and Art, Ministry of Education; Judge, Selection Committees for many literary prizes. Publications: 14 books including: G Shoffman: His Life and Work, 2 volumes, 1982; The Brenner Affair - The Fight for Free Speech, 1985; The Literature of Eretz - Israel in the Early Days of the Settlements, 1985; The First Half - The Life and Work of Dvora Baron 1888-1923, 1988; Honey from the Rock, 1989; Brenner - Nonplussed and Mentor, 1991; Burning - Poetry About Brenner, 1995; Literary Geography - Lands and Landmarks on the Map of Hebrew Literature, 1998; Reading the Generations – Contextual Studies in Hebrew Literature, 2 Volumes, 2002; Editor of 14 books. Honours: Postgraduate Scholarship, Rothschild Fund, 1973-74; Research Grants: Israel National Academy for Sciences, 1975-78, Jewish Memorial Fund, 1982, Israel Matz Fund, 1982, 1984-86, 1989, American Academy for Jewish Studies, 1984-85, 1989; Haifa Municipality Prize, 1993; Shalom Aleichem Prize, 1996; Creative Woman Prize, Wizo Prize, 1998; Bialik Prize, 1998; Israel Efros Prize, 2001. Memberships: Katz Institute for Research of Hebrew Literature; Literature Committee, Israel National Academy of Sciences and Humanities. Address: 149 Jobotinsky St, Tel-Aviv 62150, Israel.

GOVRIN Yosef, b. 18 December 1930. Ambassador; Historian. m. Hana Govrin, 1 son, 1 daughter. Education: BA, MA, PhD, Jewish History and International Relations, The Hebrew University of Jerusalem. Appointments: Israel's Ministry of Foreign Affairs, 1953-96; Diplomat, Sydney, Moscow, Buenos Aires, 1955-70; Director, East European Department, Ministry of Foreign Affairs, 1976-85; Ambassador to Romania, 1985-89; Deputy Director General of the Ministry, 1989-93; Ambassador to Austria, Slovakia, Slovenia, UNO in Vienna, 1993-95; Retired from Ministry in 1996; Research Fellow, Truman Institute for the Advancement of Peace, Hebrew University of Jerusalem. Publications: The Jewish Factor in the Relations between Nazi Germany and the USSR, Hebrew, 1986; Israeli-Soviet Relations 1953-67, Hebrew, 1990, Russian, 1994, English, 1998; Recollections of Transnistria, Hebrew, 1999; Israeli-Romanian Relations at the late Ceausescu Era 1985-1989, Hebrew 2001, English 2002; Co-editor, The First Fifty Years of Israel's Foreign Ministry, 2 volumes; Numerous essays and research papers. Honour: Israel's Prime Minister Prize, 1991. Memberships: Directorate Israel's UN Association; Yad Vashem Council and Committee for the Righteous among Nations; World Union of Jewish Studies. Address: 14 Aluf Simhoni Str, Jerusalem 92504, Israel.

GOWER David Ivon, b. 1 April 1957, Tunbridge Wells, Kent. Cricketer. m. Thorunn Ruth Nash, 1992, 2 daughters. Education: University College, London. Career: Left-hand batsman; Played for Leicestershire, 1975-89, captain, 1984-86, Hampshire, 1990-93; Played in 117 Tests for England, 1978-92, 32 as captain, scoring then England record 8,231 runs (average 44.2) with 18 hundreds; Toured Australia, 1978-79, 1979-80, 1982-83, 1986-87, 1990-91; Scored 26,339 first-class runs with 53 hundreds; 114 limited-overs internationals; Sunday Express Cricket Correspondent, 1993-95; Public Relations Consultant for cricket sponsorship National Westminster Bank, 1993-; Commentator, Sky TV, 1993-; Commentator and presenter, BBC TV, 1994-99; Columnist, Sunday Telegraph, 1995-98; Presenter, Sky TV cricket, 1999-; Columnist, The Sun, 2000-; Television: They Think It's All Over. Publications: A Right Ambition, 1986; On The Rack, 1990; The Autobiography, 1992; Articles in Wisden Cricket Monthly. Address: c/o David Gower Promotions Ltd, 6 George Street, Nottingham, NG1 3BE, England.

GOYER BUSHNO Lila Joan, b. 9 August 1931, Pomona, Missouri, USA. Poet. m. John J Bushno, 1954, 3 sons, 4 daughters. Education: AA, 1980, AS, 1989, Black Hawk College. Contributions to: Many anthologies, newspapers and magazines. Honours: Golden Poets Awards, 1985-90; Editor's Choice, 1988; Poet of Merit, 1988; Poet of the Year, International Society of Poets; World Parnassian Guild International, honorary member; Editor's Choice Award, National Library of Poetry. Address: 714 East 5th Street, Kewanee, IL 61443, USA.

GRABCO Daria, b. 14 September 1941, Republic of Moldova. Physicist. m. Alexei Grabco, 1963, 2 daughters. Education: Graduated, Chemistry, Kishinev State University, 1965; Doctor of Physics and Mathematics, 1974; DSc, Habil, Physics and Mathematics, 1993. Appointments: Junior Research Assistant, 1970, Senior Research Assistant, 1976, Leading Scientific Collaborator, 1990, Principal Scientific Collaborator, 1996, Head of Laboratory of Mechanical Properties of Crystals. Publications: 90 papers in professional journals; 130 communications at scientific meetings; 2 books; 3 preprints. Memberships: Fellow, Scientific Council of Institute of Applied Physics; President, Association for Non-destructive Testing; Fellow, Scientific Council on Scientific Degree Conferment. Address: Institute of Applied Physics,

Moldavian Academy of Sciences, Academy str 5, MD-2028, Chisinau, Republic of Moldova. E-mail: daria.grabco@phys.asm.md

GRABES Herbert, b. 8 June 1936, Krefeld. Professor of English. m. Hannelore Koch, 2 sons, 1 daughter. Education: PhD, University of Cologne, 1963; Habilitation, University of Mannheim, 1969. Appointments: Research Assistant, University of Cologne, 1962-65; Research Assistant, University of Mannheim, 1966-70; Professor of English, University of Giessen, 1970-; Vice President, University of Giessen, 1979-81. Publications: Der Begriff des a Priori in Nicolai Hartmanns Metaphysik; Fictitious Biographies; Asthetik, Was ist Literatur; The Mutable Glass, Mirror Imagery; Das englische Pamphlet I; Das amerikan, Drama 20 Jhs; Die Ästhetik des Fremden. Honours: Honorary Doctorate, University of Wisconsin, Milwaukee. Memberships: IAUPE; ACLALS; Anglistentag; Deutsche Gesellschaft für Amerikastudien; Deutsche Shakespeare Gesellschaft; Nabokov Society. Address: Sonnenstr 37, D-35444 Biebertal, Germany.

GRABOVAC David, b. 6 June 1983, Bankstown, Australia. Executive. Education: Diploma in Advertising, Macleary College; Bachelor of Arts, Media and Communications, Southern Cross University. Appointments: Executive Officer, VG Stainless Pty Ltd; Managing Director, CNET Communications Group; Dean, Regent College; Chair, The Grabovac Foundation. Publications: Book: Croatia and It's People. Honours: Justice of the Peace, New South Wales, Australia. Memberships: New South Wales Justices Association; National Trust of Australia; Royal Commonwealth Society; Australian Red Cross; Royal Society of New South Wales; Council for Education in the Commonwealth; The Claremont Institute; Life Member, Australian Croatian Cardinal Stepinac Association. Address: GPO Box 1350, Sydney, NSW 2001, Australia.

GRAÇA Ana-Liza da, b. 8 November 1974, Portugal. Public Relations and Marketing Director; Economist. Education: BA (Hons), Economics, University of Sussex, England, 1992-95; Postgraduate, Business Administration and Management (automotive focus), Portuguese Catholic University, Lisbon, 2002. Appointments: Senior HR Consultant in Investment Banking and Head of Latin American Equities, VWJ Ltd, City of London, England, 1996-98; PR Director, Aston Martin and Jaguar Portugal, Jaguar Auto Porto, Lda, 1998-99; PR and Marketing Director, Head of Lisbon Operations and Member of Board of Directors, Aston Martin and Jaguar Portugal, Jaguar Auto Lisbon SA, 2000-. Publications: Several interviews published in national media and TV interviews: the News, PR and Marketing, Brand Management programs, prime time. Honours: Best Brand, Best Car, Best Launch, 2000-; Listed in Who's Who publications and biographical dictionaries. Memberships: International Association of Business Leaders; Maecenas for National Zoo; Museum of Contemporary Art Serralves, Porto; Museum of Transport and Telecommunications, Porto; Cultural Centre of Belem, Lisbon; Who's Who in the World Historical Society; Several national charities; Sponsor of several sports events. Address: R Antonio Enes 21A, 1050-023 Lisbon, Portugal. E-mail: ldgracajagpor@mail.telepac.pt

GRACE Sherrill Elizabeth, b. Ormstown, Quebec, Canada. University Professor. 2 children. Education: BA, University of Western Ontario, 1962-65; MA, 1968-70, PhD, 1970-74, McGill University. Appointments: Teacher, Netherhall Secondary Girls School, Cambridge, England, 1967-68; Teaching Assistant, 1970-73, Special Lecturer, 1974-75, Assistant Professor, 1975-77, McGill University; Assistant Professor, 1977, Associate Professor, 1981, Professor, 1987-, Departmental Head, 1997-, University of British Columbia. Publications include: Violent Duality: A Study of Margaret Atwood, 1980; The Voyage That Never Ends: Malcolm Lowry's Fiction, 1982; Regression and Apocalypse: Studies in North American Literary Expressionism, 1989; Sursum Corda: The Collected Letters of Malcolm Lowry, 1995, 1996; Staging the North: 12 Canadian Plays, 1999; Canada and the Idea of North, 2002. Honours include: University of British Columbia President Killam Research Prize, 1990; FEL Priestley Award, 1993; University of British Columbia Jacob Biely Research Prize, 1998; Fellow, Royal Society of Canada. Memberships: International Association of University Professors of English; Modern Language Association; Association of Canadian University Teachers of English. Address: Department of English, University of British Columbia, #397-1873 East Mall, BC V6T 1Z1, Canada.

GRACIA-BENEYTO Carmen, b. 29 May 1947, Valencia, Spain. Professor; Art Historian. m. Juan Pecourt, 1 son, 2 daughters. Education: Degree, Filosofia y Letras, 1968; PhD, Geography and History, 1973, University of Valencia, Spain. Appointments: University Teacher, 1975-90, Professor, 1990-, University of Valencia, Spain; Director, Museo de Bellas Artes de Valencia, 1991-93; Director, Instituto de Arte, Institució Valenciana d'Estudios I Invstigació, 1992-95. Publications: Books: Las Pensiones de Pintura de la Diputacion de Valencia, 1987; Valencian Painter 1860-1936. From the Collection of the Council of Valencia, 1992; Història de L'Art Valencià, 1995; Arte Valenciano, 1998; La Imagen del Pensamiento: El Paisaje en Ignacio Pinazo, 2001. Honours: Honorary Director: Museo de Bellas Artes de Valencia. Memberships: Numerario Institut d'Estudis Catalans. Address: Isabel la Catolica 7, 46113 Moncada (Valencia), Spain. E-mail: carmen.gracia@uv.es

GRADE Michael Ian, b. 8 March 1943, London, England. Broadcasting Executive. m. (1) Penelope Jane Levinson, 1967, divorced 1981, 1 son, 1 daughter, (2) Hon Sarah Lawson, 1982, divorced, (3) Francesca Mary Leahy, 1998, 1 son. Education: St Dunstan's College, London, UK. Appointments: Trainee Journalist, Daily Mirror, 1960, Sports Columnist, 1964-66; Theatrical Agent, Grade Organisation, 1966; Joint Managing Director, London Management and Representation, 1969-73; Deputy Controller of Programmes (Entertainment), London Weekend TV, 1973-77; Director of Programmes and Member Board, 1977-81; President, Embassy TV, 1981-84; Controller, BBC 1, 1984-86; Director of Programmes BBC TV, 1986-87; CEO Channel Four, 1988-87; Chairman, VCI PLC, 1995-98; Director, 1991-2000, non-executive Chairman, 1995-97, Chairman, 1997-98, First Leisure Corp. Honours: CBE, Hon LLD (Nottingham), 1997; Royal TV Society Gold Medal, 1997. Memberships include: Vice President, Children's Film Unit, 1993-; Delfont Macintosh Theatres Ltd, 1994-99; Entertainment Charities Fund, 1994-; Deputy Chairman, Society of Stars, 1995-; RADA, 1996-; Royal Albert Hall, 1997-; Charlton Athletic Football Club, 1997-; Camelot Group, 2000-; Digitaloctopus, 2000-; Chair, Octopus, 2000-; Pinewood Studio Ltd, 2000-; Hemscott.NET, 2000- Address: First Leisure Corporation PLC, 7 Soho Street, London, W1V 5 FA, England.

GRADINARSKI Victor Dimitrov, b. 12 June 1955, Varna, Bulgaria. Logistics Manager. m. Nadejda Simeonova Gradinarska, 2 daughters. Education: Certificate, Arabic Language and Social Science Specialist, 1979-85; MA, State University Kliment Ohridski, Sofia, Bulgaria, 1984. Appointments: Shipping Agent, Inflot S.A., Varna, Bulgaria, 1985-88; Passport and Legal Civil Servant, Bulgarian Embassy, Tripoli, Libya, 1988-90; Vice Executive Director, Bon Marine S.A., 1990-. Honours: Listed in Who's Who publications and biographical dictionaries. Membership: Regional Association of Ship Agents and Brokers, Varna, Bulgaria. Address: Bon Marine S.A., 3 Vardar Street, 9000 Varna, Bulgaria.

Dictionary of International Biography

GRAF Steffi, b. 14 June 1969, Bruehl. Tennis Player. m. Andre Agassi, 1 son. Career: Won Orange Bowl 12s, 1981; European 14 and under and European Circuit Masters, 1982, Olympic demonstration event, Los Angeles; Winner, German Open, 1986, French Open, 1987, 1988, 1993, 1995, 1996; Australian open, 1988, 1989, 1990, 1994; Wimbledon, 1988, 1989, 1991, 1992, 1993, 1995, 1996, US Open, 1988, 1989, 1993, 1995, 1996; Ranked No 1, 1987; Official World Champion, 1988; Grand Slam winner, 1988, 1989; Olympic Champion, 1988; German Open, 1989; Youngest player to win 500 Singles victories as professional, 1991; 118 tournament wins, 23 Grand Slam titles, 1996; Won ATP Tour World Championship, 1996; Numerous Women's Doubles Championships with Gabriela Sabatini, Federation Cup, 1992; Retired, 1999. Publication: Wege Zum Erfolg, 1999. Honours: Olympic Order, 1999; German Medal of Honour, 2002. Memberships: Ambassador, World Wildlife Fund, 1984-; Founder and Chair, Children for Tomorrow; Ambassador, EXPO 2000. Address: Stefanie Graf Marketing GmbH, Mallaustrasse 75, 68219 Mannheim, Germany. E-mail: kontakt@stefanie-graf.com Website: stefanie.graf.com

GRAHAM James (8th Duke of Montrose), b. 6 April 1935, Salisbury, Rhodesia. Member of House of Lords. m. Catherine Elizabeth MacDonnell Young, 2 sons, 1 daughter. Appointments: Framer; Landowner; Ensign, Queen's Bodyguard for Scotland, Royal Company of Archers; Member of Council, National Farmers Union of Scotland, 1981-86; Chairman, Buchanan Community Council, 1982-93; Vice-Chairman, Loch Lomond and Trossachs Working Party, 1991-93; President, The Royal Highland and Agricultural Society of Scotland, 1997-98; Entered House of Lords, 1997; Elected Hereditary Peer, 1999; Opposition Whip; Opposition Spokesman for Scottish Affairs. Address: House of Lords, Westminster, London SW1A 0PW, England.

GRAHAM Robert Donald, (Bob Graham), b. 20 October 1942, Sydney, Australia. Author, Illustrator. m. Carolyn Smith, 26 August 1968, 1 son, 1 daughter. Education: Julian Ashton School of Fine Art, Sydney. Publications: Pete and Roland, 1981; Here Comes John, 1983; Here Comes Theo, 1983; Pearl's Place, 1983; Libby, Oscar and Me, 1984; Bath Time for John, 1985; First There Was Frances, 1985; Where Is Sarah?, 1985; The Wild, 1986; The Adventures of Charlotte and Henry, 1987; Crusher is Coming!, 1987; The Red Wollen Blanket, 1987; Has Anyone Here Seen William?, 1988; Bringing Home the New Baby, 1989; Grandad's Magic, 1989; Greetings From Sandy Beach, 1990; Rose Meets Mr Wintergarten, 1992; Brand New Baby, 1992; Spirit of Hope, 1993; Zoltan the Magnificent, 1994; Queenie the Bantam, 1997; Buffy, 1999; Max, 2000; Charlotte and Henry, 2000; Let's Get a Pup, 2001; Jethro Byrde, 2002; Tales from the Waterhole, 2004-. Honours: Australian Picture Book of the Year, 1988, 1991, 1993; Gold Medal, Smarties Prize, Picture Book, UK, 2000; The Boston Globe Horn Book Award, USA, 2002; Book of the Year, Early Childhood, Australia, 2002; Kate Greenaway Medal, UK, 2002. Membership: Australian Society of Authors; British Society of Authors. Address: c/o Peter Graham, 71 Yarra Street, Abbotsford 3067, Victoria, Australia.

GRAHAM-SMITH Francis (Sir), b. 25 April 1923, Roehampton, Surrey, England. Astronomer. m. Elizabeth Palmer, 3 sons, 1 daughter. Education: Natural Sciences Tripos, Downing College Cambridge; 1943-47, 1946-47; PhD (Cantab), 1952. Appointments: Telecommunications Research Establishment, Malvern, 1943-46; Research into Radio Astronomy Cavendish Laboratory, Cambridge, 1946-64, Jodrell Bank, 1964-74 and 1981-; Director, Royal Greenwich Observatory, 1976-81; Responsible for establishing the Isaac Newton Group of telescopes on La Palma, Canary Islands; Professor of Radio Astronomy, 1964-74, 1981-

90, Langworthy Professor of Physics, 1987-90, Pro-Vice-Chancellor, 1988-90, Emeritus Professor, 1990-, University of Manchester; Director, Nuffield Radio Astronomy Laboratories, Jodrell Bank, 1981-88; 13th Astronomer Royal, 1982-90. Publications: Books: Radio Astronomy, 1960; Optics (with J H Thomson), 1971, 2nd edition, 1988; Pulsars, 1977; Pathways to the Universe (with Sir ACB Lovell), 1988; Pulsar Astronomy (with A G Lyne), 1989, 2nd edition, 1998; Optics and Photonics (with T King), 2000; Introduction to Radio Astronomy (with B F Burke), 1997, 2nd edition, 2002. Honours: Fellow, 1953-64, Honorary Fellow, 1970, Downing College, Cambridge; Kt Bachelor, 1986; Royal Medal, Royal Society, 1987; DSc: Queens University Belfast, 1986, Keele University 1987, Birmingham University, 1989, Dublin University, 1990; Nottingham University, 1990, Manchester University, 1993; Glazebrook Medal, Institute of Physics, 1991. Memberships: Fellow of the Royal Society, Physical Secretary and Vice-President, 1988-94; Fellow of the Royal Astronomical Society, Secretary, 1964-71, President, 1975-77; Foreign Associate, Royal Society of South Africa, 1988; Chairman of the Governors, Manchester Grammar School, 1987-98. Address: Old School House, Henbury, Macclesfield, Cheshire SK11 9PH, England. E-mail: fgsegs@ukonline.co.uk

GRAMMENOPOULOS Filios Antoniou, b. 5 June 1923, Larnaca, Cyprus. Retired Diplomat. m. Nitsa Evriviades, 1 son, 1 daughter. Education: BA, The Open University, London, 1986-89. Appointments: East African Tobacco Co Ltd, 1945-48; British American Tobacco Co Ltd, 1948-52; Chairman, Executive Officer, Westlands Motors Ltd, Nairobi, Kenya, 1953-73; Honorary Consul of Cyprus, Nairobi, Kenya, 1968-74; High Commissioner for Cyprus to Kenya, concurrently to Uganda, Tanzania, Zambia, Seychelles, Ambassador, Sultanate of Oman and Mozambique, 1974-84. Honours: Grand Cross Order of St Mark, 1st Class; Orthodox Patriarchate of Alexandria, 1976. Memberships: Hellenic Community Trust, London; The Hellenic Centre, London. Address: 106-107 William Court, 6 Hall Road, London NW8 9PB, England. E-mail: filios.g.@aol.com

GRAÑENA Albert, b.26 September 1947, Barcelona, Spain. Physician; Haematologist. m. Asuncion Aracil, divorced, 2 sons, 1 daughter. Education: MD, 1969, PhD, 1977, Specialist, Internal Medicine, Specialist Haematology, 1981, University of Barcelona. Appointments: Assistant Physician, Hospital Clinic, Barcelona, 1970-72; Associate Professor, Escuela Farreras Valenti, Barcelona, 1974-; Specialist in Haematology, 1972-79, Senior Consultant, Haematology, Head of Bone Marrow Transplant Programme, 1979-93, Head of Haematology, 1993-, Institut Catala Oncologia; Professor, 1985-, Professor of Medicine, 1993-, University of Barcelona; Pioneer of bone marrow transplants in Spain and Europe. Publications: 450 publications in national and international professional journals; 25 book chapters; Director of 20 doctoral theses. Honours: Dr Extraordinary Prize, University of Barcelona, 1979; IX Du Pont Prize, 2000; Presidential Grant, Fundacio Josep Carreras, Barcelona, 1995-2000. Memberships: European Bone Marrow Transplantation Society; International Society of Haematology; American Society of Hematology. Address: Institut Catala Oncologia, Avda Gran Via KM 2.7, 08907 L'Hospitalet Barcelona, Spain. E-mail: a.granena@ico.scs.es

GRANIK Vladimir, b. 16 May 1934, Odessa, Ukraine. Civil Engineer. m. Galina Gaevskaya, 1 son, 1 daughter. Education: BSc, Civil Engineering Institute, Odessa, 1957; PhD, Central Research Institute of Reinforced Concrete, Moscow, 1967; Professor of Structural Mechanics, Moscow, 1972; Doctor of Technical Science, Moscow, 1989. Appointments: Engineer, Ministry of Defence, Odessa, 1957-63; Postgraduate, Central Research Institute of Structural Mechanics, Moscow, 1963-67; Associate Professor,

1967-72, Professor, 1972-88, Military Engineering Academy, Odessa; Professor, Maritime Engineering Academy, 1988-91; Visiting Professor, 1991-93, Research Associate, 1993-97, Professor, Consultant, 1997-, University of California, Berkeley, USA. Publications: The Flow of Granular Media in Tall Shells, 1988; Unified Theory of Elastic Rods, Plates, Shells, and Massive Bodies, 1991; Microstructural Mechanics of Granular Media, 1993; Doublet-Based Micromechanical Approach to Yield And Failure Criteria, 1994; A New Theory of Osmotic Pressures of Binary Solutions of Non-Electrolytes of Any Concentration, 1997; Advances in Doublet Mechanics, 1997; A Revision of Theory of Plasticity and Yield Criteria on the Basis of Thermodynamic Principles, 2001; Stochastic Dynamics of Supply and Demand in a Single Market, 2002. Address: 615 West 7th Street #205, Antioch, California 94509, USA. E-mail: vtgranik@highstream.net

GRANKIN Konstantin Nikolaevich, b. 23 November 1961, Saratov City, Russia. Astronomer. Education: MSc, Physics, Saratov State University, Saratov, Russia, 1984; PhD, Astrophysics, Main Astronomical Observatory, Russian Academy of Sciences, St Petersburg, Russia, 1995. Appointments: Assistant Astronomer, 1987-91, Junior Research Scientist, 1991-96, Senior Research Scientist, 1996-2000, Head of Department of Astrophysical Research, 2000-, Tashkent Astronomical Institute, Uzbekistan. Publications: More than 50 papers in various astronomical journals including: Astronomy and Astrophysics; Astrophysics and Space Science; Astronomische Nachrichten; Astronomy Letters. Membership: European Astronomical Society. Address: Astrophysical Research Department, Ulugh Beg Astronomical Institute of the Uzbek Academy of Sciences, Astronomicheskaya str 33, UZB-700052, Uzbekistan. E-mail: kn@astrin.uzsci.net Website: www.astrin.uzsci.net/~kgran

GRANOTT Nira, b. Petak-Tikva, Israel. Psychology Professor; Researcher. 1 son, 1 daughter. Education: MA, Tel-Aviv University, 1983; Harvard University, EdM, 1988; PhD, Massachusetts Institute of Technology, 1993. Appointments: Multimedia project director, Educational TV, Tel Aviv, 1974-80; Senior Analyst, Software Developer, Control Data Corporation, Tel Aviv, 1983-86; Assistant Professor of Psychology, University of Texas at Dallas, 1993-95, 1997-2002; Director, Microdevelopment laboratory, 1993-2002; Visiting Professor, Harvard Graduate School of Education, 1995-96; Co-founder, President, OORIM LLC, 2000-; Visiting Professor, Tufts University, 2002-. Publications: Articles include Unit of analysis, ensemble processes; Developing Learning, chapter contributed to Adult Learning and Development, 1998; Books include Microdevelopment: Transition Processes in Development and Learning, 2001. Honours: Research grant from NSF, 1999, Timberlawn Research Foundation, 1999; Texas Higher Education Coordination Board, 2000; Listed in several international biographical reference works. Memberships: American Psychological Society; European Society of Developmental Psychology; American Education Research Association; Jean Piaget Society. Address: Tufts University, Eliot Pearsons Department of Child Development, 105 College Avenue, Medford, MA 02155, USA E-mail: ngranott@aol.com

GRANT Hugh John Mungo, b. 9 September 1960, London, England. Actor. Education: BA, New College, Oxford. Career: Actor in theatre, TV and films, producer for Simian Films; Began career in the Jockeys of Norfolk (writer with Chris Lang and Andy Taylor); Films include: White Mischief, 1987; Maurice, 1987; Lair of the White Worm, 1988; La Nuit Bengali, 1988; Impromptu, 1989; Bitter Moon, 1992; Remains of the Day, 1993; Four Weddings and a Funeral, 1994; Sirens, 1994; The Englishman who went up a hill but came down a mountain, 1995; Nine Months, 1995; An Awfully Big Adventure, 1995; Sense and Sensibility,

1995; Restoration, 1996; Extreme Measures, 1996; Mickey Blue Eyes, 1998; Notting Hill, 1998; Small Time Crooks, 2000; Bridget Jones' Diary, 2001; About a Boy, 2002; Two Weeks' Notice, 2002; Love Actually, 2003. Honours include: Golden Globe Award, BAFTA Award for Best Actor, Four Weddings and a Funeral, 1995; Peter Sellers Award for Comedy; Evening Standard British Film Awards, 2002. Address: c/o Simian Films, 3 Cromwell Place, London SW7 2JE, England.

GRANT Richard E, b. 1957. Actor. m. Joan Washington, 1 daughter. Career: Actor, Theatre appearances include: Man of Mode, 1988; The Importance of Being Earnest, 1993; A Midsummer Night's Dream, 1994; TV appearances include: Honest, Decent, Legal and True, 1986; Here is the News, 1989; Suddenly Last Summer, 1992; Hard Times, 1993; Karaoke, 1996; A Royal Scandal, 1996; The Scarlet Pimpernel, 1998; Hound of the Baskervilles, 2002; Posh Nosh, 2003; Films: Withnail and I, 1986; How to Get Ahead in Advertising, 1989; Warlock, 1989; Henry and June, 1990; Mountains of the Moon, 1990; LA Story, 1991; Hudson Hawk, 1991; Bram Stoker's Dracula, 1992; The Player, 1993; The Age of Innocence, 1993; Prêt à Porter, 1995; Jack and Sarah, 1995; Portrait of a Lady, 1995; Twelfth Night, 1995; The Serpent's Kiss, 1996; The Match, 1998; A Christmas Carol, 1999; Trial and Retribution, 1999; Little Vampires, 1999; Hildegarde, 2000; Gosford Park, 2001; Monsieur 'N', 2002; Bright Young Things, 2003. Publications: With Nails: The Film Diaries of Richard E Grant, 1995; Twelfth Night, 1996; By Design - A Hollywood Novel. Address: c/o ICM, Oxford House, 76 Oxford Street, London W1N 0AX, England. Website: www.richard-e-grant.com

GRASSBY Albert Jaime, b. 12 July 1926. Politician; Author. m. Ellnor Louez, 3 February 1962, 1 daughter. Education: Arts studies, University of South West England; Special studies, agricultural extension at University of California; Attached to US Department of Agriculture in Washington DC; Studies in patterns of agricultural production and farm living, Italy, sponsored by UN FAO and Italian Department of Agriculture and Forests. Appointments: Elected Member for Murrumbidgee, New South Wales Parliament, 1965; Shadow Minister for Agriculture and Conservation, 1968-69; Elected Member for Riverina, Federal Parliament, 1969; Served on 3 Parliamentary Standing Committees: Primary Industry, Immigration, Parliamentary Broadcasting; Minister for Immigration, 1972-74; Special Advisor to Australian Government on Community Relations, 1974; Appointed Australian 1st Commissioner for Community Relations, 1975; Lecturer, institutions and colleges of advanced education and at universities including: Sydney, Melbourne, Adelaide, Perth; Served on Australian Migration Appeals Panel, 1984-86; Chairman, Australian National Consultative Committee on Peace and Disarmament, 1986-87; Special Advisor to New South Wales Government on Community Relations, 1986; Director, Australian Institute of Multiculturalism, 1985-87; Publications: Griffith of the Four Faces; The Morning After; Tyranny of Prejudice; Six Australian Battlefields; Oogeroo Nunuccal; Australia's Italians; World Perspective on Pacific Islander Migration; Republican Australia; The Australian Republic; Biography of J C Watson: First Labour Prime Minister of Australia and the World; Eight book series: Australians All, English, Italians, Irish, Greek, Chinese, Germans, Lebanese and Spanish. Honours include: AM, 1985; UN Peace Medal, 1986; Knight Commander of Order of Isabella La Catolica (Spain), 1986; Order of Merit (Ecuador), 1997; Medal of Sarajevo (Bosnia), 1998; Diploma of Appreciation of the Polish Strzelecki Foundation, 1998. Address: 73 Investigator Street, Red Hill, ACT, Australia

GRAY Douglas, b. 17 February 1930, Melbourne, Victoria, Australia. Professor of English; Writer. m. 3 September 1959, 1 son. Education: MA, Victoria University of Wellington, New Zealand, 1952; BA, 1956, MA, 1960, Merton College, Oxford. Appointment: J R R Tolkien Professor of English, Oxford, 1980-97, Emeritus, 1997-. Publications: Themes and Images in the Medieval English Religious Lyric, 1972; Robert Henryson, 1979; The Oxford Book of Late Medieval Verse and Prose (editor), 1985; Selected Poems of Robert Henryson and William Dunbar (editor), 1998. Contributions to: Scholarly journals. Honours: British Academy, fellow, 1989; Honorary LitD, Victorian University of Wellington, 1995. Memberships: Early English Text Society; Society for the Study of Medieval Languages and Literatures, president, 1982-86. Address: Lady Margaret Hall, Oxford OX2 6QA, England.

GRAY Dulcie (Winifred Catherine), b. 20 November 1920, England. Actress; Dramatist; Writer. m. Michael Denison, 29 April 1939. Education: England and Malaysia. Appointments: Numerous stage, film, radio, and television appearances. Publications: Murder on the Stairs, 1957; Baby Face, 1959; For Richer, for Richer, 1970; Ride on a Tiger, 1975; Butterflies on My Mind, 1978; Dark Calypso, 1979; The Glanville Women, 1982; Mirror Image, 1987; Looking Forward, Looking Backward (autobiography), 1991; J B Priestley, biography, 2000. Contributions to: Periodicals. Honours: Queen's Silver Jubilee Medal, 1977; Times Educational Supplement Senior Information Book Prize, 1978; Commander of the Order of the British Empire, 1983. Memberships: British Actors Equity; Linnean Society, fellow; Royal Society of Arts, fellow; Society of Authors. Address: Shardeloes, Amersham, Buckinghamshire HP7 0RL, England.

GREAVES Stuart, b. 21 March 1953, Huddersfield, England. Business and Chemical Consultant. Education: BSc, Chemistry, University of Manchester Institute of Science and Technology, Manchester, England, 1974. Appointments: Technical Manager, A H Marks & Co Ltd, Bradford, England, 1974-81; General Manager, Farmco Pty Ltd, Perth Australia, 1981-85; Managing Director, Martin Industries Ltd, Nottingham, England, 1986-96; Director of Corporate Development, Micro Flo Company, Lakeland, Florida, USA, 1996-2000; Business and Chemical Consultant, York, England, 2000-. Honours: Listed in Who's Who publications and biographical dictionaries. Memberships: Royal Society of Chemistry (Chartered Chemist), England; Royal Australian Chemical Institute (Chartered Chemist), Australia; American Chemical Society; New York Academy of Sciences; Founder Member, London Diplomatic Agency. Address: The Farmhouse, Manor Green, Bolton, York YO41 5RZ, England. E-mail: stuartgreaves@yahoo.com

GREEN Fay, b. 30 January 1954, Kent, England. Solicitor; Poet; Breeder of Rare Sheep. Education: Law Society Examinations, Honours, 1978. Appointment: Solicitor, Green & Co; Chairman Social Security Appeals Tribunal. Publications: Pure Green, 1990; Colours, 1991; No Telegrams, 1992; Fragile Ground, 1994; Poems-in-Law, 1995. Contributions to: Kent and Sussex Poetry Society Folio Competition Winners Anthologies; Law Society's Gazette; Angels of the Heart Anthology, 1992; Heart and Soul Anthology, 1996; Kentish Poems, 1996. Honours: Kent and Sussex Poetry Society, Commendations, 1992, 1994. Membership: Kent and Sussex Poetry Society; Federation of Kent Writers, committee, 1994-. Address: Charity Farmhouse, Pilgrims Way, Hollingbourne, Kent ME17 1RB, England.

GREEN Michael Frederick, b. 2 January 1927, Leicester, England. Writer. Education: BA, Honours, Open University. Publications: The Art of Coarse Rugby, 1960; The Art of Coarse

Sailing, 1962; Even Coarser Rugby, 1963; Don't Print my Name Upside Down, 1963; The Art of Coarse Acting, 1964; The Art of Coarse Golf, 1967; The Art of Coarse Moving, 1969 (TV serial, 1977); The Art of Coarse Drinking, 1973; Squire Haggard's Journal, 1976 (TV serial, 1990 and 1992); Four Plays For Coarse Actors, 1978; The Coarse Acting Show Two, 1980; Tonight Josephine, 1981; The Art of Coarse Sex, 1981; Don't Swing from the Balcony Romeo, 1983; The Art of Coarse Office Life, 1985; The Third Great Coarse Acting Show, 1985; The Boy Who Shot Down an Airship, 1988; Nobody Hurt in Small Earthquake, 1990; Coarse Acting Strikes Back, 2000. Memberships: Society of Authors; Equity; National Union of Journalists. Address: 31 Clive Road, Twickenham, Middlesex, TW1 4SQ, England.

GREEN Paul John, b. 27 July 1936, Seattle, Washington, USA. Scholar. Education: BA, Seattle Pacific College, 1957; MA, University of Washington, 1958; MLS, University of California at Berkeley, 1968; PhD, Washington State University, 1981. Appointments: Teaching Assistant, English, University of Washington, 1963-66; Instructor in English, Central Washington University, 1966-67; Research Assistant in Librarianship, University of California, Berkeley, 1967-68; Assistant Serials Librarian, University of Oregon, 1968-69; Teaching Assistant in English, Washington State University, 1974-76; Bibliographic Searching Assistant, Washington State University, 1984-2001. Publications: Contributor of numerous articles, reviews, notes and translations, bibliographies, poems, letters and an abstract; Editor, Student Writing, 1966-67; Novel: The Life of Jack Gray, (privately printed), 1991, new expanded edition, 2002; Previously unpublished literary reviews, 1997-99, 2001; Previously unpublished literary essays, 1992-2000, 2001; From Russia with Love and A Literary Potpourri, 2003; Collected Writings on the Fiction of Franz Kafka, with a Germanics Supplement, 2003; Eighteenth Century Salad with French and Italian Dressing: Swift-Voltaire, Fielding-Manzoni and Reviews Franco-Italian, and Italian, 2003. Honours: Freshman Scholarship, Seattle Pacific College, 1954-55; Non-resident Tuition Waiver, University of California, Berkeley, 1967-68; Editorial Board Member, Works and Days, 1984-94; Editorial Board Member, Recovering Literature, 1994-; Phi Sigma Iota Consultant, Language Pedagogy, China, 1997; Cavalier, World Order of Science, Education and Culture. Memberships: Smithsonian Institution; MLA; American Comparative Literature Association; Order of International Ambassadors; Academy of American Poets; International Comparative Literature Association; LFIBA; DGABIRA; Kafka Society of America; Life Member, London Diplomatic Academy; University of California Alumni Association; Arnold Bennett Hall Society, University of Oregon; Industrial Workers of the World; Sierra Club; People to People International; University of Washington Alumni Association; Oregon Shakespeare Festival; American Civil Liberties Union; Common Cause. Address: 825 Washington St #20, Eugene, OR 97401-2845, USA.

GREEN Timothy (Seton), b. 29 May 1936, Beccles, England. Writer. m. Maureen Snowball, October 1959, 1 daughter. Education: BA, Christ's College, Cambridge, 1957; Graduate Diploma in Journalism, University of Western Ontario, 1958. Appointments: London Correspondent, Horizon, and American Heritage, 1959-62; Life, 1962-64; Editor, Illustrated London News, 1964-66. Publications: The World of Gold, 1968; The Smugglers, 1969; Restless Spirit, UK edition as The Adventurers, 1970; The Universal Eye, 1972; World of Gold Today, 1973; How to Buy Gold, 1975; The Smuggling Business, 1977; The World of Diamonds, 1981; The New World of Gold, 1982, 2nd edition, 1985; The Prospect for Gold, 1987; The World of Gold, 1993; The Good Water Guide, 1994; New Frontiers in Diamonds: The

Mining Revolution, 1996; The Gold Companion, 1997; The Millennium is Gold, 1999; The Millennium is Silver, 1999. Address: 8 Ponsonby Place, London, SW1P 4PT, England.

GREENBERG Jacob, b. 29 January 1938, Odessa, Ukraine, USSR. Chemist. m. Tatyana Ilina, 24 September 1961, 2 sons. Education: Graduate, Central Musical School, Tchaikovsky State Conservatoire, Moscow, Russia, 1956; MSc, Moscow Institute of Fine Chemical Technology, 1962; PhD, 1966, DSc, 1989, Institute of General and Inorganic Chemistry, Russian Academy of Science, Moscow. Appointments: Junior Scientist, 1962-66, Research Scientist, 1966-75, Senior Scientist, 1975-89, Principal Scientist, 1989-92, Institute of General and Inorganic Chemistry, Moscow; Senior Scientist, 1993-99, Professor, 1999-, Hebrew University of Jerusalem, Israel; Visiting Lecturer, Institute of Crystal Growth, Berlin, 1997; Northwestern University, Evanston, USA, 2000; Freiburg University, Germany, 2001; Consultant, 1985-91, Platan Electronics, Moscow, 1985-91; Trucks and Tractor Company, Moscow, 1985-90; II-VI Inc PA, USA, 1996; URIGAL Technology, Rehovot, Israel, 1996-; IMARAD Imaging Systems Ltd, Rehovot, Israel, 1998-. Publications: Author and co-author, 6 books; About 150 papers; 5 Russian patents. Honours: Research work of the Year, 1967, 1976, 1988, 1991; Institute of General and Inorganic Chemistry, Russian Academy of Science, Moscow; Expo-USSR Medal, 1977, 1989. Memberships: ACS, 1994-; NYAS, 1995-; AAAS, 1995-97; Israel Association of Crystal Growth, 1999-. Address: 98/2 Nahalim Street, 98310 Maale Adumim, Israel. E-mail: jacob.greenberg@huji.ac.il

GREENBLATT Hellen, b. 15 May 1947, Frankfurt, Germany. Scientist; Educator. Education: PhD. Appointments: Senior Research Immunoparasitologist, Merck, Sharp & Dohme, Rahway, New Jersey, 1980-81; Member, Department of Microbiology and Immunology, Associate, Department of Medicine, Albert Einstein College of Medicine, Bronx, New York, 1981-84; Director, Research and New Business Development, Clinical Sciences Inc. Whippany, New Jersey, 1984-87; Senior Scientist, E I Dupont de Nemours & Company, Wilmington, Delaware, 1998-99; President, Managing Director, M-Cap Technologies International, 1990-93, Director, Technical Affairs, BTR Separations, 1993-94, Vice-president, Research and Development, 1994-97, Vice President, Product Development, 1998-2000, DuPont ConAgra Visions (DCV Inc), Wilmington, Delaware; Executive Vice President, Legacy for Life, Division of DCV Inc, Melbourne, Florida, 2000-. Publications: Book chapters, articles in scientific journals and papers presented at conferences as first author include: Compliment-Mediated Tail Loss of Schistosoma mansoni Cercariae, 1980; Genetic control of natural resistance to Trypanosoma rhodesiense in mice, 1980; Antibody Dependent Phagocytosis of Trypanosoma rhodesiense by Murine Macrophages, 1983. Address: PO Box 5941, Wilmington, DE 19808 0134. E-mail: hgreenblatt@legacyforlife.net

GREENE Jeffrey, b. 22 May 1952, Norwalk, Connecticut, USA. Professor of English; Poet. Education: BA, Goddard College, 1975; MFA, University of Iowa, 1977; PhD, University of Houston, 1986. Appointments: Assistant Professor, Associate Professor of English, University of New Haven. Publications: To The Left of the Worshipper, 1991; Glimpses of the Invisible World in New Haven, 1995; American Spirituals, 1998; French Spirits, 2003. Contributions to: New Yorker; Nation; American Scholar; Iowa Review; Antioch Review; Sewanee Review; Ploughshares; Missouri Review; Prairie Schooner; Indiana Review; Seneca Review; Ohio Review; Denver Quarterly. Honours: Discovery, The Nation Award; Mary Roberts Rinehart Grant; Brazos Prize in Poetry; 2nd Prize, National Poetry Competition; Connecticut Commission on the Arts Grant; Randall Jarrell Prize, 1996;

National Endowment for the Arts Fellowship, 1996; Samuel French Morse Prize, 1998. Memberships: Associated Writing Programs; Poetry Society of America. Address: 42 rue du Cherche Midi, 75006 Paris, France.

GREENLAND Collin Anthony Alexander, b. 8 September 1959, Kingston, Jamaica. Internal Auditor; Fraud Examiner. Education: BS, Hons, 1983; Master of Business Administration, 1991; Certified Fraud Examiner, 1996; Certified Financial Services Auditor, 1998. Appointments: Internal Auditor, Circulation's Manager, The Jamaica Record, 1989-90; Group Internal Auditor, Agricultural Development Corporation, 1990-93; Chief Internal Auditor, Caldon Finance Merchant Bank, 1994-97; Self Employed, Executive Chairman, Kaizen Management Consultancy and Investment Company, 1997-98; Chief Internal Auditor, Jamaica Tourist Board, 1998-. Publications: Numerous articles on Internal Auditing, Fraud and Management, for newspapers and journals; Editor, White Collar Journal; Persistence Perversity – Jamaica's Experience with Pyramids, Ponzis and Partners. Honours: First Place, Chapter Newsletter, IIA, 1996; Chapter Achievement Award, Silver Award by the Institute of Internal Auditors, 1998. Memberships: Institute of Internal Auditors, Jamaica Chapter; Institute of Internal Auditors, Inc; Jamaica Institute of Management; Association for the Advancement of Management; Association of Certified Fraud Examiners; National Association of Financial Services Auditors. Address: Apartment # 14, Smokey Vale Apartments, Smokey Vale, Meadowbridge, PO Box 546, St Andrew, Jamaica, W I. E-mail: cgreenland@visitjamaica.com

GREENLEAF Stephen (Howell), b. 17 July 1942, Washington, District of Columbia, USA. Attorney; Writer. m. Ann Garrison, 20 July 1968, 1 son. Education: BA, Carleton College, 1964; JD, University of California, at Berkeley, 1967; Creative Writing, University of Iowa, 1978-79. Appointments: Admitted to the Bar, California, 1968, Iowa, 1977. Publications: Grave Error, 1979; Death Bed, 1980; State's Evidence, 1982; Fatal Obsession, 1983; The Ditto List, 1985; Beyond Blame, 1986; Toll Call, 1987; Impact, 1989; Book Case, 1991; Blood Type, 1992; Southern Cross, 1993; False Conception, 1994; Flesh Wounds, 1996; Past Tense, 1997; Strawberry Sunday, 1999; Ellipsis, 2000. Honour: Maltese Falcon Award, Japan, 1993.

GREER Germaine b. 29 January 1939, Melbourne, Victoria, Australia. Writer; Broadcaster. Education: BA, Honours, Melbourne University, 1959; MA, Honours, Sydney University, 1962; PhD, Cambridge University, 1967. Appointments: Senior English Tutor, Sydney University, 1963-64; Assistant Lecturer and Lecturer, English, University of Warwick, 1967-72; Broadcaster, journalist, columnist and reviewer, 1972-; Lecturer, American Program Bureau, 1973-78; Visiting Professor, Graduate Faculty of Modern Letters, 1979, Professor of Modern Letters, 1980-83, University of Tulsa; Founder-Director, Tulsa Centre for Studies in Women's Literature, 1981; Proprietor, Stump Cross Books, 1988-; Special Lecturer and Unofficial Fellow, Newnham College, Cambridge, 1989-98. Publications: The Female Eunuch, 1969; The Obstacle Race: The Fortunes of Women Painters and Their Work, 1979; Sex and Destiny: The Politics of Human Fertility, 1984; Shakespeare (editor), 1986; The Madwoman's Underclothes (selected journalism), 1986; Daddy, We Hardly Knew You, 1989; The Change: Women, Ageing and the Menopause, 1991; Slip-Shod Sybils: Recognition, Rejection and the Woman Poet, 1995; The Whole Woman, 1999. Editor: The Uncollected Verse of Aphra Behn, 1989. Co-Editor: Kissing the Rod: An Anthology of Seventeenth Century Verse, 1988; Surviving Works of Anne Wharton (co-editor), 1997; The Whole Woman, 1999; John Wilmot, Earl of Rochester, 1999; 101 Poems by 191 Women (editor), 2001. Contributions to: Numerous articles in Listener,

Dictionary of International Biography

Spectator, Esquire, Harper's Magazine, Playboy, Private Eye and other journals. Honours: Scholarships, 1952, 1956; Commonwealth Scholarship, 1964; J R Ackerly Prize and Premio Internazionale Mondello, 1989. Address: c/o Aitken and Stone Associates Ltd, 29 Fernshaw Road, London SW10 0TG, England.

GREGORY Robert J, b. 28 August 1938, Elmira, New York, USA. Educator; Psychologist. m. Janet Elise Solomon Nicholson, 4 July 1975, 3 daughters. Education: BA, Cornell University, 1960; MA, 1964, PhD, 1968, Syracuse University. Appointments include: Vocational Evaluator, Counsellor, Placement Officer, New York State Division of Employment, Elmira, Syracuse and Cortland, New York, 1960-63; Research Scientist, Cumberland County Medical Health Center, Fayetteville, North Carolina, 1967-69; Teacher, Special Education, East Carolina University, Greenville, North Carolina, 1967-68; Consultant, 1968-75; Fellow, Institute of Human Ecology, Raleigh, North Carolina, 1969-71; Executive Director, Drug Action of Wake County Inc, Raleigh, North Carolina, 1971-73; Postdoctoral Fellow, Department of Psychiatry, Duke University Medical Center, Durham, North Carolina, 1973-75; Research Associate, Department of Anthropology, Duke University, 1975-78; Senior Extension Associate, New York State School of Industrial and Labor Relations, Cornell University, Ithaca, New York, 1978-80; Assistant Professor, Department of Counseling and Rehabilitation, Marshall University, Huntington, West Virginia, 1980-83. Publications include: A conceptual framework or process model for community psychology, 1999; Lunar and other cycles as steps toward human ecology, 1999; The ecological perspective: Streetwalking, 1999; The ecology of an aquarium, 1999; Observations on the environment, 1999; Stream Bank Rehabilitation, 2000; Advanced Studies on the Lahocla people, 2000; Parallel themes: Community psychology and Maori culture in Aotearoa, 2001; That Big Box of Photographs, 2001. Address: School of Psychology, Massey University, Palmerston North, New Zealand.

GRENNAN Eamon, b. 13 November 1941, Dublin, Ireland. Professor; Poet. 1 son, 2 daughters. Education: BA, 1963, MA, 1964, University College, Dublin; PhD, Harvard University, 1973. Appointments: Lecturer in English, University College, Dublin, 1966-67; Assistant Professor, Herbert Lehman College, City University of New York, 1971-74; Assistant Professor, 1974-83, Associate Professor, 1983-89, Professor, 1989-, Vassar College. Publications: Wildly for Days, 1983; What Light There Is, 1987; Twelve Poems, 1988; What Light There Is and Other Poems, 1989; As If It Matters, 1991; So It Goes, 1995; Selected Poems of Giacomo Leopardi (translator), 1995; Relations: New and Selected Poems, 1998; Selected and New Poems, 2000; Still Life with Waterfall, 2002. Contributions to: Anthologies and periodicals. Honours: National Endowment for the Humanities Grant, 1986; National Endowment for the Arts Grant, 1991; Guggenheim Fellowship, 1995; PEN Award for Poetry in Translation, 1997; Lenore Marshall Poetry Prize, 2003. Address: c/o Department of English, Vassar College, Poughkeepsie, NY 12604, USA.

GRESSER Sy, b. 9 May 1926, Baltimore, Maryland, USA. Stone Sculptor; Writer; Poet. 3 sons, 1 daughter. Education: BS, 1949, MA, 1972, Zoological Sciences, English and American Literature, University of Maryland; Institute of Contemporary Arts, Washington, DC, 1949-50. Appointments: Publications Consultant for various firms, 1960-; Teacher, 1965-70; Private Students. Publications: Stone Elegies, 1955; Coming of the Atom, 1957; Poems From Mexico, 1964; Voyages, 1969; A Garland for Stephen, 1971; A Departure for Sons, 1973; Fragments and Others, 1982; Hagar and Her Elders, 1989. Contributions to: Poetry Quarterly; Stand; Antioch Review; Western Humanities Review; Johns

Hopkins Review; Atavist Magazine; New York Times Book Review. Address: 1015 Ruatan Street, Silver Spring, MD 20903, USA.

GRETZKY Wayne, b. 26 January 1961, Brantford, Canada. Ice Hockey Player. m. Janet Jones, 1988, 2 sons, 1 daughter. Career: Former player with Edmonton; Played with Los Angeles Kings, 1988-96, St Louis Blues, 1996, New York Rangers, 1996-99; Retired, 1999; Most prolific scorer in National Hockey League history; Most Valuable Player (9 times). Publication: Gretzky: An Autobiography (with Rick Reilly). Honour: Hockey Hall of Fame, 1999. Address: New York Rangers, Madison Square Garden, 2 Pennsylvania Plaza, New York, NY 10121, USA.

GREVE Bent, b. 14 December 1953, Frederiksberg. Professor in Welfare State Analysis. 1 son, 1 daughter. Education: MA, Economics, Copenhagen University, 1977; PhD, Public Sector Administration (Lic scient adm), 1992; Dr Scient Adm, 2002. Appointments include: Academic Assistant, Danish Association of County Councils, 2 years; Economist, Economic Board, Danish Labour Movement, 3½ years' Head of Secretariat, Danish Union of Journalists, 3½ years; Roskilde University, 1986-, Head of Department, 1992-, Jean Monnet Professor in European Labour Market and Social Policy, 1997-; Professor, Welfare State Analysis; Danish expert to EU in freedom of worker's network, 1980-; Danish coordinator 3 Erasmus and Temous networks in: Social Security in Europe, Coordinator, Master Programme in Social Policy in Europe, 1994-, Labour Market Policy in Europe, 1995-; Teacher or lecturer in most of Europe, India, USA; Deputy member, Bureau of European Institute of Social Security, 1996-; Member, overseas editorial board of the Journal of Social Policy and Administration, 1998-; Professor in Welfare State Analysis, 2001. Publications: Numerous books and articles include: Economics of Migration in Alestalo and Kosonen (Eds): Welfare Systems and European Integration, 1996; Family Benefits Systems: Changing Policies: The Danish Case (paper), 1997; Activation: National and Supranational Buzzword - But is it really new policy? (conference paper), European University Institute, 1999; Historical Dictionary of the Welfare State; What Constitutes a Good Society; Comparative Welfare Systems; 2007: Vouchers, New Ways of Steering the Welfare State. Address: Roskilde Universitet, Universitetsvej, 4000 Roskilde, Denmark.

GRIER Pam, b. 1949, Winston-Salem, North Carolina, USA. Actress; Writer; Singer. Career: Actress, films: The Big Doll House, 1971; Women in Cages, 1971; Big Bird Cage, 1972; Black Mama, White Mama, 1972; Cool Breeze, 1972; Hit Man, 1972; Twilight People, 1972; Coffy, 1973; Scream, Blacula, Scream!, 1973; The Arena, 1973; Foxy Brown, 1974; Bucktown, 1975; Friday Foster, 1975; Sheba Baby, 1975; Drum, 1976; Greased Lightning, 1977; Fort Apache: The Bronx, 1981; Something Wicked This Way Comes, 1983; Stand Alone, 1985; The Vindicator, 1986; On the Edge, 1986; The Allnighter, 1987; Above the Law, 1988; The Package, 1989; Class of 1999, 1991; Bill and Ted's Bogus Journey, 1991; Tough Enough, Posse, 1993; Serial Killer, 1995; Original Gangstas, 1996; Escape from LA, 1996; Mars Attacks!, 1996; Strip Search, 1997; Fakin' Da Funk, 1997; Jackie Brown, 1997; Holy Smoke, 1999; In Too Deep, 1999; Fortress 2, 1999; Snow Day, 2000; Wilder, 2000; 3 A.M., 2001; Love the Hard Way, 2001; Bones, 2001; John Carpenter's Ghosts of Mars, 2001; Undercover Brother, 2002; The Adventures of Pluto Nash, 2002; Baby of the Family, 2002; TV mini-series: Roots: The Next Generations, 1979; Films: Badge of the Assassin, 1985; A Mother's Right; The Elizabeth Morgan Story, 1992; Stage appearances: Fool for Love; Frankie and Johnnie; In the Claire de Lune. Honour: Best Actress NAACP, 1986.

GRIFFITH Melanie, b. 9 August 1957, New York, USA. Actress. m. (1) Don Johnson, 1975, divorced 1976, remarried 1989, divorced 1993, 1 daughter, (2) Steve Bauer, divorced, (3) Antonio Banderas, 1996, 1 daughter. Education: Hollywood Professional School. Career: Films include: Night Moves, 1975; One On One, 1977; Roar, Body Double, 1984; Stormy Monday, 1987; Working Girl, 1988; Bonfire of the Vanities, 1991; Close to Eden, 1993; Nobody's Fool, 1994; Mulholland Falls, 1996; Lolita, 1996; Shadow of Doubt, 1998; Celebrity, 1998; Another Day in Paradise, 1998; Crazy in Alabama, 1999; Cecil B. Demented, 2000; Forever Lulu, 2000; Life with Big Cats, 2000; Tart, 2001; Stuart Little 2 (voice), 2002; TV Includes: Once an Eagle (mini-series); Carter Country (series); Steel Cowboy; She's in the Army Now. Address: Creative Artists Agency, 9830 Wilshire Boulevard, Beverly Hills, CA 90212, USA.

GRIGSBY Queen Delores Taylor-White, b. 21 August 1948, Oklahoma City, Oklahoma, USA. Consultant; Minister. m. (1) Walter Thomas White Jr, 1966, 2 sons (2) James O Grigsby, 1 son. Education: BS, Psychology, Howard University, Washington DC, 1970; Masters Degree, Counselling, Liberty University, 1988; Ordained Minister, 1989; Appointments: Housing Specialist, 1972; Housing Planner, 1972; Human Relations Consultant, 1975-76; Clinical Membership, TTAA, 1975; Owner, Taylor and Co, 1973-; Founded, Tangible Substance of God is Love Truth Church, Oklahoma, 1985; Founded, Manchild Ministries, Phoenix, Arizona, 1988; Currently Minister, Consultant. Publications: Worlds Greatest Poets: Eating While Passing By. Honours: Nellie Weaver Scholarship; Lucille McMahon Scholarship, 1968; Dartforth Leadership Award, 1968; Phillip Morris Scholarship, 1983; Golden Poet Award, 1991; International Woman of the Year, 2000; Memberships: Housing Specialist Institute; Society for Training and Development; Independent Republican; National Geographic Society; Smithsonian Associate; Williamsburg Foundation Historic Trust; History Preservation Society; Library of Congress Associates; Labor Day Foundation. Address: 1501 N E Park Pl, Oklahoma City, OK 73117, USA.

GRILLO Isaac Adetayo, 15 January 1931, Lagos, Nigeria. Medical Doctor; Cardiothoracic Surgeon. m. Arinade Adejunmobi, 5 sons, 7 daughters. Education: Bachelor of Arts, Education and Psychology, Bachelor of Science, Biology, McPherson, Kansas, USA, 1955; Doctor of Medicine, University of Kansas, 1960; Diplomate, American Board of General Surgery, 1966; Diplomate, American Board of Thoracic Surgery, 1967; Intern, Menorah Medical Center, Kansas City, Missouri, 1960-61; Resident, General Surgery, Homer G Phillips Hospital, St Louis, Missouri, 1961-65; Resident, Cardiothoracic Surgery, Olive View Hospital, California, 1965-66, Highland Hospital, 1966-67. Appointments: Physician, Fairmount Hospital, San Leandro, California, 1967-68; Lecturer to Professor of Cardiothoracic Surgery, University of Ibadan, University College Hospital, Ibadan, 1968-78, retiring as Professor, 1988; Head, Department of Surgery, University of Ibadan, University College Hospital, Ibadan, 1985-88; Senior Consultant and Head of Surgery, King Fahad Central Hospital, Gizan, Saudi Arabia, 1988-90; Senior Consultant, Assir Central Hospital, Abha, Saudi Arabia, 1991-99; Professor of Surgery, College of Medicine, King Saud University, Abha, Saudi Arabia, 1991-99; Physician and Surgeon, Salinas Valley State Prison, Soledad, California, USA, 2000-. Honours: Chemistry Scholarship and Foreign Student Scholarship, McPherson College, McPherson, Kansas, 1952-1955; Japanese Overseas Technical Co-operative Agency Scholarship, Tokyo, Japan, 1971; Fulbright-Hayes Scholarship, Presbyterian Medical Centre, 1977; Honorary Doctor of Science, McPherson College, Kansas, 1987. Memberships: Fellow, American College of Surgeons; American College of Chest Physicians; American College of Angiology; West African College of Surgeons; Nigeria

Medical Council, Surgery; International College of Surgeons; Christian Medical and Dental Association; Society of Thoracic Surgeons. Address: PO Box 367, Soledad, CA 93960, USA.

GRIMM Jane Bolles, b. 21 February 1942, San Francisco, California, USA. Artist. m. Rupert Edwin Grimm, 1 son, 1 daughter. Education: AB, Sarah Lawrence College, 1965; MFA with high distinction, California College of Arts and Crafts, 1992. Appointments: Teacher, Jewelry, Montclair Art Center, New Jersey, 1974; Sculpture, Shorthills, New Jersey; Teaching Assistant, California College of Arts and Crafts, Ceramic Department, 1991-92; Guest Lecturer, College of Siskyous, Weed, California, 1994; Guest Lecturer, California College of Arts and Crafts, 1999. Civic Activities: Board of Trustees, California College of Arts and Crafts, 1996-; Honours: Murphy Fellowship, SF Foundation, 1991; California State Fair, Award of Merit, 1994, 1999, 2000; Award of Merit Association of Clay and Glass Artists of California, 1999. Memberships: Association of Women Artists; Women's Caucus for the Arts; Pacific Rim Sculpture Group. Commissions and Creative Works: Lucent Technology, sculpture, Temple Isiah, sculpture in the collection of Berkeley Art Museum, Berkeley California; Nora Eccles Harris Museum, Washington. Address: 1895 Pacific Avenue #305, San Francisco, CA 94109, USA.

GRIMUR Marino Steindorsson, b. 25 May 1933, Vestman Isles, Iceland. Sculptor. 1 son, 1 daughter. Education: Reykjavik Art School, 1950-51; Harnarfjordur Industrial College, 1971. Career: Sculptor; Sailor; Fisherman; Group Exhibitions include: Nordic Sculpture, Copenhagen, Denmark, 1994; Vidalinskirkja, Iceland, 2002; Landsbanki, Iceland, 2002; Solo Exhibitions in Iceland include: Perlan, Reykjavik, 1992; Hofn-Harnafirdi, Hornafjudur, 1996; Safnahus Borgarfjardar, Burgarnes, 1997; Lyons Hall, Kopavogur, 2002; Ministry of Justice, Reykjavik, 2002; Customs House, Reykjavik, 2002; Numerous commissioned works include: "Herrings", Kopavogur, 1985; "Cod", Hafnarfjördur, 1990; "The Country Postman", Post and Tele of Iceland, Stadur, 1992; "Sulur", Harbour at Vestman Island, 1993; "Homeward Bound" in memory of the fishermen of Stykkisholmur, 1994; "Upphaf", for the opening of the new sporting centre at Kopavogur, 1994; "Jotnar" (Metal Sculpture), Fjardakoup, 2000. Publications: Illustrated many books of poetry including: Tone Picture Poems by Hardarson Sveinsson, 1992; Ljooblik (poems of KE Gudmundsdottir), 1993; Ur Vidjumijod Myndir, edited by Hrafn A Hardarsun, 1999. Honours: 5th Prize of the Town of Moscow, Russia, 1986; Prize, Höfdi House Summit Meeting Reagan Gorbachov Competition, 1987; 2nd Prize, Arts Festival, Reykjavik, 1988. Memberships: Association of Reykjavik Sculptors, 1980-92; Union of Icelandic Artists, 1980-92. Address: Karsnesbraut 106, 200 Kopavogur, Iceland. E-mail: hrafnh@kopavogur.is

GRINDE Kjell, b. 1 August 1929, Bergen, Norway. Civil and Structural Engineer. m. (1) Heidi, divorced, 1 son, 1 daughter, (2) Anneliv, 2 step-daughters. Education: BSc, 1954, MSc, 1956, Technical University of Norway; Diploma, Total Quality Management, Lausanne, Switzerland. Appointments: Scientific Assistant to Professor, Technical University of Norway, 1954-56; Site Engineer, Snowy Mountains Hydro-Electric Authority, Australia, 1956-58; Site Engineer, Norconsult Ethiopia, Koka Power Plant, 1958-60; Site Engineer, Assab Harbour and Water Supply, 1960-62; Chief Engineer and Resident Manager, Norconsult Nigeria, 1962-64; Marketing Director, 1964-68, Managing Director, 1968-81, Norconsult International, Oslo; Projects for World Bank, UN Agencies, Regional Banks, Developing Countries' Governments; Saga Petroleum, Oslo; Corporate Management Technical Director, projects in North Sea, Benin, Caribia, USA, 1981-91; Working Chairman, Senior Expert Group, 1991-. Publications: Professional articles; Conference papers. Honours: Honours Award for Technical Assistance to Developing Countries, Norwegian Natural Sciences Research Council, 1976. Memberships: Director, President, Federation International des Ingenieurs Conseil, 1973-80; Chairman of the Board, Norwegian Petroleum Consultants, 1975-80; Member, Executive Committee Royal Polytechnical Society, 1979-84; Director, Norwegian Export Council, 1975-80; Chairman, Drammen Technical Society, 1996-. Address: Hanna Winsnesgate 1, 3014 Drammen, Norway. E-mail: annh-gr@online.no

GRINKER Morton, b. 19 May 1928, Paterson, New Jersey, USA. Writer; Poet. m. Lynn Grinker, 28 June 1963. Education: BA, English, University of Idaho, 1952. Publications: To the Straying Aramaean, 1972; The Gran Phenician Rover, 6 volumes, 1996. Contributions to: Shig's Review; S-B Gazette; Perspectives; Or; Dust; Manhattan Review; Work; Tampa Poetry Review; Amphora; Buffalo Stamps; Hyperion; Illuminations Reader; Poems Read in the Spirit of Peace and Gladness; San Francisco Bark. Address: 1367 Noe Street, San Francisco, CA 94131, USA.

GRISEZ Germain, b. 30 September 1929, University Heights, Ohio, USA. Professor of Christian Ethics; Writer. m. Jeannette Selby, 9 June 1951, 4 sons. Education: BA, John Carroll University, University Heights, Ohio, 1951; MA and PhL, Dominican College of St Thomas Aquinas, River Forest, Illinois, 1951; PhD, University of Chicago, 1959. Appointments: Assistant Professor to Professor, Georgetown University, 1957-72; Lecturer in Medieval Philosophy, University of Virginia at Charlottesville, 1961-62; Special Assistant to Patrick Cardinal O'Boyle, Archbishop of Washington, DC, 1968-69; Consultant, Archdiocese of Washington, DC, 1969-72; Professor of Philosophy, Campion College, University of Regina, Saskatchewan, Canada, 1972-79; Archbishop Harry J Flynn Professor of Christian Ethics, Mount Saint Mary's College, Emmitsburg, Maryland, 1979-. Publications: Contraception and the Natural Law, 1964; Abortion: The Myths, the Realities, and the Arguments, 1970; Beyond the New Morality: The Responsibilities of Freedom (with Russell Shaw), 1974, 3rd edition, 1988; Beyond the New Theism: A Philosophy of Religion, 1975; Free Choice: A Self-Referential Argument (with Joseph M Boyle Jr and Olaf Tollefsen), 1976; Life and Death with Liberty and Justice: A Contribution to the Euthanasia Debate (with Joseph M Boyle Jr), 1979; The Way of the Lord Jesus, Vol I, Christian Moral Principles (with others), 1983, Vol II, Living a Christian Life (with others), 1993, Vol III, Difficult Moral Questions (with others), 1997; Nuclear Deterrence, Morality and Realism (with John Finnis and Joseph M Boyle Jr), 1987; Fulfilment in Christ: A Summary of Christian Moral Principles (with Russell Shaw), 1991. Contributions to: Many scholarly journals. Honours: Pro ecclesia et pontifice Medal, 1972; Special Award for Scholarly Work, 1981, Cardinal Wright Award for Service to the Church, 1983, Fellowship of Catholic Scholars; Various other fellowships and grants. Memberships: American Catholic Philosophical Association, president, 1983-84; Catholic Theological Society of America. Address: Mount Saint Mary's College, Emmitsburg, MD 21727, USA.

GRISHAM John, b. 8 February 1955, Jonesboro, Arkansas, USA. Author; Lawyer. m. Renée Grisham, 1 son, 1 daughter. Education: Mississippi State University; University of Mississippi Law School. Appointment: Ran one-man criminal defence practice in Southaven, Mississippi, 1981-90. Publications: The Pelican Brief; A Time to Kill; Stand in Line at a Super Crown; The Firm; The Client; The Chamber; The Rainmaker; The Runaway Jury; The Partner; The Street Lawyer; The Testament; The Brethren; A Painted House, 2001; Skipping Christmas, 2001; The Summons, 2002; The King of Torts, 2003. Address: Doubleday & Co Inc, 1540 Broadway, New York, NY 10036, USA.

GRIVAS Stathis, b. 7 March 1926, Kato Tithorea, Lokridas, Greece. Economist; Analyst; Computer Programmer. Education: Economics, Athens School of Economics and Business Science; Analyst and Computer Programmer, Greek Productivity Centre, IBM. Appointments: Employee of Hellenic Company of Chemical Products, 1953-86; Retired 1986-. Publications: Poetry: First Palpitation, 1987; Foams of Waves, 1988; Open Line, 1989; Pigeons and Hawks, 1990; Registration of Crimes, 1991; For My Little Friends (for children), 1992; Colours of Life, 1996; Fragments of Dreams, 2000; The Voice of Silence, 2000; Spreaded Leaves, 2001; It's Getting Cloudy, 2003. Honours: Recipient of Honour Diploma, Club of Greek Writers; First Prize of Honour, International Society of Greek Writers; Certificate of Merit, Metron Who's Who Publications Board; Second Prize, Cultural Agency, Johannesburg, South Africa; Honoured Member, Italian Academy El Fiorino, Florence, Italy; First Prize, International Society of Greek Writers for Contribution to Literature. Memberships: Society of Greek Writers; Phtiotians Club of Writers; International Society of Greek Writers. Address: Kato Tithorea, Lokridos 35015, Greece.

GRIXTI Jesmond, b. 8 August 1969, Malta. Composer. Education: Diploma of Fellowship, Composition, London College of Music, London, England, 1990; Certificate, Composition Class of Franco Donatoni, Accademia Musicale Chigiana Siena, 1995; Diploma Accademico di Pefezionamento, Composition Class of Franco Donatoni, Accademia Internazionale Superiore di Musica "Lorenzo Perosi", 1997; Certificate, Conducting Class of Emilio Pomarico, Civica Scuola di Musica Milano, 1999; Licenza-Conservatorio Giuseppe Verdi-Milan, 1999; Master of Music Degree, Composition with Professor Brenton Broadstock, The University of Melbourne, Australia, 2002; Currently, PhD Candidate, Composition, The University of Melbourne. Appointments: Tutor, Orchestration, 20th Century Music Techniques, Faculty of Music, The University of Melbourne. Publications: Music scores on line at www.sibeliusmusic.com. Honours: Italian Government Scholarship, 1995; The Janatha Stubbs Foundation Bursary, 2002; Grixti's music has been performed in Europe, Japan and Australia. Memberships: The Melbourne League of Composers; The Living Composers Project, USA. Address: www.sibeliumusic.com. E-mail: jes_869@hotmail.com

GROENING Matthew, b. 15 February 1954, Portland, Oregon, USA. Writer; Cartoonist. m. Deborah Lee Caplan, 2 children. Education: Evergreen State College. Appointments: Cartoonist, Life in Hell syndicated weekly comic strip, Sheridan, Oregon, 1980-; President, Matt Groening Productions Inc, Los Angeles, 1988-, Bongo Entertainment Inc, Los Angeles, 1993-; Creator, The Simpsons interludes, The Tracey Ullman Show, 1987-89; Creator, Executive Producer, The Simpsons TV show, 1989-; Founder and Publisher, Bongo Comics Group; Founder and Publisher, Zongo Comics, including Jimbo, 1995, Fleener, 1996. Publications: Love is Hell, 1985; Work is Hell, 1986; School is Hell, 1987; Childhood is Hell, 1988; Akbar and Jeff's Guide to Life, 1989; Greetings From Hell, 1989; The Postcards That Ate My Brain, 1990; The Big Book of Hell, 1990; The Simpsons Xmas Book, 1990; Greetings From the Simpsons, 1990; With Love From Hell, 1991; The Simpsons' Rainy Day Fun Book, 1991; The Simpsons' Uncensored Family Album, 1991; The Alphabet Book, 1991; Maggie Simpson's Counting Book, 1991; Maggie Simpson's Book of Colors and Shapes, 1991; Maggie Simpson's Book of Animals, 1991; The Road to Hell, 1992; The Simpson's Fun in Sun Book, 1992; Making Faces with the Simpsons, 1992; Bart Simpson's Guide to Life, 1993; The Simpsons Ultra-Jumbo Rain-Or-Shine Fun Book, 1993; Binky's Guide to Love, 1994; Love is Hell 10th Anniversary Edition, 1994; Simpsons Comics Extravaganza, 1994; Simpsons Comic Spectacular, 1994; Bartman:

The Best of the Best, 1994; Simpson Comics Simps-O-Rama, 1995; Simpsons Comics Strike Back, 1995; Simpsons Comics Wing Ding, 1997; The Huge Book of Hell, 1997; Bongo Comics.

GROISMAN Vitaly, b. 6 May 1939, B. Nicolayev, Ukraine, USSR. Physician. m. Valentina Grebennikova, 1 daughter. Education: Student, Military Navy Medical College, Odessa, USSR, 1957-59; Medical Institute, Stavropol, USSR, 1962-67. Appointments: Stomatological Surgeon, 1967-68, Head Physician, 1968-86, Stomatological Clinic, Togliatti, USSR; Assistant Director, Health Protection and Sport Avtovaz, Togliatti, 1980-82; Head Physician, Togliatti Hospital, 1982; President, Medical Scientific Firm, Togliatti, 1991; Firm "Vizavi", Russia, 1972; Founder, Pyramid Therapy; Deputy, City Duma, Togliatti, 1993. Publications: Author: Myself and the People Around, 1999; Contributor of over 90 articles to medical journals; 12 patents. Honours: Honorary Coach; Recipient, 45 Diplomas, Medals, International Acrobatics Federation, 1972-93; Named Honorary Dr of Russia, 1997. Memberships: Rotary International; New York Medical Academy; Academic Member, Russian Academy of Natural Science, 2000. Address: City Hospital #1, 68 Octyabrskaya Street, Togliatti 445009, Samarskaya Oblast, Russia. E-mail: hospital@infopac.ru

GROMAKOV Yury Alekseyevich, b. 20 December 1946, Moscow Region, Russia. Radio Engineer. m. Nina Gromakova, 2 sons, 1 daughter. Education: Radio Engineering Degree, Moscow Aviation Institute, 1971; PhD, Radio Engineering, 1998. Appointments: Engineer, Senior Engineer, Head of the Department, Radocommunications Research Institute, 1973-89; Deputy General Director of Communications, R&D Company, 1989-94; Vice-President, First Vice-President on Technical Issues, Mobile Telesystems (MTS), 1994-. Publications include: Mobile Telecommunications (monograph), 1994; Standards and Systems in Mobile Telecommunications, 1997; GSM Cellular Networks Migration to GPRS and EDGE in Russia, 2000; Aspects of Internet and Cellular Telecommunications Convergence, 2001; Patent: Telematic System, 2001. Honour: Honoured Radioman of the Russian Federation, State Prize-winner in Telecommunications, 2003. Memberships: Academician of the International Telecommunication Academy; Academician, International Academy of Sciences and Information Processes and Technologies. Address: 4 Marksistskaya Street, 109147 Moscow, Russia. E-mail: yuag@mts.ru Website: www.mts.ru

GROPSIAN Zeno, b. 13 November 1920, Sascamontana, Romania. Professor. m. Rodica, 1 daughter. Education: Chemical Engineering, 1945; Doctorate, Chemical Engineering, 1958; Consulting Professor, 1990. Appointments: Head, Chemical Engineering Department; Dean, Chemical Engineering Faculty. Publications: Metallurgy, Vacuum Technology, Heat and Mass Transfer, High Pressure, Fractals, Magnetic Liquids. Memberships: New York Academy of Sciences; Romanian Institute of Chemical Engineers. Address: Timisoara, Str Mihai Viteazul 10A, Romania.

GROS AYMERICH Jose, Zaragoza, Spain. Physician. Education: Cou, Colegio del Salvador SI, Zaragoza, 1969; MD, Universidad Autonoma de Madrid, 1976; Specialist in Medical Oncology, 1982; University Specialist in Pharmaceutical Industry Medicine, UCM, 1989. Appointments: Spanish Air Force, 1976; Jimenez Diaz Foundation, Madrid, 1978-82; Emergency Service, Social Security, 1984; Upjohn, 1984-88; Primary Care Practitioner, Social Security, 1989-. Publications: Lung Cancer Chemotherapy, 1984, Revista Par. Memberships: SEOM; ASCO; ESMO; NYAS. Address: Jazmin – 76, 3-B, E – 28033 Madrid, Spain. E-mail: jgrosay@telepolis.com

GROSHOLZ Emily Rolfe, b. 17 October 1950, Philadelphia, Pennsylvania, USA. Professor; Poet. m. Robert R Edwards, 3 sons, 1 daughter. Education: BA, Ideas and Methods, University of Chicago, 1972; PhD, Philosophy, Yale University, 1978. Appointments: Professor of Philosophy, The Pennsylvania State University, 1979-; Advisory Editor, The Hudson Review, 1984-; Life Member, Clare Hall, University of Cambridge, 1998-. Publications: Cartesian Method and the Problem of Reduction, 1991; Leibniz' Science of the Rational, 1998; Eden (Poems), 1992; The Abacus of Years (Poems), 2001. Honours: Guggenheim Fellowship, 1988-89; National Endowment for the Humanities Fellowship, 1985-85, 2004-2005; Alexander von Humboldt Foundation Grant, 1994-97; American Council of Learned Societies Fellowship, 1997. Memberships: American Philosophical Association; Philosophy of Science Association; National Council for Black Studies. Address: Department of Philosophy, 240 Sparks Building, The Pennsylvania State University, University Park, PA 16801, USA. E-mail: erg2@psu.edu

GROSSBERG Lawrence, b. 3 December 1947, New York, USA. Professor. m. Barbara Anne Claypole White, 1 son. Education: BA, University of Rochester, 1968; PhD, University of Illinois at Urbana, 1976. Appointments: Department of Communication, Purdue University, 1975-76; Department of Speech Communication, Institute of Communications Research, Unit for Criticism and Interpretative Theory, University of Illinois, 1976-94; Distinguished Professor, Department of Communication Studies, University of North Carolina, 1994-. Publications: Bringing It All Back Home: Essays on Cultural Studies; Dancing in Spite of Myself: Essays on Popular Culture; We Gotta Get Out of This Place: Popular Conservatism and Postmodern Culture. Honours: National Communication Association Distinguished Scholar; Fellow, International Communication Association. Address: Department of Communication Studies, CB 3285 Bingham Hall, University of North Carolina, Chapel Hill, NC 27599-3285, USA.

GROSSMAN Margaret Rosso, b. 17 October 1947, Illinois, USA. Professor. m. Michael, 2 sons. Education: BMus, highest honours, University of Illinois, 1969; AM, Stanford University, 1970; PhD, Musicology, 1977, JD, summa cum laude, 1979, University of Illinois. Appointments: Professor, Agricultural Law, Department of Agricultural and Consumer Economics, University of Illinois at Urbana-Champaign; Frequent Visiting Professor, Wageningen University, The Netherlands. Publications: Numerous law review articles, book chapters, books. Honours: Fulbright Research Fellow (3 awards); German Marshall Fund Research Fellow; Silver Medal, European Council for Agricultural Law; Distinguished Service Award, American Agricultural Law Association. Memberships: American Agricultural Law Association; American Veterinary Medical Law Association; European Council for Agricultural Law; Dutch Society for Agrarian Law. Address: 333 Mumford Hall, 1301 W Gregory Dr, Urbana, IL 61801, USA.

GROTRIAN Simon Herskind, b. 21 December 1961, Aarhus, Denmark. Poet. Education: Literature Studies, Universities of Aarhus and Copenhagen. Appointments: Poet, 1984-. Publications: Collections of Poems: Through My Hand, 1987; Collage, 1988; Next Heaven, 1989; Fire, 1990; Lifetraps, 1993; Snakeharvest, 1994; A Box for Lot, 1995; Magnets and Ambrosia, 1996; The Pulse of Ossian, 1997; Ten, 1998; China Letters, 1999; Life is a Cow, 2000; The Risperdal Sonnets, 2000; Prophet Stamped, 2001; Selected Poems, 2003; The Crusade of the Multiplication Table, 2004. Contributions to: Die Horen; Hjärnstorm; Poesia; Action Poetique; Blanco Móvil; Akzente; Megafon; Poet; The Journal; Ord & Bild; Quarter After Eight; Idylle, Katastrophal. Honours:

Michael Strunge Award, 1990; Harald Kidde Grant, 1990; Per Aage Brandt Award, 1994; Emil Aarestrup Medal, 1998. Address: Lemming Brovej 13B, 8632 Lemming, Denmark.

GROUT Geraldine I (Hale), b. 16 June 1923, Leominster, Massachusetts, USA. Retired Teacher. m. John M Grout. Education: Bachelor of Education; Master of Education; Doctor of Education. Licensed Nursing Home Administrator. Appointments: Secondary School Teacher, 5 years; Assistant Journal Editor, 18 years; Journal Editor, 4 years; College Professor, 9 years; Administered Nursing Home, 10 years; Currently retired. Publications: Nursing home articles; Historical articles; Articles on teaching. Honours: Fellow; Historian of 140 year old church. Memberships: Fellow, American College of Health Care Administrators; Fellow, American Academy of Medical Administrators; Life Member, Delta Pi Epsilon, Theta Chapter; Honorary Missionary Credential; Professional Member, National Business Education Association, 53 years. Address: 30 Narrow Lane, South Lancaster, MA 01561, USA.

GRUBAR Jean-Claude, b. 5 May 1944, Sars Et Rosieres, France. Professor, Psychology, Neuro-psychology. Education: Doctorate, Psychology, 1972; Doctorate, D' Etat és Lettres, 1987. Appointments: Assistant; Maître Assistant; Maître de Conferences; Professor, University Charles de Gaulle, Lille, France. Publications: 3 books; 85 articles. Honours: Chevalier de la Légion d' Honneur de l'ordre National Mérite, Palmes Académiques. Address: Résidence St Charles, 51 Rue Pascal, 59800 Lille, France.

GRUBE Michael, b. 12 May 1954, Venezuela. Violinist. m. Azucena, 1 son, 1 daughter. Education: Conservatory, Windhoek, Namibia; University, USA and Heidelberg; Professor and Doctorate, Philosophy of Music; Private studies with Max Rostal, Berne; Ivan Galamian, New York; Henryk Szeryng, Paris and Mexico; Composition and Musicology with Ewald Jammers, Heidelberg. Career: Concerts and performances with symphony and chamber orchestras world-wide: Europe, South, Central and North America, Africa, Asia, Australia, New Zealand and the Pacific Islands; Director, Master Classes and Workshops; Chairman of the Jury, 8th International Mozart Festival for string players, Pueblo, Colorado, USA; Editor of violin works, Vienna and USA. Publications: Numerous for Doblinger Edition, Vienna and Pro Musica International, USA. Honours: Numerous prizes, diplomas and awards of honorary citizenship; Guest Artist at many important festivals. Memberships: World University Round Table, Benson, Arizona, USA; Terra Firma, Caracas, Venezuela. Address: Casilla No 17-04-10343, Quito, Ecuador.

GRUNDY Isla Mary, b. 13 June 1955, Harare, Zimbabwe. Ecologist; Social Forester. Education: BSc, Zoology and Botany, University of Capetown, South Africa, 1973-75; Post-graduate certificate in Education, University of East Anglia, Norwich, 1982-83; 4th year honours, Ecology and Botany, 1987, MSc, Tropical Resource Ecology, 1988-89, Department of Biological Sciences, University of Zimbabwe; MSc, Forestry and its Relation to Land Use, 1992-93, DPhil, Forest Ecology, 1992-95, Department of Plant Sciences, University of Oxford, England. Appointments: Research Assistant, University of Zimbabwe, 1990-91; Technical Services Unit Co-ordinator, Research and Monitoring Officer, Southern Alliance for Indigenous Resources, 1996-98; Senior Lecturer, Tropical Forest Resources Group, 1998-2001; Senior Lecturer, University of Stellenbosch, South Africa, 2001-. Publications: Numerous peer reviewed publications and papers. Honours: Commonwealth Studentship, 1992-95; Editorial Board, South African Journal of Forestry, 2001; South African representative, African Network for Agroforestry Education, 1998-2001, 2001-03; ANAFE SA-RAFT Secretariat, 2001-03;

University of Stellenbosch's representative, International Union of Forestry Organisations. Address: Department of Forestry Science, University of Stellenbosch, P Bag X1, Matieland 7602, South Africa. E-mail: imgr@sun.ac.za Website: www.sun.ac.za/forestry

GRZYBKOWSKI Andrzej b. 22 January 1935, Poznań, Poland. Art Historian. m. Teresa Żmidzińska, 3 April 1967, 1 daughter. Education: BA Geography, Adam Mickiewicz University, Poznań, 1959; MA History of Art, Adam Mickiewicz University, Poznań, 1967; PhD Technological Science, Warsaw Technical University, 1976; Habilitation, University of Warsaw, 1989. Appointments: Consultant, Art History, Polish National Monument Conservation Bureau, Warsaw, 1966-74; Lecturer, Institute of the History of Architecture, Warsaw Technical University, 1974-80; Assistant Professor, 1980-90, 1997-2000, Professor, 1997-, Department of History of Art, University of Warsaw; Professor, Department of Archaeology, University of Warsaw, 2000-; Vice Director, Department of History of Art, University of Warsaw, 1981-84. Associate Professor, Institute of Conservation and Restoration of Cultural Property, Nicolas Copernicus University, Toruń, 1990-96. Publications: The Early Gothic Dominican Church in Sieradz, 1979; Medieval Chapels of Silesian Princes, 1990; Between Form and Meaning. Studies on Iconography of Gothic Architecture and Sculpture, 1997; Articles published in Zeitschrift für Kunstgeschichte; architectura Zeitschrift für Geschichte der Baukunst; Arte Medievale; Archiv für Schlesische Kirchengeschichte; Jahrbuch der Schlesien Friedrich-Wilhelms-Universität zu Breslau; Editor, Yearbook of Art History. Memberships: Art Historians in Poland, 1967; Polish Heraldry Society, 1989; Member of Board, Committee of Fine Arts, Polish Academy of Sciences. Address: Al. Niepodległości 159 m. 26, 02-555 Warsaw, Poland.

GUAJARDO Elisa, b. 13 November 1932, Roswell, New Mexico, USA. Educator. m. David R Guajardo, 1 daughter. Education: BS, 1962, MEd, 1971, Our Lady of the Lake University, San Antonio, Texas; MA, Chapman University, Orange, California, 1977. Appointments: Elementary School Teacher, 1962-63; Junior High School Teacher, 1963-70, 1972-73; District Bilingual Project Director, 1970-71; High School Counsellor, 1973-; President, Bilingual/Bicultural Parent Advisory Board, 1971-72; Reader, bilingual projects, California State Department Education, 1971-72; Visiting Lecturer, Western Washington University, 1972-73; Member, curriculum and placement councils, 1973-78, 1995-96. Publications: (ABLE) Adaptions of Bilingual/Bicultural Education, Federal Project Proposal. Honours: Alpha Chi; Listed in numerous Who's Whos and biographical publications. Memberships: National Education Association; California Teacher Association; Orange Unified Education Association; American Association of University Women. Address: 335 E Jackson Ave, Orange, CA 92867, USA.

GUEBENLIAN Shahé, b. 25 September 1920, Adana, Turkey. Journalist; International Affairs Consultant. m. Iris Kathleen Russell. Education: The English School, Nicosia, Cyprus. Appointments: Editor, Sunday Mail Weekly Magazine, Nicosia, Cyprus, 1948-53; Stringer, Part-time Correspondent, in Cyprus for the Palestine Post of Jerusalem, Al Hamishmar of Telaviv, Reuters, AFP, INS, Daily Express, Evening Standard, Observer of London, 1946-53; Cyprus and Middle East Correspondent, Reuters, 1953-63, Manager and Chief Correspondent, Reuters, Eastern and Central Africa, Nairobi, 1963-68; Manager for the whole of Africa, based in London, 1968-77; Manager for Africa, the Middle East and the Caribbean, based in London, 1969-77; Manager for Publicity and Public relations, 1977-84, Reuters; Member, Panel of Assessors, Reuters Foundation Scholarship

Dictionary of International Biography

Applicants, 1983-1999; Visiting Lecturer, International Affairs and Senior Degree Journalism, City University, London, 1984-85; Visiting Lecturer, International Journalism, School of Journalism, Berlin, 1985-94; Visiting Lecturer, News Agency Journalism and Management, All-China Journalism Syndicate, Beijing, 1985; Consultant, Cyprus News Agency, 1983-96; Consultant to UNESCO on plans to set up PanAfrican News Agency, 1994-95; Media Consultant, Armenia's Embassy, London, 1992-99; Press and Publicity Consultant, National Federation of Cypriots in Britain, 1993-99. Publications: Compiler and editor, Democracy on Trial by Mohamed Ahmed Mahgoub, 1974; Compiler and editor, Reuters Glossary of International Economic and Financial Terms, 1981; Prepared blueprints for the PanAfrican News Agency, The National News Agencies of Kenya, 1966; Kuwait, The Gulf News Agency, Bahrain and Oman, 1974-77; Islamic Features Agency, 1981; Major journalistic coverage includes: The Adolf Eichman Trial, Jerusalem, the Cyprus Emergency, several African conflicts, Non-Aligned Group Conferences, aspects of the "Wind of Change" in Africa. Honours: General Service Medal, RAF, London, 1957; Order of Menelik Insignia, Emperor of Ethiopia, 1972; Honor Award, Ohio University, USA, 1987; Journalism Award, The Reuters Foundation, London, 2000. Memberships: National Vice-President, International Friendship League, UK Branch, 1992-; Member, Manoug Parikian String Quartet (Viola) entertaining British Troops in Cyprus during WWII. Address: Penthouse B, Ross Court, Putney Hill, London SW15, 3NZ, England.

GUENEL (Genel) Leonid Samooilovitch, b. 11 August 1946, Moscow, Russia. Materials Scientist. m. Galkina Valentina Vassilyevna. 2 sons. Education: Moscow Steels and Alloys Institute, 1964-69; Magistre Diploma, 1969; Moscow D I Mendeleev Chemical Processing Institute; Postgraduate Studies, 1976-1979; DrPhil, 1980. Appointments: Engineer, Institute for Sources of Electrical Energy, 1972; Senior Engineer, Research Worker, Institute for Metal Protection from Corrosion, 1982; Chief of Sector, Chief of Department, NPO Polymerbyt, 1991; General Director, Spectroplast Ltd, 1991-. Publications: More than 70 publications in the following fields: Mechanochemistry of gluing, treatment of surface, development of new polymer based materials being produced by mechanochemical technique; Wave approach to the control strength and durability of solids, and also materials based on the approach; Liquid intermediary refrigerants and also concentrates of anti-corrosive, colouring and viscosity controlling additives to them; Polymeric compositions with decorative effects; Philosophy and cosmology which origin of matter and antimatter in the Universe is explained. Honour: The Outstanding Scholar of the 20th Century Medal, IBC, 2000. Memberships: Academician of Russian Academy for Sciences and Arts (RooAN); Academician of International Academy of Refrigeration. Address: Spectroplast Ltd, 2nd Vladimirskaya str 11, Moscow 111123, Russia. E-mail: lg@splast.ru

GUESGEN Hans Werner, b. 24 April 1959, Bonn, Germany. Associate Professor. m. Gaby, 11 August 1984, 3 daughters. Education: Dipl-Inform, University of Bonn, 1983; Dr rer nat, University of Kaiserlautern, 1988; Dr habil, University of Hamburg, 1993. Appointments: Post Doctoral Fellow, ICSI, Berkeley, California, 1989-90; Scientific Researcher, GMD St Augustin, Germany, 1983-92; Associate Professor, Computer Science Department, University of Auckland, 1992-. Publications: 2 monographs; 8 edited books, journals and reports; Over 100 refereed articles in journals, books, conference proceedings and workshop notes; Over 30 technical reports. Memberships: American Association for Artificial Intelligence. Address:

Computer Science Department, University of Auckland, Private Bag 92019, Auckland, New Zealand. E-mail: hans@cs.auckland.ac.nz

GUGLIELMI Joseph Julien, b. 30 December 1929, Marseille, France. Retired Teacher; Poet. m. Therese Bonnelalbay, deceased, 2 sons, 1 daughter. Education: Baccalaureate Philosophie-Lettres, 1950; Propedeutique lettres classiques, 1952; Primary School Teacher's Certificate, 1960. Publications: La Preparation des Titres, 1980; Aube, 1984; Fins de vers, 1986; Le Mouvement de la mort, 1988; Joe's Bunker, 1991; Principe de paysage, 1991; Kou le Dit du passage, 1992; Grungy Project, 1997; Travelogue, 2000; Le Pyromène, 2003 Contributions to: Many publications. Address: 7 rue Pihet, 75011 Paris, France

GUHA R P, b. 23 June 1929, Calcutta, India. Teacher. m. Dr Guha, 1 son, 1 daughter. Education: DLitt; PhD, Law, USA; M.H.M. Appointment: Principal; Chairman; Teacher. Publications: La Terre; Life, 2000; The World; A Bouquet; A Winsome Marrow; Selected Essays; Introduction to religion; The letter; Indian Integrates with the World Economy; Life – Part Two, 2002; A Collection of Poems, 2002; A Collection of Short Stories, 2003; The Guru, 2003. Honours: M M Academy Award; USIS Prize; Bharat Pathik Award; R S Excellency Award; Best Citizen of India Award, 2002; Listed in a Biographical Publication. Membership: Fellow, United Writer's Association. Address: Patratu School of Economics, PO PTPS (829119), PB 13, Dist Hazaribagh, Jharkhand, India.

GUI Meen-Wah, b. 2 May 1965, Malacca, Malaysia. Geotechnical Engineer; Educator. m. Chah-Chah Chen, 1 son. Education: B Eng, University of Technology Malaysia, 1989; C Dip AF, Chartered Association of Certified Accountants, 1991; PhD, University of Cambridge, England, 1996. Appointments: Geotechnical Engineer, Ove Arup & Partners, Hong Kong, 1996-97; Research Associate, Cambridge University, England, 1997-99; Visiting Scholar, Hong Kong University of Science and Technology, 1999-2000; Assistant Professor, National Taiwan University of Technology, Taipei, Taiwan, 2000-. Publications: 25 technical papers in international journals and conferences. Honours: Best Academic Performance Medal in Civil Engineering, 1989; Cambridge Commonwealth Scholarship, 1991-94; Listed in Who's Who publications and biographical dictionaries. Memberships: MIStructE; MICE; MASCE; Fellow, Cambridge Philosophical Society; Fellow, Cambridge Commonwealth Society. Address: Civil Engineering Department, NTUT, No 1, Sec 3 Zhongxiao E Road, Taipei 10643, Taiwan. E-mail: mwgui@ntut.edu.tw mwgui@yahoo.com

GUIDOIN Robert Gerard, b. 11 November 1945, La Guédeniau, France. Professor of Surgery. m. Raymonde Sylvain, 4 children. Education: Propédeutique, CSU Angers, France, 1965; BSc, Chemistry, 1967, MSc, Chemistry, 1968, PhD, Chemistry, 1970, Université de Nantes, France; DSc, Biological Engineering, Université de Technologie de Compiègne, France, 1982. Appointments include: Research Assistant, 1972-74 Teaching Assistant, 1975-76, Assistant Professor, 1976-81, Associate Professor, 1981-86, Professor of Surgery, 1986-92, 1992-2000, 2001-, Department of Surgery, Laboratory of Experimental Surgery, Laval University and Research Center, St François d'Assise Hospital, Quebec; Scientific Director, Quebec Biomaterials Institute Inc, 1992-2000. Publications: 2 thesis; 243 peer reviewed papers; 21 book chapters; 41 conference proceedings; 49 other contributions; Over 600 abstracts; numerous seminars, meetings and conferences. Honours: Honorary Faculty: University of West of China, Chengdu, China, University of Chongqing, Chongqing, China, Medical University of Varna, Varna, Bulgaria; Fellow,

Society for Biomaterials, 1996, AIMBE, 1998. Memberships: Research Committee member, Department of Surgery, Laval University; Steering Committee Member, Research Centre, PSFA, CHUW; Ethical Committee Member, CHUL, CHUQ; Member, Sciences Council of Canada, 1987-93; Founding Member, London Diplomatic Academy; Member, Granting Committees or external reviewer, various research funding agencies, MRC, FRSQ, ENSERC, NIH, Heart and Stroke Foundations. Address: Department of Surgery, Faculty of Medicine, Laval University, Quebec City, Qc G1K 7P4, Canada. E-mail: robertguidoin@hotmail.com

GUILLEMIN Roger Charles Louis, b. 11 January 1924, Dijon, France (US Citizen). Endocrinologist. m. Lucienne Jeanne Billard, 1951, 1 son, 5 daughters. Education: BA, 1941, BSc, 1942, University of Dijon; Medicine, University of Lyons, medical degree, 1949; PhD, Institute of Experimental Medicine and Surgery, Montreal, 1950. Appointments: Resident Intern, University Hospital, Dijon, 1949-51; Professor, Institute of Experimental Medicine and Surgery, Montreal; Baylor College of Medicine, Houston, Texas, 1953; Associate Director, Department of Experimental Endocrinology, Collège de France, Paris, 1960-63; Resident Fellow and Research Professor, 1970-89, Dean, 1972-73, 1976-77, Distinguished Professor, 1997-, The Salk Institute for Biological Studies, San Diego, California; Distinguished Scientist, 1989-93, Medical and Scientific Director, Director, 1993-94, 1995-97, Whittier Institute for Diabetes and Endocrinology, La Jolla; Adjunct Professor of Medicine, University of California, San Diego, 1995-97. Honours: Bonneau and La Caze Awards in Physiology, 1957, 1960; Gairdner Award, 1974; Officier, Legion d'honneur, Lasker Foundation Award, 1975; Nobel Prize for Physiology or Medicine, 1977; National Medal of Science, 1977; Barren Gold Medal, 1979; Dale Medallist, UK Society for Endocrinology, 1980. Memberships: NAS; American Academy of Arts and Sciences; American Physiological Society; Society for Experimental Biology and Medicine; International Brain Research Organisation; International Society for Research in Biology and Reproduction; Swedish Society of Medical Sciences; Academie Nacionale de Medecine; Academie des Sciences; Academie Royale de Medecine de Belgique; The Endocrine Society. Address: The Salk Institute, 10010 North Torrey Pines Road, La Jolla, CA 92037, USA.

GUILMET Glenda Jean, b. 28 March 1957, Tacoma, Washington, USA. Visual Artist. m. George M Guilmet, 1 son, 1 daughter. Education: BA, Business Administration, 1981, BA, Art, 1989, University of Puget Sound, Tacoma, Washington; Professional Photography Program, Clover Park Vocational Technical Institute, Tacoma, 1982-83. Appointment: Visual Artist, 1982-; Arts Commissioner, City of Tacoma, 1989-1992; Juror, several competitions; Photographer, Homeless Employment Partnership and Cocaine Babies Project, Support and Outreach Services, Metropolitan Development Council, Tacoma, 1990; Solo, group and internet exhibitions of work. Publications: Individual visual images appear in numerous publications. Honour: 1st Place Award, for Shadow Dance #1, Crosscurrents Art Contest (photography), 1988; Hedgebrook Invitational Residency, Hedgebrook Foundation, 2000; Listed in several who's who publications; Permanent collections in Paris, France and Seattle and Tacoma, Washington. Memberships: National Museum of Women in the Arts, Washington, DC.; En Foco: A Visual Arts Organization, Bronx, New York; Artist Trust: A Resource for Washington, Seattle; Atlatl: Native American Arts Service Organization, Phoenix, Arizona. Address: 652 Old Blyn Highway, Sequim, WA 98382, USA. E-mail: glendaguilmet@yahoo.com

GUIMARAES Romeu Cardoso, b. 29 July 1943, Belo Horizonte MG, Brazil. m. Alexandrina M Guimaraes. Education: MD, 1965; PhD, Pathology, 1970; Full Professor, Genetics, 1987. Appointments: University Federal Minas Gerais, 1966-75, 1993-; University Estadual Paulista, 1976-93; Currently working on: Origin of Life, Philosophy of Biology. Honour: Illustrious Son of Belo Horizonte. Membership: Sao Paulo Academy of Sciences; Minas Gerais Academy of Medicine. Address: Dpto de Biologia Geral, Institut Ciencias Biologicas, UFMG, 31270-901 Belo Horizonte MG, Brazil. E-mail: romeucg@mono.icb.ufmg.br

GUITTARD Charles Christian, b. 9 December 1947, Paris, France. Professor. m. Regine Lemarchand, 3 sons, 1 daughter. Education: Agregation, Classics, 1971; Ecole Normale Superieure, 1973; Docteur es Lettres, 1996. Appointments: Assistant, Sorbonne, France, 1974-75; Member, Ecole Francaise de Rome, Italy, 1975-78; Lecturer, University Tours, France, 1978-93; Lecturer, University Paris X, France, 1993-97; Professor, University Clermont-Ferrand, France, 1997-2001; Professor, Lille 3, France, 2001-. Publications: Histoire Romaine VIII, Tite-Live, 1987; Saturnales, Macrobe, 1997; Medee, Seneque, 1997; Amphitryon, Plaute, 1997; Antigone, Sophocle, 1999; De la Nature, Lucrece, 2001; Carmen et Propheties a Rome, 2003. Honours: Palmes Academiques, 1987; Military Long Services, Ministry of Defence, 1989. Memberships: Societe des Etudes Latines; Societe Ernest-Renan. Address: 1 rue Monticelli, F-75014, Paris, France. E-mail: chaguittard@aol.com

GÜLSOY Tanses Yasemin, b. Verdun, France. Advertising Executive. Education: BA, Pomona College, Claremont, California, USA, 1985; MA, Journalism and Mass Communication, New York University, New York, New York, 1988. Appointments: Research Assistant, Harry Frank Guggenheim Foundation, New York, New York, 1986-88; Advertising Copywriter, 1989-97, International Advertising Director, 1997-2001, Manajans/Thompson, Istanbul, Turkey; Founder and Owner, Tans Communications Consultancy, Istanbul, Turkey, 2001-. Publications: Why the Fight over Peace Studies, 1988; An English-Turkish Dictionary of Advertising with Turkish-English Index, 1999; 38 newspaper articles in American newspapers. Honours: Bogazici University, Business Administration Department Dean's List, 1982; Pomona College Academic Scholarship, 1982-85; Pomona College Honnold Fellowship for Graduate Study, 1985; Harry Frank Guggenheim Foundation Fellowship, 1986-88; Profiled by weekly news magazine Aktüel as one of Turkey's brightest young minds, 2002; Honours Award, Turkey's Association of Advertising Creatives, 2002; Listed in Who's Who 2003 and 2004 publications and biographical dictionaries. Memberships: American Marketing Association; Turkish Society for Opinion and Marketing Research; Turkish Association of Advertising Creatives; New York University European Alumni Group; Pomona College Alumni Volunteers; Member of Board of Directors, 1994-96, Robert College Alumni Association. Address: Adnan Saygun Cad, Dag Apt 72/10, I Ulus, 34360 Istanbul, Turkey. Website: www. tansonline.com

GUMAA Samia Ahmed, b. 20 February 1943, Cairo, Egypt. Professor of Microbiology. m. El Tigani El Musharaf, 6 daughters. Education: MBBS, Science and Medicine, University of Khartoum, 1966; Diploma, Bacteriology, University of Manchester, England, 1971; Primary MRC Path, England. Appointments: Rotating house Officer, Khartoum Civil Hospital, 1966-67; Registrar of Immunology, Manchester Royal Infirmary, Manchester Eye Hospital, St Mary's Hospital for Women and Children, Manchester, 1972; Lecturer, Senior Lecturer, 1976, Associate Professor 1977, Associate Professor of Microbiology, 1991, Professor of Microbiology, 1992-94, Head of Department of Microbiology and Parasitology, Faculty of Medicine, University of Khartoum.

Publications: Author and co-author of over 30 articles and papers in professional medical journals. Honours: Prize in Medicine, University of Khartoum, 1966; International Woman of the Year, IBC, Cambridge, England, 1998; Twentieth Century Award for Achievement, IBC, Cambridge, England, 1998. Memberships: Member, Senate, University of Khartoum; Society of Dermatologists; Society of Pathologists; Faculty Board of Medicine, University of Khartoum; Post-graduate Medical Board, Academic Board of Academy of Medical Sciences Technology. Address: Faculty of Medicine, Department of Microbiology and Parasitology, PO Box 102, University of Khartoum, Sudan.

GUN-MUNRO Sydney Douglas (Sir), b. 29 November 1916, Grenada, Windward Islands, West Indies. Medical Practitioner. 2 sons, 1 daughter. Education: MRCP, LRCP, 1942, MBBS Hons, 1943, D.O., 1952; Elected FRCS, 1985, King's College London University and King's College Hospital, London. Appointments: Medical Officer, Lewisham Hospital, 1943-46; District Medical Officer, Grenada, 1946-49; Surgeon, General Hospital St Vincent, 1949-71; District Medical Officer, Bequia, St Vincent, 1972-76; Governor, Associated State, St Vincent, 1977-79; Governor-General, St Vincent and the Grenadines, 1979-85; Retired. Honours: MBE, 1957; Kt.B, 1977; GCMG, 1979. Address: Bequia, St Vincent and the Grenadines, West Indies.

GUNN Thom(son William), b. 29 August 1929, Gravesend, England. Poet. Education: Trinity College, Cambridge. Appointments: Taught English, 1958-66; Lecturer, 1977-, Senior Lecturer, 1988-1999, University of California, Berkeley, USA. Publications: Fighting Terms, 1954; The Sense of Movement, 1957; My Sad Captains, 1961; Positives (with Ander Gunn), 1966; Touch, 1967; Moly, 1971; Jack Straw's Castle, 1976; Selected Poems, 1979; The Passages of Joy, 1982; The Occasions of Poetry (prose), 1982, expanded edition, 1985; The Man with Night Sweats, 1992; Collected Poems, 1993; Shelf Life (prose), 1993; Boss Cupid, 2000. Honours: Levinson Prize, 1955; Somerset Maugham Prize, 1959; National Institute of Arts and Letters Grant, 1964; Rockefeller Foundation, 1966; Guggenheim Fellowship, 1972; Lila Wallace/ Reader's Digest Fund Award, 1991; Forward Poetry Prize, 1992; MacArthur Fellowship, 1993; Lenore Marshall Prize, 1993; David Cohen Award, 2003. Address: 1216 Cole Street, San Francisco, CA 94117, USA.

GUNSTON Bill, (William Tudor Gunston), b. 1 March 1927, London, England. Author. m. Margaret Anne, 10 October 1964, 2 daughters. Education: University College, Durham, 1945-46; City University, London, 1948-51. Appointments: Pilot, Royal Air Force, 1946-48; Editorial Staff, 1951-55, Technical Editor, 1955-64, Flight; Technology Editor, Science Journal, 1964-70; Freelance author, 1970-; Director, So Few Ltd. Publications: Over 360 books including: Aircraft of The Soviet Union, 1983; Jane's Aerospace Dictionary, 1980, 4th edition, 1998; Encyclopaedia of World Aero Engines, 1986, 3rd edition, 1995; Encyclopaedia of Aircraft Armament, 1987; Giants of the Sky, 1991; Faster Than Sound, 1992; World Encyclopaedia of Aircraft Manufacturers, 1993; Jet Bombers, 1993; Piston Aero Engines, 1994, 2nd edition, 1998; Encyclopaedia of Russian Aircraft, 1995; Jet and Turbine Aero Engines, 1995, 2nd edition, 1997; Night Fighters, 2nd edition, 2004. Contributions to: 188 periodicals; 18 partworks; 75 video scripts; Member Association of British Science Writers. Honours: Royal Aeronautical Society, fellow; Officer of the Order of the British Empire. Address: High Beech, Kingsley Green, Haslemere, Surrey GU27 3LL, England.

GUNTER Horst, b. 23 May 1913, Leipzig, Germany. Voice Teacher; Professor of Voice; Singer (Baritone). m. 4 May 1938, 2 sons, 2 daughters. Education: Choirboy, St Thomas, Leipzig;

Musicology and Philosophy, Universities of Leipzig and Bologna; Voice, Leipzig Conservatory; Most influential teachers: Karl Straube, Fritz Polster, Emmi Leisner. Debut: Matthäus-Passion, St Thomas, Leipzig, 1939; Count in Marriage of Figaro, Schwerin State Opera, 1941. Career: Leading Lyric Baritone, Hamburg State Opera, 1950-68; Knappertsbusch and Böhm, Munich State Opera, 1958-63; Edinburgh Festival, 1952, 1956; Holland Festival, 1961; Guest Singer: Vienna State Opera, Frankfurt, with Solti; Ansbach Bach Festival, 1951-58; Numerous radio recordings: TV: 12 operas; First performance of Moses and Aaron in Hamburg, 1954; Teaching: Nordwest-deutsche Musikakademie, Detmold, 1959-65; Professor, 1963; Staatliche Musikhochschule, Freiburg, 1965-68; University of Southern California, Los Angeles, 1978-80; University of California, Los Angeles, 1981; Visiting Professor: Many US universities including Southern Methodist University, Dallas, North Texas State University, Denton, Oberlin Conservatory of Music, University of Minneapolis, University of Alaska; Musashino Academia Musicae, Tokyo, 1984, 1986, 1987, 1990, 1991, 1992; Frequent Judge, international voice competitions such as Munich, Budapest, Leipzig, s'Hertogenbosch, Los Angeles, Dallas, Osaka; Founder of EVTA, European Voice Teacher Association, 1991. Recordings include: Lohengrin; Schüchter; Moses und Aron; Zillich, Cosi fan tutte, Jochum, Don Giovanni, Klemperer, Zauberflöte, Rother, La Traviata, Wagner, Die Fledermaus; Schüchter; Weihnachts Oratorium; Karl Richter, Matthäus Passion; Kurt Redel, Zar und Zimmermann; La Bohème, Erede; CD: Dokumente einer Sängerkarriere: 18 Operatic Arias; Hansel und Gretel; Lortzing, Zar und Zimmerman; Telemann: Matthäus Passion; Wagner Lohengrin. Memberships: Honorary Member, Association Française de Professeurs de chant, 1989; Honorary Member, Association of Teachers of Staging, 1997; Association des Professeurs de chant de Suisse; Voice Teacher, International Opera Studio, Zürich, 2001; Film, Papageno's Mission, North German TV Station, Hamburg, 2001; Teacher in the USA at different universities, also in Osaka and Kyoto, Japan. Address: Unterer Heimbach 5, D-79280 Au bei Freiburg, Germany.

GUO Jin, Broadcaster. Education: Fashion Design, Harbin Radio and TV University, 1990-93; Hosting and Broadcasting, Beijing Broadcasting Institute, 1992-94. Appointments: Actress, Television Broadcasts Ltd, Hong Kong, 1995-97; Actress, Asia Television Ltd, Hong Kong, 1997-2000; Hostess, Art Horizon, China Central Television, 2000-; Chairman, China Celebrity Association, 2003-; Aiduo Troupe of China National Song and Dance Ensemble, 2003-; Inaugurator and lead singer, Spring Festival Gala, CCTV, 2002; General Artistic Supervisor, Artistic Advisor, China Federation of Literary and Art Circles Audio-visual Press, Artistic Advisor, Hong Kong Seasonal film corporation. Honours: 1st prize, Heilongjiang Province Television Hosts Competition, Heilongjiang, 1992; 3rd prize, China Youth Advertisement Model Competition, Heilongjiang, 1992; Excellent Award in Heilongjiang Province, Maggie Cup Youth Glamour TV Competition, 1992; 2nd prize, Summer in Harbin Dance Competition, Heilongjiang, 1993; Miss Aisa Pageant, 1997; Miss Photogenic; Miss Charm of Orient; Miss Most Welcome by the Media; Most Gracious Miss Asia; Film, The Extraordinary Village, winner of Eighth Spiritual "Five-one" Project Prize in Ningbo, 2003. Memberships: Honoured Advisor, Chinese Cultural Promotion Society, Honorary Director, China Audio-Video Association; Honorary Director, China Celebrity Association; Member, Hong Kong Performing Artistes Guild; Member, China Film Expert's Association; Member, China Film Performing Art Institute; Member, China Television Artists Association. Address: C17A, 12#, Tuan Jie Hu Dong Li, Chaoyang District, Beijing 100026, PR China. E-mail: kwok@public3.bta.net.cn

Dictionary of International Biography

GUPTA Rajendra Kumar, b. 18 February 1946, Alwar, Rajasthan. Remote Sensing Technologist Educator. m. Shashi, 2 children. Education: BSc, University of Rajasthan, Jaipur, India, 1965; MSc, Physics, 1967; PhD, Physics, Jawaharlal Nehru Technological University, Hyderabad, 1991. Appointments: Lecturer, Government of Rajasthan, 1967-70; Senior Scientific Assistant, 1970-72, Junior Scientific Officer, 1972-79, Indian Institute of Tropical Meteorology (IITM), Pune; Head, Systems Engineering and Meteorology Cell, National Remote Sensing Agency, Hyderabad, 1979-82; Head, Satellite Meteorology Section, 1982-88; Head, Training Group, 1988-2002; Group Director, Training and Education, 2002-; Chairman, National Symposium on Advanced Technologies in Meteorology, 1995; Organiser, UN/ESCAP Workshop on GIS and remote sensing for sustainable development, 1996; Convenor National Seminar; Main Scientific Organiser/Deputy Organiser and Editor, COSPAR Symposiums, USA, 1992, Nagoya, 1998, Warsaw, 2000, Houston, 2002, Paris, 2004; Editor, International Journal of Remote Sensing, 2001-; Chaired sessions of COSPAR Symposiums, USA, 1992, 2002, UK, 1996, Japan, 1998, Poland, 2000; Vice-Chair, COSPAR Sub-Commission A3, Paris, 2002-06; Scientist G; presenter at numerous conferences. Publications: 30 publications in international refereed journals; 22 publications in national referred journals; Contributor to numerous professional journals; Chapters to books. Honour: Editor, International Journal of Remote Sensing. Memberships: Fellow, Andhra Pradesh Academy of Sciences; Fellow, Institution of Electronics and Telecommunication Engineers; Fellow, Indian Geophysical Union; Life Member, Indian Meteorological Society; Indian Society of Remote Sensing; Indian National Cartographic Association. Address: Scientist G and Group Director-Training and Education, National Remote Sensing Agency, Balanagar, Hyderabad 5000 037, AP India.

GUPTA Vinod Kumar, b. 23 March 1954, Jaipur, India. Physician; Medical Researcher and Ethicist. m. Anjali Dhankani, 1 son. Education: MB, BS, 1977, MD, 1980, University of Rajastan, Jaipur, India; MRCP (UK) Part 1, 1988; ECFMG (USA), 1989. Appointments: Junior Resident in Medicine, All India Institute for Medical Sciences, New Delhi, India, 1977-78; Registrar in Medicine, 1978-79, Senior registrar in Medicine, 1979-80, JLN Hospital, Ajmer, India; Physician, Panacea Medical Clinic, New Delhi, India, 1980-95; General Physician and Medical Doctor, Emirates Diagnostic Clinic, Dubai, United Arab Emirates, 1985-87; Physician, Al-Rasheed Medical Clinic, Dubai, 1988-89; Physician, Dubai Police Medical Services, Dubai, 1989-. Publications: 18 publications in medical journals and books include: Ocular palsy and CIPD, 1996; A clinical review of the adaptive potential of vasopressin in migraine, 1997; Migraine-associated hypotension and autonomic ganglionitis, 1997; Does vasopressin mediate the migraine-remitting influence of warfarin, 1999. Honours include: Lala Ramchander Memorial Award, Jodhpur, India, 1970; Merit Scholarship, University of Rajastan, 1973-75; Gold Medal and Certificate of Merit, 1977, BD Khatore's Gold Medal, 1977, Dr Hiranandani Gold Medal, 1977, JLN Medical College, Ajmer, India; Rotary International Prize, 1985; Listed in Who's Who publications and biographical dictionaries. Memberships; American Association for the Advancement of Science; New York Academy of Science; American Headache Society. Address: Dubai Police Medical Services, PO Box 12005, Dubai, United Arab Emirates. E-mail: docgupta@amirates.net.ae

GURDON John Bertrand, b. 2 October 1933, Dippenhall, Hampshire, England. Molecular Biologist. m. Jean Elizabeth Margaret Curtis, 1964, 1 son, 1 daughter. Education: Graduated, Zoology, Christ Church College, Oxford, 1956; Doctorate, Embryology, Zoology Department, 1960. Appointments: Beit Memorial Fellow, 1958-61; Gosney Research Fellow, California Institute of Technology, 1961-62; Research Fellow, Christ Church, Oxford, 1962-72, Departmental Demonstrator, 1963-64, Lecturer, Department of Zoology, 1966-72; Visiting Research Fellow, Carnegie Institute, Baltimore, 1965; Scientific Staff, 1973-83, Head of Cell Biology Division, 1979-83, John Humphrey Plummer Professor of Cell Biology, 1983-2001, Medical Research Council, Molecular Biology Laboratory, University of Cambridge; Master, Magdalene College, Cambridge, 1995-2002; Fellow, Churchill College, Cambridge, 1973-95; Croonian Lecturer, Royal Society, 1976; Dunham Lecturer, Harvard Medical School, 1974; Carter-Wallace Lecturer, Princeton University, 1978; Fellow, Eton College, 1978-93. Publications: Control of Gene Expression in Animal Development, 1974. Honours: Hon DSc, 1978, 1988, 1998, 2000; Hon Dr, 1982; Albert Brachet Prize, 1968; Scientific Medal of Zoological Society, 1968; Feldberg Foundation Award, 1975; Paul Ehrlich Award, 1977; Nessim Habif Prize, 1979; CIBA Medal, Biochemical Society, 1981; Comfort Crookshank Award for Cancer Research, 1983; William Bate Hardy Triennial Prize, 1983; Charles Leopold Mayer Prize, 1984; Ross Harrison Prize, 1985; Royal Medal, 1985; Emperor Hirohito International Biology Prize, 1987; Wolf Prize for Medicine, jointly, 1989; Distinguished Service Award, Miami, 1992; Knight Bachelor, June 1995; Jean Brachet Memorial Prize, Int Soc Diffn, 2000; Conklin Medal, Society of Developmental Biology, 2001; Copley Medal Royal Society, 2003. Memberships: Honorary Foreign Member, American Academy of Arts and Sciences, 1978; Honorary Student, Christ Church, Oxford, 1985; Fullerian Professor of Physiology and Comparative Anatomy, Royal Institute, 1985-91; President, International Society for Developmental Biology, 1990-94; Foreign Associate, NAS, 1980, Belgian Royal Academy of Science, Letters and Fine Arts, 1984, French Academy of Science, 1990; Foreign Member, American Philosophical Society, 1983; Chair, Wellcome Cancer Campaign Institute, University of Cambridge, 1990-2001; Governor, The Wellcome Trust, 1995-2000; Chair, Company of Biologists, 2001-. Address: Whittlesford Grove, Whittlesford, Cambridge CB2 4NZ, England.

GURNEY A(lbert) R(amsdell), b. 1 November 1930, Buffalo, New York, USA. Professor of Literature; Dramatist; Writer. m. Mary Goodyear, 1957, 2 sons, 2 daughters. Education: BA, Williams College, 1952; MFA, Yale University School of Drama, 1958. Appointments: Faculty, 1960-, Professor of Literature, 1970-, Massachusetts Institute of Technology. Publications: Plays: Children, 1974; The Dining Room, 1982; The Perfect Party, 1986; Another Antigone, 1986; Sweet Sue, 1986; The Cocktail Hour, 1988; Love Letters, 1989; The Old Boy, 1991; The Fourth Wall, 1992; Later Life, 1993; A Cheever Evening, 1994; Sylvia, 1995; Overtime, 1995; Labor Day, 1998; The Guest Lecturer, 1999; Far East, 1999; Ancestral Voices, 1999; Human Events, 2000; Buffalo Gal, 2001; Novels: The Gospel According to Joe, 1974; The Snow Ball, 1985. Screenplay: The House of Mirth, 1972. Television Play: O Youth and Beauty (from a story by John Cheever), 1979. Opera libretto: Strawberry Fields. Honours: Drama Desk Award, 1971; Rockefeller Foundation Grant, 1977; National Endowment for the Arts Award, 1982; Theatre Award, American Academy of Arts and Sciences, 1990; Lucille Lortel Award, 1992; William Inge Award, 2000; Honorary doctorates. Address: 40 Wellers Bridge Road, Roxbury, CT 06783, USA.

GURR Andrew (John), b. 23 December 1936, Leicester, England. Professor; Writer. m. Elizabeth Gordon, 1 July 1961, 3 sons. Education: BA, 1957, MA 1958, University of Auckland, New Zealand; PhD, University of Cambridge, 1963. Appointments: Lecturer, Leeds University, 1962; Professor, University of Nairobi, 1969; University of Reading, 1976-2002. Publications: The Shakespeare Stage 1574-1642, 1970, 3rd edition, 1992; Writers in Exile, 1982; Katherine Mansfield, 1982; Playgoing in

Shakespeare's London, 1987, 3rd edition, 2004; Studying Shakespeare, 1988; Rebuilding Shakespeare's Globe, 1989; The Shakespearian Playing Companies, 1996; The Shakespeare Company 1594-1642, 2004. Editor: Plays of Shakespeare and Beaumont and Fletcher. Contributions to: Scholarly journals and periodicals. Memberships: International Shakespeare Association; Association of Commonwealth Literature and Language Studies; Society for Theatre Research; Malone Society. Address: c/o Department of English, University of Reading, PO Box 218, Reading, Berkshire RG6 2AA, England.

GURSES Metin, b. 2 April 1945, Turkey. Professor of Mathematics. m. Unsal, 1 son, 1 daughter. Education: BS, 1969, MS, 1971, PhD, 1975, Associate Professor, 1981, Physics Department, Middle East Technical University; Professor, Physics Department, Cukurova University, 1988. Appointments: Teaching Assistant, 1969-72, Instructor, 1972-76, Assistant Professor, 1976-81, Associate Professor, 1981-82, Physics Department, Middle East Technical University; Visiting Researcher, Physics Department, Yale University, 1973-75; Visiting Research Fellow, Physics Department, Princeton University, 1979; Visiting Research Fellow, Max-Planck Institute for Astrophysics, Garching, 1979-81; Visiting Scientist, Institute for Theoretical Physics, Koln University, 1987; Senior Research Scientist, Department of Mathematics, TUBITAK Basic Research Institute, 1982-88; Professor, Physics Department, Cukurova University, 1988-91; Professor, Department of Mathematics, Bilkent University, 1991-. Publications: Over 65 papers in refereed international journals. Honours: Fellow, Alexander von Humboldt, 1979-81, 1987; Sedat Simavi Science Prize, 1986; Science and Technical Research Council of Turkey Young Scientist Award, 1984. Memberships: Turkish Physical Society; International Society of General Relativity and Gravitation; Turkish Mathematical Society; Turkish Mechanics Society; American Mathematical Society; American Physical Society; Turkish Academy of Sciences; Abdus Salam Institute of Theoretical Physics. Address: Bilkent University, Matematik Bolumu, 06533 Bilkent, Ankara, Turkey.

GUSEV Vladimir K, b. 19 April 1933, Saratov, USSR. Senator. m. Klavdija Guseva, 1 son, 1 daughter. Education: Graduate, Chemical Faculty, Saratov University, 1957; Graduate, State Economic Institute of Saratov, 1969; Doctor of State; Professor; Actual Member of Academy of Natural Sciences. Appointments: From Expert on Chemical Polymer Production to General Director of Chemical Plant of Engels-city, 1959-75; First Secretary of Saratov Department Party, First Deputy of Prime-Minister, RSFSR, Deputy Prime Minister, USSR, 1975-93; Head of Committee, Duma (Parliament of the Russian Federation), 1993-2000; Senator, the Council of Federation of the Federal Assembly of the Russian Federation, 2000-. Publications: More than 200 monographs and articles on problems of the chemical industry and national economic development as well as articles on political activity. Honours: 20 State Medals; 3 Medals, State Order of Lenin; Medal, October Revolution; Medal of the Brave; Medal of the Glory. Address: The Council of Federation of the Federal Assembly of the Russian Federation, 26 Bolshay Dmitrovka Street, R 103426, Moscow, Russia.

GUTERSON David, b. 4 May 1956, Seattle, Washington, USA. Writer. m. Robin Ann Radwick, 1979, 3 sons, 1 daughter. Education: BA, 1978, MA, 1982, University of Washington. Appointment: High School Teacher of English, Bainbridge Island, Washington, 1984-94. Publications: The Country Ahead of Us, The Country Behind, 1989; Family Matters: Why Home Schooling Makes Sense, 1992; Snow Falling on Cedars, 1994; East of the Mountains, 1999. Honour: PEN/Faulkner Award for Fiction, 1995;

Barnes and Noble Discovery Award, 1995; Pacific NW Booksellers Award, 1995. Address: c/o Georges Borchardt Inc, 136 East 57th Street, New York, NY 10022, USA.

GUTHKE Jürgen Hans Friedrich, b. 16 August 1938, Halle, Germany. Psychologist. m. Ursula Guthke, 2 sons. Education: Diploma Master's Degree, 1961; Dr Phil, 1964; Dr Phil habil, 1971. Appointments: Clinical Psychologist, 1961-65; Assistant Professor, 1966-75; Associate Professor, 1975-78; Full Professor, 1978-. Publications: Assessment of intellectual learning ability, 1977; Co-author, Dynamic Assessment; Co-author, Psychodiagnostics, 1990/91. Honours: W Wundt Medal 1980; A Binet Award, 2001; H Münsterberg Award, 2001. Memberships: Scientific Boards of 5 Scientific Journals. Address: Am Fischerhaus 5B, D-04159 Leipzig, Germany. E-mail: jguthke@web.de

GUTIÉRREZ Manuel, b. 22 August 1959, Melilla, Spain. Mathematician. m. Sara García, 1 son, 1 daughter. Education includes: PhD in Mathematics, Universidad Complutense de Madrid, 1993. Appointments: Lecturer, Polytechnic University of Madrid, 1985-94; Lecturer, University of Málaga, 1994-. Publications: Several papers in international journals of geometry and optics. Membership: Real Sociedad Matemática Española, 1997. Address: Departamento Álgebra, Geometría y Topología, Facultad de Ciencias, Universidad de Málaga, 29071 Málaga, Spain. E-mail: mgl@agt.cie.uma.es

GUTU Modest, b. 14 March 1937, Lipcani, Bessarabia. Marine Zoologist. m. Olimpia Gutu, 1 son. Education: Lycée Theoretic; Faculty of Biology; PhD, Faculty of Biology, Babes-Bolyai University, Cluj. Appointments: Research Worker, 1967-91; Head of Invertebrate Zoology Department, 1990-95; Senior Research Scientist, 1991, Grigore Antipa National Museum of Natural History, Bucharest; Institute of Oceanology, Havana, 1973; Oceanographical Museum of Monaco, 1980, 1987-88; Institute of Marine Sciences at the University of Southern Mississippi, Gulf Coast Research Laboratory campus in Ocean Springs, 1999; Texas A and M University at Galveston, Department of Marine Biology, 1999; Member, 4 scientific expeditions: Caribbean Sea (twice), 1973, Indonesia Archipelago, 1991, Brazil, 1994. Publications: 4 books, over 120 scientific papers, the majority about marine crustacea fauna (the Order Tanaidacea) from diverse geographical areas, describing 111 new taxa to science (orders, families, genera and species); Co-author, Traité de Zoologie, volume 7 (3A), Crustacés Péracarides, (Monaco, 1999) and Catalogue of crustacea of Brazil (Rio de Janeiro, 1998); Editor, Results of the Zoological Expedition organized by Grigore Antipa Museum, Indonesian Archipelago (1991). Honours: 1 genus and 7 species named in his honour; 1st Prize and Trophy for 2 books; Laureate of Prize Richard, French Science Academy, 1986; Jubilee Medal Grigore Antipa Museum, 1993; Medal of International Man of Year, 1998; Listed in several biographical publications. Memberships: Romanian Society of Biological Sciences; International Commission for Scientific Exploration of the Mediterranean Sea; Crustacean Society, USA. Address: Muzeul Grigore Antipa, Soseaua Kisselef 1, 011341 Bucharest 2, Romania.

GUY Barry (John), b. 22 April 1947, Lewisham, London, England. Musician (Double Bass; Baroque Bass); Composer. Education: AGSM. Career includes: Freelance Bassist; principal, City of London Sinfonia; Academy of Ancient Music, London Classical Players until 1995; Solo recitalist; Artistic Director, London Jazz Composers Orchestra; Barry Guy New Orchestra; Plays with improvisation groups, Parker/Guy/Lytton; Guy/ Gustafsson/Strid, Cecil Taylor, Bill Dixon Quartet, Marilyn Crispell; Homburger-Guy Duo. Compositions include: Statements ll, 1972; String Quartet lll, 1973; Anna, 1974; Play, 1976; EOS for double bass and orchestra, 1977; Details, 1978; Hold Hands and Sing, 1978; Waiata, 1980; Pfiff, 1981; Flagwalk, 1974; Voyages of the Moon, 1983; RondOH!, 1985; Circular for solo oboe, 1985; The Road to Ruin, 1986; Harmos, 1987; The Eye of Silence, 1988; UM 1788, 1989; Look Up!, 1990; Theoria, 1991; After the Rain, 1992; Bird Gong Game, 1992; Mobile Herbarium, 1992; Portraits, 1993; Witch Gong Game, 1993; Witch Gong Game ll, 1994; Un Coupe De Dés, 1994; Buzz, 1994; Celebration, 1995; Ceremony, 1995; Three Pieces for orchestra, 1995; Concerto for orchestra, Fallingwater, 1996; Double Trouble Two, 1996; Holyrood, 1998; Redshift, 1998; Bubblets, 1998, Remembered Earth, 1998; Octavia, 1999; Dakryon, 1999; Inscape (Tableaux), 2000; Nasca Lines, 2001; Switch, 2001; Inachis, 2002; Folio, 2002; Aglais, 2002; Points From Now, 2003; Oort – Entropy, 2004. Recordings include: Over 100 albums including: Ode, 1972; Endgame, 1979; Incision, 1981; Tracks, 1983; Zurich Concerts, 1988; Double Trouble, 1990; Elsie jo Live, 1992; Theoria, 1992; After the Rain, 1993; Fizzles, 1993; Portraits, 1994; Vade Mecum, 1994; Imaginary Values, 1994; Witch Gong Game ll, 1994; Cascades, 1995; Obliquities, 1995; Iskra 1903, 1995; Three Pieces for orchestra, 1997; Sensology, 1997; Frogging, 1997; Natives and Aliens, 1997; Bingo, 1998, Double Trouble Two, 1998; At the Vortex, 1998; Ceremony, 1999; In Darkness Let Me Dwell; Melancholy, 2000; Nailed, 2000; Inscape-Tableaux, 2001; Odyssey, 2001; Dividuality, 2001; Symmetries, 2002; 2 of 2, 2002; Birds and Blades, 2003; Celebration, 2003; Care Charming Sleep, 2003; Ithaca, 2004; Oort-Entropy, 2004. Honours: Radcliffe Award 1st Prize, 1973; Royal Philharmonic Prize for Chamber Scale Composition, 1991; Joint Prizewinner, Hilliard Composition prize, 1994; Abendzeitung (Munich) Sterne des Jahres, 1999; Choc de l'Année, 2001. Memberships include: Musicians Union; PRS; MCPS'; BACS. Address: Postfach 52, 8477 Oberstammheim, Switzerland.

Dictionary of International Biography

H

HA Jeong Hyo, b. 25 February 1940, Jinju, Korea. Religious Leader; Philosopher; Journalist. m. Jeong Hee Choi, 2 sons. Education: College of Law, Chosun University, Korea, 1962; Senior Executive Program, Graduate School of Policy Studies, Korea University, Korea, 1997; Seminar on Politics, Oxford University, 1997; Seminar, Asia-Pacific Center, Hawaii University, 1998; Senior Executive Programme, College of Philosophy, Dyittabhawwan College, Thailand, 1998; PhD, Moscow Pedagogical State University, 1999. Appointments: Founded World Association of the Truth from Thesparldoes, Mwa Han Mwo Roo (Martial Art), 1957; Chairman, World Martial Arts Association, 1992; Chairman, World Religious Peace Conference, 1994; Chief Editor, Kyoung-In Daily, 1996; President, Korea Martial Arts Association, 1998; Chief Editor, The Law Daily, 1998; Honorary Professor, Moscow Pedagogical State University, Russia, 1999; President, Umewism Conference (Universe, Human Beings, Earth, and World-ism), 1999; Chairman, Multinational Assembly for World-wide Race Unification, 1999; Chairman, World CheTeSooDdam Campaign Conference, 1999; Founded SonBeChuChum, Beijing, China, 2002; Founded model for Hangul World of GyemCholBizGuil, 2003; Dispatched GyemCholBizGuil to about 2,300 organisations of all countires of the world, 2003. Publications: MangGyemTteulDeul/GymenCholBizGuil; The World; On the United Lineage Government; The Ideal for the Human Beings (HanNaraSaramSari); 181 volumes of Gyemgil (Bible for the Human Beings); 191 booklets on Hyun Philosophy; Common Status between the Earth and the Human Beings; MooGungShinSeo (Bible for Martial Arts); Numerous editorials and columns. Membership: Senate, Korea Mass-media Fellow Association. Address: Sung Kyuong Roo, 105-1 Changsung-Dong, Chorgro-Gu, Seoul 110-034, Republic of Korea.

HABER Marian Wynne, b. 23 August 1936, New York, USA. College Teacher. m. Julian S Haber, 1 son, 1 daughter. Education: AA, University of Florida, 1956; BA, Journalism, University of Miami, 1958; Diplomate, College Teaching, University of Miami, 1972; PhD, University of North Texas, 1987. Appointments: College newspaper advisor and instructor, Texas Wesleyan University, Fort Worth; Teacher of Journalism, Texas Christian University and University of Texas at Arlington; Reporter, Miami News and Coral Gables Times; Public Relations for Miami Beach Visitor and Convention Authority. Publications: Contributor to chapter in book: Cut Your Spending in Half; Articles in encyclopaedias; Articles for Journalism Educator and College Media Review. Memberships: Association of Women Journalists; Society of Professional Journalists. Address: 7001 Candlestick Ct, Fort Worth, TX 76133-6223, USA.

HABERLER Peter L F, b. 10 February 1941, Vienna, Austria. Physicist. m. Edit, 2 sons. Education: Bachelor of Science, Innsbruck, 1959; PhD, University of Vienna, 1966; Professor of Physics and Mathematics, 1975. Appointments: Research Associate, ICTP, Trieste, Italy, 1967; Fellow, CERNTH, 1967-69; Research Associate, Duke University, USA, 1970; Director, Hephy, Vienna, 1971-72; Professor, HTBL, Vienna, Austria, 1973-96; Member, Institute of Meteorology and Geodymanics, 1990-98. Publications: Numerous articles in scientific journals including Physics Letters B. Honour: Best Student, Erice Summer School, 1970. Memberships: New York Academy of Sciences; American Association for the Advancement of Sciences; Planetary Society; BWW, USA. Address: ZAMP, Geweyg 1a/2, A-1190 Vienna, Austria.

HABGOOD John Stapylton, Baron of Habgood Calverton, b. 23 June 1927. Retired Archbishop of York; Author. m. Rosalie Mary Ann Boston, 7 June 1961, 2 sons, 2 daughters. Education: BA, 1948, MA, 1951, PhD, 1952, King's College, Cambridge; Cuddesdon College, Oxford. Appointments: Demonstrator in Pharmacology, Cambridge, 1950-53; Fellow, King's College, Cambridge, 1952-55; Curate, St Mary Abbots, Kensington, 1954-56; Vice Principal, Westcott House, Cambridge, 1956-62; Rector, St John's Church, Jedburgh, 1962-67; Principal, Queen's College, Birmingham, 1967-73; Bishop of Durham, 1973-83; Archbishop of York, 1983-95; Pro Chancellor, University of York, 1985-90; Hulsean Preacher, University of Cambridge, 1987-88; Bampton Lecturer, University of Oxford, 1999; Gifford Lecturer, University of Aberdeen, 2000. Publications: Religion and Science, 1964; A Working Faith: Essays and Addresses on Science, Medicine and Ethics, 1980; Church and Nation in a Secular Age, 1983; Confessions of a Conservative Liberal, 1988; Making Sense, 1993; Faith and Uncertainty, 1997; Being a Person: Where Faith and Science Meet, 1998; Varieties of Unbelief, 2000; The Concept of Nature, 2002. Contributions: Theology and the Sciences, Interdisciplinary Science Reviews, 2000. Honours: Honorary DD, Universities of Durham, 1975, Cambridge, 1984, Aberdeen, 1988, Huron, 1990, Hull, 1991, Oxford, 1996, Manchester, 1996, York, 1996; Privy Counsellor, 1983; Honorary Fellow, King's College, Cambridge, 1986; Life Peer, 1995. Address: 18 The Mount, Malton, North Yorkshire YO17 7ND, England.

HABITS Willem Hermanus Antonius, b. 9 December 1926, Amsterdam, The Netherlands. Roman Catholic Priest. Education: Philosophy, Theology, Roman Catholic Major Seminary, Aalbeek, The Netherlands, 1946-52; BA, University of London, England, 1956. Appointments: Tutor, English Language and Literature, St Teresa's Seminary, Ghana, 1956-70; Tutor, Chaplain, 1970-85; Acting Head, 1970-71, Opoku Ware Secondary School, Kumasi, Ghana; School Certificate Examiner and other examinations, 1960-83. Publications: Books and articles in professional journals. Honours: Roman Catholic Ordination, 1952. Memberships: Society of African Missions; Parish Priest, Diocese of Haarlem, The Netherlands. Address: Louis Naarstig Straat 14, 1063 En Amsterdam, The Netherlands.

HACKMAN Gene, b. 30 January 1930, San Bernardino, California, USA. Actor. m. Fay Maltese 1956, divorced 1985, 1 son, 2 daughters. Education: Studied Acting, Pasadena Playhouse. Appointments: Films including: Lilith, 1964; Hawaii, 1966; Banning, 1967; Lucky Lady, 1975; Night Moves, 1976; Domino Principle, 1977; Superman, 1978; Superman II, 1980; Bat 21, 1987; The Package, 1989; The Von Metz Incident, 1989; Loose Connections, 1989; Full Moon in Blue Water, 1989; Postcards From the Edge, 1989; Cass Action, 1989; Loose Canons, 1990; Narrow Margin, 1990; Necessary Roughness, 1991; The William Munny Killings, 1991; The Unforgiven, 1992; The Firm, 1992; Geronimo, 1994; Wyatt Earp, 1994; Crimson Tide, 1995; The Quick and the Dead, 1995; Get Shorty, 1996; Birds of a Feather, 1996; Extreme Measures, 1996; The Chamber, 1996; Absolute Power, 1996; Twilight, 1998; Enemy of the State, 1998; Under Suspicion, 2000; Heist, 2001; The Royal Tenenbaums, 2001; Numerous TV appearances and stage plays. Publication: Co-author, Wake of the Perdido Star, 2000. Honours: Academy Award, Best Actor; New York Film Critics Award; Golden Globe Award; British Academy Awards; Cannes Film Festival Award; National Review Board Award; Berlin Film Award; Golden Globe for Best Actor in a Musical or Comedy, 2001. Address: c/o Barry Haldeman, 1900 Avenue of the Stars, 2000 Los Angeles, CA 90067, USA.

HADDAD Sami-Farid, b. 4 May 1922. Surgeon; Urologist. m. Huda Fawaz, 18 September 1949, 2 sons, 1 daughter. Education: BA, Med, 1941, MD, 1948, American University Beirut; FACS,

American College Surgeons, 1957; DABU, American Board Urology, 1960. Appointments: Attending Urologist, Attending Surgeon, Chief Staff, Director, Orient Hospital, Beirut, Lebanon, 1957-74; Chief Editor, Lebanese Medical Journal, 1961-69; Attending Urologist, Attending Surgeon, 1972-77, President, 1973-77, Marj'uyun Government Hospital, Marj'uyun; Chief Urologist, Chief Surgeon, 1977-81, Chief, Staff, 1979-81, Obeid Hospital, Riyadh, Saudi Arabia; Chief, Urology, Veterans Affairs Medical Centre, Phoenix, Arizona, USA, 1981-93; Clinical Associate Professor, Surgery, University Arizona, Tucson, 1987-. Publications: The prostate - Your gland, 1963; Hadith from Omar, 2nd edition, 1969; Medical Ethics Law, 1969; Barême des honoraires chirurgicaux, 1970; History of Arab Medicine, 1975; Catalogue of Medical Manuscripts, 1984; Guide to Diagnostic Imaging, vols 4, 5, 1984; At the foot of Mount Hermon, 1997; Down under the veil: A Surgeon in Saudi Arabia, 1998; A First Class Man in Every Particular, 2001; Spicelogia, 2002; From Phoenicia to Phoenix, al Hantakuwr, 2002; Twoscare and ten years of Urology, 2002, One hundred and one lascivious dreams, 2003; 1137 articles in 55 journals; 6 films and posters. Honours: Knight, 1961, Officer, 1971, Commander, 1990, National Order of the Cedars, Lebanon; Medal, Egyptian Medical Association, 1966; Merit Award, Medical Chapter, Alumni Association American University Beirut, 1982; VFW Award, 1983; Memorial Plaque, more than 45 Years Service to Community, Medical Chapter, Alumni Association American University Beirut. Memberships: Medical Alumni Association, American University Beirut, 1948-, Directory Editor 1957-68, President 1959-61; Alumni Association American University Beirut, 1948-, President 1959-61, Directory Committee Chairman and Editor 1967; International Society Urology, 1957-; Alpha Omega Alpha, 1967-; Correspondence Member, Arab Academy Damascus, 1972-; American Association History Medicine, 1981-; Phoenix and American Urological Associations, 1982-; Arizona Medical Association, 1982-; Association Military Surgeons North American, 1985-; History Science Society, 1986-; Arab American Medical Association, 1987-. Listed in: Numerous Biographical Publications. Address: 4403 E Clearwater Parkway, Paradise Valley, AZ 85253, USA.

HADFIELD Andrew David, b. 25 April 1962, Kendal, Cumbria, England. Professor of English. m. Alison Sarah Yarnold, 1 son, 2 daughters. Education: BA, 1st Class Honours, University of Leeds, England, 1984; DPhil, University of Ulster, Northern Ireland, 1988. Appointments: British Academy Postdoctoral Fellow, University of Leeds, 1989-92; Lecturer in English, 1992-96, Senior Lecturer in English, 1996-98, Professor of English, 1998-2003, University of Wales, Aberystwyth; Visiting Professor in English, Columbia University, New York, USA, 2002-2003; Professor of English, University of Sussex, England, 2003-. Publications: Literature, Politics and National Identity, 1994; Spenser's Irish Experience, 1997; Literature Travel and Colonial Writing, 1998; The English Renaissance, 2000; Shakespeare, Spenser and the Matter of Britain, 2003; Shakespeare and Renaissance Politics, 2003. Honours: Fellow of the English Association; Leverhulme Major Award, 2001-2004; Chatterton Lecture at the British Academy, 2003. Memberships: English Association; Spenser Society of America. Address: Department of English, University of Sussex, Falmer, Brighton BN1 9QN, England.

HADJISTAVROPOULOS Thomas, b. 16 March 1963, Thessaloniki, Greece. Professor of Psychology. m. Heather, 2 sons. Education: BA (First Class Honours), McGill University, 1985; MA, 1987, PhD, 1991, University of Saskatchewan. Appointments: Assistant Professor, University of British Columbia, 1992-95; Assistant Professor, University of Waterloo, 1995-96; Assistant Professor, Associate Professor, Professor, University of Regina, 1995-. Publications: Numerous scholarly articles in the areas of

pain, gerontology and ethics. Honours: Health Services Utilisation and Research Commission and Canadian Institutes of Health Research Operating Grants; Early Career Award, Canadian Pain Society; Fellow, Canadian Psychological Association; Award for Excellence in Research, University of Regina Alumni Association; Career Investigator Award, Canadian Institutes of Health Research. Memberships: International Association for the Study of Pain; Canadian Psychological Association; Canadian Pain Society; Canadian Association on Gerontology. Address: Department of Psychology, University of Regina, Regina, SK S4S OA2, Canada.

HAEBERLE Rosamond Pauline, b. 23 October 1914, Clearwater, Kansas, USA. Retired Teacher. Education: Bachelor of Science, Music Education, Kansas State College, 1936; Master of Music, Northwestern University, Evanston Illinois, 1948; Post Graduate Year, Wayne State University, Detroit, Michigan; Professional Registered Parliamentarian. Appointments: Teacher, Plevna, Kansas, 1 year; Esbon, Kansas, 4 years; Frankfurt, Kansas, 2 years, Garden City, Kansas, 1 year; 3 years Music Supervisor, Waterford Township Schools, Waterford, Michigan; 33 years (32 years music and 1 year High School English), Pontiac, Michigan. Honours: Teacher's Day Award, Michigan State Fair; Distinguished Service Award, Michigan Retired School Personnel; Award of Honor and Recognition and Citation, Michigan Federation of Music Clubs; Woman of Achievement and Woman of the Year Award, Pontiac Business and Professional Women; Excellence in Community Service; Daughter of the American Revolution; Listed in 5 Who's Who publications. Memberships: Pontiac Tuesday Musicale; Michigan Federation of Music; Business and Professional Women; American Association of University Women; Daughters of American Revolution; Oakland County Pioneer and Historical Society, Town Hall; Detroit College Women, Junior Pontiac Women, Pontiac Retired School Personnel, Past State President, Michigan Federation of Music Clubs. Address: 125 Post Oak, Wichita, KS 67201, USA.

HÄFNER Heinz, b. 20 May 1926, Munich, Germany. Psychiatrist; Researcher. m. Wiltrud Ranabauer, 3 sons, 1 daughter. Education: MD 1950, PhD, 1951, University of Munich, Germany. Appointments: Professor, Chairman, Department of Social Psychiatry, 1964-68, Professor, Chairman, Department of Psychiatry, Faculty of Clinical Medicine, 1968-94, University of Heidelberg, Germany; Director, Central Institute of Mental Health, Mannheim, 1975-94; Director, Schizophrenia Research Unit, 1994-, Central Institute of Mental Health, Mannheim, Germany; Director, WHO Collaborating Centre, Mannheim, Germany, 1980-99. Publications include: Search for the causes of schizophrenia III, 1995; New research in psychiatry, 1996; Search for the causes of schizophrenia IV, 1999; Ist es alles nur die Krankheit? 2000; Das Rätsel Schizophrenie, 2000. Honours: Hermann Simon Award, 1972; Federal Service Cross, 1983; Erik Strömgren Medal, 1988; Salomon Neumann Award, 1993; Great Order of Merit, Federation Republic of Germany, 1994; Joseph Zubin Award, American Psychopathological Association, 1997; AMDP Award, 1998; Leader of Psychiatry, WPA, 1999; German Association of Public Health Medal, 2002. Memberships: Heidelberg Academy of Sciences; German Academy of Researchers, Leopoldina; AED; WHO Expert Advisory Panel. Address: Central Institute of Mental Health, PO Box 12 21 20, 68072 Mannheim, Germany. E-mail: hhaefner@as200.zi-mannheim.de

HAGA Tatsuya, b 14 February 1941, Tokyo, Japan. Scientist. m. Kazuko Tsutsumi. Education: Bachelor Degree, Faculty of Science, Tokyo University, 1963; PhD, Department of Biochemistry, Graduate School of Science, Tokyo University, 1970. Appointments: Instructor, Tokyo University, 1969-74; Associate Professor, Hamamatsu University School of Medicine, 1974-88;

Dictionary of International Biography

Professor, Tokyo University, 1988-2001; Director and Professor Gakushuin University, Institute for Biomolecular Science, 2001-. Publications: Solubilization, purification and molecular characterization of receptors: Principles and strategy (Chapter in Receptor Biochemistry, 1990; G Protein-coupled receptors (editor). 1999. Membership: International Society of Neurochemistry. Address: Institute for Biomolecular Science, Gakushuin University, 1-5-1 Mejiro, Toshima-ku, Tokyo 1718588, Japan. E-mail: tatsuya.haga@gakushuin.ac.jp

HAGER Hermann Amadeus, b. 1 February 1955, Vienna, Austria. Artist; Painter. Education: Bachelor of Medicine, University of Norway, 1980; Doctor of Psychology and Philosophy, University of Italy, 1990. Career: Painter; Musician; Composer; Journalist; Educator; Consultant; Soul-Doctor; Reformer of Psycho-Methods; Inventor of the "Cromo-School" to help people suffering from Crom-anomolies; Advocates the company of cats as a therapy for people suffering from mental illness (and the purring of cats helps also against hypertension, the purring is the fact which enables cats to help patients); Currently working on the design of his T-Shirt Collection. Publications: Books: How to Communicate Successfully with Austrians; 100 Logical Puzzles; Geometric Colouring Book; 100 Mathematical Puzzles; Train Your Brain; Introduction to Musimetry; Many articles in different magazines. Honours: Numerous honours and awards; Listed in Who's Who publications and biographical dictionaries. Memberships: American Association for the Advancement of Science; New York Academy of Sciences. Address: Piaristengasse 5-7, 1080 Vienna, Austria.

HAGIWARA Shin-ichi, b. 12 February 1958, Japan. Physician. m. Takako Kyoden, 2 daughters. Education: Bachelor of Science, Ibaraki University, 1977-81; Doctor of Medicine, Toyama Medical and Pharmaceutical College, 1984-90, Jichi Medical School, 1990-2000. Appointments: Assistant, Jichi Medical School Hospital, 1990-2000; General Manager, Honda Engineering Health Care Centre, 2000-2004. Publications: American Journals of Respiratory and Critical Care Medicine, 2000. Membership: American Thoracic Society. Address: 4-12-10 Minamikawachimachi, Kawachigun, Tochigi 329-04 33, Japan. E-mail: shinichi_hagiwara@hondaeg.co.jp

HAGUE William Jefferson, b. 26 March 1961, Rotherham, Yorkshire, England. Politician; Management Consultant. m. Ffion Jenkins, December 1997. Education: BA, Honours, Magdalen College, Oxford, England; MBA, Insead Business School, France, 1986. Appointments: Management Consultant, McKinsey & Co, 1983-88; Elected to Parliament, Richmond, Yorkshire, England, 1989; Parlimentary Private Secretary to Chancellor of Exchequer, 1990-93; Parliamentary Under-Secretary of State, Department Social Security, 1993-94; Ministry of State, Department of Social Security, 1994-95; Secretary of State for Wales, 1995-97; Leader, Conservative Party, 1997-2001; Chair, International Democratic Union, 1999-2001; Political Adviser, JCB PLC, 2001-; Non-Executive Director, AES Eng PLC, 2001-; Member, Political Council of Terra Firma Capital Partners, 2001-. Honour: Privy Councillor, 1995. Address: House of Commons, London SW1A 0AA, England.

HAIGH Christopher, b. 28 August 1944, Birkenhead, England. Lecturer in Modern History; Writer. 2 daughters. Education: BA, Cambridge University, 1966; PhD, Victoria University of Manchester, 1969. Appointments: Lecturer in History, Victoria University of Manchester, 1969-79; Lecturer in Modern History, Christ Church, Oxford, 1979-. Publications: The Last Days of the Lancashire Monasteries, 1969; Reformation and Resistance in Tudor Lancashire, 1975; The Cambridge Historical Encyclopaedia of Great Britain and Ireland, 1984; The Reign of Elizabeth l, 1985;

The English Reformation Revised, 1987; Elizabeth l: A Profile in Power, 1988; English Reformations: Religion, Politics and Society Under the Tudors, 1993; The Plain Man's Pathways to Heaven: Kinds of Christianity in Post-Reformation England, forthcoming. Membership: Royal Historical Society, fellow. Address: c/o Christ Church, Oxford, OX1 1DP, England.

HAILEY Arthur, b. 5 April 1920, Luton, England (British and Canadian citizen). Author; Screenwriter. m. (1) Joan Fishwick, 1944, divorced 1950, 3 sons, (2) Sheila Dunlop, 1951, 1 son, 2 daughters. Education: British elementary schools. Appointments: Pilot, Flight Lieutenant, Royal Air Force, 1939-47; Flight Lieutenant, Royal Canadian Air Force Reserve, 1951; Industry and sales positions; Writer, 1956-. Publications: Runway-Zero Eight (with John Castle), 1958; The Final Diagnosis, 1959; Close-up (collected plays), 1960; In High Places, 1962; Hotel, 1965; Airport, 1968; Wheels, 1971; The Moneychangers, 1975; Overload, 1979; Strong Medicine, 1984; The Evening News, 1990; Detective, 1997. Films: Zero Hour, 1956; Time Lock, 1957; The Young Doctors, 1961; Hotel, 1966; Airport, 1970; The Moneychangers, 1976; Wheels, 1978; Strong Medicine, 1986; Detective, 2004. Honours: Royal Air Force Air Efficiency Award; Canadian Council of Artists and Authors Award, 1956; Best Canadian TV Playwright Awards, 1957, 1959; Doubleday Prize Novel Award, 1962. Memberships: Alliance of Canadian Cinema, Television and Radio Artists, honorary life member; Authors League of America; Writers Guild of America, life member. Address: Lyford Cay, PO Box N7776, Nassau, Bahamas.

HAINES Arthur Barry, b. 13 December 1921, Middlesbrough, England. Aerodynamicist. m. Lilian May Smith. Education: BSc, Honours, Mathematics, Birmingham University, England. Appointments: Aerodynamics Department, Royal Aircraft Establishment, Farnborough, England, 1941-55; Chief Aerodynamicist, 1955-80, Chief Executive, 1980-87, Aircraft Research Association, Bedford, England; Editor, 1993-2003, Consultant Editor, 2004-, Progress in Aerospace Sciences. Publications: Many reports on design of sweptback wings and wind tunnel test technology including: Scale effects of aircraft and weapon dynamics, 1994; Know your flow: The key to better prediction and successful innovation, 1998; Prediction of scale effects at transonic speeds: Current practice and a gaze into the future, 2000; Scale effects in transonic flow, 27th Lanchester Memorial Lecture, 1987. Honours: Busk Prize, Royal Aeronautical Society (on 3 occasions); Bronze Medal, Gold Medal, 1987, Royal Aeronautical Society; OBE for services to aerodynamics, 1997. Memberships: Fellow, Royal Aeronautical Society; Senior Member, AIAA. Address: 3 Bromham Road, Biddenham, Bedford MK40 4AF, England. E-mail: piashaines@kbnet.co.uk

HAKKI Sam I, b. 4 January 1952, Kurdistan. Orthopaedic Surgeon. m. Mona Thamer, 2 sons, 1 daughter. Education includes: ECFMG, Philadelphia, Pennsylvania, USA, 1976; Medical Degree, Cairo University, Egypt, 1977; PLAB (UK), 1979; The Royal College of Surgeons, London, UK, 1979-83, FRCS, 1983; Flex Exam for Licensure, Utah, USA, 1987. Appointments: Hospitals Resident and Fellow, National Health Service Accredited, UK, 1979-85; US Accredited Hospitals Resident and Fellow, 1985-91; Tenure Staff Orthopaedic Surgeon and Director of Orthopaedic Research, Bay Pines Medical Institute, Florida, USA, 1991-. Publications: Numerous presentations, research works and articles in scientific journals include most recently: Evaluation of the Clinical Practice Patterns of Innhotep in the Treatment of Acute Symptomatic Deep Venous Thrombosis (research), 2001; Efficacy of Oral Anticoagulant in the Prevention of Post-Operative Thomboembolic Disease in Hip Arthroplasty, 2001; Efficacy of Diclofenac Softgel for Knee Pain Following Arthroscopy (research), 2002; Computer Assisted Surgery in Total Knee Replacement, Aesculap Inc. (research), 2003; Prospective Data Collection in Total Hip Replacement, Wright Medical Technology (research), 2003. Honours: Honours in Surgery and Medicine; 90th Percentile, Resident's Exam conducted by the American Academy of Orthopedic Surgeons, 1990. Memberships: The American Academy of Orthopedic Surgeons; The Royal College of Surgeons, UK; American Medical Association. Address: Bay Pines VA Medical Center, 10,000 Bay Pines Blvd, Building 100, Office 3A-158, Bay Pines, FL 33744, USA. E-mail: sihakki@pol.net

HAKKINEN Mika, b. 28 September 1968, Helsinki, Finland. Racing Driver. m. Erja Honkanen. Appointments: Formerly, go-kart driver, Formula Ford 1600 driver, Finnish, Swedish and Nordic Champion, 1987; Formula 3 driver, British Champion with West Surrey racing, 1990; Formula 1 driver Lotus, 1991-93, McLaren, 1993-2001; Grand Prix wins: European, 1997, Australia, 1998, Brazil, 1998, 1999, Spain, 1998, 1999, 2000, Monaco, 1998, Austria, 1998, 2000, Germany, 1998, Luxembourg, 1998, Japan, 1998, 1999, Malaysia, 1999, Hungary, 1999, 2000, Belgium, 2000; Formula One Driver's Championship Winner, 1998, 1999; Sabbatical, 2001; Retirement from Formula One; FIA European Rally Championship, Finland, 2003. Publication: Mika Hakkinen: Doing What Comes Naturally.

HALDEMAN Joe William, b. 9 June 1943, Oklahoma City, Oklahoma, USA. Novelist. m. Mary Gay Potter, 21 August 1965. Education: BS, Physics and Astronomy, University of Maryland, 1967; MFA, English, University of Iowa, 1975. Appointment: Associate Professor, writing programme, Massachusetts Institute of Technology, 1983-. Publications: War Year, 1972; Cosmic Laughter (editor), 1974; The Forever War 1975; Mindbridge, 1976; Planet of Judgement, 1977; All My Sins Remembered, 1977; Study War No More (editor), 1977; Infinite Dreams, 1978; World Without End, 1979; Worlds, 1981; There is No Darkness (co-author), 1983; Worlds Apart, 1983; Nebula Awards 17 (editor), 1983; Dealing in Futures, 1985; Body Armour 2000 co-editor), 1986; Tool of the Trade, 1987; Supertanks (co-editor), 1987; Starfighters (co-editor), 1988; The Long Habit of Living, 1989; The Hemingway Hoax, 1990; Worlds Enough and Time, 1992; 1968, 1995; None So Blind, 1996; Forever Peace, 1997; Saul's Death and Other Poems, 1997; Forever Free, 1999; The Coming, 2000; Guardian, 2002; Camouflage, 2004. Honours: Purple Heart, US Army, 1969; Nebula Awards, 1975, 1990, 1993, 1998; Hugo Awards, 1976, 1977, 1991, 1995, 1998; Rhysling Awards, 1984, 1990, 2000; World Fantasy Award, 1993; John Campbell Award, 1998. Memberships: Science Fiction and Fantasy Writers of America; Author's Guild; Poets and Writers National Space Institute; Writers Guild. Address: 5412 North West 14th Avenue, Gainesville, FL 32605, USA.

HALE Jane Alison, b. 29 September 1948, Washington, DC, USA. Professor. m. William J Bicknell, 2 sons. Education: BA, magna cum laude, College of William and Mary, 1966-70; MST, Education, University of Chicago, 1973-74; MA, French, Stanford University, 1979-81; Exchange Student, École Normale Supérieure de Jeunes Filles, Paris, 1981-82; PhD, French, with Distinction, Stanford University, 1979-84. Appointments include: Teacher, English, (as Peace Corps Volunteer), Lycée Franco-Arabe, Abéché, Chad, 1970-72; French teacher and cross-cultural coordinator, Peace Corps Training Centre St Thomas, Virgin Islands, 1972; Second-grade teacher, Pleasant Grove Union Elementary School, Burlington, North Carolina, 1974-77; Teaching Fellow, Stanford University, 1982-83; Lecturer in French, California State University, Sacramento, 1984; Assistant Professor of French and Comparative Literature, 1985-91, Associate Professor of French and Comparative Literature, 1991-, Brandeis University; French Teacher and Consultant, Summer Institute of Intensive French,

University of Florida, 1986-88. Publications: Books: The Broken Window: Beckett's Dramatic Perspective, 1987; The Lyric Encyclopedia of Raymond Queneau, 1989; Numerous chapters and articles. Honours include: Phi Beta Kappa; Fellowships at University of Chicago, 1973-74, Stanford University, 1979-84; French Government Scholarship, 1981-82; Mrs Giles Whiting Fellowship in the Humanities, 1983-84; Fellowships, Grant, Brandeis University, 1985-90, 1989, 1990; Fulbright Senior Scholar, Senegal, 1994; Marion and Jasper Whiting Foundation Fellowship, 1995-98; Lerman-Neubauer Award for Excellence in Teaching and Counseling, 2001. Address: Brandeis University, Department of Romance and Comparative Literature, MS 024 Waltham, MA 02254, USA.

HALE Marguerite (Grete), b. 10 May 1929, Ottawa, Ontario, Canada. Business Woman. m. Reginald Britten Hale. Education: Bachelor, Journalism, Carleton University, 1954; Honorary Doctorate, University of Ottawa, 1999. Appointments: President, 1978-89, Chairman, 1989-, Morrison Lamothe Inc. (Independent family controlled Canadian frozen food processor); Directorships and Advisory Board Appointments include: Prior, Military and Hospitaller Order, St Lazarus of Jerusalem; President, Beechwood Cemetery; Executive Committee Member, Director, University of Ottawa; Friends of the National Library of Canada; Salvation Army Advisory Board (Ottawa), Member; Hospice at May Court, Chair; Canhave Children's Centre, Director; Institute of Canadian Studies, Advisory Board; Chair, Leadership, Ottawa. Publication: The Happy Baker of Ottawa, 1990. Honours: Grand Cross, Military Hospitaller Order of St Lazarus of Jerusalem; Ottawa Carleton Philanthropy Award, Outstanding Volunteer of the Year, 1997; Ottawa-Carleton Business Woman of the Year, 1997; Canadian Woman Entrepreneur of the Year Award, Lifetime Achievement Category, 1998; Ottawa Community Builder of the Year Award, 2001; Honorary Colonel, 78th Fraser Highlanders, Fort Glengarry Garrison. Memberships: Fellow, Royal Canadian Geographic Society; Fellow, Heraldry Society of Canada; Rideau Club of Ottawa; Governor, Royal Canadian Geographical Society; Chair, Community Foundation of Ottawa; Chair, Macdonald Cartier Library; Vice Sénéchale, La Chaine des Rotisseurs. Address: Bayne House, 40 Fuller Street, Ottawa, Ontario K1Y 3R8, Canada. E-mail: ghale@morrisonlamothe.com

HALL Donald (Andrew Jr), b. 20 September 1928, New Haven, Connecticut, USA. Poet; Writer; Professor of English, retired. m. (1) Kirby Thompson, 1952, divorced 1969, 1 son, 1 daughter, (2) Jane Kenyon, 1972, deceased 1995. Education: BA, Harvard University, 1951; BLitt, Oxford University, 1953; Stanford University, 1953-54. Appointments: Poetry Editor, Paris Review, 1953-62; Assistant Professor, 1957-61, Associate Professor, 1961-66, Professor of English, 1966-75, University of Michigan. Publications: Poetry: Poems, 1952; Exile, 1952; To the Loud Wind and Other Poems, 1955; Exiles and Marriages, 1955; The Dark Houses, 1958; A Roof of Tiger Lilies, 1964; The Alligator Bride: Poems New and Selected, 1969; The Yellow Room: Love Poems, 1971; A Blue Wing Tilts at the Edge of the Sea: Selected Poems 1964-1974, 1975; The Town of Hill, 1975; Kicking the Leaves, 1978; The Toy Bone, 1979; The Twelve Seasons, 1983; Brief Lives, 1983; Great Day at the Cows' House, 1984; The Happy Man, 1986; The One Day: A Poem in Three Parts, 1988; Old and New Poems, 1990; The One Day and Poems (1947-1990), 1991; The Museum of Clear Ideas, 1993; The Old Life, 1996; Without, 1998. Short Stories: The Ideal Bakery, 1987. Other: Henry Moore: The Life and Work of a Great Sculptor, 1966; Marianne Moore: The Cage and the Animal, 1970; The Gentleman's Alphabet Book, 1972; Writing Well, 1973, 7th edition, revised, 1991; Remembering Poets: Reminiscences and Opinions-Dylan Thomas, Robert Frost, T S Eliot, Ezra Pound, 1978; Goatfoot Milktongue Twinbird:

Interviews, Essays and Notes on Poetry 1970-76, 1978; To Read Literature: Fiction, Poetry, Drama, 1981, 3rd edition, revised, 1987; The Weather for Poetry: Essays, Reviews and Notes on Poetry 1977-81, 1982; Poetry and Ambition: Essays 1982-1988, 1988; Anecdotes of Modern Art (with Pat Corrigan Wykes), 1990; Here at Eagle Pond, 1990; Their Ancient Glittering Eyes, 1992; Life Work, 1993; Death to Death of Poetry, 1994; Principal Products of Portugal, 1995. Honours: Edna St Vincent Millay Memorial Prize, 1956; Longview Foundation Award, 1960; Guggenheim Fellowships, 1963, 1972; Sarah Josepha Hale Award, 1983; Poet Laureate of New Hampshire, 1984-89; Lenore Marshall Award, 1987; National Book Critics Circle Award, 1989; Los Angeles Times Book Award, 1989; Robert Frost Silver Medal, Poetry Society of America, 1991; Lifetime Achievement Award, New Hampshire Writers and Publishers Project, 1992; New England Book Award for Non-Fiction, 1993; Ruth Lilly Prize for Poetry, 1994; Honorary doctorates. Address: Eagle Pond Farm, Danbury, NH 03230, USA.

HALL Gene E, b. 19 June 1941, Rutland, Vermont, US. Professor; Dean. m. Betsey, 2 sons. Education: BS, Castleton State College, 1964; MS, Syracuse University, 1965; PhD, 1968. Appointments: Professor, Director, R and D Center for Teacher Education, University of Texas, Austin, 1968-86; Professor, Research Program Director, University of Florida, 1986-88; Professor, Educational Leadership, University of Northern Colorado, 1988-99; Professor, Dean, College of Education, 1988-92; Dean, College of Education, University of Nevada, Las Vegas, 1999-. Publications: Implementing Change: Patterns, Principles and Potholes; Introduction to the foundation of American education. Memberships: American Educational Research Association; American Association of Colleges of Teacher Education. Address: College of Education, University of Nevada, Las Vegas 4505, Maryland Parkway, Las Vegas, NV 89154-3001, USA.

HALL Jerry, b. 2 July 1956, Texas, USA. Model; Actress. m. Mick Jagger, 1990, divorced 1999, 2 sons, 2 daughters. Career: Began modelling, Paris, 1970s; Numerous TV apperances including David Letterman Show, USA; Contributing editor, Tatler, 1999-; Stage debut in William Inge's Bus Stop, Lyric Theatre, London, 1990; Films: Batman, Princess Caraboo, 1994; Diana and Me, 1996; RPM, 1996; Play: The Graduate, Gielgud Theatre, London, 2000. Publication: Tell Tales, 1985. Address: c/o Eclipse Management Production, 32 Tavistock Street, London, WC2E 7PB, England.

HALL J(ohn) C(live), b. 12 September 1920, London, England. Poet. Education: Oriel College, Oxford. Appointments: Staff, Encounter Magazine, 1955-91; Editor, Literary Executor of Keith Douglas. Publications: Poetry: Selected Poems, 1943; The Summer Dance and Other Poems, 1951; The Burning Hare, 1966; A House of Voices, 1973; Selected and New Poems 1939-84, 1985; Long Shadows: Poems 1938-2002, 2003. Other: Collected Poems of Edwin Muir, 1921-51 (editor), 1952; New Poems (co-editor), 1955; Edwin Muir, 1956. Address: 9 Warwick Road, Mount Sion, Tunbridge Wells, Kent TN1 1YL, England.

HALL Marshall (Mike) B, b. 18 June 1932, Ashland, Wisconsin, USA. Artist; Painter; Teacher. Education: Self educated; Studied with Percy Mannser, SWA. Career: Artist; Painter; Teacher. Honours: Won over fifty awards in Oregon, Washington, California and New York, from 1963- including: Honorary Degree, Society of Western Artists', for having three paintings accepted in the M H de Young Museum, San Francisco, 1965, 1967, 1968; Gold Medal, American Artists Professional League, New York, 1984. Memberships: Oregon Society of Artists'; Society of Western

Artists; The American Artists Professional League, New York. Address: 2715 NE Saratoga Street, Portland, OR 97211, 5961, USA.

HALL Peter (Geoffrey), b. 19 March 1932, London, England. Professor of Planning; Writer. m. (1) Carla Maria Wartenberg, 1962, divorced 1966, (2) Magdalena Mróz, 1967. Education: MA, PhD, St Catharine's College, Cambridge. Appointments: Assistant Lecturer, 1957-60, Lecturer, 1960-66, Birkbeck College, University of London; Reader in Geography, London School of Economics and Political Science, 1966-68; Professor of Geography, 1968-89, Professor Emeritus, 1989-, University of Reading; Professor of City and Regional Planning, 1980-92, Professor Emeritus, 1992-, University of California at Berkeley; Professor of Planning, 1992-, Director, School of Public Policy, 1995-96, University College, London. Publications: The Industries of London, 1962; London 2000, 1963, revised edition, 1969; Labour's New Frontiers, 1964; Land Values (editor), 1965; The World Cities, 1966, 3rd edition, 1984; Von Thunen's Isolated State (editor), 1966; An Advanced Geography of North West Europe (co-author), 1967; Theory and Practice of Regional Planning, 1970; Containment of Urban England: Urban and Metropolitan Growth Processes or Megapolis Denied (co-author), 1973; Containment of Urban England: The Planning System: Objectives, Operations, Impacts (co-author), 1973; Planning and Urban Growth: An Anglo-American Comparison (with M Clawson), 1973; Urban and Regional Planning: An Introduction, 1974, 2nd edition, 1982; Europe 2000, 1977; Great Planning Disasters, 1980; Growth Centres in the European Urban System, 1980; Transport and Public Policy Planning (editor with D Banister), 1980; The Inner City in Context (editor), 1981; Silicon Landscapes (editor), 1985; Can Rail Save the City? (co-author), 1985; High-Tech America (co-author), 1986; Western Sunrise (co-author), 1987; The Carrier Wave (co-author), 1988; Cities of Tomorrow, 1988; London 2001, 1989; The Rise of the Gunbelt, 1991; Technoples of the World, 1994; Sociable Cities (co-author), 1998; Cities in Civilisation, 1998; Urban Future 21 (co-author), 2000; Working Capital, 2002. Honours: Honorary Fellow, St Catharine's College, Cambridge, 1988; British Academy, fellow, 1983; Member of the Academia Europaea, 1989; Knight Bachelor, 1998; Prix Vautrin Lud, 2001. Memberships: Fabian Society, chairman, 1971-72; Tawney Society, chairman, 1983-85. Literary Agent: Peters, Fraser, Dunlap. Address: c/o Bartlett School, University College, London, Wates House, 22 Gordon Street, London WC1H 0QB, England.

HALL Sir Peter (Reginald Frederick), b. 22 November 1930, Bury St Edmunds, Suffolk, England. Director and Producer for Stage, Film, Television, and Opera; Associate Professor of Drama. m. 1) Leslie Caron, 1956, divorced 1965, 1 son, 1 daughter, (2) Jacqueline Taylor, 1965, divorced 1981, 1 son, 1 daughter, (3) Maria Ewing, 1982, divorced 1990, 1 daughter, (4) Nicola Frei, 1990, 1 daughter. Education: BA, Honours, St Catharine's College, Cambridge. Appointments: Director, Arts Theatre, London, 1955-56, Royal Shakespeare Theatre, 1960, National Theatre, 1973-88; Founder-Director-Producer, International Playwright's Theatre, 1957, Peter Hall Co, 1988; Managing Director, Stratford-on-Avon and Aldwych Theatre, London, 1960-68; Associate Professor of Drama, Warwick University, 1966-; Co-Director, Royal Shakespeare Co, 1968-73; Artistic Director, Glyndebourne Festival, 1984-90; Artistic Director, Old Vic, 1997; Wortham Chair in Performing Arts, Houston University, Texas, 1999; Chancellor, Kingston University, 2000-; Theatre, opera and film productions. Publications: The Wars of the Roses, adaptation after Shakespeare (with John Barton), 1970; John Gabriel Borkman, by Ibsen (translator with Inga-Stina Ewbank), 1975; Peter Hall's Diaries: The Story of a Dramatic Battle (edited by John Goodwin), 1983; Animal Farm, adaptation after Orwell, 1986; The Wild Duck, by

Ibsen (translator with Inga-Stina Ewbank), 1990; Making an Exhibition of Myself (autobiography), 1993; An Absolute Turkey, by Feydeau (translator with Nicola Frei), 1994; The Master Builder (with Inga-Stina Ewbank), 1995; Mind Millie For Me (new translation of Feydeau's Occupe-toi d'Amélie, with Nicola Frei), 1999; Cities in Civilization, 1999; The Necessary Theatre, 1999; Exposed by the Mask, 2000. Honours: Commander of the Order of the British Empire, 1963; Honorary Fellow, St Catharine's College, Cambridge, 1964; Chevalier de l'Ordre des Arts et Des Lettres, France, 1965; Tony Award, USA, 1966; Shakespeare Prize, University of Hamburg, 1967; Knighted, 1977; Standard Special Award, 1979; Special Award for Outstanding Achievement in Opera, 1981, and Awards for Best Director, 1981, 1987; Several honorary doctorates. Membership: Theatre Directors' Guild of Great Britain, founder-member, 1983-. Address: c/o Old Vic, Waterloo Road, London SE1 8NB, England.

HALLIWELL Geri Estelle, b. 7 August 1972, Watford, England. Singer. Career: Member, Spice Girls, -1998; Started as Touch, renamed as Spice Girls; Found manager and obtained major label recording deal; Numerous TV appearances, radio play and press interviews; UK, European and US tours; Nominated United Nations Ambassador, 1998; Solo Career, 1998-; Video and book releases. Recordings: Singles with Spice Girls: Wannabe, 1996; Say You'll Be There, 1996; 2 Become 1, 1996; Mama/Who Do You Think You Are, 1993; Spice Up Your Life, 1997; Too Much, 1997; Stop, 1998; (How Does It Feel to Be) On Top of the World, as part of England United, 1998; Move Over/Generation Next, 1998; Viva Forever, 1998; Albums: Spice, 1996; Spiceworld, 1997; Solo Singles: Look At Me, 1999; Mi Chico Latino, 1999; Lift Me Up, 1999; Bag It Up, 2000; It's Raining Men, 2001; Scream If You Want to Go Faster, 2001; Albums: Schizophonic, 1999; Scream If You Want to Go Faster, 2001. Honours: With Spice Girls, numerous music awards in polls.

HALLWORTH Grace Norma Leonie Byam, b. 4 January 1928, Trinidad, West Indies. Ex-Librarian; Author; Storyteller. m. Trevor David Hallworth, 31 October 1964. Education: Exemptions from Matriculation, 1946; Associate of Library Association, 1956; Diploma in Education, London University, 1976; Editorial Board Member, Institute of Education, University of London, 1995. Publications: Listen to this Story, 1977; Mouth Open Story Jump Out, 1984; Web of Stories, 1990; Cric Crac, 1990; Buy a Penny Ginger, 1994; Poor-Me-One, 1995; Rythm and Rhyme, 1995; Down By The River, 1997 Contributions to: Books and journals. Honours: Runner-up for Greenaway Medal. 1997. Membership: Society for Storytelling, patron, 1993-94. Address: Tranquillity, 36 Lighthouse Road, Bacolet Point, Scarborough, Tobago, West Indies.

HALPERIN John J, b. 25 January 1950, Montreal, Canada. Neurologist. m. Toula, 1 son. Education: SB, Physics, Massachusetts Institute of Technology, Cambridge, 1971; MD, Harvard Medical School, Boston, 1975. Internships, residencies and fellowships: Internal Medicine, University of Chicago Hospitals and Clinics, Chicago, Illinois, 1975-77; Neurology, Massachusetts General Hospital, Boston, Massachusetts, 1977-83; NIH NRSA Research Fellow, Neurology, Massachusetts General Hospital, 1980-82. Appointments include: Consultant in Neurology, McLean Hospital, Waltham, Massachusetts, 1980-83; Instructor, Neurology, Harvard Medical School, 1981-83; Assistant Professor, 1983-89, Associate Professor and Vice Chairman, 1989-91, SUNY, Stony Brook; Chairman, Department of Neurology, Attending Neurologist, North Shore University Hospital, 1992-; Attending Neurologist, New York Hospital, 1993-96; Associate Professor, 1992-93, Professor, 1993-96, Department of Neurology, Cornell University Medical College; Professor, Department of

Neurology, NYU School of Medicine, 1996-. Publications: 74 original reports; 7 reviews; 2 books/monographs edited; 32 book chapters; 54 abstracts. Honours: Phi Beta Kappa; Sigma Xi. Memberships: AAAS; Fellow, American Academy of Neurology; Society for Neuroscience; Long Island Neurosciences Society; Fellow, American Association of Electrodiagnostic Medicine; American Academy of Clinical Neurophysiology; American Neurologic Association; Association of University Professors of Neurology; Fellow, American College of Physicians. Address: North Shore University Hospital, Department of Neurology, Manhasset, NY 11030, USA.

HALPERN Daniel, b. 11 September 1945, Syracuse, New York, USA. Associate Professor; Poet; Writer; Editor. m. Jeanne Catherine Carter, 31 December 1982, 1 daughter. Education: San Francisco State College, 1963-64; BA, California State University at Northridge, 1969; MFA, Columbia University, 1972. Appointments: Founder-Editor, Antaeus literary magazine, 1969-95; Instructor, New School for Social Research, New York City, 1971-76; Editor-in-Chief, Ecco Press, 1971-; Visiting Professor, Princeton University, 1975-76, 1987-88, 1995-96; Associate Professor, Columbia University, 1976-. Publications: Poetry: Traveling on Credit, 1978; Seasonal Rights, 1982; Tango, 1987; Foreign Neon, 1991; Selected Poems, 1994. Other: The Keeper of Height, 1974; Treble Poets, 1975; Our Private Lives: Journals, Notebooks and Diaries, 1990; Not for Bread Alone: Writers on Food, Wine, and the Art of Eating, 1993; The Autobiographical Eye, 1993; Holy Fire: Nine Visionary Poets and the Quest for Enlightenment, 1994; Something Shining, 1998. Editor: Borges on Writing (co-editor), 1973; The American Poetry Anthology, 1975; The Antaeus Anthology, 1986; The Art of the Tale: An International Anthology of Short Stories, 1986; On Nature, 1987; Writers on Artists, 1988; Reading the Fights (with Joyce Carol Oates), 1988; Plays in One Act, 1990; The Sophisticated Cat (with Joyce Carol Oates), 1992; On Music (co-editor), 1994. Contributions to: Various anthologies, reviews, journals, and magazines. Honours: Jesse Rehder Poetry Award, Southern Poetry Review, 1971; YMHA Discovery Award, 1971; Great Lakes Colleges National Book Award, 1973; Borestone Mountain Poetry Award, 1974; Robert Frost Fellowship, Bread Loaf, 1974; National Endowment for the Arts Fellowships, 1974, 1975, 1987; Pushcaft Press Prizes, 1980, 1987, 1988; Carey Thomas Award for Creative Publishing, Publishers Weekly, 1987; Guggenheim Fellowship, 1988; PEN Publisher Citation, 1993. Address: c/o The Ecco Press, 100 West Broad Street, Hopewell, NJ 08525, USA.

HAMANO Eisaburo, b. 12 January 1947, Tokyo, Japan. m. Akiko Hamano, 1 daughter. Education: Graduate, Tokyo Institute of Technology, 1969; Postgraduate, Harvard Business School, 1998. Appointments: President, Chief Executive Officer, Toshiba Display Devices Inc., New York, USA, 1995-96; Vice-President, General Manager, CRT Division, Toshiba Corporation, Tokyo, Japan, 1997-97; Executive Quality Leader, Display Device and Component Company, 1998-2000; Board of Directors, Six Sigma Professional, Toshiba Corporation, Tokyo, Japan, 1998-2000; President, Chief Executive Officer, Corporation Vice-President, Toshiba Corporation and Display Devices and Component Company, Tokyo, Japan, 2000-2002; Corporation Vice-President, Toshiba Corporation, Tokyo, Japan, 2002-2003; Senior Executive Vice-President, Matsushita Toshiba Picture Display Company Ltd, Osaka, Japan, 2003-. Address: 1-1 Saiwai-cho Takasuki, Osaka 569-1193, Japan. E-mail: hamano.eisaburo@jp.panasonic.com

HAMBURGER Michael, (Peter Leopold), b. 22 March 1924, Berlin, Germany (British Citizen). Poet; Writer; Translator; Editor. m. Anne Ellen File, 1951, 1 son, 2 daughters. Education: MA, Christ Church, Oxford, England. Appointments: Assistant Lecturer in German, University College, London, 1952-55; Lecturer, then Reader in German, University of Reading, 1955-64; Florence Purington Lecturer, Mount Holyoke College, South Hadley, Massachusetts, 1966-67; Visiting Professor, State University of New York at Buffalo, 1969, and at Stony Brook, 1971, University of South Carolina, 1973, Boston University, 1975-77; Visiting Fellow, Wesleyan University, Middletown, Connecticut, 1970; Regent's Lecturer, University of California at San Diego, 1973; Professor (part-time), University of Essex, 1978. Publications: Poetry: Flowering Cactus, 1950; Poems 1950-51, 1952; The Dual Site, 1958; Weather and Season, 1963; Feeding the Chickadees, 1968; Penguin Modern Poets (with A Brownjohn and C Tomlinson), 1969; Travelling, 1969; Travelling I-V, 1973; Ownerless Earth, 1973; Travelling VI, 1975; Real Estate, 1977; Moralities, 1977; Variations, 1981; Collected Poems, 1984; Trees, 1988; Selected Poems, 1988; Roots in the Air, 1991; Collected Poems, 1941-94, 1995, paperback, 1998; Late, 1997; Intersections, 2000; The Take-Over, 2000; Philip Larkin: A Retrospect, 2002; From a Diary of Non-Events, 2002. Prose: Reason and Energy, 1957; From Prophecy to Exorcism, 1965; The Truth of Poetry, 1970, new edition, 1996; A Mug's Game (memoirs), 1973, revised edition as String of Beginnings, 1991; Hugo von Hofmannsthal, 1973; Art as a Second Nature, 1975; A Proliferation of Prophets, 1983; After the Second Flood: Essays in Modern German Literature, 1986; Testimonies: Selected Shorter Prose 1950-1987, 1989; Michael Hamburger in Conversation with Peter Dale, 1998. Translator: Many books, including: Poems of Hölderlin, 1943, revised edition as Hölderlin: Poems, 1952; JCF Holderlin: Selected Verse, 1961; H von Hofmannsthal: Poems and Verse Plays (with others), 1961; H von Hofmannsthal: Selected Plays and Libretti (with others), 1964; J C F Hölderlin: Poems and Fragments, 1967, new edition, enlarged, 1994; The Poems of Hans Magnus Enzenberger (with others), 1968; The Poems of Günter Grass (with C Middleton), 1969; Paul Celan: Poems, 1972, new edition, enlarged as Poems of Paul Celan, 1988, 3rd edition, 1995; Selected Poems and Fragments, 1994; Kiosk, 1997; Günter Grass: Selected Poems and Fragments, 1998; W G Sebald: After Nature, 2002. Contributions to: Numerous publications. Honours: Bollingen Foundation Fellow, 1959-61, 1965-66; Translation Prizes, Deutsche Akademie für Sprache und Dichtung, Darmstadt, 1964; Arts Council of Great Britain, 1969; Medal, Institute of Linguistics, 1977; Wilhelm-Heinse Prize, 1978; Schlegel-Tieck Prizes, 1978, 1981; Goethe Medal, 1986; Austrian State Prize for Literary Translation, 1988; Honorary LittD, University of East Anglia, 1988; European Translation Prize, 1990; Holderlin Prize, Tubingen, 1991; Petrarca Prize, 1992; Officer of the Order of the British Empire, 1992; Honorary DPhil, Technical University, Berlin, 1995; Cholmondeley Award for Poetry, 2000; Horst-Bienek Prize, Munich, 2001. Address: c/o John Johnson Ltd, Clerkenwell House, 45-47 Clerkenwell Green, London EC1 0HT, England.

HAMDALLAH Rami Waleed, b. 10 August 1958, Anabta, Tulkam, West Bank. University President. m. Rima Bustami. Education: BA, English, University of Jordan, Amman, 1980; MA, Linguistics, University of Manchester, 1982; PhD, Applied Linguistics, University of Lancaster, 1988. Appointments: Chairperson, English Department, Faculty of Arts, 1988-92, Dean, Faculty of Arts, 1992-95, Academic Vice President, Humanities, 1995-98, President, 1998-, An-Najah National University. Publications include: English Word Formation and its Pedagogical implications for TFL, 1992; Cross-Cultural Pragmatic Failure, 1992; A Contrastive Analysis of Selected English and Arabic Prepositions with Pedagogical Implications, 1993; The Role of Higher Education in the Context of an Independent Palestinian State, 1996; Linguistics Problems Facing Arab Learners of English, 1998; Problems and Approaches to Translation, with Special Reference to Arabic, 1998; A Contrastive Analysis of English and

Arabic Relativization, 1999; Numerous other articles in scientific journals. Honours: British Council Award, 1985; Lancaster University Award, 1986; Numerous other local awards. Memberships include: Steering Committee, Council of Arabic Universities for Scientific Research; Vice President, Palestinian Scientific Academy; Council of the Palestinian Universities Presidents; The Palestinian-European-American Program of Academic Cooperation; The Palestinian Constitution Committee; President, PEACE programme, 2003-05. Address: An-Najah National University, Omar Ibn Khattab Street, PO Box 7, Nablus, West Bank. E-mail: rami@najah.edu.

HAMDAN Motasem, b. 1 July 1968, Palestine. Assistant Professor of Health Policy and Management. m. Jale Hamdan, 2 sons. Education: BSc, Health Services Administration, 1994, MSc, Health Institutions Administration, 1996, School of Health Services Administration, Hacettepe University, Ankara, Turkey; PhD, Public Health, Catholic University of Leuven, Belgium, 2003. Appointments: Hospital Management Officer, Health Services Management Unit, Technical Assistance Projects, Palestinian Ministry of Health, 1996-98; Faculty and Co-ordinator of the Higher Diploma Programme in Health Management, School of Public Health, Al-Quds University, Jerusalem, 1998-99; Researcher, Centre for Health Services and Nursing Management Research, School of Public Health, Catholic University of Leuven, Belgium, 199-2003; Assistant Professor of Health Policy and Management, Co-ordinator, Health Policy and Management Programme, School of Public Health, Al-Quds University, Jerusalem, 2003-. Publications: Articles in professional journals as author and co-author include most recently: Organising Health Care within Political Turmoil: The Palestinian Case, 2003; Human resources for health in Palestine: A policy analysis. Part I: Current situation and recent developments, 2003; Human resources for health in Palestine: A policy analysis. Part II: The process of policy formulation and implementation, 2003; The dynamics of health policy development during transition and under uncertainty: what can be learned from the Palestinian experience, 2003; 4 papers presented at international conferences in Italy, Sweden, Norway and Spain. Memberships: International Association of Health Policy; International Society on Priorities in Health Care; Member of Board of Associated Editors of international refereed journal Health Policy. Address: The School of Public Health, Al-Quds University, PO Box 5100, Jerusalem. E-mail: mhamdan@med.alquds.edu

HAMMER Jane Amelia Ross, b. 9 April 1916. Philosopher; Musician. Education: BA, 1936, MA, 1937, University of North Carolina, Chapel Hill, North Carolina; Graduate, Radcliffe/Harvard, Cambridge, Massachusetts, 1938-39; New England Conservatory, violin performance pupil of Harrison Keller, 1938-39. Appointments: Philosophy Faculty, Spelman College, Atlanta, Georgia, 1946-58; Violinist, Atlanta Symphony 1947-52; Chair, OASIS, organization for successful desegregation of public schools, 1960-61; Director, Citizen Training Programs, Overseas Education Fund, U S League of Women Voters, 1962-63; Staff, LWV Education Fund registration and voting projects 1963-65; Director, Inner-City Project, 1965-67; President, Friday Morning Music Club, Inc. 1973-76; President, LWV-NPC (North Pinellas County), 1989-90; Public Representative Member, U S Department, Energy and FL Department of Health and Rehabilitative Services Committee for feasibility study of Health of Residents of the County. Publications: Logic for Living, 1951; Voting is People Power, 1967; Editor, Origin of Belief, 1972; Protector: A Life History of Richard Cromwell, 1997; Articles including: The Fight is for Fraternity. Honours: Kenan Fellowship in Philosophy, UNC-CH 1936-37, 1938-39; Delegate of UNC to Inauguration of President of Agnes Scott College, Atlanta, 1951;

Recipient of Award for Citizenship in Action on behalf of Organisations Assisting Integration in Schools (OASIS), Good Housekeeping Magazine, 1962; 500 Environmental Achiever, FUNEP, 1987; Presidential Pen for LWV-DC by President Johnson, 1965; Presidential Leadership Circle Jefferson Society, President Clinton 1995-2000; ABI World Laureate of USA, 1999, 2000. Memberships: Life Fellow, American Biographical Institute, 1993-; Life Fellow, International Biographical Association, 1996-; English Speaking Union; Women's Committee of Washington Performing Arts Society (WPAS); Hegel Society and American Philosophical Association; The Cromwell Association. Listed in: World Who's Who of Women; Who's Who in the South and Southwest, 2000-2001Millennium Edition; Who's Who in the World, 2002; Social List Green Book, DC. Address: 521 Holly Road, Edgewater, MD 21037, USA.

HAMMOND Karla Marie, b. 26 April 1949, Middletown, Connecticut, USA. Consultant; Poet. Education: BA, English, Goucher College, 1971; MA, English, Trinity College, 1973. Appointments: Executive Staff Administration, Connecticut Student Loan; Consultant, Aetna Life and Casualty; Manager, Planning and Communications, ADVO; Managing Partner, KMH Communications; Vice President, Executive Search, People Management. Contributions to: Over 185 publications in USA, Canada, England, Sweden, Italy, Japan, Australia and Greece. Honour: Nominated for Pushcart Prize. Address: 12 West Drive, East Hampton, CT 06424, USA.

HAMMOND Peter, b. 13 July 1942. Mining Supervisor. m. Diane Ivy, 12 August 1989. Education: Modules Diploma of Higher Education, 1985. Appointments: Environmental and Mining Supervisor; Public Speaker on Poetry and Literature Black Country in Colleges and Universities, Schools and Art Societies nationwide. Publications: Two in Staffordshire with Graham Metcalf, 1979; Love Poems, 1982. Contributions to: New Age Poetry; Outposts; Charter Poetry; Chase Post; Swansea Festival, 1982. Honour: School Poetry Prize, 1956. Memberships: Rugeley Literary Society; Co-Founder, Cannock Poetry Group; Poetry Society Readings. Address: 6 Gorstey Lea, Burntwood, Staffordshire W37 9BG, England.

HAMMOND-STROUD Derek, b. 10 January 1926, London, England. Concert and Operatic Baritone. Education: Studied with: Elena Gerhardt, Gerhard Hüsch, Trinity College of Music, London. Debut: London 1955, in the British Premiere of Haydn's Orfeo et Euridice. Career: Guest Artist with numerous opera companies; Principal Baritone, English National Opera, 1961-71, as Rossini's Bartolo, Verdi's Melitone and Rigoletto, Wagner's Alberich and Beckmesser; Royal Opera, Covent Garden, 1971-89; Glyndebourne, 1973-86; Broadcasts on BBC and European radio; Opera and Recital appearances: Netherlands; Denmark; Iceland; Germany; Austria; Spain; USA; Opera appearances: Metropolitan Opera, New York, 1977-89; Teatro Colón, Buenos Aires, 1981; National Theatre, Munich, 1983; Other roles included: Publio, in La Clemenza di Tito; Don Magnifico; Roles in the British premieres of La Pietra del Paragone, Der Besuch der Alten Dame, and Faninal in Der Rosenkavalier. Recordings: Many recordings for various companies including the ENO Ring of the Nibelung and Der Rosenkavalier. Honours: OBE, 1987; Honorary Member, Royal Academy of Music; Honorary Fellow, Trinity College of Music, London; Sir Charles Santley Memorial Award by Worshipful Company of Musicians. Membership: Incorporated Society of Musicians. Hobbies: Chess; Study of Philosophy. Address: 18 Sutton Road, Muswell Hill, London N10 1HE, England.

HAMNETT Katherine, b. 16 August 1948. Designer. 2 sons. Education: St Martin's School of Art. Appointments: Tuttabankem, 1969-74; Designed freelance in New York, Paris, Rome and London, 1974-76; Founder, Katherine Hamnett Ltd, 1979; Launched Choose Life T-shirt collection, 1983; Involved in Fashion Aid, 1985; Opened first Katherine Hamnett shop, London, 1986, 2 more shops, 1988; Production moved to Italy, 1989; Visiting Professor, London Institute, 1997-; International Institute of Cotton Designer of the Year, 1982; British Fashion Industry Designer of the Year, 1984; Bath Costume Museum Menswear Designer of the Year Award, 1984; British Knitting and Clothing Export Council Award for Export, 1988. Publications: Various publications in major fashion magazines and newspapers. Address: Katherine Hamnett Ltd, 202 New North Road, London N1 7BJ, England.

HAMPSHIRE Stuart (Newton) (Sir), b. 1 October 1914, Healing, Lincolnshire, England. Retired Professor of Philosophy; Writer. m. (1) Renee Ayer, 1961, deceased 1980, (2) Nancy Cartwright, 1985, 2 daughters. Education: Balliol College, Oxford. Appointments: Fellow and Lecturer in Philosophy, 1936-40, Domestic Bursar and Research Fellow, 1955-60, All Souls College, Oxford; Service in the British Army, 1940-45; Personal Assistant to the Minister of State, British Foreign Office, 1945; Lecturer in Philosophy, University College, London, 1947-50; Fellow, New College, Oxford, 1950-55; Grote Professor of Philosophy of Mind and Logic, University of London, 1960-63; Professor of Philosophy, Princeton University, 1963-70; Warden, Wadham College, Oxford, 1970-84; Professor, Stanford University, 1985-91. Publications: Spinoza, 1951; Thought and Action, 1959; Freedom of the Individual, 1965; Modern Writers and Other Essays, 1969; Freedom of Mind and Other Essays, 1971; The Socialist Idea (co-editor), 1975; Two Theories of Morality, 1977; Public and Private Morality (editor), 1978; Morality and Conflict, 1983; Innocence and Experience, 1989; Justice is Conflict, 1990. Contributions to: Philosophical journals. Honours: Honorary DLitt, University of Glasgow, 1973; Knighted, 1979. Memberships: American Academy of Arts and Sciences, fellow; British Academy, fellow. Address: 7 Beaumont Road, The Quarry, Headington, Oxford, OX3 8JN, England.

HAMPSHIRE Susan, b. 12 May 1942, London, England. Actress; Writer. m. (1) Pierre Granier-Deferre, divorced 1974, 1 son, (2) Eddie Kulukundis, 1980. Education: Knightsbridge, England. Appointments: Actress on the London stage, 1959-; Film and television appearances; Writer. Publications: Susan's Story: An Autobiographical Account of My Struggle with Dyslexia, 1982; The Maternal Instinct, 1985; Lucy Jane at the Ballet, 1987; Trouble Free Gardening, 1989; Lucy Jane on Television, 1989; Every Letter Counts, 1990; Lucy Jane and the Dancing Competition, 1990; Easy Gardening, 1992; Lucy Jane and the Russian Ballet, 1993; Rosie's First Ballet Lesson, 1995. Honours: Emmy Awards, 1970, 1971, 1973; Honorary doctorates, London University, 1984, St Andrew's University, 1986, Kingston University, 1994, Pine Manor College, Boston, Massachusetts, 1994; Officer of the Order of the British Empire, 1995. Memberships: Dyslexia Institute; Royal Society of Authors. Address: c/o Chatto and Linnit Ltd, 123a Kings Road, London SW3 4PL, England.

HAMPSON (Margaret) Daphne, b. 15 June 1944, Croydon, England. Academic. Education: BA, First Class, History and Political Institutions, University of Keele, England, 1966; D Phil, Faculty of Modern History, Oxford University, England,1974; Th M, 1976, Th D, 1983, Department of Theology, Harvard Divinity School, Harvard University, USA; MA with distinction, Continental Philosophy, Department of Philosophy, University of Warwick, England, 1994. Appointments: Instructor in British History, Department of History, University of North Carolina at Greensboro, USA, 1970-71; Teaching Fellow in Theology, Harvard University, USA, 1974; Lecturer, History of Religious Thought, Department of Philosophy, University of Stirling, Scotland, 1974-76; Lecturer,

Dictionary of International Biography

Systematic Theology, 1977, Senior Lecturer, 1994, Reader, 1999, Professor in Divinity (Post-Christian Thought), 2001-2003, School of Divinity, University of St Andrews, Scotland; Research and teaching at Oxford University in retirement, 2003-. Publications: Theology and Feminism, 1990; After Christianity, UK 1996, USA 1997, 2nd edition 2002; Swallowing a Fishbone? Feminist Theologians Debate Christianity (editor), 1996; Christian Contradictions: The Structures of Lutheran and Catholic Thought, 2001. Honours: Woodrow Wilson British Exchange Teacher, 1970-71; Knox Fellow, Harvard University, 1971-72, spring semester 1974, 1976-77; Leverhulme Research Grant, 1988-89; Visiting Academic, King's College, Cambridge, spring semester 1997, autumn semester, 1999; AHRB Research Leave Award, spring semester 2003; Visiting Fellow, Mansfield College, Oxford, Hilary and Trinity Terms 2003. Address: 27 West Street, Osney Island, Oxford OX2 0BQ, England. E-mail: daphne.hampson@theology.ox.ac.uk

HAMPSON Norman, b. 8 April 1922, Leyland, Lancashire, England. Retired University Professor. m. Jacqueline Gardin, 22 April 1948, 2 daughters. Education: University College Oxford, 1940-41, 1945-47. Publications: La Marine de l'An ll, 1959; A Social History of The French Revolution, 1963; The First European Revolution, 1963; The Enlightenment, 1968; The Life and Opinions of Maximilien Robespierre, 1974; A Concise History of the French Revolution, 1975; Danton, 1978; Will and Circumstance: Montesquieu, Rousseau and The French Revolution, 1983; Prelude to Terror, 1988; Saint-Just, 1991; The Perfidy of Albion, 1998; Not Really What You'd Call a War, 2001. Contributions to: Numerous magazines and journals. Honour: D Litt (Edinburgh), 1989. Memberships: Fellow, British Academy; Fellow, Royal Historical Society. Address: 305 Hull Road, York, Y010 3LU, England.

HAMPTON Christopher (James), b. 26 January 1946, Fayal, The Azores. Playwright. m. Laura de Holesch, 1971, 2 daughters. Education: Lancing College, Sussex, 1959-63; BA, Modern Languages, 1968, MA, New College, Oxford. Career: Resident Dramatist, Royal Court Theatre, London, 1968-70; Freelance Writer, 1970-. Publications: Tales from Hollywood, 1983; Tartuffe or The Imposter (adaptation of Moliére's play), 1984; Les Liaisons Dangereuses (adaptation of C de Laclos's novel), 1985; Hedda Gabler and A Doll's House (translations of Ibsen's plays), 1989; Faith, Hope and Charity (translator), 1989; The Ginger Tree (adaptation of Oscar Wynd's novel), 1989; White Chameleon, 1991; The Philanthropist and Other Plays, 1991; Sunset Boulevard, 1993; Alice's Adventures Underground, 1994; Carrington, 1995; Mary Reilly, 1996; The Secret Agent, 1996; Art (translator), 1996; Nostromo, 1997; An Enemy of the People (translator), 1997; The Unexpected Man (translator), 1998; Conversations After a Burial (translator), 2000; Life x Three, 2001; Three Sisters, 2003. Other: Screenplays, radio and television plays. Honours: Evening Standard Award, 1970, 1983, 1986; Plays and Players London Critics' Award, 1970, 1973, 1985; Los Angeles Drama Critics Circle Award, 1974; Laurence Olivier Award, 1986; New York Drama Critics' Award, 1987; Prix Italia, 1988; Writers Guild of America Screenplay Award, 1989; Oscar, 1989; BAFTA, 1990; Special Jury Award, Cannes Film Festival, 1995; 2 Tony Awards, 1995; Scott Moncrieff Prize, 1997; Officier, Ordre des Arts et des Lettres, 1998. Membership: Royal Society of Literature, fellow. Address: National House, 60-66 Wardour Street, London W1V 3HP, England.

HAN Ho Jae, b. 17 November 1965, Jeonnam, South Korea. Professor. m. Hyun Sook Park, 2 sons. Education: BS/DVM, Seoul National University, 1987; MS, 1989, PhD, 1993, Graduate School of Seoul National University. Appointments: Research Assistant,

Seoul National University, 1990-91; Researcher, State University of New York at Buffalo, 1992-93; Professor, Chonnam National University, 1993-; Editor, Journal of Veterinary Science, 1998-. Publications: Corresponding author, 52 papers; Co-author, 29 papers. Honours: Graduate with honours, Seoul National University, 1987; Award for Excellent Paper, 2002; Award for Young Scientist, 2003. Memberships: American Diabetes Association; Korean Society of Physiology; Korean Society of Veterinary Science; Korean Society of Nephrology. Address: College of Veterinary Medicine, Chonnam National University, 300 Yongbong-dong, Gwangju 500-757, Korea. E-mail: hjhan@chonnam.ac.kr

HAN Kihwan, b 7 April 1954, Daegu, Korea. Medical Doctor; Professor. m. Shinhyang Kim, 2 daughters. Education: MD, 1978, MSc, Medicine, 1981, PhD, 1989, Kyungpook National University, Korea. Certified Plastic Surgeon, Korean Board of Plastic and Reconstructive Surgery. Appointments: Intern, 1978-79, Resident, 1979-83, Chief, Department of Plastic and Reconstructive Surgery, 1994-, Dongsan Medical Centre, Daegu, Republic of Korea; Captain, Daegu Military Medical Centre, 1983-86; Professor, Keimyung University School of Medicine, 1986-; Visiting Professor, Harvard Medical School, Boston, USA, 1990-91. Publications: Plastic and Reconstructive Surgery, 1994; Aesthetic Plastic Surgery, 1998; Plastic Surgery for Students, 1999; Plastic Surgery in General Surgery, 2003. Memberships: Asian Pacific Cranio-Facial Association; American Cleft Palate-Craniofacial Association; American Society of Plastic and Reconstructive Surgeons. Address: Department of Plastic and Reconstructive Surgery, Keimyung University School of Medicine, Dongsan Medical Centre, 194, Dongsan-dong, Daegu 700-712 Korea. E-mail: khh@dsmc.or.kr

HAN Pao Teh, b. 19 August 1934, Shantung, China. Architect. m. Sun, Ning-Yu, 1 son, 1 daughter. Education: BS, National Cheng Kung University, 1958; March, Harvard University, 1965; MFA, Princeton University, 1967. Appointments: Architect; Chairman, Department of Architecture, Tunghai University; Dean, College of Science and Engineering, National Chung Hsing University; Director, National Museum of Natural Sciences; President, Tainan National College of the Arts, Chairman, National Culture and Arts Foundation; Columnist, China Times, China Daily; Director, Museum of World Religions. Publications: Spiritual Dimension of Architecture; Society, Culture and Architecture; The Story of Chinese Landscape Design; Recent Thought on Architecture and Culture. Honours: Education and Culture Medal; Outstanding Artist; First Golden Dragon Award of Chinese Literature and Architecture. Memberships: Chinese Association of Museums; Chinese Institute of Architecture; Chinese Institute of Urban Planning. Address: #61 Jen Ai Road, Section 2 Apt 5F-1, Taipei, Taiwan.

HAN Sheng, b. 16 February 1918, Xi-yang, Shanxi, China. Editor; Researcher. m. Ding Yu, 2 sons. Education: Industry School, Shanxi, 1936; Music Department, Lu Xun Art School on Taihang Campus. Appointments: Chief Editor, Magazine of Worker News, Taihang, Shanxi, China, 1941-47; Editor, Art Journal, Vice-Chief, Taihang Art Magazine, Taihang, Shanxi, China, 1947-49; Editor and Administrator for Arts Affairs, 1949-98, Chief Editor, 1998-, Yellow River Cultural Tribune, Taiyuan, Shaxi, China. Publications: Composed 14 plays and directed 27 Shanxi Operas; 6 books; 120 articles including: The Chinese Dramas Coming Out of Religious Rites (Research on Japan-Sino Culture, issue III); The Nuo Culture and Worship Drama in Shang Dang Area; A Collection of local dramas in Shanxi; A Collection of Opera Critiques. Honours: 2nd Prize, National Publication Exhibition, 1982; Honoured as "Peoples' Artist" by Shanxi Province, China, 1991. Memberships:

Dictionary of International Biography

China Association of Drama and Music, Vice-Chair; China Drama Literature Association, Senior Advisor; China Nuo Culture Association, Member of Standing Council. Address: 378#, Yingze da-jie, Taiyuan 030001, Shanxi, Peoples Republic of China.

HAN Younglim, b. Incheon, Republic of Korea. Professor of Shakespeare Studies. m. Sangho Shim. BA, 1980, MA, 1983, Ewha Womans University, Seoul, Republic of Korea; MLitt, 1990, PhD, 1997, University of Birmingham, England. Appointments: Lecturer, Korea University, Seoul, Republic of Korea, 1984-88; Lecturer, University of Suwon, Suwon, Republic of Korea, 1987-88; Lecturer, Ewha Womans University, Seoul, Republic of Korea, 1997; Interpreter, Birmingham City Council, West Midlands, England, 1990-93; Professor of English, Chungwoon University, Hongseong, Republic of Korea, 1998-2003; Professor of Shakespeare Studies, Kyungpook National University, Daegu, Republic of Korea, 2003-. Publications: Contributed chapters to books and articles to professional journals on Shakespeare on page, stage and film; Articles include: "Korea", The Oxford Companion to Shakespeare (ed. Michael Dobson and Stanley Wells), 2001; Author: Romantic Shakespeare: From Stage to Page, 2001. Honours: Students Scholarships, Ewha Womans University, 1977-79; Graduate Students Scholarships, Korea University, 1984-86; Overseas Research Students Awards, University of Birmingham, 1988-91; Research Fellowships, British Council, 1990-93. Memberships: International Shakespeare Conference; International Shakespeare Association; The Malone Society; Modern Language Association of America; Shakespeare Association of America; Shakespeare Association of Korea; English Language and Literature Association of Korea; Korean Association of Literature and Film; British and American Language and Literature Association of Korea; Modern British and American Drama Society of Korea; The Korean Society for Feminist Studies in English Literature. Address: Department of English Language and Literature, College of Humanities, Kyungpook National University, 1370 Sangyeok-Dong, Buk-Gu, Daegu 702-701, Republic of Korea.

HANDLEY Sandra L, b. 6 June 1938, Healdsburg, California, USA. Appraiser; Author. 1 son, 1 daughter. Education: Pacific Lutheran University, 1956-57; Senoma State University, 1968-71; Graduate Course Work, University of California-Berkeley, 1976-77. Appointments: Licensed Real Estate Appraiser; Vocational Teacher; Teacher and Counsellor, Meditation and Spiritual Life Skills; Consultant, Integrating Integrity into Business; Invited to teach University of Moscow, Russia; Real Estate and Vocational Education; State Chairperson, NRCC; Founder, ROHB; Dean of Secretarial College; Published Author. Publications: Death is Not the End; Lessons in Light; Living in Light. Honours: Woman of the Year, American Biographical Institute of International Research; Gold Medal Recipient, Small Business Council, NRCC; Teacher of the Year, Fort Bragg School District; Humanitarian of the Year; Listed in Who's Who publications and biographical dictionaries. Memberships: Appraisal Institute; ROHB. Address: 1275 Fourth Street #637, Santa Rosa, CA 95404. E-mail: slhand@msn.com

HANDY-RUFFIN Marie, b. 28 September 1916, Crittenden, Arkansas, USA. Educator. m. (1), 1 son, 1 daughter, (2) Norman William Ruffin. Education: Graduate, Business College, 1940; Music Qualification, Music College, 1941. Appointments: Educator; Family History Teacher; Real Estate Owner and Investor; Numerous political activities include: Invited by 2 prospective contenders for the US Presidency to serve on their 2000-member Founders Committee; Lobbyist, State Capitol Hill resulting in 2 new state laws and 1 national law; Invited to serve as Co-Chair for President George W Bush's Presidential Dinner, Washington DC, 2003; Chair, fund raising project for the restoration of a 114

year old mansion. Memberships: President, Conversation Club of Memphis; President, Overton Park Garden Club; Nineteenth Century Club; Scenic Hill's Women's Club; Republican Women's Club; Presidential Club; Memphis Brooks Art Museum; Dixon Art Gallery. Address: 3055 South Glengarry, Memphis, TN 38128-5105, USA

HANKIN Joseph Nathan, b. 6 April 1940, New York, USA. College President. m. Carole G Hankin, 2 sons, 1 daughter. Education: BA, Social Sciences, City College of New York, 1961; MA, History, Columbia University, 1962; DEd, Administration and Higher Education, Teachers College, Columbia University, 1967; Doctor of Letters, honoris causa, Mercy College, 1979; Doctor of Humane Letters, honoris causa, College of New Rochelle, 1996; Doctor of Pedagogy, honoris causa, Manhattan College, 2000. Appointments: Fellow, 1962-63, Lecturer, 1963-65, Department of History, City College of New York; Lecturer, Brooklyn College, City University of New York, 1963, Queens College, City University of New York, 1964; Course Assistant, Department of Higher and Adult Education, Teachers College, Columbia University, 1965; Director of the Evening Division and Summer Session, 1965-66, Director of Continuing Education and Summer Session, 1966-67, President, 1967-71, Harford Junior College; Adjunct Professor, Visiting Professor of Adult Education, Columbia University Teachers College, 1976-; President, Westchester Community College, 1971-. Publications: Numerous articles in professional journals. Honours include: Amicitia Linguarum Award for continued support of Foreign Language Study, Westchester Community College, 1996; Distinguished Alumni Award, Teachers College, Columbia University, 1997; Boy's Town of Italy, Educator of the Year Award, 1997; National Library Week Recognition Award, 2000; Certificate of Recognition of Thirty Years of Service, State University of New York, 2001; Certificate of Recognition, Association of Presidents of Public Community Colleges, 2001; Recipient, Lifetime Commitment Award, LD Access, 2001. Memberships include: American Association of University Professors; American Council on Education; American Diabetes Association; American Health Foundation; American Historical Association; American Lung Association. Address: 4 Merion Drive, Purchase, NY 10577-1302, USA.

HANKINSON Alan, b. 25 May 1926, Gatley, Cheshire, England. Writer. m. Roberta Lorna Gibson, 15 December 1951, divorced 1985, 1 son. Education: MA, History, Magdalen College, Oxford, 1949. Publications: The First Tigers, 1972; Camera on the Crags, 1975; The Mountain Men, 1977; Man of Wars, 1982; The Blue Box, 1983; The Regatta Men, 1988; A Century on the Crags, 1988; Coleridge Walks the Fells, 1991; Geoffrey Winthrop Young, 1995; Twelve Miles from a Lemon, 1996. Contributions to: Cumbria Life. Honours: Runner-Up, BP Arts Journalism, 1991; Portico Prize, 1991; Cumbria Book of the Year, 1992; Boardman Tasker Award, 1995. Address: 30 Skiddaw Street, Keswick, Cumbria CA12 4BY, England.

HANKS Tom, b. Oakland, California, USA. Actor. m. (1) Samantha Lewes, 2 children, (2) Rita Wilson, 1988, 2 sons. Career: Began acting with Great Lakes Shakespeare Festival; Appeared in Bosom Buddies, ABC TV, 1980; Films include: Splash; Bachelor Party; The Man with One Red Shoe; Volunteers; The Money Pit; Dragnet; Big; Punch Line; The Burbs; Nothing in Common; Every Time We Say Goodbye; Joe Versus the Volcano, 1990; The Bonfire of the Vanities, 1990; A League of Their Own, 1991; Sleepless in Seattle, 1993; Philadelphia, 1993; Forrest Gump, 1994; Apollo 13, 1995; That Thing You Do (also directed), 1997; Turner & Hooch, 1997; Saving Private Ryan, 1998; You've Got Mail, 1998; Cast Away, 1999; The Green Mile, 1999; Toy Story 2 (voice),

1999; From the Earth to the Moon, 1999; Road to Perdition, 2002; Catch Me If You Can, 2003. Honours: Academy Award, 1994, 1995. Membership: Board of Governors, Academy of Motion Picture Arts and Sciences, 2001-. Address: c/o CAA, 9830 Wilshire Boulevard, Beverly Hills, CA 90212, USA.

HANNAH Daryl, b. 1960, Chicago, Illinois, USA. Actress. Education: University of California at Los Angeles; Professional Training: Ballet tuition with Marjorie Tallchief, also studied with Stella Adler. Career: Film appearances include: The Fury; The Final Terror; Hard Country; Blade Runner; Summer Lovers; Splash; The Pope of Greenwich Village; Reckless; Clan of the Cave Bear; Legal Eagles; Roxanne; Wall Street; High Spirits; Steel Magnolias; Crazy People; At Play in the Fields of the Lord; Memoirs of an Invisible Man; Grumpy Old Men; Attack of the 50ft Woman; The Tie That Binds; Grumpier Old Men; Two Much; The Last Days of Frankie the Fly; Wild Flowers, 1999; My Favorite Martian, 1999; Dancing at the Blue Iguana, 2000; Cord, 2000; Speedway Junky, 2001; Jackpot, 2001; A Walk to Remember, 2002; Play: The Seven Year Itch, 2000; Directed: The Last Supper, 1994; A Hundred and One Nights, 1995. Address: c/o ICM, 8942 Wilshire Boulevard, Beverly Hills, CA 90211, USA.

HANNAH John, b. 1962, Glasgow, Scotland. Actor. m. Joanna Roth. Education: Royal Scottish Academy of Music and Drama. Career: Formerly electrician, formerly with Worker's Theatre Company; TV appearances include: McCallum; Joan; Faith; Rebus; Film appearances include: Four Weddings and a Funeral, 1994; Sliding Doors, 1998; The James Gang, 1999; The Mummy, 1999; The Mummy Returns, 2001; Pandaemonium, 2001.

HANNAH Judith Anna Challenger, b. 8 October 1948, Baltimore, Maryland, USA. Private Education Tutor. m. (1) Brian Challenger, 1968, divorced, 1994, 1 son, 1 daughter, (2) Rev W P Hannah, 2001. Education: Associate of Arts, Arlington Bible College, 1985; BS, Liberty University, 1991; MEd, Mount St Mary's College, 1996; Maryland State Teacher Certification, 1996-; Diploma, Institute of Children's Literature, Charter Oak College, 1997. Appointments: Assistant Teacher, K-4 Mill Valley School, Owing Mills, Maryland, 1984-85; Teacher, Arlington Baptist School, Baltimore, 1985-86; Nursery Teacher, Mill Valley School, 1986-87; Bookkeeper, Secretary, Challenger Engineering Inc, Finksburg, 1987-92; Assistant Director to Director, Before and After Child Care, ABC Care Inc, 1992-95; Teacher Internship for Master's degree, also long-term Substitute, Frederick County Schools, Maryland, 1995-96; Tutor, Office Manager, Learning Resources, Westminster, Maryland,1996-97; Private Tutor, President, Business Owner, A Lesson Learned Inc, Union Bridge, Maryland, 1997-; Publications: 94,520 People Can't Be Wrong, real estate article, 1981. Honours include: Delegation Member, People to People Ambassador Programme to China, 2001; People to People International, Global Peace, Egypt, 2003; Listed in several biographical dictionaries. Memberships: Volunteer, Crisis Hotline, Baltimore, 1972; Leader-Teacher, Pioneer Girls International, Arlington Baptist Church, 1975-78; Phi Lambda Theta, 1994-; Volunteers in Mission, 1997-; Emmaus, 1999-; International Dyslexia Association; Resident Member, Smithsonian Institution. Address: 48 Bucher John Road, Union Bridge, MD 21791, USA.

HANSEL William, b. 16 September 1918, Vale Summit, Maryland, USA. Professor of Physiology. m. Milbrey Downey, 2 daughters. Education: BS, University of Maryland, 1940; MS, Cornell University, 1947; PhD, 1949; Guggenheim Fellowship, University of Chicago, 1956; Lalor Foundation Fellow, Cornell University, 1960; National Science Foundation Senior Fellowship, CSIRO, Australia, 1966. Appointments: Assistant, Associate, Full

Professor, Cornell University, 1949-90; Chair, Physiology Department, 1978-83; Liberty Hyde Bailey Professor, 1983-90; Gordon D Cain Professor, Pennington Biomedical Research Centre, Louisiana State University, 1990. Publications: Around 300 publications in scientific journals. Honours: 13 national and international awards for research, including Senior Research Awards from 3 scientific societies for research in reproduction; First International Award for Lifetime Achievement in Ruminant Reproduction, 1998; Listed in numerous biographical dictionaries. Memberships: 12 professional societies, including 3 honorary societies. Address: Pennington Biomedical Research Centre, 6400 Perkins Road, Baton Rouge, LA 70808, USA. E-mail: hanselw@MHS.PBRC.edu

HANSEN-NORD Jørgen, b. 1 January 1954, Oksbøl, Denmark. Brigadier General. 1 son, 2 daughters. Education: Graduate, Danish Military Academy, 1978; Graduate, Junior Officers Command and Staff Course, 1982; Graduate, General Command and Staff Course, 1982; Graduate, Higher Command and Staff Course, Staff College, Camberley, England, 1996; Course on Legal Considerations for Military and Peace Keeping Operations, Naval Justice School, Newport, Rhode Island, USA, 1998; Senior Executive Course, George C Marshall European Center for Security Studies, Garmisch-Partenkirschen, Germany, 1999. Appointments: Danish Guard of Hussars, 1972; Advanced through ranks to Brigadier General, Danish Army; Commander, Tank Battalion, 1996; Commander, Danish Battalion for SFOR, 1997; Commanding Officer, Danish Reaction Brigade, assigned to NATO's Rapid Reaction Forces, 1997-2000; 3 staff positions, Ministry of Defence: Staff Officer 1st Division, 1986-91, Head of 1st Division, 1992-95, Deputy Permanent Secretary of State for Defence and National Armaments Director, 2000-2004; Currently, Danish National Liaison Representative to the Headquarters of Allied Command Transformation and to United States Joint Forces Command, Norfolk Virginia, USA. Honours include: Officer 1st Degree of the Order of Dannebroge; Army Commendation Medal; The UN-Medal, UNFICYP; The NATO Medal, Yugoslavia. Memberships: Former Chairman, Danish Maritime and Aeronautical Rescue Council; Chairman and member of numerous international committees. Address: 1357 Dunstan Lane, Virginia Beach, VA 23455, USA.

HANSON Albert L, b. 9 July 1952, Gainesville, Florida, USA. Physicist; Engineer. m. Anta LoPiccolo, 2 sons. Education: BS with Honors, Engineering Honors Program, North Carolina State University, 1974; MSE, 1976, PhD, 1979, University of Michigan. Appointments: Research Associate, 1979-81, from Assistant Physicist to Physicist, 1981-, Brookhaven National Laboratory, Upton, New York, USA. Publications: Contributed more than 50 articles to professional journals; 7 Reports for the US Government. Honour: Co-recipient, Research and Development 100 Award, 1988. Memberships: American Nuclear Society; American Association for the Advancement of Science; International Radiation Physics Society. Address: Brookhaven National Laboratory, Department of Energy Sciences and Technology, Building 475, Upton, NY 11973, USA. E-mail: alh@bnl.gov

HANSON Curtis, b. 24 March 1945, Los Angeles, USA. Film Director; Screenplay Writer. Career: Editor, Cinema magazine; Began film career as screenplay writer; Director, films: The Arousers, 1970; Sweet Kill (also screenplay), 1972; Little Dragons (also co-producer), 1977; Losin' It, 1983; The Bedroom Window (also screenplay), 1988; Bad Influence, 1990; The Hand That Rocks the Cradle, 1992; The River Wild, 1994; LA Confidential, 19988; The Children of Times Square (TV film); Wonder Boys, 1999; Screenplays: The Dunwich Horror, 1970; The Silent Partner, 1978; White Dog, 1982; Never Cry Wolf, 1983; Television:

Dictionary of International Biography

Hitchcock: Shadow of A Genius, 1999. Address: United Talent Agency, 9560 Wilshire Boulevard, Floor 5, Beverly Hills, CA 90212, USA.

HANSSON (Bror Rolf) Tommy, b. 21 November 1951, Södertälje, Sweden. Writer. m. Marika Bardel, 29 August 1982, 1 son, 1 daughter. Education: Cand Phil, Stockholm University, 1974; PhD, Political Science, Trinity College, Delaware, USA, 1992. Appointments: Member, Editorial Board, Idrottsbladet; Editor-in-Chief, Svenskt Skytte; Publisher, Editor, Contra Magazine; Ambassador for Peace, The Interreligious and International Federation for World Peace, 2001. Publications: Slavery in Our Time, 1989; Neutrality Myth, 1991; The October Scandal, 1991; Cold War Revisited, 1993; The War Criminal, 1998; Green Sweden, 1998; Shoot the King!, 2000; Evil Empires, 2002. Contributions to: Numerous national and international journals and magazines. Memberships: Publicist Club, Stockholm; Swedish Union of Theatre, Artists and Media, Stockholm; Member, 95 Taelghia lodge, Swedish chapter, Independent Order of Odd Fellows. Address: Rosenlundsvägen 22, 15230 Södertälje, Sweden.

HAO Kuang Tsai, b. 3 April 1961, Taiwan. Publisher of Children's Books. Education: Bachelor Degree, Department of Law, National Chengchi University, 1983. Appointments: Editor, Echo Magazine; Editor-in-Chief of Children's Books, Yuan-Liou Publishing Co Ltd; Publisher, Grimm Press, 1993-; Deputy Secretary General, National Cultural Association Taiwan, 2002-; Standing Director, The Jane Goodall Institute, Taiwan, 2002-. Publications: Contemporary books include most recently: Wings of Hope, 2000; Ill-Fortuned Mice Die Earlier, 2002; Billy and the Ball, 2003; Angie's Wings, 2003; The Giant and the Viola, 2003; Little Stone Buddha, 2003; Series include: Modern Fairy Tales, 1994; The History of Taiwan, 2001. Honours: UNICEF Prize, Illustrators of the Year; Most Creative Figure of the Year, Taiwan Kingstone Bookstore, 1995; BIB Honorary Mention of Publishing House, 1995; Member, International Selectors Committee for Bologna Illustrators Exhibition, 1996; Hsin Yi Golden Winner, Taiwan, 1998; Lecturer, "Illustrators Café", Bologna Illustrators Exhibition, 1998 and 2002; Listed in Who's Who publications and biographical dictionaries. Address: 7F, No 20 Sec 2 Hsin-Sheng Sth Rd, Taipei 106, Taiwan. E-mail: kt@cite.com.tw

HARALD V, b. 21 February 1937, Skaugum, Norway. King of Norway. m. Sonja Haraldsen, 1968, 1 son, 1 daughter. Education: Cavalry Officers Candidate School, Military Academy; Balliol College, Oxford. Career: Lived in Washington DC, 1940-45; Has participated in many international sailing competitions representing Norway at Olympic Games several times; Undertook frequent official visits abroad while Crown Prince; succeeded father, King Olav V, 1991. Address: Royal Palace, 0010 Oslo, Norway.

HARARY Keith, b. 9 February 1953, New York, USA. Research Scientist; Author; Science Journalist; Consultant. m. Darlene Moore. Education: PhD, Psychology, Graduate School of the Union Institute, 1986; BA (distinction), Psychology, Duke University, Durham, North Carolina, 1975; Specialised training in crisis and suicide intervention, individual and family counselling, Mental Health Centre, Durham, North Carolina, 1972-76. Appointments: Crisis Counselor, Durham Mental Health Centre, 1972-76; Research Associate, Psychical Research Foundation, 1973-76; Research Associate, Maimonides Medical Centre, 1976-79; Director of Counseling, Human Freedom Centre, 1979; Research Consultant, SRI International, Freelance Science Journalist, 1988-98; Editor at Large, Omni Magazine, 1995-98; President and Research Director, Institute for Advanced Psychology, 1986-. Publications: Author and co-author, numerous books and articles.

Memberships: American Psychological Association; Association for Media Psychology. Address: PO Box 2190, Portland, OR 97208-2190, USA.

HARCOURT Geoffrey (Colin), b. 27 June 1931, Melbourne, Australia. Academic; Professor Emeritus; Economist; Writer. m. Joan Margaret Bartrop, 30 July 1955, 2 sons, 2 daughters. Education: BCom, Honours, 1954, MCom, 1956, University of Melbourne; PhD, 1960, LittD, 1988, Cambridge University. Appointments: Professor Emeritus, University of Adelaide, 1988; President, Jesus College, Cambridge, 1988-89, 1990-92; Reader in the History of Economic Theory, Cambridge University, 1998; Emeritus Reader, History of Economic Theory, Cambridge, 1990-1998; Emeritus Fellow, Jesus College, Cambridge, 1998. Publications: Economic Activity (with P.H. Karmel and R.H. Wallace), 1967; Some Cambridge Controversies in the Theory of Capital, 1972; The Microeconomic Foundations of Macroeconomics (editor), 1977; The Social Science Imperialists (selected essays), 1982; Keynes and His Contemporaries: The Sixth and Centennial Keynes Seminar Held in the University of Kent at Canterbury (editor), 1985; Controversies in Political Economy (selected essays), 1986; On Political Economists and Modern Political Economy (selected essays), 1992; Post-Keynesian Essays in Biography: Portraits of Twentieth Century Political Economists, 1993; Capitalism, Socialism and Post-Keynesianism: Selected Essays, 1995; A "Second Edition" of The General Theory (editor, with P A Riach), 2 volumes, 1997; 50 Years a Keynesian and Other Essays, 2001; Selected Essays on Economic Policy, 2001; L'Economie rebelle de Joan Robinson, editor, 2001; Joan Robinson: Critical Assessments of Leading Economists, 5 volumes, editor with Prue Veu, 2002; Editing Economics: Essays in Honour of Mark Perlman, co-editor, 2002. Contributions to: Many books and scholarly journals. Honours: Economic Society of Australia, distinguished fellow, 1996; Honorary DLitt, De Montfort University, 1997; Honorary Fellow, Queen's College, University of Melbourne, 1998; Honorary DComm, Melbourne, 2003. Memberships: Fellow, Academy of the Social Sciences in Australia, 1971; President, Economic Society of Australia and New Zealand, 1974-77; Officer in the General Division of the Order of Australia (AO), 1994; Royal Economic Society. Address: Jesus College, Cambridge CB5 8BL, England.

HARDCASTLE Michael, (David Clark), b. 6 February 1933, Huddersfield, England. Author. m. Barbara Ellis Shepherd, 30 August 1979, 4 daughters. Appointment: Literary Editor, Bristol Evening Post, 1960-65. Publications: Author of over 140 children's books, 1966-; One Kick, 1986; James and the TV Star, 1986; Mascot, 1987; Quake, 1988; The Green Machine, 1989; Walking the Goldfish, 1990; Penalty, 1990; Advantage Miss Jackson, 1991; Dog Bites Goalie, 1993; One Good Horse, 1993; Soccer Captain, 1994; Puzzle, 1995; Please Come Home, 1995; Matthew's Goals, 1997; Carole's Camel, 1997; The Price of Football, 1998; Shoot-Out, 1998; Eye for a Goal, 1998; Goal-Getter, 1999; Injury Time, 1999; Rivals United, 1999; Danny's Great Goal, 1999; My Brother's a Keeper, 2000; Mine's a Winner, 2000; Sam's Dream, 2000; The Striker's Revenge, 2000; The Most Dangerous Score, 2001; Archie's Amazing Game, 2002. Contributions to: Numerous articles in magazines and journals. Honour; Member of the Order of the British Empire, 1988. Memberships: Federation of Children's Book Groups, national chair, 1989-90. Address: 17 Molescroft Park, Beverley, East Yorkshire HU17 7EB, England.

HARDIN James Michael, b. 14 March 1956, Mobile, Alabama, USA. Professor. Education: BA, magna cum laude, Mathematics, Philosophy, University West Florida, Pensacola, 1978; MS, Research Design and Statistics, Florida State University, Tallahassee, 1981; MA, Mathematics, 1984, PhD, Applied

Statistics, 1985, University of Alabama, Tuscaloosa. Appointments include: Assistant Professor, 1988-91, Associate Professor, 1991-96, Professor, Biostatistics and Biomathematics, 1996, Department of Biostatistics and Biomathematics, School of Public Health, Professor, Health Informatics, Department of Health Services Administration, School of Health Related Professions, 1996-, University of Alabama, Birmingham; Associate Professor, Nutrition Sciences, Department of Nutrition Sciences, School of Health Related Professions, 1993-, Associate Professor of Preventive Medicine, Division of Preventive Medicine, School of Medicine, 1993-, Associated Faculty of Developmental Psychology, Department of Psychology, 1993-, Associate Professor, Department of Counseling, Human Services and Foundations, School of Education, 1993-, Associate Professor, Gerontology Geriatric Medicine, Division of Gerontology and Geriatric Medicine, School of Medicine, 1994-, Professor of Medical Informatics, Division of Medical Informatics, Department of Internal Medicine, 1996-, Professor of Biostatistics and Biomathematics, 1997-, Professor of Computer Science, 1998-, Research Professor of Family and Community Medicine, School of Medicine, 2000-, Senior Scientist, Center for Aging, 2000-, University of Alabama, Birmingham, USA. Publications: Numerous articles in professional journals. Honours include: Outstanding Graduate Student, Applied Statistics, University of Alabama, 1984. Memberships: Healthcare Information and Management Systems Society; American Medical Informatics Association; Society for Clinical Trials; Society for Industrial and Applied Mathematics; Philosophy of Science Association; American Mathematics Society; Alabama Chapter, American Statistics Association; Institute of Mathematical Statistics; Biometric Society; American Statistics Association. Address: University of Alabama, Health Services Administration, 1530 3rd Avenue S, Birmingham, AL 35294-3361, USA.

HARDISH Patrick, b. Perth Amboy, New Jersey, USA. Librarian; Composer. Education: BA, Queens College, CUNY, 1976; MS, Pratt Institute, 1981; Juilliard School, 1969-72; Columbia University, graduate work, 1978-80; Bennington College composition seminar, 1980. Appointments: Library Assistant V, Columbia University, 1978-84; Co-Director and Co-Founder, Composers Concordance and its New Music Now Series, 1983-; Senior Librarian, New York Public Library, 1984-; Editorial Board, New Music Connoisseur, 1994-; Virginia Center for Creative Arts: Fellowships, 1981, 1982, 1986, 1988; Guest Composer Lectures, New York University, 2000. Publications: Reviews in music journal, Notes, 1985, 1994; Music: Sonorities IV (for saxophone), 1994; Sonorities III (for double bass), 1995; Sonorous (for saxophone quartet), 1998; 2 recordings. Honours: Meet the Composer awards, 1978, 1982 (2x), 1983, 1991, 1997; Margaret Fairbank-Jory Copying Assistance Program from the American Music Center. Memberships: St Ansgar's Scandinavian Catholic League; St George's Society of New York; American Music Center; Composers Guild of New Jersey (program committee); Music Library Association (and its New York Chapter); North American Guild of Change Ringers. Address: PO Box 36-20548, PABT, New York, NY 10129, USA. E-mail: pathardish@hotmail.com

HARDWICK David Francis, b. 24 January 1934, Vancouver, Canada. Pathologist; Professor. m. Margaret M, 1 son, 2 daughters. Education: MD, University of British Columbia, 1950-57. Appointments: Research Associate, Paediatrics, University of Southern California, 1960-62; Clinical Instructor, Pathology, 1963-65, Assistant Professor, Pathology, 1965-69, Associate Professor, Pathology, 1969-74, Professor, Pathology, 1974-99, Professor and Head, Pathology, 1976-90, Honorary Associate Professor, Paediatrics, 1972-87, Honorary Professor, Paediatrics, 1974-99, Special Advisor Planning, Medicine, 1997-, Professor Emeritus,

Pathology and Paediatrics, 1999-, University of British Columbia. Publications: Author and co-author of numerous refereed journals; books; chapters; abstracts; reports. Honours include: Certificate of Merit, Master Teacher Awards; University of British Columbia Teaching Excellence Award; Canadian Silver Jubilee Medal, 1978; President's Award for service to the University of British Columbia; LLD honoris causa, University of British Columbia, 2001; Senior Member, Canadian Medical Association, 2002; Gold Medal, International Academy of Pathology, 2002; President's Award, US and Canadian Academy of Pathology, 2004. Memberships include: BC Association of Pathologists; Canadian Association of Pathologists; Society for Paediatric Pathology; International Academy of Pathology. Address: Dean's Office, Faculty of Medicine, University of British Columbia, #317-2194 Health Sciences Mall, Vancouver, British Columbia, Canada V6T 1Z3. E-mail: david.f.hardwick@ubc.ca

HARDWICK Elizabeth, b. 27 July 1916, Lexington, Kentucky, USA. Writer; Critic; Teacher. m. Robert Lowell, 28 July 1949, divorced 1972, 1 daughter. Education: AB, 1938, MA, 1939, University of Kentucky; Columbia University. Appointments: Co-Founder and Advisory Editor, New York Review of Books, 1963-; Adjunct Associate Professor of English, Barnard College. Publications: Fiction: The Ghostly Lover, 1945; The Simple Truth, 1955; Sleepless Nights, 1979. Non-fiction: The Selected Letters of William James (editor), 1960; A View of My Own: Essays on Literature and Society, 1962; Seduction and Betrayal: Women and Literature, 1974; Rediscovered Fiction by American Women: A Personal Selection (editor), 18 volumes, 1977; Bartleby in Manhattan (essays), 1984; The Best American Essays 1986 (editor), 1986; Sight Readings: American Fictions (essays), 1998; Herman Melville, A Life, 2000. Contributions to: Periodicals. Honour: Gold Medal, American Academy and Institute of Arts and Letters, 1993. Address: 15 West 67th Street, New York, NY 10023, USA.

HARDY Alan William, b. 10 March 1951, Luton, Bedfordshire, England. Teacher; Poet. m. Sibylle Mory, 24 August 1985, 1 daughter. Education: BA, English and Italian Literature, 1973, MA, Comparative Literature, 1976, Warwick University; Dip TEFL, Christ Church College, Kent University, 1983. Appointments: English Teacher, Sir Joseph Williamson's Mathematical School, Rochester, Kent; English Language Teacher, Whitehill Estate School of English, Flamstead, Hertfordshire. Publication: Wasted Leaves, 1996. Contributions to: Orbis; Envoi; Iota; Poetry Nottingham; The Interpreter's House; South; Poetic Licence; Braquemard; Fire; Borderlines. Honour: 2nd Prize, Hastings National Poetry Competition, 1994. Address: Whitehill Estate School of English, Flamstead, St Albans, Hertfordshire AL3 8EY, England.

HARDY Robert, b. 29 October 1925. Actor; Author. m. (1) Elizabeth Fox, 1 son. (2) Sally Pearson, 2 daughters. Career: Theatre appearances include: 4 seasons of Shakespeare, Stratford-on-Avon, 2 at Old Vic; World tours include Henry V and Hamlet, USA; Numerous appearances London and Broadway theatres, 1952-; Writer and/or presenter numerous TV programmes including The Picardy Affair, The History of the Longbow, Heritage, Horses in Our Blood, Gordon of Khartoum; Other TV appearances include: Prince Hal and Henry V in Age of Kings; Prince Albert in Edward VII; Malcolm Campbell in Speed King; Winston Churchill in the Wilderness Years; Siegfried Farnon in All Creatures Great and Small; Twiggy Rathbone and Russell Spam in Hot Metal; The Commandant in the Far Pavilions; Sherlock Holmes; Inspector Morse; Middlemarch; Castle Ghosts; Gulliver's Travels; Films include: How I Won the War; Yellow Dog; Dark Places; Young Winston; Ten Rillington Place; Le Silencieux; Gawain and the

Green Knight; The Spy Who Came in From the Cold; La Gifle; Robin Hood; The Shooting Party; Paris By Night; War and Remembrance; Mary Shelley's Frankenstein; Sense and Sensibility; Mrs Dalloway; The Tichborne Claimant, 1998; An Ideal Husband, 1999; The Gathering, 2001. Publications: Longbow, 1976; The Great War Bow, 2000. Honour: Hon DLitt (Reading), 1990. Memberships: Consultant, Mary Rose Trust, 1979-, Trustee, 1991-; Trustee, Roy Armouries, 1984-; Master of Worshipful Company of Bowyers, 1988-90. Address: c/o Chatto & Linnit, 13A King's Road,, London, SW3 4PL, England.

HARE David, b. 5 June 1947, St Leonards, Sussex, England. Dramatist; Director. m. (1) Margaret Matheson, 1970, divorced 1980, 2 sons, 1 daughter, (2) Nicole Farhi, 1992. Education: Lancing College; MA, Honours, Jesus College, Cambridge. Appointments: Founder, Portable Theatre, 1968, Joint Stock Theatre Group, 1975, Greenpoint Films, 1982; Literary Manager and Resident Dramatist, Royal Court, 1969-71; Resident Dramatist, Nottingham Playhouse, 1973; Associate Director, National Theatre, 1984-88, 1989-. Plays: Slag, 1970; The Great Exhibition, 1972; Knuckle, 1974; Brassneck, 1974; Fanshen, 1976; Teeth 'n' Smiles, 1976; Plenty, 1978; Licking Hitler, 1978; Dreams of Leaving, 1980; A Map of the World, 1982; Saigon, 1983; The History Plays, 1984; Pravda, 1985; Wetherby, 1985; The Asian Plays, 1986; The Bay at Nice and Wrecked Eggs, 1986; The Secret Rapture, 1988; Paris by Night, 1989; Straples, 1990; Racing Demon, 1990; Writing Lefthanded, 1991; Heading Home, 1991; The Early Plays, 1991; Murmuring Judges, 1991; The Absence of War, 1993; Asking Around, 1993; Skylight, 1995; Mother Courage, 1995; Skylight, 1995; Ivanov, 1996; Amy's View, 1997; The Judas Kiss, 1998; The Blue Room, 1998; Via Dolorosa, 1998; My Zinc Bed, 2000; Royal Court, 2000; Via Dolorosa, 2000; The Hours, 2001; Lee Miller, 2001. Honours: John Llewellyn Rhys Award, 1974; BAFTA Award, 1978; New York Drama Critics' Circle Award, 1983; London Standard Award, 1985; Plays and Players Awards, 1985, 1990; Drama Award, 1988; Olivier Award, 1990; Critic's Circle Best Play of the Year, 1990; Time Out Award, 1990. Membership: Royal Society of Literature, fellow. Address: c/o Margaret Ramsay Ltd, 14a Goodwins Court, St Martins Lane, London WC2, England.

HAREWOOD The Earl of (George Henry Hubert Lascelles), b. 7 February 1923, London, England. Musical Administrator. m. (1) Maria Donata Stein, 1949, divorced 1967, (2) Patricia Tuckwell, 1967, 4 sons. Education: King's College, Cambridge University. Career includes: Board Directors, 1951-53, 1969-72, Administrative Executive, 1953-60, Royal Opera House, Covent Garden, London; Chairman, British Council Music Advisory Committee, 1956-66; Director General, 1958-74, Chairman, 1988-90, Leeds Musical Festival; Artistic Director, Edinburgh International Festival, 1961-65; Arts Council Music Panel, 1966-72; Artistic Advisor, New Philharmonic Orchestra, 1966-76; General Advisory Council, BBC, 1969-77; Managing Director, Sadler's Wells Opera, 1972; Managing Director, 1974-85, Chairman, 1986-95, English National Opera; Governor of BBC, 1985-87; President, British Board of Film Classification, 1985-96; Artistic Director, Adelaide Festival, 1988; Artistic Advisor, Buxton Festival, 1993-98. Publications: Editor, Opera, 1950-53; Editor and compiler, Kobbé's Complete Opera Book, 1954, 1973, 1987, 1989, 1997; Autobiography, The Tongs and The Bones, 1982; Kobbé's Illustrated Opera Books, 1989; Pocket Kobbé, 1994. Honours include: KBE, 1987. Address: Harewood House, Leeds, LS17 9LG, England.

HARINGTON Allen Abraham, b. 17 August 1956, Sasolburg, South Africa. Businessman; Director of Companies. m. Amanda Magdalena Arnold, 2 sons, 1 daughter. Appointments: President,

Celtron International Inc.; Director, Celtron International Limited; Chairman, Orbtech Holdings Limited; Director, Orbtech Tracking Systems Limited, Buddi-Trace (Pty) Ltd, Mine Work International (Pty) Ltd. Honour: Listed in Who's Who publications and biographical dictionaries. Address: 120 (a) West Road North, Morningside, Sandton, South Africa.

HARJO Joy, b. 9 May 1951, Tulsa, Oklahoma, USA. 1 son, 1 daughter. Education: BA, University of New Mexico 1976; MFA, University of Iowa, 1978; Non-degree, Film-making, Anthropology, Film Centre, 1982; Native Screenwriters Workshop, Sundance Institute, 1998; Summer Songwriting Workshop, Berklee School of Music, 1998. Appointments: Assistant Professor, Department of English, University of Colorado, 1985-88; Associate Professor, Department of English, University of Arizona, 1988-90; Professor, Department of English, University of New Mexico, 1991-97; President, Mekko Rabbit Production Inc, 1992-; Visiting Writer, UCLA Department of English, 1998; Professor, UCLA, 2001-. Publications: She Had Some Horses, 1985; Secrets from the Centre of the World, 1989; In Mad Love & War, 1990; The Woman Who Fell From the Sky, 1994; Reinventing the Enemy's Language; A Map To The Next World, poems and tales, 2000; The Good Luck Cat, children's book, 2000; How We Became Human, New and Selected Poems, W W Norton, 2002; CD: Native Joy for Real, Joy Harjo, Mekko Prod; CD: Letter from the End of the 20th Century, music and poetry with her band Joy Harjo and Poetic Justice, 1997. Honours: National Council on the Arts; The London Observer Best Book of 1997 (Reinventing the Enemy's Language); Lila Wallace Reader's Digest Writers Award, 1998-2000; Honorary Doctorate, St Mary-in-the-Woods College, 1998; First American in the Arts, Outstanding Medal of Achievement, 1998; Lifetime Achievement in the Arts, National Writers Circle of America; Western Literature Distinguished Achievement Award, 2000; Oklahoma Book Arts Lifetime Achievement, 2002. Membership: Board of Directors, Russell Moore Foundation; Board of Directors, Arts Research. Address: Mekko Productions Inc, 1140 D Alewa Drive, Honolulu, HI 96817, USA.

HARKNETT Terry, (Frank Chandler, David Ford, George G Gilman, William M James, Charles R Pike, James Russell, William Terry), b. 14 December 1936, Rainham, Essex, England. Writer. Appointments: Editor, Newspaper Features Ltd, 1958-61; Reporter and Features Editor, National Newsagent, 1961-72. Publications: (as George G Gilman), Edge series: The Godforsaken, 1982; Arapaho Revenge, 1983; The Blind Side, 1983; House of the Range, 1983; Edge Meets Steele No 3 Double Action, 1984; The Moving Cage, 1984; School for Slaughter, 1985; Revenge Ride, 1985; Shadow of the Gallows, 1985; A Time for Killing, 1986; Brutal Border, 1986; Hitting Paydirt, 1986; Backshort, 1987; Uneasy Riders, 1987. Adam Steele series: Canyon of Death, 1985; High Stakes, 1985; Rough Justice, 1985; The Sunset Ride, 1986; The Killing Strain, 1986; The Big Gunfight, 1987; The Hunted, 1987; Code of the West, 1987. The Undertaker series: Three Graves to a Showdown, 1982; Back from the Dead, 1982; Death in the Desert, 1982. As William Terry: Red Sun (novelization of screenplay), 1972. As Frank Chandler: A Fistful of Dollars (novelization of screenplay), 1972. As Charles R Pike: Jubal Cade series: The Killing Trail, 1974; Double Cross, 1974; The Hungary Gun, 1975. As William M James: Apache series: The First Death, 1974; Duel to the Death, 1974; Fort Treachery, 1975. As Terry Harknett: The Caribbean, 1972. As James Russell: The Balearic Islands, 1972. As David Ford: Cyprus, 1973. Address: Spring Acre, Springhead Road, Uplyme, Lyme Regis, Dorset DT7 3RS, England.

HARMON Maurice, b. 21 June 1930, Dublin, Ireland. Professor Emeritus; Writer; Editor. Education: BA, 1951, HDE, 1953, MA, 1955, PhD, 1961, University College, Dublin; AM, Harvard

University, 1957. Appointments: Lecturer in English, 1965-74, Associate Professor of Anglo-Irish Literature and Drama, 1975-90, Professor Emeritus, 1990-, University College, Dublin; Editor, University Review, 1970-86. Publications: Séan O'Faoláin: A Critical Introduction, 1966; Modern Irish Literature 1800-1967: A Reader's Guide, 1967; Fenians and Fenianism: Centenary Papers (editor), 1968; The Celtic Master: Contributions to the first James Joyce Symposium, 1969; Romeo and Juliet, by Shakespeare (editor), 1970; J M Synge Centenary Papers 1971 (editor), 1972; King Richard ll, by Shakespeare (editor), 1971; Coriolanus, by Shakespeare (editor), 1972; The Poetry of Thomas Kinsella, 1974; The Irish Novel in Our Time (editor with Patrick Rafroidi), 1976; Select Bibliography for the Study of Anglo-Irish Literature and Its Backgrounds, 1976; Richard Murphy: Poet of Two Traditions (editor), 1978; Irish Poetry After Yeats: Seven Poets (editor), 1979, 3rd edition, 1998; Image and Illusion: Anglo-Irish Literature and Its Contexts (editor), 1979; A Short History of Anglo-Irish Literature From Its Origins to the Present (with Roger McHugh), 1982; The Irish Writer and the City (editor), 1985; James Joyce: The Centennial Symposium (with Morris Beja et al), 1986; Austin Clarke: A Critical Introduction, 1989; The Book of Precedence (poems), 1994; Séan O'Faoláin: A Life, 1994; A Stillness at Kiawah (poems), 1996; No Author Better Served: The Correspondence of Samuel Becket & Alan Schneider, 1998; The Last Regatta (poems), 2000; The Colloquy of the Old Men (translator and editor), 2001; The Dolmen Press: A Celebration (editor), 2001; Tales of Death (poems), 2001; Poetry Ireland Review (editor), 2001-02. Address: 20 Sycamore Road, Mount Merrion, Blackrock, County Dublin, Ireland.

HARNICK Sheldon Mayer, b. 30 April 1924, Chicago, Illinois, USA. Lyricist. m. (1) Mary Boatner, 1950, (2) Elaine May, 1962, (3) Margery Gray, 1965, 1 son, 1 daughter. Education: Northwestern University. Career: Contributor to revues: New Faces of 1952; Two's Company, 1953; John Murray Anderson's Almanac, 1954; The Shoestring Revue, 1955; The Littlest Revue, 1956; Shoestring 1957, 1957; with composer Jerry Bock: Body Beautiful, 1958; Fiorello, 1959; Tenderloin, 1960; Smiling The Boy Fell Dead (with David Baker), 1961; She Loves Me, 1963; Fiddler On The Roof, 1964; The Apple Tree, 1966; The Rothschilds, 1970; Captain Jinks Of The Horse Marines (opera with Jack Beeson), 1975; Rex (with Richard Rodgers), 1976; Dr Heidegger's Fountain Of Youth (opera with Jack Beeson), 1978; Gold (cantata with Joe Raposo), 1980; Translations: The Merry Widow, 1977; The Umbrellas Of Cherbourg, 1979; Carmen, 1981; A Christmas Carol, 1981; Songs Of The Auvergne (musical; book; lyrics), 1982; The Appeasement of Aeolus, 1990; Cyrano, 1994. Address: Kraft, Haiken & Bell, 551 Fifth Avenue, 9th Floor, New York, NY 10176, USA.

HARNISCH Jörg-Henner, b. 27 February 1949, Halle/S, Germany. Scientist; Researcher; Managing Director. m. Svetlana, Baroness von Treskov, 1 son. Education: Proficiency in English Certificate, Cambridge University, 1970; Habilitation/Script, The Theories of Language and the Science of Language, 1974; 1st Staatsexamen American/British Philologies Literature, General Linguistics; American English Politics, 1975. Appointments: Lecturer at the University, Mass Media and Foreign Language Teaching, 1975; 2nd Staatsexamen in English and Politics/ Gemeinschaftskunde with very good results in the final written and oral examination, Oberprima, Oberstufe Gymnasium, 1977; Lecturer in Didactics and Methodics of English, 1978; Editor and Senior Editor, Senior Lecturer in various publishing houses, 1978; Publisher of scientific journal, USA, Great Britain, 1979-91; Director, Institute of Cultural and Economic Analyses, USA, Great Britain, 1988-2004. Publications: Various as an editor and publisher or senior editor in several publishing houses and in various

languages; Foreign Language Learning Theories & Behaviorism, 1974; Foreign Language Theories with Teaching Material, 1977; Financial and Economic Analyses of Great Britain, USA, 1994; The Philosophies of Pragmatism in the USA in the 20th Century; Language-Philosophies and the Science of Language, Charles Sanders Peirce, William James, etc, 1990; The Philosophies and Language-Philosophies of Pragmatism in the USA in the 20th Century; 2nd Habilitation Script, 1993; Intellectual Programs and Concepts for the West German Universities in the 70s and 80s, 1976, 1986; Research Program & Research Studies, Vol 1-7, 8-10 in preparation, 1990-2004; Linguistics, American Language-Philosophies of Pragmatism, Formal Logic, etc. Memberships: President, Friends of the Club of Pragmatism; International Research Committees on Sociolinguistics, Netherlands, 1992; International Communication Studies, USA, 1996; Crossroads in Cultural Studies, Finland, 1998. Address: 36037 Fulda, Rhönstrasse 13, West Germany.

HARPER Marjory-Ann Denoon, b. 6 April 1956, Blackpool, Lancashire, England. University Lecturer. m. Andrew J Shere, 22 August 1991. Education: MA, Honours, History, 1978, PhD, 1984, University of Aberdeen. Publications: Emigration from North East Scotland: Willing Exiles, 1988; Emigration from North East Scotland: Beyond the Broad Atlantic, 1988; Emigration from Scotland between the Wars: Opportunity or Exile, 1998; Adventurers and Exiles: The Great Scottish Exodus, 2003. Contributions to: History Today; British Journal of Canadian Studies; The Scottish Historical Review; Northern Scotland; Southwestern Historical Quarterly; Aberdeen Leopard; The Weekend Scotsman; Glasgow Herald; The Highlander. Memberships: Royal Historical Society, fellow; British Association of Canadian Studies. Address: School of Divinity, History and Philosophy, University of Aberdeen, Old Aberdeen AB24 3FX, Scotland.

HARRELL Margaret Ann, b. 25 September 1940, North Carolina, USA. Writer. m. Jan Mensaert, 25 February 1970. Education: BA, History, Duke University, Durham, North Carolina, USA, 1962; MA, Contemporary British and American Literature, Columbia University, 1964; Graduate Studies, C G Jung Institute, Kusnacht, Zurich, 1984-87; Energy Studies, Graduate Certificates, Basic Applications of Psycho-Dynamics, 1989-1992; Graduate, 1992, Luminessence Light Body, 1992-, Registered Teacher, Awakening Your Light Body, 2002-; Radiance: Self-Exciting, 2004-. Appointments: Assistant Editor, United Feature Syndicate, 1964; Copy Editor, Assistant Editor, Random House Publishing, 1965-68; Dance Instructor and national contest winner, double first place, 1969; Assistant to Psychologist, 1983-84; Freelance Editor, 1970-; Co-organizer, International Workshops Belgium, 1992-97; Editing Co-ordinator, 'Life, Page One' Retrospective, electronic book of essays by an international team of contributors, poems and illustrations; plus 2 music CD roms and live performance, "het Toreke" Museum, 1996-2001; Random number generator research; Frequent contributor, Exceptional Human Experience Newsletter, 2001-03; Journal, 2004. Publications include: Contributor, When The Wide Sky is Falling, (Dutch), 1993; Invocation to Masters of the Past (Romanian) 1994; The Milton Klonsky I Knew, 1995; Paper, A Call to Excelsus, Reminiscences of Dr J B Rhine and Arthur Koestler, 1995; Love in Transition, Volumes I-IV, 1996-98; Marking Time with Faulkner, 1999; Space Encounters: Chunking Down the 21st Century, Vols I-II, 2002; Inserting Consciousness into Collision, Vol III, 2003; Toward a Philosophy of Perception: The Magnitude of Human Potential – Cloud Optics, 2004; Play: Notes from The Eagles Nest, 1996. Honours: On-site Monitor, Ford Foundation Grant, 1963; 3 times Fellow MacDowell Colony for Artists, 1969, 1970, 1972. Memberships: Save the Children; American Association for the

Advancement of Science; American Society for Psychical Research; Publishers Marketing Association; Wildlife Organizations; Listed in Who's Who publications and biographical dictionaries. Address: Duraleigh Woods Apts, 4511 Mimosa Tree Lane, # 1201, Raleigh, NC 27612, USA. Website: http://www.marharrell.com

HARRELSON Woody, b. 23 July 1961, Midland, Texas, USA. Actor. m. Laura Louie, 1997, 1 child. Education: Hanover College. Career: Theatre includes: The Boys Next Door; 2 on 2 (author, producer, actor); The Zoo Story (author, actor); Brooklyn Laundry; Furthest from the Sun; On An Average Day; TV includes: Cheers; Bay Coven; Killer Instinct; Films include: Wildcats; Cool Blue; LA Story; Doc Hollywood; Ted and Venus; White Men Can't Jump; Indecent Proposal; I'll Do Anything; The Cowboy Way; Natural Born Killers; Money Train; The Sunchaser; The People vs Larry Flint; Kingpin; Wag the Dog, 1997; The Thin Red Line, 1998; EdTV, 1999; Play It to the Bone, 2000; American Saint, 2000. Address: c/o Creative Artists Agency, 9830 Wilshire Boulevard, Beverly Hills, CA 90212, USA.

HARRIS Angela Felicity (Baroness Harris of Richmond), b. 4 January 1944, St Annes-on-Sea, Lancashire, England. Member of the House of Lords. m. John Philip Roger Harris, 1 son from previous marriage. Education: Ealing Hotel and Catering College. Appointments: Member, Richmond Town Council, 1978-81, 1991-99, Mayor of Richmond, 1993-94; Member, 1979-89, Chairman, 1987-88, Richmondshire District Council; Member, 1981-2001, First Woman Chair, 1991-92, North Yorkshire County Council; Deputy Chair, Association of Police Authorities, 1997-2001; Chair, North Yorkshire Police Authority, 1994-2001; Appointed to House of Lords, 1999; Member, Refreshment Select Committee, 2000-, Member, EU Select Committee, 2000-, Chair, EU Select Sub-Committee, 2000-, House of Lords. Honours: Deputy Lieutenant of North Yorkshire, 1994; Created Liberal Democrat Life Peer, 1999. Memberships: Member, Court of the University of York, 1996-; Former Member: Service Authority, national Crime Squad, 1997-2000, Police Negotiating Board, 1995-2001; Former Justice of the Peace, 1982-98; Former, NHS Trust Non-Executive Director, 1990-97. Address: House of Lords, London, SW1A 0PW. E-mail: harrisa@parliament.uk

HARRIS Edward Allen (Ed), b. 28 November 1950, Englewood, New Jersey, USA. Actor. m. Amy Madigan. Education: Columbia University; University of Oklahoma, Norman; California Institute of Arts. Career: Stage appearances include: A Streetcar Named Desire; Sweetbird of Youth; Julius Caesar; Hamlet; Camelot; Time of Your Life; Grapes of Wrath; Present Laughter; Fool for Love; Prairie Avenue; Scar, 1985; Precious Sons, 1986; Simpatico, 1994; Taking Sides, 1996; Films include: Come, 1978; Borderline, 1978; Knightriders, 1980; Creepshow, 1981; The Right Stuff, 1982; Swing Shift, 1982; Under Fire, 1982; A Flash of Green, 1983; Places in the Heart, 1983; Alamo Bay, 1984; Sweet Dreams, 1985; Code Name: Emerald, 1985; Walker, 1987; To Kill a Priest, 1988; Jacknife, 1989; The Abyss, 1989; State of Grace, 1990; Paris Trout, 1991; Glengarry Glen Ross, 1992; Needful Things, 1993; The Firm, 1993; China Moon, 1994; Milk Money, 1994; Apollo 13, 1995; Just Cause, 1995; Eye for an Eye, 1995; The Rock, 1996; Riders of the Purple Sage, 1996; Absolute Power, 1997; Stepmom, 1998; The Truman Show, 1998; The Third Miracles, 1999; Enemy at the Gates, 2001; A Beautiful Mind, 2001; The Hours, 2002; TV films include: The Amazing Howard Hughes, 1977; The Seekers, 1979; The Aliens are Coming, 1980; The Last Innocent Man, 1987; Running Mates, 1992; The Stand, 1994. Address: 22031 Carbon Mesa Road, Malibu, CA 90265, USA.

HARRIS Emily Louise, (Emily Brown), b. 16 November 1932, New London, Connecticut, USA. Special Educator. m. John E, 10 September 1955, 1 son, 1 daughter. Education: BS, University of Connecticut, 1955; MEd, Northeastern University, 1969; Certificate, Nursing Assistant, Hebrew Rehabilitation Centre, Roslindale, Massachusetts, 1973-75; Certificate, Special Education; Reading Teacher; Supervisor, Secondary Principal Certificate. Appointments: Teacher, New Haven, Connecticut School Department, 1957-59; Teacher, Boston School Department, 1966-68; Natick, Massachusetts School Department, 1969-72; Boston School Department, 1973-. Publications: Cooking with stars; School to work; Many articles to professional journals. Honours: Teaching Award, Urban League Guild; Martin Luther King Scholarship; Zeta Phi Beta Graduate Chapter Zeta of the Year. Memberships: Alpha Delta Kappa International Honorary Sorority for Women in Education; Kappa Delta Pi Honorary Society; Prince Hall Grand Chapter Order of East Stars-past Worthy Matron, Zeta Phi Beta Sorority; Phi Delta Kappa; National Honorary Society. Address: 36 Dietz Road, Hyde Park, MA 02136, USA.

HARRIS Rolf, b. 30 March 1930, Perth, Australia. Entertainer; Singer; Musician (piano, accordion, digeridoo, wobbleboard); Artist. m. Alwen Myfanwy Wiseman Hughes, 1 March 1958, 1 daughter. Education: West Australian University. Musical Education: Piano Grade 1, AMEB. Career: International television entertainer, artist and host, Cartoon Time; Animal Hospital; Exhibition, Rolf on Art, National Gallery, London, 2002. Recordings: Numerous singles include: Tie Me Kangaroo Down Sport; Jake The Peg; Two Little Boys; Stairway To Heaven; Sun Arise; The Court of King Caractacus. Publications: 12 titles including: How To Write Your Own Pop Song; Can You Tell What It Is Yet?, autobiography. Honours: OBE; AM. Membership: Equity. Address: c/o 174-178 North Gower Street, London NW1 2NB, England.

HARRIS Rosemary (Jeanne), b. 23 February 1923, London, England. Author. Appointments: Children's Book Reviewer, The Times, London, 1970-73. Publications: The Summer-House, 1956; Voyage to Cythera, 1958; Venus with Sparrows, 1961; All My Enemies, 1967; The Nice Girl's Story, 1968 (in USA as Nor Evil Dreams, 1974); The Moon in the Cloud, 1968; A Wicked Pack of Cards, 1969; The Shadow on the Sun, 1970; The Seal-Singing, 1971; The Child in the Bamboo Grove, 1972; The Bright and Morning Star, 1972; The King's White Elephant, 1973; The Double Snare, 1974; The Lotus and the Grail: Legends from East to West (abridged edition in USA as Sea Magic and Other Stories of Enchantment), 1974; The Flying Ship, 1975; The Little Dog of Fo, 1976; Three Candles for the Dark, 1976; I Want to Be a Fish, 1977; A Quest for Orion, 1978; Beauty and the Beast (folklore), 1979; Green Finger House, 1980; Tower of the Stars, 1980; The Enchanted Horse, 1981; Janni's Stork, 1981; Zed, 1982; Summers of the Wild Rose, 1987; Love and the Merry-Go-Round, 1988; Ticket to Freedom, 1991; The Wildcat Strike, 1995; The Haunting of Joey M'basa. 1996. Honour: Library Association Carnegie Medal, 1967. Membership: Society of Authors. Address: c/o A P Watt Ltd, 20 John Street, London WC1N 2DR, England.

HARRIS Thomas, b. 1940, Jackson, Tennessee, USA. Writer. m. divorced, 1 daughter. Education: Baylor University, Texas, USA. Appointments: Worked on newsdesk Waco News-Tribune; Member, Staff, Associated Press, New York. Publications: Black Sunday; Red Dragon (filmed as Manhunter); The Silence of the Lambs (filmed). Address: St Martin's Press, 175 Fifth Avenue, New York, NY 10010, USA.

HARRIS HOLSAPPLE Linda Elizabeth, b. 20 November 1948, New Rochelle, New York, USA. Editor. m. Earle T Holsapple III, 1 son, 1 daughter. Education: Loyola Rome Center, Rome, Italy, 1970; BSc, Loyola University of Chicago, 1971; MA in Higher Educational Administration, Catholic University, Washington DC, 1973; Postgraduate studies, University of Virginia, 1975; Diploma di Merito in Italian, Wayne State University, 2000; Scola Leonardo Da Vinci, Rome, Italy, 2002. Appointments: Associate Director of Admissions, Rutgers University, Newark, New Jersey, 1973-74; Editor, Member Newsletter, Communications Specialist, 1977-85, Rutgers Community Health Plan, New Brunswick, New Jersey; Director of Business Development, SciTech Development LLC, Detroit, Michigan, 2002. Publications: Authored or collaborated on numerous articles, annual reports, brochures, newsletters, videos, television pieces. Honours: Dean's List, Loyola University, Chicago; Diploma Di Merito in Italian, Italian American Cultural Society, 2000; Certificato Di Frequenza, Scola Leonardo Da Vinci, Rome, Italy, 2002. Memberships: Descendants of the American Revolution; Girl Scouts of America. Address: 281 Kercheval Avenue, Grosse Pointe Farms, Michigan 48236, USA.

HARRISON Elizabeth Fancourt, b. 12 January 1921, Watford, Hertfordshire, England. Author. Publications: Coffee at Dobree's, 1965; The Physicians, 1966; The Ravelston Affair, 1967; Corridors of Healing, 1968; Emergency Call, 1970; Accident Call, 1971; Ambulance Call, 1972; Surgeon's Call, 1973; On Call, 1974; Hospital Call, 1975; Dangerous Call, 1976; To Mend a Heart, 1977; Young Dr Goddard, 1978; A Doctor Called Caroline, 1979; A Surgeon Called Amanda, 1982; A Surgeon's Life, 1983; Marrying a Doctor, 1984; Surgeon's Affair, 1985; A Surgeon at St Mark's, 1986; The Surgeon She Married, 1988; The Faithful Type, 1993; The Senior Partner's Daughter, 1994; Made for Each Other, 1995. Honours: Runner-up, 1970, shortlisted, 1971, 1972, 1973, Romantics Novelists Association. Memberships: Society of Authors; Romantic Novelists Association. Address: 71 Wingfield Road, Kingston on Thames, Surrey KT2 5LR, England.

HARROW Nancy, b. 3 October 1930, New York City, New York, USA. Jazz Singer; Songwriter. m. Jan Krukowski, 2 sons. Education: BA, Bennington College. Career: Club Dates and Concerts in New York City, Washington, Paris, Cologne, Stockholm, Brussels, 1961-2002; Theatre: The Marble Faun, Concert Workshop; The Salon, New York City, 1999; Jazz Puppet Show: Maya the Bee, 45 Bleecker Theater, New York City, 2000-. Creative Works: Recordings: Wild Women Don't Have the Blues, 1961, 1987, 2001; You Never Know, 1963, 1991; Anything Goes, 1979, 1991; The John Lewis Album for Nancy Harrow, 1981, 1987; Two's Company, 1984, 1991; You're Nearer, 1986, 1998; Street of Dreams, 1990; The Beatles and Other Standards, 1990; Secrets, 1992; Lost Lady, 1994; The Marble Faun: Jazz variations on a Theme by Nathaniel Hawthorne, 1999; Adventures of Maya the Bee, 2000; Winter Dreams: The Life and Passions of F. Scott Fitzgerald, 2003; Compositions (Music and Lyrics): 5 songs for Secrets; 12 songs for Lost Lady; 13 songs for The Marble Faun; 21 songs for Maya the Bee; 11 songs for Winter Dreams. Honours: Grant to compose song cycle based on the life of F Scott Fitzgerald, New York State Council on Arts, 2000; Wild Women Don't Have the Blues chosen by British Jazz awards as one of the best reissues of 2001. Membership: The Century Association. Address: 130 East End Avenue, New York, NY 10029, USA. E-mail: nancyjazz@aol.com

HARRY Deborah Ann, b. 1 July 1945, Miami, Florida, USA. Singer; Songwriter; Actress. Career: Former Playboy bunny waitress; Singer, groups: Wind In The Willows; The Stilettos; Founder, Blondie, 1974-83; Appearances include: New York punk club, CBGBs, 1974; Support to Iggy Pop, US, 1977; Solo recording career, 1981-; Actress, films including: Blank Generation, 1978; The Foreigner, 1978; Union City, 1979; Roadie, 1980; Videodrome; Hairspray; The Killbillies; Tales from the Darkside: The Movie, 1990; Intimate Stranger, 1991; Joe's Day, 1999; 200, 1999; Six Ways to Sunday, 1999; Ghost Light, 2000; Dueces Wild, 2000; Red Lipstick, 2000; TV appearances: Saturday Night Life; The Muppet Show; Tales from the Darkside; Wiseguys; Theatre: Teaneck Tanzi; The Venus Flytrap; Recordings: Hit singles: with Blondie: Denis (Denee), 1978; (I'm Always Touched By Your) Presence Dear, 1978; Picture This, 1978; Hanging On The Telephone, 1978; Heart Of Glass (Number 1, UK), 1979; Sunday Girl (Number 1, UK), 1979; Dreaming, 1979; Union City Blue, 1979; Call Me (Number 1, US and UK), 1980; Atomic, 1980; The Tide Is High (Number 1, UK and US), 1980; Rapture (Number 1, US), 1981; Island Of Lost Souls, 1982; Solo: Backfired, 1981; French Kissin' (In The USA), 1986; I Want That Man, 1989; I Can See Clearly, 1993; Albums with Blondie: Blondie, 1976; Plastic Letters, 1978; Parallel Lines (Number 1, US), 1978; Eat To The Beat (Number 1, UK), 1979; Autoamerican, 1980; The Best Of Blondie, 1981; The Hunter, 1982; Solo albums: Koo Koo, 1981; Rockbird, 1986; Def, Dumb And Blonde, 1989; Debravation, 1993; Compilations: Once More Into The Bleach, 1988; The Complete Picture, 1991; Blonde And Beyond, 1993; Rapture, 1994; Virtuosity, 1995; Rockbird, 1996; Der Einziger Weg, 1999; Contributor, film soundtracks: American Gigolo, 1980; Roadie, 1980; Scarface; Krush Groove, 1984. Publications: Making Tracks - The Rise Of Blondie (co-written with Chris Stein), 1982. Memberships: ASCAP; AFTRA; Equity; Screen Actors Guild. Current Management: Overland Productions, 156 W 56th Street, 5th Floor, New York, NY 10019, USA.

HARTCUP Adeline, b. 26 April 1918, Isle of Wight, England. Writer. m. John Hartcup, 11 February 1950, 2 sons. Education: MA, Classics and English Literature, Oxon. Appointments: Editorial Staff, Times Educational Supplement; Honorary Press Officer, Kent Voluntary Service Council. Publications: Angelica, 1954; Morning Faces, 1963; Below Stairs in the Great Country Houses, 1980; Children of the Great Country Houses, 1982, 2000; Love and Marriage in the Great Country Houses, 1984; Spello: Life Today in Ancient Umbria, 1985. Contributions to: Times Educational Supplement; Harper's; Queen; Times Higher Educational Supplement. Address: 8F Compton Road, London N1, England.

HARTER John J, b. 31 January 1926, Canyon, Texas, USA. Diplomat; Economic Analyst. m. Irene T Harter, 2 sons, 1 daughter. Education: BA, 1948, MA, 1953, University of Southern California; MA, Economics, Harvard University, 1963. Appointments: Lecturer, History, University of Southern California, 1948-53; Foreign Service Officer, US Department of State with assignments in South Africa, Chile, Thailand, Geneva, Washington, 1954-83; Oral Historian, 1983-; Declassifier, Agency for international Development, 1998-. Publications: Views on Global Economic Development, 1979; The Language of Trade, 1984; Numerous articles in Foreign Service Journal and State Magazine. Memberships: American Foreign Service Association; Diplomatic and Consular Officers Retired. Address: 4872 Admiration Drive, Virginia Beach, VA 23464-3149, USA. E-mail: jjitharter@aol.com

HARTILL Rosemary Jane, b. 11 August 1949, Oswestry, England. Writer; Broadcaster; Independent Producer. Education: BA Hons, English, University of Bristol, 1970. Appointments: BBC Religious Affairs Correspondent, 1982-88, Presenter of World Service's Meridian Books Programme, 1990-92, 1994, BBC. Publications: Emily Brontë: Poems (editor), 1973; Wild Animals, 1976; In Perspective, 1988; Writers Revealed, 1989; Were You There?, 1995; Visionary Women: Florence Nightingale, editor,

1996. Contributions to: Times Educational Supplement; Saga magazine; Guardian etc. Honours: Nominated, Sony Award for Radio Reporter of the Year, 1988 and Best Arts Radio Feature, 1990; Sandford St Martin Trust Personal Award, 1994; Honorary DLitt, University of Hull, 1995; Finalist In New York Festivals International Radio Competition, 1996; Honorary DLitt, University of Bristol, 2000. Address: Old Post Office, 24 Eglingham Village, Alnwick, Northumberland NE66 2TX, England.

HARTMANN-JOHNSEN Olaf Johan, b. 22 August 1924, Aalesund, Norway. Internist. m. (1) Mary Essil Archibald, 1956, dissolved 1968, 2 daughters, (2) Mary Eldbjørg Hestad, 1969, 1 son, 1 daughter. Education: MB, BS, University of Queensland, Australia, 1956; MD, Oslo University, 1974. Appointments: Physician: Royal Brisbane Hospital, Australia, 1956-63; Oslo University Hospital, 1964-65; Bundaberg General Hospital, 1966; Hornsby District Hospital, 1967-70; Upton Hospital, Slough, England, 1970; Blacktown District Hospital, 1971-73; Ullevål Hospital, 1974-77; Vesfn Hospital, 1977-78; Kragerø Hospital, 1978-79; Physician in Chief, St Joseph's Hospital, Porsgrunn, 1979-82; Consultant Physician, Chief Medical Officer, Nesset County, 1982-91; Government Medical Officer, 1982-91; Communal Medical Officer, Rauma County Aandalsnes, 1991-92; Staff Physician, Psychiatric Hospital, Hjelset, 1993-98; Tutor in Medicine, University of Oslo Medical School, 1975-77; Consultant in General Practice and Community Medicine, 1991-. Publications: Contribution of articles to medical journals. Honours: King Haakon VII medal; Norwegian War Service Medal; Several British Campaign Medals; Medaille de la France Liberee. Memberships: Norwegian Medical Association; College of Norwegian Internists; New York Academy of Sciences; International Churchill Society; Life Member, Royal Airforce Association; Life Member, Normandy Veterans' Association, Grimsby Branch. Address: Ranvik, 6460, Eidsvaag, Norway. E-mail: olafh-j@online.no

HARTSOUGH Gayla Kraetsch, b. 16 September 1949, Lakewood, Ohio, USA. Management Consultant. m. Jefffrey W Hartsough, 1 son. Education: BS, School of Speech, Northwestern University, 1971; EdM, Graduate School, Tufts University, 1973; MEd, School of Education, University of Virginia, 1978, PhD, Graduate School, University of Virginia, 1978. Appointments: Resource Teacher, Fairfax Public Schools, (VA), 1972-76; Graduate Assistant, University of Virginia, 1976-78; Senior Program Officer, Academy for Educational Development, Oklahoma; Management Consultant, Towers Perrin, 1980-86; President, KH Consulting Group, 1986-. Publications: Numerous articles in refereed journals and elsewhere. Honours: Outstanding Women, Entrepreneur, Century City Chamber of Commerce; Woodrow Wilson Fellow. Memberships: Former President, Organization of Women Executives; Member, Council of 100; Member, National Advisory Council, Northwestern University. Address: KH Consulting Group, 1901 Avenue of the Stars, #1900, Los Angeles, CA 90067, USA.

HARVEY Carol Josephine, b. 18 April 1941, Heckmondwike, Yorkshire, England. Professor. m. Albert Chisholm Harvey, 1 son, 1 daughter. Education: MA (Honours), Edinburgh University, 1963; L.ès L. Université de Caen, 1964; PhD, Edinburgh University, 1969. Appointments: Department of French Studies, University of Winnipeg, 1970-; Department Chair, 1983-88; Visiting Fellow, Corpus Christi College, Cambridge University (Lent term), 1989; Visiting Professor, Université de Perpignan, France, 1991-92; Université de Poitiers, France (winter term), 1995. Publications: Books: Le cycle manitobain de Gabrielle Roy, 1993; Co-author, La littérature au féminin, 1995; Co-editor, La francophonie sur les marges, 1997; Author of numerous articles, book chapters and book reviews in academic journals. Honours: Robson Award, for Excellence in Teaching, University of Winnipeg, 1980; Chevalier, Ordre des Palmes Académiques, Government of France, 1988; Social Sciences and Humanities Research Council of Canada Award, 1997-2000, 2002-2005; Clarence Atchison Award for Community Service, University of Winnipeg, 1999; Erica and Arnold Rogers Award for Excellence in Research and Scholarship, University of Winnipeg, 2000. Memberships: Canadian Society of Medievalists, Board member, 1992-96, Vice-President, 2000-2002, President, 2002-2004; International Courtly Literature Society, North American Branch, Board Member, 1997-2000; Centre d'Etudes Franco-Canadiennes de l'Ouest, Board Member, 1989-. Address: Department of French Studies, University of Winnipeg, MB R3B 2E9, Canada.

HARWOOD Eleanor May Cash, b. 29 May 1921, Maine, USA. Divorced, 1 son, 1 daughter. Education: BA, American International College, 1943; BSc, S Connecticut State University, 1955. Appointments: Ensign to Lieutenant JG USSN Waves, 1943-46; Librarian, Rathburn Memorial Library, East Haddam, Connecticut, 1955-56; Assistant Librarian, Kent Boys School, Connecticut, 1956-63; Consultant, Chester Public Library, Connecticut, 1965-71. Publications: The Independent School Library And The Gifted Child; The Age Of Samuel Johnson; Remember When?; Moosely Yours. Honours: WWII 50th Women and 50th Victory Medals; Atlantic Theater; Victory Medal; Gold Star Award for Education 1997; Eleanor Harwood College Library named for her at the Reverend Jacob Memorial Christian College, India, 2003. Memberships include: American and Connecticut Library Associations; Society of the Descendents of The Mayflower; Trustee, Chester Historical Society, 1970-72; Disabled American Veterans; American Legion Aux; Appalachian Mountain Club. Address: 10 Maple Street, Box 255, Chester, CT 06412, USA.

HASE Kazuo, b. 22 October 1954, Hiroshima, Japan. Physician. m. Kazuko, 3 sons. Education: MD, National Defence Medical College, Saitama, Japan, 1975-81; PhD, Postgraduate Course of Medicine, National Defence Medical College, Saitama, Japan, 1988-92. Appointments: Junior Resident, 1981-83, Senior Resident, 1985-87, National Defence Medical College, Tokorozawa, Japan; Medical Staff, Self-Defence Forces Sapporo Hospital, Sapporo, 1983-85; Surgeon-in-Chief, Self-Defence Forces Kumamoto Hospital, Kumamoto, Japan, 1992-94; Medical Staff, 1987-88, Surgeon-in-Chief, 1994-97, Surgical Director GI, 1997-2003, Surgical Director, 2003-, Self-Defence Forces Central Hospital, Tokyo, Japan. Publications: Articles in scientific journals include: Prognostic value of tumor "budding" in patients with colorectal cancer, 1993; Long-term results of curative rejection of "minimally invasive" colorectal cancer, 1995; Intraperitoneal exfoliated cancer cells in patients with colorectal cancer, 1998. Memberships: American Society of Colon and Rectal Surgeons; International Society of University Colon and Rectal Surgeons; American Association for the Advancement of Science; Society for Surgery of the Alimentary Tract; Japan Surgical Society; Japanese Society for Gastroenterological Surgery. Address: 3-4-24 Maehara, Koganei, Tokyo 184-0013 Japan. E-mail: kazu-h@bf6.so-net.ne.jp

HASELTON Mary M, b. 15 May 1920, Kansas City, Missouri, USA. Foreign Service Officer, Retired. m. George H Haselton, deceased. Education: Dodds School of Business, Topeka, Kansas, 1938-39; Music, Washburn University, Topeka, 1939-41; Economics, American University, Washington DC, 1943; Fine Arts, University of Texas, Austin, Texas, 1947-52; Special courses, Foreign Service Institute, Department of State, 1960-61, 1974-77; Bachelor of Liberal Arts, cum laude, Harvard University, 2001.

Appointments: War Department, Economic Defence Board, War Food Administration, Washington DC, 1941-43; Statistical Analyst, Control Staff, Quartermaster Depot, US Army, Fort Sam Houston, Texas, 1943-44; Secretary and Officer Manager for physicians, San Antonio, Texas, 1944-46; Secretary, Director of the Division of Research, International Monetary Fund, Washington DC, 1946-47; Served on boards and executive committees for Austin Symphony Orchestra Society and Texas Fine Arts Association, 1947-53; Executive Secretary and Legislative Assistant to Majority Leader, US Senate, 1953-60; Analyst, Treaty Staff of the Office of the Legal Advisor, Department of State, Commissioned as Foreign Service Officer, Assigned as Vice Consul in Zurich and Munich, 1960-64; Presented seminars with husband, United States Foreign Policy and American Government, Simon's Rock College, Great Barrington, MA, 1966-71; Re-appointed Foreign Service Officer to Office of Special Assistant to the Secretary of State for World Population Matters, 1974-79; State Department Liaison to Non-governmental Organisations at United Nations World Population Conference, Bucharest, 1974; Assigned as Deputy, American Embassy, Suva, 1977-78. Honours: National Honor Society; Sigma Alpha Iota (Music); Listed in international biographical dictionaries. Memberships: Senior Associate Member, St Antony's College, Oxford University, 1971-72. Address: 85 South Main Street, Hanover, New Hampshire, USA. E-mail: mhaselton@valley.net

HASKINS Christopher (The Rt Hon The Lord Haskins), b. 1937, Dublin, Ireland. Businessman; Member of House of Lords. m. Gilda Horsley, 5 children. Education: History (Hons), Trinity College, Dublin. Appointments: De La Rue Trainee, 1959-60; Ford Motors Dagenham Personnel, 1960-62; Manager, Belfast, 1962-68, Pioneered foods in Marks & Spencer, 1968-2002; Director, 1974, Deputy Chair, 1974, Chairman, 1980, Northern Dairies (later Northern Foods); Chairman, Express Dairies (merged with Northern Foods), 1998-2002; Member, MAFF Review of CAP, 1995; Chairman, Better Regulation Task Force, 1997-2002; Member, New Deal Task Force, 1998-2001; Member, Britain in Europe Campaign, 1998-; Non Executive Director, Yorkshire Regional Development Agency, 1998-; Advisor to the Prime Minister on Foot and Mouth "Recovery", 2001; Heading Review of Defra, 2002-2003; Chair, Selby Coalfields Task Force (Managing the impact of closure), 2002-2003; Member, CBI President's Committee, 1995-98; Member, Hampel Committee on Corporate Governance, 1996-98; Member, Irish Economic Policy Review Group, 1998; Member, Commission for Social Justice, 1992-94; Member, UK Round Table on Sustainable Development. 1995-98; Trustee, Runnymede Trust, 1989-98; Chairman, Demos Trustees, 1993-2000; Trustee, Civil Liberties, 1997-99; Trustee, Legal Assistance Trust, 1998-; Trustee, Lawes Agricultural Trust, 1999-; Director, Yorkshire TV, 2002-; Trustee, Business Dynamics, 2002; Chair, DEFRA Review Group, 2002-03; Regular speaker and writer about Europe, agriculture, regulation, corporate governance. Honours: Labour Peer, 1998; Honorary Degrees: Dublin, Hull, Essex, Nottingham, Leeds, Metropolitan, Cranfield, Huddersfield. Address: Quarryside Farm, Main Street, Skidby, Nr Cottingham, East Yorkshire HU16 5SG, England.

HASKOVA Vera, b. 4 April 1927, Pardubice, Czech Republic. Research Scientist. m. (1) Dr Milan Hasek, 1950-70; (2) Cestmir Hasek, 1978-, 1 son, 2 daughters. Education: MSc, Natural Sciences, Charles University, Prague, 1950; PhD, Biological Institute, Czechoslovak Academy of Sciences, Prague, 1955; DSc, Institute of Experimental Biology and Genetics, 1969. Appointments: Research Scientist, Institute of Experimental Biology and Genetics, Czechoslovak Academy of Sciences, 1955-66; Research Scientist, Institute of Clinical and Experimental Surgery, Prague, 1967-70; Head, Immunological Laboratory,

Institute of Clinical and Experimental Medicine, Prague, 1970-90; Research Scientist, 1991-93. Publications: 117 scientific articles; 4 monographs; others. Honours: Czechoslovak State Prize in Science, 1961; Gregory Mendel Medal; J E Purkyne Gold Medal; Many others. Memberships: Czechoslovak Academy of Sciences; Czechoslovak Biological Society; Czech Society for Immunology; The Transplantation Society. Address: Bohacova 862, Praha 4 Haje, 149 00 Czech Republic.

HASLAM Gerald William, b. 18 March 1937, Bakersfield, California, USA. Writer. m. Janice Eileen Pettichord, 1 July 1961, 3 sons, 2 daughters. Education: BA, 1963, MA, 1965, San Francisco State; PhD, Union Institute, 1980. Appointments: Instructor of English, San Francisco State College, 1966-67; Professor of English, Sonoma State University, 1967-97; Adjunct Professor, The National Faculty, 1984-, Union Graduated School, 1984-; Professor Emeritus, Sonoma State University, 1997-; Professor, The Fromm Institute, 2001-. Publications: Fiction books include: The Man Who Cultivated Fire and Other Stories, 1987; The Constant Coyote: California Stories, 1990, 1991, 1993; Condor Dreams & Other Fictions, 1994; The Great Tejon Club Jubilee, 1996; Manuel and the Madman, 2000; Straight White Male, 2000. Non-fiction includes: The Great Central Valley: California's Heartland, 1993; Workin' Man Blues: Country Music in California, 1999; Editor, anthologies including: Jack London's Golden State: Selected California Writing, 1999; Non-fiction booklets, monographs, guides and reprints; Contributor to magazines and journals, anthologies. Honours include; Laureate, San Francisco Public Library, 1998; Distinguished Achievement Award, Western Literature Association, 1999; "Coming of Age in California" named as one of 20th century's 100 best non-fiction books from the West, by San Francisco Chronicle reader's poll, 1999; Ralph J Gleason Award, 2000; Western States Book Award, 2001; Carey McWilliams Award, 2001; Sequoia, Grant of the Valley Award, 2003. Memberships include: Western Literature Association, Board of Directors, Past-president; California Studies Association, Steering Committee, founding member; CSU Emeritus and Retired Faculty Association; Yosemite Association, Board of Trustees. Address: PO Box 969, Penngrove, CA 94951, USA.

HASSAN IBN TALAL H.R.H., b. 20 March 1947, Amman. Crown Prince of Jordan. m. Sarrath Khujista Akhter Banu, 1968, 1 son, 3 daughters. Education: Christ Church, Oxford University. Appointments: Regent to the throne of Jordan in absence of King Hussein; Ombudsman for National Development, 1971-; Founder, Royal Science Society of Jordan, 1970; Royal Academy of Islamic Civilization Research (AlAlbait), 1980; Arab Thought Forum, 1981; Forum Humanum (now Arab Youth Forum), 1982; Co-Chairman, Independent Commission on International Council for Science and Technology; Honorary General of Jordan Armed Forces. Publications: A Study on Jerusalem, 1979; Palestinian Self-Determination, 1981; Search for Peace, 1984; Christianity in the Arab World, 1994. Honours: Honorary degrees from universities of Yarmouk, 1980, Bogazici (Turkey), 1982, Jordan, 1987, Durham, 1990, Ulster, 1996; Medal, President, Italian Republic, 1982; Knight of Grand Cross of Order of Self-Merit (Italy), 1983. Address: The Royal Palace, Amman, Jordan.

HASSIM Abubakr Mustapha, b. 29 April 1931, Johannesburg, South Africa. d. 14 September 2003. Professor in Obstetrics and Gynaecology. m. Cynthia Lucas, 1 son, 3 daughters. Education: BSc, 1951, MB BCh, 1955, University of Witwatersrand; DRCOG, 1958, MRCOG, 1961, London; FICS, International College of Surgeons, 1968; FACS, American College of Surgeons, 1970; FRCOG, RCOG London, 1971. Appointments: WHO Professor, Obstetrics and Gynaecology; Consultant, University Teaching Hospital, Lusaka; Professor, Obstetrics and Gynaecology,

University of Zambia School of Medicine; Senior Consultant and Chairman, Barnet and Edgware, Hospitals NHS Trust; Honorary Senior Lecturer, Royal Free Hospital, London; Retired from NHS, 1993; Currently in Consultant Practice. Publications: Co-author, Lawson's Maternity Care in Developing Countries, 2001; 21 research papers and reviews; 17 case reports; Delegate/Participant various International Congresses, 1967-93. Honours: Diploma, Royal College of Obstetrics and Gynaecology; Representative, Regional Advisory Committee, Barnet and Edgware Hospitals. Memberships: Africa Regional Council; IPPF Medical Committee; Fellow, Association of Surgeons of East Africa; Fellow, Royal Society of Medicine; British Society for Gynaecology Endoscopy, 1993; Fellow, Ford Foundation, Johns Hopkins Medical School, Baltimore; Harvard School of Medicine, Hospital de la Mujer, Mexico, 1969. Address: 16 Cressy Road, Hampstead, London, NW3 2LY, England.

HAST Sybil Dorothea Heimann, b. 8 May 1924, Shanghai, China (US Citizen). Retired Professor. 1 son, 1 daughter. Education: BA, French, Smith College, 1946; MA, French Language and Literature, University of Pittsburgh, USA, 1963; MA, German Language and Literature, University of California, Los Angeles, USA, 1966; Standard Community College Credential, 1966; 2 Diplomas, University of Barcelona, Spain, 1972. Appointments include: Assistant Professor of German, California State University, 1970-71; Language and Diction Coach, UCLA Opera Theater, 1973-93, Lecturer, 1980-93, Department of Music, University of California, Los Angeles; Founder, Artistic Director, Language and Diction Coach, Westside Opera Workshop, Santa Monica, California, 1987-95; Founder, Director, ISTMO, Santa Monica, California, 1975-; Numerous positions as Interpreter, Translator, Voice-Over Coach; Interviewer and Researcher, UCLA Oral History Program, University of California, Los Angeles, 1986-93; Consultant and Foreign Language Professor, The J Paul Getty Museum, Malibu, California, 1980-82, 1994; Professional Voice-Over Artist. Publications: Author of Poetry; In progress: Dictionary of Musical and Stage Terms in English, German, French, Spanish and Italian, Film Scripts and Children's Stories. Memberships: American Association of University Professors; Modern Language Association; Screen Actors Guild; American Federation of Television and Radio Artists; German-American Chamber of Commerce; Board Member, Annual Show Chair, Interviewer, Sunset Succulent Society. Address: River's Edge, 111 Dekoven Drive #606, Middletown, CT 06457, USA

HASTINGS Lady Selina, b. 5 March 1945, Oxford, England. Writer. Education: St Hugh's College, Oxford, England. Appointments: Daily Telegraph, books page, 1968-82; Harper's & Queen Literary Editor, 1986-94. Publications: Nancy Mitford, biography, 1985; Evelyn Waugh, 1994; Rosamond Lehmann, 2002; various children's books. Contributions to: Daily & Sunday Telegraph; Spectator; TLS; New Yorker; Harper's & Queen. Honour: Marsh Biography Award, 1993-96. Memberships: Royal Society of Literature Committee, 1994-99. Address: c/o Rogers Coleridge & White, 20 Powis Mews, London W11, England.

HASWELL Chetwynd John Drake, b. 18 July 1919, Penn, Buckinghamshire, England. Soldier; Author. m. Charlotte Annette Petter, 25 October 1947, 2 sons, 1 daughter. Education: Winchester College, 1933-37; Royal Military College, Sandhurst, 1938-39. Appointments: Soldier, 1939-60; Author, Service Intelligence, Intelligence Centre, Ashford, 1966-84. Publications: (As George Foster) Indian File, 1960; Soldier on Loan, 1961; (As Jock Haswell) The Queen's Royal Regiment, 1967; The First Respectable Spy, 1969; James II, Soldier and Sailor, 1972; British Military Intelligence, 1973; Citizen Armies, 1973; The British Army, 1975; The Ardent Queen, Margaret of Anjou, 1976; The Battle for

Empire, 1976; Spies and Spymasters, 1977; The Intelligence and Deception of the D Day Landings, 1979; The Tangled Web, 1985; The Queen's Regiment, 1986; Spies and Spying, 1986. Membership: Regimental Historian for the Queen's Regiment. Address: The Grey House, Lyminge, Folkestone, Kent CT18 8ED, England.

HATADA Kazuyuki, b. 23 December 1951, Maebashi City, Gunma, Japan. Mathematician; Educator. m. Kumiko Yoshikawa, 1 son. Education: BSc, 1974, MSc, 1976, DSc, 1979, The University of Tokyo. Appointments: Research Fellow, Faculty of Science, The University of Tokyo, 1979-80; Associate Professor (Algebra and Geometry), 1981-99, Professor (Algebra), 1999-, Department of Mathematics, Faculty of Education, Gifu University; Visiting Professor, Université Paris XI (France), autumn 1993; Visiting Professor, Nagoya University, 2001-2003. Publications: Articles for professional mathematical journals, including: Eigenvalues of Hecke operators on SL (2, Z), 1979; Congruences for eigenvalues of Hecke operators on SL (2, Z), 1981; Siegel cusp forms as holomorphic differential forms on certain compact varieties,1983; Homology groups, differential forms and Hecke rings on Siegel modular varieties, 1989; Estimates for eigenvalues of Hecke operators on Siegel cusp forms, 1996; On classical and l-adic modular forms of levels Nl**m and N, 2001. Honours: Insignia of Dedications, 1988; International Cultural Diploma of Honor, 1988; Silver Medal, 1989, Gold Medal for the first 500, 1990; The International Order of Merit, 1990; International Man of the Year, 1991-92, 1995-96; 20th Century Award for Achievement, 1993; Global Distinction Award, 1994-95; The Golden Scroll of Excellence, 1997; Albert Einstein International Academy Foundation Honoree, 1998; Man of the Year 2000; International Personality of the Year, 2001; Lifetime Achievement Award, 2002; International Scientist of the Year, 2002; American Medal of Honor, 2002; The Worldwide Honours List, 2003. Memberships: Life Member, World Institute of Achievement, Councillor, 2001, Representative, 2002, Mathematical Society of Japan; The American Mathematical Society (reviewer); Astronomical Society of Japan. Address: Department of Mathematics, Faculty of Education, Gifu University, 1-1 Yanagido, Gifu City, GIFU 501-1193, Japan.

HATEGAN Cornel, b. 17 August 1940, Ohaba-Matnic, Romania. Physicist. m. Dora, 9 October 1965, 1 daughter. Education: University Diploma Physics, University of Bucharest, 1964; Dr, Physics, Institute of Atomic Physics, Bucharest, 1973. Appointments: Assistant Researcher, Researcher, Senior Researcher, Institute of Atomic Physics, 1964-70, 1972-; Humboldt Researcher, University of Erlangen Nuremberg, 1970-71; University of Munich, 2002. Publications: Scientific papers on Atomic and Nuclear Physics. Honours: Urkunde of Humboldt Foundation; Physics Prize of Romanian Academy; Corresponding Member, Romanian Academy, elected, 1992; Fellow, Institute of Physics, London, elected, 2000. Memberships: Humboldt Club; Nuclear Physics Division of the Romanian Physical Society; New York Academy of Sciences. Address: Institute of Atomic Physics, CP MG 6, 76900 Bucharest, Magurele, Romania.

HATTERSLEY Roy, (Sydney George), b. 28 December 1932, Sheffield, England. Politician; Writer. m. Molly Loughran, 1956. Education: BSc, Economics, University of Hull. Appointments: Journalist and Health Service Executive, 1956-64; Member, City Council, Sheffield, 1957-65; Member of Parliament, Labour Party, Sparkbrook Division, Birmingham, 1964-97; Parliamentary Private Secretary, Minister of Pensions and National Insurance, 1964-67; Director, Campaign for a European Political Community, 1966-67; Joint Parliamentary Secretary, Ministry of Labour, 1967-69,

Minister of Defence for Administration, 1969-70; Visiting Fellow, Harvard University, 1971, 1972, Nuffield College, Oxford, 1984-; Labour Party Spokesman on Defence, 1972, and on Education and Science, 1972-74; Minister of State, Foreign and Commonwealth Office, 1974-76; Secretary of State for Prices and Consumer Protection, 1976-79; Principal Opposition Spokesman on the Environment, 1979-80, Home Affairs, 1980-83, Treasury and Economics Affairs, 1983-87, Home Affairs, 1987-92; Deputy Leader, Labour Party, 1983-92. Publications: Nelson: A Biography, 1974; Goodbye to Yorkshire (essays), 1976; Politics Apart, 1982; Press Gang, 1983; A Yorkshire Boyhood, 1983; Choose Freedom: The Future for Democratic Socialism, 1987; Economic Priorities for a Labour Government, 1987; The Maker's Mark (novel), 1990; In That Quiet Earth (novel), 1991; Skylark Song (novel), 1994; Between Ourselves (novel), 1994; Who Goes Home?, 1995; 50 Years On, 1997; Buster's Diaries: As Told to Roy Hattersley, 1998; Blood and Fire: The Story of William and Catherine Booth and their Salvation Army, 1999; A Brand from the Burning: The Life of John Wesley, 2002. Contributions to: Newspapers and journals. Honours: Privy Counsellor, 1975; Columnist of the Year, Granada, 1982; Honorary doctorates. Address: House of Lords, London SW1A 0PW, England.

HAUDEBOURG Brigitte, b. 5 December 1942, Paris, France. Harpsichordist; Pianofortist; Concertist; Teacher. m. Paul Cousseran, 1 son, 1 daughter. Education: Studied Piano with Marguerite Long and Jean Doyen; Harpsichord with R Veyron-Lacroix. Debut: Paris. Career: Many TV and Radio appearances in France, USA, Canada, Europe, Russia, Tunisia, Hong Kong, Bangkok, Tahiti; Artistic Director of the Festival de Musique et d'Art Baroque en tarentaise; Also responsible for a collection of rare scores for Zurfluh. Recordings: 70 Albums and CD's, including, Daquin, Dandrieu, 2 albums of suites; Devienne, for flute and harpsichord; Chevalier de St Georges, for violin and harpsichord; Jean Pierre Baur, for harp and harpsichord; W F Bach, 2 albums, No 1,3,4,5; CD's include, Louis Couperin, for harpsichord; Josse Boutmy for harpsichord, world premiere; Padre Antonio Soler; J Schobert for pianoforte; J A Benda for pianoforte; E N Mehul for pianoforte; J G Eckhard for pianoforte; L Kozeluch for pianoforte. Publications include: 2nd book of Josse Boutmy, (harpsichord). Current Management: Musilyre (Europe), Paris, France; A Declert (North America), Texas, USA. Address: 10 Avenue F Roosevelt, 92150 Suresnes, France.

HAUGAARD Erik Christian, b. 13 April 1923, Copenhagen, Denmark. Author. m. (1) Myra Seld, 23 December 1949, deceased 1981, 1 son, 1 daughter, (2) Masako Taira, 27 July 1986, deceased 1996. Publications: The Little Fishes, 1967; Orphas of the Wind, 1969; The Untold Tale, 1972; Hans Christian Andersen's Fairy Tales (translator), 1973; Chase Me Catch Nobody, 1980; Leif the Unlucky, 1982; The Samurai's Tale, 1984; Princess Horrid, 1990; The Boy and the Samurai, 1991; The Death of Mr Angel, 1992; Under the Black Flag, 1993; The Revenge of the Forty-Seven Samurai, 1995. Honours: Herald Tribune Award; Boston Globe-Horn Book Award; Jane Addams Award; Danish Cultural Ministry Award; Phoenix Award. Memberships: Authors Guild; Society of Authors; British PEN; Danish Authors Union. Address: Toad Hall, Ballydehob, West Cork, Ireland.

HAUGHEY Charles James, b. 16 September 1925. Member of Parliament, Ireland. m. Maureen Lemass, 1951, 3 sons 1 daughter. Education: Scoil Mhuire, Marino, Dublin; St Joseph's Christian Brothers School, Fairview, Dublin; BCom, University College Dublin. Appointments: Called to Irish Bar, 1949; Member, Dublin Corp, 1953-55; MP, 1957-92; Parliamentary Secretary to Minister for Justice, 1960-61; Minister for Justice, 1961-64, Agriculture, 1964-66, Finance, 1966-70, Health and Social Welfare, 1977-79;

Chairman, Irish Parliament Joint Committee on the Secondary Legislation of the European Communities, 1973-77; Taoiseach (Prime Minister), 1979-81, 1982, 1987-92; Minister for the Gaeltacht, 1987-92; Leader of the Opposition, 1981-82, 1982-87. Honours: Hon Fellow, RHA; Honorary Doctorates, Dublin City University, University of Clemont-Ferrand, University of Notre Dame. Publication: The Spirit of the Nation. Address: Abbeville, Kinsealy, Co Dublin, Ireland.

HAUSEL W Dan, b. 24 July 1949, Salt Lake City, Utah, USA. Geologist; Martial Artist. 1 son, 1 daughter. Education: BS, Geology, 1972, MS, Geology 1974, University of Utah. Appointments: Astronomy Lecturer, Hanson Planetarium, 1968-70; Research Assistant, University of Utah, 1972-74; Teaching Assistant, University of New Mexico, 1974-75; Geologist, US Geological Survey 1976-77; Geologist and Deputy Director, Wyoming Geological Survey, 1977-91; Consultant, Western Gold Exploration and Mining, 1988-89; Consultant, Chevron Gold Resources, 1990; Consultant, Fowler Gold Resources, 1992; Consultant, Bald Mountain Mining and A and E Diamond Exploration, 1993; Consultant, Echo Bay Diamond Exploration, 1994; Senior Economic Geologist, Wyoming Geological Survey, 1991-; Consultant, Western Archon, 2003. Publications: Author of more than 400 publications including books, research papers, popular magazine articles and maps on geology, diamonds, other gemstones, gold, platinum, mining history and martial arts; Artist with works displayed in several galleries and on covers of some books. Honours: Presidents Award, American Association of Petroleum Geologists, 1992; Wyoming Geological Association's Certificate of Appreciation for Outstanding Contributions, 1992; Distinguished Speaker, Laramie Lyceum, 1994; Distinguished Lecturer, Department of Geology and Geophysics, University of Wyoming, 1998; Rocky Mountain Prospector's Best Friend Award, 1998; American Biographical Institute Millennium Hall of Fame, 1998; Shorin-Ryu Instructor of the Year, 1998; Grandmaster Instructor of the Year, 1998; Kevin Bell's Karate Hall of Fame Inductee, 1998; World Karate Union Hall of Fame Inductee, 2000; International Instructor of the Year, 2001; North American Black Belt Hall of Fame Inductee, 2001; National Rock Hound and Lapidary Hall of Fame, 2001; World Martial Arts Hall of Fame Inductee, 2002; Inductee, Universal Martial Arts Hall of Fame, 2002; Latin-American Martial Arts Worldwide Hall of Fame Inductee, 2003. Membership: Wyoming Geological Association; Wyoming Professional Geologists Association; Juko Kai International; Seiyo No Shorin-Ryu Renmei; Instructor, Martial Arts, University of Wyoming; Grandmaster (9th degree black belt) of Shorin-Ryu Karate. Address: Campus Shorin-Ryu Karate, Box 3625 Wyoming Union, University of Wyoming, Laramie, WY 82071, USA.

HAUSWIRTH Otto Karl, b. 10 May 1932, Gallspach, Upper Austria. Medical Scientist. Education: MD, University of Vienna, 1958; Habilitation, University of Heidelberg, 1972. Appointments: Assistant, Hospitals Hall, Uni-Clin Vienna (intern), Atlantic City, New Jersey, USA, University Clinic Innsbruck, 1959-64; Research Assistant, Department of Pharmacology, University of Zurich, 1964-71; Grantee, Swiss National Fund and Royal Society (London), staying at University Laboratory of Physiology, Oxford (Professor D Noble), 1968-69; Associate Professor, 1973, Full Professor, 1980-97, University of Bonn; Active in anti-drug movement. Publications: Multiple contributions to professional science journals and to various books. Memberships: Swiss and German Physiological Society; British Biophysics Society; German Pharmacological Society (DGPT); Co-President, International Hippokratic Society, Zurich, 1999-; President, Austrian Hippokratic Society, Mils, 2000; International Scientific Medical

Forum on Drug Abuse (a Division of Drug Free America Foundation), 1999. Address: Schneeburgstrasse 8, A-6068 Mils, Austria.

HAUTZIG Esther, (Esther Rudomin), b. 18 October 1930, Vilna, Poland (US Citizen). Publications: Let's Cook Without Cooking (as E Rudomin), 1955; Let's Make Presents, 1961; Redecorating Your Room for Practically Nothing, 1967; The Endless Steppe, 1968; In the Park, 1968; At Home 1969; In School, 1971; Let's Make More Presents, 1973; Cool Cooking, 1974; I L Peretz: The Case Against the Wind and Other Stories (translator and adaptor), 1975; Life with Working Parents, 1976; A Gift for Mama, 1981; Holiday Treats, 1983; I L Peretz: The Seven Good Years and Other Stories (translator and adaptor), 1984; Make It Special, 1986; Christmas Goodies, 1989; Remember Who You Are, 1990; On the Air, 1991; Riches, 1992; A Picture of Grandmother, 2002; New Introduction to a facsimile edition of Vilna by Israel Cohen, 1992. Contributions to: Periodicals. Memberships: Authors Guild; Authors League of America. Address: 505 West End Avenue, New York, NY 10024, USA.

HAVE Per Dalsgaard, b. 30 July 1950, Naestved, Denmark. Veterinary Consultant. m. Varna, 2 sons, 2 daughters. Education: Cand Med Vet, DVM, 1977; PhD, 1980. Appointments: Senior Research Scientist, -1992, Head, Diagnostic Department of Virology, 1992-2002, Consultant, 2002-, Danish Veterinary Institute, Lindholm. Publications: Over 30 papers on animal virology. Honours: C O Jensens, Mindefond, 1985; Dyssegaards Legat, 1988. Memberships: EFSA Scientific Panel on Animal Health, 2003-; European Society on Veterinary Virology; FAO EUFMD Research Group, 1994-; American Association for the Advancement of Science. Address: Danish Veterinary Institute, Lindholm, DK-4771 Kalvehave, Denmark. E-mail: ph@vetinst.dk

HAVELKA Stan George, b. 8 December 1927, Litoměřice, Czech Republic. Rheumatologist. m. Vlasta Havelková. Education: MD, Medical Faculty, Charles University, Prague, 1946-51; Specialist for Paediatrics, 1954; Candidate thesis, 1962; Specialist, Internal Medicine and Rheumatology, 1965; Study stay with Professor Rodolfo Amprino, Bari, 1972; Associate Professor, Internal Medicine, Charles University, Prague, 1990; Professor of Paediatrics, Charles University, Prague, 1992. Appointments: Research Career, Research Institute of Rheumatology, Prague; President, European Society of Osteoarthrology, 1980-90; Czech Representative, Standing Committee, Paediatric Rheumatology, of EULAR, 1986-97; Chairman, Prague International Paediatric Rheumatology Symposia I-VII, 1986-99; Founder, Czech Society for Metabolic Skeletal Disease, 1995; Founder, Chief Editor, Osteological Bulletin, 1996. Publications: More than 255 medical papers; Poetry; Two musical sonnets. Honours: Czech Rheumatological Society; Czech Society for Metabolic Skeletal Disease; Australian Rheumatism Association; German Society for Osteology; Honorary President, European Society of Osteoarthrology. Memberships: Czech Republic Medical Societies. Address: Dušní 4, 110 00 Prague 1, Czech Republic.

HAVU Niilo, b. 1 May 1936, Soujärvi, Finland. Physician. m. Ulla Margareta Svedling. Education: Bachelor of Medicine, 1958, Licentiate in Medicine, 1963, MD, 1963, Uppsala, Sweden; PhD, Umeå, Sweden, 1969. Medical Diplomate, Pathology, Cytology. Appointments: Acting Professor of Pathology, 1969, Associate Professor of Pathology, 1970-86, Umeå; Acting Professor of Pathology, Linköping, Sweden, 1970-73; Head, Department of Pathology, Astra AB, Södertälje, Sweden, 1973-89; Senior Expert, Toxicology, Astra/Astrazeneca, Sweden, 1989-2001; Associate Professor of Pathology, Karolinska Institute, Stockholm, Sweden, 1986-. Publications: Author: Sulfhydryl inhibitors and pancreatic

islet tissue (thesis), 1969; Mustaschtricket som Lurade Lisbet Palme (book), 2002; About 100 scientific articles in global journals. Memberships include: Fellow, Swedish Medical Society; Fellow, Royal Society of Medicine; International Academic Society for Pathology; Nordic Society of Toxicological Pathology. Address: Häckvägen 7, S-15137 Södertälje, Sweden.

HAWDON Paul Douglas, b. 13 October 1953, Manchester, England. Artist; Painter; Printmaker. m. Helena Earl, 1 daughter. Education: St Martin's School of Art, 1978-82; Royal Academy Schools of Art, 1982-85; Italian Government Scholarship, 1985-86; Prix de Rome in Printmaking, 1988-89. Career: Painter; Printmaker; Exhibitions: Most recently: International Print Triennial, Cracow, Poland, 1994; National Print Exhibitions, 1994, 2003; Royal Academy Summer Exhibition, 1997, 2003 International Print Biennial, Taipei, 1999; Wrexham Print International, 2001, 2003; New English Art Club, 2003; The Eastern Open, 2003, 2004; The Winter Print Fair, Royal Academy of Arts; Painting in the collection of the Metropolitan Museum of Art, New York. Publications: Works featured in: You Magazine, The Mail on Sunday, Young Masters by Brian Sewell, 1985; Printmaking Today, article by Michael Blaker; Illustrations in Printmaking Today Vol 10 Nos 2 and 3, 2001. Honours: Christie's Print Prize, Royal Academy Summer Exhibition, 1985, 1990; Wingate Scholarship, 1990; Print Prize, Eastern Open, 1997, 2004; T N Lawrence Prize, 2000, St Cuthberts Mill Award, 2001, National Print Exhibition; Commended Drawing, Royal Academy Summer Exhibition, 2002. Memberships: Fellow, Royal Society of Painter-Printmakers; Printmakers Council; Chelsea Arts Club. Address: 62 Marshall Road, Cambridge CB1 7TY, England.

HAWKE Ethan, b. 6 November 1970, Austin, Texas, USA. Actor. Career: Co-founder, Malaparte Theatre Company; Theatre appearances include: Casanova, 1991; A Joke, The Seagull, 1992; Sophistry; Films include: Explorers, 1985; Dead Poets Society, 1989; Dad, 1989; White Fang, 1991; Mystery Date, 1991; A Midnight Clear, 1992; Waterland, 1992; Alive, 1993; Rich in Love, 1993; Straight to One (director), 1993; Reality Bites, 1994; Quiz Show, 1994; Floundering, 1994; Before Sunrise, 1995; Great Expectations, 1999; Gattaca, 1999; Joe the King, 1999; Hamlet, 2000; Tape, 2001; Waking Life, 2001; Training Day, 2001. Publications: Ash Wednesday, 2002. Address: Creative Artists Agency, 9830 Wilshire Boulevard, Beverly Hills, CA 90212, USA.

HAWKESWORTH Pauline Mary, b. 28 April 1943, Portsmouth, England. Secretary. m. Rex Hawkesworth, 25 October 1961, 2 daughters. Appointments: Secretarial Manager, Administrator, Ladies Athletic Club; Track and Field Judge. Publications: 2 books, 82 poems. Anthologies: Parents Enitharmon, 2000; Spirit of Wilfred Owen, 2001. Contributions to: Envoi; South; Interpreters House; Script; Iota; Poetry Nottingham International; Frogmore Press; Others. Honours: 1st Prize, Short Story, Portsmouth Polytechnic, 1981; 1st Prize, South Wales Miners Eisteddfod, 1990; 1st Prize, Hastings Open Poetry Competition, 1993; Runner-Up, Redbeck Competition, 1996; 1st Prize Tavistock and North Dartmoor, 2000; 1st Prize Newark and Sherwood Millennium Project, 2001; 2nd Prize Richmond Adult CC. Membership: Vice-President, Portsmouth Poetry Society. Address: 4 Rampart Gardens, Hilsea, Portsmouth PO3 5LR, England.

HAWKING Stephen (William), b. 8 January 1942, Oxford, England. Professor of Mathematics; Writer. m. (1) Jane Wilde, 1965, divorced, 2 sons, 1 daughter, (2) Elaine Mason, 1995. Education: BA, University College, Oxford; PhD, Trinity Hall, Cambridge. Appointments: Research Fellow, 1965-69, Fellow for Distinction in Science, 1969-, Gonville and Caius College, Cambridge; Member, Institute of Theoretical Astronomy,

Cambridge, 1968-72; Research Assistant, Institute of Astronomy, Cambridge, 1972-73; Research Assistant, Department of Applied Mathematics and Theoretical Physics, 1973-75, Reader in Gravitational Physics, 1975-77, Professor, 1977-79, Lucasian Professor of Mathematics, 1979-, Cambridge University. Publications: The Large Scale Structure of Space-Time (with G F R Ellis), 1973; General Relativity: An Einstein Centenary Survey (editor with W W Israel), 1979; Is the End in Sight for Theoretical Physics?: An Inaugural Lecture, 1980; Superspace and Supergravity: Proceedings of the Nuffield Workshop (editor with M Rocek), 1981; The Very Early Universe: Proceedings of the Nuffield Workshop (co-editor), 1983; Three Hundred Years of Gravitation (with W W Israel), 1987; A Brief History of Time: From the Big Bang to Black Holes, 1988; Black Holes and Baby Universes and Other Essays, 1993; The Nature of Space and Time (with Roger Penrose), 1996 and other essays; The Universe in a Nutshell, 2001; The Theory of Everything: The Origin and Fate of the Universe, 2002; The Future of Space Time, co-editor, 2001; On the Shoulders of Giants, 2002. Contributions to: Scholarly journals. Honours: Eddington Medal, 1975, Gold Medal, 1985, Royal Academy of Science; Pius XI Gold Medal, Pontifical Academy of Sciences, 1975; William Hopkins Prize, Cambridge Philosophical Society, 1976; Maxwell Medal, Institute of Physics, 1976; Dannie Heinemann Prize for Mathematical Physics, American Physical Society and American Institute of Physics, 1976; Honorary fellow, University College, Oxford, 1977; Trinity Hall, Cambridge, 1984; Commander of the Order of the British Empire, 1982; Paul Dirac Medal and Prize, Institute of Physics, 1987; Wolf Foundation Prize for Physics, 1988; Companion of Honour, 1989; Britannica Award, 1989; Albert Medal, Royal Society of Arts, 1999; Honorary doctorates. Memberships: American Academy of Arts and Sciences; American Philosophical Society; Pontifical Academy of Sciences; Royal Society, fellow. Address: c/o Department of Applied Mathematics and Theoretical Physics, Cambridge University, Silver Street, Cambridge CB3 9EW, England.

HAWKINS Angus Brian, b. 12 April 1953, Portsmouth, England. Historian. m. Esther Armstrong, 20 May 1980, 2 daughters. Education: BA Hons, Reading University, 1975; PhD, London School of Economics, 1980. Publications: Parliament, Party and the Art of Politics in Britain, 1987; Victorian Britain: An Encyclopaedia, 1989; British Party Politics, 1852-1886, 1998; The Political Journals of the First Earl of Kimberley, 1862-1902, 1998. Contributions to: English Historical Review, Parliamentary History, Journal of British Studies, Victorian Studies; Nineteenth Century Prose, Archive. Honours: McCann Award, 1972; Gladstone Memorial Prize, 1978. Memberships: Reform Club; Fellow, Royal Historical Society. Address: Rewley House, University of Oxford, 1 Wellington Square, Oxford, England.

HAWKINS Monica Spann, Environmental Health Scientist. Education: Bachelor of Science, Environmental Science, Howard University, Washington DC, 1991; Master of Public Health, George Washington University, Washington DC, 1997; PhD Candidate, Environmental Science and Policy, George Mason University, Fairfax, Virginia, 2005. Appointments: Cultural Diversity Co-ordinator, Campus Outreach Division, 1991-92, Membership Action Co-ordinator, Office of Grassroots Action, 1992-94, National Wildlife Federation; Analyst, ICF Incorporated, 1994-95; Environmental Protection Specialist, Special Review and Registration Division, 1995-97, Environmental Health Scientist, Health Effects Division, 1997-, Environmental Protection Agency. Publication: Co-author, Acute hazards to young children from residential pesticide exposures, 2000. Honours: 21 Century Award for Achievement; Outstanding Performance Awards, 1996, 1997, 1998, 1999; Outstanding Assistant Coach Award, The Silver Spring

Children's Track Club, 2000; Science Fair Judge Award, The Duke Ellington School of the Arts, 2001; Bronze Medal, 2001, Unsung Hero Award, 2001, US Environmental Protection Agency; Listed in Who's Who publications and biographical dictionaries. Memberships: American Public Health Association; Delta Sigma Theta Sorority Incorporated. Address: 14228 Angelton Terrace, Burtonsville, MD 20866, USA. E-mail: hawkins.monica@epa.gov

HAWN Goldie, b. 21 November 1945, Washington, USA. Actress. Divorced, 3 children. Career: debut, Good Morning, World, 1967-68; TV includes: Rowan and Martin's Laugh-In, 1968-70; Pure Goldie, Natural history documentary, 1996; Films include: Cactus Flower; There's a Girl in my Soup; Dollars; The Sugarland Express; The Girl from Petrovka; Shampoo; The Duchess and the Dirtwater Fox; Foul Play; Seems Like Old Times; Private Benjamin; Best Friends; Protocol; Swing Shift; Overboard; Bird on a Wire; Housesitter; Deceived; Death Becomes Her; The First Wives Club, 1996; Everybody Says I Love You, 1996; The Out of Towners, 1999; Town and Country, 2001; The Banger Sisters, 2003; Star and Executive Producer: Goldie Hawn Special, 1978, Private Benjamin, 1980; Executive Producer, Something To Talk About; Co-Executive Producer, My Blue Heaven, 1990. Address: Creative Artists Agency, 9830 Wilshire Boulevard, Beverly Hills, CA 90212, USA.

HAYAMI Yujiro, b. 26 September 1932, Tokyo, Japan. m. Takako, 1 son, 2 daughters. Education: BA, Liberal Arts, University of Tokyo, Japan, 1956; PhD, Economics, Iowa State University, USA, 1960. Appointments: Research Associate, National Research Institute of Agricultural Economics, 1956-66; Professor, Tokyo Metropolitan University, 1966-86; Professor Aoyama-Gakuin University, Tokyo, 1986-2000; Professor, National Graduate Institute of Policy Studies, 2000-. Publications: Agricultural Development in an International Perspective; Development Economics: From the Poverty to the Wealth of Nations; A Rice Village Saga: Three Decades of Green Revolution in the Philippines. Honours: Research Award, Agricultural Economics Society of Japan; Fellow, American Agricultural Economics Association; Honorary Life Member, International Agricultural Economics Association. Memberships: American Agricultural Economics Association; International Association of Agricultural Economists. Address: Grips-Fasid, 2-2 Wakamatsu-cho. Shinjuku-ku, Tokyo, Japan, 162-8677. E-mail: hayami@grips.ac.jp

HAYASHI Takemi, b. 8 October 1938, Nagoya, Aichi, Japan. Physics Educator. m. Mariko Tsurumi, 1 son, 1 daughter. Education: BS, 1961, MS, 1963, DSc, 1966, Nagoya University. Appointments: Research Fellow, 1966-83, Lecturer, 1983, Hiroshima University; Associate Professor, 1983-85, Professor, 1985-91, Kure National College of Technology; Professor, Kogakkan University, 1991-. Publications: Several articles in professional journals. Memberships: Physical Society of Japan; American Physical Society; American Association of Physics Teachers. Address: Kogakkan University, Kodakujimoto-cho 1704, Ise, Mie 516-8555, Japan. E-mail: hayashi@kogakkan-u.ac.jp

HAYCRAFT Anna (Margaret), (Alice Thomas Ellis, Brenda O'Casey), b. 9 September 1932. Writer. m. Colin Berry Haycraft, deceased, 1994, 5 sons, 1 deceased, 2 daughters, 1 deceased. Education: Liverpool Art College Appointments: Director, Duckworth, publishers, London; Columnist (Home life), The Spectator, 1984-90, The Universe, 1989-90, The Catholic Herald, 1990-95; The Oldie, 1995-; The Catholic Herald, 1998-2000. Publications: Natural Baby Food: A Cookery Book (as Brenda O'Casey), 1977; The Sin Eater (novel), 1977; Darling You Shouldn't Have Gone to So Much Trouble (cookery) (as Anna Haycraft with Caroline Blackwood), 1980; The Birds of the Air (novel), 1980; The 27th Kingdom (novel), 1982; The Other Side of the Fire (novel), 1983; Unexplained Laughter (novel), 1985; Home Life (collected columns from the Spectator), 1986; Secrets of Strangers (with Tom Pitt Aikens) (psychiatry), 1986; The Clothes in the Wardrobe (novel), 1987; More Home Life (collection), 1987; The Skeleton in the Cupboard (novel), 1988; Home Life III (collection), 1988; The Loss of the Good Authority (with Tom Pitt Aikens), (psychiatry), 1989; Wales: An Anthology, 1989; The Fly in the Ointment (novel), 1989; Home Life IV (collection), 1989; The Inn at the Edge of the World (novel), 1990; A Welsh Childhood (autobiography), 1990; Pillars of Gold, 1992; Serpent on the Rock, 1994; The Evening of Adam, 1994; Cat Among the Pigeons: Collected Columns from the Catholic Herald, 1994; Fairy Tale, 1996; Valentine's Day, 2000. Honours: Welsh Arts Council Award, 1977; Yorkshire Post Novel of the Year, 1983; Writers Guild Award for Best Fiction, 1991. Memberships: Fellow, Royal Literary Society, 1998.

HAYDEN Dolores, b. 15 March 1945, New York, USA. Architect; Professor; Author. m. Peter Marris, 18 May 1975, 1 daughter. Education: BA, Mount Holyoke College, 1966; Diploma, English Studies, Girton College, Cambridge, 1967; MArch, Harvard Graduate School of Design, 1972. Publications: Seven American Utopias, 1976; The Grand Domestic Revolution, 1981; Redesigning the American Dream, 1984; The Power of Place, 1995; Playing House, 1998; Line Dance, 2001; Building Suburbia, 2003; A Field Guide to Sprawl, 2004; American Yard, 2004. Contributions to: Numerous journals. Honours: National Endowment for the Humanities Fellowship, 1976; National Endowment for the Arts Fellowship, 1980; Guggenheim Fellowship, 1981; Rockefeller Foundation Fellowship, 1981; American Council of Learned Societies/Ford Foundation Fellowship, 1988. Memberships: American Studies Association; Organization of American Historians. Address: School of Architecture, Yale University, PO Box 208242, New Haven, CT 06520, USA.

HAYES Colleen Ballard, b. Kansas City, Missouri, USA. Writer; Photographer. Education: BA, English, University of Kansas, 1972. Appointments: Associate Editor, Reporter, Johnson County Sun newspapers, Johnson County, Kansas, 1967-68; Editor, Writer, press releases and public relations, Metropolitan Planning Agency, 1968-70; Writer, speeches, Freedom of Information and other letters for President of the United States, US Senators, US Representatives, midwest governors, EPA, 1972-82. Publications: Contributor, articles to: ELLE Magazine; Travel-Holiday; Country Inns Magazine, Architectural Digest publications, Confederate Veteran Magazine, The Boston Globe, The Philadelphia Inquirer, Chicago Tribune, Los Angeles Times, The Baltimore Sun, and more than 70 others; Photography published with above articles, as well as both in Odyssey, San Francisco Examiner, The Denver Post, Christian Science Monitor, The Detroit News, The Orlando Sentinel, St Petersburg Times, St Louis Post Dispatch, The Kansas City Star, San Jose Mercury News, New York Daily News, The Plain Dealer, Chicago Sun-Times, Des Moines Register, Richmond (VA) Times-Dispatch, Women's Sports and Fitness, The Calgary Herald, numerous others in US and Canada; Travelled worldwide on writing assignments; Co-author, Anthology of American Holidays; Contributor to numerous national and regional poetry anthologies; National Scholastic Magazine (recipient, writing award), Missouri Historical Review; numerous others; Lead in drama productions at regional theatres and Topeka Civic Theater; Commentator on WIBW-TV; Performed role of Medea on KTWU Public Television; Guest interview, KCUR-FM; others. Honours: 1st prize, Bethany College Creative Writing Award; numerous others; Key to City of St Joseph, Missouri; Commissioned to Honorable Order of Kentucky Colonels; Winner, City and Regional

Tennis Awards. Memberships: Jackson County Historical Society; Quantrill Historical Society; Pony Express Historical Society; St Andrew Scottish Society; Woodside Racquet Club.

HAYES Judy Ann, b. 27 July 1966, Atlanta, Georgia, USA. Poetry Writer. m. Ronald Mahoney, 2 sons, 2 daughters. Education: Phillips Medical College, Atlanta, Georgia. Appointment: Manufacturing Operative. Publications: Poetry in Library of Poetry Anthologies including: America at the Millennium 20th Century; Best Poems of the 90's; Shadows and Light. Honours: Several Editor's Choice Awards, 1996, 1997; Listed in Who's Who publications and biographical dictionaries. Memberships: Hands On Atlanta Organization; Library of Poetry. Address: 1281 Brookside Ct SE, Mableton, GA 30126, USA.

HAYS Robert Glenn, b. 23 May 1935, Carmi, Illinois, USA. Journalism Educator. m. Mary Elizabeth Corley, 21 December 1957, 2 sons. Education: BS, Journalism, 1961, MS, Journalism, 1972, PhD, 1976, Southern Illinois University. Appointments: Reporter, Granite City Press-Record, 1961-63; Public Relations Writer, 1963-66, Alumni Editor, 1966-71, Southern Illinois University; Assistant Scientist, Illinois Board of Natural Resources and Conservation, 1971-73; Journalism Faculty, Sam Houston State University, 1974-75; University of Illinois, 1975-86, 1987-; Chair, Department of Mass Communications, Southeast Missouri University, 1986-87. Publications: G-2: Intelligence for Patton, 1971, new edition, 1999; Country Editor, 1974; State Science in Illinois, 1980; Early Stories From the Land, 1995; A Race at Bay: New York Times Editorials on the 'Indian Problem', 1860-1900, 1997. Contributions to: Periodicals and journals. Honours: International ACE Award of Excellence, 1993, 1994; University of Illinois Academy of Teaching Excellence Award, 1996. Membership: Research Society of American Periodicals, founding member; Association for Education in Journalism and Mass Communications; Illinois Press Association; Investigative Reporters and Editors; Missouri Press Association; Society of Professional Journalists; National Organization for Women; American Civil Liberties Union, Chapter Steering Committee, 1991-93. Address: 2314 Glenoak Drive, Champaign, IL 61821, USA.

HAYTER Alethea Catharine, b. 7 November 1911, Cairo, Egypt. Former British Council Representative and Cultural Attache; Writer. Education: BA, MA, University of Oxford. Publications: Mrs Browning: A Poet's Work and Its Setting, 1962; A Sultry Month: Scenes of London Literary Life in 1846, 1965; Elizabeth Barrett Browning, 1965; Opium and the Romantic Imagination, 1968; Horatio's Version, 1972; A Voyage in Vain, 1973; Fitzgerald to His Friends: Selected Letters of Edward Fitzgerald, 1979; Portrait of a Friendship, Drawn From New Letters of James Russell Lowell to Sybella Lady Lyttelton 1881-1891, 1990; The Backbone: Diaries of a Military Family in the Napoleonic Wars, 1993; Charlotte Yonge, 1996; A Wise Woman: A Memoir of Lavinia Mynors from her Diaries and Letters, 1996; The Wreck of the Abergavenny, 2002. Contributions to: Oxford Companion to English Literature; Sunday Times; Times Literary Supplement; Spectator; New Statesman; History Today; Ariel; London Review of Books; Longman Encyclopedia. Honours: W.H. Heinemann Prize, Royal Society of Literature, 1963; Rose Mary Crawshay Prize, British Academy, 1968; Officer of the Order of the British Empire. Memberships: Royal Society of Literature, fellow; Society of Authors, committee of management, 1975-79; PEN. Address: 22 Aldebert Terrace, London SW8 1BJ, England.

HEALD Tim(othy Villiers), (David Lancaster), b. 28 January 1944, Dorset, England. Journalist; Writer. m. (1) Alison Martina Leslie, 30 March 1968, dissolved, 2 sons, 2 daughters, (2) Penelope

Byrne, 1999. Education: MA, Honours, Balliol College, Oxford, 1965. Appointments: Reporter, Sunday Times, 1965-67; Feature Editor, Town magazine, 1967; Feature Writer, Daily Express, 1967-72; Associate Editor, Weekend Magazine, Toronto, 1977-78; Columnist, Observer, 1990; Visiting Fellow, Jane Franklin Hall, University of Tasmania, 1997, 1999; University Tutor, Creative Writing, 1999, 2000; FRSL, 2000; Writer-in-Residence, University of South Australia, 2001. Publications: It's a Dog's Life, 1971; Unbecoming Habits, 1973; Blue Book Will Out, 1974; Deadline, 1975; Let Sleeping Dogs Lie, 1976; The Making of Space, 1999, 1976; John Steed: An Authorised Biography, 1977; Just Desserts, 1977; H.R.H: The Man Who Will be King, with M Mohs, 1977; Murder at Moose Jaw, 1981; Caroline R, 1981; Masterstroke, 1982; Networks, 1983; Class Distinctions, 1984; Red Herrings, 1985; The Character of Cricket, 1986; Brought to Book, 1988; Editor, The Newest London Spy, 1988; Business Unusual, 1989; By Appointments: 150 Years of the Royal Warrant, 1989; Editor, A Classic English Crime, 1990; Editor, My Lord's, 1990; The Duke: A Portrait of Prince Philip, 1991; Honourable Estates, 1992; Barbara Cartland: A Life of Love, 1994; Denis: The Authorised Biography of the Incomparable Compton, 1994; Brian Johnston: The Authorised Biography, 1995; Editor, A Classic Christmas Crime, 1995; Beating Retreat: Hong Kong Under the Last Governor, 1997; Stop Press, 1998; A Peerage for Trade, 2001. Contributions: Short stories: EQMM; Strand magazine; Tatler; Mail on Sunday. Memberships: Crime Writers Association, Chairman, 1987-88; PEN; Society of Authors. Literary Agent: Andrew Lownie, 17 Sutherland St, London SW1V 4JU. Address: 66 The Esplanade, Fowey, Cornwall PL23 1JA, England. E-mail: timheald@compuserve.com

HEALEY Denis (Lord Healey of Riddlesden), b. 30 August 1917, Keighley, Yorkshire, England. Politician. m. Edna May Edmunds, 1945, 1 son, 2 daughters. Education: BA, 1940, MA, 1945, Balliol College, Oxford. Appointments include: Served, World War II, 1939-45; Contested, (Labour) Pudsey and Otley Division, 1945; Secretary, International Department, Labour Party, 1945-52; Member of Parliament, South East Leeds, 1952-55, Leeds East, 1955-92; Shadow Cabinet, 1959-64, 1970-74, 1979-87; Secretary of State for Defence, 1964-70; Chancellor of the Exchequer, 1974-79; Opposition Spokesman on Foreign and Commonwealth Affairs, 1980-87; Deputy Leader, Labour Party, 1980-83. Publications: The Curtain Falls, 1951; New Fabian Essays, 1952; Neutralism, 1955; Fabian International Essays, 1956; A Neutral Belt in Europe, 1958; NATO and American Security, 1959; The Race Against the H Bomb, 1960; Labour Britain and the World, 1964; Healey's Eye, 1980; Labour and a World Society, 1985; Beyond Nuclear Deterrence, 1986; The Time of My Life (autobiography), 1989; When Shrimps Learn to Whistle (essays), 1990; My Secret Planet, 1992; Denis Healey's Yorkshire Dales, 1995; Healey's World, photographs, 2002. Honours include: Grand Cross of Order of Merit, Germany, 1979; Freeman, City of Leeds, 1992; FRSL, 1993. Membership: President, Birkbeck College, 1992-98. Address: Pingles Place, Alfriston, East Sussex BN26 5TT, England.

HEALY Terry Robin, b. 28 November 1944, Auckland, New Zealand. Research Professor of Coastal Environmental Science; Holder of the Port of Tauranga Chair of Coastal Environmental Science. m. Judy-Ann, 2 daughters. Education: BSc, 1965, MSc (Hons), 1967, University of Auckland; PhD, Monash University, 1971. Appointments: Demonstrator, Geomorphology, Department of Geology, 1969, Lecturer, Quantitative Methods, Department of Geography, 1971, University of Melbourne; Lecturer, Geomorphology, Faculty of Applied Science, University of New South Wales, 1971-73; Lecturer, Earth Sciences, 1973, Senior Lecturer, 1976, Reader, Associate Professor, 1984, Research

Professor, 1990, University of Waikato; Adjunct Professor Nanjing University China, 1995-. Publications: 196 articles in professional peer-reviewed journals and book chapters; Associate Editor, International Journal of Coastal Research; Editor-author, Muddy Coasts of the World: Process Deposits and Function, 2002. Honours: Prize for Best Paper, New Zealand Marine Sciences Society Conference, 1974; Alexander von Humboldt Research Fellowship, 1978-79, 1985-86; Japan Society for Promotion of Science Fellowship, 1989; Vice President of SCOR (Scientific Committee on Oceanic Research), 1991-96; Fulbright Research Fellowship, 1995; Monbusho Senior Fellowship, 1996; Chairperson of the Bay of Plenty Conservation Board, 1996-98; Alexander von Humboldt Preisträger Award, 1997; JSPS Short Term Senior Fellowship, 2000; Distinguished Fellowship of the Ministry of Education of China, 2003; Elected Fellow, Institution of Professional Engineers of New Zealand, 2003; Director, Coastal Education Research Foundation; Elected to Council of the University of Waikato, 2003-07; Director, Willawa Groves Ltd. Memberships: Institution of Professional Engineers of New Zealand; New Zealand Geological Society; New Zealand Marine Sciences Society; New Zealand Geophysics Society; New Zealand Hydrological Society; American Geophysical Union; New Zealand Coastal Society. Address: Coastal Marine Group, Department of Earth Sciences, University of Waikato, Hamilton, New Zealand. E-mail: trh@waikato.ac.nz

HEANEY Seamus (Justin), b. 13 April 1939, County Londonderry, Northern Ireland. Poet; Writer; Professor. m. Marie Devlin, 1965, 2 sons, 1 daughter. Education: St Columb's College, Derry; BA 1st Class, Queen's University, Belfast, 1961. Appointments: Teacher, St Thomas's Secondary School, Belfast, 1962-63; Lecturer, St Joseph's College of Education, Belfast, 1963-66, Queen's University, Belfast, 1966-72, Carysfort College, 1975-81; Senior Visiting Lecturer, 1982-85, Boylston Professor of Rhetoric and Oratory, 1985-97, Harvard University; Professor of Poetry, Oxford University, 1989-94. Publications: Eleven Poems, 1965; Death of a Naturalist, 1966; Door Into the Dark, 1969; Wintering Out, 1972; North, 1975; Field Work, 1979; Selected Poems, 1965-1975, 1980; Sweeney Astray, 1984, revised edition as Sweeney's Flight, 1992; Station Island, 1984; The Haw Lantern, 1987; New Selected Poems, 1966-1987, 1990; Seeing Things, 1991; The Spirit Level, 1996; Opened Ground: Selected Poems, 1966-1996, 1998. Prose: Preoccupations: Selected Prose, 1968-1978, 1980; The Government of the Tongue, 1988; The Place of Writing, 1989; The Redress of Poetry: Oxford Lectures, 1995; Beowulf: A New Verse Translation and Introduction, 1999; Electric Light, 2000. Honours: Somerset Maugham Award, 1967; Cholmondeley Award, 1968; W H Smith Award, 1975; Duff Cooper Prize, 1975; Whitbread Awards, 1987, 1996; Nobel Prize for Literature, 1995; Whitbread Book of the Year Award, 1997, 1999; Honorary DLitt, Oxford, 1997, Birmingham, 2000. Memberships: Royal Irish Academy; British Academy, American Academy of Arts and Letters. Address: c/o Faber & Faber, 3 Queen Square, London WC1N 3RU, England.

HEATH Edward (Richard George) (Sir), b. 9 July 1916, St Peters-in-Thanet, Kent, England. Conductor; Writer on Music. Education: Balliol College, Oxford, 1935-39; MA (Organ Scholar). Career: Has conducted the London Symphony Orchestra, Royal Philharmonic, Philharmonia, Liverpool Philharmonic, Bournemouth Symphony Orchestra, Northern Sinfonia, English Chamber Orchestra, New Queen's Hall Orchestra; Zurich Chamber Orchestra, Leningrad Conservatoire Symphony Orchestra, Georgian TV Orchestra Tbilisi, Prague Opera Chamber Orchestra, Calgary Symphony Orchestra, Berlin Philharmonic, Barcelona Symphony Orchestra, European Community Youth Orchestra, Chicago, Cleveland and Philadelphia Symphony Orchestras,

Dictionary of International Biography

Shanghai Symphony Orchestra and Central Philharmonic Orchestra of China, Peking. Recordings: Elgar Cockaigne Overture with the London Symphony Orchestra; Robert Mayer Christmas Concert 1973 with the Academy of the BBC Orchestra and BBC Singers; Carols, The Joy of Christmas with the English Chamber Orchestra and the George Mitchell Singers; Black Dyke Mills Band, 1977; Beethoven Triple Concerto with the English Chamber Orchestra and Trio Zingara; Boccherini Cello Concerto in G with Felix Schmidt and the English Chamber Orchestra, 1989. Publications: Music-A Joy for Life; Carols-the Joy of Christmas; The Course of My Life - Autobiography, 1998. Memberships: Honorary Member, London Symphony Orchestra; Vice-President, London Bach Choir; Vice-President, Oxford Bach Choir; Governor, Royal College of Music, 1960-70; President, European Community Youth Orchestra, 1977-83; Chairman, London Symphony Orchestra Trust, 1963-70; International Adviser, Praemium Imperiale Arts Awards. Address: House of Commons, Westminster, London SW1 0AA, England.

HEATH-STUBBS John (Francis Alexander), b. 9 July 1918, London, England. Poet; Writer; Translator; Editor. Education: Worcester College for the Blind; Queen's College, Oxford. Appointments: English Master, Hall School, Hampstead, 1944-45; Editorial Assistant, Hutchinson's 1945-46; Gregory Fellow in Poetry, University of Leeds, 1952-55; Visiting Professor of English, University of Alexandria, 1955-58, University of Michigan, 1960-61; Lecturer in English Literature, College of St Mark and St John, Chelsea, 1963-73. Publications: Poetry: Wounded Thammuz, 1942; Beauty and the Beast, 1943; The Divided Ways, 1946; The Swarming of the Bees, 1950; A Charm Against the Toothache, 1954; The Triumph of the Muse, 1958; The Blue Fly in His Head, 1962; Selected Poems, 1965; Satires and Epigrams, 1968; Artorius, 1973; A Parliament of Birds, 1975; The Watchman's Flute, 1978; Mouse, the Bird and the Sausage, 1978; Birds Reconvened, 1980; Buzz Buzz, 1981; Naming the Beasts, 1982; The Immolation of Aleph, 1985; Cat's Parnassus, 1987; Time Pieces, 1988; Collected Poems, 1988; A Partridge in a Pear Tree, 1988; A Ninefold of Charms, 1989; Selected Poems, 1990; The Parson's Cat, 1991; Sweetapple Earth, 1993; Chimeras, 1994; Galileo's Salad, 1996; The Torriano Sequences, 1997; The Sound of Light, 2000. Play: Helen in Egypt, 1958. Autobiography: Hindsights, 1993. Criticism: The Darkling Plain, 1950; Charles Williams, 1955; The Pastoral, 1969; The Ode, 1969; The Verse Satire, 1969. Translator: Hafiz of Shiraz (with Peter Avery), 1952; Leopardi: Selected Prose and Poetry (with Iris Origo), 1966; The Poems of Anyte (with Carol A Whiteside), 1974; The Rubaiyat of Omar Khayyam (with Peter Avery), 1979; Sulpicia, 2000. Editor: Several books, including: Faber Book of Twentieth Century Verse (with David Wright), 1953; Poems of Science (with Phillips Salman), 1984. Honours: Queen's Gold Medal for Poetry, 1973; Oscar Williams/Jean Durwood Award, 1977; Officer of the Order of the British Empire, 1989; Commonwealth Poetry Prize, 1989; Cholmondeley Award, 1989; Howard Sargeant Award, 1989; Cross of St Augustine, 1999; Fellow, English Association, 1999. Membership: Royal Society of Literature, Fellow. Address: 22 Artesian Road, London W2 5AR, England.

HECHT Anthony (Evan), b. 16 January 1923, New York, New York, USA. Poet; Professor. m. (1) Patricia Harris, 27 February 1954, divorced 1961, 2 sons, (2) Helen D'Alessandro, 12 June 1971, 1 son. Education: BA, Bard College, 1944; MA, Columbia University, 1950. Appointments: Teacher, Kenyon College, 1947-48, State University of Iowa, 1948-49, New York University, 1949-56, Smith College, 1956-59; Associate Professor of English, Bard College, 1961-67; Faculty, 1967-68, John D Deane Professor of English of Rhetoric and Poetry, 1968-85, University of Rochester, New York; Hurst Professor, Washington University, St Louis, 1971;

Visiting Professor, Harvard University, 1973, Yale University, 1977; Faculty, Salzburg Seminar in American Studies, 1977; Professor, Georgetown University, 1985-93; Consultant in Poetry, Library of Congress, Washington, DC, 1982-84; Andrew Mellon Lecturer in Fine Arts, National Gallery of Art, Washington, DC, 1992. Publications: A Summoning of Stones, 1954; The Seven Deadly Sins, 1958; A Bestiary, 1960; The Hard Hours, 1968; Millions of Strange Shadows, 1977; The Venetian Vespers, 1977; Obbligati: Essays in Criticism, 1986; The Transparent Man, 1990; Collected Earlier Poems, 1990; The Hidden Law: The Poetry of W H Auden, 1993; On the Laws of the Poetic Art, 1995; The Presumption of Death, 1995; Flight Among the Tombs, 1996; The Darkness and the Light, 2001. Co-Author and Co-Editor: Jiggery-Pokery: A Compendium of Double Dactyls (with John Hollander), 1967. Editor: The Essential Herbert, 1987. Translator: Seven Against Thebes (with Helen Bacon), 1973. Contributions to: Many anthologies; Hudson Review; New York Review of Books; Quarterly Review of Literature; Transatlantic Review; Voices. Honours: Prix de Rome Fellowship, 1950; Guggenheim Fellowships, 1954, 1959; Hudson Review Fellowship, 1958; Ford Foundation Fellowships, 1960, 1968; Academy of American Poets Fellowship, 1969; Bollingen Prize, 1983; Eugenio Montale Award, 1983; Harriet Monroe Award, 1987; Ruth Lilly Award, 1988; Aiken Taylor Award, Sewanee Review, 1988; National Endowment for the Arts Grant, 1989; Phi Beta Kappa. Memberships: Academy of American Poets, honorary chancellor, 1971-97; American Academy of Arts and Sciences; American Academy of Arts and Letters; Phi Beta Kappa. Address: 4256 Nebraska Avenue North West, Washington, DC 20016, USA.

HEDRICK Wyatt, b. 28 September 1951, Roswell, New Mexico, USA. Pharmacist. m. Marcia. Education: BS Pharmacy, 1974, University New Mexico; MSc Hospital Pharmacy, 1978, University of Houston. Appointments: Resident, Pharmacy, University of Texas, Medical Branch Hospitals, Galveston, 1977-78; Pharmacist, Memorial General Hospital, Las Cruces, New Mexico, 1978; Pharmacist, Las Palmas Medical Centre, El Paso, Texas, 1978-. Memberships: American Society of Health-System Pharmacists; Texas Society of Health-System Pharmacists; El Paso Area Society of Health-System Pharmacists. Address: 1028 Quinault Drive, El Paso, TX 79912-1223, USA.

HEEB Mary J Holzknecht, b. 20 September 1942, Louisville, Kentucky, USA. Research Biochemist. Divorced. 2 sons, 2 daughters. Education: BS Chemistry, 1966, MS Microbiology, 1968, University of Florida, Gainesville; PhD Biochemistry, Georgetown University, Washington, 1983; Postdoctoral Studies, The Scripps Research Institute, La Jolla, 1983. Appointments: Research Assistant, Department of Biochemistry, University of Florida, 1968-69; Research Assistant, Department of Pharmacology, University of Miami Medical School, 1969-72; Consultant, Department of Interior, Wrightsville Beach, North Carolina, 1972-73; Instructor, Chemistry Department, University of North Carolina, 1973-75; Group Leader, Hazleton Laboratories, Vienna, Virginia, 1975-78, 1981-83; Scientific Associate, 1988-92, Assistant Professor, 1992-99, Associate Professor, 1999-, The Scripps Research Institute, La Jolla. Publications: Author and co-author, 55 articles in professional journals, including: Binding sites for blood coagulation factor Xa and protein S involving residues 493-506 in factor Va, 1996; C-terminal residues 621-635 of protein S are essential for binding to factor Va, 1999. Honours: Wilhelm Turk prize, Austrian Society for Hematology and Oncology, 1986; Highest Score, 1/81, on American Heart Association fellowship application, California affiliate, 1986-87. Memberships: American Society for Hematology; American Association for Biochemistry and Molecular Biology; International Society for Thrombosis and Haemostasis. Address: 10550 North Torrey Pines Road, MEM 180, La Jolla, CA 92037, USA. E-mail: heeb@scripps.edu

Dictionary of International Biography

HEFNER Hugh Marston, b. 9 April 1926, Chicago, Illinois, USA. Publisher. m. (1) Mildred Williams, 1 son, 1 daughter, (2) Kimberley Conrad, 1989, 2 daughters. Education: BS, University of Illinois. Appointments: Editor-in-Chief, Playboy magazine, 1953-, Oui magazine, 1972-81; Chairman Emeritus, Playboy Enterprises, 1988-; President, Playboy Club International Inc, 1959-86. Honour: International Press Directory International Publisher Award, 1997. Address: Playboy Enterprises Inc, 9242 Beverly Boulevard, Beverly Hills, CA 90210, USA.

HEGELER Sten, b. 28 April 1923, Frederiksberg, Denmark. Psychologist. 1 son, 1 daughter. Education: Candidate for Psychology, University of Copenhagen, 1953. Publications: Peter and Caroline; Men Only; Choosing Toys for Children; What Everybody Should Know About AIDS; On Selenium; An ABZ of Love (with I Hegeler); Ask Inge and Sten; World's Best Slimming Diet; On Being Lonesome; XYZ of Love; Living is Loving. Contributions to: Aktuelt; Info; Editor, Taenk magazine. Honour: Ph-Fund and Honorary member of Danish Psychologists Association. Memberships: Danish Psychological Association; Danish Journalist Association; Danish Authors Association. Address: Frederiksberg Alle 25, DK-1820 Frederiksberg, Denmark.

HEILBRUN Carolyn (Gold), b. 13 January 1926, East Orange, New Jersey, USA. Professor of English Literature Emerita; Writer. m. James Heilbrun, 20 February 1945, 1 son, 2 daughters. Education: BA, Wellesley College, 1947; MA, 1951, PhD, 1959, Columbia University. Appointments: Instructor, Brooklyn College, 1959-60; Instructor, 1960-62, Assistant Professor, 1962-67, Associate Professor, 1967-72, Professor of English Literature, 1972-86, Avalon Foundation Professor of Humanities, 1986-93, Professor Emerita, 1993-, Columbia University; Visiting Professor, University of California at Santa Cruz, 1979, Princeton University, 1981, Yale Law School, 1989. Publications: The Garnett Family, 1961; In the Last Analysis, 1964; Christopher Isherwood, 1970; Toward a Recognition of Androgyny, 1973; Lady Ottoline's Album, 1976; Reinventing Womanhood, 1979; Representation of Women in Fiction (editor), 1983; Writing a Woman's Life, 1988; Hamlet's Mother and Other Women, 1990; The Education of a Woman: The Life of Gloria Steinem, 1995; The Last Gift of Time, 1997; Collected Stories, 1997. Honours: Guggenheim Fellowship, 1966; Rockefeller Foundation Fellowship, 1976; Nero Wolfe Award, 1981; Senior Research Fellow, National Endowment for the Humanities, 1983; Alumnae Achievement Award, Wellesley College, 1984; Award of Excellence, Graduate Faculty of Columbia University Alumni, 1984; Life Achievement Award, Modern Language Association, 1984; Many honorary doctorates. Memberships: Modern Language Association, President, 1984; Mystery Writers of America; Phi Beta Kappa. Address: c/o Department of English, Columbia University, New York, NY 10027, USA.

HEINE Susanna L, b. 17 January 1942, Prague, Czechoslovakia. University Professor. m. Peter Pawlowsky. Education: Arbitur, 1960; Mag theol, University of Vienna, 1966; Ordained Pastor, Lutheran Church, 1968; Dr theol, University of Vienna, 1973; Habilitation, University of Vienna, 1979. Appointments: Assistant, New Testament Studies, 1968-79; Dozent (Lecturer) Religious Education, 1979-82; Professor, Religious Education, 1982-90; Professor of Pastoral Theology and Psychology of Religion, University of Zurich, 1990-96; Professor of Pastoral Theology and Psychology of Religion, University of Vienna, 1996-. Publications: Leibhafter Glaube, 1976; Biblische Fachdidaktik, 1976; Women and Early Christianity, 1987, 1990; Christianity and the Goddesses, 1988, 1990; Keines Religiöses Wörterbuch, (editor) 1984; Europa in der Krise der Neuzeit (editor), 1986; Islam

Zwischen Selbstbild und Klischee (editor), 1995; Frauenbilder – Menschenrechte, 2000; Gedanken für den Tag, 2001; About 200 articles on education, psychology, feminism, history of ideas, interreligious dialogue. Memberships: European Academic Society of Theology, 1988-, Vice Chairman, 1996-2002, Science Board, Sigmund Freud Society, 1995-; World Conference, Religions and Peace, 1996-; Contact Committee for Questions concerning Islam, 1996-; Abrahamitic Friends, 1996-; Austrian Research Community on Social Ethics, 1997-; Board, International Society of Psychology of Religion, 1998-. Address: Protestant Faculty, University of Vienna, Rooseveltplatz 10, A-1090, Vienna.

HEINONEN Reijo Eljas, b. 3 October 1938, Helsinki, Finland. Professor. m. Essi Vatanen, 2 sons. Education: Master of Theology, 1965, Master of Arts, 1986, University of Helsinki; Doctor of Theology, University of Tübingen, 1972. Appointments: Acting Senior Lecturer, Teacher Training School, University of Helsinki, 1975-81; Senior Lecturer, Teacher Training Institute, University of Turku, 1981-94; Acting Associate Professor, Church History, University of Helsinki, 1987-88; Acting Professor, Historical Theology, 1994-, Professor Ordinarius, 1995-, Dean, Faculty of Theology, 2002-, University of Joensuu Publications: 5 monographs; Around 100 scientific articles on religious education, church history and ethics. Honours: Corresponding Member, Collegium Europaeum Jenense, University of Jena; Knight First Class of the Order of the Holy Lamb, Finnish Orthodox Church. Memberships: Chair, Peace-Education Institute, Helsinki, 1997-; Academic Adviser, Islam and the West. Address: Haapakatu 4, FIN-21110 Naantali, Finland. E-mail: reijo.heinonen@joensuu.fi

HEINRICH Peggy, b. 20 February 1929, USA. Writer; Poet. m. Martin R Heinrich, 4 April 1952, deceased 1976, 2 daughters. Education: BA, Hunter College, New York City, 1949. Appointment: Editor, Connecticut River Review, 1985-87. Publications: Haiga Haiku (with artist Barbara Gray), 1982; A Patch of Grass, 1984; Sharing the Woods, 1992; Forty-four Freckles, 1995. Contributions to: Connecticut Artist; Blue Unicorn; Footwork; Calliope; Poet Lore; Frogpond; Connecticut River Review; The New Renaissance; Mainichi (Tokyo) Daily News; Embers; San Fernando Poetry Journal; DeKalb Literary Arts Journal; Z Misc; Passager; Iconoclast; Basho Festival Anthology; Women and Death Anthology. Honours: Sri Chinmoy Award, Committee for Spiritual Poetry, 1980; 2nd Prize, North Carolina Haiku Society, 1984; Medal for Literary Achievement, State of Connecticut, 1985; 3rd Prize, Henderson Award, Haiku Society of America, 1994; 1st Prize, Hawaii Education Association International Haiku Contest, 1996. Memberships: Poetry Society of America; Academy of American Poets; Poets and Writers; Dramatists' Guild; Haiku Society of America; Connecticut Poetry Society. Address: 625 Gilman Street, Bridgeport, CT 06605, USA.

HEINZ Daniel, b. 19 August 1957, Vienna, Austria. Director of Archives; Lecturer. m. Irina Arefiewa. Education: Diploma in Theology, Bogenhofen Seminary, Austria, 1978; BA, 1979, MA, 1981, PhD (Religion), 1991, Andrews University, Michigan, USA. Appointments: Lecturer in Church History, Bogenhofen Seminary, Friedensau University, Germany, 1982-; Director of Archives, Euro-Africa Division, Berne, Switzerland, 1997-; Founder and Current Chairman, Institute of Adventist History, Friedensau University, Germany, 1998-; Academic Advisor, Adventist and Free Church Studies, Europe, and Member of Biblical Research Committee, Berne-Washington DC, 1990-. Publications: Adventistica, 8 volumes (editor); Glaube und Gemeinde (Encyclopaedia) (editor), forthcoming; Church, State and Religious Dissent (author), 1992; Ludwig R. Conradi, (author) 3rd edition 1998; Co-editor and author of numerous articles in the field of denominational history and free church studies. Honours: Listed

Dictionary of International Biography

in Who's Who publications and biographical dictionaries. Memberships: Association of Free Churches (Freikirchenforschung); Historical Society of Methodist Studies; Historical Society of Mennonite Studies. Address: An der Ihle 19, D-39291 Friedensau, Germany. E-mail: Daniel.Heinz@thh-Friedensau.de

HELAL Basil Hessein, b. 28 October 1927, Cairo, Egypt. Orthopaedic Surgeon. m. Susan, 3 sons, 2 daughters. Education: The English School, Cairo; The Royal London Hospital; University of London; Mastership in Orthopaedic Surgery, University of Liverpool. Appointments: Examiner, Orthopaedic Post Graduate FRCS, Royal College of Surgeons, Edinburgh; Examiner, Mastership in Orthopaedic Surgery, University of Kabangasaan, Malaysia; Examiner, Society of Physiotherapy; Examiner, Board of Examiners in Chiropody; Examiner, Society of Occupational Therapists; Orthopaedic Advisor, Royal Academy of Dancing; Orthopaedic Advisor, British Olympic Association; Lecturer, Continuing Education Programme, Australian Orthopaedic Association; Praelector, University of Strathclyde, Dundee; Orthopaedic Advisor, British Olympic Association over 5 Olympics; Honorary Consultant, Orthopaedic Surgery, Royal London Hospital, undergraduate teaching; Emeritus Consultant, Orthopaedic Surgery, Royal National Orthopaedic Hospital, postgraduate teaching; Honorary Consultant, Orthopaedic Surgery, Enfield Group Hospitals. Publications: Author, co-author and co-editor, 6 books; 117 articles in professional medical journals. Honours: Honorary Member, French Foot Society; Honorary Fellow, German Foot Society. Memberships include: Orthopaedic Foot Surgery Society; Arthritis Surgical Society; Egyptian Medical Society; British Society for Surgery of the Hand; British Association of Sport and Medicine; Royal Society of Medicine; Hunterian Society; International Orthopaedic Foot Surgery Society; International League Against Rheumatism; Yugoslav Orthopaedic Association; New Zealand Orthopaedic Association; Rheumatoid Arthritis Surgical Society; British Orthopaedic Association; International Federation of Sport Medicine. Address: Easdale, Carnaig Street, Dornoch, Sutherland IV25 3LT, Scotland.

HELLAWELL Keith, b. 18 May 1942, Yorkshire, England. Anti-Drugs Co-ordinator; Police Officer. m. Brenda Hey, 1963, 1 son, 2 daughters. Education: Dewsbury Technology College; Cranfield Institute of Technology; London University. Appointments: Miner, 5 years; Joined Huddersfield Borough Police, progressed through every rank within West Yorkshire Police to Assistant Chief Constable; Deputy Chief Constable of Humberside, 1985-90; Chief Constable of Cleveland Police, 1990-93; Chief Constable of West Yorkshire Police, 1993-98; First UK Anti Drugs Co-ordinator, 1998-2001; Adviser to Home Secretary on International Drug Issues, 2001-. Publications: The Outsider, autobiography, 2002. Memberships include: Association of Police Officers Spokesman on Drugs; Advisory Council on the Misuse of Drugs; Board, Community Action Trust; Trustee, National Society for the Prevention of Cruelty to Children; Editorial Advisory Board, Journal of Forensic Medicine. Address: Government Offices, George Street, London SW1A 2AL, England.

HEMINGWAY Wayne, b. 19 January 1961, England. Designer. m. Geraldine, 2 sons, 2 daughters. Appointments: Joint business, market stall, Camden, London; Creator of footwear, clothing and accessory label, Red or Dead, 1992; Collection retailed through 8 Red or Dead shops in England, 3 Red or Dead shops in Japan and wholesaled to international network of retailers; Joint venture with Pentland Group PLC, 1996-; Founder, Hemingway Design, 1999; Designer, new wing for Institute of Directors, 2001; Current design and consultancy projects include 700-unit housing estate, carpet design, wall covering and menswear; Chair, Prince's Trust Fashion

Initiative. Publications: The Good, the Bad and the Ugly, with Geraldine Hemingway, 1998; Kitsch Icons, 1999; Just Above the Mantlepiece, 2000. Honours: Street Designers of the Year, British Fashion Awards, 1995, 1996, 1997, 1998. Address: Red or Dead Ltd, Building 201, Courtney Road, GEC East Lane Estate, Wembley, Middlesex HA9 7PP, England.

HEMMA Sherif Mohamed Fathy, b. 27 December 1959, Alexandria, Egypt. Chief Financial Officer. m. Kamilia Ayad Wardi. Education: MBA, USA International University, San Diego, USA, 1984; Bachelors Degree of Commerce, Ain Shams University, Cairo, Egypt, 1988. Appointments: Executive positions at Brigewater Coopers; Audit Manager, CPA; Financial Planning Manager, Xerox, Egypt; Financial Manager, Bristol Myers Squibb; Deputy Finance Director, Aventis; Middle East Regional Finance Director, Phizer; Chief Financial Officer, Kabo JIL. Honours: Listed in national and international biographical dictionaries. Memberships: Chairman, Finance Forum Egypt; Member, Junior Businessmens Association. Address: 100 Osman Edn Afan St, Heliopolis, Egypt. E-mail: kabofin@soficom.com.eg

HEMMING John Henry, b. 5 January 1935, Vancouver, British Columbia, Canada. Author; Publisher. m. Sukie Babington-Smith, 1979, 1 son, 1 daughter. Education: McGill and Oxford Universities; MA; D.Litt. Appointments: Explorations in Peru and Brazil, 1960, 1961, 1971, 1972, 1986-87; Director and Secretary, Royal Geographical Society, 1975-96; Joint Chairman, Hemming Group Ltd, 1976-; Chair, Brintex Ltd., Newman Books Ltd. Publications: The Conquest of the Incas, 1970; Tribes of the Amazon Basin in Brazil (with others), 1973; Red Gold: The Conquest of the Brazilian Indians, 1978; The Search for El Dorado, 1978; Machu Picchu, 1982; Monuments of the Incas, 1983; Change in the Amazon Basin, (editor), 2 volumes, 1985; Amazon Frontier: The Defeat of the Brazilian Indians, 1987; Maracá, 1988; Roraima: Brazil's Northernmost Frontier, 1990; The Rainforest Edge (editor), 1994; The Golden Age of Discovery, 1998; Die If You Must, Brazilian Indians in the 20th Century, 2003. Honours: CMG; Pitman Literary Prize, 1970; Christopher Award, New York, 1971; Order of Merit (Peru) 1991; Order of the Southern Cross (Brazil), 1998; Honorary doctorates, University of Warwick, University of Stirling; Medals from Royal Geographical Society, Boston Museum of Science, Royal Scottish Geographical Society; Citation of Merit, New York Explorers' Club. Address: Hemming Group Ltd, 32 Vauxhall Bridge Road, London SW1V 2SS, England. E-mail: j.hemming@hgluk.com

HENDERSON Douglas James, b. 28 July 1934, Calgary, Alberta, Canada. Theoretical Physicist. m. Rose-Marie Steen-Nielsen, 3 daughters. Education: BA, 1st Class Honours, 1st place, Mathematics, University of British Columbia, 1956; PhD, Physics, University of Utah, USA, 1961. Appointments include: Assistant Professor, Associate Professor, Professor, Physics, Arizona State University, USA, 1962-69; Associate Professor, Physics, 1964-67, Professor, Applied Mathematics, Physics, 1967-69, Adjunct Professor, Applied Mathematics, 1969-85, University of Waterloo, Canada; Research Scientist, 1969-90, Research Scientist Emeritus, 1992-, IBM Almaden Research Center, San Jose, California; Research Scientist, IBM Corporation, Salt Lake City, Utah, 1990-92; Adjunct Professor, Physics, 1990-93, Adjunct Professor, Chemistry, Mathematics, 1990-95, Research Scientist, Center for High Performance Computing, 1990-95, University of Utah; Manuel Sandoral Vallarta Professor, Physics, 1988; Juan de Oyarzabal Professor, Physics, 1993-95, Juan de Oyarzabal Honorary Professor, 1996-, Universidad Autonoma Metropolitana, Mexico; Professor, Chemistry, Brigham Young University, 1995-; Many visiting positions. Publications: Over 425 research papers in scientific journals; Co-author, Statistical Mechanics and

Dynamics, 1964, 2nd edition, 1982; Co-editor, Physical Chemistry: An Advanced Treatise, 15 volumes, 1966-75; Co-author, Chemical Dynamics, 1971; Co-editor, Advances and Perspectives, 6 volumes, 1973-81; Editor, Fundamentals of Inhomogeneous Fluids, 1992. Honours include: Alfred P Sloan Foundation Fellowship, 1964, 1966; Ian Potter Foundation Fellowship, 1966; Outstanding Research Contribution Award, 1973, Outstanding Innovation Award, 1987, IBM; Corresponding Member, National Academy of Sciences of Mexico, 1990; Catedra Patrimoniales de Excelencia, Mexico, 1993-95; Premio a las Areas de Investigacion, Universidad Autonoma Metropolitana, 1996; John Simon Guggenheim Memorial Foundation Fellow, 1997; Joel Henry Hildebrand National American Chemical Society Award in Theoretical and Experimental Chemistry of Liquids, 1999. Memberships include: Fellow, American Physical Society, 1963-; Fellow, Institute of Physics, UK, 1965-; Fellow, American Institute of Chemists, 1971-; American Chemical Society; Biophysical Society; Canadian Association of Physicists; Mathematical Association of America; New York Academy of Sciences; Phi Kappa Phi; Sigma Xi; Sigma Pi Sigma. Address: Department of Chemistry, Brigham Young University, Provo, UT 84602, USA. E-mail: doug@huey.byu.edu

HENDERSON George Poland, b. 24 April 1920, London, England. Company Director. m. Shirley Prudence Ann, 2 sons. Education: University of London. Appointments: Captain, Royal Artillery, 1940-46; Commercial Reference Librarian, Guildhall Library, 1946-63; Director, Kelly's Directories Ltd, 1963-66; Director, now Chairman, CBD Research Ltd, 1966-. Publications: Current British Directories, 6 editions, 1953-71; European Companies: A Guide to Sources of Information, 3 editions, 1961-72; Directory of British Associations, 11 editions, 1965-92. Honours: Freeman, City of London, 1961. Memberships: Association of British Directory Publishers; European Association of Directory Publishers; Royal Institution of Great Britain; Royal Philatelic Society, London; Institute of Directors.

HENDERSON William James Carlaw, b. 26 September 1948, Galashiels, Selkirkshire, Scotland. Lawyer; Writer to the Signet. Education: George Heriot's School, Edinburgh; Old College, Faculty of Law, University of Edinburgh. Appointments: Trainee Solicitor, Patrick and James WS, 1971-73; Solicitor, Wallace and Guthrie, 1973-74; Solicitor, 1974-76, Partner, 1976-83, Allan McDougall and Co; Partner, Brodies WS, 1983-. Publications: 2 seminar papers, Moscow School of Political Studies, 1996, 1997; 1 monograph, 2001. Honours: Bachelor of Laws, LLB, 1971; Notary Public, 1975; Writer to the Signet, 1981. Memberships: Society of HM Writers to the Signet; Fellow, Royal Geographical Society; Secretary, 1980-83, Society of Scottish Artists; Governor, Edinburgh College of Art, 1996-99; Director, Edinburgh Printmakers Workshop, 2001-; Member, Royal Highland Yacht Club; Member, Edinburgh Sports Club. Address: 11 Inverleith Place, Edinburgh EH3 5QE, Scotland. E-mail: jimhenderson@brodies.co.uk

HENDRY Stephen Gordon, b. 13 January 1969, Edinburgh, Scotland. Snooker Player. m. Amanda Elizabeth Teresa Tart, 1995, 1 son. Appointments: Professional Player, 1985; Scottish Champion, 1986, 1987, 1988; Winner, Rothmans Grand Prix, 1987; World Doubles Champion, 1987; Australian Masters Champion, 1987; British Open Champion, 1988, 1991, 1999; New Zealand Masters Champion, 1988; Benson and Hedges Master Champion, 1989, 1990, 1991, 1992, 1993, 1996; UK Professional Champion, 1989, 1990, 1994, 1995, 1996; Asian Champion, 1989; Regal Masters Champion, 1989; Dubai Classic Champion, 1989; Embassy World Champion, 1990, 1992, 1993, 1994, 1995, 1996, 1999; Irish Masters, 1992; International Open, 1993. Publication:

Snooker Masterclass, 1994. Honours: Dr hc (Stirling), 2000; MacRoberts Trophy, 2001. Address: Stephen Hendry Snooker Ltd, Kerse Road, Stirling FK7 7SG, Scotland.

HENLEY Elizabeth Becker, b. 8 May 1952, Jackson, Mississippi, USA. Playwright. Education: BFA, Southern Methodist University. Publications: Crimes of the Heart, 1981; The Wake of Jamey Foster, 1982; Am I Blue, 1982; The Miss Firecracker Contest, 1984; The Debutante Ball, 1985, 1991; The Lucky Spot, 1987; Abundance, 1989; Beth Henley: Monologues for Women, 1992; Screenplays: Nobody's Fool, 1986; Crimes of the Heart, 1986; Miss Firecracker, 1989; Signatures, 1990; Control Freaks, 1993; Revelers, 1994. Honours: Pulitzer Prize for Drama, 1981; New York Drama Critics Circle Best Play Award, 1981; George Oppenheimer/Newsday Playwriting Award, 1981. Address: c/o The William Morris Agency, 1350 Avenue of the Americas, New York, NY 10019, USA.

HENRIQUES Eunice Ribeiro, b. 26 November 1945, Belo Horizonte, Minas Gerais, Brazil. Professor. m. Milton Mori, separated, 1 daughter. Education: BA, Federal University of Minas Gerais, Belo Horizonte, Brazil, 1969; MA, 1978, PhD, 1982 University of North Carolina, Chapel Hill, USA; Post-doctorate, Catholic University of Rio de Janeiro, Brazil, 2000. Appointments: English Language Teacher, School for Translators and Interpreters, Belo Horizonte, Brazil, 1970-71; Assistant Professor of English Methodology, Federal University of Minas Gerais, 1971-72; English Co-ordinator, Pythagoras High School, Belo Horizonte, Brazil, 1973-74; Assistant Professor, English Language and American Literature, School of Philosophy, Sciences and Letters, Belo Horizonte, Brazil, 1970-74; Portuguese Teacher Assistant, University of North Carolina, USA, 1975-82; Applied Linguistics Professor, 1983-, Department Head, Applied Linguistics, 1994-96, State University of Campinas, SP, Brazil; English Co-ordinator and Teacher of English, Catholic University of Minas Gerais (on the Web), 2000-; Foreign Language Trainer, Cendent-Mobility Intercultural Service, Chicago, Illinois USA, 2002-. Publications include: Learning and Teaching Styles in Foreign and Second Language Education, 1995; Comparing and Contrasting Brazilian and American Cultures, 2000; A Comprehensive Analysis of Students' Interlanguage, in press. Honours: Travel Grant, Institute for International Education, 1975, 1982; Student Assistantship, Latin American Bibliographical Centre, 1980-82; Teaching Assistantship, University of North Carolina, 1975-82; Listed in Who's Who publications and biographical dictionaries. Memberships: American Association of Teachers of Spanish and Portuguese, USA; Brazilian Association of Linguistics; University of North Carolina, Alumni Association, USA. Address: CP 6045 UNICAMP, Campinas, SP 13081-970, Brazil. E-mail: eunice@iel.unicamp.br

HENRY Desmond Paul, b. 5 July 1921, Almondbury, Yorkshire, England. Philosopher; Artist. m. Louise H J Bayen, 19 May 1945, 3 daughters. Education: BA Honours, Philosophy, University of Leeds, 1949; PhD, University of Manchester, 1960. Appointments: Philosophy Teacher, University of Manchester, 1949-82; Visiting Professor, Brown University, 1966, University of Pennsylvania, 1970. Publications: The Logic of St Anselm, 1967; Medieval Logic and Metaphysics, 1972; Commentary on De Grammatico, 1974; That Most Subtle Question, 1984; Medieval Meréology, 1991. Contributions to: Various publications. Membership: Manchester Medieval Society. Address: 223 Manley Rd, Chorlton-cum-Hardy, Manchester M21 ORB, England.

HENRY Lenny, b. 29 August 1958, England. m. Dawn French, 1 daughter. Appointments: Numerous tours including Loud!, 1994; Australia, 1995. Creative Works: TV includes: New Faces (debut),

Dictionary of International Biography

Tiswas, Three of a Kind, 1981-83; The Lenny Henry Show, Alive and Kicking, 1991; Bernard and the Genie, 1991; In Dreams, 1992; The Real McCoy, 1992; Chef (title role) (3 series), Lenny Hunts the Funk, New Soul Nation, White Goods, 1994; Funky Black Shorts, 1994; Comic Relief, Lenny Go Home, 1996; Lenny's Big Amazon Adventure, 1997; Lenny Goes to Town, 1998; The Man, 1998; Hope and Glory, 1999, 2000; Lenny's Big Atlantic Adventure, 2000; Lenny in Pieces, 2000, 2001; Films include: True Identity, 1991; Video: Lenny Henry Live and Unleashed, 1989; Lenny Henry Live and Loud, 1994; Toured Australia with Large! Show, 1998. Publications: The Quest for the Big Woof (autobiography), 1991; Charlie and the Big Chill (childrens book), 1995. Honours include: Monaco Red Cross Award; The Golden Nymph Award; BBC personality of the Year, Radio and TV Industry Club, 1993; Golden Rose of Montreux Award for Lenny in Pieces, 2000. Address: c/o PBJ Management Ltd, 5 Soho Square, London W1V 5DE, England.

HENSON Ray David, b. 24 July 1924, Johnston City, Illinois, USA. Lawyer, Professor of Law. Education: BS, 1947, JD, 1949, University of Illinois. Appointments: Counsel, Continental Assurance Co, and Continental Casualty Co, 1952-70; Professor of Law, Wayne State University, 1970-75; Professor of Law, 1975-95, Professor Emeritus, 1995-, University of California, Hastings College of Law. Publications: Landmarks of Law, 1960; Secured Transactions, 1973, 2nd edition, 1977; The Law of Sales, 1985; Documents of Title, 1983, 2nd edition, 1990; Various other books and numerous articles in American law reviews. Honours: Chairman, Business Law Section, American Bar Association, 1969-70; Chairman, Uniform Commercial Code Committee, American Bar Association, Illinois State Bar Association and Chicago Bar Association at various times; Member, Legal Advisory Committee, New York Stock Exchange, 1970-75. Memberships: American Bar Association; Illinois State Bar Association; Chicago Bar Association; American Law Institute; University Club, San Francisco. Address: 1400 Geary Blvd, II 2303, San Francisco, CA 94109-6561, USA.

HENTSCHEL Erwin Josef, b. 7 February 1934, Nieder-Mohrau, Sudeten. Professor. m. Eleonore, 1 daughter. Education: Dipl Biol, 1959, Dr rer nat, 1964, Facultas docendi for Animal Physiology, 1970, Dr sc nat, 1980, Dr rer nat habil, 1991, University of Jena. Appointments: Full Professor, University of Greifswald, 1988-89; Councillor, European Comparative Endocrinologists, Salzburg, 1988, Leuven, 1990; Originator, Apidology-Institute, University of Jena, 1989-97; Member, Standing Commission of Bee Biology of APIMONDIA, 33rd International Apicultural Congress in Beijing, China, 1993. Honours: Schiller Medallist, 1986; Bundesverdienstkreuz am Bande, 2000. Memberships: Deutsche Zoologische Gesellschaft. Address: Freiligrathstr 8, D-07743 Jena, Germany.

HENZE Juergen, b. 4 June 1950. Professor. m. Education: BA, Ruhr University of Bochum, Germany, 1977; PhD, 1985. Appointments: Research Fellow, Comparative Education Research Unit, Ruhr University Bochum, Germany, 1978-80; Senior Research Fellow, 1981-93; Professor, Comparative Education, Humboldt University, Berlin, Germany, 1993-. Publications: Das Erziehungs und Bildungswesen der VR China seit 1969; Berufliche Bildung des Auslands: VR China; Bildung und Wissenschaft in der Volksrepublik China zu Beginn der achtziger Jahre; Hochschulzugang in der VR China 1949-89; Many other publications and articles. Memberships: Comparative and International Education Society; European Association of China Studies; Deutsche Gesellschaft fuer Erziehungswissenschaft. Address: Humboldt University of Berlin, Geschwister Scholl Str 7, D 10099 Berlin, Germany.

HERACLEOUS Loizos Theodotou, b. 18 March 1969, Cyprus. Professor. Education: BSc, Marketing and Liberal Studies, University of Lancaster, England, 1992; MPhil, 1993, PhD, 1997, Management Studies, University of Cambridge, England. Appointments: Assistant Professor, 1996-99, Associate Professor, 2000-, School of Business, National University of Singapore; Lecturer, School of Business, Trinity College, Dublin, Ireland, 1999-2000; Editorial Board Member, Asia Pacific Journal of Management, 2000-; Editorial Board Member, Journal of Management Studies, 2003-; Senior Editor, Organization Studies, 2003-. Publications: Book: Strategy and Organization, 2003; Over 25 refereed articles in international journals including: Academy of Management Journal; Human Relations; Journal of Applied Behavioral Science. Honours: Best Paper Award, OCIS Division, Academy of Management, 1999; Listed in Who's Who publications and biographical dictionaries. Memberships: Cambridge Alumni in Management; Singapore Institute of Directors; European Group for Organization Studies; Academy of Management. Address: School of Business, National University of Singapore, 1 Business Link, Singapore 117591.

HERBERT James (John), b. 8 April 1943, London, England. Author. Education: Hornsey College of Art, 1959. Publications: The Rats, 1974; The Fog, 1975; The Survivor, 1976; Fluke, 1977; The Spear, 1978; Lair, 1979; The Dark, 1980; The Jonah, 1981; Shrine, 1983; Domain, 1984; Moon, 1985; The Magic Cottage, 1986; Sepulchre, 1987; Haunted, 1988; Creed, 1990; Portent, 1992; James Herbert: By Horror Haunted, 1992; James Herbert's Dark Places, 1993; The City, 1994; The Ghosts of Sleath, 1994; '48, 1996; Others, 1999; Once, 2001; Devil in the Dark, Craig Cabell, 2003; Nobody True, 2003. Films: The Rats, 1982; The Survivor, 1986; Fluke, 1995; Haunted, 1995. Address: c/o Bruce Hunter, David Higham Associates, 5-8 Lower John Street, London W1R 4HA, England.

HERBIG George Howard, b. 20 January 1920, Wheeling, West Virginia, USA. Astronomer. m. (1) Delia McMullin, 1943, divorced, 1968, 3 sons, 1 daughter, (2) Hannelore Tillmann, 1968. Education: Graduated, University of California at Los Angeles, 1943. Appointments: Junior Astronomer, 1948-50, Assistant Astronomer, 1950-55, Associate Astronomer, 1955-60, Astronomer, 1960-87, Assistant Director, 1960-63, Acting Director, 1970-71, Lick Observatory, California; Professor of Astronomy, University of California, Santa Cruz, 1967-87; Astronomer, 1987-2001, Astronomer Emeritus, 2001-, Institute for Astronomy, University of Hawaii. Publications: Editor of and contributor to: Non-Stable Stars, 1957; Spectroscopic Astrophysics, 1970; Approximately 220 scientific papers, articles and reviews. Honours: Warner Prize, American Astronomical Society, 1955; Medaille, University de Liege, 1969; Gold Medal, Astronomical Society for Pacific, 1980; Petrie Prize Canadian Astronomical Society, 1995. Memberships: NAS; American Academy of Arts and Sciences; Corresponding member, Societe scientifique Royale de Liege; Foreign Scientific member, Max-Planck-Institute fur Astronomie, Heidelberg; Numerous boards, commissions and consultancies. Address: Institute for Astronomy, University of Hawaii, 2680 Woodlawn Drive, Honolulu, HI 96822, USA.

HERMANN Armin Daniel, b. 26 November 1937, Neu-Sarata, South Russia. Nuclear Chemistry Engineer. m. Christine Seidel Hermann, 1970, divorced 1981, 1 son. Education: Diploma in Engineering, 1961, DSc, 1984, Technical University Dresden; PhD, Lomonossow University, Moscow, 1965. Appointments: Scientist, 1965-66, Group Leader, 1966-75, Head of Department, 1975-87, German Academy of Sciences; Project Manager, Paul Scherrer Institute, Switzerland, 1990-; Adviser, Nuclear Fuel Industry

Dictionary of International Biography

Research Group, Palo Alto, 1994-; Member, Co-ordination Council, Council of Mutual Economic Aid, Moscow, 1971-87; Nuclear Chemistry Educator, German Academy of Sciences, Technical High School, Zittau, Technical University, Dresden. Publications: Radiochemical Methods, textbook; 100 articles in scientific publications; Patentee in field of nuclear reactors. Honour: Recipient, Order Banner of Labour, governmental award. Memberships: German Chemical Society; Working Group, Nuclear Chemistry; German Society of Nuclear Technology; Swiss Union Atomic Energy; Christian Parish Control Commission. Address: Sommerhaldenstr 5A, 5200 Brugg, Aargau, Switzerland. E-mail: armin.hermann@psi.ch.

HERMANOWICZ Neal, b. 11 September 1953, Dekalb, Illinois, USA. Neurologist. m. Dagny Thorgilsdottir, 1 son, 1 daughter. Education: BS, University of Illinois, 1976; MD, Temple University School of Medicine, 1985. Appointments: Vice Chair, Department of Neurology, University of California, Irvine. Publications: Articles in medical journals. Memberships: Movement Disorders Society; Amnesty International; American Academy of Neurology. Address: 100 Irvine Hall, Irvine, CA 92697, USA.

HERNANDEZ Enrique Elbio, b. 7 October 1952, Montevideo, Uruguay. Lawyer; Military. m. Silvana Coccaro, 1 son, 2 daughters. Education: Ph, Law and Social Sciences; Ph, Diplomacy; Diploma, Economy, Professor of International Law; Professor of History of International Relations; MA, Diplomatic Studies. Appointments: Army Officer, 1971-; Professor of International Law, 1992-; Professor of History, Lawyer, 1993-. Publications: International Humanitarian Law; UN Peacekeeping Operations. Honours: UN Medal of Peace. Memberships: International Bar Association; National Geographic. Address: Solano Garcia 2525, Montevideo 11300, Uruguay.

HERREROS Jesus M, b. 1 July 1953, Torrelavega, Santander, Spain. Cardiovascular Surgeon; Professor. m. M Concepcion Arregui. 3 sons, 1 daughter. Education: Licentiate degree in Medicine, 1976, PhD, 1980, University of Navarra, Spain; Specialist in Cardiovascular and Thoracic Surgery, 1983; European Board of Thoracic and Cardiovascular Surgery, 2000. Appointments: Head, Department of Cardiac Surgery, University Hospital of Valladolid, Spain, 1995-99; Professor of Surgery, 2000-, Head, Department of Cardiovascular Surgery and Cardiology, Clinica Universitaria, 2000-, University of Navarra, Spain. Publications: Editor of 11 books; Author of 18 books; 128 articles in international journals; 237 articles in Spanish journals; 180 conferences and round-tables. Honours: Prize, Europa 2001, University of Navarra; Prize, Torrelavega Citizen, 2002. Memberships: Vice-President, Society of Cardiac Surgeons; Chancellor, Cardiac Bioassist Association; European Society for cardiovascular Surgery; International Society of Chest Physicians. Address: Cardiovascular Surgery, Clinica Universitaria Navarra, Av Pio XII 36, 31008 Pamplona, Spain. E-mail: jherreros@unav.es

HERRMANN Klaus Peter Bruno, b. 20 May 1937, Koenigszelt, Silesia. Professor. m. Rosemarie Schauer, 1 son. Education: Diploma in Physics, 1961, PhD, 1964, Habilitation, 1969, MLU Halle-Wittenberg. Appointments: Assistant, Department of Physics, 1961-69, Senior Assistant, 1970-71, MLU; Lecturer, 1973-74, Associate Professor, 1975-77, Institute of Mechanics, University of Karlsruhe; Professor of Mechanics, University of Paderborn, 1977-2002; Visiting Professor, USA, China, France, 1979-2002. Publications: Many articles in professional journals. Honours: Member of Editorial Board, Thermal Stresses, 1994; Member of Advisory Board, Acta Mechanica, 1995; Member of Advisory Board, Prikladnaja Mechanika, 1997; Associate Editor, Appl Mech Revs, 1998. Memberships: Fellow, New York Academy of Science;

European Mechanics Society; Association Applied Mathematics and Mechanics; German Association for Materials Testing; Hochschulverband. Address: Department of Mechanical Engineering, Chair of Applied Mechanics, University of Paderborn, Pohlweg 47-49, D-33098 Paderborn, Germany. E-mail: jherr1@ltm.upb.de

HERSEY Peter, b. 23 April 1938, Adelaide, South Australia. Consultant Immunologist; Professor. Education: MBBS, Adelaide, 1966; DPhil, Oxon, 1973. Appointments include: Resident Medical Officer, 1966, Registrar in General Medicine, 1969, Senior Medical Registrar, 1970, Royal Adelaide Hospital; Nuffield Dominions Trust Fellow, Nuffield Department of Clinical Medicine, Oxford, England, 1971-73; Senior Research Fellow, University of Sydney, Australia, 1974-75; Senior Staff Specialist in Immunology, Kanematsu Memorial Institute, Sydney Hospital, 1976-83; Senior Staff Specialist in Immunology and Oncology, Newcastle Mater Misericordiae Hospital, 1984-; Consultant Immunologist, Sydney Melanoma Unit, 1984-; Conjoint Professor of Oncology, University of Newcastle, 1985-; Medical and Research Director, Newcastle Melanoma Unit, 1988-. Publications: Invited speaker at national and international meetings; Over 200 articles in professional medical journals; 45 invited reviews in refereed journals and chapters in books. Honours: 8 prizes for Distinction in Surgery, Medicine, Obstetrics and Gynaecology. Memberships include: Fellow, Royal Australian College of Physicians, 1969; Australian Society for Immunology; American Association of Immunologists; Clinical Oncology Society of Australia; Australian Society for Medical Research; Society for Biological Therapy. Address: Oncology and Immunology Unit, David Maddison Building, Cnr King and Watt Streets, Newcastle, NSW 2300, Australia. E-mail: peter.hersey@newcastle.edu.au

HERSH Burton David, b. 18 September 1933, Chicago, Illinois, USA. Author; Biographer. m. Ellen Eiseman, 3 August 1957, 1 son, 1 daughter. Education: BA magna cum laude, Harvard College, 1955; Fulbright Scholar, 1955-56. Publications: The Ski People, 1968; The Education of Edward Kennedy, 1972; The Mellon Family, 1978; The Old Boys, 1992; The Shadow President, 1997. Contributions to: Many magazines. Honours: Book Find Selection, 1972; Book-of-the-Month Club, 1978. Memberships: Authors Guild; American Society of Journalists and Authors; PEN. Address: PO Box 433, Bradford, NH 03221, USA.

HERZENBERG Arvid, b. 16 April 1925, Vienna, Austria. Theoretical Physicist. m. Marjorie, 1 son, 2 daughters. Education: BSc, 1st Class Honours Physics, 1946-49, PhD, Physics, 1952, DSc, 1964, University of Manchester, England. Appointments: Assistant Lecturer to Reader in Theoretical Physics, University of Manchester, England, 1952-69; Faculty, 1970-, Emeritus Professor in Physics and Applied Physics, 1995-, Yale University, New Haven, Connecticut, USA. Publications: Articles in scientific journals: Geomagnetic Dynamos, 1958; Anomalous Scattering and the Phase Problem (with H S M Law), 1967; Core Polerization Corrections to Oscillator Strengths in Alkali Atoms, 1968; Oscillatory Energy Dependence of Resonant Electron-Molecule Scattering, 1968. Memberships: Fellow, British Physical Society; Fellow American Physical Society. Address: 6 Legrand Road, North haven, CT 06473, USA. E-mail: arvid.herzenberg@yale.edu

HESSE Axel, b. 16 July 1935, Berlin, Germany. Ethnomusicologist. m. Flora, 29 February 1964, 1 son, 1 daughter. Education; studied University of Berlin, Institute of Musicology, 1955; PhD, 1970, Postgraduate, Academy Sciences, Cuba, Doctorate 1971. Appointments: Translator; Member, International Folk Music Council, 1967; Lecturer, Ethnomusicology, Humboldt University, Germany, 1970-; Visiting Professor, National Music

School, Peru; posts in various organisations, including: Academy Sciences of Germany, Committee of GDR-Portugal, International Council Traditional Music; Director of the 1254 founded Extraordinary Music Chair Francisco Salinas, Salamanca University; Research work: Collection of German folk songs and Latin American Music; Book on Music Life in Latin America 1492-1969 (with Flora Pérez); Organisation and Chairman, Fink-Folklore Initiativkomitee; Documentary, musical field work, 1983; Founder, Ciplice Folk Sound Archives, Freyburg/Unstrut, 1989; The Multidisciplinary Salinas Colloquium on Rhythm, 1991-94; Street Musician, 1994, Arcos en Compañía, 1995; Retired, 1998, Música Peatonal 2000, steps to scientifical come-back to save his 12000 items of collected ethnic music with his daughter. Publications: The Little A-Y-O of Western Music History; 200 Years of Music in the Jesuit republic and It's Echo. Listed in: Biographical Publication. Honours: Order of International Ambassadors, 1995. Address: Calle Compañía 36, E-37002 Salamanca, Spain. E-mail: amicisdat@yahoo.com

HESTON Charlton, b. 4 October 1924, Evanston, Illinois, USA. Actor. m. Lydia Clark, 1944, 1 son, 1 daughter. Education: Northwestern University, Evanston. Appointments: 1st Broadway appearance in Antony and Cleopatra, 1948; Starred in over 50 films, 1950-. Creative Works: Films include: Julius Caesar, 1950; Dark City, 1950; The Greatest Show on Earth, 1952; The Savage, 1952; Ruby Gentry, 1952; The President's Lady, 1953; Pony Express, 1953; Arrowhead, 1953; Bad for Each Other, 1953; The Naked Jungle, 1953; Secret of the Incas, 1954; The Far Horizons, 1955; Lucy Gallant, 1955; The Private War of Major Benson, 1955; three Violent People, 1956; The Ten Commandments, 1956; Touch of Evil, 1958; The Big Country, 1958; The Buccaneer, 1958; Ben Hur, 1959; The Wreck of the Mary Deare, 1959; El Cid, 1961; The Pigeon that Took Rome, 1962; Diamond Head, 1962; 55 Days at Peking, 1962; Major Dundee, 1964; The Greatest Story Ever Told, 1965; The Agony and the Ecstasy, 1965; The War Lord, 1965; Khartoum, 1966; Counterpoint, 1967; Will Penny, 1967; Planet of the Apes, 1967; Beneath the Planet of the Apes, 1968; The Hawaiians, 1970; Julius Caesar, 1970; The Omega Man, 1971; Antony & Cleopatra, 1972; Skyjacked, 1972; The Call of the Wild, 1972; Soylent Green, 1973; The Three Musketeers, 1973; The Four Musketeers, 1974; Earthquake, 1974; Airport, 1975; Midway, 1975; Two Minute Warning, 1976; The Last hard Men, 1976; The Prince and the Pauper, 1976; Gray Lady Down, 1978; The Awakening, 1980; Mother Lode, 1981; Caine Mutiny Court Martial (also directed), 1988; Treasure Island, 1989; Almost an Angel; Solar Crisis; Wayne's World 2; True Lies, 1994; In the Mouth of Madness; Alaska; Hercules, 1997; Any Given Sunday, 1998; Town and Country, 1998; Toscano, 1999. Publications: The Actor's Life, 1979; In the Arena, 1995; Charlton Heston Presents the Bible, 1997. Honours: Academy Award, 1959; Veterans of Foreign Wars Citizenship Medal, 1982; Golden Medal of the City of Vienna, 1995; Commander Ordre des Arts et des Lettres. Memberships: National Council of Arts; Trustee, American Film Institute; Presidential Task Force on Arts and Humanities; National Rifle Association. Address: c/o Jack Gilardi, ICM, 8942 Wilshire Boulevard, Beverly Hills, CA 90211, USA.

HEUNG Vincent Che-Shing, b. 11 March 1953, Hong Kong. Tourism and Hospitality Educator. m. Cindy Chiu-Ying Mak, 1 son. Education: BSc (Hons), Hotel and Catering Administration, University of Surrey, UK, 1984; MBA, Business Administration, University of Dubuque, Iowa, USA, 1990; PhD, Marketing, University of Hong Kong, Hong Kong, 1999. Appointments: Restaurant Manager, Excelsior Hotel, Kong Kong, 1984-86; Marketing Associate, Peninsula Hotel, Hong Kong, 1986-87; Lecturer, Assistant Professor, Associate Professor of Hospitality and Tourism Management, The Hong Kong Polytechnic University,

1987-; Visiting Professor, School of Tourism, Zhejiang Forestry University, China, 2004-. Publications: Over 60 academic and professional articles in the field of hospitality and tourism management. Honours: Competitive Research Grants, 1995, 1997, 2001, 2004; Listed in Who's Who publications and biographical dictionaries. Memberships: Chartered Institute of Marketing, UK; Hotel Catering International Management Association, UK; Educational Institute AH and LA, USA. Address: School of Hotel and Tourism Management, The Hong Kong Polytechnic University, Hung Hom, Kowloon, Hong Kong. E-mail: hmvheung@polyu.edu.hk

HEWISH Antony, b. 11 May 1924, Fowey, Cornwall, England. Astronomer; Physicist. m. Marjorie E C Richards, 1950, 1 son and 1 daughter. Education: Graduated, Gonville and Caius College, Cambridge, 1948. Appointments: War Service, 1943-46; Research Fellow, Gonville and Caius College, 1951-54; Supernumerary Fellow, 1956-61; University Assistant Director of Research, 1953-61, Lecturer, 1961-69; Fellow, Churchill College, Cambridge, 1962-; Reader in Radio Astronomy, University of Cambridge, 1969-71, Professor, 1971-89, Professor Emeritus, 1989; Professor, Royal Institute, 1977; Director, Mullard Radio Astronomy Observatory, Cambridge, 1982-88; Vikram Sarabhai Professor, Ahmedabad, 1988. Publications: The First, Second, Third and Fourth Cambridge Catalogues; Seeing Beyond the Invisible, Pulsars and physics laboratories. Honours: Hamilton Prize, 1951; Eddington Medal, Royal Astronomical Society, 1968; Boys Prize, Institute of Physics, 1970; Dellinger Medal, International Union of Radio Science, Hopkins Prize, Cambridge Medal and Prize, Society Francaise de Physique, 1974; Nobel Prize for Physics, 1974; Hughes Medal, Royal Society, 1977; Vainu Bappu Prize, Indian National Science Academy, 1998. Memberships: Foreign Member, American Academy of Arts and Sciences, 1970; Member, Belgian Royal Academy of Arts and Sciences, 1989; Member, Emeritus Academia Europea, 1996; Foreign Fellow, Indian National Science Academy; 6 Honorary ScD. Address: Cavendish Laboratory, Madingley Road, Cambridge, CB3 7NQ, England.

HEWITT Heather Agnes, b. 14 July 1934, Victoria, Australia. Academic. m. John R Hewitt, 30 December 1959, 2 sons, 1 daughter. Education: BA, DipEd, University of Melbourne, 1955. Appointments: Officer in Charge of Counselling Guidance, Clinical Services, Victoria Education Department, 1957-79; Psychologist, Royal Children's Hospital, 1960-63; Lecturer, Lincoln Institute of Health Sciences, 1966-70; Lecturer, Institute of Early Childhood Development, 1978-80; Lecturer, Victoria College of Advanced Education, Burwood Campus, 1979-80; Principal, University College, University of Melbourne, 1980-99. Publications: Persons Handicapped by Rubella, 1991; Author of articles in professional journals; Editorial Board, International Journal of Rehabilitation Research, International Journal of Visual Impairment and Blindness. Memberships include: Executive Member, International Association of Deaf/Blind; Executive Member, International Council for Education of Visually Impaired, 1987-; Australian Psychological Society; Australian College of Education; Chairman, Northern Education Learning and Employment Centre. Address: 2 Kiata Drive, Mildura, Victoria 3500, Australia.

HIBBERT Christopher, b. 5 March 1924, Enderby, Leicestershire, England. Author. m. Susan Piggford, 1948, 2 sons, 1 daughter. Education: MA, Oriel College, Oxford. Appointments: Served in Italy, 1944-45; Captain, London Irish Rifles; Military Cross; Partner, firm of land agents, auctioneers and surveyors, 1948-59. Publications: The Road to Tyburn, 1957; King Mob, 1958; Wolfe at Quebec, 1959; The Destruction of Lord Raglan, 1961; Corunna, 1961; Benito Mussolini, 1962; The Battle of Arnhem, 1962; The Roots of Evil, 1963; The Court at Windsor,

1964; Agincourt, 1964; The Wheatley Diary (editor), 1964; Garibaldi and His Enemies, 1965; The Making of Charles Dickens, 1967; Waterloo: Napoleon's Last Campaign (editor), 1967; An American in Regency England: The Journal of Louis Simond (editor), 1968; Charles I, 1968; The Grand Tour, 1969; London: Biography of a City, 1969; The Search for King Arthur, 1970; Anzio: The Bid for Rome, 1970; The Dragon Wakes: China and the West, 1793-1911, 1970; The Personal History of Samuel Johnson, 1971; George IV, Prince of Wales 1762-1811, 1972; George IV, Regent and King 1812-1830, 1973; The Rise and Fall of the House of Medici, 1974; Edward VII: A Portrait, 1976; The Great Mutiny: India, 1857, 1978; The French Revolution, 1981; Africa Explored: Europeans in the Dark Continent, 1796-1889, 1982; The London Encyclopaedia (editor), 1983; Queen Victoria in Her Letters and Journals, 1984; Rome: The Biography of a City, 1985; Cities and Civilizations, 1985; The English: A Social History, 1987; Venice: Biography of a City, 1988; The Encyclopaedia of Oxford (editor), 1988; Redcoats and Rebels: The War for America 1760-1781, 1990; The Virgin Queen: The Personal History of Elizabeth I, 1990; Captain Gronow: His Reminiscences of Regency and Victorian Life (editor), 1991; Cavaliers and Roundheads: The English at War 1642-1649, 1993; Florence: Biography of a City, 1993; Nelson: A Personal History, 1994; Wellington: A Personal History, 1997; George III: A Personal History, 1998; Queen Victoria: A Personal History, 2000; The Marlboroughs: John and Sarah Churchill, 2001; Napoleon: His Wives and Women, 2002. Honours: Heinemann Award for Literature, 1962; McColvin Medal, 1989; Honorary DLitt, Leicester University, 1996. Address: c/o David Higham Associates, 5-8 Lower John Street, Golden Square, London W1F 9HA, England.

HICHENS Antony Peverell, b. 10 September 1936, Cornwall, England. Company Chairman. m. Sczerina Neomi Hobday, 1 daughter. Education: MA, Law, Magdalen College, Oxford, England; MBA, Wharton School, University of Pennsylvania, USA. Appointments: Midshipman Royal Navy Volunteer Reserve, 1954-56; Lieutenant Commander, Royal Naval Reserve, 1956-69; Called to Bar, Inner Temple, 1960; Planning Manager, Rio Tinto-Zinc Corporation, 1960-72; Finance Director, Redland plc, 1972-81; Managing Director and Chief Financial Officer, Consolidated Gold Fields plc, 1981-89; Chairman, Y J Lovell (Holdings) plc, 1989-94; Chairman, Caradon plc, 1989-98; Deputy Chairman, Candover Investments plc, 1989-2004; Member (Non-Executive), British Coal Corporation, 1992-97 Chairman LASMO plc, 2000-2001; Member, Takeover Panel, 2001-; Chairman, D S Smith plc, 1999- Honours: Reserve Decoration; Wayneflete Fellow, Magdalen College; Member, Oxford University Court of Benefactors. Membership: Brooks' Club; Naval Club. Address: Slape Manor, Netherbury, Nr Bridport, Dorset DT6 5LH, England.

HICK Graeme Ashley, b. 23 May 1966, Salisbury, Zimbabwe. Cricketer. Appointments: Right-Hand Batsman, Off-Break Bowler, Slip Fielder; Teams: Zimbabwe, 1983-86, Worcestershire, 1984-, Northern Districts, 1987-89, Queensland, 1990-91; Scored 100 aged 6 years; Youngest player to appear in 1983 World Cup and youngest to represent Zimbabwe; 65 tests for England, 1991-97, scoring 3,383 runs (average 31.32), including 6 hundreds; Scored 30,189 1st class runs (average 55.2), with 104 hundreds (including 9 doubles, 1 triple, 1 quadruple (405 not out) to 1 April 1999); Youngest to score 2,000 1st class runs in a season, 1986; Scored 1,019 runs before June 1988, including a record 410 runs in April; Fewest innings for 10,000 runs in county cricket (179); Youngest (24) to score 50 1st class hundreds; Toured Australia, 1994-95; 120 limited-overs ints for 3,846 runs (average 37.33) by December 2002; Scored 315 not out v Durham, June 2002- (highest championship innings of the season). Publication: My Early Life

(autobiography), 1992. Honours: Wisden Cricketer of the Year, 1987. Membership: England World Cup Squad, 1996. Address: c/o Worcestershire County Cricket Club, New Road, Worcester WR2 4QQ, England.

HICKS Philip, b. 11 October 1928, Leamington Spa, England. Artist; Painter. m. Jill Doreen Tweed, 1 son, 1 daughter. Education: Royal Military Academy, Sandhurst; Chelsea School of Art and Royal Academy Schools, 1949-54. Career: Part-time teacher, various schools of art, London area, 1960-86; Full-time painting, over 40 solo exhibitions, UK and abroad; Work appears in many public and corporate collections, including Tate Britain, Victoria and Albert Museum, Imperial War Museum, Contemporary Art Society, Royal College of Music, Nuffield Foundation. Publications: Mentioned in numerous journals, magazines and newspapers. Honours: British Council Award, 1977. Memberships: Arts Club, Dover Street, London; Chelsea Arts Club, London; Past Chairman and Vice President, The Artists General Benevolent Institution. Address: Radcot House, Buckland Road, Bampton, Oxfordshire OX18 2AA, England.

HIJAZY Mahmoud, b. 1939, Dar Senaid, Palestine. Consultant Dermatologist; Venereologist. m. Raedah Halawa, 2 sons, 2 daughters. Education: MBBCh, 1964; Diploma, Dermatology and Venereology, 1969; Diploma, Internal Medicine, 1970; MD (PhD), Dermatology, Venereology, 1973. Appointment: Owner and Acting Director, Dr Hijazy Medical Centre for Dermatology and Laser Surgery; Practising as a consultant Dermatologist and Venereologist; Introduced the first free international internet web site for detailed English and Arabic dermatology. Publications: The Book of Venereal Diseases, 1988; The Book of General Dermatology, 1989; The Principles of Pediatric Dermatology, 2000; Text book of Pediatric Dermatology (Arabic), 2001. Honours: Man of the Year Award, Arab American Congress, Chicago, 1971; Meritorious Achievement Award as Consultant Dermatologist, 1999; Noble Prize for Outstanding Achievement and Contribution to Humanity, United Cultural Convention, USA, 2001; Lifetime Achievement Award, IBC, England, 2001. Memberships: American Academy of Dermatology; European Academy of Dermatology and Venereology; Fellow, European Academy of Cosmetic Surgery; Fellow, Academy of Allergy and Clinical Immunology. Address: Medical Centre, Riyadh 11422, PO Box 5216, Saudi Arabia. E-mail: drmhijazy@hotmail.com

HILFIGER Tommy, b. Elmira, New York, USA. Men's Fashion Designer. m. Susie Hilfiger, 4 children. Appointments: Opened 1st store, People's Place, Elmira, 1969; Owned 10 clothes shops, New York State, 1978; Full-time Designer, 1979; Launched own sportswear label, 1984; Acquired fashion business from Mohan Muranji; Founder, Tommy Hilfiger Corporation, 1989. Honours include: Winner, From the Catwalk to the Sidewalk Award, VH-1 Fashion and Music Awards, 1995; Menswear Designer of the Year, Council of Fashion Designers of America, 1995. Memberships: Board, Fresh Air Fund, Race to Erase Multiple Sclerosis. Address: c/o Lynne Franks PR, 327-329 Harrow Road, London W9 3RB, England.

HILL Anthony Robert, b. 24 May 1942, Melbourne, Victoria, Australia. Writer; Journalist. m. Gillian Mann, 15 October 1965, 1 daughter. Publications: The Bunburyists, 1985; Antique Furniture in Australia, 1985; Birdsong, 1988; The Burnt Stick, 1994; Spindrift, 1996; The Grandfather Clock, 1996; Growing Up and Other Stories, 1999; Soldier Boy, 2001; Young Digger, 2002; The Shadow Dog, 2003. Honour: Children's Book Council of Australia Honour Book, 1995. Membership: Australian Society of Authors. Address: PO Box 85, Yarralumla, Australian Capital Territory 2600, Australia.

Dictionary of International Biography

HILL Damon Graham Devereux, b. 17 September 1960, Hamstead, London, England. Motor Racing Driver. m. Georgie Hill, 1988, 2 sons, 2 daughters. Appointments: Began motorcycle racing, 1979; Driver, Canon Williams Team, 1993; Driver, Rothmans Williams Renault Team, 1994-96; Driver, Arrows Yamaha Team, 1997; Benson and Hedges Jordan Team, 1998-99. Honours: First motor racing victory in Formula Ford 1600, Brands Hatch, 1984; First Formula One Grand Prix, Silverstone, 1992; Winner, Hungarian Grand Prix, 1993; Winner, Belgian and Italian Grand Prix, 1993, 1994; 3rd Place, Drivers' World Championship, 1993; Winner, Spanish Grand Prix, Barcelona, 1994; Winner, British Grand Prix , Silverstone, 1994; Winner, Portuguese Grand Prix, 1994; Winner, Japanese Grand Prix, 1994, 1996;French Grand Prix, 1996; Spanish Grand Prix, 1995, 1996; San Marino Grand Prix, 1995, 1996; Hungarian Grand Prix, 1995; Brazilian Grand Prix, 1996; German Grand Prix, 1996; Australian Grand Prix, 1995, 1996; Canadian Grand Prix, 1998; Belgian Grand Prix, 1998; 2nd place, Drivers' World Championship, 1994-95; World Champion, 1996; British Competition Driver of the Year, Autosport Awards, 1995; 84 Grand Prix starts; 22 wins; 20 pole positions; 19 fastest laps; 42 podium finishes; numerous racing and sports personality awards; OBE. Publications: Damon Hill Grand Prix Year, 1994; Damon Hill: My Championship Year, 1996; F1 Through the Eyes of Damon Hill. Address: c/o Clyde & Co, 51 Eastcheap, London, EC3M 1JP, England.

HILL John Richard, b. 25 March 1929, Morden, Surrey, England. Author; Editor. m. Patricia Anne, 1 son, 2 daughters. Education: Royal Naval College, Dartmouth, 1942-46; HMS Dryad, Navigation Specialist, 1954, 1959; Imperial Defence College, 1965-67; Defence Fellow, King's College, London, 1972. Appointments: Sea Appointments, Surface Ships, 1946-62; Author, 1969-; Staff Appointments, mainly Ministry of Defence, 1963-75; Defence Attaché, The Hague, 1975-77; Commodore, Defence Policy Staff, Ministry of Defence, 1977-80; Flag Officer, Admiralty Interview Board, 1981-83; Secretary, Council of the Inns of Court, 1986-93; Under Treasurer (Chief Executive) Middle Temple, 1983-94; Editor, The Naval Review, 1983-2002. Publications: The Royal Navy Today and Tomorrow, 1981; Anti-Submarine Warfare, 1984; British Sea Power in the 1980's, 1985; Maritime Strategy for Medium Powers, 1986; Air Defence at Sea, 1988; Arms Control at Sea, 1989; The Oxford Illustrated History of the Royal Navy (general editor), 1995; The Prizes of War, 1998; War at Sea in the Ironclad Age, 2000; Lewin of Greenwich, 2000; 100 articles and conference papers published in books and professional journals including: Survival; Brassey's Annual; Safety at Sea International; The Naval Review; World Survey; Navy International; Defense and Diplomacy; Nato's 15 Nations; Naval Forces; Maritime Change: Issues for Asia; Australia's Maritime Interests – Views from Overseas; Conferences in: UK, USA, Canada, Australia, Iceland, Sweden, Italy, Russia. Honours: King's Medal, Royal Naval College, Dartmouth, 1946; Mountbatten Prize for Maritime Literature, 2000. Memberships: International Institute for Strategic Studies, 1974; Royal United Services Institute, 1982; The Greenwich Forum, 1983; Society for Nautical Research, 1991, Council, 1993, Chairman, 1994-99; Navy Records Society, 1991, Council 1993, Vice-President, 1997-2000; Honorary Bencher, Middle Temple, 1994. Address: Cornhill House, The Hangers, Bishop's Waltham, Southampton SO32 1EF, England.

HILL Sonia Geraldine, b. 26 September 1939, London, England. Artist in Oils. Partner, G H Clarke, deceased 1997. Education: Maidenhead Art College, Berkshire, England, 1955-57; Studied perspective composition with A Hayward, Zambia, 1957-63. Career: Architectural Assistant, contract work, London, 1982-1990; Architectural Assistant, Victoria, London, 1991; Exhibitions: Royal Academy, 1993, 2 oil paintings sold and 2 further works accepted by the selection committee; Royal Academy, 2000, oil painting of Quinton Crisp sold, now hanging in Vancouver; Christies, 2001-2002, 2003, 3 works in oils sold (Art for Life); Exhibitions at Richmond and Paris. Publication: Painting "Jack the Lad" illustrated in Royal Academy Magazine, 1993. Honour: Fine Art, Maidenhead College, 1957; Who's Who Book of Art, 1993-2004. Memberships: Friend: Royal Academy, London, 1993-2004, The Royal Overseas League, London, 2004, The Mall Galleries, London, 2004. Address: 6a Warfield Road, Hampton TW12 2AY, England.

HILLARY Edmund Percival (Sir), b. 20 July 1919, Auckland, New Zealand. Explorer; Diplomat; Bee-farmer. m. Louise Mary Rose, 1953, deceased 1975, 1 son, 2 daughters (1 deceased). Education: University of Auckland. Appointments: Director, Field Educational Enterprises of Australia Party Ltd; President, Voluntary Service Abroad, New Zealand, 1963-64; High Commissioner to India, also accredited to Bangladesh, Bhutan and Nepal, 1985-. Career: New Zealand Garhwal Expedition to Himalayas, 1951; British Expedition to Cho Oyu, 1952; First to reach summit of Mount Everest, with Sherpa Tenzing, May 29th 1953, on British expedition, under Sir John Hunt, 1953; Leader, New Zealand Alpine Club expedition to Barun Val, 1954; New Zealand Antarctic Expedition, 1956-58; Reached South Pole, 1957; Leader, Himalayan expeditions, 1961, 1963, 1964; Built hospital for Sherpas in Nepal, 1966; Leader, expedition on Mount Herschel, Antarctica, 1967; River Ganges expedition, 1977; High Commissioner to India (also accredited to India and Nepal), 1984; Consultant to Sear Roebuck & Co, Chicago; UNICEF Special Representative of Children of the Himalayas, 1991-; Also bee-farmer. Publications: Author, High Adventure, 1955; The Crossing of Antarctica (with Sir Vivian Fuchs), 1958; No Latitude for Error, 1961; High in the Thin Cold Air (with Desmond Doig), 1963; Schoolhouse in the Clouds, 1965; Nothing Venture, Nothing Win (autobiography), 1975; From the Ocean to the Sky, 1978; Two Generations (with Peter Hillary), 1983. Honours: KG; KBE; Gurkha Right Hand (1st Class); Star of Nepal (1st Class); Cullum George Medal; Hubbard Medal, 1954; Polar Medal, 1958; Founders Gold Medal, Royal Geographical Society, 1958; James Wattle Book of the Year Award, New Zealand, 1975; Centennial Award, National Geographical Society, 1988; LLD (hon), Victoria University, British Columbia, Canada, University of Victoria, New Zealand. Address: 278A Remuera Road, Auckland 5, New Zealand.

HILLION Pierre, b. 31 January 1926, Saint-Brieuc, France. Senior Physicist. m. Jeanne Garde, deceased, 2 sons, 2 daughters. Education: Engineer, Ecole Supérieure d'Electricité, 1952; Licencié ès Sciences, 1955; Docteur ès Sciences, 1957. Appointments: Engineer, Le Materiel Electrique S-W, 1950-55; Mathematical Physicist, Army Technical Section, 1955-64; Head, Mathematical Physics Department, Laboratoire Central de l'Armement, 1964-83; Maître de Conférences, Ecole Nationale Supérieure des Techniques Avancées, 1976-88; Scientific Adviser, Centre d'Analyse de Défense, 1983-91; Senior Physicist, Institut Henri Poincaré, 1991-. Publications: About 200 papers on mathematical physics and electromagnetism in various scientific journals and several books, including: Relativité et Quanta, 1968; Essay on formal aspect of electromagnetism, 1993; Electromagnetic Waves, PIER 18, 1998. Honours: Merit for Research and Invention; Officier, Palmes Académiques; Chevalier, Ordre National du Mérite; Chevalier, Legion d'Honneur. Memberships: Société Mathématique de France; Société Internationale de Physique Mathématique; Member, New York Academy of Sciences; Académie d'Electromagnetisme. Address: 86 bis, Route de Croissy, 78110 Le Vésinet, France.

HILTON Julian K, b. 11 September 1952, London, England. Professor; Principal Investigator. m. Malika Moussaid-Hilton, 1 son, 2 daughters. Education: BA, MA, D Phil, Brasenose College, Oxford, England; Diplome d'hautes aptitudes, Université de Grenoble; Doctoral Seminar, University of München; Trainee Director, Royal Opera House Covent Garden; Trainee Director, Bayerische Staatsoper, München. Appointments include: Lecturer, 1976, Professor, 1987-91, University of East Anglia; Visiting Professor, Technische Universität, Vienna, 1988-; Director, Medica project, Advanced Informatics in Medicine (AIM) EC DGXIII, 1988-92; Consultant, World Health Organisation, Geneva, 1989-96; Director, Biotechnology in Training COMETT Pilot Project (BIT) EC DGXII, 1989-93; Expert, European Commission, 1991-93; Founder and Director, Advanced Veterinary Information System (AVIS) Project, 1992-; President, Telos Group, 1993-98; Member, European Regional Council, Association of Clinical Research Professionals; Chairman, Aleff Group, London and Tallahassee, 1999-; Founding Dean, Institute, Association of Clinical Research Professionals, 2000-2002; Principal Investigator, MiLo Project, Florida Institute of Phosphate Research, 2000-. Publications: Over 100 articles, lectures and scripts including: Books: Georg Büchner, 1982; New Directions in Theatre (general editor), 1987-; Performance, 1987; New Directions in Theatre, 1992; Plays: The Enchanted Bird's Nest, 1985; Broken Ground, 1986; The Marriage of Panurge, 1986; Courage, 1989. Honours: Key Note Lecturer, Triennial Conference of Swedish Universities, 1989; Award for Enterprise (Small Business) Anglo Dutch Chamber of Commerce, 1991; Diderot Memorial Lecture, University of Umeå, 1991; Meritorious Service Award, Association of Clinical Research Professionals, 1999. Memberships: Stiftung Maximilianeum, München, 1972; Theodor Heuss Research Fellow, Alexander von Humboldt Stiftung, 1976; Association of Clinical Research Professionals, 1996. Address: Aleff Group, 53/54 Skylines, Limeharbour, London E14 9TS, England. E-mail: jhilton@aleffgroup.com

HIMMELFARB Gertrude, b. 8 August 1922, New York, New York, USA. Professor of History Emerita; Writer. m. Irving Kristol, 18 January 1942, 1 son, 1 daughter. Education: Jewish Theological Seminary, 1939-42; BA, Brooklyn College, 1942; MA, 1944, PhD, 1950, University of Chicago; Girton College, Cambridge, 1946-47. Appointments: Professor, 1965-78, Distinguished Professor of History, 1978-88, Professor Emerita, 1988-, Graduate School of the City University of New York. Publications: Lord Acton: A Study in Conscience and Politics, 1952; Darwin and the Darwinian Revolution, 1959, revised edition, 1968; Victorian Minds: Essays on Nineteenth Century Intellectuals, 1968; On Liberty and Liberalism: The Case of John Stuart Mill, 1974; The Idea of Poverty: England in the Industrial Age, 1984; Marriage and Morals Among the Victorians and Other Essays, 1986; The New History and the Old, 1987; Poverty and Compassion: The Moral Imagination of the Late Victorians, 1991; On Looking Into the Abyss: Untimely Thoughts on Culture and Society, 1994; The De-Moralization of Society: From Victorian Virtues to Modern Values, 1995; One Nation, Two Cultures, 1999. Contributions to: Scholarly books and journals. Honours: American Association of University Women Fellowship, 1951-52; American Philosophical Society Fellowship, 1953-54; Guggenheim Fellowships, 1955-56, 1957-58; National Endowment for the Humanities Senior Fellowship, 1968-69; American Council of Learned Societies Fellowship, 1972-73; Phi Beta Kappa Visiting Scholarship, 1972-73; Woodrow Wilson Center Fellowship, 1976-77; Rockefeller Humanities Fellowship, 1980-81; Jefferson Lectureship, National Endowment for the Humanities, 1991; Templeton Foundation Award, 1997; Professional Achievement Citation, University of Chicago Alumni Association, 1998. Memberships: American Academy of Arts and Sciences; American Historical Association; American

Philosophical Society; British Academy, fellow; Royal Historical Society, fellow; Society of American Historians. Address: 2510 Virginia Avenue, NW, Washington, DC 20037, USA.

HINE Patrick, b. 14 July 1932, Chandlers Ford, Hampshire, England. Air Force Officer. m. Jill Adèle Gardner, 1956, 3 sons. Career: Fighter Pilot and Member, RAF Black Arrows and Blue Diamonds Formation Aerobatic Teams, 1957-62; Commander, No 92 Squadron, 1962-64 and 17 Squadron, 1970-71; RAF Germany Harrier Force, 1974-75; Director, RAF Public Relations, 1975-77; Assistant Chief of Air Staff for Policy, 1979-83; Commander in Chief, RAF Germany and Commander, NATO's 2nd Allied Tactical Air Force, 1983-85; Vice Chief of the Defence Staff, 1985-87; Air Member for Supply and Organisation, Air Force Board, 1987-88; Air Officer Commanding in Chief, Strike Command, Commander in Chief, UK Air Forces, 1988-; Joint Commander, British Forces in Gulf Conflict, 1990-91; with reserve force, rank of Flying Officer, 1991-; Military Adviser to British Aerospace, 1992-99. Honours: King of Arms, Order of the British Empire, 1997-.

HINGIS Martina, b. 30 September 1980, Košice, Czech Republic. Tennis Player. Appointments: 1st Tennis Tournament, 1985; Winner, French Open Junior Championship, 1993; Wimbledon Junior Championship, 1994; Competed in the Italian Open, US Open, Chase Championship (New York) and Wimbledon; Won 1st Professional Tournament, Filderstadt, Germany, 1996; Winner, Australian Open, 1997 (youngest winner of a Grand Slam title in 20th Century), 1998, 1999; Beaten Finalist, Australian Open, 2000, 2001, 2002; Winner, US Open, 1997; Beaten Finalist, US Open, 1998, 1999; Wimbledon Singles Champion, 1997; Winner, Australian Open, 1998; Won US Open, 1997, beaten finalist, 1998, 1999; Wimbledon singles champion, 1997; Swiss Federation Cup Team, 1996-98; Semi-finalist, US Open, 2001; By end of 2002 had won 76 tournament titles including five Grand Slam singles and nine doubles titles; Elected to WTA Tour Players' Council, 2002. Honours: WTA Tour Most Impressive Newcomer, 1995; Most Improved Player, 1996; Player of the Year, 1997. Address: c/o AM Seidenbaum 17, 9377 Truebbach, Switzerland.

HINOJOSA Jose, b. 23 May 1967, Seville, Spain. Paediatric Neurosurgeon. m. Raquel Terrón. Education: Faculty of Medicine, University of Valladolid; Faculty of Medicine, University Compultense, Madrid. Appointments: Department of Neurosurgery, Hospital Ramon y Catal, 1992-97; Department of Paediatric Neurosurgery, Hospital 12 de Octubre, Madrid, 1998-2003. Publications: Articles: Endoscopic Treatment of Supracelluar Arachnoid Cysts; Surgical Treatment of Trigonochepaly; Congenital Brain Tumours; Paediatric Spinal Trauma. Memberships: Spanish Society of Neurosurgery; Spanish Society of Paediatric Neurosurgery; European Society for Paediatric Neurosurgery; World Federation of Neurosurgery Societies. Address: Department of Paediatric Neurosurgery, Hospital 12 de Octubre, 28041 Madrid, Spain. E-mail: jhinojosa.hdoc@salvd.madrid.org

HINZ SORENSEN Shirley, b. 28 September 1942, Denver, Colorado, USA. Business Administration Management; Writer. m. Dale Edward Hinz. Education: Business Major, Fort Lewis College, 1961; Business Management, Barnes Business College, 1985. Appointments: Administration Assistant, United States Department of Agriculture, 1987; Administration Assistant, United States Department of Energy, 1990; Administration Assistant, United States Department of the Interior, 1991-. Publications include: A Call That Changed Our Life, short story; This Wife Remembers, poetry, 1997; Oh, The Joys of Being a Parent, short story, 2000. Honours: Outstanding Business Student, Underwood Corporation, 1960; Editors choice award, 1995, 1995; Special Publishing Award, 1996; National Merit Award, 1994; Poetry included in 15 publications; Listed in national and international biographical dictionaries. Memberships: International Society of Poets. Address: P O Box 1063, Ault, CO 80610, USA.

HIRAI Masako, b. 9 April 1949, Ashiya, Japan. Professor of English. 1 son. Education: BA, English, Kobe College, 1972; MA, English, 1974, Comp PhD, 1977, Doctor of Letters, 1999, Kyoto University, Japan. Appointments: Lecturer of English, 1977-81, Associate Professor, 1981-90, Professor of English, 1990-, Kobe College, Japan. Publications include: Sisters in Literature: Female Sexuality in Antigone, Middlemarch, Howards End and Women in Love, 1998; From Oedipus to Sons and Lovers via Hamlet, 1998. Honours: Excellent Research, at Third Competition Among Junior Scholars of the English Literary Society of Japan. Memberships: Life member, Clare Hall, Cambridge, UK; International Lawrence Society; ICLA; The George Eliot Society of UK and Japan; The English Literary Society of Japan. Address: Kobe College, 4-1 Okadayama, Nishinomiya, 662-8505, Japan.

HIRATA Tatsuya, b. 26 June 1943, Tokyo, Japan. Painter; Ceramic Artist. m. Saeko, 25 February, 2 sons, 1 deceased 29 March 1999. Education: Bachelor, French Language, French Language Department, Sophia University; Professor, Art Department, Accademia del Verbano, Italy. Creative works: Paintings; Ceramic art; Exhibitions include: France: Art Impact, Paris, 1994; Espace Branly Société Nationale des Beaux Arts, Paris 1997; Salon International de Peintures et de sculpture, Nancy, 1997; Salon de la Nationale des Beaux Arts, Paris, 2001, 2002; Triennale de Paris, 2002; Japan: Salon de l'Automne Franco-Japonais, Tokyo, 1994; USA; Galerie Montserrat, New York, 1994; Italy: Accademia Italiana "Gli Etruschi" – L'Aquilla della Liberta, Florence, 2002; Accademia Internazionale d'Arte Moderna, Rome, 2002. Honours: Accademicien del Verbano Italia, 1995; Chevalier de l'Ordre Templier, France, 1997; Academical Official Knight, Arts Department, Greci-Marino, 1998; Honorary Member, Foundation Marabello, Spain; Honorary Professor, Accademia Italiana, Gli Etruschi, 2000; Diploma di Mérite, Chevalier de la Paix, Accademia Internazionale "Il Marzocco, 2002. Memberships: Société Nationale des Beaux Arts; Society of Arts, Sciences, Lettres, Paris; Société des Artistes Français; Le Mérite et Dévoument Français; Accademia del Verbeno; Association Galleria Centro Storico, Italy; Accademia Araldia Internazionale "Il Marzocco", Italy; Accademia Italiana "Gli Etruschi", Italy; Japan International Artists Society; La Société Franco-Japonaise d'Art et d'Archéologie, Japan. Address: 2 Banchi, 2 Bancho, Chiyoda-ku, Tokyo 102-0084, Japan.

HIROTA Shigeru, b. 7 August 1960, Tokyo, Japan. Medical Educator. Education: MD, Gunma University, 1986; PhD, Niigata University, 1995. Appointments: Fellow, Gunma University, 1986-87, Niigata University, 1987-92; Vice Chairman, Akita Red Cross Hospital, 1992-95, 1996-; Visiting Professor, S IL University, USA, 1995-96. Publications: Several articles in professional journals. Memberships: AAAS; American Association of Cancer Research; Anticancer Therapeutics and Oncology Society, USA; Gastroenterology Society, Cancer; Cancer Society, France. Journal Reviewer: Gastroenterology, USA; Cancer Journal, Europe. Address: Department of Gastroenterology, Akita Red Cross Hospital, 222-1 Nawashirosawa, Saruta, Kamikitade, Akita 010-1495, Japan.

HIRSCH Gilah Yelin, b. 24 August 1944, Montreal, Quebec. Artist; Writer; Professor. Education: BA, University of California at Berkeley, 1967; MFA, University of California, Los Angeles,

1970. Career: Lecturer, Santa Monica College, 1970-73; Professor of Art, California State University, 1973-; Multidisciplinary works in varied media of writing, painting, photography and video; Art exhibited and collected internationally. Publications: Works published internationally. Honours: Numerous grants and awards. Address: 2412 Oakwood Avenue, Venice, CA 90291, USA. E-mail: gilah@linkline.com

HIRST Damien, b. 1965, Bristol, England. Artist. 2 sons. Education: Goldsmiths College, London. Creative Works: One-man exhibitions include: Institute of Contemporary Arts (ICA), London, 1991; Emmanuel Perrotin, Paris, 1991; Cohen Gallery, New York, 1992; Regen Projects, Los Angeles, 1993; Galerie Jablonka, Cologne, 1993; Milwaukee Art Museum, 1994; Dallas Museum, 1994; Kukje Gallery, Seoul, 1995; White Cube/Jay Jopling, London, 1995; Prix Eliette von Karajan, 1995; Max Gandolph-Bibliothek, Salzburg, Germany, Gasogian Gallery, New York, 1996; Bruno Bischofberger, Zurich, 1997; Astrup Fearnley, Oslo, 1997; Numerous group exhibitions world-wide. Television: Channel 4 documentary about Damien Hirst and exhibition at Gagosian Gallery, directed by Roger Pomphrey, 2000. Publications: I Want to Spend the Rest of My Life Everywhere, One to One, Always, Forever, 1997; Theories, Models, Methods, Approaches, Assumptions, Results and Findings, 2000. Honours: Turner Prize, 1995. Address: c/o Julia Royse, The White Cube Gallery, 44 Duke Street, St James's, London SW1Y 6DD, England.

HISLOP Ian David, b. 13 July 1960. Writer; Broadcaster. m. Victoria Hamson, 1988, 1 son, 1 daughter. Education: Ardingly College; BA Honours, English Language and Literature, Magdalen College, Oxford. Appointments: Joined staff, 1981-, Deputy Editor, 1985-86, Editor, 1986-, Private Eye, satirical magazine; Columnist, The Listener magazine, 1985-89; TV Critic, The Spectator magazine, 1994-96; Columnist, Sunday Telegraph, 1996-; Radio: Newsquiz, 1985-90; Fourth Column, 1992-96; Lent Talk, 1994; Gush (with Nicholas Newman), 1994; Words on Words, 1999; The Hislop Vote, 2000; A Revolution in 5 Acts, 2001; The Patron Saints, 2002; Television scriptwriting: Spitting Image, 1984-89 (with Nick Newman); The Stone Age, 1989; Briefcase Encounter, 1990; The Case of the Missing, 1991; He Died a Death, 1991; Harry Enfield's Television Programme, 1990-92; Harry Enfield and Chums, 1994-97; Mangez Merveillac, 1994; Dead on Time, 1995; Gobble, 1996; Sermon from St Albion's, 1998; Confessions of a Murderer, BBC2, 1999; My Dad is the Prime Minister, 2003; Performer: Have I Got News For You, 1990-; Great Railway Journeys, 1999; Documentaries: Canterbury Tales, 1996; School Rules, 1997; Pennies from Bevan, 1998; East to West, 1999. Publications: various Private Eye collections, 1985-; Contributor to newspapers and magazines on books, current affairs, arts and entertainment. Honours: BAFTA Award for Have I Got News for You, 1991; Editors' Editor, British Society of Magazine Editors, 1991; Magazine of the Year, What the Papers Say, 1991; Editor of the Year, British Society of Magazine Editors, 1998. Address: c/o Private Eye, 6 Carlisle Street, London W1V 5RG, England.

HISSEY Jane Elizabeth, b. 1 September 1952, Norwich, Norfolk, England. Author; Illustrator. m. Ivan James Hissey, 1 August 1979, 2 sons, 1 daughter. Education: Art Foundation Course, Great Yarmouth College of Art and Design, 1970; BA, 1974, Art Teachers Certificate, Brighton Polytechnic, 1975. Publications: Old Bear, 1986; Little Bear's Trousers, 1987; Little Bear Lost, 1989; Jolly Tall, 1990; Jolly Snow, 1991; Old Bear Tales, 1991; Little Bear's Day, Little Bear's Bedtime, 1992; Ruff, 1994; Hoot, 1996; Little Bear's Dragon, 1999; Old Bear's All-together Painting, 2000; Little Bear's Alphabet, 2000; Little Bear's Numbers, 2001; Little Bears Colours, 2002; Little Bear's Shapes, 2003; SPLASH! 2003. TV series: Old Bear Stories, 1993-98. Honours: BAFTA, Best

Dictionary of International Biography

Children's Programme, 1993. Address: c/o Hutchinson Childrens Books, Random House, 61-63 Uxbridge Road, London W5 5SA, England.

HIZIROGLU Salim, b. 21 September 1958, Turkey. Professor. Education: BS, Forest Products Engineering, Black Sea Technical University, Turkey, 1979; MS, Wood Science and Technology, University of California, Berkeley, 1985; PhD, Forest Products, Michigan State University, 1989. Appointments: Research Associate, Assistant Professor, Department of Forestry, Michigan State University, USA, 2000-2002; Assistant Professor, Department of Forestry, Oklahoma State University, USA, 2002-. Publications: Articles in scientific journals and papers presented at conferences as author and co-author include most recently: The Influence of the Surface Quality of Electrodes on the Breakdown of Sulphur Hexafluoride, 2002; Quality of Layer Thickness of Wood Composites, 2002; Fundamentals of Timber Drying, 2003. Honours: NATO Science Scholarship, 1982-86; Award for Excellence for Exceptional Programming in the area of Technical Service, Co-operative Extension Service Southern Region, 2002; Technology Transfer and Extension Award, Oklahoma Division, Ouchita Society of American Foresters. Memberships: Forest Products Society; Society of American Foresters; International Union of Forest Research Organization; Oklahoma Red Cedar Association. Address: 303-G Agricultural Hall, Department of Forestry, Oklahoma State University, Stillwater, OK 74078, USA. E-mail: hizirog@okstate.edu

HJERTÉN Stellan Vilhelm Einar, b. 2 April 1928, Forshem, Sweden. Biochemist. m. Laila Elisabet Woxström, 1 daughter. Education: PhD, Uppsala University, Sweden, 1967. Appointments: Assistant Professor, 1967-69, Professor in Biochemistry, 1969-, Uppsala University. Publications: Numerous articles of professional journals and publications. Honours: The Björkén Prize, Uppsala University, 1985; Founder's Award, Electrophoresis Society, 1988; Frederick Conference Award, 1993; The Hirai Prize, Japan, 1994; American Chemical Society Award, 1996; The Torbern Bergman Medal, Swedish Chemical Society, 1996; The Pierce Award, International Society for Molecular Recognition, 2001; The M J E Golay Award, 2002; The Rudbeck Prize, Uppsala University, Sweden, 2004; Initiator of Scandinavian Electrophoresis Society and Nordic Separation Science Society; Honorary Doctor, University Medical School, Pécs, Hungary, 1999 and Vytautas Magnus University, Kaunas, Lithuania, 2001; Listed in Historica Chromatographica, Today's Chemists at Work, American Chemical Society, 2002. Membership: Member, Editorial Board of several science journals. Address: Uppsala Biomedical Centre, Institute of Biochemistry, Box 576, SE-751 23, Uppsala, Sweden.

HJORTSBERG William Reinhold, b. 23 February 1941, New York, New York, USA. Author. Education: BA, Dartmouth College, 1962; Postgraduate Studies, Yale Drama School, 1962-63; Stanford University, 1967-68. Appointments: Adjunct Professor, Media and Theatre Arts, Montana State University, 1991-. Publications: Alp, 1969; Gray Matters, 1971; Symbiography, 1973; Toro! Toro! Toro!, 1974; Falling Angel, 1978; Tales and Fables, 1985; Nevermore, 1994; Odd Corners, 1999. Films: Thunder and Lightning, 1977; Georgia Peaches (co-author), 1980; Legend, 1986; Angel Heart, 1987. Contributions to: Various journals, magazines and newspapers. Honours: Wallace Stegner Fellowship, 1967; National Endowment for the Arts Grant, 1976; Playboy Editorial Award, 1971, 1978. Memberships: Writers Guild of America; The Authors Guild. Literary Agent: Harold Matson Company, New York City, NY, USA.

HNIKOVA Olga, b. 29 November 1931, Prague, Czechoslovakia. Medical Doctor, Paediatrician. m. Hnik Pavel, 1 son, 1 daughter. Education: Diploma, 1957, Qualifications in Paediatrics 1st Grade, 1959, 2nd Grade, 1969, PhD Diploma, 1979, Medical School, Charles University. Appointments: Assistant Professor, Paediatrics Clinic, Prague, 1965-75; Associate Professor, Paediatrics, 1990-93, Full Professor, Paediatrics, 1994-, Charles University; 3rd Medical Faculty Prague, Head of Paediatric Clinic, 1990-97. Publications: 130 articles in Czech and foreign medical magazines, mainly on paediatric endocrinology (growth disturbances, thyroid diseases); Book: Congenital Hypothyroidism (in Czech); Chapters in Czech textbooks for medical students on paediatric and adolescents endocrinopathology. Honours: Award, Introduction of mass newborn screening on congenital hypothyroidism in the whole of Czechoslovakia, 1985; Honorary Diploma for contribution in iodine deficiency elimination in the Czech Republic, 2003; Honorary member, Czech Endocrinology Society, 1991, Czech Paediatric Society, 1998, Czech Medical Society J.E. Purkinje, 2001. Memberships: European Society for Paediatric Endocrinology, 1989-; Working Group on Neonatal Screening, 1991-; International Society for Newborn Screening, 1994-; Czech Paediatric and Endocrinology Societies. Address: Children and Adolescents Clinic, Charles University, 3rd Medical Faculty, Prague, Vinohradská 159, CZ 100 81.

HO Anh Thai, b. 18 October 1960, Hanoi, Vietnam. Novelist; Diplomat. m. N B Lan, 29 January 1996, 1 son. Education: MA, International Relations, College of Diplomacy, Hanoi, 1978-83; PhD, Oriental Culture, 1988-94. Appointments: Researcher, Senior Expert, South Asia Department, Ministry of Foreign Affairs, 1983-. Publications: 8 novels and 10 collections of short stories. Contributions to: Newspapers and magazines. Honours: 1st Prize, Short Story Contest, Van Nghe Newspaper, 1985; Novel Award, Vietnam Writers' Association, 1990; Best Book Award, Union of Literature and Arts Associations, Vietnam, 1995. Memberships: Vietnam Writers' Association; Secretary General, Hanoi Writers' Association. Address: 6 Chu Van An, Hanoi, Vietnam.

HOAGLAND Edward, b. 21 December 1932, New York, New York, USA. Author; Teacher. m. (1) Amy J Ferrara, 1961, divorced 1964, (2) Marion Magid, 28 March 1968, died 1993, 1 daughter. Education: AB, Harvard University, 1954. Appointments: Faculty: New School for Social Research, New York City, 1963-64, Rutgers University, 1966, Sarah Lawrence College, 1967, 1971, City University of New York, 1967, 1968, University of Iowa, 1978, 1982, Columbia University, 1980, 1981, Bennington College, 1987-2001, Brown University, 1988, University of California at Davis, 1990, 1992, Beloit College, Wisconsin, 1995; General Editor, Penguin Nature Library, 1985-. Publications: Cat Man, 1956; The Circle Home, 1960; The Peacock's Tail, 1965; Notes from the Century Before: A Journal from British Columbia, 1969; The Courage of Turtles, 1971; Walking the Dead Diamond River, 1973; The Moose on the Wall: Field Notes from the Vermont Wilderness, 1974; Red Wolves and Black Bears, 1976; African Calliope: A Journey to the Sudan, 1979; The Edward Hoagland Reader, 1979; The Tugman's Passage, 1982; City Tales, 1986; Seven Rivers West, 1986; Heart's Desire, 1988; The Final Fate of the Alligators, 1992; Balancing Acts, 1992; Tigers and Ice, 1999; Compass Points, 2000; Numerous essays and short stories. Honours: Houghton Mifflin Literary Fellowship, 1954; Longview Foundation Award, 1961; Prix de Rome, 1964; Guggenheim Fellowships, 1964, 1975; O Henry Award, 1971; New York State Council on the Arts Award, 1972; National Book Critics Circle Award, 1980; Harold D Vursell Award, 1981; National Endowment for the Arts Award, 1982; Literary Lion Award, New York Public Library, 1988; National Magazine Award, 1989; Lannon

Dictionary of International Biography

Foundation Literary Award, 1993; Literary Lights Award, Boston Public Library, 1995; American Academy of Arts and Letters, 1982. Address: PO Box 51, Barton, VT 05822, USA.

HOANG Cuong, b. 27 March 1944, Hue, Vietnam. Composer; Violinist. m. Le Kim Thanh. 1 son, 1 daughter. Education: Intermediate Level, Carl-Maria von Weber Conservatory; Graduate, Tchaikovsky Conservatory, Moscow, Russia; Postgraduate, Chopin Conservatory, Warsaw, Poland; Professor of Music, 1992. Appointments: Violin Teacher, 1965-; Dean of Strings Department, 1984, Vice-Director, 1997, Director, 2000-, HoChiMinh City Conservatory, HoChiMinh City, Vietnam; Member of the Jury, International Violin Competition "SPOHR", Freiburg, Germany, 1997. Honours: Only student selected by a German teacher to develop musical talent, Dresden, 1959; 2nd prize for Composition, 1990, 1996, 1997, 2001 3rd Prize, 1999, 2000, Vietnamese Composer's Association. Memberships: HoChiMinh City Musicians Association; Vietnamese Composers, Musicologists and Musicians Association. Address: 112 Nguyen Du Street, Dist 1, HoChiMinh City, Vietnam. E-mail: nhacvienhcm@hcm.vnn.vn

HOBART Lady Caroline Fleur (Caroline Leeds), b. 17 May 1931, Jersey, Channel Islands. Artist. m. (1) 11th Duke of Leeds, deceased, (2) Peter Hendrick Peregrine Hoos, deceased, (3) Sir Robert Hampden Hobart, deceased. Education: Studied under Philip Lambe, RPNS; Studied under Bernard Adams, RPROINS. Career: Group Exhibitions include: Royal Society of Portrait Painters; Royal Institute of Oil Painters; Royal Society of British Artists; The Paris Salon; 1st Salon Mid Pyrenées; Roy Miles British Artists, 1991; Portraits Gagliardi Gallery, 1992; Return to Beauty, Roy Miles, 1994; One-woman shows include: Narbonne, 1990; the Abbaye de Flaran, Gers, France, 1991; Société Archéologique due Gers, 1992, 1996; Lectoure, 1993; The Gallery South Audley St, London, 1994; Recent Painting, Roy Miles, 1995; Period Homes, Olympia, 1996; Refractions, An Anglo-American exposition, London, 1997; Stair Co Galerie, MB avenue, Matignon, Paris, 1997; Gagliardi Gallery, 1999; Stair and Co, 1999; Arts and Crafts Movement, 2000; The Studio Gallery, Midhurst. Memberships: The Arts Club, Dover Street, London; Associate Lady Memberships: Royal Yacht Squadron. Address: 42 Egerton Gardens, London SW3 2BZ, England.

HOBSBAWM Eric John Ernest, b. 9 June 1917, Alexandria, Egypt (British citizen). Professor of Economic and Social History Emeritus; Writer. m. Marlene Schwarz, 1962, 1 son, 1 daughter. Education: BA, 1939, MA, 1943, PhD, 1951, University of Cambridge. Appointments: Lecturer in History, 1947-59, Reader in History, 1959-70, Professor of Economic and Social History, 1970-82, Professor Emeritus, 1982-, Birkbeck College, University of London; Fellow, King's College, Cambridge, 1949-55 (Honorary Fellow, 1971). Publications: Labour's Turning Point, 1880-1900 (editor), 1948; Primitive Rebels, 1959, US edition as Social Bandits and Primitive Rebels, 1959; The Jazz Scene, 1959, revised edition, 1993; The Age of Revolution, 1789-1848, 1962; Labouring Men, 1964; Industry and Empire: An Economic History of Britain since 1750, 1968, 1999, US edition as Industry and Empire: The Making of Modern English Society, 1968; Captain Swing (with George Rudé), 1969; Bandits, 1969, revised edition, 1981, 2000; Revolutionaries, 1973; The Age of Capital, 1848-1875, 1975; Marxism in Marx's Day (editor), 1982; The Invention of Tradition (editor with Terence Ranger), 1983; Worlds of Labour: Further Studies in the History of Labour, 1984, US edition as Workers: Worlds of Labor, 1984; The Age of Empire, 1875-1914, 1987; Politics for a Rational Left: Political Writing, 1977-1988, 1989; Echoes of the Marseillaise: Two Centuries Look Back on the French Revolution, 1990; Nations and Nationalism since 1780:

Programme, Myth, Reality, 1990, 2nd edition, 1992; Age of Extremes: The Short Twentieth Century, 1914-1991, 1994; US edition as The Age of Extremes: A History of the World, 1914-1991, 1994; On History (essays), 1997; Uncommon People: Resistance, Rebellion and Jazz, 1998; On the Edge of the New Century, 2000. Contributions to: Scholarly journals and general publications. Honours: Palmes Académiques, France, 1993; Commander, Order of the Southern Cross, Brazil, 1996; Companion of Honour, 1998; Numerous honorary degrees. Memberships: American Academy of Arts and Sciences, honorary foreign member; British Academy, fellow; Hungarian Academy of Sciences, foreign member; Academy of Sciences, Turin. Address: School of History, Birkbeck College, University of London, Malet Street, London WC1E 7HX, England.

HOBSON Fred Colby Jr, b. 23 April 1943, Winston-Salem, North Carolina, USA. Professor of Literature; Writer. m. 17 June 1967, divorced, 1 daughter. Education: AB, English, University of North Carolina, 1965; MA, History, Duke University, 1967; PhD, English, University of North Carolina, 1972. Appointments: Professor of English, University of Alabama, 1972-86; Professor of English and Co-Editor, Southern Review, Louisiana State University, 1986-89; Professor of English; Lineberger Professor in the Humanities and Co-Editor, Southern Literary Journal, University of North Carolina at Chapel Hill, 1989-. Publications: Serpent in Eden: H L Mencken and the South, 1974; Literature at the Barricades: The American Writer in the 1930's (co-editor) 1983; Tell About the South: The Southern Rage to Explain, 1984; South-Watching: Selected Essays of Gerald W Johnson (editor), 1984; The Southern Writer in the Post-Modern World, 1990; Mencken: A Life, 1994; Thirty-Five Years of Newspaper Work by H L Mencken (co-editor), 1994; But Now I See: The Southern White Racial Conversion Narrative, 1999; Faulkner's Absalom, Absalom!: Selected Essays (editor), 2002; South to the Future: An American Region in the Twenty-First Century (editor), 2002. Contributions to: Virginia Quarterly Review; Sewanee Review; Atlantic Monthly; Kenyon Review; New York Times Book Review; American Literature; Times Literary Supplement. Honours: Lillian Smith Award, 1984; Jules F Landry Award, 1994, 1999. Address: Department of English, University of North Carolina at Chapel Hill, NC 27599-3520, USA.

HOCHSCHILD Adam, b. 5 October 1942, New York, New York, USA. Writer. m. Arlie Russell, 26 June 1965, 2 sons. Education: AB cum laude, Harvard University, 1963. Appointments: Reporter, San Francisco Chronicle, 1965-66; Editor and Writer, Ramparts Magazine, 1966-68, 1973-74; Co-Founder, Editor, Writer, Mother Jones Magazine, 1974-81, 1986-87; Commentator, National Public Radio, 1982-83, Public Interest Radio, 1987-88; Regents Lecturer, University of California at Santa Cruz, 1987; Lecturer, Graduate School of Journalism, University of California at Berkeley, 1992-. Fulbright Lecturer, India, 1997-98. Publications: Half the Way Home: A Memoir of Father and Son, 1986; The Mirror at Midnight: A South African Journey, 1990; The Unquiet Ghost: Russians Remember Stalin, 1994; Finding the Trapdoor: Essays, Portraits, Travels, 1997; King Leopold's Ghost: A Story of Greed, Terror and Heroism In Colonial Africa, 1998. Contributions to: New Yorker; Harper's; New York Times; Los Angeles Times; Washington Post; Granta; Times Literary Supplement; Progressive; Village Voice; New York Review of Books; Mother Jones. Honours: Thomas Storke Award, World Affairs Council, 1987; Madeleine Dane Ross Award, Overseas Press Club of America, 1995; Lowell Thomas Award, Society of American Travel Writers, 1995; PEN/Spielvogel-Diamonstein Award for the Art of the Essay, 1998; Finalist, National Book Critics Circle Award 1999; Winner, Gold Medal, California Book Awards, 1999; J Anthony Lukas Prize, 1999; Lionel Gelber Prize,

Canada, 1999; Winner, Duff Cooper Prize, UK, 2000. Memberships: PEN; National Writers Union; National Book Critics Circle. Address: 84 Seward Street, San Francisco, CA 94114, USA.

HOCKNEY David, b. 9 July 1937, Bradford, England. Artist. Education: Bradford College of Art; Royal College of Art. Appointments: Teacher, Maidstone College of Art, 1962, University of Iowa, 1964, University of Colorado, 1965, University of California, Los Angeles, 1966, University of California, Berkeley, 1967. Creative Works: First one-man exhibition, Kasmin Galley, London, 1963; Subsequent one-man exhibitions include: Nicholas Wilder, Los Angeles, 1976; Galerie Neundorf, Hamburg, 1977; Warehouse Gallery, 1979; Knoedler Gallery, 1979, 1981, 1982, 1983, 1984, 1986; Tate Gallery, 1980, 1986, 1988; Hayward Gallery, 1983, 1985; Los Angeles County Museum, 1988; The Metro Museum of Art, New York, 1988; Knoedler Gallery, London, 1988; A Emmerich Gallery, New York, 1988, 1989; Los Angeles Louvre Gallery, Venice, 1982, 1983, 1985, 1988; Nishimura Gallery, Tokyo, Japan, 1988; Manchester City Art Galleries, 1996; National Museum of American Art, Washington DC, 1997, 1998; Museum Ludwig, Cologne, 1997; Museum of Fine Arts, Boston, 1998; Centre Georges Pompidou, Paris, 1999; Musee Picasso, Paris, 1999; Annely Juda Fine Art, 2003; National Portrait Gallery, 2003. Publications: Hockney by Hockney, 1976; David Hockney, Travel with Pen, Pencil and Ink, 1978; Photographs, 1982; China Diary (with Stephen Spender), 1982; Hockney Paints the Stage, 1983; David Hockney: Cameraworks, 1984; Hockney on Photography: Conversations with Paul Joyce, 1988; David Hockney: A Retrospective, 1988; Hockney's Alphabet, 1991; That's the Way I See It, 1993; Off the Wall: Hockney Posters, 1994; David Hockney's Dog Days, 1998; Hockney on Art: Photography, Painting and Perspective, 1998; Hockney on "Art": Conversation with Paul Joyce, 2000; Secret Knowledge: Rediscovering the Lost Techniques of the Old Masters, 2001. Honours: Numerous. Memberships include: Royal Academy, 1985. Address: c/o 7508 Santa Monica Boulevard, Los Angeles, CA 90046, USA.

HODDLE Glenn, b. 27 October 1957, England. Footballer; Football Manager. m. Christine Anne Stirling, divorced, 1 son, 2 daughters. Appointments: Player with Tottenham Hotspur, 1976-86, AS Monaco, France, 1986; (12 under 21 caps, 53 full caps on England National Team 1980-88, played in World Cup 1982, 1986); Player/Manager, Swindon Town, 1991-93 (promoted to FA Premier League 1993); Player/Manager, Chelsea, 1993-96; Coach, English National Team, 1996-99; Manager, Southampton, 2000-01; Manager, Tottenham Hotspur, 2001-. Publication: Spurred to Success (autobiography); Glenn Hoddle: The 1998 World Cup Story, 1998. Honours: FA Cup Winners Medal (Tottenham Hotspur), 1984; French Championship Winners Medal (Monaco), 1988. Address: Tottenham Hotspur Football Club Ltd, 748 High Road, Tottenham, London N17 0AD, England.

HODGE Patricia, b. Grimsby, England. Actress. m. Peter Owen, 2 sons. Education: London Academy of Music and Dramatic Art. Creative Works: Stage appearances include: No-one Was Saved; All My Sons; Say Who You Are; The Birthday Party; The Anniversary; Popkiss; Two Gentlemen of Verona; Pippin; Maudie; Hair; The Beggar's Opera; Pal Joey; Look Back in Anger; Dick Whittington; Happy Yellow; The Brian Cant Children's Show; Then and Now; The Mitford Girls; As You Like It; Benefactors; Noel and Gertie; Separate Tables; The Prime of Miss Jean Brodie; A Little Night Music; Heartbreak House, 1997; Money, 1999; Noises Off, 2000-01; His Dark Materials, 2004. Film appearances: The Disappearance; Rose Dixon - Night Nurse; The Waterloo Bridge Handicap; The Elephant Man; Heavy Metal; Betrayal; Sunset; Just Ask for Diamond; The Secret Life of Ian Fleming;

The Leading Man, 1996; Prague Duet, 1996; Jilting Joe, 1997; TV appearances: Valentine; The Girls of Slender Means; Night of the Father; Great Big Groovy Horse; The Naked Civil Servant; Softly, Softly; Jackanory Playhouse; Act of Rape; Crimewriters; Target; Rumpole of the Bailey; The One and Only Mrs Phyllis Dixey; Edward and Mrs Simpson; Disraeli; The Professionals; Holding the Fort; The Other 'Arf; Jemima Shore Investigates; Hayfever; The Death of the Heart; Robin of Sherwood; OSS; Sherlock Holmes; Time for Murder; Hotel du Lac; The Life and Loves of a She Devil; Rich Tea and Sympathy, 1991; The Cloning of Joanna May, 1991; The Legacy of Reginald Perrin, 1996; The Moonstone, 1996; The Falklands Play, 2002. Award: The Olivier Award, 2000. Address: c/o ICM, Oxford House, 76 Oxford Street, London W1R 1RB, England.

HODGES C(yril) Walter, b. 18 March 1909, Beckenham, Kent. Freelance Writer; Book Illustrator; Theatrical Historian; Designer. m. Greta, 1936, 2 sons. Education: Dulwich College; Goldsmiths' College School of Art; Hon DLitt, Sussex, 1979. Career: Stage Designer, 1929; Illustrator for advertising, magazines and children's books, 1937-99; Army, Despatches, 1940-46; Designed stage productions at Mermaid Theatre, 1951, 1964, permanent Elizabethan Stage, St George's Theatre, 1976; Mural decorations painted for Chartered Insurance Institute, UK Provident Institution; Art Director, Encyclopaedia Britannica Films, 1959-61; Reconstruction drawings for model of excavated Elizabethan Rose Theatre Museum of London, 1989-91; Consultant Designer, Globe Theatre, Alexander Mills N Carolina, USA, 1993-; Judith E Wilson Lecture in Poetry and Drama, Cambridge, 1974; Co-ordinator, Symposium for reconstruction of Globe Playhouse, 1979; Adjunct Professor, Wayne State University, USA, 1980-83; Visiting Scholar, University of Maryland, 1983. Publications: Columbus Sails, 1939; The Flying House, 1947; Shakespeare and the Players, 1948; The Globe Restored, 1953, revised edition, 1968; The Namesake, 1964; Shakespeare's Theatre, 1964; The Norman Conquest, 1966; Magna Carta, 1966; The Marsh King, 1967; The Spanish Armada, 1967; The Overland Launch, 1969; The English Civil War, 1972; Shakespeare's Second Globe, 1973; Playhouse Tales, 1974; The Emperor's Elephant, 1975; Plain Lane Christmas, 1978; The Battlement Garden, 1979; The Third Globe, editor, 1981; Enter the Whole Army: the presentation of Shakespeare's plays in the theatres of his time, 1999; Contributor to Shakespeare Survey; Theatre Notebook; The New Cambridge Shakespeare, illustrator, 1984. Honours: Kate Greenaway Medal for illustration, 1965; Honours List, Hans Christian Andersen International Award, 1966. Address: c/o 18 Parkhouse Road, Minehead, Somerset, TA24 8AD, England.

HODGSON Peter Barrie, b. 12 March 1942, Gosforth, England. Market Research Director. m. Audrone Grudzinskas, 1 son. Education: BA, St Peter's College, Oxford, England. Appointments: Senior Research Executive, Marplan Ltd, 1967-69; Senior Research Planner, Garland Compton Ltd, 1970-72; Director, Opinion Research Centre Ltd, 1973-75; Managing Director, Professional Studies Ltd, 1975-77; Director, Professional Studies Ireland Ltd, 1977-78; Managing Director, Action Research Ltd, 1977-78; Director, City Research Associates, Ltd, 1981-89; Managing Director, Travel and Tourism Research Ltd, 1978-. Publications: Articles published in: Espaces (Paris); Marketing; Journal of the Market Research Society; Journal of the Professional Marketing Research Society of Canada; Tourism Management; Journal of Travel Research; BMRA Bulletin; Synergie. Honours: Fellow, Tourism Society; Fellow, Institute of Travel and Tourism. Memberships: Council Member, Market Research Society, 1978-81; Council Member Tourism Society, 1981-84; Chairman, Association of British Market Research Companies, 1987-89; Chairman, Association of European Market Research Institutes,

1991-93; Honorary Secretary, British Market Research Association, 1998-. Address: Travel and Tourism Research Ltd, 4 Cochrane House, Admirals Way, London E14 9UD, England. E-mail: peterhodgson@whsmithnet.co.uk

HOE Susanna Leonie, b. 14 April 1945, Southampton, England. Writer. m. Derek Roebuck, 18 August 1981. Education: London School of Economics, 1980-82; BA, University of Papua New Guinea, 1983-84. Appointments: Campaign Co-ordinator, British Section Amnesty International, 1977-80; TEFL Teacher, Women's Centre, Hong Kong, 1991-97. Publications: Lady in the Chamber, 1971; God Save the Tsar, 1978; The Man Who Gave His Company Away, 1978; The Private Life of Old Hong Kong, 1991; Chinese Footprints, 1996; Stories for Eva: A Reader for Chinese Women Learning English, 1997; The Taking of Hong Kong, with Derek Roebuck, 1999; Women at the Siege, Peking 1900 (history), 2000; At Home in Paradise (Papua New Guinea, travel), 2003. Contributions to: Times (Papua New Guinea); Liverpool Post; Women's Feature Service. Honours: Te Rangi Hiroa Pacific History Prize, 1984. Membership: Honorary Research Fellow, Centre of Asian Studies, University of Hong Kong, 1991-. Address: 20A Plantation Road, Oxford OX2 6JD, England.

HOFF Johannes Nikolaus, b. 15 December 1962, Trier, Germany. Research Assistant; Lecturer. m. Ingrid Ertinger-Hoff. Education: Diploma, 1991, MA, Philosophy, 1992, Theology, Eberhard-Karls-Universität; Doctorate, Tübingen, 1999. Publications: Editor, 1 book, 1994; Author, 1 book, 1999; Many articles. Address: Hegelstr 2/1, 72072 Tübingen, Germany.

HOFFMAN Dustin Lee, b. 8 August 1937, Los Angeles, California, USA. Actor. m. (1) Anne Byrne, 1969, divorced, 2 daughters, (2) Lisa Gottsegen, 1980, 2 sons, 2 daughters. Education: Santa Monica City College. Appointments: Attendant, Psychiatric Institute; Demonstrator, Macy's Toy Department. Creative Works: Stage appearances include: Harry, Noon and Night, 1964; Journey of the Fifth Horse, 1966; Star Wagon, 1966; Fragments, 1966; Eh?, 1967; Jimmy Shine, 1968; Death of a Salesman, 1984; The Merchant of Venice, 1989; Films include: The Tiger Makes Out, 1966; Madigan's Millions, 1966; The Graduate, 1967; Midnight Cowboy, 1969; John and Mary, 1969; Little Big Man, 1970; Who is Harry Kellerman..?, 1971; Straw Dogs, 1971; Alfredo Alfredo, Papillon, 1973; Lenny, 1974; All the President's Men, 1975; Marathon Man, 1976; Straight Time, 1978; Agatha, 1979; Kramer vs Kramer, 1979; Tootsie, 1982; Ishtar, 1987; Rain Man, 1988; Family Business, 1989; Dick Tracy, 1990; Hook, 1991; Billy Bathgate, 1991; Hero, 1992; Outbreak, 1995; American Buffalo, 1996; Sleeper, 1996; Wag the Dog, 1997; Mad City, 1997; Sphere, 1997; Joan of Arc, 1999; The Messenger: the Story of Joan of Arc, 1999; Being John Malkovich, 1999. TV appearances in: Death of a Salesman, 1985. Honours include: Obie Award, 1966; Vernon Rice Award, 1967; Academy Award, 1980; New York Film Critics Award, 1980, 1988; Golden Globe Award, 1988; BAFTA Award, 1997. Address: Punch Productions, 1926 Broadway, Suite 305, NY 10023, USA.

HOFFMAN Mary Margaret Lassiter, b. 20 April 1945, Eastleigh, Hampshire, England. Writer; Journalist. m. Stephen James Barber, 22 December 1972, 3 daughters. Education: BA, 1967, MA, 1973, Newnham College, Cambridge; University College, London, 1970. Publications: 80 Children's Books including, Amazing Grace, 1991; Song of the Earth, 1995; An Angel Just Like Me, 1997; Sun, Moon and Stars, 1998; The Colour of Home, 2002; The Stravaganza Trilogy, 2002-05. Contributions to: Daily Telegraph; Guardian; Independent; Sunday Times; Specialist Children's Book Press; Editor, Armadillo Magazine, 1999-. Honour: Waldenbooks Best Children's Book Honor Award,

1991; Primary English Award, 1995; Honorary Fellow of the Library Association, 1998. Membership: Society of Authors. Address: c/o Rogers, Coleridge & White, 20 Powis Mews, London W11 1JN, England. Website: www.maryhoffman.co.uk

HOFMANN Holger Friedrich, b. 4 July 1969, Stuttgart, Germany. Researcher. Education: Stuttgart University, 1989-94; Diploma, Physics, 1994; Dr.rer.nat, 1999. Appointments: Visiting Researcher, Riken Institute, Japan, 1995, MPI, Stuttgart, 1995-96, DLR Institute of Technical Physics, 1996-99, Tokyo University, 1999-2001; JST-CREST, 2001-; Hokaido University, 2001-. Honour: Scholarship, 1990-95. Memberships: DPG; OSA. Address: Sunriver Kouwa 602, Kita 18 jou, Higashi 1, Higashi-ku, Sapporo 065-0018, Japan.

HOGWOOD Christopher (Jarvis Haley), b. 10 September 1941, Nottingham, England. Musicologist; Writer; Editor; Broadcaster. Education: BA, Pembroke College, Cambridge, 1964; Charles University, Prague; Academy of Music, Prague. Appointments: Founder-Member, Early Music Consort of London, 1967-76; Founder-Director, The Academy of Ancient Music, 1973-; Faculty, Cambridge University, 1975-; Artistic Director, 1986-2001, Conductor Laureate, 2001-, Handel and Haydn Society, Boston; Honorary Professor of Music, University of Keele, 1986-89; Music Director, 1988-92, Principal Guest Conductor, 1992-98, St Paul Chamber Orchestra, Minnesota; International Professor of Early Music Performance, Royal Academy of Music, London, 1992-; Visiting Professor, King's College, London, 1992-96; Principal Guest Conductor, Kammerorchester Basel, 2000-; Principal Guest Conductor, Orquestra de Granada, 2001-. Publications: Music at Court, 1977; The Trio Sonata, 1979; Haydn's Visits to England, 1980; Music in Eighteenth-Century England (editor), 1983; Handel, 1984; Holme's Life of Mozart (editor), 1991. Contributions to: The New Grove Dictionary of Music and Musicians, 1980, 2000. Honours: Walter Wilson Cobbett Medal, 1986; Commander of the Order of the British Empire, 1989; Honorary Fellow, Jesus College, Cambridge, 1989; Pembroke College, Cambridge, 1992; Freeman, Worshipful Company of Musicians, 1989; Incorporated Society of Musicians Distinguished Musician Award, 1997; Martinu Medal, Bohuslav Martinu Foundation, Prague, 1999; Honorary Professor of Music, Cambridge University, 2002-. Membership: Royal Society of Authors, fellow. Address: 10 Brookside, Cambridge CB2 1JE, England.

HOKIN Lowell Edward, b. 20 September, Chicago, Illinois, USA. Professor; Physician; Scientist. 2 sons, 2 daughters. Education: Student, University of Chicago, 1942-43, Dartmouth College, 1943-44, University of Louisville School of Medicine, 1944-46, University of Illinois School of Medicine, 1946-47; MD, University of Louisville, 1948; PhD, University of Sheffield, 1952. Appointments: Postdoctoral Fellow, Department of Biochemistry, McGill University, 1952-54; Faculty, 1954-57, Assistant Professor, 1955-57; Faculty, University of Wisconsin, Madison, 1957-, Professor, Physiological Chemistry, 1961-68, Professor, Pharmacology, 1968-, Professor, Chairman, Pharmacology, 1968-93; Professor Emeritus, 1999. Publications: 225 articles in professional journals; Discovered phosphoinositidie signalling. Memberships include: New York Academy of Sciences; AAAS; American Society of Pharmacology and Experimental Therapeutics; Biochemical Society, UK; American Society of Biochemistry and Molecular Biology. Address: 4120C Monona Drive, Monona, WI 53716-1147, USA.

HOLBERT James Marion Jr, b. 16 January 1945, Chattanooga, Tennessee, USA. Physician; Haematologist. m. Madeline Jane, 1 daughter. Education: BS, Duke University, Durham, North

Carolina, 1962-66, MD, University of Tennessee-Memphis, 1967-70; PhD, Biochemistry, Molecular Biology, The Health Science Center, St Jude Children's Research Hospital, University of Tennessee-Memphis, 1983-87; MBA, Fogelman College of Business & Economics, Memphis State University-Memphis, 1988-90; Postgraduate Education: Intern, Residency and Fellowship positions Baptist Memorial Hospital, Memphis, 1970-78. Appointments: Academic Appointments: Assistant Clinical Instructor, Department of Medicine, 1971-72, Clinical Assistant Professor, Department of Medicine, Division of Allergy and Immunology, 1978-85, Clinical Assistant Professor, Department of Pathology, College of Medicine, 1980-86, Clinical Associate Professor, Department of Medicine, 1985-2001; Clinical Associate Professor, Department of Pathology, College of Medicine, 1986-90, Clinical Associate Professor, Department of Paediatrics, College of Medicine, 1988-, University of Tennessee, Memphis; Hospital Appointments include: Consultant in Haematology, Department of Pathology, St Jude Children's Research Hospital, Memphis, 1980-90; Director of CytoGenetics, Department of Pathology, 1981-83, 1985-90, Co-Director of Haematology, 1982-88 Chief of Haematology, Department of Internal Medicine 1988-2002, Baptist Memorial Hospital, Memphis; Chief Executive Officer, Hematology/Immunology Consultants, PLLC, Memphis, 1993-. Publications: Books and book chapters as author and co-author: Lymphoproliferative disorders for mimicking Lymphomas and non-Hodgkins lymphomas, 1983; Neoplasms of terminal B cell differentiations: the morphological basis of functional diversity. Malignant lymphomas, 1983; Hemorrhagic and Thrombotic Abnormalities of Cancer, 1988; Complement Deficiency Syndromes, Current Practice of Medicine, 1998; 14 articles in scientific journals. Honours: Outstanding Teacher Awards, 1981-82, 1982-83, Teaching Excellence Award, 1983-84, University of Tennessee Medical Center. Memberships include: Fellowships: American Society of Clinical Pathologists, American Society of Hematology, College of American Pathologists, Royal Society of Health, London, American College of Physicians, Society of Biological Therapy. Address: 4277 Park Avenue, Memphis, TN 38117, USA. E-mail: hematob@bellsouth.net

HOLBROOK David (Kenneth), b. 9 January 1923, Norwich, England. Author. m. 23 April 1949, 2 sons, 2 daughters. Education: BA, Honours, English, 1946, MA, 1951, Downing College, Cambridge. Appointments: Fellow, King's College, Cambridge, 1961-65; Senior Leverhulme Research Fellow, 1965, Leverhulme Emeritus Research Fellow, 1988-90; Writer-in-Residence, Dartington Hall, 1972-73; Fellow and Director of English Studies, 1981-88, Emeritus Fellow, 1988, Downing College; Publications: English for Maturity, 1961; Imaginings, 1961; Against the Cruel Frost, 1963; English for the Rejected, 1964; The Secret Places, 1964; Flesh Wounds, 1966; Children's Writing, 1967; The Exploring Word, 1967; Object Relations, 1967; Old World New World, 1969; English in Australia Now, 1972; Gustav Mahler and the Courage to Be, 1975; Chance of a Lifetime, 1978; A Play of Passion, 1978; English for Meaning, 1980; Selected Poems, 1980; Nothing Larger than Life, 1987; The Novel and Authenticity, 1987; A Little Athens, 1990; Edith Wharton and the Unsatisfactory Man, 1991; Jennifer, 1991; The Gold in Father's Heart, 1992; Where D H Lawrence Was Wrong About Women, 1992; Creativity and Popular Culture, 1994; Even If They Fail, 1994; Tolstoy, Women and Death, 1996; Wuthering Heights: a Drama of Being, 1997; Getting it Wrong with Uncle Tom, 1998; Bringing Everything Home (poems), 1999; A Study of George MacDonald and the Image of Woman, 2000; Lewis Carroll: Nonsense Against Sorrow, 2001. Contributions to: Numerous professional journals. Honour: Festschrift, 1996. Honours: Founding Fellow, English Association, 2000. Membership: Society of Authors. Address: 1 Tennis Court Terrace, Cambridge CB2 1QX, England.

HOLBROOKE Richard C, b. 24 April 1941, New York, USA. Diplomat. m. (1) 2 sons, (2) Kati Morton, 1995. Education: Brown University; Woodrow Wilson School; Princeton University. Appointments: Foreign Service Officer, Vietnam and Related Posts, 1962-66; White House Vietnam Staff, 1966-67; Special Assistant to Under-Secretaries of State, Katzenbac and Richardson, Member, US Delegate to Paris Peace Talks on Vietnam, 1967-69; Director, Peace Corporations, Morocco, 1970-72; Managing Director, Foreign Policy (quarterly magazine), 1972-76; Consultant, President's Commission on Organisation of Government for Conduct of Foreign Policy, Contributing Editor, Newsweek, 1974-75; Co-ordinator, National Security Affairs, Carter-Mondale Campaign, 1976; Assistant Secretary of State for East Asian and Pacific Affairs, 1977-81; Vice President of Public Strategies, 1981-85; Managing Director, Lehman Brothers, 1985-93; Ambassador to Germany, 1993-94; Assistant Secretary of State for European and Canadian Affairs, 1994-96; Vice Chair, Credit Suisse First Boston Corporation, 1996-98; Adviser, Baltic Sea Council, 1996-98; Special Presidential Envoy for Cyprus, 1997-98, to Yugoslavia (on Kosovo crisis); Permanent Representative to UN, 1999-2000; Ambassador to UN, 1999-2001. Publications: Counsel to the President, 1991; To End a War, 1998; Several articles and essays. Honours: 12 honorary degrees; Distinguished Public Service Award, Department of Defense, 1994, 1996; Humanitarian of the Year Award, American Jewish Congress, 1998; Dr Bernard Heller, Prize, Hebrew Union College, 1999. Address: c/o Department of State, 2201 C Street NW, Washington, DC 20520, USA.

HOLDSTOCK Robert, b. 2 August 1948, Hythe, Kent, England. Writer. Education: BSc, University College of North Wales, 1970; MSc, London School of Hygiene and Tropical Medicine, 1971. Publications: Eye Among the Blind, 1976; Earthwind, 1977; Octopus Encyclopaedia of Science Fiction, 1978; Stars of Albion, 1979; Alien Landscapes, 1979; Tour of the Universe, 1980; Where Time Winds Blow, 1981; Mythago Wood, Emerald Forest, 1985; The Labyrinth, 1987; Other Edens, 1987; Lavondyss, 1988; The Fetch, 1991; The Bone Forest, 1992; The Hollowing, 1993; Merlin's Wood, 1994; Gate of Ivory, Gate of Horn, 1997; Celtika, 2001; The Iron Grail, 2002. Honours: World Fantasy Awards, 1985, 1993. Address: 54 Raleigh Road, London N8, England.

HOLENDER Barbara D, b. 15 March 1927, Buffalo, New York, USA. Poet. m. H William Holender, 8 May 1949, deceased, 1 son, 1 daughter. Education: Cornell University, 1944-46; BA, University of Buffalo, 1948. Appointments: Instructor in English, University of Buffalo, 1973-76; New York State Poets in the Schools, 1976. Publications: Shivah Poems: Poems of Mourning, 1986; Ladies of Genesis, 1991; Is This the Way to Athens?, 1996. Contributions to: New York Times; Christian Science Monitor; Literary Review; Prairie Schooner; Helicon Nine; Anthologies: New York Times Book of Verse, 1970; Sarah's Daughters Sing, 1990; 80 on the 80's, 1990; Helicon Nine Reader, 1990; Scarecrow Poetry, 1994; Lifecycles, Vol I, 1994, Vol II, 1997. Honours: Hans S Bodenheimer Award for Poetry, 1984; Western New York Writers in Residence Award, 1988. Memberships: Academy of American Poets; Poets and Writers. Address: 263 Brantwood Road, Snyder, NY 14226, USA.

HOLIČKA Ján, b. 24 June 1939, Piešťany, Slovakia. University Teacher. m. Helena Kunová, 1 son, 1 daughter. Education: Conservatory; MA, Music Teaching, Philosophical Faculty, Comenius University, 1979. Career: Debut, Slovak Radio, 1956; Over 60 performances as accordion player on Czechoslovak Radio, 1957-; Musician, Host, Presenter, Slovak Television; Numerous live performances; Founder of the band: Musica Bratislava. Recordings: Miroslav Kořínek: Concert for accordion and symphony orchestra; Jaroslav Maštalíř: Concertino for accordion and symphony orchestra; Jozef Rosinský: Suite for accordion and symphony orchestra; Bartolomej Urbanec: Variations; Suite of Strauss' waltzes. Publications: Monograph: Radio Broadcasting for Schools in Slovakia 1926-1989; Historical Study: Nonperiodical Music Publications. Honour: First Place, Competition for Czechoslovak accordion players, 1961. Memberships: Slovenská Hudobná Spoločnosť; Hudobná Mládež Slovenska. Address: Dobrovičova 16, Bratislava 811 09, Slovakia.

HOLLAND Jools (Julian), b. 24 January 1958, London, England. Musician (keyboards); Television Presenter. 1 son, 2 daughters. Career: Founder member, pianist, Squeeze, 1974-81, 1985-90; Solo artiste and bandleader: Jools Holland and his Big Band, 1982-84; Jools Holland and his Rhythm And Blues Orchestra, 1991-; Television presenter, music shows: The Tube, C4, 1981-86; Juke Box Jury, 1989; Sunday Night (with David Sanborn), 1990; The Happening, 1990; Hootenanny, 1992-; Later With Jools Holland, BBC2, 1993-; Various other television specials, including Sunday Night, NBC, 1989; Beat Route, BBC2, 1998-99; Jools Meets the Saint, 1999. Recordings: Albums: with Squeeze: Squeeze, 1978; Cool For Cats, 1979; Argy Bargy, 1980; Cosi Fan Tutti Frutti, 1985; Babylon And On, 1987; Frank, 1989; Solo albums: A World Of His Own, 1990; The Full Complement, 1991; A To Z Of The Piano, 1992; Live Performance, 1994; Solo Piano, 1994; Sex and Jazz and Rock and Roll, 1996; Lift up the Lid, 1997; The Best of Jools Holland, 1998; Sunset Over London, 1999; Hop the Wag, 2000; Small World Big Band – Friends, 2001; Small World Big Band Vol 2 – More Friends; Hit singles include: with Squeeze: Take Me I'm Yours, 1978; Cool For Cats, 1979; Up The Junction, 1979; Slap And Tickle, 1979; Another Nail In My Heart, 1980; Pulling Mussels From A Shell, 1980; Hourglass, 1987; 853 5937, 1988. Memberships: Musicians' Union; Equity; Writer's Guild. Address: Helicon Mountain Ltd, Helicon Mountain, Station Terrance Mews, London, SE3 7LP, England.

HOLLEDGE Bryan Raymond, b. 30 April 1919, Ealing, Middlesex, England. Artist; Consultant. m. Maria Haid, 27 April 1974, 2 daughters. Education: Ealing College, 1934; Ealing College of Art, 1937; H M Forces, 8th Army Royal College of Art, 1946; Graduate ARCA (London), School of Printing, 1949. Career: Lecturer, Hammersmith School of Art; Part-time teacher, St Hubert's Special School, Brook Green; Lecturer, London School of Painting and Graphic Arts; Part-time teacher, Chelsea School of Art; Graphic Designer, Metal Box, 1955; Head of Graphics, Swissco Sulzer, UK, 1958; Currently working for Controls Company; Freelance Consultant Corporate Designer, Exhibition at Whitechapel Gallery, 1953; Exhibition of wood engravings at Syon Galleries, 1960; Joint exhibition, Hampstead, London, 1991; Paintings and watercolours, London galleries; Mural for Clanline Shipping Company, 1951; Work for thesis; Painting in National Gallery exhibition for young artists. Publications: Wood engravings in Country Life magazine, 1966. Honour: Chosen by Arts Council GB, for Victory tour one man show, 1955. Memberships: Chelsea Arts Club, 1950; Royal Society of Arts, 1955; Federation of British Artists, 1980. Address: 5, The Green, Feltham, Middlesex, England.

HOLLINGHURST Alan, b. 26 May 1954, Stroud, Gloucestershire, England. Novelist. Education: BA, 1975, MLitt, 1979, Magdalen College, Oxford. Appointments: Assistant Editor, 1982-84, Deputy Editor, 1985-90, Poetry Editor, 1991-95, Times Literary Supplement, London. Publications: Novels: The Swimming-Pool Library, 1988; The Folding Star, 1994; The Spell, 1998; The Line of Beauty, 2004. Poetry: Confidential Chats with Boys, 1982. Translator: Bajazet, by Jean Racine, 1991. Honours: Somerset Maugham Award, 1988, E.M. Forster Award of the American Academy of Arts and Letters, 1990; James Tait Black

Award, 1995. Memberships: Fellow, The Royal Society of Literature. Address: c/o Antony Harwood, 103 Walton Street, Oxford, OX2 6EB, England.

HOLLOWAY James, b. 24 November 1948. Gallery Director. Education: Courtauld Institute of Art, London University, 1969-71. Appointments: Research Assistant, National Gallery of Scotland, 1972-80; Assistant Keeper of Art, National Museum of Wales, 1980-83; Deputy Keeper, Scottish National Portrait Gallery, 1983-97; Director, Scottish National Portrait Gallery, 1997-. Publications: Editor, Scottish Masters booklets for National Gallery of Scotland; Several articles; Frequent lectures on Scottish art and collections. Memberships: Curatorial Committee, National Trust for Scotland; Committee Member, Scottish Sculpture Trust; Committee Member, Scottish-Indian Arts Forum. Address: Scottish National Portrait Gallery, 1 Queen Street, Edinburgh, EH2 1JD, Scotland.

HOLLOWAY Patricia, (Patricia Pogson), b. 8 March 1944, Rosyth, Scotland. Yoga Teacher; Poet. m. (1) 1 son, 1 daughter, (2) Geoffrey Holloway, 27 August 1977. Education: National Diploma in Design, 1964; Teaching Certificate, 1971; Diploma, British Wheel of Yoga, 1987. Appointments: Draughtswoman Restorer, Ashmolean Museum, Oxford, 1964-66; Part-time Yoga Teacher; Poetry Tutor, Schools and Writing Centres, Libraries. Publications: Before the Road Show, 1983; Snakeskin, Belladonna, 1986; Rattling the Handle, 1991; A Crackle from the Larder, 1991; The Tides in the Basin, 1994; Holding, 2002. Contributions to: Anthologies, journals, reviews and magazines. Honours: 1st Prize, York Open Competition, 1985; 3rd Prize, Manchester Open Competition, 1989; 2nd Prize, National Poetry Competition, 1989; 1st Prize, BBC Kaleidoscope Competition, 1990. Memberships: Brewery Poets, Brewery Arts Centre, Kendal; Keswick Poetry Group. Address: 4 Gowan Crescent, Staveley, nr Kendal, Cumbria LA8 9NF, England.

HOLM Ian, b. 12 September 1931, Ilford, England. Actor. m. (1) Lynn Mary Shaw, 1955, 2 daughters, (2) Bee Gilbert, 1 son, 1 daughter, (3) Sophie Baker, 1982, 1 son, (4) Penelope Wilton, 1991, 1 step-daughter. Education: Royal Academy of Dramatic Arts. Creative Works: Roles include: Puck, Ariel, Lorenzo, Henry V, Richard III, the Fool (in King Lear), 1997; Lennie in The Homecoming; Moonlight, 1993; King Lear, 997; Max in The Homecoming, 2001; Films include: Young Winston; Oh!; What a Lovely War; Alien; All Quiet on the Western Front; Chariots of Fire; The Return of the Soldier; Greystoke, 1984; Laughterhouse, 1984; Brazil, 1985; Wetherby, 1985; Dance with a Stranger, 1985; Dreamchild, 1985; Henry V, 1989; Another Woman, 1989; Hamlet, 1990; Kafka, 1991; The Hour of the Pig, 1992; Blue Ice, 1992; The Naked Lunch, 1992; Frankenstein, 1993; The Madness of King George, 1994; Loch Ness, 1994; Big Night, 1995; Night Falls on Manhattan, 1995; The Fifth Element, 1996; A Life Less Ordinary, 1996; The Sweet Hereafter, 1997; Existence, 1998; Simon Magus, 1998; Esther Kahn, 1999; Joe Gould's Secret, 1999; Beautiful Joe, 1999; The Lord of the Rings, 1999; From Hell, 2000; the Emperor's New Clothes, 2000. TV appearances include: The Lost Boys, 1979; We, the Accused, 1980; The Bell, 1981; Strike, 1981; Inside the Third Reich, 1982; Mr and Mrs Edgehill, 1985; The Browning Version, 1986; Game, Set and Match, 1988; The Endless Game, 1989; The Last Romantics, 1992; The Borrowers, 1993; The Deep Blue Sea, 1994; Landscape, 1995; Little Red Riding Hood, 1996; King Lear, 1997; Alice Through the Looking Glass, 1998. Honour: Laurence Olivier Award, 1998. Address: c/o Julian Belfrage Associates, 46 Albemarle Street, London W1X 4PP, England.

Dictionary of International Biography

HOLMES Bryan John, (Charles Langley Hayes, Ethan Wall), b. 18 May 1939, Birmingham, England. Lecturer (retired); Writer. m. 1962, 2 sons. Education: BA, University of Keele, 1968. Publications: The Avenging Four, 1978; Hazard, 1979; Blood, Sweat and Gold, 1980; Gunfall, 1980; A Noose for Yanqui, 1981; Shard, 1982; Bad Times at Backwheel, 1982; Guns of the Reaper, 1983; On the Spin of a Dollar, 1983; Another Day, Another Dollar, 1984; Dark Rider, 1987; I Rode with Wyatt, 1989; Dollars for the Reaper, 1990; A Legend Called Shatterhand, 1990; Loco, 1991; Shatterhand and the People, 1992; The Last Days of Billy Patch, 1992; Blood on the Reaper, 1992; All Trails Leads to Dodge, 1993; Montana Hit, 1993; A Coffin for the Reaper, 1994; Comes the Reaper, 1995; Utah Hit, 1995; Dakota Hit, 1995; Viva Reaper, 1996; The Shard Brand, 1996; High Plains Death, 1997; Smoking Star, 1997; Crowfeeders, 1999; North of the Bravo, 2000; Pocket Crossword Dictionary, 2001; The Guide to Solving Crosswords, 2002; Jake's Women, 2002; Solving Cryptic Crosswords, 2003; Rio Grande Shoot-Out, 2004. Contributions to: Professional and academic journals. Address: c/o Robert Hale Ltd, Clerkenwell Green, London EC1R 0HT, England.

HOLMES James Christopher (Jim), b. 21 November 1948, London, England. Musician; Opera Conductor and Coach. m. Jean Wilkinson, 2 sons. Education: BA (Hons), University of Sheffield; Repetiteurs Diploma, London Opera Centre. Appointments: Principal Coach, Conductor, English National Opera, 1973-96; Numerous productions including: Pacific Overtures, London premiere; Street Scene, also BBC TV; La Belle Vivette, premiere of new version with Michael Frayn; Dr Ox's Experiment, world premiere; Arranger, National Youth Orchestra, BBC Proms; Musical Assistant to Simon Rattle, Glyndebourne Festival Opera, 1986-94; Associate Music Director, Carousel, Royal National Theatre; Conductor, BBC Concert Orchestra, London Sinfonietta, Montreal Symphony Orchestra, City of Birmingham Symphony Orchestra, Sinfonia Viva; Head of Music, Opera North, 1996-; Conductor: Gloriana, Tannhäuser, Sweeney Todd, Of Thee I Sing, Katya Kabanova, Pélleas and Melisande, Genoveva, Paradise Moscow, Cunning Little Vixen, Albert Herring; Arranger: Something Wonderful and If Ever I Would Leave You for Bryn Terfel; Guest Lecturer/Coach: National Opera Studio, Royal Northern College of Music. Publications: Numerous articles for programmes especially relating to American musical theatre; Arrangements of American musical songs for singers including: Bryn Terfel, Sally Burgess, Lesley Garrett; TV Programmes: I'm a Stranger Here Myself, Kurt Weill in America, BBC/HR; Street Scene BBC and WDR. Honours: USA Grammy Nomination for recording of Pacific Overtures; Gramophone Award for recording of Lesley Garrett, Soprano in Red. Memberships: Member, Advisory Board, Kurt Weill Complete Edition; Joint Artistic Advisor, Kurt Weill Festival, Dessau. Address: c/o Opera North, Grand Theatre, New Briggate, Leeds, W Yorkshire LS1 6NU, England.

HOLMES John Eaton (Sir), b. 29 April 1951, Preston, England. Diplomat. m. Margaret Penelope, 3 daughters. Education: BA, 1st Class Honours, Literae Humaniores (Greats), 1973, MA, 1975, Balliol College, Oxford. Appointments: Joined Foreign and Commonwealth Office, 1973: Second Secretary, British Embassy, Moscow, 1976-78; Near East and North Africa Department, 1978-82; Assistant Private Secretary to the Foreign Secretary, 1882-84; First Secretary, British Embassy, Paris, 1984-87; Deputy Head, Soviet Department, Foreign and Commonwealth Office, 1987-89; Seconded to Thomas de la Rue & Co, 1989-91; Economic and Commercial Counsellor, New Delhi, 1991-95; Diplomatic Advisor to the Prime Minister, 1996-99; British Ambassador to Portugal, 1999-2001; British Ambassador to France, 2001-. Honours: CMG, 1997; CVO, 1998; KBE, 1999. Membership: Cercle Interallie, Paris.

HOLMES-WALKER William Anthony, b. 26 January 1926, Horwich, Lancashire, England. Scientist. m. Marie-Anne Russ, 2 daughters. Education: BSc (Hons) Chemistry, 1950, PhD, Chemistry, 1953, Queen's University, Belfast, Northern Ireland; DIC, Chemical Engineering, Imperial College, London, 1954. Appointments: Technical Officer, ICI Limited, 1954-59; Head of Plastics R&D, The Metal Box Company, 1959-66; Professor of Polymer Science and Technology, Chairman of School of Materials, Brunel University, 1966-74; Director, The British Plastics Federation, 1974-81; Visiting Professor, The City University, 1981-83; Secretary General, European Brewers' Trade Association, CBMC, Brussels, 1983-87; Director, Industrial Liaison, University of Reading, 1987-90; Director, International Technology and Innovation, 1990-94; Chairman of Working Group, The Executive Committee, 1995-96; Chairman, BioInteractions Ltd, 1991-. Publications: Many articles in scientific journals and business publications; Chapter in Thermoplastics, 1969; Polymer Conversion, 1975; Best Foote Forward, 1995; Life-Enhancing Plastics, forthcoming. Honours: ERD, 1972, TD, 1980; Member, Army Emergency Reserve and TAVR, with rank of Lieutenant Colonel. Memberships: Royal Institution, 1953; FRSC, 1966; FPRI, 1969; FIM, 1972; FSA, 1989; Past Master, Skinners' Company. Address: 7 Alston Road, Boxmoor, Herts HP1 1QT, England. E-mail: anthonyhw@ntl.com.uk

HOLSTON A Frank Jr, b. 25 February 1928, Baltimore, Maryland, USA. Retired. m. Marianne, 1 son, 2 daughters. Education: AB, Fine Arts, University of Alabama, 1951; BS (equivalent), Education, Towson State University; Newspaper Intern, Syracuse University, 1958; NBC Intern, Color TV, 1959; MA, Mass Communication, Michigan State University, 1962. Appointments: Weekend commercial announcer, WBAL Radio, aged 16 years; Co-ordinator of Mass Communications, Broadcast Educator, Community College, Baltimore, 1956-89; Chairman, Faculty and Athletic Council; General Manager, WBJC-FM; Athletic Coach, Basketball and Tennis; Sports Reporter, ABC Radio Networks, 1973-89; Broadcast experience in Baltimore, Chicago, Birmingham, Tuscaloosa, Frederick and Salisbury markets; Play-by-play announcer, Johns Hopkins lacrosse and Baltimore Comets Pro Soccer, and college and high school sports; Public Address Announcer, Baltimore professional soccer team; Track Official, Anne Arundel County Schools; Announcer in sport-related activities, 1992. Publications: Master thesis, A Study of the States of Judicial Canon 35 and it's Impact on Television in the Legal Process, 1962. Honours: Listed in national and international biographical dictionaries. Memberships: Society of Professional Journalists, Maryland Chapter; Broadcast Education Association; Annapolis Shrine Club; Annapolis Bureau of Recreation; Republican Central Committee. Address: 2B1 Spa Creek Landing, Annapolis, MD 21403, USA.

HOLUBAR Karl, b. 3 June 1936, Vienna, Austria. Physician. m. Christine Bodenstein, 2 sons. Education: MD, Vienna, 1960; Residency, Dermatology, University of Vienna; Department of Dermatology, University of Amsterdam, 1968; Department of Microbiology (Immunology), State University of New York at Buffalo, USA, 1972-73; Hebrew University, Jerusalem, Israel, 1982-86. Appointments: Interim Chairman and Professor, Dermatology, University of Vienna, 1980-81; Chairman and Professor of Dermatology, Hebrew University Jerusalem, 1983-86; Professor History of Medicine, 1989-, Professor and Chairman, Institute for the History of Medicine, 1989-2001, University of Vienna. Publications: Over 500 publications, including original articles, book chapters, contributions to handbooks, special issues of journals, congress reports, posters and abstracts; 5 books: Challenge Dermatology, 1993; Sun and Skin, 1994; Med. Terminologie und ärztliche Sprache, 1997; Historical Atlas of

Dermatology, 2002; Skin in Watercolours, 2003. Honours: (with co-authors), Hoechst Award, 1969; Max Ritter Award, 1976; AESCA Award, 1979; Unilever Award, 1979; Samuel J Zakon Award (History of Dermatology), 1981; Fellow of the Royal College of Physicians; Honorary Fellow of the College of Physicians of Philadelphia. Memberships include: Royal Society of Medicine; New York Academy of Sciences; Medical Society of London; Société Internationale d'Histoire de la Médicine; Société Française d'Histoire de la Dermatologie, Vice-President; Gesellschaft der Ärzte in Wien; Austrian and German national Dermatological Societies; European Society for the History of Dermatology/Venereology, Honorary President; Numerous honorary memberships. Address: Institute for the History of Medicine, University of Vienna, Wahringer Str 25, A 1090 Vienna, Austria. E-mail: kh.histmed@univie.ac.at

HOLUTIAK-HALLICK Stephen Peter Jr, b. 3 May 1945, New York City, USA. Businessman; Educator; Retired Military Officer. m. Ann M. Bazycki, 1 son, 2 daughters. Education: Certificate, Russian Area Studies, Pennsylvania State University, 1967; Associate Science, Community College of Allegheny County; BA, Pennsylvania State University, 1967; MA, University of Manitoba, 1969; Diploma, Command-General Staff College, US Army, 1985; MBA, Mercer University, 1992. Appointments include: USAR, 1967-95 (Lt col, active duty), Translator, Interpreter, Manager, Russian Translation Department, Pullman-Swindell Inc, Pittsburgh, 1972-76; Inspector, Mechanical Engineering Department, Robert W Hunt Co, Pittsburgh, 1977-79; Administrator, Procurement Services, KHD, Humboldt Wedag, New York City, Montreal, Atlanta, 1979-82, Administrator, Project Management Services, 1982-84, Manager, Expediting and Sub-Contracts Administration, 1984-85; Staff Intelligence Officer, Forces Command Headquarters, US Army, 1985-90; Member, INF (Intermediate Nuclear Force Treaty between USA and USSR) Inspection Team, US Army, 1988; Assistant Professor, Military Science, Clemson University, South Carolina, 1990-92; Inspector General, 95th Division, 1992-95; President, TATO's Choice, Duluth, GA, 1995-; Consultant, doing business in former USSR. Publications include: Slavic Toponymic Atlas of the United States, volume I, Ukrainian, 1982; Dictionary of Ukrainian Surnames in the United States, 1994. Memberships: Reserve Officers Association; US American Security Council; Atlanta Committee on International Relations; American Name Society. Address: 2755 Kenwood Court, Duluth, GA 30096, USA.

HOLYFIELD Evander, b. 19 October 1962, Atlanta, Georgia, USA. Boxer. Career: Founder, Real Deal Record Label, 1999; Founder, Holyfield Foundation to help inner-city youth; Bronze Medal, Olympic Games, 1984; World Boxing Association Cruiserweight Title, 1986; International Boxing Federation Cruiserweight Title, 1987; World Boxing Council Cruiserweight Title, 1988; World Heavyweight Champion, 1990-92, 1993-94, 1996- (following defeat of Mike Tyson, 1996); Defended title against Mike Tyson 1997 (Tyson disqualified for biting off part of Holyfield's ear); Defended IBF Heavyweight Title against Michael Moorer, 1997; Defended WBA and IBF Titles, and Contested WBC Title, against Lennox Lewis, 1999, bout declared a draw; Lost to Lennox Lewis, November 1999; WBA heavyweight champion, 2000-01. Honours: Epsy Boxer of the Decade, 1990-2000. Address: Main Events, 390 Murray Hill Parkway, East Rutherford, NJ 07073, USA.

HOM-KIM Lillian Geraldine Lee (Hom Lee Sun Ying), b. 17 June 1919, Taishan, Canton, China. Administrator; Educator. m. Herman Hom Kim. Education: Strayer's Business College (evening school), 1938-39; Lecture Course, Social Service, YMCA, 1939; Collegiate Business Correspondence Course, 1940-41.

Appointments: Volunteer Social Service, 1936-37; Secretary, Peabody Book Shop, 1937-38; Secretary, Prisoners Aid Association, 1938-41; Secretary, Civilian Defense, Executive Division, Municipal Government, 1942-44; Secretary, Safety Director, Accident Prevention, 1944-48; Secretary, Assistant Supervisor, Administration Division, Central Payroll Bureau, Department of Finance, 1948-64; Secretary, Public Relations, Chinese Language School, 1954-70; Director, Chinese Language School, 1970-; Administrative Secretary, Section Supervisor, Administration Division, Central Payroll Bureau, 1964-77; Retired, 1977; Nominated and presented to the Executive Board, Boy Scouts of America by the Hon. Mary Arabian, served continuously, 1978-92, assigned to District Committee, 1992; Objectives of serving on Executive Board included: to increase visibility of scouting, to increase adult volunteers, to increase fund raising efforts, to improve external and internal communication; Declined re-election 1993 because of inconvenient transportation; Served on Senator Charles McC Mathia Jr's Select Immigration Committee; Recognised as outstanding specialist in immigration laws pertaining to Chinese and Asians; Advocated for repeal of the 105 Asian Quota; Solicited interest and legislative support towards the liberalisation of immigration; Congress approved more equitable immigration laws. Publications: 3 books; Bilingual news bulletin; Letters to newspaper editors; Lectures; Speeches; Several articles, short stories and essays; Television documentary. Honours: Numerous awards. Memberships: University of California, Los Angeles Alumni Association; Johns Hopkins University Alumni Association; Johns Hopkins Club; Peabody; Walters Art Gallery; Women's Civic League; Baltimore Museum of Art; Maryland Historical Society; Association of American Retired Persons; Stars Spangled Banner Foundation; Association of Senior Citizens; Association of Chinese Schools; Association of Chinese Language Teachers; National Trust for Historic Preservation; Women of Mount Vernon; Chesapeake Bay Foundation. Address: 524 Anneslie Road, Baltimore, Maryland 21212-2009, USA.

HOMAN Roger Edward, b. 25 June 1944, Brighton, England. University Professor. m. Caroline Baker. Education: BA, Religious Studies, University of Sussex, 1969; MSc, Government, London School of Economics, 1979; PhD, Sociology, University of Lancaster, 1979. Appointments: School teaching posts, 1966-67, 1969-71; Lecturer, Brighton College of Education, 1971-76; Senior Lecturer in Education, Brighton Polytechnic, 1976-92; Principal Lecturer, 1992-98, Professor of Religious Studies, 1998-, University of Brighton. Publications: 90 articles published in academic and professional journals. Honours: Fellow, Victoria College of Music, 1994. Memberships: Victorian Society; National Vice President, Prayer Book Society; Anglo-Catholic Research Society; Ecclesiological Society. Address: University of Brighton, Falmer, East Sussex, BN1 9PH, England. E-mail: r.homan@bton.ac.uk

HONAN William Holmes, b. 11 May 1930, New York, New York, USA. Journalist. m. Nancy Burton, 22 June 1975, 2 sons, 1 daughter. Education: BA, Oberlin College, 1952; MA, University of Virginia, 1955. Appointments: Editor, The Villager, New York, 1957-60; Assistant Editor, New Yorker Magazine, 1960-64; Associate Editor, Newsweek, New York City, 1969; Assistant Editor, New York Times Magazine, 1969-70; Travel Editor, 1970-72, 1973-74, Arts and Leisure Editor, 1974-82, Culture Editor, 1982-88, Chief Cultural Correspondent, 1988-93, National Higher Education Correspondent, New York Times, 1993-2000; General Assignment, New York Times, 2000-; Managing Editor, Saturday Review, 1972-73. Publications: Greenwich Village Guide, 1959; Ted Kennedy: Profile of a Survivor, 1972; Bywater: The Man Who Invented the Pacific War, 1990; Visions of Infamy: The Untold Story of How Journalist Hector C Bywater Devised the Plans that

Led to Pearl Harbour, 1991; Fire When Ready, Gridley! - Great Naval Stories from Manila Bay to Vietnam (editor), 1992; Treasure Hunt: A New York Times Reporter Tracks the Quedlinburg Treasures, 1997; Zingers (a play), 2004. Contributions to: Periodicals. Address: c/o New York Times, 229 West 43rd Street, New York, NY 10036. USA.

HONE Joseph, b. 25 February 1937, London, England. Writer; Broadcaster. m. Jacqueline Mary Yeend, 5 Mar 1963, 1 son, 1 daughter. Education: Kilkenny College, Sandford Park School, Dublin; St Columba's College, Dublin. Publications: The Flowers of the Forest, 1982; Children of the Country, 1986; Duck Soup in the Black Sea, 1988; Summer Hill, 1990; Firesong, 1997. Contributions to: Periodicals. Membership: Upton House Cricket Club. Address: c/o Aitken & Stone Ltd, 29 Fernshaw Road, London SW10, England.

HONEGGER Federico, b. 11 September 1926, Milan, Italy. Artist; Painter. m. Lucia Carminarti, 3 sons, 1 daughter. Education: Baccalaureat, College of St Michel, Fribourg, 1945; Law Degree, Catholic University, Milan, 1952; Text Prac Vereinigte Seidenwebereien AG, Germany, 1950-51. Appointments: Gaspar Honegger, Milan, 1946-59; Buying Manager, Carminarti Industries, Tessili Sp, Milan, 1960-82; President, Milan Group, Catholic Union of Italian Artists, 1982-92. Publications: Author, numerous art projects. Honours: Silver Palette, City of Milan, 1979; Top 70 winner, Art '95 New York International Competition. Memberships: Symbolicum Art Group. Address: Via Annunciata 23/2, 20121 Milan, Italy.

HONIG Edwin, b. 3 September 1919, New York, New York, USA. Retired Professor of English and of Comparative Literature; Poet; Writer; Dramatist; Translator. m. (1) Charlotte Gilchrist, 1 April 1940, deceased 1963, (2) Margot Dennes, 15 December 1963, divorced 1978, 2 sons. Education: BA, 1939, MA, 1947, University of Wisconsin at Madison. Appointments: Poetry Editor, New Mexico Quarterly, 1948-52; Instructor, Claremont College, California, 1949; Faculty, 1949-57, Assistant Professor of English, Harvard University; Faculty, 1957-60, Professor of English, 1960-82, Professor of Comparative Literature, 1962-82, Professor Emeritus, 1983-, Brown University; Visiting Professor, University of California at Davis, 1964-65; Mellon Professor, Boston University, 1977. Publications: Poetry: The Moral Circus, 1955; The Gazabos: 41 Poems, 1959; Survivals, 1964; Spring Journal, 1968; Four Springs, 1972; At Sixes, 1974; Shake a Spear with Me, John Berryman, 1974; Selected Poems 1955-1976, 1979; Interrupted Praise, 1983; Gifts of Light, 1983; The Imminence of Love: Poems 1962-1992, 1993; Time and Again: Poems 1940-97, 2000. Stories: Foibles and Fables of an Abstract Man, 1979. Non-Fiction: García Lorca, 1944, revised edition, 1963; Dark Conceit: The Making of Allegory, 1959; Calderón and the Seizures of Honor, 1972; The Poet's Other Voice: Conversations on Literary Translation, 1986. Plays: Ends of the World and Other Plays, 1984. Translations: Over 10 books, 1961-93. Contributions to: books, anthologies, reviews, journals, and periodicals. Honours: Guggenheim Fellowships, 1948, 1962; National Academy of Arts and Letters Grant, 1966; Amy Lowell Traveling Poetry Fellowship, 1968; Rhode Island Governor's Award for Excellence in the Arts, 1970; National Endowment for the Humanities Fellowship, 1975, and Grants, 1977-80; National Endowment for the Arts Fellowship, 1977; Translation Award, Poetry Society of America, 1984; National Award, Columbia University Translation Center, 1985; Decorated by the Portuguese President for translation of Pessoa, 1989; Decorated by the King of Spain for translation of Calderón, 1996. Memberships: Dante Society of America; Poetry Society of America. Address: 229 Medway Street, Apt 305, Providence, RI 02906, USA.

HONTI László, b. 27 August 1943, Lengyeltóti, Hungary. Professor. Márta Varga, 1 daughter. Education: Diploma, 1969, Hungarian, Russian and Finno-Ugric Linguistics, MA, 1970, University of Budapest; Candidate of Sciences, 1976, Doctor scientiarum, 1989, Hungarian Academy of Sciences, Budapest. Appointments: Junior Research Fellow, Senior Research Fellow, 1969-80, Head, Department of Finno-Ugric Language, 1980-88; Hungarian Academy of Sciences; Professor, University of Groningen, The Netherlands, 1988-97; Professor, University of Udine, Italy, 1997-. Publications: 7 books. Honours: Zoltain Gombocz Medal, Hungarian Linguistic Society, 1977; Critics Prize, Akademiai Kiado, 1977, 1982; Academic Prize, Hungarian Academy of Sciences, 1993. Memberships: Hungarian Linguistics Society; Societas Uralo-Altaica; Honorary Member, Finno-Ugric Society; Association for Linguistic Typology; External Member, Hungarian Academy of Sciences. Address: Dipartimento di Glottologia e Filologia Classica, University of Udine, via Mazzini 3, I-33100 Udine, Italy.

HOOK Andrew Dunnet, b. 21 December 1932, Wick, Caithness, Scotland. m. Judith Ann Hibberd, deceased, 1984, 2 sons, 1 daughter, deceased, 1995. Education: MA, University of Edinburgh, Scotland, 1954; PhD, Princeton University, USA, 1960. Appointments: Assistant Lecturer, 1961-63, Lecturer in American Literature, 1963-71, University of Edinburgh; Senior Lecturer in English, University of Aberdeen, 1971-79; Bradley Professor of English Literature, University of Glasgow, 1979-98; Visiting Fellow, English Department, Princeton University, 1999-2000; Gillespie Visiting Professor, The College of Wooster, Wooster, Ohio, 2001-2002. Publications: Scott's Waverley (editor), 1972; Charlotte Brontë's Shirley (co-editor), 1974; John Dos Passos, Twentieth Century Views (editor), 1974; Scotland and America 1750-1835, 1975; American Literature in Context 1865-1900, 1983; History of Scottish Literature, Vol II 1660-1800 (editor), 1987; Scott Fitzgerald, 1992; The Glasgow Enlightenment (co-editor), 1995; From Goosecreek to Gandercleugh: Studies in Scottish-American Literary and Cultural History, 1999; Scott's The Fair Maid of Perth (co-editor), 1999; F Scott Fitzgerald: A Literary Life, 2002. Honour: Fellow, Royal Society of Edinburgh, 2000-. Memberships: British Association for American Studies; Eighteenth Century Scottish Studies Society; Modern Languages Association; Institute of Contemporary Scotland. Address: 5 Rosslyn Terrace, Glasgow G12 9NB, Scotland.

HOOKWAY Harry Thurston (Sir), b. 23 July 1921, London, England. Administrator. m. Barbara Butler, deceased, 1 son, 1 daughter. Education: BSc, PhD, London University. Appointments: Assistant Director, National Chemical Laboratory, 1959; Director, United Kingdom Scientific Mission to North America, Scientific Attaché, British Embassy, Washington, Scientific Advisor, High Commission, Ottawa, 1960-64; Head, Information Division, DSIR, 1964-65; Chief Scientific Officer, Department of Education and Science, 1966-69; Under Secretary, Department of Education and Science, 1969-73; Deputy Chairman and Chief Executive, British Library Board, 1973-84; Pro-Chancellor, Loughborough University, 1987-93. Publications: Papers in learned and professional journals. Honours: Hon LLD; Hon D Litt; HON FLA; Hon F I Inst Sci; Gold Medal, International Federation of Library Associations; Knight Bachelor, 1978; President Library Association, 1985. Memberships: Royal Commission on Historical Monuments (England), 1981-87; Fellow, Royal Society of Arts. Address: 3 St James Green, Thirsk, North Yorkshire YO7 1AF, England.

HOOPER Michael Wrenford, b. 2 May 1941, Gloucester, England. Cleric. m. Rosemary, 2 sons, 2 daughters. Education: St David's College, Lampeter, Dyfed; St Stephen's House, Oxford. Appointments: Curate, Bridgnorth, Shropshire, 1965; Victor of

Minsterley, Rural Dean, Pontesbury, 1970; Rector and Rural Dean, Leonminster, 1981; Archdeacon of Hereford, 1997; Suffragan Bishop of Ludlow, Archdeacon of Ludlow, 2002.

HOOPLE Sally Crosby, b. 23 October 1930, Dansville, New York, USA. Professor. m. Donald G, 2 sons, 2 daughters. Education: BA, English Education, 1952, MA, English Education, 1953, Syracuse University; MA, English, New York University, 1971; PhD, English, Fordham University, 1984. Appointments: Assistant Professor, 1986-89, Associate Professor, 1989-95, Professor of Humanities, 1995-96, Maine Maritime Academy; Foreign Expert, Henan Normal University, China, 1997-98; Honorarium Instructor, China Agricultural University, Beijing, 1999, 2001. Publications include: Rationalism in The Dictionary of Art; Doors and Windows in the Age of Innocence; Chance's White-cane Garden in Jerzy Kosinski's Being There; Tabitha Tenney Humorist of the New Republic. Memberships: Melville Society; Hawthorne Society; Exeter Historical Society; Metropolitan Museum of Art; Boston Museum of Fine Art; Metropolitan Opera Guild; Castine Scientific Society; Farnsworth Museum; Maine Writers and Publishers Alliance. Address: PO Box 184, Castine, ME 04421-0184, USA. E-mail: dgramho@aol.com

HOPE Ronald (Sidney), b. 4 April 1921, London, England. Writer. Education: BA, 1941, MA, 1946, DPhil, New College, Oxford. Appointments: Fellow, Brasenose College, Oxford, 1945-47, Director, Seafarers' Education Service, London, 1947-76; Director, The Marine Society, 1976-86. Publications: Spare Time at Sea, 1954; Economic Geography, 1956; Dick Small in the Half Deck, Ships, 1958; The British Shipping Industry, 1959; The Shoregoer's Guide to World Ports, 1963; Seamen and the Sea, 1965; Introduction to the Merchant Navy, 1965; Retirement from the Sea, 1967; In Cabined Ships at Sea, 1969; Twenty Singing Seamen, 1979; The Seamen's World, 1982; A New History of British Shipping, 1990; Poor Jack, 2001. Address: 2 Park Place, Dollar, FK14 7AA, Scotland.

HOPKINS Anthony (Philip), b. 31 December 1937, Port Talbot, South Wales. Actor. m. (1) Petronella Barker, 1967, divorced 1972, 1 daughter, (2) Jennifer Lynton, 1973, divorced 2002, (3) Stella Arroyave, 2003. Education: Welsh College of Music and Drama. Career: Assistant Stage Manager, Manchester Library Theatre, 1960; Joined Nottingham Repertory Company; Royal Academy of Dramatic Art; Phoenix Theatre, Leicester; Liverpool Playhouse and Hornchurch Repertory Company. Films include: The Lion in Winter, 1967; The Looking Glass War, 1968; Hamlet, 1969; Young Winston, 1971; A Doll's House, 1972; The Girl from Petrovka, 1973; Juggernaut, 1974; Audrey Rose, 1976; A Bridge Too Far, 1976; International Velvet, 1977; Magic, 1978; The Elephant Man, 1979; A Change of Seasons, 1980; The Bounty, 1983; The Good Father, 1985; 84 Charing Cross Road, 1986; The Dawning, 1987; A Chorus of Disapproval, 1988; Desperate Hours, 1989; The Silence of the Lambs, 1990; Free Jack, 1990; One Man's War, 1990; Spotswood, 1990; Howard's End, 1991; Bram Stoker's Dracula, 1991; Chaplin, 1992; The Trial, 1992; The Innocent, 1992; Remains of the Day, 1992; Shadowlands, 1993; Legends of the Fall, 1993; The Road to Wellville, 1993; August, 1994; Nixon, 1995; Surviving Picasso, 1995; The Edge, 1996; The Mask of Zorro, 1997; Amistad, 1997; Meet Joe Black, 1997; Instinct, 1998; Titus, 1999; Hannibal, 2000; Hearts of Atlantis, 2000; Mission Impossible 2, 2001; Hannibal, 2001; The Devil and Daniel Webster, 2001; Bad Company, 2002; Red Dragon, 2002. Theatre includes: A Flea in Her Ear, 1967; A Woman Killed with Kindness, 1971; Macbeth, 1972; Equus, 1974; The Tempest, USA, 1979; Old Times, USA, 1984; The Lonely Road, 1985; King Lear, 1986. TV includes: A Company of Five, 1968; The Poet Game, 1970; War

and Peace, 1971; Lloyd George, 1972; All Creatures Great and Small, 1974; Kean, 1978; The Bunker, 1980; Othello, BBC, 1981; A Married Man, 1982; Blunt, 1985; Across the Lake, 1988; Heartland, 1988; To Be the Best, 1990; A Few Selected Exits, 1993; Big Cats, 1993. Honours include: Variety Club Film and Stage Actor Awards, 1984, 1985, 1993; BAFTA Best Actor Awards, 1973, 1991, 1994, 1995; Emmy Awards, 1976, 1981; Oscar, 1991; Laurence Olivier Awards 1985; CBE, 1987; KB, 1993; Commandeur dans l'Ordre des Arts et des Lettres, France, 1996; Honorary DLit, University of Wales, 1988; Honorary Fellowship, St David's College, Wales, 1992; 2 Los Angeles Film Critics Association, Best Actor Awards, 1993; Donesta, 1998; Numerous other awards. Address: c/o CAA, 9830 Wilshire Blvd, Beverly Hills, CA 90212, USA.

HOPKINS Antony, b. 21 March 1921, London, England. Musician; Author. m. Alison Purves, 1947, deceased 1991. Education: Royal College of Music with Cyril Smith and Gordon Jacob. Career: Lecturer, Royal College of Music, 15 years; Director, Intimate Opera Company, 1952-64; Series of radio broadcasts, Talking About Music, 1954-92. Compositions include: Operas: Lady Rohesia; Three's Company; Hands Across the Sky; Dr Musikus; Ten o'Clock Call; The Man from Tuscany; Ballets: Etude; Cafe des Sports; 3 Piano Sonatas; Numerous scores of incidental music including: Oedipus; The Love of Four Colonels; Cast a Dark Shadow; Pickwick Papers; Billy Budd; Decameron Nights. Publications include: Understanding Music, 1979; The Nine Symphonies of Beethoven, 1980; The Concertgoer's Companion, 2 volumes, 1984, 1986. Honours: Gold Medal, Royal College of Music, 1943; Italia Prize for Radio Programme, 1951, 1957; Medal, City of Tokyo for Services to Music, 1973; Commander of the British Empire, 1976. Address: Woodyard, Ashridge, Berkhamsted, Hertfordshire HP4 1PS, England.

HOPKIRK Joyce, b. 2 March 1937, England. Writer; Journalist. 1 son, 1 daughter. Appointments: Reporter, Gateshead Post, 1955; Founder Editor, Majorcan News, 1959; Reporter, Daily Sketch, 1960; Royal Reporter, Daily Express, 1961; Editor, Fashion Magazine, 1967; Woman's Editor, The Sun launch, 1969; Launch Editor, Cosmopolitan, 1971-72; Assistant Editor, Daily Mirror, 1973-78; Women's Editor, Sunday Times, 1982; Editorial Director, Elle launch, 1984; Assistant Editor, Sunday Mirror, 1985; Editor-in-Chief, She Magazine, 1986-89; Director, Editors' Unlimited, 1990-; Founder Editor, Chic Magazine, 1994. Publications: Successful Slimming, 1976; Successful Slimming Cookbook, 1978; Splash! (co-author), 1995; Best of Enemies, 1996; Double Trouble, 1997; Unfinished Business, 1998; Relative Values, 1999; The Affair, 2000. Honours: Editor of the Year, 1972, Women's Magazines Editor of the Year, 1988, British Society of Magazine Editors; Woman of Achievement Award, Women's Advertising Club of London, 1998; Co-Chairman, Periodical Publishers Association Magazine Awards, 1998. Membership: Fellow, Royal Society of Arts; Member, Competition Commission, 1999. Address: Gadespring, 109 Piccotts End, Hemel Hempstead, Hertfordshire HP1 3AT, England.

HOPPER Dennis, b. 17 May 1936, Dodge City, USA. Actor; Author; Photographer; Film Director. m. (1) Brooke Hayward, 1 daughter, (2) Doria Halprin, one daughter, (3) Katherine La Nasa, 1989, 1 son. Creative Works: Film appearances include: Rebel Without a Cause, 1955; I Died a Thousand Times, 1955; Giant, 1956; Story of Mankind, 1957; Gunfight at the O.K. Corral, 1957; Night Tide, 1958; Key Witness, 1958; From Hell to Texas, 1958; Glory Stompers, 1959; The Trip, 1961; The Sons of Katie Elder, 1962; Hang 'Em High, 1966; Cool Hand Luke, 1967; True Grit, 1968; The American Dreamer, 1971; Kid Blue, 1973; The Sky is Falling, 1975; James Dean – The First American Teenager, 1976;

Dictionary of International Biography

Mad Dog Morgan, 1976; Tracks, 1979; American Friend, 1978; Apocalypse Now, 1979; Wild Times, 1980; King of the Mountain, 1981; Human Highway, 1981; Rumble Fish, 1983; The Osterman Weekend, 1984; Black Widow, 1986; Blue Velvet, 1986; River's Edge, 1987; Blood Red, 1989; Flashback, 1989; The American Wars, 1989; Chattahoochie, 1990; Motion and Emotion, 1990; Superstar: The Life and Times of Andy Warhol, 1990; Hot Spot, 1990; True Romance, 1993; Boiling Point, 1993; Super Mario Bros, 1993; Chasers, 1994; Speed, 1994; Waterworld, 1995; Search and Destroy, 1995; Basquiat, 1996; Carried Away, 1996; Star Truckers, 1997; Blackout, 1997; Tycus, 1998; Sources, 1999; Lured Innocence, 1999; Justice, 1999; Straight Shooter, 1999; Actor, Writer, Director: Easy Rider, 1969; The Last Movie, 1971; Paris Trout, 1990; The Indian Runner, 1991; Actor, Director: Out of the Blue, 1980; Director: Colors, 1988; The Hot Spot, 1990; Catchfire, 1991; Nails, 1991; Several public exhibitions of photographs. Publication: Out of the Sixties (photographs), 1988. Honours include: Best New Director, Cannes, 1969; Best Film Award, Venice, 1971, Cannes, 1980. Address: c/o Creative Artists Agency, 9830 Wilshire Boulevard, Beverly Hills, CA 90212, USA.

HOPWOOD David Alan (Sir), b. 19 August 1933, Kinver, Staffordshire, England. Scientist. m. Joyce Lilian Bloom, 2 sons, 1 daughter. Education: BA 1st class honours, Natural Sciences, 1954, PhD, 1958, University of Cambridge; DSc, University of Glasgow, 1974. Appointments: John Stothert Bye-Fellow, Magdalene College, Cambridge, 1956-58; University Demonstrator, Assistant Lecturer in Botany, University of Cambridge, 1957-61; Research Fellow, St John's College, Cambridge, 1958-61; Lecturer in Genetics, University of Glasgow, 1961-68; John Innes Professor of Genetics, University of East Anglia, Norwich and Head of the Genetics Department, John Innes Institute, 1968-98; John Innes Emeritus Fellow, John Innes Centre, Emeritus Professor of Genetics, University of Eat Anglia, Norwich, 1998-; Visiting Research Fellow, Kosan Biosciences, Inc, 1998-. Publications: Over 270 articles on genetics, microbiology and genetic engineering in scientific publications. Honours: 3 honorary memberships; 4 honorary fellowships; Fellow, Royal Society of London; Foreign Fellowship, Indian National Science Academy; 2 honorary Doctorates of Science; Medal of the Kitasato Institute for Research in New Bioactive Compounds; Hoechst-Roussel Award for Research in Antimicrobial Chemotherapy; Chiron Biotechnology Award; Knight Bachelor; Mendel Medal of the Czech Academy of Sciences; Gabor Medal of the Royal Society. Memberships: Genetical Society of Great Britain; Society for General Microbiology; American Society for Microbiology; European Molecular Biology Organisation; Academia Europaea; Society for General Microbiology. Address: John Innes Centre, Norwich, Norfolk NR4 7UH, England. E-mail: david.hopwood@bbsrc.ac.uk

HORAK Josef, b. 24 March 1931, Znojmo, Czech Republic. International Concert Bass Clarinettist; Pedagogue. m. Emma Kovarnova. Education: Graduate, State High School of Musical and Dramatic Arts in Brno, 1952; Masterclass with K Stockhausen, P Boulez, S Gazzeloni, Days of New Music, 1965, 1966. Appointments: Czech Radio Symphonic, 1953-56; Discovered bass clarinet as a solo instrument, very first person to give bass clarinet recital, 1955; Chamber music ensemble Due Boemi di Praga with wife Emma Kovarnova on piano, 1963-; Chamber Music Lecturer, Biberach, Germany, 1969-; Professor, Music High School in Prague, 1974-79; Chamber Soloist, Czech Philharmonic, 1979-90; Soloist in international concerts on four continents; Gives masterclasses on four continents. Creative Works: Over 100 compositions recorded on LPs and CDs and has appeared on TV and radio programmes. Honours: Gold Medal competition of wind instruments, 1958; Prize Janacek Competition, 1960; Prize Hi-Fi

Festival Paris, 1965; Pick of the Year, London, 1974; Clarinet Super Record, Tokyo, 1986. Memberships: Union of Czech Interpreters; International Clarinet Association; Clarinet and Sax Society of Great Britain; Honorary Member, Jeunesse Musicales de Suisse. Address: Bubenska 39, 170 00 Prague 7, Czech Republic. E-mail: www.horakbasscl.cz

HORLOCK John Harold (Sir), b. 19 April 1928, Edmonton, England. University Administrator and Engineer. m Sheila J Stutely, 1 son, 2 daughters. Education: MA, Mechanical Sciences, 1953, PhD, Mechanical Engineering, 1955, ScD, Mechanical Engineering, 1975, Cambridge University. Appointments: Design and Development Engineer, Rolls-Royce Ltd, 1948-51; Research Fellow, St John's College Cambridge, 1954-57; Lecturer, Engineering, 1956-58; Professor of Engineering, 1967-74; Harrison Professor of Mechanical Engineering, University of Liverpool, 1958-67; Vice-Chancellor, University of Salford, 1974-80; Vice-Chancellor, 1981-90, Fellow, 1991-, Open University; Treasurer and Vice-President, Royal Society, 1992-97; Pro-Chancellor UMIST, 1995-2001; President, Association for Science Education, 1999. Publications: Books: Axial Flow Compressors, 1958; Axial Flow Turbines, 1973; Actuator Disc Theory, 1978; The Thermodynamics and Gas Dynamics of Internal Combustion Engines (co-editor), Volume I, 1982, Volume II, 1986; Cogeneration, Combined Heat and Power, 1987; Combined Power Plants, 1992; Energy for the Future, 1995; Advanced Gas Turbine Cycles, 2003. Honours include: James Clayton Prize, 1962, Thomas Hawksley Gold Medal, 1969, Arthur Charles Main Prize, 1997, Institution of Mechanical Engineers; Honorary Doctorates: Heriot-Watt University, 1980, University of Salford, 1981, University of East Asia, 1987, University of Liverpool, 1987, Open University, 1991, CNAA, 1991, De Montford University, 1995, Cranfield University, 1997; Honorary Fellowships: St John's College, Cambridge, 1989, UMIST, 1991; Knighthood, 1996; R Tom Sawyer Award, ASME, 1997; Sir James Ewing Medal, ICE, 2002; ISABE Achievement Award, 2003. Memberships: Fellow, Royal Society; Fellow of Engineering; Fellow, Institution of Mechanical Engineers; Fellow, American Society of Mechanical Engineers; Fellow, Royal Aeronautical Society, 2003; Foreign Associate, National Academy of Engineering, USA. Address: 2 The Avenue, Ampthill, Bedford MK45 2NR, England. E-mail: j.h.horlock@talk21.com

HORNSBY Bevé, b. 13 September 1915. Speech Therapist; Psychologist. Widowed, 3 sons, 1 daughter. Education: MSc, 1973, PhD, 1982, University of London; MEd, University College North Wales, 1979. Appointments: Ambulance Driver, First Aid Nursing Yeomanry (FANY) and Mechanical Transport Corps, 1939-42; Pilot, Civil Air Guard, 1938-39; Head of Speech Therapy Clinic, Kingston, 1969-71; Head, Remedial Teaching, St Thomas's Hospital, 1970-71; Head, Dyslexia Dept, St Bartholomew's Hospital, 1971-80; President, Founder, Teacher, The Hornsby International Dyslexia Centre, 1984-; Private Practice, 1984-; Lecturer on Teacher Training Courses, 1984-; Principal and Founder, Hornsby House School, 1988-. Publications: Alpha to Omega - The A to Z of Teaching Reading, Writing and Spelling, 1974, 5th edition, 1999; Alpha to Omega Flash Cards, 1975, 2nd edition 1999; Overcoming Dyslexia, 1984, 3rd edition, 1997; Before Alpha – Learning Games for the Under Fives, 1989; Alpha to Omega Activity Packs, 1990, 1993; The Alpha to Omega Activity Pack, Stage I Plus, 1998; A Walk Through Guide to Alpha to Omega, 2001; Dyslexics I Have Known. Reaching for the Stars, 2001; Numerous articles in scientific and popular journals. Honours: British Dyslexia Association, 1987; FRSA; MBE, 1997; Professorship, Cheltenham and Gloucester College of Higher Education, 1997: Fellow, College of Preceptors, 1997; Golden Award for Achievement, Help the Aged, 1997. Memberships:

Associate Member, British Psychological Society, 1983; Fellow, Royal College of Speech and Language Therapists, 1988; Chartered Psychologist, 1990; Associate, British Dyslexic Association, 1990; Trainer in Instrumental Enrichment, 1991; Honorary Member, PATOSS, for Outstanding Achievement, 1998; Fellow, Royal Society of Medicine, 2001 Address: Glenshee Lodge, 261 Trinity Road, Wandsworth, London SW18 3SN, England. E-mail: beve@dyslexia.com

HOROVITZ Michael, b. 4 April 1935, Frankfurt am Main, Germany. Writer; Poet; Editor; Publisher; Songwriter; Singer; Musician; Visual Artist; Impresario. Education: BA, 1959, MA, 1964, Brasenose, College, Oxford. Appointments: Editor and Publisher, New Departures International Review, 1959-; Founder, singer-player, director, Jazz Poetry SuperJam bandwagons, 1969-; Founder, Co-ordinator and Torchbearer, Poetry Olympics Festivals, 1980-. Publications: Europa (translator), 1961; Alan Davie, 1963; Declaration, 1963; Strangers: Poems, 1965; Poetry for the People: An Essay in Bop Prosody, 1966; Bank Holiday: A New Testament for the Love Generation, 1967; Children of Albion (editor), 1969; The Wolverhampton Wanderer: An Epic of Football, Fate and Fun, 1971; Love Poems, 1971; A Contemplation, 1978; Growing Up: Selected Poems and Pictures 1951-1979, 1979; The Egghead Republic (translator), 1983; A Celebration of and for Frances Horovitz, 1984; Midsummer Morning Jog Log, 1986; Bop Paintings, Collages and Drawings, 1989; Grandchildren of Albion (editor), 1992; Wordsounds and Sightlines: New and Selected Poems, 1994; Grandchildren of Albion Live (editor), 1996; The POW! Anthology, 1996; The POP! Anthology, 2000; The POM! Anthology, 2001; Jeff Nuttall's Wake on Paper, 2004; Jeff Nuttall's Wake on CD, 2004; A New Waste Land, forthcoming. Honours: Arts Council of Great Britain Writers Award, 1976; Arts Council Translator's Award, 1983; Poetry Book Society Recommendation, 1986; Creative Britons Award, 2000; Officer of the Order of the British Empire, 2002. Address: PO Box 9819, London, W11 2GQ, England.

HORROCKS Jane, b. 18 January 1964, Lancashire, England. Actress. Partner Nick Vivian, 1 son, 1 daughter. Education: Royal Academy of Dramatic Art. Creative Works: Stage appearances include: The Rise and Fall of Little Voice; TV appearances include: Hunting Venus (film); Red Dwarf (series); Absolutely Fabulous; The Flint Street Nativity, 1999; Film appearances: The Dressmaker, 1989; Life is Sweet, 1991; Little Voice, 1998; Born Romantic, 2001; Chicken Run (voice), 2002. Honour: Best Supporting Actress Los Angeles Critics Award, 1992. Address: Conway van Gelder Ltd, 18-21 Jermyn Street, London, SW17 6HP, England.

HORSKY Jan, b. 13 April 1940, Spinov, Czech Republic. University Professor. m. Marie Stusova, 2 sons. Education: Physics, Masaryk University, Brno, 1962; CSC degree, 1970, DSc degree, 1980, Theoretical Physics, Charles University. Junior Physics Assistant, 1963, Senior Physics Assistant, 1966, Assistant Professor, Theoretical Physics, 1973, Professor of Theoretical Physics, Brno University, 1981. Publications: Books, scientific articles, popularization articles, philosophy contributions; Member, Voluntary Fireman Union, Spinov. Honours: Man of the Year; Listed in Who's Who publications and biographical dictionaries Memberships: American Physical Society (Topical Group on Gravitation); International Society for GR and Gravitation. Address: Psenik 13, 61137 Brno, Czech Republic.

HORWITZ Angela Joan, b. 14 October 1934, London, England. Sculptress; Painter; Professor. 2 sons, 1 daughter. Education: Lycée Francais de Londres; Studied art, Marylebone Institute, 1978-90; Sir John Cass College, 1983-85; Hampstead Institute, 1990-92. Career: Fashion Designer, owner of own company, 1960-80;

Exhibitions: Grand Palais, Paris, 1985, 1986; RBA, NS, RAS, SWA, Mall Galleries, Civic Centre, Southend, SEFAS, Guildhall, Ridley Society, City of Westminster Arts Council, Alpine Gallery, Smiths Gallery Covent Garden, Wintershall Gallery; The Orangery, Hyde Park Gallery, London (Winchester Cathedral, 1992); Exhibition with City of London Polytechnic, Whitechapel, London, 1985; Salon International du Livre et de la Presse à Geneva, 1997; Miramar Hotel, 1998 and Beaux Arts, Cannes, France, 1999; Raymond Gallery, Beaux Arts, 2000; The Atrium Gallery, London, 2000; Gallery le Carre d'or, Paris, 2000; Work in permanent collections: Sculpture in stone for Winchester Cathedral; Well Woman Centre, The United Elizabeth Garrett Anderson Hospital for Women, London; Private collection: Zurich, Switzerland; National Society Ridley Arts Society. Honours: Academical Knight, Arts, Academia Internazionale Greci-Marino, 1999; Academical Knight, Department of Arts, Ordine Accademico Internatzionale, Italy. Memberships: NS, 1982; RAS, 1983; Beaux Arts, Cannes, France, 1997-2003; Landsdown Club; British Red Cross. Address: 6 Wellington House, Aylmer Drive, Stanmore, Middlesex HA7 3ES, England.

HOSHAN Ahmed H, b. 20 October 1933, Saudi Arabia. Company Chairman. m. Hessah Al Thukair, 1 son, 3 daughters. Education: Bachelor's Degree, Business Administration, UK, 1960. Appointments: Editor-in-Chief and Managing Director, Riyadh Newspaper and Yamama Press Establishment, 1966-72; Established first English Newspaper, Riyadh Daily in Saudi Arabia, 1971; Chairman, Yamama Press, 1984-86; Currently Chairman, Hoshanco. Memberships: School, Home and Office Association, Dayton, Ohio, USA; The Conference Board, New York, USA, Brussels, Belgium. Address: PO Box 59, Riyadh 11411, Saudi Arabia. E-mail: chairman@hoshanpg.com

HOSHINO Yasushi, b. 31 January 1947, Kanuma, Japan. Professor. m. Ebara Kazuko, 2 daughters. Education: Graduate, University of Tokyo, 1970; Masters degree, 1972; DEng, 1984. Appointments: Researcher, Group Leader, Manager, Nippon Telegram & Telephone Corporation, 1972-94; Professor in Nippon Institute of Technology, 1994-. Publications: Electronic Imaging Fundamentals (in Japanese); Over 20 papers in international journals. Honours: HM Charles E Ives Award from IS&T (USA); Contribution Award from China; Paper Award, Imaging Society of Japan. Memberships: Board member: Imaging Society of Japan; Society of Applied Physics of Japan. Address: 3-2-12 Maborikaigan, Yokosuka, Kanagawa, Japan.

HOSKINS Bob (Robert William), b. 26 October 1942. Actor. m. (1) Jane Livesey, 1970, 1 son, 1 daughter: (2) Linda Barnwell, 1984, 1 son, 1 daughter. Career: Several stage roles at the National Theatre; Films include: National Health, 1973; Royal Flash, 1974; Zulu Dawn, 1980; The Long Good Friday, 1980; The Wall, 1982; The Honorary Consul, 1983; Lassiter, 1984; The Cotton Club, 1984; Brazil, 1985; The Woman Who Married Clark Gable, 1985; Sweet Liberty, 1985; Mona Lisa, 1986; A Prayer for the Dying, 1987; The Lonely Passion of Judith Hearne, 1987; Who Framed Roger Rabbit?, 1987; The Raggedy Rawney (director, actor and writer), 1988; Mermaids, 1989; Shattered, 1990; Heart Condition, 1990; The Projectionist, 1990; The Favour, The Watch and the Very Big Fish, 1990; Hook, 1991, The Inner Circle, 1992; Super Mario Brothers, 1992, Nixon, 1995, The Rainbow (also director), 1996; Michael, 1996; Cousin Bette, 1996; Twenty-four-seven, 1998; The Secret Agent, 1998; Felicia's Journey, 1999; Parting Shots, 1999; Enemy at the Gates, 2001; Last Orders, 2001; TV appearances include: Omnibus – It Must be Something in the Water, 1971; Villains, 1972; Thick as Thieves, 1972; Schmoedipus, 1974; Shoulder to Shoulder, 1974; Pennies From Heaven, 1975; Peninsular, 1975; Sheppey, 1980; Flickers, 1980; Othello, 1981;

Dictionary of International Biography

The Beggers' Opera, 1983; Mussolini and I, 1984; The Changeling, 1993; World War Two: Then There Were Giants, 1993; David Copperfield, 1999; The Lost World (film), 2001; Stage: Old Wicked Songs, 1996. Honours: For Mona Lisa, New York Critics Award, Golden Globe Award, Best Actor Award, Cannes Festival, 1986. Address: c/o ICM, Oxford House, 76 Oxford Street, London, W1N 0AX, England.

HOSNEDL Stanislav, b. 7 October 1942, Domazlice, Czech Republic. University Professor. m. Miroslava, 2 sons. Education: Ing. (MSc), Mechanical Engineering, 1964; CSc (PhD), Engineering Design of Manufacturing Machines, 1984. Appointments: Head of CAE and CAD Department, Skoda Research Centre, Pilsen, Czech Republic, 1981-90; Head of Department of Machine Design, 1990-92; Associate Professor of Engineering Design of Manufacturing Machines, 1992-2001; Vice-Dean, Faculty of Mechanical Engineering, 2001-; Professor of Mechanical Engineering, University of West Bohemia, Pilsen, Czech Republic, 2001-. Publications: Handbook of Engineering Design I and II (co-author), 1999 and 2000; Design Science for Engineering Design Practice (co-author), International Conference on Engineering Design, Glasgow, 2001. Honours: ICED Award, Tampere, 1997; WDK 1980-2000 Award, Zurich, 2000. Memberships include: Founding Member and Advisory Board Member, The Design Society, Glasgow; Editorial Board Member, Journal of Engineering Design. Address: Department of Machine Design, University of West Bohemia, Univerzitni 22, 30614 Pilsen, Czech Republic. E-mail: hosnedl@kks.zcu.cz

HOSSEINI Seyyed Ali Akbar, b. 5 July 1929, Kerman, Iran. Professor. m. Fatemeh Hatami, 2 sons, 1 daughter. Education: BA, Islamic Culture, Tehran University, 1960; MA, Educational Psychology, EdS and EdD, Secondary Education, Indiana University, 1963-65. Appointments: Chancellor, Shahid Bahonar University of Kerman, 1979-80, 1994-97; Co-operation with Cultural Revolution Headquarters; The Office for the Collaboration of Theological Schools and Universities, Education Measurements Organisation, Ministry of Education, Struggle for Construction, Ministry of Culture and Islamic Guidance, Textbook Evaluation; Editor, Journal of Social Sciences and Humanities, Shiraz University, 1984-96. Publications: Over 152 articles in Persian and English; 18 volumes including translations and monographs; Numerous books and reports. Honours: Notable Researcher of Fars Province, 1980; Prominent Teacher of Shiraz University, 1991; Eminent Professor of the Country for the Year, 1997. Memberships: University Council; Graduate School Council; Humanities Specialists Committee; Research and Planning Board; Discretionary Board; The Board of Publications; Academy of Sciences of the Islamic Republic of Iran. Address: Faculty of Education, Shiraz University, Shiraz, Iran.

HOU De-Xing, b. Hunan, China. Professor. m. Hui Gao, 1 son. Education: BS, Hunan Agricultural University, China, 1981; MS, 1988, PhD, 1991, Kagoshima University, Japan. Appointments: Associate Researcher, Hunan Agricultural University, China, 1982-85; Research Scientist, Institute of Physical and Chemical Research (RIKEN), Japan, 1991-97; Associate Professor, Kagoshima University, Japan, 1997-; Guest Professor, Hunan Agricultural University, China, 2000-. Publications: Books: Scientific Terms of Animal Science (English-Japanese-Chinese), 1990; Methodology for Plant Pigment Research, 2004; Articles in scientific journals including: Nature, 1997; Nature Genetics, 1997; FEBS Letters, 1997; The EMBO Journal, 2002; Carcinogenesis, 2004. Honours: Scholar of Ministry of Science, Education and Culture, Japan, 1985-91; Fellow of Science and Technology, Agency, Japan, 1994; Investigator Award, Ministry of Agriculture, China. Memberships: American Association for the Advancement

of Science; Molecular Biology Society of Japan; Japanese Society of Nutrition and Food Science. Address: Faculty of Agriculture, Kagoshima University, Korimoto 1-21-24, Kagoshima 890-0065, Japan. E-mail: hou@chem.agri.kagoshima-u.ac.jp

HOUGHTON Eric, b. 4 January 1930, West Yorkshire, England. Teacher; Author. m. Cecile Wolffe, 4 June 1954, 1 son, 1 daughter. Education: Sheffield City College of Education, 1952. Publications: The White Wall, 1961; Summer Silver, 1963; They Marched with Spartacus, 1963; A Giant Can Do Anything, 1975; The Mouse and the Magician, 1976; The Remarkable Feat of King Caboodle, 1978; Steps Out of Time, 1979; Gates of Glass, 1987; Walter's Wand, 1989; The Magic Cheese, 1991; The Backwards Watch, 1991; Vincent the Invisible, 1993; Rosie and the Robbers, 1997; The Crooked Apple Tree, 1999. Honour: American Junior Book Award, 1964. Memberships: Society of Authors; Childrens Writers Group. Address: The Crest, 42 Collier Road, Hastings, East Sussex TN34 3JR, England.

HOUNSFIELD Godfrey Newbold (Sir), b. 28 August 1919, England. Research Scientist. Education: City and Guilds College, London; Faraday House Electrical Engineering College. Appointments: Served in Royal Air Force during World War II; Medical Systems Section, 1951-, Senior Staff Scientist, 1977-86, Consultant to Laboratories, 1986-, Inventor EMI-scanner computerised transverse axial tomography system for X-ray examinations, Central Research Laboratories of EMI (now THORN EMI); Professorial Fellow, Imaging Sciences, Manchester University, 1978. Honours: Several honorary degrees; MacRobert Award, 1972; Wilhelm-Exner Medal, Austrin Industrial Association, 1974; Wiedses des Plantes Medal, Phsikalisch-Medizinische Gesellschaft, Würzburg, 1974; Prince Philip Medal Award, City and Guilds of London Institute, 1975; ANS Radiation Award, Georgia Institute of Physics, 1975; Lasker Award, 1975; Duddell Bronze Medal, Institute of Physics, 1976; Golden Plate, American Academy of Achievement, 1976; Churchill Gold Medal, 1976; Gairdner Foundation Award, 1976; Shared Nobel Prize for Physiology or Medicine (with Professor A M Cormack), for development of computer-assisted tomography, 1979. Address: Central Research Laboratories, Dawley Road, Hayes, Middx, UB3 1HH, England.

HOUSTON Whitney, b. 9 August 1963, Newark, New Jersey, USA. Singer. m. Bobby Brown, 18 July 1992, 1 daughter. Musical Education: Singing lessons with mother, Cissy Houston. Career: New Hope Baptist Junior Choir, age 8; Nightclub performances with mother, 1978; Backing vocalist, Chaka Khan and Lou Rawls, 1978; Model, Glamour and Seventeen magazines; Actress, television shows, USA; Solo artiste, 1985-; First US and European tours, 1986; Montreux Rock Festival, 1987; Nelson Mandela Tribute concert, Wembley, 1988; National anthem, Super Bowl XXV, Miami, 1991; Speaker, HIV/AIDs rally, London, 1991; Television specials include: Welcome Home Heroes (return of Gulf troops), 1991; Whitney Houston - This Is My Life, ABC, 1992; Actress, film The Bodyguard, 1992; 87 million albums sold to date. Recordings: Singles include: You Give Good Love, 1985; Saving All My Love For You (Number 1, UK and US), 1985; How Will I Know, 1986; Greatest Love Of All (Number 1, US), 1986; I Wanna Dance With Somebody (Number 1, US and UK), 1987; Didn't We Almost Have It All (Number 1, US), 1987; So Emotional (Number 1, US), 1987; Where Do Broken Hearts Go (Number 1, US), 1988; Love Will Save The Day, 1988; One Moment In Time (Number 1, UK), 1988; I'm Your Baby Tonight (Number 1, US), 1990; All The Man That I Need (Number 1, US), 1991; Miracle, 1991; My Name Is Not Susan, 1991; I Will Always Love You (Number 1 in 11 countries), 1992; I'm Every Woman, 1993; I Have Nothing, 1993; Run To You, 1993; Queen of the Night, 1994; Why Does It Hurt So Bad, 1996; Step by Step, 1997; When You Believe, 1998; It's Not Right But It's Okay, 1999; I Learned from the Best, 1999; If I Told You That, 2000; Could I Have This Kiss Forever, 2000; Heartbreak Hotel, 2000; Whatchlookinat, 2002; One of Those Days, 2002; Albums: Whitney Houston, 1985; Whitney, 1987; I'm Your Baby Tonight, 1990; My Love Is Your Love, 1998; Whitney: The Greatest Hits, 2000; Love Whitney, 2001; Just Whitney, 2002; Film soundtrack: The Bodyguard (Number 1 in 20 countries), 1992. Also featured on: Life's A Party, Michael Zager Band; Duet with Teddy Pendergrass, Hold Me, 1984; Duet with Aretha Franklin, It Isn't, It Wasn't, It Ain't Ever Gonna Be, 1989. Honours include: 2 Grammy Awards; 7 American Music Awards; Emmy, 1986; Songwriter's Hall Of Fame, 1990; Longest-ever US Number 1 record (14 weeks), highest-ever US 1-week sales total, second best seller in US ever, all for I Will Always Love You, 1992; Numerous Gold and Platinum discs. Current Management: Nippy Inc., 2160 N Central Road, Fort Lee, NJ 07024, USA.

HOWARD Anthony Michell, b. 12 February 1934, London, England. Biographer; Reviewer; Writer. m. Carol Anne Gaynor, 26 May 1965. Education: BA, Christ Church, Oxford, 1955. Appointments: Called to the Bar, Inner Temple, 1956; Political Correspondent, Reynolds News, 1958-59; Editorial Staff, Manchester Guardian, 1959-61; Political Correspondent, 1961-64, Assistant Editor, 1970-72, Editor, 1972-78, New Statesman; Whitehall Correspondent, 1965, Sunday Times; Washington Correspondent, 1966-69, Deputy Editor, 1981-88, Observer; Editor, The Listener, 1979-81; Reporter, BBC TV News and Current Affairs, 1989-92; Obituaries Editor, The Times, 1993-99. Publications: The Making of the Prime Minister (with Richard West), 1965; The Crossman Diaries: Selections from the Diaries of a Cabinet Minister (editor), 1979; Rab: The Life of R A Butler, 1987; Crossman: The Pursuit of Power, 1990; The Times Lives Remembered (editor with David Heaton), 1993. Contributions to: Books, newspapers, and journals. Honours: Harkness Fellowship, USA, 1960; Commander of the Order of the British Empire, 1997; Hon LLD, Nottingham, 2001; Hon DLitt, Leicester, 2003. Address: 11 Campden House Court, 42 Gloucester Walk, London W8 4HU, England.

HOWARD Catherine Audrey, b. 5 February 1953, Huddersfield, England. Retired Government Officer. m. Leslie Howard, 3 April 1987. Education: Harold Pitchforth School of Commerce; Ashlar and Spen Valley Further Education Institute; Royal Society of Arts Diplomas. Appointments: Clerk, Treasury Department, 1969-70, Clerk, Housing Department, 1970-74, Elland Urban District Council; Clerk, Telephonist, Housing Department, Calderdale Metropolitan Borough Council, 1974-83; Social Work Assistant; Social Services Department, Calderdale, 1983-88. Publications: Elland in Old Picture Postcards, 1983; Poetry: Down By the Old Mill Stream, 1993; The Flamborough Longsword Dance, 1994; Sacrifice for Christianity, 1994; My Pennine Roots, 1994; The Old and the New, 1994; Having Faith, 1994; The Might of the Meek, 1995; Tough as Old Boots, 1995; Portrait of All Hallows, 1996; Childhood Memories, 1996; Old Ways in Modern Days, 1996; Northern Cornucopia, 1996; A Glimpse of Spring, 1998; Poetry From Yorkshire, 1999. Contributions to: Mercedes-Benz Gazette, 1996; Commemorative Poem presented to Bridlington Public Library on the centenary of Amy Johnson, titled Wonderful Amy, 2003. Honours: National Poet of the Year Commendations, 1996 (3 times); National Open Competition Commendations, 1996, 1997; Robert Bloomfield Memorial Awards Commendation, 1998. Address: 17 Woodlands Close, Bradley Grange, Bradley, Huddersfield, West Yorkshire HD2 1QS, England.

HOWARD Deborah (Janet), b. 26 February 1946, London, England. Architectural Historian; Writer. m. Malcolm S Longair, 26 Sept 1975, 1 son, 1 daughter. Education: BA, Honours, 1968, MA, 1972, Newnham College, Cambridge; MA, 1969, PhD, 1973, University of London. Appointments: Professor of Architectural History, University of Cambridge, 2001-; Fellow, St John's College, Cambridge; Head of Department of History of Art, University of Cambridge. Publications: Jacopo Sansovino: Architecture and Patronage in Renaissance Venice, 1975, 2nd edition, 1987; The Architectural History of Venice, 1980, 3rd edition, 1987, revised and enlarged edition, 2002; Scottish Architecture from the Reformation to the Restoration, 1560-1660, 1995; Venice and the East: The Impact on the Islamic World on Venetian Architecture 1100-1500, 2000. Contributions to: Professional journals. Honour: Honorary Fellow, Royal Incorporation of Architects of Scotland. Memberships: Fellow, Society of Antiquarians of Scotland; Fellow, Society of Antiquaries. Address: St John's College, Cambridge CB2 1TP, England.

HOWARD Elizabeth Jane, b. 26 March 1923, London, England. Author. m. (1) Peter Scott, 1941, 1 daughter, (2) James Douglas-Henry, 1959, (3) Kingsley Amis, 1965, divorced 1983. Education: Trained as Actress, London Mask Theatre School, Scott Thorndike Student Repertory. Appointments: BBC TV modelling, 1939-46; Secretary, Inland Waterways Association, 1947;Honorary Director, Cheltenham Literary Festival, 1962; Co-Director, Salisbury Festival, 1973. Publications: The Beautiful Visit, 1950; The Long View, 1956; The Sea Change, 1959; After Julius, 1965; Odd Girl Out, 1972; Mr Wrong, 1975; Getting It Right, 1982; The Cazalet Chronicles: The Light Years (1st volume), 1990, Marking Time (2nd volume), 1991, Confusion (3rd volume), 1993; Casting Off, volume 4, 1995; Falling, 1999; Slipstream: a Memoir, 2003. Other: The Lovers' Companion (anthology); Green Shades (anthology); 14 television plays; 3 film scripts. Contributions to: The Times; Sunday Times; Telegraph; Encounter; Vogue; Harper's; Queen. Honours: CBE; Yorkshire Post Novel of the Year, 1982. Memberships: Fellow, Royal Society of Literature; Authors Lending and Copyright Society. Address: c/o Jonathan Clowes, Iron Bridge House, Bridge Approach, London NW1 8BD, England.

HOWARD James Kenneth, b. 26 December 1932, London, England. Artist. m. Dora Bertolutti. Education: Hornsey School of Art, 1949-53; Royal College of Art, 1955-58; British Council Scholarship, Italy. 1958-59. Career: One-man Exhibitions: Plymouth Art Centre, 1955; New Grafton Gallery, London, 1971, 1974, 1976, 1978, 1981, 1984, 1986, 1988, 1990, 1993, 1995, 1997, 2000; Retrospective Exhibition, Plymouth City Art Gallery, 1972; Hong Kong Art Centre, Nicosia, 1978; Delhi, 1983; Lowndes Lodge Gallery, London, 1992-87; Everard Read Galley, Johannesburg, 1998; Everard Read Gallery, Cape Town, 2000; Richard Green Gallery, London, 2002, 2003, 2004. Publications: Books: The War Artists, 1983; Art Class, 1989; The Paintings of Ken Howard, 1992; Ken Howard: a Personal View, 1998, 2001; Video: Inspired by Light, 1996; A Vision of Venice in Watercolour, 1998; A Vision of Venice in Oils, 2000. Honours: First Prize, Lord Mayor of London's Art Award, 1966; Prize Winner, John Moores Exhibition, 1978; Prize Winner, Royal West of England Academy, 1981; 1st Prize, Hunting Group Awards, 1982; Critics Prize, Sparkasse, Karlsruhe; Critics Prize, New English Art Club, 2001. Memberships: President, New English Art Club; Royal Academy; Royal Water Colour Society; Royal West of England Academy; Royal Institute of Oil Painters; Royal Society of British Artists; Royal Birmingham Society of Artists; Appointed Official Artists in Northern Ireland, Imperial War Museum. Address: 8 South Bolton Gardens, London, SW4 0DH, England.

Dictionary of International Biography

HOWARD John Winston (Sir), b. 26 July 1939, Sydney, Australia. Politician. m. Alison Janette Parker, 1971, 2 sons, 1 daughter. Education: University of Sydney. Appointments: Solicitor to Supreme Court, New South Wales, 1962; Partner, Sydney solicitors' firm, 1968-74; Liberal MP for Bennelong, New South Wales Federal Parliament, 1974-; Minister for Business and Consumer Affairs, 1975-77; Minister Assisting Prime Minister, 1977; Federal Treasurer, 1977-83; Deputy Leader of Opposition, 1983-85, Leader, 1985-89; Leader, Liberal Party, 1985-89; Shadow Minister for Industrial Relations, Employment and Training, Shadow Minister assisting the Leader on the Public Service and Chairman, Manpower and Labour Market Reform Group, 1990-95; Prime Minister of Australia, 1996-. Memberships: Member State Executive, New South Wales Liberal Party, 1963-74; Vice President, New South Wales Division, Liberal Party, 1972-74; Leader, Liberal Party, 1995-. Address: Department of the Prime Minister, 3-5 National Circuit, Barton, ACT 2600, Australia.

HOWARD Peter Milner, b. 27 June 1937, Stockport, Cheshire, England. Journalist; Editor. m. Janet Crownshaw, 1 son, 1 daughter. Education: Further education, Sheffield College of Commerce and Technology. Appointments: National Service, Sergeant in Army Public Relations, GHQ Far East Land Forces, Singapore, 1958-60; Copy-boy, General Reporter, Sports Reporter/Sub-editor, Feature Writer, Sports Editor, The Star, Sheffield, 1952-75; Ministry of Defence: Press Relations for Royal Navy in UK and ships at sea, British Army, Royal Air Force in Germany, All three services in the Falklands, post fighting, Press desk work in MOD main building, Editor, Soldier, 1975-85; Jane's Information Group: Editor, Jane's Defence Weekly, Jane's Missiles and Rockets, Jane's Navy International, 3 years as Managing Editor, Military and Systems Yearbooks, 1985-2000; Freelance journalist, Editor, Jane's Defence Industry, 2001-. Memberships: Military Historical Society; International Military Music Society; Union Jack Club; Petersfield Golf Club. Address: Mildmay Cottage, Hawkley Road, West Liss, Hampshire GU33 6JL, England. E-mail: petermhoward@lineone.net

HOWARD Ron, b. 1 March 1954, Duncan, Oklahoma, USA. Film Actor; Director. m. Cheryl Alley, 1975, 2 sons, 2 daughters. Education: University of Southern California; Los Angeles Valley College. Appointments: Director, Co-Author, Star, Grand Theft Auto, 1977; Regular TV series The Andy Griffith Show, 1960-68, The Smith Family, 1971-72, Happy Days, 1974, and many other TV appearances. Creative Works: Films directed include: Night Shift, 1982; Splash, 1984; Cocoon, 1985; Gung Ho, 1986; Return to Mayberry, 1986; Willow, 1988; Parenthood, 1989; Backdraft, 1991; Far and Away (also co-producer), 1992; The Paper, 1994; Apollo 13, 1995; A Beautiful Mind, 2001; Film appearances include: The Journey, 1959; Five Minutes to Live, 1959; Music Man, 1962; The Courtship of Eddie's Father, 1963; Village of the Giants, 1965; Wild Country, 1971; Mother's Day, 1974; American Graffiti, 1974; The Spikes Gang, 1976; Eat My Dust, 1976; The Shootist, 1976; More American Graffiti, 1979; Leo and Loree (TV), 1980; Act of Love, 1980; Skyward, 1981; Through the Magic Pyramid (director, executive producer), 1981; When Your Lover Leaves (co-executive producer), 1983; Return to Mayberry, 1986; Ransom, 1996; Ed TV, 1999. Honours include: Outstanding Directorial Achievement in Motion Picture Award, Directors Guild of America, 1996; Academy Awards for Best Director and Best Film (producer), 2002; DGA Best Director Award, 2002. Address: c/o Peter Dekom, Bloom Dekom & Hergott, 150 South Rodeo Drive, Beverly Hills, CA 90212, USA.

HOWARTH Nigel John Graham, b. 12 December 1936, Manchester, England. Circuit Judge. m. Janice Mary Hooper, 2 sons, 1 daughter. Education: LLB, 1957, LLM, 1959, University

of Manchester; Bar Finals, 1st class honours, Inns of Court Law School, 1960; Macaskie Scholar, 1960, Atkin Scholar, 1961, Grays Inn. Appointments: Called to the Bar, Grays Inn, 1960; Private practice, Chancery Bar, Manchester, 1961-92; Assistant Recorder, 1983-89; Acting Deemster, Isle of Man, 1985, 1989; Recorder of Crown Court, 1989-92; Circuit Judge, 1992-. Memberships: Vice President, Disabled Living; Manchester Pedestrian Club; Northern Chancery Bar Association, Chairman, 1990-92. Address: c/o Circuit Administrator, Northern Circuit Office, 15 Quay Street, Manchester, M60 9FD, England. E-mail: nhowarth@lix.compulink.co.uk

HOWATCH Susan, b. 14 July 1940, Leatherhead, Surrey, England. Writer. Education: LLB, Kings College, University of London, 1958-61. Publications: The Dark Shore, 1965; The Waiting Sands, 1966; Call in the Night, 1967; The Shrouded Walls, 1968; April's Grave, 1969; The Devil on Lammas Night, 1970; Penmarric, 1971; Cashelmara, 1974; The Rich are Different, 1977; Sins of the Fathers, 1980; The Wheel of Fortune, 1984; Glittering Images, 1987; Glamorous Powers, 1988; Ultimate Prizes, 1989; Scandalous Risks, 1991; Mystical Paths, 1992; Absolute Truths, 1994; A Question of Integrity (published in USA as: The Wonder Worker). 1997; The High Flyer, 1999; The Heartbreaker, 2003. Contributions to: Church Times; Tablet. Honour: Winifred Mary Stanford Memorial Prize, 1992; Elected Fellow, King's College, London, 1999. Memberships: PEN; Society of Authors. Address:c/o Gillon Aitken Associates, 18-21 Cavaye Place, London SW10 9PT, England.

HOWDEN (Frank) Newton, b. 23 March 1916, Philadelphia, Pennsylvania, USA. Episcopal Priest. m Valerie, 1 son, 2 daughters. Education: AB, University of the South, Sewanee, Tennessee, 1940; M Div, General Theological College, New York City, 1943; Master of Science, University of Central Connecticut, New Britain, Connecticut; McGill University, 1954-55. Appointments: Curate, St Peter's Church, Auburn, New York, 1943-45; Vicar, St John's, Sewaren, New Jersey, 1945-48; Chaplain, US Army, 1948-51; Rector, St Luke's, St Albans, Vermont, 1951-56; Rector, Trinity, Waterbury, 1956-66; Rector, Trinity Church, Lime Rock, Lakeville, 1969-85; Assistant Professor, Waterbury Technical School, 1970-85; Retired, 1985. Publications: A Rule of Life; Holy Communion for the Sick and Shut-ins; Life Here and Hereafter. Honours: Archdeacon, 1962-64; Dean, Lichfield Deanery, 1984-85. Membership: Associate, St Margaret's Convent. E-mail: fnhowden@aol.com

HOWE Elspeth Rosamund Morton (Baroness Howe of Idlicote), b. 8 February 1932. Member of the House of Lords. m. Lord Howe of Aberavon, 1953, 1 son, 2 daughters. Education: BSc, London School of Economics, 1985. Appointments: Secretary to Principal, A A School of Architecture, 1952-55; Deputy Chairman, Equal Opportunities Commission, Manchester, 1975-79; President, Federation of Recruitment and Employment Services, 1980-94; Non-Executive Director, United Biscuits plc, 1988-94; Non-Executive Director, Kingfisher plc, 1986-2000; Non-Executive Director, Legal and General, 1989-97; Chairman, The BOC Foundation for the Environment, 1990-; Chairman, The Broadcasting Standards Commission, 1993-99. Publications: 2 pamphlets; Co-author, Women on the Board, 1990; Articles for newspapers; Lectures, speeches, television and radio broadcasts. Honours: Honorary Doctorates: London University, 1990; The Open University, 1993; Bradford University, 1993; Aberdeen University, 1994; Liverpool University, 1994; Sunderland University, 1995; South Bank University, 1995; Honorary Fellow, London School of Economics, 2001. Memberships: President, the UK Committee of UNICEF, 1993-2002; Vice Chairman, The Open University, 2001-03; Trustee, The Architectural Association;

Trustee, The Ann Driver Trust; Institute of Business Ethics; President, The Peckham Settlement; NCVO Advisory Council. Address: House of Lords, London SW1A 0PW, England. E-mail: howee@parliament.uk

HOWE Geoffrey (Lord Howe of Aberavon), b. 20 December 1926. Politician; Lawyer m. Elspeth Rosamund Morton Shand, 1953, 1 son, 2 daughters. Education: MA, LLB, Trinity Hall, Cambridge. Appointments: Lieutenant, Royal Signals, 1945-48; Chairman, Cambridge University Conservative Association, 1951; Chairman, Bow Group, 1955; Managing Director, Crossbow, 1957-60; Editor, 1960-62; Called to the Bar, Middle Temple, 1952, Bencher, 1969, Reader, 1993; Member, General Council of the Bar, 1957-61; Member, Council of Justice, 1963-70; Deputy Chairman, Glamorgan Quarter Sessions, 1966-70; Contested Aberavon, 1955, 1959; MP, Bebington, 1964-66, Reigate, 1970-74, Surrey Eeast, 1974-92; Secretary, Conservative Parliamentary Health and Social Security Committee, 1964-65; Opposition Front Bench Spokesman, 1965-66, 1974-75, 1975-79; Solicitor-General, 1970-72; Minister for Trade and Consumer Affairs, Department of Trade and Industry, 1972-74; Chancellor of the Exchequer, 1979-83; Secretary of State, Foreign and Commonwealth Affairs, 1983-89; Lord President of the Council, Leader of House of Commons, Deputy Prime Minister, 1989-90; Special Adviser on European and International Affairs to International Law Firm Jones, Day, Reavis & Pogue, 1991-2001; Herman Phleger Visiting Professor Stanford Law School, USA, 1992-93; President, Great Britain-China Centre, 1992-; International Advisory Councils, J P Morgan, 1992-2001; Chair, Framlington Russian Investment Fund, 1994-2003; Carlyle European Advisory Board, 1996-2001; Fuji Bank Advisory Council, 1999-. Publications: Conflict of Loyalty (memoirs), 1994; Various political pamphlets. Honours include: Grand Cross, Order of Merit, Portugal, 1987, Germany, 1992; Companion of Honour, 1996; Order of Ukraine for Public Service, 2001. Address: House of Lords, London SW1A 0PW, England.

HOWELL David Arthur Russell (Lord Howell of Guildford), b. 18 January 1936, London, England. Economist; Journalist; Author. m. Davina Wallace, 1 son, 2 daughters. Education: King's College, Foundation Scholar. Appointments: Member of Parliament for Guildford, 1966-97; Parliamentary Secretary, Civil Service Department, 1970-72; Minister of State, Northern Ireland, 1972-74; Secretary of State for Energy, 1979-81; Secretary of State for Transport, 1981-83; Chairman, House of Commons Foreign Affairs Select Committee, 1987-97; Chairman, UK-Japan 21st Century Group, 1989-2001; Visiting Fellow, Nuffield College, Oxford, 1991-99; Director, Monks Investment Trust, 1993-; Advising Director, UBS Warburg, 1996-2000; Chairman, Lords European Committee, Sub-Committee, 1998-2000; Director, John Laing plc, 1999-2002; Trustee, Shakespeare Globe Theatre, 2000-; Chief Opposition Spokesman on Foreign Affairs, House of Lords, 2000-. Publications: Columnist: The Japan Times; Wall Street Journal; International Herald Tribune; Books: Freedom and Capital, 1979; Blind Victory, 1986; The Edge of Now, 2000; Numerous pamphlets and articles. Honours: Privy Counsellor, 1979; Created Peer of the Realm, 1997; Grand Cordon of the Order of the Sacred Treasure, Japan, 2001. Memberships: Beefsteak Club; County Club, Guildford. Address: House of Lords, London SW1A 0PW, England. E-mail: howelld@parliament.uk

HOWELL Elmo, b. 5 August 1918, Tremont, Mississippi, USA. Retired English Teacher; Poet. Education: BA, University of Mississippi, 1940; MA, 1948, PhD, 1955, University of Florida. Appointments: Jackson State College, Jacksonville, Alabama, 1955-57; Memphis State University, 1957-83. Publications: Winter Verses, 1989; The Apricot Tree, and Other Poems, 1993; I Know

a Planted Field, 1995; Have You Been to Shubuta?, 1996. Membership: Mississippi Poetry Society. Address: 3733 Douglass Avenue, Memphis, TN 38111, USA.

HOWELLS Dawn Elizabeth b. 26 January 1954, Bedfordshire, England. Piano Recitalist. m. Clare Lange, 22 October 1977, 1 son, 1 daughter. Education: Guildhall School of Music and Drama; London Opera Centre; Private Study with Yonty Solomon. Debut: Edinburgh Festival, 1985. Career: Repetiteur, Cologne Opera House, Germany, 1978-79; Solo Recitals, 1979-; Edinburgh Festival Fringe Recitals, 1985-95, Purcell Room, 1986, St Johns Smith Square, 1989; Extensive Recitals for Children, 1991-; Piano Professor, Welsh College of Music and Drama, 1991-94; Performed Etudes of Henselt at Schwabach, Bavaria at Centenary Celebration, Complete Transcendental Etudes of Lyapunov, Complete Impromptus Fauré, 12 Etudes Saint-Saëns, Richard Rodney Bennett 5 Studies, Peter and the Wolf, Story of Babar with music and narration: Premiere of Piano Version, Little Red Riding Hood, Paul Patterson, 1993; Premiere, Twentieth Century Sidelights, Paul Pelley, 1995; Premiere, Moon Dances, Morris Pert, 1996; Premiere, Piano Tuner, Roxanna Panufnik, 1995; Partner, Belsize Music Rooms. Memberships: ISM, elected Regional Councillor, 2003; RSM. Address: 67 Belsize Lane, Hampstead, London NW3 5AX, England.

HOWLETT Neville Stanley, b. 17 April 1927, Prestatyn, Wales. Retired Air Vice-Marshal. m. Sylvia, 1 son, 1 daughter. Education: Liverpool Institute High School and Peterhouse, Cambridge, England. Appointments: Pilot Training, Royal Air Force, 1945-48; 32 and 64 Fighter Squadrons, 1948-56; RAF Staff College, 1957; Squadron Commander, 229 (Fighter) OCU, 1958-59; OC Flying Wing, RAF Coltishall, 1961-63; Directing staff, RAF Staff College, 1967-69; Station Commander, RAF Leuchars, 1970-72; Royal College of Defence Studies, 1973; Director of Operations, Air Defence and Overseas, 1973-74; Air Attaché, Washington DC, USA, 1975-77; Director, Management Support of Intelligence, 1978-80; Director General, Personal Services, 1980-82; Retired, 1982; Member, Lord Chancellors Panel of Independent Inquiry Inspectors, 1982-95; Member, Pensions Appeal Tribunal, 1988-2001. Honour: CB. Memberships: Royal Air Force Club; Royal Air Forces Association, Vice-President, 1984-, Chairman Executive Committee, 1990-97, Chairman Central Council, 1999-2001; Royal Air Force Benevolent Fund; Officers Association; Phyllis Court Club, Henley; Huntercombe Golf Club. Address: Milverton, Bolney Trevor Drive, Lower Shiplake, Oxon RG9 3PG, England.

HOYLE Trevor, b. 25 February 1940, Rochdale, England. Writer. m. 15 September 1962, 1 son, 1 daughter. Appointments: Panel Judge, Constable Novel Competition and Portico Literary Prize. Publications: Novels: The Relatively Constant Copywriters, 1972; The Adulterer, 1972; Rule of Night, 1975, 2003; Rock Fix, 1977; Seeking the Mythical Future, science fiction, 1977, 1982; Through the Eye of Time, science fiction, 1977, 1982; The Gods Look Down, science fiction, 1978, 1982; The Man Who Travelled on Motorways, 1979; Earth Cult, science fiction, 1979; The Stigma, 1980; Bullet Train, 1980; The Last Gasp, 1983, 1984, 1990; Vail, 1984, 1989; K.I.D.S., 1988, 1990; Blind Needle, 1994; Mirrorman, 1999; Film and TV adaptations: Blake's 7, 1977; Blake's 7: Project Avalon, 1979; Blake's 7: Scorpio Attack, 1981; Ghostbusters, 1985; Biggles, 1985; Civvies, 1992; Prime Suspect 2, 1992; Prime Suspect, 1993; The Governor, 1995. Contributions to: Short stories in: Transatlantic Review; Montrose Review; BBC Morning Story; New Fiction Society Magazine; New Yorkshire Writing; Fireweed; Double Space; Wordworks; Pennine Magazine; Artful Reporter; Ambit. Honours: Winner, Radio Times Drama Award, for Gigo radio play, 1991; Sony Best Actor Award, 1992; Winner, British

Dictionary of International Biography

Short Story, Transatlantic Review; Ray Mort Northern Novel Award. Membership: Society of Authors. Address: c/o Tanja Howarth 19 New Row, London, WC2N 4LA, England.

HOZUMI Motoo, b. 12 March 1933, Fukushima, Japan. Cancer Research. m. Sakiko Wakabayashi, 1 son, 2 daughters. Education: BSc, 1956, MSc, 1958, DSc, 1961, Tokyo University of Education. Appointments: Research Member, National Cancer Center Research Institute, Tokyo, 1962-64; Chief, Central Laboratory, National Cancer Center Research Institute, Tokyo, 1964-75; Research Member, Roswell Park Memorial Institute, Buffalo, New York, 1965-67; Director, Department of Chemotherapy, Saitama Cancer Center Research Institute, Japan, 1975-93; Visiting Professor, Showa University School of Medicine, Tokyo, 1988-2001; Director, Saitama Cancer Center Research Institute, 1990-93. Publications: Over 300 papers and books on cancer research. Honours: Princess Takamatsu Cancer Research Foundation Prize, Tokyo, 1974. Memberships: Japanese Cancer Association; Japanese Haematological Society; American Cancer Association; American Association for the Advancement of Science. Address: 12-288 Fukasaku, Saitama, Saitama 337, Japan.

HRABAL Antonin, b. 21 May 1957, Prilepy, Czech Republic. Physician; Researcher. Education: MD, Charles University, 1982; PhD, Costa Rica University, 1986-1998; DSc, Psychoneuroimmunology, 1998. Appointments: Researcher, 1976-88; Physician Teacher, Charles University, 1982-98; Head Physician, University Hospital, 1995-; Head of Research, University Centre, 1998-; Rector, Hippocrates University, 2000-; Chief Executive Officer, Hippokrates Corporation, 2003-. Publications: 45 articles in professional medical journals. Honours: Gold Medal for The Best Invention, 2000. Memberships: Active Member, New York Academy of Science; National Geographic Society; American Association for the Advancement of Science; International Anti-Ageing Society. Address: 45053 Casas de Mariposa, Indian Wells, CA 92210, USA E-mail: professorhrabal@yahoo.com Website: professorhrabal@hotmail.com

HŘIB Jiří Emil, b. 16 September 1942, Frýdek-Místek, Czech Republic. Plant Physiologist. m. Marie Malá, 16 January 1970, 1 daughter. Education: Engineer, 1966, PhD, 1973, University of Agriculture, Brno (now Mendel University of Agriculture and Forestry, Brno). Appointments: Scientist Aspirant, Scientific Film Laboratory, Institute of Scientific Instruments, 1967-73; Scientist, Institute of Vertebrate Zoology, 1973-74; Scientist, Institute of Botany, 1974-83; Scientist, Institute of Experimental Phytotechnics, 1984-87; Scientist, Institute of Systematic and Ecological Biology, 1987-91, Czechoslovak Academy of Sciences, Brno; Scientist, Institute of Plant Genetics, 1991-97, Principal Scientist, Institute of Plant Genetics and Biotechnology, 1997-98, External Scientific Co-worker, Institute of Plant Genetics and Biotechnology, 1999-, Slovak Academy of Sciences, Nitra. Publications: Over 100 articles in professional scientific journals; The Co-Cultivation of Wood-Rotting Fungi with Tissue Cultures of Forest Tree Species, 1990; Research films: (author) Ontogeny of the Alga Scenedesmus quadricauda, 1973; Co-author, Regeneration of the Cap in the Alga Acetabularia mediterranea, 1980. Honours: Research Board of Advisors, American Biographical Institute, 1999; Consulting Editor, Contemporary Who's Who, 2003. Memberships: Czech Society for Scientific Cinematography, Brno, 1965; Czech Botanical Society, Prague, 1967; International Association for Plant Tissue Culture and Biotechnology, 1990; International Association of Sexual Plant Reproduction Research, 1993; New York Academy of Sciences, 2001; Czechoslovak Biological Society, Brno, 2001; Czech Algological Society, Prague, 2002. Address: Ukrajinská 17, 625 00 Brno, Czech Republic.

HRIBERNIK Božidar, b. 6 November 1934, Maribor, Slovenia. Professor. m. Levina, 2 daughters. Education: Dipl. Ing., University of Ljubljana, 1957-62; MSc, University of Zagreb, 1974; Dr. Sc., University of Ljubljana, 1982. Appointments: Designer, Telephone and Lighting Appliances, 1954-57; Instructor University of Ljubljana, 1959-61; Engineering Analyst, Elektrokovina Corporation, Maribor, 1962-68; Contract Lecturer, Higher School of Engineering, Maribor, 1963-68, 1970-76; Head Development Department, Elektrokovina Corporation, 1968-74; Manager, TSN Corporation, Maribor, 1974-76; Lecturer, 1976-83, Head of Electrical Power Engineering Institute, 1980-99, Head of Research Section, 1982-86, Associate Professor, 1983-88, Vice Dean, 1983-87, Faculty of Technical Sciences, University of Maribor; Full Professor, Faculty of Technical Sciences and Department of Electrical Engineering, Computer Science and Information Technology, University of Maribor 1988-99; Dean, Department of Electrical Engineering, Computer Science and Information Technology, 1997-1999; Professor Emeritus, 2000-. Publications: Numerous articles and papers in scientific journals and conference proceedings; Book chapters and scientific reports. Memberships: member of the Committee for Economy and Technology of the Chamber of Commerce of Slovenia, 1975-80; Electrical Engineering Society of Slovenia, Honorary Member, 2000; Senior Member, IEEE; Member Senate University of Maribor; Member of the Council of Higher Education of the Government of Slovenia; Member of the Committee for Nominations in Higher Education of the Government of Slovenia. Address: University of Maribor, Faculty of Technical Sciences, Department of Electrical Engineering, Computer Science and Information Technology, Smetanova ulica 17, SI-2000 Maribor, Slovenia.

HROCH Miroslav, b. 14 June 1932, Prague, Czech Republic. University Professor in General History. 1 son. Education: MA, 1956; PhD, 1962; Habil, 1968. Appointments: Assistant Professor, 1956; Associate Professor, 1968; Professor, 1989; Director, 1990-91; Seminar of Comparative and General History, 1995-2000. Publications: (in English) Social Preconditions of National Revival, 1985, 2nd edition, 2000; In the National Interest, 2000; (in German, Catalan, Polish and Czech), 29 books and schoolbooks; 120 articles in Czech, English, German, Russian, Catalan, Polish, Greek, Norwegian, Israeli and other scientific journals on Nationalism, National Movements, 17th century, Baltic trade, revolutions. Honour: PhDhc, University Uppsala, 1997; PhDhc, Halle, 2003. Membership: Corresponding member, Finnish Academy. Address: NA Hroude 17, 100 00 Praha 10, Czech Republic.

HSIAO Ling, b. 20 February 1940, Beijing, China. Full Professor of Mathematics. m. Li Zhi-Yao, 1 son. Education: Graduate, Mathematics, Chinese University of Science and Technology, 1963. Appointments: Assistant Professor, 1963-78, Lecturer, 1978-82, Associate Professor, 1982-86, Full Professor, 1986-, Institute of Math Academia; Visiting Professor at various universities in USA or Europe including: Rutgers University, 1984, II University Roma, Italy, 1985, 1986; University Washington, Seattle, Washington, 1987-88; Indiana University, USA, 1988-89; Brown University, USA, 1991, 1994; Pisa University, Italy, 1992, ENSL France, 1993, 1996; SISSA, Italy, 1998. Publications: 2 monographs in Maths and over 95 research articles; Books: The Riemann Problem and Interaction of Waves in Gas Dynamics, Pitman Monographs and Surveys in Pure and Applied Mathematics; 1989; Quasilinear Hyperbolic Systems and Dissipative Mechanisms, World Scientific,1998. Honours: Awards for important research in natural science, presented by Academia Sinica, 1983, 1990; Honor of outstanding expert, Academia Sinica, 1992. Memberships: Chinese Mathematical Society; American Mathematical Society. Address: Academia Sinica, Institute of Mathematics, Beijing 100080, China.

Dictionary of International Biography

HSIAO Sigmund Shih-Lang, b. 10 February 1935, Taiwan. College Professor. m. Jy Hwa Ying, 2 sons. Education: BS, National Taiwan University, 1957; MSc, 1961, PhD, 1964, Tulane University. Appointments: Assistant Professor, Southeastern Louisiana College, 1964-66; Assistant Professor to Professor, University of Arizona, 1966-92; Professor, National Taiwan University, National Chung Cheng University. Publications: 50 articles in professional journals. Honours: Professor Emeritus, University of Arizona; Visiting Professor, Osaka University, Medical College. Memberships: American Psychological Association; Society for Neuroscience; Chinese Psychological Association. Address: Department of Psychology, National Chung Cheng University, Chia-Yi, Taiwan, China.

HSIEH Sung-Tsang, b. 30 September 1957, Tainan, Taiwan. Medicine. m. Whei-Min Lin, 31 January 1984, 1 son, 1 daughter. Education: MD, National Taiwan University, 1983; MPH, Harvard University, 1989; PhD, Johns Hopkins University, 1994. Appointments: Professor of Anatomy and Cell Biology, National Taiwan University, 2000-; Director, Division of Neuromuscular Disease, Department of Neurology, National Taiwan University Hospital, 1995-. Publications: Several articles in professional journals. Honours: Peter Lampert Young Investigator Award, Society for Experimental Neuropathology, 1995. Memberships: Society for Neuroscience; American Academy of Neurolology. Address: National Taiwan University, College of Medicine, Department of Anatomy and Cell Biology, 1 Jen-Ai Road, Sec 1, Taipei 10018, Taiwan.

HSU Chi Cheng, b. 1 August 1939, Pingtung, Taiwan. Retired Teacher; Writer. m. Lin Mi, 1 son, 2 daughters. Education: LLB, Soochow University; Graduate, Educational Institute, Kaohsiung Normal University. Appointments: Teacher; Journalist; Editor; Military Judge. Publications: Poetry Collections: Half-Sky Bird; With the Heart of a Buddha; A Star in the South; My Whereabouts on Both Sides of the Taiwan Strait (Bilingual, Chinese-English); Prose Collections: Excellent Seedling; Random Notes in Green Garden; In the Depths of Green Shadow; The Summer Shadow; Pearls; Experiencing the Path for Ox Carts. Honours: Prize for play writing competition, Da Wu Mt Literature; Excellent Teacher of Taiwan; Honorary Degree, LLTTD, International Poetry Translation and Research Centre. Memberships: Colleague, Large Ocean Poetry Society; Special Editor-in-Chief, Chinese Poetry International Quarterly; Member, Chinese Poetry Society; Member, The Writers Association of ROC. Address: 2F, No 5, Alley 5, Lane 710, Hsing-Fu Rd, Hsin-Chuang, Taipei County, Taiwan, ROC. E-mail: cchwr2o@yahoo.com.tw

HSU Gloria, b. 26 March 1959, Taipei, Taiwan. Piano Teacher. Education: Juilliard Pre-College, 1970-75; Peabody Conservatory, 1978-79; California State Hayward University, 1982-92. Appointments: Piano Teacher. Publications: A Family Reunited by a Concert of Fundraising, Chinese World Journal for Helping Vietnam Refugees, 1979; Rainbow Songs, Harmonization of Mother's Pieces. Honours: Winner, Greatneck Symphony Society, 1972; Winner, California Teacher's Association, 1987. Memberships: Music Teachers of California Association; National (America) Music Teachers Association. Address: 3371 Isherwood Way, Fremont, CA 94536, USA.

HSU Ping-I, b. 17 September 1961, Nan-Tong County, Taiwan. Physician. m. Hui-Chun Chen, 2 sons. Education: MD, Medicine, Taipei Medical University, Taipei, Taiwan, 1986. Appointments: Attending Physician, Kaohsiung Veterans General Hospital, 1994-; Associate Professor, Chia-Nan University of Pharmacy and Science, Tainan, Taiwan, 2001-; Associate Professor, National Defence University, Taipei, Taiwan, 2002-. Publications: Papers

in scientific journals as first author include: Eradication of H. pylori prevents ulcer development in patients with ulcer-like functional dyspepsia, 2001; Risk factors for ulcer development in patients with non-ulcer dyspepsia, 2002. Honours: Research Award, National Science Council, Taiwan, 2000; Best Paper Prize, Chung-Kung Liver Foundation, Tainan, 2001. Membership: Gastroenterological Society of Taiwan. Address: Division of Gastroenterology, Department of Internal Medicine, Kaohsiung Veterans General Hospital, 386, Ta-Chung 1st Road, Kaohsiung, Taiwan, Republic of China. E-mail: williamhsup@yahoo.com.tw

HTANG Aung, b. 4 November 1956, Matupi, Chin State, Burma. Dentist; Dental Researcher. m. Martha, 2 sons, 2 daughters. Education: BDS, 1982; PhD, Operative Dentistry, Nagasaki University, Japan, 1996. Appointments: Private Dental Practitioner, 1983-85; Civil Dental Surgeon, State Hospitals, 1985-1991; State Scholar, Japanese Ministry of Education, 1991-96; Lecturer, Institute of Dental Medicine, Yangon, 1996-; Founder, Matupi Baptist Church, Yangon. Publications: Fatigue Resistance of Composite Restorations, 1995; 6 research papers; 4 review articles; 3 case reports. Memberships: International Association for Dental Research; Myanmar Dental Association. Address: 36/801 Mahuya Street, North Dagon New Town, Yangon (Rangoon), Myanmar.

HTOO Saw Wah, b. 25 February 1943, Panglong, Southern Shan State, Myanmar. Leprologist; Dermatologist (Male); Reconstructive Surgeon. m. Naw Tha Blay, 3 sons. Education: MBBS, Myanmar, 1972; Diploma of Tropical Medicine and Hygiene, England, 1987; Leprosy Education and Reconstructive Surgery, India, 1980-81. Appointments: General Practitioner, 1972-78; Medical Superintendent, 1978-2000; Christian Leprosy and Reconstructive Surgery Hospital, Myanmar. Publication: Leprosy In Myanmar, 1992. Membership: Royal Society of Tropical Medicine and Hygiene (UK), Address: Christian Leprosy and Reconstructive Surgery Hospital, Taung Waing Road, Mawlamyine, Myanmar.

HU Kwong Yuen, b. 25 April 1955, Hong Kong, China. Bank Official. Education: Bachelor of Science, Electrical Engineering, 1979, Master of Science in Electronic Engineering, 1983, Master of Management Studies, 1997, Master of Management, 2001. Appointments: Computer Programmer, 1985-85; Insurance Underwriter, 1986-87; Banking: Bills Department Officer, 1987-89; Officer, Business Research, Credit Department, 1989-91; Officer, Credit Analysis, Credit Department, 1991-2000; Officer, Logistics for 22 Bank Branches, Logistic Department, 2000-. Publications: Antenna Propgration (thesis for MSEE), 1983; Business Classification, 1991; MIS for Local Bank in Hong Kong (thesis for MMS), 1997; Neural Network for Credit Department in Local Bank in Hong Kong (thesis for MM), 2001. Honours: Listed in Who's Who publications and biographical dictionaries. Memberships: Fellow, International Management Centre, England; Hong Kong Management Association; Associate Member, Hong Kong Institute of Engineers; Institute of Electronic and Electrical Engineers, USA. Address: Logistic Department, Chiyu Banking Corporation Ltd, 9/F 78 Des Voeux Road, Central Hong Kong, China.

HUANG Dongzhou, b. 5 November 1949, Ruijin, China. Scientist; Educator, Civil Engineer. m. Yingying Shu, 1 son. Education: BS, Civil Engineering, 1974; MS, Civil Engineering, 1985; PhD, Structural Engineering, 1989. Appointment: Professor, Civil Engineering, Fuzhou University; Senior Research Scientist, Structural Research Center, FDOT, USA; Developed finite element methods for analyzing elastic and inelastic lateral buckling of trussed-arch bridges; Developed methods for analyzing dynamic/impact factors of various types of bridges due to moving vehicles;

Found basic relationships between static and dynamic responses as well as between impact factor and lateral distribution factor; Developed a practical method for determining lateral load distribution factors of arch and beam bridges, a load capacity rating method of bridges through field test and a shear reinforcement design method for prestressed concrete beam anchorage zones; Developed a design method of end zone reinforcement for precast-prestressed concrete beams and a bridge load rating method through field test. Publications: Over 50 papers in professional journals, 2 books. Honour: 1st Prize, Best Publications. Memberships: ASCE; New York Academy of Sciences; American Association for the Advancement of Science. Address: 5416 Moores Mill Road, Tallahassee, FL 32309, USA

HUANG Hua, b. 28 May 1922, JiangXi Province, China. Director; Expert; Professor. 1 daughter. Education: Medical Doctor, Bachelor, Shanghai Medical College, 1948; Higher School Class of Physical Therapy, Health Ministry of China, 1957-58. Appointments: Director, Department of Physical Therapy, Shanghai No 6 People's Hospital, 1965-90; Director, Research Laboratory of Respiratory Diseases, 1978-90; Expert, Department of Physical Therapy, 1984-90; Director, Health Centre of TCM and Western Medicine of Pacific Rim Institute for Development and Education (PRIDE), 1991-2003. Publications: The Application of Physical Therapy on the First Case of Replantation of Completely Severed Forearm, 1964; Clinical Application of Chinese QiGong Therapy and its Mechanism, issued at the Symposium of the Fifth International Congress of Chinese Medicine and the First International Congress of QiGong, 1990. Honours: Twice Award as National Advanced Worker, 1959, 1979; Award for Paper as an Achievement of Medical Science, Tenth Anniversary of China, 1949. Memberships: Chief, Shanghai Branch of QiGong Research Association of TCM and Western Medicine, 1979-89; Chairman, Society of Physical Therapy, Shanghai Branch of the CMA, 1961-89; Council Member, Shanghai Branch of the CMA, 1961-84. Address: 7720-B El Camino Real, Ste 511, Carlsbad, CA 92009, USA. E-mail: pride9@aol.com Website: www.pridengo.org

HUANG Lie-de, b. 26 January 1922, Quan Zhou City, Fujian, China. Professor, Tongji University, Shanghai. m. Zeng Shu-Ying, 3 sons. Education: Department of Maths Physics, Fudan University, Shanghai, China, 1951. Appointment: Professor awarded by Tongji University, Shanghai, China. Publications: Many papers and articles in scientific journals include: The Solvability for Generalized Boltzmann Equation; Manned Techniques and Space Flight-Mathematical Foundation of Astronautical Dynamic Analysis; Some Aspects of Astronautical Mathematics; Some Mathematical Models for Space Science and Technology; Minimised Active Control for Flexible Space Structure; The Methods of Entrainment and Migration Controls for Chaotic Behaviour of Large (Flexible) Space Structures; Modified RBF Neural Networks Control for the Non-linear Flight of Chaotic Motion; The Effects of Boltzmann Equation for the Conjecture of the Existence of Antimatter; The Mathematical Prediction for the Existence of Dark Matter; Probe into the Nature of Dark Energy; The Mathematical Existence of Tachyons; The Mathematical Analysis and Control for AIDS Infection; An Explanation for Hawking's Black Hole of Low Mass (The Existence of Grey Hole); An Explanation for Nash Equilibrium of Non-Cooperative Game (The Reality of Semi-Cooperative Game); The Kohn-Sham Equation Method for the Simulation Calculation of Nanostructured Materials; Extension of Modern Factor Theory of Value (An Extend Formula of the New Classical Product Function). Honours: World Mathematician, 1990; Chinese Scientific Celebrity, 1992; Centuries' World Celebrity, 1997; Who's Who in the World, 1997; Outstanding Service to the Teaching Profession and Make Researches on Astronautical Mathematics, 1997; Chinese Science and Inventor, 1997; Chinese

Excellent Scientists, 1997; Outstanding Achievements to Chinese Culture, 1997; Distinguished Leadership, 1998; Outstanding Scientists, 1998; Personal Citation, 1998; Medal of Chinese Heroes, 1999; World Scientific Expert, 2000; Medal of Honor, 2000; Medal of China Outstanding Persons, 2000. Memberships: CSIAM Tsinghau University. Address: Department of Applied Mathematics, Tong Ji University, Shanghai 200092, China.

HUANG Shengyang, b. 27 August 1963, Wuhan, China. President; Chief Executive Officer. m. Yang Gu, 1 son, 1 daughter. Education: BS, Huazhong University of Science and Technology, China, 1983; MEng, 1986, Dr Eng, 1989, Dailan University of Technology, China. Appointments: Lecturer, Dailan University of Technology, 1990-91; Foreign Research Scientist, Institute of Space and Astronautics Science, Japan, 1991-94; Research Fellow, Toyota Technical Institute, Nagoya, Japan, 1994-97; Senior Engineer, Nippon Unisoft Corporation, Japan, 1997-99; Co-founder, President, Chief Executive Officer, Tricis Corporation, Japan, 2000-01; Chief Executive Officer, 2001, President, Chief Executive Officer, 2002-, PtoPA Inc, Japan. Memberships: IEEE. Address: PtoPA Inc, Aruze Takanawa Bldg, 8F 3-22-9 Takanawa, Minato-ku, Tokyo, Japan 108-0074. Website: http://www.ptopa.com

HUBEL David Hunter, b. 27 February 1926, Ontario, Canada. Neurophysiologist. m. S Ruth Izzard, 1953, 3 sons. Education: Graduated, Medicine, McGill University, Montreal, Canada. Appointments: Professor of Neurophysiology, Harvard Medical School, 1965-67; George Packer Berry Professor of Physiology and Chairman, Department of Physiology, 1967-68; George Packer Berry Professor of Neurobiology, 1968-92; John Franklin Enders University Professor, 1982-; George Eastman Professor, University of Oxford, 1991-92; First Annual George A Miller Lecture, Cognitive Neuroscience Society, 1995; Worked on the physiology of vision and the way in which the brain processes visual information. Publications: Eye, Brain and Vision, 1987; Articles in scientific journals. Honours: Lewis S Rosenstiel Award for Basic Medical Research, 1972; Friedenwald Award, 1975; Karl Spencer Lashley Prize, 1977; Louisa Gross Horwitz Prize, 1978; Dickson Prize in Medicine, 1979; Society of Scholars, Johns Hopkins University, 1980; Ledlie Prize, 1980; Joint Winner, Nobel Prize for Physiology or Medicine, 1981; New England Ophthalmological Society Award, 1983; Paul Kayser International Award of Merit in Retina Research, 1989; City of Medicine Award, 1990; Gerald Award, 1993; Charles F Prentice Medal, 1993; Helen Keller Prize, 1995. Memberships: NAS; Leopoldina Academy, Board of Syndics, Harvard University Press; Foreign Member, Royal Society, London; Senior Fellow, Harvard Society of Fellows; Fellow, American Academy of Arts and Sciences. Address: Department of Neurobiology, Harvard Medical School, 220 Longwood Avenue, Boston, MA 02115, USA.

HUCKNALL Mick, 8 June 1960, Manchester, England. Singer; Songwriter. Career: Formed early band, Frantic Elevators, 1979; Formed Simply Red, essentially a solo career with changing band members; Numerous hit singles, television appearances; Numerous tours and festival dates worldwide; Founder, Blood and Fire label, dedicated to vintage reggae tracks. Recordings: Singles: Money's Too Tight to Mention; Come To My Aid; Holding Back the Years; Jericho; Open Up The Red Box; Ev'ry Time We Say Goodbye; The Right Thing; Infidelity; Maybe Some Day; Ev'ry Time We say Goodbye; I Won't Feel Bad; It's Only Love; If You Don't Know Me By Now; A New Flame; You've Got It; Something Got Me Started; Stars; For Your Babies; Thrill Me; Your Mirror; Fairground; Remembering The First Time; Never Never Love; We're In This Together; Angel; Nightnurse; Say You Love Me; The Air That I Breathe; Ghetto Girl; Ain't That a Lot of Love;

Your Eyes; Sunrise; Albums: Picture Book, 1985; Early Years, 1987; Men and Women, 1987; A New Flame, 1989; Stars, 1991; 12"ers, 1995; Life, 1995; Fairground, 1995; Greatest Hits, 1996; Blue, 1998; Love and the Russian Winter, 1999; It's Only Love (greatest hits), 2000; Home, 2003. Address: PO Box 20197, London, W10 6YQ, England.

HUDDAR Subbarao Annappa, b. 11 July 1925, Mugabasau. Retired Primary School Teacher. m. Smt Muttammas, 3 sons, 4 + 1 daughters. Education: Mulk: Examination passed, 1944; TCH passed, 1949. Appointments: Primary schoolteacher appointment, 1945-. Memberships: Karnataka State Freedom Fighters Association, Working Committe Member. Address: Post Mugabasav, Tal Bailhongal District Belgaum, India.

HUDSON Liam, b. 20 July 1933, London, England. Psychologist; Writer. m. Bernadine Jacot de Boinod, 2 July 1965, 3 sons, 1 daughter. Education: MA, Exeter College, 1957; PhD, Cambridge University, 1961. Publications: Contrary Imaginations, 1966; Frames of Mind, 1968; The Ecology of Human Intelligence, 1970; The Cult of the Fact, 1972; Human Beings, 1975; The Nympholepts, 1978; Bodies of Knowledge, 1982; Night Life, 1985; The Way Men Think, 1991; Intimate Relations, 1995. Contributions to: Times Literary Supplement. Honour: Tanner Lectures, Yale University, 1997. Address: Flat 6, 42 Upper Brook Street, London, W1K 7QP, England.

HUETING Roefie, b. 16 December 1929, The Hague, Netherlands. Environmental Economist. m. Erna Jans Postuma, 2 daughters. Education: Doctorandus, University of Amsterdam, 1959; Dr cum laude, University of Groningen, 1974. Appointments: Public Accountant, 1959-62; Labour Market Researcher, 1962-68; Head, Department of Environmental Statistics, Stats-Netherlands, 1969-94; Advisor, 1995-2000; Advisor, Foundation Sustainable National Income Research, 2001-. Publications: What is Nature Worth to Us, 1970; New Scarcity and Economic Growth, 1980; Methodology for the Calculation of Sustainable National Income, 1992; Economic Growth and Valuation of the Environment, 2001. Honours: Decorated Officer in the Orde van Oranje Nassau, 1991; Global 500 Award, UN, 1994. Address: Roelofsstraat 6, 2596 VN, The Hague, Netherlands.

HUGHES Barry Peter, b. 29 August 1932, Wolverhampton, England. Professor. m. Pamela Anne Barker, 1 son, 2 daughters. Education: BSc honours, 1953, PhD, 1956, Civil Engineering, University of Birmingham. Appointments: Assistant Civil Engineer, Concrete Engineer, Berkeley Power Station, 1956-59; Civil Engineer, Planning Engineer, John Laing Construction Ltd, 1959-62; Lecturer, 1962-68, Senior Lecturer, 1968-73, Professor of Civil Engineering, 1974-95, Emeritus Professor, 1995-, University of Birmingham; Private Consulting, Concrete and Concrete Structures, 1989-; Visiting Professor, University of Coventry, 1999-. Publications: Numerous research and technical papers on concrete and concrete structures; 2 books. Honours: Reader in Concrete Technology, 1971, DSc, 1972, DEng, 1990, Emeritus Professor, 1995, University of Birmingham. Memberships: Institution of Civil Engineers; Institution of Structural Engineers; Concrete Society. Address: Long Barn, 8 Parkfields, Arden Drive, Dorridge, Solihull, West Midlands, B93 8LL, England. E-mail: bphughes@onetel.net.uk

HUGHES Gwyneth, b. 10 May 1929, Berkeley, California, USA. Poet; Playwright; Short Story Writer. m. Henri Lasry, 13 October 1951, 2 sons, 1 daughter. Education: BA, University of California, Berkeley, 1949. Publications: A poetry collection, Augmented Seventh; A collection of plays in verse, Escapements; 3 short story collections: After Gladys Adams, Henry's Navy Blue Hair, Within

Heart Range. Memberships: The Society of Authors (GB); Dramatists Guild (USA). Address: c/o Lasry, 106 Boulevard Diderot, 75012 Paris, France.

HUGHES Henry Richard, b. 4 July 1926, London, England. Architect. m. Anne Hill, 1 son, 2 daughters. Education: Kenton College, Nairobi, Kenya, 1938-40; Hilton College, Natal, South Africa, 1940-44; Architectural Association School of Architecture, London, 1947-53. Appointments: Kenya Regiment, attached to Royal Engineers, East Africa, 1944-46; Surveyor, African Land Settlement Board, Kenya, 1946-47; Assistant Architect, Hartford, Connecticut, USA, 1953-55; Assistant Architect, Nairobi, Kenya, 1955-57; Principal in private architectural practice, Nairobi, Kenya, 1957-86; Led Environment Liaison Centre delegation to UN Habitat Conference, Vancouver, Canada, 1976; led Environment Liaison Centre delegation to UNESCO/UNEP Conference, Tbilisi, USSR, 1977; Consultant to UN Environment Program and UN Centre for Human Settlements, Nairobi, 1978-79; Guide at Tate Gallery (now Tate Britain and Tate Modern), London, 1987-; Script Writer on art and architecture for the blind at Living Paintings Trust, 1990-; NADFAS Lecturer on art and architecture, 1995-. Publications: Books: The Habitat Handbook (with Graham Searle), 1980; In the Frame, 1989; CAPRICORN – David Stirling's Second African Campaign, 2003; Articles in professional journals and newspapers; Exhibitions: Overseas League and Imperial Institute, London, 1953; East African Institute of Architects, Nairobi, 1963; Commonwealth Arts Festival, Cardiff, 1965; German Africa Society, Bonn and Berlin, 1966; Royal Institute of British Architects: Architecture Overseas, London, 1984; Architecture by Richard Hughes 1957-86, organised by University of Nairobi Architecture Department, Gallery Watatu, Nairobi, 1986; Home, Architecture Tomorrow, RIBA, London and Bristol, 1996-. Honour: Fellow, Royal Institute of British Architects, 1969. Memberships: Member of Council, 1956-57, East African Institute of Architects; Chairman, 1958-61, Kenya Branch, Capricorn Africa Society; Governor, 1958-61, Hospital Hill School, Nairobi; Vice-President, 1962-75, Kenya Arts Society; Chairman, 1965-73, East African Institute of Architects Board of Architectural Education; Governor, 1972-74, Kenya Polytechnic; Chairman, 1972-75, Kenya Museum Society; Chairman, 1974-76, Environment Liaison Centre, Nairobi; Chairman, 1976-78, Lamu Society, Kenya; Executive Committee 1987-92, Friends of the Elderly, London; Chairman, Chiswick Quay Resident Limited, 1988-90; Board Member, 1988-98, Zebra Housing Association, London; Trustee, 1988-, Zebra Trust, London. Address: 47 Chiswick Quay, London W4 3UR, England. E-mail: richard@cquay.f9.co.uk

HUGHES John W, b. 18 February 1950, Detroit, Michigan, USA. Film Producer; Screenplay Writer; Director. m. Nancy Ludwig, 2 sons. Education: University AZ. Appointments: Copywriter, Creative Director, Leo Burnett Co; Editor, National Lampoon Magazine; Founder, President, Hughes Entertainment, 1985-. Creative Works: Films: National Lampoon's Class Reunion, 1982; National Lampoons Vacation, 1983; Mr Mon, 1983; Nate and Hayes, 1983; Sixteen Candles, 1984; National Lampoons European Vacation, 1985; Weird Science, 1985; The Breakfast Club, 1985; Ferris Bueller's Day Off, 1986; Pretty in Pink, 1986; Some Kind of Wonderful, 1987; Planes, Trains and Automobiles, 1987; The Great Outdoors, 1988; She's Having a Baby, 1988; National Lampoons Christmas Vacation, 1989; Uncle Buck, 1989; Home Alone, 1990; Career Opportunities, 1990; Dutch, 1991; Curly Sue, 1991; Only the Lonely, 1991; Beethoven, 1992; Home Alone 2: Lost in New York, 1992; Dennis the Menace, 1993; Baby's Day Out, 1993; Miracle on 34th Street, 1994; 101 Dalmations, 1996; Reach the Rock, 1998; New port South, 1999; 102 Dalmations, 2000; Just Visiting, 2001. Honours include: Commitment to

Dictionary of International Biography

Chicago Award, 1990; NATO/Sho West Producer of the Year, 1990. Address: c/o Jacob Bloom, Bloom & Dekom, 150 South Rodeo Drive, Beverly Hills, CA 90212, USA.

HUGHES Stephen Ormsby, b. 21 January 1924, Crosby, Lancashire, England. Journalist. m. M-A Raymonde Nietin, 1 son, 1 daughter. Education: St Mary's College, Crosby, England. Appointments: Pilot RAF 280 Squadron Coastal Command; Editor Sunday Ghibli, Tripoli, Libya, 1950; Reporter, Reuters, Paris, 1951-52; Editor, Atlantic Courier, Casablanca, 1952; Correspondent, Associated Press in Morocco, 1952-61; Chief Bureau, Reuters, Rabat, Morocco, 1961-94. Publications: Tight Lines and Dragonflies, 1972; La Boite de Sental (poems, translations); Morocco under King Hassan II, 2000; Antic Art (comedy play); Blue Blobbers Beware (in preparation). Honours: Atlantic Star, 1944; Commander, Ouissam Alaouite, Morocco, 1994. Memberships: Psdt Moroccan Foreign Press Association; International Union French Press; International Foreign Correspondents Association. Address: 17 Rue de Baghdad, Rabat 10000, Morocco.

HUGHES Timothy John, b. 12 June 1976, Northumberland, England. Teacher. Education: BSc (Hons), Applied Chemistry, 1998-92, PhD, Chemical Physics, 1992-98, PGCE, distinction, Secondary Science, 1998-99, University of Northumbria at Newcastle. Appointments: Analyst in Quality Control and Drug Stability, G D Searle & Co, Morpeth, Northumberland (Industrial placement year for BSc Applied Chemistry), 1990-91; Undergraduate Teaching, University of Northumbria at Newcastle, 1992-95; Home Tutor, Newcastle upon Tyne, 1996-97; Temporary Research Scientist, Sanofi (Alnwick Research Centre), Northumberland; Teacher of Chemistry, Sacred Heart School, Newcastle upon Tyne, 1999-2001; Teacher of Chemistry/Physics, The King Edward VI School, Morpeth, Northumberland, 2001-. Memberships: The Royal Society of Chemistry, 1996; The Institute of Physics, 1999; The Association of Science Education, 1998. Address: 2 Blakelaw Court, Alnwick, Northumberland, NE66 1BY, England. E-mail: Thughes@fenklestreet.fsnet.co.uk

HUGO Graeme John, b. 5 December 1946, Adelaide, SA, Australia. Professor of Geography. 1 daughter. Education: BA (Honours), Adelaide University, 1967; MA, Flinders University, 1971; PhD, ANU, 1975. Appointments: Tutor in Geography, Flinders University, 1968-71; Research Scholar, ANU, 1972-75; Lecturer in Geography, 1975-80, Senior Lecturer, 1980-85, Reader, 1985-91, Flinders University; Professor of Department of Geographical and Environmental Studies, University of Adelaide, South Australia, 1992-; Director, The National Centre for Social Applications of GIS, University of Adelaide, 1995-; Fellow, ARC Federation, 2002-07. Publications: Books include: Atlas of the Australian People, Volumes I-VIII, 1989-92; (co-author) Worlds in Motion: Understanding International Migration at the End of the Millenium, 1998; 103 refereed journal articles; 170 book chapters; Theses, conference papers, book reviews. Honours: Elected Fellow, Academy of Social Sciences, Australia, 1987; AISIST Award, Australian Urban and Information Systems Association, for contribution to GIS, 1994; Stephen Cole the Elder Prize for outstanding scholarship, University of Adelaide, 1995; Invited to visit Taiwan via Honorable Visitor Program of National Science Council of the Republic of China, 1998; Alison Furbank Communications Award, Bureau of Rural Sciences for Country Matters: Social Atlas of Rural and Regional Australia, 2000; Rothwell Prize for article, Telecommunications Journal of Australia; Geography Teachers Association of SA Award, 2002; 1.125 million ARC Federation Fellowship over 5 years for research project, 2002. Memberships: Institution of Australian Geographers; Australian Population Association; International Union for the

Scientific Study of the Population; NSW Geographical Society; Population Association of America; Royal Geographical Society of A/Asia (SA Branch); Asian Studies Association of Australia; Regional Science Association; Australian Association of Gerontology. Address: Department of Geographical and Environmental Studies, University of Adelaide, SA 5005, Australia.

HUGUENIN Nancy Hoffman, b. 12 May 1947, Franklin, Pennsylvania, USA. Behavioral Psychologist. m. Robert Louis Huguenin. Education: BS, Psychology, Pittsburgh University, 1969; MA, Psychology, 1971, PhD, 1978, Boston University, Massachusetts, USA. Appointments include: Director, Programmed Instruction Laboratory, Graduate School, 1980-85, Staff Associate, University Computing Center, 1980-81, Adjunct Assistant Professor, Psychology, 1980-87, University of Massachusetts, Amherst; Behavioural Consultant, institutions including: Department of Psychology, Monson Developmental Center, Palmer, Massachusetts, 1981-85; Bi County Collaborative, N Attleboro, Massachusetts, 1993-98; Behavioral Consultant, Walpole Publics Schools, Walpole, Massuchusetts, 1995; Greater Waltham Association of Retarded Citizens, Waltham, Massachusetts, 1995-97; Behavioral Consultant, Horace Mann Educational Associates Inc, Littleton, Massachusetts, 1996; Assabet Valley Collaborative, 1996, 1999; Charms Collaborative, Randolph, Boylston Public Schools, Boylston, Massachusetts, 1999-2000; President, Behavior Analysis and Technology Inc, Groton, Massachusetts, 1993-; Behavioral In-Service Trainer, Work, Inc, N Quincy, Massachusetts, 1997, 1999-2000; Behavioural Consultant, Institute for Professional Practice, Lunenburg, Massachusetts, USA, 1999-2000; Behavioural In-Science Trainer, Kelleher Centre, Arlington, MA, 1999; Educational Consultant, Canton, MA, 2001; Workshop Presenter, Parents of Tots, Wakefield, MA, 2001; Behavioural Consultant, Dracut, MA, 2001-2001; Behavioural In-Service Trainer, The Perkins School, Clinton, MA, 2002. Publications: Author or co-author, papers to professional journals and conference proceedings. Honours: Phi Beta Kappa, Quax, Psi Chi, University of Pittsburgh, 1969. Memberships: American Association on Mental Retardation; Association for Behavior Analysis; Association for Advancement of Behavior Therapy; American Association for the Advancement of Science; American Academy of Mental Retardation; American Psychological Association; Eastern Psychological Association. Address: Behavior Analysis & Technology Inc, 61 Long Hill Road, PO Box 327, Groton, MA 01450-0327, USA. Website: www.ba-and-t.com

HUME John, b. 18 January 1937, Londonderry, Northern Ireland. Politician. m. Patricia Hone, 1960, 2 sons, 3 daughters. Education: St Colomb's College, Londonderry; St Patrick's College, Maynooth; National University of Ireland. Appointments: Research Fellow, Trinity College; Associate Fellow, Centre for International Affairs, Harvard; Founder Member, Credit Union, Northern Ireland, President, 1964-68; Non-Violent Civil Rights Leader, 1968-69; Representative, Londonderry, Northern Ireland Parliament, 1969-72, in Northern Ireland Assembly, 1972-73; Minister of Commerce, Powersharing Executive, 1974; Representative, Londonderry in Northern Ireland Convention, 1975-76; Elected to European Parliament, 1979-; Leader, Social Democratic and Labour Party (SDLP), 1979-; Member, Northern Ireland Assembly, 1982-86; MP for Foyle, 1983-; Member for Foyle Northern Ireland Assembly, 1998- (Assembly suspended 2002). Publications: Politics, Peace and Reconciliation in Ireland. Honours include: Nobel Peace Prize (shared), 1998; Martin Luther King Award, 1999; Gandhi Peace Prize, 2002; Numerous honorary doctorates. Address: 5 Bayview Terrace, Derry BT48 7EE, Northern Ireland.

Dictionary of International Biography

HUMPHREY Mary Sandra McLeod, b. 6 August 1936, Salt Lake City, Utah, USA. Clinical Psychologist; Author. m. Brian Neil Humphrey, 1 son, 2 daughters. Education: BA, Differential Psychology, 1958, MA, Counseling Psychology, 1963, University of Minnesota. Counseling Psychologist, Minneapolis Veterans Administration Hospital, 1960; Clinical Psychologist, Anoka Metro Regional Treatment Center, 1961-92. Publications: Children's Books: A Dog Named Sleet, 1984; If You Had to Choose, What Would You Do?, 1995; It's Up to You...What Do You Do?, 1999; Keepin' it Real: A Young Teen Talks with God, 2003; MORE - If You Had to Choose What Would You Do?, 2003; Articles and stories published in: My Friend; Pockets; Touch Magazine; Once Upon a Time; Values in Action! Honours: Certifications of Commendation, State of Minnesota and National Police Officers Association of America; Award for Exemplary Leadership in Ethics Education, National Character Education Center; Listed in several biographical dictionaries. Membership: Society of Children's Bookwriters and Illustrators. Address: 19 Westwood Road, Minnetonka, MN 55305-1587, USA. E-mail: sandra305@aol.com.

HUMPHREYS Emyr Owen, b. 15 April 1919, Clwyd, Wales. Author. m. Elinor Myfanwy, 1946, 3 sons, 1 daughter. Education: University College, Aberystwyth; University College, Bangor. Publications: The Little Kingdom, 1946; The Voice of a Stranger, 1949; A Change of Heart, 1951; Hear and Forgive, 1952; A Man's Estate, 1955; The Italian Wife, 1957; A Toy Epic, 1958; The Gift, 1963; Outside the House of Baal, 1965; Natives, 1968; Ancestor Worship, 1970; National Winner, 1971; Flesh and Blood, 1974; Landscapes, 1976; The Best of Friends, 1978; The Kingdom of Bran, 1979; The Anchor Tree, 1980; Pwyll a Riannon, 1980; Miscellany Two, 1981; The Taliesin Tradition, 1983; Salt of the Earth, 1985; An Absolute Hero, 1986; Open Secrets, 1988; The Triple Net, 1988; Bonds of Attachment, 1990; Outside Time, 1991; Unconditional Surrender, 1996; The Gift of a Daughter, 1998; Collected Poems, 1999; Dal Pen Rheswm, 1999; Ghosts and Strangers, 2000; Conversations and Reflections, 2002; Old People are a Problem, 2003. Honours: Somerset Maugham Award, 1953; Hawthornden Prize, 1959; Society of Authors Travel Award, 1978; Welsh Arts Council Prize, 1983; Honorary DLitt, University of Wales, 1990; Welsh Book of the Year, 1992, 1999; Honorary Professor of English, University College of North Wales, Bangor. Membership: Fellow, The Royal Society of Literature, 1991; Cymmrodorion Medal, 2003. Address: Llinon, Penyberth, Llanfairpwll, Ynys Môn, Gwynedd LL61 5YT, Wales.

HUMPHRIES (John) Barry, b. 17 February 1934, Australia. Actor; Writer. m. (1) Rosalind Tong, 1959, 2 daughters, (2) Diane Millstead, 2 sons, (3) Lizzie Spender, 1990. Education: University of Melbourne. Appointments: Various one-man shows; film appearances. Publications: Bizarre I, 1965; Innocent Australian Verse, 1968; Wonderful World of Barry McKenzie, 1968; Bazza Pulls It Off, 1972; Adventures of Barry McKenzie, 1973; Bazza Holds His Own, 1974; Dame Edna's Coffee Table Book, 1976; Bazza Comes Into His Own, 1978; Les Patterson's Australia, 1979; Barry Humphries' Treasury of Australian Kitsch, 1980; Dame Edna's Bedside Companion, 1982; Les Patterson: The Traveller's Tool, 1985; Dame Edna: My Gorgeous Life, 1989; Women in the Background, 1996. Honour: Society of West End Managements Award, 1979. Memberships: President, Frans de Boewer Society, Belgium; Vice President, Betjeman Society, 2001-. Address: c/o The John Reid Organisation, Singes House, 32 Galena Road, London W6 0LT, England.

HUMPHRY Derek John, b. 29 April 1930, Bath, England. Journalist; Author; Broadcaster. Appointments: Messenger Boy, Yorkshire Post, London, 1945-46; Cub Reporter, Evening World, Bristol, 1946-51; Junior Reporter, Evening News, Manchester,

1951-55; Reporter, Daily Mail, 1955-61; Deputy Editor, The Luton News, 1961-63; Editor, Havering Recorder, 1963-67; Hemlock Quarterly, 1983-92, Euthanasia Review, 1986-88, World Right to Die Newsletter, 1992-94; Home Affairs Correspondent, The Sunday Times, 1966-78; Special Writer, Los Angeles Times, 1978-79. Publications: Because They're Black, 1971; Police Power and Black People, 1972; Passports and Politics, 1974; The Cricket Conspiracy, 1976; False Messiah, 1977; Jean's Way, 1978; Let Me Die Before I Wake, 1982; The Right to Die!: Understanding Euthanasia, 1986; Final Exit, 1991; Dying with Dignity, 1992; Lawful Exit, 1993; Freedom to Die, 1998; The Good Euthanasia Guide, 2004. Contributions to: New Statesman; Independent, London; USA Today. Honours: Martin Luther King Memorial Prize, UK, 1972; The Saba Medal for contribution to the World Right-to-Die Movement, 2000. Address: 24829 Norris Lane, Junction City, OR 97448-9559, USA.

HUMPHRYS John, b. 17 August 1943. Broadcaster. Divorced, 1 son, 1 daughter. Appointments: Washington Correspondent, BBC TV, 1971-77, Southern Africa Correspondent, 1977-80, Diplomatic Correspondent, 1981; Presenter, BBC Nine o'Clock News, 1981-87; Presenter, BBC Radio 4 Today Programme, 1987-, On the Record, BBC TV, 1993-, John Humphrys Interview Radio 4, 1995-. Publication: Devil's Advocate, 1999. Honours: Fellow, Cardiff University, 1998; Honorary DLitt, Dundee, 1996; Honorary MA, University of Wales, 1998; Honorary LLD, St Andrews, 1999. Address: BBC News Centre, Wood Lane, London W12, England.

HUNT Anthony James, b. 22 June 1932, London, England. Structural Engineer. m. (1) Patricia Daniels, 1957, dissolved, 1972, remarried, 1975, dissolved, 1982, 1 son, 1 daughter, (3) Diana Joyce Collett. Education: CEng, Westminster Technical College, 1961; FIStructE, 1973. Appointments: Articled via Founders' Co to J L Wheeler Consulting Engineer, 1948-51; F J Samuely and Partners, Consulting Engineers, 1951-59; Morton Lupton, Architects, 1960-62; Founded Anthony Hunt Associates, Consulting Engineers, 1962, Stood down as Chairman of Anthony Hunt Associates, became a consultant to them in 2002; Acquired by YRM plc, Building Design Consultants, 1988; Became separate limited company, 1997; Major buildings: Sainsbury Centre for the Visual Arts, Norwich, 1978, 1993; Willis Faber Dumas HQ, Ipswich, 1975; Inmos Micro Electronics Factory, Gwent, 1982; Schlumberger Cambridge Research, 1985; Waterloo International Terminal, 1993; Law Faculty, Cambridge, 1995; National Botanic Garden, Wales, 1998; New Museum of Scotland, Edinburgh, 1998; Lloyd's Register of Shipping, London, 2000; Eden Project, Cornwall, 2001; Willis Visiting Professor of Architecture, Sheffield University, 1994-. Publications: Tony Hunt's Structures Notebook, 1997; Tony Hunt's Sketchbook, 1999. Honours: FRSA, 1989; Honorary FRIBA, 1989; Gold Medallist, IStructE, 1995; Honorary DLitt, Sheffield, 1999; Graham Professor of Architecture, Graduate School of Fine Arts, University of Pennsylvania, 2002. Address: Stancombe Farm, Bisley with Lippiatt, Stroud, Gloucestershire, GL6 7NQ, England. E-mail: tony@huntprojects.freeserve.co.uk

HUNT David Roderic Notley, b. 22 June 1947, Brighton, England. Barrister. m. Alison Connell Jelf, 2 sons. Education: MA Honours, Law, Trinity College, Cambridge, 1968; Inns of Court School of Law, 1968-69. Appointments: Called to the Bar, Gray's Inn, 1969; Queen's Counsel, 1987; Recorder, 1991; Master of the Bench of Gray's Inn, 1995. Publications: Article in the Solicitor's Journal. Address: Blackstone Chambers, Blackstone House, Temple, London EC4Y 9BW, England. E-mail: davidhunt@blackstonechambers.com

HUNT Georgina, b. 15 June 1922, Reading, England. Artist. 1 son, 1 daughter. Education: DFA (Lond.), Slade School of Fine Art (William Coldstream); Hunter College, New York. Career:

Exhibited widely in the UK and internationally, including: Camden Arts Centre, 1982; Osaka International Triennale '93; The Barbican, 1998; Winchester Cathedral, 1999; Florence International Biennale '97 and '99; The Hunting Prize, 1999-2003; The London Group, 1992-2004; Flowers East/Central, 2001-2004. Publications: Works in publications including: Guy Brett, Solo Exhibition Catalogue, Camden Arts Centre, London, 1982; Judith Collins and Frances Spalding, 20th Century Painters & Sculptors, 1991; Mike Williams, Modern Painters, Winter 1994; David Buckman, The Dictionary of Artists in Britain since 1945, 1998; Who's Who in Art, 2000, 2002, 2004; The London Group, edited by Jane Humphrey, 2003. Honours: Major Award, Greater London Arts Association, 1976; 21st Century Association Prize, Osaka International Triennale, 1993; Lorenzo il Magnifico Prize for Lifetime Achievement, Florence International Biennale, 1999; Work in UK and international collections. Memberships: The London Group; Chelsea Arts Club, UCL Alumni Association. Address: 2 Camden Studios, Camden Street, London NW1 0LG, England. Website: www.thelondongroup.com

HUNT Helen, b. 15 June 1963, Los Angeles, USA. Actress. Creative Works: Stage appearances include: Been Taken; Our Town; The Taming of the Shrew; Methusalem; Films include: Rollercoaster; Girls Just Want to Have Fun; Peggy Sue Got Married; Project X; Miles From Hume; Trancers; Stealing Home; Next of Kin; The Waterdance; Only You; Bob Roberts; Mr Saturday Night; Kiss of Death; Twister; As Good As It Gets; Twelfth Night; Pay It Forward, 2000; Dr T and the Women, 2000; Cast Away, 2000; What Women Want, 2000; The Curse of the Jade Scorpion, 2001; TV includes: Swiss Family Robinson; Mad About You. Honours include: Emmy Award, 1996, 1997; Golden Globe Award, 1997; Academy Award, Best Actress, 1998. Address: c/o Connie Tavel, 9171 Wilshire Boulevard, Beverly Hills, CA 90210, USA.

HUNTER Alan James Herbert, b. 25 June 1922, Hoveton St John, Norwich, England. Author. m. Adelaide Elizabeth Cecily Cubitt, 6 March 1944, 1 daughter. Education: Royal Air Force, 1940-46. Appointments: Crime Reviewer, Eastern Daily Press, 1955-71. Publications: The Norwich Poems, 1945; Gently Go Man, 1961; Vivienne: Gently Where She Lay, 1972; The Honfleur Decision, 1980; Gabrielles Way, 1981; The Unhung Man, 1984; Traitors End, 1988; Bomber's Moon, 1994; Jackpot!, 1995; The Love of Gods, 1997; Over Here, 1998. Author of 46 crime novels featuring Chief Superintendent George Gently to 1999. Contributions to: Magazines and journals. Memberships: Society of Authors; Crime Writers Association; Authors Licensing and Collecting Society. Address: 3 St Laurence Avenue, Brundall, Norwich NR13 5QH, England.

HUNTER Holly, b. 20 March 1958, Atlanta, Georgia, USA. Actress. m. J Kaminski, divorced. Education: Career: Theatre includes: on Broadway: Crimes of the Heart; The Wake of Jamey Foster; The Miss Firecracker Contest; Other Stage Appearances include: The Person I Once Was; Battery (All New York); A Lie of the Mind (Los Angeles); Regional work; Films include: Broadcast News, 187; Raising Arizona, 1987; Once Around, 1990; The Piano and The Firm, 1993; Copycat, 1995; Crash, 1996; Living Out Loud, 1998; Time Code, 2000; O Brother Where Art Thou? 2000; When Billie Beat Bobby, 2001; Festival in Cannes, 2001; Goodbye Hello, 2002; Levity, 2003; Thirteen, 2003. Honours: 2 for TV appearances: Best Actress Emmy for Roe vs Wade, 1989; Best Actress Award, American TV Awards, 1993; Best Actress Award, Cannes Film Festival Award, 1993; Academy Award, 1994. Memberships: Director, California Abortion Rights Action League. Address: 41 Stutter Street, #1649, San Francisco, CA 94104, USA.

HURD Douglas (Richard) (Hurd of Westwell), b. 8 March 1930, Marlborough, England. Politician; Diplomat; Writer. m. (1) Tatiana Elizabeth Michelle, 1960, divorced, 3 sons, (2) Judy Smart, 1982, 1 son, 1 daughter. Education: Trinity College, Cambridge. Appointments: HM Diplomatic Service, 1952-66; Joined Conservative Research Department, 1966, Head, Foreign Affairs Section, 1968; Private Secretary to the Leader of the Opposition, 1968-70; Political Secretary to the Prime Minister, 1970-74; Member of Parliament, Conservative Party, Mid-Oxon, 1974-83, Witney, 1983-97; Opposition Spokesman on European Affairs, 1976-79; Visiting Fellow, Nuffield College, 1978-86; Minister of State, Foreign and Commonwealth Office, 1979-83, Home Office, 1983-84; Secretary of State for Northern Ireland, 1984-85, Home Secretary, 1985-89, Foreign Secretary, 1989-95; Candidate for Conservative Leadership, 1990; Deputy Chairman, NatWest Markets, 1995-98; Director Natwest Group, 1995-99; Deputy Chairman, Coutts & Co, 1998-; Chairman, Hawkpoint Advisory Committee, 1999-; Chairman British Invisibles, 1998-2000; Chairman, Prison Reform Trust, 1997-2001; Chairman, The Booker Prize Committee, 1998; Chairman, Council for Effective Dispute Resolution, 2001-; High Steward, Westminister Abbey, 2000-; Joint President, Royal Institute for Internal Affairs, 2002-. Publications: The Arrow War, 1967; Send Him Victorious (with Andrew Osmond), 1968; The Smile on the Face of the Tiger (with Andrew Osmond), 1969; Scotch on the Rocks (with Andrew Osmond), 1971; Truth Game, 1972; Vote to Kill, 1975; An End to Promises, 1979; War Without Frontiers (with Andrew Osmond), 1982; Palace of Enchantments (with Stephen Lamport), 1985; The Search for Peace (BBC TV Series), 1997; The Shape of Ice, 1998; Ten Minutes to Turn the Devil, 1999; Image in the Water, 2001. Honours: Commander of the Order of the British Empire, 1974; Privy Councillor, 1982; Spectator Award for Parliamentarian of the Year, 1990; Companion of Honour, 1995; Baron Hurd of Westwell, 1997. Address: House of Lords, London SW1A 0PW, England.

HURLEY Elizabeth, b. 10 June 1965, England. Model; Actress; Producer. 1 son. Career: Former model and spokeswoman, Estée Lauder; Head of Development for Simian Films, 1996; Films include: Aria, 1987; The Skipper, 1989; The Orchid House, 1990; Passenger '57, 1992; Mad Dogs and Englishmen, 1994; Dangerous Ground, 1995; Samson and Delilah, 1996; Produced Extreme Measures, 1996; Austin Powers: International Man of Mystery, 1996; Permanent Midnight, 1997; My Favorite Martian, 1999; EdTV, 1999; Austin Powers: The Spy Who Shagged Me, 1999; The Weight of Water, 2000; Bedazzled, 2000; Serving Sara, 2002; Double Whammy, 2002. Address: c/o Simian Films, 3 Cromwell Place, London SW7 2SE, England.

HURT John, b. 22 January 1940, Chesterfield, England. m. (1) Annette Robertson, (2) Donna Peacock, 1984, divorced 1990, (3) Jo Dalton, 1990, divorced 1995, 2 sons. Education: Lincoln Academy of Dramatic Art; Royal Academy of Dramatic Art. Appointments: Painter; Actor. Creative Works: Stage appearances include: Chips With Everything, Vaudeville Theatre, 1962; The Dwarfs, Arts, 1963; Hamp, Edinburgh Festival, 1964; Inadmissible Evidence, Wyndhams, 1965; Little Malcolm and His Struggle Against the Eunuchs, Garrick, 1966; Belcher's Luck, Aldwych, 1966; The Only Street, Dublin Festival and Islington, 1973; Travesties, Aldwych and The Arrest, Bristol Old Vic, 1974; The Shadow of a Gunman, Nottingham Playhouse, 1978; The London Vertigo, Dublin, 1991; A Month in the Country, Albery, 1994; Krapp's Last Tape, New Ambassadors Theatre, 2000, Gate Theatre, Dublin, 2001; Afterplay, Gielgud Theatre, 2002; Films include: The Elephant Man, 1980; King Ralph, 1991; Lapse of Memory, 1991; Dark at Noon, 1992; Monolith, 1994; Even Cowgirls Get the Blues, 1994; Rob Roy, 1994; Wild Bill, 1995;

Dead Man, 1996; Contact, 1997; Love and Death on Long Island, 1998; All the Little Animals, 1999; You're Dead, 1999; The Love Letter, 1999; Lost Souls, 2000; Night Train, 2000; Captain Corelli's Mandolin, 2001; Harry Potter and the Philosopher's Stone, 2001; Tabloid, 2001; Bait, 2001; Miranda, 2001; Owning Mahony, 2001; Several TV appearances. Honours: Several. Address: c/o Julian Belfrage & Associates, 46 Albemarle Street, London W1X 4PP, England.

HURT William, b. 20 March 1950, Washington, USA. Actor. m. (1) Mary Beth Hurt, (2) Heidi Henderson, 1989, 2 sons. Education: Tufts University; Juilliard School. Creative Works: Stage appearances include: Henry V, 1976; Mary Stuart; My Life; Ulysses in Traction; Lulu; Fifth of July; Childe Byron; The Runner Stumbles; Hamlet; Hurlyburly; Beside Herself, 1989; Ivanov, 1991; Films include: Altered States; Eyewitness; Body Heat; The Big Chill; Corky Park; Kiss of the Spider Woman; Children of a Lesser God; Broadcast News, 1987; A Time of Destiny, 1988; The Accidental Tourist, 1989; The Plastic Nightmare; I Love You to Death, 1990; The House of Spirits, 1990; The Doctor, 1991; Until the End of the World, 1991; Mr Wonderful, 1993; The Plague, 1993; Trial By Jury, 1994; Second Best, 1994; Jane Eyre, 1995; Secrets Shared With a Stranger; Smoke, 1995; Michael; Loved; Lost in Space, 1998; One True Thing, 1998; Dark City, 1998; The Miracle Marker, 2000; AI: Artificial Intelligence, 2001; The Flamingo Rising, 2001. Honours include: Theatre World Award, 1978; Best Actor Award, Cannes Film Festival, 1985; Academy Award, Best Actor, 1985; 1st Spencer Tracy Award, 1988. Address; c/o Hilda Quille, William Morris Agency,151 El Camino Drive, Beverly Hills, CA 90212, USA.

HURWITZ Barney, b. 6 July 1922, Poland. Chemist. m. Leah, 1 son, 2 daughters. Education: Chemist Diploma Pharmacy, Unisa University; D Phil; OFS; D Litt; FPS, South Africa; MPS, England; MI Pharmn. Appointments: Chairman, Medical Enterprises; Director of Companies; Chairman, Trademore Corp Ltd, Omnimed Pty Ltd, LSP Ltd. Honours: D Phil, hons, South Africa University; DLitt, Unisa University; Fellow, Pharmaceutical Society; South African Association of Private Hospitals; South African, Jewish Business Achiever; National Marketing Award Nominee. Address: 46 Komatie Road, Emmarentia, Johannesburg, Republic of South Africa 2195.

HUSEYNOV Vugar K, b. 20 September 1975, Armenia. Forensic Pathologist. m. Gunay R Rustamova. Education: Diploma, Azerbaijan Medical University, 1992-98; Intern Certificate, 1998-99; Postgraduate Course Diploma, 1999-2002. Appointment: Forensic Pathologist, 1998-. Publications: Medico legal age determination by facial wrinkles; Changes in the human face due to ageing in forensic medicine; Face as an object of criminalistics; Wrinkles of facial skin; Caraniofacial research at forensic medical identification of the person. Memberships: International Association of Identification; American Academy of Forensic Sciences. Address: 33, 20 January str, Apt # 58, Baku, AZ 1102, Azerbaijan.

HUSSAIN Khadim, b. 15 April 1947, Faisalabad, Pakistan. University Teacher. m. Anees, 1 son, 2 daughters. Education: BSc, 1967; MSc, Physics, 1969; PhD, Manchester University (UK), 1981. Appointments: Lecturer, Physics, Education Department, Government of the Punjab, Lahore, 1971-82; Assistant Professor, Associate Professor, Professor, Centre for Solid State Physics, 1982-2001; Professor, Physics Department, Punjab University, Lahore, 2001-. Publications: More than 40 papers published in professional scientific journals. Honours: Distinctions in SSC, BSc and MSc Exams. Membership: Fellow Royal Meteorological Society, UK. Address: Physics Department, Punjab University, New Campus, Lahore-54590, Pakistan.

HUSSEIN Queen Noor (HM), b. 23 August 1951. m. King Hussein I of Jordan, deceased 2 February 1999, 4 children. Education: BA, Architecture, Urban Planning, Princeton University, USA 1974. Appointments: Architectural and Urban Planning Projects in Australia, Iran and Jordan; Founded in Jordan, Royal Endowment for Culture and Education, 1979; Annual Arab Children's Congress, 1980; Annual International Jerash Festival for Culture and Arts, 1981; Jubilee School, 1984; Noor Al Hussein Foundation, 1985; National Music Conservatory, 1986; National Task Force for Children; Advisory, Committee for the UN University International Leadership Academy, Amman; Patron of the General Federation of Jordanian Women and the National Federation of Business and Professional Women's Clubs; Patron, Royal Society for the Conservation of Nature; Honorary President, Jordan Red Crescent; The Jordan Society, Washington DC, 1980; Patron, International Union for the Conservation of Nature and Nature Rescue, 1988; Founding Member, International Commission on Peace and Food, 1992; President, United World Colleges, 1995; Honorary President, Birdlife International, 1996; Director, Hunger Project. Honours: Numerous Honorary Doctorates, International Relations, Law, Humane Letters; International Awards and Decorations. Memberships: International Eye Foundation Honorary Board; Trustee, Mentor Foundation; General Assembly of the SOSKinderdorf International; International Council of the Near East Foundation. Address: Bab Al Salam Palace, Amman, Jordan.

HUSTON Anjelica, b. 8 July 1951, Los Angeles, California, USA. Actress. m. Robert Graham, 1992. Creative Works: Stage appearances include: Tamara, Los Angeles, 1985; TV appearances include: The Cowboy and the Ballerina, NBC-TV Film, 1984; Faerie Tale Theatre, A Rose for Miss Emily, PBS Film, Lonesome Dove, CBS Mini-Series; Films include: Sinful Davey; A Walk with Love and Death, 1969; The Last Tycoon, 1976; The Postman Always Rings Twice, 1981; Swashbuckler; This is Spinal Tap, 1984; The Ice Pirates, 1984; Prizzi's Honor, 1985; Gardens of Stone; Captain Eo; The Dead; Mr North; A Handful of Dust; The Witches; Enemies; A Love Story; The Grifters; The Addams Family; Addams Family Values; The Player; Manhattan Murder Mystery; The Crossing Guard, 1995; The Perez Family, 1995; Buffalo '66, 1997; Phoenix, 1997; Director, Bastard Out of Carolina, 1995; Phoenix, 1997; Agnes Browne, 1999; The Golden Bowl, 2001; The Royal Tenenbaums, 2002. Honours include: Academy Award, Best Supporting Actress, 1985; NY & Los Angeles Film Critics Awards, 1985. Address: c/o International Creative Management, 8942 Wilshire Boulevard, Beverly Hills, CA 90211, USA.

HUTTER Marcus, b. 14 April 1967, Munich, Germany. Education: Dipl Inform Univ, Computer Science, Technical University, Munich, 1987-92; Dr rer nat, Theoretical Particle Physics, Ludwig Maximilians University, Munich, 1992-96. Appointments: Software Developer, Steuerberatungsbuero at Markt & Technik and IABG, Munich, Germany, 1983-93; Software Developer, BrainLAB, Munich, 1996-2000; Researcher, Artificial Intelligence, IDSIA, Lugano, Switzerland, 2000-. Publications: More than 30 publications in particles physics, artificial intelligence and others. Honours: 2nd prize, Bundeswettbewerb Mathematik, 1986; 3rd prize, Bundeswettbewerb Mathematik, 1987; Patent on a new image enhancement and post-antialiasing algorithm, 2002. Memberships: Mensa. Address: IDSIA, Galleria 2, Manno-Lugano, CH-6928, Switzerland. E-mail: marcus@idsia.ch Website: http://www.idsia.ch/~marcus

HUXLEY Andrew Fielding (Sir), b. 22 November 1917, London, England. Physiologist. m. Jocelyn Richenda Gammell Pease, 1947, 1 son, 5 daughters. Education: Graduated, 1938, MA, 1941, Trinity College, Cambridge. Appointments: Operational

Dictionary of International Biography

Research in World War II, Antiaircraft Command, 1940-42, Admiralty, 1942-45; Fellow, Trinity College, Cambridge, 1941-60, 1990-; Director of Studies, 1952-60, Honorary Fellow, 1967-90, Master, 1984-90, Trinity College; Demonstrator, Department of Physiology, 1946-50, Assistant Director of Research, 1951-59, Reader in Experimental Biophysics, 1959-60 Cambridge University; Jodrell Professor of Physiology, University College, London, 1960-69; Royal Society Research Professor, 1969-83; Professor Emeritus, of Physiology, University of London, 1983-. Publications: Reflections on Muscle, 1977; Papers on nerve conduction and muscle contraction, chiefly in Journal of Physiology. Honours: Joint Winner, Nobel Prize for Physiology or Medicine, 1963; Copley Medal, 1973; Swammerdam Medal, 1997; Grand Cordon of Sacred Treasure, 1995. Membership: Fellow, Royal Society, 1955, President, 1980. Address: Manor Field, 1 Vicarage Drive, Granchester, Cambridge CB3 9NG, England.

HUXLEY Hugh Esmor, b. 25 February 1924, Birkenhead, England. Physiologist. m. Frances Frigg, 1966, 2 stepsons, 1 daughter, 1 stepdaughter. Education: Graduated, Christ's College, Cambridge, 1943; PhD, 1952. Appointments: Radar Officer, RAF Bomber Command and Telecommunications Research Establishment, Malvern, 1943-47; Research Student, Medical Research Council Unit for Molecular Biology, Cavendish Laboratory, Cambridge, 1948-52; Commonwealth Fund Fellow, Biology Department, MIT, 1952-54; Research Fellow, Christ's College, Cambridge, 1952-56; Member, External Staff, 1962-87, Joint Head, Structural Studies Division, 1976-87, Deputy Director, 1977-87, Medical Research Council Laboratory of Molecular Biology, Cambridge; Professor of Biology, 1987-97, Director, 1988-94, Professor Emeritus, 1997-, Rosenstiel Basic Medical Sciences Research Center, Brandeis University, Boston, Massachusetts; Fellow, King's College, Cambridge, 1961-67; Fellow, Churchill College, Cambridge, 1967-87; Harvey Society Lecturer, New York, 1964-65; Senior Visiting Lecturer, Physiology Course, Woods Hole, Massachusetts, 1966-71; Wilson Lecturer, University of Texas, 1968; Dunham Lecturer, Harvard Medical School, 1969; Croonian Lecturer, Royal Society of London, 1970; Ziskind Visiting Professor of Biology, Brandeis University, 1971; Penn Lecturer, University of Pennsylvania, 1971; Mayer Lecturer, MIT, 1971; Miller Lecturer, State University of New York, 1973; Carter-Wallace Lecturer, Princeton University, 1973; Pauling Lecturer, Stanford University, 1980; Jesse Beams Lecturer, University of Virginia, 1980; Ida Beam Lecturer, University of Iowa, 1981. Publications: Articles in scientific journals. Honours: Feldberg Award for Experimental Medical Research , 1963; William Bate Hardy Prize of the Cambridge Philosophical Society, 1965; Honorary DSc, 1969, 1974, 1976, 1988; Louis Gross Horwitz Prize, 1971; International Feltrinelli Prize for Medicine, 1974; International Award, Gairdner Foundation, 1975; Baly Medal, Royal College of Physicians, 1975; Royal Medal, Royal Society of London, 1977; E B Wilson Medal, American Society for Cell Biology, 1983; Albert Einstein World Award of Science, 1987; Franklin Medal, 1990; Distinguished Scientist Award, Electron Microscopy Society of America, 1991; Copley Medal, Royal Society of London, 1997. Memberships: Member, Advisory Board, Rosenstiel Basic Medical Sciences Center, Brandeis University, 1971-77; Member, Council of Royal Society of London, 1973-75, 1984-86; Member, Scientific Advisory Committee, European Molecular Biology Laboratory, 1975-81; Member, Board of Trustees, Associated Universities Inc, 1987-90; Member, Germany Academy of Science, Leopoldina, 1964; Foreign Associate, NAS, 1978; American Association of Anatomists, 1981; American Physiological Society, 1981; American Society of Zoologists, 1986; Foreign Honorary Member, American Academy of Arts and Sciences, 1965; Danish Academy of Sciences, 1971; American Society of Biological Chemists, 1976; Honorary Fellow,

Christ's College, Cambridge, 1981. Address: Rosensteil Basic Medical Sciences Research Center, Brandeis University, Waltham, MA 02254, USA.

HUXTABLE Ada Louise, b. New York, New York, USA. Architecture Critic; Writer. m. L Garth Huxtable. Education: AB, magna cum laude, Hunter College, New York City; Postgraduate Studies, Institute of Fine Arts, New York University. Appointments: Assistant Curator of Architecture and Design, Museum of Modern Art, New York, 1946-50; Contributing Editor, Progressive Architecture and Art in America, 1950-63; Architecture Critic, The New York Times, 1963-82, The Wall Street Journal, 1996-; Cook Lecturer in American Institutions, University of Michigan, 1977; Hitchcock Lecturer, University of California at Berkeley, 1982. Publications: Pier Luigi Nervi, 1960; Classic New York, 1964; Will They Ever Finish Bruckner Boulevard?, 1970; Kicked a Building Lately?, 1976; The Tall Building Artistically Reconsidered: The Search for a Skyscraper Style, 1985; Goodbye History, Hello Hamburger, 1986; Architecture Anyone?, 1986; The Unreal America: Architecture and Illusion, 1997. Contributions to: Various publications. Honours: Many honorary doctorates; Fulbright Fellowship, 1950-52; Guggenheim Fellowship, 1958; Architectural Medal for Criticism, American Institute of Architects, 1969; 1st Pulitzer Prize for Distinguished Criticism, 1970; Medal for Literature, National Arts Club, 1971; Diamond Jubilee Medallion, City of New York, 1973; Secretary's Award for Conservation, US Department of the Interior, 1976; Thomas Jefferson Medal, University of Virginia, 1977; John D and Catharine T MacArthur Foundation Fellowship, 1981-86; Henry Allen Moe Prize in the Humanities, American Philosophical Society, 1992. Memberships: American Academy of Arts and Letters; American Philosophical Society; American Academy of Arts and Sciences, fellow; New York Public Library, director's fellow; Society of Architectural Historians. Address: 969 Park Avenue, New York, NY 10028, USA.

HUY Duc Luu, b. 11 January 1958, Ha Tay, Vietnam. Chemist; Scientist. Education: BS, Hanoi National University, 1980; PhD, N D Zelinsky Institute of Organic Chemistry, Russian Academy of Sciences, 1992. Appointments: Scientist, Head of Laboratory, Fine Organic Synthesis, 1993-2003; Chemistry of Steroids, 2003-. Publications: New Methods for synthesis of corticoids from Sterols via 17-ketosteroids and 17beta-hydroxy-17alpha-ethynyl steroids. Honours: Vietnam Talent Young Science and Technology Award, 1998; Who's Who in the World, 2000. Memberships: ACS, 1996, 1997, 1998. Address: Institute of Chemistry, Vietnam Academy of Science and Technology, 18-Hoang Quoc Viet-Cau Giay- Ha Noi, Vietnam. E-mail: ldhuy@netnam.vn

HŮZL František, b. 22 September 1926, Rožnov pod Radhoštem. University Professor, MD, Expert and Research, Consultant of Occupational Health and Industrial Medicine and Toxicology. m.(1) 1951-84, (2) 1990, 1 son, 1 daughter. Education: Charles University, Prague, MD, 1951, C.Sc, 1959, DSc, 1985, Professor of Charles University, Prague, 1987; Specialist in Internal Medicine, 1956, Specialist in Working Hygiene and Occupational Disease, 1960. Diploma, Ministry of Public Health. Appointments: Assistant Specialist, Internal Clinic Faculty Hospital Charles University, Pilsen, 1955-59; Chief Department of Occupational Diseases on Toxicology at Faculty Hospital in Pilsen, 1955-86; Expert, Consultant and Researcher, Deputy Chief, Department Occupational Health, Hygiene Station, Pilsen, 1992-98; Chief, Clinic of Occupational Health and Industrial Medicine at Faculty Hospital, 1984-92; Professor, Charles University Prague, Faculty of Medicine, Pilsen, 1984-. Publications: Approximately 300 articles published in various national and international scientific journals, including most notably: Results of Prevention of Vibration

Diseases in Metallurgy Industries, in Heavy Engineering Industries and in Forestry, Charles University, Prague, 1983, and others. Honours: Honour Appreciation for the Realization of Results Research Science, Czech Agriculture Academy, 1981; Honorary Medal, J E Purkyne Society of Medicine – Occupational Health, 1983. Memberships: Member, J E Purkyne Medical Society, Prague, Czech Republic; Honorary Member of Occupational Health Society, Prague, Czech Republic. Address: B Smetana Street, No 1, Pilsen, Postal Code 30100, Czech Republic.

HWANG Hyeon-Shik, b. 13 July 1959, Kyungpook, Bonghwa, Korea. Orthodontist; Dean; Professor. m. Jung-Un Park, 2 sons. Education: DDS, 1983, MSD, 1989, PhD, 1992, Yonsei University, Seoul, Korea. Appointments: Instructor, Yonsei University, Seoul, Korea, 1990; Professor, Chonnam National University, Gwangju, Korea, 1990-; Visiting Professor, University of Pennsylvania, Philadelphia, USA, 1993-94; Visiting Professor, University of Tennessee, Memphis, USA, 1995; Director, Korean Adult Orthodontic Research Institute, Seoul, Korea, 1993-; Chairman, Department of Orthodontics, Chonnam University Hospital, Gwangju, Korea, 1994-; Director, Korean Adult Occlusion Study Centre, Seoul, Korea, 1996-; Director, Dental Science Research Institute, Gwangju, Korea, 2000-; Member of Council, Chonnam University Hospital, Gwangju, Korea, 2001-; Dean, Chonnam National University College of Dentistry, Gwangju, Korea, 2001-. Publications: Author: Book, Adult Orthodontics, 1995; Book chapter, Clark's Clinical Dentistry, 1998; Book, Lingual Orthodontics, 2000; Editor: Book, Clinical Orthodontics Yearbook 99, 1999; Book, Clinical Orthodontics Yearbook 2001, 2001. Honours: CUH Research Award, Chonnam University Hospital, 1994; Young Scientist Research Award, 1996, Outstanding Research Award, 2000, Outstanding Table Clinic Research Award, 2001, 2002, Korean Association of Orthodontists. Memberships: American Association of Orthodontists, 1990; Japan Orthodontic Society, 1991; Fellow, World Federation of Orthodontists, 1996; Member of Council, Korean Association of Orthodontists, 1996; Associate Member, European Orthodontic Society, 1997; International Association for Dental Research, 1997. Address: Department of Orthodontics, Chonnam University Hospital, Hak-Dong, Dong-Gu, Gwangju 501-757, Korea. E-mail: hhwang@chonnam.ac.kr

HWANG Kun, b. 20 December 1957, Seoul, Korea. Professor of Plastic Surgery. m. You Bong Song, 2 sons, 1 daughter. MD, College of Medicine, 1977-82, MS, 1978-88, PhD, 1989-91, Graduate School, Seoul National University, Seoul, Korea. Appointments: Intern and Resident, Department of Plastic Surgery, Seoul National University Hospital, 1986-91; Professor of Plastic Surgery, Inha University, Inchon, Korea, 1992-; Visiting Scholar, Department of Plastic Surgery, Oregon Health Science University, Oregon, USA, 1997-98. Publications: 40 articles as co-author in international journals include most recently: Treatment of condyle fracture caused by mandibular angle ostectomy, 2002; Skin thickness of Korean adults, 2002; Lateral Septoapomneurotic artery: Source of bleeding in blepharoplasty performed in Asians, 2003; Innervation of calf muscles in relation to calf reduction, 2003. Honours: Best Research Award, Inha University, 2001; Award, Korean National Police Agency, 2003; Award, Incheon Metropolitan Council, 2003; Award, Korean Medical Association, 2003. Memberships: Korean Society of Plastic and Reconstructive Surgeons; International Society of Plastic, Reconstructive and Aesthetic Surgery. Address: Department of Plastic Surgery, Inha University Hospital, 7-206 Sinheung-dong, Jung-gu, Incheon, 400-711, South Korea. E-mail: jokerhg@inha.ac.kr

HWANG Mei-shu, b. 3 February 1930, Chekiang, China. Professor; Playwright; Director; Critic. Widower, 2 sons. Education: BA, Department of English, Tamkang University, 1960;

MA, English Research Institute, National Taiwan Normal University, 1963; Associateship Certificate, Institute of Education, University of London, 1965; PhD, Theatre Arts, School of Theatre, Florida State University, 1976. Appointments: Numerous academic postings, including Professor of English and Drama, 1969-95, Director, 1976-80, Graduate School of Western Languages and Literature, Tamkang University; Editor-in-Chief, Tamkang Review, 1976-80; Consultant, Committee of Theatre Programs, National Theatre, 1987-94, Republic of China; Consultant, Committee of Theatre and Film Development, National Council for Cultural Affairs, Republic of China, 1981-; Professor, 1998-, Chair Person, 1998-2002, Department of Theatre Arts, Chinese Culture University. Publications: Numerous books, plays, translations and articles in English and Chinese, books in Chinese include, On and Off the Stage, 1980; How to Enjoy Theatre and Drama, 3rd revised edition, Taipei, 1999; Approaches to Theatre and Drama, Taipei, 2000; Plays in English include, Cathay Visions (The Empty Cage), in An Oxford Anthology of Contemporary Chinese Drama, 1997; Sesom, the Magic FOB Emperor (in English), 1999; More than 10 full-length plays in Chinese (1973-2002), all produced at home and some abroad; Director of plays and musicals including Shakespeare's King Lear, Aristophanes's Plutus and others by himself and other Chinese playwrights; Translations include works by Shakespeare, Camus, Aristophanes, Euripides, Yeats and Ingmar Bergman. Honours: Wu San-lien Award for Distinguished Achievement in Literature (for playwriting), 1984; Distinguished Professor of Tamkang University, 1986; Professor Emeritus, Tamkang University, Republic of China; 10th Liang Shih-ch'iu Literary Award for Translation, 1998; Award for Distinguished Achievement in Theatre and Drama Criticism, National Literature and Arts Association, Republic of China, 2001. Memberships: ICLA; The Chinese Comparative Literature Association, Taipei; Chinese-Taipei Theatre Association, Taipei; Member, Chinese-Taipei Film Critics' Association; Phi Tau Phi Scholastic Honour Society. Address: 1F, 3, Lane 61, Meikuei Rd, Hsintien, Taipei, Taiwan 231, Republic of China.

HWANG Seong Taek, b. 6 March 1965, Jeongju, Korea. Senior Engineer. m. Kyung-A Kim, 1 son, 1 daughter. Education: Bachelor, 1985-89, Master, 1989-90, Doctor, 1999-2002, Sogang University. Appointments: Researcher, Samsung Advanced Institute of Technology, 1993-96; Senior Engineer, 1997-2003, Project Leader, 1999-2003, Samsung Electronics. Publications: Articles in scientific journals including: Electronics Letters, vol 37, 2001; IEEE Photonics Technology Letters, vol 13, 2001; Journal of Lightwave Technology, vol 21, 2003. Honours: Chairman's Prize, Samsung Group, 1995; Who's Who in the World, 2003. Membership: IEEE. Address: 102-303, Daerim Apartment, Dokgok-dong, Pyongtaek, Gyunggi-do, Korea 459-707. Email: shwang@samsung.com

HYATT Derek James, b. 21 February 1931, Ilkley, Yorkshire, England. Artist; Teacher; Writer. m. Rosamond Joy Rockey, 1 daughter. Education: NDD Illustration, 1st class honours, Leeds College of Art, 1948-52; Part-time studies, Norwich School of Art, 1953; 1st class honours, Royal College of Art, 1954-58; Part-time courses, Film Studies, 1960, Philosophy, 1962, London University. Career: Solo exhibitions annually, throughout UK, 1958-; Visiting Lecturer, Art History and Foundation Course, Kingston School of Art, Surrey, 1959-64; Senior Lecturer, Visual Studies and Illustration Studies, Leeds Polytechnic, 1964-84; Visiting Professor, Cincinnati University, USA, 1980; Full-time artist and writer, 1984-. Publications: Numerous articles in professional art journals and magazines; Author and Illustrator, The Alphabet Stone, 1992; Co-author, Stone Fires-Liquid Clouds, The Shamanic Art of Derek Hyatt, monograph, 2001. Honours: Phil May Drawing Prize, 1954; Royal Scholar Prize, RCA, 1956;

Landscape Painting Prize, RCA, 1958; Companion of the Guild of St George, Ruskin Society, 1990; Yorkshire Arts Award, Bradford Art Gallery, Retrospective, 2001. Memberships: Artists for Nature Foundation International, Extremadura, Spain, 1998. Address: Rectory Farmhouse, Collingham, Wetherby, Yorkshire LS22 5AS, England.

HYLAND Paul, b. 15 September 1947, Poole, Dorset, England. Poet; Travel Writer. Education: BSc, Honours, Bristol University, 1968. Publications: Purbeck: The Ingrained Island, 1978; Wight: Biography of an Island, 1984; The Black Heart, 1988; Indian Balm, 1994; Backwards Out of the Big World, 1996; Discover Dorset: Isle of Purbeck, 1998; Ralegh's Last Journey, 2003; Poetry: Poems of Z, 1982; The Stubborn Forest, 1984; Getting into Poetry, 1992 , 2nd edition, 1996; Kicking Sawdust, 1995; Art of the Impossible, 2004. Honours: Eric Gregory Award, 1976; Alice Hunt Bartlett Award, 1985; Authors Foundation, 1995. Memberships: Society of Authors; Poetry Society; PEN. Address: 32 Colliton Street, Dorchester, Dorset DT1 1XH, England.

HYLLSETH Bjorn, b. 30 May 1927, Skoger, Norway. Professor Emeritus. m. Randi, 2 sons, 2 daughters. Education: BVetSci, Sydney, Australia, 1958; PhD, Virology, Royal Veterinary College, Stockholm, Sweden, 1973. Appointments: Veterinarian, Franklin Veterinary Club, New Zealand, 1958-64; Laboratory Veterinarian, National Veterinary Institute, Stockholm, 1965-73; Professor, Virology, The Norwegian School of Veterinary Science, 1973-95. Publications: Several articles in professional journals. Membership: Norwegian Veterinary Association. Address: Leanglia 48, N-1387 Asker, Norway.

HYNDE Chrissie, b. 7 September 1951, Akron, Ohio, USA. Singer; Songwriter; Musician. 1 daughter with Ray Davies, m. (1) Jim Kerr, divorced, 1 daughter, (2) Lucho Brieva, 1999. Appointments: Contributor to New Musical Express; Co-Founder, Chrissie Hynde and the Pretenders, 1978, Singer, Songwriter, Guitarist, New Band Formed, 1983; Tours in Britain, Europe & USA. Creative Works: Singles include: Stop Your Sobbing, 1978; Kid; Brass in Pocket; I Go to Sleep, 1982; Back on the Chain Gang, 1982; Middle of the Road, 1984; Thin Line Between Love and Hate; Don't Get Me Wrong; Hymn to Her; Albums include: Pretenders, 1980; Pretenders II, 1981; Extended Play, 1981; Learn to Crawl, 1985; Get Close, 1986; The Singles, 1987. Honours: Platinum and gold discs.

HYODO Haruo, b. 3 March 1928, Japan. Radiologist. m. Keiko Tomita, 1 son, 2 daughters. Education: Dokkyo University School of Medicine, Japan; Tokushima University, Japan. Appointment: Radiologist. Publications: 2 Japanese patents. Honours: Gold Medal, Honorary Member, Japanese Society of Angiography and Interventional Radiology; Japan Billiary Association; Listed in international biographical publications. Memberships: Several Japanese associations. Address: 1-9-3 Saiwai-cyo, Mibu-machi, Shimotsuga-gun, Tochigi, 321-0203 Japan. E-mail: hyodo283@green.ocn.ne.jp

HYPATIA Margaret Webster, b. 7 March 1949, Laramie, Wyoming, USA. Speaker; Author; Training Consultant. Education: BA and Secondary Teaching Certificate, University of Colorado, 1972; Graduate Diploma of Librarianship, Canberra College, Australia, 1976. Appointments: High School Teacher, 1972-82; Lecturer in Human Resource Development, University of South Australia, Flinders University and South Australian Institute of Technical and Further Education, 1983-89; Managing Director, Working Smarter Pty Ltd, improving people's performance in government, health and education through keynote speeches and seminars throughout Australia and in Asia, 1988-. Publications:

Numerous articles including recently in The Magic of Success newsletter; Topics on a project management approach to achieving organisational objectives. Memberships: National Speakers Association; Register of Management Consultants, Institute of Public Administration of Australia; Australian Institute of Project Management. Address: PO Box 434, Blackwood, SA 5051, Australia. E-mail: margaret@magicofsuccess.com.auS

HYTTINEN Seppo, b. 17 May 1937, Värtsilä, Finland. Civil Engineer; Inventor. Education: MSc, Civil Engineering, Institute of Technology, Helsinki. Appointments: Engineer, Finnish National Road Administration, Mikkeli district, 1964-92, Chief, bridge construction, 1964, Supervisor, Waterway Maintenance, 1971; Supervisor, Project Manager, highway and bridge construction, Heinola, 1987-92, Transfer to Administrative division on reserve, 1992; Retired, 2000; Private inventor, 1968-. Publications: Numerous patents for inventions in hollow floor buildings, energy-efficient heating, ventilation, bridge construction, heat pump construction, patents held in Britain, Canada, Finland, USA, Norway, Japan and Sweden. Address: Kivirannantie 6, 50100 Mikkeli, Finland.

Dictionary of International Biography

I

IBBETT Vera, b. 30 May 1929, Lower Kingswood, Surrey, England. Artist. m. Raymon Strank. Education: Reigate School of Art, 1943-46; Regent Polytehnic, 1947-48; City & Guilds of London Art School, 1948-53; Diploma, Graphic Reproduction, London College of Printing, 1960-61; Studied under John Nash R.A., 1965, Villu Toots, 1990. Career: Artist, painter and illustrator in oils, watercolour and pastel; Private commissions for animal portraits including North African charity veterinary instruction panels; Award winning seed packet designs; Book jackets, full colour illustrations; National Gallery copying transaction; Tower of London calligraphic display work; Exhibited: RA; RMS; SWA; FBA; Appeared on the TV series "The Craftsmen", 1972; Teacher, Reigate School of Art, 1975-86; Designed manuscript with illustrations and calligraphy, Flowers in Heraldry, 1972-75; Battle of Britain memorial panel for RAF Chapel Biggin Hill, 1982; Life size free standing figures for museum display, 1988; Botanical illustration for educational series, 2000; Sculptured bronze plaque commemorating working donkeys in Covent Garden, 2000; Works in private collections in UK and overseas. Publications include: Flowers in Heraldry, limited edition, The Alcuin Society, Canada, 1977; Work in Alcuin Society's Journal, Amphora, British Columbia, 1996; Works in La Revue Moderne. Honours: Awards for Lettering and Calligraphy, Worshipful Company of Painter Stainers, 1958; Elected Fellow, Society of Scribes and Illustrators, 1969; RHS Grenfell Medal for Botanical Illustration, 1970; Elected Member, RMS, 1990; RMS, Gold Bowl Honourable Mention, 1995; RHS, Silver Gilt Lindley Medal for Botanical Illustrations of Educational and Scientific Merit, 2000; Elected Honorary Member, Royal Society of Miniature Painters, 2003. Address: 89 Chipstead Lane, Lower Kingswood, Surrey KT 20 6RD, England.

ICE-T (Tracy Marrow), b. Newark, New Jersey, USA. Rap Singer; Actor. m. Darlene Ortiz, 1 child. Creative Works: Albums: Rhyme Pays, 1987; The Iceberg/Freedom of Speech; Just Watch What You Say, 1989; O G Original Gangster, 1991; Havin' a "T" Party (with King Tee), 1991; Body Count, 1992; Home Invasion, 1993; The Classic Collection, 1993; Born Dead (with Body Count), 1994; 7th Deadly Sin, 1999; Films: Breakin', 1984; New Jack City, 1991; Ricochet, 1991; Trespass, 1992; Surviving the Game, 1994; Tank Girl, 1995; Johnny Mnemonic, 1995; Below Utopia; Final Voyage, 1999; Corrupt, 1999; Leprechaun 5, 2000; Sonic Impact, 2000; The Alternate, 2000; Hip Hop 2000, 2001; Out Kold, 2001. Publication: The Ice Opinion, 1994. Address: Priority Records, 6430 West Sunset Boulevard, Los Angeles, CA 90028, USA. Website: www.mcicet.com

IDISI Park, b. 2 February 1957, Uduere-Ughelli, Nigeria. Lecturer. m. Esther Bitrus, 3 sons, 2 daughters. Education: BSc 1st class honours, 1987, MSc, 1990, Agriculture-Economics, ABU; PhD, Forest Economics, University of Ibadan, 1998. Appointments: Project Manager, IAACS Consultancy, 1985-87; Assistant Lecturer, Department of Agricultural Economics, ABU; Graduate Teaching Assistant, University of Guelph, Ontario, 1990; Lecturer I to Senior Lecturer, University of Abuja, 1993-2003; Sabbatical Appointment, PCU, Abuja, 2002-03. Publications: Bioeconomic Evaluation of Alley and Conventional Farmer Level Cropping in Humid Nigeria; Costs and Returns on Alley Farming and Conventional Cropping; Dualism Fuel in Nigeria's Niger Delta Crisis; Sustainable Mechanisms for Crude and Devastated Environments. Honours: Best Graduating Agricultural Economics Student, 1987; Research Fellow, IITA, Ibadan; AAS, Kenya, Research Fellow. Memberships: Nigerian Association of Agricultural Economists; Nigerian Economic Society; Farmers Association of Nigeria. Address: Department of Economics, University of Abuja, Nigeria. E-mail: idisi2001@yahoo.com

IDOWU Adefunke Grace, b. 29 November 1965, Nigeria. Accountant; Banker. Education: MBA, Marketing, University of Lagos; HND with distinction, Accounting, Yaba College of Technology. Appointments: Clerical Officer, Federal Ministry of Aviation, 1983; Accounts Supervisor, Nigerian National Petroleum Corporation, 1985-86; Audit Senior, Akintola Williams Deloitte and Touch, Chartered Accountants, 1988-92; Banking Officer, All States Trust Bank Ltd, 1992-94; Manager, Guaranty Trust Bank plc, 1994-98; Senior Manager, Access Bank Nigeria plc, 1998-. Honours: SWAN Prize, Institute of Chartered Accountants of Nigeria, 1990. Memberships: FCA; ISACA; ACIT; ACIB; AMNIM; ACA. Address: 5 Bailey Close, Onipanu, PO Box 3342 Shomolu, Lagos State, Nigeria. E-mail: funkeidowu@yahoo.com

IGBINOSA Igho Benjamin, b. 21 March 1952, Benin City, Nigeria. Teacher, Researcher. m. Eunice. 4 sons. Education: WASC, Edo College, Benin City, 1970; BSc, Hons, 1976, PhD, Zoology, 1983, University of Nigeria, Nsukka. Appointments: Senior Research Officer, Nigerian Institute for Oil Palm Research, 1982-85; Lecturer II, 1985-87, Edo State University, Ekpoma, Lecturer I, 1987-89; Senior Lecturer, Zoology, University of Nigeria, Nsukka, 1989-95; Reader in Zoology (Entomology), 1995-2000; Professor of Zoology (Entomology), Ambrose Alli University, Ekpoma, Nigeria, 2000; Dean, Graduate School, Ambrose Alli University, 2003-. Publications include: 4 book chapters, 25 journal articles. Honours: UNESCO Grant, Staff exchange programme within the African sub-region to visit the University of Ghana as a visiting scholar, 2001-02. Memberships: Entomological Society of Nigeria; Institute of Biology, London; Royal Entomological Society, London. Address: Department of Zoology, Ambrose Alli University, PMB 14 Ekpoma, Nigeria.

IIDA Yôichi, b. 21 August 1940, Kobe, Japan. Chemist; Molecular Biologist. m. Hiroko Yokoyama, 1 son, 1 daughter. Education: BS, University of Tokyo, 1963; MS, University of Tokyo, 1965; DSc, University of Tokyo, 1969. Appointments: Research Associate, 1965-77, Lecturer, 1977-95, Associate Professor, 1995-, Hokkaido University, Japan. Publications: Author, Seminar Book of Basic Physical Chemistry, 1992; Human Genome Project and Bioinformatics, 1995; Handbook of Multivariate Statistical Analysis and Examples, 2002; Contributor of articles to professional journals. Memberships: Physical Society of Japan; Chemical Society of Japan; Biophysical Society of Japan; Molecular Biological Society of Japan. Address: Department of Chemistry, Hokkaido University, 060-0810 Sapporo, Hokkaido, Japan. E-mail: chemjimu@sci.hokudai.ac.jp

IKARA Bashir Ahmad, b. 1944, Ikara Town, Kaduna State, Nigeria. Public Servant; Federal Commissioner. m. Sakinatu Ibrahim and Aminatu Ishak Gwamma, 4 sons, 6 daughters. Education: BA (First Class Honours), English, Ahmadu Bello University, Zaria, 1970; PhD, English, Leeds University, England, 1975; Postgraduate Diploma, Public Administration, University of Ife, 1971. Appointments: University Service: Assistant Lecturer, 1972, Lecturer II, 1974, Lecturer I, 1976, English, Bayero University, Kano, Nigeria; Executive Secretary, Centre for Nigerian Cultural Studies, 1976, Founding Head of Department, Nigerian and African Languages, 1977, Senior Lecturer/Senior Research Fellow in Languages, 1978-79, Director, Arewa House, Centre for Research and Historical Documentation, 1987-91, Research Professor of Cultural Studies, 1989-91, Ahmadu Bello University, Zaria, Nigeria; Pro-Chancellor and Chairman of the Governing Council, Igbinedion University, Okado, Edo State, Nigeria, 1999-2001; Civil Service: Assistant Secretary, Military Governor's Office, Kaduna, 1970; Executive Director, Reconstituted Kaduna State Council for Arts and Culture, 1979-83; Permanent Secretary (Political, Cabinet and Security) Military Governor's Office,

Kaduna, 1983-85; Federal Civil Service: Federal Permanent Secretary (Special Duties), Office of the President, Lagos, Nigeria, 1985-86; Special Assistant to the Chairman Technical Committee on Privatisation and Commercialisation, 1991-92; Currently, Federal Commissioner, National Population Commission, Abuja, Nigeria. Publications: Books include among others: Nigerian Languages and Cultural Development (editor), 1982, Evolution of Political Culture in Nigeria (co-editor), 1985; The Greater Future of Nigeria: A Cultural Perspective (author), 1989; Numerous journal articles, book chapters and papers presented at conferences and congresses. Honours include: Northern Nigerian Scholarship, 1966-70; Kano State Government Prize, 1970; Numerous certificates of honour and recognition; National Annual Merit Award, National Council of Arts and Culture, 1992; Man of the Year 2003, Member, Research Board of Advisors, American Biographical Institute, 2003. Memberships include among others: International Congress of African Studies; Nigerian English Studies Association; Nigerian Historical Society; Nigerian Institute of Management; Nigerian Institute of Industrialists and Corporate Administrators. Address: National Population Commission, Olusegun Obasanto Way, Zone 7, Wuse, Abuja, Nigeria. E-mail: bashirikaraacademy@yahoo.com

IKEDA Kazuyosi, b. 15 July 1928, Fukuoka, Japan. Physicist; Poet (bilingual, English/Japanese). m. Mieko Akiyama Ikeda, 20 November 1956, 1 son, 1 daughter. Education: Graduate, 1951, post graduate studies, 1951-56; Department of Physics, Kyushu University, DSc, 1957. Appointments: Assistant, 1956-60, Associate Professor, 1960-65, Department of Physics, Kyushu University; Associate Professor, 1965-68, Professor, 1988-92, Professor Emeritus, 1992-, Osaka University, Department of Applied Physics, 1965-89, Department of Mathematical Sciences, 1989-; Professor, 1992-, President, 1995-, International Earth Environment University, Japan; Board Member, Advisory Council, Ansted University, 1999-. Publications include: Mechanics without Use of Mathematical Formulae; From a Moving Stone to Halley's Comet; Statistical Thermodynamics; Invitation to Mechanics With Appendix on a Comet in Ancient Times; Basic Mechanics; Basic Thermodynamics; From Entropy to Osmotic Pressure; Graphical Theory of Relativity; over 100 papers on theoretical physics; Over 30 literary books including: Banysoo Hyakusi Collection of Poems; The World of God, Creation and Poetry; Poems on the Hearts of Creation; Mountains; North South East West; Hearts of Myriad Things in the Universe; Kazuyosi's Poetry on the Animate and the Inanimate; Poems on Love and Peace; Songs of the Soul; Hearts of Innumerous Things in Heaven and Earth; Kazuyosi's Poems on Myriad Things – For Global Brotherhood and World Peace; The World of Hearts; Peace Offerings; Men and Nature; Spring Rain; Serialised Poems of 7-5 syllables Fixed Form; Haiku; Tanka; Chinese classical fixed-form poems; Essays on Poetry. Honours include: Yukawa Commemorative Scholarship Award; Honorary D.Litt; World Decoration of Excellence Medal; Voice of Kolkata Award; Mandakini Literary Award; Hall of Fame; International Cultural Diploma of Honour; Grand Ambassador of Achievement; International Order of Merit; Cultural Doctorate in Poetical Literature; Honorary Doctor of Literature; Honorary Doctor of Environment Science; Man of the Year; Personality of the Year; International Man of the Year; One in a Million Award; Sphatica International Poet Award; Global Peace and Friendship Award; International Medal for Scientific Excellence; Chevalier Grand Cross; Golden Academy Award for Lifetime Achievement; International Eminent Poet; International Sash of Academia; Golden Scroll of Excellence; Who's Who of the Year Award; 25 Years Achievement Award; Albert Einstein Academy Award for Outstanding Achievement; Knight of San Ciriaco Order; Prize Libro d'Oro; Silver Shield of Valor; Five-Star Leader Award; Most Admired Man of the Decade, Presidential Seal of Honour; Gold

Record Achievement; Ambassador of Great Eminence; Order of Pegasus of Highest Degree; 20th Century Award; Prize Catania; Prize Pandit; International Artistic-Literary Prize of Primavera Catanase; Albert Einstein Certificate Award for Outstanding Achievement; Diploma of Honour of Institute of International Affairs; Platinum Record of Exceptional Performance; Best World Poet of Year, 1999; World Laureate; Prize Oscar 2000; International Commendation of Success in the Professions of Science and Poetry; Poet of the Millennium Award; International Scientist of the Year; International Commendation of Success; Decree of International Letters for Cultural Achievement; Outstanding Man of the 20th Century; Scientific Achievement Award; Outstanding Scientist of the 20th Century; Professional Performance Key Award; Notable Author Award; Biographical Honour Award; Torch of Gold Inspiration; Most Influential Scientist of the Decade; Michael Madhusudan Award; Voice of Kolkata Award; World Lifetime Achievement Award; Knight of Lofsensic Ursinius Order; Knight of the Universal Knights Order; NS Chandra Bose National Award; IBC Lifetime Achievement Award; Torch of Global Inspiration; Oscar 2000 Award; The 20th Century Award for Achievement; International Artistic-Literary Prize of Primavera Catanase; Ivory Eagle 2001 Award; 21st Century Award; Vice Consul; Legacy of Honor; American Medal of Honor for Significant Accomplishments in the Field of Poetry and Science; Gran Premio d'Autore; Order of International Ambassadors; Medalla al Merito of International Parliament for Safety and Peace; Companion of Honour; Knight of Templar Order; Knight of Holy Grail Order; Excellence in World Poetry Award; World Citizen of the Year; Knight Commander of Sovereign Order of Ambrosini's; International Peace Prize; Leader in Science Award; Gold Star Award; Poet of the Millennium; International Scientist of the Year 2001; Listed in over 50 Who's Who books and over 25 dedication sections. Memberships include: New York Academy of Sciences; Physical Society of Japan; Planetary Society; Director, Kansai Branch, Professors World Peace Academy; Chairman, Kansai Branch, National and Professors-Students Coalition Unification of N E W S; Chairman, Osaka Branch and Osaka University Branch; Life Patron, IBA; Deputy Director General, IBC; Deputy Governor, ABIRA; Honorary Founder and Representative for Japan of Olympoetry Movement; Senator and Minister Plenipotentiary for Japan of International Parliament for Safety and Peace; Senator and Minister Plenipotentiary for Asian States of Council of States for Protection of Life; Senator, Academy MIDI; Honorary Director, World Parnasians Guild International; Board Member, Modern Poets Society; Member, Grand Council, Confederation of Chivalry; Academician of Honour, Academy Ferdinandea; Academician of Merit, Academy Internazionali Trinacria; Charter Member, Order of International Fellowship; WIA; WLA; International Poets Academy; United Writers' Association; World Congress of Poets; Honorary Life Member, Jagruthi Kiran Foundation; Patron, Karuna India Society; Patron, Home of Letters; Patron, Katha Kathetra; Honorary Adviser, Brain Wave; Founding Charter Member, the Leading Intellectuals of the World; Founder Member, Scientific Faculty of Cambridge; Founding Member, American Order of Excellence; Chief Executive, Michael Madhusudan Academy; Founding Member, London Diplomatic Academy; Corresponding Member and Representative for Japan, Institut des Affaires Internationales; Litterateur Life Chief Patron, Metverse Muse; Founding Member, International Honour Society; Patron-in-Chief, Chetana Literary Group; Patron, Kathe Kashetere; Patron, Karuna India Society; Chief Patron, Home of Letters; Patron-in-Chief, Voice of Kolkata. Address: Nisi-7-7-11 Aomadani, Minoo-si, Osaka 562-0023, Japan.

IKONOMOVA-TCHOLAKOVA Elisavetha, b. 21 October 1929, Sofia, Bulgaria. Architect. m. Ivan Stoyanov Tcholakov, 2 sons, 1 daughter. Education: Graduate, Architecture, Politechnical

Institute, Sofia, 1952. Appointments: Strojobedinenie, Sofia, 1953-58; Designer, Head of Team, Glavproject, 1959-72; Tunisia, 1964-68; Algeria, 1972-77; Head of Team, National Institute of Monuments of Culture, 1977-90. Publications: Numerous in Edition of Architecture, Bulgaria. Honours: Kolio Fitcheto Silver Plaque, 1964; Decoration 25 years BA; Badge of Honour, NIMC; Gold Badge, Union of Architects. Memberships: Union of Architects, Bulgaria; Nicola Ficev Foundation; Architectural Council, NIMC; Reviewer, Diploma Projects at the University. Address: 15 Yanko Sakasov Str, Sofia 1504, Bulgaria.

ILEGBUNE Charles Udenze, b. 4 November 1939, Igbariam, Anambra East LGA, Nigeria. Professor of Law; Barrister; Solicitor. m. Theresa Oby Ilegbune, 1 son, 4 daughters. Education: LLB, Honours, Obafemi Awolowo University, 1963-66; LLM, PhD, London School of Economics, University of London, 1970-74; Nigerian Bar Diploma, Nigerian Law School, 1976-77. Appointments: Notary Public and Commissioner of Oaths, Nigeria, 1987; Associate Professor of Law, Chicago State University, Chicago, USA; Adjunct Professor of Law, Abia State University, Uturu, Nigeria, 1987-91; Adjunct Professor of Law, Nnamdi Azikiwe University, Awka, Nigeria, 1992-94; Dean of Law, University of Nigeria, 1987-91; Deputy Vice-Chancellor University of Nigeria, Enugu Campus, 1995-98; Professor of Law, University of Nigeria, 1988-98; Professor of Law, 1998-, Dean of Law, 1998-2000, University of Abuja; President, Nigerian Association of Law Teachers, 1988-89; Chairman, Governing Council, Nwafor Orizu College of Education, Nsugbe, Nigeria, 1988-91;President-General, Igbariam Progress Union, Nigeria, 1992-98; Chairman Board of Governors, University of Nigeria Secondary School, Enugu Campus, 1992-95; Chairman, Anambra State Panel on Land Review and Allocation, 1994; Member, Presidential Committee on Devolution of Power, 1995-98; Chairman, Board of Governors, University of Nigeria Primary School, Enugu Campus, 1995-98; National President (Nigeria) International First Aid Society, 2003-. Publications: Nigerian Business Law, co-author, book, 1983; Nigerian Hire Purchase Law, book, 2000; Numerous book chapters and articles in professional journals. Honours: Scholar of the Federal Government of Nigeria, 1964-66; Knight of the Ancient and Noble Order of the Knights of St John International, 1984; Nwaezeatuegwu Igbariam, 1944; Owelle Igbariam, 1993; Ogbuagu Igbariam, 1996. Memberships: Over 12 Professional and Academic Associations including: CLEA; NBA; INTWORLSA; ANPPCAN; IBA; ABA; NALT. Address: Faculty of Law, University of Abuja, PO Box 2340, Garki, Abuja, Nigeria. E-mail: charlesilegbune@yahoo.com

ILIESCU Ion, b. 3 March 1930, Oltenita, Romania. Hydroenergetics Engineer; Politician. m. Elena Iliescu. Education: The Energetics Institute of Moscow, Russia; Faculty of Electric Technology, The Polytechnic Institute of Bucharest, Romania. Appointments: Design Engineer, Institute of Studies and Design for Energetics, 1955-67; Minister in Charge of Youth Problems, 1967-71; Director of the Technical Publishing House in Bucharest, 1984-89; Senator, 1996-2000; President of Romania, 1990-92, 1992-96, 2000-. Publications: Global Issues. Creativity, 1992, 1994; Revolution and Reform, 1993, 1994; Romania in Europe and the World, 1994; The Revolution I Lived, 1995, 1998; Diplomatic Autumn, 1995; Moments of History, 1995, 1996; Romanian-American Dialogues, 1996; Political Life Between Violence and Dialogue, 1998; The Romanian Society – Whereto? 1999; The Romanian Revolution, 2001; Hope Reborn, 2001; Integration and Globalization. The Romanian Outlook, 2002. Membership: Scientist Academy. Address: Office of the President, Kisselef 10, Sect 1, 76238 Bucharest, Romania.

ILLSLEY Eric, b. 9 April 1955, Barnsley, South Yorkshire, England. Member of Parliament. m. Dawn Illsley, 2 daughters. Education: LLB, Law, University of Leeds. Appointments: Head of Administration, Yorkshire National Union of Mineworkers; Member of Parliament, Barnsley Central, 1987-; Member, Select Committee, on Energy, 1987, 1991, on Televising Proceedings of the House of Commons, 1988-91, on Procedure, 1991-; on Foreign Affairs, 1997-; Opposition Whip, 1991-94; Opposition spokesperson, on health, 1994-95, on local government, 1995, on Northern Ireland, 1995-97. Memberships: Member, Co-operative Party and MSF; Joint Chair, All Party Parliamentary Glass Committee; Treasurer, Yorkshire Labour Group of Members of Parliament; Member, Chairman's Panel; Vice Chair, Parliamentary and Scientific Committee; Vice Chair, Commonwealth Parliamentary Association UK Branch; Executive Committee Member, Inter Parliamentary Union. Address: House of Commons, London SW1A 0AA, England. E-mail: illsleye@parliament.uk

ILYINA Nataly V, b. 18 June 1957, Vorkuta, Russia. Geologist. Education: Graduate, Ukhta Industrial Institute (now Technical University), 1974-79; Candidate of Science (PhD), Geology, Mineralogy, 1998. Appointment: Senior Research Associate, Institute of Geology, Komi Science Centre, Ural Division of the Russian Academy of Sciences, 2001-. Publications: Book: Palynostratigraphy of the Middle Triassic in the Timan-Northern Uralian Region. Ekaterinburg: Ural Division of the RAS Press, 2001; 18 articles; 10 abstracts. Honour: The Woman of 1992-93, IBS. Memberships: Palaeontological Society of Russia; Palynological Commission of Russia. Address: Institute of Geology, Komi Science Centre, Ural Division, Russian Academy of Sciences, 54 Pervomayskaya St, 167982 Syktyvkar, Russia. E-mail: institute@geo.komisc.ru

ILYUSHIN Michael, b. 8 June 1945, Chapaevsk Kuibyshev Region, USSR. Professor; Chemistry. m. Shugalei Irina V, 1 daughter. Education: Engineer Chemist-Technologist Diploma, Leningrad Liensovet Institute of Technology (LTI), 1969; Candidate of Chemical Sciences (PhD), LTI, 1975; Doctor of Chemical Sciences, State Institute of Technology, St Petersburg, 1995. Appointments: Engineer, 1969-72; Aspirant (post-postgraduate), 1972-75; Researcher, 1975-78; Assistant Professor, 1978-93, Associate Professor, 1993-95, Professor, 1995-. Publications: 11 papers, many on explosives, in journals or other professional publications. Honours: Medal, Inventor of the USSR, 1981; Soros Associate Professor, Russia, 1997; Award for Achievement, 1998; 20th Century Award for Achievement, 1999; International Man of the Year, 1997-98, 1999-2000; International Man of the Millenium, 1999. Membership: All-Russian Chemical Society, 1972. Address: St Petersburg State Institute of Technology (Technical University), Moskovsky pr 26, 198013, St Petersburg, Russia.

IMAMURA Tohru, b. 29 September 1945, Nagoya, Japan. Physicist. m. Seiko (Kimizuka), 2 daughters. Education: Graduate, Toyama High School, 1964; BSc, Faculty of Science, University of Tokyo, 1969. Appointments: Research Officer, 1969-79, Senior Research Officer, 1979-2001, Office of International Relations, 1985-2001, National Research Laboratory of Metrology; Senior Research Scientist, National Institute of Advanced Industrial Science and Technology, 2001-. Publications: Theoretical and Applied Mechanics, 1973; Scientific papers in professional journals, 1972-. Honours: Letter of thanks for work as Chairman, Parents and Teachers Association of an elementary school; Listed in Who's Who publications and biographical dictionaries. Memberships: Acoustical Society of America; Acoustical Society of Japan; Societe Franco-Japonaise des Techniques Industrielles. Address: 5-508-2 Matsushiro, Tsukuba 305-0035, Japan. E-mail: tohru-imamura@aist.go.jp

Dictionary of International Biography

IMAN (Iman Abdul Majid), b. 25 July 1956, Model. m. (1) Spencer Haywood, divorced 1987, 1 child, (2) David Bowie, 1992. Education: Nairobi University. Appointments: Fashion Model, 1976-90; Has modelled for Claude Montana and Thierry Mugler; Signed Revlon Polish Ambers Contract (1st black model to be signed by an international cosmetics co), 1979; Numerous TV appearances; Appeared in Michael Jackson video. Creative Works: Films include: Star Trek VI: The Undiscovered Country; Houseparty II; Exit to Eden; The Deli, 1997; Omikron: The Nomad Soul, 1999. Address: c/o Elite Model Management, 40-42 Parker Street, London WC2B 5PQ, England.

IMANI Sorayga, b. 19 December 1953, Tehran, Iran. Director. m. Nasser Sammak Nejad, 1 son, 1 daughter. Education: Graduate, Economics, Tehran University. Appointment: Director of Foreign Purchasing, Department at IUP. Publications: Articles, Nashre Danesh Journal, Nagar magazine. Honours: Manager, 1st International Book Fair, Iran, 1987; Many book fairs in Iran. Memberships: Many international academic journals; Bashga Enghelab for Sport. Address: Iran University Press, No 85 Park Avenue, Tehran, Iran.

IMRAN Ayesha Iqbal Ali Khan, b. 13 February 1967, Karachi, Pakistan. Physician. m. Muhammed Imran, 2 sons, 2 daughters. Education: BA, English Literature, 1988; MBBS, 1992; Residency, Internal Medicine, 1996-99; Fellowship, Geriatrics, 2002-2003. Appointments: House Officer, Civil Hospital, Karachi, Pakistan, 1992; Research Assistant, Rush University, Chicago, Illinois, 1994-95; Resident, Internal Medicine, 1996-99, Fellow, Geriatrics, 2002-2003; Attending Geriatrician, 2003-; Research Assistant, Women's Health Initiative, African American Stroke Prevention Study. Publications: Collected data on cost-effectiveness of stroke prevention; Geriatric Evaluation Units in the United State. Honours: Gold Medal; Scholarship; Listed in Who's Who publications and biographical dictionaries. Memberships: American College of Physicians; American Medical Association; American Geriatric Society. Address: 2626 S Wellington Avenue, Westchester, IL 60154, USA. E-mail: geriatrics2@yahoo.com

IMRAN KHAN NIAZI, b. 25 November 1952, Lahore, Pakistan. Cricketer, Politician. m. Jemima Goldsmith, 1995, divorced 2004, 2 sons. Education: Aitchison College; Cathedral School, Lahore; Keble College, Oxford. Appointments: Right-Arm Fast Bowler, Mid-Order Right-Hand Batsman; Played for Lahore 1969-71, Worcestershire, 1971-76, Oxford University, 1973-75 (Captain 1974), Dawood, 1975-76, PIA, 1975-81, Sussex, 1977-88, NSW, 1984-85; 88 test matches for Pakistan, 1971-92, 48 as Captain, scoring 3,807 runs (average 37.6) and taking 362 wickets (average 22.8); Toured England, 1971, 1974, 1975, 1979, 1982, 1983, 1987; Scored 17,771 first class runs and took 1,287 first class wickets; 175 limited-overs ints, 139 as Captain (including World Cup victory); 2nd player to score a century and take 10 wickets in a Test, 1983; Only 3rd player to score over 3,000 test runs and take 300 wickets; Special representative for Sports, UNICEF, 1989; Editor-in-Chief, Cricket life, 1989-90; Founder, Imran Khan Cancer Hospital Appeal, 1991-; Founder, Movement for Justice. Publications: Imran, 1983; All-Round View (autobiography), 1988; Indus Journey, 1990; Warrior Race, 1993; Writer, Syndicated newspaper column. Honours include: Fellow, Keble College, Oxford, 1988; Hilal-e-Imtiaz, 1993. Address: c/o Shankat Khanum Memorial Trust, 29 Shah Jamal, Lahore 546000, Pakistan.

IMYANITOV Naum Solomonovich, b. 31 December 1935, Novocherkassk, Russia. Scientist. m. Kira Rozinova, 1 son. Education: MS, 1958; PhD, 1964; DSc, 1980; Diplomas: Fine Chemical Engineering, 1958; Research Chemist, 1962; Senior Research Chemist, 1967. Appointments: Research Scientist, 1958-

65; Senior Scientist, 1965-76; Department Leader, 1976-86; Chief Scientist, 1986-, VNII Neftekhim, Leningrad, St. Petersburg; Project Leader, SciVision, St Petersburg, Academic Press, 1998-2000; Project Leader, MDL Information Systems, Inc, St Petersburg, 2000-. Publications: Author, 230 articles and patents; Editor, 2 monographs. Honours: Badge, Inventor of Chechoslovakia, 1979; Badge, Inventor of USSR, 1986; Medal, Veteran of Labour, 1988. Memberships: Mendeleev Chemical Society, 1959; World Wide Club Chemical Community, 1999. Address: ul Bryantseva 18, kv 155, 195269 St Petersburg, Russia. E-mail: naum@itcwin.com

INALCIK Halil, b. 26 May 1916, Istanbul, Turkey. University Professor. m. Sevkiye, deceased 1989, 1 daughter. Education: PhD, Ankara University, 1940. Appointments: Professor of History, University of Ankara, 1942-72; University Professor, University of Chicago, 1972-86; Bilkent University, Ankara, Founder of the History Department, 1993-. Publications: The Ottoman Empire: The Classical Age, 1973; Studies in Ottoman Social and Economic History, 1985-; An Economic and Social History of the Ottoman Empire, 1994; Essays in Ottoman History, 1998. Honours: Honorary member: Middle East Studies of USA and Canada; American Historical Association. Memberships: Corresponding Member, The Royal Historical Society, 1974; Honorary, Royal Asiatic Society, 1978; Corresponding Fellow, British Academy; American Academy of Arts and Sciences, 1983; Turkish Academy of Sciences, 1995. Address: Bilkent University, History Department, 06800 Bilkent, Ankara, Turkey.

INDRIES Elena, b. 1 February 1951, Geoagiu, Romania. Editor. 1 daughter. Education: BA, University of Bucharest, 1974; PhD, 1983; Student, St Sigfrids Folkhögskola, Växjö, 1993-94; Student, Mälardalens högskola, Västerås, 1994-95; Student, Stockholm University, 1995-96; Student, Wasa Komvux, 1996-97; Student, Tensta Komvux, 1997-98; Student and editor, Rinkeby Arbetscentrum, 1998-2000. Appointments: Editorial Staff, Eminescu Publishing House, Bucharest, 1975-78; Editorial Staff, Univers Publishing House, Bucharest, 1978-91; Editor, Cahiers roumains d'études littéraires, 1981-87; Lecturer, Romanian Literature, Växjö University, 1993-; Editor, Ögat (The Eye) and Vi Också (We Too), 1998-2000; Cleaning woman, ISS, 2000-03; Retired, 2003. Publications: Stairs under Eyelids, poems, 1985; Presocratic Themes in Modern Romanian Poetry, 1985; Doctoral thesis, Dimensions of Romanian modern poetry, Bucharest, 1990; Poems and prose, Mosaik 2000, Stockholm, Sweden; Poems and articles, Rumänksa Bladet, Stockholm, 2002; 2 articles, Romania literara, 1 article, Curierul romanesc, Bucharest, 2002; Swedish poems, Dagdroppar, poetry anthology, 2002. Memberships: Romanian Writers Union, 1990; Swedish Writers Union, 2002; Political Prisoners Union in Romania, 1990. Address: Hindertorpsgr 12 Bv, 16372 Spånga, Sweden.

INGALALLI Rachappa I, b. 12 March 1948, Jodalli-Dharwad, India. Teacher; Researcher; Administrator. m. Basavanti, 2 sons. Education: BSC, 1969, MA, 1972, PhD, 1982, Karnatak University, Dharwad. Appointments: Lecturer, Logic, ASM College, Bellary, Karnatak, 1972-85; Lecturer, 1985, Reader, 1985, Professor, 1994-, Department of Philosophy, Karnatak University; Chairman of Department, 1994-96, 1999-; Chairman, Board of Studies, Philosophy, 1997-99; Chairman, Board of Examinations, Philosophy, 1997-99, 2001-2002. Publications: Books: Testimony: an Epistemological Analysis, 1988; Meaning and Knowledge, 1989; Jnana Yoga, 1989; A Study in Relation of Identity, 1990; Epistemological Analysis, 1991; Meaning and Knowledge, 1999; Modern Symbolic Logic, 2000; Epistemological Analysis, 2001; 70 articles in national and international journals. Honours: Karnatak University Scholar, 1970-72; University Grants Commission's

Teacher Fellowship, 1977-81. Memberships: Academic Council, Board of Studies; Editorial boards of several journals. Address: Department of Philosophy, Karnatak University, Dharwad 580003, India.

INGEL Lev, b. 15 May 1946, Nizhny Tagil, USSR. Geophysicist. m. Sklobovskaya (Ingel) Irina, 1 daughter. Education: Graduate, Gorky State University, 1968; PhD, Institute of Experimental Meteorology, Obninsk, 1979; Dr in Physics and Mathematics, Hydrometeo Centre, Moscow, 1998. Appointments: Engineer, Institute 'Salute', Gorky, 1969-73; Engineer, Institute of Experimental Meteorology, Obninsk, 1973-75; Scientist, Senior Scientist, Institute of Experimental Meteorology, Obninsk, 1975-. Publications: More than 130 articles in scientific journals. Honours: Grantee, International Science Foundation; Russian Foundation of Basic Research. Address: Mira St 4, Flat 45, 249038 Obninsk, Kaluga Reg, Russia.

INGLIS John, b. 27 July 1953, Glasgow, Scotland. Artist; Lecturer. m. Heather, 2 sons, 2 daughters. Education: Gray's School of Art, Aberdeen, 1970-74; Hospitalfield House, Arbroath, 1973. Career: Travelling Scholarships to Italy, 1976; One-man exhibitions, UK, USA since 1976-; Work in collections in UK, Canada, USA. Honours: Royal Scottish Academy, Keith Prize, 1976; Royal Scottish Academy, Meyer Oppenheim Prize, 1982; Royal Scottish Society of Painters in Watercolour, May Marshall Brown Award, 1996 and 2000; Scottish Arts Council Awards, 1980, 1982, 1988. Memberships: Honorary Treasurer, Royal Scottish Society of Painters in Watercolour, 1997-; Secretary, Hospitalfield Alumni Association, 2002-. Address: 84 Burnhead Road, Larbert, FK5 4BD, Scotland.

INGLIS-JONES Nigel John, b. 7 May 1935, London, England. Queen's Counsel. m. (1) Lenette Bromley-Davenport, deceased 1986, 2 sons, 2 daughters, (2) Ursula Jane Drury Culverwell, 1 son. Education: Trinity College, Oxford, 1955-58. Appointments: Subaltern, Grenadier Guards, National Service, 1953-55; Called to the Bar, 1959; Recorder of the Crown Court, 1978-93; Took Silk, 1982; Deputy Social Security Commissioner, 1993-2002; Bencher of the Inner Temple, 1981-. Publication: The Law of Occupational Pension Schemes, 1989. Honour: Queen's Counsel. Membership: MCC. Address: 35 Essex Street, Temple, London WC2R 3AR, England.

INMAN Edward Oliver, b. 12 August 1948, Oslo, Norway. Museum Director. m. Sherida Inman, 1 son, 2 daughters, 2 stepdaughters. Education: MA, Gonville and Caius College, 1969; School of Slavonic Studies, London, 1970. Appointments: Research Assistant, then Directing Staff, Imperial War Museum, London, 1972-78; Keeper, 1978-82, Director, 1982-, Imperial War Museum, Duxford, Cambridge. Honours: Order of the British Empire, 1998; Fellow, Royal Aeronautical Society, 1999. Memberships: Governor, 2nd Air Division Memorial Library, Norwich, 1994; Director, Cultural Heritage, National Training Organisation, 1998. Address: Imperial War Museum, Duxford Airfield, Cambridge, CB2 4QR, England. E-mail: einman@iwm.org.uk

INMAN Melbourne Donald, b. 1 April 1957, Sutton Coldfield, England. Barrister. m. Catherine Inman. Education: MA, Regent's Park College, Oxford; Inn's of Court, School of Law. Appointments: Called to Bar, Inner Temple, 1979; Recorder, 1996; Silk, 1998; Head of Advocacy Training and Development for the Midland Circuit, 1998; Head, 1 Fountain Court, Birmingham, 2001-. Honours: Queen's Counsel. Address: 1 Fountain Court, Steelhouse Lane, Birmingham B4 6DR, England.

INNES Brian, b. 4 May 1928, Croydon, Surrey, England. Writer; Publisher. m. (1) Felicity McNair Wilson, 5 October 1956, (2) Eunice Lynch, 2 April 1971, 3 sons. Education: BSc, King's College, London, 1946-49. Appointments: Assistant Editor, Chemical Age, 1953-55; Associate Editor, The British Printer, 1955-60; Art Director, Hamlyn Group, 1960-62; Director, Temperance Seven Ltd, 1961-; Proprietor, Brian Innes Agency, 1964-66, Immediate Books, 1966-70, FOT Library, 1970-; Creative Director, Deputy Chairman, Orbis Publishing Ltd, 1970-86; Editorial Director, Mirror Publishing, 1986-88. Publications: Book of Pirates, 1966; Book of Spies, 1967; Book of Revolutions, 1967; Book of Outlaws, 1968; Flight, 1970; Saga of the Railways, 1972; Horoscopes, 1976; The Tarot, 1977; Book of Change, 1979; The Red Baron Lives, 1981; Red Red Baron, 1983; The Havana Cigar, 1983; Crooks and Conmen, 1993; Catalogue of Ghost Sightings, 1996; The History of Torture, 1998; Death and The Afterlife, 1999; Dreams, 1999; Bodies of Evidence, 2000; Profile of a Criminal Mind, 2003; The Body in Question, 2004. Contributions to: Encyclopaedia Britannica; Grove Dictionary of Jazz; Man, Myth & Magic; Take Off; Real Life Crimes; Fire Power; The Story of Scotland; Discover Scotland; Marshall Cavendish Encyclopaedia of Science; Numerous recordings, films, radio and television broadcasts; Many photographs published. Honour: Royal Variety Command Performance, 1961. Memberships: Chartered Society of Designers; Royal Society of Literature; Royal Society of Chemistry; Royal Society of Arts; Institute of Printing; Crime Writers Association; British Actors' Equity. Address: Les Forges de Montgaillard, 11330 Mouthoumet, France.

INOUE Shintaro, b. 14 July 1952, Osaka, Japan. Biomedical Engineer; Researcher. m. Takako Hashimoto, 1 son, 1 daughter. Education: BA, 1975, MS, 1977, Osaka University, Japan; Registered Professional Engineer, Bio-Technology, Japan, 1995. Appointments: Researcher, Kyoto University, 1979-83; Researcher, University of Tokyo, 1986-87; Registered Professional Engineer, Japan, 1995-; Guest Researcher, Toyama Institute of Health, Toyama Prefecture, Japan, 2001; Deputy Director, Basic Research Laboratory, Kanebo Ltd, 2000-; Deputy Director, Kannpo Healthcare Research Laboratory, Kanebo Ltd, 2001-. Publications: Numerous original articles and reviews in international dermatological, biochemical and cosmetic journals; Reviews in books for dermatology, biotechnology and cosmetics; Patent invention of medical and cosmetic ingredients. Memberships: Institution of Professional Engineers, Japan; Society for Investigative Dermatology; Biochemistry Society, Japan; Pharmacology Society, Japan; Japanese Society of Inflammation and Regeneration; American Diabetes Association Professional Section. Address: Basic Research Laboratory, Kanebo Ltd, 5-3-28 Kotobuki Cho, Odawara, Kanagawa, 250-0002, Japan. E-mail: inoshin@oda.cos.kanebo.co.jp

IOANNOU Susan, b. 4 October 1944, Toronto, Ontario, Canada. Writer; Editor. m. Lazaros Ioannou, 28 August 1967, 1 son, 1 daughter. Education: BA, 1966; MA, 1967, University of Toronto. Appointments: Managing Editor, Coiffure du Canada, 1979-80; Associate Editor, Cross-Canada Writers' Magazine, 1980-89; Poetry Editor, Arts Scarborough Newsletter, 1980-85; Poetry Instructor, Toronto Board of Education, 1982-94, University of Toronto, 1989-90; Director, Wordwrights Canada, 1985-. Publications: Spare Words, 1984; Motherpoems, 1985; The Crafted Poem, 1985; Familiar Faces, Private Griefs, 1986; Ten Ways To Tighten Your Prose, 1988; Writing Reader-Friendly Poems, 1989; Clarity Between Clouds, 1991; Read-Aloud Poems: For Students from Elementary through Senior High School, 1993; Polly's Punctuation Primer, 1994; Where the Light Waits, 1996; A Real Farm Girl, 1998; A Magical Clockwork: The Art of Writing the Poem, 2000. Honours: Arts Scarborough Poetry Award, 1987;

Dictionary of International Biography

Media Club of Canada Memorial Award, 1990; Okanagan Short Story Award, 1997. Memberships: League of Canadian Poets; Writers' Union of Canada; Arts and Letters Club of Toronto; Canadian Poetry Association. Address: c/o Wordwrights Canada, PO Box 456, Station O, Toronto, Ontario M4A 2P1, Canada.

IOFFE Boris Lazarevich, b. 6 July 1926, Moscow, Russia. Physicist. m. Libova Nina, 1 son. Education: MS, Moscow University, 1949; PhD I, Candidate of Science, 1954, PhD II, Dr of Science, 1961, ITEP, Moscow. Appointments: Junior Scientist, 1950-55, Senior Scientist, 1955-77, Head of Laboratory, 1977-, Chairman of ITEP Scientific Council, 1990-97, Institute of Theoretical and Experimental Physics, ITEP, Moscow. Publications: Hard Processes, 1984; Osobo sekretnoe zadanie (essay), 1999; The Top Secret Assignment in: Handbook of QCD, 2001; Without Retouching, 2004; 270 scientific papers. Honours: Badge of Honour of USSR, 1954, 1974; Award of Discovery of USSR, 1986, 1990; Humboldt Award, Germany, 1994; Medal 850 Years of Moscow, 1997; The Novy Mir Magazine Prize, 1999; Listed in Who's Who publications and biographical dictionaries. Memberships: Russian Academy of Science; Fellow of American Physical Society; Executive Committee, United Physical Society of Russia. Address: Bolotnikovskaya 40-4-16, 113209 Moscow, Russia.

IOVIŢU Mariana, b. 10 April 1949, Bucharest, Romania. Professor of Economics. m. Viorel Ioviţu, 1 daughter. Education: Graduated in Political Economy, 1972; Political training classes, 1972-73; Diploma, Professor in Social Sciences, excellent, 1973; PhD, 1993. Appointments: University Assistant, 1972-76; Senior Lecturer in Economics and Health Economics, Institute of Medicine, 1976-90; Currently Professor in Economics, Department of Political Economy, Academy of Economic Studies, Bucharest; PhD Co-ordinator in Economic Science, 2000-. Publications: Economics, textbook, 1992, 1994; The transition of Eastern European countries to the market economy, doctoral thesis, 1993; Social Policy, textbook, 1994; Transition to the market economy, 1998; Economics workbook, 1999; The Theory and Practice of Welfare, 2000. Honours include: Member, Professional Women's Advisory Board, American Biographical Institute, 1999. Memberships: EAEPE; Professional Coordinator, EFTA Market and Romania Programme, 1994-95; Staff, TEMPUS Programme for Romania, 1995-98. Address: Department of Political Economy, Academy of Economic Studies, Bucharest, Romania.

IP David, b. 21 August 1960, Hong Kong. Orthopaedic Surgeon. m. Fu Nga Yue. Education: Graduate, Hong Kong University Medical School, 1985; Fellow Royal College of Surgeons of Edinburgh, 1999; Fellow, Hong Kong College of Orthopaedic Surgeons. Publications: Numerous articles in scientific journals as chief author include: Comparison of two total knee prostheses on the incidence of patella clunk syndrome; Management of forearm deformities in multiple exestoses; Early results of nexgen total knee anthroplasty; Premature fixation failure of distal fixation screws of IC nail; Rare compilation of segmental medullary tube breakage of intramedullary nailing; Orthopaedic principle in a nutshell, forthcoming. Honours: Lifetime Achievement Award, IBC; Deputy Director General, IBC; Scientific Advisor, IBC; Member, Order of International Fellowship; International Healthcare Professional of the Year Award, 2004; IBC Award of Biographical Recognition; Order of Distinction, IBC; Member, Order of Ambassadors, ABI; Winner of the Universal Award for Achievement for the Year 2004, ABI; Universal Award of Accomplishment, ABI; Outstanding Professional Award, ABI; IBC Award of Biographical Recognition; Listed in Who's Who publications and biographical dictionaries including: Who's Who in the World; Great Minds of the 21st Century; 2000 Intellectuals of the 21st Century; Leading

Intellectuals of the 21st Century; The Cambridge Blue Book. Memberships: Royal College of Surgeons of Edinburgh; Life Fellow, IBC; World Peace and Diplomacy Forum; Hong Kong College of Orthopaedic Surgeons; Overseas Member, American Association of Orthopaedic Surgeons. Address: 3B Highland Mansion, Cleveland Street, Causeway Bay, Hong Kong. E-mail: ipd8686@pacific.net.hk

IPATOV Sergei Ivanovich, b. 10 November 1952, Moscow, Russia. Applied Mathematician in Astronomy. m. Valentina Ipatova (Artioukhova), 14 June 1986, 1 son. Education: MS, Faculty of Mechanics and Mathematics, Moscow State University, 1970-75; PhD, Candidate of Physical and Mathematical Sciences, 1982; Doctor of Physical and Mathematical Sciences, 1997. Appointments: Probationer-Investigator, Keldysh Institute of Applied Mathematics of Russian Academy of Sciences, Moscow, 1975-77; Junior Scientist, 1977-87; Scientist, 1987-90; Senior Scientist, 1990-97; Leading Scientist, 1997-2003; Lecturer, Moscow State University, 1998; Visiting USA via NASA grant from July 2001; NRC Senior Research Associate in NASA Goddard Space Flight Centre, 2002-03; Visiting Senior Research Associate, George Mason University, USA, 2003-. Publications: About 200 published scientific works; Book, Migration of celestial bodies in the solar system. Honours: Listed in numerous biographical directories. Memberships: European Astronomical Society; Euro-Asian Astronomical Society; American Astronomical Society; International Astronomical Union; Committee on Space Research; Russian Academy of Natural Sciences; Russian Academy of Sciences and Arts. Address: Laboratory for Astronomy and Solar Physics, Building 21, NASA Goddard Space Flight Centre, Mail Code 685, Greenbelt, MD 20771, USA. E-mail: siipatov@hotmail.com

IREDALE John Martin, b. 10 June 1939, Workington, England. Retired Chartered Accountant; Insolvency Practitioner. m. Anne Jewell, 3 sons, 1 daughter. Appointments: Partner, W H Cork Gully & Co, 1971-99; Partner, Price Waterhouse Coopers, formerly Coopers Lybrand before merger, 1980-99. Publication: Receivership Manual. Memberships: Old Abingdonian Club; Cornhill Club; Leander; Rotary Club of Reading Abbey; Freemason; Burghfield Gun Club. Address: Holybrook Farmhouse, Burghfield Bridge, Reading, RG30 3RA, England. E-mail: martin@iredale69.fsnet.co.uk

IRELAND Kevin Mark, b. 18 July 1933, Auckland, New Zealand. Writer; Poet. m. Phoebe Caroline Dalwood, 2 sons. Appointments: Writer-in-Residence, Canterbury University, 1986; Sargeson Fellow, 1987, Literary Fellow, 1989, Auckland University. Publications: Poetry: Face to Face, 1964; Educating the Body, 1967; A Letter From Amsterdam, 1972; Poems, 1974; A Grammar of Dreams, 1975; Literary Cartoons, 1978; The Dangers of Art: Poems 1975-80, 1980; Practice Night in the Drill Hall, 1984; The Year of the Comet, 1986; Selected Poems, 1987; Tiberius at the Beehive, 1990; Skinning a Fish, 1994; Anzac Day: Selected Poems, 1997; Fourteen Reasons for Writing, 2001; Walking the Land, 2003; Other: Sleeping with the Angels (stories), 1995; Blowing My Top (novel), 1996; The Man Who Never Lived (novel), 1997; Under the Bridge and Over the Moon (memoir), 1998; The Craymore Affair (novel) 2000; Backwards to Forwards, (memoir), 2002. Honours: New Zealand National Book Award for Poetry, 1979; Commemorative Medal, 1990; Officer of the Order of the British Empire, 1992; Montana Award for History and Biography, 1999; Hon DLitt, 2000. Membership: PEN. Address: 8 Domain Street, Devonport, Auckland 9, New Zealand.

IRIZARRY-PEREZ Luis A, b. 9 June 1922, Ponce, Puerto Rico, USA. Physician. m. Gloria Pasarell, 1 son, 2 daughters. Education: Medical Technologist, Eastern School of Physician's Aides, New

York, USA, 1946; BS, University of Arkansas, 1947; Bacteriology, Arkansas State Teachers College; MD, National Autonomous University of Mexico, 1958; Internship, Damas Hospital, 1958-59. Appointments include: Director, Department of Bacteriology, St Vincent's Hospital, New York; Director, Clinical Laboratory, Director, Blood Bank, Parkview Hospital, Toledo, Ohio; Physician: Utuado Health Center, Guayanilla Health Center, Ponce Municipal Hospital, Ponce Municipal Dispensary, Emergency Room, Ponce District Hospital; Director, Guayanilla Municipal Hospital; Private Practice as Family Physician, Ponce, 1961-; Director, Diagnostic and Treatment Center of the Teachers Association, Puerto Rico; Staff Member of hospitals: Lucas, Damas and Dr Pilar; Lecturer, civic clubs, schools and on radio; Medical Examiner for free clinics; Director and Moderator, television programme "Doctor's Information Bureau"; Medical Consultant, Board of Army Recruiting Service, 1964-; Founder of Junior Chamber of Commerce in Ponce; Medical Director, International Feminine Marathons in Guayanilla; Medical Director, Fifth Central American Athletics Championships, Ponce, 1975; Numerous other civic and cultural appointments. Honours include: Physician of the Year, Southern Medical Association, 1971; Physician of the Year, Teacher's Association, 1972; Recognition, Institute of Dermatologists of Puerto Rico, 1975; Prize "Jose L Cangiano" for civic and cultural labour, 1979; Prize "Antionio Penna Salicrup", Chamber of Commerce, Ponce and South of Puerto Rico, 1988; Exalted to the "Gallery of Immortal Sports in Ponce", 1990 Recognition by the Fraternity Alpha Beta Chi, for labour in the Ponce Community, 1991; Listed in Who's Who Publications and biographical dictionaries. Memberships include: Medical Society of the Southern District; Medical Association of Puerto Rico; Southern Medical Academy; Cardiovascular Association of the South; American Medical Association; Committee, Historical Zone of Ponce; Federation of Sports Medicine, Puerto Rico; Board of Trustees, Museum Wichers-Villaronga, Ponce; Fellow, International College of Physician and Surgeons of New York; President, History of Medicine Foundation Inc. Address: PO Box 7684, Ponce, PR 00732, USA.

IRONS Jeremy, b. 19 September 1948, Isle of Wight. Actor. m. (2) Sinead Cusack, 1978, 2 sons. Creative Works: TV appearances include: Notorious Woman; Love for Lydia; Langrishe Go Down; Voysey Inheritance; Brideshead Revisited; The Captain's Doll; Tales From Hollywood, 1991; Longtitude 2000; Films: Nijinsky, 1980; The French Lieutenant's Woman, 1980; Moonlighting, 1981; Betrayal, 1982; The Wild Duck, 1983; Swann in Love, 1983; The Mission, 1986; A Chorus of Disapproval, 1988; Dead Ringers, 1988; Australia, 1989; Danny, The Champion of the World, 1989; Reversal of Fortune, 1990; Kafka, 1991; Damage, 1991; Waterland, 1992; M. Butterfly, 1994; House of the Spirits, 1994; Die Hard with a Vengeance, 1995; Stealing Beauty, 1996; Lolita, 1996; The Man in the Iron Mask, 1997; Chinese Box, 1998; Dungeons and Dragons, 2000; The Time Machine, 2001; Stage appearances: The Real Thing, Broadway, 1984; Rover, 1986; The Winter's Tale, 1986; Richard II, Stratford, 1986. Honours include: NY Critics Best Actor Award, 1988; Academy Award, 1991; Tony Award; European Film Academy Special Achievement Award, 1998. Address: c/o Hutton Management, 200 Fulham Road, London SW10 9PN, England.

IRVINE Robin Francis, b. 10 February 1950, Wales. Professor of Molecular Pharmacology. m. Sandra Jane, 2 sons. Education: MA, BA (Hons), Biochemistry, St Catherine's College, Oxford, 1972; PhD, Agricultural Research Council Unit of Developmental Botany, Cambridge, 1976. Appointments: Beit Memorial Fellow, 1975-78, Higher Scientific Officer, 1978, Senior Scientific Officer, 1980, Principal Scientific Officer, 1983, Senior Principal Scientific Officer (UG6), 1987, Deputy Chief Scientific Officer (UG5) and

Head of Development and Signalling, 1993-95, AFRC Institute of Animal Physiology, Babraham, Cambridge; Royal Society Research Professor of Molecular Pharmacology, Department of Pharmacology, University of Cambridge. Publications: Over 150 papers as author, co-author and first author published in refereed journals include: Back in the water: the return of the insitol phosphates, 2001; Inositol lipids are regulated during cell cycle progression in the nuclei of murine erythroleukaemia cells, 2001; Inositol 1,4,5-triphosphate 3-kinase A associates with F-actin and dendritic spines via its N terminus, 2001; Type IIα phosphatidylinositol phosphate kinase associates with the plasma membrane via interaction with type I isoforms, 2002. Honours: Pfizer Academic Award, 1988; Transoceanic Lecturer, The Endocrine Society, USA, 1989; FEBS Lecturer, 1993; FRS, 1993; Morton Lecturer, Biochemical Society, 1993; FIBiol, 1998; FMedSci (Founding Fellow), 1998. Memberships: Editorial Boards: Cellular Signalling, 1989-, Current Biology, 1994, Cell, 1996, Molecular Pharmacology, 2000-; Chairman, Molecular and Cellular Pharmacology Group 1999-, Council Member, 1999-, Biochemical Society; Royal Society Council, 1999-2001; Royal Society Research Fellowships Committee, 2000-. Address: Department of Pharmacology, University of Cambridge, Tennis Court Road, Cambridge CB2 1PD, England. E-mail: rfi20@cam.ac.uk

IRVING John Winslow, b. 2 March 1942, Exeter, New Hampshire, USA. Novelist. m. (1) Shyla Leary, 1964, divorced 1981, 2 sons, (2) Janet Turnbull, 1987, 1 son. Education: BA, University of New Hampshire, 1965; MFA, University of Iowa, 1967. Publications: Setting Free the Bears, 1969; The Water-Method Man, 1972; The 158-Pound Marriage, 1974; The World According to Garp, 1978; The Hotel New Hampshire, 1981; The Cider House Rules, 1985; A Prayer for Owen Meany, 1989; A Son of the Circus, 1994; Trying to Save Piggy Sneed, 1996; A Widow for One Year, 1998; My Movie Business, 1999; The Cider House Rules (screenplay), 1999; The Fourth Hand, 2001. Contributions to: New York Times Book Review; New Yorker; Rolling Stone; Esquire; Playboy. Honours: Pushcart Prize, Best of the Small Presses, 1978; National Book Award, 1980; O Henry Prize, 1981; Academy Award for Best Adapted Screenplay, 1999. Membership: Academy of Motion Picture Arts and Sciences; National Wrestling Hall of Fame. Address: c/o The Turnbull Agency, PO Box 757, Dorset, VT 05251, USA.

ISA-GONZUK Lambert, b. 6 January 1960, Dawaki, Nigeria. Water Specialist. m. Rhoda, 2 sons, 2 daughters. Education: Bachelor of Science, Chemistry, Ahmado Bello University, Nigeria, 1983; Master of Science, Water and Environmental Management, Loughborough, England, 1991; Management Certificate, Cranfield, England, 1997. Appointments: Water Chemist, 1985-92, Area Water Engineer, 1993-96; Head of Department, Water Quality Control, 1999-. Publications: Determination of Phosphorus in Some Green Leaves; Environmental Impact of Cement Works; Hydrogeology & Hydrochemistry of Jos Plateau Waters. Honours: Listed in Who's Who publications and biographical dictionaries. Membership: Plateau State Water Board, Headquarters, Industrial Area, PMB 2198, Jos, Nigeria.

ISAACS Jeremy Israel, b. 28 September 1932. Arts Administrator. m. (1) Tamara Weinreich, 1958, 1 son, 1 daughter, (2) Gillian Widdicombe, 1988. Education: Glasgow Academy; Merton College, Oxford. Appointments: TV Producer, Granada TV, 1958, Associated Rediffusion, 1963, BBC TV, 1965; Controller of Features, Associated Rediffusion, 1967; Thames TV, 1968-78; Producer, The World at War, 1974, Cold War, 1998; Director of Programmes, 1974-78; Special Independent Consultant, TV Series, Hollywood ITV, A Sense of Freedom, ITV Ireland,

TV Documentary, BBC, Battle for Crete, NZ TV, Cold War, Turner Broadcasting; CEO, Channel 4 TV Co, 1981-88; General Director, Royal Opera House, 1988-96 (director 1985-97); Chief Executive, Jeremy Isaacs Productions, 1998-. Publications: Storm Over Four: A Personal Account, 1989; Cold War, 1999; Never Mind the Moon, 1999. Honours include: Desmond Davis Award, Outstanding Creative Contribution to TV, 1972; George Polk Memorial Award, 1973; Cyril Bennett Award, 1982; Lord Willis Award, Distinguished Service to TV, 1985. Memberships include: British Film Institute; Fellow, Royal TV Society, 1978. Address: Jeremy Isaacs Productions, 8 Shelton Street, London WC2H 9JR, England.

ISEKHURE Nosakhare, b. 19 December 1950, Nigeria. Political Scientist; Journalist. m. Ekinadose Isekhure, 6 sons, 2 daughters. Education: Diploma, Journalism and Creative Writing, 1979; Bachelors degree, Political Science and Journalism, 1981-; Masters Degree, Public Administration, 1982. Appointments: Member, World Youth Parliament, Canada, 1980; Appointed Member of Board, Member, Benin Traditional Council, 1983, Bendel Radio and Television, 1984; Appointed Member of Board, BDPA; Appointed Member of the Constituent Assembly, 1988. Publications: 220 articles in newspapers; 4 books on Nigerian Politics; Book on September 11th Tragedy, forthcoming. Honours: Book Publishing Award, 1992; 22 cultural and University bodies awards; Tradomedical Award; Honorary Rotarian; Justice of the Peace. Memberships: The Rosicrucian Order; Honorary Member IBC; Honorary Rotarian; Member, BTC, Edo State, Nigeria. Address: No 7, 9, 11, Sokponba Road, Benin City, Edo State, Nigeria. E-mail: odunacommunication@yahoo.co.uk

ISHAY Jacob S, b. 13 January 1931, Podul-Iloaiei, Romania. Professor. m. Ada Brizel, 1 son, 1 daughter. Education: PhD studies, Zoology and Entomology, The Hebrew University, Jerusalem, Israel, 1964-67; Postdoctoral Studies, Department of Zoology, Frankfurt University, Germany, 1968, 1971. Appointments: Senior Lecturer, 1974-81, Associate Professor, Entomology, 1981-87, Full Professor, 1987-2000, Professor Emeritus, 2000-, Sackler School of Medicine, Tel Aviv University. Publications: Around 260 articles; 6 chapters in books; 1 book. Honours: Honorary Citizen of Texas, USA. Memberships: Israel Physiology and Pharmacology Society; American Society for Gravitational and Space Biology. Address: Department of Physiology and Pharmacology, Sackler Faculty of Medicine, Tel Aviv University, Tel Aviv 69978, Israel. E-mail: physio7@past.tau.ac.il

ISHII Shigemitsu, b. 15 April 1954, Fukuoka, Japan. University Teacher. m. Keiko Iwakami, 1 son. Education: BA, 1978, MA, 1980, Doshisha University, Japan. Appointments: Lecturer, Baika Junior College, Japan, 1982-99, Reader, Kinki University, Japan, 1999-. Publications: Rorensu Sutahn: Sterne in Japan, The Shandean 8, 1996; Tokugawa Shogun's Tristram Shandy, The Shandean 12, 2001. Memberships: The Voltaire Foundation; The British Society for Eighteenth Century Studies. Address: 4-4-34 Kita Sakurazuka, Toyonaka, Osaka 560-0022, Japan.

ISLAM Farhad Fuad, b. 5 October 1961, Rochford, England. Electronic/Computer Engineer. m. Rumaiya, 1 son. Education: BSc, 1986, MSc, 1988, Engineering (Electrical and Electronics), Bangladesh University of Engineering and Technology, Dhaka, Bangladesh; PhD, Electronics, Kyoto University, Japan, 1993. Appointments: Lecturer, Assistant Professor, Bangladesh University of Engineering and Technology, Dhaka, 1986-89; Research Engineer, Nippon Telegraph and Telephone R&D Laboratories, Tokyo, 1993-95; Research Engineer, Hewlett-Packard R&D Laboratories, Tokyo, 1995-97; Research Engineer, Canon R&D Laboratories, Sydney, Australia, 1997-2001; Research Engineer, Mitsubishi Electronics, USA, 2001-2003; Staff Engineer, Renesas Technology America, 2003-. Publications: More than 12 publications in IEEE, USA and IEICE, Japan journals and conference proceedings; 2 patents granted, USA; 9 patent applications in progress at patent offices of USA, Europe and Japan. Honours: Monbusho Scholarship, Ministry of Education, Science and Culture, Japan; Award, Nippon Telegraph and Telephone, for outstanding trial project on a distance learning system on advanced networks. Memberships: Institute of Electrical and Electronic Engineers, USA; Former Member, Institute of Electronics, Information and Communication Engineers, Japan; Former Member, Institute of Engineers, Australia. Address: Renesas Technology USA, 2635 Meridian Parkway, Durham, NC 27713, USA.

ISSA A Nourou, b. 15 September 1961, Segbana, Benin. Mathematics Teacher. m. Sylvia H Zogloba, 1 son. Education: MSc, 1988, PhD, 1993, Friendship University, Moscow, Russia. Appointments: Assistant Professor, 1995-2002, Associate Professor, 2003-, Department of Mathematics, University d'Abomey-Calavi, Contonou, Benin. Publications: Articles in scientific journals including: Journal of Mathematical Science; Quasigroups Related Systems; Reports of Mathematical Physics. Honour: Third World Academy of Science, Prize for Benin, 1998. Memberships: American Mathematical Society; Associate Member ICTP, Triest Italy, 1997-2002. Address: Department of Mathematics, University d'Abomey-Calavi, 01BP4521, Coyonou 01, Benin. E-mail: worwniss@yahoo.fr

ISSHIKI Minoru, b. 3 February 1948, Niihama City, Japan. Professor. m. Toshiko Isshiki, 1 son, 1 daughter. Education: Bachelor of Engineering, Tohoku University, 1967-71; Master of Engineering, 1971-73, Doctor of Engineering, 1973-76, Graduate School, Tohoku University. Appointments: Postdoctoral Fellow, Japan Society for the Promotion of Science, 1976-77; Assistant Professor, Department of Materials Science, 1977-91, Associate Professor, Research Institute for Mineral Dressing and Metallurgy, 1991-92, Professor, Institute for Advanced Materials Processing (From 2001, Institute of Multidisciplinary Research for Advanced Materials), 1992-, Tohoku University. Publications: Editor and co-author, Recent Development of Bulk Crystal Growth, 1998; Co-editor and co-author, Purification Process and Charaterization of Ultra High Purity Metals, 2001. Honour: Extraction and Processing Science Award, The Minerals, Metals and Materials Society. Memberships: The Japan Institute of Metals; The Japan Society of Applied Physics; Mining and Materials Processing Institute of Japan. Address: 3-2-14 Kagitori, Taihaku-ku, Sendai, 980-8577 Japan.

ITOH Chiaki, b. 4 February 1939, Akita, Japan. m. Katsuko, 1 son, 1 daughter. Education: PhD, Tokyo University of Education, Tokyo, Japan, 1966. Appointments: Lecturer, 1968-71, Assistant Professor, 1971-78, Professor, 1978-, Meiji-Gakuin University. Publication: Co-author: Unified Gauge Theory of Weak, Electromagnetic and Strong Interactions, MGU, 1973. Honours: International Man of the Year, IBC, 1994-95; The International Order of Merit, IBC, 1996; Most Admired Man of the Decade, ABI, 1995. Memberships; American Physical Society; Physical Society of Japan. Address: Department of Physics, Meiji-Gakuin University, 1518 Kamikurata Totsukaku, Yokohama 244-8539, Japan. Website: www.meijigakuin.ac.jp/~citoh/eng.htm

IVANISEVIC Goran, b. 13 September 1971, Split, Croatia. Tennis Player. Appointments: Winner, US Open Junior Doubles with Nargiso, 1987; Turned Professional, 1988; Joined Yugoslav Davis Cup Squad, 1988; Runner-up, Wimbledon Championship, 1992, 1994, 1998; Semi-Finalist, ATP World Championship, 1992; Winner, numerous ATP tournaments, include Kremlin Cup,

Moscow, 1996; Winner, Wimbledon Championship, 2001; Winner, 22 tours singles and 9 doubles titles to date. Honours include: Bronze Medal, Men's Doubles, Barcelona Olympic Games, 1992; BBC Overseas Sports Personality of the Year Award, 2001. Membership: President, Children in Need Foundation, 1995. Website: www.goranivanisevic.com

IVANOV Victor Petrovich, b. 12 May 1950, Novgorod, Russia. Deputy Head of Administration of the President of the Russian Federation. m. 1 son, 1 daughter. Education: Graduate, Leningrad Professor M. Bonch-Bruyevich Electrical Engineering Institute of Communications, 1974; Served in Soviet Army, 1974-75; Engineer, Leningrad Scientific-Production Association "Vector", 1975-77; Served in State Security Bodies, Specialisation - fight against organised crime, 1977-; Head, Directorate of Administrative Bodies, St Petersburg Mayor's Office, 1994-96; Director General, Teleplus Television Company, 1996-98; Head of Directorate, Federal Security Service of the Russian Federation, 1998-99; Deputy Director, Head of Department of Economic Security, Federal Security Service of the Russian Federation, 1999-2000; Deputy Head of Administration of the President of the Russian Federation, 2000-. Honours: Order "For Merits to the Motherland" 4th class; Order of Honour; Medal "For Merits in Combat". Address: Administration of President of Russian Federation, Staraya pl 4, 103132 Moscow, Russia.

IVANOVA-STOILOVA Tzvetanka Marinova, b. 20 June 1955, Sofia, Bulgaria. Medical Doctor. m. Orlin Stoilov, 1 son, 1 daughter. Education: Graduated as a Physician, Sofia, Bulgaria, 1979; Specialist in Anaesthesia and Intensive Care, St Petersburg, Russia, 1983; PhD, Medical Sciences, St Petersburg, Russia, 1985; Diploma of Anesthesia, UK, 1995; Fellow Royal College of Anaesthetists, UK, 1997; Certificate for Completed Training in Anaesthesia, UK, 1999. Appointments: Paediatric Anaesthetist, Emergency Institute, Sofia, Bulgaria, 1985-87; Head of Anaesthetics Department, Clinic of Plastic Reconstructive Surgery, Higher Medical School, Sofia, Bulgaria, 1987-94; Welsh School of Anaesthesia, Hospital Appointments Scheme, UK, 1994-99; Consultant in Anaesthetics and Pain Management, Lead of Pain Management Clinic, Royal Gwent Hospital, Newport, Gwent, Wales, 1999-. Publications: 43 As co-author: Book chapters in: Congenital clefts of the lip and palate, 1993; Papers in peer reviewed journals include: Combined anaesthesia for aesthetic face lifting, 1990; Ventilation parameters in cleft lip and palate children, 1990; Xenon: Recent Developments (review article), 1999; Case reports, abstracts of posters and presentations. Honours: Graduation Award for best academic achievements, 1979; British Council Travel Grant, 1991, 1992; Zeneca's Grant, 1993; Soros Foundation Travel Grant for Paediatric Anaesthesia, 1994. Memberships: British Medical Association; Royal College of Anaesthetists; Association of Anaesthetists of Great Britain and Ireland; Pain Society, British and Irish Chapters of ISAP; Welsh Pain Society; National Neuropathy Trust, UK. Address: Royal Gwent Hospital, Newport, NP20 2UB, Wales. E-mail: tzveta_stoilova@hotmail.com

IVES Kenneth James, b. 29 November 1926, St Pancras, London, England. Civil Engineer. m. Brenda Grace Tilley, 1 son, 1 daughter. Education: BSc, Engineering, 1948, PhD, 1955, DSc, Engineering, 1967, University College London. Appointments: Junior Engineer, Metropolitan Water Board, London, 1948-55; Lecturer, Reader, Professor of Civil Engineering, 1955-92, Emeritus Professor, 1992-, University College London; Postdoctoral Fellow, Harvard University, USA, 1958-59; Visiting Professor, University of North Carolina, USA, 1964; Adviser on Environmental Health, World Health Organisation, 1967-86; Visiting Professor, Delft University, Netherlands, 1977. Publications: About 120 scientific papers and

articles; 3 books: The Scientific Basis of Filtration, 1975; The Scientific Basis of Flocculation, 1978; The Scientific Basis of Flotation, 1984. Honours: Gans Medal of the Society for Water Treatment and Examination, 1966; Gold Medal, Filtration Society, 1983; Jenkins Memorial Medal, International Association for Water Pollution Research and Control, 1990; Freeze Award and Lecture, American Society of Civil Engineers, 1994; Commander of the Order of the British Empire, CBE, 1996. Memberships: Fellow, Royal Academy of Engineering; Life Fellow, Institution of Civil Engineers; Life Member, American Society of Civil Engineers; Life Member, American Water Works Association; Life Member, Water Environment Federation, USA. Address: Department of Civil and Environmental Engineering, University College London, Gower St, London WC1E 6BT, England. E-mail: ken.ives@iwahq.org.uk

IVLIEV Viktor, b. 23 September 1940, Moscow, Russia. Diplomat. m. Marina, 1 son, 1 daughter. Education: Academy of Physical Culture, Moscow, 1967; Magister, All-Union Academy of Foreign Trade, 1974, Moscow; Ph.D. Berne University, Florida, USA, 1996; Grand Doctor of Philosophy, Professor, Academician, Vice-President of International Academy of Informatisation; Senior Vice-President of European Academy of Informatisation. Appointments: Trade Representative of the Russian Federation in Belgium and Luxembourg, 1996-2002; President of Foreign Trade Society Opintorg, 1989-1996; Director of Department of Gossnab of USSR, 1981-1989; First Deputy Major of Olympic Village of XXII Olympic Games in Moscow, 1975-1981; Assistant Minister of Sports of USSR, 1966-1972; Leader of Youth Organisation, Moscow, 1963-1966. Publications: Author 200 Scientific works in field of informatisation and foreign trade. Honours: Gold Medal for great service in field of Informatisation of the World Community; Medal of UN; Laureate of international prize; European Community Order of Merit; Orders and medals USSR and Russia; Orders of Belgium; Knights Grande Cross S.O.S.J.; Order of International Ambassadors; International Order of Merit; American Order of Excellence, the Chivalrous Order of St. Andrew. Memberships: Vice-President of World Distributed University; Vice-President of International Centre of Informatisation in Belgium; Vice President, Advisory Board, Eureka-International (Association for the promotion of Science and Innovation); Senior Vice-President Academy of Security and Defence, 2002-; Head of Commander of Moscow-Russia of the Sovereign Order of Saint John of Jerusalem. Address: Serafimovicha Street 2-317, Moscow 119072, Russia.

IWAMA Hiroshi, b. 27 February 1939, Tokyo, Japan. University Professor. m. Yoko, 1 son, 1 daughter. Education: BA in Education, 1963, MA in Education, Graduate School of Waseda University, 1965, Candidate of PhD in Education, 1968, Waseda University, Japan; PhD in Educational Theory and Policy, Graduate School of Pennsylvania State University, 1990. Appointments: Associate Professor, Shibaura Junior College of Technology, Japan, 1969-76; Associate Professor of Shibaura Institute of Technology, 1977-83; Principal, Central Pennsylvania Japanese Language Supplemental School, USA, 1985-87; Professor of Kokushikan University, Tokyo, Japan, 1990-; Professor of Graduate School of Kokushikan University, 1998-. Publications: Articles in professional journals: South Africa and the New Education Fellowship, 2001; The Creation of UNESCO and the NEF, 1999; Books: Japanese Schooling, 1989; Education for Sharing, 1996. Honours: Listed in national and international biographical dictionaries. Memberships: Director, General Secretary, World Education Fellowship, Japan Section; Member, Holistic Education Society in Japan. Address: 1-26-9 Zenpukuji, Suginami-ku, Tokyo 167-0041, Japan. E-mail: hiwama@m78.com

IYEIRI Yoko, b. 10 April 1964, Fukuoka, Japan. Associate Professor. Education: BA, 1987, MA, 1989, English, Kyushu University, Japan; PhD, English, University of St Andrews, Scotland, 1993. Appointments: Lecturer, 1994-96, Associate Professor, 1996-2002, Kobe City University of Foreign Studies; Associate Professor, Kyoto University, 2002-. Publications: Negative Constructions in Middle English, 2001. Memberships: FRSA. Address: Faculty of Letters, Kyoto University, Yoshida-honmachi, Sakyo-ku, Kyoto-shi, 606-8501, Japan. Website: http://homepage3.nifty.com/iyeiri/

Dictionary of International Biography

J

JABLONSKA Stefania, b. 7 September 1920, Warsaw, Poland. Dermatologist. Education: Physician, 1943, Dr Med Sciences, 1949-50, Associate Professor, 1951, Professor, 1954, Warsaw School of Medicine. Appointments: Assistant, Senior Assistant, Assistant Professor, Associate Professor, Department of Dermatology, Warsaw School of Medicine, 1946-54; Chairperson, Warsaw Department of Dermatology, 1954-90. Publications: Over 1000 articles in international journals, several contributions to international monographs on autoimmune diseases, virology, bullous diseases; Textbooks of dermatology: 6 editions for doctors; 5 editions for students. Honours: International Awards: Robert Koch 1985; Aled Marchionini Gold Medaille, 1992; Rose Hirschler Award for Women, 1992; Ordre Nationale du Merite Republique de France, 1998; Karl Herxheimer Award, 1999; Erich Hoffmann Award, 1999; Gold Medal, Austrian Dermatology Association, 1999. Memberships: Honorary membership of 49 dermatological societies: Dermatological Investigative Associations of USA and Europe; German Academy of Sciences Leopoldina; Belgian Academy of Sciences. Address: Department of Dermatology, Warsaw School of Medicine, 02-008 Warsaw, Koszykowa 82a, Poland. E-mail: sjablonska@pro.onet.pl

JACK Ronald Dyce Sadler, b. 3 April 1941, Ayr, Scotland. University Professor. m. Kirsty Nicolson, 8 July 1967, 2 daughters. Education: MA, Glasgow, 1964; PhD, Edinburgh, 1968; DLitt, Glasgow. Appointments: Lecturer, Department of English Literature, Edinburgh University, 1965; Reader, 1978; Professor, 1987; Visiting Professor, University of Virginia, 1973-74; Director, Universities Central Council on Admissions, 1988-94; Visiting Professor, University of Strathclyde, 1993; Distinguished Visiting Professor, University of Connecticut, 1998. Publications: Scottish Prose 1550-1700, 1972; The Italian Influence on Scottish Literature, 1972; A Choice of Scottish Verse 1560-1660, 1978; The Art of Robert Burns (co-author), 1982; Sir Thomas Urquhart (co-author), 1984; Alexander Montgomerie, 1985; Scottish Literature's Debt to Italy, 1986; The History of Scottish Literature, Vol I, 1988; Patterns of Divine Comedy, 1989; The Road to the Never Land, 1991; Of Lion and Unicorn, 1993; The Poems of William Dunbar, 1997; Mercat Anthology of Early Scottish Literature, 1997, 2nd revised edition, 2000; New Oxford Dictionary of National Biography (associate editor), 2004. Contributions to: Review of English Studies; Modern Language Review; Comparative Literature; Studies in Scottish Literature. Memberships: Medieval Academy of America; Scottish Text Society. Address: David Hume Tower, George Square, Edinburgh EH8 9JX, Scotland.

JACKEVICIUS Algirdas, b. 3 August 1926, Panevezis reg, Lithuania. Surgeon. m. Marija Jackeviciene, 1 daughter. Education: MD, Vilnius University, 1948; Presentation of thesis of doctor of medicine, 1953; Surgeon, Vilnius First Hospital, 1951-1957; Habil Doctor of Medicine, Vilnius, 1969. Appointments: Senior Research Worker, Lithuanian Institute of Oncology, 1957-79; Chief of the Department of Thoracic Surgery, Lithuanian Institute of Oncology, 1979-90; Professor, 1994; Professor of the Clinic of Surgery, Lithuanian Oncology Center, 1990-2002; Professor of the Clinic of Oncology, Vilnius University, 2003- Publications: 249, 1952-2003; 6 books include: Lung Cancer, 1975; Textbook: Oncology (editor), 1992; Lung and Mediastinum Tumors, 2002. Honours: Medal: Veteran of Works, 1986; Sign of Advanced Worker of Health Service. Memberships: International Association for the Study of Lung Cancer; European Association for Cardio-Thoracic Surgery; Lithuanian Society of Thoracic and Cardio Surgeons; Lithuanian Society Against Cancer; Society of Surgeons, Vilnius.

Address: Department of Thoracic Surgery, Institute of Oncology, Vilnius University, Santariskiu 1, Vilnius 08660, Lithuania. E-mail: algirdasj@is.lt

JACKLIN Tony, b. 7 July 1944, Scunthorpe, England. Golfer. m. Vivien Jacklin, 1966, deceased 1988, 2 sons, 1 daughter, (2) Astrid May Waagen, 1988, 1 son, 1 step-son, 1 step-daughter. Appointments: Lincolnshire Open Champion, 1961; Professional, 1962-85, 1988-; Won, British Assistant Professional's Title, 1965; Won, Dunlop Masters, 1967, 1973; First British player to win British Open since 1951, 1969; US Open Champion, 1970; First British player to win US Open since 1920 and first since 1900 to hold US and British Open titles simultaneously; Greater Greensboro Open Champion, USA, 1968, 1972; Won, Italian Open, 1973, German Open, 1979, Venezuelan Open, 1979, Jersey Open, 1981, British PGA Champion, 1982 and 15 major tournaments in various parts of the world; Played in 8 Ryder Cup matches and 4 times for England in World Cup; Captain of 1983 GB and European Ryder Cup Team; Captain of European Ryder Cup Team, 1985 (1st win for Europe since 1957), 1987; BBC TV Golf Commentator; Director of Golf, San Roque Club, 1988-; Golf course designer. Publications: Golf With Tony Jacklin, 1969; The Price of Success, 1979; Jacklin's Golfing Secrets, with Peter Dobereiner; The First Forty Years, with Renton Laidlaw, 1985; Your Game and Mine, with Bill Robertson, 1999. Honours include: Honorary Fellow, Birmingham Polytechnic, 1989. Memberships include: British Professional Golfers Association. Address: Tony Jacklin Golf Academy, Plaza del Rio Office Centre, 101 Riverfront Boulevard, Suite 610, Bradenton, FL 34205, USA.

JACKMAN Brian, b. 25 April 1935, Epsom, Surrey, England. Freelance Journalist; Writer. m. (1) 14 February 1964, divorced December 1992, 1 daughter, (2) January 1993. Education: Grammar School. Appointment: Staff, Sunday Times, 1970-90. Publications: We Learned to Ski, 1974; Dorset Coast Path, 1977; The Marsh Lions, 1982; The Countryside in Winter, 1986; My Serengeti Years, editor, 1987; Roaring at the Dawn, 1996; The Big Cat Diary, 1996; Touching the Wild, 2003. Contributions to: Sunday Times; The Times; Daily Telegraph; Daily Mail; Country Living; Condé Nast Traveller; BBC Wildlife. Honours: TTG Travel Writer of Year, 1982; Wildscreen Award, 1982. Memberships: Royal Geographical Society; Fauna and Flora Preservation Society. Address: Spick Hatch, West Milton, Nr Bridport, Dorset DT6 3SH, England.

JACKSON Andrew John, b. 27 October 1962, Winchester, Hampshire, England. Temporary Clerk; Poet. Education: BA, Honours, History/English, College of Ripon and York St John, 1985-89. Appointments: Civil Service, 1982; Archaeological Assistant, Southampton and Winchester, 1984-85, 1990-91; Administrative Assistant, Benefits Agency, Winchester, 1992-94; currently on permanent contract as Students Grant Assistant, Hampshire County Council. Contributions to: Poetry Now Anthology: Love Lines, 1995; Poetry Now Anthology: Book of Traditional Verse, 1995; Poetry Now: Indelible Ink (anthology), 1995; Poetry Now magazine; Rivet magazine. Address: 100 Priors Dean Road, Harestock, Winchester, Hampshire SO22 6LA, England.

JACKSON Betty, b. 24 June 1949, Lancashire, England. Couturier. m. David Cohen, 1985, 1 son, 1 daughter. Education: Birmingham College of Art and Design. Appointments: Chief Designer, Quorum, 1975-81; Founder, Betty Jackson Ltd, 1981, Director, 1981-; Opened, Betty Jackson Retail Shop, 1991; Part-time Tutor, 1982-. Memberships: Fellow, Birmingham Polytechnic, 1989; University of Central Lancashire, 1993. Honours: Designer of the Year, 1985; Royal Designer for Industry, Royal Society of

Dictionary of International Biography

Arts, 1988, 1989; Fil d'Or, International Linen, 1989; Honorary Fellow, 1989, part time tutor, 1982-; visiting professor, 1999, RCA; Contemporary Designer of the Year, 1999. Address: Betty Jackson Ltd, 1 Netherwood Place, Netherwood Road, London W14 0BW, England.

JACKSON Colin Ray, b. 18 February 1967. Athlete. Career: Honours for 110m hurdles include: Silver Medal, European Junior Championships, 1985; Gold Medal, World Junior Championships, 1986; Silver Medal, Commonwealth Games, 1986; Silver Medal, European Cup, 1987; Bronze Medal, World Championships, 1987; Silver Medal, Olympic Games, 1988; Silver Medal, World Cup, 1989; Gold Medal, European Cup, 1989, 1993; Gold Medal, Commonwealth Games, 1990; Gold Medal, World Cup, 1992; Gold Medal (new world record), Silver Medal (relay), World Championships, 1993; Honours for 60 hurdles include: Silver Medal World Indoor Championships, 1989, 1993; Silver Medal, 1987, Gold Medal 1989, 1994, European Indoor Championships; Gold Medal, European and Commonwealth Championships, 1994; Gold Medal, European Championships, 1998, 2002; Gold Medal, World Championships, 1999; Numerous Welsh, UK, European and Commonwealth records; Most capped British athlete ever (70 vests), 2003; Total of 25 medals; Announced retirement in 2003. Honours: Hon BA, Aberystwyth, 1994; Hon BSc, University of Wales, 1999; Athlete of the Decade, French Sporting Council; Hurdler of the Century, German Athletic Association; Athlete of the Year, 1993-94; British Athletics Writers Sportsman of the Year, 1994; Sports Writers Association. Memberships: Brecon Athletics Club UK International, 1985-. Address: 4 Jackson Close, Rhoose, Vale of Glamorgan, CF62 3DQ, Wales. Website: www.mtc-uk.com

JACKSON Glenda, b. 9 May 1936, Birkenhead, Cheshire, England. Member of Parliament; Actress. m. Roy Hodges, 1958, divorced 1976, 1 son. Education: Royal Academy of Dramatic Art. Appointments: Actress, Royal Shakespeare Company; Other Theatre includes: The Investigation, Hamlet, US, 1965; Three Sisters, 1967; The Maids, 1974; Hedda Gabler, 1975; The White Devil, 1976; Antony and Cleopatra, 1978; The House of Bernada Alba, 1986; Scenes from an Execution, 1990; Mermaid, 1990; Mother Courage, 1990; Mourning Becomes Electra, 1991; Films include: Women in Love, 1969; Sunday, Bloody Sunday, Mary, Queen of Scots and The Boyfriend, 1971; A Touch of Class, 1973; The Abbess of Crewe, 1976; House Calls, 1978; Salome's Last Dance, 1988; The Rainbow, 1989; The Secret Life of Sir Arnold Bax, 1992; TV includes: Elizabeth R, 1971; The Morecambe and Wise Show; Elected Labour MP Hampstead and Highgate, 1992-; Parliamentary Under Secretary of State, Department for the Environment and Transport, 1997-99; Adviser on Homelessness, GLA, 2000-. Honours: CBE, Honorary DLitt, Liverpool, 1978; Honorary LLM, Nottingham, 1992; Honorary Fellow, Liverpool Polytechnic, 1987; 2 Academy Awards, 1971, 1974. Memberships: President, Play Matters, 1976-; Director, United British Artists, 1986-. Address: c/o House of Commons, London SW1A 0AA, England.

JACKSON Jeanett'e Jeannie, b. 30 August 1955. Business Executive. 2 sons. Education: Bachelors Degree, University of California, Los Angeles, 1991; Bachelors Degree, Modern Management, Masters Degree, Management, California State University. Appointments: Owner, Jackson MJJ Enterprizes Inc, 1980-; Independent Contractor; Lieutenant, California State Patrol Office, Oakland, San Francisco and Sacramento, 1998; R/B Security Training and Patrol Officer, 1992-. Honours include: Awards, California State Patrol; New Song Writer and Artist Singer of the Year 1990; Woman of the Year Award for Artist Singer, 1993; Notable American Women; Hall of Fame for Business Achievement; Hall of Fame for Law Enforcement; Listed in Who's

Who publications and biographical dictionaries. Memberships: National Republican Committee; National Association of Female Executives; American Biographical Institute; American Federation of Police. Address: 1783 Capitol Park Drive, Unit 298, Sacramento, CA 95833, USA.

JACKSON Jesse Louis, b. 8 October 1941, Greenville, North Carolina, USA. Clergyman; Civic Leader. m. Jacqueline Lavinia Brown, 1964, 3 sons, 2 daughters. Education: University of Illinois; Illinois Agricultural and Technical College; Chicago Theological Seminary. Appointments: Ordained to Ministry Baptist Church, 1968; Active, Black Coalition for United Community Action, 1969; Co-Founder, Operation Breadbasket, Southern Christian Leadership Conference; Coordinating Council, Conmunity Organsations, Chicago, 1966, National Director, 1966-77; Founder, Executive Director, Operation PUSH (People United to Save Humanity), Chicago, 1971-; TV Host, Voices of America, 1990-. Honours include: President's Award, National Medical Association, 1969; Humanitarian Father of the Year Award, National Father's Day Committee, 1971. Address: c/o Rainbow PUSH Coalition, 930 East 50th Street, Chicago, IL 60615, USA.

JACKSON John Ellwood, b. 3 November 1934, Cockermouth, England. Biologist; Agricultural Scientist. m. Barbara Walsh, 2 sons, 2 daughters. Education: BSc, 1st Class Honours, 1955, PhD, 1958, Nottingham University, Nottingham, England; Numerous short training courses. Appointments: Plant Physiologist, Ministry of Agriculture, Wad Medani, Sudan, 1958-65; Smuts Visiting Fellow in Commonwealth Studies, University of Cambridge, 1962-63; Research Scientist, East Malling Research Station, Kent, England, 1965-87 including: Head of Pomology Department, 1967-83, Head of Crop Production and Plant Science Division, 1983-85, Deputy Director, 1974-85, Acting Director, 1986-87; Officer in Charge, Horticultural Research Centre, Marondera, Zimbabwe, 1988-97; Consultant, FAO Rome, 1985, ICRAF Nairobi, Kenya, 1983, 1987, ICRAF Malawi, 1995; Author, 1997-. Publications: Author, Biology of Apples and Pears, 2003; More than 100 scientific papers articles and book chapters; Editor: Mineral Nutrition of Fruit Trees (co-editors D Atkinson, R O Sharples, W M Waller), 1980; Trees as Crop Plants (co-editor M G R Cannell), 1985; Dambo Farming in Zimbabwe (co-editors R Owen, K Verbeek, T Steenhuis), 1994; Smallholder Horticulture in Zimbabwe (co-editors A D Turner, M L Matanda), 1997; Acta Horticulturae Volumes 65, 114, 160, 243, 349 (Proceedings of Symposia of ISHS Working Group on Orchard and Plantation Systems). Honours: Fellow, Institute of Biology; Fellow Institute of Horticulture. Memberships: Institute of Biology; Institute of Horticulture; Tropical Agriculture Association; International Society for Horticultural Science (Past Vice-Chairman of Fruit Section, Chairman of Orchard and Plantation Systems Working Group, 1976-96). Address: The Dell, 9 Lonsties, Keswick, Cumbria CA12 4TD, England. E-mail: jellwood@primex.co.uk

JACKSON Maz, b. 6 August 1953, Norfolk, UK. Artist. Partner, Paul Hill, 2 sons, 1 daughter. Education: BA, Honours, Norwich School of Art, Norfolk, UK. Career: Tempera Painter; Exhibitions include: SGFA, Gallery 47, London, UK, 2002-2003; Cross Country, Bury Art Gallery, Suffolk, UK, 2001, Museum of Kevelaer, Germany, 2001; NYAD dfn Gallery, New York, USA, 2000-2001; EWACC International, Global Café, London, UK, 2002; ka-Boom, 2002, Fifteen (film), 2002, Documenta USA, 2002, International Fund Raiser, 2001, 2002, MONA, Detroit, USA; EWACC International, Gallery L'Espace, Paris, France, 2002; EWACC International, Circus Circus, Kobe Japan, 2002; Artists Voices, Gallery 218, Milwaukee, USA, 2003; Invited Artist, Florence Biennale, Italy, 2003; SGFA, Cork Street, London, UK, 2004; International Art Festival, Omma Centre, Chania, Crete,

2004; Amnesty International Fund Raiser, Tokyo, Japan, 2004; Selected Galleries: Royal Academy, London; Mall Galleries, London; Llewellyn Alexander Gallery, London; Art Connoisseur Gallery, London; Birmingham Art Centre, UK; Chimney Mill Gallery, Suffolk, UK. Memberships: Society of Graphic Fine Art; Society of Tempera Painters; Artworks; Eastern and Western Culture Club. Address: Friends House, Church Road, East Harling, Norfolk, NR16 2NB, England. E-mail: mazjackson@aol.com Website: www.mazjackson.com

JACKSON Michael David, (Gen Sir Mike) b. 21 March 1944, Sheffield, England. Soldier. m. Sarah Coombe, 4 May 1985, 2 sons, 1 daughter. Education: BSoc Sc, Birmingham University, 1967. Appointments: Chief of Staff Berlin Infantry Brigade, 1977-78; Co-Commander, 2nd Battalion, The Parachute Regiment, 1979-80; Directing Staff, Staff College, 1981-83; Commanding Officer, 1st Battalion, The Parachute Regiment, 1984-86; Directing Staff, Joint Services Defence College, 1987-88; Service Fellow, Wolfson College Cambridge 89; Commander, 39 Infantry Brigade, 1990-91; Director Personal Services, 1992-93; Commander 3 (UK) Division, 1994-96; Commander Multinational Division South West, Bosnia, 1996; Director, Development and Doctrine, MOD, 1996-97; Commander, Allied Command Europe Rapid Reaction Corps, 1997-1999; Commander, Kosovo Force, 1999; Commander in Chief, UK Land Force, 2000-03; Chief of the General Staff, 2003-. Honours: MBE, 1979; Freeman, City of London, 1988; CBE, 1992; CB, 1996; KCB, 1998; DS0, 1999. Membership: RUSI. Address: Office of the Chief of the General Staff, Ministry of Defence, Main Building, Whitehall, London, SW1A 2HB, England. E-mail: webmaster@dgics.mod.uk Website: www.mod.uki

JACKSON Michael Joseph, b. 29 August 1958, Gary, Indiana, USA. m. (1) Lisa Marie Presley, divorced, (2) Debbie Rowe, divorced, 2 sons, 1 daughter. Career: Lead singer, family singing group Jackson Five (later the Jacksons), 1969-75; Solo artist, 1971-; Lengthy world tours, including Bad Tour 1987; Dangerous World Tour, 1992; Film appearances: The Wiz, 1978; Captain Eo, 1986; Moonwalker, 1988; Founder, Heal The World Foundation (children's charity); Owner, ATV Music Company (including rights for John Lennon and Paul McCartney songs); Owner, MJJ record label. Compositions include: Co-writer with Lionel Richie, We Are The World, USA For Africa famine relief single, 1985. Recordings: Albums: with Jackson Five/Jacksons include: Diana Ross Presents The Jackson Five, 1969; ABC, 1970; Third Album, 1970; Goin' Back To Indiana, 1971; Maybe Tomorrow, 1971; Looking Through The Windows, 1972; Farewell My Summer, 1973; Get It Together, 1973; Skywriter, 1973; Dancing Machine, 1974; Moving Violation, 1975; Joyfull Jukebox, Music, 1976; The Jacksons, 1976; Goin' Places, 1977; Destiny, 1978; Triumph, 1980; Boogie, 1980; Live, 1981; Victory, 1984; Solo albums: Got To Be There, 1971; Ben, 1972; Music And Me, 1973; Forever Michael, 1975; The Best Of, 1975; The Wiz (film soundtrack), 1978; Off The Wall, 1979; ET - The Extra Terrestrial (film soundtrack), 1982; Thriller (Number 1 in every Western country), 1982; Bad (Number 1, UK and US), 1987; Dangerous (Number 1, US and UK), 1991; HIStory - Past, Present And Future Book I, 1995; Scream, 1995; Childhood, 1995; Invincible, 2001; Numerous solo hit singles include: Got To Be There, 1971; Rockin' Robin, 1972; Ain't No Sunshine, 1972; Ben (Number 1, US), 1972; Don't Stop Till You Get Enough (Number 1, US), 1979; Off The Wall, 1979; Rock With You (Number 1, US), 1980; One Day In Your Life (Number 1, UK), 1981; She's Out Of My Life, 1980; The Girl Is Mine, duet with Paul McCartney (Number 1, UK), 1982; Billie Jean (Number 1, US and UK), 1983; Beat It (Number 1, US), 1983; Wanna Be Startin' Somethin', 1983; Human Nature, 1983; Say Say Say, duet with Paul McCartney, 1983; Thriller, 1983; I Can't Stop Loving

You (Number 1, UK and US), 1987; Bad (Number 1, US), 1987; The Way You Make Me Feel (Number 1, US), 1988; Dirty Diana (Number 1, US), 1988; Leave Me Alone, 1989; Black And White (Number 1, UK and US), 1991; Remember The Time, 1992; Heal The World, 1992; Give In To Me, 1992; Scream (with Janet Jackson), 1995; You Are Not Alone, 1995; Earth Song, 1995; They Don't Care About Us, 1996; Ghosts, 1997; Stranger in Moscow, 1997; Blood on the Dance Floor, 1997; You Rock My World, 2001; Cry, 2001; Contributor, recordings by Minnie Ripperton; Carol Bayer Sager; Donna Summer; Paul McCartney. Publications: Moonwalk (autobiography), 1988; Dancing The Dream (poems and reflections), 1992. Honours include: Numerous Grammy Awards, 1980- (including 7 awards, 1984; Song Of The Year, 1986; Legend Award, 1993) Numerous American Music Awards, 1980- (including 11 awards, 1984; Special Award of Achievement, 1989); BRIT Awards: Best International Artist, 1984, 1988, 1989; Artist Of A Generation, 1996; Soul Train Awards, 1988-; MTV Video Vanguard Award, 1988; 2 NAACP Image Awards, 1988; Entertainer of the Decade, American Cinema Awards Foundation, 1990; First recipient, BMI Michael Jackson Award, 1990; 3 World Music Awards, 1993; Most successful album ever, Thriller (50 million copies sold worldwide); Star on Hollywood Walk Of Fame, 1984; Numerous magazine poll wins and awards; Gold and Platinum records; Honorary Director, Exeter City Football Club, 2002-. Address: c/o 10960 Wilshire Blvd, 2204 Los Angeles, CA 90024, USA.

JACKSON Peter, b. 31 October 1961, Pukerua Bay, North Island, New Zealand. Film Director. m. Frances Walsh, 1 son, 1 daughter. Films: Bad Taste, 1987; Meet the Feebles, 1989; Valley of the Stereos, 1992; Ship to Shore, 1993; Heavenly Creatures, 1994; Jack Brown Genius, 1994; Forgotten Silver, 1995; The Frighteners, 1996; The Lord of the Rings: The Fellowship of the Ring, 2001; The Lord of the Rings: The Two Towers, 2002; The Long and Short of It, 2003; The Lord of the Rings: The Return of the King, 2003. Honours: Honorary Graduation, Massey University, 2001; BAFTA Award for Best Director, 2001; Voted Man of the Year 2002, Australian Empire Magazine, 2003; Best Director Oscar for Lord of the Rings: The Return of the King, 2004. Member: New Zealand Order of Merit, 2002. Address: c/o ICM, 8942 Wilshire Boulevard, Beverly Hills, CA 90211, USA.

JACKSON Samuel L, b. 1949, Washington, USA. Actor. m. LaTanya Richardson, 1 daughter. Education: Morehouse College. Appointments: Co-Founder, Member, Just Us Theatre Company, Atlanta. Creative Works: Stage appearances: Home; A Soldier's Story; Sally/Prince; Colored People's Time; Mother Courage; Spell No 7; The Mighty Gents; The Piano Lesson; Two Trains Running; Fences; TV appearances: Movin' On, 1972; Ghostwriter, 1992; The Trial of the Moke, 1978; Uncle Tom's Cabin, 1987; Common Ground, 1990; Dead and Alive: The Race for Gus Farace, 1991; Simple Justice, 1993; Assault at West Point, 1994; Against the Wall, 1994; Films include: Together for Days, 1972; Ragtime, 1981; Eddie Murphy Raw, 1987; Coming to America, 1988; School Daze, 1988; Do The Right Thing, 1989; Sea of Love, 1989; A Shock to the System, 1990; Def by Temptation, 1990; Betsy's Wedding, 1990; Mo' Better Blues, 1990; The Exorcist III, 1990; GoodFellas, 1990; Return of the Superfly, 1990; Jungle Fever, 1991; Strictly Business, 1991; Jumpin' at the Boneyard, 1992; Patriot Games, 1992; Johnny Suede, 1992; Jurassic Park, 1993; True Romance, 1993; Hail Caesar, 1994; Fresh, 1994; The New Age, 1994; Pulp Fiction, 1994; Losing Isaiah, 1995; Kiss of Death, 1995; Die Hard With a Vengeance, 1995; The Great White Hype, 1996; A Time to Kill, 1996; The Long Kiss Goodnight; Jackie Brown; Trees Lounge; Hard Eight; Out of Sight; The Negotiator; Deep Blue Sea; Sphere; Eve's Bayou; Star Wars Episode I: The Phantom Menace, 1999; Rules of Engagement, 1999; Shaft, 2000;

Dictionary of International Biography

Unbreakable, 2000; The Caveman's Valentine, 2001; The 51st State, 2001; Changing Lanes, 2002; Star Wars Episode II: Attack of the Clones, 2002; The House on Turk Street, 2002; XXX, 2002; Basic, 2003; S.W.A.T, 2003; Country of My Skull, 2004; Twisted, 2004; Kill Bill: Vol 2, 2004. Honours include: Best Actor Award, Cannes International Film Festival; New York Film Critics Award. Address: c/o ICM, 8942 Wilshire Boulevard, Beverly Hills, CA 90211, USA.

JACKSON Victoria (Vicky), b. 6 August 1934, London, England. m. Antoine Jackson, 1 son, 1 daughter. Education: Colchester College of Further Education; Dartington College of Arts. Appointments: Professional Singer, 1969-78; Singing Teacher, 1980-83; BBC Recording Artist; Accounts Controller, Executive Director, Chief Executive Officer, 1987-. Honour: Life Fellow, International Biographical Association. Memberships: Membership Secretary, World Foundation of Successful Women; Royal Horticultural Society. Address: Withycot, Ely Road, Prickwillow, Cambridgeshire CB7 4UJ, England.

JACKSON William David, b. 15 July 1947, Liverpool, England. Freelance Journalist; Translator; Poet. m. Christa Antonie Range, 3 June 1972, 1 son, 1 daughter. Education: BA, Honours, English Language and Literature, St Catherine's College, Oxford, 1968. Publication: Then and Now, book, 2002. Contributions to: Acumen; Babel; Blithe Spirit; The Dark Horse; Haiku Quarterly; Iron; Leviathan Quarterly; Metre; Modern Poetry in Translation; Oasis; Orbis; Outposts; Oxford Poetry; Pennine Platform; Poetry Nottingham; Poetry Review; Poetry Wales; The Rialto; The Shop; Stand; Staple. Address: Clemensstrasse 66, 80796 Munich, Germany.

JACKSON (William) Keith, b. 5 September 1928, Colchester, Essex, England. Emeritus Professor. m. (1) 3 children, (2) Jennifer Mary Louch, 21 December 1990. Education: London University Teaching Certificate, 1947; BA, Honours, University of Nottingham, 1953; PhD, University of Otago, New Zealand, 1967. Publications: New Zealand Politics in Action (with A V Mitchell and R M Chapman), 1962; New Zealand (with J Harré), 1969; Editor, Fight for Life, New Zealand, Britain and the EEC, 1971; New Zealand Legislative Council, 1972; Politics of Change, 1972; The Dilemma of Parliament, 1987; Historical Dictionary of New Zealand (with A D McRobie), 1996; New Zealand Adopts Proportional Representation: Accident? Design? Evolution? (with Alan McRobie), 1998. Contributions to: Numerous professional journals. Honours: Mobil Award for Best Spoken Current Affairs Programme, Radio New Zealand, 1979; Henry Chapman Fellow, Institute of Commonwealth Studies, London, 1963; Canterbury Fellowship, 1987; Asia 2000 Fellowship, 1996. Address: 92A, Hinau Street, Christchurch 4, New Zealand.

JACKSON-LAUFER Guida Myrl Miller, (Guida Jackson), b. Clarendon, Texas, USA. Author; University Lecturer; Editor; Publisher. m. (1) Prentice Lamar Jackson, 3 sons, 1 daughter, 1954, (2) William Hervey Laufer, 1986. Education: BA, Texas Tech University, 1954; MA, California State University, 1986; PhD, Greenwich University International Institute of Advanced Studies, 1989. Appointments: Managing Editor, Touchstone Literary Journal, 1976-; Lecturer in Writing, 1986-. Publications: Passing Through, 1979; The Lamentable Affair of the Vicar's Wife, 1981; The Three Ingredients (co-author), 1981; Heart to Heart, 1988; Women Who Ruled, 1990; African Women Write (compiler), 1990; Virginia Diaspora, 1992; Encyclopaedia of Traditional Epic, 1994; Legacy of the Texas Plains, 1994. Contributions to: Encyclopaedia of Literary Epic, 1996; Women Rulers Throughout the Ages, 1999; Fall From Innocence, 1997; Numerous other books and periodicals. Address: c/o Panther Creek Press, PO Box 130233, Spring, TX 77393-0233, USA.

JACOBI Derek George, b. 22 October 1938, London, England. Actor. Education: St Johns College, Cambridge. Appointments: Birmingham Repertory Theatre, 1960-63; National Theatre, 1963-71; Prospect Theatre Company, 1972, 1974, 1976-78; Artistic Association, 1976-; Old Vic Company, 1978-79; Joined Royal Shakespeare Company, 1982; Vice-President, National Youth Theatre, 1982-; Artistic Director, Chichester Festival, 1995-. Creative Works: TV appearances include: She Stoops to Conquer; Man of Straw; The Pallisers; I Claudius; Philby; Burgess and Maclean; Tales of the Unexpected; A Stranger in Town; Mr Pye; Brother Cadfael TV series, 1994-; Films: Odessa File; Day of the Jackal; The Medusa Touch; Othello; Three Sisters; Interlude; The Human Factor; Charlotte, 1981; The Man Who Went up in Smoke, 1981; The Hunchback of Notre Dame, 1981; Inside the Third Reich, 1982; Little Dorrit, 1986; The Tenth Man, 1988; Henry V, The Fool, 1990; Dead Again, 1996; Hamlet, 1996; Love is the Devil, 1997; Gladiator, 2000; Gosford Park, 2002; Plays: The Lunatic; Lover and the Poet, 1980; The Suicide, 1980; Much Ado About Nothing; Peer Gynt; The Tempest, 1982; Cyrano de Bergerac, 1983; Breaking the Code, 1986; Richard II, 1988; Richard III, 1989; Kean, 1990; Becket, 1991; Mad, Bad and Dangerous to Know; Ambassadors, 1992; Macbeth, 1993; Hadrian VII, 1995; Playing the Wife, 1995; Uncle Vanya, 1996; God Only Knows, 2000; Director: Hamlet, 1988, 2000. Honours: Honorary Fellow, St Johns College, Cambridge; Variety Club Award, 1976; British Academy Award, 1976; Press Guild Award, 1976; Royal TV Society Award, 1976; Evening Standard Award Best Actor, 1998. Address: Chichester Festival Theatre, Oaklands Park, Chichester, West Sussex PO19 4AP, England.

JACOBSON Dan, b. 7 March 1929, Johannesburg, South Africa. Professor Emeritus; Writer. m. Margaret Pye, 3 sons, 1 daughter. Education: BA, University of the Witwatersrand; Honorary Ph.D., University of Witwatersrand. Appointments: Visiting Fellow, Stanford University, California, 1956-57; Professor, Syracuse University, New York, 1965-66; Fellow, 1981, Australian National University; Lecturer, 1975-80, Reader, 1980-87, Professor, 1988-94, Professor Emeritus, 1994-, University College, London. Publications: The Trap, 1955; A Dance in the Sun, 1956; The Price of Diamonds, 1957; The Evidence of Love, 1960; The Beginners, 1965; The Rape of Tamar, 1970; The Confessions of Josef Baisz, 1979; The Story of the Stories, 1982; Time and Time Again, 1985; Adult Pleasures, 1988; Hidden in the Heart, 1991; The God Fearer, 1992; The Electronic Elephant, 1994; Heshel's Kingdom, 1998; A Mouthful of Glass, translation, 2000; Ian Hamilton in Conversation with Dan Jacobson, interview, 2002. Contributions to: Periodicals and newspapers. Honours: John Llewelyn Rhys Memorial Award, 1958; W Somerset Maugham Award, 1964; H H Wingate Award, 1979; J R Ackerley Award, 1986; Honorary DLitt, University of the Witwatersrand, 1987; Mary Elinore Smith Prize, 1992. Address: c/o A M Heath & Co Ltd, 79 St Martins Lane, London WC2, England.

JACOBSON Howard, b. 25 August 1942, Manchester, England. Novelist. m. Rosalin Sadler, 1978, 1 son. Education: BA, Downing College, Cambridge. Appointments: Lecturer, University of Sydney, 1965-68; Supervisor, Selwyn College, Cambridge, 1969-72; Senior Lecturer, Wolverhampton Polytechnic, 1974-80; Television Critic, The Sunday Correspondent, 1989-90; Into the Land of Oz, (Channel 4), 1991; Writer/Presenter, Yo, Mrs Askew! (BBC2), 1991, Roots Schmoots (Channel 4 TV), 1993, Sorry, Judas (Channel 4 TV), 1993, Seriously Funny: An Argument for Comedy (Channel 4 TV), 1997; Columnist, The Independent, 1998-. Publications: Shakespeare's Magnanimity: Four Tragic Heroes, Their Friends and Families, 1978; Coming From Behind, 1983; Peeping Tom, 1984; Redback, 1986; In the Land of Oz, 1987; The Very Model of a Man, 1992; Roots Schmoots, 1993;

Seeing With the Eye: The Peter Fuller Memorial Lecture, 1993; Seriously Funny, 1997; No More Mister Nice Guy, 1998; The Mighty Walzer, 1999; Who's Sorry Now?, 2002; The Making of Henry, 2004. Honours: Winner Jewish Quarterly and Wingate Prize, 2000; Winner of the first Bollinger Everyman Wodehouse Prize, 2000. Membership: Modern Painters, editorial board. Address: Curtis Brown, Haymarket House, 28-29 Haymarket, London SWIY 4SP, England.

JACOBSON Raymond Earl, b. 25 May 1922, St Paul, Minnesota, USA. Electronics Company Entrepreneur; Executive. Divorced, 3 sons. Education: BE (high honours), Yale University, 1944; MBA (with distinction), Harvard University, 1948; BA Economics, Oxford University, 1950; MA, 1954. Appointments: Lt (jg) USNR, 1943-46; Lecturer, Engineering, University of California, Los Angeles, 1958-60; Chairman, General Electronic Control Inc, 1961-63; Staco Inc, Dayton, Ohio, 1961-63; President, Whitehall Electronics Inc, Dallas, 1961-63; Director, Several Electronics Companies, 1961-99; President, Maxson Electronics, Great River, New York, 1963-64; President, Jacobson Associates, California, 1964-67; Lecturer, Business Administration, University of California, Berkeley, 1965-67; Co-Founder, Chief Executive Officer, Chairman, President, Anderson Jacobson Inc, 1967-88; Chairman, CXR Telcom Inc, San Jose, 1988-93. Honours include: Prize for Excellence, Mechanical Engineering, Yale University, 1944; Rhodes Scholar, 1948; Society of Sigma Xi; Tau Beta Pi; National Honour Society; Eagle Scout. Memberships: Association of American Rhodes Scholars; Harvard Business School Association; Oxford Society; Yale Club; Yale Class of 1944 Executive Committee; Brasenose Society; Courtside Tennis Club. Address: 543 Elk River Court, Reno, NV 89511, USA.

JAEGGI Eva Maria, b. 12 February 1934, Vienna, Austria. Professor. Divorced, 1 daughter. Education: PhD, Psychology; Habilitation, Clinical Psychology, Psychoanalysis. Appointments: Assistant, Sozialforschungsstelle, Dortmund, 1957-60; Head, Student Counselling, Bochum, 1966-72; Assistant Professor, Freie University, Berlin, 1972-78; Professor, Techn University, Berlin, 1978-99. Publications: 12 books on psychotherapy and/or lifestyle; Many articles. Honours: Silbernes Ehrenzeichen der Stadt, Wien, 1995; Auzeichnung fuer die beste Lehre, 1997; Wissenschaftsbuch des Jahres, 2002. Memberships: Neue Gesellschaft fuer Psychologie; DGPT. Address: Forststr 25, D-14163, Berlin, Germany. E-mail: eva.jaeggi@tu-berlin.de

JAEKEL Torsten, b. 1 April 1961, Berlin, Germany. Marketing Manager. m. Elke, separated, 1 son, 1 daughter. Education: Diploma, University Study of Electronics, 1987. Appointments: Software Engineer, Siemens; Development Team Leader, Siemens and Tektronix; Business Development Manager, Cellware Broadband and ADVA Optical Networking; Marketing Manager, Rohde & Schwarz. Publications: Various conference publications; Articles in magazines, including News of Rohde & Schwarz. Honours: University Award, Humboldt University, 1987. Memberships: Former member, PRO-MPEG Forum; IP Datacasting Forum; FKTG Germany. Address: Alberichstr 60, 12683 Berlin, Germany. E-mail: torsten.jaekel@ftk.rohde-schwarz.com

JAFAR Muhammad Mamun, b. 5 June 1970, Kumasi, Ghana. Information Entrepreneur; Researcher. m. Umuratu Muhammad. Appointments: Founder, CEO, El-Mamun Enterprise and El-Mamun Centre; Research Board of Advisers, Board Member, American Biographical Institute; Ghana's Consulting Editor, Contemporary Who's Who of the ABI. Publications: El Mamun Business Ideas And Quotations. Honours: Research Fellow American Biographical Institute. Memberships; Meridian Club,

Honorary Member IBC Advisory Council; Listed in numerous Who's Who and biographical publications. Address: El Mamun Centre, PO Box A0. 182, Kumasi Ashanti, Ghana, West Africa. E-mail: elmamuncentre@yahoo.com

JAFFEE Annette Williams, b. 10 January 1945, Abilene, Texas, USA. Novelist. Divorced, 1 son, 1 daughter. Education: BS, Boston University, 1966. Publications: Adult Education, 1981; Recent History, 1988; The Dangerous Age, 1999. Contributions to: Ploughshares; Missouri Review; Ontario Review. Honours: New Jersey Arts Council Grant, 1986; Dodge Fellow, Yaddo, 1991. Memberships: PEN. Address: PO Box 26, River Road, Lumberville, PA 18933, USA.

JAGANNATHAN Sarangapani, b. 14 June 1965, Thuvariman, Madurai, India. Professor. m. Sandhya, 1 daughter. Education: BEng, 1986; MSc, 1989; PhD, 1994. Appointments: Director, Systems and Controls Research, Caterpillar Inc, 1994-98; Director, Intelligent Systems Laboratory, University of Texas at San Antonio, 1998-2001; Director, Embedded Systems and Networking Laboratory, University of Missouri, Rolla, 2001-. Publications: 25 journal articles; Over 70 refereed conference articles; 1 book; Several book chapters and presentations; Over 16 patents and several pending. Honours: Presidential Award for Research Excellence, 2001; NSR Cancer Award, 2000; Patent Award, 1996; Sigma Xi Award; Several Research Awards. Memberships: IEEE: ASEE: Sigma Xi; Tau Beta Pi; Eta Kappa Nu. Address: Department of Electrical and Computer Engineering, 1870 Miner Circle, Rolla, MO 65409, USA. E-mail: sarangap@umr.edu Website: www.umr.edu/~sarangapani

JAGGER Mick, b. 26 July 1943, Dartford, Kent, England. Singer; Songwriter. m. (1) Bianca Pérez Morena de Macias, 1971, divorced, 1979, 1 daughter, (2) Jerry Hall, 2 sons, 2 daughters; 1 daughter by Marsha Hunt. Education: London School of Economics. Career: Member, Rolling Stones, 1962-; Numerous tours, concerts include: National Jazz & Blues Festival, Richmond, 1963; Debut UK tour, 1963; Debut US tour, 1964; Free concert, Hyde Park, 1969; Free concert, Altamont Speedway, 1969; Knebworth Festival, 1976; Live Aid, Philadelphia, 1985; Solo tour including Japan, 1988; Steel Wheels North American tour, 1989; National Music Day Celebration Of The Blues, with Gary Moore, 1992; Voodoo Lounge World Tour, 1994-95; Bridges to Babylon Tour, 1997-98; Films include: Ned Kelly, 1970; Performance, 1970; Freejack, 1992; Bent, 1996. Compositions: Co-writer for the Rolling Stones, with Keith Richards (under the pseudonym The Glimmer Twins). Recordings: Albums include: The Rolling Stones, 1964; The Rolling Stones No 2, 1965; Out Of Our Heads, 1965; Aftermath, 1966; Between The Buttons, 1967; Their Satanic Majesties Request, 1967; Beggar's Banquet, 1968; Let It Bleed, 1969; Get Yer Ya-Ya's Out, 1969; Sticky Fingers, 1971; Exile On Main Street, 1972; Goat's Head Soup, 1973; It's Only Rock And Roll, 1974; Black And Blue, 1976; Some Girls, 1978; Emotional Rescue, 1980; Still Life, 1982; Steel Wheels, 1989; Flashpoint, 1991; Stripped, 1995; Bridges to Babylon, 1997; Solo albums: She's The Boss, 1985; Primitive Cool, 1987; Wandering Spirit, 1993; Goddess in the Doorway, 2001; Singles include: It's All Over Now; Little Red Rooster; (I Can't Get No) Satisfaction; Get Off Of My Cloud; Jumping Jack Flash; Let's Spend The Night Together; Brown Sugar; 19th Nervous Breakdown; Harlem Shuffle; Ruby Tuesday; Paint It Black; It's Only Rock'n'Roll; Start Me Up; Undercover Of The Night; Dancing In The Street (with David Bowie). Honours: with Rolling Stones include: Grammy Lifetime Achievement Award, 1986; Inducted into Rock And Roll Hall Of Fame, 1989; Q Award, Best Live Act, 1990; Ivor Novello Award, Outstanding Contribution To British Music, 1991. Address: c/o Rupert Loewenstein, 2 King Street, London SW1Y 6QL, England.

JAHN Ilse Margarete (Trommer), b. 2 February 1922, Chemnitz (Sachsen). Biologist. m. Dr Wilhelm Jahn, deceased 12 April 1945, 1 daughter. Education: Studied Biology, 1941-42, 1952-56, Diploma in Biology, 1956, Dr rer nat, 1963; University of Jena; DrScNat (habil), Humboldt University, 1979; Docent, Berlin, 1980. Appointments: Assistant Ernst-Haeckel-Haus Jena, 1956-62; Research Fellow (Editor), A-Von-Humboldt Commission, Academy of Science, Berlin, 1962-67; Curator of exposition in Museum für Naturkunde, Humboldt University, 1967-80; Docent of Museology, Humboldt University, Berlin, 1980-82. Publications: Dem Leben auf der Spur, 1969; Die Jugendbriefe Alexander von Humboldts (co-editor), 1973; Charles Darwin, 1982; Geschichte der Biologie (co-editor), 1982, 1985, 1998; Grundzüge der Biologieschichte, 1990; Darwin and Co (co-editor), 2001; 208 scientific articles and biographies. Honours: Vice-Director, Museum für Naturkunde, 1971-74; President, section/biological museums, (council of museums GDR) 1971-82; Title, Obermuseumsrat (Ministry of Culture), 1984; German Society of History and Theory of Biology; President, 1991-93. Memberships: Deutsche Akademie der Naturforscher Leopoldina, 1986-; Corresponding Member, Senckenberg Naturf Ges (SNG), 1992-; New York Academy of Sciences, 1995-; Dr h c, University of Jena, 2002. Address: Eyke-von-Repkow-Pl.2, 10555 Berlin, Germany.

JAKOBSSON Thor Edward, b. 5 October 1936, Wynyard, Sask, Canada. Research Scientist. m. Johanna Johannesdottir, 1 son, 1 daughter. Education: Cand Mag, University of Oslo and Bergen, Norway, 1964; Cand Real, Meteorology, University of Bergen, Norway, 1966; PhD, Meteorology, McGill University, Montreal, Canada, 1973. Appointments: Research Assistant, University of Bergen, Norway, 1966-68; Research Scientist, Atmospheric Environment Service, Toronto, Canada, 1973-79; Research Scientist and Project Manager, Icelandic Meteorological Office, Reykjavik, Iceland, 1979-; Adjunct Professor, University of Iceland, 1980-. Publications: Popular and scientific articles, reports and book chapters; numerous articles on various subjects in newspapers and journals. Memberships: American Meteorological Society; Canadian Meteorological and Oceanographic Society; International Biometeorological Society. Address: Espigerdi 2 (2E), IS-108 Reykjavik, Iceland, Europe.

JAMES Alan Morien, b. 20 January 1933, Newport, Monmouthshire, Wales. Retired University Teacher. m. (1) Valerie Hancox, 4 sons, 2 daughters, (2) Lorna Lloyd. Education: BSc Economics, first class honours, London School of Economics and Political Science, 1954. Appointments: Civil service, 1955-57; Assistant Lecturer, Lecturer, Senior Lecturer, Reader in International Relations, London School of Economics, 1957-73; Professor of International Relations, Keele University, 1974-98. Publications: 8 books. Honours: Rockefeller Research Fellow, Columbia University, 1968; Visiting Professor, University of Ife, 1981; Visiting Professor, Jawaharlal Nehru University, 1983; Guest Professor, National Institute for Defense Studies, Japan, 1993. Memberships: Committees of Social Science Research Council; Council for National Academic Awards; University Grants Committee. Address: 23 Park Lane, Congleton, Cheshire CW12 3DG, England.

JAMES Anthony, (A R James), b. 17 March 1931, London, England. Literary Researcher; Author. m. (1) Jacqueline, 19 April 1952, deceased, (2) Anne, 27 September 1997, 1 son, 2 daughters. Appointments: General Manager, Wimbledon Stadium, 1956-91; Secretary, NGRC Racecourse Promoters, 1989-. Publications: W W Jacobs Companion, 1990; Wimbledon Stadium - The First Sixty Years, 1993, new enlarged edition, 2000; Informing the People, 1996; W W Jacobs (biography), 1999; WW Jacobs Book: Hunter's

Field Guide, 2001. Contributions to: Book and Magazine Collector; Antiquarian Book Monthly; W W Jacobs Appreciation Society Newsletter; WWII HMSO Paperbacks Society Newsletter. Memberships: Secretary and Editor, W W Jacobs Appreciation Society, WWII HMSO Paperbacks Society. Address: 3 Roman Road, Southwick, W Sussex BN42 4TP, England.

JAMES Clive Vivian Leopold, b. 7 October 1939. Writer; Broadcaster; Journalist. Education: Sydney University; Pembroke College, Cambridge. Appointments: President, Footlights, Cambridge; TV Critic, 1972-82, Feature Writer, 1972-, The Observer; Director, Watchmaker Productions, 1994-; Lyricist for Pete Atkin; TV series including: Cinema; Up Sunday; So It Goes; A Question of Sex; Saturday Night People; Clive James on Television; The Late Clive James; The Late Show with Clive James; Saturday Night Clive; Fame in the 20th Century; Sunday Night Clive; The Clive James Show; Numerous TV documentaries including: Clive James meets Katherine Hepburn, 1986; Clive James meets Jane Fonda; Clive James meets Mel Gibson, 1998; Clive James meets the Supermodels, 1998; Postcard series, 1989-; Publications: Non-Fiction: The Metropolitan Critic, 1974; The Fate of Felicity Fark in the Land of the Media, 1975; Peregrine Prykke's Pilgrimage Through the London Literary World, 1976; Britannia Bright's Bewilderment in the Wilderness of Westminster, 1976; Visions Before Midnight, 1977; At the Pillars of Hercules, 1979; First Reactions, 1980; The Crystal Bucket, 1981; Charles Charming's Challenges on the Pathway to the Throne, 1981; From the Land of Shadows, 1982; Glued to the Box, 1982; Flying Visits, 1984; Snakecharmers in Texas, 1988; The Dreaming Swimmer, 1992; Fame, 1993; The Speaker in Ground Zero, 1999; Novels: Brilliant Creatures, 1983; The Remake, 1987; Unreliable Memoirs (autobiography), 1980; Falling Towards England: Unreliable Memoirs Vol II, 1985; Unreliable Memoirs Vol III, 1990; May Week Was in June, 1990; Brrm! Brrm! or The Man From Japan or Perfume at Anchorage, 1991; Fame in the 20th Century, 1993; The Metropolitan Critic, 1993; Criticism: Clive James on Television, 1993; The Silver Castle, 1996; 3 volumes of poetry. Address: c/o Watchmaker Productions, The Chrysalis Building, Bramley Road, London W10 6SP, England.

JAMES David Geraint, b. 2 January 1922, Treherbert, Wales. Doctor of Medicine. m. Sheila Sherlock, deceased, 2 daughters. Education: MA, MD, Jesus College, Cambridge; MRCS, LRCP, MRCP, Middlesex Hospital, University of London. Appointments: Surgeon-Lieutenant RNVR, 1946-48; Consultant Physician, Royal Navy, 1972-85; Dean of Studies, 1968-88, Consultant Physician, 1959-, Royal Northern Hospital, London; Professor of Medicine, University of London and Miami; Consultant Ophthalmic Physician, St Thomas' Hospital, London. Publications: Textbook of Infections, 1957; Colour Atlas of Respiratory Diseases, 1981; Sarcoidosis, 1985. Honours: Worshipful Society of Apothecaries, 1960-; Freeman, City of London; Honorary LLD University of Wales, 1982; FRCP, 1964; Honorary FACP, 1990. Memberships: Harvey Society, London; Osler Club, London; Medical Society, London; London Medical Ophthalmology Society; World Congress History of Medicine; RCP; Hunterian Society; World Association of Sarcoidosis; International Journal of Sarcoidosis; Postgraduate Medical Federation; Thoracic Society of France, Italy and Portugal; French National Academy of Medicine; London Glamorganshire Society; White Robed Member, Bardic Circle of Wales. Address: 41 York Terrace East, London NW1 4PT, England.

JAMES Glen William, b. 22 August 1952, London, England. Solicitor. m. Amanda Claire Dorrell, 3 daughters. Education: New College, Oxford. Appointments: Articled Clerk, 1974-76, Assistant Solicitor, 1976-83, Partner, 1983-, Slaughter and May. Publications: Various professional articles contributed to books

Dictionary of International Biography

and other publications associated with corporate and commercial law. Memberships: Law Society; City of London Solicitors' Company; Securities Institute; Royal Automobile Club. Address: c/o 1 Bunhill Row, London EC1Y 8YY, England.

JAMES Michael Leonard, b. 7 February 1941, Cornwall, England. Government Official; Writer and Broadcaster. m. Jill Tarján, 2 daughters. Education: MA, Christ's College, Cambridge; FRSA. Appointments: Entered Government Service, GCHQ, 1963; Private Secretary to Rt Hon Jennie Lee, Minister for the Arts, 1966-68; DES, 1968-71; Planning Unit of Rt Hon Margaret Thatcher, Secretary of State for Education and Science, 1971-73; Assistant Secretary, 1973; Deputy Chief Scientific Officer, 1974; Adviser, OECD, Paris and UK Governor, International Institute for Management of Technology, Milan, 1973-75; International Negotiations on Non-Proliferation of Nuclear Weapons, 1975-78; Director, IAEA Vienna, 1978-83; Adviser, International Relations, 1983-85, Consultant, 1985-2001, Commission of the European Union, Brussels; Chair, Civil Service Selection Boards, 1983-93; Chair, The Hartland Press Ltd, 1985-2001, Wade Hartland Films Ltd, 1991-2000; Feature Writer and Book Reviewer for The Times, (Resident Thriller Critic, 1990-91); Sunday Times, Guardian and Daily Telegraph, (Resident Thriller Critic, 1993-). Publications: Co-author, Internationalization to Prevent the Spread of Nuclear Weapons, 1980; Novels, as Michael Hartland: Down Among the Dead Men, 1983; Seven Steps to Treason, 1985 (South West Arts Literary Award, dramatised for BBC Radio 4, 1990); The Third Betrayal, 1986; Frontier of Fear, 1989; The Year of the Scorpion, 1991; As Ruth Carrington: Dead Fish, 1998; TV and radio include: Sonja's Report, ITV, 1990; Masterspy (interviews with KGB defector Oleg Gordievsky), BBC Radio 4, 1991. Honours: Honorary Fellow, University of Exeter, 1985-; Memberships: Governor, East Devon College of Further Education, Tiverton, 1985-91; Colyton Grammar School, 1985-90, Sidmouth Community College, 1988-; (Chair, Board of Governors, 1998-2002); Chair, Board of Governors, Axe Vale Further Education College, Seaton, 1987-91; Member, Immigration Appeal Tribunal, 1987-; Devon and Cornwall Rent Assessment Panel, 1990-; General Medical Council, Professional Conduct Committee, 2000-. Address: Cotte Barton, Branscombe, Devon, EX12 3BH, England.

JAMES P(hyllis) D(orothy) (Baroness James of Holland Park). b. 3 August 1920, Oxford, England. Author. m. Ernest Connor Bantry White, 9 August 1941, deceased 1964, 2 daughters. Appointments: Member, BBC General Advisory Council, 1987-88, Arts Council, 1988-92, British Council, 1988-93; Chairman, Booker Prize Panel of Judges, 1987; Governor, BBC, 1988-93; President, Society of Authors, 1997-. Publications: Cover Her Face, 1962; A Mind to Murder, 1963; Unnatural Causes, 1967; Shroud for a Nightingale, 1971; The Maul and the Pear Tree (with T A Critchley), 1971; An Unsuitable Job for a Woman, 1972; Innocent Blood, 1980; The Skull Beneath the Skin, 1982; A Taste for Death, 1986; Devices and Desires, 1989; The Children of Men, 1992; Original Sin, 1994; A Certain Justice, 1997; Time to be in Earnest, 1999; Death in Holy Orders, 2001; The Murder Room, 2003. Honours: Order of the British Empire; Honorary Fellow, St Hilda's College, Oxford, 1996, Downing College, Cambridge, 2000, Girton College, Cambridge, 2000; Honorary DLitt, University of Buckingham, 1992, University of Hertfordshire, 1994, University of Glasgow, 1995, University of Durham, 1988, University of Portsmouth, 1999; Honorary LitD, University of London, 1993; Dr hc, University of Essex, 1996; Grand Master Award, Mystery Writers of America, 1999. Memberships: Fellow, Royal Society of Literature; Fellow, Royal Society of Arts. Address: c/o Greene & Heaton Ltd, 37 Goldhawk Road, London W12 8QQ, England.

JAMIL Tariq, b. 9 November 1965, Pakistan. Lecturer; Engineer. Education: BSc, Electrical Engineering, NWFP University of Engineering and Technology, Pakistan, 1989; MS, Computer Engineering , 1992, PhD, Computer Engineering, 1996, Florida Institute of Technology, USA. Appointments: Graduate Teaching Assistant, Florida Institute of Technology, USA, 1994-96; Assistant Professor, Faculty of Computer Science and Engineering, GIK Institute of Engineering Sciences and Technology, Pakistan, 1997; Lecturer, School of Computer Science and Engineering, University New South Wales, Sydney, Australia, 1997-98; Lecturer, School of Computing, University of Tasmania, Launceston, Australia, 1999-2000; Assistant Professor, Information Engineering Department, Sultan Qaboos University, Muscat, Oman, 2000-. Publications include: An Investigation into the Application of Linear Feedback Shift registers for Steganography, 2002; Design of a Nibble-Size Adder for (-1+j)-base complex binary numbers, 2002; Hardware Implementation and Performance Evaluation of Complex Binary Adder Designs, 2003; Division in a Binary Representation for Complex numbers, 2003; Implementation of a CAM-based Dataflow Processor for Parallel Computations, 2004; The Rijndael Algorithm - A brief introduction to the new encryption standard, 2004. Honours include: National Talent Scholarship, 1981-89; President's Cash Award and Gold Medal, 1983, Best Graduate and Gold Medal, 1989; Quaid-e-Azam Scholarship, 1990-94; Award for Academic Excellence, IEEE, Computer Society, 1996. Memberships: IEEE, USA; Institution of Electrical Engineers, UK; Institution of Electrical and Electronic Engineers, Pakistan; Chartered Engineer, UK; Professional Engineer, Pakistan. Address: Electrical and Computer Engineering Department, Sultan Qaboos University, PO Box 33, Muscat 123, Sultanate of Oman.

JANES J(oseph) Robert, b. 23 May 1935, Toronto, Ontario, Canada. Writer. m. Gracia Joyce Lind, 16 May 1958, 2 sons, 2 daughters. Education: BSc, Mining Engineering, 1958, MEng, Geology, 1967, University of Toronto. Publications: Children's books: The Tree-Fort War, 1976; Theft of Gold, 1980; Danger on the River, 1982; Spies for Dinner, 1984; Murder in the Market, 1985. Adult books: The Toy Shop, 1981; The Watcher, 1982; The Third Story, 1983; The Hiding Place, 1984; The Alice Factor, 1991; Mayhem, 1992; Carousel, 1992; Kaleidoscope, 1993; Salamander, 1994; Mannequin, 1994; Dollmaker, 1995; Stonekiller, 1995; Sandman, 1996; Gypsy, 1997; Madrigal, 1999; Beekeeper, 2001; Flykiller, 2002. Non-Fiction: The Great Canadian Outback, 1978. Textbooks: Holt Geophoto Resource Kits, 1972; Rocks, Minerals and Fossils, 1973; Earth Science, 1974; Geology and the New Global Tectonics, 1976; Searching for Structure (co-author), 1977. Teacher's Guide: Searching for Structure (co-author), 1977; Airphoto Interpretation and the Canadian Landscape (with J D Mollard), 1984. Contributions to: Toronto Star; Toronto Globe and Mail; The Canadian; Winnipeg Free Press; Canadian Children's Annual. Honours: Grants: Canada Council; Ontario Arts Council; J P Bickell Foundation; Thesis Award, Canadian Institute of Mining and Metallurgy; Works-in-progress Grant, Ontario Arts Council, 1991; Hammett Award Nominee, International Association of Crime Writers (North American Branch). Memberships: Crime Writers Association (UK); Historical Novel Society (UK); International Association of Crime Writers (North American Branch); Crime Writers of Canada. Address: PO Box 1590, Niagara-on-the-Lake, Ontario L0S 1J0, Canada.

JANFADA Ali S, b. 1 July 1960, Urmia, Iran. Reader in Mathematics. m. Parisa M Sani, 2 sons, 1 daughter. Education: BSc, Mathematics, 1985, MSc, Mathematics (Algebra), 1989, Tabriz University, Iran; PhD, Mathematics (Algebraic Topology), Manchester University, England, 2001. Appointment: Currently Reader in Mathematics, Urmia University, Iran. Publications: Textbook: FORTRAN 77, in Persian, 1994; Articles: The group of automorphisms of non-associative communicative algebra associated with the group of automorphisms of 2-designs, 1993; The hit problem for symmetric polynomials over the Steenrod algebra, 2002; Generating H*(BO(3),F$_2$) as a module over the Steenrod algebra, 2003. Memberships: American Mathematical Society; Iranian Mathematical Society. Address: Department of Mathematics, Urmia University, PO Box 165, Urmia, Iran. E-mail: asjanfada@hotmail.com

JANKE John Eric, b. 30 March 1960, Longview, Washington, USA. Historian; Educator; Lecturer. Education: AA Degree, Lower Columbia College, 1979-82; BA degree, Central Washington University, 1982-84; BA Degree, Western Washington University, 1984-86; Fifth Year Degree, Central Washington University, 1989-91; Continuing Education, Seattle Pacific University, 1993; Masters of Education Degree, Central Washington University, 1998-99. Honours: Lettered in Golf, Robert A Long High School, Longview, Washington, 1977-79; Junior Achievement Award, Masonic Lodge, Longview, Washington, 1978; Outstanding History Student Award, Daughters of the American Revolution, Longview Chapter, 1978; Longview Education Association and School District, Outstanding Contributor Award, Future Leaders of America Conference, Portland, Oregon, 1978; Future Teacher of the Year, Lettered in Golf, Lower Columbia College, 1980-81; Special Achievement Award, Central Washington University, 1997; Film, The John Janke Story, Central Washington University, 2001. Memberships: National Education Association; Washington Education Association; Kelso Education Association. Address: 912 Elizabeth Street, Kelso, WA 98626, USA. E-mail: johnjanke@yahoo.com

JANNER Greville Ewan, Baron Janner of Braunstone, b. 11 July 1928, Cardiff, South Wales. Working Peer; Barrister; Queen's Counsel; Author; Jewish Leader. m. Myra Louise Sheink, deceased, 1 son, 2 daughters. Education: MA, Trinity Hall, Cambridge, 1946-49; Harvard Law School, 1950-51; Hon PhD, Haifa, 1984; Hon LLD, De Montfort University, Leicester, 1998. Appointments: Member of Parliament, Leicester North West, 1970-74; Member of Parliament, Leicester West, 1974-97; Chairman, Select Committee on Employment, 1992-96; Vice Chairman, British Israel and British India Parliamentary Groups; Vice President, World Jewish Congress; Founder President, Commonwealth Jewish Council; Chairman, Holocaust Educational Trust; President, Maimonides Foundation; Former President, Board of Deputies of British Jews, 1978-84; Founder, President, JSB Ltd; Former Director, Labroke plc. Publications: Author, 65 books mainly on employment and industrial relations law, presentational skills and public speaking; One Hand Alone Cannot Clap. Memberships: Magic Circle; International Brotherhood of Magicians. Address: House of Lords, London SW1A 0PW, England.

JANOW Steven, b. 12 July 1973, Rhinebeck, New York, USA. Composer; Musician (Saxophone). Education: Liberal Arts, State University of New York; Studies at North Carolina School of the Arts; Bachelor of Music, University of Hartford. Career: Performances in New York City, upstate New York. Compositions: Symphony; Saxophone Orchestra; Untitled music for brass and saxophone band; Manifesto On Music, detailing original techniques and innovations for music theory, harmony, counterpoint, instrumentation and orchestration, form, cadences and style. Honours: Ascap awards, 1998, 1999, 2000, 2001, 2002, 2003, 2004. Membership: ASCAP. Address: 69 Chestnut Street, Rhinebeck, NY 12572, USA.

JARBE Torbjorn, b. 6 May 1946, N Asum, Kristianstad, Sweden. m. 1 son, 1 daughter. Education: BA, Psychology, 1969, MS, Psychology, 1972, PhD, Psychology, 1977, University of Uppsala, Sweden; Postdoctoral, Pharmacology, University of North Carolina, Chapel Hill, North Carolina, Sponsor: Dr D E McMillan, 1977-1978. Appointments: Project Leader, University of Uppsala, Sweden, 1972-1991; Visiting Scientist, University of Medicine and Dentistry of New Jersey, New Jersey, USA, 1991; Visiting Associate Professor, 1991-92, Research Associate Professor, 1992-99, Hahnemann University, Philadelphia, Pennsylvania, USA; Research Associate Professor, College of Liberal Arts, Temple University, Philadelphia, 1999-. Publications: 14 chapters in books; Published abstracts; Institutional reports; Book reviews; Symposia-invited lectures, senior author presentation; Author and co-author of numerous articles in scientific journals. Honours include: Several honours and awards including Research Scientist Development Award, 1995-; Listed in numerous biographical dictionaries. Memberships include: College on Problems in Drug Dependence, 1993-; American Psychological Association, 1995-. Address: 2303 North Cuthbert Drive, Lindenwold, NJ 08028-2661, USA. E-mail: tjarbe@temple.edu

JARQUE Carlos Manuel, b. 18 October 1954, Mexico City, Mexico. Minister for Social Development, Mexican Government. m. Coral Lira Coria, 1 son, 2 daughters. Education: Bachelor, Actuarial Science, (Honorary Mention) Anahuac University, Mexico City; Postgraduate Diploma, Statistics, MSc, Statistics and Econometrics, London School Economics & Political Science; Postgraduate Diploma in Planning and Economic Policy, University of Oslo, Norway; PhD, Economics, Australian National University, Canberra; Postdoctorate, Economics, Harvard University. Appointments: General Director, Mexican Central Bureau of Statistics, 1983-86; Director, Department Economic Studies at TELMEX, 1982-83; Secretary, Mexican National Development Plan, 1995-2000; President, INEGI, 1988-99; President, UN Statistical Commission, 1996-98; Secretary, Sedesol, 1999-2000; Manager, Inter American Development Bank, 2000-04. Publications: Over 100 in econometrics, statistics, economics, demography, technology in journals and books. Honours: BANAMEX National Award of Science & Technology, 1979; National Award in Actuarial Science, 1982; Medal President Benito Juarez; Adolphe Quetelet Medal. Memberships: American Statistical Association; Actuaries College of Mexico; Royal Statistical Society; Econometric Society; American Economic Association; Institute of Actuaries. Address: Benjamin Franklin 197, Condesa, Mexico, D F Mexico, CP 06140.

JARRATT Alexander Anthony, b. 19 January 1924, London, England. Retired Civil Servant; Company Executive. m. Mary Philomena Keogh, 1 son, 2 daughters. Education: BCom, 1st Class Honours, Birmingham University, 1946-49. Appointments: Petty Officer Fleet Air Arm; Civil Servant Ministry of Power, 1949-64; Seconded to the Treasury, 1953-54; Cabinet Office, 1964-65; Secretary, Prices and Incomes Board, 1964-68; Deputy Under Secretary, Department of Employment and Productivity, 1968-70; Deputy Secretary Ministry of Agriculture, 1970; Chief Executive IPC and IPC Newspapers, 1970-74; Chairman and Chief Executive, Reed International, 1974-85, Director, 1970-85; Chairman Smiths Industries plc, 1985-91, Director, 1984-96; Deputy Chairman: Midland Bank plc, 1980-91, Prudential Corporation, 1987-91 and 1992-94; Non-Executive Director, ICI plc, 1975-91; President Advertising Association, 1979-83; Former Member, NEDC; Former Chairman, CBI Economic Policy Committee; Former Member, Presidents Committee, CBI; Chairman, Industrial Society, 1975-79; Henley Administrative Staff College, 1976-89; Centre for Dispute Resolution, 1990-2000, president, 2001-; Chancellor, University of Birmingham, 1983-2002. Honours: Companion of the Bath, 1968; Knight Bachelor, 1979; Honorary LLD, University of Birmingham; Honorary DSc, Cranfield; Honorary D Univ, Brunel and Essex; Honorary, CGIA; FRSA; Honorary FCGI. Address: Barn Mead, Fryerning, Essex CM4 0NP, England.

JARRE Jean-Michel, b. 24 August 1948, Lyons, France. Musician (synthesizers, keyboards); Composer; Record Producer. m. Charlotte Rampling, 1977. Musical Education: Piano and guitar from age 5; Conservatoire de Paris, with Jeanine Reuff. Career: Solo debut, Paris Opera, 1971; Youngest composer to appear, Palais Garnier, 1971; Major concerts, often including lasers and fireworks, filmed for video releases include: Beijing, China, 1981; Bastille Day, Place De La Concorde, 1979; Houston, Texas (1.3 million audience), 1986; London Docklands, 1988; La Defense, Paris (2.5 million audience), 1990; Sun City, Johannesburg, South Africa, 1993; Member of jury, First International Visual Music Awards, Midem, France, 1992. Compositions include: Oxygène Part IV, used for several television themes; Ballet and film scores include: Des Garçons Et Des Filles, 1968; Deserted Palace, 1972; Les Granges Brûlées, 1973; La Maladie De Hambourg, 1978; Gallipoli, 1979. Recordings: Albums (all self-composed and produced): Deserted Palace, 1971; Oxygène, 1977; Magnetic Fields, 1981; The Concerts In China, 1982; The Essential Jean-Michel Jarre, 1983; Zoolook, 1984; Rendez-Vous, 1986; In Concert Lyons/Houston, 1987; Revelations (Number 2, UK), 1988; Jarre Live, 1989; Waiting For Cousteau, 1990; Images - The Best Of Jean-Michel Jarre, 1991; Chronologie, 1993; Jarre Hong Kong, 1994; Cities in Concert, 1997; Oxygène 7-13, 1997; China Concert, 1999. Honours: First Western artist to play in China, 1981; Grand Prix, Academie Du Disque, Zoolook, 1985; Best Instrumental Album, Victoire de la Musique, 1986; Numerous Platinum and Gold discs worldwide. Address: c/o Dreyfus Records, 26 Avenue Kléber, 75116 Paris, France.

JARRE Maurice Alexis, b. 13 September 1924, Lyons, France. Composer. m. (1) France Pejot, 1946, 1 son, (2) Dany Saval, 1965, 1 daughter, (3) Laura Devon, 1967, (4) Khong Fui Fong, 1984. Musical Education: Conservatoire National Supéreur de Musique. Career: Musician, Radiodiffusion Française, 1946-50; Director of Music, Théatre National Populaire (TNP), 1950-63. Compositions: Symphonic music; Music for theatre and ballet include: Roland Petit's Notre-Dame de Paris (Paris Opera), 1966; Numerous film scores include: Lawrence Of Arabia, 1963; Dr Zhivago, 1965; Ryan's Daughter, 1970; Shogun, 1980; Doctors In Love, 1982; A Passage To India, 1985; The Mosquito Coast, 1987; Tai-Pan, 1987; Gaby, 1988; Gorillas In The Mist, 1989; Ghost; Dead Poets Society, 1990; Fatal Attraction; Les Vendanges de feu, 1994; Sunchaser, 1996. Honours: Officer, Légion d'Honneur, Commander des Arts et Lettres; Prix Italia, 1955, 1962; Grand Prix du Disque, Academy Charles Cross, 1962; Hollywood Golden Globe, 1965, 1984; People's Choice Award, 1988. Address: c/o Paul Kohner Inc, 9169 Sunset Boulevard, Los Angeles, CA 90069, USA.

JARSTAD John Steven, b. 7 September 1955, Seattle, Washington, USA. Ophthalmologist; Medical Doctor. m. Patricia, 1 son, 3 daughters. Education: BS, Zoology (Pre-Med), BYU, 1980; MD, University of Washington, 1984; Ophthalmology Residency, Mayo Clinic, 1988. Appointments: Outstanding Instructor in Ophthalmology, Mayo Clinic, 1987; Clinical Instructor, University of Washington, 1989-91; Visiting Professor, Ophthalmic Surgery, University of Zimbabwe, University of Indonesia, Nigeria, University of the Philippines. Publications: Invention: Jarstad Refractive Cataract Surgery; Marker, Swan Syndrome, 1987; Numerous articles on efficiency in eye surgery (Ophthalmology Management – contributing author). Honours: America's Top Ophthalmologists, 2003-2004, Consumer Research Council; Lecturer's Medal University of Indonesia; Outstanding Humanitarian Award, Washington Academy of Eye MDs. Memberships: American Academy of Ophthalmology; American Society of Cataract and Refractive Surgeons; American Medical Association; Washington Academy of Eye MDs. Address:

Evergreen Eye Centre, 34719 South Federal Way, WA 98003, USA. E-mail: drjarstad@aol.com Website: www.evergreeneye.com

JASON David, b. 2 February 1940, England. Actor. Creative Works: Theatre includes: Under Milk Wood, 1971; The Rivals, 1972; No Sex Please...We're British!, 1972; Darling Mr London (tour), 1975; Charley's Aunt (tour), 1975; The Norman Conquests, 1976; The Relapse, 1978; Cinderella, 1979; The Unvarnished Truth (Middle/Far East tour), 1983; Look No Hands! (tour and West End), 1985; Films: Under Milk Wood, 1970; Royal Flash, 1974; The Odd Job, 1978; Only Fools and Horses, 1983; Wind in the Willows, 1983; TV includes: Do Not Adjust Your Set, 1967; The Top Secret Life of Edgar Briggs, 1973-74; Mr Stabbs, 1974; Ronnie Barker Shows, 1975; Open All Hours, 1975; Porridge, 1975; Lucky Feller, 1975; A Sharp Intake of Breath, 1978; Del Trotter in Only Fools and Horses, 1981-91; Porterhouse Blue, 1986; Jackanory, 1988; A Bit of A Do, 1988-89; Single Voices: The Chemist, 1989; Amongst Barbarians, 1989; Pa Larkin in The Darling Buds of May, 1990-92; A Touch of Frost, 1992, 2001; The Bullion Boys, 1993; Micawber, 2001; Voice work: Dangermouse; Count Duckula; The Wind in the Willows. Honours include: Best Actor Award, BAFTA, 1988; BAFTA Fellowship, 2003. Address: c/o Richard Stone Partnership, 25 Whitehall, London SW1A 2BS, England.

JAWIEN Jacek, b. 28 November 1965, Krakow, Poland. Pharmacologist. Education: MD with honours, Medicine, 1990; PhD with honours, 1994, Jagiellonian University School of Medicine, Krakow, Poland. Appointments: Assistant, Department of Internal Medicine, 1990-97, Assistant Professor, Department of Pharmacology 1997-, Jagiellonian University School of Medicine, Krakow, Poland. Guest Researcher, Karolinska Institute, Stockholm, Sweden, 2001-2003. Publications: Articles in scientific journals including: Annals of the New York Academy of Sciences, 1995; Clin. Exp. Allergy, 1996; Allergy, 1997, Cardiovascular Research, 2003. Honours: Prize, Polish Foundation of Sciences, 1995; Research Award, Prime Minister of Poland, 1995; Councillor, 1998-200, Vice-President, 2000-2001, European Society for Clinical Investigation. Memberships: European Society for Clinical Investigation, 1993-; New York Academy of Sciences, 1996-. Address: Kolberga str. 14, Krakow 31-160, Poland.

JAY Peter, b. 7 February 1937. Writer; Broadcaster. m. (1) Margaret Ann Callaghan, 1961, dissolved 1986, 1 son, 2 daughters, (2) Emma Thornton, 1986, 3 sons. Education: MA, 1st class honours, Politics, Philosophy and Economics, Christ Church Oxford, 1960. Appointments: Midshipman and Sub-Lieutenant, RNVR, 1956-57; Assistant Principal, 1961-64, Private Secretary to Joint Permanent Secretary, 1964, Principal, 1964-67, HM Treasury; Economics Editor, The Time, 1967-77; Associate Editor, Times Business News, 1969-77; Presenter, Weekend World, ITV series, 1972-77; The Jay Interview, ITV series, 1975-76; Ambassador to USA, 1977-79; Director, Economist Intelligence University, 1979-83; Consultant, Economist Group, 1979-81; Chairman and Chief Executive, TV-AM Ltd, 1980-83, and TV-AM News, 1982-83; President, TV-AM, 1983-; Presenter, A Week in Politics, Channel 4, 1983-86; COS to Robert Maxwell, Chairman of Mirror Group Newspapers Ltd, 1986-89; Visiting Scholar, Brookings Institution, Washington, 1979-80; Wincott Memorial Lecturer, 1975; Copland Memorial Lecturer, Australia, 1980; Shell Lecturer, Glasgow, 1985; Governor, Ditchley Foundation, 1982-; Author and Presenter, Road to Riches, BBC TV series, 2000. Publications: The Budget, 1972; Contributor, America and the World, 1979, 1980; The Crisis for Western Political Economy and other Essays, 1984; Apocalypse 2000, with Michael Stewart, 1987; Contributor, Foreign Affairs journal, Road to Riches, or The Wealth of Man, 2000. Honours: Political Broadcaster of the Year, 1973; Harold Wincott Financial and Economic Journalist of the Year, 1973; RTS Male Personality of the Year, Pye Award, 1974; SFTA Shell International TV Award, 1974; RTS Home News Award, 1992; Honorary DH, Ohio State University, 1978; Honorary DLitt, Wake Forest University, 1979; Berkeley Citation, University of California, 1979. Address: Hensington Farmhouse, Woodstock, Oxfordshire OX20 1LH, England.

JAYACHANDRAN Divakaran, b. 10 November 1957, Kokkottukonam, Trivandrum, India. Medical Social Worker. m. S Lissa, 1 son, 1 daughter. Education: BSc, 1979, MA, Sociology, 1981, MA, Psychology, 1995; PhD in Behavioural Science in progress. Appointments: Research Scientist, Loyola College of Social Sciences, 1981-82; Psychiatric Social Worker, Medical College, Kozhirlekoda, 1982-85; Medical Social Worker (Principal) Comprehensive Epilepsy Program SCT Institute of Medical Sciences Trivandrum, 1985-. Publications: Numerous articles in medical journals. Honours: Best Scientific Paper award. Memberships: Governing Council IEA, Governing Body, State Resource Centre, Patron Epilepsy Self Group, Advisory Committee Newsletters; ISHA; ARDSI; ISSA. Address: Comprehensive Epilepsy Program, SCTIMST, Trivandrum, India.

JEANBART Jean-Clement (His Excellency Archbishop), b. 3 March 1943, Aleppo, Syria. Metropolite Greek Melkite Catholic of Aleppo; Apostolic Visitor for Western Europe. Education: St Anne Major Seminary, Jerusalem, 1961-66; Licence in Theology, St Joseph University, Beirut, 1968; Licence in Philosophy, University of Holy Spirit of Kaslik; Doctorate, Ethics and Moral Theology, Gregorian University, Rome, 1976; Licence in Canon Law, Pontifical Oriental Institute of Rome, 1977; Degree in Journalism and Public Opinion, International University, Pro Deo. Appointments: Ordained Priest, Aleppo, 1968; Editor, Diocesan Revue; Chaplain for Catholic University students; Rector, St Anne Major Seminary, Lebanon, 1977; Secretary General, Patriarchal Curia, 1982; In charge of Melkite Fund, 1989; Elected to the Metropolitan See of Aleppo, 1995; Elected Apostolic Visitor for Western Europe, 1999. Publications: Moral argumentation on the abortion problem; Biography of H B Maximos V; Numerous other studies, theological, social and religious articles published in several revues. Honours: Patriarchal Archimandrite of the See of Antioch, 1982; President, CDP, Lebanon, 1982; President, George Salem Foundation, Aleppo, 1995. Memberships: General Secretary, International Melkite Catholic Union. Address: Metropolite of Aleppo, Greek Melkite Catholic Archbishopric, PO Box 146, Aleppo, Syria.

JEE Chung, b. 27 July 1940, Seoul, Korea. Professor of Finance. m. Hye-Soon Lee, 2 sons. Education: BA, 1963, MBA, 1963, Korea University; MBA, Columbia University, USA, 1966; PhD, Korea University, 1975. Appointments: Professor of Finance, Korea University, 1969-; Dean of College and Graduate School of Business, Korea University; Board Member, Monetary Board, Korean Government, 1989-92; Chairman, Finance Advisory Council, Korean Government, 1998-2001. Publications include: International Financial Management, 1989; Investments, 2000; Principles of Finance, 2001. Memberships: President, Korean Association of Securities, 1988-90; President, Korean Association of Finance, 1990-91; President, Korean Association of Business Administration, 1996-97. Address: 250-13 Nonhyun-Dong, Hyundai Villa #B-16, Seoul 135-101, Korea. E-mail: jeechung@korea.ac.kr

JEFFS Julian, b. 5 April 1931, Wolverhampton, England. Author; Editor. m. Deborah Bevan, 3 sons. Education: Downing College, Cambridge. Appointments: Sherry Shipper's Assistant, Spain,

1956; Barrister, Gray's Inn, 1958; QC, 1975; Recorder, 1975-96; Bencher of Hon Society of Gray's Inn, 1981; Deputy High Court Judge (Chancery Division), 1981-96; Retired from practice, 1991. Publications: Sherry, 1961, 4th edition, 1992; Clerk & Lindsell on Torts, 13th edition, 1969 to 16th edition, 1989 (an editor); The Wines of Europe, 1971; Little Dictionary of Drink, 1973; Encyclopaedia of UK and European Patent Law, 1977, co-editor; The Wines of Spain, 1999. Honours: Office International de la Vigne et du Vin, 1962, 2001; Gran Orden de Canalleros del Vino; Glenfiddich Wine Writers Award, 1974 and 1978. Memberships: Member of Committee, Wine and Food Society, 1965-67, 1971-82; Chairman, Patent Bar Association, 1980-89; President, Circle of Wine Writers, 1992-96. Address: Church Farm House, East Ilsley, Newbury, Berkshire RG20 7LP, England.

JEHIEL Philippe Maurice Benoit, b. 29 September 1964, Boulogne, France. m. Sophie Cho-Le Gourierec, 1 son. Education: Ecole Polytechnique, 1984; Ecole Nationale des Ponts et Chausees, 1989; PhD in Economics, European Doctoral Programme, 1992. Appointments: Research Fellow, Centre d'Enseignement et de Recherche en Analyse Socio-Economique, 1990-; Professor of Economics, University College, London, 1997-. Publications: Numerous articles in professional journals. Memberships: Research Fellow, CEPR. Address: 2 Place Martin Nadaud, 75020 Paris, France. E-mail: jehiel@enpc.fr Website: www.enpc.fr/ceras/jehiel

JELINKOVA Jarmila, b. 13 December 1928, Prague. Medical Bacteriologist. 1 daughter. Education: Rerum Naturalium Doctor, Charles University, Prague, 1959; PhD, Academy of Sciences, Prague, 1966; Associate Professor, Medical Microbiology, Charles University, 1990. Appointments: Head, Institute of Medical Microbiology, Postgraduate Medical School, Prague. Publications: 157 articles in professional journals. Honours: Honorary Memberships, Czech and Czechoslovak Societies of Microbiology. Memberships include: President, Society for Epidemiology and Microbiology, Czech Medical Association; Czechoslovak Society for Microbiology; Advisory Panel on Bacterial Infection, World Health Organization; FEMS; IUMS; European Society of Clinical Microbiology and Infectious Diseases; International Society for Streptococcal Diseases. Address: Postgraduate Medical School, Department of Microbiology, Ruska 85, 100 05 Praha Vinohrady, Czech Republic.

JEMIRIYE Timothy Folorunso, b. 3 May 1948, Igede-Ekiti, Ekiti State, Nigeria. University Lecturer. m. 2 sons, 2 daughters. Education: BTh, Nigerian Baptist Theological Seminary, Ogbomoso/Southern Baptist Theological Seminary, Louisville, Kentucky, USA; MDiv, Queen's University, Kingston, Canada, 1980; MTh, University of Toronto, Canada, 1983; PhD, University of Ibadan, Nigeria, 1988. Appointments: Teacher, Western State School's Board, Ibadan, 1973-74; Teacher, Oyo State School's Board, Ibadan, 1974-75; Teacher, Salem Bible College, Ile-Ife, 1977-79; Graduate Assistant, University of Toronto, Emmanuel College, Ontario, Canada, 1981; University Lecturer in Religious Studies, 1989-, Acting Head, Department of Religious Studies, 1995-97, 1999-2000, Acting Dean, Faculty of Arts, 2000-02, University of Ado-Ekiti. Publications: 6 books; 2 chapters in books; 9 articles in professional journals. Honours: Kirk Prize Graduating Class Prize in New Testament, Queen's University, 1980; Grand Award Certificate, Commander, Order of Man O'War, Ondo State University, 1994; Listed in Ekiti Baptist High School at 40, 1995; Old Students Association National Merit Award, Ekiti Baptist High School, 2001. Memberships: Counseling Association of Nigeria; Nigerian Association for Biblical Studies; Nigerian Association for the Study of Religion. Address: Department of Religious Studies, University of Ado-Ekiti, PMB 5363, Ado-Ekiti, Ekiti State, Nigeria. E-mail: jefat2002@yahoo.com

JEN Tien Ming, b. 19 December 1927, Wanhsien, Szechuan, China. Educator; Consultant; Physician. m. Hua-chuan Wang, 12 April 1959, 1 son, 1 daughter. Education: BMed, National Defence Medical Centre, Taipei, 1952; MD, Department of Microbiology and Immunology, Duke University Medical Center, Durham, North Carolina, USA, 1961. Appointments: Medical Officer, Lieutenant to Retired Colonel, MC, Chinese Army, 1952-83; Assistant, Instructor, Associate Professor and Professor, Departments of Medical Biomorphics and Microbiology-Immunology, National Defence Medical Centre, Taipei, 1954-83; Director, Tri-Service General Hospital and Veterans General Hospital, Bacteriology and Serology Sections, 1955-83; Professor, Department of Microbiology and Immunology, National Defence Medical Centre, Taipei, 1974-; Researcher, Mycosis Research Laboratory, Pathology Department, Veterans General Hospital-Taipei, 1983-93; Consultant (Dermatology), Veterans General Hospital Taipei, 1993-2001. Publications: Book: Manual of Medical Mycology, Editions 1-3, 1971, 1975, 1981; Over 100 articles in professional proceedings and/or professional journals. Creative works include: In vitro drug test of Escherichia coli strains susceptible to Penicillin, 1957; Isoniazid prophylaxis of tuberculosis infection in mice, 1961; Isolation and identification of the strains of Microsporum canis, 1963; Cryptococcus neoformans var sinensis, 1965; Exophiala (Wangiella) dermatitidis able to assimilate creatinine and nitrate, 1966; Fonsecaea pedrosoi, 1968; Nocardia asteroides, 1977; In vitro drug test of Candida parapsilosis strains susceptible to Gentamicin (Gentamycin), 1985; Coccidioides immitis, 1990; Cryptococcus albidus, 1992. Honours: Model of Faithfulness and Honesty Award, Ministry of National Defence, Taiwan 1980; Model of Distinguished Service Award, Administrative Yuan, Taiwan, 1990; Excellent Physician Award, Mayor of Taipei City, Taiwan 1992. Memberships: Chinese Medical Association; Formosan Medical Association; Chinese Society of Microbiology; Chinese Society of Immunology; Mycological Society of Republic of China; Infectious Disease Society of Republic of China; Pathological Society of Republic of China; National Public Health Association, Republic of China; Taiwan Society of Cardiovascular Disease Prevention and Control; American University Club; Mycological Society of America; American Society for Microbiology; New York Academy of Sciences. Address: No 24-5, 3rd Floor, Lane 24, Kinmen Street, Taipei, Taiwan 100-17, Republic of China.

JENG Dong-Sheng, b. 5 December 1964, Taiwan. Senior Lecturer. m. Kin-Wa Kwok, 1 daughter. Education: BEng, 1987; MEng, 1989; PhD, 1992. Appointments: Lecturer, 1999-2002, Senior Lecturer, 2003-, Griffith University, Australia. Publications: 80 journals articles since 1993. Memberships: ASCE; ISOPE; AGU. Address: Griffith University School of Engineering, PMB 50 Gold Coast Mail Centre, QLD 9726, Australia. E-mail: d.jeng@griffith.edu.au

JENKINS Ivor, b. 25 July 1913, Gorseinon, South Wales. Metallurgist. m. Caroline Wijnanda James. 2 sons. Education: Folland Scholar in Metallurgy, BSc, MSc, DSc, University College of Wales, 1931-34; Industrial Bursar, GEC Research Laboratories, Wembley, England, 1934-36. Appointments: Scientific Staff, GEC Research Laboratories, Wembley, 1936-44; Deputy Chief Metallurgist, Whitehead Iron and Steel Co, Newport, Monmouthshire, Wales, 1944-46; Head of Metallurgy Department, 1946-52, Chief Metallurgist, 1952-61, GEC, Wembley; Director and Director of Research, Manganese Bronze Holdings, Ltd, 1961-69; Director of Research, Delta Metal Co and Director, Delta Metal (BW) Ltd, 1969-73; Deputy Chairman, Delta Materials Research Ltd, 1977-78; Group Director of Research, Delta metal Co Ltd and Managing Director, Delta Materials Research Ltd, 1973-78; Consultant, 1978-95; Retired, 1995. Publications: Controlled

Atmospheres for the Heat Treatment of Metals, 1946; Joint Editor, Powder Metallurgy Series, Institute of Metals, 1993-; More than 100 contributions to learned societies at home and abroad on metallurgical and related topics. Honours: Williams Prize, Iron and Steel Institute, 1946; CBE, 1970; Fellow, American Society of Metals, 1974; Platinum Medallist, Institute of Metals, 1978; Fellow, University College, Swansea, 1985. Memberships: Fellow, Royal Academy of Engineering; Institute of Metals 1932-, President, 1969-70; Iron and Steel Institute, 1937-; Fellow, Institution of Metallurgists, 1948, President, 1965-66; Fellow, Royal Society of the Arts; Honorary Member, European Powder Metallurgy Association, 1992; American Society of Metals. Address: 31 Trotyn Croft, Aldwick Fields, Bognor Regis, West Sussex PO21 3TX, England.

JENKINS Michael (Sir), b. 9 January 1936. Vice Chairman. m. Maxine Louise Hodson, 1 son, 1 daughter. Education: BA Honours, King's College, Cambridge. Appointments: Entered HM Diplomatic Service, 1959; Foreign and Commonwealth Office and British Embassies, Paris and Moscow, 1959-68; Seconded, General Electric Company, London, 1968-70; British Embassy, Bonn, 1970-73; European Commission, Brussels, 1973-83; Assistant Under-Secretary of State, Foreign and Commonwealth Office, 1983-85; Minister and Deputy Head of Mission, British Embassy, Washington, 1985-87; British Ambassador, The Netherlands, 1988-93; Executive Director and Member of Group Board, Kleinwort Benson Group, 1993-96; Vice-Chairman, Dresdner Kleinwort Wasserstein, 1996-. Publications: Arakcheev, Grand Vizier of the Russian Empire, 1969; A House in Flanders, 1992. Memberships: President's Advisory Council, Atlantic Council, 1994; Non-Executive Director, Aegon NV, 1995; Chairman of Directors, Action Centre for Europe, 1995; Chairman, British Group, Member of the European Executive Committee, Trilateral Commission, 1996-98; Adviser, Sage International, 1997; Chairman, Dataroom Ltd, 1999-2002; Non-Executive Director, EO, 2000; Chairman, MCC, 2000-02; Council of Britain in Europe, 2000-; The Pilgrims, 2001-; Advisory Council Prince's Trust, 2002-; President, Boeing UK, 2003-. Address: Dresdner Kleinwort Wasserstein, Kleinwort Benson Ltd, PO Box 560, 20 Fenchurch Street, London EC3P 3DB, England. Website: www.drkw.com

JENKINS Michael Nicholas Howard (Sir), b. 13 October 1932, Sevenoaks, Kent, England. Company Chairman. m. Jacqueline Frances, 3 sons. Education: Merton College, Oxford, 1953-56. Appointments: IBM, 1962-67; Management Consultant, Robson Morrow & Co, 1967-71; Technical Director, London Stock Exchange, 1971-77; Managing Director, European Options Exchange, 1977-80; Chief Executive, London International Futures and Options Exchange, 1981-92; Chairman, Futures and Options Association, 1992-2000; Chairman, London Commodity Exchange, 1992-96; London Clearing House, 1991- Chairman, 1996-; Deputy Chairman, Easyscreen plc, 1999-; Chairman, E. Crossnet Ltd, 1999-. Honours: OBE, 1991; Knighthood, 1997. Address: London Clearing House, Aldgate House, 33 Aldgate High Street, London EC3N 1EA, England.

JENNINGS Alex Michael, b. 10 May 1957, Upminster, Essex. Actor. Partner: Lesley Moors, 1 son, 1 daughter. Education: BA honours, Warwick University, 1978; Bristol Old Vic Theatre School, 1978-80. Career: Theatre includes: Richard II, 1990-91; The Importance of Being Ernest, 1993; Hamlet, 1997-98; Speer, 2000; The Winter's Tale, 2001; The Relapse, 2001; My Fair Lady, 2002 Films include: War Requiem, 1988; A Midsummer Night's Dream, 1996; The Wings of the Dove, 1997; The Hunley, 1998; Four Feathers, 2002; TV includes: Smiley's People; Inspector Morse; Ashenden, 1991; Inspector Alleyn Mysteries; Hard Times; Bad Blood, 1999. Honours: Best Actor for Too Clever By Half,

Dictionary of International Biography

London Theatre Critics Awards; Olivier Award, Best Comedy Performance for Too Clever By Half; Oliver Award, Best Actor for Peer Gynt; Helen Hayes Award, Best Actor for Hamlet, 1998; Hon D Litt, Warwick University, 2000; Best Actor, Evening Standard Drama Award, 2001. Address: c/o ICM, Oxford House, 76 Oxford Street, London W1N 0AX, England.

JENNINGS Elizabeth (Joan), b. 18 July 1926, Boston, Lincolnshire, England. Education: MA, St Anne's College, Oxford. Appointments: Assistant, Oxford City Library, 1950-58; Reader, Chatto & Windus Ltd, 1958-60. Publications: Poetry: Poems, 1953; A Way of Looking, 1955; A Sense of the World, 1958; Song for a Birth or a Death, 1961; Recoveries, 1964; The Mind has Mountains, 1966; The Secret Brother, 1966; Collected Poems, 1967; The Animals' Arrival, 1969; Lucidities, 1970; Relationships, 1972; Growing Points, 1975; Consequently I Rejoice, 1977; After the Ark, 1978; Selected Poems, 1980; Moments of Grace, 1980; Celebrations and Elegies, 1982; Extending the Territory, 1985; Collected Poems, 1953-86, 1986; Tributes, 1989; Times and Seasons, 1992; Familiar Spirits, 1994; A Spell of Words, 1997. Editor: The Batsford Book of Children's Verse, 1958; A Choice of Christina Rossetti's Verse, 1970; The Batsford Book of Religious Verse, 1981. Other: Let's Have Some Poetry, 1960; Every Changing Shape, 1961; Robert Frost, 1964; Christianity and Poetry, 1965; Seven Men of Vision, 1976. Contributions to: Newspapers, journals, and magazines. Honours: Arts Council Prize, 1953, and Bursary, 1969; Somerset Maugham Award, 1956; Richard Hillary Prize, 1966; W H Smith Award, 1987; Commander of the Order of the British Empire, 1992; Paul Hamlyn Award, 1997. Memberships: Society of Authors. Address: c/o David Higham Associates Ltd, 5-8 Lower John Street, London W1R 4HA, England.

JENNINGS John Michael, b. 27 August 1944, Christchurch, New Zealand. Academic Auditor. m. Cynthia Margaret Bensemann, 1 son, 1 daughter. Education: BMus with honours, University of Canterbury, New Zealand, 1966; MMus, University of Sydney, Australia, 1969; Licentiate of the Royal Schools of Music, London, 1963; Licentiate of the Trinity College of Music, London, 1965. Appointments: Assistant Lecturer, 1967-69, Lecturer, 1969-77, Senior Lecturer, 1978-2003, Dean of Arts, 1986-92, Deputy Chair, Chair, Academic Administration Committee, 1995-98, Quality Assurance Facilitator, 1998-2001, University of Canterbury; Director, New Zealand Universities Academic Audit Unit, 2002-. Publications: Articles in professional journals. Honours: University Prize Award, Commonwealth Scholarship and Fellowship Plan, 1966-67; Fellow, Institute of Registered Music Teachers in New Zealand, 1989. Memberships: Institute of Registered Music Teachers in New Zealand, 1972-; New Zealand Organisation for Quality, 1999-. Address: New Zealand Universities Academic Audit Unit, 178 Willis Street, Wellington, New Zealand. E-mail: director@aau.ac.nz Website: www.aau.ac.nz

JENNINGS Robert Yewdall (Sir), b. 19 October 1913, Idle, Bradford. Professor; Barrister; International Tribunals Judge. m. Christine Dorothy Bennett, 1 son, 2 daughters. Education: BA, 1935, LLB, 1936, Downing College, Cambridge; Choate Fellow, Harvard University Law School, 1936-37. Appointments: Assistant Lecturer, Law, London School of Economics, 1937-39; Fellow, Jesus College, Cambridge, 1939-; HM British Army, retired with rank of Major, 1940-46; University Lecturer in Law, Cambridge University, 1946-55; Senior Tutor, Jesus College, 1949-55; Whewell Professor of International Law, Cambridge University, 1955-81; Queen's Counsel, 1969; Honorary Bencher of Lincoln's Inn, 1970; Judge, 1982-96, President, 1991-94, International Court of Justice; Appointing Authority of the Iran/US Claims Tribunal,

The Hague, 1991-; Ad Hoc Judge Libya v. UK case. Publications: Editor, British Yearbook of International Law, 1959-81; The Acquisition of Territory in International Law, 1961; General Course on the Principles of International Law, 1967 Editor with Sir Arthur Watts QC, Oppenheim on International Law, 2 volumes, 1992; Collected Writings of Sir Robert Jennings, 2 volumes, 1998. Honours: Knighthood, 1982; Honorary Fellow, Jesus College, Cambridge, 1982; Honorary Fellow, Downing College, Cambridge, 1984; Honorary Fellow, London School of Economics, 1996; Honorary LLD, Cantab 1994; Honorary DCL, Oxford, 1996; Honorary DL, University of Hull, The Saarland, Leicester, Rome. Membership: Institut de droit international 1951-, President, 1983.

JENSEN Henrik Toft, b. 7 March 1945, Denmark. Rector. m. Hanne Lene, 3 daughters. Education: Cand Mag 1973. Appointments: Part-time Teacher, University of Copenhagen, 1967-73; Junior Upper Secondary School Teacher, 1973-75; Associate Professor, Roskilde University, 1975-88; Rector, Roskilde University, 1989-; Head of the National Board of Technology, 1995-2002; Head of the Steering Committee of the Institutional Evaluation Program of the European University Association (EUA), 2000-; Head of the Danish Rectors Conference, 2000-2002; Head of the International Committee of the Danish Rectors' Conference, 2002-. Publications: Books and articles include: Decentralisation and Local Government, A Danish Polish Comparative Study in Political Systems, 1988; From Centralised State to Local Government, the Case of Poland in the Light of Western European Experience, in Environment and Planning D: Society and Space, 1993. Memberships: Board Member of CAT Science Park, 1989-; Member, Administrative Board of International Association of Universities, 1996-; Member, Administrative Board, Danish Institute for Studies in Research and Research Policy, 1998-2003; Member, Advisory Research Committee of the Danish Ministry of Environment and Energy, 2000-03; Member, Board of Copenhagen IT-University, 1999-2003; Member, Board for Technology and Innovation, 2002-. Address: Roskilde University, 4000 Roskilde, Denmark.

JENSH Ronald P, b. 14 June 1938. Professor of Pathology, Anatomy and Cellular Biology. m. Ruth-Eleanor Dobson, 1962, 2 daughters. Education: BA, 1960, MA, 1962, Bucknell University; PhD, Jefferson Medical College, 1966. Appointments include: Faculty Member, Jefferson Medical College, 1966-; Faculty Member, Graduate School, Thomas Jefferson University, 1970-; Assistant Professor, Radiology and Anatomy, 1974-82, Associate Professor, Anatomy, 1974-82, Associate Professor, Radiology, 1974-91, Professor of Anatomy, 1982-94, Vice Chairman, Department of Anatomy, 1984-94, Section Chief, Microscopic Anatomy, 1988-, Associate Professor, Pediatrics, 1991-, Professor, Department of Pathology, Anatomy and Cellular Biology, 1994-, Jefferson Medical College. Publications: (author or co-author) 68 papers and books; 69 abstracts; 32 computer programs; 2 Sound and Light Programs - produced; 2 8mm movies produced, 1975; 11 photographic art exhibits including One-Man Shows, Haddonfield, New Jersey, 1987, 1988, Thomas Jefferson University, 1996; 10 photographs published, 1979-. Honours include: Phi Sigma, 1961; Psi Chi, 1961; Sigma Xi, 1967-; Phi Beta Kappa, Mu Chapter, 1986; Hon Life Member, Jefferson Medical College Alumni Association, 1994; Alumni Award, Bucknell University, Lewisburg, Pennsylvania, 1997; Borough of Haddonfield (New Jersey) "Dr Ronald Jensh Recognition Day", 31 May 1997. Memberships include: Neurobehavioral Teratology Society, President, 1985-86; American Association of Anatomists; American Association of University Professors; Teratology Society; International Association of Human Biologists; Radiation Research Society; Society for Experimental Biology and Medicine. Address: 230 East Park Ave, Haddonfield, NJ 08033-1835, USA.

Dictionary of International Biography

JEON Gyung Soo, b. 18 November 1961, Chonnam, South Korea. Associate Professor. m. Gyung Hee Cho, 1 son, 1 daughter. Education: Bachelor, Department of Chemical Engineering, Chonnam National University, 1981-85; MS, Department of Chemical Engineering, Korea Advanced Institute of Science and Technology, 1986-88; PhD, Department of Chemical Engineering, Pohang University of Science and Technology, 1991-95. Appointments: Researcher, Inorganic Chemistry Laboratory, Korea Research Institute of Chemical Technology, 1988-89; Special Researcher, Material Research Team, Kumho R&D Centre, 1989-98; Associate Professor, Department of Civil and Environmental Engineering, Chonnam Provincial College, 1998-; Visiting Scholar, Department of Chemical Engineering and Materials Science, University of Minnesota (Twin Cities Campus), USA, 2001-2002. Publications: Over 20 articles in scientific journals as author and co-author include most recently: Effects of Cure Levels on Adhesion Between Rubber and Brass in the Composites Made up of Rubber Compound and Brass-Plated Steel Cord, 2003; Boric Acid Ester as an Adhesion Promoter for Rubber Compounds to Brass-Plated Steel Cord, 2003; Effect of Cure Rate of Rubber Compound on the Adhesion to Copper-Plated Steel Cord, 2003; Adhesion of rubber compounds to nano-copper-coated iron plates as studies by AES depth profiles, 2004. Honours: President's Medal, Chonnam National University, 1985; Listed in Who's Who publications and biographical dictionaries. Membership: Life Member: Korean Institute of Chemical Engineers. Address: Department of Civil and Environmental Engineering, Chonnam Provincial College, 262 Hyanggyori, Damyangeup, Damyanggun, Chonnam 517-802, South Korea. E-mail: gjeon@namdo.ac.kr

JEONG Chan Ho, b. 10 May 1960, Daegu, Korea. Professor. m. Hae Hyung Paik, 1 son, 1 daughter. Education: BS, Geology, Kyungpook National University, 1979-83, MS, Geology, 1985-97, PhD, 1990-96, Seoul National University. Appointments: Senior Researcher, Korea Atomic Energy Research Institute, 1987-97; Professor, Department of Engineering Geology, Daejeon University, 1997-. Publications include: Effect of land use and urbanization on hydrochemistry and contamination of groundwater from Taejon Area, Korea., 2001; Mineralogical and hydrochemical effects on the adsorption removal of cesium-137 and strontium-90 by kaolinite, 2001; Mineral-water interaction and hydrogeochemistry in the Samkwang mine area, Korea, 2001. Honours: Listed in Who's Who publications and biographical dictionaries. Memberships: International Association of Hydrogeologists; Editor, Korean Society of Engineering Geology; Editor, Korean Society of Soil and Environment. Address: Yongundong 96-3, Dong-gu, Daejeon, Korea 300-716. E-mail: cchjeong@dju.ac.kr

JEONG Ji Hwan, b. 27 June 1965, Jeonjoo, Korea. Educator. m Hyun Jung Kim, 1 son. Education: BA, Department of Nuclear Engineering, Seoul National University, 1988; MS, 1990, PhD, 1995, Department of Nuclear Engineering, Korea Advanced Institute of Science and Technology. Appointments: Senior Researcher, Korea Advanced Institute of Science and Technology, 1995; Post-Doctoral Researcher, Oxford University, 1995-96; Senior Researcher, Korea Atomic Energy Research Institute, 1996-99; Cheonan College of Foreign Studies, 1999-. Publications: Numerous research papers in professional scientific journals. Honours: British Chevening Scholarship, 1995; KOSEF Post-Doctoral Fellowship. Memberships: Korean Nuclear Society; Korean Society of Mechanical Engineers; American Chemical Society. Address: Doorae Hyundae Apt 107-904, Sinbang-Dong, Cheonan. Choongnam, 330-771 Korea. E-mail: jhjeong@ccfs.ac.kr

JEONG Peter Ill-Seok, b. 1 July 1957, Korea. Mechanical Researcher. m. Qui-Oak Park, 2 sons, 1 daughter. BS, Mechanical Engineering, Busan National University, 1982; PhD, Mechanical Engineering, Choongnam National University, 1997. Appointments: Project Leader, Nuclear Power Plant Lifetime Management (PLiM), Korea Electric Power Plant Research Institute, Daejeon, Korea, 1995-; Korea Liaison of IAEA Technical Working Group on Life Management of Nuclear Power Plants, 1999-; Registered Expert on the Technology of Nuclear PLiM in IAEA Personal Database, 2001-. Publications: Nuclear Plant Lifetime Management Study (I), 1996, (II), 2001; Wolsong Unit 1 Plant Lifetime Management Study (I), 2003; Development of Ageing Management Technology, 2004; 13 scientific and domestic technical journal papers; About 80 technical papers presented at conferences; A Study on the Characteristics and relaxation of the Thermal Stratification Phenomena of Nuclear Power Plant Pressurizer Surge Line (PhD Thesis), 1997. Honours: Honoured paper Award, KNS, 2000, 2001; Honoured Paper, KSME, 2003; Listed in Who's Who publications and biographical dictionaries. Memberships: IAEA; TWG-NMNPP; KSME; KNS; KANEQ. Address: Nuclear Power Laboratory, Korea Electric Power Research Institute, 103-16 Munjidong, Yuseongku, Daejeon 305-380, Republic of Korea. E-mail: isjeong@kepri.re.kr

JERVIS Simon Swynfen, b. 9 January 1943, Yoxford, Suffolk. Art Historian. m. Fionnuala MacMahon, 1 son, 1 daughter. Education: Corpus Christi College, Cambridge, 1961-64. Appointments: Student Assistant, Assistant Keeper of Art, Leicester Museum and Art Gallery, 1964-66; Assistant Keeper, 1966-75, Deputy Keeper, 1975-89, Acting Keeper, 1989, Curator, 1989-90, Department of Furniture, Victoria and Albert Museum; Director and Marlay Curator, Fitzwilliam Museum, Cambridge, 1990-95; Director of Historic Buildings, The National Trust, 1995-2002. Publications: 7 books on furniture and design; Many articles in learned journals. Memberships: Member, 1964-, Arts Panel, 1982-95, Chairman, 1987-95, Properties Committee, 1987-95, National Trust; Member, 1966-, Council, 1977-79, 1981-83, 1986-87, Editor, 1988-92, Chairman, 1999-, Furniture History Society; Member, 1968-, Stafford Terrace Committee, 1980-90, Victorian Society; Member, Southwark Diocesan Advisory Committee, 1978-87; Member, 1982-, Council, 1987-1991, Royal Archaeological Institute; Elected Fellow, 1983, Council, 1986-88, Executive Committee, 1987-92, House Working party, 1988-, President, 1995-2001, Kelmscott Committee, 2001-, Society of Antiquaries of London; Director, 1993-, Trustee, 1996-, The Burlington Magazine; Member, 1988-, Council, Walpole Society, 1990-95; Guest Scholar, The J Paul Getty Museum, 1988-89, 2003; Member, Museums and Galleries Commission, Acceptance in Lieu Panel, 1992-2000; Trustee, The Royal Collection Trust, 1993-2001; Trustee, 1998-2002, Life Trustee, 2002-, Sir John Soane's Museum; Member, Advisory Council, National Art Collections Fund, 2002-. Address: 45 Bedford Gardens, London W8 7EF, England.

JESPERSEN Per, (Linda Clay), b. 14 January 1938, Copenhagen, Denmark. Author; Philosopher; Theologian; Teacher. m. Anne Jespersen, 28 March 1962, 1 son, 1 daughter. Education: Graduated, University of Copenhagen, 1965. Publications: Filosofi for born, 1988; Naar svanen dor, 1987; Born og filosofi, 1993. Contributions to: Philosophy, children and the schools, 1986, How to do philosophy with children, 1987, The Wonder Dough, 1988, Benjamin, 1990, Hope, 1990, A Strange Experience, 1990, It is strange, 1990, I Had a Dream, 1991, A Nightly Talk, 1991, in Analytic Teaching; Tom Finley, 2000, What is the Deepest; Wonder and Magic, 2003; Stories for Children, 2004. Membership: Danish Authors. Address: Randerup 40, 6261 Bredebro, Denmark.

JESPERSEN Vagn, b. 23 November 1918, Denmark. Consul; Industrialist; Scientist. m. Eva Ingeborg Galle, 1 son, 2 daughters. Education: School of Commercial Sciences, 1934-36;

Dictionary of International Biography

Apprenticeship, Axel B Lange, Frederikssund, 1936-38; Studies in the United States, 1946-48. Appointments: Commenced at C E Basts EFTF, Copenhagen, 1938; Member of Danish Resistance Movement, Hoiger Danske, during WWII to 1945; Appointed to various positions within C E Bast, 1949-58; Director of Research and Development, Executive Director, C E Bast, 1958-; Consul General, Principality of Monaco, 1963; Consul General for Prince Rainier III, Monaco, 1965; Member, 1963, Counsel Member, 1973, Vice-President, 1979-95, President, 1995-2000, Member of the Council, 2000-2003, Corps Consulaire Denmark; President, 1982-95; Founder, 1982, Elected President, 1982, Active President, 1982-95, Honorary President for Lifetime, 1995-, Federation Internationale des Corps et Associations Consulaires; President, Danish Association of Edible Fats, 1972; Vice President, 1973, Vice President of Honour, 1987, UNEGA, Paris; Vice President, Danish Meat Packers Association, 1976-88; President, Danish Management Society, 1979-84. Publications: Food is no Medicine and Medicine is no Food; Nutritional Observations on Solid Lipids; Founder, Thingstead Philosophy, 1981; Observations on Cholesterols; Observations on Tocopherols (E-vitamins); Editorial commentator in newspapers; Creator of new scientific proteins for medical research; Creator of biofine chemicals and scientific and commercial lipids. Honours: Danish resistance Medal, 1940-45; Sign of Recognition, Danish Resistance Movement, 1943-45; Knight, 1971, Officer, 1978, Order of Grimaldi, Monaco; Knight, 1976, Prime Grade, 1996, Order of Dannebrog; Ordem do Merito Consular Grand Cross, 1988; Golden Medal, FICAC, 1995; Golden Medal of Corps Consulaire Sweden, 2000. Memberships: Danish Microbiological Society; The Pasteur Society; Danish Society for Nutrition; Danish Biological Society; American Oil Chemists Society; New York Academy of Science; American Association for the Advancement of Science. Address: Aurehøjvej 11, DK-2900 Hellerup, Denmark.

JHA Raghbendra, b. 9 August 1953, Chaibasa, India. Economist. m. Alka Shekhar Jha, 1 son. Education: BA, Honours, Economics, 1973, St Stephen's College, MA, Economics, 1975, Delhi School of Economics, Delhi, India; M Phil, Economics, 1977, PhD, Economics, 1978, Columbia University, New York, USA. Appointments include: Preceptor, 1977-78, Instructor, 1978, Assistant Professor, 1979, Department of Economics, Columbia University, New York, USA; Assistant Professor, Williams College, Williamstown, Massachusetts, USA, 1979-83; Reader, Department of Economics, Delhi School of Economics, 1983-92; Visiting Professor, National Institute of Public Finance and Policy, New Delhi, India, 1988; Visiting Associate Professor, Queen's University, Kingston, Ontario, Canada, 1989-90, 1993-94; Professor of Economics, Indian Institute of Management, Bangalore, India, 1994-95; Visiting Faculty, University of Warwick, England, 1996; Professor of Economics, 1995-2000, Senior Professor, 2000, Indira Gandhi Institute of Development Research, Bombay, India; Rajiv Gandhi Professor and Executive Director, Australia South Asia Research Centre, The Australian National University, Canberra, Australia, 2001-; Many national and international consultancies. Publications: Author: 16 books including most recently: Modern Public Economics, 1998; Economic Reforms, Economic Growth and Anti-Poverty Strategy in India, 2001; Macroeconomics for Developing Countries, 2nd edition, 2003; Editor: Indian Economic Reforms, 2003; Numerous refereed journal articles and chapters in books. Honours include: Numerous scholarships, research and travel grants and fellowships, 1970-2005; Member, Panel of Experts, Fiscal Affairs Division, International Monetary Fund, 1996-; Special Invitee to Economic Affairs Committee, Bombay Chamber of Commerce and Industry, 1999-2000; Associate Editor, International Tax and Public Finance, 1999-; Editorial Board, International Journal of Development Issues, 2001-; Fellow, World Innovation Foundation, 2002-; Listed in Who's Who publications and biographical dictionaries. Memberships: American Economic Association; Royal Economic Society; Econometric Society; Association of Comparative Economic Studies. Address: ASARC, RSPAS, Division of Economics, Australian National University, Canberra, ACT 0200, Australia. E-mail: r.jha@anu.edu.au Website: http://rspas.anu.edu.au/people/personal/jhaxr_asarc.html

JHABVALA Ruth Prawer, b. 7 May 1927, Cologne, Germany. Writer. m. 16 June 1951, 3 daughters. Education: BA, 1948, MA, 1951, DLitt, London. Publications: The Householder, 1960; A New Dominion, 1971; Heat and Dust, 1975; Out of India, 1986; Three Continents, 1987; Poet and Dancer, 1993; Shards of Memory, 1995; East into Upper East, 1998. Honours: Booker Prize, 1975; Neil Gunn International Fellowship, 1979; John D and Catharine T MacArthur Foundation Fellowship, 1984-89; Academy Awards, 1987, 1993; American Academy of Arts and Letters Literature Award, 1992; Commander of the Order of the British Empire, 1998. Memberships: Royal Society of Literature, fellow; Authors Guild; Writers Guild of America. Address: 400 East 52nd Street, New York, NY 10022, USA.

JIANG Jia-Qian, b. 20 March 1955, China. Lecturer. m. Yi-Ping Zhu, 1 son, 1 daughter. Education: BSc, Chemical Engineering, China, 1982; PhD, Environmental Engineering, Imperial College, London, 1995. Appointments: Engineer, Chief Engineer, Head of Laboratory, Laboratory of Water and Wastewater, Shanghai Institute of Technology, China, 1982-90; Researcher, 1991-95, Research Fellow, 1995-98 Imperial College, London; Lecturer, University of Surrey, England, 1999-. Publications: Articles in scientific journals and presented at conferences as author and co-author include most recently: Progress in the development and use of ferrate (vi) salt as an oxidant and coagulant for water and wastewater treatment, 2002; Laboratory study of electro-coagulation-flotation for water treatment, 2002; Potassium ferrate(VI), a dual functional water treatment chemical, 2003; Development of an optimal poly-aluminium-iron-sulphate coagulant, 2003; Comparison of modified montmorillonite adsorbents. Part II: The effects of the type of raw clays and modification conditions on the surface properties and adsorption performance of modified clays, 2003. Honours: Excellent Paper Prize, 1984; Unwin Prize, 1997; Member, EU Research Expert Committee, 2001-; Member, UK EPSRC Peer Review College, 2003-. Memberships: Member and Chartered Chemist, The Royal Society of Chemistry, 1995-; Member, The Chartered Institution of Water and Environmental Management, UK, 1996-; Chartered Engineer, The Engineering Council, UK, 1996-. Address: School of Engineering (C5), University of Surrey, Guildford, Surrey, GU2 7XH, England. E-mail: j.jiang@surrey.ac.uk

JIANG Wen, b. 20 July 1962, Shandong, China. Cancer Researcher; Surgeon. m. Ling Jiang, 1 son, 1 daughter. Education: MBCh, Beijing University, China, 1984; MD, University of Wales College of Medicine, 1995. Appointments: Chief Resident, First Hospital, Beijing University, China, 1987-89; Research Fellow, 1989-96, Senior Research Fellow, 1996-97, Senior Lecturer, 1997-, University of Wales, College of Medicine. Publications: Books: Cancer Metastasis, 2000; Growth Factors and their Receptors in Cancer Metastasis, 2001; Over 120 articles in medical and scientific journals; Holder of patents. Honours: British Council International Fellow, 1997; Best Research Team Award, Breast Cancer Campaign, 2003. Memberships: British Association for Cancer Research; American Association for Cancer Research; European Association for Cancer Research. Address: Department of Surgery, University of Wales College of Medicine, Heath Park, Cardiff CF14 4XV, Wales. E-mail: jiangw@cf.ac.uk

JIN Moon-Seog, b. 17 April 1960, Naju, Chonnam, Korea. Professor. m. Sun-Young Park, 1 son, 1 daughter. Education: PhD, Chonnam National University, Korea, 1994. Appointment: Researcher, R&D Center, Kumho Company. Publications: 59 articles in scientific journals include: Optical Absorption of $ZnGa_2Se_4Co^{2+}$ Single Crystals. Address: Department of Physics, Dongshin University, Dae-Ho Dong 252, Naju, Chonnam 520-714, Republic of Korea. E-mail: msjin@dsu.ac.kr

JING Kuangsheng, b. 14 November 1917, Tianjing, China. Professor. m. Wang, 1 son. Education: Bachelor of Engineering, North-West Institute of Technology, 1937-41. Appointments: Professor of Mechanics, Beiyang University, Qinghua University, Jilin University of Technology, Jiangsu University of Technology Science and Technology. Publications: Books: Strength of Materials; Matrix Stucture Analysis; Theory of Elasticity; Papers: Buckling of a Prismatic Bar with Elastic Sports Under Thrust. Memberships: Council, Chinese Society of Mechanics; Vice Chairman, Jiangsu Society of Mechanics. Address: 202-19-2 Jiangsu University of Science and Technology, Zhenjiang, Jiangsu 212013, China.

JMOR Salah Abdulrahman, b. 26 June 1956, Qoratou, Khangin, Iraq. Professor of International Studies. m. Taban Ahmad, 3 sons. Education: BSc, Sulaimaniyeh University, Iraq; MA, The Graduate Institute of Development Studies, Geneva, Switzerland; MA, PhD, 1992, Graduate Institute of International Studies, Geneva University, Switzerland. Appointments: Associate Professor of International Studies, Kent State University, USA, The Center for International and Comparative Programs, Geneva; Director, Global Trade Institute; Director and Partner, Jmor & Cie, Consulting Firms; Kurdish Representative to the United National and other international organisations in Geneva. Publications: L'origine de la question Kurde, 1994; Commerce International, 1997; New European Economy, forthcoming; Numerous articles on international and European affairs. Honours: Listed in Who's Who publications and biographical dictionaries. Memberships: The State of the World Forum; Swiss Forum for International Affairs; Kurdistan National Congress. Address: 72 rue de Lausanne, 1202 Geneva, Switzerland. E-mail: sjmor@compuserve.com

JOANTA Serafim, b. 4 September 1948, Boholt, Romania. Archbishop; Metropolitain. Education: Licence, Theological Institute in Sibiu, 1970-74; Doctor of Theology, Theological Institute "St Serge", Paris France, 1982-85. Appointments: Priest, Cathedral of Alba Julia, 1975-82; Lecturer, "St Serge" Institute, Paris France, 1986-89; Auxiliary Bishop of Transylvanian Metropolitain, 1990-94; Romanian Orthodox Metropolitain for Germany and Central and North Europe. Publications: Romania. It's Hesychast Tradition and Culture (French version 1987, 1992, Romanian Version, 1992, 1994, English version, 1992, German version, 2003); More than 50 articles and homilies about theology and spirituality in Romanian, French and German. Address: Fürtherstr 166, 90429 Nürnberg, Germany. E-mail: mitropolia@mitropolia-ro.de

JOEBSTL Hans A, b. 13 June 1944, Limberg, Wolfsberg, Austria. University Professor. m. Elfriede Stampf, 1 daughter. Education: Matura, 1962; Military Service, 1962-63; Study of Forestry, 1963-68; Degree in Engineering, University of Agricultural Sciences, Vienna, 1968; DSc, 1973; Habilitation, 1977. Appointments: University Assistant, 1968-77; Docent, 1977-79; Professor of Business Management in Forestry and Timber Industries, University of Agricultural Sciences, Vienna, 1979-; Consultant in Field, 1977-; Senior Lecturer, University of Trento, Italy, 1990-99. Publications: A Model of the Permanent Forest Enterprise, 1973; Sustainable Enterprise Planning in Forestry, 1978; Cost and Performance Accounting; 2000; Managerial Economics in Forestry, 1995; Accounting in Forestry and Forest Product Industry, 2002; Rotation Period of Norway Spruce under Changed Market Conditions, 1997; In total 20 books and over 170 articles in professional journals. Honour: IUFRO Distinguished Service Award, XXI World Congress, Malaysia, 2000. Memberships: International Union of Forestry Research Organizations, Vienna, Co-ordinator of 2 Research Groups, 1987-; European Accounting Association, Brussels; Universita di Trento, Collegio dei Docenti, Italy. Address: Universität für Bodenkultur, Gregor Mendel-Straße 33, A 1180 Vienna, Austria. E-mail: hans.joebstl@boku.ac.at

JOEDODIBROTO Roehyati, b. 17 August 1929, Jakarta, Indonesia. Research Scientist. Education: Chemical Engineer, Gajah-Mada University, Yogyakarta, 1956; MSc, 1961, PhD, 1964, Pulp and Paper Technology, College of Forestry, State University of New York, Syracuse, New York, USA; Research for PhD at Department of Polymer Technology, Royal Institute of Technology, Stockholm, Sweden, 1962. Appointments: Research Assistant, Government Chemical Research Institute, Bogor, 1956-58; Head of Laboratory, Rayon and Cellulose Institute, 1964-68; Head, Research Division, Cellulose Research Institute, 1969-80; Head, Pulp Division, Institute for Research and Development of Cellulose Industries, 1981-86; Pure Research Scientist, 1987-94; Senior Principal Research Scientist, 1990; Emeritus, 1994; Lecturer, Polymer Chemistry, Institute of Textile Technology, 1964-85; Member of Examination Teams for Doctor's Degree at Bandung Institute of Technology, 1987, 1991, 1999. Publications: Book: Indonesian Natural Resources for Pulp and Paper, 2002; Articles, More than 50 in scientific journals including: Decomposition mechanism of xanthates of model compounds, 1969; Experiences in training engineering students for a better information seeking method, 1991; Pulping and papermaking properties of some woody and non-woody materials, 1992. Honours: Medal for 25 Years Service, President of the Republic of Indonesia, 1983; Medal as Senior Principal Research Scientist, Director of Indonesian Institute of Sciences, 1990; Plaque, ITB Press for Services as Editor, 1974-89. Memberships: International Association of Scientific Paper Makers; Institute of Indonesian Engineers, Chemical Engineering Chapter; Indonesian Chemical Society; Indonesian Polymer Association. Address: Jalan Kapten Tendean 4, Bandung 40141, Indonesia.

JOEL Billy (William Martin Joel), b. 9 May 1949, Bronx, New York, USA. Musician; Singer; Songwriter. m. Christie Brinkley, 23 March 1989, divorced 1994, 1 daughter. Education: LHD (honorary), Fairfield University, 1991; HMD (honorary), Berklee College of Music, 1993. Appointment: Solo Recording Artist, 1972-. Creative Works: Turnstiles; Streetlife Serenade; The Stranger, 1978; 52nd Street, 1978; Glass Houses, 1980; Songs In the Attic, 1981; Nylon Curtain, 1982; An Innocent Man, 1983; Cold Spring Harbour, 1984; Piano Man, 1984; Greatest Hits, Vols I & II, 1985; The Bridge, 1986; KOHUEPT-Live in Leningrad, 1987; Storm Front, 1989; River of Dreams, 1994; 2000 Years: Millennium Concert, 2000. Honours: 6 Grammy Awards; 10 Grammy Nominations; Grammy Legend Award, 1990; Songwriters Hall of Fame, 1992. Address: Maritime Music Inc, 2nd Floor, 280 Elm Street, Southampton, NY 11968, USA.

JOFFE Joel Goodman (Lord Joffe), b. 12 May 1932. Human Rights Lawyer; Businessman; Chairman and Trustee of Charities; National Health Services Chairman. m. Vanetta Joffe, 3 daughters. Education: B Com LLB, Witwatersrand University, Johannesburg. Appointments: Solicitor, then Barrister, Johannesburg, 1952-65; Secretary and Administrative Director, Abbey Life Assurance, London, 1965-70; Founder Director, Joint Managing Director, Deputy Chairman, Allied Dunbar Assurance, 1971-91; Founding

Trustee, Chairman, Allied Dunbar Charitable Trust, 1974-93; Chairman, Thamesdown Voluntary Services Council, 1974-1980; Trustee, Honorary Secretary, Chairman of the Executive Committee, Chair, Oxfam, 1979-; Chairman, Swindon Private Hospital plc, 1982-87; Council Member, IMPACT, 1984-; Chairman, Swindon Health Authority, 1988-93; Campaigner to protect consumers from the excesses of the Financial Services Industry, 1992-; Chairman, Swindon and Marlborough National Health Trust, 1993-95; Special Adviser to South African Minister of Transport, 1997-98; Chair of The Giving Campaign, 2000-; Trustee, J G and V L Joffe Charitable Trust. Memberships: Member, Royal Commission for the Care of the Elderly, 1997-99; Member, Home Officer Working Group on the Active Community, 1998-99. Address: Liddington Manor, Liddington, Swindon, Wiltshire SN4 0HD, England.

JOGLEKAR Prafulla, b. 12 May 1947, Dhulia, India. Professor. m. Suvarna Lagu, 2 sons. Education: BS, Mathematics, Nagpur University, 1966; MBA, Indian Institute of Management, Ahmedabad, 1968; PhD, The Wharton School, Philadelphia, USA, 1978. Appointments: Chair, Management Department, 1973-82, Director, Applied Research Center, 1979-85, Lindback Professor of Operations Management, 1991-, La Salle University. Publications: Over 30 refereed articles published. Honours: Beta Gamma Sigma; Lindback Professor; Numerous grants and awards; Summer faculty fellowships, NASA, 1993, 994, 2000, 2001. Memberships: Institute for Operations Research & Management Science; Decision Science Institute; Production and Operations Management Society. Address: La Salle University, 1900 West Olney Avenue, Philadelphia, PA 19141, USA.

JOHANNESON Steven Thor, b. 16 June 1948, Minneapolis, Minnesota, USA. Artist. m. Cynthia Joan Maurer. Education: Heatherley School of Fine Art, London, 1970-73; Studied under: Clive Leigh Duncan, David Ufland and Helen Wilson. Career: McMurray's Picture Framing Shop, London, 1970's; Cel-painter and special inker and painter, background and airbrush artist, Bajus-Jones Animation Studio, Minnesota, 1977-79; Full-time artist, 1980's-; Three-man show, Gallerie Marin, Appledore, North Devon, 1986; Regularly accepted into exhibitions at the Royal Society of Marine Artists, The Mall Galleries, London, from 1987-; One-man show, Westside Gallery, East Sheen, London, 1988; Three-man show, Mid-Cornwall Galleries, Biscovey, Par, Cornwall, 1991; Group show Gallerie Marin, Appledore, North Devon, 1992; Works accepted for the Society of Wildlife Artists Exhibition, Mall Galleries, London, 1993; Annual group shows, Gallerie Marin, Appledore, North Devon, 1994-; Two-person show, Juliet Gould Gallery, Fowey, Cornwall, 1994; Included in the 150th Anniversary Exhibition of the Heatherley School of Fine Art, Mall Galleries, London, 1996. Publications: 4 Seascapes published as prints by Pictures UK Ltd, Holmden, Cornwall, 1986; Limited edition print, Showing Off: Orcas at Evening, published by Marin Prints, Appledore, North Devon, included in 1993 Greenpeace Catalogue, 1992; Paintings regularly published as greetings cards by Gluvian Fine Art Ltd, Wadebridge, Cornwall, 1993-; Limited edition print, School's Out: Bottlenose Dolphins off Lundy Island, published by Marin Prints and included in 1995 Greenpeace Catalogue, 1994; Limited edition print, Northam Burrows, published by Marin Prints, 1995. Honour: St Cuthbert's Mill Award for the best work on paper, Royal Society of Marine Artists, 1999. Membership: Associate Member, 2001, Full Member, 2003, Royal Society of Marine Artists. Address: PO Box 1596, Sandy, OR 97055, USA. E-mail: StevenJohanneson@aol.com

JOHANSEN Bruce Elliott, b. 30 January 1950, San Diego, California, USA. College Professor. m. Patricia Ellen Keifler, 1 son. Education: BA, Communication and Political Science, 1972,

PhD, Communication and American History, 1979, University of Washington; MA, Communication and Environmental Health, University of Minnesota, 1975. Appointments: Assistant Professor, 1982-88, Associate Professor, 1988-92, Professor, 1992-, Joint Appointment, Native American Studies, 1992-, University of Nebraska at Omaha. Publications: 18 books. Honours: 3rd prize, Teaching Award, Association for Education in Journalism and Mass Communication, 1991; Robert T Reilly Diamond Alumni Professorship, University of Nebraska at Omaha, 1996-2002; University of Nebraska at Omaha Award for Outstanding Research or Creative Activity, 1997; Exemplary Service to Students Award, Project Achieve, University of Nebraska at Omaha. Address: Department of Communication, University of Nebraska at Omaha, Omaha, NE 68182, USA. E-mail: bjohansen@mail.unomaha.edu

JOHANSSON Anita Christin, b. 12 November 1940, Kiruna, Sweden. Artist. m. B W Johansson, 1 daughter. Career: Paintings characterised by bold colours, billowing lines and variations in style and technique to create a feeling of freedom. Exhibitions in Sweden, Norway, Spain, Switzerland, Japan, USA: The Swedish Place, Half Moon Bay, California, 1990; Swedish American Museum, Chicago, 1991; Galleri Smedjan vid Skabersjöslott, 1992, 1996; Galleri Valvet, Malmö, 1993, 1996, 1997, 2000; Galleri Salong Strandvägen, Stockholm, 1993; Tokyo Geijutsu Gekijyo 5F Gallery, Japan, 1994; Europ 'Art, Geneva, 1997; Galleri Belsola, Rheinfelden, Switzerland, 1997; Nordic Art Fair, Sundsvall, 1997; Konsthallen Bryggeriet, Trelleborg, 1997; Delaware River Gallery, Yardley, Pennsylvania, 1998; Galleri Svarta Soffan, Stockholm, 1998; International Contemporary Art: Private Gallery, Möhlin-Riburg, Switzerland, 1998; Galleri Hamnen, Viken, 1999; Kullander & Kullander, Malmö, 1999; International Contemporary Art: Show-Room Belvedere, St Moritz, 1999; Galerie Rote Rose, Regensberg-Zurich, 1999; Kiruna Folkets Hus I samband med Kiruna Stads 100-årsjubileum, 2000; Galleri Belsola, Rheinfelden, Switzerland, 2000; LKAB: Kiruna-Narvik, Malmberget –Luleå, 2000; Kultur Huset, Kautokeino, Norway, 2001; Galleri Stand 4, Girona, Spain, 2002. Address: Knutstorpsgatan 23, 216 22 Malmö, Sweden.

JOHANNSON Scarlett, b. 22 November 1984, New York, USA. Film Actress. North, 1994; Just Cause, 1995; If Lucy Fell, 1996; Manny & Lo, 1996; Fall, 1997; Home Alone 3, 1997; The Horse Whisperer, 1998; My Brother the Pig, 1999; Ghost World, 2000; An American Rhapsody, 2001; The Man Who Wasn't There, 2001; Eight Legged Freaks, 2002; The Girl with a Pearl Earring, 2003; Lost in Translation, 2003; The Perfect Score, 2004. Honours: BAFTA Award for Best Actress, Lost in Translation, 2004.

JOHN Elton (Sir) (Reginald Kenneth Dwight), b. 25 March 1947, Pinner, Middlesex, England. Singer; Songwriter; Musician (piano). m. Renate Blauer, 14 February 1984, divorced 1988. Musical Education: Piano lessons aged 4; Royal Academy of Music, 1958. Career: Member, Bluesology, 1961-67; Worked at Mills Music Publishers; Solo artiste, 1968-; Long-term writing partnership with Bernie Taupin, 1967-; Partnership wrote for Dick James Music; Founder, Rocket Records, 1973; Own publishing company, Big Pig Music, 1974; Performances include: Wembley Stadium, 1975; First Western star to perform in Israel and USSR, 1979; Live Aid, Wembley, 1985; Wham's farewell concert, Wembley, 1985; Prince's Trust concerts, London, 1986, 1988; Farm Aid IV, 1990; AIDS Project Los Angeles - Commitment To Life VI, 1992; Chair, The Old Vic Theatre Trust, 2002-; Film appearance, Tommy, 1975. Recordings: Hit singles include: Your Song, 1971; Rocket Man, 1972; Crocodile Rock (Number 1, US), 1973; Daniel, 1973; Saturday Night's Alright For Fighting, 1973; Goodbye Yellow Brick Road, 1973; Candle In The Wind, 1974; Don't Let The Sun Go Down On Me, 1974 (live version with

George Michael, Number 1, UK and US, 1991); Philadelphia Freedom, 1975; Lucy In The Sky With Diamonds (Number 1, US), 1975; Island Girl (Number 1, US), 1975; Pinball Wizard, from film Tommy, 1976; Don't Go Breaking My Heart, duet with Kiki Dee (Number 1, UK and US), 1976; Sorry Seems To Be The Hardest Word, 1976; Song For Guy, 1979; Blue Eyes, 1982; I Guess That's Why They Call It The Blues, 1983; I'm Still Standing, 1983; Kiss The Bride, 1983; Sad Songs (Say So Much), 1984; Nikita, 1986; Sacrifice (Number 1, UK), 1989; True Love (with Kiki Dee), 1993; Made In England, 1995; Blessed, 1995; Believe, 1995; You Can Make History, 1996; If The River Can Bend, 1998; Written in the Stars, 1999; Contributor, That's What Friends Are For, Dionne Warwick And Friends (charity record), 1986; Albums include: Elton John, 1970; Tumbleweed Connection, 1971; Friends, 1971; 17-11-70, 1971; Madman Across The Water, 1972; Honky Chateau, 1972; Don't Shoot Me, I'm Only The Piano Player, 1973; Goodbye Yellow Brick Road, 1973; Caribou, 1974; Captain Fantastic And The Brown Dirt Cowboy, 1975; Rock Of The Westies, 1975; Here And There, 1976; Blue Moves, 1976; A Single Man, 1978; Lady Samantha, 1980; 21 At 33, 1980; Jump Up!, 1982; Too Low For Zero, 1983; Breaking Hearts, 1984; Ice On Fire, 1985; Leather Jackets, 1986; Live In Australia, 1987; Reg Strikes Back, 1988; Sleeping With The Past, 1989; The One, 1992; Made In England, 1995; Big Picture, 1997; Love Songs, 1995; Aida, 1999; El Dorado, 2000; Songs From the West Coast, 2001; Elton John – Greatest Hits, 1970-2002, 2002; Achievements: Wrote music for The Lion King, 1994, stage musical The Lion King plays at six theatre worldwide, 2001. Honours include: First album to go straight to Number 1 in US charts, Captain Fantastic..., 1975; Numerous Ivor Novello Awards for: Daniel, 1974; Don't Go Breaking My Heart, 1977; Song For Guy, 1979; Nikita, 1986; Sacrifice, 1991; Outstanding Contribution To British Music, 1986; Star on Hollywood Walk Of Fame, 1975; Madison Square Gardens Honours: Hall Of Fame, 1977; Walk Of Fame (first non-athlete), 1992; American Music Awards: Favourite Male Artist, Favourite Single, 1977; Silver Clef Award, Nordoff-Robbins Music Therapy, 1979; BRIT Awards: Outstanding Contribution To British Music, 1986; Best British Male Artist, 1991; Grammy, Best Vocal Performance By A Group, 1987; MTV Special Recognition Trophy, 1987; Hitmaker Award, National Academy of Popular Music, 1989; Honorary Life President, Watford Football Club, 1989; Inducted into Songwriters Hall Of Fame (with Bernie Taupin), 1992; Q Magazine Merit Award, 1993; Officer of Arts And Letters, Paris, 1993; KBE, 1998; Dr hc Royal Academy of Music, 2002; Grammy Lifetime, Achievement Award, 2000. Address: c/o Simon Prytherch, Elton Management, 7 King Street Cloisters, Clifton Walk, London, W6 0GY, England.

JOHN Roland, b. 14 March 1940, England. Freelance Writer. Appointment: Editor, Outposts Poetry Quarterly, 1986-. Publications: Report from the Desert, 1974; Boundaries, 1976; The Child Bride's Diary (from the Chinese), 1980; Believing Words are Real, 1985; To Weigh Alternatives, 1992; A Reader's Guide to the Cantos of Ezra Pound, 1995. Contributions to: Agenda; Acumen; Envoi; Prospice; Poetry Review; South Coast Poetry Journal, USA; Printed Matter, Japan; Litteratura, Zagreb; Word and Image, Amsterdam; Outposts; Scripsi, Australia. Address: 22 Whitewell Road, Frome, Somerset BA11 4EL, England.

JOHN PAUL II, His Holiness Pope, (Karol Jozef Wojtyla), b. 18 May 1920, Wadowice, Poland. Education: Jagiellonian University, Cracow; DTh, Pontificio Ateneo Angelicum. Appointments: Ordained Priest, 1946; Professor, Moral Theology, Universities of Lubin & Cracow, 1954-58; Titular Bishop of Ombi, Auxiliary Bishop of Cracow, 1958; Vicar Capitular, 1962; Archbishop & Metro of Cracow, 1964-78; Cardinal, 1967; Elected Pope, 1978. Publications: The Goldsmith Shop (play), 1960; Love

and Responsibility, 1962; Person and Act, 1969; The Foundations of Renewal, 1972; Sign of Contradiction, 1976; The Future of the Church, 1979; Easter Vigil and Other Poems, 1979; Collected Poems (trans Jerzy Peterkiewicz), 1982; Crossing the Threshold of Hope (essays), 1994; The Place Within (trans Jerzy Peterkiewicz), 1995; The Gift and Mystery, 1996; New Hope for Lebanon, 1997; Faith and Mind, 1998; Letter to the People Well On in Years, 1999; Agenda for the Third Millennium, 1999; Incarnationis Mysterium, 2000; Novo millenio ineunte, 2000; Rosarium Virginis Mariae, 2002; Roman Triptych (poetry), 2003. Address: Palazzo Apostolico Vaticano, 00120 Città del Vaticano, Rome, Italy.

JOHNS David John, b. 29 April 1931, Bristol, England. Chartered Engineer. Education: BSc (Eng), Aero Engineering, 1950-53, MSc (Eng), 1959, University of Bristol; PhD, 1967, DSc, 1985, Loughborough University. Appointments: Apprentice up to Section Leader, Bristol Aeroplane Co Ltd, 1949-57; Technical Officer, Sir W G Armstrong Whitworth Aircraft Ltd, 1957-58; Lecturer, Cranfield College of Aeronautics, 1958-64; Reader, Professor, 1964-83, Head of Department of Transport Technology, 1972-82; Senior Pro-Vice-Chancellor, 1982-83, Loughborough University; Foundation Director, City Polytechnic of Hong Kong, 1983-89; Vice-Chancellor and Principal, University of Bradford, 1989-98; Chairman, Prescription Pricing Authority, 1998-2001; Chairman, North and East Yorkshire and Northern Lincolnshire Strategic Health Authority; Chairman, Genetics and Insurance Committee. Publications: Monograph, Thermal Stress Analyses; 126 Technical articles; 40 papers on education, training et al. Memberships: British Association for the Advancement of Science Brunel Lecturership in Engineering; Commander of the Order of the British Empire (CBE). Memberships: Chartered Engineer, Engineering Council, 1964; Fellow, Royal Aeronautical Society, 1969; Fellow, Institute of Acoustics, 1977-85; Fellow, Chartered Institute of Transport, 1977-85; Fellow, Hong Kong Institution of Engineers, 1984; Life Fellow, Aeronautical Society of India, 1986; Fellow, Royal Academy of Engineering, 1990. Address: 8 Swan Court, York Road, Harrogate, N. Yorks HG1 2QH, England. E-mail: david@johnshg1.fsnet.co.uk

JOHNSON Benjamin Sinclair Jr, b. 30 December 1961, Falmouth, Jamaica. Professional Athlete; Coach. Honours: Phil Edwards Memorial Outstanding Track Athlete, 1984, 1985, 1986, 1987; Inducted into the Canadian Amateur Hall of Fame, 1985; Olympic Champion Award, 1985; Morton Crowe Award for Male Athlete of the Year, 1985, 1986, 1987; CTFA Track Jack W Davies Outstanding Athlete of the Year, 1985, 1986, 1987; Athlete of the Month, October 1985, January 1986, August 1987, January 1988, Sports Federation of Canada; Sports Excellence Award, 1986; IAAF/Mobil Grand Prix Standings (Indoor), 1986; Lionel Connacher Award for Male Athlete of the Year, 1986, 1987; Jesse Owens International Trophy for Athletic Excellence, 1987; World Champion Award, 1987; The Tribute to Champions; Outstanding Athlete of the Year, 1986, 1987; Order of Canada, 1987. E-mail: benjohnson979@mail.com

JOHNSON Betsey Lee, b. 10 August 1942, Hartford, Connecticut, USA. Fashion Designer. m. (1) John Cale, 1966, 1 daughter, (2) Jeffrey Olivier, 1981. Education: Pratt Institute, New York; Syracuse University. Appointments: Editorial Assistant, Mademoiselle Magazine, 1964-65; Partner, Co-Owner, Betsey, Bunky & Nini, New York, 1969-; Shops in New York, Los Angeles, San Francisco, Coconut Grove, Florida, Venice, California, Boston, Chicago, Seattle; Principal Designer for Paraphernalia, 1965-69; Designer, Alvin Duskin Co, San Francisco, 1970; Head Designer, Alley Cat by Betsey Johnson (division of LeDamor Inc), 1970-74; Freelance Designer for Junior Women's

Division, Butterick Pattern Co, 1971, Betsey Johnson for Jeanette Maternities Inc, 1974-75; Designer for Gant Shirtmakers Inc (women's clothing), 1974-75, Tric-Trac by Betsey Johnson (women's knitwear), 1974-76, Butterick's Home Sewing Catalog (children's wear), 1975-; Head Designer, Junior Sportswear Co; Designed for Star Ferry by Betsey Johnson & Michael Miles (children's wear), 1975-77; Owner, Head Designer, B J Inc, Designer, Wholesale Co, New York, 1978; President, Treasurer, B J Vines, New York; Opened Betsey Johnson Store, New York, 1979. Honours include: Merit Award, Mademoiselle Magazine, 1970; Coty Award, 1971; 2 Tommy Print Awards. Memberships: Council of Fashion Designers; American Women's Forum. Address: 110 East 9th Street, Suite A889, Los Angeles, CA 90079, USA.

JOHNSON Charles (Richard), b. 23 April 1948, Evanston, Illinois, USA. Professor of English; Writer. m. Joan New, June 1970, 1 son, 1 daughter. Education: BA, 1971, MA, 1973, Southern Illinois University; Postgraduate Studies, State University of New York at Stony Brook, 1973-76. Appointments: Assistant Professor, 1976-79, Associate Professor, 1979-82, Professor of English, 1982-, University of Washington, Seattle. Publications: Faith and the Good Thing, 1974; Oxherding Tale, 1982; The Sorcerer's Apprentice: Tales and Conjurations, 1986; Being and Race: Black Writing Since 1970, 1988; Middle Passage, 1990; All This and Moonlight, 1990; In Search of a Voice (with Ron Chernow), 1991; Dreamer, 1998. Honours: Governor's Award for Literature, State of Washington, 1983; National Book Award, 1990. Address: c/o Department of English, University of Washington, Seattle, WA 98105, USA.

JOHNSON Christopher Louis McIntosh, b. 12 June 1931, Thornton Heath, England. Economic Adviser. m. Anne Robbins, 1958, 1 son, 3 daughters. Education: MA 1st class honours, Philosophy, Politics and Economics, Magdalen College, Oxford. Appointments: Journalist, 1954-76, Paris Correspondent, 1959-63, The Times and Financial Times; Diplomatic Correspondent, Foreign Editor, Managing Editor, Director, Financial Times, 1963-76; Chief Economic Adviser, 1977-91, General Manager, 1985-91, Lloyds Bank; Visiting Professor of Economics, Surrey University, 1986-90; Visiting Scholar, IMF, 1993; Specialist Adviser to the Treasury Select Committee, House of Commons, 1981-97; Chairman, British Section of the Franco-British Council, 1993-97; UK Adviser, Association for the Monetary Union of Europe, 1991-2002. Publications: Editor, Lloyds Bank Review and Lloyds Bank Economic Bulletin, 1985-91; 4 books; Newspaper articles; Lectures on the euro and other economic and financial topics. Honours: Chevalier de la Legion d'Honneur, 1996. Memberships: Member, National Commission on Education, 1991-92; Member, Council of the Britain in Europe Campaign for the Euro; Member, Council of the Institute for Fiscal Studies; Chairman, New London Orchestra; Fellow, Royal Society of Arts. Address: 39 Wood Lane, London N6 5UD, England. E-mail: johnsonc@globalnet.co.uk

JOHNSON David, b. 26 August 1927, Meir, Staffordshire, England. Historian. Education: Repton; Sandhurst. Publications: Sabre General, 1959; Promenade in Champagne, 1960; Lanterns in Gascony, 1965; A Candle in Aragon, 1970; Regency Revolution, 1974; Napoleon's Cavalry and its Leaders, 1978; The French Cavalry 1792-1815, 1989; Bonaparte's Sabres, 2003. Contributions to: The Armourer (1914: The Riddle of the Marne); Skirmish Magazine. Address: 64B John Street, Porthcawl, Mid-Glam CF36 3BD, Wales.

JOHNSON Earvin (Magic Johnson), b. 14 August 1959, Lansing, Michigan, USA. Basketball Player. m. Cookie Kelly, 1 son. Education: Michigan University. Appointments: Professional

Basketball Player, Los Angeles Lakers National Basketball Association (NBA), 1979-91, (retired), Returned to professional sport, 1992, later announced abandonment of plans to resume sporting career; Chairman, Johnson Development Corporation, 1993-, Magic Johnson Entertainment, 1997-; Vice-President, Co-Owner, Los Angeles Lakers, 1994-, Head Coach, 1994; Presenter, TV Show, The Magic Hour, 1998-. Publications: Magic, 1983; What You Can Do to Avoid AIDS, 1992; My Life (autobiography), 1992. Honours include: Named, Most Valuable Player, NBA Playoffs, 1980, 1982, 1987, NBA, 1987, 1989, 1990. Memberships include: NCAA Championship Team, 1979; National Basketball All-Star Team, 1980, 1982-89; National Basketball Association Championship Team, 1980, 1982, 1985, 1987, 1988; National AIDS Association. Address: Magic Johnson Foundation, Suite 1080, 1600 Corporate Pointe, Culver City, CA 90230, USA.

JOHNSON Harold Stephens, b. 11 February 1928, Newport, Kentucky, USA. Chaplain, Hospital and Military (Lt Col). m. Harriet E Dinsmore, 1 son, 1 daughter. Education: Diploma in Education, 1953; BSc, Elementary Education and Religion, Southern Adventist University, 1958; BD, 1965; MA, Education Immanuel Baptist Schools, 1969; DD, Mother Teresa of Calcutta Seminary, 2000; Diploma, Great Lakes Region Chaplains Service Staff College, 1990; Diploma, Southeast Region Chaplains Service Staff College, 1993; Southeast Region Staff College, 1994; United States Air Force Auxiliary National Staff College, 1994. Appointments: Pastor, Teacher and Administrator, 7th Day Adventist Church and School System (in USA, Lebanon, Iran and Africa); Vice President and Vice Principal, Laurelbrook Sanitarium and School; Chaplain, Memorial Hospital, Manchester, Kentucky; Associate Chaplain, Florida Hospital Heartland Division, Florida; Chaplain Lt Colonel, United States Air Force Auxiliary, The Civil Air Patrol. Publications: Editor, SEAU Tidings; Author, The Chaplain's Corner in The Trailblazer, The Pulse and Wings and Wheels Group 3 Civil Air Patrol, Florida Wing. Honours: Honorary D D Immanuel Schools, 1975; Honorable Order of Kentucky Colonels, 1985; VIP Award, Clay County Board of Education, 1985; Wing Chaplain of the Year for the Florida Wing, 1992, 1995; Southeast Region Chaplain of the Year, 1996; National Unit Chaplain of the Year in the Civil Air Patrol, 1997. Memberships: Adventist Chaplains Ministries, 1976; Life Member, Disabled American Veterans, 1986; Life Member, Military Chaplains Association of the USA, 1990; Life Member, Malawi Bible Society, Africa, 1997. Address: 2735 N Avocado Road, Avon Park, FL 33825-9336, USA.

JOHNSON Hugh Eric Allan, b. 10 March 1939, London, England. Author; Editor. m. Judith Eve Grinling, 1965, 1 son, 2 daughters. Education: BA, MA, King's College, Cambridge. Appointments: Feature Writer, Condé Nast Magazines, 1960-63; Editor, Wine and Food Magazine, 1962-63; Wine Correspondent, Sunday Times, 1963-67; Travel Editor, 1967; Editor, Queen Magazine, 1968-70; Wine Editor, Cuisine Magazine, New York, 1983-84; Editorial Director, 1975-90, Editorial Consultant, 1990-, The Garden; Chairman, Winestar Productions Ltd, The Movie Business, The Hugh Johnson Collection Ltd. Publications: Wine, 1966; The World Atlas of Wine, 1971, 4th edition, 1994, 5th edition with Jancis Robinson, 2001; The International Book of Trees, 1973, 2nd edition, 1994; The California Wine Book, with Bob Thompson, 1975; Hugh Johnson's Pocket Wine Book, annually, 1977-; The Principles of Gardening, 1979, revised edition, 1996; Hugh Johnson's Wine Companion, 1983, 5th edition, 2003; Hugh Johnson's Cellar Book, 1986; The Atlas of German Wines, 1986; Understanding Wine, A Sainsbury Guide, 1986; Atlas of the Wines of France, with Hubrecht Duijker, 1987; The Story of Wine, 1989, reissued, 1998; The Art and Science of Wine, with James Halliday, 1992; Hugh Johnson on Gardening, 1993; Tuscany and its Wines,

Dictionary of International Biography

2000; many articles on gastronomy, gardening and travel. Other: How to Handle a Wine, video, 1984; A History of Wine, Channel 4 TV series, 1989; Return Voyage, Star TV Hong Kong, 1992. Honours: Honorary Doctorate, University of Essex, 1998; Honorary Trustee, The American Institute for Wine, Food and the Arts, 2000; Fellow Commoner, King's, Cambridge, 2001; Chevalier De L'Ordre National Du Mérite, 2003; Hon. President, The International Wine & Food Society. Membership: President, Sunday Times Wine Club, 1973-; Founder Member, Tree Council, 1974; Circle of Wine Writers, President 1997-. Address: Saling Hall, Great Saling, Essex CM7 5DT, England.

JOHNSON Malcolm, b. 23 September 1946, Great Britain. Global Director of Respiratory Science. m. 2 children. Education: BSc, Pharmacy, School of Pharmacy, Sunderland, England, 1965-68; PhD, Department of Pharmacology, University of Newcastle upon Tyne, 1968-71. Appointments: Research Associate, Departments of Physiology and Pathology, Stanford University, California, USA, 1971-73; Senior Research Associate and Lecturer, Department of Physiology and Biochemistry, Georgetown University, Washington DC, USA, 1973-75; Research Fellow, American Heart Association, 1974-75; Senior Scientist, ICI Pharmaceuticals, Alderley Edge, Cheshire, England, 1975-84; Head of Department, Cardiovascular and Respiratory Pharmacology, Glaxo Group Research, Ware, Hertfordshire, England, 1985-93; Director of Respiratory Science, Glaxo Wellcome Research and Development, Uxbridge, Middlesex, England, 1993-2000; Global Director of Respiratory Science, GlaxoSmithKline Research and Development, Greenford, Middlesex, England, 2000-; Visiting Professor, NHLI, Imperial College, London, 2000-. Publications: Author or co-author of 172 research publications which include most recently: Effects of beta2-agonists on resident and infiltrating inflammatory cells, 2003; Blockade of LTC4 sythesis caused by additive inhibition of gIV-PLA2 phosphorylation: Effect of salmeterol and PDE4 inhibition in human eosinophils, 2003; Enhanced synergy between fluticasone propionate and salmeterol inhaled from a single inhaler versus separate inhalers, 2003. Memberships: European Respiratory Society, 1993-; American Respiratory Society, 1994-. E-mail: malcolm.w.johnson@gsk.com

JOHNSON Michael, b. 13 September 1967, Dallas, USA. Athlete. Education: Baylor University. Appointments: World Champion 200m, 1991, 400m & 4 x 400m, 1993, 200m, 400m & 4 x 400m (world record), 1995, 400m, 1997; Olympic Champion 4 x 400m (world record), 1992, 200m, 400m, 1996, World Record Holder 400m (indoors) 44.63 seconds, 1995, 4 x 400m (outdoors) 2.55.74, 1992, 2.54.29, 1993; Undefeated at 400m, 1989-97; First man to be ranked World No 1 at 200m and 400m simultaneously, 1990, 1991, 1994, 1995; World Record Holder for 400m Relay, 42.93 seconds; Olympic Champion, 200m (world record), 400m, Atlanta, 1996; Olympic Champion, 400m, Sydney 2000. Awards: Jesse Owens Award, 1994; Track and Field US Athlete of the Year (four times). Address: USA Track & Field, PO Box 120, Indianapolis, IN 46206, USA.

JOHNSON Miriam Comer, b. 14 July 1942, High Point, North Carolina. Minister; Religious Educator, Counsellor, Company Executive. m. (1) Lloyd Linwood Comer, 5 March 1983, deceased, 2 children, (2) John V Johnson, 20 July 1998. Education: Student, Howard University, 1960-63; Teaching Certificate, Divine Science School, Washington DC, 1994; Practitioners Certificate, Divine Science Federation, Denver, 1996; Ordained Minister, Divine Science Church 2001. Appointments: Manager, Advertising and Research, US News and World Report, Washington DC, 1969-77; Executive Assistant to President, Kaaren Johnson Associates, Silver Spring, Maryland, 1980-84; Course Leader, American

Management Association, Washington DC, 1983-85; Purchasing Administrator, Home Owners Warranty, Arlington, Virginia, 1984-94; Service Administrator, Federal Communications Commission, Washington DC, 1996-98; Lecturer teacher, Washington DC, 1996-; Vice-president Adams Community School Board; Teacher to Bible students in US and UK. Publications: The Open Book of Revelation, 1997; Genesis 1-5, 1998; Continuity of the Bible (lecture series), 1998; The Metaphysical Noah, 1999; Spiritual Law and the Ten Commandments, 2000; The Alpha/Omega Principle (lecture series), 2003. Honour: Who's Who in the World, Millennium Edition. Memberships: International New Thought Association; Divine Science Federation; Divine Science Ministers' Association. Address: 814 Buchanan Street, NW Washington DC 20011-7116. E-mail: mirjoh@aol.com

JOHNSON Rex Sutherland, b. 24 August 1928, Essex, England. Chartered Architect; Arbitrator; Expert Witness. m. Betty E Johnson, deceased, 2 sons. Education: Diploma of Architecture, London University. Appointments: Assistant Architect, Senior Architect, T P Bennett and Son; Junior Partner, Oliver Law and Partners, 1961-63; T P Bennett and Son, 1963-65; Associate Partner, 1965-69, Senior Partner, 1969-90, Ronald Ward and Partners; Retired, 1990; Consultant, Design 5, London. Memberships: Fellow, Royal Institute of British Architects; Fellow, Chartered Institute of Arbitrators; Founder Member, Society of Expert Witnesses. Address: Whitepines, Longmill Lane, Crouch, Nr Sevenoaks, Kent TN15 8QB, England. Email: beejons@aol.com

JOHNSON William, b. 20 April 1922, Manchester, England. University Professor. m. Heather M Thornber, 1946, 3 sons, 2 daughters. Education: BSc.Tech., UMIST, 1943; REME Commd. 1943-47; BSc Mathematics, London, 1948; DSc, Manchester University, 1960; FRS, 1982 FREng, 1983. Appointments: Professor of Mechanical Engineering, UMIST, 1960-75; Professor of Mechanics, Engineering Department, University of Cambridge, 1975-82; Visiting Professor, Industrial Engineering Department, 1984-85, United Technologies Distinguished Professor of Engineering, 1987-89, Purdue University, Indiana, USA; Visiting Professor of Mechanical Engineering and History of Science, UMIST, 1992-94. Publications (with co-author): Plasticity for Mechanical Engineers, 1962; Mechanics of Metal Extrusion, 1962; Bibliography of Slip Line Fields, 1968; Impact Strength of Materials, 1972; Engineering Plasticity, 1973; Engineering Plasticity: Metal Forming Processes, 1978; Crashworthiness of Vehicles, 1978; Bibliography of Slip Line Fields, 1982; Collected papers on Benjamin Robins, 2001-03; Record and Services Satisfactory, 2003. Honours include: Safety in Mechanical Engineering Prize, 1980, 1990; James Clayton Prize, Institution of Mechanical Engineers, 1987; Bernard Hall Prize, 1965, 1967; Silver Medal, Institute of Sheet Metal, 1987; AMPT Gold Medal, Dublin, 1995; ASME Engineer-Historian Award, 2001; Honorary DSc, Bradford University, 1976, Sheffield University, 1986, UMIST, 1995. Memberships: Foreign Fellow, Academy of Athens, 1982; Foreign Member, Russian Academy of Science, Ural Branch, 1993; Indian National Academy of Engineering, 1999; Fellow of University College, London, 1981.

JOHNSSON Bengt (Gustaf), b. 17 July 1921, Copenhagen, Denmark. Professor; Pianist; Organist. m. Esther Paustian, 1 daughter. Education: MA, Musicology, University of Copenhagen, 1947; Studies with Georg Vasarhelyi and Walter Gieseking; Degree as Organist and Church Musician, Royal Academy of Music, Copenhagen, 1945. Debut: Copenhagen, 1944. Career: Concert tours, broadcasts, Scandinavia, German Federal Republic, Switzerland, France, Netherlands; Recitals in many European countries; US tour, 1964; Organist, Danish Broadcasting, 1949-

70; Teacher, Royal Academy, Copenhagen, 1958-61; Professor, Royal Academy of Music, Aarhus, Jutland; Numerous master classes; Studied at Vatican Library, Rome, 1977, Benedictine Monastery, Montserrat, Spain, 1978, 1980-83; Spanish Cultural Department invitation to study in libraries in Barcelona and Montserrat, 1979, 1983. Recordings include: N W Gade Piano Music; Rissager, Complete Piano Works; Chamber Music of Beethoven, Brahms, Busoni; Roman Organ and Harpsichord Music from the 17th Century, 1982; Rued Langgaard: Piano Music, 1985; Catalan Organ Music, 1988. Publications include: History of the Danish School of Music until 1739, 1973; Roman Organ Music for the 17th Century; Roman Harpsichord Music from the 17th Century; Piano Music of Manuel Blasco de Nebra, 1984; 23 Piano Sonatas for Josep Galles, 1984; Editor: Heptachordum Danicum 1646 (translation, historical comments, source studies), 1977; Hans Mikkelsen Ravn: The Vatican Manuscript, 1981; Selected Sonatas of D Scarlatti including 1st edition of 4 new editions, 1985; Selected Piano Music of N W Gade, 1986; Catalan Organ Music of the 18th Century, 1986; Scarlatti Vol II, 1988, vol III, 1992; Niels W Gade: Klavierwerke, 1989; Piano Music for Franz Liszt, 1989; Selected Piano Works of Rued Langgaard, 1994. Honours: Bronze Medal Winner, Piano Music of Manuel Blasco de Nebra, International Book Messe, Leipzig, 1986. Address: Porsevænget 18, Kongens Lyngby, DK-2800 Copenhagen, Denmark.

JOHNSTON Barrie Colin, b. 7 August 1925, London, England. Retired Merchant Banker. m. Cynthia Anne, 1 son, 1 daughter. Appointments: Junior Clerk, Helbert Wagg & Co Ltd, 1939-41; War Service, Royal Marines, Commissioned, 1945, Qualified as Intelligence Officer, Served in 34th Amphibious Regiment RM in SEAC, 1943-46; Rejoined Helbert Wagg, 1946, amalgamated in 1960 to J Henry Schroder Wagg & Co Ltd; Promoted later to Assistant Director of the Bank; Created Schroder Life Assurance, on the Board for 2 years; Member of team that formed first Property Unit Trust for Pension Funds in 1966, began lecturing on Pension and Property matters, 1946-72; Director, Charterhouse Japhet, 1972-84; Chairman Chaterhouse Bank, Jersey for 5 years; Retired, 1984; Non-executive Director, Charterhouse Investment Management, 1984-86; Additional Business Interests: The Pension Fund Property Unit Trust, 1966-89; The Charities Property Unit Trust, 1967-88; The Pension Fund Agricultural Property Trust, 1976-89; Non-executive Director, T H White Ltd, 1980-87; Director, Mornington Building Society, 1988-91; Director, ML-MIM European Equity Revival Fund NV, 1990-98; Chairman, Honorary Treasurer, or Trustee of 20 charities, 1984-2003. Publications: Articles in professional magazines and newspapers; lectures to professional bodies; Book, Life's a Lottery – or is it?, 2001. Honour OBE, 1994. Memberships: Fellow, Pensions Management Institute; Associate UK Society of Investment Professionals; Honorary Fellow, Royal College of Radiologists; Honorary Member, Royal Electrical and Mechanical Engineers Institution; Fellow, Royal Society of the Arts. Address: Yew Cottage, 8 The Green, Ewell, Surrey KT17 3JN, England.

JOINES Mary Elizabeth, b. 30 July 1911, Madison, Kansas, USA. Retired Teacher; Poet. m. Glenn V Joines, 7 June 1934, 1 son, 2 daughters. Education: BS, cum laude, Home Economics, Kansas State University, 1933; 20 Graduate Hours, University of Kansas and University of Missouri; Conversational French through French Embassy, Kuwait City, Kuwait; Adult short course in Advanced Poetry, Front Range College, Westminster, Colorado. Publications: Of Home and Other Hazards, 1986; Echoes in the Wind, printed. Contributions to: Anthologies and periodicals. Honours: 257 Cash Prizes (93 of which were 1st Place, 86 were 2nd Place), 1949-; Plaque, In Appreciation of Service, Kansas Authors Club, 1981. Memberships: Ionian Literary Society; Midwest Federation of Chaparral Poets; Kansas Authors Club,

1949-85; National League of American Pen Women, 1964-; Poetry Society of Colorado, 1979-; Kentucky State Poetry Society, 1986-. Address: 8905 Oakwood Street, Westminster, CO 80031- 7504, USA.

JOKSIMOVIĆ Veliša, b. 16 October 1961, Kurjače, Serbia. Teacher of Serbian Language. m. Dobrila Milenković, 1 daughter. Education: Yugoslavian Literature and Serbian Language, Philology Faculty, University of Belgrade, 1987; Postgraduate Specialist Studies, Text Critics, 1995. Appointments: Teacher, Serbian Language and Literature, Požarevac, 1987-93; Inspector, Ministry of Culture, Republic of Serbia, 1993-96; Advisor, Ministry of Education, 1996-2003; Vice-Editor, literature magazine "Braničevo", 1995-2000. Publications: The Disaster of Aurora, 1993; The Snake Emperor, 1997; Levant Epistles, 1998; The Village of Kurjače and its School (Monograph), 2001; Eternal and Fake (essays), 2003. Honours: Literature Award, Gordana Todorović; Award of the Poet Dis "Dis ' spring". Memberships: Association of Serbian Literates; The Society of Serbian Language and Literature. Address: Tabacka carsija 12/2, 12000 Pozarevac, Serbia.

JOLLEY (Monica) Elizabeth, b. 4 June 1923, Birmingham, England. Writer; Tutor. m. Leonard Jolley, 1 son, 2 daughters. Education: Nursing Training, 1940-46. Appointment: Writer-in-Residence, Western Australia Institute of Technology, later Curtin University of Technology, Perth, 1980-. Publications: Five Acre Virgin and Other Stories, 1976; The Travelling Entertainer, 1979; Palomino, 1980; The Newspaper of Claremont Street, 1981; Mr Scobie's Riddle, 1983; Woman in a Lampshade, 1983; Miss Peabody's Inheritance, 1983; Milk and Honey, 1984; The Well, 1986; The Sugar Mother, 1988; My Father's Moon, 1989; Cabin Fever, 1990; Central Mischief, 1992; The Georges' Wife, 1993; Diary of a Weekend Farmer (poems), 1993; The Orchard Thieves, 1995; Lovesong, 1997; An Accommodating Spouse, 1998. Honours: Honorary Doctorate, Western Australia Institute of Technology, 1986; Officer of the Order of Australia, 1988; Honorary Doctor of Literature, Macquarie University, Sydney, 1995, University of New South Wales, 2000; Honorary Doctorate, University of Queensland, 1997. Address: 28 Agett Road, Claremont, Western Australia 6010, Australia.

JONAS Hilda (Klestadt), b. 21 January 1913, Düsseldorf, Germany. Concert Harpsichordist and Pianist; Teacher of Harpsichord and Piano. m. Gerald Jonas, 30 January 1938, 2 daughters. Education: Hochschule für Musik, Cologne, 1932-33; Honour Diploma, Gumpert Conservatory, 1934; Studies with Professor Michael Wittels, Cologne, Rudolf Serkin, Switzerland and Wanda Landowska, Paris, France. Career: Concert soloist and recitalist worldwide with recitals in France, Germany, Spain, Italy, Austria, Belgium, Australia, New Zealand, Hawaii, USA; Colleges, Universities, museums and art centres, Harvard, Carnegie-Mellon, Cincinnati Taft Museum, Haifa Music Museum, Milano Centro Culturale San Fedele, Empire Saal of Schloss Esterházy, Eisenstadt, Brussel's Musée Instrumental, Castello Buonconsiglio, Trento, Palais Wittgenstein, Düsseldorf, Stanford University, California, Palace of the Legion of Honour San Francisco, San Francisco State University, Goethe Institute, California West Coast from Olympia Evergreen State College to Santa Barbara, Westmont, Ventura, Monterey Peninsula Colleges, Sacramento Crocker Art Museum, Ojai Valley Art Center and other cultural centres in Marin County and San Francisco; Soloist with major symphony orchestras including: Cleveland, Cincinnati; Regular series and May festivals under Max Rudolf and Josef Krips, Honolulu, Oxford, Jerusalem, Strasbourg and elsewhere; Owner of private piano studio, Honolulu, 1938-42 and Cincinnati, 1942-75; Founder, 1965, Director, 1965-75, Harpsichord Festival Put-in-Bay, Ohio.

Recordings include: Listen Rebecca, The Harpsichord Sounds, for children of all ages; Johann Kuhnau: Six Biblical Sonatas, with text based on authentic edition; Hilda Plays Bach: Italian Concerto, Chromatic Fantasia and Fugue, Partita 1, Capriccio on the departure of his beloved brother, and others; Johann Sebastian Bach: Goldberg Variations. Contributions to: Various music magazines. Memberships: Life Member, Hadassah; Life Member, Brandeis University. Address: 50 Chumasero Drive 1-L, San Francisco, CA 94132, USA.

JONAS Manfred, b. 9 April 1927, Mannheim, Germany. Historian. m. Nancy Jane Greene, 19 July 1952, 2 sons, 2 daughters. Education: BS, City College of New York, 1949; AM, 1951, PhD, 1959, Harvard University. Appointments: Visiting Professor for North American History, Free University of Berlin, 1959-62; Assistant Professor to Professor of History, 1963-81, Washington Irving Professor in Modern Literary and Historical Studies, 1981-86, John Bigelow Professor of History, 1986-96, Union College, Schenectady, New York, USA; Dr Otto Salgo Visiting Professor of American Studies, Eötvös Lorand University, Budapest, Hungary, 1983-84. Publications: Die Unabhängigkeitserklärung der Vereingten Staaten, 1964; Isolationism in America 1935-1941, 1966, 2nd edition, 1990; American Foreign Relations in the 20th Century, 1967; Roosevelt and Churchill: Their Secret Wartime Correspondence, 1975, 2nd edition, 1990; New Opportunities in the New Nation, 1982; The United States and Germany: A Diplomatic History, 1984. Contributions to: Diplomatic History; The Historian; Mid-America; American Studies; Maryland Historical Magazine; Essex County Historical Collections; Jahrbuch für Amerikastudien. Address: Department of History, Union College, Schenectady, NY 12308, USA.

JONAS Peter (Sir), b. 14 October 1946, London, England. General and Artistic Director, Bavarian State Opera. m. Lucy Hull, 1989, divorced 2001. Education: BA honours, University of Sussex; LRAM, FRNCM, 2000, Royal Northern College of Music; CAMS, Fellow, FRCM 1989, Royal College of Music; Eastman School of Music, University of Rochester, USA. Appointments: Assistant to Music Director, 1974-76, Artistic Administrator, 1976-85, Chicago Symphony Orchestra; Director of Artistic Administration, Orchestral Association of Chicago, Chicago Symphony Orchestra, Chicago Civic Orchestra, Chicago Symphony Chorus, Allied Arts Association, Orchestra Hall, 1977-85; General Director, ENO, 1985-93; General and Artistic Director, Bavarian State Opera, 1993-; Chairman, Deutsche Opernkonferenz (Congress of German and European Opera House Directors), 1999-. Publications: with Mark Elder and David Pountney, Power House, 1992; Co-author, Eliten und Demokratie, 1999. Honours: FRSA, 1989; CBE, 1993; Honorary DrMus, Sussex, 1994; Knighted 2000; Bayerische Verdienstorden (Distinguished Service Cross), 2001; Bavarian Constitutional Medal, 2001; Queen's Lecture, Berlin, 2001. Memberships: Advisory Board, Hypo-Vereinsbank, 1994-; Board of Governors, Bayerische Rundfunk, 1999-; Board of Management, National Opera Studio, 1985-93; Council, RCM, 1988-95; Council, London Lighthouse, 1990-94. Address: Bayerische Staätsoper, Nationaltheater, Max-Joseph-Platz 2, 80539 München, Germany.

JONES Alys, b. 15 September 1944, Newborough, Anglesey, North Wales. Teacher. m. Robin Jones, 28 April 1973, 1 son, 1 daughter. Education: BA, Honours, Welsh, University College, Bangor, North Wales. Appointments: Teacher in Welsh, Maesteg Comprehensive School, 1966-67, Manchynlleth Secondary School, Powys, 1967-70, Ysgol Dyffryn Conwy, Llanrwst, 1970-74; Ysgol Glan Clwyd, Llanelwy, 1974-75. Publications: Ysbrydion y Môr, 1982; Storiau Non, 1982; Storiau Huw a'i Ffrindiau, 1987;

Dirgelwch Neuadd Henffordd, 1987; Mac Pync, 1987; Storiau Cornel y Cae, 1988; Yr Ysbryd Arian, 1989; Y Gadwyn, 1989; Jetsam, 1991; Straeon Cornel y Stryd, 1994; Cuthbert Caradog, 1998; Pwtyn Escapes, 1998; Pwtyn and Pwtan go to School, 2001; Pwtyn ar Goll, 2001; Clymau Ddoe, 2001; Pwtyn and Pwtan Meet, 2002. Contributions to: CIP; Heno Heno. Address: Llys Alaw, 18 Ystad Eryri, Bethel, Caernarfon, Gwynedd, North Wales.

JONES Catherine Zeta, b. England. Actress. m. Michael Douglas, 1 son, 1 daughter. Creative Works: Stage appearances include: The Pyjama Game; Annie; Bugsy Malone; 42nd Street; Street Scene; TV appearances include: Darling Buds of May; Out of the Blue; Cinder Path, 1994; Return of the Native, 1995; Titanic, 1996; Film appearances include: Scheherazade; Coup de Foudre; Splitting Heirs, 1993; Blue Juice, 1995; The Phantom, 1996; The Mask of Zorro, 1997; Entrapment, 1998; The Haunting, 1999; Traffic, 2000; America's Sweethearts, 2001; Chicago, 2002; Monkeyface, 2003. Honours: Best Supporting Actress, BAFTA Awards, 2003; Screen Actors Guild Awards, 2003; Academy Awards, 2003. Address: c/o ICM Ltd, Oxford House, 76 Oxford Street, London W1N 0AX, England.

JONES Clare Lynelle, b. Birmingham England. Musician. Education: MA, Oxon; ARCM (Pianoforte Teaching). Career: Debut: Wigmore Hall, Piano Accompaniment, 1977; International Recitalist in universities and musical establishments; Ballet Accompanist; Arts Educational Schools, Turnham Green; Adult Education Accompanist, Hackney Community College; Formerly sighted Braille Music Transcriber. Recording: Pianist, Andresier Ensemble, AS 1025. Memberships: Royal Society of Musicians of Great Britain; Incorporated Society of Musicians; Musicians Union. Address: 7 Regency Court, Park Road, Surbiton, Surrey KT5 8QB, England.

JONES Douglas Gordon, b. 1 January 1929, Bancroft, Ontario, Canada. Retired Professor; Poet. Education: MA, Queen's University, Kingston, Ontario, 1954. Appointment: Professor, University of Sherbrooke, Quebec, 1963-94. Publications: Poetry: Frost on the Sun, 1957; The Sun Is Axeman, 1961; Phrases from Orpheus, 1967; Under the Thunder the Flowers Light Up the Earth, 1977; A Throw of Particles: Selected and New Poems, 1983; Balthazar and Other Poems, 1988; The Floating Garden, 1995; Wild Asterisks in Cloud, 1997; Grounding Sight (poetry), 1999. Other: Butterfly on Rock: A Study of Themes and Images in Canadian Literature, 1970. Honours: President's Medal, University of Western Ontario, 1976; Governor General's Award for Poetry, 1977, and for Translation, 1993; Honorary DLitt, Guelph University, 1982. Address: 120 Hougton Street, North Hatley, Quebec JOB 2CO, Canada.

JONES George Glenn, b. 12 September 1931, Saratoga, Texas, USA. Country Singer; Musician (guitar). m. Tammy Wynette, 1969-75; Nancy Sepulveda, 1983. Career: Recording artist, 1953-; Worked under names of Johnny Williams, Hank Davis, Glen Patterson; Worked with The Big Bopper; Johnny Preston; Johnny Paycheck; Recorded duets with Gene Pitney; Melba Montgomery; Tammy Wynette; Elvis Costello; James Taylor; Willie Nelson. Compositions include: The Window Up Above, Mickey Gilley; Seasons Of My Heart, Johnny Cash, Jerry Lee Lewis. Recordings: 150 Country hits include: Why Baby Why; White Lightning; Tender Years; She Still Thinks I Care; You Comb Her Hair; Who Shot Sam?; The Grand Tour; He Stopped Loving Her Today; Recorded over 450 albums; Recent albums include: First Time Live, 1985; Who's Gonna Fill Their Shoes, 1985; Wine Coloured Roses, 1986; Super Hits, 1987; Too Wild Too Long, 1987; One Woman Man, 1989; Hallelujah Weekend, 1990; You Oughta Be Here With Me, 1990; And Along Came Jones, 1991; Friends In High Places, 1991;

Salutes Bob Wills and Hank Williams, 1992; Live At Dancetown USA, 1992; Walls Can Fall, 1992; One, 1995; I Lived to Tell It All, 1996; In a Gospel Way, 1997; It Don't Get Any Better Than This, 1998; The Cold Hard Truth, 1999; Live with the Possum, 1999; with Tammy Wynette: We Can Go Together, 1971; Me And The First Lady, 1972; Golden Ring, 1976; Together Again, 1980. Address: Razor & Tie, 214 Sullivan Street, Suite 4A, New York, NY 10012, USA.

JONES Grace, b. 19 May 1952, Spanishtown, Jamaica. Singer; Model; Actress. m. Atila Altaunbay, 1996. Education: Syracuse University. Appointments: Fashion Model, New York, Paris; Made 1st Album, Portfolio, for Island Records, 1977; Debut as Disco Singer, New York, 1977; Founder, La Vie en Rose Restaurant, New York, 1987. Creative Works: Films include: Conan the Destroyer; A View to a Kill, 1985; Vamp; Straight to Hell; Siesta; Boomerang, 1991; Albums include: Fame; Muse; Island Life; Slave to the Rhythm.

JONES Hazel Emma (Main), b. 6 April 1919. Retired Librarian. m. Clifford Henry Jones, deceased, 2 sons, 3 daughters. Education: BA, University of Melbourne, 1943; ALAA, 1974; Certificate of Graduation, Sheffield School of Interior Design, 1995. Appointments: Cataloguer, Medical Librarian, University of Melbourne, 1935-45; Catalogued at Church Grammar School, 1969; Graduate Clerk, Library, Department of Works, Australia, 1970-71; Temporary Librarian, Greenslopes Repatriation Hospital, 1971-72; Deputy Librarian to Acting Librarian, State Department of Health, 1973-84. Publications: Financial statements and annual reports. Honours: Member, Australian Institute of Librarians, 1940; Fellow, International Biographical Centre, Cambridge; Joined American Biographical Institute. Memberships: Friends of Queensland Art Gallery; Friends of the Conservatorium, 1976-; Life Member, AILIA; ARLIS/ANZ; Research Officer, IBC; ABI Genealogical Society, 1997. Address: 35 Greer Street, Bardon 4065, Brisbane, Queensland, Australia.

JONES Huw, b. 5 May 1948, Manchester, England. Broadcasting Executive. m. Siân Marylka Miarczynska, 1979, 1 son, 1 daughter. Education: BA, Modern Languages (French), MA, Oxon. Appointments: Pop Singer, Recording Artist, Television Presenter, 1968-76; Director, General Manager, Sain Recording Company, 1969-81; Chairman, Barcud Cyf (TV Facilities), 1981-93; Managing Director, Producer, Teledu'r Tir Glas Cyf (independent production company), 1982-93; First Chairman, Teledwyr Annibynnol Cymru (Welsh Independent Producers), 1984-86; Chief Executive, S4C (Welsh Fourth Channel), 1994-. Honours: Honorary Fellow, University of Wales, Aberystwyth; Member, Gorsedd of Bards National Eisteddfod of Wales; Fellow, Royal Television Society. Memberships: Chairman, Celtic Film and Television Co Ltd, 2001-; Director, Sgrin Cyf; Director, International Film Festival of Wales; Director, National Assembly of Wales Broadcasting Co Ltd; Member, British Screen Advisory Council; Member, DCMS/Skillset Audiovisual Industries Training Group. Address: S4C, Parc Ty Glas, Llanishen, Cardiff, C14 5DU, Wales. E-mail: huw_jones@s4c.co.uk

JONES James Earl, b. 17 January 1931, Mississippi, USA. Actor. m. Cecilia Hurt, 1982. Education: University of Michigan. Creative Works: Numerous stage appearances on Broadway and elsewhere including, Master Harold...And the Boys, Othello, King Lear, Hamlet, Paul Robeson, A Lesson From Aloes, Of Mice & Men, The Iceman Cometh, A Hand is on the Gate, The Cherry Orchard, Danton's Death, Fences; Frequent TV appearances; Voice of Darth Vader in films Star Wars, The Empire Strikes Back, The Return of the Jedi; Films include: Matewan; Gardens of Stone; Soul Man; My Little Girl; The Man; The End of the Road; Dr Strangelove;

Conan the Barbarian; The Red Tide; A Piece of the Action; The Last Remake of Beau Geste; The Greatest; The Heretic; The River Niger; Deadly Hero; Claudine; The Great White Hope; The Comedians; Coming to America; Three Fugitives; Field of Dreams; Patriot Games; Sommersby; The Lion King (voice); Clear and Present Danger; Cry the Beloved Country; Lone Star; A Family Thing; Gang Related; Rebound; Summer's End; Undercover Angel, 1999; Quest for Atlantis, 1999; On the Q.T., 1999; Finder's Fee, 2001; Recess Christmas: A Miracle on Third Street (voice), 2001. Honours include: Tony Award; Golden Globe Award; Honorary DFA, Princeton, Yale, Michigan. Address: Horatio Productions, PO Box 610, Pawling, NY 12564, USA.

JONES James Stuart, b. 1948, Glasgow, Scotland. Anglican Bishop. m. Sarah Jones, 3 daughters. Education: BA honours, Theology, Exeter University, 1970; PGCE, Drama and Religious Education, 1971; Theological Training, Wycliffe Hall, Oxford. Appointments: Teacher of Religious Education and Latin; Producer at Scripture Union; Reader, 1976; Deacon, 1982; Priest, 1983; Bishop, 1994; Curate and then Associate Vicar, Christ Church with Emmanuel, Clifton, Bristol; Visiting Lecturer, Media Studies, Trinity College, Bristol; Vicar of Emmanuel Church, South Croydon, 1990; Bishop of Southwark's Examining Chaplain; Bishop's Selector; Bishop of Hull, 1994; Bishop of Liverpool, 1998-. Publications: Author of books on Christian spirituality; Various articles for newspapers. Honours: Honorary Doctor of Divinity, University of Hull, 1999; Honorary Doctor of Letters, University of Lincolnshire and Humberside, 2001. Memberships: Church Pastoral Aid Society; Urban Bishops Panel of the Church of England. Address: Bishop's Lodge, Woolton Park, Liverpool L25 6DT, England.

JONES John Idris, b. 9 March 1938, Llanrhaiadr-y-Mochnant, Wales. Press Officer; Constituency Administrator. m. Denise Idris Jones, 2 sons, 1 daughter. Education: BA, Keele University, England; Cert. Ed, Leeds, England; MA, Cornell University, USA. Appointments: Lecturer in English, Yale Further Education College, Wrexham, Wales; Press Officer and Constituency Administrator, National Assembly of Wales. Publications: Barry Island and Other Poems, 1978; Renewals, 2000. Honour: Fellow of the Welsh Academy. Membership: Welsh Academy. Address: Borthwen, Llanfair Road, Ruthin, Denbighshire LL15 1DA, Wales.

JONES Linda May, b. 9 November 1937, El Dorado, Kansas, USA. Tourguide; Writer. m. Verl R Jones, 2 sons, 1 daughter. Education: University of Kansas, 1955-57; University of Colorado, 1970, 1971. Appointments: Tourguide, 1976-84, Manager of Tourguide Services, 1978-84, Queen City Tours and American Travel Brokers; Owner of Columbine Tours, 1984-92; Guide for Backyard Tours, 1992-2002; Currently, Guide for JPS Enterprises, Great Times Tours and Mountains and More Tours. Publications: Co-author, Mile High Denver, A Guide to the Queen City, 1981; Co-author, Up The Gulch, 2004; On the staff of Colorado Gambler, 1993-. Honours: Outstanding Young Women of America, 1969; Outstanding Junior Member in Colorado DAR and Southwest Division DAR, 1970. Memberships: Mt Lookout Chapter DAR; Peak to Peak Rotary Club; Gilpin County Historical Society, President, 1990-; St James United Methodist Church. Address: PO Box 615, Black Hawk, CO 80422, USA.

JONES Martin (Glyn), b. 3 June 1937, Surbiton, Surrey, England. Lecturer; Examiner; Poet. m. 1 April 1966, 1 son, 1 daughter. Education: BA, History, 1962, Postgraduate Certificate in Education, 1963, London University. Appointment: Co-Editor, Weyfarers. Publication: The Pink Shiny Raincoat, 1992; Guildford Poems, 2000. Contributions to: Outposts; New Poetry; Poetry South-East; Samphire; Weyfarers; Envoi; Poetry Nottingham.

Dictionary of International Biography

Honour: Commended, Surrey Poetry Centre Competition, 1991, Third Prize Nottingham Poetry Competition, 2002. Membership: The Poetry Society, Surrey Poetry Centre, Guildford. Address: 1 Mountside, Guildford, Surrey GU2 4JD, England.

JONES Martyn David, b. 1 March 1947, Crewe, Cheshire. Member of Parliament. divorced. 1 son, 1 daughter. Education: Liverpool College of Commerce; CIBiol, Liverpool Polytechnic; MIBiol, Trent Polytechnic. Appointments: Microbiologist, Wrexham Lager Beer Company, 1969-87; Councillor, Clwyd County Council, 1981-89; MP for Clwyd South (formerly Clwyd South West), 1987-; Opposition Spokesperson on Food, Agriculture and Rural Affairs, 1994-95; Labour Whip; 1988-92; Speaker's Panel of Chairmen, 1993-94; Chairman, Welsh Affairs Select Committee, 1997. Memberships: Council Member, Royal College of Veterinary Surgeons; SERA, Fabian Society; Christian Socialist Movement; Federation of Economic Development Authorities; Institute of Biology. Address: House of Commons, London, SW1A 0AA, England. E-mail: jonesst@parliament.uk

JONES Mike, b. 7 May 1951, Cheshire, England. Post Office Employee; Poet. Publication: Scars and Glory, 1980. Contributions to: Countryman; Outposts; Orbis; New Poetry; Envoi; Candelabrum; Artful reporter; Ipsel; Weyfarers; Chester Poets, Vols 6-12; Meridian; Allusions. Memberships: Mid Cheshire Writers Group, founder; Crewe and District Writers Group; Chester Poets. Address: Glyndwr Cottage, Birch Heath, Tarporley, Cheshire CW6 9UR, England.

JONES Peter Ivan, b. 14 December 1942, Cosham, Hampshire, England. Chairman of the Tote. m. Elizabeth Gent, 2 sons, 2 daughters. Education: BSc Economics, London School of Economics, 1964; MIPA, 1967. Appointments: Chief Executive, Boase Massimi Pollitt, 1988-89; Chief Executive, 1989-93, Director, 1989-97, Omnicom UK plc; President, Racehorse Owners Association, 1990-93; Member, Horserace Betting Levy Board, 1993-95; Director, British Horseracing Board, 1993-97; President, Diversified Agency Services, 1993-97; Chairman, Dorset Police Authority, 1997-; Director, 1995-97, Chairman, 1997-, Horserace Totalisator Board. Publications: Trainers Record, annually, 1973-87; Editor, Ed Byrne's Racing Year, annually, 1980-83. Memberships: Bridport and West Dorset Golf Club. Address: Melplash Farmhouse, Melplash, Bridport, Dorset DT6 3UH, England. E-mail: pjones@tote.co.uk

JONES Quincy, b. 14 March 1933, Chicago, Illinois, USA. Record Producer; Composer; Arranger; Musician; Conductor. m. (1) 3 children, (2) Peggy Lipton, 2 daughters. Education: Seattle University; Berklee College of Music; Boston Conservatory. Appointments: Trumpeter, Arranger, Lionel Hampton Orchestra, 1950-53; Arranger, various singers; Leader, own orchestra, concerts, TV appearances, 1960-; Music Director, Mercury Records, 1961, Vice-President, 1964. Creative Works: Solo Albums: You've Got It Bad Girl, 1973; Walking In Space, 1974; Body Heat, 1974; Mellow Madness, 1975; I Heard That!, 1976; Quintessence, 1977; Sounds And Stuff Like That, 1978; The Dude, 1981; Bossa Nova, 1983; The Q, 1984; Back On The Block, 1989. Honours: Golden Note, ASCAP, 1982; Honorary Degree, Berklee College, 1983; Over 20 Grammy Awards; Lifetime Achievement, National Academy of Songwriters, 1989; Jean Hersholt Humanitarian Award, 1995; Scopus Award; Producers' Guild of America Award, 1995; Crystal Award, World Economic Forum, 2000; Marian Anderson Award, 2001; Ted Arison Prize, National Foundation for Advancement in the Arts, 2001; Kennedy Center Honor, 2001. Address: Rogers and Cowan, 3800 Barham Boulevard, Suite 503, Los Angeles, CA 90068, USA.

JONES Russell Alan, b. 26 May 1960. Director of Operations. Education: BA Honours, British Government and Politics and History, University of Kent at Canterbury, 1978-81. Appointments: Orchestra Personnel Manager, Royal Liverpool Philharmonic Society, 1981-86; Concerts Manager, Scottish Chamber Orchestra, 1986; Chief Executive and Company Secretary, National Federation of Music Societies, 1987-97; Director of Operations, Arts and Business, 1997-. Honours: Chevalier, Coteaux des Ordre de Champagne. Memberships: Billingsgate Ward Club; Fellow, Royal Society of Arts; Member, Royal Philharmonic Society; Friends of the Phil; Kent Society; London Symphony Chorus; Lords Taverner; Musicians Benevolent Fund; National Campaign for the Arts; National Trust. Address: 12 Eastern Road, Bounds Green, London N22 4DD, England.

JONES Sally Roberts, b. 30 November 1935, London, England. Author; Publisher. Education: BA, University College of North Wales, 1957; ALA, North-Western Polytechnic, 1964. Appointments: Senior Assistant, Reference Library, London Borough of Havering, 1964-67; Reference Librarian, Borough of Port Talbot, Wales, 1967-70; Publisher, Alun Books, 1977-. Publications: Turning Away, 1969; Elen and the Goblin, 1977; The Forgotten Country, 1977; Books of Welsh Interest, 1977; Allen Raine, 1979; Relative Values, 1985; The History of Port Talbot, 1991; Pendaruis, 1992; Dic Penderyn, 1993. Honour: Welsh Arts Council Literature Prize, 1970. Memberships: Welsh Academy, chairman, 1993-97; Afan Poetry Society; Port Talbot Historical Society. Address: 3 Crown Street, Port Talbot SA13 1BG, Wales.

JONES Samuel, b. 2 June 1935, Inverness, Mississippi, USA. Composer; Conductor; Educator. m. (1) 2 daughters, (2) Kristin Barbara Schutte, 22 December 1975. Education: BA, Millsaps College, 1957; MA, PhD, Eastman School of Music, University of Rochester, 1958-60. Career: Director of Instrumental Music, Alma College, Michigan, 1960-62; Music Director, Saginaw Symphony, 1962-65; Conductor, Rochester Philharmonic, 1965-73; Founding Dean, Shepherd School of Music, 1973-79; Professor of Conducting and Composition, Rice University, 1973-97; Composer in Residence, Seattle Symphony Orchestra, 1997-; Composer in Residence, Music Alive, Meridian Symphony, 2003-04; Guest Conductor, Buffalo Philharmonic Symphonies of Detroit, Pittsburgh, Houston, Prague and Iceland. Compositions: In Retrospect; Symphony No 1 (recorded); Elegy for String Orchestra (recorded); Overture for a City; Let Us Now Praise Famous Men (recorded); Spaces; Contours of Time; Fanfare and Celebration; A Christmas Memory; A Symphonic Requiem; Variations on a Theme of Howard Hanson; The Trumpet of the Swan; Listen Now, My Children (recorded); Two Movements for Harpsichord; Canticles of Time, Symphony No 2; Symphony No 3 (Palo Duro Canyon), 1992; The Seas of God, 1992; The Temptation of Jesus (oratorio), 1995; Janus, 1998; Roundings, 1999; Eudora's Fable: The Shoe Bird, 2002; Aurum Aurorae, 2001; Chorale-Overture for organ and orchestra, 2003. Recordings: Symphony No 3 recorded by Amarillo Symphony; Roundings and Cello Sonata, Amarillo Symphony (Naxos American Classics). Address: 35247 34th Avenue S, Auburn, WA 98001, USA.

JONES Tom (Thomas Jones Woodward), b. 7 June 1940, Pontypridd, Wales. Entertainer. m. Melinda Trenchard, 1956, 1 son. Career: Former bricklayer, factory worker, construction worker; Singing debut, aged 3, later sang in clubs, dance halls, with self-formed group The Playboys; Became Tom Jones, 1963; First hit record It's Not Unusual, 1964; Appeared on radio, television; Toured US, 1965; Television show, This Is Tom Jones, 1969-71; Many international hits, albums in Top 10 charts, Europe, USA; Over 30 million discs sold by 1970; Toured continuously, television appearances, 1970s-; Score, musical play Matador; Hit single: A Boy From Nowhere, 1987; Frequent Amnesty International; Simple Truth, 1991; Rainforest Foundation, 1993; Shelter, 1993; Television series: The Right Time, 1992; Glastonbury Festival of Contemporary Performing Arts, 1992; Live stage appearance, Under Milk Wood, Prince's Trust, 1992; Performed in Amnesty International 40th Anniversary Special, 2001. Recordings: Hits include: It's Not Unusual, 1964; What's New Pussycat, 1965; Thunderball, 1966; Green Green Grass Of Home, 1966; Delilah, 1968; Love Me Tonight, 1969; Can't Stop Loving You; She's A Lady; Letter To Lucille, 1973; Say You Stay Until Tomorrow, 1976; A Boy From Nowhere, 1987; It's Not Unusual (reissue), 1987; If I Only Knew, 1994; Burning Down the House, 1999; Baby It's Cold Outside, 1999; Mama Told Me Not To Come, 2000; Sex Bomb, 2000; You Need Love Like I Do, 2000; Tom Jones International, 2002. Albums include: Green Green Grass Of Home, 1967; Delilah, 1968; This Is Tom Jones, 1969; Tom, 1970; I Who Have Nothing, 1970; Close Up, 1972; The Body and Soul Of TJ, 1973; I'm Coming Home, 1978; At This Moment, 1989; After Dark, 1989; The Lead And How To Swing It, 1994; Reload, 1999; Mr Jones, 2002; Reload 2, 2002. Honours: BRIT Award for Best British Male Solo Artist, 2000; Nodnoff Robbins Music Therapy Silver Clef Award, 2001; Q Magazine Merit Prize, 2002; BRIT Award for Outstanding Contribution to Music, 2003. Memberships: SAG; AFTRA: AGVA. Address: Tom Jones Enterprises, 10100 Santa Monica Blvd, Ste 205, Los Angeles, CA 90067, USA.

JONES Tommy Lee, b. 15 September 1946, San Saba, Texas, USA. Actor. m. (1) Kimberlea Cloughley, 1981, (2) Dawn Laurel, 2001. Education: Harvard University. Creative Works: Broadway appearances include: A Patriot for Me; Four in a Garden; Ulysses in Night Town; Fortune and Men's Eyes; TV appearances include: The Amazing Howard Hughes; Lonesome Dove; The Rainmaker; Cat on a Hot Tin Roof; Yuri Nosenko; KGB; April Morning; Films include: Love Story, 1970; Eliza's Horoscope; Jackson County Jail; Rolling Thunder; The Betsy; Eyes of Laura Mars; Coal Miner's Daughter; Back Roads; Nate and Hayes; River Rat; Black Moon Rising; The Big Town; Stormy Monday; The Package; Firebirds; JFK; Under Siege; House of Cards; The Fugitive; Blue Sky; Heaven and Earth; Natural Born Killers; The Client; Blue Sky; Cobb; Batman Forever; Men in Black, 1997; Volcano, 1997; Marshals, 1997; Small Soldiers (voice), 1998; Rules of Engagement, 1999; Double Jeopardy, 1999; Space Cowboys, 2000; Men in Black II, 2002; The Hunted, 2003; The Missing, 2003. Honours include: Emmy Award.

JONES Trevor Mervyn, b. 19 August 1942, Wolverhampton, England. Director. m. Verity Ann Bates, 1 son, 1 daughter. Education: BPharm, Honours, PhD, Kings College, London. Appointments: Lecturer, University of Nottingham; Head of Development, The Boots Co Ltd; Director, Research and Development, Wellcome Foundation; Chairman, Reneuron Holdings plc; Director of Merlin Fund, Merlin Biosciences; Director General, Association of the British Pharmaceutical Industry. Publications: Numerous scientific papers in learned journals; Books: Drug Delivery to the Respiratory Tract; Advances in Pharmaceutical Science. Honours: Honorary degrees: PhD, University of Athens; DSc, University of Nottingham; DSc, University of Strathclyde; DSc, University of Bath; Honorary Fellowships: Royal College of Physicians, Faculty of Pharmaceutical Medicine; The School of Pharmacy; Charter Gold Medal, Pharmaceutical Society; Gold Medal, Comenius University. Memberships: Fellow, Royal Society of Chemists; Fellow, Royal Pharmaceutical Society; Member, College of Pharmacy Practice; Liveryman, Worshipful Society of Apothecaries; Atheneum Club; Surrey County Cricket Club. Address: Association of the British Pharmaceutical Industry, 12 Whitehall, London SW1A 2DY, England. E-mail: tjones@abpi.org.uk

JONG Erica (Mann), b. 26 March 1942, New York, New York, USA. Author; Poet. m. (4) Kenneth David Burrows, 5 August 1989, 1 daughter. Education: BA, Barnard College, 1963; MA, Columbia University, 1965. Appointments: Lecturer in English, City College of the City University of New York, 1964-66, 1969-70; University of Maryland Overseas Division, 1967-69; Faculty, Bread Loaf Writers Conference, Middlebury, Vermont, 1982, Salzburg Seminar, Austria, 1993. Publications: Fear of Flying, 1973; How to Save Your Own Life, 1977; Fanny, Being the True History of the Adventures of Fanny Hackabout-Jones, 1980; Parachutes and Kisses, 1984; Serenissima: A Novel of Venice, (reissued as Shylock), 1987; Any Woman's Blues, 1990; Fear of Fifty: A Midlife Memoir, 1994. Poetry: Fruits and Vegetables, 1971, 2nd edition, 1997; Half-Lives, 1973; Loveroot, 1975; The Poetry of Erica Jong, 1976; At the Edge of the Body, 1979; Ordinary Miracles, 1983; Becoming Light: Poems, New and Selected, 1992; Inventing Memory, 1997. Other: Four Visions of America (with others), 1977; Witches, 1981; Megan's Book of Divorce: A Kid's Book for Adults, (reissued Megan's Two Houses), 1984; Erica Jong on Henry Miller: The Devil at Large, memoir, 1994; Lyrics: Zipless: Songs of Abandon, from the Erotic Poetry of Erica Jong, 1995. Contributions to: Various publications. Honours: Academy of American Poets Award, 1963; Bess Hokin Prize, 1971; New York State Council on the Arts Grant, 1971; Alice Faye di Castagnola Award, 1972; National Endowment for the Arts Grant, 1973; Woodrow Wilson fellow; Mother of the Year, 1982; Memberships: PEN; Authors Guild USA, Council, 1975-, President, 1991-93; Phi Beta Kappa; Poetry Society of America; Poets and Writers; Writers Guild of America (West). Address: C/o Burrows, 451 Park Avenue South, New York, NY 10016, USA.

JONJIC Anto, b. 25 May 1937, Foca, Bosnia. Medical Doctor. m. Tereza Jonjic, 27 December 1958, 1 son, 1 daughter. Education: Graduate, Medical Sciences, Medical Faculty, University of Rijeka, Croatia, 1963; Social Medical and Primary Health Care, School of Public Health Andrija Stampar, Medical Faculty Zagreb, Croatia, 1969; DSc, Medical Faculty, University of Rijeka, 1980; Assistant Professor, 1981; Professor, Social Medicine and Primary Health Care, 1987. Appointments: Professor, Social Medical and Primary Health Care, Department Social Medicine and Health Ecology, Medical Faculty, Rijeka, Croatia, 1982-, Director, Medical Faculty, 1983-87, Dean for Education, 1987-90; Director, Public Health Institute, Primorsko-Goranska Co, Rijeka, 1996-2000. Publications: 55 original science papers, 195 professional papers, 13 books. Honour: Award, Medical Faculty, Rijeka, 1986. Memberships: Medical Council, Association of the General Medicine of Croatia; Association of Social Medicine of Croatia; President, Union Medicine Against Addicted Diseases, Rijeka. Address: Mate Balote 7A, 51000 Rijeka, Croatia.

JORDAN Bill (Lord), b. 1936, Birmingham, England. m. Jean Jordan, 3 daughters. Appointments: Machine Tool Fitter, 1951; Joined engineering union, served as Shop Steward, Convenor at GKN and District President; Elected Divisional Organiser, West Midlands Division, 1977; Elected National President, Amalgamated Engineering Union, 1986; General Secretary, International Confederation of Free Trade Unions, 1994-2002. Honours: CBE; Honorary Doctorate, University of Central England, 1993; Honorary Doctorate, University of Cranfield, 1995. Memberships: General Council of the British TUC; National Economic Development Council; European Metalworkers' Federation; International Metalworkers' Federation; European Trade Union Confederation; Victim Support Advisory Committee; English Partnership; Winston Churchill Trust; Governor, London School of Economics; Governor, Ashridge Management College; RSA; Member, UN High Level Panel on Youth Employment; Member, UN Global Compact Advisory Council.

Dictionary of International Biography

JORDAN Marcus deLambert, b. 2 March 1929, Bridgetown, Barbados. Company Director. m. Grace Enid, 10 September 1960, 1 son, 1 daughter. Education: BA, University of London, 1949; Life Insurance Diploma, Canada. Appointments: Sub Editor, Barbados Advocate; School Teacher, Combermere High School; Life Underwriter, Branch Manager, Manufacturers Life Insurance Co; Senator, Government of Barbados; Honorary Consul of Cyprus to Barbados; Managing Director, Wildey Shopping Plaza Ltd; Managing Director, Lamberts Ltd; Managing Director, Bank of Nova Scotia International Ltd; Managing Director, Scotia Insurance Ltd; President of the Senate, Government of Barbados. Honour: Justice of the Peace, Government of Barbados, 1972. Memberships: Chairman, Barbados Tourist Authority; President, Junior Chamber of Commerce; Founder Member, Kiwanis Club, Barbados; Member, Commonwealth Parliamentary Association; Royal Commonwealth Society. Address: Lambert's, Dover Terrace, Christ Church, Barbados. E-mail: wildeyplaza@sunbeach.net

JORDAN Michael Jeffrey, b. 17 February 1963, Brooklyn, New York, USA. Basketball and Baseball Player. m. Juanita Vanoy, 1989, 2 sons, 1 daughter. Education: University of North Carolina. Appointments: Player, Chicago Bulls National Basketball Association (NBA), 1984-93, 1995-98, (NBA Champions, 1991, 1992, 1993, 1996, 1997, 1998), Birmingham Barons Baseball Team, 1993; Member, NCAA Championship Team, 1982, US Olympic Team, 1984, NBA All-Star Team, 1985-91; with Nashville Sounds, 1994-95; Holds record for most points in NBA Playoff Game with 63; Retired, 1998-; Came out of retirement to play for Washington Wizards, 2001-. Publications: Rare Air: Michael on Michael (autobiography), 1993; I Can't Accept Not Trying: Michael Jordan on the Pursuit of Excellence. Honours include: Seagram's NBA Player of the Year, 1987; Most Valuable Player, NBA All-Star Game, 1988; NBA Most Valuable Player, 1988, 1991, 1992, 1996, 1998; Named, World's Highest Paid Athlete, Forbes Magazine, 1992. Memberships: President, Basketball Operations, Washington Wizards, 1999-. Address: Washington Wizards, 718 7th Street NW, Washington, DC 20004, USA.

JORDAN Neil Patrick, b. 25 February 1950, Sligo, Ireland. Author; Director. 3 sons, 2 daughters. Education: BA, 1st Class Honours, History/English Literature, University College, Dublin, 1972. Appointment: Co-Founder, Irish Writers Cooperative, Dublin, 1974. Publications: Night in Tunisia, 1976; The Past, 1979; The Dream of a Beast, 1983; Sunrise with Sea Monster, 1994; Nightlines, 1995. Films as a Director: Angel, 1982; The Company of Wolves, 1984; Mona Lisa, 1986; High Spirits, 1988; We're No Angels, 1989; The Miracle, 1990; The Crying Game, 1992; Interview With the Vampire, 1994; Michael Collins, 1996; The Butcher Boy, 1997; In Dreams, 1999; The End of the Affair, 1999; Double Dawn, 2001. Honours: Guardian Fiction Prize, 1979; The London Evening Standard's Most Promising Newcomer Award, 1982; London Film Critics Circle Awards, 1984; Oscar, 1992; Los Angeles Film Critics Award, 1992; New York Film Critics Circle Award, 1992; Writers Guild of America Award, 1992; BAFTA Award, 1992; Golden Lion, Venice Film Festival, 1996; Silver Bear, Berlin Film Festival, 1997; BAFTA Award, 2000. Address: c/o Jenne Casarotto Co Ltd, National House, 60-66 Wardour Street, London W1V 3HP, England.

JORDAN Patrick William, b. 23 November 1967, Kingston Upon Thames, England. Industrial Designer; Trend Analyst. Education: BSc, honours, Mechanical Engineering, University of Bristol, 1989; MSc, Work Design and Ergonomics, University of Birmingham, 1990; PhD, Psychology, University of Glasgow, 1993. Appointments: Researcher, Lecturer, University of Glasgow, 1990-93; President, Contemporary Trends Institute, London,

England; Vice-President, Symbian, London, England; Director, Human Factors, Director Trends and Identity, Philips Design, 1993-98; Nirenberg Professor of Design, Carnegie-Mellon University, 2001-02; CEO, Contemporary Trends Institute. Commissions and Creative Works: With Philips Design and Symbian, has received many hundred commissions for the design of consumer and professional products. Publications: 5 books and over 70 refereed articles in professional and academic journals. Honours include: Presidents Medal, Ergonomics Society, 1996; Special Award, Dutch Ergonomics Society, 1996; Design Team of the Year, Philips Design, 1998; 450 design awards. Memberships: Industrial Designers Society of America; Ergonomics Society; Royal Society of the Arts; American Psychological Association; British Psychological Society; Institution of Mechanical Engineers; Institution of Electrical Engineers; Institute of Packaging. Address: Candlesby, Butleigh, Somerset BA6 8TH, England.

JORSTAD Robert, b. 15 May 1946, Bemidji, MN. Geologist. m. Mary, 1 son, 1 daughter. Education: BS, Bemidji State University, 1969; MS, 1972; PhD, University of Idaho, 1983. Appointments: Assistant, Associate, Professor of Geology; Licensed Professional Geologist. Publications: Down to Earth Software Reviews; The General Environmental and Economic Geology and Stratigraphy of East Central Illinois. Honours: Faculty Excellence Award. Memberships: Geological Society of America; National Association of Geoscience Teachers; American Association of Stratigraphic Palynologist; Society for Sedimentary Geology; American Institute of Professional Geologists. Address: Geology/Geography Department, Eastern Illinois University, Charleston, IL 61920, USA.

JORTNER Joshua, b. 14 March 1933, Poland. Professor of Chemistry. m. Ruth Thea Sanger, 1 son, 1 daughter. Education: MSc, Physical Chemistry, The Hebrew University of Jerusalem, Israel, 1951-56; PhD, Physical Chemistry, 1960. Appointments: Lecturer, 1961-63, Senior Lecturer, 1963-65, Department of Physical Chemistry, Hebrew University; Associate Professor, Physical Chemistry, 1965-66, Professor, Chemistry, 1966-, Head, Institute of Chemistry, 1966-72; Tel Aviv University; Deputy Rector, 1966-69, Acting Rector, 1969, Vice President, 1970-72, Heinemann Professor, Chemistry, 1973-2003, Vice President, 1980-86, President, 1986-95, Israel National Academy of Sciences; Vice-President, 1995-97, President, 1998-99, Past President, 2000-01, International Union of Pure and Applied Chemistry. Publications: Author and Co-author of over 680 articles in scientific journals; others. Honours: International Academy of Quantum Science Award; Weizmann Prize; Rothschild Prize; Kolthof Prize; Israel Prize in Exact Sciences; The Wolf Prize in Chemistry; Many others. Memberships: Member of learned societies including: Israel National Academy of Sciences and Humanities; International Academy of Quantum Molecular Science; Royal Danish Academy of Sciences and Letters; Polish Academy of Sciences; Russian Academy of Sciences; National Academy of Sciences of the United States of America; Others. Address: School of Chemistry, Tel Aviv University, Ramat Aviv, 69978 Tel Aviv, Israel.

JOSEPHSON Brian David, b. 4 January 1940, Cardiff, Wales. Physicist. Education: Cambridge University. Appointments: Fellow, Trinity College, Cambridge, 1962-; Research Assistant Professor, University of Illinois, 1965-66; Professor of Physics, Cambridge University, 1974-; Faculty Member, Maharishi European Research University, 1975; Helped discover the tunnelling effect in superconductivity, called the Josephson effect. Publications: Co-editor, Consciousness and the Physical World, 1980; The Paranormal and the Platonic Worlds, in Japanese, 1997; Research papers on superconductivity, critical phenomena, theory of intelligence, science and mysticism. Honours: Honorary Member,

Institute of Electrical and Electronic Engineers; Foreign Honorary Member, American Academy of Arts and Sciences; New Scientist Award, 1969; Research Corporation Award, 1969; Fritz London Award, 1970; Hughes Medal, Royal Society, 1972; Joint Winner, Nobel Prize for Physics, 1973. Address: Cavendish Laboratory, Madingley Road, Cambridge, CB3 0HE, England. E-mail: bdj10@cam.ac.uk

JOSHI Prem Chandra, b. 17 December 1941, Lucknow, India. University Teacher. m. Kamlesh, 1 son, 1 daughter. Education: BA, Lucknow, 1961; LLB, Lucknow, 1964; MAs, Sociology, Lucknow, 1966, Kanpur, 1976; Diploma in Foreign Affairs, Lucknow, 1967; Proficiency Certificates, French, Russia and Esperanto, Lucknow, 1976-69; PhD, Sociology, 1978, MA, English, 1980, Lucknow University. Appointments: Investigator, PRAI, Lucknow, 1963-64; Field Investigator, India, for Dr Khare, Wisconsin, 1967-68; Senior Inspector, RFC, Lucknow, 1965; Lecturer, Srikrishna Audyogik Inter College, Kanpur, 1972-79; Lecturer, Senior Lecturer, Senior Reader, 1979-2001; Head, Department of Sociology, Garhwal University Campus, 1988-2001; Sociology Questions Expert to the Public Service Commission, Uttaranchal State, India, 2003. Publications: Over 20 PhD research articles and papers; Radio Broadcasts on Himalayan Polyandry of Jaunsar-Bawar, 1969-78; Social Disorganisation and Problems, 1975; Himalayan Polyandry, 1984; Society and Sociology, 1985; Himalayan Ecology: The Social Reason, 1985; Sri HNB Garhwal University, 1998; Uttaranchal, 2000; Environment, 2001; Numerous projects and reports; Acted as Sociology Research Guide of several scholars for D Phil in the Garhwal University by 2002. Honours: Man of the Year, ABI, 1999; 2000 Outstanding Intellectuals of 20th Century, IBC; Deputy Director General, IBC; Outstanding Man of the 21st Century, ABI, 2001; Fellow, International Biographical Association, IBC, 2001; Selected to receive International Medal of Honor, ABI, 2001; Nominated for Membership of London Diplomatic Academy, England, 2001. Memberships: Lions Club, Tehri, 1985-87; Executive Council, HNBGU, Garhwal, 1995-96; Member, Research Board of Advisors, ABI, 2000-01; Garhwal University Teachers' Association of Tehri and Pauri, 1980-2001; Participation in academic seminars, including one on Uttaranchal, Garwal University, 2001. Address: Joshi SADAN, nr Shyam Lal Ka Bagicha, Padampur Sukhro, Kotdwar, Garhwal, Uttaranchal, India.

JOSHI Rangnath Nathrao, b. 29 July 1940, Aite Tq Bhoom district Osmanabad, Maharashtra, India. Retired Superintendent in Law and Judiciary Department; Poet; Writer; Actor; Sweet Poetry Singer; Music Director. Education: HMDs; BTMD; DLit, Colombo; DLit, Nanded; PhD, Calcutta; 16 other literary degrees. Appointments: Composer of poems and lyrics in Marathi, Hindi, English and Sanskrit, Proze and Poetry; Singer of own compositions, 2501 performances in various states and cities in India; Singer, Actor, Director, Literary researcher, artist of radio and television; Many Performances; Approved Poet of AIR; Prominent personality in various posts in several sansthas and state institutions. Publications: 7,000 poems (gits); Publications include: Sangram Tutari; Dhaktya Tuljapurchi Tuljabhavani; Bhavdhara; Shri Tuljabhavani Mahima; Gitbhavani; Dundubhi; Sachitra Gitashree; Lokmata Ahilya deviholkar; Shri Manik Prabhu Gitayan; Bhaktikaustubha; Ahilyadevi Holkar Gitayan; Shrikashi Jagadguru Charitra Gitganga; Dharmatma; Shri Mahadev Maharaj Lilamrut; Shri Sadguru Ramrang Darshan Kavya; Chan Chan bad bad gite. Honours: Six First prizes, 1953, 1974, 1976, 1980, 1999, 2001; Special Merit Certificate Pune, 1976; Numerous medals, awards, cups, certificates for literary, musical, dramatic, poetic work; International Man of the Year 2001; Presided at several literary conferences; Life member, Maharashtra Shahir Parishad Pune; Invited Chief Poet for Kavi Sammelen, arranged by Station Director

of All India Radio Aurangabad, 1981, etc; Chief guest, invitee, president, inauguarator, examiner, many literary, musical, dramatic and social institutions; Chief and Judge in numerous competitions. Memberships include: All India Rajendra Samajik Kalyan Parishad Patna 1974-; Gita Ramayan Prachar Sangha Swargashram, 1975, etc; Chief Consultant, Editor, Dharma Prbha magazine, 1984-, and others; Master in Palmistry; ShakatiPat [Kundlini] diksha Sadguru; Jyotish Maharshi. Address: 335 Kaviraj, Near Papnash Tirtha, At PO Tq, Tuljapur District, Osmanabad 413601, Maharashtra State, India.

JOSHIPURA Kamalnayan, b. 22 January 1951, Ahmedabad. Professor of Physics. m. Jagruti, 1 son. Education: MSc, 1972; PhD, 1984. Appointments: College Lecturer, 1972-84; Reader, Sardar Patel University, 1984-92; Professor, Sardar Patel University, 1992-. Publications: 75 research papers and conference abstracts on Atomic-, Molecular Physics; Over 30 articles; 2 books on physics, science. Honours: Hari Om Ashram Research award, 1991; Fellow, Gujarat Science Academy, 1993; Man of the Year, ABI, 1998. Memberships include: Life Member, Indian Physics Association; Indian Association for Physics Teachers; World Federation of Scientists. Address: Department of Physics, Sardar Patel University, Vallabh-Vidyanagar 388120, India.

JOSIPOVICI Gabriel David, b. 8 October 1940, Nice, France. Professor of English; Writer; Dramatist. Education: BA, Honours, 1st Class, St Edmund Hall, Oxford, 1961. Appointments: Lecturer in English, 1963-76, Reader in English, 1976-84, Professor of English, 1984-99, Research Professor, Graduate School of Humanities, 1999-, University of Sussex. Publications: Novels: The Inventory, 1968; Words, 1971; Mobius the Stripper: Stories and Short Plays, 1974; The Present, 1975; Migrations, 1977; The Echo Chamber, 1979; The Air We Breath, 1981; Conversations in Another Room, 1984; Contre-Jour, 1986; In the Fertile Land, Shorter Fiction, 1987; The Big Glass, 1990; In a Hotel Garden, 1993; Moo Pak, 1994; Now, 1998; Goldberg: Variations, 2002. Non-Fiction: The World and the Book, 1971; The Lessons of Modernism, 1977; Writing and the Body, 1982 The Book of God: A Response to the Bible, 1988; Text and Voice, 1992; Touch, 1996; On Trust, 1999; A Life, 2001. Contributions to: Encounter; New York Review of Books; London Review of Books; Times Literary Supplement. Honours: Sunday Times Playwriting Award, 1969; BBC nominations for Italia Prize, 1977, 1989; South East Arts Literature Prize, 1978; Lord Northcliffe Lecturer, University of London, 1981; Lord Weidenfeld Visiting Professor of Comparative Literature, University of Oxford, 1996-97; Fellow of the Royal Society of Literature, 1997; Fellow of the British Academy, 2001. Address: c/o John Johnson, Clerkenwell House, 45-47 Clerkenwell Green, London EC1R 0HT.

JOXE Daniel Pierre, b. 28 November 1934. Member of Conseil Constitutionnel. Education: Faculté de Droit de Paris, 1956; Ecole Nationale d'Administration, 1960. Appointments: Magistrate. Publications: L'Edit de Nantes, une histoire pour aujourd' hui, 1998. A propos de la France, itineraires 1, 1998. Honour: KBE. Address: Conseil Constitutionnel, 2 Rue Montpensier, 75001, Paris, France.

JOYNER-KERSEE Jaqueline, b. 3 March 1962, East St Louis, Illinois, USA. Athlete. m. Bobby Kersee, 1986. Education: University of California, Los Angeles; Training: Husband as coach. Career: Athlete in the Heptathlon; Assistant Basketball Coach, UCLA; World Record Heptathlon Scores: 7,158 points, Houston, 1986; 7,215 points, US Olympic Trial, Indianapolis, 1988; 7,291 points, Seoul, 1988; 7,044 points, Olympic Games, Barcelona 1992; Honours: 3 Olympic Gold Medals; 4 World Championships; Record erased by IAAF, 1999; With Richmond Rage in American

Dictionary of International Biography

Basketball League; Winner, IAAF Mobil Grand Prix, 1994; Chair, St Louis Sports Commission, 1996-; Jim Thorpe Award, 1993; Jackie Robinson Robie Award, 1994; Jesse Owens Humanitarian Award, 1999; Hon DHL, Spellman College, 1998, Howard University, 1999, George Washington University, 1999. Publications: A Kind of Grace, autobiography, 1997. Address: Elite International Sports Marketing Inc, 1034 South Brentwood Boulevard, Suite 1530, St Louis, MO 63117, USA.

JOZEFACKA Maria Emilia, b. 2 March 1942, Opole, Poland. Writer; Poet. Education: MA, Catholic University of Lublin, 1964; DLitt, Lodz University, 1971. Appointment: Assistant, Catholic University of Lublin, 1965-69. Publications: The Edge, 1969; The Holocaust, 1970; The Epicentre, 1971; Advent, 1982; A Bedrock, 1983; The Encounter Earth, 1988; A View from the Cross, 1992; The Whirl, The Pattern, The Choice, 1998; A Vigil, 2001. Contributions to: Reviews, magazines, radio and television. Honours: Regional Prizes, 1968, 1972, 1983, 1999, 2002; National Prize for Best Poetry Book of the Young Generation, 1971; Award, Polish Ministry of Culture and Art, 1984. Memberships: Association of Polish Writers; IBBY. Address: al Tumidajskiego nr 2B m 42, 20-247 Lublin, Poland.

JU Byeong-Kwon, b. 2 December 1962, Seoul, Korea. Researcher. m. Yun-Hi Lee, 1 daughter. Education: Bachelor's Degree, 1986; Master's Degree, 1988, Department of Electronic Engineering, University of Seoul, Korea; Doctoral Degree, Department of Electronic Engineering, Korea University, 1994. Appointment: Principal Researcher, Microsystem Center, Korea Institute of Science and Technology, 1988-. Publication: Microsystem Technology, Intervision, 2000. Honours: Best Poster Paper Award, SID, 1999; Outstanding Poster Paper Award, IDW, 2000. Memberships: SID; IEEE. Address: PO Box 131, Cheong-Ryang, Seoul, 130-650, Korea.

JUAN CARLOS I (King of Spain), b. 5 January 1938, Rome. Education: Private, Fribourg, Switzerland, Madrid, San Sebastian; Institute of San Isidro, Madrid; Colegio del Carmen; General Military Academy, Zaragoza; University Madrid. Appointments: Inaugurated as King of Spain, 1975; Named as Captain-General of the Armed Forces, 1975. Honours include: Charlemagne Prize, 1982; Bolivar Prize, UNESCO, 1983; Gold Medal Order, 1985; Candenhove Kalergi Prize, Switzerland, 1986; Nansen Medal, 1987; Humanitarian Award, Elie Wiesel, USA, 1991; Houphouet Boigny Peace Prize, UNESCO, 1995; Franklin D Roosevelt Four Freedoms Award, 1995. Memberships include: Foreign Member, Académie des sciences morales et politiques. Address: Palacio de la Zarzuela, 28071 Madrid, Spain.

JUDD Frank Ashcroft, Lord Judd, b. 28 March 1935, Sutton, Surrey, England. Specialist in International Affairs. m. Christine Willington, 2 daughters. Education: City of London School, BScEcon, London School of Economics and Political Science, 1953-56. Appointments: F/O RAF, 1957-59; Secretary General, International Voluntary Service, 1960-66; Member of Parliament, Labour, Portsmouth West, 1966-74; Portsmouth North, 1974-79; Parliamentary Private Secretary to Leader of the Opposition, 1970-72; Member of the Parliamentary Delegation to the Council of Europe and Western European Union, 1970-73 and 1997-; Shadow Navy Minister, 1972-74; Parliamentary Under Secretary of State for Defence (Navy), 1974-76; Minister of State for Overseas Development, 1976-77; Minister of State, Foreign and Commonwealth Office, 1977-79; Associate Director, International Defence and Air Fund for Southern Africa, 1979-80; Director, Voluntary Service Overseas, 1980-85; Director, Oxfam, 1985-91; Created Life Peer, 1991; Member, Sub-committee, (Environment, Agriculture, Public Health and Consumer Protection) of the

European Community Committee in the House of Lords, 1997-2001; Member, Procedure Committee and Ecclesiastical Committee in the House of Lords, 2001-; Joint Chair, Joint Working Group on Chechnya, Council of Europe; A Non-Executive Director, Portsmouth Harbour Renaissance Ltd; Honorary Senior Fellow of Saferworld; Consultant Advisor to De Montfort University. Publications: Radical Future (jointly), 1967; Fabian International Essays (jointly), 1970; Purpose in Socialism (jointly), 1973; Imagining Tomorrow (jointly), 2000. Honours: Honorary DLitt, University of Bradford, University of Portsmouth; Honorary LLD, University of Greenwich; Honorary Fellow, University of Portsmouth and Selly Oak Colleges; Freeman of the City of Portsmouth; Member of Court, London School of Economics; Member of Council, University of Lancaster. Memberships include: Royal Institute of International Affairs; The Royal Society of Arts; The British Council; The Oxfam Association; The Labour Party; The Fabian Society; President, YMCA (England); Vice-President Council for National Parks; Convenor, Social Responsibility Forum of Churches Together in Cumbria. Address: House of Lords, London SW1A 0PW, England.

JUHAS Pavol, b. 4 July 1941, Teplicany, District Kosice, SR. Civil Engineer; Professor. m. Emilia. 2 sons. Education: Ing, Civil Engineering Faculty, Technical University, 1965; PhD, Scientific Study, 1973; Doctor of Sciences, 1988; Associate Professor, 1992; University Professor, 1993. Appointments: Designer, Eastern Slovak Steel Works, 1965-68; Scientific Worker, Institute of Construction and Architecture, 1968-93; Scientific Secretary, 1980-85; Vice Director, 1985-90; Professor, Civil Engineering Faculty, 1993-; Dean, 1994-2000. Publications: Theory and design of civil engineering steel structures; Elasto plastic analyses; Global and local stability; Postcritical behaviour and load carrying capacity; Fatigue strength and lifetime of structures. Honours: Award, Slovak Academy of Sciences; Medals, Technical University; Member, Scientific Committee and Boards. Memberships: Slovak Association for Steel Structures; International Association for Bridge and Structural Engineering; Structural Stability Research Council. Address: Civil Engineering Faculty, Technical University Kosice, Vysokoskolska 4, 042 00 Kosice, Slovak Republic.

JUMONVILLE Florence M, b. New Orleans, Louisiana, USA. Librarian; Historian. Education: BA, 1971, MEd, 1976, MA, 1988, PhD, 1997, University of New Orleans; MS, Louisiana State University, 1972. Appointments: Librarian, The Historic New Orleans Collection, 1972-74, 1978-82; Librarian, 1974-78, Head Librarian, 1982-97, Belle Chasse (Louisiana) State School; Adjunct Instructor of Library Science, Louisiana State University, Baton Rouge, 1994, 1996; Head, Louisiana and Special Collections, Earl K Long Library, University of New Orleans, 1997-. Publications: Numerous articles in professional journals; 3 books; Several book chapters. Honours: Lucy B Foote Award, Louisiana Library Association, 1985; Fannie Simon Award, Special Libraries Association, Museum, Arts and Humanities Division, 1997; Elected, American Antiquarian Society, 1990; Beta Phi Mu; Phi Delta Kappa; Kappa Delta Pi. Memberships: American Library Association; American Historical Association; American Printing History Association; Association of Moving Image Archivists; Bibliographical Society of America; Society for the History of Authorship, Reading and Publishing; Ephemera Society of America; Louisiana Library Association; Southeastern Library Association; Louisiana Historical Association; Manuscript Society; many others. Address: Earl K Long Library, University of New Orleans, 2000 Lakeshore Drive, New Orleans, LA 70148, USA. E-mail: fjumonvi@uno.edu

JUNCO-TORRES Antonio, b. 2 July 1957, Las Palmas de Gran Canaria. Lecturer. Education: Licenciado en Filosofia y Letras, Psicologia, 1979. Appointments: Teacher, Deutsche Schule in Las

Palmas, Spain, 1979-88; Lecturer in Spanish, Tübingen University, Germany, 1991-. Publications: Book, Historia de Espana, 2002. Address: Romanisches Seminar, Wilhelmstr 50, 72074 Tübingen, Germany. E-mail: antonio.juncotorres@uni-tuebingen.de

JUNG Myunghee, b. 5 March 1963, Seoul, Korea. Assistant Professor. m. Eui-jung Yun, 1 son, 1 daughter. Education: BS, Computer Science and Statistics, Seoul National University, 1989; MS, Statistics, 1991, PhD, Operations Research, 1997, University of Texas, Austin. Appointments: Research Assistant, CSR in University of Texas, Austin, 1994-97; Senior Researcher, Samsung SDS Corp, Korea, 1997-98; Assistant Professor, Anyang University, Korea, 1998-. Publications: Development of High-Performance Solenoid-Type Rfi Chip Inductors Utilizing Low-Loss Al_3O_3 Core Materials, 2000; Model based simulation of multispectral images based on remotely sensed data, 2003. Membership: IEEE. Address: Department of Digital Media Engineering, Anyang University, 708-113 Anyang 5 Dong, Manan-Gu, Anyang-Shi, Kyunggi-Do 430-714, South Korea. E-mail: mhjung@aycc.anyang.ac.kr

JURGA Ludovit Milan, b. 17 July 1943, Bratislava, Slovak Republic. Physician; Oncologist; Radiotherapist. m. Jane Grünnerova, 1995. Education: MD, 1967; Assistant Professor, 1973; PhD, 1977; Associate Professor, 1979; Full Professor, 1996; DSc, 2001; European Certification in Medical Oncology, 2002. Appointments: Head, Division of Chemotherapy, 1978-89; Head of Department of Radiotherapy and Oncology, Safarik University School of Medicine, Kosice, 1989-90; Adviser in Radiotherapy, Ministry of Health Slovak Republic, Bratislava, 1990-92; Head, Department of Radiation Oncology, 1996, Vice-Dean, 1997, Faculty of Public Health, University of Trnava; Head of Department of Oncology, University Teaching Hospital, Trnava, 1997-. Publications: Clinical and oncology and radiotherapy, 2000; Textbook of Radiology, 1st and 2nd Editions, 1990-94; 200 scientific and expert papers published in Slovak, Czech and international journals, Neoplasma, Oncology. Honours: Best Paper, Published in Oncology and in Chemotherapy, Award of Slovak Medical Society, Bratislava, 1978, 1994; Premium of Literary Fund, Bratislava, 2001; Honorary membership, Slovak Oncological Society, 2003; Honorary membership, Slovak Society of Chemotherapy, 2003; Silver Medal, Slovak Medical Society, Bratislava, 2003. Memberships: European Society for Medical Oncology, Lugano, 1990; Multinational Association of Supportive Care in Cancer, St Gallen, 1993; New York Academy of Sciences, 1994; Active Member, American Society of Clinical Oncology, 2004. Address: A Zarnova 11, 917 75 Trnava, Slovakia.

Dictionary of International Biography

K

KABANOV Modest, b. 19 March 1926, St Petersburg, Russia. Psychiatrist. m. Lydia Kabanova. Education: St Petersburg Medical University, 1948. Appointments: Head Physician, District Psychoneurological Dispensary, St Petersburg, 1958-60; Head Physician, IVth City Mental Hospital, 1960-64; Director, V M Bekhterev Psychoneurological Research Institute, 1964-2002; International Programmes Director, V M Bekhterev Psychoneurological Research Institute, 2002-. Publications: Over 250 in Russian and foreign languages including 8 Monographs. Honours: Honoured Scientist of the Russian Federation. Memberships: President World Association for Dynamic Psychiatry; World Association for Psychosocial Rehabilitation; World Association for Social Psychiatry. Address: V M Bekhterev Psychoneurological Research Institute 3, Bekhterev Street, St Petersburg 192019, Russia.

KABASAWA Uki, b. 21 January 1965, Namerikawa, Japan. Physicist. Education: Bachelor Degree, 1988, Master Degree, 1990, Osaka University. Appointments: Researcher, Central Research Laboratory, 1990-96, Engineer, Electronic Device Manufacturing Equipment and Engineering Division, 1996-99, Engineer, Instruments, Beam Technology Centre, 1999-2001, Hitachi Ltd; Engineer, Hitachi High-Technologies Corporation, Naka Division, Beam Technologies Center, 2001-. Publications include: Studies of High Temperature Superconductors, volume 1, 1989, volume 6, 1990; Advances in Superconductivity VI, vol 2, 1994; Quantum Theory of Many-Body Systems, 1999; Elements of Advanced Quantum Theory, 2000; Introduction to Mesoscopic Physics (translator), 2000; The Physics of Quantum Fields (translator), 2002; The Case of the Missing Neutrinos (translator), 2002. Memberships: American Association for the Advancement of Science; New York Academy of Sciences; Physical Society of Japan; Japan Society of Applied Physics. Address: Hitachi High-Technologies Corporation, Naka Division, Beam Technology Centre, 882 Ichige, Hitachinaka-shi, Ibaraki-ken 312-8504, Japan. E-mail: kabasawa-uki@naka.hitachi-hitec.com

KABBANI Sami, b. 3 January 1937, Damascus, Syria. Professor of Surgery. m. Sally, 2 sons, 1 daughter. Education: BSc, 1958, MD, 1962, Intern, 1962-63, American University of Beirut; First Year Resident General Surgery, Cleveland Metro, General Hospital, 1963-64; 2nd and 3rd Year, Resident, St Louis University Group of Hospitals, 1963-65; Chief Resident, St John's Mercy Hospital, 1965-66; Junior to Senior Resident, Henry Ford Hospital, Detroit, 1966-68; Fellow, Cardiovascular Surgery, Texas Heart Institute, Houston, 1972-73. Appointments: Assistant Professor, 1969-74, Associate Professor, 1974-79, Director, Damascus University Cardiovascular Surgical Center, 1975-, Professor of Surgery, 1979-, Chairman, Department of Cardiovascular Surgery, 1997-, Damascus University Medical School; Cardiovascular Surgeon, Western Heart Institute, San Francisco, California, USA, 1982-83. Publications: (as author or co-author) 50 in English, 40 in Arabic, in medical journals; Numerous presentations at international meetings. Honour: First Degree Presidential Appreciation Award (for starting open-heart surgery in Syria). Memberships: Arab (Syrian) Medical Society, 1969-; American College of Surgeons; Denton A Cooley Cardiovascular Society, 1973-; Association of Thoracic and Cardiovascular Surgeons of Asia, 1978-; European Society for Cardiovascular Surgery, 1979-89; Society of Thoracic Surgeons, 1980-; California Medical Association, 1982-; San Francisco Medical Society, 1982-; Arab-American Medical Association, 1982-; American College of Cardiology, 1983-; Mediterranean Association of Cardiology and Cardiac Surgery, 1998-; American Association of Thoracic Surgery, 1999-. Address: PO Box 2837, Damascus, Syria.

KABKAB Wissam, b. 26 July 1950, Ehden, Lebanon. Teacher; Researcher. m. Hilda Ziadeh. Education: Licence in History, 1974, 1981, Lebanese University; Doctorate in History, St Esprit University, Kaslik, 1983. Publications: 10 books; 20 research papers; 11 articles; 9 indexes; Participant in several historical and religious conferences and sessions. Memberships: Lebanese Historical Association, Fanar. Address: Jounieh, PO Box 2071, Lebanon.

KAČALA Ján, b. 8 April 1937, Dobšiná, Slovakia. Professor. m. Anna Kačalová, 1 son. Education: Pedagogical University in Bratislava, 1954-58; Candidatus Scientiarum (CSc), 1968; PhDr, 1969; DrSc, 1983. Appointments: Editor-in-Chief, Kultura slova, 1971-91; Director, Ludovit Stur Linguistics Institute of the Slovak Academy of Sciences, 1981-91; Chairman, Accrediting Committee, 1995-99, Advisory Board of the Slovak Government, Head of the Slovak Language Department, Pedagogical Faculty of Comenius University, 1992-. Publications: The Second Predicate in Slovak, 1971; The Verb and Semantic Structure of the Sentence, 1989; The Syntactic System of Language, 1998. Honours: Honorable Plaque of J Dobrovsky, Czecho-Slovak Academy of Sciences, 1987; Golden Honorable Plaque of L Stur, Slovak Academy of Sciences, 1997. Memberships: Corresponding Member, Slovak Academy of Sciences, 1987-; Societas Linguistica Europaea; Slovak Linguistic Society. Address: Bagarova 4, 841 01 Bratislava, Slovak Republic.

KACZMAREK Bozydar Leon Jan, b. 11 August 1946, Jarocin, Poland. Psychologist; Neuropsychologist; Psychologist of Communications. m. Renata Kusmierzak, 1 son. Education: MA, 1969; Diplomat, 1972; PhD, 1979; DSc, 1985; Professor, 1992. Appointments: Assistant, 1974-79, Assistant Professor, 1979-86, Associate Professor, 1986-91, Head, Developmental Psychology and Neurolinguistics Department, 1986-, Director, Psychology Institute, 1991-2002, Professor, 1991-, University Maria Curie Sklodowska. Publications include: Brain Organisation of Language, 1985-93; Brain Language Behaviour, 1994, 3rd edition, 1998. Honours: Golden Cross of Merit, 1994. Membership: Polish Neurolinguistic Society. Address: 20-633 Lublin, ul Skrzatow 2 m. 10, Poland.

KADDOURA Abdul Qader, b. 17 November 1935, Damascus, Syria. m. Maiada Jouahki, 2 sons, 2 daughters. Education: BSc. Appointments: Deputy Prime Minister for Economic Affairs, Speaker of the Parliament; Member of Parliament. Publications: Articles on Economics and Policy in Baath Newspaper, 1980's; Study on Parliament in Syria, 2000. Honours: Legion d'Honneur, France; Medal of the Republic, Egypt; Star Medal, Australia. Memberships: President, Arab Parliamentary Union; Member, International Parliamentary Union. Address: Post Office Box 9143, Damascus, Syria.

KAFELNIKOV Yevgeny Aleksandrovich, b. 18 February 1974, Sochi, Russia. Tennis Player. m. 2 daughters. Education: Krasnodar Pedagogical Institute. Appointments: Started playing tennis in Sochi Children Sports School, 1982; Later with coach Anatoly Lepeshin; ATP Professional, 1992-; Won 17 ATP tournaments including Milan, St Petersburg, Gstaad, Long Island; Won French Open (singles and doubles), 1996; Won, Moscow Kremlin Cup, 1997; Won, Australian Open, 1999; Member, Russian Federation Davis Cup Championship Team, 1993; Runner-up, World Championship, Hanover, 1997; Highest ATP Rating 1st, 1999; Olympic singles champion, Sydney, 2000; Winner of 51 pro titles by 2002. Address: All-Russian Tennis Association, Luzhnetskaya nab 8, 119871 Moscow, Russia.

KAFF Albert E, b. 14 June 1920, Atchison, Kansas, USA. Journalist; Author; Columnist. m. Diana Lee-chuan Fong, 15 October 1960, 2 sons. Education: BA, Economics, University of Colorado, 1942. Appointments: Summer Reporter, Atchison (Kansas) Daily Globe, 1939-41; Reporter, Ponca City (Oklahoma) News, 1946-48, Daily Oklahoman, 1948-50; Editor, 45th Division News, Louisiana, Japan and Korea, 1950-52; Reporter, United Press, Korea, Japan, 1952-56; Bureau Manager, United Press International, Saigon, Taipei, Manila, 1956-63; Editor, United Press International, Tokyo, Hong Kong, 1963-75; Personnel Director, United Press International, New York, 1975-78; Vice President, United Press International, Hong Kong, New York, 1978-85; Managing Editor, Business and International Editor, Cornell University News Service, Ithaca, New York, 1986-93; Freelance Writer, 1993-. Publications: Fire Arrows Over Quemoy, 1967; Crash: Ten Days in October...Will It Strike Again?, 1989; Black Monday: Boraku wa Kanarazu Kuru?, 1990; Ping-Pong Diplomacy, 1997. Honour: US Army Bronze Star for Meritorious Service, 1952. Memberships: Overseas Press Club of America; Tokyo Foreign Correspondents Club; Hong Kong Foreign Correspondents Club. Address: 393 Unquowa Road, Fairfield, CT 06824, USA.

KAGAWA Noboru, b. 26 July 1957, Tokyo. Physics Educator, Researcher. m. Madoka Hashimoto, 1 son, 1 daughter. Education: BS, 1980, MS, 1982, PhD, 1989, Keio University, Tokyo. Appointments: Researcher, 1982-1989, Deputy Manager, 1989-91, Toshiba Yokohama, Japan; Lecturer, 1991-92, Associate Professor, 1992-2003, Professor, 2003, National Defence Academy, Yokosuka, Japan; Guest Researcher, National Institute of Standards and Technology, Colorado, USA, 1995-97. Publications: Various articles including Theory and Design of Stirling Engines, 1999; Regenerative Thermal Machines, Stirling and Vuilleumier Cycle Machines, for Heating and Cooling, 2000. Honours: Recipient, Best Paper Award ASME, 1992; Recipient, Best Paper Award Japan Society of Refrigeration and Air Conditioning Engineers, 2001. Memberships include: Japan Society of Mechanical Engineers; Japan Society of Refrigeration and Air Conditioning Engineers; International Stirling Engine Council, 2001; and others. Address: National Defence Academy, Department of Mechanical Systems Engineering, 1-10-20 Hashirimizi, Yokouka 239-8686, Japan. E-mail: kagawa@nda.ac.jp

KAGEYAMA Toshiyuki, b. 3 November 1966, Sendai, Miyagi, Japan. Ophthalmologist. m. Miki Ogasawara, 1 daughter. Education: Medical Degree, Tohoku University School of Medicine, 1992; Doctor of Medicine, Showa University School of Medicine, 2001. Appointments: Residency, ophthalmology, Tohoku University Hospital, 1992-95; Instructor, Ophthalmology, Showa University, Fujigaoka, 1997-2001; Assistant Professor, Showa University, Fujigaoka Hospital, 2001-02; Director of Clinic, Nanbu Clinic, Aomori, Japan. Publications: Over 30 articles on Ophthalmology. Memberships: American Academy of Ophthalmology; Japanese Ophthalmological Society; Japanese Society of Ophthalmic Surgeons.

KAIKKONEN Kaarina, b. 28 March 1952, Iisalmi. Sculptor. m. Lauri Lipasti, 1 son, 1 daughter. Education: Academy of Fine Arts, Finland, 1978-83. Appointment: Art Teacher, University of Art and Design, Helsinki. Honours: Iisalmi City Art Reward, 1979; State Art Reward, 1989; 2nd Prize in Sculpture Competition, Hyvinkää, 1996; 2nd Prize, Sculpture Competition, Espoo, 1998; Finland Art Reward, 2001; The Prize of Environmental Art, 2001. Commissions and Creative Works: Travelled Journey, Hartola Museum, 1988; The Word as the Sword, University of Joensuu, 1989; Wall, Jämsä Museum, 1993; Hope, Espoo Congregation House, 1999; Collections: Kiasma Museum for Contemporary Art; Cities of Helsinki, Joensuu, Kuopio, Mikkeli, Iisalmi, Pieksämäki;

Foundation of Jenny and Antii Wihuri; Merita Bank; Kuopio Art Museum; Helsinki Art Museum; Joensuu Art Museum; Aine Art Museum; Solo exhibitions include: Rovaniemi Art Museum, 1995; Gallery Sculptor, Helsinki, 1995; Gallery Artina, Helsinki, 1998; Maison de l'Art des Chartreux, Brussels, 1999; Galleri 21, Malmo, Sweden, 2003; Fabrica, Brighton, UK, 2003; Gallery Artina, Helsinki, Finland, 2003; Group exhibitions include: Aine Art Museum, Tornio, 1999; Wäino Aaltonen Museum, Turku, 1999; Lapinlahti Art Museum, 1999; Museum for Contemporary Art, Tampere, 1999; Mingei Museum, San Diego, USA, 1999; Museum von Pully, Lausanne, Switzerland, 1999; Malmö Konstmuseum, Sweden, 2000; Rostock Kunsthalle, Germany, 2000; New Paper Art, Crafts Council, London, UK, 2001; Konturen in Zeit und Raum, Rasttat Schloss, Germany, 2002; Yojuna, Kiasma Museum of Contemporary Art, Helsinki, 2003; 8th Havana Biennial, Wifredo Lam Center for Contemporary Art, Havana, Cuba, 2003. Address: Kymintie 16, 00560 Helsinki, Finland.

KAINBERGER Franz, b. 22 December 1957, Salzburg, Austria. Radiologist. m. Andrea, 1 son, 1 daughter. Education: Graduate, University of Innsbruck, Austria, 1983. Appointments: Associate Professor of Radiology, University of Vienna, Austria. Address: Department of Diagnostic Radiology, University of Vienna, A-1090, Vienna, Austria.

KAJI Akira, b. 13 January 1930, Tokyo, Japan (US citizen). Professor. m. Hideko Kaji, 2 sons, 2 daughters. Education: BS, University of Tokyo, 1953; PhD, Johns Hopkins University, 1958. Appointments: Research Fellow, Johns Hopkins Hospital, 1958-59; Guest Investigator, Rockefeller Institute, 1959; Research Associate, Department of Microbiology, Nashville, 1959-62; Visiting Scientist, Oak Ridge National Laboratory, Tennessee, 1962-63; Associate, 1963-64, Assistant Professor, 1964-67, Associate Professor, 1967-72, Department of Microbiology, University of Pennsylvania; Professor, Hygienic Chemistry, University of Tokyo, 1972-73; Professor, Department of Microbiology, University of Pennsylvania, 1972-; John Simon Guggenheim Scholar, Imperial Cancer Research Fund Laboratories, London, 1972-73; Visiting Professor, Fogarty International Senior Fellow, Kyoto University, Japan, 1985. Publications: 110 articles. Honours include: Special Fellowship, Japanese Government; Dazian Predoctoral Fellowship; Japan Society Fellowship. Memberships: Sigma Xi; American Society for Microbiology; British Society of Biological Chemists; American Society of Biological Chemists; Japanese Society of Biological Chemists; American Society of Chemistry; American Society of Cell Biology. Address: Department of Microbiology, University of Pennsylvania School of Medicine, 225 Johnson Pavilion, 3610 Hamilton Walk, Philadelphia, PA 19104-6076, USA. E-mail: kaji@mail.med.upenn.edu

KAKANI Shyam Lal, b. 28 October 1940, Chittorgarh, Raj, India. Researcher; Administrator. m. Sushila Devi Totla, 1 son, 3 daughters. Education: MSc, Physics, PhD, MSc, Physics, Government College, Ajmer, Affiliated to University of Rajasthan, Jaipur, India; PhD, University of Udaipur, India, 1982. Appointments: Principal Government P G College Nathwara, Government P G College, Shahpura and SMM Girls P G College, Bhilwara; Vice Principal, MLV Government Auto College, Bhilwara. Publications: 12 research monographs; Several research papers, reviews in professional journals; 93 books; 7 related to superconductivity; 39 Papers. Honours: Government of Rajasthan Merit Award, Uttar Pradesh Hindi Grandth Academy and Vigyam Parishad, Allahabad Award. Listed in: Several Biographical Publications. Memberships: Vigan Parishad, Allahabad; Indian Physics Teachers Association; High-Tc Update, Iowa State, USA;

Visiting Professor, Indian Institute of Science, Bangalore. Address: Institute of Physics, 4G45 Shastrinagar Extension, Bhilwara 311001, India.

KAKATI Dinesh Chandra, b. 1 February 1941, Soalkuchi, Assam, India. Doctor of Medicine. m. Bhabhni, 1 son, 1 daughter. Education: MBBS, Guwahati University, India, 1967; Diploma in Tropical Medicine, University of Liverpool, England, 1970; Diploma in Thoracic Medicine, Diploma in Cardiac Medicine, University of London, 1984; Diploma in Geriatric Medicine, Royal College of Physicians of London, 1985; Vocational Training Certificate, Royal College of General Practitioners, 1987; Intra-Uterine Device, Family Planning Certificate, Joint Committee on Contraception, 1987. Appointments: House Officer, Senior House Officer, Gauhati Medical College Hospital, Assam, India, 1967-68; General Medicine, Ingham Infirmary, South Shields, England, 1969; Senior House Officer, Registrar, Sunderland General Hospital, Sunderland, 1969-72; Registrar, Addenbrookes Hospital and Chesterton Hospital, Cambridge, 1972-74; Internal Medicine, University of Edinburgh, Scotland, 1973; Registrar, London Hospital and Bethnal Green Hospital, London, 1974-77; Specialist and Consultant, Oldchurch Hospital, Romford, 1977-83; Postgraduate Student, National Heart Hospital, Brompton Hospital, London Chest Hospital, London, 1983-84; Clinical Assistant, Romford Group of Hospitals based at St George's Hospital, Hornchurch, 1984-2002; General Practice Principal, Berwick Surgery, Rainham, 1997-. Publications: Numerous articles in professional journals. Honours: Class examination medals; 4th place, Guwahati University Order of Merit; Distinction, MBBS, Guwahati University. Memberships: Cultural Association of Assam in the UK; Chairman, Sankar Jayanty Celebration Committee, UK; Assamese Bihu Committee, UK; British Medical Association; Royal College of General Practitioners of London; Royal Society of Health. Address: Assam Manor, 99 Ardleigh Green Road, Hornchurch, Essex RM11 2LE, England. E-mail: kakati.dinesh@ntlworld.com

KALAGA Wojciech Henryk, b. 27 July 1949, Cracow. Academic. m. Lucyna Malik-Kalaga, 2 sons. Education: MA, 1972, PhD, 1979, Jagellonian University, Cracow; Habilitation, Poznan, 1986. Appointments: Visiting Professor, Yale University, 1983-84; Chair, Department of English and Comparative Literature, Murdoch University, 1992-94; Director of Institute of British and American Culture and Literature, 1995-; Professor, University of Silesia, 1995-; Chair, Department of Literary and Cultural Theory, University of Silesia, 1997-; Editor-in-Chief of journal: Er(r)go: Teoria-Literatura-Kultura, 1999-. Publications: Books: Mental Landscape, 1981; The Literary Sign, 1986; Nebulae of Discourse, 1997; 28 books as editor and about 100 articles. Honours: Fulbright, 1983-84; Alexander von Humboldt Grant, 1988-89; Minister of Science Award: 1981, 1987, 1998; Medal of National Education, 1999; Gold Medal of Merit, 2000. Memberships include: International Association for Semiotic Studies; International Comparative Literature Association; Member, Committee for Literary Studies, Polish Academy of Sciences; and others. Address: Ul Bedzinska 8/18, 41-205 Sosnowiec, Poland. E-mail: kalaga@us.edu.pl

KALATA Mary Ann C, b. 7 September 1962, Passaic, New Jersey, USA. Architect. Education: Bachelor of Science, Architectural Technology, New York Institute of Technology, USA. Appointments: Contemporary Landscape Architecture, Fairlawn, New Jersey; Russo & Sonder Architects, New York City; Perkins & Will Architects, New York City; Antoniades Architect & Associates, New York City, Michael J Romanik Architect, Paterson, New Jersey; Mary Ann C Kalata Architecture & Design, Clifton, New Jersey. Honours: Gold Medal in Architectural

Technology; Valedictorian, New York Institute of Technology, 1984; Graduated Summa Cum Laude. Publications: Architectural models built and used in magazine advertising. Memberships: World War II Memorial Society; National Republican Congressional Committee, Washington DC; New York Institute of Technology, 1984; ASC/AIA; United States Navy League; Slovak Catholic Sokol; National Trust for Historic Preservation. Address: 8 Baker Court, Clifton, NJ 07011, USA.

KALB Jonathan, b. 30 October 1959, Englewood, New Jersey, USA. Theatre Critic; Professor of Theatre. m. Julie Heffernan, 18 June 1988, 2 sons. Education: BA, English, Wesleyan University; MFA, Dramaturgy, Dramatic Criticism, 1985, DFA, Dramaturgy, Dramatic Criticism, 1987, Yale School of Drama. Appointments: Theatre Critic, The Village Voice, 1987-97; Chief Theatre Critic, New York Press, 1997-2001; Assistant Professor of Performance Studies, 1990-92, Assistant Professor of Theatre, 1992-95, Associate Professor of Theatre, 1996-2002, Professor of Theatre, Hunter College, City University of New York, 2003-. Publications: Beckett in Performance, 1989; Free Admissions: Collected Theater Writings, 1993; The Theater of Heiner Müller, 1998; Play by Play: Theatre Essays and Reviews, 1993-2002, 2003. Contributions to: Newspapers and journals. Honours: Fulbright Hays Grant, 1988-89; T C G Jerome Fellowship, 1989-90; George Jean Nathan Award for Dramatic Criticism, 1990-91. Memberships: Modern Language Association; PEN American Centre. Address: c/o Department of Theatre, Hunter College of the City University of New York, 695 Park Avenue, New York, NY 10021, USA.

KALINDEKAFE Meya Patricia, b. 2 May 1964, Malawi. Ecologist. m. Leonard, 2 sons, 2 daughters. Education: BSc, Biology and Chemistry, Chancellor College, University of Malawi, 1987; MSc, Ecology, University College of North Wales, Bangor, UK, 1989; Postgraduate courses: International Environmental Management, Tufts University, USA, 1994; Certificate in Watershed and Wetland Management, Mangochi, Malawi, 1996; Certificate, Hazardous Waste Management, Basel Institute of Technology, Switzerland, 1996; Certificate, Geographic Information Systems, Environmental Affairs Department in conjunction with Clarke University, USA, 1997. Appointments: Staff Associate in Biology, 1987-90, Lecturer in Ecology, 1990-2000, Senior Lecturer, 2000-, University of Malawi; Trainer of Environmental Impact Assessment, 1997-; Trustee and Country Director, African Conservation Trust, 2000-; Numerous environmental consultancies. Publications: Book chapters and reports as co-author: Climate Change Impact on Forests of Malawi: Vulnerability and Adaptation Assessment, 1999; A Landscape Ecological Approach to Sustainability: Application of the Communicative Catchment Approach to Lake Chilwa, Malawi, 1999; Land Use Histories and Fuelwood Consumption in a Highly Populated and Degraded Area in Nkhata Bay District, Malawi, 2000; Many other reports, articles and papers presented at conferences. Honours: UNEP Fellow, 1994; LEAD Fellow, Leadership for Environment and Development, Rockefeller Foundation, 1998. Memberships: Women in Science and Technology in Africa Network; Third World Organisation for Women in Science; Board Member, Wildlife Research and Management Board; Country Director, African Conservation Trust; African Conservation Foundation; Board Member, Malawi Industrial Research and Technology Development Centre. Address: Biology Department, University of Malawi, PO Box 280, Zomba, Malawi. E-mail: lkalindekafe@chanco.unima.mw

KALMBACH Gudrun, b. 27 May 1937, Grosserlach, Germany. Professor. Education: Dr rer. nat. University of Göttingen, Germany. Appointments: Assistant, University of Göttingen, Germany, 1963-66; Lecturer, University of Illinois, Urbana, USA,

Dictionary of International Biography

1967-69; Assistant Professor, University of Massachusetts, Amherst, USA, 1970-71; Assistant Professor, Pennsylvania State University, University Park, USA, 1969-75; Professor, University of Ulm, Germany, 1975-2002; Director, MINT, 2003-. Publications: 12 books; Articles in professional journals on algebra, topology, quantum structures, education; Chief Editor, Journal MINT. Honours: 4 medals; 2 titles; 2 books in honour of 60th Birthday. Memberships: AMS; AWM; DGHK; ECHA; Emmy-Noether-Verein (Chair); FDP; LDA; OIA. Address: PF 1533, D-86818 Bad Woerishofen, Germany. E-mail: gudrun.kalmbach@extern.uni-ulm.de

KALRA G L, b. 1 July 1941, Londkhor, Pakistan. Teacher; Researcher. m. Raj Kalra, 2 daughters. Education: MSc, 1962, PhD, 1967, University of Delhi. Appointments: Senior Research Fellow, University of Delhi, 1966-69; Fellow, Flinders University of South Australia, 1969-70; Fellow, University of Delhi, 1969-70; Lecturer, 1974-84; Reader, 1984-86; Associate Professor, Al Fateh University, Tripoli, 1986-87; Reader, University of Delhi, 1984-94; Professor in Physics, University of Delhi, 1994-. Publications: 48 research papers mostly in international scientific journals. Honours: Dr Vikram Sarabhai Award, 1986; Australia VC's Committee Visiting Fellowship, 1990; Offered New York Academy of Sciences Membership. Memberships: Founder Member, Astronomical Society of India; Plasma Science Society of India; Listed in Who's Who and biographical publications. Address: Department of Physics and Astrophysics, University of Delhi, Delhi 110 007, India.

KALYANE Venkat Lakshmanrao, b. 1 June 1955, Talwada (Maratha), Bhalki, India. Publication Officer. m. Sangeeta, 2 daughters. Education: BSc; B Lib Sc; MSc; DIIT, BEd, Postgraduate Diploma in Journalism and Mass Communication; MEd, Postgraduate Diploma in Higher Education, MLIS. Appointments: Senior Research Fellow, 1977-81; Research Associate, 1981-83; Technical Assistant T-II-3, 1983-88; T-4, 1989-90; Junior Scientific Officer T-6, 1990-93; Scientific Officer SD, 1993-95; Scientific Officer D, 1996-2000; Scientific Officer E, 2000-. Publications: 80 research articles; Scientometric studies on individual scientists as scholarly communication stars: Nobel laureates (C V Raman, P G de Gennes, S Chandrasekhar, Barbara McClintock, D C Hodgkin, A H Zewail, Harold W Kroto, Wolfgang Ketterle, Leland H Hartwell), Citation studies (R Chidambaram, Vikram Sarabhai), Advisory Editorial Board Member, Indian Journal of Information, Library and Society; Chief Editor, BOSLA Infoline, Selected E-LIS Editor for India. Memberships: United Writers' Association; Bombay Science Librarians' Association, Indian Science Writers' Association; Indian Library Association; Society for Information Science. Address: LISD, BARC, Trombay, Mumbai-400 085, India. E-mail: vkalyane@yahoo.com

KAMANDA Kama Sywor, b. 11 November 1952, Luebo, Congo-Kinshasa. Writer; Poet; Novelist; Playwright; Essayist; Lecturer; Storyteller. Education: State Diploma in Literary Humanities, 1968; Degree in Journalism, Journalism School, Kinshasa, Congo, 1969; Degree in Political Sciences, University of Kinshasa, 1973; HD, University of Liège, 1981. Appointments: Lecturer, various universities, schools and cultural centres; Literary Critic, various newspapers. Publications: Les Contes du griot, Volume 3 (Les Contes des veillées africaines), 1967, 1985, 1998; Les Résignations, 1986, 1997; Éclipse d'étoiles, 1987, 1997; Les Contes du griot, Volume 1, 1988, 1997; La Somme du néant, 1989, 1999; Les Contes du griot, Volume 2 (La Nuit des griots), 1991, 1996; L'Exil des songes, 1992; Les Myriades des temps vécus, 1992, 1999; Les Vents de l'épreuve, 1993, 1997; Quand dans l'âme les mers s'agitent, 1994, 1998; Lointaines sont les rives du destin,

1994, 2000; L'Étreinte des mots, 1995; Chants de brumes, 1997, 2002; Œuvre poétique, 1999; Les Contes du crépuscule, 2000; Le Sang des solitudes, 2002; Contes, 2003, 2004. Honours: Paul Verlaine Award, French Academy, 1987; Louise Labé Award Jury, 1990; Literature Award, Black African Association of French-Speaking Writers, 1991; Special Poetry Award, Academy Institute in Paris, 1992; Silver Jasmin for Poetical Originality, 1992; Special Prize, French-Speaking Countries General Council Agency, 1992; Théophile Gautier Award, French Academy, 1993; Subject of: Kama Kamanda au Pays du Conte (M C De Connick), 1993; Kama Kamanda, Poète de l'Exil (Pierrette Sartin), 1994; Kama Sywor Kamanda, chantre de la mémoire égyptienne (Isabella Cata and Frank Nyalendo), 2003. Memberships: Society of French Poets; French Society of Men of Letters; Association of African Writers; PEN Club; Association of French-Speaking Writers; International Council of French-Speaking Studies; SABAM. Address: 18 Am Moul, L-7418 Buschdorf, Luxembourg. E-mail: kamanda@pt.lu

KAMATA Kazuo, b. 27 March 1947, Shimane, Japan. Professor. m. Nobuko, 1 son, 1 daughter. Education: BEng, 1969, MEng, 1971, Yamanashi University; DrEng, PhD, Tokyo Institute of Technology, 1977. Appointments: Research Associate, Tokyo Institute of Technology, 1971-78; Associate Professor, 1978-90; Professor, 1990-, Utsunomiya University. Honours: Young Researcher Award, IEICE, 1979. Address: 2980 Ishii-machi, Utsunomiya, 321-0912, Japan.

KAMBOURELI Smaro, b. 13 October 1955, Thessaloniki, Greece. Professor; Writer. m. Robert Kroetsch, separated 1998. Education: BA (English) Aristotelian University, Thessaloniki, 1977; Fulbright Scholar, SUNY, Binghampton, New York, USA, 1977-78; MA, English, University of Manitoba, 1981; PhD, English, University of Manitoba, 1987; School of Theory and Criticism, Dartmouth College, USA, 1986. Appointments: Professor, Department of English, University of Victoria, 1987-; Guest Professor, SNDT Women's University, Bombay, India and University of Kiel, Germany; Editor, writer as critic series NeWest Press, Edmonton, Alberta, Canada. Publications: Books: A Mazing Space: Writing Canadian Women Writing (co-editor), 1986; In the Second Person (poetry), 1985; On the Edge of Genre: The Contemporary Candian Long Poem, 1991; Making a Difference: Candian Multicultural Literature (anthology-editor), 1996; Scandalous Bodies: Diasporic Literature in English Canada, 1999; Many articles, book chapters. Honours: Honorary Life Member, Manitoba Writers' Guild; Sydney Warhaft Memorial Award for Most Distinguished MA Thesis in English; Gabrielle Roy Prize for Canadian Criticism. Memberships: ACCUTE; International Council of Canadian Studies; The Writers' Union of Canada. Address: Department of English, University of Victoria, Victoria, BC V8W 3W1, Canada.

KAMEL Omar Ali, b. 9 April 1935, Cairo, Egypt. Professor. m. Eglal A Niazy, 3 sons. Education: BSc Geology and Chemistry (Hons), 1956; MSc, Mineralogy and Economic Geology, Ain Shams University, 1960; PhD, Mineralogy and Economic Geology, Moscow State University, 1963. Appointments: Head of Mineralogical Lab, Geological Survey of Egypt, 1963-75; Assistant Professor of Mineralogy and Economic Geology, Minia University, 1975-82; Professor of Mineralogy and Economic Geology, Minia University, 1975-95; Emeritus Professor of Mineralogy and Economic Geology, Minia University, 1995-. Publications: Numerous articles. Honours: Scientific mission to the Faculty of Geology, Moscow State University. Memberships: Geological Society of Egypt; Mineralogical Society of Egypt; Geological Society of Africa; Science Syndicate of Egypt. Address: Geology Dept, Faculty of Science, Minia University, Minia, Egypt. E-mail: osamaomar@link.net

Dictionary of International Biography

KAMEYAMA Michitaka, b. 12 May 1950, Utsunomiya, Japan. Professor. m. Kimiko Owashi, 29 April 1983, 1 son, 2 daughters. Education: Bachelor, Electronic Engineering, 1973, Master Electronic Engineering, 1975, Doctor, Electronic Engineering, 1978, Tohoku University. Appointments: Research Associate, 1978-81, Associate Professor, 1981-91, Professor, 1991-, Tohoku University. Publications include: A Multiplier Chip with Multiple-valued Bidirectional Current-Mode Logic Circuits, 1988. Honour: Fellow, IEEE, 1997. Address: 6-10-8, Minami-Yoshinari, Aoba-ku, Sendai, Japan. E-mail: michi@kameyama.ecei.tohoku.ac.jp

KAMIŃSKI Marcin Marek, b. 17 February 1969, Toruń, Poland. Academic Teacher. m. Grazyna Folchmann, 2 daughters. Education: MSc, Civil Engineering, 1994; PhD, Mechanics of Materials, 1997, Technical University of Lodz, Poland; Postdoctoral studies, Rice University, Houston, TX, 1999-2000. Appointments: Trainee Assistant, 1993-94, Assistant Professor, 1997-, Division of Mechanics of Materials, Technical University of Lodz; Assistant Professor, International School of Business and Economy, Lodz, Poland, 1998. Publications: More than 100 papers and articles in conference proceedings, books and refereed international journals, subjects include composite materials, engineering, numerical methods in engineering, stochastic computational mechanics, applied mechanics. Honours: Honorary Fellowship, Foundation for Polish Science, 1996, 1999-2000; Polish Academy of Science Award, 1998; Bronze Cross of Merit, 1998; John Argyris Award in Computational Mechanics, 2001. Memberships: International Association for Shell and Spatial Structures; Polish Association of Computational Mechanics; Polish Association for Composite Materials; Polish Association of Civil Engineers and Technicians; Gesselschaft fur Angewandte Mathematik und Mechanik; New York Academy of Sciences. Address: Chair of Mechanics of Materials, Technical University of Lodz, Al Politechniki 6, 93-590 Lodz, Poland. E-mail: marcinka@p.lodz.pl Website: http://kmm.p.lodz.pl/pracownicy/ Marcin_Kaminski/index.html

KAMINSKI Wlodzimierz, b. 16 April 1924, Skierniewice, Poland. Scientist; Economist. m. Krystyna Tyszkowska, 1 son. Education: MS, 1947, LLD, 1948, University of Cracow; DAgricEcon, 1961, Professor, Economic Sciences, 1973-92, doctor honoris causa, 2000, Agricultural University, Warsaw. Appointments: Researcher, Economist, 1959-92, Extraordinary Professor, 1973-80, Ordinary Professor, 1980-92, Faculty of Food Technology, Agricultural University, Warsaw; Visiting Professor, various universities and institutions; Head, Division for Spatial Research, 1983-92, Director, 1990, Institute of Agricultural and Food Economics. Publications: 24 books, over 300 publications in 8 languages. Honours: Knight, Officer and Commander Cross of Polonia Restituta, 1964, 1979, 1987; Cross of National Army, Polish Government, 1994; Croix d'Officier du Merite Agricole, French Government, 1995. Memberships: Polish Scientific Society of Food Industry; Polish Academy of Sciences; 2 committees, Association of Agricultural Economists; Hungarian Scientific Society of Food Industry; French Academy of Agriculture; International Institute of Refrigeration, Paris; New York Academy of Sciences. Address: Smolna 15, Room 11, 00375 Warsaw, Poland.

KAMIRYO Hideyuki, b. 4 December 1930, Kobe, Japan. Emeritus Professor. m. Toshiko, 2 daughters. Education: Master of Science, Management, Massachusetts Institute of Technology, USA, 1974; Master of Applied Sciences, Lincoln Agricultural College, University of Canterbury, New Zealand, 1986; International Honorary Doctor of Earth Environment Science, The Earth Environment University Round Table and the Earth Environment Academy of America, New York, USA, 1994; Dr of

Business Administration, Hiroshima Shudo University, Hiroshima, Japan, 1995; PhD, Economics, The University of Auckland, New Zealand, 2004. Appointments: Several directorships of associations and organisations before retirement in 2002; Emeritus Professor, Hiroshima Shudo University, 2003-; Director, Shibuya Kogyo Co Ltd, Kanazawa, 1981-. Publications: 28 books and many articles include: Economic Accounting: A Macro and Micro Common Approach Using National and Corporate Accounts, 1998; Growth Accounting in Discrete Time: A New Approach Using Recursive Programming, 2000; Numerical Relationships between Technological Progress and Structural Reform: To Save the Unprecedented Difficulties in the Japanese Economy at the National Institute for Research Advancement (NIRA), Tokyo; Furthering the Role of Corporate Finance in Economic Growth, Nov 2003 (PhD thesis, May 2004, at the University of Auckland, New Zealand); Basics of An Endogenous Growth Model: the Optimum CRC Situation and Conditional Convergence, 2004; Risk of Growth in My Endogenous Growth Model: Combining the Penrose Curve with the Petersburg Paradox, 2004; What Numerically Determines the Difference between Catching Up and Endless Poverty in African Countries? 2004; Endogenous Growth in China National Accounts: for Lasting Stable Growth by Region, 2004. Memberships include: American Economic Association; American Accounting Association; International Association for Research in Income and Wealth. Address: 5-28-5 Satsukigaoka, Saeki-ku, Hiroshima, Japan 7315101. E-mail: kamiryo@ms3.megaegg.ne.jp

KAMOI Kyuzi, b. 28 August 1945, Tokyo. Medical Diplomat. Education: MD, Medical School, Niigata University, 1970; PhD, 1982. Appointments: Post Doctoral Fellow, Endocrinology and Metabolism, 1972-77, Niigata University, School of Medicine; Post Doctor Fellow, Indiana University, USA, 1977-79; Nagaoka Red Cross Hospital, 1980-; Senior Consultant, Diabetes Mellitus, 1993-; Senior Consultant, Endocrine and Metabolism Diseases, 2004-. Publications: 57 original papers written in English; 94 original papers written in Japanese. Memberships: Japanese Society of Internal Medicine; The Japan Endocrine Society; The Endocrine Society; The American Society of Hypertension; The New York Academy of Sciences; The Japan Diabetes Society; The American Diabetes Society; The International Diabetes Federation; The Japan Society of Metabolism and Clinical Nutrition. Address: 3-4-36 Hanazono Nagaoka, Niigata 940-0840, Japan.

KAMU Okko, b. 7 March 1946, Helsinki, Finland. Conductor. Education: Violin studies with Väinö Arjava from 1949 and with Professor Onni Suhonen at the Sibelius Academy, Helsinki, 1952-67. Career: Leader of the Suhonen Quartet, 1964; Leader of the Finnish National Opera Orchestra, 1966-69; Conducted Britten's The Turn of the Screw in Helsinki, 1968; Guest Conductor, Swedish Royal Opera, 1969; Chief Conductor, Finnish Radio Symphony Orchestra, 1971-77; Music Director, Oslo Philharmonic, 1975-79; Music Director, Helsinki Philharmonic,1981-88; Principal Conductor, Dutch Radio Symphony, 1983-86; Principal Guest Conductor, City of Birmingham Symphony Orchestra, 1985-88; Principal Conductor, Sjaelland Symphony Orchestra (Copenhagen Philharmonic), 1988-89; Guest engagements with the Berlin Philharmonic, Suisse Romande Orchestra, Vienna Symphony Orchestra and orchestras in the USA, Far East, Australia, South America and Europe; Conducted the premieres of Sallinen's operas The Red Line and The King Goes Forth to France; Metropolitan Opera, 1983, US premiere of The Red Line; Covent Garden, 1987, in the British premiere of The King Goes Forth to France; Principal Conductor of the Helsingborg Symphony Orchestra, 1991-2000; Music Director of the Finnish National Opera, 1996-2000; Principal Guest

Dictionary of International Biography

Conductor, Singapore Symphony Orchestra, 1995-2001 and principal Guest Conductor of Lausanne Chamber Orchestra, 1999-2002. Recordings: About 70 recordings for various labels; Sallinen's Shadows, Cello Concerto and 5th Symphony. Honours: Winner, 1st Herbert von Karajan Conductors' Competition, Berlin, 1969; Member of the Royal Swedish Academy of Music. Address: Villa Arcadia, C/Mozart 7, Rancho Domingo, 29639 Benalmadena Pueblo, Spain.

KANAYAMA Masahide, b. 9 August 1962, Tokyo, Japan. Gynaecologic Surgeon. Education: BS, magna cum laude, Chemistry, Creighton University of Arts and Sciences, Omaha, USA, 1985; MD, Medical College of Wisconsin, USA, 1991; Internship and Residency, Mayo Clinic, Graduate School of Medicine, completed 1995. Appointments: Assistant Professor of Obstetrics and Gynaecology, Mount Sinai School of Medicine, New York, USA; Director, New York Endometriosis Center; Visiting Scientist, Johns Hopkins University School of Medicine. Publications: Over 30 publications include: Preventive and Therapeutic Vaccines for human papiloma-virus associated cervical cancer. Honours: Teacher of the Year, Mayo Clinic, 1993, 1993. Memberships: American College of Obstetrics and Gynaecology; American Medical Association; Japanese Medical Society. Address: 102 East 78th Street, New York, NY 10021, USA. Website: www.gynecosurgery.com

KANAZAWA Takafumi, b. 5 December 1926, Tokyo, Japan. Chemist; Educator. m. Taiko Suzuki, 1 son. Education: Bachelor of Engineering, 1948, Doctor of Engineering, 1961, University of Tokyo. Appointments: Research Associate, 1952, Lecturer, 1957, Associate Professor, 1962 Professor, 1966-90, Professor Emeritus, 1990, Tokyo Metropolitan University; Professor, Chiba Institute of Technology, 1992-. Publications: Books: Industrial Mineral Chemistry; Inorganic Phosphorous Chemistry; Inorganic Phosphate Materials; Inorganic Industrial Chemistry; Phosphorous; My Essay Technology. Honours: Science Award, The Ceramic Society of Japan; Treatise Award, The Society of Gypsum and Lime; Science Award, Japanese Association of Inorganic Phosphorous Chemistry. Memberships: The Chemical Society of Japan; The Ceramic Society of Japan; The Society of Inorganic Materials, Japan; Japanese Association of Inorganic Phosphorous Chemistry. Address: Sakura 1-62-12, Setagaya-ku, Tokyo 156-0053, Japan.

KANEDA Yasuhiro, b. 5 April 1963, Japan. Psychiatrist. m. Ikumi Yoshida, 2 sons. Education: MD, 1992, University of Tokushima Shool of Medicine, Tokushima, Japan; Licence of Physician, 1992, PhD, 1997, University of Tokushima School of Medicine; Qualified Psychiatrist, 1998; European Certificate in Anxiety and Mood Disorders, 2001. Appointments: Assistant Professor, 2000-, Medical Director, 2000-2002, Department of Neuropsychiatry, University Hospital of Tokushima; Councillor, Japanese Society of Psychosomatic Medicine, 2002-; Visiting Research Fellow, Department of Psychiatry, Vanderbilt University School of Medicine, Nashville, USA, 2002-. Publications include: Theory and practice of psychopharmacology-Schizophrenia. In Handbook of Clinical Psychopharmacology (Higuchi et al, eds), 2003; Neurotic, stress-related and somatoform disorders, In Psychiatric Medicine: Textbook of comedical staff (Nagamine I, ed), in press. Honours: Award of Tokushima Medical Association, 2000; European Certificate Award, World Federation of Societies of Biological Psychiatry, 2000; Lilly Fellowship Award, Japanese Society of Clinical Neuropsychopharmacology, 2001. Memberships: World Psychiatric Association; Collegium International Neuro-Psychopharmacologicum; International Brain Research Organisation; World Federation of Societies of Biological Psychiatry; International Society of Psychoneuroendocrinology.

Address: Department of Neuropsychiatry, The University of Tokushima School of Medicine, 3-18-15 Kuramoto, Tokushima 770-8503, Japan. E-mail: btlmnjpkan@yahoo.co.jp

KANEKO Tetsuo, b. 3 November 1953, Matsudo-Shi, Chiba-Ken, Japan. PC Operator; Physicist. Education: BS, Physics, 1977, BS, Chemistry, 1980, MS, 1984, Chuo University; Diploma, First Class Radiation Protection Supervisor, STA, 1979; Diploma, Environmental Certificate Measurer, 1982. Appointments: Assistant for Experiments, Japan Atomic Energy Research Institute, 1978-80; Radiation Protection Supervisor, Koto Microbe Laboratory Co Ltd, 1980-82; Staff Member for technical surveys, Japan NUS Co Ltd, 1985-87; Assistant for Environmental Measure, Tokyo Food Sanitation Association, 1987-93; Assistant for experiments, Seikei University, 1990-93; Part-time Lecturer, Medical Biology College, 1993-94; Technical Assistant, IAI Corporation, 1995-97; PC Operator, DIS System Trading Co Ltd, 1997-2000; Advisor, Kurakenchikuzoukeisha Co Ltd, 2000-. Publications: 8 published articles. Memberships: American Physical Society; Physical Society of Japan; Chemical Society of Japan; American Association for the Advancement of Science; New York Academy of Sciences. Address: Kogane Kazusacho 16-1, Matsudo-shi, Chiba-ken, 270-0015, Japan. E-mail: kaneko@mailaps.org

KANELLOPOULOS John, b. 12 December 1948, Athens, Greece. m. Athanasia Xenou, 31 August 1985, 2 sons. Education: DEng, National Technical University, Athens, 1979; DIC, PhD, University of London, 1979. Appointments: Lecturer, 1979-84, Assistant Professor, 1984-85, Associate Professor, 1985-90, Professor, 1990-, National Technical University of Athens. Publications: 3 books; 200 papers in international scientific journals and international conference proceedings. Honours: listed in more than 20 international biographical volumes; Numerous honours and awards from the American Biographical Institute and International Biographical Centre. Memberships: Senior Member, IEEE; MIT- based Electromagnetics Academy; JOSA; IEICE. Address: National Technical University of Athens, Department of Electrical Engineering, 9 Iroon Polytechniou Str, Zografou-15773, Athens, Greece.

KANTARIS Sylvia, b. 9 January 1936, Grindleford, Derbyshire, England. Poet; Writer; Teacher. m. Emmanuel Kantaris, 11 January 1958, 1 son, 1 daughter. Education: Diplôme d'Études Civilisation Française, Sorbonne, University of Paris, 1955; BA, Honours, 1957, Cert.Ed, 1958, Bristol University; MA, 1967, PhD, 1972, University of Queensland, Australia. Appointments: Tutor, University of Queensland, Australia, 1963-66, Open University, England, 1974-84; Extra-Mural Lecturer, Exeter University, 1974-. Publications: Time and Motion, 1975; Stocking Up, 1981; The Tenth Muse, 1983; News From the Front (with D M Thomas), 1983; The Sea at the Door, 1985; The Air Mines of Mistila (with Philip Gross), 1988; Dirty Washing: New and Selected Poems, 1989; Lad's Love, 1993. Contributions to: Many anthologies, newspapers, and magazines. Honours: National Poetry Competition Award, 1982; Honorary Doctor of Letters, Exeter University, 1989; Major Arts Council Literature Award, 1991; Society of Authors Award, 1992. Memberships: Poetry Society of Great Britain; South West Arts, literature panel, 1983-87, literary consultant, 1990-. Address: 14 Osborne Parc, Helston, Cornwall TR13 8PB, England.

KANYAMA-PHIRI George Yobe, b. 22 November 1948, Kasungu, Malawi. Professor. m. Flossie, 4 daughters. Education: BSc, Agronomy, summa cum laude, Florida A&M University, USA, 1978; MSc, Agronomy, University of California, Davis, 1981; PhD, Agronomy, Texas A&M University, College Station, Texas, 1988. Appointments: Teaching Assistant, Crop Science

Department, 1975-76, Lecturer, Pasture Agronomy and Range Management, 1981-84, 1988-92, Senior Lecturer, 1992-98, Associate Professor, 1998-2001, Professor of Crop Science, 2001-, Principal, 2000-, Bunda College of Agriculture, Lilongwe, Malawi; Dean, Faculty of Agriculture, University of Malawi, 1995-2000. Publications: 14 articles in refereed journals include most recently as co-author: Preliminary results of a stocking rate trial in Lesotho, 2002; Merino sheep responses to different stocking rates and seasonal variation under rangelands conditions in Lesotho, 2002; Farmer and Researcher Partnerships in Malawi: Developing soil fertility technologies for the near-term and far-term, 2002; Biomass production, soil nutrient status and maize yield under short term Sesbania seban Improved Fallow in Central Malawi, accepted, 2003; The Economics of Improved Fallow Agroforestry System for Smallholder Farmers in Central Malawi, accepted 2003; 18 articles published in conference and workshop proceedings; 10 articles in research bulletins; 2 book chapters; 3 monographs. Honours: Who is Who Among Students in American Universities and Colleges, 44th edition; Freshman Academic Scholarship Award; Alpha Kappa Mu Academic Honor Society; 21st Century Order of Excellence, IBA, 2003; Great Minds of the 21st Century, American Biographical Institute 2003/2004 edition. Memberships: Chairman, 1982-84, Secretary, 1989-91, Bunda College Senior Staff Association; Honorary Treasurer, Association for the Advancement of Science and Technology in Malawi, 1989-93; National Co-ordinator of the Initiative for Development and Equity in African Agriculture, Malawi, 1997-; National Co-Ordinator Farmer Innovation and Creativity Field Schools, 2002-; Member, Pesticide Control Board, 2000-; Board Member, Nkhoma Institute for Continuing Theological Training, 2002; Member, Board of Trustees of the Training Support Programme, 2003; Member, Editorial Advisory Board, Malawi Journal of Agricultural Sciences; Chairman, Malawi Human Rights Commission, 2002-. Address: Bunda College of Agriculture, PO Box 219, Lilongwe, Malawi. E-mail: gykphiri@bunda.sdnp.org.mw

KANZLER George, b. 30 March 1939, Elizabeth, New Jersey, USA. Jazz Critic; Writer. m. Margaret A Dudas, 1 daughter. Education: BA, Seton Hall University, 1960; Postgraduate, Middlebury College Breadloaf School of English, 1960; MA, New York University, 1969; Postgraduate, University of Wisconsin, 1972. Appointments: Reporter, Editor, Linden Leader, New Jersey, 1961-63; US Army, Congo, 1963-65; US Peace Corps, Nigeria, 1966-68; Assistant Professor, Ibadan Polytechnic, Nigeria, 1966-68; Jazz Disc Jockey, Nigeria Radio, 1966-68; Writer, Pop and Jazz Critic, The Star Ledger, Newark, New Jersey, 1968-2002; Contributing Editor, Hot House Jazz Magazine, 2002-. Publication: One Way to Heaven (Armchair Theatre, Nigeria Television), 1967. Honours: Newspaper Fund Fellow, 1972; Music Critics Association, Smithsonian Institute Fellow, 1974; Elector, American Jazz Hall of Fame, 1989-. Memberships: Secretary Protem, Mbari Artists' and Writers' Club, 1966-68; Voting Member (Grammys), National Association of Recording Arts and Sciences; Jazz Journalists Association; Friends of Nigeria; Board of Directors, Newark Jazz Festival, 1991-93. Address: 406 Marseille Drive, Simpsonville, SC 29680, USA. E-mail: gkjazz@usa.net

KAPSALIS John, b. 27 January 1927, Mytelene, Greece. Biochemist, Poet. m. Athena, 2 September 1956, 2 daughters. Education: BS, 1954; MS, 1955; PhD, 1959; Postdoctoral Studies, Ohio University, 1959. Appointments: Chemist, Armed Forces Food and Container Institute, Chicago, 1960-63; Head, Biochemistry Branch, US Army Natick Laboratories, 1963-87. Publications: The Odds, 1972; Twentieth and Other Centuries, 1974; The Saga of Chrysodontis Pappas, 1994; Tales of Pergamos, 1999; The Poems, 2003. Contributions to: Dark Horse; Bitterroot; Northeast Journal; Nebraska Review; Joycean Lively Arts Guild

Review Indigo. Honour: Massachusetts Artists Foundation Poetry Award, 1985. Memberships: American Poets and Fiction Writers; Academy of American Poets. Address: 5776 Deauville Lake Circle No 308, Naples, FL 34112, USA.

KAPUTKINA Ljudmila Mikhailovna, b. 15 January 1942, Moscow, Russia. Metal Physicist; Scientist; Professor. m. Efim Kaputkin, 1 son, 1 daughter. Education: Engineer, Metallurgist, Moscow Institute for Steel and Alloys, 1965; Candidate of Science, 1969; DSc, 1985; Professor, 1989. Appointments: Postgraduate, Division of Metal Science of Steel, 1965-69, Researcher, 1969-72, Senior Researcher, Laboratory of Thermomechanical Treatment, 1972-89, Professor, Division of Plastic Deformation of Special Alloys, 1989-, Scientific Leader, 1992-, Moscow Institute for Steel and Alloys. Publications include: Thermomechanical Treatment of Steels, 1983; Diagrams of Hot Forming, Structure and Properties of Steels, 1989; Tempering of Steels, 1997. Honours include: All-USSR Award; Title, Best in Profession as Researcher; D K Chernov Prize of USSR; N Anosov Prize, Russian Federation; Honoured Scientist of the Russian Federation. Memberships include: ASM; Association of Metal Scientists of Russia. Address: TMT Laboratory, Division of Plastic Deformation of Special Alloys, Moscow State Institute for Steel and Alloys, Leninsky Prospect 4, Moscow 117936, Russia.

KAR Subal, b. 27 December 1953, Shillong, India. Engineering Educator; Scientist. m. Rina Pal, 1 son. Education: BSc, 1973, Gauhati University; BTech, 1976, MTech, 1978, PhD, 1989, University of Calcutta. Appointments: Senior Research Fellow, 1980-83, Lecturer, 1983-90, University of Calcutta; Senior Lecturer, 1990-94, Reader, 1994-2002, Professor, 2002-, University of Calcutta. Publications: Research Papers published in reputed international journals and presented in International Symposium in France, USA and Japan; Patentee Microwaves. Honours: Young Scientist Award, 1995; Fulbright Tata Award, 1999-2000; Visiting Scientist to Kyoto University, Japan, 1997; Lawrence Berkeley National Laboratory, Berkeley, California, USA, 1999-2000. Memberships: Institution of Electrical and Electronics Engineers, USA; Institute of Electronics And Telecommunications Engineers, India; Indian Science Congress Association. Address: University of Calcutta, Inst of Radiophysics/ Elec, 92 APC Road, Calcutta 700009, India.

KARAEV Roman, b. 22 January 1956, Baku, USSR. Physician. Education: Physician, General Therapy Faculty, 1979, Neurologist, 1980, Medical University of Baku; Dermatologist, University of Medicine, Moscow, 1983; Doctor of Medicine, Moscow, 1997. Appointments: Physician, Clinic of Psychiatry, Baku, 1980-81; Chief of Department of Neurology, Clinic of Psychiatry, Moscow, 1981-84; Chief of Department, Medical Research Institute, 1985-89; Principal, School of Beauty Therapy, Moscow, 1996-2003. Publications: Numerous articles, 1982-2002; Manual of Beauty Therapy and Aesthetic Cosmetology, 1999; More than 15 patented inventions. Honours: Doctor of Medicine; Professor of Moscow Medical Academy, Memberships: Russian Section CIDESCO; New York Academy of Science; European Academy of Dermatology and Venearology; IAD; EACD. Address: 21 Steemiannyi Pereulok, Apt 49, 113054, Moscow, Russia. E-mail: karaev@orc.ru

KARAMANUKIAN Sirvart, b. 1 December 1912, Istanbul, Turkey (of Armenian decent). Composer; Pianist. m. 30 June 1944. Education: Istanbul Conservatory, 1939. Appointments: Professor of Piano; Compositions performed in North and South America, Europe and Middle East. Publications: Several articles in professional journals and magazines; CD released. Honour: St Sahag and St Mesrob Medal, 1992. Address: Osmansbey, Halaskargazi cd 269, Istanbul, Turkey.

KARAN Donna, b. 2 October 1948, Forest Hills, New York, USA. Fashion Designer. m. (1) Mark Karan, 1 daughter, (2) Stephen Weiss, 1983, deceased 2001. Education: Parsons School of Design, New York. Appointments: Designer, Anne Klein & Co, Addenda Co, 1968; Returned to Anne Klein, 1968, Associate Designer, 1971, Director of Design, 1974-84; Owner, Designer, Donna Karan Co, New York, 1984-96; Designer, Donna Karan International, 1996-2001; Chief Designer, LVMH, 2001-. Honours: Coty Awards, 1977, 1981; Fashion Designers of America Women's Wear Award, 1996. Membership: Fashion Designers of American. Address: Donna Karan International, 15th Floor, 5550 Seventh Avenue, New York, NY 10018, USA.

KARANDE Sunil, b. 29 July 1961, Bombay, India. Paediatrician; Researcher. Education: MBBS, 1984; DCH, 1988; MD, 1989; Diploma in Information Technology, Advanced Computing Training School, Pune, 2000. Appointments: Medical Officer, Government of India, 1990-91; Surgeon Lieutenant, Indian Navy, 1991-92; Lecturer, Paediatrics, Seth GS Medical College and KEM Hospital, Bombay, 1992-98; Associate Professor, Paediatrics, Lokmanya Tilak Municipal Medical College and Lokmanya Tilak Municipal General Hospital, Bombay, 1998-; Committee Member and Resource Person for AIDS Awareness in Junior Colleges in Mumbai, UNICEF and Mumbai Districts AIDS Control Society, 2000-. Publications: 46 indexed articles in peer reviewed journals; Written chapters in 2 books. Honours: Expert, Essential Drug List, Indian Pharmacological Society of Clinicians and Pharmacologists, 1994; First Prize, Free Paper, VII Maharashtra State Indian Academy of Paediatrics Conference, 1996; Reviewer for Indian Paediatrics, Indian Journal of Paediatrics, Journal of Postgraduate Medicine and Neurology India, indexed journals. Memberships: Member of Technical Committee: WHO/Adverse Drug Reaction Monitoring Programme, 1997-99; Life Member, Indian Academy of Paediatrics; Life Member, Indian Medical Association; Member, New York Academy of Sciences, 1996. Address: Flat 24, Joothica, 5th Floor, 22A Naushir Bharucha Road, Mumbai 400007, India. E-mail: karandesunil@yahoo.com.

KARAS Joza, b. 3 May 1926, Warsaw, Poland (Czech Nationality). Violinist; Musicologist. m. Anne Killackey, 14 February 1976, 5 sons, 1 daughter. Education: Academic Gymnasium, Prague, 1945; State Conservatory of Music, Prague, 1949; Hartt College of Music, University of Hartford, USA, 1957. Career: Violin Soloist, Recitalist, USA and Canada; Founder, Karas String Quartet. Compositions: Violin Method. Recordings: Hans Krása's Brundibár, 1993. Publication: Music in Terezín 1941-1945, 1985. Contributions to: STTH; Jewish Digest; Journal of Synagogue Music; Review of the Society for the History of the Czechoslovak Jews; Theatrical Performances during the Holocaust. Membership: Czechoslovak Society of Arts and Sciences in America. Address: 212 Duncaster Road, Bloomfield, CT 06002, USA.

KARASIN Grigory B, b. 1949, Moscow, Russia. Diplomat; Ambassador Extraordinary and Plenipotentiary. m. Olga V Karasina, 2 daughters. Education: Graduate, College of Oriental Languages, Moscow State University, 1971. Appointments: Embassy in Senegal, 1972-76; Embassy in Australia, 1979-85; Embassy in the United Kingdom, 1988-92; Director, Department of Africa, MFA, 1992-93; Director, Department of Information and Press, MFA, 1993-96; Deputy Minister of Foreign Affairs of the Russian Federation, 1996-2000; Ambassador to the Court of St James's, 2000-. Address: The Russian Embassy, 13 Kensington Palace Gardens, London W8 4QX, England.

KARAVANIĆ Ivor, b. 27 June 1965, Zagreb, Croatia. Archaeologist. m. Snježana. Education: BA, Archaeology, 1990, MA, Archaeology, 1993, University of Zagreb; PhD, Archaeology,

1999, University of Zagreb. Appointments: Research Assistant, 1991-2001; Assistant, 1993-99, Senior Assistant, 1999-2001, Assistant Professor, 2001-, Department of Archaeology, Faculty of Philosophy, University of Zagreb, 1991-. Publications include: Néandertaliens et Paléolithique supérieur dans la grotte de Vindija, co-author, 1998; Gornjopaleolitičke kamene i koštane rukotvorine iz špilje Vindije, 1994; Upper Paleolithic occupation levels and late-occurring Neanderthal at Vindija Cave (Croatia) in the Context of Central Europe and the Balkans, 1995; The Middle/Upper Paleolithic Interface and the Relationship of Neanderthals and Early Modern Humans in the Hrvatsko Zagorje, co-author, 1998; The Early Upper Paleolithic of Croatia, 1998; Neanderthal Diet at Vindija and Neanderthal Predation: The Evidence from Stable Isotopes, co-author, 2000; Stones that Speak, Šandalja in the Light of Lithic Technology (catalogue of the exhibition), co-author, 2000; Olschewian and Appearance of Bone Technology in Croatia and Slovenia, 2000; ESR and AMS-based ^{14}C dating of Mousterian Levels at Mujina Pecina, Dalmatia, Croatia, co-author, 2002; Osvit tehnologije, co-author, 2003. Honours: Fellowship, French Government, 1995, 2001; Constantin-Jireček Fellowship, 1995; Fulbright Fellowship, 1996-97; International Scientist of the Year, IBC, 2001. Memberships: National Geographic Society; Croatian Archaeological Society; Society for American Archaeology; European Association of Archaeologists; INQUA National Committee, Croatia; Serra International, Zagreb; Croatian Fulbright Alumni Association. Address: Department of Archaeology, Faculty of Philosophy, University of Zagreb, Ivana Lučića 3, 10000 Zagreb, Croatia. E-mail: ikaravan@mudrac.ffzg.hr

KAREL Jezernik, b. 11 April 1942, Doklezovje. Professor of Robotics and Control. m. Terezija Savnik, 2 sons. Education: BSc, 1968, MSc, 1974, Dr Eng, Electrical Engineering, University of Ljubjana, Slovenia. Appointments: Professor of Robotics and Control, University of Maribor, Slovenia; Dean of Electrical Faculty, Vice Rector of University of Maribor. Publication: IEEE Transaction on Industrial Electronics. Honour: Gold Medal, Rector of University of Maribor. Memberships: IEE The Institute of Electrical and Electronic Engineering USA; Electrotechnical Society of Slovenia. Address: University of Maribor, Faculty of Electrical and Computer Science Engineering, Smetanova 17, 2000 Maribor, Slovenia.

KAREV George Bentchev, b. 23 August 1943, Shoumen, Bulgaria. Medical Leader. m. Pavlina, 23 November 1969, 1 daughter. Education: MD, Medical Faculty, Varna, 1969; PhD, Medical Academy, Sofia, 1994. Appointments: Assistant Professor, Department of Medical Biology, Medical Faculty of Varna, 1969-74; Senior Assistant Professor, 1974-77; Head Assistant Professor, 1977-93; Senior Researcher, Bulgarian Academy of Sciences, 1993; Chairman, Committee on Health Care, 36th National Assembly, 1991-94; Vice Chairman, 37th National Assembly, 1994-97; Ambassador, Republic of Bulgaria, Rabat, Morocco, 1998. Publications: Parliamentary Slips by Freud; Articles to various professional journals: American Journal of Physical Anthropology, American Journal of Human Biology, Anthropologischer Anzeiger, Cortex. Honours: 11 diplomas for work with prominent students; Abroad Special Prize of Slavic Academy of Sciences. Memberships: Intl Dermatologystic Association; American Deimatoglyphic Association; European Anthropology Association; New York Academy of Sciences. Address: Embassy of Bulgaria, 4 Avenue de Meknes, BP 1301, Rabat 10000, Morocco.

KARGI Fikret, b. 2 February 1951, Malatya, Turkey. Professor. m. Hatice Aydanur, 1 son. Education: BS, MS, Chemical Engineering, Hacettepe University, Turkey, 1973; PhD, Chemical-Biochemical Engineering, Cornell University, USA, 1979.

Appointments: Assistant Professor, Lehigh University, Pennsylvania, USA, 1980-85; Associate Professor, Washington University, St Louis, Missouri, 1986-90; Professor, Dokuz Eylul University, Izmir, Turkey, 1991-. Publications: 2 textbooks (English and Turkish); Over 100 scientific-technical publications in international professional journals; Over 700 citations in SCI. Honours: Fulbright Scholarship, Cornell University, 1976-78; Engineering Science Award, Technical and Scientific Research Council of Turkey, 1997; Listed in biographical publications. Turkey. Address: Department of Environmental Engineering, Dokuz Eylul University, Buca, Izmir, Turkey.

KARR-KIDWELL P J, b. 15 July 1952, Ludlow, Massachusetts, USA. University Professor. m. David Casey Kidwell, 10 August 1980. Education: BA, University of New Hampshire, 1974; MA, 1975, PhD, 1976, The Ohio State University. Appointments: Professor, Texas Woman's University, 1977-. Publications: Youth and Adolescence: The Rising Generation, Subcultures & Contemporary Society, 1980; Poetry in anthologies. Contributions to: Journals, antologies and periodicals. Honours: Over 60 professional awards. Address: 3804 Red Oak Drive, Corinth, TX 76208, USA.

KARWOWSKI Jacek Andrzej, b. 23 March 1940, Vilna, Lithuania. Physicist. m. Anna Maria Karwowska, 2 sons, 1 daughter. Education: MSc, 1962; Doctorate, 1968; Dr hab, 1974; Professor, 1988. Appointments: Assistant, 1962-69, Adjunct, 1969-75, Docent, 1975-88, Professor, 1988-, N Copernicus University, Torun, Poland; Postdoctoral Fellow, Department of Chemistry, University of Alberta, Edmonton, Canada, 1972-73; Visiting Scientist, Max Planck Institute für Astrophysik, Garching bei München, Germany, 1-3 months yearly, 1984-2000; Visiting Professor, Consejo Superior de Investigaciones Cientificas, Madrid, Spain, 1987-88. Publications: 173 scientific papers in international journals; Co-author, 2 books. Honour: Cavalier Cross, Order of Polonia Restituta, 1994. Memberships: Polish Physical Society; European Physical Society; International Society for Theoretical Chemical Physics; Polish Chemical Society; Polish Alpine Society. Address: Instytut Fizyki, Uniwersytet Mikolaja Kopernika, ul Grudziadzka 5, PL-87100 Torun, Poland. E-mail: jka@phys.uni.torun.pl

KASER Michael Charles, b. 2 May 1926, London, England. Economist. m. Elizabeth Piggford, 4 sons, 1 daughter. Education: BA, 1946, MA, 1950, Economics, King's College, Cambridge; MA, 1960, DLitt, 1993, Oxford University. Career: Chief Scientific Advisor's Department, Ministry of Works, 1946-47; HM Foreign Service, including HM Embassy, Moscow as Second Secretary, Commercial Secretariat, 1947-51; United Nations Economic Commission for Europe, Geneva, 1951-63; Lecturer, 1963-93, Reader, 1972-93, Emeritus Fellowship, 1993-, St Antony's College; Honorary Chair, Institute for German Studies, University of Birmingham, 1993-. Publications: Author, Editor, 23 books and 350 articles in journals on the East European, Russian and Central Asian economies; Books include: Soviet Economics, 1970; Health Care in the Soviet Union and Eastern Europe, 1976; Privatisation in the CIS, 1995; The Economics of Kazakstan and Uzbekistan, 1997. Memberships: General Editor, International Economic Association, 1986-; Chairman, Councillor, 1980-92, Central Asia and Caucasus Advisory Board, Royal Institute of International Affairs; Trustee, Council of the Keston Institute and Academic Advisory Committee of Cumberland Lodge, Windsor; Former President, British Association of Former UN Civil Servants; Former President, Albania Society of Britain; Member, Advisory Group on Former Soviet and East European Studies of the Higher Education Funding Council for England, 1995-2000 Reform Club. Honours: Papal Knighthood, Order of St Gregory; Knight's Cross of the Order of Merit, Poland; Order of Naim Frasheri, Albania; Hon DSocSc, Birmingham. Address: 7 Chadlington Road, Oxford, OX2 6SY, England.

KASHIRSKY Vladimir, b. 19 October 1941, Penza, Russia. Conductor. m. Tatiana Mikheeva, 1 son, 1 daughter. Education: Kuibyshev Institute of Culture, 1973-78; Gorky State Conservatoire, 1987-91. Appointments: Conductor, Male Choir of Penza Militia; Artistic Director, The Junior Choir, Vivat; Founder, Artistic Director, Penza Academic Choir, 1984-; Founder, Artistic Director and Chief Conductor, Russian Choral and Vocal Culture Centre, Penza, 1992-96; Artistic Director, Philharmonic Society of Penza District, Chief Conductor, Symphony Capella, 2003-. Honours: Honoured Artist of the Russian Federation; The Laureate of Gubernator's Award . Address: Lunacharskogo 30, Flat 32, City Penza, Russia.

KASIPATHI Chinta, b. 17 October 1955, Rajahmundry, India. Professor of Geology. m. Hemalatha, 2 sons. Education: BSc, 1973, M Sc (Tech), 1976, PhD, 1981, Andhra University. Appointments: Research Assistant, 1976-80; Research Associate, 1980-84, Officer Pool, 1984; Lecturer, Assistant Professor, 1984-86; Reader, Associate Professor, 1986-94; Professor, 1994-; Supervised doctoral and masters theses; organised two national seminars; Consultant, several mining organisations; Adviser, national and international bodies. Publications: 98 research papers in field of Indian ore mineral studies; Editorial Board, 5 journals. Honour: Young Scientist Award, 1984; Recognised Qualified Person, Government of India. Memberships: New York Academy of Sciences; AGID; Secretary, IGC; GSI; GMMSI; IMSA; IEA; IGC, India; IMA; IGI; IAGS; SGAT; MMR; JDW; FGW; INS; AEG; ISAG; Secretary, Andhra University Geology Alumni Association; FISCA; FAPA Sc; F GARC. Address: Department of Geology, Andhra University, Visakhapatnam 530003, Andhra Pradesh, India.

KASLOW Florence, b. 6 January, Philadelphia, Pennsylvania, USA. Psychologist. m. Solis, 1 son, 1 daughter. Education: AB, Temple University, 1952; MA, Ohio State University, 1954; PhD, Bryn Mawr College, 1969. Appointments: Consultant, USA Navy, Department of Psychiatry, Naval Hospitals, San Diego, Portsmouth and Philadelphia, 1976-94; Adjunct Professor, Medical Psychology, Duke University Medical Center, North Carolina, USA, 1982-; Director, Florida Couples and Family Institute, Florida, USA, 1982-; Visiting Professor of Psychology, Florida Institute of Technology, Melbourne, Florida, USA, 1985-; President, Kaslow Associates, Palm Beach, Florida, USA. Publications include: Handbook of Relational Diagnosis, 1996; Painful Partings, Divorce and Its Aftermath, 1997; Chapter in 101 More Interventions in Family Therapy, 1998; Handbook of Couple and Family Forensic Issues, 1999; Comprehensive Handbooks of Psychotherapy, editor, 2002; Welcome Home! An international and non-traditional adaption reader, with L L Schwartz, 2003. Honours: Distinguished Family Psychologist of the Year Award, 1986; American Board of Professional Psychology, Distinguished Service and Outstanding Contribution Award, 1994; Award for Outstanding Achievement and Accomplishment in Media and Professional Psychology, 1995, American Psychology Association, Award for Distinguished Contribution to the International Advancement of Psychology, Washington DC, 2000. Memberships: American Academy of Forensic Psychology; American Association for Martial and Family Therapy, 1971-2002; American Psychological Association, 1974-; American Association of Sex Educators, Counselors and Therapists, 1977-; American Board of Family Psychology, 1992-, President, 1996-2000; Florida Psychological Association, 1981-; President, International Family Therapy Association, 1987-90; President, International Academy of Family Psychology, 1998-2002; American Academy of Clinical

Dictionary of International Biography

Sexologists, 1992-; The Academy of Clinical Psychology, 1994-; International Association of Applied Psychologists, 1994-2003; The Authors Guild Inc, 1996-2002. Address: 128 Windward Drive, Palm Beach Gardens, FL 33418, USA. E-mail: kaslowfs@worldnet.att.net

KASPAREK Karel, b. 14 June 1923, Olesnice, Czech Republic. Journalist. m. Johanna Paula Koidl. Education: Medical Studies, 1945-48, Masaryk University, Brno, Czech Republic; Economic Studies, Franz Joseph University, Innsbruck, Austria, 1949-52. Appointments: Correspondent, Radio Free Europe, Austria, 1953-58; Chairman, Radio Free Europe/Radio Liberty Works Council, 1979-87; Acting Director, RFE Czechoslovak Broadcasting Service, 1989. Publications: Political commentaries in Czech and Western media; Author, Operations of the KGB and Communist State Securities Services against Radio Free Europe and Radio Liberty, 1951-89, in progress. Honours: Letter of Appreciation from Mr William Buckley, President of Radio Free Europe/Radio Liberty, 1985; Honorary Diploma, Masaryk University, Brno Czech Republic, 1990; Honorary Diploma: In gratitude and recognition from the citizens of Olesnice for your contribution towards regaining the freedom of the nation, Town of Olesnice, 1991. Memberships: Chairman, Academic Club, Czechoslovak Christian Democratic Party (People's Party), 1946-48; American Newspaper Guild. Address: Goerresstrasse 28, 80798 Munich, Germany.

KASPAROV Garri Kimovich, b. 13 April 1963, Baku. Chess Player. m. (1) Masha Kasparova, 1 daughter, (2) Yulia Kasparova, 1 son. Education: Azerbaijan Pedagogical Institute of Foreign Languages. Appointments: Azerbaijan Champion, 1975; USSR Junior Champion, 1975; International Master, 1979, International Grandmaster, 1980; World Junior Champion, 1980; Won USSR Championship, 1981, subsequently replacing Anatoliy Karpov at top of world ranking list; Won match against Viktor Korchnoi, challenged Karpov for World Title in Moscow, 1985, the match being adjourned due to the illness of both players; Won rescheduled match to become the youngest ever World Champion; Successfully defended his title against Karpov, 1986, 1987, 1990; Series of promotional matches in London, 1987; Won Times World Championship against Nigel Short, 1993; Stripped of title by World Chess Federation, 1993. Publication: Child of Change (with Donald Trelford), 1987; London-Leningrad Championship Games, 1987; Unlimited Challenge, 1990. Honours include: Oscar Chess Prize, 1982-83, 1985-89; World Chess Cup, 1989. Membership: Professional Chess Association. Address: Mezhdunarodnaya-2, Suite 1108, Krasnopresnenskaya nab 12, 123610 Moscow, Russia. E-mail: maiavia@dol.ru Website: www.kasparovchess.com

KASUYA Hideki, b. 27 August 1961, Nagoya, Japan. Surgeon. m. Yoshie Kasuya. Education: MD, Aichi Medical University, Nagoya, Japan, 1984-90; PhD, Nagoya University School of Medicine, Nagoya, Japan, 1996-2000. Appointments: Kidney Organ Transplant Surgeon, Nagoya Red Cross Hospital, 1995-96; Vice President, Kasuya Clinic, Nagoya, Aichi, Japan, 1990-; Research Fellow, Harvard Medical School, Boston, USA, 2000-; Chief of Cancer Gene Therapy, Nagoya University School of Medicine, Department 2 of Surgery, Nagoya, Japan, 2002-. Publications: Journal of Surgeral Oncology, 1999, 2000; The Operation, 2000; Surgery, 2000; Hepato-Gastroenterology, 1997, 2001, 2002; Drugs of Today, 2003; Journal of Clinical Investigator, 2003; Annals of Surgery, 2003. Honours: Best General Surgeon of the Year, Holy Spirit International Hospital, 1990; Marquis Who's Who, 2003. Memberships: American College of Surgeons; American Association for Cancer Research; Harvard University Faculty Club Member; The Japan Surgical Association; The Japan Society for Cancer Therapy. Address: 5-20 Auchi-dori, Showa-ku, Aichi, Nagoya 466, Japan. Email: kasuya@helix.mgh.harvard.edu

KATSOURIS Andreas G, b. 1940, Meniko, Cyprus. Professor. m. Despoina, 2 daughters. Education: BA, MA, University of Athens, Greece, 1963; PhD, Greek Drama, University of Leeds, England, 1972. Appointments: Lecturer in Classics, 1973, Associate Professor, 1982, Full Professor, 1997-, University of Ioannina. Publications: 10 books; Many articles. Honours: Stipendiat, Alexander von Humboldt-Stiftung; Fellow, Center for Hellenic Studies. Address: Department of Classics, University of Ioannina, 45332 Ioannina, Greece.

KATZ Bernhard, b. 26 March 1911, Leipzig, Germany (British Citizen). Physiologist. m. Marguerite Penly, 1945, 2 sons. Education: Graduated, Medicine, University of Leipzig, 1934; PhD, 1938, Doctor of Science, 1943, University College, London. Appointments: Beit Memorial Research Fellow, Sydney Hospital, 1939-42; Royal Australian Air Force, 1942-45; Assistant Director of Research, Biophysics Research Unit, Henry Head Research Fellow, 1946-50, Reader in Physiology, 1950-51, Professor and Head of Biophysics, 1952-78, University College, London; Noted for research into the physiology of the nervous system. Publications: Electric Excitation of Nerve, 1939; Nerve, Muscle and Synapse, 1966; The Release of Neural Transmitter Substances, 1969. Honours: Knighted, 1969; Joint Winner, Nobel Prize for Physiology or Medicine, 1970. Address: Department of Physiology, University College, Gower Street, London, WC1E 6BT, England.

KATZ Naftale, b. 13 June 1940, Belo Horizonte, Brazil. Medical Doctor; Scientist. 2 sons, 2 daughters. Education: Superior, Faculty of Medicine, 1959-64; Specialization, Sanitary Engineering, 1969. Appointments: Scientific Director of the Foundation for the Support of Research of Minas Gerais State; Vice-Head, Laboratory of Schistosomiasis, Research Center "René Rachou"; Expert, World Health Organization; Supervisor, Postgraduate Course, Parasitology and Tropical Medicine Fiocruz and Faculty of Medicine, Federal University of Minas Gerais; Technical and Scientific Advisor, Foundation for the Support of Research of Rio de Janeiro and Foundation for the Support of Research of Pernambuco; Professor, FIOCRUZ; Committee, Parasitologic Diseases, Pan American Association of Infectiology. Publications: Over 240 articles in professional journals. Honours include: Medal of Merit, Municipal Legislative of Belo Horizonte City, 1994; Medal, 60 years of the Tropical Medicine Institute "Pedro Kouri", Habana, Cuba, 1997; Honorary Member, Helmintological Society of Washington, 1997; XXIII National Competition "Premio Governador do Estado", Brazilian Invention, 1998; "Health Merit" Minas Gerais Government; Medical Personality of 2002, Public Health, Medical Association of Minas Gerais. Address: Av Augusto De Lima 1715, Fiocruz - C Postal 1743, B Preto, Belo Horizonte 30190.002 MG, Brazil.

KATZ Steve, b. 14 May 1935, New York, New York, USA. Novelist; Short Story Writer; Poet; Screenwriter; Professor. m. Patricia Bell, 10 June 1956, divorced, 3 sons. Education: BA, Cornell University, 1956; MA, University of Oregon, 1959. Appointments: English Language Institute, Lecce, Italy, 1960; Overseas Faculty, University of Maryland, Lecce, Italy, 1961-62; Assistant Professor of English, Cornell University, 1962-67; Lecturer in Fiction, University of Iowa, 1969-70; Writer-in-Residence 1970-71, Co-Director, Projects in Innovative Fiction, 1971-73, Brooklyn College, City University of New York; Adjunct Assistant Professor, Queens College, City University of New York, 1973-75; Associate Professor of English, University of Notre Dame, 1976-78; Associate Professor of English 1978-82, Professor of English, 1982-, University of Colorado at Boulder. Publications: Novels: The Lestriad, 1962; The Exagggerations of Peter Prince, 1968; Posh, 1971; Saw, 1972; Moving Parts, 1977; Wier and Pouce, 1984; Florry of Washington Heights, 1987; Swanny's Ways,

1995. Short Stories: Creamy and Delicious: Eat My Words (in Other Words), 1970; Stolen Stories, 1985; 43 Fictions, 1991; Antonello's Lion, 2004. Poetry: The Weight of Antony, 1964; Cheyenne River Wild Track, 1973; Journalism, 1990. Screenplay: Grassland, 1974. Honours: PEN Grant, 1972; Creative Artists Public Service Grant, 1976; National Educational Association Grants, 1976, 1982; GCAH Book of the Year, 1991; America Award in Fiction, 1995. Memberships: Authors League of America; PEN International; Writers Guild. Address: 669 Washington Street, No 602, Denver, CO 80203, USA.

KATZENBERG Jeffrey, b. 1950, USA. Film Executive. m. Marilyn Siegal, 1 son, 1 daughter. Appointments: Assistant to Chair, CEO, Paramount Pictures, NY, 1975-77; Executive Director, Marketing, Paramount TV, California, 1977, Vice President, Programming, 1977-78; Vice President, Feature Production, Paramount Pictures, 1978-80, Senior Vice President, Production, Motion Picture Division, 1980-82, President, Production, Motion Pictures & TV, 1982-94; Chairman, Walt Disney Studios, Burbank, California, 1994-; Co-Founder, Dreamworks SKG, 1995-. Address: Dreamworks SKG, 100 Flower Street, Glendale, CA 91201, USA.

KATZNER Maurice, b. 31 March 1944, Limoges, France. Orthopaedic Surgeon. m. Michele Herrmann, 1 son, 1 daughter. Education: Baccalaurat, 1961; MD, 1970. Appointments: EHS, 1964; HIS, 1966; Assistant Professor, Mexico, 1969; Legal Expert, Delegate of the Council of Europe. Publications: 208 publications, 1968-2002. Honours: Diamant, 1972. Memberships: SICOT; SIROT; SOFCOT; SOTEST; GETO; French College of Orthopaedic Surgeons. Address: 46 Allee de la Robertsau, F-67000 Strasbourg, France.

KAUFFMAN George Bernard, b. 4 September 1930, Philadelphia, Pennsylvania. Educator. m. Ingeborg Salomon, div. 2 daughters; m. Laurie Marks Papazian, 3 stepchildren. Education: BA with honours, University of Pennsylvania, 1951; PhD, University of Florida, 1956. Appointments: Graduate Assistant, University Florida, 1951-55; Research participant, Oak Ridge Nat. Lab., 1955; Instructor, University of Texas, 1955-56; Research Chemist, Humble Oil and Refining Co. Texas, 1956, GE, Cincinnati, 1957, 1959; Assistant Professor, Chemistry, California State University, Fresno, 1956-61; Associate Professor, 1961-66, Professor, 1966, California State University; Guest, Lecturer, lecture tours, American Chemical Society, 1971; Visiting Scholar, University California, 1976; University Puget Sound, 1978; Director, Undergraduate Research Participation Program NSF. Publications: Author: Editor, numerous scientific journals including Today's Chemist at Work, 1995-; Chemical Heritage, 1996-; The Chemical Educator, 1998-; Guest Editor: Co-ordination Chemistry Centennial Symposium C3S issue, Polyhedron, 1994. Honours: Many awards including, Guggenheim Fellowship, 1972; Outstanding Professor, California State University System, 1973; Marc-Auguste Pictet Medal, Société de Physique et d'Histoire Naturelle de Genève, 1992; George C Pimentel Award, 1993; President's Medal of Distinction, 1994; Undergraduate Research Award, American Chemical Society, 1972; Laudatory Decree, Russian Academy of Sciences, 2000; Fellow, American Association for the Advancement of Science, 2002; Helen M Free Award for Public Outreach, American Chemical Society, 2002; American Chemical Society Legislative Action Honor Roll, 2003. Membership: AAAS, AAUP, Association University Pennsylvania Chemists; Mensa; Sigma Xi; Phi Kappa Phi, and others. Address: 1609 E Quincy Ave, Fresno, CA 93720-2309, USA.

KAUFMANN Myron S, b. 27 August 1921, Boston, Massachusetts, USA. Novelist. m. Paula Goldberg, 6 February 1960, divorced 1980, 1 son, 2 daughters. Education: AB, Harvard

University, 1943. Publications: Novels: Remember Me To God, 1957; Thy Daughter's Nakedness, 1968; The Love of Elspeth Baker, 1982. Address: 111 Pond Street, Sharon, MA 02067, USA.

KAUSTOVA Jarmila, b. 8 March 1945, Czech Republic. Doctor of Medicine. m. Boleslav Kausta, 1 son. Education: Medical Faculty, Charles University, 1969; Postgraduate, Medical School, Prague, 1973, 1976. Appointments: Head, Department of Diagnostics of Mycobacteria; Head, National Reference Laboratory for Mycobacterium kansasii of the Czech Republic, Regional Institute of Public Health, Ostrava. Publications: 82 in professional journals. Honours include: Medal, Societas Medica Bohemica, 1995. Memberships: Czech Society of Epidemiology and Microbiology; Czech Society of Pneumophtiseology; Czech Medical Society; New York Academy of Sciences. Address: Regional Institute of Public Health, Partyzanske Namesti 7, 70200 Ostrava N Morav, Czech Republic.

KAVALER Rebecca, b. 26 July 1930, Atlanta, Georgia, USA. Writer. m. Frederic Kavaler, 1955, 2 sons. Education: AB, University of Georgia. Publications: Further Adventures of Brunhild, 1978; Doubting Castle, 1984; Tigers in the Woods, 1986; A Little More Than Kin, 2003. Contributions to: Anthologies and magazines. Honours: Short stories included in Best of Nimrod, 1957-69; Best American Short Stories, 1972; Award for Short Fiction, Association of Writers and Poets, 1978; National Endowment for the Arts Fellowships, 1979, 1985. Membership: PEN. Address: 425 Riverside Drive, New York, NY 10025, USA.

KAWACHI Yoshiko, b. 26 July 1936, Tokyo. Professor. m. Hiroyuki. Education: BA, Tsuda College, 1959; MA, Graduate School, Keio University, 1969; PhD, Keio University, 1997. Appointments: Kyoritsu Women's College, 1969-88; Kyorin University, 1988-. Publications: Calendar of English Renaissance Drama, 1558-1642; Shakespeare and Cultural Exchange; Shakespeare's Idea of Time; Editor, Shakespeare World-wide; Japanese Studies in Shakespeare and his Contemporaries. Memberships: International Shakespeare Association; Shakespeare Society of Japan; International Association of University Professors of English. Address: 2-35-6 Mitsui-dai, Hachioji-shi, Tokyo 192-0014, Japan.

KAWAHATA Masahiro, b. 8 September 1936, Tokyo, Japan. Professor. m. Keiko Kohra, 1 son. Education: BE, Mechanical Engineering, 1960; ME, Control Engineering, 1963; PhD, Systems Engineering, 1966, University of Tokyo. Appointments: Consulting Professor, Electrical Engineering, Stanford University; Provost's Distinguished Visiting Professor, University of Southern California; Full Professor, Management Engineering, Tokai University; Visiting Professor, Industrial Engineering, University of Washington; Chairman/CEO of eCharge Co Ltd; Member of the Board of Directors, Terabeam Corporation. Publications: 130 books and articles for professional journals. Honours: Awarded by Minister of International Trade and Industry for outstanding contribution to the development of Information Society of Japan, 1986; University of Washington Pioneer Award, 1995; Honoured by MITI for outstanding contribution for Public Understanding of High Technologies, 1996; University of Southern California Provost's Distinguished Visiting Professor, 1997. Memberships: Numerous memberships including: Board of Trustees, Japan Systems Engineering Society; Board of Trustees, Japan CAI Society; Board of Trustees, Seijo University and Affiliated Schools; Secretary IEEE Tokyo Branch. Address: 3-18-2 Denenchofu Ota-ku, Tokyo 145-0071, Japan.

KAWAI Shuichi, b. 8 July 1950, Osaka, Japan. Orthodontist. m. Miho, 2 sons, 1 daughter. Education: DDS, 1976, PhD, 1980, Osaka Dental University. Appointments: Orthodontist, private practice, 1982-. Publications: Level Anchorage System: Concept and Treatment. Address: Kataoka Bldg 4F 6-19, Konya-machi, Takatsuki-city, Osaka, 569-0804, Japan.

KAWAKAMI Masaya, b. 27 April 1929, Tokyo, Japan. Professor of Medicine. m. Noriko Tsuchida, 1 son, 2 daughters. Education: MD, School of Medicine, Hokkaido University, Sapporo, Japan, 1953; Diploma, Medical Board, Japan, 1954; Doctor of Medical Science, Gunma University Maebashi, Japan, 1960. Appointments: Associate Professor, Gunma University, 1960-70; Research Associate, Georgetown University, Washington DC, USA, 1964-66; Professor, Department of Molecular Biology, School of Medicine, Kitasato University, Sagamihara, Japan, 1972-96; Honorary Professor, Kitasato University, 1996-; Director, Kitasato Institute, 1987-; Director, Future Medical Laboratory, Tokyo, 2000-; Technical Advisor, SBS Inc., 1996-. Publications: Textbook of Molecular Biology, 1975; Immune Responses, 1978; Medical Molecular Biology, 1984; Human Molecular Genetics, 1991; Gene Engineering in Medicine, 1992; Complement-activating lectin, RaRF, 1999; Role of the compliment-lectin pathway in anaphylactoid reaction, 2003. Honours: Asahi Science Award, 1959; Naito Award, 1975; Asakawa Award, Japanese Society for Bacteriology, 1999; Honorary Member, Japanese Society of Bacteriology, 2003. Memberships: Japanese Society of Bacteriology, 1956-; Japanese Society of Molecular Biology, 1980-; American Society of Microbiology, 1973-90; Liaison Officer, International Union of Microbiological Societies, Washington DC, 1973-76, 1991-94; International Complement Workshop, 1984-; Japan Society of Human Genetics, 1988-; Bioethics Committee of Japan Medical Association, 1984-92; Committee of Human Gene Therapy, Ministry of Welfare, Japan, 1986-93. Address: 2-3-3 Kamitsuruma, Sagamihara, Kanagawa 228-0802, Japan. E-mail: que02046@nifty.com

KAWAMOTO Hiroshi, b. 6 February 1945, Matsuyama City, Japan. Physicist. 1 daughter. Education: BSc, 1968, DSc, 1984, Kyoto University. Appointments: Assistant Professor, Kyoto University, 1972-84; Full Professor, Maritime Safety Academy, 1984. Honours: International Order of Merit; Listed in several Who's Who publications. Memberships: New York Academy of Sciences, 1995; AAAS, 1996; World Laureate, ABI. Address: Maritime Safety Academy, 5-1 Wakaba-cho, Kure-shi, Hiroshima 737-8512, Japan.

KAZANTZIS Judith, b. 14 August 1940, Oxford, England. Poet; Fiction Writer. 1 son, 1 daughter. Education: Honours Degree, Modern History, Oxford, 1961. Appointments: General Council, Poetry Society, member, 1991-94. Publications: Poetry Collections: Minefield, 1977; The Wicked Queen, 1980; Touch Papers (co-author), 1982; Let's Pretend, 1984; Flame Tree, 1988; A Poem for Guatemala, pamphlet, 1988; The Rabbit Magician Plate, 1992; Selected Poems 1977-92, 1995; Swimming Through the Grand Hotel, 1997; The Odysseus Papers: Fictions on the Odyssey of Homer, 1999; In Cyclops' Cave, Homeric translation, 2002; Just After Midnight, 2004; Fiction: Of Love And Terror, 2002. Contributions to: Stand; Agenda; London Magazine; Poetry London; Poetry Wales; New Statesman; Red Pepper Poetry Review; Ambit; Verse; Honest Ulsterman; Bete Noire; Key West Reader; Faber Book of Blue Verse; Virago Book of Love Poetry; Comparative Criticism; Mind Readings; Red Sky at Night. Honours: Judge, Sheffield Hallam Poetry Competition, 1995-96; Judge, Stand International Poetry Competition, 1998. Memberships: Poetry Society; English PEN; CND; Palestine Solidarity Campaign. Address: 32 St Annes Crescent, Lewes, East Sussex, England.

KAZIMIANEC Valentin, b. 13 March 1948, Lithuania. Physician and Informatics Specialist. m. 1 son. Education: Master of Physics, Honours Diploma, Vilnius University, Lithuania, 1966-71; Postgraduate study in Radioelectronics, Kaunas Institute of Radiomeasurement Technique, Lithuania, 1972-75; Doctor, Kaunas University of Technology, Lithuania, 1975; DSc, St Petersburg Electrotechnical University, Russia, 1991; Doctor Habilitus, Scientific Board of Lithuania, 1993. Appointments: Senior Researcher, 18 Engineering Physics projects, Vilnius Scientific Research Institute of Electronics, 1971-92; Expert, 3 Telecommunication projects in Lithuanian Telecom, Saving Bank and Railroads, 1993-96; Chief Inspector, Customs Department of Ministry of Finance of Lithuania, 1996-2001; Visiting Scientist, Institute of Physics and Nuclear Engineering, Bucharest, Romania, 2001; Chief Inspector, Customs Criminal Service, 2002-. Publications: Co-author of monograph on information systems for super short wave analysis; about 70 scientific articles; 2 patents; 19 scientific research reports. Honour: Senior Research Fellow, Highest Certifying Commission, Moscow, Russia, 1982; 2000 Outstanding Scientists of the 20th Century Diploma, IBC, Cambridge, England, 1999. Membership: Co-ordinating Board, St Petersburg Association of Scientists and Scholars, Russia, 1993-94; Advisory Council, IBC, Cambridge England, 1999-; Research Board of Advisors, ABI, Raleigh, USA, 1999-. Address: Liudo Giros 74-61, Vilnius 2035, Lithuania.

KAZIMLI Khanhusein, b. 1 October 1942, Azerbaijan. Economist; Accountant. m. Frangiz Kazimova, 2 sons, 3 daughters. Education: Doctor of Economic Sciences, Professor, Azerbaijan National Economic Institute (now called Azerbaijan State Economic University). Appointments: Professor of Pricing Department, Azerbaijan State Economic University; Congressman, National Assembly of Azerbaijan Republic; President, Council of CIS Appraisers' Unions. Publications: Author, Scientific articles, monographs, textbooks and lesson supplies. Honours: Honour Order, Azerbaijan Republic, 2002; Golden Pen, Media Award Laureate. Membership: Council of CIS Appraisers' Unions. Address: National Assembly, Parliament Street, Baku City, Azerbaijan Republic. E-mail: rugar_04@yahoo.com

KEANE Fergal Patrick, b. 6 January 1961, Ireland. Journalist; Broadcaster. m. Anne Frances Flaherty, 1986, 1 son. Education: Terenure College, Dublin; Presentation College, Cork. Appointments: Trainee Reporter, Limerick Leader, 1979-82; Reporter, Irish Press Group, Dublin, 1982-84; Radio Telefis, Eireann, Belfast, 1986-89 (Dublin 1984-86); Northern Ireland Correspondent, BBC Radio, 1989-91; South Africa Correspondent, 1991-94; Asia Correspondent, 1994-97; Special Correspondent, 1997-; Presenter, Fergal Keane's Forgotten Britain, BBC, 2000. Publications: Irish Politics Now, 1987; The Bondage of Fear, 1994; Season of Blood: A Rwandan Journey, 1995; Letter to Daniel, 1996; Letters Home, 1999; A Stranger's Eye, 2000. Honours: Reporter of the Year Sony Silver Award, 1992, Sony Gold Award, 1993; International Reporter of the Year, 1993; Amnesty International Press Awards; RTS Journalist of the Year, 1994; BAFTA Award, 1997; Hon DLitt, Strathclyde, 2001. Address: c/o BBC Television, Wood Lane, London W12 7RJ, England.

KEANE Ronan, b. 20 July 1932, Dublin, Ireland. Judge. m. Terry O'Donnell, 1 son, 2 daughters. Education: BA (Hons), University College, Dublin, Ireland, 1954; Barrister-at-Law, King's Inns, Dublin, 1954; John Brooke Scholar. Appointments: In Practice at Bar, 1954-79; Senior Counsel, 1970; Chairman of the Bar Council, 1975; Judge of the High Court, 1979-96; President, Law Reform Commission, 1987-92; Ordinary Judge of the Supreme Court, 1996-2000; Chief Justice of Ireland, 2000-. Publications: The Law of Local Government in the Republic of Ireland; Equity and the

Law of Trusts in the Republic of Ireland; Company Law in the Republic of Ireland (3 editions); Editor, Walsh's Planning and Development Law, 2nd edition; Many articles in learned journals including: The Irish Jurist; Dublin University Law Journal. Honours: Bencher of King's Inns, Dublin, 1979-; Honorary Bencher of Lincoln's Inns, London, 2000; Honorary Bencher, Northern Ireland Inns of Court, 2000; LLD, causa honoris, National University of Ireland, 2001. Address: 39 Richmond Park, Monkstown, Co. Dublin, Ireland.

KEARNS Gregory L, b. 3 June 1954, St Louis, Missouri, USA. Pediatric Clinical Pharmacologist. 2 sons. Education: BS, Pharmacy (Cum Laude), St Louis College of Pharmacy, 1977; Doctor of Pharmacy (PharmD), University of Cincinnati, 1979; Resident, Pediatric Clinical Pharmacy, Children's Hospital Medical Center, Cincinnati, 1977-79; Postdoctoral Fellowship, Pediatric Clinical Pharmacology, Louisiana State University School of Medicine, 1979-82; Doctor of Philosophy (PhD) in Medicine, Erasmus University of School Medicine, 2002. Appointments: Instructor of Pharmacology and Therapeutics, Instructor of Pediatrics, Louisiana State University School of Medicine, 1982-83; Visiting Research Pharmacologist, National Center for Toxicological Research, Arkansas, 1983; Assistant Professor of Pharmaceutics, Assistant Professor of Pediatrics, 1983-88, Associate Professor of Pediatrics and Adjunct Associate Professor of Pharmaceutics, 1988-95, Professor of Pediatrics and Pharmaceutics, 1995-96, University of Arkansas for Medical Sciences, Little Rock; Head, Clinical Pharmacokinetic Monitoring Service, 1985-88, Co-Director, Pediatric Clinical Research Unit, 1990-96, Arkansas Children's Hospital, Arkansas; Chief, Section of Pediatric Clinical Pharmacology, University of Arkansas for Medical Sciences and the Arkansas Children's Hospital, Little Rock, 1988-96; Visiting Research Pharmacoloigst, Naval Aerospace Medical Research Laboratory, 1991; Director, Program of Excellence in Therapeutic Medication Development, Arkansas Children's Hospital Research Center, Little Rock, Arkansas, 1992-96; Director, Arkansas Drug Care Program, Department of Pediatrics, 1992-94, Member, Arkansas Cancer Research Center, 1994-96, University of Arkansas for Medical Sciences, Little Rock; Co-Principal Investigator and Associate Director, Pediatric Pharmacology Research Unit, Arkansas Children's Hospital Research Institute, Little Rock, 1994-96; Adjunct Professor of Pediatrics, College of Medicine, University of Arkansas for Medical Sciences, Little Rock, Arkansas, 1996; Marion Merrell Dow Professor of Pediatric Clinical Pharmacology, University of Missouri at Kansas City and the Children's Mercy Hospital, Kansas City, Missouri, 1996-; Chief, Division of Pediatric Clinical Pharmacology and Medical Toxicology, 1996-; Program Director and Co-Principal Investigator, Pediatric Pharmacology Research Unit, 1996-, Program Director, Center for Pediatric Clinical Pharmacology and Therapeutics, 1999-, Children's Mercy Hospital, Kansas City, Missouri; Professor of Pediatrics and Pharmacology, Colleges of Medicine and Pharmacy, University of Missouri at Kansas City, 1996-. Publications: Numerous peer-reviewed publications on original research, case reports and articles. Honours: Smith, Kline and French Award, 1977; O J Cloughy Fellowship, St Louis College of Pharmacy, 1977; Rho Chi Society, University of Cincinnati, 1979; Young Investigator Award in Pediatrics, 1982; Marion Merrell Dow endowed chair in Pediatric Clinical Pharmacology, 1996; Distinguished Alumnus for Service to the Profession Award, 1997; Invited speaker and lecturer, USA, Germany, Holland; Kansas City's Top Doctors Award, 2000; Distinguished Alumnus, School of Pharmacy, University of Cincinnati, 2001; Nominated to serve as Commissioner of the US Food and Drug Administration, 2002; 3rd HKA Visser Lectureship, Erasmus University Medical Center and Sophia Children's Hospital, The Netherlands, 2003; John and Marion Kraemer Research Award, Children's Mercy

Hospital, 2003; Special Consultant, Royal College of Pediatrics, 2003. Memberships: Society for Pediatric Research; Regent of American College of Clinical Pharmacology; American Board of Clinical Pharmacology; Government Affairs Committee, American Society of Clinical Pharmacology and Therapeutics; Corresponding Member, European Society for Developmental Pharmacology; Special Government Employee, Division of Clinical Pharmacology, Center for Drug Evaluation and Research, US Food and Drug Administration; Therapeutic Drug Network Data and Safety Monitoring Board, Cystic Fibrosis Foundation; Research Alliance for Children's Health; US Pharmacopeia Council of Experts. Address: The Children's Mercy Hospital, 2401 Gillham Road, Kansas City, MO 64108, USA. E-mail: gkearns@cmh.edu

KEATING Henry Reymond Fitzwalter, b. 31 October 1926, St Leonards-on-Sea, Sussex, England. Author. m. 1953, 3 sons, 1 daughter. Education: BA, Trinity College, Dublin. Publications: The Perfect Murder, 1964; Inspector Ghote Trusts the Heart, 1972; The Lucky Alphonse, 1982; Under a Monsoon Cloud, 1986; Dead on Time, 1989; The Iciest Sin, 1990; The Man Who (editor), 1992; The Rich Detective, 1993; Doing Wrong, 1994; The Good Detective, 1995; The Bad Detective, 1996; Asking Questions, 1996; The Soft Detective, 1997; Bribery, Corruption Also, 1999; Jack the Lady Killer, 1999; The Hard Detective, 2000; Breaking and Entering, 2000; A Detective in Love, 2001; The Dreaming Detective, 2003; Detective at Death's Door, 2004. Contributions to: Crime books reviews, The Times, 1967-83. Honours: Gold Dagger Awards, 1964, 1980, Diamond Dagger Award, 1996, Crime Writers Association. Memberships: Crime Writers Association, chairman, 1970-71; Detection Club, president, 1986-2001; Royal Society of Literature, fellow; Society of Authors, chairman, 1982-84. Address: 35 Northumberland Place, London W2 5AS, England.

KEATING Paul John, b. 18 January 1944. Australian Politician. m. Anna Johanna Maria Van Iersel, 1975, 1 son, 3 daughters. Education: De La Salle College, Bankstown, New South Wales. Appointments: Research Officer, Federal Municipal & Shire Council Employees Union of Australia, 1967; MP for Blaxland, 1969-96; Minister for Northern Australia, 1975; Shadow Minister for Agriculture, 1976, for Minerals & Energy, 1976-80, for Resources & Energy, 1980-83; Shadow Treasurer, 1983; Federal Treasurer of Australia, 1983-91; Deputy Prime Minister, 1990-91; Prime Minister of Australia, 1991-96. Publication: Engagement: Australia Faces the Asia Pacific, 2000. Memberships: Chairman, Australian Institute of Music, 1999-; Board of Architects of New South Wales, 2000-. Address: GPO Box 2598, Sydney, NSW 2001, Australia.

KEATON Diane, b. 5 January 1946, CA, USA. Education: Student at Neighbourhood Playhouse, New York. Career: Theatre in New York includes: Hair, 1968; The Primary English Class, 1976; Films include: Lovers and Other Strangers, 1970; The Godfather, 1972; Sleeper, 1973; Annie Hall, 1977; Manhattan, 1979; Shoot the Moon, 1982; Crimes of the Heart, 1986; Baby Boom, 1988; The Godfather III, 1991; Manhattan Murder Mystery, 1993; Father of Bride II, 1995; Marvins's Room, 1996; The First Wives Club, 1996; The Only Thrill, 1997; Hanging Up (also director), 1999; The Other Sister, 1999; Town and Country, 1999; Sister Mary Explains It All, 2001; Director: Heaven, 1987; Wildflower, 1991; Unsung Heroes, 1995. Publications: Reservations, Still Life, editor. Address: c/o John Burnham, William Morris Agency, 151 El Camino, Beverly Hills, CA 90212, USA.

KEATON Michael, b. 9 September 1951, Pittsburgh, USA. Actor. m. Caroline MacWilliams, divorced, 1 son. Education: Kent State University. Appointments: With Comedy Group, Second City, Los Angeles; TV appearances include: All in the Family; Maude; Mary

Tyler Moore Show; Working Stiffs; Report to Murphy; Roosevelt and Truman (TV film); Body Shots (producer), 1999. Creative Works: Films: Night Shift, 1982; Mr Mom, 1983; Johnny Dangerously, 1984; Touch and Go, 1987; Gung Ho, 1987; Beetlejuice, 1988; Clean and Sober, 1988; The Dream Team, 1989; Batman, 1989; Much Ado About Nothing, 1992; My Life, The Paper, 1994; Speechless, 1994; Multiplicity, Jackie Brown, 1997; Desperate Measures, 1998; Jack Frost, 1998; A Shot at Glory, 2000; Quicksand, 2001; First Daughter, 2004. Address: c/o ICM Management, 8942 Wilshire Boulevard, Beverly Hills, CA 90211, USA.

KEATS Reynold Gilbert, b. 15 February 1918, Pt Pirie, South Australia, Australia. Emeritus Professor of Mathematics. m. Verna Joy, 2 daughters. Education: Diploma in Accountancy, 1939; BSc, 1948, PhD, 1966, University of Adelaide. Appointments: Clerk, Savings Bank of South Australia, 1934-40; Private to Lieutenant, 2/48th Battalion, Australian Imperial Forces, 1940-45; Visiting Research Scientist, Royal Aircraft Establishment, Farnborough, England, 1948-51; Scientific Officer, Australian Government Department of Supply, Melbourne, Victoria, 1951, 1952; Senior Scientific Officer, 1952-57, Principal Scientific Officer, 1957-61, Australian Government Department of Supply, Weapons Research Establishment, Salisbury, South Australia; Senior Lecturer, University of Adelaide, South Australia, 1961-67; Professor of Mathematics, 1968-83, Dean, Faculty of Mathematics, 1971-76, 1980-83, Member of Council, 1977, 1978, Deputy Chairman of Senate, 1977, 1978, Emeritus Professor, 1983-, Honorary Professor, 1984-88, University of Newcastle, New South Wales. Honours: Fellow, Australian Society of Certified Practising Accountants, 1952; Fellow, Institute of Mathematics and its Applications, 1973; Honorary DMath, University of Waterloo, Ontario, Canada, 1979; Chartered Mathematician, Institute of Mathematics and its Applications, 1993; Fellow, Australian Mathematical Society, 1995; Fellow, Australian Computer Society, 1997. Membership: The Legacy Club of Newcastle. Address: 39 Woodward St, Merewether, NSW 2291, Australia.

KEAY John (Stanley Melville), b. 18 September 1941, Devon, England. Author. Education: BA, Magdalen College, Oxford, 1963. Publications: Into India, 1973; When Men and Mountains Meet, 1977; The Gilgit Game, 1979; India Discovered, 1981; Eccentric Travellers, 1982; Highland Drove, 1984; Explorers Extraordinary, 1985; The Royal Geographical Society's History of World Exploration, 1991; The Honourable Company, 1991; Collins Encyclopaedia of Scotland, 1994; Indonesia: From Sabang to Meranke, 1995; The Explorers of the Western Himalayas, 1996; Last Post, 1997; India: A History, 2000; The Great Arc, 2000; Sowing the Wind, 2003. Address: Succoth, Dalmally, Argyll, Scotland.

KEEFFE Barrie (Colin), b. 31 October 1945, London, England. Playwright. m. (1) Dee Truman, 1969, divorced 1979, (2) Verity Bargate, 1981, deceased 1981, 2 stepsons, (3) Julia Lindsay, 1983, divorced 1993. Appointments: Writer; Actor; Director; Journalist; Dramatist-in-Residence, Shaw Theatre, London, 1977, Royal Shakespeare Company, 1978; Associate Writer, Theatre Royal Stratford East, London, 1986-91; Board of Directors, Soho Poly Theatre, 1976-81; Associate Director, Soho Poly Theatre, 1989-; Board of Directors, Theatre Royal, Stratford East, 1981-89; Ambassador, United Nations, 50th anniversary year, 1995. Publications: Plays: A Mad World, My Masters, 1977, revised version, 1984; Methuen, 1977; Gimme Shelter, 1977; Barbarians, 1977; Frozen Assets, 1978, revised version, 1987; Sus, 1979; Heaven Scent, 1979; Bastard Angel, 1980; Black Lear, 1980; She's So Modern, 1980; Chorus Girls, 1981; A Gentle Spirit (with Jules Croiset), 1981; The Long Good Friday (screenplay), 1984; Better

Times, 1985; King of England, 1986; My Girl, 1989; Not Fade Away, 1990; Wild Justice, 1990; I Only Want to Be With You, 1997; Barrie Keeffe Plays, Volume 1, 2001; Shadows on the Sun, 2001; Novels: Gadabout, 1969; No Excuses, 1983; Journalism: Numerous articles contributed to national newspapers, including Sunday Times; The Independent; The Guardian; Evening Standard. As Director: The Gary Oldman Fan Club, 1998. Radio Plays: Good Old Uncle Jack, 1975; Pigeon Skyline, 1975; Self-Portrait, 1977; Paradise, 1990; On the Eve of the Millennium, 1999; Tales, 2000; Feng Shui and Me, 2000; The Five of Us, 2002. Television Plays: Gotcha, 1977; Champions, 1978; Hanging Around, 1978; Waterloo Sunset, 1979; No Excuses Series, 1983; King, 1984; Honours: French Critics Prix Revelation, 1978; Giles Cooper Award, Best Radio Plays, 1978; Edgar Allan Poe Award, Mystery Writers of America, 1982; Ambassador for United Nations 50th Anniversary, 1995. Address: 110 Annandale Road, London SE10 0JZ, England.

KEEGAN John (Desmond Patrick) (Sir), b. 15 May 1934, London, England. Editor; Writer; Defence Correspondent. m. Susanne Everett, 1960, 2 sons, 2 daughters. Education: BA, 1957, MA, 1962, Balliol College, Oxford. Appointments: Senior Lecturer in Military History, Royal Military Academy, Sandhurst, 1960-86; Fellow, Princeton University, 1984; Defence Editor, Daily Telegraph, 1986-; Delmas Distinguished Professor of History, Vassar College, 1997. Publications: The Face of Battle, 1976; Who's Who in Miltary History (co-author), 1976; World Armies (editor), 1979, new edition, 1982; Six Armies in Normandy, 1982; Zones of Conflict (co-author), 1986; The Mask of Command, 1987; The Price of Admiralty, 1988, reissued as Battle at Sea, 1993; The Times Atlas of the Second World War, 1989; Churchill's Generals (editor), 1991; A History of Warfare, 1993; Warpaths: Travels of a Military Historian in North America, 1995; War and Our World: The Reith Lectures, 1998; The Penguin Book of the War: great miltary writings (editor), 1999. Honours: Officer of the Order of the British Empire, 1991; Duff Cooper Prize, 1994; Honorary Doctor of Law, University of New Brunswick, 1997; Honorary Doctor of Literature, Queen's University, Belfast, 2000; Knighted, 2000; Honorary Doctor of Letters, University of Bath, 2001. Address: The Manor House, Kilmington, near Warminster, Wilts BA12 6RD, England.

KEEN Richard, b. 29 March 1954, Rustington, Sussex, England. Queen's Counsel. m. Jane Carolyn Anderson, 1 son, 1 daughter. Education: Beckman Scholar, University of Edinburgh. Appointments: Admitted to Faculty of Advocates (Scottish Bar), 1980; Counsel to DTI in Scotland, 1986-93; Queen's Counsel, 1993-; Chairman, Appeal Committee, Institute of Chartered Accountants Scotland (ICAS), 1996-. Address: The Castle, Elie, Fife KY9 1DN, Scotland. E-mail: rskeenqc@compuserve.com

KEHINDE Elijah Oladunni, b. 13 November 1953, Ogbomoso, Nigeria. Professor of Surgery. m. Funmilola, 3 daughters. Education: MBBS, University of Ibadan Medical School, Nigeria, 1974-79; Diploma in Urology (London), 1987; Fellow, Medical College of Surgeons of Nigeria, 1990, Fellow, Royal College of Surgeons, England, 1990; MD, University of Leicester, UK (by thesis), 1998. Appointments: House Officer, Senior House Officer, Nigeria, 1979-83; Registrar in Surgery, 1983-84, Senior Registrar in Urology, 1984-86, University College Hospital, Ibadan, 1983-86; Registrar (Surgery/Urology), hospitals in England, 1987-88; Senior House Officer (General Surgery), Harrogate District Hospital, UK, 1988-89; Senior House Officer (Renal Transplant/ Urology), Royal Free Hospital, London, 1989; Registrar (Surgery/ Urology), Edith Cavell Hospital, Peterborough, 1989-90; Research Fellow/Registrar, Renal Transplant Surgery/Urology, Leicester General Hospital, UK, 1990-94; Consultant Urologist, West Dorset General Hospital, UK, 1994; Assistant Professor, Head of

Urological Surgery, Consultant Urological/Transplant Surgeon, Sultan Qaboos University, Muscat, Sultanate of Oman, 1994-98; Assistant Professor of Urological Surgery, Kuwait University, Consultant Urological Surgeon, 1998-2003, Associate Professor, 2003-, Mubarak Al Kabeer University Teaching Hospital, Jabriya, Kuwait. Publications: 3 theses; 4 chapters in books; Numerous papers in professional journals. Listed in: Biographical Publications. Memberships include: Medical Protection Society (UK); British Medical Association; British Association of Urological Surgeons; British Transplantation Society; American Urological Association. Address: Department of Surgery, Faculty of Medicine, Kuwait University, PO Box 24923, Safat 13110, Kuwait.

KEIGER John Frederick Victor, b. 7 December 1952, Wembley, England. University Professor. Education: Institut d'etudes Politiques d'Aix-en Provence, University of Aix Marseille III, France, 1971-74; PhD, University of Cambridge, 1975-78. Appointments: Professor, Salford University, Manchester; Director, The European Studies Research Institute, Salford University. Publications: France and the Origins of the First World War; Europe 1848-1914 (19 volumes in British Documents on Foreign Affairs, Reports and Papers from the Foreign Office Confidential Print), 1988-92; Raymond Poincaré, 1997; France and the World Since 1870, 2001. Contributions to: Times Higher Education Supplement; History; International History Review. Honour: Fellow, Royal Historical Society, UK. Address: European Studies Research Institute, Salford University, Manchester M5 4WT, England.

KEIGHTLEY Richard Charles, b. 2 July 1933, Aldershot, England. Army Major General. m. Caroline Rosemary Butler, 3 daughters. Education: Royal Military Academy Sandhurst, 1951-53; Army Staff College, 1963; National Defence College, 1971-72; Royal College of Defence Studies, 1980. Appointments: Various Regimental and Staff appointments, 1953-70; Commander, 5th Royal Inniskilling Dragoon Guards, 1972-75; Colonel GS, 1st Division, 1977; Commander 33 Armoured Brigade, 1978-79; Brigadier General Staff, UK Land Forces, 1981; GOC Western District, 1982-83; Commandant, Royal Military Academy Sandhurst, 1983-87; Chairman, Dorset Healthcare NHS Trust, 1995-97; Chairman, Dorset Health Authority, 1988-95, 1998-2001; Chairman, Southampton University Hospitals NHS Trust, 2002-. Honour: CB, 1987. Memberships: President, Dorset County Royal British Legion; President, Dorset Relate; Member, St John Council for Dorset. Address: Kennels Farmhouse, Tarrant Gunville, Dorset DT 11 8JQ, England.

KEILLOR Elaine, b. 2 September 1939, London, Canada. Ethnomusicologist; Pianist. m. Vernon McCaw. Education: ARCT, Royal Conservatory of Music, piano, youngest ever awarded, 1951; BA, 1970, MA, 1971, PhD, 1976, University of Toronto. Appointments: Numerous appearances as pianist in recital, chamber ensembles and with orchestra; Lecturer, York University, 1975-76; Instructor, Queen's University, 1976-77; Assistant Professor, Carleton University, 1977-82; Associate Professor, 1982-95; Visiting Professor, McMaster University, 1984; Professor, Carleton University, 1995-. Publications: Piano Music I, Ottawa, 1983; Piano Music II, Ottawa, 1986; Music for Orchestra II, Ottawa, 1994; John Weinzweig and His Music, 1994; Music for Orchestra III, Ottawa, 1995; Pianist on 10 CDs, 1993-2002. Honours: Chappell Award (for outstanding young pianist in Commonwealth), 1958; Merit Award, Carleton University, 1981; Canadian Women's Mentor Award, Arts and Culture category inaugural recipient, 1999; The Helmut Kallmann Prize for Distinguished Service relating to music libraries and archives, 2004. Memberships: Association for Canadian Studies; Society for Ethnomusicology; International Alliance for Women in Music; Society for American Music;

Canadian University Music Society. Address: SSAC: Music, Carleton University, 1125 Colonel By Drive, Ottawa, ON K1S 5B6, Canada.

KEILLOR Garrison, (born Gary Edward Keillor), b. 7 August 1942, Anoka, Minnesota, USA. Writer; Radio Host. Education: BA, University of Minnesota, 1966. Appointments: Creator-Host, national public radio programmes, A Prairie Home Companion and American Radio Company. Publications: Happy to Be Here, 1982; Lake Wobegon Days, 1985; Leaving Home, 1987; We Are Still Married: Stories and Letters, 1989; WLT: A Radio Romance, 1991; The Book of Guys, 1993; Wobegon Boy, 1997; Lake Wobegon Summer 1956, 2001. Children's Books: Cat, You Better Come Home, 1995; The Old Man Who Loved Cheese, 1996; Sandy Bottom Orchestra, 1997; ME by Jimmy (Big Boy) Valente as Told to Garrison Keillor, 1999. Contributions to: Newspapers and magazines. Honours: George Foster Peabody Award, 1980; Grammy Award, 1987; Ace Award, 1988; Best Music and Entertainment Host Awards, 1988, 1989; American Academy and Institute of Arts and Letters Medal, 1990; Music Broadcast Communications Radio Hall of Fame, 1994; National Humanities Medal, 1999. Address: c/o Minnesota Public Radio, 45 East 7th Street, St Paul, MN 55101, USA.

KEINÄNEN Matti Tapio, b. 1 January 1953, Kuopio, Finland. Docent. m. Kristina, 2 sons, 1 daughter. Education: Licentiate of Medicine, 1977; Doctor of Medicine and Surgery, 1981; Specialist in Psychiatry, 1985; Psychoanalytic Psychotherapy Training, 1986; Specialist-level Psychotherapy Training, 1992; Advanced Specialist-level Individual Psychotherapy Training, 1997; Docent in Psychiatry, Turku University, 2002; Family Therapy Training, Finnish Mental Health Society, 1987; Licentiate Psychotherapist, 1995; Licentiate Advanced Specialist-level Individual Psychotherapist, 1998, National Authority for Medicolegal Affairs; Supervising Member, Finnish Balint-Group Organisation, 1999; Docent in Clinical Psychology, Jyväskylä University, 2000. Appointments: Psychiatrist, Finnish Student Health Service, Turku; Docent in Psychiatry, Turku University; Docent in Clinical Psychology, Jyväskylä University. Publications: Articles on biological basic study of psychiatry, family research and symbolic function research in individual psychoanalytic psychotherapy. Memberships: Finnish Medical Association; Finnish Psychiatric Association; International Semiotic Association; Finnish Psychodynamic Psychotherapy Association; Finnish Adolescent Psychiatry Association; Finnish Balint-Group Association. Address: Finnish Student Health Service, Kirkkotie 13, FIN-20540 Turku, Finland.

KEIR James Dewar, b. 30 November 1921, Edinburgh, Scotland. Retired Barrister. m. Jean Mary Orr, 2 sons, 2 daughters. Education: MA, Christ Church, Oxford, 1948; Inner Temple, 1949-50; Yarborough-Anderson Scholar, Inner Temple, 1950. Appointments: Legal Adviser, 1954-66, Secretary, 1966-73, United Africa Co Ltd; Deputy Head, Legal Services, Unilever Ltd, 1973-76; Joint Secretary, Unilever plc and Unilever NV, 1976-84; Chairman, 1969-72, President, 1980-82, Bar Association Commerce, Finance and Industry; Member, Monopolies and Mergers Commission, 1987-92; Director, Open University Educational Enterprises, 1983-88; Chairman, Pharmacists Review Panel, 1986-97; Chairman, Professional Committee, Royal College of Speech and Language Therapists, 1993-2000. Honour: Queen's Counsel, 1980. Membership: Caledonian Club. Address: 15 Clay's Close, East Grinstead, West Sussex RH 19 4DJ, England. E-mail: jamesdewarkeir@aol.com

KEITEL Harvey, b. 13 May 1939, USA. Actor. m. Lorraine Bracco, divorced, 1 daughter. Education: Actors Studio. Appointments: US Marines. Creative Works: Stage appearances:

Dictionary of International Biography

Death of a Salesman, Hurlyburly; Films: Mean Streets; Alice Doesn't Live Here Anymore; That's the Way of the World; Taxi Driver; Mother Jugs and Speed Buffalo Bill and the Indians; Welcome to LA; The Duelists; Fingers; Blue Collar; Eagle's Wing; Deathwatch; Saturn 3; Bad Timing; The Border; Exposed; La Nuit de Varennes; Corrupt; Falling in Love; Knight of the Dragon Camorra; Off Beat; Wise Guys; The Men's Club; The Investigation; The Pick-up Artist; The January Man; The Last Temptation of Christ; The Two Jakes; Two Evil Eyes (The Black Cat); Thelma & Louise; Tipperary; Bugsy; Reservoir Dogs; Bad Lieutenant; Mean Streets; The Assassin; The Young Americans; The Piano; Snake Eyes; Rising Sun; Monkey Trouble; Clockers; Dangerous Game; Pulp Fiction; Smoke; Imaginary Crimes; Ulyssees' Gaze, 1995; Blue in the Face, 1995; City of Industry; Cop Land, 1996; Head Above Water; Somebody to Love, 1996; Simpatico, 1999; Little Nicky, 2000; U-571, 2000; Holy Smoke, 2000. Address: c/ o William Morris Agency, 151 South El Camino Drive, Beverly Hills, CA 90212, USA.

KEITH Penelope Anne Constance, b. 2 April 1940, Sutton, Surrey, England. Actress. m. Rodney Timson, 1978. Education: Webber Douglas School, London. Creative Works: Stage appearances include: Suddenly at Home, 1971; The Norman Conquests, 1974; Donkey's Years, 1976; The Apple Cart, 1977; The Millionairess, 1978; Moving, 1980; Hobson's Choice, 1982; Captain Brassbound's Conversation, 1982; Hay Fever, 1983; The Dragon's Tail, 1985; Miranda, 1987; The Deep Blue Sea, 1988; Dear Charles, 1990; The Merry Wives of Windsor, 1990; The Importance of Being Ernest, 1991; On Approval, 1992; Relatively Speaking, 1992; Glyn and It, 1994; Monsieur Amilcar, 1995; Mrs Warren's Profession, 1997; Good Grief, 1998; Star Quality, 2001; Film appearances include: Rentadick; Take a Girl Like You; Every Home Should Have One; Sherlock Holmes; The Priest of Love; TV appearances include: The Good Life (Good Neighbors in USA), 1974-77; Private Lives, 1976; The Norman Conquests, 1977; To the Manor Born, 1979-81; On Approval, 1980; Spider's Web; Sweet Sixteen; Waters of the Moon; Hay Fever; Moving; Executive Stress; What's My Line?, 1988; Growing Places; No Job for a Lady, 1990; Law and Disorder, 1994; Next of Kin; Coming Home, 1999. Honours include: Best Light Entertainment Performance, British Academy of Film & TV Arts, 1976; Best Actress, 1977; Show Business Personality, Variety Club of Great Britain, 1976; BBC TV Personality, 1979; Comedy Performance of the Year, Society of West End Theatre, 1976; Female TV Personality; TV Times Awards, 1976-78; BBC TV Personality of the Year, 1978-79; TV Female Personality, Daily Express, 1979-82. Address: London Management, 2-4 Noel Street, London W1V 3RB, England.

KELEMEN József-Imre, b. 9 November 1934, Reghin, Mures county, Romania. Physician; Pathologist. m. Melinda Eröss, 2 daughters. Education: University of Medicine, 1958; Specialisation in General Pathology, 1965; Postgraduate Specialisation in human and experimental neuropathology, 1969, Budapest, Pécs, Hungary; Humboldt Research Fellowships, Max Planck Institute of Psychiatry, 1971, Berlin Institute of Neuropathology, 1991-92. Appointments: General Medical Practice, 1958-62; Senior Research Fellow, Research Station of Romanian Academy of Sciences, Teacher, Histology and Pathology, Medical University Tirgu-Mures, 1962-75; Head, Department of Pathology, Harghita County State Hospital, Miercurea Ciuc, Romania, 1975-. Publications: Over 140 scientific works in neurohistology, general pathology, neuropathology; Chapter in Medical Researches; First description of intraorganic vegetative microganglion in a rabbit's kidney; 11 Methods for Experimental and Human Neurohistology. Honours: Medal for Eminent Work, 1969; 10 Certificates of Innovation in Neurohistology, Romanian Academy of Sciences,

1963-71; Medal of Sanitar Merit, 1972. Memberships: International Society of Neuropathology; Hungarian Society of Neuropathology; International Brain Research Organization; Active Member, New York Academy of Sciences, 1998-; Active Member, Commun Corporation, Hungarian Academy of Sciences, 2000. Address: Head, Department of Pathology, Hargita County Hospital, str Tudor Vladimirescu 50, RO 530180, Miercurea Ciuc, Romania.

KELLAS John Gordon, b. 13 March 1925, Lismore, New South Wales, Australia. Education: Matriculation, 1943; PhC, Queensland, 1948. Career: Accountancy firm, 1943-44 (15 months); Pharmacy Apprenticeship, Brisbane, 1944-47; Dispensed in approximately 120 different pharmacies and hospitals, 1944-62: Queensland: Brisbane, Townsville, Surfer's Paradise, Burleigh Heads, Gin Gin, Mt Morgan, Sarina, Ingham, Ravenshoe, Ayr, Boonah, Charleville, Gladstone, Mareeba, Gordonvale, Murgon, Monto, Warwick, Cairns, Toowoomba, Rockhampton, Bundaberg, Mackay Maryborough; Queensland Public Hospitals: Brisbane General, Kingaroy, Maryborough, Bundaberg, Rockhampton, Mackay; New South Wales: Sydney, Newcastle, Lismore, Grafton Hospital, Casino, Kyogle, Murwillumbah, Maitland and Maitland Hospital at night, Singleton, Wee Waa, Gulgong, Narrandera, Jerilderie, Laurieton, Bowraville, Broken Hill, Bonalbo, The Entrance, Wyong, North Shore Hospital, Albury; Victoria: Melbourne, Barham, Stawell, Ararat, Jeparit, Bendigo, Geelong (Hospital), Repat Heidelberg Hospital, Dandenong, Cowes, Bacchus Marsh, Moe, Beaufort, Warragul, South Melbourne, Preston, Prahran, Reservoir, Essenden Nidre, Black Rock, Clayton, Murrumbeena, Tecoma, Footscray, Springvale, Richmond, Highton, West Ivanhoe, South and West Dandenong, Mt Eliza, Euroa; South Australia: Adelaide, Hamley Bridge, Port Pirie, Cleve, Tailem Bend, Burra, Yankalilla, Penola, Maitland, Nurioopta, Jamestown, Peterborough, Crystal Brook; Northern Territory: Darwin Hospital; Western Australia: Perth; Retired, present registrations: Queensland and New South Wales; Farmer and Grazier from 1963 to retirement. Honours: Honours and awrds, American Biographical Institute, International Biographical Centre, UK. Membership: World Nations Congress 2003, ABI, USA. Address: 260 Ainsworth Road, Leeville, Via Casino, NSW 2470, Australia.

KELLER Evelyn Fox, b. 20 March 1936, New York, New York, USA. Professor of History and Philosophy of Science; Writer. 1 son, 1 daughter. Education: BA, Brandeis University, 1957; MA, Radcliffe College, 1959; PhD, Harvard University, 1963. Appointments: Professor of Mathematics and Humanities, Northeastern University, 1982-88; Senior Fellow, Cornell University, 1987; Member, Institute for Advanced Study, Princeton, New Jersey, 1987-88; Professor, University of California at Berkeley, 1988-92; Professor of History and Philosophy of Science, Massachusetts Institute of Technology, 1992-. Publications: A Feeling for the Organism: The Life and Work of Barbara McClintock, 1983, 2nd edition, 1993; Reflections on Gender and Science, 1985, new edition, 1995; Women, Science and the Body (editor with Mary Jacobus and Sally Shuttleworth), 1989; Conflicts in Feminism (editor with Marianne Hirsch), 1990; Keywords in Evolutionary Biology (editor with Elisabeth Lloyd), 1992; Secrets of Life, Secrets of Death: Essays on Language, Gender, and Science, 1992; Refiguring Life: Metaphors of Twentieth Century Biology, 1995; Feminism and Science (editor with Helen Longino), 1996; The Century of the Gene, 2000; Making Sense of Life, 2002. Contributions to: Scholarly journals. Honours: Distinguished Publication Award, Association for Women in Psychology, 1986; Alumni Achievement Award, Brandeis University, 1991; Honorary Doctorates, Holyoke College, 1991, University of Amsterdam, 1995, Simmons College, 1995, Rensselaer Polytechnic Institute, 1995, Technical University of Lulea, Sweden, 1996; John D and

Catharine T MacArthur Foundation Fellowship, 1992-97; Numerous honorary degrees. Address: c/o Program in Science, Technology and Society, Massachusetts Institute of Technology, 77 Massachusetts Avenue, Cambridge, MA 02139, USA.

KELLMAN Steven G, b. 15 November 1947, Brooklyn, New York, USA. Professor; Author. Education: BA, State University of New York, Binghamton, 1967; MA, 1969, PhD, 1972, University of California, Berkeley. Appointments: Assistant Professor, Bemidji State College, 1972-73; Lecturer, Tel-Aviv University, 1973-75; Visiting Lecturer, University of California, Irvine, 1975-76; Assistant Professor, 1976, Associate Professor, 1980-85, Professor, 1985-, Ashbel Smith Professor, Comparative Literature, 1995-2000, University of Texas, San Antonio; Visiting Associate Professor, University of California, Berkeley, 1982; President, Board of Directors, Gemini Ink Literary Centre, 1998-2002; Co-editor, Magill's Literary Annual, 2000-. Publications include: The Self-Begetting Novel, 1980; Loving Reading: Erotics of the Text, 1985; The Plague: Fiction and Resistance, 1993; Perspectives on Raging Bull, editor, 1994; Into the Tunnel: Readings of Gass's Novel, co-editor, 1998; Leslie Fiedler and American Culture, co-editor, 1999; The Translingual Imagination, 2000; Torpid Smoke: The Stories of Vladimir Nabokov, co-editor, 2000; Masterplots II: American Fiction Series, co-editor, 2000; UnderWords: Perspectives on Don DeLillo's Underworld, co-editor, 2002; Switching Languages: Translingual Writers Reflect on Their Craft, editor, 2003; Contributions to magazines and journals. Honours: Fulbright Senior Lecturer, Tbilisi State University, 1980; H L Mencken Award, 1986; Fulbright-Hays Grant to China, 1995; NEH Summer Seminar, South Africa, 1996; John Sawyer Fellow, Longfellow Institute, Harvard, 1997; Fulbright Distinguished Chair, University of Sofia, 2000. Memberships: Board Director, National Book Critics Circle, 1996-2002; PEN American Center; Modern Language Association. Address: 302 Fawn Drive, San Antonio, TX 78231-1519, USA.

KELLY Anthony, b. 25 January 1929, Hillingdon, Middlesex, England. Consultant. Education: BSc, 1st class, Physics, University of Reading, 1949; PhD, Trinity College, Cambridge, 1953; ScD, University of Cambridge, 1968. Appointments: Research Associate, University of Illinois, 1953-55; ICI Fellow, University of Birmingham, 1955; Assistant Professor, Associate Professor, The Technological Institute, Northwestern University, Chicago, 1956-59; University Lecturer, University of Cambridge, 1959-67; Superintendent, 1967-69, Deputy Director, 1969-75, National Physical Laboratory, Middlesex; Seconded to ICI plc, 1973-75; Consultant to many international companies, 1973-; Vice Chancellor and Chief Executive, University of Surrey, 1975-94; Founder, Surrey Research Park, 1979; Director, Johnson Wax UK Ltd, 1981-96; Director, QUO-TEC Ltd, 1984-2000; Director, NPL Management Ltd, 1994-2001; Distinguished Research Fellow, Department of Materials Science and Metallurgy, University of Cambridge, 1994-. Publications: 200 papers in scientific and technical journals; Numerous books; Many lectures. Honours include: CBE, 1988; Gold Medal, American Society of Materials, 1991; Platinum Medal, Institute of Materials, 1992; Knight of St Gregory, 1992; Deputy of Lieutenant for the County of Surrey, 1993; DUniv, University of Surrey, 1994; Honorary Fellow, Institution of Structural Engineers, 1996; Hon DSc, University of Birmingham, 1997; Honorary Fellow, Institution of Civil Engineers, 1997; Acta Metallurgica Gold Medal, 2000; Honorary DEng, Hanyang University, Korea, 2001; Honorary Doctor of Science, University of Reading, 2002. Memberships: Institute of Metals; British Non-Ferrous Metals Research Association; Engineering Materials Requirements Board, Department of Trade and Industry; European Association of Composite Materials; Royal National Institute for the Deaf; Institute of Materials. Address: Churchill College, Cambridge, CB3 0DS, England. E-mail: ak209@cam.ac.uk

KELLY Patrick Joseph, b. 19 September 1941, Lackawanna, New York, USA, Neurosurgeon; Educator. m. Carol Huey, 2 sons, 1 daughter. Education: BS, University of Michigan, 1962; MD, SUNY Buffalo, 1966. Appointments: Intern, US Naval Hospital, Philadelphia, 1966-67; Lieutenant Commander, US Navy, 1968-70; Resident in Internal Medicine, Northwestern University, Chicago, 1970-72; From Assistant Professor to Associate Professor, University of Texas Medical School, Galveston, 1972-79; Associate Professor, SUNY Buffalo, 1979-84; Professor, Consultant, Mayo Medical School, Mayo Clinic, Rochester, Minnesota, 1984-93; Professor, Chairman, Neurosurgery Department, New York University Medical Center, 1993-; Consultant, Advisory Board Member, Jet Propulsion Laboratory, NASA, Pasadena, California, 1994. Publications: Tumor Stereotaxis (author), 1991; Computers in Stereotactic Neurosurgery (co-editor and contributor), 1992; Book chapters and over 260 articles in medical journals. Honours include: Citizen of the Year, Buffalo Evening News, 1982; Best Doctors in America: Good Housekeeping, 1993, Town & Country, 1992, American Health, 1996, Top 100, Irish American Magazine, 1996, 1999; Best Doctors in New York, New York magazine, 1999, 2000, 2001, 2002; Profiled America's Top Doctors and Top Doctors, New York Metropolitan Area 2000-2002, Castle Connolly Guide; Inducted Boys and Girls Clubs of America Hall of Fame, 2001. Memberships: Fellow, ACS; American Society for Stereotactic Neurosurgery; American Association of Neurological Surgeons, Van Wagenen Fellow, 1977; Academy of Neurological Surgery; Society of Neurological Surgeons; Société Neurochurgic de Lange Française. Address: New York University Medical Center, 530 1st Avenue, New York, NY 10016-6401. E-mail: kelly@brainscans.com

KELLY Tom, b. 22 May 1947, Jarrow, Tyne and Wear, England. College Lecturer; Poet. m. (1) Carol Kelly, 20 December 1969, deceased 1992, 1 daughter, (2) Linda Kelly, 1 September 1995. Education: BA, Honours. Appointment: Lecturer, Further Education College. Publications: The Gibbetting of William Jobling, 1972; Still With Me, 1986; John Donne in Jarrow, 1993; Their Lives, 1993; Riddle of Pain, 1995. Contributions to: Stand; Iron; Orbis; Rialto; Staple; Hybrid; Samphire; Working Titles; Purple Patch; Oasis; Sepia; First Time; Exile; Intoprint; Tees Valley Writer; Krax; Harry's Hand; Foolscap; Eavesdroppper; Here Now; Tourism; Reid Review; Iota; Pennine Platform; Poetry Nottingham; Westwords; Third Half; Overspill. Address: Thorneyholme, 11 Thorneyholme Terrace, Blaydon, Tyne and Wear NE21 4PS, England.

KELMAN James, b. 9 June 1946, Glasgow, Scotland. Author; Dramatist; Essayist. m. Marie Connors, 2 daughters. Publications: The Busconductor Hines, 1984; A Chancer, 1985; A Disaffection, 1989; How Late it Was, How Late, 1994; Translated Accounts, 2001; You Have to be Careful in the Land of the Free, 2004. Short Stories: An Old Pub Near the Angel, 1973; Short Tales from the Nightshift, 1978; Not Not While the Giro and Other Stories, 1983; Lean Tales, 1985; Greyhound for Breakfast, 1987; The Burn, 1991; Busted Scotch, 1997; The Good Times, 1998. Plays: The Busker, 1985; In the Night, 1988; Hardie and Baird, The Last, 1990; One, Two – Hey, 1994; The Art of the Big Bass Drum, Radio 3, 1998; Essays, Some Recent Attacks, 1991; And The Judges Said..., 2002; CD, Seven Stories, 1997. Screenplay: The Return, 1990. Honours: Cheltenham Prize, 1987; James Tait Black Memorial Prize, 1989; Writers Guild Award; Booker Prize, 1994. Address: c/o Rodgers, Coleridge and White Ltd, 20 Powis Mews, London W11 1JN, England.

KELSALL Malcolm Miles, b. 27 February 1938, London, England. Professor of English. m. Mary Emily Ives, 5 August 1961. Education: BA, Oxon, 1961; BLitt, Oxon, 1964; MA, Oxon, 1965. Appointments: Staff Reporter, The Guardian newspaper, 1961; Assistant Lecturer, Exeter University, 1963-64; Lecturer, Reading University, 1964-75; Professor, University of Wales, Cardiff, 1975-. Publications: Editor, Sarah Fielding, David Simple, 1969; Editor, Thomas Otway, Venice Preserved, 1969; Christopher Marlowe, 1981; Congreve: The Way of the World, 1981; Studying Drama, 1985; Byron's Politics, 1987; Editor, Encyclopedia of Literature and Criticism, 1990; The Great Good Place: The Country House and English Literature, 1992; Editor, J M Synge, The Playboy of the Western World, 1997; Editor, William Congreve, Love For Love, 1999; Jefferson and the Iconography of Romanticism, 1999; Literary Representations of the Irish Country House, 2003. Contributions to: Byron Journal; Essays in Criticism; Irish University Review; Theatre Research International; Review of English Studies; Studies in Romanticism. Honours: Elma Dangerfield Prize, 1991; British Academy Warton Lecturer, 1992. Address: School of English, Cardiff University, PO Box 94, Cardiff CF10 3XB, Wales.

KEMP Hubert Bond Stafford (Hugh), b. 25 March 1925, Cardiff, Wales. Orthopaedic Surgeon. m. Moyra Ann Margaret Odgers, 3 daughters. Education: BSc, University of South Wales, 1942; St Thomas Medical School, University of London; MRCS, 1947, LRCP, 1947, FRCS, 1970; FRCS Ed, 1960, MB BS, London, 1949, MS, London, 1969. Appointments: Second Assistant, 1961-64, First Assistant, 1964-65, Professorial University, Orthopaedics and Traumatology, Nuffield Orthopaedic Centre, University of Oxford; University Lecturer, Orthopaedics and Traumatology; Tutor, General Surgery, Oxford Medical School; Senior Lecturer, 1965-74; Consultant, Royal National Orthopaedic Hospital, Stanmore and London, 1965-92; Hunterian Professor, RCS, 1969; Visiting Professor, VII Congress, Society Latino America de Orthopaedica y Traumatologica, 1971; Honorary Senior Lecturer, 1974-92; University Teacher in Orthopaedics; Honorary Consultant, St Luke's Hospital for the Clergy, 1975-90; Consultant, The Middlesex Hospital, 1984-90; Honorary Consultant, Royal National Orthopaedic Hospital Trust, 1992-. Publications: Orthopaedic Diagnosis, 1984; Chapters in textbooks. Honours: Robert Jones Gold Medal and British Orthopaedic Association Prize, 1964, 1969. Memberships: British Orthopaedic Association; British Orthopaedic Research Society; International Skeletal Society; British Orthopaedic Oncological Society; British Hip Society; International Muculo-Skeletal Oncological Society; British Medical Association; Royal Society of Medicine. Address: Red Lodge, 55 Loom Lane, Radlett, Hertfordshire WD7 8NX, England.

KEMP Terence James, b. 26 June 1938, Watford, Hertfordshire, England. Professor. m. Sheila Therese, 1 son, 2 daughters. Education: BA, 1961, MA, DPhil, 1963, Jesus College, Oxford. Appointments: DSIR Research Fellow, Cookridge Laboratory, University of Leeds, 1962; Assistant Lecturer, 1966-66, Lecturer, 1966-70, Senior Lecturer in Chemistry, 1970-74, Reader in Chemistry, 1974-80, Professor of Chemistry, 1980-, Pro-Vice Chancellor, 1983-89, University of Warwick. Publications: Introductory Photochemistry, 1971; Dictionary of Physical Chemistry, 1992; 230 original scientific articles. Honours: Meldola Medal, Royal Institute of Chemistry, 1967; Order of Merit, Polish People's Republic, 1978; Nagroda, 2nd prize, Marie Curie-Slodowska Society for Radiation Research, 1992. Address: Department of Chemistry, University of Warwick, Coventry CV4 7AL, England. E-mail: t.j.kemp@warwick.ac.uk

KENDALL Bridget, b. 27 April 1956, Oxford, England. Journalist. Education: Lady Margaret Hall, Oxford, 1974-78; Harvard, USA, 1978-80; St Antony's College, Oxford, 1980-83; Voronegh State University, 1976-77; Moscow State University, 1981-82. Appointments: Trainee, BBC World Service, 1983; Presenter and Producer, Newsnight, BBC2, 1983-84; Producer, Reporter, Editor, BBC World Service Radio, 1984-89; BBC Moscow Correspondent, 1989-93; BBC Washington Correspondent, 1994-98; BBC Diplomatic Correspondent, 1998-. Publications: Co-author, David the Invincible, annotated translation (classical Armenian philosophy), 1980; Kosovo and After: The future of spin in the digital age (Jubilee Lecture for St Antony's College, Oxford), 2000; Co-author, The Day that Shook the World (BBC correspondents on September 11th 2001), 2001. Honours: British Council Scholar to USSR, 1976-77, 1981-82; Harkness Fellow, USA, 1978-80; Sony Award, Reporter of the Year (Bronze Award), 1992; James Cameron Award for distinguished journalism, 1992; Voice of the Listener and Viewer Award, 1993; MBE, 1994; Honorary Doctorate, University of Central England, Birmingham, 1999; Honorary Doctorate in Law, St Andrew's University, 2001; Honorary Doctorate in Law, Exeter University, 2002. Memberships: Advisory Board, Russian and Eurasian Programme at Chatham House, Royal Institute of International Affairs, 2000-; Member of Council, Royal United Services Institute, 2001-; Member of Advisory Council, European Research Institute, University of Birmingham. Address: BBC Television Centre, Wood Lane, London W12, England.

KENDALL Roy O, b. 21 May 1912, Ingalls, Gray County, Kansas, USA. Retired US Federal Civil Service Employee. m. Conway (Connie) Alford Montgomery, deceased 1991, 2 sons, 1 deceased. Education: Louisiana State University, 1936-37; Trinity University, 1951-56. Appointments: Pre-retirement: Administrative, dealing with acquisitions, storage and distribution of military supplies and equipment; Pre and post retirement: Basic biological research of lepidoptera; Several honorary positions, Research Associate, Welder Wildlife Foundation, Florida State College of Arthropods; Technical Consultant, Texas Parks and Wildlife Department. Publications: Lepidopterists' Society Commemorative Volume, xvii, 1945-73; 40 articles on lepidoptera life histories in professional journals. Honours: John Abbot Award, 1984; Floyd E Potter Jr Award, 1989; Honorary Leadership Recognition, Bronze Portrait Plaque on entrance wall of Entomology building, Texas A and M University, 1994; 2 books dedicated to him by the authors: A Field Guide to Butterflies of Texas by Raymond W Neck, 1996 and Butterflies of West Texas Parks and Preserves by Roland H Wauer, 2002; 9 Lepidoptera patronyms described honouring him and his late wife. Memberships: Lepidopterists' Society (international); Southern Lepidopterists' Society; Journal of Research on Lepidoptera. Address: 5598 Mt McKinley Drive NE, San Antonio, TX 78251, USA.

KENNEDY Alexander, b. 20 April 1933, Manchester, England. Retired Consultant Histopathologist. Education: MB ChB, Liverpool, 1956; MD, Liverpool, 1964; MRCPath, 1967; FRCPath, 1985. Appointments: House Office, Stanley and Royal Liverpool Children's Hospitals, 1956-58; Short Service Commission, Royal Air Force Medical Branch, 1958-61; Pathologist, RAF Hospital, Wroughton, 1958-61; Lecturer, University of Liverpool, 1961-67; Visiting Assistant Professor, University of Chicago, 1968; Senior Lecturer, University of Sheffield, 1969-77; Consultant Histopatholgist, 1977-97, Retired, 1997-, Northern General Hospital, Sheffield. Publications: 4 books; Over 50 articles in professional journals; Abstracts, letters and other publications. Memberships: Pathological Society of Great Britain and Ireland; British Thoracic Society; British Division of

Dictionary of International Biography

the International Academy of Pathology; Trent Regional Thoracic Society; Sheffield Medico-Chirurgical Society. Address: 16 Brincliffe Gardens, Sheffield, S11 9BG, England. E-mail: sandy.kennedy@care4free.net

KENNEDY Alison Louise, b. 22 October 1965, Dundee, Scotland. Writer. Education: BA Hons, Theatre Studies and Drama, Warwick University, England. Appointments include: Community Arts Worker for Clydebank & District, 1988-89; Writer in Residence, Hamilton & East Kilbride Social Work Department, 1989-91; Writer in Residence for Project Ability, Arts & Special Needs, 1989-95; Book Reviewer for Scotsman, Glasgow Herald, BBC, STV, Telegraph, 1990-; Writer in Residence, Copenhagen University, 1995; Editor of New Writing Scotland, 1993-95; Booker Prize Judge, 1996. Publications: Night Geometry and the Garscadden Trains, 1991; Looking for the Possible Dance, 1993; Now That You're Back, 1994; So I Am Glad, 1995; Tea and Biscuits, 1996; Original Bliss, 1997; The Life and Death of Colonel Blimp, 1997; Everything You Need, 1999; On Bullfighting, 2000; Indelible Acts, 2002; Paradise, 2004. Film/Drama includes: Delicate, performance piece for Motionhouse dance company, 1995; Ghostdancing, BBC TV drama/documentary, writer and presenter, 1997; True, performance project for Fierce Productions and Tramway Theatre. Address: c/o Antony Harwood Ltd, 103 Walton Street, Oxford, OX2 3EB, England.

KENNEDY D James, b. 3 November 1930, Augusta, USA. Senior Minister. m. Anne Lewis, 1 daughter. Education: BA, University of Tampa, 1958; MDiv, cum laude, Columbia Theological Seminary, 1959; MTh, summa cum laude, Chicago Graduate School of Theology, 1969; DD, Trinity Evangelical Divinity School, 1969; PhD, New York University, 1979; DSac Lit, Christian Bible College, 1985; Litt D, California Graduate School of Theology, 1986; D Sac Theol, Southwest Baptist University, 1987; Doc Hum Let, Campbell University, 1992. Appointments: Senior Minister, Coral Ridge Presbyterian Church, 1959-; President, Evangelism Explosion International, 1962-; Founder, Westminster Academy, 1971-; Founder, WAFG-FM Radio Station, 1974-; President, Coral Ridge Ministries Media Inc, 1974-; Chancellor, Knox Theological Seminary, 1990-; Founder, D James Kennedy Center for Christian Statesmanship, 1995-; Founder, Center for Reclaiming America, 1996-; President, Creation Studies Institute, 2004-. Publications; 63 books including: Evangelism Explosion, 1970; Truths That Transform, 1974, 1996; Why I Believe, 1980, 1996; What if Jesus had Never Been Born?, 1994; New Every Morning, 1996; Skeptics Answered, 1997; What if the Bible had Never Been Written?, 1998; Led by the Carpenter, 1999; Today's Conflict, Tomorrow's Crisis, 2000; Solving Bible Mysteries, 2000; God's Absolute Best for You, 2001; Back to Basics, 2001; Why Was America Attacked?, 2001; What if America Were a Christian Nation Again?, 2003; Christ's Passion: The Proven and the Promise, 2003; What's Wrong with Same-Sex Marriage?, 2004; My Father's World, 2004. Honours: Books written about him: The Kennedy Explosion, by Russell Chandler, 1971, D James Kennedy: The Man and His Ministry, by Dr Herbert Lee Williams, 1990, 1999; George Washington Honor Medal Award, 1971,76,80; Clergyman of the Year, 1984; International Clergyman of the Year, 1986; Man of the Year, 1988; Philip Award, 1988; National John Calvin Award, 1989; DAR Founders Medal Award, 1998; 1000 Leaders of World Influence, 2000; International Man of the Year, 1999-2000; National Religious Broadcasters 2003 Television Program of the Year Award; National Religious Broadcasters 2004 Best Radio Teaching Program of The Year Award. Memberships: Numerous including: Council for National Policy; Institute of Contemporary Christianity; National Christian Heritage Foundation; Committee to Restore American Values; Evangelism Explosion International; Christian Educators

Association. Address: Coral Ridge Presbyterian Church, 5555 N Federal Highway, Ft Lauderdale, Florida 33308 3294, USA. Website: www.crpc.org

KENNEDY (George) Michael (Sinclair), b. 19 February 1926, Manchester, England. Music Critic; Author. m. (1) Eslyn Durdle, 16 May 1947, deceased 2 January 1999, (2) Joyce Bourne, 10 October 1999. Education: Berkhamsted School. Appointments: Staff, 1941-, Northern Music Critic, 1950-, Northern Editor, 1960-86, Joint Chief Music Critic, 1986-89, The Daily Telegraph; Music Critic, The Sunday Telegraph, 1989-. Publications: The Hallé Tradition: A Century of Music, 1960; The Works of Ralph Vaughan Williams, 1964, revised edition, 1980; Portrait of Elgar, 1968, 3rd edition, 1987; Elgar: Orchestral Music, 1969; Portrait of Manchester, 1970; A History of the Royal Manchester College of Music, 1971; Barbirolli: Conductor Laureate, 1971; Mahler, 1974, revised edition, 1990; The Autobiography of Charles Hallé, with Correspondence and Diaries (editor), 1976; Richard Strauss, 1976, revised edition, 1995; The Concise Oxford Dictionary of Music (editor), 1980, revised edition, 1995; Britten, 1981, revised edition, 1993; The Hallé 1858-1983, 1983; Strauss: Tone Poems, 1984; The Oxford Dictionary of Music (editor), 1985, 2nd edition, revised, 1994; Adrian Boult, 1987; Portrait of Walton, 1989; Music Enriches All: The First 21 Years of the Royal Northern College of Music, Manchester, 1994; Richard Strauss, Man, Musician, Enigma, 1999; The Life of Elgar, 2004. Contributions to: Newspapers and magazines. Honours: Fellow, Institute of Journalists, 1967; Honorary MA, Manchester, 1975; Officer of the Order of the British Empire, 1981; Fellow, Royal Northern College of Music, 1981; Commander of the Order of the British Empire, 1997; Companion, Royal Northern College of Music, 1999; Hon MusD, Manchester, 2003. Address: The Bungalow, 62 Edilom Road, Manchester M8 4HZ, England.

KENNEDY Iain Manning, b. 15 September 1942, Northampton, England. Company Director. m. Ingrid Annette, 2 daughters. Education: Pembroke College, Cambridge, 1961-64. Appointments: Joined staff, 1969, Production Director, 1976, Chief Executive, 1998, Chairman, 2001, Church and Co plc; Chairman, SATRA, 1989; Governor, University College, Northampton, 1998; Retired, 2001. Honours: OBE, 2002. Address: 3 Townsend Close, Hanging Houghton, Northampton, NN6 9HP, England. E-mail: 106252.351@compuserve.com

KENNEDY Jane Hope, b. 28 February 1953, Loughborough, England. Architect. m. John Maddison, 2 sons. Education: Dip Arch, Manchester Polytechnic; Registered Architect, RIBA. Appointments: British Waterways Board, 1978-80; Assistant, David Jeffcoate Architect, 1980-81; Self-employed, 1981-86; Norwich City Council Planning Department, 1986-88; Architect, 1988-, Partner, 1992-, Purcell Miller Tritton; Surveyor to the fabric of Ely Cathedral, 1994-. Memberships: Institute of Historic Building Conservation; Fellow, Royal Society of Arts; Architect Accredited in Building Conservation. Address: Purcell Miller Tritton, 46 St Mary's Street, Ely, Cambridgeshire CB7 4EY, England. E-mail: janekennedy@pmt.co.uk

KENNEDY Nigel, b. 28 December 1956, England. Violinist. Partner, Eve Westmore, 1 son. Education: Yehudi Menuhin School; Juilliard School of Performing Arts. Creative Works: Chosen by the BBC as the subject of a 5 year documentary on the development of a soloist following his debut with the Philharmonic Orchestra, 1977; Appeared with all the major British orchestras; Appearances at all the leading UK Festivals and in Europe at Stresa, Lucerne, Gstaad, Berlin & Lockenhaus; Debut at the Tanglewood Festival with the Boston Symphony under André Previn, 1985, at MN with Sir Neville Marriner, at Montreal with Charles Dutoit; Given

Dictionary of International Biography

concerts in the field of jazz with Stephane Grappelli at Carnegie Hall and Edinburgh, runs his own jazz group; Recordings include: Elgar Sonata with Peter Pettinger; Tchaikovsky; Sibelius; Vivaldi; Mendelssohn; Bruch; Walton Viola & Violin Concertos; Elgar Concerto with London Philharmonic Orchestra. Publication: Always Playing, 1991. Honours include: Best Classical Disc of the Year Award, London, 1985; Hon DLitt, Bath, 1991. Memberships include: Senior Vice President, Aston Villa FC, 1990-. Address: c/o Russells Solicitors, Regency House, 1-4 Warwick Street, London W1R 5WB, England.

KENNEDY P Lynn, b. 5 October 1963, Greeley, Colorado, USA. Alexander Regents Professor. m. Julie Ann Ritschard, 2 sons, 1 daughter. Education: Associate of Arts, Agriculture, Northeastern Junior College, Sterling, Colorado, 1984; BSc, with high distinction, Agricultural Economics, Colorado State University, Fort Collins, Colorado, 1987; MSc, Agricultural Economics, University of Oxford, England, 1988; PhD, Agricultural and Applied Economics, University of Minnesota, St Paul, Minnesota, 1994. Appointments: Research Assistant, University of Minnesota, 1990-94; Teaching Assistant, University of Minnesota, 1993; Visiting Assistant Professor, Humboldt University, 1995-97; Assistant Professor, 1994-99, Associate Professor, 1999-2003, Professor, 2003-, Department of Agricultural Economics and Agribusiness, Louisiana State University. Publications: Author and co-author: 3 books; 7 chapters or essays in books; 30 articles in refereed journals. Honours: Rotary Foundation Graduate Scholarship, University of Oxford; Teaching Merit Honor Roll, The Honor Society of Agriculture, 1996-2000; Alpha Lambda Delta Freshman Honor Society Award, 1999; Teaching Award of Merit, Gamma Sigma Delta, 2001; Joseph E Sedberry, Junior Foundation Award, 2001; Class Ten of the ESCOP/ACOP Leadership Development Program, 2000-01; Outstanding Teacher, LSU Ag Alumni Association, 2002; LSU Distinguished Faculty Award, 2003; Research Award of Merit, Gamma Sigma Delta, 2003. Memberships: American Agricultural Economics Association; International Agricultural Trade Research Consortium; International Association of Agricultural Economists; International Food and Agribusiness Management Association; Northeastern Agricultural and Resource Economics Association; Southern Agricultural Economics Association; Western Agricultural Economics Association. Address: 101 Ag Admin Bldg, Department of Agricultural Economics and Agribusiness, Louisiana State University and Agricultural and Mechanical College, Baton Rouge, LA 70803-5604, USA. E-mail: lkennedy@agcenter.lsu.edu

KENNEDY Peter Graham Edward, b. 28 March 1951, London, England. Professor of Neurology. m. Catherine Ann Kennedy, 1 son, 1 daughter. Education: University College London and University College Hospital Medical School, 1969-74; MB BS, 1974; PhD, 1980; MD, 1983; FRCP (London), 1988; FRCP (Glasgow), 1989; DSc, 1991; FRSE, 1992; MPhil, 1993; MLitt, 1995; FRCPath, 1996; FMedSci, 1998. Appointments: Honorary Research Assistant, MRC Neuroimmunology Project, University College, London, 1978-80; Registrar, then Senior Registrar, National Hospital for Nervous Diseases, London, 1982-84; Visiting Assistant Professor of Neurology, Johns Hopkins University Hospital, USA, 1985; Senior Lecturer, Neurology and Virology, University of Glasgow, 1986-87; Burton Professor of Neurology, University of Glasgow and Consultant Neurologist, Institute of Neurological Sciences, Southern General Hospital, Glasgow, Scotland, 1987-. Publications: Numerous articles in learned journals on Neurology and Neurovirology; Books: Infections of the Nervous System (with R T Johnson), 1987; Infectious Diseases of the Nervous System (with L E Davis), 2000. Honours include: BUPA Medical Foundation Doctor of the Year Research Award, 1990; Linacre Medal and Lectureship, Royal College of Physicians,

London, 1991; TS Srinivasan Gold Medal and Endowment Lecturer, Madras, 1993; Fogarty International Scholar-in-Residence, National Institutes of Health, Bethesda, USA, 1993-94; James W Stephens Honored Visiting Professor, Department of Neurology, University of Colorado Health Sciences Center, Denver, USA, 1994. Memberships: Association of Physicians of Great Britain and Ireland; Corresponding Member, American Neurological Association; Association of British Neurologists; Fellow of the Royal Society of Edinburgh; Founder Fellow, Academy of Medical Sciences; Secretary, International Society for Neurovirology; Chairman, EFNS Scientist Panel on Infections including AIDS; Member Editorial Boards several medical journals. Address: Glasgow University Department of Neurology, Institute of Neurological Sciences, Southern General Hospital, Glasgow G51 4TF, Scotland. E-mail: P.G.Kennedy@clinmed.gla.ac.uk

KENNEFICK Christine Marie, b. 4 July 1962, Washington DC, USA. Materials Scientist. Education: BSc, 1984, MSc, 1986, Stanford University; PhD, Cornell University, 1991. Appointments: National Research Council Associate, NASA Lewis Research Center, Cleveland, Ohio, 1991-93; Guest Scientist, Max-Planck Institute, Stuttgart, Germany, 1994-96; ASEE Postdoctoral Fellow, US Army Research Laboratory, Aberdeen, Maryland, 1997-98; Senior Research Associate, Air Force Research Laboratory, Dayton, Ohio, 1998-2000; Visiting Assistant Professor, Shippensburg University, Pennsylvania, 2001-02. Honours: BSc with Distinction and in Departmental Honors Program; International Woman of Year, IBC, 1998-2001; Outstanding Woman of the Twentieth Century, ABI, 1999; Listed in biographical publications. Memberships: Life Fellow, International Biographical Association; Fellow, Deputy Governor, American Biographical Institute; New York Academy of Sciences; American Physical and Materials Research Societies; International Order of Merit; Order of International Ambassadors. Address: 2029 Turtle Pond Drive, Reston, VA 20191, USA.

KENNEL Charles Frederick, b. 20 August 1939, Cambridge, Massachusetts, USA. University Administrator. m. Ellen Lehman, 1 son, 1 daughter. Education: AB, Astronomy, Harvard College, 1959; PhD, Astrophysical Sciences, Princeton University, 1964. Appointments: Assistant Research Physicist, 1960-61, Senior Staff Member, 1964-65, Principal Research Scientist, 1966-67, AVCO-Everett Research Laboratory; Member, 1972-, Acting Associate Director, 1976-77, Institute of Geophysics and Planetary Physics, Associate Professor, 1967-71, Professor, 1971-93, Chair, 1983-86, Department of Physics, Founding Member, 1987, Associate Director, 1991-92, Acting Director, 1992-93, Institute for Plasma and Fusion Research, Executive Vice Chancellor, 1996-98, University of California, Los Angeles; Associate Administrator, National Aeronautics and Space Administration, Mission to Planet Earth Program, 1993-96; Director, Vice Chancellor of Marine Sciences, Scripps Institution of Oceanography, University of California, San Diego, 1998-. Publications: Numerous articles in professional journals. Honours include: NASA Group Achievement Award, 1990, 1993; Aurelio Peccei Prize, Environmental Science, Accademia Lincei, Rome, 1996; NASA Distinguished Service Medal, 1996; James Clerk Maxwell Prize, American Physical Society, 1997; Hannes Alfven Medal, European Geophysical Society, 1998. Memberships include: American Physical Society; American Geophysical Union; American Association for the Advancement of Science; International Academy of Astronautics; National Academy of Sciences; American Philosophical Society; American Academy of Arts and Sciences; DSc (Hon), University of Alabama. Address: Scripps Institution of Oceanography, 9500 Gilman Drive, La Jolla, CA 92093-0210, USA.

Dictionary of International Biography

KENNET 2nd Baron, (Wayland Hilton Young), b. 2 August 1923, England. Politician; Writer; Journalist. m. Elizabeth Ann Adams, 24 January 1948, 1 son, 5 daughters. Education: Trinity College, Cambridge. Appointments: Royal Navy, 1942-45; Staff, Foreign Office, 1946-47, 1949-51; Delegate, Parliamentary Assemblies, Western European Union and Council of Europe, 1962-65; Editor, Disarmament and Arms Control, 1962-65; Parliamentary Secretary, Ministry of Housing and Local Government, 1966-70; Opposition Spokesman on Foreign Affairs and Science Policy, 1971-74; Member, European Parliament, 1978-79; Chief Whip, 1981-83, Spokesman on Foreign Affairs and Defence, 1981-90, Social Democratic Party, House of Lords; Vice President, Parliamentary and Scientific Committee, 1989-. Publications: As Wayland Young: The Italian Left, 1949; The Deadweight, 1952; Now or Never, 1953; Old London Churches (with Elizabeth Young), 1956; The Montesi Scandal, 1957; Still Alive Tomorrow, 1958; Strategy for Survival, 1959; The Profumo Affair, 1963; Eros Denied, 1965; Thirty-Four Articles (editor), 1965; Existing Mechanisms of Arms Control, 1965. As Wayland Kennet: Preservation, 1972; The Futures of Europe, 1976; The Rebirth of Britain, 1982; London's Churches (with Elizabeth Young), 1986; Northern Lazio; An Unknown Italy (with Elizabeth Young), 1990; Parliaments and Screening, 1995. Address: 100 Bayswater Road, London, W2 3HJ, England.

KENSIT Patsy (Jude), b. 4 March 1968, London, England. Film Actress. m. (1) Dan Donovan, (2) Jim Kerr, divorced, 1 son, (3) Liam Gallagher, divorced, 1 son. Creative Works: Films include: The Great Gatsby; The Bluebird; Absolute Beginners; Chorus of Disapproval; The Skipper; Chicago Joe and The Showgirl; Lethal Weapon II; Twenty-One; Prince of Shadows; Does This Mean We're Married; Blame It On the Bellboy; The Turn of the Screw; Beltenebros; Bitter Harvest; Angels and Insects; Grace of My Heart; Human Bomb; Janice Beard; Pavillions, 1999; Best; Things Behind the Sun, 2000; Bad Karma; Who's Your Daddy, 2001; The One and Only, 2001; TV appearances: Great Expectations; Silas Marner; Tycoon: The Story of a Woman; Adam Bede; The Corsican Brothers (US TV); Aladdin; Emmerdale. Address: c/o Steve Dagger, 14 Lambton Place, London, W11 2SH, England. E-mail: daggerents@aol.com

KENTFIELD Graham Edward Alfred, b. 3 September 1940, Buckhurst Hill, Essex. Retired Central Banker. m. Ann Hewetson, 2 daughters. Education: BA (Lit. Hum. 1st Class), St Edmund Hall, Oxford, 1963. Appointments: Head of Monetary Policy Forecasting, 1974-76, Governor's Speechwriter, 1976-77, Editor, Quarterly Bulletin, 1977-80, Senior Manager, Banking and Money Supply Statistics, 1980-84, Adviser, Banking Department, 1984-85; Deputy Chief Cashier, 1985-91, Chief Cashier and Chief of Banking Department, 1991-94, Chief Cashier and Deputy Director, 1994-98, Bank of England. Honour: Fellow of Chartered Institute of Bankers, 1991; Memberships: Bank of England Director BACS Ltd, 1988-95; Bank of England Director, Financial Law Panel, 1994-98; Bank of England Representative, Council of Chartered Institute of Bankers, 1991-98; Bank of England Representative, APACS Council, 1991-98; Member, Building Societies Investor Protection Board, 1991-2001; Member, Deposit Protection Board (Banks), 1991-98; Chairman, Insolvency Practices Council, 2000-; Honorary Treasurer, Society for the Promotion of Roman Studies, 1991-; Trustee, 1994- Chairman, 2000-, Chartered Institute for Bankers Pension Fund; Trustee, Overseas Bishoprics Fund, 1998-; Member, Council of London University, 2000-. Address: 27 Elgood Avenue, Northwood, Middlesex, HA6 3QL, England.

KENWRIGHT Bill, b. 4 September 1945, England. Theatre Producer. Education: Liverpool Institute. Appointments: Actor, 1964-70; Theatre Producer, 1970-; Director, Everton Football Club. Creative Works: Plays directed include: Joseph and The Amazing Technicolor Dreamcoat, 1979; The Business of Murder, 1981; A Streetcare Named Desire, 1984; Stepping Out, 1984; Blood Brothers, 1988; Shirley Valentine, 1989; Travels With My Aunt, 1993; Piaf, 1994; Lysistrata, 1993; Medea, 1993; Pygmalion, 1997; A Doll's House; An Ideal Husband; The Chairs, 2000; Blood Brothers; Ghosts; The Female Odd Couple. Address: Bill Kenwright Ltd, 106 Harrow Road, London, W2 1RR, England.

KENYON Michael, b. 26 June 1931, Huddersfield, Yorkshire, England. Author. 3 daughters. Education: Wadham College, Oxford, 1951-54; MA (Oxon), History. Publications: May You Die in Ireland, 1965; The 100,000 Welcomes, 1970; Mr Big, 1973; The Rapist, 1976; A Healthy Way to Die, 1986; Peckover Holds the Baby, 1988; Kill the Butler!, 1991; Peckover Joins the Choir, 1992; A French Affair, 1992; Peckover and the Bog Man, 1994. Contributions: 35 articles to Gourmet Magazine. Membership: Detection Club. Address: 164 Halsey Street, Southampton, NY 11968, USA.

KENYON Ronald James, b. 24 May 1951, Penrith, England. Chartered Accountant. m. Ann Christine Kenyon, 1 son, 1 daughter. Education: Trent Polytechnic, Nottingham; Foundation Course, Institute of Chartered Accountants. Appointments: Pricewaterhouse, Leeds, 1968-69; Chartered Accountant, 1974-, Partner, 1980-, F T Kenyon and Son, Kyle and Kenyon, Kyle Saint and Co, Saint and Co; Chairman, Cumberland Society of Chartered Accountants, 1991. Publications: Rock Climbing in the North of England, 1978; Rock Climbing Guide to Borrowdale, 1986, 1990. Honours: Fellow, Institute of Chartered Accountants; Vice President, Fell and Rock Climbing Club. Memberships: Fell and Rock Climbing Club; Eden Valley Mountaineering Club; Penrith Agriculture Society; Eden Sports Council; Penrith Partnership; Penrith Mountain Rescue Team, 1967-92.

KENZHEGUZIN Marat, b. 30 May 1939, Blagoveshenka, Kazakhstan. Economist. m. Raida Kenzheguzina, 2 sons. Education: Excellent Diploma II, 1957-62, PhD, Economics, 1962-65, Institute of National Economy "G V Plekhanov", Moscow; Dr degree in Economics, 1982; Professor, Department of Economic Management Mechanisms, Moscow, 1989. Appointments: Senior Scientist, Scientific Research Institute of Economics, Gosplan, Kazakh SSR, 1965-68; Head, Department of Economic Cybernetics, Kazakh Scientific Research Institute of Economics and Agriculture Organisation, 1968-79; Director, Kazakh Branch, All-Union State Technological Project Institute on Calculation Mechanism and Calculating Works, Central Statistics Association, USSR, 1979-85; Pro-Rector, 1985-88, Rector, 1988-94, Republican High School of Agriculture Industrial Complex Management; Pro-Rector on Science, Kazakh State Academy of Management, 1994-95; Director, Institute of Economics, Ministry of Education and Science, Republic of Kazakhstan, 1995-. Publications: More than 300 scientific works including 20 monographs and books which include most recently: Reformation of Kazakhstani economy: problems and their solution, 1997; Securities market of Kazakhstan: problems of formation and development, 1998; Market economy of Kazakhstan: problems of coming-into-being and development, 2 volumes, 2001; Kazakhstani economy on the way of reforms, 2001; Export-transit potential of Kazakhstan: mechanism of realisation, 2002; Decentralisation of governmental management, 2003; Tax regulation of gas transporting system, 2003. Honour: Award for Contribution into Scientific Development of the Republic of Kazakhstan. Memberships include: Academician, International Academy of Euro-Asia; Academician, International Academy of Informatization; Chairman, Scientific-Co-ordinating Committee on Economics; Presidium, Higher Attestation Committee, Republic

Dictionary of International Biography

of Kazakhstan; Scientific Expert Council, Inter-parliamentary Assembly, Euro-Asian Community. Address: 29 Kurmangazy str, Almaty, Republic of Kazakhstan. E-mail: ieconom@academset.kz Website: www.ieconom.academset.kz

KER David Peter James, b. 23 July 1951. Art Dealer. m. Alexandra Mary Ker, 1 son, 1 daughter. Education: Eton, 1964-69. Appointments: Founder and Sole Proprietor, David Ker Fine Art, 1980-; Director, Parc St Roman, SA, 1977-79; Director, Oceanic Development Co, Bahamas, Ltd, 1979-80; Director, Ker Management Ltd, 1980-; Director, Belgrave Frames Ltd, 1986-92; Director, John Paravicini Ltd, 1988-92; Director, James Roundell Ltd, 1995-; Director, Dickinson Roundell Inc, USA, 1998-; Managing Director, Simon Dickinson Ltd; Director, Simon Dickinson Inc; Director, Humphrey Butler Ltd, 2000-. Memberships: Member, Executive Committee Member, Society of London Art Dealers, 1986; Chairman, Eton Society. Address: 58 Jermyn Street, London SW1Y 6LX, England.

KERNICK Robert Charles, b. 11 May 1927, Istanbul. Wine Merchant. m. Adelaide Anne Elizabeth White, 1 son, 1 daughter. Education: Blundells and Sidney Sussex, Cambridge. Appointments: Director, Grandmetropolitan Ltd, 1972-75; Managing Director, International Distillers and Vintners, 1972-75; Clerk of the Royal Cellars, 1979-92; Chairman, Corney and Barrow Ltd, 1981-88; Clerk of the Prince of Wales's Cellar, 1992-99. Honours: Commander of the Royal Victorian Order; Chevalier de l'Ordre du Merite Agricole. Memberships: Merchant Taylors' Company; Leathersellers' Company; Cavalry and Guards Club; MCC; Swinley Forest Golf Club. Address: 79 Canfield Gardens, London NW6 3EA, England.

KERR Deborah Jane, b. 30 September 1921, Dumbarton, Scotland. Actress. m. (1) Anthony Bartley, divorced, 2 daughters, (2) Peter Viertel, 1960, 1 step-daughter. Education: Northumberland House, Bristol. Career: Open Air Theatre, Regent's Park, London, 1939; Films include: Contraband, Jenny (Major Barbara, 1940); Love on the Dole, 1940; The Day Will Dawn, 1941; Black Narcissus, 1945; The Huckester, 1946; If Winter Comes, 1947; The Prisoner of Zenda, 1948; King Solomon's Mines, 1950; Dream Wife, 1952; From Here to Eternity, 1953; The King and I, 1956; An Affair to Remember, 1957; Beloved Infidel, 1960; the Innocents, 1961; The Night of the Iguana, 1963; Marriage on the Rocks, 1965; Gypsy Moths, 1968; Reunion at Fairborough, 1984; Theatre includes: Heartbreak House, 1943; Tea and Sympathy, 1953, US 1954-55; Souvenir, 1975; Overheard, 1981; The Corn is Green, 1985; TV includes: A Song at Twilight, 1981; Ann & Debbie and A Woman of Substance, 1984; Hold the Dream, 1986. Honours: NY Drama Critic's Award, 2 in 1947, 1957, 1960; Hollywood For Press Association Award, 1956; The King and I, 1958; Variety Club of Great Britain Award, 1961; BAFTA Special Award, 1991; 6 nominations for Academy Awards. Address: Klosters, 7250 Grisons, Switzerland.

KERR Ralph William Francis Joseph (Lord), b. Jedburgh, Scotland. Company Director. m. Marie Claire Black, 4 sons, 2 daughters. Education: Ampleforth College, Yorkshire. Appointments: Director, Grange Estates, Newbattle, Ltd; Sotheby's Representative, Derbyshire, UK; President, 1994-2000, Vice President, 1992-94, 2000-, St Johns Ambulance, Derbyshire; President, Treetops Hospice; President, Melbourne Male Voice Choir. Honours: Member of the Royal Company of Archers, HM Queen's Bodyguard in Scotland. Memberships: Boodles Club; Brooks' Club; Jedforest Club; Derby County Club. Address: Melbourne Hall, Melbourne, Derby, DE73 1EN, England. E-mail: melbhall@globalnet.co.uk

KERSEY John, b.10 December 1972, Enfield, Middlesex. Educational Consultant; Concert Pianist; Music Critic. Education: Foundation Music Scholar and eleven times prizeman, The Latymer School, London; Graduated with congratulatory triple First as top pianist of his year, Royal College of Music; Further studies, Christ's College, Cambridge, Collège de France, Paris; Master of Music in Performance Studies, Royal College of Music, 1997; Doctor of Philosophy, Knightsbridge University, Denmark, 2003; Répétiteurs' Course, English National Opera; Fellow, Norwich School of Church Music; Fellow, Curwen College of Music. Appointments: Professional début as concert pianist, Purcell Room, aged seventeen; has subsequently performed throughout Britain and Europe, appeared on radio and television and made several recordings as soloist and collaborative artist; Geoffrey Parsons Junior Fellow, Royal College of Music, 1997-98; Lecturer and tutor in Music at institutions including the Guildhall School of Music and Drama; Birkbeck College, University of London; Morley College, London; South Bank University, London; Honorary President for the UK, Accademia Superiore di Studi di Scienze Naturali e Psicobiofisiche Prof Ambrosini – Diandra International University and Academy, Italy, Brazil, Spain and USA; Honorary Visiting Professor of Music, Parthasarathy International Cultural Academy, Madras, India; Honorary Member of Advisory Council and Honorary Representative for the UK, Ansted University, Malaysia and British Virgin Islands; Honorary President, Association of British Music Colleges and Societies of Musicians, 2003-04; Head of Information Technology and Music, Mander Portman Woodward Independent Fifth and Sixth-Form College, London; Examiner, Curwen College of Music and Central Academy of Music, London; Deputy Member of the National Assembly, British Parliamentary Group, International States Parliament for Safety and Peace, Italy; Vice-Delegate for England, President of the English National Office and Vice-President of the English National Delegation, World University Roundtable, Arizona, USA; Director and Fellow, London Society for Musicological Research; Honorary Secretary –General and Life Fellow, Institute of Arts and Letters, London; President, St Katherine's Institute of Theology and Religious Studies. Publications: Critic, International Piano; Tempo; Hi-Fi News and Record Review; International Record Review; Times Higher Education Supplement; Major contributor of articles on music and literature, Routledge Encyclopaedia of Contemporary Italian Culture, 2000; Academical Dress of Music Colleges and Societies of Musicians in the UK (with Nicholas Groves), 2002; A History of the Central School of Religion, 2003; Numerous articles; Various compositions; Consultant for films and radio programmes on musical subjects. Honours: Honorary Major, Hungarian National Guard; Knight, The International Knightly Order of St George (Hungary); Knight of Grace, Sovereign Order of St John of Jerusalem (Malta); Knight Grand Cross, Knights of Holy Mary of Angels, and General Lieutenant, Corps of Volunteers of Assistance and of Peace, California, USA; Chevalier Grand Cross, Order of St Cornelius the Centurion, New Jersey, USA; Medal of Honour for Science and Art, Austrian Albert Schweitzer Society; Friedrich Silcher Medal in Bronze, Friedrich Silcher Vocalists' Foundation, Hessen, Germany; Medal of the Hungarian Freedom Fighters of the Hungarian National Guard; Doctor of Music honoris causa, Ansted University, 2003; Doctor of Philosophy in Arts and Letters (for distinguished achievements), Accademia Superiore di Studi di Scienze Naturali e Psicobiofisiche Professor Ambrosini – Diandra International University and Academy, 2003; Cultural Doctorate in Philosophy of Music, World University Roundtable, Arizona, USA, 2001; Honorary Fellow in Music, Independent Contemporary Music Awards; Honorary Fellow: Central Academy of Music, North and Midlands School of Music; Academy of St Cecilia; Central Institute, London; Honorary Secretary General, Life Fellow, Institute of Arts and Letters, London; Fellow and

Member, Governing Council, Metropolitan College of Music; Fellow, Director, London Society for Musicological Research; Honorary Member, International Writers and Artists Association, Ohio, USA; Over 12 awards whilst at the RCM, including Sir Percy Buck Award; Sir Arthur Bliss Solo Piano Prize; Bernard Stevens Performance Prize; Marjorie and Arnold Ziff Prize for an Outstanding Diploma Recital; Ernst Pauer Prize. Memberships: Fellow: Royal Society of Arts, Society of Antiquaries of Scotland, Guild of Musicians and Singers, Faculty of Liturgical Musicians, Irish Guild of Organists and Choristers, Cambridge Society of Musicians; Freeman, City of London; Liveryman, Worshipful Company of Musicians; Founder Member, World University, Arizona, USA; Doctoral Member, World University Roundtable, Arizona, USA. Address: BM3816, London WC1 3XX, United Kingdom. Website: www.johnkersey.org

KERSHAW David Robert, b. 1953, Dunedin, New Zealand (British and New Zealand subject). Solicitor. m. Christine Anne Sexton, 3 sons, 1 daughter. Education: MA (Hons) Law, Trinity College, Cambridge; College of Law. Appointments: Partner, Corporate Department, Ashurst Morris Crisp, 1986-; Specialisation: company law, mergers and acquisitions, corporate finance, insolvency and restructuring. Memberships: Chairman, Ashurst Morris Crisp Opinions Committee; Freeman, City of London Solicitors Company; Member, Company Law Sub-Committee, City of London Law Society; Founder Member, Oxford University Anglo German Law Conference. Address: Broadwalk House, 5 Appold Street, London, EC2A 2HA, England.

KERSHAW Walter, b. 7 December 1940, Rochdale, England. Artist. Partner, Gillian Halliwell, 1 son, 1 daughter. Education: BA (Hons), Durham University, Durham, England, 1962. Career: Self employed freelance artist and international mural painter of large external images; Exhibitions and murals for: The British Council, Brazil and Germany, 1983-95; Trafford Park, Manchester, England, 1978-92; Manchester United FC, 1988; Sarajevo International Art Festival, 1996; Leonard Cheshire Foundation, 2002-2004. Honours: BA Honours Fine Art, Dunelm, 1962; Gulbenkian Foundation, Lisbon, 1978-80; British Council, Brazil, 1983-85. Memberships: Littleborough Cricket Club; The Conservative Party. Address: The Studio, Todmorden Road, Littleborough OL15 9EG, England.

KERTÉSZ Sándor, b. 29 October 1940, Kaposvar, Hungary. Painter; Teacher. m. Eva Szabo, 2 sons. Education: Degree, Szeged Teacher Training College, 1961. Career: Primary School Teacher, 1961-82; Art Teacher, Táncscis Mihály Secondary School, Kaposvaŕ, Hungary, 1982-98. Publications: Collective Exhibitions in foreign countries including Poland, Romania, Bulgaria, Yugoslavia, Austria, Germany, France, The Netherlands, Italy; One-Man Exhibitions: Tornio, Finland, 1991; Wien, Austria, 1993; Szeged, Pécs, Kaposvaŕ, Szekszard, Mohacs, Nagyatad, Hungary; Art Competitions: New York, USA, 1995; Pisa, Italy, 1990, 91, 92. Honours: Székely Bertalan Prize, 1986; Award of the Art of Somogy County, 1992; Standard Quality Nivo Prize, 6 times; Hungarian Culture Award from the Hungarian Educational Minister, 1987, 1998. Memberships: Association of the Somogy County Artists, Kaposvar; Association of the Hungarian Artists, Budapest. Address: Szanto U-23, 7400 Kaposvar, Hungary.

KESSNER Dolly Eugenio, b. 7 November 1946, Hanapepe, Kauai, Hawaii, USA. Professor; Pianist; Theorist; Composer. m. Daniel Aaron Kessner, 29 June 1968, 2 sons. Education: BA, cum laude, Music Education; MA, Composition, University of California, Los Angeles; PhD, Music Theory, University of Southern California; Studied Piano with Aube Tzerko, Composition, Henri Lazarof, Leon Kirchner, Robert Linn, Music

Theory, Robert Moore, William Thomson. Appointments: Professor, Chair, Music and Dance Department, Moorpark College; Concert Pianist, European, US and West Coast Premieres; Soloist, Orquesta Sinfonica de El Salvador, San Salvador, Filarmonica Marea Neagra, Constanza, Romania, Moorpark Symphony Orchestra, California. Compositions: Five Piano Pieces, 1980; Toccata for Piano, 1992. Recordings: Lyric Piece for Piano and Orchestra; Equali II, for Piano Celeste and Three Percussionists. Publication: Article, Structural Coherence in Twentieth Century Music: The Linear-Extrapolation Paradigm, 1993. Honours: Grant, The Fund for US Artists; University of Southern California Graduate Merit Fellowship in Music; Meritorious Performance and Professional Promise Award, California University, Northridge. Memberships: College Music Society; Association for Technology in Music Instruction. Address: 10955 Cozycroft Avenue, Chatsworth, CA 91311, USA.

KETTANI M Ali, b. 27 September 1941, Fes, Morocco. Professor. m. Nuzha, 3 sons, 1 daughter. Education: Diploma, Electrical Engineering, Swiss Federal Institute of Technology, Lausanne; PhD, Electrical Engineering, Carnegie-Mellon University, Pittsburgh, USA, 1966. Appointments: Assistant Professor, Electrical Engineering Department, University of Pittsburgh, 1966-68; Associate Professor, Electrical Engineering Department, University of Petroleum & Minerals, Dhahram, Saudi Arabia, 1969-75, Professor, 1975-81; Visiting Professor, Michigan Institute of Technology, USA, 1975; Director General, IFSTAD (Oil), Jeddah, Saudi Arabia, 1981-89; Director, Ecole Superieure de Management, Casablanca, Morocco, 1990-; Rector, Founder, President of the Board, Universidad Islamica Averroes, Cordoba, Spain. Publications: 15 books and over 100 articles in professional journals. Memberships: Founding Member, Vice President, Islamic Academy of Sciences, Amman, Jordan; Member of several scientific organizations. Address: Universidad Islamica Averroes, 3 Calleja de la Hoguera, 14003 Cordoba, Spain.

KETTLEY John Graham, b. 11 July 1952, Halifax, West Yorkshire, England. Presenter; Weather Consultant. m. Lynn, 2 sons. Education: BSc honours, Applied Physics, Coventry University. Appointments: Meteorological Office, 1970-2000; National BBC TV broadcast meteorologist, Domestic TV manager and lead presenter, 1985-2000; Appearances on numerous TV series; Ambassador for Cricket World Cup, 1999; Presenter and host, Triangular NatWest One-day International cricket, 2001; Freelance presenter and weather consultant, John Kettley Enterprises; Contract weather presenter and sporting features for BBC Radio 5Live, 2001-. Publications: Several articles for cricket journals, travel and leisure brochures; Foreword, Rain Stops Play, book by Andrew Hignell, 2002. Memberships: Lord's Taverner, 1990-; Institute of Broadcast Meteorology, 1995-; Fellow, Royal Meteorological Society, 2001-. Address: c/o PVA Management, Hallow Park, Hallow, Worcester WR2 6PG, England. E-mail: johnkettley@bbc.co.uk

KEVELAITIS Egidijus, b. 27 July 1961, Kaunas, Lithuania. Medical Doctor. m. Sigita, 2 sons. Education: MD, 1985; PhD, 1988; DSc, 1993; Docent diploma, 1994. Appointments: Assistant Professor, Department of Physiology and Pathophysiology, Kaunas Medical Institute, 1985-88; Senior Lecturer, Department of Physiology and Pathophysiology, Kaunas Medical Academy, 1988-92; Associate Professor, Department of Physiology, 1992-2001, Professor, Department of Physiology, 2001-, Chairman, Department of Physiology, 2002-, Kaunas Medical University. Publications: Articles to medical journals; Editor, textbook: Human Physiology, 1999, 2002; Journal, Medicina, 2001-. Honours: Award, Lithuanian Academy of Sciences, 1984; Research Fellowship, European Society of Cardiology, 1997. Memberships:

Dictionary of International Biography

Lithuanian Physiological Society, Vice-President, 1992-; European Society of Cardiology; New York Academy of Sciences; Danish Society of Pharmacology. Address: Department of Physiology, 9 Mickeviciaus, Kaunas Medical University, 3000 Kaunas, Lithuania.

KEYES Gregory James, b. 26 December 1952, Warrigul, Victoria, Australia. International Presenter. m. Evelyn Keyes, 1 son, 1 daughter. Education: BA, 1997; MBA, 1999; PhD, Doctor of Business and Leadership Studies, 2001; Master of Science, Exercise Science, 2003. Appointments: Chief Executive Officer, Global Lifestyle Organisation Web; Chief Executive Officer, Global Aquatic Instructor Network; Chief Executive Officer, Absolute Concepts of Entertainment; Chief Executive Officer, Ready Steady Live Consulting; Professor, St Regis On-Line University, 2003-. Publications: Aquatics – The Umbilical into Lifestyle Wellness and Advancement, 2003; The Star of Communication Stratagem, 2003; Ready Steady Live – Adventurism into Lifestyle Development; The most unique Vehicle ever created – You!; Concept creations: TAR – Total Audience Reality Concept; Keyes Core of Concept Creativity Method; Keyes Scopes of Excellence Appraisal System; Keyes "EGA" Scale of Exertion, Goal and Achievement System; Keyes Scale of Stress Rationality Method; Keyes Combat-A-Size System (A combination method course of Self Defence mixed with Education on Body Awareness/Fitness Exercise Prescription/Performance and Weight Loss Methodology). Honours: National Medal, Australia, 1988; Global Award Aquatics, USA, 2002; Emma Award, Aquatics Europe, 2003. Address: Triangeldreef 48, Etten-Leur 4876EH, The Netherlands. E-mail: gregkeyesphd@planet.nl

KEZAR Dennis Dean Jr, b. 29 June 1968, Oxford, England. Professor. Education: BA, University of the South, 1990; MA, 1992, PhD, 1997, University of Virginia. Appointments: Assistant Professor of English, University of the South; Assistant Professor of English, Vanderbilt University, 1997-. Publications: Guilty Creatures (book), 2001; 10 articles in professional journals. Honours: DuPont Fellowship, Advanced Graduate Scholarship; University Research Council Fellowship. Memberships: ODK; PBK; Renaissance Society of America. Address: 416 North Petway, Franklin, TN 37064, USA.

KHAN Mohammad Mohabbat, b. 16 January 1949, Dhaka, Bangladesh. Teacher; Constitutional Post Holder. m. Rokeya Khan, 2 sons. Education: BA (Hons), 1968, MA, 1970, University of Dhaka, Bangladesh; MPA, Syracuse University, USA, 1974; MPA, 1976, PhD, 1976, University of Southern California, USA. Appointments: Associate Professor, University of Benin, Nigeria, 1981-82; Professor, Department of Public Administration, University of Dhaka, Bangladesh, 1983-; Professor, Yarmouk University, Jordan, 1991-92; Member Bangladesh Public Service Commission, 1999-. Publications: 12 books; 6 monographs; 150 chapters and articles in edited books and national and international professional journals. Honours: Awarded in many categories by IBC and ABI. Memberships: American Society for Public Administration; Commonwealth Association for Public Administration and Management; International Political Science Association; International Institute of Administration Science. Address: Department of Public Administration, University of Dhaka, Dhaka-1000, Bangladesh. E-mail: mmkhan@bangla.net

KHANNA Atul, b. 21 November 1960, Hyderabad, India. Consultant Plastic Surgeon. m. Sunanda, 2 sons. Education: MBBS, Osmania University, Hyderabad, India, 1983; FRCS, Royal College of Physicians, 1989; FICS, International College of Surgeons, 1994; MBA, Open Business School, Open University, 1994; FRCS (Plast), Intercollegiate Board of Plastic Surgery, 1997; Dip Eur B(Plast), European Board of Plastic Reconstructive and Aesthetic

Surgery, 1998. Appointments: Specialist Registrar in Plastic Surgery, Nottingham City Hospital NHS Trust, Nottingham, England, 1998; Locum Consultant in Plastic Surgery, University Hospital Birmingham NHS Trust, Selly Oak Hospital, Birmingham, England, 1998-99; Consultant Plastic Surgeon, College Tutor in Surgery, Sandwell General Hospital, Lyndon West Bromwich, England, 1999-; Private Practice, BUPA Hospital, Little Aston, Birmingham, England. Publications: Articles in peer-reviewed journals include most recently: Overview of trends in burns and scalds related mortality in the last 20 years at the Birmingham Burns Unit, 2001; Current attitudes to fluid resuscitation in the UK, 2001; Unilateral Mydriasis during Blepharoplasty, 2001; A novel method of ring removal from a swollen finger, 2001. Honours: National Merit Scholarship Holder, 1974; State Merit Scholarship Holder, 1976. Memberships: Society of Expert Witnesses; British Burns Association; British Association of Aesthetic Plastic Surgeons; British Association of Plastic Surgeons; Honorary Secretary, West Midlands Specialist Advisory Committee in Plastic Surgery, 2002-; Chairman, Birmingham Division, British Medical Association, 2003-. Address: Department of Plastic Surgery, Sandwell General Hospital, Lyndon, West Bromwich, West Midlands, B71 4HJ, England. E-mail: atulkhanna@doctors.org.uk

KHANNA Kapil Mohan, b. 15 April 1934, Chiniot. Teacher; Researcher. m. Kanta, 3 sons, 1 daughter. Education: BSc Hons; MSc Hons; PhD; FICC. Appointments: Professor, Head, Department of Physics, Dibrugarh University, 1967-72; Professor, Head, Department of Physics, BIT Ranchi, 1972-76; Professor, Head, Department of Materials Science, NIFFT RANCHI, 1976-95; UNESCO Expert, Physics, 1987-89; Professor, Head, Department of Physics, MOI University, Kenya, 1995-. Publications: 105 Research Publications; 4 Advance Books on Physics. Honours: Punjab University Medal, 1956; Associate Member, ICTP Trieste, Italy. Memberships: Indian Physics Association; Indian Cryogenic Council; International Centre for Mechanical Sciences. Address: Department of Physics, MOI University, P O Box 3900 Eldoret, Kenya.

KHANTHAVIT Anya, b. 20 May 1962, Thailand. Finance Professor. m. Kwanjai Khanthavit, 1 daughter. Education: BBA, Thammasat University, Thailand,1983; MSc, State University of New York, USA, 1985; PhD, New York University, USA, 1992. Appointment: Professor of Banking and Finance, Thammasat University, Bangkok, Thailand. Publication: Scale and Scope Economies at Large banks: Technological and Regulatory Effects. Honours: Prince Viwatanajai Fellow; TRF Senior Researcher. Membership: Financial Management Association. Address: Faculty of Commerce and Accounting, Thammasat University, Bangkok 10200, Thailand. E-mail: akhantha@tu.ac.th

KHARE Mukesh, b. 1 January 1956, Varanasi, India. Engineer; Professor. m. Lekha, 2 sons. Education: Bachelor of Engineering, University of Roorkee, 1973-77; Master of Engineering, 1977-79; PhD, University of Newcastle Upon Tyne, England, 1984-89. Appointments: Assistant Design Engineer, Irrigation Design Organisation, 1979-81; Assistant Environmental Engineer, Pollution Control Board, 1981-84; Fellow, Council of Scientific and Industrial Research, National Environmental Engineering Research Institute, 1989-90; Demonstrator, University of Newcastle Upon Tyne, 1984-89; Assistant Professor, Indian Institute of Technology, Delhi, 1990-96; Lecturer, University of Technology, Lae, Papua New Guinea, 1996-97; Assistant Professor, Indian Institute of Technology, 1997-99; Associate Professor, Civil Engineering, Indian Institute of Technology, 2000-. Publications: Soil aggressiveness towards buried water pipelines; Computer aided simulation of efficiency of an electrostatic precipitator; Emission control from coke ovens in TATA steel;

Dictionary of International Biography

Evaluating indoor air quality using CO_2 as a surrogate index; Book: Modelling Vehicular Exhaust Systems (in Advances in Transportation series), 2002; 49 publications in total. Honours: National Merit Scholarship; Best Outgoing Student; Best Solo Singer; University Grant Fellowship; National Scholarship for Study Abroad; Overseas Research Student Award, UK. Memberships: FRD, South Africa; NRC, South Africa; Research Management Group, USA; Research Board of Advisors, ABI, USA; Consultant to Associates in Rural Development (ARD) Inc, USA; Principal Investigator (India), International Consortium on rapidly urbanising regions, Arizona State University, USA; Member, Civil Engineering Department Board, Delhi; Fellow, IWWA; Author: Institute Water Quality Monitoring Program; Coordinator, Indo-French Unit in water and waste technologies (IFUWWT), Delhi; others. Address: Indian Institute Tech, Civil Engineering Dept Hauz Khaz, New Delhi 110016, India.

KHARE Shabd Sharan, b. 7 April 1947, Allahabad, UP, India. University Pro-Vice Chancellor. m. Urmila Khare, 2 sons. Education: MSc, Mathematics, 1968; PhD, Mathematics, 1977. Appointments: Lecturer, Allahabad University, 1968-71; Lecturer, Gorakhpur University, 1972-75; Lecturer, 1976-78, Reader, 1979-85, Professor, 1986-98, Dean of Science Faculty, 1998-2001, North Eastern Hill University, Shillong, India; Pro-Vice Chancellor, North Eastern Hill University, Tura, India, 2001-. Publications: 23 research papers in international journals of repute. Honours: Gold Medallist, BSc; Silver Medallist, MSc Mathematics; Fulbright Fellow, 1986; Commonwealth Fellow, 1987; Fellow, National Academy of Science, Allahabad, India, 1994. Memberships: Allahabad Mathematical Society; Indian Mathematical Society. Address: North Eastern Hill University, Tura Campus, Chandmari, Tura, Meghalaya 794002, India. E-mail: kharess@rediffmail.com

KHARISSOV Boris Ildusovich, b. 19 January 1964, Uglegorsk, Russia (Mexican citizenship, 2003). Researcher; Chemist. m. Oxana V Kharissova, 2 daughters. Education: Department of Chemistry, 1986, PhD, 1993, Moscow State University, Russia. Appointments: Engineer, Moscow Institute of Chemical Technology, Russia, 1986-89; Researcher, Moscow State University, 1989-94; Researcher and Professor, Autonomous University Nuevo León, Monterrey, Mexico, 1994-; Participated in recovery work at Chernobyl, 1987; Worked on projects for Mexican National Agency for Science and Technology, 1996, 1998, 2003-; Expert on scientific projects for the Foundation for Research and Technology of Argentina, 2001; Guest Editor, 3 special issues of the international journals, Polyhedron and Journal of Co-ordination Chemistry dedicated to inorganic and co-ordination chemistry in Latin America, 2000, 2001, 2003. Publications: More than 50 published and accepted articles; 3 monographs: Direct Synthesis of Co-ordination Compounds, co-author, 1997; Direct Synthesis of Co-ordination and Organometallic Compounds, co-author and co-editor, 1999; Synthetic Co-ordination and Organometallic Chemistry, co-author and co-editor, 2003; 2 patents; Attended many international scientific congresses. Honours: National Researcher of Mexico, 1999; Best Research Work in the UANL, 2002; Listed in biographical dictionaries. Membership: Mexican Academy of Inorganic Chemistry; Regular Member, Mexican Academy of Sciences, 2002-. Address: A P 18-F, CP 66450 Ciudad Universitaria UANL, San Nicolás de los Garza, NL, Mexico. E-mail: bkhariss@hotmail.com

KHATAMEE Masood, b. 12 February 1936, Mashad, Iran. Physician. m. Mahin, 3 daughters. Education: MD, Shiraz University School of Medicine, Shiraz, Iran, 1955-61. Appointments: Teaching Assistant, 1962-65, Clinical Instructor 1965-66, New York University School of Medicine; Assistant Attending, 1966-, Assistant Research Scientist, 1996-97, Beth Israel North Hospital, New York Medical Center; Faculty Member, University of Tehran, 1968-70; Director of Training, Family Planning Unit, Ministry of Health, 1969-70; Medical Director, Solaimanih Community Health Center, Tehran, 1969-70; Chairman, Iranian Women's Association, Family Planning Sub-committee, 1969-70; Assistant Attending, Lenox Hill Hospital, New York, 1971-; Assistant Attending, Bellevue Hospital Center, New York, 1971-; Clinical Instructor, 1971-74, Clinical Assistant Professor, 1972-77, Clinical Associate Professor, 1977-97, Clinical Professor, 1997-, Obstetrics and Gynecology, New York University School of Medicine; Executive Director, Fertility Research Foundation, New York, 1989-. Publications: Numerous presentations and articles in professional scientific journals; 2 books; Television and radio interviews. Honours: 9 times winner, Physician's Recognition Award, American Medical Association, 1971-95; Diplomat, American Board of Obstetrics and Gynecology, 1973; ACOG Recognition Award, 1977, 1980, 1988, 1990; Honorary Professorship, World Conference on Family Health and Population, Turkey, 1986; Citation Award, Shiraz University School of Medicine, 1988-89; Citation Award, Lenox Hill Hospital, 1995; Citation Award for 35 years distinguished service, Bellevue Hospital, 1996; Citation Award for 25 years of service, 1996; Citation, Canadian Iranian Engineers Society, 2001; Honorary Member, Iranian Infertility Society; 2001 Wall Street Businessman of the Year; Gold Medallist, Republican Congressional Committee; 35 Year Service Award, NYU School of Medicine, 2003. Memberships: American Society of Reproductive Medicine; Fellow, Federation of International Gynecologists and Obstetricians; Fellow, International College of Surgeons; Founder, Board of Directors, Shiraz University School of Medicine Alumni Society Inc, USA; Iranian American Republican Council. Address: 875 Park Ave, New York, HY 10021, USA. Website: www.frfbaby.com

KHATIB Hisham, b. 5 January 1936, Palestine. International Consultant. m. Maha, 21 August 1968, 2 sons, 1 daughter. Education: BSc, Engineering, 1959, University of Cairo; BSc, Economics, 1967, PhD, Engineering, 1974, University of London. Appointments: Energy Expert, Arab Fund, 1976-80; Director General, Jordan Electricity Authority, 1980-84; Minister of Energy, 1984-90, Minister of Planning, 1993-95, Government of Jordan. Publications: 1 history book: Palestine and Egypt under the Ottomans; 3 books on engineering and economics. Honours: Achievement Medal, Institute of Electrical Engineers, UK, 1998; Decorated in Italy, Indonesia, Austria, Jordan, Vatican. Memberships: Fellow, IEE (UK); Fellow, IEEE (USA). Address: PO Box 925 387, Amman 11190, Jordan.

KHAZANOV Anatoly M, b. 13 December 1937, Moscow, Russia. Social/Cultural Anthropologist. m. Irina Khazanov, 1 son. Education: MA, 1960, PhD, 1966, Moscow State University; Dr Sci, Academy of Sciences, USSR, 1976. Appointments: Senior Scholar, Academy of Sciences, USSR, 1975-81; Professor, Department of Sociology and Social Anthropology, Hebrew University of Jerusalem, 1985-90; Professor, Department of Anthropology, 1990-97, Ernest Gellner Professor of Anthropology, 1997-, University of Wisconsin, Madison, USA. Publications: The Social History of the Scythians, Main Problems of the Ancient Nomads of the Eurasian Steppes, in Russian, 1975; Nomads and the Outside World, 1984; After the USSR: Ethnicity Nation and Nationalism in the Commonwealth of Independent States, 1995. Honours: Guggenheim Fellow; Rockefeller Foundation Fellow; Honorary member, Central Eurasian Studies Society; Corresponding Member, International Institute for the Studies of Nomadic Civilisations, UNESCO. Membership: Fellow, British Academy. Address: University of Wisconsin – Madison, Department of Anthropology, 1180 Observatory Drive, Madison, WI 53706, USA. E-mail: khazanov@facstaff.wisc.edu

KHINTIBIDZE Elguja, b. 7 June 1937, Georgia. Philologist. m. Mzia Menabde, 2 sons. Education: Student of Tbilisi State University, 1955-60; Postgrad Student, 1960-63; Cand Philol, 1963; DrPhilol, 1971; Professor, 1973; Corresponding Member, Georgian Academy Sciences, 1997. Appointments: Assistant Professor, 1966, Professor, 1973, Deputy Dean Philology Department, 1965-66, The Dean of Philology Department, 1976-85, Vice Rector, Tbilisi State University, 1985-93; Director, Centre of Georgian Studies, 1992-; Head, Laboratory of Georgian-Foreign Literature Contacts, 1993-; Head, Chair of Old Georgian Literature, 2000-. Publications: 180 scholarly works including 14 monographs; Georgian-Byzantine Literary Contacts, 1996; The Designation of Georgians and Their Etymology, 1998; Georgian Literature in European Scholarship, 2001; Georgian Literature in European Scholarship, 2001. Honours: Ivane Javakhishvili Prize, 1983; International Order of Merit, 1994. Memberships: Membre Titulaire de Société Internationale pour l'Etude de la Philosophie Médiévale (Belgique Louvan La Neuve). Address: Side Street Ateni 18A Apt 13, Tbilisi 380079, Georgia.

KHONG Dien, b. 12 January 1944, Vinh Phu Province, Vietnam. Ethnologist; Socio-Cultural Anthropologist. m. Vu Thi Kim Thoa, 2 sons, 2 daughters. Education: BA, Ethnology, Faculty of History, National University of Bulgaria, Sophia, 1972; PhD, Historical Science, Supreme Examination Council of the USSR, 1987. Appointments: Head of the Department of Maps, Demography and Ethno-ecology, 1983-90, Deputy Director, Institute of Ethnology, 1990-95, Director, Institute of Ethnology/Anthropology, 1995-; Member, 1991-, Chairman, 1995-, Scientific Council, Institute of Ethnology; Editor-in-Chief, Ethnology/Anthropology Review, 2000-. Publications include: Books: Author: Population and ethno-population in Vietnam, 1995; Population and ethno-demography in Vietnam, 2002; Co-author: Ethnic minorities in Vietnam in the context of industrialisation and modernisation, 2000; Present urgent issues of seasonable and practical ethnic relationships, 2001; 16 book chapters; 27 articles in scientific journals and conference proceedings include most recently: The ethnology of Vietnam, integration and development, 2001; Vietnam's regional and ethnic diversity: State efforts to reconcile cultural aspects, 2001; Some social features of the Trieng minority groups in Quang Nam Province, 2002. Honours: Medal of task for ethnic groups and mountainous development; Medal of task for science and technology; Medal of task for Science and Technique Associations; Medal of task for Social Sciences and Humanities. Memberships: Executive Committee, 1991-, Vice-President, 2000-, Vietnamese Ethnology Association; Folk Cultures Association of Vietnam. Address: The Institute of Anthropology, 27 Tran Xuan Soan Street, Hanoi, Vietnam. E-mail: khongdienvdt@hn.vnn.vn

KHOO Boo-Chai, b. 24 April 1929, Singapore. Medical Doctor. m. Cheng Lui, 2 sons. Education: Anglo Chinese School, 1946; MBBS, University of Singapore, 1954. Appointments: Medical Officer, General Surgery Unit, Singapore General Hospital, 1954-58; Resident, Plastic Surgery Unit, Tokyo Metropolitan Police Hospital, Japan, 1959-61; Private Practice, Plastic Surgery, Singapore, 1962-; Deputy Editor, Chinese Journal of Plastic and Reconstructive Surgery. Publications: Clinics in Plastic Surgery: Plastic Surgery in non-Caucasian; Aesthetic Surgery for the Oriental; Oriental Eye Surgery; Concepts of Oriental Beauty; Surgery for the Oriental Eyelid; Sculpturing the Nasal Tip and Lobule Region; Many others. Memberships: American Society of Plastic and Reconstructive Surgeons; Israel Association of Plastic Surgeons; Association of Plastic Surgeons of India; International Society Aesthetic Plastic Surgery; Oriental Society Aesthetic Plastic Surgery; Singapore Medical Association. Address: 05-12 Parkway Parade Medical Centre, Singapore 449 269.

KHORANA Har Gobind, b. 9 January 1922, Raipur, Punjab Region, India (US Citizen). Chemist. m Esther Elizabeth Sibler, 1952, 1 son, 2 daughters. Education: Bachelor's Degree, 1943, Master's Degree, 1945, Chemistry, Punjab University; Doctorate, Liverpool University; Postdoctoral work in Zurich, Switzerland. Appointments: Organic Chemist, working with Sir Alexander Todd, Cambridge, 1950-52; Organic Chemist, National Research Institute, Canada, 1952-60; Professor and Co-Director, Institute of Enzyme Chemistry, University of Wisconsin, 1960-64; Conrad A Elvehjem Professor in Life Sciences, 1964-70; Andrew D White Professor at Large, Cornell University, 1974-80; Alfred P Sloan Professor, 1970-97, Professor Emeritus and Senior Lecturer, 1997-, Massachusetts Institute of Technology. Publications: Some Recent Developments in the Chemistry of Phosphate Esters of Biological Interest, 1961; Articles on Biochemistry in various journals. Honours: Joint Winner, Nobel Prize for Physiology or Medicine, 1968; Louisa Gross Horwitz for Biochemistry, 1968; American Chemical Society Award for creative work in Synthetic Chemistry, 1968; Lasker Foundation Award, 1968; American Academy of Achievement Award, 1971; Willard Gibbs Medal, 1974; Gairdner Foundation Annual Award, 1980; National Medal of Science, 1987; Paul Kayser International Award of Merit, 1987; Numerous honorary degrees and international awards. Memberships: NAS; Foreign Academician, USSR Academy of Sciences; Foreign Member, Royal Society, London; Pontifical Academy of Sciences. Address: Departments of Biology and Chemistry, Massachusetts Institute of Technology, 77 Massachusetts Avenue, Room 68-680, Cambridge, MA 02139, USA.

KIDD Jodie, b. 1979, Surrey, England. Fashion Model. Education: St Michael's School, W Sussex. Appointments: Modelled for numerous fashion magazines, also top international catwalk model for designers include: Gucci, Prada, Karl Lagerfeld, Yves Saint Laurent, Chanel, John Galliano, Calvin Klein, Yohji Yamamoto; Make-up Model for Chanel, 1999 season. Honours: Former National Junior Athletics Champion; Holder, Under 15s High Jump Record for Sussex; Many awards as junior show jumper. Address: c/o IMG Models, Bentinck House, 3-8 Bolsover Street, London, W1P 7HG, England.

KIDMAN Fiona (Judith) (Dame), b. 26 March 1940, Hawera, New Zealand. Writer; Poet. m. Ernest Ian Kidman, 20 August 1960, 1 son, 1 daughter. Appointments: Founding Secretary/Organiser, New Zealand Book Council, 1972-75; Secretary, 1972-76, President, 1981-83, New Zealand Centre, PEN; President, 1992-95, President of Honour, 1997-, New Zealand Book Council. Publications: Novels: A Breed of Women, 1979; Mandarin Summer, 1981; Paddy's Puzzle, 1983, US edition as In the Clear Light, 1985; The Book of Secrets, 1987; True Stars, 1990; Ricochet Baby, 1996; The House Within, 1997; The Best of Fiona Kidman's Short Stories, 1998. Short stories: Unsuitable Friends, 1988; The Foreign Woman, 1994; Poetry: Honey and Bitters, 1975; On the Tightrope, 1978; Going to the Chathams, Poems 1977-1984, 1985; Wakeful Nights: Poems Selected and New, 1991. Other: Search for Sister Blue (radio play), 1975; Gone North (with Jane Ussher), 1984; Wellington (with Grant Sheehan), 1989; Palm Prints (autobiographical essay), 1995; New Zealand Love Stories: An Oxford Anthology, 1999. Contributions to: Periodicals. Honours: Scholarships in Letters, 1981, 1985, 1991, 1995; Mobil Short Story Award, 1987; Queen Elizabeth II Arts Council Award for Achievement, 1988; Officer of the Order of the British Empire, 1988; Victoria University Writing Fellowship, 1988; President of Honour, New Zealand Book Council, 1997; Dame Companion of the New Zealand Order of Merit, for services to literature, 1998. Memberships: International PEN; Media Women; New Zealand

Book Council, president, 1992-95; Patron, Cambodia Trust Aotearoa. Address: 28 Rakau Road, Hataitai, Wellington 3, New Zealand.

KIDMAN Nicole, b. 20 June 1967, Hawaii, USA, Australian nationality. Actress. m. Tom Cruise, 1990, divorced 2001, 1 adopted son, 1 adopted daughter. Education: St Martin's Youth Theatre, Melbourne; Australian Theatre for Young People, Sydney. Appointments: Goodwill Ambassador, UNICEF. Acting début in Australian film aged 14; Actress, TV mini-series, Vietnam, 1987; Bangkok Hilton, 1989. Creative Works: Films: The Emerald City; The Year My Voice Broke; Flirting; Dead Calm, 1990; Days of Thunder, 1990; Billy Bathgate, 1991; Far and Away, 1992; Malice, 1993; My Life, 1993; Batman Forever, 1995; To Die For, 1995; Portrait of a Lady, 1996; The Peacemaker, Eyes Wide Shut, 1998; Practical Magic, 1999; Moulin Rouge, 1999; The Others, 2000; Moulin Rouge, 2001; Birthday Girl, 2001; The Hours, 2001; Dogville, 2003; Cold Mountain, 2003; The Human Stain, 2003; Birth, 2003; The Interpreter, 2004; Alexander the Great, 2004. Play: The Blue Room, 1998-99. Honours: Best Actress Award, Australian Film Institute; Actress of the Year, Australia; Seattle International Film Festival Award, 1995; London Film Critics Award, 1996; Best Actress, Golden Globe Award, 1996; BAFTA Nominee, 1996; Best Actress in a Musical, Golden Globe Award, 2001; Best Dramatic Actress, Golden Globe Award; 2003; BAFTA Award for Best Actress in a Leading Role, 2003; Academy Award for Best Actress, 2003. Address: c/o Ann Churchill-Brown, Shanahan Management, PO Box 478, Kings Cross, NSW 2011, Australia.

KIE Francois, b. Paris, France. Music Producer (Piano, Keys, Informatic); President of Universe Melody Inc. Education: Lycee Pasteur; Schola Cantorum; Sorbonne; ENA; Jeanine Rueff (Prix de Rome, Conservatoire National de Paris – CNMP; Jen-Louis Florentz (CNMP). Career: Professor, Musical Institute of Professional Formation, IMFP, Salon de Provence, 1985-91; JAM, Regional School, Montpellier, 1988-96; Reporter, French Radio USA and Tam-Tam Radio (Des notes au Net); Worked with: Michel Magne, Pierre Vassiliu, Ivan Jullien, Michel Barrot, Hal Singer, Big al Downing, Dominique Dipiazza, Michel Petrucciani, Soriba Kouyaté, Philippe Gaillot, Mike Stern, Branscombe Richmond, Dom Famularo, Robin Dimaggio, Joe Porcaro, Linda Martinez, Danielle Lopresti; Group Member: Petrucciani Quartet; Cocoverde, Colors and Light; Laurie "Jam" Orchestra; Branscombe Richmond and the Renegade Posse; Danielle Lopresti and the Masses Band; Main Concerts: Opening Miles Davis, Nimes, 1986; Festival Radio France, Montpellier, 1992-93; Opening Ahmad Jamal, Marseille, 1994; Opening, Charlie McCoy, European Festival Country of Mirandes, 1997-98; Show HARIBO FRANCE, Branscombe Richmond and Lorenzo Lamas, 1998-2001; Danielle Lopresti "Say it records", Kulak's Woodshed, Los Angeles, 2004; Films and Video: Actor in Sandy, Sandy Stevenson, Michel Galabru, 1983; TV Michel Drucker, Sacrée Soirée, 1986; Clip M6, Colors and Light, 1995; Main Compositions: Kids, Laurie, Louisiane, Rap on Jazz, Take no Jazz, Kietronic, Tekila Remix, Scorpion Dance King, Elise; Main Recordings: The First, P & M, Petrucciani; Brassens Inspiration, Kie; Runaway Heart, Jan Ryan and Big Al Downing; Kanakassi and Bamana, S Kouyaté and P Gaillot; Creative Visualisation, Kie; Scorpion Dance King, B Richmond, & Kie; Kietronic, Kie & Eddy B. Memberships: SACEM; ASCAP; PAS (Percussive Arts Society). E-mail: kie@kieworld.com Website: kieworld.com

KIEFER Claus, b. 25 April 1958, Karlsruhe, Germany. Theoretical Physicist. Education: Diplom (Master) in Physics, 1984; PhD, Physics, 1988; Habilitation, 1995. Appointments: Postdoctoral, Heidelberg University, 1988-89; Postdoctoral, Zurich

University, 1989-93; Science Assistant and Lecturer, Freiburg University, 1993-2001; Full Professor, University of Cologne, 2001-; Many invited visits to universities including: Cambridge, Alberta. Publications: Author, Quantum Gravity, 2004; Co-author, Decoherence and the Appearance of a Classical World in Quantum Theory, 1996, second edition, 2003; Co-Editor, Black-Holes Theory and Observation, 1998; Around 50 articles in internationally renowned journals. Memberships: Vice-President, Gravity Section, German Physics Society, 1996-, President, 2000-2004. Address: University of Cologne, Institute for Theoretical Physics, Zülpicher Str 77, 50937 Cologne, Germany.

KIEHL Reinhold, b. 8 October 1947, Worms, Germany. Chemist; Biochemist; Human Biologist. m. Ilse Gertraud Schoyerer, divorced, 2 daughters. Education: BEng, Engineering School, Mannheim, 1971; MS, Chemistry, University of Heidelberg, 1974; DSc, 1977; MEng, Fachhochschule, Mannheim, 1982. Appointments: Registered Eco-Audit Specialist, Research Fellow Max Planck Institute, Heidelburg, 1977; Postdoctoral Fellow Scripps Clinic, La Jolla, 1977-79; Assistant Professor, Ruhr University, Bochum, 1979-85; Associate Professor, Bielefeld University, 1985-87; Head of Laboratory And Research, Clinic Neukirchen, 1987-94; Professor, Director; Freelance Workshop And Course Instructor, 1995-. Publications: Over 50 articles to professional journals. Memberships: American Heart Association; Max Planck Society; Royal Society of Chemistry; AAAS; British Society of Allergy and Clinical Immunology; International Union of Pure and Applied Chemistry; New York Academy of Science. Address: RKI Institut(e) (Lab Research Molecular Med/Biol), Saliterweg 1, 93437 Furth Im Wald, Germany. Website: www.rki-i.com

KIHARA Noriyasu, b. 22 October 1934, Fukayama City, Hiroshima-Ken, Japan. Author; Professor. m. Hiroko, 4 children. Education: Lecturer, Kyushu Sangyou University, 1963-67; BA, Literature, Kita Kyushu University, 1958; MA, Literature, Kyushu University, 1960; PhD, Social Science, Iond University, 2001. Appointments: Lecturer, Assistant Professor, Fukuoka Women's Junior College, 1967-70; Lecturer, Assistant Professor, Full Professor, Kinki University's Kyushu School of Engineering, 1971-. Publications: Atomic Dome; An Angel in White; Parent's Headache Street; The Key Word and Key Sentence, Volume 2; Editor, Man Language Culture, Volume 3 academic journal, Japan Anthropological Linguistic Association. Honours: Literature Award, Association of the Study of Japanese Spiritual Culture; Deputy Director General, Life Fellow, International Biographical Centre. Memberships: Japanese Centre of International PEN; Vice President, Japan Anthropological Linguistic Association; Director, Association of the Study of Japanese Spiritual Culture. Address: 53-17 Igisu, Iizuka City, Fukuoka-Ken, 820-0053, Japan.

KIHARA Yasuki, b. 8 February 1955, Hiroshima, Japan. Cardiologist. m. Miho Yukitoshi, 1 son, 2 daughters. Education: BSc, 1973-75, MD (School of Medicine), 1975-79, PhD, Graduate School of Medicine, 1982-86, Kyoto University, Japan; Speciality Board, Internal Medicine, Japan Society of Internal Medicine, 1985; Speciality Board of Cardiology, Japanese Circulation Society, 1992. Appointments: Residencies, Tenri Hospital, Nara, 1979-82; Clinical Fellow, Kyoto University, 1986; Research Fellow in Medicine, 1986-87, Instructor, 1987-89, Harvard Medical School; Assistant Professor, Toyama Medical and Pharmaceutical University, 1989-93, Kyoto University Graduate School of Medicine, 1993-2002; Visiting Professor, Case Western Reserve University, 1999-; Visiting Professor, Boston university, 1999-; Visiting Scholar, Stanford University, 2001-; Director, Outpatient Clinic, Department of Cardiovascular Medicine, Kyoto University Hospital, 1998-; Associate Professor, Kyoto University Graduate

School of Medicine, 2002-. Publications: Articles in medical journals. Honours: Research Awards: Yamanouchi Foundation, Tokyo, 1986, (Fellowship) American Heart Association, Massachusetts Affiliate, 1987-88, Japan Heart Foundation, 1992, Yokohama Foundation, Nagoya, 1992; R I Bing Award, International Society for Heart Research, 1989; Sagawa Young Investigator Award, Cardiovascular System Dynamics Society, Kobe, 1992; Pfizer Health Research Award, 1999; Sigma Xi. Memberships: Fellow, American College of Cardiology; Councilor, Japan Society of Ultrasonics in Medicine; Japan Society of Internal Medicine; Japan Circulation Society; American Association for the Advancement of Science; International Society for Heart Research. Address: Department of Cardiovascular Medicine, Kyoto University Graduate School of Medicine, 54 Shogoin, Sakyo, Kyoto 606-8507, Japan.

KIKUCHI Shiro, b. 25 March 1957, Kawasaki, Japan. Surgeon. m. Rie Firuhashi, 1 son, 1 daughter. Education: MD, 1981, PhD (Doctor of Medical Science, 1993, Kitasato University School of Medicine, Kanagawa, Japan. Appointments: Resident, Department of Surgery, Kitasato University Hospital, Kanagawa, Japan, 1981-83; Resident, Department of Surgery, National Cancer Center, Tokyo, Japan, 1983-86; Clinical Fellow, Department of Surgery, Moabit Hospital, Berlin, Germany, 1988-91; Chief of Surgery, Department of Surgery, Izu-shimoda Hospital Shizuoka, Japan, 1991-94; Assistant Professor, Department of Surgery, Kitasato University School of Medicine, Kanagawa, Japan, 1994-. Publications: Hepatogastroenterology, World Journal of Surgery, Langenbeck's Archives of Surgery, Anticancer Research, 2000; Anticancer Research, In Vivo, 2001; Anticancer Research, 2002; Hepatogastroenterology, 2003. Memberships: Japan Surgical Society; Japanese Society of Gastroenterological Surgery; International Society of Surgery; International Association of Surgeons and Gastroenterologists. Department of Surgery, Kitasato University School of Medicine, 1-15-1, Kitasato, Sagamihara-shi, Kanagawa 228-8555, Japan.

KILICMAN Adem, b. 3 February 1966, Hatay, Turkey. Lecturer. m. Arini Nuran Idris, 2 sons. Education: BSc, 1989, MSc, 1991, Hacettepe University, Turkey; PhD, Leicester University, England, 1995. Appointments: Research Assistant, 1990-96; Assistant Professor, 1996-97; Lecturer, 1997-2001; Associate Professor, 2001-. Publications: 53 papers, 14 technical reports; 3 books. Honours: Excellent Service Awards, 1999, 2000; Distinguished Young Researcher Award, 2001; Outstanding Researcher Award, 2002. Memberships: American Mathematical Society; New York Academy of Sciences; Malaysian Mathematical Society; Reviewer American Mathematical Society; Reviewer, ZDM; Reviewer, Computing Reviews. Address: Department of Mathematics, University Putra Malaysia, 43400 UPM, Serdang, Selangor, Malaysia. E-mail: akilic@fsas.upm.edu.my

KILLOUGH (Karen) Lee, b. 5 May 1942, Syracuse, Kansas, USA. Science Fiction Writer. Publications: A Voice Out of Ramah, 1979; The Doppelganger Gambit, 1979; The Monitor, the Miners, and the Shree, 1980; Aventine, 1981; Deadly Silents, 1982; Liberty's World, 1985; Spider Play, 1986; Blood Hunt, 1987; The Leopard's Daughter, 1987; Bloodlinks, 1988; Dragon's Teeth, 1990; Bloodwalk, 1997; Bridling Chaos, 1998; Blood Games, 2001; Wilding Nights, 2002. Memberships: Science Fiction and Fantasy Writers of America; Mystery Writers of America; Sisters In Crime. Address: PO Box 1167, Manhattan, KS 66505, USA.

KILMER Val, b. 31 December 1959, Los Angeles, USA. Actor. m. Joanne Whalley, divorced, 1 son, 1 daughter. Education: Hollywood's Professional's School; Juilliard. Creative Works: Stage appearances include: Electra and Orestes, Henry IV Part

One, 1981; As You Like It, 1982; Slab Boys, 1983; Hamlet, 1988; Tis Pity She's A Whore, 1992; TV Films: Top Secret, 1984; Real Genius, 1985; Top Gun, 1986; Willow, 1988; Kill Me Again, 1989; The Doors, 1991; Thunderheart, 1991; True Romance, 1993; The Real McCoy, 1993; Tombstone, 1993; Wings of Courage, 1995; Batman Forever, 1995; Heat, 1995; The Saint, 1996; The Island of Dr Moreau, 1996; The Ghost and the Darkness, 1996; Dead Girl, 1996; Joe the King, 1999; Pollock, 2000; Red Planet, 2000; The Salton Sea, 2002; Run for the Money, 2002; Masked and Anonymous, 2003; Wonderland, 2003; The Missing, 2003; Spartan, 2004; Mind Hunters, 2004. Address: c/o CAA, 9830 Wilshire Boulevard, Beverly Hills, CA 90212, USA.

KIM Chul Sung, b. 5 July 1950, Seoul, Korea. Professor of Physics. m. Sung Hee Choi, 1 son, 1 daughter. Education: BS, Physics, 1972, MS, Physics, 1974, PhD, Physics, 1982, Yonsei University, Korea. Appointments: Professor, Air Force Academy, Seoul, Korea, 1977-80; Professor, Kookmin University, 1980-; Director, Natural Science Institute, 1991-93; Director, Centre of Inter-university Facility, 1993-2001; Visiting Professor, Johns Hopkins University, Baltimore, USA, 1987-88. Publications: 220 papers in the field of Mössbauer and magnetic materials. Honours: Best Paper Award, Korean Physical Society, 1991; Best Paper Award, 1999, Outstanding Research Paper Award, 2002, Korean Magnetics Society. Memberships: General Affairs, 1997-2000, Editor-in-Chief, Vice President, 2001-, Korean Magnetics Society; Treasurer, 1997-99, Director, 2003-, Korean Physical Society; American Physical Society; Mössbauer Century Club; IEEE; IBAME. Address: Department of Physics, Kookmin University, Seoul 136-702, Republic of Korea. E-mail: cskim@phys.kookmin.ac.kr, Website: http://phys.kookmin.ac.kr/~cskim (also, www.cskim.net)

KIM David Sang Chul, b. 9 November 1915, Seoul, Korea (came to USA, 1959). Publisher; Evangelist; Retired Seminary President. m. Eui Hong Kang, 6 January 1942, 5 children. Education: BA, English Literature, Chosen Christian College, Seoul, 1939; Postgraduate, University of Wales, 1954-55, West Conservative Baptist Seminary, 1959-61, University of Oregon, 1962-63; MA, University of Oregon, 1965; Postgraduate, Pacific School of Religion, Berkeley, California, 1965-66; PhD, Pacific Columbia University, 1988. Appointments: Staff Member, Chosen Rubber Industry Association, Seoul, 1939-45; Financial Assistant, US Military Government, Kunstan City, Korea, 1945-48; Government Official Ministry of Finance, Ministry of Foreign Affairs, Government of Republic of Korea, Seoul, 1948-59; Charter Member, Unification Church, Seoul, 1954; 1st Mission to England, 1954-55; Mission, Evangelical Unification Church, US, 1959-70; Counselling Supervisor Clearfield Job Corps Centre, Clearfield, Utah, 1966-70; Founder, President, Owner, The Cornerstone Press (Now Rose of Sharon Press), 1978-85. Publications: Individual Preparation for His Coming Kingdom: Interpretation of the Principle, 1964; Victory Over Communism and the Role of Religion, 1972; Papers in this field; Editor (book series) Day of Hope in Review, Part 1, 1972-74, 1974, Part 2 1974-75, 1975, Part 3 1976-81, 1981; Executive Producer (radio broadcast) The Unification Hour, 1975-2001, True Love Journey, 1993-2001. Honours: Byzantine Golden Medal American Institute, Patristic Byzantine Studies Inc, 1992; Special Award, for Distinguished Dedicated Service, Unification Church International, 1996; President Emeritus, Board of Trustees, Unification Theological Seminary, USA, 2000; Listed in several Who's Who publications. Memberships: Charter Member, Trustee, World Relief Friendship Foundation Inc (now International Relief Friendship Foundation Inc), 1974-; President, International One World Crusade Inc, 1975-; Founder, President, United Faith, Inc, Portland, Oregon, 1970-; President, Unification Theological Seminary, 1974-94; Charter

Member, Trustee, National Council Churches and Social Action, 1976-96; Advisor Financial Supporter, Global Congress of World Religions Inc, 1978-96; Global Education Research and Development Fund Inc, 1981-96; Charter Member, International Religious Foundation Inc, 1982-; Founder, President, Marriage and Family Institute of America, 1994-; Chairman, Inaugurated for the Family Federation, Unification and World Peace, Netherlands, 1996-; Cheon Il Guk Owner Award, Family Federation for World Peace and Unification, Seoul, Korea, 2003. Address: 12 South Randolph Avenue, Poughkeepsie, NY 12601-5122, USA.

KIM Deok Won, b. 5 September 1952, Seoul, Korea. Professor. m. Lim Misula, 1 son, 1 daughter. Education: BE, Seoul National University, Korea, 1976; MS, Northwestern University, USA, 1980; PhD, University of Texas at Austin, USA, 1986. Appointments: Assistant Professor, Yonsei University, 1987-96; Associate Professor, 1996-2001; Professor, 2001-; Editorial Board, Yonsei Medical Journal, 1996-; Editor in Chief, Journal of Korean Society of Medical and Biological Engineering (KOSOMBE), 1996-97; Academic Director, KOSOMBE, 1998-99; Chairman, Department of Medical Engineering, 1999-. Publications: Development of a frequency dependent type apex locator with automatic compensation, 1998; Measurement of leg arterial compliance of normal and diabetics using impedance plethysmography, 1999; A nominvasive estimation of hypernasality using a linear predictive model, 2001; Objective evaluation of treatment effects on port-wine stains using Lab color coordinates, 2001; Root canal length measurement in teeth with electrolyte compensation, 2002; Optimum electrode configuration for detection of arm movement using bio-impedance, 2003; Development and evaluation of an automated stainer for acid-fast bacilli, 2003; An improved approach for measurement of stroke volume during treadmill exercise, 2003. Honours: Recipient, Medison Biomedical Engineering Award, 1996; IEEK Distinguished Service Award, 2003. Memberships: New York Academy of Sciences; IEEE; The Biomedical Engineering Society. Address: Dept of Medical Engineering, Yonsei University College of Medicine, CPO Box 8044, Seoul, Korea. E-mail: kdw@yumc.yonsei.ac.kr

KIM Gyu Ug, b. 14 November 1960, Seoul, Korea. Professor. m. Tae Jeong Jeon, 1 son, 1 daughter. Education: BS, 1983; MS, 1985; PhD, 1988. Appointments: Senior Scientist, Korea Research Institute of Standards and Science, 1988-96; Visiting Scientist, Electrotechnical Laboratory, Japan, 1990-91; Professor, Kumoh National Institute of Technology, 1996-; Subgroup Leader, Center for Controlling of Optical Chaos, 2002-03; Director, Research Institute, Max Engineering Co Ltd, 2003-. Publications: Articles in scientific journals which include: Journal of Applied Physics, 1988; The Review of Laser Engineering, 1991; Journal of the Optical Society of America, 1992, 2003; Physics Review, 1994; Chinese Journal of Lasers, 2001; Optics Letters, 2003; Journal of the Korean Physical Society, 2003. Honours: Listed in Who's Who publications and biographical dictionaries. Memberships: Korean Physical Society; Optical Society of Korea; Optical Society of America. Address: 188 Shinpyung-Dong, Kumi, Kyungbuk, 730-701, Korea. E-mail: gukim@mail.kumoh.ac.kr

KIM Ho Yeon, b. 8 July 1966, Seoul, Korea. Professor of Economics. m. Hee Jeong Kim, 1 son. Education: BA, University of California, Berkeley, 1989; MA, Cornell University, 1992; PhD, University of Pennsylvania, 1995. Appointments: Research Assistant, University of Pennsylvania, 1993-94, Postdoctoral Fellow, Simon Fraser University, 1996-97; Research Fellow, Korea Development Institute, 1997-98; Assistant Professor, Sungkyunkwan University, 1998-. Publications: Impact of trade

liberalization on the location of firms: NAFTA and the automobile industry; The effects of regulations on land transactions: The case of Korea. Honours: Full Fellowship, University of Pennsylvania, 1992, 1994; Best Teacher Award, Department of Economics, Sungkyunkwan University, 2001. Memberships: Regional Science Association International; Korean Economic Association. Address: Department of Economics, Sungkyunkwan University, Myungryun-dong, Chongro-gu, Seoul 110-745, Korea. E-mail: hokim@hanmail.net

KIM Hyun-Tak, b. 7 July 1958 (lunar calendar), Dogae, Korea; h. Pohang. Solid State Physicist. m. Eun-Hee Lee, 1 son, 1 daughter. Education: Bachelor, Physics, Pusan National University, 1982; Master, Theoretical Solid-State Physics, Seoul National University, 1984; PhD, Applied Physics, University of Tsukuba, Japan, 1995. Appointments: Researcher, Technical Institute, HanKook Tire Co, 1984-85; Head of Development Department, SystemBase Co, 1986-92; Research Associate (mon-bu-kyo-kan), University of Tsukuba, Japan, 1995-98; Senior Researcher, Electronics and Telecommunications Research Institute, 1998-. Principal Achievements: Successfully demonstrated the first-order metal-insulator transition (called Mott transition) with band filling by an extending of the Brinkman-Rice picture, establishing the justification of a fractional charge using the concept of measurement. The fractional charge revealed the most important unsolved problems, such as the 2-dimensional density of states with band filling, the intrinsic superconducting gap, pairing symmetry, and an extension of the Ambegaokar-Baratoff theory for the mechanism of high-T_c superconductivity. Observed the Mott transition with electric field for the first time near a critical on-site Coulomb energy $U/U_c=1$ in VO_2 Mott insulator (an important problem) and fabricated a transistor using the Mott transition (opened horizon of a metal transistor). Publications: Principal papers: Instability of local charge-density-wave potential energy in $BaBiO_3$, Phys Rev B54 (1996) 90; Extended Brinkman-Rice picture and its application to high-T_c superconductors, in New Trends in Superconductivity (Editor J F Annet and S Kruchinin, Kluwer, 2002), Nato Science Series Vol II/67, p137, http://arXiv.org/abs/cond-mat/0110112; Analysing intrinsic superconducting gap by means of measurement in Bi-2212 superconductors, J Phys Soc Jpn 71 (2002) 2106, http://arXiv.org/abs/cond-mat/0203497; http://arXiv.org/abs/cond-mat/0301097; Explanation of small IcRn values observed in inhomogeneous superconductors, Physica C 399 (2003) 48, http://arXiv.org/abs/cond-mat/0301097, http://arXiv.org/abs/cond-mat/0306421; Pairing symmetry analysed by means of measurement in inhomogeneous high-Tc superconductors, "Horizon in superconductivity researches", (NovaScience Co, 2003); Mechanism and observation of Mott transition in VO2 based transistor, http://arXiv.org/abs/cond-mat/0305632, http://arXiv.org/abs/cond-mat/0308042. Switching field-effect transistor using abrupt metal-insulator transition, (USA, Patent, Appl No: 10/188,522, Pub No: US2003/0054615 A1), 2002. Memberships: Korean Physical Society; Japan Physical Society; American Physical Society. Honours: Most Influential Scientist of the Decade, ABI, 2002; Great Minds of the 21st Century, ABI, 2002; Deputy Governor, ABI, 2002; 2000 Outstanding Intellectuals of the 21st Century, IBC, 2002; 500 Founders of the 21st Century, IBC, 2002; IBC Fellow, 2002; Living Legends, IBC, 2003; 1000 Great Asians, IBC, 2003. Address: Semiconductor Basic Research Laboratory, ETRI, Daejeon 305-350, Korea. E-mail: kimht45@hotmail.com

KIM Jeong-Kyun, b. 29 August 1960, Kwang-Ju, South Korea. Senior Scientist. m. Eun-Young Jang, 2 sons, 1 daughter. Education: BS, Materials and Metallurgical Engineering, Chunnam National University, Korea, 1987; MS, Materials and Metallurgical

Engineering, Korea Advanced Institute of Science and Technology, Korea, 1990; PhD, Materials Engineering, University of Wisconsin-Milwaukee, 1997. Appointments: Researcher, Korea Atomic Energy Research Institute, 1990-92; Research Assistant, 1992-97, Post Doctoral Research, 1997-98, Research Assistant, 1998-2000, University of Wisconsin-Milwaukee; Senior Scientist, MER Corporation, Tucson, Arizona, 2000-. Publications: 17 papers in journals; 13 papers in proceedings. Honours: Listed in national and international biographical dictionaries; M Schiel Award for Honourable Mention in Metallography, 1997; M Schiel Award for Excellence in Metallography, 2000. Address: 5584 N Lydell Ave, #14, Milwaukee, WI 53217, USA. E-mail: jkkim40@hotmail.com

KIM Jong Il, b. 16 February 1942, Mount Paekdu, Korea. Leader of the Democratic People's Republic of Korea; General Secretary of the Workers' Party of Korea; Chairman of the National Defence Commission of the Democratic People's Republic of Korea. Education: Graduated, Kim Il Sung University, Pyongyang. Career: Officer, Section Chief, Deputy Director, Director, Department of the Central Committee of the Worker's Party of Korea, 1964-73; Member, Central Committee of the Workers' Party of Korea, 1972; Secretary, Central Committee of the Workers' Party of Korea, 1973; Member, Political Commission, Central Committee of the Workers' Party of Korea, 1974; Member, Presidium, Political Bureau, Central Committee and Member, Central Military Commission of the Workers' Party of Korea, 1980; Deputy, Supreme People's Assembly of the Democratic People's Republic of Korea, 1982; First Vice-Chairman, National Defence Commission, Democratic People's Republic of Korea, 1990-93; Chairman, National Defence Commission, Democratic People's Republic of Korea, 1993-; Supreme Commander, Korean People's Army, 1991-; Marshal, Democratic People's Republic of Korea, 1992-; General Secretary, Worker's Party of Korea, 1997. Publications: Kim Jong Il Selected Works, 14 volumes; For the Completion of the Revolutionary Cause of Juche, 10 volumes. Honours: 3 times, The Hero of the Democratic People's Republic of Korea; 3 times, The Kim Il Sung Order; The Kim Il Sung Prize; Many other domestic and foreign orders and medals, honorary titles and titles of doctorate. Address: The Central Committee of the Workers' Party of Korea, Pyongyang, Democratic People's Republic of Korea.

KIM Ki Hang, b. 5 August 1936, Pyong-Nam, Korea. Distinguished Professor of Mathematics. m. Myong-Ja Hwang, 1 son, 1 daughter. Education: BSc, 1960, MSc, 1961, Mathematics, University of Southern Mississippi; MPhil, 1970, PhD (Dissertation guided by Gian-Carlo Rota of MIT), 1971, Mathematics, George Washington University. Appointments: Instructor of Mathematics, University of Hartford, 1961-66; Lecturer of Mathematics, George Washington University, 1966-68; Associate Professor of Maths and Chairman, St Mary's College of Maryland, 1968-70; Associate Professor of Mathematics, University of North Carolina at Pembroke, 1970-74; Distinguished Professor of Mathematics, Alabama State University, 1974-. Publications: 7 books and over 150 articles in Mathematics; Mathematical Social Sciences, Editor-in-Chief, 1981-94. Honours: 6 National Science Foundation research grant awards. Memberships: Korean Academy of Science and Technology. Address: 416 Arrowhead Drive, Montgomery, AL 36117, USA.

KIM Kyeong Uk, b. 20 August 1951, Jeomchon, Korea. Professor. m. Jung Sook Kang, 2 daughters. Education: BS, 1975, MS, 1978, Seoul National University, Korea; PhD, University of Illinois, USA, 1981. Appointments: Research Scholar, International Rice Research Institute, 1976-77; Professor, Seoul National University, Korea, 1981-; Visiting Scholar, Cornell University, USA, 1986-87; Visiting Scholar, Technical University of Munich, 1990-91. Publications Articles in professional scientific journals include: Analysis of transmission load of agricultural tractors, 2000; Analysis of tractor transmission and driving axle loads, 2001; Development of a seedling pick-up device for vegetable transplanters, 2002. Honours: Academic Award, Korean Society for Agricultural Machinery, 1996; Agricultural Science and Technical Award, Ministry of Agriculture, 1998. Memberships: Korean Society for Agricultural Machinery; American Society of Agricultural Engineers. Address: School of Bioresources and Material Engineering, College of Agriculture and Life Science, Seoul National University, San 50-51, Shillin-dong, Kwanak-ku, 151-742 Seoul, Korea. E-mail: kukim@plaza.snu.ac.kr

KIM Min-Huei, b. 25 August 1951, Yecheon-koon, Kyungbuk, Korea. Professor of Electrical Engineering. m. Hyeon-Jung Kim, 2 daughters. Education: BA, 1974, MA, 1980, Department of Electrical Engineering, Yeungnam University, Taegu, Korea; PhD, Department of Electrical Engineering, Chung-Ang University, Seoul, Korea, 1989. Appointments: Professor, Yeungnam College of Science and Technology, Taegu, Korea, 1978-; Advisor, Industrial Advancement Administration, Korea Government, Teagu, Korea, 1988-93; Research Professor, University of Tennessee, USA, 1993-95; Organising Committee Director, Vice-President, Korea Institute of Power Electronics, 1999-. Publications: Author: Electrical Machinery, 1979, 2003; Electromagnetics, 1986; Power Electronics, 1993; Instrument Engineering, 1996; Digital Power Electronics, 2003; More than 80 articles. Memberships: Life Member: KIEE, KIPE; Senior Member, IEEE. Address: Chungsan Town 101/301. #1269-1, Jisan-dong, Susang-gu, Taegu Metropolitan, Republic of Korea. E-mail: mhkim@ync.ac.kr

KIM Pill Soo, b. 5 May 1961, Seoul, Korea. Professor. m. 1 son, 1 daughter. Education: BS, 1984, MS, 1986, PhD, 1994, Electrical Engineering, Dongguk University, Seoul, Korea. Appointments: Lecturer, Dongguk University, 1989-99; Professor, Chungcheong College, Cheongju, Korea, 1992-96; Professor, Daelim College, Anyang, Korea, 1996-. Publications: 100 technical papers, 6 patents and 13 books: include Automotive Electricity, 1998; Electromagnetics, 1998; Automotive Electricity Experiment, 1999; Automotive Laws and Regulations of Korea, 1999; Automotive Electronic Control, 1999; Automotive Inspection, 2000; Fundamentals of Automotive Electricity and Electronics, 2000; Experiments of Automotive Electronic Control, 2001; Car Oscilloscope, 2001; Basic Fundamentals of Electric and Electronics, 2001; Practice for Automotive Electronic Control, 2002; Problems for National and Technical Qualification Certificates of Automobiles, 2002; A Guide for Used Car Appraisal – Series I, 2002; Basic Automotive Electricity, 2003. Honours: Founder Award, IBC, 2001; Gold Record, ABI 2001; International Order of Merit, IBC, 2001; Noble Prize, United Cultural Convention, 2001; International Peace Prize, United Cultural Convention, 2002; World Citizen of the Year, 2002, Man of the Year, 2002, ABI; International Scientist of the Year, 2002, IBC; Man of the Year, 2002, 2003, ABI; International Educator of the Year, IBC, 2003; The Da Vinci Diamond Award, IBC, 2004; Listed in several biographical dictionaries. Memberships: IEEE; IEE of Japan; Korea IEE; European Power Electronics; International Association of Science and Technology for Development; SAE of Japan; SAE of Korea; New York Academy of Sciences; London Diplomatic Academy; The Planetary Society; World Order of Science-Culture-Engineering; International Association of Business Leaders. Address: Department of Automotive Engineering, Daelim College, 526-7 Bisan-dong, Dongan-ku Anyang-si, Kyunggi-do 431-715, Korea. E-mail: pskim@daelim.ac.kr

Dictionary of International Biography

KIM Sang-Koo, b. 8 April 1940, Jinju City, Gyungsangnamdo, Republic of Korea. Professor. m. Soon-Ja Park, 1 son, 3 daughters. Education: BA, Seoul National University, Republic of Korea, 1960-64; Master of Arts, Pusan National University, Republic of Korea, 1973-77; PhD, Kyemyung University, Republic of Korea, 1983-88. Appointments: Professor, English Department, 1979-, Director, Institute for the Humanities, 2000-, Pusan National University, Republic of Korea; President, New Korean Association of English Language and Literature, 2001-2003; Vice-President, Committee Board of Institute for the Humanities of Korea, 2004-. Publications: Books: The Crying of Lot 49 (editor), 1994; American Literary Naturalism (editor), 2001; Trends in Contemporary American/English Literature, 2002; Article: The Philosophical Literary Constructions of M Blanchot and G Bataille, 2000. Honours: Annual Achievements Award, 1976; Distinguished Research Award, 1999; Listed in Who's Who publications and biographical dictionaries. Memberships: MLA; New Korean Association of English Language and Literature; Society of English Language and Literature. Address: 1310-21 Yunsandong, Yunjeku, Pusan 607-805, Republic of Korea. E-mail: kskoo@pusan.ac,kr

KIM Su Gwan, Professor; Dentist; Researcher; Educator. Appointments: Associate Professor, Director, Department of Oral and Maxillofacial Surgery, Chosun University, Korea. Publications: Over 250 publications in scientific journals and books include: The use of particulate dentin-plaster of Paris combination with/without platelet-rich plasma in the treatment of bone defects around implants, 2002. Honours: Presidential Award, 5 times, 1999-2003; Scientific Research Award, 7 times. Address: 421 Seosuk-dong, Dong-gu, Gwangju-City, Korea 501-825. E-mail: sgckim@mail.chosun.ac.kr

KIM Suk-Joon, b. 15 June 1950, Seoul, Korea. m. Jung-Sook Choi Kim, 1 son, 1 daughter. Professor. Education: BE, SNU, 1973; MPA, SNU, 1975; MA, University of California, Los Angeles, 1985; PhD, Political Science, UCLA, 1987. Appointments: Professor, Ewha Womans University, 1979-; Visiting professor, Harvard University, 1998; Visiting professor, Oxford University, 1999; Dean, Graduate School of Information Science, Ewha Womans University, 1993-98; President, The Korean Association for Public Administration, 2003-04; President, Citizens United for Better Society. Publications: The State, Public Policy and NIC Development, 1988; Crisis in the Korean Capitalist State, 1991; The Rise of the Neo-Mercantile Security State in Korea, 1992; The Korean Industrialising State, 1992; The Political Economy of State Change in Korea, 1994; The State and Change, 1995; The State and Public Policy of the American Military Government in Korea, 1996; State Capacity and Economic Statecraft, 2002; Modern Korean Presidency I, 2002; The Politics of Governance in Korea, 2002. Honours: Phi Beta Kappa; Korean Association for Public Administration Book Award. Memberships: The Presidential Commission on Policy Planning; Republic of Korea; Administrative Reform Committee, ROK; KAPA; KAPS; KPSA. Address: 752-12 Sinbong Yi, Sujieup, Yonginsi, Seoul 449-840, South Korea. E-mail: ksj@mm.ewha.ac.kr

KIM Un Bae, b. 11 September 1959, Seoul, Korea. Professor of Theology. m. Hyun, 1 daughter. Education: BA, Theology, Sahmyook University, 1982; M Div, 1986, D Min, 1993, Andrews University. Appointments: Church Ministry, 1986-98; Professor, Department of Theology, Sahmyook University, 1999-. Publications: A Discipleship Strategy for the Local Seventh-Day Adventist Churches in Korea, 1993; A Reasonable Approach to Christian Truth, 2003, Contemporary Popular Culture and Christian Responsibility: A Korean Adventist Perspective. Memberships: The Adventist Theological Society; Korea Association of Christian

Studies; The Korean Society for Practical Theology. Address: Sahmyook University, Department of Theology, Cheongnyangni PO Box 118, 130-650, Seoul, Korea. E-mail: ubkim@syu.ac.kr

KIM Young Ho, b. 16 February 1958, Kimhae, Kyungnam, South Korea. Professor. m. Do Youn Jun, 2 daughters. Education: BS, 1976-80, MS, 1980-82, PhD, 1982-85, Kyungpook National University, Taegu, South Korea. Appointments: Instructor, Taegu Health College, 1981-82; Teaching and Research Assistant, 1982-86, Instructor, College of Natural Sciences, 1986-88, Assistant Professor, 1988-94, Associate Professor, 1994-99, Professor, 1999-, Chairman, 1995-97, Department of Microbiology, College of Natural Sciences, Kyungpook National University, South Korea; Visiting Fellow, Gerontology Research Center, National Institute of Aging, NIH, Baltimore, USA, 1989-92; Visiting Professor, Enzyme Institute, Tokushima University, Japan, 2003. Publications: Articles in scientific journals include: Murine T lymphocyte proliferation induced by interleukin-2 correlates with a transient increase in $p56^{kk}$ kinase activity and tyrosine phosphorylation of 97-kDa protein, 1993; Negative regulatory role of overexpression of PLC gamma 1 in the expression of early growth response 1 gene in rat 3Y1 fibroblast, 2002; Characterization of human phosphorine aminotranferase involved in the phosphorylated pathway of L-serine biosynthesis, 2003. Honours: Best Promotion of Research Award, Korean Society for Applied and Industrial Microbiology, 1987; Visiting Fellowship, NIH, USA, 1989-92; Best Research Paper Award, Korean Society for Microbiology and Biotechnology. Memberships: Society for Leukocyte Biology; American Society for Microbiology; Japanese Society for Molecular Biology. Address: Department of Microbiology, College of Natural Sciences, Kyungpook National University, Taegu 702-701, South Korea. E-mail: ykim@knu.ac.kr

KIMURA Genki, b. 3 January 1937, Shimonoseki City, Japan. Microbiologist. m. Yoshiko Kunigoshi, 2 sons. Education: MD, School of Medicine, 1961; PhD, 1966, Graduate School, Kyushu University, Fukuoka, Japan; Internship in Medical Practice, St Luke's International Hospital, Tokyo, Japan. Appointments: Research Associate, Microbiology, Kyushu University School of Medicine, 1966-67; Associate Professor, Microbiology, Tottori University School of Medicine, Yonago, Japan, 1967-74; Visiting Scientist, Salk Institute, USA, 1968-70; Professor, Virology, Tottori University School of Medicine, 1974-77; Professor, Cancer, Kyushu University School of Medicine, 1977-82; Professor, Virology, Medical Institute of Bioregulation, Kyushu University, 1982-2000; Non-Resident Lecturer, Kyushu University, 2002-. Publications: Author of 163 original research papers in the fields of virology, cancer research, cell biology, somatic cell genetics and study of host-defence against viral infection. Honours: Fellow, Eleanor Roosevelt International Cancer Research Fellowship, American Cancer Society, 1968; Asahi Science Promotion Award, 1973. Memberships: Councillor, Japanese Society for Virology; Japanese Cancer Society; New York Academy of Sciences; Life Member, Association of UICC Fellows. Address: 4-2-15 Torikai, Jonan-ku, Fukuoka 814-0103 Japan.

KIMURA Masashi, b. 26 January 1966, Japan. Research Scientist. Education: Biological Sciences, 1986-89, Graduate School, 1989-93, University of Tsukuba; PhD, Science, 2000. Appointment: Gifu University School of Medicine, 1993-. Publications: Articles in scientific journals including: Journal of Biological Chemistry, 1997, 1999; Cancer Research, 1999; Molecular Cell Biology, 2002. Membership: Molecular Biology Society of Japan; American Society of Cell Biology. Address: Department of Molecular Pathobiochemistry, Gifu University School of Medicine, Tsukasamachi 40, Gifu 500-8705, Japan.

KINCAID John, b. 5 May 1946, Philadelphia, Pennsylvania, USA. Professor; Director. 2 daughters. Education: BA, Political Science, Temple University, Philadelphia, Pennsylvania, USA, 1967; MA, Urban Affairs, University of Wisconsin, Milwaukee, Wisconsin, 1968; PhD with distinction, Political Science, Temple University, Philadelphia, Pennsylvania, USA, 1981. Appointments include: Instructor, 1969-70, Adjunct Professor, 1976-77, Urban Studies, Saint Peter's College, Jersey City, New Jersey, USA; Assistant Professor, 1979-84, Associate Professor, 1984-94 (on leave 1987-94), Political Science, University of North Texas, Denton, Texas, USA; Executive Director, US Advisory Commission on Intergovernmental Relations, Washington DC, 1988-94; Robert B and Helen S Meyner Professor of Government and Public Service, 1994-, Director Robert B and Helen S Meyner Center for the Study of State and Local Government, 1994-, Acting Head, Department of Government and Law, 1997-98, Lafayette College, Easton, Pennsylvania, USA. Publications: Books: Political Culture, Public Policy and American States (editor and contributor), 1982; Covenant, Polity and Constitutionalism (co-editor and contributor), 1983; Competition among States ad Local Governments: Efficiency and Equity in American Federalism (co-editor and contributor), 1991; The Covenant Collection: From Federal Theology to Modern Federalism (co-editor), 2000; American Federalism: A Reference of History, Theory and Policy (editor), 2005; Numerous articles in professional journals, book chapters, book reviews and papers presented at conferences and symposia; Editor, Publius: The Journal of Federalism, 1986-; Editor, Politics and the Governments of the American States, 50 book series, 1989-; Editor, The Federalism Report, 2000-. Honours include: Grantee numerous research and academic program grants, 1979-; Elected Fellow, National Academy of Public Administration, 1991-; Distinguished Federalism Scholar, American Political Science Association, 2001. Memberships: Academy of Political Science; American Political Science Association; American Society for Public Administration; International Political Science Association; IPSA Comparative Federalism Study Group; National Academy of Public Administration. Address: Robert B and Helen S Meyner Center for the Study of State and Local Government, 002 Kirby Hall of Civil Rights, Lafayette College, Easton, PA 18042-1785, USA. E-mail: meynerc@lafayette.edu

KINDERSLEY Tania, b. 30 January 1967, London, England. Writer. Education: MA, Christ Church, Oxford. Publications: Goodbye, Johnny Thunders, 1997; Don't Ask Me Why, 1998; Elvis Has Left the Building, 2001; Nothing to Lose, 2002. Address: Home Farm, Aboyne, Aberdeenshire AB34 5JP, Scotland. E-mail: pulch66@totalscne.co.uk

KINDL Milan, b. 14 May 1954, Zatec, Czech Republic. Lawyer; Writer. 1 son. Education: Graduate, Law Faculty, Charles' University, Prague, Czech Republic, 1973-78; PhD, 1989; JuDr, 1980. Appointments: Judge, 1980-87; Vice-Director, Institute of State and Law, Czech Academy of Sciences, 1990-99; Dean, Law Faculty, West Bohemian University, 1999-; Editor-in-Chief, Lawyer, the oldest magazine for lawyers in the world, 1992-. Publications: 4 Novels: Affairs of CV; Night Guest; The Best Short Cut; Disservice; Monographs: Taxes and Duties; Encyclopaedia of Ecological Law; Law Adviser I-II; Ecological Crime; About 100 articles. Memberships: International Council for Ecological Law; Board of Directors, Czech Bar Association; Convocation of Law Faculty, Charles' University. Address: Zborovska 1315, Chomutov 43001, Czech Republic. E-mail: houdkof@fpr.zcu.cz Website: www.kindl-partwer/.cz

KING B B, b. 16 September 1925, Itta Bena, MI, USA. Singer; Musician. Education: Selftaught Guitar. Appointments: Member, Elkhorn Singers; Played with Sonny Boy Williamson, 1946;

Regular broadcast slot, The Sepia Swing Show, Radio WDIA; 300 Performances a Year, 1950s-70s; Numerous worldwide tours. Creative Works: Singles: Three O'Clock Blues; You Didn't Want Me; Please Love Me; You Upset Me Baby; Sweet Sixteen; Rock Me aby; The B B Jones; The Thrill is Gone. Honours: Grammy Awards, 1971, 1982; Best Traditional Blues Recording, 1984, 1986, 1991, 1992; Rock'n'Roll Hall of Fame, 1987; NARAS, 1988; Songwriters Hall of Fame, 1990; Gibson Guitars, 1991; Star in Hollywood Walk of Fame, 1990; MTV Video Award, with U2, 1989; Q Inspiration Award, 1992. Membership: Co-Chairman, Foundation for the Advancement of Inmate Rehabilitation & Recreation. Address: 1414 6th Avenue, New York, NY 10019, USA.

KING Billie Jean, b. 22 November 1943, California, USA. Tennis Player. m. Larry King, 1965, divorced. Education: Los Angeles State University. Career: Amateur status, 1958-67; Professional, 1967-; Championship Titles: Australia, 1968; South Africa, 1966, 1967, 1969; Wimbledon 20 Titles, 10 doubles, 4 mixed and 6 singles, 1966, 1967, 1968, 1972, 1973, 1975, Italy, 1970; Federal Republic of Germany, 1971; France, 1972; Winner, 1/046 singles tournaments, 1984; Other: Sports Commentator ABC-TV, 1975-78; Founded Women's Tennis Association, 1973; Publisher of Women's Sports, 1974-; US Tennis Team Commissioner, 1981-; CEO World Team Tennis, 1985-; US Federation Cup Team Captain, 1995-; Women's Olympic Tennis Coach, 1996, 2000; Virginia Simms Championship Series Consultant. Publications: Tennis to Win, 1970; Billie Jean, w K Chapin, 1974; We Have Come a Long Way: The Story of Women's Tennis, 1988. Honour: Top Woman Athlete of the Year, 1973. Address: c/o World Team Tennis, 445 North Wells, Suite 404, Chicago, IL 60610, USA.

KING Carole, b. 9 February 1942. Singer; Songwriter. Career: Songwriter in partnership with Gerry Goffin; Worked with artists including: Eric Clapton; Crosby & Nash; Branford Marsalis; David Sanborn; Numerous concerts and tours; Actress in theatre including: Starring role, Mrs Johnstone, Broadway production, Blood Brothers, 1994; Environmental activist for natural forest preservation; Presently studying European traditional music. Compositions: Hit songs include: Will You Love Me Tomorrow; Take Good Care Of My Baby; Go Away Little Girl; The Locomotion; Up On The Roof; Chains; One Fine Day; Hey Girl; I Feel The Earth Move; Natural Woman; Smackwater Jack; You've Got A Friend; Now And Forever (For film, A League Of Their Own); Soundtrack, animated film, Really Rosie. Recordings include: Albums: The City, 1968; Writer, 1970; Tapestry, 1971; Rhymes And Reasons, 1972; Music, 1972; Fantasy, 1973; Wrap Around Joy, 1974; Thoroughbred, 1975; Really Rosie, 1975; Simple Things, 1977; Welcome Home, 1978; Greatest Hits, 1978; Touch The Sky, 1979; Pearls, 1980, 1994; One To One, 1982; Speeding Time, 1983; City Streets, 1989; For Our Children, 1991; A League Of Their Own, 1992; 'Til Their Eyes Shine, 1992; Colour Of Your Dreams, 1993; In Concert, 1994; Time Gone By, 1994; A Natural Woman, 1994; Carnegie Hall Concert, 1996; Goin' Back, 1998; Love Makes the World, 2001; Single: Anyone at All, 1999. Honours include: Inducted Songwriters' Hall Of Fame, 1987; Rock And Roll Hall Of Fame, 1990; National Academy of Songwriters' Lifetime Achievement Award, 1988; Grammy Awards; Multi-Platinum, Platinum and Gold albums; Academy Award Nomination, Now And Forever. Memberships: AFTRA; AMPAS: NARAS; NAS; SAG; AFofM. Address: 11684, Ventura Boulevard, #273, Studio City, CA 91604, USA.

KING Cynthia, b. 27 August 1925, New York, New York, USA. Writer. m. Jonathan King, 26 July 1944, deceased 1997, 3 sons, 1 deceased. Education: Bryn Mawr College, 1943-44; University of Chicago, 1944-46; New York University Writers Workshop,

1964-67. Appointments: Associate Editor, Hillman Periodicals, 1946-50; Managing Editor, Fawcett Publications, 1950-55; Creative Writing Teacher, The Awty School, Houston, 1974-75. Publications: In the Morning of Time, 1970; The Year of Mr Nobody, 1978; Beggars and Choosers, 1980; Sailing Home, 1982. Contributions to: Book Reviews: New York Times Book Review; Detroit News; Houston Chronicle; LA Daily News; Short Fiction: Good Housekeeping, Texas Stories and Poems, Quartet. Honours: Michigan Council for the Arts, Artists Grant, 1986; Winner, Detroit Women Writers Spring Reading Series for Skaters – a New York Memoir, 2002. Memberships: Authors Guild; Poets and Writers; Detroit Women Writers, President 1979-81. Address: 228 River Street, Bethel, VT 05032, USA. E-mail: tonibking@aol.com

KING Francis Henry, (Frank Cauldwell), b. 4 March 1923, Adelboden, Switzerland. Author; Drama and Literary Critic. Education: BA, 1949, MA, 1951, Balliol College, Oxford. Appointment: Drama Critic, Sunday Telegraph, 1978-88. Publications: Novels: To the Dark Tower, 1946; Never Again, 1947; An Air That Kills, 1948; The Dividing Stream, 1951; The Dark Glasses, 1954; The Firewalkers, 1956; The Widow, 1957; The Man on the Rock, 1957; The Custom House, 1961; The Last of the Pleasure Gardens, 1965; The Waves Behind the Boat, 1967; A Domestic Animal, 1970; Flights, 1973; A Game of Patience, 1974; The Needle, 1975; Danny Hill, 1977; The Action, 1978; Act of Darkness, 1983; Voices in an Empty Room, 1984; Frozen Music, 1987; The Woman Who Was God, 1988; Punishments, 1989; Visiting Cards, 1990; The Ant Colony, 1991; Secret Lives (with Tom Wakefield and Patrick Gale), 1991; The One and Only, 1994; Ash on an Old Man's Sleeve, 1996; Dead Letters, 1997; Prodigies, 2001; The Nick of Time, 2003. Short Stories: So Hurt and Humiliated, 1959; The Japanese Umbrella, 1964; The Brighton Belle, 1968; Hard Feelings, 1976; Indirect Method, 1980; One is a Wanderer, 1985; A Hand at the Shutter, 1996. Other: E M Forster and His World, 1978; A Literary Companion to Florence, 1991; Autobiography: Yesterday Came Suddenly, 1993. Honours: Somerset Maugham Award, 1952; Katherine Mansfield Short Story Prize, 1965; Officer, 1979, Commander, 1985, of the Order of the British Empire. Memberships: English PEN, president, 1976-86; International PEN, president, 1986-89, vice-president, 1989-; Royal Society of Literature, fellow. Address: 19 Gordon Place, London W8 4JE, England. E-mail: fhk@dircon.co.uk

KING Larry, b. 19 November 1933, Brooklyn, USA. Broadcaster. m. (1) Alene Akins, 1 daughter, (2) Sharon Lepore, 1976, (3) Julia Alexander, 1989, 1 son, (4) Shawn Southwick, 1997. Appointments: Disc Jockey, various radio stations, Miami, Florida, 1957-71; Freelance Writer, Broadcaster, 1972-75; Radio Personality, Station WIOD, Miami, 1975-78; Writer, Entertainment Sections, Miami Herald, 7 years; Host, The Larry King Show, 1978-, 1990 Goodwill Games, WLA-TV Let's Talk, Washington DC; Columnist, USA Today, Sporting News; Appeared in films, Ghostbusters, 1984, Lost in America, 1985. Publications: Mr King, You're Having a Heart Attack (with B D Colen), 1989; Larry King: Tell Me More, When You're From Brooklyn, Everything Else is Tokyo, 1992; On the Line (jointly), 1993; Daddy Day, Daughter Day (jointly), 1997. Honours: Several broadcasting and journalism awards. Address: c/o CNN Larry King Live, 820 1st Street NE, Washington, DC 20002, USA.

KING Margaret Leah, b. 16 October 1947, New York, New York, USA. Professor of History; Author. m. Robert E Kessler, 2 sons. Education: BA, History, Sarah Lawrence College, 1967; MA, History, Stanford University, 1968; PhD, 1972. Appointments: Assistant Professor, California State College, Fullerton, 1969-70; Assistant Professor, Brooklyn College, 1972-76; Associate Professor, 1976-86; Professor, Brooklyn College and Graduate Center, CUNY, 1987-. Publications: Western Civilization: A Social and Cultural History; The Death of the Child Valerio Marcello; Women of the Renaissance; Venetian Humanism in an Age of Patrician Dominance; Her Immaculate Hand: Selected Works by and about the Women Humanities of Quattrocento Italy; Many others. Honours: Leonard and Claire Tow Distinguished Professor, 2000-02; Helen and Howard R Marraro Prize; Distinguished Guest Professor, University of Toronto; Tow Award for Distinction in Scholarship; Favourite Teacher, Brooklyn College; NEH Fellowship; Gladys Krieble Delmas Foundation Grant; Leonard and Claire Tow Distinguished Professor, 2000; Many others. Memberships: American Historical Association; Renaissance Society of America; Historical Society. Address: 324 Beverly Road, Douglaston, NY 11363, USA.

KING Mervyn Allister, b. 30 March 1948, Chesham Bois, England. Economist; Central Banker. Education: BA honours, King's College, Cambridge. Appointments: Junior Research Officer, 1969-73; Kennedy Scholarship, Harvard University, 1971-72; Research Officer, 1972-76; Lecturer, Faculty of Economics, Cambridge, 1976-77; Fellow, St John's College, Cambridge, 1972-77; Esmee Fairbairn Professor of Investment, University of Birmingham, 1977-84; Visiting Professor of Economics, Harvard University, 1982-83; Massachusetts Institute of Technology, 1983-84; Visiting Professor of Economics, Harvard University, and Senior Olin Fellow, National Bureau of Economic Research, 1990; Professor of Economics, London School of Economics, 1984-95; Chief Economist and Executive Director, Bank of England, 1991-98; Visiting Professor of Economics, London School of Economics, 1996-; Deputy Governor, Bank of England, 1998-2003; Governor, Bank of England, 2003-. Publications: Indexing for Inflation, 1975; Public Policy and the Corporation, 1977; The British Tax System, 1978, 5th edition, 1990; The Taxation of Income from Capital, 1984; Numerous articles in various journals. Honours include: Stevenson Prize, Cambridge University, 1970; Medal of the University of Helsinki, 1982; Honorary Fellow, St John's College, Cambridge, 1997; Honorary degrees from Birmingham and London Guildhall and City (London) Universities; Other activities: Advisory Council, London Symphony Orchestra, 2001-2003; Chairman of OEDC's Working Party 3 Committee, 2001-2003; Member, Group of Thirty, 1997-; President of Institute for Fiscal Studies, 1999-2003; Visiting Fellow, Nuffield College, Oxford, 2002-2003;. Address: Bank of England, Threadneedle Street, London EC2R 8AH, England.

KING Peggy, b. 25 April 1941, Hong Kong, China. Company President and Vice-President. m. Herbert King, 1 son, 1 daughter. Education: BA, Seattle University, USA, 1964; MA, University of Washington, USA, 1966. Appointments: President, King Real Estate International Inc, Houston, Texas, USA, 1979-; Vice-President, Totalmed, Houston, Texas, USA, 1997-. Publications: Column writer for: East & West Magazine; Southwest Journal; Southern Chinese News and Chinese Daily News; How to Invest in Real Estate; How to Balance Your Career and Your Family; The Similarity Between American Indian and Chinese Culture. Honours: Outstanding American Chinese Woman Award, Houston Texas, 1983; Excellence 2000 Awards (1989) at the White House, Washington DC; Business Leader of the Year, 1995; Distinguished Service Award, Science Engineering and Technology Conference at Houston, 2001; International Who's Who of Professionals, 2000; IBC Woman of the Year, 2004. Memberships: Board of Directors of SETS, 2001-2004; Better Business Bureau; United States Chamber of Commerce; National Association of Realtors; Houston Symphony League; Republican Women's League of the USA; Women's Tennis Club of the USA; International Who's Who of Professionals. E-mail: peggyking@totalmed-usa.com

Dictionary of International Biography

KING Stephen Edwin, (Richard Bachman), b. 21 September 1947, Portland, Maine, USA. Author. m. Tabitha J Spruce, 1971, 2 sons, 1 daughter. Education: University Maine. Appointments: Teacher, English, Hampden Academy, Maine, 1971-73; Writer-in-Residence, University of Maine, Orono, 1978-79. Publications: Carrie, 1974; Salem's Lot, 1975; The Shining, 1977; The Stand, 1978; The Dead Zone, 1979; Firestarter, 1980; Danse Macabre, 1981; Cujo, 1981; Christine, 1983; Pet Sematary, 1983; The Talisman (w Peter Straub), 1984; Cycle of the Werewolf, 1985; It, 1986; The Eyes of the Dragon, 1987; Misery, 1987; The Tommyknockers, 1987; The Dark Half, 1989; Four Past Midnight, 1990; Needful Things, 1991; Gerald's Game, 1992; The Girl Who Loved Tom Jordan, 1999; Hearts in Atlantis, 1999; Storm of the Century (adapted to mini-series), 1999; Riding the Bullet, 2000; On Writing, 2000; Dreamcatcher, 2001; Everything's Eventual, 2002; The Dark Tower Stories: Volume 1: The Gunslinger, 1982, Volume 2: The Drawing of the Three, 1984. Short Story Collections: Night Shift, 1978; Different Seasons, 1982; Skeleton Crew, 1985; Gerald's Game, 1992; Dolores Claiborne, 1993; Nightmares & Dreamscapes, 1993; Insomnia, 1994; As Richard Bachman: Thinner, 1984; The Bachman Books: Rage, The Long Walk, Roadwork, The Running Man, 1985; Numerous other short stories. Memberships: Authors Guild of America; Screen Artists Guild; Screen Writers of America; Writers Guild. Address: 49 Florida Avenue, Bangor, ME 04401, USA. Website: www.stephenking.com

KING Thomas, b. 1 June 1934, China. Physician; Physiologist. m. Amy, 2 daughters. Education: MB ChB, 1959, MD, 1963, University of Edinburgh. Appointments: Associate Professor of Medicine and Biophysics, Cornell University; Lecturer, Department of Medicine, University of Hong Kong; Fellow, Nuffield Foundation, Welsh National Medical School; Senior Tutor, Registrar, Queens University and Royal Victoria Hospital, Belfast. Publications include: The Physiology of Respiration and Pulmonary Function Tests. Part II. Tests of pulmonary function, 1977; Abnormalities of Blood Gas Exchange in Chronic Obstructive Pulmonary Diseases, 1977; Peripheral bronchial involvement in relapsing polychondritis: Demonstration by thin-section CT, 1989; Academia versus Clinic: Practice patterns in the diagnosis of pulmonary embolism at a large teaching hospital, 1994; Recent advances in the understanding and management of asthma, 1994. Honours: Fellow, Royal College of Physicians, London; Wu Chung Visiting Professor, University of Hong Kong; Harris Visiting Professor; Taiwan Pulmonary Academic Award, NIH, USA. Memberships: American Physiologic Society; American College of Chest Physicians; Medical Research Society of UK; American Federation of Clinical Research; American Thoracic Society. Address: Cornell University, Weill Medical College, 1300 York Avenue, NY 10021, USA.

KINGETSU Toshiki, b. 4 April 1949, Kobe, Japan. Materials Physicist; Researcher. m. Yukiko Hori, 1 son. Education: BEng, MEng, 1979, DEng, 1982, Osaka University. Appointments: Postdoctoral Associate, Cornell University, 1982-83; Senior Researcher, Nisshin Steel Company Limited, 1988-93, 2000-; Chief Researcher, Rrgaku Corporation, 1997-99. Publications: 80 articles in professional journals. Membership: Materials Research Society. Address: 6-13-17 Takakuradai, Suma, Kobe, Hyogo 654 0081, Japan.

KINGSLEY Ben, b. 31 December 1943, England. Actor. m. 3 sons, 1 daughter. Appointments: RSC, 1970-80, National Theatre, 1977-78; Associate Artist, RSC. Creative Works: Stage appearances include: A Midsummer Night's Dream; Occupations; The Tempest; Hamlet (title role); The Merry Wives of Windsor; Baal; Nicholas Nickleby; Volpone; The Cherry Orchard; The

Country Wife; Judgement; Statements After An Arrest; Othello (title role); Caracol in Melons; Waiting for God; TV appearances include: The Love School, 1974; Kean; Silas Marner; The Train, 1987; Murderous Amongst Us, 1988; Anne Frank; Several plays: Films: Gandhi, 1982; Betrayal, 1982; Harem, 1985; Turtle Diary, 1985; Without A Clue, 1988; Testimony, 1988; Pascali's Island, 1988; Bugsy, 1991; Sneakers, 1992; Innocent Moves, 1992; Dave, 1992; Schindler's List, 1993; Death and the Maiden, 1994; Species, 1995; Twelfth Night, 1996; Photographing Fairies, 1997; The Assignment, 1998; Weapons of Mass Destruction, 1998; Sweeney Todd, 1998; The Confession, 1999; Sexy Beast, 1999; Rules of Engagement, 1999; What planet Are You From? 1999; Spooky House, 1999; A.I., 2000; Triumph of Love, 2000; Anne Frank, 2000; Tuck Everlasting, 2001; Sound of Thunder, 2002; Suspect Zero, 2002; House of Sand and Fog, 2002. Honours include: 2 Hollywood Golden Globe Awards, 1982; NY Film Critics Award; 2 BAFTA Awards; Los Angeles Film Critics Award, 1983; Best Actor, British Industry Film Awards, 2001; Screen Actors' Guild Award for Best Actor, 2002. Address: c/o ICM, 76 Oxford Street, London W1N 0AX, England.

KINGSOLVER Barbara, b. 8 April 1955, Annapolis, Maryland, USA. Author; Poet. m. (1) Joseph Hoffmann, 1985, divorced 1993, 1 daughter, (2) Steven Hopp, 1995, 1 daughter. Education: BA, DePauw University, 1977; MS, University of Arizona, 1981. Appointments: Research Assistant, Department of Physiology, 1977-79, Technical Writer, Office of Arid Land Studies, 1981-85, University of Arizona, Tucson; Journalist, 1985-87; Author, 1987-; Founder, Bellwether Prize to recognize a first novel of social significance, 1997. Publications: The Bean Trees (novel), 1988; Homeland and Other Stories, 1989; Holding the Line: Women in the Great Arizona Mine Strike of 1983 (non-fiction), 1989; Animal Dreams (novel), 1990; Pigs in Heaven (novel), 1993; Another America (poems), 1994, new edition, 1998; High Tide in Tucson: Essays from Now or Never, 1995; The Poisonwood Bible (novel), 1998; Prodigal Summer (stories), 2000; Small Wonder, 2002; Last Stand, 2002. Contributions to: Many anthologies and periodicals. Honours: Feature-Writing Award, Arizona Press Club, 1986; American Library Association Awards, 1988, 1990; PEN Fiction Prize, 1991; Edward Abbey Ecofiction Award, 1991; Los Angeles Times Book Award for Fiction, 1993; PEN Faulkner, 1999; American Booksellers Book of the Year, 2000; National Humanities Medal, 2000; Governor's National Award in the Arts, Kentucky, 2002; John P McGovern Award for the Family, 2002; Physicians for Social Responsibility National Award, 2002; Academy of Achievement Golden Plate Award, 2003. Address: PO Box 31870, Tucson, AZ 85751, USA.

KINNO Yoshinori, Medical Doctor. Education: City University, Yokohama, Japan, 1987; Diplomate: Japanese Board of Radiology, Japanese Board of Nuclear Medicine, Japanese Board of Hyperthermia Oncology. Appointments: Resident, Japanese Railways Tokyo General Hospital, 1987; Resident, 1987-89, Staff, 1989-90, Yokohama City University, Japan; Kanagawa Cancer Centre, Yokohama, 1990-94; Chief, Department of Radiology, Kanagawa Cardiovascular and Respiratory Disease Centre, Yokohama, 1994-97; Head, Department of Radiology, Yokohama Minamikyousai Hospital, 1997-. Publication: Gadopentetate Dimeglumine as an alternative contrast material for use in angiography, 1993. Honour: Prizewinner, Image Interpretation Session, Japan Radiological Society, 1999, 2002. Memberships: Board of Directors, Japan Society of Angiography and Interventional Radiography; Japan Radiological Society; Japanese Society of Nuclear Medicine; Japanese Society of Hyperthermia Oncology. Address: 1-21-1 Mutuurahigashi, Kanazawaku, Yokohama, 236-0037 Japan.

Dictionary of International Biography

KINNOCK Glenys, b. 7 July 1944, Roade, Northamptonshire, England. Member of European Parliament, South Wales East. m. Neil Kinnock, 1 son, 1 daughter. Education: BA, Dip Ed, University College, Cardiff, 1962-66. Appointments: Primary and Secondary School Teacher, 1966-93; European Parliamentary Labour Party Spokesperson and Government Link on Development and Co-operation, Co-President of the African, Caribbean and Pacific States ACP-EU Joint Parliamentary Assembly; Member of European Parliament, South Wales East, 1994-99; Member of European Parliament, Wales, 1999-. Publications: Books: Voices for One World, 1987; Eritrea – Images of War and Peace, 1989; Nambia - Birth of a Nation, 1991; Could Do Better – Where is British Education in the European League Tables?; By Faith and Daring, 1993. Honours: Honorary Fellow, University of Wales College, Newport; Honorary Doctorates from: Thames Valley, Brunel and Kingston Universities; Fellow, Royal Society of Arts. Memberships: NUT; GMB; President, One World Action; Patron, Saferworld; Council Member, Voluntary Service Overseas; Patron, Drop the Debt Campaign; Vice President, Parliamentarians for Global Action; Board Member, International AIDS Vaccine Initiative; Board Member, World Parliamentarian Magazine; President, Coleg Harlech; Patron, Welsh Woman of the Year; Vice President, South East Wales Racial Equality Council; Vice President, St David's Foundation; Special Needs Advisory Project, Cymru; UK National Breast Cancer Coalition Wales; Community Enterprise Wales and Charter Housing; Patron, Burma Campaign UK; Crusaid; Elizabeth Hardie Ferguson Trust; Medical Foundation for Victims of Torture; National Deaf Children's Society; Council Member, Britain in Europe. Address: 1 Bridge View, Cwmfelinfach, Newport, South Wales NP1 7HG, Wales.

KINNOCK Neil Gordon, b. 28 March 1942, England. Politician. m. Glenys Elizabeth Parry, 1967, 1 son, 1 daughter. Education: Pengam University College, Cardiff. Appointments: President, University College Cardiff Students Union, 1965-66; Tutor, Organizer, Industrial & Trade Union Studies, Workers' Educational Association, 1966-70; MP for Bedwellty, 1970-83, for Islwyn, 1983-95; Member, Welsh Hospital Board, 1969-71; Parliamentary Private Secretary to Secretary of State for Employment, 1974-75; Member, National Executive Committee, Labour Party, 1974-94; Leader of Labour Pty, 1983-92; Leader of the Opposition, 1983-92; EC Commissioner with Responsibility for Transport, 1995-99; President, Cardiff University, 1998-; Vice-President, European Commission, 1999-2004. Publications: Wales and the Common Market, 1971; Making Our Way, 1986; Thorns and Roses, 1992; Numerous contributions in periodicals, newspapers and books including The Future of Social Democracy, 1999. Honours: Several honorary doctorates. Address: European Commission, 200 rue de la Loi, 1049 Brussels, Belgium.

KINSKI Natassja, b. 24 January 1961, West Berlin, Germany. Actress. m. I Moussa, 1984, 1 son, 1 daughter; 1 daughter with Quincy Jones. Career: Debut in Falsche Bewegung, 1975; Films include: Stay as You Are, 1978; Cat People, 1982; Moon in the Gutter, 1983; Unfaithfully Yours; Paris; Texas and the Hotel New Hampshire, 1984; Magdalene, 1989; Terminal Velocity, 1994; One Night Stand, 1997; Sunshine, 1998; Town and Country, 1999; The Claim, 2000; The Day the World Ended, 2001; An American Rhapsody, 2001. Address: c/o Peter Levine, William Morris Agency, 151 South El Camino Drive, Beverly Hills, CA 90212, USA.

KIPLE Kenneth F, b. 29 January 1939, Iowa, USA. Professor. m. 1 son, 4 daughters. Education: BA, University of South Florida, 1965; PhD, University of Florida, 1970. Appointments: Instructor, Department of Social Studies, University of Florida, 1969-70; Assistant Professor, 1970-76, Associate Professor, 1976-81,

Professor of History, 1981-94, Distinguished University Professor, 1994-, Department of History, Bowling Green State University. Publications include: Blacks in Colonial Cuba 1774-1899, 1976; Another Dimension to the Black Diaspora: Diet, Disease and Racism, 1981; The Caribbean Slave: A Biological History, 1984; The African Exchange: Toward a Biological History of Black People, 1988; The Cambridge World History of Human Disease, 1993; Biological Consequences of the European Expansion 1450-1800, 1997; Plague, Pox, Pestilence: Disease in History, 1997; The Cambridge World History of Food, 2 volumes, 2000. Honours: Several. Address: Department of History, Bowling Green State University, 1001 East Wooster Street, Bowling Green, OH 43403-0001, USA.

KIRBY Gordon William, b. 20 June 1934, Wallasey, Cheshire, England. Chemist; Emeritus Professor. m. Audrey Jean Rusbridge, div 1983, 2 sons. Education: Liverpool Technical College, 1950-52; Exhibitioner, 1953-54, Minor Scholar, 1954-55, Dunlop Research Student, 1955-58, BA, 1955, MA, 1959, PhD, 1958, ScD, 1971, Gonville and Caius College, Cambridge. Appointments: 1851 Exhibition Senior Studentship, 1958-60, Assistant Lecturer, 1960-61, Lecturer, 1961-67, Imperial College, London; Professor of Organic Chemistry, Loughborough University of Technology, 1967-72; Regius Professor of Chemistry, 1972-96, Professor of Chemistry, 1997, currently Emeritus Professor of Chemistry, University of Glasgow. Publications: Research papers mainly in the Journals of the Royal Society of Chemistry; Co-editor, Progress in the Chemistry of Organic Natural Products, 1971-. Honours: Schuldam Plate, Gonville and Caius College, Cambridge, 1956; Corday-Morgan Medal and Prize, Royal Society of Chemistry, 1969; Tilden Lecturership and Medal, Royal Society of Chemistry, 1974-75. Memberships: FRSC and C.Chem, 1970; FRSE, 1975; Member, American Chemical Society; Member, Royal Philosophical Society of Glasgow. Address: Department of Chemistry, University of Glasgow, G12 8QQ, Scotland.

KIRK Raymond Maurice, b. 31 October 1923, Beeston, Nottinghamshire, England. Surgeon, retired. m. Margaret Schafran, 1 son, 2 daughters. Education: King's College, London; Charing Cross Hospital, London; University of London. Appointments: Ordinary Seaman to Lieutenant RNVR, 1942-46; House Surgeon and Casualty Officer, Charing Cross Hospital, 1952; Lecturer in Anatomy, King's College, London, 1952-53; House Surgeon and Resident Surgical Officer, Royal Postgraduate Medical School, Hammersmith Hospital, London, 1953-56; Registrar and Senior Registrar, Charing Cross Hospital, 1956-60; Senior Surgical Registrar, Royal Free Hospital, 1961; Consultant Surgeon, Willesden General Hospital, 1962-72; Consultant Surgeon and Honorary Senior Lecturer, Royal Free Hospital, 1964; Part-time Lecturer in Anatomy and Developmental Biology, University College, London; Honorary Consulting Surgeon, Honorary Senior Lecturer, Royal Free Hospital and Royal Free and University College, London School of Medicine, 1989-. Publications: Author and co-author, 8 books; Numerous articles and chapters in professional medical journals. Memberships: Royal College of Surgeons of England; Court of Examiners; Royal Society of Medicine; Hunterian Society; Medical Society of London; Association of Surgeons of Poland; Association of Surgeons of Sri Lanka. Address: 10 Southwood Lane, Highgate Village, London N6 5EE, England. E-mail: kirk@rfc.ucl.ac.uk

KIRK-GREENE Anthony (Hamilton Millard), b. 16 May 1925, Tunbridge Wells, England. m. Helen Sellar, 1967. University Lecturer; Fellow; Writer; Editor. Education: BA, 1949, MA, 1954, Clare College, Cambridge; MA, Oxford University, 1967. Appointments: Senior Lecturer in Government, Institute of Administration, Zaria, Nigeria, 1957-62; Professor of Government,

Ahmadu Bello University, Nigeria, 1962-65; University Lecturer and Fellow, St Antony's College, Oxford, 1967-, Director, Foreign Service Programme, 1986-90, Oxford University; Associate Professor, Stanford University (Oxford Campus), 1992-99; Associate Editor, New Dictionary of National Biography, 1996-2003. Publications: A Biographical Dictionary of the British Colonial Service, 1939-66, 1991; Diplomatic Initiative: A History of the Foreign Service Programme, 1994; On Crown Service, 1999; Britain's Imperial Administrators, 2000; The British Intellectual Engagement with Africa in the 20th Century (co-editor), 2000; Glimpses of Empire, 2001. Contributions to: Various reference books and scholarly journals. Honours: Member of the Order of the British Empire, 1963; Hans Wolff Memorial Lecturer, 1973; Fellow, Royal Historical Society, 1985; Festschrift, 1993; Leverhulme Emeritus Fellowship, 1993; Companion of the Order of St Michael and St George, 2001. Memberships: Royal African Society; International African Institute; Britain – Nigeria Association, Council Member, 1985-; African Studies Association of UK, President, 1988-90; Vice President, Royal African Society, 1992-. Address: c/o St Antony's College, Oxford OX2 6JF, England.

KIRKHOPE Timothy John Robert, b. 29 April 1945, Newcastle upon Tyne, England. Solicitor. m. Caroline Maling, 4 sons. Education: Law Society College of Law, Guildford, Surrey. Appointments: Qualified as Solicitor, 1973; Partner, Wilkinson Maughan, now Eversheds, Newcastle upon Tyne, 1977-87; Conservative, Member of Parliament, Leeds North East, 1987-97; Government Whip, 1990-95; Vice Chamberlain to HM the Queen, 1995; Under Secretary of State, Home Office, 1995-97; Business Consultant, 1997-; Member of European Parliament, Yorkshire and the Humber, 1999-; Spokesman on Citizens Rights, Justice and Home Affairs, 1999-; Chief Whip, Conservative Delegation, 1999-2001; Member, Future of Europe Convention, 2002-. Memberships: Fountain Society; Northern Counties Club; Dunstanburgh Castle Golf Club; Newcastle Aero Club, private pilot. Address: c/o ASP 14E, 246 European Parliament, Rue Wiertz, B-1047 Brussels, Belgium. E-mail: tkirkhope@europarl.eu.int

KIRSZENSTEIN-SZEWINSKA Irena, b. 24 May 1946, Leningrad, Russia. Athlete. m. 2 sons. Education: Warsaw University. Appointments: Athlete, 1961-80 (100m, 200m, long jump, 4 x 100m relay, 4 x 400m relay); Took part in Olympic Games, Tokyo, 1964, Munich, 1972; 10 times world record holder for 100m, 200m, 400m; President, Polish Women's Sport Association, 1994-; Polish Athletic Association, 1997-; Vice President, Polish Olympic Committee, 1988, Polish Olympians Association, 1993, World Olympians Association, 1995-; Member, Council European Athletic Association, 1995-, Women's Committee, International Association of Athletics' Federation, International Olympic Committee, 1998-, President, Irena Szewinska Foundation-Vita-Aktiva, 1998, IOC Coordination Committee, Athens, 2004-. Honours include: Gold Cross of Merit, 1964; Officer Cross, Order of Polonia Restituta, 1968; Commander's Cross, Order of Polonia Restituta, 1972, with Star, 1999; Order of Banner of Labour, 2nd class, 1976. Address: Polish Athletic Association, ul Ceglowska 68/70, 01-809 Warsaw, Poland.

KIRTON Jennifer Carol Myers, b. 16 September 1949, Berwick, Pennsylvania, USA. Artist. m. Timothy Lee Kirton, 2 sons, 1 daughter. Education: Registered Nurse, Orange Memorial Hospital School of Nursing, Orlando, Florida; Art mentors include Charles Turzak, Don Haris, Joy Postell and Jean Schupert. Appointments: Group and solo exhibitions of art works; Art judge and juror; Artistic demonstrations and lectures. Publications: Numerous articles in popular journals; Logo designs. Honours include: First,

second and third place, First Annual Art Works juried show, 2000. Memberships: Leesburg Association of Artists; National Museum of Women in the Arts; Founding Member, Florida Committee of National Museum in the Arts, Florida; Past President, Orange County League of Artists. Address: 4700 Meadowland Drive, Mount Dora, FL 32757, USA. E-mail: kirtonart@aol.com

KIRUNDA Ezra, b. 21 February 1942, Nawango, Uganda. Mathematician; Educator. m. Rosemary, 2 daughters. Education: MSc, 1970, PhD, 1973, Mathematics, Friendship University, Moscow, Russia; Postgraduate diploma, Population Studies, University College, Cardiff, Wales, 1981. Appointments: Lecturer, Department of Mathematics, Makerer University, Kampala, Uganda, 1973-76; Lecturer, Department of Mathematics and Statistics, University of Nairobi, Kenya, 1976-80; Lecturer, 1981-84, Senior Lecturer, 1984-85, and Head, Department of Mathematics, University of Swaziland; Associate Professor of Mathematics, University of Transkei, South Africa, 1985-86; Professor and Head, Department of Mathematics and Computer Science, University of Venda, Republic of South Africa, 1986-. Memberships: South Africa Mathematical Society; South African Mathematical Education Reform Network. Address: PO Box 11814, Bendor Park, Polokwane 0699, South Africa.

KISA Jack Jacob, b. 12 June 1937, Maragoli, Kenya. Economist. m. Priscilla Wesa, 3 daughters. Education: BSc (Hons), Economics, University of London, England, 1964; Diploma, International Development, York University, Toronto, Canada, 1969; MPA, Economic Development, Harvard University, USA, 1971. Appointments: Senior Economist, Principal Economist, Ministry of Finance and Planning, Kenya Government; Director, World Employment Programme in Africa, UN; Economist, Senior Economist, The World Bank. Publications: Numerous publications in professional journals. Honours: Shell BP Prize for Best Economics Student; Who's Who in the World, 1998, 2000-01, 2002. Memberships: American Economic Association; Karen Country Club. Address: 15 Ngong View Rise, Karen, PO Box 24204, Nairobi 00502, Kenya.

KISELOVA Natalia, b. 15 August 1971, Minsk, Belarus. Philologist. 1 daughter. Education: University Diploma of Belarussian and Russian Philology, 1993; Doctor of Slavic Languages, 2000; Doctor of Philosophy, 2003. Appointments: Scientific Researcher, Institute of Linguistics, Belarussian Academy of Sciences, 1993-99; University Tutor, Slovak and Polish, Philological Faculty, Belarussian State University, 1997-99; University Tutor, Slavic Languages, Matej Bel University, Banska Bystica, Slovakia, 1999-. Publications: 3 monographs in the field of Areal lingustics and Slavic literatures, 200, 2002, 2003; 2 university textbooks, 2000, 2000; More than 40 articles in scientific publications; 2 books of poetry, 2000, 2002; Translations of poetry, 2000. Honour: Nominated as Woman of the Year 2003, American Biographical Institute. Membership: Editorial Board, scientific magazine: Filologicka Revue, Slovakia, Executive Redactor; Slovak Society of Interpreters; The Society of Slavic Unity. Address: Ruzova 11, 97553, Banska Bystrica, Slovakia. E-mail: natkis@pobox.sk

KISHORE KUMAR Rajagopal, b. 19 March 1963, Kollegal, India. Paediatrician. m. Vidya, 1 son, 1 daughter. Education includes: MBBS, Gulbarga University, India, 1986; DCH, 1988, MD Paed, 1989, Mysore University, Mysore, India; PLAB Test, General Medical Council, London, UK; DCH Royal College of Physicians, London, UK, 1991; MRCP Pt I and 2, Royal College of Physicians, Dublin, Ireland, 1992-93; US Medical Licensing Examination, USA, 1994-95; Fellow, Royal Australasian College of Physicians, 1999; Fellow, Royal College of Physicians, Dublin,

2000. Appointments: House Officer, Senior House Officer and Registrar in 4 hospitals in India, 1985-90; Numerous appointments in the UK include: Senior House Officer, Paediatrics, Ashford Hospital, Middlesex, 1991; Senior House Officer in Neonatal Paediatrics, Dudley Road Hospital, Birmingham, 1992; Registrar in Paediatrics and Paediatric Endocrinology, 1993-94, Registrar in Paediatric Nephrology, 1994, Royal Victoria Infirmary, Newcastle upon Tyne; Consultant Paediatrician, Whiston Hospital, Merseyside, 1994-95; Appointments in Australia: Fellow Neonatal Intensive Care Unit, Monash Medical Centre, Melbourne, 1995-96; Senior Paediatric Registrar Intensive Care Unit, Sydney Children's Hospital, 1996; Senior Paediatric Registrar, NSW NETS, 1996; Lecturer in Paediatrics, 1997-2001, Senior Lecturer in Paediatrics and Child Health, 2001- University of Tasmania; Consultant Paediatrician and Neonatologist, 1996-2001, Visiting Medical Officer in Paediatrics, 2001-, Honorary Head, Department of Paediatrics, 2002-, North West Regional Hospital, Burnie, Tasmania. Publications: 41 publications and articles in medical journals include most recently: How safe is hepatitis B vaccination at birth?, 2000; Not every child who coughs has asthma, 2000; Urinary tract infection in children – Tips for a family physician, 2001; Bronchiolitis (book chapter), 2001. Honours include: Gold Medal, All India Medicos Society; Elected Secretary, Tasmanian Branch, Australian Medical Association for 2 years, 2000-2002; Honorary Referee, Journal of Post Graduate Medicine, India, 2000; Elected Member, Rostrum Club, Burnie, 2000. Memberships include: Indian Academy of Paediatrics, Royal College of Paediatrics and Child Health, UK; Associate Member, American Academy of Paediatrics; Australian Medical Association; Indian Medical Association; New York Academy of Sciences. Address: PO Box 1625, Subiaco, WA 6904, Australia. E-mail: kishkum@hotmail.com

KITANO Hirohisa, b. 28 January 1931, Toyama, Japan. Tax Law Educator. m. Hachie Aoyama, 3 sons. Education: LLB, Ritsumeikan University, Kyoto, Japan, 1955; LLM, Waseda University, Tokyo, 1962; LLD, Ritsumeikan University, 1974. Appointments: Staff, Bureau of Tax, Ministry of Finance, Tokyo, 1955-60; Lecturer, University of Toyama, 1962-89; Lecturer University of Tokyo, 1963-64, 1977-79; Assistant Professor, 1964-66, Associate Professor, 1966-71, Professor, 1971-2001, Professor Emeritus, 2001-, Nihon University, Tokyo; Chief, Nihon University Comparative Law Institute, 1996-98, President, Nihon University Law Library, 1998-99; Visiting Scholar, University of California, Berkeley, 1975-76. Publications: Structures of Modern Tax Law, 1972; Rights of Taxpayers, 1981; Japanese Constitution and Public Finance 1983; Taxpayers Fundamental Rights, 1991; Theory of Business Tax Law, 1994; Japanese General Consumption Tax, 1996; Study of Tax Professional, 1997; Fundamental Theory of Science of Tax Law, 2003. Honours: Onoazusa Prize, Waseda University, 1962; Nihon University Award, 1977, 1995; Prize, Japan Association of Tax Consultants, 1973, 1977; Honorary Professor, Southwest University of Political Science and Law, China, 2000. Memberships: President, Japan Taxpayers Association, 1977-; Director, Japan Civil Liberties Union, 1978-2002; Tokyo Bar Association, 1981-; President, Japan Association of Public Financial Law, 1991-2000; President, Japan Democratic Lawyers Association, 1993-; President, Japan Association of Science of Taxation, 1995-; Science Council of Japan, 1994-2003; Vice-president, Japan Lawyers International Solidarity Association, 1995-. Address: 5-9-25 Kitamachi, Kokubunji, Tokyo 1850001, Japan.

KITCHELL Kenneth Francis Jr, 24 October 1947, Brockton, Massachusetts, USA. Professor of Classics. m. Theresa Barre, 1 daughter. Education: BA, magna cum laude, Classics, College of the Holy Cross, Worcester, Massachusetts, 1969; MA, Classical

Studies, Loyola University of Chicago, 1972; Hetty Goldman Fellow, American School of Classical Studies, 1972-73; PhD, Classical Studies, Loyola University of Chicago, 1977. Appointments include: Instructor, Louisiana State University, 1976-78, Assistant Professor, 1978-83, Associate Professor, 1983-94, Gertrude Smith Professor, Director of Summer Programme, American School of Classical Studies, Summer 1989; Co-Director, Programme in Greece for Vergilian Society of America, Summer 1990; Full Professor, 1994-99, Named Distinguished Alumni Professor, 1997; Visiting Professor, University of Massachusetts, 1998-99; Full Professor, 1999-. Publications: Books, monographs include: A Trilogy on the Herpetology of Linnaeus's Systema Naturae X (co-author), Smithsonian Herpetological Service Vol 100, 1994; Entering the Stadium. Approaches to Ancient Greek Athletics, editor and contributor for Classical Bulletin, thematic issue, fall 1998; 2 large volumes, Albertus Magnus De Animalibus: A Medieval Summa Zoologica (co-author), 1999; Albert the Great: A Selectively Annotated Bibliography (1900-2000) (co-author), 2004; 50 articles and chapters. Honours: George Deer Teaching Award, finalist, Spring 1980; American Philological Association Award for Excellence in the Teaching of Classics, 1983; LSU Student Government Association Faculty Award, 1991; Robert L (Doc) Amborski Distinguished Honors Professor Award, 1993; Hewlett Teaching Fellow, University of Massachusetts, Amherst, 2000. Memberships include: Vice President for Education (elected post), American Philological Association, 1998-2002; President, American Classical League, 2002-. Address: Department of Classics, Herter 529, University of Massachusetts, Amherst, MA 01003, USA. E-mail: kkitchel@classics.umass.edu

KITE Thomas O Jr, b. 9 December 1949, Austin, Texas, USA. Golfer. m. Christy Kite, 2 sons, 1 daughter. Appointments: Won Walker Cup, 1971; Turned Professional, 1972; Won Ryder Cup, 1979, 1981, 1983, 1985, 1987, 1989, 1993; European Open, 1980, US Open, Pebble Beach, CA, 1992; LA Open, 1993; 10 US PGA Wins; Appointed Captain, US Team for 1997 Ryder Cup, Valderrama, Spain; Joined Sr PGA Tour 2000; Numerous wins including The Countryside Tradition, 2000; MasterCard Championship, 2002; Spokesman for Chrysler Jr Golf Scholarship Programme. Address: c/o PGA Tour, 112 Tpc Boulevard, Ponte Vedra Beach, FL 32082, USA.

KITIS Eliza, b. 27 February 1946, Thessaloniki. Professor; Linguistics. m. George Kitis, 2 sons. Education: MA, Theoretical Linguistics, University of Essex, England, 1975; PhD, Philosophy of Language, University of Warwick, England, 1982. Appointments: Lecturing at Department of English, Aristotle University, Thessaloniki, Greece, 1981-. Publications: Names of periodicals, Journal of Pragmatics, 1987, 1997, 1999; Word and Image, 1997; Pragmatics and Cognition, 2000, many others. Honours: Various studentships, Department of Education and Science, England; Major 3 year studentship, 1976. Memberships: LAGB, IASS, AIMAV, ESSE, HASE, ICLA; IPrA. Address: Department of English, Aristotle University, Thessaloniki 54124, Greece. E-mail: ekitis@enl.auth.gr

KITT Eartha Mae, b. 26 January 1928, South Carolina, USA. Actress; Singer. m. William MacDonald, 1960, divorced, 1 daughter. Career: Soloist, Katherine Graham Dance Group, 1948; Night Club Singer, 1949-; Theatre Work includes: Dr Faustus, Paris, 1951; New Faces, 1952; Timbuktu, 1978; Blues in the Night, 1985; The Wizard of Oz, 1998; The Wild Party, 2000; Films include: New Faces, 1953; Accused, 1957; Anna Lucasta, 1958; Synanon, 1965; Up the Chastity Belt, 1971; Boomerang, 1991; Fatal Instinct, 1993; Numerous TV appearances. Publications: Thursday's Child, 1956; A Tart is Not a Sweet, Alone with Me, 1976; I'm Still Here, 1990; Confessions of a Sex Kitten, 1991.

Dictionary of International Biography

Publications: Thursday's Child, 1956; A Tart is Not a Sweet, Alone with Me, 1976; I'm Still Here, 1990; Confessions of a Sex Kitten, 1991; Down to Earth (jointly), 2000; How to Rejuvenate: It's Not Too Late (jointly), 2000. Honour: National Association of Negro Musicians Woman of the Year, 1968. Address: c/o Eartha Kitt Productions, Flat 37, 888 7th Avenue, New York, NY 10106, USA.

KITTLEMAN Martha Adrienne, b. 31 December 1936, Houston, Texas, USA. Caterer; Decorator; Florist. m. Edmund Taylor Kittleman, 3 sons, 2 daughters. Education: BA, University of Mississippi; 2 years, University of Tulsa; UNC; Silver Jubilee, Oxford University, England, 1977; Correspondence degrees, Floristry, Interior Decorating, Antiques. Appointments: Owner, Chef, Adrienne's Tea Room, Bartlesville, Oklahoma, 1979; Head Cook, Bluestem Girl Scout Council, Bartlesville, 1993; Head Cook, Washington/Nowata Counties Community Action Fund Inc (WNCCAF), Dewey, Oklahoma, 1993; Supervisor, Aftercare Program, St John School, Bartlesville, 1994-95; Gourmet Cook, International Mozart Festival, Bartlesville, 1998; Sampler, Auntie Anne's Pretzels, Bartlesville, 1998; Director Associate of RBC; Abundant Health Associates, Independent Member of RBC. Honours: Advisory Council, IBC; Nominee, Woman of the Year, IBC; Member, Society of Descendants of Knights of the Most Noble Order of the Garter; Listed in biographical dictionaries. Memberships: Bartlesville Choral Society; Eucharistic Minister; Magna Carta Dames; Plantagenet Society; Delta Delta Delta Sorority. Address: 110 Fleetwood Place, Bartlesville, OK 74006, USA. E-mail: aewkm7p8@aol.com

KITTREDGE William Alfred, (Owen Rountree), b. 14 August 1932, Portland, Oregon, USA. Professor; Writer. 1 son, 1 daughter. Education: BS, Agriculture, Oregon State University, 1954; MFA, University of Iowa, 1969. Appointment: Professor Emeritus of English, University of Montana. Publications: We Are Not In This Together, 1982; Owning It All, 1984; Hole in the Sky, 1992; Who Owns the West?, 1996; Portable Western Reader (editor), 1998; Balancing Water, 2000; The Nature of Generosity, 2000; Southwestern Homelands, 2002. Contributions to: Time; Newsweek; New York Times; Wall Street Journal; Esquire; Outside; Paris Review. Address: 143 South 5th East, Missoula, MT 59801, USA.

KIVELÄ Sirkka-Liisa, b. 14 January 1947, Temmes, Finland. Professor. m. Mauri Akkanen. Education: Medical Doctor, 1971; Doctor of Philosophy, 1983; Associate professor in Family Medicine, 1984; Specialist in Family Medicine, 1976; Specialist in Geriatrics, 1985. Appointments: Chief Physician, Posio Health Centre, 1971-80; Senior Lecturer in Geriatrics, Tampere University, 1980-88; Professor in Public Health, Oulu University, 1988-90; Professor in Family Medicine, Oulu University, 1990-2000; Professor in Family Medicine, Turku University, 2000-. Publications: Over 300 scientific articles in English and Finnish; 40 publications for medical education. Honours: Eeva Jalavisto Prize, 1996; Sv Aa og Magda Friederichens Prize, 1999. Address: University of Turku, Department of Family Medicine, Lemminkaisenkatu 1, 20014 University of Turku, Finland. Website: www.utu.fi/med/yleislaak/kivela.html

KIWERSKI Jerzy Edward, b. 24 June 1937, Warsaw, Poland. Physician. m. Szymczak Dorota, 1 son, 3 daughters. Education: Physician, 1963; Doctor of Medical Sciences, 1971; Habilitation, 1975; Professor of Medicine, 1984. Appointments: Head and Chairman, Rehabilitation Clinic, Warsaw Medical University, 1982-; Regional Consultant in Rehabilitation, 1981-2002; National Consultant in Rehabilitation, 2002-; Vice President, 1990, President, 1999, Committee of Rehabilitation, Polish Academy of Sciences; Director, Metropolitan Rehabilitation Center, 1991-98;

President, Polish Society of Rehabilitation, 1992-99; Honorary Member, Polish Society of Rehabilitation, 2002-; New York Academy of Sciences, 1993; Vice-President, Polish Society of Biomechanics, 1994-2000. Publications: 17 handbooks; Over 520 articles in national and international periodicals; Over 330 lecture and congress papers. Honours: Ministry of Health Awards; President of Warsaw Award, National Orders; Outstanding Man of 21st Century, ABI; 2000 Outstanding Intellectuals of the 20th Century, IBC; Man of the Year 2001, ABI; Listed in several biographical publications. Memberships: International Medical Society of Paraplegia; European Spine Society; International Rehabilitation Medical Association; European Board of Physical Medicine and Rehabilitation. Address: Chyliczki, Orchidei 4, 05-500 Piaseczno, Poland.

KLAUER Karl Christoph, b. 30 October 1961, Bad Kreuznach, Germany. University Professor. m. Susanne. Education: Diploma in Mathematics, 1984, Diploma in Psychology, 1985, PhD in Psychology, 1988, Hamburg University; Habilitation, FU Berlin, 1992. Appointments: Assistant Lecturer, Hamburg University, 1985-88; Assistant Professor, FU Berlin, 1988-94; Professor, Heidelberg University, 1994-96; Professor, Bonn University, 1996-. Publications: Numerous articles in professional journals. Honours: Heinz-Heckhausen Jungwissenschaftlerpreis, 1990; Heisenberg Scholarship, 1993; Award for Outstanding Research of the International Federation of Classification Societies, 1993; Award for Distinguished Contributions to Psychological Assessment, 1995. Memberships: German Psychological Society; American Psychological Association; American Psychological Society; International Classification Societies; Society of Experimental Social Psychology; European Association of Experimental Social Psychology. Address: Psychology Institute, Bonn University, Roemerstr 164, 53117 Bonn, Germany. E-mail: christoph.klauer@uni-bonn.de

KLEBANOV Iakov Mordukhovich, b. 9 September 1949, Samara, Russia. Professor; Researcher. m. Olga R Klebanova, 1 son. Education: Mechanical Engineer, 1971; PhD, Engineering Science, Solid Mechanics, 1975; Doctor of Science Degree, Solid mechanics, 1989; Professor's Certificate, 1992. Appointments: Mechanical Engineer, 1971; Assistant Professor, 1977-81, Associate Professor, 1981-90, Department of Machine Components, Professor, Department of Machine Design Theory, 1990-94, Head of Mechanics Department, 1994-, Deputy Director, Institute of Mechanics and Technology, 2000-, Samara State Technical University. Publications: Uniqueness of solutions of non-homogenous and anisotropic problems of non-linear viscoelasticity, 1996; Constitutive equations of creep under changing multiaxial stresses, 1999; A parallel computational method in steady power-law creep, 2001. Honours: Fellowship Grants by EPSRC, UK, German Academic Exchange Service; International Collaboration Award, NSF, USA; Best Paper Award, 8th International ANSYS Conference. Memberships: Russian Academy of Quality Problems; European Mechanics Society. Address: PO Box 4038 Samara, 443110 Russia. E-mail: klebanov@samgtu.ru

KLEIN Calvin Richard, b. 19 November 1942, New York, USA. Fashion Designer. m. (1) Jayne Centre, 1964, 1 daughter, (2) Kelly Rector, 1986. Education: Fashion Institute of Technology, New York. Appointments: Own Fashion Business, 1968; President, Designer, Calvin Klein Ltd, 1969-; Consultant, Fashion Institute of Technology, 1975-. Honours: Coty Award, 1973, 1974, 1975; Coty Hall of Fame; FIT President's Award, Outstanding Design Council of Fashion Designers of America. Memberships: Council of Fashion Designers. Address: Calvin Klein Industries Inc, 205 West 39th Street, NY 10018, USA.

Dictionary of International Biography

KLEMP Harold, b. USA. Ministry Writer; Lecturer. Education: Colleges in Milwaukee, Fort Wayne, Indiana. Appointments: US Air Force; Radio Intercept Operator, Goodfellow AFB, Texas. Publications: The Wind of Change; Soul Travelers of the Far Country; Child in the Wilderness; The Living Word, Books 1 and 2; The Book of ECK Parables, vols 1-4; The Spiritual Exercises of ECK; Ask the Master, Books 1 and 2; The Dream Master; We Come as Eagles; The Drumbeat of Time; The Slow Burning Love of God; The Secret of Love; Our Spiritual Wake-Up Calls; A Modern Prophet Answers Your Questions About Life; The Art of Spiritual Dreaming, 1999; Autobiography of a Modern Prophet, 2000; How to Survive Spiritually in Our Times, 2001; The Spiritual Laws of Life, 2002; Past Lives, Dreams and Soul Travel, 2003; The Language of Soul, 2003; Your Road Map to the ECK Teachings: ECKANKAR Study Guide, 2 vols, 2003. Address: c/o Eckankar, PO Box 27300, Minneapolis, MN 55427, USA.

KLEVER Paul, b. Germany. Scientist; Educator; Businessman. Education: M Eng, Department of Chemical and Mechanical Engineering, University of Applied Sciences, Cologne, Germany; MSc, Chemical Engineering, Technical University of Berlin, Germany; Master of Business Administration, Trinity University, Texas, USA; Doctorate of Science in Chemistry, Vasile Goldis Western University, Arad, Romania; PhD, Business Economics, Harvard Business School, Massachusetts, USA; Numerous training and business courses. Appointments: Project Engineer and Manager, Turbon Tunzi Klimatechnik, Berlin and Bergisch Gladbach, Germany; Researcher, Engineering, Technical University of Dortmund, Germany; President, K + K Publishing GmbH, Bonn, Germany; Sales Manager Computer Systems, Control Data GmbH, Hamburg, Germany; Sales Manager Computer Systems, Computervision GmbH, Hamburg, Director Marketing and Key Account Sales Manager, McDonnel Douglas Information Systems Group, Frankfurt, Cologne and London; President, Data Business Partnership GmbH, Dusseldorf and Frankfurt, Germany; Director, Lexington Asset Trust & Holdings Corp, Palm Beach, Chicago, New York, USA and London, UK; Visiting Professor, Vasile Goldis Western University, Arad, Romania; Vice-Rector and Honorary Professor, Albert Schweitzer International University, Madrid, Spain; Official Representative to the United Nations Geneva, International Commission on Distance Education, Geneva and Madrid. Publications: Numerous articles, research papers and technical journals; Presented numerous papers in his areas of expertise. Honours: Honorary PhD, University at Jefferson City, Missouri, USA; Honorary Doctorate of science in Economics, Moscow State University, Moscow, Russia. Memberships: Chamber of Commerce, Boca Raton, Florida, USA; Grand Commander, Sovereign Order of the Knights of Justice, UK and Malta; Royal Yachting Association and Coastal Skipper, UK; Grand Commander, World Order of Science, Education and Culture, Belgium and UK; Diplomatic Counsellor, London Diplomatic Academy, UK; Jagruthi Kiran Foundation, Netaji National Award for Excellence, India.; The Augustan Society, California, USA Address: Cologne, Germany; London, UK. E-mail: euroclass@gmx.net

KLINE Kevin Delaney, b. 24 October 1947, St Louis, USA. Actor. m. Phoebe Cates, 1989, 1 son, 1 daughter. Education: Indiana University; Julliard School of Drama. Appointments: Founding Member, The Acting Co, NY, 1972-76. Creative Works: Films include: Sophie's Choice; Pirates of Penzance; The Big Chill, 1983; Silverado, 1985; Violets Are Blue, 1985; Cry Freedom, 1987; A Fish Called Wanda, 1988; January Man, 1989; I Love You to Death, 1989; Soapdish, 1991; Grand Canyon, 1991; Consenting Adults, 1992; Chaplin, 1992; Dave, 1993; Princess Caraboo, 1994; Paris Match, 1995; French Kiss, 1995; Fierce Creatures, 1996; The Ice Storm, 1997; In and Out, 1997; A

Midsummer Night's Dream, 1999; Wild Wild West, 1999; The Anniversary Party, 2001; Life as a House, 2001; Orange County, 2002; The Emperor's Club, 2002; The Hunchback of Notre Dame II (voice), 2002; De-Lovely, 2004; Theatre includes: Numerous Broadway appearances in On the Twentieth Century, 1978; Pirates of Penzance, 1980; Arms and the Man, 1985; Several off-Broadway appearances including Richard III, 1983; Henry V, 1984; Hamlet (also director), 1986, 1990; Much Ado About Nothing, 1988; Measure for Measure, 1995; The Seagull, 2001. Honours include: Tony Award, 1978, 1980; Academy Award, Best Supporting Actor, 1989. Address: c/o William Morris Agency, 1325 Avenue of the Americas, New York, NY 10019, USA.

KLINGER Michael, b. 10 November 1930, Baltsi, USSR. Theoretical Physicist. m. Irina Ashkinazy, 1 son. Education: PhD, 1953, DSci, 1964, USSR. Appointments: Associate Professor, University Chernovits, USSR, 1953-56; Researcher, 1956-60, Senior Scientist, 1960-86, Leading Scientist, Principal Scientist, Professor, 1986-94, Ioffe Phys-Tech Institute, St Petersburg; Professor, Bar-Ilan University, Israel, 1994-. Publications: 246 articles; 12 reviews; 2 monographs in Russian and English. Honours: Fellow, Trinity College, Cambridge, England. Memberships: Russian Physical Society; Israel Physical Society. Address: Department of Physics, Bar-Ilan University, 52 900 Ramat-Gan, Tel Aviv, Israel. E-mail: klingem@mail.biu.ac.il

KLINKOWITZ Jerome, b. 24 December 1943, Milwaukee, Wisconsin, USA. Author; Professor of English. m. (1) Elaine Plaszynski, 29 January 1966, (2) Julie Huffman, 27 May 1978, 1 son, 1 daughter. Education: BA, 1966, MA, 1967, Marquette University; University Fellow, 1968-69, PhD, 1970, University of Wisconsin. Appointments: Assistant Professor, Northern Illinois University, 1969-70; Associate Professor, 1972-75, Professor of English, 1975-, University Distinguished Scholar, 1985-, University of Northern Iowa. Publications: Literary Disruptions, 1975; The Life of Fiction, 1977; The American 1960s, 1980; The Practice of Fiction in America, 1980; Kurt Vonnegut, 1982; Peter Handke and the Postmodern Transformation, 1983; The Self Apparent Word, 1984; Literary Subversions, 1985; The New American Novel of Manners, 1986; Rosenberg/Barthes/Hassan: The Postmodern Habit of Thought, 1988; Short Season and Other Stories, 1988; Their Finest Hours: Narratives of the RAF and Luftwaffe in World War II, 1989; Slaughterhouse-Five: Reinventing the Novel and the World, 1990; Listen: Gerry Mulligan/An Aural Narrative in Jazz, 1991; Donald Barthelme: An Exhibition, 1991; Writing Baseball, 1991; Structuring the Void, 1992; Basepaths, 1995; Yanks Over Europe, 1996; Here at Ogallala State U.., 1997; Keeping Literary Company, 1997; Vonnegut in Fact, 1997; Owning a Piece of the Minors, 1999; With the Tigers over China, 1999; You've Got to Be Carefully Taught, 2001; The Vonnegut Effect, 2004; Pacific Skies, 2004; The Enchanted Quest of Dana and Ginger Lamb, forthcoming. Contributions to: Over 250 essays to Partisan Review, New Republic, Nation, American Literature; Short stories to North American Review, Chicago Tribune, San Francisco Chronicle. Honours: PEN Syndicated Fiction Prizes, 1984, 1985. Memberships: PEN American Center; Modern Language Association. Address: Department of English, University of Northern Iowa, Cedar Falls, IA 50614-0502, USA.

KLINSMANN Jurgen, b. 30 June 1964, Germany. Footballer. m. Debbie, 1995, 1 son. Appointments: Started career with Stuttgarter Kickers, before moving to Stuttgart, 1984-89; Member, Winning Team, World Cup, 1990, UEFA Cup with Inter Milan, 1991 and Bayern Munich, 1996; With Inter Milan, 1989-92; AS Monaco, 1992-94; Tottenham Hotspur, 1994-95, 1997-98, played for Bayern Munich, 1995-97, Sampdoria, 1997; International Ambassador for SOS Children's Villages in partnership with FIFA;

Founder, children's care charity AGAPEDIA; Vice President, Soccer Solutions. Honour: Footballer of the Year, 1988, 1994; English Footballer of the Year, 1995. Address: Soccer Solutions LLC, 744 SW Regency Place, Portland, OR 97225, USA. Website: www.soccersolutions.com

KLONER Robert, b. 8 October 1949, Buffalo, New York, USA. Physician; Scientist; Cardiologist. m. Judith Astei, 2 daughters. Education: Honours Program in Medical Education, 1971, PhD, Experimental Pathology, 1974, MD, 1975, Northwestern University; Postgraduate education, internship, residency, cardiology, fellowship, Brigham and Women's Hospital, Harvard Medical School, 1975-80. Appointments: Assistance Professor of Medicine, 1974-84, Associate Professor of Medicine, 1984, Harvard Medical School; Professor of Medicine, Wayne State University, 1985-88; Professor of Medicine, University of Southern California, 1988-. Publications: Over 625 articles, chapters and monographs; Editor or co-editor,19 books. Honours: Established Investigator of the American Heart Association, 1981-86; American Society of Clinical Investigation. Memberships: American Heart Association; American College of Cardiology; International Society of Heart Research. Address: Heart Institute, Good Samaritan Hospital, 1225 Wilshire Blvd, Los Angeles, CA 90017, USA. E-mail: rkloner@goodsam.org

KLYATIS Lev Matusovich, b. 4 March 1933, Kiev, Ukraine. Engineering Scientist. m. Nallya Klyatis, 1 son, 1 daughter. Education: BS, Mechanical Engineering, Dnepropetrovsk Agricultural Institute, Ukraine, 1958; PhD, Engineering Technology, Belorussia Scientific Agricultural Institute, 1963. Doctor of Technical Sciences, Leningrad Agricultural University, 1982; Full Life Professor, All-USSR Science Association "Autoelectronic"; Habilitated Dr-Ing, Latvia State University of Agriculture, 1993; Academician, Academy for Quality, Russian Federation, 1998. Appointments: Test Engineer, Senior Test Engineer, Principal Engineer, All-USSR Governmental Test Centres, 1958-65; Principal Special, Head of Department, All-USSR, Ministry of Agriculture, 1965-73; Head of Reliability Department (part-time), All-USSR Institute of Agricultural Mechanics, 1965-72; Lead Scientist, Head, Engineering Department, All-USSR Agrochemical Institute, 1973-86; Head Reliability Department, All-USSR Farm Machinery Industry Institute, 1986-90; Professor, Moscow University of Agricultural Engineering, 1990-92; Member of the Board of Directors, International Association for Arts and Sciences, 1994-; Head of Reliability Department, Eccol Inc.,1997-; USA Expert for the International Electrotechnical Commission (IEC), 2000-. Publications: Over 200 publications, books articles and papers in 8 languages; Over 30 patents; Books include: Accelerated Testing of Farm Machinery, 1985; Successful Accelerated Testing, Part I, 2002. Honours: 12 Certificates of Appreciation, Education, Achievements and Service, 1995-; American Society for Quality, Research Grant, 1998, Special Service Award, 2002; Allen Chop Award in Reliability, USA, 2003; Listed in Who's Who publications and biographical dictionaries. Memberships: SAE International, 1997-; Senior Member, American Society for Quality, 1995; Society of Reliability Engineers, 2002-. Address: 72 Montgomery Street #1311, Jersey City, NJ 07302, USA.

KLYUSOV Anatoly, b. 2 July 1940, Jenisejsk, Russia. Chemistry Researcher. m. Lubov, 2 sons. Education: Degree, Engineering, Technical Institute, St Petersburg, 1963; PhD, Mendeleev Chemical and Technical Institute, Moscow, 1973; DSc, Mendeleev Chemical and Technical University, 1993; Professorial Degree, 1995. Appointments: Master Cement Plant, St Petersburg, 1963-64; Head of Laboratory, Industrial Institute, Tyumen, 1964-68; Oil and Gas Geological Institute, Tyumen, 1968-75; Scientific Research Institute Gas Industry, Tyumen, 1975-94; Head of Chair, Professor, Academy of Architecture and Civil Engineering, Tyumen, 1994-95; Head of Laboratory, All Russian Scientific Research Institute for Gas Technology, Moscow, 1995-. Publications: 10 scientific reviews, 190 scientific articles and 43 patents in the field of Arctic oil and gas cements. Honours: Honoured Inventor of Russia, Presidium of the Supreme Soviet of RSFSR,1987; Russian State Prize Winner, 1989; Four State Awards; 10 silver medals of the Exhibition of National Economic Achievement. Memberships: Academician, President of the Regional Office, International Informatization Academy, 1994; New York Academy of Sciences, 1995; Fellow Cchem FRSC, 1998. Address: Brateevskaya st 16, Korp 6, KV 343, Moscow 115408, Russia.

KMEŤ Stanislav, b. 6 March 1957, Přerov, Slovakia. Civil Engineer. m. Alena Kneslova, 1 daughter. Education: College Kovakska, Košice, 1976; MSc, Civil Engineering, Technical University of Košice, 1982; PhD, Civil Engineering, Slovak Technical University, Bratislava, 1989. Appointments: Assistant Professor, Associate Professor, Professor, Faculty of Civil Engineering, Technical University of Košice, Slovakia. Publications: Author of 2 books; 60 journal papers; Over 100 conference papers. Honours: Awards of the Civil Engineering Faculties of the Universities of: Bratislava, Prague, Košice, Miscolc. Membership: International Association for Spatial Structures. Address: Technical University of Košice, Faculty of Civil Engineering, Vysokoskolska 4, 04200 Košice, Slovak Republic. E-mail: stanislav.kmet@tuke.sk

KNAPMAN Roger Maurice, b. 20 February 1944, Crediton, Devon, England. Chartered Surveyor. m. Carolyn Eastman, 1 son, 1 daughter. Education: Royal Agricultural College, Cirencester, England. Appointments: Conservative Member of Parliament for Stroud, 1987-97; Parliamentary Private Secretary to the Minister of State for the Armed Forces, 1991-93; Junior Government Whip, 1995-96; Senior Government Whip and Lord Commissioner of the Treasury, 1996-97; Political Advisor to UK Independence Party, 2000-. Address: Coryton House, Coryton, Okehampton, Devon, EX20 4PA, England.

KNAPP-FISHER John Arthur, b. 2 August 1931, London, England. Artist; Author. m. Sheila Bassett, divorced, 1 son, 1 daughter. Education: Eastbourne College; Graphic Art, Maidstone College of Art. Career: Designed in the theatre; Opened Studio/ Gallery, 1967; Painted and exhibited from his seagoing vessel home for five years; Works in watercolour, mixed media and oil colour on paper and board; Gallery exhibitions include: London: The Royal Academy of Arts; Agnews; Langton; Marjorie Parr, Upper Grosvenor; Bankside; Business Art Galleries (at the RA); Fry; CCA Galleries; Pump House; New Academy Gallery; Outside London: Royal West of England Academy; Royal Cambrian Academy; Haverfordwest Museum; National Eisteddfod; Aberystwyth Art Centre; Oriel-Welsh Arts Council; Century Henley; Touring Dyfed Museums; Beaux Arts, Bath; Camarthen College of Art; National Museum of Wales; Trevigan Cottage 25th Anniversary Exhibition, 1992; Lichfield Cathedral, Artist in Residence, 1995; Senecio Press Gallery; Martin Tinney Gallery; Albany Gallery, Cardiff; Attic, Swansea; Tenby Museum & Art Gallery (A Retrospective 1958-1998); Tidal Wave Gallery, Hereford; Abroad: Galleries in Johannesburg, Cape Town, Toronto, Paris; Collections: National Museum of Wales; National Library of Wales; Tenby Museum; West Wales Association for the Arts; Withybush Hospital Haverfordwest; Swansea University; Beecroft Art Gallery (Southend); Barclays Bank (Ipswich); National Bank of Nova Scotia; BBC Wales, Cardiff; Numerous private collections world-wide. Publications: A History of Fire Arms (author and illustrator), 1952; Article: Vikings Voyage, 1972/73; John Knapp-

Dictionary of International Biography

Fisher's Pembrokeshire written and illustrated by the artist, 1995; Churches of Pembrokeshire by Michael Fitzgerald (illustrator); Included in: Cymru Cynfas (Wales on Canvas) Fifteen Contemporary Artists by Hywel Harries, 1983; Welsh Painters Talking by Tony Curtis, 1997; Numerous TV appearances. Honours: Elected Member, Royal Cambrian Academy, 1992; Prizewinner for contribution to Art in the Community, The W C W James OBE Memorial Trust, 1997. Membership: Royal Cambrian Academy. Address: Trevigan Cottage, Croesgoch, Haverfordwest, Pembrokeshire SA62 5JP, Wales.

KNEZKOVA-HUSSEY Ludmila, b. 22 April 1956, Mukacevo, Ukraine. Concert Pianist. m. Bernard Hussey, 1 daughter. Education: Graduate, Special Music School, Lvov, Ukraine; Bachelor degree, Moscow Music College (Russia), 1975; Master degree, Tchaikovsky Conservatory in Moscow, Russia, 1980; PhD, Academy of Music in Prague, Czech Republic, 1989; Studied in France with Professor Ringeissen, 1986, 1987, Germany with Professor Detlef Kraus and Professor Rolf-Dieter Arens, 1989, 1990, Banff Centre of Fine Arts, Canada with Professor Gyorgy Sebok, 1992. Appointments: Soloist with West Bohemian Symphony Orchestras, Czech Republic, 1984-90; Soloist with Karlovy Vary Symphony Orchestra, Czech Republic, 1980-92; Piano Professor, Teplice Conservatory, Czech Republic, 1985-90; Concert Performer in numerous countries around the world and teaching master classes in 50 countries; Concerts broadcast in Europe and Canada; Founder, Developer, Artistic Director, Ludmila Knezkova-Hussey International Piano Competition, 1993. Compositions: Works for solo piano, string orchestra, concerto and symphony orchestra; Symphonic work, St Andrews Anthology premiered at the St Andrews Summer Festival, St Andrews, New Brunswick, Canada, 2001; Double concerto for piano and voice, Tabula Rosa, 2002 Honours include: Smetana International Piano Competition and Czechoslovakia National Piano Competition (1st prize); Best Performer, Weimar, Germany, 1988; Scholarship Banff Centre School of Fine Arts, Canada, 1992; New Brunswick, Merit Award, Canada, 1995; Founder, Ludmila Knezkova-Hussey International Piano Competition, named as one of the 2000 Outstanding Intellectuals of the 20th Century, England, 2000, also one of the 1000 World Leaders of Influence, USA, 2000; International Order of Merit, IBC, 2000; Selected by McLeans Magazine as one of 50 people who have contributed greatly to Canada, 2001; Recipient of the 2001 Excellence Award for the Arts, Canada; Paul Harris Fellow, International Rotary Club. 2002; Subject of TV Documentary, Flying on the Moon – the Ludmila Story, 2002. Memberships: Czech Musicians Association; New Brunswick Musicians Association; American Federation of Musicians; Juno Awards Association, Canada. Address: 155 Allison Crescent, Bathurst, NB E2A 3B4 Canada.

KNIGHT Daniel (formerly Nicolino Giacalone), b. 28 November 1956, Montreal, Canada; British National, 1998. Singer (Bass/Bass-Baritone); Voice Teacher; Artistic and Musical Director. Education: Piano with step-father Karl Steiner; Marianopolis College, 1974-76; McGill University, 1976-78; Conservatoire de Musique, Quebec, 1977-79; BFA, Concordia University, 1980-82; Studied singing with Benjamin Luxon, Vera Rozsa, James Bowman, Rita Streich, Max van Egmond, Arno Niifof, Daniel Ferro, and Emma Kirkby. Debut: Director, Dido and Aeneas, Waltham Abbey, 1995; Singing, St John's Smith Square, London, 1997; BBC Radio debut, Glenn Gould, Bach. Career: Teacher, Singing, Privately, Masterclasses in Canada, USA, Ireland, England, 1974-; Singing, Modern World Premiere Singing Title Role of full staged complete performance of H Purcell's Dioclesian, Dartington and Croatia with Paul Goodwin conducting, 1995, 19th and 20th Century Austrian Lieder to mark Austria's Thousand Years, 1996; Artistic Director, Founding Member,

Handel Opera Company, 1995; Recital and Voice Masterclass, Houston, Texas, 1999; Musical Director, Artistic Director and Chairman of Handel Opera Co Ltd. Recordings: Music of the Second Generation, 1995; Dioclesian by H Purcell, 1995; Baroque Opera Arias for Bass, 1997. Publication: A Scarlatti Cantatas and Serenatas, 1997; Articles on singing in NODA London News. Honours: Pauline Donalda Memorial Scholarship, Montreal Opera, 1981; CBC National Competition Winner, 1985; Dartington International Scholarship, 1995. Membership: National Association of Singing Teachers; British Actors Equity; British Voice Association. Address: 2nd Floor, 68 Old Brompton Road, London SW1 3LD, England. Website: www.danielknight.net

KNIGHT Gregory, b. 4 April 1949, Blaby, Leicestershire, England. Member of Parliament; Solicitor. Education: College of Law, London. Appointments: Member of Parliament for Derby North, 1983-97; Assistant Government Whip, 1989-90; Lord Commissioner of the Treasury, 1990-93; Government Deputy Chief Whip, 1993-96; Minister of State for Industry, Department of Trade and Industry, 1996-97; MP for East Yorkshire, 2001-; Shadow Deputy Leader, House of Commons, 2001-03; Shadow Minister for Culture, 2003; Shadow Minister for Railways and Aviation, 2003-. Publications: Westminster Words, 1988; Honourable Insults, 1990; Parliamentary Sauce, 1993; Right Honourable Insults, 1998. Honour: Privy Councillor, 1995. Memberships: Member of Conservative Party, 1966-; Member of Law Society, 1973; Member, Bridlington Conservative Club, 2001-. Address: House of Commons, Westminster, London SW1A 0AA. E-mail: secretary@gregknight.com

KNIGHT Peter, b. 12 August 1947, Bedford, England. Professor. m. Christine Knight, 2 sons, 1 daughter. Education: BSc, 1968, DPhil, 1972, University of Sussex. Appointments: Research Associate, University of Rochester, USA, 1972-74; SRC Research Fellow, Sussex University, 1974-76; Jubilee Research Fellow, Royal Holloway College, 1976-78; SERC Advanced Fellow, 1978-83, Lecturer, 1983-87, Reader, 1987-88, Professor, 1988-, Head of Quantum Optics and Laser Science Group, 1992-2001, Head of Physics Department, 2001-, Imperial College, London. Publications: Over 300 scientific papers in international journals; 1 textbook, Concepts of Quantum Optics, 1983. Honours: Fellow, Royal Society; Fellow, Institute of Physics; Fellow, Optical Society of America; Thomas Young Medal, Institute of Physics; Einstein Medal and Prize, Eastman Kodak Co; Parsons Medal, Royal Society and Institute of Physics; Elected Vice President, 2002, President Elect, 2003, Optical Society of America. Memberships: Royal Society; Optical Society of America; Institute of Physics. E-mail: p.knight@ic.ac.uk

KNOPFLER Mark, b. 12 August 1949, England. Guitarist; Songwriter. m. Lourdes Salomone, 1983. Education: Leeds University. Appointments: Former Journalist, Yorkshire Evening Post; Founder, Dire Straits, 1977, Guitarist; 1st Concert, 1977; Group has toured worldwide. Creative Works: Albums include: Making Movies; Brothers in Arms; On Every Street; Songs include: Romeo and Juliet; Money For Nothing; Calling Elvis; Toured with Eric Clapton and recorded with Chet Atkins; Founder, Notting Hillbillies. Honours include: Ivor Novello Award; Grammy Award. Address: c/o Damage Management, 16 Lambton Place, London W11 2SH, England.

KNOWLES Evelyn, b. 14 April 1931, London, England. City Councillor. 1 son, 2 daughters. Education: BA Honours, Psychology, Ealing College of Higher Education. Appointments: President, Cambridge MS Society; Chair, Cambridge Citizens Advice Bureaux; Cambridge City Councillor, 1986-; Director, St Lukes Community Centre, 1989-98; Mayor of Cambridge, 2000-

Dictionary of International Biography

01; Non-executive Director, Cambridge Primary Care Trust. Memberships: Fellow, Royal Society of Arts; Member, Liberal Democrat Party; Chair, Liberal Democrat Council Group; Member, Fawcett Society; Friends of the Earth. Address: 21 Primary Court, Cambridge, CB4 1NB, England.

KNOX (Alexander John) Keith, b. 27 November 1933, Belper, Derbyshire, England. Electronic Engineer (retired); Record Producer. m. Ingrid Zakrisson Knox, 1 son. Education: BSc, Physics and Maths, Southampton University, London; Brighton College of Advanced Technology; Course with Richard Goodman, Decision Mathematics for Management. Appointments: Electronic Engineer, with EMI, 1957-59, Brush Clevite Company, Hythe, Hampshire, UK, 1959-62; Redifon Ltd, Crawley, Sussex, UK, 1962-64; Amplivox Ltd, Wembley, Middlesex, UK, 1964-65, Transitron Electronic SA, Switzerland, 1965-67; Transitron Electronic Sweden AB, 1967-72; Freelance sound record producer, Caprice Records/Sonet Records/WEA-Metronome Records (Stockholm), Storyville Records (Copenhagen), 1971-85; Manager for music group, "Sevda", 1971-74; Manager for music group "Music for Xaba", 1972-73; Marketing and liaison engineer, Sonab AB, Solna, Sweden, 1972-74; Support Engineer, Royal Institute of Technology (KTH), Stockholm, Sweden, 1975-98; English language copywriter for advertising agency, Andersson and Lembke AB, Sundbyberg, Sweden, 1974-75; Executive Producer, Silkheart Records, Stockholm, Sweden, 1986-. Publications: (biography) Jazz Amour Affair, 1986; Numerous articles for jazz publications and underground press. Address: Silkheart Records, Dalagatan 33, SE 11323 Stockholm, Sweden.

KNOX David Laidlaw (Sir), b. 30 May 1933, Lockerbie, Dumfriesshire, Scotland. Member of Parliament, retired. m. Margaret Eva Mackenzie, 2 stepsons, 1 deceased. Education: BSc Honours, Economics, London University. Appointments: Production Manager, printing industry, 1956-62; Internal Company Management Consultant, 1962-70; Parliamentary Adviser, Chartered Institute of Management Accountants, 1980-97; Member of European Legislation Select Committee, 1976-97; Member of Speakers Panel of Chairmen, 1983-97; Member of Parliament for Leek, 1970-83; Vice Chairman, Conservative Party, 1974-75; Member of Parliament for Staffordshire Moorlands, 1983-97; Chairman, London Union of Youth Clubs, 1998-99; Deputy Chairman, London Youth, 1999-. Publications: 4 pamphlets. Honours: Knighted, 1993. Memberships: Past member, Federation of Economic Development Authorities; Past member, Industry and Parliament Trust; Past member, One World Trust; Honorary Fellowship, Staffordshire University; Member, Conservative Party; Member, Conservative Group for Europe; Member, Tory Reform Group. Address: The Mount, Alstonefield, Ashbourne, Derbyshire, DE6 2FS, England.

KNOX-JOHNSTON Robin (Sir), b. 17 March 1939. Marina Consultant. m. Suzanne Singer, 1962, 1 daughter. Appointments: Merchant Navy, 1957-67; First Person to sail single-handed non-stop around the World, 1968-69; Managing Director, St Katharine's Yacht Haven Ltd, 1975-76; Director, Mercury Yacht Harbours Ltd, 1970-73; Rank Mariner International, 1973-75; Troon Marina Ltd, 1976-83; National Yacht Racing Centre Ltd, 1979-86; Knox-Johnston Insurance Brokers Ltd, 1983-; Managing Director, St Katherine's Dock, 1991-93; Chairman, Clipper Ventures plc; Set record for sailing circumnavigation, 1994. Publications: A World of My Own, 1969; Sailing, 1975; Twilight of Sail, 1978; Last But Not Least, 1978; Bunkside Companion, 1982; Seamanship, 1986; The BOC Challenge 1986-1987, 1988; The Cape of Good Hope, 1989; History of Yachting, 1990; The Columbus Venture, 1991; Sea, Ice and Rock, 1992; Beyond Jules Verne, 1995. Honours: CBE, 1969; Sunday Times Golden Globe, 1969; Book of the Sea

Award; Knighthood, 1995; Dr Sci, ME Maritime Academy. Memberships: Trustee, National Maritime Museum, 1993; Trustee, National Maritime Museum, Cornwall, England; Sports Council Lottery Panel, 1995; Fellow, Royal Institute of Navigation; Member, English Sports Council, 1999; President Sail Training Association, 1992-2001. Address: St Francis Cottage, Torbryan, Newton Abbot, Devon TQ12 5UR, England.

KNUDSEN Dagfinn Andreas, b. 11 April 1942, Drevja, Norway. Metallurgist. m. Karin Nilssen, 1 daughter. Education: Engineering Degree, Metallurgical Techniques, Trondheim Tekniske Skole, 1967. Appointments: Assistant Engineer, Årdal Verk, ÅSV, 1967-72; Project Engineer, Sunndal Verk, ÅSV, 1972-86; Process Engineer, Franzefoss Bruk, 1986; Service Engineer, Østlandsmeieriet, 1989; Service Engineer, Autodisplay AS, 1991. Publications: Articles in technical journals; Essay on sensational journalism, 1991; about industrial culture, employees management, company and loyalty; Essay on Norway's fishing industry. Address: Rådhusgata 29, N 8657 Mosjøen, Norway.

KO Yiu Fai, b. 17 December 1962, Hong Kong. Company Executive. Education: BSc (Hons), Electronic Engineering; PhD, Electronics Engineering, Thesis: Digital Cellular Mobile Radio Links and Networks. Appointments: Personal Communications Research Engineer, Unitel, UK, 1990-91; Senior Cellular Engineer, Mercury One 2 One, UK, 1992-94; Senior Consultant, 1994-95, Technical Director, 1996-2000, Technical R&D Director, 2000-2001, Chief Technology Architect, 2001-, Actix Ltd. Publications: Co-author of book: Mobile Phone Communications, 1992, 1999; Contributor of articles to international professional and trade journals. Honour: Recipient of US West Chairman's Award, 1994. Memberships: Institute of Electrical and Electronics Engineers; Institution of Electrical Engineers. Address: 6 St Edmund's Square, London, SW13 8SA, England. E-mail: yiufai@drko.freeserve.co.uk

KOBAK Kira, b. 5 June 1936, St Petersburg, Russia. Scientist; Educator. Widow, 1 son. Education: MS, 1959, PhD, Biology Sciences, 1965, St Petersburg Forestry Academy; Doctor of Science, Geographical Sciences, Institute of Geography, Russian Academy of Sciences, Moscow, 1990. Appointments: Forest Engineer, Forest Inventory Enterprises, St Petersburg, 1959-61; Scientist, Main Geophysics Observatory, St Petersburg, 1966-62; Scientist, Komarov Botanical Institute, St Petersburg, 1972-74, Associate Professor, St Petersburg Forestry Academy, 1974-82; Leading Scientist, State Hydrological Institute, St Petersburg, 1982-; Professor, Yan Kokhanovski University, Kilce, Poland, 1996-. Publications: More than 140 articles; Author: Atmospheric CO_2 1982; Biotical components of carbon cycle, 1988; Co-author of 8 books including: Microbiology, 1985; Anthropogenic climate change, 1987; Prospects for future climate, 1990. Honour: Medal, 300 Years of St Petersburg. Membership: Russian Botanical Society; New York Academy of Sciences. Address: State Hydrological Institute, 23 Second Line, 199053 St Petersburg, Russia.

KOBAYASHI Junko, b. September 1960, Kobe, Japan. Concert Pianist. Education: Osaka College of Music; Essen Musik Hochschule, Germany; Studied with Maria Curcio and Louis Kentner. Debut: Royal Festival Hall, London, 1988. Career: The Purcell Room Recitals, 1983-93; Appearances in England, Germany, France, Denmark, Bulgaria, USA, Venezuela, Zambia and Japan; Played with orchestras such as the London Philharmonic Orchestra, the Osaka Philharmonic Orchestra, the New Philharmonic Orchestra, The Academy of St Nicholas; Broadcasts on BBC Radio 3, WKAR Televion, USA, ZDF Television, Germany. Contributions: Essays to Kansei Music newspaper.

Memberships: Founder-Chairman, Takemitsu Society, 1997-. Address: 26 Sandown Road, West Malling, Kent ME19 6NS, England.

KOCH Blaise Edward, b. 20 November 1952, East London, South Africa. Actor; Director; Lecturer; Author; Motivational Speaker; Dialogue Coach. Education: Performer's Diploma, London School of Mime Certificate. Career: Actor, The Space Theatre, 1973-76, CABAB, 1976, Baxter Theatre, Cape Town, 1976-77, Don Hughes Organisation, 1977; Pieter-Dirk Uys Productions, 1977-78, London School of Mime, 1979, PACT, Pretoria, South Africa, 1982, NAPAC, Durban, South Africa, 1982-83; Regional SAFTU Representative, 1984-; Actor, Director, PACOFS, Bloemfontein, South Africa, 1983-90; Lecturer, 1989-; Senior Actor, CAPAB, Cape Town, South Africa, 1990-95; Lecturer, University of Cape Town, South Africa; Director; Senior Lecturer, Drama Department, University of Stellenbosch, South Africa, 1998-; Currently: Freelance Performer; Professional Adjudicator for University and Drama Eisteddfods; Regional Representative-Theatre Benevolent Fund; Bilingual Dialogue Coach "Egoli - Place of Gold"; Aids Campaigner and Motivational Speaker, 2003; Directed World Premier of Pieter-Dirk Uys's HIV infancy play, Auditioning Angels, 2003. Publication: Autobiography, In, Around, Through & Out, 2002. Honours Include: Three Leaf Best Supporting Actor in Kennedy's Children; Scholarship, London School of Mime, 1979; SAA Merit Award, PACOFS, 1987; AA Vita Award for Direction of Blood Knot by Athol Fugard; Fleur du Cap Awards, 1991, 1994 1995, 1999; Best Contribution to a Musical – Performance, Clarence in "Boy Meets Boy", 2001; Vita Award for Best Production, Elephant Man, 1999; Kay-Oscar for performance in television Richelieu advertisement; Listed in Who's Who publications and biographical dictionaries; 6 Nominations, Naledi Awards for "Auditioning Angels" and "Offbeat Broadway", 2004; Universal Award of Accomplishment, American Biographical Institute, 2004. Memberships: SAFTU; Theatre Benevolent Fund. Address: c/o 22 Engelwold Drive, Saxonwold, Gauteng , South Africa 2196. E-mail: perryer@icon.co.sa

KOCH-BRANDT Claudia, b. 21 January 1952, Halle, Germany. Professor of Biochemistry. m. Hans Peter Brandt, 1 son, 1 daughter. Education: Graduate, Pharmaceutical Sciences, 1976, PhD, Biochemistry, 1980, Venia Legendi, 1985, University of Frankfurt. Appointments: DFG Fellow, EMBL Heidelberg, 1980-84; Staff Member, EMBL Heidelberg, 1984-85; Assistant Professor, University of Frankfurt, 1985-91; Professor, University of Mainz, 1991-. Publications: Over 40 articles in professional journals. Honours: Heinz Maier-Leibnitz Award, Minister for Science and Education, 1984; Research Grants, DFG, Ministry of Research and Technology, Fonds Chemistry Industry, 1985-. Memberships: German Society of Biological Chemistry; German Society of Cell Biology; German Society of Pharmacological Toxicology; German Pharmaceutical Sciences; American Association for the Advancement of Sciences; American Association of Cell Biology. Address: Institute of Biochemistry, Becherweg 30, 55099 Mainz, Germany.

KOÇO Eno, b. 1 April 1943, Tirana, Albania. Musician; Conductor; Musicologist. m. Raimonda, 1 son, 1 daughter. Education: Violinist, 1966 Conductor, 1977, Tirana Conservatory; Degree of Doctor of Philosophy, University of Leeds, 1998. Appointments: Violinist, Tirana Opera Orchestra, 1966-72; Conductor, Tirana Music School, 1972-78; Conductor, Albanian Radio and Television Symphony Orchestra, 1976-91; Principal Conductor of the Orchestra, School of Music, University of Leeds, 1992-2004; Conductor, York Symphony Orchestra, 1993-95; Conductor, Harrogate Philharmonic Orchestra, 1994-97; Principal

Conductor, Yorchestra, 1994-2002. Publications: Treatise on Orchestration, 1977; Albanian Musical Life in the 1930s, 2000; Albanian Urban Lyric Song in the 1930s, 2002; Korçare Distinctive Song, 2003; Albanian Urban Lyric Song in the 1930s, 2004; Several articles in Albanian and English published in professional journals; Numerous recordings of Albanian and Western music, instrumental and vocal. Honours: Honoured Artist of Albania, conducting award, 1984. Address: 106 Church Avenue, Leeds LS6 4JT, England. E-mail: enokoco1@hotmail.com

KODIROV Bekmurod Amanovich, b. 20 November 1948, Sherabad District, Uzbekistan. Teacher; Pedagogist. m. Kodirova Jamila, 3 sons, 2 daughters. Education: Diploma, 1970, Diploma, Candidate of Pedagogical Sciences, 1979, Termez State University; Diploma, Doctor of Pedagogical Sciences, Moscow, 1992. Appointments: Journalist, 1970-71; Military Service, 1971-72; Teacher, 1972-84, Dean, Faculty of Pedagogics and Physical Training, 1984-, Termez State University. Publications: Over 320 scientific articles in 10 languages; 8 monographs. Honours: Dotsent, 1983; Academician Award of Active Public Education, 1987. Memberships: International Academy of Pedagogics, 1995; International Association of Peoples Pedagogics. Address: Termez 732006, Festival Street, Proezd 4/8, Surkhandarya Region, Republic of Uzbekistan. Email: kulmatov@online.ru

KOEGLER Hans-Herbert, b. 13 January 1960, Darmstadt, Germany. Professor of Philosophy. Education: MA, 1986, PhD, 1991, J W Goethe University, Frankfurt. Appointments: Dissertation Fellow, German Fellowship Foundation, 1987-91; Research Fellow, Visiting Scholar, Northwestern University, New School for Social Research, University of California at Berkeley, 1989-90; Assistant Professor of Philosophy, Department of Philosophy, 1991, Assistant Professor, Unit for Criticism and Interpretative Theory, 1994, University of Illinois at Urbana-Champaign; Honorary Faculty Associate, University of Catamarca, Argentina, 1996; Visiting Professor as NEH Fellow, University of Boston, 1997; Assistant Professor of Philosophy, Department of History and Philosophy, 1997, Associate Professor, 1999, University of North Florida, Jacksonville; Visiting Professor as NEH Fellow, University of Arizona, 2000. Publications: Die Macht des Dialogs, 1992; Michel Foucault: Ein antihumanistischer Aufklarer, 1994, 2004; The Power of Dialogue: Critical Hermeneutics After Gadamer and Foucault, 1999; Empathy and Agency: The Problem of Understanding in the Human Sciences, 2000. Contributions to: Journals, anthologies, periodicals, reviews and magazines. Address: c/o Department of Philosophy, University of North Florida, 4567 St Johns Bluff Road South, Jacksonville, FL 32224-2645, USA.

KOEHLER Colleen Mary, b. 6 July 1972, Belleville, Illinois, USA. Accountant. Education: Bachelor of Science, Accounting and Management, McKendree College, Lebanon, Illinois, 1998; Masters of Science, Taxation, Fontbonne University, St Louis, Missouri, 2002. Appointments: Accountant, Ralston Purina Co, St Louis; Accountant, Drury Development Corporation, St Louis. Honours: Listed in national and international biographical dictionaries; Management Award, McKendree College; Outstanding Student of Science in Taxation Award. Memberships: Illinois CPA Society; American Institute of Certified Public Accountants; Sigma Beta Delta Honor Society. Address: Nestle Purina Co, Checkerboard Square, Saint Louis, MO 63101, USA. E-mail: colleen.koehler:ddcmail.com

KOGAN Norman, b. 15 June 1919, Chicago, Illinois, USA. Professor Emeritus of Political Science. m. Meryl Reich, 18 May 1946, 2 sons. Education: BA, 1940, PhD, 1949, University of Chicago. Appointments: Faculty, University of Connecticut, 1949-

Dictionary of International Biography

88; Visiting Professor, University of Rome, 1973, 1979, 1987. Publications: Italy and the Allies, 1956; The Government of Italy, 1962; The Politics of Italian Foreign Policy, 1963; A Political History of Postwar Italy, 1966; Storia Politica dell' Italia Repubblicana, 1982, 2nd edition, revised and expanded, 1990; A Political History of Italy: The Postwar Years, 1983. Contributions to: Yale Law Journal; Il Ponte; Western Political Quarterly; Journal of Politics; Comparative Politics; Indiana Law Journal. Honour: Lifetime of Achievement Award, 2003. Address: 13 Westwood Road, Storrs, CT 06268, USA.

KOH Hwee-Ling, Pharmacist; Educator; Consultant. Education: BSc (Hons), Pharmacy, National University of Singapore, 1990; MSc, Pharmacy, National University of Singapore, 1992; PhD, University of Cambridge, England, 1996. Appointments: Pre-Registration Pharmacist, Singapore General Hospital, 1990; Pharmacist Guardian Pharmacy, Singapore, 1992; Research Assistant, 1991, Lecturer, 1996-2000, Assistant Professor, 2001-, National University of Singapore. Publications: Articles in medical and scientific journals including: Journal of Orthopaedic Research, 1996; Drug Safety, 2000; Journal of Sep. Science, 2002; Journal of Alternative and Complementary Medicine, 2003; Drug Discovery Today, 2003; Journal of Chromatography A, 2003. Honours: Prime Ministers Book Prize, Ministry of Education, Singapore, 1983; EDB, Glaxo Human Resource Development Scholarship, Economic Development Board, 1992-96; Herchel Smith Endowment Fund Scholarship, UK, 1992-96; Fellow, Japan Society for Promotion of Science, 1998. Memberships: American Association of Pharmaceutical Scientists; Pharmaceutical Society of Singapore; International Society for Magnetic Resonance in Medicine, USA; Pharmaceutical Sciences Group, Royal Pharmaceutical Society of Great Britain; Food Advisory Committee, Ministry of Environment, Singapore; Traditional Chinese Medicine Task Force. Address: Department of Pharmacy, Faculty of Science, National University of Singapore; 18 Science Drive 4, Singapore 117543, Republic of Singapore. E-mail: phakohhl@nus.edu.sg

KOJIĆ-PRODIĆ Biserka, b. 29 August 1938, Čakovec, Croatia. Scientist. m. Dragutin Kojić, 1 daughter. Education: BSc, 1961, MSc, 1963, PhD, Chemistry, 1968, Faculty of Science, University of Zagreb, Croatia. Appointments: Head of Laboratory for Chemical and Biological Crystallography, Rudjer Bošković Institute, Zagreb, Croatia; Senior Scientist, Visiting Scientist: University of Uppsala, University of Utrecht, Medical Foundation of Buffalo, Texas Christian University, Fort Worth, USA. Publications: 225 scientific articles in international journals; Chapter in Encyclopaedia of Agrochemicals, 2002. Honours: National Science Award, 1971; National Academy of Science and Art Award, 1997; DAAD Visiting Science Award, 1995, 2000. Memberships: Croatian Crystallographic Association; Croatian Biochemical Society; International Union of Crystallography; European Academy of Science. Address: Rudjer Bošković Institute, POB 180, HR-10002 Zagreb, Croatia. E-mail: kojic@rudjer.irb.hr

KOKOT Franciszek, b. 24 November 1929, Olesno Sl. Physician. m. Malgorzata Skrzypczyk, 4 sons. Education: Medical Studies, 1948-53; MD, 1957; PhD, 1962; Associate Professor, 1962-69; Extraordinary Professor, 1969-82; Ordinary Professor, 1982-. Appointments: Technician, Department of Chemistry, 1949-50, Department of Pharmacology, 1950-57, Assistant Senior Assistant, Department of Internal Medicine, Assistant Professor, Associate Professor, 1957-74, Professor, Head of Department of Nephrology, 1974-2000, Rector, 1982-84, Silesian School of Medicine. Publications: Over 700 scientific publications; Several chapters in 30 textbooks. Honours: Honorary Member, 7 foreign societies of

Nephrology, L Pasteur Medal (Strasbourg), 1985; Dr hc of the Medical School of: Wroclaw, 1990, Katowice, 1993, Szczecin, 1995, Kosice, 1997, Lublin, 1997; Warsaw, 1999; Jagiellonian University, Cracow, 1999, Medical Academy of Bialestok, 2001; F Volhard Golden Medal, 1991; International Distinguished Medal, 1991. Memberships: International Society of Nephrology; European Society of Nephrology; President, Polish Society Nephrology, 1989-98. Address: Al Korfantego 8/162, 40-004 Katowice, Poland.

KOKOTT Julia B, b. 18 June 1957, Frankfurt, Germany. Professor of Law. m. Rainer Sturies, 3 sons, 2 daughters. Education: LLM, American University, 1983; Dr iuris utriusque, University of Heidelberg, 1985; SJD, Harvard, 1990. Appointments: Visiting Professor of Law, Berkeley, 1991; Professor of Law, Augsburg, 1993; Professor of Law, Heidelberg, 1994; Professor of Law, Dusseldorf, 1995-99; Professor of Law, St Gallen, 1999-. Honours: Otto Hahn Medal, Max Planck Society. Memberships: German Advisory Council on Global Change, 1996-. Address: Monchhofstr 42, DE-69120 Heidelberg, Germany. Website: www.rwa.unisg.ch/kokott

KOLACHEV Boris, b. 4 April, Kimri Tver Region, Russia. Educator. m. Sinizina Galina, 2 daughters. Education: Engineer, 1952; Candidate of Science, 1955; Doctor of Science, 1967; Professor, 1968. Appointments: Assistant, 1955-58, Senior Lecturer, 1959-68, Full Professor, 1968-90, Honoured Professor, 1990-, Moscow Institute of Aircraft and Technology; Expert, High Certification Committee, USSR Government, 1975-92. Publications: 28 books. Honours: Honoured Man of Science and Technology; State Prize Winner; Honoured Professor. Memberships: New York Academy of Science; Permanent Working International Committee on Hydrogen Treatment of Materials. Address: Andropov Avenue 41/8 - 106, 142800 Stoopino, Moscow Region, Russia.

KOLB Felix Oscar, b. 12 November 1921, Vienna, Austria. Physician. m. Susan Goldberger, 1 son, 1 daughter. Education: AB, University of California, Berkeley, 1938-41; MD, University of California, School of Medicine, 1940-43. Appointments: 1st Lt Capt, Medical Corps, US Army, 1944-46; Resident Internal Medicine, University of California, School of Medicine, 1946-49; Senior Resident, Internal Medicine, New England Center, Boston, Massachusetts, 1949-50; Graduate Assistant in Medicine (Endocrine Service of Dr Fuller Albright) at Massachusetts General Hospital, Harvard Medical School, Boston, Massachusetts, 1950-51; Attending Physician, UC Moffitt-Long Hospital, San Francisco, 1951-98; Assistant Chief, Associate Chief, Senior and Emeritus, Department of Medicine, UC/Mount Zion, 1952-98; Private Consultative Practice, Endocrinology and Metabolism, 1952-; Clinical Instructor in Medicine, UCSF, 1952-53; Assistant Clinical Professor of Medicine and Assistant Research Physician, Metabolic Research Unit, 1953-59; Assistant Director, Metabolic Research Unit and Associate Clinical Professor of Medicine and Associate Research Physician, 1959-68; Research Physician and Associate Director, Metabolic Research Unit, 1968-82; Clinical Professor of Medicine, UCSF, 1968-2000; Clinical Professor Emeritus, 2000-; Chairman, Division of Endocrinology, Mount Zion Hospital, San Francisco, 1969-76; Consulting Physician, various hospitals, San Francisco, 1985-. Publications: Over 160 publications; Book chapters; Text books; Book reviewer and abstractor; Referee for several professional journals. Honours: Honour Student Society, UC Berkeley, 1939; Alpha Omega Alpha, 1943; Listed in Who's Who publications and biographical dictionaries Memberships include: American Medical Association; Endocrine Society; American Diabetes Association; American Society Bone and

Mineral Research; American Federation for Clinical Research. Address: 9 Starboard Court, Mill Valley, CA 94941, USA. E-mail: fokolb@pol.net

KOLLER James, b. 30 May 1936, Oak Park, Illinois, USA. Writer; Poet; Artist. m. 2 sons, 4 daughters. Education: BA, North Central College, Naperville, Illinois, 1958. Publications: Poetry: Two Hands, 1965; Brainard and Washington Street Poems, 1965; The Dogs and Other Dark Woods, 1966; Some Cows, 1966; I Went To See My True Love, 1967; California Poems, 1971; Bureau Creek, 1975; Poems for the Blue Sky, 1976; Messages-Botschaften, 1977; Andiamo, 1978; O Didn't He Ramble-O ware er nicht unhergezogen, 1981; Back River, 1981; One Day at a Time, 1981; Great Things Are Happening-Grossartoge Dige passieren, 1984; Give the Dog a Bone, 1986; Graffiti Lyriques (with Franco Beltrametti), graphics and texts, 1987; Openings, 1987; Fortune, 1987; Roses Love Sunshine, 1989; This Is What He Said, graphics and texts, 1991; In the Wolf's Mouth, poems 1972-88, 1995; Travaux de Voirie, 1997; The Bone Show, 1999; Dopo Giorni Di Pioggia, 1999; Iron Bells, 1999; Close to the Ground, 2000; Looking for His Horses, 2003; Crows Talk to Him, 2003. Prose: Messages, 1972; Working Notes 1960-82, 1985; Gebt dem alten Hund'nen Knochen (Essays, Gedichte and Prosa 1959-85), 1986; The Natural Order, essay and graphics, 1990; Like It Was (selected poetry, prose and fiction), 2000; The Man Who Knows, co-translator, 2003. Fiction: If You Don't Like Me You Can Leave Me Alone, UK edition, 1974, US edition, 1976; Shannon Who Was Lost Before, 1975; The Possible Movie, 1997. Address: PO Box 629, Brunswick, ME 04011, USA.

KOLTOVER Vitaliy Kiva, b. 15 May 1944, Orekhovo-Zuyevo, Russia. Biophysicist. 1 son. Education: MS, Physics, Kiev State University, 1966; PhD, Physics and Mathematics, Institute of Chemical Physics, Moscow, 1971; DSc, Biophysics, Moscow, 1988. Appointments: Plant Physiology Institute, Kiev, Ukraine, 1966-68; Predoctoral Fellow, Junior Scientist, Senior Scientist, Head Bioreliability Group Institute of Problems of Chemical Physics, 1968-. Publications: Books and articles in professional journals on reliability, aging, radiation ecology, metallofullerenes. Honours: Outstanding Achievement Diploma of President of Russian Academy of Sciences. Memberships: International Union of Radioecology; New York Academy of Sciences; American Academy of Anti-Aging Medicine, Expert Consultant, Russian Foundation for Basic Research. Address: Institute of Problems of Chemical Physics, Russian Academy of Sciences, Chernogolovka 142432, Moscow, Russia.

KOMAR Kathleen Lenore, b. 11 October 1949, Joliet, Illinois, USA. Professor; Vice-Chair of Academic Senate. m. Ross Shideler. Education: BA, English, University of Chicago, 1971; Study, universities of Bonn and Freiburg, 1971-72; MA, 1975, PhD, 1977, Comparative Literature, Princeton University. Appointments: Assistant Professor, 1977-84, Associate Professor, 1984-90, Professor, 1990-, Department of Comparative Literature and Department of Germanic Languages, Chair of Program in Comparative Literature, 1986-89, Director, Humanities Cluster Program, 1991-92, Associate Dean, Graduate Division, UCLA, 1992-2002. Publications: Books: Pattern and Chaos: Multilinear Novels by Dos Passos, Döblin, Faulkner and Koeppen, 1983; Transcending Angels: Rainer Maria Rilke's "Duino Elegies", 1987; Lyrical Symbols and Narrative Transformations (Co-editor), 1998; Reclaiming Klytemnestra, 2003; Numerous articles. Honours: Phi Beta Kappa, 1971; Honours: Fellowships, grants and teaching awards; Invited member, Advisory Council on Comparative Literature, Princeton, 1992-96, 1994-96, 1996-2000; Advisory Board, American Comparative Literature Association, 1992-95; 1999-2003; Vice President, American Computer Literature

Association, 2003-05. Address: University of California at Los Angeles, Royce Hall 212 UCLA; Los Angeles, CA 90095-1536, USA.

KOMESU Okifumi, b. 31 December 1931, Okinawa, Japan. Professor of English. m. Tomiko, 3 daughters. Education: BA, Muskingum College, New Concord, Ohio, 1955; MA, 1960, PhD, 1968, Michigan State University. Appointments: Professor of English, 1969, Chair, English Department, 1974-83, Director of the Libraries, 1987, Emeritus Professor of English, 1997, University of the Ryukyus. Publications: Numerous articles, books and papers, in English and Japanese, including, The Double Perspective of Yeats' Aesthetic, 1984; Mimesis and Extasis: Conflicting Claims of Art (in Japanese), 1984; The Literary Work of Art: Studies on the Creative Process from the Cultural Perspective (in Japanese), 1998. Honours: Research Fellowship, American Council of Learned Societies, ACLS, 1972; The Okinawa Times Publishing Culture Award, 1992; The Okinawa Times Cultural Award, 2002. Memberships: International Association for the Study of Irish Literature, IASIL, International Association of the University Professors of English, IAUPE. Address: 4-7-2 Kakazu, Ginowan, Okinawa 901-22, Japan.

KONG Cheol-Won, b. 7 September 1970, Seoul, Korea. Researcher. m. Hee-Jung Kim, 2 daughters. Education: BS, Pusan National University, Korea; MS, 1995, PhD, 2000, KAIST, Taejon, Korea. Appointments: Researcher, Korea Aerospace Research Institute; Development of composite tanks for Korea sounding rocket; Research about postbuckling of composite structures with damage; Research about NDT of composite structures. Publications: Articles in scientific journals: Postbuckling Strength of Stiffened Composite Plates; Testing and Analysis of Downscaled Composite Wing Box; Design of Composite Pressure Vessels with Metallic and Plastic Liners. Honour: Ministerial Citation, Ministry of Science and Technology, 2003. Membership: Korean Society for Composite Materials. Address: Korea Aerospace Research Institute, PO Box 113, Yusang, Taejon 305-600, Korea. E-mail: kcw@kari.re.kr

KONTSEVOY Mikhail Grigorievich, b. 16 October 1922, Lubin Village, Biransk Region, Russia. Agronomist. 2 daughters. Education: Graduate, Timiriazev Agricultural Academy, 1952; Defended Dissertation, 1957; Assistant Professor, 1961; Professor, 1985. Appointments: Chief Agronomist, Souzsortsemovosch, Moscow, 1956-57; Member of Staff, Plant-Growing Department, Tzhevsk State Agricultural University, Russia, 1957-. Publications: 99 articles; 2 monographs; 6 booklets: Sea-Buckthorn; Fruit and Berry Crops in Prenrals Region; Fruit Growing; New Crops in Ural Garden; All about Berries. Honours: Outstanding Worker of Higher Education, 1985; Honoured Scientist of the Udmurt Republic. Address: H 16 Agricultural Academy, Kiriva Str. Igevsk, 426018 Russia.

KONURALP Cüneyt, b. 21 February 1967, Ankara, Turkey. Physician; Cardiovascular Surgeon. m. Zeynep, 1 son. Education: BS, Bahçelievler Deneme Lisesi, Ankara, 1984; MD, Ankara University School of Medicine, 1990; Cardiovascular Surgery Specialist, Siyami Ersek Thoracic and Cardiovascular Surgery Center, Istanbul, 1996. Appointments: Resident, 1990-96, Staff Surgeon, 1996, Cardiovascular Surgery Department, Siyami Ersek Thoracic and Cardiovascular Surgery Center, Istanbul, Turkey; Clinical Fellow, Cardiothoracic Surgery Department, 1996-98, 1999-2000, Cardiothoracic Transplantation Department, 1998-99; Texas Heart Institute, St Luke's Episcopal Hospital, Houston, Texas; Staff Surgeon, Cardiovascular Surgery Department, Siyami Ersek Thoracic and Cardiovascular Surgery Center, Istanbul Turkey, 2000-. Publications: 28 congress presentations; 47

published scientific articles; 2 invited reviews; 13 abstracts; 3 book chapters; 2 invited talks; 1 patent pending. Honours include: Superior Performance on Track and Field, Turkish Ministry of Youth and Sport, 1986; Grant, Turkish Society of Cardiology, 2001; Winner, Edip Kürklü Award, Turkish Heart Foundation, 2001; Runner-up, C Walton Lillehei Young Investigator's Award, European Association for Cardio-Thoracic Surgery, 2001; Best Paper Prize, World Society of Cardio-Thoracic Surgeons, 2002; International Health Professional of the Year Award, IBC, 2003; Award of Biographical Recognition, IBC, 2004; Lifetime Achievement Award, IBC, 2004; Universal Award of Accomplishment, ABI, 2004; International Scientist of the Year, IBC, 2004; Member, Research Board of Advisors, ABI; Scientific Advisor, IBC. Memberships include: Fellow, International College of Surgeons; Fellow, American College of Chest Physicians; Fellow, American Heart Association; Fellow, European Society of Cardiology; Fellow, American College of Cardiology; Life Fellow, International Biographical Association; Turkish Medical Association; Cardiovascular Surgery Network; Denton A Cooley Cardiovascular Surgery Society; International Society for Heart and Lung Transplantation; Society of Thoracic Surgeons; Turkish Society of Cardiology; World Heart Federation; Heart Failure Society of America; Turkish Society of Perfusionists; Turkish Society of Thoracic and Cardiovascular Anaesthesia and Intensive Care; European Society for Artificial Organs; American Stroke Association; European Association for Cardio-Thoracic Surgery; Turkish Society of Cardiovascular Surgery; Galatasaray Sports Club. Address: Ayşe Çavuş Sokak, No 7/6, Huri Apt Suadiye, Istanbul 34740, Turkey. E-mail: ckonuralp@usa.net

KOO Christine, b. 30 October 1951, Shanghai, China. Solicitor. Education: LLB with honours, University of Hong Kong Law School, 1979; MCI Arb, Royal Melbourne Institute of Technology, Australia, 1986-87. Appointments: Non-Executive Director, China Life Trustees Ltd, 1998-; Non-Executive Director, Bank of East Asia (Trustees) Ltd, 1999-; Non-Executive Director, Tai Ping Trustees (HK) Ltd, 1999-; Non-Executive Director, Zurich Financial Services Pension and Trustees (HK) Ltd, 1999-2000; Investment Advisor, Investment Advisory Board of Bank of Communications (Hong Kong Branch), 1999-; Non-Executive Director, Hong Kong Dance Company Ltd, 2001-; Principal Partner, Christine M Koo & Ip, Solicitors and Notaries. Publications: Articles in professional journals. Honours: Honorary Legal Adviser, Actuarial Society of Hong Kong, Chinese Life Assurance Association of Hong Kong, FLMI Society of Hong Kong, Insurance Institute of Hong Kong Ltd, Hong Kong General Insurance Agents Association Ltd, Hans Andersen Club. Memberships: Inland Revenue Ordinance; Law Society of Hong Kong. Address: Room 3105, Bank of America Tower, 12 Harcourt Road, Hong Kong. E-mail: hristinekoo@cmkoo.com.hk Website: www.cmkoo.com.hk

KOOIJMAN Arthur, b. 11 December 1955, Heerlen. Translator; Linguist; Publisher. Education: BA, Philosophy, 1985; MA, Dutch Linguistics, 1986. Appointments: Head of Dutch Translation Department, Aldus Europe, Edinburgh, 1988-93; Freelance Translator, 1993-. Publications: Marsmans Woorden, 2000; Uit de Donkere Kamer, 2000; Rupert Brooke 1914 Translation of poems, 2000; Many articles in journals such as Onze Taal. Address: Saharadreef 3, 3564 CV Utrecht, Netherlands. E-mail: kooyman@planet.nl

KOONTZ Dean R(ay), (David Axton, Brian Coffey, Deanna Dwyer, K R Dwyer, John Hill, Leigh Nichols, Anthony North, Richard Paige, Owen West), b. 9 July 1945, Everett, Pennsylvania, USA. Writer. m. Gerda Ann Cerra, 15 October 1966. Education: BS, Shippensburg University, 1966. Publications: Star Quest, 1968; The Fall of the Dream Machine, 1969; Fear That Man, 1969; Anti-Man, 1970; Beastchild, 1970; Dark of the Woods, 1970; The Dark Symphony, 1970; Hell's Gate, 1970; The Crimson Witch, 1971; A Darkness in My Soul, 1972; The Flesh in the Furnace, 1972; Starblood, 1972; Time Thieves, 1972; Warlock, 1972; A Werewolf Among Us, 1973; Hanging On, 1973; The Haunted Earth, 1973; Demon Seed, 1973; Strike Deep, 1974; After the Last Race, 1974; Nightmare Journey, 1975; The Long Sleep, 1975; Night Chills, 1976; Prison of Ice, 1976, revised edition as Icebound, 1995; The Vision, 1977; Whispers, 1980; Phantoms, 1983; Darkfall, 1984; Twilight Eyes, 1985; The Door to December, 1985; Strangers, 1986; Watchers, 1987; Lightning, 1988; Midnight, 1989; The Bad Place, 1990; Cold Fire, 1991; Hideaway, 1992; Dragon Tears, 1992; Mr Murder, 1993; Winter Moon, 1993; Dark Rivers of the Heart, 1994; Strange Hideways, 1995; Intensity, 1995; Tick-Tock, 1996; Fear Nothing, 1998; False Memory, 1999; From the Corner of the Eye, 2000. Contributions to: Books, journals, and magazines. Honours: Daedalus Award, 1988; Honorary DLitt, Shippensburg University, 1989. Address: William Morris Agency, 1325 Avenue of the Americas, New York, NY 10019, USA.

KOOŸMANS Pieter Hendrik, b. 6 July 1933, Heemstede, The Netherlands. Judge. m. Adriana Verhage, 2 sons, 2 daughters. Education: BEcon, 1955; LLM with honours, 1957; PhD with honours, International Law, 1964. Appointments: Professor, Public International Law and European Law, Free University, Amsterdam, 1965-73; State Secretary for Foreign Affairs, 1973-77; Professor, Public International Law, University of Leiden, 1978-92, 1995-97; Minister of Foreign Affairs, 1993-94; Judge, International Court of Justice, 1997-. Publications: The Doctrine of the Legal Equality of States; A Bird's Eye View on Public International Law; Numerous articles. Memberships: Institut de Droit International; International Law Association. Address: International Court of Justice, Peace Palace, Carnegieplein 2, 2517KJ, The Hague, The Netherlands.

KOPECKÝ Miloslav, b. 4 May 1928, Prague, Czechoslovakia. Astrophysicist. m. Františka née Matysová, 1927-94, 2 sons. Education: Charles University, Prague, 1947-51; RNDr (rerum naturalium doktor), 1953; DrSc (doctor of physical mathematical science), 1969; Corresponding Member, Czechoslovak Academy of Sciences, 1977. Appointments: Worker of the Astronomical Institute, Ondrejov, 1949-93; Head of the Solar Department, 1971-75; Vice-Director of the Institute, 1975-90; Pensioner, Emeritus Worker of the Institute, 1993-. Publications: Over 200 scientific papers; 4 scientific monographs. Honours: State Prize, 1961; State Distinction, 1988; Various medals from different academies of sciences, universities. Membership: International Astronomical Union; Astronomische Gesellschaft. Address: 25165 Ondrejov 234, Czech Republic.

KOPELMAN Roni, b. 6 July 1978, Staten Island, New York, USA. Biochemist. Education: BA, Skidmore College, New York, 2000; MA, 2002, PhD, 2004, University of Washington. Appointments: Chief Technology Officer, AquaStasis. Publications: A Novel Approach to Attachment of Organo Metallic Probes to Nucleic Acids, 1998; Optically Tunable Metal Spirooxazine Complexes: Magnetism and Photophysics, 2003; Tunable photochromism of Spirooxazines via Metal Complexation, 2003; Materials and Devices for Information Technology, 2004. Honours: Herbert B Jones Foundation Grand Prize, Centre for Technology Entrepreneurship; Best Technology, VW Business School, 2004. Memberships: Sigma Xi, Scientific Research Society. Address: 2900 First Ave, Apt N107, Seattle, Washington, DC 98121, USA. E-mail: raki@u.washington.edu

Dictionary of International Biography

KOPP Maria, b. 14 January 1942, Budapest, Hungary. Doctor of Medicine; Psychologist. m. Arpad Skrabski, 2 daughters. Education: MD, Semmelweis University of Medicine, Budapest, 1968; Psychologist, Eötvös L University, Budapest, 1977; Specialisation in clinical psychology, 1984. Appointments: National Institute of Occupational Health Organiser of Clinical Epidemiology Research Group, 1968-73; Head, Clinical Epidemiology Research Group, Semmelweis University of Medicine, 1973-82; Head, Psychophysiology and Clinical Epidemiology Research Group, Head of Outpatient Behaviour Medical Department, Institute of Psychiatry, Semmelweis University of Medicine, 1982-93; Director, Institute of Behavioural Sciences, Semmelweis University Medicine, 1993-. Publications: Behavioural Sciences Applied to a Changing Society, 1996; 165 scientific papers. Honours: Nyiro Prize, Hungarian Psychiatric Association; Lege Artis Medicinae Prize, 1997. Memberships: President, Hungarian Psychophysiology and Health Psychology Society; Hungarian Representative; International Society Behavioural Medicine; Hungarian Representative, European Society Health Psychiatry. Address: Nagyvarad tér 4, H-1089 Budapest, Hungary.

KOPTAGEL Yuksel, b. 27 October 1931, Istanbul, Turkey. Pianist; Composer. m. Danyal Kerven, 30 December 1964. Education: Private studies with composer Djemal Rechid; Graduated, Real conservatorio de Music, Madrid, 1955; Diplome Superieur, Schola Cantorum, Ecole Superieure de Musique, Paris, 1958; Certificates on Composition and Spanish Music Interpretation, Santiago, 1959. Debut: First public concert, Istanbul, aged 5. Career: Concerts in Europe (Spain, France, Italy, Switzerland, Czechoslovakia, Germany) USA, India, Pakistan, Russia; Compositions published by Max Eschig, Paris and Bote Bock, Berlin; International concert career with European Orchestras, 1953-; Member of Jury, Schola Cantorum, Paris; Participant, numerous music festivals. Address: Caddebostan Plajyolu 21/32, 34728 Istanbul, Turkey.

KOPYLOV Yury Mikhailovich, b. 3 April 1946, Medvedovskaya Station, Russia. Mayor of Vladivostok City. m. Ludmila Grigoryevna, 1 son, 1 daughter. Education: Diploma with Honours in Production Engineering of Fish products, Far Eastern Maritime College, Nakhodka Town, Primorsky Province, USSR, 1961-65; Diploma of Engineer-Economist, Far Eastern Technical Institute of Fishery, Vladivostok, USSR, 1972-77; Diploma in Political Science, Moscow Higher Party School, 1982-85; Candidate of Economic Science, 2002. Appointments: Promoted from Probationer to Captain's Mate on Production Management, Vostokrybholodflot Fishery Co, 1966-70; Executive positions in party organisations of Youth Communist League, Leninist Young Communist League of the Soviet Union and Communist Party of the Soviet Union Committees, 1970-90; Director, Commercial Management and Foreign Economic Relations Division, Primorsky Agricultural Union, 1990-91; Director General, Poisk Commodity Exchange, 1991-92; Director General, Pallada Co, 1992-96; First Deputy Mayor of Vladivostok, City Manager, 1996-98; Acting Mayor of Vladivostok, 1998-2000; Mayor of Vladivostok City, 2000-. Publications include: Local Government: Trends and Potential, 2002; Regional Integration Processes in Primorsky Territory Development, 2002; Free Economic Zones: Global Experience and Prospects of Development in Russia, 2003; Globalism and Social-Economic Transformations in Regional Estimation, 2003. Honours: Commemorative Medal, 330 Years of Russian Fleet; Honorary Reward, Veteran of Honour; Award of Merit, Russian Ministry of Emergency Situations; Commemorative Medal, 70 Years of USSR Armed Forces; Reward of Russian Federation Ministry of Justice, Criminal Correction System. Membership: Full Member, Peter the First Academy of Sciences

and Arts, St Petersburg, Russia. Address: Apt 5, Bld 18, Praporschika Komarova St, Vladivostok, Russia 690000. E-mail: kopilov@vlc.ru

KORDA Petr, b. 23 January 1968, Prague, Czech Republic. Tennis Player. m. Regina Rajchrtova, 1992, 1 son, 2 daughters. Appointments: Coached by his father until 18 years old; Coached by Tomas Petera, 1991-; Winner, Wimbledon Junior Doubles, 1986; Turned Professional, 1987; Winner, Stuttgart Open, 1997, Australian Open, 1998, Qatar Open, 1998; Member, Czechoslovak Davis Cup Team, 1988, 1996; Retired, 1999, after winning 20 professional titles including 10 singles titles; Currently plays in Seniors Tour; Winner, Honda Challenge, 2002; Chairman, Board of Supervisors, Karlštejn golf resort.

KORDIĆ Snježana, b. 29 October 1964, Osijek, Croatia. Educator and Researcher of South Slavic Languages. m. Atila Rusić, 3 October 1992. Education: Diploma, Croatian or Serbian Language and South Slavic Literature, Joseph George Strossmayer's University of Osijek, 1988; Postgraduate Study of Linguistics, Zagreb University, 1992; DPhilol Sci, Zagreb University, 1993; Habilitation in Slavic Philology, Westfälische Wilhelms-University, Münster, Germany, 2002. Appointments: Teacher, Second School, Sisak, 1988-90; Researcher of Linguistics, Pedagogical Faculty, Osijek University, 1990-91; Lecturer, Department of Journalism, Faculty of Political Science, Zagreb University, 1991-92; Researcher and University Assistant, Modern Croatian Language, Faculty of Philosophy, Zagreb University, 1991-95; Lecturer and Scientific Contributor of German Association of Researchers, Faculty of Philology, Ruhr University of Bochum, Germany, 1993-98; University Docent for South Slavic Languages, Slavic and Baltic Department, Faculty of Philosophy, Westfälische Wilhelms University of Münster, Germany, 1998-2004. Publications: Author, Relativna rečenica, 1995; Serbo-Croatian, 1997; Kroatisch-Serbisch: Ein Lehrbuch für Fortgeschrittene mit Grammatik, 1997; Der Relativsatz im Serbokroatischen, 1999; Wörter im Grenzbereich von Lexikon und Grammatik im Serbokroatischen, 2001; Riječi na granici punoznačnosti, 2002; Contributions articles in professional journals; Contributor in Linguistics Bibliography of Permanent International Committee of Linguistics. Memberships: Presidency, Croatian Society of Philology, 1991-93; Croatian Applied Linguistics Society, 1991-93; Editorial Board, Journal Suvremena lingvistika, 1991-93; International Slavic Committee for Sociolinguistics, 1993-96; German Association of Researchers, 1998-; German Association of University Educators of Slavic Languages and Literatures, 2002-. Address: Westfälische Wilhelms-Universität Münster, Slavisch-Baltisches Seminar, Bispinghof 3A, D-48143 Münster, Germany.

KORNBERG Arthur, b. 3 March 1918, Brooklyn, New York, USA. Biochemist. m. (1) Sylvy R Levy, deceased 1986, 3 sons, (2) Charlene W Levering, 1988, deceased 1995. Education: Pre-Medical Course, College of the City of New York, BS, 1937; Medical Degree, University of Rochester School of Medicine, 1941. Appointments: Commissioned Officer, US PUBLIC Health Service, 1941-42; National Institutes of Health, Bethesda, Maryland, 1942-52; Professor and Chairman, Department of Microbiology, Washington University School of Medicine, 1953-59; Executive Head, 1959-69, Professor, 1959-88, Professor Emeritus, 1988-, Department of Biochemistry, Stanford University School of Medicine, Palo Alto; Made the first synthetic molecules of DNA; Synthesized a biologically active artificial viral DNA. Publications: For the love of Enzymes: the odyssey and a biochemist (autobiography), 1989; Numerous original research papers and reviews on subjects in biochemistry, particularly enzymatic mechanisms of biosynthetic reactions. Honour: Joint Winner, Nobel Prize in Medicine and Physiology, 1959; Several honorary degrees; numerous other awards. Memberships: NAS; American Philosophical Society; American Academy of Arts and Sciences, Foreign member, Royal Society, 1970. Address: Department of Biochemistry, Stanford, University Medical Center, Stanford, CA 94305, USA.

KORNBERG Hans Leo, b. 14 January 1928, Herford, Germany (British Citizen). Professor of Biochemistry. Education: BSc, 1949, PhD, 1953, Sheffield University. Appointments: John Stokes Research Fellow, University of Sheffield, 1952-53; Member, Medical Research Council Cell Metabolism Research Unit, University of Oxford, 1955-61; Lecturer in Biochemistry, Worcester College, Oxford, 1958-61; Professor of Biochemistry, University of Leicester, 1961-75; Sir William Dunn Professor of Biochemistry, University of Cambridge, 1975-95; University Professor and Professor of Biology, Boston University, Massachusetts, USA, 1995-; Fellow, 1975-, Master, 1982-95, Christ's College, Cambridge. Publications: Numerous articles in scientific journals. Honours: Commonwealth Fund Fellow, Yale University and Public Health Research Institute, New York, 1953-55; Colworth Medal, Biochemical Society, 1963; Warburg Medal, Gesellschaft für biologische Chemie der Bundersrepublik, 1973; Honorary member of: Society of Biological Chemistry (USA), 1972; Japanese Biochemical Society, 1981; American Academy of Arts and Sciences, 1987; Honorary FRCP, 1989; Numerous honorary fellowships and degrees. Memberships: German Academy of Sciences, Leopoldina, 1982; Foreign associate, NAS, 1986; Academie Europaea, 1988; Fellow, American Academy of Microbiology, 1992; Foreign member, American Philosophical Society, 1993; Foreign member, Accademia Nazionale dei Lincei, Italy, 1997. Address: The University Professors, Boston University, 745 Commonwealth Avenue, Boston, MA 02215, USA.

KORNFELD Robert Jonathan, b. 3 March 1919, Newtonville, Massachusetts, USA. Dramatist; Writer; Poet. m. Celia Seiferth, 23 August 1945, 1 son. Education: AB, Harvard University, 1941; Attended, Columbia University, Tulane University, New York University, New School for Social Research, Circle-in-the-Square School of Theatre, and Playwrights Horizons Theatre School and Laboratory. Appointment: Playwright-in-Residence, University of Wisconsin, 1998. Publications: Plays: Great Southern Mansions, 1977; A Dream Within a Dream, 1987; Landmarks of the Bronx, 1990; Music For Saint Nicholas, 1992; Hot Wind From the South, 1995; The Hanged Man, 1996. Plays produced: Father New Orleans, 1997; The Queen of Carnival, 1997; The Celestials, 1998; Passage in Purgatory, Shanghai, China, 2000. Other: Fiction and poetry. Contributions to: Various publications. Honours: Numerous awards and prizes; Visiting Artist, American Academy, Rome, 1996. Memberships: Authors League; Dramatists Guild; National Arts Club; New York Drama League; PEN. Address: The Withers Cottage, 5286 Sycamore Avenue, Riverdale, NY 10471, USA.

KOROLEV Mikhail Antonovich, b. 12 September 1931, Alma-Ata. Statistician. m. E Letalina-Koroleva, 1957, 1 daughter. Education: Moscow Plekhanov Institute of National Economy. Appointments: Assistant, Moscow Plekhanov Institute of National Economy, 1954-56; Assistant Dean, Department Head, 1956-66, Rector, 1966-72, Professor, 1967-, Moscow Institute of Economics and Statistics; Deputy, First Deputy Director, 1972-85, Director, 1985-87, Central Statistics Board of USSR; Vice-Chair, 1976-79, 1989-91, Chair, Statistical Commission of UN, 1979-81; President, USSR State Committee on Statistics, 1987-89; Advisor to Prime Minister of USSR, 1991; President, Interstate Statistical Committee, CIS, 1992-. Publications: 20 books, numerous articles. Honour: PhD on Economics; Professor, Honorary Scientist, member, International Informatics Academy. Membership:

International Statistical Institute. Address: Interstate Statistical Committee of the Commonwealth of Independent States, Build 1, 39 Myasnitskaya Street, 107450 Moscow, Russian Federation.

KOROTKOV Leonid Viktorovich, b. 19 January 1965, Zavitinsk, Amurskaya Region, Russia. Governor of the Amurskaya Region. m. Tatyana Arkadievna Korotkova, 2 sons. Education: Diploma in Journalism, The Far East State University, 1987; Economist, Finance Academy under the Government of the Russian Federation, 1999. Appointments: Journalist on Amurskaya Pravda (a regional paper in Blagoveshchensk), 1988; Member of the Council of Federation of the Federal Assembly of the Russian Federation, 1993; Deputy of the First Convocation, Russian Federation State Parliament (Duma), 1995; Deputy of the Third Convocation, Russian Federation State Parliament (Duma), 1999; Governor of the Amurskaya Region, 2003. Honours: Awarded 3 State Medals of the Russian Federation, 1987, 2002, 2003; World Wildlife Foundation's title "Guardian of the Planet Earth", 2003. Membership: Journalist Association of the Russian Federation. Address: The Amurskaya Region Administration, Lenin Street 135, Blagoveshchensk, 675023 Amurskaya Region, Russia. E-mail: governor@amurrobl.ru

KORZENIK Diana, b. 15 March 1941, New York, New York, USA. Professor Emerita; Painter; Writer. Education: Oberlin College; BA, Vassar College; Master's Programme, Columbia University; EdD, Graduate School of Education, Harvard University. Appointments: Professor Emerita, Massachusetts College of Art, Boston. Publications: Chapter in Art and Cognition (editors, Leondar and Perkins), 1977; Drawn to Art, 1986; Art Making and Education (with Maurice Brown), 1993; The Cultivation of American Artists (co-editor with Sloat and Barnhill), 1997; The Objects of Art Education, 2004. Contributions to: Professional journals and to magazines. Honours: Boston Globe L L Winship Literary Award, 1986; National Art Education Association Lowenfeld Award, 1998. Memberships: Friends of Longfellow House, founder, board member; American Antiquarian Society; Massachusetts Historical Society. Address: 7 Norman Road, Newton Highlands, MA 02461, USA.

KOSHANOV Amenzhol, b. 11 October 1934, Kazakhstan. Economist. m. Rausham Koshanova. Education: Diploma, Moscow State University "M V Lomonosov", 1957; Doctoral Diploma, Moscow, 1980; Professor, Moscow, 1984. Appointments include: Academician-Secretary, Department of Social Studies and the Humanities of the National Academy of Sciences of the Republic of Kazakhstan, 1994-. Publications: Monographs: Mixed Economics: the transformational model of the development of Kazakhstan, 1997; Relations of Property in the Market Transformation of Kazakhstan, 2003; Competitionable Import Substitution and the International Market, 2003; Relations of Property and Functionability of Foreign Enterprises, 2003; Article: National Economic Interests of the Republic of Kazakhstan and Globalisation in Society and Economics, 2003. Honours: Academician of the National Academy of Sciences of Kazakhstan; State Honour: Meritorious Science and Technology Worker of Kazakhstan. Memberships: Academician, Asia-European International Economical Academy, Kazakhstan; Member of the Presidium of Kazakh Economists' Association. Address: Institute of Economy, Kurzmangazy 29, Almaty 480100, Republic of Kazakhstan. E-mail: koshanov@ok.kz

KOSOWSKI Stanisław Wincenty, b. 27 July 1940, Zarki, Cracow, Poland. Physicist. Divorced, 2 sons, 2 daughters. Education: Master of Physics, Jagiellonian University, Cracow, 1963; Doctor of Technological Sciences, 1967; Habilitated Doctor of Technological Sciences, Institute of Fundamental Technological

Research, Polish Academy of Sciences, 1973. Appointments: Adjunct, IFTR-PAS, 1968-74, docent, 1974-85; Unemployed, 1985-95; Non-paid creative work, 1995-; Pension, voluntary work, 1995-; Published new theory of distant variable stars brightness, 1995. Publications: Balcerowicz Plan; Wałesa Casus; Presidential Election '95'; 40 scientific articles on physics and astrophysics; Hypothesis on the rotational motion of planets and its development; Model of propagation of light in transparent media, among others; Articles expounding several new ideas on economics; 3000 unpublished short poems; Several unpublished poems about America, 2001-03. Address: ul Pereca 2m 1214, 00-849 Warsaw, Poland.

KOSYRZ Zdzislaw, b. 3 January 1930, Jaworzno, Poland. Educator. m. Lidia Kolodziej, 1 son, 1 daughter. Education: Master of Pedagogy, University of Warsaw, Poland, 1960; Doctor of Science, 1967; Habilitation, 1973; Lecturer, 1955-65, Reader, 1955-70; Associate Professor, 1983; Professor, 1989. Appointments: Educational Institute of Teachers, Warsaw, 1975-80; College of Education, Bydgoszoz, 1981-89; Military Academy, Warsaw, 1983-90; College of Agriculture and Education, Siedlce, 1994-99; College of Special Education, 1994-2002; Mazowiecka College of Humanities and Education, Lowicz, 1994-90; Academy of Special Education, Warsaw, 1999-2002; College of Education, Warsaw, 2000; Academy of Humanities and Economics, Lodz, 2002. Publications: Shaping Patriotic and Defensive Attitudes (co-author), 1983; Patriotic Education of University Students, 1985; Interpersonal Education, 1993; Tutor Personality (5 editions), 2000; More than 200 academic articles; Supervisor of more than 22 doctoral theses on arts and humanities. Honours: Knight, Polnia Restituta Order; Polish Teacher badge of Merit; National Education Commission Medal. Memberships: Polish Pedagogical Association, 1984-; Polish Association of Psychic Hygiene, 1990-2002; Committee of Pedagogical Sciences, Polish Academy of Sciences, 1971-90; Polish Association of Suicide Science. Address: ul Mila 17/19, 00-174 Warsaw, Poland.

KOSZEWSKI Andrzej, b. 26 July 1922, Poznań, Poland. Composer; Musicologist. m. Krystyna Jankowska, 9 September 1959, 1 daughter. Education: Diploma Musicology, University of Poznań, 1950; Diplomas, Composition and Theory of Music, State Higher Schools, Poznań, 1948, 1953, Warsaw, 1958. Appointments: Lecturer, State Music Schools, Poznan, 1948-78; Professor of Composition, Academy of Music, Poznań, 1978-; Full Professor of Composition, 1985-. Creative works: Contributor of publications on Chopinology and Musical Education; Numerous compositions especially for choir performed and recorded at important festivals and competitions in Europe, Asia, America, Africa, Australia, South America. Honours: Awards, Ministry of Culture and Arts, Poland, 1967, 1973, 1977, 1978, 1982, 1988; Prize, Prime Minister of Poland, 1982; Prize, Polish Composers' Union, Warsaw, 1986; Artistic Prizes, Province and City of Poznań, 1968, 1986, 1994. Memberships: Polish Composers' Union; Chopin Society; Authors Society ZAIKS. Address: ul Poznańska 37/9, 60-850 Poznań, Poland. .

KOSZTOLNYIK Zoltan J, b. 15 December 1930, Heves, Hungary. Professor Emeritus of History. m. Penelope South Kosztolnyik, 2 daughters. Education: BA, St Bonaventure University, 1959; MA, Fordham University, 1961; PhD, New York University, 1968. Appointments: Instructor in History, 1967-68, Assistant Professor, 1968-72, Associate Professor, 1972-81; Professor of History, 1981-2003; Professor Emeritus, 2003-; Texas A and M University; Guest Professor of Medieval History, Janus Pannonius University, Hungary. Publications: Five Eleventh Century Hungarian Kings, 1981; From Coloman the Learned to Bela III (1095-1196): Hungarian domestic policy and its impact upon foreign affairs, 1987; Hungary in the 13th Century, 1996; Hungary under the early Arpads, 890's to 1063, 2002; Over 50 articles, and over 50 book reviews published in scholarly journals. Honours: New York University Founders Day Award, 1969; Phi Kappa Phi, 1979-; TAMU/College of Liberal Arts Distinguished Teaching Award, 1995. Memberships: Medieval Academy of America; American Historical Association; American Catholic Historical Association. Address: Department of History, Texas A&M University, College Station, TX 77843-4236, USA.

KOTKER (Mary) Zane, (Maggie Strong), b. 2 January 1934, Waterbury, USA. Writer. m. Norman Kotker, 7 June 1965, 1 son, 1 daughter. Education: MA, Columbia University, 1959-60. Publications: Bodies in Motion (novel), 1972; A Certain Man (novel), 1976; White Rising (novel), 1981; Mainstay (as Maggie Strong), 1988; Try to Remember (novel), 1997; Mainstay (as Maggie Strong), 1997. Honour: National Endowment for the Arts, 1972. Address: 160 Main Street, Northampton, MA 01060, USA.

KOTTEK Alfred Viktor, b. 23 November 1934, Iglau. International Civil Servant. 2 sons. Education: Studies of Paleontology, Universities of Tübingen, Berlin, Athens, 1955-63; DSc, 1963; Graduate, German Institute for Development Policy, Berlin, 1966. Appointments: Research Fellow, Paleontology, University Athens, 1963-65; Chief Project Section for Latin America, German Development Service, 1966-67; Head, Latin American Program, International Organization for Migration, 1967-75; IOM Chief of Mission, Portugal, 1975-83; Jordan and Iraq, 1991; IOM Regional Representative, East Asia, Hong Kong, 1983-93; Central Europe, Vienna, 1993-96; Country Representative, Germany, IOM/Organisation for Security and Co-operation in Europe, 1996-97; Election Observer, European Union, Cambodia, 1998; Country Representative, Indonesia for IOM/United Nations, 1999. Publications: The sequence of ammonites in the Greek Toarcium; Pictures of change, Murals in Portugal; Poetry, 10 pages in an anthology; Ancient China's Bronze Way into the Money Economy, Vienna, 1996. Honours: Scheffel Prize for German Literature; Medal of City of Angra; Medal of City of Braganca; Citation: Director of IOM; Kyrgyzstan: Border Guard Medal; Others. Memberships: Burg Waldeck Association; Palaeontological Society; Society for Literature; Maison Internationale des Intellectuels; German Press Association; Friends of the National Library of Austria; others. Address: 2301 Bauhinia Bldg, 535 Nicola Street, Vancouver, BC V6G 3G3, Canada.

KOTTIS PETRAKI Athena, b. Sparta, Greece. University Professor. m. George Kottis. Education: BA, Athens University of Economics, 1961; MSc, Economics, London School of Economics, London, 1964; PhD, Economics, Wayne State University, USA, 1970. Appointments: Professor, Athens University of Economics and Business, 1977-; Member, Board of Governors, Greek Mortgage bank, 1989-92; Member, European Employment Observatory, 1997-99; Consultant with various duties to: European Commission, The World Bank, The OECD and other organisations. Publications: About 50 articles in international economic journals; 10 textbooks on economics. Honour: Prize, Greek Society of Literary Writers. Memberships: American Economic Association; Greek Economic Association. Address: 14 Loukianou Street, Athens 10675, Greece.

KOUBA Vaclav, b. 16 January 1929, Vrabi, Czech Republic. Epizootiologist. m. Anna Holcapkova, 1 son, 1 daughter. Education: Diploma, Veterinary Medicine, 1953, PhD, 1961, Habil Docent 1966, DrSc, 1978, Professor, Epizootiology, 1988, University of Veterinary Medicine, Brno, Czech Republic. Appointments: Lecturer, 1952-56, University of Veterinary Medicine, Brno, Czech Republic; National Chief Epizootiologist,

Prague, 1956-78; Visiting Professor, University of Havana, 1967-71; Animal Health Officer (Research/Education), Senior Animal Health Officer, FAO-UN, Rome, Italy, 1978-85; Professor, Founder of faculty and Institute of Tropical Veterinary Medicine, Brno, 1985-88; Chief, Animal Health Service, Food and Agriculture Organisation of the United Nations, Rome, 1988-91; Visiting Professor, Mexico City, 1993; Visiting Professor, University of Kosice, 1993-98; Visiting Professor, University of Prague, 1999-; Founder of modern epizootiology; Achievements as leading specialist: Eradication of bovine brucellosis, 1964, bovine tuberculosis, 1968, Teschen disease, 1973 and foot and mouth disease, 1975 in Czechoslovakia; Foot and mouth disease in Mongolia, 1964; African swine fever in Cuba, 1971; Myiasis Cochliomyia hominivorax in Northern Africa, 1991 regaining free status of the whole Eastern hemisphere; First isolation of Aujeszky disease virus in Czechoslovakia, 1954. Publications include: General Epizootiology textbooks; FAO-WHO-OIE World Animal Health Yearbook, editor; Over 700 articles on epizootiology; Software: Epizoo, Epizmeth, Epiztext, electronic textbook. Honours: Polar Star Order, Mongolian Government; Outstanding Work Order, Czechoslovak Government; Veterinary Public Health Expert, World Health Organization, Geneva; Informatics Expert, International Office of Epizootics, Paris; Honourable President, Cuban Veterinary Scientific Society. Memberships: World Veterinary Association, Education Committee; International Society of Veterinary Epidemiology and Economics; World Association for the History of Veterinary Medicine. Address: PB 516, 17000 Praha 7, Czech Republic.

KOUL Sarswati, b. 15 February 1974, India. Researcher; Postdoctoral Student. Education: Bachelors Degree with Honours, Chemistry and Genetics, 1992; Masters Degree, Chemistry, 1996; Bachelors Degree in Education (Psychology and Chemistry), 1998; Diploma in Computer Programming, 2002; PhD, Applied Chemistry and Polymer Technology, 2003. Appointments: Research Associate, GE-NPL Project; Research Assistant, ISRO, Aerospace project; Junior Research Scientist, SRI Industry (India) in electron-beam radiation epoxy project; Postdoctoral Student, Electrical Department, Waterloo University, Ontario, Canada. Publications: 10 publications in national and international journals; 1 Indian and US Patent; 1 technical report on radiation in polymeric composites. Honours: Young Scientist Award in Material Science for best investigation in conducting polymers, ISCA, India, 2001; Best Thesis of the Year, 2003; Exchange Indo-European Fellowship for 6 months in France. Memberships: Indian Chemical Society; Student Member, IUPAC; MRS; American Chemical Society; Student Member, NACE. Address: Department of Electrical and Computer Engineering, Faculty of Engineering, University of Waterloo, 200 University Avenue West, Waterloo, ONT N2L 3G1, Canada. E-mail: sarrkoul@yahoo.com

KOUMAKIS George, b. 13 April 1937, Heracliou, Crete. Associate Professor. m. Efstathia, 26 December 1971, 1 son, 3 daughters. Education: Diploma of Philosophy and Philology, University of Athens, 1960; Master of Arts, Philosophy, University of Bonn, Germany, 1967; PhD, 1970. Appointment: Associate Professor, Greek, English, German and French Language, University of Ioannina. Publications: Numerous books and articles in professional journals. Honours: Prize of Municipality, Heracliou, Crete, for book, Nikos Kazantzakis; Scholarship, DAAD; United Cultural Convention's International Peace Prize, 2003; Participated in many Greek, international and world congresses. Memberships: Greek Philosophical Association; American Philosophical Association. Address: Keramikou str 6, 15125 Maroussi, Athens, Greece.

KOVACHEV Ljubomir, b. 26 November 1942, Dimitrovgrad, Bulgaria. Surgeon. m. Anelia Panteleeva, 1 son. Education: MD, Higher Medical Institute, Sofia, 1972; MD, Surgery, Medical Academy, Sofia, 1978; PhD, Highest Certifying Commission, Sofia, 1985. Appointments: Registrar in Surgery, in hospitals of Dulovo and Pernik, 1972-75; Assistant Professor, 1976-85, Associate Professor, 1986-2002, Head of Department, 1987-2002, Dean of Foreign Students, 1987-93, Higher Medical Institute, Pleven. Publications: Professional journals. Honours: Man of the Year, ABI, 1998; Listed in biographical publications. Membership: Eurosurgery. Address: George Kochev Street 39, Entr D, Ap 2, 5800 Pleven, Bulgaria.

KOVACS George, b. 30 October 1943, Budapest. Professor. m. Noemi Farago, 2 sons, 1 daughter. Education: Electrical Engineer, 1966; Dr Techn, 1976, PhD, 1978, Technical University of Budapest; Dr, Hungarian Academy, Hungarian Academy of Sciences, 1996. Appointments: Visiting Researcher in USA, 1972-73, Russia, 1977-79, Germany, 1983; Visiting Professor in Mexico, 1986, Italy, 1994; Computer and Automation Institute, Head of CIM Research Laboratory, 1990-; Professor at the Technical University, Budapest, 1995-. Publications: Over 250 mostly in English on automation, manufacturing, artificial intelligence. Honours: Excellent Innovator, 1991; Best Researcher, 4 times. Memberships: IEEE; IFAC; IFIP. Address: 1025 Budapest, Verecke ut 116, Hungary.

KOVE Miriam, b. 17 February 1941, Chotin, Bassarabia. Psychoanalytic Psychotherapist. Divorced, 2 daughters. Education: BA, Sir George University, Montreal, Canada, 1962; MS, Education, Hunter College, 1976; Certificate in Psychoanalytic Psychotherapy, New Hope Guild Centres, New York, 1979; M of SW, Adelphi University, 1983; Diplomate, American Board of Examiners, NYC, 1991-. Appointments: Private practice, 25 years; Faculty Supervisor, New Hope Guild Centres Training Programme; Adjunct Lecturer, Early Childhood, Kingsborough. Publications: Articles to professional journals; Presentations; 2 books. Honours: Presenter, National Conference of the Society of Clinical Social Work, Chicago; Who's Who Among Human Service Professionals; Who's Who in American Women. Memberships: National Association of Social Work; American Board of Examiners in Clinical Social Work. Address: 320 E 25th St, #8EE, New York, NY 10010, USA.

KOVENSKY Barbara Jane, b. 24 October 1945, Cambridge, USA. Chemist. m. Sheldon, 2 daughters. Education: BA, Chemistry, Wheaton College, 1967; MSc, Food Chemistry, University of Toronto, 1972. Appointments: Head, Instrumentation Methodology and Analytical Research Laboratories, RP Scherer Corporation, Detroit, 1968-70; Technical Consultant, Smith, Miller and Patch (Canada) Ltd and Sterile Pharmaceutical Ltd, Toronto, 1971-72; Director, Quality Control, Sterile Pharmaceutical Ltd, Toronto, 1972-75; Director, Envirolab Division, Surveyor, Nenniger and Chenevert (SNC), Montreal, 1975-76; Manager, Organic Analysis Division, Technitrol Canada Ltd, 1967-83; Vice President, Technitrol Expertise Incorporated, Downsview, Ontario, 1983-98; President, Experchem Laboratories Incorporated, Downsview, 1998-. Publications: Several articles in professional journals. Honours: Listed in several biographical dictionaries including: Who's Who of Canadian Women; Who's Who in Canadian Business. Memberships: Order of Professional Chemists; Association of the Chemical Profession of Ontario; Canadian Institute of Food Science and Technology; Canadian Cosmetic, Toiletry and Fragrance Association; Association of Official Analytical Chemists; Fellow, IBA. Address: Experchem Laboratories Incorporated, 1111 Flint Road Units 40-41, Downsview, Ontario M3J 3C7, Canada.

KOWALSKI Luiz Paulo, b. 16 August 1956, Curitiba, Brazil. Physician. m. Ivonete S G Kowalski, 2 daughters. Education: Medical Doctor, 1979; Medical residency, 1980-84; Master Degree, 1986; PhD, 1989; Free Professor of Oncology, 1996. Appointments: Director, Head and Neck Surgery Department, Hospital Do Cancer A C Camargo; Professor, Post Graduate Courses in Oncology, University of São Paulo and Fundacao Antonio Prudente. Publications: 107 peer-reviewed articles in international journals; 90 articles in Brazilian journals; 5 books. Honours: Presidential Citation, American Head and Neck Society; Senior Lecturer, Eastman Dental Institute, University College of London, England. Memberships: American Head and Neck Society; Brazilian Head and Neck Society; Brazilian College of Surgeons. Address: Rua Professor Antonio Prudente 211, 01509-900 São Paulo, Brazil. E-mail: lp_kowalski@ual.com.br

KOZÁK János, b. 20 December 1945, Kenderes, Hungary. Professor. m. Erzsébet Barna, 3 sons, 2 daughters. Education: Agricultural Engineer, 1968, Professional Agricultural Engineer, 1975, Agricultural Doctor of the University, 1979, University of Agricultural Sciences, Gödöllő, Hungary; Candidate of Economy (PhD), The Hungarian Committee of Scientific Qualifications, Budapest, Hungary, 1988; Habilitation, Szent István University, Gödöllő, Hungary 1998. Appointments: Assistant, Co-operative Farm, Aranykalász, Törökszentmiklós; Manager, Farm Machinery Institute, Gödöllő, 1970; Chief Animal Breeder, Co-operative Farm, Lenin, Kunság Népe, Kunhegyes, 1970-78; Assistant Professor, Professor, University of Agricultural Sciences, Gödöllő, 1978-99; Professor, Szent István University, Gödöllő, 2000-. Publications: Books: Vertical relations and possibilities for the improvement of interest in goose production; Miscellaneous poultry breeding; Examination of environmental conditions in the light of European Union requirements; Poultry Industry in Hungary; Works on technologies, market regulation and animal welfare. Honour: Outstanding Worker of Agriculture Award, Ministry of Agriculture and Food Industry. Memberships: World's Poultry Science Association Working Group No 8 Waterfowl, Hungarian Branch; Technical Commission of International Down and Feather Bureau; Chairman, Hungarian Standard National Technical Committee MSZT/MB 626, Feather and Down; Poultry Breeding Department, Association of Hungarian Foodstuffs Industry Science; World Rabbit Science Association, Hungarian Branch; Hungarian Association of Agricultural Economists; World Council of Hungarian University Professors; Association of Hungarian Specialists; Public Body of the Hungarian Academy of Sciences. Address: Szent István University; Department of Pig and Poultry Breeding; Páter Károly u 1, H-2103 Gödöllő, Hungary. E-mail: jkozak@fau.gau.hu

KOZLOV Victor Vasilievich, b. 8 July 1944, Moscow, Russia. Company Director. m. Anna Vasilievna Kozlova, 1 daughter. Education: Moscow Institute of Chemical Machines Construction; All Union Academy of Foreign Trade; Candidate of Economic Sciences (PhD). Appointments: Engineer, Ministry of Heavy Power-producing and Transport Engineering Industry, Moscow, 1970-73; Engineer, Expert, Deputy Chief of Department, State Committee of Economic Relations of the USSR, Moscow, 1974-79; Expert, Chief of Representative Office, Atomenergoexport, Helsinki, Finland, 1979-83; Director, New Engineering Office, Deputy Chief of Foreign Trade Society Atomenergoexport, State Committee of Economic Relation of the USSR, Moscow, 1984-87; Deputy Chief of Personnel Management, Headquarters, State Committee of Economic Relations of USSR, Moscow, 1987-90; Chairman, Atomenergoexport, Ministry of Foreign Trade, USSR, 1990-94; Director General, JSC Atomenergoexport, 1994-98; Director General, Atomenergoexport and Atomstroyexport, 1998-. Publications: Co-author: Internal Labour Market in Condition of

Transformation of Company's Corporate Culture, 2001; Author, Corporate Culture: Experience, Problems and Development Prospects, 2001. Honours: Medal, For distinguished labour achievements; Medal of Afghanistan "The 10th Anniversary of April Revolution"; Order of Friendship. Membership: Supervisory Board for Some Banks and Organizations. Address: 35 bld 3, Malaya Ordynka, 115184, Moscow, Russia. E-mail: post@atomstroyexport.ru

KOZLOV Vladislav, b. 15 February 1936, Kramatorsk, Donetch Region, USSR. Radiochemist; Historian; Artist; Painter. m. Inna Kozlova, 2 daughters. Education: Graduate, Radiochemistry, Leningrad University, 1958; Graduation Certificate, Drawing, Painting, History of Art, Stroganov Art High School, 1963; Doctor of Chemical Science, Professor, 1964. Appointments: Senior Scientific Researcher, Aerospace Technology, Atomic Submarine Engineering, 29 years; Participated in many years control over the consequences of 50-megatonne thermonuclear tests on Novaya Zemlya; President, Centre "Our Heritage", 1987-. Publications: Author of more than 200 articles and books on radiochemistry; 66 articles and books on history of arts, problems of state development and monarchy include: Illustrated album, Russian Emperor Dynasty, 1993; The Brilliant Europe of XVII Century, 2001. Honours include: 2 Honorary Diplomas and Prizes, Mendeleyev Chemical Society; 14 prizes in the field of new (special technologies); Pushkin Medal, Russia Philological Academy; Government Awards: Silver Medal in honour of the 300th Anniversary of the Russian Fleet, 1996; Honorary Diploma, For Services to the Motherland, President of Russia, 2002; Medal, 40 years of U Gagarin's Flight, 2003; Presented album, The Russian Emperor Dynasty to HM Queen Elizabeth II; Presented book, The Brilliant Europe of XVII Century to 7 European monarchs and professors of the Swedish Royal Academy. Memberships: Academician, Russian Academy of Sciences and Arts, 2003-; Honorary Member, Russian Philological Academy, 2003. Address: Ul Kirova dom 13 kv 50, Himki Moscow Region, 141400 Russia. E-mail: sla77@mail.ru

KOZLOVA Ariadna, b. 28 May 1957, Russia. Senior Researcher. Education: Physics Educator, Orekhovo-Zuevo Pedagogical Institute, 1974-78; Mathematics Educator, Orekhovo-Zuevo, 1981-83; PhD, High Temp Institute, Academy of Sciences, Moscow, 1991; Postdoctoral, Moscow, 1993-96. Appointments: Teacher, Physics, Adelino, Ryazan Region, Russia, 1978-79; Senior Technician, EORRIB Electrogorsk, Moscow, 1979-80; Teacher, Physics and Mathematics, School, Electrogorsk, Russia, 1980-81; Tutor, Dept of Physics, Orekhovo-Zuevo Pedagogical Institute, 1981-83; Engineer, Department of Physics, 1983-84; Corresponding Postgraduate, 1984-88, Research Worker, Department of Physics, 1987-93; Postdoctoral Student, 1993-96, Research Worker, Department of Physics, Moscow Aviation Institute. Publications include: High Power Laser-Science and Engineering, 1996; Solar Ultraviolet Radiation, (Modelling, Measurements, Effects), 1997; Surface Diffusion: Atomistic and Collective Processes, 1997. Memberships: New York Academy of Sciences; National Geographic Society; Russian Pushkin Society. Address: Moscow Aviation Institute, Volokolamskoye shosse 4, 125 871 Moscow, Russia.

KRAGGERUD Egil, b. 7 July 1939, S Höland, Norway. Professor. m. Beate, 3 sons, 1 daughter. Education: Oslo University, 1958-64. Appointments: Lecturer, 1967; Dr of Philosophy, 1968; Professor, Classical Philology, 1969-; Co-editor, Editor, Symbolae Osloenses, 1972-94; Professor Emeritus, 2002. Publications: Aeneisstudien; Der Namensatz der taciteischen Germania; Horaz und Actium; Numerous articles in English and German. Honours: Thorleif Dahl's Literary Award. Memberships: Norwegian

Dictionary of International Biography

Academy of Science and Letters; The Royal Norwegian Society of Sciences and Letters; Academia Europea. Address: Bygdöy alle 13, 0257 Oslo, Norway.

KRAJEWSKI Joyce, b. 17 November 1952, Cuyahoga. Educator. Divorced. Education: Business and Marketing, Cuyahoga Community College, 1970s, 1990s; Toastmasters qualifications, CTM, ATM, Bronze, Silver and Gold, 1994-2000; Certified, Registered and Qualifies Health and Fitness Specialist, National Academy for Health and Fitness, 1997; Teachers Aide Certificate Diploma, 1998; American Red Cross, different subjects: Child abuse, Disaster, Church nurse; Many different workshops and adult education programmes. Appointments: Television Workshop Inc, voiceover, 1985; Professional Sales Training, Kirlins, 1993; Animal Disaster Team, 1995; Greater Cleveland Chapter of Sweet Adelines, 1996; Volunteer work, hospital, library, churches and others. Honours: Cleveland Advertising Club, Runner Up, 1986; Certificate of Thanks, Outstanding Volunteer Service, 1996; Nominated Olympic Games Torch Relay, 1996; Finalist, Manhattan Model Search, 1996; Table Topics Toastmaster, 1997. Membership: Toastmaster International. Address: 19603 Libby Rd, Cleveland, OH 44137, USA.

KRAJICEK Richard, b. 6 December 1972, Rotterdam, Netherlands. Tennis Player. m. Daphne Dekkers, 1999, 1 son, 1 daughter. Appointments: Started playing tennis, 3 years; Reached semi-finals, Australian Open, 1992; Wimbledon Men's Singles Champion, 1996; Won 20 titles to date Address: ATP Tour, 201 ATP Tour Boulevard, Ponte Vedra Beach, FL 32082, USA.

KRÁLÍK Jan, b. 21 March 1947, Lázně Toušeň, Czechoslovakia. Writer on Music. Education: Graduation in Mathematics, 1970, Philosophical Faculty, 1974, Doctorate in Mathematics, 1983, PhD, 1994, Charles University of Prague; Singing with J O Masák since 1970 and N Kejřová, 1972-83; Theory of Music, Institute of Theatre, Prague, 1977-79. Career: Studies on music and criticism, publishing, 1971-; Radio broadcaster, 1972-; Lecturer on music, 1973-. Recordings: Albums, 1978-; CD, 1989; TV, 1996; DVD, 2003. Publications: Beethoven, 1978; Verdi, 1981; Wagner, 1983; Dvořák, 1985; Smetana, 1990; Novotná, 1991; The Complete Destinn, 1994; Červená, 1999. Contributions to: Gramorevue; Hudební rozhledy; Harmonie; The Record Collector; Libretti for 4 children's operas composed by O Kvech. Honours: Preis der Deutschen Schallplatten-kritik, 1995. Memberships: Jeunesses Musicales, 1972, Czech President, 1993-95; Czech Chamber Music Society, 1989; Established Emmy Destinn Club in 1992. Address: Mlýnská 29, 250 89 Lázně Toušeň, Czech Republic.

KRALJ Božo, b. 7 May 1932, Maribor, Slovenia. Doctor; Professor of Gynecology. m. Majda, 1 son, 1 daughter. Education: Graduated, Medical Faculty Ljubljana, 1956; Masters Degree, 1974; Doctors Degree, 1974. Appointments: Professor, Gynecology and Obstetrics, School of Midwifery, 1962-84; Full Professor, Gynecology and Obstetrics, Medical Faculty, Ljubljana, 1989; Director, Department of Gynecology and Obstetrics, 1991-98; Dean, University College for Health Sciences, 1998-. Publications: Author of 2 chapters, book, Urogynecology and Urodynamic; More than 300 Bibliographics units, published in international journals and collections of scientific papers. Honours: Honorary document of town Ljubljana; Golden symbol of University of Ljubljana; Honorary recognition, Society of Gynecologists and Obstetrics, Jugoslavija and Makedonija; Honourable member, Italian Society for Obstetrics and Gynecology. Memberships: Member, 7 international journals; Vice-president, president, IUGA; Member of Executive Boards: EUGA,

EAGO, ESGO, European Academy of Science and Arts. Address: Samova 11 b, 1000 Ljubljana, Slovenija. E-mail: bozo.kralj@vsz.uni.lj.si

KRAMER Stephen Ernest, b. 12 September 1947, Hampton Court, England. Circuit Judge. m. Miriam Leopold, 1 son, 1 daughter. Education: BA, 1969, MA, 1987, Keble College, Oxford; Université de Nancy, France. Appointments: Called to the Bar (Gray's Inn), 1970; Assistant Recorder, 1987-91, Recorder of the Crown Court, 1991-; Standing Counsel (Crime) to HM Customs and Excise South Eastern Circuit, 1989-95; Member, Bar Council, 1993-95, Committee, South Eastern Circuit, 1997-2000; Chairman Liaison Committee, Bar Council/Institute of Barristers' Clerks, 1996-99; Committee Member, 1993-98, Acting Vice Chairman, 1998-99, Vice Chairman, 1999-2000, Chairman, 2000-2001, Criminal Bar Association; Queen's Counsel, 1995; Bencher Gray's Inn, 2001-; Head of Chambers, 2 Hare Court Temple, London, 1996-2003; Circuit Judge, 2003-.

KRARUP Bertel, b. 20 April 1947, Copenhagen, Denmark. Rector. m. Elisabeth Dahlerup, 2 sons, 2 daughters. Education: Studies in Music Theory and Music History, Copenhagen University; Diploma, 1973, Masters Degree in Music Pedagogy, 1975, Royal Danish Academy of Music. Appointments: Teacher in Music Theory, Copenhagen University, 1975-83; Teacher, 1974-, Assistant Professor, 1980-, Rector, 1989-, Carl Nielsen Academy of Music, Odense; Artistic Co-Leader of Contemporary Music Festival, Musikhøst, 1988-; President, Association of Baltic Academies of Music, 2000-. Publications: Numerous articles on contemporary music and 20th century composers in various professional music journals. Honours: The Funen Jazz Award, 1999; Knight's Cross of the Order of Dannebrog. Memberships: Member, Danish Council of Arts, 2003-. Address: Linde Alle 13, DK-5230 Odense M, Denmark. Website: www.dfm.dk

KRASILNIKOV Nikolay, b. 22 January 1927, Irkutsk, USSR. Communications Educator; Researcher. m. Olga Krasilnikova, 1 son. Education: Graduate, Leningrad Politechnical Institute, 1950; PhD, Leningrad Institute of Aviation Instrument Making, 1952; DSc, Academy of Communication, Leningrad, 1964; Diploma of Professor, 1965. Appointments: Engineer, Institute of Television, Leningrad, 1950-54; Assistant Professor, 1954-57, Head of Department of Transmitting and TV Devices, Leningrad Institute of Aviation Instrument Making, 1957-1994; Professor, State University of Aerospace Instrumentation, Saint Petersburg, 1994-. Publications: 181 including 5 monographs, 1961, 1976, 1986, 1999, 2001; Articles in professional journals. Honours: Medal for Leningrad Defence, 1944; Honoured Scientific and Technical Worker of Russia, 1992; Honoured Professor of State University of Aerospace Instrumentation, St Petersburg, 1997. Memberships: Fellow, Science and Technology Society of Radio Engineering, Electronics and Communications, 1951; New York Academy of Sciences, 1995. Address: State University of Aerospace Instrumentation, 67 Bolshaia Morskaia, 190000 Saint Petersburg, Russia.

KRAUSE Dorothy, b. 22 September 1940, Alabama, USA. Professor Emeritus; Artist; Digital Imaging. m. Richard Krause, 1 daughter. Education: BA, Montevallo University, 1957-60; MA, University of Alabama, 1961-62; DEd, Pennsylvania State University, 1965-68; Harvard University, 1980. Appointments: Associate Professor, Virginia Commonwealth University, 1969-74; Associate Professor, 1974-75, Dean, 1975-82, Vice President, 1982-85, Professor, 1985-2000, Massachusetts College of Art. Publications: Taking Technology to the heARTland; Digital Portfolio: Cube with a Pseudoview; Just Press Print. Commissions and Creative Works: Federal Reserve Bank of Boston; Artist In

Dictionary of International Biography

Residence, Kodak Center for Creative Imaging; Smithsonian American Art Museum; Work/Tank Think/Shop: Media for the New Millennium; Massachusetts College of Art; Littleton Studios; Herman Miller. Honours: 1st Annual Photo District News Digital Photography Award, 1995; SoHo Photo Gallery, 1996; Computerworld/Smithsonian Technology in the Arts Award, 1998; Kodak Innovators Award, 2000; Kodak Innovator Award, 2000; IDAA Award, 2003. Memberships: The Boston Printmakers; American Print Alliance, Photographic Resource Center; Women's Caucus for Art; College Art Association; American Computing Machinery Special Interest Group, Graphics. Address: 32 Nathaniel Way, PO Box 421, Marshfield Hills, MA 02051, USA.

KRAVCHENKO Peter, b. 21 June 1921, Kyiv, Ukraine. Designer of Special Effects. m. Valentyna Ponomarenko, 1 son, 1 daughter. Education: Diploma, Kyiv State Taras Shevchenko Art School; Diploma, Institute of Commercial Art, Australia; Diploma, School of Television Skill, Australia. Appointments: Visual Artist, Designer of Special Effects, Wardrobe Department, TV Studio, ABN 2, 20 years; Director, Board of Directors of Ukrainian Studies Foundation in Australia; Participated in art exhibitions in Australia and Ukraine. Publications: Many articles published as Approbated Correspondent, Ukrainian Weekly, The Free Thought; Book: Costumes of Ukraine, 1999. Honours: Honourable Diplomas from: President of Ukraine; Mayor of Kyrv, Ukraine; Council Ukrainian Organisation in Australia; International Charity Funds: Spiritual Legacy, Ukrainian Khata. Memberships: Honorary Member, National Society of Artists in Ukraine; International Charity Fund, Spiritual Heritage, Kyiv; Co-founder, Member and Secretary, Ukrainian Artists Society in Australia. Address: 57 Georges Avenue, Lidcombe, New South Wales, Australia 2141.

KREMER Erhard K, b. 19 January 1953, Löhnberg, Germany. Professor. Education: Diploma, Mathematics, University of Giessen, Germany, 1977; PhD, Mathematics, University of Hamburg, Germany, 1979; Habilitation, Mathematics, University of Hamburg, Germany, 1983. Appointments: Scientific Assistant, 1977-80, University Assistant, 1981-83, Professor of Applied Mathematical Statistics, 1983-, Mathematics Department, University of Hamburg, Germany; Mathematical Referent, Bavarian Re in Munich, Germany, 1980-81; President, Non-profit Association on Applied Mathematical Statistics and Risk Theory, Hamburg, 1986-98; Deputy Governor, American Biographical Institute Research Association, Raleigh, USA, 1996-; Consular Representative of the United Cultural Convention, 2001-. Publications: About 150 mathematical articles, notes, books and further. Honours: Man of the Year, ABI, 1995, 1996; Most Admired Man of the Year, ABI, 1995; Most Admired Man of the Decade, ABI, 1995; 20th Century Award for Achievement, IBC, 1995; Gold Record of Achievement, 1995; Who's Who of the Year, 1995; World Lifetime Achievement Award, 1996; Personality of Year, ABI, 1996; 2000 Millennium Medal of Honour, ABI, 1998; Platinum Record for Exceptional Performance, ABI, 1998; Outstanding Man of the 20th Century, ABI, 1999; Outstanding Man of the 21st Century, ABI, 2000; Presidential Seal of Honor, ABI, 2000; International Intellectual of the Year, IBC, 2001; World Citizen of the Year 2002, ABI, 2002; International Scientist of the Year, IBC, 2002; Lecturer, world-wide, including: Hamburg, 1981, Prague, 1982, Tel Aviv, 1986, Berlin, 1988, Rio de Janeiro, 1988, New York, 1989, Quebec, 1989, Cairo, 1991, Munich, 1992, Tokyo, 1994, Athens, 1996, Cairns, 1997; Peking, 1998; Washington, 2001; Listed in international biographical dictionaries. Memberships: International Actuarial Association; German Mathematicians Association; German Actuarial Association; German University Union; Order of International Ambassadors. Address: Max Tau Strasse 34, 22529 Hamburg, Germany.

KRENEK Mary, b. 8 December 1951, Wharton, Texas, USA. Researcher; Educator; Army Reserve Officer. Education: AA, Wharton County Junior College, 1972; BA, Texas A & I University, Corpus Christi, 1974; MA, St Mary's University, San Antonio, 1992; Czech Language Certificate, Charles University, Prague, Czech Republic, 1994. Appointments: Certificate, Secondary and Elementary Teacher, Texas; Polygraph Examiner, San Antonio, Texas 1979-81; Industry Contractor Market, Political and Social Research, San Antonio and Houston, 1982-; Substitute Teacher, Teacher, San Antonio School District, 1981-82, Houston School District, 1991-98, 2001-; Delegate, Texas Democrat Convention, 1971-72; 1st Lieutenant, US Army, 1975-78; Lieutenant Colonel, USAR, 1978-; Retired USAR, 2003; Associate, J C Penney Co Inc, 1994-2000; Instructor, Government, Wharton County Junior College, Wharton, Texas, 1997-2000. Memberships: National Association of Self-Employed; Reserve Officers Association, Secretary-Treasurer, Alamo Chapter, (Junior Vice-President Department Texas), St Mary's University Alumni Association; Alumni Association Presidential Classroom for Young Americans; Pi Sigma Alpha; Political Science Honor Society; American Legion; Czech Ex Students Association of Texas; Wharton County Historical Museum Association; Women in Military Service for America Memorial Foundation (Charter); Houston Czech Cultural Center; American Political Science Association; Point/ Counterpoint (Local Houston Chapter); Elected, Secretary of the Board of Directors, Egypt Plantation Museum. Address: Box 310, Egypt, TX 77436, USA.

KRICHMAR Sava I Krichmar, b. 11 December 1928, Odessa, Ukraine. Chemist. 1 daughter. Education: Physical Chemist, Dnepropetrovsk University, 1950; Doctor of Chemical Science, 1969; Professor, 1979. Appointments: Engineer, Nitrogenfertilizer works, Dneprodzerginsk, 1950; Manager, Laboratory, Institute of Nitrogen, 1959; Chief, Department of Chemistry, Industrial Institute, 1972; Professor, Main Scientist, Technical University, Kherson, 1994. Publications: More than 280 publications; Polarization Mechanism of the Smoothing by Electrochemical Burnishing of the Metals; Coulometric Detector for Gas Chromatography; Polarographic Analysis with Polymicroelectrode; Passage of Gas Convectional Barrier; Preparation of Calibrational Limiting Diluting of Gas Mixtures; Association within the Classical Theory of Fetus Formation of New Phase. Honours: Medal, Inventor of USSR; Medal, Veteran of Work; IBC Outstanding People of the 21st Century Medal; Soros Grant. Memberships: New York Academy of Sciences; American National Geographic Society. Address: Bereslavskoe Street 24, Technical University, Kherson 73008, Ukraine.

KRIKLER Dennis, b. 10 December 1928. Cardiologist. m. Education: MB, ChB, with honours, 1951, MD, 1973, University of Cape Town. Appointments: House Physician and House Surgeon, 1952, Medical Registrar, 1954-55, Senior Medical Registrar, 1957-58, Groote Schurr Hospital, Cape Town; Registrar and Tutor, University of Cape Town, 1953; Fellow in Medicine, Lahey Clinic, Boston, USA, 1956-57; Consultant Physician, Salisbury Area Hospital, Rhodesia, 1958-66; Clinical Assistant, Westminster Hospital, 1966-68; Clinical Tutor, North London Postgraduate Medical Centre, 1969-73; Consultant Physician, Prince of Wales's General Hospital and St Ann's General Hospital, London, 1967-73; Consultant Cardiologist, King Edward Memorial Hospital and Ealing Hospital, 1973-89; Consultant Cardiologist and Reader in Cardiovascular Diseases, Hammersmith Hospital and Royal Postgraduate Medical School, 1973-94. Publications: Numerous articles in professional medical journals. Honours include: Freeman of the City of London, 1990; Medal of Honour, European Society of Cardiology, 1990; Silver Medal, British Cardiac Society, 1992; Chevalier dans l'Ordre National de la

Legion d'Honneur, France, 1999. Memberships: Fellow, American College of Cardiology; Honorary Member, Societa' di cultura Medica Vercellese; Honorary Member, Societa di Medical de Levante, Valencia; Committee Member, British Cardiac Society; Ex-Officio Councillor; Corresponding Member, Societe Francaise de Cardiologie; Honorary Fellow, Council on Clinical Cardiology; Fellow, American Heart Association. Address: 55 Wimpole Street, London W1G 8YL, England.

KRIM Fateh, b. 22 October 1954, Setif, Algeria. Professor. m. Saifi Salima. 1 son, 1 daughter. Master of Electrical Engineering, 1978; Engineer, Ecole Centrale, Lyon, France, 1979; PhD, Electrical Engineering, University of Grenoble, France, 1983. Appointments: Chairman, Laboratory of Industrial Control, Vice-President of University, Head of Department, University of Setif; Head of Design Department, CIT Alcatel, Paris, France. Publications: 80 papers in journals and international conferences. Honours: IEEE Senior Member; Commemorative Medal of Honor, 2000, American Order of Excellence, 2000, ABI World Laureate Plaque, 2001, American Biographical Institute. Memberships: IEEE; Academy of Sciences of New York. Address: University of Setif, Department of Electronics, 19000 Setif, Algeria. E-mail: krim_f@ieee.org Website: www.chez.com/krim

KRISHNAIAH CHETTY Oleti V, b. 7 August 1944, Madanapalle, India. Professor. m. Manjulavani Oleti, 1 son, 1 daughter. Education: Bachelor of Engineering (Mech), 1966; Master of Technology (Production Science and Technology), 1971; PhD, 1980. Appointments: Lecturer, 1974-82, Assistant Professor, 1982-91, Professor, 1991-, Manufacturing Engineering Section, Department of Mechanical Engineering, Indian Institute of Technology, Madras, Chennai, India; Professor of Production Engineering and Management, The University of the West Indies, Trinidad, West Indies, 1994-96. Publications: 141 technical papers. Honours: 8 Technical Paper Awards. Memberships: Society of Manufacturing Engineers, USA; Water Jet Technology Association, USA; Fellow, Institution of Engineers, India. Address: Manufacturing Engineering Section, Department of Mechanical Engineering, Indian Institute of Technology, Madras, Chennai, 600 036 India. E-mail: ovk@iitm.ac.in

KRISHNAKUMAR Jayalakshmi, b. 20 April 1958, Delhi, India. University Professor. m. Velamur Krishnakumar, 1 son, 1 daughter. Education: BA, Economics, 1979; MA, Econometrics, 1981; PhD, Econometrics and Statistics, 1987. Appointments: Currently: Professor of Econometrics, University of Geneva, Switzerland; Invited Professor, University of Neuchâtel, Switzerland; Project Head for research projects funded by Swiss National Science Foundation. Publications: Articles in leading international journals including: Econometric Theory; Journal of Econometrics; Empirical Economics; Author of book; Contributor to books; Editor of book; Participant and speaker and session-chairperson in many international conferences. Memberships: Econometric Society; Swiss Statistical Association; Scientific Committee of Geneva Foundation; Vedantic Centre; Interreligious Platform of Geneva. Address: Department of Econometrics, University of Geneva, 40, Bd du Pont d'Arve, CH-1211 Geneva 4, Switzerland. E-mail: jaya.krishnakumar@metri.unige.ch

KRISTENSSON-HALLSTROM Inger, b. 17 November 1955, Hasselholm, Sweden. Associated Professor. m. Per Hallstrom, 2 sons, 1 daughter. Education: RN, 1977; Paediatric Nurse, 1984; PhD, 1998; Associate Professor, 2002. Appointments: Senior Lecturer, 1999-2002, Associated Professor, 2002-, Department of Nursing, The Vandal Institute Medical Faculty, Lund University, Sweden. Publications: Articles in professional medical journals. Honours: Quality Award, University Hospital, Lund, 1996.

Memberships: EANS; European Association of Nursing Science. Address: Department of Nursing, Lund University, Baravagen 3 Skane, Lund 221 00, Sweden. E-mail: inger.hallstrom@omv.lu.se

KRISTIN Anton, b. 2 August 1956, Bratislava, Slovakia. Zoologist; Animal Ecologist. 1 son, 1 daughter. Education: Rerum Naturaliae Doctor, 1980; PhD, 1985; Senior Scientist Degree, 1992. Appointments: Department of Ecology and Zoology, Comenius University, 1980-82; Institute of Agrochemical Technology, 1982-85; Institute of Forest Ecology of the Slovak Academy of Sciences, 1985-. Publications: 219 scientific articles, -2003. Honour: Professor Ferianc Medal for Ornithology. Membership: European Ornithologists Union Committee. Address: Zvolen, Kremnicka 13, SK – 960 06, Slovakia.

KROEGER Knut, b. 16 March 1962, Krefeld, Germany. Physician. m. Ute, 3 sons, 1 daughter. Education: Diploma of Medicine, 1989; Thesis, 1990; Diploma of Health Economy, 2000; University Lecturing Qualification, 2003. Appointment: Vice-Director, Department of Angiology, University of Essen, Germany, 1996-. Publications: Contributor of articles to professional journals. Memberships: German Society of Cardiology; German Society of Angiology; American Society of Angiology; International Union of Angiology; American College of Angiology. Address: Department of Angiology, University of Essen, Hufelandstrasse 55, 45122 Essen, Germany.

KRONDAHL Hans, Professor Emeritus; Fibre Artist; Fabric Designer. Education: Graduate, University College of Arts Crafts and Design, Stockholm, Sweden; Further studies in Europe and the Far East. Appointments: Teacher, Fibre Art and Textile Design in art schools, 1960-; Working in own studio for Tapestry Weaving and Fabric Design, 1963-; Senior Lecturer, Head of Textile Department, University College of Arts Crafts and Design, Stockholm, Sweden, 1977-78; Head of Textile Design Department, National College of Art and Design, Oslo, Norway, 1978-79; Head of Textile Design Department, HDK College, 1981-88, Professor of Textile Art, 1988-94 Gothenburg University, Sweden, 1981-88; Worked as UNIDO Expert in Textile Design, Indonesia, 1979-80; Exhibits in Sweden and abroad most recently works included in "Katja of Sweden", Kulturen Museum, Lund, 2002-2003; Permanent representation in museum collections in Europe and USA; Tapestries, front curtains, rugs, carpets, ecclesiastical textiles and vestments commissioned for the public environment. Publications: Works included in: The Lunning Prize Exhibition Catalogue, 1986; Svenska Textilier 1890-1990, by Jan Brunius, etc, 1994 ; Contemporary Textile Art by Charles S Talley, 1982; Fiberarts Magazine, 1996. Address: Smedjegatan 8, S 21421 Malmö, Sweden.

KRONE Cheryl Anne, b. 25 May 1948, Renton, Washington, USA. Research Scientist; Consultant. Education: BA, 1978, MS, 1981, PhD, 1984, University of Washington, Seattle, Washington, USA. Appointments: Visiting Scientist, University of Hawaii, Honolulu, Hawaii, 1983; Lecturer, University of Washington, 1983-84; Research Chemist, National Oceanic and Atmospheric Administration, Seattle, Washington, USA, 1984-98; Consultant, CK Consulting Services, Renton, Washington, USA, 1998-; Deputy Director and Senior Research Scientist, Applied Research Institute, Palmerston North, New Zealand, 1998-. Publications: Book chapters in: CRC Carcinogens and Mutagens in the Environment, 1982; American Chemical Society, Xenobiotics in Feeds and Foods, 1983; 40 peer-reviewed articles in medical and nutrition journals. Honour: Phi Beta Kappa, elected 1978. Memberships: American Chemical Society; Institute of Food Technologists; Sigma Xi; New Zealand Association of Scientists. Address: PO Box 1969, Palmerston North, New Zealand. E-mail: cakrone@ u. washington.edu.

Dictionary of International Biography

KROPACHEV Nikolay, b. 8 February 1959, Leningrad, Russia. Lawyer; Judge. m. Natalia Alexandrovna Sidorova, 1 son. Education: Graduate, Law Faculty, 1981, PhD Student, 1981-84, PhD (Candidate of Law), Law Faculty, 1985, Doctor of Law Degree, 2000, St Petersburg State University. Appointments: Assistant (Junior) Lecturer, 1985-92, Senior Lecturer, 1992-, Dean of the Special Law Faculty, 1992-98, Dean of the Law Faculty, 1998- St Petersburg State University; Chairman, St Petersburg Charter Court, 2000-. Publications: Mechanism of Criminal Law Regulation, 1989; Penal Law (textbook), 1989; Criminology (textbook), 1992, 2005; Criminal Law on a Contemporary Stage, 1992; Russian Criminal Legislation (complete analysis), 1996; Criminal Law Legislation. Mechanism and System, 1999. Honours: F Koni Medal, Ministry of Justice, 1999; Russian President's Prize, 2002; Order of Honour, 2004. Memberships: Vice-President, Interregional Association of Law Schools, 1996; President, St Petersburg and Lenningrad Region Association of Lawyers. Address: Faculty of Law, St Petersburg State University, 22 aya liniya 7, R-199026 VO St Petersburg, Russia. E-mail: office@jurtak.spb.ru

KROYER Gerhard Th., b. 20 August 1951, Vienna, Austria. University Professor. 1 daughter. Education: Diploma Engineer, Technical Chemistry, 1976, Doctor, Technical Sciences, 1979, University of Technology, Vienna. Appointments: University Assistant, 1980-88, Associate Professor, 1988-97, Institute of Food Chemistry and Technology, Professor, 1997-, Institute of Chemical Engineering, University of Technology, Vienna; University Lecturer, Institute of Nutritional Sciences, University of Vienna, 1991-; Scientific Consultant, Food Industry Companies, 1988-. Publications: Co-author, 3 scientific books; More than 100 publications in scientific journals; Numerous presentations at international congresses, meetings and symposia in the field of food chemistry, food technology, functional food, food supplements, food additives, food contaminants, nutrition, food and environment, nutrient bio-availability and cosmetics. Honours: Several stipendia and awards from scientific and commercial organisations. Memberships: Austrian Nutrition Society, 1990; Austrian Society of Chemists, 1990; New York Academy of Science, 1997; Institute of Food Technology, 1994; Founder Diplomatic Councellor, London Diplomatic Academy, 2000; International Diplomatic Academy, 2003; American Biographical Institute, 2003. Address: Franz Lisztstrasse 28, A-7092 Winden, Austria. E-mail: gkroyer@mail.zserv.tuwien.ac.at

KRUG Arno, b. 16 February 1935, Schneidemuhl, Germany. Surgeon. m. Christine, 3 sons, 1 daughter. Education: MD, Berlin-Marburg, 1959; PhD, Surgery, 1972, Professor, 1978, Kiel. Appointments: Chief Surgeon, City Hospital, Hof/Saale, Germany, 1978-98; Retired, 1998-. Publications: Blood supply of the myocardium after temporary coronary occlusion; Alteration in myocardial hydrogen concentration: a sign of irreversible cell damage; The extent of ischemic damage in the myocardium of the cat after permanent and temporary coronary occlusion. Memberships: German Society of Surgery. Address: Theodor-Fontane-Str 20, D-95032 Hof/Saale, Germany. E-mail: arnokrug@yahoo.de

KRUG Edward Charles, b. 24 August 1947, New Brunswick, New Jersey, USA. Biogeochemist. m. Nancy Wegner. Education: BSc, Environmental Science, 1975, MSc, Soil Chemistry, 1978, PhD, Soil Science, 1981, Rutgers University. Appointments: Assistant Soil Scientist, Connecticut Agricultural Experiment Station, Connecticut, 1981-85; Associate Professional Scientist, Illinois State Water Survey, 1985-90; Independent Consultant, Minnesota, 1991-2000; Biogeochemist, Office of the Chief, Illinois State Water Survey, 2000-. Publications: Numerous articles in professional journals; 10 book chapters. Honours: Frank G Helyar

Award, Rutgers University, 1973; Excellence in Review Award, Journal of Environmental Quality, 1991; Listed in several biographical publications. Memberships: American Geophysical Union; Soil Science Society of America; International Society of Soil Science; Certified Professional Soil Scientist; American Society of Agronomy. Address: Illinois State Water Survey, 2204 Griffith Dr, Champaign, IL 61820, USA. E-mail: ekrug@uiuc.edu

KRUGER Richard Alan, b. 8 July 1942, Bloemfontein, South Africa. Scientist. m. Yvonne Athalie Kruger, 2 daughters. Education: BSc, 1966; MSc, 1973; DSc, 1976. Appointments: Senior Chemist, South African Railways and Harbours, 1971-76; Chief Senior Research Scientist, National Physical Research Laboratory, CSIR, 1976-80; Manager, Coal Ash Programme, Foundation for Research Development, 1980-88; Manager, New Business Development, Ash Resources, 1988-; Technical Director, Sphere-Fill, 1997-. Publications: Over 60 articles in various international journals. Honours: Alexander Von Humboldt Research Fellow; Commonwealth of Kentucky, Honorable Colonel; United Nations Consultant. Memberships: Pr Sci Nat, honorary member; South African Ceramic Society; American Coal Ash Association; World Wide Coal Ash Council. Address: PO Box 75826, Lynnwood Ridge, Pretoria 0040, South Africa. E-mail: richonne@mweb.co.za

KRUMMACHER Christoph, b. 27 May 1949, Berlin, Germany. Professor. m. Elisabeth Ebersbach, 3 sons. Education: Church Music Diplomas, Master, Dresden, 1969, Leipzig, 1975; Dr theol, Rostock, 1991. Appointments: Cathedral Organist, Brandenburg, 1975-80; University Organist and Docent, University of Rostock, 1980-92; Professor, 1992, Rector, 1997-, University of Music and Theatre, Leipzig; International career as an organist. Publications: Many articles on organ playing and church music; Organ CDs. Honours: Kulturpreis Hausenstadt, Rostock, 1991. Memberships: Saxon Academy of Sciences; Executive Committee, German Church Music Conference; Executive Committee, Silbermann-Society. Address: University of Music and Theatre, Grassistr 8, D-04107 Leipzig, Germany.

KRUSE Penny Thompson, b. 7 June 1963, USA. College Professor; Musician. m. Steven Kruse. Education: Bachelor of Music with distinction, Violin, Northwestern University School of Music, 1985; Master of Music in Violin, Yale University School of Music, 1987; Doctor of Musical Arts in Violin, University of Missouri-Kansas City, 1999. Appointments: Escher Sting Quartet Residency, Gladstone Academy for Visual and Performing Arts Elementary Magnet School, 1989-91; Escher String Quartet Residency, Music at Penn's Woods, Pennsylvania State University, 1989-91; Chamber Music Coach, Theory Teacher, Master Class Teacher, Eastern Music Festival, Greensboro, North Carolina, 1993-; Assistant Professor of Violin, Head of String Area, William Jewell College, Liberty, Missouri, 1992-2000; Assistant Professor of Violin, 2000- Assistant Dean for Graduate Studies, 2001-2003, College of Musical Arts, Bowling Green State University, Bowling Green, Ohio; Over 50 solo and duo concert appearances in America, and abroad; Member, Kruse Duo, Violin-Viola Duo, 1990-; Founding Member, Kansas City Chamber Soloists, 1989-91; Member William Jewell Trio, 1992-2000. Publications: Articles in professional journals: Finding harmony between East and West, 2003; Remembering Joseph and Lillian Fuchs, 2003. Honours: Numerous honours include most recently: professor of the year, 2001; Invited Performer, College Music Society, Toronto, Canada, 2000; Selected Presenter, College Music Society, Kansas City Missouri, 2002; Selected performer, International Viola Congress, Kronberg, Germany, 2003. Memberships: American String Teachers Association with National School Orchestra Association; College Music Society; Music Educators National Conference;

Dictionary of International Biography

Music teachers National Association; Pi Kappa Lambda; Sigma Alpha Iota. Address: College of Musical Arts, Bowling Green State University, Bowling Green, OH 43403, USA.

KRUSOS Denis Angelo, b. 27 October 1927, New York, USA. Communications Company Executive. m. Catherine Bezas, 1 son, 1 daughter. Education: BS, City College of New York, 1949; MS, Newark College of Engineering, 1951; JD, St John's University, 1968. Appointments include: US Army, 1946-47; Development Engineer, Missile Division, Republic Aviation and Fairchild Engineering Corporation, 1952-56; Senior Engineer, Arma Division, American Bosch Arma Corporation, 1956-60; Founder Director, Automational Labs, Inc, Mineola, NY, 1955-56; Founder, Chairman of the Board, Director, Integrated Electronic Corporation, Huntingdon Station, NY, 1966-83; Chairman of the Board, Color Q Inc, Dayton, Ohio, 1969-92; Founder, President, Director, Panafax Corporation, Woodbury, NY, 1977-82; Founder, Chairman of the Board, Director, Visual Sciences, Inc, 1969-83; Founder, Chairman of the Board, Chief Executive Officer, Director, CopyTele, Inc, Melville, NY, 1982-. Memberships: Senior Member IEEE; Member, New York Bar Association; American Bar Association and Suffolk Bar Association. Address: CopyTele, Inc, 900 Walt Whitman Road, Melville, NY 11747-2293, USA.

KRYSTAL ALLEN Kathleen Joan, b. 12 March 1952, Lackwanna, New York. Artist; Picture Framer. Divorced, 1 son, 1 daughter. Education: Buffalo State University, Buffalo, NY, 1972; College of Marin, Kentford, CA, 2001-03. Career: Exhibiting Artist, 1980-2003; Vice President, Board of Directors, Stinson Beach Montessori School, 1983-84; Vice President, Board of Directors, 1986-90, President, Board of Directors, 1990, Stinson Beach Community Center, Stinson Beach, California; Realtor, Oceanic Reality, Stinson Beach, California, 19991-95; Picture Framer, 1996-2000; Designer, Picture Framer, The Painters Place, Larkspur, California, 2000-03. Publications: Works appear on the internet. Honours: Best in Class, Watermedia, Marin Co Fair, San Rafael, California, 1996; Best Fair Theme, Marin Co Fair, San Rafael, California, 2003. Memberships: Marin Arts Council; Bolinas Museum; Point Reyes Open Studios; Marin Watercolor Society; Coastal Marin Artists. Address: PO Box 184, Inverness, CA 94937-0184, USA. E-mail: krystal@krystalallen.com

KSICOVA Danuse, b. 26 April 1932, Brno, Czechoslovakia. Professor, Slavonic Literature. m. Evzen Petrov, deceased, 1 daughter. Education: Faculty of Arts, Russian and Czech Philology, 1951-56, PhD, 1969, CSc, 1970, DSc, 1991, Professor, 1995, Brno University. Appointments: Lecturer, 1956, Senior Lecturer, 1961, Associated Professor, 1990, Professor, 1995, Masaryk University in Brno, Czech Republic, Faculty of Arts, the Institute of Slavonic Studies. Publications: Author, 6 books include: The Romantic and Neoromantic Long Poems, 1983; (in Russian) Russian Poetry at the Turn of the Century, 1990; Art Nouveau - Word and Image, 1998; K D Balmont, The Soul of the Czech Lands, 2001; Co-author, 4 books including: East Slavonic-Czech Literary Relationships until the Foundation of Czechoslovakia, 1997; Editor, Anthology of Lermontov's Poetry, 1976, Litteraria Humanitas, I, II, IV, VI, XII, 1991-98, 2003; The Drama of the Russian Symbolism 1.(K D Balmont, V Y Bryosov), 1, 2001, 2. (D S Merezhkovsky), 2003; Dictionary of Russian, Ukrainian and Belorussian Writers, 2001; Symbolism on the MCHAT Scene, K S Stanislavsky's Conception of Direction, 2003; Over 220 studies, 180 articles, reviews and transmissions, translations of 25 TV, theatre plays, essays and Russian poetry. Honours: Silver Plaque of Brno University, 1982; Memorial Plaque of Brno Skauting, 1990. Address: 616 00 Brno-16, E Machové 37, Czech Republic.

KUAN Tung-kuei, b. 5 March 1931, Yutu, Jiang-hsi, China. Historian. m. Pao-chen Wang, 1 son, 4 daughters. Education: BA, Department of History, National Taiwan University, 1956; Visiting Scholar, Harvard University, USA, 1965-67. Appointments: Assistant, 1956-60, Assistant Research Fellow, 1960-67, Associate Research Fellow, 1967-73, Research Fellow, 1973-98, Head, Anthropology Section, 1974-95, Institute Director, 1989-95, Retired 1998; Part-time Research Fellow, 1998- Institute of History and Philology, Academia Sinica; Programme Officer, National Science Council, 1973-77; Professor: Tung-hai University, 1976-85, National Taiwan Normal University, 1977-2003, National Taiwan University, 1987-94. Publications: Monograph, Marriage and Mortuary Customs of the Magpie MIAO Data and MIAO Texts (co-author Professor Ruey Yih-fu), 1962; More than 50 articles on Chinese minorities and the ancient history of China. Honours: Annual Award, National Science Council, 1960-65, 1967-95. Memberships: Historians Association; Ethnogists Association. Address: The Institute of History and Philology, Academia Sinica, 130 Academia Sinica Road, #2, 11529 Taipei, Taiwan.

KUBICA Benedyct Piotr, b. 19 October 1958, Katowice, Poland. Signalling Engineer. m. Anna Kryj, 2 daughters. Education: MSc, Engineering, Silesian Technical University, Gliwice, Poland, 1982. Appointments: Maintenance Polish Railway, signalling and telecommunications, Tarnowskie Gory, Poland, 1982-84; Design Engineer, Railway Design Office, Katowice, Poland, 1984-91; Technical Fellowship for Signalling Engineers, Coras Iompair Eireann, Irish Rail, Dublin, 1991-92; Software Engineer, Westinghouse Rail Systems, Chippenham, England, 1992-. Publications: Automatyka Kolejowa Magazine. Honours: Best Computer Program Award, Transport Engineers Association, Computer Club, 1989. Memberships: IEEE; Association for Computing Machinery (ACM); New York Academy of Sciences. Address: Westinghouse Rail Systems, Mainline Systems, PO Box 79, Pew Hill, Chippenham, Wiltshire, SN95 1JD, England. E-mail: b.kubica@computer.org

KUBIK Gerhard, b. 10 December 1934, Vienna. Cultural Anthropologist; Ethnomusicologist; Psychoanalyst. m. Lidiya Malamusi. Education: PhD, University Vienna, 1971; Habilitation with the work Theory of African Music, 1980. Appointments: Field work since 1959 in 16 countries of sub-Saharan Africa, since 1974 also in Venezuela and Brazil, leading to the world's most comprehensive collection of documented recordings of African music and oral literature; Present status, University Professor. Publications: 260 works, including several books. Honours: Twice a recipient of a Körner Foundation Prize in Vienna; Life affiliation to the Centre for Social Research, University of Malawi; Elected to Honorary Fellowship of the Royal Anthropological Institute of Great Britain and Ireland, London, 1995. Memberships: Sigmund Freud Museum, Vienna; Centre for Black Music Research, Chicago; Royal Anthropological Institute of Great Britain and Ireland, London; Oral Literature Research Programme, Blantyre, Malawi. Address: Burghardtgasse 6/9, A 1200 Vienna, Austria.

KUBILIUS Jonas, b. 27 July 1921, District Jurbarkas, Lithuania. Mathematician. m. Valerija Pilypaité, 1 son, 1 daughter. Education: Diploma with Honours, Vilnius University, 1945; Candidate of Science, Leningrad University, 1951; DSc, Steklov Institute, Moscow, 1957. Appointments: Laboratory Assistant, Assistant Professor, 1945-48, Associate Professor, Professor, 1951-, Rector, 1958-92, Vilnius University; Member, Praesidium, Academy of Sciences of Lithuania, 1962-92; People's Deputy of USSR, 1989-91; Member of Parliament of Lithuania, 1992-96. Publications: Probability methods in the Number Theory (7 editions), 1959; Real Analysis, 1970; Probability and Statistics (2 editions), 1980; Limit

Theorems, 1988; Book of Essays, 1996; Antanas Baranauskas and Mathematics, 2001; Several hundred papers. Honours: State Prize in Sciences, 1958, 1980; Dr hc, Greifswald, Prague, Latvian, Salzburg universities, several orders. Memberships: Founder and President, Lithuanian Mathematical Society, 1962-; President, Lithuanian-USA Association, 1991-. Address: Faculty of Mathematics and Informatics, Vilnius University, Naugarduko 24, Vilnius LT-2006, Lithuania.

KUBOTA Hiroshi, b. 9 November 1961, Yamanashi, Japan. Cardiovascular Surgeon. m. Yumiko Iwaki, 1 son. Education: MD, Tsukuba University, Ibaraki, 1986; Diplomate, 1995, 1995; Certified Specialist of Surgery, 1990; Specialist of Cardiac Surgery, 1994. Appointments: Intern, Tokyo University, 1986-87; Resident, Tokyo Metropolitan Police Hospital, 1987-90, Tokyo University, 1990-94; Instructor, Tokyo University, 1994-97; Special Intern, Clermont-Ferrand University, France, 1996-98; Instructor, 1998-2001, Assistant Professor, 2001-2003, Tokyo University; Assistant Professor, 2002-2003, Associate Professor, 2003, Kyorin University. Publications: Articles in medical journals as author: Successful management of massive pulmonary tumour embolism from renal cell carcinoma, 1996; Mid-term results of rotation-advancement flap method for correction of partial anomalous pulmonary veneous drainage into the superior vena cava, 1996; Successful treatment of Tetralogy of Fallot with pulmonary atresia using a pulmonary homograft, 1997; Surgical correction of the hypoplastic aortic arch by the subclavian free flap method in the neonate, 1998. Honours: Grant-in-aid for Scientific Research, Japanese Ministry of Education, 1999, 2000, 2001-, granted for arrhythmia treatment, Japanese Heart Foundation; Pfizer, 2000. Memberships: Asian Society for Cardiovascular Surgery; Japan Surgical Society; Japanese Association for Thoracic Surgery; Japanese Circulation Society; Japanese College of Cardiology. Address: Department of Cardiovascular Surgery, University of Kyorin, 6-20-2 Shinkawa, Mitaka, Tokyo 181-8611, Japan. E-mail: kub@kyorin-u.ac.jp

KUBOTA Kiyoshi, b. 1 December 1952, Tokyo, Japan. Physician. m. Noriko Yamada, 26 July 1991, 1 daughter. Education: BMed, Hokkaido University, Sapporo, Japan, 1978. Appointments: Residency, Hokkaido University Hospital, 1978-83; Research Fellow, Division of Clinical Pharmacology, National Medical Centre, 1983-89; Research Fellow, University of California, San Francisco, 1989-91; Honorary Research Fellow, Drug Safety Research Unit, UK, 1991-96; Associate Professor, Department of Pharmacoepidemiology, Faculty of Medicine, University of Tokyo, 1996-. Publications: Science papers in: British Journal of Clinical Pharmacy, 1986, 1991, 1994; Journal of Pharmaceutical Sciences, 1990-95; European Journal of Clinical Pharmacology, 1991-96, 2001; Pharmacoepidemiology and Drug Safety, 1993, 1994, 2001, 2002. Membership: International Society for Pharmacoepidemiology, USA, 1995-. Address: Department of Pharmacoepidemiology, Faculty of Medicine, University of Tokyo, 7-3-1 Hongo, Bunkyo-ku, Tokyo 113-8655, Japan.

KUCHITSU Kozo, b. 7 September 1927, Tokyo, Japan. Chemistry Professor. m. Sachiko Yamamoto, 2 sons, 1 daughter. Education: BSc, Chemistry, 1951, DSc, Science, 1958, The University of Tokyo, Tokyo, Japan. Appointments: Assistant, 1956-61, Lecturer, 1961-62, Associate Professor, 1962-69, Professor, 1969-88, Department of Chemistry, Dean, Faculty of Science, Professor Emeritus, 1988-, The University of Tokyo; Professor, 1988-93, Professor Emeritus, 1993-, Nagoya University of Technology; Professor, Josei University, 1993-2003. Publications: Books: Quantities, Units and Symbols in Physical Chemistry (co-author), 1988, 1993; Landolt Börnstein, Structure Data of Free Polyatomic Molecules II/25, A-D (editor and author), 1998-2003.

Honours: The Chemical Society of Japan Award, 1982; Medal with Purple Ribbon, Japanese Government, 1992; The Order of the Sacred Treasure, The Gold and Silver Star, The Japanese Government, 1999. Memberships: Honorary Member, Chemical Society of Japan, Crystallographic Society of Japan; Life Member, Physical Society of Japan; IUPAC Fellow. Address: 4-34-10-401 Hakusan, Bunkyo-ku, Tokyo 112-0001, Japan. E-mail: kuchitsu@cc.tuat.ac.jp

KUCZMARSKI Susan Smith, b. 24 April 1951, Portland, Oregon, USA. Consultant; Author. m. Thomas Dale Kuczmarski, 3 sons. Education: BA, Colorado College, 1969-73; MIA, School of International Affairs of Columbia University, 1973-75; MEd, 1979, EdD, 1979, Teachers College, Columbia University. Appointments: Research Intern, United Nations Institute for Training and Research (UNITAR); Research Intern for Academy for Educational Development; Associate Editor, Journal of International Affairs; Instructor at: National Louis University, Northwestern University, Concordia University, Dominican University, Colorado College, University of Illinois at Chicago, Columbia University; Education Director, Constitutional Rights Foundation; Ex Vice President, Kuczmarski and Associates. Publications: Co-author: Values-Based Leadership: Rebuilding Employee Commitment, Performance and Productivity, 1995; The Family Bond: Inspiring Tips for Creating and Closer Family, 2000; The Secret Flight of the Teenager: A Parent's Guide to Stepping Back and Letting Go, 2002. Honours: International Fellows Program, Columbia University; Fellow, School of International Affairs, Columbia University. Memberships: Committee on Foreign Affairs, Chicago; Trustee, Edward Lowe Foundation, 1986-98; Trustee, Chicago City Day School, 1996-; Trustee, Naked Eye Theatre, 2003-. Address: Kuczmarski and Associates, 1165 N Clark St, Suite #700, Chicago, IL 60610, USA.

KUDRYAVTSEV Victor Alexandrovich, b. 9 May 1961, Yerevan, Armenia. IT Company Executive. m. Ekaterina Kudryavtseva Potapova, 2 sons, 2 daughters. Education: Degree, Mechanical Engineering, Moscow Bauman Higher Technical School, 1986. Appointments: Organiser and Executive, Impulse Youth Association, computers, software and hardware packages, 1987; Co-Founder, IVK Cooperative, 1988; Co-Founder, Chairman of the Board, Inforum Science and Production Cooperative, 1988; Co-Founder, Chairman of the Board, Inforum Ltd, 1989-91; Co-Founder, Inforum MB Co (renamed Inforum Cacao Ltd, 1994), 1991-94; Co-Chairman of the Board of Directors, Inforum Group, Chairman of the Board of Directors, ZAO Inforum Prom, 1994-. Address: Kostomarovsky per 3, 107120 Moscow, Russia. E-mail: victor@vk-firm.ru

KUHN Alfred Karl, b. 19 January 1933, Basel, Switzerland. Chemical Engineer. m. Elizabeth A Bierwert, 1 son. Education: Diploma, (MS), 1956. Appointments: Research and Development Engineer, Brown Boveri, 1957-62; Lummus Process Engineer, 1975; ANG Process Engineer, Manager, Director, 1975-84; Process Development Manager, ANG and DGC, 1985-97; Retired, 1997; Part-time Consultant, 1998-. Honours: Distinguished Service Award, 1996. Membership: GEP. Address: 7425 South Houstoun Waring Circle, Littleton, CO 80120, USA.

KUHRT Gordon Wilfred, b. 15 February 1941, Madras, South India. Clergyman. m. Olive, 3 sons. Education: BD, Honours, London University, 1960-63; Oakhill Theological College, 1965-67; Doctor in Professional Studies, Middlesex University, 2001. Appointments: Religious Education Teacher, 1963-65; Curate, St Illogan, Truro, England, 1967-70; Curate, Holy Trinity, Wallington, England, 1970-73; Vicar of Shenstone, Lichfield, England, 1973-79; Vicar of Emmanuel, South Croydon, England, 1979-89; Rural

Dean, Croydon Central, 1981-86; Honorary Canon of Southwark Cathedral, 1987-89; Archdeacon of Lewisham, 1989-96; Chief Secretary of the Advisory Board for Ministry, 1996-98; Director of Ministry, Ministry Division, Archbishop's Council, 1999-. Publications: Handbook for Council and Committee Members, 1985; Believing in Baptism, 1987; Doctrine Matters (editor), 1993; To Proclaim Afresh (editor), 1995; Issues in Theological Education and Training, 1998; Clergy Security, 1999; An Introduction to Christian Ministry, 2000; Ministry Issues for the Church of England – Mapping the Trends, 2001. Membership: Fellow of the College of Preachers. Address: Ministry Division, Archbishops' Council, Church House, Great Smith Street, London SW1P 3NZ, England. E-mail: gordon.kuhrt@mindiv.c-of-e.org.uk

KUKLA Lubomir, b. 21 August 1955, Brno, Czech Republic. Paediatrician. Divorced. 1 daughter. Education: MD, 1980; Degree in Paediatrics, 1985; PhD, Paediatrics, 1987; MPH cum laude, 1996. Appointments: Research Worker, Paediatrics, 1980; Research Worker, Social Paediatrician, 1987; Head, Department of Preventive and Social Paediatrics, Research Institute Child Health, Director National Centre for project: European Longitudinal Study Pregnancy and Childhood, Temporary Adviser WHO for Czech Republic, ELSPAC, 1989; International Co-ordinator, Executive Committee of ELSPAC, 1997-. Publications: Head Author, book in English, book in Czech; 2 book chapters in English, several in Czech; Over 40 journal publications; Over 80 Lectures in international congresses and conferences; Over 20 posters. Honours: FIBA, 1999; 3 Key Awards, ABI. Memberships: ESSOP; European Science Foundation; ISPCAN; Secretary General, Czech Society for Social Paediatrics, Czech Medical Association J E Purkyne; Czech Paediatric Society of Czech Medical Association J E Purkyne; Science Council of Ministry of Health of Czech Republic; Scientific Commission for Paediatrics and Genetics of International Grant Agency of Ministry of Health of Czech Republic; Executive Board; Editorial Board, Journal of Czech Physicians; Member Research Board of Advisors, ABI; Active member, New York Academy of Sciences, 2002-; Distinguished Professor, BWW Society, 2003-. Address: Masaryk University, Medical Faculty, Department of Preventive and Social Paediatrics, Bieblova 16, 613 00 Brno, Czech Republic.

KULENOVIC Indira, b. 7 April 1957, Sarajevo, Bosnia and Herzegovina. Physician; Specialist in Internal Medicine; Endocrinologist. Education: MD, Medical Faculty, University of Sarajevo, 1982; Postgraduate Study, Basics of Medical Investigation, University of Sarajevo, 1982-84; Residency, Internal Medicine, Department of Endocrinology, Diabetes and Metabolic Disorders, University Medical Centre, Sarajevo, 1984-88; Advanced Course in Endocrinology, London, UK, 1987; Postgraduate Study in Endocrinology, Medical Faculty, University of Zagreb, Croatia, 1989-90; Master of Science, 1995; PhD, 2001. Appointments: Department of Internal Medicine, Section of Endocrinology, Diabetes and Metabolic Disorders, Clinical Centre, University of Sarajevo, 1982-2002; Local Supervisor, WHO nutritional surveys carried out in Sarajevo, 1994-95; Part-time Project Co-ordinator for Elderly and Hospital Twinning Project, WHO Regional Office for Bosnia and Herzegovina, Sarajevo Field Office, 1996-97; Assistant Professor, Department of Internal Medicine, Section of Endocrinology, University of Sarajevo, 2002-; Medical Officer, Organisation for Security and Co-operation in Europe, Mission to Bosnia and Herzegovina, 2002-. Publications: 38 articles in medical journals and presented at conferences as author and co-author include: Nutritional status and food security: Winter nutrition monitoring in Sarajevo 1993-94, 1995; The Impact of war on Sarajevans with non-insulin dependent diabetes mellitus, 1996; Evaluation of insulin usage in non-insulin dependent diabetes, 1999; Body mass and blood pressure control in patients with type

1 diabetes mellitus with different insulin regimes, 2001; Risk factors for the development of persistent proteinuria in patients with type 2 diabetes mellitus, 2002. Honour: Honorary Title of Primarius, Federal Ministry of Health of Bosnia and Herzegovina, 1996. Membership: Association of Physicians of Bosnia and Herzegovina; Association of Diabetologists and Endocrinologists of Bosnia and Herzegovina; European Association for the Study of Diabetes. Address: Bjelave 70, 71000 Sarajevo, Bosnia and Herzegovina. E-mail: indirak@oscehih.org

KULIK Igor Orestovich, b. 19 November 1935, Kharkov, Ukraine. Physicist. m. Tamara P Narbut, 4 June 1960, 2 sons. Education: MS 1959, PhD 1962, Kharkov State University; DSc, B Verkin Institute, Low Temperature Physics, Kharkov, 1973. Appointments: Research Associate, 1960-70, Head of Department of Theoretical Physics, B Verkin Institute of Low Temperature Physics, 1970-93; Professor, Department of Physics, Bilkent University, Ankara, Turkey, 1993-. Publications: Josephson Effect in Superconductive Tunnelling Structures, 1970, 1972; Quantum Mesoscopic Phenomena and Mesoscopic Devices in Microelectronics, 2000; Approximately 250 papers in various journals. Honours: N Ostrovskii Award in Science, Ukraine, 1970; State Award in Science and Technology, Ukraine, 1978. Memberships: Corresponding Member, Ukrainian Academy of Science, 1978-; New York Academy of Science, 1995-; American Physical Society, 1993-; Associate Editor, Soviet Journal of Low Temperature Physics, 1991-94. Address: Department of Physics, Bilkent University, Ankara 06533, Turkey. E-mail: kulik@fen.bilkent.edu.tr

KULIKOV Anatoly, b. 4 September 1946, Aygursky, Stavropol Region, Russia. Deputy of the State Duma. m. Valentina Kulikova, 2 sons, 1 daughter. Education: Vladikavkaz Military School of Internal Troops of the Ministry of the Interior, 1966; Frunze Military Academy, 1974; Military Academy of the General Staff of the Armed Forces, 1990; Candidate of Economic Sciences, 1992; Doctor of Economic Sciences, 1994. Appointments: Head of Administration of Internal Troops, Caucus Region, Russia, 1990-92; Deputy Minister of the Interior, Head of Internal Troops, 1992-95; Minister of the Interior, 1995-98; Chief Scientific Employee and Chairman of the Council of Security for the Russian Academy of Sciences, 1998-99; Deputy of the State Duma, Chairman of the Subcommittee on Legislation, 1999-2003; Deputy of the State Duma, Deputy Chairman of the Committee on Security, 2003-; Chairman of the Board of the World Anticriminal and Antiterrorist Forum; General of the Army. Publications: 4 mongraphs; 3 books; More than 200 scientific articles. Honours: Order of Merit for Fatherland; Order for Personal Courage; Order for Service in the Armed Forces; Order for Honour; More than 20 Medals. Memberships: Commission of the European Council Parliament Assembly; Academician, Russian Academy of Natural Sciences; Member, Academy of Military Sciences. Address: Okhotny Ryad 1, Moscow, 103265 Russia. E-mail: askulikov@duma.gov.ru

KULKARNI Ashok Balkrishna, b. 8 August 1948, Bijapur, Karnataka, India. University Professor. m. Lalita Kulkarni, 1 son, 1 daughter. Education: BSc, First Class, Agra University, 1966; MSc, First Class, Karnatak University, 1969; PhD, Kurukshetra University, 1979; Diploma, Marketing Management, First Class, First Rank, Punjabi University, 1984. Appointments: Lecturer, SDPG College, Meerut University, 1972-83; Reader, Physics, 1983-87, Professor, Applied Electronics, 1987-, Professor and Chairman, Department of Applied Electronics, 1987-93, 1995-97, 1999-2001, 2001-03, Gulbarga University; Member, University Syndicate, 1995-96, 2003-04. Publications: Over 140, many in international and national refereed journals; Original contributions in nuclear reaction mechanisms, material science, microwave

Dictionary of International Biography

antenna systems, fuzzy logic controllers, P-C based instrumentation, fibre optic communications. Honours: Throughout National Scholar; Bursar Agra University; Research Fellowships: CSIR and Department of Atomic Energy; Listed in numerous Who's Whos and biographical dictionaries. Memberships: Fellow, IETE; IACG; ISTE; Academic Council. Gulbarga University, 1987-. Address: Department of Applied Electronics, Gulbarga University, Gulbarga 585 106, Karnataka, India. E-mail: kulkarniab2@rediffmail.com

KULMATOV Rashid Anorovich, b. 1 July 1946, Denav, Surkhandarya, Uzbekistan. University Vice-Rector. m. Zainab Kulmatova, 2 sons, 1 daughter. Education: Tashkent State Pharmaceutical Institute, 1965-70. Appointments: Currently Vice-Rector, Termez State University. Publications: 2 scientific monographs; More than 150 scientific articles in fields of ecology and chemistry. Memberships: International ECOSAN Foundation: International Water Resources Protection Committee; Environmental Protection Committee. Address: At-termizi Street 21/11, Termez 732011, Surkhandarya Region, Republic of Uzbekistan. Email: nauka@uzpak.uz

KUME Haruki, b. 5 May 1964, Fukushima Prefecture, Japan. Medical Doctor. m. Yoko Kume, 1 son. Education: MD, 1989, PhD, 2000, Faculty of Medicine, University of Tokyo, Japan, 1989. Appointments: Associate Professor, International University of Health and Welfare, 2000; Lecturer, University of Tokyo, 2003; Medical Doctor, Urology; Researcher, Molecular Biology. Publications: Articles in medical journals: Genetic Identification of Bilateral Primary of Metastatic Renal Cell Carcinoma, 2000; Bilateral testicular tumour in Neurofibromatosis type 1, 2001. Address: Higashi-Nakano 5-6-4, Nakano-ku, Tokyo 164-6003, Japan. E-mail: kume@kuc.bigle

KUNDT Wolfgang Helmut, b. 3 June 1931, Hamburg, Germany. Astrophysics Professor. m. Ulrike Schümann, 1 son, 1 daughter. Education: Dipl Phys, 1956, Promotion, 1959, Habilitation, 1965, Hamburg University, under Pascual Jordan. Career: Professor, Hamburg, Bielefeld, Bonn; Visiting Scientist: Pittsburgh, Pennsylvania; Edmonton; Cern; Kyoto; Boston; Bangalore; Linz. Publications: Over 250 articles on astrophysics, geophysics and biophysics; 6 books including: Astrophysics: a Primer, 2001. Honours: NASA Group Achievement Award, 1975. Memberships: AG; EPS. Address: Institut für Astrophysik der Universität, Auf Dem Hügel 71, D-53121, Bonn, Germany. E-mail: wkundt@astro.uni-bonn.de

KUNERT Günter, b. 6 March 1929, Berlin, Germany. Poet; Author; Dramatist. m. Marianne Todten. Education: Hochschule für angewandte Kunst, Berlin-Weissensee. Publications: Poetry: Wegschilder und Mauerinschriften, 1950; Erinnerung an einen Planeten: Gedichte aus Fünfzehn Jahren, 1963; Der ungebetene Gast, 1965; Verkündigung des Wetters, 1966; Warnung vor Spiegeln, 1970; Im weiteren Fortgang, 1974; Unterwegs nach Utopia, 1977; Abtötungsverfahren, 1980; Stilleben, 1983; Berlin beizeiten, 1987; Fremd daheim, 1990; Mein Golem, 1996; Erwachsenenspiele, autobiography, 1997; Nachtvorstellung, poems, 1999. Novel: Im Namen der Hüte, 1967. Other: Der ewige Detektiv und andere Geschichten, 1954; Kramen in Fächen: Geschichten, Parabeln, Merkmale, 1968; Die Beerdigung findet in aller Stille statt, 1968; Tagträume in Berlin und andernorts, 1972; Gast aus England, 1973; Der andere Planet: Ansichten von Amerika, 1974; Warum schreiben?: Notizen ins Paradies, 1978; Ziellose Umtriebe: Nachrichten von Reisen und Daheimsein, 1979; Verspätete Monologe, 1981; Leben und Schreiben, 1983; Vor der Sintflut: Das Gedicht als Arche Noah, 1985; Die letzten Indianer Europas, 1991. Honours: Heinrich Mann Prize, 1962; Heinrich

Heine Prize, Düsseldorf, 1985; Hölderlin Prize, 1991; Georg-Trakl Prize, Austria, 1997. Memberships: Deutsche Akademie für Sprache und Dichtung e.v., Darmstadt. Address: Schulstrasse 7, D-25560 Kaisborstel, Germany.

KÜNG Hans, b. 19 March 1928, Lucerne, Switzerland. Professor of Ecumenical Theology Emeritus; Author. Education: Gregorian University, Rome; Institut Catholique, Paris; Sorbonne, University of Paris. Appointments: Ordained Roman Catholic Priest, 1954; Practical Ministry, Lucerne Cathedral, 1957-59; Scientific Assistant for Dogmatic Catholic Theology, University of Münster/Westfalen, 1959-60; Professor of Fundamental Theology, 1960-63, Professor of Dogmatic and Ecumenical Theology, 1963-80, Director, Institute of Ecumenical Research, 1963-96, Professor of Ecumenical Theology, 1980-96, Professor Emeritus, 1996-, University of Tübingen; President, Foundation Global Ethic, Germany, 1995, Switzerland, 1997; Various guest professorships and lectureships throughout the world. Publications: The Council: Reform and Reunion, 1961; That the World May Believe, 1963; The Council in Action, 1963; Justification: The Doctrine of Karl Barth and a Catholic Reflection, 1964, new edition, 1981; Structures of the Church, 1964, new edition, 1982; Freedom Today, 1966; The Church, 1967; Truthfulness, 1968; Infallible?: An Inquiry, 1971; Why Priests?, 1972; On Being a Christian, 1976; Signposts for the Future, 1978; The Christian Challenge, 1979; Freud and the Problem of God, 1979; Does God Exist?, 1980; The Church: Maintained in Truth, 1980; Eternal Life?, 1984; Christianity and the World Religions: Paths to Dialogue with Islam, Hinduism and Buddhism (with others), 1986; The Incarnation of God, 1986; Church and Change: The Irish Experience, 1986; Why I Am Still A Christian, 1987; Theology for a Third Millennium: An Ecumenical View, 1988; Christianity and Chinese Religions (with Julia Ching), 1989; Paradigm Change in Theology: A Symposium for the Future, 1989; Reforming the Church Today, 1990; Global Responsibility: In Search of a New World Ethic, 1991; Judaism, 1992; Mozart: Traces of Transcendence, 1992; Credo: The Apostles' Creed Explained for Today, 1993; Great Christian Thinkers, 1994; Christianity, Its Essence and History, 1995; Islam, in preparation; A Dignified Dying; A plea for personal responsibility (with Walter Jens) 1995; A Global Ethic for Global Politics and Economics, 1997; The Catholic Church, A Short History, 2001; Tracing the Way, Spiritual Dimensions of the World Religions, 2002; My Struggle for Freedom, Memoirs I, 2003. Honours: Oskar Pfister Award, American Psychiatric Association, 1986; Göttingen Peace Award, 2002; Many honorary doctorates. Address: Waldhäuserstrasse 23, 72076 Tübingen, Germany.

KUNJAPPU Joy, b. 18 January 1951, Trichur, India. Research Chemist. m. Mercy Joseph, 1 son, 1 daughter. Education: MSc, 1972; PhD, 1985; DSc, 1996. Appointments: Lecturer, Chemistry, Star Tutorial College, Trichur, 1972-74; Scientific Officer, Bhabha Atomic Research Centre, India, 1974-87, 1989-94; Associate Research Scientist, Postdoctoral, Columbia University, New York, 1987-89, 1994-96; Research Chemist, Polytex Environmentalinks, New York, 1997-98; Consultant, Chemical Sciences, 1999-; Consultant and Adjunct Faculty, Yeshiva University, New York, 2001-; Visiting Professor of Chemistry, Barnard College of Columbia University, New York, 2000-; Adjunct Research Scientist, Chemistry Department, Columbia University, New York, 2004-. Publications: 80 including research articles; Book: Essays in Ink Chemistry, 2002; Poems in Malayalam. Honours: Deputy Director General, International Biographical Association; Advisor to the American biographical Institute; Netaji Subash Chandra Bose Award for Excellence in Surface Science, 2004. Memberships: Association for Surface Scientists; New York Academy of

Sciences; American Chemical Society, USA; Association for the Advancement of Medical Instrumentation, USA. Address: 200W, 106th St, #5A, New York, NY 10025, USA.

KÜNNAP Ago, b. 23 July 1941, Tallinn, Estonia. Professor. m. Ene Räst, 3 sons. Education: BA, 1965, PhD, 1969, Dr philol hab, 1974, Tartu University; PhD, Helsinki University, 1971. Appointments: Lecturer, 1968-76, Professor, 1976-92, Full Professor, 1992-, Finno-Ugric languages, University of Tartu, Estonia; Lecturer, Estonian Language, University of Oulu, Finland, 1968-69; Lecturer, Estonian Language, 1969-71, Lecturer, Samoyed languages, 1973-74, Lecturer, Estonian and Samoyed languages, 1985-91, Guest Professor, 2000, University of Helsinki, Finland; Guest Professor, Uralic languages, University of Lund, Sweden, 1998; Guest Professor, Uralic languages, University of Hamburg, Germany, 1998-99; Guest Professor, Uralic languages, University of Naples, Italy, 2001. Publications: 6 books; 401 articles. Honours: Honorary Consul, Republic of Hungary in Tartu, Estonia; White Star V, ESTREP. Memberships: President, Estonian Committee of Hungarology. Address: Kaunase 17-7/EE-50704 Tartu, Estonia. Email: kunnap@ut.ee

KUNTZSCH Matthias, b. 22 September 1935, Karlsruhe, Germany. Conductor (Symphony and Opera). m. Sylvia Anderson, 18 May 1966, 1 son, 1 daughter. Education: Studied Piano, Horn, Conducting, Hochschule fur Musik und Theatre, Hannover; Master courses, Mozarteum, Salzburg, under Lovro von Matacic, Hermann Scherchen, Herbert von Karajan, and Zermatt under Pablo Casals, Karl Engel. Career: Conductor, Jeunesse Musicale Orchestra, Braunschweig, 1957; Musical Assistant, Hannover Opera, 1958; Kapellmeister, Opera Braunschweig, 1959; Assistant to Wolfgang and Wieland Wagner, Bayreuth Festival, 1962-64; Principal Conductor, Bonn Opera, 1962-64; Mannheim Opera, 1964-66; Hamburg State Opera, 1966-69, Staatskapellmeister, Munich State Opera, 1969-73; Generalmusikdirektor, Lübeck Opera and Symphony, 1973-77; Generalmusikdirektor and Operndirektor, Saarbrücken State Opera and Symphony, 1977-85; Guest conductor: Amsterdam, Paris, Brussels, London, Madrid, Bologna, Trieste, Milano, Venezia (Tristan and Isolde, Ring der Nibelungen, Rosenkavalier, Mozart Operas) and in Stuttgart, Frankfurt, Düsseldorf, Hannover, Berlin, Rio de Janeiro, Teheran, etc; Conductor, International Youth Festival Orchestra, Bayreuth, 1981-86; Principal Guest Conductor and Artistic Advisor, Basque National Symphony, San Sebastian, Spain, 1986-89; 1989, moved to USA to conduct concerts with Utah Symphony, Colorado Symphony, Colorado Springs Symphony, Bufallo Philharmonic, NHK Tokyo and others and operas with San Diego Opera, Columbus Opera, Portland Opera, Utah Opera, Colorado Opera, Puerto Rico Opera, Sacremento Opera, Vancouver Opera; Conducted world premieres of operas, Humphrey Searle's Hamlet, Hamburg, 1968 and Gian Carlo Menotti's Help Help the Globolinks, Hamburg, 1968; Günther Bialas's Aucassin et Nicolette, Munich, 1969; Detlev Mueller-Siemens's Genoveva, Germany TV ZDF; Professorship for conducting Opera at Hochschule für Music Hamburg, 1974 and Hochschule für Musik Frankfurt, 1993 Currently regular Guest Conductor with Utah Symphony, Utah Opera and Colorado Symphony; Since 1991, Music Director, Bay Area Summer Opera Theatre Institute. Recordings: With soloists Ruggiero Ricci, Eugene List and others. Address: 123 Nantucket Cove, San Rafael, CA 94901, USA.

KUNUGI Tomoaki, b. 15 September 1953, Kofu, Yamanashi, Japan. University Professor. m. Keiko Kishi, 1 son, 2 daughters. Education: BE, 1977, ME, 1979, Chemical Engineering, Keio University; PhD, Quantum Engineering and System Science, The University of Tokyo, 1996. Appointments: Japan Atomic Energy Research Institute, 1979-98; Professor, Tokai University, 1998-

99; Professor, Kyoto University, 1999-. Publications: MARS for Multiphase Calculation, 2001; Direct Numerical Simulation of Carbon Dioxide Gas Absorption Caused by Turbulent Free Surface Flow, 2001; Approaches to Fusion Science to Global Warming from the Perspective of Thermofluid Research, 2002. Honours: Technical Visualization Award, Flow Visualization Society of Japan, 1987; 2002 International SFT Award, Société Française de Thermique, 2002. Memberships: Japan Society of Mechanical Engineers; Atomic Energy Society of Japan; Visualization Society of Japan. Address: Yoshida, Sakyo, Kyoto 606-8501, Japan. E-mail: kunugi@nucleng.kyoto-u.ac.jp

KUO Cheng-Hsiung, b. 24 January 1955, Taiwan. Engineering Educator. m. Yueh-Er Jenny Jeng, 1 son, 1 daughter. Education: BS, 1978, MS, 1980, Department of Mechanical Engineering, National Cheng-Kung University, Taiwan; PhD, Department of Mechanical Engineering and Mechanics, Lehigh University, Pennsylvania, USA, 1988. Appointments: Registered Professional Engineer, 1983; Associate Researcher, China Steel Corporation, Kaohsiung, Taiwan, 1989-91; Associate Professor, 1991-98, Professor, 1998-2003, National Chung Hsing University. Publications: Articles in scientific journals as co-author include: Non-uniform Recovery of Vortex Breakdown over Delta Wing in Response to Blowing Along Vortex Core, 1996; Self-sustained Oscillation Induced by Horizontal Cover Plate above the Cavity, 2000. Honours: Listed in Who's Who publications and biographical dictionaries. Memberships: Micro System Technology Association, Taiwan. Address: 10F No 95 May-Tsun South Road, Taichung 402, Taiwan.

KUPEK Emil, b. 16 October 1959, Zadar, Croatia. Epidemiologist. 1 daughter. Education: BSc, Clinical Psychology, 1984, MSc, Developmental Psychology, 1991, University of Belgrade, Yugoslavia; PhD, Public Health Medicine, Imperial College School of Medicine at St Mary's, University of London, England, 1997. Appointments: Assistant Professor, Department of Psychology, University of Belgrade, Yugoslavia, 1988-91; European Science Foundation Visiting Grant, Department of Experimental Psychology, University of Oxford, England, 1991-92; Research Posts in Statistics and Computing, St Mary's Hospital Medical School, Imperial College, London, 1992-95; Visiting Professor, Research Fellowship, 1997-99, Professor of Epidemiology, 1999-, Department of Public Health, Universidade Federal de Santa Catarina, Florianópolis, Brazil. Publications: Over 40 articles in international scientific journals as author and co-author on developmental psychology, anthropology, HIV/AIDS, methodology and statistics and other fields of medicine include most recently: Demographic and socio-economic determinants of community and hospital services costs for people with HIV/AIDS in London, 1999; Comparability of trends in condom use for different countries: Some methodological issues with secondary data analysis, 2000; The reduction of HIV transfusion risk in southern Brazil in the 1990's, 2001; Effectiveness of a mass immunisation campaign against serogroup C meningococci in children in the federal state of Santa Catarina, Brazil, 2001; Clinical, provider and sociodemographic predictors of late initiation of antenatal care in England and Wales, 2002. Honours: European Science Foundation Fellowship; Visiting Professor Fellowship, Brazilian Ministry of Education. Membership: American Association for the Advancement of Science. Address: Department of Public Health, Universidade Federal de Santa Catarina/CCS, 88040-900 Florianopolis-SC, Campus Universitario – Trindade, Brazil.

KUPKA Valerij, b. 23 December 1962, Khomut, Ukraine. Teacher. m. Ivana, 7 August 1993, 1 son, 1 daughter. Education: MA, 1988; Diploma in Russian Language and History; PhD, 2000. Appointments: Postgraduate, Russian Department, Safarik

Dictionary of International Biography

University, Presov, 1990-94; Research Assistant, 1994-. Publications: Inconstancy, 1994; Skomoroshina, 1995; A Fly in the Ear, 1998; Lisa Quieter than a Monastery, 2001. Contributions to: Ticha Voda; Tvorba; Gumanitarny Fond; Romboid; Cirk; Olme. Membership: Slovak Writers Community; Ruthenian Writers Community. Address: Vazecka 12, 080 05 Presov, Slovakia.

KURACHI Akemi, b. 29 August 1951, Kyoto, Japan. Professor; Psychologist. Education: PhD, University of Illinois at Urbana-Champaign, USA, 1982. Appointments: Post-Doctoral Fellow, Stanford University, California, 1982-83; Research Co-ordinator, Institute for Child Behaviour and Development, University of Illinois at Urbana, 1983-84; Assistant and Associate Professor, Ritsumeikan University, Kyoto, 1986-93; Associate Professor, 1993-2000, Professor, 2000-, Hiroshima University; Board of Directors, Journal Support Network, Hiroshima, 1994-. Publications: A Path Leading Beyond Cultural Diversity, 1992; Change From Within: A New Development for Transcultural Communication, 1998; Analysis of Volunteers' and Teachers' Cultural Stereotypes: Perspectives on Perceptions and Awareness, 2003. Honours: Recipient, Letitia Walsh Fellowship, University of Illinois, Urbana, 1981; University Fellowship, University of Illinois, 1981-82; Awards for the Promotion of Education for International Understanding, 1986, 2001. Memberships: American Educational Research Association; Japanese Society of Transcultural Psychiatry; Intercultural Education Society. Address: Hiroshima University, Graduate School of Education, 1-1-1 Kagamiyama, Higashi-hiroshima, Hiroshima 7398524, Japan.

KURIHARA Ryoko, b. 30 July 1953, Ichikawa, Japan. Professor. Education: BA, Tokyo University of Education, 1978; MA, Sarah Lawrence College, 1985. Appointments: Lecturer, Sagami Women's University, Sagamihara, Japan, 1988-98; Lecturer, Nihon Women's University, Ikata, Japan, 1997-98; Lecturer, 1998-2001, Associate Professor, 2001-, Iwate Prefectural University, Takizawa, Japan; Lecturer, Graduate School, Tohoku University, Sendai, Japan, 1998-; Lecturer, Iwate University, Morioka, Japan, 2002-. Publications: Books: American Woman Suffrage Movement (author), 1993; The Japanese Woman Suffrage Movement in Comparison with the American Movement (author), 2001; American Study and Gender (co-author), 1997; How to Know America (co-author), 2002; Women's America Refocusing the Past, 2 volumes (co-translator), 2000. Memberships: American Studies Association of Japan; Election Committee, 1995-96, Women's Studies Association of Japan. Address: 5-5-25-504 Honcho Toda, Saitama, 335-0023 Japan. E-mail: ryoko@js7.so-net.jp

KUROSE Ryoichi, b. 6 July 1970, Fukuoka, Japan. Research Scientist. m. Chiaki, 1 daughter. Education: BA, 1993, MA, 1995, Dr Eng, 1998, Kyushu University, Fukuoka. Appointments: Research Scientist, Central Research Institute of Electric Power Industry, 1998-; Visiting Associate Professor, Gunma University, 2001-. Publications: Advances in Turbulence; Journal of Fluid Mechanics; Internal Journal of Multiphase Flow; Fuel, Combustion and Flame; ASME Journal of Fluids Engineering. Honours: Research Fellow, Japan Society for the Promotion of Science, 1995-98; Young Engineers Award, The Japan Society of Mechanical Engineers, 2000. Memberships: The Society of Chemical Engineers; The Japan Society of Mechanical Engineers; The Combustion Institute; The American Physical Society; many others. Address: Central Research Institute of Electric Power Industry, 2-6-1 Nagasaka, Yokosuka, Kanagawa 240-0196, Japan.

KURTZ Katherine Irene, b. 18 October 1944, Coral Gables, Florida, USA. Author. m. Scott Roderick MacMillan, 9 April 1983, 1 son. Education: BS, University of Miami, 1966; MA, University of California, Los Angeles, 1971. Publications: Deryni Rising,

1970; Deryni Checkmate, 1972; High Deryni, 1973; Camber of Culdi, 1976; Saint Camber, 1978; Camber the Heretic, 1981; Lammas Night, 1983; The Bishop's Heir, 1984; The King's Justice, 1985; The Quest for Saint Camber, 1986; The Legacy of Lehr, 1986; The Deryni Archives, 1986; The Harrowing of Gwynedd, 1989; Deryni Magic: A Grimoire, 1990; King Javan's Year, 1992; The Bastard Prince, 1994; Two Crowns for America, 1996; King Kelson's Bride, 2000; St Patrick's Gargoyle, 2001; In the King's Service, 2003; With Deborah Turner Harris: The Adept, 1991; Lodge of the Lynx, 1992; The Templar Treasure, 1993; Dagger Magic, 1994; Death of an Adept, 1996; The Temple and the Stone, 1998; The Temple and the Crown, 2001. With Robert Reginald: Codex Derynianus, 1998. Editor: Tales of the Knights Templar, 1995; On Crusade, 1998; Crusade of Fire, 2002; Deryni Tales, 2002; Various short stories. Honours: Edmund Hamilton Memorial Award, 1977; Balrog Award, 1982. Memberships: Authors Guild; Science Fiction Writers of America. Address: Holybrooke Hall, Kilmacanogue, Bray, County Wicklow, Ireland.

KUSHNER Aileen, b. 26 January 1947, Brooklyn, New York, USA. Registered Nurse. Divorced, 2 sons, 1 daughter. Education: AS, 1983; BSN, 2000. Appointments: Nurse Liaison, Department of Physical Medicine and Rehabilitation, 1997-2002; Nurse Liaison, Quality Management, 2002-2003; Head Nurse, Medical/Surgical Units, 2003-. Honours: Sigma Theta Tau, Molloy College; Green Key Honours Society, SUNY Farmingdale. Address: 3042 Lowell Avenue, Wantagh, NY 11793-3221, USA.

KUTCHER Ashton (Christopher), b. 7 February 1978, Ceder Rapids, Iowa, USA. Actor. Education: Biochemical Engineering Student, University of Iowa. Career: Sweeper, General Mills plant; Modeling. Film Appearances include: Coming Soon, 1999; Down To You, 2000; Reindeer Games, 2000; Dude Where's My Car?, 2000; Texas Ranger, 2001; Just Married, 2003; My Boss's Daughter, 2003; Cheaper by the Dozen, 2003; The Butterfly Effect, 2004. TV Appearances include: Just Shoot Me, 1997; That 70's Show, 1998; Grounded for Life, 2002; The Tonight Show with Jay Leno, 2003; RI:SE, 2003; Entertainment Tonight, 1981; Celebrities Uncensored, 2003; The Bernie Mac Show, 2004; T4, 2004. Honours: Young Artist Award, 1999; Sierra Award, 2000; MTV Movie Award, 2001; Razzie Award, 2004.

KÜTHEN Hans-Werner, b. 26 August 1938, Cologne, Germany. Musicologist. m. Annette Magdalena Leinen, 1 son. Education: Studied Musicology, Bonn University; Bologna; MA 1980; PhD 1985; Bonn University. Appointments: Editor, Beethoven Archives, 1968-2003. Publications: On Beethoven: Essay, Kammermusik mit Bläsern, 1969; Article Beethoven Herder, Das Grosse Lexikon der Musik, 1978; Complete edition: Ouverturen und Wellingtons Sieg, 1974; Critical Report, separately, 1991; Klavierkonzerte I, 1984; Klavierkonzerte II (nos 4 and 5), with Critical Report separately; Klavierkonzerte III, 2004; Klavierkonzerte Nos 1-5 Henle Studien-Editionen, 1998-2003; same in practical edition for 2 pianos, 1988-99. Contributions to: International professional publications including: Beethoven Yearbooks, Bonner Beethoven-Studien, congress reports, scholarly periodicals; International Congress of the Gesellschaft für Musikforschung, Freiburg i.Br, 1993: Gradus ad partituram; Erscheinungsbild und Funktionen der Solostimme in Beethovens Klavierkonzerten, Congress Report, 1999; Ein unbekanntes Notierungsblatt Beethovens aus der Entstehungszeit der Mondscheinsonate, Prague, 1996; Rediscovery and reconstruction of an authentic version of Beethoven's Fourth Piano Concerto for pianoforte and 5 strings, see Beethoven Journal Vol 13 No 1, San José, 1998; Co-editor: Beethoven im Herzen Europas. Leben und Nachleben in den Böhmischen Ländern, Prague, 2000; Editor, Congress Report Bonn 2000: Beethoven und die Rezeption der Alten Musik, Bonn 2002; On Viadana: Article V in Herder-Lex, 1982, id in Lexikon für Theologie und

Dictionary of International Biography

Kirche, Herder, 2000. Memberships: Gesellschaft für Musikforschung; Patron of the Verein Beethoven-Haus Bonn; VG Musikedition. Address: Am Hofgarten 7, D-53113 Bonn, Germany.

KUTILEK Miroslav, b. 8 October 1927, Trutnov, Czech Republic. Professor of Soil Science and Soil Physics. m. Xena Radova, 1 son, 1 daughter. Education: Ing, CTU, Prague, 1946-51; CSc, 1952-55; DrSc, 1966. Appointments: Associate Professor, CTU Prague, 1968-73; Reader, University of Khartoum, Sudan, 1965-68; Professor, CTU, Prague, 1973-90, 1992-93; Deputy Dean, 1974-85; Visiting Professor, Institute de Mechanique, Grenoble, France, 1979-80, 1985, 1991; Visiting Professor, University of California, 1981-82; Visiting Professor, Technische Universitat, Braunschweig, 1989; Professor, Bayreuth University, Fachbereich Geookologie, Germany, 1990-92. Publications: Research papers in journals; Scientific Books in Czech; Four books on Soil Science, Soil Hydrology, Porous Materials; Scientific books and monograph chapters in English; Others; Seven fiction books in Czech. Honours: Felber's Award, Technical Sciences; Mendel's Award, Biological Sciences; Honorary Member, IUSS. Memberships: International Soil Science Society; New York Academy of Sciences; International Commission on Irrigation and Drainage; International Council of Scientific Unions; European Cultural Club; Others. Address: Nad Patankou 34, 160 00 Prague 6, Czech Republic.

KUTTNER Paul, b. 20 September 1922, Berlin, Germany. Publicity Director; Author. m. Ursula Timmermann, 1963, divorced, 1970, 1 son. Education: Bryanston College, Blandford, Dorset, 1939-40. Appointments: Child Actor, aged nine, in films including: "Kameradschaft" (directed by G W Pabst); "Emil und die Detektive" (based on Erich Kästner's international juvenile best-seller, opposite Fritz Rasp); "M" (directed by Fritz Lang, starring Peter Lorre), Germany, 1931; US Publicity Director for the Guinness Book of World Records, 1964-89; Publicity Director, Sterling Publishing Co Inc, 1989-98. Publications: Translator of nine American books from German into English, 1963-76; The Man Who Lost Everything, 1976 (Best Seller in Spanish Language Edition, 1982); Condemned, 1983; Absolute Proof, 1984; The Iron Virgin, 1985; History's Trickiest Questions, 1990; Arts & Entertainment's Trickiest Questions, 1993; Science's Trickiest Questions, 1994; The Holocaust: Hoax or History? - The Book of Answers to Those Who Would Deny the Holocaust, 1997; Autobiography: "Struggling Non-Stop", 2005. Contributions to: Der Weg; London Week. Address: Apt 5C, 37-26 87th Street, Jackson Heights, NY 11372, USA.

KWEON Soon-Yong, b. 12 August 1968, Seochon-kun, Chungnam, South Korea. Materials Science and Engineering Educator. m. Kyoung-Hee Lee, 1 son, 1 daughter. Education: BS, 1991, MS, 1993, PhD, 2002, Korea Advanced Institute of Science and Technology, Taejon, South Korea. Appointments: Senior Engineer, Hynix Semiconductor Inc, Ichon-si, South Korea, 1999-2003; Professor, Chungju National University, Chungju-si, South Korea, 2004-. Publications: Various patents and papers related to FeRAM device; Development of 256kb, 1Mb, 4Mb, 16Mb (2003) FeRAM device. Honours: Listed in Who's Who publications and biographical dictionaries. membership: Korean ceramic society. Address: 123, Geomdan-ri, Iryu-myeon, Chungju-si, Chungbuk 380-702, South Korea. E-mail: sykweon@kungju.ac.kr

KWON Soon-Kyoung, b. 14 October 1940, Anjoo, Korea. Professor. m. Sin-Kang Park, 1 son, 1 daughter. Education: BS, Seoul, 1962; MS, Seoul, 1964; PhD, Munster, Germany, 1975. Appointments: Assistant Professor, 1978-82, Associate Professor, 1982-87, Professor, 1987-, Vice President, 1992-93, Dean, College Pharmacy, 1998-2000; President, 2001, Duk-Sung Women's University. Publications: Medicinal Chemistry, 1985; The World of Drugs, 1988; Medicinal Chemistry, 1996, 1999; The Advices of Drugs and Health, 2000. Honours: Prize for Distinguished Scientist, 1980; Golden Tower Prize for Distinguished Pharmacist, 1992; Prize for Commentator on Pharmaceutical Affairs, 1997; Dong-Am prize in pharmacy, Korean Pharmaceutical Industry News, 2001. Memberships: American Chemical Society; Pharmaceutical Society of Korea; Korean Chemical Society; Korean Society of Applied Pharmacology. Address: Sooyoo-dong 572-25, Kangbook-Ku, Seoul 142-880, Korea.

KYLBERG Jan Peter Henrik, b. 29 November 1938, Stockholm, Sweden. Film Director. m. Margaret Wickham, divorced, 2 sons, 2 daughters. Education: Institution of Physical Chemistry, Stockholm Royal Institute of Technology. Appointments: Film Director; Composer; Artist. Publications: Films: Kadens, 1960; En Kortfilm av Peter Kylberg, 1963; Paris D-Moll, 1964; Jag, 1966; Konsert för Piano, Två Ansikten Och En Fortsättning, 1968; Opus 25, 1978; Du, 1985; F42, 1990; I Ställes För Ett Äventyr, 1996. Honours: Four film awards; Many diplomas. Address: Angsklockevagen 50B, 181 57 Lidingo, Sweden.

KYNASTONE Vivien Rebecca, b. 11 November 1957, Bishop Auckland, County Durham, England. Company Executive. Education: BA (Hons) Philosophy, Lancaster University, 1979; MA, Business Studies and Japanese, 1981; PhD, 1983, University of Ulster; Macroeconomics Diploma, London School of Economics, 1984. Appointments: Outlets Researcher, Hodorle Inc, Smolian, Bulgaria, 1983-86; Export Contracts Director, Baines & Redfearn, 1986-90; Liaisons Controller, Singleton Moray, 1990-; Proprietor and Founder, Unst Langoustine Farm, 1995-. Publications: Rural Balkan Porcelain, 1989; The Z-Men, 1990 The Long Future of the Exotic African Languages, 1991; The Brazil Debacle, 1990; The Stevenage Williwaw, 1992; North Korea – Culture and Powerhouse, 1993; How to Kill a Rat with an Oboe, 1994; Untidy Position, 1995; Beethoven's Unbegun Symphony, 1996; The Selkirk Triple, 1997; The Samovar Creed, 1999; Paulo's Picnic, 2000; Fazackerley Mills, 2001. Memberships: Consultant and Speaker, Lerwick Rotary Club; Highlands and Islands Development Board; Aberdeen University Society for the Furtherance of the Gaelic Language. Address: Aadnesen House, Baltasound, Shetland, ZE2 4NG, Scotland. E-mail: cefims@soas.ac.uk

KYONI Kya Mulundu, b. 9 April 1948, Mukulakulu, Katanga, Democratic Republic of Congo. Lecturer. m. Ngongo Muzinga Mukenwendo, 2 sons, 1 daughter. Education: Humanities Greco-Latines, 1969; Licence/Philologie romane, UOC Lubumbashi, 1975; Diploma, History, Diploma, Classical Philology, Vienna University, 1984. Appointments: Lycee Lubusha, 1975-77; French and Latin Teacher, Institut Mapinduzi, 1977-80; Studies at the Vienna University, Austria, 1981; Lecturer, Kiluba, Institut fur Afrikanistic, Vienna University, 1985; Lecturer, Francophonie, Institut fur Romanische Sprachen, Wirtschaftsuni, Vienna, 1985. Publications: Biography of President Moïse Kapenda Tshombe; Articles on Katanga; Biographies of politicians from Katanga; History of Katanga. Address: 22 Langobardenst, 126/5/1, A-1220 Vienna, Austria. E-mail: kya-mulundu.kyoni@chello.at

KYTE Peter Eric, b. 8 May 1945, Rawalpindi, Pakistan. Barrister. m. Virginia Cameron, 1 son, 1 daughter. Education: MA, Trinity Hall, Cambridge, 1968. Appointments: Teacher of Classics and French, 1964-65; Manager, Charter Consolidated Ltd, London, Mauritania and Congo, 1968-73; Account Executive, Merrill Lynch, London and New York, 1973-74; Joined Chamber of Daniel Hollis QC, now Hollis Whiteman Chambers, 1974-; Recorder, 1991; Queen's Counsel, 1996; Legal Assessor for the General

Medical Council. Honours: Recommended as Leading Silk in the field of Criminal Fraud in Chambers Guide to the Legal Profession, 2000-01. Memberships: New York Stock Exchange; Chicago Board of Trade; Gray's Inn; Criminal Bar Association; Aula Club. Address: Forge House, Lower Heyford, Oxfordshire, OX25 5NS, England. E-mail: peterkyte@u-net.com

KYUNG Hee-Moon, b. 27 January 1957, Kyungpook, Korea. Professor. m. Myung-Hee Kim, 1 son, 1 daughter. Education: DDS, Dental School, 1974-80, MS, Graduate Course, 1981-83, Kyungpook National University; PhD, Graduate Course, Kyunghee University, 1986-89. Appointments: Full-time Instructor to Professor, Dental School, Kyungpook National University, 1986-; Visiting Professor, Osaka University, Japan, 1991-92; Visiting Professor, The University of British Columbia, Canada, 1996-97; Dean, Dental School, Kyungpook National University, 2001-2003. Publications: The growth of rat mandibles following mandibular retractive force, 1989; Longitudinal data of cranofacial growth from lateral cephalometrics in Korean with normal occlusion, 2002; The mushroom bracket positioner for lingual orthodontics, 2002; development of orthodontic micro-implants for intraoral anchorage. Honours: Best Presentation Awards, 4th European Society of Lingual Orthodontist's Meeting, 2002; Best Presentation Awards, 13th Congress of Brazilian Orthodontists, 2002. Memberships: Korean Association of Orthodontists; Japanese Association of Orthodontists; American Association of Orthodontists; Tweed Foundation; European Society of Lingual Orthodontists. Address: Department of Orthodontics, School of Dentistry, Kyungpook National University, 101 Dong In Dong, Jung Gu, Daegu, Korea, 700-422. E-mail:hmkyung@knu.ac.kr

Dictionary of International Biography

L

LA PLANTE Lynda, b. England. Television Dramatist. m. Richard La Plante. Education: Royal College of Dramatic Art. Appointments: Former Actress. Creative Works: Appeared in The Gentle Touch, Out, Minder; TV dramas include: Prime Suspect, 1991; Civvies; Framed; Seekers; Widows, series; Comics, 2 part drama, 1993; Cold Shoulder 2, 1996; Cold Blood; Bella Mafia, 1997; Trial and Retribution, 1997-; Killer Net, 1998; Mind Games, 2000. Publications include: Entwined; Cold Shoulder; The Governor; She's Out; Cold Heart, 1998; Sleeping Cruelty, 2000. Address: La Plante Productions Ltd, Paramount House, 162-170 Wardour Street, London, W1V 3AT, England.

LA SALA Gaspare, b. 18 December 1970, Lucerne, Switzerland. Investment Banker. m. Julie Cynthia Dysart, 1 son. Education: Master of Mathematics, University of Zurich, Switzerland, 1996-96; Trader, Treasury Department, UBS Warburg, Zurich, 1996-97; Trader, Fixed Income Derivatives, UBS Warburg, London, UK, 1997-98; Senior Trader, Fixed Income Derivatives, UBS Warburg, Zurich, 1998-. Honours: Graduation with honours, High School of Lucerne, 1990; Graduation with honours, University of Zurich, 1995. Address: UBS Warburg, Europastrasse 1, CH-8152 Opfikon, Zurich, Switzerland. E-mail: gaspare.lasala@ubsw.com

LAAR Mart, b. 22 April 1960, Tallinn, Estonia. Prime Minister. m. Katrin Laar, 1981, 1 son, 1 daughter. Education: MA, Philosophy, BA, History, Tartu University. Appointments: Member, Supreme Council, 1990-92; Member, Constitutional Assembly, 1992; Prime Minister of Estonia, 1992-94, 1999-2002; National Coalition Fatherland Party Chairman, 1992-95; Member of Parliament, Riikogu, VII Session, 1992-95; Member of Parliament, Riigikogu, VIII Session, 1995-98; Chairman, Pro Patria, 1998-; Prime Minister, Republic of Estonia, 1999. Publications: Variety of Estonian and English language books and publications on history. Honours: The Year's Best Young Politician in the World Award, 1993; European Tax Payer Association Year Prize, 2001; European Bull, Davastoeconomic Forum, Global Link Award, 2001; Adam Smith Award, 2002. Memberships: Chairman, Jaan Tonisson Institute; Estonian Christian Democratic Union; Pen Club; Estonian University Students Society. Address: State Chancellery, Lossi Plats 1a, Tallinn 15161, Estonia.

LABAR Boris, b. 9 April 1907, Zadar, Croatia. Doctor of Medicine. m. Žegka, 2 sons. Education: Board Examination in Internal Medicine, 1976; Master of Science, 1978; PhD in Medicine, 1982; Assistant Professor of Medicine, 1984; Professor of Medicine, 1990; Board Examination in Haematology, 1992. Appointments: Faculty member, 1976-, Head, BMT Unit, 1982-85, Head, Department of Haematology, 1985-, Dean, School of Medicine, 2000-, Department of Medicine, Clinical Hospital Center, Zagreb. Publications: 393 publications, 82 in cc journals; 845 citations. Honours: City of Zagreb for BMT, 1984; Award for the Best Scientific Paper, Croatian Academy of Medical Science, 1998. Memberships: Leukaemia and Lymphoma Group, EORTC; EBMTG; European Haematology Association; American Society for Haematology; IBHTR; ESO; Croatian Medical Association. Address: Division of Haematology, Department of Medicine, Clinical Hospital Center, School of Medicine, Kispaticeva 12, 10 000 Zagreb, Croatia. E-mail: boris.labar@inet.hr Website: www.inet.hr

LACEY Miriam, b. 3 November 1948, California, USA. Professor. 2 daughters. Education: BS, 1970, MS, 1975, Utah State University; PhD, University of Utah, 1980. Appointments: Professor. Publications: After a Peak Experience – The Impact of Executive Sudden Termination; Creating High Performance/High Commitment Organizations; Tacit Knowledge and Lean Building. Honours: Phi Beta Kappa; Beta Gamma Sigma; Milton Bennion Scholar. Memberships: Organization Development Network; International Organization for Development Association; Organization Development Institute; Faculty, Executive Programs, Pepperdine University. Address: 13792 Typee Way, Irvine, CA 92620-3272, USA.

LACEY Nicholas Stephen, b. 20 December 1943, London, England. Architect. m. (1) Nicola, (2) Juliet, 2 sons, 3 daughters. Education: MA, Emmanuel College Cambridge; AADipl, Architectural Association, London. Appointments: Partner, Nicholas Lacey and Associates, 1971-83; Partner, Nicholas Lacey and Partners, 1983-. Honours: Winner, Wallingford Competition; Winner, Crown Reach (Millbank) Competition; Joint Winner, Arunbridge Competition; Prize Winner, Paris Opera House Competition; RIBA Regional Awards; Civic Trust Awards. Memberships: Royal Institute of British Architects (RIBA); Architecture Club; Athenaeum; Royal Dorset Yacht Club. Address: Reeds Wharf, 33 Mill Street, London SE1 2AX, England. E-mail: nicholaslacey@lineone.net

LACHELIN Gillian Claire Liborel, b. 5 February 1940, Reigate, Surrey, England. Emeritus Consultant in Obstetrics and Gynaecology. Education: MA, MB, BChir, 1964, MRCOG, 1969, MD (London), 1981, FRCOG, 1982, Cambridge University and St Thomas' Hospital Medical School. Appointments: Reader and Consultant in Obstetrics and Gynaecology, 1977-2000, Emeritus Reader and Consultant in Obstetrics and Gynaecology, 2000-, University College London and University College Hospitals Trust. Publications: Numerous articles on reproductive endocrinology; Books: Miscarriage: The Facts; Introduction to Clinical Reproductive Endocrinology. Memberships: Committee on Safety of Medicines, 1993-96; Society for Gynecologic Investigation (USA), 1982-. Address: Department of Obstetrics and Gynaecology, Royal Free and University College Medical School, 88-96 Chenies Mews, London WC1E 6HX, England.

LACHINOV Mikhail, b. 31 March 1957, Gorkovskaya Region, Russia. Engineer; Economist. 1 son, 1 daughter. Education: M Eng, Moscow Civil Engineering University, 1979; PhD, 1987; Master of Economics, State Financial Academy of the Russian Federation Government, 1991; Postgraduate Courses, London School of Business, Holborn College, London, England, 1994. Appointments: Professor of Economics, Moscow State Civil Engineering University, 1995-2002; Head, Director, Institution of Civil Engineers representation in Russia, 1996-2003; Deputy Director, Economics, "Mospromstroi" Construction Corporation, 2002-. Publications: Textbook: Foreign Economic Relations in Construction, 2001; More than 30 scientific articles. Honours: Medal, Krasnoyarsk Region Development Award; Medal, For International Links Development. Memberships: Fellow, Institution of Civil Engineers (UK); Fellow, Russian Society of Civil Engineering; Chartered Engineer. Address: Flat 19, Building 10, Pokrovskyi Blvd 4/17, 101000 Moscow, Russia. E-mail: lachinov@rambler.ru

LACHOWICZ Tadeusz Zygmunt, b. 11 December 1919, Drohobycz. Physician; Microbiologist; Chemist. m. Wanda Jadwiga Schmager, deceased. Education: MD, 1948, Master's degree in Chemistry, 1951, Jagiellonian University; Candidate of Medical Sciences, 1958; Lecturer, 1960; Extraordinary Professor, 1968; Ordinary Professor, 1974. Appointments: Assistant, Adjunct, State Institute of Hygiene, 1946-50; Lecturer in Epidemiology, Military Service, Chief of Laboratory; Chief of the Microbiological Department in District Laboratory, 1954-63; Chief of Microbiology Department, Military Institute of Hygiene, 1963-65; Chief of the

Dictionary of International Biography

Centre, 1965-1980, Retired, 1980. Publications: 135 experimental works, 2 manuals, 2 patents, over 100 interviews to radio, press and television; Investigations on Staphylococcins, 1962; Purification and properties of Staphylococcin A, 1968; The use of Immunofluorescence Adsorption Test for Titrating Tetanus Anatoxins, 1968. Honours: Awards of Ministry of Military Affairs, I, II, II, Grade, 1971, 1977, 1980; Awards of City of Krakow, 1973, 1978; Knight Cross, 1963; Man of the Year, ABI, 1991, 1992, 1993, 1995, 1999, 2000 with Commemorative Medal; ABI Laureate of Poland, 1999; Key of Success Medical Excellence from ABI, 2000; Man of the Year, 1991-92, 1995-96, IBC; International Order of Merit, 1994; Scroll of Legend, Medal, Living Legends, IBC, 2003; Honorary Member, IBC, 2003; International Register of Profiles, 12th Edition, 2003; International Peace Prize, United Cultural Convention United States of America; The First Five Hundred, IBC, 2003; International Medal of Honour, IBC, 2003. Memberships: International Society of Pathology of Infectious Diseases; Polish Physician Society; International Biographical Association; American Biographical Institute's Research Association. Address: Krowoderskich Zuchow 23m44, 31-271 Krakow, Poland.

LĀCIS Romans, b. 1 January 1946, Kuldiga, Latvia. Doctor; Heart Surgeon. m. Aleksandra, 1 son, 3 daughters. Education: Therapeutic Faculty, 1974-70, Postgraduate Course, General Surgery Department, 1970, Dissertation of Medical Science Candidate, 1974, Riga Institute of Medicine; Professor's Degree in Cardiac Surgery, Vilnius State University, 1987; Training: Moscow, 1975, 1980; Vilnius, 1983, 1986, 1987; Lincoping, 1985; Hanover, 1990; Chicago, Boston, USA, 1991. Appointments: Assistant, General Surgery Department, 1971-74, Head of Research Laboratory of Cardiovascular Surgery, 1971-92, Riga Institute of Medicine; Professor of Cardiac Surgery, Latvian Academy of Medicine, Riga Stradins University, 1992-; Head, Department of Surgery of Acquired Heart Disease, 1974-98; Chief, Centre of Cardiac Surgery, P Stradins University, Riga, 1998-. Publications: 189 publications in the field of: Myocardial revascularisation, heart valve surgery, heart valve bioprostheses, biomechanics of heart valve, cardiac tumours, surgical treatment of atrial fibrillation. Honours: Diploma for first heart transplantation in Latvia, Latvian Prime Minister, 2002; Diploma for first heart transplantation in Latvia, Latvian Academy of Science, 2002; Man of the Year 2002; Listed in Who's Who publications and biographical dictionaries. Memberships: International Society of Cardiovascular Surgery; European Association of Cardiothoracic Surgery; Honorary Member, Academy of Science, Latvia. Address: str Ozolciema 16/6-40, Riga LV-1058, Latvia.

LACOMBE Michel Pierre Louis, b. 29 October 1929, Paris, France. Surgeon. m. Denise Anne-Marie Augis, 1 son, 1 daughter. Education: Medical Studies in Paris, 1951-; Houseman at Paris Hospitals, 1953-58; Senior Registrar at Paris Hospital, 1958-60; Doctor of Medicine, 1960. Appointments: Associate Surgeon, Clinique Chirugicale Universitaire in Geneva (Switzerland), 1960-61; Researcher, CNRS (Centre National de la Recherche Scientifique), 1964-66; Chief Surgeon, Paris Hospitals, 1966; Surgeon in Chief, Beaujon Hospital, 1973; Consulting Surgeon, Beaujon Hospital, 1995; Associate Professor, 1966; Professor of Surgery, University Paris VII (Faculty of Medicine Xavier Bichat), 1973. Publications: 300 articles in field of organ transplantation and vascular surgery; 10 didactic books; 2 films on cardiac transplantation, renal transplantation. Honour: Prizewinner, National Academy of Medicine of France, for works in field of organ transplantation, 1980. Memberships: European Society of Cardiovascular Surgery and International Society for Cardiovascular Surgery (European Chapter); French Society of

Transplantation; French Society of Vascular Surgery; National Academy of Surgery of France. Address: 49 rue Guersant 75017 Paris, France.

LACROIX Christian Marie Marc, b. 16 May 1951, Arles, France. Fashion Designer. m. Francoise Roesenstiehl, 1989. Education: Université Paul Valéry, Montpellier; Université Paris, Sorbonne; Ecole du Louvre. Appointments: Assistant, Hermès, 1978-79, Guy Paulin, 1980-81; Artistic Director, Jean Patou, 1981-87, Christian Lacroix, 1987-, Emilio Pucci, 2002-; Design for Carmen, Nîmes, France, 1988, for L'as-tu revue?, 1991, for Les Caprices de Marianne, 1994, for Phèdre a la Comèdie Francaise, 1995; Created costumes for Yoyaux, Opera Garnier, 2000; Decorated the TGV Mediterranee, 2001. Publications: Pieces of a Pattern, 1992; Illustrations for albums, Styles d'aujourd'hui, 1995; Journal d'une collection, 1996. Honours include: Des d'or, 1986, 1988; Prix Balzac, 1989; Goldene Spinnrad Award, Germany, 1990; Chevalier, Arts es Lettres, 1991; Prix Moliere, for costumes in Phèdre, 1996. Membership: Council, Fashion Designers of America. Address: 73 rue de Faubourg Saint Honoré, 75008 Paris, France.

LADER Malcolm Harold, b. 27 February 1936, Liverpool, England. Psychopharmacologist. m. Susan Ruth, 3 daughters. Education: Liverpool University, 1953-59; London University, 1960-66; Open University, 2001-. Appointments: External Staff, Medical Research Council, 1966-2001; Honorary Consultant, Maudsley Hospital, 1970-2001; Professor of Psychopharmacology, Institute of Psychiatry, University of London, 1978-2001; Emeritus Professor of Psychopharmacology, Kings College, London, 2001-; Trustee, Psychiatry Research Trust, 2002-; Advisor to H.M.Government in several capacities. Publications: 15 authored books; 20 edited books; 650 scientific articles on psychopharmacology, psychiatry and ethics. Honours: Honorary Fellow, Society for the Study of Addiction; Honorary Fellow, British Association of Psychopharmacology; Honorary Fellow, American College of Psychiatrists; OBE, 1996; Fellow Academy of Medical Sciences, 2000. Memberships: Royal Society of Medicine; Royal College of Psychiatrists. Address: 16 Kelsey Park Mansion, 78 Wickham Road, Beckenham, BR3 6QH, England. E-mail: m.lader@iop.kcl.ac.uk

LADYMAN Stephen John, b. 6 November 1952, Ormskirk, Lancashire, England. Member of Parliament. m. Janet Ladyman, 2 stepsons, 1 daughter, 1 stepdaughter. Education: BSc, Applied Biology, Liverpool Polytechnic; PhD, Strathclyde University. Appointments: Research Scientist, MRC Radiobiology Unit, 1979-85; Head of Computing, Kennedy Institute, 1985-91; Head, Computer Support, Pfizer Central Research, 1991-97; Member of Parliament, South Thanet, 1997-; Treasurer, All Party British Fruit Industry Group, 2000-; Chair, All Party Parliamentary Group on Autism, 2000-; Liaison MP for The Netherlands, 2001-; Chair, All Party British-Dutch Group, 2001-; Parliamentary Private Secretary to the Minister for the Armed Forces, 2001-. Address: House of Commons, London SW1A 0AA, England. E-mail: ladymans@parliament.uk

LAGERFELD Karl-Otto, b. 1938, Hamburg, Germany. Fashion Designer. Education: Art School, Hamburg. Appointments: Fashion Apprentice, Balmain and Patou, 1959; Freelance Designer, associated with Fendi, Rome, 1963-, Chloe, Paris, 1964-83, Chanel, Paris, 1982-, Isetan, Japan; Designer, Karl Lagerfeld's Women's Wear, Karl Lagerfeld France Inc, 1983-; First collection under own name, 1984; Honorary Teacher, Vienna, 1983; Costume Designer for film, Comédie d'Amour, 1989. Publications: Lagerfeld's Sketchbook, 1990; Karl Lagerfeld Off the Record, 1995. Honours include: Golden Thimble, 1986. Address: Karl Lagerfeld France Inc, 75008 Paris, France.

Dictionary of International Biography

LAGOS Ricardo, b. 2 March 1938, Santiago, Chile. Politician. m. Luisa Durán, 5 children. Education: University of Chile; Duke University, North Carolina, USA; PhD. Appointments: Professor, 1963-72, former Head, School of Political and Administrative Sciences, former Director, Institute of Economics, General Secretary, 1971, University of Chile; Chairman, Alianza Democrática, 1983-84; Chairman, Partido por la Democracia, 1987-90; Minister of Education, 1990-92; Minister of Public Works, 1994; President of Chile, 2000-. Publications: Numerous books and articles on economics and politics. Address: Office of the President, Palacio de la Moneda, Santiago, Chile.

LAGRAVENESE Richard, b. 30 October 1959, Brooklyn, New York, USA. Film Screenplay Writer, Director and Producer. m. Ann Weiss, 1986, 1 daughter. Education: Emerson College; BFA, New York University. Appointments: Producer, The Ref, film, 1994; Director, Living Out Loud, film, 1998. Creative Works: Screenplays: Rude Awakening, 1991; The Fisher King, 1991; The Ref, 1994; A Little Princess, 1995; The Bridges of Madison County, 1995; The Horse Whisperer, 1998; Living Out Loud (also Director), 1998; Unstrung Heroes; Defective Detective, 2002. Honours: Independent Film Project Writer of the Year. Address: c/o Kirsten Bonelli, 8383 Wilshire Boulevard, Suite 340, Beverly Hills, CA 90211, USA.

LAGUEUX Maurice, b. 19 December 1940, Montreal, Canada. Professor. m. Gisèle Houle, 1 son, 1 daughter. Education: License Philosophy, University of Montreal, 1961-63; PhD, Philosophy, University of Paris, Nanterre, 1963-65; MA Economics, McGill University, 1968-70. Appointments: Invited Professor, University of Ottawa, 1976-77; Professor, 1965-, Full Professor, 1982-, Department of Philosophy, University of Montreal. Publications: 2 books; More than 20 book chapters; 40 articles in various journals. Honours: General Governor's prize, Le marxisme des années soixante. Memberships: Canadian Philosophical Association; European Society for History of Economic Thought; History of Economic Society; Canadian Society of Aesthetics; Société de Philosophie du Québec. Address: Department of Philosophy, University of Montreal, CP 6128, Succ. Centre-ville, Montreal H3C 3J7, Canada. E-mail: maurice.lagueux@umontreal.ca

LAGZDINS Viktors, b. 28 August 1926, Riga, Latvia. Writer. m. Dzidra Reita, 6 June 1952, 1 daughter. Education: Pedagogic School, Liepaja, 1947; Diploma of Education, Faculty of Philology, Riga Pedagogic Institute, 1958. Appointments: Teacher, 1947-58; Writer, 1955-; Journalist on the Editorial Staff of a Daily Newspaper, Liepaja, 1958-63, and Monthly magazine, Riga, 1963-82. Publications: Parbaude, English translation as The Test, 1959; Indianu Virsaitis Drossirdigais Kikakis, 1963; Kedes Loks, 1972; Nakts Mezazos, English translation as A Night at Elk Farm, 1976; Zili Zala, English translation as The Blue and The Green, 1986. Membership: Writers' Union of Latvia, 1959-, chairman of the prose section, 1979-80. Address: Agenskalna iela 22-48, Riga, LV-1046, Latvia.

LAHMAM BENNANI Abdelhak, b. 1945, Fes, Morocco. Agronomist; Chief Engineer; Administrator. m. Benabdallah Najat, 1 son, 3 daughters. Education: Certificate of Advanced Studies, MPC, Faculty of Science, Rabat, 1967; Diploma, General Agronomy, Hassan II Institute of Agronomy and Veterinary Science, Rabat, 1970; Agricultural Engineer, Agricultural and Food Industries, IAV Hassan II-Centre for Study and Research in the Food Industry, Brussels, Belgium, 1972; Doctorat ès Sciences Sociales, Analysis and Development of Projects, IAE, Lille, France, 1994; CIHEAM Advanced Courses, Development of New Food Crops, 1997, International Strategic Management of Agricultural

Food Produce Enterprises, 1999. Appointments: Head, Office of Technical Studies, Investment Services, 1972-73, Departmental Head, Studies and Vocational Guidance, 1973-74, Board of Economic Affairs and Agricultural Industry; Head, Department of Agricultural Industry, Board of Agricultural Land Improvement, 1974-80, Head, Department of Agricultural Industry, Board of Vegetable Production, 1980-93, Ministry of Agriculture and Agrarian Reform; Board of Directors, companies: Les Dattes de Zagora, 1977-93, Sucrerie Nationale de Betteraves du Loukkos, 1981-87, Sucrerie de Beni Mellal, 1981-98; Board of Directors, Moroccan Institute of Packing and Drying, 1981-94; Head, Division for Projects on Land Improvement and Agricultural Industry, Department of Vegetable Production, 1993-; Board of Directors, Office for Port Administration, 1998-. Publications: Survie et conservation des fleurs coupées et plantes ornementales, 1993; Guide pour la réalisation d'un entrepôt frigorifique moderne, French edition, 1995; Gestion de la qualité dans la chaîne du froid des fruits et légumes, 1998; Several others on refrigeration of produce; Development strategy of canned products, 2001. Memberships: Secretary General, Association Nationale du Froid; Assistant Treasurer, Association pour la Promotion de l'Agriculture, l'Halieutique et l'Industrie; Académie Marocaine de Gastronomie. Address: Hay Riad, Secteur 2, Bloc B11, BP 6433, Madinat al Irfane, Rabat, Morocco. E-mail: ficopam@ficopam.ma

LAHOOD Julie Ann, b. 31 May, Martins Ferry, Ohio, USA. Owner of Historic Properties. Education: Education: St Mary Academy, Monroe, Michigan; Theatre, Classical Studies, Fine Arts, Loyola University, Chicago, Illinois; Fashion Merchandising and Modelling, Ray College of Design, Chicago. Appointments: Junior Executive, SAKS, Fifth Avenue, Chicago and Detroit; Junior Executive, Department Manager, Bonuit Teller, Chicago; Owner of Historic Properties, Monroe, Michigan, (home of General Custer and last battle of War of 1812). Publications: Contributed to Anthology of Best Poems and Poets, International Society of Poets, 2001, 2002, 2003; Poetry appears on www.poetry.com, International Society of Poets. Honours: Tri-state region and vocal awards, Ohio, North Virginia and surrounding area; Runner Up, Miss Toledo Beauty Pageant, aged 17 years; Distinguished Member, International Society of Poets; Editor's Choice Awards, Best Poems of 2001-02; Best Poems and Poets, 2003-04; Who's Who in America, 58th Edition, 2004; Who's Who in the World, 2004; Who's Who of American Women, 24th edition, 2004-05. Memberships: Monroe Michigan Historic Society; Chicago Historic Society; National Right to Life, Washington DC; National Air and Space Museum; Roman Catholic, Member of Holy Name Cathedral, Chicago; St Patrick Church, St Charles; Humane Society of the United States; Smithsonian Institute. Address: 707 Monroe Av, St Charles, IL 60174, USA.

LAHOUD Emile (General), b. 1936, Baabdate, Lebanon. Politician; Naval Officer. m. Andrée Amadouni, 2 sons, 1 daughter. Education: Brumana High School; Cadet Officer, Military Academy, 1956; Naval Academy courses, UK, USA, 1958-80. Appointments: Ensign, 1959, Sub-Lieutenant, 1962, Lieutenant, 1968, Lieutenant-Commander, 1974, Commander, 1976, Captain, 1980, Rear-Admiral, 1985, General, 1989; Commander of Second Fleet, 1966-68, First Fleet, 1968-70; Staff of Army Fourth Bureau, 1970-72; Chief of Personal Staff of General and Commander of Armed Forces, 1973-79; Director of Personnel, Army Headquarters, 1980-83; President of Military Office, Ministry of Defence, 1983-89; General and Commander of Armed Forces, 1989-; President of Lebanon, 1998-. Publications: Procedure and Modus Operandi, 1998. Honours: Medal of Merit and Honour, Haiti, 1974; Lebanese Medal of Merit, General Officer, 1989; War Medals, 1991, 1992; Dawn of the South Medal, 1993; National

Unity Medal, 1993; Medal of Esteem, 1994; Grand Cordon, Order of the Cedar, Lebanon, 1993; Commandeur, Légion d' Honneur, France, 1993; Order of Merit, Senior Officer Level, Italy, 1997; Grand Cross of Argentina, 1998; Order of Hussein ibn Ali, Jordan, 1999; Necklace of Independence, Qatar, 1999. Address: Presidential Palace, Baabda, Lebanon. E-mail: opendoor@presidency.gov.lb

LAI Dae, b. 7 December 1944, Da Jiang Village, Xiang Dong District, Ping Xiang City, Jing Xi Province, China. Mining Engineer. 3 sons. Education: Graduate, Jiang Xi Coal Mine College, 1962. Appointments: Ping Xiang Mineral Bureau, Deep Actual Measurement Technique in Coal Mining, 1962-1999; Technician Engineer, 1962-83; Expert, Senior Engineer, Zong Engineer, 1984-95. Honours: Awards include entry in Dictionary of Prominent Chinese Scientists and Technicians, 1996; Worldwide Consultative Expert, 1998; World VIP, 1998; Scientific and Technology for Progress in China, 1999; Present of Talent Musical Notation of China, 1999; Outstanding Achievement mine pressure for Research Accomplishment (International Prize, Jiang Xi Province 1st Prize); Thesis: A Test of Composite Support and An Approach to Working Resistance (international prize, Province 1st Prize); Project: QZJ-1 Type Composite Support to Working Resistance (international prize); Approach for affirming the support to the working resistance of face in Da Chao seam in An Yuan Mine (Pingmine 1st Prize, province 1st Prize, Ptoi): Mine Support Pressure and On the Spot Actual Measurement Summary of Technique at Ping Mine. Membership: Coal Mine Inst of China.

LAI Shih-Kung, b. 15 November 1957, Taiwan. Professor. m. Chiung-Ku Lee, 15 October 1993. Education: BSE, Urban Planning, National Cheng Kung University, 1979; MCRP, City and Regional Planning, Ohio State University, 1985; PhD, Regional Planning, University of Illinois at Urbana-Champaign, 1990. Appointment: Director, Centre for Land Management and Technology, Associate Professor, Professor, Department of Real Estate and Built Environment, National Taipei University. Publication: Meanings and Measurements of Multiattribute Preferences, 1996; Omega, Environment and Planning B, Decision Sciences. Honour: Research awards of National Science Council, Republic of China, 1993-2003. Memberships: American Planning Association; INFORMS; Chinese Planning Association. Address: 67, Section 3, Min Sheng East Road, Taipei, Taiwan, Republic of China. E-mail: lai@mail.ntpu.edu.tw

LAIDLAW Christopher Charles Fraser (Sir), b. 9 August 1922. Business Executive. m. Nina Mary Prichard, 1952, 1 son, 3 daughters. Education: St John's College, Cambridge. Appointments: War Service, Europe, Far East, Major on General Staff, 1939-45; With British Petroleum Co Ltd, 1948-83: Representative, Hamburg, 1959-61, General Manager, Marketing Department, 1963-67, Director, BP Trading, 1967, President, BP Belgium, 1967-71, Director of Operations, 1971-72, Chairman, BP Germany, 1972-83, Managing Director, BP Co Ltd, 1972-81, Deputy Chairman, BP Co Ltd, 1980-81, Chairman, BP Oil Ltd, 1977-81, Chairman, BP Oil International 1981; Director, Commercial Union Assurance Co, 1978-83, Barclays Bank International Ltd, 1980-87, Barclays Bank, 1981-88; Chairman, ICL, 1981-84; President, ICL France, 1983; Director, Amerada Hess Corporation, 1983-94; Director, Barclays Merchant Bank, 1984-87; Chairman, Boving and Co, 1984-85; Chairman, UK Advisory Board, 1984-91, Director, 1987-94, INSEAD; Director, Amerada Ltd, 1985-98; Chairman, Bridon PLC, 1985-90; Director, Daimler-Benz UK Ltd, 1994-99. Honours: Honorary Fellow, St John's College, Cambridge. Memberships: President, German Chamber of Industry and Commerce, 1983-86; Master, Tallow Chandlers Company, 1988-89; Vice-President, British-German Society, 1996-. Address: 49 Chelsea Square, London SW3 6LH, England.

LAINE Cleo (Clementina Dinah Dankworth), b. 28 October 1927, Southall, Middlesex, England. Singer. m. (1) George Langridge, 1947, 1 son, (2) John Philip William Dankworth, 1958, 1 son, 1 daughter. Appointments: Joined, Dankworth Orchestra, 1953; Lead, Seven Deadly Sins, Edinburgh Festival and Sadler's Wells, 1961; Acting roles in Edinburgh Festival, 1966, 1967; Founder, Wavendon Stables Performing Arts Centre, 1970; Many appearances with symphony orchestras; Frequent tours and TV appearances and productions including Last of the Blonde Bombshells, 2000. Publications: Cleo: An Autobiography, 1994; You Can Sing If You Want To, 1997. Honours include: Woman of the Year, 9th Annual Golden Feather Awards, 1973; Edison Award, 1974; Variety Club of GB Show Business Personality Award, 1977; TV Times Viewers' Award for Most Exciting Female Singer on TV, 1978; Grammy Award, Best Jazz Vocalist, Female, 1985; Best Actress in a Musical, 1986; Theatre World Award, 1986; Lifetime Achievement Award, 1990; Vocalist of the Year, British Jazz Awards, 1990; Lifetime Achievement Award, USA, 1991; ISPA Distinguished Artists Award, 1999. Memberships include: National Association of Recording Merchandisers. Address: The Old Rectory, Wavendon, Milton Keynes MK17 8LT, England.

LAING William Peter, b. 8 October 1948. Geologist. m. Susan Kay Turner, 1 son, 1 daughter. Education: BSc (Honours, 1st Class), Sydney University; PhD, University of Adelaide. Appointments: Exploration Geologist, Hastings Exploration, NL, 1970-72; Senior Geologist, CRA Exploration Pty Ltd, 1979-82; Senior Lecturer, Geology, James Cook University, 1983-89; Managing Director, Principal Consultant, Laing Exploration Pty Ltd, 1989-01; Honorary Research Fellow, James Cook University, 1993-01; over one hundred Geology Consultancies, Australia, Pacific, Asia, South America, North America, Africa. Publications: Numerous scientific papers in international journals; Transactions of the Institute of Mining and Metallurgy, Benchmark Papers in Geology, 1975-01; Monographs: Structural Geology in Drillcore; Ore Systems Analysis, 1989-2004; Co-designer, Drillcore Orientometer (international export), 1989; Musical recordings (LP, audio cassette, CD), folk bands: Hammer'n'Tap, 1981; Threepenny Bit, 1988; Mango Jam, 1996, 2001; Warttle and Gum, 1983-2004; Producer and Artistic Director, SOCOG Sea Change Concert, Queensland, 1998. Honours: Honorary Research Fellow, James Cook University, 1993; Australia Day Award, Thuringowa City, 1997; Producer and Artistic Director, Event of the Year, Townsville City Council, 1998. Memberships: Fellow, Society of Economic Geologists; Fellow, Australasian Institute of Mining and Metallurgy; Fellow, Australian Institute of Geoscientists; Geological Society of Australia; Australian Society of Exploration Geophysicists; Scientists for Global Responsibility, Convenor, North Queensland Branch, 1986-90; North Queenslanders for Reconciliation, 1997-01; Amnesty International, 2002-04. Address: 11 McLauchlan Crescent, Kelso, Qld 4815, Australia.

LAINSON Ralph, b. 21 February 1927, Upper Beeding, Sussex, England. Parasitologist. m. Zéa Constante Lins-Lainson, 1 son, 2 daughters. Education: BSc, 1947-51, London University; PhD, 1952-55, DSc, 1964, University of London, London School of Hygiene and Tropical Medicine. Appointments: Lecturer, Department of Medical Protozoology, London School of Hygiene and Tropical Medicine, 1955-59; Director, Leishmaniasis Unit, Baking Pot, Cayo, Belize, Central America, 1959-62; Research Worker, London School of Hygiene and Tropical Medicine, 1962-65; Director, Wellcome Parasitology Unit, Instituto Evandro Chagas, Belém, Pará, Brazil, 1965-92. Publications: 350 articles

Dictionary of International Biography

in scientific journals and textbooks of parasitic diseases, particularly Leishmaniasis, Malaria and Toxoplasmosis. Honours: Chalmer's Medal, Royal Society of Tropical Medicine and Hygiene, 1971; Manson Medal, Royal Society of Tropical Medicine and Hygiene, 1984; Fellow, Royal Society of London, 1982; Associate Fellow, Third World Academy of Sciences, 1989; OBE, 1996. Memberships: Honorary Member, London School of Tropical Medicine and Hygiene; Honorary Member, British Society of Parasitology; Honorary Member, Royal Society of Tropical Medicine and Hygiene; Honorary Member, Society of Protozoologists. Address: Avenida Visconde de Souza Franco 1237, Apto 902, 66053-000, Belém, Pará, Brazil. E-mail: ralphlainson@iec.pa.gov.br

LAIRD Gavin Harry (Sir), b. 14 March 1933, Clydebank, Scotland. Trade Union Official. m. Catherine Gillies Campbell, 1956. Appointments: Shop Stewards Convener, Singer, Clydebank, 7 years; Regional Officer, 1972-75, Executive Councillor for Scotland and North-West England, 1975-82, General Secretary, Union Section, 1992-95, Amalgamated Engineering Union, formerly Amalgamated Union of Engineering Workers; Scottish Trades Union Congress General Council, 1973-75; Part-time Director, Highlands and Islands Development Board, 1974-75; Part-time Director, British National Oil Corporation, 1976-86; Trades Union Congress General Council, 1979-82; Industrial Development Advisory Board, 1979-86; Chairman, The Foundries Economic Development Committee, 1982-85; Arts Council, 1983-86; Director, Bank of England, 1986-94; Non-Executive Director, Scottish TV Media Group PLC, 1986-99; Non-Executive Director, Britannia Life, 1988-; Non-Executive Director, GEC Scotland, 1991-99; Non-Executive Director, Edinburgh Investment Trust, 1994-; Chairman, Greater Manchester Buses North, 1994-96; Armed Forces Pay Review Body, 1995-98; Employment Appeal Tribunal, 1996-; Non-Executive Director, Britannia Investment Managers Ltd and Britannia Fund Managers Ltd, now Britannia Asset Managers Ltd, 1996-; Chairman, Murray Johnstone Venture Capital Trust 4, 1999-; Murray Johnstone Private Acquisition Partnership Advisory Committee, 1999-. Honours: Commander, Order of the British Empire. Memberships: Trustee, John Smith Memorial Trust; Advisory Board, Know-How Fund for Poland, 1990-95; Trustee, Anglo-German Foundation, 1994-; President, Kent Active Retirement Association, 1999-; Vice-President, Pre-Retirement Association of Great Britain and Northern Ireland, 1999-; Editorial Board, European Business Journal. Address: 9 Cleavedon House, Holmbury Park, Bromley BR1 2WG, England.

LAJTHA George, b. 10 March 1930, Budapest, Hungary. Engineer. m. Judith Brebovszky, 26 July 1958, 1 son. Education: MEE, Technical University of Budapest, 1952; PhD, Hungary Academy of Sciences, 1963. Appointments: Research Fellow, 1952, Head, Telecom Department, 1963, Science Vice Director, 1974, Advisor, General Director, 1986, PO Research Section; Editor-in-Chief, Periodical Hungarian Telecom, 1990-2001; Editor in Chief, Hiradastechn, 2001-. Publications include: Theory and Planning Telecom Network; Optical Telecom Systems and Elements. Honours: Virag-Pollak Award, 1967, 1975; Jaky Award, 1977; Puskas Award, 1981, 1990; Eotvos Award, 1981; Bekesy Gyorgy Memorial Medal, 1985; Szechenyi Award, 1992; Denis Gabor Award 2001. Memberships: Science Telecom Association; Hungarian Standardisation Body; Chairman Telecom Committee, Hungarian Academy of Science; General Assembly Delegate. Address: Budafoki-ut 10/A, H-1111 Budapest, Hungary.

LAKATANI Sani, Politician. Appointments: Leader, Niue People's Party; Prime Minister of Niue, 1999-2001; Minister for External Affairs, Finance, Customs and Revenue, Economic and Planning Development and Statistics, Business and Private Sector Development, Civil Aviation, Tourism, International Business Company and Offshore Banking, Niue Development Bank, 1999-2001; Chancellor, University of the South Pacific, Fiji, 2000-03; Deputy Premier and Minister for Planning, Economic Development and Statistics, the Niue Devt Bank, Post, Telecommunication and Information Computer Technology Development, Philatelic Bureau and Numismatics, Shipping, Investment and Trade, Civil Aviation and Police, Immigration and Disaster Management, 2002-. Address: c/o Office of the Prime Minister, Alofi, Niue, South Pacific.

LAKER Frederick Alfred (Sir), b. 6 August 1922. Business Executive. m. (4) Jacqueline Harvey. Appointments: Short Bros, Rochester, 1938-40; General Aircraft, 1940-41; Served with Air Transport Auxiliary, 1941-46; Aviation Traders, 1946-60; British United Airways, 1960-65; Chairman, Managing Director, Laker Airways Ltd, 1966-82; Director, Skytrain Holidays, 1982-83; Director, Sir Freddie Laker Ltd, 1982-; Director, Northeastern International Airlines Inc, USA, 1984-; Chairman, Managing Director, Laker Airways Bahamas Ltd, 1992-. Honours: Honorary Fellow, University of Manchester Institute of Technology, 1978; Honorary DSc, City University, 1979; Honorary DSc, Cranfield Institute of Technology, 1980; Honorary LLD, Victoria University of Manchester, 1981. Memberships: Jockey Club, 1979-; Chairman, Guild of Air Pilots and Navigators Benevolent Fund. Address: Princess Tower, West Sunrise, Box F-4207, Freeport, Grand Bahama, Bahamas.

LAKES Diana. Artist. m. Roderic Lakes. Appointments: Watercolour and acrylic artist; Exhibitions across USA, Italy, South America, China and Korea, 1987-; Paintings housed in numerous public and private collections, and museum collections in France and Canada. Publications: Newspaper articles and reproduction of paintings in public and professional journals. Honours: Listed in national and international biographical dictionaries. Memberships: Wisconsin Watercolor Society. Address: 1225 Edgehill Drive, Madison, WI 53705, USA.

LAKIZA Sergij, b. 25 October 1951, Uzghorod, Ukraine. Chemist. m. Tanya Tsarenko, 1 son, 1 daughter. Education: Chemical Department, Uzghorod State University, 1974; Doctor Degree, Inorganic Chemistry, 1978. Appointments: Chemical Department, 1968-74, Postgraduate, 1974-77, Uzghorod State University; Institute for Problems of Materials Science, 1978-. Publications: Several articles in professional scientific journals. Address: Frantsevich Institute for Problems of Materials Science, Krzizanovskogo 3, 03142 Kyiv, Ukraine.

LAKSHMIKANTHAM Vangipuram, b. 8 August 1926, Hyderabad, India. US citizen, 1966. Educator. m. Soroja Bukkapatnam, 22 February 1942, 3 children. Education: MA, Osmania University, Hyderabad, 1955; PhD, 1958. Appointments: Faculty member, University of California at Los Angeles, 1960-61; Mathematics Research Centre, University of Wisconsin, Madison, 1961-62; Member, Research Institute, Advanced Studies, Baltimore, 1962-63; Associate Professor, University of Alberta, Calgary, Canada, 1963-64; Professor, Chairman, Department of Mathematics, Marathwada University, Aurangabad, India, 1964-66; University of Rhode Island, Kingston, 1966-73; University of Texas, Arlington, 1973-88; Professor, Head, Department of Mathematical Sciences, Florida Institute of Technology, Melbourne, 1989-. Publications: Author, 35 books; Founder, Editor: Journal of Nonlinear Analysis, Series A and Series B; Realworld Problems, Nonlinear Studies; Stochastic Analysis and Applications; Mathematical Problems in Engineering; Hybrid Systems and Applications; Associate Editor, other journals; Contributor, over 450 research articles to professional publications.

Dictionary of International Biography

Memberships: American Mathematical Society; Indian Mathematical Society; Society of Industrial and Applied Mathematics; National Academy of Science, India; Founder, International Federation of Nonlinear Analysts. Address: Florida Institute of Technology, Department of Applied Mathematics, 150 W University Blvd, Melbourne, FL 32901-6982, USA.

LALITHA Mukkai Kesavan, b. 11 March 1946, Kerala, India. Professor. m. N Balasubramanian, 2 sons, 1 daughter. Education: MBBS, 1969; MD, Microbiology, 1975. Appointments: Demonstrator in Microbiology, 1970-71; Junior Lecturer, 1972-75; Senior Lecturer, 1976-79; Reader, 1979-82; Associate Professor, 1982-84; Professor of Microbiology, 1984-. Publications: Over 100 article in peer-reviewed journals. Honours: Yedanapalli Award, 1987; Silver Jubilee Annual Oration Award, 1992; Gujarat Cancer Society Award, 1998; Senior Training Fellowship Award, 1996; Presidential Oration, Antimicrobial Resistance-Experience over Two Decades, 2001; B C Roy Award for Excellence in Medical Education, 2001. Memberships include: Life Member and President, Indian Association of Medical Microbiologists; European Society for Clinical Microbiology and Infectious Diseases; American Society for Microbiology; Hospital Infection Society of India. Address: Department of Clinical Microbiology, Christian Medical College and Hospital, Vellor 632 004, Tamilnadu, India. Email: mkl_micro@yahoo.com

LALL Dharam Bir (Bill), b. 16 April 1933, Bannu, India. Chartered Accountant. m. Shashi, 1 daughter. Education: Chartered Accountant, 1964; Chartered Management Accountant, 1965. Appointments: KPMG, Dunlop and PriceWaterhouse, Milan, Italy; Senior Executive Officer, Ministry of Defence and Department of Trade and Industry, -1992; Own accountancy practice, 1992-. Honours: Chairman, Newham Asian Business Association, 1993-95; Chairman, Newham Chamber of Commerce, 2000-02; Vice Chairman, London East Ethnic Business Association, 2001-; Board Member, East London Business Alliance, 1998-2002; UK College of Life Coaching. Memberships: Business Mentoring Academy; Board Member, Regulatory and Monitoring Board of Chartered Institute of Management Accountants, 1998-; Executive Committee Member, Institute of Business Advisers, London Board, 2001-; Honorary Doctor of Business Administration, University of East London, 2003. Address: Woodlands, 17 Stradbroke Drive, Chigwell, Essex IG7 5QV, England. E-mail: lall888@aol.com

LALLAAICHA (HRH Princess), Diplomatist. Appointments: Moroccan Ambassador to UK, 1965-69; Moroccan Ambassador to Italy and accredited to Greece, 1969-73. Honours: Grand Cordon, Order of the Throne of Morocco. Membership: President, Moroccan Red Crescent. Address: c/o Ministry of Foreign Affairs, ave Franklin Roosevelt, Rabat, Morocco.

LALLY Margaret, b. Cleveland, Ohio, USA. Associate Professor of English; Poet. m. Thomas R Lally, 21 October 1961, deceased, 2 sons. Education: BA, English, 1972, MA, English, 1974, PhD, English Literature, 1982, Case Western Reserve University. Appointments: Graduate Assistant and Lecturer, Case Western Reserve University, 1975-83; Lecturer in English, University of Akron, Ohio, 1982-87; Professor, Citadel, Military College of South Carolina, USA, 1987-. Publication: Juliana's Room, 1988; The Virgin and the Gipsy: Rewriting the Pain, in Aging and Gender in Literature: Studies in Creativity (book chapter), 1993. Contributions to: Kenyon Review; Ohio Review; Literary Review; Hudson Review. Honours: Individual Artist's Award, Ohio Arts Council, 1984; Nomination, Los Angeles Times Book Prize, 1989. Membership: Poet's Prize Committee, Poets and Writers; Associated Writing Programs. Address: P O Box 30494, Charleston, SC 29417, USA.

LALOV Ivan, b. 4 October 1938, Lovech, Bulgaria. Professor of Physics. Education: MSc, 1961, PhD, Physics, 1977, DSc, Physics, 1988, Sofia University. Appointments: Assistant Professor, 1961-69, Senior Assistant, 1969-76, Chief Assistant, 1976-80, Associate Professor, 1980-91, Professor, 1991-, Dean, Faculty of Physics, 1991-93, Rector, 1993-99, Sofia University; Minister of Education, Science and Technology, February-May, 1997. Publications: textbook: Electromagnetic Phenomena, 1986, 1993; First Great Unification: Electricity, Magnetism, Optics, 2001; 75 scientific papers on Condensed Matter Physics in international journals. Honours: Great Honour Medal Soca University, Japan, 1995. Memberships: President, Union of Physicists, Bulgaria, 1992-2001; President, Bulgarian-Korean Society, 1995-99; President, Rectors Conference, 1993-98; Vice-President, Bulgarian Tourist Union, 1997-98, President, 1999-2002; President of the Association of Bulgarian Renaissance Towns, 1999-; President, Balkan Physical Union, 2003-. Address: Faculty of Physics, 5 J Bourchier Str, 1164 Sofia, Bulgaria.

LAM Cheuk-Sum, b. 16 July 1961, Hong Kong. Medical Doctor. m. Yuk-Lin Tsui, 3 sons. Education: MBBS (HK), 1985; MRCP (UK), 1989; FHKCP, 1992; FHKAM (Med), 1993; MAIS (City U), 1997; FRCP (Edin), 2001. Appointments: Medical Officer, 1986-91; Senior Medical Officer and Cardiologist, 1991-. Publications: 22 articles in professional scientific journals including: Angioplasty-midCAB combination for the treatment of coronary artery disease, 2000; Prevalence of Strongyloidiasis in potential renal transplant recipients, 2000; Parasitic Infestations in end-stage renal transplant patients in Hong Kong, 2000. Memberships: Hong Kong College of Cardiology; Men's Health Forum; Asian Pacific Society of Atherosclerosis; Hong Kong Medical Informatics Association. Address: Flat B, 4/F, One Robinson Place, 70 Robinson Road, Hong Kong. E-mail: lamcs1@i-cable.com

LAM Heung Young (Tsun Wha), b. 26 January 1936, Shanmei, Guangdong, China. Poet; Writer; Journalist; Publisher. Education: Doctor of Literature, Literature Academy of the World Research Center for Celebrity Culture of USA. Appointments: Editor-in-chief, Hong Kong Literature; Marketing Manager, The Spirit of China magazine; Marketing Manager, Hong Kong & Macau Back to Motherland Books Agency Company Ltd; Director, Grace Publishing Company; Editor, Shenxing Times, Huanan Jingji Journal, Ming Pao Daily News and Comic Daily. Publications: Crisscross magazine; A Colourful World magazine; Collections of poems: Tropical Wind & Rain; Love Song Under the Bauhinia Trees; The Blossom Season of the Bauhinia Trees; The Sound of Waves at Repulse Bay; Selected Poems of Tsun Wha; Collections of prose: The Harbour of Hong Kong Glittering in Spring Flowers & Autumn Moon; Lyric Prose on Hong Kong; A Sketch of Hong Kong; Love of Ocean – Starry Night – Plum Blossom; Create a Happy Life; A Guide to Famous Cities and Scenic Spots in China; Hong Kong Scenic Spots, Antiquities & Historical Anecdotes; The Beautiful Scenery of Hong Kong; The Art of War Advocated by the Hundred Schools of Thought in Ancient China vs Modern Enterprises; The Science Fictional Prophecy in a Classical Novel of Chinese Gods & Heroes vs Modern Technology; Novels: The Romance of Rose; Drifting Duckweed and Wandering Waves. Honours: 10 national and overseas prizes in literary creation. Memberships: Chairman, International Association of Chinese Arts & Culture; Vice Chairman, Hong Kong Prose Poetry Society; Board Member, Hong Kong Poets Association, Hong Kong Literature Development Association, Overseas Chinese Artists Association of United States and International Intelligent Merchant Society; Secretary, Chinese P.E.N. Centre of Hong Kong; Member, Federation of Hong Kong Writers; Hong Kong Writers Association; Shenzhen Writers Association; Reviewer, Hong Kong Arts

Development Council; Editorial Board Member, Contemporary Poetry. Address: PO Box 73464, Kowloon Central Post Office, Kowloon, Hong Kong.

LAMB Allan Joseph, b. 20 June 1954, Langebaanweg, Cape Province, South Africa. Cricketer. m. Lindsay Lamb, 1979, 1 son, 1 daughter. Education: Abbotts College. Appointments: Mid-Order Right-Hand Batsman; Teams: Western Province, 1972-82, 1992-93, OFS, 1987-88, Northamptonshire, 1978-95, Captain 1989-95; Qualified for England 19 82 and played in 79 Tests, 1982-92, 3 as Captain, scoring 4,656 runs, average 36.0, including 14 hundreds; Toured Australia, 1982-83, 1986-87, 1990-91; Scored 32,502 1st Class Runs, 89 hundreds; 1,000 15 times; 122 limited-overs internationals; Director, Lamb Associates Event Management Company, Grenada Sports Ltd; Contributor, Sky Sports Cricket. Publication: Silence of the Lamb, autobiography, 1995. Address: Lamb Associates, First Floor, 4 St Giles Street, Northampton NN1 1JB, England.

LAMB Andrew (Martin), b. 23 September 1942, Oldham, Lancashire, England. Writer on Music. m. Wendy Ann Davies, 1 April 1970, 1 son, 2 daughters. Education: Corpus Christi College, Oxford, 1960-63; MA, Honours, Oxford University. Publications: Jerome Kern in Edwardian London, 1985; Ganzl's Book of the Musical Theatre (with Kurt Ganzl), 1988; Skaters' Waltz: The Story of the Waldteufels, 1995; An Offenbach Family Album, 1997; Shirley House to Trinity School, 1999; 150 Years of Popular Musical Theatre, 2000; Leslie Stuart: Composer of Florodora, 2002. Editor: The Moulin Rouge, 1990; Light Music from Austria, 1992; Leslie Stuart: My Bohemian Life, 2003. Contributions to: The New Grove Dictionary of Music and Musicians; The New Grove Dictionary of American Music; The New Grove Dictionary of Opera; Gramophone; Musical Times; Classic CD; American Music; Music and Letters; Wisden Cricket Monthly; Cricketer; Listener; Notes. Memberships: Fellow, Institute of Actuaries; Lancashire County Cricket Club. Address: 12 Fullers Wood, Croydon CR0 8HZ, England.

LAMB Bernard Charles, b. 8 June 1942, London, England. Geneticist; Lecturer. m. Brenda Strong. Education: BSc, 1st Class Honours in Botany, 1963, PhD in Genetics, 1966, DSc, 2000, Bristol University. Appointments: Gosney Postdoctoral Fellow and Fulbright Travel Scholar, Biology Division, California Institute of Technology, Pasadena, USA, 1966-67; SRC/NATO Postdoctoral Fellow, Genetics Department, University of Leicester, England, 1967-68; Lecturer in Genetics, Botany Department, 1968-84, Senior Lecturer in Genetics, Department of Pure and Applied Biology, 1984-88, Imperial College of Science and Technology; Reader in Genetics, Department of Biological Sciences, Imperial College, London, 1988-. Publications: Many scientific papers in genetics journals; Author and co-author: Judging Wine and Beer, 1990; How to Write About Biology, 1994; English for Technology, 1995; The Opinions and Practices of Teachers of English, A National Survey of Teachers of English to 11-18 Year Olds, 1997; The Applied Genetics of Plants, Animals, Humans and Fungi, 2000. Memberships: The Genetics Society; Fellow, The Genetics Society of America; Fellow, Institute of Biology; Trustee, The Vitiligo Society; Chairman, London Branch, The Queen's English Society; Chairman, Richmond Wine Guild; The National Guild of Wine and Beer Judges; United Kingdom Vineyards Association; External Examiner, Jaffna University, Sri Lanka. Address: Department of Biological Sciences, Sir Alexander Fleming Building, Imperial College London, London SW7 2AZ, England. E-mail: b.lamb@imperial.ac.uk

LAMB Timothy Michael, b. 24 March 1953, Hartford, Cheshire, England. Company Chief Executive. m. Denise Ann Lamb, 1 son, 1 daughter. Education: The Queen's College, Oxford, 1971-74.

Appointment: Chief Executive, England and Wales Cricket Board, 1996-. Memberships: Lord's Taverners; Ashridge Alumni. Address: England and Wales Cricket Board, Lord's Ground, London NW8 8QZ, England.

LAMB Willis Eugene Jr, b. 12 July 1913, Los Angeles, California, USA. Physicist. m. (1) Ursula Schaefer, 1939, deceased 1996, (2) Bruria Kaufman, 1996. Education: University of California; PhD. Appointments: Instructor, 1938, Professor of Physics, 1948-52, Columbia University, New York City; Loeb Lecturer, Harvard University, 1953-54; Professor of Physics, Stanford University, Stanford, California, 1951-56; Wykeham Professor of Physics and Fellow, New College, University of Oxford, England, 1956-62; Henry Ford II Professor of Physics, 1962-72, J Willard Gibbs Professor of Physics, 1972-74, Yale University, USA; Professor of Physics and Optical Sciences, 1974-, Regents Professor, 1990-, University of Arizona, Tucson; Senior Alexander von Humboldt Fellow, 1992-94. Honours: Rumford Premium, American Academy of Arts and Sciences, 1953; Honorary ScD, University of Pennsylvania, 1953; Co-recipient, Nobel Prize in Physics, 1955; Research Corporation Award, 1955; Guggenheim Fellow, 1960; Honorary LHD, Yeshiva University, 1964; Honorary ScD, Gustavus Adolphus College, 1975; Honorary ScD, Columbia University, 1990; Humboldt Fellowship, 1992; Honorary Fellow, Royal Society of Edinburgh. Memberships: National Academy of Sciences. Address: Optical Sciences Center, University of Arizona, Tucson, AZ 85721, USA.

LAMBERT Nigel Robert Woolf, b. 5 August 1949, London, England. Barrister; Queens Counsel. m. Roamie Elisabeth Sado, 1 son, 1 daughter. Education: College of Law, London. Appointments: Called to the Bar, Gray's Inn, 1974; Ad eundem Member of Inner Temple, 1986; Chairman, South Eastern Circuit, Institute of Barristers Clerks Committee; Assistant Recorder, 1992-96; Recorder, 1996-; Queens Counsel, 1999; Chairman, North London Bar Mess, 2001-. Memberships: Life Vice President, Cokethorpe Old Boys Association; North London Bar Mess Committee, 1991-; Criminal Bar Association, Committee, 1993-2000; Member, Bar Council, 1993-2000; Member, South Eastern Circuit, Executive Committee, 2001-; Inner Temple Bar Liaison Committee, 2002-. Address: 2-4 Tudor Street, London EC4Y 0AA, England. Email: nigellambertqc@hotmail.com

LAMBERT Richard Peter, b. 23 September 1944. Journalist. m. Harriet Murray-Browne, 1973, 1 son, 1 daughter. Education: Balliol College, Oxford; BA Oxon. Appointments: Staff, 1966-2001, Lex Column, 1972, Financial Editor, 1978, New York Correspondent, 1982, Deputy Editor, 1983, Editor, 1991-2001, Financial Times; Lecturer and Contributor to The Times, 2001-; External Member, Bank of England Monetary Policy Committee, 2003-. Honours: Hon DLitt, City University, London, 2000; Princess of Wales Ambassador Award, 2001; World Leadership Forum Business Journalist Decade of Excellence Award, 2001. Memberships: Director, London International Financial Futures Exchange; AXA Investment Mans, International Rescue Committee, UK; Chair, Visiting Arts; Governor, Royal Shakespeare Co; UK Chair, Franco-British Colloque; Member, UK-India Round Table; Member, International Advisory Board, British-American Business Inc. Address: Bank of England, Threadneedle Street, London EC2R 8AH, England.

LAMINE LOUM Mamadou, b. Senegal. Politician. Appointments: Formerly Minister of Economics, Finance and Planning, Senegal; Prime Minister of Senegal, 1998-99. Memberships: Parti Socialiste. Address: Office of the Prime Minister, ave Leopold Sedar Senghor, Dakar, Senegal.

LAMONT Norman Stewart Hughson (Baron Lamont of Lerwick in the Shetland Islands), b. 8 May 1942, Lerwick, Shetland, Scotland. Politician; Writer; Businessman. m. Alice Rosemary White, 1971. Education: BA Economics, Fitzwilliam College, Cambridge. Appointments: Personal Assistant to Duncan Sandys MP, 1965; Staff, Conservative Research Department, 1966-68; Merchant Banker, N M Rothschild and Sons, 1968-79; Director, Rothschild Asset Management; Conservative Member of Parliament for Kingston-upon-Thames, 1972-97; Parliamentary Private Secretary to Norman St John Stevas, 1974, Opposition Spokesman on Prices and Consumer Affairs, 1975-76, Opposition Spokesman on Industry, 1976-79, Parliamentary Under-Secretary of State, Department of Energy, 1979-81, Minister of State, Department of Trade and Industry, 1981-85, Minister of State, Department of Defence Procurement, 1985-86, Financial Secretary to Treasury, 1986-89, Chief Secretary to Treasury, 1989-90, Chancellor of the Exchequer, 1990-93; Non-Executive Director, N M Rothschild and Sons Ltd, 1993-95; Chairman, Archipelago Fund, Food Fund and Indonesia Investment Trust, 1995-; Chairman, Conservatives Against a Federal Europe, 1998; Vice-Chairman, International Nuclear Safety Commission; Vice-President, Bruges Group; House of Lords Select Committee on European Union; Director, Balli Group PLC. Publications: Sovereign Britain, 1995; In Office, 1999. Honour: Life Peeerage, 1998; Privy Councillor. Memberships: Chairman, Cambridge University Conservative Association, 1963; President, Cambridge Union, 1966. Address: c/o Balli Group plc, 5 Stanhope Gate, London, W1Y 5LA, England.

LAMPARD Dulcie Irene, b. 30 May 1923, Albany, Western Australia. Writer. Publications: Ride!, 1985, Saddle Up!, 1994. Honours: Australian Christian Bookshop of the Year Awards, 1980, 1984, 1988. Address: 1045 Mayo Road, Wooroloo, Western Australia 6558, Australia.

LAMPI Rauno Andrew, b. 12 August 1929, Gardner, Massachusetts, USA. Food Scientist; Engineer. m. Betty, 3 sons, 1 daughter. Education: BS, 1951, MS, 1955, PhD, 1957, Food Technology, University of Massachusetts. Appointments: Technical Director, New England Apple Products; Manager, Food Technology Section, Central Engineering, FMC Corporation; Research Physical Scientist, US Army Natick R and D Centre; Physical Science Administrator, N Labs; Independent Food Scientist/Engineer. Publications: Over 80, including 5 book chapters: 3 patents. Honours: US Army Exceptional Civilian Service Medal; Institute of Food Technology's Industrial Achievement Award; Institute of Food Technology Riester-Davis Award. Memberships: Institute of Food Technology. Address: 20 Wheeler Road, Westborough, MA 01581, USA.

LAMPITT Dinah, b. 6 March 1937, Essex, England. Author. m. L F Lampitt, 28 November 1959, deceased, 1 son, 1 daughter. Education: Regent Street Polytechnic, London. Publications: Sutton Place Trilogy: Sutton Place, 1983; The Silver Swan, 1984; Fortune's Soldier, 1985; To Sleep No More, 1987; Pour the Dark Wine, 1989; The King's Women, 1992; As Shadows Haunting, 1993; Banishment, 1994; Writing as Deryn Lake: Death in the Dark Walk, 1995; Death at the Beggar's Opera, 1996; Death at the Devil's Tavern, 1997; Death on the Romney Marsh, 1998; Death in the Peerless Pool, 1999; Death at Apothecaries' Hall, 2000; Death in the West Wind, 2001; Death at St James's Palace, 2002; Death in the Valley of Shadows, 2003. Serials: The Moonlit Door; The Gemini Syndrome; The Staircase; The Anklets; The Wardrobe. Contributions to: Numerous short stories to women's magazines. Memberships: Society of Authors; Crime Writers Association. Address: c/o Vanessa Holt Ltd, 59 Crescent Road, Leigh-on-Sea, Essex, SS9 2PF, England.

LANARO Clara Maria Laura Marrama, b. 26 October 1920, Aquila, Italy. Music Teacher. m. David H Lanaro, 2 sons. Education: Private Schools of Music, 1933-37; Liceo Musicale "L D'Annunzio", 1937-42; Degrees: Solfeggio, Theory, Organ, Harmony, Music History, 1936-39; Diploma of Piano, 1942. Appointments: Piano Teacher to Undergraduates, Liceo "L D'Annunzio, 1943; Piano Teacher, San Francisco, USA, 1948-51; Teaching piano free of charge to American children in Tangier, to study American child and family as a possible influence on her new ways in music; Inventor, 1964-71; Patented Teaching Toy comprising Moveable Tangible Music Symbols and teaching elements contained in The Grand Staff XL and the Staff XL, 1971; Copyrighted 2 volumes containing the Moveable Tangible Music Symbols the Grand Staff and more, 1972; Reconfirmed copyrights of 1972 declaring:- Greatly Amplified, 2000; Preparing for presentation of "Time Signature in Super Learning", 2001. Publications: Not yet published: Time Signature in Super Learning; The Grand Staff XL; The Staff XL. Honours: Graduate with the Highest Marks ever given, 1942; Invited to Represent the USA in Seville; Listed in Who's Who publications. Address: 1183 Ayala Drive, Sunnyvale, CA 94086, USA.

LANCE Betty Rita Gomez, b. 28 August 1923, Costa Rica. Professor Emeritus; Writer; Poet. 2 sons. Education: Teaching Diploma, Universidad Nacional, Costa Rica, 1941; BA, Central Missouri State University, Warrensburg, 1944; MA, University of Missouri, Columbia, 1947; PhD, Washington University, St Louis, 1959. Appointment: Professor Emeritus of Romance Languages and Literatures, Kalamazoo College. Publications: La Actitud Picaresca en la Novela Espanola del Siglo XX, 1969; Vivencias, 1981; Bebiendo Luna, 1983; Vendimia del Tiempo, 1984; Hoy Hacen Corro las Ardillas (short story), 1985; Alas en el Alba, 1987; Siete Cuerdas, 1996. Contributions to: Americas; Letras Femeninas; Caprice; and others. Memberships: Poets and Writers of America, USA; Asociacion de Escritores de Costa Rica; Asociacion Prometeo de Poesia, Madrid; Academia IberoAmericana De Poesia, Madrid. Address: 1562 Spruce Drive, Kalamazoo, MI 49008, USA.

LANCHAVA Omar, b. 3 November 1942, Jvarisa, Tqibuli District, Georgia. Historian; Archaeologist. m. Darejan Jmukhadze, 1 son, 1 daughter. Education: Kutaisi State Pedagogical Institute, 1969; Institute of History, Ethnography and Archaeology, Georgian Academy of Sciences, 1972; Candidate, Historical Sciences, 1975; Doctor of Historical Sciences, 1995. Appointments: Head, Department of Archaeology; Vice Rector, Education and Science, Kutaisi State University; Head, Kutaisi Expedition, Archaeological Research Centre; Participated in archaeological excavations, Ancient Colchis, Western Georgia. Archaeopolis Kutaisi, Vani and Rodopolis, 1965-. Publications: Toward the Ancient History of Kutaisi, 1975; Kutaisi from Ancient Times till the 13th Century, 1994; Kutaisi Within the System of the Polis of Egrisi-Lazica, 1995; 70 articles. Honours: Order of Honour, 2003. Memberships: Scientific Council, Archaeological Research Centre of Georgia; Academy of Ecological Sciences; Academy of Education Sciences. Address: Tamar Mepe str 59, Kutaisi 4600, Georgia. E-mail: irpdd@sanetk.net.ge

LANCHBERY John Arthur, b. 15 May 1923, London, England. Conductor; Composer. m. Elaine Fifield, 1951, divorced 1960, 1 daughter. Education: ARAM, FRAM, Royal Academy of Music. Appointments: Served, Royal Armoured Corps, 1943-45; Musical Director, Metropolitan Ballet, 1948-50; Sadler's Wells Theatre Ballet, 1951-57; Conductor, 1957-59, Principal Conductor, 1959-72, Royal Ballet; Musical Director, Australian Ballet, 1972-77; Musical Director, American Ballet Theatre, 1978-80; Composer and Arranger, ballet music, Pleasuredrome, 1949, Eve of St Agnes,

1950, House of Birds, 1955, La Fille Mal Gardée, 1960, The Dream, 1964, Don Quixote, 1966, Giselle, 1968, La Sylphide, 1970, Hoffman, 1972, Merry Widow, 1975, Month in the Country, 1976, Mayerling, 1978, Rosalinda, 1979, Papillon, 1979, La Bayadère, 1980, Peer Gynt, 1981, The Sentimental Bloke, 1985, Le Chat Botté, 1985, A Midsummer Night's Dream, 1985, Hunchback of Notre Dame, 1988, Figaro, 1992, Robinson Crusoe, opéra comique, 1986, Madame Butterfly, 1995, Dracula, 1997, Snow Maiden, 1998, Cleopatra, 2000, Mr Toad, 2000; For films, Tales of Beatrix Potter, 1971, Don Quixote, 1972, The Turning Point, 1977, Nijinsky, 1980, Evil Under the Sun, 1982, Birth of a Nation, 1992, The Iron Horse, 1994. Honours: Bolshoi Theatre Medal, 1961; Carina Ari Medal, Stockholm, 1984; Queen Elizabeth II Coronation Award, Royal Academy of Dancing, 1989. Address: 71 Park Street, St Kilda West, VIC 3182, Australia.

LANDAU Jacob, b. 20 March 1924. University Professor. m. Zipora Marcus, 1 son, 1 daughter. Education: MA, Hebrew University of Jerusalem, 1946; PhD, School of Oriental and African Studies, University of London, 1949; Postdoctoral Studies, Harvard University, 1955-56. Appointments: Lecturer, Professor, Chaired Professor in the politics of the modern Middle East, Hebrew University of Jerusalem, 1956-93; Visiting Professor, US and European universities. Publications: 21 books; Editor, 12 books; 600 papers in professional journals; Several chapters in books; Most recent book: Politics of Language in the Ex-Soviet Muslim States (with B Kellner-Heinkele), 2001. Honours include: Itzhak Ben-Zvi and Itzhak Gruenbaum awards; Special Citation for Life Research in Middle Eastern Studies, Israeli Political Science Association; Medal, Bosphoros University, Istanbul. Memberships: Israel Oriental Society; Israeli Association of Political Science; Middle East Studies Association of North America; Turkish Society of History; Centre International des Etudes Pré-Ottomanes et Ottomanes; European Association of Arabists and Islamists. Address: 6 Beyt Eshel Street, 93227 Jerusalem, Israel.

LANDSBERGIS Vytautas, b. 18 October 1932, Kaunas, Lithuania. Musicologist; Politician. m. Grazina Rucyte, 1 son, 2 daughters. Education: J Gruodis Music School, 1949, Ausra gymnasium, Kaunas, 1950; Lithuanian Music Academy, Vilnius, 1955. Appointments include: Chairman, 1988-90, Honorary Chairman, 1991-, Lithuanian Reform Movement, Sajudis; President of the Supreme Council of the Republic of Lithuania (Head of State), 1990-92; Member of Seimas (Parliament), Republic of Lithuania and Leader of Opposition, 1992-96, member, Lithuanian Delegation to Parliamentary Assembly of Council of Europe and to the Baltic Assembly, 1992-96, 2000-; Chairman, Lithuanian Conservative Party, 1993-2003; President, Seimas (Parliament) Republic of Lithuania, 1996-2000; Candidate, Presidential elections, 1997; Member of the Seimas (Parliament) of the Republic of Lithuania, 2000; Observer to the European Parliament, 2003-04, and MEP, 2004. Publications: Books: (in Lithuanian) The Hope Regained, 1990, 1991; The Case of Freedom, 1992; The Cross-roads, 1995; Autobiography, Years of Decision (in German and Lithuanian), 1997, Lithuania Independent Again (in English), 2000; Numerous others include: Monographs on the artist and composer M K Ciurlionis, 1965, 1971 (in Russian), 1976, 1986, 1992 (in English); Intermezzo (poems), 1991, 2004; Waves Give Me the Road. Pictures of Kačergne (memories of the kid), 2004; Together. The Council of the Baltic States 1990-92 (in English), 1996; Edition of Documents: The Act of 11 March. Facsimiles, 2000; The Heavy Freedom (in Lithuanian) volumes I-III, 2000; The Cousin Mathew. The Book on Stasys Lozoraitis from His Letters and Messages (in Lithuanian), 2002, 2003; Koenigsberg and Lithuania, 2003; Unknown Documents on January 13 (in Lithuanian), 2003, 2004. Honours include: Norwegian People's

Peace Prize, 1991; Fondation de Future (France), 1991; Hermann-Ehlers-Preis, Germany, 1992; Legion of Honour Order 2nd Class, France, 1997; Order of Grand Duke Vytautas, 1st Class, Lithuania, 1998; Vibo Valentia Testimony Prize, Italy, 1998; Royal Norwegian Order of Merit (Grand Cross), 1998; Grand Cross Order of the Republic of Poland, 1999; UNESCO Medal, 1999; Order of Merit (Grand Cross) of the Order of Malta, 1999; Grand Croix de l'Ordre de l'Honneur of Greece, 1999; Truman-Reagan Freedom Award (USA), 1999; Pleiade Ordre de la Frankophonie (France), 2000; Three Stars Order, 2nd Class, Latvia, 2001; Order of the Cross of St Mary's Land, 1st Class, Estonia, 2002; Order of Grand Duke Vytautas with Golden Collar, 2003; Nine Honorary doctorates, including University of Sorbonne. Memberships: Lithuanian Composers Union; European St Sebastian's Order of Knights; Chairman: M K Ciurlionis Society; M K Ciurlionis International Competition. Address: Traidenio 34-15, LT 2004 Vilnius, Lithuania.

LANE Roumelia, b. 31 December 1927, Bradford, West Yorkshire, England. Writer. m. Gavin Green, 1 October 1949, 1 son, 1 daughter. Publications: Numerous books, including: Sea of Zanj; Rose of the Desert; Cafe Mimosa; Harbour of Deceit; Desert Haven; Bamboo Wedding; Night of the Beguine; The Chasm; The Nawindi Flier. Television and film scripts: Stardust; The Chasm; Tender Saboteur; Chantico; Turn of the Tide; Gilligan's Last Gamble; Where Are the Clowns?; Death From the Past. Contributions to: Various journals and magazines. Honour: Listed in several biographical publications. Memberships: Society of Authors of Great Britain; Writers Guild of Great Britain; Writers Guild of America (East and West). Address: Casa Mimosa, Santa Eugenia, Majorca, Beleares, Spain.

LANEVE Cosimo Raffaele, b. 14 January 1940, Taranto, Italy. Professor. m. Emilia Salvatore, 1 son, 1 daughter. Education: Degree in Pedagogy, University of Bari, Italy, 1964. Appointment: Professor of Education, Universita degli Studi di Bari, Italy. Publications: Books: Rhetoric and Education. 1981; Language and Person, 1987; Elements of Didactic, 1998; Cultural Drifts and Pedagogic Criticism, 2001; Didactic Between Theory and Practice, 2003. Honours: Recipient, Peschara, 1997; Abroed, 1996. Membership: Italian Society of Pedagogy. Address: Universita degli Studi di Bari, Piazza Umberto I –1, 70120 Bari, Italy.

LANG Helmut, b. 10 March 1956, Vienna, Austria. Fashion Designer. Career: Established own studio, Vienna, 1977; Opened made-to-measure shop, Vienna, 1979; Developed ready-to-wear collections, 1984-86; Presented Helmut Lang's Women's Wear, 1986, Helmut Lang's Menswear, 1987-, Paris Fashion Week; Started licensed business, 1988; Professor, Masterclass of Fashion, University of Applied Arts, Vienna, 1993-; Helmut Lang Underwear, 1994; Helmut Lang Protective Eyewear, 1995. Honours: Council of American Fashion Designers of the Year Award, 1996. Address: c/o Michele Montagne, 184 rue St Maur, 75010 Paris, france.

LANG Ian (Bruce) (Lang of Monkton, Baron of Merrick and the Rhinns of Kells in Dumfries and Galloway), b. 27 June 1940. Politician. m. Sandra Montgomerie, 1971, 2 daughters. Education: Sidney Sussex College, Cambridge. Appointments: Director, Rose, Thomson, Young and Co (Glasgow) Ltd, 1966-75; Trustee, Savings Bank of Glasgow, 1969-74, West of Scotland Savings Bank, 1974-83; Member, Queen's Bodyguard for Scotland, Royal Company of Archers, 1974-; Director, Hutchison and Craft Ltd, 1975-81, Hutchison and Craft (Underwriting Agents) Ltd, Lloyd's, 1976-81; Director, P MacCallum and Sons Ltd, 1976-81; Director, Glasgow Chamber of Commerce, 1978-81; Conservative Member of Parliament for Galloway, 1979-83, for

Galloway and Upper Nithsdale, 1983-97; Assistant Government Whip, 1981-83; Lord Commissioner of HM Treasury, 1983-86; Parliamentary Under-Secretary of State, Department of Employment, 1986; Parliamentary Under-Secretary, 1986-87; Minister of State, 1987-90, Scottish Office; Secretary of State for Scotland and Lord Keeper of the Great Seal of Scotland, 1990-95; President of Board of Trade, 1995-97; Director, Marsh and McLennan, 1997-, Director, Second Scottish National Trust, 1997-; Director, Lithgows, 1997-; Chairman, Murray Ventures Investment Trust PLC, 1998-; Deputy Lieutenant, Ayrshire and Arran, 1998; Member, House of Lords Select Committee on the Constitution, 2001-. Publication: Blue Remembered Years, 2002. Address: House of Lords, London SW1A 0AA, England.

LANG k d (Kathryn Dawn Lang), b. 2 November 1961, Consort, Alberta, Canada. Singer; Composer; Actress. Career: Played North American clubs with own band, 1982-87; Performed at closing ceremony, Winter Olympics, Calgary, 1988; Headlining US tour, 1992; Royal Albert Hall, 1992; Earth Day benefit concert, Hollywood Bowl, 1993; Sang with Andy Bell, BRIT Awards, 1993; Television includes: Late Night With David Letterman; Wogan; The Arsenio Hall Show; The Tonight Show; Top Of The Pops; Subject, South Bank Show documentary, ITV, 1995; Film appearance, Salmonberries, 1991. Recordings: Albums: A Truly Western Experience, 1984; Angel With A Lariat, 1986; Shadowland, 1988; Absolute Torch and Twang, 1990; Ingénue, 1992; Even Cowgirls Get The Blues (soundtrack), 1993; All You Can Eat, 1995; Drag, 1997; Australian Tour, 1997; Invincible Summer, 2000; Live By Request, 2001; Features on soundtrack to Dick Tracy; Hit singles include: Crying (duet with Roy Orbison); Constant Craving; Mind Of Love; Miss Chatelaine; Just Keep Me Moving; If I Were You. Honours: Canadian CMA Awards: Entertainer Of Year, 1989; Album Of Year, 1990; Grammy Awards: Best Female Country Vocal Performance, 1990; Best Pop Vocal, 1993; Album of the Year, Ingénue, 1993; American Music Award: Favourite New Artist, 1993; Songwriter Of The Year, with Ben Mink, 1993; BRIT Award, Best International Female, 1995.

LANG Wendy Frances, b. 15 February 1938. Cleveland, Ohio. Photographer. Education: BA, Antioch College, Ohio, 1961; MA, Stanford University Graduate School, 1963; Institute des Hautes Etudes de L'Amerique Latine, Paris, 1964-65; Los Angeles City College, 1973-77; Abram Freeman Occupation Center, 1981; California State University, 1981-82. Appointments: Self Employed, Photographer, 1969-; Assistant Administrator, G Ray Hawkins Gallery, 1979; Taught Photography, Los Angeles City College Community Services, 1979-82, Otis School of Design, 1994-96; Coordinator, The Photography Museum, Los Angeles, California, 1980-81; Interpreter, Pasadena City College Hearing Impaired Program, 1981-83; Freelance Photographer, Otis School of Design, 1984-96; Freelance Interpreter, GLAD, Otis School. Publications: Manuscripts Magazine, Article; Wolf Magazine of Letters; Minolta Contact Sheet; Communication Arts; Hispanic-American Report; Worldmark Encyclopedia. Commissions and Creative Works: Group Exhibitions, Soho/Cameraworks, Los Angeles; Friends of Photography, Carmel; Steps Into Space, Los Angeles; San Francisco Camerwork, Herbert Asherman Gallery, Ohio; Butler Institute of American Art, Ohio; 6th St Gallery, Illinois; Canton Institute of Art, Downey Museum of Art, Los Angeles; Status Gallery, Los Angeles; 10eme Recontres Internationales de la Photographie, France; Clarence Kennedy Gallery, MA. Memberships: Society for Photographic Education; Friends of Photography; Center for Creative Photography; Museum of Photography. Address: 1231 Kipling Avenue, Los Angles, CA 90041 1616, USA.

LANGE Jessica, b. 20 April 1949, Cloquet, Minnesota, USA. Actress. m. Paco Grande, 1970, divorced, 1 daughter with Mikhail Baryshnikov; 1 son, 1 daughter with Sam Shepard. Education: University of Minnesota; Mime, Etienne DeCroux, Paris. Appointments: Dancer, Opera Comique, Paris; Model, Wilhelmina Agency, New York. Creative Works: Films include: King Kong, 1976; All That Jazz, 1979; How to Beat the High Cost of Living, 1980; The Postman Always Rings Twice, 1981; Frances, 1982; Tootsie, 1982; Country, 1984; Sweet Dreams, 1985; Crimes of the Heart, 1986; Everybody's All American, 1989; Far North, 1991; Night and the City, 1993; Losing Isaiah, 1994; Rob Roy, 1994; Blue Sky, 1994; A Thousand Acres, 1997; Hush, 1998; Cousin Bette, 1998; Titus, 1999; Play: Long Day's Journey Into Night, 2000; Star Showtime TV Production, Cat On A Hot Tin Roof, 1984. Honours include: Theatre World Award, Golden Globe, 1996. Address: c/o CAA, Ron Meyer, 9830 Wilshire Boulevard, Beverly Hills, CA 90212, USA.

LANGHAM John Michael, b. 12 January 1924, Stroxton, UK. Chartered Engineer. m. Irene Elizabeth Morley, 2 sons, 1 daughter. Education: MA (Cantab), Mechanical Sciences Tripos, Queen's College, Cambridge, England; Administrative Staff College. Appointments: Engineer Officer, Royal Navy, 1944-46; Various Appointments, 1947-67, Executive Director, 1967-80, Stone-Platt Industries, plc; Director, BPB Industries plc, 1976-92; Chairman: Vacu-Lug traction Tyres Ltd, 1973-95; Chairman, Langham Industries, Ltd, 1980-; External Appointments: Member, CBI Council, 1967-79; Chairman, CBI Production Committee, 1970-79; Member, Executive Board, British Standards Institute, 1969-76; Deputy Chairman, Quality Assurance Council, 1971-79; Member, General Council, 1974-82, Member, Management Board, 1979-82, Vice-President, Executive Committee, 1978-82, E.E.F; Principal and Vice Chancellor, University of Dundee, 2000-; Honorary Professor, Warwick Business School, 1996; Honorary Professor, Johns Hopkins University, 2000-. Publications: Presented British Exchange Paper to 21st International Foundry Congress, Italy; Article: The Manufacture of Marine Propellers with Particular Reference to the Foundry. Honours: Commander of the Order of the British Empire (CBE); Diploma, Institute of British Foundrymen, 1954, 1963; British Foundry Medal and Prize, 1955; Award of American Foundrymen's Society, Detroit Congress, 1962, Dorset Business Man of the Year, 1996; Hon FCGI, 2000; Hon Fellow, Royal College of General Practitioners, 2001. Memberships: Fellow, Institution of Mechanical Engineers; Fellow, Institute of Marine Engineers; Fellow, Institute of British Foundrymen, Companion of the Institute of Management. Address: Bingham's Melcombe, Dorchester, Dorset DT2 7PZ, England.

LANGTON Daniel Joseph, b. 6 September 1927, New Jersey, USA. College Professor. m. 1 February 1949, 1 son. Education: St Paul's and Hayes; San Francisco State College; University of California. Appointments: High School Teacher, 1963-67; College Teacher, 1967-. Publications: Querencia; The Hogarth-Selkirk Letters; The Inheritance; Life Forms. Contributions to many periodicals. Honours; London Prize; Browning Award; Devins Award. Memberships: Poetry Society of America; American Academy of Poets. Address: Box 170012, San Francisco, CA 94117, USA.

LANKA Vaclav, b. 25 October 1941, Hredle, near Rakovník, Czech Republic. Teacher. 1 son. Education: Diploma, Faculty of Natural Science, Charles University, Prague, 1974; Diploma Biologist. Appointments: Teacher, to 1994; Vice-Mayor, Town of Rakovník, 1994-98; Currently Teacher. Publications: Co-author, books: Amphibians and Reptiles, 11 editions, 6 languages, 1985; Wolfgang Böhme, 1999; Handbuch der Reptilien und Amphibien Europas, Vol 3/IIA; Monographs: Dice Snake, Natrix tessellata,

1975; Variabilität und Biologie der Würfelnatter, Natrix tessellata LAURENTI, 1976; Several hundred popular articles on nature and ecology; Several hundred specialist and popular lectures. Membership: Entomological Society of the Czech Republic, 1956-; Species Survival Commission, International Union for the Conservation of Nature and Natural Resources. Address: Jilská ul. 1061, 269 01 Rakovník, Czech Republic.

LANSBURY Angela Brigid, b. 16 October 1925, United Kingdom. Actress. m. (2) P Shaw, 1949, 1 son, 1 step-son, 1 daughter. Education: School of Singing and Dramatic Art, London; School of Drama and Radio, New York. Career: with MGM, 1943-50; Freelance, 1951-; Films include: Gas Light, National Velvet, 1944; The Picture of Dorian Gray, 1945; If Winter Comes, The Three Musketeers, 1948; Kind Lady, 1951; Please Murder Me, 1956; The Reluctant Debutante, 1958; Blue Hawaii, 1961; The Greatest Story Ever Told, The Amorous Adventures of Moll Flanders, 1965; Bedknobs and Broomsticks, 1971; Death on the Nile, 1978; The Mirror Crack'd, The Lady Vanishes, 1980; The Pirates of Penzance, 1982; The Company of Wolves, 1983; Voice of Mrs Potts in Beauty and the Beast, 1991; Theatre includes: Broadway debut in Hotel Paradiso, 1957; Mame, New York Winter Garden, 1966-68; Gypsy, 1974; Anna, The King and I, 1978; Sweeny Todd, 1979; TV includes: Madeira! Madeira!, The Ming Llama, Lace, Murder She Wrote, 1984-96; The Shell Seekers, 1989; Miss Arris Goes to Paris, 1992; Mrs Santa Claus, 1996; South by Southwest, 1997; A Story to Die For, 2000. Publication: Positive Moves, co-author and video. Honours include: Academy Award Nomination, Best Supporting Actress, 1944; Nomination, Academy Award, The Manchurian Candidate; Pudding Theatre Woman of the Year, 1968; Antoinette Perry Awards for Mame, 1968; Dear World, 1969; Gypsy, 1975; Sweeney Todd, 1982; Sarah Siddons Awards, 1974, 1980; BAFTA Lifetime Achievement Award, 1992; CBE; National Medal of Arts, 1997; Nomination, 16 Emmy Awards; Winner, 6 Golden Globe Awards, nominated 8 Golden Globe Awards. Address: c/o MCA Universal, 100 Universal City Plaza, Universal City, CA 91608, USA.

LANSING Sherry, b. 31 July 1944, Chicago, Illinois, USA. Business Executive. m. (2) William Friedkin, 1991. Education: BS, Northwestern University, Evanston, Illinois. Appointments: Mathematics Teacher, Public High Schools, Los Angeles, California, 1966-69; Model, TV commercials, Max Factor Co and Alberto-Culver, 1969-70; Appeared in films Loving and Rio Lobo, 1970; Executive Story Editor, Wagner International, 1970-93; Vice-President for Production, Heyday Productions, 1973-75; Executive Story Editor, then Vice-President for Creative Affairs, MGM Studios, 1975-77; Vice-President, then Senior Vice-President for Production, Columbia Pictures, 1977-80; President, 20th Century Fox Productions, 1980-83; Founder, Jaffe-Lansing Productions, Los Angeles, 1982-; Produced films including Racing with the Moon, 1984, Firstborn, 1984; Fatal Attraction, 1987; The Accused, 1989; Black Rain, 1990; School Ties, 1992; Indecent Proposal, 1993; Chairperson, Paramount Pictures, 1992-. Address: Paramount Pictures Corporation, 555 Melrose Avenue, Los Angeles, CA 90038, USA.

LAPHAM Lewis H, b. 8 January 1935, San Francisco, California, USA. Writer. m. 3 children. Education: BA, Yale University, 1956; Cambridge University. Appointments: Reporter, San Francisco Examiner, 1957-59; New York Herald Tribune, 1960-62; Editor, Harper's Magazine, 1976-81, 1983-; Syndicated newspaper columnist, 1981-87; Lecturer in universities including Yale, Stanford, Michigan, Virginia and Oregon; Host, Author, six-part documentary series, America's Century, 1989; Host, Executive Editor, Book Mark, 1989-1991; Appearances on American and British television, National Public Radio and Canadian Public

Radio. Publications: Fortune's Child (essays), 1980; Money and Class in America, 1988; Imperial Masquerade, 1990; The Wish for Kings, 1993; Hotel America: Scenes in the Lobby of the Fin-de-Siècle, 1995; Waiting for the Barbarians, 1997; The Agony of Mammon, 1999; Theater of War, 2002; 30 Satires, 2003; Gag Rule, 2004. Contributions to: Monthly essay for Harper's magazine as "Notebook"; Commentary; National Review; Yale Literary Magazine; Elle; Fortune; Forbes; American Spectator; Vanity Fair; Parade; Channels; Maclean's; London Observer; New York Times; Wall Street Journal. Honour: National Magazine Award for Essays, 1995. Address: c/o Harper's Magazine, 666 Broadway, New York, NY 10012, USA.

LAPIN Boris A, b. 10 August 1921, Kharkov, Ukraine. Pathologist. m. Yakovleva, 1 son, 1 daughter, deceased. Education: Graduate, Moscow Medical Institute, MD, 1949; Candidate of Medical Science, 1953; Doctor of Medical Science, 1960; Professor, 1962. Appointments: Researcher, Laboratory of Pathomorphology, 1952-53; Deputy Director, 1953-57; Director, Institute of Experimental Pathology and Therapy, 1958-92; Director, Institute of Medical Primatology, 1992-; Advisor to the Presidium, Academy of Medical Science, 1992-. Publications: Over 600. Honours: 9 Orders, 17 Medals of World War II and for achievements in national medicine and healthcare; V Timakov Prize, 1984; Premium of the Government of RF, 1997; State Premium of the Russian Federation, 2002. Memberships: Several. Address: Institute of Medical Primatology, Russian Academy of Medical Sciences, 354376 Sochi-Adler, Veseloye 1, Russia.

LAPOLT Eda Marie, b. 11 March 1956, Monticello, New York, USA. Library Clerk; Poet. Education: AAS Degree, Secretarial Science with Word Processing, Orange County Community College, 1983. Publication: Expressions from the Heart, 1998. Contributions to: National Library of Poetry; Poetry in Motion; Poet's Corner; True Romance Magazine. Honours: 6 Editor's Choice Awards, National Library of Poetry. Memberships: National Poet's Association; International Society of Poets. Address: 21 Nelshore Drive, Monticello, NY 12701, USA.

LAPORTE Adrienne Aroxie, b. 29 September 1938, Oceanside, Long Island, New York, USA. Registered Nurse. Education: Diploma, Nursing, St John's Episc Hospital, 1960; BA, Behavioural Sciences, Lesley College, 1986; MA, Counseling, Liberty University, 1994; Registered Nurse, New York, Florida, Massachusetts, Louisiana, Alabama; Certificate, Psychiatric, Mental Health Nurse, American Nurses Credentialing Board. Appointments: Supervisors, Creedmoor State Hospital, Queens Village, New York, 1960-66; Lieutenant Colonel, Nursing Corps, US Army, 1966-87; Supervisor, Psychiatric Unit, University Hospital of Jacksonville, 1977-79; Parkwood Hospital, New Bedford, 1980-84; Taunton State Hospital, 1985-87; Director, Nursing Care Unit, Jacksonville Beach, Florida, 1987-90; Mental Health Resources, Jacksonville, Florida, 1990-92; Bradford Adult and Adolescent, Pelham, Alabama, 1992-93, 1994-95; Program Director, Bowling Green Hospital, Mandeville, Louisiana, 1993; Staff Builders Home Health Agency, New Bedford, Massachusetts, 1996-. Honours: Vietnam decorated Bronze Star, Legion of Merit. Memberships: ACA; VFW; International Nurses Society of Addictions, Florida Nursing Association; American Legion. Address: 47 Little Oak Road, New Bedford, MA 02745-2021, USA.

LAPTEV Vladimir, b. 28 April 1924, Moscow, Russia. Professor of Law. m. Maya Lapteva, 2 sons. Education: Graduate, Law Department, Moscow Institute for Foreign Trade, 1949. Appointments: Chief of Section of Economic Law, Institute of State and Law of Russian Academy of Sciences, Moscow, 1959; Chief,

Centre of Entrepreneurial and Economic Law, 1992; Chief scientific researcher of the Institute, 1997; Head of Chair of Entrepreneurial Law of Academic Law University, Moscow, 1997. Publications: More than 350 scientific books and articles in field of economic and entrepreneurial law. Honour: Professor, Doctor of Law, Honoured Scientist of Russian Federation. Membership: Russian Academy of Sciences. Address: Institute of State and Law, Znamenka 10, Moscow.

LAQUEUR Walter (Ze'ev), b. 26 May 1921, Breslau, Germany. History Educator. m. (1) Barbara Koch, 29 May 1941, deceased, 2 daughters, (2) Susi Wichmann, 1995. Appointments: Journalist, Freelance Author, 1944-55; Editor, Survey, 1955-65; Co-Editor, Journal of Contemporary History, 1966-; Member, Center for Strategic and International Studies, Washington, DC. Publications: Communism and Nationalism in the Middle East, 1956; Young Germany, 1961; Russia and Germany, 1965; The Road to War, 1968; Europe since Hitler, 1970; Out of the Ruins of Europe, 1971; Zionism, a History, 1972; A Reader's Guide to Contemporary History (co-editor), 1972; Confrontation: The Middle East and World Politics, 1974; Weimar: A Cultural History 1918-1933, 1974; Guerrilla, 1976; Terrorism, 1977; Fascism: A Reader's Guide (editor), 1978; The Missing Years, 1980; The Terrible Secret, 1980; Farewell to Europe, 1981; Germany Today: A Personal Report, 1985; World of Secrets: The Uses and Limits of Intelligence, 1986; The Long Road to Freedom: Russia and Glasnost, 1989; Thursday's Child Has Far to Go, 1993; The New Terrorism: Fanaticism and the Arms of Mass Destruction, 1999. Honours: 1st Distinguished Writer's Award, Center for Strategic and International Studies, 1969; Inter Nations Award, 1985. Address: Center for Strategic and International Studies, 1800 K Street North West, Washington, DC 20006, USA.

LARA Brian Charles, b. 2 May 1969, Santa Cruz. Cricketer. Appointments: Started playing cricket aged 6; Played football for Trinidad Under 14; Played cricket for West Indies Under-19; Captain, West Indies Youth XI against India, scoring 186; Left-Hand Batsman; Teams: Trinidad and Tobago, 1987-, Captain 1993-; Warwickshire, 1994, Captain 1988; Making world record 1st class score of 501 not out, including most runs in a day, 390, and most boundaries in an innings, 72, v Durham, Edgbaston, 1994; 90 Tests for West Indies 1990-2002, 18 as Captain, scoring 7,572 runs, average 50.49, including 18 hundreds, highest score 375, world record v England, St John's, Antigua, 1994; Has scored 16,737 1st class runs, 45 hundreds, to 2002, including 2,066 off 2,262 balls for Warwickshire, 1994, with 6 hundreds in his first 7 innings; Toured England, 1991, 1995; 203 One Day Internationals, -2002 for 7,549 runs (average 42.65). Honours: Federation of International Cricketers' Associations International Cricketer of the Year, 1999. Publication: Beating the Field, autobiography, 1995. Address: c/o West Indies Cricket Board, PO Box 616, St John's, Antigua.

LARGE Andrew McLeod Brooks (Sir), b. 7 August 1942, Goudhurst, Kent, England. Banker and Regulatory Official. m. Susan Melville, 1967, 2 sons, 1 daughter. Education: University of Cambridge; Euorpean Institute of Business Administration, Fontainebleau; MA, Economics; MBA. Appointments: British Petroleum, 1964-71; Orion Bank Ltd, 1971-79; With Swiss Bank Corporation, 1980-89, as Managing Director, 1980-83, Chief Executive, Deputy Chairman, 1983-87, Group Chief Executive, 1987-88, SBCI London; Board, Swiss Bank Corporation, 1988-90; Non-Executive Director, English China Clays, 1991-96; Chairman, Large, Smith and Walter, 1990-92; Chairman, Securities and Investments Board, 1992-97; Member, Board on Banking Supervision, 1996-97, Deputy Governor, 2002-, Bank of England; Deputy Chairman, 1997-2002, Director, 1998-2002, Barclays

Bank; Chairman, Euroclear, 1998-2000. Address: Bank of England, Threadneedle Street, London EC2R 8AH, England. Website: www.bankofengland.co.uk

LARROUTUROU Bernard, b. 24 September 1958, Clermont-Ferrand, France. Scientist. m. Marie-Hélène Cancelloni, 6 sons, 2 daughters. Education: PhD in Applied Mathematics, Paris 13 University, 1987. Appointments: Researcher, INRIA, 1983-89; Member, Vice President and President, Evaluation Board, INRIA, 1989-96; Head, CERMICS, 1990-96; President, Applied Mathematics Department, Ecole Polytechnique, 1996-99; Professor, Applied Mathematics, Ecole Polytechnique, 1993-99; President, Board of Directors, Simulog, 1996-98; President, Board of Directors, Inria-Transfert, 1998-; President, CEO, INRIA, 1996-2003; Head, Director of CNRS, 2003-. Publications: Over 100 publications in international reviews, book chapters and communications. Honours: Laplace Prize, French Academy of Sciences, 1980; Prize, Peccot Foundation, College de France, 1989; Blaise Pascal Prize, French Academy of Sciences, 1989; First Cray France Award, 1991; CISI-Ingenierie Award for scientific computing, 1995; Chevalier, Ordre national du merite, 1998; Chevalier, Ordre national de la Legion d'honneur, 2003. Memberships: Scientific Board, Renault, 1995-99; Board of Directors: Simulog, 1996-; Ilog, 1996; Bull and O2 Technology, 1996-97; Realviz, 1999; Thomson SA, 1999, 2000; Trusted-Logic, 1999-; Renault, 2000-; Member, Advisory Board, I-Source Gestion, 1998-. Address: CNRS, 3 rue Michel-Ange, 75794 Paris, Cedex 16, France.

LARSEN Marianne, b. 27 January 1951, Kalundborg, Denmark. Poet. Publications: Several volumes of poems, 1971-; Free Compositions, 1991. Contributions to: Many Danish and foreign magazines. Honours: Adam Oehelagers Prize, 1980; Emil Aarestrup Prize, 1982; Beatrice Prize, 1989; Martin Andersen Nexo Prize, 1990; Egmont Fond Prize, 1991; Henrik Pontopidan Prize, 2003. Membership: Danish Ministry of Cultural Affairs Committee for Rewarding Poets and Writers with State Aid. Address: Worsaesvej 20, 2 tv, 1972 Frederiksbourg C, Denmark.

LARSON Jane Warren, b. 2 June 1922, San Francisco, California, USA. Science Reporter; Ceramist. m. Clarence, deceased, 2 sons. Education: Swarthmore, 1939-41; University of Rochester, 1942-43; BA, cum laude, English, Anna Mahler, 1957-58; Antioch Masters of Fine Arts in Ceramics, 1982; Travel Europe, Egypt, Japan, Indonesia; Courses in Nuclear Calutron and Associated Sciences. Appointments: Science Reporter, Artist, County Schools. Publications: These are our voices; Language in Ceramics; Clay tales from the bedding plane; Chemistry in Art; Stalking the wild tile; It Is Time for Durable Records. Honours: Phi Beta Kappa; Poetry and Short Story Prizes; Award of the Year, Tile Heritage Foundation, 2001; Others. Memberships: Cosmos Club of Washington DC; Eistophos Science Club; Kiln Club; Ceramic Guild. Address: 9707 Old Georgetown Rd, #1420, Bethesda, MD 20814, USA.

LASHKARIPOUR Gholam Reza, b. 10 October 1954, Nehbandan, Iran. Professor. m. Najmeh Rezanezhad-Joulaei, 2 sons, 1 daughter. Education: BSc, Geology, University of Ferdowsi, Iran; MSc, Engineering Geology, Tarbiat Modaress, Iran; PhD, Civil Engineering, University of Newcastle upon Tyne, England. Appointments: Head of Geology Department, Professor of Geology, University of Sistan and Baluchestan, Iran. Publications: 73 papers. Honours: First Position in Research among all Academic Members, University of Sistan and Baluchestan, 2000, 2001, 2002. Memberships: International Association of Engineering Geology; International Society of Rock Mechanics. Address: Department of Geology, University of Sistan and Baluchestan, Zahedan, 98135-655 Iran. E-mail: lashkarg@hamoon.usb.ac.ir

Dictionary of International Biography

LASKA Vera, b. 21 July 1928, Kosice, Czechoslovakia. Professor of History; Lecturer; Columnist; Author. m. Andrew J Laska, 5 November 1949, 2 sons. Education: MA, History, 1946, MA, Philosophy, 1946, Charles University, Prague; PhD, History, University of Chicago, 1959. Appointments: Professor of History, Regis College, Weston, Massachusetts, 1966-; Fulbright Professor, Charles University, Prague, 1993. Publications: Remember the Ladies; Outstanding Women of the American Revolution, 1976; Franklin and Women, 1978; Czechs in America 1633-1977, 1978; Benjamin Franklin the Diplomat, 1982; Women in the Resistance and in the Holocaust, 1983, 2nd edition, 1988; Nazism, Resistance and Holocaust: A Bibliography, 1985; Two Loves of Benjamin Franklin (in Czech), 1994. Contributions to: Over 350 articles and book reviews in newspapers and professional journals. Honours: Kidger Award for Excellence in History, 1984; George Washington Honor Medal in Communication, 1990; Fulbright Professor, Prague, 1992-93. Address: 50 Woodchester Drive, Weston, MA 02493, USA.

LASKOWSKI Leonard Francis Jr, b. 16 November 1919, Milwaukee, USA. Microbiologist. m. Frances Bielinski, 1 June 1946, 3 sons. Education: BS, 1941, MS, 1948, Marquette University; PhD, St Louis University, 1951; Diplomate, American Board of Microbiology. Appointments: Served with MC AUS, 1942-46; Instructor, Bacteriology, Marquette University, 1946-48; Faculty Member, 1951-, Professor of Pathology and Internal Medicine, Division of Infectious Diseases, 1969-90, Professor Emeritus, 1990-, Associate Professor of Internal Medicine, 1977-90, St Louis University School of Medicine; Assistant Deputy Chief, Public Health Laboratory, St Louis Civil Defense, 1958-; Health and Technology Training Co-ordinator for Latin American projects, Peace Corps, 1962-66; Director, Clinical Microbiology Section, St Louis University Hospital Laboratories, 1965-; Consultant, Clinical Microbiology, Firmin Desloge Hospital, St Louis University Group Hospitals, St Mary's Group Hospitals; Consultant, Bacteriology, Veterans Hospitals; Consultant, St Elizabeth Hospital, St Louis County Hospital, St Francis Hospital. Publications: Contributor of articles to professional journals. Memberships: Fellow, American Academy of Microbiology; Member, Society of American Bacteriologists; New York Academy of Sciences; Missouri Public Health Associations; AAUP; Medical Mycology Society of America; Alpha Omega Alpha. Address: 6229 Robertsville Road, Villa Ridge, MO 63089-2617, USA.

LATHAM Cecil Thomas, b. 11 March 1924, Gravesend, Kent, England. Retired. m. Ivy Frances, 1 son, 1 daughter. Appointments: War Service, Royal Navy, 1942-45; Assistant Clerk, Maidstone, 1945, Leicester, 1948-54, Bromley, 1954-63; Deputy Clerk to the Liverpool Justices, 1963-65; Clerk to the Manchester City Justices, 1965-76; Stipendiary Magistrate, now called Circuit Judge, for Greater Manchester, 1976-94. Publications: Various articles in legal journals; 2 booklets; Editor: Stone Justices Manual 101st-109th edition; Family Law Reports, 1980-1986; Family Court Reporter, 1987-1999. Honours: OBE, 1976; Honorary MA, Manchester University, 1984. Memberships: Law Society; Magistrates' Courts' Rule Committee; Criminal Law Revision Committee; Royal Commission on Criminal Procedure, 1978-81. Address: 12 Oakside Nay, Oakwood, Derby DE21 2UH, England.

LATIS Cecilia Popescu. Teacher; Translator; Literary and Art Critic. Education: Exam, Faculty of Philology, 1971, First Grade, 1983-85, Doctor of Humanist Sciences, 1999, University "Al I Cuza", Iasi, Romania; Certificat d'Études Européennes, University of Bucharest and le Centre Européen de Culture, le Collège d'Europe, Brüges, Belgium, 1991; Diplomat of Courses for Pedagogy "Waldorf", Sibiu, Brasov, Cluj-Napoca, Suceava, 1991-96; Courses d'Initiate for Computer, 2000, 2003-04. Appointments:

French and Romanian Teacher, High School "Spiru Haret"; Consultant Teacher, Study of Learning Methods and Curriculum Studies, Teachers and Curriculum Studies, Teachers Training College; Methodic Professor, French Language Group, ISJ; Translator; Literary Critic; Art Critic. Publication: Polifonii creatorare; Thesis: Architectures parallèles: Marguerite Yourcenar – Vintila Horia & L'Attitude antiguerrière dans la littérature française entre 1870-1920; Many studies in the national and international press, 1985-. Honours: National Prize 'Mioritza', Journal of Targoviste, 1993; Gradation of Merit, 1998; Gradation of Merit, 2002; National Prize 'Mihail Eminescu of Oravitza', 2001; Honorary Member, Club 'Mihail Eminescu', Timisoara, 2001; Woman of the Year, ABI, 2003. Memberships: UNICEF, 1992; Société Internationale d'Études Yourcenariennes, 1996; International Biographical Centre, Cambridge, 2004. Address: Boulevard George Enescu nr 15, Bl T33 Sc B Et 3 Ap 11, Suceava 720246 PO Box 7, Romania. E-mail: cecilia_latis@yahoo.fr

LATYSHEV Pyotr Mikhailovich, b. 30 August 1948, Khmelnitsky, Ukraine. Politician; Security Officer. m. 2 sons. Education: Omsk Higher School of Ministry of Internal Affairs, Academy of Ministry of Internal Affairs. Appointments: Inspector, the Head, Perm Division for the Fight against Economic Crime, 1970-86; Head, Department of Internal Affairs, Perm oblast, 1986-91; People's Deputy of the Russian Federation, 1990-93; Member of the Committee of Supreme Soviet on Law and the Fight against Crime, 1993; Head, Department of Internal Affairs Krasnador Territory, 1991-94; Deputy Minister of Internal Affairs Russian Federation, 1994-2000; Plenipotentiary Representative of the President of the Russian Federation in the Urals Federal District, 2000-. Honours: State Orders. Address: Office of the Plenipotentiary Representative of the President of the Russian Federation in the Urals Federal District, Oktyabrskaya pl 3, 620031 Yekaterinburg, Russia. Website: www.uralfo.ru

LAUDA Andreas-Nikolaus, b. 22 February 1949, Vienna. Racing Driver. m. Marlene Knaus, 1976, 2 sons. Appointments: Competed in hill climbs, 1968, later in Formula 3, Formula 2, Sports Car Racing; Winner, 1972 John Player Brit Formula 2 Championship; Started Formula 1 racing in 1971; World Champion, 1975, 1977, 1984, runner-up, 1976; Founder, Owner, Own Airline, Austria. Creative Works: Grand Prix Wins: 1974 Spanish, Ferrari, 1974 Dutch, Ferrari, 1975 Monaco, Ferrari, 1975 Belgian, Ferrari, 1975 Swedish, Ferrari, 1975 French, Ferrari, 1975 US, Ferrari, 1976 Brazillian, Ferrari, 1976 South African, Ferrari, 1976 Belgian, Ferrari, 1976 British, Ferrari, 1977 South African, Ferrari, 1977 German, Ferrari, 1977 Dutch, Ferrari, 1978 Swedish, Brabham-Alfa Romeo, 1978 Italian, Brabham-Alfa Romeo; Retired, 1979; Returned to racing, 1981; Won US Formula 1 Grand Prix, British Grand Prix, 1982, Dutch Grand Prix, 1985; Retired, 1985; Chair, Lauda Air, -2000; CEO Ford's Premier Performance Division, 2001-02; Head, Jaguar Racing Team, 2001-02. Honours include: Victoria Sporting Club International Award for Valour, 1977. Address: Sta Eulalia, Ibiza, Spain.

LAUDER Leonard Alan, b. 19 March 1933, New York City, New York, USA. Business Executive. m. Evelyn Hausner, 1959, 2 sons. Education: Wharton School, University of Pennsylvania. Appointments: Joined, 1958, Executive Vice-President, 1962-72, President, 1972-, Chief Executive Officer, 1982-, now also Chairman, Estee Lauder Inc, cosmetics and fragrance company, New York; Trustee, University of Pennsylvania, 1977-; President, Whitney Museum of American Art, 1977-; Trustee, Aspen Institute for Humanistic Studies, 1978-; Governor, Joseph H Lauder Institute of Management and International Studies, 1983-. Address: Estee Lauder Inc, 767 Fifth Avenue, New York, NY 10153, USA.

Dictionary of International Biography

LAUGHTON Anthony Seymour (Sir), b. 29 April 1927. Oceanographic Scientist. m. (1) Juliet A Chapman, 1957, dissolved 1962, 1 son, (2) Barbara C Bosanquet, 1973, 2 daughters. Education: King's College, Cambridge; John Murray Student, Columbia University, New York, 1954-55; PhD. Appointments: Served Royal Naval Volunteer Reserve, 1945-48; Oceanographer, 1955-88, later Director, National Institute of Oceanography, later Institute of Oceanographic Sciences; Member, 1974-, Chairman, 1986-, Joint IOC-IHO Guiding Committee, GEBCO, ocean charts; Member, 1981-, Chairman, 1995-, Governing Body, Charterhouse School; Council, University College, London, 1983-93; Co-ordinating Committee for Marine Science and Technology, 1987-91; Trustee, Natural History Museum, 1990-95. Publications: Papers on marine geophysics. Honours: Silver Medal, Royal Society of Arts, 1958; Prince Albert the 1st of Monaco Gold Medal, 1980; Founders Medal, Royal Geographical Society, 1987; Murchison, Geological Society, 1989. Memberships: Fellow, Royal Society; President, Challenger Society for Marine Science, 1988-80; President, Society for Underwater Technology, 1995-97; President, Hydrographic Society, 1997-99. Address: Okelands, Pickhurst Road, Chiddingfold, Surrey GU8 4TS, England.

LAURELL Göran Frans Emanuel, b. 19 January 1954, Stockholm, Sweden. Medical Doctor; Otolaryngologist. m. Birgitta, 1 son, 1 daughter. Education: MD, 1983, PhD, 1991, Karolinska Institute. Appointments: Associate Professor, Karolinska Institute, 1996; Consultant, Department of Otolaryngology, Karolinska Hospital, 1997. Memberships: Swedish Medical Association; Association of Research in Otolaryngology, USA. Address: Department of Otolaryngology and Head and Neck Surgery, Karolinska Hospital, SE-17176 Stockholm, Sweden. E-mail: goran.laurell@ks.se

LAUREN Ralph, b. 14 October 1939, Bronx, New York, USA. Couturier. m. Ricky L Beer, 1964, 3 sons. Appointments: Salesman, Bloomingdale's, New York, Brooks Brothers, New York; Assistant Buyer, Allied Stores, New York; Representative, Rivetz Necktie Manufacturers, New York; Neckwear Designer, Polo Division, Beau Brummel, New York, 1967-69; Founder, Polo Menswear Company, New York, 1968-, Ralph Lauren's Women's Wear, New York, 1971-, Polo Leathergoods, 1978-, Polo Ralph Lauren Luggage, 1982-, Ralph Lauren Home Collection, 1983-; Chair, Polo Ralph Lauren Corporation, 66 stores in USA, over 140 worldwide. Honours: Several fashion awards, including: American Fashion Award, 1975; Council of Fashion Designers of America Award, 1981. Address: Polo Ralph Lauren Corporation, 650 Madison Avenue, New York, NY 10022, USA.

LAURENT Pierre-Henri, b. 15 May 1933, Fall River, Massachusetts, USA. Historian; Educator. m. Virginia Brayton, 2 sons, 2 daughters. Education: AB, Colgate University, 1956; AM, 1960, PhD, 1964, Boston University. Appointments: Instructor, Boston University, 1961-64; Assistant Professor, Sweet Briar College, 1964-66; Visiting Professor, University of Wisconsin at Madison, 1966-67; Associate Professor, Tulane University, 1967-70; Associate Professor, 1970-75, Professor, 1975-2003, Professor Emeritus, 2003-, Tufts University. Publications: Co-editor, State of European Union, 1998; NATO and the European Union, 1999. Honours: Belgian-American Educational Foundation Fellow, 1962; NATO Research Fellow, 1967; National Endowment for Humanities Fellow, 1969; Paul-Henri Spaak Foundation Fellow, 1976-77; Fulbright/EC Research Scholar, 1992-93; Fulbright Chair in US/EU Relations, College of Europe, 1998. Memberships: American Historical Association; American Association of University Professors; European Union Studies Association. Address: East Hall, Department of History, Tufts University, Medford, MA 02155, USA.

LAURENTS Arthur, b. 14 July 1917, New York, New York, USA. Dramatist; Writer; Director. Education: BA, Cornell University, 1937. Publications: Plays: Home of the Brave, 1946; The Bird Cage, 1950; The Time of the Cuckoo, 1952; A Clearing in the Woods, 1956; Invitation to a March, 1960; The Enclave, 1973; Scream, Houston, 1978; The Hunting Season, 1995; The Radical Mystique, 1995; Jolson Sings Again, 1995; My Good Name, 1997; Big Potato, 2000; Venecia, 2001; Claude Lazlo, 2001. Musical Plays: West Side Story, 1957; Gypsy, 1959; Anyone Can Whistle, 1964; Do I Hear a Waltz?, 1964; Hallelujah Baby, 1967; Nick and Nora, 1991; Memoir, Original Story By, 2000. Screenplays: The Snake Pit, 1948; Rope, 1948; Caught, 1948; Anna Lucasta, 1949; Anastasia, 1956; Bonjour Tristesse, 1958; The Way We Were, 1973; The Turning Point, 1977. Novels: The Way We Were, 1972; The Turning Point, 1977. Honours: Tony Awards, 1967, 1984; Drama Desk Awards, 1974, 1978; Golden Glove Award, 1977; Writers Guild of America, 1977; Best Director Award, 1985. Memberships: Academy of Motion Picture Arts and Sciences; Authors League; Dramatists Guild; PEN; Screenwriters Guild; Theatre Hall of Fame. Address: c/o William Morris Agency, 1325 Avenue of the Americas, New York, NY 10019, USA.

LAURIE Hugh, b. 11 June 1959, Oxford, England. Actor; Comedian. m. Jo, 2 sons, 1 daughter. Education: Cambridge University. Appointments: President, Footlights, Cambridge University; TV Appearances include: with Stephen Fry, A bit of Fry and Laurie, 1989-91; Jeeves and Wooster, 1990-92; Film Appearances include: Peter's Friends; Cousin Bette, 1998; Maybe Baby, 2000; Stuart Little, 2000. Publications: Fry and Laurie 4, (with Stephen Fry), 1994; The Gun Seller, 1996. Address: Hamilton Asper Ltd, Ground Floor, 24 Hanway Street, London W1P 9DD, England.

LAURITSEN René, b. 15 August 1973, Aarhus, Denmark. Board Member; Director. Education: BEcon; IT administrator education. Appointments: Founder, ScanRen, Copenhagen, Denmark, 1996-97; Founder, BestSellerPublishing, 1997; Founder, Chief of Product Development, PharmaTech, 1998-2000; Product development and programming, Investorsuniverse, 2000-01; Founder, Real Estate Company, 2002-. Publications: 3 books. Honour: Ordained reverend, 2002. Address: Wilstersgade 33A, Isal-8000, Aarhus, Denmark.

LAVATELLI Carla, b. 21 August 1928, American born in Rome, Italy. Sculptor; Weaver; Carver. Career: Invited to work at Officina Cidonio with Moore Arp and Noguchi, Pietrasanta, 1966; Carves in alabaster, wood and stone; Patented (by son, Carlo Lavatelli) a sun-controlled plaza, the fountain with a permanent shadow; Invented Sculpture to wear in 1967, purchased by Benjamin Gallery and shown at the Albright Knox Museum, Buffalo, New York; Figurative Artist until 1966, makes portrait heads, the last one of Princess Grace of Monaco with her 3 children and of Mr and Mrs Spingold for the lobby of the Spingold Theater, Brandeis University; Works as independent artist with self funding and studio in Soho, New York for 35 years also Via Margutta, Rome and the Working Place, Sculpture Garden Museum, Tuscany. Creative Works include: Installations: Picasso Museum of Photography, France; Einstein Institute of Advanced Studies, Princeton; Tapestry, Annenberg Theater, Palm Desert Museum, Palm Springs, California; Renoir Museum, 1995; Several installations, "For Peace", The Window of Hope Tapestry for the 20th Anniversary of Pope John Paul II, Vatican City, 1998; Numerous public collections including: College of William and Mary, Williamsburg; Palm Desert Museum Tapestry; Museum of Modern Art, San Francisco; Centennial of Cathedral of St John the Divine, New York City, Grace Cathedral, San Francisco, 1998; Recent projects pending approval: La Fontaine de la Vie, Bordeaux, 2002; Matisse

Museum, Place Furstenberg, Paris, 2003; Commissions: Carla Lavatelli Plaza: Place du Banc des Amis, Mougins, France; Born From Water, Grace Cathedral, San Francisco; Lavatelli Golden Pond, Botanical Gardens, Freiburg, Germany; Prince Rainier's Palace, Monaco; Shah of Iran's Palace and Museum of Modern Art; Spingold Theater, Brandeis University; Stanford University, Stanford, California; Sculpture dedicated by President Ford, invited to visit the White House; The Sciences Plaza, Brown University, Providence, Rhode Island; John Upjohn Pharmaceuticals, Kalamazoo, Michigan; United Nations 50th Anniversary; President of Italy, Giovanni Leone; National Museum, Pinacoteca Di Stato, Rome, Italy; Horace Kadoree, Hong Kong; Sandoz pharmaceuticals, New Jersey; New Enterprise Associates, San Francisco; Mimi and Bernard Landau Collection, Geneva, Switzerland; A Ferrari with the Soul, painted right wing of Ferrari Formula One, 2001; One Woman Exhibitions include: Hakone Open Air Museum, Japan; Phillips Collection, Washington DC; Iolas, New York City; Palm Beach Gallery, Florida; Gimpel, New York City; Gallery Motte, Paris and Geneva; Gallery Carpine, Rome, Italy; Benjamin Gallery, Chicago; Sari Heller, Beverley Hills, California; Pecci Museum, Prato, Italy. Publications: Subject of numerous collected works; The Plaza of Carla Lavatelli in Mougins, Place du Banc des Amis; Book of Days, 1995; The Work of Carla Lavatelli, by Carla Lavatelli (1970-84), purchased by Museums and Galleries throughout the world including the Metropolitan, Museum of Modern Art, New York, The Tate Museum, London and The Pompidou in Paris; Living Art, Art Vivant, Arte Viva, 2001; My Alabaster World, 2002; Recent projects, 2003; Forthcoming; The Power of Hope, 50 years of letter: Good, Bad, Useless; My Family, a biography. Honours: La Quinzane du Livre d'Art, Centre Georges Pompidou, Paris, 1985; Gold Medal for Outstanding Contribution to the Life of the City, City of Mougins, France, 1995. Address: The Working Place, Sculpture Garden, CP114-55041 Camaiore (Lucca), Italy. E-mail: carla@lavatelli.org Website: www.lavatelli.org

LAVENDER Justin, b. 4 June 1951, Bedford, England. Opera Singer. m. Louise Crane, 1 son, 1 daughter. Education: Queen Mary College, University of London; Guildhall School of Music and Drama. Career: Operatic Tenor; Leading roles with most of the world's major opera houses, 1980-; Concert engagements with major orchestras and conductors worldwide; Numerous recordings, most recently Pierre Bezuhov in Prokofiev's War and Peace. Publications: Regular contributions to The Irish Examiner, original articles and book reviews, 1996-; Contributions to various professional journals. Membership: Newlands Rowing Club. Address: c/o Athole Still International Management Ltd, 25-27 Westow Street, London SE19 3RY, England.

LAVER Rod(ney) George, b. 9 August 1938, Rockhampton, Queensland, Australia. Tennis Player. m. Mary Benson, 1966, 1 son. Education: Rockhampton High School. Career: Played Davis Cup for Australia, 1958, 1959, 1960, 1961, 1962, and first open Davis Cup, 1973; Australian Champion, 1960, 1962, 1969; Wimbledon Champion, 1961, 1962, 1968, 1969; USA Champion, 1962, 1969; French Champion, 1962, 1969; First player to win double Grand Slam, 1962, 1969; Professional from 1963; First Player to win over 1,000,000 US $ in prize money. Publications: How to Play Winning Tennis, 1964; Education of a Tennis Player, 1971. Honours: Member, Order of the British Empire; Melbourne Park centre court renamed Rod Laver Arena in his honour, 2000. Address: c/o Tennis Australia, Private Bag 6060, Richmond South, VIC 3121, Australia.

LAVIELLE Lisette, b. 14 April 1941, Mulhouse, France. Researcher. m. Jean-Pierre Lavielle, 2 daughters. Education: Graduate, Chemical Engineering, École Nationale Supérieure de Chimie, Mulhouse, 1964; Doctor of Engineering, University of Strasbourg, France, 1968; DSc, University of Haute-Alsace, Mulhouse, 1971. Appointments: Research Associate, Thin Films Laboratory, CNRS, École Nationale Supérieure de Chimie, Mulhouse, 1964-70; Research Associate, Mineral Chemistry Laboratory, CNRS, Mulhouse, 1971-76; Engineer, European Society of Propulsion, Vernon, 1978-79; Research Associate, Macromolecular Chemistry Laboratory, CNRS, Rouen, 1980-81; Research Associate, Centre for Physical Chemistry Solid Surfaces, CNRS, Mulhouse, 1981-94; Research Associate, General Photochemistry Laboratory, CNRS, 1995-2001. Publications: Polymer Surface Dynamics, chapter, 1987; Polymer Characterisation by Inverse Gas Chromotography, chapter, 1989; UV Phototreatment of Polymer Film Surface: Self-Organization and Thermodynamics of Irreversible Processes, chapter, 1999. Honour: Recipient, Emilio Noelting Prize, École Nationale Supérieure de Chimie de Mulhouse, 1964. Memberships: French Society of Chemistry; French Society of Physics. Address: 6 rue la Fayette, 68100 Mulhouse, France.

LAVRIK Alexandr S, b. 5 April 1954, Pjatigorsk, Russia. Geologist; Geophysicist. m. Elena V Lavrik, 2 sons. Education: Graduated, Moscow State University, Geological Faculty, 1980. Appointments: Engineer, team for specialized processing, Central Geophysical Expedition, 1980-86, Chief Geophysicist, Contract for Geological-Geophysical Studies in India, 1986-89, Senior Engineer, Chief Engineer, Group for Specialised Processing, 1989-95, Chief Geologist, 1995-, Central Geophysical Expedition. Publications: 24 scientific publications and 2 patents pertaining to development of processing procedures and integrated interpretation techniques. Memberships: SEG; EAGO; EAGE; SPWLA. Address: Central Geophysical Expedition, Bldg 3, 38 Navodnogo Opolcheniya Str, Moscow, 12398 Russia. E-mail: lavrik@cge.ru

LAW Chun-Kong, b. 24 June 1959, Hong Kong. Professor. m. Shuk-kwan Susan Leung, 2 sons. Education: BSc, MPhil, The Chinese University of Hong Kong, Hong Kong; PhD, University of Pittsburgh, USA. Appointments: Associate Professor, 1992-98, Professor, 1998-, Chairman, 2000-2003, Department of Applied Mathematics, National Sun Yat-sen University. Publications: Articles in professional journals as co-author include: Archive for Rational Mechanics and Analysis, 1998; Inverse Problems, 1998, 1999, 2001; Transactions AMS, 2002. Honours: Andrew Mellon Predoctoral Fellowship, University of Pittsburgh, 1990-92; Research Grant Award for Young Investigators, National Science Council, Taiwan, 1997-98; Research Award, National Science Council, Taiwan, 1994-2000. Memberships: Mathematics Society, Taiwan; American Mathematics Society. Address: Department of Applied Mathematics, National Sun Yat-sen University, Kaohsiung, Taiwan 804, ROC.

LAW Jude, b. 29 December 1972, London, England. Actor. m. Sadie Frost, 1997, divorced 2003, 2 sons, 1 daughter. Appointments: National Youth Music Theatre; Co-founder Natural Nylon (production company); Stage appearances include: Joseph and the Amazing Technicolour Dreamcoat; Les Parents Terribles; Film appearances include: Shopping; Wilde; Gattaca; Midnight in the Garden of Good and Evil; Bent; Music From Another Room; The Wisdom of Crocodiles; eXistenZ; The Talented Mr Ripley; Final Cut; Enemy at the Gates; Artificial Intelligence: AI; Road to Perdition; Cold Mountain. Address: c/o Julian Belfrage Associates, 46 Albemarle Street, London, W1S 4DF, England.

LAWRENCE Jerome, b. 14 July 1915, Cleveland, Ohio, USA. Playwright; Lyricist; Biographer. Education: BA, Ohio State University, 1937; Graduate Studies, University of California at Los Angeles, 1939-40. Appointments: Partner, 1942-, President,

1955, Lawrence and Lee Inc, New York City and Los Angeles; Professor of Playwriting, University of Southern California, New York University, Baylor University, Ohio State University. Publications: Look, Ma, I'm Dancin' (co-author), musical, 1948; Inherit the Wind (with Robert E Lee), 1955; Auntie Mame (with Lee), 1957; The Gang's All Here (with Lee), 1960; Only in America (with Lee), 1960; Checkmate (with Lee), 1961; Mame (co-author), musical, 1967; Dear World, musical, 1969; Sparks Fly Upward (co-author), 1969; The Night Thoreau Spent in Jail (with Lee), 1970; Live Spelled Backwards, 1970; The Incomparable Max (with Lee), 1972; The Crocodile Smile (with Lee), 1972; Actor: The Life and Times of Paul Muni, 1974; Jabberwock (with Lee), 1974; First Monday in October (with Lee), 1975; Whisper in the Mind (with Lee and Norman Cousins), 1987. Memberships: Dramatists Guild; Authors League. Address: 21056 Las Flores Mesa Drive, Malibu, CA 90265, USA.

LAWRENCE Karen Ann, b. 5 February 1951, Windsor, Ontario, Canada. Writer. m. Robert Gabhart, 18 December 1982, 1 son. Education: BA, Honours, University of Windsor, 1973; MA, University of Alberta, 1977. Publications: Nekuia: The Inanna Poems, 1980; The Life of Helen Alone, 1986; Springs of Living Water, 1990. Honours: W H Smith/Books in Canada First Novel Award, 1987; Best First Novel Award, PEN, Los Angeles Center, 1987. Memberships: Writers' Union of Canada; Association of Canadian Radio and Television Artists. Address: 2153 Pine Street, San Diego, CA 92103, USA.

LAWRENCE Margaret Elizabeth, b. Richmond, Victoria, Australia. Retired Writer; Television and Radio Producer. Widow. Education: Intermediate Certificate, Swinburne Technical College. Appointments: Manager, TV and Radio Producer for an advertising agency, 20 years; Founder and Editor of 2 Yachting Magazines; Victorian Correspondent for Modern Boating; Sculptor; Painter; News Reporter and Broadcaster for regional ABC Radio/TV; Volunteer Broadcaster, Community Radio Stations 101.3 and 101.5; Founding Chairman, Noosa Federation of the Arts Incorporated, 1989; President, Friends of the Queensland Conservatorium of Music, 4 years; First Australian female reporter into Japan after the Second World War to film and record documentaries and interviews for Australian radio and television, working with Japanese film and recording crews; Crewmember on "Gretel", skippered by Jock Sturrock when she broke the Melbourne-Devonport race record by 2hrs 58mins. Publications: Founder and Editor of 2 yachting magazines: Royal Brighton Yacht Club, Starboard and Ocean Racing Club of Victoria, Blue Water; Victorian Correspondent for Modern Boating; Articles in Advertising Age, Short History of Strauss, plus many editorials on the arts. Honours: Silver Medal, New York TV and Film Industry Award; Bronze Medal, Chicago TV and Film Industry Award; Gold Logie (grand prix), Australian Film and TV Awards; Cultural Award, Noosa Shire; 2003 Citizen of the Year Award, Noosa Shire. Memberships: Noosa Federation of the Arts Inc; Community Auditorium Working Group, Noosa Council; Executive Member, Noosa Sister Cities and Friendship Links Association; Sunshine Beach Surf Life Saving Club; Life Member, Noosa Yacht and Rowing Club; Noosa Heads Bowls Club; Community Radio 101.3, Noosa; Community Radio 101.5, Caboolture. Address: 3/3 Pilchers Gap, Sunshine Beach, Qld 4567, Australia. E-mail: meglaw@sun.big.net.au

LAWSON Charles Nicholas, b. 4 May 1940, Crawley, Sussex, England. Publisher. m. Marion Victoria Lawrence, 1 son, 1 daughter. Education: Wellington College, Berkshire, England, 1967-71; Surrey County Technical College, 1971-73, Cambridge College of Arts and Technology, 1973-74. Appointments: Production Director, Hawthorne Press Ltd, 1982-88; Chief

Executive, Snipe Publishing, 1988-; Director, Eddison Press Ltd, 1986-; Director, Academy of Children's Writers Ltd, 1986-. Memberships: International Platform Association; Cambridge Business and Professional Club; University of Cambridge Club; National Trust. Address: The Poplars, 90 Aldreth Road, Haddenham, Ely, Cambridgeshire CB6 3PN, England.

LAWSON David Douglas Alexander, b. 20 June 1965, London, England. Writer; Poet. Education: Trinity College, Glenalmond, Scotland, 1979-83; Trinity College, Cambridge, 1984-87; Trinity College, Oxford, 1987-90. Contributions to: Haiku Hundred. Honour: Powell Prize. Memberships: Cambridge/Oxford; School of Poets, Edinburgh. Address: Pittarrow, Perth Road, Abernethy, Tayside PH2 9LW, Scotland.

LAWSON Dominic Ralph Campbell (Hon), b. 17 December 1956, London, England. Journalist; Editor. m. (1) Jane Fiona Wastell Whytenead, 1982, divorced 1991, (2) Hon Rosamond Monckton, 1991, 2 daughters. Education: Christchurch, Oxford; BA Oxon. Appointments: World Tonight and The Financial World Tonight, BBC, 1979-81; Staff, Energy Correspondent, Lex Columnist, 1987-90, Columnist, 1991-94 The Financial Times; Deputy Editor, 1987-90, Editor, 1990-95, The Spectator; Editor, The Spectator Cartoon Book; Columnist, Sunday Correspondent, 1990; Columnist, Daily Telegraph, 1994-95; Editor, The Sunday Telegraph, 1995-. Publications: Korchnoi, Kasparov, 1983; Britain in the Eighties, co-author, 1989; The Spectator Annual, editor, 1992, 1993, 1994; The Inner Game, editor, 1993. Honours: Editor of the Year, Society of Magazine Editors, 1990. Memberships: Fellow, Royal Society of Arts. Address: The Sunday Telegraph, 1 Canada Square, Canary Wharf, London E14 5AR, England.

LAWSON Lesley (Twiggy), b. 19 September 1949, London. England. Model; Singer; Actress. m. (1) Michael Whitney Armstrong, 1977, deceased, 1983, 1 daughter, (2) Leigh Lawson, 1988. Career: Model, 1966-70; Manager, Director, Twiggy Enterprises Ltd, 1966-; Own musical series, British TV, 1975-76; Founder, Twiggy and Co, 1998-; Made several LP records; Appearances in numerous TV dramas, UK and USA; Appeared in films including The Boy Friend, 1971, There Goes the Bride, 1979, Blues Brothers, 1981, The Doctor and the Devils, 1986, Club Paradise, 1986, Harem Hotel, Istanbul, 1988, Young Charlie Chaplin, TV film, 1989, Madame Sousatzka, 1989, Woundings, 1998; Appeared in plays: Cinderella, 1976; Captain Beaky, 1982; My One and Only, 1983-84; Blithe Spirit, Chichester, 1997; Noel and Gertie, USA, 1998; If Love Were All, New York, 1999; Blithe Spirit, New York, 2002; Play What I Wrote, 2002; Mrs Warren's Profession, 2003. Publications: Twiggy: An Autobiography, 1975; An Open Look, 1985; Twiggy in Black and White, co-author, 1997. Honours: 2 Golden Globe Awards, 1970. Address: c/o Peters Fraser and Dunlop, Drury House, 34-43 Russell Street, London WC2B 5HA, England. E-mail: postmaster@pfd.co.uk

LAWSON Nigel (Lawson of Blaby, Baron of Newnham in the County of Northamptonshire), b. 11 March 1932, London, England. Politician. m. (1) Vanessa Salmon, divorced. 1980, deceased. 1985, (2) Thérèse Mary Maclear, 1980, 2 sons, 4 daughters, 1 deceased. Education: Christ Church, Oxford; MA Oxon. Appointments: Sub-Lieutenant, Royal Naval Volunteer Reserve, 1954-56; Editorial Staff, Financial Times, 2956-60; City Editor, Sunday Telegraph, 1961-63; Special Assistant to Prime Minister, 1963-64; Columnist, Financial Times and Broadcaster, BBC, 1965; Editor, The Spectator, 1966-70; Regular Contributor to Sunday Times and Evening Standard, 1970-71, The Times, 1971-72; Fellow, Nuffield College, Oxford, 1972-73; Special Political Adviser, Conservative Party Headquarters, 1973-74; Member of Parliament for Blaby, Leicestershire, 1974-92; Opposition Whip,

1976-77; Opposition Spokesman on Treasury and Economic Affairs, 1977-79; Financial Secretary to the Treasury, 1979-81; Secretary of State for Energy, 1981-83; Chancellor of the Exchequer, 1983-89; Non-Executive Director, Barclays Bank, 1990-98; Chairman, Central European Trust, 1990-; Adviser, BZW, 1990-91; Non-Executive Director, Consultant, Guinness Peat Aviation, 1990-93; Director, Institute for International Economics, Washington DC, 1991-; International Advisory Board, Creditanstalt Bankverein, 1991-; International Advisory Board, Total SA, 1994-; Advisory Council, Prince's Youth Business Trust, 1994-; President, British Institute of Energy Economics, 1995-; Chairman, CAIB Emerging Russia Fund, 1997-; Privy Councillor. Publications: The Power Game, co-author, 1976; The View from No 11: Memoirs from a Tory Radical, 1992; The Nigel Lawson Diet Book, co-author, 1996; Various pamphlets. Memberships: President, British Institute of Energy Economics, 1995-; Governing Body, Westminster School, 1999-. Honours: Finance Minister of the Year, Euromoney Magazine, 1988; Honorary Student, Christ Church, Oxford, 1996. Address: House of Lords, London SW1A 0PW, England.

LAYARD Peter Richard Grenville (Baron of Highgate in the London Borough of Haringey), b. 15 March 1934, Welwyn Garden City. Economist. m. Molly Meacher, 1991. Education: BA, Cambridge University; MSc, London School of Economics. Appointments: Schoolteacher, London County Council, 1959-61; Senior Research Officer, Robbins Committee on Higher Education, 1961-64; Deputy Director, Higher Education Research Unit, 1964-74, Lecturer, 1968-75, Head, Centre for Labour Economics, 1974-90, Reader, 1975-80, Professor of Economics, 1980-99, Director, Centre for Economic Performance, 1990-, London School of Economics; Consultant, Centre for European Policy Studies, Brussels, 1982-86; University Grants Committee, 1985-89; Chairman, Employment Institute, 1987-92; Ch-Chairman, World Economy Group, World Institute for Development Economics Research, 1989-; Economic Adviser to Russian Government, 1991-97. Publications: Cost Benefit Analysis, 1973; Causes of Poverty, co-author, 1978; Microeconomic Theory, co-author, 1978; More Jobs, Less Inflation, 1982; The Causes of Unemployment, co-editor, 1984; The Rise in Unemployment, co-editor, 1986; How to Beat Unemployment, 1986; Handbook of Labour Economics, co-editor, 1987; The Performance of the British Economy, co-author, 1988; Unemployment: Macroeconomic Performance and the Labour Market, co-author, 1991; East-West Migration: the alternatives, co-author, 1992; Post-Communist Reform: pain and progress, co-author, 1993; Macroeconomics: a text for Russia, 1994; The Coming Russian Boom, co-author, 1996; What Labour Can Do, 1997; Tackling Unemployment, 1999; Tackling Inequality, 1999. Honours: Created Life Peer, 2000. Memberships: Fellow, Econometric Society. Address: 45 Cholmeley Park, London N6 5EL, England.

LAZZARI Carlo Giuseppe, b. 11 May 1957, Caracas, Venezuela. Clinical Psychologist. Education: MD, University of Rome, Italy, 1982; MSc, Drexel University, Philadelphia, Pennsylvania, USA, 1985; Diploma, Infectious Diseases, 1993; PhD, Work and Organisational Psychology, 1997, Diploma in Labour and Industrial Relations, 2000, University of Bologna, Italy. Appointments: Research Assistant, Drexel University, Pennsylvania, USA, 1984-86; Clinical Assistant, Institute of Psychiatry, University of London, England, 1986-87; Research Assistant, National Institutes of Health, USA, 1989-90; Research Fellow, Institute of Infectious Diseases, University of Bologna, 1987-98; Consultant, Ronald McDonald House Charities, 1998-2001. Publications: Author of 35 books including: Counselling in Medicine; Counselling of Terminally Ill People; HIV/AIDS Counselling; Work Counselling During Harassment and Mobbing; Ethical Economy; Poetry and Psychology. Honours: Listed in Who's Who publications and biographical dictionaries. Membership: New York Academy of Science. Address: via Raiale 112, 65128 Pescara, Italy. E-mail: sianca@micso.net Website: www.micso.com/esi

LE Tuan Hung, b. 15 October 1960, Vietnam. Composer; Performer; Musicologist. Education: Graduate Diploma, Information Services, Royal Melbourne Institute of Technology, 1992; Bachelor of Music, University of Melbourne, 1986; Doctor of Philosophy, Musicology, Monash University, 1991. Career: Freelance Composer, Performer and Musicologist, 1987-; Program Director, Music, Australia Asia Foundation, 1994-. Compositions: Reflections, 1990; Spring, 1991; Prayer for Land, 1991; Longing for Wind, 1996; Calm Water, 1996; Water Ways, 1997; Scent of Memories, 1998; Three Musical Poems, 2002; On the Wings of a Butterfly, 2004. Recordings: Quivering String, 1992; Musical Transfigurations, 1993; Landscapes of Time, 1996; Echoes of Ancestral Voices, 1997; Scent of Time, 2002. Publications: Dan Tranh Music of Vietnam: Traditions and Innovations, 1998; Numerous articles in magazines, reviews and journals. Honour: Overseas Fellowship, Australian Academy of Humanities, 1993. Memberships: Australasian Performing Rights Association. Address: PO Box 387, Springvale, Vic 3171, Australia.

LÊ Vu Hoàng, b. 12 December 1956, Dam Doi-Ca Mau, Vietnam. Film Director. m. Phan Thi Ngoc Lan, 2 sons. Education: Bachelor of Science Degree, 1999; Bachelor of Journalism Degree, 2003. Appointment: Ca Mau Radio and Television Station, Ca Mau City, Vietnam, 1977-. Publications: Book, The Land and People of Ca Mau Province; Documentary Films: Drop of Honey; The Quiet in the Current of Life; Bright Eyes – Bright Heart. Honours: Medal for the Profession of Journalism of Vietnam; Medal for the Profession of Broadcasting and Television of Vietnam. Memberships: Journalist, Videopersons, Film Directors in Vietnam. Address: 62/5 Lam Thanh Mau Street, Ca Mau City, Ca Mau Province, Vietnam.

LE BLANC Matthew, b. 25 July 1967, Newton, Massachusetts, USA. Actor. m. Melissa McKnight, 2003, 1 daughter, 2004. Education: Newton High School; Trained as Carpenter. Television Includes: TV 101, 1988; Top of the Heap, 1991; Vinnie and Bobby, 1992; Red Shoes Diaries, 1993; Friends, 1994; Reform School Girl, 1994; Red Shoes Diaries 7,1997; Joey, 2004; Commercials, Levi's 501 jeans, Coca Cola, Doritos, Heinz Ketchup. Films include: Lookin' Italian, 1994; Ed, 1996; Lost in Space, 1998; Charlie's Angels, 2000; All the Queens Men, 2001; Charlie's Angels: Full Throttle, 2003. TV Guest Appearances include: Just the Ten of us, 1989; Monsters, 1990; Married... with Children, 1991; The Rosie O'Donald Show, 1996; The Tonight Show with Jay Leno, 1996; Entertainment Tonight, 2003; Opera Winfrey Show, 2003; Celebrities Uncensored, 2003; Tonight with Jay Leno, 2004. Honours: TV Guide Award, 2000; Teen Choice Award, 2002. Address: c/o United Talent Agency, 9560 Wilshire Boulevard, Suite 500, Beverly Hills, CA 90212, USA.

LE BRAS Michel, b. 16 January 1947, Meaux, France, Research Engineer. m. Michèle Guilbert, 2 sons, 1 daughter. Education: Philosophical Dissertation in Structural Engineering, 1977; Doctorate in Physical Sciences, 1997. Appointments: Ingénieur de Recherche Hors Classe, École Nationale Supérieure de Chimie de Lille, 1979-; Senior Lecturer, Chemistry (CNAM Lille). Publications: Editor, 3 books, 3 journals (special issue); 2 extended abstracts; 114 papers in international journals; 41 chapters in books; 21 other papers; 158 communications in conferences; 3 French patents, 1 international patent. Membership: International Editorial Board, Polym Polym Composites (RAPRA p46); Journal of Fire

Science. Address: Laboratoire des Procédés d'Elaboration de Revêtements Fonctionnels, ENSCL, BP 108, 59652 Villeneuve d'Ascq Cedex, France.

LE BRUN Christopher Mark, b. 20 December 1951, Portsmouth, England. Artist. m. Charlotte Verity, 2 sons, 1 daughter. Education: DFA, Slade School of Fine Art, 1970-74; MA, Chelsea School of Art, 1974-75. Career: Visiting Lecturer: Brighton Polytechnic, 1975-82, Slade School of Fine Art, 1978-83, Wimbledon School of Art, 1981-83; Professor of Drawing, 2000-02, Chair, Education Committee RA, 2000-, Royal Academy; Member, Advisory Committee, Prince of Wales's Drawing Studio, 2000-; Trustee: Tate Gallery, 1990-95, National Gallery, 1996-2003, Dulwich Picture Gallery, 2000-; Numerous one-man and group exhibitions internationally since 1979; Public Collections include: Tate Gallery, British Museum, Victoria and Albert, MOMA, New York; British Council; National Portrait Gallery; Scottish National Gallery of Modern Art; Walker Art Gallery. Publications: Works feature in: 50 Etchings, 1991; Christopher Le Brun, 2001. Honours: John Moores Liverpool Prizewinner, 1978, 1980; Gulbenkian Printmakers Commission, 1983; DAAD Fellowship, Berlin, 1987-88. Membership: Royal Academician (RA), 1996. Address: c/o Marlborough Fine Art, 6 Albemarle Street, London, W1X 4BY, England.

LE MARCHANT Francis Arthur (Sir), b. 6 October 1939, Hungerton, UK. Artist; Farmer. Education: Byam Shaw School of Drawing and Painting; Certificate, RAS, Royal Academy Schools. Career: One man exhibitions include: Museum of Art and Science, Evansville, USA; Agnews; Roy Miles Fine Art; Group exhibitions include: Royal Academy Summer Exhibitions; Leicester Galleries; Spink; Bilan de l'Art Contemporain, Paris; Spink; Collections include: Government Art Collections, 2 paintings; Financial Times; The Museum of Evansville, USA; University of Evansville, USA; Collection of the late Mrs Anne Kessler. Honour: Silver Medal, Bilan de l'Art Contemporain, Paris. Memberships: Savile Club; Reynolds Club (Alumni Association of Royal Academy Schools). Address: c/o HSBC, 88 Westgate, Grantham, Lincolnshire NG31 6LF, England.

LEA-JONES Julian, b. 2 December 1940, Bristol, England. Avionics Researcher; Writer; Presenter. m. Diane Susan Parsons, 22 December 1962, 1 son, 1 daughter. Education: College Certificates; Diplomas for Telecommunications and Business Management Studies. Appointments: Contributing Author, Editor, The Templar, 1980-; Past Joint Editor, Alha Journal, Avon Past, 1986; European Commission Evaluator for Aeronautics (panellist). Publications: St John's Conduit: An Account of Bristol's Medieval Water Supply, 1985; Survey of Parish Boundary Markers and Stones for Eleven of the Ancient Bristol Parishes, 1986; Yesterday's Temple, 1987; Bristol Past Revisited, 1989; Bristol Faces and Places, 1992; Papers for the 37th International Medieval Congress, University of Leeds, England, 2002: The making and maintaining of a 13c lead water conduit – The Carmelite's Friary Pipe, Bristol England, sponsor: The Association Villard de Honnecourt for the Interdisciplinary Study of Medieval Technology, Science & Art (Selected for the 2004 Ashgate Medieval Technology Series); The Loving Cup – The Ceremony and its Derivation, for the 37th International Medieval Congress, Kalamazoo, Michigan, USA, 2002; Contributions to: Newspapers, journals, radio and television. Memberships: West of England Writers Association; Temple Local History Group, founder, life member; Bristol History Research Exchange, archivist. Address: 33 Springfield Grove, Henleaze, Bristol BS6 7XE, England. Website: www.history4u.info

LEACH Henry (Conyers) (Admiral of the Fleet Sir), b. 18 November 1923. Naval Officer. m. Mary Jean McCall, 1958, deceased 1991, 2 daughters. Education: Royal Naval College,

Dartmouth. Appointments: Served cruiser Mauritius, South Atlantic and Indian Ocean, 1941-42, battleship Duke of York, 1943-45, destroyers, Mediterranean, 1945-46; gunnery, 1947; Gunnery appointments, 1948-51; Gunnery Officer, cruiser Newcastle, Far East, 1953-55; Staff appointments, 1955-59; Commanded destroyer Dunkirk, 1959-61; Captain, 27th Squadron and Mediterranean, frigate Galatea, 1965-67; Director of Naval Plans, 1968-70; Commanded Commando Ship Albion, 1970; Assistant Chief of Naval Staff, Policy, 1971-73; Flag Officer, First Flotilla, 1974-75; Vice-Chief of Defence Staff, 1976-77; Commander-in-Chief and Allied Commander-in-Chief, Channel and Eastern Atlantic, 1977-79; Chief of Naval Staff, First Sea Lord, 1979-82; First and Principal ADC to the Queen, 1979-82; Deputy Lieutenant; Chairman, 1987-98, Honorary Vice-President, 1991-, Council, King Edward VII Hospital; Governor, Cranleigh School, 1983-93; Chairman, 1983-98, Honorary Vice-President, 1999-, St Dunstan's; Governor, St Catherine's, 1987-93. Publications: Endure No Makeshifts, autobiography. Honours: Knight Grand Cross, Order of the Bath; Honorary Freeman, Merchant Taylors, Shipwrights, City of London. Memberships: Royal Bath and West of England Society, President, 1993, Vice-President, 1994-; Royal Naval Benevolent Society, President, 1984-93; Sea Cadet Association, President, 1984-93; Patron, Meridian Trust Association, 1994-; Patron, Hampshire Royal British Legion, 1994-. Address: Wonston Lea, Wonston, Winchester, Hants SO21 3LS, England.

LEAHY John H G (Sir), b. 7 February 1928, Worthing, Sussex, England. Retired Diplomatist. m. Elizabeth Anne Pitchford, 1954, 2 sons, 2 daughters. Education: Clare College, Cambridge; Yale University; MA. Appointments: Joined Diplomatic Service, 1951; Third Secretary, Singapore, 1955-57; Second Secretary, then First Secretary, Paris, 1958-62; First Secretary, Tehran, 1965-68; Counsellor, Paris, 1973-75; Attached to Northern Ireland Office, Belfast, 1975-76; Ambassador to South Africa, 1979-82; Deputy Under-Secretary for Africa and Middle East, Foreign and Commonwealth Office, 1982-84; High Commissioner to Australia, 1984-88; Director, The Observer, 1989-92; Pro-Chancellor, City University, 1991-97; Non-Executive Director, 1993-98, Chairman, 1994-97, Lonrho PLC; Chairman, Governors Committee, Tonbridge School, 1994-99. Honours: Knight Commander, Order of St Michael and St George; Honorary DCL, City University, 1997; Officier, Légion d'Honneur, France. Memberships: Franco-British Council, Chairman, 1989-93; Master, Skinners Company, 1993-94; Chairman, Britain-Australia Society, 1994-97. Address: Manor Stables, Bishopstone, Near Seaford, East Sussex BN25 2UD, England.

LEAPER David John, b. 23 July 1947, York, England. Professor of Surgery. m. Francesca Ann, 1 son, 1 daughter. Education: MBChB with honours, University of Leeds Medical School, 1970; MD, 1979, ChM, 1982. Appointments: House Officer, Leeds General Infirmary, 1970-71; MRC Fellow, 1971-73; Registrar, Leeds General Infirmary and Scarborough, 1973-76; Senior Registrar in Surgery, CRC Fellow, Westminster and Kings College Hospitals, London, 1976-87; Professor of Surgery, University of Hong Kong, 1988-90; Senior Lecturer in Surgery, University of Bristol, 1981-95; Professor of Surgery, University of Newcastle, 1995-. Publications: Books: International Surgical Practice; Oxford Handbook of Clinical Surgery; Oxford Handbook of Operative Surgery; Series: Your Operation; Member, Editorial Board of surgical journals; Papers on wound healing, surgical infections, colorectal and breast cancer. Honours: Fellow, Royal College of Surgeons of England, 1975, of Edinburgh, 1974, of Glasgow, 1998; Hunterian Professor, 1981-82; Zachary Cope Lecturer, 1998; Fellow, American College of Surgeons, 1998; Past Member, Court of Examiners, Royal College of Surgeons of England;

Dictionary of International Biography

Intercollegiate Fellowship Examiner, 2002. Memberships: Founder Member, Past Recorder and Past President, European Wound Management Association; Surgical Infection Society of Europe; Past Vice President, Section of Surgery, Royal Society of Medicine; Past Committee Member, Surgical Research Society; Member, Specialist Advisory Committee, Higher Surgical Training, UK. Address: 33 Peverell Avenue East, Poundbury, Dorchester, Dorset DT1 3RH, England. E-mail: profdavidjohnleaper@doctors.org.uk

LEAPMAN Michael Henry, b. 24 April 1938, London, England. Writer; Journalist. m. Olga Mason, 15 July 1965, 1 son. Appointment: Journalist, The Times, 1969-81. Publications: One Man and His Plot, 1976; Yankee Doodles, 1982; Companion Guide to New York, 1983; Barefaced Cheek, 1983; Treachery, 1984; The Last Days of the Beeb, 1986; Kinnock, 1987; The Book of London (editor), 1989; London's River, 1991; Treacherous Estate, 1992; Eyewitness Guide to London, 1993; Master Race (with Catrine Clay), 1995; Witnesses to War, 1998; The Ingenious Mr Fairchild, 2000; The World for a Shilling 2001; Inigo, 2003. Contributions to: Numerous magazines and journals. Honours: Campaigning Journalist of the Year, British Press Award, 1968; Thomas Cook Travel Book Award, Best Guide Book of 1983; Garden Writers Guild Award, 1995; Times education Supplement Senior book Award, 1999. Memberships: Society of Authors; Royal Society of Arts, National Union of Journalists; Garden Writers' Guild. Address: 13 Aldebert Terrace, London SW8 1BH, England.

LEAVER Christopher (Sir), b. 3 November 1937, London, England. Business Executive. m. Helen Mireille Molyneux Benton, 1975, 1 son, 2 daughters. Appointments: Commissioned, Royal Army Ordnance Corps, 1956-58; Member, Retail Food Trades Wages Council, 1963-64; Justice of the Peace, Inner London, 1970-83; Council, Royal Borough of Kensington and Chelsea, 1970-73; Court of Common Council, Ward of Dowgate, 1973, Sheriff, 1979-80, Lord Mayor, 1981-82, City of London; Justice of the Peace, City, 1974-93; Board, Brixton Prison, 1975-78; Governor, Christ's Hospital School, 1975; Governor, City of London Girls School, 1975-78; Board of Governors, 1978-, Chancellor, 1981-82, City University; Chairman, Young Musicians Symphony Orchestra Trust, 1979-81; Trustee, Chichester Festival Theatre, 1982-97; Church Commissioner, 1982-83, 1996-; Chairman, London Tourist Board Ltd, 1983-89, Trustee, London Symphony Orchestra, 1983-91; Deputy Chairman, 1989-93, Chairman, 1993-94, Vice-Chairman, 1994-2000, Thames Water PLC; Adviser to Secretary of State on Royal Parks, 1993-96; Non-Executive Director, Unionamerica Holdings, 1994-97; Chairman, Eastbourne College. Honours: Knight Grand Cross, Order of the British Empire; Knight, Order of St John of Jerusalem; Honorary Colonel, 151 Regiment, Royal Corps of Transport (Volunteers), 1983-89; Honorary Colonel, Royal Corps of Transport, 1988-91; Honorary Liveryman, Farmers Company; Fellow, Chartered Institute of Transport; Honorary Freeman, Company of Water Conservators; Freeman, Company of Watermen and Lightermen; Order of Oman. Memberships: Vice-President, Playing Fields Association. Address: c/o Thames Water PLC, 14 Cavendish Place, London W1M 0NU, England.

LEAVER Peter Lawrence Oppenheim, b. 28 November 1944. Lawyer; Football Executive. m. Jane Rachel Pearl, 1969, 3 sons, 1 daughter. Education: Trinity College, Dublin; Called to Bar, Lincoln's Inn, 1967. Appointments: Member, Committee on Future of the Legal Profession, 1986-88, Council of Legal Education, 1986-91, General Council of the Bar, 1987-90; Chairman, Bar Committee, 1989, International Practice Committee, 1990; Director, Investment Management Regulatory Organisation, 1994-2000; Recorder, 1994-; Bencher, 1995; Queen's Counsel; Chief

Executive, Football Association Premier League, 1997-99; Deputy High Court Judge. Memberships: Chartered Institute of Arbitrators; Member, Dispute Resolution Panel for Winter Olympics, Salt Lake City, 2002. Address: 5 Hamilton Terrace, London NW8 9RE, England.

LEAVITT Thomas Whittlesey, b. 8 January 1930, Boston, Massachusetts, USA. Art Museum Director. m. Michele Chisholm Leavitt. Education: AB, Middlebury College, 1951; MA, Boston University, 1952; PhD, Harvard University, 1958. Appointments: Director, Pasadena Art Museum California, USA, 1957-63; Director, Santa Barbara Museum of Art, California, USA, 1963-68; Director, A W White Museum of Art, Cornell University, Ithaca, New York, USA, 1968-73; Director, H F Johnnson Museum of Art, Cornell University, Ithaca, New York, USA, 1973-91. Publications: Catalogues: New Renaissance in Italy, 1958; American Painting in the 19th Century, 1960; The Photograph as Poetry, 1961; Piet Mondrian, 1965; Earth Art, 1969; G L Brown, 1973; Albert Bierstadt, 1964; Brücke, 1970; Seymour Lipton, 1973; The Beleaguered Director (Art in America), 1971. Honours: Professor Emeritus, Cornell University, 1991; Distinguished Service Award, American Association of Museums, 1997. Memberships: American Association of Museums, President, 1982-85; Association of Art Museum Directors, President, 1977-78; Independent Sector, Trustee, 1980-84; National Endowment for the Arts, Director of Museum Program, 1970-72. Address: 25 Waterway, Saunderstown. RI 02874, USA.

LEBED Aleksander Ivanovich (Lieutenant General), b. 20 April 1950, Novocherkassk, Russia. Army Officer. m. 2 sons, 1 daughter. Education: Ryazan Higher School of Airborne Troops; M Frunze Military Academy. Appointments: Platoon then Company Commander, Ryazan Higher Airborne Troops Commanding School, 1973-81; Battalion Commander, Afghanistan, 1981-82; Regimental Commander, 1985-86; Deputy Commander, Airborne Troops Formation, 1986-88; Commander, Tula Airborne Troops Division, 1989-92; Stood guard with paratrooper battalion at Supreme Soviet building during attempted coup, August, 1991; Deputy Commander, Airborne Troops and Military Education Institute, 1991; Commander, 14th Russian Army, Pridniestr Republic, 1992-94; Deputy Chairman, National Council, Congress of Russian Communities, 1995-96; Member, State Duma, 1995-96; Candidate, Presidential Election, 1996; Secretary, Security Council of Russia, 1996; Started negotiations with Chechen separatists; Founder, Russian People's Republican Party; Governor, Krasnoyarsk Territory; Member, Council of Russian Federation, 1998-. Publications: It is a Pity for the Power, 1995; My Life and My Country, 1997; Ideology of Common Sense, 1997. Honours: Several military orders. Address: House of Administration, Mira prospect 110, 660009 Mrasnoyarsk, Russia.

LEBED Aleksey Ivanovich, b. 14 April 1955, Novocherkassk, Rostov Region, Russia. m. Yelizaveta Vladimirovna, 1 son, 1 daughter. Education: Ryazan Higher School of Airborne Troops; Military Academy; Saint Petersburg State University. Appointments: Served in the Soviet Army, 1979-88; Served in Afghanistan, 1982, Pskov, 1991; Military operations, various parts of USSR, 1980-92; Regimental Commander, 300th Paratroop Regiment, 1995-96; State Duma Deputy, 1996-; Head of Government, Republic of Khakassia, 1996-2001; Member, Council of Russian Federation, 1996-; Member, Congress of Russian Communities. Honours: Order of the Red Star; Medal for Courage; Honoris Causa Degree, Khakassia Kalanov State University; Peter the Great Prize, 2001. Address: House of Government, Prospect Lenina 67, R-665019 Abakan, Russia. E-mail: pressa@khakasnet.ru

Dictionary of International Biography

LEBEDA Aleš, b. 13 April 1951, Brno, Czechoslovakia. m. Hana Lebedová, 2 sons. Education: Dipl Ing, MSc, Horticulture, University of Agriculture, Brno, Czechoslovakia, 1970-75; Postgraduate study, Mycology, Charles University, Prague, Czechoslovakia, 1977-78; PhD, Plant Pathology, Research Institute for Crop Production, Prague, 1981-82; DrSc, Agricultural and Forestry Plant Pathology, 1993, Associate Professor, 1994, Professor, 1999, Mendel University of Agriculture and Forestry, Brno. Appointments: Head of Plant Pathology Laboratory, Research Institute for Vegetable Growing and Breeding, Olomouc, 1975-91; Lecturer, 1984-97; Vice Mayor, village of Smržice, 1990-98; Head of Plant Pathology Laboratory, SEMO, Vegetable Breeding Station, Smržice, 1991-94; Associate Professor, 1994-99, Professor of Botany, 1999-, Palacký University, Olomouc-Holice. Publications: Author and co-author, numerous books, proceedings, booklets; 600 scientific and professional papers; Over 500 citations in international and domestic journals; Co-author, 2 lettuce and 5 green pea cultivars. Honours: Zenit Gold Plaque, Czechoslovak Academy of Agricultural Sciences; Golden Medal for Scientific Activity, Czechoslovak Academy of Agricultural Sciences; Rudolf Hermanns Foundation Award in Viticultural and Horticultural Sciences; Horticulture Research International, Visiting Fellow Award; Golden Medal of Palacký University; 1st Class Medal for Research, Ministry of Education of the Czech Republic. Memberships include: International Society for Plant Pathology; Czech Scientific Society for Mycology; Czechoslovak Biological Society; Genetic Society of Gregor Mendel; Czechoslovak Scientific Horticultural Society; Czech Academy of Agricultural Science; many others. Address: Palacký University, Faculty of Science, Department of Botany, Šlechtitelů 11, 783 71 Olomouc-Holice, Czech Republic. E-mail: lebeda@prfholnt.upol.cz

LEBEDEV Aleksei A, b. 28 August 1930, Ivanovo, Russia. Pharmacologist. Education: Graduate, State Medical Institute of Ivanovo, 1953; Aspirant, 1955-57; Candidate of Medical Sciences, 1955; Doctor of Medical Sciences, 1964; Professor of Pharmacology, 1965. Appointments: Assistant Professor, 1957-62, Associate Professor of Pharmacology, 1962; Chief of Pharmacological Chair, 1964-2000, Professor of Pharmacology, 2000-, Samara State Medical University, Russia; Created scientific school, Pharmacology of the Kidney, Samara (11 scholars became Doctors of Medical Science and 28 became candidates of Medical and Biological Sciences). Publications: 240 scientific works include: Autotransplantation of the Kidney, 1971; Diuretics and blood circulation, 1984; Pharmacology of the Kidney, 2002. Honours: Honoured Scientist of Russia, 1980; Order of International Friendship, USSR, 1986; Selected and named as Soros Professor, 1994 and 1996; Medal of Order for Merit to Fatherland, 2000; Honoured Professor of Samara State Medical University, 2000; Honoured Professor of Medical Academy of Ivanovo, 2001. Memberships: Chairman, Samara Region Society of Pharmacologists; Russian Board of Scientific Pharmacological Society; Editorial Staff, Experimental and Clinical Pharmacology Journal; Academician, International Eurasian Academy of Sciences; Chairman, Scientific Student Society, Samara State Medical University, 1970-2003. Address: Sadovaya, 208, 4, Samara, 443001 Russia. E-mail: lebedcard@sama.ru

LECHEVALIER Hubert Arthur, b. 12 May 1926, Tours, France. Microbiologist. m. Mary Jean Pfeil, 2 sons. Education: Licence ès Sciences, 1947, MS, 1948, Laval University, Quebec, Canada; PhD, Rutgers University, New Brunswick, New Jersey, 1951. Appointments: Assistant Professor, Microbiology, College of Agriculture then Waksman Institute, Rutgers University, 1951-56; Associate Professor, Microbiology, 1956-66, Professor, Microbiology, 1966-91, Associate Director, 1980-88, Waksman

Institute of Microbiology, Rutgers University; Professor Emeritus, Rutgers, The State University of New Jersey, 1991-. Publications: Author or co-author of over 140 scientific papers, co-author or co-editor of 10 books including: A Guide to the Actinomycetes and Their Antibiotics, 1953; Antibiotics of Actinomycetes, 1962; Three Centuries of Microbiology, 1965, reprint 1974; The Microbes, 1971; 4 US patents. Honours include: Honorary Member, the Société Française de Microbiologie 1972-; Charles Thom Award (jointly with Mary P Lechevalier), 1982; DSc, Laval University, 1983; Bergey Trust Award for contributions to bacterial taxonomy, 1989; New Jersey Inventors Hall of Fame, 1990; Honorary member of the Society for Actinomycetes, Japan, 1997. Address: 131 Goddard-Nisbet Rd, Morrisville, VT 05661-8041, USA. E-mail: hubartlech@msn.com

LEDEN Ido Lorenz, b. 4 July 1942, Lund, Sweden. Medical Doctor. m. Birgitta, 2 daughters. Education: Certified and Medical Licencure, 1971; Qualified Speciality, Internal Medicine, 1976, Rheumatology, 1978. Appointments: Head, Rheumatology Section, 1981-2002, Staff Member, 2002-, Central Hospital, Kristianstad. Publications: Several articles in rheumatology, internal medicine, paleopathology and history of medicine. Honours: Trafvenfelt Silver Medal, Swedish Society of Medicine, 1993. Address: Rheumatology Section, Central Hospital, 291 85 Kristianstad, Sweden.

LEE Anne W M, b. 21 February 1952, Hong Kong. Doctor. Education: MB BS, Hong Kong, 1976; DMRT, England, 1982; FRCR, England, 1983; FHKCR, Hong Kong, 1992; FHKAM, Hong Kong, 1993. Appointments: Medical and Health Officer, 1977-85, Senior Medical and Health Officer, 1985-91, Consultant, 1991-93, Institute of Radiology and Oncology, Queen Elizabeth Hospital, Hong Kong; Consultant, 1993-94, Chief of Service, 1995-, Department of Clinical Oncology, Pamela Youde Nethersole Eastern Hospital, Hong Kong. Publications: Numerous articles in professional journals. Memberships: Hong Kong Head and Neck Society; Hong Kong College of Radiologists; Hong Kong Society of Radiation Therapy and Oncology; Hong Kong Chemotherapy Society; Asia Oceanian Clinical Oncology Association; Hong Kong Paediatric Haematology and Oncology Study Group; American Association for the Advancement of Science. Address: Department of Clinical Oncology, Pamela Youde Nethersole Eastern Hospital, 3 Lok Man Road, Chaiwan, Hong Kong.

LEE Chan-Yun, b. 19 July 1952, Hwa-Liang, Taiwan. Technical Staff Member Associate Professor of Physics. m. Chia-Li Grace Yang, 1 son, 2 daughters. Education: BS, Physics, Soochow University, 1974; MS, Physics, University of Southern California, 1980; PhD, Physics, University of Notre Dame, 1994. Appointments: Assistant Professor, Physics, TIT, 1982-86; Associate Professor, Physics, TIT, 1986-88; Chairman, Physics Section, TIT, 1986-88; Consultant, TSD, 1983-88; Director, TNSM, 1986-88; Senior Engineer, LRC, 1994-99; Professor, Physics, SJCC, 1998-2000; Key Account for South Asia Area, LRC, 1997-99; Technical Staff, 1999-, West Coast Process Co-ordinator, 2000, TEA. Publications: Over 20 articles published in professional journals. Honours: 27th Science and Technology Personnel Research Award, 1988; Excellent Researchers Prize, 1986, 1987; Outstanding Academic Publication Prize, 1987, 1988. Memberships: Chinese Physics Association; American Vacuum Association. Address: 471 Via Vera Cruz, Fremont, CA 94539-5325, USA.

LEE Chong-Won, b. 26 February 1948, Kunsan, Korea. Professor. m. Namdeuk Woo, 1 son, 1 daughter. Education: BS, Mechanical Engineering, 1970, MS, Mechanical Engineering, 1972, Seoul National University; MS in Applied Mechanics, Yale University,

1975; PhD, Mechanical Engineering, University of California, Berkeley, 1980. Appointments: Instructor, Korea Military Academy, 1972-74; Visiting Professor, The University of Michigan, Ann Arbor, 1985-86, 2003; Professor, Korea Advanced Institute of Science and Technology, 1980-; Director, Centre for Noise and Vibration Control, KAIST, 1989-1998. Publications: Author and co-author of over 150 journal papers and over 110 international conference papers; Author of: Vibration Analysis of Rotors, 1993. Honours include: THE KAIST Award for Excellence in Teaching, 1997; Mayor's Award for Honouring the city of Daejeon in memory of the 50th Anniversary for Establishment of the Korean Government, 1998; Fellow, The Korean Academy of Science and Technology, 1999-2018; Fellow, American Society of Mechanical Engineers International, 2001-; Member, The National Academy of Engineering of Korea, 2003-2018. Memberships: Numerous memberships including President, 2001-2002, Vice President, 1995-2000; Korean Society for Noise and Vibration Engineering. Address: Department of Mechanical Engineering, Korea Advanced Institute of Science and Technology, Science Town, Daejeon 305-701, Korea. E-mail: cwlee@novic.kaist.ac.kr

LEE Christopher Frank Carandini, b. 27 May 1922, London, England. Actor; Author; Singer. m. Birgit Kroenke, 1961, 1 daughter. Education: Wellington College. Appointments: Served RAF, 1941-46; Mentioned in Despatches, 1944; Film industry, 1947-; Appeared in over 200 motion pictures; Films include: Moulin Rouge, 1953; The Curse of Frankenstein, 1956; Tale of Two Cities, 1957; Dracula, 1958; The Hound of the Baskervilles, 1959; The Mummy, 1959; Rasputin the Mad Monk, 1965; The Wicker Man, 1973; The Three Musketeers, 1973; The Private Life of Sherlock Holmes, 1973; The Four Musketeers, 1975; The Man with the Golden Gun, 1975; To the Devil a Daughter, 1976; Airport 77, 1977; Return from Witch Mountain, 1977; How the West Was Won, 1977; Caravans, 1977; The Silent Flute, 1977; The Passage, 1978; 1941, 1978l Bear Island, 1978; The Serial, 1979; The Salamanda, 1980; An Eye for an Eye; Goliath Awaits; Charles and Diana; The Return of Captain Invincible; The Howling Z; Behind the Mask; Roadstrip; Shaka Zulu; Mio my Mio; The Girl Un Metier du Seigneur; Casanova; The Disputation (TV); Murder Story; Round the World in 80 Days (TV); Return of the Musketeers; Outlaws; Gremlins II, 1989; Sherlock Holmes; Rainbow Thief; L'Avaro; Wahre Wunde, 1990; Young Indy, 1991; Cybereden, 1991; Death Train, 1992; The Funny Man, 1993; Police Academy, Mission in Moscow, 1993; A Feast at Midnight, 1994; The Stupids, 1995; Moses, 1995; Jinnah, 1997; Sleepy Hollow, 1999; The Lord of the Rings, 2000, 2001, 2003; Star Wars II, 2000, 2002. Publications: Christopher Lee's Treasury of Terror, Christopher Lee's Archive of Evil, 1975; Christopher Lee's Great Villains, 1977; Tall Dark and Gruesome, 1977, 1997. Honours: Officier, Ordre des Arts et des Lettres, 1973; Commander, St John of Jerusalem, 1997. Address: c/o London Management, 2-4 Noel Street, London, W1V 3RB, England.

LEE Dong Chun, b. 25 August 1960, Korea. Professor. m. 2 daughters. Education: BS, Department of Computer Science, Chonbuk National University, 1984; MS, Department of Computer Science, Kwangwoon University, Seoul, 1987; PhD, Department of Computer Science, Yonsei University, Seoul, 2001. Appointments: Assistant Professor, 1991-94, Associate Professor, 1995-2000, Dean of Computer Centre, 1994-98, Professor, 2000-, Department of Computer Science, Howon University. Publications: Numerous articles in professional scientific journals; Book chapter, Agent-based Approaches in Economic and Social Complex Systems, 2001; Book chapter, Agents and Web Intelligence System, 2003. Honours: Best Researcher, Korea Information Assurance Society, 2002. Memberships: IEEE; ISCA; ICICE; IEE; IEICE; International Journal Referee. Address: 727 Wolha-ri, Impi Kunsan, Chonbuk, South Korea. E-mail: ldch@sunny.howon.ar.kr

LEE Elhang Howard, b. 19 December 1947, Seoul, Korea. Professor. m. Namsoo Chang, 1 son, 1 daughter. Education: BSEE, Seoul National University, 1970; MSc, Yale University, 1972; MPhil, Yale University, 1975; PhD, Yale University, 1977. Appointments: Research Fellow, Yale University, 1977-78; Research Fellow, Princeton University, 1979-80; Research Specialist, Monsanto Company, 1980-84; Senior Scientist and Team Leader, AT&T Bell Laboratories, 1984-90; Vice President, Electronics Telecom Research Institute, 1990-98; Professor and Dean, Graduate School of Information and Telecommunications Sciences, Inha University, Korea. Publications: 1 book; Over 250 scholarly journal papers and articles; Over 100 worldwide talks and speeches; Plenary Speeches and Keynote Speeches. Honour: National Medal of Honour, Korea, 1996; Distinguished Academic Award, KPS, 1995; Fellow, Optical Society of America; Fellow, IEEE; Fellow, IEE, Royal Chartered UK, 1997; President, IEEE/LEOS Korea Chapter, 1993-98; Sigma Xi; IEEE Third Millennium Leadership Award, 2000; Outstanding Academic Achievement Award, KIEE, 2000; King Sejong Award, President, Korea, 2003. Memberships: Fellow, Korean Academy of Science and Technology; AAAS, USA; New York Academy of Science; Fellow, Korean Physical Society; Fellow, Optical Society of Korea; Chair, Advisor, International Conferences, USA, Europe, Russia, Asia-Pacific Region; Vice President, Optical Society of Korea; Vice-President, Technology Innovation Society of Korea. Address: School of Information and Communication Engineering, Inha University, Inchon 402-751, South Korea.

LEE Eun Hwa, b. 3 September 1971, South Korea. Lawyer. m. Olivier Ravel. Education: Bachelor of Arts, International Relations, with honours and distinction, 1992, Master of Arts, Sociology, 1992, Stanford University, USA; Juris Doctor, Georgetown, USA, 1996. Appointments: Jean Monnet Fellow, SOLLAC SA, Paris, 1992-93; Dean Acheson Legal Stagiaire, Court of Justice of the European Communities, Luxembourg, 1996; Associate, Rosenman & Colin LLP, New York, USA, 1997-98; Associate, Weil Gotshal & Manges LLP, London, 1998-2000; Associate, Debevoise & Plimpton LLP, New York and Paris, 2001-. Publications: Co-author: Update, Going Private, 1998; Author, pamphlet, A Practical Guide to the Dean Acheson Legal Stage program, 1996; Individual Development Accounts and Illinois Women's Business Development Center in State Support for Women-Owned Businesses, 1996; Korean Women's Development Institute (Honours Thesis), 1992. Honours: Awards at Stanford University; Staff Award and Scholarship, World Affairs Council, 1992; Academic Dean's List, Georgetown, 1994-96. Memberships: New York Bar; International Bar Association; World Association of International Studies; Cap and Gown Women's Honors Society. Address: Debevoise & Plimpton LLP, 21 ave George V, 75008 Paris, France. E-mail: ehlee@debevoise.com

LEE Hong-Koo, b. 9 May 1934, Seoul, Korea. Politician; Political Scientist. m., 1 son, 2 daughters. Education: Seoul National University; Emory University; Yale University; PhD. Appointments: Assistant Professor, Emory University, USA, 1963-64; Assistant Professor, Case Western Reserve University, 1964-67; Assistant Professor, Associate Professor, Professor of Political Science,1968-88, Director, Institute of Social Sciences, 1979-82, Seoul National University, Korea; Fellow, Woodrow Wilson International Center for Scholars, Smithsonian Institution, Washington DC, 1973-74; Fellow, Harvard Law School, 1974-75; Minister of National Unification, Korea, 1988-90; Special Assistant to President, 1990-91; Ambassador to UK, 1991-93;

Dictionary of International Biography

Commission on Global Governance, 1991-95; Senior Vice-Chairman, Advisory Council for Unification, Chairman, Seoul 21st Century Committee, The World Cup 2002 Bidding Committee, 1993-94; Deputy Prime Minister, Minister of National Unification, 1994; Prime Minister, 1994-95; Chairman, New Korea Party, 1996; Ambassador to USA, 1998-. Publications: An Introduction to Political Science; One Hundred Years of Marxism; Modernization. Address: Embassy of the Republic of South Korea, 2450 Massachusetts Avenue NW, Washington, DC 20008, USA. E-mail:korinfo@koreaemb.org

LEE Hung, b. 21 November 1954, Taiwan. Professor. m. Colleen McCann, 1 son, 1 daughter. Education: BSc, honours, Biochemistry, University of British Columbia, 1977; PhD, Biochemistry, McGill University, 1982. Appointments: Research Associate, Division of Biological Sciences, National Research Council, Canada, 1983-86; Assistant Professor, Department of Environmental Biology, 1986-91, Adjunct Professor, School of Engineering, 1992-, Associate Professor, Department of Environmental Biology, 1991-99, University of Guelph; Visiting Professor, Biotechnology Laboratory, University of British Columbia, 1992-93; Affiliated Network Investigator, Protein Engineering Network Center of Excellence, 1998-; Professor, Department of Environmental Biology, University of Guelph, 1999-; Regional Associate Editor for the journal, Environmental Toxicology, 2000-; Network Investigator, Canadian Water Network Centre of Excellence, 2001-. Publications: 128 original research papers, 23 original review papers, 12 book chapters, 1 patent, 170 conference abstracts, 12 non-refereed technical reports, 4 disclosures. Honours include: Canadian MRC Studentship, McGill University, 1978-82; Research Excellence Citation, Imperial Oil Limited, 1990; Presidential Distinguished Professor Award, University of Guelph, 2002-04. Memberships: American Society for Microbiology; Society for Industrial Microbiology. Address: Department of Environmental Biology, University of Guelph, Guelph, Ontario N1G 2W1, Canada.

LEE Jon, b. 5 March 1934, Seoul, Korea. Research Scientist. m. Janet Adams Lee, 2 sons, 2 daughters. Education: BS, Chemical Engineering, Seoul National University, 1956; MS, 1958, PhD, 1962, Chemical Engineering, Ohio State University. Appointments: Chemical Engineer, Materials Laboratory, 1962-64, Applied Mathematician, Aerospace Research Laboratory, 1964-76, Research Scientist, Flight Dynamics Laboratory, 1976-, USAF Research Laboratory, Wright-Patterson AFB, Dayton. Publications: 40 articles in scientific journals; 30 articles for conference proceedings; Contribution to encyclopedia chapter; Web book, 10 Lessons in Fractals, Complex Geometry, and Chaos (http://mathforum.org/te/exchange/hosted/lee/). Honours: Phi Lambda Upsilon; Sigma Xi; General Foulois Award of Flight Dynamics Laboratory; Scientific Achievement Award of the Department of Air Force. Memberships: American Academy of Mechanics; American Physical Society; Society of Industrial and Applied Mathematics; Society of Engineering Science. Address: Air Force Research Laboratory, Wright-Patterson AFB, Dayton, OH 45433, USA. E-mail: jon.lee@wpafb.af.mil

LEE Kenneth B, b. 17 January 1926, US citizen born in Korea. Educator; Author. m. Alice, 2 sons, 1 daughter. Education: BA, Economics and History, Korea University, 1949; MA, International Economics, Monterey Institute of International Studies, California, 1969; Graduate Studies, Stanford and New York University, 1952-72; PhD, University of Southern California, 1974. Appointments: Founder and Member of Board of Directors, International Language and Culture Foundation; President, Korea-America Association, 1952-; Chief, Research Division, Chairman and Dean, Defense Language Institute, Monterey, California, 1979-86;

Professor of Social Science, Chapman University, Orange County, California, 1975-85; Private tutor, 3 ancient Asian languages, 8 languages overall. Publications: Relationship of Economy and Higher Education in Post-war Japan, Dissertation; Chief Editor, Korea-America Scholastic Journal; Author, Korea and East Asia, 1997. Honours: Lifetime Achievement Award, 500 Founders of the 21st Century, Who's Who of the 21st Century, International Biographical Centre; 500 Leaders of World Influence; Greatest Minds of 21st Century, American Biographical Institute; US Government Awards for Excellent Services. Memberships: Asian Studies Society; Member, Phi Delta Kappa Society; Founder and Director of the Board, International Language and Cultural Foundation, 1983. Address: PO Box 135, / 9, Overlook Place, Monterey, CA 93942-0135, USA.

LEE Martin Chu Ming, b. 8 June 1938, Hong Kong. Politician; Barrister. m. Amelia Lee, 1969, 1 son. Education: BA, University of Hong Kong. Appointments: Queen's Counsel; Justice of the Peace; Hong Kong Legislative Council, 1985-; Basic Law Drafting Committee, 1985-90; Hong Kong Law Reform Commission, 1985-91; Chairman, Hong Kong Consumer Council, 1988-91; Founder, 1989, Leader, 1990-, United Democrats of Hong Kong; Chairman, Democratic Party, 1994-; Goodman Fellow, University of Toronto, 2000. Publications: The Basic Law: some basic flaws, co-author, 1988. Honours: International Human Rights Award, American Bar Association, 1995; Prize for Freedom, Liberal International, 1996; Democracy Award, National Endowment for Democracy, USA, 1997; Honorary LLD, Holy Cross College, 1997; Honorary LLD, Amherst College, USA, 1997; Statesmanship Award, Claremont Institute, USA, 1998; Schuman Medal, European Parliament, 2000. Memberships: Chairman, Hong Kong Bar Association, 1980-83. Address: Democratic Party of Hong Kong, 4th Floor, Hanley House, 776-778 Nathan Road, Kowloon, Hong Kong Special Administrative Region, China. E-mail: oml@martinlee.org.hk Website: www.martinlee.org.hk

LEE Minhyung, b. 3 July 1965, South Korea. Professor. m. Jungin Kim, 1 son, 1 daughter. Education: BA, 1989, MS, 1991, Mechanical Engineering, Seoul National University; PhD, Mechanical Engineering, University of Texas at Austin, USA, 1995. Appointments: Researcher, KIST, Korea, 1991-92; Postdoctoral Fellow, IAT, Austin, Texas, USA, 1995-96; Assistant Professor, US Naval Postgraduate School, Monterey, California, 1996-98; Head of Mechanical Engineering, Sejong University, Korea, 1998-. Publications: An Engineering Impact Model for Yawed Projectiles, 2000; A New Wave Technique for Free Vibration of a String with Time-Varying Length, 2002. Honours: Academic Prize, Daeyang Foundation, 2001. Memberships: American Society of Mechanical Engineers; KSHE; KIMST; SNAK. Address: 98 Kwanjin-Gu, Kunja-Dong, Sejong University, Seoul, 143-747, Korea. E-mail: mlee@sejong.ac.kr Website: http://dasan.sejong.ac.kr./mlee

LEE Rosa, b. 1 February 1957, Hong Kong. Fine Artist; Painter. m. Mark A S Graham, 1 son. Education: BA honours, Sussex University, 1975-79; BA honours, St Martin's School of Art, 1983-86; RCA (MA), Royal College of Art, 1986-88. Appointments: Fine Artist and Painter; Solo and group exhibitions throughout England and in Canada; Works in public and private collections. Publications: Contributions to catalogues, professional and public journals. Honours: ABTA Award, Commonwealth Festival Prizewinner, 1986; RCA Mario Dubsky Travel Award, 1987; Visiting Fellow in Painting, Winchester School of Art, 1988-89; Prizewinner, John Moores 16, Liverpool, 1989; Greater London Arts Award, 1989; British Council Award, 1993; British Council Award, 2002; London Arts Grant, 2002. Memberships: Fellow, Royal Society of Arts, 2001. Address: 14 Oak Village, London NW5 4QP, England. E-mail: rosa.lee@virgin.net

Dictionary of International Biography

LEE Sang-Hie, b. 21 November 1939, Seoul, Korea. Professor of Music; Pianist Pedagogue; Arts Higher Education Administrator. 1 son, 1 daughter. Education: BA degree in piano performance, Ewha Womans University, 1961, Korea; PhD Higher Education, University of Michigan, 1995; MM in piano performance, American Conservatory of Music, Chicago, 1966; EdD in piano performance and pedagogy, University of Georgia, 1977. Debut: Rome, Italy, 1980. Career: Assistant Professor of Music, Grambling State University, 1977-81; Assistant Professor of Music, State University of New York, 1981-82; Assistant/Associate Professor of Music, University of Alabama, 1983-91; Associate Dean, College of Fine Arts, 1995-98, Associate Professor of Music, School of Music, University of South Florida, 1995-. Publications: Music Pedagogy, 1987; Using the Personal Computer to Analyse Piano Performance, 1989; Pianist's Hand Ergonomics and Touch Control, 1990; Pianist's Biomechanics and the Implications in Teaching, 1990; TV movie White Tiger; Ergonomie de la main du pianist et controle du toucher, 1996; Uses of Computer Technology in Piano Research, 1997. Contributions: The Piano Quarterly, 1981; The Pianist's Reference Guide, 1982; Pianographie, 1982; MENC Handbook of Research on Music Teaching and Learning, 1992. Honours: Korean National Scholarship, 1958-61; Pi Kappa Lambda, 1976; Kappa Kappa Delta, 1976; Rackham Merit Fellowship, 1992-94; Distinguished Alumna Award, 1997. Memberships: Society for Research in Psychology of Music; Society for Music Perception and Cognition; International Council of Fine Arts Deans; Association for Study of Higher Education. Address: School of Music, University of South Florida, FAH 110 4202 East Fowler Avenue, Tampa, FL 33620-7350, USA.

LEE Sang Hee, b. 30 September 1960, Youngdong-gun, Chungbuk, Korea. Professor. m. Hye Jeong Song, 1 son. Education: BS, 1988, MS, 1990, PhD, 1993, Seoul National University, Korea. Appointments: Private First Class, Republic of Korea Army, 1981-84; Research Associate, Genetic Engineering Institute, Seoul National University, Korea, 1990-92; Postdoctoral Research Associate, University of Wisconsin-Madison, Wisconsin, USA, 1993-95; Associate Professor, Youngdong University, Chungbuk, Korea, 1995-2003; Professor, Department of Biological Science, Myongji University, Kyunggido, Korea, 2003-; Evaluator, Korea Institute of S&T Evaluation and Planning, 2003-; Consultant, Small and Medium Business Administration, Cheongju, Chungbuk, 2001-; Director-General of Research and Development, MB Biotech, Inc; Director of BioGree Program, Rural Development Administration, Korea. Publications: Articles in scientific journals and first author and corresponding author include most recently: Dissemination of SHV-12 and characterization of new AmpC-type beta-lactamase genes among clinical isolates of Entereobacter species in Korea, 2003; Characterization of bla$_{CMY-10}$ a novel, plasmid-encoded AmpC-type beta-lactamase gene in a clinical isolate of Enterobacter aerogenes, 2003; Crystallization and preliminary X-ray crystallographic analyses of CMY-1 and CMY-10, plasmidic class C beta-lactamases with extended substrate spectrum, 2004. Memberships: Korean Society for Molecular and Cellular Biology, 1999-; Microbiological Society of Korea, 1999-; Korean Society of Microbiology and Biotechnology; American Society of Microbiology, 2001-; Member of Evaluators, Korean Broadcasting System, Korea, 2003-. Address: Department of Biological Science, Myongji University, San 38-2 Namdong, Yongin, Kyunggido, 449-728, Republic of Korea. E-mail: sangeeLEE@mju.ac.kr

LEE Sang Jun, b. 4 January 1954, Kyungpook, Korea. Molecular Biologist. Education: BSc, 1977, MSc, 1982, Kyungpook National University, Taegu, Korea; PhD, Sydney University, Sydney, Australia, 1992. Appointments: Postdoctoral, University of Medicine and Dentistry of New Jersey, New Jersey, USA, 1991-92; Researcher, Yeungnam University, Taegu, Korea, 1993-94;

Senior Researcher, 1994-, Director, 2003-, National Fisheries Research and Development Institute, Korea. Publications: Articles in scientific journals include: A noble technique for the effective production of short peptide analogs from concatametic short peptide multimers, 2000; Algalytic activity of α-mannosidase on harmful marine microalgae, 2000. Address: Biotechnology Research Center, National Fisheries Research and Development Institute, Pusan 619-902, Republic of Korea.

LEE Sanghack, b. 11 February 1958, Seoul, Korea. Professor of Economics. m. Kyounghee Kim, 1 son, 1 daughter. Education: BA, Economics, Seoul National University, Korea, 1980; PhD, Economics, State University of New York (SUNY), Buffalo, New York, USA, 1989. Appointments: Junior Economist, Bank of Korea, 1980-85; Research Instructor, SUNY at Buffalo, 1989-90; Associate Research Fellow, KIEP, 1990-91; Professor of Economics, Kookmin University, 1991-. Publications: Scientific papers in journals. Memberships: Korea International Economic Association; Korea Economic Association. Address: School of Economics, Kookmin University, Seoul 136-702, South Korea.

LEE Seung-Goo, b. 1 February 1959, Seoul, Korea. Theologian; Educator. m. Hyun-Sook Kim Lee, 1 son, 1 daughter. Education: BA, Chongshin College, 1982; MEd, Seoul National University, 1984; MDiv, Hapdong Theological Seminary, 1987; MPhil, 1985, PhD, 1990, The University of St Andrews. Appointments: Research Fellow, Yale University Divinity School, 1990-92; Professor of Systematic Theology, Westminster Graduate School of Theology, 1992-98; Associate Professor, Systematic Theology, Kukje Theological Seminary, 1999-; Vice President for Academic Affairs, Kukje Theological Seminary, 2003-. Publications include: Books in Korean: Interviews with Modern British Theologians, 1992; Studies in Reformed Theology: Toward a Reformed Theology in Korea, 1995; What is the Church? 1996; The Genuine Christian Comfort: Exposition of the Heidelberg Catechism I, 1998; Studies in Reformed Theology: Toward a Reformed Theology in Korea, II, 1999; The Holy Spirit and the Church, 2001; A Theological Perspective on Cloning, 2003; What is the Christian World-View? 2003; 25 translations into Korean; 31 book articles and chapters in Korean; 2 book articles and chapters in English; 3 book reviews and 4 articles translated into Korean. Address: 1577-5 Shillim 1 Dong, Kwan-ak District, Seoul, Korea 151-5525. E-mail: wminb@hitel.net

LEE Spike (Shelton Jackson Lee), b. 20 March 1957, Atlanta, Georgia, USA. Film Maker; Actor. m. Tonya Lewis, 1993, 1 daughter. Education: Morehouse College; Atlanta University; New York University; Institute of Film and TV. Appointments: Wrote Scripts for Black College; The Talented Tenth; Last Hustle in Brooklyn; Produced, Wrote, Directed, Joe's Bed-Stuy Barbershop; We Cut Heads; Has directed music videos; TV Commercials; Films include: She's Gotta Have It, 1985; School Daze, 1988; Do the Right Thing, 1989; Love Supreme, 1990; Mo' Better Blues, 1990; Jungle Fever, 1991; Malcolm X, 1992; Crooklyn; Girl 6; Clockers, 1995; Girl 6; Get on the Bus; 4 Little Girls; He Got Game, 1998; Summer of Sam, 1999; Tales from the Hood, 1995; Bamboozled, 2000; The Original Kings of Comedy, 2000; Lisa Picard is Famous, 2001; A Huey P Newton Story, 2001; The 25th Hour, 2003. Publications: Spike Lee's Gotta Have It: Inside Guerilla Filmmaking, 1987; Uplift the Race, 1988; The Trials and Tribulations of the Making of Malcolm X, 1992; Girl 6; Get on the Bus, 1996. Honours: Cannes Film Festival Prize for Best New Film; Dr h c, New York University, 1998. Address: Forty Acres and a Mule Filmworks, 124 De Kalb Avenue, Brooklyn, New York, NY 11217, USA.

Dictionary of International Biography

LEE Tzong-Ru, b. 28 December 1964, Kaohsiung, Taiwan, Republic of China. Professor. m. Hui-Chueh Chen, 2 sons. Education: B in Management, 1987, MA, Industrial Engineering, 1989, Chiao-Tung University, Hsin-Chu City, Taiwan; PhD, Industrial Engineering, Texas A&M University, College Station, USA, 1995. Appointments: Researcher, Texas Instruments, Dallas, USA, 1994-2000; Associate Professor, Department of Agricultural Marketing, 2000-, Professor, Department Head, Marketing Department, National Chung-Hsing University, Taichung, Taiwan. Publications: 80 papers published in Simulation Practice and Theory, Agricultural Systems, International Journal of Physical Distribution and Logistics Management, Aquaculture Economics and Management. Honours: Outstanding Research Award, Northeast Decision Science Institute, 1998; Listed in several Who's Who and biographical publications; Editor, International Journal of Supply Chain. Memberships: Phi-Tau-Phi; Operations Research, Council of Logistics, USA. Address: Department of Marketing, National Chung-Hsing University, 250 KuoKuang Road, Taichung, Taiwan, Republic of China. E-mail: trlee@dragon.nchu.edu.tw

LEE William Johnson, b. 13 January 1924, Oneida, Tennessee, USA. Attorney. m. Marjorie Young Lee, 20 August 1949, 2 sons. Education: Akron University; Denison University; Harvard University Graduate School; Ohio State University Law School; Admitted, Ohio Bar, Florida Bar, Federal US District Court Northern and Southern Districts, Ohio and Southern District of Florida. Appointments: Research Assistant, Ohio State University Law School, 1948-49; Served USAF; Attorney Examiner, Assistant State Permit Chief, State Permit Chief, Assistant State Liquor Control Director, Liquor Purchases Chief, Ohio Department Liquor Control, 1951-57; Assistant Counsel, Hupp Corporation, 1957-58; Lawyer in general practice, Acting Municipal Judge, Ohio, 1959-62; Part-time Instructor, College Business Administration, Kent State University, 1961-62; Papy and Carruthers Law Firm, Florida, 1962-63; Special Counsel, City Attorney's Office, Fort Lauderdale, Florida, 1963-65; Private practice in law, Fort Lauderdale, 1965-66; Assistant Attorney General, Office of Attorney General, State of Ohio, 1966-70; Administrator, State Medical Board, Ohio, 1970-85; Member, Editorial Board, Ohio State Law Journal; Member, Federated State Board's National Commission for Evaluation of Foreign Medical Schools, 1981-83; Member, Flex 1/Flex 2 Transitional Taskforce, 1983-84. Publications: Several articles. Honours: Wall of Tolerance, Montgomery, Alabama, USA; Outstanding People of 20th Century. Memberships: Broward County Bar Association; Akron Bar Association; Columbus Bar Association; Franklin County Trial Lawyers Association; American Legion; Phi Kappa Tau; Pi Kappa Delta; Delta Theta Phi; Experimental Aviation Association South West Florida; Association of Trial Lawyers of America. Address: 704 Country Club Drive, Apple Valley, Howard, OH 43028, USA.

LEE Young Woo, b. 9 March 1937, Ulsan City, Korea. Neuroscientist; Neurosurgeon; Biomedical Engineer. m. Kyung Ja Kim, 1 son, 1 daughter. Education: MD, School of Medicine, 1962, MSc, Medicine, 1965, PhD, 1973, Graduate School, Pusan National University, Pusan, Korea; Rotating Internship, 1962-63, Residency, General Surgery, 1963-65, Residency, Neurosurgery, 1965-67, Pusan National University Hospital, Pusan, Korea; Fellowship, Neurosurgery, Long Island College Hospital, Brooklyn, New York, USA, 1980-81. Appointments: Army Service, 1967-70; Instructor, Assistant Professor, Associate Professor, Professor, 1971-2002, Chairman, Department of Neurosurgery, 1975-2002, Pusan National University School of Medicine and Pusan National University Hospital, Pusan, Korea; Honorary Professor, Pusan National University, 2002-; Honorary Superintendent, Dong-Rae Bong Seng Hospital and Chairman of Department of Neurosurgery in Bong Seng Hospital, 2002-; Research Fellow, Department of Neurology, University of Alabama in Birmingham School of Medicine and Medical Center, USA, 1974-75; Fellowship, Department of Neurosurgery, Montreal Neurological Institute, McGill University, Montreal, Canada, 1998-99. Publications: Over 150 articles in scientific journals as author and co-author include most recently: Clinical Analysis Spondylolisthesis Treated with Pediatric Screw Instrumentation, 1998; Clinical Analysis of Thoracolumbar and Lumbar Spine Fracture Treated with Instrumentation; 1999; Prognosis of Surgically Treated Acute Subdural Hematoma, 2003; Chemical Hypoxia-Induced Cell Death in Human Glioma Cells: Role of Reactive Oxygen Species and Lipid Peroxidation; Role of Oxidative Stress in Amyloid-β Peptide-induced Death of Human Glioma Cells; H_2O_2-Induced Cell Death in Human Glioma Cells: Role of Lipid Peroxidation and PARP Activiation, 2001; Underlying Mechanism of Cisplatin-induced Apoptosis in PC-12 Cells, 1998; Modulation of Immune Responses by Capsaicin in Mice, 2000; Books in collaboration: Neurosurgery, 1989, 1996, 2001; The Great Medical Encyclopedia, 1991. Honours include: Military Medal in Vietnam War, President of the Republic of Korea, 1968; 2 Medals, Vietnam Government, 1969; Pfizer's Medical Company Prize, 1997; Madison Biomedical Prize, Korean Society of Biomedical Engineering, 1999; Educational Prizes, 2001, Korean Teacher Association, Pusan Teacher Association; Research Prize, Korean Neurosurgical Society, 2001. Numerous Memberships include: Korean Medical Association; Korean Neurosurgical Society; International College of Surgeons; Korean Society of Medical and Biological Engineering; New York Academy of Sciences; Korean Brain Tumour Study Group; Korean Society for Brain and Neural Science (Neuroscience); Korean Veterans Society. Address: Department of Neurosurgery, Pusan National University School of Medicine, 1-10 Ami-Dong, Seo-Ku, Pusan 607-753, Korea.

LEE Yuan Tseh, b. 29 November 1936, Hsinchu, Taiwan. Professor of Chemistry. m. Bernice W Lee, 1963, 2 sons, 1 daughter. Education: National Taiwan University; National Tsinghua University, Taiwan; University of California, Berkeley; PhD. Appointments: Assistant Professor, 1968-71, Associate Professor, 1971-72, Professor of Chemistry, 1973-74, James Franck Institute and Department of Chemistry, University of Chicago, Illinois, USA; Professor of Chemistry, 1974-94, Professor Emeritus, 1994-, University of California, Berkeley; Head, Academia Sinica, 1994. Publications: Articles in professional journals. Honours: Sloan Fellow, 1969; Guggenheim Fellow, 1976; Miller Professorship, 1981; E O Lawrence Award, US Department of Environment, 1981; Co-recipient, Nobel Prize for Chemistry, 1986; Many other awards and prizes. Memberships: American Academy of Arts and Sciences. Address: Department of Chemistry, University of California, Berkeley, CA 94720, USA.

LEE Yun-Bae, b. 29 May 1952, Mokpo, Chun-nam, Korea. Professor. m. 1 son, 1 daughter. Education: BS, 1980, MS, Graduate School, 1983, Kwang Woon University, Seoul, Korea; PhD, Soongsil Graduate School, 1993. Appointments: Dean, College of Information Science, Chosun University, 1997-99; Vice-president, Korea Information Processing Society, 2003-2004; President, Homan – Jeju Division, Korea Information Processing Society, 2001-2004. Publications: Author 110 technical papers and editor of 24 books in the field of information security, artificial intelligence, database and computer vision. Honour: Meritorious Services, KISS, 1995. Memberships: Korea Information Science Society; Korea Information Processing Society. Address: School of Computer Engineering, Chosun University, #375 Seosuk-dong, Dong-ku, Gwangju 501759, Korea. Website: http://cspost.chosun.ac.krl~yblee

Dictionary of International Biography

LEEDY Emily Louise Foster, b. 24 September 1921, Jackson, Ohio, USA. Educator: Administrator. m. William N Leedy, 1 son. Education: MEd, Ohio University; Postgraduate work, Counselling and Administration: Ohio University, Ohio State University, Michigan State University, Case Western Reserve University. Appointments: Teacher, Frankfort Public Schools, 1941-46, Ross County Schools, 1948-53, Chilicothe Public Schools, 1953-56, Berea City Schools (Dean of Girls), 1956-57, (Visiting Teacher), Parma City Schools, 1957-59, Ohio; Counsellor, Professional Staff Experimental Program, Flossmoor Public Schools, Illinois, 1959-60; Teaching Fellow, 1960-62, Assistant Professor of Education, 1962-64, Ohio University; Counsellor, Associate Professor of Education, Cuyahoga Community College, Cleveland, 1964-66; Dean of Women, 1966-67, Associate Dean of Student Affairs, 1967-69, Cleveland State University; Director of Guidance, Cathedral Latin School, Cleveland Public Schools, 1969-71; Director, Women's Division, Ohio Bureau of Employment Services, 1971-83. Honours include: Delta Kappa Gamma, Tau Chapter presents annually the Emily L Leedy Scholarship, 1974-; Award, Agriculture, Home Economics and Natural Resources College Council, Ohio State University Certificate of Merit, 1981; Special Award, National Association of Commissions for Woman, Washington DC, 1983; National Association of Women Deans, Counselors and Administrators, Meritorious Service Award, Boston, Massachusetts, 1983. Memberships Include: American Personnel and Guidance Association; Cleveland Counselors Association, President, 1966, Secretary-Treasurer, 1969; National Vocational Guidance Association. Address: 580 Lindberg Blvd, Berea, OH 44017-1418, USA.

LEES Andrew John, b. 27 September 1947, Liverpool, England. Professor of Neurology. m. Juana Luisa Pulin Perez Lopez, 1 son, 1 daughter. Education: Royal London Hospital Medical College, University of London; Post Graduate Training, L'Hopital Salpetriere, Paris, University College London Hospitals, National Hospital for Neurology and Neurosurgery. Appointments: Consultant Neurologist, National Hospital for Neurology and Neurosurgery; Professor of Neurology, Institute of Neurology; Director, Reta Lila Weston Institute of Neurological Science; Appeal Steward to the British Boxing Board of Control. Publications: Ray of Hope, authorised biography of Ray Kennedy; Tic and Related Disorders; 820 articles in peer reviewed medical journals. Honours: Charles Smith Lecturer, Jerusalem, 1999; Cotzias Lecturer 2000, Spanish Neurological Association. Memberships: Member, Royal Society of Medicine; Fellow, Royal College of Physicians; President, European Section of the Movement Disorders Society; Editor-in-Chief, Movement Disorders. Address: The Reta Lila Weston Institute for Neurological Studies, The Windeyer Building, 46 Cleveland Street, London, W1T 3AA, England. E-mail: a.lees@ion.ucl.ac.uk

LEES David (Bryan) (Sir), b. 23 November 1936, Aberdeen, Scotland. Business Executive. m. Edith Bernard, 1961, 2 sons, 1 daughter. Education: Chartered Accountant. Appointments: Articled Clerk, 1957-62, Senior Audit Clerk, 1962-63, Binder Hamlyn and Co, Chartered Accountants; Chief Accountant, Handley Page Ltd, 19640-68; Financial Director, Handley Page Aircraft Ltd, 1969; Chief Accountant, 1970-72, Deputy Controller, 1972-73, Director, Secretary, Controller, 1973-76, GKN Sankey Ltd; Group Finance Executive, 1976-77, General Manager Finance, 1977-82, GKN Ltd; Finance Director, 1982-87, Group Managing Director, 1987-88, Chairman, 1988-, Chief Executive Officer, 1988-97, GKN PLC; Commissioner, Audit Commission, 1983-90; Council Member, 1988-, Chairman, Economic Affairs Committee, 1988-94, Member, President's Committee, currently, Confederation of British Industry; Governor, Shrewsbury School, 1986-; Listed Companies Advisory Committee, 1990-97; Director,

1991-, Chairman, Courtaulds, 1996-98; Director, Bank of England, 1991-99; National Defence Council, 1995-; European Round Table, 1995-2002; Panel on Takeovers and Mergers, 2001-; Governor, Sutton's Hospital in Charterhouse, 1995-; Director, Royal Opera House, 1998-; Currently Chairman, Tate and Lyle PLC. Honours: Officer's Cross, Order of Merit, Germany, 1996; Founding Societies Centenary Award for Chartered Accountants, 1999. Memberships: Companion, British Institute of Management; Fellow, Institute of Chartered Accountants; Fellow, Royal Society of Arts; President, Engineering Employers Federation, 1990-92; President, Society of Business Economists, 1994-99. Address: Tate and Lyle PLC, Sugar Quay, Lower Thames Street, London EC3R 6DQ, England.

LEGGE-BOURKE Victoria Lindsay, b. 12 February 1950, Witchford, Cambridgeshire, England. Business Executive. Education: Benenden and St Hilda's College, Oxford. Appointments: Social Attaché, British Embassy, Washington, USA, 1971-73; Director, Junior Tourism LTD, 1974-81; Lady-in-Waiting, HRH The Princess Royal, 1974-86; Extra Lady-in-Waiting, HRH The Princess Royal, 1986-; Special Assistant, 1983-89, Head of Protocol, 1991-94, American Embassy, London; Council of the American Museum in Britain, 1995-; Executive Director, 1995-98, Executive Director of Cultural and Social Affairs, 1999-, Goldman Sachs International; Governor of the English Speaking Union, 1996-99; Director, Lehman Brothers, 1998-99. Honours: LVO, 1986; Meritorious Honor Award, US State Department, 1994. Membership: The Pilgrims. Address: 72 Albany Mansions, Albert Bridge Road, London SW11 4PQ, England. E-mail: victoria.legge-bourke@gs.com

LEGH Davis Piers Carlis (The Hon), b. 21 November 1951, Compton, England. Chartered Surveyor. m. Jane Wynter Bee, 2 sons, 2 daughters. Education: Eton, Royal Agricultural College, Cirencester. Appointments: Senior Partner, John German, 1994-99; Senior Partner, Germans, 1999-2000; Chairman, Fisher, German Chartered Surveyors, 2000-. Honour: FRICS. Memberships: Chairman, Taxation Committee, CLA. 1993-97; Chairman, East Midlands Region Country Land and Business Association (CLA), 2002-. Address: Cubley Lodge, Ashbourne, Derbyshire DE6 2FB, England.

LEGRIS Manuel Christopher, b. 19 October 1964, Paris, France. Ballet Dancer. Education: Paris Opera School of Dancing. Career: Member, Corps de Ballet, 1980, Danseur Etoile, 1986-, Paris Opéra; Major roles, Paris Opéra, include Arepo, Béjart, 1986, In the Middle Somewhat Elevated, Forsythe, 1987, Magnificat, Neumeier, 1987, Rules of the Game, Twyla Tharp, 1989, La Belle au Bois Dormant, Nureyev, 1989, Manon, MacMillan, 1990, Dances at the Gathering, Robbins, 1992; In Hamburg created Cinderella Story and Spring and Fall, Neumeier; Appearances, Bolshoi Ballet, Moscow, La Scala, Milan, Royal Ballet, London, New York City Ballet, Tokyo Ballet, Stuttgart Ballet, elsewhere. Honours: Gold Medal, Osaka Competition, 1984; Prix du Cercle Corpeaux, 1986; Nijinsky Prize, 1988; Benois de la Danse Prize, 1998; Chevalier des Arts et des Lettres, 1998; Nijinsky Award, 2000. Address: Théâtre National de l'Opéra de Paris, 8 rue Scribe, 75009 Paris, France.

LEHMAN Maria, b. 6 September 1960, Buffalo, New York, USA. Civil Engineer. m. Carl, 3 sons. Education: BS, Civil Engineering, 1981; Registered Professional Engineer, New York. Appointments: Project Manager, De Leuw Cather & Company; Transportation Group Leader, Project Manager, URS, 1994-97; Corporate Director, QA/QC URS, 1997-2000; Commissioner of Public Works, Erie County, 2000-. Honours: Edmund Friedman Young Engineer of the Year, 1990; Buffalo Business 40 Under 40,

1994; Outstanding Public Works Official of the Year, 2003; Governor's Award for Excellence in Business, 2003; SUNY at Buffalo, Engineering Alumna of the Year. Memberships: American Society of Civil Engineers; National Society of Professional Engineers; Tau Beta Pi; Chi Epsilon; Highway Users Alliance. Address: Erie County Department of Public Works, 95 Franklin Street, Buffalo, NY 14202, USA

LEHMANN Charlotte, b. 16 January 1938, Zweibrücken, Germany. Singer (Soprano); Professor. m. Ernst Huber-Contwig, 21 June 1965, 1 son. Education: Academy of Music and University of Saarland, Saarbrücken, with Sibylle Ursula Fuchs, then private study with Paul Lohmann, Wiesbaden. Career: Sang at concerts in Europe and America; Broadcasts, all German radio stations, France Musique, Schweizerischer Rundfunk, RTB Brussels, NL Hilversum, Turkish Radio, others; Television performances on ARD and ZDF; Started teaching at Hanover Music Academy, 1972; Appointed to Chair of Voice, Würzburg Academy of Music, 1988-2003; Has taught winners of international prizes, including Lioba Braun, Thomas Quasthoff and Maria Kowollik; Has led international master classes in Brazil, Chile, England, Bulgaria, Japan and Luxembourg; Has regularly given courses at the Haus Marteau music centre, Lichtenberg-Bayreuth; Editor, Bach and Mozart arias for all voice parts, for publishers Bärenreiter-Verlag; International jury service; Lectures. Recordings: Works of Bach, Mozart, Schumann, Wolf, Fauré, Debussy, Hindemith, Schönberg, other composers. Honours: Prizewinner, L'Amour du Chant International Competition and UFAM, Paris; German Record Critics Prize for Debussy and Schönberg recording, 1982. Membership: President, 1995-2000, Honorary President, 2000-, Bundesverband Deutscher Gesangspädagogen. Address: Gellertstrasse 55, 30175 Hannover, Germany.

LEIBOWITZ Annie, b. 2 October 1949, Connecticut, USA. Photographer. Education: San Francisco Art Institute. Career: Photographed rock'n'roll stars and other celebrities for Rolling Stone magazine, 1970s; Chief Photographer, Vanity Fair, 1983-; Proprietor, Annie Leibovitz Studio, New York; Celebrity portraits include studies of John Lennon, Mick Jagger, Bette Midler, Louis Armstrong, Ella Fitzgerald, Jessye Norman, Mikhail Baryshnikov, Arnold Schwarzenegger, Tom Wolfe; Retrospective exhibition, Smithsonian National Portrait Gallery, Washington DC, 1991. Publications: Photographs 1970-90, 1992; Women, with Susan Sontag, 2000. Honours: Innovation in Photography Award, American Society of Magazine Photographers, 1987. Address: Annie Leibowitz Studio, 55 Vandam Street, New York, NY 10013, USA.

LEIGH Elisabeth Sarah, b. 14 July 1939, London, England. Writer; Lecturer. Education: BA, French and Italian, Somerville College, Oxford; Piccolo Teatro School of Mime, Milan; Central School of Speech and Drama, London. Appointments: Researcher, Producer, Director, BBC Television, 1963-68; Producer, Director, Yorkshire Television, 1969; Independent documentary film producer/director, films for BBCTV, Thames TV and Yorkshire TV, 1969-82; Contributor, food and magazine features, Sunday Times, 1984-91; Novelist, 1989-; Lecturer in Creative Writing, City of Westminister College, London, 1999-. Publications: 5 novels; Sunday Times Guide to Enlightened Eating; Articles for Sunday Times, Elle and Evening Standard. Honours: British Association for the Advancement of Science: Experiment in Time, 1969; BISFA Award, Call for Help, 1971; Argos Award for Consumer Journalism, 1987. Memberships: Society of Authors. Address: c/o David Higham Associates, 5-8 Lower John Street, London W1R 4HA, England.

LEIGH Jennifer Jason, b. 5 February 1962, Los Angeles, California, USA. Actress. Career: Appeared in Walt Disney TV movie The Young Runaways, age 15; Other TV films include The Killing of Randy Webster, 1981, The Best Little Girl in the World, 1981; Film appearances including Eyes of a Stranger, 1981, Fast Times at Ridgemont High, 1982, Grandview, USA, 1984, Flesh and Blood, 1985, The Hitcher, 1986, The Men's Club, 1986, Heart of Midnight, 1989, The Big Picture, 1989, Miami Blues, 1990, Last Exit to Brooklyn, 1990, Crooked Hearts, 1991, Backdraft, 1991, Rush, 1992, Single White Female, 1992, Short Cuts, 1993, The Hudsucker Proxy, 1994, Mrs Parker and the Vicious Circle, 1994, Georgia, 1995, Kansas City, 1996, Washington Square, 1997, eXistenZ, 1999; The King is Alive, 2000; The Anniversary Party, 2001; Crossed Over, 2002; Road to Perdition, 2002; In The Cut, 2003; Stage appearances including Sunshine, Off-Broadway, 1989. Address: c/o Elaine Rich, 2400 Whitman Place, Los Angeles, CA 90211, USA.

LEIGH Mike, b. 20 February 1943, Salford, Lancashire, England. Dramatist; Film and Theatre Director. m. Alison Steadman, 1973, divorced 2001, 2 sons. Education: Royal Academy of Dramatic Arts; Camberwell School of Arts and Crafts; Central School of Art and Design; London Film School. Publications: Plays: The Box Play, 1965; My Parents Have Gone to Carlisle, The Last Crusade of the Five Little Nuns, 1966; Nenaa, 1967; Individual Fruit Pies, Down Here and Up There, Big Basil, 1968; Epilogue, Glum Victoria and the Lad with Specs, 1969; Bleak Moments, 1970; A Rancid Pong, 1971; Wholesome Glory, The Jaws of Death, Dick Whittington and His Cat, 1973; Babies Grow Old, The Silent Majority, 1974; Abigail's Party, 1977, also TV play; Ecstasy, 1979; Goose-Pimples, 1981; Smelling a Rat, 1988; Greek Tragedy, 1989; It's a Great Big Shame!, 1993. TV films: A Mug's Game, Hard Labour, 1973; The Permissive Society, The Bath of the 2001 F A Cup, Final Goalie, Old Chums, Probation, A Light Snack, Afternoon, 1975; Nuts in May, Knock for Knock, 1976; The Kiss of Death, 1977; Who's Who, 1978; Grown Ups, 1980; Home Sweet Home, 1981; Meantime, 1983; Four Days in July, 1984; Feature films: Bleak Moments, 1971; The Short and Curlies, 1987; High Hopes, 1988; Life is Sweet, 1990; Naked, 1993; Secrets and Lies, 1996; Career Girls, 1997; Topsy Turvy, 1999; All or Nothing, 2002. Radio Play: Too Much of a Good Thing, 1979. Honours: Golden Leopard, Locarno Film Festival, 1972; Golden Hugo, Chicago Film Festival, 1972; George Devine Award, 1973; Evening Standard Award, 1981; Drama Critics Choice, London, 1981; Critics Prize, Venice Film Festival, 1988; Honorary MA, Salford University, 1991; Northampton, 2000; OBE, 1993; Best Director Award, Cannes Film Festival, 1993; Palme D'Or, Cannes Film Festival, 1996; Honorary DLitt, Stafford, 2000, Essex, 2002. Address: The Peters, Fraser and Dunlop Group Ltd, 503/4 The Chambers, Chelsea Harbour, London SW10 0XF, England.

LEISTNER Lothar E E, b. 23 July 1927, Aue, Germany. Food Microbiologist. m. Kai-Min Leistner, 2 sons, 1 daughter. Education: Dr Med Vet (DVM), Berlin, Germany, 1954. Appointments: Federal Centre for Meat Research, Germany, 1954-59; American Meat Institute Foundation, USA, 1959-61; Institute Pasteur de Lille, France, 1961-62; Euratom, France, 1962-63; Iowa State University, USA, 1963-66; Federal Centre for Meat Research, Germany, 1966-92; International Food Consultant, 1992-. Publications: Author, co-author, 1200 scientific publications including 65 chapters of books and 8 books; Specialist on food microbiology, food preservation and food toxicology. Honours: Elected member, Academy of Agricultural Science of Russia, 1991; Appointed permanent consultant Chinese Meat Research Center, 1991; International Award American Meat Science Association,

1992; Rievel-Medaille of the Federal Centre for Meat Research, Germany, 1993. Address: An den Weinbergen 20, D-95326 Kulmbach, Germany.

LEITE Ascendino, b. 21 June 1915, Conceição, PB, Brazil. Writer; Journalist. Widower, 1 son, 4 daughters. Education: Self-Taught. Appointments: Government Official, Retired. Publications include: Literary Criticism: Estética do modernismo Notal Provincianas; Fiction: A Viuva Branca, O Salto Mortal. A Prisão O Brasileiro; Translations: Armancia (Stendhal); Uma Visa (Maupassant); Poetry: Visoés do Vale; Os Juizes; Por Uma Saudade Azul; Poemas do Fim Comun; A Flor da Terra; Poesia Reunida; Aforismos da Precisão; Articles in literary journals. Honours: Rio Branco Medal, Itamarati; Ordem do Infante, Portuguese Government; Epitácio Pessoa Medal, Paraiba, Brazil; Tamandaré Medal, Brazil. Memberships: Academia Carioca de Letras; Instituto Histório de Petrópolis; Instituto Histórico da Paraiba; I H de R G Norte; Academia Paraibana de Letras. Address: Caixa Postal 3065, Tambaú, Joao Pessoa, Paraiba, Brazil, CEP 58039-970

LEITH Prudence Margaret, b. 18 February 1940, Cape Town, South Africa. Caterer; Author. m. Rayne Kruger, 1 son, 1 daughter. Education: Haywards Heath, Sussex; St Mary's, Johannesburg; Cape Town University; Sorbonne, Paris; Cordon Bleu School, London. Appointments: Started Leith's Good Food, 1965; Leith's Restaurant, 1969; Cookery Correspondent, Daily Mail, 1969-73; Managing Director, Prudence Leith Ltd, 1972-94; Chair, Leith's Ltd, 1994-96; Opened Leith's School of Food and Wine, 1975; Added Leith's Farm, 1976; Cookery Correspondent, Daily Express, 1976-80; Cookery Editor, The Guardian, 1980-85; Columnist, 1986-90; Subject of TV Documentaries by BBC and Channel 4; Presented Series Tricks of the Trade, BBC1; Government National Institute of Economic and Social Research; Vice Patron, Women in Finance and Banking; Chair, UK Committee, New Era Schools Trust, 1994 British Food Heritage Trust, 1997-; Director, Halifax Plc, 1995-; Whitbread PLC, 1995; Argyll Group, 1989-96; Woolworths, 2001-; Governor, Kingsmead City Technical College; Reader, Queen's Anniversary Prizes; Patron, Prue Leith College of Food and Wine, Johannesburg, 1997-. Publications include: Leith's All Party Cook Book, 1969; Parkinson's Pie, 1972; Cooking for Friends, 1978; The Best of Prue Leith, 1979; Leith's Cookery Course, 1979-80; The Cook's Handbook, 1981; Prue Leith's Pocket Book of Dinner Parties, 1983; Dinner Parties, 1984; Leith's Cookery School, 1985; Entertaining with Style, 1986; Confident Cooking, 1989-90; Leith's Cookery Bible, 1991; Leith's Complete Christmas, 1992; Leith's Book of Baking, 1993; Leith's Vegetarian Cookery, 1993; Leith's Step by Step Cookery, 1993; Leaving Patrick (novel), 1999; Sisters (novel), 2001. Honours: Honorary Fellow, University of Salford, 1992; Visiting Professor, University of North London, 1993; Business Woman of the Year. Memberships: Royal Society of Arts; Vice-President, Restaurateurs Association of Great Britain; National Council for Vocational Qualifications; UK Skills, Stamp Committee. Address: 94 Kensington Park Road, London, W11 2PN, England.

LELAS Vesna, b. 28 July 1947, Zagreb, Croatia. University Professor. m. Tihomir Lelas, 2 daughters. Education: Faculty of Technology, University of Zagreb, 1972; Master of Science, University of Zagreb, 1980; PhD, Faculty of Food Technology and Biotechnology, University of Zagreb, 1985. Appointments: Assistant, 1973-86, Assistant Professor, 1986-91, Associate Professor, 1991-97, Vice Dean for Education, 1995-99, Professor, 1997-, Vice Dean for Science, 1999-2001, Faculty of Food Technology and Biotechnology, University of Zagreb. Publications: 6 book chapters; 50 scientific articles; 4 professional articles.

Honours: Honour of Science 'Danica', 1998. Memberships: Croatian Academy of Engineering; Institute of Food Technologists, USA; PBN Club. Address: Faculty of Food Technology and Biotechnology, Pierottijeva 6, 10000 Zagreb, Croatia. E-mail: vlelas@pbf.hr

LEMPER Ute, b. 4 July 1963, Munster, Germany. Singer; Dancer; Actress. Education: Max Reinhardt-Seminar, Vienna. Appointments: Leading Role, Viennese Production of Cats, 1983; Appeared in Peter Pan, Berlin, Cabaret, Düsseldorf and Paris; Chicago, 1997-99; Life's A Swindle tour, 1999; Punishing Kiss tour, 2000; Albums include: Ute Lemper Sings Kurt Weill, 1988; Vol 2, 1993; Threepenny Opera, 1988; Mahoganny Songspiel, 1989; Illusions, 1992; Espace Indécent, 1993; City of Strangers, 1995; Berlin Cabaret Songs, 1996; All that Jazz/The Best of Ute Lemper, 1998; Punishing Kiss, 2000; Film appearances include: L'Autrichienne, 1989; Moscou Parade, 1992; Coupable d'Innocence, 1993; Prêt à Porter, 1995; Bogus, 1996; Combat de Fauves; A River Made to Drown In; Appetite. Honours: Moliere Award, 1987; Laurence Oliver Award; French Culture Prize, 1993. Address: c/o Oliver Gluzman, 40 rue de la Folie Regnault, 75011 Paris, France.

LENARCIC Leonid Alojzij, b. 24 July 1932, Ljubljana. Architecture; Planning. Education: Diploma, Faculty of Architecture, University of Belgrade; Diploma in Planning, Architectural Association School of Architecture, London. Appointments: Architect-Planner, member of team designing Central Zone of New Belgrade, 1959; Architect in charge (Group Leader), Architects Department, Institute for Testing Materials and Constructions, Belgrade, 1960-67; Professional Officer Grade B, Greater London Council PTDept, 1968-72; Senior Researcher with Magistracy, Urban Planning Institute of Slovenia, 1972-96. Civic Activities: Environmental Protection (see International Directory of Environment-Behaviour-Design Researches). Publications: Percepcijski aspekti mestne vizualne oblike (Aspects of Urban Visual Form, 1974); Numerous articles in professional journals on urban planning theory, urban environment and spatial planning. Honours: Silver Plaque for Outstanding Contributions, Yugoslav League for Protection and Advancement of the Human Environment; Sixth Belgrade Triennial of World Architecture; 100 Buildings Representative of Belgrade Architecture in the 20th Century; Museum of Contemporary Art, 2000; Listed in national and international biographical publications. Memberships: Association of Urban and Spatial Planners of Slovenia; Association of Architects of Slovenia. Commissions and Creative Works: National Competition for Centre of New Belgrade, 1st Place, 1958; Centre of New Belgrade project, 1959; Residential Building PTT Zdr. Celara, Belgrade, 1967; Residential buildings "A" and "B" Neighbourhood Unit 21, New Belgrade, 1967; Urban Development Plan "Potamisje", Pancevo, 1991. Address: Scapinova 1/B, 1000 Ljubljana, Slovenia.

LENDL Ivan, b. 7 March 1960, Czechoslovakia, US citizen, 1992. Retired Professional Tennis Player. m. Samantha Frankel, 1989, 5 daughters. Appointments: Winner, Italian Junior Singles, 1978; French Junior Singles, 1978; Wimbledon Junior Singles, 1978; Spanish Open Singles, 1980, 1981; South American Open Singles, 1981; Canadian Open Singles, 1980, 1981; WCT Tournament of Champion Singles, 1982; WCT Masters Singles, 1982; WCT Finals Singles, 1982; Masters Champion, 1985. 1986; French Open Champion, 1984, 1986, 1987; US Open Champion, 1985, 1986, 1987; US Clay Court Champion, 1985; Italian Open Champion, 1986; Australian Open Champion, 1989, 1990; Finalist Wimbledon, 1986; Held, World No 1 Ranking for a Record 270 weeks; Named World Champion, 1985, 1986, 1990; Retired, 1994. Publication: Ivan Lendl's Power Tennis. Honours: Granted

American Citizenship, 1992; ATP Player of the Year, 1985, 1986, 1987; Inducted, International Tennis Hall of Fame, 2001. Memberships: Laureus World Sports Academy. Address: c/o Laureus World Sports Academy, 15 Hill Street, London W1 5QT, England.

LENEY Sheila Joan, b. 23 November 1930, Norbury, London, England. Artist. m. Edward William, deceased, 2 sons, 1 daughter. Education: Art and Needlework, Croydon School of Art, 1947-49. Career: Botanical Artist and Embroiderer; Exhibitions: The Mall Galleries; Westminster Gallery; Linnean Society; Knapp Gallery; Hampton Court; McEwan Gallery, Scotland; Galleries in Surrey and Sussex; Works in Private Collections; Designs for the Medici Society. Memberships: Society of Botanical Artists, 1987-2000; Society of Graphic Fine Art, 1988-95. Address: Invermene, 107 Newton Wood Road, Ashtead, Surrey KT21 1NW, England.

LENGYEL Alfonz, b. 21 October 1921, Godollo, Hungary. Professor. m. Hongying Liu. Education: Law Degree, Miskolc Law Academy, 1948; BA, 1958, MA, 1959, Art History, San Jose State College; Doctorate, Institute of Art and Archaeology, University of Paris, 1964; Internship, Ecole du Louvre, Paris, 1964-65. Appointments: Assistant Professor, Art History, San Jose State College, 1961-63; Lecturer, University of Maryland, 1963-68; Professor, Wayne State University, 1968-72; Professor, Northern Kentucky University, 1972-77; Founder, Dean, Institute of Mediterranean Art and Archaeology, Cincinnati, Ohio, 1977-82; Coordinator, Rosemont College, 1982-85; Professor, Eastern College, St Davids, 1985-87; Member, Advisory Board, US Department of Interior, 1987-91; Advisory Professor, Fudan University, Shanghai, 1987-; Consulting Professor, Xian Jiaoting University, China, 1988-; Founder, American Director, Sino-American Field School of Archaeology. Publications: Public Relations for Museums; Archaeology for Museologists; Chinese Chronological History. Honours: Honorary Doctorate in Law; Gold Medal, Brazil Academy of Humanities; Certificate in Merit, Classical Archaeology; Director's Award, UPAO. Memberships: New York Academy of Sciences; International Academy of Sciences and Letters; Michigan Academy of Sciences, Letters and Arts; Institute of Social Murumbi; American Associations of Museums; International Council of Museums, ICOM/UNESCO; Member, Governing Board of the Museum of Asian Art, Sarasota, Florida, USA; Others. Address: 4206-73rd Terrace East, Sarasota, FL 34243, USA.

LENNARD-JONES John Edward, b. 29 January 1927, Great Britain. Emeritus Professor of Gastroenterology. m. 4 sons. Education: BA, 1947, MA, 1951, MB BChir, 1953, MD, 1965, Cambridge University; MRCP, London, 1956; FRCP, London, 1968; FRCS, England, 1992; DSc (Hon), Kingston University, 1999. Appointments include: Senior House Officer, Medical Professorial Unit, Manchester Royal Infirmary, 1954-56; Medical Registrar, Central Middlesex Hospital, London, 1956-58; Medical Registrar, University College Hospital, London, 1958-59; Scientific Staff, Medical Research Council, University College Hospital Medical School, London, 1959-61; Senior Medical Registrar, Department of Gastroenterology, 1961-63; Member, Medical Research Council, Gastroenterology Research Unit, 1963-74, Central Middlesex Hospital, London; Consultant Gastroenterologist, St Mark's Hospital, 1965-92; Consultant Physician, University College Hospital, 1965-74; Professor of Gastroenterology, The Royal London Hospital Medical College, 1974-87; Emeritus Professor of Gastroenterology, University of London, 1987-; Honorary Consulting Gastroenterologist, The Royal London Hospital, 1988-; Emeritus Consultant Gastroenterologist. St Mark's Hospital, 1992-; Honorary Senior Research Fellow, United Guy's and St Thomas's Medical and

Dental School, London, 1996-2000. Publications 4 books (joint author); Many book chapters; Numerous scientific papers, reports and other contributions on gastroenterology, clinical nutrition, general medicine. Honours include: Cunning Prize in Medicine, Corpus Christi College, Cambridge, 1953; Trotter Medal in Clinical Surgery, Filliter Exhibition in Pathology, Tuke Silver Medal in Clinical pathology, 1952; Aichison Scholarship, Magrath Scholarship in Medicine, Fellowes Gold Medal in Medicine, Alexander Bruce Gold Medal in Surgical Pathology, Sir Thomas Lewis Essay Prize, 1953, University College Hospital, London; Research Prize, Central Middlesex Hospital, 1964; Honorary Fellow, Royal Society of Medicine, 1994; Medal for Outstanding Contribution to Clinical Nutrition, British Association for Parenteral and Enteral Nutrition, 1995; Fellow, University College, London, 1995. Honorary Memberships include: British Society of Gasteroenterology (numerous offices, 1965-); Ileostomy Association; Life President, National Association for Colitis and Crohn's Disease; Trustee, Chairman, 1997-, Sir Halley Stewart Trust. Address: 72 Cumberland Street, Woodbridge, Suffolk, IP12 4AD, England.

LENNARTSSON Olof Walter, b. 27 October 1943, Sweden. Physicist. m. Nancy Karllee, 1 son. Education: MEng, 1969, PhD, Plasma Physics, 1974, Royal Institute of Technology, Stockholm, Sweden. Appointments: NAS/NRC Research Associate, 1974-76; Docent, Royal Institute of Technology, Sweden, 1976-78; Staff Scientist, Lockheed Martin Missiles and Space, 1979-. Publications: Numerous articles in scientific journals and books. Memberships: American Geophysical Union; American Institute of Physics. Address: Lockheed Martin Space Systems Co, Advanced Technology Center, ADCS, B255, 3251 Hanover Street, Palo Alto, CA 94304, USA.

LENNOX Annie, 25 December 1954, Aberdeen, Scotland. Singer; Lyricist. m. (1) Rahda Raman, March 1984, divorced, (2) Uri Fruchtmann, 1 son, 1 daughter. Musical Education: Royal Academy Music. Career: Member, with Dave Stewart, The Catch, 1977; Re-named The Tourists, 1979-80; Formed Eurythmics with Dave Stewart, 1980-89; World-wide concerts include Nelson Mandela's 70th Birthday Tribute, Wembley, 1988; Solo artiste, 1988-; Eurythmics reformed, 1999; TV includes: Documentary, Diva, BBC2, 1992; Unplugged concert, MTV, 1992; Actress, film Revolution, 1985; 10 million albums sold to date. Creative works: Recordings: with the Tourists: The Tourists; Reality Affect; Luminous Basement; with Eurythmics: In The Garden, 1982; Sweet Dreams (Are Made Of This), 1983; Touch (Number 1, UK), 1984; 1984 (For The Love Of Big Brother), 1984; Be Yourself Tonight, 1985; Revenge, 1986; Savage, 1988; We Too Are One (Number 1, UK), 1989; Eurythmics Greatest Hits (Number 1, UK), 1991; Eurythmics Live 1983-89, 1992; Solo: Diva (Number 1, UK), 1992; Medusa (Number 1, UK), 1995; Bare, 2003; Contribution to: Red Hot And Blue, 1990; Rock The World, 1990; Hit singles include: with the Tourists: I Only Want To Be With You, 1979; So Good To Be Back Home, 1979; with Eurythmics: Sweet Dreams (Are Made Of This) (Number 1, US), 1983; Love Is A Stranger, 1983; Who's That Girl?, 1983; Right By Your Side, 1983; Here Comes The Rain Again, 1984; Sex Crime (1984), from film 1984, 1984; Would I Lie To You?, 1985; There Must Be An Angel (Playing With My Heart), (Number 1, UK), 1985; Sisters Are Doing It For Themselves, duet with Aretha Franklin, 1985; It's Alright (Baby's Coming Back), 1986; When Tomorrow Comes, 1986; Thorn In My Side, 1986; Missionary Man, 1986; You Have Placed A Chill In My Heart, 1988; I Changed the World Today, 2000; Feels Like I'm Seventeen Again, 2000; Solo: Put A Little Love In Your Heart, with Al Green, from film soundtrack Scrooged, 1988; Why, 1992; Walking On Broken Glass, 1992; Little Bird/ Love Song For A Vampire, from film Bram Stoker's Dracula, 1993;

Dictionary of International Biography

No More I Love Yous, 1995; Whiter Shade Of Pale, 1995; Waiting In Vain, 1995; Something So Right, with Paul Simon, 1995; Videos: Eurythmics Live; Sweet Dreams; Savage. Honours: Grammy Awards; BRIT Awards; Ivor Novello Awards; Rolling Stone Readers Poll Winner, Best Female Singer, 1993. Address: 19 Management, Unit 32, Ransomes Dock, 35-37 Parkgate Road, London SW11 4NP, England.

LEONĂCHESCU Nicolae, 9 July 1934, Stroeşti-Argeş Village, Romania. Thermo-Engineer. m. Nicolina, 1 son, 1 daughter. Education: Technical University of Civil Engineering, Bucharest, 1957; Doctorate in Thermodynamics, 1968. Appointments: Assistant, 1957-62; Lecturer, 1962-68; Associate Professor, 1968-77; Visiting Professor, Technical University, Dresden, Germany, 1971; Professor, 1977-2001; Founder and President, Cultural-Scientific 'Stroeşti-Argeş' Society, 1972-92; Founder and President, Romanian Thermodynamic Society, 1990-98; Chief Editor, TERMOTEHNICA Review, 1993-98; Visiting Professor, University of Moscow, 1977; Visiting Professor, University of Strasbourg, France, 1991; Visiting Professor, University of Chambery, France, 1994; MP, House of Deputies, 1996-2004; Secretary BP House of Deputies, 2001-2004; Deputy Chairman, Committee on European Integration, 2000-2002; Deputy Chairman, Committee on Environment, House of Deputies. Publications include: More than 430 scientific articles and materials; 30 books; 2 patents. Honours: Professor Emeritus, 1981; Prize, CNOP, 1986; Prize, "Dimitrie Leonida", 1995; SRT, 1999; Doctor Honoris Causa, Craiova University, 2004; Listed in Who's Who publications and biographical dictionaries. Memberships include: Romanian Thermodynamic Society; Cultural Scientific 'Stroeşti-Argeş' Society. Address: Str Cobălcescu 41B, Ap 8, Sector 1, 010193 Bucharest 1, Romania. E-mail: nleonachescu@cdep.ro

LEONARD Elmore (John, Jr), b. 11 October 1925, New Orleans, Louisiana, USA. Novelist. m. (1) Beverly Cline, 30 August 1949, 3 sons, 2 daughters, divorced 7 October 1977, (2) Joan Shepard, 15 September 1979, deceased, 13 January 1993, (3) Christine Kent, 15 August 1993. Education: BA, University of Detroit, 1950. Publications: 33 novels including: Hombre, 1961; City Primeval, 1980; Split Images, 1981; Cat Chaser, 1982; Stick, 1983; Labrava, 1983; Glitz, 1985; Bandits, 1986; Touch, 1987; Freaky Deaky, 1988; Killshot, 1989; Get Shorty, 1990; Maximum Bob, 1991; Rum Punch, 1992; Pronto, 1993; Riding the Rap, 1995; Out of Sight, 1996; Pagan Babies, 2000. Other: The Tonto Woman and Other Western Stories, 1998; Screenplays: Cuba Libre, 1998; Be Cool, 1999. Honours: Edgar Allan Poe Award, 1984, and Grand Master Award, 1992, Mystery Writers of America; Michigan Foundation for the Arts Award for Literature, 1985; Honorary degrees in Letters from Florida Atlantic University, 1995, University of Detroit Mercy, 1997. Memberships: Writers Guild of America; PEN; Authors Guild; Western Writers of America; Mystery Writers of America. Address: c/o Michael Siegel, Brillstein-Grey Entertainment, 9150 Wilshire Boulevard, Beverly Hills, CA 90212, USA.

LEONARD Hugh, (John Keyes Byrne), b. 9 Nov 1926, Dublin, Ireland. Playwright. m. Paule Jacquet, 1955, 1 daughter. Publications: Plays: The Big Birthday, 1957; A Leap in the Dark, 1957; Madigan's Lock, 1958; A Walk on the Water, 1960; The Passion of Peter Ginty, 1961; Stephen D, 1962; The Poker Session, 1963; Dublin 1, 1963; The Saints Go Cycling In, 1965; Mick and Mick, 1966; The Quick and the Dead, 1967; The Au Pair Man, 1968; The Barracks, 1969; The Patrick Pearse Motel, 1971; Da, 1973; Thieves, 1973; Summer, 1974; Times of Wolves and Tigers, 1974; Irishmen, 1975; Time Was, 1976; A Life, 1977; Moving Days, 1981; The Mask of Moriarty, 1984. Television: Silent Song,

1967; Nicholas Nickleby, 1977; London Belongs to Me, 1977; The Last Campaign, 1978; The Ring and the Rose, 1978; Strumpet City, 1979; The Little World of Don Camillo, 1980; Kill, 1982; Good Behaviour, 1982; O'Neill, 1983; Beyond the Pale, 1984; The Irish RM, 1985; A Life, 1986; Troubles, 1987; Parnell and the Englishwoman, 1988; A Wild People, 2001. Films: Herself Surprised, 1977; Da, 1984; Widows' Peak, 1984; Troubles, 1984. Publications: Home Before Night, autobiography, 1979; Out After Dark, autobiography, 1988; Parnell and the Englishwoman, 1989; I, Orla! 1990; Rover and other Cats, a memoir, 1992; The Off-Shore Island, novel, 1993; The Mogs, for children, 1995; Magic, 1997; Fillums, 2003. Honours: Honorary DHL (RI); Writers Guild Award, 1966; Tony Award; Critics Circle Award; Drama Desk Award; Outer Critics Award, 1978; Doctor of Literature, Trinity College, Dublin, 1988. Address: 6 Rossaun Pilot View, Dalkey, County Dublin, Ireland.

LEONARD Ray Charles (Sugar Ray), b. 17 May 1956, Wilmington, North Carolina, USA. Boxer. m. Juanita Wilkinson, 1980, divorced 1990, 2 sons. Appointments: Amateur Boxer, 1970-77; won 140 of 145 amateur fights; World amateur champion, 1974; US amateur athletic union champion, 1974; Pan-American Games Gold Medallist, 1975; Olympic Gold Medallist, 1976; Guaranteed Record Purse of $25,000 for first professional fight, 1977; Won, North American Welterweight title from Pete Ranzany, 1979; Won World Boxing Council Version of World Welterweight title from Wilfred Benitez, 1979; Retained title against Dave Green, 1980; Lost it to Roberto Duran, Montreal, 1980; Regained title from Duran, New Orleans, 1980; Won Junior Middleweight title, World Boxing Association, 1981; Won, WBA World Welterweight title from Tommy Hearns to become undisputed World Champion, 1981; Drew rematch, 1989; 36 professional fights, 33 wins, lost 2, 1 draw; Retired from boxing, 1982; returned to ring, 1987; Won World Middleweight title; Lost to Terry Norris, 1991; retired, 1991, 1997; returned to ring, 1997; Lost International Boxing Council Middleweight title fight to Hector Camacho, 1992; Commentator, Home Box Office TV Co; Motivational speaker. Address: Suite 303, 4401 East West Highway, Bethesda, MD 20814, USA.

LEONARD Todd Jay, b. 16 November 1961, Shelbyville, Indiana, USA. University Professor. Education: BA with Honors and Distinction, Humanities, 1985, MA, History, 1987, Purdue University, Indiana, USA; Diploma, Teaching English as a Foreign Language, English Language Centre, London, England, 1993; PhD, Social Science, Empresarial University of Costa Rica, 2004. Appointments include: Visiting Professor, La Universidad de las Americas, Costa Rica, 1987; Visiting Lecturer, 1988, Course Coordinator, 1988-89, Department of Foreign Languages and Literatures, Purdue University, Indiana, USA; Assistant English Teacher, Japan Exchange and Teaching Programme, 1989-92; Associate Professor of English, Hirosaki Gakuin University, Japan, 1992-; Part-time Lecturer, Faculty of Education, 1993-; Part-time Lecturer, Faculty of Liberal Arts, 1993-, Hirosaki University, Japan; English Language Committee Member, National Entrance Examination, Daigaku Nyushi Center, Tokyo, 1998-2002; Ordained Minister, Universal Spiritualist Association, Muncie, Indiana, 2003. Publications: Academic books include: East Meets West: Understanding Misunderstandings between ALTs and JTEs, 1999; Orbit English Reading, 2004; ESL related textbooks include: Team-Teaching Together: A Bilingual Resource Handbook for JTES and AETS; East Meets West: An American in Japan, 1998; Trendy Traditions! A Cross-Cultural Skills-Based Reader of Essays on the United States, 2001; Business as Usual: An Integrated Approach to Learning English, 2004; Numerous academic articles and book reviews. Honours include: Dean's List, Purdue University; Outstanding and Distinguished Graduate Instructor, Purdue University, 1987; Rotary Scholar, La Universidad de Costa

Rica, 1987; Governor Appointed Trustee for the Committee on Foreigners Living in Aomori, Aomori Foundation for International Relations, 1991-92; Pi Sigma Alpha; Sigma Delta Pi; Phi Alpha Theta; Phi Kappa Phi. Memberships include: Japan Association for Language Teachers; Modern Language Journal Association; Japan Association of Comparative Culture; Life Member Purdue Alumni Association. Address: Jyonan 4-3-19, Hirosaki-shi, Aomori-ken 036-8232 Japan. E-mail: tleonard@infoaomori.ne.jp Website: www.toddjayleonard.com

LEONHARDT Joyce LaVon, b. 17 December 1927, Aurora, Nebraska, USA. Poet. Education: BS, Union College, Lincoln, 1952. Appointments: High School Teacher, 1952-76; Junior College Instructor, 1981-90. Contributions to: Several books of poems. Honours: Honourable Mention Certificates; Golden Poet; Silver Poet. Membership: World of Poetry. Address: 1824 Atwood Street, Longmont, CO 80501, USA.

LEONI Tea, b. 25 February 1966, New York, USA. Actress. m. David Duchovny, 1997, 1 son, 1 daughter. Career: Film appearances in Switch, 1991, A League of Their Own, 1992, Wyatt Earp, 1994, Bad Boys, 1995, Flirting with Disaster, 1996, Deep Impact, 1998, There's No Fish Food in Heaven, 1999; The Family Man, 2000; Jurassic Park III, 2001; Hollywood Ending, 2002; People I Know, 2002; House of D, 2004; Appeared in TV sitcoms Naked Truth, 1995, Flying Blind, 1995. Address: c/o ICM, 8942 Wilshire Boulevard, Beverly Hills, CA 90211, USA.

LEONIDOPOULOS Georgios, b. 19 April 1958, Kalamata, Messinia, Greece. Electrical, Computer and Electronics Engineer; Researcher; Educator. Education: Diploma, Electrical and Computer Engineering, Patra University, Greece, 1981; Postgraduate, Iowa State University, USA, 1982, Wayne State University, USA, 1983; MSc, 1984; PhD, Electronic and Electrical Engineering, Strathclyde University, Glasgow, Scotland, 1988. Appointments: Trainee Electrical Engineer, Public Electricity Co, Kalamata, Greece, 1979; Teaching Assistant, Strathclyde University, Scotland, 1984-87; Engineering Educator, Secondary School, Kalamata, Greece, 1991-94; Professor, Engineering, Institute of Technology, Kalamata, Greece, 1994-97; Professor, Engineering, Electrical Engineering Department, Institute of Technology, Lamia, Greece, 1997-. Publications include: A method for locating polymeric insulation failure of underground cables, 1998; On the convergence of three series, 1998; Root investigation of third degree algebraic equation, 1998; A mathematical method for solving a particular type of linear differential equations using complex symbolism, 2000; Trigonometric form of the quadratic algebraic equation solution, 2000; Greenhouse dimensions estimation and short time forecast of greenhouse temperature based on net heat losses through the polymeric cover, 2000; Greenhouse daily sun-radiation intensity variation, daily temperature variation and heat profits through the polymeric cover, 2000; Test methods of the four basic mathematical operations, 2001. Honours: Referee of research articles; Patentee in field; Examiner for Greek postgraduate scholarships; Selectee, Euratom research position, Joint European Torus, Culham, Oxford, England, 1990; Head of Electrical Engineering Department, 2000-03; Listee, expert evaluator of European Commission's scientific research and development programmes; European programme Socrates, Greece, 2000-; Grant, Schilizzi Foundation, 1987; Grant, Empeirikeion Foundation, 1994. Memberships: New York Academy of Sciences; IEEE; National Geographic Society; AMSE. Address: Kilkis 11, Kalamata 24100, Messinia, Greece. E-mail: georgiosleonidopoulos@yahoo.gr

LEONOV Aleksey Arkhipovich (Major-General), b. 30 May 1934, Listianka, Kamerovo Region, Russia. Cosmonaut. m. Svetlana Leonova, 2 daughters. Education: Chuguevsky Air Force

School for Pilots; Zhukovsky Air Force Engineering Academy; Cosmonaut Training, 1960. Appointments: Pilot, 1956-59; Member, CPSU, 1957-91; Participant, space-ship Voskhod 2 flight, becoming first man to walk in space, 1965; Pilot Cosmonaut of USSR; Chairman, Council of Founders, Novosti Press Agency, 1969-90; Deputy Commander, Gagarin Cosmonauts Training Centre, 1971; Participant, Soyuz 19-Apollo joint flight, 1975; Major-General, 1975; Deputy Head, Centre of Cosmonaut Training, 1975-92; Director, Cheteck-Cosmos Co, 1992-; Vice-President, Investment Fund Alfa-Capital, 1997-; Vice President, Alpha Bank, 2000. Honours: Honorary DrScEng; Hero of the Soviet Union, 1965, 1975; Hero of Bulgaria; Hero of Vietnam; Order of Lenin, twice; USSR State Prize, 1981. Memberships: Co-Chairman, Board, International Association of Cosmonauts. Address: Alfa-Capital, Academician Sakharov Prospect 12, 107078 Moscow, Russia.

LÉOTARD François Gérard Marie, b. 26 March 1942, Cannes, France. Politician. m. (1) France Reynier, 1976, (2) Isabelle Duret, 1992, 1 son, 1 daughter. Education: Faculté de Droit, Paris; Institut d'Etudes Politiques, Paris; Ecole Nationale d'Administration. Appointments: Secretary of Chancellery, Ministry of Foreign Affairs, 1968-71; Administration, Town Planning, 1973-76; Sous-Préfet, 1974-77; Mayor of Fréjus, 1977-92, 1993-97; Deputy to National Assembly, for Var, 1978-86, 1988-92, 1995-97, 1997-2002; Conseiller-Général, Var, 1980-88; Secretary, 1982-88, President, 1988-90, 1995-97, Honorary President, 1990-95, Général Parti Républican; Vice-President, 1983-84, President, 1996-, Union pour la Démocratie Française; Minister of Culture and Communications, 1986-88; Member, Municipal Council, Fréjus, 1992; Minister of National Defence, 1993-95; With EU Special Envoy to Macedonia, 2001-; Inspector General de Finances pour l'extérieur, 2001-. Publications: A Mots Découverts, 1987; Culture: Les Chemins de Printemps, 1988; La Ville aimée: mes chemins de Fréjus, 1989; Pendant la Crise, le spectacle continue, 1989; Adresse au Président des Républiques françaises, 1991; Place de la République, 1992; Ma Liberté, 1995; Pour l'honneur, 1997; Je vous hais tous avec douceur, 2000; Paroles d'immortels, 2001. Honours: Chevalier, Order Nationale du Mérite. Address: Nouvelle UDF, 133 bis rue de l'Université, 75007 Paris, France.

LEROY Miss Joy, b. 8 September 1927, Riverdale, Illinois, USA. Miss LeRoy - Model; Narrator; Designer; Author. Education: Texas Technological College, Lubbock, 1946; BS (Honours), Purdue University, Lafayette, Indiana, 1949. Further studies include sewing, theatre, computer programming, fine arts, music. Appointments: Model, sales representative for Jacques and sales representative for the book department at Loebs, Lafayette; Window trimmer, Marshall Fields and Co, 1952-53, and sales and display representative, Emerald House, 1954-55, Evanston, Illinois; Turned professional in field of design, modelling and narrating; Model and narrator for companies including: American Motors Corp (Auto and Kelvinator); Speedway Petroleum Co; Ford Motor Company (Auto and Tractor); The Sykes Co; Coca Cola Co; Hoover Vacuum Co; General Motors (Chevrolet and Oldsmobile) J L Hudson; Jam Handy Organization; Boston, 1962-70 as a model for "Copley 7" and a tour guide, model, free lance writer for The Christian Science Monitor and The Christian Science Publishing Society; later, Special Events Co-ordinator for Opening of the Sheraton Hotel and Prudential Insurance Co; From 1976 to 2002 travelled around the seven continents. Publications: Articles in field of fashion writing, creative ideas for Youth, and educational Puzz-its, copyright from 1986-. Honours: Numerous include: Congressional Certificate of Appreciation, 1991; Republican National Hall of Honour, 1992; Republican Presidential Legion of Honour, Republican Presidential Task Force, Wall of Honour, 1993; Republican Senatorial Medal of Freedom, Order of Liberty

National Republican Committee, Republican Presidential Legion of Merit and National Republican Senatorial Order of Merit, 1993; Republican Campaign Council, 1994; Ronald Wilson Reagan Eternal Flame of Freedom, 1995; Grand Club, Republican Party of Florida, 1996; International Women of the Year, 1996-98; Woman of the Year, 1998-99, 2001, 2002; Presidential Task Force Medal of Merit, Republican Party, 1997; Distinguished 20th Century Republican Leader, 1998; Republican Senatorial Millennium Medal of Freedom, World Laureate of England, Deputy Director General in1999; Presidential Roundtable Representative from Florida, 2000 to 2004, Ronald Wilson Reagan Founder's Wall, 2002; ABI: 2000 Notable American Women; Deputy Governor and Continental Governor; Millennium Medal of Honour and Presidential Medal of Honour; a Noble Member of the Order of International Ambassadors; International Order of Merit, 2000; Presidential Seal of Honor, 2000; American Order of Excellence, 2000; Secretary-General and Noble Prize, and International Peace Prize, United Cultural Convention, 500 Leaders of Influence, Hall of Fame, 2001; Leading Intellectuals of the World; IBC: 2000 Outstanding Intellectuals of the 20th and 21st Century; 500 Founders of the 21st Century; Honours List and American Medal of Honor, 2002; International Medal of Honour, IBC, 2003; Outstanding People of the 21st Century and Who's Who in the 21st Century Medals, 2003; Intellectual of the Year; Charter Member, International Honour Society, 2002; One Thousand Great Americans, 2003; International Register of Profiles, 2003; Vice Consul, 2002; Lifetime Achievement Award, IBC, 2002; Congressional Medal of Excellence, ABI, 2002; World Lifetime Achievement Award, ABI, 2003; Republican Senetorial Medal of Freedom and Star "The highest honor the Republican members of the US Senate can bestow", 2003; International Visual Artist of the Year and International Hall of Fame, 2004, World Academy of Letters, with honours. Address: Apt 2104, 2100 S Ocean Lane, Fort Lauderdale, FL 33316-3827, USA.

LESLIE John, b. 11 July 1923, Philadelphia, USA. Artist; Designer; Photographer; Sculptor. m. (1) Kathryn Elizabeth Frame, (2) Mary Frances Huggins, 3 children. Education: Graduate, Commercial Art, Murrell Dobbins Tech, Philadelphia, 1941; Postgraduate, Fleisher Art Memorial, Philadelphia, 1939-42, Philadelphia Museum School of Industrial Art, 1944, Philadelphia Musical Academy, 1965-67, Pennsylvania State University, 1982-. Appointments include: Staff Artist, Philadelphia Daily News, 1942; Founder, Creative Director, Graphic Advertising Displays Inc, Philadelphia, 1944; Collaborative Designer, Gimbel Brothers Thanksgiving Day Parade and Fashion Show Stage Set Designer, Philadelphia, 1945; Artist, Muralist, Bonwit Teller, Philadelphia, 1944-46; President, Art Director, Dupiex Display and Manufacturing Company Inc, Philadelphia, 1947-54; President, Designer, Leslie Creations Inc, Lafayette Hill, 1954-65; President, Founder, Mail Order Methods Inc, Lafayette Hill, Pennsylvania, 1954-57; President, World Treasures, Seven Seas House Inc, Lafayette Hill, Pennsylvania, 1960-65; President, Lions, Lafayette Hill, 1960-71; Founder, Creative Director, Kopy Kat Inc, franchised Instant Printing Centers in 31 States, Ft Washington, 1968-77; Art Director, Designer, Jesse Jones Industries Inc, Philadelphia, 1978-79; Co-Founder, Art Director, Galerie Marjole Inc, Sanatoga, 1987-89; Lecturer, 1987-; Fine Art Spokesman, Radio and Television, 1989-. Honours: Numerous. Memberships: Woodmere Art Museum, Philadelphia; Boca Grande, Florida, Art Alliance; New York Oil Pastel Association; US Army's 8th Armored Division Association; National AMVETS; Les Amis de Veterans Français. Commissions and Creative Works: Designer, Mannequettes, 3-D miniature human figures with cylindrical wooden heads and paper sculptured clothing; Plasti-Coil: An expandable-retractable coil of multicoloured plastic tubing wound over a soft wire core, both used in major department store windows interiors across the USA;

The Crystal Mall: a climate controlled glass atrium enclosing entire existing downtown shopping districts; US Veterans of WWII Memorial Hall of Honor; First avant-garde A Frame Home on US Atlantic Coast; Creator, Inventor: Functional Metal Sculpture – a collection of occasional furniture pieces; Numerous exhibitions and works in public and private collections. Address: Blueberry Hill, 6318 Zeno Circle, Port Charlotte, FL 33981, USA.

LESLIE Peter Evelyn (Sir), b. 24 March 1931, Oxford, England. Banker. m. Charlotte Chapman-Andrews, 1975, 2 stepsons, 2 stepdaughters. Education: New College, Oxford; MA Oxon. Appointments: Joined Barclays Bank DCO, 1955, serving in Sudan, Algeria, Zaire, Kenya and Bahamas; General Manager, 1973-76, Director, 1979-91, Barclays Bank Ltd; Chairman, British Bankers Association Executive Committee, 1978-79; Member, 1978-81, Chairman, 1987-92, Export Guarantees Advisory Council; Senior General Manager, Barclays Bank International, 1980-83; Chief General Manager, 1985-87, Managing Director, 1987-88, Deputy Chairman, 1987-91, Barclays Bank PLC; Governor, 1983-2001, Chairman, 1994-2001, Stowe School; Chairman, Committee, London and Scottish Clearing Bankers, 1986-88; Council for Industry and Higher Education, 1987-91; Chairman, Overseas Development Institute, 1988-95; Board of Banking Supervision, Bank of England, 1989-94; Chairman, Commonwealth Development Corporation, 1989-95; Chairman, Queen's College, London, 1989-94; Curator, University Chest, Oxford, 1990-95; Deputy Chairman, Midland Group, 1991-92; Council, Ranfurly Library Service, 1991-94; Council, Royal Institute of International Affairs, Chatham House, 1991-97; Oxford University Audit Committee, 1992-2001; Board, International Institute for Environment and Development, 1992-95; Chairman, NCM UK, 1995-98; Supervisory Board, NCM Holding NV, Amsterdam, 1995-2000. Memberships: Fellow, Institute of Bankers; Fellow, Linnean Society. Address: 153 Sutherland Avenue, London W9 1ES, England.

LESSING Doris May, b. 22 October 1919, Kermanshah, Persia. Writer. m. (1) Frank Charles Wisdom, 1939, divorced 1943, 1 son, 1 daughter, (2) Gottfried Anton Nicholas Lessing, 1945, divorced 1949, 1 son. Publications: Novels: The Grass Is Singing 1950; Children of Violence, 1952; A Proper Marriage, 1954; A Ripple from the Storm, 1965; The Four-Gated City, 1969; Retreat to Innocence, 1956; The Golden Notebook, 1962; Briefing for a Descent into Hell, 1971; The Summer Before the Dark, 1973; The Memoirs of a Survivor, 1974; Canopus in Argos: Archives, 1979-1983; The Diary of a Good Neighbour, 1983; If the Old Coul, 1984; The Diaries of Jane Somers, 1984; The Good Terrorist, 1985; The Fifth Child, 1988; Love, Again, 1996; Mara and Dann, 1999; Ben, in the World, 2000; The Old Age of El Magnifico, 2000; The Sweetest Dream, 2001; Short stories: Collected African Stories, 2 volumes, 1951, 1973; Five, 1953; The Habit of Loving, 1957; A Man and Two Women, 1963; African Stories, 1964; Winter in July, 1966; The Black Madonna, 1966; The Story of a Non-Marrying Man and Other Stories, 1972; A Sunrise on the Veld, 1975; A Mild Attack of Locusts, 1977; Collected Stories, 2 volumes, 1978; London Observed: Stories and Sketches, 1992; Non-fiction includes: Going Home, 1957, 1968; Particularly Cats, 1967; Particularly Cats and More Cats, 1989; African Laughter: Four Visits to Zimbabwe, 1992; Under My Skin, 1994; Walking in the Shade, 1997. Plays: Each to His Own Wilderness, 1958; Play with a Tiger, 1962; The Singing Door, 1973; Other publications include: Fourteen Poems, 1959; A Small Personal Voice, 1974; Doris Lessing Reader, 1990. Honours: 5 Somerset Maugham Awards, Society of Authors, 1954-; Prix Médicis for French translation, Carnet d'or, 1976; Austrian State Prize for European Literature, 1981; Shakespeare Prize, Hamburg, 1982; W H Smith Literary Award, 1986; Palermo Prize and Premio

Dictionary of International Biography

Internazionale Mondello, 1987; Grinzane Cavour Award, Italy, 1989; Woman of the Year, Norway, 1995; Los Angeles Times Book Prize, 1995; James Tait Memorial Prize, 1995; Premi Internacional Catalunya, Spain, 1999; David Cohen Literary Prize, 2001; Principe de Asturias, Spain, 2001; PEN Award, 2002. Memberships: Associate Member, American Academy of Arts and Letters, 1974; National Institute of Arts and Letters, USA, 1974; Member, Institute for Cultural Research, 1974; President, Book Trust, 1996-. Address: c/o Jonathon Clowes Ltd, Iron Bridge House, Bridge Approach, London NW1 8BD, England.

LESTER Adrian Anthony, b. 14 August 1968, Birmingham, England. Actor. Education: Royal Academy of Dramatic Art, London. Career: Theatre appearances including Cory in Fences, Garrick, 1990, Paul Poitier in Six Degrees of Separation, Royal Court and Comedy Theatre, 1992, Anthony Hope in Sweeney Todd, Royal National Theatre, 1994, Rosalind in As You Like It, Albery and Bouffes du Nord, 1995, Company, Albery and Donmar, 1996; Hamlet, Bouffes du Nord and Young Vic, 2001; TV appearances: For the Greater Good; In the Dark; The Tragedy of Hamlet; Hustle; Film appearances include Ray in The Affair, 1995, Up on the Roof, Primary Colors, 1997, Storm Damage, Love's Labour's Lost, 1999; Dust, 2001; Final Curtain, 2001; Tomorrow, 2002. Honours: Time Out Award, 1992, 1995; Olivier Award, 1996. Memberships: Amnesty International; Greenpeace. Address: c/o Artists Rights Group (ARG), 4 Great Portland Street, London W1W 8PA, England.

LESTER Anthony Paul (Baron Lester of Herne Hill in the London Borough of Southwark), b. 3 July 1936, London, England. Lawyer. m. Catherine Elizabeth Debora Wassey, 1971, 1 son, 1 daughter. Education: Trinity College, Cambridge; BA, Cantab; LLM, Harvard Law School; Called to Bar, Lincoln's Inn, 1963, Bencher, 1985. Appointments: Special Adviser to Home Secretary, 1974-76, to Northern Ireland Standing Advisory Commission on Human Rights, 1975-77; Appointed Queen's Counsel, 1975; Member, Board of Overseers, University of Pennsylvania Law School, Council of Justice, 1977-90; Member, Court of Governors, London School of Economics, 1980-94; Honorary Visiting Professor, University College London, 1983-; Board of Directors, Salzburg Seminar; President, Interights, 1996-2000; Recorder, South-Eastern Circuit, 1987-93; Co-Chair, Board, European Roma Rights Center; Governor, British Institute of Human Rights; Chair, Board of Governors, James Allen's Girls' School, 1987-93; Chair, Runnymede Trust, 1990-93; Governor, Westminster School, 1998-; Member, Advisory Committee, Centre for Public Law, University of Cambridge, 1999-; International Advisory Board, Open Society Institute, 2000-; Parliamentary Joint Human Rights Commission, 2001-; Foreign Honorary Member, American Academy of Arts and Sciences, 2002. Publications: Justice in the American South, 1964; Race and Law, co-author, 1972; Butterworth's Human Rights Cases, editor-in-chief; Halsbury's Laws of England Title Constitutional Law and Human Rights, 4th edition, consultant editor, contributor, 1996; Human Rights Law and Practice, co-editor, 1999; Articles on race relations, public affairs and international law. Honours: Honorary degrees and fellowships, Open University, University College, London University, Ulster University, South Bank University; Liberty Human Rights Lawyer of the Year, 1997. Address: Blackstone Chambers, Blackstone House, Temple, London EC4Y 9BW, England.

LESTER Bijou Yang, b. 2 April 1950, Sinchu, Taiwan. College Professor. m. David Lester, 1 son, 1 daughter. Education: BA, 1971, MA, 1974, National Taiwan University; AM, 1975, PhD, Economics, 1981, University of Pennsylvania. Appointments: Economist, Economic Planning Council, ROC, 1973-74; Summer

Intern, The World Bank, 1977; Economist, Wharton Econometric Forecasting Association, 1981-83; Assistant Professor, Villanova University, 1983-85; Visiting Assistant Professor, Richard Stockton State College, 1985-86; Visiting Assistant Professor, Trenton State College, 1986-87; Assistant Professor, 1987-94, Associate Professor, 1995-, Drexel University. Publications: Co-author with D Lester: The Economy and Suicide, 1997; Suicide and Homicide in the 20th Century, 1998; 26 papers in economics journals; 68 papers in other social science journals; 11 book chapters. Honours: Thesis Grant, International Institute for Applied System Analysis, Vienna, Austria, 1978; University Research Scholar Award, Drexel University, 1991-92; 1999 Irwin/McGraw-Hill Distinguished Paper Award, Annual Conference of the Mid-West Business Association; The E-Commerce Research Grant from the Safeguard Scientific Center for Electronic Commerce Management, Drexel University, 1999; Editorial Board, Journal of Socio-Economics, 2001-. Memberships: American Economic Association, 1981-; Committee on the Status of Women in the Economics Profession, 1987-; Treasurer, Society for the Advancement of Behavioural Economics, 1992-. Address: 5 Stonegate Ct, RR41, Blackwood, NJ 08012-5356, USA.

LESTER Richard, b. 19 January 1932, Philadelphia, USA. American Film Director. m. Deirdre V Smith, 1956, 1 son, 1 daughter. Education: William Penn Carter School; University of Pennsylvania. Appointments: TV Director, CBS, 1952-54; ITV, 1955-59; Composer, 1954-57; Film Director, 1959-; Films directed: The Running, Jumping and Standing Still Film, 1959; It's Trad ad, 1962; The Mouse on the Moon, 1963; A Hard Day's Night, 1963; The Knack, 1965; Help!, 1965; A Funny Thing Happened on the Way to the Forum, 1966; How I Won the War, 1967; Petulia, 1969; The Bed Sitting Room, 1969; The Three Musketeers, 1973; Juggernaut, 1974; The Four Musketeers, 1974; Royal Flash, 1975; Robin and Marian, 1976; The Ritz, 1976; Butch and Sundance: The Early Days, 1979; Cuba, 1979; Superman II, 1980; Superman III, 1983; Finders Keepers, 1984; The Return of the Musketeers, 1989; Get Back, 1990. Honours: Academy Award Nomination, 1960; Grand Prix, Cannes Film Festival, 1965; Best Director, Rio de Janeiro Festival, 1966; Gandhi Peace Prize, Berlin Festival, 1969; Best Director, Tehran Festival, 1974. Address: c/o Creative Artists Agency, 9830 Wilshire Boulevard, Beverley Hills, CA 90212, USA.

LETSIE III, King of Lesotho, b. 17 July 1963, Morija, Lesotho. Monarch. Education: National University of Lesotho; Universities of Bristol, Cambridge and London. Appointments: Principal Chief of Matsieng, 1989; Installed as King of Lesotho, 1990, abdicated, 1995, reinstated after father's death, 1996-; Patron, Prince Mohato Award. Address: Royal Palace, Masero, Lesotho.

LETTE Kathy, b. 11 November 1958, Sydney. Australian Author. m. Geoffrey Robertson, 1990, 1 son, 1 daughter. Education: Sylvania High School, Sydney. Publications: HIT and MS, 1984; Girl's Night Out, 1987; The Llama Parlour, 1991; Foetal Attraction, 1993; Mad Cows, 1996; Puberty Blues, 1997; Plays: Wet Dreams, 1985; Perfect Mismatch, 1985; Grommitts, 1988; I'm So Sorry For You, I Really Am, 1994; Radio: I'm So Happy For You, I Really Am; Essays: She Done Him Wrong, 1995; The Constant Sinner in Introduction to Mae West, 1995; Altar Ego, 1998; Nip 'n Tuck, 2001. Address: c/o Ed Victor, 6 Bayley Street, London, WC1B 3HB, England.

LETTERMAN David, b. 12 April 1947, Indianapolis. American Broadcaster. m. Michelle Cook, 1969, divorced 1977. Education: Ball State University. Appointments: Radio and TV Announcer, Indianapolis; Performer, The Comedy Store, Los Angeles, 1975-; TV Appearances include: Rock Concert, Gong Show; Frequent guest host, The Twilight Show; Host, David Letterman Show, 1980; Late Night with David Letterman, 1982; The Late Show with David Letterman, CBS, 1993-; TV Scriptwriting includes, Bob Hope Special; Good Times; Paul Lynde Comedy Hour; John Denver Special. Publications: David Letterman's Book of Top Ten Lists, 1996. Honours: Recipient, Six Emmy Awards. Address: Late Show with David Letterman, Ed Sullivan Theater, 1697 Broadway, New York, NY 10019, USA.

LETTS Quentin Richard Stephen, b. 6 February 1963, Cirencester, Gloucestershire, England. Journalist. m. Lois Rathbone, 1 son, 1 daughter. Education: Trinity College, Dublin; Jesus College, Cambridge. Appointments: Daily Telegraph, 1988-95, 1997-2000; New York Bureau Chief, The Times, 1995-97; Parliamentary Sketchwriter, Daily Mail, 2000-. Membership: The Savile Club. Address: Scrubs' Bottom, Bisley, Gloucestershire GL6 7BU, England.

LEU Paul, b. 26 June 1927, Carja-Murgeni, Romania. Educator and Researcher. m. Magdalena Leu, 2 sons, 1 daughter. Education: Philology Graduate (Head of Promotion), Al I Cuza University, Iasi, Romania, 1954; Diploma in Teaching Language, Literature and Literature Theory. Appointments: Teacher, 1949-96; Associate Professor, 1965; Lecturer, 1968; Extensive researches into subjects including: literary history, ethnography, history of music, teaching and history of teaching, history of Bucovina during Austria's domination, also researches into the unpublished works of S Fl Marian, Ciprian Purumbescu, Iraclie Porumbescu and others. Publications: 29 books include most recently: Romanian Folk Stories II, III and IV, 1996; The S Fl Marian Academician - Monograph, 1998; S Fl Marian, Facerea lumii, 1998; S Fl Marian, Legende botanice, 1999; Founder of the Romanian Ethnography – Monograph I and II, 1998-99; S Fl Marian Plantele noastre, 2000; Colegiul National Stefan cel Mane Suceava – Monography, Etapia austriaeă, 2000; Iraclie Prumbescu - Monograph, 2000; Quo vadis romane!, 2001; Gr-or KK Obergymnasium din Suceava, in intampinarea unirii Bucovinei cu Romania, 2003; S Fl Marian, Cosmogeneza, 2004; 500 articles, documents and book reviews; Script for the short TV Movie, Remember Ciprian Porumbescu, 1996. Honours: Front Ranking Teacher Award, Romanian Ministry of Education, 1964; Second Degree Teacher Diploma, 1965; First Degree teaching Diploma, 1976; A Pen on Two Continents, summary of Paul Leu's works by Octavian Nestor; Listed in Who's Who publications and biographical dictionaries. Membership: Member and President, Society of Romanian Language and Literature. Address: 7217 175th Street, Unit #113, NE, Kenmore, WA 98028, USA. E-mail: paulleu@hotmail.com

LEUNG Ares, b. 18 August 1960, Hong Kong. Physician. Education: MB BS, 1984. Appointments: Director, Prestige Medical Centre, Hong Kong; Head, Department of Obstetrics and Gynaecology, Union Hospital, Hong Kong. Memberships: Fellow, Royal College of Obstetrics and Gynaecology; Fellow, Hong Kong College of Obstetrics and Gynaecology. Address: Department of Obstetrics and Gynaecology, Union Hospital, 18 Fu Kin Street, Tai-Wai, Shatin, New Territories, Hong Kong. E-mail: aresleung@medscape.com

LEUNG Kam Tim, b. 21 June 1931, China. Educator. Education: Sun Yat-sen University, 1953. Appointments: Teacher, secondary schools, college and universities, mainland China, 1953-95; Tutor, Open University of Hong Kong, 1997-99; Part-time Tutor, Hong Kong University, 2001. Publications: 30 articles in top journals. Honours: Senior Lecturer Certificate, Educational Department of Guangdong Province, China, 1987; Listed in national and international biographical publications. Memberships: Regular Member, International Association of Chinese Linguistics, 1994-. Address: PO Box 91360, Tsim Sha Tsui Post Office, Kowloon, Hong Kong.

LEVENE Peter Keith (Baron of Portsoken in the City of London) b. 8 December 1941, Pinner, Middlesex, England. Business Executive; Justice of the Peace. m. Wendy Ann Levene, 1966, 2 sons, 1 daughter. Education: BA, University of Manchester. Appointments: Joined, 1963, Managing Director, 1968, Chair, 1982, United Scientific Holdings; Member, South-East Asia Trade Advisory Group, 1979-83; Personal Adviser to Secretary of State for Defence, 1984; Alderman, 1984, Sheriff, 1995-96, Lord Mayor, 1998-99, City of London; Chair, European NATO National Armaments Directors, 1990-91; Special Adviser to Secretary of State for the Environment, 1991-92; Chair, Docklands Light Railway Ltd, 1991-94; Chair, Public Competition and Purchasing Unit, H M Treasury, 1991-94; Chair, Wasserstein Perella and Co Ltd, 1991-94; Adviser to Prime Minister on Efficiency, 1992-97; Special Adviser to President of Board of Trade, 1992-95; Chair, Chief Executive Officer, Canary Wharf Ltd, 1993-96; Senior Adviser, Morgan Stanley and Co Ltd, 1996-98; Chair, Bankers Trust International, 1998-99; Chair, Investment Banking Europe, Deutsche Bank AG, 1999-2001; Vice Chair, Deutsche Bank, UK, 2001-02; Chair, Lloyds of London, 2002-. Honours: Honorary Colonel Commandant, Royal Corps of Transport, 1991-93; Master, Worshipful Company of Carmen, 1992-93; Honorary Colonel Commandant, Royal Logistics Corps, 1993-; Fellow, Queen Mary and Westfield College, London University, 1995; Knight Commander, Order of St John of Jerusalem; Commander, Ordre National du Mérite, 1996; Honorary DSc, City University, 1998; Knight Commandants Order of Merit, Germany, 1998; Middle Cross Order of Merit, Hungary, 1999; Knight Commander, Order of the British Empire. Memberships: Fellow, Chartered Institute of Transport; Companion, Institute of Management; Defence Manufacturers Association, Council, 1982-85, Vice-Chair, 1983-84, Chair, 1984-85. Address: 1 Great Winchester Street, London EC2N 2DB, England. E-mail: peter.k.levene@db.com

LEVER Bernard Lewis, b. 1 February 1951, Manchester, UK. Judge. m. Anne Helen Ballingall, 2 daughters. Education: MA, The Queen's College, Oxford. Appointments: Called to the Bar, Middle Temple, 1975; Barrister, Northern Circuit, 1975-2001; Recorder, 1995-2001; Standing Counsel to the Inland Revenue, 1997-2001; Circuit Judge, 2001. Honour: Neale Exhibitioner, Oxford University. Membership: Vincent's Club. Address: Manchester Crown Court, Minshull Street, Manchester M1 3FS, England.

LEVER Tresham Christopher Arthur Lindsay (Sir) (3rd Baronet), b. 9 January 1932, London, England. Naturalist; Writer. m. Linda Weightman McDowell Goulden, 6 November 1975. Education: Eton College, 1945-49; BA, 1954, MA, 1957, Trinity College, Cambridge. Publications: Goldsmiths and Silversmiths of England, 1975; The Naturalized Animals of the British Isles, 1977; Naturalized Mammals of the World, 1985; Naturalized Birds of the World, 1987; The Mandarin Duck, 1990; They Dined on Eland: The Story of the Acclimatisation Societies, 1992; Naturalized Animals: The Ecology of Successfully Introduced Species, 1994; Naturalized Fishes of the World, 1996; The Cane Toad: The History and Ecology of a Successful Colonist, 2001; Naturalized Reptiles and Amphibians of the World, 2003. Contributions to: Books, Art, Scientific and general publications. Memberships: Fellow, Linnean Society of London; Fellow, Royal Geographical Society; World Conservation Union Species' Survival Commission; Council of Ambassadors, WWF (UK); Honorary Life member Brontë Society, 1988. Address: Newell House, Winkfield, Berkshire SL4 4SE, England.

Dictionary of International Biography

LEVEY Geoffrey Brahm, b. 16 February 1959, Brisbane, Australia. BA, University of Queensland, 1981; M Soc Sci, Hebrew University of Jerusalem, 1991; AM, 1992, PhD, 1999, Brown University. Appointments: Junior Research Fellow, Human and Social Sciences, St Anne's College, Oxford, England, 1993-95; Hakoah Lecturer in Jewish Studies and Political Science, 1996-98, Founding Director, Programme in Jewish Studies, 1996-, Senior Lecturer, Politics and International Relations, 1998-, University of New South Wales, Australia. Publications: Journals: Political Theory; British Journal of Political Science; Political Studies; Philosophy of the Social Sciences; Studies in Contemporary Jewry; Encyclopaedias: Encyclopaedia of American Religion and Politics; Encyclopaedia of Modern Jewish Culture. Book: Jews and Australian Politics, 2004. Honours: Dean's Fellow, Brown University, 1988-89; Golda Meir Fellow, Hebrew University Jerusalem, 1990-91; Australian Research Council, 1997; British Academy Visiting Fellow, 2001. Memberships: American Political Science Association; Life Member, University of New South Wales Union; Life Member, University of Sydney Union. Address: School of Politics and International Relations, University of New South Wales, Sydney 2052, Australia.

LEVEY Michael (Vincent) (Sir), b. 8 June 1927, London, England. Writer. m. Brigid Brophy, deceased 1995, 1 daughter. Education: Exeter College, Oxford. Appointments: Assistant Keeper, 1951-66, Deputy Keeper, 1966-68, Keeper, 1968-73, Deputy Director, 1970-73, Director, 1973-87, National Gallery, London; Slade Professor of Fine Art, Cambridge, 1963-64, Oxford, 1994-95. Publications: Six Great Painters, 1956; National Gallery Catalogues: 18th Century Italian Schools, 1956; The German School, 1959; Painting in 18th Century Venice, 1959, 3rd edition, 1994; From Giotto to Cézanne, 1962; Dürer, 1964; The Later Italian Paintings in the Collection of HM The Queen, 1964, revised edition, 1991; Canaletto Paintings in the Royal Collection, 1964; Tiepolo's Banquet of Cleopatra, 1966; Rococo to Revolution, 1966; Bronzino, 1967; Early Renaissance, 1967; Fifty Works of English Literature We Could Do Without (co-author), 1967; Holbein's Christina of Denmark, Duchess of Milan, 1968; A History of Western Art, 1968; Painting at Court, 1971; The Life and Death of Mozart, 1971, 2nd edition, 1988; The Nude: Themes and Painters in the National Gallery, 1972; Art and Architecture in 18th Century France (co-author), 1972; The Venetian Scene, 1973; Botticelli, 1974; High Renaissance, 1975; The World of the Ottoman Art, 1976; Jacob van Ruisdael, 1977; The Case of Walter Pater, 1978; The Painter Depicted, 1981; Tempting Fate, 1982; An Affair on the Appian Way, 1984; Pater's Marius the Epicurean (editor), 1985; Giambattista Tiepolo, 1986; The National Gallery Collection: A Selection, 1987; Men at Work, 1989; The Soul of the Eye: Anthology of Painters and Painting (editor), 1990; Painting and Sculpture in France 1700-1789, 1992; Florence: A Portrait, 1996; The Chapel is on Fire (memoir), 2000; The Burlington Magazine, anthology, 2003. Contributions to: Periodicals. Honours: Hawthornden Prize, 1968; Knighted, 1981; Honorary Fellow, Royal Academy, 1986; Banister Fletcher Prize, 1987; Lieutenant, Royal Victoria Order, 1965. Memberships: Ateneo Veneto, foreign member; British Academy, fellow; Royal Society of Literature, fellow. Address: 36 Little Lane, Louth, Lincolnshire LN11 9DU, England.

LEVI Kurt (Adolf Israel), b. 3 May 1926, Stuttgart, Germany. Holocaust Survivor; Manager. m. (1) Vicky Vickland, 1950, divorced, (2) Lucille Walker, 1956, divorced, 1 daughter, (3) Idamaria Strobel, 1980, divorced, 2 sons, 1 daughter, (4) Dora Martha Martinez Diaz De Leon, 1998. Education: San Francisco City College and State University. Appointments include: With Combat Infantry, Okinawa, Korea 38th Parallel, 1944-46; Electrician, Manager Distributor, College Supplementary;

Manager, Night-club, Stuttgart, Germany; Sales Manager, Beringer Winery; Active in Civil Rights Movement and Peace Organisation, US, Mexico and Nicaragua, 1970-; Author of 120 poems; Autobiography on travels in 34 countries. Publications: Contributor of articles and poems to professional journals. Memberships: Chairman, Mill Valley Freeze; Leader, Nicaragua Children's Park, Masaya, 1989; Desarollo Rural De Mexico. Address: Apdo 58 B, Monturra 211, Vista Alegre 20292, Ags Ags 211 CP, Mexico. E-mail: lapazconamor@prodigy.net.mx

LEVI-MONTALCINI Rita, b. 22 April 1909, Turin, Italy. Neuroscientist. Education: Graduated, Medicine, University of Turin, 1936. Appointments: Neurological research in Turin and Brussels, 1936-41, in Piemonte, 1941-43; In hiding in Florence during German occupation, 1943-44; Medical Doctor working among war refugees, Florence, 1944-45; Resumed academic positions at University of Turin, 1945; Worked with Professor Viktor Hamburger, 1947, Associate Professor, 1956, Professor, 1958-77, St Louis, USA; Director, 1969-78, Guest Professor, 1979-89, Guest Professor, Institute of Neurobiology, 1989-, Institute of Cell Biology of Italian National Council of Research, Rome. Publications: In Praise of Imperfection: My Life and Work, 1988. Honour: Joint Winner, Nobel Prize for Medicine, 1986. Address: Institute of Neurobiology, CNR Viale Marx 15, 00137, Rome, Italy.

LÉVI-STRAUSS Claude, b. 28 November 1908, Brussels, Belgium. Anthropologist; University Professor; Writer. m. (1) Dina Dreyfus, 1932, (2) Rose Marie Ullmo, 1946, 1 son, (3) Monique Roman, 1954, 1 son. Education: University of Paris-Sorbonne. Appointments: Professor, University of São Paulo, Brazil, 1935-39; Visiting Professor, New School of Social Research, New York, USA, 1942-45; Cultural Counsellor, French Embassy, USA, 1946-47; Associate Director, Musée de l'Homme, Paris, France, 1949-50; Director of Studies, Ecole Pratique des Hautes Etudes, Paris, 1950-74; Professor, 1959-82, Honorary Professor, 1983-, Collège de France. Publications: La vie familiale et sociale des indiens Nambikwara, 1948; Les structures élémentaires de la parenté, 1949; Tristes tropiques,, 1955; Anthropologie structurale, 1958; Le totémisme aujourd'hui, 1962; La pensée sauvage, 1962; Le cru et le cuit, 1964; Du miel aux cendres, 1967; L'origine des manières de table, 1968; L'homme nu, 1971; Anthropologie structurale deux, 1973; La voie des masques, 1975, 1979; Le regard éloigné, 1983; Paroles données, 1984; La potière jalouse, 1985; De près et de loin, co-author, 1988; Histoire de Lynx, 1991; Regarder, écouter, lire, 1983; Saudades do Brasil, 1994. Honours: Dr hc, Brussels, Harvard, Yale, Chicago, Columbia, Oxford, Stirling, Zaire, Mexico, Uppsala, Johns Hopkins, Montreal, Québec and Visva-Bharati University, India; Prix Paul Pelliot, 1949; Huxley Memorial Medal, 1965; Viking Fund Gold Medal, 1966; Gold Medal, Centre National de la Recherche Scientifique, 1967; Erasmus Prize, 1973; Aby M Warburg Prize, 1996; Grand Croix, Légion d'Honneur; Commandeur, Ordre National du Mérite, des Palmes Académiques, des Arts et des Lettres. Memberships: Académie Française; Foreign Member, Royal Academy of the Netherlands, Norwegian Academy of Sciences and Letters, American Academy of Arts and Sciences, American Academy and Institute of Arts and Letters, British Academy; Foreign Associate, National Academy of Sciences, USA; Honorary Member, Royal Anthropological Institute, American Philosophical Society, London School of Oriental and African Studies. Address: 2 rue des Marronniers, 75016 Paris, France.

LEVICK William Russell, b. 5 December 1931, Sydney, Australia. Neuroscience Researcher. m. Patricia Lathwell, 1 son, 1 son deceased, 1 daughter. Education: BSc, honours, 1953, MSc, 1954, MBBS, honours, 1957, University of Sydney. Appointments:

Dictionary of International Biography

C J Martin Travelling Fellow, Cambridge University, University of California, Berkeley, 1963-64; Professorial Fellow, 1967-83, Professor, 1983-96, Australian National University, Canberra. Honours: Fellowship, Australian Academy of Sciences, 1973, Optical Society of America, 1977, Royal Society of London, 1982. Memberships: Society for Neuroscience; Australian Neuroscience Society; Australian Physiological and Pharmacological Society. Address: 33 Quiros Street, Red Hill, ACT 2603, Australia.

LEVIN Ira, b. 27 August 1929, New York, New York, USA. Novelist; Dramatist. m. (1) Gabrielle Aronsohn, 20 August 1960, divorced January 1968, 3 sons, (2) Phyllis Finkel, 1979, divorced 1981. Education: Drake University, 1946-48; AB, New York University, 1950. Appointments: US Army, 1953-55. Publications: Novels: A Kiss Before Dying, 1953; Rosemary's Baby, 1967; This Perfect Day, 1970; The Stepford Wives, 1972; The Boys From Brazil, 1976; Silver, 1991; Son of Rosemary, 1997. Plays: No Time for Sergeants, 1956; Interlock, 1958; Critic's Choice, 1961; General Seeger, 1962; Drat! The Cat! 1965; Dr Cook's Garden, 1968; Veronica's Room, 1974; Deathtrap, 1979; Break a Leg, 1981; Cantorial, 1990. Contributions to: Television and films. Honours: Edgar Allan Poe Awards, Mystery Writers of America, 1953, 1980. Memberships: American Society of Composers, Authors and Publishers; Authors Guild; Authors League of America; Dramatists Guild. Address: c/o Harold Ober Associates, 425 Madison Avenue, New York, NY 10017, USA.

LEVIN Robert A, b. 25 September 1948, Baltimore, Maryland, USA. Glass Artist; Sculptor. m. Wanda Levin, 2 daughters. Education: BFA, Denison University, Granville, Ohio, 1971; MFA, Southern Illinois University, Carbondale, Illinois, 1974; Penland School of Crafts, Penland, North Carolina. Appointments: Glassblowing Instructor, 1975-76, Resident Glass Artist, 1976-80, Penland School of Crafts, North Carolina; Artist in Residence, ArtPark, Lewiston, 1987; Visiting Assistant Professor in Glass, Rochester Institute of Technology, Rochester, New York, Spring, 1988; Numerous workshops and lectures, 1976-; Independent studio glass artist, 1980-; Visiting Glass Instructor, Wanganui College, New Zealand, 1990; Reading Tutor, Burnsville, North Carolina, 1990-96; Board of Directors: Penland School, 1991-95; Glass Art Society, 1991-94; Arthur Morgan School, 1992-98; Visiting Panelist, NC Arts Council. 1992-93; Exhibitions include: Hot and Cool: Contemporary Glass Works, touring via Exhibits USA, 1999; (solo) Blue Spiral Gallery, Asheville, NC, 1999; Steninge World Exhibition of Art Glass 1999, Stockholm, Sweden, 1999; Ogden Museum of Southern Art, New Orleans, LA, 2001; Knoxville Museum of Art, Knoxville, TN, 2002; Grounds for Sculpture, Hamilton, NJ, 2002; Center for Southern Craft and Design, New Orleans, LA, 2003; Commissions and Creative Works: Collections in USA, Denmark, Germany, Spain, Japan, Europe. Honours: Grants, fellowships and awards include: Steuben project Award, GAS Conference, Corning Glass Center, 1991; Created award for NC Governor's Entrepreneurial Schools Awards, 1994, 1995, 1996, 1997, 1998, 1999; Southern Arts Federation/NEA Regional Visual Arts Fellowship, 1995; North Carolina Arts Council Fellowship, 1996. Memberships include: American Crafts Council; Glass Art Society. Address: 699 Upper Browns Creek Road, Burnsville, NC 28714, USA.

LEVINE Larry (Aaron Laurence), b, 26 July 1925, Edmonton, Alberta, Canada. Professor Emeritus of Economics. m. Fay, 2 sons, 3 daughters. Education: BA, University of Alberta, 1949; MA, University of Toronto, 1950; PhD, University of London, London School of Economics and Political Science, 1954. Appointments: Director of Natural Resource Economics Section, Government of Ontario, Department of Economics, 1955-56; Professor of Economics, 1956- (currently Professor Emeritus), University of

New Brunswick, Fredericton, New Brunswick, Canada. Publications: Book: Industrial Retardation in Britain 1880-1914, 1967; The Era of Leontief – and Who?, "A Suggested Interpretation", 1974. Memberships: Royal Economic Society; American Economic Association; Canadian Economic Association. Address: Department of Economics, University of New Brunswick, Fredericton, New Brunswick, Canada, E3B 5A3.

LEVINSON Barry, b. 6 April 1942, Baltimore, Maryland, USA. American Screenwriter; Director. m. Diana. Education: American University. Appointments: Wrote and acted on TV Comedy Show, Los Angeles; Later worked on Network TV; Wrote and appeared, The Carol Burnett Show; Worked on film scripts for Silent Movie and High Anxiety; TV work includes: Writer, Tim Conway Comedy Hour; The Marty Feldman Comedy Machine; The Carol Burnett Show; Executive Producer, Harry 30 Minutes of Investigative Ticking; Diner; Homicide; Life on the Street; Films directed: Diner; The Natural; Young Sherlock Holmes; Tin Men; Good Morning Vietnam; Rain Man; Disclosure, 1995; Director, Producer, Avalon; Bugsy; Toys; Jimmy Hollywood, 1994; Sleepers, 1996; Wag the Dog, 1997; Sphere, 1998; Liberty Heights, 2000; An Everlasting Piece, 2001; Bandits, 2001; Writer: Diner; Tin Men; Avalon; Co-wrote screenplays with Valerie Curtin for: And Justice for All; Inside Movies; Best Friends; Unfaithfully Yours; Toys; Liberty Heights; Actor: Quiz Show, 1994. Honours: Emy Awards, 1974, 1975; Academy Award, 1988. Address: c/o Baltimore/Spring Creek Pictures, Building 133-208, 4000 Warner Boulevard, Burbank, CA 91522, USA.

LEVITAS Valery, b. 3 April 1956, Kiev, Ukraine. Researcher; Educator. m. Natasha Levitas, 20 January 1993, 2 sons. Education: MS honours, Mechanical Engineering, Kiev Institute of Technology, 1978; PhD, Materials Science, Institute of Superhard Materials, Kiev, 1981; DSc, Continuum Mechanics, Institute of Electronic Machine Building, Moscow, 1988; DEng habil, Continuum Mechanics, University of Hannover, Germany, 1995; Registered Professional Engineer, Texas, 2001. Appointments: Leader, Research Group, 1982-95, Associate Research Professor, 1984-88, Research Professor, 1989-95, Consultant, 1995-, Institute for Superhard Materials, Ukrainian Academy of Sciences, Kiev; Humboldt Research Fellow, 1993-95, Visiting and Research Professor, 1995-99, University of Hannover, Germany; Associate Professor, 1999-2002, Professor, 2002-, Director, Center for Mechanochemistry and Synthesis of New Materials, 2002-, Texas Tech University, Lubbock, 2002-; President, Firm "Material Modeling", Lubbock, 2002-; Consultant, Los Alamos National Laboratory, 2001-. Publications include: Large Elastoplastic Deformations of Materials at High Pressure, 1987; Thermomechanics of Phase Transformations and Inelastic Deformations in Microinhomogeneous Materials, 1992; Large Deformation of Materials with Complex Rheological Properties at Normal and High Pressure, 1996; Continuum Mechanical Fundamentals of Mechanochemistry, 2004. Honours: Medal, Ukrainian Academy of Sciences, 1984; Alexander von Humboldt Foundation Fellowship, Germany, 1993-95; International Journal of Engineering Sciences Distinguished Paper Award, 1995; Richard von Mises Award, Society of Applied Mathematics and Mechanics, 1998. Memberships: International Association for the Advancement of High Pressure Science and Technology; American Society of Mechanical Engineers; American Physical Society; Society of Engineering Science; Society of Applied Mathematics and Mechanics. Address: Texas Tech University, Department of Mechanical Engineering, Lubbock, TX 79409-1021, USA.

LEVITT Arthur, Jr, b. 3 February 1931, Brooklyn, New York, USA. Business Executive. m. Marylin Blauner, 1955, 1 son, 1 daughter. Education: Williams College. Appointments: Assistant

Promotion Director, Time Inc, New York, 1954-59; Executive Vice-President, Director, Oppenheimer Industries Inc, Kansas City, 1959-62; Joined, 1962, President, 1969-78, Shearson Hayden Stone Inc, now Shearson Lehmann Bros Inc, New York; Chair, Chief Executive Officer, Director, American Stock Exchange, New York, 1978-89; Chair, Levitt Media Co, New York, 1989-93; Chair, New York City Economic Development Corporation, 1990-93; Chair, Securities and Exchange Commission, 1993-2001; Various directorships and other business and public appointments. Honours: Honorary LLD, Williams College, 1980, Pace, 1980, Hamilton College, 1981, Long Island, 1984, Hofstra, 1985. Address: Securities and Exchange Commission, 450 Fifth Street NW, Washington, DC 20001, USA.

LEVY Alain M, b. 19 December 1946, France. Record Company Executive. Education: Ecole des Mines, France; MBA, University of Pennsylvania. Appointments: With CBS, Assistant to the President, CBS International, New York, 1972, Vice-President, Marketing for Europe, Paris, 1973, Vice-President, Creative Operations for Europe and Manager, CBS Italy, 1978; Managing Director, CBS Disques, France, 1979; Chief Executive Officer, PolyGram, 1984; Executive Vice-President, PolyGram Group, France and Federal Republic of Germany, 1988; Manager, US Operations PolyGram Group, 1990-; President, Chief Executive Officer, Member, Board of Management, PolyGram USA, 1991-; Member, Group Management Committee, Philips Electronics, 1991-; Majority Shareholder, PolyGram USA, 1991-98; Chair, Bd EMI Group plc, 2001-, Chair and CEO, EMI Recorded Music, 2001-. Address: EMI Group plc, 4 Tenterden Street, Hanover Square, London W1A 2AY, England.

LEVY John Court (Jack), b. 16 February 1926, London, England. Engineer; Consultant; Managing Director. m. Sheila F Krisman, 2 sons, 1 daughter. Education: BSc, Engineering, Imperial College of Science and Technology, London, England, 1943-46; MS, University of Illinois, USA, 1953-54; PhD, University of London, 1961. Appointments: Stress Analyst, Boulton Paul Aircraft, 1946-48; Assistant to Chief Engineer, Fullers Ltd, 1948-52; Lecturer, Senior Lecturer, Reader, 1952-66, Head (Professor) of Mechanical and Manufacturing Engineering, 1966-83, City University, London; Director, Engineering Profession at Engineering Council, 1983-90; Consulting Engineer, 1990-97; Consultant to Engineering Council, 1997-; Managing Director, Levytator Ltd, 2000-. Publications: Most recent publications include: UK Manufacturing – Facing International Challenge, 1994; Co-author, Sustaining Recovery, 1995; The University Education and Industrial Training of Manufacturing Engineers for the Global Market, 1996; UK Developments in Engineering Education, Including the Matching Section, 1998; Keynote address at international conference, The Impact of Globalization on Engineering Education and Practice, Balaton, Hungary, 1999. Honours: OBE, 1984; Member, Board of Governors, Middlesex University, 1990-; Freeman of City of London, 1991; Honorary Doctorates, City University, London, University of Portsmouth, Leeds Metropolitan University. Memberships: Fellow, Royal Academy of Engineering; Fellow, Institution of Mechanical Engineers; Fellow, Royal Aeronautical Society; Fellow, City and Guilds of London Institute; Fellow, Royal Society of Arts; Fellow, Institution of Engineers of Ireland. Address: 18 Woodberry Way, Finchley, London N12 0HG, England. E-mail: jack.levy@btclick.com

LEVY Joseph Bruno, b. 8 November 1930, Milan, Italy. Retired Company Director. Divorced, 1 son, 1 daughter. Education: BSc, Chemistry, 1950, BSc Tech, Engineering, 1951, BSc Tech, Industrial Administration, 1952, University of Manchester, England; MSc, Chemistry, University of Massachusetts, USA, 1954; MA, Chemistry, 1956, PhD, Physics and Physical Chemistry,

1958, University of Princeton, USA; MHE, International Human Ecology Foundation, Buenos Aires, Argentina, 1994; BSc, Psychology, University Del Salvador, Buenos Aires, Argentina, 1999. Appointments: Assistant Director, 1957-76, Director, 1980-87, Textile Fibres, DuPont Argentina; Director General, DuPont Italiana, 1976-78; Group Director, DuPont Mexico, 1978-80. Publications: Several in: American Dyestuff Reporter, USA; Journal of the Textile Research Institute; Textile Research Journal, USA; Fashion, Argentina; DuPont News, Argentina and New Mexico; Modern Packaging, Argentina; Magazine of the Argentine Fly Fishing Association, Argentina; Símbolo, Argentina. Honours include: Full Member, New York Academy of Science, New York, NY, USA, 1982; Full Life member, Sigma Xi, Honorary Research Organization, USA, 1958; Honorary President, International Human Ecology Foundation, Buenos Aires, Argentina, 1993. Memberships: New York Academy of Science, USA; Sigma Xi, USA; International Human Ecology Foundation, Argentina; Scientific and Medical Network, England; Society for Scientific Exploration, USA; American Association for the Advancement of Science, USA; Freemason, England; Freemason, Argentina. Address: Av. Del Libertador 356, (21º A), Ciudad Autónoma de Buenos Aires, C1001ABQ – República Argentina. Email: joelevy@speedy.com.ar

LEVY Ralph David, b. 3 August 1951, London, England. Teacher of Theology. Education: BA (Honours), University of York, 1974; BA, Ambassador University, Pasadena, California, 1977; MA, California State University, Los Angeles, 1987; PhD, Union Institute and University, Cincinnati, Ohio, 1995. Appointments: Assistant Professor of Theology, English and Spanish, Ambassador University, Pasadena, California and Big Sandy, Texas, 1981-96; Teacher of Spanish and ESL, Texas Secondary Schools, 1996-98; Teacher of Theology, Ambassador Bible Center, Cincinnati, Ohio, 1999-. Publications: The Symbolism of the Azazel Goat, 1998. Membership: Greater Cincinnati Council on World Affairs. Address: 250H Postoak, Milford, OH 45150-8737, USA.

LEW Julian D M, b. 3 February 1948, South Africa. Lawyer; Queen's Counsel. m. Margot Gillian, 2 daughters. Education: LLB honours, University of London, 1969; Doctorat special en droit international, Catholic University of Louvain, Belgium, 1977; Fellow, Chartered Institute of Arbitrators. Appointments: Called to Bar in England, 1970; Admitted Solicitor, 1981; New York State Bar, 1985; Visiting Professor, Head of School of International Arbitration, Centre for Commercial Law Studies, Queen Mary, University of London; Partner and Head of the International Arbitration Practice Group, Herbert Smith. Publications: Numerous books and articles on international commercial arbitration and international trade. Memberships: Chairman, Committee on arbitration practice guidelines of Chartered Institute of Arbitrators, 1996-2001; Chairman, Committee on Intellectual Property Disputes and Arbitration, International Chamber of Commerce, 1995-99; Member, Council of the ICC Institute of World Business Law; Director and Member of Court, London Court of International Arbitration. Address: Herbert Smith, Exchange House, Primrose Street, London EC2A 2HS, England. E-mail: julianlew@herbertsmith.com

LEWIN Michael Zinn, b. 21 July 1942, Cambridge, Massachusetts, USA. Writer; Dramatist. 1 son, 1 daughter. Education: AB, Harvard University, 1964; Churchill College, Cambridge, England. Appointment: Co-Editor, Crime Writers Association Annual Anthology, 1992-94. Publications: Author of 18 novels including: Called by a Panther, 1991; Underdog, 1993; Family Business, 1995; Rover's Tales, 1998; Cutting Loose, 1999; Family Planning, 1999; Eye opener, 2004. Other: Various radio plays, stage plays and short stories Contributions to: Indianapolis

for New York Times Sophisticated Traveller. Honours: Maltese Falcon Society Best Novel, 1987; Raymond Chandler Society of Germany Best Novel, 1992; Mystery Masters Award, 1994. Memberships: Detection Club; Crime Writers Association; Mystery Writers of America; Private Eye Writers Association; Authors Guild. Address: Garden Flat, 15 Bladud Buildings, Bath BA1 5LS, England.

LEWIN Russell Mark Ellerker, b. 21 March 1958, Woolwich, England. Solicitor. 2 sons. Education: BA, Jurisprudence, 1980, MA, Jurisprudence, 1990, St John's College, Oxford. Appointments: Articled Clerk, 1981-83, Solicitor, 1983-, Partner, 1990, Recruitment Partner, 1994-98, European Regional Council, 1997-, Policy Committee, 1998-, Managing Partner, 1998, Baker & McKenzie, London. Publications: Various articles on topics of Intellectual Property and EU Competition Law. Memberships: City of London Solicitors' Guild; Academy for Chief Executives; Liberal Democrats. Address: c/o Baker & McKenzie, 100 New Bridge Street, London EC4V 6JA, England. E-mail: russell.lewin@bakernet.com

LEWING Anthony Charles, (Mark Bannerman) b. 12 July 1933, Colchester, England. Author. m. Françoise Faury, 2 July 1966, 1 son, 1 daughter. Appointments: Royal Army Pay Corps, 1951-89; Civil Service, 1989-95. Publications: Grand Valley Feud, 1995; The Beckoning Noose, 1996; Escape To Purgatory, 1996; The Early Lynching, 1997; Renegade Rose, 1997; Ride Into Destiny, 1997; Goose Pimples, 1997; Man Without A Yesterday, 1998; Trail To Redemption, 1998; Blood To Cross, 1998; Short Story World, 1999; Comanchero Rendezvous, 1999; The Cornish Woman, 1999; Frank Riddle – Frontiersman, 1999; Pinkerton Man, 2000; Galvanized Yankee, 2001; Railroaded, 2001; Lust To Kill, 2003; The Frontiersman, 2004; Blind Trail, 2004; Bender's Boot, 2004; The Saga of Nelly's Nipple, 2004. Contributions to: Over 300 short stories in magazines, newspapers and anthologies. Address: Greenmantle, Horseshoe Lane, Ash Vale, Surrey, GU12 5LJ, England.

LEWIS (Joseph) Anthony, b. 27 March 1927. Writer; Journalist. m. (1) Linda Rannells, divorced 1982, 1 son, 2 daughters, (2) Margaret H Marshall. Education: BA, Harvard College. Appointments: Sunday Department, New York Times, 1948-52; Reporter, Washington Daily News, 1952-55; Legal Correspondent, Washington Bureau, New York Times, 1955-64; Nieman Fellow, Harvard Law School, 1956-57; Chief London Correspondent, New York Times, 1965-72; Editorial Columnist, 1969-2001; Lecturer in Law, Harvard Law School, 1974-89; James Madison Visiting Professor, Columbia University, 1983-. Publications: Gideon's Trumpet, 1964; Portrait of a Decade: The Second American Revolution, 1964; Make No Law: The Sullivan Case and the First Amendment, 1991; Written into History, editor, 2001; Articles in American law reviews. Honours: Pulitzer Prize for National Correspondence, 1955, 1963; Heywood Broun Award, 19955; Overseas Press Club Award, 1970; Presidential Citizens Medal, 2001; Hon DLitt: Adelphi University, New York, 1964, Rutgers University, 1973, New York Medical College, 1976, Williams College, Massachusetts, 1978, Clark University, Massachusetts, 1982; Hon LLD: Syracuse, 1979, Colby College, 1983, Northeastern University, Massachusetts, 1987; Georgetown University, 2003; Honorary Doctor of Humanities, Oberlin College, 2003. Memberships: Governor, Ditchley Foundation, 1965-72; American Academy of Arts and Sciences, 1991. Address: 1010 Memorial Drive, Cambridge, MA 02138, USA.

LEWIS Arnold, b. 13 January 1930, New Castle, Pennsylvania, USA. Architectural Historian; Art Historian; Professor. m. Beth Irwin, 24 June 1958, 2 sons, 1 daughter. Education: BA, Allegheny College, 1952; MA, 1954, PhD, 1962, University of Wisconsin; University of Bonn, 1959-60; University of Munich, 1960. Appointments: Wells College, Aurora, New York, 1962-64; College of Wooster, Ohio, 1964-96. Publications: American Victorian Architecture, 1975; Wooster in 1876, 1976; American Country Houses of the Gilded Age, 1983; American Interiors of the Gilded Age (with James Turner and Steven McQuillin), 1987; An Early Encounter with Tomorrow: Europeans, Chicago's Loop, and the World's Columbian Exposition, 1997. Contributions to: Journal of the Society of Architectural Historians. Honours: Founder's Award, JSAH, 1974; SAH Western Reserve Book Award, 1977; Barzun Prize in Cultural History, American Philosophical Society, 1998. Memberships: College Art Association; Society of Architectural Historians, director, 1979-82. Address: c/o Department of Art, College of Wooster, Wooster, OH 44691, USA.

LEWIS Bernard, b. 31 May 1916, London, England. Professor Emeritus of Near Eastern Studies; Writer. m. Ruth Helene Oppenhejm, 1947, divorced 1974, 1 son, 1 daughter. Education: BA, 1936, PhD, 1939, University of London; Diplôme des études semitiques, University of Paris, 1937; War Service, 1940-45. Appointments: Professor of History of the Near and Middle East, University of London, 1949-74; Visiting Professor, University of California at Los Angeles, 1955-56, Columbia University, 1960, Indiana University, 1963, University of California at Berkeley, 1965, Collège de France, 1980, École des Hautes Études en Sciences Sociales, Paris, 1983, University of Chicago, 1985; Class of 1932 Lecturer, Princeton University, 1964; Visiting Member, 1969, Member, 1974-86, Institute for Advanced Study, Princeton, New Jersey; Gottesman Lecturer, Yeshiva University, 1974; Cleveland E Dodge Professor of Near Eastern Studies, 1974-86, Professor Emeritus, 1986-, Princeton University; Douglas Robb Foundation Lecturer, University of Auckland, 1982; Andrew D White Professor-at-Large, Cornell University, 1984-90; Sackler Fellow, Tel Aviv University; Director, Annenberg Research Institute, Philadelphia, 1986-90; Tanner Lecturer, Brasenose College, Oxford, 1990; Merle Curti Lecturer, University of Wisconsin, 1993. Publications include: The origins of Ismailism: A Study of the Historical Background of the Fatimid caliphage, 1940; A Handbook of Diplomatic and Political Arabic, 1947; The Arabs in History, 1950; Co-editor, Encyclopedia of Islam, 1956-86; Istanbul and the Civilization of the Ottoman Empire, 1963; Editor and Translator, Islam, from the Prophet Muhammad to the Capture of Constantinople, 2 volumes, 1974; The World of Islam: Faith, People, Culture, 1976; The Muslim Discovery of Europe, 1982; Semites and Anti-Semites, 1986, 1999; The Political Language of Islam, 1988; Race and Slavery in the Middle East: An Historical Enquiry, 1990; The Shaping of the Modern Middle East, 1994; Cultures in Conflict: Christians, Muslims and Jews in the Age of Discovery, 1995; The Middle East: Two Thousand Years of History from the Rise of Christianity to the Present Day, 1995; The Future of the Middle East, 1997; The Multiple Identities of the Middle East, 1998; A Middle East Mosaic: Fragments of life, letters and history, 2000; Music of A Distant Drum: Classical Arabic, Persian, Turkish and Hebrew Poems, 2001; What Went Wrong? Western Impact and Middle Eastern Response, 2002; The Crisis of Islam: Holy War and Unholy Terror, 2003. Contributions to professional journals. Honours: Citation of Honour, Turkish Ministry of Culture, 1973; Harvey Prize, Technion-Israel Institute of Technology, 1978; Jefferson Lecturer in the Humanities, National Endowment for the Humanities, 1990; Ataturk Peace Prize, 1998; 14 honorary doctorates. Memberships: Fellow, University College, London, 1976; Fellow, British Academy; Member, American Philosophical Society; Member, American Academy of Arts and Sciences; Associate Member, Institut d'Égypte; Corresponding

Dictionary of International Biography

Member, Institut de France; Honorary Member, Turkish Academy of Sciences. Address: Department of Near Eastern Studies, 110 Jones Hall, Princeton University, Princeton, NJ 08544, USA.

LEWIS Bernard Walter, b. 24 July 1917, Lincoln, England. Flour Miller. m. Joyce Ilston Storey, 1943, 1 son, 1 daughter. Education: University of Manchester. Appointments: Joined King's Own Regiment, served in Middle East, 1940-46; RASC, 1941; Captain, 1942; Major, 1943; Chairman and Managing Director, Green's Flour Mills Ltd, 1955-90; General Tax Commissioner, 1957-93; Chairman, Dengie and Maldon Essex Bench, 1970-88; Chairman, Maldon Harbour Commissioners, 1978-2001; Chairman, Flour Advisory Bureau, 1979-88; President, National Association of British and Irish Millers, 1985-86; Chairman, Edward Baker Holdings Ltd, 1983-89; Retired, 1989. Honour: CBE, 1973. Memberships: Financial Board, Conservative Party, 1966-75; Chairman, Board of Governors, Plume School, 1968-83; Liveryman, Worshipful Company of Bakers, 1973. Address: Roughlees, 68 Highlands Drive, Maldon, Essex CM9 6HY, England.

LEWIS Carl, b. 1 July 1961, Birmingham, Alabama, USA. American Athlete. Education: University of Houston. Appointments: Bronze Medal, Long Jump, Pan-American Games, 1979; Won World Cup Competition, 1981; First World Championships (with 8.55 metres); Achieved World Record 8.79 metre jump, 1983; Gold Medals, Olympic Games, 100 metres, 200 metres, Long Jump, 4x100m, 1984; 65 Consecutive wins in Long Jump, 1985; Silver Medal, 200 metres; Gold Medal, 100 metres, Olympic Games, 1988; Jumped 8.64 metres, New York, 1991; World Record, 100 metres 9.86 seconds, 1991; Gold Medal, Long Jump, Olympic Games, 1992; Gold Medal for long jump (27ft. 10.75 in), Olympic Games, 1996; Retired, 1997; Attached to Trialtir, 1997. Honours: Track and Field News Athlete of the Decade, 1980-89; Athlete of the Century, IAAF, 1999. Address: c/o Carl Lewis International Fan Club, P O Box 57-1990, Houston, TX 77257-1990, USA.

LEWIS David K(ellogg), b. 28 September 1941, Oberlin, Ohio, USA. Professor of Philosophy; Writer. m. Stephanie Robinson, 5 September 1965. Education: BA, Swarthmore College, 1962; MA, 1964, PhD, 1967, Harvard University. Appointments: Assistant Professor of Philosophy, University of California, Los Angeles, 1966-70; Faculty, 1970-73, Professor of Philosophy, 1973-, Princeton University; Fulbright Lecturer, Australia, 1971; John Locke Lecturer, Oxford University, 1984; Kant Lecturer, Stanford University, 1988. Publications: Convention: A Philosophical Study, 1969; Counterfactuals, 1973; Philosophical Papers, 2 volumes, 1983, 1986; On the Plurality of Worlds, 1986; Parts of Classes, 1991; Papers in Philosophical Logic, 1998; Papers in Metaphysics and Epistemology, 1999; Papers in Ethics and Social Philosophy, 2000. Honours: Matchette Prize for Philosophical Writing, 1972; Fulbright Research Fellow, New Zealand, 1976; Santayana Fellow, Harvard University, 1988; Doctor of Letters, University of Melbourne, 1995; Doctor of the University, University of York, 1999. Memberships: American Association of University Professors; Australian Academy of the Humanities; British Academy; National Association of Scholars; American Academy of Arts and Sciences. Address: c/o Department of Philosophy, Princeton University, Princeton, NJ 08544, USA.

LEWIS Denise, b. 27 August 1972, West Bromwich, England. Athlete. Career: Specialises in heptathlon; Commonwealth Heptathlon Record Holder (6,736 points), 1977; Fifth European Junior Championships, 1991; Gold Medal, Commonwealth Games, 1994; Gold Medal, European Cup, 1995; Bronze Medal, Olympic Games, 1996; Silver Medal, World Championships, 1997; Gold

Medal, European Championships, 1998; Gold Medal, Commonwealth Championships, 1998; Silver Medal World Championship, 1999; New Commonwealth Record (6,831 points), 2000; Gold Medal, Olympic Games, 2000. Publications: Denise Lewis: Faster, Higher, Stronger, autobiography, 2001. Honours: British Athletics Writers Female Athlete of the Year, 1998, 2000; Sports Writers Association Sportswoman of the Year, 2000. Address: c/o MTC (UK) Ltd, 20 York Street, London, W1U 6PU, England. E-mail: info.mtc-uk.com

LEWIS Edward B, b. 20 May 1918, Wilkes-Barre, USA. Professor of Biology. m. Pamela Harrah, 1946, 3 sons, 1 deceased. Education: Minnesota University; California Institute of Technology; PhD. Appointments: Instructor, 1946-48, Assistant Professor, 1948-49, Associate Professor, 1949-56, Professor, 1956-88, Thomas Hunt Morgan Professor of Biology Emeritus, 1988-; Rockefeller Foundation Fellow, Cambridge University, England, 1947-48; Guest Professor, Institute of Genetics, Copenhagen University, Denmark, 1975-76. Honours: Honorary PhD, Umeå University, Sweden, 1981; Thomas Hunt Morgan Medal, Gairdner Foundation International Award, 1987; Co-recipient, Wolf Prize for Medicine, 1989; Rosentiel Medical Research Award, 1990; National Medal of Science, USA, 1990; Co-recipient, Albert Lasker Basic Medical Research Award, 1991; Louisa Gross Horwitz Prize, 1992; Honorary DSc, Minnesota University, 1993; Co-recipient, Nobel Prize for Medicine, 1995. Memberships: Genetics Society of America, Secretary, 1962-64, Vice-President, 1966-67, President, 1967; National Academy of Sciences; American Academy of Arts and Sciences; American Philosophical Society; Foreign Member, Royal Society, 1989; Honorary Member, Genetical Society of Great Britain, 1990. Address: 805 Winthrop Road, San Marino, CA 91108, USA.

LEWIS Esyr ap Gwilym, b. 11 January 1926, Clydach Vale, Glamorgan, Wales. Retired Judge. m. Elizabeth Hoffmann, 4 daughters. Education: Exhibitioner and Foundation Scholar, Trinity Hall, Cambridge, 1947-50. Appointments: Army Intelligence Corps, 1944-47; Called to Bar at Gray's Inn, 1951; Law Supervisor, Trinity Hall, Cambridge, 1951-57; Queens Counsel, 1971; Recorder, Crown Court, 1972-84; Deputy High Court Judge, 1978-84; Official Referee, London Official Referees Courts, 1984-98; Senior Official Referee, 1994-98; Leader, Welsh Circuit, 1978-82; Member, Criminal Injuries Compensation Board, 1977-84. Publications: Articles in legal publications. Honour: Queen's Counsel. Memberships: Fellow, Chartered Institute of Arbitrators; Vice-President, Academy of Experts; Honorary Fellow, Society of Advanced Legal Studies; Bencher of Gray's Inn, 1978-, Treasurer, 1997. Address: 2 South Square, Gray's Inn, London WC1R 5HT, England.

LEWIS Jack (Baron Lewis of Newnham), b. 13 February 1928, Barrow, England. Professor of Chemistry. m. Elfreida M Lamb, 1951, 1 son, 1 daughter. Education: Universities of London and Nottingham; PhD. Appointments: Lecturer, University of Sheffield, 1954-56; Lecturer, Imperial College, London, 1956-57; Lecturer-Reader, 1957-61, Professor of Chemistry, 1967-70, University College, London; Professor of Chemistry, University of Manchester, 1961-67; Professor of Chemistry, University of Cambridge, 1970-95; Fellow, Sidney Sussex College, Cambridge, 1970-77; Warden, Robinson College, Cambridge, 1975-. Publications: Papers in scientific journals. Honours include: Honorary Fellow, Sidney Sussex College, Cambridge; Honorary Fellow, Royal Society of Chemistry; 21 honorary degrees; Davy Medal, Royal Society, 1985; Chevalier, Ordre des Palmes Académiques; Commander Cross of the Order of Merit, Poland. Memberships: Fellow, Royal Society; Foreign Associate, National Academy of Sciences, USA; Foreign Member, American

Philosophical Society, 1994; Foreign Member, Accademia Nazionale dei Lincei, 1995; Numerous committees. Address: Robinson College, Grange Road, Cambridge CB3 9AN, England.

LEWIS Jerry (Joseph Levitch), b. 16 March 1926, Newark, New Jersey, USA. Comedian; Writer; Director; Producer; Actor. m. (1) Patti Palmer, 1944, divorced, 5 sons, (2) SanDee Pitnick, 1983, 1 daughter. Career: Comedian, night-clubs, then with Dean Martin, 500 Club, Atlantic City, New Jersey, 1946; Professor of Cinema, University of Southern California; Film debut with Dean Martin in My Friend Irma, 1949; Other films, many also as producer and director, include My Friend Irma Goes West, 1950, That's My Boy, 1951, The Caddy, 1952, Sailor Beware, 1952, Jumping Jacks, 1953,; The Stooge, 1953, Scared Stiff, 1953, Living It Up, 1954, Three Ring Circus, 1954, You're Never Too Young, 1955, Partners, 1956, Hollywood or Bust, 1956, The Delicate Delinquent, 1957, The Sad Sack, 1958, Rock a Bye Baby, 1958, The Geisha Boy, 1958, Visit to a Small Planet, 1959, The Bellboy, 1960, Cinderfella, 1960, It's Only Money, 1961, The Errand Boy, 1962, The Patsy, 1964, The Disorderly Orderly, 1964, The Family Jewels, 1965, Boeing-Boeing, 1965, Three On a Couch, 1965, Way Way Out, 1966, The Big Mouth, 1967, Don't Raise the Bridge, Lower the River, 1968, One More Time, 1969, Hook, Line and Sinker, 1969, Which way to the Front?, 1970, The Day the Clown Cried, 1972, Hardly Working, 1979, King of Comedy, 1981, Slapstick of Another Kind, 1982, Smörgåsbord, 1983, How Did You Get In?, 1985, Mr Saturday Night, 1992, Funny Bones, 1995; Appeared in play, Damn Yankees, 1995, on tour, 1995-97; Television appearances including Startime, The Ed Sullivan Show and the Jazz Singer. Publications: The Total Film-Maker, 1971; Jerry Lewis in Person, 1982. Address: Jerry Lewis Films Inc, 3160 W Sahara Avenue, C-16, Las Vegas, NV 89102, USA. Website: www.jerrylewiscomedy.com

LEWIS Jerry Lee, b. 29 September 1935, Ferriday, Louisiana, USA. Singer; Musician (piano); Entertainer. m. 6 times. Career: Appeared on Louisiana Hayride, 1954; Film appearances: Jamboree, 1957; High School Confidential, 1958; Be My Guest, 1965; Concerts include: National Jazz & Blues Festival, 1968; Rock'n'Revival Concert, Toronto, 1969; First appearance, Grand Ole Opry, 1973; Rock'n'Roll Festival, Wembley, 1974; Numerous appearances with own Greatest Show On Earth; Subject of biographical film, Great Balls Of Fire, 1989. Recordings: Hit singles include: Whole Lotta Shakin' Goin' On', 1957; Great Balls Of Fire, 1958; Breathless, 1958; High School Confidential, 1958; What I'd Say, 1961; Good Golly Miss Molly, 1963; To Make Love Sweeter For You, 1969; There Must Be More To Love Than This, 1970; Would You Take Another Chance On Me?, 1971; Me And Bobby Gee, 1972; Chantilly Lace, 1972. Albums include: Jerry Lee Lewis, 1957; Jerry Lee's Greatest, 1961; Live At The Star Club, 1965; The Greatest Live Show On Earth, 1965; The Return Of Rock, 1965; Whole Lotta Shakin' Goin' On, 1965; Country Songs For City Folks, 1965; By Request - More Greatest Live Show On Earth, 1967; Breathless, 1967; Together, with Linda Gail Lewis, 1970; Rockin' Rhythm And Blues, 1971; Sunday Down South, with Johnny Cash, 1972; The Session, with Peter Frampton, Rory Gallagher, 1973; Jerry Lee Lewis, 1979; When Two Worlds Collide, 1980; My Fingers Do The Talking, 1983; I Am What I Am, 1984; Keep Your Hands Off It, 1987; Don't Drop It, 1988; Great Balls Of Fire! (film soundtrack), 1989; Rocket, 1990; Young Blood, 1995; Many compilations; Contributor, film soundtracks: Roadie, 1980; Dick Tracy, 1990. Honours include: Inducted into Rock'n'Roll Hall Of Fame, 1986; Star on Hollywood Walk Of Fame, 1989. Address: Warner Bros Records, 75 Rockefeller Plaza, New York, NY 10019, USA.

LEWIS Juliette, b. 21 June 1973, Fernando Valley, California. Film Actress. Appointments: TV Appearances include: Homefires (mini-series); I Married Dora, 1988; Too Young to Die (movie), 1989; A Family for Joe, 1990; Films include: My Stepmother is an Alien, 1988; Meet the Hollowheads, 1989; National Lampoons Christmas Vacation, 1989; Cape Fear, 1991; Crooked Hearts, 1991; Husbands and Wives, 1992; Kalifornia, 1993; One Hot Summer, That Night, 1993; What's Eating Gilbert Grape, 1993; Romeo is Bleeding, 1994; Natural Born Killers, 1994; Mixed Nuts, 1994; The Basketball Diaries, 1995; Strange Days, 1995; From Dusk Till Dawn, 1996; The Evening Star, 1996; The Audition, Full Tilt Boogie, 1997; The Other Sister, 1999; The 4th Floor, 1999; Way of the Gun, 2000; My Louisiana Sky, 2001. Address: c/o Willia, Morris Agency, 151 El Camino Boulevard, Beverley Hills, CA 80212, USA.

LEWIS Lennox, b. 2 September 1965, Heavyweight Boxer. Career: Defeated Jean Chanet to win European Heavyweight Title, Crystal Palace, 1990; Defeated Gary Mason to win British Heavyweight Title, Wembley, 1991; Commonwealth Heavyweight; WBC Heavyweight, 1992; WBC World Champion, 1993-94, 1997-; Defended WBC Title, and challenged for World Boxing Association (WBA) and International Boxing Federation (IBF) Titles against Evander Holyfield, 1999, Bout declared a draw; Undisputed World Heavyweight Champion, 1999-2001 (lost WBC and IBF titles when defeated by Hasim Rahman, 2001); Defeated Frank Bruno, 1993; Founder, Lennox Lewis College, Hackney, London, 1994; regained title of world heavyweight champion from Hashim Rahman, November 2001; retained title of undisputed world heavyweight champion after beating Mike Tyson, June 2002-; 40 professional wins (20 losses, 1 draw, 31 knock-outs); Film appearance in Ocean's Eleven, 2002. Publications: Lennox Lewis, autobiography, 1993; Lennox, 2002. Honour: Honorary Doctorate, University of London, 1999. Address: Office of Lennox Lewis, Suite 206, Gainsborough House, 81 Oxford Street, London, W1D 2EU, England. E-mail: rose@lennoxlewis.com

LEWIS Peter Tyndale, b. 1929, London, England. Retail Businessman. m. Deborah Anne Collins, 1 son, 1 daughter. Education: Christ Church, Oxford, 1949-52. Appointments: 2nd Lieutenant, Coldstream Guards, 1948-49; Pilot Officer, RAFVR, 1951-52; Barrister, Middle Temple, 1955-59; Joined John Lewis Partnership, 1959; Director, John Lewis Department Stores, 1967-71; Chairman, John Lewis Partnership plc and John Lewis plc, 1972-93. Honours: Companion, Institute of Management; Fellow, Royal Society of Arts. Memberships: Executive Committee, Industrial Society, 1968-79; Executive Committee, Design Council, 1971-74; Chairman, Retail Distributors Association, 1971-72; Governor, Windlesham House School, 1979-95; Governor, NIESR, 1983-2000; Trustee, Bell Educational Trust, 1987-97; Governor, Queen's College, Harley Street, 1994-2000; Trustee, Southampton University Development Trust, 1994-. Address: 34 Victoria Road, London W8 5RG, England.

LEYGRAF Hans, b. 7 September, 1920, Stockholm, Sweden. Concert Pianist; Music Educator. m. Margarethe Stehle, 1 son, 1 daughter. Education: Piano with Gottfried Boon, Stockholm, Sweden, 1928-38; Piano with Anna Hirzel-Langenhan, Schloss Berg, Thurgau, Switzerland, 1938-41; Composition, Conducting, Music Academy, Stockholm, Sweden, 1936-40; Composition, Conducting, Music Academy, Munich, Germany, 1941-42. Career: Concert Pianist in more than 30 countries, 1938-; Piano Teacher, Music Academy, Darmstadt, Germany, 1954-62; Visiting Piano Teacher, Edsberg Music School, Stockholm, Sweden, 1958-70; Piano Teacher, Music University, Hannover, Germany, 1962-85; Piano Professor, University Mozarteum, Salzburg, Austria, 1972-; Visiting Piano Professor, Music University of Berlin, 1988-97.

Recordings: 5 CDs: Mozart, all piano sonatas, 1982-85; 3 CDs, Schubert, 3 recitals, 1994. Honours: Litteris et Artibus, Stockholm, Sweden, 1977; Das österreichische Ehrenkreuz, Vienna, Austria, 1984; Das grosse silberne Ehrenzeichen, Vienna, Austria, 1994. Memberships: Swedish Academy of Music, Stockholm, 1961; Honorary Member, University of Mozarteum, Salzburg, 1988-; Honorary Doctor, University of Luleå, Sweden, 2003. Address: Am Irrsee 15, A-4893 Zell am Moos, Austria.

LI Ching-Chung, b. 30 March 1932, Changshu, China. Professor of Electrical Engineering and Computer Science. m. Hanna Wu Li, 2 sons. Education: BSEE, National Taiwan University, 1954; MSEE, 1956, PhD, 1961, Northwestern University. Appointments: Professor, Electrical Engineering, University of Pittsburgh, 1967-; Professor, Computer Science, University of Pittsburgh, 1977-. Publications: Over 200 papers. Memberships: Fellow, IEEE; Biomedical Engineering Society; Pattern Recognition Society. Address: 2130 Garrick Drive, Pittsburgh, PA 15235-5033, USA.

LI Hua, b. 25 August 1960, Wuhan, People's Republic of China. Research Scientist; Division Manager. m. Dong-Ping Yuan, 1 daughter. Education: BSc, 1982, MSc, 1987, Wuhan University of Technology; PhD, National University of Singapore, 1999. Appointments: Managing Director, Wuhan University of Technology Press, 1990-94; Research Scholar, Senior Research Engineer, Institute of High performance Computing, National University of Singapore, 1994-2000; Postdoctoral Associate, University of Illinois Urbana-Champaign, USA, 2000-2001; Research Scientist, Division Manager, Institute of High Performance Computing, Singapore, 2001-. Publications: Vibration analysis of a rotating truncated circular conical shell, 1997; A new hybrid meshless differentiated order reduction (hM-DOR) method with application to shape control of smart structures via distributed sensors/outactors, 2003. Honour: NUS Research Scholarship for PhD Programme. Memberships: China Society for Vibration Engineering; China Society of Mechanics. Address: Blk 612 #09-302, Clementi West St 1, Singapore 120612. E-mail: lihua@ihpc.a-star.edu.sg

LI Lingwei, b. 1964. Badminton Player. Career: Participant in international championships; Won Women's Singles Title, 3rd World Badminton Championships, Copenhagen, 1982; Won Women's Singles and Women's Doubles, 5th ALBA World Cup, Jakarta, 1985; Won Women's Singles, World Badminton Grand Prix finals, Tokyo, 1985; Won Women's Singles at Dunhill China Open Badminton Championship, Nanjing, and Malaysian Badminton Open, Kuala Lumpur, 1987; Won Women's Singles at World Grand Prix, Hong Kong, China Badminton Open, and Danish Badminton Open, Odense, 1988; Won Women's Singles, All-England Badminton Championships, 1989; Winner, Women's Singles, 6th World Badminton Championships, Jakarta. Honours: Elected 7th in list of 10 Best Chinese Athletes. Address: China Sports Federation, Beijing, People's Republic of China.

LI Yanmin, b. 25 October 1959, Shandong, China. Banker. m. Liwen Gao, 2 daughters. Education: BSc, Physics, Qufu Normal University, Shandong, China, 1978-82; MSc, Theoretical Physics, Northeast University, Shenyang, China, 1982-84; PhD, Theoretical Physics, Institute of Physics, Chinese Academy of Sciences, 1985-87; PhD, Finance, Business School, Warwick University, England, 1996-2002. Appointments: Research Associate, Institute of Theoretical Physics, Academia Sinica, China, 1988-89; Research Fellow, International Centre for Theoretical Physics, Trieste, Italy, 1989-91; Research Fellow, Warwick University, England, 1991-94; Visiting Scientist, Max Planck-Institut für Physik Komplexer Systemer, Dresden, Germany, 1994-95; Senior Research Fellow, Department of Physics, Warwick University, England, 1995-97;

Senior Research Fellow, Centre for Quantitative Finance, Imperial College, London, England, 1997-99; Associate Director, Tokyo-Mitsubishi International, London, England, 1999-. Publications: Over 40 research papers published in physical and financial journals as author and co-author include most recently: Thermodynamic properties of a band Jahn-Teller system, 1998; Scaling behaviour of transaction costs in optimally hedging options, 1999; A new algorithm for constructing implied binomial trees: Can the implied model fit any volatility smile? 2000/2001; Hedging option portfolios without using Greeks, 2002. Honours: Regular Member of the Centre for Advanced Science and Technology, Beijing, China, 1987; Honorary Professorship, Qufu Normal University, China, 1989; Kingston University Industrial Fellow, 2003. Memberships: American Physical Society; Institute of Physics, UK. Address: 52 Rokeby Gardens, Woodford Green IG8 9HR, England.

LI-LAN, b. 28 January 1943, New York, New York, USA. Artist. Appointments: Regional Council, Parrish Art Museum, Southampton, New York, 1984-87; Artists Advisory Board, East Hampton Center for Contemporary Art, East Hampton, New York, 1989-90. Publications: Canvas With an Unpainted Part: An Autobiography, Tokyo, Japan, 1976; Texts in exhibition catalogues and books, numerous articles. Commissions and Creative Works: Collections in numerous museums including: Virginia Museum of Fine Arts, Richmond, Virginia; The Parrish Art Museum, Southampton, New York; William Benton Museum of Art, Storrs, Connecticut; Arkansas Arts Center, Little Rock; Seibu Museum of Art, Tokyo Japan; Ohara Museum of Art, Kurashiki, Japan; Other collections include: Estee Lauder Inc, Mobil Oil Corporation, Lifetime TV, Chermayeff and Geismer Associates, New York; Gap Inc, Flagship Store, Oahu, Hawaii; Art For Peace Collection, Fischer Pharmaceuticals Ltd, Tel Aviv, Israel; Seattle First National Bank, Washington; Security Pacific National Bank, Los Angeles, California; Weatherspoon Art Gallery, Greensboro, North Carolina; Solo exhibitions in USA, Japan, Taiwan include: Robert Miller Gallery, New York, 1978; OK Harris Gallery, New York, 1983, 1985, 1987; The William Benton Museum of Art, Storrs, Connecticut, 1990; Lin & Keng Gallery, Taipei, Taiwan, 1995, 1997, 2001; Art Projects International, New York, New York, 1994, 1996; DoubleVision Gallery, Los Angeles, California, 2003; Nabi Gallery, New York, 2004; Numerous group exhibitions in USA, Japan and Taiwan. Honours: Artists Grant, Artists Space, New York, 1988, 1990; Certificate of Merit: Chinese American Cultural Pioneer, New York City Council, 1993.

LIANG Xue-Zhang, b. 1 December 1939, Pingdu, Shandong, China. University Professor. m. Feng-Jie, 2 sons, 1 daughter. Education: Diploma, 1962; Postgraduate thesis and diploma, 1965. Appointments: Assistant, 1965; Lecturer, 1978; Associate Professor, 1983; Professor, 1990; PhD Supervisor, 1993. Publications: Articles in journals: Lagrange representation of multivariate interpolation, 1989; On the convergence of Hakopian interpolation and cubature, 1997; On the integral convergence of Kergin interpolation on the disk, 1998; Solving second kind integral equation by Galrrkin methods with continous orthogonal wavelets, 2001; The application of Cayley-Bacharach theotem to bivariate Lagrange interpolation, 2004. Honours: Natural Science Award, China, 1982; Scientific and Technical Progress Award, Education Committee of China, 1988. Membership: Jilin Province Expert Association of China. Address: Institute of Mathematics, Jilin University, Changchun, Jilin 130012, China.

LIAO Lawrence Manzano, b. 11 April 1959, Cebu City Philippines. Biological Oceanographer. m. Claudette Y Go. Education: BSc Marine Biology, University of San Carlos, 1980; MSc Marine Biology, University of the Philippines, 1987; PhD

Biology, University of North Carolina at Chapel Hill, 1995. Appointments: Assistant Professor, 1996-98, Associate Professor, 1998-2000, Professor, 2000-, University of San Carlos; Visiting Professor, Zamboanga State College of Marine Sciences and Technology, 1997-99; Assistant Editor, The Philippine Scientist, 1996-. Publications: Articles in professional scientific journals. Honour: Dr William C Coker Fellowship, the University of North Carolina at Chapel Hill. Memberships: American Society of Plant Taxonomists, International Phycological Society; Korean Society for Phycology; National Research Council of the Philippines; Phycological Society of America. Address Department of Biology, University of San Carlos, 6000 Cebu City, Philippines. E-mail: phycologist@lycos.com

LIBERMAN Anatoly, b. 10 March 1937. Professor. m. Sofya Slavina, 1 son. Education: BA, summa cum laude, Hertzen Pedagogical Institute, Leningrad, USSR, 1954-59; Candidate of Philological Sciences (PhD), Leningrad University, 1965; Doctor of Philological Sciences (Habilitation), Academy of Sciences of the USSR, 1971. Appointments: School Teacher, Leningrad Region, USSR, 1959-62; Instructor, Leningrad Polytechnical Institute, 1962-65; Junior Research Fellow, 1965-72, Senior Research Fellow, 1972-75, Institute of Linguistics, Academy of Sciences of the USSR; Hill Visiting Professor, 1975-76, Associate Professor, 1976-78, Professor, 1978-, University of Minnesota, Minneapolis, USA; Visiting Professor: Harvard; Sapientia, Rome; University of Freiburg, Germany. Publications: Over 450 publications in the areas of general and Germanic linguistics, medieval literature, folklore, Russian literature and poetic translation; Books include: On the Heights of Creation: The Lyrics of Fedor Tyutchev, 1993; Word Heath, 1994; Germanic Accentology, 1982; N S Trubetzkoy, Studies in General Linguistics and Language Structure, 2001. Honours: Guggenheim Fellowship, 1982; Fulbright Research Fellowship, 1988; Festschrift: Germanic Studies in Honor of Anatoly Liberman, 1997; Fellowship, American Council of Learned Societies, 2001-2002; Fesler-Lampert Professorship, 1999-2002; Prizes for the best book and best paper and numerous awards from the University of Minnesota. Memberships: Society for the Advancement of Scandinavian Study; Dictionary Society of North America; National Organization for Scholars; Association of Literary Scholars and Critics. Address: University of Minnesota, Department of German, Scandinavian and Dutch, Minneapolis, MN 55454, USA. E-mail: liber002@umn.edu

LICARY Cheryl, b. 15 March 1951, Beloit, Wisconsin, USA. Education. 1 son, 1 daughter. Education: BA, Music Education, Luther College, Decorah, Iowa, USA, 1972; Master of Science in Teaching, Kodály Emphasis, University of Wisconsin, 1976; 30 post graduate credits, various universities. Appointments: Vocal Music and Department Chairperson, School District of Beloit, Wisconsin, USA, 30 years; Organist and Choir Director, Our Saviour's Lutheran Church; Choral Adjudicator and Clinician. Publication: Beyond Ratings: Enriching the Solo and Ensemble Experience, Wisconsin School Music Association, 2003. Honours: Rotary Educator Recognition, 2001; Wisconsin Award for Excellence in Music Teaching, 2003; Choirs have appeared twice in Carnegie Hall on public radio – Garrison Kiellor; Listed in Who's Who publications and biographical dictionaries. Memberships: American Choral Directors Association; Wisconsin School Music Association; Wisconsin Choral Directors Association; Music Educators National Conference; American Guild of Organists. Address: 1305 11th Street, Beloit, WI 53511, USA. E-mail: clicary@sdb.k12.wi.us

LICHFIELD 5th Earl of, Thomas Patrick John Anson, b. 25 April 1939. British Photographer. m. Lady Leonora Grosvenor, 1975, divorced 1986, 1 son, 2 daughters. Education: Sandhurst.

Appointments: Army Service, Grenadier Guards, 1957-62; Photographer. Publications: The Most Beautiful Women, 1981; Lichfield on Photography, 1981; A Royal Album, 1982; Patrick Lichfield's Unipart Calendar book, 1982; Patrick Lichfield Creating the Unipart Calendar, 1983; Hot Foot to Zabriske Point, 1985; Lichfield on Travel Photography, 1986; Not the Whole Truth, 1986; Lichfield in Retrospect, 1988; Queen Mother: The Lichfield Selection, 1990; Elizabeth R: a Photographic Celebration of 40 Years, 1991. Honours: Hon DL, Stafford, 1996. Memberships: Fellow, British Institute of Professional Photographers; Fellow, Royal Photographic Society. Address: Shugborough Hall, Stafford, England. E-mail: lichfield@lichfieldstudios.co.uk

LIDDELL-GRAINGER David Ian, b. 26 January 1930. Landowner. m. (1) Anne Mary Sibylla, 14 December 1957, dissolved 1982, 4 sons, 1 daughter, (2) Christine, Lady de la Rue, 2 sons, 1 deceased. Education: College of Estate Management, London. Appointments: Scots Guards, 1948-50; Farmer; County Councillor, 1958-73; Council Member: Scottish Gas Council; RNLI; Scottish Scout Association; National Trust for Scotland; Royal Agricultural Society of England; Scottish Landowners Federation; Deputy Chairman, Timber Growers UK, 1985-88; Area Commissioner, Scouts Scottish Borders; Trustee, Shackleton Preservation Trust; President, Berwick-on-Tweed Wildlife Trust. Memberships: Member, Queen's Body Guard for Scotland, Royal Company of Archers, 1955-83; DL, 1962-85; Grand Master Mason of Scotland, 1969-74; Knight of St John, 1974; Hospitaller Order of St John, Scotland, 1977-82; FSA, Scotland; Member, Regional Advisory Committee Forestry Commission. Address: Ayton Castle, Berwickshire, TD14 5RD, Scotland.

LIEBERMAN Herbert Henry, b. 22 September 1933, New Rochelle, New York, USA. Novelist; Playwright; Editor. m. Judith Barsky, 9 June 1963, 1 daughter. Education: AB, City College of New York, 1955; AM, Columbia University, 1957. Publications: The Adventures of Dolphin Green, 1967; Crawlspace, 1971; The Eighth Square, 1973; Brilliant Kids, 1975; City of the Dead, 1976; The Climate of Hell, 1978; Nightcall from a Distant Time Zone, 1982; Night Bloom, 1984; The Green Train, 1986; Shadow Dancers, 1989; Sandman Sleep, 1993; The Girl with the Botticelli Eyes, 1996. Honours: 1st Prize for Playwriting, University of Chicago, 1963; Guggenheim Fellowship, 1964; Grand Prix de Litterature Policiere, Paris, 1978. Memberships: Mystery Writers of America; International Association of Crime Writers. Address: c/o Georges Borchardt, 136 East 57th Street, New York, NY 10022, USA.

LIEBERMAN Louis Stuart, b. 23 May 1938, Swan Hill, Victoria, Australia. Barrister; Solicitor; Director. m. Marjorie Cox, 2 sons, 1 daughter. Education: New South Wales Barristers and Solicitors Admission Board; Studied and worked as Articled Law Clerk; Qualified as a Solicitor, New South Wales and High Court and Barrister and Solicitor, Victoria; Diploma in Law (SAB). Appointments include: Senior Partner, Harris Lieberman & Co Barristers and Solicitors, 1974-76; Chair, House of Representatives Standing Committee on Aboriginal and Torres Strait Islander Affairs; Parliamentary Secretary to Leader of Opposition, Commonwealth Parliament; Shadow Minister for Health, Further Education, Water Resources, Property and Services; Minister for Planning, Assistant Health, Minerals and Energy, Mines; Member for Benambra, Legislative Assembly, Parliament of Victoria, 1976-92, retired; Member for Indi, House of Representatives, Commonwealth of Australia, 1993-2001, retired; Director, Hume Building Society Ltd. Memberships: Fellow, Australian Institute of Company Directors; Law Society of New South Wales; Law Institute, Victoria; Australian War Memorial Foundation; Patron

Bandiana Military Museum; La Trobe University Council; Wodonga Technical College Council; Rotary. Address: PO Box 151, Wodonga, Victoria, Australia 3689.

LIEW Wee Liik, b. 17 April 1967, Kuching, Sarawak, Malaysia. Consultant Cardiothoracic Surgeon. 1 daughter. Education: Bachelor of Medicine, Bachelor of Surgery, Bachelor of Arts of Obstetrics, Queen's University, Belfast, Northern Ireland, 1991; Fellow, Royal College of Surgeons, Edinburgh, 1995; Fellow, Royal College of Surgeons, Ireland, 1995. Appointments: House Officer, Manchester, England, 1991-92; Lecturer, University of Manchester, 1992-93; Senior House Officer, Manchester, England, 1993-94; Senior Registrar, The London Chest Hospital, 1994-97; Consultant Cardiothoracic Surgeon, Normah Medical Specialist Centre, 1998-. Publication: Co-author: Helicobacter Pylori and Upper Gastrointestinal Bleed in Heart Valve Surgery, 1998. Honours: Young Investigator Award in Cardiovascular and Thoracic Surgery, Sydney, Australia, 1997; Listed in Who's Who publications and biographical dictionaries. Memberships: Chapter of Cardiothoracic Surgery, College of Surgeons, Academy of Medicine, Malaysia; New York Academy of Science. Address: No 1374 Kenyalang Park, Jalan Sim Kheng Hong Selatan 3, 93300 Kuching, Sarawak, Malaysia. E-mail: liewwliik@hotmail.com

LIFSHITZ Fima, b. 24 April 1938, Mexico City, Mexico. Paediatrician; Endocrinologist. m. Jere Ziffer, 1985, 2 sons. Education: BS, Yavne College, Mexico City, 1955; MD, National University, Mexico City, 1961, Diplomate, American Board of Pediatrics; Diplomate, American Board of Pediatric Endocrinology. Appointments: Professor of Pediatrics, Cornell University Medical Centre, New York City, 1975-91; Associate Director Pediatrics, 1977-90, Vice Chairman, Department of Pediatrics, 1990-91, North Shore University Hospital, Manhasset, New York; Professor of Pediatrics, SUNY Health Science Center, Brooklyn, 1991-; Chairman, Department of Pediatrics, Maimonides Medical Center, Brooklyn, 1991-97; Chief of Staff, 1997-2001, Chief of Nutrition Sciences, 2000-02, Miami Children's Hospital, Florida; Professor, Pediatrics, University of Miami, Florida; Senior Nutrition Scientist, Sansum Medical Research Institute, Santa Barbara, 2003-. Memberships: International Society of Pediatric Nutrition; American College of Endocrinology; Lawson-Wilkins Pediatric Endocrine Society; Society for Pediatric Research; American College of Physician Executives. Honours: Man of the Year, Juvenile Diabetes Foundation, 1996; Fellow, American Academy of Pediatrics. Address: 1040 Alston Road, Santa Barbara, CA 93108, USA. E-mail: mchdfl@aol.com

LIGAA Urtnasangiin, b. 10 March 1932, Galt sum, Khovsgol aimag, Mongolia. Botanist; Economic Botanist. m. Norjingiina Ninjil, 1 son, 4 daughters. Education: BS, Biological Sciences, Mongolian State University, Ulaanbaatar, Mongolia. 1951-56; Chemistry and Pharmacology of Medicinal Plants, Veterinary Institute and Institute of Medicinal Plants, Budapest, Hungary, 1965-66; Postgraduate Botany, Economic Botany, (PhD), V L Komarov Botanical Institute, Academy of Sciences of Leningrad (St Petersburg), Russia, 1969-72. Appointments: Veterinary, State Farm "Erentsav", 1956-63; Scientific Researcher, Agricultural Institute of Mongolian Academy of Sciences, 1964-68; Scientific Researcher, Chief Scientist, Leading Scientist, Chief Advisor for Economic Botany Sector, Member, Academic Council, Institute of Botany, Mongolian Academy of Science, 1973-92; Teacher, Traditional Medicine Institute "Mamba Datsan", 1993-94; Leading Scientist, National Institute of Mongolian Traditional Medicine, 1995-97; Teacher of Medicinal and Useful Plants, 1998-2000; Senior Leading Scientist, Project Executor, 2001-, Mongolian State University of Agriculture. Publications: 21 books and numerous papers to specialist journals, conferences and seminars. Address: Ulaanbaatar 46, POB 743, Mongolia.

LILIENTHAL Alfred M(orton), b. 25 December 1913, New York, New York, USA. Author; Historian; Attorney; Lecturer. Education: BA, Cornell University, 1934; LLD, Columbia University School of Law, 1938. Appointment: Editor, Middle East Perspective, 1968-85. Publications: What Price Israel? 1953; There Goes the Middle East, 1958; The Other Side of the Coin, 1965; The Zionist Connection I, 1978; The Zionist Connection II, 1982. Contributions to: Numerous journals. Honour: National Press Club Book Honours, 1982. Memberships: University Club; Cornell Club; National Press Club; Capital Hill Club. Address: 800 25th St North West # 806, Washington, DC 20037, USA.

LILLEY Peter Bruce (Right Honourable), b. 23 August 1943, Kent, England. Politician. m. Gail Ansell, 1979. Education: Clare College, Cambridge; MA, Cantab. Appointments: Chairman, Bow Group, 1973; Member of Parliament for St Albans, 1983-97, for Hitchin and Harpenden, 1997-; Economic Secretary, 1987-89, Financial Secretary, 1989-90, to Treasury; Secretary of State for Trade and Industry, 1990-92, for Social Security, 1992-97; Opposition Front Bench Spokesman for Treasury, 1997-98; Deputy Leader of the Opposition, 1998-99; Former Director, Greenwell Montague, Oil Analyst. Publications: The Delusion of Incomes Policy, co-author, 1977; The End of the Keynesian Era, 1980; Thatcherism: The Next Generation, 1990; Winning the Welfare Debate, 1996; Patient Power, 2000; Common Sense on Cannabis, 2001; Taking Liberties, 2002. Honours: Privy Councillor. Address: House of Commons, London SW1A 0AA, England.

LIM In-Taek b. 16 July 1962, Ulju-Gun, Ulsan, South Korea. Electronics and Communications Educator. m. Hyo-Young Kim, 3 children. Education: BS, University of Ulsan, Ulsan, Korea, 1980-84; MS, Seoul National University, Seoul, Korea, 1984-86; PhD, University of Ulsan, Ulsan, Korea, 1994-98. Appointments: Information Processing Engineer No 1, Human Resources Development Service of Korea, 1983; Senior Researcher, Samsung Electronics Co, Suwon, Korea, 1986-93; Professor, Dong Pusan College, Korea, 1993-98; Editor, Korea Information Processing Society, Seoul, Korea, 2002-; Consultant, Small and Medium Business Administration, Daejun, Korea, 2000-. Publications: Articles in scientific journals including: IEEE Transactions on Consumer Electronics; IEICE Transactions on Communications; ETRI Journal; Editor, Korea Information Processing Society Review; Research projects include: Medium Access Control Protocol for TDMA-Based; Technical support in developing wireless interfaces for monitoring camera based on internet; A Design of MAC Protocol for Integrated Voice/Data Services; Design of a Vitual Learning Support System for Internet-Based Institution; A study on the instruction design with ICT; Patents: Medium access control scheme; Dynamic slot allocation scheme for real time variable bit rate services in the wireless ATM networks. Memberships: IEEE; Korean Institute of Maritime Information and Communication Science; Korean Institute of Communications Sciences; Korea Information Science Society. Address: Pusan University of Foreign Studies, San 55-1 Uan-Dong, Busan Nam-Gu 608738 Republic of Korea. E-mail: itlim@taejo.pufs.ac.kr

LIM Jong-Sik, b. 17 November 1968, Hwasun, Jeonnam, Republic of Korea. Electronic Engineer; Educator; Patent Examiner. m. Kyoung-Sun Park, 1 son, 1 daughter. Education: Bachelor, Electronic Engineering, 1991, Master, Electronic Engineering, 1993, Sogang University, Seoul, Republic of Korea; PhD, Electrical Engineering and Computer Science, Seoul National University, Republic of Korea, 2003. Appointments: Senior Research Engineer, Electronics and Communication Research Institute, Daejeon, Republic of Korea, 1993-99; Lecturer, Woosong Technical College, Daejeon, Republic of Korea, 1997; Lecturer,

Dictionary of International Biography

Graduate School, Soongsil University, Seoul, Lecturer, Graduate School, Soonchunhyang University, Asan, Republic of Korea, 2003; Patent Examiner, Korean Intellectual Property Office, 2003-. Publications: Almost 100 papers for domestic and international journals and conferences including KEES, IEEE, IEE, IEICE, in the research field of microwave circuits; 4 patents; 5 patents pending. Honours: Excellent Paper Award, 1993, Excellent Engineer Award, 1998, Electronics and Communications Research Institute; Design Paper Contest Award, Hewlett Packard, 1999; Brain Korea 21 Paper Award, Seoul National University, 2001; Human Technology Paper Award, Samsung Company, 2002. Memberships: Life Member, Alpha Sigma Nu (αΣN); IEEE; IEICE; Korean Electromagnetic Engineering Society. Address: Green APT 305-706, Songgang-Dong 199, Yusong-Gu, Daejeon 305-751, Republic of Korea. E-mail: paransim@krpost.net

LIM Kok Peng, (Fang Ran), b. 6 March 1943, Singapore. Writer. m. Meng Cheng Ng. Education: Graduate, Chong Cheng High School, 1962; Studied at St Thomas English School, 1963. Appointments: Manager, Equatorial Wing Publishing House; Chief Editor, Equatorial Wind Literary Quarterly; Instructor, Creative Writing, Nanyang Art Academy, 1996; Chief Editor, Echo (Prose magazine). Publications: Grass Under the Rock (collection of poems); Those that Wrapped by Indocalamus Leaves (collection of poems); Selected Verses by Fang Ran (Chinese and English); Black Horse (collection of fiction); Big City Small Story (collection of fiction); The Sky is No Longer Blue (collection of prose); Collection of Fang Ran's Verses and Criticisms. Honours: Judge (novels) of the 7th Country-wide literary award held by the Chinese Association of the University of Malaya; Special Invited Advisor of A Dictionary of Introduction to the Poetry of Overseas Chinese; Senior Advisor of A Dictionary of the World-Wide Poet; Literary Creation Competition Award of Excellence (Poetry), Singapore, 1975; Literary Creation Competition Award of Excellence (Poetry and Prose), Singapore, 1977; 2nd Prize, World Chinese Odes and Part Time Award, 1993; 2nd Prize, Hong Kong Dragon Cultural Award, 2000. Address: Blk 170 Stirling Road, #15-1145, Singapore 140170, Singapore. E-mail: ahbah@signet.com.sg

LIMERICK, Sylvia Countess of; Sylvia Rosalind Pery; CBE (1991), b. 7 December 1935, Cairo, Egypt. m. 6th Earl of Limerick, deceased 2003, 2 sons, 1 daughter. Education: MA, Lady Margaret Hall, Oxford. Appointments include: Research Assistant, Foreign and Commonwealth Office, 1959-62; Volunteer, British Red Cross, 1962-66; President and Chairman, Kensington and Chelsea Division, British Red Cross, 1966-72; Member of Board of Governors, St Bartholomew's Hospital, 1970-74; Vice Chairman, Foundation for the Study of Infant Deaths, 1971-; President, 1972-79, Vice President, 1979-99, UK Committee for UNICEF; Vice-Chairman, Community Health Council, 1974-77; Member, Committee of Management, Institute of Child Health, London, 1976-96; Member Area Health Authority, Kensington, Chelsea and Westminster, 1977-82; Council Member, King Edward's Hospital Fund for London, 1977-; Vice President, 1978-84, President, 1984-2002, Community Practitioners and Health Visitors' Association; Trustee, Child Accident Prevention Trust, 1979-87; President, 1973-84, Vice President, 1985-90, National Association for Maternal and Child Welfare; Reviewed National Association of Citizens' Advice Bureau for H M Government, 1983; Vice-Chairman, 1984-85, Chairman of Council, 1985-95, Chairman Emeritus, 1995-97; British Red Cross Society; Advisory Board, Civil Service Occupational Health Service, 1989-92; Board Member, Eastman Dental Hospital Special Health Authority, 1990-96; Trustee, Voluntary Hospital of St Bartholomew, 1991-; Vice President, International Federation of Red Cross and Red Crescent Societies, 1993-97; Vice Chairman, Institute of Neurology/Hospital for Neurology and Neurosurgery Joint Research Ethics Committee,

1993-; Non-Executive Director, University College London Hospitals NHS Trust, 1996-97; Chairman, CMO's Expert Group to Investigate Cot Death Theories, 1994-98; Trustee, Child Health Research Appeal Trust, 1995-; Chairman, Committee of Management, Eastman Dental Institute, 1996-99; Chairman, Eastman Dental Research Foundation, 1996-2002; Chairman, CPHVA Charitable Trust, 1997-2002; Patron, Child Advocacy International, 1998-; Honorary Vice President, British Red Cross Society, 1999-; Patron, CRUSE. Publications: Co-author, Sudden Infant Death: patterns, puzzles and problems, 1985; Over 60 articles in medical journals; Articles on International Red Cross and Red Crescent Movement. Honours: CBE, 1991; Hugh Greenwood Lecturer, Exeter University, 1987; Hon D Litt, Council for National Academic Awards, 1990; Samuel Gee Lecturer, RCP, 1994; European Women of Achievement Humanitarian Award, 1995; Hon LLD, University of Bristol, 1998. Memberships: Fellow, Royal Society of Medicine, 1977-; Hon MRCP, 1990, Hon FRCP, 1994, Royal College of Physicians; Freeman Honoris Causa, Worshipful Company of Salters, 1992; Honorary Fellow, Institute of Child Health, London, 1996; Honorary Member, 1986-, Honorary Fellow, 1996, Royal College of Paediatrics and Child Health; Freeman, Worshipful Company of World Traders, 2003; Order of the Croatian Star, 2003. Address: 30A Victoria Road, London W8 5RG, England. E-mail: srlimerick@aol.com

LIN Foong-Yi, b. 2 November 1966, Selangor, Malaysia, Physician; Paediatrician. Education: BA, Biology, Barnard College, Columbia University, New York, New York, USA, 1984-89; Doctor of Medicine, Dartmouth Medical School, Hanover, New Hampshire, USA, 1990-94; Brown University Medical School, Providence, Rhode Island, USA, 1991-94; Residency in Paediatrics, Hasbro Children's Hospital, Brown University Program in Paediatrics, Providence, Rhode Island, USA, 1994-97. Appointments: Paediatric Consultant, Department of Neonatology, Kent County Hospital, Warwick, Rhode Island, USA, 1995-97; Paediatric Consultant, The Westerly Hospital, Westerly, Rhode Island, 1997-; Paediatric Consultant, Department of Paediatrics, Hasbro Children's Hospital, Providence, Rhode Island, USA, 1998-; Clinical Instructor in Paediatrics, Brown University Medical School, Providence, Rhode Island, USA. Publication: Articles in peer reviewed journals as co-author: Factors Influencing the Utilization Practices in the Pediatric Emergency Room, 1994; Transient Non-Ketotic Hyperglycinemia And Defective Seratonin Metabolism In A Child With Neonatal Seizures, submitted. Memberships: American Academy of Pediatrics; American Medical Association; Rhode Island Medical Society. Address: 45 Wells Street, Suite 201, Westerly, RI 02891, USA. E-mail: fy_lin@msn.com

LIN Ho-Mu, b. 12 July 1938, Kaohsiung, Taiwan, Republic of China. Professor of Chemical Engineering. m. Su-Jung Lin, 2 sons. Education: BS, Chemical Engineering, National Taiwan University, 1962; Postgraduate Diploma in Chemical Engineering and Chemistry, Tokyo Institute of Technology, 1966; PhD, Chemical Engineering, Oklahoma State University, 1970. Appointments: Senior Lecturer, Research Associate, Department of Chemical Engineering, Oklahoma State University, 1970-73; Research Fellow, Department of Chemical Engineering, Rice University, 1974-75; Technical Director, Senior Engineer, Thermodynamics Laboratory, Department of Chemical Engineering, 1975-87; Senior Fellow, Department of Food Science, 1988-92; Senior Fellow, Laboratory of Renewable Resources Engineering, 1992-94, Purdue University; Senior Scientific Adviser, BIOS Industrial, Canada, 1987-; Special Chair, Department of Chemical Engineering, National Taiwan University, 1994; Special Chair, Department of Chemical Engineering, National Taiwan Institute of Technology, 1994-97; Professor, Chairman, Department of Chemical

Dictionary of International Biography

Engineering, 1997-2001, Vice President, 2001-, National Taiwan University of Science and Technology, Taipei. Publications: 150 in technical journals; 3 US patents; 2 book chapters. Honours include: UNESCO Fellowship; American Petroleum Fellowship; Outstanding Research Achievement Awards; Chinese Institute of Engineers Distinguished Professor; ChIChE Award; Special Chair, National Science Council, Taiwan. Memberships include: Sigma Xi; Omega Chi Epsilon; American Institute of Chemical Engineers; American Chemical Society; Chinese Institute of Chemical Engineers; Chinese Canadian Academic and Professional Society. Address: Department of Chemical Engineering, National Taiwan University of Science and Technology, 43 Kee-Lung Road, Sec 4, Taipei 106, Taiwan, Republic of China. E-mail: hml@ch.ntust.edu.tw

LIN Kelvin, b. 31 October 1953, Singapore. Audio Consultant. m. Gina Ler Chay Ling, 2 sons, 1 daughter. Education: Fellow, Trinity College of London, UK, 1977; Fellow, Royal Academy of Music, UK, 1979; Fellow, Institute of Audio Engineering, USA, 1982. Appointments: Manager, Carrington Harlowe Productions, 1975-78; Manager, Celebrity Productions, 1978-79; Director, Kelvin Lin & Associates, Singapore, 1979-97; President and Principal Consultant, Lin Asia, 1997-. Honours: Listed in International Who's Who of Professionals and Who's Who in the World. Membership: Charter Member, Entertainment Investors Association of Singapore, President, 1990-92. Address: 14 Almond Street, Singapore 677856. E-mail: linasia@singnet.com.sg

LIN Yvonne Y, b. Taipei, Taiwan. Japanese Language Teacher. 1 son, 1 daughter. Education: BA Gakushuin University, Tokyo Japan; BS, University of California, Davis, California; MS, Purdue University, W Lafayette, Indiana. Appointments: Japanese Drill Master, Mililani High School, Mililani, Hawaii; Japanese, Conversation Instructor, Wahiawa Community School for Adults, Hawaii, 1996-97; Japanese Drill Master, McKinley High School, Honolulu, Hawaii, 1997-98 Substitute and Part-time Japanese Teacher, Punahou School, Honolulu, Hawaii,1998-; Japanese Teacher, St Francis School, Honolulu, Hawaii, 1998-. Memberships: National Council of Japanese Language Teachers; Hawaii Association of Language Teachers; Hawaii Association of Teachers of Japanese. Address: St Francis School, 2707 Pamoa Road, Honolulu, HI 96822-1886, USA. Website: www.stfrancis-oahu.org

LINDSAY (John) Maurice, b. 21 July 1918, Glasgow, Scotland. Poet; Writer; Editor. m. Aileen Joyce Gordon, 3 August 1946, 1 son, 3 daughters. Education: Glasgow Academy, 1928-36; Scottish National Academy of Music, 1936-39. Appointments: Programme Controller, 1961-63, Production Controller, 1963-66, Chief Interviewer, 1966-67, Border Television; Director, The Scottish Civic Trust, 1967-83; Consultant, 1983-2002, Honorary Trustee, 2000-, The Scottish Civic Trust; Editor, Scottish Review, 1975-85; Honorary Secretary General, Europa Nostra, 1983-90; President, Association for Scottish Literary Studies, 1982-83. Publications: The Advancing Day, 1940; Predicament, 1942; No Crown for Laughter, 1943; The Enemies of Love: Poems, 1941-45, 1946; Selected Poems, 1947; At the Wood's Edge, 1950; Ode for St Andrew's Night and Other Poems, 1951; The Exiled Heart: Poems, 1941-56, 1957; Snow Warning and Other Poems, 1962; One Later Day and Other Poems, 1964; This Business of Living, 1971; Comings and Goings, 1971; Selected Poems, 1942-72, 1973; The Run from Life: More Poems, 1942-72, 1975; Walking Without an Overcoat: Poems, 1972-76, 1977; Collected Poems, 2 volumes, 1979, 1993; A Net to Catch the Wind and Other Poems, 1981; The French Mosquito's Woman and Other Diversions, 1985; Requiem for a Sexual Athlete and Other Poems and Diversions, 1988; The Scottish Dog, with Joyce Lindsay, 1989; The Theatre

and Opera Lover's Quotation Book, with Joyce Lindsay, 1993; News of the World: Last Poems, 1995; Speaking Likenesses, 1997; Worlds Apart, poems, 2000; Glasgow: Fabric of a City, 2000. Other: Editions of poetry, plays, etc. Honours: Territorial Decoration; Commander of the Order of the British Empire, 1979; DLitt, University of Glasgow, 1982. Memberships: Association of Scottish Literary Studies; Honorary Fellow, Royal Incorporation of Architects in Scotland. Address: Park House, 104 Dumbarton Road, Bowling, G60 5BB, Scotland.

LINDSAY Kathryn Elizabeth, b. 15 February 1953, Renfrew, Ontario, Canada. Research Ecologist. m. Timothy Holden Freemark, 1 son, 2 daughters. Education: BSc, honours, Biology, Queens University, Kingston, Ontario, 1977; PhD, Biology, Carleton University, Ottawa, 1984; Loeb Fellowship, Harvard University, Cambridge, 1998-99. Appointments: Research Associate, University of Illinois, Champaign, 1980-83; Strategic Grants Officer, Natural Sciences and Engineering Research, Council of Canada, Ottawa, 1984-86; Pesticides Evaluation Officer, 1986-88, Research Scientist, 1988-, National Wildlife Research Center, Canadian Wildlife Service. Publications: Many articles in professional journals. Honours: Research Grant, Natural Sciences and Engineering Research Council of Canada, 1998-2002. Memberships: Ecological Society of America; Society of Conservation Biology; International Association of Landscape Ecology; Society of Canadian Ornithologists. Address: National Wildlife Research Centre, Canadian Wildlife Service, Environment Canada, Ottawa, ON K1A 0H3, Canada.

LINDSAY Oliver John Martin, b. 30 August 1938, Lincolnshire, England. Author; Editor; Historian. m. Lady Clare Giffard, 1 son, 2 daughters. Education: Royal Military Academy, Sandhurst, UK; Staff College, Camberley, UK; National Defence College, Latimer, UK. Appointments: Regular Soldier, Grenadier Guards and on the Staff, 1957-93; Retired in rank of Colonel; Trust Director and Fund Raiser, Treloar Trust for disabled children, 1993-99; Editor, Guards Magazine, 1993-. Publications: Books: The Lasting Honour: the Fall of Hong Kong 1941, 1978; At the Going Down of the Sun: Hong Kong and South East Asia 1941-45, 1981; A Guards General: the Memoirs of Sir Allan Adair (editor), 1986; Once a Grenadier, 1986; Articles published in three continents. Honours: CBE; FRHist S; Member of the Queen's Body Guard for Scotland, Royal Company of Archers. Membership: Boodles Club. Address: Church Farm, Beer Hackett, Sherborne, Dorset DT9 6QT, England.

LINDSAY Robert, b. 1951, Ilkeston, Derbyshire, England. Actor. m. Cheryl Hall, divorced; 1 daughter with Diana Weston; 2 sons with Rosemarie Ford. Education: Royal Academy of Dramatic Art. Career: Stage career commenced at Manchester Royal Exchange; Appeared in Me and My Girl, London, Broadway and Los Angeles, 1985-87; Appeared as Henry II in Anouilh's Beckett, London, 1991, Cyrano de Bergerac, London, 1992; Film appearances in Bert Rigby, You're a Fool, Loser Takes All, Strike It Rich, Fierce Creatures, 1996; Television appearances including Edmund in King Lear, Granada, Wolfie in comedy series Citizen Smith, Michael Murray in serial GBH, Channel 4, 1991; My Family, BBC, 2000-; Other recent performances in Genghis Cohn, Jake's Progress, Goodbye My Love, 1996, Oliver, 1998, Richard III, 1998, Fagin in Oliver Twist, 1999. Honours: Olivier, Tony and Fred Astaire Awards for performance in Me and My Girl; Olivier Award for Best Actor in a Musical, 1998. Address: Hamilton Asper Management, Ground Floor, 24 Hanway Street, London W1P 9DD, England.

LINDSTRÖM Lars Ernst Simon, b. 8 September 1943, Lund, Sweden. Professor of Education. m. Barbara Lindström, 1 son, 1 daughter. Education: BA, 1966, MA, 1970, Lund University,

Sweden; Certificate as a Psychologist, 1972; PhD, Education, Stockholm University, Sweden, 1986. Appointments: Lecturer, Stockholm School of Social Work, 1973-76; Assistant Professor, University College of Arts, Crafts and Design, Stockholm, 1976-90; Research Associate, 1990-94, Professor of Education, 1995-, Stockholm Institute of Education, Stockholm University; Visiting Scholar, Harvard University, Massachusetts, USA, 1991; Visiting Professor, Linköping University, Sweden, 1999; External Evaluator for the Norwegian Ministry of Education, 2001. Publications: Author, Managing Alcoholism: Matching Clients to Treatments, 1992; Editor: Nordic Visual Arts Research, 1998; The Cultural Context, 1999; Contributed articles to professional journals including: Addiction; Journal of Art and Design Education; Arts Education Policy Review. Memberships: Scientific Advisor, National Swedish Board of Health and Welfare; Governing Board, Stockholm Institute of Education; Editorial Board, Comenius-Jahrbuch, Germany. Address: Stockholm Institute of Education, Box 34103, S-10026 Stockholm, Sweden. E-mail: lars.lindstrom@lhs.se

LINEKER Gary Winston, b. 30 November 1960, Leicester, England. Former Footballer; Television Host. m. Michelle Denise Cockayne, 1986, 4 sons. Career: Debut as professional footballer, Leicester City, 1978; Everton, 1985; Represented England, 1986 World Cup, Mexico, 1990 World Cup, Italy; Captain, England, 1991-92; FC Barcelona, Spain, 1986-89; Transferred to Tottenham Hotspur, 1989-92; 80 international caps; Scored 48 goals, June 1992; Grampus Eight Team, Japan, 1994; Presenter, Match of the Day, BBC TV, 1995-. Honour: MA, Leicester, 1992, Loughborough, 1992; OBE, 1992. Address: c/o SFX Sports Group, 35/36 Grosvenor Street, London W1K 4QX, England.

LING Sergey Stepanovich, b. 7 May 1937. Politician and Agronomist. m. 3 children. Education: Belarus Agricultural Academy; Higher CPSU School, CPSU Central Committee. Appointments: Agronomist Sovkhoz, Lesnoye Kopylsk District; Chief Agronomist Sovkhoz, Chief Agronomist, Krynitsa Kopylsk District; Deputy Director, Lyuban Production Co; Chief, Soligorsk Production Agricultural Administration; Deputy Chairman, then Chairman, Slutsk District Executive Committee, Secretary, Smolevichi District CPSU Committee, 1960-72; Chief, Agricultural Division, Secretary, Minsk Regional Belarus Communist Party Committee, 1972-82; First Deputy Chairman, then Chairman, Executive Committee, Minsk Regional Soviet, 1982-86; Chairman, Belarus State Committee on Prices, Deputy Chairman, State Planning Committee, 1986-90; Head, Agricultural Division, Secretary, Central Committee, Belarus Communist Party, 1990-91; Deputy Chairman, Belarus Council of Ministers, State Committee on Economics and Planning, 1991-; Deputy Prime Minister, 1994-96, Acting Prime Minister, 1996-97, Prime Minister, 1997-2000, Belarus. Address: c/o Council of Ministers, pl Nezavisimosti, 220010 Minsk, Belarus.

LINGARD Joan Amelia, b. 8 April 1932, Edinburgh, Scotland. Author. 3 daughters. Education: General Teaching Diploma, Moray House Training College, Edinburgh. Publications: Children's Books: The Twelfth Day of July, 1970; Frying as Usual, 1971; Across the Barricades, 1972; Into Exile, 1973; The Clearance, 1974; A Proper Place, 1975; The Resettling, 1975; Hostages to Fortune, 1976; The Pilgrimage, 1976; The Reunion, 1977; The Gooseberry, 1978; The File on Fraulein Berg, 1980; Strangers in the House, 1981; The Winter Visitor, 1983; The Freedom Machine, 1986; The Guilty Party, 1987; Rags and Riches, 1988; Tug of War, 1989; Glad Rags, 1990; Between Two Worlds, 1991; Hands Off Our School!, 1992; Night Fires, 1993; Dark Shadows, 1998; A Secret Place, 1998; Tom and the Tree House, 1998. Novels: Liam's Daughter, 1963; The Prevailing Wind, 1964; The Tide

Comes In, 1966; The Headmaster, 1967; A Sort of Freedom, 1968; The Lord on Our Side, 1970; The Second Flowering of Emily Mountjoy, 1979; Greenyards, 1981; Sisters by Rite, 1984; Reasonable Doubts, 1986; The Women's House, 1989; After Colette, 1993; Lizzie's Leaving, 1995; Dreams of Love and Modest Glory, 1995; Dark Shadows, 1998; A Secret Place, 1998; Tom and the Tree House, 1998. Honours: Scottish Arts Council Bursary, 1967-68; Preis der Leseratten ZDF, Germany, 1986; Buxtehuder Bulle, Germany, 1987; Scottish Arts Council Award, 1994; MBE, 1998. Memberships: Society of Authors in Scotland, chairman, 1982-86; Scottish PEN; Director, Edinburgh Book Festival. Address: David Higham Associates Ltd, 5-8 Lower John Street, Golden Square, London W1R 4HA, England.

LINKLATER Richard, b. 30 July 1960, Houston, Texas, USA. Film Director. Appointments: Founder, Director, own film company, Detour Films, Austin, Texas; Founder, Artistic Director, Austin Film Society; Director, films, Slacker, 1991, Dazed and Confused, 1993; Before Sunrise, 1995, Suburbia, 1997, The Newton Boys, 1998; Waking Life, 2001; Tape, 2001; Live From Shiva's Dance Floor, 2003; The School of Rock, 2003; Before Sunset, 2004; $5.15/Hr, 2004. Honours: Silver Bear, Berlin Film Festival, 1995.

LINSCOTT Gillian, b. 27 September 1944, Windsor, England. Journalist; Writer. m. Tony Geraghty, 18 June 1988. Education: Honours Degree, English Language and Literature, Somerville College, Oxford University, 1966. Appointments: Journalist, Liverpool Post, 1967-70; Northern Ireland Correspondent, Birmingham Post, 1970-72; Reporter, The Guardian,1972-79; Sub Editor, BBC Radio News, Local Radio Parliamentary Reporter, 1979-90; Freelance Writer, 1990-. Publications: A Healthy Body, 1984; Murder Makes Tracks, 1985; Knightfall, 1986; A Whiff of Sulphur, 1987; Unknown Hand, 1988; Murder, I Presume, 1990; Sister Beneath the Sheet, 1991; Hanging on the Wire, 1992; Stage Fright, 1993; Widow's Peak, 1994; Crown Witness, 1995; Dead Man's Music, 1996; Dance on Blood, 1998; Absent Friends, 1999; The Perfect Daughter, 2000; Dead Man Riding, 2002; The Garden, 2002; Blood on the Wood, 2003. Honours: Herodotus Award, The Historical Mystery Appreciation Society, 1999; Ellis Peters Historical Dagger, Crime Writers Association, 2000. Memberships: Society of Authors; Crime Writers Association. Address: Wood View, Hope Under Dinmore, Leominster, Herefordshire HR6 0PP, England.

LIOTTA Ray, b. 18 December 1955, Newark, New Jersey, USA. Actor. m Michelle Grace, 1997, 1 daughter. Education: BFA, University of Miami. Career: Various television appearances including Another World, NBC, 1978-80, Hardhat & Legs, CBS movie, 1980, Crazy Times, ABC pilot, 1981, Casablanca, NBC, 1983, Our Family Honour, NBC, 1985-86, Women Men – In Love there Are No Rules, 1991; The Rat Pack, 1998; Point of Origin, 2002; Film appearances in The Lonely Lady, 1983, Something Wild, 1986, Arena Brains, 1987, Dominick and Eugene, 1988, Field of Dreams, 1989, Goodfellas, 1990, Article 99, 1992, Unlawful Entry, 1992, No Escape, 1994, Corrina, Corrina, 1994, Operation Dumbo Drop, 1995, Unforgettable, 1996, Turbulence, 1997, Phoenix, 1997, Copland, 1997, The Rat Pack, 1998, Forever Mine, 1999, Muppets From Space, 1999; Blow, 2001; Heartbreakers, 2001; Hannibal, 2001; John Q, 2002; A Rumor of Angels, 2002; Narc, 2002. Address: c/o Endeavour Talent Agency, 9701 Wilshire Boulevard, 10th Floor, Beverly Hills, CA 90212, USA.

LIOU Michelle, b. 20 May 1956, Kaohsiung, Taiwan. Researcher. Education: PhD, University of Pittsburg, USA, 1985. Appointment: Research Fellow, Institute of Statistical Science, Academia Sinica,

1985-2003. Publication: Co-author: Bridging functional MR images and scientific inference: Reproducibility maps, 2003. Honours: Distinguished Research Award, National Science Council, Republic of China, 1999; New Perspective in FMRI Research Award, Journal of Cognitive Neuroscience, USA, 2003. Memberships: Chinese Psychological Association; Chinese Measurement Association; Chinese Statistical Association. Address: Institute of Statistical Science, Academia Sinica, Taipei 115, Taiwan. E-mail: mliou@stat.sinica.edu.tw

LIOU Shyhnan, b. 1 January 1963, Taiwan. Associate Professor. m. Fei-Pin Tai, 2 sons. Education: Bachelor, Department of Psychology, 1987, Master, Institute of Psychology, 1989, PhD, Institute of Psychology, 1998, National Taiwan University. Appointments: Specialist, Industrial Technology Research Institute, 1987-90; Instructor, National Tsing Hua University, 1990-94; Assistant Professor, National Chung Cheng University, 1994-. Publications: Articles in professional journals including: International Journal of Technology Management; Chinese Journal of Psychology; Journal of Technology Management; Gifted Education Quarterly; Journal of Labor Studies; Journals of Management and Systems; International Journal of Psychology. Honours: Distinguished thesis award, Technology Management Research Award; Dragon Thesis Award; Listed in Who's Who publications and biographical dictionaries. Memberships: International Association of Applied Psychology; International Union of Psychology; Chinese Psychology Association; Chinese Society of Management Technology; Academy of Human Research Development; American Psychology Association. Address: 160 San-Hsing, Ming-Hsiung, Chia-Yi, Taiwan. E-mail: labsnil@ccu.edu.tw

LIPCZUK Ryszard, b. 29 January 1948, Teremiec, Poland. Germanic Scholar; Linguist. m. Joanna Gosek, 1 son, 1 daughter. Education: MA, German Philology, Warsaw, Poland, 1970; Doctor, Warsaw, 1977; Habilitation, Poznan, 1986; DAAD Scholarship, Leipzig, 1973-74; Alexander von Humboldt Foundation Scholar: Münster, 1981-82; Mannheim, 1987, Kiel, 1998, Leipzig, 2000; Full Professor, 2002-. Appointments: Assistant, 1970, Reader, Adjunct, 1977, Associate Professor, 1990, Chair German Department, Nicholas Kopernicus University , Torun, Poland; Associate Professor, 1993, Head of Institute, 1993-97, Head of the Chair of German Language, 1993-, Institute of Germanic Philology, University of Szczecin, Poland; Co-ordinator, Tempus Phare JEP Project (participants: Szczecin, Poland, Giessen, Germany, Antwerp and Brussels, Belgium), 1998-2001. Publications: Books include: Verbale Tautonyme lateinischer Herkunft im deutsch-polnischer Relation, 1987; Wörter fremder Herkunft im deutschen und polnischen Sportwortschatz, 1989; Co-author, Lexikon der modernen Linguistik; Textbooks for German as a foreign language; Numerous articles. Honour: Award, Polish Minister of Education, 1989. Memberships: International Association for Germanic Studies; Polish Association for Germanic Studies, Member Board of Governors, 1991-96; Societas Humboldtiana Polonorum; Polish Association of Linguistics, Scientific Associations, Szczecin; Member, Editorial Board, international bibliographical periodical, Germanistik. Address: Institute for Germanic Philology, ul. Rycerska 3, 70-537 Szczecin, Poland. E-mail: ryszard_lipczuk@interia.pl Website: http://germ.univ.szczecin.pl/~lipczuk

LIPKA Cezary, b. 9 June 1964, Parczew, Poland. Publicist; Teacher. Education: Master's Degree Diploma, Wood Technology Faculty, Warsaw Agricultural University SGGW, 1983-88; Diploma, Bible Course, Faculty of Philosophy, SJ Cracow, 1993-97; Journalist (collaboration), 1996-2002; Diploma, Post-Graduate Pedagogical Study, Papacy Faculty of Theology, 2001-03.

Appointments: Technologist, Furniture Factory, Zamo, 1988-89; Assistant Teacher, Warsaw Agricultural University SGGW, 1990-96; Businessman, Telwa Trading, 1997-98; Teacher at numerous secondary schools, 1994-2004. Publications: Saint Stephen, King of Hungary, 1996; Saint Vatzlav, the Patron of the Czech Kingdom, 1997; Saint Sogismund, King of Burgundy, 1998; Saint Ladislas, King of Hungary, 1999; Stephen Bathory, a Transylvanian Prince on the Polish Trone, 2000; Saint Benedict and His Legacy, 2001; Waiting for a Catastrophe – Consideration about the Church, 2000; Future of Slovakia: The interview with Rudolf Schuster, 1999. Memberships: Soli Deo Board, 1991-; The Conservative-Monarchist Club, Poland, 1994-2003; Gymnastic Society (Falcon), 1995. Address: 22-400 Zamo, Kamienna 19m.8, Poland. E-mail: cezarylipka@poczta.onet.pl

LIPWORTH Maurice Sydney (Sir), b. 13 May 1931, Johannesburg, South Africa. Barrister; Businessman. m. Rosa Liwarek, 1957, 2 sons. Education: BCom, LLB, University of Witwatersrand. Appointments: Practising Barrister, Johannesburg, 1956-64; Non-Executive Director, Liberty Life Association of Africa Ltd, 1956-64; Executive, Private Trading Companies, 1964-67; Executive Director, Abbey Life Assurance PLC, 1968-70; Vice-President, Director, Abbey International Corporation Inc, 1968-70; Co-Founder, Director, 1970-88, Deputy Managing Director, 1977-79, Joint Managing Director, 1979-84, Deputy Chairman, 1984-88, Allied Dunbar Assurance PLC; Director, J Rothschild Holdings PLC, 1984-87; Director, BAT Industries PLC, 1985-88; Deputy Chairman of Trustees, 1986-93, Chairman, 1993-, Philharmonia Orchestra; Chairman, Monopolies and Mergers Commission, 1988-92; Non-Executive Director, Carlton Communications PLC, 1993-; Deputy Chairman, Non-Executive Director, National Westminster Bank, 1993-2000; Chairman, Financial Reporting Council, 1993-2001; Non-Executive Director, 1994-99, Chairman, 1995-99, Zeneca Group PLC; Member, Senior Salaries Review Body, 1994-; Trustee, South Bank Ltd, 1996-. Honours: Honorary Queen's Council, 1993. Memberships: Chairman, Bar Association for Commerce, Finance and Industry, 1991-91; European Policy Forum. Address: 41 Lothbury, London EC2P 2BP, England.

LISSENKO Vadim Andrejevitch, b. 25 December 1937, Leningrad (St Petersburg), Russia. Structural Engineer; Restorer; Architect; Educator. m. Sofia Markevitch. Education: MS, Civil Engineering and Architecture, 1960, PhD, 1967, Odessa Civil Engineering Institute; Translator, Kiev State Institute, 1969; Restoration, Reconstruction, Architecture, Academy of Architecture, Paris, 1974; Doctor of Sciences, Professor of Architecture and Restoration, Kharkov State University of Civil Engineering, Ukraine, 1990. Appointments: Chief Architect, Odessa State Design and Project Institute of Civil Engineering, 1960-63; Professor, Odessa State Institute of Civil Engineering, 1963-69; Professor, King Institute, Phnom-Phen, Cambodia, 1969-70; Head of the Chair, Architectural Constructions, Restoration and Reconstruction, Odessa State Academy of Building and Architecture, 1971-present; Senior researcher, CSTB France, Paris, 1973-74; Dean, Architectural Faculty, Odessa State Academy of Building and Architecture, 1974-75; Major architectural and restoration works include: Planetarium, Odessa, 1960; Restoration of the western façade of Anghkor-Watt, Cambodia, 1969; Restoration of the Lutheran Church, Odessa, 1984; Reconstruction of Izmail Fortress, 1988; Rehabilitation of Odessa Opera House, 1991-95; Rehabilitation of San Domenico Convent, Italy, 2000-2002. Publications: More than 200 scientific works include: Recommendation on use of ZKP for conservation and restoration of monuments and historical stone and concrete buildings, 1984; Restoration of deformation and accidents of buildings and structures, 1984; Handbook of Architecture, 1988; Bases of architectural designing, volume I, 1989, volume II, 1995; Preservation of the Architectural and Historical Heritage of Odessa, 1998; Repair of concrete constructions by epoxy structures, 2001. Honours: 2 Gold Medals; Prizes, Exhibition of Achievements, National Economic EANE of the USSR and Ukrainian SSR. Memberships: Academician, Building Academy of Ukraine; Academician, Engineering Academy of Ukraine; Academician, International Engineering Academy, Moscow; New York Academy of Sciences; Regional Council's People's Deputy; Volley-ball Regional Committee. Address: p/b 215, 9/4 Liapounov St, 270026, Odessa, Ukrain. E-mail: lis@vad.intes.odessa.ua

LISTE Hartmut Manfred Heinz, b. 20 August 1947, Berlin, Germany. Language Professor. Education: Russian, Czech, Slovac and French Languages, Humboldt University, Berlin, 1966-1971; Diplom Philologe, Humboldt University, Berlin, 1971-1973; Dr Phil, 1975. Appointments: Scientific assistant, Humboldt University, Berlin, 1971-1973; Researcher, Professor of Languages, Humboldt University, Berlin, 1973-. Publications: Pocket Education Manual of the Czech Language, 1980, 2nd edition, 1983, 3rd edition, 1985, 4th edition, 1987, 5th edition, 1990; Pocket Dictionary Czech-German, 1986, 2nd edition, 1987, 3rd edition, 1990. Memberships: Trade Union Education Sciences; Evangelical German Church. Address: Schivelbeiner Strr 26, D-10439, Berlin, Germany. E-mail: hartmut.liste@rz.hu-berlin.de

LISTER Richard Percival, b. 23 November 1914, Nottingham, England. Author; Poet; Painter. m. Ione Mary Wynniatt-Husey, 24 June 1985. Education: BSc, Manchester University. Publications: Novels: The Way Backwards, 1950; The Oyster and the Torpedo, 1951; Rebecca Redfern, 1953; The Rhyme and the Reason, 1963; The Questing Beast, 1965; One Short Summer, 1974. Poetry: The Idle Demon, 1958; The Albatross, 1986. Travel: A Journey in Lapland, 1965; Turkey Observed, 1967; Glimpses of a Planet, 1997. Biography: The Secret History of Genghis Khan, 1969; Marco Polo's Travels, 1976; The Travels of Herodotus, 1979. Short Stories: Nine Legends, 1991; Two Northern Stories, 1996. Contributions to: Punch; New Yorker; Atlantic Monthly. Honour: Royal Society of Literature, fellow, 1970. Address: Flat 11, 42 St James's Gardens, London W11 4RQ, England.

LITTEN Nancy Magaret, b. 30 September 1951, Dartford, Kent, England. Musician. m. Clinton Davis, 2 sons, 1 daughter. Education: LRAM Violin (Teacher's), 1970, LRAM Piano (Teacher's), 1971, Royal Academy of Music; Cert Ed, Exeter, 1972; ATCL Voice (Performer's), 2001. Appointments: Accompanist and Piano Teacher, Kent Centre for Young Instrumentalists, 1993-; Piano and Keyboard Teacher, Benenden School, 1995-; Teacher of Choirs, Keyboard and Strings, Kent Music School, 1997-; ABRSM Examiner, 1998-; Founder, Director, Kent Keyboard Orchestra, 1999-; Freelance Accompanist and Adjudicator. Publications: Involved in the Federation of Music Services new schemes of work, A Common Approach, 2002, keyboard section. Honours: Elizabeth Stokes Open Piano Scholarship, 1968; Janet Duff Greet Prize for most deserving British scholar, 1970, 1971. Membership: Incorporated Society of Musicians. Address: Springfield, 39 Ashford Road, Maidstone, Kent ME14 5DP, England.

LITTLE RICHARD (Richard Penniman), b. 5 December 1935, Macon, Georgia, USA. Singer; Musician (piano). Education: Theological college, 1957. Career: R&B singer, various bands; Tours and film work with own band, The Upsetters; Gospel singer, 1960-62; World-wide tours and concerts include: Star Club, Hamburg, Germany, with Beatles, 1962; European tour, with Beatles, Rolling Stones, 1963; UK tour with Everly Brothers, 1963; Rock'n'Revival Concert, Toronto, with Chuck Berry, Fats Domino,

Jerry Lee Lewis, Gene Vincent, Bo Diddley, 1969; Toronto Pop Festival, 1970; Randall Island Rock Festival, with Jimi Hendrix, Jethro Tull, 1970; Rock'n'Roll Spectaculars, Madison Square Garden, 1972-; Muhammad Ali's 50th Birthday; Benefit For Lupus Foundation, Universal City, 1992; Westbury Music Fair, 1992; Giants Of Rock'n'Roll, Wembley Arena, 1992; Film appearances: Don't Knock The Rock, 1956; Mr Rock'n'Roll, 1957; The Girl Can't Help It, 1957; Keep On Rockin', 1970; Down And Out In Beverly Hills, 1986; Mother Goose Rock'n'Rhyme, Disney Channel, 1989. Recordings: Albums: Here's Little Richard, 1957; Little Richard Is Back, 1965; Greatest Hits, 1965; Freedom Blues, 1970; The King Of Rock'n'Roll, 1971; God's Beautiful City, 1979; Lifetime Friend, 1987; Featured on: Folkways - A Vision Shared (Woody Guthrie tribute), 1988; For Our Children, 1991; Shake It All About, 1992; Little Richard and Jimi Hendrix, 1993; Shag on Down by the Union Hall,1996; Hit singles include: Tutti Frutti, 1956; Long Tall Sally, 1956; The Girl Can't Help It, 1957; Lucille, 1957; She's Got It, 1957; Jenny Jenny, 1957; Keep A Knockin', 1957; Good Golly Miss Molly, 1958, Baby Face, 1959; Bama Lama Bama Loo, 1964. Honours include: Inducted, Rock'n'Roll Hall of Fame, 1986; Star, Hollywood Walk Of Fame, 1990; Little Richard Day, Los Angeles, 1990; Penniman Boulevard, Macon, named in his honour; Platinum Star, Lupus Foundation Of America, 1992; Grammy Lifetime Achievement Award, 1993.

LITTLECHILD Wilton, b. 1 April 1944, Hobbema, Alberta, Canada. Lawyer (Barrister and Solicitor). m. Helen, 1 son, 2 daughters. Education: Diploma in Sports and Recreation, Royal Life Saving Society, 1962; Bachelors Degree in Physical Education, 1967; Masters Degree in Physical Education, 1975; Bachelors Degree in Law, 1976. Appointments: Queen's Counsel and Indigenous Peoples' Counsel of the Legal Profession; Sports Consultant and Coach, swimming and hockey; International Red Cross Youth Volunteer; Barrister and Solicitor, own law firm; Member of Parliament, House of Commons, Canada and Indigenous Parliament of the Americas; Appointed to United Nations Forum on Indigenous Issues. Publications: Tom Longboat – Canada's Outstanding Indian Athlete; Indian Hockey Council – Alberta on Ice; To Run with Longboat. Honours: Order of Canada; Inducted into 4 Sports Halls of Fame; Honorary Chief of the Maskwacîs Cree Nation and Treaty No 6; Most Outstanding Indian Athlete of the Year in Canada, 1967, 1975; 4 Lifetime Achievement Awards, Sports and Law (Indigenous Bar Association); 10 Athlete of the Year Awards. Memberships: Law Society of Alberta; Indigenous Bar Association; Canadian Bar Association; Canadian Legion; Former Parliamentarians Association; W.I.N. Sports Inc. Address: Box 370, Hobbema, Alberta, Canada T0G 1N0. E-mail: jwlittle@incentre.net

LITTLEJOHN Joan Anne, b. 20 April 1937, London, England. Creative Artist. Education: Royal College of Music, 1955-59; Postgraduate Study, Howells and Others; LRAM, 1957; GRSM, 1958. Appointments: Freelance Composer, Musicologist, Photographer, 1959-; Administrative Staff, Royal College of Music, 1960-83; Piano Teacher, Harrow School, 1972-73. Publications: Poems and Music. Honours: RVW Trust and Patrons Fund Awards in the 1970's; Recipient Howells' Composing Piano, 1984; Award of Merit, Golden Poet Award, 1985 and Silver Poet Award, 1986; Millennium Medal of Honour, 1998; Archives destined for The Nation, to be housed at The Devon Record Office. Memberships: PRS; ABIRA. Address: Shepherds Delight, 49 Hamilton Lane, Exmouth, Devon EX8 2LW, England.

LITTLEMORE Christopher Paul, b. 8 March 1959, Warwickshire, England. Architect. m. Jane Evelyn Chalk, 1 son, 1 daughter. Education: BA (Hons), B.Arch, Manchester University, 1977-83; MSc, Conservation of Historic Buildings, Bath

University, 1998-99. Appointments: Associate, 1986, Director, 1989, The Charter Partnership, Architects. Membership: Royal Institute of British Architects. Address: Meadow House, Broad Chalke, Nr Salisbury, Wilts, England. E-mail: cplittlemore@charter.eu.com

LITTON Andrew, b. 16 May 1959, New York City, New York, USA. Orchestral Conductor; Pianist. Education: Mozarteum, Salzburg; Juilliard School of Music; MM. Appointments: Assistant Conductor, La Scala, Milan, 1980-81; Exxon-Arts Endowment Assistant Conductor, then Associate Conductor, National Symphony Orchestra, Washington DC, 1982-86; Principal Guest Conductor, 1986-88, Principal Conductor, Artistic Adviser, 1988-94, Conductor Laureate, 1994-, Bournemouth Symphony Orchestra; Music Director, Dallas Symphony Orchestra, 1994-; Guest Conductor, many leading orchestras world-wide including Chicago Symphony, Philadelphia, Los Angeles Philharmonic, Pittsburgh Symphony, Toronto Symphony, Montreal Symphony, Vancouver Symphony, London Philharmonic, Royal Philharmonic, London Symphony, English Chamber, Leipzig Gewandhaus, Moscow State Symphony, Stockholm Philharmonic, RSO Berlin, RAI Milan, Orchestre National de France, Suisse Romande, Tokyo Philharmonic, Melbourne Symphony and Sydney Symphony orchestras; Opera debut with Eugene Onegin, Metropolitan Opera, New York, 1989; Conducted Leoncavallo, La Bohème and Falstaff, St Louis Opera, Hansel and Gretel, Los Angeles Opera, 1992, Porgy and Bess, Royal Opera House, Covent Garden, 1992, Salome, English National Opera, 1996; Music Consultant to film The Chosen. Publications: Recordings including Mahler Symphony No 1 and Songs of a Wayfarer, Elgar Enigma Variations, complete Tchaikovsky symphony cycle, complete Rachmaninov symphony cycle, Shostakovich Symphony No 10, Gershwin Rhapsody in Blue, Concerto in F, Bernstein Symphony No 2, Brahms Symphony No 1; As piano soloist and conductor, Ravel Concerto in G. Honours: Winner, William Kapell Memorial US National Piano Competition, 1978; Winner, Bruno Walter Conducting Fellowship, 1981; Winner, BBC-Rupert Foundation International Conductors Competition, 1982; Honorary DMus, Bournemouth, 1992. Address: c/o IMG Artists Europe, Media House, 3 Burlington Lane, London W4 2TH, England.

LIU Hsi-wen Daniel, b. 18 October 1958, Tainan, Taiwan. Philosopher; Teacher. m. Yun-chi Ivy Wang, 2 sons. Education: BA, Philosophy, 1984, MA, Philosophy, 1988, Tunghai University, Taichung; PhD, Cognitive Science, University of Edinburgh, UK, 1999. Appointments: Postdoctoral Researcher, Institute of Philosophy, National Tsing Hua University, Hsinchu, Taiwan, 1999-2000; Assistant Professor, Division of Humanities, Providence University, Taichung, Taiwan, 2000-; Part-time Assistant Professor, Logic Course, Centre for General Education, National Tsing Hua University, 2000-2002; Reviewer, Twenty Fourth and Twenty Fifth Annual Conferences of the Cognitive Science Society, 2002, 2003. Publications: Articles in professional journals: The Model Control of Situated Representation, 2000; Animat mechanicalism: On the mechanisms of interactions between cognitive architectures and the environment, 2000; An Ethical Consideration of Life for Future Generations: The Formation of Norms for Germ-line Gene Therapy, 2001; 11 papers presented at national and international conferences; Translations into Chinese: Dictionary of the History of Ideas vol. 2 (Philosophy and Religion), 1987; The Cambridge Dictionary of Philosophy, 2002. Honours: 3 Research Projects funded by the National Science Council, Taiwan, 2001, 2002, 2003. Memberships: Cognitive Science Society; Philosophy of Science Association; International Society of Artificial Life; Taiwan Philosophical Association. Address: Division of Humanities, Providence University, 200 Chung-chi Road, Shalu, Taichung County 433, Taiwan. E-mail: hwliu@pu.edu.tw Website: http://www1.pu.edu.tw/~hwliu

LIU Michel Jean-Marie, b. 3 July 1937, Shanghai, China. University Professor. m. Marie-Thérèse Delaporte, 2 sons, 1 daughter. Education: Doctorat d'Etat ès-Sciences, Nuclear Physics, Université de Paris-Orsay, 1970; Graduate, International Business Administration Teaching Program, Northwestern University, Chicago, USA, 1971; Doctorat d'Etat ès-Lettres et Sciences Humaines, Institut d'Etudes Politiques de Paris, 1986. Appointments: Professor in Social Sciences, Program Director of the Doctoral Studies in Industrial Engineering, Ecole Centrale de Paris, 1974-1988; Director, Organization Sociology Research Centre, CERSO, 1991-2000; Professor of Sociology, Paris IX Dauphine University, Director of the Doctoral Program, Organization Dynamics and Social Changes, 1991-. Publications: 5 books; 5 articles in professional journals. Membership: French Language Sociologists International Association; Cybernetic, Cognitive and Technical Systems Science Association. Address: CERSO, Université Paris Dauphine, Place du Maréchal de lattre de Tassigny, Paris 75775 cedex 16 France. E-mail: michel.liu@dauphine.fr

LIU Shi-Yue, b. Tientsin, China. Music Archaeologist; Poet; Pianist; Musicologist; Writer. Education: Diploma, University of Logic and Language, China, 1983; Self-studies in piano, violin, composition; Advanced studies in piano with V Askenazy by correspondence, 1965, with J Squier in Tientsin, 1982; Self-culture in Music Archaeology, Musicology, 1983; Self-culture in Rock Art, 1985, Ecology, 1998. Appointments: Appearances include: Tientsin TV, 1986-99; Tianjin Radio, 1986-98; Hong Kong TV, 1986; Hong Kong Radio, 1986; ANSA, 1986; TASS, 1986; AP, 1986; VOA, 1986; Reuter, 1986; French Agency, 1986; TV Telefilm "Liu Shi-Yue", 1986-99; Central Radio Peking, 1987; CCTV, 1989; Tianjin Radio, 2003. Publications: Report on Archaeological Finds of Bone Flutes in China, 1985; Okay, Vanquish All Things At Once, 1985, 1988; Bone Flutes of Hemudu in Chekiang, China, 1988; Apollo and Pianist, 1993; Human Ecology Past and Present, 1999; The Site of Old Stone Age in Mongolia, 1999. Honours: Lu Hsun Literature and Art Prize, 1988; Hua Xia Yi Qi Award for Telefilm Liu Shi-Yue, Music Archaeologist, 1991; Diploma, Outstanding Service to Culture and Art, State Council of People's Republic of China, 1992; Certificate of IBA, IBC, 1993; 9 Gold Coins of Fellow Research, ABI, USA, 1994-96; Certificate, IBC Advisory Council, 1995; Academician Certificate of Orient Famous Person Institute, 1999; Certificate, World Cultural Celebrity Achievement Prize, 1999; Certificate of World Artist, Hong Kong and America, 1999; Favorite Son of China, 1999; Certificate, World Culture and World Art Research Center, Hong Kong, 1999. Memberships: International Council for Traditional Music (UNESCO); ICTM Study Group on Music Archaeology (UNESCO); Director, Overseas Chinese Artists Association of USA; Research of World Culture and Art Center; Advisor of Hong Kong Academy of Sciences; IBC; ABI. Address: 87, Changsha Road, Tientsin 300050, China.

LIU Zhaorong, b. 1 July 1937, Zuoquan County, Shanxi Province, China. Educator. m. Shaohua Zhao, 1 son, 3 daughters. Education: Mathematical Department, Harbin Teachers' College. Appointment: Teacher, Yuci Railway Middle School, 1962-95. Publications: The Proof of Goldbach's Conjecture; Numerous other mathematical research papers. Honours: Listed in Who's Who publications and biographical dictionaries. Membership: American Mathematical Society. Address: #168 Anning Street, Yuci District, Jinzhong City, Shanxi Province 030600, P R China. E-mail: qingqingcao830@yahoo.com

LIVELY Penelope Margaret, b. 17 March 1933, Cairo, Egypt. Writer. m. Jack Lively, 27 June 1957, 1 son, 1 daughter. Education: Honours Degree, Modern History, Oxford University, England.

Publications: Fiction: The Road to Lichfield, 1977; Nothing Missing But the Samovar, and Other Stories, 1978; Treasures of Time, 1979; Judgement Day, 1980; Next to Nature, Art, 1982; Perfect Happiness, 1983; Corruption and Other Stories, 1984; According to Mark, 1984; Moon Tiger, 1986; Pack of Cards: Stories 1978-86, 1987; Passing On, 1989; City of the Mind, 1991; Cleopatra's Sister, 1993; Spider Web, 1998. Non-Fiction: The Presence of the Past: An Introduction to Landscape History, 1976. Children's Books: Astercote, 1970; The Whispering Knights, 1971; The Driftway, 1972; Going Back, 1973; The Ghost of Thomas Kempe, 1974; Boy Without a Name, 1975; Fanny's Sister, 1976; The Stained Glass Window, 1976; A Stitch in Time, 1976; Fanny and the Monsters, 1978; The Voyage of QV66, 1978; Fanny and the Battle of Potter's Piece, 1980; The Revenge of Samuel Stokes, 1981; Uninvited Ghosts and Other Stories, 1984; Dragon Trouble, Debbie and the Little Devil, 1984; A House Inside Out, 1987; Heat Wave, 1996; Beyond the Blue Mountains: Stories, 1997; Spiderweb, 1998; A House Unlocked, 2001; In Search of A Homeland: The Story of the Aeneid, 2001; The Photograph, 2003. Contributions to: Numerous journals and magazines. Honours: Officer of the Order of the British Empire, 1989; Commander of the British Empire, 2002; Several honorary degrees and literary awards. Address: c/o David Higham Associates, 5-8 Lower John Street, Golden Square, London W1R 4HA, England.

LIVESLEY Brian, b. 31 August 1936, Southport, Lancashire, England. Medical Practitioner. m. Valerie Anne Nuttall, 1 son, 2 daughters. Education: MB, ChB, Leeds University Medical School, 1960. Appointments: Clinical Training and Teaching posts, University and District Hospitals, Leeds, Manchester and Liverpool, 1961-69; Harvey Research Fellow, King's College Hospital Medical School, London, 1969-72; Consultant Physician, Geriatric Medicine, Southwark, London, 1973-88; University of London's Foundation Professor in the Care of the Elderly, Honorary Consultant Physician in General and Geriatric Medicine, Chelsea and Westminster Hospital NHS Trust, London, 1988-2001; North West Thames Regional Adviser, Postgraduate Education, British Postgraduate Medical Federation, 1990-96; Invited Expert on the care of elderly persons for several Police Constabularies and HM Coroner's offices, 1999-. Publications: Over 150 professional publications. Honours: Freeman of the City of London, 1975; Officer Brother, 1992, Knight, 1994, Most Venerable Order of St John of Jerusalem. Memberships: Worshipful Society of Apothecaries of London; Royal Society of Medicine; Royal College of Physicians of London; British Medical Association. Address: PO Box 295, Oxford OX2 9GD, England. Email: brian.livesley@btinternet.com

LIVINGSTONE Kenneth Robert, b. 17 June 1945, London, England. Politician. m. Christine Pamela Chapman, 1973, divorced 1982. Education: Phillipa Fawcett College of Education. Appointments: Technician, Cancer Research Unit, Royal Marsden Hospital, 1962-70; Joined, 1969, Member, Regional Executive, 1974-86, National Executive Council, 1987-89, 1997-, Northern Ireland Select Committee, 1997-99, Labour Party; Councillor, Borough of Lambeth, 1971-78; Councillor, Borough of Camden, 1978-82; Councillor, 1973-86, Leader, 1981-86, Greater London Council; Member of Parliament for Brent East, 1987-; Elected Mayor of London, 2000-2004, Re-elected 2004-. Publications: If Voting Changed Anything They'd Abolish It, 1987; Livingstone's Labour, 1989. Memberships: Zoological Society of London, Council, 1994-, Vice-President, 1996-98. Address: Greater London Authority, Romney House, Marsham Street, London, SW1P 3PY. E-mail: mayor@london.gov.uk

LIVINGSTONE Laureen, b. 3 February 1946, Dumbarton, Scotland. Singer (Soprano); Teacher. 1 son, 1 daughter. Education: Royal Scottish Academy of Music, 1963-66; London Opera Centre,

1967-69; DipMusEd; RSAM. Career: Wide variety of operatic, concert and TV appearances in UK and abroad; BBC Proms; Recitals including Wigmore Hall and 1st BBC Lunchtime recital in 1976; Guest appearances with London Symphony Orchestra, Hallé, English Sinfonia, Northern Sinfonia, Scottish National and Scottish Chamber Orchestras; Operatic roles include: Zerlina, Pamina, Gretel, Lucia in Rape of Lucretia with Scottish Opera, Susanna, Sophie and Vrenchen in A Village Romeo and Juliet with English National Opera North, Gilda in Rigoletto and Sophie in Der Rosenkavalier for English National Opera, 1988; Major roles with the New Sadler's Wells Opera, Handel Opera and others; Engagements abroad include Woglinde at Teatro di San Carlo, Naples, 1980 and Gilda for Royal Flemish Opera in Antwerp, 1985; Professor of Singing at Trinity College of Music, London. Recordings: Several recital programmes for BBC; Countess Maritza; Gianetta in The Gondoliers, 1st colour production for BBC TV; Ninetta in L'Amour des Trois Oranges, BBC TV, 1980; Elsie in The Yeoman of the Guard, Channel 5 video; Amore in Il Ritorno d'Ulisse in Patria, Glyndebourne, video 1973. Honours: Caird Scholarship, 1967; Winner, Peter Stuyvesant Scholarship, 1969. Address: 12 Pymmes Brook Drive, New Barnet, Hertfordshire EN4 9RU, England.

LJUBENOV Todor Todorov, b. 31 March 1942, Sofia, Bulgaria. Physician; Radiotherapist; Oncologist. m. Dimitra Furnadjieva Ljuenova, 1 daughter. Education: Graduate, Medical University, Sofia, Bulgaria, 1969; Postgraduate School, Berlin-Buch, Germany, 1970-71; MD, Berlin, 1970; Specialisation, Medical University, Geneva, Switzerland, 1984. Appointments: Lecturer, School of Radiology, 1976-80, Chief Assistant Professor, Department of Nuclear Medicine and Radiotherapy, Faculty of Medicine, Medical University, Sofia, 1973-2003; Collaborator in Cyclophasotron, Joint Institute for Nuclear Research, Dubna, Russia, 2002. Honours: Listed in Who's Who publications and biographical dictionaries. Publications: Chapters in books and articles in scientific journals including: Handbook of Rentgenology and Radiology, 1985; The British Journal of Radiology, 1992; Oral Oncology vol II, 1991; Radiobiology, Radiotherapy, 1988; Diabolisme in Medical Mundi parts I, II, III, 1999-2003. Memberships: Member Elect, American Diabetes Society, 2001. Address: 8 Nikolai Pavlovich Street, 1142 Sofia, Bulgaria.

LLEWELLIN (John) Richard (Allan), b. 30 September 1938, Haverfordwest, South Wales. Bishop. m. Jennifer Sally House, 1 son, 2 daughters. Education: Clifton College, Bristol; Theological studies, Westcott House and Fitzwilliam College, Cambridge, 1961-64. Appointments: Articled to Messrs Farrer and Co of Lincoln's Inn Fields; Solicitor, Messrs Field Roscoe and Co, London; Assistant Curate, Radlett, Hertfordshire, 1964-68; Assistant Priest, Johannesburg Cathedral, South Africa, 1968-71; Vicar of Waltham Cross, 1971-79; Rector of Harpenden, 1979; Bishop of St Germans, 1985; Bishop of Dover and Bishop in Canterbury, 1992; Bishop at Lambeth and Head of Staff to the Archbishop of Canterbury, 1999-. Address: Lambeth Palace, London, SE1 7JU, England. Email: richard.llewellin@lampal.c-of-e.org.uk

LLOVERAS Jean-Jacques, b. 3 September 1956, Toulouse, France. Doctor. Education: MD, 1983; Nephrology, 1985. Appointments: Medical Doctor. Publications: Cycloprine in heart transplantation; Treatment of cardiac rejection. Address: 15 Avenue A Briand, 31400 Toulouse, France.

LLOYD Christopher, b. 22 October 1938, Stamford, Connecticut, USA. Actor. m. Carol. Education: Neighbourhood Playhouse, New York. Appointments: Film Debut, One Flew Over the Cuckoo's Nest, 1975; Films include: Butch and Sundance: The

Early Days; The Onion Field; The Black Marble; The Legend of the Lone Ranger; Mr Mom; To Be or Not to Be; Star Trek III: The Search for Spock; Adventures of Buckaroo Banzai; Back to the Future; Clue; Who Framed Roger Rabbit?; Track 29; Walk Like a Man; Eight Men Out; The Dream Team; Why Me?; Back to the Future, Part II; Back to the Future, Part III; The Addams Family; Twenty Bucks; Dennis the Menace; Addams Family Values; The Pagemaster; Camp Nowhere; The Radioland Murders; Things To Do in Denver When You're Dead; Cadillac Ranch; Changing Habits; Dinner at Fred's; Baby Geniuses; My Favorite Martian; Man on the Moon; Chasing Destiny, 2000; When Good Ghouls Go Bad, 2001; Wit, 2001; Wish You Were Dead, 2003; Interstate 60, 2003; TV includes: Taxi; Best of the West; The Dictator; Tales from Hollywood Hills; Pat Hobby - Teamed with Genius; September Gun; Avonlea; Alice in Wonderland. Honours: Winner, Drama Desk and Obie Awards, Kaspar, 1973. Address: The Gersh Agency, 252 North Canon Drive, Beverly Hills, CA 90210, USA.

LLOYD Clive Hubert, b. 31 August 1944, British Guiana, now Guyana. Cricketer. m. Waveney Benjamin, 1 son, 2 daughters. Career: Left-Hard Batsman, Right-Arm Medium-Paced Bowler; Played for British Guiana and Guyana, 1963-83; Played, 1968-86, Captain, 1981-83, 1986, for Lancashire; 110 Tests for West Indies, 1966-85, with record 74 as Captain, scoring 7,515 runs, averaging 46.6, including 19 centuries; Toured England, 1969, 1973, 1975 in World Cup, 1976, 1979 in World Cup, 1980, 1983 in World Cup, 1984; Scored 31,232 first-class runs including 79 centuries; Director, Red Rose Radio PLC, 1981; Executive Promotions Officer, Project Fullemploy, 1987-; West Indies Team Man, 1988-89, 1996-; International Cricket Council Referee, 1992-95. Publications: Living for Cricket, co-author, 1980; Winning Captaincy, co-author, 1995. Honours: Commander, Order of the British Empire. Address: c/o Harefield, Harefield Drive, Wilmslow, Cheshire SK9 1NJ, England.

LLOYD David Dilsworth Talbott, b. 9 May 1930, Montclair, New Jersey, USA. Professor Emeritus. m. Maureen Doody, 2 sons and 1 stepson, 3 daughters. Education: BA, Montclair State Teacher's College, New Jersey, 1952; MA, University of Michigan, Ann Arbor, Michigan, 1957; PhD (not completed) University of Michigan and Temple University. Appointments include: Instructor and Head of Theater Wing, Glassboro State Teachers College, now Rowan University, 1959-2000; Chair of Journalism and Creative Writing, 1997-2000, now an adjunct at Rowan and Gloucester County College. Publications: Author and Illustrator of: The Circle, 1974; Author and Illustrator of Snowman, 2nd edition, 1999; Zen Poems, 2002; others. Honours include: 12 place awards for water colours; New Jersey's 1st prize for watercolour, 2000. Memberships: Former Chair, New Jersey Poetry Society; Former President, Gloucester Co Art League and others. Address: 17 Fourth Avenue, Pitman, NJ 08071-1419, USA.

LLOYD (David) Huw (Owen), b. 14 April 1950, London, England. Family Doctor. m. Mary Eileen, 1 son, 3 daughters. Education: Gonville and Caius College, Cambridge, 1968-71; Guy's Hospital, London, 1971-74; Somerset Vocational Training Scheme, 1976-79. Appointments: Principal, Cadwgan Surgery, Old Colwyn; Clinical Governance Lead, Conwy Local Health Group. Memberships: Fellow, Royal College of General Practitioners; Chairman, Mental Health Task Group, RCGP; Deputy Chairman, North Wales Local Medical Committee; Member, Welsh Council, RCGP; General Practitioners Committee, Wales. Address: Maes yr Onnen, Abergele Road, Llanddulas; Abergele LL22 8EN, Wales. E-mail: huwlloyd@welshnet.co.uk

LLOYD Elisabeth Anne, b. 3 September 1956, Morristown, New Jersey, USA. Professor. Education: BA Science and Political Theory, University of Colorado, Boulder, 1980; PhD, Princeton University, 1984. Appointments: Assistant Professor, Department of Philosophy, University of California, San Diego, 1985-88; Assistant Professor, Department of Philosophy, 1988-90, Associate Professor, 1990-97, University of California, Berkeley; Affiliated Faculty, History and Philosophy of Science Programme, University of California, Davis, 1990-98; Professor, Department of Philosophy, University of California, Berkeley, 1997-99; Professor, Department History and Philosophy of Science, 1998-, Chair, Department of History and Philosophy of Science, 2000-; Tanis Chair of History and Philosophy of Science, 2001-, Indiana University, Bloomington. Publications: 2 books; 38 articles in professional journals; 4 book reviews; numerous presentations and invited lectures; Articles and books in progress. Honours: University of California: Resident Fellow and Fellow, UC Humanities Research Institute; National Science Foundation Scholar's Award; Humanities Graduate Research Assistance Fellowship; Several grants; Regents Summer Faculty Fellowship; Princeton University: National Science Foundation Graduate Fellow; Garden State Graduate Award; University of Colorado: Phi Beta Kappa; Van Ek Award. Memberships include: American Philosophical Association; Philosophy of Science Association; International Society for the History, Philosophy and Social Studies of Biology. Address: History and Philosophy of Science Department, Goodbody Hall 130, Indiana University, Bloomington, IN 47405-2401, USA. E-mail: ealloyd@indiana.edu

LLOYD Geoffrey (Ernest Richard) (Sir), b. 25 January 1933, London, England. Emeritus Professor of Ancient Philosophy and Science; Writer. m. Janet Elizabeth Lloyd, 1956, 3 sons. Education: BA, 1954, MA, 1958, PhD, 1958, King's College, Cambridge. Appointments: Fellow, 1957, Senior Tutor, 1969-73, King's College, Cambridge; Assistant Lecturer in Classics, 1965-67, Lecturer in Classics, 1967-74, Reader in Ancient Philosophy and Science, 1974-83, Professor of Ancient Philosophy and Science, 1983-2000, Cambridge University; Bonsall Professor, Stanford University, 1981; Sather Professor, University of California at Berkeley, 1984; Visiting Professor, Beijing University and Academy of Sciences, 1987; Master, Darwin College, 1989-2000; Professor at Large, Cornell University, 1990-96; Zhu Kezhen Visiting Professor, Institute for the History of Natural Science, Beijing, 2002. Publications: Polarity and Analogy, 1966; Early Greek Science: Thales to Aristotle, 1970; Greek Science After Aristotle, 1973; Magic, Reason and Experience, 1979; Science, Folklore and Ideology, 1983; Science and Morality in Greco-Roman Antiquity, 1985; The Revolution of Wisdom, 1987; Demystifying Mentalities, 1990; Methods and Problems in Greek Science, 1991; Adversaries and Authorities, 1996; Aristotelian Explorations, 1996; The Way and the Word (with N Jivin), 2002; In the Grip of Disease, Studies in the Greek Imagination, 2003; Editor: Hippocratic Writings, 1978; Aristotle on Mind and Senses (with G E L Owen), 1978; Le Savoir Grec (with Jacques Brunschwig), 1996, English edition, 2000. Contributions to: Books and journals. Honours: Sarton Medal, 1987; Honorary Fellow, King's College, Cambridge, 1990; Honorary Foreign Member, American Academy of Arts and Sciences, 1995; Knighted, 1997. Memberships: British Academy, fellow; East Asian History of Science Trust, chairman, 1992-; International Academy of the History of Science, 1997. Address: 2 Prospect Row, Cambridge CB1 1DU, England.

LLOYD John Nicol Fortune, b. 15 April 1946. Journalist. m. (1) Judith Ferguson, 1974, divorced 1979, (2) Marcia Levy, 1983, divorced 1997, 1 son. Education: MA, University of Edinburgh. Appointments: Editor, Time Out, 1972-73; Reporter, London Programme, 1974-76; Producer, Weekend World, 1976-77; Industrial Reporter, Labour Correspondent, Industrial and Labour Editor, Financial Times; 1977-86; Editor, 1986-87, Associate

Editor, 1996-, New Statesman; Other Financial Times assignments, 1987-, including Moscow Correspondent, 1991-95; Freelance journalist, 1996-. Publications: The Politics of Industrial Change, co-author, 1982; The Miners' Strike: Loss Without Limit, co-author, 1986; In Search of Work, co-author, 1987; Counterblasts, contributor, 1989; Rebirth of a Nation: an Anatomy of Russia, 1998; Re-engaging Russia, 2000; The Protest Ethic, 2001. Honours: Journalist of the Year, Granada Awards, 1984; Specialist Writer of the Year, IPC Awards, 1985; Rio Tinto David Watt Memorial Prize, 1997. Address: New Statesman, Victoria Station House, 7th Floor, 191 Victoria Street, London SW1E 5NE, England. E-mail: info@newstatesman.co.uk

LLOYD Kathleen Annie, (Kathleen Conlon, Kate North), b. 4 January 1943, Southport, England. Writer. m. Frank Lloyd, 3 August 1962, divorced, 1 son. Education: BA, Honours, King's College, Durham University. Publications: Apollo's Summer Look, 1968; Tomorrow's Fortune, 1971; My Father's House, 1972; A Twisted Skein, 1975; A Move in the Game, 1979; A Forgotten Season, 1980; Consequences, 1981; The Best of Friends, 1984; Face Values, 1985; Distant Relations, 1989; Unfinished Business, 1990; As Kate North: Land of My Dreams, 1997; Gollancz, 1997. Contributions to: Atlantic Review; Cosmopolitan; Woman's Journal; Woman; Woman's Own. Membership: Society of Authors. Address: 26A Brighton Road, Birkdale, Southport PR8 4DD, England.

LLOYD PARRY Eryl, b. 28 April 1939, Waterloo, Liverpool, England. Chairman of Employment Tribunals. m. Nancy Kathleen Lloyd Parry, 3 sons, 1 daughter. Education: St Peter's College, Oxford; Appointments: Part-time Chairman, Employment Tribunals in the Liverpool region, 1977; Vice-President, Merseyside and Cheshire Rent Assessment Panel, 1985; Full-time Chairman, Employment Tribunals in the Manchester region, 1992. Publications: Poems, articles, plays and reviews variously published and performed. Honours: MA (Oxon); Diploma in Public and Social Administration, Oxon; Barrister, Lincoln's Inn. Memberships: Southport Dramatic Society; Formby Theatre Club; Sefton Theatre Company; Sussex Playwrights' Club; Honorary Life Member, Liverpool Bar Cricket Club; Amnesty International. Address: Office of Employment Tribunals, 1st Floor Cunard Building, Pier Head, Liverpool L3 1TS, England.

LLOYD WEBBER Andrew, (Baron Lloyd Webber of Sydmonton) b. 22 March 1948, London, England. Composer. m. (1) Sarah Jane Hugill, 1971, divorced 1983, 1 son, 1 daughter, (2) Sarah Brightman, 1984, divorced 1990, (3) Madeleine Gurdon, 1991, 2 sons, 1 daughter. Education: Magdalen College, Oxford; Royal College of Music, FRCM, 1988. Career: Composer and producer, musicals; Composer, film scores; Deviser, board game, And They're Off; Owner, Really Useful Group. Compositions: Musicals: Joseph And The Amazing Technicolour Dreamcoat (lyrics by Tim Rice), 1968; Jesus Christ Superstar (lyrics by Tim Rice), 1970; Jeeves (lyrics by Alan Ayckbourn), 1975; Evita (lyrics by Tim Rice), 1976; Tell Me On A Sunday (lyrics by Don Black), 1980; Cats (based on poems by T S Eliot), 1981; Song And Dance, 1982; Starlight Express (lyrics by Richard Stilgoe), 1984; The Phantom Of The Opera (lyrics by Richard Stilgoe and Charles Hart), 1986; Aspects Of Love (lyrics by Don Black and Charles Hart), 1989; Sunset Boulevard (lyrics by Don Black and Christopher Hampton), 1993; By Jeeves (lyrics by Alan Ayckbourn), 1996; Whistle Down The Wind (lyrics by Jim Steinman), 1996; The Beautiful Game (book and lyrics by Ben Elton), 2000; Bombay Dreams, 2002; Film Scores: Gumshoe, 1971; The Odessa File, 1974; Jesus Christ Superstar, 1974; Others: Requiem, 1985; Variations On A Theme Of Paganini For Orchestra, 1986; Amigos Para Siempre (official theme for 1992 Olympic Games), 1992; When Children Rule The World (official theme for the opening ceremony 1998 Winter Olympics). Publications: Evita (with Tim Rice), 1978; Cats: The Book of the Musical, 1981; Joseph And The Amazing Technicolour Dreamcoat (with Tim Rice), 1982; The Complete Phantom of the Opera, 1987; The Complete Aspects of Love, 1989; Sunset Boulevard: From Movie to Musical, 1993; Restaurant Columnist, the Daily Telegraph, 1996-99. Honours include: 5 Laurence Olivier Awards; 6 Tony Awards; 4 Drama Desk Awards; 3 Grammy Awards; Triple Play Award, ASCAP, 1988; Knighthood, 1992; Praemium Imperiale Award, 1995; Richard Rogers Award, 1996; Oscar, Best Song, (with Tim Rice), 1997; Honorary Life Peer, 1997; Critics Circle Award Best Musical, 2000. Address: 22 Tower Street, London WC2H 9NS, England.

LLOYD WEBBER Julian, b. 14 April 1951, London, England. Cellist. m. (1) Celia M Ballantyne, 1974, divorced 1989, (2) Zohra Mahmoud Ghazi, 1989, divorced, 1999, son, (3) Kheira Bourahla, 2001. Education: Royal College of Music. Appointments: Debut, Queen Elizabeth Hall, 1972; Debut, Berlin Philharmonic Orchestra, 1984; Appears in major international concert halls; Undertaken concert tours throughout Europe, North and South America, Australasia, Singapore, Japan, Hong Kong and Korea; Numerous TV appearances and broadcasts in UK, Netherlands, Africa, Germany, Scandinavia, France, Belgium, Spain, Australasia, USA; Recordings include: World Premieres of Britten's 3rd Suite for Solo Cello; Bridges Oration Rodrigo's Cello Concerto; Holst's Invocation; Gavin Bryar's Cello Concerto; James MacMillan's Kiss on Wood; Sullivan's Cello Concerto; Vaughan Williams' Fantasia on Sussex Folk Tunes; Andrew Lloyd Webber's Variations; Elgar's Cello Concerto; Dvorak Concerto; Saint Saens Concerto; Lalo Concerto; Walton Concerto; Britten Cello Symphony. Publications: Frank Bridge, Six Pieces, 1982; Young Cellist's Repertoir, 1984; Travels with my Cello, 1984; Song of the Birds, 1985; Recital Repertoire for Cellists, 1986; Short Sharp Shocks, 1990; The Great Cello Solos, 1992; The Essential Cello, 1997; Cello Moods, 1999. Honours: British Phonographic Industry Award for Best Classical Recordings, 1986; Crystal Award Economic Forum, 1998. Address: c/o IMG Artists Europe, Lovell House, 616 Chiswick High Road, London, W4 5RX, England. Website: www.julianlloydwebber.com

LLOYD-JONES Sir (Peter) Hugh (Jefferd), b. 21 September 1922, St Peter Port, Jersey, Channel Islands. Classical Scholar. m. (1) Frances Hedley, 1953, divorced 1981, 2 sons, 1 daughter, (2) Mary R Lefkowitz, 1982. Education: Christ Church, Oxford; MA (Oxon), 1947. Appointments: Fellow, Jesus College, Cambridge, 1948-54; Fellow, Corpus Christi College, Oxford, 1954-60; Regius Professor of Greek and Student of Christ Church, Oxford, 1960-89. Publications: The Justice of Zeus, 1971, 2nd edition, 1983; Blood for the Ghosts, 1982; Supplementum Hellenisticum (with P J Parsons), 1983; Sophoclis Fabulae (with N G Wilson), 1990; Sophoclea (with N G Wilson), 1990; Academic Papers, 2 volumes, 1990; Greek in a Cold Climate, 1991; Sophocles (editor and translator), 3 volumes, 1994-96; Sophocles: Second Thoughts (with N G Wilson), 1997. Contributions to: Numerous periodicals. Honours: Honorary DHL, University of Chicago, 1970; Honorary PhD, University of Tel Aviv, 1984; Knighted, 1989; Honorary DPhil, University of Thessalonica, 1999; Göttingen, 2002. Memberships: British Academy, fellow; Academy of Athens, fellow; Corresponding Member; American Academy of Arts and Sciences; American Philosophical Society; Rheinisch-Westfälische Akademie; Bayerische Akademie der Wissenschaften; Accademia di Lettere, Archeologia e Belle Arti, Naples. Address: 15 West Riding, Wellesley, MA 02482, USA.

LO Wen-Lin, b. 1 January 1958, Kaohsiung, Taiwan. Dermatologist. m. Yung-Jung Ho, 1 son, 1 daughter. Education: MD, National Yang-Ming Medical College, Taipei, 1982. Appointments: Resident, Dermatology, 1984-89, Attending Physician, 1989-91, Veterans General Hospital, Taipei; Lecturer, National Yang-Ming Medical College, 1989-91; Attending Physician, 1991-93, Section Chief, 1993-94, Chutong (Taiwan) Veterans Hospital; Private Practice, 1994-. Publications: Contributor of articles in professional journals. Memberships: Fellow, American Academy of Dermatology; Asian Dermatological Association; International Society of Dermatology; Chinese Dermatological Society; Laser Medicine Society. Address: 2/F #2 Lane 14, Chung Shan North Sec 7, Taipei 111, Taiwan.

LO VERSO Girolamo, b. 1947, Palermo, Italy. Professor; Psychotherapist. m. Giuseppina Ustica, 1 son, 1 daughter. Education: Doctor, 1970; Specialist in Psychology, 1973; Specialist in Psychotherapy, 1978; Specialist in Group Analysis, 1980. Appointments: Chief, Psychology, Psychiatric Service, 1976; University Assistant, 1980, Professor of Clinical Psychology, 1991, Professor of Psychotherapy, 2004-, University of Palermo, Italy. Publications: Articles in scientific journals and 25 books as author and co-author include: Le Relazioni Soggettuali, 1994; La Psicodinamica Dei Gruppi, (with F DiMaria) 1995; Gruppi, (with F DiMaria) 2002; La Psiche Mafiosa (with G Lococo), 2003. Honours: Listed in Who's Who publications and biographical dictionaries. Memberships: Group Analytic Society; Society for Psychotherapy Research. Address; via Vincenzo di Marco 9, 90143 Palermo, Italy. E-mail: girolamo.loverso@tin.it

LOACH Kenneth, b. 17 June 1936, Nuneaton, England. Film Director. m. Lesley Ashton, 1962, 3 sons (one deceased), 2 daughters. Education: St Peter's Hall, Oxford. Appointments: BBC Trainee, Drama Department, 1963; Freelance Film Director, 1963-; Films include: Poor Cow, 1967; Kes, 1969; In Black and White, 1970; Family Life, 1971; Black Jack, 1979; Looks and Smiles, 1981; Fatherland, 1986; Hidden Agenda, 1990; Riff Raff, 1991; Raining Stones, 1993; Ladybird Ladybird, 1994; Land and Freedom, 1995; Carla's Song, 1996; My Name is Joe, 1998; Bread and Roses, 2001; The Navigators, 2001; Sweet Sixteen, 2002; 11.09.01 UK Segment, 2002; TV includes: Diary of a Young Man, 1964; Three Clear Sundays, 1965; The End of Arthur's Marriage, 1965; Up the Junction, 1965; Coming Out Party, 1965; Cathy Come Home, 1966; In Two Minds, 1966; The Golden Vision, 1969; The Big Flame, 1970; After a Lifetime, 1971; The Rank of File, 1972; Auditions, 1980; A Question of Leadership, 1980; The Red and the Blue, 1983; Questions of Leadership, 1983; Which Side are You On?, 1984; The View from the Woodpile, 1988; Time to Go, 1989; Dispatches: Arthur Scargill, 1991; The Flickering Flame, 1996; Another City, 1998. Honours: Hon DLitt, St Andrews; Staffordshire University, Bristol; Dr hc, Royal College of Art, 1988; Honorary Fellow, St Peter's College, Oxford. Address: c/o Parallax Pictures, 7 Denmark Street, London, WC2H 8LS, England.

LOADES David Michael, b. 19 January 1934, Cambridge, England. Retired Professor of History; Writer. m. Judith Anne Atkins, 18 April 1987. Education: Emmanuel College, Cambridge, 1955-61, BA, 1958, MA, PhD, 1961, LittD, 1981. Appointments: Lecturer in Political Science, University of St Andrews, 1961-63; Lecturer in History, University of Durham, 1963-70; Senior Lecturer, 1970-77, Reader, 1977-80, Professor of History, 1980-96, University College of North Wales, Bangor; Director, British Academy John Foxe Project, 1993. Publications: Two Tudor Conspiracies, 1965; The Oxford Martyrs, 1970; The Reign of Mary Tudor, 1979; The Tudor Court, 1986; Mary Tudor: A Life, 1989; The Tudor Navy, 1992; John Dudley: Duke of Northumberland, 1996; Tudor Government, 1997; England's Maritime Empire,

2000; The Chronicles of the Tudor Queens, 2002; Elizabeth I, 2003. Editor: The Papers of George Wyatt, 1968; The End of Strife, 1984; Faith and Identity, 1990; John Foxe and the English Reformation, 1997; John Foxe: an historical perspective, 1999; with C S Knighton, The Anthony Roll of Henry VIII, 2000; Letters from the Mary Rose, 2002. Contributions to: Journals. Memberships: Royal Historical Society, fellow; Society of Antiquaries of London, fellow. Address: The Cottage, Priory Lane, Burford, Oxon OX18 4SG, England.

LOCKERBIE D(onald) Bruce, b. 25 August 1935, Capreol, Ontario, Canada. Scholar; Writer. Education: AB, 1956, MA, 1963, New York University. Appointments: Scholar-in-Residence, Stony Brook School, New York, 1957-91; Visiting Consultant at American Schools in Asia and Africa, 1974; Visiting Lecturer/Consultant to American universities. Publications: Billy Sunday, 1965; Patriarchs and Prophets, 1969; Hawthorne, 1970; Melville, 1970; Twain, 1970; Major American Authors, 1970; Success in Writing (with L Westdahl), 1970; Purposeful Writing, 1972; The Way They Should Go, 1972; The Liberating Word, 1974; The Cosmic Center: The Apostles' Creed, 1977; A Man under Orders: Lt Gen William K Harrison, 1979; Who Educates Your Child?, 1980; The Timeless Moment, 1980; Asking Questions, 1980; Fatherlove, 1981; In Peril on the Sea, 1984; The Christian, the Arts and Truth, 1985; Thinking and Acting Like a Christian, 1989; Take Heart (with L Lockerbie), 1990; College: Getting In and Staying In (with D Fonseca), 1990; A Passion for Learning, 1994; From Candy Sales to Committed Donors, 1996; Dismissing God, 1998. Honours: DHL, Eastern College, 1985; Taylor University 1993. Address: PO Box 26, Stony Brook, NY 11790, USA.

LOCKHEAD Gregory Roger, b. 8 August 1931, Boston, Massachusetts, USA. Psychologist. m. Jeanne Hutchinson, 1 son, 2 daughters. Education: BS, Tufts University, 1958; PhD, Johns Hopkins University, 1965. Appointments: Research Staff, IBM Research Centre, 1958-61; Instructor, Johns Hopkins University, 1961-64; Assistant Professor, 1965; Associate Professor, 1968; Professor, Department of Psychology, Duke University, 1972; Research Associate, University of California at Berkeley; Scholar, Stanford University; Visiting Professor, Oxford University, England; Visiting Professor, Florida Atlantic University; Chair, Department of Psychology, Duke University, 1991-97. Publications: 1 edited book and around 60 articles in professional journals. Honours: NIMH Research Fellow; Numerous research grants; ATA-NSF Scientific Lecturing Fellow. Memberships: American Psychological Association; American Psychological Society; International Society of Psychophysics; Sigma Xi; Society of Experimental Psychologists. Address: Department of Psychological and Brain Sciences, Duke University, Durham, NC 27708, USA.

LODER Robert Reginald (Robin), b. 12 November 1943, Titchfield, Hampshire, England. Landowner. m. Jane Royden, 2 sons, 2 daughters. Education: MA, Trinity College, Cambridge. Appointments: Owner, Leonardslee Gardens; High Sheriff of West Sussex, 2000-01. Address: Leonardslee Gardens, Lower Beeding, Horsham, West Sussex RH13 6PP, England. E-mail: gardens@leonardslee.com

LODGE David John, b. 28 January 1935. Honorary Professor of Modern English Literature. m. Mary Frances Jacob, 1959, 2 sons, 1 daughter. Education: BA, honours, MA (London); PhD, Birmingham; National Service, RAC, 1955-57. Appointments: British Council, London, 1959-60; Assistant Lecturer, 1960-62, Lecturer, 1963-71, Senior Lecturer, 1971-73, Reader of English, 1973-76, Professor of Modern English Literture, 1976-87, Honorary Professor, 1987-2000, Emeritus Professor, 2001-,

University of Birmingham; Harkness Commonwealth Fellow, 1964-65; Visiting Associate Professor, University of California, Berkeley, 1969; Henfield Writing Fellow, University of East Anglia, 1977. Publications: Novels: The Picturegoers, 1960; Ginger, You're Barmy, 1962; The British Museum is Falling Down, 1965; Out of the Shelter, 1970, revised edition, 1985; Changing Places, 1975; How Far Can You Go?, 1980; Small World, 1984; Nice Work, 1988; Paradise News, 1991; Therapy, 1995; Home Truths, 1999; Thinks...., 2001; Consciousness and the Novel, 2002. Criticism: Language of Fiction, 1966; The Novelist at the Crossroads, 1971; The Modes of Modern Writing, 1977; Working with Structuralism, 1981; Write On, 1986; After Bakhtin (essays), 1990; The Art of Fiction, 1992; The Practice of Writing, 1996. Honours: Yorkshire Post Fiction Prize, 1975; Hawthornden Prize, 1976; Whitbread Book of the Year Award, 1980; Sunday Express Book of the Year Award, 1988; Chevalier de L'Ordre des Arts et des Lettres, 1997; CBE, 1998. Address: Department of English, University of Birmingham, Birmingham B15 2TT, England.

LODGE Henry S, b. 20 October 1958, Boston, Massachusetts, USA. Physician. m. Teresa Goetz, 2 daughters. Education: BA, Magna Cum Laude, University of Pennsylvania, 1981; MD, Columbia University College of Physicians and Surgeons, 1985; Intern, Internal Medicine, 1985-86, Resident, Internal Medicine, 1986-88, Columbia Presbyterian Medical Center; Certificate of Added Qualification in Geriatrics, 1989. Appointments: Instructor in Clinical Medicine, 1988-89, Assistant Clinical Professor of Medicine, 1989-, Columbia University College of Physicians and Surgeons; Attending Physician, Presbyterian Hospital of the City of New York, 1989-; Chairman and Chief Executive Officer, New York Physicians LLP, a 23 physician, multi-speciality group practice; Consulting Internist, The McKeen Behavioral Program@CPMC; Student Advisor, 1988-; Residency Advisor, 1990-; 3rd Year Clinical Preceptor in Medicine, 1988-. Honours: Robert F Loeb Graduation Award for Excellence in Clinical Medicine; Castle and Connelly Survey, Best Doctors in New York; New York Magazine, Best Doctors in New York; Woodward and White, Best Doctors in America; Listed in Who's Who publications and biographical dictionaries. Memberships: American College of Physicians; American Medical Association; CMPC Society of Practitioners, Executive Committee, 1998-, Vice President, 2002-2003; New York Clinical Society, President 2001; Fellow, New York Academy of Science. Address: 1 West 85th Street, #6B, New York, NY 10024, USA.

LODGE Oliver Raymond William Wynlayne, b, 2 September 1922, Painswick, Goucestershire, England. Retired Barrister. m. Charlotte Young, deceased, 1990, 1 son, 2 daughters. Education: Officer Cadet, Royal Fusiliers, 1942; BA, 1943, MA, 1947, King's College, Cambridge. Appointments: Called to the Bar by Inner Temple, 1945; Practiced at Chancery Bar, 1945-74; Admitted ad eundam to Lincoln's Inn, 1946; Member of Bar Council, 1952-56, 1967-71; Member of Supreme Court Rules Committee, 1968-71; Bencher of Lincoln's Inn, 1973; Permanent Chairman of Industrial Tribunals, 1975-92, Part-time Chairman, 1992-94; Regional Chairman of London South Region of Industrial Tribunals, 1980-92; General Commissioner of Income Tax for Lincoln's Inn District, 1983-91; Treasurer of Lincoln's Inn, 1995. Publications: Editor, 3rd edition, Rivington's Epitome of Snedl's Equity, 1948; Editor, article on Fraudulent and Voidable Conveyances in 3rd edition of Halsbury's Laws of England, 1956. Memberships: Garrick Club; Bar Yacht Club. Address: Southride House, Hindon, Salisbury, Wiltshire SP3 6ER, England.

LOEDOLFF Cecilia Van Der Bijl, b. 11 March 1951, De Aar, Republic of South Africa. Curator; Art Consultant. m. Hendrik. Education: BA, University of Pretoria, 1971; Higher Educational

Diploma, 1972. Career: Joined Absa, 1988; Responsible for Absa Group Art Acquisitions and Strategic Direction of Art Funding, 1989-. Publications: Art book on Absa's art collection; Various booklets and catalogues; Article on the Absa Group art collection in De Arte, 1998. Honours: Quality Award, 1997; Business Arts South Africa Award, 2000. Memberships: Vice Chairman, Association of Arts, Pretoria. Address: cecilel@absa.co.za

LOFTHOUSE Geoffrey (Lord Lofthouse of Pontefract), b. 18 December 1925, Featherstone, England. Deputy Speaker, House of Lords. m. Sarah, deceased, 1 daughter. Education: Leeds University, 1954-57. Appointments: Member, Pontefract Health Council, 1962; Mayor of Pontefract, 1967-68; Leader, Pontefract Borough Council, 1969-73; First Chairman, Wakefield MDC, 1973; Chairman, Housing Committee, 1973-79; Elected Member of Parliament for Pontefract and Castleford, 1978; Elected Deputy Speaker of the House of Commons, 1992-97; Elected Deputy Speaker of the House of Lords, 1997-; Chairman of Wakefield Health Authority, 1998. Publications: A Very Miner MP (autobiography), 1985; Coal Sack to Woolsack (autobiography), 1999. Honours: Knighthood, 1995; Peerage, 1997. Memberships: Member of the Imperial Society of Knights Bachelor; Appointed Magistrate, 1970; President, British Amateur Rugby League Association. Address: 67 Carleton Crest, Pontefract, West Yorkshire WF8 2QR, England.

LOGANI Mahendra, b. 15 May 1941, Sialkot, India. Scientist. m. Shashi Prabha Logani, 1 son, 1 daughter. Education: BS, 1957, MS, 1961, PhD, 1967, Aligarh University, Aligarh, India. Appointments: Lecturer, Chemistry, Dharam Samaj College, Aligarh, India, 1961-64; Assistant Professor of Dermatology, 1972-76, Associate Professor of Dermatology, 1977-, Professor of Biomedical Physics, 1994-, Temple University Medical School. Publications: Articles in professional journals and books. Honours: Postdoctoral Fellowship, Sloan Foundation, 1968-69; Visiting Scientist: University of Padova, Italy, 1980; University of Nagoya Japan, 1980; Oak Ridge National Laboratory, USA, 1981-82. Memberships: Bioelectromagnetic Society; AAS; Sigma Xi. Address: Center for Biomedical Physics, Temple University School of Medicine, 3440 N Broad Street, Philadelphia, PA 19140, USA. E-mail: mklogani@hotmail.com

LOGUE Christopher (John), b. 23 November 1926, Portsmouth, Hampshire, England. Poet; Writer; Dramatist. m. Rosemary Hill, 1985. Education: Prior College, Bath. Publications: Poetry: Wand and Quadrant, 1953; Devil, Maggot and Son, 1954; The Weakdream Sonnets, 1955; The Man Who Told His Love: 20 Poems Based on P Neruda's "Los Cantos d'amores", 1958, 2nd edition, 1959; Songs, 1960; Songs from "The Lily-White Boys", 1960; The Establishment Songs, 1966; The Girls, 1969; New Numbers, 1969; Abecedary, 1977; Ode to the Dodo, 1981; War Music: An Account of Books 16 to 19 of Homer's Iliad, 1981; Fluff, 1984; Kings: An Account of Books 1 and 2 of Homer's Iliad, 1991, revised edition, 1992; The Husbands: An Account of Books 3 and 4 of Homer's Iliad, 1994; Selected Poems (edited by Christopher Reid), 1996; All Day Permanent Red, 2003. Plays: The Lily-White Boys (with Harry Cookson), 1959; The Trial of Cob and Leach, 1959; Antigone, 1961; War Music, 1978; Kings, 1993. Screenplays: Savage Messiah, 1972; The End of Arthur's Marriage, 1965; Crusoe (with Walter Green), 1986. Other: Lust, by Count Plamiro Vicarion, 1955; The Arrival of the Poet in the City: A Treatment for a Film, 1964; True Stories, 1966; The Bumper Book of True Stories, 1980. Editor: Count Palmiro Vicarion's Book of Limericks, 1959; The Children's Book of Comic Verse, 1979; London in Verse, 1982; Sweet & Sour: An Anthology of Comic

Verse, 1983; The Children's Book of Children's Rhymes, 1986. Honour: 1st Wilfred Owen Award, 1998. Address: 41 Camberwell Grove, London SE5 8JA, England.

LOHSE Andrea, b. 28 April 1964, Kellinghusen, Schleswig-Holstein, Germany. Lawyer. Education: First State Examination, Christian-Albrechts University, Kiel, 1988; Dr iur, LLD, Christian-Albrechts University, Kiel, 1991; Second State Examination, after 3 years practical training in judicial or other legal work, Schleswig-Holstein, 1993. Appointments: Research Assistant, Christian-Albrechts University, 1984-89; Stagaire, trainee, Commission, European Community, Direction General IV, Brussels, 1989-90; Administrative Assistant, ERASMUS, student exchange, program, 1990-93, Academic Assistant, civil law, 1993-94, Christian-Albrechts University; Lecturer, Academy of the Savings Banks, Kiel, 1991-94; Academic Assistant, civil, business and competition law, Free University Berlin, 1994-2001. Publications: Indonesian law concerning prohibition of monopolistic practices and unfair business competition, 2000, 2001; Law in Cases: Antitrust Law and Unfair Business Competition Law, 2001; The Prohibition of Cartels and the EEC Umbrella Regulation, 2001; Corporate Governance – the duties of the members of the management and supervisory board, 2004. Honours: Scholarships: Schleswig-Holstein, 1989-90, University Association Schleswig-Holstein, 1992; Faculty Award, Law, Christian-Albrechts University, 1992; Kieler Doctores Juris Association, 1993; Furtherance Honor, Hermann-Ehlers-Foundation, 1992; Scholarship, German Research Foundation, 2002-03. Membership: Protestant Church, 1964-. Address: Hengeler Mueller, Bockenheimer Landstrasse 51, D-60325 Frankfurt am Main, Germany. E-mail: andrea.lohse@hengeler.com

LOJDA Ladislav, b. 18 January 1926, Litohor, Czech Republic. Senior Research Worker. m. Jirina Simova, 8 September 1951, 2 sons. Education: Diploma, Veterinary Medicine, 1950; DVM, 1950; Candidate of Science, 1968. Appointments: Veterinary General Practitioner, 1950-56; Special, Reproduction of Domestic Animals, 1956-58; Regional Veterinary Special, 1958-62; Introduced the health progeny testing (Animal hereditary health control) and matched it with breeding selection, Czechoslovakia, 1958-62; Senior Research Worker, 1962-92. Publications include: Heredopathology of Reproduction in Domestic Animals, 1971; Methods of Chromosomal Study, 1977; Cytogenetics of Animals, 1989; History and Perspectives of Genetic Prevention in Veterinary Medicine, 1996. Honours: Listed in numerous national and international biographical dictionaries; Many others. Memberships: Genetic Society, Academy of Sciences, Brno; Cytogenetic Society, Academy of Sciences, Praha; Czech Biology Society, Academy of Sciences, Brno. Address: Listi 7, 61400 Brno, Czech Republic.

LOLLOBRIGIDA Gina, b. 4 July 1927, Sibiaco. Italian Actress. m. Milko Skofic, 1949, 1 son. Education: Liceo Artistico, Rome. Appointments: First Screen Role, Pagliacci, 1947; Appeared in numerous films including: Campane a Martello, 1948; Cuori Senza Frontiere, 1949; Achtung, bandit!, 1951; Enrico Caruso, 1951; Fanfan la Tulipe, 1951; Altri Tempi, 1952; The Wayward Wife, 1952; Les belles de la nuit, 1952; Pane, amour e fantasia, 1953; La Provinciale, 1953; Pane, amour e gelosia, La Romana, 1954; Il Grande Gioco, 1954; La Donna piu Bella del Mondo, 1955; Trapeze, 1956; Notre Dame de Paris, 1956; Solomon and Sheba, 1959; Never So Few, 1960; Go Naked in the World, 1961; She Got What She Asked For, 1963; Woman of Straw, 1964; Le Bambole, 1965; Hotel Paradiso, 1966; Buona Sera Mrs Campbell, 1968; King, Queen, Knave, 1972; The Bocce Showdown, 1990; Plucked, Bad Man's River; The Lonely Woman; Bambole. Publications: Italia Mia, 1974; The Philippines. Address: Via Appia Antica 223, 00178 Rome, Italy.

LOMAS Herbert, b. 7 February 1924, Yorkshire, England. Poet; Critic; Translator. m. Mary Marshall Phelps, 29 June 1968, 1 son, 1 daughter. Education: BA, 1949, MA, 1952, University of Liverpool. Appointments: Teacher, Spetsai, Greece, 1950-51; Lecturer, Senior Lecturer, University of Helsinki, 1952-65; Senior Lecturer, 1966-72, Principal Lecturer, 1972-82, Borough Road College. Publications: Chimpanzees are Blameless Creatures, 1969; Who Needs Money?, 1972; Private and Confidential, 1974; Public Footpath, 1981; Fire in the Garden, 1984; Letters in the Dark, 1986; Trouble, 1992; Selected Poems, 1995; A Useless Passion, 1998. Translations: Territorial Song, 1991; Contemporary Finnish Poetry, 1991; Fugue, 1992; Wings of Hope and Daring, 1992; The Eyes of the Fingertips are Opening, 1993; Black and Red, 1993; Narcissus in Winter, 1994; The Year of the Hare, 1994; Two Sequences for Kuhmo, 1994; In Wandering Hall, 1995; Selected Poems, Eeva-Lisa Manner, 1997; Three Finnish Poets, 1999; A Tenant Here, 1999. Contributions to: London Magazine and other reviews, journals, and magazines. Honours: Prize, Guinness Poetry Competition; Runner Up, Arvon Foundation Poetry Competition; Cholmondeley Award; Poetry Book Society Biennial Translation Award; Knight First Class, Order of the White Rose of Finland, 1991; Finnish State Prize for Translation, 1991. Memberships: Society of Authors; Finnish Academy; Finnish Literary Society; President, Suffolk Poetry Society, 1999-. Address: North Gable, 30 Crag Path, Aldeburgh, Suffolk IP15 5BS, England.

LOMAX Alan, b. 31 January 1915, Austin, Texas, USA. Ethnomusicologist; Writer. m. E Harold, 1937, 1 daughter. Education: Harvard University, 1932-33; BA, University of Texas at Austin, 1936; Graduate Studies in Anthropology, Columbia University, 1939. Appointments: Folk Song Collector, US and Europe; Director, Bureau of Applied Social Research, 1963, Cantometrics Project, Columbia University, 1963. Publications: American Folk Song and Folk Lore: A Regional Bibliography (with S Cowell), 1942; Mr Jelly Roll, 1950, 2nd edition, 1973; Harriett and Her Harmonium, 1955; The Rainbow Sign, 1959; Cantometrics: A Handbook and Training Method, 1976; Index of World Song, 1977; The Land Where the Blues Began, 1993. Editor: American Ballads and Folksongs (with John Lomax), 1934; Negro Folk Songs as Sung by Leadbelly (with John Lomax), 1936; Our Singing Country (with John Lomax), 1941; Folk Song: USA (with John Lomax), 1947, 4th edition, 1954; Leadbelly: A Collection of World Famous Songs (with John Lomax), 1959, 2nd edition, 1965; The Folk Songs of North America in the English Language, 1960; The Penguin Book of American Folk Songs, 1966; Hard-Hitting Songs for Hard-Hit People, 1967; Folk Song Style and Culture, 1968. Honours: National Medal of Arts, 1986; National Book Critics Circle Award, 1993. Memberships: American Association for the Advancement of Science; American Folklore Society, fellow; American Anthropological Association. Address: c/o Association for Cultural Equity, 450 West 41st Street, 6th Floor, New York, NY 10036, USA.

LOMBARDI Adolph V, Jr, b. 12 January 1956, Philadelphia, USA. Orthopaedic Surgeon. m. Anne T Lombardi, 1 son, 2 daughters. Education: BS, Biology, St Joseph's University, Philadelphia, 1973-77; MD, Temple University School of Medicine, Philadelphia, 1977-81. Appointments: Internship, Temple University School of Medicine, Philadelphia, 1981-82; Residency, Albert Einstein Medical Centre, Philadelphia, 1982-86; Shriners Hospital, Philadelphia, 1984; Thomas Jefferson University Hospital, Philadelphia, 1985; Fellowship, Ohio State University, 1986; Fellowship, National Hospital for Orthopaedics and Rehabilitation, Virginia, 1987; Clinical Assistant Professor, Orthopaedic Surgery, Ohio State University, current; Clinical Assistant Professor, Biomedical Engineering, Ohio State University, current; Chairman, Department of Surgery, New Albany

Dictionary of International Biography

Surgical Hospital. Publications: Numerous books and articles. Honours: Peer Appreciation Award; Award of Recognition as Editor of yearbook; Student Government; Physician's Recognition Award in Continuing Medical Education. Memberships include: Examiner for American Board of Orthopaedic Surgery; AAOS; American College of Surgeons: International College of Surgeons; The Knee Society; The Hip Society; Association for Arthritic Hip and Knee Surgery; many others. Address: Emilia's Estate, 17 New Albany Farms Road, New Albany Farms; New Albany, Ohio 43054, USA. E-mail: lombardiav@joint-surgeons.com

LOMU Jonah, b. 12 May 1975, Auckland, New Zealand. Rugby Football Player; Athlete. m. (1) Tanya Rutter, divorced, (2) Fiona Taylor, 2003. Appointments: Bank Officer, ASB Bank of New Zealand; Youngest Ever Capped All Black; Wing; International Debut, New Zealand versus France, 1994; Semi Finalist at World Cup, South Africa, 1995; Affilliated to Rugby Union; Ran 100m in 10.7 Seconds; With All Blacks, 1999-. Website: www.jonahlomu.com

LONDON Herbert Ira, b. 3 March 1939, New York, USA. President of a Think Tank; Professor. m. Vicki, 3 daughters. Education: BA, Columbia, 1960; MA, Columbia, 1961; PhD, NYU, 1966. Appointments: Professor of Social Studies, 1967-; Dean, Gallatin School, NYU, 1972-94; John M Olin Professor of Humanities, NYU, 1994-; President, Hudson Institute, 1997-. Honours: Honorary degrees from University of Aix-Marseilles and Grove City College; Martin Luther King Humanitarian Award; Peter Shaw Memorial Award for Exemplary Writing; Templeton Award for Great Professors, 1997; American Maritain Association Award, 1998. Memberships: Council of Foreign Relations; Hudson Institute Board of Trustees; National Association of Scholars; Merrill Lynch Assets Management. Address: 10 West Street, New York, NY 10004, USA.

LONDOÑO VELEZ Maria Victoria, b. 20 May 1956, Cali, Colombia. Educator; Social Development Director. 1 son. Education: BA, Philosophy, University of Valle, Colombia, 1985; MA, Education, Harvard University, USA, 1992; Graduate, Distance Education, London University, England, 1987. Appointments: Media Consultant, Ministry of Education, Colombia, 1984-86; Media Consultant, Ministry of Education, Paraguay, OAS, 1986; Director, Social Development Department, Government of Valle, 1995-97; Director, Education Department , Carvajal Foundation, 1988-94, 1998-2003; Director of Science, Cultural and Education Centre, Colombia, 2002-. Publications: Philosophy for 5th Grade Media Education, 1985; Gurnard in the Broken Sky, language and education in children's narratives, 2001; CD Rom, Travel Case, language and education for teachers, 2002; Designer, didactic material, Let's Do an Active Education, 1993 and Ecological Kit, 1993. Honours: Co-winner, World Award for a Literacy Campaign, UNESCO/IRA, 1986; Recipient Scholarship, Harvard-FES, 1991; Finalist, National Award Colombia Ministry of Culture, 1995. Memberships: Board Director, Universidad del Valle Cali/Colombia, 1999-2003; Board Director, Corporation for Basic Education, Colombia, 1991. Address: Carrera 12 # 1-56, Barrio San Antonio, Cali, Colombia. E-mail: viclon@fundacioncarvajal.org.co

LONERAGAN Owen William, b. 26 March 1924, Maylands, Western Australia. Forestry; Esperanto. m. Joan Edith Shaw, 2 sons, 1 daughter. Education: Arts I, 1946, Science I and II, 1947-48, University of Western Australia; Australian Forestry School, Canberra, 1949-50, Diploma, 1951;BSc, 1954, MSc, 1963, University of Western Australia. Appointments: Junior, Health Department, Western Australia, 1940-41; Australian Military Forces, 1942; RAAF attached RAF aircrew Wireless Operator,

1943-45; Clerk, Commonwealth Repatriation Commission, Perth, 1945-46; University Trainee, Commonwealth Reconstruction Training Scheme, 1946-51; Professional Forester, Forests Department, Western Australia, Forest Assessor, Jarrahdale, 1951-52; Assistant Divisional Forest Officer, Dwellingup-Pemberton, 1952-60; Research Silviculturist, Manjimup-Como, 1961-79; Senior RS, 1980-84; Regeneration and treatments, Growth and Ecology of Jarrah, Karri, Sandalwood, Forest Parks and Reserves. Publications include: Review of Sandalwood Research, 1990; Karri Phenological Studies, 1979; Co-author, Vegetation Complexes, 1980; Ecology of Jarrah, 1986. Honours: War Medals, 1939-45; University of Western Australia Hackett Bursary, 1947; Forests Department of Western Australia Bursary, 1949-50; United Nations Association of Australia Peace Award, 1996; Deputy Director General, IBC. Memberships include: Life Member, Institute of Foresters of Australia; Life Member, United Nations Association of Australia (WA), President, 1982-85; UN Year of the Tree and inaugural member of Greening Australia (WA), 1982; Tree Society (WA); RAAF Association (WA); Returned Services League, (WA); Australian Conservation Foundation (WA); Life Member, Esperanto League (WA), Honorary Treasurer, 1976-85, 1997-2002; Multicultural Education Council (WA), 1978-80; Life Member, Australian Esperanto Association, Honorary Treasurer, 1986-95, Esperanto Examination Certificates Elementa, 1985, Meza, 2002; Vice President, Australia-Bangladesh Aid Inc, 1987; Inaugural member, World Peace and Diplomacy Forum, International Biographical Centre, 2003; Deputy Director General for Oceania, IBC, 2004. Address: 26 Second Avenue, Claremont, WA 6010, Australia.

LONG Derek Albert, b. 11 August 1925, Gloucester, England. Scientist; Author; Antiquarian. m. Moira Hastings (Gilmore), 3 sons. Education: MA, D Phil, Jesus College, Oxford. Appointments: Fellow, University of Minnesota, USA, 1949-50; Research Fellow, Spectroscopy, University of Oxford, 1950-55; Lecturer, Senior Lecturer, Reader in Chemistry, University College, Swansea, 1956-66; Professor of Structural Chemistry, 1966-92, Professor Emeritus, 1992-, Chairman of the Board of Physical Sciences, 1976-79, Director, Molecular Spectroscopy Unit, 1982-88, University of Bradford; OECD Travelling Fellow, Canada and USA, 1964; Leverhulme Research Fellow, 1970-71; Visiting Professor: Reims, Lille, Bordeaux, Paris, Bologna, Florence, Keele; Chairman, Second International Conference on Raman Spectroscopy, Oxford, 1970; Co-Director, NATO Advanced Studies Institute, Bad Winsheim, 1982; Member, Italian-UK Mixed Commission for Implementation of Cultural Convention, 1985; Vice Chairman, Euro Laboratory for Non-Linear Spectroscopy, Florence, 1986-92; Founder, Editor, Editor-in-Chief, Emeritus Editor, 2000-, Journal of Raman Spectroscopy. Publications: Books (sole author): Raman Spectroscopy, 1977; The Raman Effect, 2002; Books (joint editor): Essays in Structural Chemistry, 1971; Specialist Periodical Reports in Molecular Spectroscopy (vols 1-6), 1973-79; Non-Linear Raman Spectroscopy and Its Chemical Applications, 1988; Proceedings Eleventh International Conference on Raman Spectroscopy, 1988; About 200 papers in scientific journals relating to Raman Spectroscopy; Other papers: Sevres Service des Arts Industriels, 1997; The Goodmanham Plane, 2002. Honours: Fellow, Royal Society of Chemistry, Chartered Chemist; Foreign Member, Lincei Academy, Rome, Italy; Honorary, Docteur es Sciences, Reims, France. Membership: Oxford and Cambridge Club. Address: 19 Hollingwood Rise, Ilkley, W Yorks, LS29 9PW, England. E-mail: profdalong@debrett.net

LONG Lynn Lamberton, b. 1 February 1949, Orlando, Florida, USA. Professor; Therapist. m. Richard Long, 2 sons. Education: MA, 1982; EdS, 1988; PhD, 1992; Marriage and Family Therapy, Counsellor Education. Appointment: Chair, Department of

Counsellor Education, Stetson University, Florida. Publications: Co-author: Counselling and Therapy for Couples, 1998; Sexuality Counselling for Couples, 2005. Honours: Outstanding Alumni Award, Rollins College. Address: 4138 Pecan Lane, Orlando, FL 32812-7993, USA. E-mail: llongphd@aol.com

LONGFORD Countess of, (Elizabeth Pakenham), b. 30 August 1906, London, England. Author. m. F A Pakenham, 1931, deceased 2001, 4 sons, 3 daughters. Education: MA, Lady Margaret Hall, Oxford. Publications: Points for Parents, 1956; Catholic Approaches (editor), 1959; Jameson's raid, 1960, new edition, 1982; Victoria RI, 1964; Wellington: Years of the Sword, 1969; Wellington: Pillar of State, 1972; The Royal House of Windsor, 1974; Churchill, 1974; Byron's Greece, 1975; Life of Byron, 1976; A Pilgrimage of Passion: The Life of Wilfrid Scawen Blunt, 1979; Louisa: Lady in Waiting (editor), 1979; Images of Chelsea, 1980; The Queen Mother: A Biography, 1981; Eminent Victorian Women, 1981; Elizabeth R, 1983; The Pebbled Shore (autobiography), 1986; The Oxford Book of Royal Anecdotes (editor), 1989; Darling Loosy: Letters to Princess Louise 1856-1939 (editor), 1991; Poet's Corner: An Anthology (editor), 1992; Royal Throne: The Future of the Monarchy, 1993. Honours: James Tait Black Memorial Prize for Non-Fiction, 1964; Yorkshire Post Prize, 1969; Honorary DLitt, Sussex University, 1970; Commander of the Order of the British Empire, 1974. Membership: Women Writers and Journalists, honorary life president, 1979-. Address: 18 Chesil Court, Chelsea Manor Street, London SW3 5QP, England.

LONGLEY Adrian Reginald, 27 September 1925, Harrogate, Yorkshire, England. m. Sylvia Margaret, 3 daughters. Education: MA (Honours), History, Trinity College, Cambridge, 1947-49; Law School, 1955-58. Appointments: Military Service, Rifle Brigade, 1944-47, Middle East, 1946-47, Acting Captain, 1947; School Master, Aysgarth, Yorkshire, Copthorne, Sussex; Solicitor, Freshfields, London, 1959-69; Associate, White Brooks & Gilman, Solicitors, Winchester, 1970-72; Legal Adviser, National Council for Voluntary Organisations, 1972-90; Consultant to various charities including: Campaign to Protect Rural England (formerly Council for the Protection of Rural England), Memorial Gates Trust, 1998-; Consultant to Arlingtons Sharmas Solicitors London, 1992-. Publications: Contributions to: Law Society Gazette; Solicitors' Journal; Sunday Times; CAF/ICFM Fund Raising Series; Charities: The Law and Practice (Sweet and Maxwell); Butterworth's Encyclopaedia of Forms and Precedents; ACSA Charities Administration Manual; Charity Law and Practice Review; Charity Finance Handbook. Honour: OBE, 1991.Memberships: Trustee: Cyril Wood Memorial Trust; Menerva Educational Trust; Russian European Trust; Committee Member: Goodman Committee on Charity Law and Voluntary Organisations, 1974-76; NCVO Committees on Malpractice in Fundraising for Charity, Report, 1986; Effectiveness and the Voluntary Sector, Report, 1990; Standards Committee, Institute of Fundraising, 1991-; Honorary Fellow, Institute of Fundraising; Member of the Law Society; Royal Commonwealth Society; Cavalry and Guards Club; MCC. Address: c/o Arlingtons Sharmas, 6 Arlington Street, St James's, London SW1A 1RE, England. E-mail: arl@arlingtons.co.uk

LONGMAN (James Edward) Ford, b. 8 December 1928, Watford, Hertfordshire, England. Doctor. m. Dilys Menai, 2 sons, 3 daughters. Education: BSc, University of London; University of Leeds. Appointments: RAF Radar and Wireless School and Education Branch, 1947-49; Ministry of Health, Board of Control and Office Ministry for Science, 1949-62; Honorary Secretary, Watford Council of Churches and Lay Preacher, 1950-62; Assistant Director, Joseph Rowntree Memorial Trust, 1962-70; Director, Social Services, Yorkshire (Regional) Council and 7 other regional bodies, 1970-75; Member, Lord Chancellor's Advisory Committee on Crown Courts; Chairman of the Board, HM Borstal, Wetherby; Chairman, All-Party United World Trust for Education and Research; Executive Member, National Peace Council and NCSS; Member, Yorkshire and Humberside Regional Economic Planning Council, 1965-72; Founder and Director, Community Development Trust, 1968-76; HM Inspector of Community Education, 1975-83; County councillor, North Yorkshire, 1985-97; Deputy leader, Liberal Democrat Group, 1989-93; Member, Executive Committee, Association of CCs 1993-95. Honours: Life Fellow and Honorary Professor, Community Development, University of Victoria; Honorary DD; Honorary LLD; Honorary DPhil; FRAI; FREconS: FRGS; Baron Ordre Royal de la Couronne de Bohème; Knight Order of Holy Grail; Knight Commander, Lofsensichen Ursinius-orden; Knight Templar Order of Jerusalem. Memberships: Society of Friends; Local Preacher, Methodist Church; Green Democrats; Liberal Democrat Christian Forum; Vice-chairman and chaplain, Ryedale Motor Neurone Disease Association. Joint Founder: Christian Industrial Leadership Schools; St Leonard's Housing Association, York Abbeyfield Society, Regional Studies Association. Address: Toby's Cottage, Slingsby, York YO62 4AH, England.

LONGMORE Andrew Centlivres, b. 25 August 1944, Liverpool, England. Judge. m. Margaret McNair, 1 son. Education: Lincoln College, Oxford. Appointments: Called to Bar, 1966; Queen's Counsel, 1983; Recorder of Crown Court, 1992; High Court Judge, 1993; Lord Justice of Appeal, 2001. Publications: Co-editor, 6th, 7th, 8th and 9th edition of MacGillirray's Law of Insurance. Honours: Knight, 1993; Privy Councillor, 2001. Memberships: Middle Temple, 1962-. Address: Royal Courts of Justice, London WC2A 2LL, England.

LONGO Jeannie Michèle Alice, b. 31 October 1958, Annecy, France. Cyclist. m. Patrice Ciprelli, 1985. Education: Institut d'Etudes Commerciales, Grenoble; University of Limoges. Career: French Cycling Champion, 1979-86; Winner, 13 world titles including World Champion, Road, 1985, 1987, World Champion, 1988, 1989, World Champion, Against the Clock, Spain, 1997; Winner, Tour of Colorado, 1987, 1987, Tour of Colombia, 1987, 1988, Tour of Norway, 1987, Tour de France, 1987; Silver Medal, World Track Race, 1987; Holder, several world records including World Record for 3 km, Covered Track, Grenoble, 1992; Winner, French Cycle Racing Championship, 1992; Silver Medallist, Olympic Games, Barcelona, 1992; Gold Medallist, Olympic Games, Atlanta, 1996; Consultant, France Télévision, 1999-. Honours: Médaille d'Or, La Jeunesse et des Sports; Medaille d'Or, Académie des Sports. Address: Fédération Française de Cyclisme, 5 rue de Rome, 93561 Rosny-sous-Bois, France.

LONGUET-HIGGINS Hugh Christopher, b. 11 April 1923, Lenham, Kent, England. Theoretical Chemist. Education: Doctorate, Balliol College, Oxford, 1947. Appointments: Research Fellow, Balliol College, 1947-48; Research Associate, University of Chicago, 1948-49; Lecturer, Reader, Theoretical Chemistry, Victoria University of Manchester, 1949-52; Professor of Theoretical Physics, King's College, London University, 1952-54; Fellow, Corpus Christi College and Professor of Theoretical Chemistry, Cambridge University, 1954-67; Royal Society Research Professor, 1968-74, Sussex University, 1974-89; Professor Emeritus, 1989-, Edinburgh University. Developed the application of precise mathematical analyses to chemical problems. Publications: The Nature of Mind, 1972; Mental Processes, 1987; About 200 papers in scientific journals. Honours: Honorary Fellow, Balliol College, Oxford; Honorary Fellow, Wolfson College, Cambridge; Dr hc, York, 1973, Essex, 1981, Bristol, 1983, Sussex, 1989, Sheffield, 1995. Memberships: Foreign Member, American

Dictionary of International Biography

Academy of Arts and Sciences; Foreign Associate, NAS; Life Fellow, Corpus Christi College, Cambridge. Address: Centre for Research on Perception and Cognition, Laboratory of Experimental Psychology, University of Sussex, Falmer, Brighton, BN1 9QG, England.

LOPEZ Jennifer, b. 24 July 1970, Bronx, New York. Actress; Dancer; Singer. m. (1) Ojani Noa, 1997, (2) Cris Judd, 2001, (3) Marc Anthony, 2004. Appointments: Album: On the 6; J Lo, 2001; Film appearances include: My Little Girl, 1996; My Family – Mia Familia, 1995; Money Train, 1995; Jack, 1996; Blood and Wine, 1996; Anaconda, 1997; Selena, 1997; U-Turn, 1997; Out of Sight, 1998; Thieves, 1999; Pluto Nash, 1999; The Cell, 2000; The Wedding Planner, 2000; Angel Eyes, 2001; Enough, 2002; Maid in Manhattan, 2002; Gigli, 2003; TV appearances include: Second Chances; Hotel Malibu; Nurses on the Line; The Crash of Flight 7. Honours: Golden Globe, 1998; MTV Movie Award, 1999. Address: United Talent Agency, 9560 Wilshire Boulevard, 5th Floor, Beverley Hills, CA 90212, USA.

LOPEZ GARCIA Angel, b. Madrid, Spain. Telecommunication Engineer. m. Maria Del Mar, 2 daughters. Education: Telecommunication Engineer, ETSIT, Madrid, Spain, 1980-1986. Appointments: Systems Analyst, Siemens S A, 1986-1989; Project Leader, Sener S A, 1989-1991; Project Leader, Indra Sistemas S A, 1991-. Honours: Graduate with honours, Telecommunication Engineering. Address: Caleruega, 73, 28033, Madrid, Spain. E-mail: algarcia@indra.es

LÓPEZ-COBOS Jesús, b. 25 February 1940, Toro, Spain. Orchestral Conductor. Education: DPhil, Madrid University; Composition, Madrid Conservatory; Conducting, Vienna Academy. Appointments: Worked with major orchestras including London Symphony, Royal Philharmonic, Philharmonia, Concertgebouw, Vienna Philharmonic, Vienna Symphony, Berlin Philharmonic, Hamburg NDR, Munich Philharmonic, Cleveland, Chicago Symphony, New York Philharmonic, Philadelphia, Pittsburgh; Conducted new opera productions at La Scala, Milan, Covent Garden, London, Metropolitan Opera, New York; General Musikdirektor, Deutsche Oper, Berlin, 1981-90; Principal Guest Conductor, London Philharmonic Orchestra, 1981-86; Principal Guest Conductor, Artistic Director, Spanish National Orchestra, 1984-89; Music Director, Cincinnati Symphony Orchestra, 1986-; Music Director, Lausanne Chamber Orchestra, 1990-2000; Orchestre Français des Jeunes, 1998-2001. Publications: Recordings including: Bruckner symphonies; Haydn symphonies; Donizetti's Lucia di Lammermoor; Rossini's Otello; Recital discs with José Carreras. Honours: 1st Prize, Besançon International Conductors Competition, 1969; Prince of Asturias Award, Spanish Government, 1981; Founders Award, American Society of Composers, Authors and Publishers, 1988; Cross of Merit, 1st Class, Federal Republic of Germany, 1989. Address: c/o Terry Harrison Artists, The Orchard, Market Street, Charlbury, Oxon OX7 3PJ, England.

LOPUSHANSKAYA Sophiya P, b. 16 March 1926, Poltava, Ukraine. Professor of Linguistics. Widow, 1 son. Education: Russian Philology, Moscow State University, 1950; Candidate of Science, Russian Philology, Leningrad State Pedagogical Institute; PhD, Philology, Moscow State Pedagogical Institute, 1976. Appointments: Director, Academical Research Institute of Russian Language History, Volgograd State University, Russia; Member of Presidium of Head Council in Philology, Commissioner in Co-ordination Council, Ministry of Education, Russian Federation. Publications: 174 publications (10 books) include: Development and Functioning of Old Russian Verb, 1990; The History of Course Book of the Russian Language, 1998; Cyril and Methodius

Traditions in Russia at the End of the 20th Century, 1999. Honours: Doctor of Philology; PhD; Academician of Humanitarian Academy of Liberal Arts; Honorary Scientist of the Russian Federation; Medals: Labour Veteran, USSR, 1987; Honourable Worker of High Professional Education in Russia; "A S Pushkin" for Efforts in Propagation of Russian, International Association of Teaching Russian Language and Literature, 1996. Memberships: Co-ordination Council of Testing Russian Language Proficiency of Foreign Students, Ministry of Education, Russian Federation. Address: Tulaka St, 2-68, Volgograd 400119, Russia. E-mail: sophiya.lopushanskaya@volsu.ru

LOREN Sophia, b. 20 September 1934, Rome, Italy. Actress. m. Carlo Ponti, 1957 (marriage annulled 1962, m. 1966), 2 sons. Education: Scuole Magistrali Superiori. Appointments: First Screen Appearance, as an extra in Quo Vadis; Appeared in many Italian and other Films including: E Arrivato l'Accordatore, 1951; Africa sotto i Mari (first leading role); La Tratta delle Bianche, La Favorita, 1952; Aida, 1953; Il Paesedei Campanelli, Miseria e Nobilta, Il Segno di Venere, 1953; Tempi Nostri, 1953; Carosello Napoletano, 1953; L'Oro di Napoli, 1954; Attila, 1954; Peccatoche sia una canaglia, la Bella Mugnaia, La Donna del Fiume, 1955; Boccaccio, 1970; Matromonio All; Italiana; American Films include: The Pride and the Passion, 1955; Boy on a Dolphin, Ledgend of the Lost, 1956; Desire Under the Elms, 1957; That Kind of Woman, 1958; Houseboat, 1958; The Key, 1958; The Black Orchid, 1959; The Millionairess, 1961; Two Women, 1961; El Cid, 1961; Yesterday, Today and Tomorrow, 1963; The Fall of the Roman Empire, 1964; Lady L, 1965; Judith, 1965; A Countess from Hong Kong, 1965; Arabesque, 1966; More than a Miracle, 1967; The Priest's Wife, 1970; Sunflower, 1970; Man of La Mancha, 1972; Brief Encounter, (TV), 1974; The Verdict, 1974; The Cassandra Crossing, 1977; A Special Day, 1977; Firepower, 1978; Brass Target, 1979; Blood Feud, 1981; Mother Courage, 1986; Two Women, 1989; Pret a Porter, 1995; Grumpier Old men; Chair, National Alliance for Prevention and Treatment of Child Abuse and Maltreatment. Publications: Eat with Me, 1972; Sophia Loren on Women and Beauty, 1984. Honours: Venice Festival Award for the Black Orchid, 1958; Cannes Film Festival Award for Best Actress, 1961; Honorary Academy Award, 1991; Chevalier Legion d'Honneur; Goodwill Ambassador for Refugees, 1992. Address: Chalet Daniel, Burgenstock, Luzern, Switzerland.

LORENTZEN Bent, b. 11 February 1935, Stenvad, Denmark. Composer. m. Edith Kaerulf Moeller, 2 August 1958, 1 son, 3 daughter. Education: Royal Academy of Music, Copenhagen, 1960. Career includes: Performances throughout Europe of works including Euridice, Die Music kommt mit äusserst bekannt vor!, Eine Wundersame Liebesgeschichte, Stalten Mette, Toto, Fackeltanz, Samba, Pianoconcerto Nordic Music Days, Saxophone Concerto, two choral songs to Enzensberger, 1991, Bill and Julia (opera), The Magic Brilliant, (The Danish National Opera), 1993; The Scatterbrain (Royal Theatre), 1995; Pergolesi's Home Service; Carnaval. Compositions include: Quadrata; Purgatorio, choral; Granite; Quartz; Syncretism; Quartetto Barbaro; Wunderblumen; Flamma; Zauberspiegel; Dunkerblau; Farbentiegel; Blütenweiss; Contours; Colori; Concerto for oboe; Cello Concerto; Hunting Concerto; Double Concerto; Samba; Paradiesvogel; Graffiti; Carnaval; Purgatorio; Ich bin eine Rose; 3 Madrigals; 5 Motets; Genesis; Canon I-V for 2 accordeons; New Choral Dramatics; Ammen Dammen Des; 9 east pieces for Strings, 2002; Round; Spirals; Circles; 5 easy Piano Pieces, Flood of Paradise; Olof Palme for mixed choir; Comics; 3 Latin Suites; Venezia; Tordenskiold; Der Steppenwolf, opera, 2000; Fourteen Danish Love songs, 2003; Stabat Mater, 2001; Circus, 2002. Recordings include: 5 easy Piano Pieces; The Bottomless Pit; Visions; Cloud-Drift; Mambo, Intersection, Puncti, Triplex, Groppo, Nimbus, Cruor, Goldranken;

Nachtigall; Abgrund; Die Musik kommt mir äusserst bekannt vor!; Syncretism; A Wonderous Love Story; Sol; Luna; Mars; Mercurius; Jupiter; Venus; Saturnus; Umbra, Colori, Paesaggio, Dunkelblau, Round, Cyclus I-IV; Piano and oboe concertos; Regenbogen; Comics; Lines; Tears; Orfeo Suite; Intrada; Alpha and Omega; Comics; Stabat Mater; Fanfare I and II; Umbra. Publications: Ej Sikkelej, 1967; Recorder System, 1962-64; Musikens AHC, 1969; Mer om Musiken, 1972; Introduction to Electronic Music, 1969. Honours: Prix Italia, 1970; First prize, Nyon Film Festival, 1973, as well as awards in Poland, Austria, and Messiaen-prize, Bergamo, 1988; Composer of the Year, 1990; Recording Award 1991 for Piano Concerto; Carl Nielsen Award, 1995; Finalist in A New Opera for Prague, 2000; Composer's Prize (Edition Wilhelm Hansen). Memberships: Danish Composers Society. Address: Sotoften 37, 2820 Genofte, Denmark.

LORENZ Kuno, b. 17 September 1932, Vachdorf, Germany. University Teacher. m. Karin Lindemann, 21 December 1965, 2 sons. Education: Staatsexamen: Mathematics, Physics, Bonn, 1957; DrPhil, Philosophy, Kiel, 1961; Habilitation: Philosophy, Erlangen-Nuremberg, 1969. Appointments: Visiting Fellow, Princeton University, 1957-58; Professor, Philosophy, University of Hamburg, 1970-74; University of Saarland, Saarbrucken, 1974-; Emeritus, 1998-. Publications: Elemente der Sprachkritik, 1970; Co-author, Dialogische Logik, 1978; Einfuhrung in die Philosophische Anthropologie, 1990; Indische Denker, 1998. Memberships: Academia Europaea, 1992-. Address: Fachrichtung 3.1, Universitat des Saarlandes, D-66041, Saarbrucken, Germany.

LOUBSER J A (Bobby), b. 25 July 1949, Cape Town, South Africa. Dean; Professor. m. Minnie Le Roux, 3 sons, 1 daughter. Education: Licentate in Theology, MA in Classical Greek, Doctor of Theology, University of Stellenbosch. Appointments: Minister of Religion, 1978-89; Head of Department, Professor in New Testament, 1990-; Dean of Faculty, 2003-. Publications: Author, 3 academic books and 10 popular books; 2 chapters in academic books; Numerous academic articles in professional journals. Honours: Travel Award, Senate of the University of Zululand, 1995; Centre for Science Development Research Award, 1995; National Research Foundation of South Africa, Overseas Study Award, 2000. Memberships: Association for the Study of Religion in South Africa; New Testament Society of South Africa; Biblical studies Society of South Africa; Theological Society of South Africa; South African Academy for Science and Art; South African Association for Conflict Intervention; South African Academy of Religion; Society for Biblical Literature; American Academy of Religion. Address: PO Box 128, Mtunzini 3867, KZN, South Africa. Website: www.uzulu.ac.za/the/the.htm

LOUIS Alan, b. 23 November 1965, South Africa. Entrepreneur. m. Almie Louis, 2 sons. Education: B Com, 1st Class Honours, 1988; M Com, Cum Laude, 1989; PhD, Commerce, 1993. Appointments: Chief Executive Officer, The Louis Group of Companies which has in excess of 60 international subsidiary companies and manages in excess of 800 international corporate companies. Publications: South Africa's Blue Book of Business; Today Magazine, Business Academy; Monthly articles in Cape Times. Honours: PhD, Commerce; Chief Executive Officer of South Africa's Leading Companies; Gold Medallist, South African Ironman; Top Business Manager and Business Mentor; Listed in Who's who publications and biographical dictionaries. Membership: South Africa's Estate Agency Group; IATA Address: Louis Group Building, 2 Boundary Road, Century City, Cape Town 7441, South Africa. E-mail: alan@louisgroupint.com Website: www.louisgroupint.com

LOUISY Calliopa Pearlette, b. 8 June 1946, St Lucia, West Indies. Governor General. Education: BA, University of the West Indies, 1969; MA, Laval University, 1975; PhD, University of Bristol, 1994. Appointments: Principal, St Lucia A Level College, 1981-86; Dean, 1986-94, Vice Principal, 1994-95, Principal, 1996-97, Sir Arthur Lewis Community College; Governor General, 1997. Publications: The Changing Role of the Small State in Higher Education; Globalisation and Comparative Education: A Caribbean Perspective; Nation Languages and National Development in the Caribbean: Reclaiming Our Own Voices. Honours: Student of the Year, 1968; Grand Cross of the Order of St Lucia, 1997; International Woman of the Year, 1998, 2001; Grand Cross of the Order of St Michael and St George, 1999; Honorary Degree of Doctor of Law (LL.D) University of Bristol, 1999 and University of Sheffield; Dame of Grace of the Most Venerable Order of the Hospital of St John of Jerusalem, 2001; Listed in International Biographical Dictionaries. Membership: Fellow, Royal Society of Arts, 2000. Address: Government House, Morne Fortune, Castries, St Lucia, West Indies.

LOUSADA Peter Allen, b. 30 March 1937, Amesbury, Wiltshire, England. Businessman. m. Jane Gillmor, 2 sons, 1 daughter. Appointments: Pilot Officer, RAF, National Service, Canada, 1956-58; Advertising and Marketing, Unilever group companies Lintas, Gibbs, 1958-64; Director, Middle East, Bristol-Myers International Inc, Teheran, 1965-69; Vice President, Canada Dry Corporation, including operations in Africa and Europe, 1970-86; Director, Schweppes International, 1986-90; Chairman, Cadbury Schweppes, Portugal, 1988; Supervisory Board Apollinaris and Schweppes, 1988-90; Vice President, Cadbury Beverages Europe, 1986-90, Board of Management, BSDA, 1988-96; Founder Member, International Soft Drinks Council, Washington DC, 1994-95; Director, UNESDA-CISDA, 1988-95; Elected President, Berlin, 1990; Senior Vice President, Cadbury Beverages, 1990-96; Chairman, Faraday Consulting, 1997-2003; Non-Executive Chairman, Canadean Ltd, 1997-2003; Commander, St John Ambulance, 1999-, Deputy Lieutenant, 2003-, Bedfordshire. Memberships: Honorary Member, BSDA; Honorary Member, UNESDA-CISDA; Woburn Golf Club; RAF Club. Address: Well Cottage, Bow Brickhill, Milton Keynes, MK17 9JU, Buckinghamshire, England.

LOVE Courtney, b. 1965. Singer; Musician (guitar); Actress. m. Kurt Cobain, 24 February 1992, deceased, 1 daughter. Career: Member, Faith No More, 1 year; Founder, singer/guitarist, Hole, 1991-; Tours include: Support tour to Nine Inch Nails; Reading Festival, 1994, 1995; Film appearances: Straight To Hell; Sid And Nancy; Feeling Minnesota; The People vs Larry Flynt; Man on the Moon; Beat, 2000; Julie Johnson, 2001; Trapped, 2002. Recordings: Albums: Pretty On The Inside, 1991; Live Through This, 1994; Celebrity Skin, 1998. Singles: Doll Parts, 1994; Ask for It, 1995; Celebrity Skin, 1998; Malibu, 1998; Awful, 1999. Address: c/o Q-Prime Inc, 729 7th Avenue, 14th Floor, New York, NY 10019, USA.

LOVELL (Alfred Charles) Bernard (Sir), b. 31 August 1913, Oldland Common, Gloucestershire, England. Professor of Radio Astronomy Emeritus; Writer. m. Mary Joyce Chesterman, 1937, deceased 1993, 2 sons, 3 daughters. Education: University of Bristol. Appointments: Professor of Radio Astronomy, 1951-80, Professor Emeritus, 1980-, University of Manchester; Director, Jodrell Bank Experimental Station, later Nuffield Radio Astronomy Laboratories, 1951-81; Various visiting lectureships. Publications: Science and Civilisation, 1939; World Power Resources and Social Development, 1945; Radio Astronomy, 1951; Meteor Astronomy, 1954; The Exploration of Space by Radio, 1957; The Individual and the Universe, 1958; The Exploration of Outer Space, 1961;

Discovering the Universe, 1963; Our Present Knowledge of the Universe, 1967; The Explosion of Science: The Physical Universe (editor with T Margerison), 1967; The Story of Jodrell Bank, 1968; The Origins and International Economics of Space Exploration, 1973; Out of the Zenith, 1973; Man's Relation to the Universe, 1975; P M S Blackett: A Biographical Memoir, 1976; In the Centre of Immensities, 1978; Emerging Cosmology, 1981; The Jodrell Bank Telescopes, 1985; Voice of the Universe, 1987; Pathways to the Universe (with Sir Francis Graham Smith), 1988; Astronomer By Chance (autobiography), 1990; Echoes of War, 1991. Contributions to: Professional journals. Honours: Officer of the Order of the British Empire, 1946; Duddell Medal, 1954; Royal Medal, 1960; Knighted, 1961; Ordre du Mérite pour la Recherche et l'Invention, 1962; Churchill Gold Medal, 1964; Gold Medal, Royal Astronomical Society, 1981; Many honorary doctorates. Memberships: American Academy of Arts and Sciences, honorary foreign member; American Philosophical Society; International Astronomical Union, vice-president, 1970-76; New York Academy; Royal Astronomical Society, president, 1969-71; Royal Society, fellow; Royal Swedish Academy, honorary member. Address: The Quinta, Swettenham, Cheshire CW12 2LD, England.

LOVELL Walter Benjamin, b. 7 January 1947, Cottonwood, Arizona, USA. Teacher; Director of Bands. m. Karen Lynn Bird, 1 son, 5 daughters. Education: AA, Eastern Arizona College, 1966; BME, 1969, MM, 1975, Northern Arizona University; PhD, Music Education, Hamilton University, 2001. Appointments: Director of Bands, Kingman High School, Arizona, 1968-70; Assistant Director of Bands, Phoenix Union High School, 1970-71; Director of Bands: Carl Hayden High School, Phoenix, Arizona, 1971-73; Mohave High School, Bullhead City, Arizona, 1973-78; Elko High School, Nevada, 1978-; Conductor of competitive performances with Elko High School Band including: University of Nevada-Las Vegas Band Competition, 1988 Weber State University, Ogden, Utah, 1990-97, 2002; University of Utah, 1995; Boise State University, Idaho, 1990-97; Presidential Inaugural Parade, Washington, 1981; North Nevada Youth Band Tour of Great Britain, 1982; Fiesta Bowl Parade, Phoenix, 1985; Hollywood Christmas Parade, 2002; Associate Director, All Arizona Bi-Centennial Band, 1976. Compositions: For concert bands: Suite for Band, 1975; Tranquillity, 1988; For jazz bands: Maybe Tuesday, 1974; Sunday Afternoon, 1987. Honours include: Gubernatorial Proclamation for Elko High School Band, 1981, 1983, 1986, 1988, 1990, 1992, 1994, 1996, 1998; Proclaimed The Pride of Nevada, 1995, 1996, 2000; Proclaimed Nevada's Musical Ambassador, 1998, 2000; National School Band Achievement Awards, 1981, 1982; Distinguished Service Award, Nevada-Reno Bands, 1986; Distinguished Bandmaster of America Award, 1981; Nevada State Marching Band Champion Award, 1983-86, 1992-94, 1997, 1999, 2001; Nevada Music Educator of the Year, 1999; Nevada Broadcasters Hall of Fame, 2001; Class AA Regional Champion, 2001. Memberships: National Band Association (Citation of Excellence, 1987); Nevada Music Educators Association; Music Educators National Conference; Nevada Music Educators Association; International Association of Jazz Educators. Address: 940 West Sage Street, Elko, NV 89801-2763, USA. E-mail: bandguy@frontiernet.net

LOWE Gordon, b. 31 May 1933, Halifax, England. University Professor. m. Gwynneth Hunter, 2 sons. Education: BSc, ARCS, 1954, PhD, DIC, 1957, Royal College of Science, Imperial College, London University; MA, Oxford University, 1960. Appointments: University Demonstrator, 1959-65, Weir Junior Research Fellow, University College, 1959-61, Official Fellow, Tutor in Organic Chemistry, Lincoln College, 1962-99, University Lecturer, 1965-88, Sub-Rector, Lincoln College, 1986-89, Aldrichian Praelector in Chemistry, 1988-89, Professor of Biological Chemistry, 1989-

2000, Emeritus Professor of Biological Chemistry, Supernumerary Fellow, 2000-, Oxford University; Director, Founder, Scientific Consultant, Pharminox Ltd, 2002-. Publications: Around 240 articles in learned journals. Honours: CChem, FRSC, 1981; Charmian Medal for Enzyme Chemistry, Royal Society of Chemistry, 1983; FRS, 1984; DSc, Oxon, 1985; Royal Society of Chemistry Award for Stereochemistry, 1992. Memberships: Fellow, Royal Society, London; Fellow, Royal Society of Chemistry, London. Address: 17 Norman Avenue, Abingdon, Oxfordshire, OX14 2HQ, England. E-mail: gordon.lowe@chem.ox.ac.uk

LOXLEY Thomas Edward, b. 20 January, 1940, Pennsylvania, USA. Engineering Scientist. Education: BS, Engineering Science, Case Institute of Technology, 1961; Postgraduate work in energy conservation, systems analysis, structural design, hydraulics, geophysics and oceanography. Appointments: Mechanical Engineer, Naval Weapons Laboratory, 1961-65; Mechanical Engineer, Watervliet Arsenal, 1965-68; Systems Engineer, International Hydrodynamics Ltd, 1968-69; President, Manned Submersible System Co, 1969-71; Mechanical Engineer, Naval Surface Weapons Centre, 1971-75; Assistant Professor, Virginia Polytechnic Institute and State University, 1975-78; Founded, Inverted Cave Education, 1978. Publications: 5 books; several professional papers. Honours: Recognition by US National Bureau of Standards, 1980; 1 patent. Memberships: International Council for Building Research Studies and Documentation; American Society of Heating, Refrigeration and Air-Conditioning Engineers. Address: Inverted Cave Education, 680 Canal Street, No 402, Beaver, PA 15009, USA. E-mail: proftloxley@yahoo.com

LOYD Francis Alfred (Sir), b. 5 September 1916, Berkhamsted, England. Colonial Service Officer. m. (1) Katharine Layzell, deceased 1981, 2 daughters, (2) Monica Murray Brown. Education: Trinity College, Oxford, England. Appointments: Appointed to Colonial Service, 1938; District Officer, Kenya, 1939; Military Service, East Africa, 1940-42; Private Secretary to Governor of Kenya, 1942-45; District and Provincial Commissioner, 1945-62; Commonwealth Fund Fellowship to USA, 1953-54; Permanent Secretary, Governor's Office, 1962-63; H.M. Commissioner for Swaziland, 1964-68; Director, London House for Overseas Graduates, 1969-79; Chairman, Oxfam Africa Committee, 1979-85. Honours: MBE, 1951; OBE, 1954; CMG, 1961; KCMG, 1965. Memberships: Vincent's Club (Oxford). Address: 53 Park Road, Aldeburgh, Suffolk IP15 5EN, England.

LOYOLA Angel Miguel, b. 12 June 1948, Yauco, Puerto Rico, USA. Doctor of Medicine. m. Melba Santos, 2 sons, 3 daughters. Education: BS, Chemistry, Catholic University of Puerto Rico, 1968; Doctor in Medicine, University of Puerto Rico School of Medicine, 1979. Appointments: Private Practitioner, Internal Medicine, 1983-; Active Faculty Member, Damas Hospital, Ponce, Hospital Metropolitano, 1983-; Physician Advisor, PSRO Ponce, 1984; Medical Director, CMS Yauco, 1984-86; Medical Education Director, Yauco Hospital, 1985-87; Medical Director, Union Carbide Caribe, 1990-95; President, Medical Faculty, Bella Vista Hospital, 1998-2000; Instructor, Internal Medicine, Ponce School of Medicine, 2000-; Co-ordinator, Internal Medicine, Pontificia Universidad Catolica Madre y Maestra, 2000-. Memberships: American College of Physicians Executives; American Society of Internal Medicine; American College of Medicine; American Geriatric Society; American College of Physicians & Surgeons; Sociedad Médica del Sur. Address: PO Box 3048, Yauco, PR 00698, USA.

LU Ruihua, b. 26 December 1938, Chaozhou, Guangdong, China. Professor. m. Ying Wei, 1 son, 1 daughter. Education: Bachelor of Science, Physics, 1963, Master of Science, Molecular

Dictionary of International Biography

Spectroscopy, 1966, Zhongshan (Sun Yat-sen) University, Guangzhou, China. Appointments: Factory Director, Foshan Analytical Instrument Factory, 1983; Mayor of Foshan City, Guangdong, China, 1985-91; Executive Vice-Governor of Guangdong, 1991-96; Governor of Guangdong, 1996-2003; Member of Standing Committee of 10th National People's Congress of People's Republic of China; Professor, Supervisor of PhD Students and Honorary Dean, School of Business, Zhongshan (Sun Yat-sen) University, Guangzhou, China, 2003-. Publications: To Build A City Using Technology, 1986; Inspiration From Option Theory, 1998; Dialogues With Economic Advisors included in The Foreign Consultants' Brainstorming (1), (11), (111), International Consultative Conference on the Future Economic Development of Guangdong Province, 2000, 2001 and 2002. Honours: National Outstanding Achievement Award in Mechanical Industry, China, 1978; Award for Contribution to the Chinese International Management Programme, Fontainebleau, Insead Euro-Asia Centre, France, 1983; Honorary Fellow, Universita deli Studi di Ferrara, Italy, 2001. Address: Office of the People's Government of Guangdong Province, Guangzhou, Guangdong, People's Republic of China. E-mail: lrh_gd@hotmail.com

LUBETZKI Isabelle Korn, b. 3 December 1951, Paris, France. Medical Doctor. m. Marcel Korn, 2 sons, 1 daughter. Education: MD, University of Paris V, France, 1976; Specialist in Neurology, Israel, 1984; MD, Israel, 1992. Appointment: Head of the Neurological Service, Bikur Cholim Hospital, Jerusalem, Israel, 1990-. Memberships: Corresponding Member, American Academy of Neurology; Israeli Paediatric Neurology Association; Israeli Neurological Association. Address: Neurological Service, Bikur Cholim Hospital, 5 Strauss Street, POB 492, Jerusalem 91004, Israel. E-mail: kl@md.huji.ac.il

LUCAS George, b. 14 May 1944, Modesto, California, USA. Film Director. Education: University of South California. Appointments: Warner Brothers Studio; Assistant to Francis Ford Cappola, The Rain People; Director, Documentary on making The Rain People; Formed, Lucasfilm Ltd; Director, Co-Author, Screenplay Films THX-1138, 1970; American Graffiti, 1973; Director, Author, Star Wars, 1977; Director, Author, To Prequel The Phantom Menace, 1999; Executive Producer, More American Graffiti, 1979; The Empire Strikes Back, 1980; Raiders of the Lost Ark, 1981; Return of the Jedi, 1982; Indiana Jones and the Temple of Doom, 1984; Howard the Duck, 1986; Labyrinth, 1988; Willow, 1988; Tucker: The Man and His Dream, 1988; Co-Executive Producer, Mishima, 1985; Indiana Jones and the Last Crusade, 1989; Star Wars Episode I: The Phantom Menace, 1999; Star Wars Episode II: Attack of the Clones, 2002; Executive Producer, The Young Indiana Jones Chronicles (TV series), 1992-93; Radioland Murders, 1994. Honours: Dr hc, University of South California, 1994; Irving Thalberg Award, 1992. Address: Lucasfilm Ltd, P O Box 2009, San Rafael, CA 94912, USA.

LUCAS Suzanne, b. 10 September 1915, Calcutta, India. Artist; Watercolourist; Miniaturist. m. Louis Lucas. Education: Grenoble, Munich and Edinburgh Universities; Language Studies, Rome, Florence, Venice; Reimann Schule (of Art), Berlin, Paris. Career: Exhibitions: Cooling Galleries, 1954; Sladmore Galleries, 1973; Mall Galleries, 1975, 1979; Liberty's Exhibition Hall, 1977; Annual Exhibition, Royal Horticultural Society; Royal Academy; Paris Salon; Royal Institute of Painters in Water Colour; Sponsored and Directed First World Exhibition of Miniatures, 1995; First Woman President of a Royal Society, Royal Society of Miniature Painters, Sculptors and Gravers, 1980-2004, Golden Jubilee Member, 1954-2004, presented Gold Memorial Bowl and Armorial Bearings as gifts to the society. Publications: Articles for Bonhams; In Praise of Toadstools Volumes I and II (large luxury editions, richly

illustrated); Articles in The Artist; The Royal Society of Miniature Painters, Sculptors and Gravers One Hundred Years. Honours: Medaille de la France Libre for War Services in Egypt; 13 Gold Medals for extensive paintings of botanical subjects, Royal Horticultural Society; Diploma of Merit, Università delli Arti, Italy; Hunting Group Prize Gold Memorial Bowl, 2000. Memberships: President, Royal Society of Miniature Painters, Sculptors and Gravers; Fellow, Linnean Society of London; Founder President, Society of Botanical Artists (started world-wide botanical movement in art); Royal Automobile Club. Address: Ladymead, Manor Road, Mere, Wiltshire BA12 6QH, England.

LUGOVETS Alexander A, b. 24 October 1946, Vladivostok, Russia. Shipping Industry Executive. m. Galina M Lugovets, 2 daughters. Education: Far Eastern Maritime Academy, 1970; Khabarovsk Higher Party School, 1982; Ministerial Academy of Economics, 1991; Doctor of Transportation, 2001. Appointments: Merchant Marine Officer, FESCO, 1970-75; Vladivostok City Council, 1978-81; FESCO Management, 1981-87; Vice President FESCO, 1987-97; First Vice Minister of Transportation, Russian Federation, 1997-2000; President, Chief Executive Officer, FESCO, 2000-; Philosophy Doctor, Engineering Sciences, Professor, Far Eastern maritime Academy, 2002-; Senior State Councillor, Russian Federation; 1997-. Publications include: Books: Shipping Company Management, Vladivostok, 2001; Sea Transport as a System in Russian Transportation, Moscow, 2003; 60 published scholarly and professional articles on shipping issues; 2 registered inventions. Honours: Order of Honour, Russian Federation; 6 professional medals. Memberships: President, Primorye Regional Society, Russia – Japan. Address: 78 Krasnogo Znameny Av, ap 60, Vladivostock 690014, Russia. E-mail: mico@vvo.ru

LUGTON Charles Michael Arber, b. 5 April 1951, Johannesburg, South Africa. Government Civil Servant. m. Elizabeth Joyce Graham, 2 sons. Education: St John's College, Johannesburg; The Edinburgh Academy; University of Edinburgh. Appointments: Private Secretary to Permanent Under Secretary of State, Scottish Office, 1976-78; Head of Branch, Police Division, 1978-83; Head of Town and Country Planning Policy Branch, 1983-87; Head of Public Health Division, 1988-90; Head of Criminal Justice and Licensing Division, Scottish Home and Health Department, 1990-95; Principal Private Secretary to the Secretary of State for Scotland, 1995-97; Director of Corporate Development, 1998-99; Head of Constitution and Parliamentary Secretariat, Scottish Executive, 1999-. Memberships: Governor, Merchiston Castle School, Edinburgh; Board Member, Civil Service Healthcare Society Limited. Address: Scottish Executive, St Andrew's House, Regent Road, Edinburgh EH1 3DG, Scotland. E-mail: michael.lugton@scotland.gov.uk

LUK FONG Yuk Yee Pattie, b. 16 August 1951, Hong Kong. Educator. m. Hing Sun Luk, 2 sons. Education: M Ed, University of Hong Kong, 1981; MA, Education, The Chinese University of Hong Kong, 1993; PhD, University of Canberra, Australia, 2002; Certificate of Family Therapy. Appointments: Graduate Mistress, Ming Kei College, 1973-78; Teaching Consultant, University of Hong Kong, 1978-80; Lecturer and Senior Lecturer of Granham College of Education, Hong Kong, 1980-87; Senior Lecturer, Sir Robert Black College of Education, Hong Kong, 1987-90; Senior and Principal Lecturer, Northcote College of Education, Hong Kong, 1990-95; Senior Lecturer, Hong Kong Institute of Education, Hong Kong, 1995-. Publications: Articles in professional journals include: Competing Contexts for Developing Personal and Social Education in Hong Kong, 2001; A search for new ways in describing parent-child relationships; voices from principals, teachers, guidance professionals, parents and pupils, forthcoming.

Dictionary of International Biography

Honours: Listed in Who's Who publications and biographical dictionaries. Memberships: American Counseling Association; Hong Kong Counselling Associations. Address: 10 Lo Ping Road, Tai Po, New Territories, Hong Kong.

LUKE Garry Alec, b. 19 February 1954, Aberdeen, Scotland. Research Scientist. m. Jane Knowles Murray. Education: BSc, Zoology, 1980, MSc, Biochemistry, 1986, PhD, Endocrinology, 1989, Faculty of Medicine, University of Aberdeen; MBA, Heriot-Watt University, Edinburgh, 1997; MA, University of St Andrews, 2000-. Appointments: Research Assistant, Department of Obstetrics and Gynaecology, University of Aberdeen, 1983-89; Research Fellow, Glasgow Dental Hospital and School, University of Glasgow, 1989-90; Research Fellow, School of Biomedical Sciences, University of St Andrews, 1990-. Publications: Numerous articles in scientific journals. Memberships: Institute of Biology; European Communities Biologists Association. Address: 5 Carr Crescent, Crail, Anstruther, Fife, KY10 3XR, Scotland. E-mail: garryluke@hotmail.com

LUKE William Ross, b. 8 October 1943, Glasgow, Scotland. Chartered Accountant. m. Deborah Jacqueline Gordon Luke, 3 daughters, 1 deceased. Appointment: Senior Partner, Luke, Gordon & Co, Chartered Accountants, 1983-. Honours: Metropolitan Police Commendation, 1983; Life Vice-President, London Scottish Rugby Football Club, 1995-. Memberships: Fellow, Institute of Chartered Accountants in England and Wales; Member, London Scottish Rugby Football Club; Member, Caledonian Society of London; Qualified Sub-Aqua Open Water Diver (PADI). Address: 105 Palewell Park, London SW14 8JJ, England.

LUKOSEVICIUS Viktoras, b. 9 August 1939, Kaunas, Lithuania. University Teacher. m. Emilija Lukoseviciene, 2 sons. Education: Diploma Engineer of Geodesy, Kaunas Polytechnical Institute, Lithuania, 1962; PhD, Engineering, Institute of Surveying, Aerial Photography and Cartography, Moscow, 1966; Associate Professor, Kaunas Polytechnical Institute, 1970. Appointments: Head of Basic Science Department, 1967-70, Head of Civil Engineering Department, 1970-81, KPI; Vice Dean and Associate Professor, Panevezys Faculty, Kaunas University of Technology, 1981-87, Head of Civil Engineering Department, Associate Professor and Faculty Council Chair of Panevezys Campus, Kaunas University of Technology, 1988-2001; Head of Civil Engineering Department, Associate Professor of Panevezys Institute, KTU, 2002-. Publications: Over 60 scientific articles; Participant in conferences in USA, Brazil, Sweden, Norway, Russia. Honours: Certificate, Governor of State of Ohio, USA for outstanding contribution of the continued success of the Columbus National Program, 1995; Fellowship Winner, NATO and Italy National Science Competition, 1996. Memberships: Senate Member, Kaunas University of Technology, 1992-2001; Council Member, KTU, Panevezys Institute, Faculty of Technology; International Association for Continuing Engineering Education; Association for the Advancement of Baltic Studies; Council Member, Lithuanian Liberal Society, 1992-2004; Candidate, Lithuanian Republic Parliament, 1992,1996; Board Member, Panevezys Department, Lithuanian Scientists Union; President, Panevezys Lithuanian and Swedes Society. Address: Statybininku 56-66, Lt 37348 Panevezys, Lithuania.

LULO Drita, b. 20 December 1954, Berlin, Germany. Project Engineer. 1 son. Education: Graduate, Civil Industrial Engineering, Faculty of Construction, 1977; Doctor of Technical Sciences, 1993. Appointments: Engineer, Tirana Engineering Works, Tirana, Albania, 1977-80; Project Engineer, Chief of Department, Institute of Building Technology Studies, 1981-92; Co-owner and Director, Technoprojekt Building Company, Tirana, 1993-2002.

Publications: Scientific articles in journals including: The Bulletin of Technical Sciences; The Bulletin of Economic Problems. Membership: Institute of Building Studies. Address: Str "Ismail Qemali" P. 27/1, Tirana, Albania.

LUMLEY Joanna, b. 1 May 1946, Kashmir, India. Actress. m. (1) Jeremy Lloyd, divorced, (2) Stephen Barlow, 1 son. Career: TV includes: Release; Comedy Playhouse; Satanic Rites of Dracula, 1973; Coronation Street; General Hospital, 1974-75; The New Avengers, 1976-77; Steptoe & Son; Are You Being Served?; Sapphire & Steel, 1978; Absolutely Fabulous, 1992-94, 1996, 2001; Class Act, 1994; Joanna Lumley in the Kingdom of the Thunder Dragon, 1997; Coming Home, 1998; A Rather English Marriage, 1998; Nancherrow; Dr Willoughby MD; Mirrorball, 1999; Giraffes on the Move, 2001; Up In Town, 2002; Films include: Some Girls Do; Tam Lin; The Breaking of Bumbo; Games That Lovers Play; Don't Just Lie There, Say Something; On Her Majesty's Secret Service; Trail of the Pink Panther; Curse of the Pink Panther; That Was Tory; Mistral's Daughter; A Ghost in Monte Carlo; Shirley Valentine; Forces Sweetheart; Innocent Lies; James and the Giant Peach; Cold Comfort Farm; Prince Valiant; Parting Shots; Mad Cows; Maybe Baby; The Cat's Meow; Ella Enchanted; Theatre includes: Blithe Spirit, 1986; Vanilla, 1990; The Letter, 1995; all in London. Publications: Stare Back and Smile, memoirs, 1989; Girl Friday, 1994; Joanna Lumley in the Kingdom of the Thunder Dragon, 1997. Honours: OBE; Hon DLitt, Kent, 1994; D University, Oxford Brookes, 2000; BAFTA Award, 1992, 1994; Special BAFTA, 2000. Address: c/o Caroline Renton, 23 Crescent Lane, London SW4, England.

LUMSDEN David (James) (Sir), b. 19 March 1928, Newcastle upon Tyne, England. Musician. m. Sheila Gladys Daniels, 28 July 1951, 2 sons, 2 daughters. Education: Selwyn College, Cambridge; MA, 1955; DPhil, 1957. Career: Fellow, Organist at New College Oxford; Rector, chori, Southwell Minster; Founder and Conductor of Nottingham Bach Society; Director of Music, Keele University; Visiting Professor at Yale University; Principal: Royal Scottish Academy of Music and Drama and Royal Academy of Music, London; Hugh Porter Lecturer at Union Theological Seminary, New York, 1967; Director, European Union Baroque Orchestra, 1985-. Publications: An Anthology of English Lute Music, 1954; Thomas Robinson's Schoole Musike 1603, 1971. Contributions to: The Listener; The Score; Music and Letters; Galpin Society Journal; La Luth et sa Musique; La musique de la Renaissance. Honours: Knight, 1985; Honorary Fellow, Selwyn College, Cambridge, 1986; Honorary DLitt, Reading, 1990; Honorary Fellow of Kings College, London, 1991; Honorary Fellow, New College, Oxford, 1996. Memberships: Incorporated Society of Musicians, President, 1984-85; Royal College of Organists, President, 1986-88; Incorporated Association of Organists, President, 1966-68; Honorary Editor, Church Music Society, 1970-73; Chairman, National Youth Orchestra of Great Britain, 1985-94; Chairman, Early Music Society, 1985-89; Board, Scottish Opera, 1977-83; Board, ENO, 1983-88. Address: Melton House, Soham, Cambridgeshire CB7 5DB, England.

LUNA Charita Abao, b. 3 September 1940, Tagatong, Carmen, Agusan Norte, Philippines. Teacher. m. Sisenando O Luna, 2 sons, 2 daughters. Education: BSE and AB, Mathematics, University of Bohol, Tagbilaran City, Philippines, 1964; MAT, Mathematics, Marikina Institute of Science and Technology, 1978; PhD, De La Salle University, Manila, 1989. Appointments: Instructor, 1972-84, Associate Professor, 1984-92, Professor, 1992-99, College Professor, 1999-, Mindano Polytechnic State College, Cagayan de Oro City, Philippines. Publications: Metacognitive Strategies in Simple Integral Calculus Problem Solving; Elementary and Secondary Mathematics Teachers Competency in Cagayan de Oro

Dictionary of International Biography

City; Mathematical Power and Communication; Effect of Seminar Workshop with Reward on Participant's Achievement Scores. Honours: Outstanding Faculty Member, 1984-85; Plaque of Recognition as Member of MPSC Board of Trustees, 1997-2002; Fulbright Scholarship Award, 1999; Plaque of Recognition in Science and Engineering, 2002-2003. Memberships: Mathematical Society of the Philippines; American Mathematical Society; National Council of Teachers of Mathematics; MAA; MSM; SIAM. Address: 29 Venus Street, Hillside Subdivision, Macasandig, Cagayan de Oro City 9000, Philippines. E-mail: charita.luna@eudoramail.com

LUNAN (Charles) Burnett, b. 28 September 1941, London, England. Medical Practitioner. m. Helen Russell Ferrie, 2 sons, 1 daughter. Education: MB ChB, 1965, MD, 1977, University of Glasgow. Appointments: Research Fellow, MRC Unit, Strathclyde University, UK, 1971-72; Lecturer, University of Aberdeen, UK, 1973-75; Senior Lecturer, University of Nairobi, Kenya, 1975-77; Consultant Obstetrician, Gynaecologist, North Glasgow University NHS Trust, 1977-; Consultant to WHO, Bangladesh, 1984-85; Short term Consultant to WHO, ODA, Bangladesh, 1988-94. Publications: Various chapters and articles on female sterilisation, infection in pregnancy, diabetes in pregnancy, Caesarean section, health care in the developing world. Honours: MRCOG, 1970, FRCOG, 1983, Royal College of Obstetricians and Gynaecologists, London; FRCS, 1985, Royal College of Physicians and Surgeons of Glasgow. Memberships: Secretary, 1978-82, Vice President, 1998-2002, President, 2002-, Glasgow Obstetrical and Gynaecological Society; Treasurer, 1982-90, Vice President, 1990-91, President, 1991-92, Royal Medico-Chirurgical Society of Glasgow. Address: Princess Royal Maternity, 16 Alexandra Parade, Glasgow G31 2ER, Scotland.

LUNCEFORD Joe Elbert, b. 20 January 1937, Slate Springs, MS, USA. Professor. m. (1) deceased, 2 sons, (2) Stacey DeAnn Cruse. Education: BA, Mississippi College, 1962; BD, New Orleans Baptist Theological Seminary, 1966; PhD, Baylor University, 1979. Appointments: Assistant Professor, Georgetown College, 1981-86; Associate Professor, 1986-94; Professor, 1994-; Deacon, Faith Baptist Church, Georgetown. Publications: Commentary on 1-2 Peter, 1-2-3, John, Jude; Orphans in Ancient Israel; Articles. Honours: Cawthorne Excellence in Teaching Award, 1997. Memberships: Society of Biblical Literature; National Association of Baptist Professors of Religion. Address: 1088 Graves Pike, Stamping Ground, KY 40379, USA.

LUNKIM Tongkhojang, b. 1 January 1937, Kamu village, Manipur, India. Doctor of Theology; Minister. m. Chongnu, 2 sons, 4 daughters. Education: D Div, M Div, Serampore College (University); M Theol, Fuller Theological Seminary, USA. Appointments: Administrative Secretary, Kuki Christian Church, 1979-; Kuki Bible Translator, 1964-72; President, Kuki Baptist Convention, 1958-59, General Secretary, 1959-68; Chairman, Kuki Movement for Human Rights, 1996-; Co-worker, Disaster Emergency Service Incorporation, and Senior Minister of Imphal Christian Church, 1982-. Address: K C C Office, PO Imphal 795001, Manipur, India.

LUO Hongbo, b. 11 March 1946, Jiang Su Province, China. Research Fellow. 2 daughters. Education: BA, Beijing Broadcasting University, 1970; Economics and History, Calabria University and Sienna University, Italy, 1979-80. Appointments: Vice Chairman, Secretary General, Chinese Association of Italian Studies; Deputy Director, Institute of European Studies, Professor and Director, Department of European Studies of the Graduate School, Chinese Academy of Social Sciences. Publications: Many publications including 10 monographs. Memberships: Council Member, Chinese

Association of European Studies; Executive Member, China-Europe Forum. Address: 5 Jianguomennei Dajie, The Institute of European Studies, Chinese Academy of Social Sciences, Beijing 100732, Peoples Republic of China. E-mail: luohgbo46@hotmail.com

LUO Kai Hong, b. 13 April 1964, Sichuan, China. Professor of Computational Fluids and Combustion. m. Evguenia Gloukhova, 1 son. Education: B Eng, 1985, M Eng, 1987, Huazhong University of Science and Technology, China; PhD, Computational Fluid Dynamics and Combustion, Engineering Department, Cambridge University, England, 1991. Appointments: Postdoctoral Scientist, Mechanical Engineering Department, Imperial College London, 1991-93; Postdoctoral Scientist, Areo Engineering Department, 1993-95, Lecturer, 1995-98, Senior Lecturer, 1998-2000, Reader 2000-2002, Professor, 2002-, Engineering Department, Queen Mary, University of London. Publications: Over 80 scientific and technical papers in international journals, conferences and books which include most recently as co-author: Vortex dynamics in spatio-temporal development of reacting plumes, 2002; Numerical simulation of particle dispersion in a spatially-developing mixing layer, 2002; Direct numerical simulation of an impinging jet, 2002. Honours: Sugden Award, 2000, Gaydon Prize, 2002, The Combustion Institute (British Section). Memberships: Senior Member, American Institute of Aeronautics and Astronautics; Member, American Society of Mechanical Engineers; Combustion Institute. Address: Engineering Department, Queen Mary, University of London, London E1 4NS, England. E-mail: k.h.luo@qmul.ac.uk

LUO Zhi-Shan, b. 20 August 1936, Da-pu, Guangdong, China. Teacher; Researcher of Mechanics. m. Wang Xiu-Yin, 2 sons. Education: Graduate, Tianjin University, China, 1958. Address: Assistant, 1958-79, Lecturer, 1979-85, Associate Professor, 1986-93, Director, Laboratory of Mechanics, 1984-85; Director, Teaching and Research Section, 1985-86, Professor of Mechanics, 1993-, Tianjin University; Visiting Professor, Mechanical Engineering, University of Hong Kong, 1992; Technical Consultant, Shanton Jingyi Machinery Co, Shanton, China, 1992-94, Hong Kong Press Publications, 1996-97; Chief Engineer, Director of Research, Tianjin Xingu Intelligent Optical Measuring Technique Company, 2000-. Publications: The Principle and Application of Sticking Film Moire Interferometry; Ultra-high Sensitivity Moiré Interferometry for Subdynamic Tests in Normal Light Environment; Research of Instrumentation and Intellectualization for Moiré Interferometry; Ultra-High Sensitivity Moiré Interferometry by the Aid of Electronic-liquid Phase Shifter and Computer; Moiré Interferometer of Intelligent Mode and Its Application; New Computer Adjusted-and-Processing Moiré Interferometer's Applied Research to Mechanical Property Measure of Concrete. Honours: Medal of Gold, 2nd Invention Exhibition of China, 1986; Advanced Award of Science and Technology, China Education, 1986, 1997; Medal of Gilding, 15th International Exhibition of Invention and New Technique, Geneva, 1987; National Award of Invention, China, 1987. Memberships: China Mechanics Society; China Invention Society; Society for Experimental Mechanics, Inc. Address: Four Season Village, 29-5-401, Tianjin University, Tianjin 300072, China. E-mail: lzstju@public.tpt.tj.cn

LUONGO C Paul, b. Winchester, Massachusetts, USA. Public Relations Executive. Education: BS, Suffolk University Boston; MBA, Babson College; Graduate, Bentley College, Cambridge school of Radio-TV Broadcasting (Grahm Junior College); Attended Harvard University and Berklee College of Music. Appointments: Young and Rubicam Inc, New York; Founded C Paul Luongo Company (Press-Public Relations), 1964-; Clients include: Federated Securities Corporation, Pittsburgh; Charles Schwab & Co Inc, San Francisco; Carnegie Mellon University, Pittsburgh; Sullivan and Worcester, Boston, New York and Washington DC; Visible Genetics Inc, Toronto; L Roy Papp Associates, Arizona; Datek Online, New York; The Brookstone Company, New Hampshire; The Cadillac Supernetwork; Dataram Corporation, New Jersey; Bingham Legg Advisers, LLC, Boston; Regularly featured on NBC-TV Today Show; The Merv Griffin Show; WABC-TV Good Morning New York!; Numerous other TV shows and local and regional radio and TV shows in USA and Canada; Contributing Editor of Travel Smart, New York; Columnist for the Boston Metro (newspaper). Publications: America's Best 100; Columns: Public Relations Today, Communications Today, C Paul on PR written for: The Boston Sunday Herald American, New England Advertising Week, Bay State Business and other New England newspapers and magazines. Honours: Honorary Degree, Grahm Junior College; Listed in Who's Who publications and biographical dictionaries. Memberships: Japan-America Society; Boston Stockbrokers Club; Friend of the Boston Pops; Advertising Club of Greater Boston; Royal Ontario Museum, Toronto, Canada; Neighborhood Association of the Back Bay Inc; The Back Bay Association; The Boston Center for International Visitors; Preservation Society of Newport County, Rhode Island; James Beard Foundation, New York; Founding Member, Anthony Spinazzola Memorial Scholarship Foundation, Boston University; Former Board Member, General Alumni Association, Suffolk University, Boston. Address: 441 Stuart Street, Boston, MA 02116, USA.

LURAGHI Raimondo, b. 16 August 1921, Milan, Italy. Professor Emeritus. m. 24 June 1950, 1 son, 1 daughter. Education: MD, University of Turin, 1946; PhD, University of Rome, 1958. Appointments: Professor of History, Junior College, 1954-64; Professor of American History, 1964-, Emeritus Professor, 1995-, University of Genoa. Publications: Storia della Guerra Civile Americana, 1966; Gli Stati Uniti, 1972; The Rise and Fall of the Plantation South, 1975; Marinai del Sud, 1993; A History of the Confederate Navy 1861-1865, 1995. Contributions to: Italian, French, American and Chinese historical magazines. Membership: Italian Association for Military History, president. Address: Corso Regina Margherita 155, 10122 Torino, Italy.

LURIE Alison, b. 3 September 1926, Chicago, Illinois, USA. Professor of English; Author. 3 sons. Education: AB, magna cum laude, Radcliffe College, 1947. Appointments: Lecturer, 1969-73, Adjunct Associate Professor, 1973-76, Associate Professor, 1976-79, Professor of English, 1979-, Cornell University. Publications: Love and Friendship, 1962; The Nowhere City, 1965; Imaginary Friends, 1967; Real People, 1969; The War Between the Tates, 1974; V R Lang: Poems and Plays, With a memoir by Alison Lurie, 1975; Only Children, 1979; Clever Gretchen and Other Forgotten Folktales (juvenile), 1980; The Heavenly Zoo (juvenile), 1980; The Language of Clothes (non-fiction), 1981; Fabulous Beasts (juvenile), 1981; Foreign Affairs, 1984; The Truth About Lorin Jones, 1988; Don't Tell the Grownups: Subversive Children's Literature, 1990; Women and Ghosts, 1994; The Last Resort, 1998; Familiar Spirits, 2001. Contributions to: Many publications. Honours: Guggenheim Fellowship, 1966-67; Rockefeller Foundation Grant, 1968-69; New York State Cultural Council Foundation Grant, 1972-73; American Academy of Arts and Letters Award, 1984; Pulitzer Prize in Fiction, 1985; Radcliffe College Alumnae Recognition Award, 1987; Prix Femina Etranger, 1989; Parents' Choice Foundation Award, 1996. Address: c/o Department of English, Cornell University, Ithaca, NY 14853, USA.

LURKIN Paul, b. 29 April 1935, Brussels, Belgium. University Teacher; Chartered Accountant. m. Madeleine Bomblet, 1 son, 1 daughter. Education: Degree in Applied Economics, 1957, Degree in Business Teaching, University of Louvain, Belgium, 1961; CPA, 1967; Chartered Accountant, 1976; Commissaire aux Comptes, France, 1996. Appointments: Assistant Professor, University of Louvain, 1960-69; Professor in Accountancy, ICHEC, Brussels, 1967-; President, UEC, European Accountants, 1983, 1984; President, European Accountants Congress, 1983, 1989; Member of the Board, Belgian Institute of CPA, 1976-95; Vice-President, French International Accountants Federation; Visiting Professor, University Robert Schuman, Strasbourg, HEC Tunis, University of Bukavu, Congo, Lille II, France. Publications: Author books: Le Droit Comptable Belge, 1977, 1981; Analyse et Interpretation des Etats Financiers, 1985; Vademecum Belgian Accounting; Articles on evaluation of companies, auditing, non-profit organisations. Honour: Chevalier, Ordre de Leopold, Belgium. Memberships: Vice-president, AFECA, Vannes, France; Belgian Institute of CPA; Belgian Institute of Accountants. Address: Place Vander Elst 2 Bg, 1180 Brussels, Belgium.

LUSCOMBE Lawrence Edward, b. 10 November 1924, Torquay, England. Anglican Bishop. m. Doris Luscombe, deceased, 1 daughter. Education: Kings College, London, 1963-64; LLD, 1987, MPhil, 1991, PhD, 1993, University of Dundee. Appointments: Indian Army, 1942-47; Chartered Accountant, Partner, Galbraith, Dunlop and Co, later Watson and Galbraith, 1952-63; Rector, St Barnabas, Paisley, 1966-71; Provost of St Paul's Cathedral, Dundee, 1971-75; Bishop of Brechin, 1975-90; Primus of the Scottish Episcopal Church, 1985-90. Publications: The Scottish Episcopal Church in the Twentieth Century; A Seminary of Learning; Matthew Luscombe, Missionary Bishop; The Representative Man. Honours: Chaplain, Order of St John; Honorary Research Fellow, University of Dundee; Honorary Canon, Trinity Cathedral, Davenport, Iowa, USA. Memberships: Institute of Chartered Accountants of Scotland; Society of Antiquaries of Scotland; Royal Society of Arts. Address: Woodville, Kirkton of Tealing, By Dundee, DD4 0RD, Scotland.

LUSHCHAK Volodymyr Ivanovych, b. 18 September 1956, Ivano-Frankivsk, Ukraine. Biochemist. m. Ljudmyla, 1 son, 2 daughters. Education: PhD Student, Biological Department, Moscow State University, 1982-87; DSc Chernivtsi University, Ukraine. Appointments: Artist in wood, 1973-74; Service in Army, 1974-76; Student, Moscow State University, 1976-82; Part-time Technician, Biochemical Laboratory, Moscow State University, 1980-82; Part-time Junior Research Fellow, Biological Faculty, Moscow State University, 1982-86; Scientific Secretary of Director of Karadag Branch of Institute of Biology of Southern Seas, Ukrainian Academy of Sciences, 1987-89; Research Fellow, Karadag Branch of IBSS, 1989-91; Head of Fish Biochemistry Laboratory, National Academy of Sciences Ukraine, 1991-99; Visiting Professor, Biology Department, Carleton University, Canada, 1993; Visiting Researcher, Cellular Biology Department, University of Brasilia, 1996-97; Professor of Biochemistry, Department of Biology, Precarpathian University, Ukraine, 1999-2002; Professor, Head of Biochemistry Department, Natural Sciences Faculty, Precarpathian University, Ukraine, 2002-. Publications: Author of numerous articles in professional scientific journals. Honours: Listed in international biographical dictionaries; several scientific and scholarly grants. Address: Department of Biology, Natural Sciences Faculty, Vassyl Stefanyk Prekarpathian University, Ministry of Higher Education and Science of Ukraine, 57 Shevchenka Str, Ivano-Frankivsk, 76025, Ukraine. E-mail: lushchak@pu.if.ua

LUTTWAK Edward N(icholae), b. 4 November 1942, Arad, Romania (US citizen, 1981). Political Scientist; Author. m. Dalya Iaari, 14 December 1970, 1 son, 1 daughter. Education: Carmel College, England; BSc, London School of Economics and Political Science, 1964; PhD, Johns Hopkins University, 1975. Appointments: Associate Director, Washington Center of Foreign Policy Research, District of Columbia, 1972-75; Visiting Professor of Political Science, Johns Hopkins University, 1973-78; Senior Fellow, 1976-87, Research Professor in International Security Affairs, 1978-82, Arleigh Burke Chair in Strategy, 1987-, Director, Geo-Economics, 1991-, Center for Strategic and International Studies, Washington, DC; Nimitz Lecturer, University of California, Berkeley, 1987; Tanner Lecturer, Yale University, 1989. Publications: A Dictionary of Modern War, 1971, new edition with Stuart Koehl, 1991; The Grand Strategy of the Roman Empire: From the First Century A.D. to the Third, 1976; The Economic and Military Balance Between East and West 1951-1978 (editor with Herbert Block), 1978; Sea Power in the Mediterranean (with R G Weinland), 1979; Strategy and Politics: Collected Essays, 1980; The Grand Strategy of the Soviet Union, 1983; The Pentagon and the Art of War: The Question of Military Reform, 1985; Strategy and History, 1985; On the Meaning of Victory: Essays on Strategy, 1986; Global Security: A Review of Strategic and Economic Issues (editor with Barry M Blechman), 1987; Strategy: The Logic of War and Peace, 1987; The Endangered American Dream: How to Stop the United States from Becoming a Third World Country and How to Win the Geo-Economic Struggle for Industrial Supremacy, 1993; Turbo-Capitalism: Winners and Losers in the Global Economy, 1999; La renaissance de la puissance aerienne stategique, 1999; Che cos'é davvero la democrazia (with Susanna Creperio Verratti); Il Libro delle Liberta, 2000; Strategy Now (editor), 2000. Contributions to: Numerous books and periodicals. Address: c/o Center for Strategic and International Studies, Georgetown University, 1800 K Street North West, Washington, DC 20006, USA.

LYKLEMA Johannes, b. 23 November 1930, Apeldoorn, The Netherlands. Professor. m. 2 children. Education: Studies in Chemistry and Physics, State University of Utrecht, 1948-55; PhD, Utrecht, 1956; Honorary Doctorate, Universite Catholic, Louvain-la-Neuve, Belgium, 1988, Royal Institute of Technology, Stockholm, Sweden, 1997. Appointments: Military Service, 1956-58; Science Co-Worker, University of Utrecht, 1958-61; Visiting Associate Professor, University of South California, Los Angeles, USA, 1961-62; Professor, Physical and Colloid Chemistry, Wageningen Agricultural University, 1962-; Visiting Professor, University of Bristol, England, 1971, Australian National University, Canberra, 1976, University of Tokyo, Japan, 1988; Visiting Professor, University of Florida, Gainesville, USA, 1997-. Publications: Over 300 articles in professional journals. Honours: Nightingale Award for Medical Electronics, 1963; Gold Medal, Centre for Marine Research, Ruder Boskovic, Zagreb, 1986; Knight in the Order of the Dutch Lion, 1991; Koninklijke Shell Prize, 1995; Thomas Graham Prize, 1995. Memberships: 90 national and local committees; 95 international. Address: Wageningen University, Department of Physical Chemistry and Colloid Science, De Dreijen 6, 6703 HB Wageningen, The Netherlands.

LYNCH Annette Peters, b. 23 October 1922, Marion, Indiana, USA. Retired College Professor. Poet. m. Thomas Millard Lynch, 24 August 1949, 2 sons, 2 daughters. Education: BA, Indiana University, 1944; MA, 1945, PhD, Occidental College, Los Angeles, 1960. Appointments: Professor, Indiana University, 1945-49, Glendale College, 1949-50, Occidental College, 1950-55, Mount San Antonio College, 1955-93. Publication: Ways Around the Heart. Contributions to: Alderbaran; Athena Incognito;

California State Poetry Quarterly; Calapoyya Collage; Christian Science Monitor; Facet; Galley Sail Review; Inside English; Maryland Poetry Review; Toyon; Underpass; Wisconsin Review; Blue Unicorn; Cloverdale Review; Forum; Gaia; New Los Angeles Poets; Onthebus; Psychopoetica; Tempo; Voices. Honours: Anthology of Magazine Verse, 1986-88; 2nd Prize, Annual California Quarterly National Contest, 1992; Outstanding Faculty Emeritus, Mount San Antonio College, 1993. Memberships: Academy of American Poets; Poetry Society of America; California State Poetry Society. Address: 833 Garfield Avenue, South Pasadena, CA 91030, USA.

LYNCH David, b. 20 January 1946, Missoula, Montana, USA. Film Director. m. (1) Peggy Reavey, 1967, divorced, 1 daughter, (2) Mary Fisk, 1977, divorced, 1 son. Education: Hammond High School, Alexandria; Corcoran School of Art, Washington, DC; School of Museum of Fine Arts, Boston; Pennsylvania Academy of Fine Arts, Philadelphia. Appointments: Films include: The Grandmother, 1970; Eraserhead, 1977; The Elephant Man, 1980; Dune, 1984; Blue Velvet, 1986; Wild at Heart, 1990; Storyville, 1991; Twin Peaks; Fire Walk With Me, 1992; Lost Highway, 1997; Crumb, 1999; The Straight Story, 1999. TV includes: Twin Peaks, 1990; Mulholland Drive, 2000. Honours: Fellow, Centre for Advanced Film Study, American Film Institute, Los Angeles, 1970; Dr hc, Royal College of Art; Golden Palm, Cannes. Address: c/o CAA, 9830 Wilshire Boulevard, Beverly Hills, CA 90212, USA.

LYNCH John, b. 11 January 1927, Boldon, England. Professor Emeritus; Historian. Education: MA, University of Edinburgh, 1952; PhD, University of London, 1955. Appointments: Lecturer in History, University of Liverpool, 1954-61; Lecturer, Reader and Professor of Latin American History, University College, London, 1961-74; Professor of Latin American History and Director of Institute of Latin American Studies, University of London, 1974-87. Publications: Spanish Colonial Administration 1782-1810: The Intendant System in the Viceroyalty of the Río de la Plata, 1958; Spain Under the Habsburgs, 2 volumes, 1964, 1967, 2nd edition, revised, 1981; The Origins of the Latin American Revolutions 1808-1826 (with R A Humphreys), 1965; The Spanish American Revolutions 1808-1826, 1973, 2nd edition, revised, 1986; Argentine Dictator: Juan Manuel de Rosas 1829-1852, 1981; The Cambridge History of Latin America (with others), Vol 3, 1985, Vol 4, 1986; Bourbon Spain 1700-1808, 1989; Caudillos in Spanish America 1800-1850, 1992; Latin American Revolutions 1808-1826: Old and New World Origins, 1994; Massacre in the Pampas, 1872: Britain and Argentina in the Age of Migration, 1998; Latin America between Colony and Nation, 2001. Honours: Encomienda Isabel La Católica, Spain, 1988; Doctor, Honoris Causa, University of Seville, 1990; Order of Andres Bello, 1st Class, Venezuela, 1995. Membership: Royal Historical Society, fellow. Address: 8 Templars Crescent, London N3 3QS, England.

LYNDEN-BELL Donald, b. 5 April 1935. Astrophysicist. Education: Graduated, Clare College, Cambridge; PhD, 1960. Appointments: Harkness Fellow, California Institute of Technology and Hale Observatories, 1960-62; Visiting Associate, 1969-70, Research Fellow, then Fellow and Director of Studies in Mathematics, Clare College, Cambridge, 1960-65; Assistant Lecturer, Applied Mathematics, Cambridge University, 1962-65; Principal Scientific Officer, later Senior Principal Scientific Officer, Royal Greenwich Observatory, Herstmonceux, 1965-72; Professor of Astrophysics, University of Cambridge, 1972-; Director, Institute of Astronomy, Cambridge, 1972-77, 1982-87, 1992-94; Visiting Professorial Fellow, Queen's University, Belfast, 1996-. Publications: Numerous papers in scientific journals; Monthly Notices of Royal Astronomical Society. Honours: Honorary DSc, Sussex, 1987; Eddington Medal, 1984; Gold Medal, Royal

Astronomical Society, 1993; Catherine Wolf George Medal, 1998; J J Carty Award, NAS, 2000; Russell Lecturer, American Astronomical Society, 2000. Membership: Fellow, Royal Astronomical Society; Foreign Associate, NAS. Address: Institute of Astronomy, The Observatories, Madingley Road, Cambridge, CB3 0HA, England.

LYNDON SKEGGS Barbara Noel, b. 29 December 1924, London, England. Retired. m. Michael Lyndon Skeggs, 2 sons, 2 daughters. Appointments include: Served 6 months in Aircraft Factory and 2½ years in the WRNS during World War II; Joined Conservative Party, holding various constituency positions over the years, 1945-; Manager of Ford Primary School, 1963-88; Appointed Justice of the Peace, 1966-94; Conservative County Councillor for Crookham, 1968-81; Appointed Tax Commissioner, 1984-94; Appointed Deputy Lieutenant for Northumberland, 1988-; Appointed High Sheriff of Northumberland, 1994-95. Honours: Freeman of the City of London, 1973; Badge of Honour for Distinguished Service, BRCS, 1987; MBE, 1990. Memberships: Berwick Infirmary Management Committee, 1966-74; Area Health Authority, 1974-90; Northumberland Family Practitioner Committee, 1980-90; Northumberland Magistrates Committee, 1980-94; Ford and Etal PCC, 1961-96; Board of Northern Opera, 1971-81. Address: Dalgheal, Evanton, Ross-shire IV16 9XH, Scotland.

LYNN Vera (Margaret Lewis) (Dame), b. 20 March 1917. Singer. m. Harry Lewis, 1941, 1 daughter. Career: Debut performance, 1924; Appeared with Joe Loss, Charlie Kunz, 1935; Ambrose, 1937-40; Applesauce, Palladium, London, 1941; Became known as the Forces Sweetheart, 1939-45; Radio show Sincerely Yours, 1941-47; Tour of Burma, entertaining troops, 1944; 7 Command performances; Appearances, Europe; Australia; Canada; New Zealand; Performed at 50th Anniversary of VE Day Celebrations, London, 1995; Own television shows: ITV, 1955; BBC1, 1956; BBC2, 1970; First British artist to top Hit Parade. Numerous recordings include: Auf Wiederseh'n (over 12 million copies sold). Publication: Vocal Refrain (autobiography), 1975. Honours: Order of St John; LLD; MMus. Address: c/o Anglo-American Enterprises, 806 Keyes House, Dolphin Square, London SW1V 3NB, England.

LYON Martin, b. 10 February 1954, Romford, Essex, England. Librarian; Poet. Education: BA, 1976. Appointments: Principal Library Assistant, University of London. Contributions to: Acumen; Agenda; Orbis; Outposts Poetry Quarterly; Pen International; Spokes. Honour: Lake Aske Memorial Award. Address: 63 Malford Court, The Drive, South Woodford, London E18 2HS, England.

LYSSOIVAN Anatoli Ivanovich, b. 21 June 1946, Berlin, Germany. Researcher in Fusion Plasmas. m. Tatyana Lysoyvan, 1 daughter. Education: BS and MS Degrees, Diploma, Physics, 1971, PhD Degree, Diploma, Radio Frequency Plasma Physics, 1986, Kharkov University, Kharkov, Ukraine. Appointments: Junior Research Staff, Research Staff, Senior Research Staff, Radio Frequency Heating Group Leader, Institute for Plasma Physics, NSC KIPT, Kharkov, Ukraine, 1973-95; Research Scientist in Fusion Plasmas, Laboratory for Plasma Physics, ERM/KMS, Brussels, Belgium, 1995-. Publications: Co-author of numerous papers published in scientific journals including, Soviet Journal of Plasma Physics, 1981; Nuclear Fusion, 1986, 1990, 1992; Plasma Physics Controlled Fusion, 1990; Journal of Nuclear Materials, 1997; Proceedings of 22-24th, 26th, 28th, 30th EPS Conference on CFPP, 1995-97, 1999, 2001, 2003. Membership: Physical Society for Students, 1965-71; Belgian Physical Society, 2001-. Address: Laboratory for Plasma Physics – ERM/KMS, Av de la Renaissance 30, 1000 Brussels, Belgium.

Dictionary of International Biography

M

MA Liming, b. 4 June 1935, Gaixian County, Liaoning Province. Medical Entomologist. m. Dai Qinying, 3 daughters. Education: Graduated from Jilin Medical School, 1956. Appointments: Physician, Plague Control Station of Daan County, Jilin Province, 1956-61; Associate Chief Physician, First Institute of Endemic Diseases Research of Jilin Province, 1961-. Publications: Published 310 pieces of articles on biology and taxonomy of fleas, ticks, mites and rodents; Author: Investigation Report on some Ecological Habits of Fleas in North China; Printed a volume of Collection of Articles. Address: First Institute of Endemic Diseases Research of Jilin Province, 85 Haiming West Road, Baicheng City, Jilin Province, 137 000 China.

MAASS Marie Denise, b. 7 July 1958, Santiago, Chile. Engineer; Strategist. 2 daughters. Education: Human Physiology Course, School of Medicine, University of Chile, Santiago, 1982; Industrial and Electronic Engineering, Catholic University, Santiago, 1978-86; Research Fellow, postdoctoral research on MRI Processing, Imperial College, London, 1994-96; MSc, Business Administration, London Business School, 1996-98. Appointments: SNITEM, Paris France, 1987-88; R&D Engineer, Telsa Informatique, Paris, France, 1988-90; Advisor of the Board on equipment needs, Stock Exchange, Santiago, Chile; In Charge of Negotiations, French Exchange Program, Santiago, Chile, 1990-91; Head of US TDP Program, Ministry of Health, Santiago, Chile; Head of Strategy, Chilectra Metropolitana, Santiago, Chile, 1990-93; Executive, Price Waterhouse Coopers, London, England, 1997-99; Consultant in Ethics, Business Philosophy and Strategy, 2000-04. Publications: 4 papers presented at conferences and symposia. Honours: Two votes of distinction, School of Engineering, Chile, 1986; Award for outstanding contribution to the biomedical field, International Youth in Achievement, Cambridge, 1986; Award for outstanding leadership, Institute of Electronic and Electrical Engineers, 1994. Memberships: LBS Alumni Association; AMBA (UK). Address: 27 Chemin des Buissonnets, 14100 Lisieux, France. E-mail: marie.maas@wanadoo.fr

MACCARTHY Fiona, b. 23 January 1940, London, England. Biographer; Cultural Historian. m. David Mellor, 1966, 1 son, 1 daughter. Education: MA, English Language and Literature, Oxford University, 1961. Appointments: Reviewer, The Times, 1981-91, The Observer, 1991-98. Publications: The Simple Life: C R Ashbee in the Cotswolds, 1981; The Omega Workshops: Decorative Arts of Bloomsbury, 1984; Eric Gill, 1989; William Morris: A Life for our Time, 1994; Stanley Spencer, 1997; Byron Life and Legend, 2002. Contributions to: Times Literary Supplement; New York Review of Books. Honours: Royal Society of Arts Bicentenary Medal, 1987; Honorary Fellowship, Royal College of Art, 1989; Wolfson History Prize, 1995; Honorary D Litt, University of Sheffield, 1996; Senior Fellowship, Royal College of Art, 1997; Fellow, Royal Society of Literature, 1997; Honorary Doctorate, Sheffield Hallam University, 2001. Memberships: PEN Club; Royal Society of Literature. Address: The Round Building, Hathersage, Sheffield S32 1BA, England.

MACCORMACK Geoffrey Dennis, b. 15 April 1937, Canterbury, Kent, UK. Retired Professor of Law. 1 daughter. Education: University of Sydney, Australia, 1954-60; University of Oxford, England, 1960-65. Appointment: Professor of Jurisprudence, University of Aberdeen, 1971-96. Publications: Traditional Chinese Law, 1990; The Spirit of Traditional Chinese Law, 1996. Address: School of Law, King's College, University of Aberdeen, Old Aberdeen AB24 3UB, Scotland. E-mail: g.maccormack@abdn.ac.uk

MACDONALD Angus D, b. 9 October 1950, Edinburgh, Scotland. Headmaster. m. Isabelle M Ross, 2 daughters. Education: MA (Hons), Cambridge University, 1969-71; Dip Ed, Edinburgh University, 1971-72. Appointments: Assistant Teacher, Alloa Academy, 1972-73; Assistant Teacher, King's School, Paramatta, 1978-79; Assistant Teacher, Edinburgh Academy, 1973-82; Head of Geography, 1982, Deputy Principal, 1982-86, George Watson's College; Headmaster, Lomond School, 1986-. Honour: Exhibition to Cambridge University. Membership: Chairman, Clan Donald Lands Trust. Address: 8 Millig Street, Helensburgh, Argyll & Bute, Scotland.

MACDONALD Hugh Ian, b. 27 June 1929, Toronto, Ontario, Canada. Professor, University Administrator. m. Dorothy Marion, 2 sons, 3 daughters. Education: B Com, University of Toronto, 1952; MA, Oxford University, 1954; B Phil, Oxford University, 1955; LL D, University of Toronto, 1974; D Univ, The Open University, 1998; D Litt, The Open University of Sri Lanka, 1999; D Litt, Dr B R Ambedkar Open University of Hyderabad, 2001; FCOL (The Commonwealth of Learning), 2004-. Appointments: Lecturer, Economics, University of Toronto, 1955; Dean of Men, 1956; Assistant Professor, Economics, 1962; Chief Economist, Government of Ontario, 1965; Deputy Provincial Treasurer, 1967; Deputy Treasurer and Deputy Minister of Economics, 1968; Deputy Treasurer, Deputy Minister of Economics and Intergovernmental Affairs, 1972; President, York University, 1974-84; Director, York International, 1984-94; President Emeritus, Professor of Economics and Public Policy, 1994-. Publications: Various Publications. Honours: Governor General's Medal; Cody Trophy; Canadian Centennial Medal; Queens Silver Jubilee Medal; Officer of the Order of Canada; Knight of Grace of the Order of St Lazarus of Jerusalem; Citation of Merit, The Court of Canadian Citizenship; Medal of the Dominican Republic; Commemorative Medal for the 125th Anniversary of Confederation of Canada; Award of Merit, Canadian Bureau for International Education; Honorary Life Member, Canadian Olympic Association; Vanier Medal for distinction in public service and excellence in public administration, Institute of Public Administration, Canada, 2000; Queen's Golden Jubilee Medal, 2002. Memberships: Director Canadian Rhodes Scholars Foundation; Past Chairman, The Commonwealth of Learning; Chairman, Balliol Annual Fund Appeal in Canada; Advisory Board, International Master of Business Administration Program, York University; Many other Memberships. Address: York University, Rm N207, Schulich School of Business, 4700 Keele Street, Toronto, Ontario, M3J 1P3, Canada.

MACDONALD Simon Gavin George, b. 5 September 1923, Beauly, Inverness-shire, Scotland. University Professor of Physics, retired. m. Eva Leonie Austerlitz, 1 son, 1 daughter. Education: First Class Honours, Mathematics and Natural Philosophy, Edinburgh University, 1941-43, 1946-48; PhD, St Andrews University, 1953. Appointments: Junior Scientific Officer, Royal Aircraft Establishment, Farnborough, 1943-46; Lecturer in Physics, 1948-57, Senior Lecturer in Physics, 1962-67, University of St Andrews; Senior Lecturer in Physics, University College of the West Indies, Jamaica, 1957-62; Senior Lecturer in Physics, 1967-72, Dean, Faculty of Science, 1970-73, Professor of Physics, 1973-88, Vice-principal, 1974-79, University of Dundee. Publications: 3 books; Numerous articles in scientific journals on x-ray crystallography. Honours: Fellow, Institute of Physics, 1958; Fellow, Royal Society of Edinburgh, 1972; Chairman, Dundee Repertory Theatre; Chairman, Federation of Scottish Theatres. Address: 7a Windmill Road, St Andrews, Fife KY16 9JJ, Scotland.

MACDOUGALL Ruth Doan, b. 19 March 1939, Laconia, New Hampshire, USA. Writer. m. Donald K MacDougall, 9 October 1957. Education: Bennington College, 1957-59; BEd, Keene State

College, 1961. Publications: The Lilting House, 1965; The Cost of Living, 1971; One Minus One, 1971; The Cheerleader, 1973; Wife and Mother, 1976; Aunt Pleasantine, 1978; The Flowers of the Forest, 1981; A Lovely Time Was Had By All, 1982; Snowy, 1993; Fifty Hikes in the White Mountains, 1997; Fifty More Hikes in New Hampshire, 1998; The Cheerleader: 25th Anniversary Edition, 1998; A Woman Who Loved Lindbergh, 2001; Henrietta Snow, 2004. Contributions to: Book Reviewer: New York Times Book Review; Newsday; Others. Honours: Winner, PEN Syndicated Fiction Project, 1983, 1984, 1985. Membership: National Writers Union. Address: 285 Range Road, Center Sandwich, NH 03227, USA. Website: www.ruthdoanmacdougall.com

MACDOWELL Andie, b. 21 April 1958, South Carolina, USA. Film Actress. m. (1) Paul Qualley, divorced, 1 son, 2 daughters, (2) Rhett DeCamp Hartzog, 2001. Appointments: TV appearances include: Women and Men 2, In Love There are No Rules, 1991; Sahara's Secret; Films include: Greystoke, 1984; St Elmo's Fire, 1985; Sex, Lies and Videotape, 1989; Green Card, 1990; Hudson Hawk, 1991; The Object of Beauty, 1991; The Player, 1992; Ruby, 1992; Groundhog Day, 1993; Short Cuts, 1993; Bad Girls, 1994; Four Weddings and a Funeral, 1994; Unstrung Heros, 1995; My Life and Me, 1996; Multiplicity, 1996; The End of Violence, 1997; Town and Country, 1998; Shadrack, 1998; The Scalper, 1998; Just the Ticket, 1998; Muppets From Space, 1999; The Music, 2000; Harrison's Flowers, 2000; Town and Country, 2001; Crush, 2001; Ginostra, 2002. Address: c/o ICM 8942 Wilshire Boulevard, Beverly Hills, CA 90211, USA.

MACDOWELL Douglas Maurice, b. 8 March 1931, London, England. Professor of Greek; Writer. Education: BA, 1954, MA, 1958, DLitt, 1992, Balliol College, Oxford. Appointments: Assistant Lecturer, Lecturer, Senior Lecturer, Reader in Greek and Latin, University of Manchester, 1958-71; Professor of Greek, 1971-2001, Professor Emeritus, Honorary Research Fellow, 2001-, University of Glasgow. Publications: Andokides: On the Mysteries (editor), 1962; Athenian Homicide Law, 1963; Aristophanes: Wasps (editor), 1971; The Law in Classical Athens, 1978; Spartan Law, 1986; Demosthenes: Against Meidias (editor), 1990; Aristophanes and Athens, 1995; Antiphon and Andocides (with M Gagarin), 1998; Demosthenes: On the False Embassy (editor), 2000. Honours: Fellow, Royal Society of Edinburgh, 1991; Fellow, British Academy, 1993. Address: Department of Classics, University of Glasgow, Glasgow G12 8QQ, Scotland.

MACEK Karel, b. 31 October 1928, Prague, Czechoslovakia. Analytical Biochemist. m. Olga Haaszová, 2 sons. Education: Dr rerum naturalium, Charles University, Prague, 1951; Postdoctoral studies Universities of Goettingen, 1957, Munich, 1966, London, 1968; DrSc, Technical University, Pardubice, 1983. Appointments: Head of Laboratories, Research Institute of Pharmacy and Biochemistry, Prague, 1950-68; Associate Professor, Academy of Arts, Prague, 1958-68; Associate Professor, Technical University, Pardubice, 1968; Associate Professor, Medical University, Prague, 1970-71; Visiting Professor, University of Rome, 1968-69; Head of Laboratories, Internal Clinic, Charles University of Prague, 1971-77; Leading Scientist, Physiological Institute, Academy of Science, Prague, 1977-91; Editor, Journal of Chromatography (Amsterdam), 1977-96. Publications: Author or editor, 18 books on chromatography; Chapters in 10 books on chromatography; Editor of 14 symposia proceedings; 160 scientific papers in professional international journals. Honours: Cvet Award, USSR, 1978; Hanuš Award, Czechoslovakia, 1978; Tswett Award in chromatography, USA, 1985; Purkyně Award, Czechoslovakia, 1988; Michaelis Award in clinical chemistry, GDR, 1988; Stass Award in toxicology, Germany, 1991. Memberships: Chairman

Chromatography Section, Czechoslovak Chemical Society, 1960-93; Honorary Member, Czechoslovak Chemical Society, 1996-; Vice-President, Society for Research in Connective Tissue, Czech Republic, 1997-. Address: Lukešova 16, CZ-14200 Prague 4, Czech Republic.

MACGREGOR John Roddick Russell (Lord MacGregor of Pulham Market), b. 14 February 1937, Glasgow, Scotland. Politician; Businessman. m. Jean Mary Elizabeth Dungey, 1 son, 2 daughters. Education: MA, First Class Honours, St Andrew's University; LLB, King's College, London. Appointments: University Administrator, 1961-62; Editorial Staff, New Society, 1962-63; Hill Samuel & Co, 1968-79; Director, Hill Samuel and Co, 1973-79; Deputy Chairman, Hill Samuel Bank Ltd, 1994-96; Non-Executive Director: Slough Estates plc, 1995-, Associated British Foods plc, 1994, Unigaze plc, 1996-, Friends Provident plc, 1998-; Political Career: Special Assistant to Prime Minister, 1963-64; Head, Opposition Office, 1965-68; Member of Parliament for South Norfolk, 1974-2001; Lord Commissioner of the Treasury, 1979-81; Parliamentary Under Secretary of State for Industry with particular responsibility for small businesses, 1981-83; Minister of State for Agriculture, Fisheries and Food, 1983-85; Chief Secretary to the Treasury, 1985-87; Minister for Agriculture, Fisheries and Food, 1987-89; Secretary of State for Education, 1989-90; Lord President of the Council and Leader of the Commons, 1990-92; Secretary of State for Transport, 1992-94; Member of the House of Lords, 1991-. Honours: OBE, 1971; PC, 1985; Honorary Fellow, King's College, London, 1990; Honorary LLD, University of Westminster, 1995. Address: House of Lords, London SW1A 0PW, England.

MACHIDA Curtis A, b. 1 April 1954, San Francisco, USA. Molecular Neurobiologist. Education: AB, University of California, Berkeley, 1976; PhD, Oregon Health Sciences University, 1982. Appointments: Postdoctoral Fellow, Biochemistry, Oregon Health Sciences University, 1982-85; Postdoctoral Fellow, Vollum Institute, 1985-88; Assistant Scientist, 1988-95, Assistant Professor, 1989-95; Associate Scientist, Associate Professor, 1995-2002 Neuroscience, Oregon National Primate Research Center, Oregon Health Sciences University; Research Associate Professor, Integrative Biosciences, Oregon Health Sciences University, 2002-; Adjunct Faculty, Biochemistry and Biophysics, Oregon State University. Publications: Over 100 articles and abstracts in professional journals; Patent holder; Editor, Adrenergic Receptor Protocols; Editor, Viral Vectors for Gene Therapy: Methods and Protocols; Member, Editorial Boards, Molecular Biotechnology; Frontiers in Bioscience. Honours include: NIH First Award; AHA Established Investigator Award; NIH Grant Recipient. Memberships: AAAS; ASM; ASBMB; ASGT; AHA Scientific Council. Address: Department of Integrative Biosciences, School of Dentistry, Oregon Health Sciences University, 611 SW Campus Drive, Portland, OR 97239, USA.

MACINNES Patricia, b. 7 April 1954, Quantico, Virginia, USA. Writer. Education: BA, San Diego State University, 1977; MFA, Writing, University of Montana, Missoula, 1981. Publication: The Last Night on Bikini, 1995. Contributions to: Journals. Honours: Wallace Stegner Writing Fellowship, Stanford University, 1984; Nelson Algren Award for Short Fiction, 1987; Writing Fellowship, Provincetown Fine Arts Work Center, 1988-89; Ludwig Vogelstein Grant, 1989. Address: c/o Mary Jack Wald Associates, 111 East 14th Street, New York, NY 10003, USA.

MACKERRAS Sir (Alan) Charles, b. 17 November 1925, Schenectady, New York, USA. Orchestral Conductor. m. Helena Judith Wilkins, 22 August 1947, 2 daughters. Education: Sydney Grammar School, Sydney Conservatorium of Music, Studies with

Vaclav Talich, Prague Academy of Music, 1947-48. Appointments: Principal Oboist, Sydney Symphony Orchestra, 1943-46; Oboist, Sadler's Wells Opera Orchestra, 1947; Staff Conductor, Sadler's Wells Opera, 1948-54; Freelance conductor, orchestras in Britain, European Continent, USA, Australia, 1957-66; First Conductor, Hamburg State Opera, 1966-69; Musical Director, Sadler's Wells Opera, later English National Opera, 1970-77; Chief Guest, Conductor, BBC Symphony Orchestra, 1976-79; Chief Conductor, Sydney Symphony Orchestra, Australian Broadcasting Company, 1982-85; Principal Guest Conductor, Royal Liverpool Philharmonic, 1986-88; Scottish Chamber Orchestra, 1992-95; Conductor Laureate, 1995-; Musical Director, Welsh National Opera, 1987-92; Conductor Emeritus, 1992-; Principal Guest Conductor, San Francisco Opera, 1993-96; Conductor Emeritus, 1996-; Royal Philharmonic Orchestra, 1993-96; Czech Philharmonic Orchestra, 1997-2003; Music Director, Orchestra of St Luke's, 1998-2001, Music Director Emeritus, 2001-; Principal Guest Conductor, Philharmonia Orchestra, 2002-; President, Trinity College of Music, 2000-. Publications: Ballet arrangement of Pineapple Poll, 1951 (Sullivan) and The Lady and the Fool, 1954 (Verdi); Reconstruction of Arthur Sullivan's lost cello concerto, 1986; Contributed 4 appendices to Charles Mackerras: a musicians' musician, by Nancy Phelan, 1987; Numerous articles in musical journals and magazines. Honours: CBE, 1974; Knighthood, 1979; AC (Companion of Order of Australia), 1997; Medal of Merit, Czech Republic, 1996; CH, 2003; Hon RAM, 1969; Hon FRCM, 1987; Honorary Fellow, Royal Northern College of Music, Manchester, 1999; Honorary Fellow, Trinity College of Music, London, 1999; Honorary Fellow, Saint Peter's College, Oxford, 1999; Cardiff University, 2003; Honorary DMus: Hull, 1990, Nottingham, 1991, Brno (Czech Republic), York and Griffith (Brisbane), 1994, Oxford, 1997; Prague Academy of Music, 1999; Napier University, 2000; Melbourne and Sydney, 2003; Janacek Academy of Music, Brno, 2004. Address: 10 Hamilton Terrace, London NW8 9UG, England.

MACKERRAS Colin Patrick, b. 26 August 1939, Sydney, Australia. Academic. m. Alyce Barbara Brazier, 2 sons, 3 daughters. Education: BA, Melbourne, 1961; BA, Honours, Australian National University, 1962; M Litt, Cambridge, England, 1964; PhD, Australian National University. Appointments: Foreign Expert, Beijing Institute of Foreign Languages, Beijing, China, 1964-66, 1985, 1995-96; Research Scholar, 1966-69, Research Fellow, 1969-73, Senior Research Fellow, 1973, Department of Far Eastern History, Australian National University; Foundation Professor, China Studies, 1974-, Chairman, 1979-85, Head, 1988-89, School of Modern Asian Studies, Co-Director, Key Centre for Asian Languages and Studies set up jointly at Griffith University and the University of Queensland, 1988-96, Head, School of Modern Asian Studies (later Asian and International Studies), 1996-2000, Griffith University, Australia. Publications: Books as single-author include: The Chinese Theatre in Modern Times from 1840 to the Present Day, 1975; China's Minorities: Integration and Modernization in the Twentieth Century, 1994; Western Images of China, Revised Edition, 1999; The New Cambridge Handbook of Contemporary China, 2001; China's Ethnic Minorities and Globalisation, 2003; Numerous edited books, books with one or more authors, chapters in books, articles, book reviews. Honours: International Visitor to the USA, Department of State, USA, 1997; Gold Citation, Media Peace Prize, United National Association of Australia (shared), 1981; Twentieth Century Award for Achievement, International Biographical Centre, Cambridge, England, 1993; Albert Einstein (1879-1955) International Academy Foundation Cross of Merit Award, 1993; Elected Fellow, Australian Academy of the Humanities, 1999; Australia-China Council Award, Australian Minister of Foreign Affairs, 1999; 2000 Millennium Medal of Honor, American Biographical Institute; Award for

Excellence in Teaching, Individual Teacher of the Year Category, Griffith University, 2000; Centenary Medal for distinguished service to education and international relations, Governor General of Australia, 2003. Memberships: Fellow, Australian Academy of the Humanities; Member and Former President, Asian Studies Association of Australia. Address: 19 Allambee Crescent, Capalaba, Queensland 4157, Australia. E-mail: colinmackerras@hotmail.com

MACKESY Piers Gerald, b. 15 September 1924, Cults, Aberdeenshire, Scotland. Historian; Writer. Education: BA, Christ Church, Oxford, 1950; DPhil, Oriel College, Oxford, 1953; DLitt, Oxford, 1978. Appointments: War Service: Lieutenant, The Royal Scots Greys, N.W. Europe, 1943-7; Harkness Fellow, Harvard University, 1953-54; Fellow, 1954-87, Emeritus, 1988-, Pembroke College, Oxford; Visiting Fellow, Institute for Advanced Study, Princeton, New Jersey, 1961-62; Visiting Professor, California Institute of Technology, 1966. Publications: The War in the Mediterranean 1803-1810, 1957; The War for America 1775-1783, 1964, 1993; Statesmen at War: The Strategy of Overthrow 1798-1799, 1974; The Coward of Minden: The Affair of Lord George Sackville, 1979; War without Victory: The Downfall of Pitt 1799-1802, 1984; British Victory in Egypt, 1801: The End of Napoleon's Conquest (Templer Medal), 1995. Memberships: National Army Museum, council member, 1983-92; Society for Army Historical Research, council member, 1985-94; British Academy, fellow, 1988. Address: Westerton Farmhouse, Dess, by Aboyne, Aberdeenshire AB34 5AY, Scotland.

MACKIERNAN Francis Joseph, b. 3 February 1926, Co Leitrim, Ireland. Catholic Bishop. Education: BA (Honours), 1947, BD, (Honours), 1950, Higher Diploma in Education, 1953, St Patrick's College, Maynooth and University College, Dublin. Appointments: Teacher of Classics, St Malachy's College, Belfast, 1951-52; Teacher of Classics and Irish, St Patrick's College, Cavan, 1952-62; President, St Felim's College, Ballinamore, Co Leitrim, 1962-72; Bishop of Kilmore, 1972-88; Retired, 1988. Publications: Bishops and Priests of the Diocese of Kilmore 1136-1988, 1988; St Mary's Abbey, Cavan, 2000; Many historical articles in Breifne, Journal of the Breifne Historical Society, 1958-. Membership: Editor of Breifne Journal, Secretary, Breifne Historical Society. Address: 5 Brookside, Cavan, Ireland.

MACKINTOSH Cameron Anthony, b. 17 October 1946, Enfield, England. Theatre Producer. Education: Prior Park College, Bath. Appointments: Stage Hand, Theatre Royal, Drury Lane; Assistant Stage Manager; Worked with Emile Littler, 1966; Robin Alexander, 1967; Producer, 1969-; Chair, Cameron Mackintosh, 1981-; Director, Delfont Mackintosh, 1991-; Productions: Little Women, 1967; Anything Goes, 1969; Trelawney, 1972; The Card, 1973; Winnie the Pooh, 1974; Owl and the Pussycat Went to Sea, 1975; Godspell, 1975; Side by Side by Sondheim, 1976; Oliver!, 1977; Diary of a Madam, 1977; After Shave, 1977; Gingerbread Man, 1978; Out on a Limb, 1978; My Fair Lady, 1979; Oklahoma!, 1990; Tomfoolery, 1980; Jeeves Takes Charge, 1981; Cats, 1981; Song and Dance, 1982; Blondel, 1983; Little Shop of Horrors, 1983; Abbacadabra, 1983; The Boyfriend, 1984; Les Miserables, 1985; Cafe Puccini, 1985; Phantom of the Opera, 1986; Follies, 1987; Miss Saigon, 1989; Just So, 1990; Five Guys Named Moe, 1990; Moby Dick, 1992; Putting it Together, 1992; The Card, 1992; Carousel, 1993; Oliver!, 1994; Martin Guerre, 1996; The Fix, 1997; Oklahoma!, 1999; The Witches of Eastwick, 2000; My Fair Lady, 2001. Honours: Observer Award for Outstanding Achievement; Laurence Oliver Award, 1991; Knighted. Address: Cameron Mackintosh Ltd, 1 Bedford Square, London, WC1B 3RA, England.

MACKLIN Elizabeth, b. 28 October 1952, Poughkeepsie, New York, USA. Poet. Education: BA in Spanish, State University of New York at Potsdam, 1973; Graduate School of Arts and Sciences, New York University, 1975-78. Appointment: Editorial Staff, 1974-99, Query Editor, 1981-99, The New Yorker Magazine; Poetry Editor, Wigwag Magazine, 1989-91; Freelance Editor and Writer, 2000-. Publication: A Woman Kneeling in the Big City, 1992; You've Just Been Told, poems, 2000. Contributions to: Nation; New Republic; New York Times; New Yorker; Paris Review; Threepenny Review. Honours: Ingram Merrill Foundation Award in Poetry, 1990; Guggenheim Fellowship, 1994; Amy Lowell Poetry Travelling Scholarship, 1998-99. Memberships: Authors Guild; PEN American Center, executive board, 1995-96. Address: 207 West 14th Street, 5F, New York, NY 10011, USA.

MACKMIN Michael, b. 20 April 1941, London, England. Psychotherapist; Poet; Editor. Divorced, 2 daughters. Education: BA, 1963; MA, 1965. Appointment: Editor, The Rialto. Publications: The Play of Rainbow; Connemara Shore. Address: PO Box 309, Aylsham, Norwich NR11 6LN, England.

MACLAINE Shirley, b. 24 April 1934, Richmond, Virginia, USA. Film Actress; Writer; Film Director. m. Steve Parker, 1954, 1 daughter. Education: Grammar School; Lee High School, Washington. Appointments: Chorus Girl and Dancer; Films include: The Trouble with Harry Artists and Models; Around the World in 80 Days; Hot Spell; The Matchmaker; Can-Can; Career; The Apartment; Two for the Seesaw; The Children's Hour; Irma La Douce; What a Way to go; The Yellow Rolls-Royce; Gambit; Woman Times Seven; The Bliss of Mrs Blossom; Sweet Charity; Two Mules for Sister Sara; Desperate Characters; The Possessions of Joel Delaney; The Turning Point, 1977; Being There, 1979; Loving Couples, 1980; The Change of Seasons, 1981; Slapstick, 1981; Terms of Endearment, 1984; Out on a Limb, 1987; Madame Sousatzka, 1989; Steel Magnolias, 1989; Waiting for the Light, 1990; Postcards from the Edge, 1990; Used People, 1993; Wrestling Ernest Hemingway, 1994; Guarding Tess, 1994; Mrs Westbourne, 1995; The Evening Star, 1995; Mrs Winterbourne, 1996; Revues: If My Friends Could See Me Now, 1974; To London with Love, 1976; London, 1982; Out There Tonight, 1990; TV Film: The West Side Waltz, 1994; Video: Shirley MacLaines's Inner Workout, 1989; Producer and Co-director, The Other Half of the Sky - A China Memoir, 1973. Publications: Don't Fall From Here, 1975; Out on a Limb, 1983; Dancing in the Light, 1985; It's all in the playing, 1987; Going Within, 1989; Dance While You Can, 1991; My Lucky Stars, 1995; The Camino, 2000. Honours: Star of the Year Award, Theatre Owners of America, 1967; Best Actress Award, Desperate Characters, Berlin Film Festival, 1971; Academy Award, Best Actress, 1984; Golden Globe Award, Best Actress, 1989; Lifetime Achievement Award, Berlin Film Festival, 1999. Address: MacLaine Enterprises Inc, 25200 Malibu Road, Suit 101, Santa Monica, CA 90265, USA.

MACLAVERTY Bernard, b. 14 September 1942, Belfast, Northern Ireland. Novelist; Dramatist. m. Madeline McGuckin, 1967, 1 son, 3 daughters. Education: BA, Honours, Queen's University, Belfast, 1974. Publications: Bibliography: Secrets and Other Stories, 1977; Lamb (novel), 1980; A Time to Dance and Other Stories, 1982; Cal (novel), 1983; The Great Profundo and Other Stories, 1987; Walking the Dog and Other Stories, 1994; Grace Notes (novel), 1997; The Anatomy School (novel), 2001. For Young Children: A Man in Search of a Pet, 1978; Andrew McAndrew, 1988, US edition, 1993. Radio Plays: My Dear Palestrina, 1980; Secrets, 1981; No Joke, 1983; The Break, 1988; Some Surrender, 1988; Lamb, 1992. Television Plays: My Dear Palestrina, 1980; Phonefun Limited, 1982; The Daily Woman, 1986; Sometime in August, 1989. Screenplays: Cal, 1984; Lamb,

1985; Bye-Child, 2003. Drama Documentary: Hostages, 1992, US edition, 1993; Television Adaptation: The Real Charlotte by Somerville and Ross, 1989. Honours: Northern Ireland and Scottish Arts Councils Awards; Irish Sunday Independent Award, 1983; London Evening Standard Award for Screenplay, 1984; Joint Winner, Scottish Writer of the Year, 1988; Society of Authors Travelling Scholarship, 1994; Shortlisted, Saltire Society Scottish Book of the Year, 1994, 2001; Grace Notes awarded The Saltire Scottish Book of the Year Award, 1997; A Scottish Arts Council Book Award; Shortlisted for: The Booker Prize; the Writers Guild Best Fiction Book; The Stakis Scottish Writer of the Year; The Whitbread Novel of the Year; Creative Scotland Award, the Scottish Arts Council, 2003; Nominated, BAFTA Best Short Film for Bye-Child, 2004.

MACLEAY John (Iain) Henry James, b. 7 December 1931, Inverness Scotland. Retired Clergyman. m. Jane Speirs Cuthbert, 1 son, 1 daughter. Education: BA, 1954, MA, 1960, St Edmund Hall, Oxford; College of the Resurrection, Mirfield, Yorkshire. Appointments: Deacon, 1957; Priest, 1958; Curate, St John's, East Dulwich, England, 1957-60; Curate, 1960-62, Rector, 1962-70, St Michael's, Inverness, Scotland; Priest-in-Charge, St Columba's, Grantown-on-Spey with St John the Baptist, Rothiemurchus, Scotland, 1970-78; Canon, St Andrew's Cathedral, Inverness, 1977-78; Rector of St Andrew's, Fort William, 1978-99; Synod Clerk of Argyll and the Isles, Canon of St John's Cathedral, Oban, 1980-87; Dean of Argyll and the Isles, 1987-99; Honorary Canon of Oban, 2001. Address: 47 Riverside Park, Lochyside, Fort William PH33 7RB, Scotland.

MACLEOD Alison, b, 12 April 1920, Hendon, Middlesex, England. Writer. Publications: The Heretics (in US as The Heretic), 1965; The Hireling (in UK as The Trusted Servant), 1968; City of Light (in UK as No Need of the Sun), 1969; The Muscovite, 1971; The Jesuit (in US as Prisoner of the Queen), 1972; The Portingale, 1976; The Death of Uncle Joe, 1997. Address: 63 Muswell Hill Place, London N10 3RP, England.

MACNAB Roy Martin, b. 17 September 1923, Durban, South Africa. Retired Diplomat. m. Rachel Heron-Maxwell, 6 December 1947, 1 son, 1 daughter. Education: Hilton College, Natal, South Africa; MA, Jesus College, Oxford, 1955; DLitt et Phil, University of South Africa, 1981. Publications: The Man of Grass and Other Poems, 1960; The French Colonel, 1975; Gold Their Touchstone, 1987; For Honour Alone, 1988. Co-Editor: Oxford Poetry, 1947; Poets in South Africa, 1958; Journey Into Yesterday, 1962. Editor: George Seferis: South African Diary, 1990; The Cherbourg Circles, 1994. Contributions to: Times Literary Supplement; Spectator; Poetry Review; History, Today. Honour: Silver Medal, Royal Society of Arts, 1958. Address: c/o Barclays Private Bank, 59 Grosvenor Street, London W1X 9DA, England.

MACNICHOL Marianne, b. Jacksonville, Florida, USA. Community College Educator. Education: BFA, Ballet Major, Theatre Minor, 1963, BA, History Major, English Minor, 1963, Texas Christian University. MA, Interdisciplinary Humanities, 1971, MA, English, 1973, PhD, Interdisciplinary Humanities, 1982, Florida State University. Appointments: Duval County School System, 1963-70, 1971-72, 1974-78; Adjunct, Florida Community College at Jacksonville, 1974-2001; Full-time St John's River Community College, 1978-2003; Retired from college in drop programme, June 2003; Rehired full-time, August 2003. Honours: Sarah Herndon Award for outstanding teaching in the humanities, 1974; International Executive Club, 2001; Award, National Institute for Staff and Organizational Development, 2002; 2000 Notable American Women; Woman of the Year 2003; Listed in Who's Who publications and biographical dictionaries. Memberships: Florida

Association of Community Colleges; Cummer Museum; Metropolitan Museum of New York. Address: PO Box 65279, Orange Park, FL 32065, USA.

MACPHERSON Elle, b. 29 March 1963, Killara, Australia. Model; Actress; Business Executive. m. G Bensimon, divorced 1990, 1 son with Arpad Busson. Career: Founder, Elle Macpherson Intimates, and Macpherson Men lingerie and underwear companies; Released fitness video, Stretch and Strengthen, The Body Workout, 1995; Chief Executive, Elle Macpherson Inc; Co-owner, Fashion Café, New York; Films: Sirens; Jane Eyre; If Lucy Fell; The Mirror Has Two Faces; Batman and Robin; The Edge; Beautopia; With Friends Like These. Address: c/o Artistmanagement Associates Inc, 414 East 52nd Street, Penthouse B, New York, NY 10022, USA.

MACQUEEN Hector Lewis, b. 13 June 1956, Ely, Cambridgeshire, England. Professor of Law. m. Frances Mary, 2 sons, 1 daughter. Education: LLB Honours, 1974-78, PhD, 1985, University of Edinburgh. Appointments: Lecturer, Senior Lecturer, Reader, 1979-94, Professor of Private Law, 1994-, Faculty of Law, Dean of the Faculty of Law, 1999-, University of Edinburgh; Visiting Professor, Cornell University, USA, 1991, Utrecht University, Netherlands, 1997; Director, The David Hume Institute, 1991-99. Publications: Copyright, Competition and Industrial Design, 1989, 2nd edition, 1995; Common Law and Feudal Society in Medieval Scotland, 1993; Studying Scots Law, 1993, 2nd edition, 1999; Contract Law in Scotland (with J M Thomson), 2000; Numerous articles in learned and professional journals and collections. Honour: Fellow of the Royal Society of Edinburgh. Memberships: Chair, Scottish Records Advisory Council, 2001-; Literary Director, Stair Society, 1999-; Heriots FP Cricket Club. Address: Faculty of Law, University of Edinburgh, Edinburgh EH8 9YL, Scotland. E-mail: hector.macqueen@ed.ac.uk

MACRAE (Alastair) Christopher (Donald) (Summerhayes) (Sir), b. 3 May 1937, Burleigh, Gloucestershire, England. Retired Diplomat. m. Mette Willert, 2 daughters. Education: BA Hons, Lincoln College, Oxford; Henry Fellow, Harvard University, USA. Appointments: Royal Navy, 1956-58; Second Secretary, Dar es Salaam, Tanzania, 1963-65; Middle East Centre for Arab Studies, 1965-67; Second Secretary, Beirut, Lebanon, 1967-68; Principal, Near East Department, Foreign and Commonwealth Office, 1968-70; 1st Secretary and Head of Chancery, Baghdad, Iraq, 1970-71; 1st Secretary and Head of Chancery, Brussels, Belgium, 1972-76; On loan to European Commission, 1976-78; Ambassador to Gabon, 1978-80, concurrently to Sao Tome and Principe; Head of West Africa Department, Foreign and Commonwealth Office, and Non-resident Ambassador to Chad, 1980-83; Political Counsellor, Paris, France, 1983-87; Head of Mission, Tehran, Iran, 1987; Assistant Under Secretary, Cabinet Office, 1988-91; British High Commissioner to Nigeria, 1991-94 and concurrently Ambassador to Benin; British High Commissioner to Pakistan, 1994-97; Secretary General Order of St John, 1997-2000. Honours: CMG, 1987; KCMG, 1993; KStJ, 1997. Memberships: Royal Commonwealth Society; Board Member, Aga Khan Foundation (UK); Chairman, Pakistan Society; President St John Ambulance, Ashford District. Address: 4 Church Street, Wye, Kent TN25 5BJ, England. E-mail: christophermacrae@btinternet.com

MACY William H, b. 13 March 1950, Miami, Florida, USA. Actor. Education: Goddard College, Vermont. Appointments: Co-founder, St Nicholas Theatre Company; Atlantic Theatre Company; Stage appearances include: The Man in 605, 1980; Twelfth Night; Beaurecrat; A Call from the East; The Dining Room; Speakeasy; Wild Life; Flirtations; Baby With the Bathwater; The Nice and the Nasty; Bodies Rest and Motion; Oh Hell!; Prairie du Chien; The

Shawl; An Evening With Dorothy Parker; The Dining Room; A Call From the Sea; The Beaver Coat; Life During Wartime; Mr Gogol and Mr Preen; Oleanna; Our Town; Play director: Boy's Life; Film appearances include: Without a Trace; The Last Dragon; Radio Days; Somewhere in Time; Hello Again; House of Games; Things Change; Homicide; Shadows and Fog; Benny and Joon; Searching for Bobby Fischer; The Client; Oleanna; The Silence of the Lambs; Murder in the First; Mr Holland's Opus; Down Periscope; Fargo; Ghosts of Mississippi; Air Force One; Wag the Dog; Pleasantville; A Civil Action; Psycho; Magnolia; State and Maine; Panic; Focus; Jurassic Park III; Welcome to Collinwood; The Cooler; Stealing Sinatra; Out of Order; Film director: Lip Service; TV appearances include: Chicago Hope; The Murder of Mary Phagan; Texan; A Murderous Affair; The Water Engine; Heart of Justice; A Private Matter; The Con; A Slight Case of Murder.

MADDEN John, b. 8 April 1949, Portsmouth, England. Film Director. Appointments: TV includes: Inspector Morse; Prime Suspect IV; Ethan Frome; Films: Mrs Brown, 1997; Shakespeare in Love, 1998; Captain Corelli's Mandolin, 2001. Honours: Academy Award for Best Film; BAFTA Award for Best Film, 1998.

MADDOCK Beatrice Louise, b. 13 September 1934, Hobart, Tasmania. Artist. Education: Diploma, Fine Art, Hobart Technical College, 1956; Postgraduate Studies, Slade School, University College, London, 1959-61. Appointments: Lecturer, Art, Launceston Teacher's College, Tasmania, 1962-63; Lecturer, Ceramics and Printmaking, Launceston Technical College, Tasmania, 1965-69; Lecturer, Printmaking, National Gallery School, Melbourne, 1970-72; Senior Lecturer, Printmaking, Victorian College of the Arts, Melbourne, 1973-81; Head, School of Art, Tasmanian College of Advanced Education, Launceston, 1983-84; Full-time Practising Artist, Victoria and Tasmania, 1985-. Civic Activities: Member, Visual Arts Board, Australia, 1979-80; Chairperson, Ritchies Mill Art Centre, Launceston, 1984-85; Member, Council of Australian National Gallery, Canberra, 1985-88; Member, Launceston Art Co-operative, 1993-97. Publications: Decoy: A Lithograph by Jasper Johns, Art Bulletin of Victoria, 1973-74; Graduate Diploma in Fine Arts, Art Network, 1980; Forty Days on the Icebird, Antarctic Journey, 1988; The Makings of a Trilogy, Art Bulletin of Victoria, 1990; Saying and Seeing, Siglo No 6, Hobart, 1996. Honours: Creative Arts Fellow, Australian, National University, 1976; IVth Prize, International Print Biennale, Poland, 1974; Honour member, Order of Australia, 1991; Clemenger Award, Contemporary Australian Art, 1993. Commissions and Creative Works: 30 solo exhibitions, Tasmania, Melbourne, Sydney, Ballarat, Canberra, 1964-99; 82 major group exhibitions in Australia, SE Asia, USA, Canada, New Zealand, Yugoslavia, Poland, Hungary, UK, Japan, Norway, Italy, Germany, India, South America, 1964-99. Address: P O Box 171, Mowbray Heights, Tasmania 7248, Australia.

MADDOCKS Morris Henry St John, b. 28 April 1928, Elland, West Yorkshire, England. Bishop. m. Anne. Education: MA (Cantab), Trinity College, Cambridge, 1956; Chichester Theological College. Appointments: Curate, St Peter's Ealing, London, 1954-55; Curate, St Andrew's, Uxbridge, 1955-58; Vicar, Weaverthorpe, Helperthorpe and Luttons Ambo, 1958-61; Vicar, St Martin's-on-the-Hill, Scarborough, 1961-71; Bishop of Selby, 1972-83; Co-founder, with Anne Maddocks, The Acorn Christian Healing Trust, 1983; Adviser to the Archbishops of Canterbury and York for the ministry of health and healing, 1983-95; Assistant Bishop, Diocese of Chichester, 1987-; Canon of Chichester Cathedral, 1992. Publications: Books: The Christian Healing Ministry, 1981; The Christian Adventure, 1983; Journey to Wholeness, 1986; A Healing House of Prayer, 1987; Twenty

Dictionary of International Biography

Questions About Healing, 1988; The Vision of Dorothy Kerin, 1991. Honour: Cross of St Augustine, 1995. Membership: Founding Life President (with Anne Maddocks), The Acorn Christian Foundation. Address: 3 The Chantry, Cathedral Close, Chichester, West Sussex PO 19 1PZ, England.

MADNI Asad Mohamed, b. 8 September 1947, Bombay, India. Company President. m. Gowhartaj A, 1 son. Education: AAS, RCA Institutes Inc, 1968; BS, 1969, MS, 1972, University of California, Los Angeles; PhD, California Coast University, 1987; Certificate Program in Engineering Management, Caltech, 1987; Executive Institute, Stanford University, 1984; Program for Senior Executives, MIT, Sloan School of Management, 1990. Appointments: Senior Instructor, Pacific States University, 1969-71; Senior Engineer, Pertec Corporation, 1973-75; President and General Manager, Systron Donner Microwave/Instrument Divisions, 1975-1990; President, Chief Executive Officer and Chairman, Systron Donner Corporation, 1990-92; President and Chief Executive Officer, BEI Sensors and Controls, 1992-93; President and Chief Executive Officer, BEI Sensors and Systems, 1993-2000; President and COO, BEI Technologies Inc., 2000-. Publications: Over 90 refereed publications; 24 patents issued, 16 patents pending. Honours: Numerous honours and awards from industry, academia, government and professional societies including: IEEE Millennium Medal; IEEE MTT-S Medal, AOC Gold Certificate of Merit; Joseph F Engelberger Best Paper Award, 2000 World Automation Congress, 2000; Distinguished Alumni Award, California Coast University, 2001; Professional Achievement Award Medal, University of California, Los Angeles, 2002; George Washington Engineer of the Year Award, Los Angeles Council of Engineers and Scientists, 2003; Distinguished Engineering Achievement Award, Engineers' Council, 2004; Listed in several biographical dictionaries. Memberships: Fellow, IEEE; Fellow, IEE; Fellow IAE; Fellow, NYAS; Life Fellow, IBA; Fellow AAAS; Life Senior Member, AIAA; Life Member, AOC; Member, SAE. Address: 3281 Woodbine Street, Los Angeles, CA 90064, USA.

MADONNA (Madonna Louise Veronica Ciccone), b. 16 August 1958, Bay City, Michigan, USA. Singer; Songwriter; Actress. m. (1) Sean Penn, 1985, divorced 1989; 1 daughter with Carlos Leon, (2) Guy Ritchie, 2000, 1 son. Education: University Of Michigan, 1976-78. Career: Dancer, New York, 1979; Actress, 1980-; Solo singer, 1983-; Film appearances include: Vision Quest, 1985; Desperately Seeking Susan, 1985; Shanghai Surprise, 1986; Who's That Girl, 1987; Bloodhounds On Broadway, 1990; Dick Tracy, 1990; A League Of Their Own, 1992; Evita, 1996; The Next Best Thing, 2000; Swept Away, 2002; Die Another Day, 2002; Numerous worldwide concerts, 1983-; Major appearances include: Live Aid, Philadelphia, 1985; Don't Bungle The Jungle, ecological awareness benefit, 1989; Television includes: In Bed With Madonna, documentary, 1991; Stage performance, Speed The Plow, Broadway, 1988; Up For Grabs, Wyndhams Theatre, 2002; Owner, Maverick record label. Compositions include: Co-writer, own hits: Live To Tell; Open Your Heart; Justify My Love; Co-writer, Each Time You Break My Heart, Nick Kamen, 1986. Recordings: Hit singles include: Holiday, 1983; Lucky Star, 1984; Borderline, 1984; Like A Virgin, 1984; Material Girl, 1985; Crazy For You, 1985; Angel, 1985; Into The Groove, 1985; Dress You Up, 1985; Gambler, 1985; Live To Tell, 1986; Papa Don't Preach, 1986; True Blue, 1986; Open Your Heart, 1986; La Isla Bonita, 1987; Who's That Girl, 1987; Causin' A Commotion, 1987; The Look Of Love, 1987; Like A Prayer, 1989; Express Yourself, 1989; Cherish, 1989; Dear Jessie, 1989; Oh Father, 1990; Keep It Together, 1991; Vogue, 1991; I'm Breathless, 1991; Hanky Panky, 1991; Justify My Love, 1991; Rescue Me, 1991; This Used To Be My Playground, 1992; Erotica, 1992; Deeper And Deeper, 1992; Bad Girl, 1993; Fever, 1993; Rain, 1993; Frozen, 1998;

Ray of Light, 1998; Power of Goodbye, 1998; Nothing Really Matters, 1999; Beautiful Stranger: theme song from Austin Powers: The Spy Who Shagged Me, 1999; American Pie, 2000; Music, 2000; Don't Tell Me, 2000; What It Feels Like For A Girl, 2001; Die Another Day, 2002; American Life, 2003. Albums: Madonna, 1983; Like A Virgin, 1985; True Blue, 1986; Who's That Girl?, film soundtrack, 1987; You Can Dance, 1988; Like A Prayer, 1989; I'm Breathless, 1990; The Immaculate Collection, 1990; Dick Tracy, film soundtrack, 1990; Erotica, 1992; Bedtime Stories, 1994; Something To Remember, 1995; Evita, film soundtrack, 1996; Ray of Light, 1997; Music, 2000; American Life, 2003. Publications: Sex, 1992; The English Roses, 2003; Mr Peabody's Apples, 2003. Honours include: Numerous MTV Video Awards, including Vanguard Award, 1986; American Music Awards: Favourite Female Video Artist, 1987; Favourite Dance Single, 1991; Oscar, Best Song, 1991; Juno Award, International Song Of The Year, 1991; Grammy Award, Best Longform Music Video, 1992; Numerous awards from Billboard, Vogue and Rolling Stone magazines. Address: c/o Norman West Management, 9348 Civic Centre Drive, Beverly Hills, CA 90210, USA.

MADSEN Michael, b. 25 September 1958, Chicago, USA. Actor. m. Jeannine Bisignano, 1 son. Appointments: Began acting career, Steppenwolf Theatre, Chicago; Appeared in plays including: Of Mice and Men; A Streetcar Named Desire; Appeared in Broadway Production of A Streetcar Named Desire, 1992; Films: Wargames, debut, 1983; The Natural; Racing with the Moon, 1984; The Killing Time, 1987; Shadows in the Storm; Iguana, 1988; Blood Red, 1989; Kill Me Again, 1990; The Doors, 1991; The End of Innocence, 1991; Thelma and Louise, 1991; Fatal Instinct, 1992; Inside Edge, 1992; Reservoir Dogs, 1992; Straight Talk, 1992; Almost Blue, 1992; Free Willy, 1993; A House in the Hills, 1993; Money for Nothing, 1993; Trouble Bound, 1993; Wyatt Earp, 1993; The Getaway, 1994; Dead Connection, 1994; Species; Free Willy II: The Adventure Home, 1995; The Winner, 1996; Red Line, 1996; Mulholland Falls, 1996; Man with a Gun, 1996; The Last Days of Frankie the Fly, 1996; Rough Draft, 1997; The Marker, 1997; Donnie Brasco, 1997; Catherine's Grove, 1997; Papertrail, 1997; The Girl Gets Moe, 1997; Executive Target, 1997; The Thief and the Stripper, 1998; Supreme Sanction, 1998; The Florentine, 1998; Species II, 1998; Detour, 1999; Code of the Dragon, 2000; The Ghost, 2000; High Noon, 2000; LAPD Conspiracy, 2001; LAPD To Protect and Serve, 2001; TV: Our Family House, 1985-86; Special Bulletin, 1983; War and Remembrance, 1988; Montana, 1990; Baby Snatcher, 1992; Beyond the Law, 1994. Address: Grant and Tane, 9100 Wilshire Boulevard, Beverley Hills, CA 90212, USA.

MAEGAARD Jan Carl Christian, b. 14 April 1926, Copenhagen, Denmark. Musicologist; Composer. m. Kirsten, divorced 1988, 2 daughters. Education: Music theory, composition, music history, piano, double bass, 1945-50, conducting 1952, Royal Danish Conservatory of Music; Musicology, University of Copenhagen, 1951-57; State certificate as music teacher in music theory and music history, 1953; Studies in Los Angeles, 1958-59, 1964; Dr phil, 1972. Appointments: Freelance musician, 1949-56; Music critic, various newspapers, 1952-60; Teacher, Royal Danish Conservatory of Music, 1953-58; Teaching Assistant, University of Copenhagen, 1959-61, Associate Professor, 1961-71, Full Professor, 1971-96; Guest Professor, State University of New York, Stony Brook, 1974; Professor of Music, University of California, Los Angeles, 1978-81; Guest lecturer at institutions at home and abroad including Universities in Oslo, 1965, 1985, 1987, Vancouver, 1981, Santa Barbara, 1981, Riverside (California), 1981, Poznan and Warsaw, 1986, Akademie der Künste, Berlin, 1986. Publications: Books include: Musikalsk Modernisme, 1964, 1971; Studien zur Entwicklung des dodekaphonen Satzes bei

Dictionary of International Biography

Arnold Schönberg, 1972; Præludier til Musik af Schönberg, 1976; Musikalsk analyse efter Forte-meloden (editor), 1988; Begreber I musikhistorien frem til ca. 1600, 1999; (co-author) Kuhlau. Kanons, 1996; Numerous articles; contributions to reference works; Printed music includes: Progressive Variations Viol, vcl Op 96, Engstrøm & Sødring musikforlag, Copenhagen, 1993; Concerto for cello and orchestra, Op 98, Danish Radio, 1993; Jeu mosaïque for harp and orchestra, Op 99, Samf, 1995; Partita for cello solo, Op 103, Engstrøm & Sødring musikforlag, Copenhagen, 1997. Honour: Knight of Dannebrog 1st Degree. Memberships include: Royal Danish Academy of Sciences and Letters, 1986; Norwegian Academy of Science and Letters, 1988. Address: Duevej 14, 6, 2000 Frederiksberg, Denmark.

MAEHLER Herwig Gustav Theodor, b. 29 April 1935, Berlin, Germany. Emeritus Professor of Papyrology. m. Margaret, 2 daughters. Education: Classics and Classical Archaeology, Universities of Hamburg, Tübingen and Basel, 1955-61; PhD, University of Hamburg, 1961; Postdoctoral British Council Fellowship, Oxford University, England, 1961-62; Habilitation, Freie Universität, Berlin, 1975. Appointments: Research Assistant, University of Hamburg, 1962-63; Research Assistant, Hamburg University Library, 1963-64; Keeper of Greek Papyri, Egyptian Museum, West Berlin, 1964-79; Reader in Papyrology, 1979-81, Professor of Papyrology, 1981-2000, Professor Emeritus, 2000-, University College, London. Publications: Die Auffassung des Dichterberufs im frühen Griechentum bis zur Zeit Pindars, 1963; Die Handschriften der S Jacobi-Kirche in Hamburg, 1967; Urkunden römischer Zeit, 1968; Papyri aus Hermupolis, 1974; Die Lieder des Bakchylides Part I, 1982, Part II, 1997; Greek Bookhands of the Early Byzantine Period (with G Cavallo), 1987; Editions of Bacchylides, 1970 and Pindar, 1971, 1975, 1989; About 120 articles in learned journals. Honours: Corresponding Member, German Archaeological Institute, 1979; Fellow, British Academy, 1986; Fellow, Accademia Nazionale dei Lincei, Rome 2001; Honorary Fellow, University College London, 2001; Honorary PhDs: University of Helsinki, 2000, University of Budapest, 2001, Rome II Tor Vergata, 2003. Address: Department of Greek and Latin, University College London, Gower Street, London, WC1E 6BT, England. E-mail: hgt.maehler@virgin.net

MAELAND Johan Andreas, b. 22 February 1934, Hordaland, Norway. Professor of Medicine. 3 sons. Education: MD, 1959; PhD, 1969; Certified Specialist in Medical Microbiology and Dermatology. Appointments: Intern and Resident, Assistant Professor, University of Buffalo, USA, 1971-72; Professor of Microbiology and Head of Department of Microbiology, 1975-, Dean, Medical Faculty, 1978-80, University Hospital, Trondheim, Norway. Publications: 110 scientific articles mostly in international journals. Honour: Schering Corporation Prize, 1984. Memberships: ESCMID; American Society of Microbiology; Scandinavian and National Medical Associations. Address: Havstadvn 15A, N-7021 Trondheim, Norway.

MAES Michael H J, b. 10 March 1954, Ghent. Professor; Psychiatrist. m. Steyaert Carine, 2 daughters. Education: MD, 1979; Psychiatrist, 1986; PhD, 1991. Appointments: Assistant Professor of Psychiatry, University of Antwerp, Belgium, 1986-91; Assistant Professor of Psychiatry, CWRU, Cleveland, Ohio, USA, 1991-96; Director, Clinical Research, Centre of Mental Health, Antwerp, 1995-; Adjunct Professor, Vanderbilt University, Nashville, Tennessee, USA, 1997-; Professor of Psychiatry, Department of Psychiatry, University of Maastricht, The Netherlands, 1999-. Publications: 350 articles in international journals. Honours: ECNP Award, 1991; The Klerman Award for Outstanding Research, NARSAD, 1998; Prize, Rimauz-Bartier, FWO, 1999; Listed in Several Biographical Publications.

Memberships: World Psychiatric Association; Society of Biological Psychiatry. Address: Department of Psychiatry and Neuropsychology, University Hospital of Maastricht, Postbus 5800, AZ 6202, Maastricht, The Netherlands. E-mail: crc.mh@skynet.be

MAGA Othmar, b. 30 June 1929, Brno, Czechoslovakia. Conductor. Education: Studied at the Stuttgart Hochschule für Musik, 1948-52; Tubingen University, 1952-58; Accademia Chigiana at Siena with Paul van Kempen, 1954-55; Further studies with Sergiu Celibidache, 1960-62. Career: Conducted the Göttingen Symphony Orchestra, 1963-67, Nuremberg Symphony, 1968-70; General Music Director at Bochum, 1971-82; Artistic Director of the Odense Symphony Orchestra, Denmark, and Permanent Conductor of the Orchestra of the Pomeriggi Musicali de Milano, 1987-90; Also Professor at the Folkswangschule at Essen; Guest Conductor with leading orchestras in Europe and Japan; From 1992-96 Chief Conductor of the KBS-Symphony Orchestra in Seoul, Korea; Guest Conductor with leading orchestras in Europe, Japan and America. Address: Merlos 19, 36323 Grebenau, Germany.

MAGEE Bryan, b. 12 April 1930, London, England. Writer. m. Ingrid Söderlund, 1 daughter. Education: MA, Keble College, Oxford University, 1956; Yale University, 1955-56. Appointments: Theatre Critic, The Listener, 1966-67; Lecturer in Philosophy, Balliol College, Oxford, 1970-71; Visiting Fellow, All Souls College, Oxford, 1973-74; Regular Columnist, The Times, 1974-76; Member of Parliament for Leyton, 1974-83; President, Critics Circle of Great Britain, 1983-84; Honorary Senior Research Fellow, 1984-94, Visiting Professor, 1994-2000, King's College, London; Honorary Fellow, Queen Mary College, London, 1988-; Fellow, Queen Mary and Westfield College, London, 1989-; Visiting Fellow: Wolfson College, Oxford, 1991-94, New College, Oxford, 1995, Merton College, Oxford, 1998, St Catherine's College, Oxford, 2000, Peterhouse College, Cambridge, 2001. Publications: Go West Young Man, 1958; To Live in Danger, 1960; The New Radicalism, 1962; The Democratic Revolution, 1964; Towards 2000, 1965; One in Twenty, 1966; The Television Interviewer, 1966; Aspects of Wagner, 1968; Modern British Philosophy, 1971; Popper, 1973; Facing Death, 1977; Men of Ideas, 1978, reissued as Talking Philosophy, 2001; The Philosophy of Schopenhauer, 1983; The Great Philosophers, 1987; On Blindness, 1995, reissued as Sight Unseen, 1998; Confessions of a Philosopher, 1997; The Story of Philosophy, 1998; Wagner and Philosophy, 2000; Clouds of Glory, 2003. Contributions to: Numerous journals. Honour: Silver Medal, Royal Television Society, 1978. Memberships: Critics Circle; Society of Authors; Arts Council of Great Britain and Chair, Music Panel, 1993-94; Honorary Fellow, Keble College, Oxford, 1994-; Silver Medal, Royal TV Society. Address: Wolfson College, Oxford OX 2 6UD, England

MAGER Peter Paul, b. 18 June 1946, Klostergeringswalde, Saxony, Germany. m. Christine, 2 daughters. Education: Approbation in Medicine, Leipzig, 1973; MD, 1974; Mathematics in Chemistry, 1975, Degree in Pharmacology and Toxicology, 1978, Halle; DSc, 1982; Degree in Educational and Didactic Methodology in University Teaching, 1983; Facultas docendi, 1990; Dr med habil, 1991. Appointments: Assistant, Pharmacology and Toxicology, University of Greifswald, 1973-75; Assistant in Internal Medicine, Doesen/Saxony, 1975-76; Senior Researcher, Institute of Pharmacy, University of Halle, 1976-80; Head of Research Group of Pharmacochemistry, University of Leipzig, 1980-; Co-ordinator, Research Programme, FMC Co, Princeton, New Jersey, USA, 1984-90; Consultant, Clinical Pharmacology, Leipzig, 1985-90; Consultant, Biostructure SA, France, 1991-94; Managing Director, Institute of Pharmacology and Toxicology,

University of Leipzig, 1993-95; Professor, 1996. Publications: Co-editor and Referee of scientific periodicals; Around 200 papers in scientific periodicals and handbooks; 3 monographs. Honour: Leibniz Award. Memberships include: New York Academy of Sciences; American Association for the Advancement of Science; Affiliate, International Union of Pure and Applied Chemistry; German Society of Pharmacology and Toxicology; Medicinal Chemistry Division, Computer Chemistry Division, German Chemical Society; Deutsche Hochschulverband. Address: Institute of Pharmacology and Toxicology, Haertelstr 16-18, Leipzig D-04107, Germany. E-mail: magp@server3.medizin.uni-leipzig.de

MAGNUSSON Magnus, b. 12 October 1929, Reykjavik, Iceland. Writer; Broadcaster. m. Mamie Baird, 1954, 1 son, 3 daughters. Education: Edinburgh Academy; Jesus College, Oxford. Appointments: Assistant Editor, Scottish Daily Express; The Scotsman; Presenter, various TV and radio programmes including: Chronicle; Mastermind; Pebble Mill and One; BC, The Archaeology of the Bible Lands; Tonight; Cause for Concern; All Things Considered; Living Legends; Vikings!; Birds for All Seasons; Editor, The Bodley Head Archaeologies; Popular Archaeology, 1979-80; Chair, Ancient Monuments Board for Scotland, 1981-89; Cairngorms Working Party, 1991-93; NCC for Scotland, 1991-92; Scottish National Heritage, 1992-99; Rector, Edinburgh University, 1975-78; Member, UK Committee for European Year of the Environment, 1987; Board of Trustees, National Museum of Scotland, 1985-89; President, RSPB, 1985-90; Honorary Vice President, Age Concern Scotland; RSSPCC; FSA, Scotland, 1974. Publications: Introducing Archaeology, 1972; The Clacken and the Slate, 1974; Hammer of the North, 1976; BC, The Archaeology of the Bible Lands, 1977; Landlords or Tenant?; A View of Irish History, 1978; Iceland, 1979; Vikings! Magnus on the Move, 1980; Treasures of Scotland, 1981; Lindisfarne: The Cradle Island, 1984; Iceland Saga, 1987; I've Started So I'll Finish, 1997; Rum: Nature's Island, 1997; Magnus Magnusson's Quiz Book, 2000; Scotland: The Story of a Nation, 2000; Contributions to various historical and novelty books; Introductions to numerous books on historical, geographical and cultural themes; Editor: Echoes in Stone, 1983; Readers Digest Book of Facts, 1985; Chambers Biographical Dictionary, 1990; Others. Honours: Honorary Fellow, Oxford, 1990; Honorary FRIAS, 1987; FRSGS, 1991; Dr hc, Edinburgh, 1978; Hon D Univ, York, 1981; Paisley, 1993; Hon D Litt. Strathclyde, 1984, Naiper, 1984; Glasgow, 2001, Glasgow Caledonian, 2001; Iceland Media Award, 1985; Silver Jubilee Medal, 1977; Medlicott Medal, 1989; Knight of Order of the Falcon, Iceland, 1975; Commander, 1986; Honorary KBE. Address: Blairhaith House, Balmore-Tottance, Glasgow, G64 4AX, Scotland.

MAGNUSSON Tomas Herbert, b. 1 April 1949, Linköping. Dentist. m. Annica Birgitta Hedmo, 3 daughters. Education: L D S, 1974; Odont Dr, PhD, 1981; Docent, Reader, 1986; Certified Specialist in Stomatographic Physiology, 1993. Appointments: General Practitioner, Jokkmokk, Sweden, 1974-1979; Assistant Professor, University of Göteberg, Sweden, 1979-1980; Head, Senior Consultant, Lulea, Sweden, 1980-1988; Senior Consultant, 1988-2000, Head, Senior Consultant, 2000-, Jonkoping, Sweden. Publications: Published more than 60 scientific papers in peer review national and international journals mainly in the field of temporomandibular disorders; One out of two authors of four textbooks and author of four separate book chapters, all in the field of temporomandibular disorders. Honours: The Forsberg Dental Foundation Award for extraordinary clinical achievements, 1990; The Henry Beyron Award for unique research, 2000; Corresponding member, Finnish Dental Society, 2002. Memberships: Swedish Dental Association; Swedish Dental Society; Swedish Academy of Temporo Mandibular Disorders;

Board member and past president of the Society of Oral Physiology. Address: The Institute for Postgraduate Dental Education, Box 1030, SE-55111 Jonkoping, Sweden. E-mail: tomas.magnusson@ltjkpg.se

MAGUIRE Adrian Edward, b. 29 April 1971, Ireland. Jockey. m. Sabrina, 1995, 1 daughter. Education: Kilmessan National School; Trim Vocational School. Appointments: Champion Pony Race Rider, 1986; Champion Point to Point Rider, 1990-91; Champion Conditional Jockey, 1991-92; Winner of the Following Races: Cheltenham Gold Cup; Irish Grand National; Galway Plate; Imperial Cup; Greenalls Gold Cup; Queen Mother Champion Chase; King George VI Chase; Triumph Hurdle and Cathcort Chase; Holds record for most Point to Point winners in a season; Most winners in a season for a conditional jockey (71), 1991-92; Retired due to neck injury having won over 1,000 races, 2002. Address: The Jockey Club (Jockey Section), 42 Portman Square, London, W1H 0EM, England.

MAHAJAN Harpreet, b. November 1953, Simla, India. Computer Consultant; Teacher. Education: BSc, University of Delhi, India, 1973; MA, Political Science, 1975, MPhil, International Affairs, 1976, PhD, International Affairs, 1980, Jawaharlal Nehru University, India; MPhil, Political Science, Columbia University, 1983. Appointments: Executive Director of Information Technology, School of International and Public Affairs, Columbia University, 1995-; Adjunct Associate Professor, School of International Public Affairs, Columbia University, 1993-; Director of Information Technology, Institute for Social and Economic Research and Policy, Columbia, 1998-2002; Consultant, Institute for Social and Economic Research and Policy, 2002-03. Publications: Arms Transfers to India, Pakistan and the Third World, 1982; Peace and Disputed Sovereignty, 1985; Computers: Personal Computers, 2003. Honours: President's Fellow, Political Science, Columbia University, 1980-81; Fellow, Political Science, Columbia, 1978-80; Research Fellow, Delhi University, 1975-79; Listed in national and international biographical dictionaries. Address: 420 W 118th Street, #1514 IAB, Columbia University, New York, NY 10027, USA. Website: www.sipa.columbia.edu

MAHECHA GÓMEZ Jorge Eduardo, b. 8 August 1948, La Palma, Cundinamarca, Colombia. Physicist. m. Clara Inés Botero, 2 sons. Education: BSc, Physics, University of Antioquia, Medellin, Colombia, 1973; MSc Physics, 1979, PhD Physics, 1995, University of Belgrade, Yugoslavia. Appointment: Professor of Physics, Institute of Physics, University of Antioquia, Medellin, Colombia. Publications: Books: Advanced Classical Mechanics; Computational Packages in Science and Engineering; Course on Atomic Doubly Excited States, editor; Articles include: On Riemann Zeta Function; Confined one-electron atom; One-electron atom near metal surfaces; Confined electron hole-systems; Coulomb 3-body systems. Honours: Associate Fellowship, The Abdus Salam, International Centre for Theoretical Physics, Trieste, Italy, 1987-93, 1995-2001. Memberships: Sociedad Mexicana de Fisica; Sociedad Colombiana de Fisica; American Physical Society. Address: Institute of Physics, University of Antioquia, Calle 67 No 53-108, AA 1226, Medellin, Colombia. E-mail: mahecha@fisica.udea.edu.co

MAHJOUB Bechir Mohamed, b. 18 June 1935, Mahdia, Tunisia. Professor. m. Aicha Zouari, 2 sons, 1 daughter. Education: Licence de Mathématiques, Institut des Hautes Études de Tunis, 1960; Diplôme D'Études Supérieures, University of Tunis, 1963; Doctorat d'État es Sciences Mathématiques, Paris Sorbonne, 1970. Appointments: Professor of Mathematics, University of Tunis, 1974-; Director General, Higher Education of Tunisia, 1977-88; Delegate of Tunisia at UNESCO, 1988-92; Professor, University of Qatar, 1992-2000. Publications: Book: Cours D'Analyse, 1983; Numerous articles on mathematics published in the proceedings of the Academy of Sciences of Paris and in the annals of the Institute Henri Poincare. Honours: Officier de l'Ordre de la Republique, Tunisia, 1978; Officier de la Légion d'Honneur, France, 1983; Officier de l'Ordre National du Merite, France, 1984. Memberships: Société Mathématique de Tunisie; Association Tunisienne des Sciences Mathématiques. Address: 9 rue des Narcisses, 1004 Elmenzah 5, Tunisia. E-mail: b.mahjoub@planet.tn

MAHMOUD Samia Aly, b. 12 November 1940, Cairo, Egypt. Food Legumes Scientist. m. Salah El Din Aly, 2 sons. Education: BSc, Agronomy, 1962, MSc, Genetics, 1968, PhD, Genetics, 1973, Ain Shams University; Diploma in Agriculture, University of Illinois, USA, 1976. Appointments: Specialist, Food Legumes Research Programme, 1962-67; Assistant Researcher, 1968-72; Associate Researcher, 1974-78; Senior Researcher, 1979-86; Associate Professor of Genetics, 1980-85, Head of Botany Department, 1982-85, Professor of Genetics, 1987-92, Girls College of Education, Saudi Arabia; Visiting Professor, 1986; Chief of Research, 1987; Leader, Food Legumes Research Programme, Filed Crop Institution, Agricultural Research Centre, Giza, Egypt, 1995-2000; Co-ordinator, Food Legumes research Programme, Nile Valley and Red Sea Research and Contributor to Technology Transfer Programmes and Field Days for Extensions, Farmers and Postgraduates. Publications: Over 40 scientific publications as co-author include most recently: Screening for Faba Bean Necrotic Yellows Virus Resistance in the Faba bean, 1998; Selection of drought tolerance Faba bean genotypes, 1999; Trends in support for research and development of cool season food legumes in the developing countries, 1999. Honours: Named on of the three best trainees in the USA, AID, 1976; Award of Excellence, Girl's College of Education, Saudi Arabia, 1987-92; Award of Distinction and Recognition, 2002, Award of Excellence, 2002, University of Maryland, USA; Listed in Who's Who publications and biographical dictionaries. Memberships include: Faba Bean Export System Project, 1999-2001; Member and Contributor, International Conference on Soybean Production Under Newly Reclaimed Lands, Egypt, 1998; Arbitration Committee of Scientific Production and Activities; Egyptian Society of Genetics and Cytology; Egyptian Society of Agronomy; Egyptian Society of Plant Breeding; American Society of Agronomy. Address: 9 Hamadan St, Off Murad St, Giza 12211, Egypt.

MAHY Marcus John, b. 8 February 1961, Southampton, England. Trust Company Managing Director. Education: TEC/BSc, Aerospace Engineering, 1981; MBA, Business Administration, 1990; Registered Trust and Estate Practitioner, 1992; Member, Offshore Institute, 1992. Appointments: Manager, Coutts & Co, Bermuda; General Manager, State House Trust Co Ltd; President and Managing Director, Landmark Trust (Bermuda) Limited. Publications: Author book, Inside the MIG29; Numerous articles. Memberships: Offshore Institute; Society of Trust and Estate Practitioners. Address: Landmark Trust (Bermuda) Limited, 95 Front Street, Hamilton, Bermuda HM 12. E-mail: mmahy@smithlaw.bm

MAIKASUWA Salisu Abubakar, b. 4 March 1958, Keffi Local Government Area, Nigeria. Civil Servant. m. Fatima and Hajara, 3 sons. Education: BSc, Sociology, 1980; MSc, Public Administration and Policy Analysis, 1984. Appointments: Ministry of the Federal Capital Area Abuja: Assistant Secretary II, Establishments; Principal Personnel Officer, Corporate Affairs; Chief Personnel Officer, Special Duties; Chief Personnel Officer, Public Accounts (The Presidency, Nigeria); Assistant Director, Special Assistant to the Director General/Clerk, National Assembly; Deputy Director/Special Assistant to the Clerk, National

Assembly. Publications: The Impact of Local Government Reforms on the Chieftancy Institution of Keffi Emirate of Nasarawa State (BSc Research Project); The Nature and Problems of Local Government Administration in Federal Capital Territory, Abuja (MSc Research Project). Honours: Pilot of True Service to the Nation Award, National Association for Democratic Youth; Abuja Developers Award, Nigerian Union of Journalists. Address: Office of the Special Assistant to the Clerk of National Assembly, PMB 141, 3 Arms Zone, Abuja, Nigeria.

MAILER Norman (Kingsley), b. 31 January 1923, Long Beach, California, USA. Writer. m. (1) Beatrice Silverman, 1944, divorced 1951, 1 daughter, (2) Adele Morales, 1954, divorced 1962, 2 daughters, (3) Lady Jeanne Campbell, 1962, divorced 1963, 1 daughter, (4) Beverly Rentz Bentley, 1963, divorced 1980, 2 sons, 1 daughter, (5) Carol Stevens, divorced, 1 daughter, (6) Norris Church, 1980, 1 son. Education: BS, Harvard University. Publications: The Naked and the Dead, 1948; Barbary Shore, 1951; The Deer Park, 1955 (dramatised 1967); Advertisements for Myself, 1959; Deaths for the Ladies (poems), 1962; The Presidential Papers, 1963; An American Dream, 1964; Cannibals and Christians, 1966; Why are We in Vietnam?, 1967; The Armies of the Night, 1968; Miami and the Siege of Chicago, 1968; Moonshot, 1969; A Fire on the Moon, 1970; The Prisoner of Sex, 1971; Existential Errands, 1972; St George and the Godfather, 1972; Marilyn, 1973; The Faith of Graffiti, 1974; The Fight, 1975; Some Honourable Men, 1976; Genius and Lust: A Journey Through the Writings of Henry Miller, 1976; A Transit to Narcissus, 1978; The Executioner's Song, 1979; Of Women and Their Elegance, 1980; The Essential Mailer, 1982; Pieces and Pontifications, 1982; Ancient Evenings, 1983; Tough Guys Don't Dance, 1983; Harlot's Ghost, 1991; How the Wimp Won the War, 1991; Oswald's Tale, 1995; Portrait of Picasso as a Young Man, 1995; The Gospel According to the Son, 1997; The Time of Our Time, 1998; The Spooky Art: Thoughts on Writing, 2003; Why Are We At War? 2003. Contributions to: Numerous journals and magazines. Honours: National Book Award for Arts and Letters, 1969; Pulitzer Prize for Non-Fiction, 1969; Award for Outstanding Service to the Arts, McDowell Colony, 1973. Memberships: PEN, president, 1984-86; American Academy of Arts and Letters. Address: c/o Rembar, 19th West 44th Street, New York, NY 10036, USA.

MAILLET Jeanne, b. 14 August 1931, Le Touquet, France. Poet. m. Bernard Maillet, 2 daughters. Education: Institut Etudes Litteraires, Nice, 1951; Licence es Lettres, Faculty Aix Marseille, 1955. Career: Established a poetry circle, Saint-Pol-Sur-Ternoise, 1978-. Publications: 17 poetry books, 1977-; Stories and poems for children. Honours: Numerous poetry prizes. Memberships: Rosati (Arras); Society of French Poets, Paris; PEN Club of Monaco. Address: 17 rue d'Egmont, 62130 Saint-Pol-Sur-Ternoise, France.

MAIYEKOGBON Seth Abel, b. 8 August 1941, Mopa, Mopamuro Local Government Area, Kogi State, Nigeria. Management Consultant. m. Alice Ajoke, 5 sons, 1 daughter. Education: BSc, Economics, Polytechnic of Central London (now Westminster University), England, 1965; Post Graduate Diploma, Personnel Management and Project Evaluation. Appointments: Provincial Commercial Officer in charge of Kano and Katsina Provinces, Northern Nigeria Government, 1965-67; Various capacities, Ministry of Trade and Industry, Kwara State, 1967-76; General Manager, Salcom Limited, Ilorin, Kwara State, 1976-78; Established Alma Industrial and Management Consultants, 1978-; Trained National Youth Service Corps; Organiser in-plant courses for companies including: Nigeria Sugar Company Limited, Nigeria Paper Mill Limited, Bacita and United Textiles Mill Limited; Member, Finance Committee, ECWA Headquarters, Jos, Nigeria,

1981-83; Member, Governing Council, Lagos State Polytechnic, 1979-82; Member, Lagos State Continuing Education Board, 1982-83 Management Consultant to National Directorate of Employment, Small Scale Industrial Programme, Federal Ministry of Labour and Productivity, 1985-2002, currently involved in organising, management and technical workshops in collaboration with federal and state agencies and the organised private sector in Nigeria. Publications: Over 85 papers in technical and management journals, columnist on management, business and management, Sunday Herald, Kwara State, Nigeria; Contributor to current affairs programmes including View Point and X-Ray. Honours: Nominee APBN Merit Awards, Institute of Management Consultants of Nigeria, 2000; Appointed to Think Tank of Afenifere; Listed in several biographical dictionaries for outstanding professional achievements. Memberships: Institute of Personnel Management of Nigeria, Chairman, Kwara State Branch, 1982-85, National Vice President, 1984-85; Fellow, Institute of Management Consultants of Nigeria, President, 1983-84; Fellow, Institute of Administrative Management of Nigeria; Nigeria Institute of Management; Nigeria Economic Society, University of Ibadan, Vice Chairman, Kwara State Chapter; Nigeria Institute of Training and Development, Chairman, Kwara State Chapter. Address: Alma Industrial and Management Consultants, 147/208 Ibrahim Taiwo Road, PO Box 396, Ilorin, Kwara State, Nigeria.

MAJOR Clarence, b. 31 December 1936, Atlanta, Georgia, USA. Poet; Writer; Artist; Professor. m. (1) Joyce Sparrow, 1958, divorced 1964, (2) Pamela Ritter. Education: BS, State University of New York at Albany, 1976; PhD, Union Graduate School, 1978. Appointments: Editor, Coercion Review, 1958-66, Writer-in-Residence, Center for Urban Education, New York, 1967-68, Teachers and Writers Collaborative-Teachers College, Columbia University, 1967-71, Aurora College, Illinois, 1974, Albany State College, Georgia, 1984, Clayton College, Denver, 1986, 1987; Associate Editor, Caw, 1967-70, Journal of Black Poetry, 1967-70; Lecturer, Brooklyn College of the City University of New York, 1968-69, 1973, 1974-75, Cazenovia Collge, New York, 1969, Wisconsin State University, 1969, Queens College of the City University of New York, 1972, 1973, 1975, Sarah Lawrence College, 1972-75, School of Continuing Education, New York University, 1975; Columnist, 1973-76, Contributing Editor, 1976-86, American Poetry Review; Assistant Professor, Howard University, 1974-76, University of Washington, 1976-77; Visiting Assistant Professor, University of Maryland at College Park, 1976, State University of New York at Buffalo, 1976; Associate Professor, 1977-81, Professor, 1981-89, University of Colorado at Boulder; Editor, 1977-78, Associate Editor, 1978-, American Book Review; Professor, 1989-, Director, Creative Writing, 1991-, University of California at Davis. Publications: Poetry: The Fires That Burn in Heaven, 1954; Love Poems of a Black Man, 1965; Human Juices, 1965; Swallow the Lake, 1970; Symptons and Madness, 1971; Private Line, 1971; The Cotton Club: New Poems, 1972; The Syncopated Cakewalk, 1974; Inside Diameter: The France Poems, 1985; Surfaces and Masks, 1988; Some Observations of a Stranger in the Latter Part of the Century, 1989; Parking Lots, 1992; Configurations: New and Selected Poems 1958-1998, 1998; Waiting for Sweet Baby, 2002. Fiction: All-Night Visitors, 1969; new version, 1998; NO, 1973; Reflex and Bone Structure, 1975; Emergency Exit, 1979; My Amputations, 1986; Such Was the Season, 1987; Painted Turtle: Woman with Guitar, 1988; Fun and Games, 1990; Dirty Bird Blues, 1996. Other: Dictionary of Afro-American Slang, 1970; The Dark and Feeling: Black American Writers and Their Work, 1974; Juba to Jive: A Dictionary of African-American Slang, 1994; Necessary Distance: Essays and Criticism, 2001; Come by Here: My Mother's Life, 2002. Editor: Writers Workshop Anthology, 1967; Man is Like a Child: An Anthology of Creative Writing by Students, 1968; The

New Black Poetry, 1969; Calling the Wind: Twentieth Century African-American Short Stories, 1993; The Garden Thrives: Twentieth Century African-American Poetry, 1995. Honours: Fulbright-Hays Exchange Award, 1981-83; Western States Book Award, 1986; Pushcart Prize, 1989. Address: c/o Department of English, University of California at Davis, Davis, CA 95616, USA.

MAJOR John, b. 29 March 1943. Politician; Former Member of Parliament. m. Norma Major, 1970, 1 son, 1 daughter. Education: Associate, Institute of Bankers. Appointments: Various executive positions, Stand Chartered Bank, UK and overseas, 1965-80; Served, Lambeth Borough Council, 1968-71, including Housing and Finance Committees, also Chairman, Accounts Committee and Housing Committee, 1969; Contested Camden, St Pancras North, February and October 1974; Member, Board, Warden Housing Association, 1975-93; Member of Parliament for Huntingdonshire, 1979-83, for Huntingdon, 1983-2001; Parliamentary Private Secretary to Ministers of State, Home Office, 1981-83; Assistant Government Whip, 1983-84; Lord Commissioner of Treasury, Senior Government Whip, 1984-85; Parliamentary Under-Secretary of State, Department of Health and Social Security, 1985-86; Minister of State, Social Security and the Disabled, 1986-87; Chief Secretary to the Treasury, 1987-89; Secretary of State for Foreign and Commonwealth Affairs, 1989; Chancellor of the Exchequer, 1989-90; Elected Leader, Conservative Party, 1990; Prime Minister, 1st Lord of the Treasury, Minister for the Civil Service, 1990-97. Memberships: Parlimentary Consultant to Guild of Glass Engravers, 1979-83; President, Eastern Area Young Conservatives, 1983-85; National Asthma Campaign, 1998-; Chair, Carlyle Group, 2001-; Non-Executive Director, Mayflower Corporation, 2000-; Member, Main Committee, MCC, 2001-; Honorary Master of the Bench of the Middle Temple, 1992. Publications: The Autobiography, 1999. Address: House of Commons, London, SW1A 0AA, England.

MAJOR Malvina (Lorraine) (Dame), b. 28 January 1943, Hamilton, New Zealand. Opera Singer (Soprano). m. Winston William Richard Fleming, 16 January 1965, deceased 1990, 1 son, 2 daughters. Education: Grade VIII, Piano, Singing, Theory, Convent at Ngaruawahia, Waikato; Singing continued under Dame Sister Mary Leo, St Mary's Music School, Auckland, 1960-65 and Ruth Packer, Royal College of Music, London, London Opera Centre, UK, 1965-67. Debut: Camden Town Festival, 1968 in Rossini's La Donna del Lago. Career includes: Performances as: Belle, Belle of New York, New Zealand, 1963; Pamina, Magic Flute, London Opera Centre, 1967; 1st non Mormon Soloist to sing with Mormon Tabernacle Choir, 1987; Matilda in Elisabetta Regina d'Inghilterra, Camden Town, 1968; Rosina, Barber of Seville, Salzburg (conductor, Claudio Abbado), 1968-69; Gala Concert, King and Queen of Belgium, Centenary Antwerp Zoological Society, 1969; Marguerite, Gounod's Faust, Neath and London, 1969; Bruckner's Te Deum, conductor Daniel Barenboim, 1968; Cio Cio San, Madam Butterfly; Widow, The Merry Widow; Gilda in Rigoletto; Tosca; Constanze in Die Entführung; Arminda in La Finta Giardiniera, Brussels, 1986; Donna Elvira, Don Giovanni, Brighton Festival, 1987; Donna Anna in Don Giovanni at Sydney, Australia, 1987; Operas include recent productions of Rosalinda (Die Fledermaus) and Lucia di Lammermoor, Mimi in La Bohème and Constanze in New York and Australia; Sang Arminda at Lausanne, 1989, Constanze with the Lyric Opera of Queensland; Season 1992-93 with Lucia at Adelaide, Arminda at Salzburg, Violetta and Gilda at Wellington; Sang in Eugene Onegin and Don Giovanni with Wellington City Opera, 1997. Recordings: To The Glory of God, 1964; L'amico Fritz, opera (Caterina), 1969; Songs for All Seasons, Mahler Symphony No 4, 1970; Scottish Soldiers Abroad, 1975; Alleluia, 1974; Operatic Arias, conductor John Matheson, 1987; La Finta Giardiniera, Brussels. Contributions

Dictionary of International Biography

to: London Sunday Times (article by Desmond Shawe-Taylor). Honours: New Zealand Mobil Song Quest, 1963; Melbourne Sun Aria, Australia, 1964; Kathleen Ferrier Scholarship, London, 1966; OBE, 1985; DBE, 1991; Honorary D Litt, 1993; Honorary D Waik, 1993. Address: P O Box 4184, New Plymouth, New Zealand.

MAKAROV Valery, b. 25 May 1937, Novosibirsk, Russia. Scientist. m. Nina Pakhomova, 1 son, 1 daughter. Education: Moscow State Economic University, 1960; PhD, Academy of Sciences, 1965; Professor of Economics, 1970. Appointments: Director, Central Economics and Mathematics Institute, Moscow, Russia, 1985-; Rector, New Economic School, 1992-. Publication: Mathematical Economic Theory (Advanced Books in Economics), 1995. Honours: State Award of USSR, 1980; Kantorovich Award, 1995; State Order of Merit, 1997.Memberships: Fellow, Econometric Society, 1978; Full Member, Russian Academy of Sciences, 1990. Address: Central Institute of Economics and Mathematics, Nakhimovsky Prospect 47, 117418 Moscow, Russia. E-mail: makarov@cemi.rssi.ru

MAKARUK Hanna E, b. Warsaw, Poland. Theoretical Physicist. m. Robert M Owczarek. Education: MS, Physics, Warsaw University, 1989; XLIV Postgraduate Course in Computational Mathematics, Institute of Computer Sciences and Institute of Mathematics of Polish Academy of Sciences, 1991; Doctor of Technical Sciences, Polish Academy of Sciences, Institute of Fundamental Technological Research, 1994. Appointments: Research Assistant, Polish Academy of Sciences, 1989-94; Associate Professor, Polish Academy of Sciences, Institute of Fundamental Technological Research, 1994-96 (on leave, 1996-); Director-Funded Postdoctoral Fellowship, Los Alamos National Laboratory, Theoretical Division, 1996-98; Technical Staff Member, Los Alamos National Laboratory, 1999-. Publications: 30 journal papers and book chapters. Honours: Long-term Fellowship for Priority Area Research in Japan, Japan Society for Promotion of Science, 1995; Grant, Polish State Committee for Scientific Research, 1995; Kosciuszko Foundation Fellowship, New York, 1996. Memberships: International Society for Interaction of Mechanics and Mathematics; Society for Industrial and Applied Mathematics; American Mathematical Society; Institute of Physics; American Nuclear Society; National Association of Environmental Professionals; Polish Physical Society; Polish Society of Applied Electromagnetics. Address: 59 Coryphodon Lane, Jemez Springs, NM 87025, USA.

MAKES Yozua, b. Jakarta, Indonesia. Lawyer. m. Dewi Julia Pramitarini, 1 son, 3 daughters. Education: SH, University of Indonesia, Faculty of Law; LLM, School of Law, University of California, Berkeley, USA; Master in Management, Asian Institute of Management, Philippines. Appointments: Founding Partner, Makes & Partners Law Firm, Jakarta, Indonesia; Partner, Kartini Muljadi & Rekan, Jakarta, Indonesia; Head Corporate Finance, Lubis Hadiputranto Ganie Surowidjojo, Jakarta, Indonesia; Partner, Mulya Lubis & Partners, Jakarta, Indonesia; Expert Staff to: Minister of Defence, Former Minister of the Co-operatives, Medium and Small Scale Industries; Qualified to act as a Receiver or Administrator of companies declared bankrupt. Publications: Speaker, lecturer and author of various publications including: Building Value in Asia, 2000; Search Report on Indonesian Economics Law Infrastructure (edited by Faisal Basri). Memberships include: National Committee on Corporate Governance; Member of Team to Formulate General Outlines of Indonesian State Policy, 1998; Board of Experts, Indonesian Public Listed Companies Association; Board of Trustees, Jakarta Art Foundation. Address: Makes & Partners Law Firm, Menara Batavia, 7th Fl, Jalan KH Mas Mansyur Kav 126, Jakarta 10220, Indonesia. E-mail: makes@makeslaw.com

MAKINDE Amos Morakinyo, b. 3 November 1954, Ado-Ekiti, Nigeria. University Senior Lecturer. m. Foluke, 2 sons, 1 daughter. Education: BSc (Hons), Biology, 1980, MSc, Botany, 1984, Unife; PhD, Botany, Obafemi Awolowo University (Unife), 1991. Appointments: Lecturer, Adeyemi College, Ondo, 1985-94; Botany Lecturer, Obafemi Awolowo University, Ile Ife, 1994-. Publications: Articles in scientific journals including: New Botanist, 1993; Nigerian Journal of Botany, 1993; Experientia, 1994; Journal of Agriculture, Science and Technology, 1994; NJB, 1999; African Journal of Science, 1999. Honour: Reviewer of journal papers for: Nigerian Journal of Botany, Journal of Agriculture Science and Technology, Environtropica. Memberships: Botanical Society of Nigeria; Nigerian Field Society; Board of Studies, Institute of Agriculture Research and Training, Obafemi Awolowo University, Ibadan. Address: Department of Botany, Obafemi Awolowo University, Ile Ife, Nigeria.

MAKOWER Peter, b. 12 September 1932, Greenwich, London, England. Architect; Town Planner. m. Katharine Chadburn, 2 sons, 1 daughter. Education: The Royal Engineers, 1951-52; Territorial Army, 1952-56; Master of Arts, Trinity College, University of Cambridge, 1959; Diploma in Architecture, The Polytechnic, London, 1959; Diploma in Town Planning, University of London, 1969. Appointments: Architect, 1959-62, Associate, 1962-82, Frederick Gibberd Partners, London; Executive Architect, Chapman Taylor Partners, 1982-85; Solo Principal, Peter Makower Architects and Planners, 1985-99. Publications: The World is Not Enough – an account of the filming of part of the river chase in the Bond film of that name; The Boater, The Quarterly Magazine of the Thames Vintage Boat Club, 2000. Honours: Conservation and Design Award, London Borough of Richmond upon Thames and the Mortlake with East Sheen Society; Lay Reader, Church of England. Memberships: Associate, 1961-70, Fellow, 1970-, Royal Institute of British Architects; Royal Town Planning Institute, 1972-. Address: 89 Hartington Road, Chiswick, London W4 3TU, England.

MAKTOUM H H Sheikh Maktoum bin Rashid al, b. 1941. Ruler of Dubai. m. 1971. Appointments: Succeeded his father Sheikh Rashid bin Said al Maktoum, as 5th Sheikh, 1990; Prime Minister, United Arab Emirates, 1971-79, 1991-; Deputy Prime Minister, 1979-90; Vice-President, 1990-. Address: Ruler's Palace, Dubai, United Arab Emirates.

MAKTOUM Sheikh Mohammed bin Rashid al, b. 1948. Crown Prince of Dubai; Race Horse Owner. Appointments: Trained in British Army and RAF; Minister of Defence, Dubai; with Brothers Sheikh Maktoum al Maktoum, Sheikh Hamden al-Maktoum and Sheikh Ahmed al-Maktoum has had Racing interests in UK, 1976-; first winner, Hatta, Goodwood, 1977; with Brothers now owns studs, stables, country house and sporting estates in Newmarket and elsewhere in UK; Worldwide racing interests based at Delham Hall Stud, Newmarket; Horses trained in England, Ireland and France; Director, Godolphin Racing, Dubai; f Racing Post (daily), 1986; Owner, Balanchine, winner, Irish Derby, 1994; Winner, numerous classic races, Leading Owner, 1985-1989, 1991-93. Address: Ministry of Defence, PO Box 2838, Dubai, UAE.

MALAMBUGI Angolwisye Isakwisa, b. 30 June 1946, Ileje, Tanzania. Pastor; Lecturer. m. Elizabeth, 4 sons, 3 daughters. Education: Diploma of Theology, Makerere University, Uganda, 1972-75; Bachelor of Divinity, Makumira Lutheran Theological College, Tanzania, 1979-80; Master of Theology, Presbyterian Theological Seminary, Seoul, Korea, Certificate in Mission Studies, OMSC, Newhaven, USA, 1994-95. Appointments: Principal Utengule Bible College, 1981-83; Vice-Chairman, Moravian Church in Tanzania, SW province, 1984-88; Chairman, Moravian

Church in Tanzania SW province, 1988-94; Lecturer, Mbeyamoravian Theological College, 1995-; Part-time Lecturer, Open University of Tanzania (Philosophy and Religious Studies), 1999-; Proprietor, African Drum Herald Booksellers and Stationery. Publications: Article: Hebrew Words in Swahili Language, in Tam Tam AACC, Nairobi. Honours: Deputy Governor, American Biographical Institute and Research Association; Researcher of the Year, ABI, 2001. Memberships: Ecumenical Association of Third World Theologians; American Biographical Institute (Board of Directors); Society of Biblical Literature, USA; General Committee of All Africa Conference of Churches 1992-2003; Old Testament Society of South Africa, 1998; Association of Biblical Scholars in East Africa, 2000; Founder, Mbeya Multidevelopment Centre (NGO); Founder, Halleujah-Hossana Christian Ministries. Address: PO Box 1133, Mbeya, Tanzania.

MALBRÁN María del Carmen, b, 9 October 1941, General Villegas, Argentina. University Researcher. m. Jorge Alberto Serdarevich, 1 daughter. Education: Professor of Special Education, Ministry of Education, Argentina, 1963; Educational Psychologist, University of La Plata Argentina, 1969; Master of Education, University of Puerto Rico, USA, 1972. Appointments: Postgraduate Teacher; Senior Researcher, University of Buenos Aires, National University of La Plata. Publications: Papers published in national and international journals on matters relating to cognitive psychology and inclusive education; Abstracts and articles. Honours: Pemio Credit Suisse (Science and Letters); Fellowship, University of Peace; Fellowship, Finnish Foreign Ministry. Memberships: Council Member, International Association for the Study of Intellectual Disability. Address: Av Rivadavia 3049 4° "H", C1203 AAC, Buenos Aires, Argentina. E-mail: malbranserdarevich@infovia.com.ar

MALFITANO Catherine, b. 18 April 1948, New York City, New York, USA. Singer (Soprano). Education: High School of Music and Art; Manhattan School of Music; With violinist father and dancer/actress mother; Voice with Henry Lewis. Debut: Nannetta in Falstaff, Central City Opera, 1972. Career: With Minnesota Opera, 1973, New York City Opera, 1973-79, debut as Mimi/La BohÈme; Netherlands Opera: Susanna in Figaro, 1974, Eurydice, 1975, Mimi, 1977; Tosca 1998; Salzburg Festival: Servilia in Tito, 1976, 1977, 1979, 3 Hoffmann roles, 1981, 1982, Salome, 1992, 1993, Elvira in Giovanni, 1994, 1995, 1996; Jenny in Mahagonny, 1998; Met debut as Gretel, 1979, returning for many other roles; Vienna Staatsoper: Violetta, 1982, Manon, 1984, Grete in Schreker's Der Ferne Klang, 1991, Salome and Butterfly, 1993; Wozzeck, 1997; Maggio Musicale Florence: Suor Angelica, 1983, Jenny in Weill's Mahagonny, 1990, Salome, 1994; Teatro Comunale, Florence: Antonia in Hoffmann, 1980-81, Mimi, 1983, Faust, 1985, Butterfly, 1988, Poppea, 1992; Munich: Berg's Lulu, 1985, Mimi, 1986, Daphne, 1988; Covent Garden: Susanna, Zerlina, 1976, Butterfly, 1988, Lina (Stiffelio), Tosca, Tatyana, 1993, Salome, 1995, 1997; Berlin Deutsche Oper: Butterfly, 1987, Amelia in Boccanegra, Mimi, Susanna, 1989, Salome, 1990; Berlin Staatsoper, Marie (Wozzeck), 1994, Leonore (Fidelio), 1995; Geneva: Fiorilla (Turco), 1985, Poppea, Manon, 1989, Leonore, 1994; La Scala: Daphne, 1988, Butterfly, 1990; Wozzeck, 1997; Lyric Opera, Chicago: Susanna, 1975, Violetta, 1985, Lulu, 1987, Barber's Cleopatra, 1991, Butterfly, 1991-92, Liu, 1992; McTeague/Bolcom, 1992; Makropulos Case, 1995-96; 3 Roles/Il Trittico, 1996; Salome, 1996; Butterfly 1997, 1998; Mahagonny, 1998; View from Bridge/Bolcom, 1999; Macbeth, 1999; World premiere roles created: Conrad Susa's Transformations, 1973, Bilby's Doll (Carlisle Floyd), 1976, Thomas Pasatieri's Washington Square, 1976, William Bolcom's McTeague, 1992. Recordings: Rossini Stabat Mater, conductor Muti; Gounod Roméo et Juliette,

conductor Plasson; Strauss's Salome, conductor Dohnányi; Music for Voice and Violin with Joseph Malfitano; Tosca - Zubin Mehta; Others; Videos include Tosca with Domingo; Stiffelio with Carreras and Salome. Honours: Emmy, Best Performance in Tosca film; Honorary Doctorate De Paul University, Chicago.

MALICK Terrence, b. 30 November 1943, Ottawa, Illinois, USA. Film Director. Education: Center for Advanced Film Study; American Film Institute. Appointments: Films: Bedlands; Days of Heaven, 1978; The Thin Red Line, 1998; The Moviegoer. Honours: New York Film Critics Award, National Society of Film Critics Award, 1978; Cannes Film Festival Award, 1978; Golden Berlin Bear Award, 1999; Chicago Film Critics Association Award, 1999; Golden Satellite Award, 1999. Address: c/o DGA, 7920 Sunset Boulevard, Los Angeles, CA 90046, USA.

MALIK Hafeez, b. 17 March 1930, Lahore, Pakistan. Professor of Political Science. m. Lynda P, 2 sons, 1 daughter. Education: Graduate Diploma, Journalism, University of Punjab, Lahore, Pakistan, 1952; MS, Journalism, Syracuse University, 1955; MS, Political Science, 1957; PhD, Political Science, 1961. Appointments: Assistant Professor, Political Science, Villanova University, 1961-63; Associate Professor, 1963-67; Professor, 1967-; Editor, Journal of South Asian and Middle Eastern Studies, Villanova University, 1977-; Many visiting professor positions. Publications: Encyclopedia of Central Asia; Encyclopedia of Pakistan; Fifty Years of Pakistan; The Roles of the United States, Russian and China in the New World Order; Soviet Pakistan Relations and Current Dynamics; Central Asia, Its Strategic Importance and Future Prospects; Many other publications. Honours: 4 grants received to organize international conferences and seminars. Memberships: Association for Asian Studies; Pi Sigma Alpha; American Association of University Professors; American Political Science Association; Pakistan Historical Association; Pakistan Council, The Asia Society, New York; The National Seminar on Pakistan, Bangladesh of Columbia University. Address: Villanova University, 416-421 SAC, Villanova, PA 19085, USA.

MALKOVICH John, b. 9 December 1953, Christopher. m. Glenne Headley, 1982, divorced, 1 daughter, 1 son by Nicoletta Peyran. Education: Eastern Illinois and Illinois State University. Appointments: Co-Founder, Steppenwolf Theatre, Chicago, 1976; Theatre appearances include: True West, 1982; Death of a Salesman, 1984; Burn This, 1987; Director, Balm in Gilead, 1984-85; Arms and the Man, 1985; Coyote Ugly, 1985; The Caretaker, 1986; Burn This, 1990; A Slip of the Tongue, 1992; Libra, 1994; Steppenwolfe, 1994; Film appearances include: Places in the Heart, 1984; The Killing Fields, 1984; Eleni, 1985; Making Mr Right, 1987; The Glass Menagerie, 1987; Empire of the Sun, 1987; Miles from Home, 1988; Dangerous Liaisons, 1989; Dangerous Liaisons, 1989; Jane, La Putaine du roi, 1989; Queen's Logic, 1989; The Sheltering Sky, 1989; The Object of Beauty, 1991; Shadows and Fog, 1992; Of Mice and Men, 1992; Jennifer Eight; Alive; In the Line of Fire, 1993; Mary Reilly, 1994; The Ogre, 1995; Mulholland Falls, 1996; Portrait of a Lady, 1996; Con Air; The Man in the Iron Mask, 1997; Rounders, 1998; Tune Regained, 1998; Being John Malkovich, 1999; The Libertine, 1999; Ladies Room, 1999; Joan of Arc, 1999; Shadow of the Vampire, 2000; Je Rentre à la Maison, 2001; Hotel, 2001; Knockaround Guys, 2001; The Dancer Upstairs, director and producer, 2002; Ripley's Game, 2003; Johnny English, 2003; Executive Producer, The Accidental Tourist. Address: c/o Artists Independent Network, 32 Tavistock Street, London, WC2E 7PB, England.

MALLARD John Rowland, b. 14 January 1927, Northampton, England. Professor of Medical Physics and Medical Engineering. m. Fiona Lawrance, 1 son, 1 daughter. Education: BSc honours, Physics, University College, Nottingham, 1947; PhD, Magnetism, 1952, DSc, Medical Physics, 1972, University of Nottingham. Appointments: Assistant Physicist, Radium Institute, Liverpool, 1951-53; Senior then Principal Physicist, 1953-56, Head, Department of Physics, 1956-62, Hammersmith Hospital, London; Reader, Medical Physics, Postgraduate Medical School, University of London, 1962-64; Reader, Biophysics, St Thomas's Hospital Medical School, London, 1964-65; Professor of Medical Physics, Head of Department of Bio-Medical Physics and Bio-Engineering, University of Aberdeen and Grampian Health Board, 1965-92. Publications: Over 240 papers, review articles and lectures in medical and scientific journals. Honours include: OBE, 1992; Royal Society Wellcome Gold Medal, 1984; Royal Society Mullard Gold Medal, 1990; Honorary DSc, University of Hull, 1994; Norman Veall Prize Medal, British Nuclear Medicine Society, 1995; Honorary DSc, University of Nottingham, 1996; Keith of Dunottar Silver Medal, Royal Scottish Society of Arts, 1996; Honorary DSc, University of Aberdeen, 1997. Memberships include: Fellow: Royal Society of Edinburgh; Royal Academy of Engineering; Institution of Electrical Engineers; Institute of Physics; Royal College of Pathologists; Honorary Fellow: Institute of Physics and Engineering in Medicine; British Institute of Radiology; British Nuclear Medicine Society; Founder Fellow, International Society of Magnetic Resonance and Medicine; Founder President, International Union of Physics and Engineering in Medicine. Address: 121 Anderson Drive, Aberdeen, AB15 6BG, Scotland. E-mail: h.parry@biomed.abdn.ac.uk

MALLET Philip Louis Victor, b. 3 February 1926, London, England. Member of HM Diplomatic Service (Retired). m. Mary Moyle Grenfell Borlase, 3 sons. Education: Balliol Colllege, Oxford, England. Appointments: Army, 1944-47; HM Foreign Diplomatic Service, 1949-82; Served in Iraq, Cyprus, Aden, Germany, Tunisia, Sudan and Sweden; British High Commissioner in Guyana and non-resident Ambassador to Suriname, 1978-82. Honour: CMG. Address: Wittersham House, Wittersham, Kent TN30 7ED, England.

MALLEY Raymond Charles, b. 22 December 1930, Cambridge, Massachusetts, USA. Retired Senior Foreign Service Officer; Industrial Executive. m. (1) Rita Ann Masse, 26 May 1951, deceased June 1989, 3 sons, (2) Josette Lucile Vidril Murphy, 11 August 1995. Education: AA, 1950, BS, 1952, Boston University, USA; MA Equivalent, University of Geneva, Switzerland, 1955; MA, PhD ABD, Fletcher School, Law and Diplomacy, Tufts University and Harvard University, Massachusetts, 1956. Appointments: Major, US Air Force, 1952-54; Active Reserve, 1954-70; Economist, Financial Analyst, Texaco Inc, New York City, 1957-61; Foreign Service Officer, US Department of State/AID, Washington and foreign posts, 1961-82; Director, US Trade and Development Programme, Washington, 1980; Vice President, Silopress Inc, Sioux City, Iowa, 1982-87; President, Silopress Canada Inc, 1984-87; Consultant, Adviser, Labat-Anderson International, Arlington, Virginia, 1988-93; Senior Group Adviser, North and South American representative, Halla Business Group, Seoul (Korea), New York City, Washington, 1991-; Chairman, Halla America Inc, 1996-2001. Memberships: Member, Executive Board, College of Management, Long Island University, Brookville, New York, 1994-; Member, Acadian Cultural Society; American Foreign Service Association; Diplomatic and Consular Officers Retired; US Professional Tennis Registry; Harvard Club. Address: 6224 Loch Raven Dr, McLean, VA 22101-3133, USA.

MALONE Robert R, b. 8 August 1933, McColl, South Carolina, USA. Art Professor. m. Cynthia, 1 son. Education: Furman University, Greenville, 1951-53; BA, University of North Carolina, Chapel Hill, 1953-55; MFA, University of Chicago, 1957-58; Postgraduate, University of Iowa, 1959. Appointments: Lambuth College, Jackson, 1959-61; Wesleyan College, 1961-68; West Virginia University, Morgantown, 1968-70; Southern Illinois University, Edwardsville, 1970-. Publications: Several articles in professional journals. Honours: Over forty regional and national awards. Commissions and Creative Works: International Graphic Arts Society, New York City, 1966; Lakeside Studio, Michigan, 1971-79; Illinois Art Council, Chicago, 1973; Art and Architecture Program, State of Illinois, 1994. Address: 600 Chapman Street, Edwardsville, IL 62025, USA.

MALONE Vincent, b. 11 September 1931, Liverpool, England. Bishop. Education: BSc, Liverpool University, 1959; Cert Ed, 1960, Dip Ed, 1962, Cambridge University. Appointments: Chaplain to Notre Dame Training College, Liverpool, 1955-59; Assistant Priest, St Anne's, Liverpool, 1960-61; Assistant Master, Cardinal Allen Grammar School, Liverpool, 1961-71; Chaplain to Liverpool University, 1971-79; Administrator (Dean), Liverpool Metropolitan Cathedral, 1979-89; Auxiliary Bishop of Liverpool, 1989-. Membership: Fellow, College of Preceptors. Address: 17 West Oakhill Park, Liverpool L13 4BN, England. E-mail: vmalone@onetel.net.uk

MALONEY Simone, b. 11 September 1936, Manchester, New Hampshire, USA. Accountant, Tax Services. m. Anthony B Maloney, 3 sons. Education: BS, Accounting, Southern University of New Hampshire, 1981. Appointments: Certified Tax Professional; Practitioner of Taxation; Receptionist, Telephone Operator, Accounting Supervisor, Travelers Insurance Co, Manchester, New Hampshire, 1966-76; Auditor, 1976-79; Private Practice as Accountant and Bookkeeper and Tax Services, Manchester, 1981-; Volunteer: Boy Scouts of America; 1980 Campaign to re-elect Robert Shaw as Mayor of City of Manchester, 1985; Presidential Campaign, Congressman Phil Crane, 1980; Campaign Congressman Bill Zeliff, 1990; Candidate for Alderman, City of Manchester, 1983; Office Manager, 1983-84, Treasurer, 1985-86 for Campaign Congressman Bob Smith; Elected Selectman Ward 2, 1992-95, appointed Moderator, 1996, elected Moderator, 1997-, Manchester. Honour: Bella Duperron Award, Manchester Republican Party, 2003. Memberships: Secretary, Greater Manchester Federated Republican Women's Club, 1987; Treasurer, Manchester Republican Committee, 1989-92, 1996-; Secretary, Chairman, Ward 2 Republican Committee, 1987-88; National Society of Tax Professionals; National Federated Republican Women; Smithsonian Institute. Address: 171 Russell St, Manchester, NH 03104-3770, USA.

MALOUF (George Joseph) David, b. 20 March 1934, Brisbane, Queensland, Australia. Poet; Novelist. Education: BA, University of Queensland, 1954. Appointments: Assistant Lecturer in English, University of Queensland, 1955-57; Supply Teacher, London, 1959-61; Teacher of Latin and English, Holland Park Comprehensive, 1962; Teacher, St Anselm's Grammar School, 1962-68; Senior Tutor and Lecturer in English, University of Sydney, 1968-77. Publications: Poetry: Bicycle and Other Poems, 1970; Neighbours in a Thicket: Poems, 1974; Poems, 1975-1976, 1976; Wild Lemons, 1980; First Things Last, 1981; Selected Poems, 1981; Selected Poems, 1959-1989, 1994. Fiction: Johnno (novel), 1975; An Imaginary Life (novel), 1978; Child's Play (novella), 1981; The Bread of Time to Come (novella), 1981, republished as Fly Away Peter, 1982; Eustace (short story), 1982; The Prowler (short story), 1982; Harland's Half Acre (novel), 1984; Antipodes (short stories), 1985; The Great World (novel), 1990;

Remembering Babylon (novel), 1993; The Conversations at Curlow Creek (novel), 1996; Dream Stuff (stories), 2000. Play: Blood Relations, 1988. Opera Libretti: Voss, 1986; Mer de Glace; Baa Baa Black Sheep, 1993. Memoir: Twelve Edmondstone Street, 1985. Editor: We Took Their Orders and Are Dead: An Anti-War Anthology, 1971; Gesture of a Hand (anthology), 1975. Contributions to: Four Poets: David Malouf, Don Maynard, Judith Green, Rodney Hall, 1962; Australian; New York Review of Books; Poetry Australia; Southerly; Sydney Morning Herald. Honours: Grace Leven Prize for Poetry, 1974; Gold Medals, Australian Literature Society, 1975, 1982; Australian Council Fellowship, 1978; New South Wales Premier's Award for Fiction, 1979; Victorian Premier's Award for Fiction, 1985; New South Wales Premier's Award for Drama, 1987; Commonwealth Writer's Prize, 1991; Miles Franklin Award, 1991; Prix Femina Etranger, 1991; Inaugural International IMPAC Dublin Literary Award, 1996; Neustadt Laureat, 2000. Address: 53 Myrtle Street, Chippendale, New South Wales 2008, Australia.

MALPAS James Spencer, b. 15 September 1931, Wolverhampton, England. Medical Practitioner. m. Joyce May Cathcart, 2 sons. Education: St Bartholomew's Hospital Medical College, University of London, England 1949-55; Postgraduate, Royal Postgraduate Medical School, Hammersmith Hospital, London, 1960, Nuffield Department of Medicine, Oxford, England, 1962-65. Appointments: Medical Specialist, Royal Airforce, 1957-60; House Physician, Hammersmith Hospital Royal Postgraduate Medical School, 1960-61; Lecturer in Medicine, Oxford University, 1962-65; Dean of the Medical College, 1969-72, Director, ICRF Department of Medical Oncology, 1976-85, Clinical Director, ICRF, 1985-90, Professor of Medical Oncology, 1979-95, Vice President, Medical College, 1987-95, St Bartholomew's Hospital; Professor Emeritus, London University, 1995-; Elected Master of the London Charterhouse, 1996-2001; Currently Trustee, St Bartholomew's London Charitable Foundation. Publications: Over 200 peer-reviewed articles on adult and paediatric cancer and haematology; Co-editor, Myeloma Biology and Management, 3rd edition 2003; Editor, Cancer in Children, 1996. Honours include: Lockyer Lecture, Royal College of Physicians, 1978; Skinner Medal, Royal College of Physicians, 1986; Freeman of the City of London, 1988; Subhod-Mitra Gold Medal, Delhi, India, 1991; Medicus Hippocraticus Prize, Greece, 1996, Memberships: Member of many medical societies; Fellow, Royal College of Physicians; Fellow, Royal College of Radiology; Fellow, Royal College of Paediatricians and Child Health; Fellow, Royal Institution of Great Britain and Northern Ireland. Address: 253 Lauderdale Tower, Barbican, London EC2Y 8BY, England. E-mail: gmalpas@supamet.com

MALPAS John Peter Ramsden, b. 14 December 1927, Colombo, Ceylon. Stockbroker. m. Rosamond Margaret Burn, 3 sons. Education: MA (Oxon), P.P.E., New College Oxford. Appointments: Imperial Chemical Industries, 1951-56; Chase, Henderon and Tennant, 1956-58; Deputy Chairman, Quilter Goodison, 1959-87; London Stock Exchange, 1961-88; Non Executive Director, Penny & Giles International, 1988-92; Management Board, 1988-, Honorary Treasurer, 1988-98, Royal Hospital for Neuro Disabilities; Non Executive Director, West Wittering Estate, 1998. Honour: MA (Oxon). Memberships: Itchenor Sailing Club; Ski Club Great Britain. Address: 48 Berwyn Road, Richmond, Surrey TW10 5BS, England. E-mail: peter.malpas@ukgateway.net

MALTBY Per Eugen, b. 3 November 1933, Oslo, Norway. Astrophysicist. m. Elisabet Ruud, 1 son, 1 daughter. Education: Cand Real, University of Oslo, 1957; Dr Philosophiae, 1964. Appointments: Research Fellow, California Institute of Technology,

1960-61, Senior Research Fellow, 1964-65; Amanuensis, University of Bergen, 1961-63; Universitetslektor, försteamanuensis, University of Oslo, 1963-67, Dosent, 1967-82, Chairman, Astronomy Department, 1975-77, Professor, 1983-; Visiting Scientist, CSIRO, Sydney, 1974-75; Chairman, Norwegian Council for Natural Science Research, 1978-80. Memberships: Norwegian Academy of Science and Letters; International Astronomical Union; American Astronomical Society; European Physics Society; Norwegian Physics Society. Address: Institute of Theoretical Astrophysics, University of Oslo, PO Box 1029, Blindern, N-0315 Oslo, Norway.

MAMET David Alan, b. 30 November 1947, Chicago, USA. Playwright; Director. m. (1) Lindsay Crouse, 1977, divorced, (2) Rebecca Pidgeon, 1991. Education: Goddard College, Plainfield, Vermont. Appointments: Artist in Residence, Goddard College, 1971-73; Artistic Director, St Nicholas Theatre Company, Chicago, 1973-75; Guest Lecturer, University of Chicago, 1975, 1979; New York University, 1981; Associate Artistic Director, Goodman Theatre, Chicago, 1978; Associate Professor of Film, Columbia University, 1988; Director, House of Games, 1986; Things Change, 1987; Homicide, 1991; Play, A Life in the Theatre, 1989. Publications: The Duck Variations, 1971; Sexual Perversity in Chicago, 1973; The Reunion, 1973; Squirrels, 1974; American Buffalo, 1976; A Life in the Theatre, 1976; The Water Engine, 1976; The Woods, 1977; Lone Canoe, 1978; Prairie du Chien, 1978; Lakeboat, 1980; Donny March, 1981; Edmond, 1982; The Disappearance of the Jews, 1983; The Shawl, 1985; Glengarry Glen Ross, 1984; Speed-the-Plow, 1987; Bobby, Guild in Hell, 1989; The Old Neighborhood, 1991; Oleanna, 1992; Ricky Jay and his 52 Assistants, 1994; Death Defying Acts, 1996; Boston Marriage, 1999; Screenplays: The Postman Always Rings Twice, 1979; The Verdict, 1980; The Untouchables, 1986; House of Games, 1986; Things Change, 1987; We're No Angels, 1987; Oh Hell!, 1991; Homicide, 1991; Hoffa, 1991; Glengarry Glen Ross, 1992; The Rising Sun, 1992; Oleanna, 1994; The Edge, 1996; The Spanish Prisoner, 1996; Wag the Dog, 1997; Boston Marriage, 2001; Childrens' books: Mr Warm and Cold, 1985; The Owl, 1987; The Winslow Bay, 1999; Essays: Writing in Restaurants, 1986; Some Freaks, 1989; On Directing Film, 1990; The Hero Pony, 1990; The Cabin, 1992; A Whore's Profession, 1993; The Cryptogram, 1994; The Village (novel), 1994; Passover, 1995; Make-Believe Town: Essays and Remembrances, 1996; Plays, 1996; Plays 2, 1996; The Duck and the Goat, 1996; The Old Religion, 1996; True and False, 1996; The Old Neighbourhood, 1998; Jafsie and John Henry, 2000; State and Maine, (writer, director), 2000. Honours: Outer Critics Circle Award, for contributions to American Theatre, 1978; Honorary DLitt (Dartmouth College), 1996; Pulitzer Prize for Drama, New York Drama Critics Award. Address: c/o Howard Rosenstone, Rosenstone/Wender Agency, 38 East 29th Street, 10th Floor, New York, NY 10016, USA.

MANABE Syukuro, b. 21 September 1931, Japan. Research Scientist. m. Nobuko Nakamura, 26 February 1962, 2 daughters. Education: BA, 1953, MA, 1955, DSc, 1958, University of Tokyo. Appointments: Research Meteorologist, General Circulation Research Section, US Weather Bureau, Washington, DC, 1958-63; Senior Research Meteorologist, Geophysical Fluid Dynamics Laboratory, Environmental Science Services Administration, Washington, DC, 1963-68; Senior Research Meteorologist, Geophysical Fluid Dynamics Laboratory, National Oceanic and Atmospheric Administration, Princeton, New Jersey, 1968-97; Director, Global Warming Research Program, Frontier Research System for Global Change, Tokyo, Japan, 1997-2001; Visiting Research Collaborator, Program in Atmospheric and Oceanic Sciences, Princeton University, USA, 2002-. Publications: Over

Dictionary of International Biography

140 papers in professional journals. Honours: Rossby Research Medal, American Meterological Society; Revelle Medal, American Geophysical Union; Milankovich Medal, European Geophysical Society; Blue Planet Prize, Asahi Glass Foundation; Asah Prize, Asahi Newspaper Publishing Co; Volvo Prize, Volvo Prize Foundation. Memberships: US National Academy of Sciences; Academia Europaea; Royal Society of Canada; Honorary Member, American Meteorological Society; Honorary Member, Japan Meterological Society; Fellow, American Geophysical Union; Fellow, AAAS. Address: 6 Governors Lane, Princeton, NJ 08540, USA.

MANDAL Anil Kumar, b. 2 January 1958, West Bengal, India. Doctor. m. Vijaya Kumari Gothwal. Education: MBBS, NRS Medical College, Calcutta, India, 1983. MD, All India Institute of Medical Sciences, New Delhi, 1987; Diplomate, National Board for Practice of Ophthalmology, 1987. Appointments: Junior Ophthalmologist, 1990, Assistant Ophthalmologist, 1991-94, Associate Ophthalmologist, 1994-97, Head, Children's Eye Care Center, 1997-, Professor of Ophthalmology, 1998-, L V Prasad Eye Institute, Hyderabad. Publications: In professional journals. Honours: Best Resident, Ophthalmologic Research Association, AIIMS, New Delhi, 1990; Best Thematic Film, All India Ophthalmological Society, India, 1997; Professor P Siva Reddy Gold Medal, All India Ophthalmological Society, 1997. Memberships: Life Member, All India Ophthalmological Society; Elected International Member, American Academy of Ophthalmology; International Member, Association for Research and Vision in Ophthalmology. Address: LV Prasad Eye Institute, L V Prasad Marq, Banjara Hills, Hyderabad 500 034 AP, India.

MANDALIEV Angel Ivanov, b. 19 July 1936, Plovdiv, Bulgaria. Neurologist; Psychiatrist. m. Gudrun Metzinger, 1 son, 1 daughter. Education: Music School and Opera Studio, 1953-59; Graduate, Faculty of Medicine, Plovdiv, Bulgaria, 1961; Specialist of Neurology, Sofia, Bulgaria, 1967; Specialist of Neurology and Psychiatry, Freiburg, West Germany, 1984. Appointments: Psychiatrist, Silistra, 1962-65; Neurologist, Pasardjik, 1966-75, Plovdiv, 1976-80; Psychiatrist, Bad Dürkheim, Baden-Baden, Germany, 1980-84; Neurologist, Bad Berleburg, Passau, Germany, 1985-93; Consultant, Neurology and Psychiatry, Winterberg, Germany, 1994-. Publications: 25 international publications in English, French, German, Italian, Russian and Bulgarian since 1972; Epidemiological studies about potential adverse effect of industrial and environmental pollution and agents of abuse upon the nervous system; Studies about neurological rehabilitation and the medicine of ancient Thrace. Honours: 3 First Prizes for Poetry, Pen Club of Young Writers of Bulgaria; 1st Prize for Sculpture, Young Artists Competitions. memberships: New York Academy of Sciences; German Society of Neurology; German Society of Clinical Electrophysiology; Christian Democratic Party; American Association for the Advancement of Science; AMIEV; Academia Internationale di Medicina Sociale e Medicina Legale. Address: Espeweg 89, 57319 Bad Berleburg, Germany. E-mail: dr.mandaliev@gmx.de

MANDELA Nelson Rolihlahla, b. 1918, Umtata, Transkei. President (retired); Lawyer. m. (1) Evelyn Mandela, divorced 1957, 4 children, 2 deceased, (2) Winnie Mandela, 1958, divorced 1996, 2 daughters, (3) Graca Machel, 1998. Education: University College, Fort Hare; University of Witwatersrand. Appointments: Legal Practice, Johannesburg, 1952; On trial for treason, 1956-61 (acquitted); Sentenced to 5 years imprisonment, 1962; Tried for further charges, 1963-64, sentenced to life imprisonment; Released, 1990; President, African National Congress, 1991-97; President of South Africa, 1994-99; Chancellor, University of the North, 1992-; Joint President, United World Colleges, 1995-. Publications:

No Easy Walk to Freedom, 1965; How Far We Slaves Have Come: South Africa and Cuba in Today's World, co-author, 1991; Nelson Mandela Speaks: Forging a non-racial democratic South Africa, 1993; Long Walk to Freedom, 1994. Honours: Jawaharlal Nehru Award, India, 1979; Simon Bolivar Prize, UNESCO, 1983; Sakharov Prize, 1988; Liberty Medal, USA, 1993; Nobel Peace Prize (Joint Winner), 1993; Mandela-Fulbright Prize, 1993; Honorary Bencher, Lincoln's Inn, 1994; Tun Abdul Razak Award, 1994; Anne Frank Medal, 1994; International Freedom Award, 2000; Honorary QC, 2000; Honorary Freeman of London; Numerous honorary doctorates. Address: c/o ANC, 51 Plein Street, Johannesburg 2001, South Africa.

MANDELBROT Benoit B, b. 20 November 1924, Warsaw, Poland (French Citizen). Mathematician. Education: Graduated, Ecole Polytechnique, Paris, 1947; MS, California Institute of Technology, 1948; PhD, Sorbonne, Paris, 1952. Appointments: Staff Member, Centre National de la Recherche Scientifique, Paris, 1949-57; Institute of Advance Study, New Jersey, 1953-54; Assistant Professor of Mathematics, University of Geneva, 1955-57; Junior Professor of Applied Mathematics, Lille University; Professor of Mathematical Analysis, Ecole Polytechnique, Paris; Research Staff Member, IBM Thomas J Watson Research Centre, New York, 1958; IBM Fellow, 1974; Abraham Robinson Professor of Mathematical Science, 1987-99, Sterling Professor, 1999-, Yale University, New Haven, Connecticut; Visiting Professor, Harvard University, 1962-64, 1979-80, 1984-87; Devised the term Fractal to describe a curve or surface. Publications: Logique, Langage et Théorie de l'Information, co-author, 1957; Fractals: Form, Chance and Dimension, 1977; Fractal Geometry of Nature, 1982; Fractals and Scaling in Finance: Discontinuity, Concentration, Risk, 1997; Fractales, hasard et finance, 1997; Multifractals and Low-Frequency Noise: Wild Self-Affinity in Physics, 1998; Gaussian Self-Similarity and Fractals, 2000; Nel mondo dei frattali, 2001; Globality, The Earth, Low-frequency Noise and R/S, 2002; Fractals, Graphics and Mathematical Education, with M L Frame, 2002; Fractals in Chaos and Statistical Physics, 2003; Numerous scientific papers; Editorial Boards, several journals. Honours: Several honorary degrees; Numerous awards and medals including Chevalier, L'Ordre de la Légion d'Honneur, 1989; L F Richardson Medal for Geophysics, 2000; Procter Prize of Sigma Xi, 2002; Japan Prize for Science and Tech, 2002. Address: Mathematics Department, Yale University, New Haven, CT 06520, USA.

MANDELL Gordon Keith, S, b. 6 March 1947, New York City, New York, USA. Aerospace Engineer. Education: BS, Aeronautics, Astronautics, 1969, MS, Aeronautics, Astronautics, 1970, Massachusetts Institute of Technology. Appointments: Staff Member, Fluid Dynamics Research Laboratory, Massachusetts Institute of Technology, 1970-72; Consulting Aerospace Engineer, 1973-76; Federal Aviation Administration Designated Engineering Representative, 1976-82; Federal Aviation Administration Aerospace Engineer, determining compliance of aircraft designs with safety standards, 1982-. Publications: Missile Recovery by Extensible Flexwing, 1966; Numerous articles in Model Rocketry magazine, 1968-72; Co-author, Lenticular Re-entry Vehicle, 1970; Co-author, editor, book, Topics in Advanced Model Rocketry, 1973. Honours: Louis de Florez Award; James Means Memorial Prize; Grumman Scholar, Massachusetts Institute of Technology, 1965-69; National Science Foundation Fellow, Massachusetts Institute of Technology, 1969-70; Admitted to: Tau Beta Pi; Sigma Gamma Tau; Sigma Xi. Memberships: National Association of Rocketry; National Space Society; Planetary Society; Team Seti. Address: Post Office Box 671388, Chugiak, AK 99567-1388, USA.

MANDELSON Peter Benjamin, b. 21 October 1953, England. Politician. Education: St Catherine's College, Oxford. Appointments: Joined TUC, with Economic Department, 1977-78; Chair, British Youth Council, 1978-80; Producer, London Weekend TV, 1982-85; Director of Campaigns and Communications, Labour Party, 1985-90; MP for Hartlepool, 1992-; Opposition Whip, 1994-97, Shadow Frontbench Spokesman on Civil Service, 1995-96, on Election Planning, 1996-97; Chair, General Election Planning Group, 1995-97; Minister without Portfolio, 1997-98; Secretary of State for Trade and Industry, 1998; for Northern Ireland, 1999-2001 (resigned); Vice-Chair, British Council, 1999-. Publications: Youth Unemployment: Causes and Cures, 1977; Broadcasting and Youth, 1980; The Blair Revolution: Can New Labour Deliver? 1996. Memberships include: Council, London Borough of Lambeth, 1979-82; International Advisory Committee, Centre for European Policy Studies, 1993-; Trustee, Whitechapel Art Gallery, 1994-; Panel 2000, 1998-. Address: House of Commons, London SW1A 0AA, England.

MANEA Norman, b. 19 July 1936, Suceava, Romania. Writer. m. Cella Boiangiu, 28 June 1969. Education: MS, Engineering, Institute of Construction, Bucharest, 1959. Publications: In English: October, eight o'clock, 1992, On Clowns 1992-; Compulsory Happiness, 1993; The Black Envelope, 1995; The Hooligan's Return, 2003. Others: Captivi, 1970; Atrium, 1974; Anii de ucenicie ai lui August Prostul, 1979. Contributions to: New Republic; Partisan Review; Paris Review; Lettre Internationale; Vuelta; Akzente; Neue Rundschau; Sinn und Form. Honours: Guggenheim Fellowship, 1992; John D and Catharine T MacArthur Foundation Fellowship, 1992. Membership: American PEN. Address: 201 West 70th Street, Apt 10-I, New York, NY 10023, USA.

MANESCU, Maria, b. 2 October 1943, Ocnita, Romania. Engineer. m. Manescu Mihai, 1 son. Education: Diploma, Engineer, University Politechnica, Bucharest, 1965; DEng, Technological Equipment, 1987. Appointments: Design Engineer, Technological Equipment, 1965-78; Assistant, University Petrol-Gaze, Ploiesti, 1978-81; Lecturer, 1981-90, Professor, 1996-, University Valahia, Târgoviste. Publications include: Calculation of main line tensions; Industrie application of the descriptive geometry. Honours: Diploma of Honour, Invention Show Room, 1993. Membership: Founder Member, Scientists Foundation. Address: Str Aleena Trandafirilor, Bl P5, Apt 8, Târgoviste, Romania.

MANFREDI Roberto, b. 22 June 1964, Bologna, Italy. Researcher. Education: MD, 1988; Infectious Disease Specialist, University of Bologna, 1992. Appointments: Researcher, Grantee, 1986-91, Medical Assistant, Infectious Diseases, 1991-93, Associate, 1993-, Contract Professor of Infectious Diseases, Postgraduate School of Infectious Diseases, 1996-, University of Bologna; Board of Associate Professors of Infectious Diseases, 2003. Publications: Over 1200 scientific publications in textbooks, congress proceedings and professional journals; 9 monographs. Honours: L Concato Award, University of Bologna, 1988; F Schiassi Award, 1989; G Salvioli Award, University of Bologna, 1991; FESCI Young Investigator Award, 2000. Memberships: International Society of Infectious Diseases; Italian Society for Infectious and Parasite Diseases; European AIDS Clinical Society; Editorial Board and Reviewer of many scientific journals. Address: Via di Corticella 45, I-40128, Bologna, Italy.

MANILOW Barry (Pinkus), b. 17 June 1946, Brooklyn, New York, USA. Singer; Musician (piano); Songwriter. Education: Advertising, New York City College; Musical Education: NY College Of Music; Juilliard School Of Music. Career: Film Editor, CBS-TV; Writer, numerous radio and television commercials;

Member, cabaret duo Jeanne and Barry, 1970-72; MD, arranger, producer for Bette Midler; Solo entertainer, 1974-; Numerous world-wide tours; Major concerts include: Gala charity concert for Prince and Princess of Wales, Royal Albert Hall, 1983; Arista Records 15th Anniversary concert, Radio City Music Hall, 1990; Royal Variety performance, London, 1992; Television film Copacabana, 1985; Numerous television specials and television appearances; Broadway show, Barry Manilow At The Gershwin, 1989; West End musical, Copacabana, 1994. Recordings: Albums include: Barry Manilow, 1973; Barry Manilow II, 1975; Tryin' To Get The Feelin', 1976; This One's For You, 1977; Barry Manilow Live (Number 1, US), 1977; Even Now, 1978; Manilow Magic, 1979; Greatest Hits, 1979; One Voice, 1979; Barry, 1981; If I Should Love Again, 1981; Barry Live In Britain, 1982; I Wanna Do It With You, 1982; Here Comes The Night, 1983; A Touch More Magic, 1983; Greatest Hits Volume II, 1984; 2.00 AM Paradise Café, 1984; Barry Manilow, Grandes Exitos En Espanol, 1986; Swing Street, 1988; Songs To Make The Whole World Sing, 1989; Live On Broadway, 1990; The Songs 1975-1990, 1990; Because It's Christmas, 1990; Showstoppers, 1991; The Complete Collection And Then Some, 1992; Hidden Treasures, 1993; The Platinum Collection, 1993; Singin' with the Big Bands, 1994; Another Life, 1995; Summer of '78, 1996; Manilow Sings Sinatra, 1998; Hit singles include: Mandy (Number 1, US), 1975; Could It Be Magic, 1975; I Write The Songs (Number 1, US), 1976; Tryin' To Get The Feelin', 1976; Weekend In New England, 1977; Looks Like We Made It (Number 1, US), 1977; Can't Smile Without You, 1978; Copacabana (At The Copa), from film Foul Play, 1978; Somewhere In The Night, 1979; Ships, 1979; I Made It Through The Rain, 1981; Let's Hang On, 1981; Bermuda Triangle, 1981; I Wanna Do It With You, 1982. Honours: Grammy Awards: Song Of The Year, I Write The Songs, 1977; Best Male Pop Vocal Performance, Copacabana (At The Copa), 1979; Emmy Award, The Barry Manilow Special, 1977; American Music Awards, Favourite Male Artist, 1978-80; Star on Hollywood Walk Of Fame, 1980; Tony Award, Barry Manilow On Broadway show, 1976; Academy Award Nomination, Ready To Take A Chance Again, 1978; Hitmaker Award, Songwriters Hall Of Fame, 1991; Named, Humanitarian of the Year, Starlight Foundation, 1991; Platinum and Gold records. Address: Arista Records, 6 W 57th Street, NY 10019, USA.

MANN (Colin) Nicholas Jocelyn, b. 24 October 1942, Salisbury, Wiltshire, England. Dean. m. (1) Joëlle Bourcart, 1 son, 1 daughter, divorced, (2) 1 daughter. Education: BA 1st class, Modern and Medieval Languages, 1964, MA, PhD, 1968, King's College, Cambridge. Appointments: Research Fellow, Clare College, Cambridge, 1965-67; Lecturer in French, University of Warwick, 1967-72; Visiting Fellow, All Souls College, Oxford, 1972; Fellow and Tutor in Modern Languages, 1973-90, Emeritus Fellow, 1991-, Pembroke College, Oxford; Director of the Warburg Institute and Professor of the History of the Classical Tradition, University of London, 1990-2001, Senior Research Fellow of the Warburg Institute, 2002-; Dean of the School of Advanced Study and Professor of Renaissance Studies, University of London, 2002-. Publications: Books and articles on Petrarch and other topics in professional journals. Honours: CBE, 1999; Member of many advisory and editorial boards. Memberships: Vice-President and Foreign Secretary, 1999-, British Academy; Council of Contemporary Applied Arts; Council of the Museum of Modern Art, 1984-92. Address: School of Advanced Study, University of London, Senate House, Malet Street, London WC1E 7HU, England. E-mail: nicholas.mann@sas.ac.uk

MANN Jessica, b. England. Writer. Publications: A Charitable End, 1971; Mrs Knox's Profession, 1972; The Only Security, 1973; The Sticking Place, 1974; Captive Audience, 1975; The Eighth

Dictionary of International Biography

Deadly Sin, 1976; The Sting of Death, 1978; Funeral Sites, 1981; Deadlier Than the Male, 1981; No Man's Island, 1983; Grave Goods, 1984; A Kind of Healthy Grave, 1986; Death Beyond the Nile, 1988; Faith, Hope and Homicide, 1991; Telling Only Lies, 1992; A Private Inquiry, 1996; Hanging Fire, 1997; The Survivor's Revenge, 1998; Under a Dark Sun, 2000. Contributions to: Daily Telegraph; Sunday Telegraph; Various magazines and journals. Memberships: Detection Club; Society of Authors: PEN; Crime Writers Association. Address: Lambessow, St Clement, Cornwall, England.

MANN Michael K, b. Chicago, USA. Producer; Director; Writer. Education: University of Wisconsin; London Film School. Appointments: Executive Producer, (TV) Miami Vice, Crime Story, Drug Wars: Camarena Story, Drug Wars: Cocaine Cartel, Police Story, Starsky & Hutch. Creative Works: Films directed include: The Jericho Mile, 1981; The Keep, 1981; Manhunter, 1986; Last of the Mohicans, 1992; Heat, 1995; The Insider, 1999. Honours include: 2 Emmy Awards. Memberships: Writers Guild; Directors Guild. Address: c/o Creative Artists Agency, 9830 Wilshire Boulevard, Beverly Hills, CA 90212, USA.

MANNERS Gerald, b. 7 August 1932, Ferryhill, County Durham, England. Economic Geographer. m. Joy Edith Roberta Turner, 2 sons, 2 daughters. Education: BA, 1954, MA, 1958, Undergraduate and Scholar, First Class Geographical Tripos, St Catharine's College Cambridge. Appointments: Commissioned Officer, Royal Air Force, 1955-57; Lecturer, Geography, University College, Swansea, 1957-67; Visiting Scholar, Resources for the Future Inc., Washington DC, USA, 1964-65; Reader in Geography, University College London, 1968-80; Visiting Associate, Joint Center for Urban Studies, Harvard University and Massachusetts Institute of Technology, 1972-73; Visiting Fellow, Centre for Resource and Environmental Studies, Australian National University, 1991; Professor of Geography, 1980-97, Emeritus Professor, 1997-, University College London. Publications include: The Geography of Energy, 1964; South Wales in the Sixties, 1964; Spatial Policy Problems of the British Economy, 1971; The Changing World Market for Iron Ore 1950-1980, 1971; Regional Development in Britain, 1972; Minerals and Men, 1974; Coal in Britain: an Uncertain Future, 1981; Office Policy in Britain, 1986. Honours include: Governor, 1978-95, Chairman, 1986-95, Vice-President, 1995-99, Sadler's Wells Foundation; Trustee, Eaga Charitable Trust; Specialist Adviser to the House of Lords Select Committee on Sustainable Development, 1994-95; Trustee, 1977-, Chairman, 1996-, City Parochial Foundation and the Trust for London; Specialist Adviser, House of Commons Environmental Audit Committee. Memberships: Fellow, Royal Geographical Society (with the Institute of British Geographers); British Institute of Energy Economics; Regional Studies Association, Address: 338 Liverpool Road, London N7 8PZ, England. E-mail: g.manners@ucl.ac.uk

MANNERS Wendy, b. 18 February 1956, Greenfield, Massachusetts, USA. Insurance Executive. Education: Bachelor of Science, Smith College, Northampton, Massachusetts, 1978; Certified Employee Benefits Specialist, Wharton School of Pennsylvania, 1992. Appointments: Manager, Group Medical Claims, Director, Product Development, Employee Benefits, Phoenix Home Life Insurance Company, Hartford, Simsbury, Connecticut, USA, 1979-93; Assistant Vice-President, Integrated Benefits, Hartford Financial Services Co., Hartford, Connecticut, USA, 1993-. Publications: Articles in professional journals including: Worker's Compensation Perspectives, 1997; The Hartford Agent, 1997; Managed Disability Solutions, 1997, BNA, 1997, 1999; National Underwriter, 1998; Nevada Business Journal, 2000; Employee Benefit News, 1998, 1999, 2000, 2001; Risk

and Insurance, 2000, Risk report, 2003; Numerous papers presented at conferences. Honours: Second and Third Annual National Cancer Policy Summit Attendee; Washington Business Group on Health, Thought Leader; Washington Business Group on Health Council on Health Disparities; Winner, The Hartford's Excellence at Work Award and Service Objective Achievement Award; Flame Award for outstanding sales program, 1998; Telly Award for media marketing materials, 1998; Winner, Integrated Benefits Institute Chairman's Award for contributions to improving health and productivity management, 2002. Memberships: Integrated Benefits Institute; Disability Management Employer Coalition. Address: 140 Elwell Heights, Wilmington VT 05363, USA. E-mail: wnedymvt1@aol.com

MANNING Jane Marian, b. 20 September 1938, Norwich, Norfolk, England. Singer (Soprano); Lecturer. m. Anthony Payne. Education: Royal Academy of Music, London; Scuola di Canto, Cureglia, Switzerland. Career: Freelance solo singer specialising in contemporary music; More than 350 world premiers including operas; Regular appearances in London, Europe, USA, Australia, with leading orchestras, conductors, ensembles and at major festivals; Lectures and master classes at major universities in USA including Harvard, Princeton, Cornell, Stanford; UK universities and leading conservatories in Europe and Australia; Visiting Professor, Mills College, Oakland, USA, 1981, 1984, 1986; Artistic Director, Jane's Minstrels, 1988-; Artist-in-Residence, universities in USA, Canada, Australia and New Zealand; Currently Visiting Professor, Royal College of Music, London; Honorary Professor, Keele University, 1996-2002; Many CDs, radio broadcasts worldwide. Publications: Books, New Vocal Repertory – An Introduction; New Vocal Repertory 2; Chapter on the vocal cycles in A Messiaen Companion; Numerous articles and reviews in newspapers and professional journals. Honours: Special Award, Composers Guild of Great Britain; FRAM, 1980; Honorary Doctorate, University of York, 1988, OBE, 1990; FRCM, 1998. Memberships: Vice-President, Society for the Promotion of New Music; Chairman, Nettleford Trust (Colourscape Festival); Executive Committee, Musicians Benevolent Fund; Royal Philharmonic Society; Incorporated Society of Musicians. Address: 2 Wilton Square, London N1 3DL, England. E-mail: jane@wiltonsq.demon.co.uk

MANSEL LEWIS David Courtenay (Sir), b. 25 October 1927, London, England. Lord-Lieutenant of Dyfed (Retired). m. Lady Mary Rosemary Marie-Gabriel Montagu-Stuart-Wortley, 1 son, 2 daughters. Education: Keble College, Oxford, England. Appointments: Welsh Guards, 1946-49; Lieutenant RARO, 1948; High Sheriff Carmarthenshire, 1965; JP, 1969; DL, 1971; HM Lieutenant, 1973-74; HM Lieutenant of Dyfed, 1974-79; Lord-Lieutenant of Dyfed, 1979-2002. Honour: Fellow, Trinity College Carmarthen, 1997. Memberships: President, West Wales, TAVRA, 1979-90; President Mid and West Wales TAVRA, 1979-90; Wales TAVRA, 1999; Patron, Carmarthen Royal British Legion, 1974-; President, Dyfed SSAFA, 1986-2003; Founder President, Llanelli Branch Welsh Guards Association, 1974-; Patron Wales Gurkha Villages Aid Trust, 1998-; President, Dyfed Branch Magistrates' Association, 1979-02; President, St Johns Council for Dyfed; Sub Prior St John Priory for Wales, 1998-02; Patron, Dyfed Branch British Red Cross Society; President, Carmarthenshire Association Boy Scouts; President, Carmarthen-Cardigan Branch Country Landowners Association, 1977-91 and of Dyfed Branch 1991-; Chairman South Western Division Royal Forestry Society, 1963-93; Chairman South Wales Woodlands, 1969-85; President, Dyfed Wildlife Trust, 1978-02; Patron Carmarthenshire Federation of Young Farmers' Clubs; Member Court of Governors UCW Aberystwyth 1974-02; Member Committee, 1974-99, Member Council, 1987-91, Member Court of Governors, 1987-91, National

Museum of Wales; Previously served on Music Committee of Wales Arts Council and on Board of Welsh National Opera; President, Burry Port Operatic Society; President, Llanelli Art Society, 1956-; Founder President, Gwyl Llanelli Festival, 1979; Trustee, Llandovery College, 1985, Chairman, 2000. Founder, Carmarthen-Cardigan Committee of the Sail Training Association, 1968-; Regional Chairman Sail Training Association South Wales, President, Burry Port, RNLI, 1982-1985; Founder Commodore Burry Port Yacht Club, 1966; Patron Tall Ships Council of Wales, 1991-; President, The Welsh Association of Male Voice Choirs, 1997-; Patron, The Commonwealth Games for Wales, 1998-; Chairman Llanelli Millennium Coastal Park Trustees, 1999-. Address: Stradey Castle, Llanelli, Dyfed SA15 4PL, Wales.

MANSELL Nigel, b. 8 August 1953, Upton-on-Severn, England. Racing Driver. m. Rosanne Perry, 2 sons, 1 daughter. Appointments: Began in Kart-racing, then Formula Ford, Formula 2, 1978-79, first Grand Prix, Austria, 1980; Winner, South African Grand Prix, 1992; Member, Lotus Grand Prix Team, 1980-84, Williams Team, 1985-88, 1991-92, Ferrari Team, 1989-90, Newman-Haas IndyCar Team, 1992-95, McLaren Team, 1995; Winner of 31 Grand Prix; Surpassed Jackie Stewart's British Record of 27 wins; World Champion, 1992; PPG IndyCar World Series Champion, 1993; Editor-in-Chief, Formula One Magazine, 2001. Publications: Mansell and Williams (with Derick Allsop), 1992; Nigel Mansell's IndyCar Racing (with Jeremy Shaw), 1993; My Autobiography (with James Allen), 1995. Honours include: Honorary DEng, Birmingham, 1993; OBE, 1990; BBC Sports Personality of the Year, 1986, 1992; Special Constable for 12 years; Awarded Honorary Fellowship of Centre for Management of Industrial Reliability, Cost and Effectiveness (MIRCE), 1997; Awarded Grand Fellowship of the MIRCE Akademy, 2000; Appointed President, UK Youth Charity, 2002. Address: c/o Nicki Dance, Woodbury Park Golf & Country Club, Woodbury Castle, Woodbury, Exeter, Devon EX5 1JJ, England.

MANSER Martin Hugh, b. 11 January 1952, Bromley, England. Reference Book Editor. m. Yusandra Tun, 1979, 1 son, 1 daughter. Education: BA, Honours, University of York, 1974; MPhil, C.N.A.A., 1977. Publications: Concise Book of Bible Quotations, 1982; A Dictionary of Everyday Idioms, 1983, 2nd edition, 1997; Listening to God, 1984; Pocket Thesaurus of English Words, 1984; Children's Dictionary, 1984; Macmillan Student's Dictionary, 1985, 2nd edition, 1996; Penguin Wordmaster Dictionary, 1987; Guinness Book of Words, 1988; Dictionary of Eponyms, 1988; Visual Dictionary, Bloomsbury Good Word Guide, 1988; Printing and Publishing Terms, 1988; Marketing Terms, 1988; Guinness Book of Words, 1988, 2nd edition, 1991; Bible Promises: Outlines for Christian Living, 1989; Oxford Learner's Pocket Dictionary, 2nd edition, 1991; Get To the Roots: A Dictionary of Words and Phrase Origins, 1992; The Lion Book of Bible Quotations, 1992; Oxford Learner's Pocket Dictionary with Illustrations, 1992; Guide to Better English, 1994; Chambers Compact Thesaurus, 1994; Bloomsbury Key to English Usage, 1994; Collins Gem Daily Guidance, 1995; NIV Thematic Study Bible, 1996; Chambers English Thesaurus, 1997; Dictionary of Bible Themes, 1997; NIV Shorter Concordance, 1997; Guide to English Grammar, 1998; Crash Course in Christian Teaching, 1998; Dictionary of the Bible, 1998; Christian Prayer (large print), 1998; Bible Stories, 1999; Editor: Millennium Quiz Book, 1999; I Never Knew That Was in the Bible, 1999; Pub Quiz Book, 1999; Trivia Quiz Book, 1999; Children's Dictionary, 1999; Compiler, Lion Bible Quotation Collection, 1999; Common Worship Lectionary, 1999; The Eagle Handbook of Bible Promises, 2000; The Westminster Collection of Christian Quotation, 2001; Wordsworth Crossword Companion, 2001; Biblical Quotations: A Reference Guide, 2001; NIV Comprehensive Concordance, 2001; 365 Inspirational Quotations,

2001; Writer's Manual, 2001; The Facts On File Dictionary of Proverbs, 2001; Dictionary of Foreign Words and Phrases, 2002; Getting to Grips with Grammar, 2003; A Treasury of Psalms, 2003; Dictionary of Classical and Biblical Allusions, 2003; The Joy of Christmas, 2003. Address: 102 Northern Road, Aylesbury, Bucks HP19 9QY, England.

MANSFIELD Eric Arthur, b. 14 April 1932, Southend, Essex, England. RAF Officer; Consulting Engineer. m. Marion Byrne, 1 son, 1 daughter. Education: RAF Apprenticeship, 1949-52; MA, St John's College, Cambridge, England; RAF Flying and Training to Wings Standard, 1957-58; MSc, Southampton University, 1962-63; RAF Staff College, 1968-69. Appointments: Tours with RAF Chief Scientist, Exchange with USAF, 1963-68; Nimrod Aircraft Engineering Authority and OC Engineering Wing, RAF Cottesmore, 1969-74; Chief Electrical Engineer, HQ RAF Germany, 1974-78; Staff, HQ 18 Group, 1978-82; Staff, Ministry of Defence, 1983-86; Staff, NATO HQ AFSOUTH, 1986-88; Staff, RAF Support Command, 1986-89; Association of Consulting Engineers, 1989-94; Independent Consultant, 1994-95; Retired, 1995. Memberships: Royal Aeronautical Society; Chartered Engineer. Address: 33 Chalgrove End, Stoke Mandeville, Bucks HP22 5UH. E-mail: ericandmarion@eamansfield.freeserve.co.uk

MANSFIELD Janet Winifred, b. 19 August 1934, Sydney, Australia. Artist; Author. m. Dr Colin Mansfield, 23 September 1955, 1 son, 3 daughters. Education; Training in Ceramics, National Art School, ESTC, 1964, 1965. Appointments: Editor, Ceramics Art and Perception, 1990-; Ceramics Technical, 1995-; Invited speaker, juror; 33 solo exhibitions including Australia, Japan, 1985, 1988, 1997, New Zealand, 1972, 1973, 1986, 1968-; Exhibitions including: Gallery le Vieux-Bourg, Switzerland, 1992; Kunst & Keramiek, Holland, 1993; Museum in Oslo, Lillehammer, Norway, 1993; Mino Kami City Festival, Japan, 1994; Contemporary Ceramics, London, UK, 1994; Faenza Museum of Ceramics, Italy, 1995; The Scottish Gallery, Edinburgh, Scotland, 1995, 2000; Galerie b15, Munich, 1996; Green Gallery, Tokyo, 1996; Vessel Exhibition, ANU, 1996; Saga Prefectural Museum, 1996; Galerie Hadewrk, Munich, 1997; Tachikichi Gallery, Kyoto, 1997; Gres au sel, Touring France, 1997; Other exhibitions in countries including: USA, Germany, Hungary, Czech Republic, Denmark, Korea. Honours: Australia Ceramic Society Award, 1986; OAM, 1987; Australia Council Emeritus Award, 1990; Award of the Ceramic Art Foundation, USA, 1999. Memberships: Vice President, International Academy of Ceramics. Address: 120 Glenmore Road, Paddington, NSW 2021, Australia.

MANSFIELD Michael, b. 12 October 1941, London, England. Barrister. m. (1) Melian Mansfield, 1967, divorced 1992, 3 sons, 2 daughters, (2) Yvette Mansfield, 1992, 1 son. Education: Keele University. Appointments: Began Practising, 1967; Founder, Tooks Court Chambers, 1984; Speciality, Civil Liberties Work; Professor of Law, Westminster University, 1996. Creative Works: Films for BBC TV: Inside Story, 1991; Presumed Guilty. Publication: Presumed Guilty. Honours: Honorary Fellow, Kent University; Several Honorary Degrees. Membership: Patron Acre Lane Neighbourhood Chambers, Brixton, 1997-. Address: Tooks Court Chambers, 14 Tooks Court, Cursitor Street, London EC4Y 1JY, England.

MANSOUR Mohamed, b. 30 August 1928, Dumyat, Egypt. Professor of Automatic Control ETH. m. Zeinab Fattouh, 2 sons, 2 daughters. Education: BSc, 1951, MSc, 1953, University of Alexandria; DSc techn, ETH Zurich, with Silver Medal, 1965. Appointments: Lecturer, ETH, 1966-67; Assistant Professor, Queen's University, Canada, 1967-68; Professor, Automatic Control and Head of Institute of Automatic Control ETH, 1968-

93; Dean of Electrical Engineering, ETH, 1976-78; Chair of Intelligent Control, Tokyo Institute of Technology, 1995. Publications: 200 scientific articles; Editor, 6 books; Editorial board, 6 international journals, systems and control encyclopaedia; Book series: Interdisciplinary System Research. Honours: Dedication of World Automation Congress, 1996; Honorary Chairman of International Conferences; Life Fellow IEEE; Associate Fellow TWAS; Gullemin-Cauer Award IEEE; IFAC Outstanding Service Award; IFAC Adviser; Honorary degrees from 3 Chinese universities. Memberships: Council Member and Treasurer, International Federation of Automatic Control, IFAC; President, Swiss Society of Automatic Control and honorary member; Chairman of Engineering Committee of Third World Academy of Science, TWAS; Delegate of TWAS to the United Nations; Adviser to UNESCO; Chairman of Awards Committee, Control System Society IEEE. Address: Obere Heslibachstr 20, 8700 Küsnacht/ZH, Switzerland.

MANTEL Hilary (Mary), b. 6 July 1952, Derbyshire, England. Author. m. Gerald McEwen, 23 September 1972. Education: London School of Economics; Sheffield University; Bachelor of Jurisprudence, 1973. Publications: Every Day is Mother's Day, 1985; Vacant Possession, 1986; Eight Months on Ghazzah Street, 1988; Fludd, 1989; A Place of Greater Safety, 1992; A Change of Climate, 1994; An Experiment in Love, 1995; The Giant, O'Brien, 1998; Giving up the Ghost, 2003; Learning to Talk, 2003. Contributions to: Film column, Spectator, 1987-91; Book reviews to range of papers. Honours: Shiva Naipaul Prize, 1987; Winifred Holtby Prize, 1990; Cheltenham Festival Prize, 1990; Southern Arts Literature Prize, 1990; Sunday Express Book of the Year Award, 1992; Hawthornden Prize, 1996. Memberships: Royal Society of Literature, fellow; Society of Authors. Address: c/o A M Heath & Co, 79 St Martin's Lane, London WC2, England.

MANVILLE Stewart Roebling, b. 15 January 1927, White Plains, New York, USA. Archivist; Curator. m. Ella Viola Brandelius-Ström Grainger, 17 January 1972. Education: Hunter College Opera Workshop, 1950-52; Akademie für Musik und Darstellende Kunst, Vienna, 1952-53; BS, Columbia University, 1962. Appointments: Assistant Stage Director, European Opera Houses, 1952-57; Editor, 1959-63; Archivist of Percy Grainger's music, curator of the Percy Grainger House in White Plains New York, 1963-. Publications: Manville-Manvel Genealogy, 1948-; Seeing Opera in Italy, 1955; Seeing Opera in Central Europe, 1956. Memberships include: Soc des Antiquaires de Picardie; National Trust for Historic Preservation; Westchester County Historical Society; St Nicholas Society of New York. Address: 46 Ogden Ave, White Plains, NY 10605-2323, USA.

MAO Zai-Sha, b. 3 July 1943, Chengdu, China. Research Chemical Engineer. m. Junxian Zhou, 2 daughters. Education: BEng, Department of Chemical Engineering, Tsinghua University, Beijing, China, 1966; MS, Institute of Chemical Metallurgy, Chinese Academy of Sciences, Beijing, China, 1981; PhD, Department of Chemical Engineering, University of Houston, Texas, USA, 1988. Appointments: Research Professor, Institute of Process Engineering, Chinese Academy of Sciences; Professor, Graduate School, Chinese Academy of Sciences; Associate Editor in Chief, Chinese Journal of Chemical Engineering, Beijing; Associate Editor in Chief, Chinese Journal of Process Engineering, Beijing. Publications: 77 papers in peer-reviewed journals; 55 conference presentations; 5 patents on multiphase chemical reactor design. Honours: Best Fundamental Paper, South Texas Section, AIChE, USA, 1992; Excellent Postgraduate Adviser, Graduate School, Chinese Academy of Sciences, Beijing, 2001. Memberships: Member, Chemical Industry and Engineering Society of China. Address: Institute of Process Engineering, CAS, PO Box 353, Beijing 100080, China.

MAR AND KELLIE (Earl of) Jamie, b. 10 March 1949, Edinburgh, Scotland. Peer. m. Mary. Education: Diploma in Social Work, Moray House College of Education, 1968-71; Certificate in Building, Inverness College, 1987-88. Career: Social Work, 20 years; Building Work, 4 years; Hereditary Peer, 1994-99; Life Peer, 2000-. Honours: Life Peerage: Lord Erskine of Alloa Tower, 2000. Memberships: Chairman, Clackmannanshire Heritage Trust; Non-Executive Director, Clackmannanshire Enterprise; Select Committee on the Constitution, 2001-. Address: Hilton Farm, Alloa FK10 3PS, Scotland.

MARADONA Diego Armando, b. 1960, Lanus, Argentina. Footballer. m. Claudia Villafane, 2 daughters. Appointments: Boca Juniors, Argentina, 1982; Barcelona Football Club; Naples Football Club, 1984-91, Sevilla (Spain), 1992, Boca Juniors, 1997, Badajoz, 1998-; Founder, Maradona Producciones; Former Ambassador for UNICEF; Banned from football for 15 months after drugs test; Convicted by Naples Court on charges of possession of cocaine, 14 month suspended sentence and fine of 4 million lira, 1991; Federal Court in Buenos Aires ruled he had complied with the treatment; Suspended for 15 months for taking performance-enhancing drugs in World Cup Finals, 1994; Indicted for shooting an air rifle at journalists, 1994; Resigned as coach of Deporto Mandiyu, 1994; Captain of Argentina, 1993. Honour: Footballer of the Century Award, Féderation Internationale de Football Association (France), 2000. Membership: President, International Association of Professional Footballers, 1995-.

MARAI Ibrahim Fayez Mahmoud, b. 10 January 1930, Geiza, Egypt. Academic Staff Member; Professor. m. Wafaa Mohamed Amin Salama, 2 sons, 1 daughter. Education: BSc in Agriculture, 1950, MSc in Animal Production, 1960, PhD in Animal Production, 1964, Cairo University. Appointments: Teacher in Agriculture Secondary Schools, 1950-60; Demonstrator, Lecturer, Assistant Professor, 1960-76, Head, Department of Animal Production, 1972-82, Professor, 1976-, Vice-Dean, 1982-85, Faculty of Agriculture, Zagazig University, Zagazig. Publications: More than 235 scientific papers and 22 scientific articles; Editor and author, books: New Techniques in Sheep Production, 1987, Spanish edition, Nuevas Técnicas de Producción Ovina, 1994; Pollution in Livestock Production Systems, 1994. Honours: Several listings. Memberships: Head, City Council, Hesseneya, Sharkia, 1968-72; Head, Building and Construction Co-operative, Zagazig University, 1985-92; Head, Egyptian Rabbit Science Association, 1998-2000; New York Academy of Sciences, 1996-. Address: Department of Animal Production, Faculty of Agriculture, Zagazig University, Zagazig, Egypt. E-mail: elamierfayes@yahoo.com

MARAMA Andrew Viva, b. 10 March 1965, Zomba, Malawi. Architect. m. Svetlana, 3 daughters. Education: Diploma in Cartography, 1984-85; MSc, Architecture, 1985-91; Dip Architecture, 1991-92. Appointments: Architect, Ministry of Lands and Housing, Tanzania, 1991; Senior Architect, Covell Matthews Partnership, 1992-96; Managing Partner, MD Initiative, Malawi, 1997-. Publications: Stabilised Soil Blocks for Walling; Construction Materials in Malawi. Honours: Outstanding Professional Award; Paul Harris Fellow. Memberships: Corporate Member, Architects Association of Tanzania; Malawi Institute of Architects; Associate, American Institute of Architects. Address: PO Box 31112, Lilongwe 3, Malawi. E-mail: marama@eomw.net

MARBER Patrick, b. 19 September 1964, London, England. Playwright; Director. 1 son. Education: BA, English Language & Literature, Wadham College, Oxford University, 1983-86. Publications: Plays: Dealer's Choice, 1995; After Miss Julie, 1996; Closer, 1997; Howard Katz, 2001. Honours: Writer's Guild Award

Dictionary of International Biography

for Best West End Play, 1995; Evening Standard Award for Best Comedy, 1995; Evening Standard Award for Best Comedy, 1997; Critic's Circle Award for Best Play, 1997; Olivier Award for Best Play, 1997; New York Critics' Award for Best Foreign Play, 1999. Address: c/o Judy Daish Associates, Ltd, 2 St Charles Place, London W10 6EG, England.

MARC Jeyaraj, b. 6 May 1956, India. Minister of the Church; Bishop. m. Sheela, 1 son, 2 daughters. Education: Diploma, Technology in Automobile Engineering, 1974; Christian Faith Course from Florida Beacan College, USA, 1992. Appointments: Surveyors Engineer, 1974-75; Service Manager, 1975; Fulltime Ministry, 1975; President and Founder, Mission Evangelistic Association, 1981-2001; Ordained by World Wide Missions, 1979; Ordained by Columbus Cathedral, USA, 1986 and by Elijah Ministries Inc, Canada, 1999. Publications: Baptism Book in English and in Hindi; Answers to Your Questions. Honours: Doctor of Divinity, World International Bible College, India, 1994; Doctor of Divinity, World Wide Missions of India, 1998; Consecrated as Bishop, 6 February 2000. Address: PO Box 30, Dumka (SP), Jharkhand, India 814101.

MARCEAU Marcel, b. 22 March 1923, Strasbourg, France. Mime Artist. m. (1) Huguette Mallet, divorced, 2 sons, (2) Ella Jaroszewicz, 1966, divorced, (3) Anne Sicco, 1975, divorced, 2 daughters. Education: Lille and Strasbourg Lycees. Appointments: Director, Compagnie de Mime Marcel Marceau, 1948-64; Annual world tours and numerous TV appearances world-wide; Created Don Juan (mime drama), 1964, Candide (ballet), Hamburg, 1971; Creator of the character "Bip"; Director, Ecole de Mimodrame Marcel Marceau, 1978-. Creative Works: Mimes include: Le manteau, Exercices des style (both filmed); Mort avant l'aube; Le joueur de flute; Moriana et Galvau; Pierrot de Montmartre; Les trois perruques. Publications: Les sept péchés capitaux; Les reveries de Bip; Alphabet Book; Counting Book; L'histoire de Bip; The Third Eye; Pimporello, 1987. Honours: Académie des Beaux Arts, 1991; Officier, Légion d'honneur; Commander, Ordre nationale du Mérite; Commander, des Arts et des Lettres; Honorary Degrees from Princeton and Oregon Universities, 1987; Grand Officier du Merite, 1998. Address: c/o Compagnie de Mime Marcel Marceau, 32 rue de Londres, 75009 Paris, France.

MARCEAU Sophie (Sophie Danièle, Sylvie Maupu), b. 17 November 1966, Paris, France. Actress. 1 son, 1 daughter. Creative Works: Stage appearances include: Eurydice, 1991; Pygmalion, 1993; Films: La Boum, 1981; La Boum 2, 1982; Fort Saganne, 1984; Joyeuses Pâques, 1985; L'Amour Braque, 1985; Police, 1985; Descente aux Enfers, 1986; Chouans!, 1987; L'Etudiante, 1988; Mes Nuits Sont Plus Belles Que Vos Jours, 1989; Pacific Palisades, 1989; Pour Sacha, 1991; La Note Bleue, 1991; Fanfan, 1993; La Fille de D'Artagnam, 1994; Braveheart, 1995; Beyond the Clouds, 1995; Firelight, 1988; Anna Karenine, 1996; Marquise, 1997; The World is Not Enough, 1998; La Fidelité, 1999; Belphégor, 2001; Alex and Emma, 2003; Je reste! 2003; Les Clefs de bagnole, 2003. Publication: Menteuse, 1996. Address: c/o Artmedia, 10 avenue George V, 75008 Paris, France.

MARCHI Lorraine, b. 5 June 1923, San Francisco, California, USA. Health Care Executive. m. (1) Robert L Fastie, deceased, (2) Gene Marchi Snr, divorced, 2 sons, 2 daughters. Education: Stanford University, California; University of California, Berkeley; Honorary doctorate, State University of New York, 2002. Appointment: Founder and CEO, National Association for Visually Handicapped. Publications: Several articles in professional journals. Honours: L HD, State University of New York, 2002; Listed in numerous biographical publications. Address: 22 West 21st Street, New York, NY 10010, USA. E-mail: staff@navh.org

MARCU Aurora, b. 2 April 1942, Bestepe, Tulcea County, Romania. Biologist; Zoologist. m. Marcu Ioan Dan, 1 son. Education: Doctor in Biology, Biology Faculty, Zoology Section of "Al I Cuza" University, Iasi, Romania. Appointments: Biology Teacher, Highschool, Tarqu Bujor, Galati County, 1966-67; Biologist, Galati Water Works, 1967; Biologist, Museum Curator, Natural Science Museum, Galati, 1967; Manager, Natural Science Museum Complex, Galati, 1990-. Publications: 19 scientific works include: Flora of the Earth - Galati Botanical Garden, 1998; 4 articles and essays. Memberships: EASZA; IZE; SOR; AMNR (Romanian Naturalist Museum Curators Association); AER; Romanian Entomology Association. Address: Romania, Galti County Str, Domnesca nr 91, Galati, cod 6200.

MARCUS DeLAMBERT Jordan, b. 2 March 1929, Barbados. Managing Director. m. Grace Enid, 1 son, 1 daughter. Education: Life Insurance Diploma, Canada, Harrison College, 1941-48; Inter BA, University of London, 1949. Appointments: Sub Editor, Barbados Advocate; School Teacher, Combermere High School; Life Underwriter, Branch Manager, Manufacturers Life Insurance Co; Senator, Government of Barbados; Honorary Consul of Cyprus to Barbados; Managing Director, Wildey Shopping Plaza Ltd; Lamberts Ltd; Bank of Nova Scotia International; Scotia Insurance; President of the Senate, Government of Barbados. Membership: Chairman, Barbados Tourism Authority; Founding member of Kiwanis Club, Barbados, Member, Commonwealth Parliamentary Association, Royal Commonwealth Society. Address: Lambert's, Dover Terrace, Christ Church, Barbados. Website: wildeyplaza@sunbeach.net

MARDER Todd Benjamin, b. 14 November 1955. Professor of Inorganic Chemistry. Education: BSc, Chemistry, Massachusetts Institute of Technology, USA, 1976; PhD, Inorganic Chemistry, University of California, Los Angeles, 1981. Appointments: Postdoctoral Fellow, University of Bristol, School of Chemistry, England, 1981-83; Visiting Research Scientist, E I DuPont DeNemours & Co Inc, Central Research and Development Department, Wilmington, Delaware, USA, 1983-85; Assistant Professor, 1985-89, Associate Professor, 1989-93, Professor of Inorganic Chemistry, 1993-97, Adjunct Professor, 1997-2000, University of Waterloo, Waterloo, Ontario, Canada; Professor of Inorganic Chemistry, 1997-, Head of Inorganic Teaching Section, 1998-2003, Member of the Centre for Molecular and Nanoscale Electronics, 2000-, Sir Derman Christopherson Foundation Fellow, 2003-2004, University of Durham, Durham, England; Numerous visiting research posts, fellowships, and professorships 1987-2003. Publications: 140 papers published; 29 invited lectures at conferences; Over 140 invited lectures at universities, industrial and government research centres world-wide; Over 170 submitted conference presentations. Honours include: Member, Sigma Xi, 1981-; Ichikizaki Fund for Young Chemists Travel Award, 1991; Rutherford Memorial Medal for Chemistry, The Royal Society of Canada, 1995; Leverhulme Study Abroad Fellowship, 2003-2004; Sir Derman Christopherson Foundation Fellow, University of Durham, 2003-2004. Memberships: Fellow, Royal Society of Chemistry, UK; American Chemical Society; Chemical Institute of Canada; American Association for the Advancement of Science; New York Academy of Sciences; British Liquid Crystal Society; British Crystallographic Association. Address: Department of Chemistry, University of Durham, South Road, Durham DH1 3LE, England. E-mail: todd.marder@durham.ac.uk

MARDI Shalva, b. 10 May 1933, Georgia, Former USSR. Medical Doctor; Professor. m Rosa-Maria Mardi, 1 son, 1 daughter. Education includes: BC, College of the City of Kutaisi, USSR, 1953; Medical Doctor, National Russian Academy of Medicine, Moscow, 1959; Professor of Oncology, Cand med sci, Academy

Dictionary of International Biography

of Medical Sciences, St Petersburg, Russia, 1963; Doctor of Science in Medicine, Academy of Medical Sciences, Kiev, Ukraine, USSR, 1968; PhD, Moscow, 1968. Appointments include: Clinical Professor of Oncology, Tbilisi, Georgia, USSR, 1970; Numerous Visiting and Guest Professorships including: Tel-Aviv; Munich; Vienna; Milan; Houston, Texas; Buffalo, New York; Tokyo; Basel; Zurich; Rio de Janeiro, Brazil; Moscow; Paris; London; Kiev; St Petersburg; University Hospitals and Clinics; Director of Skin Institute of Skin Treatment, Kiron, Israel; President of Scientific, Medical Pharmaceutical and Cosmetic Laboratory, Binningen, Switzerland; Head of Department and Professor of Dermatological Division, SOLCO-Basel AG, Switzerland; Chief Scientist and Consultant, Rishardson-Meryll Company, USA, Basotherm AG, Germany; ABIC and TEVA Pharmaceuticals, Israel. Publications: More than 250 Scientific publications, books, monographs; 12 international new patents in medicine and for the invention of Mardi's Shark Caviar as an alternative for natural Beluga Caviar and as a food supplement for preventing cancer diseases as well as for the development of new lines in cosmeto-dermatology: Marditalia and Mardisrael global projects for United Nations and World Health Organisation: Stop and Solve Skin Cancer Epidemics, 2003. Honours: Numerous United Nations, international and national prizes, honour awards, medals and diplomas in scientific medicine. Memberships include: UNO, American, including: USA, European and Asian Scientific Academies and Societies of Onco-Dermatology. Address: 3 Bleicherweg, Binnigen, CH-Y102 Switzerland. E-mail: shavla33@bluewin.ch

MAREE Jacobus Gideon, b. 7 December 1951, Koekenaap, South Africa. Professor. 1 son. Education: BA; HEd; BEd; MEd; DEd (Career Counselling); PhD, Didactics of Mathematics; DPhil, Psychology. Appointments: Teacher, Head of Department, Department of Education, (CAPE), 1976-85; Lecturer, 1985-86; Senior Lecturer, 1987-92, Associate Professor, 1993-95, Professor, 1996-, University of Pretoria. Publications: Make Your Child Brighter; Become an Ace at Maths; Trial Match; Kickstart for Maths; Lifeskills and Career Counselling Outcomes-Based Assessment; Editor; 58 articles in refereed journals. Honours: Academic Colours, University of Pretoria, 1985, 1997; Medal of Honour, Education Association of South Africa, 2001; C-rated researcher with the National Research Foundation; Exceptional Achiever Status as a Researcher, University of Pretoria, 2003. Memberships: Psychological Society of South Africa; South African Society for Clinical Hypnosis; Association for Maths Education in South Africa; Editor, Perspectives in Education (ISI listed; nationally accredited). Address: 1300 Arcadia Street, Hatfield, 0083 Pretoria, South Africa. E-mail: jgmaree@hakuna.up.ac.za

MARGRETHE II H.M. (Queen of Denmark), b. 16 April 1940, Denmark. m. Count Henri de Laborde de Monpezat (now Prince Henrik of Denmark), 1967, 2 sons. Education: University of Copenhagen; University of Aarhus; University of Cambridge; University of Sorbonne, Paris; London School of Economics. Appointments: Illustrator, The Lord of the Rings, 1977, Norse Legends as Told by Jorgen Stegelmann, 1979, Bjarkemaal, 1982; Poul Oerum's Comedy in Florens, 1990; Cantabile poems by HRH the Prince Consort, 2000. Publications: (trans) All Men are Mortal (with Prince Henrik), 1981; The Valley, 1988; The Fields, 1989; The Forest (trans), 1989. Honours include: Hon LLD, Cambridge, 1975, London, 1980; Honorary Bencher, Mid Temple, 1992; Honorary Fellow, Girton College, Cambridge, 1992; Medal of the Headmastership, University of Paris, 1987; Hon KG, 1979. Address: Amalienborg Palace, 1257 Copenhagen K, Denmark.

MARGULIS Lynn, b. 5 March 1938, Chicago, Illinois, USA. Scientist; Professor. 3 sons, 1 daughter. Education: AB, Liberal Arts, University of Chicago, 1957; MS, University of Wisconsin,

1960; PhD, University of California, Berkeley, 1965. Appointments: Research Associate, Brandeis University, 1963-65; Elementary Science Study Consultant, 1963-67; US Peace Corps-Colombia Instructor, 1965-66; Adjunct Assistant Professor, 1966-67, Assistant Professor, 1967-71, Associate Professor, 1971-77, Professor, 1977-88, University Professor, 1986-88, Boston University; Visiting Professor, University of California, San Diego, 1980; Co-administrator, NASA, Planetary Biology Internship Program, 1981-; NASA, Planetary Biology Microbial Ecology, 1980, 1982, 1984; Visiting Professor, Universidad Autónoma de Barcelona, 1985, 1986; Visiting Scholar, Marine Science Research Center, SUNY, Stony Brook, 1986; Distinguished University Professor, Department of Botany, 1988-93, Distinguished University Professor, Department of Biology, 1993-97, University of Massachusetts, Amherst; Visiting Professor, Boston University Marine Program, 1994-99; Visiting Professor, George Mason University, 1995; Distinguished University Professor, Department of Geosciences, University of Massachusetts, Amherst, 1997-. Publications: Many publications and articles to professional journals; Author: Symbiosis in Cell Evolution, 2nd edition; Co-author: Acquiring Genomes: A Theory of the Origins of Species and more than 14 other books. Honours: US National Medal of Science, 1999; Collegium Helveticum Fellow, Zurich, 2001; Alexander von Humboldt Prize, German Government, 2002; Hanse Wissenschaft-Kolleg Fellow, 2002. Memberships: National Academy of Sciences; Russian Academy of Natural Science; American Academy of Arts and Science; World Academy of Arts and Sciences. Address: Department of Geosciences, University of Massachusetts, 611 North Pleasant Street, Amherst, MA 01003-9297, USA.

MARINELLI Carlo, b. 13 December 1926, Rome, Italy. Musicologist; Discologist; Discographer. 1 son, 1 daughter. Education: Degree in Letters, La Sapienza University of Rome, 1948. Career: Founder and Editor, Microsolco magazine, 1952-59; Professor, History of Music, 1970-98, Associate, 1985-98, Associate, History of Modern and Contemporary Music, 1992-98, Department of Comparative Cultures, Faculty of Letters, University of L'Aquila; Professor, Discography and Musical Videography, 1998-2002, DAMS, Faculty of Letters, University of Bologna; Honorary Member, International Association of Sound and Audiovisual Archives; President, Institute for Research on Musical Theatre, Rome. Publications: Discographies of Mozart, Rossini, Monteverdi, Donizetti, Bellini, Verdi, Puccini; Editor, catalogues of Italian audiovisual and sound sources of Mozart and Rossini; Editor: Notizie Videoarchivio Opera e Balletto, Notizie Archivio Sonoro Musica Contemporanea, IRTEM "Quaderni"; Le cantate profane di J S Bach, 1966; La musica strumentale da camera di Goffredo Petrassi, 1967; Lettura di Messiaen, 1972; Cronache di musica contemporanea, 1974; L'opera ceca, l'opera russa, l'opera in Polonia e Ungheria, 1977; Opere in disco. Da Monteverdi a Berg, 1982; Di Goffredo Petrassi, un'antologia, 1983; Prolegomeni ad una nuova disciplina scientifica: Discografia e videografia musicale, 1998; Prolegomena to a new scientific discipline: musical discography and videography, 2000; I documenti musicali sonori e visivi quali fonti di conoscenza, informazione e transmissione, 2002; Sound and Visual Musical Documents as Sources of Knowledge, Information and Transmission, 2002; Rilettura digitale come alterazione di documenti sonori originali, 2004; Discological Critical Edition: Giovanni Paisiello, Il re Teodoro in Venezia, 1994. Discographies: Faust e Mefistofele nelle opere sinfonico-vocali, 1986; Le opere di Mozart su libretti di Da Ponte, 1988; Mozart Singspiele, 1993; Mozart, Opere serie italiane, 1995; Monteverdi, Balli e Madrigali in genere rappresentativo, 1996; De Falla, Atalantida, 1996; Rossini, Il barbiere di Siviglia, 1998; Verdi, Rigoletto, Il trovatore, La traviata, 1999; Monteverdi, Opere teatrali, 2000; Rossini, Opere teatrali 1820-1829, 2001; Verdi, Don Carlo, Otello, Falstaff, 2002; Verdi, Oberto, Giorno di regno, Nabucco, Lombardi, Ernani, Due Fascari, 2003; Verdi, Don Carlos, La forza del destino, 2003, Verdi, Aida, 2004; Operatic Discography Encyclopaedia, 2004. Memberships: President, Associazione Italiana Archivi Sonori Audiovisivi; Board Member, Internationales Musik Zentrum, 1993-95; Chairman, Discography Committee, IASA, 1996-99; International, American, Australian, French, Spanish and Italian Musicological Societies; International Association of Music Libraries; Association of Recorded Sound Collectors; Australasian Sound Recording Association; Association Française Archives Sonores; Associazione Italiana Studi Nord Americani; Associazione Docenti Universitari Italiani Musica. Address: Via Francesco Tamagno 67, I-00168 Rome, Italy. E-mail: carlomarinelli@mclink.it Website: www.carlomarinelli.it

MARITIME George, b. 19 February 1942, Yonkers, New York, USA. Poet. Education: Syracuse University; Sarah Lawrence College. Appointment: Director, Folk Music Hall of Fame. Publications: Columbus, 1991; The Cricket's Song: The Story of John Keats, 1992; The Ballad of Christopher Marley, 1994. Contributions to: New Press; Herald Statesman. Honour: Award, Composers, Artists and Authors of America. Memberships: Marlowe Society of America; New York Shelley Society; Melville Society; Marlowe Lives Association. Address: 44 Cherwing Road, Bryn Mawr Knolls, Yonkers, NY 10701, USA.

MARKHAM Jehane, b. 12 February 1949, Sussex, England. Poet; Playwright. 3 sons. Education: Central School of Art, 1969-71. Publications: The Captain's Death; Ten Poems, 1993; Virago New Poets, 1993; Twenty Poems, 1999; Between Sessions and Beyond the Couch, 2002; In The Company of Poets, 2003. Radio Plays: More Cherry Cake, 1980; Thanksgiving, 1984; The Bell Tar; Frost in May. Television Play: Nina, 1978. Theatre Plays: One White Day, 1976; The Birth of Pleasure, 1997. Contributions to: Women's Press; Longmans Study; Sunday Times; BBC 2 Epilogue; Bananas Literary Magazine; Camden Voices; Independent; Observer; Acorn; Ambit; New Statesman. Memberships: Poetry Society; Highgate Literary and Scientific Society; NFT.

MARKHAM Richard, b. 23 June 1952, Grimsby, England. Concert Pianist. Education: Piano privately with Shirley Kemp and Max Pirani; National Youth Orchestra of Great Britain; Royal Academy of Music, London, 1969-73. Career: Concert Pianist; Tours in over 40 countries as David Nettle/Richard Markham Piano Duo, 1977-; Examiner for Associated Board of the Royal Schools of Music, 1984-. Recordings include: Nettle and Markham in America; Nettle and Markham in England; Nettle and Markham in France. Honours: ARCM, 1967; LRAM, 1968; Nora Naismith Scholarship, 1969; Bronze Medal, Geneva International Competition, 1972; Countess of Munster Musical Trust Awards, 1973, 1974; Frederick Shinn Fellowship, 1975; Gulbenkian Foundation Fellowship, 1976-78; ARAM 1983; MRA Award for Excellence, 1985. Memberships: Incorporated Society of Musicians; RAM Club; Friend of Stonewall. Address: The Old Power House, Atherton Street, London SW11 2JE, England. E-mail: nettleandmarkham@debrett.net

MARKÓ Béla, b. 8 September 1951, Târgu-Secuiesc, Romania. 2 sons, 1 daughter. Education: Graduate, Faculty of Hungarian and French Language and Literature, Babeş-Bolyai University, Cluj-Napoca, Romania, 1974. Appointments: Member, Gaál Gábor Literary Club, 1970-74, President, 1971-73; Teacher, 1974-76; Editor, Igaz Szó (literary periodical), 1976-89; Chief Editor, Látó (literary periodical) 1990-; Founding Member, DAHR (Democratic Alliance of Hungarians in Romania), Mureş County, 1989;

Senator, 1990-, reelected, 1992, 1996, 2000; President, DAHR, 1993, reelected, 1995, 1999. Publications: 21 books of verse including Notes on a Happy Pear Tree in English and Hungarian and Comme un échiquier fermé, in French; 3 volumes of essays, speeches and interviews. Honours: Literary awards: Romanian Writers Association; Hungarian Writers Association; Hungarian PEN, Romania; DAHR (Democratic Alliance of Hungarians in Romania). Address: RO-540099 Târgu Mureş, str Ulciorului 4, jud Mureş, Romania.

MARKOPOULOS Joannis, b. 14 October 1948, Thessaloniki, Greece. Chemical Engineer; Assistant Professor. m. Evangelina Charlotte Brigitte Jahnel, 2 sons. Education: Dipl-Ing, Chemical Engineering, Technical University of Darmstadt, Germany, 1973; Dr-Ing, Physical Chemistry, University of Thessaloniki, Greece, 1981. Appointments: Research Assistant, 1976-81, Lecturer, 1983, Assistant Professor, 1988-, University of Thessaloniki, Greece. Publications: In Greek: Introduction to Electrochemistry, 1990; Mass transfer, 1992; Membrane Separation Processes, 1997; Articles in international scientific journals and conferences; Articles concerning education, philosophy and philosophy of science in journals, periodicals and newspapers; 3 books of poetry. Honours: Distinguished Writing Award, Hellenic Club of Writers, Athens, 1995; Reviewer, international scientific journals. Memberships: University Senate, 1991-93; Technical Chamber of Greece; Greek Association of Chemical Engineers; German Chemical Association; American Chemical Society; Greek Philosophical Society; International Association of Greek Philosophy. Address: Megalou Alexandrou Avenue 45, 54643 Thessaloniki, Greece. E-mail: jonimark@vergina.eng.auth.gr

MARKOV Veselin Dimov, b. 15 December 1951, Popov, Bulgaria. Artist. Education: Studied with the Bulgarian Sculptor Luibomir Prahov, 1977-86; Studied with Stephan Hinkov, 1987-93. Career: One-man exhibition, Sculpture Outdoors, Sea Park, Varna, Bulgaria (destroyed by the Communist regime), 1982; Outdoor installation, Water Dragon (today considered onset of contemporary art in Bulgaria), 1983; Magic Space Tangra, indoor installation, camera obscura, Dordreht, Holland, 1986; Retired from public art life, 1986; Created Art group, Var(t)na, One-man exhibition, Paper and Colour, Issued own art newspaper "Bezmer", 1996; Indoor installation, Focus in Focus, 1998; Jordan River-Ilindenzi, outdoor sculpture used in traditional religious rituals of local citizens, 2000; Temple, outdoor installation 600/450 metres, Avion Spotlights, storm clouds, 2002; Temple of Light, outdoor installation; World Academic Forum Project, 2004. Publications: Frequent articles about his works in Art in Bulgaria Magazine and in world-wide internet sites. Honours: Numerous international awards and nominations. Memberships: Bulgarian and international professional organisations. Address: 4 Vega Street, Zvezdica 9027, Varna, Bulgaria. E-mail: vesselin_dimov@yahoo.com

MARKS James G Jr, b. 19 May 1945, Trenton, New Jersey, USA. Professor of Dermatology. m. 1 child. Education: BA, Biology, Wilkes College, Wilkes-Barre, Pennsylvania, 1963-67; Temple University School of Medicine, Philadelphia, Pennsylvania, 1967-71; Intern, Geisinger Medical Centre, Danville, 1971-72; Dermatology Resident, Wilford Hall, USAF Medical Centre, San Antonio, Texas, 1975-78; Dermatopathology, Armed Forces Institute of Pathology, Washington DC, 1978. Appointments: Staff Dermatology, The Milton S Hershey Medical Centre, Pennsylvania State University College of Medicine, 1980-; Professor of Dermatology, Division of Dermatology, 1991-, Director, Dermatology Resident Programme, 1997-, Chief, Division of Dermatology, 1998-2001, The Milton S Hershey Medical Centre, Pennsylvania State College of Medicine; Chair, Department of Dermatology, 2002. Publications: Co-author and editor of books:

Principles of Dermatology, 2000; Handbook of Contact Dermatitis, 2000; Contact and Occupational Dermatology, 2002; Several articles in professional medical journals. Honours include: Roerig Pharmaceutical Challenges in Dermatology Educational Exhibition Award, American Academy of Dermatology Annual Meeting, New Orleans, 1982; US Patent Award, 1998; President, American Society of Contact Dermatitis, 2001. Memberships: American Academy of Dermatology; Society for Investigative Dermatology; Association of Military Dermatologists; Dermatology Foundation; Philadelphia Academy of Dermatology; Philadelphia Dermatology Society; North American Contact Dermatitis Group; American Contact Dermatitis Society; European Society of Contact Dermatitis; World Fragrance Research Team; Agromedicine Consortium. Address: Hershey Medical Centre, M.C. HU14, PO Box 850, Hershey, PA 17033-0850, USA. E-mail: jmarks@psu.edu

MARKS Michael A, b. 29 July 1958, Brooklyn, New York, USA. Chiropractic Physician. m. Julie, 2 sons. Education: BS, 1980; DC, 1988. Appointment: Chiropractic Physician, 1988-. Honour: Expert Medical Advisor for the State of Florida. Memberships: FCA; American Academy of Spine Physicians. Address: 8903 Glades Road, Suite A-11, Boca Raton, FL 33434, USA. E-mail: jmboca@aol.com

MARKWELL John Robert, b. 31 July 1948. Information Technology Management; Applied Research & Development. m. Deborah D Walker, 17 December 1977, 1 son, 1 daughter. Education: BS, Physics, James Cook University, North Queensland, 1970; Diploma in Information Processing, University of Queensland, 1972; International Executive Programme, INSEAD, France, 1991; Senior Executive Business Study Course, Tsinghua University, Beijing, 1996. Appointments: Shift Supervisor, University of Queensland Computer Centre, 1972; Trainee Programmer, Systems Programmer, Principal Programmer (Systems & Communications), TAB of Queensland, 1972-77; Director, Hong Kong Jockey Club Systems (Australia) Pty Ltd, 1992-97; Systems Analyst/Designer, Software Manager, Software Development Manager, Systems Development Manager, Information Systems Controller, Head, Information Technology, Royal Hong Kong Jockey Club, 1978-93; Director of Information Technology, Hong Kong Jockey Club, 1994-97; Director of IT & Technology, New World Telephone Ltd, 1997-98; Executive Chair, DASCOM Australia P/L, 1999-2000; Managing Director, TECASA P/L, 2000-. Honour: Global 100 Top Users of Information Technology, to RHKJC by Computerworld, 1985; International Order of Merit, 2004. Memberships: HKMA Telecomms Users Group, Executive Committee, Honorary Treasurer, 1983-85; Committee, Information Technology Training, Vocational Training Council, Hong Kong, 1988-95; Co-opted Member, Sub-Committee on Information Technology of Committee on Science & Technology, Trade & Industry/Central Government Office, Hong Kong, 1988-91; Honorary Information Technology Adviser to Urban Council, 1990-95; Advisory Committee for Centre of Computing Services & Telecommunications, Hong Kong University of Science & Technology, 1991-97; Hong Kong Country Club, Finance Committee, 1994-98, General Committee, 1995-97; Departmental Advisory Committee for Department of Computer Science, City University, Hong Kong, 1995-97; Advisory Committee on Computing, Department of Computing, Hong Kong Polytechnic, 1995-97; Hong Kong Jockey Club; Hong Kong Country Club; Multihull Yacht Club Queensland Inc. Address: TECASA Pty Ltd, Suite 368, Locked Bag 1, Robina Town Centre, QLD 4230, Australia.

MAROVIC Pavao, b. 26 January 1954, Split, Croatia. University Professor; Civil Engineer. m. Vladica Herak, 1 son. Education: Faculty of Civil Engineering, University of Zagreb, 1972-77; Graduate, Civil Engineer, 1977; PhD, Faculty of Civil Engineering, University of Zagreb, 1987. Appointments: Teaching Assistant, 1978-88, Assistant Professor, 1988-92, Head of Department, Testing and Technology of Materials, 1988-91, Vice Dean of the Faculty, 1991-94, President, University Assembly, 1991-93, Associated Professor, 1992-96, Vice Rector, 1994-98, Professor, 1996-, Head of the Chair for Strength of Materials, Testing of Structures, 1998-, Dean of the Faculty, 2000-, University of Split; Associated Member, Croatian Academy of Technical Sciences, 2000. Publications: Nonlinear Calculations of R/C Structures; Nonlinear Engineering Computations; International Congress of Croatian Society of Mechanics; Symposium on The Use of Computers in Civil Engineering; Co-editor of 25 Croatian Conference proceedings and approximately 160 scientific and professional papers in journals and conference proceedings; many others. Honours: Rector's Student Award; Plaque of the CAD/CAM Congress; Decorated by the President of the Republic of Croatia; County Splitsko-dalmatinska Yearly Award for Science; 2000 Outstanding Scientists of the 20th Century Silver Medal, International Biographical Centre; World Lifetime Achievement Award, American Biographical Institute. Memberships: International Association for Computer Methods and Advances in Geomechanic; International Association for Bridge and Structural Engineering; Central European Association for Computational Mechanics; European Scientific Association of Material Forming; National Geographic Society; Croatian Society of Mechanics; Croatian Society of Structural Engineers; Many others. Address: Faculty of Civil Engineering and Architecture, University of Split, Matice hrvatske 15, HR-21000 Split, Croatia.

MARQUIS Max, (Edward Frank Marquis), b. Ilford, Essex, England. Author. m. (1) 1 son, (2) Yvonne Cavenne, 1953. Appointments: News Writer and Reader, RDF French Radio, 1952; Sub Editor, Columnist, Continental Daily Mail, 1952, Evening News, London, 1955; Chief British Correspondent, L'Equipe, Paris, 1970; Football Commentator, Broadcaster, Télévision Suisse-Romande, 1972. Publications: Sir Alf Ramsey: Anatomy of a Football Manager, 1970; The Caretakers, 1975; A Matter of Life, 1976; The Shadowed Heart, 1978; The Traitor Machine, 1980; Body Guard to Charles, 1989; Vengeance, 1990; The Twelfth Man, 1991; Deadly Doctors, 1992; Elimination, 1993; Undignified Death, 1994; Written in Blood, 1995; Death of a Good Woman, 1998. Address: c/o Rupert Crew Ltd, 1A Kings Mews, London WC1N 2JA, England.

MARSDEN Simon Neville Llewelyn (Sir), b. 1 December 1948, Lincoln, Lincolnshire, England. Photographer; Author. m. Caroline Stanton, 1 son, 1 daughter. Education: Sorbonne, Paris. Career: Professional photographer and author; Photographs in the following collections: J Paul Getty Museum, California, USA; Victoria and Albert Museum, London; Bibliothéque Nationale, Paris, France; The Cleveland Museum of Art, USA; The Maryland Historical Society, Baltimore, USA; The University of Arizona, USA; Flanders Field Museum, Ypres, Belgium. Publications: In Ruins: The Once Great Houses of Ireland, 1980; The Haunted Realm – Ghosts, Witches and Other Strange Tales, 1986; Visions of Poe - A Personal Selection of E A Poe's Stories and Poems, 1988; Phantoms of the Isles – Further Tales from the Haunted Realm, 1990; The Journal of a Ghosthunter – In search of the Undead from Ireland to Transylvania, 1994; Beyond the Wall – The Lost World of East Germany, 1999; Venice - City of Haunting Dreams, 2002. Memberships: Chelsea Arts Club; The Arthur Machen Society. Address: The Presbytery, Hainton, Market Rasen, Lincolnshire LN8 6LR, England. E-mail: info@marsdenarchive.com

Dictionary of International Biography

MARSDEN-SMEDLEY Christopher, b. 9 February 1931, London, England. Retired Architect. m. Susan Penelope King, 2 sons 1 daughter. Education: BA, (Arch), University College, London, 1956. Appointments: Partner, 1961-96, Senior Partner, 1990-96, Nealon Tanner Partnership; High Sheriff, Avon, 1994-95; Deputy Lieutenant, Somerset, 2000. Publications: Burrington, Church and Village; Articles in various architectural papers. Honours: ARIBA, 1959; FRIBA, 1969. Memberships: Honorary Secretary, Bristol Civic Society, 1966-71; Governor, 1969-75, Chairman, 1972-75, Fairfield School; Committee Member, 1974-97, Chairman, 1988-97, Vice President, 1997-, Bristol Age Care; President, Bristol Commercial Rooms, 1988; Trustee, Wells Cathedral, 1997-; Committee Member, 1997-, President 2000-2001, Canynges Society. Address: Church Farm, Burrington, Near Bristol BS40 7AD, England.

MARSH Eric M, b. 25 July 1943, Preston, England. Hotelier. m. Elizabeth Margaret, 2 sons, 2 daughters. Education: National Diploma in Hotelkeeping and Catering, Courtfield Catering College, Blackpool, Lancashire, England, 1960-63. Appointments: Dorchester Hotel, London, 1963-68; Rank Hotels, London, 1968-73; Director and General Manager, Newling Ward Hotels, St Albans, Hertfordshire, England, 1973-1975; Tenant of Cavendish Hotel from Chatsworth Estate, 1975-; Managing Director, Paludis Ltd (Trading as Cavendish Hotel), 1975-; Managing Director of Eudaemonic Leisure Ltd (Trading as George Hotel), 1996-; Managing Director, Cavendish Aviation Ltd (Operating at Gamston Airfield), 1975-. Publications: Several articles in Caterer and Hotelkeeper magazine and Pilot magazine. Memberships: Institute of Marketing; Institute of Advanced Motorists; Director, Committee Member, British Aerobatic Association. Address: Cavendish Hotel, Baslow, Derbyshire DE45 1SP, England. E-mail: info@cavendish-hotel.net

MARSH Francis Patrick, b. 15 April 1936, Birmingham, England. Consultant Physician. m. Pamela Anne Campbell, 1 son, 2 daughters. Education: BA, Natural Science Tripos, Gonville and Caius College, 1957; London Hospital Medical College, 1957-60; MB BChir, Cambridge, 1960; MA, Cambridge, 1961; MRCP, London, 1963; FRCP, London, 1976. Appointments: House Physician, 1960-61, House Surgeon, 1961, The London Hospital; Senior House Officer in Medicine, Kent and Canterbury Hospital, 1961-62; Registrar in Medicine, Royal Free Hospital, 1962-63; Registrar in Medicine, The London Hospital, 1963-65; Research Fellow, 1965-67, Lecturer, Senior Registrar, 1967-70, The London Hospital and London Hospital Medical College; Honorary Consultant Physician, Bethnal Green Hospital, 1970-71; Senior Lecturer in Medicine, The London Hospital Medical College, now St Bartholomew's and the Royal London School of Medicine and Dentistry, 1970-2001; Consultant Nephrologist, Barts and the London NHS Trust, 1971-2001; Dean of Medical Studies and Governor, The London Hospital Medical College, 1990-95; Board of Directors, American University of the Caribbean, 2000-; Honorary Senior Lecturer in Medicine, Bartholomew's and the Royal London School of Medicine and Dentistry, 2001-; Emeritus Consultant Nephrologist, Barts and the London NHS Trust, 2001-. Publications: Around 80 original research papers; Author, 26 book chapters; Editor, Postgraduate Nephrology; Refereed many medical journals and for regional and national prizes. Memberships include: Joint Formulary Committee, British National Formulary; Renal Association; Specialist Advisory Committee on Renal Disease; North East Thames Regional Medical Advisory Committee; North East Thames Regional Committee for Hospital Medical Services; Council of the Section of Medicine, Experimental Medicine and Therapeutics (Royal Society of Medicine); Central Committee for Hospital Medical Services. Address: Butchers End, 20 Butchers Lane, East Dean, West Sussex, PO18 0JF, England. E-mail: frank.marsh@virgin.net

MARSH Laurie Peter. Consultant; Property Restoration. Education: National Service RASC and Intelligence Corps, 1950-51, commissioned; Reserve Captain, 1954. Appointments: Chairman, Chief Executive Officer, Raincheque Ltd sold to Blacketts Stores plc, Director of plc, 1956; Chairman, Chief Executive Officer, Wadey Davison and L P Marsh (Properties) Ltd, Director, Greenaways (Builders), London, 1958; Chairman, Booty Jewellery, London, 1962; Director, Tigon Film Group, 1969; Acquired Classic Cinemas, 1971; Chairman, Town and District Properties plc and Laurie Marsh Group plc, 1971; Aquired Essoldo Cinema Group and part Rank cinemas, expanded multiple cinemas; LMG expanded into Europe, name changed to Intereuropean Prop Holdings plc, 1974; Chairman and Director, theatre group with Brian Rix and Ray Cooney, acquired 6 London theatres and 1 on Broadway, New York, 1976; Elected Vice President, 1978, President, 1979, Cinematograph Exhibitors Association; Sold IPH plc to ACC Leisure Group, Lord Grade, 1980; Chairman, Cosgrove Hall Properties Inc, New York, 1980; Chairman, Theatre Royal Bath; Restored theatres in London and New York, 1981; Chairman, F and GP LAMDA, UK National Charity, 1991; Founder, Libertas Charity Group, Chairman, Soundalive Tours Group (now International Heritage Group), 1986-98; Non-Executive Chairman, Cole Kitchen Theatre Group, 1994; Non-Executive Chairman, London Crystal Cleaners and Capital Property Services, 1999; Consultant to major property groups; Property restoration, theatre, financial consultancy. Address: 30 Grove End Road, St John's Wood, London NW8 9LJ, England. E-mail: lauriemarsh@tandemlodge.freeserve.co.uk

MARSHALL Albert Selwyn, b. 26 September 1934, Tatsfield, Surrey, England. Retired Diplomat. m. Joan Margaret Lashwood, deceased, 1985, 1 son, 1 daughter. Education: Kent Horticultural College, Kent, England. Appointments: Royal Corps of Signals, Korea, Suez Canal, Cyprus, 1952-57; Foreign Office, 1957-61; Communications Officer, UK Mission to UN, New York, 1961-64; Archivist, British Embassy, Prague, 1954-65; ECO, British High Commission, Kingston, Jamaica, 1965-68; Foreign and Commonwealth Office, London, England, 1968-72; Management Officer, British Embassy, Addis Ababa, Ethiopia, 1972-75; British Vice-Consul, Belgrade, Yugoslavia, 1975-77; HM Vice-Consul, Tokyo, Japan, 1977-81; Foreign and Commonwealth Office, London, England, 1981-86; Management Officer, British Embassy, Washington DC, USA, 1986-90; HM Consul, Tel Aviv, Israel, 1990-94; Retired, 1994. Honour: MBE, 1968. Memberships: Treasurer, Merrow Horticultural Society; Volunteer, National Trust, Polesden Lacey. Address: 4 Tansy Close, Guildford, Surrrey GU4 7XN, England. E-mail: albert@asmarshall.freeserve.co.uk

MARSHALL Fray Francis, b. 27 August 1944, New York, USA. Urologist. m. Lindsay, 1 son, 1 daughter. Education: BA with distinction, 1965, MD, 1969, University of Virginia; Surgery Internship, 1969-70, Surgery Residency, 1970-72, University of Michigan; Urology Residency, Harvard University, Massachusetts General Hospital, 1972-75. Appointments: Assistant Professor, Associate Professor, Professor of Urology, Johns Hopkins School of Medicine, 1976-98; Professor and Chairman, Department of Urology, Emory University School of Medicine, 1999-. Address: Department of Urology, Emory University, 1365 Clifton Road, Atlanta NE, GA 30322, USA.

MARSHALL-ANDREWS Robert, b. 10 April 1944, London, England. Member of Parliament; Queen's Counsel; Writer. m. Gillian Diana, 1 son, 1 daughter. Education: University of Bristol; Gray's Inn. Appointments: Member of Bar, 1967; Recorder, Crown Court, 1982; Queen's Counsel, 1987; Deputy High Court Judge, 1996; Bencher, Gray's Inn, 1996; Member of Parliament, 1997-. Publications: Numerous political articles in national (UK) newspapers and publications: Novels: Palace of Wisdom, 1989; A Man Without Guilt, 2002. Honours: Winner Observer Mace, 1967; Spectator Parliamentary Award, 1997. Address: House of Commons, London SW1A 0AA, England.

MARSTON Jeffery Adrian Priestley, b. 15 December 1927, London, England. Surgeon. m. Sylvie Colin, 2 sons, 1 daughter. Education: MA (Oxon), 1952, DM MCh, 1963, Magdalen College, Oxford; St Thomas' Hospital Medical School; Harvard University; FRCS (Eng), 1958. Appointments: Training Posts at St Thomas' Hospital, St Mark's Hospital, 1959-65; Consultant Surgeon, The Middlesex Hospital, The Royal Northern Hospital, 1970-85, University College Hospital, 1985-92; Consultant Vascular Surgeon, The Manor House Hospital, 1974-93, The National Heart Hospital, 1985-91, The Royal National Orthopaedic Hospital, 1985-91; Emeritus Consultant Surgeon, University College London Hospitals, 1993-; Dean, Royal Society of Medicine. Publications: Books: Intestinal Ischaemia, 1977, Contemporary Operative Surgery, 1979; Vascular Disease of the Gut, 1980; Visceral Artery Reconstruction, 1984; Splanchnic Ischaemia and Multiple Organ failure, 1989; Hamilton Bailey: A Surgeons Life, 1999; Over 130 papers on vascular surgery and gasto-enterology. Honours: MD (honoris causa), Université de Nice, 1983; Gimbernat Prize, University of Barcelona, 1986; Honorary Fellow, Collegio Brasileiro de Cirugões; Honorary Fellow, College of Physicians and Surgeons of Pakistan; Chevalier d'Honneur, Ordre National du Mérite de la République Française. Memberships include: Vice-President, Royal College of Surgeons of England; President, Association of Surgeons of Great Britain and Ireland; President Vascular Surgery Society; British Medical Association; Royal Society of Medicine; Association of Surgeons; Medical Society of London; Membre d'Honneur, Association Française de Chirurgie; Socio de Honor, Asociación Española de Cirugía. Address: 4 Hereford Square, London SW7 4TT, England. E-mail: amar576837@aol.com

MARTEN Richard Hedley Westwood, b. 24 January 1943, Leeds, England. Barrister. m. Fiona Sinclair, divorced, 2 sons, 1 daughter. Education: Magdalene College, Cambridge, 1961-65. Appointments: Head of Chambers, 1995-; Bencher of Lincoln's Inn, 2000. Publication: Testamentary Disposition of Chattels, 2001; Contentious Probate Claims, 2003. Honour: Thomas More Bursar of Lincoln's Inn. Memberships: Brooks's; St James's; Butterflies Cricket Club; Academy Club. Address: 11 New Square, Lincoln's Inn, London WC2A 3QB, England.

MARTIN Angus, b. 6 February 1952, Argyll, Scotland. Postman; Poet. m. Judith Honeyman, 28 March 1986, 3 daughters. Publication: The Larch Plantation. 1990; The Song of the Quern, 1998. Contributions to: Weekend Scotsman; Lines Review; Chapman; Poetry Wales; PEN New Poetry; New Writing Scotland; An Canan; Northwords; The Dark Horse. Honour: Scottish Arts Council Spring Award. Address: 13 Saddell Street, Campbeltown, Argyll PA28 6DN, Scotland.

MARTIN Archer John Porter, b. 1 March 1910, London, England. Biochemist. m. Judith Bagenal, 1943, 2 sons, 3 daughters. Education: Graduated, 1932, PhD, 1935, Peterhouse, Cambridge University. Appointments: Dunn Nutritional Laboratories, 1936-38; Wool Industries Research Association, Leeds, 1938; Head, Biochemistry Division, Research Department, Boots Pure Drug Company, Nottingham, 1946-48; Staff, Medical Research Council; Lister Institute of Preventive Medicine, Head, Division of Physical Chemistry, National Institute for Medical Research, 1952-56, Chemical Consultant, 1956-59; Director, Abbotsbury Laboratory, 1959-70; Extraordinary Professor, Eindhoven Technological University, Holland, 1964-74; Consultant, Wellcome Research

Laboratories, University of Sussex, 1970-73; Invited Professor of Chemistry, Ecole Polytechnique, Lausanne, Switzerland, 1980; Developed paper chromatography. Honours: Berzelius Gold Medal of Swedish Medical Society, 1951; Joint Winner, Nobel Prize for Chemistry, 1952; John Scott Award, 1958; Leverhulme Medal, 1963; Kolthoff Medal, 1969; Callendar Medal, 1971; Randolf Major Medal, Connecticut University, 1979; Fritz Pregl Medal, Austria, 1985; Order of the Rising Sun, 2nd Class, Japan; Several honorary degrees.

MARTIN Bill, b. 9 November 1938, Govan, Glasgow, Scotland. Songwriter; Music Publisher. m. Jan, 1 son, 3 daughters. Musical Education: Royal Scottish Academy of Music Certificate. Career: Songwriter; First song, Kiss Me Now, released 1963; Writing partnership with Tommy Scott, 1964-65; Writing partnership with Phil Coulter, 1965-83; Martin-Coulter publishing company, 1970-; Producer of musical, Jukebox, 1983; Producer, publisher and writer, Angus Publications; Acquisitions and Back Catalogue Consultant, SONY/ATV Music, 2000-. Honours: 20 Gold albums; 4 Platinum albums; 3 Ivor Novello Awards; 3 ASCAP Awards; First British Winner, Eurovision Song Contest with Puppet on a String, 1967; Rio de Janeiro Award of Excellence, 1967, 1969; Antibes Song Festival Award for the Best Song, 1971; Japanese Yamaha Best Song Award, 1978; Variety Club Silver Heart, 1979; Scotland's Songwriter of the Decade, 1980. Memberships: BASCA; PRS; Society of Distinguished Songwriters; Freeman of the City of London; Freeman of the City of Glasgow; Member, Worshipful Company of Distillers; Member, MCC; Past Golf Captain, Royal Automobile Club; Member, St George's Hill Golf Club. Address: 14 Graham Terrace, Belgravia, London SW1W 8JH, England. E-mail: bill.puppetmartin@virgin.net

MARTIN David (Alfred), b. 30 June 1929, London, England. Professor of Sociology Emeritus; Priest; International Fellow; Writer. m. (1) Daphne Sylvia Treherne, 1953, 1 son, (2) Bernice Thompson, 30 June 1962, 2 sons, 1 daughter. Education: DipEd, Westminster College, 1952; External BSc, 1st Class Honours, 1959, PhD, 1964, University of London; Postgraduate Scholar, London School of Economics and Political Science, 1959-61. Appointments: Assistant Lecturer, Sheffield University, 1961-62; Lecturer, 1962-67, Reader, 1967-71, Professor of Sociology, 1971-89, Professor Emeritus, 1989-, London School of Economics and Political Science; Ordained Deacon, 1983, Priest, 1984; Scurlock Professor of Human Values, Southern Methodist University, Dallas, 1986-90; Senior Professorial Fellow, later International Fellow, Institute for the Study of Economic Culture, Boston University, 1990-; Various visiting lecturerships. Publications: Pacifism, 1965; A Sociology of English Religion, 1967; The Religious and the Secular, 1969; Tracts Against the Times, 1973; A General Theory of Secularisation, 1978; Dilemmas of Contemporary Religion, 1978; Crisis for Cranmer and King James (editor), 1978; The Breaking of the Image, 1980; Theology and Sociology (co-editor), 1980; No Alternative (co-editor), 1981; Unholy Warfare (co-editor), 1983; Divinity in a Grain of Bread, 1989; Tongues of Fire, 1990; The Forbidden Revolution, 1996; Reflections on Sociology and Theology, 1997; Does Christianity Cause War?, 1997; Pentecostalism: The World Their Parish, 2000; Christian Language and the Secular City, 2002; Christian Language and its Mutations. Honours: Honorary Assistant Priest, Guildford Cathedral, 1983-; Honorary Professor, Lancaster University, 1993-2002; Sarum Lecturer, Oxford University, 1994-95; Honorary Doctor of Theology, Helsinki, 2000. Membership: International Conference of the Sociology of Religion, president, 1975-83. Address: Cripplegate Cottage, 174 St John's Road, Woking, Surrey GU21 1PQ, England.

Dictionary of International Biography

MARTIN Diana Joan, b. Jackson Heights, New York, USA. University Administrator. m. Thomas Creola, 1 daughter. Education: BA, Honours, University of Florida, USA, additional study, University of Maryland, USA and Munich, Germany; Newspaper Fund Fellowship, California State University at Fullerton; M Ed, Florida Atlantic University, USA; PhD, The University of South Florida. Appointments: Director of Admissions/Career Program Director, Prospect Hall College, Fort Lauderdale, Florida, 1973-79; Director of Development and Alumni Affairs, Webber College, Babson Park Florida, 1979-84; Director of University Development, University of North Florida, Jacksonville, Florida, 1984-86; Director of Development, Trinity University, San Antonio, Texas, 1986-90; Executive Director, ACCD Foundation and Executive Director of Development, Community Relations and Public Relations (Institutional Advancement), Alamo Community College District, San Antonio, Texas, 1990-96; Vice-President for Institutional Advancement, Lees-McRae College, Banner Elk, North Carolina, 1996-99; Vice-President and Capital Campaign Director, Jacksonville University, Jacksonville, Florida, 1999-2000; Vice-President for Advancement, North Georgia College and State University and Director NGCSU Foundation Inc, Dahlonega, Georgia, 2000-2002; President, Funding STAR Inc, 2002-; University Faculty, 2002-. Publications: Public/Private Partnership Philanthropy, 1986; Events in Support of the Annual Fund, 1990. Honours: Phi Kappa Phi National Honor Society; Keynote Speaker, Fourth Annual Women's Leadership Conference, International Women's Day, 2000; USF Alumni Scholars Award; Bouvier Award for Excellence in Writing; Newspaper Fund Fellowship Award; Listed in Who's Who publications and biographical dictionaries. Memberships include: American Association of University Administrators; Association of Fundraising Professionals; American Association of University Women; Association of Governing Board of Colleges and Universities; Ex-officio Board Member, Dahlonega-Lumpkin County Chamber of Commerce; Georgia Education Advancement Council; Women and Leadership Committee; Board of Trustees, Episcopal Children's Services. Address: 43 Hyalite Road West, Dahlonega, GA 30533, USA. E-mail: dmartin@linkamerica.net

MARTIN George (Henry), b. 3 January 1926, England. Music Industry Executive; Producer; Composer. m. (1) Sheena Rose Chisholm, 1948, 1 son, 1 daughter, (2) Judy Lockhart Smith, 1966, 1 son, 1 daughter. Education: Guildhall School of Music and Drama. Appointments: Sub-Lieutenant, RNVR, 1944-47; Worker, BBC, 1950, EMI Records Ltd, 1950-65, Chair, 1965-; Built AIR Studios, 1969; Built AIR Studios, Montserrat, 1979; Completed new AIR Studios, Lyndhurst Hall, Hampstead, 1992; Co-merged with Chrysalis Group, 1974, Director, 1978-; Chair, Heart of London Radio, 1994-; Scored the music of 15 films. Publications: All You Need is Ears, 1979; Making Music, 1983; Summer of Love, 1994. Honours include: Ivor Novello Awards, 1963, 1979; Grammy Awards, 1964, 1967 (two), 1973, 1993, 1996. Address: c/o AIR Studios, Lyndhurst Hall, Hampstead, London, NW3 5NG, England.

MARTIN Graham Dunstan, b. 21 October 1932, Leeds, Yorkshire, England. Educator; Writer. m. (1) Ryllis Eleanor Daniel, 21 August 1954, 2 sons, 1 daughter, (2) Anne Moone Crombie, 14 June 1969, 2 sons. Education: Oriel College, Oxford, 1950-54; Manchester University, 1955; Linacre House, Oxford, 1963-64. Appointments: Assistant Teacher, French, English, Spanish, various secondary schools, 1956-65; Assistant Lecturer, French, 1965-67, Lecturer, 1967-82, Senior Lecturer, 1982-2000, Edinburgh University. Publications: Remco Campert; Love and Protest; Le Cimetiere Marin; Anthology of Contemporary French Poetry; Louise Labé: Sonnets; J-C Renard: Selected Poems; Jules Laforgue, 1998; Non-Fiction Books: Language, Truth and Poetry;

The Architecture of Experience; Shadows in the Cave; Inquiry into the Purposes of Speculative Fiction; Novels for children: Giftwish; Catchfire; Novels for adults: The Soul Master; Time-Slip; The Dream Wall; Half a Glass of Moonshine; Numerous articles in periodicals including, British Journal of Aesthetics, Chapman, The European Legacy, Forum for Modern Language Studies, French Studies; Contributions to: Lines; London Magazine; Modern Poetry in Translation; Prospice; 2 Plus 2; New Edinburgh Review; Lost Voices of World War One. Memberships: Fellow, Society of Antiquaries, Scotland; Society of Authors. Address: 21 Mayfield Terrace, Edinburgh, EH9 1RV, Scotland.

MARTIN Joan, b. 14 May 1949, Figures, Catalonia, Spain. Professor of Botany. Education: Licenciate, Pharmacy, 1975; PhD, 1988. Appointments: Auxiliar Professor, 1977-95, Associate Professor, 1995-2000, Interine (provisional) Professor, 2000-03, Definitive Functionary Professor , 2003, University of Barcelona. Publications: The Apertural Sporoderm of Pollen Grains in Euphorbia; A Correlation Study between Airbourne Pollen and Pollinosis in Humans; Phylogeny of Subtribe Artemisilnae; Cytogenetic and Isozymic Characterization of the Endemic Species Artemisia Molinieri; Pollen Diameter and Fertility in Nine Species of Puccinellia (poaceae); Pollen Studies in Centaureinae. Honours: Elected member and Member of Faculty Council New York Academy of Sciences; Member, Academic Staff University of Barcelona. Memberships: New York Academy of Sciences; American Association for the Advancement of Science; Planetary Society; Organization for the Phyto-Taxonomic Investigation of the Mediterranean Area. Address: Moline Street, 1, 1st 2nd, 08006 Barcelona, Spain. E-mail: villodhe@farmacia.far.ub.es

MARTIN Michael John, b. 3 July 1945. Politician. m. Mary McCay, 1 son, 1 daughter. Education: St Patrick's Boys' School, Glasgow, Scotland. Appointments: Glasgow City Councillor, 1973-79; Member of Parliament, Glasgow, Springburn, 1979-; Deputy Speaker and Deputy Chairman of Ways and Means, 1997-2000; Speaker of the House of Commons, 2000-. Address: Speaker's House, House of Commons, London SW1A 0AA.

MARTIN Philip (John Talbot), b. 28 March 1931, Melbourne, Victoria, Australia. Retired Senior Lecturer; Poet. Education: BA, University of Melbourne, 1958. Appointments: Tutor to Senior Tutor in English, University of Melbourne, 1960-62; Lecturer in English, Australian National University, 1963; Lecturer to Senior Lecturer, Monash University, 1964-88. Publications: Poetry: Voice Unaccompanied, 1970; A Bone Flute, 1974; From Sweden, 1979; A Flag for the Wind, 1982; New and Selected Poems, 1988. Other: Shakespeare's Sonnets: Self Love and Art (criticism), 1972; Lars Gustafsson: The Stillness of the World Before Bach (translator), 1988. Contributions to: 7 anthologies, 1986-98; Age; Australian; Carleton Miscellany; Helix; Meanjin; New Hungarian Quarterly; Poetry USA; Quadrant; Southerly; Times Literary Supplement. Address: 25/9 Nicholson Street, Balmain 2041, New South Wales, Australia.

MARTIN Ricky, (Enrique Martin Morales), b. 24 December 1971, Puerto Rico. Singer; Actor. Career: Joined group Menudo, aged 13; Numerous tours and recordings; Left Menudo, 1989; Acted in Mexican soap opera Alcanzur una Estrella II; Began releasing Spanish language albums; Role as bartender in General Hospital; Won the role of Marius in Broadway production of Les Miserables; Dubbed voice in Spanish version of Disney film Hercules; Released first English Language album including a duet with Madonna; Numerous television appearances and tour dates. Recordings: Singles: Maria, 1996; 1 2 3 Maria, 1997; Cup of Life, 1998; La Bomba, 1999; Livin' La Vida Loca, 1999; She's All I Have Had, 1999; Shake Your Bon-Bon; Story, with Christine

Aguilera; Albums: Ricky Martin, 1991; Me Amarás, 1993; A Medio Vivir, 1995; Vuelve, 1998; Ricky Martin, 1999; Sound Loaded, 2000; La Historia, 2001. Honour: Grammy Award, Best Latin Pop Album, 1999. Address: c/o Sony Music Latin, 550 Madison Avenue, New York, NY 10022, USA.

MARTIN Steve, b. 1945, Waco, Texas, USA. Actor; Comedian. m. Victoria Tennant, 1986, divorced. Education: Long Beach State College; University of California, Los Angeles. Appointments: TV Writer, several shows; Nightclub Comedian; TV Special, Steve Martin: A Wild and Crazy Guy, 1978. Creative Works: Recordings: Let's Get Small, 1977; A Wild and Crazy Guy, 1978; Comedy is Not Pretty, 1979; The Steve Martin Bros; Film appearances include: The Absent Minded Waiter; Sgt Pepper's Lonely Hearts Club Band, 1978; The Muppet Movie, 1979; The Jerk, 1979; Pennies From Heaven, 1981; Dead Men Don't Wear Plaid, 1982; The Man With Two Brains, 1983; The Lonely Guy, 1984; All of Me, 1984; Three Amigos, 1986; Little Shop of Horrors, 1986; Roxanne, 1987; Planes, Trains and Automobiles, 1987; Parenthood, 1989; My Blue Heaven; L.A. Story; Grand Canyon; Father of the Bride; Housesitter, 1992; Leap of Faith, 1992; Twist of Fate, 1994; Mixed Nuts, 1994; Father of the Bride 2; Sgt Bilko, 1995; The Spanish Prisoner; The Out of Towners; Bowfinger, 1999; Joe Gould's Secret, 2000; Novocaine, 2002; Bring Down the House, 2003; Cheaper By The Dozen, 2003. Honours: Grammy Award, 1977, 1978; National Society of Film Critics Actor's Award. Address: ICM, 8942 Wilshire Boulevard, Beverly Hills, CA 90211, USA.

MARTIN Todd, b. 8 July 1970, Hinsdale, Illinois, USA. Tennis Player. Education: Northwestern College. Appointments: Winner, New Haven Challenger, 1989; Turned professional, 1990; Semi-Finalist, Stella Artois Grass Court Championships, London, 1993; Champion, 1994, Champion (doubles with Pete Sampras), 1995; Finalist, Australian Open, 1994, Grand Slam Cup, Munich, 1995; Semi-Finalist, US Open, 1994, Wimbledon, 1994, 1996, Paris Open, 1998; Champion, Scania Stockholm Open, 1998; Winner of 13 pro titles by end of 2002. Honours include: Adidas/ATP Tour Sportsmanship Award, 1993, 1994; ATP Tour Most Improved Player, 1993. Memberships: US Davis Cup Team, 1994-99; President, ATP Players' Council, 1996-97. Address: c/o Advantage International, 1751 Pinnacle Drive, Suite 1500, McLean, VA 22102, USA.

MARTIN Victoria Carolyn, b. 22 May 1945, Windsor, Berkshire, England. Writer. m. Tom Storey, 28 July 1969, 4 daughters. Education: Winkfield Place, Berks, 1961-62; Byam Shaw School of Art, 1963-66. Publications: September Song, 1970; Windmill Years, 1975; Seeds of the Sun, 1980; Opposite House, 1984; Tigers of the Night, 1985; Obey the Moon, 1987. Contributions to: Woman; Woman's Own; Woman's Realm; Woman's Journal; Good Housekeeping; Woman's Weekly; Redbook; Honey, 1967-87. Address: Newells Farm House, Lower Beeding, Horsham, Sussex RH13 6LN, England.

MARTIN Vivian, b. Detroit, Michigan. Opera and Concert Singer. m. Education: Conservatoire de Fountainebleau, France; Detroit Conservatory of Music; France; New York; Munich; Berlin; Detroit. Debut: Operatic debut, Leonardo, Verdi's La Forza Del Destino, 1971. Career: Major opera roles including Leonora, Verdi's Il Trovatore; Rezia, Weber's Oberon; Selika, Meyerbeer's L'Africane; Bess, Gershwin's Porgy and Bess, more than 500 times; Major opera houses and concert halls in Europe, Asia, USA, South America; TV and radio appearances; Toured and soloist with numerous orchestras; Symphonies in Sweden, Berlin, Munich, Nurenberg; Philharmonic orchestras in Germany, Slovenska Philharmonia, Detroit Symphony Orchestra; Sang in Tivoli Garden, Copenhagen, Denmark; Grosser Konzert Saal, Vienna, Austria;

Théâtre des Champs Elysees, Paris, France, Kongress Saal, Munich, Germany; Participated in World of Gershwin; Festival with concerts with St Petersburg National Symphony Orchestra in Shostakovich Philharmonic Hall, St Petersburg; Moscow Symphony Orchestra in Tschaikovsky, Moscow, Russia. Honours: First prize and Jean Paul award, Conservatoire de Fountainbleau, 1953; Eighteen singing scholarships and awards. Memberships: AFTRA; American Guild of Music Artists; Actors Equity Association; Wayne State University Alumni Association; Alpha Kappa Alpha. Address: c/o Dr Gösta Schwark International APS, Opera-Concert-Theatre, 18 Groennegade, 1 Floor, DK-1107 Copenhagen, Denmark.

MARTIN-QUIRK Howard Richard Newell, b. 8 August 1937, Sanderstead, Surrey, England. Architectural Historian. m. Mitzi Quirk. 1 son. Education: BA (Cantab), 1959, MA, 1961, Christs College, Cambridge University; BSc, Bartlett School of Architecture, London University, 1967; MSc, University College, London, 1985. Appointments: Architectural Assistant, Greater London Council, 1966-67; Senior Research Assistant, Kingston College of Art, 1967-70; Director of Undergraduate Studies, School of Architecture, Kingston Polytechnic, 1970-94; Principal Lecturer and Director of History, School of Architecture, Kingston University, 1994-; Chief Oenologist, Chiddingstone Vineyards, 1971-83; Partner, Martin Quirk Associates Architects, 1980-90; Freelance Writer and Journalist. Publications: Meaning and Metaphore in Architecture, 1983; The Crime of the Century (with Kinglsey Amis), 1989; Fame in Architecture, 2001; Articles and reviews in many architectural publications. Honours: Silver Medal, International Wine and Spirit Society, 1991. Memberships: Society of Architectural Historians; Victorian Society; Wagner Society; Architectural Association; NATFHE; Ecclesiological Society. Address: The Old Coach Road, Chiddingstone, Kent TN8 7BH, England. E-mail: howardmartinquirk@hotmail.com

MARTINEZ Conchita, b. 16 April 1972, Monzon, Spain. Tennis Player. Appointments: Turned Professional, 1988; Reached last 16, French Open, 1988, quarter-finals, French Open, 1989, 1990, 1991, 1992, 1993, semi-finals, Italian Open, 1991, French Open, 1994, Australian, French and US Opens and Wimbledon, 1995, French and US Opens, 1996, quarter-finals, Olympic Games, 1992; With Arantxa Sanchez-Vicario, won Olympic Doubles Silver Medal, 1992; Won, Italian Open, 1993, Hilton Head (SC), Italian Open, Stratton (Vt), 1994; Wimbledon Singles Champion, 1994; by end of 2002 had won 42 WTA tour titles. Honours: WTA Tour Most Impressive Newcomer, 1989; Most Improved Player, Tennis Magazine, 1994; ITF Award of Excellence, 2001; International Tennis Hall of Fame, 2001.

MARTINEZ Richard Isaac, b. 16 August 1944, Havana, Cuba. Science Administrator. 1 son, 1 daughter. Education: BSc, Chemistry, McGill University, Montreal, Canada, 1964; PhD, Physical Chemistry, University of California, Los Angeles, 1976. Appointments: Teaching Assistant, McGill University, Montreal, Canada, 1964-65; Teaching and Research Assistant, San Diego State University, San Diego, California, 1965-67; Chemist, Shell Chemical Company, Torrance, California, 1967-70; Postgraduate Research Chemist, University of California, Los Angeles, 1971-76; Research Chemist, National Institute of Standards and Technology, Gaithersburg, Maryland, 1976-92; National Institute of General Medical Sciences, Bethesda, Maryland, 1992-. Publications: 45 refereed journal articles and invited book chapters in well-respected internationally acclaimed science journals and book series on physical, analytical and organic chemistry; Chemical physics; Reaction mechanisms; Mass spectrometry; 2 US patents. Honours: Doctoral Fellowship, University of California, Los Angeles, 1970-73; NRC Postdoctoral Research Associate,

Dictionary of International Biography

National Academy of Sciences, 1976-78; Bronze medal, US Department of Commerce, 1981; I-R 100 Award for patented Flue-Gas Desulfurization Process, 1983; President and Chairman of Board of Directors, Bethesda-Chevy Chase Jewish Community Group, 1991-93; Fellow, 1995-96, Senior Fellow, 1996-, Council for Excellence in Government; Listed in Who's Who in the World, 18th Edition, and numerous Who's Who publications. Memberships: American Chemical Society; Society for the Advancement of Chicanos and Native Americans in Science. Address: National Institute of General Medical Sciences, 45 Center Dr, Bethesda, MD 20892-6200, USA. E-mail: rm63f@nih.gov

MARTINEZ-LAGE Juan F, b. 4 July 1944, Almeria, Spain. Medical Doctor. m. Presen Azorin, 4 sons, 2 daughters. Education: MD, University of Madrid, 1968. Appointments: Neurosurgical Registrar, Newcastle-upon-Tyne, 1975-76; Neurosurgeon, 1976-, Chief, Section of Pediatric Neurosurgery, 1998-2003, Chief of the Regional Service of Neurosurgery, 2003-, University Hospital Murcia; Assistant Professor of Neurosurgery, University of Murcia, 2003-. Publications: Pediatric Neurosurgery, 2001; Chapters in books, several articles in professional medical journals. Honours: Researcher, European Community, 1993-; Temporary Adviser, OMS, Geneva, 1999-; Listed in national and international biographical dictionaries. Memberships: ESPN; SENEP; ISPN; EANS; SENEC. Address: Alfonso X El Sabio 14, E-30008 Murcia, Spain.

MARTINO Donald, b. 16 May 1931, Plainfield, New Jersey, USA. Composer; Clarinetist; Educator. m. Lova Harvey, 1 son, 1 daughter. Education: BM, Syracuse University, 1952; MFA, Princeton University, 1954; Fulbright Scholar, Italy, 1956. Appointments: Assistant Professor, Yale University, 1959-69; Chairman of Composition, New England Conservatory, 1969-79; Professor of Music, Brandeis University, 1979-82, Harvard University, 1982-92; Retired. Publications: Many compositions in all genres. Honours: Fulbright Scholar; Guggenheim Grantee; Pulitzer Prize. Memberships: American Academy of Arts and Sciences; American Academy of Arts and Letters. Address: 11 Pembroke Street, Newton, MA 02458, USA. E-mail: dantinfo@dantalian.com

MARTINS Herbert Ernst, b. 27 January 1950, St Veit/Glan, Austria. Economist. m. Doris Martins, 2 daughters. Education: Master of Economics, University of Vienna, Austria, 1972; Doctor of Economics, Vienna School of Economics and Business Administration, Austria, 1975; Fulbright Scholar Postgraduate, University of Oregon, USA, 1975, University of Chicago, USA, 1976. Appointments: Research Associate, University of Chicago, USA, 1976-77; Secretary to Minister of State for Economic Affairs, Austria, 1978; Deputy Director for Foreign Economic Policy Co-ordination, 1987-91, Director for Multilateral Economic Affairs, 1991-, Federal Chancellery, Department for Co-ordination, Vienna, Austria; Lecturer in Economics, Vienna School of Economics and Business Administration, 1987-96; Member of the Bureau of the Senior Economic Advisors of the UNO Economic Commission for Europe, 1989-90; Minister Counsellor, Permanent Delegation of Austria to the Organisation for Economic Co-operation and Development (OECD), Paris, France, 1990; Member, OECD Committee for International Investment and Multinational Enterprises, 1990-94. Publication: Book, "The Dangerous Force – Unemployment, Inflation and Social Justice – on Poverty and Wealth", 2001. Honours: Recipient of various scholarships and grants, 1969-75; Fulbright Scholarship, 1975. Memberships: Austrian Economic Association; Austrian Association for Foreign Policy and International Relations; Austrian Association for Public Finance; Austrian Society for the United Nations; Austrian Society

for Political and Strategic Studies. Address: Bundeskanzleramt, Ballhausplatz 2, A-1014 Vienna, Austria. E-mail: herbert.martins@bka.gv.at

MARTY Bobby, (Etienne Martens), b. 4 October 1937, Brugge (Bruges), Belgium. m. Suffys Nicole, 8 September 1963, 1 son, 1 daughter. Education: Private lessons, Dirigent Pol Horna; Bass Guitar & 1 Year Piano, age of 12 years. Career: Andrex; Ensemble Pol Horna; The Shamrocks; Luc Rène and the Jumps; Own show with the Bobby Marty Dancers, 1980-; Radio's in Belgium & France; TV in France; Concerts with trio Tea for Three, own songs and music of the 60s, played bass, singer. Compositions: Houtem Mijn Dorpje; De Bruggeling; Adieu Jacques Brel; La Maison Du Bonheur; Mon Amour; Ma Guitare et Quelques Chansons; Une Belle Nuit D'Hiver; Au Rendez-Vous des Artistes. Recordings: 18 singles; 1 LP; 2 compilation CD's in France with other French artists; 3 solo CDs: Bobby Marty International (6 languages); Bobby Marty sings Elvis and Country Dreams. Publications: Flash, own magazine, 1989-. Honours: Golden Record, Rose Des Neiges; Silver Record for Johnny Laat je Jodel nog eens Horen (composition of Johnny Hoes). Address: Molenwalstraat 8A, 8630 Houtem-Veurne, Belgium.

MASLANKA Julian Józef, b. 5 March 1930, Lukawiec. Polish Scholar-Historian of Slavonic Culture. m. Barbara, 1 son, 1 daughter. Education: MA, 1955, Doctors degree, 1963, Assistant Professor, 1968, Associate Professor, 1979, Full Professor, 1986, Jagellonian University in Krakow. Appointments: Visiting Professor, Université Nancy II, 1975-81; Institut de Polonais; Editor, periodical, Ruch Literacki; Editor, An International Writers Lexicon (Slownik pisarzy siriata), 2004. Publications: Books: Z D Chodakowski, 1965; Slowianskie mity historyczne, 1968; Literatura a dzieje bajeczne, 1984, 1990; Z dziejow literatury I kultury, 2001; Editor, writings of A Mickiewicz; Editor, An International Writers' Lexicon, 2004 (in Polish: Slownik pizarzy swiata). Memberships: Secretary of Philology Division, Polska Akademia Umiejetnosci (Krakow). Address: ul H Wieniawskiego 8A, 31-436 Krakow, Poland.

MASON Roy (Lord Mason of Barnsley), b. 18 April 1924, England. Member of the House of Lords. m. Marjorie Sowden, 2 daughters. Education: TUC Scholarship, London School of Economics; D University, Hallam University, Sheffield. Appointments: Coal Miner, 1938-53; Labour Candidate for Bridlington, 1951-53; Member of Parliament for Barnsley, 1953-83, Barnsley Central, 1983-87; Opposition Spokesman on Defence and Post Office Affairs, 1960-64; Minister of State for Shipping, Board of Trade, 1964-67; Minister of Defence Equipment, 1967-68; Postmaster General, 1968; Minister of Power, 1968-69; President, Board of Trade, 1969-70; Principal Spokesman on Board of Trade Affairs, 1970-74; Member, Council of Europe and Western European Union, 1973; Secretary of State for Defence, 1974-76; Secretary of State for Northern Ireland, 1976-79; Principal Opposition Spokesman on Agriculture, Fisheries and Food, 1979-81. Publication: Paying the Price, autobiography. Honours: PC, 1968; Peerage, 1987. Memberships: Yorkshire Miners' Council, 1949-53; Council of Europe, 1970-71; Yorkshire Group of Labour MPs, 1970-74, 1981-84; Miners' Group of MPs, 1973-74, 1980-81; Railway and Steel Union MPs, 1979-80; National Rivers Authority, 1989-92. Address: 12 Victoria Avenue, Barnsley, South Yorkshire, S70 2BH, England.

MASSEY Alan Randolph Charles, b. 6 June 1932, Berkshire, England. Librarian; Poet. m. Gillian Elizabeth Petty, 30 September 1974. Publications: Trajectories in the Air; The Fire Garden. Contributions to: Agenda; Poetry Review; Workshop; Expression. Membership: Poetry Society. Address: 41 Albany Road, Windsor, Berkshire SL4 1HL, England.

Dictionary of International Biography

MASSEY Roy Cyril, b. 9 May 1934, Birmingham, England. Cathedral Organist. m. Ruth Carol Craddock. Education: University of Birmingham, 1953-56; Private tuition under Sir David Willcocks, Worcester Cathedral. Appointments: Accompanist, City of Birmingham Choir, 1953-60; Church and School appointments, 1956-65; Warden, Royal School of Church Music, 1965-68; Organist and Master of the Choristers, Birmingham Cathedral, 1968-74; Organist and Master of the Choristers, Hereford Cathedral, 1974-2001. Publication: The Organs of Hereford Cathedral (in Hereford Cathedral, a history), 2000. Honours: Honorary Fellowship, Royal School of Church Music, 1971; Lambeth Degree, Doctor of Music, 1991; MBE for Services to Music, 1997; Honorary Fellowship, Guild of Church Musicians, 2000; President, Royal College of Organists, 2003-. Address: 2 King John's Court, Tewkesbury, Gloucestershire GL20 6EG, England. E-mail: drroymassey@ukonline.co.uk

MASSIER Paul F, b. 22 July 1923, Pocatello, Idaho, USA. Retired. m. (1) Miriam Parks, 1948, deceased 1975, 2 daughters, (2) Dorothy Hedlund Wright, 1978. Education: Mechanical Engineering Certificate, University of Idaho Southern Branch, 1943; BS, Mechanical Engineering, University of Colorado, 1948; MS, Mechanical Engineering, Massachusetts Institute of Technology, 1949. Appointments: Engineer, Construction and Maintenance Department, Pan American Refining Corporation, Texas City, Texas, 1948; Design Engineer, Maytag Co, Newton, Iowa, 1949-50; Research Engineer, Boeing Co, Seattle, Washington, 1950-55; Senior Research Engineer, Group Supervisor, Member, Technical Staff, Task Manager, Jet Propulsion Lab, California Institute of Technology, Pasadena, California, 1955-88; retired, 1989; Continued as Member of Technical Staff until 1994. Publications: Author, Co-author of 39 professional technical articles in journals. Honours: Engineering Professional Achievement Award, Idaho State University; Basic Noise Research Team Award, NASA; Apollo Achievement Award, NASA; AIAA, Sustained Service Award; Life Member Service Award, California Parent Teachers Association; Layman of the Year Award, Arcadia Congregational Church; Military Unit Citation Award; Listed in numerous Who's Who and biographical publications. Memberships: New York Academy of Sciences; Planetary Society; American Institute of Aeronautics and Astronautics; Research Society of Sigma Xi; Order of Engineers; California Parent Teachers Association; IBA; ABI Research Association; International Board and Life Member, Bukovina Society of The Americas. Address: 764 Lava Falls Drive, Las Vegas, NV 89110, USA.

MASTERS Roger D, b. 8 June 1933, Boston, Massachusetts, USA. Research Professor; Nelson A Rockefeller Professor Emeritus. Education: AB, Summa cum Laude, Harvard College, 1955; MA, University of Chicago, 1958; Auditor, Institut d'Etudes Politiques, Paris, 1958-59; PhD, University of Chicago, 1961. Appointments: Private to SP3, US Army, 1955-57; Instructor to Assistant Professor, Department of Political Science, Yale University, New Haven, 1961-67; Associate Professor to Professor, 1967-, Departmental Chair, 1986-89, Nelson A Rockefeller Professor of Government, 1992-98, Acting Departmental Chair, January-June 1993, Department of Government, Dartmouth College, Hanover; Chair, Executive Committee, Gruter Institute for Law and Behavioural Research, 1995-98; Council, Association for Politics and the Life Sciences, 1997-; Cultural Attaché, US Embassy, Paris, France, 1969-71; Visiting Lecturer, Yale Law School, 1988; Adjunct Professor, Vermont Law School, 1993, 1994. Publications: Translator, Editor or co-editor, numerous books including: Collected Writings of Rousseau; Author, The Nation is Burdened: American Foreign Policy in a Changing World, 1967; The Political Philosophy of Rousseau, 1968; The Nature of Politics,

1989; Beyond Relativism: Science and Human Values, 1993; Machiavelli, Leonardo and the Science of Power, 1996; Fortune is a River: Leonardo da Vinci and Niccolò Machiavelli's Magnificent Dream to Change the Course of Florentine History, 1998; Over 150 scholarly articles and journalistic essays in English, French and German including contributions to scientific journals on toxins, health and behaviour. Honours: Fulbright Fellowship to France, 1958-59; Joint Yale-SSRC Fellowship, 1964-65; John Simon Guggenheim Fellowship, 1967-68; John Sloan Dickey Third Century Professor of Government, Dartmouth College, 1979-85; Director d'Etudes Associé, Ecole des Hautes Etudes en Sciences Sociales, Paris, France, 1986; Government Consultant; Companion of Honour, IBC. Memberships: Association for Politics and the Life Sciences; American Political Sciences Association; President, Foundation for Neuroscience and Society. Address: Box 113, South Woodstock, VT 05071, USA.

MASTERSON Kleber Sanlin, Jr, b. 26 September 1932, San Diego, California, USA. Physicist; Military Operations Researcher. m. Sara Cooper Masterson, 2 sons. Education: BS (Engineering), US Naval Academy, 1954; MS (Physics), US Naval Postgraduate School, 1960; PhD (Physics), University of California at San Diego, 1963; Graduate, Advanced Management Programme, Harvard Business School, 1980. Appointments: Commanding Officer, USS Preble; Antiship Missile Defence Project Manager; Assistant Deputy Commander; Naval Sea Systems Command for Anti-Air and Surface Warfare Systems; Chief, Studies Analysis and Gaming Agency; Office of the Joint Chiefs of Staff; Retired as Rear Admiral, US Navy, 1950-82; Vice President, Partner, Booz, Allen and Hamilton, 1982-92; Senior Vice President, Science Applications International Corporation, 1992-96; President, The Riverside Group Ltd, 1994-; President, Military Operations Research Society, 1988-89; President, Massachusetts Society of the Cincinnati, 2001-04; Assistant Secretary-General, The Society of the Cincinnati, 2001-04; Treasurer General, The Society of the Cincinnati, 2004-. Publications: Numerous articles and invited presentations; Created NELIAC ALGOL compiler, 1958-59. Honours: Defence Superior Service Medal; Legion of Merit with 2 gold stars for subsequent awards; Navy Commendation Medal with Combat 'V' and 2 gold stars. Memberships: American Physical Society; Society of Sigma Xi; Society of the Cincinnati. E-mail: skidmasterson@compuserve.com

MATA-SEGREDA Julio F R, b. 3 August 1948, San José, Costa Rica. Professor. m. Luisa Díaz-Sánchez, 2 sons, 3 daughters. Education: BSc, Chemistry, 1970, Licentiate, Chemistry, 1971, University of Costa Rica; PhD, Chemistry, University of Kansas, USA. Appointments: Instructor, 1975, Professor, 1984, University of Costa Rica; Invited Researcher, Ritsumeikan University, Kyoto, Japan, 1982; Invited Researcher, University of Kansas, USA, 1986-87; Invited Professor, University of the Andes, Merida, Venezuela, 1991. Publications: 65 scientific papers in professional journals; Some book chapters. Honours: National Science Award, 1981; Fullbright Fellowship, 1986; Matsumae Fellowship and Medal, Tokyo, Japan, 1982; Fellow, National Academy of Science, 1994. Memberships: Physical Chemistry Section of the American Chemical Society; Costa Rican Association of Philosophy and History of Science; National Academy of Science, Costa Rica. Address: School of Chemistry, University of Costa Rica, 2060 Costa Rica. E-mail: jmata@cariari.ucr.ac.cr

MATEJČÍK Viktor, b. 1 January 1951, Bratislava, Slovak Republic. Neurosurgeon. Education: MD, Comenius University, Bratislava, 1969-75; PhD, 1980-85; Certificate of Pedagogy, 1985-87. Appointments: Neurosurgeon, Faculty of Medicine, Bratislava, 1975-; Attestation from Surgery, 1980; Attestation from Neurosurgery, 1990. Publications: Articles in Journal of

Neurosurgery, Injury, Bratislava Medical Journal, Acta Medica Martiniana, Acta Chirurgiae Plasticae, etc. Memberships: Neurosurgical Society; Neurological Society; Society of Medical Jurisprudence. Address: Department of Neurosurgery, Comenius University, Derer's Faculty Hospital, Limbova 5, 833 05 Bratislava, Slovak Republic.

MATHESON Michael, b. 8 September 1970, Glasgow, Scotland. Member of the Scottish Parliament. Education: BSc, Occupational Therapy, Queen Margaret College, Edinburgh, 1988-92; BA, Diploma in Applied Social Sciences, Open University, 1992-96. Appointments: Community Occupational Therapist, Stirling Council, Central Regional Council and Highland Regional Council, 1992-99; Member of the Scottish Parliament, 1999-. Memberships: State Registered Occupational Therapist, Council for Professions Supplementary to Medicine; Member, Ochils Mountain Rescue Team; Member, Scottish Parliament Justice Committee; Convenor, Cross Party Group on Disability; Vice Convenor, Cross Party Group on Cuba. Address: The Scottish Parliament, Edinburgh, EH99 1SP, Scotland. E-mail: michael.matheson.msp@scottish.parliament.uk

MATHUR Anil Kumar, b. 12 June 1954, Gorakhpur, UP, India. Veterinary Scientist. m. Sandhya Mathur, 2 sons. Education: BSc, BVSc&AH, Agra University; MVSc, PhD, Gynaecology and Obstetrics. Appointments: Deputy Veterinary Superintendent, Amul Dairy, Anand, Gujrat, 1981-; Scientist, S-1, Animal Reproduction, Division of Fur Animal Breeding, Garsa, Kullu, 1982-83; Senior Scientist, Central Sheep and Wool Research Institute, Avikanagar, Rajasthan, 1989-96; Senior Scientist, Project Directorate on Cattle, Meerut, UP, 1996-; Principal Scientist, P D Cattle, Meerut, 1998. Publications: Over 60 research and scientific articles in foreign and Indian journals. Honour: ICAR Junior Research fellowship, 1978-79. Memberships: Life Member: Indian Society for Study on Animal Reproduction, Society of Animal Physiologists of India, Indian Science Congress Association, Indian Society for Study of Reproduction and Fertility; Indian Society for Advancement of Canine Practice, Lucknow. Address: D-6, Awho Colony, Mawana Road, Meerut, UP, India. E-mail: director@pdcattle.up.nic.in

MATIOR Rahman, b. 8 February 1942, Akua Village, Mymensingh District, Bangladesh. Teacher. m. Begum Nurunnatar, 2 sons, 3 daughters. Education: BSc, 1964; MSc, 1967. Appointments: Teacher, 1964-2001; Retired 2001; Involved in politics, 1964-. Honours: Man of the Year 2003, American Biographical Institute, North Carolina; Bangabandhu Award, 2000. Memberships: President, District Awami League; Research Board of Advisors, American Biographical Institute. Address: House No 8, Road Natakgharlane, District Mymensingh, 2200 Bangladesh

MATOUŠEK Jiří, b. 4 April 1930, Příbram, Czech Republic. Chemical Engineer. m. Dagmar Matoušková, 1 son, 1 daughter. Education: Dipl Eng (Chem), Czech Technical University, Prague and Military Technical Academy, Brno, 1954; PhD (CSc), Military Technical Academy, Brno, 1958; DSc, Military Academy of Chemical Protection, Moscow, 1967; Associate Professor, Special Technology, Military Academy, Brno, 1966; Professor, Organic Chemistry, Palacký University, Olomouc, 1983. Appointments: Assistant Professor, Military Technical Academy, Brno, 1954-59; Head of Department, 1959-63; Director, NBC Defence R & D Establishment, Brno, 1963-71; Deputy Head, Department of Toxicology, Purkyne Medical Research Institute, Hradec Králové, 1971-81; Director for Research, NBC Defence R & D Establishment, Brno, 1981-89; Senior Research Fellow, Academy of Science, Prague, 1989-90; Professor of Toxicology, Masaryk

University, Brno, 1990-; Visiting Professor International Institute for Peace, Vienna, 1990-; Director Institute of Environmental Chemistry and Technology, Brno University of Technology, 1992-2000. Publications: Over 490 articles in professional and scientific journals; About 130 research reports, 90 patents and improvement suggestions, mostly realised in production and use; More than 410 conference papers, mostly international; 21 books and 31 chapters in monographs dealing with chemistry and analysis of toxic agents, chemical and biological disarmament, verification, conversion, ecological, environmental and other global problems, mostly in English but also in German, French, Russian, Czech and Slovak. Honours: 7 state and military orders and medals; Memorial Medal of Masaryk University, 1991; Memorial Medal of Brno University of Technology, 1999; American Medal of Honor, 2002. Memberships: International Network of Engineers and Scientists; World Federation of Scientific Workers; Pugwash Conferences; Accredited Representative of World Federation of Scientific Workers at UNO and conference of NGOs; Chairman, Scientific Advisory Board, Organisation for the Prohibition of Chemical Weapons; Many other professional organisations. Address: Krásného 26, CZ-636 00 Brno, Czech Republic. E-mail: matousek@recetox.muni.cz

MATSUFUJI Toru, b. 30 April 1928, Fukuoka-ken, Japan. College Teacher. m. Kazue, 2 daughters. Education: Masters Degree, Hiroshima Bunrika University, 1949-52; Postgraduate Course, Edinburgh University, Scotland, 1984-85; Cultural Doctorate Course, Japan School of the World University, Arizona, USA, 1989-90. Appointments: Seinan Jo Gakuin, Oshimo Gakuen, Horoshima Jo Gakuin High School and College, 1952-69; Notre Dame Seishin University, 1969-94; Professor, 1985, retired 1994, University of Science Okayama, Kurashiki University of Science and the Arts; Junsei Junior College, 1970-. Publications: Carlyle: His Moral Energy – Twinkling of Truth Literature of Soul, 1983; Carlyle: Literature of Awakening Insight – with Ruskin's Morality of Pious Sincerity, 1991; My View of Life (in Japanese), 1992; My Advice Words to Youth (in Japanese), 1999. Honours: Cultural Doctorate, World University, Arizona, USA; Doctor of Divinity Honoris Causa, Romano Byzantine College, Minnesota, USA. Memberships: English Literary Society of Japan; Japan Association of College English Teachers; English Literary Association of Hiroshima University; Okayama Church. Address: Apolon-sha, Kamigyo-ku, Kyoto City, Japan.

MATSUKA Mitsuo, b. 27 March 1942, Tokyo. Professor, m. Yoko Okada, 1 son, 1 daughter. Education: BA, Tamagawa University, 1964; Dr. Sci., Tokyo University, 1969. Appointments: Lecturer, 1969, Associate Professor, 1971, Professor, 1982, Faculty Agriculture, Tamagawa University; Dean, Graduate School Agriculture, 1997; Vice Director, Research Institute, 2001. Publications: Biology of Insects, Japan; Asian Bees and Beekeeping, editor. Memberships: Japan Society Applied Entomology Zoology; President, Society Biological Science Education Japan; International Bee Research Association; President, Asian Apicultural Association. Address: Faculty Agriculture, Tamagawa University, Machida-shi, Tokyo 194-8610, Japan.

MATSUMOTO Takeo, b. 11 August 1932, Kitakyuushuu, Japan. Crystallographer; Mineralogist. m. Yuriko Kawamura, 2 sons. Education: BSc, 1957, MSc, 1959, Doctor of Science, 1962, Tokyo University. Appointments: Assistant, Tokyo University, 1962; Associate Professor, Kanazawa University, 1968; Professor, Kanazawa University, Faculty of Science, 1986; Professor Emeritus, 1998-. Publications: 2 monographs; 90 papers. Memberships: International Union of Crystallography; International

Mineralogical Association. Address: Department of Earth Sciences, Faculty of Science, Kanazawa University, Kakumachi, Kanazawa, 920-1192, Japan.

MATSUO Chie Nakago, b. 8 January 1962, Nishinomiya, Japan. Orthodontist. m. Toshihiko Matsuo. Education: DDS (Doctor of Dental Science), Osaka Dental University, 1987; PhD, 1996. Appointments: Okayama University Dental School, 1987-96; Kyoyama Dental Centre, 1996-. Publications: Articles in American Journal of Orthodontics; Dentofacial Orthopedics. Honour: Board Certified Orthodontist, 1993. Membership: Japan Orthodontic Society. Address: Kyoyama 2-3-3-301, Okayama City 700-0015, Japan. E-mail: chie-boo@d7.dion.ne.jp

MATSUOKA Yoshiyuki, b. 2 June 1955, Shimonoseki, Japan. Professor. m. Naoko, 1 son. Education: BA, Engineering, Waseda University, Japan, 1979; MA, Engineering, 1982, PhD, Engineering, 1997, Chiba University, Japan. Appointments: Planner, Designer, Nissan Motor Co, Ltd, 1982-96; Assistant Professor, 1996-98, Associate Professor, 1998-2003, Professor, 2003-, Keio University, Japan; Lecturer, Tokyo Institute of Technology, 2001-; Visiting Research Fellow, Illinois Institute of Technology, USA, 2002-2003. Honours include: Prize for Best Papers, Japan Society for the Science of Design, 2001; Liberty Mutual Best Paper Award, 2003; Best Paper Award, Japan Society for Design Engineering, 2004. Memberships include: Director, Councillor, Japanese Society for the Science of Design; Councillor, Japan Ergonomics Society; Committee Member, Japan Society of Mechanical Engineers; ASME; ACM; IEEE. Address: 951-27 Nurumizu, Atsugi, 243-0033 Japan.

MATSUSHIMA Hitoshi, b. 4 June 1960, Tokyo, Japan. Economics Educator. m. Satoko Matsushima, 1 son. Education: BA, Economics, 1983, MA, Economics, 1985, PhD, Economics, 1988, University of Tokyo. Appointments: Assistant Professor of Economics, 1989, Lecturer in Economics, 1989-92, Associate Professor of Economics, 1992-94, Institute of Socio-Economic Planning, University of Tsukuba, Japan; Associate Professor of Economics, 1994-2002, Professor of Economics, 2002-, Faculty of Economics, University of Tokyo. Publications: Articles in professional journals as author and co-author: A New Approach to the Implementation Problem, 1988; Efficiency in Repeated Games with Imperfect Monitoring, 1989; Efficiency in Partnerships, 1991; Virtual Implementation in Iteratively Undominated Strategies: Complete Information, 1992; Bayesian Monotonicity with Side Payments, 1993; Private Observation, Communication and Collusion, 1998; Multimarket Contact, Imperfect Monitoring and Implicit Collusion, 2001. Honours: Hyoe-Ouch Award, University of Tokyo, 1983; Nakahara Prize, Japanese Economic Association, 2004. Membership: Fellow of the Econometric Society, 2003-. Address: Faculty of Economics, University of Tokyo, 7-3-1 Hongo, Bunkyo-ku, Tokyo 113-8654, Japan.

MATTESSICH Richard, b. 9 August 1922, Trieste, Italy. Professor Emeritus. m. Hermine. Education: Mech Engineer Diploma, 1940; Dipl Kaufmann, 1944; Dr rer pol, 1945; Dr honoris causa, 1998. Appointments: Research Fellow, Austrian Institute of Economic Research, 1945-47; Lecturer, Rosenberg College, Switzerland, 1947-52; Department Head, Mount Allison University, Canada, 1953-58; Associate Professor, University of California, Berkeley, 1959-67; Professor, Ruhr University, Bochum, 1965-66; Professor, University of British Columbia, 1967-88; Professor, University of Technology, Vienna, 1976-78; Professor Emeritus, University of British Columbia, 1988-. Publications: Books: Accounting and Analytic Methods, 1964; Simulation of the Firm, 1964; Instrumental Reasoning and Systems

Methods, 1978; Modern Accounting Research, 1984; Accounting Research in the 1980's, 1991; Critique of Accounting, 1995; Foundational Research in Accounting, 1995; The Beginnings of Accounting, 2000. Honours: Ford Founding Fellow, USA, 1961, 62; Erskine Fellow, New Zealand, 1970; Killam Senior Fellow, Canada, 1971; Literary Awards, AICPA, 1972, CAAA, 1991. Memberships: Accademia Italiana di Econ Aziendale, 1980-; Austrian Academy of Science, 1984-; Life member, American Accounting Association; Life member, Academy of Accounting Historians; Officially Nominated for the Nobel Prize in Economics, 2002. Address: c/o Faculty of Commerce and Business Administrator, University of British Columbia, Vancouver, British Columbia, Canada V6T 1Z2. E-mail: richard.mattessich@sauder.ubc.ca

MATTHEW Christopher Charles Forrest, b. 8 May 1939, London, England. Novelist; Journalist; Broadcaster. m. Wendy Mary Matthew, 19 October 1979, 2 sons, 1 daughter. Education: BA, Honours, MA, Honours, St Peter's College, Oxford. Appointments: Editor, Times Travel Guide, 1972-73. Publications: A Different World; Stories of Great Hotels, 1976; Diary of a Somebody, 1978; Loosely Engaged, 1980; The Long-Haired Boy, 1980; The Crisp Report, 1981; Three Men in a Boat, annotated edition, with Benny Green, 1982; The Junket Man, 1983; How to Survive Middle Age, 1983; Family Matters, 1987; The Amber Room, 1995; A Nightingale Sang in Fernhurst Road, 1998; Now We Are Sixty, 1999; Knocking On, 2000; Now We Are Sixty (And a Bit), 2003. Contributions to: Many leading newspapers; Columnist for Punch, 1983-88; Restaurant Critic for English Vogue, 1983-86; Book and TV reviewer for Daily Mail. Membership: Society of Authors. Address: 35 Drayton Gardens, London SW10 9RY, England.

MATULIONIS Arvydas, b. 1 April 1940, Kupiskis, Lithuania. Professor of Physics. m. Ilona, 3 sons, 1 daughter. Education: Diploma in Physics, Vilnius University, Lithuania, 1961; Candidate of Science, Physics and Mathematics, 1967, DSc, Physics and Mathematics, 1981, Vilnius University, Lithuania; Doctor Habilitus, Nature Science, Lithuania, 1993. Appointments: Research Associate, Institute of Optics, University of Rochester, USA, 1969-70; Senior Research Associate, 1972-74, Head of Laboratory, 1974-91, Associate Professor (part-time), 1983-85, Professor of Physics and Principal Research Associate, 1991-95, Professor of Physics and Head of Fluctuation Research Laboratory, 1995-, Semiconductor Physics Institute, Vilnius; Professor of Physic (part-time), Vytautas Magnus University, Kaunas, Lithuania, 1991-95. Publications: Over 160 in professional journals; Monograph: H L Hartnagel, R Katilius, A Matulionis, Microwave Noise in Semiconductor Devices, John Wiley and Sons, New York, 2001. Honours: Lithuanian National Award in Science, 1983, 1995. Memberships: Lithuanian Physical Society; International Advisory Committee, International Conference on Noise and Fluctuations; International Advisory Committee, European Workshop on Compound Semiconductor Devices and Integrated Circuits (WOCSDICE). Address: Fluctuation Research Laboratory, Semiconductor Physics Institute Vilnius, 11 A Gostauto, Vilnius 01108, Lithuania.

MATUSZEWSKI Roman, b. 28 February 1951, Gostynin, Poland. Logician. m. Grazyna Lach, 3 sons. Education: Engineer, 1973, MSc, Mechanics, 1975, Warsaw Technical University, Poland; PhD, Computer Science, Shinshu University, Japan, 2000. Appointments: Research Professor, Mathematics & Logic, Warsaw University, Bialystok, 1976-; Researcher, University Catholique de Louvain, Belgium, 1984-90; Researcher, Shinshu University, Nagano, Japan, 1996. Publications: Several articles in professional journals. Honours: Merit Cross, Republic of Poland, 1981.

Dictionary of International Biography

Memberships: Academy of Sciences of Nature and Society, Moscow; American Mathematical Society. Address: University of Bialystok, Mizar Project, Plac Uniwersytecki 1, 15-420 Bialystok, Poland.

MATYJASZEWSKI Krzysztof, b. 8 April 1950, Konstantynow, Poland. Professor. m. Malgorzata, 1 son, 1 daughter. Education: MSc, BS, Technical University of Moscow, 1972; PhD, Polish Academy of Sciences, 1976; Habilitation, Polytechnical University of Lodz, Poland, 1985. Appointments: Research Associate, Polish Academy of Sciences, 1978-89; Visiting Professor, University of Paris, 1985; Professor, 1985-98, Department Head, Chemistry, 1994-98, J C Warner Professor of Natural Sciences, 1998- Carnegie Mellon University; Adjunct Professor, Polish Academy of Sciences, 2000-; Adjunct Professor, Department of Chemical and Petroleum Engineering, University of Pittsburgh, 2000-; Editor, Progress in Polymer Science; Member numerous editorial boards. Publications: Books: Cationic Ring-Opening Polymerization, 1980; Cationic Polymerizations, 1996; Controlled Radical Polymerization, 1998; Controlled Living Radical Polymerization, 2000; Handbook of Radical Polymerization, 2001. Honours: Presidential Young Investigator Award, 1989; Creative Polymer Chemistry Awards, 1995; Elf Chair of French Academy of Sciences, 1998; Humboldt Award for Senior US Scientist, 1999; Fellow, American Chemical Society, 2001; Pittsburgh Award, American Chemical Society, 2001; Polymer Chemistry Award, American Chemical Society, 2002.Memberships: American Chemical Society; Polish Chemical Society. Address: Department of Chemistry, Carnegie Mellon University, 4400 Fifth Ave, Pittsburgh, PA 15213. E-mail: km3b@andrew.cmu.edu

MAUELSHAGEN Franz Matthias, b. 4 October 1967, Bonn, Germany. Historian. Education: MA, Philosophy, History and Law, University of Bonn, 1994; PhD, History, University of Zurich, Switzerland, 2000. Appointments: Research Assistant, Institute of Contemporary History, Germany, 1995; Freelancer, Haus der Geschichte der Bundesrepublik Deutschland, 1996-98; Doctoral Scholarship, German National Merit Foundation, 1997-99; Research Fellow, University of Bielefeld, 2000-03. Publications: Monograph; Numerous articles. Honours: German Youth Team Chess Championships, 1986. Memberships: Verband der Historiker Deutschlands; European Society for Environmental History; Bielefeld School for Historical Research. Address: Faculty of History, Philosophy and Theology, University of Bielefeld, Universitatsstrasse 10, Postfach 10 01 31, 33501 Bielefeld, Germany. E-mail: f.mauelshagen@web.de Website: www.geschichte.uni-bielefeld.de/fmauelsh/

MAUGER Anthony, b. 8 September 1945, Halifax, Yorkshire, England. Entrepreneur; Former International Banker. m. Yvonne Le Messurier Parkes, 2 sons, 1 daughter. Education: Templeton College, Oxford, England, 1985. Appointments: Standard Chartered Bank, 1964-95, rising to various senior management positions including: Head of International Banking, 1987-92; Head of Sovereign Debt, 1989-93; Global Head, Financial Institutions, 1992-93; General Manager, East Asia, 1993-95; Director, 1993-95: Institute of International Finance, Washington, USA; SIFDA, Geneva, Switzerland; Standard Chartered Merchant Bank, Singapore; Standard Chartered Bank, Sydney, Australia; Commissioner, PT Standard Chartered Bank, Brunei; Chairman, International Creditor Banks Steering Committee, 1993; Representative for Europe, Investec Bank, South Africa, 1996-97; Cofounder, Mauger Family Trust, Alderney, Channel Islands, 2000; Managing Director Mauger Family Investment Fund, 2002. Publication: Sovereign Debt Restructuring: The Practical Background, 1986. Honours: Associate, Chartered Institute of Bankers; Fellow of Royal Society of Arts. Memberships: Chartered

Institute of Bankers, London; Guincho Club, Portugal; South Eastern Bull Terrier Club. Address: 2 La Brecque Phillippe, St Annes, Alderney, Channel Islands.

MAUPIN Armistead, b. 13 May 1944, Washington, District of Columbia, USA. Writer. Education: BA, University of North Carolina at Chapel Hill, 1966. Appointments: Reporter, News and Courier, Charleston, 1970-71, Associated Press, 1971-72; Columnist, Pacific Sun, San Francisco, 1974, San Francisco Chronicle, 1976-77. Publications: Tales of the City, 1978; More Tales of the City, 1980; Further Tales of the City, 1982; Babycakes, 1984; Significant Others, 1987; Sure of You, 1989; 28 Barbary Lane, 1990; Back to Barbary Lane, 1991; Maybe the Moon, 1992; The Night Listener, 2000. Other: Libretto for the musical Heart's Desire, 1990. Television Programme: Armistead Maupin's Tales of the City, 1993. Contributions to: Periodicals. Honours: Best Dramatic Serial Award, Royal TV Society, 1994; George Foster Peabody Award, 1994. Address: 584 Castro Street, # 528, San Francisco, CA 94114, USA.

MAVOR Elizabeth (Osborne), b. 17 December 1927, Glasgow, Scotland. Author. Education: St Andrews, 1940-45; St Leonard's and St Anne's College, Oxford, England, 1947-50. Publications: Summer in the Greenhouse, 1959; The Temple of Flora, 1961; The Virgin Mistress: A Biography of the Duchess of Kingston (US edition as The Virgin Mistress: A Study in Survival: The Life of the Duchess of Kingston), 1964; The Redoubt, 1967; The Ladies of Llangollen: A Study in Romantic Friendship, 1971; A Green Equinox, 1973; Life with the Ladies of Llangollen, 1984; The Grand Tour of William Beckford, 1986; The White Solitaire, 1988; The American Journals of Fanny Kemble, 1990; The Grand Tours of Katherine Wilmot, France 1801-3 and Russia 1805-7, 1992; The Captain's Wife, The South American Journals of Maria Graham 1821-23, 1993. Address: Curtis Brown Ltd, 28-29 Haymarket, London SW1Y 4SP, England.

MAXWELL DAVIES Peter (Sir), b. 8 September 1934, Manchester, England. Composer. Education: Royal Manchester College of Music; Mus B (Hons), Manchester University, 1956. Musical Education: Studies with Goffredo Petrassi in Rome, 1957; Harkness Fellowship, Graduate School, Princeton University, studied with Roger Sessions, Milton Babbitt, Earl Kim. Career: Director of Music, Cirencester Grammar School, 1959-62; Founder and co-director (with Harrison Birtwistle) of the Pierrot Players, 1967-71; Founder, Artistic Director, Fires of London, 1971-87; Founder, Artistic Director, St. Magnus Festival, Orkney Islands, Scotland, 1977-86; Artistic Director, Dartington Summer School of Music, 1979-84; President, Schools Music Association, 1983-; President, North of England Education Conference, 1985; Visiting Fromm Professor of Composition, Harvard University, 1985; Associate Composer/Conductor, Scottish Chamber Orchestra, 1985-94; President, Composer's Guild of Great Britain, 1986-; President, St Magnus Festival, Orkney Islands, 1986-; President, National Federation of Music Societies, 1989-; Major retrospective festival as South Bank Centre, London, 1990; Conductor/ Composer, BBC Philharmonic, 1992-; Associate Conductor/ Composer, Royal Philharmonic Orchestra, 1992-; President, Cheltenham Arts Festival, 1994-; Composer Laureate of Scottish Chamber Orchestra, 1994-; President, Society for the Promotion of New Music, 1995-. Compositions: Stage: Operas Taverner 1962-70; The Martydom of St Magnus 1976-77; The Two Fiddlers 1978; The Lighthouse, 1979; Theatre Pieces: Notre Dame des Fleurs 1966; Vesalii Icones 1969; Eight Songs for a Mad King 1969; Nocturnal Dances, ballet 1969; Blind Man's Buff 1972; Miss Donnithorne's Maggot 1974; Salome, ballet 1978; Le Jongleur de Notre Dame 1978; Cinderella 1980; The Medium 1981; The No 11 Bus 1983-84; Caroline Mathilde, ballet, 1990;

Operas: Resurrection 1987 and The Doctor of Myddfai 1996. Orchestra and Ensemble: Alma Redemptoris Mater for 6 wind instruments 1957; St Michael, sonata for 17 wind instruments 1957; Prolation 1958; Ricercar and Doubles for 8 instruments 1959; 5 Klee Pictures 1959, rev 1976; Sinfonia 1962; 2 Fantasias on an In Nomine of John Taverner 1962-64; 7 In Nomine 1963-65; Shakespeare Music 1965; Antechrist 1967; Stedman Caters 1968; St Thomas Wake 1969; Worldes Blis 1969; Renaissance Scottish Dances 1973; Ave Maris Stela 1975; 4 Symphonies 1973-76, 1980, 1984, 1988; Runes from a Holy Island 1977; A mirror of Whitening Light 1977; Dances from Salome, 1979; The Bairns of Brugh 1981; Image Reflection, Shadow 1982; Sinfonia Concertante 1982; Sinfonietta Accademica 1983; Kirkwall Circle 1984; An Orkney Wedding, with Sunrise 1985; Jimmack the Postie, overture 1986; 10 Strathclyde Concertos for Violin 1985, Trumpet 1987, Oboe 1988, Clarinet 1990, Violin and Viola, 1991, Flute 1991, Doublebass 1992, Bassoon, 1993, Chamber Ensemble 1994, Orchestra 1995; Vocal: 5 Motets 1959; O Magnum Mysterium 1960; Te Lucis ante Terminum 1961; Frammenti di Leopardi, cantata 1962; Veni Sancte Spiritus 1963; Revelation and Fall; The Shepherds' Calendar 1965; Missa super L'Homme Arme 1968, rev 1971; From Stone to Thorn 1971; Hymn to St Magnus 1972; Tenebrae super Gesualdo 1972; Stone Litany 1973; Fiddlers at the Wedding 1974; Anakreontika 1976; Kirkwall Shopping Songs 1979; Black Pentecost 1979; Solstice of Light 1979; The Yellow Cake Review, 6 cabaret songs 1980; Songs of Hoy 1981; Into The Labyrinth for tenor and orchestra 1983; First Ferry to Hoy 1985; The Peat Cutters 1985; House of Winter 1986; Excuse Me 1986; Sea Runes, vocal sextet 1986; Hymn to the Word of God, for tenor and chorus, 1990; The Turn of the Tide for orchestra and children's choir, 1992; Chamber music includes: String Quartet 1961; The Kestrel Paced Round the Sun 1975; Sonatina 1981; The Pole Star 1982; Sea Eagle 1982; Sonata for violin and cimbalon 1984; Piano Sonata 1981; Organ Sonata, 1982; Latest works: Sails in St Magnus I-III, 1997-98; Job, oratorio for chorus, orchestra and soloists, 1998; A Reel of Seven Fishermen for orchestra, 1998; Sea Elegy, for chorus, orchestra and soloists, 1998; Roma Amor Labyrinths, 1998; Maxwell's Reel with Northern Lights, 1998; Swinton Jig, 1998; Temenos with Mermaids and Angels, for flute and orchestra, 1998; Spinning Jenny, 1999; Sails in Orkney Saga III: An Orkney Wintering, for alto saxophone and orchestra, 1999; Trumpet Quintet, for string quartet and trumpet, 1999; Mr Emmet Takes a Walk, 1999; Horn Concerto, 1999; Orkney Saga IV: Westerly Gale in Biscay, Salt in the Bread Broken, 2000, Symphony No 7, 2000; Antarctic Symphony, Symphony No 8, 2000; Canticum Canticorum, 2001; De Assumtione Beatae Mariae Virginis, 2001; Crossing Kings Reach, 2001; Mass, 2002; Naxos Quartet No 1, 2002; Piano Trip, 2002; Naxos Quartet No 2, 2003. Honours: Many honours including: Fellow, Royal Northern College of Music, 1978; Honorary Member, Royal Academy of Music, 1979; Honorary Member, Guildhall School of Music and Drama, 1981; CBE, 1981; Knight Bachelor, for services to music, 1987; L'officier dans L'Ordre des Arts et des Lettres, France, 1988; First Award, Association of British Orchestras, outstanding contribution and promotion of orchestral life in UK; Gulliver Award for Performing Arts in Scotland, 1991; Fellowship, Royal Scottish Academy of Music and Drama, 1994; Charles Grove Award, outstanding contribution to British Music, 1995; Member of the Bayerische Akademie der Schönen Künste, 1998. Current Management: Judy Arnold. Address: c/o 50 Hogarth Road, London SW5 0PU, England.

MAY Brian James, b. 7 January 1945. Retired Teacher; Poet. m. 29 July 1967, 1 son, 2 daughters. Education: BA, 1967; MA, 1971; PGCE, 1973; MA, Education, 1991. Appointments: Assistant Warden, Adult Education, Dartington, 1968-70; Head of Drama, Arthur Terry School, Birmingham, 1970-81; Tutor, Open University, 1973-; Head of English, Swanshurst School, Birmingham, 1981-83; Head of Arts Faculty, Chamberlain College, 1983-88; Vice Principal, Josiah Mason College, 1988-93. Contributions to: Orbis; Illuminations; Christ's College Magazine; Times Educational Supplement; Poetry Now. Membership: Fellow, College of Teachers. Address: 3 Holte Drive, Sutton Coldfield, Birmingham B75 6PR, England.

MAY Geoffrey John, b. 7 May 1948, London, England. Chartered Engineer. m. Sarah, 2 sons. Education: MA, Double First Class Honours, Natural Sciences Tripos, Materials Science, Fitzwilliam College, University of Cambridge; PhD, Department of Metallurgy and Materials Science; Fellow of the Institute of Metals; Chartered Engineer. Appointments: Research Officer, Central Electricity Generating Board, 1973-74; Technical Manager, Chloride Silent Power Ltd, 1974-78; Design and Development Manager, Chloride Technical Ltd, 1978-82; Technical Director, 1982-86, Operations Director, 1986-88, Tungstone Batteries Ltd; General Manager, Brush Fusegear Ltd, 1988-90; Managing Director, Barton Abrasives Ltd, 1990-91; Group Director of Technology, Hawker Batteries, 1991-97; Group Director of Technology, BTR Power Systems, 1997-2000; Chief Technology Officer, Fiamm SpA, 2000-. Publications: Numerous publications in technical and trade journals and conference proceedings. Address: Troutbeck House, Main Street, Swithland, Loughborough, Leicestershire LE12 8TJ, England. E-mail: geoffrey.may@fiamm.com

MAY Julian, b. 10 July 1931, Chicago, Illinois, USA. Writer. m. Thaddeus E Dikty, 1953, 2 sons, 1 daughter. Publications: Over 250 books including: The Many Colored Land, 1981; The Golden Torc, 1982; The Nonborn King, 1983; The Adversary, 1984; Intervention, 1987; Black Trillium, 1990; Jack the Bodiless, 1991; Blood Trillium, 1992; Diamond Mask, 1994; Magnificat, 1996; Sky Trillium, 1997; Perseus Spur, 1998; Orion Arm, 1999; Sagittarius Whorl, 2001; Conqueror's Moon, 2003. Address: Box 851 Mercer Island, WA 98040, USA.

MAY Robert McCredie (Baron May of Oxford), b. 1 August 1936, Professor. Education: BSc, PhD, Theoretical Physics, Sydney University. Appointments: Gordon MacKay Lecturer, Applied Mathematics, Harvard University; Senior Lecturer in Theoretical Physics, Personal Chair in Physics, Sydney University; Class of 1877 Professor of Zoology, 1973, Chairman of the Research Board, 1977-88, Princeton University, USA; Royal Society Research Professor, 1988; Chief Scientific Adviser, UK Government, 1995-2000; Head, UK Officer of Science and Technology, 1995-2000; Joint Professorship, Department of Zoology, Oxford University and Imperial College, London; Fellow, Merton College, Oxford University; President, The Royal Society, 2000-05. Publications: Numerous books; Several hundred papers in major scientific journals; Broader contributions to scientific journalism in newspapers, radio and TV. Honours: Knighthood, 1996; Companion of the Order of Australia, 1998; Crafoord Prize, Royal Swedish Academy; Swiss-Italian Balzan Prize; Japanese Blue Planet Prize. Memberships: Foreign Member, US National Academy of Sciences; Overseas Fellow, Australian Academy of Sciences. Address: Department of Zoology, University of Oxford, South Parks Road, Oxford, OX1 3PS, England. E-mail: robert.may@zoo.ox.ac.uk

MAYAGOITIA Jesus, b. 4 May 1948, Mexico City. Sculptor. m. Rosa Marques, 1 daughter. Education: BA, Visual Arts, National School of Arts, National University of Mexico, 1974-77. Career: Since 1974 participation in more than 100 exhibitions with other artists in galleries, museums and cultural centres in Mexico, Poland, France, Japan, Argentina, Belgium and USA; Individual Exhibitions: Virtual Plans and Volumes, San Carlos Academy,

Mexico DF, 1978; Cultural Festival in Tepoztian Morelos, 1992; Auditorium, Underground Station, Mexico DF, 1994; ITESM Campus, State of Mexico, 1995; Geometric Abstraction, ITESM Campus Laguna Coah, 1997; House of the Lake, Mexico DF, 1999; House of the Tithe, Celaya Gto, 2000; Cultural Centre of the National Polytechnic Institute, Mexico DF, 2000; Lopez Quiroga Gallery, 2001; Museo Luis Nishizawa, Toluca, State of Mexico, 2002; Abstract Art Museum, Manuel Felguerez, Zacatecas, 2002; Four Seasons, Mora Institute, Mexico DF, 2003; Geometric Poem, ITESM Campus, Mexico City, 2004. Publications: Works featured in: Nueva Plastica Mexicana, 1997; Diccionario de Escultores Mexicanos del Siglo XX, 1999; Abstract Museum of Art, Manuel Felguerez, Artes de Mexico y del Mundo SA de CV, 2002; Mexico en el Mundo de las Colecciones de Arte, 1999; Mexico Eterno, 1999; 1900-2000 Un Siglo de Arte Mexicano, 1999; Mexican Sculpture, Instituto Nacional de Bellas Artes. Honours: 1st Prize, Sculpture, National Contest for Art Students, Cultural House, Aguascalientes, 1977; Third Place, First Trienal of Sculpture, Mexico DF, 1979; First Place, Artistic Teaching, National Institute of Fine Arts, 1979; Special Prize, Second Trienal of Sculpture, Mexico DF, 1982; Second Place in Sculpture, Torre Lomas Building, 1984; Grand Prize, Henry Moore, Utsukushi-gahara, Japan, 1987. Membership: Sistema Nacional de Ceadores (National Creators System), 1997-. Address: Peten No 151-301, Col. Narvarte CP 03020, Mexico DF. E-mail: jmayagoitiad@prodigy.net.mx

MAYALL Richard Michael (Rik), b. 7 March 1958, England. Comedian; Actor; Writer. m. Barbara Robin, 1 son, 2 daughters. Education: University of Manchester. Creative Works: Theatre includes: The Common Pursuit, 1988; Waiting for God, 1991-92; The Government Inspector, 1995; Cell Mates, 1995; TV includes: The Young Ones (also creator and co-writer), 1982, 1984; The Comic Strip Presents, 1983-84, 1992; George's Marvellous Medicine, 1985; The New Statesman, 1987-88, 1990, 1994; Bottom, 1990, 1992, 1994; Rik Mayall Presents, 1992-94; Wham Bham Strawberry Jam!, 1995; The Alan B'Stard Interview with Brian Walden, 1995; In the Red, 1998; The Bill, 1999; Jonathan Creek, 1999; The Knock, 2000; Murder Rooms, 2000; Tales of Uplift and Moral Improvement, 2000; Films include: Whoops Apocalypse, 1982; Drop Dead Fred, 1990; Horse Opera, 1992; Remember Me, 1996; Bring Me the Head of Mavis Davis, 1996; Guest House Paradiso, 1999; Merlin – The Return, 1999; Kevin of the North, 2000; Jesus Christ, Super Star, 2000; Several voices for animations; Live Stand Up includes: Comic Strip, 1982; Kevin Turvey and Bastard Squad, 1983; Rik Mayall, Ben Elton, Andy De La Tour, UK tour and Edinburgh Fringe 1983; Rik Mayall and Ben Elton, 1984-85, Australian tour 1986, 1992; Rik Mayall and Andy De La Tour, 1989-90; Rik Mayall and Adrian Edmondson, UK tours, 1993, 1995, 1997, 2001. Honours include: BAFTA, Best New Comedy, 1990; British Comedy Awards, Best New Comedy, 1992, Best Comedy Actor, 1993. Address: c/o The Brunskill Management Ltd, Suite 8A, 169 Queen's Gate, London SW7 5HE, England.

MAYER Daniel C, b. 28 May 1956, Graz, Austria. Mathematician; Physicist. Education: PhD, Karl-Franzens University, Graz, Austria, 1983; MA, University Regensburg, Germany, 1998. Appointments: Assistant, Karl-Franzens University, Graz, Austria, 1982-90; Research Assistant, University of Manitoba, Winnipeg, Canada, 1990-91; Controlling Software Engineer, Schelling, Schwarzach, Austria, 1991-94; Teacher, Michaeli Gymnasium, Munich, 1994-99; Web and GIS System Analyst, Infonova and Daimler Chrysler, Graz, 1999-. Publications: Articles in numerous professional journals; Reviewer for Mathematical Reviews, 1992-. Honour: Recipient, Erwin Schrödinger Grant, Austrian Science Foundation, Vienna, 1990-

91. Memberships: Austrian Mathematical Society, 1983-; American Mathematical Society, 1990-. Address: Naglergasse 53, A-8010 Graz, Austria. E-mail: daniel.mayer@algebra.at Website: http://www.algebra.at

MAYER Sydney L, b. 2 August 1937, Chicago, USA. Publisher. m. Charlotte W M Bouter. Education: BA, MA, University of Michigan; MPhil, Yale University. Appointments: Lecturer, University of Maryland, USA, 1966-77; Visiting Assistant Professor, University of Southern California, 1969-74; UK Director, University of Maryland, 1972-73; Managing Director, Bison Books Ltd, 1973-95; President, CEO, Brompton Books Corporation, 1982-98; President, Twin Books Corporation, 1985-98; Chairman, Twin Films Ltd, 1997-. Publications: 22 books including: The World of Southeast Asia (with Harry J Benda), 1971; The Two World Wars (with William J Koenig), 1976; Signal, 1975; World War Two, 1981; hundreds of articles. Honours: Angell Society, University of Michigan, 1989; Honorary Fellow, Oriel College, Oxford, 1993; Fulbright Advisory Board, London, 1993-. Address: 2 Shrewsbury House, 42 Cheyne Walk, London, SW3 5LN, England.

MAYNARD John David, b. 14 May 1931, Carshalton, England. Consultant Surgeon. m. (1) Patricia Gray, 2 sons, 2 daughters, (2) Gillian Mary Loveless, 1 son. Education: MB BS, Charing Cross Hospital, London, 1954; FRCS, England, 1961; MS, Guy's Hospital, London, 1966. Appointments include: House Surgeon, Charing Cross Hospital, 1954; House Physician, Putney Hospital, 1954; Resident Anaesthetist, Charing Cross Hospital, 1955; Junior Specialist in Surgery, QAM Hospital, 1956; Demonstrator in Anatomy, London Hospital, 1958-59; Accident and Emergency Surgeon, Putney Hospital, 1959; Clinical Assistant, St Marks Hospital, 1962-64; Assistant Curator, Pathology Museum, Guy's Hospital, 1962-69; Curator, 1969-96; Consultant Surgeon, Guy's Hospital, 1967-92; Lecturer on Surgery, London University, 1967-96; Lecturer in Surgery, Guy's Hospital Dental School, 1985-96; Consultant Surgeon Emeritus, Guy's Hospital, 1992-; RCS Adviser to her Majesty's Prison Service on surgical services for Prisoners in England and Wales, 1995-; Surgical Adviser to the Director of the Museums at the Royal College of Surgeons, 1996-. Publications: Numerous articles in professional medical journals and chapters in 5 surgical books. Honours: Gold Medal in Medicine and Surgery, 1953; Prize in Dermatology, 1955; Research Prize, South West Metropolitan Regional Hospital Board. Memberships: Member, Council of the Royal Society of Medicine, 1997-; Member, Society of Expert Witnesses, 1999-; The Law Society Directory of Expert Witnesses, 2000-. Address: 14 Blackheath Park, London SE3 9RP, England.

MAYNE Richard (John), b. 2 April 1926, London, England. Writer; Broadcaster. m. Jocelyn Mudie Ferguson, 2 daughters. Education: MA, PhD, Trinity College, Cambridge, 1947-53. Appointments: Rome Correspondent, New Statesman, 1953-54; Assistant, Tutor, Cambridge Institute of Education, 1954-56; Official of the European Community, Luxembourg and Brussels, 1956-63; Personal Assistant to Jean Monnet, Paris, 1963-66; Paris Correspondent, 1963-73, Co-Editor, 1990-94, Encounter; Visiting Professor, University of Chicago, 1970; Director, Federal Trust, London, 1971-73; Head, UK Offices of the European Commission, London, 1973-79; Film Critic, Sunday Telegraph, London, 1987-89, The European, 1990-98. Publications: The Community of Europe, 1962; The Institutions of the European Community, 1968; The Recovery of Europe, 1970; The Europeans, 1972; Europe Tomorrow (editor), 1972; The New Atlantic Challenge (editor), 1975; The Memoirs of Jean Monnet (translator), 1978; Postwar: The Dawn of Today's Europe, 1983; Western Europe: A Handbook (editor), 1987; Federal Union: The Pioneers (with John Pinder),

1990; Europe: A History of its Peoples (translator), 1990; History of Europe (translator), 1993; A History of Civilizations (translator), 1994; The Language of Sailing, 2000; In Victory, Magnanimity, in Peace, Goodwill: a History of Wilton Park, 2003; Cross Channel Currents: 100 Years of the Entente Cordiale, co-editor, 2004. Contributions to: Newspapers and magazines. Honour: Scott-Moncrieff Prize for Translation from French, 1978; Officier de L'Ordre des Arts et des Lettres, 2003. Memberships: Society of Authors; Royal Institute of International Affairs; Federal Trust for Education and Research. Address: Albany Cottage, 24 Park Village East, Regent's Park, London NW1 7PZ, England.

MAZID Muhammad Abdul, b. 31 December 1952, Mymensingh, Bangladesh. Public Servant. m. 25 April 1976, 2 sons, 1 daughter. Education: BSc, 1972, MSc, 1973, Bangladesh Agricultural University; MSc, Kagoshima University, Japan, 1978; PhD, Tokyo University of Agriculture, 1980; Postdoctoral, Kagoshima University, Japan, 1983. Appointments: Lecturer, 1976-79, Assistant Professor, 1979-85, Bangladesh Agricultural University; Chief Scientific Officer, Bangladesh Fisheries Research Institute, 1985-89; Additional Director, 1989-92, Director, 1992-97, Director General, 1997, Ministry of Fisheries and Livestock. Publications: Over 100 in professional national and international journals. Honours: 20th Century Achievement Award, ABI; Award for Fisheries Research and Technology Development by Prime Minister, Government of the People's Republic of Bangladesh, 1997; Award for Scientific Printing and Publication, Prime Minister, Government of the People's Republic of Bangladesh, 1999. Memberships: World Fish Nutrition Society, USA; Asian Fisheries Society, Manila; ICLARM, Manila; International Network of Genetics in Aquaculture, Manila; Fellow of Zoological Society of Bangladesh, Dhaka University. Address: Bangladesh Fisheries Research Institute, PO Kewotkhali, Mymensingh 2201, Bangladesh.

MBONDJI MBONDJI Pierre, b. 1 January 1946, Kake, Cameroon. Entomologist. m. Marie Madeleine Mouelle, 3 sons, 2 daughters. Education: Diploma, Chemistry, Physics and Biological Sciences, 1967; Diploma, Tropical Meteorology and Hydrology; Diploma, Biology, Microbiology and Plant Physiology, 1968; Agricultural Engineer, Yaounde, 1970; MSc, Paris, 1972; Doctorate, Paris, 1979; Doctor of Sciences, Yaounde, 2001. Appointments: Head, Stimulant Crops Department, 1976-2000; Head, Engineering and Planning Department, 1984-93; Deputy Director of Research, 1993-98; Director, Regional Centre for Bananas and Plantains, 1999-2001; Director, Coca Growing Support, 2002. Publications: Pests of Cocoa and Coffee in the Cameroon, 1984; Observations on the Biology of Phosphorus Virescens, 1984; Epidemiological Study on Hypothenemus hampei, 1988; Eco-biological observations on the Antestiopsis lineaticollis intricata in Cameroon, 1999; Biological data on Sphaerocoris annulus (F) in Cameroon, 2000; Numerous articles in professional journals. Honours: Chevallier of the Order of Valour; President's Awards, Zone Chairman's Awards, Lion's Club International. Memberships: Entomological Society of France; African Association of Insect Scientists; Advisory Group for Cocoa Economy; African Coffee Network; President, Cameroon Entomological Society. Address: PO Box 8206, Institute of Agronomic Research for Development, Yaounde, Cameroon. E-mail: mbondji_aphag@yahoo.fr

McALEESE Mary Patricia, b. 27 June 1951, Belfast, Northern Ireland. President of Ireland. m. Martin, 1976, 1 son, 2 daughters. Education: LLB, The Queen's University, Belfast, 1969-73; BL, Inn of Court of Northern Ireland, 1973-74; MA, Trinity College, Dublin, 1986; Diploma in Spanish, Institute of Linguistics, 1991-94. Appointments: Reid Professor, Criminal Law, Criminology and

Penology, Trinity College, Dublin, 1975-79, 1981-87; Current Affairs Journalist, Presenter, Irish National TV, 1979-81; Part-time Presenter, -1975; Director, Institute of Professional Legal Study, Queen's University of Belfast, 1987-97; Pro-Vice Chancellor, 1994-97; President, Ireland, 1997-. Publications: The Irish Martyrs, 1995; Reconciled Beings, 1997. Honours: Several honorary degrees; Silver Jubilee Commemoration Medal, Charles University, Prague. Memberships: European Bar Association; International Bar Association; Inns of Court, North Ireland; King's Inn, Dublin; Former Member: Institute of Advanced Study; Irish Association of Law Teachers; Society of Public Teachers of Law; British and Irish Legal Technology Association. Address: Áras an Uachtaráin, Phoenix Park, Dublin 8, Ireland. E-mail: webmaster@aras.irigov.ie

McCARTHY Cormac, (Charles McCarthy Jr), b. 20 July 1933, Providence, Rhode Island, USA. Author; Dramatist. m. Lee Holleman, 1961, divorced 1 child, (2) Anne deLisle, 1967, divorced. Publications: Novels: The Orchard Keeper, 1965; Outer Dark, 1968; Child of God, 1974; Suttree, 1979; Blood Meridian, or The Evening Redness in the West, 1985; All the Pretty Horses, 1992; The Crossing, 1994; Cities of the Plain, 1998. Plays: The Gardner's Son, 1977; The Stonemason, 1994. Honours: Ingram Merrill Foundation Grant, 1960; William Faulkner Foundation Award, 1965; American Academy of Arts and Letters Travelling Fellowship, 1965-66; Rockefeller Foundation Grant, 1966; Guggenheim Fellowship, 1976; John D and Catharine T MacArthur Foundation Fellowship, 1981; National Book Award, 1992; National Book Critics Circle Award, 1993. Address: 1011 N Mesa Street, El Paso, TX 79902, USA.

McCARTHY Joseph, b. 28 November 1938, Lowell, Massachusetts, USA. Plastic Reconstructive Surgeon. m. Karlan von L Sloan, 6 June 1964, 1 son, 1 daughter. Education: AB, Harvard University, 1960; MD, Columbia University College of Physicians and Surgeons, 1964. Appointments: Lawrence D Bell Professor of Plastic Surgery and Director of Institute of Reconstructive Plastic Surgery, NY Medical Center; Attending Plastic Surgeon and Chief of Service, New York University; Visiting Plastic Surgeon and Director of Service, Bellevue Hospital Center; Attending Surgeon, Manhattan Eye, Ear and Throat Hospital; Attending Surgeon, Veterans Administration Hospital. Publications include: Books: Reconstructive Plastic Surgery, 2nd edition, 1977; Proceedings on 2nd International Conference on the Diagnosis and Treatment of Craniofacial Anomalies, 1979; Clinics Plastic Surgery, 1979; Plastic Surgery, 1990; Distraction of the Craniofacial Skeleton, 1998; 251 papers and 125 chapters in medical journals; 185 presentations and visiting professorships. Honours include: Joseph Garrison Parker Award, Columbia University College of Physicians and Surgeons, 1964; Sir James Carreras Award, International Variety Clubs, 1990; 1st Prize, American Society of Maxillofacial Surgeons, 1991; Senior Basic Science Award, Plastic Surgery Educational Foundation Scholarship Contest, 1996; Trusler Visiting Professor, University of Indiana, 2000; Theograj Memorial Lecture, Medical College of Virginia, 2001; 50th Anniversary Award Recipient, National Foundation for Facial Reconstruction, 2001; Honorary Award, University of Zurich, 2003. Memberships include: President, International Society of Craniofacial Surgeons, 1989-91; Vice President, 1996-97, President, 1998-99, Trustee, 2000, American Association of Plastic Surgeons; Board of Directors, 1999-, Chairman, Medical Advisory Board, 1999-, The Smile Train; Parliamentarian, American Society of Maxiofacial Surgeons, 2000. Address: Institute of Reconstructive Surgery, 722 Park Avenue, New York, NY 10021, USA. E-mail: joseph.mccarthy@med.nyu.edu

McCARTIN Brian J, b. 26 August 1951, Providence, Rhode Island, USA. Professor of Applied Mathematics. 1 son. Education: BS, 1976, MSc, 1977, Applied Mathematics, University of Rhode Island; PhD, Applied Mathematics, New York University (Courant Institute of Mathematical Sciences), 1981; BM, Music Theory (summa cum laude), Hartt School of Music, 1994. Appointments include: Science Analyst, Pratt & Whitney Aircraft, 1977-81; Various appointments, Middlesex Community College, 1982-83, University of Hartford, 1982-84, Central Connecticut State University, 1982-84, University of Connecticut, 1985; Adjunct Associate Professor, Computer Scientist, Hartford Graduate Centre, 1984-89; Senior Research Mathematician, United Technologies Research Centre, 1981-89; United Technologies Research Centre, 1989-93; Professor, 1989-92, Chairman, 1989-91, Computer Scientist, Hartford Graduate Centre; Founder, President, Chief Scientist, Computational Mathematics Consultants, 1992; Associate Professor, Applied Mathematics, University of Bridgeport, 1992-93; Professor, Applied Mathematics, Kettering University, 1993-. Publications: 115 in professional journals, conference proceedings. Honours include: Phi Kappa Phi; Alpha Chi; Pi Kappa Lambda; Pi Mu Epsilon (URI Chapter); Kappa Mu Epsilon; Invited Lecturer, Workshop on Computational Electromagnetics, Institute for Computer Applications in Science and Engineering, NASA Langley Research Centre, June 12-16, 1995; Distinguished Visiting Professor of Applied Mathematics, Department of Mathematical Sciences, New Jersey Institute of Technology, March 24-28, 1997; Kettering University Outstanding Researcher Award, 2000; Kettering University Outstanding Teaching Award, 2001; Michigan Section of the Mathematical Association of America Award for Distinguished Teaching, 2004. Memberships: Mathematical Association of America (MAA); Society for Industrial and Applied Mathematics (SIAM). Address: 2310 Crestbrook Lane, Flint, MI 48507-2209, USA. E-mail: bmccarti@kettering.edu

McCARTNEY (James) Paul (Sir), b. 18 June 1942, Liverpool, England. Singer; Songwriter; Musician. m. (1) Linda Eastman, 12 March 1969, deceased 1998, 1 son, 2 daughters, 1 stepdaughter, (2) Heather Mills, 2002, 1 daughter. Education; Self-taught in music. Appointments: Member, The Quarrymen, 1957-59, The Beatles, 1960-70; Founder, Apple Corporation Ltd; Founder, MPL Group of Companies; Founder, Wings, 1970-81; Solo Artiste, 1970-; International tours, concerts, TV, radio, films; Founder, Liverpool Institute of Performing Arts, 1995. Creative Works: Numerous albums with The Beatles. Solo Albums: McCartney, 1970; Ram, 1971; McCartney II, 1980; Tug of War, 1982; Pipes of Peace, 1983; Give My Regards to Broad Street, 1984; Press to Play, 1986; All the Best, 1987; Flowers in the Dirt, 1989; Tripping the Light Fantastic, 1990; Unplugged, 1991; Choba b CCCP, 1991; Paul McCartney's Liverpool Oratorio, 1991; Off the Ground, 1993; Paul is Live, 1993; Flaming Pie, 1997; Standing Stone, symphonic work, 1997; A Garland for Linda, composition with 8 other composers for a capella choir, 2000; Paul McCartney: The Music and Animation Collection, DVD, 2004. Publications: Paintings, 2000; The Beatles Anthology (with George Harrison and Ringo Starr), 2000; Sun Prints (with Linda McCartney), 2001; Many Years From Now, autobiography, 2001; Blackbird Singing: Poems and Lyrics 1965-1999, 2001. Honours: MBE, 1965; Numerous Grammy Awards; 3 Ivor Novello Awards; Freeman, City of Liverpool, 1984; Doctorate, University of Sussex, 1988; Guinness Book of Records Award, 1979; Q Merit Award, 1990; Knighted, 1997; Fellowship, British Academy of Composers and Songwriters, 2000. Address: c/o MPL Communications, 1 Soho Square, London W1V 6BQ, England.

McCARTNEY Stella, b. 1972. Fashion Designer. Education: Central St Martins College of Art and Design. Appointments: Work with Christian Lacroix at age 15 and later with Betty Jackson;

Work experience in Fashion Department, Vogue magazine; After graduation, set up own design company in London; Chief Designer for Chloe, Paris; Designed collection for Gucci, 2001; VH/1 Vogue Fashion and Music Designer of the Year, 2000. Address: Gucci Group, via Don Lorenzo Perosi, 6 Casellina di Scandici, 50018 Florence, Italy. Website: www.stellamccartney.com

MccGWIRE Michael Kane, b. 9 December 1924, Madras, India. Retired Commander of the Royal Navy and Professor; Writer. m. Helen Jean Scott, 22 November 1952, 2 sons, 3 daughters. Education: Royal Naval College, Dartmouth, 1938-42; BSc, University of Wales, 1970. Appointments: Commander, Royal Navy, 1942-67; Professor, Dalhousie University, 1971-79; Senior Fellow, Brookings Institution, Washington, DC, 1979-90; Visiting Professor, Global Security Programme, Cambridge University, 1990-93; Honorary appointments: Fellow, Social and Political Sciences, Cambridge University, 1993-; Senior Fellow, Foreign Policy Studies, Dalhousie University, 1996-; Professor of International Politics, University of Wales, 1997-. Publications: Military Objectives and Soviet Foreign Policy, 1987; Perestroika and Soviet National Security, 1991; NATO Expansion and European Security, 1997; Editor: Soviet Naval Developments, 1973; Soviet Naval Policy, 1975; Soviet Naval Influence, 1977. Contributions to: 40 books; numerous journals. Honour: Officer of the Order of the British Empire. Address: Hayes, Durlston, Swanage, Dorset BH19 2JF, England.

McCLURE Gillian Mary, b. 29 October 1948, Bradford, England. Author; Illustrator. 3 sons. Education: BA, Combined Honours in French, English and History of Art, Bristol University; Teaching Diploma, Moray House. Publications: 16 children's books, 1974-03. Honours: Shortlisted for Smarties Award and Highly Commended in Kate Greenaway Award, 1985. Membership: CWIG Society of Authors, committee member, 1989-; PLR Advisory Committee, 1992. Address: 9 Trafalgar Street, Cambridge CB4 1ET, England.

McCOLGAN Elizabeth, b. 24 May 1964, Dundee, Scotland. Athlete. m. Peter McColgan, 1 daughter. Education: Coached by Grete Waitz. Appointments: Gold Medal Commonwealth Games 10,000 m, 1986, 1990; Silver Medal, Olympic Games 10,000m, 1988; Silver Medal, World Indoor Championships 3,000m, 1989; Bronze Medal, Commonwealth Games, 3,000m, 1990; Gold Medal, World Championships 10,000m, 1991; Gold Medal, World Half Marathon Championships, 1992; First in New York City Marathon, 1991; First in Tokyo Marathon, 1992; Third in London Marathon, 1993; Fifth in 1995; First in 1996; Second in 1997, 1998; Retired, 2001; Runs own fitness centre and coaches young athletes in Dundee. Address: c/o Marquee UK, 6 George Street, Nottingham NG1 3BE, England.

McCONAUGHEY Matthew, b. 4 November 1969, Ulvade, Texas, USA. Actor. Education: University of Texas, Austin. Appointments: Film appearances include: Dazed and Confused; The Return of the Texas Chainsaw Massacre; Boys on the Side; My Boyfriend's Back, 1993; Angels in the Outfield, 1994; Scorpion Spring; Submission, 1995; Glory Daze; Lone Star; A Time to Kill, 1996; Larger Than Life, 1997; Amistad; Contact; Making Sandwiches; Last Flight of the Raven; Newton Boys; South Beach; EdTV, 1999; U-571, 2000; The Wedding Planner, 2001; Reign of Fire, 2001; Frailty, 2001; 13 Conversations About One Thing, 2001; Tiptoes, 2003; How to Lose a Guy in Ten Days, 2003. Address: c/o Warner Brothers Incorporated, 4000 Warner Boulevard, Suite 1101, Burbank, CA 91522, USA.

McCONNELL Charles Stephen, b. 20 June 1951, Yorkshire, England. Chief Executive. m. Natasha Valentinovna, 1 son, 1 daughter. Education: BA honours, Politics, MPhil, Community

Development. Appointments: Youth and Community Worker, Dobroyd Community School, Yorkshire, 1974-75; Action Research Worker in Community Education, Scottish Local Government Research Unit, Strathclyde, 1975-77; Lecturer, Community Education, Dundee College of Education, 1977-84; Senior Policy Development Officer, National Consumer Council, London, 1984-87; Deputy Director, Action Resource Centre, London, 1987-88; Assistant Director, Community Development Foundation, London, 1988-89; European and Public Affairs Director, London, 1989-93; Chief Executive, Scottish Community Education Council, 1993-99; Director, Secretary General, International Association for Community Development, 1998-2002; Chief Executive, Community Learning Scotland, 1999-2002; Chairman, UK National Training Organisation for Community Learning and Development, 2000-2002. Publications: Author, editor, co-editor, over 15 books; Many other articles, research and conference papers. Membership: Fellow, Royal Society of Arts. Address: Corrieway House, Easter Balgedie, Kinross, Perthshire, KY13 9HQ, Scotland. E-mail: charlie.mcconnell@virgin.net

McCORMICK John Owen, b. 20 September 1918, Thief River Falls, Minnesota, USA. Professor of Comparative Literature Emeritus; Writer. m. Mairi MacInnes, 4 February 1954, 3 sons, 1 daughter. Education: BA, 1941, MA, 1947, University of Minnesota; PhD, Harvard University, 1951. Appointments: Senior Tutor and Teaching Assistant, Harvard University, 1946-51; Lecturer, Salzburg Seminar in American Studies, Austria, 1951-52; Professor of American Studies, Free University of Berlin, 1952-53, 1954-59; Professor of Comparative Literature, 1959-, now Emeritus, Rutgers University, New Brunswick, New Jersey. Publications: Catastrophe and Imagination, 1957, 1998; Versions of Censorship (with Mairi MacInnes), 1962; The Complete Aficionado, 1967, 2nd edition, 1998; The Middle Distance: A Comparative History of American Imaginative Literature, 1919-1932, 1971; Fiction as Knowledge: The Modern Post-Romantic Novel, 1975, 1998; George Santayana: A Biography, 1987; Sallies of the Mind: Essays of Francis Fergusson (editor with G Core), 1997; Seagoing: Memoir, 2000. Contributions to: Numerous magazines, journals and reviews. Honours: Longview Award for Non-Fiction, 1960; Guggenheim Fellowships, 1964-65, 1980-81; National Endowments for the Humanities Senior Fellow, 1983-84; American Academy and Institute of Arts and Letters Prize, 1988. Address: 31 Huntington Road, York YO31 8RL, England.

McCOY Earl D, b. 14 May 1948, Hamilton, Ohio, USA. Professor. m. Cheryl D S McCoy, 1 son, 1 daughter. Education: BSc, Florida University, 1970; MSc, University of Miami, 1973; PhD, Florida University, 1977. Appointments: Biological Intern, Merritt Island National Wildlife Refuge, 1969; Instructor, Organization for Tropical Studies, 1977; Marsh Ecologist, Florida Medical Entomology Laboratory, University of Florida, 1977-78; Assistant Professor, 1978-83, Board of Directors, Center for Urban Ecology, 1982-, Associate Professor, 1983-89, Professor, 1989-, University of South Florida; Visiting Faculty Member, Mountain Lake Biological Station, University of Virginia, 1981-87. Publications: Numerous articles in professional journals. Honours: Outstanding Teacher Award, Florida State Legislature, 1994; Provost's Faculty Excellence Award, University of South Florida, 1995; Professional Excellence Award, Florida State Legislature, 1998. Address: Department of Biology, University of South Florida, Tampa, FL 33620-5150, USA.

McCULLAGH Sheila Kathleen, b. 3 December 1920, Surrey, England. Writer. Education: Bedford Froebel College, 1939-42; MA, University of Leeds, 1949. Publications: Pirate Books, 1957-95; Tales and Adventures, 1961; Dragon Books, 1963-70; One, Two, Three and Away, 1964-2000; Tim Books, 1974-83 and 2004;

Into New Worlds, 1974; Hummingbirds, 1976-92; Whizzbang Adventurers, 1980; Buccaneers, 1980-84; Where Wild Geese Fly, 1981; Puddle Lane, 1985-90; The Sea Shore and 5 other information books, 1992. Honour: Member of the Order of the British Empire, 1986. Membership: Society of Authors. Address: 27 Royal Crescent, Bath, NE Somerset, BA1 2LT, England.

McCULLOCH Nigel Simeon (The Right Reverend Bishop of Wakefield), b. 17 January 1942, Anglican Bishop. m. Celia Hume, 2 daughters. Education: Selwyn College, Cambridge; Cuddesdon College, Oxford. Appointments: Assistant Curate, Ellesmere Port, 1966-70; Chaplain and Director of Studies in Theology, Christ's College, Cambridge, 1970-73; Diocesan Missioner, Norwich, 1973-78; Rector of St Thomas's, Salisbury, 1978-86; Archdeacon of Sarum, 1979-86; Bishop of Taunton, 1986-92; Bishop of Wakefield, 1992-; Member of the House of Lords, 1997-; Lord High Almoner to H.M. The Queen, 1997-. Publications: A Gospel to Proclaim; Barriers to Belief; Credo Columnist for the Times, 1996-2000. Honour: MA. Memberships: Chairman, Sandford St Martin Religious Broadcasters Awards; National Chaplain, The Royal British Legion; National Chaplain, The Royal School of Church Music. Address: Bishop's Lodge, Wakefield WF2 6JL, England. E-mail: bishop@wakefield.anglican.org

McCULLOUGH Colleen, b. 1 June 1937, Wellington, New South Wales, Australia. Writer. m. Ric Robinson, 1984. Education: Holy Cross College, Woollahra, Sydney University; Institute of Child Health, London University. Appointments: Neurophysiologist, Sydney, London and Yale University Medical School, New Haven, Connecticut, USA, 1967-77; Relocated to Norfolk Island, South Pacific, 1980. Publications: Tim, 1974; The Thorn Birds, 1977; An Indecent Obsession, 1981; Cooking with Colleen McCullough and Jean Easthope, 1982; A Creed for the Third Millennium, 1985; The Ladies of Missalonghi, 1987; The First Man in Rome, 1990; The Grass Crown, 1991; Fortune's Favorites, 1993; Caesar's Women, 1996; Caesar, 1997; The Song of Troy, 1998; Roden Cutler, V.C. (biography), 1998; Morgan's Run, 2000. Honour: Doctor of Letters (honoris causa), Macquarie University, Sydney, 1993. Address: "Out Yenna", Norfolk Island, Oceania (via Australia).

McCULLOUGH Kathryn Taylor Baker, b. 5 January 1925, Trenton, Tennessee, USA. Emeritus Diplomate in Clinical Social Work. m. (1) John R Baker, 30 September 1972, deceased, (2) T C McCullough, 14 May 1988. Education: BS, University of Tennessee, 1945; University of Chicago, 1950; Vanderbilt University, 1950-51; MSW, University of Tennessee, 1954. Appointments: Home Demonstration Agent, Hardeman Co, Tennessee, University of Tennessee Agricultural Extension Service, 1946-49; Dyer Co, Tennessee, 1949-50; Director, Medical Social Work Department, Le Bonheur Children's Hospital, 1954-57; Chief Clinical Social Worker, Clinic for Mentally Retarded Children, University of Tennessee, Department of Pediatrics, 1957-59; Clinical Social Worker, Children's Medical Center, Tulsa, Oklahoma, 1959-60; Director, Medical Social Work Department, University of Tennessee, College of Medicine, 1960-69; Associate Professor, Social Work, University of Tennessee, College of Medicine and College of Social Work, 1960-85; Director, Community Services Regional Medical Program, College of Medicine, 1969-76; Director, Regional Clinic Program Child Development Center, College of Medicine, 1976-85; Social Worker, Admissions Board, Arlington Development Center, 1976-98; Advisory Council, 1997-2003, Field Representative, 2003-, AGAPE Child and Family Service; Gibson Co. Utility Commission, 1990-98, President, Chair of the Board, 1990-94; Child Abuse Panel, Tennessee Department of Children's Services, 1999-2003; Steering Committee, National Association of Social Workers,

1999-2002; Board of Visitors, University of Tennessee, College of Social Work, 2000-; Former Board of Directors, State of Tennessee or Shelby Co, Tennessee: American Heart Association; American Cancer Society, American Lung Association, United Cerebral Palsy, Goodwill Industries; AGAPE Child and Family Services; Health and Welfare Planning Council; Greater Shelby Co Head Start; Greater Memphis Day Care Association. Publications: 14 Books (reference books on community service). Honours: Licenced Social Worker State of Tennessee Charter Licence to Present; Emeritus Diplomate in Clinical Social Work recognised by American Board of Examiners. Memberships: National Association of Social Workers; Tennessee Conference on Social Welfare; American Association of University Professors, AAUP; Life Fellow, American Association on Mental Retardation; Church of Christ; Life Member, Sigma Kappa Sorority. Address: 627 Riverside Yorkville Road, Trenton, TN 38382-9513, USA.

McDAID Perry, (Phoenix Martin, Pam Louis), b. 10 October 1959, Derry City, Ireland. Writer. Education: BA, Social Sciences, Open University. Publications: Victims and Angels, 1999; Indaba, 2002. Contributions to: Anchor Books; Reach; Abbey Books; Dragonheart Press; Dragon Chronicle; Poetry Now; Banksnotes; Quill Books; Triumph House; Voice and Verse; Women's Words; Quantum Leap; Poetic Hours; Poetic Circle of Friends. Honours: Top 20 Living Poets, Dragonheart Press, 1997; Winner, Lost Poet, 1997; Winner, Wisbech OPC, 1998; Prizewinner, Sense of Sussex OPC, 1998; 2nd and 3rd Prizes, International ISP Competition, 1999. Memberships: Distinguished Member, International Society of Poets; Capricorn Guild of Poets. Address: The Crobie, Derry, Ireland.

McDANIEL David, b. 12 May 1952, Clarksburg, West Virginia. Cosmetic Dermatologist. m. Sheila. Education: Undergraduate, Degree received, BS cum laude Chemistry, 1974; MD, 1978, Internship, Pathology, Anatomic, 1979, Residency, Dermatology, 1980-83, West Virginia University Medical School, Morgantown, West Virginia, USA. Appointments: Clinical Instructor of Internal Medicine, Dermatology, Eastern Virginia Medical School, 1986-91; Assistant Professor of Clinical Dermatology, 1991-, Assistant Professor of Clinical Plastic Surgery, 1992-, Eastern Virginia Medical School; Adjunct Assistant Professor, Department of Biological Sciences, Old Dominion University; Command Consultant, Department of Plastic Surgery, Naval Medical Centre, Portsmouth, 1994-; Medical Director, Anti-Aging Research and Consulting. Publications: Author and co-author of numerous articles in medical journals; 4 patents issued and additional pending. Lectures, conferences. Honours: Phi Lambda Upsilon, National Chemistry Honorary – Undergraduate; Mountain, Undergraduate Men's Honorary. Address: 933 First Colonial Road, Suite 113, Virginia Beach, VA 23454, USA. E-mail: mail@lasercenterofvirginia.com

McDERMOTT Patrick Anthony, b. 8 September 1941, Ripley, Surrey, England. Her Majesty's Diplomatic Service, Retired. m. (1) 2 sons, (2) Christa Herminghaus, 2 sons. Education: Clapham College, London. Appointments: Foreign and Commonwealth Office, London, 1961-63; Mexico City, 1963-66; New York, 1966-71; Belgrade, 1971-73; Foreign and Commonwealth Office, London, 1973; Bonn, 1973-76; Paris, 1976-79; Foreign and Commonwealth Office, London, 1979-83; HM Consul-General and Economic and Financial Adviser to the British Military Government, West Berlin, 1984-88; Foreign and Commonwealth Office, London, 1988-89; Counsellor, Paris, 1990-95; Foreign and Commonwealth Office, London, 1996-97; HM Consul General, Moscow, 1998-2001; Retired, 2001-; Management Consultant, Diplomatic Consulting, 2001-02; Deputy Bursor, Ampleforth

College, 2002-. Honours: Member, Royal Victorian Order, 1972; Freeman of the City of London, 1986. Address: Linkfoot House, 10 Acres Close, Helmsley, York YO62 5DS, England.

McDONALD Catherine Donna, b. 20 December 1942, Vancouver, British Columbia, Canada. Writer; Arts Administrator. m. Robert Francis McDonald, 28 August 1965. Education: BA, 1964. Publications: Illustrated News: Juliana Horatia Ewing's Canadian Pictures 1867-1869; The Odyssey of the Philip Jones Brass Ensemble; Lord Strathcona; A Biography of Donald Alexander Smith; Milkmaids and Maharajas: A History of 1 Palace Street. Contributions to: Periodicals and journals. Address: 10 Chelwood Gardens, Richmond, Surrey TW9 4JQ, England.

McDONALD Forrest, b. 7 January 1927, Orange, Texas, USA. Distinguished University Research Professor; Historian; Writer. m. (1) 3 sons, 2 daughters, (2) Ellen Shapiro, 1 August 1963. Education: BA, MA, 1949, PhD, 1955, University of Texas. Appointments: Executive Secretary, American History Research Centre, Madison, Wisconsin, 1953-58; Associate Professor, 1959-63, Professor of History, 1963-67, Brown University; Professor, Wayne State University, 1967-76; Professor, 1976-87, Distinguished University Research Professor, 1987-, University of Alabama, Tuscaloosa; Presidential Appointee, Board of Foreign Scholarships, Washington, DC, 1985-87; Advisor, Centre of Judicial Studies, Cumberland, Virginia, 1985-92; James Pinckney Harrison Professor, College of William and Mary, 1986-87; Jefferson Lecturer, National Endowment for the Humanities, 1987. Publications: We the People: The Economic Origins of the Constitution, 1958; Insull, 1962; E Pluribus Unum: The Formation of the American Republic, 1965; The Presidency of George Washington, 1974; The Phaeton Ride, 1974; The Presidency of Thomas Jefferson, 1976; Alexander Hamilton: A Biography, 1979; Novus Ordo Seclorum, 1985; Requiem, 1988; The American Presidency: An Intellectual History, 1994; States' Rights and the Union 1776-1876, 2000. Contributions to: Professional journals. Honours: Guggenheim Fellowship, 1962-63; George Washington Medal, Freedom's Foundation, 1980; Frances Tavern Book Award, 1980; Best Book Award, American Revolution Round Table, 1986; Richard M Weaver Award, Ingersoll Foundation, 1990; First Salvatori Award, Intercollegiate Studies Institute, 1992; Salvatori Book Award, Intercollegiate Studies Institute, 1994; Mount Vernon Society Choice, One of the Ten Great Books on George Washington, 1998. Memberships: American Antiquarian Society; Philadelphia Society; The Historical Society. Address: PO Box 155, Coker, AL 35452, USA.

McDONALD Trevor, b. 16 August 1939, Trinidad. Broadcasting Journalist. m. 2 sons, 1 daughter. Appointments: Worked on newspapers, radio and TV, Trinidad, 1960-69; Producer, BBC Caribbean Service and World Service, London, 1969-73; Reporter, Independent TV News, 1973-78; Sports Correspondent, 1978-80; Diplomatic Correspondent, 1980-87; Newscaster, 1982-87; Diplomatic Editor, Channel 4 News, 1987-89; Newscaster, News at 5.40, 1989-90; News at Ten, 1990-99; ITV Evening News, 1999-2000; ITV News at Ten, 2001-; Chairman, Better English Campaign, 1995-97; Nuffield Language Inquiry, 1998-2000; Governor, English-Speaking Union of the Commonwealth, 2000; President, European Year of Languages, 2000. Publications: Clive Lloyd: a biography, 1985; Vivian Richard's biography, 1987; Queen and Commonwealth, 1989; Fortunate Circumstances, 1993; Favourite Poems, 1997; World of Poems, 1999. Honours: Hon DLitt, Nottingham, 1997; Dr hc, Open University, 1997; Honorary Fellow, Liverpool John Moores University, 1998; Newscaster of the Year, TV and Radio Industries Club, 1993, 1997, 1999; Gold Medal, Royal Television Society, 1998; Richard Dimbleby Award for Outstanding Contribution to Television, BAFTA, 1999; Knighted; OBE. Address: c/o ITN, 200 Gray's Inn Road, London, WC1 8XZ, England.

McDONNELL Kilian Perry, b. 16 September 1921, Great Falls, Montana, USA. Priest; Monk; Theologian. Education: BA, St John's University, Collegeville, Minnesota, 1947; Licentiate in Theology, University of Ottawa, Ontario, Canada, 1960; STD, Theological Faculty, Trier, Germany, 1964. Appointments: Professor of Theology, Graduate School, St John's University, Collegeville, Minnesota, 1964-92; Founder, 1967, Executive Director, 1967-73, President, 1973- Institute for Ecumenical and Cultural Research, Collegeville, Minnesota; Consultor for the Pontifical Council for Promoting Christian Unity, Vatican, Rome, 1987-2002. Publications: 12 books as author and co-author include: John Calvin, The Church and The Eucharist, 1967; The Baptism of Jesus in the Jordan: The Trinitarian and Cosmic Order of Salvation, 1996; The Otherhand of God: The Holy Spirit as the Universal Touch and Goal, 2003; Swift, Lord, You Are Not: The Experience of the Word of God (poetry), 2003; Numerous articles in Catholic and scholarly journals on aspects of theology and religion. Honours: Pro Pontifice et Ecclesia, a Papal award for ecumenism, 1983; Pax Christi Award, St John's University, Collegeville,1985; John Courtney Murray Award, Catholic Theological Society of America, 1993; Honorary Degree of Doctor in Humane Letters, Loyola University, Chicago, 1999; James Fitzgerald Award for Ecumenism, National Association of Diocesan Ecumenical Officers, 2001. Memberships: Catholic Theological Society; Academy of American Poets; Society for Pentecostal Studies. Address: St John's Abbey, Collegeville, MN 56321, USA. E-mail: kmcdonnell@csbsju.edu

McDONOUGH David Fergus, b. 7 June 1953, Eastbourne, Sussex. Public Relations. Education: MA honours, Merton College, Oxford, 1972-75. Appointments: Special Adviser, Basil Feldman, now Lord Feldman, 1975-79; Managing Director, McDonough Associates Ltd, 1980-90; Senior Consultant, 1990-2000, Director, 2001, Deputy Chairman, 2002-03, Bell Pottinger Consultants; Chairman, The McDonough Partnership, 2003. Honours: OBE, 1998; Officer of the Order of St John, 2002; Fellow, Royal Society of Arts. Memberships: White's; Boodles; The Hurlingham Club. Address: 18 Mimosa Street, London SW6 4DT, England. Email: david@mcdonoughpartnership.co.uk

McDORMAND Frances, b. 23 June 1957, Illinois, USA. Actress. m. Joel Coen, 1 son. Education: Yale University, School of Drama. Appointments: Stage Appearances include: Awake and Sing, 1984; Painting Churches, 1984; The Three Sisters, 1985; All My Sons, 1986; A Streetcar Named Desire, 1988; Moon for the Misbegotten, 1992; Sisters Rosenweig, 1993; The Swan, 1993; Films include: Blood Simple, 1984; Raising Arizona, 1987; Mississippi Burning, 1988; Chattaboochee, 1990; Darkman, 1990; Miller's Crossing, 1990; Hidden Agenda, 1990; The Butcher's Wife, 1991; Passed Away, 1992; Short Cuts, 1993; Beyond Rangoon, 1995; Fargo, 1996; Paradise Road, 1997; Johnny Skidmarks, 1997; Madeline, 1998; Talk of Angels, 1998; Wonder Boys, 1999; Almost Famous, 2000; The Man Who Wasn't There, 2001; Upheaval, 2001; Laurel Canyon, 2002; City By the Sea, 2003; Something's Gotta Give, 2003; Catwoman, 2004; Has appeared in several TV series. Honours: Screen Actors' Guild Award, 1996; London Film Critics' Circle Award, 1996; Independent Spirit Award, 1996; American Comedy Award, 1997; LA Film Critics Award, 2000. Address: c/o William Morris Agency, 1325 Avenue of the Americas, New York, NY 10019, USA.

McDOUGALL Bonnie Suzanne, b. 12 March 1941, Sydney, Australia. Professor of Chinese. m. H Anders Hansson, 1 son. Education: BA honours, 1965, MA honours, University Medal,

1967, PhD, 1970, University of Sydney. Appointments: Lecturer in Oriental Studies, University of Sydney, 1972-76; Research Fellow, East Asian Research Center, Harvard University, 1976-79; Associate in East Asian Studies, John King Fairbank Center, Harvard University, 1979-80; Visiting Lecturer on Chinese, Harvard University, 1977-78; Editor and Translator, Foreign Languages Press, Peking, 1980-83; Teacher of English, College of Foreign Affairs, Peking, 1984-86; Senior Lecturer in Chinese, University of Oslo, 1986-87; Professor of Modern Chinese, University of Oslo, 1987-90; Professor of Chinese, University of Edinburgh, 1990-. Publications: Numerous books and articles on Chinese Literature. Memberships: Association for Asian Studies; European Association of Chinese Studies; British Association of Chinese Studies; Universities' China Committee in London; Scots Australian Council. Address: Scottish Centre for Chinese Studies, School of Asian Studies, University of Edinburgh, 8 Buccleuch Place, Edinburgh EH8 9LW, Scotland.

McDOWALL David Buchanan, b. 14 April 1945, London, England. Writer. m. Elizabeth Mary Risk Laird, 19 April 1975, 2 sons. Education: MA, 1966-69, M.Litt, 1970-72, St John's College, Oxford. Appointments: Subaltern, Royal Artillery, UK and Hong Kong, 1963-70; British Council, Bombay, Baghdad and London Headquarters, 1972-77; Contributions Officer, United Nations Relief and Works Agency for Palestine Refugees in the Near East, 1977-79; Consultant to voluntary agencies re development in Middle East, 1979-84; Full-time Writer, 1984-. Publications: Lebanon: A Conflict of Minorities, 1984 Palestine and Israel: The Uprising and Beyond, 1989; An Illustrated History of Britain, 1989; Europe and the Arabs: Discord or Symbiosis?, 1992; Britain in Close Up, 1993, 1998; The Palestinians: The Road to Nationhood, 1994; A Modern History of the Kurds, 1996; Richmond Park: The Walker's Historical Guide, 1996; Hampstead Heath: The Walker's Guide (co-author Deborah Wolten), 1998; The Kurds of Syria, 1998; The Thames from Hampton to Richmond Bridge: The Walkers Guide, 2002. Contributions to: World Directory of Minorities, Middle East section, 1997. Honour: The Other Award. Address: 31 Cambrian Road, Richmond, Surrey TW10 6JQ, England.

McDOWELL Malcolm, b. 13 June 1943, Leeds, England. Actor. m. (1) Mary Steenburgen, 1980, 1 son, 1 daughter, (2) Kelley Kuhr, 1992. Appointments: Began career with Royal Shakespeare Company, Stratford, 1965-66; Early TV appearances in such series as Dixon of Dock Green; Z Cars; Stage Appearances: RSC, Stratford, 1965-66; Entertaining Mr Sloane, Royal Court, 1975; Look Back in Anger, New York, 1980; In Celebration, New York, 1984; Holiday Old Vic, 1987; Another Time, Old Vic, 1993; Films Include: If..., 1969; Figures in a Landscape, 1970; The Raging Moon, 1971; A Clockwork Orange, 1971; O Lucky Man, 1973; Royal Flash, 1975; Aces High, 1976; Voyage of the Damned, 1977; Caligula, 1977; The Passage, 1978; Time After Time, 1979; Cat People, 1981; Blue Thunder, 1983; Get Crazy, 1983; Britannia Hospital, 1984; Gulag, 1985; The Caller, 1987; Sunset, 1987; Sunrise, 1988; Class of 1999, Il Maestro, 1989; Moon 44; Double Game; Class of 1999; Snake Eyes, Schweitzer; Assassin of the Tsar, 1991; The Player; Chain of Desire; East Wind; Night Train to Venice; Star Trek: Generations, 1995; Tank Girl, 1995; Kids of the Round Table; Where Truth Lies; Mr Magoo, 1998; Gangster No 1, 2000; TV include: Our Friends in the North. Address: c/o Markham and Froggatt, 4 Windmill Street, London, W1P 1HF, England.

McELLISTREM Marcus T, b. 19 April 1926, St Paul, Minnesota, USA. Emeritus Professor of Physics. m. Eleanor, 1 son, 5 daughters. Education: BA, St Thomas College, St Paul; MS, 1952, PhD, 1956, University of Wisconsin, Madison.

Appointments: Research Associate, Indiana University, 1955-57; Assistant Professor, 1957-60, Associate Professor, 1960-65, Professor, 1965-, University of Kentucky; Director, Accelerator Laboratory, University of Kentucky, 1974-. Publications: 95 articles in professional journals. Honours: Distinguished Professor, Arts and Sciences, 1981-82; Kentucky Distinguished Scientist Award, 1992; President, Kentucky Academy of Sciences, 1997. Memberships: Fellow, American Physical Society; Kentucky Academy of Sciences. Address: Department of Physics and Astronomy, University of Kentucky, Lexington, KY 40506-0055, USA.

McENROE John Patrick, b. 16 February 1959, Wiesbaden, Federal Republic of Germany. Lawn Tennis Player. m. (1) Tatum O'Neil, 1986, 2 sons, 1 daughter, (2) Patty Smyth, 2 daughters, 1 step-daughter. Education: Trinity High School, New Jersey; Stanford University, California. Appointments: Amateur Player, 1976-78; Professional, 1978-93; USA Singles Champion, 1979, 1980, 1981, 1984; USA Doubles Champion, 1979, 1981, 1989; Wimbledon Champion (doubles), 1979, 1981, 1983, 1984, 1992 (singles) 1981, 1983, 1984; WCT Champion, 1979, 1981, 1983, 1984, 1989; Grand Prix Champion, 1979, 1983, 1984; Played Davis Cup for USA, 1978, 1979, 1980, 1982, 1983, 1984, 1985; Only Player to have reached Wimbledon semi-finals (1977) as pre-tournament qualifier; Semi Finalist, 1989; Tennis Sportscaster, USA Network, 1993; Member, Men's Senior's Tours Circuits, 1994; Winner, Quality Challenge, Worldwide Senior Tennis Circuit, 1999; Owner, John McEnroe Gallery. Publications: You Cannot Be Serious, autobiography, 2002. Honour: International Tennis Hall of Fame, 1999. Address: c/o John P McEnroe Sr, Paul Weiss Rifkind Wharton and Garrison, 1285 Avenue of the Americas, New York, NY 10019, USA.

McEWAN Ian, b. 21 June 1948, Aldershot, Hampshire, England. Author. m. (1) Penny Allen, 1982, divorced, 1995, 2 sons, 2 step daughters, (2) Annalena McAfee, 1997. Education: Woolverstone Hall; University of Sussex; University of East Anglia; Hon D Phil, Sussex, 1989; East Anglia, 1993. Publications: First Love, Last Rites, 1975; In Between the Sheets, 1978; The Cement Gardens, 1978; The Imitation Game, 1980; The Comfort of Strangers, 1981; Or Shall we Die?, 1983; The Ploughman's Lunch, 1983; The Child in Time, 1987; Soursweet (screenplay), 1987; A Move Abroad, 1989; The Innocent, 1990; Black Dogs, 1992; The Daydreamer, 1994; The Short Stories, 1995; Enduring Love, 1997; Amsterdam (novel), 1998; Atonement, 2001. Honours: Somerset Maugham Prize, 1975; Primo Letterario, Prato, 1982; Whitbread Fiction Prize, 1987; Prix Femina, 1993; Booker Prize, 1998; Shakespeare Prize, 1999; National Book Critics Circle Award, 2003. Address: c/o Jonathan Cape, Random Century House, 20 Vauxhall Bridge Road, London SW1V 2SA, England. Website: www.ianmcewan.com

McFALL John, b. 1944, Member of Parliament. m. Joan McFall, 3 sons, 1 daughter. Education: BSc honours, Chemistry; BA honours, Education; MBA. Appointments: School teacher, Assistant Head Teacher, -1987; Member of Parliament for Dumbarton, 1987-; Opposition Whip with responsibility for Foreign Affairs, Defence and Trade and Industry, 1990; Deputy Shadow Secretary of State for Scotland with responsibility for Industry and Economic Affairs; Employment and Training; Home Affairs, Transport and Roads; Highland and Islands, 1992-97; Lord Commissioner, 1997-98; Parliamentary Under Secretary of State, Northern Ireland Office, 1998-99; Chairman of the Treasury Select Committee, 2001. Memberships: British/Hong Kong Group; British/Italian Group; British/Peru Group; Retail Industry Group; Roads Study Group; Scotch Whisky Group; Parliamentary and Scientific Committee; Select Committee on Defence; Select Committee on Sittings of the House; Executive Committee

Parliamentary Group for Energy Studies; Information Committee; Executive Committee Parliamentary Group for Energy Studies. Address: House of Commons, London SW1A 0AA, England. E-mail: mcfallj@parliament.uk

McGEACHIE Daniel, b. 10 June 1935, Barrhead, Glasgow, Scotland. Journalist; Company Director. m. Sylvia Andrew, 1 daughter. Appointments: Journalist, Scotland and Fleet Street, 1955-60; Foreign Correspondent, Daily Express, 1960-65; Parliamentary Correspondent, Diplomatic and Political Correspondent, Daily Express, 1965-75; Political Advisor, Conoco UK Ltd, 1975-77; Director, General Manager, Government and Public Affairs, Conoco UK Ltd, 1977-2000. Honours: OBE for services to Industry and Government relations, 1992. Memberships: Council member, Industry-Parliament Trust; Member, Parliamentary Energy Studies Group; Company member, Royal Institute of International Affairs; Member, Reform Club. Address: 27 Hitherwood Drive, London SE19 1XA, England. Email: danmcgeachie@ukgateway.net

McGEOCH Ian Lachlan Mackay, b. 26 March 1914, Helensburgh, Scotland. Naval Officer. m. Eleanor Somers Farrie, 2 sons, 2 daughters. Education: Nautical College, Pangbourne, England. Appointments: Cadet, Royal Navy, 1931; Commanded HMS submarine Splendid, 1942-43; Commanded HMS Fernie, 1946-47; Naval Liaison Officer, RAF Costal and Bomber Commands, 1955-57; Commanded HMS Adamant and third submarine flotilla, 1957-58; Director, Undersurface Warfare Division Naval Staff, 1959-60; Imperial Defence College, 1961; Commanded HMS Lion, 1962-64; Flag Officer, Submarines and NATO Commander Submarines, Eastern Atlantic, 1965-67; Vice Admiral, Flag Officer Scotland and Northern Ireland, and NATO Commander Northern Sub-Area, Eastern Atlantic and Commander Nore Sub-Area, Channel, 1968-70; Director, Midar Systems Ltd, 1986-. Publications: Editor, The Naval Review, 1972-80; Co-author: The Third World War: a future history, 1978; The Third World War: the untold story, 1982; Author: An Affair of Chances, 1991; The Princely Sailor: Mountbatten of Burma, 1996. Honours: Companion of Distinguished Service Order, 1943; Mentioned in Despatches, 1944; Distinguished Service Cross, 1944; Companion of the Most Honourable Order of the Bath, 1966; Knight Commander of the Most Honourable Order of the Bath, 1969; MPhil, Edinburgh University, 1975. Memberships: The Queen's Bodyguard for Scotland, Royal Company of Archers; Member, Honourable Company of Master Mariners; Fellow, Royal Institute of Navigation; Fellow, Nautical Institute; Naval Member, Royal Yacht Squadron; Life Vice Commodore, Royal Naval Sailing Association; Member, Royal Cruising Club; Royal, Harwich Yacht Club. Address: Hill House, High Street, Ixworth, Bury St Edmunds, Suffolk IP31 2HN, England.

McGEOWN Mary Graham, b. 19 July 1923, Lurgan, Northern Ireland. Physician. m. Joseph Maxwell Freeland, deceased, 3 sons. Education: MD, 1950, PhD, 1953, FRCPE, 1969, MRCPE, 1967, Queen's University of Belfast. Appointments include: Research Fellow, Royal Victoria Hospital Belfast, 1956-58; Consultant Nephrologist, Belfast Hospitals, 1962-88; Physician in administrative charge of the Renal Unit, Belfast City Hospital, 1968-88; Chairman UK Transplant Management Committee, 1983-90; Honorary Reader, 1972-88, Professorial Fellow, 1988-, Queens University, Belfast. Publications: Numerous articles and chapters in the field of calcium metabolism, kidney diseases treatment, kidney transplantation; Books: Clinical Management of Electrolyte Disorders, 1983; Clinical Management of Renal Transplantation, 1992. Honours include: CBE; Honorary Member, Renal Association, British Transplantation Society, European Dialysis and Transplantation Association, European Dialysis and Transplant

Dictionary of International Biography

Nurses Association; Honorary DSc, University of Ulster, 1983; Honorary DMSc, Queen's University of Belfast, 1991. Memberships: Association of Physicians; European Dialysis and Transplantation Association; American Society of Artificial Internal Organs; British Association of Urological Surgery; International Society of Nephrology. Address: 14 Osborne Gardens, Belfast BT9 6LE, Northern Ireland.

McGOUGH Roger, b. 9 November 1937, Liverpool, England. Poet. m. Hilary Clough, 1986, 3 sons, 1 daughter. Education: St Mary's College, Crosby; BA and Graduate Certificate of Education, Hull University. Appointments: Fellow of Poetry, University of Loughborough, 1973-75; Writer-in-Residence, West Australian College of Advanced Education, Perth, 1986. Publications: The Mersey Sound (with Brian Patten and Adrian Henri), 1967; Strictly Private (editor), 1982; An Imaginary Menagerie, 1989; Blazing Fruit (selected poems 1967-87), 1990; Pillow Talk, 1990; The Lighthouse That Ran Away, 1991; You at the Back (selected poems 1967-87, Vol 2), 1991; My Dad's a Fire Eater, 1992; Defying Gravity, 1992; The Elements, 1993; Lucky, 1993; Stinkers Ahoy!, 1994; The Magic Fountain, 1995; The Kite and Caitlin, 1996; Sporting Relations, 1996; Bad, Bad Cats, 1997; Until I Met Dudley, 1997; The Spotted Unicorn, 1998; The Ring of Words (editor), 1998; The Way Things Are, 1999; Everyday Eclipses, 2002; Good Enough to Eat, 2002; Moonthief, 2002; Wicked Poems (editor), 2002; Collected Poems of Roger McGough, 2003; What on Earth Can It Be? 2003. Honours: Honorary Professor, Thames Valley University, 1993; Officer of the Order of the British Empire, 1997; Honorary MA, 1998; Cholmondeley Award, 1998; Fellow, John Moores University, Liverpool, 1999. Address: c/o The Peters, Fraser and Dunlop Group Ltd, Drury House, 34 – 43 Russell Street, London WC2B 5HA, England.

McGREGOR Ewan, b. 31 March 1971, Perth, Scotland. Actor. m. Eve Mavrakis, 1995, 2 children. Education: Guildhall School of Music and Drama. Appointments: Formerly with Perth Repertory Theatre; Theatre include: What the Butler Saw; Little Malcolm and his Struggle against the Eunuchs, Hampstead Theatre Club, 1989; TV includes: Lipstick on Your Collar; Scarlet and Black; Kavanagh QC; Doggin Around; Tales from the Crypt; ER; Films include: Being Human; Family Style; Shallow Grave; Blue Juice; The Pillow Book; Trainspotting; Emma; Brassed Off; Nightwatch; The Serpent's Kiss; A Life Less Ordinary; Velvet Goldmine; Star Wars Episode I: The Phantom Menace; Little Voice; Rogue Trader; Eye of the Beholder; Nora; Moulin Rouge, 2001; Black Hawk Down, 2002; Stars Wars Episode II: Attack of the Clones, 2002; Down with Love, 2003; Young Adam, 2003; Faster, 2003; Big Fish, 2003. Honours: Best Actor Dinard Film Festival, 1994; Best Actor, Berlin Film Festival; Empire Award; Variety Club Awards; Film Critics' Awards. Address: c/o Peters, Fraser and Dunlop, Drury House, 34-43 Russell Street, London, Wc2B 5HA, England.

McGREGOR Ralph, b. 11 February 1932, Leeds, England. Professor Emeritus. m. Maureen McGaul, 2 sons, 1 daughter. Education: BSc, First Class Honours, 1953, PhD, Applied Chemistry, 1957, University of Leeds, England. Appointments: Science Teacher, Roundhay High School, Leeds, 1956-58; Courtaulds Research Fellow, University of Manchester Institute of Science and Technology, 1958-59; Lecturer in Polymer and Fibre Science, UMIST, 1959-68; Visiting Senior Researcher, Ciba A G, Basel Switzerland, 1965-66; Senior Scientist, Fibers Division, Allied Chemica Corporation, Petersburg, Virginia, USA, 1968-70; From Professor to Cone Mills Distinguished Professor in Textile Chemistry, North Carolina State University, USA, 1970-98; Visiting Senior Researcher, Swiss Federal Institute of Technology, Zurich, Switzerland, 1998-99. Publications: Over 100 refereed papers in a wide range of scientific journals; Research monograph: Diffusion and Sorption in Fibres and Films, 1974. Honours: Le Blanc Medal of Leeds University as the outstanding undergraduate student in the Faculty of Technology; Perkin Travel Grants, Sweden, 1962, Switzerland,1965-66; Research Medal, Worshipful Company of Dyers, 1976; Honorary Doctor of Science, University of Leeds, 1979; National Science Foundation Grant, Japan, 1981; Grant from Tokyo Institute of Technology, Japan, 1986; Olney Medal, American Association of Textile Chemists, 1984; Grant for collaborative research, Swiss Federal Institute of Technology, 1993, renewed 1998-99. E-mail: rmcgrago@bellsouth.net

McGUINNESS Martin, b. Derry, Northern Ireland. Politican. m. 4 children. Appointments: Took part in secret London Talks between Secretary of State for Northern Ireland and Irish Republicans Army (IRA), 1972; Imprisoned for six months during 1973, Irish Republic, after conviction for IRA membership; Elected to North Ireland Association, Refused Seat; Stood against John Hume in General Elections of 1982, 1987, 1992; MP for Mid-Ulster, House of Commons, 1997-; Member, Ulster-Mid, Northern Ireland Association, 1998-2000, Association suspended 11 February 2000; Minister of Education, 1999-2000; Spokesperson for Sinn Féin; Member of National Executive; Involved in Peace Negotiations with British Government. Address: Sinn Féin, 51-55 Falls Road, Belfast, BT12 4PD, Northern Ireland.

McGUIRE John L, b. 3 November 1942, Kittanning, Pennsylvania, USA. Research Executive. m. Pamela Hale, 2 daughters. Education: BS, Butler University, Indianapolis, Indiana, 1965; MA, PhD, Biochemistry and Physiology, Princeton University, Princeton, NJ, 1968-69; Postdoctoral Fellow, The Population Council. Appointments: Adjunct Professor of Obstetrics, Gynaecology and Reproductive Endo, University of Medicine and Dentistry of New Jersey; Adjunct Professor, Department of Obstetrics and Gynaecology, Eastern Virginia School of Medicine; Adjunct Associate Professor, Department of Clinical Pharmacology, MS Hershey School of Medicine; Assistant in Instruction, Princeton University, 1968-69; Pharmacologist, 1969-72; Section Head, Molecular Biology, 1972-75; Executive Director of Research, 1975-80; VP of Preclinical R&D, 1980-88, Ortho Pharmaceutical Corp, Raritan, New Jersey, USA; Senior Vice President, Research and Development Worldwide, R W Johnson Pharmaceutical Research Institute, Raritan, New Jersey, 1988-92; Corp Vice President, Business Development, Johnson & Johnson, New Brunswick, New Jersey, 1992-2004; President, Ferring Research Institutes, Copenhagen, Denmark, 2004-. Publications: Over 200 publications and Patents. Honour: Johnson Medal for Research and Development. Memberships: Biochemical Society of Great Britain; Royal Society of Medicine; The American Physiological Society; Society Experimental Biology and Medicine; American Society of Pharmacology and Experimental Therapeutics; American Society of Clinical Pharmacology and Therapeutics; Society of Gynaecological Investigation. Address: Ferring Pharmaceuticals, Copenhagen, Denmark.

McGURN Barrett, b. 6 August 1914, New York, New York, USA. Author. m. Janice Ann McLaughlin, 5 sons, 1 daughter. Education: AB, Fordham University, 1935. Appointments: Reporter, New York Herald Tribune, 1935-66, Bureau Chief, Rome, Paris, Moscow, 1946-62; US Foreign Service, Rome, Saigon; Foreign Service Officer, State Department, Washington, 1966-72; Communications Director, US Supreme Court, 1973-82; Communications Director, Archdiocese of Washington, 1983-89. Publications: Decade in Europe, 1958; A Reporter Looks at the Vatican, 1962; A Reporter Looks at American Catholicism, 1967; America's Court, The Supreme Court and the People, 1997; The Pilgrim's Guide to Rome for the Millennium, 1999; Yank,

Dictionary of International Biography

Voice of the Greatest Generation, 2004. Honours: Best US Foreign Correspondent, Long Island University Award, New York, 1956; Best US Foreign Correspondent, Overseas Press Club, 1957; Honorary Doctorate of Letters, Fordham University, New York, 1958; Grand Knight, Italian National Order of Merit, 1962; Pulitzer Prize Nomination, 1966; US State Department Meritorious Honour Award, 1972. Memberships: Overseas Press Club of America, President, 1963-65; Association of Foreign Correspondents in Italy, President, 1961, 1962; National Press Club, Washington DC; Cosmos Club, Washington DC. Address: 5229 Duvall Drive, Bethesda, MD 20816, USA. E-mail: jmcgurn@erols.com

McILWAIN Clara Evans, b. 5 April 1919, Jacksonville, Florida, USA. Economist; Teacher. m. Ivy, deceased, 1 son, 3 daughters. Education: BS, District of Columbia, University of Education, History, Geography, 1939; MS, Agricultural Economics, University of Florida, 1972. Appointments: Statistician, Agricultural Economicst; Programme Analyst, US Department of Agriculture, 1960-79; Adjunct Professor, Patman College, 2003. Publications: Steps to Eloquence with the Wonder of God; Blazing the Trail to the Kingdom of God. Honours: Scholarship, University of Florida, 1970; Member, Omega Phi Epsilon Honor Society in Economics. Memberships: Omicron Delta Epsilon, Toastmasters International; American Agricultural Economics Association. Address: 6612, Denny Place, McLean, VA 22102, USA. E-mail: phyllis52003@yahoo.com

McINERNEY Jay, b. USA. Writer. m. (1) Linda Rossiter, (2) Merry Raymond, (3) Helen Bransford, 1991, 1 son, 1 daughter. Education: Williams University. Publications: Bright Lights, Big City, 1984; Ransom, 1986; Story of My Life, 1988; Brightness Falls, 1992; The Last of the Savages, 1996; Model Behaviour, 1998; How It Ended, 2000.

McINTOSH Ronald Robert Duncan, b. 26 September 1919, Whitehaven, England. Public Service. m. Doreen Frances MacGinnity. Education: MA, Balliol College, Oxford. Appointments: Merchant Navy, 1939-45; Counsellor, British High Commission, New Delhi, 1957-61; Deputy Secretary, Cabinet Office, 1968-70; Director General, National Economic Development Office, 1973-77; Director, SG Warburg and Co and other companies, 1978-89; Chairman, APV plc, 1982-89. Honours: KCB; Honorary DSc, Aston University. Memberships: Co-chairman, British Hungarian Round Table, 1980-84; Chairman, Danish-UK Chamber of Commerce, 1990-92; Chairman, British Health Consortium for the former Soviet Union, 1992-97. Address: The Thatched Cottage, Throwley, Faversham ME13 0PN, England.

McINTYRE Ian (James), b. 9 December 1931, Banchory, Kincardineshire, Scotland. Writer; Broadcaster. m. Leik Sommerfelt Vogt, 1954, 2 sons, 2 daughters. Education: BA, 1953, MA, 1960, St John's College, Cambridge; College of Europe, Bruges, Belgium, 1953-54. Appointments include: National Service, Commissioned in the Intelligence Corps, 1955-57; BBC Current Affairs Talks Producer, 1957; Editor, At Home and Abroad, 1959; Programme Services Officer, Independent Television Authority, 1961-62; Director of Information and Research, Scottish Conservative Central Office, 1962-70; Writer, Broadcaster, 1970-76, Controller, Radio 4, 1976-78, Controller, Radio 3, 1978-87, British Broadcasting Corporation; Associate Editor, The Times, London, 1989-90. Publications: The Proud Doers: Israel After Twenty Years, 1968; Words: Reflections on the Uses of Language, editor, contributor, 1975; Dogfight: The Transatlantic Battle over Airbus, 1992; The Expense of Glory: A Life of John Reith, 1993; Dirt and Deity: A Life of Robert Burns, 1996; Garrick, 1999.

Honour: Winner, Theatre Book Prize, 1999. Memberships; Union Society, Cambridge; Beefsteak Club. Address: Spylaw House, Newlands Avenue, Radlett, Hertfordshire WD7 8EL, England.

McINTYRE James Archibald, b. 2 September 1926, Stranraer, Scotland. Retired Farmer. m. Hilma Wilson Brown, 1 son, 2 daughters. Education: Oxford University, 1944, 6 months short army course. Commissioned 12 H Royal Lancers, 1945-47; West of Scotland Horticultural College, 1948-49. Appointments: Council Member, 1962-72, President, 1969, National Farmers Union, Scotland; Member, 1973-, Chairman, 1985-95, Dumfries and Galloway Health Board; Board Member, NFU Mutual Insurance, 1983-93. Honours: JP, 1989; OBE, 1989; CBE, 1995; O St J, 1979; C St J, 2000. Memberships: National Farmers Union, Scotland, 1950-; Member, Order of St John, 1972-. Address: Glenorchy, Broadstone Road, Stranraer, Scotland.

McINTYRE Michael Edgeworth, b. 28 July 1941, Sydney, Australia. Scientist. m. Ruth Hecht, 2 step-sons, 1 step-daughter. Education: BSc Hons (1st class), Mathematics, University of Otago, New Zealand, 1963; PhD, Geophysical Fluid Dynamics, University of Cambridge, England, 1967. Appointments: Assistant Lecturer, Mathematics, University of Otago New Zealand, 1963; Postdoctoral Research Associate, Department of Meteorology, Massachusetts Institute of Technology, USA, 1967-69; Assistant Director of Research in Dynamical Meteorology, 1969-72, University Lecturer, 1972-87, Reader, Atmospheric Dynamics, 1987-93, Professor, Atmospheric Dynamics, 1993-, Department of Applied Mathematics and Theoretical Physics, University of Cambridge; Co-Director, Cambridge Centre for Atmospheric Science, 1992-2003; Principal Investigator, UK Universities' Global Atmospheric Modelling Programme, Natural Environmental Research Council, 1990-; Senior Consultant, Jet Propulsion Laboratory, Pasadena, California, USA, 1991-; Scientific Steering Committee, STRATEOLE experiment (quasi-Lagrangian tracers in the Antarctic stratospheric vortex), 1992-. Publications: Author and co-author of over 100 articles in learned scientific journals and conference proceedings, including most recently: On shear-generated gravity waves that reach the mesosphere, 1999; Potential-vorticity inversion on a hemisphere, 2000; Balance and the slow quasimanifold: some explicit results, 2000; Balance, potential-vorticity inversion, Lighthill radiation and the slow quasimanifold, 2001; Some fundamental aspects of atmospheric dynamics with a solar spin-off, 2002; Wind-generated water waves: two overlooked mechanisms?, 2004; Solar tachocline dynamics: eddy viscosity, anti-friction, or something in between?, 2003; Remote recoil: a new wave-mean interaction effect, 2003. Honours include: Research Fellowship, St John's College, Cambridge, 1968-71; Adams Prize, University of Cambridge, 1981; Carl-Gustaf Rossby Research Medal, American Meteorological Society, 1987; Distinguished Sackler Lecturer, University of Tel Aviv, Israel, 1995; Julius Bartels Medal, European Geophysical Society, 1999. Memberships include: Academia Europaea, 1989-; Fellow of the Royal Society, 1990-; Fellow, American Meteorological Society, 1990-; Fellow, American Association for the Advancement of Science, 1999. Address: Department of Applied Mathematics and Theoretical Physics, Centre for Mathematical Sciences, Wilberforce Road, Cambridge, CB3 0WA, England. Website: www.atm.damtp.cam.ac.uk/people/mem

McISAAC Ian, b. 13 July 1945. Chartered Accountant. m. (1) Joanna Copland, dissolved, 1 son, 1 daughter, (2) Debrah Ball, 1 son, 1 daughter. Education: Charterhouse scholar. Appointments: Partner, Touche Ross (UK), 1979-88; Touche Ross (Canada), 1983-85; Chief Executive, Richard Ellis Finanacial Services, 1988-91; Partner, Deloitte and Touche (formerly Touche Ross), 1991-; Global Head, Reorganisation Service, 1999-, UK Chairman,

Emerging Markets, 2000-; Chairman, Society of Turaround Professionals, Director, Care International (UK). Honours: Freeman of the City of London; Member of the Worshipful Company of Chartered Accountants; ACA, 1969; FCA, 1979. Memberships: City of London Club; Hurlingham Club; Royal Mid-Surrey Golf Club; High Post Golf Club; OCYC. Address: 28 Hereford Square, London SW7. E-mail: imcisaac@deloitte.co.uk

McKEE Patrick A, b. 30 April 1937, Tulsa, Oklahoma. Professor of Medicine. m. Sarah Jane Grant, 2 sons, 3 daughters. Education: Doctorate of Medicine, University of Oklahoma College of Medicine, 1958-62. Appointments: George Lynn Cross Professor of Medicine, Laureate Chair of Molecular Medicine; Scientific Director, Warren Medical Research Center Institute, University of Oklahoma Health Sciences Center. Publications: Incidence and significance of cryofibrinogenemia; The sunbunit polypeptides of human fibrinogen; The natural history of congestive heart failure; Phylogeny of baboonfibrin-fibrinolysis; Effects of the spleen on canine factor VIII; Activation of human plasmagen; Structure of human fibrin stabilizing factor; Structure-function studies of human Von Willebrand factor; Many others. Honours: Phi Eta Sigma; B C Barclay Scholarship; McClure Scholarship; Sword and Key Scholastic Honour Society; Student Research Achievement Award; Physician of the Year; George Lynn Cross Professor of Medicine; Laureate Chair of Molecular Medicine. Memberships: Alpha Omega Alpha; American Clinical and Climatological Society; American Society for Clinical Investigation; American Medical Association; American Heart Association; Association of American Physicians; Many others. Address: BSEB-321, PO Box 26901, W K Warren Medical Research Center, Oklahoma City, OK 73190, USA.

McKEEVER Paul Edward, b. 3 December 1946, Pasadena, California. Professor. m. Mary Olivia, 1 son, 2 daughters. Education: BS Biology, Brown University, Providence Rhode Island, 1964-68; MD, University of California, 1972; PhD, Medical University of South Carolina, 1976. Appointments: Anatomic Pathology Intern and Cardiopulmonary Trainee, University of California, 1972-73; Neuropathology Fellow and Anatomic Pathology Resident, Medical University of South Carolina, 1973-6; Research Associate, 1976-79, Consultant in Neuropathology, 1976-83, Clinical Associate Professor, 1978-83, Neuropathologist, 1979-83, Pathology Consultant, 1980-83, Bethesda, Maryland; Chief, Department of Pathology, 1983-, Staff Physician, 1983-, Associate Professor, 1983-99, Director, Nerve and Muscle Biopsy Service, 1985-89, Director, Neurohistology Laboratory, 1996, Professor, University of Michigan, 1999-. Publications: Numerous books and articles. Honours include: Mosby Book Award, 1972; Who's Who in the East, 1978; American Men and Women of Science, 1980. Memberships: International Academy of Pathology; American Association of Neuropathologists; Society for Neuroscience; American Association of Pathologists; Children's Oncology Group; Histochemical Society, Publications Committee, Future Directions Committee. Address: Pathology Department, University of Michigan, Box 0602, 1301 Catherine St, Rm M5228, Ann Arbor, MI 48109-0602, USA.

McKELLEN Ian Murray (Sir), b. 25 May 1939, Burnley, Lancashire, England. Actor. Education: Bolton School; St Catherines College, Cambridge. Appointments: First stage appearance, Roper (A Man for All Seasons), Belgrade Theatre, Coventry, 1961; Numerous other parts including: Royal National Theatre: Bent, Max; King Lear, Kent; Richard III, world tour then US tour, 1990-92; Napoli Milionaria, 1991; Uncle Vanya, 1992; An Enemy of the People, 1997; Peter Pan, 1997; The Seagull, Present Laughter, The Tempest, West Yorkshire Playhouse, 1998-99; Dance of Death, Broadhurst Theatre, New York, 2001; Films include: Alfred the Great, 1969; The Promise, 1969; A Touch of Love, 1969; Priest of Love, 1981; The Keep, 1982; Plenty, Zina, 1985; Scandal, 1988; The Ballad of Little Jo, 1992; I'll do Anything, 1992; Last Action Hero, 1993; Six Degrees of Seperation, 1993; The Shadow, 1994; Jack and Sarah, 1994; Restoration, 1994; Richard III, 1995; Bent, 1996; Swept From Sea, 1996; Apt Pupil, 1997; Gods and Monsters, 1998; X-Men, 1999; Lord of the Rings: The Fellowship of the Ring, 2001; Lord of the Rings: The Two Towers, 2002; X-Men 2, 2003; Emile, 2003; Lord of the Rings: The Return of the King, 2003; TV appearances include: David Copperfield, 1965; Ross, 1969; Richard II; Edward II; Hamlet, 1970; Hedda Gabler, 1974; Macbeth; Every Good Boy Deserves Favour, Dying Day, 1979; Acting Shakespeare, 1981; Walter; The Scarlet Pimpernel, 1982; Walter and June, 1983; Countdown to War, 1989; Othello, 1990; Tales of the City, 1993; Cold Comfort Farm, 1995; Cameron Mackintosh Professor of Contemporary Theatre Oxford University, 1991. Publications: William Shakespeare's Richard III, 1996. Honours: Clarence Derwent Award, 1964; Hon D Litt, 1989; Variety and Plays and Players Awards, 1966; Actor of the Year, Plays and Players, 1976; Society of West End Theatres Award for Best Actor in a Revival, 1977, for Best Comedy Performance, 1978, for Best Actor in a New Play, 1979; Tony Award, 1981; Drama Desk, 1981; Outer Critics Circle Award, 1981; Royal TV Society Performer of the Year, 1983; Laurence Olivier Award, 1984, 1991; Evening Standard Best Actor Award, 1984, 1989; Screen Actor's Guild Award for besting supporting Actor, 2000. Address: c/o ICM 76 Oxford Street, London, W1N 0AX, England.

McKENDRICK Melveena Christine, b. 23 March 1941, Crynant, Neath, Wales. Hispanist. m. Neil McKendrick, 2 daughters. Education: BA 1st class honours, Spanish, King's College, London; PhD, Girton College, Cambridge, 1967. Appointments: Jex-Blake Research Fellow, 1967-70, Tutor, 1970-83, Senior Tutor, 1974-81, Director of Studies in Modern Languages, 1984-95, Girton College, Cambridge; Lecturer in Spanish, 1980-92, Reader in Spanish Literature and Society, 1992-99, Professor of Spanish, Golden-Age Literature, Culture and Society, 1999-, University of Cambridge; British Academy Reader, 1992-94, Visiting Professor, University of Victoria, 1997; Fellow of the British Academy, 1999-. Publications: Author and co-author, numerous books; Articles on Early Modern Spanish theatre in many journals. Memberships: General Board, Cambridge University, 1993-97; Humanities Research Board, British Academy, 1996-98; Arts and Humanities Research Board, 1998-99; Consultant Hispanic Editor, Everyman, 1993-99; Editorial board, Donaire, 1994-; Revista Canadiense de Estudios Hispanicos, 1995-; Bulletin of Hispanic Studies, Glasgow, 1998-. Address: The Master's Lodge, Gonville and Caius College, Cambridge, CB2 1TA, England.

McKENDRICK Neil, b. 28 July 1935, Formby, Lancashire, England. Historian. m. Melveena Jones, 2 daughters. Education: BA 1st class honours, History, 1956, MA, 1960, Christ's College, Cambridge; FRHistS, 1971. Appointments: Research Fellow, 1958, Christ's College Cambridge; Assistant Lecturer in History, 1961-64, Lecturer, 1964-95, Secretary to Faculty Board of History, 1975-77, Chairman, History Faculty, 1985-87, Cambridge University; Fellow, 1958-96, Lecturer in History, 1958-96, Director of Studies in History, 1959-96, Tutor, 1961-69, Gonville and Caius College; Lectures: Earl, University of Keele, 1963; Inaugural, Wallace Gallery, Colonial Williamsburg, 1985; Chettyar Memorial, University of Madras, 1990. Publications: Author and Editor of numerous publications; Author of articles in learned journals. Memberships: Tancred's Charities, 1996; Sir John Plumb Charitable Trust, 1999-; Properties Committee, National Trust,

Dictionary of International Biography

1999-; Vice President, Cains Foundation in America, 1998-; Glenfield Trust, 2001-. Address: The Master's Lodge, Gonville and Caius College, Cambridge, CB2 1TA, England.

McKENZIE Dan Peter, b. 21 February 1942, Cheltenham, England. Earth Scientist. m. Indira Margaret, 1 son. Education: BA, MA, PhD, King's College, University of Cambridge. Appointments: Senior Assistant in Research, 1969-75, Assistant Director of Research, 1975-79, Reader in Tectonics, 1979-84, Royal Society Professor of Earth Sciences, Department of Earth Sciences, University of Cambridge. Publications: Author of various papers in learned journals. Honours: Honorary MA, University of Cambridge, 1966; Fellow, Royal Society, 1976; Foreign Associate, US National Academy of Sciences, 1989; Balzan Prize (with F J Vine and D H Matthews), International Balzan Foundation, 1981; Japan Prize (with W J Morgan and X Le Pichon), Technological Foundation of Japan, 1990; Royal Medal of the Royal Society, 1991; Crafoord Prize, 2002. Address: Bullard Laboratories, Madingley Road, Cambridge CB3 0EZ, England.

McKENZIE Jane A, b. 7 July 1932, USA. Thanatologist. Education: BA, Latin and Education, Alverno College, Milwaukee, Wisconsin, 1960; MA, Administration, Clarke College, Dubuque, Iowa, 1971; Study and research into Comparative Education in England, France, Switzerland, Germany, Costa Rica, USA, 1972-82; Study in Liberation Theology, USA, Costa Rica, Mexico, 1983-88; Study of medicinal herbs and plants in Peru, Mexico, USA, 1983-88; AAS, Maxima cum Laude, Hospice and Grief Counselling, Elizabeth Kubler-Ross Hospice Training Institute, Northern New Mexico Community College, El Rito, New Mexico, 1992; Hospice and Palliative Care Study Seminar, Mt Edgecombe Hospice, St Austell, Cornwall, England, 1996. Appointments include: Elementary School Teacher and Principal various schools, 1951-71; Administrative Assistant and Elementary Supervisor, Diocesan Schools, Rockford, Illinois, 1972-75; Professor and Department Chairperson, Colegio St Clare San Jose, Costa Rica, 1976-81; Program Director for homeless pregnant women, Transitional Housing for House of Ruth, Washington DC, 1983-87; Administrative Assistant and Spiritual Director, Cuernavaca Center for International Dialogue and Development, Mexico, 1987-88; Executive Director, St Elizabeth Shelter, Santa Fe, New Mexico, 1988-91; Management Team, Heart of the Hills, Hospice/Hospice Kerrville, Kerrville, Texas, 1992-95; Chaplain and Bereavement Therapist, Family Hospice, Kerville, Texas, 1995-99; Chaplain and Bereavement Therapist, Vistacare Family Hospice, Kerrville, Texas, 1999-2000; Aftercare Grief Therapist, Altstadt-Tyborski-Ermenc-Mcleod Funeral Service, Milwaukee, Wisconsin, 2000-2003; Catholic Chaplain, Thanatologist, Kerrville VA Hospital, Texas, 2003-; Established the Death, Dying and Bereavement Center (now Thanatology Resource Center); Co-founded two children's centres, Kyle's Korner and My Good Mourning Place. Publications: Articles: When the Casseroles Stop Coming and the Kids Have All Gone Home; Cappellanus/Chapelain/Chaplain; Hints, Help and Hope for the Holidays, parts I and II. Memberships: Phi Theta Kappa Honor Society; APSL Latin Honor Society; National Hospice and Palliative Care Organization; Association for Death Education and Counseling; American Academy of Bereavement; National Association of Catholic Chaplains Emeritus. Address: 805 Loop 534 Unit 111, Kerrville, TX 78028, USA. E-mail: jan_ard@webtv.net

McKENZIE Kathleen Julianna, b. 20 January 1957, South Bend, Indiana. m. Myron Roy McKenzie, 1 son, 1 daughter. Education: Studied under the following painting mentors: Richard Borden, 1979-82; Arthur Getz, 1987-90; Curt Hanson, 1992-. Publications: Listed in Encyclopedia of Living Artists in America, 7th, 9th and 11th Editions; New England Artists' Directory, 2001; International Encyclopaedic Dictionary of Modern and Contemporary Art, Italy,

2003-2004. Honours: 3rd Place, Mystic Outdoor Art Festival; Connecticut Women Artists Inc; Woman of the Year 2003, American Biographical Institute; Listed in several international biographies of artists and Who's Who publications. Memberships: International Peace and Diplomacy Forum; American Biographical Institute Research Association Deputy Governors. Address: 1655 Mountain Road, Torrington, CT 06790, USA.

McLANE Wilhelmina, b. 30 September 1912, Franklin, Ohio, USA. Music Educator. m. E S Vinnell. Education: BM, MMus, Cincinnati Conservatory of Music; Studied with Nadia Boulanger, Conservatory of the Palais de Fontainbleu, Paris, France; Piano Pedagogy with Louise Robyn and Ethel Lyon, American Conservatory, Chicago, Illinois. Career: Adjudicator, National Guild of Piano Teachers, American Scholarship Association; Currently, Organist, United Methodist Church, Springboro, Ohio, USA; Private Piano and Organ Teacher. Honours: George Ward Nicholas Scholarship; Springer Postgraduate Award of Merit. Membership: Special Active Member, Dayton Ohio Music Club. Address: 1618 Gage Drive, Middletown, OH 45042, USA.

McLEAN Don, b. 2 October 1945, New Rochelle, New York, USA. Singer; Instrumentalist; Composer. m. Patrisha Shnier, 1987, 1 son, 1 daughter. Education: Villanova University; Iona College. Appointments: President, Benny Bird Corporation Inc; Member, Hudson River Slope Singers, 1969; Solo concert tours throughout USA, Canada, Australia, Europe, Far East; Numerous TV appearances; Composer of film scores for Fraternity Row; Flight of Dragons; Composer of over 200 songs including Prime Time; American Pie; Tapestry; Vincent; And I Love You So; Castles in the Air; Recordings include: Tapestry, 1970; American Pie, 1971; Don McLean, 1972; Playin' Favourites, 1973; Homeless Brother, 1974; Solo, 1976; PrimeTime, 1977; Chain Lightning, 1979; Believers, 1982; For the Memories, Vol I, Vol II, 1986; Love Tracks, 1988; Headroom, 1991; Don McLean Christmas, 1992; Favourites and Rarities, 1993; The River of Love, 1995; Numerous compilation packages. Publications: Songs of Don McLean, 1972; The Songs of Don McLean, Vol II, 1974. Honours: Recipient of many gold discs in USA, Australia, UK and Ireland; Israel Cultural Award, 1981. Address: Benny Bird Co, 1838 Black Rock Turnpike, Fairfield, Connecticut 06432, USA.

McMANUS Jonathan Richard, b. 15 September 1958, Heywood, England. Barrister. Education: First Class Honours in Law, Downing College, Cambridge, 1978-81; Called to the Bar, 1982; Appointments: Commenced practice at the bar, 1983; Government A panel of Counsel, 1992-1999; QC, 1999. Publication: Education and the Courts, 1998. Honour: Maxwell Law Prize, Cambridge, 1981. Memberships: Administrative Law, Bar Association; National Trust; English Heritage; Friend of the Royal Opera House. Address: 4 and 5, Gray's Inn Square, Gray's Inn. London WC1R 5AH, England.

McMICKLE Robert Hawley, b. 30 July 1924, Paterson, New Jersey, USA. Physicist. m. Gwendolyn Gill, 3 sons, 2 daughters. Education: BA, Physics, Oberlin College, 1947; MS, Physics, University of Illinois, 1948; PhD, Physics, Pennsylvania State University, 1952. Appointments: Research Physicist, BF Goodrich Company, Brecksville, Ohio, 1952-59; Professor, Physics, Robert College, Istanbul, Turkey, 1959-71, University of the Bosphorus, Istanbul, Turkey, 1971-79; Schreiner College, Kerrville, Texas, 1979-80; Luther College, Decorah, Iowa, 1980-81; Adjunct Professor, Physics, Memphis State University, Tennessee, 1981-83; Accreditation Co-ordinator, Northeast Utilities, Seabrook, New Hampshire, 1983-94, Retired, 1994. Publications include: Diffusion Controlled Stress Relaxation, 1955; The Compressions of Several High Molecular Weight Hydrocarbons, 1958; Introduction to

Modern Physics, 1979. Honours include: Fellowship, American Petroleum Institute, 1950-52; Research grant, Optics, Innovative Systems Research Inc, Pennsauken, New Jersey, 1976; Distinguished Service Award, University of the Bosphorus, Istanbul, Turkey, 1989. Memberships: American Association of Physics Teachers; Physical Society of Turkey; Sigma Xi. Address: 3032 Fernor Street, Allentown, PA 18103, USA.

McMILLAN James (Coriolanus), b. 30 October 1925. Journalist. m. Doreen Smith, 7 April 1953, 3 sons, 1 daughter. Education: MA, Economics, University of Glasgow. Publications: The Glass Lie, 1964; American Take-Over, 1967; Anatomy of Scotland, 1969; The Honours Game, 1970; Roots of Corruption, 1971; British Genius (with Peter Grosvenor), 1972; The Way We Were 1900-1950 (trilogy), 1977-80; Five Men at Nuremberg, 1984; The Dunlop Story, 1989; From Finchley to the World - Margaret Thatcher, 1990. Address: Thurleston, Fairmile Park Road, Cobham, Surrey KT11 2PL, England.

McQUAIN Jeffrey Hunter, b. 23 November 1955, Frederick, Maryland, USA. Writer; Researcher. Education: AA in General Education, Montgomery College, 1974; BA, 1976, MA, 1977, in English, University of Maryland; PhD in Literary Studies, American University, 1983. Appointment: Researcher to William Safire, New York Times, 1983-. Publications: Books: The Elements of English, 1986; Guide to Good Word Usage, 1989; Power Language, 1996; Coined by Shakespeare, 1998; Never Enough Words, 1999; Coined by God, 2003; The Bard on the Brain, 2003. Contributions to: New York Times Magazine. Honours: Words From Home Award to Power Language, 1996. Membership: Modern Language Association. Literary Agent, David Hendin. Address: Box 4008, Rockville, MD 20849, USA.

McQUEEN Alexander, b. London. Education: St Martin's School of Art, London; Appointments: London Tailors, Anderson and Shepherd, Gieves and Hawkes; Theatrical Costumiers, Berman and Nathans; Des Koji Tatsuno; Romeo Gigli, Rome; Final Collection, St Martin's, 1992 established his reputation; Subsequent shows include: The Birds; Highland Rape; The Hunger; Dante; La Poupee; It's a Jungle Out There; Untitled; Aquired Italian manufacturing company Onward Kashiyama; Chief Designer, Givenchy, Paris, 1996-2000, of Gucci, 2000-. Honours: Designer of the Year, London Fashion Awards, 1996, 2000; Joint Winner, with John Galliano, 1997; Special Achievement Award, London Fashion Awards, 1998. Address: c/o Gucci Group NV Rembrandt Tower, 1 Amstelplein, 1096 MA Amsterdam, The Netherlands. Website: www.gucci.com

McRAE Hamish Malcolm Donald, b. 20 October 1943, Barnstaple, Devon, England. Journalist; Author. m. Frances Anne Cairncross, 10 September 1971, 2 daughters. Education: Fettes College, Edinburgh, 1957-62; Honours Degree, Economics and Political Science, Trinity College, Dublin, 1966. Appointments: Editor, Euromoney, 1972, Business and City, The Independent, 1989; Financial Editor, The Guardian, 1975; Associate Editor, The Independent, 1991. Publications: Capital City - London as a Financial Centre (with Frances Cairncross), 1973, 5th edition, 1991; The Second Great Crash (with Frances Cairncross), 1975; Japan's Role in the Emerging Global Securities Market, 1985; The World in 2020, 1994. Contributions to: Numerous magazines and journals. Honours: Financial Journalist of the Year, Wincott Foundation, 1979; Special Merit Award, Amex Bank Review Essays, 1987; Columnist of the Year, Periodical Publishers Association Awards, 1996. Address: 6 Canonbury Lane, London N1 2AP, England.

McVIE J Gordon, b. 13 January 1945, Glasgow, Scotland. Director Cancer Intelligence; Professor. Education: BSc (Hons), Pathology, 1967, MB, ChB, 1969, University of Edinburgh, Scotland; ECFMG, USA, 1971; Accreditation in Internal Medicine and Medical oncology, Joint Committee on Higher Medical Training, 1977; MD, Edinburgh, 1978; FRCPE, Edinburgh, 1981; FRCPS, Glasgow, 1987; DSc (Hon), University of Abertay, Dundee, Scotland, 1996; DSc (Hon), University of Nottingham, England, 1997; FRCP, 1997; FMedSci, 1998; DSc (Hon), University of Portsmouth, England; FRCSE, Edinburgh, 2001. Appointments: House Officer, Royal Infirmary, Edinburgh and Royal Hospital for Sick Children, Edinburgh, 1969-1970; Medical Research Council Research Fellow, Department of Pathology and Therapeutics, Edinburgh University; 1970-1971; Temporary Lecturer in Therapeutics, 1971-73, Lecturer in Therapeutics, 1973-76, Edinburgh University; Honorary Registrar, 1971-73, Honorary Senior Registrar, 1973-76, Lothian Health Board, Scotland; Senior Lecturer, The Cancer Research Campaign Department of Clinical Oncology, University of Glasgow, 1976-1980; Honorary Consultant in Medical Oncology, Greater Glasgow Health Board, 1976-1980; Head, Clinical Research Unit, Consultant Physician, and Chairman, Division of Experimental Therapy, The National Cancer Institute, Amsterdam, The Netherlands, 1980-84; Clinical Research Director, The National Cancer Institute of the Netherlands, 1984-1989; Scientific Director, 1989-1996, Director General, 1996-2002, The Cancer Research Campaign; Director General, Cancer Research UK, 2002-; Director, Cancer Intelligence, 2003-. Publications: Extensive within this field; Membership of numerous medical editorial boards. Honours: Gunning Victoria Jubilee Prize in Pathology, 1967; Honeyman Gillespie Lecturer in Oncology 1977; Visiting Fellow, Department of Medical Oncology, University of Paris, 1978; Visiting Fellow, Netherlands Cancer Institute, Amsterdam; Consultant, Carcinogenesis of Cytostatic Drugs, International Agency, Research in Cancer, WHO, Lyon, 1980; Visiting Professor, University of Sydney, NSW, Australia; Visiting Professor, British Postgraduate Medical Federation, London University; 1990-96; Chairman, UICC Fellowships Program, 1990-98; President, European Organisation for Research and Treatment of Cancer, 1994-97; First European Editor of Journal of the National Cancer Institute, 1994-; Visiting Professor, University of Glasgow, 1996-; Semmelweis Medal for Excellence in Science. Memberships: European Organisation for Research on Treatment of Cancer (EORTC), 1979-; Numerous advisory committees and examination boards including: Member, Steering Committee, Alliance of World Cancer Research Organisations, 1999; Cancer Research Funders Forum, 1999-2001; Member, AACR Membership Committee, 2000-01; Member, AACR Clinical Cancer Research Committee, 2001-. Address: Cancer Intelligence, 4 Stanley Rd, Cotham, Bristol BS6 6NW, England. E-mail: gordonmcvie@doctors.org.uk

McWHIRTER George, b. 26 September 1939, Belfast, Northern Ireland. Writer; Poet; Translator; Professor. m. Angela Mairead Coid, 26 December 1963, 1 son, 1 daughter. Education: BA, Queen's University; MA, University of British Columbia. Appointments: Co-Editor-in-Chief, 1977, Advisory Editor, 1978-, Prism International Magazine; Professor, University of British Columbia, 1982-. Publications: Catalan Poems, 1971; Bodyworks, 1974; Queen of the Sea, 1976; Gods Eye, 1981; Coming to Grips with Lucy, 1982; Fire Before Dark, 1983; Paula Lake, 1984; Cage, 1987; The Selected Poems of José Emilio Pacheco (editor and translator), 1987; The Listeners, 1991; A Bad Day to be Winning, 1992; A Staircase for All Souls, 1993; Incubus: The Dark Side of the Light, 1995; Musical Dogs, 1996; Fab, 1997; Where Words Like Monarchs Fly (editor and translator), 1998; Ovid in Saskatchewan, 1998; Eyes to See Otherwise: The Selected poems of Homero Aridjis, 1960 – 2000 (co-editor and translator); The Book of Contradictions (poems), 2001. Contributions to:

Numerous magazines and journals. Honours: McMillan Prize, 1969; Commonwealth Poetry Prize, 1972; F R Scott Prize, 1988; Ethel Wilson Fiction Prize, 1988; Killan Prize for Teaching, UBC, 1998; League of Canadian Poets' National Chapbook Competition, for Ovid in Saskatchewan, 1998. Memberships: League of Canadian Poets; Writers' Union of Canada; PEN; Literary Translators Association of Canada. Address: 4637 West 13th Avenue, Vancouver, British Columbia V6R 2V6, Canada.

MEACHER Michael Hugh (Rt Hon), b. 4 November 1939, Hemel Hempstead, Hertfordshire, England. Member of Parliament. m. Lucianne Sawyer, 2 sons, 2 daughters. Education: Greats, Class 1, New College, Oxford; Diploma in Social Administration, London School of Economics. Appointments: Lecturer, Social Administration, York and London School of Economics, 1966-70; Member of Parliament for Oldham West, 1970-; Minister for Industry, 1974-75; Minister for the Department of Health and Social Security, 1975-76; Minister for Trade, 1976-79; Member of the Shadow Cabinet, 1983-97; Minister for the Environment, 1997-. Publications: Taken for a Ride (about the care of the elderly), 1972; Socialism with a Human Face, 1982; Diffusing Power, 1992. Memberships: Labour Party; Fabian Society; Child Poverty Action Group. Address: House of Commons, Westminster, London, SW1A 0AA, England.

MEDVED Alphonse Anthony, b. 8 August 1910, Schoenstein, Austria. m. Isabel Margaret McFarlane, 4 September 1933, 2 sons. Education: BA, University of Wisconsin, 1932; BD, Colgate Rochester Divinity School, 1936; Courses, University of Maryland. Publication: ELUL, 1965. Publication: J of K, Judah of Kerioth (novel), 2003; Contributions to: Poetry Journal; Motive Magazine; Christian Century; National Library of Poetry; Anthology of New England Writers; Thirteen Poetry Magazine; Amherst Society; Anemone; Threshold of a Dream. Honours: 1st Prize, Annual Contest, Indiana State Federation of Poetry Clubs, 1992. Memberships: New England Writers; Vermont Poetry Society; Monadnock Writers Group; Poetry Society of America. Address: 38 Fort Hill Road, Putney, VT 08346, USA.

MEEK Elizabeth R, b. 7 May 1953, London, England. Artist. 2 daughters. Career: Exhibitions include: The Royal Academy; The Royal Miniature Society; The Society of Women Artists; The Hunting Observer Exhibition at the Mall Galleries, the Smith Gallery, Yorkshire, and Espace Pierre Cardin Paris; The Llewellyn Alexander Gallery; the Société des Artistes Miniature et Arts Precieux de France; Barbican and Jersey Arts Centre; The Hilliard Society; The British Painters; Chelsea Arts Society; One-Woman Exhibition, The National Fine Arts Museum, Valetta, Malta. Publications: Works included in: The Techniques of Painting Miniatures by Sue Burton; A Book to Celebrate the 100th Year of the Royal Miniature Society by Suzanne Lucas; Listed in the Dictionary of Artists of the SWA for 1955-1996 which is housed in the Archives of the Victoria and Albert Museum; Who's Who in Art; Various magazines and newspapers. Honours include: Bell Award for the Best Portrait, Hilliard Society, 1992, 1997, 2002; Runner-up, Gold Memorial Bowl, Royal Miniature Society, 1992, 1994; Suzanne Lucas, Best in Exhibition Award, Hilliard Society, 1993, 1994; Gold Memorial Honourable Mention, Royal Miniature Society, 1993; The Gold Memorial Bowl (Hors Concours), Royal Miniature Society, 1995; Mundy Sovereign Award, Best Portrait, Royal Miniature Society, 1995, 1999; Best Group Award, Royal Miniature Society, 1999; President's Choice Award, Royal Miniature Society, 2002. Memberships: Hilliard Society, 1994; President, Society of Women Artists, 2000-; Elected Fellow, Royal Society of Arts; President, Royal Society of Miniature Painters, Sculptors and Gravers, 2004-. Address: 482 Merton Road, Southfields, London SW18 5AE, England. E-mail: elizabethmeek@msn.com

MEFED Anatoly Egorovich, b. 7 December 1938, Gorodische, Bryansk, Russia. Physicist; Researcher of NMR in solids; Consultant. m. Lyudmila Ivanovna Putilova, 1 daughter. Education: Graduate, Moscow University, 1962; PhD, Russian Academy of Sciences, 1972. Appointments: Professor, Physics and Maths, Institute Radioengineering and Electronics Russian Academy of Sciences, Fryazino, 1989; Professor, Kazan State University, 1989. Publications: Author and co-author: Discovery, A New Physical Law in Spin Thermodynamics in Solids, 1968; Contribution to more than 80 research papers to professional journals. Honours: Recipient USSR diploma for discovery of a new physics law in spin thermodynamics in solids, 1987; USSR inventor medal Russian Academy of Sciences; Listed in biographical publications. Membership: New York Academy of Sciences, Russian Academy of Natural Sciences. Address: Russian Academy of Sciences Institute of Radioengineering & Electronics, Vvedenskogo Sq, 141190 Fryazino, Moscow, Russia. E-mail: aem228@ire216.msk.su

MEGRELISHVILI Richard, b. 1 January 1934, Tbilisi, Georgia. Coding Theorist. m. Tinatin Chimakadze, 1 daughter. Education: Faculty of Energetics, Georgian Technical University, 1957; Aspirant, Institute of Automation and Telemechanics, Academy of Sciences, USSR, 1960-63; Candidate of Technical Sciences, 1966; Doctor of Technical Sciences, 1997. Appointments: Scientific Collaborator, Institute of Electronics, Automation and Telemechanics, Academy of Sciences, Georgian SSR, 1957-66; Chief, Department of Physical Cybernetics Problems, Laboratory of Javakhishvili, Tbilisi State University, 1967-; Professor, Department of Computer Systems, 1997. Publications: More than 50 Scientific Articles; Estimation of signal number in a class of correcting codes; The method for correction of multiple burst errors in cyclic codes. Memberships: Scientific Board, Editorial Board, Faculty of Applied Mathematics and Computer Sciences of the University. Address: Tsereteli St 5 Apt 2, Tbilisi, 380012, Georgia.

MEGYERI Lajos, b. 5 May 1935, Bačko Gradište, Serbia & Monte Negro. Composer; Conductor; Professor. m. Toth Maria, 5 September 1959, 1 daughter. Education: Music Academy, Composing Line, Belgrade. Career: Professor, Music School, Subotica; Conductor, Music Director, National Theatre Orchestra, Subotica, 1977-81; Appearances in Germany, 1968, 1970, USA, 1972, Holland, 1973; Author's Concerts in Subotica, 1969, 1995, 2000. Compositions: Quatuor, for strings quartet, 1961; Symphonic Movement with Introduction, for symphony orchestra, 1963; Suite, 1959; Adagio, 1959; Capriccio, 1959; Variation, 1960; Scherzo, 1960; Sonatina, 1960; Scherzettino, 1961; Intermezzo, 1969; Ecloga, 3 Miniature, In Spring, Miniatur-Suite I, Remembrance, Miniatur-Suite II, 1975; for piano; Missa Hungarica, for mixed choir and organ, 1995; The Ortolan Flew Off, for mixed choir 'a capella', 1997; The Duck and the Frogs, for voice and piano, 1969; 12 Miniatures for Accordeon, 1968; Prelude and Scherzo, for accordion, 1967; The Rascal, children's musical, 1979. Recordings: Piano Album - Author's LP, 1991; Quatuor, for string quartet, CD, 1998; Three Piano Pieces: Ecloga, In Spring, Remembrance, CD, 1998; Piano Album, CD, 2000; Sonatina, for piano, CD, 2001; Missa Hungarica, for mixed choir and organ, CD, 2000; The Ortolan Flew Off, for mixed choir 'a capella', CD, 2000; Prelude and Scherzo, for woodwind quartet, CD, 2000; Adagio, for string orchestra, 2002; Piano Album, DVD, 2004. Publications: Piano Album, 1989, 1990; Miniaturen für Accordeon, 2002. Honours: 1st Prize, Accordion Trio, World Festival, Luzern, 1968; 1st Prize, Gold Medal, Accordion Orchestra, Grand Prix European de L'Accordeon, France, 1972. Memberships: Organization of Composers in Serbia & Monte Negro; Alliance of Estrade Artists. Address: Nušićeva 2a, 24000 Subotica, Serbia & Monte Negro.

MEH Duska, b. 18 March 1964, Slovenia. Medical Doctor. Education: MD, 1989; MSc, 1992; PhD, 1995. Appointment: Scientific Councillor, Institute for Rehabilitation and Medical Faculty, Ljubljana. Publications: Several articles in professional journals; Editor, Medicinski Razgledi, medical journal, 1983-89. Honour: Presern's Award, Student Research: INABIS 2000 Science On Line's Award for the best presentation on 6th Internet World Congress for Biomedical Sciences. Memberships: Medical Association of Slovenia; Medical Chamber of Slovenia; International Association for the Study of Pain; American Diabetes Association; World Federation of Neurology; International Federation of Clinical Neurophysiology and its European Chapter; Slovenian Neuroscience Association; International Brain Research Organisation. Address: Jarska c. 36, SL 1000, Ljubljana, Slovenia.

MEHANDJIEV Marin Roussev, b. 8 March 1927, Sofia, Bulgaria. Chemical Engineer; Ecologist. m. Krassimira Kercheva-Mehandjieva, 1 son, 1 daughter. Education: MSc, Diploma Engineer, Chemistry, Polytechnic of Sofia, 1949; Associate Professor Degree, Non-Ferrous Metallurgy, Polytechnic of Sofia, 1970; PhD, High Chemical Institute in Bourgas, 1971; Associate Professor Degree in Non-Equilibrium Thermodynamics of Accumulation Processes, Institute of Physical Chemistry of Bulgarian Academy of Sciences, 1989; PhD, International Relations, Alabama University, 1999; Professor, Human Rights and Environment, International Association of Lecturers. Appointments: Consultant: UNESCO, UNICEF, ECOSOC/UNO, 1999; Academician World Peace Academy, USA, 1999. Publications: More than 400 scientific publications, including 18 monographs. Honours: Doctor of Philosophy Honoris Causa, Political Science, International Academy of Culture and Political Science, USA, 1999; Honorary Member, Spanish Association of Professionals in Occupational Health and Environment, Spain, 1998; Honorary Member, Ansted University Board of Advisory Council, Malaysia, 1999; Man of the Year, 1998-99, International Biographical Centre, Cambridge, England, 1998; Honorary-Citizen of the Museum-town Koprivhtitsa, Bulgaria, 2001; Nominee, Nobel Prize Award for Chemistry, 2004, by Ansted University, England for his contribution to non-equilibrium thermodynamics of accumulation processes and its applications, particularly the carcinogenic theory based on the proper protective mechanism of cellular tissues. Memberships include: Founding Member, Balkan Union of Oncology, 1995-; Corresponding Member, Ukrainian Ecological Academy of Sciences, 1995-; Active Member, New York Academy of Sciences, 1996-; Lecturer in Ecological Modelling in South-Western University, N Rilski, Blagoevgrad, 1995-; High Council of Environmental Experts in the Ministry of Environment and Water of Bulgaria, 1997-; President, Foundation, Science and Environmental Analyses, 1998-; Member, International Administration, World University Roundtable, Benson, Arizona, USA, 1999; Academician, Central European Academy of Science and Art, 2000-; Academician, Romanian Ecological Academy, 2000-; Founding Member, Scientific Vice-President and Academician, Balkan Academy of Sciences, New Culture and Sustainable Development, D Jersov, 2001-; Corresponding Member, Royal Academy of Pharmacy, Spain, 2002-; Honourable Academician, Academia Mundial de Ciencias, Technologia, Education y Humanidades, Valencia, Spain, 2003-. Address: Ent A Ste 26, Compl Nadejda Bl 533, 1229 Sofia, Bulgaria.

MEHTA Ratti, b. 25 November 1924, Bombay, India. Concert Pianist; Pianoforte Teacher. m. Jal Mehta. Education: Licentiate, Royal Schools of Music, London, 1942; Licentiate, Trinity College, London, 1943; Licentiate, Royal Academy of Music, London, 1948; Associate, Royal College of Music, London, 1948; Special Certificate, Royal Academy of Music, London. Career includes: Numerous Concerts and Performances including, Soloists with Orchestra: Bombay Symphony, Jules Craen, 1945; Royal Academy, Ernest Reed, 1950; Royal Academy, Clarence Raybould, 1950; Bombay City, Vere Da Silva, 1957; Violin/Piano: Sonate Recital, Bombay; Solo Piano Forte: Cama Oriental Institute, Bombay, 1944; International Musikfestwechen, Lucerne, 1951; BBC, London, 1953, 1954; Radio Paris, 1953; Channing Hall, Highgate, London, 1954; C J Hall, Bombay, 1956; The Taj, Bombay, 1959; Invitee/Participant, Meisterkurses held by Maestro Edwin Fischer, Lucerne, Switzerland, 1951, 1953. Honours: Bronze Medal, Royal Academy of Music; Scholarship, Associated Board of Music, London, 1945; Listed in Who's Who publications. Memberships: Vice President, 1985-87, President, 1988-89, Concerts Committee Chairperson, 1956-93, Time and Talents Club, Bombay; Member, Willingdon Sports Club, 1957-; Member, Royal Bombay Yacht Club, 1986-1996. Address: Chheda Sedan, Flat 12N, 5th Floor, 115 Churchgate Reclamation, Bombay 400 020, India.

MEINARDUS Otto Friedrich August, b. 29 September 1925, Hamburg, Germany. Coptologist; Professor. m. Eva Zimmermann, 1 son, 1 daughter. Education: Studies at Hamburg University, London University, Richmond College; BD, Concordia Seminary, St Louis, Missouri, 1949; STM, 1950, PhD, 1955, Boston University; Postdoctoral Studies, Harvard University; FICS, Institute of Coptic Studies, Cairo, 1960. Appointments: Methodist Minister: Christchurch, New Zealand, 1950-51, Adelaide, South Australia, 1951, Peabody, Massachusetts, 1952-56, Maadi Church, Cairo, 1956-68, St Andrew's Church, Athens, Greece, 1968-75; Professor, American University, Cairo, 1956-68; Professor, Athens College, Athens, Greece, 1968-72; Minister, Evangelical Church, Rheinland, 1975-84. Publications: Christian Egypt, Ancient and Modern, 1965, 1977; Monks and Monasteries of the Egyptian Deserts, 1961, 1989, 1992; 2000 Years of Coptic Christianity, 1999; Coptic Saints and Pilgrimages, 2002; Christian Egypt and Life, 1990; St Paul in Greece, 1972; St John of Palmos, 1974; many others. Honours: BD; STM; PhD; FICS. Memberships: German Archaeological Society. Address: Stettiner Str 11, D-25479 Ellerau, Germany.

MELLERS Wilfrid (Howard), b. 26 April 1914, Leamington, Warwickshire, England. Professor of Music (retired); Composer; Author. m. (1) Vera M Hobbs, (2) Pauline P Lewis, 3 daughters, (3) Robin S Hildyard. Education: Leamington College, 1933; BA, 1936, MA, 1938, Cambridge University; DMus, University of Birmingham, 1960. Appointments: Staff Tutor in Music, University of Birmingham, 1948-60; Andrew Mellon Professor of Music, University of Pittsburgh, 1960-63; Professor of Music, University of York, 1964-81; Visiting Professor, City University, 1984-. Publications: Music and Society: England and the European Tradition, 1946; Studies in Contemporary Music, 1947; François Couperin and the French Classical Tradition, 1950, 2nd edition, revised, 1987; Music in the Making, 1952; Romanticism and the 20th Century, 1957, 2nd edition, revised, 1988; The Sonata Principle, 1957, 2nd edition, revised, 1988; Music in a New Found Land: Themes and Developments in the History of American Music, 1964, 2nd edition, revised, 1987; Harmonious Meeting: A Study of the Relationship between English Music, Poetry, and Theatre, c.1600-1900, 1965; Caliban Reborn: Renewal in Twentieth-Century Music, 1967; Twilight of the Gods: The Music of the Beatles, 1973; Bach and the Dance of God, 1980; Beethoven and the Voice of God, 1983; A Darker Shade of Pale: A Backdrop to Bob Dylan, 1984; Angels of the Night: Popular Female Singers of Our Time, 1986; The Masks of Orpheus: Seven Stages in the Story of European Music, 1987; Le Jardin Retrouvé: Homage to Federico Mompou, 1989; Vaughan Williams and the Vision of Albion, 1989, new enlarged edition, 1997; The Music of Percy Grainger, 1992; Francis Poulenc, 1994; Between Old Worlds and New: Occasional Writings on Music by Wilfrid Mellers, 1998;

Singing in the Wilderness, 2001; Celestial Music, 2002. Contributions to: Reference works and journals. Honours: Honorary DPhil, City University, 1981; Officer of the Order of the British Empire, 1982. Membership: Sonneck Society, honorary member. Address: Oliver Sheldon House, 17 Aldwark, York, YO1 7BX, England.

MELLOR D(avid) H(ugh), b. 10 July 1938, England. Professor of Philosophy; Writer. Education: BA, Natural Sciences and Chemical Engineering, 1960, PhD, 1968, ScD, 1990, M in English, 1992, Pembroke College, Cambridge; MSc, Chemical Engineering, University of Minnesota, 1962. Appointments: Research Student in Philosophy, Pembroke College, 1963-68, Fellow, Pembroke College, 1965-70, University Assistant Lecturer in Philosophy, 1965-70, University Lecturer in Philosophy, 1970-83, Fellow, 1971-, and Vice-Master, 1983-87, Darwin College, University Reader in Metaphysics, 1983-85, Professor of Philosophy, 1986-99, Professor Emeritus, 1999-, Pro-Vice-Chancellor, 2000-01, Cambridge University; Visiting Fellow in Philosophy, Australian National University, Canberra, 1975; Honorary Professor of Philosophy, University of Keele, 1989-92. Publications: The Matter of Chance, 1971; Real Time, 1981; Cambridge Studies in Philosophy, (editor), 1978-82; Matters of Metaphysics, 1991; The Facts of Causation, 1995; Real Time II, 1998; numerous articles on philosophy of science, metaphysics and philosophy of mind. Contributions to: Scholarly journals. Memberships: Aristotelian Society, president, 1992-93; British Academy, fellow; British Society for the Philosophy of Science, president, 1985-87. Address: 25 Orchard Street, Cambridge CB1 1JS, England.

MELLY (Alan) George (Heywood), b. 17 August 1926, Liverpool, England. Jazz Singer; Critic. m. (1) Victoria Vaughn, 1955, divorced 1962, (2) Diana, 1963, 1 son, 1 stepdaughter. Career: Assistant, London Gallery, 1948-50; Singer, Mick Mulligan's Jazz Band, 1949-61; Cartoon strip writer with Trog, 1956-71; As critic for The Observer: Pop Music, 1965-67; Television, 1967-71; Films, 1971-73; Film scriptwriter, Smashing Time, 1968; Take A Girl Like You, 1970; Singer, John Chilton's Feetwarmers, 1974-; Concerts include: Royal Festival Hall; Royal Albert Hall; Edinburgh Festival; Television includes: Subject, This Is Your Life. Recordings: 30 albums; George Melly and John Chilton's Feetwarmers: Best of Live; Anything Goes; Frankie & Johnny; Puttin' On The Ritz. Publications: I Flook, 1962; Owning Up, 1965; Revolt Into Style, 1970; Flook By Trog, 1970; Rum Bum And Concertina, 1977; The Media Mob (with Barry Fantoni), 1980; Tribe Of One, 1981; Great Lovers, (with Walter Dorin), 1981; Mellymobile, 1982; Scouse Mouse, 1984; It's All Writ Out For You, 1986; Paris And The Surrealists (with Michael Woods), 1991; Don't Tell Sybil: An Intimate Memoir of E L T Mesens, 1997. Honours: Critic Of The Year, IPC National Press Awards, 1970; Fellow, John Moores University; Doctor, Middlesex and Glamorgan University; President, British Humanist Society, 1972-74; BT British Jazz Awards, 1998; Award for Lifetime Acheivement For Jazz. Address: 82 Frithville Gardens, Shepherds Bush, London W12 7JQ, England.

MELVILLE Bryan Niel, b. 5 September 1937, Salisbury, Rhodesia. Quantity Surveyor. Appointments: Jacks Burns partnership, Salisbury, Rhodesia, 1954-61; J B Fauder & Co, Gatooma, Rhodesia, 1961-67; General Construction Ltd, Limbe, Malawi, 1967-69; Hawkins Leshnick, Pridgeon & Veale, Salisbury, 1969-71; De Leeuw, Van Der Laan and Partners, Pretoria, South Africa, 1971-75; LTA Civil Engineering Ltd, Johannesburg, South Africa, 1975-78. Honours: 2000 Outstanding Intellectuals of the 21st Century, IBC; Nominated for Man of the Year and The Worldwide Honours List; Listed in Who's Who publications and biographical dictionaries. Address: PO Box 1153, Christenburg, Bethlehem 9700, Republic of South Africa.

MELZER John T S, b. 9 September 1938, Ashland, Ohio, USA. Translator. Education: AB, Auburn University, USA, 1961; AM, University of Virginia, USA, 1964; PhD, Tulane University, USA, 1978; Appointments: Professor, Georgetown College, Kentucky, USA, 1964; Professor, Columbus State University, Georgia, USA, 1964-67; Professor, University of West Alabama, 1977; Director of Historical Research, Saint Augustine Restoration Commission, Saint Augustine, Florida, 1968; Drilling Fluids, Consultant, 1979-; Scholar-in-Residence, Professor, English Translex Institute, Miraflores, Lima, Peru, 1985-92; Investigador Ad Honorem, National Institute of Culture, Peru, 1989; Editor-in-Chief, Oakbowery Books, Auburn, Alabama, 1994. Publications: 4 journal articles; 18 newspaper articles on Peru and 3 newspaper articles on the Persian Gulf; Books: Fourteen Days to Field Spanish, 1985; Bastion of Commerce in the City of Kings the Consulado de Comercio de Lima 1593-1887, 1991; Oilfield Spanish, Thousands of Words and Terms, A Vocabulary of Walk-Around Rig-Spanish, 1997. Honours: Tau Kappa Alpha, National Forensics Honor Fraternity; Investigador Ad Honorem, National Institute of Culture of Peru; Honorary Diploma, University National Federico Villarreal, Lima, Peru, 1990; Consejo Nacional de Ciencia y Tecnologia Peru, Grant for publication of book in English, Spanish and German, 1991. Memberships: SAR; Alpha Phi Omega; Delta Tau Delta; Tau Kappa Alpha. Address: 74 Curtis Street, Camp Hill, AL 36950, USA. E-mail: oilfieldspanish2003@yahoo.com

MENDES Sam, b. 1 August 1965, England. Theatre Director. m. Kate Winslet, 1 son. Education: Magdalen College School; Oxford University; Peterhouse, Cambridge University. Appointments: Artistic Director, Minerva Studio Theatre, Chichester; Artistic Director, Donmar Warehouse, 1992-2002. Creative Works: Plays directed include: London Assurance, Chichester; The Cherry Orchard, London; Kean, Old Vic, London; The Plough and the Stars, Young Vic, London, 1991; Troilus and Cressida, RSC, 1991; The Alchemist, RSC, 1991; Richard III, RSC, 1992; The Tempest, RSC, 1993; National Theatre debut with The Sea, 1991; The Rise and Fall of Little Voice, National and Aldwych, 1992; The Birthday Party, 1994; Othello (also world tour); Assassins, Translations, Cabaret, Glengarry Glen Ross, The Glass Menagerie, Company, Habeas Corpus, The Front Page, The Blue Room, To the Green Fields Beyond, (all at Donmar Warehouse) 1992-2000; Uncle Vanya and Twelfth Night, Donmar Warehouse, 2002; Oliver!, London Palladium; Cabaret, The Blue Room, Broadway, New York; Gypsy with Bernadette Peters, Broadway. Films: American Beauty, 1999; The Road to Perdition, 2002. Honours include: Commander of the British Empire; Critics' Circle Award, 1989, 1993, 1996; Olivier Award for Best Director, 1996; Tony Award, 1998; LA Critics' Award, Broadcast Critics' Award, Toronto People's Choice Award, Golden Globe Award, 1999; Shakespeare Prize, Academy Award for Best Director (also Best Film) for American Beauty, 2000; The Hamburg Shakespeare Prize; Oliver Award for Best Director (also Special Award), 2003. Address: 26-28 Neal Street, London, WC2H 9QQ, England. E-mail: mleigh@scampltd.com

MÉNDEZ RODRÍGUEZ José Manuel, b. 19 March 1955, Reinosa, Spain. Professor of Logic. 2 sons. Education: BA, History, 1978, BA, Philosophy, 1979, PhD, 1983, University of Salamanca, Spain. Appointments: Assistant Lecturer, 1980, Associate Professor, 1981, Professor, 1988-, University of Salamanca. Publications: Several articles in professional journals. Honours: 1st Class Distinction, Philosophy, University of Salamanca 1979; Award with Special Distinction. Philosophy, University of Salamanca, 1983. Address: Departmento de Filosofia, Universidad de Salamanca, Edificio FES, Campus Unamuno, 37007 Salamanca, Spain.

Dictionary of International Biography

MENEM Carlos Saul, b. 2 July 1935, Anillaco, La Rioja, Argentina. Politician. m. (1) Zulema Fatima Yoma, 1966, divorced, 1 son, deceased, 1 daughter, (2) Cecilia Bolocco, 2001. Education: Cordoba University. Appointments: Founder, Juventud Peronista, Peron Youth Group, La Rioja Province, 1955; Defended political prisoners following 1955 Coup; Legal Advisor, Confederacion General del Trabajo, La Rioja Province, 1955-70; Candidate, Provincial Deputy, 1958; President, Partido Justicialista, La Rioja Province, 1963-; Elected Govenor, La Rioja, 1973, re-elected, 1983, 1987; Imprisoned following military coup, 1976-81; Candidate for President, Argentine Republic for Partido Justicialista, 1989; President of Argentina, 1989-2001; Vice President, Conference of Latin-American Popular Parties, 1990-; Arrested for alleged involvement in illegal arms sales during his presidency, June 2001, charged, July 2001, placed under house arrest for five months; Presidential Candidate, 2003. Publications: Argentine, Now or Never; Argentina Year 2000; The Productive Revolution, with Eduardo Duhalde. Address: Casa de Gobierno, Balcarce 50, 1064 Buenos Aires, Argentina.

MENGERSEN Kerrie, b. 19 January 1962, Sydney, Australia. Statistician. m. Gerard Davis, 1 son, 2 daughters. Education: BA, First Class Honours, 1985, PhD, Statistics, 1989, University of New England, Australia; Graduate Certificate in Tertiary Education, QUT, Australia, 1996. Appointments: Statistical Consultant, Siromath Pty Ltd, 1987-88; Assistant Professor, Bond University, 1989-90; Lecturer, Senior Lecturer, Central Queensland University, 1991-92; Visiting Associate Professor, Colorado State University, USA, 1993; Lecturer, Senior Lecturer, QUT, 1994-2000; Professor and Head of Discipline, University of Newcastle, 2001-2004. Publications: In the last 5 years: 2 edited books; 9 book chapters; 26 papers in international refereed journals; 12 refereed articles in conference proceedings. Honours: ISI Top 10 Citation; Listed in Who's Who publications and biographical dictionaries. Memberships: Statistical Society of Australia; International Society for Bayesian Analysis; Institute of Mathematical Statistics; International Biometrics Society. Address: University of Newcastle, University Drive, Callaghan, Newcastle, NSW 2308, Australia. E-mail: kerrie.mengersen@newcastle.edu.au

MENINGAUD Jean-Paul, b. 18 October 1966, Alicante, Spain. Plastic Surgeon. m. Caroline, 1 son, 1 daughter. Education: MD, 1997; PhD, 2002. Appointments: Head, Department of Maxillofacial and Plastic Surgery, Teaching Hospital of Villeneuve-Saint-Georges, France. Publications: Ethics and aims of cosmetic surgery, medicine and law, 2000; Depression, anxiety and quality of life among facial cosmetic surgery patients, 2001, 2003; Ethical Assessment of clinical research publications, 2001. Honours: Who's Who in the World, 2003-04. Memberships: International Association of Oral and Maxillofacial Surgeons. Address: Department of Maxillofacial Surgery, 40 Allee de la Source, CHIV, 94190, Villeneuve-Saint-Georges, France. E-mail: meningaud@noos.fr Website: www.meningaud.com

MENKEN Alan, b. 22 July 1949, New York, USA. Composer. Education: New York University. Creative Works: Theatre music including: God Bless You Mr Rosewater, 1979; Little Shop of Horrors, with Howard Ashman; Kicks; The Apprenticeship of Duddy Kravitz; Diamonds; Personals; Let Freedom Sing; Weird Romance; Beauty and the Beast; A Christmas Carol; Film music includes: Little Shop of Horrors, 1986; The Little Mermaid, 1988; Beauty and the Beast, 1990; Lincoln, 1992; Newsies, 1992; Aladdin, 1992; Life with Mikey, 1993; Pocahontas, with Stephen Schwartz, 1995. Honours include: Several Academy Awards, 1989, 1993, 1996; Golden Globe Award, 1996. Address: The Shukat Company, 340 West 55th Street, Apt 1A, New York, NY 10019, USA.

MENNEN Ulrich, b. 1 July 1947, Barberton, Mpumalanga, South Africa. m. Johanna Margaretha Louw, 2 sons, 1 daughter. Education: MBChB, University of Pretoria, 1970; FRCS, Glasgow, 1978, Edinburgh, 1978; FCS (SA) Ortho, 1979; MMed, Orthopaedics, University of Pretoria, 1979; PhD, Orthopaedics, 1983. Appointments include: Senior Surgeon, 1980, Principal Surgeon, 1981; Associate Professor and Principal Surgeon, 1983, Orthopaedics, Pretoria Academic Hospital; Microsurgery Fellow, Duke University Medical Centre, Durham, North Carolina, 1983; Professor and Head, Department of Hand- and Microsurgery, Medical University of Southern Africa, 1985-; Honorary Head, Hand Surgery Unit, Pretoria Academic Hospital; Head, Department of Orthopaedic Surgery, Medical University of Southern Africa, 1990-91; Visiting Professor, Hong Kong, Australia, USA, Vietnam, Iran, South Korea, Botswana, Ethiopia, Uganda, Tanzania; Private Hand Surgery Practice, 1992-; Founder and Member, Pretoria Hand Institute, Jakaranda Hospital, 1997-. Publications: Chirurgiese Sinopsis, 1978; Co-author, Surgical Synopsis, 1983; Editor, The Hand Book, 1988, second edition, 1994; Co-editor, Principles of Surgical Patient Care, vols 1 and 2, 1990, second edition, 2003; The History of South African Society for Surgery of the Hand 1969-1994, 1994; Numerous articles in professional journals and book chapters. Honours include: Registrar's Prize for Best Paper, 1978, 1979; G F Dommisse Orthopaedic Registrar Prize, 1979; Mer-National Literary Prize, for article, 1982; Smith and Nephew Literary Award, South African Orthopaedic Association, 1985; Chamber of Mines Research Grant, 1987; Glaxo Literary Award, 1990; Finalist, Wellcome Medal for Medical Research, 1990; Research Excellence Award, Faculty of Medicine, MEDUNSA, 1997; Masimanyane Award, Engineering Association, 1997; South African Bureau of Standards Design Institute Award, Overall Chairman's Award for Excellence, 1997; Numerous other literary prizes; Originator and developer of the Mennen Clamp-on Bone Fixation System. Memberships include: South African Medical Association; SA Orthopaedic Association; SA Association for Arthritis and Rheumatic Diseases; Cripples Research Association of South Africa; International Member, American Society for Surgery of the Hand; Executive Member and Past President, South African Society for Surgery of the Hand; Founding Member, South African Society for Hand Therapy; Executive Member, Secretary-General, International Federation of Societies for Surgery of the Hand. Address: 374 Lawley Street, Waterkloof, 0181, Pretoria, South Africa.

MÉRAUD Jacques Adrien, b. 22 May 1926, Lyons, France. Economist. m. Nicole Rupied, 2 sons, 2 daughters. Education: Diploma, Engineer, Ecole Polytechnique, 1949; Diploma, Ecole Nationale de la Statistique et de l'Administration Economique (ENSAE), 1951; Diploma, Institute of Statistics of the University of Paris (ISUP), 1951. Appointments include: Professor, Short term economic forecasts, ENSAE, 1956-95; Professor, Ecole des Hautes Etudes en Sciences Sociales (EHESS), Chair of Statistics and Economic Forecasts, 1962-92; Inspector General, National Institute of Statistics and Economic Studies (INSEE), 1973-92; Director, Centre of Studies on Income and Costs (CERC), 1966-76. Publications (in French) include: Productivity, growth, employment, 1984; To Reinvent the Growth, 1993; Public Expenditure in France, With International Comparisons, 1994; Local Collections and the National Economy, 1997; Employment, Growth and Money: For a New Policy, 1998. Honours: Officer of the Legion of Honour; Officer of the Ordre National du Mérite; Holder of the Palmes Académiques; 2 Prizes of the French Academy des Sciences Morales et Politiques, 1985, 1990. Memberships: National Economic and Social Council, 1979-94; General Council of the Bank of France, 1989-91; International Statistical Institute, 1972-; Vice-President, 1985-86, President, 1987, French Statistical Society. Address: 125 Boulevard de la Reine, 78000, Versailles, France.

Dictionary of International Biography

MERCER Ian Dews, b. 25 January 1933, Wolverhampton, England. Rural Conservator, retired. m. (1) Valerie Jean, 4 sons, 1 deceased, (2) Pamela Margaret Gillies, 1 step son, 1 step daughter. Education: BA honours, Geography, University of Birmingham. Appointments: National Service, Sub-Lieutenant RNR, 1954-56; Assistant, Preston Montford Field Centre, 1956-57; Assistant Warden, Juniper Hall Field Centre, 1957-59; Warden, Slapton Ley Field Centre, 1959-68; Lecturer, St Lukes College, Exeter, 1968-70; Warden, Malham Tarn Field Centre, 1970-71; County Conservation Officer, Devon County Council, 1971-73; Chief Officer, Dartmoor National Park Authority, 1973-90; Chief Executive, Countryside Council for Wales, 1990-95; Professor of Rural Conservation, University of Wales, Bangor, 1991-; Secretary General, Association of National Park Authorities, 1996-2001; Governor, University of Plymouth, 1996-; Chairman, South West Forest Partnership, 2002-. Publications include: Several papers in professional journals; Book chapters; Crisis and Opportunity: Report by chair of public inquiry into Foot and Mouth Disease in Devon, 2002. Honours: Honorary LLD, Exeter, 1994; CBE, 1995; Honorary DSc, Plymouth, 1995; Honorary Fellow, Landscape Institute, 1997; Fellow, Royal Agricultural Societies, 1999. Memberships: British Ecological Society; President, Field Studies Council; President, Devon Wildlife Trust; Devon and Cornwall Regional Committee National Trust; World Commission on Protected Areas. Address: Ponsford House, Moretonhampstead, Devon, TQ13 8NL, England. E-mail: ian.mercer@freeuk.com

MEREDITH William (Morris), b. 9 January 1919, New York, New York, USA. Poet; Retired Professor of English. Education: AB, Princeton University, 1940. Appointments: Instructor in English and Woodrow Wilson Fellow in Writing, Princeton University, 1946-50; Associate Professor in English, University of Hawaii, 1950-51; Associate Professor, 1955-65, Professor in English, 1965-83, Connecticut College, New London; Instructor, Bread Loaf School of English, Middlebury College, Vermont, 1958-62; Consultant in Poetry, Library of Congress, Washington, DC, 1978-80. Publications: Poetry: Love Letters from an Impossible Land, 1944; Ships and Other Figures, 1948; The Open Sea and Other Poems, 1958; The Wreck of the Thresher and Other Poems, 1964; Winter Verse, 1964; Year End Accounts, 1965; Two Pages from a Colorado Journal, 1967; Earth Walk: New and Selected Poems, 1970; Hazard, the Painter, 1975; The Cheer, 1980; Partial Accounts: New and Selected Poems, 1987. Non-Fiction: Reasons for Poetry and the Reason for Criticism, 1982; Poems Are Hard to Read, 1991. Editor: Shelley: Poems, 1962; University and College Poetry Prizes, 1960-66, 1966; Eighteenth-Century Minor Poets (with Mackie L Jarrell), 1968; Poets of Bulgaria (with others), 1985. Translator: Guillaume Apollinaire: Alcools: Poems, 1898-1913, 1964. Honours: Yale Series of Younger Poets Award, 1943; Harriet Monroe Memorial Prize, 1944; Rockefeller Foundation Grants, 1948, 1968; Oscar Blumenthal Prize, 1953; National Institute of Arts and Letters Grant, 1958, and Loines Prize, 1966; Ford Foundation Fellowship, 1959-60; Van Wyck Brooks Award, 1971; National Endowment for the Arts Grant, 1972, and Fellowship, 1984; Guggenheim Fellowship, 1975-76; International Vaptsarov Prize for Literature, Bulgaria, 1979; Los Angeles Times Prize, 1987; Pulitzer Prize in Poetry, 1988. Memberships: Academy of American Poets, chancellor; National Institute of Arts and Letters. Address: 6300 Bradley Avenue, Bethseda, MD 20817, USA.

MERELLI Raimo Wilhelm, b. 5 October 1947, Karvia, Finland. Company Director. m. Katri Vähämaki, 4 December 1976, 1 son, 1 daughter. Education: Commercial College, Kauhava; MBA, Washington University. Appointments: Director, several companies in Finland, 1971-. Honours: Defence Medal and Blue Cross of Finland and other military medals; Knight Order of Cross of Constantin The Great; Knight Commander Order of St Eugen of Trebizond; Gold Medal, Central Chamber of Commerce, Finland; Accademician of Accademia Angelina Constantiniana de Arte, Lettere e Scienzi. Membership: Finland-Liechtenstein Society. Address: PO Box 495, 00101 Helsinki, Finland.

MERI Lennart, b. 29 March 1929, Tallinn, Estonia. President of the Republic of Estonia; Professor. m. Helle Meri, 2 sons, 1 daughter. Education: Graduate, Historian, cum laude, Tartu University, 1953. Appointments: Dramatist, Vanemuine Theatre, 1953-55; Professor, Tartu Art School; Producer, Estonian Radio, 1955-61; Script Writer, 1963-68, Producer, 1968-71, 1986-88, Tallinnfilm; Foreign Relations Secretary, Estonian Writers Union, 1985-87; Estonian Popular Front and National Heritage Preservation Association, 1980's; Founder, Director, Estonian Institute, 1988-90; Ministry of Foreign Affairs, Estonia, 1990-92; Ambassador of Estonia to Finland, 1992; President, Republic of Estonia, 1992-96, re-elected, 19962001. Publications include: Kobrade ja karakurtide jälgedes (Following the Trails of Cobras and Black Widows), 1959; Virmaliste väraval (At the Gate of Northern Lights), 1974; Tulen maasta, jonka nimi on Viro (Coming From the Country Called Estonia), 1995. Address: Pilviku str 3, Tallin, Estonia.

MERZHANOV Victor Korpovich, b. 15 August 1919, Tombov, Russia. Pianist; Organist. 1 daughter. Education: Graduate and Postgraduate, Moscow State Conservatoire "P. I. Chaikovsky", 1941. Appointments: Teacher, 1947, Reader, 1951, Professor, 1964, Head of the Chair of Piano Faculty, 1985-2000, Moscow Conservatoire; Judge at prominent competitions including: Queen Elisabeth, Brussels, European Piano Forum in Berlin, European Epta Kongress and other musical competitions, 1960-; Masterclasses in France, Germany, Greece, Israel, Italy, Poland, USA, Yugoslavia and Japan, 1960-; Professor, Higher Musical School Warsaw, 1973-78; Vice President, Russian Musical Society, 1984; President, Russian Rachmaninov Society, 1996; Honourable President of Russian Branch of European Pianist-Teachers Association, 1996; Honourable Doctor of the Byelorussian Academy of Music, 2003. Creative Works: 2000 chamber solo and symphony concerts in 298 cities of 30 countries, 1946-; 28 gramophone records, 5 CDs in Russia, USA, Italy and Japan; Created new modern edition of, Well-tempered Clavier, by Bach. Honours: Laureate I of the Prize of All-Union competition of pianists; Laureate of International Competition of Chopin; Orders, For Outstanding Public Service to Polish Culture, For Outstanding Public Service to Poland; Order of Peoples Friendship, Russian Government. Memberships: Russian Musical Society; Russian Rachmaninov Society; European Pianist-Teachers Association. Address: Sadovo Spasskaia St 21-183, Moscow, 107078 Moscow, Russia. E-mail: vicira@rol.ru

MESSERE Kenneth Charles, b. 16 April 1928, Richmond, Surrey, England. Freelance Writer; Consultant for IMF, OECD, World Bank; Former Head of Fiscal Affairs Division, OECD. m. (1) Mary Humphrey, 1954, divorced 1982; (2) Brunehilde Lequesne, 1984-. Education: MA, Philosophy, Politics, Economics, Oxford University, 1951. Appointments: Assistant Principal and Principal, British Customs and Excise, London, 1951-64; Principal Administrator and Head of Fiscal Affairs Division, OECD, (Organisation for Economic Corporation and Development) Paris, 1964-91; Consultant, OECD, IMF, World Bank in East Europe, North Africa, Latin America, writer and editor of books and articles, 1991-2002. Publications: Vth World International Correspondence Chess Championship, 1971; Tax Policy in OECD countries: Choices and Conflicts, 1993; Tax policy: theory and practice in OECD countries, 2003. Honours: International Correspondence Chess Master, 1971; Order of British Empire, 1991. Address: 8 rue Eugène Delacroix, 75116 Paris, France.

METCALF John Wesley, b. 12 November 1938, Carlisle, England. Writer. m. Myrna Teitelbaum, 3 sons, 2 daughters. Education: BA, Bristol University, 1960. Appointments: Writer-in-Residence, University of New Brunswick, 1972-73, Loyola of Montreal, 1976, University of Ottawa, 1977, Concordia University, 1980-81, University of Bologna, 1985. Publications: The Lady Who Sold Furniture, 1970; The Teeth of My Father, 1975; Girl in Gingham, 1978; Kicking Against the Pricks, 1982; Adult Entertainment, 1986; How Stories Mean, 1993; Shooting the Stars, 1993; Freedom from Culture, 1994; Forde Abroad, 2004; An Aesthetic Underground, 2004. Contributions to: Many publications in Canada and USA. Honour: Canada Council Arts Awards, 1968-69, 1971, 1974, 1976, 1978, 1980, 1983, 1985. Address: 128 Lewis Street, Ottawa, Ontario K2P 0S7, Canada.

MEYER Conrad John Eustace, b. 2 July 1922, Bristol, England. Retired Roman Catholic Priest. m. Mary Wiltshire. Education: Pembroke College, Cambridge; Westcott House, Cambridge; Ordained Priest in the Roman Catholic Church, 1995. Appointments: War Service, 1942-46; Lieutenant (S), Chaplain, RNVR, retired 1954; As Anglican: Diocesan Secretary for Education, 1960-69; Archdeacon of Bodmin, Truro Diocese, 1969-79 Honorary Canon, Truro Cathedral, 1960-79; Provost, Western Division of Woodard Schools, 1970-92; Examining Chaplain to the Bishop of Truro, 1973-79; Area Bishop of Dorchester, Oxford Diocese, 1979-87; Honorary Assistant Bishop, Truro Diocese, 1990-94; As Roman Catholic: Honorary Canon, Plymouth Roman Catholic Cathedral, 2001. Memberships: Formerly Chairman of Appeal Committee, Vice-Chairman of Society, 1989-90, Vice-President, 1990-, Society for Promoting Christian Knowledge (SPCK); Chairman, Cornwall Civil Aid and County Commissioner, 1993-96; Honorary Fellow, Institute for Civil Defence and Disaster Studies. Address: Hawk's Cliff, 38 Praze Road, Newquay, Cornwall TR7 3AF, England.

MEYER Heinrich H D, b. 13 July 1950, Holtrup, Germany. Biochemist. m. Susanna, 1 son, 3 daughters. Education: Diploma in Biochemistry, Dr rer nat; Dr agr habil, Professor of Physiology. Appointments: Full Professor, Technical University, Munich; Regular Consultant of UN organisations, the EU and research institutes. Publications: About 300 on endocrinology, enzyme immunoassay development, wildlife biology, comparative physiology, reproduction, doping control and growth regulation. Honours: German Endocrine Society, 1982; H W Schumann Foundation, 1989; Society of Nutrition, 1992. Memberships: Various societies on endocrinology, biochemistry and nutrition. Address: Meisenstrasse 12, D-85416 Langenbach, Germany.

MEYER Siri, b. 5 June 1952, Oslo, Norway. Professor. Education: Mag. Art, 1983, Dr. Art, 1993, University of Bergen, Bergen, Norway. Appointments: Associate Professor, 1991-98, Professor, 1998-, Department of Art History, University of Bergen, Bergen, Norway; Director, Centre for the Study of European Civilisation, University of Bergen, 1993-2004. Publications: Pippi Longstockings Gives the Lessons, Essays on the Language of Power and the Power of Language, 1995; A Craving for Reality. Travelling in Himalaya, 2002; The Empire is Calling. An Essay on the Anatomy of Power, 2003. Membership: Commission on Power of Democracy appointed by the Government of Norway; Editor of the book series: Cultural Texts. Address: Nygårdsgt 2A, 5015 Bergen, Norway. E-mail: siri.meyer@sek.vib.no

MEYERS Carol, b. 26 November 1942, Wilkes-Barre, Pennsylvania, USA. University Professor; Archaeologist. m. Eric Meyers, 2 daughters. Education: AB (Honours), Wellesley College, 1960-64; MA, 1966, PhD, 1975, Near Eastern and Judaic Studies, Brandeis University. Appointments include: Assistant Professor,

1977-84, Associate Professor, 1984-90, Professor, 1990-, Mary Grace Wilson Professor of Religion, 2002-, Department of Religion, Duke University; Co-director, Duke University, Summer Program in Israel, 1980-; Research Faculty, Women's Studies, Duke University, 1983-; Co-Director, Joint Sepphoris Project, 1984-; Associate Director, Women's Studies Program, Duke University, 1986-98; Member, Center of Theological Inquiry, Princeton, 1991-; Co-director, Sepphoris Regional Project, 1992-; Consultant, "Mysteries of the Bible", Cable Television, by Christy Connell Roos Entertainment Group, 1993; For Film Roos, 1993-94, 1995-96, 1996-97; Consultant Lilith Publications Network, 1994-; Visiting Faculty, MA program in Judaic Studies, University of Connecticut, 1994-; Consultant, Dreamworks (Spielberg et al) production, Prince of Egypt, 1997-98; Senior Adviser, Sepphoris Acropolis Project, 1999-; Consultant, Israel/Hebrew Bible Series (NOVA/WGBH Boston), 2000-; Consultant, BBC Network Current Affairs documentary on Jesus' family tree, 2003; Consultant, Oxford University Press, for Oxford Bible Atlas, 2002-03; Editorial Board, Women's Commentary on the Torah; Editorial Advisor, Cambridge Dictionary of Jewish Religion, History and Culture; Editorial Board, Jewish Women: A Comprehensive Historical Encyclopaedia; Associate Editor, Bulletin of the American Schools of Oriental Research; Acting Director, Duke University Judaic Studies Program, 2004. Publications: Books include: Discovering Eve: Ancient Israelite Women in Context, 1988; Co-author, Haggai-Zechariah 1-8, 1987; Co-author, Sepphoris, 1992; Co-author, Zechariah 9-14, 1993; Community, Identity and Ideology: Social Science Approaches to the Hebrew Bible (co-editor), 1996; Sepphoris in Galilee: Cross Currents of Culture (co-editor), 1996; Co-author, Families in Ancient Israel, 1997; Women in Scripture: A Dictionary of Named and Unnamed Women in the Hebrew Bible, the Apocryphal/Deuterocanonical Books, and the New Testament (editor), 2000; Hundreds of articles in professional journals, contributions to other works, papers, cassettes, videos. Honours include: Many grants, fellowships, biographical entries, Fachberiech Evangelische Theologie, Johann Wolfgang Goethe Universität, Frankfort am Main, Research Associate, 1995; International Corresponding Fellow, Ingeborg Rennert Center for Jerusalem Studies, Bar Ilan University, Israel, 1998-; Wellesley College Alumnae Achievement Award, 1999; Education Endowment Award, Women's Institute for Continuing Jewish Education, 2001. Address: 3202 Waterbury Drive, Durham, NC 27707, USA.

MEYERS Mary Ann, b. 30 September 1937, Sodus, New York, USA. Foundation Executive; Author. m. John Matthew Meyers, 1 son, 1 daughter. Education: BA, magna cum laude, Syracuse University, 1959; MA, 1965, PhD, 1976, University of Pennsylvania. Appointments: Editorial Assistant, Ladies Home Journal, 1959-62; Editor and Assistant Director, News Bureau, 1962-65, Assistant to President, 1973-75 University of Pennsylvania; Director of College Relations, Editor of Horizons, Lecturer in Religion, Haverford College, 1977-80; Secretary of the University, Lecturer in American Civilization, University of Pennsylvania, 1980-90; President, Annenburg Foundation, 1990-92; Vice President, Moore College of Art and Design, 1995-97; Senior Fellow, John Templeton Foundation, 1997-. Publications: Author: A New World Jerusalem: The Swedenborgian Experience in Community Construction, 1983; Art, Education and African American Culture: Albert Barnes and the Science of Philanthropy, 2004; Co-author: Death in America, 1975; Gladly Learn, Gladly Teach, 1978; Coping with Serious Illness, 1980; Religion in America, 1987. Honours: Elected Member, Phi Beta Kappa; Awards for Excellence, Women in Communications Inc, 1973, 1974; Award for Public Affairs Reporting, Newsweek/ Council for Advancement and Support of Education, 1977; Silver Medal, Council for Advancement and Support in Education, 1986.

Memberships: Board of Advisors, Peter Gruber Foundation; Secretary and Director, American Academy of Political and Social Science; Cosmopolitan Club; Sunday Breakfast Club. Address: 217 Gypsy Lane, Wynnewood, PA 19096, USA.

MEYLAN Raymond, b. 22 September 1924, Geneva. Flautist; Musicologist. m. Anne-Marie Bersot, 28 July 1959, 1 daughter. Education: University of Lausanne, 1947; DLitt, University of Zurich, 1967; Studied at Conservatoire of Geneva, 1943 and in Paris with Marcel Moyse, 1948; Accademia Chigiana, Sienna, with Ruggero Gerlin, 1949-51. Debut: 1944. Career: Solo Flute, Ass Alessandro Scarlatti, 1951-54; Pomeriggi Musicali, Milan, 1954-58; Orchestra of Radio Beromünster, Zurich, 1958-70; Basler Orchester Gesellschaft, Basle, 1971-89; Lecturer in Musicology, University of Zurich, 1969-77; Conductor, Orchestre Académique de Zurich, 1969-77, Orchesterverein Liestal, 1977-91; Studies in archaeology of flutes, 1972-. Compositions: Le Choix, for voice, choir, flute, vibraphone and marimba, 1979; Notre Dame de Lausanne, for wind, 1986; Bourrasque, for large orchestra in ampitheatre, 1987; Cinq Miniatures, for flute and guitar, 1987; Assonances, for scattered orchestra, 1988. Recordings: Flute Concertos by Danzi, Widor and Reinecke; Salieri, in Virtuoso Oboe; Bernard Reichel, VDE Gallo; Beethoven, 10 themes and variations, op 107; Telemann, triple concerto, with Zagreber Solisten, A Janigro, Amadeo and The Bach Guild. Publications: L'énigme de la musique des basses danses du quinzième siècle, 1969; The Flute, 1974; Publications on Attaingnant, Mazzocchi, A and D Scarlatti, Sarri, JC and JS Bach, Nardini, Fischer, Schwindl, Kozeluh, Bellini, Donizetti, Böhm, d'Alessandro, other works forthcoming. Contributions to: Musical and scholarly journals; Musical dictionaries. Membership: Swiss Association of Musicians; Swiss Musicological Society; French Society of Musicology. Address: Buchenstr 58, 4142 Münchenstein, Switzerland.

MGBENU Emmanuel Nwaka, b. 24 January 1941, Kano, Nigeria. University Professor. m. Chinwe Mgbenu, 2 sons, 2 daughters. Education: BSc, Physics, 1964, PhD, Nuclear Physics, 1969, University of London. Appointments: Post Doctoral Research Fellow, Northern Polytechnic, London, 1969; Lecturer, Fourah Bay College, Sierra Leone, 1969-73; Lecturer, Senior Lecturer, University of Ibadan, 1973-81; Professor, Abia State University, 1981-99; Professor, Imo State University, 1999-; Head of Department, 1981-90, Dean, 1992-97, 2000-, Imo State University. Publications: Books: Electromagnetism and Modern Physics for Physical Sciences, 1993; Waves, Optics and Thermal Physics, 1995; Modern Physics, 1995; Many articles published in local and international journals in the specialist areas of nuclear physics, solid state physics and solid state electronics. Honours: Eastern Nigeria Government University Scholarship, 1961-64; Commonwealth Scholarship, 1965-68; Fellowship of the Nigerian Institute of Physics, 1998. Memberships: Life Member, Council Member, 1996-2000, Nigerian Institute of Physics; Science Association of Nigeria. Address: Department of Physics and Industrial Physics, Imo State University, PMB 2000, Owerri, Nigeria.

MGBOH Angela M N, b. 10 December 1940, Enugu, Nigeria. Retired Civil Servant. m. Vincent O Mgboh, 1 son, 4 daughters. Education: Certificate in Education, 1963; Diploma in Education, Backward Children, 1966; BA (Hons), Education, History, 1975; Masters Degree in Education, 1980; PhD, Education, 1988. Appointments: Director, Exams Dev Centre, Enugu, Nigeria; Permanent Secretary, Ministry of Education, Enugu, Nigeria; Head of Service, Enugu State, Nigeria; Consultant, Economic Affairs Unit, Government House, Enugu, Nigeria; Chairman, State Primary Education Board, Enugu State, Nigeria. Publications: Education

of Backward Children in Nigeria; Anambra State Common Entrance Examination as a predictor of Academic Achievement in Schools; The Development and Validation of Instruments for the Continuous Assessment of Pupils Achievement in Lower Primary Maths. Honours: National Honours Award, Member of the Federal Republic of Nigeria (MFR); Meritorious Service Award, Office of HOSF, Abuja, Nigeria. Memberships: Catholic Women's Organisation; National Council of Women's Societies in Nigeria; Belle Afrique; Eke Women's Association. Address: Road 9, House 15A, Trans-Ekulu, PO Box 2538, Enugu, Enugu State, Nigeria.

MGEMANE Isaac Lizo Sheperd, b. 6 July 1934, Orange Free State, South Africa. Physician; Musician; Composer. 1 son, 1 daughter. Education: MB, ChB, Oslo, 1968; Diploma in Music, Oslo Correspondence School of Music, 1975; Private studies. Appointments: Medical Officer, Sweden, 1970-72; District Assistant, Selje, 1970; Hospital Training, Fredrikstad, 1969, Ulleval and Riks Hospitals, 1970-71, Aker Hospital, Oslo, 1972, Falkoping, 1973; Probationer, Hoyanger Hospital, 1970, Molde Fylkes Hospital, 1971, Legevakt, Oslo, 1973-78, Moss Legevakt, 1979-83; Private Practice, Oslo and Mosslegev. Publications: Poliklinikk Medisin, 1977; Teach Yourself Guitar and Improvisation, 1980; A Method in Violin Playing, 1986; An Introduction to Keyboards and Piano Playing, 2001; Concerto No 1 in C major, for piano and orchestra, 2001; Composer of 6 violin concerto and 3 piano concertos in C, D, and A majors; Concertos 2 and 3 for the piano and orchestra, 2002. Honours: Gold Medal, 1986; Order of Merit, 1994; Platinum Record, 1996; Hall of Fame, 1998; Outstanding Man of the 20th century, 1999-2000; Man of the Millennium, IBC, 1999-2000; 2000 Millennium Medal of Honor, 2000; Universal Award of Accomplishment, 2000. Memberships: Methodist Church; Musicians Union of South Africa; Pan African Congress; Research Council, IBC. Address: PO Box 21982, 1820 Zakariya Park, Johannesburg, South Africa.

MIANO Eliphelet, b. 18 November 1932, Meru, Kenya. Civil Engineer. m. Zipporah Murugi, 2 sons, 3 daughters. Makerere University, Kampala, Uganda, 1950-52; University of Alberta, Canada, 1961-65. Appointments: Engineering Assistant, 1953-61, Civil Engineer, 1965-67, Mowlem Construction Company; East African Engineering Consultants, 1967-; Appointed Director, 1969, Chairman, 1978. Honours: Elder of the Order of Burning Spear (EBS), Republic of Kenya, 1985. Memberships: Fellow, Institution of Engineers of Kenya; Association, Consulting Engineers of Kenya. Address: PO Box 21045, Nairobi, Kenya.

MICHAEL Alun Edward, b. 22 August 1943, Wales, England. m. 2 sons, 3 daughters. Education: Keele University. Appointments: Journalist, South Wales Echo, 1966-71; Youth and Community Worker, Cardiff, 1972-84; Area Community Education Officer, Grangetown and Butetown, 1984-87; Member, Cardiff City Council, 1973-89; Member, House of Commons, Labour and Co-op, for Cardiff South and Penarth, 1987-; Opposition Whip, 1987-88; Opposition Frontbench Spokesman on Welsh Affairs, 1988-92, on Home Affairs and the Voluntary Sector, 1992-97; Ministry of State, Home Office, 1997-98; Secretary of State for Wales, 1998-99; 1st Secretary, National Assembly for Wales, 1999-2000; Minister of State for Rural Affairs and Urban Quality of Life, Department for the Environment, Food and Rural Affairs, 2001-; Member, National Assembly for Wales for Mid and West Wales, 1999-. Memberships include: Vice President, YHA. Address: House of Commons, London, SW1A 0AA, England.

MICHAEL George (Georgios Kyriacos Panayiotou), b. 25 June 1963, Finchley, London, England. Singer; Songwriter; Producer. Career: Singer, The Executive, 1979; Singer, pop duo Wham! with Andrew Ridgeley, 1982-86; Solo artiste, 1986-; Worldwide appearances include: Live Aid, with Elton John, Wembley, 1985; Prince's Trust Rock Gala, 1986; Wham's 'The Final' concert, Wembley, 1986; Nelson Mandela's 70th Birthday Tribute, 1988; Rock In Rio II Festival, Brazil, 1991; A Concert For Life, tribute to Freddie Mercury, Wembley Stadium, 1992; Elizabeth Taylor AIDS Foundation Benefit, Madison Square Garden, New York, 1992; Dispute with Epic record label, and parent company Sony Entertainment, 1992-95; Television special, Aretha Franklin: Duets, 1993. Recordings: Albums: with Wham!: Fantastic, 1983; Make It Big, 1984; The Final, 1986; Solo albums: Faith, 1987; Listen Without Prejudice, Vol 1, 1990; Older, 1996; Older and Upper, 1998; Ladies and Gentlemen: The Best of George Michael, 1998; Songs from the Last Century, 1999; Patience, 2004; Contributor, Duets, Elton John, 1991; Two Rooms, 1992; Hit singles include: with Wham!: Wham Rap, 1982; Young Guns (Go For It), 1982; Bad Boys, 1983; Club Tropicana, 1983; Wake Me Up Before You Go Go, 1984; Last Christmas, 1984; Careless Whisper, 1984; Everything She Wants, 1984; Freedom, 1985; I'm Your Man, 1985; The Edge Of Heaven, 1986; Solo: A Different Corner, 1986; I Knew You Were Waiting For Me, duet with Aretha Franklin, 1987; I Want Your Sex, 1987; Faith, 1987; Father Figure, 1988; One More Try, 1988; Monkey, 1988; Kissing A Fool, 1988; Praying For Time, 1990; Freedom 90, 1990; Don't Let The Sun Go Down On Me, duet with Elton John; Too Funky, 1992; Five Live EP, 1993; Somebody To Love, with Queen, 1993; Jesus To A Child, 1995; Fast Love, 1996; Star People, 1997; You Have Been Loved, 1997; Outside, 1998; As, with Mary J Blige, 1999; If I Told You That, with Whitney Houston, 2000; Freeek!, 2002; Shoot the Dog, 2002; Amazing, 2004; Contributor, Do They Know It's Christmas?, Band Aid, 1985; Nikita, Elton John, 1985. Publication: Bare, with Tony Parsons (autobiography). Honours include: BRIT Awards: Best British Group, 1985; Outstanding Contribution to British Music, 1986; Best British Male Artist, 1988; Best British Album, 1991; Ivor Novello Awards: Songwriter Of The Year, 1985, 1989; Most Performed Work (Careless Whisper), 1985; Hit Of The Year (Faith), 1989; Grammy, with Aretha Franklin, 1988; Nordoff-Robbins Silver Clef Award, 1989; American Music Awards: Favourite Pop/Rock Male Artist, Soul R&B Male Artist, Favourite Album, 1989; ASCAP Golden Note Award, 1992. Address: c/o Connie Filipello Publicity, 17 Gosfield Street, London W1P 7HE, England.

MICHAEL H M King, b. 25 October 1921, Romania. King of Romania. m. Princess Anne of Bourbon-Parma, 1948, 5 daughters. Appointments: Declared heir apparent, ratified by Parliament 1926; Proclaimed King, 1927, deposed by his father, 1930; Succeeded to the throne of Romania following his father's abdication, 1940; Led coup d'etat against pro Nazi dictator Ion Antonescu, 1944; Forced to abdicate following communist takeover of Romania, 1947; Subsequently ran chicken farm in Hertfordshire, England; Went to Switzerland as a Test Pilot, 1956; Worked for Lear Incorporated; Founder, Electronics Company; Stockbroker; Deported from Romania on first visit since exile, 1990; Returned to Romania, 1992; Romanian citizenship and passport restored, 1997; Undertook official mission for Romania's integration into NATO and EU 1997. Honours: Order of Victoria, USSR, 1945; Chief Commander, Legion of Merit, USA, 1946; Honorary KCVO. Address: Villa Serena, Versoix, Geneva, Switzerland.

MIDDLETON Stanley, b. 1 August 1919, Bulwell, Nottingham, England. Novelist. m. Margaret Shirley Charnley, 22 December 1951, 2 daughters. Education: University College, Nottingham; BA, London University; Cert Ed, Cambridge University; MEd, Nottingham University. Appointments: H M Forces, 1940-46; Head of English, High Pavement College, Nottingham; Judith E Wilson Visiting Fellow, Emmanuel College, Cambridge. Publications: A Short Answer, 1958; Harris's Requiem, 1960; A

Serious Woman, 1961; The Just Exchange, 1962; Two's Company, 1963; Him They Compelled, 1964; The Golden Evening, 1968; Wages of Virtue, 1969; Brazen Prison, 1971; Holiday, 1974; Still Waters, 1976; Two Brothers, 1978; In a Strange Land, 1979; The Other Side, 1980; Blind Understanding, 1982; Entry into Jerusalem, 1983; Daysman, 1984; Valley of Decision, 1985; An After Dinner's Sleep, 1986; After a Fashion, 1987; Recovery, 1988; Vacant Places, 1989; Changes & Chances, 1990; Beginning to End, 1991; A Place to Stand, 1992; Married Past Redemption, 1993; Catalysts, 1994; Toward the Sea, 1995; Live and Learn, 1996; Brief Hours, 1997; Against the Dark, 1997; Necessary Ends, 1999; Small Change, 2000; Love in the Provinces. Honours: Co-Recipient, Booker Prize, 1974; Honorary MA, Nottingham University; Honorary MUniv, Open University; Honorary DLitt, De Montfort University; FRSL; Honorary DLitt, Nottingham Trent University, 2000. Membership: PEN. Address: 42 Caledon Road, Sherwood, Nottingham NG5 2NG, England.

MIDLER Bette, b. 1 December 1945, Paterson, New Jersey, USA. Singer; Actress; Comedienne. m. Martin von Haselberg, 1984, 1 daughter. Education: Theatre studies, University of Hawaii. Career: As actress: Cast member, Fiddler On The Roof, Broadway, 1966-69; Salvation, New York, 1970; Rock opera Tommy, Seattle Opera Company, 1971; Nightclub concert performer and solo artiste, 1972-; Numerous television appearances include: Ol' Red Hair Is Back, 1978; Bette Midler's Mondo Beyondo, HBO, 1988; Earth Day Special, ABC, 1990; The Tonight Show, NBC, 1991; Now, NBC, 1993; Films include: Hawaii, 1965; The Rose, 1979; Jinxed!, 1982; Down And Out In Beverly Hills, 1985; Ruthless People, 1986; Outrageous Fortune, 1987; Big Business, 1988; Beaches, 1988; Stella, 1990; Scenes From A Mall, 1990; For The Boys (also co-producer), 1991; Hocus Pocus, 1993; Own company, All Girls Productions, 1989-. Recordings: Albums include: The Divine Miss M, 1972; Bette Midler, 1973; Songs For The New Depression, 1976; Broken Blossom, 1977; Live At Last, 1977; Thighs And Whispers, 1979; The Rose, film soundtrack, 1979; Divine Madness, film soundtrack, 1980; No Frills, 1984; Beaches, film soundtrack, 1989; Some People's Lives, 1991; Best Of, 1993; Bette Of Roses, 1995; Experience the Divine, 1997; Bathhouse Betty, 1998; From a Distance, 1998. Singles include: The Rose; Wind Beneath My Wings (Number 1, US), from Beaches soundtrack, 1989; From A Distance, 1991. Publications: A View From A Broad; The Saga Of Baby Divine. Honours: After Dark Award, Performer Of The Year, 1973; Grammy Awards: Best New Artist, 1973; Best Female Pop Vocal Performance, The Rose, 1981; Record Of The Year, Song Of The Year, Wind Beneath My Wings, 1990; Special Tony Award, 1973; Emmy, Ol' Red Hair Is Back, 1978; Golden Globe Awards: The Rose, 1979; For The Boys, 1991; Oscar Nomination, Best Actress, The Rose, 1980; Contributor, We Are The World, USA For Africa, 1985; Oliver And Company, 1988. Address: c/o All Girls Productions, Animation Bldg #3B-10, 500 South Buena Vista, Burbank, CA 91521, USA.

MIGENES Victor, b. 10 August 1959, New York, USA. Astronomer. m. Sonia N Migenes, 2 daughters. Education: BSc, Physics, University of Puerto Rico, 1981; PhD, Astronomy and Astrophysics, University of Pennsylvania, USA, 1989. Appointments: Postdoctoral Research Appointment, University of Manchester, Joddrell Bank, England, 1989-92; Postdoctoral Research Appointment, ATNF-CSIRO, Australia, 1992-95; Postdoctoral Research Appointment, National Astronomical Observatory of Japan, 1995-97; Research Professor, University of Guanajuato, Mexico, 1997-. Publications: Over 40 papers and 400 citations. Honours: Fontaine Fellowship, University of Pennsylvania, 1982-84; Ella Nichols Pawling Fellowship, University of Pennsylvania, 1982-85; Sistema de Investigadores,

CONACVT, Mexico. Memberships: American Astronomical Society, Astronomical Society of Australia; International Astronomical Union. Address: University of Guanajuato, Department of Astronomy, PO Box 144, Guanajuato, GTO 36000, Mexico. E-mail: vmigenes@astro.ugto.mx

MIHĂILĂ Marian-Ioan, b. June 1954, Romania. International Lawyer. Education: Graduate, Faculty of Law, Bucharest, Romania; Postgraduate studies, Humanitarian International Law and Human Rights Law, 1993-94; The Summer School of Porec-Croatia-speciality, The euroregional co-operation, 1999; Studies in Public International Law, 1999-2002; Doctor in International Law, "Al. I Cuza" Academy, Faculty of Law, Bucharest, 2002. Appointments: Lecturer, Public and Private International Law, Human Rights Law, European Community Law, Faculty of Administrative and Economic Sciences, "Eftimie Murgu" University of Reşiţa; Lecturer, Masters Course, Romanian Humanitarian Law Society; Organiser, International Scientific Seminars on the Protection of Cultural Property in Romania, 1999-. Publications include: The Protection of Cultural Property in International Law, 1995; Co-author: Human Rights in the United Nations System, 1997; Co-author: Yugoslavia- The Last Emergency Signal for Saving the Cultural Property with International Value, 2000; Co-author: European Community Law, 2000; The Juridical Protection of Human Rights, 2001; Nations of Public and Private International Law, 2001; Co-author: The European Community Offices, the transfrontier co-operation in the International Law and the Regional development, 2002; Co-author: The International Law of the Community, 2002; The Protection of Cultural Property in the International Law, 2003; La Protection des Biens Culturels dans le droit international, French edition, 2003. Memberships: President, Branch Reşiţa, Romanian Humanitarian Law Association, 1994-; President, Romanian Society for the Protection of Cultural Property, 1996-; President, League of National Societies for the Protection of Cultural Property, 2003-2004. Address: P-ţa 1 Decembrie 1918, bl. 4, sc. B, ap 11, cod: 320067, Caraş Severin County, Romania. E-mail: srpbcromania@yahoo.fr

MIHĂILESCU Petru Şerban, b. 8 March 1944, Bucharest, Romania. Engineer. m. Doina Mihăilescu, 1 daughter. Education: Graduate, Bucharest Polytechnic School, 1966; Graduate, National Defence College, 2001; Candidate for PhD in the field of Central Public Administration Management. Appointments: Secretary of State, Ministry of Transport, 1992-96; Member of Romanian Parliament, 1996-2000; Minister for Co-ordinating the General Secretariat of Government, Member of Romanian Parliament, 2000-. Publications: More than 20 scientific works, articles and socio-political studies published in Romania and abroad. Honours: Star of Romania, Officer Degree; Légion d'honneur, Officer Degree. Membership: Vice-President, Democrat Social Party of Romania (Government Party). Address: Piata Victoriei 1, Bucharest, Romania. E-mail: sgg@gov.ro Website: www.sgg.ro

MIHALTAN Florin Dumitru, b. 26 October 1954, Sibiu, Romania. Pneumologist. m. Monica Mihaltan. Education: Faculty of Medicine, Bucharest, Romania, 1973-79; Specialist in Pneumology, 1982-91. Appointments: Associate Professor of Pneumology, 2000-; Vice-President, Romanian Society of Pneumology; Vice-President, NGO "Aer Pur". Publications: Author of 200 papers published in Romanian Review; 20 papers published in International Review; 6 books published in Romania. Honour: Silver Medal, Romanian Red Cross. Memberships: Chest; French Society of Pneumology; American College of Angiology. Address: Str. Daniel Barcianu Nr 34, Sect III, Bucharest, Romania. E-mail: mihaltan@starnets.ro

MIKHAILOV Viacheslav Fedorovich, b. 16 June 1928, Chimkent, Kazakhstan. Physicist. m. Ludmila Ilinichna, 2 sons, 1 daughter. Education: Kazakhstan State University, Almaty, 1957; Postgraduate course, Kaz St University, Experimental Physics Chairman and JINR Dubna, 1961. Appointments: Student, 1953-57, Assistant exp phys chairman, 1957-59, Postgraduate, 1959-61, Kazakhstan State University; Senior Research Worker, 1st Nuclear Physics Academy of Sciences, Kazakhstan, Almaty, 1961-70; Senior Research Worker, High Energy Physics Institute, Academy of Sciences, Almaty, 1970-95. Publications: Books: Courants, amers, écueils en microphysique, 1993; Fondation Louis de Broglie, Paris; Advanced Electromagnetism, World Scientific, Singapore, 1995; Over 100 articles in various physical journals. Address: Sadovaya 8, 480082 Almaty 82, Kazakhstan.

MIKHAILOVA Maria V, b. 17 January 1945, Moscow, Russia. Philologist. Education: Student, Philological Faculty, Moscow State University, 1964-69; Postgraduate Course, 1969-72; PhD, 1974; DH, 1996. Appointments: Lecturer, Russian Literature of the end of the XIXth Century – the beginning of the XXth Century, 1969-82, Assistant Professor, 1982-98, Professor, 1998-, Philological Faculty, Department of Russian Literature of the XXth Century, Moscow State University. Publications: History of Russian Literary Criticism of the end XIXth Century – the beginning of the XXth Century, 1985; The Fate of Women Writers in Literature at the Beginning of the XXth Century, 1996; Articles in the Dictionary of Russian Women Writers, 1994; Prefaces and commentaries to books of fiction; Editor, feminist magazine: Preobrazhenie, 1993-99. Honour: The Best Philologist of Moscow State University, 1996. Memberships: Moscow Union of Writers; Member of numerous dissertation boards. Address: Malaya Gruzinskaya Str. 28, Flat 162, 123557 Moscow, Russia. E-mail: mary12@rol.ru

MIKHAILUSENKO Igor Georgievich, b. 20 April 1932, Moscow, Russia. Translator; Poet; Journalist. Education: Graduate, Maurice Thorez Foreign Languages Institute, Moscow, 1958; Higher Education Diploma, Translator from Russian into English. Appointments: Various posts as translator and English-language speaker; USSR Travel Agency, Intourist; Various assignments as a free-lance journalist; Poetry writer. Publications: Contributor to numerous publications including Dostoinstvo newspaper, 1995-2003; Many poems set to music, which became popular songs; Articles include: Tribute to Third Millennium (book), 2001; Memoirs of Moscow's Man (book); Poet's Dreams (book), 2001; A Peaceful Travel – USA Through Foreign Eyes, (book), 2001; What I Wish (Oh I Wish) I Had Said (book), 2002; Poems That Mirror My Soul, (book), 2003; Poems about Flowers (book), 2004. Honours: Many awards and citations for international peace efforts, including Badge of Honour, Moscow Peace Committee, 1982; Recognised by the United Poets Laureate International, 1987; Award, Editors of Fine Arts Press, Knoxville, USA, for noteworthy contribution to book: Rainbows and Rhapsodies and his excellence in poetry, 1988; Laureate Man of Letters, awarded the Laurel Wreath, 1997; Listed in several prestigious international biographical directories. Memberships: Laurel Leaves, Official Organ of the United Poets Laureate International; Board of Directors, International Writers and Artists Association. Address: Bolshaya Gruzinskaya Street, House 63, Apartment 87, Moscow 123056, Russia. E-mail: vitaigor@list.ru Website: http://mikhailusenko.tripod.com

MIKKOLA Kari Juhani, b. 13 May 1959, Salla, Finland. Process Operator; Writer on Science. Education includes: Short course in Theology, State Church Facility ERSTA, Stockholm, Sweden, 1976; Degree in Electricity Automation, 1977; Deacon's Studies, Swedish State Church, 1 year; Home Nurse School, Härnösand, 1979; Short course in Theology, Lekmanna School, Sigtuna, 1980;

Manufacturing course, Forest Industry Centre, Markaryd, 1980; Russian History, University of Linköping, 1996; Currently studying Russian and Latin. Appointments: Currently Process Operator, Smurfit Aspa Bruk AB, Sweden; Independent Researcher in Astronomy, Astrophysics. Cosmology, Archaeology, Quantum Physics, Social Anthropology, Culture, Chemistry, Theology, Bible history; Diplomatic Councillor of the London Diplomatic Academy; Co-Founder, American Order of Excellence Society. Publications: Numerous, especially in theology and science. Honours: His Excellency Ambassador, Knight, International Order of Ambassadors; Citation of Meritorious Achievements in Natural Science; Citation of Meritorious Achievements in Astronomy and Astrophysics; Member, London Diplomatic Academy (LDA); Co-founder, Diplomatic Council, LDA; American Order of Excellence, 2000; International Peace Prize Award, 2003; Cabinet Member, World Peace and Diplomacy Forum, UK, 2003; Many others. Memberships: National Geographic Society, USA; Society for Popular Astronomy, England; American Association for the Advancement of Science; New York Academy of Sciences; Member, London Diplomatic Academy (LDA); Co-founder, Diplomatic Council, LDA; European Life Scientists' Organization; Community of Scientists, USA; Member, Global Benefits Administration Corporation, USA, 2002. Address: Parkvägen 3, 69673 Aspa Bruk, Sweden. E-mail: kari.mikkola@swipnet.se

MIKLOS Tomas, b. 29 May 1938, Mexico City. Management and Planning Consultant; Future Studies. m. Monique, 1 son, 1 daughter. Education: Chemical Engineer (UNAM), 1959; PhD, Mathematics, Sorbonne, 1963; Master Degree in Psychoanalysis (CIEP), 1978. Appointments: Consultant, Government Human and Social Council; Latin American Institute for Educational Communication; General Coordinator, Adult Forming Network, RED-RED and RE.FORM.AD; General Director, CREFAL, International Agency: UNESCO, OEA, Mexican Government, General Director, Fund Javier Barros Sierra, Prospective Research Centre; General Director, National Institute for Advanced Assessment. Publications: Prospective Planning, 1991; Interactive Planning, 1994; Basics for Planning, 1999; Alternative Learning and Competency Based Education, 1999. Honours: Benito Juarez Medal; Honorary Mention, National Institute for Public Administration. Memberships: WFS; NYAAS; SMGH; ANHG; ANI. Address: Cerrada Del Rayo 20, La Herradura, 11002 Mexico City, Huixquilucan, Mexico.

MIKULICH Mikalai U, b. 3 July 1960, Minskaya Region, Belarus. Professor. 1 son. Education: teacher of Belarusian and Belarusian Literature, M Gorky State Pedagogical Institute, Minsk, 1978-82; Postgraduate Studies, 1982-86, Course of Studies for Degree of Doctor of Sciences, 1992-96, Institute of Literature, Belarusian Academy of Sciences. Appointment: Assistant Professor, Head of Department, Department of Belarusian Literature, Grodno Yanka Kupala State University, 1986-92, 1996-. Publications: 10 monographs and brochures and more than 190 articles include: Maxim Tank and Modern Belarusian Lyrics, 1994; Milestones of the Century, 1995; Maxim Tank: At the Crossroads of the Century, 1999. Honours: Prize Winner, Literary Competition, Grodnenskaya Region, 2000; Member, Research Board of Advisors, American Biographical Institute, 2002-. Memberships: Research Council, Institute of Literature, Belarusian Academy of Sciences, 1992-96; Scientific Council, Grodno State University, 1996-2001; Union of Belarusian Writers, 2001-. Address: Praspect Klyatskova, D5 kv 34, Grodno, Republic of Belarus 230020.

MILES Elizabeth Jane, b. 13 March 1927, Upper Fairmount, Maryland, USA. Social and Mental Health Worker; Deaconess of Methodist Church; Director of Christian Education. Education: AA, St Mary's College, St Mary's City, Maryland, 1947; BA, Scannett College, Nashville, Tennessee, 1951; Master's Degree,

Vanderbilt University, Nashville, Tennessee, 1951. Appointments: Deaconess Methodist Church, Social Work, Baltimore Conference; Founder, Homecoming Inc, for mental patients and homeless from institutions, appointed by Governor Millard Tawes of Maryland, served as Director for 26 years; Appointed to Commission of Aging Board of Somerset County, Maryland; Consultant, Mental Health, Oxford, England; Currently, Member, Board of Directors, Christian County Retreat, Bradenton, Florida. Honour: Honoured with a banquet on retirement after 26 years as Founder and Director of Homecoming Inc. Memberships: American Association of University Women; National Historic Trust. Somerset County Commission of Aging; Smithsonian Preservation; Methodist Church. Address: Fishing Island Blvd, Upper Fairmount, MD 21867, USA.

MILES Sarah, b. 31 December 1941, England. Actress. m. Robert Bolt, 1967, divorced 1976, re-married 1988, deceased 1995. Education: Royal Academy of Dramatic Art, London. Creative Works: Films include: Those Magnificent Men in Their Flying Machines, 1964; I Was Happy Here, 1966; The Blow-Up, 1966; Ryan's Daughter, 1970; Lady Caroline Lamb, 1972; The Hireling, 1973; The Man Who Loved Cat Dancing, 1973; Great Expectations, 1975; Pepita Jiminez, 1975; The Sailor Who Fell From Grace With the Sea, 1976; The Big Sleep, 1978; Venom, 1981; Hope and Glory, 1987; White Mischief, 1988; The Silent Touch; Theatre appearances include: Vivat! Regina!; Asylum, 1988; TV appearances: James Michener's Dynasty; Great Expectations; Harem; Queenie; A Ghost in Monte Carlo; Dandelion; Dead Ring Around the Moon; The Rehearsal. Publications: Charlemagne, play, 1992; A Right Royal Bastard, memoirs, 1993; Serves Me Right, memoirs, 1994; Bolt From the Blue, memoirs, 1996.

MILICESCU Viorica-Maria, b. 26 April 1938, Barlad, Romania. Dental Physician, University Professor. m. Stefan Milicescu, 1 son, 1 daughter. Education includes: MD Graduate, 1960; Postgraduate Course in Orthodontics, 1963-64; Specialist in Orthodontics and ODF, 1964; Assistant Professor, 1966; PhD, 1976, Bucharest Faculty of Stomatology, Carol Davila University. Appointments: Medical Appointments: Stomatologist Doctor, Rural Obligatory Stomatological Assistance, 1960-61; Orthodontics Specialist Doctor, Stomatological Department, Ploiesti, Prahova, 1964-65; Dan Teodorescu Stomatological Hospital, Bucharest, Romania, 1965-; University Appointments: Lecturer, 1991, Senior Assistant Professor, 1993, Professor, 1998, Professor and Head of Department, 1999-2002, Department of Orthodontics and ODF, Bucharest Faculty of Stomatology, Carol Davila University, Bucharest; Professor and Head of Orthodontics and ODF, Titu Maiorescu University, Faculty of Stomatology, Bucharest, 1998-; Senior Assistant Professor, Department of Orthodontics and ODF, Ovidius University of Constanta, Faculty of Stomatology, 1995-96; Associate Professor, Senior Associate Professor, Professor, Head of Postgraduate Orthodontic and ODF Courses, Bucharest, 1986-; Head, Orthodontics Advisory Board, Romanian Ministry of Health and Romanian College of Doctors (National Order of Doctors), 1999. Publications: More than 320 works in fields including: unusual and pathological growth and development, craniofacial embriology, congenital malformations and genetic diseases, craniofacial alterations in endocrinopathies, gellemarity, rickets, pulmonary and osteoarticular tuberculosis; Book: Craniofacial growth and general development in children during the period of mixed dentition, 2001. Honours include: Silver Medal, René Descartes University, Paris, France, 1996; Medal, Medical Association of the Danubian Countries, 1996; Silver Jubilee Diploma, Carol Davila University, 1998; Excellence Diploma, European Society of Dental Pharmacology and Dental Materials, 2002; Award, Romanian National Association of Orthodontist, 2002; Woman of the Year 2003, ABI. Memberships include: World

Federation of Orthodontists; European Academy of Implantology; Medical Association of the Danubian Countries; European Orthodontic Society; Romanian Medical Association; National Romanian Association of Orthodontists, Founder Member; Balkan Medical Union, 1967; Balkanic Stomatological Society, 1996; Association Stomatologique Internationali (ASI), 1969; Association of Stomatologists with Free Practice, Founder Member, 1998. Address: Faculty of Stomatology, Department of Orthodontics and ODF, Bucharest, Romania. E-mail: stefmili@xnet.ru

MILLAR Oliver Nicholas (Sir), b. 26 April 1923, Standen, Hertfordshire, England. Surveyor Emeritus of the Queen's Pictures. m. Delia Mary Dawnay, 1 son, 3 daughters. Education: Academic Diploma in the History of Art, Courtauld Institute of Art, University of London. Appointment: Assistant, Surveyor of the King's Pictures, 1947-49, Deputy Surveyor of the Kings Pictures, 1949-72; Surveyor of the Queen's Pictures, 1972-88; Director of the Royal Collection, 1987-88; Surveyor Emeritus, 1988-; Trustee, National Portrait Gallery, 1972-95; Member, Reviewing Committee on Export of Works of Art, 1975-87; Executive Committee, National Art Collections Fund, 1986-98; Trustee, National Heritage Memorial Fund, 1989-97; Chairman, Patrons of British Art, 1989-90. Publications: Gainsborough, 1949; English Art 1625-1714 (with Dr M D Whinney), 1957; Ruben's Whitehall Ceiling, 1958; Tudor, Stuart and Early Georgian Pictures in the Collection of HM the Queen, 1963; Later Georgian Pictures in the Collection of HM the Queen, 1969; Inventories and Valuations of the King's Goods, 1972; The Queen's Pictures, 1977; Victorian Pictures in the Collection of H M the Queen, 1992; Van dyck: A Complete Catalogue of the Painting (with others), 2004; Numerous catalogues and articles in magazines and journals. Honours: MVO, 1953; CVO, 1963, KCVO, 1973; GCVO, 1988; FBA, 1970. Memberships: MCC; FSA; Corresponding Fellow: Ateneo Veneto, Venice; Koninklikje Academie voor Wetenschappen Letteren en Schone Kunsten, Belgium. Address: The Cottage, Ray's Lane, Penn, Bucks HP10 8LH, England.

MILLER Annie C, b. 22 December 1947, Greenville, North Carolina, USA. Teacher. 1 son, 1 daughter. Education: BS, Elizabeth City State University, 1970; MA, University of the District of Columbia, 1977. Appointments: Social Studies Teacher; Community Service Worker. Honours: Fellow, UK Kellogg Foundation, Partners of America, 1998; Fulbright Scholars Scholarship, 2001; International teacher of the Year, World Affairs Council, DC, 2001; Listed in Who's Who publications and biographical dictionaries. Memberships: Board Member, Teenlife Choices; Missionary, True Deliverance Church; Southern Poverty Center; Wildlife. Address: 531 42nd Street NE, Washington DC 20019, USA.

MILLER Arthur, b. 17 October 1915, New York, USA. Playwright. m. (1) Mary Grace Slattery, 1940, 1 son, 1 daughter, (2) Marilyn Monroe, 1956, (3) Ingeborg Morath, 1962, 1 son, 1 daughter. Education: University of Michigan. Publications: The Man Who Had All the Luck, 1943; Situation Normal, 1944; Focus, 1945; All My Sons, 1947; Death of a Salesman, 1949; The Crucible, 1953; AView From the Bridge, 1955; A Memory of Two Mondays, 1955; Collected Plays, 1958; The Misfits, screenplay, 1959; After the Fall, 1964; Incident at Vichy, 1964; I Don't Need You Any More, short stories, 1967; The Price, play, 1968; In Russia, with Inge Morath, 1969; The Creation of the World and Other Business, play, 1972; Up From Paradise, 1974; Chinese Encounters, 1979; The American Clock, 1980; Playing for Time, play, 1981; Elegy for a Lady, play, 1983; Some Kind of Love Story, play, 1983; Salesman in Beijing, journal, 1984; Two Way Mirror, 1985; Danger: Memory!, plays, 1986; The Archbishop's Ceiling, 1986; Timebends: A Life, autobiography, 1987; Everybody

Wins, screenplay, 1989; The Ride Down Mount Morgan, 1990; The Last Yankee, 1990; Broken Glass, 1994; Homely Girl, novella, 1995; The Crucible, screenplay, 1995; Mr Peters' Connection, play, 2000; Echoes Down the Corridor, essays, 2000. Honours include: Kennedy Centre Award, 1984; National Medal of Arts, 1993; Olivier Award, 1995; Professor of Contemporary Theatre, University of Oxford, 1995-; Hon DLitt, University of East Anglia, 1984, University of Oxford, 1995, Harvard University, 1997; Dorothy and Lillian Gish Prize, 1999; Antoinette Perry Lifetime Achievement Award, 1999; Prix Moliere, 1999; Praemium Imperiale Award, Japan Art Association, 2001; Prince of Asturias Prize for Literature, 2002; Jerusalem Prize, Israel, 2003. Memberships include: President, International PEN Club, 1965-69; Fellow, St Catherine's College, Oxford. Address: c/o ICM, 40 West 57th Street, New York, NY 10019, USA.

MILLER Jeanne-Marie, b. 18 February 1937, Washington DC, USA. Graduate Professor Emerita of English. m. Nathan J Miller. Education: BA, 1959, MA, 1963, PhD, 1976, English, Howard University. Appointments: Instructor, 1963-76, Graduate Assistant Professor, 1976-79, Graduate Associate Professor, 1979-92; Assistant Director, Institute for the Arts and the Humanities, 1973-75, Assistant for Academic Planning, Office of the Vice President for Academic Affairs, 1976-90; Director, Graduate Studies Program in English, 1991-97; Graduate Professor of English, 1992-97; Professor Emerita of English, 1997-, Howard University. Publications: 80 articles in variety of academic books and journals. Honours: Fellow, Ford Foundation, 1970-72; Fellow, Southern Fellowships Fund, 1972-74; Grantee, Howard University Faculty Research Grant, 1975, 1976-77, 1994-95, 1996-97; Grantee, American Council of Learned Societies, 1978-79; National Endowment for the Humanities, 1981-84; Pi Lambda Delta. Memberships: American Association of Higher Education; American Studies Association; College Language Association; National Council of Teachers of English; Modern Language Association; American Association of University Women; Corcoran Gallery of Art Association; Founder Member, John F Kennedy Memorial Centre for the Performing Arts; Washington Opera Society; Associate, Metropolitan Museum of Art; Metropolitan Opera Guild; Ibsen Society of America; Drama League of New York; Folger Shakespeare Library; Shakespeare Theatre Guild. Address: 504 24th Street, NE, Washington DC 20002-4818, USA.

MILLER Jonathan (Wolfe), b. 21 July 1934, London, England. Theatre, Film, and Television Director; Writer. m. Helen Rachel Collet, 1956, 2 sons, 1 daughter. Education: MB, BCh, St John's College, Cambridge, 1959. Appointments: Theatre, film, and television director; Resident Fellow in the History of Medicine, 1970-73, Fellow, 1981-, University College, London; Associate Director, National Theatre, 1973-75; Visiting Professor in Drama, Westfield College, London, 1977-; Artistic Director, Old Vic, 1988-90; Research Fellow in Neuropsychology, University of Sussex. Publications: McLuhan, 1971; Freud: The Man, His World, His Influence (editor), 1972; The Body in Question, 1978; Subsequent Performances, 1986; The Don Giovanni Book: Myths of Seduction and Betrayal (editor), 1990. Honours: Silver Medal, Royal Television Society, 1981; Commander of the Order of the British Empire, 1983; Albert Medal, Royal Society of Arts, 1990; Honorary Doctor of Letters, University of Cambridge. Memberships: Royal Academy, fellow; American Academy of Arts and Sciences. Address: c/o IMG Artists, Media House, 3 Burlington Lane, London W4 2TH, England.

MILLER Linda, b. 22 January 1948, Kansas City, USA. Teacher. Education: BS, Secondary Education, University of Kansas, 1970; MA, Secondary Education, University of Virginia, 1978; EdD,

Secondary Education and Social Studies, 1991. Appointments: Teacher, Turner Unified School District #202, Kansas City, 1970-72, Fairfax County Public Schools, 1972-86, Department of Teacher Education, University of Virginia, 1986-87; Teacher, Fairfax County Public Schools, 1987-2002; Community College of Southern Nevada, 2003. Publications: Several articles in professional educational journals. Honours include: American Bar Association High School Award, 1991; DAR History Award, 1992, 1993; University of Virginia Secondary Teacher of the Year, 1997; Virginia Historical Society Teacher of the Year Award, 1998; Teaching Excellence Award, 1998; George Washington Freedom Foundation Award, 1998; Global Teacher of the Year, National Peace Corps Association, 1999; 2002 National Peace Educator, Peace Corps Association; 2002 World History Teaching Prize; 2003 National Endowment for the Humanities Leadership Award. Memberships: National Council for the Social Studies; Organization of American History; American Legal History Society; American Historical Society. Address: 2319 Great Elk Drive, Henderson, NV 89052, USA.

MILLER Michael Dawson, b. 12 March 1928, London, England. Solicitor; Insurance Manager. m. Gillian Margaret Gordon, 3 daughters. Appointments: Regular, Parachute Regiment, 1946-49; Parachute Regiment TA, 1949-55; 1st Regiment Hon. Artillery Company TA, 1957-63; Articled Clerk to Solicitor, 1949-53; Practice as a Solicitor, 1953-55; Executive, 1955-61, Partner, 1962-90, Thos R Miller & Son, Mutual Insurance Managers; Partner, Thos R Miller & Son (Bermuda), 1969-90; Directorships: Shipowners Assurance Management, Montreal, 1973-84, A/B Indemnitas, Stockholm, 1980-90, Thomas R Miller War Risks Services Ltd, 1985-90; Technical Adviser, Planning Board for Ocean Shipping, 1970-; National Shipping Advisory Committee, 1970-90; Arbitrator, London Maritime Arbitrators Association, 1963-. Publications: Marine War Risks, 1990, 2nd edition, 1994, supplement, 1999; Uncommon Lawyer, 2001; Wars of the Roses, forthcoming; Numerous articles in journals and conference proceedings include: Shipowners Liabilities, Singapore Seminar, 1980; Shipping, 4th Arm of Defence, Hong Kong, 1982; Shipping Under Fire, Athens, 1987. Honour: Silver Medal, Hellenic Merchant Marine. Memberships: Liveryman, Worshipful Company of Solicitors of the City of London, 1974-; Liveryman, Worshipful Company of Shipwrights, 1977-; Royal Bermuda Yacht Club, 1970-; Royal Ocean Racing Club, 1983-; Royal Thames Yacht Club, 1992-; Hurlingham Club, 1964-; City of London Club, 1974-. Address: 52 Scarsdale Villas, London W8 6PP. E-mail: mllmd@aol.com

MILLER Ronald Jay, b. 8 August 1944, Los Angeles, California, USA. Artist; Film Maker. m. Sherie Miller. Education: Sculpture Classes, Valley College, Van Nuys, California; Scholarship, Chouinard Art Institute, Los Angeles. Career: Freelance Fine Artist (watercolor), 1965-; Director at Large, National Watercolor Society, 1996; 4th Vice President, 1997, 2nd Vice President, 1998-99, President, 2000, National Watercolor Society; Teacher, Unique Art Exchange, North Hollywood; Director of Photography, Television and Motion Pictures; 39 years of motion picture industry experience including and 10 year's experience as a gaffer in commercials and music video's; Exhibitions: Charles and Emma Frye Museum, Seattle, Washington; National Academy of Design, New York; Otis Art Institute, Los Angeles, California; Laguna Beach Museum of Art, Laguna Beach, California; Downey Museum, Downey, California; Pacificulture-Asia Museum, Pasadena, California; San Bernardino County Museum, Redlands, California; The Noyes Museum of Art, Oceanville, New Jersey; Many solo and group exhibitions; Represented in the Archives of American Art, Smithsonian Institution;. Publication: Author: When Landscape is a Calling, Watercolour Magic Magazine, 2000.

Honours: Buzza Cardoza Award, California National Watercolor Society; Several others. Membership: President, 2000, Board of Directors, 1995-2001, National Watercolor Society, Los Angeles; Life Signature Member, National Watercolor Society, 2001. Address: 12773 Willard Street, North Hollywood, CA 91605, USA.

MILLER Stanley Lloyd, b. 7 March 1930, Oakland, California, USA. Chemist. Education: Graduated, University of California, 1951; PhD, University of Chicago, 1954. Appointments: Postdoctoral Jewett Fellow, California Institute of Technology, 1954-55; Instructor in Biochemistry, Assistant Professor, Department of Biochemistry, Columbia College of Physicians and Surgeons, 1955-60; Assistant Professor, Associate Professor, Professor of Chemistry, University of California at San Diego, 1960-. Publications: The Origins of Life on the Earth, with L E Orgel, 1974. Memberships: NAS; Honorary Councillor, Higher Council of Scientific Research of Spain; Oparin Medal, International Society for the Study of the Origin of Life. Address: University of California, San Diego, Department of Chemistry, La Jolla, CA 92093-0317, USA.

MILLINGTON Barry (John), b. 1 Nov 1951, Essex, England. Music Journalist; Writer. Education: BA, Cambridge University, 1974. Appointments: Music Critic, Times, 1977-2001; Reviews Editor, BBC Music Magazine; Artistic Director, Hampstead and Highgate Festival. Publications: Wagner, 1984, revised edition, 1998; Selected Letters of Richard Wagner (translator and editor with S Spencer), 1987; The Wagner Compendium: A Guide to Wagner's Life and Music (editor), 1992; Wagner in Performance (editor with S Spencer), 1992; Wagner's Ring of the Nibelung: A Companion (editor with S Spencer), 1993. Contributions to: Articles on Wagner to New Grove Dictionary of Opera, 1992, New Grove Dictionary of Music and Musicians, 2nd edition, 2001; Newspapers and magazines. Membership: Critics' Circle. Address: 50 Denman Drive South, London NW11 6RH, England.

MILLIS James Michael, b. 22 February 1959, Nashville, Tennessee, USA. Surgeon. m. Janet Lynn Cassel, 1 son, 1 daughter. Education: BA, Emory University, 1981; MD, University of Tennessee Centre for Health Sciences, 1985. Appointments: General Surgery Residency, 1985-87, 1989-92, Transplant Research Fellowship, 1987-89, Transplant Clinical Fellowship, 1992-94, Instructor of Surgery, 1992-94, University of California at Los Angeles; Assistant Professor of Surgery, 1994-97, Associate Professor of Surgery, 1997-2002, Professor of Surgery, 2002-, University of Chicago. Publications: Over 100 articles for professional medical journals. Honours: Chief, Section of Transplantation, University of Chicago; Director, Liver Transplantation, University of Chicago; Listed in biographical reference publications. Memberships: SUS; American College of Surgeons; ASTS; AST; AASLD; AAS. Address: 5841 S Maryland Ave, MC5027, Department of Surgery, Section of Transplantation, Chicago, IL 60637, USA.

MILLS Hayley Catherine Rose Vivien, b. 18 April 1946, London, England. Actress. m. Roy Boulting, 1971, divorced 1977, 2 sons. Education: Elmhurst Ballet School; Ist Alpine Vidamanette. Creative Works: Films include: Tiger Bay, 1959; Pollyanna, 1960; The Parent Trap, 1961; Whistle Down the Wind, 1961; Summer Magic, 1962; In Search of the Castaways, 1963; The Chalk Garden, 1964; The Moonspinners, 1965; The Truth About Spring, 1965; Sky West & Crooked, 1966; The Trouble with Angels, 1966; The Family Way, 1966; Pretty Polly, 1967; Twisted Nerve, 1968; Take a Girl Like You, 1970; Forbush and the Penguins, 1971; Endless Night, 1972; Deadly Strangers, 1975; The Diamond Hunters, 1975; What Changed Charley Farthing?, 1975; The Kingfisher Caper,

Dictionary of International Biography

1975; Appointment with Death, 1987; After Midnight, 1992; TV appearances include: The Flame Trees of Thika, 1981; Parent Trap II, 1986; Good Morning Miss Bliss; Murder She Wrote; Back Home; Tales of the Unexpected; Walk of Life, 1990; Parent Trap III, IV, Amazing Stories; Numerous stage appearances. Publication: My God, with Marcus Maclaine, 1988. Honours include: Silver Bear Award, Berlin Film Festival, 1958; British Academy Award; Special Oscar, USA. Address: c/o Chatto & Linnit, Prince of Wales Theatre, Coventry Street, London W1V 7FE, England.

MILLS John, b. 22 February 1908, North Elmham, Suffolk, England. Actor. m. Mary Hayley Bell, 1941, 1 son, 2 daughters. Creative Works: Stage appearances include: Noel Coward's Cavalcade, 1931; Words and Music, 1932; Give Me A Ring, 1933; Jill Darling, 1934; Red Night, 1936; A Midsummer Night's Dream; She Stoops to Conquer; The Damascus Blade, 1950; Figure of Fun, 1951; Powers of Persuasion, 1963; Veterans, 1972; At the End of the Day, 1973; Good Companions, musical, 1974; Great Expectations musical, 1975; The Petition, 1986; Pygmalion, 1987; When the Wind Blows, TV play, 1987; Film appearances include: Operation Crossbow; The Wrong Box; The Family Way; Chuka; Cowboy in Africa; Adam's Woman; Lady Hamilton; Oh! What a Lovely War; Run Wild, Run Free; A Black Veil for Lisa; Ryan's Daughter; Dulcima; Young Winston; Oklahoma Crude; The Human Factor; Trial by Combat; The Big Sleep; Thirty-Nine Steps; Zulu Dawn; Dr Strange; Love Boat; Quatermass, TV; Young at Heart, TV, 1980-82; A Woman of Substance, TV; The Masks of Death, TV; Murder with Mirrors, TV; Gandhi, 1980; Sahara, 1983; A Woman of Substance; Tribute to Her Majesty, film documentary, 1986; A Tale of Two Cities, TV, 1989; Ending Up, TV, 1989; Harnessing Peacocks, 1993; The Big Freeze; Martin Chuzzlewit, TV, 1994. Publications: Up in the Clouds Gentlemen Please, 1980; Book of Famous Firsts, 1984; Still Memories (autobiography), 2000. Honours: Numerous. Address: c/o ICM Ltd, 76 Oxford Street, London W1R 1RB, England.

MILNER Arthur David, b. 16 July 1943, Leeds, England. Professor of Cognitive Neuroscience. Education: BA, 1965, MA, 1970, University of Oxford, England; Dip Psych, London, 1966; PhD, Experimental Psychology, University of London, 1971. Appointments: Research Worker, Institute of Psychology, London, 1966-70; Lecturer and Senior Lecturer in Psychology, 1970-85, Reader in Neuropsychology, 1985-90, Head Department of Psychology, 1983-88, 1994-97, Professor of Neuropsychology, 1990-2000, Dean, Faculty of Science, 1992-94, Honorary Professor of Neuropsychology, 2000-, University of St Andrews, Scotland; Professor of Cognitive Neuroscience, University of Durham, 2000-, Academic Director of Applied Psychology, 2000; Honorary Research Fellow, North Durham Health Care Trust, 2002-. Publications: Co-author and/or editor or co-editor of 6 books; Author and co-author of over 100 chapters in books and articles in refereed journals; Numerous invited lectures and workshops. Honours: Fellow, Royal Society of Edinburgh, 1992; Leverhulme Trust Research Fellow, 1998-2000; FC Donders Lecturer, Max-Planck-Institut, Nijmegen, 1999; Member, Scientific Council, Helmholtz Instituut, Netherlands, 2002-. Memberships: Experimental Psychology Society; International Neuropsychological Symposium; International Association of Attention and Performance; Royal Society of Edinburgh; European Brain and Behaviour Society. Address: Wolfson Research Institute, University of Durham, Queen's Campus, Stockton-on-Tees TS 17 6BH, England. E-mail: a.d.milner@durham.ac.uk

MILOS Jon, b. 16 February 1930, Sutjeska, Yugoslavia (Romanian parents). Writer; Poet; Translator. Divorced, 1 son, 1 daughter. Education: Graduate, Faculty of Philosophy, University of Belgrade, 1955; Studies in Paris, France 1955-56; Licence ès lettres in Philology, Sorbonne, Paris, 1963; Student, École des Hautes Études, Paris, 1963-64. Appointments: Writer, Journalist, Translator, Belgrade, Yugoslavia, 1956-59; Teacher, French, Romanian, Serbo-croatian and Swedish, Colleges of Education, Malmö and Lund Sweden, 1964-; Editor, Journal, The Candle, 1973-80; Established Romanian Orthodox Church in Malmö with Father Dr Alexandru Ciurea, 1975; From 1977 publishes articles studies and essays in literary journals in Sweden, Romania and Yugoslavia. Publications: 20 volumes of poetry in Romanian include: Buds, 1953; The Everlasting Dawn, 1977; The Fire's Roots, 1994; At the Table of Silence (anthology of Romanian poetry), 1998; Love's Sky 2nd edition, 2001; Poetry in English: Through the Needle's Eye, 1990; In Secure Hands, 1999; 4 volumes of poetry in Swedish; 4 volumes of poetry in Serbian; 1 volume of poetry in Macedonian; Translations of books and poetry: 17 from Romanian into Swedish; 5 from French into Swedish; 9 from Serbian into Swedish; 2 from the languages of former Yugoslavia into Swedish; 3 from Croatian into Swedish; 2 from Slovenian into Swedish; 1 from Macedonian into Swedish; Numerous volumes from Swedish into Macedonian, Serbian and Romanian. Honours: Prize of the Writer's Association of Romania, 1998; Mihai Eminescu Prize, Romanian Academy, 1998; Doctor, honoris causa, University of Oradea, 1999; Honorary Citizen of Cluj-Napoca, Romania, 1999; Commodore of Trustful Service, National Order for Culture, 2002; First ever Citizen of Honour of Romania, 2002. Memberships include: Writers Association, Sweden, 1978; Writers Association of Yugoslavia, 1989; Writers Association of Macedonia, 1989; Writers Association of Romania, 1990; PEN Sweden, 1992. Address: Ö. Rönneholmsvägen 6B, 21147 Malmö, Sweden. E-mail: poetjonmilos@yahoo.se

MIŁOSZ Czesław, b. 30 June 1911, Szetejnie, Lithuania. (US citizen, 1970). Poet; Novelist; Critic; Essayist; Translator; Professor of Slavic Languages and Literatures Emeritus. m. (1) Janina Dlusta, 1943, deceased 1986, (2) Carol Thigpen, 1992, deceased 2002. Education: M Juris, University of Wilno, 1934. Appointments: Programmer, Polish National Radio, Warsaw, 1934-39; Diplomatic Service, Polish Ministry of Foreign Affairs, 1945-50; Visiting Lecturer, 1960-61, Professor of Slavic Languages and Literatures, 1961-78, Professor Emeritus, 1978-, University of California at Berkeley. Publications: Poetry: Poems, 1940; Poems, 1969; Selected Poems, 1973, revised edition, 1981; Selected Poems, 1976; The Bells in Winter, 1978; The Separate Notebooks, 1984; Collected Poems, 1990; Provinces: Poems 1987-1991, 1991; Facing the River: New Poems, 1995; Roadside Dog, 1998. Novels: The Seizure of Power, 1955; The Issa Valley, 1981. Non-Fiction: The Captive Mind (essays), 1953; Native Realm: A Search for Self-Definition (essays), 1968; The History of Polish Literature, 1969, revised edition, 1983; Emperor of the Earth: Modes of Eccentric Vision, 1977; Nobel Lecture, 1981; Visions From San Francisco Bay, 1982; The Witness of Poetry (lectures), 1983; The Land of Ulro, 1984; The Rising of the Sun, 1985; Unattainable Earth, 1986; Beginning With My Steters: Essays and Recollections, 1992; Striving Towards Being (correspondence), 1997; Collected Works, 1999; It, 2000; Poetic Treatise with Author's Commentary, 2001; The Second Space, 2002; Orpheus and Euridice, 2002. Editor and Translator: Postwar Polish Poetry: An Anthology, 1965, revised edition, 1983. Honours: Prix Littéraire Européen, Les Guildes du Livre, Geneva, 1953; Marian Kister Literary Award, 1967; Guggenheim Fellowship, 1976; Neustadt International Literary Prize, 1978; Nobel Prize for Literature, 1980; National Medal of Arts, 1990; Order of the White Eagle, Poland, 1994; Order of Gedyminas, Lithuania, 1997; Several honorary doctorates. Memberships: American Academy and Institute of Arts and Letters; American Academy of Arts and Sciences; American Association for the Advancement of Slavic Studies; Polish Institute of Letters and Sciences in America. Address: c/o Department of Slavic Languages and Literatures, University of California at Berkeley, Berkeley, CA 94720, USA.

MIN Soo-Hong, b. 25 March 1928, Seoul, Korea. Professor. m. Ryung-Ja Cheung, 2 sons. Education: BS, College of Engineering, Seoul National University, 1951; MS, Graduate School, University of Alabama, USA, 1964; PhD, Graduate School, Pusan National University, 1975. Appointments: Professor, Air Force Academy, 1953; Professor, 1957, Dean, College of Engineering, 1966, Pusan National University; Director, Office of Research Co-ordination, Ministry of Science and Technology, 1967; Director General, Office of Atomic Energy, Republic of Korea, 1971; Director, Inha University, 1971-93; President, Halla Institute of Technology, Halla University, 1995-. Publications: Metallic Materials; Materials Science. Honour: Medal of Wharang Silver Star, 1953. Memberships: President, Korean Society of Mechanical Engineers, 1985-86; Vice President, Korean Federation of Science & Technological Societies, 1990-96; President, Korean Professional Engineers Association, 1993-95; Senior Fellow, Korean Academy of Science & Technology, 1994-. Address: 2-906 Hannam Heights Apt, 220-1 Oksu-dong, Songdong-ku, Seoul 133-100, Korea.

MINAKAMI Motoyuki, b. 9 January 1957, Hitoyoshi-shi, Kumamoto-ken, Japan. Researcher. Education: Bachelor of Engineering, Civil Engineering Department, 1979, Doctor of Philosophy, 2004, Hokkaido University, Japan. Appointments: Senior Researcher, Research Centre for Advanced Information Technology, 2002-; Visiting Senior Research Fellow, Transportation Research Group, University of Southampton, England, 2001. Publication: Article in JSSC, Journal of Constructional Steel, 2003. Honours: Yoshimachi Prize, 1979, Hiroi Isami Prize, 1979, Hokkaido University, Japan. Memberships: ASCE; ASME; JSCE. Address: 1 Asahi, Tsukuba-shi, Ibaraki-ken, 305-0804, Japan.

MINGHELLA Anthony, b. 6 January 1954, Isle of Wight, England. Director; Playwright. m. Carolyn Choa, 1 son, 1 daughter. Education: St John's College; University of Hull. Appointments: Drama Lecturer, University of Hull. Creative Works: TV include: Inspector Morse, 1st series, screenplay; Films directed include: Truly; Madly; Deeply; Mr Wonderful; The English Patient, 1997; The Talented Mr Ripley, 2000. Honours include: Hon DLitt, University of Hull, 1997; First Honorary Freeman, Isle of Wight, 1997.Publications: Whale Music, 1983; Made in Bangkok, 1986; Jim Henson's Storyteller, 1988; Interior-Room, Exterior-City, 1989; Plays: One, 1992; Driven to Distraction: A Case for Inspector Morse, 1994; Two, 1997; The English Patient, screenplay, 1997. Website: www.bfi.org.uk

MINNELLI Liza, b. 12 March 1946, USA. Singer; Actress. m. (1) Peter Allen, 1967, (2) Jack Haley Jr, 1974, (3) Mark Gero, 1979, divorced 1992, (4) David Gest, 2002, divorced. Creative Works: Films: Charlie Bubbles, 1968; The Sterile Cuckoo, 1969; Tell Me That You Love Me; Junie Moon, 1971; Cabaret, played Sally Bowles, 1972; Lucky Lady, 1976; A Matter of Time, 1976; New York, New York, 1977; Arthur, 1981; Rent-a-Cop, 1988; Arthur 2: On the Rocks, 1988; Sam Found Out, 1988; Stepping Out, 1991; Parallel Lives, 1994; TV specials: Liza; Liza With a Z, 1972; Goldie and Liza Together, 1980; Baryshnikov on Broadway, 1980; A Time to Live, 1985; My Favourite Broadway: The Leading Ladies, 1999; Theatre: The Best Foot Forward, 1963; Flora, the Red Menace, 1965; Chicago, 1975; The Act, 1977-78; Liza at the Winter Garden, 1973; The Rink, 1984; Victor-Victoria, 1997; Recordings: Liza with a Z; Liza Minnelli: The Singer; Liza Minnelli: Live at the Winter Garden; Tropical Nights; The Act; Liza Minnelli: Live at Carnegie Hall; The Rink; Liza Minnelli at

Carnegie Hall; Results, 1989; Maybe This Time, 1996; Minelli on Minelli, 2000. Honours include: Academy Award, Best Actress; Hollywood Foreign Press Golden Globe Award; British Academy Award; David di Donatello Award. Address: Angel Records, 810 7th Avenue, Floor 4, New York, NY 10019, USA.

MINOGUE Kylie (Ann), b. 28 May 1968, Melbourne, Victoria, Australia. Singer; Actress. Appointments: Actress, Australian TV dramas: Skyways, 1980; The Sullivans, 1981; The Henderson Kids, 1984-85; Neighbours, 1986-88; Film Appearances: The Delinquents, 1989; Streetfighter, 1994; Biodome, 1995; Sample People, 1998; Cut, 1999; Moulin Rouge, 2001; As Singer, biggest selling single of decade in Australia, Locomotion, 1987; Highest UK chart entry for female artist, Locomotion, 1988; Highest album chart entry, Australia, UK, Kylie, 1988; First ever artist with 4 Top 3 singles from an album; First female artist with first 5 singles to receive Silver discs; Performances worldwide. Creative Works: Albums: Kylie, 1988; Enjoy Yourself, 1989; Rhythm of Love, 1990; Let's Get To It, 1991; Kylie - Greatest Hits, 1992; Kylie Minogue, 1994; Kylie Minogue, 1997-98; Light Years, 2000; Fever, 2001; Body Language, 2004. Singles: Locomotion, 1987; I Should Be So Lucky, 1988; Je Ne Sais Pas Pourquoi, 1988; Especially For You, 1988; Never Too Late, 1989; Confide In Me, 1994; Put Yourself In My Place, 1995; Where Is The Feeling, 1995; Where The Wild Roses Grow, 1995; Some Kind of Bliss, 1997; Did it Again; Breathe, 1998; GBI (German Bold Italic), 1998; Spinning Around, 2000; On A Night Like This, 2000; Please Stay, 2000; Can't Get You Out of My Head, 2001; In Your Eyes, 2002; Love at First Sight, 2002; Red Blooded Woman, 2004. Honours: Numerous Platinum, Gold and Silver Discs; 6 Logies (Australia); 6 Music Week Awards (UK); 3 Smash Hits Awards (UK); 3 Australian Record Industry Association Awards; 3 Japanese Music Awards; Irish Record Industry Award; Canadian Record Industry Award; World Music Award; Australian Variety Club Award; MO Award (Australian Showbusiness); Amplex Golden Reel Award; Diamond Award, (Belgium); Woman of the Decade (UK); MTV, Australian Female Artist of the Year, 1998; Pop Release of the Year, Light Years, ARIA; Best International Solo Female Artist and Best International Album, 2002. Address: c/o Terry Blamey Management, P O Box 13196, London SW6 4WF, England.

MINQUET Jean-Paul Louis, b. 13 February 1948, Béziers, France. Professor of Finance, 1 son, 1 daughter. Education: Masters in Economic Science, University of Paris, Panthéon-Sorbonne, 1966-72; MBA, HEC, Jouy-en-Josas, France, 1969-72; PhD, University of Haute Normandie, Rouen, France, 1977-84. Appointments: Professor, European Graduate School of Management, Paris, France, 1994; Professor, Ecole Supérieure des Affaires, Graduate School of Management, Beyrouth, Lebanon, 2000-; Visiting Professor, Universidad Argentina de la Empresa, Buenos Aires, 1995-, Instituto Tecnologico y de Estudios, Monterrey, Mexico, 1999, Centre International d'Etudes du Sport, Neuchâtel, Switzerland, 1998-; Financial Expert, FIFA (International Football Federation), Zurich, Switzerland, 2000; Member, Appeal Commission of Control of the Management, French Federation of Football, Paris , France, 2000-; Expert, ANVAR (French Agency for Innovation); Administrator, Mattim Council. Publications: Books: Economic Management of the Firm, 1978; Regulation of the Future Markets, 1985; Corporate Finance (co-author) Volume I, 1990; Corporate Finance (co-author), Volume II, 1992; For a Humanism of Sport (co-author), 1994; Sport Management: Theory and Practice, 1997; Numerous articles in professional journals. Honours: Officer, Order of French Courtesy; Listed in Who's Who publications and biographical dictionaries. Memberships: Editorial Committee Member, ACCOMEX Review. Address: 6 allée des Camélias, 95230 Soisy sous Montmorency, France. E-mail: minquet@escp.eap.net

Dictionary of International Biography

MIPUN Jatin, b. 1 August 1952, Gondhia Mishing Gaon, India. Civil Servant. m. Nilima Mipun, 3 sons. Education: PhD, Sociology, Dibrugarh University, Assam, India, 1983. Appointments: Lecturer, Dhemaji College, 1976; Adhoc Lecturer, Dibrugarh University, 1977-78; District Research Officer, 1979; Assam Civil Service, 1980; Indian Police Service, 1983; Currently, Director, State Fire Service Organisation, Assam, India. Publications: Dopark Nishar Bahit (poetry); Asam Darsham (essay); Miksijih (novel); Kangkanor Prithirit (short story); Tani Agom (short story); Mipak Nagbo (short story); The Mishings (Miris) of Assam, Development of a New Life Style; Chief Editor, Bartapakhili Magazine. Honours: Axam Xahitya Xobha Ambikagiri Roychoudhury Award for novel Mikisijih; Sayed Abdul Malik Agrodoot Award for contribution to to Assamese Literature; Bharatjyoti Award for Social Service, 2003. Memberships: President, Satadal; Pararkuchi Unnazan Krishi Unnayan Sarmittee; Sarada Devi Trust; Adviser, Brihattan Dimaria Krishi Unnayan Sarmittee. Address: Patarkuchi. PO Basistha, Guwahati-781029, Assam, India. E-mail: jatinmipun@rediff.com

MIRREN Helen, b. 26 July 1945, London, England. Actress. m. Taylor Hackford, 1997. Creative Works: Roles include: The Faith Healer, Royal Court, 1981; Antony & Cleopatra, 1983, 1998; The Roaring Girl, RSC, Barbican, 1983; Extremities, 1984; Madame Bovary, 1987; Two Way Mirror, 1989; Sex Please, We're Italian, Young Vic, 1991; The Writing Game, New Haven, Connecticut, 1993; The Gift of the Gorgon, NY, 1994; A Month in the Country, 1994; Orpheus Descending, 2001; Dance of Death, New York, 2001; Films include: Age of Consent, 1969; Savage Messiah, O Lucky Man!, 1973; Caligula, 1977; The Long Good Friday, Excalibur, 1981; Cal, 1984; 2010, 1985; Heavenly Pursuits, 1986; The Mosquito Coast, 1987; Pascali's Island, 1988; When the Whales Came, 1988; Bethune: The Making of a Hero, 1989; The Cook, the Thief, his Wife and her Lover, 1989; The Comfort of Strangers, 1989; Where Angels Fear to Tread, 1990; The Hawk, The Prince of Jutland, 1991; The Madness of King George, 1995; Some Mother's Son, 1996; Killing Mrs Tingle, 1998; The Pledge, 2000; No Such Thing, 2001; Greenfingery, 2001; Gosford Park, 2001; TV include: Miss Julie; The Apple Cart; The Little Minister; As You Like It; Mrs Reinhardt; Soft Targets, 1982; Blue Remembered Hills; Coming Through; Cause Celebre; Red King, White Knight; Prime Suspect, 1991; Prime Suspect II, 1992; Prime Suspect III, 1993; Prime Suspect: Scent of Darkness, 1996; Painted Lady, 1997; The Passion of Ayn Rand, 1998. Honours include: BAFTA Award, 1991; Emmy Award, 1996; Screen Actor's Guild Award for Best Supporting Actress, 2001. Address: c/o Ken McReddie Ltd, 91 Regent Street, London W1R 7TB, England.

MIRYALA Muralidhar, b. 26 November 1963, Karvena, India. Scientist. m. Radha Rani, 1 son, 1 daughter. Education: BSc, 1984, MSc, 1987, BEd, 1998, PhD, 1992, Osmania University, India. Appointments: Post doctoral Research fellow, 1993-94, Part-time Lecturer in Physics, 1993-95, Young Scientist, 1995, Department of Physics, Osmania University, India; Visiting Scientist, 1996-97, Chief Research Scientists, 1998-, SRL-ISTEC, Japan. Publications: 170 Research Publications; 8 articles in edited books; 25 invited talks; Patentee in field (6); Reviewer for number of superconductivity journals; Evaluated PhD theses, others. Honours: Young Scientist Award, 1995; Director's Award SRL-ISTEC, 1998; PASREG Award for Excellence, 1999; Best Presentation Award, IWCCII, 2003; Director's Award, SRL-ISTEC, 2003; Listed in several biographical publications. Memberships: Minerals, Metals and Materials Society (TMS) USA; Founder member of ASSSI, India. Address: Superconductivity Research Laboratory SRL-ISTEC, 3-35-2 Iiokashinden, Morioka, Iwate 020-0852, Japan. E-mail: miryala1@istec.or.jp

MIRZA Qamar, b. 19 March 1927, Ferozepur, India. Librarian. Education: BA, 1947; Certificate in LSc, 1951; Registration Exam Library Association, London, 1953-54; Masters degree in LSc, 1968-69. Appointments: Assistant Librarian, Northumberland County Library, 1954-62; Deputy Librarian, University of Peshawar, Pakistan, Teacher at Department of LSc, 1962-68, 1971-74; Graduate Librarian, Western Institute of Technology, Australia, 1975-76; Librarian, Umm Al-Qura University, Makkah, Saudi Arabia, 1977-98. Publications: Perspective of Past, Present and Future of L-Services in the University of Peshawar, in Pakistan Librarianship, 1963-64; Islamic Subject Headings in LC Subject Headings, 1992. Honours: Beta Phi Mu. Memberships: Life Member, Pakistan Library Association. Address: 17/46 Wahdat Colony, Disposal Road, Gujranwala, Pakistan.

MIRZAYANOVA Ludmila, b. 6 August 1957, Azerbaijan. Educational Psychologist. m. Rim Mirzayanov, 2 sons. Education: Qualification, Teacher of English and French, Minsk Foreign Languages Training Institute, 1979; Practical Psychologist, Special advancement and retraining course, Minsk State Teachers' Training Institute, 1990; Course, Academy of Postgraduate Education, Minsk, 1997; Candidate of Sciences, Pedagogical Psychology; Reader in Psychology, 2001. Appointments: Teacher at Day Care Centre and at Kamen School, 1979-81; Senior Pioneer Leader, Nesvizh Boarding School, 1983; Social Organiser Pioneer House, 1983-85; Teacher, Educational Science and Psychology, 1985-95, Vice-Principal in charge of Research Work, 1997-, Baranovichi State Teachers' Training College. Publications: Guide, Adaptation of the first year student. Solving the problem by means of diagnostics school for groups' tutors, 1996; Guide, Didactic theatre in future teacher training for creative pedagogical activities, 1999; Monograph, Forestalling adaptation to pedagogical profession, 1999; Monograph, Forestalling adaptation of students to pedagogical activities (crises, adapting means), 2003; Guide, Lesson of Psychology, 2003. Honours: Badge of Excellence, BSSR Education System, 1991; The 3rd Prize of the Belarus President's Social Welfare Fund for personal contribution to educating gifted students, 1999; Personal Grant, President of Belarus for outstanding contribution to education development, 2002. Memberships: Director, Research Laboratory on the Forestalling Adaptation of Educational Work; Organiser of international conferences on the problem of forestalling adaptation. Address: 153 A, Apt 84 Telman Str, Baranovichi, 225417, Belarus. E-mail: mirz@aport2000.ru

MIRZOEFF Edward, b. 11 April 1936, London, England. Television Producer. m. Judith Topper, 3 sons. Education: MA (Oxon), Open Scholarship in Modern History, The Queen's College, Oxford. Appointments: Market Researcher, Social Surveys (Gallup Poll) Ltd, 1959-58; Public Relations Executive, Duncan McLeish and Associates, 1960-61; Assistant Editor, Shoppers' Guide, 1961-63; BBC Television, 1963-2000; Executive Producer, Documentaries, 1983-2000; Freelance TV Producer, Director, 2000-; Director and Producer of many film documentaries including: Metro-land, 1973; A Passion for Churches, 1974; The Queen's Realm: A Prospect of England, 1977; The Front Garden, 1977; The Ritz, 1981; The Englishwoman and the Horse, 1981; Elizabeth R, 1992; Torvill and Dean: Facing the Music, 1994; Treasures in Trust, 1995; John Betjeman - The Last Laugh, 2001; Series Editor: Bird's-Eye View, 1969-71; Year of the French, 1982-83; In at the Deep End, 1983-84; Just Another Day, 1983-85; Editor, 40 Minutes, 1985-89; Executive Producer of many documentary series including: The House, 1992, Full Circle with Michael Palin, 1997; The 50 Years War: Israel and the Arabs, 1998; Children's Hospital, 1998-99. Honours: CVO, 1993; CBE, 1997; BAFTA Award for Best Documentary, 1981; BAFTA Awards for Best Factual Series, 1985, 1989; BFI TV Award, 1988; Samuelson Award, Birmingham Festival, 1988; British Video

Award, 1993; BAFTA Alan Clarke Award for Outstanding Creative Contribution to Television, 1995; International EMMY, 1996; Royal Philharmonic Society Music Award, 1996; British Press Guild Award for Best Documentary Series, 1996. Memberships: Vice-Chairman TV, 1991-95, Chairman, 1995-97, Trustee, 1999-, British Academy of Film and Television Arts (BAFTA); Trustee, 1999-, Vice Chair, 2000-02, Chair, 2002-, Grierson Memorial Trust; Board Member, Director's and Producer's Rights Society, 1999-; Salisbury Cathedral Council, 2002-. Address: 9 Westmoreland Road, London, SW13 9RZ, England.

MISHCHENKO Alexey M, b. 27 January 1949, USSR. Company Executive. m. Nadezhda Mishchenko, 1 son, 1 daughter. Education: University Degree in Microelectronics, USSR, 1973; PhD, Optic Components, USSR, 1989; Academician, International Telecommunications Academy, Moscow, Russia, 1998. Appointments: Various executive position in FORA Communications; ZAO Lucent Technologies, Russia, JV AT&T St Petersburg and Dalnya Svyaz; Currently: Chief Executive Officer, OJSC Vimpelcom Region, Russia and First Vice-President of OJSC Vimpelcom (NYSE-VIP). Publications: Articles in professional journals on fibre optics, Moscow, USSR, 1980-98. Honours: Successful Labour Medal, USSR Government, Moscow, 1972; Friendship of People Order, USSR Government, Moscow, 1985; Listed in Who's Who publications and biographical dictionaries. Address: #10/14 8 Marta Street, Moscow, Russia 127083, Russia. E-mail: tpashchenko@beeline.ru Website: www.beeline.ru

MISHIMA Hiroyuki, b. 8 January 1952, Koriyama, Fukushima, Japan. Professor. m. Amiko Tanaka, 1 son, 2 daughters. Education: BSc, Tokai University, Tokyo, 1974; PhD, Nihon University, Tokyo, 1986. Appointments: Teacher, High School, Shimizu, Japan, 1974-75; Prefectural High School, Gyoda, Japan, 1975-77; Assistant, 1977-78, Instructor, 1978-95; Assistant Professor, 1995-2003, Nihon University School of Dentistry at Matsudo; Visiting Assistant Professor, University of South Carolina, 1991-92; Professor, Kochi Gakuen College, 2003-. Publications: (in journals and proceedings) Tooth Enamel IV, 1984; Tooth Enamel V, 1989; Mechanisms and Phylogeny of Mineralization in Biological Systems, 1992; Biomineralization 93, 1994; Dental Morphology 98, 1999; Neanderthal Burials Excavations of the Dederiyeh Caves, Afrin, Syria, 2002; Biomineralization, 2004. Memberships: International Association for Dental Research; Japanese Association of Anatomists; Japanese Association of Oral Biology; Microscopy Society of America; New York Academy of Sciences; Society of Vertebrate Palaeontology. Address: Kochi Gakuen College, 292-26 Asahitenjinmachi, Kochi, 780-0955 Japan.

MISHRA Raghu Nath (HEH Mt Hon Lord), b. 7 April 1947, Amwa Digar, UP, India. Distinguished Professor; Agriculturist. m. Miss Abha, 30 January 1973, 2 sons. Education: BSc Electrical Engineering, 1st Class Honours I, 1969; MTech, 1971; PhD, 1975; MA, Engineering Education, 1985; DCTech, 1988; DSc, DCS Business Management, DD, LLD, DIL magna cum laude, 1992; DSc, Telematics and Communication, DSc Cybernetics, DCE, 1993; Muniv 1994. Appointments: Senior Research Assistant, Indian Institute of Technology (IIT), Kanpur, 1973-75; Assistant Professor, 1975-87, University Professor, 1977-, Associate Professor, 1987-97, Professor 1997-, Head, Computer and Information Technology, 2002-, College of Technology, GBUAT, PantNagar. Publications include: Application of Memory Gradient Methods to Economic Load Dispatching Problem, 1972; Univariate or One-Dimensional Search Techniques for Power Flow Optimisation Problems, 1973; Estimation, Detection and Identification Methods in Power System Studies, 1975;

International System of Units, 1978; Memory Gradient Method via Bridge Balance Convergence, 1979; Assumptions in Theory of Ballistic Galvanometer, Hybrid Algorithm for Constrained Minimisation, Convergence of Nonlinear Algorithms, 1980. Honours: National Scholarship, Board of High School and Intermediate Education, Uttar Pradesh, 1963-69; Trainee as Student Engineer, Hindustan Steel Limited (now, Steel Authority of India Limited), summer vacations, 1967, 1968; Lala Balak Ramji Kohinoor Memorial Gold Medal; The RBG Modi Medal; NVR Nageswar Iyer Prize, BH University, 1969; Institute Scholarship, IIT Kanpur, 1969-73; International Register of Profiles, 1982; International Biographical Roll of Honour, 1983, 1984, 1985; CSIR registration as Instrumentation/Technologist, 1983; Men of Achievement, certificate of merit, 1984; First Five Hundred medal, plaque, 1985; Commemorative Medal of Honour, Pewter, 1986, Gold, 1993, Research Fellow Gilt Silver Coins, 1994, 1995; IBC Paperweight and Letter Opener, 1987; IBC Certificate of Appreciation, Member of Merit for Life, Confederation of Chivalry, 1988; International Leaders in Achievement, medal, International Who's Who of Intellectuals, Dictionary of International Biography, medals, 1990; Who's Who in Australasia and Far East, medals, Count of San Ciriaco, 1991; KLUO, KtT, 1992; Baron of Bohemian Crown (Royal Order), General Knighthood (NOBLE, JUST and CHILVALROUS) Medal for merit for life, CSC, CU, MIDI pins, Coptic Cross, Capt AM, 1993; KHG, 1994; Bharat Gaurav, 1998; Eminent Personalities of India, proclamation, 1999; Expert, Union Public Service Commission in Electrical Engineering for Civil Services (preliminary) and Engineering Services Examinations, 1994-2001; Dictionary of International Biography 30th Anniversary Edition Certificate, 2002; Uttaranchal Public Service Commission Specialist in Computer Science for Civil Services (preliminary) examinations, 2002; Invitation for founding membership of the Academic Council of the London Diplomatic Council of the London Diplomatic Academy, 2002; Expert, Union Public Service Commission in Electronics and Telecommunication Engineering for Engineering Services Examinations, 2003-; Nominations for Lifetime of Scientific Achievement Award, Dictionary of International Biography 31st Edition, Order of Excellence, Man of the Year for Strength of Character and Achievement, World Medal of Honor for Strong Character and personal dignity, International Peace Prize for Positive Peace and Justice, 2003; Member of the Board of Studies of Vikram University, Ujjain, 2004. Listed in numerous international biographical publications including 1000 Great Scientists, 2000 Outstanding Scientists of the 20th Century, 2000 Outstanding Scientists of the 21st Century. Memberships: Deputy, International States Parliament for Safety and Peace, 1992-2002; Lifelong Member, World Academy Association of the Masters of the Universe; Lifelong Fellow, Australian Institute for Co-ordinated Research; ABI; ABI Research Association; International Advisor, Life Member, Indian Society for Technical Education; IIT Kanpur Alumni Association; Indian Alumni of the World University; Academy of Ethical Science; Indian Citizens Association; International Cultural Correspondence Institute; MIDI. Address: College of Technology Computer Department, GBP University of Agriculture and Technology, PantNagar, Uttaranchal-263 145, India.

MISRA Sri Prakash, b. 29 June 1957, Mughalsarai, India. Medical Doctor. m. Vatsala Misra, 1 son, 1 daughter. Education: MB BS, 1980; MD, 1984; DM, 1988. Appointment: Assistant Professor, Gastroenterology, 1990-98; Associate Professor, 1997-99; Professor, 1999-. Publications: Over 100 in professional medical journals. Honours: Basanti Devi Amir Chand Prize, Indian Council of Medical Research, 1988; Hoechst Om-Prakash Memorial Award, Indian Society of Gastroenterology, 1992; SN Gupta Award, Association of Physicians of India, 1995; N N Gupta

Dictionary of International Biography

Award, Association of Physicians of India, 1996; Olympus-Mitra Award, Indian Society of Gastroenterology, 1996; Gold Medal, Social and Preventive Medicine; Fellow, National Academy of Sciences, India, 1996; International GI Training Grant Award, American College of Gastroenterology; Postdoctoral Fellow, Mayo Clinic, Rochester, USA, 1997; Sisco-Pentax Oration, Society of Gastrointestinal Endoscopy of India, 1998; Searle Oration, Association of Physicians of India, 1999; Fellow, American College of Gastroenterology, 1999; Dr R M Kasliwal Award, National Academy of Medical Sciences, 2000; Council Member, National Academy of Sciences, India, 2000-01; Fellow, Royal College of Physicians of Edinburgh, 2000; Dr Shurvir Singh Visiting Professor, Association of Physicians of India, 2001; Fellow, Indian College of Physicians, 2003; Professor M P Mehrotra Oration, API, 2003. Memberships: Indian Society of Gastroenterology; Indian Association for Study of the Liver; Indian Academy of Gastroenterology; Society of Gastrointestinal Endoscopy of India; Association of Physicians of India; Indian Medical Association. Address: 4/411, MLN Medical College Campus, Department of Gastroenterology; 211 001 Allahabad, India.

MITCHELL Adrian, (Volcano Jones, Apeman Mudgeon, Gerald Stimpson), b. 24 October 1932, London, England. Poet; Writer; Dramatist; Lyricist. 2 sons, 3 daughters. Education: Christ Church, Oxford, 1953-55. Appointments: Granada Fellow, University of Lancaster, 1968-70; Fellow, Wesleyan University, 1972; Resident Writer, Sherman Theatre, 1974-75, Unicorn Theatre for Children, 1982-83; Judith Wilson Fellow, University of Cambridge, 1980-81; Fellow in Drama, Nanyang University, Singapore, 1995; Dylan Thomas Fellow, UK Festival of Literature, Swansea, 1995. Publications: Novels: If You See Me Coming; The Bodyguard; Plays: Plays with Songs, 1995; Out Loud; Heart on the Left; Blue Coffee; All Shook Up; For children: Robin Hood and Maid Marian; Nobody Rides the Unicorn; Maudie and the Green Children; also adaptions of numerous foreign plays; Television: Man Friday, 1972; Daft as a Brush, 1975; Glad Day, 1978; Pieces of Piece, 1992; Poetry: Paradise Lost and Paradise Regained; 5 programmes of Brecht's poetry, 1998; Radio plays: Animals Can't Laugh; White Suit Blues; Anna on Anna; Plays: Tyger Tyger Two; Man Friday; Mind Your Head; A Seventh Man, White Suit Blues; Uppendown Money; Hoagy; In the Unlikely Event, Satie Day/Night; The Pied Piper; The Snow Queen; Jemima Puddleduck; The Siege; The Heroes; The Lion, The Witch and the Wardrobe; The Mammoth Sails Tonight; Who Killed Dylan Thomas; Films: Man Friday, 1975; The Tragedy of King Real, 1982; Music: The Ledge, opera libretto, 1961; Houdini, opera libretto, 1977; Start Again, oratorio, 1998. Contributions to: Newspapers, magazines, and television. Honours: Eric Gregory Award; PEN Translation Prize; Tokyo Festival Television Film Award; Honarary Doctorate, North London University, 1997. Memberships: Royal Society of Literature; Society of Authors; Writers Guild. Address: c/o Peters, Fraser and Dunlop Group Ltd, Drury House, 34-43 Russell Street, London WC2B 5HA, England.

MITCHELL David John, b. 24 January 1924, London, England. Writer. m. 1955, 1 son. Education: Bradfield College, Berkshire; MA, Honours, Modern History, Trinity College, Oxford, 1947. Appointment: Staff Writer, Picture Post, 1947-52. Publications: Women on the Warpath, 1966; The Fighting Pankhursts, 1967; 1919 Red Mirage, 1970; Pirates, 1976; Queen Christabel, 1977; The Jesuits: A History, 1980; The Spanish Civil War, 1982; Travellers in Spain, 1990; The Spanish Attraction, editor, 2001. Contributions to: Newspapers and magazines. Membership: Society of Authors. Address: 20 Mountacre Close, Sydenham Hill, London SE26 6SX, England.

MITCHELL George John, b. 20 August 1933, Waterville, USA. Politician; Lawyer. 1 daughter. Appointments: Called to Bar, 1960; Trial Attorney, US Department of Justice, Washington, 1960-62; Executive Assistant to Senator Edmund Muskie, 1962-65; Partner, Jensen & Baird, Portland, 1965-77; US Attorney for Maine, 1977-79; US District Judge, 1979-80; US Senator from Maine, 1980-85; Majority Leader, US Senate, 1988-95; Special Advisor to President Clinton for Economic Initiatives in Ireland, 1995; Chancellor designate, Queen's University, Belfast, 1999-; Adviser, Thames Water, 1999-. Memberships: Chair, Maine Democratic Committee, 1966-68; Member, National Committee, Maine, 1968-77; Chair, Committee on Northern Ireland, 1995. Honours: Hon LLD, Queens University, Belfast, 1997; Honorary KBE, 1999; Shared, Honphouet-Boigny Peace Prize, 1999; Presidential Medal of Freedom, 1999; Tipperary International Peace Award, 2000. Address: c/o Verner, Liipfert, Bernhard, 901 15th Street, NW, #700, Washington, DC 20005, USA.

MITCHELL J J, b. 2 January 1965, Hampshire, England. Musician; Graphic Artist. m. Runi Delgado, divorced. Education: BA, Creative Arts, Plymouth Brethren Community College, 1986; Postgraduate Course, Graphic Art and Production, New York. Appointments: Typesetter, Leftfield Publishing and Printing, New Orleans, Louisiana, 1988-89; Bass Guitarist, Melonheads, 1989; Singer, Bass Guitarist, Plankton, 1990-91; Graphic Designer, Metro Publications, 1991-94; Chief Designer, X-L Art Publications, 1995-98; Director, Chief Designer, Plasma Comix. Memberships: Musicians Union; Equity; Star Trek Fan Club. Address: 4357 Sunscape Lane, Raleigh, NC 27613, USA.

MITCHELL Jerome, b. 7 October 1935, Chattanooga, Tennessee, USA. Retired Professor; Writer. Education: BA, Emory University, 1957; MA, 1959, PhD, 1965, Duke University. Appointments: Assistant Professor, University of Illinois, 1965-67; Associate Professor, 1967-72, Professor, 1972-97, University of Georgia; Fulbright Guest Professor, University of Bonn, 1972-73; Visiting Exchange Professor, University of Erlangen, 1975; Richard Merton Guest Professor, University of Regensburg, 1978-79. Publications: Thomas Hoccleve: A Study in Early 15th Century English Poetic, 1968; Hoccleve's Works: The Minor Poems, 1970; Chaucer: The Love Poet, 1973; The Walter Scott Operas, 1977; Scott, Chaucer and Medieval Romance, 1987; Old and Middle English Literature, 1994; More Scott Operas, 1996. Contributions to: Various scholarly journals. Address: PO Box 1268, Athens, GA 30603, USA.

MITCHELL Joni (Roberta Joan Anderson), b. 7 November 1943, Fort Macleod, Alberta, Canada. Singer; Songwriter. m. (1) Chuck Mitchell, 1965, (2) Larry Klein, 1982, 1 daughter by Brad McGrath. Education: Alberta College. Creative Works: Albums include: Song to a Seagull; Clouds; Ladies of the Canyon, 1970; Blue, 1971; For the Roses; Court and Spark, 1974; Miles of Aisles; The Hissing of Summer Lawns, 1975; Hejira, 1976; Don Juan's Reckless Daughter; Mingus, 1979; Shadows and Light, 1980; Wild Things Run Fast, 1982; Dog Eat Dog, 1985; Chalk Mark in a Rain Storm, 1988; Night Ride Home, 1991; Turbulent Indigo, 1994; Hits, 1996; Misses, 1996; Taming the tiger, 1998; Both Sides Now, 2000; Travelog, 2002; Songs include: Both Sides Now; Michael From Mountains; Urge for Going; Circle Game; TV includes: Joni Mitchell: Intimate and Interactive. Publication: Joni Mitchell: The Complete Poems and Lyrics. Honours include: Jazz Album of the Year, Rock-Blues Album of the Year, Downbeat Magazine, 1979; Juno Award, 1981; Century Award, Billboard Magazine, 1996; Polar Music Prize, Sweden, 1996; Governor General's Performing Arts Award, 1996; National Academy of Songwriters Lifetime Achievement Award, 1996; Rock and Roll Hall of Fame, 1997; National Academy of Popular Music-

Songwriters Hall of Fame, 1997. Address: c/o S L Feldman & Associates, 1505 West 2nd Avenue, Suite 200, Vancouver, BC V6H 3Y4, Canada.

MITCHELL Julian, b. 1 May 1935, Epping, Essex, England. Author; Dramatist. Education: BA, Wadham College, Oxford, 1958. Appointment: Midshipman, Royal Naval Volunteer Reserve, 1953-55. Publications: Imaginary Toys, 1961; A Disturbing Influence, 1962; As Far as You Can Go, 1963; The White Father, 1964; A Heritage and Its History (play), 1965; A Family and a Fortune (play), 1966; A Circle of Friends, 1966; The Undiscovered Country, 1968; Jennie Lady Randolph Churchill: A Portrait with Letters (with Peregrine Churchill), 1974; Half-Life (play), 1977; Another Country (play), 1982, (film), 1984; Francis (play), 1983; After Aida (play), 1985; Falling Over England (play), 1994; August (adaptation of Uncle Vanya) (play), 1994, (film), 1995; Wilde (film script), 1997. Contributions to: Welsh History Review; Monmouthshire Antiquary. Address: 47 Draycott Place, London SW3 3DB, England.

MITCHELL William Joseph, b. 4 January 1936, Bristol, England. Catholic Priest. Education: MA, Jurisprudence, Corpus Christi College, Oxford, 1956; Seminaire S. Sulpice, Paris France, 1956-61; Ordained Priest, 1961; License in Canon Law, Pontifical Gregorian University, Rome, 1963. Appointments: Curate, Pro-Cathedral, Bristol, 1963-64; Secretary to the Bishop of Clifton, 1964-75; Parish Priest, St Bernadette, Bristol, 1975-78; Rector, Pontifical Beda College, Rome, 1978-87; Parish Priest, St John's, Bath, 1988-90; Parish Priest St Anthony's, Bristol, 1990-96; Parish Priest, St Mary-on-the-Quay, Bristol, 1996-97; Dean of Clifton Cathedral, 1997-2000; Parish Priest, St Michael's Tetbury, Gloucestershire, 2001-; Judicial Vicar and Episcopal Vicar for Matrimonial Matters, 2002-. Honours: Prelate of Honour (Monsignor), Pope John Paul I, 1978-; Canon of Cathedral Chapter, Diocese of Clifton, 1987-; Vicar General, Diocese of Clifton, 1987-2001; Judicial Vicar and Episcopal Vicar for Matrimonial Matters, 2002-. Membership: Chaplain to the Knights of the Holy Sepulchre, 2003. Address: St Michael's Presbytery, 31 Silver Street, Tetbury, Gloucestershire, GL8 8DH, England. E-mail: billmitchell@tetbury31.freeserve.co.uk

MITCHELL William Marvin, b. 3 March 1935, Atlanta, Georgia, USA. Physician; Pathologist. m. Shirley Ann Crowell, 3 sons. Education: BA, Biology, 1957, MD, 1960, Vanderbilt University, Nashville Tennessee; PhD, Biochemistry, Johns Hopkins University, Baltimore, Maryland. Appointments: Intern, Internal Medicine, 1960-61, Doctoral Candidate, Biochemistry, Department of Biology, 1961-66, Johns Hopkins University; Assistant Professor of Microbiology, 1966-70, Assistant Professor of Medicine, 1969-76; Associate Professor of Microbiology, 1970-74, Associate Professor of Pathology, 1974-78, Professor of Pathology, 1978-, Vanderbilt University School of Medicine, Nashville, Tennessee. Publications: Over 200 peer reviewed articles as co-author in scientific journals include: Antibody dependent enhancement of human immunodeficiency virus type 1 infection, 1988; Complement-mediated, antibody-dependent enhancement of human immunodeficiency virus type 1 (HIV-1) infection in vitro accelerates viral RNA and protein synthesis and infectious virus production, 1989; Neutralization and enhancement in vitro and in vivo HIV and SIV infection, 1990; Antibodies to the primary immunodominant domain of human immunodeficiency virus type 1 (HIV-1) glycoprotein 41 enhance HIV-1 infection in vitro, 1990. Honours: Borden Award in Research, 1960; Eleanor Roosevelt Scholar, 1976-77; Career Development Award, NIH, 1972. Address: Department of Pathology, Vanderbilt University, Nashville, TN 37232, USA. E-mail: bill.mitchell@vanderbilt.edu

MITSUSHIMA Dai, b. 14 March 1965, Osaka, Japan. Physiologist. m. Emi Narui. Education: Doctor of Veterinary Medicine, 1990; PhD, 1996. Appointments: Research Associate, 1990-93, Honorary Fellow, 1993, University of Wisconsin-Madison, USA; Lecturer, 1994-2000, Assistant Professor, 2002-, Yokohama City University School of Medicine. Publications: Articles as first author in scientific journals including: Proceedings of the National Academy of Science, USA, 1994; Journal of Neuroscience, 1996; Endocrinology, 1997; Neuroscience, 2002. Honours: Young Investigator Award, Physiological Society of Japan, 2000; Young Investigator Award, Japan Neuroscience Society, 2002. Memberships: Society for Neuroscience; Japan Neuroscience Society; Physiological Society of Japan; Japanese Society of Veterinary Science. Address: Department of Neuroendocrinology, Yokohama City University Graduate School of Medicine, 3-9 Fukuura Kanazawaku, Yokohama 236-0004, Japan. E-mail: dm650314@med.yokohama-cu.ac.jp

MITZOV Simeon, b. 31 January 1938, Vrav, Vidin Region, Bulgaria. Civil Culture Engineer. m. Maria Janeva Mitzovna, 1 son, 1 daughter. Education: Forestry University, Sofia, 1956-61; Environmental Studies Specialisation, Bulgarian Science Academy, Sofia, 1967. Appointments: Head of Aforestation Department, Director of Technical Department, Director of Civil Engineering Department, Director of Production Department, Director of Civil Engineering and Environment Department of Sunny Beach "Balkan Tourist", Nature Park Nesebar, 1961-66. Publications: Author of over 40 publications on environment and nature protection; Book: A Lifetime is not enough for a Forest. Honours: Enlisted among 100 Famous Forest Engineers of Bulgaria; "Kolyo Ficheto" State Award for Construction; Ministry of Tourism Award; Ministry of Forests Award; A number of Government awards and medals. Memberships: Founder and President, Bulgarian Blue Flag Movement; Board Member, Foundation for Environmental Education with headquarters in England. Participant in three Global Symposia "Religion, Science and Environment" under the patronage of the Ecumenical Patriarch Bartholomew I. Address: 1A "Vasil Levski" Street, 8200 Pomorie, Bourgas Region, Bulgaria. E-mail: smitzov@yahoo.com

MIURA Akihiko, b. 17 September 1971, Saitama, Japan. Safety Engineer. m. Sachiko. Education: Bachelor's Degree, Electro and Electrical Engineering, Science University of Tokyo, 1995; Master's Degree, Plasma Physics, Tokyo Institute of Technology, 1997. Appointment: Assistant Senior Researcher, Power Reactor and Nuclear Fuel Development Corporation (now Japan Nuclear Cycle Development Institute), 1997-. Publications: Articles in scientific journals: Spread behaviour of explosion in enclosed space; Reflection and Diffraction Phenomena of Blast Wave Propagation in Nuclear Fuel Cycle Facility. Honours: Best Paper of the 4th International Symposium on Hazards, Prevention and Mitigation of Industrial Explosions. Memberships: Atomic Energy Society of Japan; Japan Explosives Society. Address: 4-33 Muramatsu, Tokai-mura, 319-1106 Ibaraki, Japan. E-mail: amiura@tokai.jnc.go.jp

MIYAKE Issey, b. 22 April 1939, Tokyo, Japan. Fashion Designer. Education: Tama Art University; Tokyo and La Chambre Syndicale de la Couture Parisienne, Paris. Appointments: Assistant Designer to Guy Laroche, Paris, 1966-68, to Hubert de Givenchy, Paris, 1968-69; Designer, Geoffrey Beene (ready-to-wear firm), New York, 1969-70; Founder, Miyake Design Studio, Tokyo, 1970; Director, Issey Miyake International, Issey Miyake and Associates, Issey Miyake Europe, Issey Miyake USA, Issey Miyake On Limits, Tokyo; Executive Advisor, Planner, First Japan Culture Conference, Yokohama, 1980. Creative Works: Works exhibited in Paris, Tokyo and MIT, appears in collections of Metro Museum of Art, New York and Victoria and Albert Museum,

Dictionary of International Biography

London. Honours: Japan Fashion Editors Club Awards, 1974, 1976; Mainichi Design Prize, 1977; Pratt Institute Award, New York, 1979; Dr.h.c. Royal College of Art, 1993.

MIYAKOSHI Naohisa, b. 22 April 1965, Akita, Japan. Physician; Orthopaedic Surgeon. m. Miwako Yoshida Miyakoshi, 1 son, 1 daughter. Education: MD, Medical Science, 1990, PhD, Bone Metabolism, 1996, Akita University, Japan. Appointments: Resident, Akita University Medical Centre, 1990-91; Senior Resident, Taihei Children's Hospital, 1991-92; Clinical Fellow, Akita Rosai Hospital, 1992-93; Clinical Fellow, 1993-, Instructor, 1998-, Akita University Medical Centre. Publications: 4 book chapters; 10 review articles; 76 original articles in medical science. Honours include: Travel Grant Award, American Society for Bone and Mineral Research, 2000; Outstanding Poster Award, Japanese Society for Bone and Mineral Research, 2001. Memberships: Japanese Orthopaedic Association; Japanese Society for Bone and Mineral Research; American Society for Bone and Mineral Research; Japan Spine Research Society and 8 others. Address: Department of Orthopaedic Surgery, Akita University, School of Medicine, 1-1-1 Hondo, Akita 010-8543, Japan.

MIYAZAKI Koichi, b. 7 December 1949, Yokohama, Japan. Professor in Economics. m. Mizuyo Muto. Education: BA, 1972, Yokohama National University; MA, 1974, University Tokyo. Appointments: Professor in Economics, Hosei University, 1986-. Memberships: American Economic Association; Japanese Economic Association; Tokyo Centre for Economic Research. Address: 350-1-108 Katakura-Machi, Hachioji-Shi, Tokyo 192-0914, Japan.

MIYOSHI Kazuhisa, b. 15 February 1946, Kobe, Japan. Scientist; Engineer. m. Sumiko, 2 sons, 2 daughters. Education: BS, Engineering, Osaka Institute of Technology, 1968; MS, 1970, PhD, 1975, Engineering, Osaka University. Appointments: Faculty Member, Kanazawa University, 1970-78; Research Associate, NRC-NASA, 1976-78; Research Scientist, NASA Glenn Research Center, Cleveland, Ohio, 1979-. Publications: Over 200. Honours: Space Flight Awareness Award; Superior Accomplishment Award; NRC-NASA Associateship Programs Award; Technology Transfer Awards; JSPS Invitation Fellowship Award. Memberships: AVS; STLE; ACerS; JAST. Address: NASA Glenn Research Center, 21000 Brookpark Road, MS106-5, Cleveland, OH 44135, USA.

MIZRAHI Isaac, b. 14 October 1961, Brooklyn, New York, USA. Fashion Designer. Education: Parsons School of Design. Appointments: Apprenticed to Perry Ellis, 1982, full-time post, 1982-84; Worked with Jeffrey Banks, 1984-85, Calvin Klein, 1985-87; Founder, own design firm in partnership with Sarah Hadad Cheney, 1987; First formal show, 1988, First spring collection, 1988; First menswear line launched, 1990, Announced closure of firm, 1998. Address: 104 Wooster Street, New York, NY 10012, USA.

MIZUNO Hirobumi, b. 28 April 1931, Ureshino, Saga Prefecture, Japan. Professor. Education: BSc, Mathematics, Waseda University, Japan; MSc, 1955, DSc, 1965, Mathematics, University of Tokyo. Appointments: Lecturer, Meiji University, Tokyo, 1959-66; Associate Professor, 1966-70, Professor, 1970-97, University of Electro-Communication; Professor, Meisei University, 1998-2003. Publications: Fundamentals of Information Algebra, 1980; Fundamentals of Information Mathematics, 1996; Articles in professional journals. Memberships: The Mathematical Society of Japan; American Mathematical Society. Address: 5-9-19-110 Himonya, Meguru-ku, Tokyo 152-0003, Japan.

MO Timothy (Peter), b. 30 December 1950, Hong Kong. Writer. Education: Convent of the Precious Blood, Hong Kong; Mill Hill School, London; BA, St John's College, Oxford. Publications: The Monkey King, 1978; Sour Sweet, 1982; An Insular Possession, 1986; The Redundancy of Courage, 1991; Brownout on Breadfruit Boulevard, 1995; Renegade or Halo², 1999. Contributions to: Periodicals. Honours: Gibbs Prize, 1971; Geoffrey Faber Memorial Prize, 1979; Hawthornden Prize, 1983; E M Forster Award, American Academy of Arts and Letters, 1992; James Tait Black Memorial Prize, 1999. Address: c/o Chatto & Windus, 20 Vauxhall Bridge Road, London SW1V 2SA, England.

MOAGAR-POLADIAN Gabriel, b. 23 September 1965, Bucharest, Romania. Senior Researcher Physics. Education: MSc, 1985-90, PhD, 1992-99, Faculty of Physics, Bucharest University. Appointments: Research Scientist, SC Optoelectronica SA, work on infrared detectors, 1990-92; Research Scientists, SC Biotechnos, SA work on physical characterization of cells suspensions 3, 1992-94; Senior Researcher, National Institute of Microtechnology, work on optoelectronics, sensors and microsystems, 1994-. Publications: 23 articles and papers published/presented in international journals and conferences. Honours: Invited to join IEEE, American Association for the Advancement of Science, New York Academy of Sciences. Memberships: Romanian Physical Society; European Physical Society, European Optical Society, Optical Society of America. Address: Aleea Fuiorului Nr 6 bloc Y3A sc 1 et 6 ap 27, Sector 3, Bucharest, Romania.

MOCUMBI Pascoal Manuel, b. 10 April 1941, Maputo, Mozambique. Medical Doctor. m. Adelina Isabel Bernadino Paindane, 3 January 1966, 2 sons, 2 daughters. Education: MD, University of Lausanne, 1973; Diploma, Health Planning, Institut Planification Sanitaire, University of Dakar, 1975. Appointments: Chief Medical Officer, Sofala Province, 1976-80; Minister of Health, 1980-87; Foreign Minister, 1987-94; Prime Minister, 1994-. Publications: Co-author, Manual de Obstetricia Pratica, Intervencoes Obstétricas; Health for All by the Year 2000?, 1996. Honours: National decorations; International decorations, Brazil, Chile. Memberships: Mozambique Medical Association; Mozambique Public Health Association; Mozambique Family Development Association. Address: Praça da Marinha, Maputo, Mozambique. E-mail: dgpm.gov@teledata.mz

MODEL Anselm, b. 14 January 1942, Goerlitz-Weinhuebel. Physician; Philosopher. Education: Medicine, University of Freiburg, Germany and Vienna, Austria; Philosophy, Sociology, University of Freiburg; MD, 1972; PhD, 1986; Research works and clinical training in several institutions and hospitals. Appointments: Private Practice, Physical and Rehabilitation Medicine, Pain Treatment, Chiropraxis, Freiburg, Germany, 1997-. Publications: Several articles in professional journals. Memberships: Gottfried-Wilhelm-Leibniz Association; Allgemeine Gesellschaft für Philosophie in Deutschland; Deutsche Gesellschaft zum Studium des Schmerzes; Deutsche Gesellschaft für manuelle Medizin; Vereinigung Süddeutscher Orthopaeden; Deutsche Ärztegesellschaft für Akupunktur; Zentralverband der Ärzte für Naturheilverfahren. Address: Kirchbergstr 16, D-79111, Freiburg, Germany.

MODI Om Prakash, b. 25 January 1956, Nawadih (Bihar), India. Scientist. m. Sunita Modi, 1 son, 1 daughter. Education: BSc Engg, Metallurgy, BIT Sindri (RU), 1981; MTech, Metallurgy, 1983, PhD, Materials & Metallurgy, 1994, IIT Kanpur. Appointments: Scientist B, 1983-88, Scientist C, 1988-93, Scientist E-1, 1993-98, Scientist EII, 1998- Regional Research Laboratory. Publications: 50 research papers in international reviewed journals on microstructure, mechanical and wear properties of materials. Honours: Best paper (Presentation/Award in National Conference on Industrial Tribology, Delhi, Tribology Society of India; Indian National Science Academy, New Delhi, Fellowship; Honorary Visiting Research Fellow, University of Hertfordshire, Hatfield, UK; Listed in several Who's Who publications. Memberships: Life member, Indian Institute of Metals, Calcutta, India; Life Fellow, Institution of Engineers, India; Life Fellow, Tribology Society of India; Member, Research Board of Advisors, American Biographical Institute, 1999. Address: Regional Research Laboratory, Hoshangabad Road, Bhopal (MP) 462026, India. E-mail: om_prakashmodi@hotmail.com

MOE Janet Anne Mangan, b. 24 May 1946, Sacramento, California, USA. Educator; Organist. m. Edward E Moe, deceased 2002, 1 son, 1 daughter. Education: BA, California Lutheran University, 1968; Standard Secondary Teaching Credential, California State University at Sacramento, 1969; Certification in Orff Schulwerk Levels I, II and III, University of California, Santa Cruz, 1987; Cross-cultural Language and Academic Development Certificate, California State University at Sacramento, 1996; Master of Science in Educational Administration and Preliminary Administrative Credential, National University, 2001. Appointments: Elementary School Teacher, Gloria Dei School, 1969-73; Elementary Music Specialist, Sacramento City Unified School District, 1982-; All City Elementary Honor Choir Co-ordinator, 1999-01; Choral Director, Sierra Mountain Music Camp, 2001; Member of the task force to restore music and the fine arts to Sacramento City Unified School District, 1999-2000; Organist Gloria Dei Lutheran Church, 1970-2002; Organist the Lutheran Church of the Good Shepherd (Sacramento), 2003-. Publications: The effectiveness of Music in Teaching Character Education (proposal as partial fulfilment of Masters Thesis), National University, 2000. Honours: Honorary Service Award, PTA Bear Flag School, 1992; Outstanding Music Educator Award, 1996, 2003; Member, California Music Educators' Association Board Capitol Section. Memberships: California Teachers' Association; National Education Association; California Music Educators' Association; Music Educators' National Conference; National Audubon Society; Evangelical Lutheran Church in America. Address: PO Box 109, Elk Grove, CA 95759-0109, USA. E-mail: janmoe@comcast.net

MOECK Walter Francis, b. 18 March 1922, Milwaukee, Wisconsin, USA. Musician; Symphony Conductor. m. Barbara, 2 sons, 1 daughter. Education: BM, Eastman School of Music, 1947; MM, University of Iowa. Career: Musical Director and Conductor of: the University of Alabama Symphony Orchestra; Alabama Pops Symphony Orchestra; Birmingham Ballet; Los Angeles Repertoire Symphony; Westlake Symphony; San Fernando Valley Theatre of Performing Arts; San Carlo Opera Company; American Philharmonia; Guest Conductor: Philadelphia Symphony; New Orleans Philharmonic; Burbank Symphony, Bakersfield Philharmonic and many others; Musical Director and conductor, Fine Arts Orchestra, Scottsdale/Phoenix, and the Sun City Concert Band, Sun City, Arizona. Honours: Many state and national honours before the age of 16; Life Fellow, International Institute of Arts and Letters, Zurich, Switzerland, 1963; Medal of Merit, President George Bush, 1990; Honorary Doctorate Degree, Fine Arts and Music, London Institute of applied Research, London, England, 1993; International Man of the Year, 1993, International Biographical Centre. Memberships: President's task Force; National Republican Congressional Committee; National Republican Senatorial Committee. Address: 14507 Trading Post Drive, Sun City West, AZ 85375, USA.

MOEN Ragnar, b. 2 November 1935, Porsgrunn, Norway. Chemist. m. (1) Helene Roholt Moen, 2 sons, (2) Nora Starrs. Education: Diplom-Chemiker, 1961, Dr Rer Nat, 1963, Aachen, Germany. Appointments: Research Chemist, Exxon Research; Chief Chemist, Marcal Paper Mills; Physical Vapour Deposition of Titanium Nitride, General Magnaplate; Chemistry Teacher, Union College; Science Teacher, Hamburg School System, Germany; Science Teacher (Captain), Valley Forge Military Academy; Science Teacher, Berkeley Institute; Speaker at American Chemical Society's National Meeting, Miami Beach, Florida, April 1967; Guest Speaker, Ole Bull Music Festival, Galeton, Pennsylvania, 1998-. Publications: Magnetic Nonequivalence of a Thiophosphate Ester, 1966; Determination of 2-Substituted 5-Norbornenes by Nuclear Magnetic Resonance Spectroscopy, 1967. Honour: Listed in biographical dictionaries. Memberships: American Chemical Society; Sons of Norway. Address: 1 Higa Terrace, Union, NJ 07083, USA.

MOFFAT Gwen, b. 3 July 1924, Brighton, Sussex, England. Author. m. Gordon Moffat, 1948, 1 daughter. Publications: Space Below My Feet, 1961; Two Star Red, 1964; On My Home Ground, 1968; Survival Count, 1972; Lady With a Cool Eye, 1973; Deviant Death, 1973; The Corpse Road, 1974; Hard Option, 1975; Miss Pink at the Edge of the World, 1975; Over the Sea to Death, 1976; A Short Time to Live, 1976; Persons Unknown, 1978; Hard Road West, 1981; The Buckskin Girl, 1982; Die Like a Dog, 1982; Last Chance Country, 1983; Grizzly Trail, 1984; Snare, 1987; The Stone Hawk, 1989; The Storm Seekers, 1989; Rage, 1990; The Raptor Zone, 1990; Pit Bull, 1991; Veronica's Sisters, 1992; The Outside Edge, 1993; Cue the Battered Wife, 1994; The Lost Girls, 1998; A Wreath of Dead Moths, 1998; Running Dogs, 1999; Private Sins, 1999; Quicksand, 2001; Retribution, 2002. Contributions to: Newspapers and magazines. Memberships: Crime Writers Association; Mystery Writers of America; Sierra Club; Pinnacle Club. Agent: c/o Juliet Burton, 2 Clifton Avenue, London W12 9DR, England. Website: http://www.twbooks.co.uk/authors/gmoffat.html

MOH Sangman, b. 20 February 1963, Republic of Korea. Professor. m. Keumsook Yoon, 2 sons. Education: PhD, Information and Communications University, Republic of Korea, 2002. Appointments: Project Leader, Electronics and Telecommunications Research Institute, Republic of Korea, 1991-2002; Professor, Chosun University, Republic of Korea, 2002-. Publications: Professional papers and articles contributed to professional journals; Overseas and domestic patents in field. Honours: Registered Professional Engineer, Republic of Korea, 1993; Best Paper Award, Institute of Electronics Engineers of Korea, 1995; Ministerial Award, Ministry of Information and Communications, Republic of Korea, 2001; Listed in Who's Who publications and biographical dictionaries. Memberships: Institute of Electrical and Electronics Engineers; Association for Computing Machinery. Address: Department of Internet Engineering, Chosun University, 375 Seoseok-dong, Dong-gu, Gwangju 501-759, Republic of Korea. E-mail: smmoh@chosun.ac.kr

MOHAMMED Tarek Uddin, b. 19 November 1965, Noakhali, Bangladesh. Researcher. m. Samina Hasanat, 1 son. Education: BSc, Civil Engineering, Bangladesh University of Engineering and Technology, Bangladesh, 1989; M Eng, Asian Institute of Technology, Bangkok, Thailand, 1994; D Eng, Tokyo Institute of Technology, Japan, 1997. Appointments: Lecturer, Bangladesh Institute of Technology, Chittagong, 1990-92; Research Associate, Asian Institute of Technology, Bangkok, Thailand, 1994; Deputy Manager, NEWJEC Inc, Osaka, Japan, 1998-2000; Special Researcher, Port and Airport Research Institute, Japan, 2000-. Publications: More than 50 papers in journals and proceedings of

Dictionary of International Biography

international conferences; Journals include: American Concrete Institute Materials Journals; ASCE Materials Journal; American Concrete Institute Concrete International; Cement and Concrete Research Journal; Journal of Japan Concrete Institute; Journal of Japan Society of Civil Engineers. Honours: Young Researcher Award, Japan Concrete Institute, 2002; Listed in Who's Who publications and biographical dictionaries. Memberships: Japan Society of Civil Engineers; Japan Concrete Institute; American Concrete Institute; Institute of Engineers of Bangladesh; Japan Society of Professional Engineers. Address: Port and Airport Research Institute, 3-1-1Nagase, Yokosuka Shi, Japan 239-0826. E-mail: tarek@pari.go.jp

MOHAN Brij, b. 9 August 1939, Mursan, India. Professor. m. Prem Sharma, 1 son, 1 daughter. Education: MSW, Agra University, 1960; PhD, Social Work, Lucknow University, 1964. Appointments: Lecturer and Research Supervisor/scholar, Lucknow University, 1960-75; Academic Specialist, University of Wisconsin, OSHKOSH, 1975-76; Associate Professor, 1976-81, Professor, 1981-, Louisiana State University (LSU); Dean, LSU School of Social Work, 1981-86. Publications: Global Development, 1992; Eclipse of Freedom, 1993; Democracy of Unfreedom, 1996; Unification of Social Work, 1999; Social Work Revisited, 2002; The Practice of Hope, 2003. Honours: Alumni Distinguished Faculty Award, LSU school of Social Work, 1997; LSU Distinguished Faculty Award, 1999. Memberships: IASSW; IUCISD; NASW; AAUP; CSWE. Address: 1573 Laycester Drive, Baton Rouge, LA 70808, USA. E-mail: dialog@cox.net

MOHANTA Guru Prasad, b. 12 June 1960, Talkunda, Orissa. University Professor. m. Reena, 1 son, 1 daughter. Education: Intermediate in Science, Utkal University, 1978; BPharmacy, Jadavpur University, Calcutta, 1982; MPharmacy, Jadavpur University, Calcutta, 1984; PhD Annamalai University, 2001. Appointments: Demonstrator, College of Pharmaceutical Sciences, Orissa, 1982-83; Lecturer, V L College of Pharmacy, Raichur-Karanataka, 1984-85; Lecturer, Annamalai University, Tamil Nadu, 1985-94; Reader, 1994-2003, Professor, 2003-, Annamalai University, Tamil Nadu. Publications: Numerous articles in professional journals. Honours: National Rural Talent Scholarship, 1972-76; Merit Scholarship, 1976-78; Orissa Government Stipend, 1978-82; UGC Student Fellowship, 1982-84; WHO funding, 2002 and 2004. Memberships: Life Member, Indian Pharmaceutical Association; Life Member, Indian Society for Technical Education; Fellow, Institution of Chemists (India); Life Member, Indian Hospital Pharmacist's Association. Address: Department of Pharmacy, Annamalai University, PO, Annamali Nagar, Tamil Nadu, 608002, India.

MOIR (Alexander) (Thomas) Boyd, b. 1 August 1939, Bolton, Lancashire, England. Medical Practitioner; Scientist. m. Isobel May Shechan, deceased, 1 son, 2 daughters. Education: MBChB, BSc, 1970; PhD, Edinburgh University. Appointments: Rotating Intern, New York City, USA; 1964-65; Scientific Staff, 1965-67, Clinical Scientific Staff, 1968-73, Medical Research Council; Senior Medical Officer, 1972-77, Principal Medical Officer, 1977-85, Director of Chief Scientist Organisation, 1986-96, Scottish Health Department; Currently, Honorary Appointments, Edinburgh and Glasgow Universities; Consultancy and Clinical Services. Publications: Publications on Neuroscience, Pharmacology, Biochemistry, Toxicology, Research Management, Public Health. Honours: FRCP (Edin); FRCP (Glasgow); FRCPath; FFPHM; FIBiol; FIFST; MFOM; MFPM; FRSS. Memberships: UK Royal Colleges of Physicians and their Faculties; Royal College of Pathologists; Institute of Biology; Association of Chemists and

Biochemists; Pharmacology Society. Address: 23 Murrayfield Gardens, Edinburgh EG 12 6DG, Scotland. E-mail: boyd_moir@msn.com

MOJTABAI Ann Grace, b. 8 June 1937, New York, New York, USA. Author; Educator. m. Fathollah Motabai, 27 April 1960, divorced 1966, 1 son, 1 daughter. Education: BA, Philosophy, Antioch College, 1958; MA, Philosophy, 1968, MS, Library Science, 1970, Columbia University. Appointments: Lecturer in Philosophy, Hunter College, 1966-68; Briggs-Copeland Lecturer on English, Harvard University, 1978-83; Writer in Residence, University of Tulsa, 1983-. Publications: Mundome, 1974; The 400 Eels of Sigmund Freud, 1976; A Stopping Place, 1979; Autumn, 1982; Blessed Assurance, 1986; Ordinary Time, 1989; Called Out, 1994; Soon, 1998 Contributions to: New York Times Book Review; New Republic; Philosophy Today; Philosophical Journal. Honours: Radcliffe Institute Fellow, 1976-78; Guggenheim Fellowship, 1981-82; Richard and Hinda Rosenthal Award, American Academy and Institute of Arts and Letters, 1983; Lillian Smith Award, Southern Regional Council, 1986; Award in Literature, American Academy of Arts and Letters, 1993. Memberships: Mark Twain Society; PEN; Texas Institute of Letters; Phi Beta Kappa. Address: 2102 South Hughes, Amarillo, TX 79109, USA.

MOKRÝ Jaroslav, b. 14 October 1964, Czech Republic. Histologist. m. Michaela Mokra, 1 son. Education: MD, 1990; PhD, 1995; Associate Professor, 1999. Appointment: Head, Department of Histology & Embryology, Charles University, Medical Faculty, Hradec Králové. Honours: Rector's Prize, Charles University, 1987, 1990; Young Histochemist Award, IFSHC, Kyoto, 1996; Eastern European Award, European Tissue Culture Society, Mainz, 1997. Memberships: Czech Anatomical Society; Czech Society for Histochemistry and Cytochemistry; Czech Society of Neuroscience; Czech Medical Chamber; Czechoslovak Biological Society. Address: Department of Histology and Embryology, Charles University, Simkova 870, 500 01 Hradec Králové, Czech Republic.

MÖLDER Leevi, b. 4 July 1933, Tudulinna, Estonia. Professor of Chemical Engineering. m. Maila Vägi, 1961, 2 sons, 1 daughter. Education: MSc, Chemical Engineering, 1957, PhD, 1963, Tallinn Technical University. Appointments: Researcher, 1957-62, Associate Professor, 1962-73, Professor, 1973-85, 1992-2000, Emeritus Professor, 2001-, Tallinn Technical University; Head of Department, Institute of Chemistry, Estonian Academy of Sciences, 1983-97; Vice Chairman, Council Oil Shale, Estonian Academy of Sciences, 1989-99; Chairman, Commission on Liquid Fuels Quality Specification, Ministry of Economics, Tallinn, 1994-97; Consultant, RAS Kiviter Chemical Co, Kohtla-Jarve, Estonia, 1995-98. Publications: Technology of Heavy Chemicals, co-author, 1970; English-Estonian-Russian Dictionary of Chemistry, co-author, 1998; 203articles in professional journals; 11 inventions. Honours: Mente et manu Medal, Tallinn Technical University, 1983, 1993; Paul Kogerman Medal, Estonian Academy of Sciences, 1987; White Star Order of Merit, 2004; Listed in numerous biographical publications. Memberships: American Society for Testing and Materials; Estonian Chemical Society; Union of Estonian Scientists; Estonian Society for Nature Conservation. Address: Tallinn Technical University, 5 Ehitajate tee, Tallinn 19086, Estonia. E-mail: leevi.molder@ttu.ee

MOLNÁR Péter Pál, b. 2 March 1951, Pécs, Hungary. Physician; Pathologist; Neuropathologist. Divorced. Education: BS, 1969; MD, 1975; Board Certification, Pathology, 1979; PhD, Medicine, 1987; Board Certification, Neuropathology, 1989; Dr Sci, Hungarian Academy of Sciences, 1999. Appointments:

Postdoctoral Fellow, Pathology, University Medical School, Department of Pathology, Debrecen, Hungary, 1975-79; Full Professor, 1995-; Visiting Fellow, NCI, NIH, Bethesda, Maryland, 1979-82; Visiting Professor, Northwestern University, Chicago, USA, 1992-95, 2000-; Director, Professor Tadashi Hirano Centre, Hungarian-Japanese Electron Microscopic Centre, University Medical School, Debrecen, 1994-. Publications: Numerous articles in professional journals; Several abstracts and book chapters. Honours: University Educational Award, 1975; Arányi Lajos Memorial Note; Outstanding Educator, 1994; Dr Med Habil, 1995; Selected as a member of the American Association for Cancer Research; Honorary Board Member, (for distinguished standing) Research Board 2000, American Biographical Institute, 2000; Listed in 2000 Outstanding Intellectuals of the 20th Century, International Biographical Centre, Cambridge; Co-ordinator, Hungarian National Paediatric Neuro-Oncology Program, 2001. Memberships include: Hungarian Society of Biophysics; Hungarian Society of Pathology, Board of Directors, 1995; European Society of Clinical Investigation; European Society of Pathology; International Society of Neuropathology, Councillor, Hungarian Section, 1995; Hungarian Society of Biology; Hungarian Society for Microscopy; European Association of Neuro-Oncology, Board of Directors, 1996; International Academy of Pathology, Board of Directors, Hungarian Division, 1996; Society for Ultrastructural Pathology, Alabama, USA; New York Academy of Sciences; Society of Neuro-Oncology, USA; Research Board of Advisors of the American Biographical Institute; American Association for the Advancement of Science; Association for Neuro-Oncology, USA; Society for Neuro-Oncology of Hungary; British Society of Neuropathology; Editorial Board, Journal of Neuro-Oncology; Member, IBRO; The Hungarian Society of Paediatric Oncology. Address: University of Debrecen, Clinical and Health Sciences Centre (DE-OEC), Department of Pathology, Hungarian-Japanese EM Centre (HJEMC), Debrecen, Nagyerdei krt 98, POB 24, H-4012 Hungary. E-mail: molnarp@jaguar.dote.hu

MONCAYO-MEDINA Alvaro, b. 14 May 1941, Pasto, Colombia. Doctor in Medicine. Education: Doctor in Medicine, Javeriana University, Bogotoa, Colombia, 1969; Specialist in Public Health, Antioquia University, Medellin, 1972; Epidemiologist, Centers for Disease Control, Atlanta, Georgia, USA, 1971. Appointments: Chief Epidemiological Analysis, Ministry of Health, Colombia; Adviser in Epidemiology, Pan American Health Organisation; Chief, Trypanosomiases Control, World Health Organisation, Geneva, Switzerland, 1979-2001. Publications: More than 30 scientific articles on epidemiology of communicable diseases and on Chargas' Disease epidemiology and control. Honours: Honorary Epidemiologist of the State of California, 1972; Carlos Chagas Award (Extraordinary), Rio de Janeiro, Brazil, 2000; Memberships: Colombia Academy of Medicine; Academy of Medicine, Argentina; Royal Society of Tropical Medicine and Hygiene, London, England; International Epidemiological Society. Address: Calle 70 No 5-60, Bogota, Colombia. E-mail: amoncayo@uniandes.edu.co

MONDY Nell Irene, b. 27 October 1921, Pocahontas, Arkansas, USA. Professor Emeritus of Food Science, Nutrition and Toxicology. Education: BS, BA, Ouachita University, 1943; MA, Biochemistry, Texas University at Austin, 1945; PhD, Cornell University, 1953. Appointments include: Assistant, Associate and Full Professor, Nutritional Sciences, Food Science, Toxicology, Cornell University, 1953-92; Consultant, Holmen Brenderi, Norway, 1973; Consultant, S & B Shokuhin Co, Japan, 1979, Consultant, American Cyanamid, 1984; Visiting Scientist, International Institute of Tropical Agriculture, Ibadan, Nigeria, 1983-84; Consultant, Proctor and Gamble, Cincinnati, Ohio, 1985; Consultant, Frito-Lay, Rhinelander, Wisconsin, 1988; Visiting

Scholar, Inter University center, Food Science and Technology, Gadjah Mada University, Indonesia, 1989; New York State Potato Advisory Committee, 1990; Consultant, Endico Potatoes Inc, New York, 1990; Consultant, General Mills, Minneapolis, Minnesota, 1991; Consultant, ETA, Britannia Brands, New Zealand Ltd, 1991; Professor Emeritus, Cornell University, 1992-. Publications: Numerous articles in professional journals; Numerous conference proceedings; Book, Experimental Food Chemistry, 1980; Book: You Never Fail Until You Stop Trying. A Pioneer Woman Chemist, 2001. Honours include: Danforth Award, 1954, 1958; National Science Foundation Award, 1959; NATO Award, 1960; Distinguished Alumni Award, Ouachita Baptist University, 1960; Honorary Life Member, Potato Association of America, 1983; Centennial Achievement Award, Ouachita Baptist University, 1986; Honorary Life Member, Graduate Women in Science, 1986; E F Stier Award, Institute of Food Technologists, 1997; Outstanding Alumni Award, Cornell University College of Agriculture and Life Sciences, 2000; Graduate Women in Science, Award of National Recognition, 2001. Memberships include: American Chemical Society; Elected Fellow, American Association for the Advancement of Science; Fellow, Institute of Food Technologists; Fellow, American Institute of Chemists; New York Academy of Sciences; Potato Association of America; American Society of Plant Physiologists; European Association for Potato Research; Graduate Women in Science; American Association of University Women; International Platform Association; Institute of Food Technologists; Charter Member, Liberty Hyde Bailey Leadership Society (Ag & Life Science Cornell), 2004. Address: 126 Honness Lane, Ithaca, NY 14850, USA. E-mail: niml@cornell.edu

MONETTE Madeleine, b. 3 October 1951, Montreal, Quebec, Canada. Author. m. William R Leggio, 27 December 1979. Education: MA, Literature, University of Quebec. Publications: Le Double Suspect, 1980; Petites Violences, 1982; Fuites et Poursuites, 1982; Plages, 1986; L'Aventure, la Mesaventure, 1987; Amandes et melon, 1991; Nouvelles de Montreal, 1992; La Femme furieuse, 1997; Nouvelles d'Amérique, 1998; Doubly Suspect, tr Louise von Flotow, 2000; Lignes de Métro, 2002. Contributions to: Periodicals. Honours: Robert-Cliche Award, 1980; Grants, Canadian Council of Arts, the Conseil des Arts et des Lettres du Quebec, Fonds Gabrielle-Roy. Memberships: Quebec Writers Union; PEN. Address: 2 Charlton Street, 11K, New York, NY 10014, USA.

MONEY David Charles, b. 5 October 1918, Oxford, England. Retired Schoolmaster; Writer. m. Madge Matthews, 30 November 1945, 1 son. Education: Honours Degree, Chemistry, 1940; Honours Degree, Geography, 1947, St John's College, Oxford University. Publications: Human Geography, 1954; Climate, Soils and Vegetation, 1965; The Earth's Surface, 1970; Patterns of Settlement, 1972; Environmental Systems (series), 1978-82; Foundations of Geography, 1987; Climate and Environmental Systems, 1988; China - The Land and the People, 1984, revised edition, 1989; China Today, 1987; Australia Today, 1988; Environmental Issues - The Global Consequences, 1994; China in Change, 1996; The Vocation of Bachan Singh, 1997; Weather and Climate, 2000. Honour: Geographical Association, honorary member. Memberships: Farmer's Club; Royal Geographical Society, fellow. Address: 52 Park Avenue, Bedford MK40 2NE, England.

MONEY Keith, b. 1934, Auckland, New Zealand. Author; Artist; Photographer. Publications: Salute the Horse, 1960; The Horseman in Our Midst, 1963; The Equestrian World, 1963; The Art of the Royal Ballet, 1964; The Art of Margot Fonteyn, 1965; The Royal Ballet Today, 1968; Fonteyn: The Making of a Legend, 1973; John Curry, 1978; Anna Pavlova: Her Life and Art, 1982; The Bedside

Book of Old Fashioned Roses, 1985; Some Other Sea: The Life of Rupert Brooke, 1988-89; Margot, assoluta, 1993; Fonteyn and Nureyev: The Great Years, 1994. Other: Screenplays. Contributions to: Anthologies, journals, and magazines. Address: Fair Prospect Farm, Mahurangi West Road, RD3 Warkworth, New Zealand.

MONTAGU OF BEAULIEU Edward John Barrington Douglas-Scott-Montagu, 3rd Baron, b. 20 October 1926, London, England. Museum Administrator; Author; Elected Peer. m. (1) Elizabeth Belinda, 1959, divorced, 1974, 1 son, 1 daughter, (2) Fiona Herbert, 1974, 1 son. Education: St Peter's Court, Broadstairs; Ridley College, St Catharines, Ontario; New College, Oxford. Appointments: Founder, Montagu Motor Car Museum, 1952, world's first Motor Cycle Museum, 1956, National Motor Museum, Beaulieu, 1972; Founder-Editor, Veteran and Vintage magazine, 1956-79; Chairman, Historic Buildings and Monuments Commission, 1983-92; Free-lance motoring journalist; Hereditary Peer, 1947-99, Elected Peer, 1999-, House of Lords. Publications: The Motoring Montagus, 1959; Lost Causes of Motoring, 1960; Jaguar: A Biography, 1961, revised edition, 1986; The Gordon Bennett Races, 1963; Rolls of Rolls-Royce, 1966; The Gilt and the Gingerbread, 1967; Lost Causes of Motoring: Europe, 2 volumes, 1969, 1971; More Equal Than Others, 1970; History of the Steam Car, 1971; The Horseless Carriage, 1975; Early Days on the Road, 1976; Behind the Wheel, 1977; Royalty on the Road, 1980; Home James, 1982; The British Motorist, 1987; English Heritage, 1987; The Daimler Century, 1995; Wheels within Wheels, 2000. Memberships: Federation of British Historic Vehicle Clubs, president, 1989-; Federation Internationale des Voitures Anciennces, president, 1980-83; Historic Houses Association, president, 1973-78; Museums Association, president, 1982-84; Union of European Historic Houses, president, 1978-81; Guild of Motoring Writers. Address: Palace House, Beaulieu, Brockenhurst, Hants SO42 7ZN, England.

MONTEIRO George, b. 23 May 1932, Cumberland, Rhode Island, USA. Professor; Poet. 1 son, 2 daughters. Education: AB, Brown University, 1954; AM, Columbia University, 1956; PhD, Brown University, 1964. Appointments: Instructor to Professor, Brown University, 1961-. Publications: The Coffee Exchange, 1982; Double Weavers Knot, 1990. Contributions to: Denver Quarterly; Centennial Review; NEDGE, New England Journal of Medicine; James River Review. Address: 59 Woodland Drive, Windham, CT 06280, USA.

MONTGOMERIE Colin, b. 23 June 1963, Glasgow, Scotland. Golfer. m. Eimear Wilson, 1 son, 2 daughters. Education: Baptist University, Texas, USA. Career: Professional Golfer, 1987-; Member, Walker Cup team, 1985, 1987, Ryder Cup team, 1991, 1993, Dunhill Cup Team, 1988, 1991, 1992, World Cup Team, 1988, 1991; Leader, European Tour Merit, 1993, European Order of Merit, 1994; 28 tournament wins as at end December 2002; Signed contract to play Ben Hogan irons and golf balls from 2003. Honours: Winner: Scottish Stroke Play, 1985; Scottish Amateur Championship, 1987; European Tour Rookie of the Year, 1988; Portuguese Open, 1989; Scandinavian Masters, 1991, 1999, 2001; Heineken Dutch Open, 1993; Volvo Masters, 1993; Spanish Open, 1994; English Open, 1994; German Open, 1994; Peugeot Open de Espana, 1995; Murphy's English Open, 1995; Volvo German Open, 1995; Trophee Lancome, 1995; Alfred Dunhill Cup, 1995; 2nd, Dubai Desert Classic, 1995; Dubai Desert Classic, 1996; Murphy's Irish Open, 1996, 1997, 2001; Coanon European Masters, Million Dollar Challenge, 1996; World Cup Individual, 1997; Andersen Consulting World Champion, 1997; Compaq European Grand Prix, 1997; King Hassan II Trophy, 1997; World Championship of Golf, 1998; PGA Championship, 1998, 1999, 2000; German Masters, 1998; British Masters, 1998; Benson and

Hedges International Open, 1999; BMW International Open, 1999; Cisco World Matchplay, 1999; Skins Game, US, 2000; Novotel Perrier Open de France, 2000; Ericsson Australian Masters, 2001; Volvo Masters Andalucia, TCL Classic, 2002. Member: winning European Ryder Cup team, 1995. Address: c/o IMG, Pier House, Strand-on-the-Green, London, W4 3NN, England.

MONTGOMERY John Warwick, Baron of Kiltartan, Lord of Morris, Comte de St Germain de Montgommery, b. 18 October 1931, Warsaw, New York, USA. m. (1) Joyce Ann Bailer, 14 August 1954, 2 daughters, (2) Lanalee de Kant, 26 August 1988, 1 adopted son. Education: AB, Philosophy with distinction, Cornell University, 1952; BLS, 1954, MA, 1958, University of California at Berkeley; BD, 1958, MST, 1960, Wittenberg University, USA; PhD, University of Chicago, USA, 1962; Docteur de l'Universite, mention Theologie Protestante, University of Strasbourg, France, 1964; LLB, La Salle Extension University, 1977; Diplome cum laude, International Institute of Human Rights, Strasbourg, 1978; MPhil in Law, University of Essex, England, 1983; Dr (hon), Institute of Religion and Law, Moscow, 1999; LLM, 2000, LLD, 2003, Cardiff University, Wales; Bar: Virginia, 1978; California, 1979; DC, 1985; Washington State, 1990; US Supreme Court, 1981; England & Wales, 1984; Licenced Real Estate Broker, California; Certificate, Law Librarian; Diplomate, Medical Library Association; Ordained to ministry, Lutheran Church, 1958; Librarian, general reference service, University of California Library, Berkeley, 1954-55; Instructor, Biblical Hebrew, Hellenistic Greek, Medieval Latin, Wittenberg University, Springfield, Ohio, 1956-59; Head Librarian, Swift Library of Divinity and Philosophy, member Federated Theological Faculty, University of Chicago, 1959-60; Associate Professor, Chairman, Department of History, Wilfred Laurier University, Ontario, Canada, 1960-64; Professor, Chairman, Division of Church History, History of Christian Thought, Director, European Seminar Programme, Trinity Evangelical Divinity School, Deerfield, Illinois, 1964-74; Professor, Law and Theology, International School of Law, Washington DC, 1974-75; Theology consultant, Christian Legal Society, 1975-76; Director of Studies, International Institute of Human Rights, Strasbourg, France, 1979-81; Founding Dean, Professor Jurisprudence, Director of European Programme, Simon Greenleaf University School of Law, Anaheim, California, 1980-88; Distinguished Professor of Theology and Law, Director, European Programme, Faith Evangelical Lutheran Seminary, Tacoma, Washington, 1989-91; Principal Lecturer, Reader in Law, 1991-93, Professor of Law and Humanities, Director, Centre of Human Rights, 1993-97, Emeritus Professor, 1997-, Luton University, England; Distinguished Professor of Apologetics, Law, and History of Christian Thought, Vice President, Academic Affairs, UK and Europe, Trinity College and Theological Seminary, Newburgh, Indiana, 1997-; Distinguished Professor of Law, Regent University, Virginia, 1997-99; Senior Counsel, European Centre for Law and Justice, 1997-2001; Visiting Professor, Concordia Theological Seminary, Springfield, Illinois, 1964-67; DePaul University, Chicago, 1967-70; Honorary Fellow, Revelle College, University of California, San Diego, 1970; Rector, Freie Fakultaten Hamburg, Federal Republic of Germany, 1981-82; Lecturer, Research Scientists Christian Fellowship Conference, St Catherine's College, Oxford University, 1985; International Anti-Corruption Conference, Beijing, China, 1995; Pascal Lecturer on Christianity and the University, University of Waterloo, Ontario, Canada, 1987; A Kurt Weiss Lecturer, Biomedical Ethics, University of Oklahoma, 1997; Adjunct Professor, Puget Sound University School of Law, Tacoma, Washington, 1990-91; Worldwide Advocacy Conference lecturer, Inns of Court School of Law London, 1998; Law and Religion Colloquium lecturer, University College, London, 2000; numerous other functions. Publications: Author, 50 books, most recently: The Transcendental

Holmes, 2000; The Repression of Evangelism in Greece, 2000; Christ Our Advocate, 2002; Tractatus Logico-Theologicus, 2002; Editor, Contributing Editor, Film and TV series; Contributor of articles to academic, theological, legal encyclopaedias and journals, and chapters to books. Honours: Ordre des chevaliers du Saint-Sepulcre Byzantin; Phi Beta Kappa; Phi Kappa Phi; Beta Phi Mu; Awards: National Lutheran Educational Conference Fellow, 1959-60; Canada Council Postdoctoral Senior Research Fellow, 1963-64; American Association of Theological Schools Faculty Fellow, 1967-68; Recipient Angel Award, National Religious Broadcasters, 1989, 1990, 1992; Fellow: Trinity College, Newburgh, Indiana; Royal Society of Arts, England; Victoria Institute, London; Academie Internationale des Gourmets et des Traditions Gastronomiques, Paris; American Scientific Affiliation; Society for Advanced Legal Studies, UK. Memberships: European Academy of Arts, Sciences and Humanities; Literature Academy, France; Heraldry Society, UK (Advanced Certificate); Lawyers' Christian Fellowship (Honorary Vice-President); National Conference of University Professors; International Bar Association; World Association of Law Professors; Middle Temple and Lincoln's Inn; American Society for International Law; Union Internationale de Avocats; National Association of Realtors; ALA; Tolkien Society of America; New York C S Lewis Society; American Historical Society; Society for Reformation Research; Creation Research Society; Tyndale Fellowship, England; Stair Society, Scotland; Presbyterian Historical Society, Northern Ireland; American Theological Library Association; Bibliographical Society, University of Virginia; Evangelical Theological Society; International Wine and Food Society; Societe des Amis des Arts; Chaine des Rotisseurs; Athenaeum Club; Freeman of the City of London and Liveryman of the Scriveners' Company; Wig and Pen; Players' Theatre Club; Sherlock Holmes Society of London; Societe Sherlock Holmes de France; Club des Casseroles Lasserre, Paris. Address: Church Lane Cottage, 3-5 High Street, Lidlington, Bedfordshire, MK43 0RN, England. E-mail: 106612.1066@compuserve.com

MOOK Sarah, b. 29 October 1929, Brooklyn, New York, USA. Chemist. Education: BA, Hunter College, 1952; Graduate Coursework, Columbia University, 1954-57; Coursework, University of Hartford, 1958-59; Language Course, Columbia University, 1962-65. Appointments: Cartographic Aide, US Geological Survey, 1952-54; Research Assistant, Columbia University, 1954-57; Analytical Chemist, Combustion Engineering, 1957-59; Research Scientist, Radiation Applications Inc, 1959-62; Chemist, Marks Polarised Corp, 1962-64; Senior Chemist, NRA Inc, 1964-74; Clinical Technologist, Coney Island Hospital, 1974-84; Supervisor, 1984-89, Principal Chemist, 1989-95, Bellvue Hospital; Retired, 1995-. Publications: Several professional articles. Memberships: American Chemical Society; American Association for the Advancement of Science; American Association for Clinical Chemistry; New York Academy of Science. Address: 2042 East 14th Street, Brooklyn, NY 11229, USA.

MOOLLAN Cassam Ismael (Sir), b. 26 February 1927, Port Louis, Mauritius. Legal Consultant; Arbitrator. m. Rassoolbibie Adam Moollan, 1 son, 2 daughters. Education: LLB, London School of Economics and Political Science, University of London, 1947-50; Barrister at Law, Lincoln's Inn, London, 1951. Appointments: Private Practice at Mauritian Bar, 1951-55; District Magistrate, 1955-58; Crown Counsel, 1958-64; Senior Crown Counsel, 1964-66; Solicitor General, 1966-70; Puisne Judge Supreme Court, 1970; Senior Puisne Judge, Supreme Court, 1978; Chief Justice of Mauritius, 1982-88; Acting Governor General on several occasions every year, 1984-88; Retired, 1989. Publications: Editor, Mauritius Law Reports, 1982-88. Honours: Queen's Counsel, 1969; Knight Bachelor, 1982; Chevalier dans l'Ordre

National de la Legion d'Honneur, France, 1986. Address: 22 Hitchcock Avenue, Quatre Bornes, Mauritius. E-mail: sircassam@chambers.sirhamid.intnet.mu

MOORE Brian C J, b. 10 February 1946. Professor of Auditory Perception. Education: BA, 1968, MA, 1971, Natural Sciences, PhD, Experimental Psychology, 1971, University of Cambridge, England. Appointments: Lecturer, Psychology, University of Reading, England, 1971-73; Fulbright-Hayes Senior Scholar and Visiting Professor, Department of Psychology, Brooklyn College of CUNY, 1973-74; Lecturer, Psychology, University of Reading, 1974-77; Lecturer, Experimental Psychology, University of Cambridge, 1977-89; Fellow, Wolfson College, Cambridge, 1983-; Visiting Researcher, University of California at Berkeley, USA, 1985; Reader in Auditory Perception, 1989-95, Professor of Auditory Perception, 1995-, University of Cambridge. Publications: Books include most recently: An Introduction to the Psychology of Hearing, 4th edition, 1997, 5th edition, 2003; Cochlear Hearing Loss, 1998; New Developments in Hearing and Balance (co-editor), 2002; Over 77 book chapters and papers in conference proceedings; Over 298 publications in refereed journals. Honours include: T S Littler Prize, British Society of Audiology, 1983; Honorary Fellow, British Society of Hearing Aid Audiologists, 1999; Invitation Fellowship, Japanese Society for the Promotion of Science, 2000; Carhart Memorial Lecturer, American Auditory Society, 2003; Silver Medal, Acoustical Society of America, 2003. Memberships: Experimental Psychology Society; Fellow, Acoustical Society of America; Cambridge Philosophical Society; British Society of Audiology; American Speech-Language-Hearing Association; Audio Engineering Society; Acoustical Society of Japan; American Auditory Society; Association for Research in Otolaryngology; American Academy of Audiology; Fellow, Academy of Medical Sciences; Fellow, Royal Society. Address: Department of Experimental Psychology, University of Cambridge, Downing Street, Cambridge CB2 3EB, England. Website: http://hearing.psychol.cam.ac.uk

MOORE Dahrl Elizabeth, b. 27 January 1923, Newark, New Jersey, USA. Retired Librarian; Genealogist. m. Frank J Moore, Jr, 2 sons, 1 daughter. Education: BA, Latin American Studies, History, George Mason University, 1974; MLS, MA, University of South Florida, 1980; MA, History, Florida Atlantic University, 1986. Appointments: Interlibrary Loan Librarian, George Mason University, Fairfax, Virginia, 1974-77; Interlibrary Loan Librarian, 1984-89, Serials Acquisitions Librarian, 1989-2002, Florida Atlantic University, Boca Raton, Florida; President, Zonta International Boca Raton Chapter, 1983-85; President, Palm Beach County Genealogical Society, 1993-95, 1995-97; Book Review Editor, 1987-93; Education Chair, 1997-2002; Lecturer on various genealogical subjects, 1994-; Teacher, Genealogy for Librarians, University of South Florida, Boca Raton, 1997. Publications: Entry in Biographical Dictionary of the American Left, Mary Van Kleeck, 1986; Thesis: Mary Van Kleeck: a biographical sketch and annotated bibliography of her writings, 1986; Article: More on More: Jacob More (1710-1754) and after of Cumberland County, New Jersey, 1990; Historical and Genealogical Holdings in the State of Florida: a directory, 1992; Librarians Genealogical Notebook, 1998; Web article: Genealogy for Librarians, 2000. Honours: Phi Kappa Phi; Phi Alpha Theta; Beta Phi Mu; Alpha Chi. Memberships: IFLA, Genealogical and Local History Committee, 2001-2002; National Genealogical Society; New England Historical and Genealogical Society; American Library Association. Address: 10988 Ravel Court, Boca Raton, FL 33498, USA. E-mail: dahrl@att.net

Dictionary of International Biography

MOORE David Moresby, b. 26 July 1933, Barnard Castle, County Durham, England. Professor Emeritus of Botany. m. Ida Elizabeth Shaw, 2 sons. Education: BSc, Honours, Botany, 1954, PhD, 1957, DSc, 1984, University College and Botany Department, University of Durham. Appointments: Research Officer, Genetics Section, Division of Plant Industry, CSIRO, Canberra, ACT, Australia, 1957-59; Research Fellow, Department of Botany, University of California at Los Angeles, 1959-61; Lecturer, Genetics, Department of Botany, University of Leicester, England, 1961-68; Reader, Plant Taxonomy, 1968-76, Professor of Botany, 1976-94, Reading University, England. Publications: About 100 articles on taxonomy, geography, cytogenetics of plants; 19 books include: Vascular Flora of the Falkland Islands, 1968; Plant Cytogenetics, 1976, Flora Europaea Check-List and Chromosome-Number Index, 1982; Green Planet, 1982; Flora of Tierra del Fuego, 1983; Garden Earth, 1991. Honours: Botany Field Prize, University of Durham, 1954; British Association Studentship, University of Durham; Plaque for services to Magellanic Botany, Instituto de la Patagonia, Punta Arenas, Chile, 1976; Premio Perito Francisco P Moreno, Sociedad Argentina de Estudios Geográficos, 1985; Enrique Molina Gold Medal, University of Concepción, Chile. Memberships: Botanical Society of the British Isles; Editorial Committees: Webbia, Italy, Polish Botanical Journal, Anales del Instituto de la Patagonia, Flora de Chile. Address: 26 Eric Avenue, Emmer Green, Reading, Berks, RG4 8QX, England.

MOORE Demi, b. 11 November 1962, Roswell, New Mexico, USA. Actress. m. Bruce Willis, divorced 2000, 3 daughters. Career: Started in TV, also Model; Films include: Blame it on Rio; St Elmo's Fire; One Crazy Summer; About Last Night...; Wisdom; The Seventh Sign; Ghost; Mortal Thoughts, also co-producer; The Butcher's Wife; A Few Good Men; Indecent Proposal; Disclosure; The Scarlet Letter; Striptease, 1995; The Juror, 1996; GI Jane, 1996; The Hunchback of Notre Dame, 1996; Now and Then, produced & acted, 1996; Deconstructing Harry, 1997; Austin Powers: International Man of Mystery, producer, 1997; Passion of Mind, 2000; Airframe; Charlie's Angels: Full Throttle, 2003; Theatre: The Early Girl; TV: General Hospital, Bedroom. Honour: Theatre World Award for The Early Girl. Address: c/o Creative Artists Agency, 9830 Wilshire Boulevard, Beverly Hills, CA 90212, USA.

MOORE Julianne, b. 1961, USA. Actress. Education: Boston University School for Arts. Creative Works: Stage appearances include: Serious Money, 1987; Ice Cream with Hot Fudge, 1990; Uncle Vanya; The Road to Nirvana; Hamlet; The Father; Film appearances include: Tales From the Darkside, 1990; The Hand That Rocks the Cradle, 1992; The Gun in Betty Lou's Handbag, 1992; Body of Evidence, 1993; Benny & Joon, 1993; The Fugitive, 1993; Short Cuts, 1993; Vanya on 42nd Street, 1994; Roommates, 1995; Safe, 1995; Nine Months, 1995; Assassins, 1995; Surviving Picasso, 1996; Jurassic Park: The Lost World, 1997; The Myth of Fingerprints, 1997; Hellcab, 1997; Boogie Nights, 1997; The Big Lebowski, 1998; Eyes Wide Shut, The End of The Affair, 1999; Map of the World, 1999; Magnolia, 1999; Cookie's Fortune, 1999; An Ideal Husband, 1999; Hannibal, 2000; The Shipping News, 2000; Far From Heaven, 2002; The Hours, 2002; TV appearances include: As the World Turns, series; The Edge of Night, series; Money, Power Murder, 1989; Lovecraft, 1991; I'll Take Manhattan; The Last to Go; Cast a Deadly Spell. Honours: Best Actress, Venice Film Festival, 2002. Address: c/o Creative Artists Agency, 9830 Wilshire Boulevard, Beverly Hills, CA 90212, USA.

MOORE Patrick Alfred Caldwell (Sir), b. 4 March 1923, England. Astronomer; Broadcaster; Writer. Appointments: Served with RAF during World War II; Officer, Bomber Command, 1940-45; Presenter, TV Series, The Sky at Night, 1957-; Radio Broadcasts; Director, Armagh Planetarium, Northern Ireland, 1965-68; Freelance, 1968-; Composer, Perseus and Andromeda (opera), 1975; Play, Quintet, Chichester, 2002. Publications: Over 170 books and numerous articles include: Moon Flight Atlas, 1969; Space, 1970; The Amateur Astronomer, 1970; Atlas of the Universe, 1970; Guide to the Planets, 1976; Guide to the Moon, 1976; Can You Speak Venusian?, 1977; Guide to the Stars, 1977; Guide to Mars, 1977; Atlas of the Universe, 1980; History of Astronomy, 1983; The Story of the Earth, 1985; Halley's Comet, 1985; Patrick Moore's Armchair Astronomy, 1985; Stargazing, 1985; Exploring the Night Sky with Binoculars, 1986; The A-Z of Astronomy, 1986; Astronomy for the Under Tens, 1987; Astronomers' Stars, 1987; The Planet Uranus, 1988; Space Travel for the Under Tens, 1988; The Planet Neptune, 1989; Mission to the Planets, 1990; The Universe for the Under Tens, 1990; A Passion for Astronomy, 1991; Fireside Astronomy, 1992; Guinness Book of Astronomy, 1995; Passion for Astronomy, 1995; Stars of the Southern Skies, 1995; Teach Yourself Astronomy, 1996; Eyes on the Universe, 1997; Brilliant Stars, 1998; Patrick Moore on Mars, 1999; Yearbook of Astronomy AD 1000, 1999; Data Book of Astronomy, 2001. Honours include: Officer of the Order of the British Empire, 1968; Numerous Honorary Degrees; Honorary Member, Astronomic-Geodetic Society of the Soviet Union, 1971; Royal Astronomical Society's Jackson-Gwilt Medal, 1977; CBE, 1987; Fellow, Royal Society, 2001; Knight Bachelor, 2001; Minor Planet No 2602 is named in his honour; BAFTA Special Award, 2002. Memberships: Royal Astronomical Society; Member, British Astronomical Association, President, 1982-84; Athenaeum; Life Member, Sussex Cricket Club; Lord's Taverners. Address: Farthings, 39 West Street, Selsey, Sussex PO20 9AD, England.

MOORE Roger, b. 14 October 1927, London, England. Actor. m. (1) Doorn van Steyn, divorced, (2) Dorothy Squires, 1953, divorced, (3) Luisa Mattioli, 2 sons, 1 daughter. Education: Royal Academy of Dramatic Arts. Appointment: Special Ambassador for UNICEF, 1991-. Creative Works: Films include: Crossplot, 1969; The Man With the Golden Gun, 1974; That Lucky Touch, 1975; Save Us From Our Friends, 1975; Shout At The Devil, 1975; Sherlock Holmes in New York, 1976; The Spy Who Loved Me, 1976; The Wild Geese, 1977; Escape to Athens, 1978; Moonraker, 1978; Esther, Ruth and Jennifer, 1979; The Sea Wolves, 1980; Sunday Lovers, 1980; For Your Eyes Only, 1980; Octopussy, 1983; The Naked Face, 1983; A View to a Kill, 1985; Key to Freedom, 1989; Bed and Breakfast, 1989; Bullseye!, 1989; Fire, Ice and Dynamite, 1990; The Quest, 1997; TV appearances include: The Alaskans; The Saint, 1962-69; The Persuaders, 1972-73; The Man Who Wouldn't Die, 1992; The Quest, 1995. Publication: James Bond Diary, 1973. Address: c/o ICM Ltd, 76 Oxford Street, London W1R 1RB, England.

MOORE Terence, b. 24 December, 1931, London, England. Retired Businessman. m. Tessa Catherine, 2 sons, 1 daughter. Education: BSc, Economics, London; AMP, Harvard, USA. Appointments: Various positions, Shell International, 1948-64; Economics Analyst, Investment Banking, 1964-65; Various positions, 1965-87, Managing Director, Supply and Trading, 1979-87, Chief Executive Officer, Conoco Ltd, 1987-95; Currently, Trustee Institute of Petroleum; Chairman, Thorpes YD Management Co Ltd; Merchant Court Freehold Ltd; Non-executive Director, Conoco Pension Funds Ltd; James Fisher & Sons plc. Publications: Various technical and business articles. Honour: CBE. Memberships: Fellow, Institute of Petroleum; Associate, Chartered Insurance Institute; Associate, Institute of Chartered Shipbrokers; Friend: Royal Academy of Art, Tate Gallery, Imperial War Museum, National Trust. Address: 67 Merchant Court, 61 Wapping Wall, London EW1 3SJ, England. E-mail: terrymoore@terrymoore.demon.co.uk

Dictionary of International Biography

MOORE Willis Henry Allphin, b. 14 December 1940, New York, New York, USA. Educator. 2 sons, 1 daughter. Education: BA, Letters, University of Oklahoma, 1962; M Education Administration, University of Hawai'i, 1971; Certificate in Church Music, Virginia Theological Seminary, Alexandria, Virginia. Appointments: Adjunct Faculty, Chaminade University, Honolulu, Hawai'i; Instructor, Department of Public Safety, Hawai'i; Editor and Manager, Hawai'i Geographic Society; Education Co-Ordinator, Bernice P Bishop Museum, Honolulu, Hawai'i; Lecturer on Geography and Natural History, US National Audubon Society and various other venues in USA and Canada. Publications: Hawai'i Parklands: Guide to the Parks and Natural History of Hawai'i, 1988; Total Solar Eclipse Over Hawai'i, 1991; Christmas Comes to Hawai'i: A History of the Anglican Church in Hawai'i, 1999; Many articles in newspapers, magazines and newletters including: The Hololulu Advertiser; The Honolulu Star-bulletin; Honolulu Weekly; Sierra Magazine; The Historiographer (National Episcopal Historians and Archivists). Honours: Top 10 Senior Men, University of Oklahoma, 1962; President's Religious Leadership Award, 1962; Listed in Who's Who publications and biographical dictionaries. Memberships: National Society for Arts and Letters; Corrections Education Association; National Episcopal Historians and Archivists; Hawaiian Historical Society; Sierra Club; Professional Travel Film Lecturers Association. Address: PO Box 37214, Honolulu, HI 96837-0214. E-mail: willishamoore@hotmail.com

MOORHOUSE Geoffrey, b. 29 November 1931, Bolton, Lancashire, England. Author. m. (1) Janet Marion Murray, 1956, 2 sons, 2 daughters, 1 deceased, (2) Barbara Jane Woodward, 1974, divorced, 1978, (3) Marilyn Isobel Edwards, 1983, divorced, 1996. Appointments: Editorial Staff, Bolton Evening News, 1952-54, Grey River Argus, New Zealand, Auckland Star, and Christchurch Star-Sun, 1954-56, News Chronicle, 1957, Guardian, Manchester, 1958-70. Publications: The Other England, 1964; The Press, 1964; Against All Reason, 1969; Calcutta, 1971; The Missionaries, 1973; The Fearful Void, 1974; The Diplomats, 1977; The Boat and the Town, 1979; The Best-Loved Game, 1979; India Britannica, 1983; Lord's, 1983; To the Frontier, 1984; Imperial City: Rise and Rise of New York, 1988; At the George, 1989; Apples in the Snow, 1990; Hell's Foundations: Town, Its Myths and Gallipoli, 1992; Om: Indian Pilgrimage, 1993; A People's Game: Centenary History of Rugby League Football 1895-1995, 1995; Sun Dancing: Medieval Vision, 1997; Sydney, 1999; The Pilgrimage of Grace: the rebellion that shook Henry VIII's throne, 2002. Contributions to: Newspapers and magazines. Honours: Cricket Society Award, 1979; Fellow, Royal Society of Literature, 1982; Thomas Cook Award, 1984; Nominated Booker Prize, 1997. Membership: Royal Society of Literature, fellow. Address: Park House, Gayle, near Hawes, North Yorkshire DL8 3RT, England.

MORAES Dominic, b. 19 July 1938, Bombay, India. Writer; Poet. m. Leela Naidu, 1970. Education: Jesus College, Oxford. Appointments: Managing Editor, Asia Magazine, Hong Kong, 1972-; Consultant, United Nations Fund for Population Activities, 1973-. Publications: A Beginning, 1957; Gone Away, 1960; My Son's Father (autobiography), 1968; The Tempest Within, 1972-73; The People Time Forgot, 1972; A Matter of People, 1974; Voices for Life (essays), 1975; Mrs Gandhi, 1980; Bombay, 1980; Ragasthan: Splendour in the Wilderness, 1988; Collected Poems 1957-87, 1988; Serendip (poems), 1980; Never At Home (autobiography), 1994; In Cinnamon Shade (poems), 2001. Honour: Hawthornden Prize, 1957. Address: 12 Sargent House, Allan Marg, Mumbai 400039, India.

MORDAUNT David Haydn, b. 1 November 1969, Surrey, England. Engineer. m. Jodie, 1 son. Education: BSc, First Class Honours, Chemical Physics, 1991, PhD, Chemistry, 1994,

University of Bristol, England. Appointments: Principal Laser Engineer, Coherent Inc; Director Surgical Research and Development, Vice-President, Research and Development, Lumensis Inc; President, Chief Executive Officer and Founder, OptiMedica Inc. Publications: Author of 34 peer-reviewed articles in scientific journals; 2 review articles; 2 text-book and professional book chapters; 6 US Patents (some pending). Honours: Harrison Medal, Royal Society of Chemistry; Royal Society Fellow; NATO Research Fellow; Marie Curie Research Fellow; Max-Planck Fellow. Listed in Who's Who publications and biographical dictionaries. Address: OptiMedica Inc, 23116 Summit Road, Los Gatos, CA 95033, USA. E-mail: mordauntbiz@aol.com

MOREIRA Alberto, b. 29 June 1962, Sao Jose Dos Campos, Brazil. Scientist. m. 14 November 1992, 1 son, 1 daughter. Education: BSEE, ITA, Sao Jose dos Campos, Brazil, 1980-84; MSEE, 1985-86; PhD, Electrical Engineering, Technical University of Munich, Germany, 1988-93. Appointments: Consultant, Research Assistant, Technology Institute of Aeronautics, ITA, 1985-86; Scientist, German Aerospace Centre, Institute for Radio Frequency Technology, 1987-91; Leader of the Group SAR Signal Processing, 1992-95; Leader, Department SAR Technology, German Aerospace Centre, 1996-2001; Leader, Microwaves and Radar Institute, 2001-. Publications: 150 publications in international journals, conference papers and technical reports; 9 patents. Honours: PhD thesis with honours; NASA Certificate in appreciation of an outstanding contribution; DLR Scientific Award; IEEE, Transactions Prize Paper Award; IEEE, Young Radar Engineer of the Year; IEEE Fellow. Memberships: IEEE; VDE; The Electromagnetics Academy. Address: German Aerospace Centre, Microwaves and Radar Institute, Postfach 1116, 82230 Wessling, Germany. E-mail: alberto.moreira@gmx.net

MORET Jean-Marc, b. 6 June 1942, Geneva, Switzerland. Professor. Education: Classical Maturity, Type A, Collège Calvin, 1961; Bachelor in Arts, Greek, Latin and French, 1965, PhD, Classical Archaeology, 1974, University of Geneva. Appointments: Assistant, Classical Archaeology, University of Bâle, 1974-78; Lecturer, Classical Archaeology, University of Fribourg, 1978-81; Lecturer, Classical Archaeology, University of Geneva, 1981-; Professor of Classical Archaeology, University of Lyon II, 1999-; Excavation in Italy and Syria. Memberships: Honorary member, German Institute, 2001-; Honorary Member, French Society for Classical Archaeology, 2003-. Address: 11A Sous Caran, CH-1222-Genève, Switzerland.

MORGAN Jacqui, b. 22 February, New York City, USA. Illustrator; Painter; Educator. Widow. Education: BFA, Honours, Pratt Institute, Brooklyn, 1960; MA, Hunter College, CCNY, 1977. Appointments; Textile Designer, M Lowenstein & Sons, New York City, 1966-; Associate Professor, Pratt Institute, Brooklyn; Guest Lecturer, University of Queensland, Syracuse University, Warsaw TV and Radio; NYU; Parsons School of Design (New York), School of Visual Arts (New York), Virginia Commonwealth University; Instructor, The Fashion Institute of Technology; Commissions and Creative Works: One person shows include: Krannert Museum, University of Illinois, 1998; Art Gallery at Marywood University, Scranton, Pennsylvania, 1998; One Person and group shows in several countries; Collections: Smithsonian Institution; Museum of Warsaw. Publications: Author, Illustrator: Watercolor for Illustration; Produced 3 instructional watercolour videos; Series of prints, 1995; Articles in professional journals. Honours: Over 200 awards from various organisations including: Society of Illustrators, Federal Design Council, Commercial Arts Magazine, Print Magazine, American Institute of Graphic Arts, New York Art Directors Club. Memberships: Graphic Artists

Guild; Society of Illustrators. Address: Apt 11C 176 E 77th Street, New York, NY 10021, USA. Website: www.jacquimorganstudio.com

MORGAN Rex Henry, b. Devon, England. Educator; Author. m. Mary Elizabeth Cottrell, 29 March 1958, 2 sons, 1 daughter. Education: Commonwealth School, University of Sydney, Australia; DiptTG, Teachers Guild of New South Wales; ATCL; LTCL, Trinity College, London, England; Associate, Royal Photographic Society; Honorary MSc, Brooks Institute, California, USA. Appointments: Founder, Pittwater House Schools, New South Wales, 1962; Freelance Broadcaster, Lecturer, Author, Editor, Shroud News; Led Hermes expeditions, and to Jordan, Israel. Publications include: Perpetual Miracle, 1983; Jubilee Picture Book, 1987; Frank Mason's Churt, 1988; Shroud Guide, 1983; The Hermes Adventure, 1985; With Man and Beast on the Oregon Trail, 1993; The History of Bathurst 1815-1915 (ed), 1994; Byzantine Frescoes (ed), 1994; Cappadocian Frescoes (ed), 1996; Catacombs and the Early Church (ed), 1998; Castle, Kitbag and Cattle Truck (introduction), 2001. Contributor: to numerous booklets, papers, articles, broadcasts. Honours: Dux of Course, Teachers Guild of New South Wales; Justice of the Peace, New South Wales; Fellow, Australian College of Education; MBE, 1969; Commonwealth of Australia Recognition Award for Senior Australians, 2000; HRH Princess Sirindhorn Badge of Recognition, Thailand, 2000; Board Member, Winitsuksa School Thailand, 1999-; National President, Friends of the Duke of Edinburgh's Award, Australia, 2000-; Member of the Order of Australia, 2002; Australian Centenary Medal, 2003. Memberships include: Fellow, Royal Geographical Society; Fellow, Royal Society of Arts; President, South East Asia Research Centre for the Holy Shroud, 1986; President, Rex Morgan Festival Committee, 1992-; South East Asia Writers' Award Committee, Thailand, 1995; Rex Morgan Foundation, 1999-. Address: Abercrombie House, Bathurst, NSW 2795, Australia.

MORGAN Robin Richard, b. 16 September 1953, Stourbridge, England. Editor; Journalist; Author. 2 sons, 1 daughter. Appointments: Insight Editor, Sunday Times; Features Editor, Sunday Times; Editor, Sunday Express; Editor, Sunday Times Magazine; Editorial Director Designate, Readers Digest; Editor, Sunday Times Magazine, 1995-. Publications: The Falklands War, co-author, 1982; Bullion, co-author, 1983; Rainbow Warrior, co-author, editor, 1986; Manpower, editor, 1986; Ambush, co-author, 1988; Book of Movie Biographies, co-editor, 1997. Honours: Campaigning Journalist of the Year, 1982, 1983. Address: Sunday Times Magazine, 1 Pennington Street, London E1 9XW, England.

MORGAN William Bruce, b. 20 December 1926, Fairfield, Iowa, USA. Naval Architect. m. Mary Maxine Gillam, 2 daughters. Education: BS, Marine Engineering, US Merchant Marine Academy, 1950; MS, Hydraulic Engineering, University of Iowa, 1951; Dr of Engineering, University of California at Berkeley, 1961. Appointments: David Taylor Model Basin, Bethesda, Maryland: Hydraulic Engineer, 1951-52; Naval Architect, 1952-58; Naval Architect Supervisor, 1958-62; Head, Propeller Branch, 1962-70; David Taylor Ship R&D Centre: Head, Hydromechanics Division, 1970-79; Head, Hydromechanics Directorate (name change in 1992: Naval Surface Warfare Centre, Canderock Division), 1979-2001; Retired. Publications: 32 papers; 2 book chapters; 13 reports. Honours: Numerous works related awards. Memberships: American Society of Mechanical Engineers; American Society of Naval Engineers; Society of Naval Architects and Marine Engineers; NAE; Schiffbantechnische Gesellschaft; Sigma Xi; Honorary Member, Chinese Society of Naval Architects and Marine Engineers. Address: 110 Upton Street, Rockville, MD 20850, USA. E-mail: wbmorgan@erols.com

MORGAN William Richard, b. 27 March 1922, Cambridge, Ohio, USA. Mechanical Engineer. m. Marjorie Eleanor Stevens, 17 February 1946, 1 son, 1 daughter. Education: BSME, Ohio State University, 1944; MSME, Purdue University, 1950; PhD, Mechanical Engineering, 1951. Appointments: Licensed Professional Engineer, Ohio; Power Plant Design Engineer, Curtiss Wright Corp, Columbus, Ohio, 1946-47; Instructor and Westinghouse Research Fellow, Purdue University; West Lafayette Indiana, 1947-51; Supervisor, Experimental Mechanical Engineering, GE, Cincinnati, 1951-55; Manager, Controls Analysis Development, Aircraft Gas Turbine Division, GE, 1955-59; Manager, XV5A vertical take-off and landing aircraft programme, GE, 1959-65; Manager, Acoustic Engineering, Flight Propulsion Division, GE, 1965-69; Manager, quiet engine programme 1969-71; President, Cincinnati Research Corporation, 1971-73; Vice President, SDRC International, Cincinnati, 1973-79; Engineering and Management Consultant, Cincinnati, 1979-. Publications: Numerous papers presented in seminars and symposia and articles in professional journals. Memberships: ASME; Sigma Xi; Pi Tau Sigma; Pi Mu Epsilon. Address: 312 Ardon Ln, Cincinnati, OH 45215, USA.

MORINAGA Masahiko, b. 20 August 1946, Osaka, Japan. Professor. m. Kazue, 1 son, 1 daughter. Education: BS, 1969, MS, 1971, Kyoto University, Japan; PhD, Northwestern University, USA 1978. Appointments: Lecturer, 1979-83, Associate Professor, 1983-91, Professor 1991-94, Toyohashi University of Technology; Professor, Nagoya University, 1994-. Honours: The Meritorious Award of the Japan Institute of Metals, 1989; The Nagai Science Award, 1991; Memorial Lecture for the Korean Institute of Metals, 1997; The Science Award of the DV-Xα Society of Japan, 2001. Memberships: The Minerals, Metals and Materials Society; The Japan Institute of Metals; Iron and Steel Institute of Japan; Physical Society of Japan; DV-Xα Society of Japan. Address: Department of Materials Science and Engineering, Graduate School of Engineering, Nagoya University, Furo-cho, Chikusa-ku, Nagoya 464-8603, Japan. E-mail: morinaga@numse.nagoya-u.ac.jp

MORISSETTE Alanis, b. 1 June 1974, Ottawa, Canada. Singer. Career: Solo recording artiste; Appeared on Canadian cable TV, aged 10; Signed contract as songwriter with MCA Publishing aged 14; Concerts include: Twix Mix Jamboree, with David Bowie, Birmingham NEC, 1995; 16 million albums sold. Recordings: Albums: Alanis, 1991; Now Is The Time, 1992; Jagged Little Pill, 1995; Space Cakes (live), 1998; Supposed Former Infatuation Junkie, 1998; Alanis Unplugged (live), 1999; Under Rug Swept, 2002. Singles: Fate Stay With Me; You Oughta Know, 1995; One Hand In My Pocket, 1995; Ironic, 1996. Film: Dogma, 1999. Honour: BRIT Award, Best International Newcomer, 1996; Four Grammy Awards, including Album of the Year and Best Rock Album; Best Female Award, MTV European Music Awards, 1996.

MORITZ Ralf, b. 2 May 1941, Leipzig, Germany. University Professor. m. Marlies Ludwig, 1 son. Education: Diploma, Philosophy and Sinology, Leipzig University, 1963, Peking, 1966; Doctor's Degree, Leipzig, 1969; Habilitation, 1980. Appointments: Assistant Professor, Leipzig University, 1966-69; Fellow, Academy of Social Sciences, Berlin, 1969-80; Lecturer, 1981-84, Professor 1984-, Vice-Director for African and Middle East Studies, 1983-86, Director, Asian Department, 1988-93, Director of East Asia Institute, 1994-98, 2001-, Leipzig University. Publications: Confucius. Analects (editor, translator), 1982; How and why did philosophy arise in different regions of the world? (co-editor, co-author), 1988; The Philosophy of Ancient China (author), 1990; Sinological Traditions in the Mirror of New Researches (editor, co-author), 1993; Middle German Studies of East Asia (book series, editor), 1998; The Confucianism (co-editor, co-author), 1998. Memberships: German Society for Chinese Studies; European Association for Chinese Studies. Address: Kurt-Weill-Str 7, D-04347 Leipzig, Germany. E-mail: moritz@rz.uni.leipzig.de

MORLEY John, b. 12 September 1942, Beckenham, England. Painter; Wood Engraver. m. Diana Howard, 1 daughter. Education: Beckehnam School of Art, 1957-62; Ravensbourn College of Art, 1962-63; Royal Academy Schools, 1963-66; David Murray Landscape Scholarship, 1965-66. Career: Teacher, Epsom School of Art, Westminster School, Suffolk College, Lowestoft College of Further Education, 1974-76; Exhibitions include: One-man Exhibitions: Charleston Festival, Sussex, 1975; Royal Academy of Art, London, 1975; Festival Gallery, Bath, 1977; Piccadilly Gallery, London, 1982, 1985, 1989, 1992, 1999, 2002; Kew Gardens Gallery, Royal Botanic Gardens, Kew, 1991; Numerous Group Exhibitions include most recently: Eastern Open Competition, King's Lynn, Norfolk, 1996; 50th Aldeburgh Festival Art Exhibition, 1997; The Discerning Eye, The Mall Galleries, London (by invitation), 1999-2001; Painting at Charlecote, The National Trust, Charlecote Park, Warwick, 2000; Painters and Sculptors of East Anglia, Messum's London, 2001. Publications: Illustrations: Nine Poems, Eve Machin: Brotherhood of Ruralists, 1987; The Secret Garden, Brotherhood of Ruralists, 1989; Great Tew, Simon Rae: Brotherhood of Ruralists, 1989; Laelia Anceps (Orchid) The Plantsman Vol II part I, 1989; A Broad Canvas: Art in East Anglia Since 1880, by Ian Collins, 1990; Art & Design "The Ruralists", edited by Christopher Martin, 1991. Honours: Arts Council Award, Great Britain; Winner, A Christmas Card Competition, Royal Academy, 1982; BBC TV Omnibus Film "A Week in the Country" devoted to John Morley, 1982; Winner, Award for Christmas Card Design, British and American Tobacco (Export), 1985; Herbert Baker Scholarship, President and Council of the Royal Academy, 1985; Numerous art exhibition prizes. Memberships: Elected Brother of the Art Workers Guild; Elected Member, Society of Wood Engravers. Address: c/o Piccadilly Gallery, 43 Dover Street, London W1S 4NU, England. Website: www.johnmorley.info

MORRIS Alisa (Sonja Christina), b. 21 December 1925. Freelance Writer. m. Desmond Morris, 1 daughter. Education: Ecole le Vivre. Publications: Emotions, poetry, 1972; The Future was Yesterday, play, 1972. Honours: 12 Golden Poets Awards, World of Poetry; Poem exhibited in Museum of Tolerance; Poem exhibited in Astara magazine; 5 letters from Mother Teresa; Work read on New York and Southampton TV and radio, 1991-92; Honorary Charter Member, American Society of Poetry, 1993; Poets Fantasy Award, 2000; Award for outstanding support of poetry, American Poetry Association, 2001; Achievement in Poetry Award for outstanding achievement and short stories, Drury's Publications, 2000, 2003; Recognition for Poetry, Editor's Choice Award for outstanding merit in poetry, Famous Poetry Society, 2003; Nominated for International Poet of Merit, Honoured Member, International Society of Poets, 2004; Posed for painter, Sir Agustus John; First Prize, Globe Magazine Short Story Contest; Appeared in movies for MGM and Warner Brothers; Owned Art Gallery, New York City; Owned Esmeralda Club, London, England; Listed in biographical dictionaries; Certificate of Achievement for Outstanding Achievement in Poetry, Famous Poetry Society, 2004. Address: PO Box 142, Lennox Hill, New York City, NY 10021, USA.

MORRIS Desmond John, b. 24 January 1928, Purton, Wiltshire, England. Zoologist; Author; Broadcaster; Artist. m. Ramona Baulch, 30 July 1952, 1 son. Education: BSc, Birmingham University, 1951; DPhil, Oxford University, 1954. Appointments: Zoological Research Worker, University of Oxford, 1954-56; Head

of Granada TV and Film Unit, Zoological Society of London, 1956-59; Curator of Mammals, Zoological Society of London, 1959-67; Director, Institute of Contemporary Arts, London, 1967-68; Privately engaged writing books, 1968-73; Research Fellow, Wolfson College, Oxford, 1973-81; Privately engaged writing books and making television programmes, 1981-2004. TV series: Zootime, 1956-67; Life, 1965-67; The Human Race, 1982; The Animals Roadshow, 1987-89; The Animal Contract, 1989; Animal Country, 1991-96; The Human Animal, 1994; The Human Sexes, 1997; Solo exhibitions (paintings): Art galleries across England and in Holland, Belgium, France, USA and Ireland. Publications include: The Biology of Art, 1962; The Big Cats, 1965; Zootime, 1966; The Naked Ape, 1967; The Human Zoo, 1969; Patterns of Reproductive Behaviour, 1970; Intimate Behaviour, 1971; Manwatching, 1977; Animal Days, 1979; The Soccer Tribe, 1981; Bodywatching: A Field Guide to the Human Species, 1985; Catwatching, 1986; Dogwatching, 1986; Catlore, 1987; The Human Nestbuilders, 1988; The Animal Contract, 1990; Animal-Watching, 1990; Babywatching, 1991; Christmas Watching, 1992; The World of Animals, 1993; The Naked Ape Trilogy, 1994; The Human Animal, 1994; The World Guide to Gestures, 1994; Bodytalk: A World Guide to Gestures, 1994; Catworld: A Feline Encyclopaedia, 1996; The Human Sexes: A Natural History of Man and Woman, 1997; Illustrated Horsewatching, 1998; Cool Cats: The 100 Cat Breeds of the World, 1999; Body Guards: Protective Amulets and Charms, 1999; The Naked Ape and Cosmic Behaviour (with Kaori Ishida), 1999; The Naked Eye, 2000; Travels in Search of the Human Species, 2000; Dogs: a Dictionary of Dog Breeds, 2001; Peoplewatching, 2002; The Silent Language (in Italian), 2004; The Nature of Happiness, 2004; The Naked Woman, 2004. Contributions to: Many journals and magazines. Honour: Honorary DSc, Reading University, 1998. Membership: Scientific Fellow, Zoological Society of London. Address: c/o Jonathan Cape, Random Century House, 20 Vauxhall Bridge Road, London SW1V 2SA, England.

MORRIS Gareth Charles Walter, b. 13 May 1920, Clevedon, Somerset, England. Flautist. m. Patricia Mary Murray, 1 son, 3 daughters. Education: Privately; Royal Academy of Music, London. Career: Soloist and Chamber Musician; Professor of Flute, Royal Academy of Music, London, 1945-85; Principal Flautist, Philharmonia Orchestra, London, 1948-72; International Adjudicator in flute playing; First performance of numerous works for flute. Publications: Flute Technique, 1991; Numerous articles in journals and dictionaries. Honours: Associate, Royal Academy of Music; Fellow, Royal Academy of Music; Fellow, Royal Society of Arts. Memberships: Royal Society of Musicians; Royal Society of Arts; Member of Council of Honour, Royal Academy of Music. Address: 4 West Mall, Clifton, Bristol, England.

MORRIS Mali, b. 5 February 1945, North Wales. Artist. Education: BA, University of Newcastle upon Tyne; MFA, University of Reading. Career: Senior Lecturer, Chelsea College of Art and Design; External Examiner, Royal College of Art; Exhibits nationally and internationally; Solo exhibitions: Ikon Gallery, Birmingham, 1979; 2 at Nicola Jacobs Gallery, London; 1 with Kapil Jariwala, London; 5 with Francis Graham-Dixon, London; 9 other solo exhibitions in Manchester, Newtown, Nottingham, Jarrow, Sunderland, Winchester, Luxembourg and Japan; Group exhibitions include: John Moores, Walker Art Gallery, Liverpool, 1980, 1989 and 2002; Whitechapel Gallery, London; The Serpentine Gallery, London; The Hayward Gallery, London; The Barbican, London; Recent group shows include: Four British Painters, Antwerp; Slow Burn, Mead Gallery, Coventry; Small is Beautiful in Flowers West, Santa Monica, USA; Happy the World so Made, Nunnery Gallery, London, 2001; British Abstract Painting 2001, Flowers East, London; Spica Museum, Tokyo, 2004; Works in private, corporate and public collections including: Arts Council of Great Britain; The British Council; The Contemporary Art Society; Whitworth Art Gallery, Manchester. Publications: Mali Morris Painting, 1994; Mali Morris, 2000; Many exhibition catalogues. Honours: Lorne Award; British Council Travel Awards; DAIWA Anglo-Japanese Foundation Travel Award; Chelsea College of Art Research Awards; Hatton Scholarship; GLAA Major Award; Elephant Trust Award. Membership: Art in Perpetuity Trust (APT). Address: APT Studios, 6 Creekside, London SE8 4SA, England.

MORRIS Richard Francis Maxwell, b. 11 September 1944, Sussex, England. Chief Executive. m. Marian Sperling, 9 April 1983, 2 daughters. Education: New College, Oxford, 1963-66; College of Law, London, 1967. Appointments: Solicitor, Farrer & Co, 1967-71; Banker, Grindlay Brandts, 1971-75; Director, Invicta Radio plc, 1984-92; General Manager, Corporate Finance, SG Warburg & Co, 1975-79; Managing Director, Edward Arnold Ltd. 1987-91; Finance Director, Joint Managing Director, Hodder & Stoughton, 1979-91; Founder, Almaviva Opera, 1989-; Trustee, Governor, Kent Opera, 1985-90; Director, Southern Radio plc, 1990-92; Chief Executive, Associated Board of the Royal Schools of Music, 1993-; Trustee, Director, Kent Music School, 2001-; Member, Executive Committee, Chairman, Music Education Council, 1995-; Trustee, Council for Dance Education and Training, 1999-. Honours: Honorary RCM; Honorary RNCM; MA (Oxon). Memberships: Incorporated Society of Musicians; Music Masters and Mistresses Association. Address: 24 Portland Place, London W1B 1LU, England. E-mail: rmorris@abrsm.ac.uk

MORRIS Richard Graham Michael, b. 27 June 1948, Worthing, Sussex, England. Neuroscientist. m. Hilary Ann Lewis, 2 daughters. Education: MA, Trinity Hall, University of Cambridge, 1966-69; DPhil, Sussex University, 1969-73. Appointments: Senior Scientific Officer, British Museum, Natural History, Researcher, BBC Television, Science and Features Department, 1973-75; Lecturer, Psychology, 1977-86, MRC Research Fellow, 1983-86, University of St Andrews; Reader in Neuroscience, 1986-93, Professor of Neuroscience, 1993-, Director, Centre for Neuroscience, 1993-97, Chairman, Department of Neuroscience, 1998-, University of Edinburgh; Editorial roles in various scientific journals, 1990-. Publications: Over 150 papers in academic journals; Neuroscience: The Science of the Brain (booklet for secondary school children); Parallel Distributed Processing: Implications for Psychology and Neurobiology (editor), 1989. Honours: Fellow, Academy of Medical Sciences, 1998-; Decade of the Brain Lecturer, 1998; Zotterman Lecturer, 1999; Forum Fellow, World Economics Forum, 2000; Life Sciences Co-ordinate OST Foresight Project on Cognitive Systems, 2002-03; Yngve Zotterman Prize, Karolinska Institute, 1999; Henry Dryerre Prize, Royal Society of Edinburgh, 2000. Memberships: Experimental Psychology Society, Honorary Secretary, 1984-88; British Neuroscience Association, Chairman, 1991-95; Society for Neuroscience, USA; European Brain and Behaviour Society. Address: Department of Neuroscience, University of Edinburgh, 1 George Square, Edinburgh EH8 9JZ, Scotland.

MORRIS William (Bill), b. 1938, Jamaica. Trade Union General Secretary. m. Minetta, deceased 1990, 2 sons. Appointments include: Joined engineering company, Hardy Spicers, Birmingham; Joined T&G, 1958; Elected Shop Steward, Hardy Spicers, 1962; Involved in first industrial dispute, 1964; Elected Member, T&G's General Executive Council, 1972; District Officer, T&G, Nottingham/Derby District, 1973; Northampton District Secretary, T&G, 1976; National Secretary of the Passenger Service Trade Group, T&G, 1979; Deputy General Secretary, T&G, 1986-92; Elected General Secretary, 1991, re-elected, 1995-2003; Member, TUC General Council, 1988-2003; Member, TUC Executive

Committee, 1988-; Member, Commission for Racial Equality, 1980-87; Member, Executive Board of the International Transport Worker's Federation, 1986; Member, New Deal Task Force, 1997-2000; Member, Court of the Bank of England, 1998-; Member of Committee for Integrated Transport, 1999-; Member, Governing Councils, Luton University and Northampton University; Chancellor, University of Technology, Jamaica, 1999-. Honours: Numerous Honorary Degrees; Honorary Professorship, Thames Valley University , 1997; Honorary Fellowship, Royal Society of Arts, 1992; Honorary Fellowship City & Guilds London Institute, 1992; Order of Jamaica, 2002; Public Figure of the Year, Ethnic Multicultural Media Awards, 2002. Memberships: Board of Fullemploy, 1985-88; Trustee, 1987-90, Advisory Committee, 1997- Prince's Youth Business Trust. Address: 156 St Agnells Lane, Grove Hill, Hemel Hempstead, Hertfordshire, HP2 6EG, England.

MORRISON Anthony James (Tony Morrison), b. 5 July 1936, Gosport, England. Television Producer; Writer. m. Elizabeth Marion Davies, 30 July 1965, 1 son, 1 daughter. Education: BSc, University of Bristol, 1959. Appointments: Partner, South American Pictures; Director, Nonesuch Expeditions Ltd. Publications: Steps to a Fortune (co-author), 1967; Animal Migration, 1973; Land Above the Clouds, 1974; The Andes, 1976; Pathways to the Gods, 1978; Lizzie: A Victorian Lady's Amazon Adventure (co-editor), 1985; The Mystery of the Nasca Lines, 1987; Margaret Mee: In Search of Flowers of the Amazon (editor), 1988; QOSQO: Navel of the World, 1997; Peru: Country of Contrasts, 2003. Address: 48 Station Road, Woodbridge, Suffolk IP12 4AT, England. E-mail: Morrison@Southamericanpictures.com

MORRISON Charles Edward, b. 4 March 1944, Billings, Montana, USA. Researcher; Educator. m. Chieko, 2 sons, 2 daughters. Education: PhD, Johns Hopkins University. Appointments: Professional Lecturer, Johns Hopkins School for Advanced International Studies, 1977-80; Legislative Assistant to the late Senator William V Roth Jr, 1972-80; Senior Research Associate, Japan Center for International Exchange, Tokyo, 1980-84, 1985-92; Special Assistant to President, 1986-92, Director, Program on International Politics and Economics, 1992-95, President, 1998-, East-West Center; Director, Asia Pacific Economic Council, Study Center and Chair, US Consort of APEC Study Centers, 1996-98; Founding member, US-Asia Pacific Council, 2003-. Publications: Wide range of books, book chapters, reports and other publications in the field of international relations. Memberships: Various advisory committees and councils. Address: East West Centre, 1601 East West Rd, Honolulu, HI 96848-1601, USA.

MORRISON Errol York St Aubyn, b. 21 September 1945, Kingston, Jamaica. Physician; University Professor. m. Fay Esme Whitbourne, 5 daughters. Education: MD, Royal University of Malta, 1969; MSc (Lond), 1971; PhD, University of the West Indies, 1979; FRCP (Glasg), 1986; FACP, 1990; FRSM (UK), 1995. Appointments: Professor of Biochemistry and Endocrinology; Pro Vice Chancellor and Dean, School for Graduate Studies and Research, University of the West Indies. Publications: Over 110, mainly on diabetes related research. Honours: The American Diabetes Association; Harold Rifkin Award, for Outstanding Services in the field of diabetes, 1998; Fulbright Scholarship, 1994; Gold Musgrave Medal for distinguished eminence in the field of Medical Sciences, Jamaica; National Honour, Order of Jamaica for distinguished services to Medicine, Biochemistry and the Social Sciences. Memberships: New York Academy of Sciences; Caribbean Academy of Sciences. Address: The Vice Chancellery, University of the West Indies, Kingston 7, Jamaica.

Dictionary of International Biography

MORRISON Toni (Chloe Anthony), b. 18 February 1931, Lorain, Ohio, USA. Novelist. m. Harold Morrison, 1958, divorced 1964, 2 children. Education: Howard University; Cornell University. Appointments: Teacher, English and Humanities, Texas Southern University, 1955-57, Howard University, 1957-64; Editor, Random House, New York, 1965-; Associate Professor of English, State University of New York, 1971-72; Schweitzer Professor of the Humanities, 1984-89; Robert F Goheen Professor of the Humanities, Princeton University, 1989-. Publications: The Bluest Eye, 1970; Sula, 1974; Song of Solomon, 1977; Tar Baby, 1983; Beloved, 1987; Jazz, 1992; Playing in the Dark: Whiteness and the Literary Imagination, 1992; Nobel Prize Speech, 1994; Birth of a Nation'hood: Gaze, Script and Spectacle in the O J Simpson Trial, 1997; The Big Box (poems), 1999. Honours include: Pulitzer Prize and Robert F Kennedy Book Award, for Beloved, 1988; Nobel Prize for Literature, 1993; Commander, Ordre des Arts et des Lettres; National Medal of Arts, 2000. Membership: Council, Authors' Guild. Address: c/o Suzanne Gluck, International Creative Management, 40 57th Street West, NY 10019, USA.

MORRISON Van (George Ivan Morrison), b. 31 August 1945, Belfast, Northern Ireland. Singer; Songwriter; Composer; Musician. 1 daughter. Career: Founder, lead singer, Them, 1964-67; Solo artiste, 1967-; Appearances include: Knebworth Festival, 1974; The Last Waltz, The Band's farewell concert, 1976; Played with Bob Dylan, Wembley Stadium, 1984; Self Aid, with U2, Dublin, 1986; Glastonbury Festival, 1987; Prince's Rock Trust Gala, 1989; Performance, The Wall, by Roger Waters, Berlin, 1990; Concert in Dublin, with Bono, Bob Dylan, 1993; Phoenix Festival, 1995. Recordings: Singles include: Gloria; Brown-Eyed Girl; Moondance; Domino; Wild Night; Albums include: Blowin' Your Mind, 1967; Astral Weeks, 1968; Moondance, 1970; His Band And Street Choir, 1971; Tupelo Honey, 1971; St Dominic's Preview, 1972; Hard Nose The Highway, 1973; It's Too Late To Stop Now, 1974; TB Sheets, 1974; Veedon Fleece, 1974; This Is Where I Came In, 1977; A Period Of Transition, 1977; Wavelength, 1978; Into The Music, 1983; Bang Masters, 1990; Common One, 1980; Beautiful Vision, 1982; Inarticulate Speech Of The Heart, 1983; Live At The Opera House Belfast, 1984; A Sense Of Wonder, 1984; No Guru, No Method, No Teacher, 1986; Poetic Champions Compose, 1987; Irish Heartbeat, 1988; Best Of..., 1990; Avalon Sunset, 1989; Enlightenment, 1990; Hymns To The Silence, 1991; Too Long In Exile, 1993; Best Of..., Vol 2, 1993; A Night in San Francisco, 1994; Days Like This, 1995; Songs of the Mose Allison: Tell Me Something, 1996; The Healing Game, 1997; The Skiffle Sessions: Live in Belfast, 1998, 2000; Brown Eyed Girl, 1998; The Masters, 1999; Super Hits, 1999; Back on Top, 1999. Also recorded on albums: with The Band: Cahoots, 1971; The Last Waltz, 1978; with John Lee Hooker: Folk Blues, 1963; Mr Lucky, 1991; with Bill Wyman: Stone Alone, 1976; with Jim Capaldi: Fierce Heart, 1983; with Georgie Fame: How Long Has This Been Going On, 1996. Honours include: Inducted into Rock And Roll Hall Of Fame, 1993; BRIT Award, Outstanding Contribution to British Music, 1994; Q Award, Best Songwriter, 1995.

MORT Graham Robert, b. 11 August 1955, Middleton, England. Poet. m. Maggie Mort, 12 February 1979, 3 sons. Education: BA, University of Liverpool, 1977; PGCE, St Martin's College, Lancaster, 1980; PhD, University of Glamorgan, 2000. Appointment: Creative Writing Course Leader, Open College of the Arts, 1989-2000. Publications: A Country on Fire; Into the Ashes; A Halifax Cider Jar; Sky Burial; Snow from the North; Starting to Write; The Experience of Poetry, Storylines; Circular Breathing; A Night on the Lash. Contributions to: Numerous literary magazines and journals. Honours: 1st Prizes, Cheltenham Poetry Competition, 1979, 1982; Duncan Lawrie Prizes, Arvon Poetry Competition, 1982, 1992, 1994; Major Eric Gregory Award, 1985; Authors Foundation Award, 1994. Memberships: Society of Authors; National Association of Writers in Education. Address: 2 Chapel Lane, Burton-in-Lonsdale, Carnforth, Lancs LA6 3JY, England.

MORTIMER John (Clifford), Sir, b. 21 April 1923, Hampstead, London, England. Author; Barrister; Playwright. m. (1) Penelope Fletcher, 1949, 1 son, 1 daughter, (2) Penelope Gollop, 2 daughters. Education: Brasenose College, Oxford. Appointments: Called to the Bar, 1948; Master of the Bench, Inner Temple, 1975; Member, Board of National Theatre, 1968-; Chairman, Council Royal Society of Literature, 1989; Chairman, Council Royal Court Theatre, 1990-; President, Howard League for Penal Reform, 1991-. Publications: Novels: Charade, 1947; Rumming Park, 1948; Answer Yes or No, 1950; Like Men Betrayed, 1953; Three Winters, 1956; Will Shakespeare, 1977; Rumpole of the Bailey, 1978; The Trials of Rumpole, 1979; Rumpole's Return, 1981; Rumpole and the Golden Thread, 1983; Paradise Postponed, 1985; Rumpole's Last Case, 1987; Rumpole and the Age of Miracles, 1988; Rumpole a la Carte, 1990; Clinging to the Wreckage (autobiography), 1982; In Character, 1983; Character Parts (interviews), 1986; Summer's Lease, 1988; The Narrowing Stream; Titmuss Regained, 1990; Dunster, 1992; Rumpole on Trial, 1992; The Best of Rumpole, 1993; Murderers and Other Friends (autobiography), 1993; Rumpole and the Angel of Death, 1995; Rumpole and the Younger Generation, 1996; Felix in the Underworld, 1997; Rumpole's Return, 1997; The Third Rumpole Omnibus, 1997; The Sound of Trumpets, 1998; The Summer of a Dormouse (autobiography), 2000; Rumpole Rests His Case, 2001; Rumpole and the Primrose Path, 2002; Numerous plays and translations. Honours include: British Academy of Writers' Award, 1979, 1980. Address: A D Peters Ltd, 5th Floor, The Chambers, Chelsea Harbour, Lots Road, London SW10 0XF, England.

MOSIMANN Anton, b. 23 February 1947, Switzerland. Chef; Restaurateur. m. Kathrin Roth, 1973, 2 sons. Appointments: Apprentice, Hotel Baeren, Twann; Worked in Canada, France, Italy, Sweden, Japan, Belgium, Switzerland, 1962-; Cuisinier, Villa Lorraine, Brussels, Les Prés d'Eugénie, Eugénie-les-Bains, Les Frères Troisgros, Roanne, Paul Bocuse, Collonges au Mont d'Or, Moulin de Mougins; Joined Dorchester Hotel, London, 1975, Maitre Chef des Cuisines, 1975-88; Owner, Mosimann's, 1988-, Mosimann's Party Service, 1990-, The Mosimann Academy, 1995-, Creative Chefs, 1996-, Château Mosimann, 2001-; Numerous TV appearances. Publications: Cuisine a la Carte, 1981; A New Style of Cooking: The Art of Anton Mosimann, 1983; Cuisine Naturelle, 1985; Anton Mosimann's Fish Cuisine, 1988; The Art of Mosimann, 1989; Cooking with Mosimann, 1989; Anton Mosimann – Naturally, 1991; The Essential Mosimann, 1993; Mosimann's World, 1996. Honours: Freedom of the City of London, 1999; Royal Warrant from HRH the Prince of Wales for Caterers, 2000; Numerous others. Address: c/o Mosimann's, 11B West Halkin Street, London SW1X 8JL, England.

MOSQUERA Aydeé, b. 15 July 1996, Bogotá, Colombia. Chiropractor. Education: Bachelor of Science, Chemistry and Biology, Bogotá, Colombia, 1987; Chiropractic, Bournemouth, England, 1993. Appointment: Chiropractor, Cartagena, Spain. Memberships: British Chiropractic Association; Spanish Chiropractic Association. Address: Calle Asdrubal No 3 Bajo, Cartagena, Murcia, Spain.

MOSS Kate, b. 16 January 1974, Addiscombe, England. Model. 1 daughter. Career: Modelled for Harpers and Queen; Vogue; The Face; Dolce & Gabana; Katherine Hamnett; Versace; Yves St Laurent; Exclusive world-wide with Calvin Klein, 1992-99.

Publication: Kate, 1994. Film: Unzipped, 1996; Honour: Female Model of the Year, VH-1 Awards, 1996. Address: Storm Model Management, 1st Floor, 5 Jubilee Place, London SW3 3TD, England.

MOSS Norman Bernard, b. 30 September 1928, London, England. Journalist; Writer. m. Hilary Sesta, 21 July 1963, 2 sons. Education: Hamilton College, New York, 1946-47. Appointments: Staff Journalist with newspapers, news agencies and radio networks. Publications: Men Who Play God - The Story of the Hydrogen Bomb, 1968; A British-American Dictionary, 1972, 5th edition, revised, 1994; The Pleasures of Deception, 1976; The Politics of Uranium, 1982; Klaus Fuchs: The Man Who Stole the Atom Bomb, 1987; Managing the Planet, 2000; 'Nineteen Week. America, Britain and the Fateful Summer of 1940', 2003 Honour: Magazine Writer of the Year, Periodical Publishers Association, 1982. Memberships: International Institute of Strategic Studies; Society of Authors. Address: 21 Rylett Crescent, London W12 9RP, England.

MOSS Stirling, b. 17 September 1929, London, England. Racing Driver. m. (1) Katherine Stuart Moson, 1957, dissolved 1960, (2) Elaine Barbarino, 1964, 1 daughter, dissolved 1968, (3) Susie Paine, 1980, 1 son. Education: Haileybury and Imperial Service College. Appointments: British Champion, 1951; Built Own Car, The Cooper-Alta, 1953; Drove in HWM Formula II Grand Prix Team, 1950, 1951, Jaguar Team, 1955; Leader, Maserati Sports & Grand Prix Teams, 1956, Aston Martin Team, 1956; Member, Vanwall, Aston Martin, Maserati Teams, 1958; Events include New Zealand, Monaco Grand Prix, Nurburgring 1,000km, Argentine 1,000km. UK, Pescara, Italy, Moroccan Grand Prix; Managing Director, Stirling Moss Ltd; Director, 28 companies; Journalist; Lecturer; President, Patron, 28 Car Clubs. Publications: Stirling Moss, 1953; In the Track of Speed, 1957; Le Mans 59, 1959; Design and Behaviour of the Racing Car, 1963; All But My Life, 1963; How to Watch Motor Racing, 1975; Motor Racing and All That, 1980; My Cars, My Career, 1987; Stirling Moss: Great Drives in the Lakes and Dales, 1993; Motor Racing Masterpieces, 1995; Stirling Moss, autobiography, 2001. Honours include: Honorary FIE, 1959; Gold Star, British Racing Drivers Club, 10 times, 1950-61; Driver of the Year, Guild of Motoring Writers, 1954; Sir Malcolm Campbell Memorial Award, 1957. Address: c/o Stirling Moss Ltd, 46 Shepherd Street, Mayfair, London W1Y 8JN, England. E-mail: stirlingmossltd@aol.com

MÖSSBAUER Rudolf Ludwig, b. 31 January 1929, Munich, Germany. Physicist. Education: Graduated, Munich Institute of Technology, 1952; PhD, 1958; Postgraduate Research, Max Planck Institute for Medical Research, Heidelberg, 1958. Appointments: Professor of Physics, California Institute of Technology, Pasadena; Concurrent Professorship, Munich Institute of Technology; Discovered the Mössbauer Effect. Publications: Papers on Recoilless Nuclear Resonance Absorption and on Neutrino Physics. Honour: Nobel Prize for Physics, 1961. Address: Fachbereich Physik, Physik Department E 15, Technische Universität Menchen, D-85747 Garching, Germany. E-mail: beatrice.vbellen@ph.tum.de

MOTION Andrew, b. 26 October 1952, England. Biographer; Poet; Poet Laureate of the United Kingdom, 1999-. m. (1) Joanna J Powell, 1973, dissolved 1983, (2) Janet Elisabeth Dalley, 1985, 2 sons, 1 daughter. Education: Radleigh College and University College, Oxford. Appointments: Lecturer in English, University of Hull, 1977-81; Editor, Poetry Review, 1981-83; Poetry Editor, Chatto & Windus, 1983-89, Editorial Director, 1985-87; Professor of Creative Writing, University of East Anglia, Norwich, 1995-; Chair, Literary Advisory Panel Arts Council of England, 1996-

98; Poet Laureate of the United Kingdom, 1999-. Publications: Poetry: The Pleasure Steamers, 1978; Independence, 1981; The Penguin Book of Contemporary British Poetry (anthology), 1982; Secret Narratives, 1983; Dangerous Play, 1984; Natural Causes, 1987; Love in a Life, 1991; The Price of Everything, 1994; Selected Poems, 1996-97, 1998; Horn to Eternity, autobiography, 2000; Public Property, 2001; Criticism: The Poetry of Edward Thomas, 1981; Philip Larkin, 1982; William Barnes Selected Poems (ed), 1994; Salt Water, 1997; Biography: The Lamberts, 1986; Philip Larkin: A Writer's Life, 1993; Keats, 1997; Wainewright the Poisoner, novel, 2000; The Invention of Dr Cake, novel, 2003. Novels: The Pale Companion, 1989; Famous For the Creatures, 1991. Honours include: Rhys Memorial Prize, 1984; Somerset Maugham Award, 1987; Whitbread Biography Award, 1993; Honorary DLitt, Hull, 1996, Exeter, 1999, Brunel, 2000, APU, 2001, Open University, 2002. Address: Department of English and American Studies, University of East Anglia, Norwich NR4 7TJ, England.

MOUKHA Vladimir Dmitrievich, b. 26 January 1935, Chemal, Gorny Altay, Russia. Academician; Agronomist; Rector. m. Melania Andreevna Moucha, 1 son. Education: Candidate of Agricultural Sciences, 1967, Doctor of Agricultural Sciences, 1981, Kharkhov Agricultural Institute. Appointments: Senior Technician, Soil Scientist, 1958, Engineer, Soil Scientist, 1958, Head of Soil Expedition, 1959-60, Ukrainian Research Soil Science Institute; Senior Laboratory Worker, 1960, Assistant, 1960, Assistant Professor, 1967, Professor, 1982, Soil Science Chair, Kharkov V Dokuchayev Agricultural Institute; Teacher, Konakri Polytechnical Institute, Konakri, Guinea, Africa, 1966-70; Poltava Agricultural Institute, Poltava, Ukraine, 1982-88; Rector, Head of Soil Science and Agrochemistry Chair, Kursk State Ivanov Agricultural Academy, 1988-. Publications: Over 200 scientific writings on soil science, crop growing, agrochemistry, agroecology, and others. Honours: Medal for Valiant Labour, 1970; Honoured Worker of RF Science, 1993; 30 Years Victory in the Great Patriotic War of 1941-45, 1995; Honoured Worker of Higher Education in Russia, 1997; Order of Friendship, 1998; Honoured Worker of Science and Education of Kursk Region, 1999; Knight of Science and Art, Russian Academy of Natural Sciences, 2000. Memberships: Russian Writer's Union; Russian Academy of Natural Sciences; Russian Ecological Academy; International Academies of Informatics and Agrarian Education. Address: Kursk State Agricultural Academy, 70 K Marx St, Kursk 305021, Russia. E-mail: academy@kgsha.ru Website: www.kgsha.ru

MOULDEN Stanley Jeremy, b. 10 December 1937, Burton, The Wirral, Cheshire, England. Educator; Company Director. m. Raquel Poblete, 2 sons. Education: B Ed, Liverpool, 1959; M Ed, London, 1960; D Ed, Albert Einstein International, Yugoslavia, 1993; PhD, UNLV, 1994. Appointments: Deputy Headmaster, Wells Cathedral Junior School, 1961-64; Headmaster, Markham College Lower School, Lima, Peru, 1964-78; Headmaster, Miami Shores Preparatory School, Florida, USA, 1973-74; Founder and Provost, Newton College, Lima, Peru; Chief Executive Officer and President, Nicoa, Inventrex, USA, Sabre, Ivertemb, Proinco, Peru. Honours: MBE, H M Queen Elizabeth II, 1997; Park in Barranco, Peru named after him. Membership: Canning Club, St James Square; Fellow, Royal Geographical Society; New York Academy of Sciences. Address: Las Redes 234, Las Lagunas de la Molina, Lima 12, Peru. E-mail: drsjmouldon@hotmail.com

MOULE Ros, b. 18 March 1941, Swansea, Wales. Lecturer and Writer. 1 son, 1 daughter. Education: BA, University College of Swansea, 1962; PGCE, London Institute of Education, 1963. Appointments: Lecturer, American and European Studies, University of London, 1970-75; Lecturer, Kingston College of Further Education, Surrey, 1975-87, Swansea College, 1991-2001.

Contributions to: Poetry Wales; Poetry Digest; Merlin; Westwords; Anglo Welsh Review. Honours: West Wales Writers Umbrella Annual Competition; Swansea Writers Circle Competition; Currently Chairperson of the Tibetan Yungdrung Bön Study Centre (UK) SCO 23439 (Charity Number). Address: 15 Admirals Walk, Sketty, Swansea, West Glamorgan SA2 8LQ, Wales.

MOUNT William Robert Ferdinand, b. 2 July 1939, London, England. Novelist; Journalist; Editor. m. Julia Lucas, 20 July 1968, 2 sons, 1 daughter. Education: BA, Christ Church, Oxford, 1961. Appointments: Political Editor, 1977-82, 1985, Literary Editor, 1984-85, Spectator; Head of Prime Minister's Policy Unit, 1982-84; Political Columnist, The Times, 1984-85, Daily Telegraph, 1985-90; Editor, Times Literary Supplement, 1991-2002; Fellow, 1991, Council, 2002-, RSL; Senior Columnist, The Sunday Times, 2002-. Publications: Very Like a Whale, 1967; The Theatre of Politics, 1972; The Man Who Rode Ampersand, 1975; The Clique, 1978; The Subversive Family, 1982; The Selkirk Strip, 1987; Of Love and Asthma, 1991; The British Constitution Now, 1992; Umbrella, 1994; The Liquidator, 1995; Jem (and Sam), 1998; Fairness, 2001. Contributions to: Spectator; Encounter; National Interest; Politique Internationale. Honour: Hawthornden Prize, 1992; Honorary Fellow, University of Wales, Lampeter, 2002. Address: 17 Ripplevale Grove, London N1 1HS, England.

MOUSTAFA Sohair Abd Allah, b. 25 December 1953, Egypt. Professor. Education: BSc, Cairo University, 1975; MSc, 1985, PhD, 1992, Suez Canal University. Appointments: Assistant and Associate Professor of Zoology, Faculty of Science, Suez Canal University, Ismailia, Egypt, 1992-2001; Associate Professor of Zoology, Faculty of Education for Girls, Saudi Arabia, 2001-02; Professor of Zoology, Faculty of Science, Suez Canal University, 2004. Publications: Numerous articles in professional journals. Honours: PhD joint supervision scholarship sponsored by the Egyptian Government and accomplished between Egypt and the USA; Listed in national and international biographical dictionaries including Who's Who in Science and Engineering 6th edition. Memberships: American Physiological Society; American Diabetes Association; Egyptian Society for Zoology; Egyptian German Society for Zoology; Egyptian British Society for Biological Sciences. Address: Department of Zoology, Faculty of Science, Suez Canal University, Ismailia, Egypt. E-mail: sohabdulla@hotmail.com

MOYNIHAN Daniel Patrick, b. 16 March 1927, Tulsa, Oklahoma, USA. Retired United States Senator; Writer. m. Elizabeth Therese Brennan, 29 May 1955, 2 sons, 1 daughter. Education: City College of New York, 1943; BA, Tufts University, 1948; MA, 1949, PhD, 1961, Fletcher School of Law and Diplomacy. Appointments: Special Assistant, 1961-62, Executive Assistant, 1962-63, to the US Secretary of Labor; Assistant Secretary of Labor, 1963-65; Fellow, Center for Advanced Studies, Wesleyan University, 1965-66; Professor of Education and Urban Politics, 1966-73, Senior Member, 1966-77, Professor of Government, 1973-77, Kennedy School of Government, Harvard University; Assistant for Urban Affairs, 1969-70, Counsellor, 1969-70, Consultant, 1971-73, to the President of the US; US Ambassador to India, 1973-75; US Permanent Representative to the United Nations, 1975-76; US Senator (Democrat) from the State of New York, 1977-2001. Publications: Beyond the Melting Pot (with Nathan Glazer), 1963; The Defenses of Freedom: The Public Papers of Arthur J Goldberg (editor), 1966; Equal Educational Opportunity (co-author), 1969; On Understanding Poverty: Perspectives for the Social Sciences (editor), 1969; The Politics of a Guaranteed Income, 1973; Coping: On the Practice of Government, 1974; Ethnicity: Theory and Experience (editor with Nathan Glazer), 1975; A Dangerous Place (with S Weaver),

1978; Counting Our Blessings: Reflections on the Future of America, 1980; Loyalties, 1984; Family and Nation, 1986; Came the Revolution: Argument in the Reagan Era, 1988; On the Law of Nations, 1990; Pandaemonium: Ethnicity in International Politics, 1993; Miles to Go: A Personal History of Social Policy, 1996; Secrecy: The American Experience, 1999. Contributions to: Professional journals. Honours: Meritorious Service Award, US Department of Labor, 1965; Centennial Medal, Syracuse University, 1969; International League for Human Rights Award, 1975; John LaFarge Award for Interracial Justice, 1980; Medallion, State University of New York at Albany, 1984; Henry Medal, Smithsonian Institution, 1985; SEAL Medallion, Central Intelligence Agency, 1986; Laetare Medal, University of Notre Dame, 1992; Thomas Jefferson Award, 1993; Numerous honorary doctorates. Address: c/o United State Senate, 464 Russell Senate Building, Washington, DC 20510, USA.

MTHOKO November Ananias, b. 22 November 1943, Onyaanya, Namibia. Teacher; Administrator. m. Ndahambelela, 1 son, 2 daughters. Education: Secondary School Teacher's Diploma, Nkrumah Teacher's College, in Association with the University of Zambia, 1972; BA, Hons, Adult Education, University of Lagos, Nigeria, 1980. Appointments: School teacher, Zambia, 1971-73; Teacher, Namibia Health and Education Centres, 1976-77, 1980-81; Executive Director, UNIN-Namibian Extension Unit 1981-90; Director, Lifelong Learning Programmes, Ministry of Basic Education, Sport and Culture, Namibia, 1990-. Publications: Co-author of several course textbooks, including Basic Agriculture Course; English Course; Primary Health Care Course for the Namibian Extension Unit Students, 1980-85; Junior Secondary Geography of Namibia, 1990; Graded Reader for the National Literacy Programme of Namibia, 1998; Co-author, Unity in Diversity: A Culture Booklet for Adult Basic Education in Namibia, 2000; Co-author: Unity in Diversity: A Culture Booklet for Adult Basic Education in Namibia, 2000; Farming with Animals and Fish in Namibia, 2001; Co-author, Supplementary Reader for Adult Literary Programme, 2002. Memberships: International Diabetic Federation, Belgium, 1992-; New York Academy of Sciences, 1998-; National Geographic Society, Washington DC, 1984-. Address: PO Box 776, 89 Bach Strasse Windhoek West, Windhoek 9000, Namibia.

MUELLER Kathryn Lucile, b. 14 February 1951, Lincoln, Nebraska, USA. Occupational Medicine Physician. m. Rex Logemann, 1 son, 1 daughter. Education: BA, MD, 1977, University of Nebraska; MPH, Medical College of Wisconsin, 1994. Appointments: Assistant Professor, 1987-98, Associate Professor, Emergency Medicine and Preventive Medicine, University of Colorado, Health Sciences Center; Medical Director, Colorado Division of Worker's Compensation, 1991-; Residency Director, Occupational Medicine, University of Colorado. Publications: Acceptance and self-reported use of national occupational practice guidelines (co-author), 2000; numerous other book chapters on practical guidelines. Honours: President, Rocky Mountain Academy of Occupational Medicine; National Leadership Award, Central State Occupational Medicine Association. Membership: Fellow and Board of Directors, 2000-, American College of Occupational and Environmental Medicine. Address: University of Colorado Health Sciences Center, 4200 E 39th Avenue B119, Denver, CO 80122. E-mail: kathryn.Mueller@uchsc.edu

MÜHLEIS Daniela, b. 27 April 1955, St Gallen, Switzerland. Singer; Musician (guitar, piano). m. Hans Georg Huber, 26 September 1986, 1 adopted daughter. Education: Commercial school, commercial association, St Gallen. Musical Education: Music Lessons: guitar, piano. Career: Joined Cargo, 1979; National

Country and Western Festival in Zürich, Open-Air Festival, St Gallen, 1981; Swiss finals, European Song Contest; Debut album, 1983; Band renamed, Daniela Mühleis and Band, 1984; Successful concerts, Switzerland, Italy; Country Festivals; Swiss television: Sonntagsmagazin, 1989; Holansky kapr Country Music Festival, Prague, 1989; International Country Festival, Geiselwind, 1990; German Cable TV: Offener Kanal Dortmund, 1991; PORTA Country Festival, Czechoslovakia, 1992; International Visagino Country Festival, Lithuania, 1993; Lithuanian television; Swiss TV: Country Roads; Video clip produced in Malta, 1994; Television: Switzerland, Malta; Own radio show in St Gallen, Country Music, 1984-97; Nominated by European Country Music Association as European Female Vocalist, 1998; Winner, International Rising Star Award, by North America Country Music Association International, 1999. Recordings include: Albums: Stage-fright, 1983; Die Sieger des 1 Country und Western Festivals Zürich, 1986; Far Away, 1987; Animals, 1990: Far Away, 1991; Better Life, 1993; Open Minds, 1997. Honours: Winner, Modern Country Music section, Swiss Country Open Air, 1985; SRI Selection, 1997. Memberships: CMA, USA; CMFS, Switzerland; ECMA; NACMAI, USA; ECMA, Europe. Address: Lehnackerstrasse 9a, CH-9033 Untereggen, Switzerland.

MUIR Richard, b. 18 June 1943, Yorkshire, England. Author; Photographer. Education: 1st Class Honours, Geography, 1967, PhD, 1970, University of Aberdeen. Appointment: Editor, National Trust Regional Histories and Countryside Commission National Park Series; Co-founder, Editor, LANDSCAPES journal, 2000-. Publications: Over 40 books, including: Modern Political Geography, 1975; Hedgerows: Their History and Wildlife (with N Muir), 1987; Old Yorkshire, 1987; The Countryside Encyclopaedia, 1988; Fields (with Nina Muir), 1989; Portraits of the Past, 1989; The Dales of Yorkshire, 1991; The Villages of England, 1992; The Coastlines of Britain, 1993; Political Geography: A New Introduction, 1997; The Yorkshire Countryside: A Landscape History, 1997; Approaches to Landscape; New Reading the Landscape, 2000; Landscape Detective, 2002; Encyclopaedia of Landscape, 2004; Ancient Trees, Living Landscapes, forthcoming. Contributions to: Academic journals and general periodicals. Honour: Yorkshire Arts Literary Prize, 1982-83; Honorary Research Fellow, Department of Geography and Environment, University of Aberdeen. Address: 20 Stray Walk, Harrogate, Yorkshire HG2 8HU, England.

MUJALLID Mohammad Ibrahim, b. 20 November 1959, Makkah, Saudi Arabia. Assistant Professor of Anatomy. m. Khalidah, 6 daughters. Education: BSc, 1984, MSc, 1990, King Abdul Aziz University, Saudi Arabia; PhD, University of Birmingham, England, 1996; Specialised Course, Electron Microscopy, Royal Microscopical Society, School of Electron Microscopy, University of Manchester, England, 1995. Appointment: Assistant Professor of Anatomy, Department of Biological Sciences, Faculty of Science, King Abdul Aziz University, Saudi Arabia, 1996-. Publications: Book Chapter: Co-author, Lethal and sub-lethal effects of copper upon fish: a role for ammonia toxicity, 1996; Co-author, Lethal and sub-lethal effect of copper on fishes, 1997; Ultra structural Changes in the Gills of Brown Trout, Salmo trutta, Seasonally Acclimated to 5° & 15° C, Following Exposure to Copper in Soft Acidic Water, in press. Honours: Diploma of Membership of the Institute of Science and Technology, 1992; Listed in Who's Who publications and biographical dictionaries. Memberships: Fellow, Royal Microscopical Society; Microscopy Society of America; Histochemical Society; International Society of Stereology; American Association of Anatomists. Address: Department of

Biological Sciences, Faculty of Science, King Abdul Aziz University, PO Box 80203, Jeddah 21589, Saudi Arabia. E-mail: mmujallid@kaau.edu.sa

MULDER Johannes (Jan) W F, b. 28 June 1919, Arnhem, The Netherlands. Emeritus Professor of Linguistics. m. Dora Kodong, deceased 15 July 2001, 2 sons. Education: Student of Sinology, University of Djakarta, Indonesia, 1950-51; BA (equivalent), Chinese and Japanese Linguistics and Literature, University of Leiden, The Netherlands, 1954; Doctoral Degree, 1958; MA Oxon, 1962; DPhil, Oxon, 1966; Fellow of St Cross College, Oxon. Appointments: Bibliographical Secretary, The Linguistic Survey of Asia, sponsored by the American State Department, 1959-61; Far Eastern Librarian, 1961-64, Senior Librarian, 1964-68, Oriental Institute, Oxford, England; Concurrently, Lectured in Linguistics at Oxford University and supervised research students; Senior Lecturer, 1968-72, Personal Chair in Linguistics, 1972-84, Emeritus Professor, 1984-, St Andrews University, Scotland; Visiting Professorships: Mahidol University, Thailand, 1984-85, Albert Ludwigs Universität, Freiburg, West Germany, 1985-86, 1989-90. Publications: Books: Sets and Relations in Phonology: an axiomatic approach to the description of speech, 1968; The Strategy of Linguistics: Papers on the theory and methodology of axiomatic functionalism (in collaboration with SGJ Hervey), 1980; Theory of the linguistic sign (in collaboration with SGJ Hervey), 1972; Foundations of axiomatic linguistics, 1989; Author and co-author of numerous articles in professional journals and conference proceedings; Initiator of the Linguistic Theory called Axiomatic Functionalism. Honours: Member Queen's College Oxford; Fellow, St Cross College, Oxford; Honorary President, Societé Internationale de Linguistique Fonctionelle, 1984; 21st Century Award for Achievement, IBC, Cambridge, 2000-2001; American Medal of Honor for contribution to functional linguistics, ABI, USA, 2003. Memberships: Leiden Linguistic Circle, Chairman, 1959-61; Member Editorial Board, La Linguistique, 1976-; Societé Internationale de Linguistique Fonctionelle; President 1977-84. Address: Winterdijkweg, 4A, 3950 Kaulille, Belgium. E-mail: jfwmulder@yahoo.co.uk

MULDOON Paul, b. 20 June 1951, Portadown, County Armagh, Northern Ireland. Poet; Writer; Dramatist; Professor in the Humanities. m. Jean Hanff Korelitz, 1987. Education: BA, English Language and Literature, Queen's University, Belfast, 1973. Appointments: Producer, 1973-78, Senior Producer, 1978-85, Radio Arts Programmes, Television Producer, 1985-86, BBC Northern Ireland; Judith E Wilson Visiting Fellow, University of Cambridge, 1986-87; Creative Writing Fellow, University of East Anglia, 1987; Lecturer, Columbia University, 1987-88; Lecturer, 1987-88, 1990-95, Director, Creative Writing Programme, 1993-, Howard G B Clark Professor in the Humanities, 1998-, Princeton University; Professor of Poetry, University of Oxford, 1999-04; Writer-in-Residence, 92nd Street Y, New York City, 1988; Roberta Holloway Lecturer, University of California at Berkeley, 1989; Visiting Professor, University of Massachusetts, Amberst, 1989-90, Bread Loaf School of English, 1997-. Publications: Poetry: Knowing My Place, 1971; New Weather, 1973; Spirit of Dawn, 1975; Mules, 1977; Names and Addresses, 1978; Immram, 1980; Why Brownlee Left, 1980; Out of Siberia, 1982; Quoof, 1983; The Wishbone, 1984; Meeting the British, 1987; Madoc: A Mystery, 1990; Incantata, 1994; The Prince of the Quotidian, 1994; The Annals of Chile, 1994; Kerry Slides, 1996; New Selected Poems, 1968-94, 1996; Hopewell Haiku, 1997; The Bangle (Slight Return), 1998; Hay, 1998; Poems 1968-98, 2001. Theatre: Monkeys (television play), 1989; Shining Brow (opera libretto), 1993; Six Honest Serving Men (play), 1995; Bandanna (opera libretto), 1999. Essays: To Ireland, I, 2000. Translator: The Astrakhan Cloak, by Nuala Ni Dhomhnaill, 1993; The Birds, by

Aristophanes (with Richard Martin), 1999. Editor: The Scrake of Dawn, 1979; The Faber Book of Contemporary Irish Poetry, 1986; The Essential Byron, 1989; The Faber Book of Beasts, 1997; Moy Sand and Gravel, 2002. Children's Books: The O-O's Party, 1981; The Last Thesaurus, 1995; The Noctuary of Narcissus Batt, 1997. Contributions to: Anthologies and other publications. Honours: Eric Gregory Award, 1972; Sir Geoffrey Faber Memorial Awards, 1980, 1991; Guggenheim Fellowship, 1990; T S Eliot Prize for Poetry, 1994; American Academy of Arts and Letters Award, 1996; Irish Times Poetry Prize, 1997; Pulitzer Prize for Poetry, 2002. Memberships: Aosdana; Poetry Society of Great Britain, president, 1996-; Royal Society of Literature, fellow; American Academy of Arts and Sciences, 2000. Address: Creative Writing Programme, Princeton University, Princeton, NJ 08544, USA.

MÜLLER-WERDAN Ursula, b. 14 June 1961, Sonthofen, Germany. Physician. m. Karl Werdan. Education: MD, 1986, Doctors Diploma, 1988, University of Munich; Habilitation, University of Halle-Wittenberg, 1999. Appointments: Assistant Lecturer, Resident, University of Munich, 1987-96; Assistant Lecturer, Academic Fellow, 1996-99, Senior Consultant, Senior Lecturer, 1999-, University of Halle-Wittenberg. Publications: 2 monographs; Several original papers in scientific journals. Honours: Several awards dedicated to members of her scientific group. Memberships: National and international societies of internal medicine, cardiology and intensive care. Address: Department of Medicine III, University of Halle-Wittenberg, Ernst-Grube-Strasse 40, D-06097 Halle, Germany. E-mail: ursula.mueller-werdan@medizin.uni-halle.de

MULLIGAN Kevin T, b. 7 May 1955, New York, New York, USA. Director Engineering Services. m. Eileen, 1 son, 2 daughters. Education: BS, Biochemistry, Marquette University, 1977; MBA, Fairleigh Dickinson University, 1982. Appointments: Director Packaging, Director Engineering, Director New product Development, Tyco Healthcare, Mansfield, New Hampshire, USA. Publication: Article in Packaging Magazine; 10PP Packaging Article. Honours: Package of the Year Award, 1991; Listed in Who's Who publications and biographical dictionaries. Membership: 10PP; Packaging Institute. Address: 152 High Street, Hingham, MA 02043, USA. E-mail: Kevin.mulligan@tycohealthcare.com

MULVAGH Jane Mary E, b. 1 September 1958, Lancashire, England. Historian; Writer. m. Anthony Bourne, 2 daughters. Education: MA, Girton College, Cambridge (first student to propose and have accepted, the study of fashion textiles and dress for history faculty). Appointments: Freelance Journalist contributing to The Financial Times, The Daily Telegraph, The Art Newspaper, The Independent; Writer, Historian, Condé Nast, Vogue, 1980-89; Teacher, MA, Journalism, Central St Martin's College of Art, London, 1995-2000. Publications: Books: Vogue History of Twentieth Century fashion, 1989; Costume Jewellery in Vogue, 1989; Newport Houses (Architecture), 1989; Vivienne Westwood: An Unfashionable Life, 1998; Over 1000 articles in: The Financial Times, Telegraph, Vogue, The Independent; The Times; The Sunday Times; The Art Newspaper on subjects including: fashion, art wildlife, falconry; Lectures at venues including: The Victoria and Albert Museum and Oxford University; Regular TV slot on fashion and news, 1990. Memberships: University Women's Club; Biographers Club; Former member, NUJ. E-mail: jane@arbourne.com

MULVIHILL Maureen E, b. Detroit, Michigan, USA. Scholar; Author; Professor. m. Daniel R Harris. Education: PhB, Montieth College, Wayne State University, Detroit, Michigan; MA, Department of English, Wayne State University, Detroit, Michigan;

PhD, Department of English, University of Wisconsin-Madison, 1982; Postdoctoral training: Yale Center for British Art, Yale University, New Haven, Connecticut; Rare Book School, Columbia University, New York City. Appointments: Academic Appointments: Visiting Professor: Mercy College Manhattan; St Joseph's College, Clinton Hill, Brooklyn, New York; Fordham College, Lincoln Center, New York City; New York University, Washington Square Campus, New York City; Non-Academic Appointments: Consulting Writer (financial): Gruntal & Co Inc., Wall St, New York City; Bank of New York, Wall Street, New York City; Saatchi & Saatchi, New York City; Securities Industry Automated Corp, New York City. Publications: Books: Poems by Ephelia, 1992, 2nd edition 1993; Ephelia, 2003; Thumbprints of Ephelia: The End of an Enigma in Restoration Attribution, Text, Image, Sound (e-monograph: ReSoundings, 2001, updated 2003, http://www.millersville.edu/~resound/ephelia/Millersville U., PA); Articles in journals and essay collections including most recently: The Female Spectator, 2002; Seventeenth Century News, 2003; Profiles of women writers in: Encyclopaedia of Continental Women Writers, 1989; Dictionary of British and American Women Writers, 1987; An Encyclopaedia of British Women Writers, 1998; Book and exhibition reviews in journals including: New Hibernia Review, The Oscholars (online journal), Scriblerian, Eighteenth Century Studies; Irish Literary Supplement; Restoration and Eighteenth Century Theatre Research; Seventeenth Century News. Honours: NEH Fellow, Johns Hopkins University; Women's Caucus List of Honoured Scholars and Teachers, and also Juror, James Clifford Committee, American Society for Eighteenth Century Studies; Scholarships: Wayne State University, Detroit; University of Wisconsin-Madison; Guest Speaker: McMaster University, Canada; American Irish Historical Society; New York City; Utah State University; Southwest Texas State University; New York University; Honors Institute, New Jersey Institute of Technology, Georgian Court College, New Jersey; Frances Hunter Award, Princeton Research Forum, New Jersey, 1993, 1995,1997. Memberships: American Society for Eighteenth Century Studies; Society for the History of Authorship, Reading and Publishing; Renaissance Society of America; The James Joyce Society of New York City; International Association of Anglo-Irish Literatures; American Conference for Irish Studies. Address: One Plaza St West, Park Slope, Brooklyn, NY 11217-3742, USA. E-mail: mulvihill@nyc.rr.com

MUNDA Ivka Maria, b. 7 July 1927, Ljubljana, Slovenia. Scientific Official. Education: Diploma, Biology, Chemistry; PhD, Marine Biology, University of Ljubljana, 1963; PhD, Marine Botany, University of Gothenbourg, Sweden, 1963. Appointments: Assistant, Biological Institute, Medical Faculty, University of Ljubljana; National Research Association, University of Trondheim; Water Research Institute, Oslo; Yearly Grants, Icelandic Research Foundation, Reykjavik, Iceland, for Algological Research; Scientific Official, Hydrobiologist Instituute, Yerseke, Holland, 1964-65; Scientific Official, Biological Institute, Centre for Scientific Research of the Slovene Academy of Science and Arts, 1966-; Grants from the Alexander von Humboldt Foundation, Bonn, Germany, 1975-76. Publications: 125 scientific papers, marine algal ecology, geographic distribution and biochemistry, international journals. Honours: Slovene Award, Boris Kidrič; 20th Century Achievement Award, International Biographical Centre; New Century Award, The Europe 500; 1000 Leaders of World Influence; Leading Intellectuals of the World, 2000-2001; Presidential Award, 500 Great Minds; Order of International Ambassadors; American Medal of Honour, Profiles of Excellence. Memberships: British Phycological Society; Phycological Society of America; International Phycological Society; COST; CIESM; Deutsche Botanische Geselschaft; The New York Academy of Sciences; Board of Governors, American Biographical Institute; Research Board of Advisors, ABI; The Planetary Society; Deputy

Dictionary of International Biography

Director General, Biographical Centre, Cambridge; Secretary General, United Cultural Convention, USA; Scientific Advisor to the Director General, IBC; The BWW Society, USA. Address: Centre for Scientific Research, Slovene Academy of Science and Arts, Novi trg 2, 1000 Ljubljana, Slovenia.

MUNERA Héctor Augusto, b. 16 October 1943, Medellin, Columbia. Engineer and Physicist. m. Liliana Parra, divorced, 1 son, 2 daughters. Education: Chemical Engineer, University of Antioquia, Medellin, Columbia, 1966; MSc, Radiation Studies, University of Surrey, Guildford, England, 1971; Magister, Systems Engineering, National University, Bogota, Columbia, 1974; PhD, Nuclear Engineering, University of California, Berkeley, USA, 1978. Appointments: Chief of Division, Colombian Institute of Nuclear Affairs, 1967-75, Member, Board of Directors, 1997-98; Partner and CEO, Tecnicontrol and Dinatec, Bogota, 1978-83, 1986-88; Postdoctorate in Risk Analysis, Swiss Federal Institute of Technology, ETH, Zurich, Switzerland, 1984-85; Scientific Researcher, International Centre of Physics, CIF, Bogota, Columbia, 1989-; Professor of Physics, Department of Physics, National University, Bogota, Colombia, 2000. Publications: Circa 40 papers on foundations of decision making under uncertainty; Circa 30 papers on inertia, space-time and electrodynamics, probability and uncertainty; Circa 40 papers on applied nuclear physics and engineering. Honours: First Graduate Gold Medal, Institution of Nuclear Engineers, London, 1970; Distinction in MSc degree, University of Surrey; Certificates of Recognition for Outstanding Papers: Colombian Association for Operational Research, 1972; Colombian Society of Chemical Engineers, 1973; American Nuclear Society, 1988. Memberships: Institution of Nuclear Engineers, London; American Nuclear Society, USA; Society for Risk Analysis (USA); Colombian Society of Physics. Address: Apartado Aereo 84893, Bogota, Colombia, South America.

MUNJIZA Antonio, b. 2 February 1960, Trogir, Croatia. Reader in Computational Mechanics. m. Yasna. Education: Dipl Ing – Civ Eng, Structural Engineering, University of Split, 1979-94; MSc, Structural Dynamics, University of Zagreb, 1987-89; Specialisation in Earthquake Engineering, Tohoku University, Sendai, Japan, 1989-90; PhD, University of Wales, Swansea, 1990-92; Postdoctoral Study, Intelligent Systems Engineering Laboratory, Massachusetts Institute of Technology, USA, 1992-93. Appointments: Construction Engineer, 1984-85; Structural Engineer and Lecturer, 1985-89; Research Assistant and PhD Student, Swansea, Wales, 1990-92; Research Engineer, Massachusetts Institute of Technology, 1992-93; Senior Research Assistant, University of Wales, Swansea, 1993-95; Lecturer in Engineering, 1995-, Reader in Computational Mechanics and Software Engineering, 2003-, Department of Engineering, Queen Mary, University of London. Publications: Over 80 publications including, books, journal papers, keynote lectures, plenary lectures, invited lectures, seminars and workshops; Refereed journal papers include most recently as first author and co-author: 3D dynamics of discrete element systems comprising irregular discrete elements, 2003; Experimental validation of a computationally efficient beam element for combined finite-discrete element modelling of structures in distress, 2003; Comparison of experimental and numerical results for gravitational deposition of identical cubes, in press, 2004; The combines finite-discrete element method for structural failure and collapse, in press, 2004. Honours: 2 University Awards for Outstanding Grades, Award for Highest Overall Average Grades, University of Split; Best Student in Class of 30, University of Zagreb; Numerous research grants. Address: 26 Peel Road, South Woodford, London E18 2LG, England. E-mail: a.munjiza@qmul.ac.uk

MUNRO Alice, b. 10 July 1931, Wingham, Ontario, Canada. Author. m. (1) James Armstrong Munro, 29 December 1951, divorced 1976, 3 daughters, (2) Gerald Fremlin, 1976. Education: BA, University of Western Ontario, 1952. Publications: Dance of the Happy Shades, 1968; A Place for Everything, 1970; Lives of Girls and Women, 1971; Something I've Been Meaning to Tell You, 1974; Who Do You Think You Are?, 1978, US and British editions as The Beggar Maid: Stories of Flo and Rose, 1984; The Moons of Jupiter, 1982; The Progress of Love, 1986; Friend of My Youth, 1990; Open Secrets, 1994; Selected Stories, 1996; The Love of a Good Woman, 1998; Hateship, Friendship, Courtship, Loveship, Marriage, 2001. Honours: Governor-General's Awards for Fiction, 1968, 1978, 1986; Guardian Booksellers Award, 1971; Honorary DLitt, University of Western Ontario, 1976; Marian Engel Award, 1986; Canada-Australia Literary Prize, 1994; Lannan Literary Award, 1995; W H Smith Literary Award, 1996; National Book Critics Circle Award, 1998. Address: The Writers Shop, 101 5th Avenue, New York, NY 10003, USA.

MUNSHI Ajay Praful, b. 22 October 1950, Broach, Gujarat, India. Doctor; Surgeon. m. Angana, 1 son, 1 daughter. Education: MBBS, 1973; MS, 1977; FACS, 1985; PhD, 1994. Appointments: Registrar, 1974-77; Assistant Professor, 1979-90; Associate Professor, 1990-91. Publications: Over 56 articles in national and international journals. Honours: Dr M D Desai Gold Medal; Dr H D Joshi Trophy; Best Paper Award; Best Research Paper Award; Rotary International President's citation; National Pulse-Polio Committee of Rotary International Award; PhD degree, Gujarat University. Memberships: All India Society of Gastrointestinal Endoscopy; Indian Society of Gastroenterology and Surgical Gastroenterology; Indian Society of Occupational Health; National Biomedical Engineering Society; Gujarat State Surgeons' Associations; Ahmedabad Surgeons' Association; Society for Clinical and Experimental Hypnosis; All India Surgeons' Association; Gujarat Cancer Society; All India Urology Society; Member, Indian Science Congress; Vice President, National Board of Examiners. Address: 51 Pritam Nagar, Ellis Bridge, Ahmedabad 380 006, India. E-mail: dt_ajaymunshi@yahoo.com

MUNTER Rein, b. 23 December 1936, Tallinn, Estonia. Professor. m. Helge-Liis, 1 son, 1 daughter. Education: BSc, Tallinn Technical University, 1960; PhD, Tallinn Technical University, 1968; DSc, Kiev Institute of Water Chemistry, 1991. Appointments: Engineer and Research Fellow, Institute of Chemistry, 1960; PhD Student, 1962-65; Assistant, 1965-69; Senior Lecturer, 1969-74; Associate Professor, 1975-91; Professor, 1991; Head, Chemical Engineering Department and Department of Environmental Chemistry, Institute of Chemistry, Tallinn Technical University. Publications: 70 international publications. Honours: Active Member of New York Academy of Sciences, 1994-; Board Member of International Ozone Association; Estonian State Science Award for Research of Advanced Water Treatment Processes, 2001. Memberships: TDA; Board Member, Journal: Ozone: Science and Engineering, USA. Address: Vilde Str 68-43, Tallinn 13421, Estonia. E-mail: rmunt@edu/ttu.ee

MURCHISON Duncan George. Consultant. Education: BSc Honours, Geology, University of Durham, 1952; PhD, University of Durham, 1957. Appointments: Geologist, Royal Dutch Shell, 1957-58; Research Associate, 1958-60, Lecturer, 1960-63, University of Durham; Lecturer, 1963-71, Senior Lecturer, 1971-77, Reader in Geochemistry, 1971-76, Professor of Organic Petrology, 1976-93, Dean of the Faculty of Science, 1980-83, Head of the Department of Geology, 1982-86, Pro-Vice-Chancellor, 1986-90, Acting Vice-Chancellor, 1991, Pro-Vice-Chancellor, 1992-93, Chairman of numerous university committees, University of Newcastle. Publications: Author and Co-author, books and articles in professional scientific journals. Honours: Fellowship, Royal Society of Edinburgh, 1973; Honorary Fellow, Royal Microscopical Society, 1979; Thiessen Medal of the International Committee for Coal Petrology, 1987; Honorary Fellow, International Committee for Coal Petrology, 1994; Honorary Lifetime Member, Society for Organic Petrology, 2002. Memberships: Royal Society of Edinburgh; Geological Society of London, Vice-President, 1995-97, Treasurer, 2000-; Royal Microscopical Society, President, 1976-78; International Committee for Coal Petrology, President, 1979-83; Edinburgh Geological Society; Yorkshire Geological Society. Address: School of Civil Engineering and Geosciences, Drummond Building, University of Newcastle, NE1 7RU, England. E-mail: duncan@dmurchison.freeserve.co.uk

MURDOCH Keith Rupert, b. 11 March 1931, Melbourne, Australia (American citizen, 1985-). Publishing and Broadcasting Executive. m. (1) Patricia Booker, divorced, 1 daughter, (2) Anna Maria Torv, 28 April 1967, divorced, 2 sons, 1 daughter, (3) Wendy Deng, 1999. Education: MA, Oxon, Worcester College, Oxford, England, 1953. Appointments: Chairman, News American Publishing Inc, 1974-; Chairman, Chief Executive Officer, News Corporation Ltd, Sydney, Australia, 1991-; Chairman, 20th Century Fox, 1985-; Joint Chairman, Managing Director, Ansett Transport Industries Ltd; Chairman & Managing Director, News International plc, UK; Director, News Ltd Group and Associate Corporation, Australia; Director, Wm Collins plc, UK, 1989-; Chief Executive Officer, Sky Television, 1989-; Chair BskyB, 1999; United Technologies Corporation; Owner, numerous newspapers, magazines and TV stations in UK, US and Australia. Honours: AC, 1984; Commander of the White Rose, First Class, 1986; Knight of St Gregory the Great, 1998. Address: News Ltd, 2 Holt Street, Surry Hills, Sydney, NSW 2010, Australia.

MURDOCH Lachlan Keith, b. 8 September 1971, Australia. American citizen. Business Executive. m. Sarah O'Hare, 1999. Education: Princeton University. Appointments: Reporter, San Antonio Express News, The Times (UK); Sub-Editor, The Sun (UK); General Manager, Queensland Newspapers Pty Ltd, 1994-95; Executive Director, News Ltd, 1995; Director, Beijing PDN Xinren Information Technology Co Ltd, 1995-; Deputy Chair, Star Television, 1995-; Deputy Chief Executive, News Ltd, 1995-96; Director, The Herald & Weekly Times Ltd, 1996-, News Corporation, 1996-; Deputy COO, 2000-, Independent Newspapers Ltd (NZ), 1997-; Executive Chair, Chief Executive Officer, News Ltd, 1997; Senior Executive Vice-President, US Print Operations News Corporation, 1999-. Address: News Ltd, 2 Holt Street, Surry Hills, NSW 2010, Australia.

MURIN Gustav, b. 9 April 1959, Bratislava, Slovakia. Author. m. Jana, 2 daughters. Education: BSc, 1983, MSc, 1984, PhD, 1991, Comenius University, Bratislava. Publications: Author: The Case of a Buried Cemetery, in Czech, 1989; Summer Favors Lovers, 1990; Comebacks from Light, 1990; Substitutional End of the World, 1992; Instinct Contra Culture, 1994; Orgasmodromes, 1997; How Are You, 1998; Animals, Me and Other, 1998; Sex Contra Culture, in Czech, 1999; Substitutional End of the World, in Czech, 1999; Just Like the Gods, 2001; You Will Become Gods, in Czech, 2002; Co-author, 10 different story collections in Slovakia and 6 abroad; Author, 11 radio-dramas, TV documents, TV play and script for art movie; Author of more than 990 articles in 39 major Slovak, Czech and international newspapers and magazines; Numerous translations. Honours: Best Slovak story, 1979; Best Czech and Slovak story, 1981; Best Czech and Slovak novella, 1986; Special prize in Slovak radio drama, 1988; Honorary Fellow in Writing, University of Iowa, 1995; E E Kisch Award, 2003; Active participation in international literary conferences.

Memberships: Member, 1993-, Secretary, 1995-97, President, 2000-04, Slovak Centre of the PEN International; Member, Slovak Centre of Roma Club, 1994-; Member, Slovak Syndicate of Journalists, 1995-. Address: J Hagaru 17, 831 51 Bratislava, Slovak Republic. E-mail: murin@m2.fedu.uniba.sk

MURPHREY Elizabeth, b. 22 March 1947, Rocky Mount, North Carolina, USA. Historian; Librarian. Education: BA, History of International Studies, The University of North Carolina at Greensboro, 1969; MA, History, 1971, PhD, History, 1976, Duke University; Master's in Library Science, University of North Carolina, Chapel Hill, 1993. Appointments: College Professor, Wake Forest, North Carolina, A&T State University, Fayetteville State University, Elizabeth City State University, 8 years; Intelligence Research Specialist, US Army, 8 years; Academic Librarian, Florida International University, 5 years. Publications: Editor, Microfilm Edition, Socialist Party of America Papers and 2 hardcover descriptions of them; 5 entries, Historical Dictionary of World War II France: The Occupation, Vichy and The Resistance (editor Bertram Gordon); Article in Proceedings of the French Colonial Historical Society; Classified studies for the US Army. Honours: Phi Beta Kappa; Phi Alpha Theta; History Department's Departmental Award for Excellence in Teaching, Fayetteville State University, 1990; Listed in Who's Who publications and biographical dictionaries. Memberships: American Historical Association; Society for French Historical Studies; Society for Historians of American Foreign Relations; World History America. Address: 424 Windmeadows Street, Altamonte Springs, FL 32701, USA. E-mail: emurphrey@hotmail.com

MURPHY Eddie (Edward Regan), b. 3 April 1951, Brooklyn, New York, USA. Film Actor. m. (2) Nicole Mitchell, 2 sons, 1 daughter. Creative Works: Films include: 48 Hours, 1982; Trading Places, 1983; Delirious, 1983; Best Defence, 1984; Beverly Hills Cop, 1984; The Golden Child, 1986; Beverly Hills Cop II, 1987; Eddie Murphy Raw, 1987; Coming to America, 1988; Harlem Nights, 1989; 48 Hours 2, 1990; Boomerang, 1992; Distinguished Gentleman, 1992; Beverly Hills Cop III, 1994; The Nutty Professor, 1996; Dr Dolittle, 1998; Holy Man, 1998; Life, 1998; Bowfinger, 1999; Toddlers, 1999; Pluto Nash, 1999; Nutty Professor II: The Klumps; Dr Dolittle 2, 2001; Showtime, 2002; I-Spy, 2003; Daddy Day Care, 2003; The Haunted Mansion, 2003; Shrek 2 (voice), 2004; Tours with own comedy show; Comedy Albums: Eddie Murphy, 1982; Eddie Murphy: Comedian, 1983; How Could It Be, 1984; So Happy, 1989; Recorded 7 albums of comedy and songs. Honours include: Numerous awards and nominations. Address: c/o Jim Wiatt, ICM, 8942 Wilshire Boulevard, Beverly Hills, CA 90211, USA.

MURRAY Bill, b. 21 September 1950, Evanston, Illinois, USA. Actor; Writer. m. Margaret Kelly, 1980, 2 son. Education: Loyola Academy; Regis College, Denver; Second City Workshop, Chicago. Appointments: Performer, Off-Broadway National Lampoon Radio Hour; Regular Appearances TV Series Saturday Night Live; Appeared in Radio Series Marvel Comics' Fantastic Four; Co-Producer, Director, Actor, Quick Change, 1990; Writer, NBC-TV Series Saturday Night Live, 1977-80; Films: Meatballs, 1977; Mr Mike's Mondo Video, 1979; Where the Buffalo Roam, 1980; Caddyshack, 1980; Stripes, 1981; Tootsie, 1982; Ghostbusters, 1984; The Razor's Edge, 1984; Nothing Lasts Forever, 1984; Little Shop of Horrors, 1986; Scrooged, 1988; Ghostbusters II, 1989; Quick Change, 1990; What About Bob?, 1991; Mad Dog and Glory, 1993; Groundhog Day, 1993; Ed Wood, 1994; Kingpin, 1996; Larger Than Life, 1996; Space Jam, 1996; The Man Who Knew Too Little, 1997; With Friends Like These, 1998; Veeck as in Wreck, 1998; Rushmore, 1998; Wild Things, 1998; The Cradle Will Rock, 1999; Hamlet, 1999; Company Man,

1999; Charlie's Angels, 2000; The Royal Tenenbaums, 2001; Osmosis Jones, 2001; Lost in Translation, 2003. Honours include: Emmy Award, Best Writing for Comedy Series, 1977; BAFTA Award for Best Actor, 2004. Address: c/o William Carroll Agency, 139 N San Fernando Road, Suite A, Burbank, CA 91502, USA.

MURRAY Kevin Ian, b. 9 June 1954, Bulawayo, Rhodesia (Zimbabwe). Businessman; Specialist, Strategic Communications and Reputation Management. m. 1 son, 1 daughter. Education: Numerous leadership and management courses include: Louis Allen Management Course; The Leadership Challenge; Managing Corporate Affairs (Henley); Institute of Director's Diploma in Company Direction, 1994-95. Appointments: South African Infantry, 1 year; Active Service, annual civilian force tours of duty, Transvaal Scottish Regiment, 10 years; Court Reporter, Crime Reporter, Foreign Correspondent, Argus Company, London, Air Correspondent and Transport Editor, Head of General Assignments Team, News Editor, The Star, Johannesburg, South Africa, 1973-81; Group Publications Editor and PR Executive, Barlow Rand Limited, Johannesburg, 1981-82; Managing Editor, Leadership SA Magazine, Director, Marketing and Advertising, CMP, Churchill Murray Publications, Johannesburg, 1982-85; Managing Director, Kestrel Publications (subsidiary), Managing Director, Shearwater Communications, Oxfordshire, England, 1985-88; PR Manager, Bayer UK Ltd, UK Group Public Relations Manager, Bayer plc, 1988-92; Director Corporate Communications, Director Corporate Affairs, UK Atomic Energy Authority, 1992-96; Director of Communications, British Airways plc, 1996-98; Senior Consultant, 1998-99, Managing Director, 1999-2000, Chief Executive, 2001-03, Bell Pottinger Communications; Chairman, Chime Communications Public Relations Division, 2003-. Honours: International Awards for Public Relations Work; National Awards in South Africa and the United Kingdom. Address: 22 Springlines, Wanborough, Swindon SN4 0ES, England. E-mail: kmurray@chime.plc.uk

MURRAY Noreen Elizabeth, b. 26 February 1935, Read, Nr Burnley, Lancashire, England. Scientist; University Teacher. m. Kenneth Murray. Education: BSc, Botany, King's College, London, 1953-56; PhD, Microbial Genetics, University of Birmingham, 1956-59. Appointments: Research Associate, Department of Biological Sciences, Stanford University, 1960-64; Research Fellow, Botany School, Cambridge, 1964-67; Member, MRC Molecular Genetics Unit, 1968-74, Lecturer, 1974-80, Department of Molecular Biology, University of Edinburgh; Group Leader, European Molecular Biology Laboratory, Heidelberg, Germany, 1980-82; Reader, Department of Molecular Biology, 1982-88, Professor of Molecular Genetics (Personal Chair), 1988-2001, Professor Emeritus 2002-, University of Edinburgh. Publications: Numerous publications in scientific journals, including early papers in the field of genetic engineering. Honours: Member, European Molecular Biology Organisation, 1980; Fellow Royal Society, 1982; Fellow Royal Society of Edinburgh, 1989; Member, Academica Europaea, 1989; Royal Society Gabor Medal, 1989; Society of General Microbiology Fred Griffiths Lecturer, 2001; CBE for services to science, 2002; Honorary DSc, UMIST, Birmingham and Warwick. Memberships: Genetics Societies of UK and USA; UK Societies of Biochemistry and General Microbiology; President, Genetics Society of UK, 1987-90; Trustee, Darwin Trust of Edinburgh, 1990-; Member of Board, International Genetics Federation, 1998-2002; Council Member of BBSRC, 1994-98; Council Member, The Royal Society, 1992-93, 2002-2004; Member of the Athenaeum Club, 2001. Address: Mortonhall Road, Edinburgh, EH9 2HW, Scotland. E-mail: noreen.murray@ed.ac.uk

MURRAY Richard Henry, b. 20 September 1936, St Paul, Minnesota, USA. Senior Executive. m. Diann Murray, 1 son, 2 daughters. Education: Harvard University, USA, 1958; Harvard Law School, 1961. Appointments: Partner and Head of Litigation Department, Oppenheimer Law Firm, St Paul, Minnesota, USA, 1961-73; General Counsel, Touche Ross, New York, USA, 1973-86; Executive Director, Touche Ross International, New York, 1986-89; Chairman and Chief Executive Officer, Minet Professional Services, London, England, 1989-94; General Counsel, Deloitte Consulting, New York, 1994-2002; Global Director of Legal and Regulatory Affairs, Deloitte Touche Tohmatsu, New York, 1994-2002; Chief Claims Strategist, Swiss Re, New York and Zurich, 2002-; Director, Corporate Performance Project (a joint initiative of the World Economic Forum and Deloitte Touche Tohmatsu); Special Advisor to the Asia Business Council; Member of APEP, the Institute of International Insurance and the Republican Presidential Roundtable. Memberships: Formerly: Director, Executive Committee and Lecturer, Institute of Management Development, Lausanne, Switzerland, 1984-93; Advisory Board Member, Princess Grace Foundation, Monaco, 1983-90; Task Force Member of the Group of Thirty, Washington DC, 1994 and 1996; Risk and Insurance Management Society, USA, 1985-89; British Assurance Association, London, 1989-94; Member of Lloyds (London), 1989-94; Chairman, Professional Responsibility Committee of the Large Global Accountancy Firms, 1999-2002. Address: Swiss Re, 55 East 52nd Street, 44th Floor, New York, NY 10055, USA E-mail: richard_murray@Swissre.com

MURRAY Roderick Charles, b. 29 January, Johannesburg, South Africa. Company President and Chief Executive Officer. m. Yvonne Edna Bennett, 1 son, 1 daughter. Education: BS, Witwatersrand Technical College, 1962; MBA, California Coast University, 1992. Appointments: Packaging Chemist, South African Breweries; Marketing Director, Metal Box; Vice-President, Klockner Packaging Machinery; President and Chief Executive Officer, PPi Technologies Inc, Sarasota, Florida. Publications: New Product Launch – Remember Technology; Stand Up Pouch – 21st Century and On; Over 40 patents in flexible packaging. Membership: Institute of Packaging Professionals. Address: 1610 Northgate Boulevard, Sarasota, FL 34234, USA. Website: www.ppitechnologies.com

MURRELL Janice Marie, b. 29 November 1937, St Louis, Missouri, USA. Concert Opera Artiste. Education: Certificate, Kroeger Institute of Music Masters, 1971; Juillard School of Music, Certificate, 1979; Washington University Music Department, Citation, 1972. Appointments: International Concert, Opera Presentations; Young Audience, Director introducing Young Artiste; Assistant Music, Drama Director of St Louis CVPA Arts School Singer, Actress Summer Stock Theaters. Publications: Book, Young Only Once; World distributed poetic works; Articles, international publications. Honours: London International Musicians Museum, St Louis Symphony Chair Award, Dame Dr Title, White House Award; Metropolitan Opera Anniversary PIN Award. Memberships: Metropolitan Opera; St Louis Symphony Orchestra; International Poetry Society; White House Committee; Emily's List, Association of Women Senators, Washington DC. Address: 5556 Riverview Blvd, St Louis, MO 63120, USA.

MURSELL (Alfred) Gordon, b. 4 May 1949, Guildford, England. Priest in Church of England. m. Anne. Education: Pontifical Institute of Sacred Music, Rome, 1966-67; Brasenose College, Oxford, 1967-71; Cuddesdon College, Oxford, 1971-73; BA, History; BA, Theology; ARCM, Organ Performance; BD, Theology. Appointments: Curate, Walton, Liverpool, 1973-77; Vicar, St John's East Dulwich, London, 1977-86; Tutor, Salisbury-

Wells Theological College, Salisbury, 1986-91; Team Rector, Stafford, 1991-99; Provost, 1999-2002, Dean, 2002-, Birmingham Cathedral. Publications: The Theology of Carthusian Life, 1989; Out of the Deep: Prayer as Protest, 1989; The Wisdom of the Anglo-Saxons, 1997; The Story of Christian Spirituality (editor), 2001; English Spirituality (2 volumes), 2001. Address: 103a Selly Park Road, Birmingham, B29 7LH, England. E-mail: gordonmursell@beeb.net

MURUGESAN A G, b. 10 April 1960, Ariyapuram, India. Teacher; Researcher; Consultant. m. V Rathiha, 1 daughter. Education: BSc, 1980; MSc, 1982; Diploma in Gandhian Thought, 1984; Diploma in World Religions, 1988; PhD, Industrial Toxicology, 1988; DSc, 1998. Appointments: Senior Research Fellow, Assistant Professor in Biology, SPK College, Alwarkurichi, 1987-88; Scientist Pool Officer, M S University, 1992-98; Senior Assistant Professor, SPK Centre for Environmental Sciences, M S University, 1998-. Publications: 31 book chapters; 25 popular articles; 225 research papers. Honours: Best Research Paper Presentation Award; Man of the Year, 1998, 2001; Great Minds of the 21st Century; Distinguished Leadership Award. Memberships: Fellow, Academy of Environmental Biology; Academy of Zoology; Exnora International; Academy of Sciences for Animal Welfare; Society of Environmental Sciences; Society of Toxicology; Founder-Director, Academy of Sustainable Agriculture and Environment; Member, Board of Studies in Environment, Microbiology and Biotechnology; Adviser, Biotechnology Co-ordination Committee of Pollution Control Board; Member, Steering Committee on Tamirabanai River Water Partnership Programme; Member, Public Hearing Committee of Tamil Nadu Pollution Control Board; Co-ordinator, Green Squad, Co-editor, Journal of Environment and Ecoplanning; Operating several research and consultancy projects. Address: Manonmaniam Sundaranar University, SPK Centre for Environmental Sciences, Alwarkurichi, 627412 India.

MUSIL Robert Kirkland, b. 27 October 1943, New York, USA. Director. m. Caryn McTighe, 15 June 1968, 2 daughters. Education: BA, Yale University, 1964; MA, 1966, PhD, 1970, Northwestern University; MPH, 2001, Johns Hopkins University. Appointments: Instructor, Defence Information School, Fort Benjamin, Harrison, Indiana, 1969-71; Co-Director, CCCO, Agency for Military and Draft Counseling, Philadelphia, 1971-74; Director, Military Affairs Project, Centre for National Security Studies, Washington DC, 1974-75; Assistant Professor, English and American Studies, Temple University, Philadelphia, 1976-78; Producer, Host, Consider the Alternatives Radio, Philadelphia, 1978-92; Executive Director, SANE Education Fund, Philadelphia and Washington DC, 1984-88; Executive Director, Professionals Coalition for Nuclear Arms Control, Washington DC, 1988-92; Director, Policy and Programmes, Physicians for Social Responsibility, Washington DC, 1992-95; Executive Director, CEO, 1995-; Adjunct Professor, American University, School of International Service, 1996-. Memberships: American Public Health Association; American Academy of Arts and Sciences. Honours: Major Armstrong Award, Radio Ex, Armstrong Foundation, Columbia University, 1988, 1989. Address: 8600 Irvington Avenue, Bethesda, MD 20817, USA.

MUSIL Rudolf, b. 5 May 1926, Brno, Czech Republic. University Professor. m. Ing Liba Kochová, 26 July 1952, 2 sons. Education: RNDr, 1952, CSc, 1960, Habil, 1966, DSc, 1968, Full Professor, 1980, Education, Masaryk University, Charles University. Appointments: Full Professor, Institute of Geological Sciences, Faculty of Science, Masaryk University, Brno. Publications: Personalities of the Faculty of Science, 1997; Climatic Comparison of Terrestrial and Marine Sediments, 1997; Ende des Pliozäns und

Unteres bis Mittleres Pleistozän, 1997. Honours: Silver Medal, National Museum, 1968; Silver Medal, Humboldt Universität, Berlin; Medal, Moravian Museum, 1968; Medal, Slaskie University, Poland, 1983; Medal, Velkopolskie Towarzystwo, 1983; Silver Medal, Academy, 1986; Gold Medal, Masaryk University, 1997. Memberships: Czech Society of Geology and Mineralogy; Czech Society of Speleology; National Committee, INQUA; Czech Committee of Stratigraphy; International Commission on History of Geological Sciences. Address: Kotlárska Str 2, 61137 Brno, Czech Republic. E-mail: rudolf@sci.muni.cz

MÜSSIG Ricarda, b. 24 June 1925, Wuppertal, Germany. Children and Family Therapist. m. Siegfried Müssig, 1 son, 2 daughters. Education: Studies: Geology, Palaeontology: Diploma, 1952; Doctorate, 1953, analytical children and youth therapist, 1971; Further subjects: Spanish, Music, Psychology. Appointments: Scientific Assistant of the Geological Institute, University of Heidelberg, 1952-54; Freelance, journals and broadcasting companies, 1960s; Private practice, 1971-; Lecturer, Institute for Analytical Children and Youth Therapy, Heidelberg, 1972-73, Institute for Social Education, Karlsruhe, 1974-75; Editor of Kontext, 1985-89. Publications: On geology, palaeontology, analytical children and family therapy, psychoanalysis and human ethology, including: The Head-Legs-Scheme is the Mother Scheme; Economic Threat Behaviour; Three Phases of Prenatal Development Psychology; The Incest Taboo, the Forgotten Eleventh Commandment; Monographs: Imaginative Methods in Couples and Family Therapy; The Mother Scheme and Images of Men - Inherited, Learnt, Constructed, now in search of a publisher; The Cultural and Spiritual Heritage of the Upper Paleolithic. Memberships: ISHE; Pro Familia; BvPPF. Address: Analytische Kinder-und Jugendlichen Psychotherapeutin, Familientherapeutin, Neustadter Str 7, 76187 Karlsruhe, Germany.

MUSTAFA Abu Salim, b. 28 June 1952, India. Professor. m. Khalida Salim, 2 son, 3 daughters. Education: PUC, 1970; PMC, 1971; BSc, honours, 1972; MSc, 1974; PhD, 1979. Appointments: Assistant Professor, 1989-92, Associate Professor, 1992-96, Professor, 1996-; Consultant, 1989-. Publications: 190 scientific articles. Honours: Graduate Program Director, Research Awards, 1996, 2000, 2002; Invited Speaker, several international conferences. Memberships: International Immunology Society; International Infectious Disease Society; European Mycobacteriological Society; Fellow, Royal College of Pathologists, England; American Biographical Institute. Address: Microbiology Department, 4th Ring Road, PO Box 24923, Safat 13110, Kuwait.

MUSTAFA Walid Said, b. 10 October 1942, Al-Bireh, Palestine. Geographer; Educator. m. Valentina Korenda, 2 sons, 1 daughter. Education: BA, Geography, Damascus University, 1965; PhD, Kiev State University, Ukraine, 1972. Appointments: Lecturer, Department of Geography, Jordan University, Amman, Jordan, 1973-78; Acting Head, Department of Geography, Al-Najah University, Nablus, Palestine, 1979-80; Head, Research Centre, Department of Occupied Territory, Palestinian Liberation Organisation, Amman, Jordan, 1980-94; Senior Researcher and Lecturer, Department of History, Geography and Political Science, Bir Zeit University, Palestine, 1994-95; Dean of Students, 1996-2001, Lecturer, Department of Humanities, 2001-, Bethlehem University, Palestine. Publications: Author: Bethlehem, The Story of the City, 1990; Jerusalem, Population and Urbanization, 1850-2000, English edition, 2000; Co-author: Collective Destruction of Palestinian Villages and Zionist Colonization, 1881-1982, 1987; Collective Books: Palestinian Encyclopaedia – General Edition, 1984; Toward Palestinian Strategy for Jerusalem, 1998; Palestinian Perspectives, 1999; Editor: Abu-Shusheh Village, 1995; Biet

Jibreen Village, 1995; Biet-Nabala Village, 1998; Translator: The Death of a Little Girl and Other Stories, 1980; Gorbachev, MC, Perestroika – For Us and The World, 1990. Honours: Assistant Professor, 1973; Associate Professor, 1999. Memberships: Palestinian National Council, 1987-; Central Committee, Palestinian People's Party, 1982-98; Vice-President, Board of Trustees, Arab Thought Form, Jerusalem, 1998-; Board of Trustees, Applied Research Institute, Jerusalem, 1999-; Board of Trustees, Palestinian Human Rights Monitoring Group, 2000. Address: Bethlehem University, Frier Street, PO Box No 9, Bethlehem, Palestine. E-mail: wshmustafa@yahoo.com

MUSTEATA Gheorghe, b. 26 May 1937, Riscani, Moldova. Doctor; Surgeon; Assistant Professor. m. Larisa Musteata, 1 son. Education: MD Degree, Medical Diploma with Honours, General Medicine Department, 1955-61; Medical Education Programme, Speciality of Surgery, Chair of Faculty Surgery, 1962-63; Postgraduate Course on Surgery, PhD Degree, Doctor of Sciences in Medicine Diploma, Chair of Faculty Surgery, 1963-65, Chisinau State Medical Institute, Moldova. Appointments: Assistant Professor, Chair of Surgery No 2; Vice-Dean, Clinical Department, Vice-Dean, General Medicine Department, till 2000; State Medical and Pharmaceutical University "N. Testemitanu". Publications: 80 articles and abstracts in national and international peer-reviewed periodicals; 9 innovations. Honours: "N. Testemitanu" Medal, University Senate; Medal for "Development of Virgin Lands", Supreme Council. Memberships: Moldavian Scientific Surgery Society; Scientific Council of the General Medicine Department, State Medical and Pharmaceutical University "N. Testemitanu"; Methodical Committee on Surgery of the Ministry of Health. Address: Testemitanu St II, Apt 49, 2025 Chisinau, Republic of Moldova. v_musteata@hotmail.com

MUSTEATA Larisa, b. 30 December 1948, Calarasi, Moldova. Doctor; Haematologist; Assistant Professor. m. Gheorghe Musteata, 1 son. Education: MD Degree, Medical Diploma with Honours, General Medicine Department, Chisinau State Medical Institute, Moldova, 1966-72; Fellowship Postgraduate Course, Chair of Haematology, Central Institute for Postgraduate Medical Education, Moscow, Russia, 1977; PhD Degree, Doctor of Sciences in Medicine Diploma, Central Institute of Haematology and Transfusion Medicine, Moscow, Russia, 1988. Appointments: Assistant Professor, Education Chief, Chair of Haematology and Oncology, State Medical and Pharmaceutical University "N. Testemitanu"; Head of the 1st Haematology Department, Member, Specialized Scientific Council, Institute of Oncology of Moldova. Publications: 115 articles and abstracts in national and international peer-reviewed periodicals; 26 innovations; 1 invention; Combined Chemotherapy-Radiotherapy in I – IIE Stages of non-Hodgkin's Lymphomas, 1997; Primary Gastric MALT-Lymphomas, 2000. Honours: Diplomas of Honour, University Senate and Institute of Oncology. Memberships: Moldavian Scientific Society of Haematology and Transfusion Medicine; Moldavian Scientific Society of Oncology; Specialized Scientific Council, Institute of Oncology of Moldova; Methodical Committee on Haematology, Ministry of Health. Address: Institute of Oncology, Division of Haematology/State Medical and Pharmaceutical University "N. Testemitanu", Chair of Haematology and Oncology, Testemitanu St 30, 2025 Chisinau, Republic of Moldova. E-mail: v_musteata@hotmail.com

MUTINDA Charles John Masaku, b. 22 December 1958, Kenya. Research Scientist. m. Cyndy Kenyajui, 2 sons, 1 daughter. Education: BSc, Agriculture, University of Nairobi, Kenya, 1980-84; MSc, Genetics and Plant Breeding, University of Wales, Aberystwyth, Wales, 1987-89; PhD, Genetics and Plant Breeding, University of Nairobi, Kenya, 1992-96; Numerous postgraduate

courses include: Diploma, Maize Improvement, Elbatan, CIMMYT Headquarters, Mexico, 2001. Appointments: Assistant Agricultural Officer II, Ministry of Agriculture and Livestock Development, 1984-87; Assistant Maize Breeder, Kenya Agricultural Research Institute, 1984-87 (on secondment); Assistant Agricultural Officer I, Ministry of Agriculture and Livestock Development, 1987; Research Officer II (Maize Breeder), 1987-89, Research Officer I (Maize Breeder), 1989-97, Senior Research Officer, 1997-, Kenya Agricultural Research Institute. Publications: 16 articles as co-author in professional scientific journals and presented at conferences including most recently: performance of pigs maintained on QPM and ordinary maize, 2002; Accelerated technology development: the case of maize varieties in moist transitional zone, 2002; Development and dissemination of improved maize cultivars in Kenya, 2002; Meeting challenges in the development and deployment of insect resistant maize using novel technologies: the Irma approach, 2003. Honours: Awards for 2 papers presented at conferences, 2002. Memberships: Plant Breeders Association of Kenya; Founder Member, ARPPIS Scholars Association; Association of African Insect Scientists; National Performance Trial and Variety Release Committees, Kenya. Address: Kenya Agricultural Research Institute, Regional Research Centre, PO Box 27, Embu, Kenya. E-mail: kariembu@salpha.co.ke

MWANZA Frederick Kamnongona, b. 20 September 1936, Patauke, Zambia. Management Consultant. m. Stella Kelie Lungu, 5 sons, 5 daughters. Education: Chartered Institute of Secretaries, now The Institute of Chartered Secretaries and Administrators, England, 1966. Appointments: First Zambian Group Company Secretary, INDECO Ltd, parent holding company of State investment in industry and commerce in various sectors of the economy; Managing Director, NIEC Ltd, Director and Chairman of its subsidiaries, 1966-75; Management Consultant, MFK Management Consultancy Services, Lusaka, Zambia, 1976-. Publications: Author, Chasing the Winds and Dependency Syndrome on Political Economy; Numerous articles to the print media on social, economic, political and religious questions. Honours: Listed in national and international biographical dictionaries. Memberships: Institute of Chartered Secretaries and Administrators; St Ignatius Parish of the Catholic Commission for Justice and Peace. Address: Luangwa House, Cairo Road, Lusaka, Zambia.

MWENDA Kenneth Kaoma, b. 5 January 1969, Livingstone City, Zambia. Lawyer; Diplomat. Education: LLB, Zambia, 1990; BCL/MPhil, Oxford, 1994, Gr Dip, LCCI, 1991; Adv Dip, IoC; AHCZ; MBA, Hull, 1995; DBA, Pacific Western, 1996; PhD, Pacific Western, 1999; DCL, Trinity; Gr Cert, Warwick, 1998; PhD, Warwick, 2000; FCI; FRSA; Rhodes Scholar; Professor of Corporate Law. Appointments: Staff Development Fellow, Lecturer in Law, University of Zambia, 1991-95; Lecturer in Law, University of Warwick, UK, 1995-98; Visiting Professor of Law, University of Miskolc, Hungary, 1997; Young Professional, Counsel, Legal Department, 1998-99; Projects Officer, 2000-2003, Senior Projects Officer, 2003-, The World Bank; Visiting Professor, University of Zambia School of Law, Lusaka, 2001-02. Publications: Books: Legal Aspects of Corporate Capital and Finance, 1999; Banking Supervision and Systemic Bank Restructuring: An International and Comparative Legal Perspective, 2000; The Dynamics of Market Integration: African Stock Exchanges in the New Millennium, 2000; Contemporary Issues in Corporate Finance and Investment Law, 2000; Zambia's Stock Exchange and Privatisation Programme: Corporate Finance Law in Emerging Markets, 2001; Banking and Micro-Finance Regulation and Supervision: Lessons from Zambia, 2002; Principles of Arbitration Law, 2003; Frontiers of Legal Knowledge: Business and Economic Law in Context, 2003; More than 60 published journal and law review articles.

Dictionary of International Biography

Honours: Law Association of Zambia Best Student in Jurisprudence Prize, 1990; Selected to World Bank's Young Professionals Programme, 1998; University of Yale Law Faculty Fellowship, 1998; International Cultural Diploma of Honour, American Biographical Institute, 2001; Outstanding Professional Award in Corporate Law, ABI, 2001; International Commendation of Achievement and Success in Corporate Law, ABI, 2001; Listed in numerous biographical dictionaries and Who's Who publications. Memberships: Fellow, Royal Society of Arts of England; Fellow, Institute of Commerce of England; International Bar Association; Law Association of Zambia; British Association of Lawyers for the Defence of the Unborn. Address: The World Bank, 1818 H Street NW, Washington DC 20433, USA. E-mail: kmwenda@worldbank.org

MYCKA Katarzyna, b. 27 October 1972, Leningrad, Russia. Musician (Marimba soloist). Education: Piano Diploma, Music School in Gdansk, Poland, 1979-85; Diploma with Distinction,1985-91; Gdansk Academy of Music, 1991-95; Postgraduate Study, Music Academy, Stuttgart, Germany, 1993-95; Studied at Mozarteum, Salzburg, Austria, 1993-98; Soloist Class, Stuttgart Music Academy, 1995-97; Master's Degree in Music. Career: Winner in numerous competitions, First Prize Opole Percussion Competition, Poland, 1991; Prize, CIEM, Geneva, 1992; First Prize and Audience Prize Solo Marimba Competition, Luxembourg, 1995; First Prize First World Marimba Competition, Stuttgart, 1996; Final Round, International Percussion Competition ARD, Munich, 1997; Scholarship for Young Artists, Rotary Club, Stuttgart, 1997; Promotional Scholarship, Foundation of the Arts, Baden Wurttemberg, 1998; Festival Artist, First World Marimba Festival, Osaka, Japan, 1998; Numerous recordings for radio and TV in Germany and Poland; Masterclasses in Germany, USA, Poland, Switzerland, Luxembourg; Concerts in USA, Japan and Europe; Soloist with Stuttgart Philharmonic, Bejin Symphony Orchestra, Rubinstein Philharmonie, Camerata Israeli, WKO Heilbronn and Vienna Chamber Orchestra. Recordings: Solo CD, Katarzyna Mycka: Marimba Spiritual, 1997; Solo CD, Katarzyna Mycka: Marimba Dance, 1999; Solo CD, Katarzyna Mycka: Marimba Concerto, 2001. Honour: Ambassador of Polish Percussive Arts, Polish Percussive Arts Society, 1999. Memberships: Percussive Arts Society, USA; Percussion Creative, Germany; Founder of the International Katarzyna Mycka Marimba Academy. Address: Bodelschwinghstr 7A, 70597 Stuttgart, Germany.

MYERS Mike, b. 25 May 1963, Toronto, Ontario, Canada. Actor; Writer. m. Robin Ruzan, 1993. Creative Works: Stage appearances: The Second City, Toronto, 1986-88, Chicago, 1988-89; Actor and Writer, Mullarkey & Myers, 1984-86; TV show, Saturday Night Live, 1989-94; Films: Wayne's World, 1992; So I Married an Axe Murderer, 1992; Wayne's World II, 1993; Austin Powers: International Man of Mystery, 1997; Meteor, 1998; McClintock's Peach, 1998; Just Like Me, 1998; It's A Dog's Life, 1998; 54, 1998; Austin Powers: The Spy Who Shagged Me, 1998; Pete's Meteor, 1999; Austin Powers: Goldmember, 2002; Shrek (Voice), 2003; Cat in the Hat, 2003; Shrek 2 (Voice), 2004. Honours: Emmy Award for outstanding writing in a comedy or variety series, 1989; MTV Music Award, 1998; Canadian Comedy Award, 2000; American Comedy Award, 2000; Blockbuster Entertainment Award, 2000; Teen Choice Award, 2000; MTV Music Award, 2003; AFI Star Award, 2003. Address: c/o Creative Artists Agency, 9830 Wilshire Boulevard, Beverly Hills, CA 90212, USA.

MYERS Theldon, b. 4 February 1927, Illinois, USA. Composer; Arranger; Music Educator. m. Christine Petty, 15 Oct 1948, 2 sons, 1 daughter. Education: BS, Northern Illinois University; MA, California State University at Fresno; DMA, Peabody Conservatory, Johns Hopkins University; Woodwind study with Emerson Both, Russell Howland, Jerome Stowell, Santy Runyon and Marcel Jean; Composition study with Sandor Veress, Stefan Grové and Arthur Bryon and with Nadia Boulanger at Conservatoire Américain, France. Career: Music Educator; Woodwind performer and recitalist, Illinois and California; Faculty Member, Music Department, Towson University, 1963-93; Professor Emeritus of Theory and Composition. Compositions: Concertino for Orchestra; String Quartet, 1966; Symphony, 1969; Clarinet Sonata; Saxophone Sonatine; The Joy of Christmas, for band; And The Lord Promised, for chorus; People, Look East, for orchestra; Concertino for Band; Toccata-Fantasy. Recordings: Configuration; Concertino for Orchestra; Symphony 1969; Elegy; Cadenza and Lament, for clarinet and band; Festival Fantasia, for organ; String Quartet, 1966; Studies for Piano; The Wind Doth Blow, piano variations; Fanfare for a New Millennium, for orchestra; Toccata, Fantasy for orchestra. Publications: Numerous compositions and arrangements for band; Compositions and arrangements for string orchestra; Compositions for chorus; Compositions for solo instruments and for chamber groups. Contributions to: Numerous journals including: Gluck's Reforms, 1973; Henry Cowell, 1975. Honours: ASCAP Standard Award, yearly since 1988; Baltimore Chamber Orchestra commission, 1987, 1996; 1999. Memberships: Phi Kappa Phi; MENC; Phi Mu Alpha; ASCAP; Susquehanna Symphony Orchestra, Board of Directors and Composer-in-Residence. Address: 604-E Squire Lane, Bel Air, MD 21014, USA.

Dictionary of International Biography

N

N'DOUR Youssou, b. 1959, Dakar, Senegal. Musician; Singer; Songwriter. Career: Member, Sine Dramatic, 1972; Orchestre Diamono, 1975; The Star Band (houseband, Dakar nightclub, the Miami Club), 1976-79; Founder, Etoile De Dakar, 1979; Reformed as Super Etoile De Dakar, 1982-; International tours include support to Peter Gabriel, US tour, 1987. Recordings: Albums: A Abijan, 1980; Xalis, 1980; Tabaski, 1981; Thiapathioly, 1983; Absa Gueye, 1983; Immigres, 1984; Nelson Mandela, 1985; The Lion, 1989; African Editions Volumes 5-14, 1990; Africa Deebeub, 1990; Jamm La Prix, 1990; Kocc Barma, 1990; Set, 1990; Eyes Open, 1992; The Best Of Youssou N'Dour, 1994; The Guide, 1995; Gainde - Voices From The Heart Of Africa (with Yande Codou Sene), 1996; Immigrés/Bitim Rew, 1997; Inedits 84-85, 1997; Hey You : The Essential Collection, 1988-1990; Best of the 80's, 1998; Special Fin D'annee Plus Djamil, 1999; Joko: From Village to Town, 2000; Batay, 2001; Le Grand Bal, Bercy, 2000; Le Grand Bal 1 & 2, 2001; Birth of a Star, 2001; Et Ses Amis, 2002; Nothing's in Vain, 2002; Hit Single: Seven Seconds, duet with Neneh Cherry, 1995; How Come Shakin' the Tree, 1998; Recorded with: Paul Simon, Graceland, 1986; Lou Reed, Between Thought and Expression, 1992; Otis Reading, Otis! The Definitive Otis Reading, 1993; Manu Dibango, Wafrika, 1994; Cheikh Lo, Ne La Thiass, 1996; Alan Stivell, I Dour, 1998. Address: Youssou N'Dour Head Office, 8 Route des Almadies Parcelle, BP 1310, Dakar, Senegal. E-mail: yncontact@yahoo.fr Website: www.youssou.com

NABADE Mohammad Kabir, b. 11 November 1960, Birnin Kebbi, Nigeria. Architect. m. Saratu Ibrahim and Maryam Ibrahim, 5 sons, 3 daughters. Education: BSc (Hons), Architecture, 1985; MSc, Architecture, 1988. Appointments: Pupil Architect, 1985; Assistant Lecturer, 1988, Senior Lecturer, 1992, Director, 1994, Deputy Rector, 1996, Rector, 1999-, Waziki Umaru Polytechnic, Birnin Kebbi, Kebbi State, Nigeria. Publications: Active and Passive Design Principles in Solar Architecture and Building Performance Overview of Energy Utilisation and Biogas Digester; Emerging Issues and Challenges, Design and Construction of 10m³ Biogas Digester. Honours: Merit Award, Youth Council, NASU; NANS (Norai West); MESA Rotaract; NACES. Memberships: ANIA; MARCHES; MNIM; MNISEARTH; FICEN. Address: Waziki Omaru Polytechnic, Birnin Kebbi, PMB 1034 Birnin Kebbi, Kebbi State, Nigeria.

NAGARJUNA Settivari, b. 10 May 1961, Somala, Andhra Pradesh, India. Metallurgist. m. Kusuma Latha, 21 October 1988, 1 son, 1 daughter. Education: BTech, Metallurgical Engineering, 1984; PhD, Metallurgical Engineering, 1996. Appointments: Engineer Trainee, M/S Mishra Dhatu Nigam Ltd, 1984-85; Scientist, Defence Metallurgical Research Laboratory, 1985-. Publications: several technical papers in international reputed journals. Honours: Young Metallurgist Award, Government of India, 1991; Best Technical Paper Award, Director, Defence Metallurgical Research Laboratory, 1996; Listed in several Who's Who publications. Memberships: Life Member, Indian Institute of Metals; Life Member, Materials Research Society of India. Address: Defence Metallurgical Research Laboratory, Kanchanbagh-PO, Hyderabad 500058, India.

NAGASHIMA Hideki, b. 28 November 1963, Matsue, Japan. Orthopedic Surgeon. m. Kiyoe, 3 sons. Education: MD, Tottori University School of Medicine, 1982-88; PhD, Tottori University Graduate School of Medicine, 1990-94. Appointments: Resident, Orthopedic Surgery, 1988-89, Assistant Professor, Department of Orthopedic Surgery, Faculty of Medicine, 1994-, Tottori University; Visiting Professor, Miami Project to Cure Paralysis, University of

Miami, School of Medicine, USA, 1998. Publications: 15 articles in professional medical journals. Memberships: The Japanese Orthopedic Association; The Japan Spine Research Society. Address: Department of Orthopedic Surgery, Faculty of Medicine, Tottori University, 36-1 Nishi-Machi, Yonago, Tottori 683-8504, Japan. E-mail: hidekin@grape.med.tottori-u.ac.jp

NAGATSUKA Ryuji, b. 20 April 1924, Nagoya, Japan. Professor; Writer. m. 20 July 1949. Education: Graduated, French Literature, University of Tokyo, 1948. Appointments: Professor, Nihon University, 1968-. Publications: Napoleon tel qu'il était, 1969; J'étais un kamikaze, 1972; George Sand, sa vie et ses oeuvres, 1977; Napoleon, 2 volumes, 1986; Talleyrand, 1990. Contributions to: Yomiuri Shimbun. Honours: Prix Pierre Mille, 1972; Prix Senghor, 1973. Membership: Association Internationale des Critiques Littéraires, Paris. Address: 7-6-37 Oizumigakuen-cho, Nerima-ku, Tokyo, Japan.

NAGY Gergely, b. 9 June 1957, Budapest, Hungary. Architect. Education: Architectural Faculty, Technical University, Budapest, 1981, Postgraduate Degree, Protection of Architectural Monuments, 1987; PhD, Theory of Architecture, 1994. Appointments: Leading Designer, 1981-97, Part Section Leader, 1984-91, Section Leader, 1991-97 (Planning Office of Budapest); Director, Manager, Pannonterv, 1997-. Publications: Our Garden City, The Wekerle, 1994; Market Halls in Budapest, 1997; Garden Cities in Europe –Wekerle Estate, 1997; Central Market Hall in Budapest, Hüvösvölgy, 1999; Inner City - Budapest, 2002; World Heritage Sites of Hungary, 2003; Famous Hungarian Architects, 2004. Memberships: Secretary General, National Committee of ICOMOS of Hungary; Chamber of Hungarian Architects; Association of Hungarian Architects; Scientific Association of the Building Industry. Commissions and Creative Works: Reconstruction of Wekerle Garden City, 1987-92 Reconstruction of Architectural Monuments: Reconstruction of Central Market Hall, Budapest, 1992-94; Reconstruction of Apponyi Castle in Högyész-Thermal Hotel, 1999-2000; New Buildings: Agricultural Laboratory Building, 1987-90; Office Building, Budapest, 1986-90; Frama Envelope Factory, Budapest, 1996-97; Residential Building, Budapest, 1997-98; Citroën Showroom and Service, Budapest, 2000. Address: 1114 Budapest XI, Szabolcska u 7, Hungary.

NAHYAN Zayed bin Sultan an- (Sheikh), b. 1926. Ruler of Emirate of Abu Dhabi. m. Appointments: Appointed as personal representative to Ruler of Abu Dhabi (his brother), Al Ain, 1946; Ruler of Abu Dhabi, 1966-; President, Federation of United Arab Emirates, 1971-; Helped establish Gulf Co-operative Council. Address: Presidential Palace, Abu Dhabi, United Arab Emirates.

NAIPAUL V(idiadhar) S(urajprasad) (Sir), b. 17 August 1932, Chaguanas, Trinidad. Author. m. (1) Patricia Ann Hale, 1955, deceased 1996, (2) Nadira Khannum Alvi, 1996. Education: Queen's Royal College, Trinidad; BA, Honours, English, University College, Oxford, 1953. Publications: Novels: The Mystic Masseur, 1957; The Suffrage of Elvira, 1958; Miguel Street, 1959; A House for Mr Biswas, 1961; Mr Stone and the Knights Companion, 1963; The Mimic Men, 1967; A Flag on the Island, 1967; In a Free State, 1971; Guerrillas, 1975; A Bend in the River, 1979; The Enigma of Arrival, 1987; A Way in the World, 1994. Other: The Middle Passage, 1962; An Area of Darkness, 1964; The Loss of El Dorado, 1969; The Overcrowded Barracoon, and Other Articles, 1972; India: A Wounded Civilization, 1977; The Return of Eva Perón, 1980; Among the Believers, 1981; Finding the Centre, 1984; A Turn in the South, 1989; India: A Million Mutinies Now, 1990; A Way in the World, 1994; Beyond Belief: Islamic Excursions Among the Converted Peoples, 1998; Letters Between a Father and Son, 1999; Reading and Writing: a Personal

Dictionary of International Biography

Account, 2000; Half a Life, 2001. Contributions to: Journals and magazines. Honours: John Llewelyn Rhys Memorial Prize, 1958; Somerset Maugham Award, 1961; Hawthornden Prize, 1964; W H Smith Award, 1968; Booker Prize, 1971; Honorary Doctor of Letters, Columbia University, New York City, 1981; Honorary Fellow, University College, Oxford, 1983; Honorary DLitt, University of Cambridge, 1983, University of Oxford, 1992; Knighted, 1990; British Literature Prize, 1993; Nobel Prize for Literature, 2001. Memberships: Royal Society of Literature, fellow; Society of Authors. Address: c/o Gillon Aitken Associates, 29 Fernshaw Road, London SW10 0TG, England.

NAKAMURA Shigehisa, b. 4 October 1933, Nagasaki. Scientist (Geophysics). Education: BSc, 1958, MSc, 1960, DEng, 1976, Kyoto University. Appointments: Kyoto University, 1963-97; Senior Visiting Fellow, University of Hawaii, USA, 1978; Visiting Scientist, CSIRO, Perth, Australia, 1980-81; Director, Shirahama Oceanographic Observatory, Kyoto University. Publications: Two books and The Planetary Earth in the 21st Century, 1999. Honours: Prix de la Franco-Japonaise Sociéte d'Oceanographie, 1983. Memberships: IBA; ABI; AGU; PACON International. Address: Famille Villa A-104, Minato, Tanabe 646-0031, Japan.

NAKAMURA Tsukasa, b. 28 November 1926, Yamanashi Prefecture, Japan. Professor Emeritus. m. Miyoji Sakamoto, 1 son, 1 daughter. Education: Bachelor of Arts, Yamanashi Normal School, Kofu, Japan, 1947; Master of Science, Tokyo University of Literature and Science, Tokyo, Japan, 1950; Doctor of Science, Tokyo University of Education, Tokyo, Japan, 1969. Appointments: Professor, Faculty of Education, Councillor, 1983-87, Director, University Library, 1987-89, Yamanashi University, Kofu, Japan; Director, Kofu Study Center, University of the Air, Kofu, 1994-97. Publications: Book: Birds of Yamanashi, 1977; Articles in scientific journals include: Migratory activities in caged Emberiza rustica exposed to different artificial lights and temperatures; Influence of Photoperiod Duration on Fecal Androgen Content in Migratory Reed Bunting Emberiza schoeniclus and Non-Migratory Meadow Bunting Emberiza civides Males, 1996. Honours: Japan Ornithology Prize, Ornithological Society of Japan, 1969; Prince Hitachi Prize, Japanese Association for the Protection of Birds, 1989; Yamashina Yoshimaro Prize, Yamashina Institute for Ornithology, Chiba Japan, 1994. Address: 1286-2 Yamamiya, Kofu, Yamanashi Prefecture, 400-0075 Japan. E-mail: tnaka@ccn.yamanashi.ac.jp

NAKASHIMA Toshio, b, 6 September 1920, Japan. Professor. m. Sumiko Asakura, 1 son, 1 daughter. Education: DAgric, Hokkaido University, 1952; Exchange Program, University of Massachusetts, USA, 1959-60. Appointments: Assistant, Faculty of Agriculture, 1950, Lecturer, 1959, Assistant Professor, 1961, Professor, 1972-84, Member of University Senate, 1977-79, Hokkaido University; Professor, Hokkaido Musashi Women's Junior College, 1984-93. Publications: Over 50 scientific papers on ecology of Scarabaeidae and Ambrosia beetles; New Applied Entomology, textbook; Photographic Explanation of the Habits of Several Ambrosia Beetles, textbook. Honours: Emeritus Professor, Hokkaido University, 1984; The Order of the Rising Sun, 3rd Class, The Emperor of Japan, 1995. Memberships: Japanese Society of Applied Entomology and Zoology; Past Member of Senate, Japanese Society of Applied Entomology and Zoology, The Entomological Society of Japan; Japanese Society of Sericultural Science; Vice-Chairman, Drainage Canal of Chitose River; Past Vice-Chairman, Development of Tokachi River; Committee of Environmental Impact Assessment on Otarunai Dam. Address: D-206 Fureaino Machi, Noukendai, 3-51-1, Kanazawa-Ku, Yokohama, 236-0057, Japan.

NAKASHIMA Tsutomu, b. 22 March 1950, Ichinomiya City, Japan. Professor of Otorhinolaryngology. m. Mikiko, 1 son, 1 daughter. Education: Graduate, Nagoya University School of Medicine, 1974. Appointment: Professor of Otorhinolaryngology, Nagoya University School of Medicine, Japan, 1994-. Publication: Disorders of cochlear blood flow, 2003. Address: Department of Otorhinolaryngology, Nagoya University School of Medicine, 65, Tsurumaincho, Shomo-ku, Nagoya 466-8550, Japan.

NAKATA Yukifumi, b. 20 October 1930, Japan. Vascular Surgeon. m. Koyuki Suguro, 3 daughters. Education: Nagoya Medical Department, 1957; Doctor of Medicine, 1967. Appointments: Lecturer, Nagoya University Medical Department, 1979; Subdirector, Prefectural Owari Hospital, 1980; Director, Nagoya Quarantine, 1988; Director, Meitou Senior Health Institution, 1998. Publications: Vascular lesions due to obstruction of the vasa vasorum, 1966; An experimental study on the vascular lesions caused by obstruction of the vasa vasorum, 1967; Onset and clinicopathological course in Buerger's disease, 1976. Honour: The Fourth Order of Merit, Japan, 2001. Memberships: International Cardiovascular Society; Japanese College of Angiology. Address: 470-0154 Aichiken Aichigun, Tougou Cho, Wagougaoka 2-15-6, Japan.

NAKIB Khalil Adib, b. 10 August 1944, Sidon, Lebanon. Assistant Professor. m. Joumana Shammaa', 1 son, 1 daughter. Education: BA, Public Administration, American University of Beirut, 1966; Master of Public Administration, New York University, USA, 1968; PhD, Public Administration, Florida State University, USA, 1972. Appointments: Executive Director, Lebanon Family Planning Association, 1973-76; Lecturer and Assistant Professor, American University of Beirut, 1976-80, 1986-; Lecturer in Management, The Lebanese University, 1976-77, 1979-80, 1985-87; Lecturer in Management, Beirut University College, 1977-78, 1986-94; Technical Specialist, 1977-84, Head of Section, 1984-90, Secretary of the Board, 1990-2003, Investment Co-ordinator, 2003-, Council for Development and Reconstruction. Publications: Bureaucracy and Development, A Study about the Lebanese Administration (in Arabic), 1976; Traditionalism and Change among Lebanese Bureaucrats, 1976. Memberships: Vice President, National Institute of Investment Guarantee, 1993-; Member, Board of Directors, Development Studies Association. Address: Yasminah Building, Jal-al-Bahr, Ras Beirut, Beirut, Lebanon. E-mail: khalilnakib@hotmail.com

NAM Charles Benjamin, b. 25 March 1926, Lynbrook, New York, USA. Demographer; Sociologist. m. Marjorie Tallant, deceased, 1 son, 1 daughter. Education: BA, Applied Statistics, New York University, 1950; MA, Sociology, 1957, PhD, Sociology, 1959, University of North Carolina. Appointments: Staff, 1950-53, Branch Chief, 1957-63, US Bureau of the Census; Professor, Florida State University, 1964-95; Professor Emeritus and Author, Research Associate, Centre for Demography and Population Health, Florida State University, 1995-. Publications: 12 books; Over 100 articles and chapters. Honours: Fellow, American Association for the Advancement of Science; Fellow, American Statistical Association. Memberships: American Association for the Advancement of Science; Population Association of America, Past President; American Statistical Association; Society for the Study of Social Biology; American Sociological Association; International Union for the Scientific Study of Population. Address: 820 Live Oak Plantation Road, Tallahassee, FL 32312-2413, USA. E-mail: charlesnam@earthlink.net

NAM Ngo Quang, b. 12 November 1942, Thai Binh, Vietnam. Painter; Writer; Poet; Architect; Journalist. m. Phan Kim Binh, 1 son, 1 daughter. Education: Diploma, 1967-73, Higher studies leading to title of Academical Painter, 1985-86, Academy of Fine Art, Prague, Czechoslovakia. Appointments: Director of Culture, President of Literature and Art, Vinh Phu Province, Vietnam, 1978-90; Director of Administrative Bureau of Culture and Information Ministry, 1990-98; Director, Fine Art Department of Vientnam, 1998-2003. Publications: Merry Day's Century (long poem), 1975; Stream and Blood (novel), 1982; Palmaceous's Forest (poem book), 1990; Refrain of a Song of Bull's Words (poem book), 1994; Charm of a Moonlight (poem and fine art book), 1999; Swan's Century Book, 2001. Honours: 17-11 Award, Academy of Fine Art, Prague, Czechoslovakia; Hung Vuong Award, Vietnam, 1985. Memberships: Fine Art Association of Vietnam; Journalists Association of Vietnam; Literature and Art of Hanoi. Address: Fine Art Department, 38 Cao Ba Quat, Quan Ba Dinh, Hanoi, Vietnam.

NAN Sheli, b. New York, USA. Pianist; Harpsichordist; Percussionist; Composer; Educator. Education: Studied with Vivian Rivkin; Juilliard School of Music; University of Wisconsin; Conservatorio Luigi Cherubini, Italy. Career: The Music Studio, 1975-; Rhythmtwisters, 1997-; Performances include: International Festival of Spanish Keyboard Music, Almeira Spain; 2 concerts of original music one on harpsichord, one on piano, Cuba, 2003; Concert "Afro-Baroque" premiered: The Historic Meeting of Queen Maria Barbara of Spain and King Odukogbe of Africa, sponsored by the San Francisco Early Music Society and the University of California at Berkeley; North American premiere of Suite: 2 Love Letters and a Prayer, Music Sources, Berkeley, California, 2004; Performance of Sarah and Hagar by the Los Angeles Jewish Symphony, 2004; Compositions: La Musica Nos Cuenta Una Historia; Sarah and Hagar for string symphony and 2 sopranos (libretto and music); 2 Love Letters and a Prayer; Over 50 other compositions for piano, harpsichord, guitar, voices, chamber music and string orchestra. Recordings: Old Age Meets New Age: Sheli Nan at the Harpsichord; Undercurrents, by The Elixirs; Heart-Felt Piano Music; Acoustic Piano Excursions; Sarah and Hagar; Music for a Vanished Tribe; The Last Gesture and Other Works for harpsichord; CD's Old Age Meets New Age: Sheli Nan at the Harpsichord; Undercurrents, by The Elixirs; Palomino: Sheli Nan plays Original Jazz and Latin Piano. Publications: The Essential Piano Teachers' Guide: The Sheli Nan Method; Bienvenidos! Welcome to the Musical World of Sheli Nan!; La Musica Nos Cuenta Una Historia; The Composers Tool Kit. Memberships: ASCAP; SFMS; Music Sources. Address: PO Box 5173, Berkeley, CA 94705, USA.

NARANG Gopi Chand, b. 1 January 1931, Dukki, Baluchistan, India. Professor. m. Manorma Narang, 9 December 1973, 2 sons. Education: Honours, 1st in 1st Class, Urdu, 1948, Honours, 1st in 1st Class, Persian 1958, Punjab University; MA, 1st in 1st Class, Urdu, 1954, PhD, 1958, Diploma in Linguistics, 1st Division, 1961, University of Delhi; Postdoctoral courses in Acoustic Phonetics and Transformational Grammar, Indiana University, USA, 1964. Appointment: Professor of Urdu Language and Literature, Delhi University, 1986-95; Acting Vice Chancellor, Jamia Millia University, 1981-82; Vice-Chairman, Urdu Academy, Delhi, 1996-99; President, Sahitya Akademi, National Academy of Letters, 2003-; Vice-chairman, National Council for Promotion of Urdu Language, 2000-; Visiting Professor, Wisconsin University, 1963-63, 1968-70; Norway University, Oslo, 1998. Publications: Karkhandari Dialect of Delhi Urdu, 1961; Puranon Ki Kahaniyan, 1976; Anthology of Modern Urdu Poetry, 1981; Urdu Afsana, Riwayat aur Masail, 1982; Safar Ashna, 1982; Usloobiyat-e-Mir, 1985; Saniha-e-Karbala bataur Sheri Istiara, 1987; Amir Khusrau ka Hindavi Kalaam, 1988; Adabi Tanqeed aur Usloobiyat, 1989; Rajinder Singh Bedi (anthology), 1990; Urdu Language and Literature: Critical Perspectives, 1991; Sakhtiyat, Pas-Sakhtiyat, Mashriqi Sheriyat, 1993; Balwant Singh (anthology), 1995;

Hindustan ke Urdu Musannifin aur Shoara, 1996; Urdu Postmodernism, a Dialogue, 1998. Honours: Padma Bhushan, Highest Civilian Award by the President of India, 1992; Sahitya Akademi Award, 1995; Rockefeller Foundation Fellowship for Residency at Belagio, Italy, 1997. Address: D-252 Sarvodaya Enclave, New Delhi 110017, India.

NARAYANAN Arumugakannu, b. 31 December 1938, Nagercoil, India. m. Kamala Devi, 2 sons, 1 daughter. Education: BSc, Chemistry, 1958; BSc, Agriculture, 1961; MSc, 1963; PhD, 1966. Appointments: Attache de Recherch, CNRS, Paris; Plant Physiologist, USAID, New Delhi; Pool Officer, TNAU, Coimbatore; Plant Physiologist, ICRISAT, Hyderabad; Professor, Crop Physiology, Acharya NGR Agricultural University, Hyderabad; Principal, Agricultural College, Bapatla; Professor, University Head, Plant Physiology; Retired; Emeritus Scientist, ICAR, Sugarcane Breeding Institute, Coimbatore; Secretary, Organic Agriculture Scientific Society for Integrated Services (OASIS). Publications: 69 articles in professional journals. Honours: Fellow, Indian Society of Plant Physiology; AP State Best Teacher Award; Academy of Agricultural Science Award. Memberships: Patron, Plant Physiology Club, APAU; Member, Indian Society of Plant Physiology; Member, Society of Plant Physiology and Biochemistry. Address: D No 19, Phase 5 Maharani Ave, Vadavalli, Coimbatore 641041, Tamil Nadu, India. E-mail: prof_narayanan_a@hotmail.com

NARAYANAN Kocheril Raman, b. 27 October 1920, Uzhavoor, Kottayam, Kerala, India. President of India. Education: MA, Engl Literature, University of Travancore; BSc, Economics, 1st class honours, London School of Economics. Appointments: Lecturer, University of Travancore, 1943; Journalist, The Hindu, Madras & Times of India, Bombay; Indian Foreign Service, 1949, serving in Indian Embassies in Rangoon, Tokyo, London, Canberra and Hanoi; Educator, Economic Administration, Delhi School of Economics, 1954-55; Joint Director, Orientation Centre for Foreign Technicians; India's Ambassador to Thailand, 1967-69, Turkey, 1973-75, China, 1976-78; Secretary, Ministry of External Affairs, 1976, retired; Vice Chancellor, Jawaharlal Nehru University, 1979-80; India's Ambassador to USA, 1980-84; MP, 1985-92; Union Minister of State for Planning, 1985, External Affairs, 1985-86, Science and Technology, Atomic Energy, Space, Electronics and Ocean Development and Vice-President, Council of Science and Industrial Research, 1986-89; Vice-President of India, 1992-97; President of India, 1997-2002. Publications include: India and America: Essays in Understanding; Images and Insights; Non-Alignment in Contemporary International Relations. Honours: Several honorary degrees. Memberships include: President, Indian Council for Cultural Relations, Indian Institute of Public Administration, Ramakrishna Mission Institute of Cultures, Calcutta; Patron, International Award for Young People, India. Address: Office of the President, Rashtrapati Bhavan, New Delhi 110 004, India.

NARMANIA Vladimer, b. 18 February 1952, Zugdidi, Georgia. Mathematician. m. Maia Kiria, 1 son, 1 daughter. Education: Graduate, Moscow Lomonosov State University, 1975; Candidate Degree, Physics and Mathematical Science, 1981. Appointments: Scientist, Tbilisi Institute of Mathematics, Georgia, 1981-89; Chief Employee, Georgian Scientific Academy, Samegrelo Region, 1989; Docent, Mathematics Department, Tbilisi State University, Zugdid Branch, 1996. Publications: Articles published in the journals of the Georgian Scientific Academy. Honours: Listed in Who's Who publications and biographical dictionaries; Nominee, 21st Century Award for Achievement, International Scientist of the Year 2002, International Biographical Centre. Address: Samegrelo Regional Scientific Centre, 4 David Agmashenebeli St, 2100 Zugdidi, Georgia. E-mail: tekle3@rambler.ru

Dictionary of International Biography

NAROTZKY Norman David, b. 14 March 1928, Brooklyn, New York, USA. Artist. m. Mercedes Molleda, 10 March 1957, 2 daughters. Education: High School of Music and Art, New York City, New York, 1941-45; Art Students League, New York City, 1945-49; BA, Brooklyn College, 1949; Cooper Union Art School, New York City, 1949-52; Atelier 17, Paris, 1954-56; Kunstakademie, Munich, 1956-57; New York University Institute of Fine Arts, 1957-58; BFA, Cooper Union Art School, 1979. Appointments: 53 solo exhibitions in Europe and USA. Creative Works: Group shows at Brooklyn Museum; National Gallery, Oslo; Salon de Mai and Salon des Réalités Nouvelles, Paris; VI Bienal Sao Paulo, Brazil; Museum of Modern Art, New York; Baltimore Museum of Art; San Francisco Museum of Art; Whitney Museum of Art, New York; Palazzo Strozzi, Florence; Haus Der Kunst, Munich; Fundació Miro, Barcelona; Work in the collection of museums in Europe and USA. Publications: 9 original colour etchings for limited edition artist's book, The Raven, by Edgar Allan Poe; Several articles in professional journals and magazines. Honours: Cooper Union Award for Excellence in Graphic Arts, 1952; Award, Texas Watercolor Society, San Antonio, Texas, 1954; Wooley Foundation Fellowship, 1954; French Government Fellowship, 1955; Fulbright Fellowship, 1956; Philadelphia Museum Purchase Prize, 1956; 1st Prize, Hebrew Educational Society, Brooklyn, 1959; Award, 2nd Mini Print International Cadaques, 1982; Painting Grant, Generalitat de Catalunya, 1983; Grand Prize, II Bienal D'Art Fc Barcelona, 1987; Listed in national and international biographical dictionaries. Memberships: Art Students League, New York; Cercle D'Art Sant Lluc, Barcelona; Catalan Association of Visual Artists. Address: Putxet 84, 08023 Barcelona, Spain. E-mail: narotzky@compuserve.com Website: www.narotzky-art.com

NASCIMENTO Marcelino Pereira do, b. 1 August 1962, Brazil. Mechanical Engineer. m. Adriana Aparecida Palandi do Mascimento. Education: Graduated in Mechanical Engineering, 1991; Master of Science, 1999; Doctor of Mechanical Engineering, 2003. Appointments: Specialist on effects of surface treatments such as shot peening process, electroless nickel/hard chromium electroplating and welding process on the structural integrity of high strength steels used in aircraft. Publications: Articles in scientific journals and presented at conferences including: Plating and Surface Finishing, 2001; Surface and Coating Technology, 2001; International Journal of Fatigue, 2001; Materials Research, 2002; SAE Brazil International Conference on Fatigue, 2001; Eighth International Fatigue Congress, 2002; 14th European Congress on Fatigue, 2002. Honours: First Time Author Award Plating and Surface Finishing, Abner Brenner Award, American Electroplaters and Surface Finishers, 2001; Silver Medal Award for Outstanding Paper published in Plating and Surface Finishing, Abner Brenner Award, American Electroplaters and Surface Finishers, 2001. Membership: Brazilian Society of Materials Research. Address: State University of São Paulo, 333 Ariberto Pereira da Cunha Ave, Guaratinguetá City, São Paulo State, Brazil. E-mail: pereira@feg.unesp.br Website: www.feg.unesp.br

NASIR Babar Murad, b. 25 October 1955, Karachi, Pakistan. Consultant. Education: BSc, 1st Class Honours, Electronics, 1975, D Phil, 1979, University of Sussex, England. Appointments: Lecturer, University of Ibadan, Nigeria, 1979-80; Principal System Analyst, NWDB, Nigeria, 1981; Researcher A, University of Greenwich, England, 1984-86; Postdoctoral Research Fellow, King's College, University of London, England, 1986-88; Research Fellow, Birkbeck College, University of London, 1989-90. Publications: Sole author 1994-98 of: 14 Colloquium Digest Articles, IEE; 1 UK Patent; 4 International conference proceedings articles. Honours: Nominated Man of the Year 2003, American Biographical Institute; Nominated as recipient of American Medal of Honor, 2003; Listed in Who's Who publications and biographical dictionaries. Membership: IEE. Address: 14 Cool Oak Lane, London NW9 7BJ, England. E-mail: bmnasir@talk21.com

NASR Seyyed Hossein, b. 7 April 1933, Tehran, Iran. University Professor. m. Soussan Daneshvary, 1 son, 1 daughter. Education: BS, MIT, 1954; MSc, Harvard University, 1956; PhD, History of Science and Philosophy, 1958. Appointments: Professor of Philosophy and History of Science, 1958-79, Dean of Faculty of Letters, 1968-72, Vice Chancellor, 1970-71, Tehran University; Visiting Professor, Harvard University, 1962, 1965; Aga Khan Professor of Islamic Studies, American University of Beirut, 1964-65; President, Aryamehr University, 1972-75; Founder, 1st President, Iranian Academy of Philosophy, 1974-79; Distinguished Visiting Professor, University of Utah, 1979; Professor of Religion, Temple University, 1979-84; University Professor, The George Washington University, 1984-; A D White Professor-at-Large, Cornell University, 1991-97. Publications: Over 300 books and articles in journals throughout the world. Honours: Royal Book Award of Iran, 1963; Honorary Doctorate, University of Uppsala, 1977; Honorary Doctorate, Lehigh University, 1996; Gifford Lecturer; Volume of Living Philosophers, 2001, dedicated to Seyyed Hossein Nasr. Memberships: Institut International de Philosophie; Greek Academy of Philosophy; Royal Academy of Jordan. Address: The George Washington University, Gelman Library, 709-R, 2130 H Street, NW Washington, DC 200152, USA.

NASSAR Eugene Paul, b. 20 June 1935, Utica, New York, USA. Professor of English; Writer; Poet. m. Karen Nocian, 30 December 1969, 1 son, 2 daughters. Education: BA, Kenyon College, 1957; MA, Worcester College, Oxford, 1960; PhD, Cornell University, 1962. Appointments: Instructor in English, Hamilton College, 1962-64; Assistant Professor, 1964-66, Associate Professor, 1966-71, Professor of English, 1971-, Utica College, Syracuse University; Director, Ethnic Heritage Studies Center. Publications: Wallace Stevens: An Anatomy of Figuration, 1965, 2nd edition, 1968; The Rape of Cinderella: Essays in Literary Continuity, 1970; Selections from a Prose Poem: East Utica, 1971; The Cantos of Ezra Pound: The Lyric Mode, 1975; Wind of the Land: Two Prose Poems, 1979; Essays: Critical and Metacritical, 1983; Illustrations to Dante's Inferno, 1994; A Walk Around the Block: Literary Texts and Social Contexts, 1999; Local Sketches, 2003. Editor of several books. Contributions to: Various publications. Address: 918 Arthur Street, Utica, NY 13501, USA.

NASTASE Ilie, b. 19 July 1946, Bucharest, Romania. Tennis Player. m. (1) 1 daughter, (2) Alexandra King, 1984. Appointments: National Champion (13-14 age group), 1959, (15-16 age group) 1961, (17-18 age group) 1963, 1964; Won, Masters Singles Event, Paris, 1971, Barcelona, 1972; Boston, 1973, Stockholm, 1975; Winner, Singles, Cannes, 1967, Travemunde, 1967, 1969, Gauhati, 1968, Madras, 1968, 1969, New Delhi, 1968, 1969, Viareggio, 1968, Barranquilla, 1969, Coruna, 1969; Budapest, 1969, Denver, 1969, Salisbury, 1970, Rome, 1970, Omaha, 1971, 1972, Richmond, 1971, Hampton, 1971, Nice, 1971, 1972, Monte Carlo, 1971, 1972, Baastad, 1971, Wembley, 1971, Stockholm, 1971, Istanbul, 1971, Forest Hills, 1972, Baltimore, 1972; Madrid, 1972, Toronto, 1972, S Orange, 1972, Seattle, 1972, Roland Garros, 1973, US Open, 1973; Winner, Doubles, Roland Garros (with Ion Tiriac), 1970; Played 130 matches for the Romanian team in the Davis Cup. Publication: Breakpoint, 1986. Honours: ILTF Grand Prix, 1972, 1973; Best Romanian Sportsman of the Year, 1969, 1970, 1971, 1973. Address: Clubul Sportiv Steaua, Calea Plevnei 114, Bucharest, Romania.

Dictionary of International Biography

NATAL'IN Boris, b. 27 July 1950, Fergana, Uzbekistan, USSR. Geologist. m. Irina Natalina, 2 sons, 1 daughter. Education: MS, St Petersburg University, 1972; PhD, Far East Branch, Academy of Sciences of the USSR, 1981. Appointments: Far East Institute of Mineral Resources, 1972; Senior Researcher, Head of Department, Leading Researcher, Institute of Tectonics and Geophysics, Far East Branch of the Academy of Science of the USSR, 1973-92; Professor of Geology, Istanbul Technical University, 1992-. Publications: 70 articles; 7 maps; 3 books. Honour: Outstanding Young Scientist Diploma of the All Union Exhibition of Achievement in Industry, 1981. Memberships: Geological Society of America; American Geophysical Union; Tectonic Committee of Russia. Address: Istanbul Technical University, Maden Fakultesi, Jeoloji Bolumn, Maslak, 34446 Istanbul, Turkey.

NAUGHTIE (Alexander) James, b. 9 August 1951, Aberdeen, Scotland. Journalist. m. Eleanor Updale, 1986, 1 son, 2 daughters. Education: University of Aberdeen; Syracuse University. Appointments: Journalist, The Scotsman (newspaper), 1977-84, The Guardian, 1984-88, Chief Political Correspondent; Presenter, The World at One, BBC Radio, 1988-94, The Proms, BBC Radio and TV, 1991-, Today, BBC Radio 4, 1994-, Book Club, BBC Radio 4, 1998-. Publication: The Rivals, 2001. Honour: LLD, Aberdeen. Membership: Council, Gresham College, 1997-. Address: BBC News Centre, London W12 7RJ, England.

NAVRATILOVA Martina, b. 18 October 1956, Prague, Czech Republic (now American Citizen). Tennis Player. Career: Defected to the US in 1975, professional Player since; Titles: Wimbledon Singles, 1978, 1979, 1982, 1983, 1984, 1985, 1986, 1987, 1990; Doubles: 1976, 1979, 1982, 1983, 1984, 1985; Avon, 1978, 1979, 1981; Aust, 1981, 1983, 1985; France, 1982, 1984; US Open, 1983, 1984, 1986, 1987; Finalist at Wimbledon, 1988, 1989; Federation Cup for Czechoslovakia, 1973, 1974, 1975; 54 Grand Slam Titles (18 Singles, 37 Doubles); World Champion, 1980; Ranked No 1, 1982-85; 8 Wimbledon Titles, 1993; Women's Record for Consecutive wins, 1984; 100th Tournament win, 1985; only player to win 100 Matches at Wimbledon, 1991; Record 158 singles victories, 1992; 1,400 Victories, 1994; 167 Singles Titles, 1994; Made comeback in 2000 (in doubles only); Winner, Mixed Doubles, Australian Open, 2003 (oldest winner of a grandslam title). Appointments: President, Women's Tennis Association, 1979-80; Designs own fashionwear. Publications: Being Myself, 1985; The Total Zone (with Liz Nickles, novel, 1994); The Breaking Point (with Liz Nickles), 1996; Killer Instinct, (with Liz Nickles), 1998. Address: IMG, 1360 E 9th Street, Cleveland, OH 44114, USA.

NAZDRATENKO Yevgeny Ivanovich, b. 16 February 1949, Severokurilsk, USSR. Mining Engineer. m. Galina I Nazdratenko, 2 sons. Education: Master of Economics, Dalnevostochny Technological Institute, The Far East Technological University. Appointments: President, Vostok Mining Company, Primovskaya, Gornorudnaya Kompania, 1990-93; Governor of Primorsky Kray, 1993-2001; Chairman, State Committee for Fisheries of the Russian Federation, 2001-. Publications: Articles in various Russian newspapers and magazines. Honours: Man of the Year 2002, Russian Biographical Institute; Order, For Personal Courage; Order, For Services to the Fatherland. Membership: Member of the Board, St Andrew Apostle Foundation. Address: 12 Rozhdestvensky Blvd, Moscow 103031, Russia. Website: www.gkr.ru

NAZEM Nasser, b. 12 January 1949, Shahreza, Iran. Cardiovascular Surgeon. m. Mina Bahrami, 3 daughters. Education: MD, distinction, 1968; Speciality of General Surgery, 1980; Sub-Speciality of Cardiovascular Diseases, 1989. Appointments: Cardiovascular Surgeon, Assistant Professor, Iran Medical Sciences University; General Surgeon; Chief Editor, Journal of Cardiovascular Diseases in Iran. Publications: Several articles in professional journals. Honours include: Prize, Director of Tehran University, 1967. Memberships: Iran Medical Council; International Society of Surgeons, Japan; Iranian College of Surgeons; International Board, Journal of Current Surgery. Address: Apt 17B, Hormozan Comp Building 8, Phase 2, Hormozan Street, Shahrak-E-Gharb, 19395 Tehran, Iran.

NEAL Adrian, b. 30 June 1967, Ashby-de-la-Zouch, Leicestershire, England. University Lecturer. m. Melanie Joan. Education: BSc (Honours), Geology, University of Hull, 1985-88; MSc, Sedimentology and its Applications, 1988-89, PhD, 1990-94, University of Reading. Appointments: Lecturer, 1994-2001, Senior Lecturer, 2001-, Environmental Science, University of Wolverhampton. Publications: Numerous articles in professional scientific journals. Memberships: Fellow, Geological Society of London; European Union for Coastal Conservation; International Geographical Union Commission on Coastal Systems; Quarternary Research Association; Coastal Education and Research Foundation; British Geomorphological Research Group. Address: Grooms Cottage, The Gardens, Penylan Lane, Oswestry, Shropshire, SY10 9AA, England. E-mail: a.neal@wlv.ac.uk

NEESON Liam, b. 5 June 1952, Ballymena, Northern Ireland. Actor. m. Natasha Richardson, 1994, 1 son. Education: St Mary's Teachers College, London. Appointments: Forklift Operator; Architect's Assistant. Creative Works: Theatre includes: Of Mice and Men, Abbey Theatre Co, Dublin; The Informer, Dublin Theatre Festival; Translations, National Theatre, London; The Plough and the Stars, Royal Exchange, Manchester; The Judas Kiss; Films include: Excalibur; Krull; The Bounty; The Innocent; Lamb; The Mission; Duet for One; A Prayer for the Dying; Suspect Satisfaction; High Spirits; The Dead Pool; The Good Mother; Darkman; The Big Man; Under Suspicion; Husbands and Wives; Leap of Faith; Ethan Frome; Ruby Cairo; Schindler's List; Rob Roy; Nell; Before and After; Michael Collins; Les Misérables, 1998; The Haunting; Star Wars: Episode 1 – The Phantom Menace; Gun Shy, 1999; Gangs of New York, 2000; K19: The Widowmaker, 2002; Love Actually, 2003; TV includes: Arthur the King; Ellis Island; If Tomorrow Comes; A Woman of Substance; Hold the Dream; Kiss Me Goodnight; Next of Kin; Sweet As You Are; The Great War. Honours include: Best Actor, Evening Standard Award, 1997. Address: c/o ICM, 8942 Wilshire Boulevard, Beverly Hills, CA 90211, USA.

NEGI Gorkhu Ram, b. 1 April 1960, Suroo 15/20, India. Lecturer in Indian and European History. Education: MA, History, 1982; Postgraduate Diploma in Adult Education, 1985; MPhil, History, 1986; PhD, History, 2003. Appointments: Lecturer in History (ad-hoc), Government College, Rampur Bushahr, 1985-86; Lecturer in History (10+2), Senior Secondary School, 1986-87; Lecturer in History, College Cadre, Government Post Graduate College, Rampur Bushahr HP, 1987-. Publications: Research paper, History of Christian Missionary Activities and their Impact on Himachal Pradesh 1840-1947 AD, 1995; The Himalaya Mission with Special Reference to the Contribution of American Missionaries and Samuel Evans Stokes, 1997; The Moravian Missionaries and their contribution to the cause of tribals in Himachal Pradesh, published in the book, Tribal Development: Appraisal and Alternatives by Institute of Tribal Studies, Himachal Pradesh University, Shimla, 1998; The Moravian Brethren in India: with Special Emphasis on their Activities in the North-Western Himalayas', 2000; Christianity in Punjab: with Special Emphasis on Christian Missionaries Activities in Kangra and Lahaul, AD 1854-1940, 2002. Memberships: Life Member, Himachal Pradesh, History Congress; Life Member, American Studies Research Centre, Library Osmania

Dictionary of International Biography

University Campus, Hyderabad, India; Church History Association of India; Governing Body Member, Indian Confederation of Indigenous and Tribal People; Member, Rotary Club, Rampur Bushahr, Rotary International District 3080; Attended Conference organised by the Society for Threatened Peoples, Bonn, Germany, 1995; Visits to Netherlands, Belgium, Luxembourg. Address: Government Post Graduate College, Rampur Bushahr, District Shimla, Himachal Pradesh-172001, India.

NEGNEVITSKY Michael, b. 14 September 1956, Minsk, Russia. Electrical Engineer; Researcher; Educator. m. Svetlana, 1 son. Education: BEE, 1st class honours, 1978; PhD, 1983; MBA, 1988. Appointments: Senior Research Fellow, Senior Lecturer, Byelorussian University of Technology, Minsk, 1984-91; Senior Lecturer, Professor, University of Tasmania, Australia, 1993-. Publications: 4 books, 9 chapters in books, over 200 papers in professional journals; 4 patents for inventions. Memberships: Institution of Engineers, Australia; Institute of Electric and Electronic Engineers, USA; New York Academy of Sciences. Address: University of Tasmania, Department of Electrical and Electronic Engineering, GPO Box 252-65, Hobart 7001, Australia.

NEGRI SEMBILAN Yang di-Pertuan Besar, Tuanku Jaafar ibni Al-Marhum Tuanku Abdul Rahman, b. 19 July 1922, Malaysia. Malaysian Ruler. m. Tuanku Najihar binti Tuanku Besar Burhanuddin, 1943, 3 sons, 3 daughters. Education: Malay College; Nottingham University. Appointments: Entered Malay Administrative Service, 1944; Assistant District Officer, Rembau, 1946-47; Parti, 1953-55; Chargé d'Affaires, Washington DC, 1947; 1st Permanent Secretary, Malayan Permanent Mission to UN, 1957-58; 1st Secretary, Trade Counsellor, Deputy High Commissioner, London, 1962-63; Ambassador to United Arab Republic, 1962; High Commissioner, concurrently in Nigeria and Ghana, 1965-66; Timbalan Yang di-Pertuan Agong (Deputy Supreme Head of State), 1979-84, 1989-94; Yang di-Pertuan Agong (Supreme Head of State), 1994-99.

NEHORAI Arye, b. 10 September 1951, Haifa, Israel. Professor. m. Shlomit, 1 son, 1 daughter. Education: BSc, Technion, Israel, 1976; MSc, Technion, Israel, 1979; PhD, Stanford University, 1983. Appointments: Research Engineer, Systems Control Technology Inc, 1983-85; Assistant Professor, Yale University, 1985-89; Associate Professor, Yale University, 1989-95; Professor, University of Illinois, Chicago, 1995-. Publications: More than 80 journal papers; 100 conference papers. Honours: University Scholar, University of Illinois; IEEE Signal Processing Society Senior Award for Best Paper, 1989; Fellow, IEEE; Fellow, Royal Statistical Society; Editor in Chief, IEEE Transactions on Signal Processing, 2000-2002; Vice President, Publications, IEEE Signal Processing Society, 2003-. Memberships: IEEE; Royal Statistical Society. Address: ECE Department, University of Illinois at Chicago, 851 S Morgan Street, Chicago, IL 60607, USA. E-mail: nehorai@ece.uic.edu

NEIL Andrew, b. 21 May 1949, Paisley, Scotland. Publisher; Broadcaster; Columnist; Media Consultant. Education: MA, University of Glasgow. Appointments: Conservative Party Research Department, 1971-73; Correspondent, The Economist, 1973-83; UK Editor, 1982-83; Editor, Sunday Times, 1983-94; Executive Chairman, Sky Television, 1988-90; Executive Editor and Chief Correspondent, Fox News Network, 1994; Contributing Editor, Vanity Fair, New York, 1994-; Freelance Writer and Broadcaster, 1994-; Publisher, (Chief Executive and Editor-in-Chief), The Scotsman, Edinburgh, The European, London, Sunday Business, London, 1996-; Consultant, NBC News, 1997-; Anchorman, BBC TV's Despatch Box, ITV's Thursday Night Live; BBC Radio's Sunday Breakfast, 1998-2000; Lord Rector, University of St Andrews, 1999-2002; Fellow, Royal Society for Arts, Manufacture and Commerce. Publications: The Cable Revolution, 1982; Britain's Free Press: Does It Have One?, 1988; Full Disclosure (autobiography), 1996: British Excellence, 1999, 2000, 2001. Address: Glenburn Enterprises Ltd, PO Box 584, London SW7 3QY, England.

NEILL Sam, b. 14 September 1947, Northern Ireland. Actor. m. Noriko Watanabe, 1 daughter. 1 son by Lisa Harrow. Education: University of Canterbury. Creative Works: Toured for 1 year with Players Drama Quintet; Appeared with Amamus Theatre in roles including Macbeth and Pentheus in The Bacchae; Joined New Zealand National Film Unit, playing leading part in 3 films, 1974-78; Moved to Australia, 1978, England, 1980; TV appearances include: From a Far Country; Ivanhoe; The Country Girls; Reilly: Ace of Spies; Kane and Abel (mini-series); Submerged (film), 2001; Framed (film), 2002; Dr Zhivago (mini-series), 2002; Films: Sleeping Dogs, 1977; The Journalist; My Brilliant Career; Just Out of Reach; Attack Force Z; The Final Conflict (Omen III); Possession; Enigma; Le Sand des Autres; Robbery Under Arms; Plenty; For Love Alone; The Good Wife; A Cry in the Dark; Dead Calm; The French Revolution; The Hunt for Red October; Until the End of the World; Hostage; Memoirs of an Invisible Man; Death in Brunswick; Jurassic Park; The Piano; Sirens; Country Life; Restoration; Victory; In the Month of Madness; Event Horizon; The Horse Whisperer; My Mother Frank; Molokai; The Story of Father Damien; Bicentennial Man; The Dish, 2000; Monticello; The Zookeeper, 2001; Jurassic Park III, 2001; Dirty Deeds, 2002; Perfect Strangers, 2002. Address: c/o ICM, 8942 Wilshire Boulevard, Beverly Hills, CA 90211, USA.

NELSON Marcella May, b. 11 October 1928, Schaunavon, Saskatchewan, Canada. Retired Civil Servant. Education: High School Graduate; Extensive additional training for civil service career. Appointments: 37 years with State of Idaho; Retired from Department of Employment, 1984; Full-time Volunteer with the Chamber of Commerce and 3 arts organisations in Sandpoint, Idaho. Honours: State Employee, 1968; Chamber of Commerce Volunteer of the Month, 1987, 2000; Citizen of the Year, 1990; Retiree of the Year 1985 and 2003, International Association of Personnel in Employment Security; Woman of Distinction, Women's Forum of North Idaho, 1999; Woman of Wisdom, Sandpoint, Idaho, 2000. Memberships: Membership Co-ordinator, Chamber of Commerce; Other Membership Committees include: Government Affairs, Auction, Winter Carnival, Boat Show. Address: PO Box 54, Sandpoint, ID 83864, USA.

NELSON Nigel David, b. 16 April 1954, London, England. Journalist; Writer; Broadcaster. 3 sons, 2 daughters. Education: Sutton Valence School, Kent, England; Department of Journalism, Harlow College. Appointments: Crime Reporter, Kent Evening Post; Reporter, Daily Mail; Royal Correspondent; Daily Mail; New York Correspondent; Daily Mail; Feature Writer, TV Critic, Sunday Mirror; Political Editor, Sunday People. Publications: If I Should Die, film biography of Rupert Brooke For Burfield-Bastable Productions, 1986; The Porton Phial, a political thriller, 1991; The Honeytrap, short story, 1991. Honour: Commended, Young Journalist of the Year, 1974. Address: Sunday People, 1 Canada Square, Canary Wharf, London E14 5AP, England.

NETANYAHU Benjamin, b. 21 October 1949. Politician; Businessman. m. 3 children. Education: BSc, 1974, MSc, 1976, MIT. Appointments: Managing Consultant, Boston Consulting Group, 1976-78; Executive Director, Jonathan Institute, Jerusalem, 1978-80; Senior Manager, Rim Inds, Jerusalem, 1980-82; Deputy Chief of Mission, Israeli Embassy, Washington DC, 1982-84; Permanent Representative to UN, 1984-88, Deputy Minister of Foreign Affairs, 1988-91, Deputy Minister, PM's Office, 1991-92; Leader, Likud, 1993-99; Minister of Foreign Affairs, 2002-

03, of Finance, 2003-. Publication: A Place Among the Nations: Israel and the World, 1993; Fighting Terrorism, 1995; A Durable Peace, 2000. Address: Ministry of Finance, POB 13191, 1 Rehov Kaplan, Kiryat Ben-Gurion, Jerusalem 91008, Israel.

NETANYAHU Benzion, b. 25 March 1910, Warsaw, Poland. Historian; Educator; Editor. m. Cela Segal, 3 sons. Education: MA, Hebrew University, Jerusalem, 1933; Ph.D., Dropsie College, Philadelphia, Pennsylvania, USA, 1947. Appointments: Editor, Hebrew daily Hayarden, 1934-35; Editor, Political Library, 1936-39; Member, Jabotinsky Delegation to US, 1940; Head, public campaign and political activities, New Zionist Organisation of America, 1941-48; General Editor, Editor-in-Chief, ten volumes, Encyclopaedia Hebraica, 1949-62; Professor of Modern Hebrew Literature and Medieval Jewish History, Dropsie College, 1962-68; Professor of Jewish History and Hebrew Literature, Denver University, 1968-71; Professor of Judaic Studies, Cornell University, 1971-78; Professor Emeritus, Judaic Studies, 1978-. Publications include: Max Nordau, 4 studies, 1937-54; Theodor Herzl, two studies, 1937, 1962; Israel Zangwill, 1938; Leo Pinsker, 1944; Vladimir Jabotinsky, 3 Studies, 1981-2004; Don Isaac Abravanel: Statesman and Philosopher, 1953, 1998; The Marranos of Spain, 1966, 1999; The Cabbalistic Works ha-Kanah and ha-Peliah, 1975; The Origins of the Inquisition in Fifteenth Century Spain, 1995, 2001; Toward the Inquisition: Essays on Jewish and Converso History in Late Medieval Spain, 1998; The Old-New Controversy about Spanish Marranism, 2000; Causas y fines de la Inquisición española, 2001; The Founding Fathers of Zionism, 2004; Numerous editorial works. Memberships: American Academy for Jewish Research, Fellow, 1965-; Real Academia de Bellas Artes y Ciencias Históricas de Toledo, Académico; The University of Valladolid, Doctor Honoris Causa, 2001. Address: 4 Haportzim Street, Jerusalem 93662, Israel.

NETHERLANDS, HRH Prince of the (Bernhard Leopold Frederik Everhard Julius Coert Karel Godfried Pieter), Prince zur Lippe-Biesterfeld, b. 29 June 1911, Germany. m. Juliana Louise Emma Marie Wilhelmina, 4 daughters. Education: University of Lausanne; University of Munich; University of Berlin. Appointments include: Member, State Council; Chief Netherlands Liaison Officer with British Forces; Colonel later Major-General, Chief of Netherlands Mission to War Office; Supreme Commander, Netherlands Armed Forces, 1944; Council for Military Affairs of the Realm; Member, Joint Defence Army, Admiralty & Air Force Councils; Inspector-General, Armed Forces; Administrative General, Royal Netherlands A F General (Army), 1954-78; Honorary Air Marshal, RAF, 1964; Honorary Commander, NZAF, 1973; Member of Board, Netherlands Trade and Industries Fair; Founder, Regent, Prince Bernhard Fund for the Advancement of Arts and Sciences, Netherlands; Regent Praemium Erasmianum Foundation; Founder President, World Wildlife Fund International. Memberships include: President, World Wildlife Fund, Netherlands, Rhino Rescue Trust; Chair, Achievement Board, ICBP; Honorary Member, Royal Aeronautical Society, Royal Institute of Naval Architects, Aeromedical Society, Royal Spanish Academy. Address: Soestdijk Palace, Baarn, Netherlands.

NETTER Petra S, b. 1 April 1937, Hamburg, Germany. Professor of Psychology. m. Karl Joachim Netter. Education: Diploma in Psychology; Medical Exam as Physician; PhD, Psychology; MD, Medicine; Habilitation. Appointments: Research Fellow, Medical Statistics, 1968-75; Associate Professor of Psychology, University of Düsseldorf, 1975-77; Associate professor and Section Head of Medical Psychology, University of Mainz, 1977-79; Full Professor of Personality Psychology, University of Giessen, 1979-. Publications: 180 in different psychological, psychiatric and neuroscience journals; Co-editor, Anxiety and Psychotropic Drugs (book in German). Honour: Honorary Member, German Society

of Psychophysiology. Memberships: CINP; EBPS; ISSID; EAPP; AGNP; DGPA; DGPs; DGPM; Biological Psychiatry Germany. Address: Department of Psychology, University of Giessen, Otto Behaghel-strasse 10F, D 35394, Giessen, Germany. E-mail: petra.netter@psychol.uni-giessen.de

NEUBAUER Peter B, b. 5 July 1913, Krems, Austria. Psychoanalyst. Education: MD, 1938; Child Analyst, 1964. Appointments: Clinical Professor of Psychiatry, New York University, 1970-; Former Director, Child Development Center; Chairman Emeritus, Center for Psychoanalytic Training and Research. Publications: Numerous articles in professional journals. Memberships: Sigmund Freud Gesellschaft, Vienna; Sigmund Freud Archives; American Psychoanalytic Association; International Psychoanalytic Association; American Academy of Child Psychiatry. Address: 33 East 70th Street, New York, NY 10021, USA.

NEUFELD Karl H, b. 16 February 1939, Warendorf, Germany. Professor of Theology. Education: Lic phil, 1965, Lic Theol, 1970, Lyon-Fouvière; Dr theol, Catholic Institute of Paris, 1975; Dr theol habil, Innsbruck University, 1980; Dr phil, München-Hochschule für Philosophie, 1983. Appointments: Assistant of K Rahner, 1971-73; Professor of Theology, Rome Pont University Gregoriana, 1978-1989; Professor of Theology, Innsbruck, 1990-. Publications: Books and articles about French Theology; Studies about the work of Ad Von Harnack, Philosophy and Theology, History of Thought and History of Theology, Theology of Religions. Honours: Honorary member, Direct Committee of Istituto di Scienze Religiouse, Trento, Italy. Memberships: ASS Internationale Card Henri de Lubac, Paris; German Cercle of Theologians, Dt Hochschulverband. Address: Sillgasse 6, P'fach 569 A- 6021, Innsbruck, Austria.

NEVES A Ferdinando Dos Santos, b. 13 October 1932, Porto, Portugal. University Professor. m. Rita Ciotta Neves, 2 sons. Education: MA, Philosophy and Theology, 1953-59; Doctor in Philosophy, 1980; Doctor in Applied Social Sciences, 1983. Appointments: Professor, University of Paris, 1973-79; Professor, University of Lisbon, 1973-79; Founder, Professor and Rector, Universidade Lusofona de Humanidades e Tecnologias, Lisbon, 1991-. Publications include: Ecumenismo en Angola, 1968; Negritude e Revolicão en Angola, 1973; As Colonias Portugueses e o sen Futuro, 1974; Para una Critica da Razão Lusofona: Onze Teses Sobre a Lusofonia, 2000; Introducão as Pensamento Contemporanes, 1997. Address: Universidade Lusofona de Humanidades e Tecnologias, Av Campo Grande, 376-1749-024, Lisbon, Portugal. E-mail: reitoria@@ulusofona.pt Website: www.ulusofona.pt

NEW Anthony Sherwood Brooks, b. 14 August 1924, London, England. Retired Architect; Writer. m. Elizabeth Pegge, 11 April 1970, 1 son, 1 daughter. Education: Northern Polytechnic School of Architecture, 1941-43, 1947-51. Publications: Observer's Book of Postage Stamps, 1967; Observer's Book of Cathedrals, 1972; A Guide to the Cathedrals of Britain, 1980; Property Services Agency Historic Buildings Register, Vol II (London), 1983; A Guide to the Abbeys of England and Wales, 1985; New Observer's Book of Stamp Collecting, 1986; A Guide to the Abbeys of Scotland, 1988. Memberships: Society of Antiquaries, fellow; Royal Institute of British Architects, fellow; Institution of Structural Engineers. Address: 45A Woodbury Avenue, Petersfield, Hants, GU32 2ED, England

NEWELL Mike, b. 1942, St Albans, England. Film Director. m. Bernice Stegers, 1979, 1 son, 1 daughter. Education: University of Cambridge. Appointments: Trainee Director, Granada TV, 1963. Creative Works: TV work includes: Big Breadwinner Hog (series),

1968; Budgie (series); Thirty Minute Theatre and other TV plays; Director, European Premiere of Tennessee Williams' The Kingdom of the Earth, Bristol Old Vic; Films: The Man in the Iron Mask, 1976; The Awakening, 1979; Bad Blood, 1980; Dance with a Stranger, 1984; The Good Father, 1985; Amazing Grace and Chuck, 1986; Soursweet, 1987; Common Ground, 1990; Enchanted April, 1991; Into the West; Four Weddings and a Funeral, 1994; An Awfully Big Adventure, 1994; Donnie Brasco, 1997; Pushing Tin, 1998; Photographing Fairies (executive producer), 1997; 200 Cigarettes, 1999; Best Laid Plans, 1999; High Fidelity, 2000; Traffic, 2000. Honours include: BAFTA Award, Best Director, 1995. Address: c/o ICM, Oxford House, 76 Oxford Street, London, W1N 0AX, England.

NEWING Peter, b. 10 May 1933, Littlebourne, Canterbury, England. Clerk in Holy Orders. m. Angela Newing. Education: Cert Ed, Birmingham, Worcester College of Education, 1953-55; BA and Long Prize (Proxime Accesit), St John's College, Durham, 1960-65; B Ed, Bristol University, 1976; BSc, State University of New York, USA, 1985; Ed D, Pacific Western University, USA, 1988; Diploma, Religious Studies, Cambridge University, 1991. Appointments: National Service, RAF, London, 1951-53; Science Teacher, Bedfordshire County Council, 1955-60; Curate of Blockley with Aston Magna, 1965-69; Deacon, 1965, Priest, 1966, Gloucester; Priest in Charge of Taynton and Tibberton, 1969-75; Lecturer, Gloucestershire College of Arts and Technology, University of Gloucestershire, 1972-82; Tutor, Open University, 1975-76; Rector of Brimpsfield, Elkstone and Syde, 1975-95; Rector of Brimpsfield, Daglingworth, The Duntisbournes, etc., 1995-2001; Curate of Redmarley, Bromesberrow, Dymock etc., 2001-03; Honorary Curate, 2003-. Publications: Pamphlet, The Literate's Hood and Hoods of the Theological Colleges of the Church of England, 1959; Various articles on church bells. Honours: Fellow Society of Antiquaries, Scotland, 1959; Fellow Royal Society of Arts, London, 1960; Fellow The College of Preceptors, London, 1995. Memberships: Bishop of Gloucester's Visitor to Church Schools, 1976-94; Member of Court, University of Bristol, 1977-; Member, Gloucester Diocesan Synod, 1982-2001, re-elected 2003-; Member, Gloucester Diocesan Board of Finance, 1982-; Member, Gloucester Diocesan Board of Patronage, 1985-93, 2001-; Member, Panel of Advisers Incumbents (Vacation of Benefices) Measure 1977, 1985-; Member, Central Council of Church Bellringers, 1985-. Address: The Rectory, Albright Lane, Bromesberrow, Ledbury, Herefordshire HR8 1RU, England.

NEWKIRK Herbert William, b. 23 November 1928, Jersey City, New Jersey, USA. Materials Scientist. m. Madeleine Dorothy, 2 sons, 1 daughter. Education: AA, Pre-Engineering, Jersey City Junior College, 1948; BSc, Polytechnic Institute of Brooklyn, 1951; PhD, Ohio State University, 1956. Appointments: Chemist, General Electric, Hanford Research Laboratories, 1956-59; Chemist, RCA, David Sarnoff Research Center, 1959-60; Group Leader, Materials Scientist, Lawrence Livermore National Laboratory, 1960-92; Consultant and Participating Guest, Environmental Restoration Division, Lawrence Livermore National Laboratory; Visiting Research Professor, Aachen Technical Institute and Philips Laboratories, Aachen, Germany, Philips Laboratories, Eindhoven, Netherlands, 1969-71. Publications: Over 50 publications and articles on various topics of materials science; 2 inventions. Honours: First Prize and Best of Show – Ceramographic Exhibit, American Ceramic Society, 1965; Research and Development 100 Magazine Award for Technologically Most Significant Invention, 1991; William L Dickinson High School Scholastic Hall of Fame, 2001. Memberships: American Association of Crystal Growth; Treasurer, Northern California Section; Phi Lambda Upsilon; Sigma Xi Fraternity. Address: 1141 Madison Avenue, Livermore, CA 94550, USA. E-mail: newkirk01@aol.com

NEWMAN Jay, b. 28 February 1948, Brooklyn, New York, USA. Philosophy Professor. Education: BA, Brooklyn College, 1968; MA, Brown University, 1969; PhD, York University, 1971. Appointments: Lecturer, 1971-72, Assistant Professor, 1972-77, Associate Professor, 1977-82, Professor of Philosophy, 1982-, University of Guelph. Publications: Non-Fiction: Foundations of Religious Tolerance, 1982; The Mental Philosophy of John Henry Newman, 1986; Fanatics and Hypocrites, 1986; The Journalist in Plato's Cave, 1989; Competition in Religious Life, 1989; On Religious Freedom, 1991; Religion vs Television: Competitors in Cultural Context, 1996; Religion and Technology: A Study in the Philosophy of Culture, 1997; Inauthentic Culture and Its Philosophical Critics, 1997; Biblical Religion and Family Values, 2001. Honours: Several grants; Distinguished Alumnus Award, Brooklyn College, 1988. Memberships: Royal Society of Canada, fellow; Canadian Theological Society, president, 1990-91. Address: 313-19 Woodlawn Road East, Guelph, Ontario N1H 7B1, Canada.

NEWMAN John Kevin, b. 17 August 1928, Bradford, Yorkshire, England. Classics Educator. m. Frances M Stickney, 8 September 1970, 1 son, 2 daughters. Education: BA, Lit Humaniores, 1950, BA, Russian, 1952, MA, 1953, University of Oxford; PhD, University of Bristol, 1967. Appointments: Classics Master, St Francis Xavier College, Liverpool, 1952-54, Downside School, Somerset, 1955-69; Faculty, 1969-, Professor of Classics, 1980-, University of Illinois, Urbana; Editor, Illinois Classical Studies, 1982-87. Publications: Augustus and the New Poetry, 1967; The Concept of Vates in Augustan Poetry, 1967; Latin Compositions, 1976; Golden Violence, 1976; Dislocated: An American Carnival, 1977; Pindar's Art, 1984; The Classical Epic Tradition, 1986; Roman Catullus, 1990; Lelio Guidiccioni, Latin Poems, 1992; Augustan Propertius, 1997; Co-author with A V Carozzi, Horace-Bénédict de Saussure, 1995; De Saussure on Geography, 2003. Honours: Silver Medals, Vatican, Rome, for original Latin Poems 1960, 1962, 1965, 1997. Membership: Senior Common Room, Corpus Christi College Oxford, 1985-86. Address: 703 West Delaware Avenue, Urbana, IL 61801, USA.

NEWMAN Nanette, b. Northampton, England. Actress. m. Bryan Forbes, 2 daughters. Education: Italia Conti School; Royal Academy of Dramatic Art. Appointments: Varied Career in Films, Stage and TV. Creative Works: Appearances in Films including: The Wrong Box; The Stepford Wives; The Raging Moon; International Velvet; The Endless Game; The Mystery of Edwin Drood; Talk Show, The Fun Food Factory; TV Series, Stay With Me Till Morning; Comedy Series, Let There Be Love, Late Expectations. Publications: God Bless Love, That Dog, The Pig Who Never Was, Amy Rainbow, The Root Children; The Fun Food Factory; Fun Food Feasts; My Granny Was a Frightful Bore; The Cat Lovers Coffee-Table Book; The Dog Lovers Coffee-Table Book; The Cat and Mouse Love Story; The Christmas Cookbook; Pigalev; The Best of Love; Archie; The Summer Cookbook; Small Beginnings; Bad Baby; Entertaining with Nanette Newman and Her Two Daughters Sarah and Emma; Charlie The Noisy Caterpillar; Sharing; Cooking for Friends; Spider the Horrible Cat; There's A Bear in the Bath; A Bear in the Classroom; Take 3 Cooks; To You With Love, 1999; Up to the Skies and Down Again, 1999; Bad Baby Good Baby, 2002. Honours include: Best Actress Award, Variety Club; Best Actress, Evening News. Address: Chatto & Linnit Ltd, 123 King's Road, London SW3 4PL, England.

NEWMAN Paul, b. 26 January 1925, Cleveland, USA. Actor. m. (1) Jacqueline Witte, 1949, 1 son (deceased 1978), 2 daughters, (2) Joanne Woodward, 1958, 3 daughters. Education: Kenyon College; Yale University School of Drama. Appointments: Military Service, 1943-46. Creative Works: Stage appearances include: Picnic, 1953-54; Desperate Hours, 1955; Sweet Bird of Youth,

1959; Baby Want a Kiss, 1964; Films include: The Rack, 1955; Somebody Up There Likes Me, 1956; Cat on a Hot Tin Roof, 1958; Rally Round the Flag, Boys, 1958; The Young Philadelphians, 1958; From the Terrace, 1960; Exodus, 1960; The Hustler, 1962; Hud, 1963; The Prize, 1963; The Outrage, 1964; What a Way to Go, 1964; Lady L, 1965; Torn Curtain, 1966; Hombre, 1967; Cool Hand Luke, 1967; The Secret War of Harry Frigg, 1968; Butch Cassidy and the Sundance Kid, 1969; WUSA, 1970; Pocket Money, 1972; The Life and Times of Judge Roy Bean, 1973; The Mackintosh Man, 1972; The Sting, 1973; The Towering Inferno, 1974; The Drowning Pool, 1975; Buffalo Bill and the Indians, 1976; Silent Movie, 1976; Slap Shot, 1977; Absence of Malice, 1981; The Verdict, 1982; Harry and Son (director), 1984; The Color of Money, 1986; Fat Man and Little Boy, 1989; Blaze, 1989; Mr and Mrs Bridge, 1990; The Hudsucker Proxy, 1994; Nobody's Fool, 1994; Message in a Bottle, 1999; Director: Rachel, Rachel, 1968; The Effect of Gamma Rays on Man in the Moon Marigolds, 1973; The Shadow Box, 1980; When Time Ran Out, 1980; Fort Apache: The Bronx, 1981; The Glass Menagerie, 1987; Super Speedway, 1997; Where the Money Is, 1998; Twilight, 1998; Where the Money Is, 2000; The Road to Perdition, 2001. Honours include: Best Actor, Academy of Motion Pictures, Arts and Sciences, 1959, 1962, 1964; Honorary Academy Award, 1986. Address: Newman's Own Inc, 246 Post Road East, Westport, CT 06880, USA.

NEWMAN TURNER Roger, b. 29 April 1940, Radlett, Hertfordshire, England. Naturopath; Osteopath; Acupuncturist. m. Birgid Rath, 1 son, 1 daughter. Education: ND (Naturopathic Diploma) and DO (Diploma in Osteopathy), 1963; BAc, 1973, British College of Acupuncture. Appointments: Private practice, Naturopathy, Osteopathy and Acupuncture, 1963-; Editor, British Journal of Acupuncture, 1982-93; Trustee, Tyringham Foundation, 1985-; President, British Acupuncture Association, 1990-92; Chairman, Research Council for Complementary Medicine, 1993-97, Trustee, 1983-; Served on many committees and editorial boards for complementary and integrated medicine. Publications include: Diets to Help Control Cholesterol, 1973; Naturopathic Medicine, 1984, 2000; Hay Fever Handbook, 1988; Banish Back Pain, 1989; Editorial advisor and contributor to various encyclopaedias of natural health care including Readers Digest; Numerous journal articles. Memberships: General Council and Register of Naturopaths; General Osteopathic Council; Fellow, British Acupuncture Council. Address: 1 Harley Street, London W1G 9QD, England. E-mail: roger@naturomed.co.uk

NEWTON-JOHN Olivia, b. 26 September 1948, Cambridge, England. Singer; Actress. m. Matt Lattanzi, 1984, 1 daughter. Career: Moved to Australia, aged 5; Singer in folk group as teenager; Local television performer with Pat Carroll; Winner, National Talent Contest, 1964; Singer, actress, 1965-; Represented UK in Eurovision Song Contest, 1974; Music For UNICEF Concert, New York, 1979; Film appearances include: Grease, 1978; Xanadu, 1980; Two Of A Kind, 1983; It's My Party, 1995; Sordid Wives, 1999; Own clothing business, Koala Blue, 1984-. Recordings: Albums: If Not For You, 1971; Let Me Be There, 1974; Music Makes My Day, 1974; Long Live Love, 1974; If You Love Me Let Me Know (Number 1, US), 1974; Have You Ever Never Been Mellow, 1975; Clearly Love, 1975; Come On Over, 1976; Don't Stop Believin', 1976; Making A Good Thing Better, 1977; Greatest Hits, 1978; Grease (film soundtrack), 1978; Totally Hot, 1979; Xanadu (film soundtrack), 1980; Physical, 1981; 20 Greatest Hits, 1982; Olivia's Greatest Hits Vol 2, 1983; Two Of A Kind, 1984; Soul Kiss, 1986; The Rumour, 1988; Warm And Tender, 1990; Back To Basics: The Essential Collection 1971-92, 1992; Gaia - One Woman's Journey, 1995; More than Physical, 1995; Greatest Hits, 1996; Olivia, 1998; Back with a Heart, 1998; Highlights from the Main Event, 1999; Greatest Hits: First

Impressions, 1999; Country Girl, 1999; Best of Olivia Newton John, 1999; Love Songs: A Collection: Hit singles include: If Not For You, 1971; What Is Life, 1972; Take Me Home Country Roads, 1973; Let Me Be There, 1974; Long Live Love, 1974; If You Love Me (Let Me Know), 1974; I Honestly Love You (Number 1, UK), 1974; Have You Never Been Mellow (Number 1, US), 1975; Please Mr Please, 1975; Something Better To Do, 1975; Fly Away, duet with John Denver, 1976; Sam, 1977; You're The One That I Want, duet with John Travolta (Number 1, US and UK, third-best selling single in UK), 1978; Summer Nights, duet with John Travolta (UK Number 1, 9 weeks), 1978; Hopelessly Devoted To You (Number 2, UK), 1978; A Little More Love, 1979; Deeper Than The Night, 1979; I Cant Help It, duet with Andy Gibb, 1980; Xanadu, with ELO (Number 1, UK), 1980; Magic (Number 1, US), 1980; Physical (US Number 1, 10 weeks), 1981; Make A Move On Me, 1982; Heart Attack, 1982; Twist Of Fate, from film soundtrack Two Of A Kind, 1983; Back with a Heart, 1998; Grease (Remix), 1998; I Honestly Love You, 1998; Physical Remix 1999, 1999. Honours include: OBE; Grammy Awards: Record of the Year, 1974; Best Country Vocal Performance, 1974; Best Pop Vocal Performance, 1975; Numerous American Music Awards, 1975-77, 1983; CMA Award, Female Vocalist Of Year (first UK recipient), 1975; Star on Hollywood Walk Of Fame, 1981; Numerous other awards from Record World; Billboard; People's Choice; AGVA; NARM; Goodwill Ambassador, UN Environment Programme, 1989. Address: MCA, 70 Universal City Plaza, North Hollywood, CA 91608, USA.

NG Choi-Keung, b. 1 August 1948, Hong Kong. Cardiac Surgeon. m. Paula Völlenklee, 2 sons, 1 daughter. Education: Doctorate of Medicine, General Surgery Board Certified, Cardiac Surgery Board Certified, Associate Professor of Cardiac Surgery, University of Innsbruck, Austria. Appointments: Cardiac Surgery Consultant, University of Innsbruck, Austria, 1984; Cardiac Surgery Consultant, University Hospital, Singapore, 1987-88; Cardiac Surgery Consultant, University Hospital, Zurich, Switzerland, 1989-90; Cardiac Surgery Consultant and Department Deputy Head, General Hospital Wels, Austria, 1990-; Vice-President, International College of Angiology, 2003-. Publications: Clinical research in Electrophysiology of cardiac arrhythmias and treatments; Article: Mitral valve valvuloplasty techniques have been presented in numerous top journals; Book: Modern Mitral Valve Repair, 2003. Honour: Award, Austrian Society of Cardiology, 1991. Memberships: Austrian Society of Cardiovascular and Thoracic Surgery; European Society of Cardiology; International Society for Heart Transplantation; American Heart Association; New York Academy of Science; International Society of Cardiac-Thoracic-Surgeons. Address: Hunterterweg 9-D, A-4600 Wels, Austria. E-mail: choi.keung.ng@liwest.at

NGAN KEE Warwick D, b. 27 September 1960, New Zealand. Professor; Medical Practitioner. m. Rosemary Rainbow, 1 son, 3 daughters. Education: BHB, 1982; MBChB, 1985; FANZCA, 1993; MD, FHKCA, 1996;FHKAM (Anaesthesiology), 1996; MD, 1998. Appointment: Professor, Department of Anaesthesia and Intensive care, The Chinese University of Hong Kong. Publications: Over 70 articles in peer-reviewed medical journals. Honour: Gilbert Brown Prize, Australian and New Zealand College of Anaesthetists, 1997. Memberships: Treasurer, Obstetric Anaesthesia Society of Asia and Oceania; Executive Member, Obstetrics Special Interest Group, Australian and New Zealand College of Anaesthetists. Address: Department of Anaesthesia and Intensive Care, The Chinese University of Hong Kong, Shatin, Hong Kong.

NGOKA Uzochukwu Anozie, b. 29 July 1969, Owerri, Imo State, Nigeria. Electrical Engineer. m. Helen Victory Anyanwu. Education: Bachelors of Engineering, Electrical and Electronics

Engineering, Federal University of Technology, Owerri, Nigeria, 1986-91; Industrial Training: Production Department, Golden Guinea Breweries Ltd, Umuahia, 1988; Transmitter Department, Imo Broadcasting Corporation, 1989; Instrument and Telecoms Department, Port Harcourt Refining Company, 1990. Appointments: Access Control Systems, El-ethel Tech Co, Port Harcourt, 1996; Project Engineer, El-ethel Tech Co Ltd, 1998-; Consultant: Bonnedo Engineering Ltd; Chedeyo Ventures Ltd; International Consolidated Ltd; Numerous research works, projects and inventions developed. Honours: Indigenous Innovators Grant Loan. Memberships: Nigerian Society of Engineers. Address: 146 Royce Road, PO Box 6440, Owerri, Imo State, Nigeria. E-mail: uzngoka@yahoo.co.uk

NGUYEN Huy Sinh, b. 10 May 1952, Hung Yen, Vietnam. Professor of Physics; Teacher; Researcher. 2 sons. Education: Graduated, Eötvös Loránd Scientific University, Budapest, Hungary, 1974; PhD, Physics, Vietnam National University, 1990. Publications: 74 papers in scientific journals in physics, -2003. Memberships: International Union of Crystallography Society (IUce); New York Academy of Sciences. Address: Cryogenic Laboratory, Vietnam National University, 334 Nguyen Trai, Thanh Xuan, Hanoi, Vietnam. Email: nhsinh@netnam.vn

NGUYEN Toan Khoa, b. 20 November 1956, Nha Trang, Vietnam. Catholic Priest. Education: Bachelor of Theology, 1991; Master of Theology, 1998. Appointments: Parish Priest, St Joseph's Church, Belmore, New South Wales, Australia; Priest-in-Charge, Vietnamese Catholic Chaplaincy; Member of College of Consultors to the Archbishop of Sydney; Member of the Council of Priests, Archdiocese of Sydney. Publications: Various articles in bulletins, newspapers and magazines. Address: 763 Canterbury Road, Belmore, NSW 2192, Australia. E-mail: tknsb67@vietcatholicsydney.net Website: www.vietcatholicsydney.net

NÍ ÚRDAIL Meidhbhín Antoin, b. 13 June 1966, Cork, Ireland. University Lecturer. m. Jürgen Uhlich. Education: BA, First Class Honours, Irish and English, 1987, Higher Diploma in Education, Irish, 1988, MA, 1991, University College, Cork, Ireland; Dr Phil, Albert-Ludwigs-Universität, Freiburg, Germany, 1997. Appointments: Tutor, Research Assistant, Albert-Ludwigs-Universität, Freiburg, Germany, 1991-96; Temporary full-time College Lecturer, Department of Early and Medieval Irish, 1996-97, Temporary full-time College Lecturer, Departments of Early and Medieval Irish and Modern Irish, 1997-98, University College, Cork, Ireland; Temporary full-time College Lecturer, Department of Modern Irish, University College, Dublin, Ireland, 1998-99; National University of Ireland Post-doctoral Fellow in Irish/Celtic Studies, 1999-2001; Scholar, School of Celtic Studies, Dublin Institute for Advanced Studies, 2001-2002; Lecturer, Department of Modern Irish, University College Dublin, 2002-. Publications: Monograph: The scribe in eighteenth- and nineteenth-century Ireland: motivations and milieu, 2000; Numerous articles in academic journals and book chapters. Memberships: The Brian Merriman Society; Eighteenth-Century Ireland Society; Early Irish Society, Trinity College, Dublin; Irish Texts Society. Address: Department of Modern Irish, John Henry Newman Building, University College Dublin, Belfield, Dublin 4, Ireland. E-mail: meidhbhin.niurdail@ucd.ie

NICHOLS John (Treadwell), b. 23 July 1940, Berkeley, California, USA. Writer; Photographer. 1 son, 1 daughter. Education: BA, Hamilton College, New York, 1962. Publications: The Sterile Cuckoo, 1965; The Wizard of Loneliness, 1966; The Milagro Beanfield War, 1974; The Magic Journey, 1978; A Ghost in the Music, 1979; If Mountains Die, 1979; The Nirvana Blues, 1981; The Last Beautiful Days of Autumn, 1982; On the Mesa,

1986; American Blood, 1987; A Fragile Beauty, 1987; The Sky's the Limit, 1990; An Elegy for September, 1992; Keep It Simple, 1993; Conjugal Bliss, 1994; Dancing on the Stones, 1999; An American Child Supreme, 2001; The Voice of the Butterfly, 2001. Address: Box 1165, Taos, NM 87571, USA.

NICHOLS Mike (Michael Igor Peschowsky), b. 6 November 1931, Berlin, Germany. Stage and Film Director. m. (1) Patricia Scot 1957, (2) Margot Callas, 1974, 1 daughter, (3) Annabel Nichols, (4) Diane Sawyer, 1988. Education: University of Chicago. Creative Works: Shows Directed: Barefoot in the Park, New York, 1963; The Knack, 1964; Luv, 1964; The Odd Couple, 1965; The Apple Tree, 1966; The Little Foxes, 1967; Plaza Suite, 1968; Films Directed: Who's Afraid of Virginia Woolf?, 1966; The Graduate, 1967; Catch-22, 1969; Carnal Knowledge, 1971; Day of the Dolphin, 1973; The Fortune, 1975; Gilda Live, 1980; Silkwood, 1983; Heartburn, 1985; Biloxi Blues, 1987; Working Girl, 1988; Postcards From the Edge, 1990; Regarding Henry, Wolf, 1994; Mike Nicholas, 1995; The Birdcage, 1998; Primary Colors, 1998; What Planet Are You From?, 2000; All the Pretty Horses, 2000; Plays Directed: Streamers, 1976; Comedians, 1976; The Gin Game, 1978; Lunch Hour, 1980; The Real Thing, 1984; Hurlyburly, 1984; Waiting for Godot, 1988; Death and the Maiden, 1992; Blue Murder, 1995; The Seagull, 2001; Producer, Annie, 1977. Honours include: Tony Awards; National Association of Theatre Owners' Achievement Award. Address: c/o Mike Ovitz, CAA, 9830 Wilshire Boulevard, Beverly Hills, CA 90212, USA.

NICHOLS Peter Richard, b. 31 July 1927, Bristol, England. Playwright. m. Thelma Reed, 1960, 1 son, 3 daughters (1 deceased). Appointments: Actor, 1950-55; Teacher, Primary and Secondary Schools, 1958-60; Arts Council Drama Panel, 1973-75; Playwright-in-Residence, Guthrie Theater, Minneapolis, 1976. Publications: Television Plays: Walk on the Grass, 1959; Promenade, 1960; Ben Spray, 1961; The Reception, 1961; The Big Boys, 1961; Continuity Man, 1963; Ben Again, 1963; The Heart of the Country, 1963; The Hooded Terror, 1963; When the Wind Blows, 1964, later adapted for radio; The Brick Umbrella, 1968; Daddy Kiss It Better, 1968; The Gorge, 1968; Hearts and Flowers, 1971; The Common, 1973. Films: Catch Us If You Can, 1965; Georgy Girl, 1967; Joe Egg, 1971; The National Health, 1973; Privates on Parade, 1983. Stage Plays: A Day in the Death of Joe Egg, 1967; The National Health, 1969; Forget-me-not Lane, 1971; Chez Nous, 1973; The Freeway, 1974; Privates on Parade, 1977; Born in the Gardens, 1979, televised, 1986; Passion Play, 1980; Poppy (musical), 1982; A Piece of My Mind, 1986; Blue Murder, 1995; So Long Life, 2000. Autobiography: Feeling You're Behind, 1984; Diary, 1969-77; 2000. Honours: Standard Best Play Awards, 1967, 1969, 1983; Evening Standard Best Comedy, Society of West End Theatre Best Comedy, Ivor Novello Best Musical Awards, 1977; Society of West End Theatre Best Musical, 1982; Tony Award, 1985; Fellow, Royal Society of Literature. Address: 22 Belsize Park Gardens, London NW3 4LH, England.

NICHOLSON Geoffrey Joseph, b. 4 March 1953, Sheffield, England. Writer. Education: MA, English, Gonville and Caius College, Cambridge, 1975; MA, Drama, University of Essex, Colchester, 1978. Publications: Street Sleeper, 1987; The Knot Garden, 1989; What We Did On Our Holidays, 1990; Hunters and Gatherers, 1991; Big Noises, 1991; The Food Chain, 1992; Day Trips to the Desert, 1992; The Errol Flynn Novel, 1993; Still Life with Volkswagens, 1994; Everything and More, 1994; Footsucker, 1995; Bleeding London, 1997; Flesh Guitar, 1998; Female Ruins, 1999; Bedlam Burning, 2000; The Hollywood Dodo, 2004. Contributions to: Ambit magazine; Grand Street; Tiger Dreams; Night; Twenty Under 35; A Book of Two Halves; The Guardian, Independent; Village Voice; New York Times Book

Review; Salon.Com. Honour: Shortlisted, Yorkshire Post 1st Work Award, 1987; Shortlisted, The Whitbread Prize, 1998. Address: c/o A P Watt, 20 John Street, London EC1N 2DR, England.

NICHOLSON Jack, b. 22 April 1937, Neptune, New Jersey, USA. Actor; Film Maker. m. Sandra Knight, 1961, divorced 1966, 1 daughter. Career: Films include: Cry-Baby Killer, 1958; Studs Lonigan, 1960; The Shooting; Ride the Whirlwind; Hell's Angels of Wheels, 1967; The Trip, 1967; Head, 1968; Psych-Out, 1968; Easy Rider, 1969; On a Clear Day You Can See Forever, 1970; Five Easy Pieces, 1971; Drive, He Said, 1971; Carnal Knowledge, 1971; The King of Marvin Gardens, 1972; The Last Detail, 1973; Chinatown, 1974; The Passenger, 1974; Tommy, 1974; The Fortune, 1975; The Missouri Breaks, 1975; One Flew Over the Cuckoo's Nest, 1975; The Last Tycoon, 1976; Goin' South, 1978; The Shining, 1980; The Postman Always Rings Twice, 1981; Reds, 1981; The Border, 1982; Terms of Endearment, 1984; Prizzi's Honor, 1984; Heartburn, 1985; The Witches of Eastwick, 1986; Ironweed, 1987; Batman, 1989; The Two Jakes, 1989; Man Trouble, 1992; A Few Good Men, 1992; Hoffa, 1993; Wolf, 1994; The Crossing Guard, 1995; Mars Attacks! The Evening Star, Blood and Wine, 1996; As Good As It Gets, 1997; The Pledge, 2000; About Schmidt, 2002; Anger Management, 2003. Honours: Academy Award, Best Supporting Actor, 1970, 1984; Academy Award, Best Actor, 1976; Cecil B De Mille Award, 1999; Kennedy Center Honor, 2001; Commander des Arts et des Lettres; Golden Globe for Best Dramatic Actor, 2003. Address: 12850 Mulholland Drive, Beverly Hills, CA 90210, USA.

NICHOLSON Michael Thomas, b. 9 January 1937, Romford, Essex, England. Foreign Correspondent. m. Diana Margaret Slater, 16 December 1968, 2 sons, 2 daughters (second adopted, 2000). Education: Leicester University MA. Appointments: Publications: Partridge Kite, 1978; Red Joker, 1979; December Ultimatum, 1981; Across the Limpoto, 1985; Pilgrims Rest, 1987; Measure of Danger, 1991; Natasha's Story, 1993. Contributions to: Economist; Daily Mail; Express; Spectator; Times; Daily Telegraph. Honour: OBE, 1991. Address: Grayswood House, Grayswood, Surrey GU27 2DR, England.

NICKERSON John Mitchell, b. 1 July 1937, Lewiston, Maine, USA. University Professor. Education: BA, The University of Maine, 1959; MA, Washington State University, 1966; PhD, University of Idaho, 1971. Appointments: Faculty Member, now Professor and Chair, Political Science/Public Administration, The University of Maine at Augusta, Maine. Publications: A Study of Policy Making: The Dynamics and Adaptability of the US Federal System; The Control of Civil Disturbance. Honours: Pi Alpha Alpha, The National Honor Society for Public Affairs and Administration; Pi Sigma Alpha, The National Honor Society for Political Science. Memberships: Academy of Political Science; American Academy of Political and Social Science Association; American Society for Public Administration. Address: The University of Maine at Augusta, 46 University Drive, Augusta, ME 04330, USA. E-mail: john.nickerson@maine.edu

NICKLAUS Jack William, b. 21 January 1940, Columbus, Ohio, USA. Professional Golfer. m. Barbara Jean Bash, 1960, 4 sons, 1 daughter. Education: Ohio State University. Career: Professional, 1961-; Winner: US Amateur Golf Championship, 1959, 1961; US Open Championship, 1962, 1967, 1972, 1980; US Masters, 1963, 1965, 1966, 1972, 1986; US Professional Golfers' Association, 1963, 1971, 1973, 1975, 1980; British Open Championship, 1966, 1970, 1978; 6 times, Australian Open Champion; 5 times, World Series winner; 3 times individual winner, 6 times on winning team, World Cup; 3 times, US representative in Ryder Cup matches; 97 tournament victories; 76 official tour victories; 58 times second, 36 times third; Won US Senior Open, USA; 136 tournament

appearances, 1996; Played in 154 consecutive majors, 1999; Designer of golf courses in USA, Europe, Far East; Chairman, Golden Bear International Inc; Captain, US team which won 25th Ryder Cup, 1983 Co-chair, The First Tee's Capital Campaign, More Than A Game, 2000. Publications: My 55 Ways to Lower Your Golf Score, 1962; Take a Tip From Me, 1964; The Greatest Game of All, autobiography, 1969; Lesson Tee, 1972; Golf My Way, 1974; The Best Way to Better Your Golf, vols 1-3, 1974; Jack Nicklaus' Playing Lessons, 1976; Total Golf Techniques, 1977; On and Off the Fairway, autobiography, 1979; The Full Swing, 1982; My Most Memorable Shots in the Majors; My Story, 1997. Honours: Athlete of the Decade Award, 1970s; Hon LLD, St Andrew's, 1984; 5 times US PGA Player of the Year; Golfer of the Century, 1988. Address: 11780 US Highway #1, North Palm Beach, FL 33408, USA.

NICKOLAYEV Nickolay, b. 9 April 1947, Latvia. Professor; Physician. m. Viya, 1 son. Education: Latvian Medical Academy, 1972; Tianjin International University of Traditional Chinese Medicine, 1989. Appointments: Head, International Training Course for Traditional Chinese Medicine; Constant Director of International Association for Integrated Medicine; Honorary Member, ICMART Scientific Committee. Publications: Over 300 scientific articles on Chinese traditional medicine; 10 monographs on medical acupuncture. Honours: President and Vice-President, Latvian Association for Medical Acupuncture and Related Techniques, ICMART; Senior Advisor, World Federation of Chinese Medicine. Memberships: ICMART; WFCM; WFAS; PEFOTS. Address: Nr 102, Dubultu Ave, Jurmala, LV-2008, Republic of Latvia. E-mail: polaris_lv@inbox.lv

NICKS Stevie (Stephanie Nicks), b. 26 May 1948, California, USA. Singer; Songwriter. Appointments: Songwriter with Lindsey Buckingham; Recorded album, Buckingham Nicks, 1973; Joined Group, Fleetwood Mac, 1973. Creative Works: Albums with Fleetwood Mac: Fleetwood Mac, 1975; Rumours, 1977; Tusk, 1979; Fleetwood Mac Live, 1980; Mirage, 1982; Tango in the Night, 1987; Behind the Mask, 1990; 25 Years - The Chain, 1992; Solo albums include: Bella Donna, 1981; The Wild Heart, 1983; Rock a Little, 1985; Time Space, 1991; Street Angel, 1994; Composer of Songs Rhiannon, Landslide, Leather and Lace, Dreams, Sara, Edge of Seventeen, If Anyone Falls (with Sandy Stewart), Stand Back (with Prince Rogers Nelson), I Can't Wait (with others), The Other Side of the Mirror, Time Space, Street Angel, Seven Wonders (with Sandy Stewart). Address: WEA Corporation, 79 Madison Avenue, Floor 7, New York, NY 10016, USA.

NICOL Donald MacGillivray, b. 4 February 1923, Portsmouth, England. Historian; Professor Emeritus. m. Joan Mary Campbell, 1950, 3 sons. Education: MA, 1948, PhD, 1952, Pembroke College, Cambridge. Appointments: Scholar, British School of Archaeology, Athens, 1949-50; Lecturer in Classics, University College, Dublin, 1952-64; Visiting Fellow, Dumbarton Oaks, Washington, DC, 1964-65; Visiting Professor of Byzantine History, Indiana University, 1965-66; Senior Lecturer and Reader in Byzantine History, University of Edinburgh, 1969-70; Koraës Professor of Modern Greek and Byzantine History, Language and Literature, 1970-88, Assistant Principal, 1977-80, Vice Principal, 1980-81, Professor Emeritus, 1988-, King's College, University of London; Editor, Byzantine and Modern Greek Studies, 1973-83; Birbeck Lecturer, University of Cambridge, 1976-77; Director, Gennadius Library, Athens, 1989-92. Publications: The Despotate of Epiros, 1957; Meterora: The Rock Monasteries of Thessaly, 1963, revised edition, 1975; The Byzantine Family of Kantakouzenos (Cantacuzenus) ca 1100-1460: A Genealogical and Prosopographical Study, 1968; Byzantium: Its Ecclesiastical

History and Relations with the Western World, 1972; The Last Centuries of Byzantium 1261-1453, 1972, 2nd edition, 1993; Church and Society in the Last Centuries of Byzantium, 1979; The End of the Byzantine Empire, 1979; The Despotate of Epiros 1267-1479: A Contribution to the History of Greece in the Middle Ages, 1984; Studies in Late Byzantine History and Prosopography, 1986; Byzantium and Venice: A Study in Diplomatic and Cultural Relations, 1988; Joannes Gennadios - The Man: A Biographical Sketch, 1990; A Biographical Dictionary of the Byzantine Empire, 1991; The Immortal Emperor: The Life and Legend of Constantine Palaiologos, Last Emperor of the Romans, 1992; The Byzantine Lady: Ten Portraits 1250-1500, 1994; The Reluctant Emperor: A Biography of John Cantacuzene, Byzantine Emperor and Monk c. 1295-1383, 1996; Theodore Spandounes: On the Origin of the Ottoman Emperors (translator and editor), 1997. Contributions to: Professional journals. Membership: British Academy, fellow. Address: 4 Westberry Court, Pinehurst, Grange Road, Cambridge, CB3 9BG, England.

NICOL Michael George, b. 17 November 1951, Cape Town, South Africa. Writer; Journalist. 1 son, 1 daughter. Education: BA, Honours, University of South Africa, 1993. Appointments: Reporter, To The Point, Johannesburg, 1974-76, The Star, Johannesburg, 1976-79; Editor, African Wildlife, Johannesburg, 1979-81; Freelance Journalist, 1981-85; Assistant to the Editor, Leadership, Cape Town, 1986-88; Writer, Journalist, 1989-. Publications: Among the Souvenirs (poetry), 1979; The Powers That Be (novel), 1989; A Good-Looking Corpse (history), 1991; This Day and Age (novel), 1992; This Sad Place (poetry), 1993; Horseman (novel), 1994; The Waiting Country (memoir), 1995; The Ibis Tapestry (novel), 1998; Bra Henry (novella for young adults), 1998; The Invisible Line: The Life and Photography of Ken Oosterbroek (biography), 1998; Sea-Mountain, Fire City; Living in Cape Town (Memoir), 2001. Contributions to: The Guardian; New Statesman; London Magazine. Honour: Ingrid Jonker Award, 1980. Address: c/o Apwatt, 20 John Street, London WC1N 2DR, England.

NICOLESCU Ovidiu, b. 10 November 1943, Ploiesti, Romania. Professor. m. Florica, 1 son, 1 daughter. Education: MBA, Academy of Economic Studies, 1966; PhD, Economic Research Institute, 1979. Appointments: Researcher, Institute of Economic Research, 1966-74; Professor, Academy of Economic Studies, 1970-2003; Director, Manager, International Management and Marketing Institute, 1990-2003; President, Romanian National Council SME's, 1992-2003. Publications: 55 books; 371 papers and articles in national and international books, journals and reviews. Honours: Virgil Madgearu Prize, Romanian Academy of Science, 1996; Medalia Didactica, International Association for Simulations and Games (ISAGA), 1990; Victor Slavescu Prize, Romanian Academy of Science, 1992; Doctor Honoris Causa, University North East, 1992; OMNIA prize for the Best Romanian Economist, 2003. Memberships: European Foundation of Entrepreneurship Research, Brussels; World Association for Case Research and Applications, USA; The University Council for Management Education Transfer, Sweden; IESE, Alumni Association, Barcelona; World Association for Small and Medium Enterprises, India; European Council for Small Business, Brussels; Union Europeene de l'Artisanat et des Petites et Moyennes Entreprises, Brussels; Academy d'Avignon for European Entrepreneurship, France. Address: Anghel Saligny nr 6, Ap 12, Bucharest, Romania. E-mail: manager@pcnet.ro

NIELSEN Ron, b. 1 November 1932, Poland. Nuclear Scientist. m. Lorna, 2 September 1982, 1 son, 1 daughter. Education: MSc; DSc. Appointments: Research Fellow, Institute of Nuclear Research, Poland, 1956-63; Research Fellow, Department of

Nuclear Physics, Australian National University, Australia, 1964-67; Fellow, Department of Nuclear Physics, Australian National University, Australia, 1967-89; Visiting Fellow, Department of Physics, Birmingham University, England, 1970-71; Visiting Professor, Laboratorium für Kernphysik, Zürich, Switzerland, 1975-76; Visiting Professor, Max-Planck-Institut für Kernphysik, Heidelberg, Germany, 1983-84; Host of regular weekly radio programmes on environmental issues and on the progress of science and technology. Publications: Numerous articles in professional journals; Books include, The 21st Century, Reaching to the Sky, 1999, 2nd Edition, 2000; The 21st Century: The Seven Thunders, 2001, 2nd Edition, 2002. Honours: Honorary Member, IBC Advisory Council; Peaceful Use of Atomic Energy Award, 1959; 20th Century Achievement Award, 1998; Millennium Medal of Honour, 2000. Memberships: Fellow, Australian Institute of Physics; Active Member, New York Academy of Sciences. Address: 4 Murdoch Place, University Shores, Robina, QLD 4226, Australia.

NIEUW AMERONGEN Arie van, Professor of Oral Biochemistry. Education: MSc, Biochemistry, 1970; PhD, Biochemistry, 1974, Vrije Universiteit, Amsterdam. Appointments: Assistant Professor, Dental Faculty, Department of Oral Biochemistry, 1974-78, Associate Professor, 1974-90, Chairman of Department, 1984, Professor of Oral Biochemistry, 1990-, Vrije Universiteit, Amsterdam; Head of the Subdepartment of Oral Biochemistry, 1984-; Chairman, Department of Basic Dental Sciences, 1999-; Chairman, Dutch Dental Research School, 2000-; Supervisor of 22 PhD Students; Organised 2 international congresses: 5th European Symposium on the Application of Saliva in Clinical Practice and Research, Egmond aan Zee, 1999; 6th European Symposium on Saliva, Egmond aan Zee, 2002 . Publications: First author, 100 papers; Co-author 140 papers; Books: Saliva and Salivary Glands, 1988; Saliva and Oral Health, 1994; Saliva and Dental Elements, 1999; Faith and Science, 2001; Saliva, Salivary Glands and Oral Health, 2003. Memberships: Member of the Editorial Boards: Journal of Dental Research, 1998-2001; Journal of Odontology, 2000-2002; 6 Patents. Address: Free University, Department of Oral Biochemistry, VD Boechorststraat 7, 1081 BT Amsterdam, The Netherlands.

NIGAM Prakash Kumar, b. 10 October 1923, Bhainsdahi, M.P. India. Electrical Engineer/Writer. m. Kanta Nigan, 2 sons, 1 daughter. Education: Bachelor of Science, Nagpur University, India, 1944; BS in Electrical Engineering, University of Wisconsin, USA, 1948. Appointments: Testing Engineer, G.E., USA, 1948-49; Electrical Engineer, Assistant Superintendent, Tata Electric Co. Bombay, India, 1950-60; Chief Power Engineer, HEC, Ranchi, India, 1968; Electrical Engineer with United Engineers, Crawford and Russel, Ebasco, New York, Commonwealth Associates, Bechtel Giffels in USA, 1968-81; Consulting Engineer, Accro and ADSC in US, 1983. Conference: Thermo Electric Plants as complement to Hydro-Electric Development in Bombay-Poona Region for World Power Conference, 1952. Publications include: Book, Reflections on History of the World in 20th Century, to be published 2004; 30 articles in newspapers, 1994-2003. Honours: Scholarship for Advance Studies in USA from J N Tata Endowment, Bombay, India. Memberships: Rotary International Club; Lions Club; A.I.E.E. Address: 43/44 Vijay Nagar Colony, Lalghati, Bhopal, India, 462032.

NIGG Joseph Eugene, b. 27 October 1938, Davenport, Iowa, USA. Editor; Writer. m. (1) Gayle Madsen, 20 August 1960, divorced 1979, 2 sons, (2) Esther Muzzillo, 27 October 1989. Education: BA, Kent State University, 1960; MFA, Writers Workshop, University of Iowa, 1963; PhD, University of Denver, 1975. Appointments: Assistant Editor, Essays in Literature, 1974-75; Associate Editor, Liniger's Real Estate, 1979-85; Fiction Editor,

Dictionary of International Biography

Wayland Press, 1985-92. Publications: The Book of Gryphons, 1982; The Strength of Lions and the Flight of Eagles, 1982; A Guide to the Imaginary Birds of the World, 1984; Winegold, 1985; The Great Balloon Festival, 1989; Wonder Beasts, 1995; The Book of Fabulous Beasts 1998; The Book of Dragons and Other Mytical Beasts. Contributions to: Various journals and magazines. Honours: Non-Fiction Book of the Year Awards, Colorado Authors League, 1983, 1985, 1989, 1996, 2003; Mary Chase Author of the Year. Memberships: Colorado Authors League; Writers Guild. Address: 1114 Clayton Street, Denver, CO 80206, USA.

NIGHY William (Bill) Francis, b. 12 December 1949, Caterham, Surrey, England. Actor. m. Diana Quick, 1 daughter. Education: St John Fischer School, Purley, Surrey, England. Career: National Theatre: A Map of the World and Skylight by David Hare; Pravda by David Hare and Howard Brenton; The Seagull by Chekov; Arcadia by Tom Stoppard; Mean Tears by Peter Gill; Blue Orange by Joe Benhall; A Kind of Alaska and Betrayal by Harold Pinter; Films: Still Crazy; Lawless Heart; Lucky Break; Love Actually; Underworld; Capture the Castle; TV: Absolute Hell; The Maitlands; The Lost Prince; The Men's Room; Numerous radio performances. Honours: Evening Standard Peter Sellars Comedy Award, 1998; Barclays Bank Theatre Award, Best Actor; BAFTA Award for Best Supporting Actor, 2004. Address: c/o Markham & Froggatt Ltd, Julian House, 4 Windmill Street, London W1P 1HF, England.

NIKOLEISHVILI Avtandil, b. 27 August 1948, Vani, Georgia. Philologist; Literary Critic. m. Manana Zivzivadze, 1 son, 1 daughter. Education: Graduated, Department of History and Philology, Kutaisi Pedagogical Institute, 1974-; PhD, Georgian Literature, 1983. Appointments: Chancellor, Kutaisi State University; Chairman, Department of Georgian Language and Literature. Publications: 25 books including 12 monographic works; 120 articles and essays published in various academic journals; 2 books of poetry. Honour: Georgian Writers' Association Award. Memberships: Gelati Research Academy; International Academic Society; Georgian Writers' Association. Address: 5 Rodzevichi Street, Kutsisi 384000, Georgia. E-mail: geo-gelati@hotmail.com

NIKS Inessa, b. 6 November 1938, St Petersburg, Russia. Piano Teacher; Musicology Teacher. m. Mikhail Niks, deceased, 1 son, 1 daughter. Education: Studied Piano, Special Music School for Gifted Children, St Petersburg, 1948-56; Master in Musicology, Diploma with Distinction, St Petersburg Conservatory, 1956-61. Career: Teacher of Musicology and Piano, Music College, Novgorod, Russia, 1961-64; Teacher of Musicology and Piano, Music School, St Petersburg, 1966-76; Head of Musicology Department, Pskov Music College, 1976-79; Owner, piano and musicology studio, Redlands, California, 1983-; Co-Founder, Niks Hand Retraining Center, 1991-. Publications: Numerous articles in specialist music journals concerning newly developed piano technique; Co-Inventor of Hand Guide, piano training device, 1991; Manual, Play Without Tension, supplement to piano training device, 1998; Manual, Type Without Tension, 2000. Honours: Silver Medal, 1983, Bronze Medal, 1984, International Piano Recording Competition; Finalist, Audio-Visual Piano, 1995. Memberships: Music Teachers' Association of California, 1983-; European Piano Teachers' Association, 1985-; The National League of American Pen Women, 2002-. Address: Niks Hand Retraining Centre, 1434 Fulbright Ave, Redlands, CA 92373, USA. Website: www.nikstechnique.com

NIMOY Leonard, b. 26 March 1931, Boston, Massachusetts, USA. Actor; Director. m. (1) Sandi Zober, 1954, divorced, 1 son, 1 daughter. (2) Susan Bay, 1988. Education: Boston College; Antioch University. Appointments: US Army, 1954-56; TV

appearances include: Star Trek, 1966-69; Eleventh Hour; The Virginian; Rawhide; Dr Kildare; Film appearances include: Old Overland Trail, 1953; Satan's Satellites, 1958; Valley of Mystery, co-producer, 1967; Catlow, co-producer, 1971; Invasion of the Bodysnatchers, co-producer, 1978; Star Trek - The Motion Picture, co-producer, 1979; Star Trek: The Wrath of Khan, co-producer, 1982; Star Trek III: The Search for Spock, Director, 1984; Star Trek IV: The Voyage Home, Director, 1986; Star Trek V: The Final Frontier, 1989; Star Trek VI: The Undiscovered Country; Director, Three Men and a Baby, 1987, The Good Mother, 1988, Funny About Love, 1990, Holy Matrimony, 1994; The Pagemaster (voice), 1994; Carpati: 50 Miles, 50 Years, 1996; A Life Apart: Hasidism in America (voice), 1997; David, 1997; Brave New World, 1998; Sinbad, 2000; Atlantis: The Lost Empire, 2001. Publications: I Am Not Spock, autobiography, 1975; We Are All Children, 1977; Come Be With Me, 1979; I am Spock, 1995. Address: c/o Gersh Agency Inc, 222 North Cannon Drive, Beverly Hills, CA 90210, USA.

NINA Jaine Manuel Simões, b. 28 November 1951, Lisbon, Portugal. Physician. m. Maria da Conceição Rogado Barão da Cunha, 1 son, 1 daughter. Education: MD, University of Lisbon, Portugal, 1975; Diploma, Higiene and Medicina Tropical, Institute of Hygiene and Tropical Medicine, Lisbon, 1979; PhD, Medicine, University of London, UK, 1995; Diploma, Research Tropical Medicine and Hygiene, University of London, UK, 1996. Appointments: Junior Resident, 1979-81, Resident, 1981-87, Hospital Egaz Moniz, 1979-81; Internal Medicine Specialist, 1987-92, Internal Medicine Consultant, 1992-93, Hospital Santarem; Invited Assistant, 1983-99, Invited Junior Professor, 1999-4, Deputy Director, 2001-2004, Clinical Division Director, 2003-, Invited Associate Professor, 2004-, Institute of Hygiene and Tropical Medicine, Lisbon, Portugal; Inf Dis Consultant, Hospital Egas Moniz, 1993-. Publications: Book chapter in Immunology and Molecular Biology of Parasitic Infections, 3rd edition; Articles in scientific journals including: Research Microbiology; Acta Tropica; VIII International AIDS Conference Abstract Book; XIV International AIDS Conference Abstract Book; International Immunology; New England Journal of Medicine. Honours: Treaty of Windsor Research Program Grant, 1988; DRTM&H, 1996. Memberships: Portuguese Medical Association; Royal Society of Tropical Medicine & Hygiene; International AIDS Society; American Association for the Advancement of Science; Associação Port Estudo Clinico Sida. Address: Director, Divisão Clinica, Instituto de Higiene & Medicina Tropical, Rua da Junqueira 96, 1349-008 Lisbon, Portugal. E-mail: jnina@ihmt.unl.pt

NIR Isaac, b. 1916, Radom, Poland (Immigrated from Poland, 1936). Professor Emeritus. m. Barbara. Education: MSc, Biology, 1936-42, PhD, Biochemistry, 1943-46, MD, Medicine, 1951-57, The Hebrew University of Jerusalem, Israel. Appointments include: Served in Haganah, 1936-46; Israeli Army, Chemed Science Troops, 1947-49; Founder and Director, Institute for Standardisation and Control of Pharmaceuticals, Ministry of Health, Jerusalem, 1953-62; Head, WHO Unit on Safety in Chemicals in Human Consumption, Geneva, Switzerland, 1957-60; Visiting Associate Professor, University of Chicago, 1963-65; Visiting Professor, 1965-70, Associate Professor, 1970-78, Head, Department of Applied Pharmacology, School of Pharmacy, 1975-76, Professor, 1978-85, Professor Emeritus, 1985-, The Hebrew University of Jerusalem; Head, Department of Clinical Pharmacology, Ministry of Health, Jerusalem, 1965-81; Scientific Consultant on Drugs, Kupat Cholim Clalit, 1966-76; Visiting Scientist, Max-Planck Institute, Göttingen, Germany, 1971-75; Visiting Scientist, NIH, Bethesda, Maryland, USA, 1981-82; Visiting Scientist, Rudolf Magnus Institute for Neurosciences, Utrecht, The Netherlands, 1983-84; Honorary Visiting Professor, Hong Kong Institute (each summer), 1984-89; Visiting Scientist,

Dictionary of International Biography

Brain Research Institute, Frankfurt, Germany, 1984. Publications: 245 scientific papers in scientific journals including as co-author: The effect of exogenous melatonin on the hypophysial-pituitary-adrenal axis in intact and prealectomised rats under basal and stress-induced conditions, 1993; The antigonadotrophic effect of melatonin in Syrian hamsters id modulated by prostaglandin, 1994; Circadian melatonin, TSH, prolactin and cortisol levels in serum of young adults with autism, 1995; Effects of long-term administration of melatonin and a putative antagonist on the ageing rat, 1995; Co-editor, 2 scientific books; Author and co-author 5 book chapters. Honours: Israel Chemical Society Prize, 1948; Annual Faculty Prize, Chicago Medical School; Israel Medical Association Prize, 1977; Hebrew University's Medal, 1986. Memberships include: Permanent Panel Member, Expert Advisory Committees on Drugs and Chemicals in use by Humans, WHO, Geneva, 1965-85; High Toxicologic Committee, Ministry of Defence, Israel, 1967-70; Scientific Committee, International Symposium on Endocrine Aspects of the Pineal Gland, Nova Scotia, 1984; International Society of Neuroendocrinology; New York Academy of Sciences; Council. European Study Group on the Pineal Gland. Address: Gelber 1, Jerusalem 96755, Israel.

NIRENBERG Marshall Warren, b. 10 April 1927, New York, New York, USA. Biochemist. Education: Graduated, Biology, 1948, Master's Degree, 1952, University of Florida; PhD, Biological Chemistry, University of Michigan, 1957. Appointments: National Institute of Health (Arthritic and Metabolic Diseases), 1957-62, Head, Laboratory of Biochemical Genetics, 1962-; Laboratory of Biochemical Genetics, National Heart, Lung and Blood Institute, Bethesda, Washington, DC; Work in deciphering the chemistry of the genetic code. Honour: Honorary Member, Harvey Society; Molecular Biology Award, National Academy of Sciences, 1962; Medal, Department of Health, Education and Welfare, 1963; Modern Medicine Award, 1964; National Medal for Science, President Johnson, 1965; Joint Winner, Nobel Prize for Physiology or Medicine, 1968; Louisa Gross Horwitz Prize for Biochemistry, 1968. Memberships: New York Academy of Sciences; AAAS; NAS; Pontifical Academy of Sciences, 1974; Deutsche Leopoldina Akademie der Naturforscher; Foreign Associate, Academy des Sciences, France, 1989. Address: Laboratory of Biochemical Genetics, National Heart, Lung and Blood Institute, Building 36, Room IC06, Bethesda, MD 20892, USA.

NISH Ian Hill, b. 3 June 1926, Edinburgh, Scotland. Retired Professor. m. Rona Margaret Speirs, 29 December 1965, 2 daughters. Education: University of Edinburgh, 1943-51; University of London, 1951-56. Appointments: University of Sydney, New South Wales, Australia, 1957-62; London School of Economics and Political Science, England, 1962-91. Publications: Anglo-Japanese Alliance, 1966; The Story of Japan, 1968; Alliance in Decline, 1972; Japanese Foreign Policy, 1978; Anglo-Japanese Alienation 1919-52, 1982; Origins of the Russo-Japanese War, 1986; Contemporary European Writing on Japan, 1988; Japan's Struggle with Internationalism, 1931-33, 1993; The Iwakura Mission in America and Europe, 1998; Japanese Foreign Policy in the Inter-War Period. Honours: Commander of the Order of the British Empire, 1990; Order of the Rising Sun, Japan, 1991. Memberships: European Association of Japanese Studies, president, 1985-88; British Association of Japanese Studies, president, 1978. Address: Oakdene, 33 Charlwood Drive, Oxshott, Surrey KT22 0HB, England.

NISHIKAWA Masao, b. 15 July 1933, Tokyo. University Professor. m. Junko Monna, 1 son. Education: Graduate, University of Tokyo, 1956; Graduate, Graduate School, University of Tokyo, 1962; Studied at the Graduate Schools of the Universities of Pennsylvania and Columbia University, 1959-62. Appointments:

Assistant, University of Tokyo, 1962-66; Professor, Tokyo Woman's Christian University, 1966-68; Professor, University of Tokyo, 1968-94, emerited, 1994-; Professor, Senshu University, 1994-2004. Publications: Der Erste Weltkrieg und die Sozialisten, 1999; Nationalisme et post-nationalisme du Japon, 2002; Numerous publications in Japanese. Honour: Viktor-Adler-Preis, Austrian State Award. memberships: AHA; HS. Address: Kichijoji Minami-cho 3-2-10, Musashino-shi, Tokyo, 180-0003 Japan. E-mail: nismamus@parkcity.ne.jp

NISHIMATSU Yuichi, b. 16 January 1932, Japan. Consultant Engineer; Professor Emeritus, University of Tokyo. m. Teiko Kawaguchi, 2 daughters. Education: Graduate, Department of Mining, University of Tokyo, 1954; DEng, University of Tokyo, 1969. Appointments: Research Engineer, Coal Research Institute, Tokyo, 1957; Professor, Department of Mining, University of Tokyo, 1976; Professor Emeritus, 1992-. Publications: Several articles in professional journals. Honours: 4 Prizes, Excellent Research Papers. Membership: Engineering Academy of Japan. Address: 31-9-1003 Honcho, Wako City, Saitama 351-0114, Japan.

NISHIMURA Akira, b. 7 February 1938, Osaka, Japan. Management Accountant. m. Junko, 2 sons. Education: Masters Degree, 1963, PhD, 1966, Graduate School of Economics, Kyoto University, Japan; Doctor of Economics, Kyushu University, 1990. Appointments: Lecturer, Osaka University of Economy, 1967; Assistant Professor, 1971, Professor, 1982, Dean of Faculty of Economics, 1996-98, Professor Emeritus, Kyushu University; Professor, Kyushu Sangyo University, 2001-. Publications: Transplanting Japanese Management Accounting and Cultural Relevance (article), 1995; Accounting in the Asia-Pacific Region (editor), 1999; Management Accounting: Feed Forward and Asian Perspectives. Honour: Awards of prominent work (book), Japanese Association of Management Accounting, 2002. Memberships: Executive Director, Japanese Association of Management Accounting; Director, International Centre for the Study of East Asian Development. Address: 7-18-8 Miwadai Higashi, Fukuoka, Japan. E-mail: anishi@ip.kyusan-u.ac.jp

NISHIMURA Hiroyuki, b. 14 February 1945, Yokohama, Japan. University Professor. m. Kikuko Nishimura, 1 daughter. Education: Bachelor of Agriculture. Tokyo Nohko University, 1967; Master of Agriculture, Department of Agricultural Chemistry, Nagoya University, 1969. Appointments: Instructor, Department of Agric Chem, Hokkaido University, 1969; Postdoctoral Fellow, Department of Chemistry, University of California, Berkeley, 1975-77; Associate Professor, Department of Agric Chem, Hokkaido University, 1988; Professor, Department of Bioscience and Technology, Hokkaido Tokai University, 1988. Publications: Vinyldithiims in Garlic and Japanese Domestic Allium (A victorialis: Chapter 9 in M Huang et al (Editors); Food Phytochemicals for Cancer Prevention I, ACS Symposium Series 546, 1994; Identification of Allelochemicals in Eucalyptus citriodora and Polygomum sachlinense: Chapter 5 in Inderjit et al Allelopathy, ACS series 582, 1993. Honour: Research Incentive Awards at Agricultural Chemical Society of Japan, 1985. Memberships: Agricultural Chemical Society of Japan; International Allelopathy Society; Solar Energy Society of Japan. Address: Department of Bioscience and Technology, School of Engineering, Hokkaido Tokai University, Sapporo 005-8601, Japan.

NISPEROS Nestor M, b. 29 April 1928, Manila, Philippines. Professor; Consultant. m. Josefina T Buenaseda, 3 sons, 2 daughters. Education: AB, Political Science, 1951, MPA, Public Administration, 1964, University of the Philippines; PhD, Public and International Affairs, University of Pittsburgh, USA, 1969.

Appointments: Chief, Research Analysis Division, National Intelligence Co-ordinating Agency, Office of the President of Manila, 1961-; Senior Executive Development Officer, Philippine Executive Academy, Faculty Member, University of the Philippines, Manila, 1964-; Seconded to Department of Foreign Affairs, National Defence; Retired, 1988-; Consultant, Strategic and International Studies and Executive Development. Publications: Philippine-Soviet Relations Policy Question, 1970; The Sabah Question, 1987; The Changing International Environment Challenge to Leadership, 1990; The Bases Question, 1990. Honours: Fellow, International Development Fellowships, East-West Center, USA, 1964-67; Fellow, National Defense College of the Philippines, 2002-; Executive Director, Executive Developments Academy, 1971-73; Delegate with full powers, Philippines-Malaysia Talks on Sabah, Bangkok, 1968. Memberships: Board Member, National Defense Course Foundation; Life Member, Upsilon Sigma Phi; Life Member, GSPIA Society, USA. Address: 28 Road 8 Corner Road 2 Extension, Project 6, Quezon City, 1100 Metro, Manila, Philippines. E-mail: nestornisperos@yahoo.com

NISSEL Siegmund (Walter), b. 3 January 1922, Munich, Germany. Violinist. m. Muriel, 5 April 1957, 1 son, 1 daughter. Education: External Matriculation, Honours Degree, London University; Private violin study with Professor Max Weissgarber until 1938, then with Professor Max Rostal in London. Debut: With Amadeus Quartet at Wigmore Hall in London, 1948. Career: Founder Member of the Amadeus Quartet; innumerable BBC Radio and TV and ITV appearances; International concert career; Quartet disbanded in 1987 after the death of the violist Peter Schidlof. Recordings: Mozart, Beethoven, Schubert and Brahms Quartets; Benjamin Britten; Brahms Sextets; etc. Honours: Honorary DMus, London and York Universities; OBE; Verdienstkreuz für Musik in Germany and Austria; Honorary LRAM. Memberships: ISM; ESTA. Address: 11 Highgrove Point, Mount Vernon, Frognal Rise, London NW3 6PZ, England.

NISTOREANU Gheorghe, b. 26 June 1946, Moinesti, Romania. University Professor of Law. m. Florenta Elena Nistoreanu, 1 daughter. Education: Bachelor of Law, 1969, Doctor's Degree, 1984, University of Bucharest; Professor of Law, Romanian Police Academy Faculty of Law, 1990; Conferred the right to supervise and direct candidates for doctor's degree, 1991. Appointments: Teaching Assistant, 1970, University Lecturer, 1976, Professor, 1990, Dean, 1992, Faculty of Law, Romanian Police Academy; Secretary of Juridical Committee, Romanian national Council for Academic Evaluation and Accreditation, 1993; Associate Professor, numerous Romanian Universities. Publications: Over 34 scientific treatises, courses of lectures and monographs: The Security Measures in Romanian Penal Law; Legal Representation in Criminal Proceedings; Penal Law (university course); Criminology; Criminal Proceedings (university course); Author of 71 studies and articles in scientific reviews. Honours: Simion Bonmutiu Award, Romanian Union of Jurists, 1998; Title of Excellency, Vasile Gololis University, Anool, Romania, 1999; V Songoroz Award, Romanian Union of Jurists, 2002. Memberships: Vice-President, Romanian Nation Group, International Association of Penal Law; Vice-President, Romanian Society of Criminology; Honorary President, ANTJ of Romania. Address: B-dul Jan Miholoche Nr 109, Bloc 134, Sc B, Et 4, Ap 61, Sector 1, Bucharest, 011 177 Romania. E-mail: bnpnistoreanu@xnet.ro

NIVARTHI Raju, b. 16 June 1964, India. Researcher. m. Aparna, 1 son, 1 daughter. Education: BS, 1984; MS, 1986; PhD, 1996. Appointments: Doctoral Fellow, School of Life Sciences, University of Hyderabad, India, 1987-93; Research Scientist, Department of Anesthesiology, New York University Medical Centre, New York, 1993-99; Scientist, Wyeth-Ayerst Research,

Pearl River, New York, 1999-2001; Senior Scientist, Manager, Bristol-Myers Squibb, Syracuse, New York, 2001-. Publications: Numerous articles in professional journals. Honours include: Junior Research Fellowship, CSIR, India, 1987, Senior Research Fellowship, 1990; Certificate of Merit, Pharmacia Biotech and Science Prize for Young Scientists, 1998; Post Doctoral Training Fellowship, National Institute of Drug and Abuse (National Institute of Health), 1998; cGMPs for Pharmaceutical QC and R and D laboratories, School of Pharmacy, University of Wisconsin, 1999; Listed in numerous Who's Who and biographical publications. Memberships: American Association for the Advancement of Science; American Chemical Society; American Society of Anesthesiologists; American Society for Biochemistry and Molecular Biology; International Anaesthesia Research Society; International Society for the Study of Xenobiotics; New York Academy of Sciences. Address: 161 North Way, Camillus, NY 13031, USA.

NIXON Colin Harry, b. 9 March 1939, Putney, London. Civil Servant (retired). m. Betty Morgan, 2 September 1967, 3 daughters. Education: Diploma in Sociology, London University, 1968. Appointments: Civil Servant, 1960-99; Disablement Resettlement Officer, 1974-83; ACAS Conciliation Officer, 1983-99. Publications: Roads, 1975; Geography of Love, 1977; With All Angles Equal, 1980; The Bright Idea, 1983; Included in anthologies: Spongers, 1984; Affirming Flame, 1989; Poetry Street 3, 1991; Red Candle Treasury, 1948-1998, 1998; The Art of Haiku 2000, 2000. Contributions to: Outposts; Tribune; Countryman; Cricketer. Honours: George Camp Memorial Poetry Prize, 1975, 1983; 1st Prize, Civil Service Poetry, 1979; Runner-up in Voting for Small Press Poet, 1986. Address: 72 Barmouth Road, Wandsworth Common, London SW18 2DS, England.

NJALSSON Gunnar Kari Alexander, b. 11 January 1968. Special Researcher in Space Law and Public Administration (IT Policy); Writer; Composer. Education: Commercial Diploma, Marketing and Accounting, Swedish Commercial College, Helsinki, Finland, 1994; Bachelor of Social Sciences with honours, Public Administration and Economics, Swedish School of Social Sciences, Helsinki, 1997; Master of Social Sciences with honours, Public Administration, University of Helsinki, 1997; Confirment of ac title politices magister, Faculty of Social Sciences, University of Helsinki, 2000; Proficiency Certificate in Spanish, English, Finnish, Norwegian, Danish and Portuguese, University of Helsinki, 2002; Postgraduate Training with honours, Science and Technology Administration, Universidad Nacional de Quilmes, Argentina, 2002; Postgraduate Certificate of Doctoral Studies with Honours, Public Administration (IT Policy), 2003, University of Helsinki; DLL, International Law (Space Law), in progress. Appointments: Various postings in the public and private sectors in the US, Mexico and Iceland, 1985-88; Assistant, Bellona Environmental Fund, Oslo, Norway, 1988; Civil Servant for Finnish State, Education and Justice Sectors, 1989-96; Economics Assistant, Leif Höegh Ltd, Oslo, Norway, 1996- 97; Economist, BMG Finland, Helsinki, 1997-99; Lecturer, Policy Evaluation and IT Policy, Swedish School of Social Sciences, Helsinki, 1998-; Founder and Patent/Trademark Holder, SPACEPOL – International Research Network for Space and IT Policy (www.spacepol.com), Espoo, Finland, 1998-; Writer, literary debut (Swedish) Finland, 1999; Governing Member, Writer's Guild of Espoo, Finland, 2000-; Expert Member (Legal), Working Group on Earth Observation, Space Affairs, Finnish Centre for Technological Development (TEKES), Helsinki, 2001-; Appointed Member, Municipal Committees on Social, Cultural and Educational Affairs for Swedish-speaking Citizens, Espoo, 2001-; Dp Member, Municipal Zoning Board, Espoo, 2001-03; Appointed Delegate, Swedish Regional Federation of Southern Finland, 2001-03; Composer, various Latin and Jazz theme song orchestrations including "Novela

Policial, Summer 1977" and "A Question of Life or Death" (often with producers Alex Ojasti and Maki Kolehmainen) 2003-; Special Researcher in Space Law, Institute of Air and Space Law, Faculty of Law, University of Lapland, Rovaniemi, Finland, 2003-; Periodic Consulting Expert, Argentine Congressional Working Group on Research and Development, Buenos Aires, 2003. Publications: Siaren (The Seer), 1999; Editorials and articles in Swedish, English, Finnish and Spanish on the subjects of IT policy, space law, welfare policy and separation of religion and state in democracies. Honours: Membership, Alpha Lambda Delta, 1985; University of Texas at El Paso, 4.0 GPA scholarship, 1986; Comradery Award, Gyllenberg-Helsingforsaftongymnasium, 1991; Nominee, City of Espoo Literary Award for novel "Siaren", 2000; Finnish Ministry of Education Literary Scholarship, 2000; Nylands Fraternity; Ella and Georg Erhnrooth, E J Sariola, Otto A Malm, Oskar Öflund and Swedish Cultural Foundation Academic Scholarships, 2000-03; Outstanding Scholar Award, IBC, 2002. Memberships: Sociedad Argentina de Analisis Politico; Nylands Nation Fraternity; Emerald Club Finland; Clan McKeown; Fellow, International Biographical Association; Finnish Union of University Researchers and Teachers; Irish Music Rights Organisation (IMRO); 98th Percentile Member, International High IQ Society; Fellow, International Institute of Space Law. Address: SPACEPOL – International Research Network for Space and IT Policy, PO Box 25, FIN-02631 Espoo, Finland.

NOAKES Vivien, b. 16 February 1937, Twickenham, England. Writer. m. Michael Noakes, 9 July 1960, 2 sons, 1 daughter. Education: MA, D Phil, English, Senior Scholar, Somerville College, Oxford. Publications: Edward Lear: The Life of a Wanderer, 1968, 4th edition, 2004; For Lovers of Edward Lear, 1978; Scenes from Victorian Life, 1979; Edward Lear 1812-1888, The Catalogue of the Royal Academy Exhibition, 1985; The Selected Letters of Edward Lear, 1988; The Painter Edward Lear, 1991; The Imperial War Museum Catalogue of Isaac Rosenberg, 1998; The Daily Life of the Queen: An Artists Diary, 2000. The Poems of Isaac Rosenberg, 2004. Contributions to: Times; Times Literary Supplement; Daily Telegraph; New Scientist; Punch; Harvard Magazine; Tennyson Research Bulletin; Memberships: Fellow, Royal Society of Literature; Member, Society of Authors; PEN. Literary Agent: Watson, Little Ltd, Capo di Monte, Windmill Hill, London NW3 6RJ, England. Address: 146 Hamilton Terrace, London NW8 9UX, England. E-mail: mail@vivien-noakes.co.uk

NOBBS David Gordon, b. 13 March 1935, Orpington, Kent, England. Writer. m. (1) Mary Jane Goddard, 18 November 1968, 2 stepsons, 1 stepdaughter, divorced 1998, (2) Susan Sutcliffe, 4 August 1998, 1 stepdaughter. Education: Marlborough College, 1948-59; BA, English, St John's College, Cambridge, 1955-58. Publications: Novels: The Itinerant Lodger, 1965; Ostrich Country, 1967; A Piece of the Sky is Missing, 1968; The Fall and Rise of Reginald Perrin, 1975; The Return of Reginald Perrin, 1977; The Better World of Reginald Perrin, 1978; Second From Last in the Sack Race, 1983; A Bit of a Do, 1986; Pratt of the Argus, 1988; Fair Dos, 1990; The Cucumber Man, 1994; The Legacy of Reginald Perrin, 1995; Going Gently, 2000; TV: The Fall and Rise of Reginald Perrin; Fairly Secret Army; A Bit of a Do; The Life and Times of Henry Pratt; Love On a Branch Line; Gentlemen's Relish. Address: 10 Iron Bridge House, Bridge Approach, London NW1 8BD, England.

NOBLE Weston H, b. 30 November 1922, Riceville, Iowa, USA. Music Educator; Band and Choir Director. Education: BA, Luther College, Decorah, Iowa, 1943; Master of Music Degree, University of Michigan, 1953. Career: Service with US Army, European Theatre, WWII, 1943-46; Director of Band and Choir, Luverne High School, Luverne, 1946-48; Department of Music Luther College, Decorah, Iowa, 1948-; Professor of Music and Director

of Choir and Band, Luther College; Guest Director at numerous festivals in 49 US States; Conductor of All-State groups in bands, choirs and orchestras; Appearances as conductor of Luther College Nordic Choir, Luther College Concert Band and festival groups at venues including: the Orchestra Hall Chicago, the Carnegie Hall and Lincoln Center, New York, the J F Kennedy Center, Washington, DC, the Music Center of Los Angeles, the Orchestra Hall, Minneapolis the Mormon Tabernacle, Salt Lake City, Bolshoi Hall, Moscow, Glinka Chapel, St Petersburg; 8 concert tours of Europe including: Norway, Romania, the former USSR, Hungary, Poland; Adjudicator, International Festival of the Three Cities, Vienna, Budapest, Prague; Band Consultant and Guest Director, Association for International Cultural Exchange, Vienna; Bridges of Song Music Festival, Tallinn, Estonia with 25,000 participants; Guest Adjudicator at the Federacao de Coros do Rio Grande do Sul, Porto Alegre, Brazil. Honours include: Honorary Doctorates: Augustana College, Sioux falls, South Dakota, 1971; St Olaf, Northfield, Minnesota, 1996; Outstanding Music Educator of the United States, National Federation of High School Associations; First Recipient, Weston H Noble Award for Lifetime Achievement in the Choral Art, North Central Division of American Choral Directors; Judge Henry and Helen Graven Award, Wartburg College, Waverly, Iowa; Presidential Award, Illinois Music Educators Association; Robert Lawson Shaw Citation, American Choral Directors Association; St Olaf Medallion awarded by the King of Norway. Address: 602 Mound, Apt 4, Decorah, IA 52101, USA.

NODA Mitsuru, b. 3 September 1956, Osaka, Japan. Psychologist. m. Mika Takeshima. Education: BA, Literature, 1983, Master in Literature (Psychology), 1985, Waseda University, Japan. Appointments: Clinical Psychologist, Itsukaich Public Health Center, 1984-92; Full-time Lecturer, 1992-, Head of the Department of Psychology, 2002-03; Dean of the First College Clusters including the Departments of Psychology, Mental Health, Health Welfare, 2004-, Edogawa University Health and Welfare Technical College, Japan; Part-time Lecturer, Rissho University, Japan, 1996-. Publications: Co-author textbook: Kukan ni kiru, 1995; Imeji no Sekai, 2001; Kodomo to Hoiku no Shinrigaku, 2003; Jikken de manabu Hattatsu shinrigaku, 2004; Human Science, 2004. Honours: Listed in Who's Who publications and biographical dictionaries. Memberships: APA; Society for Research in Child Development; Japanese Psychological Association. Address: Yachiyo TY Plaza A-206, Kayada 1057, Yachiyo-City, Chiba 276-0043, Japan.

NOGUCHI Makoto, b. 22 April 1934, Ishioka-shi, Ibaraki-ken, Japan. University Professor. m. Yoko, 3 sons, 1 daughter. Education: MA, Religious Studies, University of Tokyo, Japan, 1970; MA, New Testament, University of Durham, England, 1997. Appointments: Pastor, Ishioka Church of Christ, 1967-2004; Professor, Ibaraki Christian University, 1968-2005. Publications: Introductory Biblical Greek, 1999; A Study of ΠΡΟΩΡ?ΣΝ in Rom.8:29, 2001; The Anti-Terrorism Strategy and the Bible, 2002. Memberships: Japanese Association of Religious Studies; Japan Society of Christian Studies; Japan Society of New Testament Studies; Japan Evangelical Theological Society. Address: 4-8-10 Fuchu, Ishioka-shi, Ibaraki-ken, 315-0013 Japan.

NOLAN David Joseph, b. 27 June 1946, Boston, USA. Author, Historian. 1 son, 1 daughter. Education: University of Virginia, Charlottesville, 1963-65. Appointments: Field Secretary, Virginia Students Civil Rights Committee, 1965-66; Editor, New South Student Magazine, 1967-69; Freelance Author and Lecturer, 1969-. Publications include: Fifty Feet in Paradise The Booming of Florida, 1984; The Houses of St Augustine, 1995. Honour: Author Award from Council for Florida Libraries, 1985. Memberships: Marjorie Kinnan Rawlings Society; Fort Mose Historical Society. Address: 30 Park Terrace Drive, St Augustine, FL 32080, USA.

NOLTE Nick, b. 1942, Omaha, USA. Film Actor. m. Rebecca Linger, 1984, divorced 1995, 1 son. Education: Pasadena City College; Phoenix City College. Creative Works: Films: Return to Macon County, 1975; The Deep, 1977; Who'll Stop the Rain, 1978; North Dallas Forty, 1979; Heartbeat, 1980; Cannery Row, 1982; 48 Hours, 1982; Under Fire, 1983; The Ultimate Solution of Grace Quigley, 1984; Teachers, 1984; Down and Out in Beverly Hills, 1986; Weeds, 1987; Extreme Prejudice, 1987; Farewell to the King, 1989; New York Stories, 1989; Three Fugitives; Everybody Wins; Q & A, 1990; Prince of Tides, 1990; Cape Fear, 1991; Lorenzo's Oil, 1992; Blue Chips, 1994; I'll Do Anything, 1994; Love Trouble, 1994; Jefferson in Paris, 1994; Mulholland Falls, 1996; Mother Night, 1996; Afterglow, 1997; Affliction, 1998; U-Turn; Breakfast of Champions, 1998; The Thin Red Line, 1998; The Golden Bowl, 2000; Investigating Sex, 2001; Double Down, 2001; The Good Thief, 2003; Northfork, 2003; Hulk, 2003; Numerous TV and theatre appearances. Address: 6153 Bonsall Drive, Malibu, CA 90265, USA.

NOOR AL-HUSSEIN, H.M. Queen of Jordan, b. Lisa Najeeb Halaby, 23 August 1951. m. King Hussein I of Jordan, 1978, deceased 1999, 4 children. Education: Princeton University. Appointments: Architechtural and Urban Planning Projects, Australia, Iran, Jordan, 1974-78; Founder, Royal Endowment for Culture and Education, Jordan, 1979, Annual Arab Childrens Congress, Jordan, 1980, Annual International Jerash Festival for Culture and Arts, Jordan, 1981, Jubilee School, Jordan, 1984, Noor Al-Hussein Foundation, Jordan, 1985, National Music Conservatory, Jordan, 1986; Chair, National Task Force for Children; Advisory Committee, UN University International Leadership Academy, Amman; Patron, General Federation of Jordanian Women, National Federation of Business and Professional Womens Clubs, Royal Society for Conservation of Nature and various cultural, sporting and national development organisations. Publication: Leap of Faith: Memoirs of an Unexpected Life, 2002. Honours: Numerous honorary doctorates, international awards and decorations. Memberships include: Honorary President, Jordan Red Crescent; Founding Member, International Commission on Peace and Food, 1992; President, United World Colleges, 1995. Address: Royal Palace, Amman, Jordan.

NORBECK Jack C, b. 8 December 1940, Greensburg, Pennsylvania, USA Education: University of Connecticut, Ratcliffe Hicks School of Agriculture, 1964; Dale Carnegie, 1967; Opticians Institute, 1971. Appointment: President, Norbeck Research (educational library exhibits on steam and draft animals), 1978-; Lectured on North American steam traction engines and work horses; Owner one of largest private collections of photographs of operational steam traction engines and draft horses still working farmlands; Gymnast for the University of Connecticut. Publication: Author, The Encyclopedia of American Steam Traction Engines; 60 magazine covers; over 75 magazine articles; Over 200 photo educational exhibits world-wide. Honours: International Man of the Year, International Biographical Centre, Cambridge; Order of International Ambassadors Medal, ABI, 2000; Winner, numerous medals for proficiency on side horse; One Thousand Great Americans Medal, 2000; Gold Record of Achievement, American Biographical Institute, 2001; American Medal of Honor, American Biographical Institute 2001; Noble Prize, American Biographical Institute, 2001; Listed in biographical publications including Who's Who in Gymnastics. Memberships: Historical Steam Associations; American Society of Agricultural Engineers; The Author's Guild;

Union Historical Fire Society; YMCA; American Legion; USA Gymnastics. Address: 117N Ruch Street, 8 Coplay, PA 18037 1712, USA.

NORDLING Carl Olof, b. 16 December 1919, Helsinki, Finland. Architect. m. Margit Ester Karlsson, 2 sons. Education: Architect's Diploma, 1939; several advanced courses in Urban Planning, Statistics, Real Estate Valuation and others. Appointments: Research Assistant, Urban Planning, Royal Institute of Technology, Stockholm, 1944-47; Professor, pro tem, 1946; Consultant in Private Practice, Stockholm, 1948-53; Architect, Vattenbyggnadsbyrån, Stockholm, 1953-74; Researcher, Faktainformation A-Z, Lidingo, Sweden, 1974-. Publications include: A New Theory on the Cancer-Inducing Mechanism, 1953; Origin of a Depression, 1967; K Voprosu o tselya I zadachakh krestovogo Birgera Jarla v Finlandiyu v 1240g, 1976; Defence or Imperialism? An Aspect of Stalin's Military and Foreign Policy 1933-1944, 1984; The Death of King Charles XII – The Forensic Verdict, 1988; The Creation of Finnish and the Finns, 1995; The Finland-Swedes, 2002; In the Shade of Overlord, 2002; Scientists Against Science, 2004. Membership: Economic Union, Sweden. Address: Sporrvagen 16, S 181 41 Lidingo, Sweden. E-mail: carl.o.nordling@swipnet.se Website: http://home.swipnet.se/ nordling

NORMAN Barry Leslie, b. 21 August 1933, London, England. Writer; Broadcaster. m. Diana Narracott, 1957, 2 daughters. Appointments: Entertainments Editor, Daily Mail, London, 1969-71; Weekly Columnist, The Guardian, 1971-80; Writer and Presenter, BBC 1 Film, 1973-81, 1983-88, The Hollywood Greats, 1977-79, 1984, The British Greats 1980, Omnibus, 1982, Film Greats, 1985, Talking Pictures, 1988; Barry Norman's Film Night, BSkyB, 1998-2001; Radio 4 Today, 1974-76, Going Places, 1977-81, Breakaway, 1979-80. Publications: Novels: The Matter of Mandrake, 1967; The Hounds of Sparta, 1968; End Product, 1975; A Series of Defeats, 1977; To Nick a Good Body, 1978; Have a Nice Day, 1981; Sticky Wicket, 1984. Non-Fiction: Tales of the Redundance Kid, 1975; The Hollywood Greats, 1979; The Movie Greats, 1981; Talking Pictures, 1987; 100 Best Films of the Century, 1992, 1998; And Why Not? 2002. Thriller: The Birddog Tape, 1992; The Mickey Mouse Affair, 1995; Death on Sunset, 1998. Honours: British Association of Film and Television Arts Richard Dimbleby Award, 1981; Magazine Columnist of the Year, 1991; Honorary DLitt, University of East Anglia, 1991, University of Hertfordshire, 1996; Magazine Columnist of the Year, 1991; Commander of the Order of the British Empire, 1998. Address: c/ o Curtis Brown Ltd, Haymarket House, 28-29 Haymarket, London SW1Y 4SP, England.

NORMAN David Bruce (Percival Arthur), b. 20 June 1952, Ilfracombe, Devon, England. University Academic; Museum Director. m. Christine, 1 son, 1 daughter. Education: BSc (Hons), Microbiology and Zoology, University of Leeds, 1973; PhD, Vertebrate Palaeontology, University of London, King's College, 1977. Appointments: Royal Society European Postdoctoral Fellowship, Brussels, 1977-78; Lecturer, School of Biology, Queen Mary College, London, 1978-82; Lecturer, Brasenose College, Oxford, 1983-87; Departmental Lecturer, Department of Zoology, Oxford University, 1982-87; Honorary Research Associate, University Museum, Oxford, 1987-92; Head of Palaeontology Division, Nature Conservancy Council, 1987-92; Visiting Lecturer, Department of Zoology, University of Cambridge, 1988-91; Associate Editor, 1982-, Editor, 1989-96, Zoological Journal, Linnean Society; Visiting Lecturer, Department of Zoology, Oxford University, 1990-91; Curator, Sedgwick Museum of Geology/Earth Sciences, Cambridge, 1992-; Director, Sedgwick Museum of Earth Sciences, Cambridge, 1994-; Visiting Lecturer, Institute of Palaeontology, University of Uppsala, Sweden, 1995-98; Asher

Dictionary of International Biography

Tunis Distinguished Research Fellow in Palaeobiology, Smithsonian Institution, Washington DC, USA, 2000-2002; Fellow, Director of Studies, Christ's College, Cambridge, 2002-. Publications: Over 70 articles as author and co-author in refereed journals including most recently: Primates and Engineering Principles: applications to craniodental mechanisms in ancient terrestrial predators, 2002; Dinosaurs: are they a metaphor for progress? 2002; Ornithischian dinosaurs from the Lower Cretaceous (Berriasian) of England, 2002; Author, 20 books and book chapters on dinosaurs and palaeontology; Numerous other science based articles. Honours include: Distinguished Lecturer, Carnegie Museum, Pittsburgh, USA, 1988; Honorary MA, Wagner Free Institute, Philadelphia, USA, 1991; Golden Trilobite Award, The Paleontological Society, USA, 1996; Palaeontological Medal, Natural History Museum, Salas, Burgos, Spain. Memberships: Fellow, 1982-, Vice-President, 1999-2001, Linnean Society; Palaeontological Association; Society of Verebrate Palaeontology; Society for the History of Natural History; Cambridge Philosophical Society. Address: Sedgwick Museum, Department of Earth Sciences, Downing Street, Cambridge CB2 2EQ, England.

NORMAN Gregory John, b. 10 February 1955, Queensland, Australia. Professional Golfer. m. Laura, 1 July 1981, 1 son, 1 daughter. Career: Professional, 1976-; Numerous major victories including: Doral Ryder Open, 1990, 1993, 1996; South African Open, 1996; Players Championship, 1994; PGA Grand Slam of Golf, 1993, 1994; British Open, 1986, 1993; Canadian Open, 1984, 1992; Australian Masters, 1981, 1983, 1984, 1989, 1990; New South Wales Open, 1978, 1983, 1986, 1988; Australian Open, 1980, 1985, 1987; European Open, 1986; World Match-Play, 1980, 1983, 1986; Australian Team, Dunhill Cup, 1985, 1986. Publications: My Story, 1982-83; Shark Attack, 1987-88; Greg Norman's Instant Lessons, 1993; Greg Norman's Better Golf, 1994. Honours: Inducted into World Golf Hall of Fame, 2001. Address: Great White Shark Enterprises Inc, PO Box 1189, Hobe Sound, FL 33475-1189, USA.

NORMAN Shane Henry, b. 12 September 1946, Cork, Ireland. Risk Analyst. m Claudia Maria Villabona Mattos, 1 son. Education: MA (Hons), Modern History, Lincoln College, Oxford, 1964-67. Appointments: Analyst and Account Executive, James Capel & Co, London (now HSBC Securities), 1968-80; Associate Director, James Capel (Far East) Ltd, 1978; Investment Manager, National Employers' Mutual, 1980-82; Investment Director, NM Rothschild & Sons (Hong Kong)Ltd, 1982-88, Deputy Managing Director, 1985-88; Managing Director, Pierson, Heldring & Pierson (Hong Kong) Ltd, 1988-92; Founder and Managing Director, Muskerry Farran Ltd, Hong Kong, 1992-96; Co-Founder and Research Director, RCP & Partners SA, which has developed a form of risk measurement called Fiduciary Rating for institutional asset management, 1996-, Established and managed offices in Hong Kong, 1996-99, Germany, 1999-2000, UK, 2000-. Publications: Article: What part should Asia-Pacific investments play in a pension fund portfolio? 1984; Compiler/Editor, The FT Guide to Investment Managers in Asia, 1997-2000. Memberships: Ocean Cruising Club, 1969-; Executive Committee, Hong Kong Association of Deposit-taking Companies, 1984-92; Committee on Unit Trusts, Securities & Futures Commission, Hong Kong, 1986-92. Address: 3 Ennismore Gardens, London, SW7 1NL, England. E-mail: shane.norman@btinternet.com

NORODOM RANARIDDH Prince, b. 2 January 1944, Cambodia. m. 1968, 2 sons, 1 daughter. Appointments: President, United National Front for an Independent, Neutral, Peaceful & Co-operative Cambodia; Co-Chair, Provisional National Government of Cambodia; Minister of National Defence, Interior and National Security, 1993; Member, National Assembly, 1993-; Co-Prime Minister, Member, Throne Council, 1993; 1st Prime Minister of Royal Government of Cambodia, 1993-97; Chair, National Development Council, 1993-97; Found guilty of conspiracy with Khmer Rouges to overthrow the government, sentenced to 30 years imprisonment; In Exile; Returned from exile 1998; Professor of Public Law.

NORODOM SIHANOUK Samdech Preah, b. 31 October 1922, Cambodia. King of Cambodia. m. Princess Monique, 14 children (6 deceased). Education: Saigon; Vietnam; Paris; Military Training, Saumur, France. Appointments: Elected King, 1941, Abdicated, 1955; Prime Minister, Minister of Foreign Affairs, 1955, 1956, 1957; Permanent Representative to UN, 1956; Elected Head of State, 1960; Took Oath of Fidelity to Vacant Throne, 1960; Deposed by Forces of Lon Nol, 1970; Resided, Peking; Established, Royal Government of National Union of Cambodia, (GRUNC) 1970; Restored as Head of State when GRUNC forces overthrew Khmer Republic, 1975, Resigned, 1976; Special Envoy of Khmer Rouge to UN, 1979; Founder, National United Front for an Independent Neutral, Peaceful and Co-operative Kampuchea, 1981-89; President, Tripartite National Cambodian Resistance, in exile 13 years, retured to Cambodia, 1991-93; Crowned King of Cambodia, 1993-; Colonel in Chief, Armed Forces, 1993-. Publications: L'Indochine vue de Pékin (with Jean Lacouture), 1972; My War With the CIA (with Wilfred Burchett), 1973; War and Hope: The Case for Cambodia, 1980; Souvenirs doux et amers, 1981; Prisonnier des Khmers Rouges, 1986; Charisme et Leadership, 1989. Address: Khemarindra Palace, Phnom Penh, Cambodia.

NORTON Hugh Edward, b. 23 June 1936, London, England. Business Executive. m. (1) Janet M Johnson, 1965, deceased, 1 son, (2) Joy Harcup, 1998. Education: Winchester College; Trinity College, Oxford. Appointments: Joined British Petroleum Company, 1959, Exploration Department, 1960, in Abu Dhabi, Lebanon & Libya, 1962-70, subsequently held appointments in Supply, Central Planning; Policy Planning, Regional Directorate Mid E & International & Government Affairs departments; Managing Director, BP's Associate Companies, Singapore, Malaysia, Hong Kong, 1978-81, Director of Planning, 1981-83, Regional Director for Near East, Middle East & Indian Sub-Continent, 1981-86, Director of Administration, 1983-86, Managing Director, CEO, BP Exploration Co, 1986-89, Chair, 1989-95, Managing Director, British Petroleum Co PLC, 1989-95; Chair, BP Asia Pacific Private Co Ltd, 1991-95; Director, Inchcape PLC, 1995-, Standard Chart PLC, 1995-, Lasmo PLC, 1997-. Memberships: Council, Royal Institute of Economic Affairs, 1991-. Address: c/o BP Asia Pacific Pte Ltd, BP Tower, 25th Storey, 396 Alexandra Road, 0511 Singapore.

NORWICH John Julius (The Viscount Norwich), b. 15 September 1929, London, England. Writer; Broadcaster. m. (1) Anne Clifford, 5 August 1952, 1 son, 1 daughter, (2) Mollie Philipps, 14 June 1989. Education: University of Strasbourg, 1947; New College, Oxford, 1949-52. Appointments: Writer, Royal Navy, 1947-49; Foreign Office, 1952-64; Third Secretary, British Embassy, Belgrade, 1955-57; Second Secretary, British Embassy, Beirut, 1957-60; First Secretary, Foreign Office, London, 1961; British delegation to Disarmament Conference, Geneva, 1960-64; Writer, Broadcaster, 1964-; Chairman: British Theatre Museum, 1966-71; Venice in Peril Fund, 1970-; Executive Committee, National Trust, 1969-95; Franco-British Council, 1972-79; Board, English National Opera, 1977-81. Publications: Mount Athos, 1966; Sahara, 1968; The Normans in the South, 1967; The Kingdom in the Sun, 1970; A History of Venice, 1977; Christmas Crackers 1970-79, 1980; Glyndebourne, 1985; The Architecture of Southern England, 1985; A Taste for Travel, 1985; Byzantium: The Early Centuries, 1988; More Christmas Crackers 1980-89, 1990; Venice: A Traveller's Companion (editor), 1990; The Oxford

Illustrated Encyclopaedia of the Arts (editor), 1990; Byzantium, the Apogee, 1991; Byzantium: The Decline and Fall, 1995; A Short History of Byzantium, 1997; Shakespeare's Kings, 1999; Still More Christmas Crackers 1990-99, 2000. Honours: Commander, Royal Victorian Order; Commendatore, Ordine al Merito della Repubblica Italiana; Award, American Institute of Architects. Memberships: Fellow, Royal Society of Literature; Fellow, Royal Geographical Society; Fellow, Royal Society of Arts. Address: 24 Blomfield Road, London W9 1AD, England.

NOTO Aldo, b. 3 March 1964, Bronx, New York, USA. Patent Attorney. Education: BSEE, US Coast Guard Academy, 1985; BS, Mathematics, State University of New York, 1985; Juris Doctor, 1990, Master of Law in Intellectual Property, 1993, George Washington University. Appointments: LT, US Coast Guard Officer, 1985-2000; LLP, Dorsey and Whitney, 2000-. Publications: Software patents procuring and engineering, Patent Resource Group, 2000-03 editions. Honours: US Coast Guard Ensign; USCG Lt JG; USCG, LT. Memberships: US Patent and Trademark Office Patent Bar; Virginia State Bar; District of Columbia Bar; American Intellectual Property Law Association; US International Trade Association Trial Lawyers. Address: 600 North Oxford Street, Arlington, VA 22203, USA.

NOVAK Maximillian Erwin, b. 26 March 1930, New York, New York, USA. University Professor. m. Estelle Gershgoren, 21 August 1966, 2 sons, 1 daughter. Education: PhD, University of California, 1958; DPhil, St John's University, Oxford, 1961. Appointments: Assistant Professor, University of Michigan, 1958-62; Assistant Professor to Professor, University of California, Los Angeles, 1962-. Publications: Economics and the Fiction of Daniel Defoe, 1962; Defoe and the Nature of Man, 1963; Congreve, 1970; Realism Myth and History in the Fiction of Daniel Defoe, 1983; Eighteenth Century English Literature, 1983; Stoke Newington Defoe. Volume 1, 1999. Editor: The Wild Man Within, 1970; English Literature in the Age of Disguise, 1977; California Dryden, Vols X and X111, 1971, 1984; Passionate Encounters, 2000; Daniel Defoe: Master of Fictions, 2001. Contributions to: Professional journals. Address: Department of English, University of California, Los Angeles, CA 90095, USA.

NOVÁKOVÁ Hana, b. 7 June 1931, Chlumec n.C., Czech Republic. Pedagogue. m. Jiři Novák. Education: Diploma of Engineer, Technical University of Agriculture, Prague, Czech Republic, 1954; PhD, Martin-Luther University, Halle-Wittenberg, Germany, 1975. Appointments: Lecturer, Technology Education, Charles University, Prague, 1967-69, 1988-89; Main Editor, Production and School (teachers' magazine), 1972-90; Scientific Assistant, 1955-63, Deputy Head and Head, 1963-77, Department of Technology Education, Research Institute of Pedagogy; Programme Specialist, Ministry of Education, 1977-88; Deputy Director, Research Institute of Pedagogy, 1988-90; Director, Pedagprogram, 1991-. Publications: Co-ordinator and editor of international projects: Priority Components of General Education for the 21st Century in the Potential Future Countries of the European Community in the European Context with the View to Technology Education, 1993; Production of Training Materials Concerning Education of a Free Demoćratic Personality Equipped with Technology and Ecological Literacy and Prepared for a New Culture of Creativity, Competence and Co-operation and Care in the Four New Democracies of Central Europe, 1995; The Contribution of Technology and Vocational Education to Higher Flexibility and Adaptability for Young People on Labour Market and for Lifelong Education in the Four New Democracies of Central Europe, 1997; The Development of New Approaches in Technology and Vocational Education in the Countries in Transition – the Countries of Central Europe and South Africa, an International

Pilot Project, 2003; Textbooks on agricultural technology, teachers' guides , monographs on philosophy on technology education; Main author and author in over 30 books; 300 pedagogical articles published in the Czech Republic and abroad; Papers presented at conferences in 24 countries. Honours: Outstanding Teacher in Adult Education, 1955; Outstanding Programme Specialist, Ministry of Education, 1979; Meritorious Programme Specialist, Ministry of Education, 1986; Award, University of Blagoievgrad, Bulgaria, 1989; International PATT Award for outstanding contribution to technology education, 1995. Memberships: Pupils Attitude Towards Technology; World Association for Educational Research; IOSTE; IASE; Czech Pedagogical Association. Address: Konevova 241, 130 00 Prague 3, Czech Republic.

NOVIK Gotfrid, b. 15 September 1935, Ludza, Latvia. Petrophysicist; Researcher. m. Nina Varijchuk, 1 son. Education: Diploma, Mining Engineer, 1959; Candidate of Technical Sciences, 1965; Doctor in Technical Sciences, 1970; D.hab, Geology, 1995. Appointments: Head, Department of Chemistry, Mining University, Moscow, 1973-94; Professor, Head of Department of Natural Sciences, Rezekne University, Latvia, 1994-. Publications include: Foundation of Rock Physics. Membership: New York Academy of Sciences; Water Environment Federation. Address: Maskavas Str 9/2-18, LV-4604 Rezekne, Latvia.

NOVOTNA Jana, b. 2 October 1968, Brno, Czech Republic. Tennis Player. Appointments: Won US Open Junior Doubles, 1986; Turned Professional, 1987; Won 1st Title, Adelaide, 1988; Olympic Silver Medal, Doubles wih Helena Sukova, 1988; Won Australian and US Open Mixed Doubles with Pugh, 1988; Won 6 Women's Doubles Titles, 1989;With Sukova, won Australian Open, French Open, Wimbledon Doubles, 1990; Reached Quarter Finals, French Open, 1991; Won 7 Doubles Titles with Savchenko Neiland, 1992; Won Singles Titles, Osaka and Brighton, 1993; Singles Titles, Leipzig, Brighton, Essen, 1994; Won Wimbledon Singles and Doubles, 1998; Announced retirement, 1999. Honours: Olympic Bronze Medal in Singles, Silver Medal in Doubles, Atlanta, 1996.

NOVOTNÝ Miroslav, b. 11 May 1922, Tovačov, Czech Republic. Mathematician. m. Věra Zábojníková, 2 daughters. Education: RNDr, Masaryk University, Brno, 1948; DrSc, Charles University, Prague, 1962. Appointments: Reader, Technical University and Military Academy, Brno, 1947-53; Associate Professor, 1953-63, Professor, 1963-72, 1990-, Masaryk University, Brno; Leading Research Fellow, Mathematical Institute, Czechoslovak Academy of Sciences, 1972-90. Publications: Over 100 scientific articles and 1 book. Honours: Award for Collaboration, Polish and Czechoslovak Academies, 1988; B Bolzano Gold Medal, Czechoslovak Academy of Sciences, 1992. Memberships: Czechoslovak Union of Mathematicians and Physicists. Address: Faculty of Informatics, Masaryk University, Botanická 68a, 602 00 Brno, Czech Republic.

NOWACKI Zbigniew, b. 19 January 1940, Kutno, Poland. Professor; Electrical Engineer. m. Maria, 1 son. Education: MSc, Electrical Engineering, 1962; PhD, Electrical Drive Control, 1970; DSc, 1982, Professor, 1991. Appointments: Electrical Engineer, Factory of Transformers and Traction Apparatus, 1962-65; Teacher, 1966, Vice Dean, Electrical Faculty, 1987-93, Head, Electrical Drive Division, 1983-, Technical University of Lodz. Publications: Over 80 articles, 3 books: Suboptimal Control of an Induction Motor with Respect to a Modified Quadratic Performance Index, 1981; Electrical Drive in Question and Answers, 1986; Pulses Width Modulation in Variable Frequency Drives, 1991; 4 books for students. Honours: 2 Awards, Ministry of Education, 1970, 1981. Memberships: Senior Member, Institute of Electrical and

Electronic Engineers; European Power Electrics and Drive Association; PTETiS. Address: Konstytucyina 9/43, 90-155 Lodz, Poland.

NOWAK Grzegorz, b. 29 March 1969, Jedrzejow, Poland. Physician. Education: MD, Medical University, Lodz, Poland, 1994; PhD, Karolinska Institute, Stockholm, Sweden, 2003. Appointments: Internship, Central Clinical Hospital, Warsaw, Poland, 1994-95; Research Fellow, Okayama University, Okayama, Japan, 1995-97; Research Fellow, 1997-2002, Clinical, Research Assistant, 2002-, Karolinska Institute, Stockholm, Sweden. Address: Karolinska Institute, Department of Transplantation Surgery, Stockholm 14816, Sweden.

NUNN Trevor Robert, b. 14 January 1940, Ipswich, England. Theatre Director. m. (1) Janet Suzman, 1969, 1 son, (2) Sharon Lee Hill, 1986, 2 daughters, (3) Imogen Stubbs, 1994, 1 son, 1 daughter. Education: Downing College, Cambridge. Appointments: Trainee Director, Belgrade Theatre, Coventry; Associate Director, Royal Shakespeare Company, Director Emeritus, 1986-; Founder, Homevale Ltd, Awayvale Ltd; Artistic Director, Royal National Theatre, 1996-2001. Creative Works: Productions include: The Merry Wives of Windsor, 1979; Once in a Lifetime, 1979; Juno and the Paycock, 1980; The Life and Adventures of Nicholas Nickleby, 1980; Cats, 1981; All's Well That Ends Well, 1981; Henry IV (pts I and II), 1981, 1982; Peter Pan, 1982; Starlight Express, 1984; Les Misérables, 1985; Chess, 1986; The Fair Maid of the West, 1986; Aspects of Love, 1989; Othello, 1989; The Baker's Wife, 1989; Timon of Athens, 1991; The Blue Angel, 1991; Measure for Measure, 1991; Heartbreak House, 1992; Arcadia, 1993; Sunset Boulevard, 1993; Enemy of the People, 1997; Mutabilitie, 1997; Not About Nightingales, 1998; Oklahoma, 1998; Betrayal, 1998; Troilus and Cressida, 1999; The Merchant of Venice, 1999; Summerfolk, 1999; Love's Labour's Lost, 2002; TV: Antony and Cleopatra, 1975; Comedy of Errors, 1976; Every Good Boy Deserves Favour, 1978; Macbeth, 1978; Shakespeare Workshops Word of Mouth, 1979; The Three Sisters, Othello, 1989; Porgy and Bess, 1992; Oklahoma!, 1999; Films: Hedda, Lady Jane, 1985; Twelfth Night, 1996; Operas: Idomeneo, 1982; Porgy and Bess, 1986; Cosi Fan Tutte, 1991; Peter Grimes, 1992; Katya Kabanova, 1994; Sophie's Choice, 2002. Publications: British Theatre Design, 1989. Honours: Numerous. Address: Royal National Theatre, Upper Ground, South Bank, London SE1 9PX, England.

NURLANOVA Nailya, b. 20 December 1949, Petropavlovsk, Kazakhstan. Economist. Education: Excellent Diploma, 1967-71, Training, 1971-73, PhD, Economics, 1973-76, Almaty Institute of National Economy, Kazakhstan; Certificate, KMPGs Course on Foreign Investment Privatisation in Kazakhstan, 1994; Dr Degree in Economics, 1999; Certificate, Programme of Governmental Accounts and Financial Management, Institute of Government Accounts and Finance, New Delhi, India, 2001; Professor's Degree, 2002. Appointments: Junior Scientist, Kazakh Branch of Scientific Research Institute of Labour, 1976-81; Junior Scientist, 1981-87, Senior Scientist, 1987-92, Head of Department of Regional Economic Problems, 1992-95, Institute of Economics, Academy of Sciences, Republic of Kazakhstan; Deputy Director, Institute of Economics, Ministry of Education and Science, Republic of Kazakhstan, 1995-. Publications: More than 125 scientific works on the problems of macro and regional economics include: Personal monograph: Formation and using of investments in Kazakhstan's economy: strategy and mechanism, 1998; More than 20 monographs and books as co-author include: Investments on the securities market of Kazakhstan: opportunities, efficiency and risk, 1998; Regional policy of republic of Kazakhstan: economic mechanism of realisation, 1998; Market economy of Kazakhstan: problems of coming-into-being and development (2

volumes), 2001. Memberships include: Academician, International Academy of Euro-Asia; Chairman, Dissertational Council, Institute of Economics, Ministry of Education and Science; Deputy Chairman, Scientific Co-ordinational Centre on Economics; Editorial Board, Journal, Economics and Statistics. Address: 29 Kurmangazy Str, Almaty, Republic of Kazakhstan. E-mail: ieconom@academset.kz

NUTTALL Mark Antony, b. 5 July 1962, Chester, England. Henry Marshall Tory Professor. m. Anita Dey-Nuttall, 1 son. Education: MA, First Class Honours, University of Aberdeen, 1982-86; PhD, Arctic Anthropology, University of Cambridge (Jesus College), 1986-90. Appointments: Research Fellow, Social Anthropology, University of Edinburgh, 1990-92; Lecturer, Social Anthropology, Brunel University, 1992-95; Research Associate in Arctic Anthropology, Scott Polar Research Institute, University of Cambridge and Affiliate Assistant Professor of Anthropology, University of Alaska Fairbanks, 1994-95; Lecturer in Sociology, 1995-99, Senior Lecturer in Sociology, 1999-2000, Professor of Social Anthropology, 2000-2003, University of Aberdeen; Henry Marshall Tory Professor, Department of Anthropology, University of Alberta, Canada, 2003-. Publications: Authored books and edited collections: Arctic Homeland: kinship, community & development in northwest Greenland, 1992; White Settlers: the impact of rural repopulation in Scotland (with C Jedrej), 1996; Protecting the Arctic: indigenous peoples and cultural survival (in Studies in Environmental Anthropology vol 3), 1998; The Arctic: environment, people, policy (co-editor with T V Callaghan), 2000; Cultivating Arctic Landscapes: knowing and managing animals in the circumpolar North (co-editor with D G Anderson), 2003; Encyclopaedia of the Arctic (editor) 3 vols, 2004; The Russian North in Global Context (co-editor with S Crate), in press. Honour: Honorary Professor of Sociology, University of Aberdeen, 2004-. Memberships: Fellow, Royal Anthropological Institute, 1989-; Fellow, Royal Geographical Society, 1990-; Association of Social Anthropologists of the Commonwealth, 1991-; Senior Associate Scientist, Stefansson Arctic Institute, Akureyri, Iceland, 2002-; Fellow, Arctic Institute of North America, Calgary, Canada (elected 2002); Senior Associate, Scott Polar Research Institute, University of Cambridge, 1996-. Address: Department of Anthropology, University of Alberta, Henry Marshall Tory Building 13-15, Edmonton, Canada, T6G 2H4. E-mail: mnuttall@ualberta.ca

NUTTING Cherie, b. 24 April 1949, Newton, Massachusetts, USA. Photographer. Divorced. Education: Graduated, Spanish Literature, magna cum laude, University of Massachusetts, 1977; Graduate Courses, School of Visual Arts, New York, 1982-83; New England School of Photography, 1978-80. Appointments: Teacher, Brimmer and May School, Chestnut Hill, Massachusetts, 1977-80; Worked in collaboration with the late Paul Bowles on a book of text and photographs published November 2000, 1986-99; Manager and Photographer for The Master Musicians of Jajouka, 1988-96; Organised and co-ordinated the recording of the Rolling Stones, Continental Drift for Steel Wheels CD and BBC film: The Rolling Stones in Morocco, 1989; Photographer, manager and location assistant for recording: Apocalypse Across the Sky by The Master Musicians of Jajouka, 1991; Photographer, manager, design assistant and co-producer for Pipes of Pan CD and book with The Rolling Stones; Organised music for Bernardo Bertolucci's Sheltering Sky and Croneberg's Naked Lunch (Jajouka Music); Photographer, manager, locations assistant and co-producer for Peter Gabriels recording: Jajouka Between the Mountains, 1996; Exhibition: Rizzoli Gallery, San Francisco, 2000; The June Bateman Gallery, New York, NY, 2002. Publications: Pipes of Pan, in collaboration with Polygram and the Rolling Stones; Paul Bowles: Yesterday's Perfume; Book with Bachir Attar, The Master Musicians of Jajouka, in progress; Contributions to numerous magazines; Designs for several album covers. Honour:

NEH Adviser, study of Haitian girls under Duvalier, 1980. Commissions and Creative Works: Photographs of Paul Bowles in Kunst Museums in Berne and Zurich. Address: PO Box 1691, New York, NY 10009, USA.

NWAKA Geoffrey Iheanyichukwu, b. 13 November 1941, Abajah, Nigeria. University Professor. m. Justina Oputa, 3 sons, 1 daughter. Education: University of Ibadan, 1964-66; BA, Honours, History, 1967, University of Nigeria Nsukka; MA, 1972, University of Birmingham, England; PhD, Dalhousie University, Halifax, Canada, 1975. Appointments: Lecturer, University of Nigeria and University of Calabar, 1975-81; Senior Lecturer, 1981-88, Professor, 1988-, Imo State University (now Abia State University), Nigeria. Publications: Published widely in African History and Urban Studies in professional journals, edited books and international conferences. Honours: Research Fellowships to Nordic Africa Institute, Sweden, 1988-89, to Flinders University, South Australia, 1992, to University of Economics, Vienna, Austria, 1993 and to several other countries in Europe. Memberships include: International Society of City and regional Planners; International Federation of Housing and Planning; SID; IIAAS; HSN. Address: Dean, Postgraduate Studies, Abia State University, PMB 2000, Uturu, Nigeria. E-mail: geoffreynwaka@yahoo.com

NWANKPA Emmanuel Chukwuemeka, b. 19 August 1947, Barakin Ladi, Plateau State, Nigeria. Lawyer. m. Agnes Ilemobade Nwankpa, 2 sons, 1 daughter. Education: Government College, Umuahai, Nigeria, 1965-66l University of Ife, Ile-Ife, Nigeria, 1973-77; Nigerian Law School, Lagos, Nigeria, 1978-79; Advanced Leadership Training Course, Haggai Institute, Singapore, 1991. Appointments: Co-ordinator, Intercession, International Christian Chamber of Commerce; Member, Council of Reference Cook Foundation Discipleship Programme, USA; Co-Ordinator, AD 2000 & Beyond Movement, United Prayer Track, Africa Region; Chairman, Board of Trustees, Intercessors for Nigeria; Co-ordinator, Intercessors for Africa, 1981-; Conference Speaker, Ministered in over 40 countries on 5 continents during the last 25 years; member Governing Council, College of Education (Technical) Arochukwu, Abia State, Nigeria, 1993-97; International Director, Sundoulos African Leadership Training Programme (SALT), 1997-; Member, Governing Council, 2000-2003, Pro-Chancellor and Chairman, Governing Council, 2003 for 4 year tenure, Abia State University, Uturu, Abia State, Nigeria. Publications: Translated into the Kingdom of Christ, 1981; Introducing Jesus Christ, 1994; Redeeming the Land – Interceding for the Nations, 1994; The Lord is a Man of War – A Manual for Spiritual Warfare, 1996, German and French editions, 1996. Memberships: International Christian Chamber of Commerce; Alumni Haggai Institute, Singapore. Address: Abia State University, PMB, 2000, Uturu, Abia State, Nigeria.

NWAUBANI Chukwuma Hope (Chief, Sir), b. 1 August 1940, Umuahia, Nigeria. Chartered Accountant. m. Patricia U Nwaubani, 3 sons, 2 daughters. Education: BA, Economics, Durham, 1966; FCCA, 1973; FCA, 1974; FCTI, 1983; FREcons, 1974; MBIM, 1976. Appointments: Worked in different capacities in both public and private sectors in accounting consultancy and top management positions in Nigeria, Sierra Leone and England, 1966-; Lectured in many universities. Publications: Many articles in international journals and newspapers. Honours: Abia State Government Merit Award of Oke Oji, 1998; Chieftancy Titles, 1987, 2001. Memberships: Prominent Social Clubs in Nigeria; Knight of Saint Mulumba (KSM), 1997. Address: Chuks Nwaubani & Co (Chartered Accountants), 26 Macaulay Street, PO Box 635, Umuahia, Abia State, Nigeria. E-mail: Chukshopen@yahoo.com

NWOSU Ikechi Nwachukwu, b. 24 November 1949, Amakama, Nigeria. Clergyman; Bishop. m. Nne Patience Nwosu, 1 son, 2 daughters. Education: Dip Th (College), Dip Th (WAATI), Trinity Theological College, Umuahia, Nigeria, 1975-78; BD, Theology, University of London, 1979-82; PGC Th, Theology, Wycliffe Hall, Oxford University, England, 1982-83; PhD, New Testament, Ridley Hall, Cambridge, England, 1995. Appointments: Ordained Priest, 1978; Chaplain to the Dean, 1978-91, Bishop's Chaplain, 1987-92; Diocese of Aba, Church of Nigeria; Cathedral AFF Chaplain, St Michael's Cathedral, Aba, 1985-91; Arch Deacon, St Stephen's Cathedral, Umuahia, 1995-98; Board of Governors, 1995-, Registrar, 1996-97, Rector, 1997-99, Trinity Theological College, Umuahia, Nigeria; Cathedral Administrator, 1995-96; Canon Theologian, 1996, Adviser on Mission/Evangelism, 1997-, Diocese of Umuahia; Director for Spiritual Growth, Ibru Centre, Anglican Communion, 1999-2003; Chairman, Abia State Pilgrims Board, State House, 2003; Bishop, Diocese of Umuahia, Anglican Communion, Nigeria, 2003-. Publications: The feeding of the five thousand and the four Evangelists, 1988; New Birth: A New testament Phenomenon that applies to the Old Testament, 1997; Alex Uremu Ibru: The Daniel from the lions Den (contributor), 2002; Columnist and writer, Guardian Newspaper Ltd, Nigeria. Honours: Harris Bolton Award, Best all round Student, Trinity Theological College, 1978; Wycliffe Hall Scholar, Wycliffe Hall, Oxford, 1980-81; Christian Sacrifice Award, Parishes of the Sampfords, Near Cambridge, 1994; Ridley Hall Scholar, Ridley Hall, Cambridge, 1992-95. Memberships: Trinity College Governing Council; Church of Nigeria Doctrinal and Theological Committee; Abia State of Nigeria Pilgrims Board; Board of Governors, Ibru Ecumenical Retreat. Address: Bishops Court, c/o St Stephen's Cathedral, Umuahia, Abia State, Nigeria.

NYBERG Tore Samuel, b. 4 January 1931, Uppsala, Sweden. Professor Emeritus. m. Nurbaiti Pamuntjak. Education: fil. Kand., Uppsala, 1956; fil. lic., Lund, 1960; fil.dr., Lund, 1965; exam. theol. Munich, 1969; dr phil. habil., Augsburg, 1981. Appointments: Alexander von Humboldt Research Fellow, Munich, 1967-69; Lecturer, Assistant Professor, Professor of Medieval History, Odense University (now University of Southern Denmark), 1970-2001; Professor Emeritus, 2001-; Visiting Professor, Augsburg, 1984; Director, International Birgittine Center, Farfa, Italy, 1993-94. Publications: Birgittinische Klostergründungen des Mittelalters, 1965; Dokumente und Untersuchungen zur innern Geschichte der drei Birgittenklöster Bayerns 1420-1570, 1972-74; Die Kirche in Skandinavien, 1986; Monasticism in North-Western Europe 800-1200, 2000. Honours: Birgitta-Price, Birgittastiftelsen, Vadstena, Sweden; teol.dr.hc, Uppsala University, Sweden, 2003. Memberships: Commission International d'Histoire Ecclésiastique Comparée; Det Kongelige Samfund for Fæderneslandetshistorie, Copenhagen. Address: Centre for History, University of Southern Denmark, Campusvej 55, DK-5230 Odense M, Denmark. E-mail: tny@hist.sdu.dk

NYE Robert, b. 15 March 1939, London, England. Author; Poet; Dramatist; Editor. m. (1) Judith Pratt, 1959, divorced 1967, 3 sons, (2) Aileen Campbell, 1968, 1 daughter. Publications: Fiction: Doubtfire, 1967; Tales I Told My Mother, 1969; Falstaff, 1976; Merlin, 1978; Faust, 1980; The Voyage of the Destiny, 1982; The Facts of Life and Other Fictions, 1983; The Memoirs of Lord Byron, 1989; The Life and Death of My Lord Gilles de Rais, 1990; Mrs Shakespeare: The Complete Works, 1993; The Late Mr Shakespeare, 1998. Children's Fiction: Taliesin, 1966; March Has Horse's Ears, 1966; Wishing Gold, 1970; Poor Pumpkin, 1971; Out of the World and Back Again, 1977; Once Upon Three Times, 1978; The Bird of the Golden Land, 1980; Harry Pay the Pirate, 1981; Three Tales, 1983; Lord Fox and Other Spine-Chilling Tales, 1997. Poetry: Juvenilia 1, 1961; Juvenilia 2, 1963; Darker Ends,

1969; Agnus Dei, 1973; Two Prayers, 1974; Five Dreams, 1974; Divisions on a Ground, 1976; A Collection of Poems, 1955-1988, 1989; 14 Poems, 1994; Henry James and Other Poems, 1995; Collected Poems, 1995, 1998. Plays: Sawney Bean (with Bill Watson), 1970; The Seven Deadly Sins: A Mask, 1974; Penthesilea, Fugue and Sisters, 1976. Translator: Beowulf, 1968. Editor: A Choice of Sir Walter Raleigh's Verse, 1973; The English Sermon, 1750-1850, 1976; The Faber Book of Sonnets, 1976; PEN New Poetry 1, 1986; First Awakenings: The Early Poems of Laura Riding (co-editor), 1992; A Selection of the Poems of Laura Riding, 1994. Contributions to: Magazines and journals. Honours: Eric Gregory Award, 1963; Guardian Fiction Prize, 1976; Hawthornden Prize, 1977. Membership: Royal Society of Literature, fellow. Address: 2 Westbury Crescent, Wilton, Cork, Ireland.

NYIRI Ferenc (Baron), b. 25 August 1964, Hodmezovasarhely. Basstrombone Player. Education: Academy of Music, Franz Liszt, Szeged, 1985. Appointment: Symphony Orchestra of Pec, 1985. Publications: Journal of Hungarian Trombone-Tuba Association. Honours: Competition of Trombone, III Prize, 1984, II Prize, 1985; Price of Artisjus, 2001. Address: Ipoly sor 11/B. H 6724 Szeged, Hungary.

NYSTRÖM Stig Henning Mikael, b. 14 July 1924, Helsinki, Finland. Professor of Neurosurgery; Artist. m. Maire Sauna-aho. Education: MA, History of Art, University of Helsinki, 1948; École Nationale Supérieure des Beaux Arts, Paris, 1948-49, 1951; MD, 1960, Specialist in Neurosurgery, 1962, Assistant Professor qualification, 1966, Competence for Extraordinary Chair in Neurosurgery, 1974, University of Helsinki; Scientist, Oath as Officer of Instruction, Harvard University, USA, 1963-64; Neurosurgery Fellow, Massachusetts General Hospital, Boston, 1963-64; Clinical and Research Fellow, Montreal Neurological Institute, Canada, 1965. Appointments: Assistant Head Neurosurgeon, University Central Hospital, Helsinki, 1971-75; First Ordinary Professor of Neurosurgery in Finland, 1975-89, Head, Department of Neurosurgery, 1975-89, University of Oulu; Physician-in-Chief as short locum tenens, Oulu University Central Hospital, summers 1976, 1977; 32 exhibits of oil paintings in Finland, France, Italy and USA, 1989-2003; Represented in museums, public or private art collections in Finland, France, Spain and USA. Publications: Internal spring clip, 1959, 1962; Tumour vessels, 1960, 1965; High energy proton beams, 1964; 1966; Shape Factor Intensity Analysis, 1985; On-line evoked potential analyser and CO_2-YAG-laser, 1988; Intraoperative holographic ultrasound, 1989; Art from the years 1929-1999, 1999. Honours: Art scholarship, French Government 1953; Invitation and Grants, National Institute of Health, USA, for research at Harvard University and Massachusetts General Hospital, 1963-64; Honorary Nyström Lecture sponsored by Oulu Medical Research Foundation, 1979-; Knight, Order of the White Rose of Finland, 1st Class, 1984; American Medal of Honor for Contributions to Medicine, 2002; Volume Dedicated in Honour, Annals of Clinical Research, Supplement 47, 1986; Cultural Diploma for creative art and Key of Success for Excellence in Arts, Raleigh, USA, 2000; Lifetime Achievement Award for Pictorial Art, IBC, 2001; International Scientist of the Year 2002 in Experimental Op-Art, IBC; Premio Oscar della Pittura, Firenze, Premio Alba della pittura, Ferrara, Italy, 2003. Memberships: Honorary Member, Societas Neurochirurgica Fennica, 1990; Member of the International Order of Merit and of the American Order of Excellence, 2000; Finland's Artists Association; Corresponding Academician and Professor of Art, Academia Greci-Marino, Verbano, Italy; Arts sur Scène Association, Asnières-sur-Seine, Grand-Paris. Address: Bulevardi 34 A 8, 00120 Helsinki, Finland.

Dictionary of International Biography

O

Ó hEOCHA Padraig Aonghus, b. 17 January 1930, Co Waterford, Ireland. Consulting Civil Engineer. m. Lucy Moran, 2 sons, 3 daughters. Education: BE, Civil Engineering, University College, Cork, Ireland, 1951. Appointments: Engineer, O'Connell & Harley, Consulting Engineers, Cork, Ireland, 1951-53; Engineer, Delap & Waller, Consulting Engineers, Dublin, Ireland, 1954-57; Engineer, George Wimpey & Co Ltd, London, England, 1957-58; Senior Engineer, Tarmac Civil Engineering Ltd, Wolverhampton, England, 1958-59; Founder, Director, DeLeuw, Chadwick, Ó hEocha, Consulting Engineers, Dublin, Ireland, 1959-90; Deputy Chairman, Ewbank, Preece, Ó hEocha, Consulting Engineers, 1990-95; Consultant, Mott MacDonald EPO, Dublin, 1995-2000. Publications: Articles in transactions and professional journals include: A Major Road and Bridges Project in Nigeria, 1979-80; Ro-Ro Facilities – The Design and Construction of the B&I Terminal at Pembroke Dock, 1984-85; Aspects of Engineering Projects Overseas, 1989; Dublin Transportation System Report, 1992; Major Contract versus Project Management in Road Projects – A Consulting Engineer's Perspective, 1993. Honours: Auditor, 1949-50, Gold Medal for Debate, 1950, Irish Language Society, University College, Cork, 1949-50; Vice-President, Students' Council, University College Cork, 1950-51; Board Director, Gael-Linn, 1965-75; President, Association of Consulting Engineers of Ireland, 1975-76; Chairman, Ring College Dungarvan, Co Waterford, Ireland, 1976-; Institution Prize (Premier Prize) for learned paper, 1980, Smith Testimonial for learned paper, 1985, Institution of Engineers of Ireland. Memberships: Fellow, Institution of Engineers of Ireland; Fellow, Institution of Civil Engineers; Member, Royal St George Yacht Club; Member, Killiney Golf Club. Address: St Arnaud, Killiney Avenue, Killiney, Co Dublin, Ireland. E-mail: pa.oheocha@eircom.net

O'BAIRE Marika Helene, b. 3 October 1947, US Army Base, Manilla, Philippines. Psychiatric Nurse; Author; Entrepreneur. Fiancé, Pieter Kark, 3 sons, 1 daughter. Education: University of Connecticut School of Fine Arts, 1965-66; Nursing Diploma, State University of New York – Albany, Ellis Hospital School of Nursing, 1974-77; Russell Sage College, Troy, New York, 1975-80; Ontological Design Course, Alameda, California, 1984-93; 4 courses short of a Masters Degree in Humanities, California State University at Dominguez Hills, 1997-2000; Licensed Avatar Master/Wizard Star's Edge International, 1999-; University of Dundee College of Medicine and Dentistry Department of Nursing Masters Programme, 2000. Appointments: Ellis Hospital Neuro Constant Care Unit, 1977-78; Staff Nurse in Acute Psychiatry, Samaritan Hospital, New York, 1978-80; Staff Nurse, Paediatric Intensive Care Unit, Albany Medical Center, New York, 1980-84; Researcher, Commission on Quality Care for the Mentally Disabled, Albany, 1984; Staff Nurse, Columbia-Greene Medical Center, Catskill, New York, 1984-89; Night Charge Nurse, Conifer Park, Scotia, New York, 1991-92; Nursing Educator, St Clare's Hospital, Schenectady, New York, 1992-96; Adjunct Clinical Educator, Albany Medical Center, South Vermont College, Bennington, 1997-2001; Community Hospice, Saratoga, 1998-; Favorite Nurses, Colonie, New York, 2001-; Business Owner and President, Future Design and Create What You Prefer. Publications: Future Joyous (novel), 2002; Dragon (novel), forthcoming; About Love (collected short stories); Mabel, published in Gates to the City, Albany's Tricentennial Literary Anthology; My Song (poem), American Anthology, 1986. Honours: Daughters of the American Revolution Award for Citizenship, 1963; Disabled Veterans Award for the Spirit of Americanism, 1977; International Health Professional, 2004. Memberships: Upstate Independent Filmmakers/Screenwriters; Avatar Master/Wizard Community;

China-US Friendship Organization International; Sierra Club; Childreach Plan International. Address: 7 Center St, Cazanovia, NY 13035-1123, USA. E-mail: mobaire@yahoo.com

O'BRIEN Beajae, b. 4 December 1935, Oshkosh, Wisconsin, USA. Artist. m. John W O'Brien, 1 son, 1 daughter. Education: University of Wisconsin, Madison, Wisconsin; Satellite of University of Wisconsin at Oshkosh, Wisconsin; DUC Concord, California; C Costa College, San Pablo, California; New York Art Workshop, New York City; Study with George McNiel, New York City; Private study with Irene Gilliwater, New York City; 10 years Private Study, Orinda, California. Appointments: Owner, Beajae Fine Arts; Employee Moraga Gallery; Art Participant, Design Connection, Oakland, California; Participant, International Experimental Artist, National College, Cleveland, Ohio; Solo Art Shows, 1995-. Publications: Works featured in: Best of Watercolor, 1996; Painting Texture, 1997; Best of Drawing and Sketching, 1998; Collected Best of Water Color, 2002. Honours: Rockport Publishers Award; National Collage Award, 1997; California Art Festival Award, 1998; National Collage Merit Award, 1998; 1st Place Bay Area Festival, 1999; 1st Place Art and Wine Festival, 1999; Cash Award, National Collage Society, 2000; National Collage Society Award, 2001; Listed in Who's Who publications and biographical dictionaries. Memberships: International Society of Experimental Artists; National Collage Society; NE Collage Society; Lamorinda Arts Alliance; Collage Artist of America; Intuitive Layering Group; National Museum of Women in the Arts. Address: 34 Sea Pines, Moraga, CA 94556, USA.

O'BRIEN Conor Cruise, (Donat O'Donnell), b. 3 November 1917, Dublin, Ireland. Writer; Editor. m. (1) Christine Foster, 1939, divorced 1962, 1 son, 1 daughter, (2) Máire MacEntee, 1962, 1 adopted son, 1 adopted daughter. Education: BA, 1940, PhD, 1953, Trinity College, Dublin. Appointments: Member, Irish diplomatic service, 1944-61; Vice-Chancellor, University of Ghana, 1962-65; Albert Schweitzer Professor of Humanities, New York University, 1965-69; Member, Labour Party, Dublin North-east, Dail, 1969-77, Senate, Republic of Ireland, 1977-79; Visiting Fellow, Nuffield College, Oxford, 1973-75; Minister for Posts and Telegraphs, 1973-77; Pro-Chancellor, University of Dublin, 1973-; Fellow, St Catherine's College, Oxford, 1978-81; Editor-in-Chief, The Observer, 1979-81; Visiting Professor and Montgomery Fellow, Dartmouth College, New Hampshire, 1984-85; Senior Resident Fellow, National Humanities Center, North Carolina, 1993-94. Publications: Maria Cross, 1952; Parnell and His Party, 1957; The Shaping of Modern Ireland (editor), 1959; To Katanga and Back, 1962; Conflicting Concepts of the UN, 1964; Writers and Politics, 1965; The United Nations: Sacred Drama, 1967; Murderous Angels (play), 1968; Power and Consciousness, 1969; Conor Cruise O'Brien Introduces Ireland, 1969; Albert Camus, 1969; The Suspecting Glance (with Máire Cruise O'Brien), 1970; A Concise History of Ireland, 1971; States of Ireland, 1972; King Herod Advises (play), 1973; Neighbours: The Ewart-Biggs Memorial Lectures 1978-79, 1980; The Siege: The Saga of Israel and Zionism, 1986; Passion and Cunning, 1988; God Land: Reflections on Religion and Nationalism, 1988; The Great Melody: A Thematic Biography and Commented Anthology of Edmund Burke, 1992; Ancestral Voices, 1994; On the Eve of the Millennium, 1996; The Long Affair: Thomas Jefferson and the French Revolution, 1996; Memoir: My Life and Themes, 1998. Honours: Valiant for Truth Media Award, 1979; Honorary doctorates. Memberships: Royal Irish Academy; Royal Society of Literature. Address: Whitewater, Howth Summit, Dublin, Ireland.

O'BRIEN Edna, b. 15 December 1936, Tuamgraney, County Clare, Ireland. Author; Dramatist. m. 1954, divorced 1964, 2 sons. Education: Convents; Pharmaceutical College of Ireland.

Publications: The Country Girls, 1960; The Lonely Girl, 1962; Girls in Their Married Bliss, 1963; August is a Wicked Month, 1964; Casualties of Peace, 1966; The Love Object, 1968; A Pagan Place, 1970; Night, 1972; A Scandalous Woman, 1974; Mother Ireland, 1976; Johnnie I Hardly Knew You, 1977; Mrs Reinhardt and Other Stories, 1978; Virginia (play), 1979; The Dazzle, 1981; Returning, 1982; A Christmas Treat, 1982; A Fanatic Heart, 1985; Tales for Telling, 1986; Flesh and Blood (play), 1987; Madame Bovary (play), 1987; The High Road, 1988; Lantern Slides, 1990; Time and Tide, 1992; House of Splendid Isolation, 1994; Down by the River, 1997; James Joyce: A Biography, 1999; Wild Decembers, 1999; In the Forest, 2002; Iphigenia (play), 2003. Honours: Yorkshire Post Novel Award, 1971; Los Angeles Times Award, 1990; Writers' Guild Award, 1993; European Prize for Literature, 1995; American National Arts Gold Medal. Address: David Godwin Associates, 14 Goodwin Court, Covent Garden, London WC2N 4LL, England.

O'BRIEN Francis J, Jr, b. 7 December 1946, Providence, Rhode Island, USA. Scientist. m. Julianne Jennings, 1 son, 2 daughters. Education: BA, Rhode Island College, 1972; MA, Med, MPhil, Columbia University, 1977; PhD, Columbia University, 1980. Appointments: Statistician, US Government Research, 1980-87; Senior Scientist, US Navy, 1987-; Former President, Aquid Neck Indian Council, 1996-2002. Publications: 23 US patents; Numerous articles and proceedings papers; 6 Books. Honours: Who's Who in the East; Who's Who in Science and Engineering; Kappa Delta Pi; Pi Lambda Theta. Memberships: Mensa; Intertel; New York Academy of Sciences; Rhode Island Historical Society; Rhode Island Indian Council. Address: 12 Curry Avenue, Newport, Rhode Island, 02840-1412, USA. E-mail: moondancer_nuwc@hotmail.com

O'BRIEN Stephen, b. 1 April 1957, East Africa. Member of Parliament. m. Gemma, 2 sons, 1 daughter. Education: MA (Hons) Law, Emmanuel College, Cambridge, 1976-79; Final Professional Examination, College of Law, Chester, 1979-80. Appointments: Solicitor, Senior Managing Solicitor, Freshfields Solicitors, City of London, 1981-88; Executive Assistant to the Board, 1988-89, Director of Corporate Planning, 1989-94, Director, International Operating Group, 1994-98, Deputy Chairman, Director, Redland Tile & Brick Ltd (Northern Ireland), 1995-98, Group Committee Member, 1990-98, Group Secretary and Director, Corporate Affairs, 1991-98, Redland PLC; International Business Consultant, 1998-; Member of Parliament for Eddisbury, South West Cheshire, 1999-; Parliamentary Private Secretary to the Chairman of the Conservative Party, 2000-2001; Opposition Whip (Front Bench), 2001-2002; Shadow Paymaster General, 2002-03; Shadow Secretary of State for Industry, 2003-. Memberships: CBI, Elected Member, South East Regional Council, 1995-98; Scottish Business in the Community, Council of Members, 1995-98; BMP Construction Products Association, 1995-99. Address: House of Commons, London SW1A 0AA. E-mail: obriens@parliament.uk

O'CONNOR Sinead, b. 8 December 1966, Dublin, Ireland. Singer. m. John Reynolds, divorced, 1 son, 1 daughter. Education: Dublin College of Music. Appointments: Band Member, Ton Ton Macoute, 1985-87. Creative Works: Singles include: Heroin, 1986; Mandinka, 1987; Jump in the River, 1988; Nothing Compares 2 U, 1990; Three Babies, 1990; You Do Something to Me, 1990; Silent Night, 1991; My Special Child, 1991; Visions of You (with Jan Wobble's Invaders of the Heart), 1992; Emperor's New Clothes, 1992; Secret Love, 1992; Success Has Made a Failure of Our Home, 1992; Albums include: The Lion and the Cobra, 1987; I Do Not Want What I Haven't Got, 1990; Am I Not Your Girl?, 1992; Universal Mother, 1994; Gospeloak, 1997; Sean-Nós Nua, 2002; Video films: Value of Ignorance, 1989; The Year of the Horse, 1991; TV film: Hush-a-Bye-Baby. Honours include: MTV

Best Video, Best Single Awards, 1990; Grammy Award, Best Alternative Album, 1991. Address: c/o Principle Management, 30-32 Sir John Rogerson Quay, Dublin 2, Ireland.

O'DONNELL Chris, b. 1970, Winnetka, Illinois, USA. Actor. m. Caroline Fentress, 1997, 1 daughter. Creative Works: Films include: Men Don't Leave, 1990; Fried Green Tomatoes, 1991; Scent of a Woman, 1992; School Ties, 1992; The Three Musketeers, 1993; Blue Sky, 1994; Circle of Friends, 1995; Mad Love, 1995; Batman Forever, 1995; The Chamber, In Love and War, Batman and Robin, Cookie's Fortune, 1998; The Bachelor, 1998; Vertical Limit, 2000; 29 Palms, 2002; Kinsey, 2004. Address: c/o Kevin Huvane, CAA, 9830 Wilshire Boulevard, Beverly Hills, CA 90212, USA.

O'DONNELL Peter, (Madeleine Brent), b. 11 April 1920, London, England. Author. Education: Catford Central School, London. Appointments: Writer of Strip Cartoons, Garth, 1953-66, Tug Transom, 1954-66, Romeo Brown, 1956-62, Modesty Blaise, 1963-2001. Publications: Modesty Blaise, 1965; Sabre-Tooth, 1966; I, Lucifer, 1967; A Taste for Death, 1969; The Impossible Virgin, 1971; Pieces of Modesty (short stories), 1972; The Silver Mistress, 1973; Murder Most Logical (play), 1974; Last Day in Limbo, 1976; Dragon's Claw, 1978; The Xanadu Talisman, 1981; The Night of Morningstar, 1982; Dead Man's Handle, 1985; Cobra Trap, 1996 (under Peter O'Donnell). As Madeleine Brent: Tregaron's Daughter, 1971; Moonraker's Bride, 1973; Kirkby's Changeling, 1975; Merlin's Keep, 1977; The Capricorn Stone, 1979; The Long Masquerade, 1981; A Heritage of Shadows, 1983; Stormswift, 1984; Golden Urchin, 1986. Address: 49 Sussex Square, Brighton BN2 1GE, England.

O'DONNELL Thomas Vianney, b. 23 July 1926, Wellington, New Zealand. Professor. m. Mary Jean Lynch, 1 son, 3 daughters. Education: BMedSc, University of Otago, 1946; MBChB (NZ), 1949; MD (NZ), 1959; Fellow, Royal Australasian College of Physicians, 1963; Fellow, Royal College of Physicians, London, 1972. Appointments: Faculty of Medicine, University of Otago, Dunedin, New Zealand, 1960-66; Professor, 1970-; Foundation Professor and Head, Department of Medicine, University of Otago, Wellington School of Medicine, 1973-86; Dean of Medical School and Professor of Medicine, University of Otago, 1986-92; Emeritus Professor, University of Otago, 1992. Publications: Over 90 papers in scientific medical publications relating particularly to cardiopulmonary medicine, occupational respiratory health and medical education. Honours: CBE, 1989; Nuffield Commonwealth Travelling Fellowship, 1956; Thoracic Society of Australia and New Zealand Society Medal, 1994. Memberships: Asthma Foundation of New Zealand; Wellington Medical Research Foundation; Thoracic Society of Australia and New Zealand; New Zealand Federation of Sports Medicine; Cardiac and Thoracic Societies of New Zealand; American Thoracic Society. Address: 32a Simla Crescent, Khandallah, Wellington, New Zealand. E-mail: todonnel@paradise.net.nz

O'DONOGHUE (James) Bernard, b. 14 December 1945, Cullen, County Cork, Ireland. University Teacher of English; Poet. m. Heather MacKinnon, 23 July 1977, 1 son, 2 daughters. Education: MA in English, 1968, BPhil in Medieval English, 1971, Lincoln College, Oxford. Appointments: Lecturer and Tutor in English, Magdalen College, Oxford, 1971-95; Fellow and University Lecturer in English Wadham College, Oxford, 1995-. Publications: The Courtly Love Tradition, 1982; Razorblades and Pencils, 1984; Poaching Rights, 1987; The Weakness, 1991; Seamus Heaney & the Language of Poetry, 1994; Gunpowder, 1995; Here Nor There, 1999. Contributions to: Norton Anthology of Poetry; Poetry Ireland Review; Poetry Review; Times Literary Supplement. Honours: Southern Arts Literature Prize, 1991;

Dictionary of International Biography

Whitbread Poetry Award, 1995. Memberships: Poetry Society, London, 1984-; Fellow, Royal Society of Literature, 1999; Fellow, English Society, 1999; Association of University Teachers. Address: Wadham College, Oxford OX1 3PN, England.

O'HALLORAN James, b. 12 July 1932, Callan, County Kilkenny, Ireland. Priest; Educator. BA, London University, 1959; Post Graduate Diploma, Education, Oxford University, 1967; B Div, St Patrick's College, Maynooth, Ireland, 1979; MA, La Salle University, Philadelphia, USA, 1989. Appointments: Principal and Teacher, St Patrick's Primary and Secondary School, Malta, 1963-66, Salesian High School, Manzini, Swaziland, 1967-71; Curriculum Consultant, Amalgamated University of Botswana, Lesotho and Swaziland, Examining Board, 1967-71; Professor of English Literature and Education, Catholic University, Quito, Ecuador, 1972-78; Latin American Delegate, World Congress of Salesian Co-operators, 1976; Member, Ecuadorian Preparatory Team Puebla CELAM Conference, 1978; Visiting Lecturer, Theology: Kenya: Karen College, Nairobi, 1981; Kenyatta College, Nairobi, 1981, GABA Pastoral Centre, Eldoret, 1994-95, Tangaza Seminary, Nairobi, 1994; Sierra Leone: Kenema Pastoral Centre, 1981-91, Milton Margay College, Freetown, 1982; Fourah Bay University, 1982; England: Selly Oak Colleges, Birmingham University, 1982; Australia: Notre Dame University, Perth, 1992; Thailand: Tamkaenjam Buddhist Centre, 1992; South Africa: Ave Maria Pastoral Centre, Tzaneen, 1997-; Malawi: St John the Baptist Seminary, Mangochi, 2003; Lecturer, Theology, All Hallows College, Dublin, Ireland, 1993-; Milltown Institute, Dublin, Ireland, 1993-; Church of Ireland Theological College (Anglican), Dublin, 1996-; Kimmage Missionary Institute, Dublin, Ireland, 1997-; Co-ordinator, Ecumenical European Team Third International Consult. Small (Basic) Christian Communities, Cochabamba, Bolivia, 1999; Animating Team, European Conference Small Christian Communities, Iona, Scotland, 1999. Publications: Living Cells, (theology) 1984; The Least of These (short stories), 1991; When the Acacia Bird Sings (novel), 1999; Remember José Inga (novel), 2003; Small Christian Communities, Vision and Practicalities (theology), 2003; The Brendan Book of Prayer, 2003; Columnist Irish Sunday Independent, 1984; Articles in professional journals. Honours: Swaziland Independence Medal, Government of Swaziland, 1969; Honorary Chieftanship, Sunyani, Ghana, 1982; Research Grant, Misereor, 1987-88; Listed in Who's Who publications and biographical dictionaries. Memberships: Irish Missionary Union; Conference of Religious of Ireland; Affiliated, National Council of Priests of Ireland. Address: Salesian House, St Teresa's Rd, Crumlin, Dublin 12, Ireland. E-mail: ohallo@gofree.indigo.ie

O'KANE Stephen Granville, b. 26 April 1951, Harrow, Middlesex, England. Writer; Researcher. Education: BA, Politics, History (subsidiary), University of Nottingham, England, 1970-73; MA, Political Thought, University of Keele, England, 1973-75; PhD, Christianity and Socialism in British thought, University of London, London School of Economics, 1975-79; Reading ability in French, 1989-93; Numerous computer courses, 1978-98; Business Enterprise Programme and Extended Business Training, 1989-91. Career: Owing to ill health (asthma and ME/CFS) became researcher and writer rather than pursue an institutional career; Writings and research on the confluence between ethical and political issues and the implications of that for ethics itself, 1979-; Research into political affairs in individual members of the European Union, 1988-; Part-time Adult Education Teacher, Clerical and Market Research work, 1980-81, 1984-86, 1993; Set up own website (http://www.stgok.mistral.co.uk) adjusted to RNIB guidelines for people with sight difficulties; Supporter of Project Discover which aims to use computer technology to express the emotions of disabled people, 1995-. Publications: Book, Politics and Morality under Conflict, 1994; Book in progress, Ethics and

Radical Freedom (proposed publication 2005); Several articles for The Radical Quarterly, 1987-90; 2 articles in FSI News/ Business News (Sussex), 1989, 1990; Article, What Right to Private Property? In Economy and Society, 1997; Paper, Ethical Systems and Expansion in Information Circulation, 2003. Memberships: British Society for Ethical Theory; Brighton and Hove Friends of the Earth, 1995-. Address: Flat 168, Wick Hall, Furze Hill, Hove BN3 1NJ, England. E-mail: stgok@mistral.co.uk

O'MEARA Mark, b. 13 January 1957, Goldsboro, North Carolina, USA. Golfer. Education: Long Beach State University. Career: Professional Golfer, 1980-; Ryder Cup Team, 1985, 1989, 1991, 1997; Won US Amateur Championship, 1979, Greater Milwaukee Open, 1984, Bing Crosby Pro-American, 1985, Hawaii Open, 1985, Fuji Sankei Classic, 1985, Australian Masters, 1986, Lawrence Batley International, 1987, AT&T Pebble Beach National Pro-American, 1989, 1990, 1992, 1997, H-E-B TX Open, 1990, Walt Disney World/Oldsmobile Classic, 1991, Tokia Classic, 1992, Argentine Open, 1994, Honda Classic, 1995, Bell Canada Open, 1995, Mercedes Championships, 1996, Greater Greensboro Open, 1996, Brick Invitational, 1997, US Masters, 1998, British Open, 1998, World Matchplay 1998; Best Finish 2002, 2nd in Buick Invitational and 2nd in Buick Open. Honour: All-American Rookie of the Year, Long Beach State University, 1981; PGA Tour Player of the Year, 1998. Address: c/o PGA, Box 109601, Avenue of Champions, Palm Beach Gardens, FL 33410, USA.

O'NEAL Ryan, b. 20 April 1941, Los Angeles, USA. m. (1) Joanna Moore, divorced, 1 son, 1 daughter, (2) Leigh Taylor-Young, divorced, 1 son, 1 son with Farrah Fawcett. Career: Numerous TV appearances; Films include: The Big Bounce, 1969; Love Story, 1970; The Wild Rovers, 1971; What's Up, Doc? 1972; The Thief Who Came To Dinner, 1973; Paper Moon, 1973; Oliver's Story, 1978; The Main Event, 1979; So Fine, 1981; Partners, 1982; Irreconcilable Differences, 1983; Fever Pitch, 1985; Tough Guys Don't Dance, 1986; Chances Are, 1989; Faithful, 1996; Hacks, 1997; Burn Hollywood Burn, 1997; Zero Effect, 1998; Coming Soon, 1999; Epoch, 2000; People I Know, 2002; Malibu's Most Wanted, 2003.

O'NEAL Shaquille Rashaun, b. 6 March 1972, Newark, USA. Basketball Player. m. Shaunie Nelson, 2 children, 2 children from previous relationships. Education: Los Angeles University. Appointments: Center Orlando Magic, 1992-96; Los Angeles Lakers, 1996-. Creative Works: Films: Blue Chips, 1994; Kazaam, 1996; Music: has released five rap albums; Own record label, Twism. Memberships: National Basketball Association All-Star Team, 1993; Dream Team 11, 1994. Address: c/o Los Angeles Lakers; 3900 West Manchester Boulevard, Inglewood, CA 90306, USA.

O'NEILL Joseph D, b. Bayonne, New Jersey, USA. Lawyer. Education: AB, Allegheny College; JD, New York Law School. Appointments: Admitted to Bar, New Jersey and US District Court, District of New Jersey, 1968; US Supreme Court, 1974; US Court of Appeals, Third Circuit, 1999. Publications: Articles in professional legal journals include: Author: Assignment of Counsel to Indigents in Municipal Court: A Suggested Plan, 1971; The Criminal Case: Preparation and Control, 1978; Our Most Formidable Challenge, 1988; What ATLA is Doing for You, 1989; Lawyers Have Rights Too, 1989; Co-author with Thomas Westerman, MD, Demonstrating Objective Testing of Subjective Symptoms in ENT Cases, 1988; Demonstrating Soft Tissue Injury Without Supportive Medical Tests, Hot Tips in Tort Law, 1990; Don't let Juries Confuse Neurosis and Malingering, Hot Tips in Tort Law II, 1991; Themes for Damages, Hot Tips in Tort Law III, 1992; Attorney Conducted Voir Dire: We Need It, 1994; Getting Cases, Keeping Them and Enhancing Your Awards, Million Dollar

Tips for Million Dollar Advocates, 1999; Lecturer for: Association of Trial Lawyers of America, National College of Advocacy, Association of Trial Lawyers of America-New Jersey, New Jersey State Bar Association and various state and county bar associations and law schools. Honours: In 2000 become the only lawyer in the history of South Jersey ever to argue and win a case before the United States Supreme Court. Apprendi v. New Jersey 530 US 466, 120S Ct 2348, 147 L Ed 2d 435, 2000; Outstanding Contribution and Leadership Award, National Association of Defense Lawyers, 1977-78; Listed in Who's Who publications and biographical dictionaries. Memberships: Cumberland County (Chairman, Medical-Legal Committee, 1985), New Jersey State (Member, Board of Directors, Certified Trial Attorneys Section, 1988-90) and American (Member, Trial Techniques Committee and Products Liability Committee, Tort and Insurance Practice Section, 1980-) Bar Associations; The Association of Trial Lawyers of America (National Governor, 1992-98); National Association of Criminal Defense Lawyers (Member, National Hotline Panel of Homicide Case Experts); Association of Criminal Defense Lawyers of New Jersey; The Association of Trial Lawyers of America – New Jersey (President , 1988-89, Member Board of Governors, 1979-, President Elect 1987-88, First Vice-President, 1986-87, 2nd and 1st Vice-President, 1985-86, Treasurer, 1984-85, Secretary, 1983-84, Trustee, ATLA Legal PAC-NJ, 1988-90, Chairman, 1992-95); Advocate American Board of Trial Advocates; Fellow, Rosco Pound-American Trial Lawyers Foundation; Certification as a Civil and Criminal Trial Specialist by the National Board of Trial Advocacy; Certified Criminal and Civil Trial Attorney, Supreme Court of New Jersey, Board on Trial certification; President, Cumberland County Legal Aid Society, 1974-97; Member, New Jersey Automobile Arbitration Panel; Member of Panel, American Arbitration Association; Member, Million Dollar Advocates Forum. Address: O'Neill & Coant, PC, 30 W Chestnut Avenue, PO Box 847, Vineland, NJ 08362, USA. E-mail: joneillesq@mindspring.com

O'SULLEVAN Peter John (Sir), b. 3 March 1918. Racing Correspondent; Commentator. m. Patricia Duckworth, 1951. Education: College Alpin, Switzerland. Appointments: Chelsea Rescue Service, 1939-45; Editorial work and manuscript reading with Bodley Head Publisher; Racing Correspondent, Press Association, 1945-50, Daily Express, 1950-86, Today, 1986-87; Race Broadcaster, 1946-98; Chair, Osborne Studio Gallery, 1999-. Publication: Calling the Horses: A Racing Autobiography, 1989. Honours include: Derby Award, Racing Journalist of the Year, 1971; Racehorse Owner of the Year Award, Horserace Writers Association, 1974; Sport on TV Award, Daily Telegraph, 1994; Services to Racing Award, Daily Star, 1995; Lester's Award, Jockeys' Association, 1996; Special Award, TV and Radio Industries Club, 1998. Address: 37 Cranmer Court, London SW3 3HW, England.

O'SULLIVAN Sonia, b. 28 November 1969, Cobh, Ireland. Athlete. Education: Accounting Studies, Villanova, USA. Career: Gold Medal 1500m, Silver Medal 3000m, World Student Games, 1991; Holds 7 national (Irish) records; Set new world record (her first) in 2000m, TSB Challenge, Edinburgh, 1994, new European record in 3000m, TSB Games London, 1994; Gold Medal in 3000m European Athletic Championships, Helsinki, 1994; Winner, Grand Prix 3000m, 2nd overall, 1993; Silver Medal, 1500m World Championships, Stuttgart, 1993; Gold Medal, 5000m World Championships, Gothenburg, 1995; Gold Medal, World Cross Country Championships 4km, 8km, 1998; Gold Medal, European Championships 5000m, 10,000m, 1998; Silver Medal, 5,000m 2000 Olympic Games; Silver Medal, 5,000m, 10,000m European Championships, 2002. Publications: Running to Stand Still.

Honours: Female Athlete of the Year, 1995; Texaco Sports Star of the Year (Athletics), 2002. Address: c/o Kim McDonald, 201 High Street, Hampton Hill, Middlesex TW12 1NL, England.

O'TOOLE Peter Seamus, b. 2 August 1932, Eire, Ireland. Actor. 1 son, 2 daughters. Education: RADA (Diploma), Associate, RADA. Career: Joined Bristol's Old Vic Theatre, played 73 parts, 1955-58; West End debut in Oh My Papa, 1957; Stratford Season, 1960; Stage appearances in, Pictures in the Hallway, 1962; Baal, 1963; Ride a Cock Horse, Waiting for Godot, 1971; Dead Eye Dicks, 1976; Present Laughter, 1978; Bristol Old Vic Theatre Season, 1973; Macbeth Old Vic, 1980; Man and Superman, 1982-83; Pygmalion, 1984, 1987; The Applecart, 1986; Jeffrey Barnard is Unwell, 1989, 1991, 1999; Films include: Kidnapped, 1959; The Day They Robbed the Bank of England, 1959; Lawrence of Arabia, 1960; Becket, 1963; Lord Jim, 1964; The Bible, 1966; What's New Pussycat?, 1965; Night of the Generals, 1967; Great Catherine, 1967; The Lion in Winter, 1968; Goodbye Mr Chips, 1969; Brotherly Love, 1970; Country Dance, 1970; Murphy's War, 1971; Under Milk Wood, 1972; The Ruling Class, 1972; Man of La Mancha, 1972; Rosebud, 1974; Man Friday, 1975; Foxtrot, 1975; Caligula, 1977; Power Play, 1978; Stuntman, 1978; Zulu Dawn, 1978; The Antagonists, 1981; My Favourite Year, 1981; Supergirl, 1984; Club Paradise, 1986; The Last Emperor, 1986; High Spirits, 1988; On a Moonlit Night, 1989; Creator, 1990; King Ralph, 1990; Wings of Fame, 1991; Rebecca's Daughters, 1992; Our Song, 1992; Civies, 1992; Fairytale: the True Story, 1997; Coming Home, 1998; The Manor, 1998; Molokai: The Story of Father Damien, 1999; Global Heresy, 2002; The Final Curtain, 2002; Bright Young Things, 2003; Troy, 2004. Publications: The Child, 1992; The Apprentice, 1996. Honours: Commander of the Order of Arts and Letters, France; Outstanding Achievement Award, 1999. Address: c/o William Morris Agency, Stratton House, Stratton Street, London, W1X 5FE, England.

OAKES Philip, b. 31 January 1928, Burslem, Staffordshire, England. Author; Poet. Appointments: Scriptwriter, Granada TV and BBC, London, 1958-62; Film Critic, The Sunday Telegraph, London, 1963-65; Assistant Editor, Sunday Times Magazine, 1965-67; Arts Columnist, Sunday Times, London, 1969-80; Columnist, Independent on Sunday, London, 1990, Guardian Weekend, London, 1991-. Publications: Unlucky Jonah: Twenty Poems, 1954; The Punch and Judy Man (with Tony Hancock), screenplay, 1962; Exactly What We Want (novel), 1962; In the Affirmative (poems), 1968; The God Botherers, US edition as Miracles: Genuine Cases Contact Box 340 (novel), 1969; Married/Singular (poems), 1973; Experiment at Proto (novel), 1973; Tony Hancock: A Biography, 1975; The Entertainers (editor), 1975; A Cast of Thousands (novel), 1976; The Film Addict's Archive, 1977; From Middle England (memoirs), 1980; Dwellers All in Time and Space (memoirs), 1982; Selected Poems, 1982; At the Jazz Band Ball (memoirs); Shopping for Women (novel), 1994. Address: Fairfax Cottage, North Owersby, Lincolnshire LN8 3PX, England.

OAKLEY Ann (Rosamund), b. 17 January 1944, London, England. Professor of Sociology and Social Policy; Writer. 1 son, 2 daughters. Education: MA, Somerville College, Oxford, 1965; PhD, Bedford College, London, 1974. Appointments: Research Officer, Social Research Unit, Bedford College, London, 1974-79; Wellcome Research Fellow, Radcliffe Infirmary, National Perinatal Epidemiology Unit, Oxford, 1980-83; Deputy Director, Thomas Coram Research Unit, 1985-90, Director, Social Science Research Unit, 1990-, Professor of Sociology and Social Policy, 1991-, University of London. Publications: Sex, Gender and Society, 1972; The Sociology of Housework, 1974; Housewife, 1974, US edition as Women's Work: A History of the Housewife, 1975; The Rights and Wrongs of Women (editor with Juliet Mitchell), 1976; Becoming a Mother, 1980; Women Confined,

Dictionary of International Biography

1980; Subject Women, 1981; Miscarriage (with A McPherson and H Roberts), 1984; Taking It Like a Woman, 1984; The Captured Womb: A History of the Medical Care of Pregnant Women, 1984; Telling the Truth about Jerusalem, 1986; What Is Feminism (editor with Juliet Mitchell), 1986; The Men's Room, 1988; Only Angels Forget, 1990; Matilda's Mistake, 1990; Helpers in Childbirth: Midwifery Today (with S Houd), 1990; The Secret Lives of Eleanor Jenkinson, 1992; Social Support and Motherhood: The Natural History of a Research Project, 1992; Essays on Women, Medicine and Health, 1992; Scenes Originating in the Garden of Eden, 1993; Young People, Health and Family Life (with J Brannen, K Dodd and P Storey), 1994; The Politics of the Welfare State (editor with S Williams), 1994; Man and Wife, 1996; The Gift Relationship by Richard Titmuss (with John Ashton), 1997; Experiments in Knowledge: Gender and Method in the Social Sciences, 2000; Overheads, 2000; Gender on Planet Earth, 2002. Contributions to: Professional journals; Many chapters in academic books. Honours: Hon DLitt, Salford, 1995; Honorary Professor, University College, London, 1996-; Honorary Fellow, Somerville College, Oxford, 2001-. Address: c/o Tessa Sayle Ltd, 11 Jubilee Place, London SW3, England.

OBIORAH Edwin, b. 26 June 1960, Ifitedunu, Nigeria. Attorney. Education: B Phil, 1981; BD, 1985; PGDE, 1989; LLB, 1990; BL, 1991; LLM, 1992; LLM, 1995; JSD, 1997. Appointments: Director, Pastor, Catholic Diocese of Akwa, Nigeria, 1985-90; Associate Attorney, Law Firm, Ben Nwazojie SAN, 1991-94; Associate Attorney, Harris, Beach & Wilcox, LLP, 1997-99; Managing Attorney at Law at Law Office of Edwin S C Obiorah, JSD, 1999-. Publications: Eco-Justice: A New Paradigm in Environmental Jurisprudence; Consideration: A Pillar in Contractual Relations?; Epilesia: Its Nexus with Justice and Prudence; The Learned and the Moral Problems of Contemporary Society. Honours: 1st Class Honours from Urban University Rome, Italy, 1985; Fellow of Cornell IAD, 1995; Listed in Who's Who publications and biographical dictionaries. Memberships include: New York State Bar; Monroe County Bar; Nigerian bar; Catholic Clergy Organisation. Address: Akwa Catholic Secretariat, PMB 5021, Akwa, Nigeria.

ODELL Robin Ian, b. 19 December 1935, Totton, Hampshire, England. Writer. m. Joan Bartholomew, 19 September 1959. Publications: Jack the Ripper in Fact and Fiction, 1965; Exhumation of a Murder, 1975; Jack the Ripper: Summing-up and Verdict (with Colin Wilson), 1977; The Murderers' Who's Who (with J H H Gaute), 1979; Lady Killers, 1980; Murder Whatdunit, 1982; Murder Whereabouts, 1986; Dad Help Me Please (with Christopher Berry-Dee), 1990; A Question of Evidence, 1992; Lady Killer, 1992; The Long Drop, 1993; Landmarks in Twentieth Century Murder, 1995; The International Murderer's Who's Who, 1996. Contributions to: Crimes and Punishment; The Criminologist. Honours: FCC Watts Memorial Prize, 1957; International Humanist and Ethical Union, 1960; Edgar Award, Mystery Writers of America, 1980. Memberships: Paternosters; Our Society. Address: 11 Red House Drive, Sonning Common, Reading RG4 9NT, England.

ODENDAAL André, b. 4 May 1954, Queenstown, South Africa. History Professor; Writer; Museum Director. m. Zohra Begum Ebrahim, 1 son, 2 daughters. Education: BA, 1974-76; BA (Hons), History, cum laude, 1977; MA, History, cum laude, 1981, University of Stellenbosch, South Africa. DPhil, History, St John's College, Cambridge, UK, 1984. Appointments: Professor and Founding Director, Mayibuye Centre for History and Culture in South Africa, University of Western Cape, 1992; Founding Director, Robben Island Museum (the first official heritage institution of democratic South Africa), 1998. Publications: Vukani Bantu! The beginnings of black protest politics in South Africa to

1912, 1984; The Story of an African Game: Black cricketers and the unmasking of one of cricket's greatest myths, South Africa, 1850-2003, 2003; 5 other books on the history of apartheid and resistance. Honours: Sanlam Prize for Literature (Third Place), 1985; President's Award for Sport, 2002. Address: 1 Sunningdale Road, Kenilworth, Capetown, South Africa. E-mail: andreodendaal@absamail.co.za

ODOM John Yancy, b. 22 September 1948, Jackson, Mississippi, USA. Human Resource Development Consultant. m. Annie Perkins, 1 daughter. Education: BA, English, Lane College, Jackson, Tennessee, 1969; MS, Educational Administration, 1973, PhD, Educational Administration, 1978, University of Wisconsin-Madison. Appointments: Teacher of English, Beloit, Wisconsin Schools, 1969-73; Affirmative Action Officer, 1973-76, Director, Department of Human Relations, 1976-80; Madison Schools, Wisconsin; Middle School Principal, Madison, Wisconsin, 1980-85; Academic Specialist, University of Wisconsin, 1985-86; President, Odom & Associates LLC, 1985-. Publications: The Diversity Movement has Legs; Educational Administration and Human Relations: An Integration (doctoral dissertation), 1978; My People My Power; Saving Black America: An Economic Plan for Civil Rights, 2001. Honours: Martin Luther King Humanitarian of the Year, Human Rights Award of Madison, Wisconsin; Listed in Who's Who publications and biographical dictionaries. Address: Post Office Box 56155, Madison, WI 53705, USA. E-mail: jyodom@charter.net Website: www.odom.ws

ODORA HOPPERS Catherine A, b. 3 July 1957, Gulu, Uganda. Academic; Assistant Professor. m. Wim Hoppers, 1 son, 2 daughters. Education: BA, Education, 1981, Master's Degree, Social Science, International and Comparative Education, 1992, Stockholm, Sweden; PhD, International and Comparative Education, 1998. Appointments: Assistant Professor, University of Pretoria, South Africa, 2001-2004; Visiting Professor, Stockholm University, Sweden, 2003-; Chief Research Specialist, South Africa, Human Sciences Research Council; Deputy Director, Centre for Education Policy Development, South Africa; Adviser, Team Leader, Mentor on National Initiative on Indigenous Knowledge and the Integration of Knowledge Systems, South African Parliament, Ministry for Science and Technology. Publications: Several publications including: Indigenous Knowledge and the Integration of Knowledge Systems: Towards a Philosophy of Articulation; Poverty, Power, Partnerships: a Post Victimology Perspective. Honours: Member of the Academy of Science of South Africa; Adviser to UN bodies at OAU level; Adviser to professorial bodies; Listed in Who's Who publications and biographical dictionaries. Memberships: Academy of Science, South Africa; Several academic journals; Boards of Organisations. Address: Stottingsgrand 1, Bv, 12945 Hagersten, Stockholm, Sweden.

ODUARAN Akpovire Bovadjera, b. 20 March 1955, Ughelli, Delta State, Nigeria. Professor of Adult Education. Education: B Ed (Honours), History, University of Benin, Benin City, Nigeria, 1978; MA, Adult Education, University of Ife (now Obafemi Awolowo University) Ile-Ife, Nigeria, 1983; PhD, Adult and Community Education, University of Ibadan, Nigeria, 1986; Certificate in Advanced Christian Leadership, Haggai Institute, Hawaii, USA, 1997. Appointments include: Graduate Assistant, 1981-83, Assistant Lecturer, 1983-85, Lecturer II, 1985-87, Lecturer I, 1987-90, Senior Lecturer, 1990-93, Professor of Adult and Community Education, 1993-97, University of Benin, Nigeria; Associate Professor of Adult Education, 1997-2000, Professor of Adult Education, 2000-, Head, Department of Adult Education, 2002-, University of Botswana, Gaborone, Botswana. Publications: Books as author: An Introduction to Community Development, 1994; Social Welfare and Social Work Education for Africa, 1996;

Dictionary of International Biography

The Essentials of Adult Learning, 1996; Effective Adult Learning and Teaching, 2000; Literacy Programmes Development and Evaluation Process in Africa (co-author), 1995; 20 contributions to books and monographs; Over 35 articles in refereed journals; Numerous conference and seminar papers. Honours: Federal Government of Nigeria Scholar, 1980-88; Distinguished Alumnus Award, University of Benin; Professional Associate, The Continuum, Centre for Continuing Education, University of East London, UK, 2003; Listed in Who's Who publications and biographical dictionaries. Memberships: International Association for Community Development; Nigerian National Council for Adult Education; Nigerian Institute on Substance Abuse; Curriculum Organisation of Nigeria; Community Education and Research Society of Nigeria; Botswana Educational Research Association; International Consortium for Intergenerational Program (ICIP); Botswana Adult Education Association. Address: Department of Adult Education, University of Botswana, Gaborone, Botswana. E-mail: oduarana@mopipi.ub.bw

OFUYA Thomas Inomisan, b. 4 November 1954, Kano, Nigeria. Teacher; Researcher. m. Olayinka Oshinowo, 2 daughters. Education: BSc, Agriculture, 1976, PhD, Plant Science, Entomology, 1984, University of Ife, Nigeria. Appointments: Lecturer II, 1985 to Full Professor, 1999-, Federal University of Technology, Akure, Nigeria. Publications: Over 70 articles in peer-reviewed science journals; Editor, 1 book; Editor-in-chief, international journal, 1996-. Honours: Alexander Von Humboldt Research Fellowship, 1991; Royal Society London Research Fellowship, 1993; COSTED Research Fellowship, 1998; IFS/ DANIDA Award, 1998. Memberships: Entomological Society of Nigeria; Science Association of Nigeria; Nigerian Society for Plant Protection. Address: Department of Crop, Soil and Pest Management, The Federal University of Technology, PMB 704, Akure, Nigeria. E-mail: tomofuya@yahoo.com

OGG James Elvis, b. 24 December 1924, Centralia, Illinois, USA. Microbiologist. m. Betty Jane Ackerson, 1 son, 1 daughter. Education: BS, Microbiology, Chemistry, University of Illinois, 1949; PhD, Microbiology, Genetics, Cornell University, 1956. Appointments include: Active, Reserve, US Army, 1943-53; Bacteriologist, 1950-53, Consultant, 1953-56, Medical Microbiologist, 1956-58, Biological Laboratories, Fort Detrick, MD, 1953-56; Professor, Department of Microbiology, 1958-85, Assistant Dean, Graduate School, 1965-66, Department Head, 1967-77, Emeritus Professor, 1985-, Colorado State University, Fort Collins; Director, Advanced Science Education Program, National Science Foundation, 1966-67; Academic Administration Advisor, Institute of Agriculture and Animal Science, Tribhuvan University, Nepal, 1988-91; Deputy Team Leader, Nepal Agricultural Research Study, 1991-93; Consultant, Advisor, several bodies. Publications: Over 80 including: Genetics, radiation resistance and physiology of possibly diploid strains of Escherichia coli; Virulence factors of Yersina pestis; Ovine Vibriosis Vaccine; Coccoid (non-culturable forms) of Campylobacter; Transduction and bacteriophage conversion of Campylobacter species; Bacteriophage-induced changes in serotypes of Vibrio cholera; Transduction and transfection in Vibrio cholerae; Vibrio cholerae in ruminants, birds, and surface waters of Colorado; Toxins of Clostridium haemolyticum. Honours: Fellow, American Association for the Advancement of Science; Fellow, American Academy for Microbiology; Fulbright-Hays Senior Lectureship, Nepal, 1976-77, 1981. Memberships include: American Society for Microbiology; Fulbright Association; American Legion; Phi Kappa Phi. Address: 1442 Ivy Street, Fort Collins, CO 89525, USA. E-mail: www.jeogg@lamar.colostate.edu

OGG James George, b. 25 November 1952, Frederick, Maryland, USA. Professor of Geology. m. Gabriele Marie Dürr, 2 sons. Education: BSc, Hons, 1975, MSc, Planetary Geology, 1975, California Institute of Technology, Pasadena; PhD, Oceanography, Scripps Institution of Oceanography, University of California at San Diego, La Jolla, 1981; Postdoctoral Fellowship, 1981-83. Appointments: Adjunct Assistant Professor, Department of Geology and Geophysics, University of Wyoming, Laramie, 1984-85; Assistant Researcher, Scripps Institution of Oceanography, 1986-; Assistant Professor, 1986-90, Associate Professor, 1990-95, Full Professor, 1995-, Department of Earth and Atmospheric Sciences, Purdue University, West Lafayette, Indiana; Consultant, various petroleum companies, 1992-. Publications: Over 80 refereed journal articles, as author or co-author on geological time-scale calibration, paleoceanography, paleomagnetism and magnetostratigraphy, cyclic climate and associate sediments; Around 50 contributions to cruise volumes of Deep Sea Drilling Project and Ocean Drilling Programme; Coordinator, Geological Time Scale 2004; Secretary General of International Commission on Stratigraphy. Honours include: Finalist, Westinghouse Science Talent Search, 1971; Top Award, Tomorrow's Scientist and Engineers Award, National Science Teachers Association, 1971; Numerous visiting professorships and keynote presentations. Memberships: International Subcommission on Jurassic Stratigraphy, International Union of Geological Sciences; Oxfordian-Kimmeridigan Working Group, 1985-; Kimmeridigian-Tithonian Bounday Working Group, 1989-; Committee on Quantitative Stratigraphy, 1987-; Geological Society of America; American Geophysical Union; American Association for the Advancement of Science. Address: Department of Earth and Atmospheric Sciences, Purdue University, West Lafayette, IN 47907, USA. Email: jogg@purdue.edu

OGG Wilson Reid, b. 26 February 1928, Alhambra, California, USA. Social Scientist; Philosopher; Lawyer; Poet; Lyricist; Educator. Education: AA, 1947; AB, 1949; JD, University of California, 1952; Hon DD, Universal Life Church, 1969; Doctorate, Religious Humanities, 1970. Appointments: Psychology Instructor, US Armed Forces Institute, Taegu, Korea, 1953-54; English Instructor, Taegu English Language Institute, 1954; Trustee Secretary, 1st Unitarian Church of Berkeley, 1957-58; Research Attorney, Continuing Education of the Bar, University of California, 1958-63; Vice President, International House Association, 1961-62; President, Board Chairman, California Society for Psychical Study, 1963-65; Private Law Practitioner, 1955-; Director, Admissions, International Society for Philosophical Enquiry, 1981-84. Publications: Poetry publications in numerous journals and anthologies. Honours: Commendation Ribbon W Medal Pendant; Cultural Doctorate, World University. Memberships: American Bar Association; State Bar of California; American Mensa; The Triple Nine Society; Parapsychological Association; International House Association; Faculty Club of the University of California at Berkeley; New York Academy of Sciences; Scientific Faculty, Cambridge, England; London Diplomatic Academy; International Platform Association; San Francisco Bar Association; American Association for the Advancement of Science; American Society of Composers, Authors and Performers. Address: Pinebrook at Bret Harte Way, 8 Bret Harte Way, Berkeley, CA 94708, USA. E-mail: wilsonogg@cal.berkeley.edu Website: www.wilsonogg.com

OGRODNICK Margaret Jean, b. 2 August 1956, Edmonton, Alberta, Canada. Professor. Education: BA, Philosophy, MA, Political Science, University of Alberta, Canada; PhD, Political Science, York University, Toronto. Appointment: Political Scientist in Political Theory. Publications: Nietzsche as Critic of Rousseau: Squaring off on Nature, 1995; Instinct and Intimacy: Political Philosophy and Autobiography in Rousseau, 1999. Memberships:

American Political Science Association; Canadian Political Science Association; Rousseau Association. Address: Department of Political Studies, University of Manitoba, Winnipeg, MB R3T 5V5, Canada. E-mail: ogrodnic@ms.umanitoba.ca

OGUN Oluremi, b. 10 October 1957, Owo Nigeria. Economics Educator. Education: BSc (Honours), Economics, 1981, MSc, Economics, 1983, PhD, Economics, 1990, University of Ibadan, Nigeria; ACIB, London, 1991. Publications: Several journal articles, 1 book. Honours: African Economic Research Consortium (AERC) Research Grant, 1992, 1994, 1996; Research Fellowship, 1994; Special Service Award, Institute for New Technology, UN University, Maastricht, 1992; African Technology Policy Studies (ATPS) Research Grant, 1995; Listed in numerous biographical dictionaries. Memberships: Nigerian Economics Society, Life Member and Secretary Oyo State Chapter, 1993; AERC; ATPS; West African Economics Association; Chartered Institute of Bankers, London; Economic Development Association; Association of Third World Studies. Address: Department of Economics, University Ibadan, Nigeria.

OHANJANYAN Karen, b. 19 July 1957, Stepanakert, Nagorno-Karabakh. Co-ordinator, Nagorno-Karabakh Committee of Helsinki Initiative 92. Education: Master Degree, Systems Technical Engineer, 1975-80, Masters degree, Medical Cybernetics, 1978-80, Yerevan Polytechnic University, Yervan, Armenia; Doctor of Philosophy (PhD), International Academy of Culture and Political Science, Brussels, Belgium, 2000. Appointments: Secretary "Krunk" Committee (which led the Karabakhian movement during Soviet times), Stepanakert, Nagorno-Karabakh, 1988-90; Co-ordinator, Nagorno-Karabakh Committee of Helsinki Initiative 92, Stepankert, Nagorno-Karabakh, 1992-; MP, Nagorno-Karabakh Parliament, 1995-2000; Representative, Findhorn Foundation (Scotland) in Armenia and Nagorno-Karabakh, 2000-; Representative of International Human Rights and Religious Freedom Organisation (Geneva, Switzerland), in Armenia, 2002-; President, Armenian Human Rights Agency, Yerevan, Armenia, 2002-; Director of Peace House, Stepanakert, Nagorno-Karabakh, 2003-; Participant in numerous international conferences; Promoted the release of more than 500 Azeri and Armenian prisoners of war and hostages, 1992-2002. Publications: The Links between Conflict Transformation and Different Levels of Perception of Security, 1998; Democracy is not Stagnation but a Development Process, 2000; The End of Moral Era, 2002; Evolution of a Human being from Homo Sapiens to the Creator, 2002. Honours: Peace and Human Rights Award, Interchurch Peace Council, The Hague, Netherlands, 2000; Certificate of Honor, Institute of International Affairs, Brussels, Belgium, 2002; Certificate of Honor, International Academy of Culture and Political Science, Brussels, Belgium, 2002. Memberships: Member of International Co-ordination Committee, Prague, Czech Republic, Helsinki Citizens' Assembly, 1992-; Co-ordination Committee, Agency of Development of Initiatives, Ljubljana, Slovenia, 1996-98; Regional Representative, Amnesty International, UK, in Nagorno- Karabakh, 1998-; Representative of Links (UK) in Nagorno-Karabakh, 1999-; Member, State of the World Forum, New York, USA, 1999-; Member, Co-existence Initiative, New York, USA, 1999-. Address: Apt 7, 5 Garegin Nzhdehi Street, Yerevan, Armenia, 375006. E-mail: karandje@hca.nk.am

OHMORI Mukon, b. 15 September 1925, Tochigi, Japan. Artist; Calligrapher; Advisor on Clinical Educational Psychology. m. Teruko Uehara. Education: Graduate, National Yokohama Institute of Technical College, 1947, Tokyo Scientific College, 1962, Japanese Calligraphic College, 1987. Appointments: Teacher, Sumida Technical High School, 1952-84; Juror, 1990, Director, 1993-, All-Japanese Calligraphic Exhibition's Association; Title of Especially Recognised Excellent Artist, Committee to Develop

Art-Culture between Japan and France and Le Sermadiras Artistes and Ateliers, France, 1993; Publications: Mechanical Design and Drafting, 1966; Exercises in Mechanical Design and Drafting, 1971; Principal Treatises: The Catastrophic Phenomenon in Senior High School Students, 1979; The Heuristic Learning In Mechanical Design and Drafting, 1983. Honours: Prizes, All-Japanese Calligraphic Exhibition's Association, 1991, 1992, 1994, 1995, 1997; Special Prize, Director of Tourism Representative Office of California State Government, Japan, 1994; Grand Art Prize, Department of Art Cultural Exchange of Tai-Yuan City, China, 1998; Special Prize, Sankei Art Exhibition, Japan, 1998; International Order of Merit and Gold Star Award, IBC, 2000; Universal Award of Cultural Accomplishments, 2000. Memberships: Fellowship and Honours List, International Biographical Centre, England; Le Sermadiras Artistes and Ateliers, France. Commissions and Creative Works: One Man Shows of Art and Calligraphy: London, England, 1994, 1995; Tokyo, Japan, 1990, 1992, 1995; New York, USA, 1996, 1998; All Japanese Calligraphic Exhibitions Association; Asian Cultural Exchanging Association; Japanese Mechanical Design and Drafting Academy; Japanese Educational Psychological Academy. Address: 64-2 Ohyaguchi Matsudo-shi, Chiba 270, Japan.

OHSETO Shinji, b. 17 June 1967, Tokyo, Japan. Associate Professor. m. Miki Kato, 2 sons. Education: BS, Tokyo Institute of Technology, Tokyo, Japan, 1991; MA, University of Tsukuba, Ibaraki, Japan, 1993; PhD, Osaka University, Oskaka, Japan, 2000. Appointments: Assistant Professor of Economics, 1995-97, Associate Professor of Economics, 1997-98, Ritsumeikan University, Kyoto, Japan; Associate Professor of Economics, Tokyo Metropolitan University, Tokyo, Japan, 1998-. Publications: Articles in: Economic Studies Quarterly, 1994; Mathematical Social Sciences, 1997; Social Choice and Welfare, 1999, 2002; Economic Theory, 1999; Games and Economic Behavior, 2000; International Journal of Game Theory, 2000; Economic Theory, forthcoming; Japanese Economic Review, forthcoming. Memberships: Game Theory Society; Society for Social Choice and Welfare; Japanese Economic Association. Address: Tokyo Metropolitan University, Faculty of Economics, 1-1 Minamiosawa, Hachioji, Tokyo 192-0397, Japan.

OHTO Yasuhiro, b. 25 October 1951, Tokyo, Japan. Professor. Education: Bachelor of Education, Yokohama National University, Yokohama, Japan, 1972-76; Master of Education, 1976-78, Doctor of Education, 1978-82, University of Tsukuba, Tsukuba, Japan. Appointments: Postdoctoral Fellow, Japan Society for the Promotion of Science, 1982-83; Lecturer, 1983-85, Associate Professor, 1985-95, Tokyo Gakugei University, Japan; Associate Professor, 1995-98, Professor, 1998-, Chair of Doctoral Program in Education, 2002-, University of Tsukuba, Japan. Publications: Books: History of Education in Japan (co-author), 1995; People's History of Education in Japan (co-author), 1996; Studies of the Japanese Educational History in the Middle Ages (author), 1998; Der Herbartianismus (co-author), 1998; Social History of Education in Japan (co-author), 2002. Honour: The 1st Ishikawa Ken Award, Society for the Historical Studies of Japanese Education, 1988. Memberships: Japan Society for the Study of Education; Society for the Historical Studies of Japanese Education; Director, Japan Society for the Historical Studies of Education. Address: 1130-63, Kashio-cho, Totsuka-ku, Yokohama, Kanagawa 244-0812, Japan. Website: bamberg@c3-net.ne.jp

OIDA Akira, b. 21 December 1942, Fukui City, Japan. Engineering educator. m. Naoko Kaseda, 1 son, 1 daughter. Education: Bachelor of Agriculture, 1965, Master of Agriculture, 1967, Doctor of Agriculture, 1976, Kyoto University. Appointments: Assistant Professor, 1967-84, Associate Professor, 1989-99, Professor, 1999-, Kyoto University; Lecturer, 1984-85,

Associate Professor, 1985-89 Niigata University, Japan; Guest Professor, Technische Universität München, 1976-78, 1995-96, Jilin University of Technology, Changchun, 1979, Qingdao University, Qingdao, People's Republic of China, 2002; Dispatched expert, JICA, Bogor, Indonesia, 1992, Jordan, 1996; Guest Scholar, Wageningen Agricultural University, 1996, 2001. Publications: 7 books, including Dynamics Between Vehicle, Machine and Soil, 1993; 246 papers and articles contributed to specialist refereed journals. Honours: JSAM, Academic Award, 1986; ISTVS, Best paper, 1990, 1996, 1999; CIGR, Best Paper, 2000; United Cultural Convention, International Peace Prize, 2002. Memberships: International Society for Terrain-Vehicles Systems; Associate Editor, 1992, National Secretary, 1999; Councillor, 1992, Director, 2001, Editor, 2001, Kansai Branch President, 2003, JSAM; Member of Editorial Board, 1992, Vice President, 2002, Asian Association for Agricultural Engineering; Japanese Society for Terramechanics, President, 1999; Fellow, American Biographical Institute, 2000. Address: 1-17-10 Hieidaira Ohtsu 520-0016, Japan.

OKAJIMA Idzumi, b. 15 May 1974, Japan. Researcher. Education: Bachelor of Engineering, Muroran Institute of technology, 1997; Dr of Engineering, Shizuoka University, 2005 (expected date of graduation). Appointments: Researcher, Hokkaido Environmental Development Corporation, Japan, 1997-98; Researcher, National Institute of Materials and Chemical Research, 1998-2000; researcher, Nagasaki Ryoden Technica Corporation, Japan, 2000-. Publications: Handbook of applications of supercritical fluids to food industry, Science Forum, 2002; Decomposition of epoxy resin and recycling of CFRP with sub and supercritical water, 2002. Address: 3-5-1 Johoku, Hamamatsu, Shizuoka 432-8561, Japan. E-mail: okaji20@hotmail.com

OKAZAKI Motoaki, b. 17 July 1937, Tokyo, Japan. Researcher. m. Keiko Yamaguchi, 3 daughters. Education: BS, Keio University, 1961. Appointments: Staff, Yokoyama-Kogyo Kanagawa-ken, 1961-63; Senior Engineer, Japan Atomic Energy Research Institute, Tokai-mura, Japan, 1963-97. Publications: Development of Two-Phase Flow Analysis Code by 2V2T Model, Derivation of Basic Equations, 1986; Analysis of Density Wave Instability in a Boiling Flow Using a Characteristic Method, 1994. Honours: Listed in several biographical publications. Memberships: Fellow, Japan Society of Mechanical Engineers; Fellow Atomic Energy Society of Japan. Address: 29-10 Ichigaya Sanai-cho, Shinjuku-ku, Tokyo, F162-0846, Japan.

OKAZAWA Hidehiko, b. 18 October 1961, Nagano, Japan. Radiologist; Nuclear Medicine Specialist. m. Chiseko, 1 son, 2 daughters. Education: MD, 1988, Faculty of Medicine, PhD, 1996, Graduate School of Medicine, Kyoto University. Appointments: Resident, Kyoto University Hospital, 1988-89; Radiologist, Shiga Medical Centre, Moriyama, Japan, 1989-92; Postdoctoral Fellow, Brain Imaging Centre, Montreal Neurological Institute, Canada, 1996-98; Medical Imaging Researcher, Shiga Medical Centre, 1999-2002; Associate Professor, Fukui Medical University, 2003-. Publications: Co-author of articles in professional medical journals including: Journal of Cerebral Blood Flow and Metabolism; Journal of Nuclear Medicine; Journal of Neurochemistry; Brain. Honour: 40th Annual Award, Japanese Society of Nuclear Medicine. Memberships: Society of Nuclear Medicine; International Society for Cerebral Blood Flow and Metabolism; European Association of Nuclear Medicine; Japanese Society of Nuclear Medicine; Japan Radiological Society. Address: Biomedical Imaging Research Centre, Fukui Medical University, 23-3 Shimaizuki, Matsuoka-cho, Fukui, 910-1193, Japan. E-mail: okazawa@fmsrsa.fukui.med.ac.jp

OKEN Robert J, b. 15 October 1929, New York, USA. Neuroscientist; Researcher; Consultant. Divorced. Education: BA, 1949, PhD, 1958, New York University. Appointments: Vice President, Director, Oken Fabrics Inc, 1959-68, 1971-73; Researcher, Consultant, US Army and Navy, 1955-56; Researcher, Consultant, Teller Environmental Systems, 1969-70; Scientific Advisor, Lifer Environmental Group, 1984-87; Businessman, R A Siegel Galleries, New York, 1978-87; Volunteer, Dover Medical Center, 1989-90; Researcher and Consultant, to Director, New York State Institute for Basic Research, 1991-93; Researcher, Consultant, Gerex Biotech Inc, 1994-98; Neuroscience Research, 1998-. Publications: Research papers in numerous medical journals and reviews. Honours: Phi Beta Kappa; Achievement Award, Dover Medical Center; Listed in several biographical dictionaries. Memberships: New York Academy of Sciences; New York Neuropsychology Group; American Chemical Society; American Association for Advancement of Science; MENSA; INTERTEL. Address: PO Box 412, Hopatcong, NJ 07843, USA. E-mail: robertjoken@nac.net.

OKOKO Enobon Etim, b. 11 May 1962, Ikot Eyo, Akwa Ibom State, Nigeria. Town Planner. m. Peace Okoko, 3 sons, 1 daughter. Education: Bachelor of Science, First Class Honours, University of Maiduguri, Nigeria, 1984; Master of Urban and Regional Planning, University of Ibadan, Nigeria, 1987; PhD, Federal University of Technology, Akure, Nigeria, 2002. Appointments: Lecturer, Town and Regional Planning Department, Federal Polytechnic, Nasarawa, Nigeria, 1988-91; Senior Lecturer, Urban and Regional Planning Department, Federal University of Technology, Akure, Nigeria, 1991-. Publications: Book: Quantitative Techniques in Urban Analysis, 2001; 3 book chapters; Over 20 articles in learned journals. Honours: Principal's Prize for Best Student of the Year in WASCE Examination, 1978; Dean's Prize for Best Student of the Year, Faculty of Social and Management Sciences, University of Maiduguri, 1984; Listed in Who's Who publications and biographical dictionaries. Memberships: Associate Member, Royal Geographical Society, London; Member, Society for Environment Management and Planning; Corporate Member, Nigerian Institute of Town Planners; Member, International Geographical Union, Commission on Modelling Geographical Systems (United Kingdom); Registered Town Planner, 2000. Address: Department of Urban and Regional Planning, School of Environmental Technology, Federal University of Technology, PMB 704, Akure, Ondo State, Nigeria. E-mail: enookoko@yahoo.com

OKRI Ben, b. 15 March 1959, Minna, Nigeria. British Author; Poet. Education: Urhobo College, Warri, Nigeria; University of Essex, Colchester. Appointments: Broadcaster and Presenter, BBC, 1983-85; Poetry Editor, West Africa, 1983-86; Fellow Commoner in Creative Arts, Trinity College, Cambridge, 1991-93. Publications: Flowers and Shadows, 1980; The Landscapes Within, 1982; Incidents at the Shrine, 1986; Stars of the New Curfew, 1988; The Famished Road, 1991; An African Elegy, 1992; Songs of Enchantment, 1993; Astonishing the Gods, 1995; Birds of Heaven, 1995; Dangerous Love, 1996; A Way of Being Free, 1997; Infinite Riches, 1998; Mental Fight, 1999; In Exilus (play), 2001. Contributions to: Many newspapers and journals. Honours: Commonwealth Prize for Africa, 1987; Paris Review/Aga Khan Prize for Fiction, 1987; Booker Prize, 1991; Premio Letterario Internazionale Chianti-Ruffino-Antico-Fattore, 1993; Premio Grinzane Cavour, 1994; Crystal Award, 1995; Honorary DLitt, Westminster, 1997, Essex, 2002; Premio Palmi, 2000. Memberships: Society of Authors; Royal Society of Literature; Vice-president, English Centre, International PEN, 1997-; Board, Royal National Theatre of Great Britain, 1999-. Address: c/o Vintage, Random House, 20 Vauxhall Bridge Road, London SW1 2SA, England.

Dictionary of International Biography

OKUMURA Meinoshin, b. 22 November 1958, Osaka, Japan. Researcher in Medical Science; Surgeon. m. Sachiko Nishiyama, 1 son, 1 daughter. Education: MD, 1984, PhD, 1993, Osaka University School of Medicine. Appointments: Postdoctoral Fellow, Howard Hughes Medical Institute, Washington University in St Louis, 1993-96; Assistant Professor, Osaka University School of Medicine, 1996-2002; Staff Surgeon, National Kinki-Chuo Hospital for Chest Diseases, Osaka, Japan, 2002-. Publications: Articles in medical journals include: Clinical and functional significance of WHO classification on human thymic epithetical neoplasms: a study of consecutive 146 tumors, 2001; The World Health Organization histologic classification system reflects the oncologic behavior of human thymoma. A clinical study of 273 patients, 2002. Honour: Ozawa Award, Scholarship of Alumni Association, Osaka University School of Medicine, Department of Surgery, 2000. Memberships include: Japan Surgical Society; Japanese Association of Thoracic Surgery. Address: National Kinki-Chuo Hospital for Chest Diseases, 1180 Nagasone-cho, Sakai City, Osaka 591-8555 Japan. E-mail: m-okumura@kch.hosp.go.jp

OKWAN Joseph E K, b. 10 February 1948, Abakrampa. Farmer; Public Relations Officer. m. Margaret Yawson, 3 sons, 4 daughters. Education: Diploma, Bible Knowledge (Religion), 1971; RSA, Intermediate, 1975. Appointments: Teacher, Secondary/Comm Institution, as Head of English and Religious Department, 1975-83; Assistant Public Relations Officer, Ghana National Mobilization Programme, 1991-. Address: Methodist Church, PO Box 1, Abakrampa Via Cape Coast, Ghana.

OLADEJI Oladayo Akinwumi, b. 19 March 1962, Ogbomoso, Nigeria. Banker. m. Olatoun Motunrayo, 3 sons. Education: BSc, Business Administration, 1983; MSc, Finance, 1986; ACA, 1992. Appointments: Senior Manager, Head of Capital Markets, First City Merchant Bank Ltd, 1990-98; Assistant General Manager, Head of Investment Banking, Equatorial Trust Bank Ltd, 1998-99; General Manager, Trans International Bank Plc, 1999-. Honour: Nigerian National Merit Award (Undergraduate Level), for Best Academic Performance, 1983. Memberships: Institute of Chartered Accountants of Nigeria; Nigeria Finance Association; Nigeria Institute of Management. Address: Trans International Bank plc, Oba Adebimpe Road, Ibadan, Nigeria.

OLAIYA Samuel Ayodele, b. 8 August 1938, Ode-Ekiti, Nigeria. Teacher; Researcher. m. Adefunke Olaiya, 4 sons, 2 daughters. Education: MSc, Industrial Planning, 1969, PhD, Economics, 1972, Kiev Institute of National Planning, USSR; Certificate in Industrial Training, North East London Polytechnic, England 1979; Certificate in Management and Training, Leeds, England, 1991. Appointments: Director, Training, Industrial Training Fund, Nigeria; Director, Special Duties, The Presidency, Abuja, Nigeria; Currently, Senior Lecturer, University of Ado-Ekiti, Nigeria. Publications: Training for Industrial Development in Nigeria; Prerequisites for a Profitable Business. Honours: Citation, Department of Industrial Organisation, Kiev Institute of National Planning, 1972; Citation for Good Service Award, Industrial Training Fund, Nigeria; Award as Effective Manager of the Year, 1990/91, University of Jos, Nigeria. Memberships: Nigerian Institute of Management; Nigerian Economic Society. Address: Department of Economics, University of Ado-Ekiti, PMB 5363, Ado-Ekiti State, Nigeria.

OLARU Paul Christian, b. 29 June 1952, Bucharest, Romania. Physical Metallurgy Research Scientist. m. Irina, 1 daughter. Education: Master's Degree, Polytechnic University, Bucharest, 1977; Diploma I, University of Beijing, China, 1983, Diploma II, University of Taiyuan, China, 1984; Expert, Aircraft Materials I,

1983, II, 1984; PhD, cum laude, Physical Metallurgy, 1998. Appointments: Head Technology Engineer, Sidex SA, Galati, Romania, 1977-81; Scientific Research Engineer III, Metav SA, Bucharest, 1981-83; Head, Heat Treatment Department, Aerofina SA, Bucharest, 1983-89; Expert Engineer I, Usam SA, Bucharest, 1990-96; PhD Manager AQ , Faur SA, Bucharest, 1996-2002; Project Manager, Research, Inav SA, Bucharest, 2002-. Publications: 30 scientific works published: EUROMAT 99, Munich, Germany, 1999; Sunriver, Oregon, USA, 1999; EUROMAT, Tours, France, 2000; ICCE/8, Tenerife, Spain, 2001; Rex & GG, RWTH, Aachen, Germany, 2001; ASM International, Iasi, Romania, 2001. Honours: National Romanian Research Prize II, 1998, National Romanian Research Prize I, 1999, S & R Ministry; Honourable Mention, EUROMAT, Tours France, 2000; Honourable mention, Rex & GG, Conference, RWTH, Aachen, Germany, 2001. Memberships: ASM International, 1994; HTS International, USA, 1994; TMS, USA, 1996; AGIR, Romania, 1993; DGM, Germany, 2001. Address: E Caragiani No 48, Bl 13G, Sc 3, Apt 40, 14215 Bucharest, Romania. E-mail: inav@fx.ro

OLARU Radu, b. 12 February 1949, Botosani, Romania. Electrical Engineer. m. 26 July 1978, 2 sons. Education: University degree, Faculty of Electrical Engineering, 1972, PhD, 1994, Technical University, Iasi. Appointments: Engineer in industry, Suceava, 1972-74; Engineer, Scientific Researcher, Institute of Research and Development of Technical Physics, Iasi, 1974-79; Assistant Professor, 1979-87, Lecturer, 1987-95, Associate Professor, 1995-99, Professor, 1999-, Technical University, Iasi. Publications: 3 books, 1997, 2003, 2004; 8 papers in world's leading journals; 60 papers published in Romania and abroad; 19 patents. Honours: 2 Silver Medals, International Exhibition of Inventions, Iasi, 1992, 1996; Biographical listing in several who's who publications. Memberships: Romanian Association of Measurements, 1990-94; Fellow, Faculty of Electrical Engineering Council, 1996-2000. Address: Technical University of Jasi, Faculty of Electrical Engineering, 53 Mangeron Blvd, 6600 Jasi, Romania.

OLATUNJI-BELLO Ibiyemi Ibilola, b. 23 April 1964, Lagos, Nigeria. Lecturer. m. Tunji Bello, 1 son, 2 daughters. Education: BSc (Hons), Physiology, University of Ibadan, Nigeria, 1985; MSc, Physiology, 1987, PhD, Physiology, 1998, University of Lagos, Nigeria. Appointments: Assistant Lecturer, 1988-91, Lecturer II, 1991-96, Lecturer I, 1996-99, Senior Lecturer, 1999-, Department of Physiology, College of Medicine of the University of Lagos, Nigeria. Publications: 23 articles include: Effect of acute acetyl-l-camitine treatment on daytime melatonin synthesis in the rat, 1997. Honours: Staff Enhancement Fellow to the USA, Nigerian Government, 1994; Recipient, 1999-2000, 2nd Best Teacher in Physiology Department of College of Medicine of the University of Lagos; Fellow, Swedish International Development Agency, 2000. Memberships: New York Academy of Sciences; Physiological Society of Nigeria; Lagos University Medical Society. Address: Department of Physiology, College of Medicine of the University of Lagos, PMB 12003 Lagos, Nigeria. E-mail: yemibello@lycos.com

OLAZABAL Jose Maria, b. 5 February 1966, Spain. Professional Golfer. Career: Member, European Ryder Cup team, 1987, 1989, 1991, 1993, 1997, Kirin Cup Team, 1987, Four Tours World Championship Team, 1989, 1990, World Cup Team, 1989, Dunhill Cup Team, 1986, 1987, 1988, 1989, 1992; Winner, Italian Amateur Award, 1983, Spanish Amateur Award, 1983, European Masters-Swiss Open, 1986, Belgian Open, 1988, German Masters, 1988, Tenerife Open, 1989, Dutch Open, 1989, Benson & Hedges International, 1990, Irish Open, 1990, Lancome Trophy, 1990, Visa Talhoyo Club Masters, 1990, California Open, 1991, Turespana Open de Tenerife, 1992, Open Mediterrania, 1992, US Masters, 1994, 1999, Dubai Desert Classic, 1998; Benson &

Hedges International Open 2000, French Open, 2001, Buick Invitational, 2002; Tour victories include: NEC World Series of Golf, 1990; The International, 1991; US Masters, 1994, 1999; Dubai Desert Classic, 1998; Golf course designer. Address: PGA Avenue of Champions, Palm Beach Gdns, FL 33418, USA. Website: www.aboutgolf.com/jmo

OLDFIELD Bruce, b. 14 July 1950, England. Fashion Designer. Education: Sheffield City Polytechnic; Ravensbourne College of Art; St Martin's College of Art. Appointments: Founder, Fashion House, Producing Designer Collections, 1975; Couture Clothes for Individual Clients, 1981; Opened Retail Shop, Couture & Ready-to-Wear, 1984; Managing Board, British Knitting & Clothing Export Council, 1989; Designed for films, Jackpot, 1974, The Sentinel, 1976; Vice-President, Barnardo's, 1998; Govenor, London Institute, 1999-; Trustee, Royal Academy, 2000-. Publication: Seasons, 1987. Exhibition: Retrospective, Laing Galleries, Newcastle-upon-Tyne, 2000. Honours: Fellow, Sheffield Polytechnic, 1987, Royal College of Art, 1990, Durham University, 1991; Hon DCL (Northumbria), 2001. Address: 27 Beauchamp Place, London SW3, England.

OLDKNOW Antony, b. 15 August 1939, Peterborough, England. Poet; Fiction Writer (Ghost Stories), Literary Translator; Professor. Education: BA, University of Leeds, 1961; Postgraduate Diploma, Phonetics, University of Edinburgh, 1962; PhD, University of North Dakota, USA, 1983. Appointments: Editor, Publisher, Scopcraeft Press Inc, 1966-; Travelling Writer, The Great Plains Book Bus, 1979-81; Writer-in-Residence, Wisconsin Arts Board, 1980-83; Poetry Staff, Cottonwood, 1984-87; Professor of Literature, Eastern New Mexico University, 1987-; Associate Editor, Blackwater Quarterly, 1993. Publications: Lost Allegory, 1967; Tomcats and Tigertails, 1968; The Road of the Lord, 1969; Anthem for Rusty Saw and Blue Sky, 1975; Consolations for Beggars, 1978; Miniature Clouds, 1982; Ten Small Songs, 1985; Clara d'Ellébeuse (translated novel), 1992; The Villages and Other Poems (translated book), 1993. Contributions to: Anthologies, reviews, journals, and magazines. Address: Department of Languages and Literature, Eastern New Mexico University, Portales, NM 88130, USA.

OLECH Adam Henryk, b. 20 February 1953, Bielsko-Bial~a, Poland. Academic Teacher. m. Halina Olech, 1 daughter. Education: MA, 1977, Phd, 1988, Jagiellonian University, Cracow. Appointments: Silesian University, 1977-79; Częstochowa Institute of Technology, 1979-86; Pedagogical University of Częstochowa, 1986-. Publications include: Monograph: Language, expressions and meanings. K Ajdukiewicz's semiotics. Honours: President, Polish Philosophical Society, Częstochowa Branch; Chief, Department of Philosophy, Pedagogical University of Częstochowa. Memberships: Polish Philosophical Society; European Society for Analytic Philosophy. Address: ul Gombrowicza 6/16, 42-224 Częstochowa, Poland.

OLIVAN-GONZALVO Gonzalo, b. 18 September 1961, Zaragoza, Spain. Paediatrician; Consultant; Researcher. m. Brigitte Gracia-Martinez, 1 son. Education: MD Degree, Medicine and Surgery Faculty, Zaragoza University, 1985; Medicine and Surgery License, Ministry of Education and Science, Madrid, 1985; Paediatrics Residency, University Clinic Hospital, Zaragoza, 1986-89; Childcare Specialist Physician Qualification, Ministry of Public Health and Consumption, Madrid, 1987; Paediatrics Specialist Physician Qualification, Ministry of Education and Science, Madrid, 1990; Paediatrics Continuing Education Certificates: SPARS, 1986-95, SPEH-AEP, 1995-2000, SEPEAP-SEICAP, 1999-2001, AAP, 1994-96 and 2000-02. Appointments: Director, Manager, Dr Oliván International Adoption Paediatric Centre, Zaragoza, Spain, 1991-; Private Practice, Quirón Clinic, Zaragoza,

Spain, 1991-; High Health Career Government Employee, Aragón Autonomous Community Administration, Spain, 1992-; Head, Paediatrics and Adolescent Medicine Services, Aragón Social Services Institute, Spain, 2000-; Paediatrics Consultant, Health National Institute, 1990-91, Euromutua Health Insurance, 1992-, MAZ Hospital, 1992-2000, Social Security Military Foundation, 1998-2001; Advisor and Collaborator Children Today Journal, Madrid, 2002-, Globus Communication Editorial Group, Madrid, 2001-03; Childcare Professor, Department of Health, Social Welfare and Work, Aragón Public Administration Institute, 1994; Paediatrics Professor, Nursing Provincial School, 1986. Publications: More than 180 papers in international and national professional journals on topics including: Child abuse and neglect, international adoption, foster and residential care, immigration, ethnic minorities, juvenile delinquency, adolescence and behaviour, infectious and parasitic diseases, growth and nutrition, dysmorphology and bone dysplasias. Honours: Zaragoza Medical University Archives Award, Clinical research area, 1990; PharmaDirect Award, Clinical Paediatric Dermatology, 1994; Physician Recognition Award, American Academy of Pediatrics, 1994-96, 2000-02; Critic referee for Annals of Paediatrics, Official Publication of the Spanish Paediatric Association, 2001, 2003; Expert for Special Commission on International Adoption of Spanish Senate, 2003; Partner, Daphne Project "Childhood, disability and violence: empowering disability organisations to develop prevention strategies", The Daphne Programme, 2000-03, of the European Commission; Listed in Who's Who publications and biographical dictionaries. Memberships: Spanish Association of Paediatrics; Aragón, La Rioja and Soria Paediatric Society, Childhood Accidents Prevention Working Group, 1989-92, Child Abuse and Neglect Prevention Working Group, 1992-95; Founding Member, Medical Sciences Academy of Aragón; Spanish Society of Extra-Hospital Paediatric and Primary care; International Society for Prevention of Child Abuse and Neglect; Spanish Society of Social Paediatrics. Address: Paediatrics and International Adoption Centre, Av de las Torres 93, Zaragoza 50007, Spain. E-mail: g.olivan@comz.org Website: www.visualcom.es/olivan-pediatra

OLIVEIRA Carlos A, b. 1 December 1942, Barras-Piauí, Brazil. Medical Doctor. Widowed, 3 daughters. Education: MD, Faculdade Nacional de Medicina, Rio de Janeiro, 1966; Specialist in Otolanyngology, American Board of Otolaryngology, Chicago Illinois, 1979; Doctor of Philosophy, Otolaryngology, University of Minnesota Graduate School, Minneapolis, Minnesota, USA, 1977; Postdoctoral Fellowship, Harvard Medical School, Boston, Massachusetts, USA, 1989. Appointments: Associate Professor, 1977-97, Professor and Chairman, Department of Otolanyngology, 1997-, Brasilia University Medical School, Brasilia, Brazil. Publications: 82 scientific articles published in Brazil, 14 scientific articles in international journals including, Annals of Otology, Rhinology & Laryngology; Archives of Otolaryngology; Laryngoscope; International Tinnitus Journals. Honours: Physician Recognition Award, American Medical Association, 1977; International Scientist of the Year, IBC. Memberships: Prosper Menière Society; Schuknecht Society, Boston, Massachusetts, USA; Neuroquilibriumetric Society, Bad Kinssingen, Germany; Brazilian Otolaryngology Society. Address: Avda W-3 Sul Quadra 716, Bloco E, Sala 202, Brasilia DF, Brazil. E-mail: oliv@abordo.com.br

OLIVERA NUNES Jorge Manuel Costa de, b. 16 June 1941, Lisbon, Portugal. Civil Engineer. m. Clara de Jesus Martinho do Nacimento de Oliveira Nunes, 1 son. Education: BSc (Eng) (Civil), University of Wittwatersrand, Johannesburg, South Africa, 1969; Registered Professional Engineer, South Africa, 1974; Chartered Civil Engineer, 1979; Registered European Engineer, European

Union, 1990. Appointments: Engineer in Training, C A Rigby & Partners, Johannesburg, South Africa, 1969-71; Engineer in Training, Engineer, Senior Engineer, Keeve Steyn Incorporated, Johannesburg, South Africa, 1971-80; Senior Engineer, Ledingham, Reed, Hunt Incorporated, Johannesburg South Africa, 1980-81; Senior Engineer, Principal Engineer, Keeve Steyn Incorporated, 1981-91; Senior Engineer, Lillicrap Crutchfield (Pty), Johannesburg, South Africa, 1991-98; Principal Structural Engineer, Head of Structural Division, Black & Veatch Africa, Johannesburg, South Africa, 1998-. Publications: Paper on the design and construction aspects of the Dome at Northgate, Randburg, Johannesburg, included in Tubular Structures 1X, proceedings of the Ninth International Symposium and Euro Conference on Tubular Steel Structures, Dusseldorf, Germany, 2001. Honours: Transvaal Concrete Man of the Year, 1987; Listed in Who's Who publications and biographical dictionaries. Memberships: Fellow, Institution of Civil Engineers, London; Fellow, American Society of Civil Engineers; Fellow, South African Institution of Civil Engineers, Committee Member, 1997-, Vice Chairman, 2000-2001, Chairman, 2002-2003, Wittwatersrand Branch; Member Ordem dos Engenheiros, Lisbon, Portugal. Address: 9A Arbroath Road, Bedfordview 2007, Johannesburg, Gauteng, South Africa.

OLIVER Colin, b. 13 March 1946, Tasburgh, Norfolk, England. Primary School Headteacher; Poet. m. Carole Oliver, 5 September 1968, 1 son, 1 daughter. Education: Education Diploma, University of London Goldsmiths' College. Appointment: Headteacher, Wickambrook Primary School, Suffolk, 1985-1999. Publications: In the Open, 1974; Seeing, 1980; Ploughing at Nightfall, 1993; Stepping into Brilliant Air, 1996; Speaking Trees, 1999. Contributions to: Guardian; Iron; Lines Review; Middle Way; Oasis; Resurgence; PN Review; Haiku Hundred anthology; Salmon; Smiths Knoll; Staple; Frogmore Papers; Workshop New Poetry; Mountain Path (India). Memberships: Poetry Society, UK; British Haiku Society. Address: 45 Westfield, Clare, Sudbury, Suffolk, England.

OLMSTEAD Andrea Louise, b. 5 September 1948, Dayton, Ohio, USA. Musicologist. m. Larry Thomas Bell, 2 January 1982. Education: BM, Hartt College of Music, 1972; MA, New York University, 1974. Appointments: Faculty, The Juilliard School, 1972-80; Boston Conservatory, 1981-. Publications: Roger Sessions and His Music, 1985; Conversations With Roger Sessions, 1987; The New Grove 20th Century American Masters, 1987; The Correspondence of Roger Sessions, 1992; Juilliard: A History, 1999. Contributions to: Journal of the Arnold Schoenberg Institute; American Music; Musical Quarterly; Tempo; Musical America; Perspectives of New Music; Music Library Association Notes. Honours: National Endowment for the Humanities Grants; Outstanding Academic Book Choice, 1986. Memberships: Sonneck Society; Pi Kappa Lambda. Address: 73 Hemenway Street, Apt 501, Boston, MA 02115, USA.

OLSEN Arild Karl, b. 31 January 1938, Gildeskaal, Norway. Senior Consultant Surgeon. m. Bärbel Grossmann, 2 sons, 1 daughter. Education: MD, Kiel University, Germany, 1965; Specialised in general surgery, 1977; Gastroenterological Surgery, 1984. Appointments: Medical Officer, Flatanger, Norway, 1966-70, Namdal Hospital, Namsos, Norway, 1970-73, Central Hospital, Stavanger, Norway, 1973-80; Captain, Norwegian Army Medical Corps, 1968; Consultant Surgeon, Aker University Hospital, Oslo, 1981-84; Consultant Surgeon, 1984-86, Senior Consultant Surgeon, 1986-, Central Hospital, Stavanger. Publications: About 30 publications including: Intraoperative Ultrasonography and the Detection of Liver Metastases in Patients with Colorectal Cancer,

1990; Laparoscopic Ultrasound (LUS) in Gastrointestinal Surgery, 1999. Memberships: IGSC; HPBA; CICD. Address: Svaberget 50, N-4029 Stavanger, Norway. Email: arildkolsenc2i.net

OMELCHENKO Nickolay Victorovich, b. 26 June 1951, Kazakhstan, USSR. Professor of Philosophy. m. Svetlana, 2 daughters. Education: Diploma, Philosophy, 1978, Postgraduate studies, 1978-81, PhD, 1984, Moscow State University by the name of MV Lomonosov. Appointments: Assistant Professor, 1982-87, Senior Lecturer, 1987-92, Associate Professor, 1992-99, Philosophy Department, Dean, History and Philosophy Faculty, 1996-2000, Full Professor, Social Philosophy Department, 1999-, Dean, Philosophy and Social Technologies Faculty, 2000-, Volgograd State University, Russia. Publications: 65 including: Human Creativity and the Teaching of Philosophy, The Mansfield-Volgograd Anthology, 2000; participation in conferences. Honours: Exchange Professor, Mansfield University, Pennsylvania, USA, 1997; Academician of Academy for Humanities, St Petersburg, Russia, 1998-; Fulbright Scholar-in-Residence, Mansfield University, Pennsylvania, USA, 2001-02; included in international biographical directories. Memberships: Russian Philosophical Society, 1978-; International Erich Fromm Society, Germany, 1993-; Society for Philosophy of Creativity, USA, 1998-. Address: Volgograd State University, 2nd Prodolnaya Street 30, Volgograd 400062, Russia. E-mail: nomelchenko@mail333.com

OMOKANYE Akim Tunde, b. 30 October 1963, Kano, Nigeria. Research Agronomist. 1 son. Education: BSc, Agriculture, 1988, MSc, Animal Science, 1998 Ahmadu Bello University, Zaria, Nigeria; PhD, Farming Systems, University of Western Sydney, Australia, in progress, date of completion 2003. Appointments: Graduate Assistant, 1988-89, Assistant Research Fellow, 1989-98, Research Fellow II, 1998-, National Animal Production Research Institute, Shika, Nigeria; PhD Student, University of Western Sydney, Australia, 2000-2003. Publications: 21 peer-reviewed journal articles; 17 papers in conference proceedings; 11 conference abstracts and posters; 2 newsletter articles. Honours: Roll of Honour, Nigerian Society for Animal Production; International Postgraduate Research Scholarship, UWS, Australia; Listed in Who's Who publications and biographical dictionaries. Memberships: American Association for the Advancement of Science; Nigerian Society for Animal Production; Tropical Grassland Congress, Australia; International Farming Systems Association. Address: College of Science, Technology and Environment, School of Environment and Agriculture, University of Western Sydney, Building J4, Locked bag 1797, Penrith South DC, NSW 1797, Australia. E-mail: a.omokanye@uws.edu.au

ONDAATJE Michael, b. 12 September 1943, Colombo, Sri Lanka. Author. 2 sons. Education: Dulwich College, London; Queen's University; University of Toronto. Publications include: Poetry: The Dainty Monsters, 1967; The Man With Seven Toes, 1968; There's a Trick with a Knife I'm Learning to Do, 1979; Secular Love, 1984; Handwriting, 1998; Fiction: The Collected Works of Billy the Kid; Coming Through Slaughter; Running in the Family; In the Skin of a Lion; The English Patient; Handwriting; Anil's Ghost, 2000. Honour: Booker Prize for Fiction, 1992; Prix Medicis, 2000. Address: 2275 Bayview Road, Toronto, Ontario N4N 3MG, Canada.

ONDOH Tadanori, b. 3 January 1935, Okayama, Japan. Director, Space Earth Environment Laboratory. m. Takako Seki. Education: BSc, 1958, MSc, 1960, DSc, 1965, Geophysical Institute, Kyoto University. Appointments: NRC-NAS Research Associate, NASA Goddard Space Flight Center, USA, 1968-70; Chief, Space Physics Sec Radio Research Laboratories, Ministry of Posts and Telecommunications, 1975; Director, Space Science Office, MPT,

Dictionary of International Biography

1984; Director, Communications Research Laboratory, MPT, 1988; Deputy Director General for Asia, IBC, England; LFIBA. Publications: Over 100 scientific research papers for international professional journals; Geospace Environment Science, in Japanese, 2000; Science of Space Environment, in English, 2001. Honours: Tanakadate Gold Medal, Japanese Society for Geomagnetism and Geoelectricity, 1973; Distinguished Scientist Gold Medal, Minister Science and Technology, Japan, 1993. Memberships: American Geophysical Union, 1961-; SGEPSS, 1960-; COSPAR Associate, 1994-. Address: 5186 Kitano, Tokorozawa, Saitama 359-1152, Japan.

ONEGA JAÉN Susana, b. 17 November 1948, Madrid, Spain. Professor of English Literature. m. Francisco Curiel Lorente, 2 sons. Education: Degree, 1975, PhD, 1979, English Philology, University of Zaragoza; Numerous certificates for aptitude in English, French, Italian and German, Madrid, Cambridge, Heidelberg, 1967-77. Appointments: Teacher of English, Official School of Languages, Madrid, 1968-69; Untenured Lecturer, 1975-77, Untenured Associate Professor, 1977-83; Tenured Associate Professor, 1983-86, Full Professor, 1986, Vice-Head of Department, 1989-90, 1995-97, Head of Department, 1987-89, 1991-93, 1993-95, 1997-99, Department of English, University of Zaragoza; Head of Research Team (financed by the Ministry of Education) 1991-95, 1995-98, 1998-2001, (financed by the Ministry of Science and Technology), 2001-04; Research Manager for The Philologies and Philosophy, Ministry of Science and Technology, 2001-03. Publications: Books include: Análisis estructural, método narrativo y "sentido" de The Sound and the Fury de William Faulkner, 1980; Estudios literarios ingleses II: Renacimiento y barroco (editor and author of introduction), 1986; Form and Meaning in the Novels of John Fowles, 1989; Telling Histories: Narrativizing History/Historicizing Literature (editor and author of introduction), 1995; Narratology: An Introduction (co-editor and co-author of introduction), 1996; Peter Ackroyd: The Writer and his Work, 1998; Metafiction and Myth in the Novels of Peter Ackroyd, 1999; London in Literature: Visionary Mappings of the Metroplis (co-editor and co-author of Introduction), 2002; Refracting the Canon in Contemporary British Literature and Film (co-editor and co-author of introduction), 2004; Numerous articles in professional journals, book chapters, conference papers and translations. Honours: Extraordinary Prize for Degree in Philosophy and Letters, University of Zaragoza, 1976; Extraordinary Prize for Doctorate in Philosophy and Letters, University of Zaragoza, 1980; Enrique García Díez Award, 1990; Honorary Research Fellowship, Birkbeck College, University of London, 1995-96. Memberships: Spanish Association for Anglo-American Studies, 1977-; European Association for American Studies, 1977-; European Society for the Study of English, 1990-; International Association of University Professors of English, 1995-; National Federation of Associations of Spanish University Professors, 1997-2002; Corresponding Fellow, The English Association, 2003-; Association of Women Researchers and Technologists, 2003-. Address: Dpto de Filología Inglesa y Alemana, Facultad de Filosofía y Letras, 50009 Universidad de Zaragoza, Spain. E-mail: sonega@unizar.es

ONES Saime Ulker, b. 20 March 1939, Ankara, Turkey. Paediatrics Educator. m. Somer Ones, 1 son, 1 daughter. Education: MD, Medical School, Istanbul, Turkey, 1963. Appointments: Researcher, Institute of Immunobiology, Paris, 1967-68; Assistant Professor, 1968-72, Associate Professor, 1973-79, Professor of Paediatrics, 1980-97, Director, Department of Clinical Immunology, Allergy and Infectious Diseases, 1997-, Director, Department of Paediatric Allergy and Chest Diseases, 1998, Director, Department of Paediatrics, 2000-, School of Medicine, Istanbul, Turkey; Editor, Journal of Infectious Diseases and Clinical Microbiology, Expressions on Allergen Specific Immunotherapy,

1996. Publications: Articles in professional journals include most recently: The serum and sputum ECP levels in children with asthma and chronic bronchitis, 1999; Egg and milk allergy in asthmatic children: assessment by Immulite allergy food panel, skin prick tests and double-blind placebo-controlled food challenge, 1999; Childhood Asthma Perception in Turkey Under Real-Life Environment (CAPTURE) Study, 2001. Honour: Grantee, Institute of Immunobiology, Broussais Hospital, Paris France, 1967-68. Memberships: European Academy of Allergy and Clinical Immunology; European Society of Immunology; American Academy of Allergy, Asthma and Immunology; Turkish Paediatric Respiratory Tract Diseases Society; Turkish Paediatric Association. Address: Tavukcu Fethi sok No 33-35 Arma Apt., Osmanbey 80260, Istanbul, Turkey. E-mail: sones@tnn.net

ONUIGBO Macaulay Amechi, b. 17 March 1958, Enugu, Nigeria. Nephrologist; Transplant Physician. m. Nnonyelum, 3 September 1988, 3 children. Education: MB BS, 1981, MSc, Medical Biochemistry, 1988, University of Nigeria; Combined Residency/Nephrology Fellowship, University of Nigeria Teaching Hospital, Enugu, Nigeria, 1985-89. Appointments: Renal Registrar, Queen Elizabeth Hospital, Birmingham, England, 1988; Diplomate in Nephrology, West African College of Physicians, 1989; Senior Lecturer/Assistant Professor of Medicine/Nephrology, University of Nigeria, Enugu, 1990-94; ISN Nephrology Research Fellow, University of Texas Health Science Center, Houston, Texas, USA, 1994-96; Resident, Greater Baltimore Medical Center, 1997-2000; Clinical Fellow in Nephrology, University of Maryland, Baltimore, 2000-02; Diplomate, Internal Medicine, American Board of Internal Medicine, 2000; Diplomate in Nephrology, American Board of Internal Medicine, 2002; Transplant Specialist Faculty/Speaker, Wyeth-Ayerst Laboratories, USA, June 2002; Nephrologist and Transplant Physician, Luther Midelfort, Mayo Health System, Eau Claire, Wisconsin, 2002-. Publications: Co-author, Handbook of Physiology, book chapter, 1999; Contributed over 70 articles to professional publications. Membership: Co-founder, Cream Circle League (a philanthropic organisation), Enugu, Nigeria, 1990. Address: 856 Kari Drive, #3, Eau Claire, WI 54701, USA. E-mail: onuigbo.macaulay@mayo.edu

ONYEAMA Charles Dillibe Ejiofor, b. 6 January 1951, Enugu, Nigeria. Publisher; Author; Journalist. m. (1) Ethel Ekwueme, 15 December 1984, 4 sons, (2) Theodora Okwu, 27 December 1995, 2 daughters. Education: Eton College, Windsor, Berkshire, England; Premier School of Journalism, Fleet Street, London, England. Appointments: Board of Directors, Star Printing and Publishing Co Ltd, 1992-94; Udi Local Government Council, Enugu State, Caretaker Committee, Councillor, 1994-96; Managing Director, Delta Publications (Nigeria) Ltd. Publications: Nigger at Eton, 1972; John Bull's Nigger, 1974; Sex is a Nigger's Game, 1975; The Book of Black Man's Humour, 1975; I'm the Greatest, 1975; Juju, 1976; Secret Society, 1977; Revenge of the Medicine Man, 1978; The Return, 1978; Night Demon, 1979; Female Target, 1980; The Rules of the Game, 1980; The Story of an African God, 1982; Modern Messiah, 1983; Godfathers of Voodoo, 1985; African Legend, 1985; Correct English, 1986; Notes of a So-Called Afro-Saxon, 1988; A Message To My Compatriots, 1996; The Boomerang, 1998; The New Man, 2003; The Joys of Ibo Humour, 2003. Contributions to: Books and Bookmen; Spectator; Times; Daily Express; Sunday Express; Drum; West Africa; Roots; Guardian; Evening News. Address: 8B Byron Onyeama Close, New Haven, PO Box 1172, Enugu, Enugu State, Nigeria.

OOSTEN Louis Harm, b. 4 December 1940, Driebergen, Netherlands. Minister. m. Hiltje Schaafsma, 1 son, 1 daughter. Education: Certificate, Municipal Administration, 1963; Certificate for Secondary education, Dutch Politics (Constitutional Law),

Dictionary of International Biography

1967; Certificate, Dutch Palaeography, 1967; Degree, Theological Faculty, Rijks Universiteit Utrecht, 1976. Appointments: Official, Town Hall, Zeist, Netherlands; Minister, Dutch Reformed Church, Wouterswoude, Netherlands, 1976-84, Hedel, Netherlands, 1984-92, Sint Anthoniepolder/Maasdam, Netherlands, 1992-; Founder, Reformatorische Dagblad (daily newspaper), 1971; Chairman, Stichting Reformatorische Publicatie; Founder and Secretary, Stichting Evangelisatie Limburg; Chairman, Regional, Ring Binnenmaas of Dutch Reformed Ministers. Publications: Author: Ontdekkende Prediking, 1980; Wat is een oprecht geloof? 1988; Wat gelooft gij van de Kerk, 1988; Goddelijke Waarheden, 1994; Bewaar Uw Kerk, 1996; Editor: Ach, leefde Luther nog maar (Dr A Zahn), 1999; Waarom ik in de gevestigde Kerk blijf (A Mond), 2000; Het recht der Hervormde Gezindheid (Mr G Groen van Prinsterer), 1996; Articles in newspapers and magazines. Memberships: Dutch Reformed Church; Association of Dutch Reformed Ministers; Regional Commission for Church Order; Dutch Society of Genealogy; Fries Genootschap (Frisian Society for History and Language). Address: Dutch Reformed Manse, Polderdijk 77, 3299 LM Maasdam/Sint Anthoniepolder, Netherlands.

OPDAHL-MEYER Helen Bernadine, b. 2 March 1929, Sioux County, Iowa, USA. Financial Services Executive; Advertising and Public Relations Director. m. (1) W Thomas Logan, divorced, 1 stepson (2) William James Meyer, deceased, 1 adopted son. Education: Portraiture, Costume Design, Illustration; School of Minneapolis Institute of Art, 1946-49; NASD Registered Representative, 1980. Appointments: Advertising Artist, Writer, Manager, Lawton Company, Cincinnati, Ohio, 1949-51; Illustrator, Account Executive, Simons Advertising, New York City, New York, 1951-53; Assistant Advertising Manager, Max Wiesen Inc, New York City, New York, 1953-54; Assistant Advertising Manager, Mays Department Store, Brooklyn, New York, 1954-55; Advertising, Public Relations Director, Dayton's-Fantle's, Sioux Falls, South Dakota, 1955-66; Commercial Illustrator and Continuity Writer, Electronic Media, 1967-76; Regional Promotion Director and Shopping Mall Developer, Developers Diversified, Cleveland, Ohio, 1977-79; Financial Services Executive, Meyer Insurance and Investment, Worthington, Minnesota, 1980-. Publications: Numerous professional papers and articles on advertising, public relations and financial services. Honours: Listed in Who's Who publications and biographical dictionaries. Memberships: Charter Member, Advertising Artists Guild, 1960-66, Director, 1963-64; Charter Treasurer, President, Zonta International, Sioux Falls, 1957-66; Public relations and promotions Staff, American Cancer Society, Worthington, Minnesota, 1972-77. Address: 29744 290 Street, Worthington, MN 56187, USA.

OPIE Iona, b. 13 October 1923, Colchester, England. Writer. m. Peter Opie, 2 September 1943, deceased, 2 sons, 1 daughter. Publications: A Dictionary of Superstitions (with Moira Tatem), 1989; The People in the Playground, 1993; With Peter Opie: The Oxford Dictionary of Nursery Rhymes, 1951, new edition, 1997; The Oxford Nursery Rhyme Book, 1955; The Lore and Language of Schoolchildren, 1959; Puffin Book of Nursery Rhymes, 1963; A Family Book of Nursery Rhymes, 1964; Children's Games in Street and Playground, 1969; The Oxford Book of Children's Verse, 1973; Three Centuries of Nursery Rhymes and Poetry for Children, 1973; The Classic Fairy Tales, 1974; A Nursery Companion, 1980; The Oxford Book of Narrative Verse, 1983; The Singing Game, 1985; Babies: an unsentimental anthology, 1990; Children's Games with Things, 1997. Honours: Honorary MA, Oxon, 1962, Open University, 1987, DLitt, University of Southampton, 1987, University of Nottingham, 1991, Doctorate, University of Surrey, 1997; CBE, 1998; FBA, 1998. Address: Mells House, Liss, Hampshire GU33 6JQ, England.

OPIK Lembit, b. 2 March 1965, Bangor, County Down, Northern Ireland. Member of Parliament. Education: BA, Philosophy, Bristol University. Appointments: President, Bristol Students Union, 1985-86; Member, National Union of Students National Executive, 1987-88; Brand Assistant, 1988-91, Corporate Training and Organisation Development Manager, 1991-96, Global Human Resources Training Manager, 1997, Proctor and Gamble; Elected to Newcastle City Council, 1992; Elected as MP for Montgomeryshire, 1997; Party Spokesperson on Northern Ireland and Young People, 1997; Spokesperson for Wales, Leader of the Welsh Liberal Democrats, Member of Shadow Cabinet, 2001-. Publications: Articles on politics in newspapers and magazines; Weekly column in Shropshire Star, The Week in Politics. Honours: Nominated for Channel 4 House Magazine New MP of the Year, 1998; Nominated for Country Life Rural MP of the Year, 1999. Memberships: Agriculture Select Committee, 1998-2001; Co-Chair, All Parliamentary Middle Way Group; Member, Spinal Injuries Association; Speaks on behalf of British Gliding Association; Chair, All Party Parliamentary Motorcycle Group; President, Shropshire, Astronomical Society. Address: House of Commons, London, SW1A 0AA, England. E-mail: opikl@parliament.uk

ORALLO Francisco, b. 17 February 1958, Lugo, Spain. Professor. Education: BSc, with Special Distinction, Pharmacy, 1980; PhD, with Special Distinction, Pharmacy. Appointments: Predoctoral Fellow, 1981-84, Assistant Professor, 1984-86, Professor, Head of Cardiovascular Research, 1987-, Department of Pharmacology, School of Pharmacy, University of Santiago de Compostela, Spain; Postdoctoral Fellow, Department of Pharmacology, School of Medicine, Universidad Autónoma, Madrid, 1987-88, University Louis Pasteur, Strasbourg, France, 1991-92. Publications: Contributor of articles in professional journals. Honours: Eloy Diez Award, Pharmaceutical College, Pontevedra, Spain, 1984; SEQT Award, Spanish Society of Therapeutic Chemistry, Madrid, 1987; Dr Esteve Honorable Mention, Dr Esteve Foundation, Barcelona, 1992; Dolores Trigo Award, School of Pharmacy, University of Santiago, 1993; Xunta de Galicia Research Award, Education Department, Galicia Autonomous Government, 1996; Spanish Society of Pharmacology, Almirall Prodesfarma Research Award, 2003. Memberships: American Society for Pharmacology and Experimental Therapeutics (ASPET); American Association for the Advancement of Science; New York Academy of Sciences; Spanish Society of Pharmacology; Spanish Society of Therapeutic Chemistry; Pharmaceutical Society of Latin Mediterranean. Address: Dr Maceira 5-2 A, 15706 Santiago Compostela, Spain.

ORLOFF Harold David, b. 24 November 1915, Winnipeg, Manitoba, Canada. Chemist. m. Leah Orloff, 1 son, 2 daughters. Education: BSc, Honours, 1937, MSc, 1939, University of Manitoba; PhD, McGill University, 1941. Appointments: Research Chemist, Canadian Board of Grain Commissioners, 1938; Research Scientist, H Smith Paper Mills, 1941-48; Associate Director of Research, Ethyl Corporation, 1948-82; Adjunct Professor of Chemistry, University of Detroit, Michigan, USA, 1957. Publications include: Articles and papers in Pulp and Paper Magazine, Canada, 1946; Journal of the American Chemical Society, 1951, 1953, 1954; Chemical Reviews, 1954; Industrial Engineering and Chemistry, 1961; Botyu Kagaku, 1956; Proceedings of the 7th World Petroleum Congress, 1967; Zeolites, 1984; Poultry Science, 1985; Over 50 patents; Co-inventor, Arborite Plastics, also Secondary Chemical Recovery System for use in kraft pulp production. Honours: Isbister Scholar, University of Manitoba, 1934-37; Research Fellow, McGill University, 1940-41; Weldon Memorial Gold Medal, Senior Award of Canadian Pulp and Paper Association, 1948. Memberships: American

Dictionary of International Biography

Chemical Society; Sigma Xi; Pulp and Paper Associations, USA, Canada. Address: 2903 Victoria Circle, Apt D3, Coconut Creek, FL 33066, USA.

ORMAN Stanley, b. 6 February 1935, London, England. Consultant. m. Helen Hourman, 1 son, 2 daughters. Education: BSc, 1st Class Honours, Chemistry and Physics, 1957, PhD, Chemistry, 1960, Kings College, London; Fulbright Fellow, Brandeis University Massachusetts, USA, 1960-91. Appointments: Scientist Ministry of Defence, 1961-82, positions held include: Chief Weapons Systems Engineer Chevaline, 1980-82, Minister, British Embassy, Washington, USA, 1982-84, Deputy Director Atomic Weapons research Establishment, 1984-86, Founding Director General, SDI Participation Office, 1986-90; Under Secretary of State, UK Ministry of Defence, 1982-90; Chief Executive Officer, General Technology Systems, USA, 1990-96; Chief Executive Officer, Orman Associates, 1996-. Publications: Author book: Faith in G.O.D.S – Stability in Nuclear Age, 1991; Over 120 published papers and articles on chemistry, corrosion science, adhesion and defence issues including over 80 articles on missile defence; Participation in workshops and presentations at over 70 international conferences on defence issues. Honours: Captained London University Track Team, 1956-57; Represented Britain in World Student Games, 3rd in 100m and 7th in Long Jump, 1956; Jelf Medalist, King's College, London, 1957. Address: 17825 Stoneridge Drive, North Potomac, MD 20878, USA. E-mail: or2withdog@aol.com

ORME John David, b. 1 June 1952, Portland, Oregon, USA. Professor. Education: BA, History, University of Oregon, 1974; MA, 1978, PhD, 1982, Government, Harvard University. Appointments: Visiting Professor, Dickinson College, 1982-83; Assistant, Associate, then, after 1995, Full Professor at Oglethorpe University in Politics; Research Fellow, Center for Science and International Affairs, Harvard University, 1990-92. Publications: Political Instability and American Foreign Policy, 1989; Security in East Central Europe, 1991; Deterrence, Reputation and Cold War Cycles, 1992; The Unexpected Origins of Peace, 1996; The Utility of Force in a World of Scarcity, 1997-98; The War that Never Happened, 2001; The Paradox of Peace, 2004. Honours: Phi Beta Kappa; Donald C Agnew Award for Distinguished Service, 2001; Listed in Who's Who Among America's Teachers. Memberships: American Political Science Association; International Studies Association. Address: Oglethorpe University, 4484 Peachtree Road NE, Atlanta, GA 30319, USA. E-mail: jorme@oglethorpe.edu

ORMOND Julia, b. 1965, England. Actress. m. Rory Edwards, divorced. Education: Farnham Art School; Webber Douglas Academy. Appointments: Worked in Repertory, Crucible Theatre, Sheffield, Everyman Theatre, Cheltenham; On tour with Royal Exchange Theatre, Manchester; Appeared in Faith, Hope and Charity, Lyric, Hammersmith; Treats, Hampstead Theatre; West End Debut in Anouilh's The Rehearsal; My Zinc Bed, 2000. Creative Works: TV appearances: Traffik (Channel 4 series); Ruth Rendell Mysteries; Young Catherine, 1990; Films: The Baby of Macon; Legends of the Fall; First Knight; Sabrina; Smilla's Sense of Snow, 1997; The Barber of Siberia, 1998; The Prime Gig, 2000; Resistance, 2003. Address: c/o CAA, 9830 Wilshire Boulevard, Beverly Hills, CA 90212, USA.

ORMSBY Frank, b. 30 October 1947, Enniskillen County, Fermanagh, Northern Ireland. Poet; Writer; Editor. Education: BA, English, 1970, MA, 1971, Queen's University, Belfast. Appointment: Editor, The Honest Ulsterman, 1969-89. Publications: A Store of Candles, 1977; Poets from the North of Ireland (editor), 1979, new edition, 1990; A Northern Spring, 1986; Northern Windows: An Anthology of Ulster Autobiography (editor), 1987; The Long Embrace: Twentieth Century Irish Love Poems (editor), 1987; Thine in Storm and Calm: An Amanda McKittrick Ros Reader (editor), 1988; The Collected Poems of John Hewitt (editor), 1991; A Rage for Order: Poetry of the Northern Ireland Troubles (editor), 1992; The Ghost Train, 1995; The Hip Flask: Short Poems from Ireland (editor), 2000. Address: 33 North Circular Road, Belfast BT15 5HD, Northern Ireland

ORNA Rav-Hon, b. 2 May 1946, Israel. Poet; Writer. m. Uzi, 3 sons, 1 daughter. Education: MA, Hebrew Literature and Philosophy. Appointments: Chairman, Committee for Foreign Affairs of the Hebrew Association of Writers in Israel, 1988-90; Member, Executive Community, Hebrew Association Writers in Israel, 1990-99. Publications: Ceof-Hachol; Negiot Shel CochHavim; Firebird; Brucha Ani; A'ahavat Horef. Honours: Tel-Aviv Prize for Culture and Literature (2 times); The Presidents Prize. Memberships: Hebrew Writers Association; Party for Human Rights; Sidha-Yoga, Kabbalah. Address: Hanarkisim 1 Cfar-Sirkin 49935, Israel.

OROPEZA Rubén, b.23 May 1930, Zacatlan-Pue, Mexico. Physician. m. Joyce E Oropeza, 1 son, 2 daughters. Education: BS, 1948, MD cum laude, 1954, National University of Mexico; Surgical Residency, Masters Degree, Surgery, University of Minnesota Hospitals, USA, 1954-59; Fellow, Surgical Oncology, Memorial Sloan Kettering, 1959-62. Appointments: Attending Surgeon Chairman, Department of Gynaecology and Head and Neck Cancer, Cancer Hospital, Mexico, City, Mexico1962-64; Attending Surgeon, Pack Medical Group, New York, USA, 1964-68; Assistant Professor of Surgery, New York University Medical Center, New York, 1967-98; Assistant Professor of Surgery, Columbia University, New York, 1967-2003; Hospital affiliations: Beth Israel Hospital, 1964-97; Cabrini Hospital, 1964-2000; New York University Hospital, 1967-98; Bellvue Hospital, 1967-98; Veterans Hospital, New York, 1967-98; Harlem Hospital, Columbia University, 1972-2003; North General Hospital, 1997-2003; Active Member Cancer Program/Cancer Registry, 1972-2003, Co-ordinator Cancer Program, 2002-, Harlem Hospital. Publications: Books: Early Diagnosis and Detection of Cancer, 1962; Between Puffs: History of Tobacco in Pre-Columbian Cultures, in press; Book chapters: Melanomas of special anatomical sites, 1977; Melanomas of the gastrointestinal tract, 1982; Journal articles as first author and co-author include most recently: Limb Salvage in Recurrent Synovial Sarcoma of the Right Ankle and Lower Leg, 2002; Benign Phyllodes Tumor of the Male Breast, 2002; Impact of Cancer Screening Program on Breast Cancer Stage at Diagnosis in a Medically Underserved Urban Community, 2003. Honours: Cum Laude, Medical School, University of Mexico; Masters Degree of Surgery, University of Minnesota. Memberships include: Surgical Oncological Society (James Ewing Society); New York Cancer Society; American College of Surgeons; Head and Neck Society; New York County Society; Mexican Cancer Society. Address: 301 Fieldstone Terrace, Wyckoff, NJ 07481, USA. E-mail: oropezar@nychhc.org

ORSHER Stuart, b. 19 October 1949, Philadelphia, Pennsylvania, USA. Physician; Attorney. m. Gladys George, 2 sons. Education: BA, Humanities, Villanova University, 1971; MD, Hahnemann Medical College, 1975; JD, Fordham University School of Law, 1982. Appointments: Physician in Private Medical Practice; President, New York County Medical Society, 1987; President, New York State Medical Society, 1997; Attending Physician, Lennox Hill Hospital, New York City, New York, USA. Memberships: New York State Bar Association; New York State Medical Society; American Medical Association. Address: 3 East 79th Street, New York, NY 10021, USA.

Dictionary of International Biography

ÖRVELL Claes Gunnar, b. 22 April 1945, Stockholm, Sweden. Physician; Virologist. m. Eva Reimert, 2 sons, 3 daughters. Education: MD, 1973, PhD, 1977, Karolinska Institutet. Appointments: Researcher, Department of Virology, Karolinska Institutet, 1978-79; Researcher, Virology, National Bacteriological Laboratory, 1980-92; Associate Professor, Karolinska Institutet, 1988-; Senior Physician, Stockholm City Council, 1992-. Publications: Numerous articles on virological diseases and the subject structure of viruses to professional journals. Honours: International Order of Merit; MOIF; Deputy Director General, IBC; Lifetime Achievement Award; Presidential Seal of Honour, 2001; World Biographee Day, 2001; United Cultural Convention Prize, 2001; FAOE, 2001; Continental Governor, ABI, 2001; Ambassador of Grand Eminence, ABI, 2002; Minister of Culture, ABI, 2003. Memberships: New York Academy of Sciences; Society of General Microbiology; Continental Governor, ABI. Address: Department of Clinical Virology, Huddinge University Hospital, F68, 14186 Stockholm, Sweden. E-mail: claes.orvell@hs.se

OSBORN John Holbrook (Sir), b. 14 December 1922, Sheffield, England. Semi-retired: Politician; Industrialist; Scientist; Soldier. m. (1) Molly Suzanne Marten, divorced 2 daughters, (2) Joan Mary Wilkinson, deceased, (3) Patricia Felicity Read. Education: MA Cantab, Part II Tripos Metallurgy, Trinity Hall, Cambridge University, England, 1943; Diploma in Foundry Technology, National Foundry College, Wolverhampton Technical College, 1949. Appointments: Royal Corps Signals, 1943-74; Battery Commander, Royal Artillery TA, 1948-55; Assistant Works Manager, Production Controller, Cost Controller, 1947-51, Company Director, 1951-79, Samuel Osborn and Company Limited, Sheffield, England; Conservative Candidate and Member of Parliament, Sheffield Hallam, 1959-87; Parliamentary Private Secretary to Minister for Commonwealth Relations, 1962-64; Joint Honorary Secretary, Conservative 1922 Committee, 1968-87; Former Chairman, Conservative Transport Committee, All-Party Road Study Group, Parliamentary Group Energy Studies; All-Party Channel Tunnel Group; Member of the European Parliament, 1975-79; Former Member of the Interim Licensing Authority; Chairman, Friends of Progress, 1990-94. Publications: Co-author: Conservative publications: Export of Capital; Trade not Aid; Change or Decay; A Value Added Tax; European Parliamentary publications: Help for the Regions; Energy for Europe; Also a Parliamentary and Scientific Committee report. Honours: Knight Bachelor, Birthday Honours 1983, for Public and Political Services; Chairman, Business in Development Committee, UK Chapter of Society of International Development, 1990-1995, attached to Worldaware; Member Executive, 1968-75, 1979-82, Life Member, 1987, IPU, UK branch; Life Member, CPA, UK branch, 1987-; Officer, 1960-87, Life Member, 1987, Parliamentary and Scientific Committee; European Atlantic Group Committee, 1990-; Member, Royal Institute of International Affairs, 1985-; Member, Conservative Group for Europe, European Movement, 1975-; Council Member, 1963-79, Life Member, Industrial Society; Junior Warden-Searcher, Assistant Searcher, Freeman, 1987-, Company of Cutlers in Hallamshire. Memberships: Fellow, Royal Society for Encouragement of the Arts, Manufacture and Commerce, 1966-; Trustee of many Sheffield Charitable Trusts; President, 1960-96, Honorary Patron, Sheffield Institute of Advanced Motorists; Fellow, Institute of Directors, 1955-; Fellow, Institute of Materials, 1947-. Address: Newlands, 147 Hawton Road, Newark, Nottinghamshire, NG24 4QG, England. E-mail: j.h.osborn147@ntlworld.co.uk

OSBORNE Judith Barbour, b. 14 October 1950, Winnipeg, Manitoba, Canada. Artist; Art Educator. m. Frederick S Osborne Jr. Education: BFA, Philadelphia College of Art, University of the Arts, 1974; MFA, Pennsylvania Academy of Fine Arts, 1997. Appointments: Principal, Barbour Calligraphics, Philadelphia, 1976-2003; Director of Publications and Publicity, Philadelphia Conference on the Calligraphic Arts, 1982; Adjunct Faculty Member, University of the Arts, Philadelphia, 1982-85, 1992, 2000; Drexel University, Philadelphia, 1991-2002; Innovations, 7th international calligraphy conference, New York City, 1987; Evening Speaker, Writing Beyond Words, 19th international calligraphy conference/east, Guilford, Connecticut, 1999; Exhibition Co-ordinator: Calleidoscope, 13th international calligraphy conference, Trenton, New Jersey, 1993; Guest Curator, Kamin Gallery, University of Pennsylvania, 1993, 1995; Exhibition Juror, Philadelphia Calligraphers' Society, 1989, 1991, 1994, 1995, 1998; Philadelphia Sketch Club, 2002. Creative Works: Solo exhibitions include: Rourke Art Gallery, Moorhead, Minnesota, 1999; Philadelphia Art Alliance, 2000; Living Arts of Tulsa, Oklahoma, 2000; Artists' House, Philadelphia, 1998, 2001, 2002; Group shows include: National Arts Club, New York City, 1990; Pennsylvania State Museum, Harrisburg, 1994, 2000, 2001; Nexus Foundation for Today's Art, Philadelphia, 1997; Collaborator, Sophia Osborne Dance Associates, 1999-2001; Delaware Center for the Contemporary Arts, 2002; Tenri Cultural Institute, New York City, 2002; Shanxi Art Museum, Xian, China, 2003; Ice House Gallery, Berkeley Springs, West Virginia, 2004; Permanent collections include: Blue Cross; Federal Reserve Bank of Philadelphia. Publications: Writer, Art Matters, 1997-2001; Letter Arts Review, 2003; Catalogue essay, Philadelphia Sketch Club, 2002; Listed in national and international biographical dictionaries. Honours: Best of Show, Abington Art Center, Pennsylvania, 1990; Fellowship Prize, Pennsylvania Academy of Fine Arts, 1997; Recipient, Independence Foundation Fellowship, 2001. Listed in: Several Biographical Dictionaries. Memberships: College Art Association; Philadelphia Calligraphers' Society, board member, publications editor, 1980-85; Institute of Noetic Sciences. Address: 11 Mitchel Terrace, Ivoryton, CT 06442-1042, USA. E-mail: fojo5@earthlink.net

OSBORNE Michael John, b. 25 January 1942, Eastbourne, England. University Vice Chancellor. m. Dawn. Education: BA, Oxford, 1965; MA, 1968; Dr Philos, DLit, Katholieke University, Leuven, Belgium, 1978; Hon D Litt, Athens, 2001. Appointments: Lecturer, Classics, University of Bristol, England, 1965-66; Lecturer, Senior Lecturer, Classics and Archaeology, University of Lancaster, England, 1966-82; Professor, Head of Classical Studies, University of Melbourne, Australia, 1983-89; Pro Vice Chancellor, Vice President, Academic Board, University of Melbourne, 1988-89; Vice Chancellor, President, La Trobe University, 1990-; Chair, Academic Board, 1990-; Professor, Peking University, 2003-. Publications: Naturalization in Athens; Lexicon of Greek Personal Names; The Foreign Residents of Athens; The Inscriptions of Athens in the Hellenistic Period; Author of many chapters in books and articles for learned journals. Honours: Hon D Litt, Athens; Laureate, Belgian Royal Academy of Sciences, Letters and Fine Arts; Professor Emeritus, University of Melbourne; Japan Foundation Fellow; Honorary Professor, Yunnan University, China; Honorary Professor, Kunming Medical University, China; Honorary Professor, Yunnan Normal University, China; Honorary Professor, Yunnan Agricultural University, China; Honorary Professor, Sichuan University, China; Honorary Professor, Harbin Medical University, China; Aristotle Award for Services to Hellenic Study; Honorary Distinction of Republic of Cyprus for Services to Hellenic Culture; Fellow, Australian Academy of Humanites; Honorary Fellow, Hungarian Academy of Engineering; Corresponding Member, Academy of Athens; Fellow, Australian Institute of Management; Alexander S Onassis Fellowship; Centenary Medal, Australia. Memberships include: Australian Vice-Chancellors' Committee (AVCC), 1990-; Board of Directors, AVCC; Chair, AVCC Standing Committee for Student

Dictionary of International Biography

Affairs; Chair, AVCC Standing Committee for International Affairs; Australian International Education Foundation Council, 1997-98; Board of Directors, Graduate Careers Council of Australia; Board of Directors International Development Programme; Board of Directors, Business Higher Education Round Table; President, University Mobility Program in Asia Pacific, 2001-; President, International Network of Universities. Address: Office of the Vice Chancellor, La Trobe University, Bundoora, VIC 3086, Australia.

OSENI Wahab Lanre, b. 21 August 1963, Ojoku, Nigeria. Bank Manager. m. Titilayo Hamdat, 2 sons, 2 daughters. Education: BSc Honours, Economics, 1986; Masters degree, Managerial Psychology, 1999. Appointments: Clerical Officer, Federal Office of Statistics, 1980; Research Officer II, NTA News V/Island, Lagos, 1989; Manager, Bank Examination, Central Bank of Nigeria, 1989-. Publications: Economics for Beginners in Nigeria, 1995; Economics for Beginners, revised edition, unpublished, 2003. Honours: Listed in national and international biographical dictionaries. Memberships: Associate, Institute of Personnel Management of Nigeria, 1996; Associate, Institute of Public Administration of Nigeria, 2001. Address: Bank Examination Department, CBN, Tinubu-Lagos, c/o H/O-P/O PO Box 15970, Ibadan, Nigeria. E-mail: lanrewajuoseni@yahoo.com

OSMAN Ahmed, b. 3 January 1930, Ouja, Morocco. President of the Rassemblement National des Independents. m. Ahlam Benosman, 1 son, 1 daughter. Education: Master's Degree in Public and Private Law, University of Bordeaux, France, 1956. Appointments: Ambassador in Bonn, Germany, 1961; Ambassador in Washington, DC, USA, 1968; Minister, 1970-71; Director of the Royal Cabinet, Morocco, 1971-72; Prime Minister of Morocco, 1972-79; President of the Parliament of Morocco, 1984-92; President of the Rassemblement National des Independents (RNI Political Party). Publications: Speeches and articles on political, economical and social issues, constitutional institutions; Conferences and press conferences. Honours: Great Officer of the Throne Order. Memberships: Interaction Council (former Heads of State and Prime Ministers); President, RNI; President, NGO "ANGAD". Address: Allée des Princesses, Rabat, Morocco.

OSTOJIĆ Negoslav, b. 9 September 1948, Ivanjica, Yugoslavia. Economist. m. Olga Dondur, 1 daughter. Education: BA, MA, Faculty of Economics, Belgrade. Appointments: Adviser, Institute for International Scientific Educational, Cultural and Technical Co-operation, Republic of Serbia, Belgrade; Executive Director, South-South Corporation Agency, Belgrade; Executive Director, European Centre for Peace and Development of the University for Peace, established by United Nations, Belgrade. Publications include: International Financing of Economic Development; Doing Business with Yugoslavia; Yugoslav Potentials for Scientific and Technical Co-operation; Directory, Corporate Research, Consulting and Engineering; Small and Medium-Size Enterprises in Developing Countries; SMEDC, Technical-Technological Development Marketing; Numerous articles in the field of economics, international relations, banking, financing and contemporary management. Memberships: Society of International Development; Scientific Society of Economists; General Co-ordination of World Scientific Banking Meeting. Address: European Centre for Peace and Development, Terazije 41, 11000 Belgrade, Yugoslavia. Email: ecpd@Eunet.yu

OSTROM Gladys Marion Snell, b. 1 November 1935, Schenectady, New York, USA. Expressive Arts Therapist. m. Andrew Griswold Ostrom, 4 sons, 1 daughter. Education: Certificate Student, Famous Writers School, Connecticut, 1970; Famous Artist School, Connecticut, 1979; MA, Education, Psychology, Beacon College, Washington DC, 1983; PhD; Expressive Therapy, National Institute of Expressive Therapy,

Hawaii, 1992; PhD, Imagery Therapy, Summit University of Louisiana, 1994. Appointments: Expressive Arts Therapist; Certified Expressive Therapist; Therapist National Expressive Therapy Association; Faculty Member, National Institute for Expressive Therapy; Executive Director, GoCo, 1983-; Provost, Summit University of Louisiana, 1994-2000; Provost, University for Integrated Learning, 2000-; Executive Director, Creative Artistic Training; Cato's Publishing, 1997-; Director, Middle Grove Management, 1999. Publications: The Funny Book, 1976; Touch-Me Letters, 1979; Creative Artistic Training, 1994; Leggys in Letter-Land, 2002; Articles to journals. Honours: PhD; FIBA; MOIF; DDG. Memberships: The National Expressive Therapy Association; The National Institute for Expressive Therapy; American Society for the Study of Mental Imagery. Address: 2887 Shaw Road, Middle Grove, NY 12850, USA.

OSUKA Atsuhiro, b. 16 October, 1954, Gamagori, Aichi, Japan. Professor of Chemistry. m. Keiko, 2 daughters. Education: Graduate , 1977, Master Course, 1979, PhD Degree, 1982, Kyoto University. Appointments: Assistant Professor, 1974, Ehime University; Assistant Professor , 1984, Associate Professor, 1986, Professor, 1996, Kyoto University. Publications: Fully Conjugated Porphyin Tapes with Electronic'Absorption Bands That Reach into Infrared, 2001. Honours: Chemical Society of Japan, Young Award, 1988; Japanese Photochemistry Association Award, 1999. Memberships: Chemical Society of Japan; American Chemical Society; American Photobiology Association. Address: Department of Chemistry, Graduate School of Science, Kyoto University, Kyoto 6060-8502, Japan. E-mail: osuka@kuchem.kyoto-u.ac.jp

OSWALD Angela Mary Rose (Lady), b. 21 May 1938, London, England. Lady-in-Waiting. m. Sir Michael Oswald, 1 son, 1 daughter. Appointments: Extra Woman of the Bedchamber to H M Queen Elizabeth the Queen Mother, 1981-83; Woman of the Bedchamber to H M Queen Elizabeth the Queen Mother, 1983-2002. Honours: LVO, 1993; Freeman of the City of London, 1995; CVO, 2000. Address: The Old Rectory, Weasenham St Peter, King's Lynn, Norfolk, PE32 2TB, England.

OSWALT Sally W. Hundt, b. 17 April 1917, Bangor, Wisconsin, USA. Beautician. 2 sons, 2 daughters, 2 deceased. Education: Graduate, Milwaukee School of Cosmetology, 1941; Bachelor of Political Science, University of Wisconsin-La Crosse, 1991 (aged 72). Appointments: Owner and Operated Beauty Salon for 1958-; Elected to County Board, 1974-76, 1984-90, 1992-94; State of Wisconsin Pharmacy Internship Board, 1980-85; Board of Directors, Community Credit Union, 1985-90; La Crosse County Health Board, 1986-2002; Regional Planning Committee, 1988-2003; ; Board of Directors, Diocese of La Crosse Cemetery Association, 1995-; Vice-Chair, La Crosse County Republican Women, 2003-; Chapel Restoration; School Restoration. Publications: Essays and items for Op-Ed page, La Crosse Tribune; Unpublished poetry. Honours: Woman of the Year in Government/Politics, Y.W.C.A.,1984; Member of Group Award to Business and Professional Woman, 1998. Memberships: Business and Professional Women; League of Women Voters; Republican party; Blessed Sacrament Church and Choir; Volunteer at Nursing Homes. Address: 2116 Pine Street, La Crosse, WI 54601-3811, USA.

OTTO Claude, b. 20 March 1952, Strasbourg, France. Assistant Professor. m. Isabel Ayala-Andres, 1 son, 1 daughter. Education: Degree in Arts, 1973; Master of Arts, 1974; PhD, 1977. Appointments: Assistant Professor, University of Strasbourg, France; Assistant Professor, University of Saarland, Germany. Publications: Numerous articles on linguistics in many European journals and scientific works. Membership: New York Academy of Sciences; Fellow of various societies in Germany and France. Address: 25 Avenue Christian Pfister, F-67100 Strasbourg-Meinau, France.

OTTOVÁ-LEITMANNOVÁ Angela, b. 14 January 1952, Slovakia (former Czechoslovakia). Professor in Biophysics. m. H Ti Tien, 1 son, 1 daughter. Education: MSc, Humboldt University, Berlin, Germany, 1974; PhD, Biophysics, 1977; Associate Professor, 1989; DrSc, 1995, Professor, 2001. Appointments: Humboldt University, 1972-77; Slovak Academy of Sciences, 1977-81; Slovak Technical University, 1981-; Visiting Associate Professor, 1991-2001, Visiting Professor, Biophysics, Michigan State University, East Lansing, 2001-. Publications: Over 150 in professional journals. Honours: Several. Memberships: Union of Slovak Mathematicians and Physicists; Slovak Medical Society; Slovak Cybernetic Society at Slovak Academy of Sciences; Slovak Academy of Sciences. Address: Department of Physiology, Michigan State University, Biomedical and Physical Sciences Building, East Lansing, MI 48824, USA.

OUATTARA Moussa, b. 2 April 1955, Bobo-Dioulasso, Burkina Faso. Professor. m. Agnès, 3 sons, 1 daughter. Education: Licence in mathematics, 1981; Master of mathematics, 1982; PhD, mathematics, Montpellier, France; Doctorat d'Etat es Sciences Mathématiques, 1991. Appointments: Assistant, 1988-91; Assistant Lecturer, 1991-92; Senior Lecturer, 1992-2000, Professor, 2000-; Vice-Dean of the Faculty, 1994-95; Vice-Rector, 1995-97; Rector of the University, 1997-2001. Publications: More than 25 publications in professional journals and book chapters include most recently as co-author: Autour de la condition d'Engel dans les algèbres de Bernstein, 2000; Sur les sous-algèbres monogènes d'algèbres d'évolution stationnaire, 2002; Sur une classe d'algèbres d'Evolution, 2002. Honour: Chevalier de l'Ordre des Palmes Académiques, 1999. Memberships: African Mathematical Union; American Mathematical Society; Executive Board Member, Association of African Universities. Address: Department of Mathematics, UFR-SEA, University of Ouagadougou, 03 BP 7021, Burkina Faso. E-mail: ouatt.mouss@fasonet.bf

OULD EL JOUD Dahada, b. 31 December 1961, Tidjikja, Mauritania. Epidemiologist. m. Varh Mint El Ghoth. 3 sons, 1 daughter. Education: Medical Training, URSS, 1984; Master in Public Health, Rabat, Morocco, 1993; Degree in Biostatistics, ULB, Brussels, Belgium, 1997; PhD, Epidemiology, Paris, France, 2001. Appointments: Head Doctor of Public Health Region, Inchiri, 1984-86, Tensoueïlim (Nouakchott), 1987, Toujourine, 1988-89; Ministry of Public Health, 1990-93; Head of Statistics Service, Ministry of Health, 2002. Publications: Articles in medical journals include as first-author and co-author: Evaluation of the quality of care for severe obstetric haemorrhage in three French Regions, 2001; Dystocia: a study of its frequency and risk factors in 7 cities of West Africa, 2001; Epidemiological features of uterine rupture in West Africa, 2002; Co-author Cultural Health Assessment, C E D'Avanzo and E M Geissler, 3rd edition, 2003. Address: BP 4036, Nouakchott, Mauritania. E-mail: dahada@voila.fr

OUZTS Eugene Thomas, b. 7 June 1930, Thomasville, Georgia, USA. Minister; Secondary Educator. m. Mary Olive Vineyard. Education: MA, Harding University, 1957; Postgraduate: Murray State University, University of Arkansas, Arizona State University, University of Arizona; Northern Arizona University. Appointments: Certificated Secondary Teacher, Arkansas, Missouri, Arizona; Ordained Minister Church of Christ, 1956; Minister in various Churches in Arkansas, Missouri, Texas, -1965; Teacher, various public schools, Arkansas, Missouri, 1959-65; Teacher, Arizona, 1965-92; Minister in Arizona Church of Christ, Clifton, Morenci,

Safford and Duncan, 1965-. Honours: Civil Air Patrol, Arizona Wing Chaplain of Year, 1984; Thomas C Casaday Unit Chaplain, 1985; Arizona, Wing Safety Officer, 1989; Arizona Wing Senior Member, 1994; Meritorious Service Award, 1994; Southwestern Region Senior Member, 1995; Exceptional Service Award, 1997; Life Fellowship, IBA, Cambridge, England. Memberships: Military Chaplains Association; Disabled American Veterans; Air Force Association; American Legion; Elks; Board, Arizona Church of Christ Bible Camp; Airport Advisory Board, Greenlee County, Arizona; Civil Air Patrol/Air Force Auxiliary (Chaplain, 1982, 1st Lieutenant advanced through grades to Lieutenant Colonel, 1989); Assistant Wing Chaplain. Address: 739 E Cottonwood Road, Duncan, Arizona 85534-8108, USA.

OVERMIER James Bruce, b. 2 August 1938, Queens, New York, USA. Professor of Psychology. m. Judith Ann Smith, 1 daughter. Education: AB, Chemistry, Kenyon College, 1960; MA, Psychology, Bowling Green State University, 1962; MA, 1964; PhD, 1965, Psychology, University of Pennsylvania. Appointments: Professor of Psychology, University of Minnesota, 1965-; Visiting Professor, University of Hawaii, 1974, 1976, 1982, 1986, Kwansei Gakuin University, 1993, University of Seville, 1997, 2000; Professor II, University of Bergen, Norway, 1992-2006. Publications: Over 200 peer articles, chapters and books. Honours: National Academy of Science Exchange Fellow, 1972; Fulbright Hays, 1980; Fogarty Fellow, 1984; Norwegian Marshall Fellow, 1987; Honorary DSc, Kenyon, 1990; Fellow, Society of Experimental Psychologists, 1992; Sigma Xi National Distinguished Lecturer (1999-2001); Quad-L Award, University of New Mexico, 1999; CT Morgan Award, 2001; Gantt Medal, 2003. Memberships: President or Member of Board of Directors of: American Psychological Association; American Psychological Society; Pavlovian Society; International Union of Psychological Sciences; Society for General Psychology. Address: Department of Psychology, Elliott Hall, University of Minnesota, 75 E River Road, Minneapolis, MN 55455, USA.

OWEN Gordon P, b. 28 June 1953, London, England. Voluntary Sector Fundraising Consultant; Trust Company Secretary. m. Janice Joel, 2 sons. Education: Diploma in Psychology; HND, Business Studies; NVQ Desktop Publishing and Word Processing. Appointments include: Principal, Messrs G Owen & Co, 1972-; Part-time Proprietor, Rent-A-Bar Service, 1981-2003; Principal Administrative Officer, London Borough of Newham, 1976-93; Projects/Fundraising Administrator and PR Officer, 1993-2002, Newham Youth Trust (Limited), London; Founder and Developer, Newnham Youth Lodge Hostel Project, 1979-94; Never-Land (Children's Adventure), 1993-; Corporate Customer Services Manager , Technologic LSI (Europe) Limited, London, 1998; Customer Services Executive, Barclays Bank Corporate International and Offshore, 1999; Office Utilisation Consultant, 1999; Regional Administrator, CVS Volunteering Partners, 1999-2002; Senior Co-ordinator, Newham Night Shelter, 1998-2004; Fundraising and Development Officer, Barking and Dagenham CVS, 2002-2004. Honour: Queens Jubilee Award, 2002. Memberships include: Chairman, St Bartholomew's Social Club, 1976-79; St Bartholomew's Development Committee, 1977-84; St Bartholomew's District Church Council, 1977-87, 1998-; Parish Councillor, 1978-; Newham Deanery Synod, London, 1980-81, 1982-84; Chairman, Newham Youth Leaders Association, 1979-85; London Borough of Newham Education Committee Youth Panel, 1983-84, 1985-88; Newham Voluntary Agencies Council, Children and Young People Steering Committee, 1981-83; Founder, Developer, Newham Youth Lodge Hostel Project, 1979-94; Metropolitan Police Newnham Volunteer Cadet Corps, 1996-; Parochial Church Council, Parish of East Ham, London, 1977-87, 2000-; Parish Warden, 1999- Fete Chairperson and Co-ordinator, Friends of Barking Church of England School PTA, 1993-94;

Dictionary of International Biography

Institute of Charity Managers; British Apple Systems Users Group Royal Horticultural Society; Cyclists Touring Club; British Mountain Bike Federation; CoachVille; TrainingZone; Former memberships: National Youth Bureau; National Association of Youth Clubs; London Union of Youth Clubs; Individual and Commercial Member, The Carnival Guild; The National Camping and Caravanning Club; Conway Owners Club; National Union of Licensed Victuallers Association; Shop Steward, 1982-84, 1986-93, Convenor, Branch Officer/Information Technology Officer and Metropolitan Regional Representative, UNISON formerly NALGO, Newham Branch; The London Bungee Club. Address: Owen House, 60 Beccles Drive, Barking, Essex IG11 9HY, England. E-mail: gordonowen1@yahoo.com Website: http://www.cvreferral.com/19/109659.html

OWEN Stephen John, b. 6 December 1953, Stratford-on-Avon, England. Poet. m. Louise Owen, 1 son, 3 daughters. Education: Department of Arabian and Hebrew, Department of Philosophy and History of Science, Leeds University; Department of Open Studies, Warwick University. Appointments: Forester, 1973-74; Editor, Omnibus (Leamington Spa), 1978-80; Fine Arts Worker, 1982-84; Editor, 4th Dimension and The Crack, 1989-97; Reader in Poetry, Oxford, 2003. Publications: Published poetry in: Depixol Junkies; Bark, Belfast poetry magazines; Articles on philosophy of religion in Green Spirituality; Articles in, NSF Today, Crack; Poems published in: Moonstone and Purple Patch, 2001, Borderlines, Anglo-Welsh Poetry Broadsheet; Currently publishing in: The Magazine, The Journal, The Cosmographs, volumes I – V: Poetic meditations on Archetypalmythology; Poetry performance at Purple Patch Convention, West Midlands, 2001; Existential Soap Opera, The Tall Tree, written as serial for Perceptions magazine, 2001-2002. Honours: 2nd Prize, Belfast (NSF) Poetry Competition; 2 Arts Council Grants for 4th Dimension Award; Golden Angel Award – 2 stars, for community poetry, Birmingham, England, 1996. Memberships: British Astronomical Association; British Interplanetary Society; Fellow, Theosophical Society, England; Labour Party; Founder member, Walter Savage Landor Society, Warwick. Address: 18 Humphries Street, Warwick CV34 5RA, England. E-mail: astrognosis@amserve.net

OWENS Agnes, b. 24 May 1926, Milngavie. Fiction Writer. m. Patrick Owens, 30 August 1964, 3 sons, 4 daughters. Publications: Gentlemen of the West, 1985; Lean Tales, 1985; Like Birds in the Wildnerness, 1986; A Working Mother, 1994; People Like That, 1996; For the Love of Willie, 1998; Bad Attitudes, 2003. Honour: Short Leet for Scottish Writer of the Year Award (Stakis Prize), 1998.Membership: Scottish Pen Centre. Address: 21 Roy Young Avenue, Balloch, Dunbartonshire, G83 8ER, Scotland.

OWENS John Edwin, b. 13 June 1948, Widnes, Cheshire, England. Political Scientist. m. Margaret Owens, 1 October 1971, 1 son, 1 daughter. Education: BA Honours, University of Reading, 1973; University of Warwick, 1973-75; PhD, University of Essex, 1982. Appointments: Lecturer, Central London Polytechnic, 1978-85; Lecturer, University of Essex, 1985-86; Senior Lecturer, 1986-98, Reader, 1998-2002, Professor, United States Government and Politics, 2002-, University of Westminster, London; Member, Editorial Boards, Presidential Studies Quarterly; The Journal of Legislative Studies and Politics and Policy. Publications: After Full Employment, with John Kearne, 1986; Congress and the Presidency: Institutional Politics in a Separated System, with Michael Foley, 1996; The Republican Takeover of Congress, with Dean McSweeney, 1998; Leadership in Context, with Erwin C Hargrove, 2003. Contributions to: British Journal of Political Science; Political Studies; Politics and Policy; American Review of Politics; Roll Call; Times Higher Educational Supplement; The Journal of Legislative Studies. Memberships: Political Studies Association, UK; Legislative Studies Section, American Political

Science Association; International Political Science Association. Address: The Centre for the Study of Democracy, The University of Westminster, 100 Park Village East, London NW1 3SR, England.

OWUSU-NSIAH Nana Stephen, b. 24 March 1945, Berekum, Ghana. Accountant; Lawyer. m. Agnes Owusu-Nsiah, 3 sons, 2 daughters. Education: Diploma in Accounting, Legon, Ghana, 1975; BSc, Administration, Legon, Ghana, 1978; MBA, Legon, Ghana, 1981; Barrister-at-Law, Ghana School of Law, 1990. Appointments: Regional Paymaster, Tamale, Ghana, 1979; Finance and Budget Officer, Police Headquarters, 1981; Chief Internal Auditor, Police Headquarters, 1982; Paymaster General and Controller, 1984; Quartermaster General, 2001; Director of Immigration, 2001; Inspector General of Police, 2002. Honours: Traditional Ruler: Mawerehene of Berekum (Divisional Chief responsible for maintenance of peace), Brong Ahafo Region, Ghana. Memberships: Ghana Bar Association; Chartered Institute of Administrators. Address: Ghana Police Service, Police Headquarters, PO Box 116, Accra, Ghana.

OYEBADE Eunice Funke, b. 20 October 1953, Ondo, Nigeria. University Administrator. m. Bayo Oyebade, 1 son, 3 daughters. Education: B Ed, University of Ibadan, 1978, M Ed, University of Benin, 1985, PhD, Ondo State University (now University of Ado-Ekiti), 2000. Appointments: Administrative Officer I, 1982, Assistant Registrar, 1985, Senior Assistant Registrar II, 1988, Senior Assistant Registrar I, 1991, Principal Assistant Registrar, 1994, Deputy Registrar, 1998, Registrar, 2001-, Federal University of Technology, Akure, Nigeria. Publication: A Study of the Causes of Staff-Authority Conflict in the Higher Institutions of Ondo State – Nigeria in Educational Perspective a Journal of the Faculty of Education, Lagos State University, Lagos, Nigeria. Honours: Distinguished Award of Excellence in the Nigerian Public Service; Certified and Distinguished Educational Administrator. Memberships: Fellow, Society of Educational Administrators of Nigeria; Fellow, Chartered Institute of Public Administrators of Nigeria; International Member, AUA, UK; Honorary Fellow, The Institute of Administrative Management of Nigeria. Address: No 1 Anuoluwapo Oyebade Close, Stateline Street, off FUTA Road, Akure, Ondo State, Nigeria. E-mail: registrar@futa.edu.ng

OZ Amos, b. 4 May 1939, Jerusalem, Israel. Author; Professor of Hebrew Literature. m. Nily Zuckerman, 5 April 1960, 1 son, 2 daughters. Education: BA cum laude, Hebrew Literature, Philosophy, Hebrew University, Jerusalem, 1965. Appointments: Teacher, Literature, Philosophy, Hulda High School and Givat Brenner Regional High School, 1963-86; Visiting Fellow, St Cross College, Oxford, England, 1969-70; Writer-in-Residence, Hebrew University, Jerusalem, 1975, 1990; Visiting Professor, University of California, Berkeley, USA, 1980; Writer-in-Residence, Professor of Literature, The Colorado College, Colorado Springs, 1984-85; Writer in Residence, Visiting Professor of Literature, Boston University, Massachusetts, 1987; Full Professor of Hebrew Literature, Ben Gurion University, Beer Sheva, Israel, 1987-; Writer-in-Residence, Tel Aviv University, 1996; Writer in Residence, Visiting Professor of Literature, Princeton University, (Old Dominion Fellowship), 1997; Weidenfeld Visiting Professor of European Comparative Literature, St Anne's College, Oxford, 1998. Publications include: Where the Jackals Howl (stories), 1965; My Michael (novel), 1968; Under This Blazing Light (essays), 1978; Black Box (novel), 1987; Don't Call It Night (novel), 1994; All Our Hopes (essays) 1998; The Same Sea, 1999. Honours include: Holon Prize, 1965; Wingate Prize, London, 1988; Honorary Doctorate, Tel Aviv University, 1992; Cross of the Knight of the Legion D'Honneur, 1997; Honorary Doctorate, Brandeis

University, USA, 1998; Israel Prize for Literature, 1998; Freedom of Speech Prize, Writers' Union of Norway, 2002. Address: c/o Deborah Owen Ltd, 78 Narrow Street, London E14, England.

OZAWA Takeo, b. 14 February 1932, Yokohama, Japan. Material Scientist. m. Hisae, 30 June 1957, 1 son, 1 daughter. Education: BSc 1955, MSc 1957, DSc 1980, University of Tokyo. Appointments: Researcher, 1957-70, Section Chief, 1970-87, Electrotech Laboratory, AIST, MITI; General Manager, Tsakuba Research Center, Daicel Chemical Industries Ltd, 1987-97; Professor, Chiba Institute of Technology, Department of Electrical Engineering, 1997-2002; Retired 2002; Part-time Professor, Chiba Institute of Technology Department of Electrical Engineering, 2002-03. Publications: Over 100 original papers. Honours: Mettler Award, North American Thermal Analysis Society, 1981; Best Energy Storage Paper, American Society of Mechanical Engineering, 1986; Kurnakov Medal, Kurnakov Institute of General and Inorganic Chemistry, 1984; ICTAC-TA Instruments Award, 2000. Memberships: President, International Confederation for Thermal Analysis and Calorimetry, 1992-96; Japan Society for Chemistry; Japan Institute for Electrical Engineers; Japan Society for Polymer Science. Address: 18-6 Josuishin-machi 1-chome, Kodaira, Tokyo 187-0023, Japan.

OZICK Cynthia, b. 17 April 1928, New York, New York, USA. Author; Poet; Dramatist; Critic; Translator. m. Bernard Hallote, 7 September 1952, 1 daughter. Education: BA, cum laude, English, New York University, 1949; MA, Ohio State University, 1950. Appointment: Phi Beta Kappa Orator, Harvard University, 1985. Publications: Trust, 1966; The Pagan Rabbi and Other Stories, 1971; Bloodshed and Three Novellas, 1976; Leviation: Five Fictions, 1982; Art and Ardor: Essays, 1983; The Cannibal Galaxy, 1983; The Messiah of Stockholm, 1987; Metaphor and Memory: Essays, 1989; The Shawl, 1989; Epodes: First Poems, 1992; What Henry James Knew, and Other Essays on Writers, 1994; Portrait of the Artist as a Bad Character, 1996; The Cynthia Ozick Reader, 1996; Fame and Folly, 1996; The Puttermesser Papers, 1997; The Best American Essays, 1998; Quarrel and Quandary, 2000. Contributions to: Many anthologies, reviews, quarterlies, journals, and periodicals. Honours: Guggenheim Fellowship, 1982; Mildred and Harold Strauss Living Award, American Academy of Arts and Letters, 1983; Lucy Martin Donnelly Fellow, Bryn Mawr College, 1992; PEN/Spiegel-Diamonstein Award for the Art of the Essay, 1997; Harold Washington Literary Award, City of Chicago, 1997; John Cheever Award, 1999; Lotos Club Medal of Merit, 2000; Lannan Foundation Award, 2000; National Critics' Circle Award for Criticism, 2001; Koret Foundation Aard for Literary Studies, 2001; Many honorary doctorates. Memberships: American Academy of Arts and Letters; American Academy of Arts and Sciences; Authors League; Dramatists Guild; PEN; Phi Beta Kappa. Address: c/o Alfred A Knopf Inc, 201 East 50th Street, New York, NY 10022, USA.

Dictionary of International Biography

P

PÄÄSUKE Mati, b. 2 April 1954 Viljandi, Estonia. Professor. m. Maive Pääsuke, 1 son. Education: Diploma Physical Education, 1976, PhD, Physiology, University of Tartu, Estonia. Appointments: Researcher, 1981-88, Associate Professor, 1989-2001, Dean of Faculty of Exercise and Sports Sciences, 1989-98, Head, Institute of Exercise Biology and Physiotherapy, 1998-; Professor of Kinesiology and Biomechanics, 2002-, University of Tartu, Estonia. Publications: Over 40 articles in international refereed journals including: Acta Orthopaedica Scandinavica; Acta Physiologica Scandinavica; Annals of Anatomy, Ageing: Clinical and Experimental Research; European Journal of Applied Physiology; Electromyography and Clinical Neurophysiology; Pediatric Exercise Science. Honours: Listed in Who's Who publications and biographical dictionaries. Memberships: Estonian Physiological Society; Estonian Federation of Sports Medicine; International Society of Biomechanics in Sports. Address: Institute of Exercise Biology and Physiotherapy, University of Tartu, 5 Jakobi Street, 51014 Tartu, Estonia. E-mail: mati.paasuke@ut.ee Website: www.ut.ee/KKKB

PACA Jan, b. 20 August 1945, Prague, Czech Republic. Bioengineer. m. Jana Novotná, 31 October 1975, 1 son, 1 daughter. Education: MSc, Technical University, Prague, 1968; PhD, 1975, DSc, 1993, Professor, 1995, University of Chemical Technology, Prague. Appointments: Designer, Vienna, 1969; Researcher, Research Institute Fat Industry, Prague, 1969-70; Assistant Professor, 1973-90; Referee, NSF, Washington DC, USA, 1976-78; Associate Professor, 1990-95; Senior Reader, Technical University, Prague, 1983-91; Full Professor, University of Chemical Technology, 1995-; Senior Reader, Charles University, Prague, 1995-96; Senior Reader, Fachhochschule Magdeburg, 1997; Senior Reader, Universidade Federal do Parana, Curitiba, 2001 and 2003. Publications: 152 original science papers; 21 Review papers; 11 Patents; 6 Textbooks and books; 4 edited and co-author of books; Co-author, 5 books; 281 lectures, papers, posters. Honours: Best Science Article in Journal Folia Microbiologica, 1977; Diploma for lecture at Czech Microbiology Society, 1980; Diploma for textbooks, 1986, 1988. Memberships: Science Council, Czech Academy of Science, 1992-95; Science Council, University of Chemical Technology, Prague, 1991-; Head, Committee of Czech Microbiology Society, Prague, 1989-96; Vice President, FEANI for Czech Republic, 1995-2000; Member, Committee for Professional Development, FEANI, 1995-; New York Academy of Science, 1997-; Air & Waste Management Association, Pennsylvania, USA, 2002-; Member, Editorial Board of Engineering in Life Sciences, Wiley, 1998-; Brazilian Archives of Biology and Technology, 2001-. Address: University of Chemical Technology, Department Ferment Chemistry and Bioengineering, 166 28 Prague 6, Technicka 5, Czech Republic.

PACINO Al (Alfredo James), b. 25 April 1940, New York, USA. Actor. Education: The Actors Studio. Appointments: Messenger, Cinema Usher; Co-Artistic Director, The Actors Studio Inc, New York, 1982-83; Member, Artistic Directorate Globe Theatre, 1997-. Creative Works: Films include: Me, Natalie, 1969; Panic in Needle Park, 1971; The Godfather, 1972; Scarecrow, 1973; Serpico, 1974; The Godfather Part II, 1974; Dog Day Afternoon, 1975; Bobby Deerfield, 1977; And Justice For All, 1979; Cruising, 1980; Author! Author!, 1982; Scarface, 1983; Revolution, 1985; Sea of Love, 1990; Dick Tracy, 1991; The Godfather Part III, 1990; Frankie and Johnny, 1991; Glengarry Glen Ross, 1992; Scent of A Woman, 1992; Carlito's Way, 1994; City Hall, 1995; Heat, 1995; Donny Brasco, 1996; Looking For Richard, 1996; Devil's Advocate, 1997; The Insider, 1999; Chinese Coffee, 1999; Man of the People, 1999; Any Given Sunday, 1999; Insomnia, 2002; Simone, 2002; People

I Know, 2002; The Recruit, 2003; Gigli, 2003. Honours include: Tony Award, 1996; British Film Award; National Society of Film Critics Award. Address: c/o Rick Nicita, CAA, 9830 Wilshire Boulevard, Beverly Hills, CA 90212, USA.

PACKER Kerry Francis Bullmore, b. 17 December 1937, Sydney, New South Wales, Australia. Publishing and Broadcasting Executive. m. Roslyn Weedon, 30 August 1963, 1 son, 1 daughter. Appointments: Chairman, Consolidated Press Holdings Ltd, 1974-; Director, Publishing & Broadcasting Ltd, 1994-. Memberships: Royal Sydney Golf Club; Australian Golf Club; Elanora Co Club; Tattersall's Athaeneum (Melbourne) Club. Address: Consolidated Press Holdings Ltd, 54 Park Street, Sydney, NSW 2000, Australia.

PACZYNSKI Georges, b. 30 March 1943, Grenoble, France. Musician (drums). m. Sophie Tret, 24 April 1995, 1 daughter. Musical Education: Self-taught. Career: Represented France, Festival of Montreux, Festival of Zurich, 1968; Broadcasts, France Culture, with Black And Blue, 1981, 2002; Founded trio with Jean-Christophe Levinson and Jean-François Jenny-Clark, 1984; Professor, Conservatoire National de Cergy-Pontoise and Conservatoire National Superieur de Lyon; Founded new trio with Philippe Macé and Ricardo del Fra, 1996 and a new trio with Yves Torchinsky and Edouard Ferlet, 2000. Compositions: 29 pieces for percussion and piano, Paris, Zurfluh, 1985-2002. Recordings: Eight Years Old, 1992; Levin's Song, 1994. Publications: Thesis: Baudelaire Et La Musique, 1973; La Genèse Du Rythme Et L'Anthropologie Gestuelle, 1984; Book: Rythme Et Geste, Les Racines Du Rythme Musical, 1988; Une Histoire de la Batterie de Jazz, Vol 1, 1997; Une Histoire De La Batterie de Jazz, Vol 2, 2000; L'Art de travailler un thème de jazz à la batterie; L'Art de travailler les accords du jazz au piano, 2003; Une Histoire de la Batterie de Jazz, Vol 3, 2004. Honours: Medal of the Society of Encouragement For Progress, 1989. Address: Georges Paczynski, 6 rue de Vaureal, 95000 Cergy-Village, France.

PADMANABHAN Krishnan, b. 11 May 1964, Trivandrum City. Research and Development Officer. Education: MSc, Eng, Materials Engineering, Indian Institute of Science, Bangalore, 1991; PhD, Materials Engineering, Indian Institute of Science, Bangalore, 1995. Appointments: Postdoctoral Fellow, Nanyang Technological University, Singapore, 1996-98; Guest Researcher, University of Delaware and National Institute of Standards and Technology, USA, 1998-99; Guest Faculty, IIT, Madras, 1999; Research Fellow, Singapore MIT Alliance, 2000-02; Consultant, CEO, KALPANA. Publications: Over 50 articles in international refereed journals; Proceedings at international conferences and workshops; Many oral and poster presentations, short articles, lectures and seminars. Address: New No 40, 14th Cross Street, New Colony, Chromepet, Chennai 600044, India.

PAGLIA Camille (Anna), b. 2 April 1947, Endicott, New York, USA. Professor of Humanities; Writer. Education: BA, State University of New York at Binghamton, 1968; MPhil, 1971, PhD, 1974, Yale University. Appointments: Faculty, Bennington College, Vermont, 1972-80; Visiting Lecturer, Wesleyan University, 1980; Visiting Lecturer, Yale University, 1980-84; Assistant Professor, 1984-87, Associate Professor, 1987-91, Professor of Humanities, 1991-2000, Philadelphia College of the Performing Arts, later the University of the Arts, Philadelphia; University Professor and Professor of Humanities and Media Studies, 2000-. Publications: Sexual Personae: Art and Decadence from Nefertiti to Emily Dickinson, 1990; Sex, Art, and American Culture: Essays, 1992; Vamps and Tramps: New Essays, 1994; Alfred Hitchcock's "The Birds", 1998. Contributions to: Journals and periodicals and Internet communications. Address: c/o Department of Liberal Arts, University of the Arts, 320 South Broad Street, Philadelphia, PA 19102, USA.

Dictionary of International Biography

PAHANG H.R.H. Sultan of, b. 24 October 1930, Istana Mangga Tunggal, Pekan, Malaysia. m. Tengku Hajjah Afzan binti Tengku Muhammad, 1954. Education: Malay College, Kuala Kangsar; Worcester College, Oxford; University College, Exeter. Appointments: Tengku Mahkota (Crown Prince), 1944; Captain, 4th Battalion, Royal Malay Regiment, 1954; Commander, 12th Infantry Battalion of Territorial Army, 1963-65, Lieutenant-Colonel; Member, State Council, 1955; Regent, 1956, 1959, 1965; Succeeded as Sultan, 1974; Timbalan Yang di Pertuan Agong (Deputy Supreme Head of State), Malaysia, 1975-79, Yang di Pertuan Agong (Supreme Head of State), 1979-84, 1985; Constitutional Head, International Islamic University, 1988. Honours include: DLitt, Malaya, 1988, LLD, Northrop, USA, 1993. Address: Istana Abu Bakar, Pekan, Pahang, Malaysia.

PAI Kochikar Pushpalatha b. 12 March 1946, Kundapura, India. Paediatric Surgeon. m. K Ganesh Pai, 1 son, 1 daughter. Education: MBBS, Bangalore Medical College, Bangalore, India, 1972; MD (pathology), Kasturba Medical College, Manipal, India, 1976. Appointments: Tutor in Pathology, Kasturba Medical College, Manipal, 1972-76; Pathologist, Fr Muller's Hospital, Mangalore, 1977-83; Lecturer, 1983-85, Assistant Professor, 1985-88, Reader, 1988-90, Associate Professor, 1990-92, Professor of Pathology, 1992-, Kasturba Medical College, Mangalore, India. Publications: 29 papers published in national and international journals include most recently: Hepatoprotective influence of selenium in experimental liver cirrhosis, 2001; Fine needle aspiration diagnosis in HIV related lymphadenopathy in Mangalore, 2002; Extensive squamous metaplasia in nodular goiter-FNAC diagnosis – A case report, 2002; FNAC as a Diagnostic Tool in Paediatric Tumours, 2002; Book chapter: Necrotising Enteritis in Infancy and Childhood in Tropical Paediatric Surgery, 1998; Numerous papers presented at conferences. Honours: Undergraduate and Postgraduate Examiner in Pathology, Mangalore University, Rajive Ghandi University, Karnataka, MGR University, Tamilnadu, Manipal Academy of Higher Education, Karnataka; Distinguished Alumni Award, Kasturba Medical College, Mangalore, 1990; Selected as Participant, 31st National Course on Educational science for Teachers of Health Professionals, Pondicherry, 1994. Memberships: Life member, Karnataka Chapter, Indian Association of Pathologists and Microbiologists; Indian Association of Pathologists and Microbiologists. Address: "Laxmi Ganesh", Near Mangala Nursing Home, Kadri Road, Mangalore 575 003, India. E-mail: pushpalathapai@yahoo.co.in

PAICHADZE Sergei A, b. 7 June 1936, Batumi, Georgia. Bibliologist. m. Larisa A Kozhevnikova, 1 son, 1 daughter. Education: Library Institute, 1956-61; Postgraduate, 1967-70; PhD, 1971; DSc, 1992; Professor, 1994. Appointments: Instructor, Dean, Proctor, Institute of Culture, Chabarovsk, 1971-86; Researcher, 1986-93; Head, Bibliology Group, 1995-2002; Senior Researcher, State Public Scientific Technician Library of the Siberian Branch of the Russian Academy of Sciences, 2002-; Member, Editorial Board of 2 scientific journals; Deputy Head of the PhD Council; Member, Committee on Complex Book Study, World Culture Council, RAS. Publications: 200 publications, monographs and articles in professional journals; 12 successful PhD students. Honour: Laureate, All-Russian Competitions of Scientific Works. Address: ul Voschod 15, 630200 Novosibirsk, Russia.

PAIGE Elaine, b. 5 March 1948, Barnet, England. Singer; Actress. Education: Aida Foster Stage School. Creative Works: West End theatre appearances in Hair, 1968, Jesus Christ Superstar, 1973, Grease (played Sandy), 1973, Billy (played Rita), 1974, Created roles of Eva Peron in Evita, 1978 and Grizabella in Cats, 1981, Abbacadabra (played Carabosse), 1983, Chess (played Florence), 1986, Anything Goes (played Reno Sweeney), 1989, Piaf, 1993-94, Sunset Boulevard (played Norma Desmond), 1995-96, The

Misanthrope (played Célimène), 1998; The King and I, 2000; 14 solo albums, 4 multi-platinum albums, 8 consecutive gold albums. Honours include: Society of West End Theatres Award, 1978; Variety Club Award, 1986; British Association of Songwriters, Composers & Authors Award, 1993; Lifetime Achievement Award, National Operatic and Dramatic Association, 1999. Address: c/o EP Records, M M & M Pinewood Studios, Pinewood Road, Iver, Bucks SL10 0NH, England.

PAISLEY Ian Richard Kyle, b. 6 April 1926, Ireland. Politician; Minister of Religion. m. Eileen E Cassells, 1956, 2 sons, 3 daughters. Education: South Wales Bible College; Reformed Presbyterian Theological College, Belfast. Appointments: Ordained, 1946; Minister, Martyrs Memorial Free Presbyterian Church, 1946-; Moderator, Free Presbyterian Church of Ulster, 1951; Founder, The Protestant Telegraph, 1966; Leader (co-founder), Democratic Unionist Party, 1972; MP (Democratic Unionist), 1974-, (Protestant Unionist 1970-74), resigned seat, 1985 in protest against the Anglo-Irish Agreement; Re-elected, 1986; MP (Protestant Unionist) for Bannside, Co Antrim, Parliament of Northern Ireland (Stormont), 1970-72, Leader of the Opposition, 1972, Chair, Public Accounts Committee, 1972; Member, Northern Ireland Assembly, 1973-74, elected to Second Northern Ireland Assembly, 1982; Member, European Parliament, 1979-; MP for Antrim North, Northern.Ireland Assembly, 1998-2000; Member, Political Committee European Parliament Northern Ireland Assembly, 1998-. Publications include: Jonathan Edwards, The Theologian of Revival, 1987; Union with Rome, 1989; The Soul of the Question, 1990; The Revised English Bible: An Exposure, 1990; What a Friend We Have in Jesus, 1994; Understanding Events in Northern Ireland: An Introduction for Americans, 1995; My Plea for the Old Sword, 1997; The Rent Veils at Calvary, 1997; A Text a Day Keeps the Devil Away, 1997. Address: The Parsonage, 17 Cyprus Avenue, Belfast BT5 5NT, Northern Ireland.

PAL Dulal Chandra, b. 25 October 1940, Bangladesh (East Pakistan). Scientist; Indian Medicinal Plants Expert; Expert on Tribal Medicine; Social Worker. 1 son, 1 daughter. Education: MSc; PhD; FBS; FEs; FIAT; MNASc; BA (Special); German (Cert), Russian (Cert), Hindi (Pragya). Appointments: Lecturer, Botany, Degree College; Scientist, Government of India; Guest Professor, Botany, Vidya Sagar University, WB; Advisor, Compendium Government WB; Advisor, India Agri-Hort Society; Member, IPR India Chapter. Publications: 12 books; 180 scientific papers; 20 popular articles. Honours: Fellow: Botanical Society; Ethnobotanical Society; Indian Angiosperm; Taxonomy; Hersberger Medal, 2003. Memberships: National Academy of Science; Indian Botanical Society; Indian Science Congress Association.

PALADUGU Ramamohana Rao, b. 25 November 1937, Chinaogirala, Andhra Pradesh, India. Educator; Researcher. m. Seetaramamma Nagabhiru, 1 son, 1 daughter. Education: BSc (Hons), 1958; MSc, 1960; PhD, 1966, Delhi University; German Certificate, 1964; German Diploma, 1965; MA Status, Sydney Sussex College, 1969; Postdoctoral Research Fellow, 1967-71, University of Cambridge. Appointments: Assistant Lecturer, 1964-67, Research Associate, 1971-75, Delhi University; Assistant Professor, H P University, Shimla, 1975-78; Lecturer, Reader, 1978-83, Professor, 1984-, UGC Fellow, 1999-2001, Emeritus Professor, 2002-, Head, Department of Botany and Microbiology, 1991-93, Nagarjuna University, Nagarjunanagar; Founder Director and Founder Head Centre for Biotechnology, 1993-97, Nagarjuna University; Visiting Professor, Central University, Caracas, Venezuela, 1980; Visiting Professor, Uppsala University, Sweden, 1982-84; Visiting Professor, University of Paris, 1986-87. Publications: About 150 publications in national and international

Dictionary of International Biography

journals in the field of reproductive botany. Honour: Best Professor award, Andhra Pradesh State, 1997-98. Memberships: Life member, International Society of Plant Morphologists, Delhi; Foundation life member, Editorial Advisory Board member, Joint Secretary, Assistant Editor, Orchid Society, India. Address: 4-5-16/E 'Seetaaramam', Navabharatnagar 2nd Lane, Ring Road, Guntur 522006, Andhra Pradesh, India.

PALEY Grace, b. 11 December 1922, New York, New York, USA. Author; Poet; Retired University teacher. m. (1) Jess Paley, 20 June 1942, divorced, 1 son, 1 daughter, (2) Robert Nichols, 1972. Education: Hunter College, New York City, 1938-39; New York University. Appointments: Teacher, Columbia University, Syracuse University, Sarah Lawrence College, City College of the City University of New York. Publications: Fiction: The Little Disturbances of Man: Stories of Women and Men at Love, 1968; Enormous Changes at the Last Minute, 1974; Later the Same Day, 1985; The Collected Stories, 1994. Poetry: Long Walks and Intimate Talks (includes stories), 1991; New and Collected Poems, 1992. Other: Leaning Forward, 1985; Three Hundred Sixty-Five Reasons Not to Have Another War: 1989 Peace Calender (with Vera B Williams), 1988; Just as I Thought, 1998; Begin Again (poems), 2000. Contributions to: Books, anthologies and magazines. Honours: Guggenheim Fellowship, 1961; National Institute of Arts and Letters Award, 1970; Edith Wharton Citation of Merit as the first State Author of New York, New York State Writers Institute, 1986; National Endowment for the Arts Senior Fellowship, 1987; Vermont Governor's Award for Excellence in the Arts, 1993. Membership: American Academy of Arts and Letters. Address: Box 620, Thetford Hill, VT 05074, USA.

PALIN Michael Edward, b. 5 May 1943, Sheffield, Yorkshire, England. Freelance Writer and Actor. m. Helen M Gibbins, 1966, 2 sons, 1 daughter. Education: BA, Brasenose College, Oxford, 1965. Appointments: Actor, Writer: Monty Python's Flying Circus, BBC TV, 1969-74; Ripping Yarns, BBC TV 1976-80; Writer, East of Ipswich, BBC TV, 1986; Films: Actor and Joint Author: And Now for Something Completely Different, 1970; Monty Python and the Holy Grail, 1974; Monty Python's Life of Brian, 1978; Time Bandits, 1980; Monty Python's The Meaning of Life, 1982; Actor, Writer, Co-Producer, The Missionary, 1982; Around the World in 80 Days, BBC, 1989; Actor: Jabberwocky, 1976; A Private Function, 1984; Brazil, 1984; A Fish Called Wanda, 1988; Contributor, Great Railway Journeys of the World, BBC TV, 1980; Actor, Co-Writer, American Friends, film, 1991; Actor, GBH, TV Channel 4, 1991; Actor, Fierce Creatures, 1997; Michael Palin's Hemingway Adventure, BBC, TV, 1999. Publications: Monty Python's Big Red Book, 1970; Monty Python's Brand New Book, 1973; Dr Fegg's Encyclopaedia of All World Knowledge, 1984; Limericks, 1985; Around the World in 80 Days, 1989; Pole to Pole, 1992; Pole to Pole - The Photographs, 1994; Hemingway's Chair, 1995; Full Circle, 1997; Full Circle - The Photographs, 1997; Michael Palin's Hemingway Adventure, 1999; Sahara, 2002; For Children: Small Harry and the Toothache Pills, 1981; The Mirrorstone, 1986; The Cyril Stories, 1986. Honours: Writers Guild, Best Screenplay Award, 1991; Dr hc (Sheffield), 1992, (Queen's, Belfast), 2000. Address: 34 Tavistock Street, London WC2E 7PB, England.

PÁLMADÓTTIR Elín, b. 31 January 1927, Reykjavik, Iceland. Journalist; Writer. Education: Philosophy, English and French, University of Iceland; Cand. Phil, University of Iceland, 1948. Appointments: Secretary, Ministry of Foreign Affairs, Iceland, 1947; Research Assistant, United Nations Headquarters, New York, 1949; Secretary, Embassy of Iceland in Paris, 1950-52; Professional Journalist, writing articles for foreign and local press, 1953-; Reporter, Staff Columnist and Storywriter, Morgunbladid (most important daily newspaper in Iceland), 1958-97; Deputy

Commissioner for Iceland for EXPO 67 Montreal, Canada, 1967; Elected Councillor, Municipality of Reykjavik, 1970-82; Vice-President, National Council of Iceland for the Protection of Nature, 1984-90. Publications: Books: Gerdur, biography of a sculptor, 1985; Fransi Biskvi, Les Pecheurs d'Islande, on the French fishermen fishing cod around Iceland for centuries, 1989; Með Fortídina í Farteskinu, historical novel about four generations, 1996; Eins og ég Man ?að (As I Remember it), autobiography, 2003. Honours: Nominated for the Literary Prize, Association of Icelandic Publishers, 1989; Honorary Degree, Union of Icelandic Journalists on its 90 Years Anniversary, 1992; Honorary Decoration, Icelandic Society for Science and Nature, 1993; Order of the Falcon for achievements in journalism and literature, President of Iceland; Ordre National du Merit, President of France, 1999. Address: Grandavegur 47, 107 Reykjavik, Iceland. E-mail: epa@mbl.is

PALMER Arnold Daniel, b. 10 September 1929, Latrobe, USA. Golfer; Business Executive. m. Winifred Walzer, 1954, 2 daughters. Education: Wake Forest University, North Carolina. Appointments: US Coast Guard, 1950-53; US Amateur Golf Champion, 1954; Professioanl Golfer, 1954-;Winner, 92 professional titles, including British Open 1961, 1962, US Open 1960, US Masters 1958, 1960, 1962, 1964, Candadian PGA 1980, US Seniors Championship 1981; Member, US Ryder Cup Team, 1961, 1963, 1965, 1967, 1971, 1973, Captain 1963; 1975; President, Arnold Palmer Enterprises; Board of Directors, Latrobe Area Hospital. Publications: My Game and Yours, 1965; Situation Golf, 1970; Go for Broke, 1973; Arnold Palmer's Best 54 Golf Holes, 1977; Arnold Palmer's Complete Book of Putting, 1986; Playing Great Golf, 1987; A Golfer's Life (with James Dodson), 1999; Playing by the Rules, 2002. Honours: LLD, Wake Forest National College of Education; DHL, Florida Southern College; Athlete of the Decade, Associated Press, 1970; Sportsman of the Year, Sports Illustrated, 1960; Hickok Belt, Athlete of the Year, 1960. Address: PO Box 52, Youngstown, PA 15696, USA.

PALMER Frank Robert, b. 9 April 1922, Westerleigh, Gloucestershire, England. Retired Professor; Linguist; Writer. m. Jean Elisabeth Moore, 1948, 3 sons, 2 daughters. Education: MA, New College, Oxford, 1948; Graduate Studies, Merton College, Oxford, 1948-49. Appointments: Lecturer in Linguistics, School of Oriental and African Studies, University of London, 1950-52, 1953-60; Professor of Linguistics, University College of North Wales, Bangor, 1960-65; Professor and Head, Department of Linguistic Science, 1965-87, Dean, Faculty of Letters and Social Sciences, 1969-72, University of Reading. Publications: The Morphology of the Tigre Noun, 1962; A Linguistic Study of the English Verb, 1965; Selected Papers of J R Firth, 1951-1958 (editor), 1968; Prosodic Analysis (editor), 1970; Grammar, 1971, 2nd edition, 1984; The English Verb, 1974, 2nd edition, 1987; Studies in the History of Western Linguistics (joint editor) 1986; Semantics, 1976, 2nd edition, 1981; Modality and the English Modals, 1979, 2nd edition, 1990; Mood and Modality, 1986, 2001; Grammatical Roles and Relations, 1994; Grammar and Meaning, 1995 (editor) 1995. Contributions: to Professional journals. Memberships: Academia Europaea; British Academy, fellow; Linguistic Society of America; Philological Society. Address: Whitethorns, Roundabout Lane, Winnersh, Wokingham, Berkshire RG41 5AD, England.

PALTROW Gwyneth, b. 1973, Los Angeles, USA. Actress. m. Chris Martin, 2003, 1 daughter. Education: University of California, Santa Barbara. Creative Works: Films include: Flesh and Bone, 1993; Hook; Moonlight and Valentino; The Pallbearer; Seven; Emma, 1996; Sydney; Kilronan; Great Expectations, 1998; Sliding Doors, 1998; A Perfect Murder, 1998; Shakespeare in Love, 1998;

The Talented Mr Ripley, 1999; Duets, 1999; Bounce, 2000; The Intern, 2000; The Anniversary Party, 2001; The Royal Tenenbaums, 2001; Shallow Hal, 2001; Possession, 2002; View From the Top, 2003; Sylvia, 2003. Honours include: Academy Award, Best Actress, 1998. Address: c/o Rick Kurtzman, CAA, 9830 Wilshire Boulevard, Beverly Hills, CA 90212, USA.

PALVA Ilmari Pellervo, b. 5 May 1932, South Pirkkala, Finland. Physician; Haematologist. m. Seija Kaivola, 9 June 1956, 1 son, 3 daughters. Education: MD, 1956, PhD, 1962, University of Helsinki. Appointments: Registrar, 1959-63, Consultant, 1964-65, Department of Medicine, University Hospital, Helsinki; Instructor, University of Helsinki, 1963-64; Associate Professor, Internal Medicine, University of Oulu, 1965-74; Professor, Internal Medicine, University of Kuopio, 1974; Acting Professor, Medical Education, University of Tampere, 1975-76; Consultant, City Hospitals, Tampere, 1976-92, Retired, 1992. Publications: Over 250 scientific papers in professional journals. Honours: Knight of 1st Order, Finnish White Rose, 1986; Honorary Member, Finnish Society of Haematology, 1992. Memberships: Finnish Medical Association; Finnish Society of Internal Medicine; Finnish Society of Haematology; International Society of Haematology; American Society of Hematology. Address: Oikotie 8, FIN 33950 Pirkkala, Finland.

PÁLYI István, b. 25 June 1932, Mezötúr, Hungary. Research Scientist. m. Vilma Szeidel. Education: BS, Biology, Chemistry, 1954, PhD, Cell Biology, 1964, József Attila University, Szeged, Hungary; Candidate of Science, Tumor Cell Biology, 1970, Doctor of Science, 1985, Hungarian Academy of Sciences. Appointments: Postdoctoral Fellow, 1954-64, Research Associate, 1964-70, Research Institute of Oncopathology, Head, 1964-79, Senior Scientist, 1970-79, Tissue Culture Laboratory, Head, Department of Cell Biology, 1979-, Secretary Scientific Council, 1984-92, Vice Director of Research, 1986-91, Director of Research, 1992-95, National Institute of Oncology, Budapest, Hungary; Visiting Professor of Biology, József Attila University, Szeged, 1988-; Retired, 1999-. Publications: 252 publications in national and international scientific journals including Cancer Chemotherapy, Proceedings of the National Academy of Science of the USA; Drugs of the Future. Honours: CNRS Fellowship, Paris, 1963; Eleanor Roosevelt International Cancer Fellowship, International Union Against Cancer, 1971-72; Award of Papolczy Fund, 1981; Award for Scientific Work, Hungarian Ministry of Health and Welfare, 1982. Memberships include: European Association for Cancer Research; European Organisation for Research and Treatment of Cancer; New York Academy of Sciences; International Society for Preventive Oncology; Hungarian Cancer Society; European Tissue Culture Society. Address: National Institute of Oncology, Rath Gyorgy Str 7-9, H-1122 Budapest, Hungary. E-mail: palyi@oncol.hu

PAMINA (Pamina Lydia Knowles-Missonnier), b. 2 March 1951, Paris, France. Diseuse. m. Marc Missonnier. Education: Dance, Institut Jacques Dalcroze, Paris, training in classical dancing from Nina Tikanova, master classes on the art of Isadora and Elizabeth Duncan by Yvonne Hoenig, 1960-67; Drama, coverage of the French classical repertory and the art of the diseuse under Charlotte Mutel, Fanny Robiane and Blanche Ariel, 1962-69; Music, Conservatoire National Supérieur de Musique, Paris, followed by tuition under Pierre Lantier and singing under Geneviève Touraine, 1965-73. Career: Deviser of scholarly tributes to humorous fin-de-siècle and 20th-century French diseuses and singers and reinterpreter of their repertoire; performances premiered in France and repeated in the UK under the patronage of the Limouse Foundation; Principle performances include: La Chanson de sa vie, for the Bibliothèque Nationale Yvette Guilbert exhibition, 1994-95, performing with Irène Aïtoff; Les années 30,

1996; Chansons d'Yvette Guilbert, 1997; Autour du Chat Noir, Musée de l'Armée, 1999; L'Esprit du Chat Noir révélé par Yvette Guilbert, Musée de l'Armée, 1999; A la rencontre de Marie Dubas, Théâtre du Renard, 2001; Du Chat Noir au Musée Carnavalet avec l'irrespecteuse Yvette Guilbert, Musée Carnavalet, 2002; Aimons la vie, Nouveau Théâtre Mouffetard, 2003. Publications: Lectures on the history of French song, delivered with Blanche Ariel, 1973-87; Report on Yvette Guilbert's connections with the Société Baudelaire, 1994; Aimons la vie, a filmed portrayal of Marie Dubas as seen by writers and artists of her day, 2001; Interviews for various publications and channels including France-Culture, 2002; Featured in several articles in magazines and books including: Femmes Artistes International, 2000, 2001, 2003; Mémoires de la Chanson by Martin Pénet, volume 1, 2000, volume 2, 2004. Honour: Grand Prix des Rencontres Internationales des Arts et Lettres for the 1994-95 Yvette Guilbert tribute, La Chanson de sa vie. Memberships: Association des Anciens Elèves du Conservatoire National Supérieur de Musique de Paris; Executive Committee, Société Baudelaire; Founding President, Association L'Esprit du Chat Noir; Consultant on the history of French song for various institutions including: Centre Duncan-France, Editions Fortin. Address: c/o Association L'Esprit du Chat Noir, 24 rue Saint-Séverin, 75005 Paris, France. E-mail: esprit.chat.noir@free.fr

PANAYOTOVA Marinela, b. 12 April 1961, Nikopol, Bulgaria. Chemistry Educator. m Vladko Panayotov, 1 son. Education: MSc, Inorganic and Analytical Chemistry, University "St K Ohridsky", Sofia, Bulgaria, 1984; PhD, Physical Chemistry, Bulgarian Academy of Sciences, 1990; MSc, Environmental Technology and Management, TEMPUS (JEP 1918-92), EC, 1994. Appointments: Chemist, University "St K Ohridski", 1984-85; PhD Student, 1985-90, Assistant Professor, Department of Chemistry, 1990-2001, Reader in Corrosion Protection, 1991-, Reader in General Chemistry, 1992-, Reader in Physical Chemistry, 1997-, Associate Professor, Physical Chemistry, 2001-, University of Mining and Geology, Sofia, Bulgaria. Publications: Over 70 including: 2 textbooks; 2 manuals for students and 1 edited book. Honours: Gold Medal University "St K Ohridski", 1984; Diploma, Institute of Electronics Bulgarian Academy of Sciences; Diploma, College of Mining, Bulgaria; 2 Gold Medals, EastWestEuroIntellect, Bulgaria. Memberships: Licensed Expert, Environmental Protection (Water, Ministry of Environment and water, 1996-; Union of Chemists of Bulgaria; The Balkan Centre of Ecology; SAFERELNET (EC NET). Address: Department of Chemistry, University of Mining and Geology, 1700 Sofia, Bulgaria. E-mail: marichim@mgu.bg

PANCHENKO Yurii Nikolayevich, b. 6 April 1934, Kharkov, Ukraine. Chemist. m. Larisa Grigoriyevna Tashkinova, 1 son. Education: Department of Chemistry, MV Lomonosov Moscow State University, 1959; PhD, Chemistry (Molecular Spectroscopy), 1970. Appointments: Junior Researcher, Karpov Physico-Chemical Institute, 1959-61; Junior Researcher, 1961-77, Senior Researcher, 1977-, Department of Chemistry, Moscow State University. Publications: Numerous articles in professional journals. Honours: Silver Medal, Medal of Eötvös Lorand Budapest University. Membership: Fellow, World Association of Theoretically Oriented Chemists. Address: Laboratory of Molecular Spectroscopy, Division of Physical Chemistry, Department of Chemistry, MV Lomonosov Moscow State University, Vorobiovy gory, Moscow 119899, Russia.

PANDEY Jagdish, b. 9 February 1928, Bararhi, PS Dehri-on-Sone Dist Rohtas, Bihar, India. Retired Chief Engineer, Irrigation Department, Government of Bihar. m. Smt Manorma, 4 sons, 3 daughters. Education: Fellow, Institution of Engineers, India, FIE, 1987; Chartered Engineer, India, 1988. Appointments: Assistant Engineer, Executive Engineer, Superintending Engineer, Chief

Engineer, Irrigation Department, Government of Bihar, India. Publications: Rural Development and Small Scale Industries; Bihar and Small Scale Industries; Problem of Pollution and Science of the Modern Age; Sanskrit Language and Indian Civilisation; Saint Tulsidas and His Devotion; Problem of Unemployment and its Solution in India; Condition of Women and their Problem in India. Honours: Best Citizen of India Award; Man of Achievement Award, International Publishing House, New Delhi; Man of the Year 1998, American Biographical Institute, ABI, USA; Distinguished Leadership Award, Research Board of Advisors, ABI, 1999; Rising Personalities of India Award for Outstanding Services, Achievements and Contribution, International Penguin Publishing House; 20th Century Bharat Excellence Award, Glory of India Award, Friendship Forum of India, New Delhi; National Udyog Excellence Award, International Institute of Education and Management; National Gold Star Award, International Business Council; Jewel of India Award, International Institute of Education and Management; Outstanding Intellectuals of the 20th Century, International Biographical Centre, Cambridge, England; The Millennium Achiever 2000, All India Achievers' Conference, New Delhi; Mahamana Madan Mohan Malvia Samman; Honour by Sanatan Brahman Samaj North Bihar Muzaffarpur (India); Eminent Personalities of India Award, Board of Trustees of International Biographical Research Foundation India in Recognition of Superb Achievements within the Community of Mankind during 20th Century; Vijay Rattan Award and Certificate of Excellence, India International Friendship Society; Bibhuti Bhushan Award, Jagatguru-Shankaracharya of Gobardhan Pith Puri; Sajio Maha Manav Award, National President Sanatan Samaj; Bharat Jyoti Award for outstanding services achievements and contribution, International Institute of Success Awareness, Delhi; Rashtriya Nirman Award, International Business Council; Honorary Member, Research Board of Advisors, ABI, USA, 1999; Life Time Achievement Award, National and International Compendium Delhi; Gold Medals, Friendship Forum of India; Rashitriya Ratan Shiromani Award, Modern India International Society; Gold Medal and Man of the Year, 2003; Great Achiever of India Award, FNP; Pride of India Award, International Institute of Education and Management; 21st Century Excellence Award, International Business Council; Rashtra Shresth Nidhi Award, Delhi; Eminent Citizen of India Award for outastanding achievements in chosen field of activity, NIC; International Gold Star Award, Taranath Ranabhat M P , Rt Hon Speaker, Pratinidhi Sabha (House of Representatives of Nepal), Kathmandu, 2004; Vijay Shree Award for most religious and spititual activities, International Business Council; Goswami Tulsidal Award for excellent achievements and selfless services to the nations, Industrial Technology Development Prominent Citizens of India Award, 2004; Vikas Shree Award for outstanding achievements in chosen Field of Activity, IIEM; Rashtra Prabha Award for Meritorious Accomplishments in Diverse Fields of Activities that immensely Contributed for the Nation's Progress; Rashtra Nirman Ratna Award for unmatched services to Mother India to enhance her prestige and honour. Memberships: Fellowship of Institution of Engineers, India; Chartered Engineer, India; President, Sanskrit Sanjivan Samaj; President, Jagjiwan Sanatorium Shankerpuri; President, Sur Mandir; President, Durga Puja Samiti Patna; President, Sanatan Brahman Samaj Bihar; Vice President, Sanatan Brahman Samaj India; President, Hindi Sahitya Sammelan Bihar Patna; Chief Patron, Subordinate Engineers Association, Bihar, Patna, India; Patron, Sangrakshak Mandal Pragya Samiti, Bihar, Patna; Member, International Bhojpuri Sammelan, Bihar, Patna; President, Ganga Sewa Sangh, Bihar, Patna. Address: Rajendra Nagar, Road No 6/C, Patna 800 016, Bihar, India.

PÁNEK Jaroslav, b. 23 January 1947, Prague, Czech Republic. Historian. m. Markéta Pánková, 2 daughters. Education: Graduated, History, Archive Science, Slavonic Studies, Charles University, Prague, 1970; PhD, Czechoslovak Academy of Sciences, 1980; DrSci, Historical Institute, Czech Academy of Sciences, 1991; Associate Professor, Charles University, 1992, Professor, Masaryk University, Brno, 1996. Appointments: Director, District Archive, Benesov, nr Prague, 1970-75; Research Fellow, Institute of History, Czechoslovak Academy of Sciences, 1976-93; Associate Professor, Early Modern History, Faculty of Arts and Philosophy, Charles University, 1993-96; Professor of History, Universities of Prague and Brno, 1996-; Pro-Rector, Charles University, 1997-2000; Director of Institute of History, 1998-. Publications: Books include: Oton Berkopec: Life and Work, 1976; Estates Opposition in Bohemia and Moravia and its Struggle against the Habsburgs, 1982; The Lives of the Last Rozmberks, 2 volumes, 1985; The Expedition of the Czech Nobility to Italy 1551-1552, 1987; Last Rozmberks: The Magnates of the Czech Renaissance, 1989; Jan Amos Komensky-Comenius, 1990; Slovenian Culture in the Czech Republic, 1997; Vilém of Rozmberk: A Politician of Conciliation, 1998; Czech Historiography in the 1990s, 2001 (editor); Bohemian Land Codes and Beginnings of Constitutionalism in Central Europe, 2001 (co-editor); My Life was Determined by History, 2002; Czechs and Poles in One Thousand Years of Common History, 2002; Historians Against the Abuse of History, 2002 (with J Pešek); A Handbook of Encyclopaedia of Czech History, 2003 (editor). Honours: Jacob Gallus Award, Slovenia, 1991; Comenius Medal, 1992, 1998; Medal, Université Libre de Bruxelles, Belgium, 1998; Jubilee Medal of Charles University, 1998; Medal of Université de Montpellier, France, 1999; Jubilee Medal, Comenius University, Bratislava, Slovakia, 1999; Golden Medal, Charles University, Prague, 2000; Tadeusz Manteuffel Medal, Polish Academy Institute of History, Warsaw, Poland, 2003. Memberships: Association of Czech Historians, President, 1996-2002; Czech National Committee of Historians, President, 2002-; Collegium Carolinum, 1998; Many scientific associations and editorial boards. Address: Parlérova 9, 16900 Prague, Czech Republic.

PANT Dipak Raj, b. 17 July 1958, Lamjung, Nepal. Anthropologist; Economist. m. Bettina Castiglioni, deceased, 1 daughter. Education: BA, Banaras Hindu University, Varanasi, India; MPhil, PhD, Gregorian University, Holy See, Rome. Appointments: Associate Professor of Anthropology, Tribhuvan University, Kathmandu, Nepal, 1987-91; Professor of International Studies, University of Trieste, Italy, 1991-93; Visiting Professor of Development Studies, University of Padua, Italy, 1993-98; Professor of Comparative Economics and Anthropology, LIUC, Italy, 1995-. Publications: 3 books. Honours: Doctor in Philosophy, summa cum laude, Gregorian University; Senior Fellow, Society for Applied Anthropology, USA. Memberships: Italian National Association of Ethnology and Anthropology; Society for Applied Anthropology. Address: Università Cattaneo, Corso Matteotti-22, 21053 Castellanea (VA), Italy. E-mail: drpant@liuc.it

PAPADAKIS Nikolas, b. 5 April 1935, Greece. Professor of Neurosurgery. 2 daughters. Education: Graduate, Medical School of Thessaloniki, Greece 1959; American Board of Neurosurgery, 1969. Appointments: Assistant Professor of Neurosurgery, Harvard Medical School, USA, 1973-81; Professor of Neurosurgery, Patras Medical School, Greece, 1984-2001; Chairman of Neurosurgery, Errikos Dunan Hospital, Athens, Greece, 2001-. Publications: About 120 publications in recognised scientific journals and presentations during conferences all related to neurosurgery. Honours: Kentucky Colonel; George Papandreou Society Award; Medical Society of Rethymnon Award. Memberships: American Association of Neurological Surgeons; American College of Neurosurgery; Alumni of Massachusetts General Hospital; Greek Society of Neurosurgery. Address: Markou Botsari 76, Chania, Crete 73136, Greece. E-mail: papneuro@ath.forthnet.gr

PAPADOPOULOS Stylianos G, b. 4 May 1933, Corinth, Greece. Professor of Patrology. m. Soteria Tektonidou, 1 son, 2 daughters. Education: BD, School of Theology, University of Athens, 1955; Ecole Pratique des hautes Etudes, Sorbonne, Paris, 1956-57; Institut Catholique, Paris, 1956-57; Institut Russe de Théologie Orthodoxe, Paris, 1956-57; Faculty of Philosophy, Munich, 1957-59; Theological Faculty, Munich, 1957-59; PhD, School of Theology, University of Athens, 1967. Appointments: Assistant Professor, 1970, Associate Professor of Patrology, 1972, Full Professor of Patrology, 1978, Head of Faculty of Theology, School of Theology, 1986-87, 1997-99, University of Athens; Visiting Professor, Faculties of Theology, Bucharest, Sibiu, Romania, Moscow, St Petersburg, Russia, Beograd, Presov, Slovakia, Beyrouth, Liban, Sofia, Bulgaria, Coptic School of Theology, Egypt. Publications include: 35 books, 600 articles, Greek translations of Thomas Aquinas; Contribution to History of Byzantine Theology; Theology and Language, 1987; Patrology, vol I, 1987, Vol II, 1999; The Orthodox March: Church and Theology in the Third Millennium, 2000; J Chrysostomus, Vol I: His Life, His Activities, His Works and Vol II: His Theology, 1999. Honours: Dr hc (Oradea); Listed in Who's Who and biographical publications. Address: Sifnou 23, Agia Paroskevi, Athens, Greece.

PAPITASHVILI Alexander Michael, b. 20 October 1949, Orjonikidze, USSR. Physician. Education: Graduate, Tbilisi State Medical University, Georgia, 1972; PhD, Moscow Central State Research Scientific Institute of Obstetrics and Gynaecology, 1976; Professor, Tbilisi State Medical University, 1990, Professor, Tbilisi Medical College "Vita", 1994. Appointments: Research Worker, Moscow Central State Research Scientific Institute of Obstetrics and Gynaecology, 1973-76; Associate Professor, Department of Obstetrics and Gynaecology, Tbilisi State Medical University, Georgia, 1990-; Professor, Tbilisi Medical College "Vita", 1994-. Publications: 135 scientific publications in the field of reproduction, obstetrics and gynaecology, prenatal and perinatal medicine, ultrasound in medicine, medical demography, mathematical modelling in medicine; Author of certified method of sonohysterosalpingology, 1979. Honour: Winner, Ukrainian Davidenkow Medical Prize, 1997. Memberships: President, Georgian Association of Scientists and Specialists, Department of Medicine; Secretary General, Georgian Association of Prenatal and Perinatal Medicine; Board Member, Russian Association of Ultrasound in Medicine; American Institute of Ultrasound in medicine, 1997-2000. Address: 16-A, Irakli Abashidze Str, Apt #8, Tbilisi, 0179 Georgia. E-mail: ampsnpge@ hotmail.com

PARDALA Antoni Jerzy, b. 28 January 1949, Piolunka, Poland. University Lecturer. m. Teresa Stanek, 15 July 1972, 1 son, 1 daughter. Education: Master of Mathematics, 1971; Doctoris Degree, Mathematical Sciences, Cracow, 1981; Dr Degree, Pedagogical Sciences, Moscow, 1994. Appointments: Institute of Mathematics, Pedagogical University, Rzeszow, 1971-95; Professor, Department of Mathematics, Rzeszow University of Technology, 1995-. Publications: 45 research works in Polish, English and Russian, including 2 monographs, 1 published translation into Russian. Honours: Chancellor's Awards for research works, Pedagogical University, Rzeszow, 1982, 1983, 1986, 1988, 1989, 1994, Rzeszow University of Technology, 1996-98. Membership: Polish Mathematics Association. Address: Department of Mathematics, Rzeszow University of Technology, ul W Pola 2, 35959 Rzeszow, Poland.

PARER Julian Thomas, b. 2 September 1934, Melbourne, Australia. Professor. m. Robin M W Parer. Education: BAgrSc, University of Melbourne, 1959; MRurSc, University of New England, 1962; PhD, Oregon State University, 1965; MD, University of Washington, Seattle, 1971. Appointments: Associate Staff, Cardiovascular Research Institute, University of California, San Francisco, 1976-; Professor, 1982-, Director, Maternal-Fetal Medicine Fellowship Training Program, 1983-2002, Director, Division of Perinatal Medicine and Genetics, 1999-2002, Department of Obstetrics, Gynecology and Reproductive Sciences, University of California, San Francisco. Publications: Numerous articles in professional journals. Memberships include: American College of Obstetricians and Gynecologists; American Physiological Society; Fetal and Neonatal Physiological Society; Perinatal Society of Australia and New Zealand; Society for Gynecologic Investigation. Address: University of California, 505 Parnassus Avenue, San Francisco, CA 94143-0550, USA.

PARISESCU Vasile, (Parizescu), b. 25 October 1925, Braila, Romania. Fine Artist; Officer Engineer. m. Victoria, 1 daughter. Education: Bachelor of Art, Faculty of Philology and Philosophy, University of Bucharest, 1949; The Military School of Artillery, 1947; The Military technical Academy, 1953, The Fine Art School, Bucharest, 1973; Independent study of paintings with Dumitru Ghiata, Rudolph Schweitzer Cumpana and Gheorghe Vanatoru. Career: Painter; Scientist; General of the Brigade, Romanian Army; Command appointments in the Romanian Army in the field of armours and auto-drivers technology; 17 personal exhibitions in Romania and abroad; Several national and group exhibitions; Many participations at international exhibitions including: Moscow, 1987, Rome, 1990, 1999, Paris 2000, Wiene, 2003; Paintings in collections and museums in Romania, Austria, England, Canada, Switzerland, France, Germany, Netherlands, USA, Greece, Cyprus, Sweden, Turkey, Japan, Yugoslavia, Italy. President of the Society of Art Collectors of Romania; Director of the magazine, Pro Arte. Publications: 26 books in the field of science and technology; Over 1000 articles on science, technology and art; Monography Albums, Vasile Parizescu, 1995, 2001; The Encyclopaedia of Romanian Contemporary Artists, 1999, 2003; The Encyclopaedia of Great Personalities from Romanian History, Science and Culture, 5th volume, 2004; Several TV and Radio appearances. Honours: Laureate of the National First Prize for Science, 1979; The First National Prize, Republican Art Exhibitions, 1981, 1983, 1985, 1987; Laureate with diploma and medal, International Art Festival, Moscow, 1987; First Prize, National Salon of Art, Botosani, Romania, 1988; Cultural Diploma and Plaquette, City of Bucharest, 1988; Honoured Citizen of the city of Orăila, 1994; Albo D'Oro Prize and selected as Effective Senator of the International Academy of Modern Art, Rome, 1999. Memberships: President of Honour, Fine Arts Society, Bucharest; Member of the National Commission of Museums and Collections; National expert for modern and contemporary art. Address: Bd. Nicole Balcescu nr 3, Bloc Dunarea 3, scara 1, ap 12, cod 70111, sector 1 Bucharest, Romania.

PARK Dae-Hwan, b. 9 May 1955, Chunnam, Korea. m. 1 son, 2 daughters. Education: BA, Chosun University; MA, Hankuk University of Foreign Studies; PhD, Chungnam National University. Appointments: Dean, College of Foreign Studies, Chosun University; Vice-President, Korean Association of German Language and Literature; Member, Presidential Commission on Policy Planning, Republic of Korea. Publications Committee Member, Korean Association of German Language and Literature Education. Publications include: A Study of Duerrenmatt's Writings, 1991; The Distance Technique in Duerrenmatt's Plays, 1991; The Image of Women in Kafka's Works, 1996; The Characteristics of Women in Grimm's Tales, 1999; The Characteristics of Women in Boell's Works, 2001; The Characteristics of Women in Hesse's Works, 2002. Honours: Plaque of Appreciation, South Korea Minister of Domestic Affairs; Plaque of Appreciation, LCDI (NGO) in Cambodia. Memberships: Korean Association of German Language and Literature; Korean

Dictionary of International Biography

Association of German Language and Literature Education. Address: 2-1503 Samick Ceramic Apts, Hakdong, Donggu, Gwangju, Korea.

PARK Jin-Young, b. 23 February 1962, Seoul, Korea. Orthopaedic Surgeon. m. In-Hwa Hwang, 2 sons. Education: MD, 1986, PhD, 1997, Seoul National University, Korea; Clinical fellow, Columbia University, USA, 1998. Appointments: Orthopaedic Surgeon, Department of Orthopaedics, College of Medicine Dankook University, Korea; Editor in Asia, Journal of Shoulder and Elbow Surgery; Commissioner, Korean Olympic Committee; Board of Trustees, Korean Shoulder and Elbow Society; Corresponding member, American Shoulder and Elbow Society. Publications: Books: Anatomy for the Orthopaedic Surgeon, 1st edition, 1996, 2nd edition, 1998; How Much Painful Is Your Shoulder, 2001; Article: A serial comparison of arthroscopic repair for partial and full TRCT, 2004. Honours: Travelling Fellow, Korean Shoulder and Elbow Society; GOTS Fellow, Korean Orthopaedic Sports Medicine Society. Memberships: Korean Shoulder and Elbow Society; Korean Orthopaedic Association. Address: Dankook University College of Medicine, Department of Orthopaedics, 16-5 Anseo-dong, Cheonan City, Chongnam Province, 330-715 Republic of Korea.

PARK Kwangsung, b. 4 January 1960, Suncheon, Korea. Professor of Urology. m. Sulhyun Kim, 1 daughter. Education: MD, Chonnam National University Medical School, 1983; PhD, Chonnam National University Graduate School, 1993. Appointments: Professor of Urology, Chonnam University Hospital, Korea; Board of Directors, International Society for the Study of Women's Sexual Health, 2001-2003; Editorial Board, International Journal of Impotence, 2003; Researcher, The Journal of Sexual Medicine, 2003. Publications: Diabetes induced alteration of clitoral hemodynamics and structure in the rabbit (co-author), 2002; Textbook of Andrology (Korean) (a chief editor), 2003. Honours: Jean-Paul Ginestie Prize, 1996, Newman Zorgniotti Prize, 2000, International Society for Impotence Research. Memberships: Korean Medical Association; Korean Urological Association; Korean Andrological Society; American Urological Association; International Society for Impotence Research. Address: Department of Urology, Chonnam University Hospital, 8 Hak-dong, Gong-ku, Gwangju 501-757, Republic of Korea. E-mail: kpark@chonnam.ac.kr

PARK Nicholas W, b. 1958, Preston, Lancashire, England. Film Animator. Education: Sheffield Art School; National Film & TV School, Beaconsfield. Appointments: Aardman Animations, 1985, partner, 1995-. Creative Works: Films include: A Grand Day Out, 1989; Creature Comforts, 1990; The Wrong Trousers, 1993; A Close Shave, 1995; Chicken Run (co-director), 2000. Honours: BAFTA Award, Best Short Animated Film, 1990; Academy Award, 1991, 1994. Address: Aardman Animations Ltd, Gas Ferry Road, Bristol BS1 6UN, England.

PARK Roy H Jr, b. 1938, Raleigh, North Carolina, USA. Media Executive. m. Tetlow Parham, 1961, 1 son, 1 daughter. Education: BA, Journalism, University of North Carolina, Chapel Hill, 1961; MBA, Cornell University Johnson Graduate School of Management, 1963. Appointments: Senior Account Executive, Review Board Executive, Advertising Planning Director, Personnel Group, Head, J Walter Thompson Co, New York City and Miami, 1963-70; Vice President, Marketing and Account Management, Kincaid Advertising Agency, 1970-71; Vice President, General Manager, Park Outdoor Advertising, Ithaca, New York, 1971-75; Vice President, Advertising and Promotion, Park Broadcasting Inc, Ithaca, New York and Managing Editor, Park Communications, 1976-81; Managing Director, Ag Research Advertising Agency, Ithaca, 1976-84; Vice President, General Manager, Park Outdoor

Advertising, 1981-84; President, CEO, Director, Park Outdoor Advertising, New York Inc, 1984-; Chairman, Outdoor Advertising Council of New York Inc, 1992-96; Director, Park Communications Inc, 1993-95; Director, Senior Vice President, RHP Incorporated and RHP Properties Inc, 1994-96; Trustee, Vice President, Park Foundation Inc, 1995-2003; President and Chairman, Triad Foundation Inc, 2003-; Trustee, Cornell University, 1999-; Advisory Council, Cornell Johnson Graduate School of Management, 1996-; Board of Visitors, University of North Carolina School of Journalism and Mass Communications, 1994-; Director, Boyce Thompson Institute Inc, 1995-2002; Vice-Chairman, Chairman Compensation Committee, 2002-. Publications: Numerous articles in magazines and newspapers including: Seventeen, The American Way, The Rural New Yorker, The Raleigh News & Observer, The Chapel Hill Weekly, The Raleigh Times, The Durham Morning Herald. Listed in: Numerous Biographical Publications. Memberships include: North Carolina Society of New York; Ithaca Yacht Club; Ithaca Country Club; Boca Bay Pass Club. Address: Park Outdoor Advertising of New York Inc, Ithaca, USA.

PARK (Rosina) Ruth (Lucia), b. Australia. Author; Playwright. Publications: The Uninvited Guest (play), 1948; The Harp in the South, 1948; Poor Man's Orange, US edition as 12 and a Half Plymouth Street), 1949; The Witch's Thorn, 1951; A Power of Roses, 1953; Pink Flannel, 1955; The Drums Go Bang (autobiographical with D'Arcy Niland), 1956; One-a-Pecker, Two-a-Pecker, US edition as The Frost and the Fire, 1961; The Good Looking Women, 1961; The Ship's Cat, 1961, US edition as Serpent's Delight, 1962; Uncle Matt's Mountain, 1962; The Road to Christmas, 1962; The Road Under the Sea, 1962; The Muddle-Headed Wombat series, 11 volumes, 1962-76; The Hole in the Hill, US edition as The Secret of the Maori Cave, 1964; Shaky Island, 1962; Airlift for Grandee, 1964; Ring for the Sorcerer, 1967; The Sixpenny Island, US edition as Ten-Cent Island, 1968; Nuki and the Sea Serpent, 1969; The Companion Guide to Sydney, 1973; Callie's Castle, 1974; The Gigantic Balloon, 1975; Swords and Crowns and Rings, 1977; Come Danger, Come Darkness, 1978; Playing Beatie Bow, 1980; When the Wind Changed, 1980; The Big Brass Key, 1983; The Syndey We Love, 1983; Missus, 1985; My Sister Sif, 1986; The Tasmania We Love, 1987; Callie's Family: James, 1991; A Fence Around the Cuckoo, 1992; Fishing in the Styx, 1993; Home Before Dark, 1995; Ruth Park's Sydney, 2000. Address: c/o Society of Authors, PO Box 1566, Strawberry Hills, New South Wales 2021, Australia.

PARK Ta-Ryeong, b. 20 January 1961, Dongkwangyang, Korea. Professor. m. Hyung-Ji Kim, 3 sons. Education: BS, 1983, MS, 1985, Seoul National University; PhD, Michigan State University, 1991. Appointments: Senior Lecturer, 1991-93, Assistant Professor, 1993-97, Associate Professor, 1997-2002, Professor, 2002-, Hoseo University, Korea. Publications: Articles and papers to professional journals. Memberships: American Physical Society; Korean Physical Society. Address: Hoseo University, Department of Physics, Asan Choongnam 336-795, Korea.

PARK Yoo Hwan, b. 11 July 1964, Mokpo, Korea. Professor of Internal Medicine. m. Na Yoon Jung, 1 son, 1 daughter. Education: Bachelor of Medicine (MD), 1982-88, MS, 1989-90, Chosun University College of Medicine, Gwangju, Korea; PhD, Chosun University, Gwangju, Korea, 1991-93; Internship, 1988-89, Residency, Internal Medicine, 1989-92, Chosun University Hospital, Gwangju, Korea; Fellowship Training Programme, Haematology/Oncology Department of Internal Medicine, Seoul National University Hospital, 1996; Training Programme for Endoscopy, PDT, Laser Therapy, PA Hertzen Moscow Research Oncological Institute, Moscow, Russia, 2002. Appointments: Full Time Instructor, 1995-96, Assistant Professor, 1997-99, Associate

Dictionary of International Biography

Professor, 2000-2002, College of Medicine, Chosun University, Gwangju, Korea; Head of Endoscopy, PDT, Laser Therapy Department, Chief of Homeopathy Department, Cheomdan Medical Centre, Gwangju, Korea, 2003-; Professor College of Oriental Medicine, Dongshin University, Naju, Korea. Publications: 14 articles in scientific medical journals include most recently: Inducibility of Superoxide Dismutase and Metalloprothionein in the Liver and Kidney of Mice by paraquat with Age, 2001; Effect of Tamoxifen ˙on Ion Channel in Mouse Proximal Colonic Myocytes, 2002; Effect of Arachiodonic Acid on ATP-sensitive K+ Current in Murine Colonic Smooth Muscle Cells, 2002; Molecular Mechanism of Anticancer Activity of Heptplatin Against Cisplastin-resistant Gastric Cancer Sublines, 2002. Honour: Superior Graduate of Honours, The Korean Medical Association, 1988. Memberships: Korean Society of Internal Medicine; Korean Cancer Association including Korean Cancer Study Group; Korean Society of Gastrointestinal Endoscopy; Special Board of Hemato-oncology; American Society of Clinical Oncology. Address: #665 Sangam Dong, Gwangsan-gu, Cheomdan Medical Center, Gwangju, South Korea. E-mail: hurricainpark@hanmail.net

PARK Young Jun, b. 6 December 1974, Pusan, Republic of Korea. Researcher. Education: BS, Department of Environmental Engineering, Pusan University, Republic of Korea, 1993-97; MS, 1997-99, PhD, 1999-2002, School of Environmental Science and Engineering, Pohang University of Science and Technology, Republic of Korea. Appointment: Section Head, Samsung Engineering Co Ltd, Republic of Korea. Publications: Articles as first author in scientific journals including: Journal of the Korea Society of Waste Management, 2000, 2003; Ceramics International, 2002, 2003; Journal of Hazardous Materials, 2002. Honours: Listed in Who's Who publications and biographical dictionaries. Memberships: Korea Society of Waste Management; Korean Society of Environmental Engineers; The Korean Engineer's Society of Pyrolysis and Melting; The Korean Hydrogen and New Energy Society. Address: 39-3 Sungbok-dong, Yongin-City, Gyonggi Province, Republic of Korea. E-mail: juni@postech.ac.kr

PARKASH Anand, b. 12 November 1943, Ladwa. Engineer. m. Madhu, 1 son, 2 daughters. Education: BSc, Engineering, Pb Engineering College, Punjab University, 1965; Post Graduate Diploma, Engineering, 1971; Certificate, Investment Planning Project Evaluation, Indian Institute of Economic Growth, 1976; Diploma, United Nations and International Understanding, Institute of UN Studies, 1976; Upanished Vishard, Bhartiya Vidya Bhawan, Bombay, 1987; Post Graduate Diploma, Journalism, 1988. Appointments: Lecturer, Education Department, Government of Punjab, 1965-70; Post Graduation, 1970-71; Adviser, Co-operatives and Architects, 1971; SDO, Haryana Ware Housing Corporation, 1971-72; SDO, HSAM Board, 1972; Executive Engineer, 1976-78; Superintending Engineer, HSAM Board, 1978-90; Chief Engineer, 1990-96; Chief Project Engineer, 1996-2001; Director, Ladakh Foods Ltd, 2002; Director, Srigen Ltd, 2002. Publications: Modernisation of Grain Markets in Haryana; Page Make Up Problems; Relevance of Upanishadic Teachings to Modern World; Terse Caption Writer; Reactions Writer; Many others. Honours: 1st position in Matriculation in the School; 1st position in Journalism; Winner, Sports, Swimming, Water Polo, Basket Ball, College Level; Many others. Memberships: Institution of Engineers; Indian Council of Arbitrators; Indian Group of International Association for Bridges and Structural Engineers; Indian Standard Bureau; Indian Road Congress; Indian Institute of Economic Growth Delhi University; Indian Water Works Association; Many others. Address: House No 12, Sector 27A, Chandigarh Chd, India.

PARKER Alan William (Sir), b. 14 February 1944, London, England. Film Director; Writer. m. Annie Inglis, 1966, divorced 1992, 3 sons, 1 daughter. Education: Owen's School, Islington, London. Appointments: Advertising Copywriter, 1965-67; TV Commercial Director, 1968-78; Writer, Screenplay, Melody, 1969; Chair, Director's Guild of Great Britain, 1982-, British Film Institute, 1998-; Member, British Screen Advisory Council, 1985-. Creative Works: Writer, Director: No Hard Feelings, 1972; Our Cissy, 1973; Footsteps, 1973; Bugsy Malone, 1975; Angel Heart, 1987; A Turnip Head's Guide to the British Cinema, 1989; Come See the Paradise, 1989; The Road to Wellville, 1994; Director: The Evacuees, 1974; Midnight Express, 1977; Fame, 1979; Shoot the Moon, 1981; The Wall, 1982; Birdy, 1984; Mississippi Burning, 1988; The Commitments, 1991; Evita, 1996; Angela's Ashes, 1998; The Life of David Gale, 2003. Publications: Bugsy Malone, 1976; Puddles in the Lane, 1977; Hares in the Gate, 1983; Making Movies, 1998. Honours include: BAFTA Michael Balcon Award for Outstanding Contribution to British Film; National Review Board, Best Director Award, 1988; Lifetime Achievement Award, Director's Guild of Great Britain; BAFTA Award, Best Director, 1991; CBE. Address: c/o Creative Artists Agency, 9830 Wilshire Boulevard, Beverly Hills, CA 90212, USA.

PARKER Gordon, b. 28 February 1940, Newcastle upon Tyne, England. Author; Playwright. Education: Newcastle Polytechnic, 1965-68. Appointment: Book Reviewer, BBC Radio and ITV. Publications: The Darkness of the Morning, 1975; Lightning in May, 1976; The Pool, 1978; Action of the Tiger, 1981. Radio plays: The Seance, 1978; God Protect the Lonely Widow, 1982. Address: 14 Thornhill Close, Seaton Delaval, Northumberland, England.

PARKER Michael Richard, b. 13 July 1949, Weymouth, Dorset, England. Professor of English Literature. m. Aleksandra Gajewska, 19 March 1978, 3 daughters. Education: BA Hons, University of Reading, England, 1967-70; Certificate for Education, University of Southampton, England, 1970-71; MA, University of Lódz, 1977-79; MPhil, University of Manchester, England, 1984-87; PhD, University of Liverpool, 1989-97. Appointments: Assistant for English, Ruffwood School, later Head of English; Lecturer in English, University of Lódz, Poland, 1977-79; Head of English, St Nicholas RC High School, 1979-86; Head of English, Holy Cross Sixth Form College, Bury, 1986-90; Senior Lecturer in English, Liverpool Hope University College, 1990-99; Principal Lecturer, later Professor of English Literature, University of Central Lancashire, 1999-. Publications: Poems: Of Old, 1971; One Way Traffic, 1976; Critical Study: Seamus Heaney: The Making of the Poet, 1993; The Hurt World: Short Stories of the Troubles (editor), 1995; Postcolonial Literatures: A New Casebook (co-editor), 1995; Contemporary Irish Fictions: Themes, Tropes, Theories (co-editor), 2000; Chapter in: The Achievement of Ted Hughes, editor Keith Sagar, 1983; Contemporary Writing & National Identity, editor, Tracy Hill & William Hughes, 1995; Irish Encounters, editors, Alan Marshall and Neil Sammells, 1998; Well Dreams: Critical Essays on John Montague, 2004. Articles include: Shadows to Glass: Self-Reflexivity in the Fiction of Deirdre Madden, Irish University Review, 2000; Reckonings: The Political Contexts for Northern Irish Literature 1965-68, Irish Studies Review, 2002; Changing Skies: The Role of Native and American Narratives in the Politicisation of Seamus Heaney's Early Poetry, Symbiosis, 2002; Northern Odyssey: John Montague's The Cry and its Political Contexts, New Hibernia Review, 2003. Contributions to: TLS, Guardian, Irish Times, Irish Studies Review, Irish University Review, Honest Ulsterman Hungarian Journal of English and American Literature; Articles/Reviews: Honest Ulsterman; PN Review; New Hibernia Review, Translations: TLS; Verse; PN Review. Honours: Fellowship, Institute of Irish Studies, University of Liverpool, 1993-; Visiting Fellow, Academy for Irish Cultural

Dictionary of International Biography

Heritages, University of Ulster, 2005. Memberships: BAIS; IASIL. Address: Department of Humanities, University of Central Lancashire, Preston, PR1 2HE, England. E-mail: mrparker@uclan.ac.uk

PARKER Sarah Jessica, b. 25 March 1965, Nelsonville, Ohio, USA. Actress. m. Matthew Broderick, 1997, 1 son. Creative Works: Stage appearances include: The Innocents, 1976; The Sound of Music, 1977; Annie, 1978; The War Brides, 1981; The Death of a Miner, 1982; To Gillian on Her 37th Birthday, 1983-84; Terry Neal's Future, 1986; The Heidi Chronicles, 1989; How to Succeed in Business Without Really Trying, 1996; Once Upon a Mattress, 1996; Film appearances include: Rich Kids, 1979; Somewhere Tomorrow, 1983; Firstborn, 1984; Footloose, 1984; Girls Just Want to Have Fun, 1985; Flight of the Navigator, 1986; LA Story, 1991; Honeymoon in Vegas, 1992; Hocus Pocus, 1993; Striking Distance, 1993; Ed Wood, 1994; Miami Rhapsody, 1995; If Lucy Fell, 1996; Mars Attacks!, 1996; The First Wives Club, 1996; Extreme Measures, 1996; Til There Was You, 1997; A Life Apart: Hasidism in America, 1997; Isn't She Great, 1999; Dudley Do-Right, 1999; State and Main, 2000; Numerous TV appearances include: Equal Justice, 1990-91; Sex and the City, 1998-2003. Honours: Golden Globe for Best Actress in a TV Series, 2001. Address: Creative Artists Agency, 9830 Wilshire Boulevard, Beverly Hills, CA 90212, USA.

PARKES Roger Graham, b. 15 October 1933, Chingford, Essex, England. Novelist; Scriptwriter. m. Tessa Isabella McLean, 5 February 1964, 1 son, 1 daughter. Education: National Diploma of Agriculture. Appointments: Staff Writer, Farming Express and Scottish Daily Express, 1959-63; Editor, Farming Express, 1963; Staff Script Editor, Drama, BBC-TV, London, 1964-70. Publications: Death Mask, 1970; Line of Fire, 1971; The Guardians, 1973; The Dark Number, 1973; The Fourth Monkey, 1978; Alice Ray Morton's Cookham, 1981; Them and Us, 1985; Riot, 1986; Y-E-S, 1986; An Abuse of Justice, 1988; Troublemakers, 1990; Gamelord, 1991; The Wages of Sin, 1992. Contributions to: Daily Express; Sunday Express. Honour: Grand Prix de Littérature, Paris, 1974. Memberships: Writers Guild of Great Britain; Magistrates Association. Address: Cartlands Cottage, Kings Lane, Cookham Dean, Berkshire SL6 9AY, England.

PARKINSON Michael, b. 28 March 1935, Yorkshire, England. TV Presenter; Writer. m. Mary Heneghan, 3 sons. Appointments: The Guardian, Daily Express, Sunday Times, Punch, Listener; Joined Granada TV Producer, Reporter, 1965; Executive Producer and Presenter, London Weekend TV, 1968; Presenter, Cinema, 1969-70, Tea Break, Where in the World, 1971; Hosted own chat show "Parkinson", BBC, 1972-82, 1998-, "Parkinson One to One", Yorkshire TV, 1987-90; Presenter, Give Us a Clue, 1984-, All Star Secrets, 1985, Desert Island Discs, 1986-88, Parky, 1989, LBC Radio, 1990; Help Squad, 1991, Parkinson's Sunday Supplement, Radio 2, 1994, Daily Telegraph, 1991-; Going for a Song, 1997-; Parkinson's Choice, Radio 2, 1999-2000. Publications: Football Daft, 1968; Cricket Mad, 1969; Sporting Fever, 1974; George Best: An Intimate Biography, 1975; A-Z of Soccer, co-author, 1975; Bats in the Pavilion, 1977; The Woofits, 1980; Parkinson's Lore, 1981; The Best of Parkinson, 1982; Sporting Lives, 1992; Sporting Profiles, 1995; Michael Parkinson on Golf, 1999; Michael Parkinson on Football, 2001. Honours: Sports Feature Writer of the Year, British Sports Journalism Awards, 1995, 1998; Yorkshire Man of the Year, 1998; BAFTA Award for Best Light Entertainment, 1999; Media Society Award for Distinguished Contribution to Media, 2000. Address: J W International, 74 Wimpole Street, London W1M 7DD, England.

PARR John Brian, b. 18 March 1941, Epsom, England. University Researcher. m. Pamela Harkins, 2 daughters. Education: BSc (Econ), University College London, University of London, 1959-62; PhD, University of Washington, Seattle, USA, 1962-67. Appointments: Assistant Professor of Regional Science, 1967-72, Associate Professor of Regional Science, 1972-75, University of Pennsylvania, USA; Lecturer, Senior Lecturer in Urban Economics, 1975-80, Reader in Applied Economics, 1980-89, Professor of Regional and Urban Economics, 1989-, University of Glasgow. Publications include: Regional Policy: Past Experience and New Directions (co-edited book), 1979; Market Centers and Retail Location: Theory and Applications (co-authored book), 1988; Numerous refereed articles in professional journals include: Outmigration and the depressed area problem, 1966; Models of city size in the urban system, 1970; Models of the Central Place System: A More General Approach, 1978; A note on the size distributions of cities over time, 1985; The economic law of market areas: A further discussion, 1995; Regional economic development: an export-stages framework, 1999; Missing elements in the analysis of agglomeration economies, 2002. Honours: Guest, Polish Academy of Sciences, Warsaw, Poland, 1977; Speaker, August Lösch Commemoration, Heidenheim an der Brenz, Germany, 1978; Speaker at the Ehrenpromotion (award of honorary doctorate) of Professor Dr Martin Beckmann, University of Karlsruhe, Germany, 1981; Participant in Distinguished Visitors Program, University of Pennsylvania, Philadelphia, 1983; Academician, Academy of Learned Societies for the Social Sciences, 2002; Moss Madden Memorial Medal, 2003. Memberships: Royal Economic Society; Scottish Economic Society; Regional Science Association International and British and Irish Section; Regional Studies Association; Member of various editorial boards of scientific journals. Address: Department of Urban Studies, University of Glasgow, Glasgow G12 8QQ, Scotland.

PARR Robert G, b. 22 September 1921, Chicago, Illinois, USA. Professor. m. Jane Bolstad, 1 son, 2 daughters. Education: AB, magna cum laude, Brown University, 1942; PhD, Physical Chemistry, University of Minnesota, 1947; Dhc, University of Leuven, 1986; Jagiellonian University, 1996. Appointments include: Assistant Professor, Chemistry, University of Minnesota, 1947-48; Assistant Professor, Professor, Chemistry, Carnegie Institute of Technology, 1948-62; Visiting Professor, Chemistry, Member, Center of Advanced Study, University of Illinois, 1962; Professor of Chemistry, Johns Hopkins University, 1962-74; Chairman, Department of Chemistry, 1969-72; William R Kenan Junior Professor of Theoretical Chemistry, University of North Carolina; Wassily Hoeffding Professor of Chemical Physics, 1990-. Publications: Over 200 scientific articles, 2 books. Honour: Langmuir Award, American Chemical Society; Award in Chemical Sciences, National Academy of Sciences. Memberships include: International Academy of Quantum Molecular Science; National Academy of Sciences; American Academy of Arts and Sciences; Indian National Science Academy. Address: Chemistry Department, University of North Carolina, Chapel Hill, NC 27599, USA.

PARRINDER (John) Patrick, b. 11 October 1944, Wadebridge, Cornwall, England. Professor of English; Literary Critic. 2 daughters. Education: Christ's College, 1962-65, Darwin College, 1965-67, Cambridge; MA, PhD, Cambridge University. Appointments: Fellow, King's College, Cambridge, 1967-74; Lecturer, 1974-80, Reader, 1980-86, Professor of English, 1986-, University of Reading. Publications: H G Wells, 1970; Authors and Authority, 1977, 2nd edition, enlarged, 1991; Science Fiction: Its Criticism and Teaching, 1980; James Joyce, 1984; The Failure of Theory, 1987; Shadows of the Future, 1995. Editor: H G Wells: The Critical Heritage, 1972; Science Fiction: A Critical Guide, 1979; Learning from Other Worlds, 2000. Contributions to:

Dictionary of International Biography

London Review of Books; Many academic journals. Honour: President's Award, World Science Fiction, 1987; Fellow, English Association, 2001. Memberships: H G Wells Society; Science Fiction Foundation; Society of Authors. Address: School of English and American Literature, University of Reading, PO Box 218, Reading, Berkshire RG6 6AA, England.

PARTON Dolly Rebecca, b. 19 January 1946, Sevier County, Tennessee, USA. Singer; Composer. m. Carl Dean, 1966. Creative Works: Films include: Nine to Five, 1980; The Best Little Whorehouse in Texas, 1982; Rhinestone, 1984; Steel Magnolias, 1989; Straight Talk, 1991; The Beverly Hillbillies; Albums include: Here You Come Again, 1978; Real Love, 1985; Just the Way I Am, 1986; Heartbreaker, 1988; Great Balls of Fire, 1988; Rainbow, 1988; White Limozeen, 1989; Home for Christmas, 1990; Eagle When She Flies, 1991; Slow Dancing with the Moon, 1993; Honky Tonk Angels, 1994; The Essential Dolly Parton, 1995; Just the Way I Am, 1996; Super Hits, 1996; I Will Always Love You and Other Greatest Hits, 1996; Hungary Again, 1998; Grass is Blue, 1999; Best of the Best –Porter 2 Doll, 1999; Halos and Horns, 2002. Composed numerous songs including: Nine to Five. Publication: Dolly: My Life and Other Unfinished Business, 1994. Honours include: Vocal Group of the Year Award (with Porter Wagoner), 1968; Vocal Duo of the Year, All Music Association, 1970, 1971; Nashville Metronome Award, 1979; Female Vocalist of the Year, 1975, 1976; Country Star of the Year, 1978; Peoples Choice, 1980; Female Vocalist of the Year, Academy of Country Music, 1980; East Tennessee Hall of Fame, 1988. Address: RCA, 6 West 57th Street, New York, NY 10019, USA.

PARTRIDGE Derek William, b. 15 May 1931. London, England. Retired Diplomat. Appointments: HM Diplomatic Service: Foreign Office, London, England, 1951-54, Oslo, 1954-56, Jedda, 1956, Khartoum, 1957-60, Sofia, 1960-62, Manila, 1962-65, Djakarta, 1965-67, FCO, 1967-72, Brisbane, 1972-74, Colombo, 1974-77; Head, Migration and Visa Department, FCO, 1981-83; Head, Nationality and Treaty Department, FCO, 1983-86; British High Commissioner, Freetown, Sierra Leone, 1986-91; Liberal Democrat Councillor, London Borough of Southwark, 1994-2002. Honours: CMG, 1987. Memberships: National Liberal Club; Royal African Society. Address: 16 Wolfe Crescent, Rotherhithe, London SE16 6SF, England.

PARVEZ Tariq, b. 5 April 1952, Multan, Pakistan. Oncologist. m. Kaniz Akhter, 2 sons, 1 daughter. Education: BSc, 1975, MBBS, 1976, MCPS, 1988, DMRT, 1988, MD, 1994. Appointments: GDMO Pakistan Army, 1976-79; Demonstrator, AIMC, Lahore, 1979-85; SMO Radiotherapy Mayo Hospital, Lahore, 1987-88; Head of Radiotherapy and Oncology, SGRH Lahore and AIMC, Lahore, 1988-97; Head of Radiotherapy and Oncology Services, Hospital Lahore, 1997-2001; Consultant Oncologist, KFH, Almadina Almunawra, KSA, 2001-. Publications: 7 books on cancer; 55 research papers; 1 booklet on breast cancer; 150 articles. Honour: President of Pakistan Gold Medal for Cancer Research; Year 2000 Millennium Medal of Honour; Medal Outstanding People of the 20th Century; Award and Dedication, Who's Who of Intellectuals; Distinguished Leadership Award; Certificate of Merit; Medal, Outstanding People of the 20th Century; Hall of Fame Award. Memberships: PSCP; Fellow, Association of UICC Fellows; Several national and international organizations and associations. Address: PO Box 3643, King Fahad Hospital, Al Medina Al Munawarah, Kingdom of Saudi Arabia. E-mail: tariq_parvez52@hotmail.com

PASCALLON Pierre, b. 12 November 1941, Gap, France. Economist; Educator. m. (1) Laurette Gaulin, 1968, deceased, (2) Christine-Claire Fourgeaud, 1999, 1 daughter. Education: Licence University, Aix en Provence, France, 1967; Doctorate, 1970. Appointments: Professor, Economic Sciences, Faculte de Sciences, Economics, Clermont-Ferrand, France, 1970-; Adjunct Director, 1970-76; Vice-President, 1976. Publications: Contributor, articles to professional journals. Honours: Order Palmes Academiques; Chevalier dans l'ordre de la Legion d'Honneur. Memberships: Rotary Club; Club Participation et Progres. Address: 9 Place Saint-Avit, 63500 Issoire, France.

PASCOE Frank Diggory (Digs), b. 28 March 1939, Pietermaritzburg, South Africa. Engineer; Conservationist. m. Anne, 1 son, 4 daughters, 1 foster daughter. Education: Diploma, Industrial Welfare and Psychology, 1961; Degree, Electrical Engineering, 1962; Diploma, Conservation, Ecology, 1982; Diploma, National Engineers. Appointments: Developed self help schemes, small mining and tourism ventures, Zambia, 1964-71; Discovered world's largest deposit of emeralds, Zambia, 1966; Developed Jewellery Manufacturing and Exports SA, 1972-84; Travelled to USA and Brazil to study self-help schemes and community projects, 1984-85; Property Developer, shopping centre and office complex in "whites only" area for black business men, South Africa, 1986-96; Developed Lake Game viewing and Gemstone/Geology trails to assist local communities to create tourism ventures and related businesses, 1996-99. Publications include: Thesis: Automatic Control of Tumbling Ball Mills; Paper: Development of Information Lay-byes along a National Heritage Route; Present research: Origin of Man sites in Northern KwaZulu Natal/Museum of The Elephant – Africa's Power Icon. Honours: President, Zululand Agricultural & Industrial Show Society, 1998; Chairman, Provincial Roads & Tourism Committee; Eshowe Tourism Association; Regional Honorary Conservation Officers Group; Vice Chairman, Maputaland Tourism & Development Association; Executive; Regional Council Development Committee, Maputaland Biosphere reserve; Board Member, Community Radio Station, Eshowe Career Guidance College, Tourism Association of KwaZulu Natal Province; Space for Elephants Founding Trustee; Chief Executive Officer, Space for Elephants Foundation; Development of Museum & Research Centre for Post Graduate Students; Delegate, Africa Tourism Conference, Lusaka, Zambia, 1994; Trans Frontier Parks – Kingdom of KwaZulu Natal; Outstanding work in the Tourism Community; Promoting Tourism "Off the Beaten track"; TANK Provincial Tourism Development Award. Membership: Rotary International. Address: PO Box 86, Eshowe 3815, Kwa Zulu Natal, Republic of South Africa. E-mail: digspascoe@zulukingdom.co.za

PASKALEV Atanas, b. 30 August 1946, Haskovo, Bulgaria. Civil Engineer. m. Maria Paskaleva, 2 sons. Education: Civil Engineering and Geodesy, University of Architecture, Sofia, 1967-71; Doctorate in Sanitary Engineering, 1988. Appointments: President, Bulgarian Association on Water Quality; Managing Director, Aquapartner Ltd. Publications: Water Quality Data Sharing on the Bulgarian-Romanian Reach of the Danube River Basin (the need for harmonisation of legislation), 1997; Utility Regulation in Bulgarian Water, 2000. Honours: People's Republic of Bulgaria, Ministerial Council Higher Testimonial Commission PhD Diploma, 1988; Listed in Who's Who publications and biographical dictionaries. Memberships: President, Bulgarian National Association on Water Quality; Bulgarian International Water Association, London, UK. Address: 51 Kn Maria Louiza Blvd, floor 4, 1202 Sofia, Bulgaria. E-mail: waterql@tea.bg Website: www.bnawq.org

PASTERKAMP Jan Sjoerd, b. 14 September 1944, Zaandam, Holland. Minister; Missionary. m. Jacoba Catharina Goede, 3 sons. Education: Bachelor of Christian Ministries; Studies for Masters in Christian Ministries (unfinished due to leaving Australia and return to Holland). Appointments: Missionary, Papua, New Guinea,

Dictionary of International Biography

1966-86; Senior Pastor, Australia, 1986-92; Senior Minister/Pastor, Holland, 1992-2003. Publications: 1 Bible Study book; 2 Pastoral Handbooks; Many articles in various Christian publications; 5 years editor of Herstel Magazine (Restore), Holland. Honour: Honorary Diploma in Theology, Zion Bible College, Auckland, New Zealand. Membership: Christian Union (Political). Address: c/o Kandelaar Church, Nieuwe Binnenweg, 326-3021, GU Rotterdam, Holland. E-mail: jansjoerd@kandelaar.nl

PASUPULETI Devakinanda V Raja, b. 27 August 1953, Machilipatnam, India. Neurologist; Physician. b. Bhanumathi, 1 son, 3 daughters. Education: MBBS, India, 1975; Psychiatry Residency, 1981-84; MD, Neurology, 1984-87; EMG Fellowship, 1987-88; FAAEM, 1991; FACP, 2003. Appointments: Clinical Professor, MSU, USA; Director of Neurology; Past Chairman, Department of Neurology; Past Board Member, local medical society; Teaching Neurologist; Assistant Editor, Medical Society Bulletin. Publications: Numerous articles in medical journals; Author, Happiness for Everyone, 2004. Honours: Scout Gold Medal, President of India, 1969; Best Teaching Award, Medical Students of Michigan State University, USA. Memberships: American Medical Association; American Academy of Neurology; Michigan Neurological Association; American College of Physicians; American College of Family Physicians; Genessee County Medical Society. Address: 2370 South Linden Road, Rochelle Center, Flint, MI 48532, USA. E-mail: dpasupu1@hurleymc.com

PATEL Davbhai Jethabhai, b. 5 June 1944, Sapawada, Idar, Sabarkantha (GS), India. Agricultural Scientist. m. Daxaben, 1 son. Education: MSc, Agriculture; PhD, Nematology. Appointments: Senior Research Assistant, 1967-71, Instructor in Plant Protection, 1971-74, Nematologist, 1974-85, Professor of Nematology, 1985-97, Principal, BA College of Agriculture, Anand, 1997-98; Principal, C P College of Agriculture, SKNagar, 1999; Principal BA College of Agriculture, 1999-; Director of Campus, Gujarat Agricultural University, Anand, 2002-. Publications: Scientific, 110 in national and 98 in international journals; 42 popular articles; 1 book chapter; 3 bulletin/folder/leaflets. Honours: Plant Protection Association of India Award for Best Paper on Plant Protection in Field Crops, Central Plant Protection Training Institute, Hyderabad, 1986; Best Research Paper, Hari Om Ashram Perit Shri Bhaikaka Inter-University Smarak Trust Award, Sardar Patel University, 1993; Fellow, Phytopathological Society of India, Division of Mycology and Plant Pathology; IARI, New Delhi; Fellow, Plant Protection Association of India, Central Plant Protection Training Institute, Hyderabad; Hexamar Research and Development Award, Bioved Research Society, Allahabad, 1986; Sardar Patel Agricultural Research Award, Ministry of Agriculture, Co-operation and Rural Development, Government of Gujarat; Fellow, Indian Society of Tobacco Science, Central Tobacco Research Institute, Rajahmundry. Memberships: Life members of 19, annual member of 5 scientific organisations. Address: Principal, BA College of Agriculture, Gujarat Agricultural University, Anand 388 110, Gujarat, India.

PATERSON Howard Cecil, b. 16 March 1920, Edinburgh, Scotland. Retired. Widower, 1 son. Education: Edinburgh College of Art, 1937-39. Appointments: Army Service, Royal Artillery, 1939-45; Personnel Section Officer, 1945-49; TA, 1949-70; Retired as Lieutenant Colonel, 1970; Assistant Personnel Manager, Jute Industries Ltd, 1949-51; Deputy Director, Scottish Country Industries Development Trust, 1951-66; Senior Director, Scottish Tourist Board, 1966-81; Independent Tourism Consultant, Tourism Advisory Services, 1981-2000; Chairman, Taste of Scotland Scheme, 1984-86; Chairman, Scottish International Gathering

Trust, 1981-91; Vice-Chairman, 1982-89, Chairman, 1989-90, Scottish Aircraft Collection Trust; Vice-Chairman, John Buchan Society, 1990-95; Chairman, 1990-2003, Honorary Life President, 2003-, Trekking and Riding Society of Scotland. Publications: Tourism in Scotland, 1969; The Flavour of Edinburgh, 1986. Honours: Territorial Decoration (TD) with two clasps; Front Line Britain medal; Polish Medal, Custodian of Places of National Remembrance. Memberships: Royal Scots Club, Edinburgh; Scottish Reserve Forces and Cadets Association; Royal Artillery Association; Royal Artillery Institution; Founder Member, Firepower; Royal Artillery Museum, Woolwich; City of Edinburgh Artillery Officers Association; 52 Lowland Division Officers Club; Reserve Forces Association; Friend of Historic Scotland; Life Fellow, Royal Society for the Protection of Birds; Fellow, Society of Antiquaries in Scotland; Life Member, National Trust for Scotland; Friend, National Botanic Gardens of Scotland; Art Fund; Friend of the National Galleries of Scotland; Member, Scottish Borders Music and Arts Guild; Scottish Landowners Federation; Countryside Alliance; British Association for Shooting and Conservation; Scottish Association of Country Sports; World Wildlife Fund; Country Club UK; West Linton Historical Association; West Linton Music Society. Address: Dovewood, Carlops Road, West Linton, Peeblesshire EH46 7DS, Scotland.

PATEY-GRABOWSKA Alicja Wanda, (Alicja Wanda Grabowska-Steffen), b. 24 July 1939, Warsaw, Poland. Poet; Teacher; Editor. m. Jan Steffen, 9 December 1978, 1 son. Education: MA, Polish Philology, Warsaw University. Publications: From the Circle, 1968; Adam Ewa, 1975; A Tree From the Inside, 1979; A Lullaby, 1981; You and I, 1982; A Wound of the Earth, 1983; Here Am I Women, 1984; Zoo, 1988; Przed Snem, 1990; Imprints of Time, 1997. Contributions to: Anthologies, children's books and periodicals. Honours: 1st Prize for Theatrical Play, 1985; Silver Wreath, Accademia Internazionale di Pontzen, Naples, 1989; Award, Accademia La Crisalide, Italy, 1997; Award, Polish Ministry of Culture, 1997. Memberships: Society of Authors; Accademia Internazionale di Pontzen, Naples; Academia La Crisalide, Italy; Societe Europenne de Culture. Address: Orlowicza 6m 30, 00-414 Warsaw, Poland.

PATON David Romer, b. 5 March 1935, Grandhome, Aberdeen, Scotland. Chartered Surveyor. m. Juliette Burney, 2 sons. Education: London School of Economics; Keble College, Oxford. Appointments: Chartered Surveyor, 1970-. Honours: OBE; CStJ; DL; Honorary degree, DBA; Fellow, Royal Institution of Chartered Surveyors; Fellow, Society of Antiquaries, Scotland. Memberships: Aberdeen Harbour Board; Scottish Council Development and Industry; North East Scotland Preservation Trust; Order of St John; Prince's Scottish Youth Business Trust; Don District Salmon Fishery Board; Aberdeen Civic Society; Macmillan Cancer Relief; many others. Address: Grandhome, Danestone, Aberdeen AB22 8AR, Scotland. E-mail: davidpaton@btconnect.com

PATTEN Brian, b. 7 February 1946, Liverpool, England. Poet; Writer. Appointment: Regents Lecturer, University of California at San Diego. Publications: Poetry: The Mersey Sound: Penguin Modern Poets 10, 1967; Little Johnny's Confession, 1967; The Home Coming, 1969; Notes to the Hurrying Man: Poems, Winter '66-Summer '68, 1969; The Irrelevant Song, 1970; At Four O'Clock in the Morning, 1971; Walking Out: The Early Poems of Brian Patten, 1971; The Eminent Professors and the Nature of Poetry as Enacted Out by Members of the Poetry Seminar One Rainy Evening, 1972; The Unreliable Nightingale, 1973; Vanishing Trick, 1976; Grave Gossip, 1979; Love Poems, 1981; New Volume, 1983; Storm Damage, 1988; Grinning Jack: Selected Poems, 1990; Armada, 1996; The Utterly Brilliant Book of Poetry (editor), 1998. Editor: Clare's Countryside: A Book of John Clare, 1981; The Puffin Book of 20th Century Children's Verse, 1991;

Dictionary of International Biography

The Story Giant, 2001. Children's Books: Prose: The Jumping Mouse, 1972; Mr Moon's Last Case, 1975; Emma's Doll, 1976; Jimmy Tag-along, 1988; Grizzelda Frizzle, 1992; Impossible Parents, 1994; Beowulf, a version, 1999. Poetry: Gargling With Jelly, 1985; Thawing Frozen Frogs, 1990; The Magic Bicycle, 1993; The Utter Nutters, 1994; The Blue and Green Ark, 1999; Juggling with Gerbils, 2000; Little Hotchpotch, 2000; Impossible Parents Go Green. Contributions to: Journals and newspapers. Honour: Special Award, Mystery Writers of America, 1977; Arts Council of England, Writers Award, 1998; Freedom of the City of Liverpool, 2000; Honorary Fellow, John Moores University, 2002. Membership: Chelsea Arts Club. Address: c/o Puffin Penguin Books, 27 Wrights Lane, London W8 5TZ, England.

PATTERSON Amy J, b. 30 September 1937, West, Texas, USA. English Instructor. m. Leslie A Patterson, 1 son, 2 daughters. Education: AA, Navarro College, 1982; BA, 1984, MA, 1986, Stephen F Austin State University. Appointments: Graduate Assistant, Stephen F Austin State University, 1984-86; English Teacher, Nacogdoches High School, 1986-87; English Instructor, Navarro College, 1987-. Publications: Between the Walnut Tree and the Fountain: Perspective of the earthly life in Hawthorne's "An Old Woman's Tale," 1984; Tolstoy's De-glorification of Passion in Anna Karenina, 1986. Honours: NISOD Recipient, National Institute for Staff and Organizational Development, 1993; Recipient of Cook Center Mini-grant, 2001. Memberships: Alpha Delta Kappa (now); Sigma Tau Delta, Phi Theta Kappa (in school). Address: English Department, Navarro College, Corsicana, TX 75110, USA.

PATTERSON Percival Noel James, b. 10 April 1935, Dias Hanover, Jamaica. Politician; Lawyer. 1 son, 1 daughter. Education: BA, English, University of West Indies, 1958; BLL, London School of Economics, 1963. Appointments: Joined People's National Party, 1958; Party Organiser, People's National Party, 1958; Vice President, People's National Party, 1969; Minister of Industry, Trade and Tourism, 1972; Deputy Prime Minister and Minister of Foreign Affairs and Foreign Trade, 1978-80; Chairman, People's National Party, 1983; Deputy Prime Minister and Minister of Development, Planning and Production, 1989-90; Deputy Prime Minister and Minister of Finance and Planning, 1990-99; President and Party Leader, People's National Party, 1992; Prime Minister, 1992-. Honours: Sir Hughes Parry Prize for excellence in the Law of Contract; Leverhulme Scholarship, London School of Economics; Appointed to Privy Council of the United Kingdom, 1992; Honorary Doctor of Letters, Northeastern University, 1994; Honorary Degree of Doctor of Laws, Brown University, 1998; Numerous foreign awards include: Order of Jose Marti, Cuba, 1997; Order of the Volta, Ghana, 1999; Food and Agriculture Organisation Agricola Medal, Jamaica, 2001; Juan Mora Fernandez Great Silver Cross, Costa Rica, 2001. Address: Office of the Prime Minister, 1 Devon Road, Kingston 6, Jamaica. E-mail: jamhouse@cwjamaica.com

PATZELT Gerald, b. 3 February 1931, Rumburg, Bohemia. Geologist. m. Heike Herr, 27 July 1962, deceased, 2 daughters. Education: Diploma, Geology, University of Halle and Greifswald, 1953; Dr.rer.nat, University of Leipzig, 1968. Appointments: Mining Geologist, 1954; Geologist, Geological Service of the GDR; Natural Science, Museum of Mühlhausen; Retired. Publications: 40 articles in professional journals on stratigraphy and tectonics of Albania, the Harz Mountains and Thuringia; 4 booklets. Memberships: Gesellschaft für Geowissenschaften; Thüringischer Geologischer Verein. Address: Felchtaer Str 26, D-99974 Mühlhausen, Germany.

PAUL Dieter, b. 22 September 1938, Freital, Germany. Chemist. m. Christa, 2 sons. Education: Graduated as Chemist, 1962; Dr rer nat, TH Leuna-Merseburg, 1966; Dr habil, University of Leipzig, 1972. Appointments: Scientist, Institute of Polymer Chemistry, Teltow, 1964-91; Visiting Scientist, Instituto de Quimica y Biologia La Habana, 1979-83; Scientist, GKSS Research Centre Geestacht, Germany, 1992-; Director, Institute of Chemistry and Professor, University of Hamburg, Germany, 1994-2002. Publications: Author and co-author of about 200 publications and 60 patent applications in the field of applied polymer research, membranes and biomaterials. Honour: Order of Merit of the Federal Republic of Germany. Memberships: German Society of Chemistry; German Society of Biomaterials; Member of various scientific boards. Address: Wolfswerder 25, 14 532 Kleinmachnow, Germany.

PAULLI Gianfranco, b. 14 February 1948, Soresina, Italy. Sculptor; Painter. m. Maria Lucia Manfredini, 1 son. Education: Diplomas of Art Master, Istituto d' Arte Stagi Peitrasanta di Lucca, Italy, 1973. Appointments: Restorer of ancient marbles for the Holy See of Rome, and other locations world-wide; Commissioned to create various sculptural and monumental pieces. Publications: Various articles for the art magazine, Arte Rivista; Cavaliere della Republica Italiano, autobiography. Honours include: "Accademico", Accademia Tibernia, Rome, 1971; L'Ambrogino d'Oro, Città di Milano, 1979; Award Arcole d'Ore, Milano, 1980; Spiga Italica (Italic Spike, Palazzo Pignatelli, 1983; Appointed, Cavaliere dell'Ordine di S Silvestro Papa, 1990; Acknowledgement, La lanterna d'argento Palazzo Ducale, Genova, 2002. Listed in numerous biographical publications. Memberships: Accedemia Tiberina, Rome, 1978-. Address: Via G Verdi 2, 26011 Casalbuttano CR, Italy. E-mail: bosiorag@tin.it

PAVAROTTI Luciano, b. 12 October 1935, Modena, Italy. Singer (Tenor). m. (1) Adua Veroni, 1961, 3 daughters, (2) Nicoletta Mantovani, 2003, 1 daughter. Education: DMus, Istituto Magistrale; Tenor Range. Career: Debut, Rodolfo in La Bohème, Reggio nell' Emilia, 1961; Edgardo in Lucia di Lammermoor, Miami, USA, 1965; Appearances incl: Staatsoper Vienna, Royal Opera House of London, 1963, La Scala European tour, 1963-64; La Scala, 1965, Metropolitan Opera House, New York, 1968, Paris Opéra and Lyric Opera of Chicago, 1973; Many recitals and concerts worldwide, 1973-; Appeared in MGM film, Yes, Giorgio, 1981; Sang Manrico in TV simulcast from the Metropolitan Opera House, 1988; New production of Rigoletto, 1989, Nemorino in L'Elisir d'Amore at Covent Garden, 1990; Concert at Glasgow, 1990; Sang Manrico at 1990 Maggio Musicale Florence and appeared with 2 other tenors at World Cup Concert, Caracalla; Concert performances of Otello at Chicago, 1991; Sang Otello and Nemorino in New York, 1991-92; Debut as Verdi's Don Carlos at opening of 1992-93 season, La Scala; Returned to Covent Garden as Cavaradossi, 1999; Radames, 2001; Tosca at Covent Garden, 2002; Metropolitan Opera as Arvino in I Lombardi 1994; Sang Gustavus (Ballo in Maschera) at Covent Garden, 1995, Metropolitan Opera House, 1997. Creative works: Recordings include: La Bohème, Madame Butterfly, Beatrice di Tenda, Lucia di Lammermoor, La Fille du Régiment, Maria Stuarda, Un Ballo in Maschera, Luisa Miller, Macbeth, Mefistofele, Idomeneo, Aida, Norma, Tosca, Otello. Publication: Pavarotti: My Own Story, with William Wright. Honours include: Honorary Degree, Pennsylvania, 1979; Grand Officier, Italy; Noce d'Oro National Prize; Luigi Illica International Prize; First Prize Gold Orfeo (Academie du Disque Lyrique de France); Kennedy Center Honor, 2001. Address: Via Giardini 941, 41040 Saliceta, Modena, Italy.

PAVAZZA Radoslav, b. 30 August 1945, Split, Croatia. Professor of Mechanics. Education: BS, Naval Architecture, Belgrade, 1972; MS, Naval Architecture, Zagreb, 1984; PhD, Naval Architecture,

Zagreb, 1991. Appointments: Naval Architect, Split Shipyard, Croatia, 1972-74; Assistant, Mechanics Department, Split University, Croatia, 1974-84; Naval Architect, Croatia Register of Shipping, Croatia, 1984-85; Assistant, Mechanics Department, 1985-92, Assistant Professor of Mechanics, 1992-2000, Professor of Mechanics, 2000-, Split University, Croatia. Publications: Author and co-author, articles in professional journals; Research in the theory of thin-walled structures and theory of elasticity. Honours: Listed in Who's Who publications and biographical dictionaries. Membership: Croatian Society of Mechanics. Address: Faculty of Electrical Engineering, Mechanical Engineering and Naval Architecture, University of Split, R Boškovića bb, 21000 Split, Croatia. E-mail: radoslav.pavazza@fesb.hr

PAVEL Abraham, b. 21 October 1948, Creaca, Salaj County, Romania. Jurist of Law; Policeman. m. Viorica, 1 daughter. Education: The Ministry of the Interior Active Service Officers School, 1972; Bucharest School of Law, 1974; Postgraduate Courses in Criminology, 1979; PhD, Law, 1995. Appointments: Director, Penal Investigation Directorate (Romanian National Police General Inspectorate), 1995-97; Inspector General of the Romanian Police, 1997-; Professor, Advanced Training Centre, 1997-99; Director, Analysis, Strategies and Resources Planning Independent Services with the Ministry of the Interior Main Staff, 1999-2000; Secretary of State, Ministry of the Interior, 2001-2003; President, National Anti-Drug Agency Romania, Ministry of the Interior, 2003-. Publications: Author and co-author of more than 40 publications and papers on law, police and social assistance including: Police, Community and Transition; Crimes Stipulated by Special Laws; Democratic Values and Human Rights Observance in Police Work; Introduction to Probation; Human Rights; Children's Rights. Memberships: International Policeman Associations; National Criminology Society; International Criminology Society; Romanian Journalist Association; Chairman, Romanian Chapter of the Europe 2000 International Association; Honorary Member, Foreign Students Association, Higher Police School Saint Cry au Mont D'Or, Lyon, France. Address: Coltei Street Ho 25, Apartment 20, Sector 3, Bucharest, Romania. E-mail: abraham-pavel@mi.ro

PAVEY Donald Adair, b. 25 July 1922, Wandsworth, London, England. Researcher into Colour Aesthetics. Education: Painting, 1943-46, Design Research, 1974-75, Royal College of Art; British School at Athens, under Professor Jenkins, 1953; Art History, 1954-56, Psychology, 1956-59, London University Extra Mural; Perugia University (Stranieri), 1971-72. Appointments: Senior Lecturer, Art Research for BA Honours and M Phil, Kingston College of Art/University, 1960-83; Director of Micro Academy (www.microacademy.co.uk), 1996; Director of Colour Academy (www.coloracademy.co.uk), 2001. Publications: Methuen Handbook of Colour and Colour Dictionary (editor), 1861, 1967, 1978; ATHENE, Journal of the Society for Education through Art (editor), 1972-82; Art-Based Games, 1979; Juegos de Expresion Plastica, 1982; The Revolution in Child Art, 1983; The Artists' Colourmen's Story, 1985; ProMICAD System for Empowerment, 2001; Trowbridge: Lifetime Careers, 2001; On Colours (translation from Thylesius 1528), 2003; Colour and Humanism, 2003; Psycho Box (advisor and contributor), 2004. Honours: ARCA Medal of Special Distinction, Royal College of Art, London, 1946; FRSA, Fellow of the Royal Society of Arts, London, 1955; Diploma Award for colour research, London University City Literary Institute, 1957; Medal, Accademia Tommaso Campanella, 1971; Founder, Colour Reference Library, Royal College of Art, 1975; Founder, National Art Education Archive, Leeds University at the RCA, 1983; Freedom of the City of London, Guild of Painter Stainers, 1985; Isaac Newton Medal, Colour Group (Great Britain) City University, London, 1986. Memberships: Fellow of the Royal Society of Arts, London; Colour Group (Great Britain) City University, London; Design Research Society. Address: Studio House, 30 Wayside, London SW14 7LN, England. E-mail: studio@coloracademy.co.uk

PAVLICHENKOV Igor Mikhailovitch, b. 4 December 1934, Reutov City, Moscow Region, Russia. Physicist; Theoretician. m. Olga Yavorskaya, 11 November 1972, 1 son. Education: Physics, Moscow University, 1958; Candidate of Physics, JINR, Dubna, 1964; DPhys, Kurchatov Institute, 1982. Appointments: Junior Researcher, 1958-83, Senior Researcher, 1983-87, Leading Researcher, 1987-93, Principal Researcher, 1993-, Kurchatov Institute. Publications: Several research papers in professional journals. Honours: I V Kurchatov Annual Prize, 1988, 1994. Memberships: Russian Nuclear Research Programme Committee, Moscow, 1986-90; Several scientific boards. Address: Russian Research Centre, Kurchatov Institute, 123182 Moscow, Russia.

PAVLOTSKI Vladimir Yakovlevich, b. 3 September 1925, Ashgabat, Turkmenistan. Artist. Education: Graduate, Odessa School of Art, 1951. Career: Served in 724 Red Banner Aviation Regiment, WWII, liberation of Minsk and capture of Berlin; Artist Painter, 1950-; Head, Military Patronage and Marine Commission, Turkmenistan Union of Artists; Member, Central Military Patronage Commission, cultural patronage of the marine and inland water transport. Organiser, Open Picture Gallery, Krasnovodsk (now Turkmenbashi City), 1969; Organiser, Open Picture Gallery, Board of Troops of Central Asia Frontier Region, 1978; Member, Central Board of the Soviet-Polish Friendship Society, 1987; Organiser, Turkmen-Polish Friendship Clubs, 1987; Elected Vice-President, Turkmen-Polish Friendship Society, 1992; Organiser, Days of Culture of Poland, Ashgabat, 1999; Organiser of Exhibition, "Asia in Posters of Polish Artists", 1997; Organiser, Personal Jubilee Exhibition dedicated to the 80th Anniversary of Poland's Independence, Ashgabat, 1998. Exhibitions: 35 personal exhibitions in Ashgabat, Turkmenistan, Moscow, Russia, Warsaw, Poland, other Russian and Polish cities and Bergen, Norway; Pictures in collections: Museums of Ashgabat, Turkmenbashi, Tretyakov Gallery, Museum of Asia and Pacific Ocean, Warsaw; Polish Army Museum, Warsaw; Museum of Radom City; Bergen City Museum, Norway; Exhibition Foundations of the Ministry of Culture of Turkmenistan, Russia and Poland; Works in private collections in many countries of the world. Honours include: Patriotic War Order; 15 Soviet and Polish Medals; 6 Soviet, Turkmen and Polish Government Awards for creative and public activities; Golden Honorary Badge and Gold Medal, Central Board, Soviet-Polish Friendship Society; Jubilee Medal, Museum of Asia and the Pacific Ocean, Warsaw; Honoured Art Worker of Turkmenistan; Honoured Culture Worker of Poland; Honorary Consul of Poland in Turkmenistan; Byashim Nurali Prize Laureate of Turkmenistan Artists Union. Memberships: Turkmenistan Artists Union; International Artists Federation of Russia. Address: Kravchenko Street 8, Apartment 78, 117313 Moscow, Russia.

PAXMAN Jeremy Dickson, b. 11 May 1950, Leeds, England. Journalist; Author. Education: St Catherine's College, Cambridge. Appointments: Journalist, Northern Ireland, 1973-77; Reporter, BBC TV Tonight and Panorama Programmes, 1977-85; Presenter, BBC TV Breakfast Time, 1986-89, Newsnight, 1989-, University Challenge, 1994-, Start the Week, Radio 4, 1998-2002. Publications: A Higher Form of Killing (co-author), 1982; Through the Volcanoes, 1985; Friends in High Places, 1990; Fish, Fishing and the Meaning of Life, 1994; The Compleat Angler, 1996; The English, 1998; The Political Animal, 2002; Numerous articles in newspapers and magazines. Honours include: Royal TV Society Award, International Reporting; Richard Dimbley Award, BAFTA, 1996, 2000; Interview of the Year, Royal TV Society, 1997, 1998; Voice of the Viewer and Listener Presenter of the Year, 1994,

1997; Dr h c, Leeds, Bradford, 1999; Variety Club Media Personality of the Year, 1999; Fellow, St Edmund Hall, Oxford, St Catharine's College, Cambridge, 2001. Address: c/o BBC TV, London W12 7RJ, England.

PEARCE Ann Philippa, b. Great Shelford, Cambridgeshire, England. Children's Writer. m. Martin James Christie, 9 May 1963, 1 daughter. Education: MA, University of Cambridge. Appointments: Script Writer, Producer, School Broadcasting, Radio, 1945-58; Children's Editor, André Deutsch Ltd, 1960-67. Publications: Minnow on the Say, 1954; Tom's Midnight Garden, 1958; Mrs Cockle's Cat, 1961; A Dog So Small, 1962; The Children of the House (with Sir Brian Fairfax-Lucy), 1968, reissued as The Children of Charlecote, 1989; The Squirrel Wife, 1971; What the Neighbours Did and Other Stories, 1972; The Shadow Cage and Other Stories of the Supernatural, 1977; The Battle of Bubble and Squeak, 1978; The Elm Street Lot, 1979; The Way to Sattin Shore, 1983; Lion at School and Other Stories, 1985; Who's Afraid? and Other Strange Stories, 1986; Emily's Own Elephant, 1987; The Toothball, 1987; Freddy, 1988; Old Belle's Summer Holiday, 1989; Here Comes Tod, 1992; Dread and Delight: A Century of Children's Ghost Stories (editor), 1995; The Rope and other stories, 2000; Amy's Three Best Things, 2003. Contributions to: Times Literary Supplement; Guardian. Honours: Carnegie Medal, 1959; New York Herald Tribune Spring Festival Prize, 1962; Whitbread Prize, 1979; Honorary Doctor of Letters, University of Hull, 1995; Officer of the Order of the British Empire, 1997. Membership: Society of Authors; Fellow, Royal Society of Literature, 1994. Address: c/o Laura Cecil, 17 Alwyne Villas, London N1 2HG, England.

PEARSALL Derek Albert, b. 28 August 1931, Birmingham, England. Emeritus Professor of English. m. Rosemary Elvidge, 30 August 1952, 2 sons, 3 daughters. Education: BA, 1951, MA, 1952, University of Birmingham. Appointments: Assistant Lecturer, Lecturer, King's College, University of London, 1959-65; Lecturer, Senior Lecturer, Reader, 1965-76, Professor, 1976-87, University of York; Visiting Professor, 1985-87, Gurney Professor of English, 1987-2000, (Emeritus), Harvard University, Cambridge, Massachusetts, USA. Publications: John Lydgate, 1970; Landscapes and Seasons of the Medieval World (with Elizabeth Salter), 1973; Old English and Middle English Poetry, 1977; Langland's Piers Plowman: An Edition of the C-Text, 1978; The Canterbury Tales: A Critical Study, 1985; The Life of Geoffrey Chaucer: A Critical Biography, 1992; John Lydgate (1371-1449): A Bio-bibliography, 1997; Chaucer to Spenser: An Anthology of Writings in English 1375-1575, 1999; Gothic Europe 1200-1450, 2001; Arthurian Romance: A Short Introduction, 2003. Memberships: Early English Text Society, council member; Medieval Academy of America, fellow; New Chaucer Society, president, 1988-90; American Academy of Arts and Sciences, fellow. Address: 4 Clifton Dale, York YO30 6LJ, England.

PECHAN Paul Michael, b. 13 July 1954, Bystrica, Slovakia. Scientist. Education: BSc, University of Waterloo, Ontario, Canada; PhD, Cambridge University, England. Appointments: Research Fellow, University of California, 1984-85; Research Fellow, Canada Agricultural Department, Ottawa, 1985-88; Group Leader, Max Planck Institute, Munich, 1988-95; Scientist, Technical University, Munich, 1995-. Publications: Numerous research publications, abstracts and guest lectures; Author; Producer of science documentaries. Honours: Alexander Von Humboldt Fellow; Visiting Professor, Agricultural University Prague; Vice President, Pias, Prague, 1992-97. Memberships: New Jersey Academy of Sciences; Sigma Xi. Address: Lehrstuhl für Pflanzenbau, 85350 Freising-Weihenstephan, Technical University, Munich, Germany.

PEDERSEN K George, b. 13 June 1931, Alberta, Canada. Educator. m. Penny, 1 son, 1 daughter. Education: Diploma, BC Provincial Normal School, 1952; BA, University of British Columbia, 1959; MA, University of Washington, 1964; PhD, University of Chicago, 1969. Appointments: Teacher, Vice President and Principal, various public schools, 1952-65; Academic appointments at University of Toronto, 1968-70, University of Chicago, 1970-72; Dean and Academic Vice President, University of Victoria, 1972-79; President, Simon Fraser University, 1979-83; President, University of British Columbia, 1983-85; President, University of Western Ontario, 1985-94; Interim President, University of Northern British Columbia, 1995; Founding President, Royal Roads University, 1995-96. Publications: The Itinerant Schoolmaster; Several book chapters; Innumerable articles. Honours: 10 major scholarships; Fellow, Canadian College of Teachers, Commonwealth Medal, 1992; Officer, Order of Canada, 1993; Order of Ontario, 1994; Order of British Columbia, 2002; Queens Jubilee Medal, 2002; LLD, McMaster University, 1996; DLH, Emily Carr Institute of Art and Design, 2003; LLD, Simon Fraser University, 2003; Fellow, Royal Society for the Advancement of the Arts; many others. Address: 2232 Spruce St, Vancouver, BC V6H 2P3, Canada.

PEETA Srinivas, b. Guntur, India. Educator. m. Uma. Education: BTech, Indian Institute of Technology, Madras, 1988; MSCE, California Institute of Technology, 1989; PhD, University of Texas, Austin, 1994. Appointment: Assistant Professor, 1994-2000, Associate Professor, 2000-, School of Civil Engineering, Purdue University. Publications: Several articles in professional journals. Honours include: Best International Dissertation Award in Transportation Science, INFORMS, 1994; National Science Foundation Career Award, 1997; Wansik Excellence in Research Award, Civil Engineering, Purdue University, 2004. Memberships include: Omega Rho; Tau Beta Pi; Sigma Xi; Institute for Operations Research and Management Science; Transportation Science Technical Section, INFORMS; American Society of Civil Engineers; Associate Editor of the Journal, Networks and Spatial Economics; Editorial Board, Intelligent Transportation Systems Journal; Editorial Board, Transportation Research, Part B; Member, Technical Committee on Transportation Systems, International Federation of Automatic Control; Member, Transportation Research Board (TRB), Committee on Network Modeling; Member, TRB Committee on Travel Behavior and Values; Chair, TRB Sub-committee on Route Choice and Spatial Behavior. Address: Purdue University, School of Civil Engineering, 550 Stadium Mall Drive, West Lafayette, IN 47907-2051, USA.

PELÉ (Edson Arantes do Nascimento), b. 23 October 1940, Tres Coracoes, Minas Gerais State, Brazil. Football Player; Author. m. Rosemeri Cholbi, 1966, divorced 1978, 1 son, 2 daughters. Education: Santos University. Appointments: Football Player at Bauru, Sao Paulo, Bauru Athletic Club; Joined Santos FC, 1955; 1st International Game v Argentina; Played in World Cup, 1958, 1962, 1966, 1970; Retired with New York Cosmos; Chair, Pelé Soccer Camps, 1978-; Director, Santos FC, 1993-; Special Minister for Sports, Government of Brazil, 1994-; Director, Soccer Clinics. Publications: Eu Sou Pelé, 1962; Jogando com Pelé, 1974; My Life and the Beautiful Game, 1977; Pelé Soccer Training Program, 1982; The World Cup Murders (novel), 1988. Honours: 3 World Cup Winner medals; 2 World Club Championship medals; 110 international caps; 97 goals for Brazil; 1,114 appearances for Santos, 1,088 goals; 9 league championship medals; 4 Brazil Cup medals; Goodwill Ambassador for 1992; UN Conference on Environment and Development, Rio De Janeiro; International Peace Award, 1978; WHO Medal, 1989; Honorary KBE, 1997; FIFA World Footballer of the Century, 2000. Address: 75 Rockefeller Plaza, New York, NY 10019, USA.

PELLING John Arthur, b. 9 August 1930, Hove, Sussex, England. Clergyman; Artist. m. Françoise Coutinet, divorced, 4 sons. Education: Brighton College of Arts and Crafts, 1946; ARAC, Painting, Royal College of Art, 1950-54; Trained as Anglican Priest, Chichester Theological College, 1955-58. Appointments: National Service: Instructor, Royal Army Ordnance Corps, Aldershot, 1949-50; Deacon, Parish of St Helen, Hangleton, Hove, Sussex, 1958; Ordained Priest, 1959; Senior Curate, St Mary Abbots, Kensington, London and Priest-in-Charge, Christ Church, Kensington, 1961; Visiting Tutor, teaching life painting and drawing and pictorial composition, Sir John Cass College of Art, London, 1962; Vicar, St Saviour's Church, Shepherds Bush, London, 1973; Visiting Chaplain, Royal Academy of Dramatic Art, 1976; Chaplain, Anglican Church, Nice, France, 1979; Lived and taught painting in Monte Carlo, 1983-94; Returned to London, 1995. Exhibitions: First one man exhibition, Drian Gallery, London, 1965; Subsequently several one man exhibitions: Drian Gallery, Moyen Gallery, Manchester and Sussex Universities; Brighton, Summer Exhibitions, Royal Academy and Free Painters; Eton Art Gallery, Windsor, 1983; Association Internationale des Arts Plastiques, UNESCO, Monte Carlo; "The Splitting Image", Air Gallery, London, 1998; "Double Exposure", Air Gallery, London, 2001; Works in collections: Nuffield Foundation; The Victoria de Sica Private Collection; Other private collections; National Collection of Modern Art, Gdansk, Poland; Paintings include: Series of paintings "Vulnerability", Monte Carlo, 1983-94; Last known portrait of novelist Graham Greene from life, 1989; Fourteen Stations of the Cross, Church of St Thomas the Apostle, Hanwell, England, 2003; Reredos "The Annunciation", Church of St Gabriel, North Acton, England, 2004; Commissioned for Stations of the Cross, Church of St Andrew, North Weald, Epping, England, 2004. Honours: Associate of the Royal College of Art; Ordained Anglican Priest, 1959; Member of the Jury in artistic capacity for the International Annual Firework Competition, Monte Carlo. Memberships: Chelsea Arts Club, London; Church of England "Forward in Faith". Address: 44 Redcliffe Road, London SW10 9NJ, England.

PELLOW Andrew Charles Henry (Newman), b. 29 September 1944, Nettlestone, Isle of Wight, England. Musician; Writer. Education: Diploma, History of Church Music, Williams School, 1986. Appointments: Organist, Nettlestone Methodist Chapel, 1956-93; Clerk, Legal Cashier, John Robinson & Jarvis, 1961-66, Robinson, Jarvis & Rolf, 1967-90; Freelance Piano Teacher, Accompanist, Calligrapher, 1990-; Organist, Choir Master, St Helen's (IW) Parish Church, 1993; Organist, Choir Master, Sandown Parish Church, Christ Church, Broadway, 1994-97; Director of Music, Organist, Choir Master, Parish and Priory Church of St Mary-the-Virgin, Carisbrooke, 1997-99; Freelance Organist, 1999-; Sub-Deacon with Traditional Anglican Church in Britain, St Barnabas Mission, Isle of Wight, 2004. Publications: Robella Ruby (poems), 1985; Numerous poems in anthologies; Several articles in professional magazines and newsletters; Periodic letters and concert critiques in local press. Honours: AILCA, 1984; Winner, Piano, Organ, Composition, Speech, Poetry and Prose, Isle of Wight and Portsmouth Musical Competition Festivals, 1989-2003; Twice winner, thrice runner-up Isle of Wight County Press/ Tritone Singers Annual Carol Competition, 1996, 1998, 2000, 2001 and 2002; LGMS, 1996; 1st Prize, Poetry, Poetry Today, 1998; Elected a Fellow of the Academy of St Cecilia, 2001; Granted Life Membership of the Central Institute, London (MCIL), 2002; Piano-Oxford Musical Festival, 2003, 2004; Ceremonially admitted to CIL, 2003. Memberships: Executive Trustee, 1998-2003, Official Accompanist, 1994-, Isle of Wight Musical Competition Festivals; Friend of Winchester Cathedral; Guild of Musicians and Singers; Isle of Wight Organists' Association; St Thomas's (Ryde) Heritage Centre Trust; Zion Chapel Trust; Isle of Wight Morris Minor Owners' Club, 1998-; Company Secretary, Primary Flats

(Carisbrooke) Management Company Ltd, 1999-; Parochial Church Council, St Michael and All Angels, Swanmore, 2000-03; Ryde Arts Festival (Planning), 2002-. Address: 2 Radley Cottages, Nettlestone Hill, Nettlestone, Nr Sea View, Isle of Wight, PO34 5DW, England.

PENA Lorenzo, b. 29 August 1944, Alicante, Spain. University Professor. m. Teresa Alonso, 19 February 1969. Education: American Studies Diploma, Liège University, Belgium, 1978; PhD, Philosophy, Liège University, 1979; Bachelor of Law, Spanish Open University, Madrid, Spain, 2002. Appointments: Professor of Philosophy, Pontifical University of Ecuador, 1973-75, 1979-83; Professor, University of Léon, Spain, 1983-87; Senior Science Researcher, CSIC (Spanish Institute of Advanced Study), 1987-; Visiting Position, Australian national University, Research School of Social Sciences, 1992-93. Publications: Rudiments of Mathematical Logic (Madrid), 1991; Philosophical Findings, 1992. Honours: National Prize for Literary Creation in the Humanities, Madrid, 1988. Memberships: Australian Association of Philosophy; Mind Association; Aristotelian Society; European Society of Analytical Philosophy. Address: Spanish Institute for Advanced Study, Department of Philosophy, Pinar 25, E28006 Madrid, Spain.

PENASO Anthony Makinano, b. 28 July 1972, Anda, Bohol, Philippines. Mathematician; Educator. m. Abigail Noemis Tescon-Penaso. Education: BS, Education (Mathematics) summa cum laude, 1992; MA, Teaching Mathematics, 1997; DSc, Mathematics Education magna cum laude, 1999; PhD, Mathematics, 2002; Ed D, Educational Planning and Management, 2004. Appointments: Instructor, 1992-2001, Associate Professor, 2001-, Director of Instruction, 2002-2003, Vice President for Research and Extension, 2003-, Central Mindanao University; Visiting Professor, Northern Mindanao State Institute of Science and Technology, 2002-2003; Visiting Professor, Mindanao Polytechnic State College, 2003-. Publications: Book: Methods of Research, 2001; Capturing A Unified Definition of Chaos, 2001; Chaos in Travelling Waves of Lattice Dynamical Systems, 2002; A Non-Chaotic Introduction to Chaos Theory, 2002. Honours: University Academic Excellence Award, 1988-1992; First to Graduate summa cum laude in CMU's History; Bronze Service Award, 1997, Silver Service Award, 2001, Boy Scouts of the Philippines; Fulbright Scholarship, Pennsylvania State University, USA, 2000-2001; Outstanding Research Paper Award, 2001; ICTP-UNESCO-IAEA Fellow, The Abdus Salam International Centre for Theoretical Physics, Trieste, Italy, 2002. Memberships: American Mathematical Society; Canadian Mathematical Society; Society for Industrial and Applied Mathematics; Fulbright Association; Mathematical Society of the Philippines; Philippines Council of Mathematics Teacher Educators; Southeast Asia Mathematical Society. Address: 106 Mancono St, Central Mindanao University, University Town, Musuan, Bukidnon, Philippines. E-mail: anpen@eudoramail.com

PENICK John Edgar, b. 2 January 1944, Langley, Virginia. Educator. m. Nell Ann Inman, 1 son, 1 daughter. Education: BS, Zoology and Chemistry, 1966, MA, Junior College Teaching of Biology, 1969, University of Miami; PhD, Science Education, Biology, Florida State University, 1973. Appointments: Head, Science Department, Miami Jackson High, 1967-70; Teacher, Biology and Botany, Miami-Dade Junior College, Summer 1968; Science Methods, Plant Physiology, Florida State University, 1970-73; Assistant Professor and Director of Teacher Education, Loyola University, Chicago, 1973-75; Professor, 1982, Chair, 1981-82, 1990-92, University of Iowa, 1975-97; Professor and Head of Mathematics, Science and Technology Education, North Carolina State University, 1998-; Consultant, Lecturer, international institutions including, UNESCO, World Bank, in countries including Taiwan, Indonesia, Belize, Venezuela, Europe, New

Zealand, Trinidad, USSR, Malaysia, Thailand, Philippines, Singapore, Australia, Jamaica. Publications: 185 articles, 38 books and monographs; 50 reviews; Numerous presented papers. Honours: Fellowships, awards include: Outstanding Science Educator in the United States, AETS, 1987; President, National Association of Biology Teachers, USA, 1989; Burlington Northern Foundation Faculty Achievement Award, University of Iowa, 1992; AETS Award for Outstanding Mentor, 1997; President, AETS, 2002; Epsilon Pi Tau; Distinguished Service Citation, 2003; President, National Science Teachers Association, USA, 2003-04; Listed in Several Biographical Dictionaries. Memberships include: Board of Directors, National Science Teachers Association; Association for the Education of Teachers in Science; Sigma Xi; Phi Delta Kappa; Board of Directors of ICASE, NABT and Council of Scientific Society Presidents (CSSP). Address: 326 Poe Hall, Box 7801, North Carolina State University, Raleigh, NC 27695-7801, USA.

PENN Sean, b. 17 August 1960, Burbank, California, USA. Actor. m. (1) Madonna, 1985, (2) Robin Wright, 1996, 2 children. Creative Works: Theatre appearances include: Heartland; Slab Boys; Hurlyburly, 1988; Film appearances: Taps, 1981; Fast Times at Ridgemont High, 1982; Bad Boys, 1983; Crackers, 1984; Racing with the Moon, 1984; The Falcon and the Snowman, 1985; At Close Range, 1986; Shanghai Surprise, 1986; Colors, 1988; Judgement in Berlin, 1988; Casualties of War, 1989; We're No Angels, 1989; State of Grace, 1990; Carlito's Way, 1993; Dead Man Walking, 1996; U Turn, 1997; She's So Lovely, 1997; Hurlyburly, 1998; As I Lay Dying, 1998; Up at the Villa, 1998; The Thin Red Line, 1998; Sweet and Lowdown; Being John Malkovich; The Weight of Water; The Pledge, 2000; Up at the Villa, 2000; I am Sam, 2001; Mystic River, 2004; Director, Writer: The Indian Runner, 1991, The Crossing Guard, 1995. Honours include: Best Actor Award, Berlin Film Festival, 1996; Oscar for Best Actor, Mystic River, 2004. Address: William Morris Agency, 151 South El Camino Drive, Beverly Hills, CA 90212, USA.

PENROSE Roger, b. 8 August 1931, Colchester, Essex, England. Mathematician. Education: University College, London; Doctorate, Cambridge University, 1957. Appointments: Worked with father in the devising of seemingly impossible geometric figures; Lecturing and Research posts in Britain and the USA; Professor of Applied Mathematics, Birkbeck College, London, 1966-73; Rouse Ball Professor of Mathematics, Oxford University, 1973-98; Professor Emeritus, 1998- Important contributions to the understanding of astrophysical phenomena, especially Black Holes. Publications: Techniques of Differential Topology in Relativity, 1973; Spinors and Space-time, with W Rindler, volume I, 1984, volume II, 1986; The Emperor's New Mind, 1989; The Nature of Space and Time, with S Hawking, 1996; The Large, the Small and the Human Mind, 1997; White Mars, with B Aldiss, 1999; articles in scientific journals. Honours: Adams Prize, 1966-67; Dannie Heinemann Prize, 1971; Eddington Medal, 1975; Royal Medal, 1985; Wolf Foundation Prize for Physics, 1988; Dirac Medal and Prize, Institute of Physics, 1989; Einstein Medal, 1990; Science Book Prize, 1990; Naylor Prize, London Mathematics Society, 1991; 8 Dr h c; Hon D University, 1998. Memberships: London Mathematical Society; Cambridge Philosophical Society; Institute for Mathematics and its Applications; International Society for General Relativity and Gravitation; Fellow, Birkbeck College, 1998; Institute of Physics, 1999; Foreign Associate, National Academy of Sciences, USA, 1998. Address: Mathematical Institute, 24-29 St Giles, Oxford, OX1 3LB, England.

PENZAR Ivan, b. 17 December 1928, Gola, Koprivnica, Croatia. Professor. m. Branka, 2 sons, 1 daughter. Education: BSc, 1951, MSc, 1962, PhD, 1970, Physics of Atmosphere, Faculty of Sciences, University of Zagreb. Appointments: Research Assistant, 1951, Assistant Professor, 1972, Associate Professor, 1984, Full Professor, 1986, Physical Meteorology, Physics of Atmosphere, Dynamics of Atmosphere, Measurements in Meteorology, Basics of Geophysics at Faculty of Sciences, Agroclimatology, University of Zagreb and Osijek, Croatia and University of Mostar, Bosnia and Herzegovina. Publications: 81 scientific papers; 99 other papers; 7 books dealing with solar irradiation, climatology, interaction between the physics of the sea and atmosphere and history of Croatian Meteorology. Honours: The Order of Croatian Danica, with figure of Ruger Boschovich. Memberships: International Solar Energy Society; European Association for Atmosphere Pollution; Croatian Committee for Geodessy and Geophysics; Scientific Council on Energetic, Croatian Academy of Science and Arts. Address: Grskoviceva 9, 10000 Zagreb, Croatia.

PENZIAS Arno Allan, b. 26 April 1933, Munich, Germany (US Citizen). Radio Engineer. m. (1) Anne Barras, 1954, 1 son, 2 daughters, (2) Sherry Chamovelevit, 1996. Education: Bachelor of Physics, City College of New York, 1954; Master's Degree, 1958, Doctorate, 1962, Columbia University, New York. Appointments: Staff Member, Radio Research Department, 1961-72, Head, Technical Research Department, 1972-74, Head, Radiophysics Research Department, 1974-76, Executive Director of Research and Communication Science, Radio Research Laboratories, Bell Telephone Company; Lecturer, Department of Astrophysical Science, Princeton University, 1967-82; Associate, Harvard College Observatory, 1968; Visiting Professor, Princeton University, 1972; Adjunct Professor, State University of New York at Stony Brook, 1975; Trustee, Trenton State College, New Jersey, 1976; First to detect isotropic cosmic microwave background radiation. Honours: Henry Draper Medal, National Academy of Sciences, 1977; Herschel Medal, Royal Astronomical Society, 1978; Joint Winner, Nobel Prize for Physics, 1978; Pender Award, 1992; International Engineering Consortium Fellow Award, 1997; Numerous other prizes and awards. Memberships: National Academy of Engineering; American Astronomical Society; World Academy of Arts and Science; Fellow, AAAS; American Physical Society. Address: AT&T Bell Laboratories, 600 Mountain Avenue, Murray Hill, NJ 07974, USA.

PEPPÉ Rodney Darrell, b. 24 June 1934, Eastbourne, East Sussex, England. Author; Artist. m. Tatjana Tekkel, 16 July 1960, 2 sons. Education: Eastbourne School of Art, 1951-53, 1955-57; London County Council Central School of Art, 1957-59; NDD, Illustration (special subject) and Central School Diploma. Appointments: Art Director, S H Benson Ltd, 1960-64; J Walter Thompson & Co Ltd, 1965-65; Consultant Designer to Ross Foods Ltd, 1965-72; Free-lance Graphic Designer, Illustrator, 1965-98; Children's Author and Illustrator, 1968; Toymaker and Automatist. Publications: The Alphabet Book, 1968; Circus Numbers, 1969; The House That Jack Built, 1970; Hey Riddle Diddle!, 1971; Simple Simon, 1972; Cat and Mouse, 1973; Odd One Out, 1974; Henry series, 1975-78; Rodney Peppé's Moving Toys, 1980; The Mice Who Lived in a Shoe, 1981; Run Rabbit, Run!, 1982; The Kettleship Pirates, 1983; Little Toy Board Book series, 1983; The Mice and the Flying Basket, 1985; The Mice and the Clockwork Bus, 1986; Thumbprint Circus, 1988; Huxley Pig series, 1989-90; The Animal Directory, 1989; The Mice on the Moon, 1992; The Mice and the Travel Machine, 1993; The Magic Toybox, 1996; Gus and Nipper, 1996; Hippo Plays Hide and Seek, 1997; Angelmouse Series, 2000; Automata and Mechanical Toys, 2002; Toys and Models, 2003. Contributions to: Periodicals. Membership: Society of Authors. Address: Stoneleigh House, 6 Stoneleigh Drive, Livermead, Torquay, Devon TQ2 6TR, England.

Dictionary of International Biography

PEPPERCORN David James Creagh, b. 25 August 1931, London, England. Consultant. m. (1) 3 daughters, (2) Serena Sutcliffe. Education: MA, Trinity College, Cambridge. Appointments: International Distillers and Vintners, Director of Morgan Furze, Peter Dominic and Gilbey Loudenne, 1962-74, Wine Consultant, 1974-93; Wine Standards Board, 1987-93; Private Liquor Brands Ltd and French Wine Farmers, 1993-99; Consultant, Ascot Wine Management SA, 2000; Director, AWM Fine Wine Fund Ltd, 2000. Publications: Drinking Wine, with Brian Cooper, 1979; Pocket Guide to Wines of Bordeaux, translations into French, Danish, Swedish, German and Japanese, 1986; Bordeaux, 1991; Guide to Wines of Bordeaux, also German edition, 2002, 2004; Bordeaux Section of Wine Report by Tom Stevenson, 2004. Honours: Master of Wine, 1962; Chairman of Institute of Masters of Wine, 1968-70; Chevalier dans l'Ordre des Arts et des Lettres, 1988; Andre Simon Memorial Prize, 1983; Silver Medal, GAD, 1987. Memberships: Garrick Club; Saintsbury Club; MCC; Vintners Company. Address: 2 Bryanston Place, London, W1H 2DE, England.

PERAK H.H. Sultan of, Sultan Azlan Muhibbuddin Shah ibni Al-Marhum Sultan Yussuf Ghafarullahu-Lahu Shah, b. 19 April 1928, Batu Gajah. Malaysian Ruler. m. Tuanku Bainun Mohamed Ali, 1954, 2 sons, 3 daughters. Education: Malay College; University of Nottingham. Appointments: Called to Bar, Lincoln's Inn; Magistrate, Kuala Lumpur; Assistant State Secretary, Perak; Deputy Public Prosecutor; President, Sessions Court, Seremban and Taiping; State Legal Advisor, Pahang and Johre; Federal Court Judge, 1973; Chief Justice of Malaysia, 1979; Lord President, 1982-83; Raja Kechil Bongsu (6th in line), 1962, Raja Muda (2nd in line), 1983; Sultan of Perak, 1984-; Yang di-Pertuan Agong (Supreme Head of State), 1989-94; Pro-Chancellor, University of Saina Malaysia, 1971, Chancellor, University of Malaya, 1986; Honorary Colonel-in-Chief, Malaysian Armed Forces Engineers Corps; Manager, Malaysian Hockey Team, 1972; President, Malaysian Hockey Federation, Asian Hockey Federation; Vice-President, International Hockey Federation, Olympic Council of Malaysia.

PERES Constanze, b. 9 March 1957, Koblenz, Germany. Professor. m. Wolfgang Holler, 1 son. Education: Baccalaureate, Philosophie, 1977; PhD, Philosophy, 1982; Professor, Dresden, 1994; Research Fellow, Deutsche Forschungsgemeinschaft (DFG). Appointments: Professor of Philosophy, Hochschule für Bildende Künste, Dresden, 1994; Guest Lecturer, Hochschule für Philosophie, S.J., Munich, 1995-. Special fields: Aesthetics, Metaphysics; Epistemology. Publications: Books and numerous papers (in German), contributed to specialist journals, including most recently: Auseinandersetzungen mit Metaphysik, 2000. Schönheit als ontosemantische Konstellation, 2000; Ontosemantische Komplexität ästhetischer Zeichen – Goodmans Symbalisierungstheorie und Baumgartens Ästhetik, In: Sign Processes in Complex Systems – Zeichenprozesse in komplexen Systemen. Proceedings des 7 Internationalen Kongresses für Semiotik der International Association for Semiotic Studies (IASSL), CD-Rom, 2003. Memberships: Allgemeine Gesellschaft für Philosophie Deutschland (AGPhD); Gottfried Wilhelm Leibniz Gesellschaft; Deutsche Gesellschaft für Aesthetik. Address: Hochschule für Bildende Künste, Dresden, D-01288 Dresden, Germany. E-mail: peres@serv1.hfbk-dresden.de

PEŘINOVÁ Vlasta Anna, b. 16 October 1943, Ostravice, Czech Republic. Professor. m. Jan Peřina, 1 son, 1 daughter. Education: Graduate, Faculty of Natural Sciences, 1965, Rerum Naturalium Doctor, Mathematical Analysis, 1967, PhD, Mathematical Analysis, 1981, Associate Professor, 1992, Professor, General Physics and Mathematical Physics, 1995; Palacký University Olomouc, Czech Republic; DSc, General Physics and Mathematical Physics, Charles University, Prague, Czech Republic, 1990. Appointments: Research Worker, Computational Centre, 1966-68, Scientific Worker, Laboratory of Optics, 1968-84, Senior Scientific Worker, Joint Laboratory of Optics of Palacký University and Czechoslovak Academy of Sciences, 1984-90; Leading Scientific Worker, Laboratory of Quantum Optics, 1990-95; Professor, Department of Optics, 1995-, Faculty of Natural Sciences, Palacký University, Olomouc, Czech Republic. Publications: Monograph: Phase in Optics, 1998; Book Chapters in Modern Nonlinear Optics, 1993, Progress in Optics volume 33, 1994, volume 40, 2000, volume 43, 2002; Modern Nonlinear Optics part 1, 2001; Numerous articles in professional scientific journals. Honour: Collective Prize, Ministry of Education, Prague, 1991. Memberships: Union of Czech Mathematicians and Physicists, 1967-; International Society of Optical Engineering - SPIE, 1991. Address: Department of Optics, Faculty of Natural Sciences, Palacký University, Třída Svobody 26, 771 46, Olomouc, Czech Republic. E-mail: perinova@optnw.upol.cz

PERKINS David Rhede, b. 25 April 1955, Pietermaritzburg, South Africa. General Medical Practitioner. m. Margaret Wenda Vere Benstead-Smith, 1 son, 4 daughters. Education: MB, ChB, University of Capetown Medical School, South Africa, 1979; Diploma in Diving and Submarine Medicine, South African Navy Medical Centre, 1981; Diploma, Community Medicine, University of Stellenbosch, South Africa, 1989; Advanced Cardiac Life Support, South African Resuscitation Council, 2000; Advanced Trauma Life Support, South African Trauma Society, 2001; Member College of Family Practitioners (South African Colleges of Medicine), 2001. Appointments include: Intern, 1980, Registrar, 1981-85 (2 year interruption for military conscription), Groote Schur Hospital, Capetown; South African Defence Force, Medical Services then Special Forces Units, 1981-83; Senior Registrar, Groote Schur Hospital, Capetown, 1985-86; Medical Officer, Cape Divisional Council (later Western Cape Regional Services Council), 1986-89; Medical Officer of Health, Stellenbosch and Paarl Health Districts, 1990-93; Special Projects, Western Cape Regional Services Council and associated institutions and NGO's active in the restructuring of South Africa into a democratic state, 1994; Private General Medical Practice in South Africa, 1995-2002; Provincial Chairperson, South African National Tuberculosis Association; Cochrane Collaboration Reviewer (Infectious Diseases Group); Private General Medical Practice, Australia, 2002-; General Practice in Roma, Queensland, 2002-2003; General Practice in Rosalie Shire, Queensland, 2003-. Publications: Articles in scientific journals and presented at conferences as author and co-author include: Vaccine-Induced Remission of Severe Chronic Arthritis, 1998; Twice Weekly vs Daily Chemotherapy for Childhood Tuberculosis, 2000; Research Priorities for Tuberculosis in Developing Countries: including Anthropological Aspects, 2001. Honours include: Pro Patria Medal (Military), 1982; Mayor's Award for Outstanding Community Service, Somerset West, 1993; Nominee, Nelson Mandela Award for Health and Human Rights, 1996, 1997; Cochrane Scholarship, 2000. Memberships include: Royal Australian College of General Practitioners; Fellow, Australian College of Rural and Remote Medicine; Australian Medical Association, Queensland; South African Medical Association. Address: 93 Mocatta Street, Goombungee, Queensland, 4354, Australia. E-mail: dr.david.perkins@bigpond.com.au

PERKINS George Burton, b. 16 August 1930, Lowell, Massachusetts, USA. Professor; Writer. m. Barbara Miller, 9 May 1964, 3 daughters. Education: AB, Tufts College, 1953; MA, Duke University, 1954; PhD, Cornell University, 1960. Appointments: Teaching Assistant, Cornell University, 1957-60; Assistant Professor, Farleigh Dickinson University, 1963-66; Lecturer, American Literature, University of Edinburgh, 1966-67; Professor,

Eastern Michigan University, 1967-2001; General Editor, Journal of Narrative Technique, 1970-92. Publications: Writing Clear Prose, 1964; The Theory of the American Novel, 1970; Realistic American Short Fiction, 1972; American Poetic Theory, 1972; The American Tradition in Literature (with B Perkins), 9th edition, 1988; The Practical Imagination (with Frye and Baker), 1985; Contemporary American Literature (with B Perkins), 1991; Benet's Reader's Encyclopedia of American Literature (with Perkins and Leininger), 1991; Kaleidoscope (with B Perkins), 1993; Women's Work (with Perkins and Warhol), 1994; The Harper Handbook to Literature (with Frye, Baker and Perkins), 1997; A Season in New South Wales, 1998. Contributions to: Professional journals. Honours: Duke University Fellow, 1953-54; Cornell University Fellow, 1954-55; Phi Kappa Phi, 1956; Distinguished Faculty Award, Eastern Michigan University, 1978; Fellow, Institute for Advanced Studies in the Humanities, University of Edinburgh, 1981; Senior Fulbright Scholar, University of Newcastle, Australia, 1989. Memberships: Various professional organisations. Address: 1316 King George Boulevard, Ann Arbor, MI 48108, USA.

PERLMAN Kato Lenard, b. 18 July 1928, Budapest, Hungary. Research Chemist; Senior Scientist. m. David Perlman, deceased. Education: Dipl Chem, Eotvos Lorand University, Budapest, Hungary, 1950; PhD, Organic Chemistry, Eotvos Lorand University, Budapest, Hungary, 1960. Appointments: Research Chemist, Chinoin Pharmaceutical Company, 1950-54; Research Staff Member, Research Institute for Pharmaceutical Industry, Budapest, Hungary, 1954-62; Research Associate, Research Staff Member, Princeton University, New Jersey, USA, 1963-68; Research Associate, McArdle Laboratories, University of Wisconsin, USA, 1968-69; Research Associate, School of Pharmacy, University of Wisconsin, USA, 1969-72; Associate Scientist, School of Pharmacy, University of Wisconsin, USA, 1972-81; Research Associate, Biochemistry Department, University of Wisconsin-Madison, USA, 1981-87; Senior Scientist, Biochemistry Department, University of Wisconsin-Madison, USA, 1987-95; Distinguished Service Emerita, 1995-. Publications: 49 scientific publications; 40 US patents; 6 Hungarian patents. Memberships: American Chemical Society; British Chemical Society. Address: 1 Chippewa Ct, Madison, WI 53711, USA. E-mail: kperlman@facstaff.wisc.edu

PEROT (Henry) Ross, b. 27 June 1930, Texarkana, Texas, USA. Industrialist. m. Margot Birmingham, 1956, 4 children. Education: US Naval Academy. Appointments: US Navy, 1953-57; IBM Corporation, 1957-62; Founder, Electron Data Systems Corporation, 1962, Chair of Board, CEO, 1982-86; Director, Perot Group, Dallas, 1986-; Founder, Perot Systems Corporation, WA, 1988-, Chair, 1988-92, 1992-, Board Member, 1988-; Chair, Board of Visitors, US Naval Academy, 1970-; Candidate for President of USA, 1992, 1996; Founder, Reform Party, 1995. Publications: Not For Sale at Any Price, 1993; Intensive Care, 1995. Address: The Perot Group, PO Box 269014, Plano, TX 75026, USA.

PERRY OF SOUTHWARK Baroness (Pauline Perry), b. 15 October 1931. Life Peer, 1991. m. George Walter Perry, 3 sons, 1 daughter. Education: MA, Girton College, Cambridge. Appointments: Teacher, English secondary school and Canadian and American high schools, 1953-54, 1959-61; High School Evaluator, New England, USA, 1959-61; Research Fellow, University of Manitoba, 1956-57; Lecturer in Philosophy, University of Manitoba, 1957-59; University of Massachusetts, Salem, 1960-62; Part time Lecturer in Education, University of Exeter, 1962-66; Tutor for In-Service Training, Berkshire, 1966-70; Part time Lecturer in Education, Department of Educational Studies, Oxford University, 1966-70; HM Inspector of Schools, 1970-86; Staff Inspector, 1975; Chief Inspector, 1981; Director, South Bank Polytechnic, 1987-92; Vice-Chancellor, S Bank

University, 1992-93; President, Lucy Cavendish College, Cambridge University, 1994-2001; Alexander Stone Lecturer in Rhetoric, Glasgow, 1999. Publications: Case Studies in Teaching, 1969; Case Studies in Adolescence, 1970; Your Guide to the Opposite Sex, 1970; The Womb in Which I Lay, 2003; Contributions to: Advances in Teacher Education, 1989; Women in Education Management, 1992; Public Accountability and Quality Control in Higher Education, 1990; The Future of Higher Education, 1991; Technology: the challenge to education, 1992; What is Quality in Higher Education?, 1993; Education in the Age of Information, 1993; School Inspection, 1995; Women and Higher Education, 1996; Against the Tide: women leaders in American and British higher education, 1996; Higher Education Reform, 2000; Articles in various educational journals; Freelance journalism for radio and TV. Honours: Freeman, City of London, 1992; Liveryman, Bakers' Company, 1992; Honorary FCollP, 1987; Honorary FRSA, 1988; Honorary Fellow, Sunderland Polytechnic, 1990; Honorary LLD: Bath, 1991; Aberdeen, 1994; Honorary DLitt: Sussex, 1992; South Bank, 1994; City, 2000; DUniv, Surrey, 1995; Honorary DEd, Wolverhampton, 1994; Honorary Member, Pedagogical Academy, Swedish Academy of Science, 1992; Honorary Fellow, Girton College, Cambridge, 1994; Honorary Fellow, CGLI, 2000; Honorary Fellow, Lucy Cavendish College, Cambridge, 2001. Memberships: Committee on International Co-operation in Higher Education, British Council, 1987-97; ESRC, 1988-91; Governing Body, Institute of Development Studies, Sussex University, 1987-94; Board, South Bank Centre, 1992-95; NI Higher Education Council, 1992-94; National Advisory Council on Education and Training Targets, 1992-95; Prime Minister's Advisory Panel on Citizen's Charter, 1993-97; Overseas Project Board, 1993-98; House of Lords Select Committee on Science and Technology, 1992-95, 2003-; House of Lords Select Committee on relationships between local and central government, 1995-96; House of Lords Select Committee on Scrutiny of Delegated Powers, 1995-98; Royal Society Project Science Board of Patrons, 1995-2000; Joint Select Committee of Commons and Lords on Human Rights, 2000-03; House of Lords Select Committee on Stem Cell Research, 2001-02; Select Committee on Religious Offences, 2002-03; Chairman: DTI Export Group for Education and Training Sector, 1993-98; Judges Panel on Citizen's Charter, 1997-2003; Inquiry into the Crown Appointments Commission for the Church of England, 1999-2002; Advisor on Police Training to Home Office, 1991-93; Rector's Warden, Southwark Cathedral, 1990-94; MInstD; CIMgt, 1994; Member, Court University of Bath, 1991-99; Trustee, Cambridge University Foundation, 1997-; Pro-Chancellor, University of Surrey, 2001-; Vice President, C&G, 1994-99. Address: House of Lords, London, SW1A 0PW, England.

PERRY Walter Laing Macdonald, (Lord Perry of Walton) b. 16 June 1921, Dundee, Scotland. Physician; Scientist. m. (1) Anne Grant, 1946, 3 sons, (2) Catherine Crawley, 1971, 2 sons, 1 daughter. Education: MB, ChB, 1943, MD, 1948, DSc, 1958, St Andrews University. Appointments: Staff, Medical Research Council, 1947-52; Director, Department of Biological Standards, 1952-58; Professor of Pharmacy, 1958-68, Vice Principal, 1967-68, University of Edinburgh; Founding Vice Chancellor, Open University, 1969-81; Chairman, 1980-96, Pres, 1996- Videotel International. Publications: Open University, 1975; A Short Guide to Distance Education, 1987; Numerous articles in learned journals. Honours: OBE, 1957; Sykes Gold Medal, 1958; Knighted, 1974; FRCP; FRCPE; FRSE; FRS; Welcome Gold Medal, 1995; Fellow, University College, London and Open University; 10 Honorary Doctorates. Memberships: British Pharmaceutical Commission, 1952-68; British Pharmaceutical Society, 1948-; President, Research Defence Society, 1994-; Royal Society of Edinburgh, 2000. Address: 2 Cramond Road South, Edinburgh EH4 6AD, Scotland.

Dictionary of International Biography

PESCI Joe, b. 9 February 1943, USA. Film Actor. Creative Works: Films include: Death Collector, 1976; Raging Bull, 1980; I'm Dancing as Far as I Can, 1982; Easy Money, 1983; Dear Mr Wonderful, 1983; Eureka, 1983; Once Upon a Time in America, 1984; Tutti Dentro, 1984; Man On Fire, 1987; Moonwalker, 1988; Backtrack, 1988; Lethal Weapon II, 1989; Betsy's Wedding, 1990; Goodfellas, 1999; Home Alone, 1990; The Super, 1991; JFK, 1991; Lethal Weapon III, 1992; Home Alone II, 1992; The Public Eye, 1992; My Cousin Vinny, 1992; A Bronx Tale, 1993; With Honours, 1994; Jimmy Hollywood, 1994; Casino, 1995; 8 Heads in a Duffel Bag, 1997; Gone Fishing, 1997; Lethal Weapon 4, 1998. Honours include: Academy Award, Best Supporting Actor, 1991.

PESEK Jiri R V, b. 19 April 1936, Prague, Czech Republic. Geologist. m. Jarmila Dobiasova, 2 daughters. Education: Graduate, Faculty of Science, Charles University, 1959; Postgraduate Study, 1962-66; PhD, 1967. Appointments: Institute of Geology Exploration, 1959-60; Assistant Professor, 1967-88, Associate Professor, 1988-91, Professor of Economic Geology, 1991-, Faculty of Science, Charles University. Publications: 16 books and textbooks, about 280 papers in professional journals. Honours: Gold Medal, Faculty of Science; Commemorative Medal, Charles University. Memberships include: Czech Geological Society, Sub-Commission on Carboniferous Stratigraphy. Address: Charles University, Faculty of Science, 12843 Prague 2, Albertov 6, Czech Republic.

PETERLE Alojz, b. 5 July 1948, Cuznja, Slovenia. Politician; Economist. m. Branka, 1 son, 2 daughters. Education: Graduate, History and Geography, University of Ljubljana, Slovenia; 2 years study Economics, Faculty of Economics, Ljubljana, Slovenia. Appointments: Member of Parliament, National Assembly, 1990, 1992, 1996, 2000; Prime Minister, first democratically elected Slovene Government, 1990-92; Deputy Prime Minister and Minister of Foreign Affairs, 1993; Chairman, Parliamentary Commission for European Affairs, 1996; Re-elected Minister of Foreign Affairs, 2000; President, Christian Democrats of Slovenia, 1990-2000; Vice-President, European Union of Christian Democrats, 1996-99; Chairman, European State Legislative Leaders Foundation, 2000; Elected Representative of the National Assembly to the European Convention, 2002-; Member of Presidency of the National Assembly to the European Convention, 2002-; Currently: Chairman, Committee for European Affairs; Member of Slovenian Delegation to the Joint Parliamentary Committee of the EU; Member Committee on Foreign Policy; member Constitutional Commission; Chairman of Council of the Nova Slovenja Party, 2001-. Address: The National Assembly of the Republic of Slovenia, Subiceva 4, 1000 Ljubljana, Slovenia.

PETERS Catherine Lisette, b. 30 September 1930, London, England. Lecturer; Writer. m. (1) John Glyn Barton, 14 January 1952, 3 sons, (2) Anthony Storr, 9 October 1970. Education: BA, 1st Class Honours, 1980, MA, 1984, University of Oxford. Appointments: Editor, Jonathan Cape, 1960-74; Lecturer in English, Somerville College, Oxford, 1981-92. Publications: Thackeray's Universe, 1987; The King of Inventors: A Life of Wilkie Collins, 1991; Charles Dickens, 1998; Byron, 2000. Contributions to: Books and journals. Memberships: Wilkie Collins Society; Society of Authors; Royal Society of Literature, fellow; International PEN. Address: 45 Chalfont Road, Oxford OX2 6TJ, England.

PETERS Evelyn Joan Jones, b. 25 March 1927, Anchorage, Alaska, USA. Professional Artist. m. Frederick W Peters, deceased, 1 son, 1 daughter. Education: Diploma (Honours), Eugene High School, 1945; University of Oregon, Eugene, 1945-50; Oregon State College, Corvallis, Oregon, 1955-56. Appointments:

Technical Secretary, Los Alamos National Laboratory, Los Alamos, 1958-70; Senior Secretary, EG&G, Los Alamos, 1970-71; Professional Artist, 1974-; Official Coast Guard Artist, 1988-; Retired Executive Director, NWNM Arts Council, Farmington, New Mexico, 1998-2003. Civic Activities: Hill Country Arts Foundation, 1984-90; Highland Lakes Arts Council, Marble Falls, Texas, 1986; NWNM Arts Council, Farmington, 1997-. Publications: 39 paintings in reproduction including 8 in limited editions: Forever Yesterday, 1982; Granbury Station, 1983; Flying Home, 1992; Journey to Yesterday, 1985; Lily's Place, 1984; Prairie Peddler, 1988; Thistle Hill, 1988; The Welcome Light, 1988. Honours: Purchase Awards: Granbury Station, 1983, Welcome Light, 1988; USCG Geo Gray Award for painting, Polar Lights, 1993; Gold Cup (1st place) ABI International Competition, 1993; Top 200 Arts for the Parks, 2000; Woman of the Year, 1991, 1992, 1995; Recipient, International Peace Prize, United Cultural Convention, USA, 2003. Membership: National Acrylic Painters Association (US and UK). Commissions and Creative Works: USCG: Captain of her Destiny (Cdr Beverly Kelley USCG), 1997; To Fly with the Eagles, 1994; Flying Home, Alaska Aviation Heritage Museum, Anchorage, 1992; A Special Evening, Church of Christ Scientist, the Mother Church, Boston, Massachusetts, 1992; Also many private commissions. Address: Painter of Western Americana, 1646 16th Avenue SE, Rio Rancho, NM 87124, USA

PETERS Lenrie, b. 1 September 1932, Bathurst, Gambia. Physician; Poet; Writer. Education: BA, Trinity College, Cambridge, 1956; University College Hospital, London. Appointments: Surgeon, Victoria Hospital, Gambia, 1969-72; Surgeon in private practice, Gambia, 1972-; Chairman, West African Examinations Council, 1988-90. Publications: Poems, 1964; Satellites, 1967; Katchikali, 1971; Selected Poetry, 1981. Novel: The Second Round, 1965. Contributions to: Many anthologies. Address: Westfield Clinic, PO Box 142, Banjul, Gambia.

PETERS Mercedes, b. New York City, USA. Education: MS, 1953; PhD, 1989. Appointments: Faculty Postgraduate Center For Mental Health, Object Relations Institute; Supervisor, Faculty Director, Education Consultant, Jewish Board of Family and Children's Services Psychotherapy; Staff, SR, Community Service Society, 1975-; Private Practice of Psychoanalysis. Publications: Depression Among Blacks, Analytic Neutrality; The Black Persona, Culture As Object. Memberships: National Association for The Advancement of Psychoanalysis; Chair, UN Committee of WOPECNAAP; Member, Postgraduate Psychoty Society. Address: 142 Joralemon Street, Brooklyn, NY 11201-4709, USA.

PETERSEN Poul Henning, b. 3 March 1939, Snostrup, Denmark. Reader Animal Science and Animal Health. m. Pernille Bock. Education: BSc, Agriculture, 1967, PhD, Agriculture, 1972, Junior Research Fellow, 1968-70, Senior Research Fellow, 1976-79, The Royal Veterinary and Agricultural University (KVL), Frederiksberg, Denmark; Post Doctoral Studies, Ohio State University, USA, 1974-75; Practical Agriculture, Denmark, Iceland, France, Israel. Appointments: Assistant Professor, 1970-72, Associate Professor, 1972-79, Docent (Reader), 1989-, Head of Department of Animal Science and Animal Health, 1979-87, 1990-92, The Royal Veterinary and Agricultural University, Denmark. Publications: Articles in refereed journals as co-author include: Estimation of genetic and phenotypic parameters for clinical mastitis, somatic cell production deviance and protein yield in dairy cattle using Gibbs sampling, 1998; Pheotypic characterisation of three strains on indigenous goats in Tanzania, 2000; Genetic parameters for average daily yield, area of M Longissimus Dorsi, feed efficiency and feed intake capacity in young bulls of dairy populations, 2000; Genetic correlations between beef traits measured on young performance test bulls and their daughters yield, 2000; Simulations on cooperative breeding between Nordic red dairy cattle populations with diverse objectives, 2002. Memberships: Programme Committee, Research Programme, Genetics, breeding and reproduction, Danish Ministry of Agriculture, 1992-97; Board, Danish Institute of Animal Science, 1990-97; Cattle Research Committee, Danish Institute of Animal Science, 1991-2001; Chairman, 1999-,Committee for Planning Postgraduate Courses in Animal Breeding, Nordic Association of Agricultural Researchers. Address: Department of Animal Science and Animal Health, The Royal Veterinary and Agricultural University (KVL), Grønnegårdsweg 3, DK-1870 Frederiksberg C, Denmark. E-mail: php@kvl.dk

PETERSON Richard Byron, b. 10 May 1933, Sioux City, Iowa, USA. University Professor. m. Barbara B Peterson, 1 son, 1 daughter. Education: BA, Augustana College, Illinois, 1955; MA, University of Illinois, 1957; PhD, University of Wisconsin, 1966. Appointments: Ekco-Alcoa Containers Inc Personal Assistant, 1959-63; Assistant Professor, 1966-71; Associate Professor, 1971-78, Professor, 1978-, School of Business, University of Washington, Seattle, Washington 98195-3200, USA. Publications: Books include: The Modern Grievance Procedure in the United States, 1988; Managers and National Culture: A Global Perspective (editor), 1993; Advances in International Comparative Management (co-editor), 1998, 2000; Numerous research publications and articles and papers. Honours include: Phi Kappa Phi; Chair, International Management Division of Academy of Management, 1986-87; Distinguished Visiting Professor, Australian Graduate School of Management, University of New South Wales, 1988; Editorial Board, Journal of International Business Studies, 1987-88, 1989-90, 1991-92, 1993-94, 1995-96, 1997-98, 1999-2000. Memberships: Academy of Management; Industrial Relations Research Association (IRRA); Academy of International Business; International Industrial Relations Association. Address: 4737-49th NE, Seattle, WA 98105, USA.

PETOUKHOV Vladimir Kirillovich, b. 27 July 1946, Kischinjow, Moldovia. Geophysicist. m. Tatiana Petoukhova, 1 son, 1 daughter. Education: Master of Science, Moscow State University, Moscow, Russia, 1971; Doctor, Institute of Atmospheric Physics, Moscow, Russia, 1975. Appointments: Lead Scientist, Institute of Atmospheric Physics, Moscow, Russia, 1990; Professor, Hydrometeorological Institute, Leningrad, Russia, 1991; Visiting Professor, International Institute for Applied System Analysis, Laxenburg, Austria, 1992-94; Visiting Professor, 1995-2002, Project Leader, 2003-, Potsdam Institute for Climate Research, Potsdam, Germany, 1990. Publications: Statistical-Dynamical Modelling of the Large-Scale Climate Processes, 1991; Simulation of Modern and Glacial Climates with a Coupled Global Model of Intermediate Complexity, 1998; Climate System Model of Intermediate Complexity Part I: Model Description and Performance for Present Climate, 2000. Honours: Great Minds of the 21st Century, American Biographical Institute; The Contemporary Who's Who, 2002/2003. Membership: EGS. Address: Bisamkiez 22, Potsdam 14478, Germany. E-mail: petukhov@pik-potsdam.de

PETRAKIS Emmanuel, b. 24 December 1934, Alexandria, Egypt. Educationalist; Social Psychologist. Education: Diploma in Journalism, The Regent Institute, London, 1952; Higher Institute of Social Studies, Alexandria, Egypt, 1953-54; English Proficiency Diploma, Cambridge University, 1961; TEFL Diploma, International Teacher Training Institute, London, 1965; Diploma in Psychology, London College of Applied Sciences, 1968; Institute of Advanced Study in Rational Psychotherapy, 1968-74; Doctorate in Social Sciences, International Open University for Complementary Medicines, Colombo, Sri Lanka, 1993; various

other courses, seminars and training workshops. Appointments: Chief Editor, The Middle East Observer, 2 years; Instructor in Educational Psychology for teachers by the Cameroonian Ministry of Education; Freelance editor and contributor to numerous publications; Psychological Consultant to national and multinational companies; Founder and Executive Director of Vie Nouvelle, French Alps (residential seminar centre), 1970-72; Founder and Executive Director, International Institute of Social Sciences, Athens, Greece; Psychological Counsellor and Psychotherapist in clinical practice, France, 1975-80; Workshop Leader; English Teacher and TEFL Specialist, in Egypt, UK, Australia, Cameroon, India, Thailand and Greece, 35 years. Publications: 12 books: Poetry of Our Times; The Dance of Life; Bible Prophecies, World Events and the Coming Civilisation, etc; plus many articles. Honours: Diplome d'Honneur; Académie des Poètes de Paris; Delegate for Greece of Universal Alliance (UK) and World University (USA); New consciousness promoter for a fraternal world community. Address: c/o Mrs Mary Fantoudis, Le Fructidor No 6, 1 rue Andre Chenier, 13090 Aix-en-Provence, France.

PETRIC Nedjeljka, b. 15 May 1928, Visiting Full Professor. m. Bartul Petric, 2 sons. Education: Education: Graduate, Technical Faculty, University of Zagreb, 1954; PhD, Chemical Science, University of Zagreb, 1972. Appointments: Dean, Faculty of Chemical Technology, 1983-87. Publications: 56 scientific articles in fields of chemical engineering and religion and science. Honours: Order of Danica Hrvatska with the figure of R Boskovic for distinguished services in science, from President of the Republic of Croatia; Listed in numerous biographical publications. Memberships: New York Academy of Sciences. Address: Faculty of Chemical Technology, Teslina 10/V, 21000 Split, Croatia.

PETROV Valery Danilovich, b. 13 February 1946, Moscow, Russia. Consultant; Educator; Researcher. Education: Honoured Diploma in Physics of Semiconductors, Moscow Technical University, Moscow Power Institute, 1970. Appointments: Engineer, Chief Engineer, Scientist, Chief Scientist, Head of Laboratory, Moscow, 1971-89; Consultant, Educator, Germany, 1992-. Made contributions to several scientific fields: Physics, Photochemistry, Volumic Imaging, Human Vision; Lectures on computer- and laser-based systems of volumic and quasi-volumic imaging; Proposed a novel concept and mechanism of volumic human and animal vision, in 1995; Postulated the conceptual notion of volumic view as a basis of volumic data acquisition, 1995; Invented momental holography, 1976-78, the technique was used in space, resulting in the first ever holograms and interferograms made in microgravity conditions, 1981-83; Obtained first holograms outdoors and recorded first holograms in violet part of visible spectrum; Inventor, several devices for non-destructive testing and measurement of deformations and vibrations, 1996-99; Several compact devices for industrial applications and physical research, including those capable of working outdoors in brightly lit natural environments, 1999-2002; Novel bathless techniques for ultra-high resolution silver-halide media, 1996-97; Introduced instantaneous spray-jet holography and holographic interferometry, 1990-2002; Invented dynamic – sliding holographic method permitting to process tremendous amounts of data – over 100 GB per second, 2001-03; Proposed holographic minirobot for investigations of Mars, 2003. Publications: Over 100 research papers published in refereed journals and conference proceedings; Over 60 communications at international scientific conferences. Honours: Several Diplomas and Medals from IBC and from Marquis Who's Who in the World; Best Paper Award, from Toyota, 1999; Listed in numerous biographical publications. Membership: FIBA. Address: Postfach 3350, D-89023, Ulm, Germany.

Dictionary of International Biography

PETTIFER Julian, b. 21 July 1935, Malmesbury, England. Freelance Writer; Broadcaster. Education: St John's College, Cambridge, 1955-58. Appointments: TV Reporter, Writer, Presenter: Southern TV, 1958-62; Tonight, 1962-64, 24 Hours, 1964-69, Panorama, 1969-75, BBC; Presenter, Cuba - 25 Years of Revolution, series, 1984, Host, Busman's Holiday, 1985-86, ITV; Numerous TV documentaries including: Vietnam War Without End, 1970; The World About Us, 1976; The Spirit of 76, 1976; Diamonds in the Sky, 1979; Nature Watch, 5 series, 1981-90; Automania, 1984; The Living Isles, 1986; Africawatch, 1989; Missionaries, 1990; BBC Assignment, 1993-94; BBC Correspondent, 1994-95; Crossing Continents 2000-. Publications: Diamonds in the Sky: A Social History of Air Travel (co-author), 1979; Nature Watch, 1981; Automania, 1984; The Nature Watchers, 1985; Missionaries, 1990; Nature Watch, 1994. Honour: Reporter of the Year Award, Guild of Television Directors and Producers, 1968. Memberships: Royal Society for Nature Conservation, vice-president, 1992-; Royal Society for the Protection of Birds, president, 1994-2000. Address: c/o Curtis Brown, 28/29 Haymarket, London SW1Y 4SP, England.

PETTOROSSI Alberto, b. 21 October 1947, Portorecanati, Italy. University Teacher. Education: Degree, Electronic Engineering, Rome University, Italy, 1971; Master in Computer Science, Syracuse University, New York, USA, 1978; PhD, Computer Science, Edinburgh University, Scotland, 1984. Appointments: Research Assistant, Rome University, 1971-75; Italian Air Force, 1972-73; Research Worker, Italian National Research Council, 1975-88; Associate Professor, Theoretical Computer Science, Rome University, 1988-. Publications: Over 110 articles in professional journals or conferences. Honour: Prize, Polish Mathematical Society, 1988. Membership: ACM. Address: University of Roma Tor Vergata, c/o IASI-CNR, Viale Manzoni 30, I-00185 Roma, Italy.

PETTY William Henry, b. 7 September 1921, Bradford, Yorkshire, England. Retired Educator; Poet. m. Margaret Elaine Bastow, 31 May 1948, 1 son, 2 daughters. Education: Peterhouse, Cambridge, 1940-41, 1945; MA, Cantab, 1950; BSc, London, 1953; D Litt, Kent, 1983. Appointments: Administrative, Teaching, and Lecturing posts, London, Doncaster, North and West Ridings of Yorkshire, Kent, 1945-73; Chief Education Officer, Kent, 1973-84; Chairman of Governors, Christ Church University College, Canterbury, 1992-94. Publications: No Bold Comfort, 1957; Conquest, 1967; Springfield: Pieces of the Past, 1994; Genius Loci (with Robert Roberts), 1995; The Louvre Imperial, 1997; Interpretations of History, 2000; No-One Listening, 2002. Contributions to: Various anthologies, 1954-2004, reviews, quarterlies, and journals. Honours: Cheltenham Festival of Literature Prize, 1968; Camden Festival of Music and the Arts Prize, 1969; Greenwood Prize, Poetry Society, 1978; Lake Aske Memorial Award, 1980; Commander of the Order of the British Empire, 1981; Swanage Festival of Literature Prize, 1995; Ali Competition Prize, 1995; Kent Federation of Writers Prize, 1995; White Cliffs Prize, 2000; Otaker/Faber Competition, 2003; Envoi Competition, 2004. Membership: Poetry Society; English Association. Address: Willow Bank, Moat Road, Headcorn, Kent TN27 9NT, England.

PETUKHOV Michail Alexeyevich, b. 12 January 1935, Krasnoyarsk Region, Russia. Mechanical Engineer. m. Alexandrovna Lubov, 1 son. Education: Doctor of Pedagogical Sciences; Professor of the Chair of Pedagogical Sciences. Appointments: Sub-Unit Leader, Military College; Assistant Commanding Officer, Chief of Military College Chair, Military Academy; Chief of Chair of Institute of Advanced Teaching Studies; Assistant Director of Scientific Methodical Centre; Chief of Pedagogy Chair, Ulyanovsk State Pedagogical University.

Publications: Over 60 publications include: Scientific foundations of professional-technological system of special subject teaching (monograph), 2000; Professional-technological system of special subject teaching (manual), 2001; Foundations of professional pedagogical activity (manual) 2002; Axiological foundations of competent approach to professional formation of pedagogical university graduate (article), 2002. Honours: 15 Honorary Diplomas; 8 Medals; 1 Order for Services to Motherland in Armed Forces. Address: Fl 19, Lenin St 57/24, 432063 Ulyanovsk, Russia. E-mail: u1gpu@mv.ru

PEYTON Kathleen Wendy, (Kathleen Herald, K M Peyton), b. 2 August 1929, Birmingham, England. Writer. m. Michael Peyton, 1950, 2 daughters. Education: ATD, Manchester School of Art. Publications: As Kathleen Herald: Sabre, the Horse from the Sea, 1947; The Mandrake, 1949; Crab the Roan, 1953. As K M Peyton: North to Adventure, 1959; Stormcock Meets Trouble, 1961; The Hard Way Home, 1962; Windfall, 1963; Brownsea Silver, 1964; The Maplin Bird, 1964; The Plan for Birdsmarsh, 1965; Thunder in the Sky, 1966; Flambards Trilogy, 1969-71; The Beethoven Medal, 1971; The Pattern of Roses, 1972; Pennington's Heir, 1973; The Team, 1975; The Right-Hand Man, 1977; Prove Yourself a Hero, 1977; A Midsummer Night's Death, 1978; Marion's Angels, 1979; Flambards Divided, 1981; Dear Fred, 1981; Going Home, 1983; The Last Ditch, 1984; Froggett's Revenge, 1985; The Sound of Distant Cheering, 1986; Downhill All the Way, 1988; Darkling, 1989; Skylark, 1989; No Roses Round the Door, 1990; Poor Badger, 1991; Late to Smile, 1992; The Boy Who Wasn't There, 1992; The Wild Boy and Queen Moon, 1993; Snowfall, 1994; The Swallow Tale, 1995; Swallow Summer, 1995; Unquiet Spirits, 1997; Firehead, 1998; Swallow the Star, 1998; Blind Beauty, 1999; Small Gains, 2003. Honours: New York Herald Tribune Award, 1965; Carnegie Medal, 1969; Guardian Award, 1970. Address: Rookery Cottage, North Fambridge, Chelmsford, Essex CM3 6LP, England.

PFEIFFER Michelle, b. 29 April 1957, Santa Ana, California, USA. Actress. m. (1) Peter Horton, divorced 1987, 1 adopted daughter, (2) David E Kelly, 1993, 1 son. Career: Films include: Grease 2; The Witches of Eastwick; Scarface; Married to the Mob; The Fabulous Baker Boys; Tequila Sunrise; Dangerous Liaisons, 1989; Frankie and Johnnie, 1990; Batman Returns, 1992; The Age of Innocence, 1993; Wolf, 1994; Dangerous Minds, 1997; Up Close and Personal, 1997; To Gillian on Her 37th Birthday, 1997; One Fine Day, 1997; A Thousand Acres, 1997; Privacy, 1997; The Story of US, 1999; The Deep End of the Ocean, 1999; A Midsummer Night's Dream, 1999; Being John Malkovitch, 1999; What Lies Beneath, 2000; I am Sam, 2001; White Oleander, 2002; Sinbad: Legend of the Seven Seas (voice), 2003; TV includes: Delta House; Splendour in the Grass. Address: c/o ICM, 8942 Wilshire Boulevard, Beverly Hills, CA 90211, USA.

PHAM Hoang V, b. 6 January 1934, Vietnam (refugee to USA, 1975). Medical Doctor. m. Hong Ngoc Thai, 4 sons. Education: Graduate, Saibon Medical School, 1962; Military Service, 1962-68; Director, Rehabilitation Centre, South Vietnam, 1968-75; Fellowship, New York University, 1972; Retrained in USA. Appointments: Acupuncturist, established own practice in California, 1978. Honours: Acupuncturist of the Year, 1995, 1997, 1999, 2001; Listed in international biographical dictionaries. Memberships: Founding Member, American Academy of Medical Acupuncture; ICMA; CMA. Address: 9600 Bolsa Avenue, Suite F, Westminster, CA 92683, USA.

PHAM Randal Tanh Hoang, b. 24 November 1960, Saigon, Vietnam. Surgeon. Education: Bachelor Degree, Arts and Sciences, 1983; Master in Health and Medical Sciences, 1986, Doctor of Medicine, 1988, University of California Berkeley and University of California San Francisco, USA. Appointment: Clinical Assistant Professor, Department of Ophthalmology, Division of Plastic and Reconstructive Surgery, Stanford University, California, USA. Publication: Treatment of vascular lesions with combined dynamic precooling, postcooling, thermal quenching and ND: yag 1,064 nm laser, 2001. Honours: Best Clinical Science Award, American Society for Laser Medicine and Surgery, 2001; Best Abstract Presentation, International Society for Cosmetic Laser Surgeons, 2002. Membership: Fellow, American College of Surgeons. Address: Aesthetic & Refractive Surgery Medical Center, 455 O'Connor Drive, Ste 190, San Jose, CA 95128, USA. Website: www.lasernews.com

PHAN Giuong Van, b. 2 February 1943, Le Thuy, Vietnam. Linguist; Educator. m. Dung Kim Pham, 4 children. Education: BA, University of Saigon, Vietnam, 1971; M Ed, University of Sydney, Australia, 1985; PhD, Linguistics; DipEd (Vietnam); Dip TEFL, Sydney University, Australia. Appointments: Vietnamese and English Teacher in High Schools, 1964-67; Cabinet Officer, Ministry of Education, Vietnam, 1969-72, 1974-75; Lecturer in English, English Language Centre, Vietnam, 1974-75; Lecturer, English, Polytechnic Institute, Vietnam, 1979-80; Part-time English Teacher for adult migrants, NSW-AMES, Australia, 1981-84; Lecturer, Vietnamese, Department of Humanities, 1985-92, Senior Lecturer, Vietnamese, 1992-95, Associate Professor, 1995-, Department of Asian Studies and Languages, Victoria University of Technology, Australia; General Co-ordinator, Vietnamese Language Faculty, Victoria School of Languages, 1987-; Numerous visiting lectureships in Vietnam, China, USA, 1991-; Editor-in-Chief, Viet Literature Magazine, Australia, 1998-; Chair, Setting and Marking for International Baccalaureate, Vietnamese, 2002-; Director, Vietnamese Heritage Project, 2002-. Publications: 22 books include: Vietnamese for Beginners, 1991; Vietnamese Phrase book, 2002; Vietnamese English Dictionary, 2002; 5 book chapters; More than 50 articles to Vietnamese newspapers and magazines in Vietnam, Australia, Canada, USA; Numerous papers presented at national and international conferences. Honours: Medal for educational and cultural services, Minister of Education of Vietnam, 1974; Victorian Achiever of the Year Award, Australia Day Committee, Victoria, 1991; Order of Australia Medal, 2000. Memberships: Australian Journalists' Association; International PEN, Melbourne Centre; Fellowship of Australian Writers; Linguistics Society of Australia; Modern Language Teachers' Association; Return Services League, Australia; Vietnamese Teachers' Association of Victoria; The Order of Australia Association, Australia. Address: Victoria University, Faculty of Arts, PO Box 14428 MCMC, Melbourne 8001 VIC, Australia. E-mail: giuong.phan@vu.edu.au

PHELAN Tom (Thomas J.), b. 5 November 1940, Mountmellick, County Laois, Ireland. Novelist. m. Patricia Mansfield, 14 September 1991, 2 sons. Education: BA, Philosophy, St Patrick's Seminary, Carlow, 1965; Master Degree, Seattle University, 1977. Appointments: Priest; Assistant Professor of English, Harriman College, New York; Insurance Arbitrator; Carpenter. Publications: In the Season of the Daisies, 1993; Iscariot, 1995; Saying Goodbye (short story), 1995; In the Vatican Museum (short story), 1998; Derrycloney (novel), 1999; My Life as a Priest (essay), 2004; The Clothing of the King, forthcoming. Honour: Selected for Discover Great New Writers, series sponsored by Barnes & Noble. Memberships: Authors Guild; Irish Writers Union; Poets and Writers. Address: Long Island, NY, USA. Website: http://members.aol.com/glanvil2

PHILLIPS Barnet IV, b. 5 July 1948, USA. Attorney. m. Sharon W Phillips, 2 daughters. Education: BA, Yale University, USA, 1970; JD, Fordham University, USA, 1973; LLM, New York University, 1977. Appointments: Hughes Hubbard & Reed, New

York, New York, USA; Currently, Partner, Skadden, Arps, Slate, Meagher & Flom LLP, New York, New York, USA. Publications: Co-author, Structuring Corporate Acquisitions – Tax Aspects, BNA, 2nd edition, 1997; Associate Editor, Fordham Law Review, Fordham University; Graduate Editor, Tax Law Review, New York University. Membership: American Bar Association. Address: 6 Hycliff Road, Greenwich, CT 06831, USA. E-mail: bphillip@skadden.com

PHILLIPS Daniel Anthony, b. 24 February 1938, Boston, Massachusetts, USA. Private Trustee. m. Diana Walcott Phillips, 1 son, 1 daughter. Education: AB Cum Laude, Harvard College, 1960; MBA, Harvard Business School, 1963. Appointments: Assistant to President, 1963-69, Vice-President, 1970-92, President, Chief Executive Officer, Director, 1992-2002; Former Chairman, President and Director, 2002-2003; Past Chair, Board of Directors, 1994-96, Director, 1991-, Alliance for Children and Families; President, 1988-98, Treasurer, 2002-, American Memorial Hospital, Rheims, France; Trustee and Member of Finance Committee, Cambridge Homes; Board of Directors, 1996-, Chair, 1997-98, Secretary Treasurer, Ways to Work, 1999-, Families International Inc; Past President, 1986-89, Honorary Trustee, Family Service of Greater Boston; Trustee, French Library and Cultural Center, 2003-; Treasurer and Director, Grime-King Foundation for the Elderly, Inc; Member, Corporate Advisory Board, Jobs for the Future; Governor and Trustee, Co-Chair of Capital Campaign, New Bedford Oceanarium; Corporator, George H and Irene L Walker Home for Children, Inc; Vice-President and Treasurer, Frederick E Weber Charities Corporation; Vice-Chair and Director, member, Executive Committee, Chair, Community Investments Committee, Chair, Foundations, Member, Leadership Council for Children and Youth, United Way of Massachusetts Bay. Honours: Recipient, HHA Award, Harvard Alumni Association, 1995; Grand Medal of Reims, 1998; Regional Champagne-Ardenne Medal, 1998; Chevalier, Legion of Honour, 2002. Memberships: Member, Advisory Board of the Corporate Resource Committee, The Boston Club; Past President and Treasurer, Charles Square Condominium Association; Member, Advisory Board, CEO's for Fundamental Change in Education; Elected Director, 1986-89, Vice-President, 1989093, Member, Executive Committee, 1989-93, 1996-2002, First Vice-President, 1996-97, President, 1997-98, Harvard Alumni Association; Secretary, Harvard College Class of 1960; Treasurer and Member of Executive Committee, Association of Harvard College Secretaries and Treasurers; Treasurer and Director, Land a Hand Society; Member, Garden Under Glass Council, Massachusetts Horticultural Society; Member Executive Corporate Council, YWCA Boston. Address: Fiduciary Trust Company, 175, Federal Street, Boston, MA 02110, USA.

PHILLIPS Edward John, b. 17 July 1937, Bristol, Pennsylvania, USA. Computer Scientist; Writer. Education: BA, Maths, Temple University, 1963; Stockbrokers licence, Texas, USA, 1992. Appointments: Planetary Research Programmer, Jet Propulsion Laboratory, Pasadena, California, 1969-78; Brain Research Programmer, University of California Medical School, Los Angeles, 1979-80; Science Systems Engineer, Elect Data Systems, Riverside, California and Dallas, Texas, 1980-85; Senior Systems Analyst, US Navy Corona, California, 1986-89; Computer Scientist, Riverside, California, 1989-92; Dallas, Texas, 1992-93; Levittown, Pennsylvania, 1993-. Publications: The Computer and Statistics; The Prediction of Failure in Automobile Components and Systems; Sam Grey in the Heartland; Timeless Mystery; The Song Beyond Memory. Honour: Man of the Year, American Biographical Institute, 2000; Leonardo da Vinci, Vitruvian Man, 2000; 20th Century Achievement Award. Memberships: Academy of American Poets; Broadcast Music Inc, London Diplomatic

Academy, 1994-; Mathematical Association of America. Address: 80 Indian Red Road, Levittown, PA 19057, USA. E-mail: edwardphillips@londondiplomatic.com

PHILLIPS Edward O, b. 26 November 1931, Montreal, Quebec, Canada. Teacher; Writer. Education: BA, McGill University, 1953; LL.L, University of Montreal, 1956; AMT, Harvard University, 1957; MA, Boston University, 1962. Publications: Sunday's Child, 1981; Where There's a Will, 1984; Buried on Sunday, 1986; Hope Springs Eternal, 1988; Sunday Best, 1990; The Landlady's Niece, 1992; The Mice Will Play, 1996; Working on Sunday, 1998; No Early Birds, 2001; A Voyage on Sunday, 2004. Contributions to: Short stories to various Canadian journals. Honour: Arthur Ellis Award, 1986. Memberships: Canadian Writers Union; PEN. Address: 1455 Sherbrooke St W, # 1502, Montreal, QC, H3G 1L2, Canada.

PHILLIPS Fred (Sir), b. 14 May 1918, St Vincent. Queen's Counsel. m. Gloria, 3 sons, 2 daughters. Education: Barrister, Middle Temple, 1956; LL.B, London, 1957; MCL (Master of Civil Law), McGill University, 1968; LLD, Hon, University of the West Indies, 1989. Appointments: Cabinet Secretary, Federal Government of the West Indies, 1960-62; Administrator, St Kitts, Nevis, Anguilla, 1966-67; Governor, St Kitts, Nevis, Anguilla, 1967-69; Chief Legal Adviser in the Caribbean for Cable and Wireless, 1969-97. Publications: Freedom in the Caribbean: A Study in Constitutional Change, 1977; The Evolving Legal Profession in the Commonwealth, 1978; West Indian Constitutions: Post Independence Reforms, 1985; Caribbean Life and Culture: A Citizen Reflects, 1991; Numerous papers in journals. Honours: Commander of the Royal Victorian Order, (CVO); Knight Bachelor, 1967. Address: PO Box 3298, St John's, Antigua. E-mail: fredp@candes.ag

PHILLIPS Richard England, b. 13 December 1950, Los Angeles, California, USA. University Professor. m. Alicia Luna Phillips, 1 son, 1 daughter. Education: BA, magna cum laude, Spanish, University of California, Irvine, 1973; MA, Spanish, University of California, Santa Barbara, 1975; PhD, Art History, University of Texas, Austin, 1993. Appointments: Assistant Instructor, University of Texas, Austin, 1989-91; Professor of Art History, Savannah College of Art & Design, 1992-93; Department of Human Services, State of Texas, Austin, 1993-95; Assistant Professor of Art History, Virginia Commonwealth University, Richmond, 1995-2000. Assistant Professor of Art History, University of Texas-Pan American, Edinburg, Texas, 2000-. Publications: Several articles in professional journals. Honours: Samuel H Kress Dissertation Travel Grant; VCU Research Grant. Memberships: Association for Latin American Art; Society of Architectural Historians; College Art Association. Address: Art Department, The University of Texas-Pan American, 1201 W University Drive, Edinburg, TX 78541, USA.

PHILP Peter, b. 10 November 1920, Cardiff, Wales. Writer. m. 25 September 1940, 2 sons. Publications: Beyond Tomorrow, 1947; The Castle of Deception, 1952; Love and Lunacy, 1955; Antiques Today, 1960; Antique Furniture for the Smaller Home, 1962; Furniture of the World, 1974; The Real Sir John (play), 1995. Contributions to: Times; Antique Dealer and Collectors Guide; Antique Collecting; Antique Furniture Expert (with Gillian Walkling), 1991; Antiques Trade Gazette, 1992-. Honours: Arts Council Award, 1951; C H Foyle Award, 1951. Membership: Society of Authors. Address: 77 Kimberley Road, Cardiff CF23 5DP, Wales.

PIASECKI Krzysztof Maciej, b. 15 October 1952, Poznan, Poland. Lecturer; Researcher. m. Małgorzata, 1 son, 1 daughter. Education: MSc, 1976, Dr Math., 1981, University Adam

Mickiewiz, Poznan, Poland; Dr Sc. Econ., University of Economics, Poznan, Poland, 1991. Appointments: Assistant: Industrial Institute of Agricultural Machinery, Poznan, Poland, 1976-79; Assistant, 1979-81, Tutor, 1981-91, Professor, 1991-, University of Economics, Poznan, Poland. Publications: Books: Decisions and reliable forecast (Polish), 1991; Mathematics Assisting Management, 1994, 1997, 1999, 2002; Article: Probability of fuzzy events defined as denumerable measure (English), 1985. Address: University of Economics, al Niepodleglosci 10, 60-967 Poznan, Poland. E-mail: piasecki@novci1.ae.poznan.pl

PICARD Barbara Leonie, b. 4 December 1917, Richmond, Surrey, England. Author. Publications: Ransom for a Knight, 1956; Lost John, 1962; One is One, 1965; The Young Pretenders, 1966; Twice Seven Tales, 1968; Three Ancient Kings, 1972; Tales of Ancient Persia, reprinted, 1993; The Iliad, 1991; The Odyssey, 1991; French Legends, Tales and Fairy Stories, 1992; German Hero-sagas and Folk-tales, 1993; Tales of the Norse Gods, 1994; Selected Fairy Tales, 1994; The Deceivers, 1996; The Midsummer Bride, 1999; Numerous other publications. Address: Oxford University Press, Great Clarendon Street, Oxford, England.

PICCARDI Luigi, b. 3 December 1961, Prato, Italy. Geologist. m. Cristina Poccianti, 1 son, 1 daughter. Education: BSc, Geology, cum laude, University of Firenze, Italy, 1988; Professional Habilitation Geologist, Italy, 1988; European School of Tectonics, ICTP Trieste, Italy, 1991; PhD, Tectonics, University of Firenze, Italy, 1993. Appointments: Consulting Geologist, 1988-94; Researcher, Italian National Research Council, Firenze, 1994-; Chairman, European COST Action 625, 2003-. Publications: Articles as author and co-author in scientific journals and conference proceedings including: Geophysical Journal International, 1999; Geology, 2000; 1st Joint GSA-GSL Meeting, 2001; Tectonophysics, 2004 in press. Honours: Visiting Professor, University of St Joan, Argentina, 1993; Listed in Who's Who publications and biographical dictionaries. Memberships: Ordine Nazionale Geologi, 1989; Italian Group of Structural Geology, 1992; Ordine Geologi Toscana, 1993; International Quaternary Association, 1995. Address: CNR Institute of Geosciences and Earth Resources, via G La Pira 4, 50121 Firenze, Italy.

PICCIONE Nicolas Antonio, b. 18 September 1925, Buenos Aires, Argentina. Economic and Financial Consultant. m. Betti Raquel Saigg, 2 sons, 1 daughter. Education: Degree in Public Accounting, 1953, Economics Licentiate, 1963, Doctor of Economic Sciences, 1968, Buenos Aires University, Argentina; Financial Administration, Executives Institute, Mexico City, Mexico, 1968. Appointments: Accounting Auditor, Manufacturing Tabacos Piccadoro SA, Buenos Aires, 1954-60; Trustee and Administration Manager, Industria Autom, Santa Fe DKW-Auto Union Arg. SA. 1960-63; Administration Manager and Accountant, Kellogg Co, Argentina SA, 1968-71; General Manager, Inst. Obra Social Ministry, 1972-74; Economic and Financial Consultant, Sind.Gr.Empr.Pub. 1975-91; Trustee, Buenos Aires Catering, SA Arg (Swizzer Co). Publications: Author: Economic/Financial Administration, 1968, 3rd edition, 1988; Economic/Financial Administration of Enterprises; Added value Tax, 1974; Articles in professional journals. Honours: Titular Professor in MBA Programme; Titular Professor, Financial Management, Belgrano University, Buenos Aires, Argentina, 1977-95; Titular Professor Master, Business Administration, Salvador University, Buenos Aires, Argentina, 1988. Memberships: Fellow, Finances and Development International Monetary Fund; Member Public Finance Commission. Address: Avda Santa Fe No 3858 – 7th "A" City of Buenos Aires, Republic of Argentina 1425. E-mail: nicoap24@hotmail.com

PICKERING Paul Granville, b. 9 May 1952, Rotherham, England. Novelist; Playwright. m. Alison Beckett, 11 December 1983, 1 daughter. Education: BA, Honours, Psychology, Leicester University. Appointments: Thomson Graduate Training Scheme; Latin American, Middle East and USA Correspondent for Now! Magazine; Columnist, Times, Sunday Times, Punch. Publications: Wild About Harry, 1985; Perfect English, 1986; The Blue Gate of Babylon, 1989; Charlie Peace, 1991. Anthologies: Winters Tales (contributed short story), 1989; Hakakawa, Japan (short story), Oldie Magazine, 1999; Plays: After Hamlet, New Grove Theatre, London, 1994; Beach, 1998; Walk Her Home, Louvre, Paris, 1999, plus film and web event 2002; Contributions to: The Times, Literary Review; New Society; Sunday Correspondent. Honours: Sports Colours, University of Leicester; Included in Best of Young British Novelists, W.H. Smith Top 10, 1989; British Council reading tour of France, 1993. Membership: Society of Authors; Fellow of the Royal Geographical Society; Holland Park Lawn Tennis Club. Address: Mic Cheetham Literary Agency, 11-12 Dover Street, London W1X 3PH, UK. E-mail: ryetrip@aol.com

PICKERING Thomas Reeve, b. 5 November 1931, Orange, New Jersey, USA. Diplomat. m. Alice Stover Pickering, 1 son, 1 daughter. Education: AB, 1953, LLD, 1983, Bowdoin College, Brunswick, Maine, USA; MA, Fletcher School of Law and Diplomacy, Medford, Massachusetts, USA, 1954; MA, University of Melbourne, Carlton, Victoria, Australia, 1956. Appointments: US State Department: Consul, Zanzibar, 1965-67; Deputy Chief of Mission, Dar es Salaam, Tanzania, 1967-69; Deputy Director of Political Military Affairs, 1969-73; Executive Secretary, Department of State, 1973-74; Ambassador to Jordan, 1974-78; Assistant Secretary of State for Oceans, Environment and Science, 1978-83; Ambassador to Nigeria, 1983-85; Ambassador to El Salvador, 1983-85; Ambassador to Israel, 1985-88; Ambassador and Representative to the United Nations, New York, 1989-92; Ambassador to India, 1992-93; Ambassador to Russia, 1993-96; President, Eurasia Foundation, Washington DC, 1996-97; Under Secretary for Political Affairs, US Department of State, 1997-2001; Senior Vice President, International Affairs, The Boeing Company, 2001-. Honours: President Superior Achievement Award, 1985, 1987; Department of State Superior Honor Award, 1996. Memberships: International Institute of Strategic Studies, London; Council on Foreign Relations, New York; Aspen Institute; Carnegie Corporation of New York; United Nations Association, New York; Eurasia Foundation Board, Washington DC; Council on Competitiveness, Washington DC; Policy and Global Affairs Committee, National Academy of Science, Washington DC; Stimson Center, Washington DC. Address: 2318 Kimbro Street, Alexandria, VA 22307, USA.

PIERCE Gregory Robert, b. 10 December 1952, Brooklyn, New York. Finance Professor. m. Linda Egan, 1 son, 1 daughter. Education: BS, Electrical Engineering, 1974, MBA, Organizational Behaviour, 1976, Pennsylvania State University. Appointments: Chief Finance Offices, Licom Technologies Inc, 1993-1996; Director, Honours Core Program, Instructor in Finance, Sineal College of Business, Pennsylvania State University, 1996-. Publications: IME Inc, A New Course for Integrating Design, Manufacturing and Production into the Engineering Curriculum, 2003. Address: 601 H Business Administration Building, University Park, PA 16802, USA. E-mail: grp@psu.edu

PIERCE Mary, b. 15 January 1975, Montreal, Canada. Tennis Player. Career: Turned Professional, 1989; Moved to France, 1990; Represented France in Federation Cup, 1991; 1st Career Title, Palermo, 1991; Runner-up, French Open, 1994; Winner, Australian Open, 1995, Tokyo Nichirei, 1995; Semi-Finalist, Italian Open, Candian Open, 1996; Finalist, Australian Open singles, 1997,

doubles with Martina Hingis, 2000; Winner of singles and doubles, with M Hingis, French Open, 2000; Highest singles ranking No 3; Winner of doubles, with M Hingis, Pan Pacific; French Federation Cup team, 1990-92, 1994-97; French Olympic team, 1992, 1996; 24 WTA Tour singles and doubles titles (by end 2002); France's (rising star) Burgeon Award, 1992; WTA Tour Comeback Player of the Year, 1997. Address: c/o WTA, 133 First Street North East, St Petersburg, FL 33701, USA.

PIERIDES Demetrios Zeno, b. 30 June 1937, Cyprus. President, Pierides Foundation. Divorced, 1 son. Education: BSc, Economics, University of Lausanne, Switzerland, 1956-60. Appointments: Companies Chairman in 38 shipping, travel, hotel and insurance companies; President, Pierides Foundation (13 museums and art galleries in Cyprus and Greece); Vice President, University of Cyprus; Director, Bank of Cyprus, Nicosia and Athens. Publications: A score of interviews, articles on arts and economy. Honours: Knight First Class, Royal Order of VASA, Sweden; Commander, Royal Order of Polar Star, Sweden; Academy of Athens Highest Award; Gold Medal of Republic of Cyprus; Governor, European Cultural Foundation; Commander of Arts and Letters, France; Commander of National Order of Merit, France; Doctor Honoris Causa, Faculty of Philosophy, University of Athens; Commander of Order of Merit, Italy; Gold Medal, Municipality of Larnaca, Cyprus; Gold Cross Order of Honour, Greece. Membership: Rotary Club. Address: 4 Zeno Kitiefs Str, 6300 Larnaca, Republic of Cyprus.

PIES Ronald, b. 6 December 1952, Rochester, New York, USA. Physician. Education: AB, Cornell University, 1974; MD, SUNY Upstate Medical Center, 1978. Publications: Ruach, 1976; Absence, 1976; Voices, 1978; Missing Children, 1986; In Greens, 1990; Riding Down Dark, 1992; Consultation Request, 1992; Feinmann's Books, 1993; The Road Test, 1993; Styx, 1993; Sitting Shiva, 1994; The Camera, 1994; Spellcheck for a Blighted Fetus, 1995; Sedating the Bard, 1995; Yazowitz on Yom Kippur, 1996; Old Ladder Black, 1996; Purple Loosestrife, 1997; Reflections, 1997; Sophie Fein Goldberg Stein, 1997; Summer of the Quiet Son, 1998; Hunting Season; Butterflies, 1998; Cabbage Soup. Contributions to: Literary Review; Vital Signs; Nightshade Press; Kaleidoscope; Oasis; New Jersey Review; Voices West; Poetpourri; Comstock Review; Rockhurst Review; Midstream; Stoneflower; Moment. Address: Tufts University, Department of Psychiatry, Box 1007, 750 Washington Street, Boston, MA 02111, USA.

PIGGOTT Lester Keith, b. 5 November 1935, England. Former Jockey; Trainer. m. Susan Armstrong, 1960, 2 daughters. Career: Rode over 100 winners per year in UK alone in several seasons, 1955-; Rode 3000 winners in UK, 1974; Champion Jockey, 9 times, 1960, 1964-71; Numerous rides in France; Equalled record of 21 Classic victories, 1975; Won 29 English classic victories, 1985; 4349 winners 1985; Retired, 1985; Winner of numerous races including: Derby, 9 times; St Leger, 8 times; Prix de l'Arc de triomphe, 3 times; Washington DC International, 1968, 1969, 1980; Trainer, 1985-87; Sentenced to 3 years imprisonment for tax fraud, 1987, released after 12 months; Returned to racing, 1990; retired as Jockey, 1995; Record 30 classic wins, 1992. Publication: Lester: The Autobiography of Lester Piggott, 1995. Address: Beech Tree House, Tostock, Newmarket, Suffolk, England.

PIKE Edward Roy, b. 4 December 1929, Perth, Western Australia. Physicist. Education: BSc, Mathematics, 1953, BSc, Physics, 1954, PhD, Physics, 1957, University College, Cardiff, Wales. Appointments: Fellow, American Society for Testing Materials, University College, Cardiff, 1954-58; Research Assistant, University of Wales, Cardiff, 1957-58; Instructor, Massachusetts Institute of Technology, USA, 1958-60; Senior

Dictionary of International Biography

Scientific Officer to Chief Scientific Officer, Royal Signals and Radar Establishment, Malvern, England, 1960-86; Visiting Professor of Mathematics, Imperial College of Science and Technology, London, 1984-85; Non-Executive Director, Richard Clay plc (Printers), 1984-86; Clerk Maxwell Professor of Theoretical Physics, King's College, London, 1986-; Head of School of Physical Sciences and Engineering, King's College, London, 1991-94; Chairman, Stilo Technology Ltd (Publishing and World Wide Web software), 1995-2002; Chairman, 2000-02, Non-Executive Director, 2002-, Stilo International plc. Publications: 300 papers and 10 books in the fields of theoretical physics, X-Ray diffraction, statistics, imaging and optics, inverse problems, compact disc technology. Honours: Charles Parsons Prize, Royal Society, 1975; McRobert Award, Confederation of Engineering Institutions, 1977; Annual Achievement Award, Worshipful Company of Scientific Instrument Makers, 1978; Civil Service Award to Inventors, 1980; Guthrie Medal and Prize, Institute of Physics, 1995; Fellow, University College Cardiff; Fellow King's College London; Fellow of the Institute of Mathematics and Applications; Fellow of the Institute of Physics; Fellow of the Optical Society of America; Fellow of the Royal Society. Address: Physics Department, King's College London, Strand, London WC2R 2LS, England.

PIKE Lionel John, b. 7 November 1939, Bristol, England. University Professor; Organist. m. Jennifer Marguerite Parkes, 2 daughters. Education: BA, Class I, Music, B Mus, MA, D Phil, Pembroke College, Oxford; FRCO; ARCM. Appointments: Organist, 1969-, Lecturer in Music, 1965-80, Senior Lecturer in Music and College Organist, 1980-2004, Professor of Music, 2004-, Royal Holloway College (University of London), UK. Publications: Beethoven, Sibelius and "The Profound Logic", 1978; Hexachords in Late Renaissance Music, 1998; Vaughan Williams and the Symphony, 2003; The Works of Henry Purcell, volumes 14 and 17 (editor); Many articles, compositions, reviews and CD's. Honours: Book: Beethoven, Sibelius and "The Profound Logic", named by Choice Magazine as one of the three best academic books in any subject for the year 1978-79; Limpus Prize for FRCO. Memberships: Royal College of Organists; Havergal Brian Society; Robert Simpson Society; RVW Society; Chaine des Rotisseurs. Address: Music Department, Royal Holloway (University of London), Egham Hill, Egham, Surrey TW20 0EX, England. E-mail: lionel.pike@rhul.ac.uk

PILCH Herbert Leo, b. 13 February 1927, Wehlau, East Prussia, Germany. University Professor. m. Annegret Harms. 1 son, 1 daughter. Education: University of Kiel, 1946-49; University of Birmingham, England, 1949-50; PhD, 1951, State Examination in English, French and Russian, 1952, venia legendi, 1957, University of Kiel. Appointments: Assistant, Department of English, University of Kiel, 1952-53; Research Fellow, Linguistics Department Yale University, 1953-54; Research Fellow, Deutsche Forschungsgemeinschaft (Research Work in Celtic at Aberystwyth, Wales), 1954-57; Deputy Professor, University of Cologne, 1959-60; Associate Professor, University of Frankfurt/Main, 1960-61; Full Professor, University of Freiburg I Br, 1961-; Visiting Professor: Monash University, 1969, University of Basel, 1974-77, University of Massachusetts, 1977-78, University of Brest, Brittany, 1986. Publications: Der Untergang des Präverbs ge-im Englischen, 1951; Layamons 'Brut', 1960; Phonemtheorie I, 1964, 1968, 1974; Altenglishe Grammatik, 1970; Altenglischer Lehrgang, 1970; Empirical Linguistics, 1976; Co-editor, Altenglishe Literatur, 1979; Co-editor, Sound, Sense, and System; Herbert Pilch and Postwar German Studies in English Linguistics, 1987; Manual of English Phonetics, 1994; Over 100 articles on English, German, Slavic and Celtic linguistics and literature. Honours: D.Litt, St Andrews University, 1984; Dr honorary, Iasi, Romania, 1993.

Memberships: Fellow, International Society of Phonetic Sciences, 1978; President, Societas Linguistica Europaea, 1990-91; Foundation Member, Société de Linguistique fonctionelle, 1975; World Linguistic Circle, member of executive committee, 1978. Address: Albet-Ludwigs-U Eng Sem 1, Postfach, D-79085 Freiburg, Germany.

PILCHER Rosamunde, b. 22 September 1924, Lelant, Cornwall, England. Writer. m. Graham Pilcher, 4 children. Publications: April, 1957; On My Own, 1965; Sleeping Tiger, 1967; Another View, 1969; The End of the Summer, 1971; Snow in April, 1972; The Empty House, 1973; The Day of the Storm, 1975; Under Gemini, 1977; Wild Mountain Thyme, 1978; The Carousel, 1981; Voices in Summer, 1984; The Blue Bedroom and Other Stories, 1985; The Shell Seekers, 1988; September, 1989; Flowers in the Rain, 1991; Coming Home, 1996; Winter Solstice, 2000. Contributions to: Woman and Home; Good Housekeeping. Honour: Romantic Novelists Association Award, 1996. Address: Penrowan, Longforgan, by Dundee DD2 5ET, Scotland.

PILGER John Richard, b. Sydney, Australia. Journalist; Author; Film Maker. 1 son, 1 daughter. Appointments: Journalist, Sydney Daily/Sunday Telegraph, 1958-62; Reuters, London, 1962; Feature Writer, Columnist, Foreign Correspondent, Chief Foreign Correspondent, Daily Mirror, London, 1963-86; Columnist, New Statesman, London, 1991-; Freelance Contributor, The Guardian, The Independent, New York Times, Melbourne Age, The Nation, South China Morning Post, Aftonbladet, Sweden; Documentary film maker, Granada TV, 1969-71, Associated Television, 1972-80, Central and Carlton Television, 1980-. Publications: The Last Day, 1975; Aftermath: The Struggle of Cambodia and Vietnam, 1983; The Outsiders, 1983; Heroes, 1986; A Secret Country, 1989; Distant Voices, 1992; Hidden Agendas, 1998; The New Rulers of the World, 2002; Tell Me No Lies, editor, 2004; Films: 58 documentary films include: The Quiet Mutiny, 1970; Cambodia Year Zero, 1979; The Last Dream, 1988; Death of a Nation, 1994; Inside Burma, 1996; Apatheid Did Not Die, 1998; Welcome to Australia, 1999; Paying the Price: Killing the Children of Iraq, 2000; Palestine Is Still The Issue, 2002; Breaking the Silence: Truth and Lies in the War on Terror, 2003; Feature film: The Last Day, 1983. Honours: Descriptive Writer of the Year, 1966; Journalist of the Year, 1967, 1979; International Reporter of the Year, 1970; Reporter of the Year, 1974; Reporters Sans Frontiers, France; US Television Academy Award, Emmy, 1991; British Television Academy Award, 1990; Honorary Doctorates: DLitt, Staffordshire University, DPhil, Dublin City University, Ireland, DArts, Oxford Brookes University; DLaws, St Andrews University; DLitt, Kingston University; DUniv, The Open University. Address: 57 Hambalt Road, London SWX 9EQ, England. E-mail: jpmarheine@hotmail.com

PILLER Laurence William, b. 9 March 1927, Plymouth, Devon, England. Clinical Technologist. m. Jane Rosemary Cousins, 1 son, 1 daughter deceased. Education: Training in Cardiac and Respiratory Technology, 1950-54; Qualified as Associate of the Society of Cardiac Technicians of Great Britain, 1953; Qualified as Member of the American Cardiology Technologists Association, 1961. Appointments: Cardiac Laboratories, National Heart Hospital and Institute of Cardiology, University of London, 1950-54, Senior Technician, 1954; Technical Advisor, Honeywell Controls Ltd, London, 1954-56; Assisted in first open heart operation in Britain, Post Graduate Medical School, Hammersmith, London, 1954; Member of Staff, Groote Schuur Hospital and the University of Capetown, South Africa, 1956-92; Assisted Professor Barnard and Dr Brian Kennelly during 5 surgical arrhythmia mapping procedures of the heart, 1963; Assisted at diagnostic procedures of the first heart transplantation patient, 1967; Chief Technician, Cardiac Clinic, Groote Schuur Hospital, 1969;

Technical Assistant to Physicians at NASA and University of Texas Medical School, 1975; Chief Technologist, Special Grade, 1979; Registered Clinical Technologist, Cardiology South African Medical and Dental Council, 1980; Attended numerous conferences and symposia in Europe and America, 1973-90; Final Subject Examiner, Department of Education for the National Diploma of Clinical Technology, 1991. Publications: Books: A Manual of Cardio-pulmonary Technology, 1964; Instrumentation Theory of Cardiac Technology, 1970; Essential Cardiac Technology for the Student Health Care Professional, 1996; The Cardiac Clinic, Groote Schure Hospital. 1951-1972 The Schrire Years, 1999; Over 30 articles in medical journals and presented at conferences. Honours: Honorary Fellowships, Society of Cardiological Technicians of Great Britain, 1958, South African Society of Clinical Technologists, 1987; Honorary Life Memberships: South African Heart Foundation, 1974, Southern Africa Cardiac Society; Most Distinguished Technologists Award, Head of Department of Medicine, University of Capetown, 1992; BTech, Clinical Technology, Academic Board, ML Sultan Technikon, Durban South Africa, 1997. Memberships include: American Cardiology Technologist Association; Associate Member, Institute of Electrical and Electronic Technician Engineers, GB; American Society of Cardio-pulmonary Technologists; American Society of Cardiovascular Professionals. Address: 10 Morkel Road, Bergvliet, Capetown 7845, South Africa.

PINCHER (Henry) Chapman, b. 29 March 1914, Ambala, India. Author. m. (1), 1 daughter, 1 son, (2) Constance Wolstenholme, 1965. Education: BSc Honours, Botany, Zoology, 1935. Appointments: Staff, Liverpool Institute, 1936-40; Royal Armoured Corps, 1940; Defence, Science and Medical Editor, Daily Express, 1946-73; Assistant Editor, Daily Express, Chief Defence Correspondent, Beaverbrook Newspapers, 1972-79. Publications: Breeding of Farm Animals, 1946; A Study of Fishes, 1947; Into the Atomic Age, 1947; Spotlight on Animals, 1950; Evolution, 1950; It's Fun Finding Out (with Bernard Wicksteed), 1950; Sleep and How to Get More of It, 1954; Sex in Our Time, 1973; Inside Story, 1978; Their Trade is Treachery, 1981; Too Secret Too Long, 1984; The Secret Offensive, 1985; Traitors - the Labyrinth of Treason, 1987; A Web of Deception, 1987; The Truth about Dirty Tricks, 1991; One Dog and Her Man, 1991; Pastoral Symphony, 1993; A Box of Chocolates, 1993; Life's a Bitch!, 1996; Tight Lines!, 1997. Novels: Not with a Bang, 1965; The Giantkiller, 1967; The Penthouse Conspirators, 1970; The Skeleton at the Villa Wolkonsky, 1975; The Eye of the Tornado, 1976; The Four Horses, 1978; Dirty Tricks, 1980; The Private World of St John Terrapin, 1982; Contamination, 1989. Honours: Granada Award, Journalist of the Year, 1964; Reporter of the Decade, 1966; Honorary DLitt, University of Newcastle upon Tyne, 1979; King's College, London, fellow, 1979. Address: The Church House, 16 Church Street, Kintbury, Near Hungerford, Berkshire RG15 0TR, England.

PINGULI Edmond, b. 7 October 1948, Tirana, Albania. Projecting Engineer. m. Eva, 2 sons. Graduate, Civil Industrial Engineering, Faculty of Construction Engineering, 1971; Master of Technical Sciences, 1985; Docent Scientific Degree and Doctor of Technical Sciences, 1990; Professor, 1994. Appointments: Applicant Engineer, 1971-72, Chief Engineer, 1972-80, Works for Construction of the Fierza Hydro-Power Station; Projecting Engineer, Chief of Department, Ditector of Institute of Building Technology Studies, 1981-92; Owner, Tecnoproject Building Company, Tirana, 1993-2002. Publications: Numerous scientific articles in professional journals, 1972-92. Memberships: Staff of the Scientific Board, Institute of Building Studies; Board of Polytechnic University of Tirana; Board of the Ministry of Construction. Address: Str Ismail Qemali – P 27/1, Tirana, Albania.

PINSON William Meredith Jr, b. 3 August 1934, Fort Worth, Texas, USA. Minister; Pastor; Executive. m. Bobbie Judd Pinson, 2 daughters. Education: BA, University of North Texas, 1955; Miv, 1959, ThD, 1963, Southwestern Baptist Seminary; Postdoctoral Study, Columbia University, 1969-70; Postgraduate study, University of Edinburgh, Scotland, 1956-57. Appointments: Associate Director, Christian Life Commission, Baptist General Convention of Texas, 1957-63; Professor of Christian Ethics, Southwestern Baptist Seminary, 1963-75; Pastor, First Baptist Church, Wichita Falls, Texas, 1975-77; President, Golden Gate Seminary, Mill Valley, California, 1977-82; Executive Director, Baptist General Convention of Texas, 1982-2000; Executive Director Emeritus, BGCT, 2000-; Distinguished University Professor, Dallas Baptist University, 2000-; Director, Texas Baptist Heritage Centre, 2000-; Distinguished Visiting Professor, Baylor University, 2001-. Publications include: The Local Church in Ministry; Ready to Minister; How to Deal with Controversial Issues; The Biblical View of the Family; Co-author: Decision Making. Honours: Outstanding Alumnus Award, University of North Texas; Outstanding Alumnus Award, Southwestern Baptist Seminary; Several honorary doctorates; Listed in numerous biographical dictionaries. Memberships include: Association of Baptist Schools and Colleges; Baptist World Alliance. Address: Baptist General Convention of Texas, 333 North Washington, Dallas, TX 75246, USA.

PINTER Harold, b. 10 October 1930, London, England. Playwright. m. (1) Vivien Merchant, 1956, 1 son, (2) Lady Antonia Fraser, 1980. Appointments: Actor, English and Irish Provincial Repertory, 1949-58; Playwright, 1957-; Associate Director, National Theatre, 1973-83; Director, United British Artists, 1983-85; Joint Editor, Publisher, Greville Press, 1988-; Board Member, Cricket World, 1989-. Film: Mansfield Park, 1999; Plays: The Room, 1957; The Dumb Waiter, 1957; The Birthday Party, 1957; A Slight Ache, 1958; The Hothouse, 1958; The Caretaker, 1959; A Night Out, 1959; Night School, 1960; The Dwarfs, 1960; The Collection, 1961; The Lover, 1962; Tea Party (TV play), 1965; The Homecoming, 1964; The Basement (TV play), 1966; Landscape, 1967; Silence, 1968; Night (1 act play), 1969; Old Times, 1970; Monologue (1 act play), 1972; No Man's Land, 1974; Betrayal, 1978; Family Voices, 1980; Other Places, 1982; A Kind of Alaska, 1982; Victoria Station, 1982; One for the Road, 1984; Mountain Language, 1988; The New World Order, 1991; Party Time, 1991; Moonlight, 1993; Ashes to Ashes, 1996; Celebration, 2000; Remembrance of Things Past, 2000; Screenplays: The Caretaker, 1962; The Servant, 1962; The Pumpkin Eater, 1963; The Quiller Memorandum, 1965; Accident, 1966; The Birthday Party, 1967; The Go-Between, 1969; Langrishe Go Down, 1970; A la Recherche du Temps Perdu, 1972; The Last Tycoon, 1974; The French Lieutenant's Woman, 1980; Betrayal, 1981; Victory, 1982; Turtle Diary, 1984; The Handmaid's Tale, 1987; Reunion, 1988; The Heat of the Day, 1988; The Comfort of Strangers, 1989; The Trial, 1989; Plays directed: The Man in the Glass Booth, 1967, 1968; Exiles, 1970, 1971; Butley, 1971, 1973; Close of Play, 1979; Quartermaine's Terms, 1981; Incident at Tulse Hill, 1982; The Trojan War Will Not Take Place, 1983; The Common Pursuit, 1984; Sweet Bird of Youth, 1985; Circe and Bravo, 1986; Vanilla, 1990; The New World Order, 1991; Party Time, 1991, 1992; Oleanna, 1993; Ashes to Ashes, 1995; Twelve Angry Men, 1996; The Late Middle Classes, 1999; Celebration, 2000; The Room, 2000; No Man's Land, 2001; Television: A Night Out, 1960; Huis Clos, 1965; The Basement, 1967; Rogue Male, 1976; Lanerishe, Go Down, 1978; The Birthday Party, 1987; Breaking the Code, 1997; Catastrophe, 2000; Wit, 2000. Publications: Poems and Prose 1949-77, 1978; The Proust Screenplay (with Joseph Losey and Barbara Bray), 1978; Collected Poems and Prose, 1986; 100 Poems by 100 Poets (co-editor), 1986; The Dwarfs (novel), 1990; Various Voices: Prose, Poetry, Politics 1948-98, 1999. Honours

Dictionary of International Biography

include: Chilean Order of Merit, 1992; David Cohen British Literature Prize, 1995; Special Olivier Award, 1995; Moliere d'Honneur, Paris, 1997; Sunday Times Award for Literary Excellence, 1997; BAFTA Fellowship, 1997; RSL Companion of Literature, 1997; Critics' Circle Award for Distinguished Service to the Arts, 2000; Brianza Poetry Prize, Italy, 2000; South Bank Show Award, 2001; S T Dupont Golden Pen Award, 2001; Premio Fiesole ai Maestri del Cinema, Italy, 2001; Laurea ad honorem, University of Florence, 2001; World Leaders Award, Toronto, 2001; Hermann Kesten Medallion; German PEN, Berlin, 2001. Address: c/o Judy Daish Associates, 2 St Charles Place, London W10 6EG, England.

PINZÁS Juana Rosa, b. 13 June 1949, Lima, Peru. Educational Psychologist. m. José Carlos Vera, 2 daughters. Education: BA, Humanities, Catholic University of Peru, 1971; Licensed Psychologist, Catholic University of Peru, 1973; MSc, Social Psychology, London School of Economics and Political Science, London, England, 1974; MSc, Research Methods, Strathclyde University, Scotland, 1975; PhD, Educational Psychology, Catholic University of Nijmegen, The Netherlands, 1993. Appointments: Principal Professor, Catholic University of Peru and University of Lima; Editorial Board, Revista Psicologia, Catholic University of Peru; Consultant, Ministry of Education, Psychologist/Counselor, Roosevelt School; Research Team on Reading Comprehension and Assessment, University of Lima; The Reading Spot Director, Children's Library. Publications: Books: Leer Pensando; Lectura y Metacognicion; Leer mejor para escribir mejor; Se aprende a leer leyendo; Organizadores graficos; Chapter: Higher Education in Peru: A 3rd World Perspective. Honours: Fulbright Scholar, 1985; Top People in Peru, several years to present, 2003. Memberships: AERA; EARLI; IRA; APA; AEPI; SIP; Colegio de Psicologos del Peru. Address: Los Cedrones 398, Urb. Los Sirius, La Molina, Lima 12, Peru. E-mail: jrpinzas@terra.com.pe

PIPPARD Alfred Brian (Sir), b. 7 September 1920, London, England. Physicist. m. Charlotte Frances Dyer, 3 daughters. Education: Clare College Cambridge, 1938-41. Appointments: Demonstrator, Lecturer, Reader in Physics, 1946-60, John Humphrey Professor of Physics, 1960-71, Cavendish Professor of Physics, 1971-82, Cambridge University; President, Clare Hall, Cambridge, 1966-73. Publications: Elements of Classical Thermodynamics, 1957; Cavendish Problems in Classical Physics, 1962; Dynamics of Conduction Electrons, 1965; Forces and Particles, 1972; Physics of Vibration, 2 volumes, 1978, 1983; Response and Stability, 1985; Magnetoresistance, 1989; Many papers in Proceedings of the Royal Society and other journals. Honours: Hughes Medal, Royal Society, 1959; Holweck Medal, 1961; Dannie-Heinemann Prize, 1969; Guthrie Prize, Institute of Physics, 1970; Knight Bachelor, 1975. Memberships: Fellow, Clare College, Cambridge, 1947-66; Fellow of the Royal Society, 1956-; Honorary Fellow, Clare College, 1973-; Honorary Fellow, Clare Hall, 1973; President, Institute of Physics, 1974-76; Honorary Fellow, Institute of Physics. Address: 30 Porson Road, Cambridge CB2 2EU, England.

PIQUET Nelson, b. 17 August 1952, Rio de Janeiro, Brazil. Racing Driver. m. (1) Maria Clara, (2) Vivianne Leao, 1 son. Appointments: 1st Grand Prix, Germany, 1978; Member, Ensign Grand Prix Team, 1978, BS McLaren Team, 1978, Brabham Team, 1978-85, Williams Team, 1986-87, Lotus Team, 1988-89, Benetton Team, 1990; Winner of 23 Grand Prix; Formula One World Champion, 1981, 1983, 1987.

PIRIE David Tarbat, b. 4 December 1946, Dundee, Scotland. Dramatist; Writer. m. Judith Harris, 21 June 1983, 1 son, 1 daughter. Education: University of York; University of London. Appointments: Tutor; Film Critic, Editor, Time Out Magazine,

1980-84. Publications: Heritage of Horror, 1974; Mystery Story, 1980; Anatomy of the Movies, 1981; The Patient's Eyes, 2001. Films: Rainy Day Women, 1984; Wild Things, 1988; Black Easter, 1993; Wildest Dreams, 1995; Element of Doubt, 1996. Television: Never Come Back, BBC serial, 1989; Ashenden, BBC serial, 1990; Natural Lies, serial, 1991; The Woman in White, 1997; Murder Rooms: The Dark Beginnings of Sherlock Holmes, 2000; Murder Rooms 2: The Safe House. Contributions to: Various journals. Honours: Drama Prize, New York Festival, 1985; Best TV Network Series Prize, 1990, Best TV Feature Film Prize, 1996, Chicago Film Festival; BAFTA Nomination, Best TV Serial, The Woman in White, 1997. Membership: Soho House, London 1990. Address: c/o The Agency (UK) Ltd, 24 Pottery Lane, London W11, England.

PIRK Jan, b. 20 April 1948, Prague, Czechoslovakia. Cardiac Surgeon. m. Blanka Navratilová, 2 sons. Education: MD, Charles University, Prague, 1972; DSc, Czech Academy of Science, 1988; Professor of Surgery, Charles University, Prague, 2000-. Appointments: Department of Surgery Hospital Nymburk, 1972-74; Head of Cardiac Surgery, Institute for Clinical and Experimental Medicine, 1974-; Fellow, Cardiac Surgery, Ochsner Medical Foundation, New Orleans, 1983-84; Consultant, Odense University Hospital, Denmark, 1990-91. Publications: Over 100 in European and US journals. Memberships: European Association for Cardio-Thoracic Surgery, Councillor; Society of Cardio-Thoracic Surgery, USA. Address: Institute for Clinical and Experimental Medicine, Prague 4, Vidensá 800, Czech Republic.

PISARCHIK Alexander N, b. 3 June 1954, Minsk, Belarus. Physicist. m. Liudmila Kotashova, 1 son, 4 daughters. Education: MS, Belorussian State University, 1976; PhD, Institute of Physics, Minsk, 1990. Appointments: Visiting Professor, University Libre, Brussels, 1992; Visiting Professor, Universitat Autonoma de Barcelona, 1993-94, 1997-99; Visiting Professor, University of Iceland, Reykjavik, 1995; Senior Researcher, Institute of Physics, Minsk, 1996-99; Research Professor, Centro de Investigaciones en Optica, Leon, Gto, Mexico, 1999-. Publications: Contributor, articles to professional journals including Physics review A and E; Physics review Letters; Physica D; Physics Letters A; Optical Communications. Honours: First Prize, National Academy of Science, Minsk, 1999. Memberships: European Physical Society, 1994-; Academia Mexicana de Optica, 2000-; Society for Industrial and Applied Mathematics, 2001-; Mexican National System of Researchers (SNI, level 2), 2001-; Mexican National System of Evaluators on Science and Technology (SINECYT), 2002-. Address: Centro de Investigaciones en Optica AC, Loma del Bosque # 115, Col Lomas del Campestre, 37150 Leon, Guanajuato, Mexico. E-mail: apisarch@foton.cio.mx

PISPAS Asterios (Stergios), b. 16 October 1967, Athens, Greece. Chemist. m. Tserepa Charikleia, 1 son. Education: BS, Chemistry, 1989, PhD, Polymer Chemistry, 1994, University of Athens, Greece. Appointments: Post Doctoral Fellow, Department of Chemistry, University of Alabama, Birmingham, USA, 1994-95; Research Associate, Department of Chemistry, University of Athens, Greece, 1997-. Publications: Over 70 research publications in refereed journals; Over 70 announcements in Scientific Conferences; Co-author, 1 book on Block Copolymers. Honours: American Institute of Chemists Foundation Award for Outstanding Postdoctoral Fellow, 1995. Memberships: Greek Chemists Association; Greek Polymer Society. Address: Department of Chemistry, University of Athens, Panepistimiopolis, 15771 Zografou, Athens, Greece. E-mail: pispas@chem.uoa.gr

PIT Chamnan, b. 27 December 1951, Preyveng Province, Cambodia. University Rector. m. Seng Solydet, 3 sons, 1 daughter. Education: BA, Khmer Literature, University of Preyveng Province,

1969-73; Higher Secondary Education Professional Certificate, Ecole Normale Superieur, 1973-74; MEd, Adult Education, UTC, Australia, 1997-98. Appointments: Director of Foreign Languages School, Phnom Penh University, 1982-88; Vice Rector, 1988-99, Rector, 2000-, The Royal University of Phnom Penh. Publications: Language and Education in Cambodia, 1997; Teacher in a Changing World, 2003; English Language Teaching Development in Cambodia Past, Present and Future. Honours: Award of Highest Honor, 2001, Education and Culture Award, 2002, Soka University, Japan. Memberships: Member, Australian Alumni Association of Cambodia, 1998-. Address: Royal University of Phnom Penh, Russian Federation Bld, Phnom Penh, Cambodia. E-mail: pitch@camnet.com.kh

PITCHER Harvey John, b. 26 August 1936, London, England. Writer. Education: BA, 1st Class Honours, Russian, University of Oxford. Publications: Understanding the Russians, 1964; The Chekhov Play: A New Interpretation, 1973; When Miss Emmie was in Russia, 1977; Chekhov's Leading Lady, 1979; Chekhov: The Early Stories, 1883-1888 (with Patrick Miles), 1982; The Smiths of Moscow, 1984; Lily: An Anglo-Russian Romance, 1987; Muir and Mirrielees: The Scottish Partnership that became a Household Name in Russia, 1994; Witnesses of the Russian Revolution, 1994; Chekhov: The Comic Stories, 1998. Contributions to: Times Literary Supplement. Address: 37 Bernard Road, Cromer, Norfolk NR27 9AW, England.

PITCHES Douglas Owen, b. 6 March 1930, Exning, Suffolk, England. Poet. m. Barbara Joyce Budgen, 7 August 1954. Education: BA, Honours, Open University, 1979. Publications: Poems, 1965; Prayer to the Virgin Mary (Chaucer Translation), 1965; Man in Orbit and Down to Earth, 1981; Art Demands Love Not Homage, 1992. Contributions to: Orbis; Outposts; Envoi; Tribune; Anthologies: Responding; New Voices; Another 5th Poetry Book and others. Address: 14 Linkway, Westham, Pevensey, East Sussex BN24 5JB, England.

PITMAN Jennifer Susan, b. 11 June 1946, England. Racehorse Trainer. m. (1) Richard Pitman, 1965, 2 sons, (2) David Stait, 1997. Career: National Hunt Trainer, 1975-99; Director, Jenny Pitman Racing Ltd, 1975-99; Racing and Media Consultant, 1999-; Winners include: Corbiere, Welsh National, 1982, Grand National, 1983; Burrough Hill Lad, Welsh National, 1984, Cheltenham Gold Cup, 1984, King George VI Gold Cup, 1984, Hennessy Gold Cup, 1984; Smith's Man, Whitbread Trophy, 1985; Gainsay, Ritz Club National Hunt Handicap, 1987, Sporting Life Weekend Chase, 1987; Garrison Savannah, Cheltenham Gold Cup, 1991; Wonderman, Welsh Champion Hurdle, 1991; Don Valentino, Welsh Champion Hurdle, 1992; Royal Athlete, Grand National, 1995; Willsford, Scottish National, 1995. Publications: Glorious Uncertainty (autobiography), 1984; Jenny Pitman: The Autobiography, 1999; On the Edge, 2002; Double Deal, 2002; The Dilemma, 2003. Honours include: Racing Personality of the Year, Golden Spurs, 1983; Commonwealth Sports Award, 1983, 1984; Piper Heidsieck Trainer of the Year, 1983-84, 1989-90; Variety Club of Great Britain Sportswoman of the Year, 1984. Address: Owls Barn, Kintbury, Hungerford, Berkshire, RG17 9XS, England.

PITT Brad, b. 18 December 1963, Shawnee, Oklahoma, USA. Film Actor. m. Jennifer Aniston. Creative Works: TV appearances include: Dallas (series); Glory Days (series); Too Young to Die? (film); The Image (film); Films include: Cutting Glass, 1989; Happy Together, 1989; Across the Tracks, 1990; Contact, 1991; Thelma and Louise, 1991; The Favor, 1992; Johnny Suede, 1992; Cool World, 1992; A River Runs Through It, 1992; Kalifornia, 1993; Legend of the Fall, 1994; 12 Monkeys, 1995; Sleepers, 1996; Mad Monkeys, 1996; Tomorrow Never Dies, 1996; Seven Years

in Tibet, 1997; The Devil's Own, 1997; Meet Joe Black, 1998; Fight Club, 2000; Snatch, 2000; The Mexican, 2001; Spy Game, 2001; Ocean's Eleven, 2001; Confessions of a Dangerous Mind, 2002; Sinbad: Legend of the Seven Seas (voice), 2003; Troy, 2004. Address: Creative Artists Agency, 9830 Wilshire Boulevard, Beverly Hills, CA 90212, USA.

PLATER Alan Frederick, b. 15 April 1935, Jarrow on Tyne, County Durham, England. Writer; Dramatist. m. (1) Shirley Johnson, 1958, divorced 1985, 2 sons, 1 daughter, (2) Shirley Rubinstein, 1986, 3 stepsons. Education: King's College, Durham, 1953-57; University of Newcastle. Career: Full time writer, for stage, screen, radio, television, anthologies and periodicals, 1960-; Written extensively for radio, TV, films and theatre, also for The Guardian, Listener, New Statesman, etc; Plays include: The Fosdyke Saga; Films include: It Shouldn't Happen to a Vet; Keep the Aspidistra Flying; TV series include: Z Cars; Softly Softly; TV adaptions include: Barchester Chronicles; The Fortunes of War; A Very British Coup; Campion; A Day in Summer; A Few Selected Exits; Oliver's Travels; Dalziel and Pascoe. Publications: The Beiderbecke Affair, 1985; The Beiderbecke Tapes, 1986; Misterioso, 1987; The Beiderbecke Connection, 1992; Oliver's Travels, 1994; and others. Honours: Various stage, radio and television drama awards; Honorary Fellow, Humberside College of Education, 1983; Honorary DLitt (Hull), 1985; Hon DCL (Northumbria), 1997; Royal TV Society Writers' Award, 1988; BAFTA Writers' Award, 1988. Memberships: Royal Society of Literature, fellow; Royal Society of Arts, fellow; Co-chair, 1986-87, President, 1991-95, Writer's Guild of Great Britain. Address: c/o 200 Fulham Road, London SW10 9PN, England.

PLATH James Walter, b. 29 October 1950, Chicago, Illinois, USA. Writer; Editor; Educator. 3 sons, 2 daughters. Education: BA, English, California University at Chicago, 1980; MA, English, 1982, PhD, English, 1988, University of Wisconsin-Milwaukee. Appointments: Professor of English, Illinois Wesleyan University. Publications: Conversations With John Updike, 1994; Courbet, On The Rocks, 1994; Remembering Ernest Hemingway, 1999. Contributions to: Anthologies, reviews, periodicals, journals, quarterlies, magazines and newspapers. Honours include: Fulbright Scholar; Editors Award, Council of Literary Magazines and Presses, 1990. Memberships: Academy of American Poets; Fitzgerald Society; Fulbright Association; Hemingway Society; Illinois College Press Association; Society of Midland Authors. Address: c/o Department of English, Illinois Wesleyan University, Bloomington, IL 61702-2900, USA.

PLATT Jan Kaminis, b. 27 September 1936, St Petersburg, Florida, USA. County Official. m. William R Platt, 1 son. Education: BA, Florida State University, 1958; Postgraduate, University of Florida Law School, 1958-59, University of Virginia, 1962, Vanderbilt University, 1964. Appointments include: Public School Teacher, Hillsborough County, Tampa, Florida, 1959-60; Field Director, Girl Scouts Suncoast Council, Tampa, 1960-62; City Councilman, Tampa City Council, 1974-78; County Commissioner, Hillsborough County, 1978-94, 1996-; Chairman, Hillsborough County Board County Commissioners, 1980-81, 1998-99; Chairman, Tampa Bay Regional Planning Council, 1982; Chairman, Hillsborough Area Regional Transit Authority, 2002-03; Co-Chairman, National Association of Counties Energy and Land Use Steering Committee; Board, Florida Aquarium, 2003-; Board Member, 1984-94, 2001-03, Hillsborough County Hospital Authority, Tampa; Chairman of numerous other local government and community committees. Honours: Numerous awards and honours include most recently: Freedom to Read Roll of Honor, American Library Association, 1999; Community Service Award, Tampa Bay Muslim Alliance, 2000; Liberty Bell Award, Hillsborough County Bar Association, 2000; Black Bear Award,

Tampa Bay Sierra Club, 2001; Jan Kaminis Platt Regional Library Dedicated, 2000; Listed in Who's Who publications and biographical dictionaries. Memberships include: President, Suncoast Girl Scout Council; President, Tampa Bay Area Phi Beta Kappa Alumni; President, Hillsborough County Head Start Foundation; Vice-President, Hillsborough County Bar Auxiliary; Chair, Friends of the Library Development Committee; Board, Sierra Club of Tampa Bay; Board, Tampa Audubon Society; Board, Tampa Historical Society; Member, American Association of University Women. Address: 3531 Village Way, Tampa, FL 33629-8914, USA.

PLAWES Sidney, b. 8 December 1957, New York, New York, USA. Physician. m. Deborah, 2 sons, 3 daughters. Education: Graduate with honours, Mathematics, Brooklyn College, 1978; Graduate, Albert Einstein School of Medicine, 1983. Appointment: Physician of Internal Medicine and Cardiology. Publications: Articles in medical journals including: Annals of Thoracic Surgery, 1989. Membership: American Medical Association. Address: 2270 Kinball St, Brooklyn, NY 11234, USA. E-mail: cnt531@hotmail.com

PLESKO Ivan, b. 13 June 1930, Selpice, Slovakia. Physician. m. Anna, 2 daughters. Education: MD, Comenius University, Bratislava, 1955; PhD, 1964; DSc, Slovak Academy of Sciences, Bratislava, 1987; Associate Professor, 1968. Appointments: Research Assistant, 1955-68; Assistant Professor, Epidemiology, Comenius University, Bratislava, 1968-76; Host Researcher, Institute Pasteur, Paris, 1968-; Assistant Professor, University of Constantine, Algery, 1971-73; Head, Department of Epidemiology, Cancer Research Institute, Slovak Academy of Sciences, 1976-; Head, National Cancer Registry of Slovakia, 1996-. Publications: Atlas of Cancer Occurrence in Slovakia; Epidemiology of Lung Cancer; Atlas of Cancer Mortality in Central Europe; More than 130 papers in professional journals. Honours: Jesenius Medal, Research in medical sciences; Golden Medal, Research and Art; Gold medal of Health Promotion Foundation, Warsaw, Poland; Gold medal of the Slovak Medical Society; others. Memberships: League Against Cancer, Slovakia; International Association of Cancer Registries; Science Council; Czech National Cancer Registry; European Institute of Oncology. Address: Pri Suchom mlyne 62, 811 04 Bratislava, Slovakia.

PLESKOV Vladimir Mikhailovich, b. 25 February 1942, Usviaty, Russia. Biochemist. m. Natalya Lysova, 1 daughter. Education: MD, 1st State Medical Institute, 1965; PhD, Institute of Experimental Medicine, Leningrad, 1987. Appointments: Chief, Clinical Laboratory, Marine Hospital, Health Ministry, Leningrad, 1987-89; Currently Senior Scientist, Laboratory of Pathomorphology, Influenza Research Institute, Russian Academy of Sciences, St Petersburg. Publications: Author experimentally argumented hypothesis of pathogenesis of autoimmune demielinizating diseases of nervous system, mechanism of viral persistence in atherosclerotic plaques and of the data concerning the problem of tumor growth rate decreasing based on the restriction of transport into cells of some metabolites which take part in cell membranes formation; More than 100 in scientific journals. Honours: Member, National Geographic Society; Member, New York Academy of Sciences; Academic of Russian Academy of Sciences. Address: Ispytatelei pr 11-164, 197341 St Petersburg, Russia.

PLESNIČAR Stojan Josip, b. 5 February 1925, Gorica, Italy. Oncologist; Educator; Consultant; Editor. m. Ljudmila Mila Gec, 2 sons. Education: MD, University of Ljubljana, Slovenia, 1954. Appointments: Intern, General Hospital, Koper, 1955-57; Resident, Institute of Oncology, Ljubljana, 1958-63; Assistant Professor, The Faculty of Medicine, Ljubljana, 1964-72; Research Fellow,

Karolinska Sjukhuset, Stockholm, Sweden, 1973-76; Professor of Oncology, Chairman of Oncology, 1982-95, University of Ljubljana, 1976-; Head, Department of Oncology and Radiotherapy, 1976-80; Founder and Head, Department of Tumour Biology, 1982-95; Lecturer, European School of Oncology, Milan, Italy, 1985-90; Visiting Professor and Fulbright Senior Researcher, University of Nebraska Medical School, Omaha, USA, 1981, 1982; Research Experience: Study of Tumour Metastases; Director, Institute of Oncology, Ljubljana, 1982-86; Lecturer, School of Environmental Sciences, University Polytechnic, Nova Gorica, Slovenia, 1997-. Publications: Cancer – A Preventable Disease, 1990, honourable mention, 1994; Textbook of Oncology and Radiotherapy, in Slovenian, 1977; Guest Editor: Cancer in the Emerging World, 2001; Co-founder, Editor-in-Chief, Member of Editorial Board, Radiology and Oncology, 1990-, recognition of merits Federative Cancer Society, 1990; Co-ordinating Editor, Challenge-ESO Newsletter, 1994-; Lecturer in field; Member of the Editorial Board, Cancer Letter, Oxford, England; Seminars in Oncology, Philadelphia, USA. Honours: Recipient, Golden Medal, Slovenian Cancer Society, 1992; Listed in Who's Who publications and biographical dictionaries. Memberships: The Djerba Group, 1995; American Association for Cancer Research; New York Academy of Sciences; European Society of Medical Oncology; Medical Association of Slovenia; Slovenia Cancer Research Foundation, co-founder, 1993; Academic Association for Third University in Slovenia, president; Member of the Senate, newly founded Faculty of Medicine, University of Maribor, Slovenia, 2002; Nomination for Membership of the Slovenian Academy of Sciences and Arts, 2001;Lion's Club Ljubljana, district governor, 1998-99. Address: Tesarska St, No 6, 1001 Ljubljana, Slovenia. E-mail: stojan.plesnicar@mf.uni-lj.si

PLISCHKE Elmer, b. 15 July 1914, Milwaukee, Wisconsin, USA. Professor Emeritus. m. Audrey Seihr, 1 son, 1 daughter. Education: PhB, Marquette University Milwaukee, 1937; MA, American University, Washington DC, 1938; PhD, Clark University, Worcester, Massachusetts, 1943. Appointments: District Supervisor and State Director, Wisconsin Historical Records Survey, 1940-42; Executive Secretary, Wisconsin War Records Commission, 1942; US Navy, 1943-46; Assistant Professor, De Pauw University, 1946-48; Assistant Professor, Associate Professor, Professor, Head of Department of Government and Politics, University of Maryland, 1948-79; Special Historian, Historical Division of the Office of the US High Commissioner for Germany, 1950-52; Professor Emeritus, 1979-; Adjunct Professor, Gettysburg College, 1979-85. Publications: 30 books and monographs; Forewords for 5 books; Over 80 articles in journals; 30 encyclopaedia articles; Several book reviews. Honours include: Establishment of The Elmer Plischke Award in Political Science, Munich Centre of University of Maryland, 1961; Recognition Award, University of Maryland chapter of Pi Sigma Alpha, 1966; Knight of Mark Twain, 1970; Diploma for Distinguished Achievement, Men of Achievement 1974; Fellowship Research Grant, Earhart Foundation, 1982-83, 1985-86; Special Research Grant, Gettysburg College, 1984-85. Memberships: Charter Member, Committee for the Study of Diplomacy, 1969-; Member, Institute for the Study of Diplomacy, Georgetown University, 1980-; Member, Pennsylvania Political Science Association, 1981-; Member, Torch Club, 1983-. Address: 227 Ewell Avenue, Gettysburg, PA 17325, USA.

PLISCHKE Le Moyne W, b. 11 December 1922, Greensburg, Pennsylvania. Research Chemist. m. Joan Harper. Education: BS, Waynesburg College, Pennsylvania, 1948; MS, West Virginia University, 1952. Appointments: Instructor, Waynesburg College, Pennsylvania, 1948-49; Research Chemist, US Naval Ordnance Test Station, California, 1952-53; Assistant Professor of Chemistry, Commonwealth University, Virginia, 1953-54; Research Chemist,

Dictionary of International Biography

E I Dupont, New Jersey, 1955-57; Research Chemist, Monsanto, Florida, 1957-. Publications: 18 US patents; 51 foreign patents. Honours: Monsanto Achievement Award. Memberships: American Chemical Society. Address: 2100 Club House Drive, Lillian, AL 36549-5402, USA. E-mail: plis123@gulftel.com

PLOTKIN Stanley A, b. 12 May 1932, New York, USA. Consultant; Emeritus Professor. m. Susan Lannon, 2 sons. Education: BA, New York University, 1948-52; MD, State University of New York College of Medicine, Brooklyn, 1952-62; MA, University of Pennsylvania, 1974. Appointments: Rotating Internship, Cleveland Metropolitan Hospital, 1956-57; Senior Assistant Surgeon, Epidemic Intelligence Service, USPHS, 1957-60; Instructor in Paediatrics, 1959-61, Associate in Paediatrics, 1964-65, Assistant Professor of Paediatrics, 1966-71, Associate Professor of Paediatrics, 1971-74, Professor, 1974-91, Professor of Microbiology, 1981-91, Associate Chairman, Department of Paediatrics, 1986-88, Professor Emeritus of Paediatrics, 1991-, University of Pennsylvania; Associate Member, 1960-61, Associate Member, 1963-74, Member, 1974-77, Professor, 1977-91, Professor Emeritus of Virology, 1991-, Wistar Institute of Anatomy and Biology; Resident in Paediatrics, 1961-62, Associate Physician, 1965-73, Director, Division of Infectious Diseases, 1969-90, Senior Physician, 1973-91, Chief, Infection Control Department, 1978-90, President, Medical Staff, 1984-86, Children's Hospital of Philadelphia; Resident in Paediatrics, Hospital for Sick Children, London, 1962-63; Medical and Scientific Director, Pasteur Mérieux Connaught Vaccines, Paris, 1991-97; Medical and Scientific Consultant, Aventis Pasteur, 1997-. Publications: 623 articles in professional scientific journals. Honours include: Listed in national and international biographical dictionaries; James D Bruce Award for Preventative Medicine, 1987; Distinguished Physician Award, Paediatric Infectious Diseases Society, 1993; Clinical Virology Award, Pan American Group for Rapid Viral Diagnosis, 1995; French Legion of Honour Medal, Chevalier, 1998; Distinguished Alumnus Award, Children's Hospital of Philadelphia, 2001; Sabin Foundation Gold Medal, 2002. Memberships include: Fellow, American Academy of the Advancement of Science; Society for Paediatric Research; American Society for Microbiology; Infectious Diseases Society of America; American Epidemiologic Society; American Association of Immunologists; American Society for Virology. Address: 4650 Wismer Road, Doylestown, PA 18901, USA. E-mail: stanley.plotkin@aventis.com

PLOWRIGHT Joan Anne, b. 28 October 1929, Brigg, Lancashire, England. Actress. m. (1) Roger Gage, 1953, (2) Sir Laurence (later Lord) Olivier, 1961, 1 son, 2 daughters. Education: Old Vic Theatre School. Appointments: Member, Old Vic Company, toured South Africa, 1952-53. Creative Works: Plays and films include: Richard Wagner, 1982; Cavell, 1982; Britannia Hospital, 1981; Brimstone and Treacle, 1982; The Cherry Orchard, 1983; The Way of the World, 1984; Mrs Warren's Profession, 1985; Revolution, 1985; The House of Bernardo Alba, 1986; Drowning by Numbers, 1987; Uncle Vanya, 1988; The Dressmaker, 1988; The Importance of Being Earnest, 1988; Conquest of the South Pole, 1989; And a Nightingale Sang, 1989; I Love You to Death, 1989; Avalon, 1990; Time and the Conways, 1991; Enchanted April, 1991; Stalin, 1991; Denis the Menace, 1992; A Place for Annie, 1992; A Pin for the Buterfly, 1993; Last Action Hero, 1993; Widow's Peak, 1994; On Promised Land, 1994; Return of the Natives, 1994; Hotel Sorrento, 1994; A Pyromaniac's Love Story, 1994; The Scarlet Letter, 1994; Jane Eyre, 1994; If We Are Women, 1995; Surviving Picasso, 1995; Mr Wrong, 1995; 101 Dalmatians, 1996; The Assistant, 1996; Shut Up and Dance, 1997; Tom's Midnight Garden, 1997; It May Be the Last Time, 1997; America Betrayed, 1998; Tea with Mussolini, 1998; Return to the Secret Garden, 1999; Frankie and

Hazel, 1999; Bailey's Mistake, 2000; Global Heresy, 2000. Publications: And That's Not All, autobiography, 2001. Honours include: Best Actress, Tony Award, 1960; Best Actress, Evening Standard Award, 1964; Variety Club Award, 1976; Variety Club Film Actress of the Year Award, 1987; Golden Globe Award, 1993; 18th Crystal Award for Women in Film, USA, 1994. Address: c/o The Malthouse, Horsham Road, Ashurst, Steying, West Sussex BN44 3AR, England.

PLUMMER Ora Beatrice, b. 25 May 1940, Mexia, Texas, USA. Registered Nurse. 1 son, 2 daughters. Education: BS, University of New Mexico, College of Nursing, 1961; MS, Nursing Education, University of California, School of Nursing, 1966. Appointments: Staff Nurse, Alba, New Mexico, Staff Nurse-Supervisor, Hollywood, California, 1961-62; Instructor, University of New Mexico, College of Nursing, Alba, New Mexico, 1968-69; Assistant Professor, University of Colorado School of Nursing, 1974-76; Staff Associate III, WICHEN, Boulder, Colorado, 1976-78; Nurse Surveyor, Training, Colorado Department of Health, 1979-92, 2000-2003. Publications: Effect of Nursing Reassurance on Patient Vocal Stress Levels, 1976; Demonstration Model for Patient Education, 1977; Long-Term Care: Implication for Medical Practice, 1988; Project Manager Report of Statistical Findings, 1989. Honours: Alpha Tau Delta, University of California at Los Angeles, 1965-66; Phi Delta Kappa, 1974-78; Florence Nightingale Nominee, 2003; Listed in Who's Who publications and biographical dictionaries. Memberships: Board of Directors, State Institutional Abuse Review; Team Member, Gerontological Advisory Committee, Metro State College, 1989-92. Address: Colorado Department of Health, 4300 Cherry Creek Drive South, Denver CO 80246 1523, USA.

PLUMMER William T, b. 25 March 1939, Baltimore, Maryland, USA. Optical Physicist. m. Susan W Plummer, 2 daughters. Education: AB, Physics, 1960, PhD, Physics, 1965, Johns Hopkins University. Appointments: Captain, US Army Reserve, 1965-67; Assistant Professor, Astronomy, University of Massachusetts, Amherst, 1967-69; Polaroid Corporation, 1969-2001; Scientist, Senior Scientist, Engineering Fellow, Senior Director; President, WTP Optics Inc, 2002-. Publications: Over 40 in professional journals; 94 US Patents. Honours: David Richardson Medal, 1980; Joseph Fraunhofer Award, 1997; Robert M Burley Prize, 1997; Elected Member, National Academy of Engineering, 1999. Memberships: Optical Society of America; SPIE. Address: 129 Arena Terrace, Concord, MA 01742-4413, USA.

PODDAR Sitaram, b. 17 March 1932, Patna City (Bihar), India. Medical Doctor; Lecturer; Researcher; Author; Social Worker. m. (1) divorced, 2 sons, 2 daughters, (2) Damayanti Poddar, 26 July 1978, 1 son, 1 daughter. Education: MB, BS, 1959, MS (General Surgery), 1962, MSc (Anatomy), 1965, Patna University. Appointments: Demonstrator, Anatomy, Patna Medical College, 1963-67; Lecturer, Anatomy, Patna Medical College, 1967-73; Lecturer, Human Biology and Anatomy, University of Sheffield, 1973-75; Teaching Fellow, Anatomy, University of Texas at Houston, 1974; Lecturer, Anatomy, 1975-78, Senior Lecturer, Anatomy, 1978-97, University of the West Indies; Retired, 1997. Publications: Several research articles on mammalian salivary glands and histochemistry of mucosubstances; 6 books on anatomy; Several self-instructional monographs on various topics of anatomy. Honours: Honorary Citizen of Houston and Goodwill Ambassador, 1974; Jewel of the Society Award for exceptional services to society, Shri Marwari High School, Patna City, 1988; The Jamaica Physiotherapy Association Outstanding Contribution Award, 1989; Chairman's Award for Outstanding Contribution, The National Council for Indian Culture in Jamaica, 1999; International Diploma of Honor; Universal Award of Accomplishment, American Biographical Institute, 2001; World Citizen of the Year 2002; Order of International Ambassadors, ABI, 2002; 2000 Outstanding Intellectuals of the 21st Century; International Order of Merit; 500 Leaders of Influence; Outstanding Speaker of the 21st Century; International Directory of Distinguished Leadership Hall of Fame; 500 Founders of the 21st Century; Life-Time Achievement Award; Life-time Deputy Governor, American Biographical Institute Research Association; Recipient of 2001 Noble Prize, United Cultural Convention, USA; January 28 to be permanently known as International Sitaram Poddar Day as a World Biographee; Outstanding Chief Editor Award, Prema Satsangh of Jamaica, 2002; International Peace Prize, United Cultural Convention, USA, 2003; Eminent Educationist and Scholarship in his name, Marwari High School, 2003; Founding Cabinet Member, World peace and Diplomacy Forum, 2003. Memberships: Former Member: Anatomical Society of Great Britain and Ireland; American Association of Anatomists; Association for the Study of Medical Education, UK; Advisory Editorial Board, West Indian Medical Journal; Founder Patna City Shishu Bhawan School, 1964; Co-Founder, Secretary, National Council for Indian Culture in Jamaica, 1998; Past Vice-President, Club India, Jamaica; Life Member, Anatomical Society of India; Life Fellow, International Biographical Centre; Life Fellow, American Biographical Institute. Address: 5 Gerbera Drive, Mona Heights, Kingston 6, Jamaica, West Indies.

PODRAZA-KWIATOWSKA Maria, b. 19 January 1926, Kolomyja, Poland. Professor of Philology. m. Jerzy Kwiatkowski, 1 son, 1 daughter. Education: Master's Degree, 1951; PhD, 1964; Habilitation, 1970. Appointments: Research Worker, Institute of Literary Research, Polish Academy of Sciences, 1951-74; Docent, 1974-82, Professor of Philology, 1982-, Jagellonian University, Cracow, Poland; Visiting Professor, University of Mainz, Germany, 1991-92. Publications: Books include: Harmonies and Dissonances of Young Poland, 1969; Symbolism and Symbols, 1975; Somnambulists, Decadents, Heroes, 1985; Literature of Young Poland, 1992; Freedom and Transcendence, 2001. Honours; Prize, Ministry of Higher Education, 1976, 1986, 1993; Prize of Voivode, Cracow, 1994; Prize of the Town of Cracow, 2001. Memberships: International Comparative Literature Association (Polish Section); Polish Academy of Arts and Sciences; Association of Polish Writers. Address: Aleja Mickiewicza 13/2, 31-120 Cracow, Poland

POGRIBNY Wlodzimierz, b. 19 November 1938, Sahnovszchyna, Ukraine. Professor; Scientific Researcher. m. Iryna Pogribna, 3 daughters. Education: PhD, Institute of Electrical Dynamics, Academy of Science, Kiev, 1970; DSc, Institute of Radiotechnology and Electronics, Academy of Science, Moscow, 1986; Professor, State Committee of Education of USSR, Moscow, 1990. Appointments: Research Scientist, Lviv Physical-Mechanical Institute, Lviv, 1960-87; Head of Chair, National University, Lviv Polytechnic, 1987-96; Professor, Institute of Telecommunications, University of Technology and Agriculture, Bydgoszcz, Poland, 1996-. Publications: Author, 5 books; Author, over 300 other scientific works and 80 inventions in field of Signal Processing. Honours: Man of the Year 2000. Memberships: International Academy of Information, 1993-; IEEE, 2004; SPIE, 1999-. Address: Institute of Telecommunications of UTA, 7 Kaliskiego Ave, Bydgoszcz, PL 85-796, Poland. E-mail: pohry@atr.bydgoszcz.pl

POITIER Sidney, b. 20 February 1927, Miami, Floria, USA. Actor. m. (1) Juanita Hardy, 4 daughters, (2) Joanna Shimkus, 2 daughters. Appointments: Army service, 1941-45; Actor with American Negro Theatre, 1946; Member, 1994-2003, President, 1994-2003, Board of Directors, Walt Disney Company; Ambassador to Japan from the Commonwealth of the Bahamas; Actor, films including: Cry the Beloved Country; Red Ball Express; Go, Man, Go; Blackboard Jungle, 1955; Goodbye My Lady, 1956;

Edge of the City, Something of Value, 1957; The Mark of the Hawk, The Defiant Ones, 1958; Porgy and Bess, 1959; A Raisin in the Sun, Paris Blues, 1960; Lilies of the Field, 1963; The Long Ships, 1964; The Bedford Incident, 1965; The Slender Thread, A Patch of Blue, Duel at Diablo, 1966; To Sir With Love, In the Heat of the Night, 1967; Guess Who's Coming to Dinner, 1968; For the Love of Ivy, 1968; The Lost Man, 1970; They Call Me Mister Tibbs, 1970; The Organization, 1971; The Wilby Conspiracy, 1975; Shoot to Kill, 1988; Deadly Pursuit, 1988; Separate But Equal, TV, 1992; Sneakers, Children of the Dust, TV, 1995; To Sir With Love II, TV, 1996; Actor, director, Buck and Preacher, 1972; Warm December, 1973; Uptown Saturday Night, 1974; Let's Do It Again, 1975; A Piece of the Action, 1977; One Man, One Vote, 1996; Director, Stir Crazy, 1980; Hanky Panky, 1982; Got For It, 1984; Little Nikita, 1987; Ghost Dad, 1990; Sneakers, 1992; The Jackal, 1997. Publication: This Life, 1980. Honours: Silver Bear Award, Berlin, 1958; NT Film Critics Award, 1958; Academy Award, Oscar, Best Actor of 1963; Cecil B De Mille Award, 1982; Life Achievement Award, American Film Institute, 1992; Kennedy Centre Honours, 1995; Honorary KBE; Honorary Academy Award for Lifetime Achievement, 2002. Address: c/o CAA, 9830 Wilshire Boulevard, Beverly Hills, CA 90210, USA.

POLAY Bruce, b. 22 March 1949, Brooklyn, New York, USA. Musician. m. Louise Phillips, 17 December 1983, 2 sons, 3 daughters. Education: BM, Composition, University of Southern California, 1971; MA, Composition, California State University, 1976; DMA, Instrumental Music, Arizona State University, 1989. Appointments: Music Director, Southern California Philharmonia, 1971-81; Conductor, Phoenix Symphony Guild Youth Orchestra, 1981-83; Assistant Conductor, Arizona State University Symphony Orchestra, 1981-83; Music Director, Conductor, Knox-Galesburg Symphony, 1983-; Professor of Music, Chair, Music Department, Knox College, 1983-. Creative Works: Numerous commissions, Compositions include: Encominm, 1986; Concerto for Tenor Trombone, 1990; Cathedral Images, 1992; Semi-Suite for Piano Trio, 2001; Illumination for Orchestra, 2004; Several recordings for CD's; US Guest Conductor, Piano Soloist and Recitalist in Romania, Spain, Russia, Belarus, United Kingdom, USA. Honours: Illinois Orchestra of the Year, 1986-87, 1998-99; 2 Mellon Foundation Travel Grants; ASCAP Standards Awards, 1993-2004; 2 Lilly Foundation Grants; Illinois Conductor of the Year, 1997-98 and 2004-05; Exceptional Achievement Award, Knox College. Memberships: ASCAP; American Music Centre; Phi Kappa Phi; Illinois Council of Orchestras; Board of Directors, Barlow Endowment for Music Composition, Brigham Young University; Advisory Board, Foundation for New Music. Address: 1577 N Cherry Street, Galesburg, IL 61401-1820, USA.

POLENSKY-KSIAZEK Henryk, b. 12 April 1953, Miechow, Poland. Pilot. m. Anna Zachwieja, 1989, 2 son, 1 daughter. Education: Pilot College, Deblin, 1974; American Flight Academy, Oklahoma, USA, 1992. Appointments: Airforce Pilot, Instructor, 1972-82; Pilot, Flygtjänst, Sweden, 1987; Pilot, Greenlandair, 1988-89; Pilot, Euroflight, Sweden, 1990-92; Managing Director, Polensky Inc, 1994; Pilot, PLL LOT Warsaw, Poland, 1997-2003; Flight Operations Manager, Globe Airlines, Poland, 2003-. Publication: Book, Flight to Freedom, 2000. Honour: Member, Bronze Medal Winner, Polish Team, World Helicopter Championships. Membership: Pilots Association. Address: Solståndsg 30, 41509 Gothenburg, Sweden. E-mail: ksiazek@post.utfors.se

POLIAKOFF Stephen, b. 1952, London, England. Dramatist; Director. m. Sandy Welch, 1983, 1 son, 1 daughter. Education: Westminster School; University of Cambridge. Theatre: Clever Soldiers, 1974; The Carnation Gang, 1974; Hitting Town, 1975;

City Sugar, 1976; Strawberry Fields, 1978; Shout Across the River, 1978; The Summer Party, 1980; Favourite Nights, 1981; Breaking the Silence, 1984; Coming into Land, 1987; Playing with Trains, 1989; Sienna Red, 1992; Sweet Panic, 1996; Blinded by the Sun, 1996; Talk of the City, 1998; Remember This, 1999; Films: Hidden City, 1992; Close My Eyes, 1992; Century, 1995; The Tribe, 1998; Food of Love, 1998; TV plays include: Caught on a Train; She's Been Away; Shooting the Past, 1999; Perfect Strangers, 2001; The Lost Prince, 2003. Publications: Plays One, 1989; Plays Two, 1994; Plays Three; Sweet Panic; Blinded by the Sun; Talk of the City; Shooting the Past; Remember This. Honours include: Best British Film Award, 1992; Critic's Circle Best Play Award; Prix Italia; BAFTA Award; Venice Film Festival Prize. Address: 33 Donia Devonia Road, London N1 8JQ, England.

POLKA Pavel, b. 9 April 1957, Prague, Czech Republic. Foreign Relations Officer. Education: Autodidact; Private studies and consultations. Career: Founder, The Czech Handel Society, 1990; Chief Manager, Masterworks of Baroque Opera - George Frideric Handel and his Contemporaries, 1996-; Six Handel opera productions; Productions of Vivaldi's Orlando finto pazzo and Alessandro Scarlatti's L'Amor Generoso (modern world premières). Publications: A Handel monograph, Prague, 1991; The title in English, The Triumph of Time and Truth. Contributions: Händel-Jahrbuch, Halle, Germany; Newsletter of the American Handel Society, College Park, Maryland, USA; Zpravodaj SSH, Prague; Händel-Hausmitteilungen, Halle, Germany; Handel News, London; articles in Czech newspapers. Honours: Czech Music Fund Awards, 1984, 1985, 1986, 1987, 1988. Memberships: The Czech Handel Society, chairman; The George Frideric Handel Society, Halle, Germany; The Czech Music Society; The Joseph Haydn European Cultural Centre Foundation, Czech Republic. Address: Na Maninách 11/795, 170 00 Praha 7, Czech Republic.

POLLACK Sydney, b. 1 July 1934, Lafayette, Indiana, USA. Film Director. m. Claire Griswold, 1958, 1 son, 2 daughters. Education: Neighbourhood Playhouse Theatre School, New York. Appointments: Assistant to Sanford Meisner, 1954; Acting Instructor, 1954-57, 1959-60; Army service, 1957-59; Executive Director, The Actors Studio, West Coast branch; Theatre appearances: The Dark is Light Enough, Broadway, 1954; A Stone for Danny Fisher, 1955; TV appearances include: Aloa Presents; Director, The Chrysler Theatre, Ben Casey, for TV, 1962-63; Director, films: The Slender Thread, 1965; This Property is Condemned, 1966; The Scalphunters, 1967; Castle Keep, 1968; They Shoot Horses Don't They, 1969-70; Jeremiah Johnson, 1971-72; The Way We Were, 1972-73; The Yakuza, 1974; Three Days of the Condor, 1974-75; Bobby Deerfield, 1976; The Electric Horseman, 1978-79; Absence of Malice, 1981; Tootsie, 1982; Producer, Song Writer, 1984; Out of Africa, producer, 1985; Havana, 1989; The Firm, 1993; Sabrina, 1996; Producer: The Fabulous Baker Boys, 1989; The Last Ship, 1990; King Ralph, co-executive producer; Dead Again, executive producer; Presumed Innocent, 1990; Sense and Sensibility executive producer; The Talented Mr Ripley, 1999; Co-producer: Bright Lights, Big City, 1988; Actor: The Player; Death Becomes Her; Husbands and Wives; A Civil Action; Eyes Wide Shut. Address: Mirage Enterprises, De Mille Bldg, 110, 5555 Melrose Avenue, Los Angeles, CA 90212, USA.

POLLARD Jane, (Jane Jackson, Dana James), b. 22 November 1944, Goole, Yorkshire, England. Author. m. (3) Michael Pollard, 2 June 1992, 2 sons, 1 daughter. Publications: Historical Romances: Harlyn Tremayne, 1984; The Consul's Daughter, 1986; Contemporary Romance: Doctor in The Andes, 1984; Desert Flower, 1986; Doctor in New Guinea, 1986; Rough Waters, 1986; The Marati Legacy, 1986; The Eagle and the Sun, 1986; Heart of Glass, 1987; Tarik's Mountain, 1988; Snowfire, 1988; Pool of

Dreaming, 1988; Dark Moon Rising, 1989; Love's Ransom, 1989; A Tempting Shore, 1992; Bay of Rainbows, 1993; Mystery: Deadly Feast, 1997; Historical Romance: A Place of Birds, 1997; The Iron Road, 1999; Eye of the Wind, 2001; Tide of Fortune, 2004. Contributions to: Falmouth Packet; West Briton; Western Morning News; Woman's Way; Radio Cornwall; BFBS Gibraltar, GIB TV; Mammoth Book of Men O' War: Stories from the Glory Days of Sail, 1999, volume 2: Hearts of Oak, 2001. Memberships: Romantic Novelists Association; Society of Authors; Historical Novel Society. Literary Agent: Dorian Literary Agency, Upper Thornehill, 27 Church Road, St Marychurch, Torquay TQ1 4QY. Address: 32 Cogos Park, Comfort Road, Mylor, Falmouth, Cornwall TR11 5SF, England.

POLUBOTKO Aleksey, b. 11 January 1950, Leningrad, Russia. Physicist; Theorist. 1 daughter. Education: Diploma, Physical Faculty, Leningrad State University, 1967-73; Postgraduate, Leningrad Physico-Technical Institute of Russian Academy of Sciences, 1978-82; PhD, 1983. Appointments: Senior Engineer, Physical Faculty, Leningrad State University, 1973-74; Senior Engineer, Leningrad Electrotechnical Institute; 1974-78; Engineer, Theoretical Department, 1980-83, Junior Scientific Worker, Theoretical Department, 1983-87, Laboratory of Physico-Chemical Properties of Semiconductors, 1987-88, Scientific Researcher, Laboratory of Physico-Chemical Properties of Semiconductors, Leningrad Physico-Technical Institute, 1988-; Visiting Associate Professor, Tohoku University, Japan, 1993; Visiting Postdoctoral Fellow, Northwestern University, Evanston, Illinois, 1997; Visiting Professor, Xiamen University, Xiamen, China, 2000. Publications: Several articles in professional journals maily about SERS (Surface Enhancement of Raman Scattering) theory and the theory of zero-gap magnetic semiconductors. Honours include: 2 Silver medals, Leningrad Championships in orienteering and marathon orienteering, 1971; 2 Bronze medals, Leningrad Championships in marathon orienteering, 1972, 1973. Address: A F Ioffe Physico-Technical Institute, Politechnicheskaya 26, 194021 St Petersburg, Russia.

POLYAKOV Valeriy Ivanovich, b. 18 July 1956, Bryansk, Russia. Head of the City of Bryansk. m. Tamara Polyakova. Education: Bryansk Machine Building Institute, 1985; Branch of Oryol Academy of State Service, 2001; Candidate of Technical Sciences. Appointments: Director General of the Plant "Litiy", 1991-2001; Chairman, Bryansk City Council of People's Deputies, 2001-2002; Head of the City and City Management, Bryansk City Administration, 2002-. Honours: Medal , Second Class, for Services to the Homeland; Title, Honoured Machine Builder; The Order of Friendship. Memberships: Congress of Russian Municipalities; International Assembly of Capitals and Cities of the CIS; Congress of Local and Regional Authorities of Europe; International Association "Twin-Cities". Address: Lenin Avenue 35, Bryansk 241002, Russia. E-mail: root@gorod.bryansk.ru Website: www.bryansk.032.ru

POLYANIN Andrei Dmitrievitch, b. 1 November 1951, Beijing, China. Mathematician; Mechanic. Education: MSc, Faculty of Mechanics and Mathematics, Moscow State University, 1974; PhD, Institute for Problems in Mechanics, 1981, DSc, Institute for Problems in Mechanics, 1986, Russian Academy of Sciences. Appointments: Trial Researcher, 1975, Junior Researcher, 1976, Researcher, 1981, Senior Researcher, 1987, Professor, 1992, Institute for Problems in Mechanics, Russian Academy of Sciences; Editor of Book Series, "Differential and Integral Equations and their Applications", Taylor & Francis Inc, London, 1998; Editor of Website, EqWorld, "The World of Mathematical Equations" (http://eqworld.ipmnet.ru), 2004. Publications: 33 books in English, Russian, German and Bulgarian include; Handbook of Exact Solutions for Ordinary Differential Equations, 1995, 2003;

Handbook of Integral Equations, 1998; Handbook of Linear Mathematical Physics Equations, 2001; Handbook of Nonlinear Mathematical Physics Equations, 2002; Handbook of Linear Partial Differential Equations for Engineers and Scientists, 2002; Handbook of Nonlinear Partial Differential Equations, 2004; Over 120 science articles and 3 patents. Honours: Chaplygine Prize of Russian Academy of Sciences, 1991; International Man of the Year 2000-2001, IBC; Award, Ministry of Education of the Russian Federation, 2001; Listed in numerous biographical dictionaries. Memberships: Russian National Committee on Theoretical and Applied Mechanics, 2001; Research Board of Advisors of the American Biographical Institute, 2000; Editorial Board of the Journal Theoretical Foundations of Chemical Engineering, 2001; Editorial Advisors of the Research Signpost (India). Address: Institute for Problems in Mechanics, Russian Academy of Sciences, Vernadsky ave 101, Bldg 1, 119526, Moscow, Russia.

POMBEIRO Armando José Latourrette, b. 9 June 1949, Porto, Portugal. Professor of Chemistry. 2 sons, 1 daughter. Education: Chemical Engineering, Instituto Superior Tecnico, Portugal, 1971; DPhil, University of Sussex, England, 1976. Appointments: Assistant, 1971, Auxiliary Professor, 1975, Associate Professor, 1979, Full Professor, 1989, Instituto Superior Tecnico. Publications: 2 books; 40 book chapters and review articles; Over 260 articles in scientific journals; 7 patents; 10 didactic publications; 17 other publications including science and technology systems, biographies. Memberships: Full member, Academy of Sciences of Lisbon, 1988-, Vice President of Class of Sciences, 1999-2000, Vice General Secretary, 1998, Secretary of Class of Sciences, 1998-2001, Directorate, 1998-, Commission for Publications; Secretary General, Academy of Sciences, 2001-; European Academies' Science Advisory Council (EASAC), 2001-; Fellow, Royal Society of Chemistry, 1986-; New York Academy of Sciences, 1995; Higher Council for Science and Technology, 1995; Higher Council for Science, Technology and Innovation, 2004-; Physical and Engineering Science and Technology Panel, 1999, Advisory Panel on ASI Programme, 1995-98, NATO Science Programme; Member, European Academies Science Advisory Council, 2001-; Member, External Evaluation Commission of the Portuguese Universities, 2002-; Member and Co-Founder, Portuguese Electrochemical Society, President, 1988-89, 1994-95, Vice President, 1990-91, Secretary, 1983-87; Member and Co-Founder, Iberoamerican Society of Electrochemistry and National Representative, 1992-96; International Society of Electrochemistry; Affiliate Member, IUPAC; Portuguese Chemical Society. Address: Centro de Quimica Estutural, Complexo Interdisciplinar, Instituto Superior Tecnico, Av Rovisco Pais, 1049-001 Lisboa, Portugal. E-mail: pombeiro@ist.ut.pt

POMPILI Claudio, b. 12 May 1949, Gorizia, Italy. Composer. Education: BMus, University of Adelaide, 1983; Study with Richard Meale and Tristram Cary in Australia (1980-82) and with Franco Donatoni and Salvatore Sciarrino in Italy (1984-85); IRCAM studios, Paris, 1984. Career includes: Faculty Member, University of Adelaide, 1983-84, University of New England, 1987-97; Associate Professor and Director, Conservatorium of Music, University of Wollongong, 1998-2001; Commissions from Duo Contemporain, Perihelion and others. Compositions include: Medieval Purity in a Bed of Thorns, for tape, 1981-84; The Star Shoots a Dart, for flute, clarinet, violin and cello, 1985; Polymnia Triptych for soprano and large ensemble, 1986; Songs for Ophelia for soprano, 1989; Scherzo alla Francescana, for double bass, 1990; Trio for violin, guitar and double bass, 1990; Zeitfluss: teuflicher kontrapunkt, for wind quintet, 1990; Lo spazio stellato si riflette in suoni, for baroque flute, 1990; Ah, amore che se n'ando nell'aria, for clarinet, viola and cello, 1991; String Quartet, 1992; El viento lucha a obscura con tu sueno, 1993; Fra l'urlo e il tacere, for bass

clarinet, 1993. Honours include: Adolf Spivakovsky Scholarship, 1990. Address: 264 Milne Road, Modbury Heights, SA 5092, Australia.

PONASENKOV Evgeni, b. Moscow. Historian; Politologist; Singer. Education: Moscow Lomonosov University; School of Belcanto, Moscow. Appointment: Professor of International University of Perjavin in Moscow. Publications: Books: Napoleon, 1995; Russian Vocal School, 2000; Article in Vlast-kommersant: Iraq Problem, 2003. Honours: Grand Prix, Russian Vocal Festival of 2000; Listed in Who's Who publications and biographical dictionaries. Memberships: Russian Americanist Association; President, Russian Napoleonic Association. Address: 64 K1 Koroschevskoe Schosse, 123007 Moscow, Russia. E-mail: ponasenkov@mtn-net.ru

PONG David Bertram Pak-Tang, b. 28 September 1939, Hong Kong. Professor. m. Barbara Mar, 3 daughters. Education: St Paul's College, Hong Kong, 1951-60; BA, Hons, School of Oriental and African Studies, University of London, 1963; PhD, School of Oriental and African Studies, 1969. Appointments: Research Fellow, Institute of Historical Research, University of London, 1965-66; Fellow, Far Eastern History, School of Oriental and African Studies, University of London, 1966-69; Assistant Professor, History, University of Delaware, 1969-73; Associate Professor, History, 1973-89; Research Fellow, Research School of Pacific Studies, Institute of Advanced Studies, Australian National University, 1978-82; Professor, 1989-; Chair, Department of History, 1992-98; Director, East Asian Studies Programme, 1989-. Publications: Taiwan haifang bing kaishan riji; A Critical Guide to the Kwangtung Provincial Archives Deposited at the Public Record Office of London; Ideal and Reality: Social and Political Change in Modern China, 1860-1949; Shen Pao-chen and China's Modernization in the Nineteenth Century; Shen Baozhen pingzhuan; Zhongguo Jindaihua de changshi; Resisting Japan: Mobilization for War in China, 1935-45; Many Articles. Honours: Research Fellowship, Institute of Historical Research, University of London, 1965-66; American Council of Learned Societies Research Fellowship, 1973-74; Research Fellow, Research School of Pacific Studies, Institute of Advanced Studies, Australian National University, 1978-82; Phi Kappa Phi Honor Society, 1999; Honorary Research Fellow, Modern History Research Centre, Hong Kong Baptist University, 2002-. Memberships: Association for Asian Studies; Society for Qing Studies; History Society of 20th-Century China; Modern Chinese History Society of Hong Kong; Chinese Military History Society; Phi Kappa Phi Honor Society. Address: Department of History, University of Delaware, Newark, DE 19716, USA.

PONIATOWSKA Irena, b. 5 July 1933, Góra Kalwaria, Poland. Musicologist. m. Andrzej Poniatowski, 14 November 1953, deceased 1994, 1 daughter. Education: Diploma, Musicology, Warsaw University, 1962; PhD, 1970; Qualification to Assistant Professor, 1983; Habil; Qualification to Professor, 1994. Career: Tutor, 1970, Vice Director, 1974-79; Assistant Professor, 1984, Extraordinary Professor, 1991, Ordinary Professor, 1996, Institute of Musicology, Vice Dean, Faculty of History, 1986-90, 1993-99, Warsaw University; President, Council, 1976-86, Vice President, 1986-91, Chopin Society; President: Congress, Musica Antiqua Europae Orientalis, Poland, 1988, 1991, 1994, 1997, 2000, 2003; Polish Chopin Academy, 1994-; Chopin Congress, 1999; President, Programm Council of Institut Fryderyk Chopin, 2001-; Editor of many encyclopaedias including: Polish Encyclopaedia of Music, Volumes I, II, III, IV, 1979; Various offices in Union of Polish Composers, Section of Musicologists. Publications: Beethoven Piano Texture, 1972; The Chronicle of the Important Musical Events in Poland 1945-72, 1974; Piano Music and Playing in XIX Century Artistic and Social Aspects,

Dictionary of International Biography

1991; Dictionary of Music for Schools, 1991, 2nd edition, 1997; History and Interpretation of Music, 1993, 2nd edition, 1995; Editor, Musical Work: Theory History, Interpretation, 1984; Maria Szymanowska 25 Mazurkas, 1993; Editor, Chopin in the Circle of his Friends, Vols I-V, 1995-99; 24 Préludes de Frédéric Chopin op 28; Facsimile edition with commentaries, 1999; I Polonaise Brillante op 4 (violin and piano) of H Wieniawski, urtext and critical edition, 2000; Chopin and his Work in the Context of Culture, Vols 1-2, 2003; Many articles in collective works. Contributions to: Muzyka; Ruch Muzyczny; Rocznik Chopinowski; Chopin Studies; Res Facta; Barok; Hudobny Život; Quadrivium; Music Towards Tradition: Ideas, work, reception, (studies edited by Sz Paczkowski, 2004), dedicated to I Poniatowska for her 70th anniversary. Address: Filtrowa 63-38, 02-056 Warsaw, Poland.

POOL Adam de Sola, b. 5 November 1957, Palo Alto, California, USA. Venture Capitalist. m. Kristina Gjerde, 1 son. Education: BA, University of Chicago, 1981; MA, University of California, 1982; MBA, Massachusetts Institute of Technology. Economist, First National Bank of Chicago, 1980; Research Officer, 1982-83, International Officer, 1983-86, Assistant Vice President, 1986, Industrial Bank of Japan, New York; Associate, Corporate Finance, Salomon Brothers Inc, New York, 1987, 1988-92; Principal Banker, 1992-94, Senior Banker, 1994-95, European Bank for Reconstruction and Development; Chief Investment Officer, Yamaichi Regent ABC Polska, 1995-97; Owner, PP Investments, 1998-. Publications: Published photographer. Memberships: Board member: Relpol Centrum SA; Finesco SA; Korte-Organica RT; Honorary Member, Yale Club. Address: ul Piaskowa 12c, 05-510 Konstanin, Poland. E-mail: pool@eip.com.pl

POPA Anghel, b. 25 March 1946, Vatra Dornei, Judeţul Suceava, Romania. Professor of History. 1 son. Education: Graduate, Faculty of History, Al.I.Cuza University, 1971; Doctors Degree, History, 1982. Appointments: Professor of History, High School. Publications: Over 90 articles and studies in magazines of history; 4 books dealing with problems of modern history in Romania. Honours: Magazin Istoric Cultural Foundation of Bucharest; The Cultural Bukovina's Foundation of Suceava. Memberships: Sever Zotta Romanian Institute of Genealogy and Heraldry of IAŞI; A.D.Xenopol History Foundation, IAŞI. Address: Str Rândunicii Nr 2, Bl, G-4, Sc C, Et 4, Ap 20, Câmpulung Moldovenesc 5950, Judeţul Suceava, Romania.

POPIELA Tadeusz, b. 23 May 1933, Nowy Sącz, Poland. Surgeon. m. Mieczysława Popiela, 1 son, 1 daughter. Education: Medical Faculty, Jagiellonian University, 1950-55; Dr Deg, 1961; Habilitation, 1965; Professor of Medicine, 1972. Appointments: Research Assistant, Department of Surgery, 1955-65; Assistant Professor, 1965-71; Head, Surgical Unit of Gastroenterology, 1971-76; 3rd Department and Clinic of General Surgery, Jagiellonian University; Rector, Medical Faculty, Jagiellonian University, 1972-81; Professor, Head, 1st Department of General and GI Surgery, Jagiellonian University, 1976-2003; Head, Intraoperative Radiotherapy and Chemotherapy Ward of the 1st Department of General and GI Surgery, 2003-. Publications: 11 monographies; 401 articles; 707 contributions at congresses. Honours: President's Best Poster Prize; CICD World Congress, Jerusalem, 1986; 2 First Prizes, International Gastric Cancer Congress, Kyoto, 1995; Doctor Honoris Causa, Pomeranian Medical University, 2002, Wroclaw Medical University, 2003. Memberships: Honorary member, JE Purkyne Czech Medical Association; Honorary member, German Society of Surgery; President, ESS, 2000; National delegate, ISS, CICD; Deputy Secretary, Executive Office Member, EAES; AGA; Society of Polish Surgeons; American College of Surgeons; IGSC; EDS; IGCA, council member; IHPE; ESES; Polish Academy of Sciences; Polish Academy of Arts and Sciences; State Committee

for Scientific Research. Address: 1st Department of General and GI Surgery, Jagiellonian University, 40 Kopernika St, 31-501 Kraków, Poland. E-mail: mspopiel@cyf-kr.edu.pl

POPIOLEK-RODZIŃSKA Irena, b. 17 May 1939, Zdołbunów, Poland. Artist; Art Educator. m. Stanisław Rodziński, 1 daughter. Education: MA, Academy of Fine Arts, Cracow, Poland, 1965; Professor, 1995. Appointments: Professor, Secondary School, Clothes Industry, Cracow, Poland, 1965-75; Inspector, Provincial School Superintendent's Office, Cracow, 1975-78; Professor, Pedagogical Academy, Cracow, 1978-97; High School Philosophy and Pedagogics Ignatianum, Cracow, 1993-; University of Rzeszow, 1997-; Exhibitions: More than 50 solo exhibitions in Poland including: Cracow, Warsaw, Katowitce, Rzeszow, Wroclaw and abroad in: Germany, Holland, Italy, Austria; Represented in permanent collections in numerous museums in Poland, Australia, Canada, Germany, Holland, Austria and USA. Honours Numerous awards include: Drawing Biennale, Belgrade; Picture of the Year, Ars Aquae, Katowice. Membership: Union of Polish Artists. Address: ul Heleny 14/106, 30-837 Krakow, Poland.

POPOV Alexandr Vassilievich, b. 9 May 1947, Rostov Region, Russia. Engineer. m. Natalia Yevgenievna, 1 son, 1 daughter. Education: Engineer of Electronic Equipment, Radiotechnical Institute of Taganrog, 1973; Teacher of Communism Science, Higher Communist Party School of Rostov-on-Don, 1988; Academician, Russian Academy for Humanitarian Sciences, 2000; Doctor of Sociology, 2002. Appointments: Head of Chair of Regional Studies, Rostov State University; Chairman of Rostov Regional Council of People's Deputies, -1994; Chairman of Legislative Assembly of the Rostov Region, 1994-. Publications: Regions' Management – Rostov-on-Don, 2001; Problems of regional development ideologies formation (co-author), 2002. Honours: Order of Friendship; Medal for Labour Merit. Memberships: Member of Council for Interaction between Federal Council of Federal Assembly of the Russian Federation with Legislative Representative Authorities of the Russian Federation Subjects (Russian Legislators' Council). Address: Legislative Assembly of the Rostov Region, Sotsialisticheskaya Str. 112, Rostov-on-Don, 344050 Russia. E-mail: zsrnd@donpac.ru

POPOV Lubomir Savov, b. 7 December 1952, Plovdiv, Bulgaria. Design Educator. Education: Master of Architecture, University of Architecture, Civil Engineering and Geodesy, Sofia, Bulgaria, 1978; PhD, Sociology, Bulgarian Academy of Sciences, 1992; PhD, Architecture, University of Wisconsin-Milwaukee, USA, 1998. Appointments: Research Specialist, Sofia State University, Bulgaria; Research Specialist, Bulgarian Academy of Sciences, 1985-88, 1992-93; Teaching Assistant, 1993-97, Postdoctoral Position, 1998-99, University of Wisconsin-Milwaukee, USA; Assistant Professor, Bowling Green State University, USA, 1999-. Publications: Monographs: Facility programming as Sociospatial Planning, 1999; The Culture of Facility Programming Clients, 2001; The Architectural Student Culture, 2003; 17 refereed papers and many conference presentations; Research areas: facility programming, planning and post-occupancy evaluation, environment and behaviour, design methodology. Honours: Recipient of Fellowships from several institutions. Memberships: Environmental Design Research Association; Interior Design Educators Council; Design Research Society; Union of Architects in Bulgaria; Phi Delta Kappa International. Address: 301 Johnson Hall, Bowling Green State University, Bowling Green, OH 43403, USA.

POPOV-PERGAL Katarina, b. 6 December, 1947, Novi Sad, Yugoslavia. Associate Professor. m. Miroslav Pergal, 1 son. Education: Diploma, Chemistry, 1972, Specialist in Chemistry, 1974, Faculty of Science, University of Novi Sad; Dr Chem Sci,

University of Belgrade, 1988. Appointments: Secondary School Teacher of Chemistry, High School in Vrbas, Yugoslavia, 1972-74; Associate in Organic Chemistry, 1974-81, Assistant in Organic Chemistry, 1981-93, Research Associate in Organic Chemistry, 1993-98, Assistant Professor in Organic Chemistry Heterocyclic Compounds for postgraduate students, 1995-98, Faculty of Science, University of Novi Sad; Assistant Professor of Chemistry, 1998-2001; Associate Professor of Chemistry, Faculty of Forest Science, University of Belgrade, 2001-. Publications: 44 scientific papers for journals, 3 patents, 52 communications and section lectures at domestic and international scientific meetings, 2 textbooks, 23 finished scientific projects. Honours: Fellowship Award of the Second International Conference on Heteroatom Chemistry, Albany, New York, USA, 1989; Letter of Gratitude of Chemical Society of Vojvodina, 2000. Memberships: Serbian Chemical Society, 1972-; Associate Member, 1986-2001, Member (MRSC), Royal Society of Chemistry, 2001-; International Society Heterocyclic Chemistry, 1988-; Affiliated Member, International Union of Pure and Applied Chemistry, 1989-; International Member of the American Association for the Advancement of Science, 1994-; New York Academy of Sciences, 1997-; Deputy Director General, International Biographical Centre, 1998-; Member of the Research Board of Advisors, The American Biographical Institute, 1999. Address: Francuska 43, YU-11000 Belgrade, Yugoslavia. E-mail: pergal@eunet.yu

PORFIRIEV Boris, b. 20 August 1955. Researcher; Teacher. m. Natalia, 28 April 1983, 1 daughter. Education: MS, Moscow State University, 1977; PhD, Russian Academy of Science, 1981; DSc, 1990; Diploma, Professor, Russian Ministry of Education, 1996. Appointments: Student, Moscow State University, 1972-77; Junior Researcher, 1977-81; Researcher, 1981-85; Senior Researcher, 1985-95; Leading Researcher, 1995-2000; Professor, Academy of Management, 1996-2001; Chief Researcher, Russian Academy of Science, 2001-03; Director, Center for Risk and Crisis Research, Institute for International Economic and Political Studies, Russian Academy of Science, 2004-. Publications: More than 180 publications including 14 books. Honours: Russian President's Award to Distinguished Scientists, 1997-2000; Russian Academy of Sciences Award to Distinguished Scientists, 2000-2002. Memberships: First Vice-President, International Research Committee for Disasters (IRCD) of International Sociological Association; European Sociological Association; European Academy for Crisis Management (ECMA), Governors Council. Address: Rostovskaya Naberezhnaya 3-128, 119121 Moscow, Russia.

PORIES Muriel Helen, b. 19 December 1925, Milwaukee, Wisconsin, USA. Inventor. m. (formerly) Walter J Pories, 4 daughters. Education: BS, 1951; MA, 1979; JD, 1985. Appointments: President, owner, Mar-Bruc Inc, 1985-; Inventor, Product on the market, 2004; Adjunct Professor, American College of Law, Anaheim, California, 2002; Co-inventor, E-Z Cycle Lite. Publications: That's Because We Love You, 1976; A Program for Dropout Reduction, 1978. Honours: Jurisprudence Award, 1983; Listed in Biographical Publications. Memberships: Alumni, American College of Law; American Association of University Women. Address: 231 Cozumel, Laguna Beach, CA 92651, USA.

PORTER George (Lord Porter of Luddenham), b. 6 December 1920, Stainforth, Yorkshire, England. Physical Chemist. m. Stella Brooke, 2 sons. Education: Graduated, Leeds University, 1941; Emmanuel College, Cambridge. Appointments: Radar Officer, Royal Navy, 1941-45; Demonstrator, Physical Chemistry, 1949-52, Assistant Director of Research, 1952-54, University of Cambridge; Professor of Physical Chemistry, 1955-63, Firth Professor and Head of Department of Chemistry, 1963-66,

University of Sheffield; Professor of Chemistry, 1963-66, Director, 1966-85, Fullerian Professor of Chemistry, 1966-88, The Royal Institution, London; Professor Emeritus, 1988-. Publications: Chemistry for the Modern World, 1962; Progress in Reaction Kinetics; Numerous scientific papers; BBC TV series: Laws of Disorder, 1965; Time Machines, 1969-70; Natural History of a Sunbeam, 1976; Chemistry in Microtime, 1996. Honours include: Nobel Prize for Chemistry, shared with Professor R G W Norrish, 1967; Life Peerage, Lord Porter of Luddenham, 1990; Longstaff Medal of RSC, 1981; Michael Faraday Award, 1991. Address: Departments of Chemistry and Biochemistry, Imperial College, London, SW7 2AY, England.

PORTER Rockne, b. 13 March 1932, Crossplains, Tennessee, USA. Business Executive. m. Judy. Education: BS, Middle Tennessee State University, 1957; MA, Peabody College (now part of Vanderbilt University), 1963. Appointments: ITT Corporation, 1961-80; Various international positions, 1981-86; Director, Industrial Product Marketing Asia, Alcatel Trade International (Joint venture with ITT), 1987-89; Director of Industrial Product Marketing Asia, Tuthill Asia Ltd, 1990-; Managing Director, Corporate Director, Tuthill Tohin Machinery Ltd, Yixing, China. Publications; 5 in journals, related to Japanese industrial training, based on MA thesis. Memberships: American Chamber of Commerce, Japan, 1963-67, Chairman, Joint Venture and Licensing Committee, 1965; American Japan Society, 1968-72; American Society of Training Directors, Japan, 1962-68; Reserve Officers Association (Major-AUS retired), 1992-; Lifetime Tokyo American Club. Address: 3060 Lebanon Road, Nashville, TN 37214-2219, USA.

PORTILLO Michael Denzil Xavier (Rt Hon), b. 26 May 1953. Politician; Member of Parliament. m. Carolyn C Eadie, 1982. Education: Peterhouse, Cambridge University, England. Appointments: Ocean Transport and Trading Co, 1975-76; Conservative Research Department, 1976-79; Special Adviser to Secretary of State for Energy, 1979-81; Kerr McGee Oil (UK) Ltd, 1981-83; Special Adviser to Secretary of State of Trade and Industry, 1983, to Chancellor of Exchequer, 1983-84; Member of Parliament for Enfield, Southgate, 1984-97; Social Security, 1987-88, Minister of State, Department of Transport, 1988-90; Minister of State for Local Government and Inner Cities, 1990-92; Chief Secretary to the Treasury, 1992-94; Secretary of State for Employment, 1994-95, for Defence, 1995-97; Shadow Chancellor, 2000-01; Freelance writer and broadcaster, 1997-; Adviser to Kerr McGee Corporation, 1997-; Director (non-executive), BAE Systems, 2002-; Member, International Commission for Missing Persons in former Yugoslavia. Publications: Clear Blue Water, 1994; Democratic Values and the Currency, 1998. Address: c/o Conservative Party, 32 Smith Square, London, SW1P 3HH, England.

PORTO Mucio Joao, b. 23 April 1962, Patos de Minas, Brazil. Medical Doctor; Plastic Surgeon. m. Valeria M D Porto, 2 daughters. Education: Graduate in Medicine, UFG; General Surgery, Hospital das Forcas Aramadas; Plastic Surgery at PUC-RJ Service. Appointments: Invited Professor, University of Brazil, Brasilia; General and Plastic Surgeon, FHDF, Brasilia; Director, Clinica, Mucio Porto, Brasilia. Publications: Articles in medical journals include: The use of meme prosthesis in mammary augmentation; Simetrisation of contralateral breast in breast reconstruction. Honours: President, Bazilian Society of Aesthetic Medicine; Resident-in-Chief, Clinico Ivo Pitanguy. Memberships: Brazilian Society of Plastic Surgery; Brazilian College of Surgeons; American Academy of Cosmetic Surgery; Brazilian Society of Aesthetic Medicine. Address: SHIS, QL 20-02-12 Lago Sul, Brasilia DF, Brazil 71650125. E-mail: wwwmucioporto@aol.com Website: www.mucioporto.com.br

PORTWAY Christopher (John), b. 30 October 1923, Halstead, Essex, England. Writer. m. Jaroslava Krupickova, 4 April 1957, 1 son, 1 daughter. Publications: Journey to Dana, 1955; The Pregnant Unicorn, 1969; All Exits Barred, 1971; Corner Seat, 1972; Lost Vengeance, 1973; Double Circuit, 1974; The Tirana Assignment, 1974; The Anarchy Pedlars, 1976; The Great Railway Adventure, 1983; Journey Along the Spine of the Andes, 1984; The Great Travelling Adventure, 1985; Czechmate, 1987; Indian Odyssey, 1993; A Kenyan Adventure, 1993; Pedal for Your Life, 1996; A Good Pair of Legs, 1999; The World Commuter, 200l; Flat Feet & Full Steam, forthcoming. Contributions to: Motoring and Leisure Magazine; Holiday Magazine; Glasgow Herald; Saga Magazine; Heathrow International Traveller. Honour: Winston Churchill Fellow, 1993. Membership: Fellow, Royal Geographical Society; Founder Member, British Guild of Travel Writers. Address: 22 Tower Road, Brighton BN2 2GF, England.

POSADA Brenda Dalila, b. 10 November 1965, San Francisco, USA. Attorney; Solicitor. 1 son. Education: Bachelor of Arts, Political Science and French (double degree), 1987; Juris Doctorate, School of Law, 1990, University of San Francisco; Certificate, Universite de la Sorbonne, France, 1985; International Law, Henry Dunant Institute, Geneva, Switzerland, 1989. Appointments: Admitted: US District Court, Northern District of California; US District Court, Central District of California; US Court of Appeals, Ninth Circuit; US District Court, Eastern District of California. Publication: Author: A Deceased Plaintiff's Right to Pain and Suffering Damages: Till Death Us Do Part?, 1993. Honours: Listed in Who's Who publications and biographical dictionaries. Memberships: State Bar of California; Member: Lawyer Pilots' Bar Association; California Trial Lawyers' Association. Address: Sterns & Walker, 901 Clay Street, Oakland, CA 94577. E-mail: posadab@cs.com

POSNER Gerald, b. 20 May 1954, San Francisco, California, USA. Attorney; Writer. m. Trisha D Levene, April 1984. Education: BA, University of California, 1975; JD, Hastings College of Law, 1978. Publications: Mengele: The Complete Story, 1986; Warlords of Crime, 1988; Bio-Assassins, 1989; Hitler's Children, 1991; Case Closed, 1993; Citizen Perot, 1996; Killing the Dream, 1998; Motown 2003; Why America Slept, 2003. Contributions to: New York Times; New Yorker; Chicago Tribune; US News & World Report. Honour: Pulitzer Finalist, 1993. Memberships: National Writers Union; Authors Guild; PEN. Address: 1521 Atton Road, Suite 442, Miami Beach, FL 33139, USA.

POSPÍŠIL Jaroslav, b. 19 February 1935, Charváty, Czech Republic. Professor. Education: MSc, 1957; MEng, 1964; RNDr, 1968; PhD, 1968; DSc, 1992; Graduated in Physics and Mathematics, Palacký University, Olomouc, Electrical Engineering, Technical University, Brno. Appointments: Researcher, Optics, Institute of Industrial Sciences, Tokyo University; Professor, Optics and Quantum Electronics, Head, Department of Applied Physics, Palacký University, Olomouc. Publications: over 240 research papers in professional journals mainly in the field of transfer, statistical and informational properties of optical, photographical, optoelectrical and human vision systems. Honours: Gold Medal, Palacký University, 1995; Merit Member and Honorary Member, Union of Czech Mathematicians and Physicists, 1996 and 2002. Memberships: International Society for Optical Engineering; Union of Czech Mathematicians and Physicists; Czech Committee, International Commission for Optics; Optics and Electronics Division of European Physical Society; Czech and Slovak Society for Photonics; Czech Society for Metrology. Address: Ovesná 10, 77900 Olomouc, Czech Republic.

POSPISIL Leopold, b. 10 March 1925, Brno, Czech Republic. Microbiologist. m. Alena, 1 son. Education: MD, Faculty of Medicine, Masaryk University, 1949; PhD, 1956; Associate Professor, 1963; DSc, 1975; Professor, 1983. Appointments: Lecturer, 1956-63, Assistant Professor, 1963-83, Professor, 1983-89, Head, Department of Microbiology, 1989-93, St Ann Hospital, Faculty of Medicine, Brno. Publications: 354 original papers. Honours: MVDr.h.c, Veterinary and Pharmaceutical University, Brno, 1995. Memberships: Czech Microbiology Society; Veterinary Research Institute. Address: Lucni 32, 61600 Brno, Czech Republic.

POSTELNICU Tiberiu, b. 15 June 1930, Campina, Romania. Professor. m. Viorica-Maria, 1 son, 1 daughter. Education: MS, 1952, PhD, 1957, Mathematical Faculty, University of Bucharest; Fellowship, Humboldt Foundation, University of Bonn, Germany, 1969-70. Appointments: Assistant and Associate Professor, Mathematics Faculty, University of Bucharest, 1951-59; Senior Researcher, Head of the Department Statistical Inference, Institute for Mathematical Statistics, 1969-; Professor, Head of Department of Mathematics, Academy of Economic Studies, 1974-77; Head of Department of Biostatistics, Medical University, Bucharest, 1990-2001. Publications: Theorems on binary responses to combination of stimuli, 1992; Limiting forms of probability mass functions, 1993; Specific numerical taxonomy methods in biological classification, 1994; Statistical nonlinear models in cell biology, 1998; Sample size for survival studies, 2000; Histogram computing program, 2002; Patterns in journal citation data, 2003. Honours: Gheorghe Lazar Award for monograph: Mathematical Methods in Medicine and Biology, Romanian Academy, 1972. Memberships: American Mathematical Society; International Statistical Institute; International Association for Statistical Computing; Italian Statistical Society; New York Academy of Sciences; International Biometric Society. Address: Institute for Mathematics Statistics of the Academy, Calea 13 Septembrie Nr 13, RO 050711, Bucharest 5, Romania. E-mail: tposteln@k.ro

POSTLETHWAITE Pete, b. 16 February 1946, Lancashire, England. Actor. Career: Theatre includes: Macbeth, Bristol; Films include: The Last of the Mohicans; In the Name of the Father; Romeo and Juliet; Alien 3; Dragonheart; Distant Voices; Still Lives; Brassed Off; The Lost World; Jurassic Park; Amistad; The Serpent's Kiss; Among Giants; The Divine Ryans; TV includes: Between the Lines; Lost for Words; Butterfly Collectors. Address: c/o Markham and Froggatt Ltd, 4 Windmill Street, London, W1P 1HF, England.

POTT Francis (John Dolben), b. 25 August 1957, Oxfordshire, England. Composer; Pianist. m. Virginia Straker, 19 September 1992, 1 son, 1 daughter. Education: Music Scholar, Winchester College and Magdalene College, Cambridge; Composition with Robin Holloway, Hugh Wood; Piano with Hamish Milne, London; MA, MusB, University of Cambridge; Fellow, London College of Music, 2003. Career: Secondary Education (Music), 1980-86; Tutor in Compositional Techniques, University of Oxford, 1987-89; Lecturer in Music, St Hugh's College, Oxford, 1988; Director of Foundation Studies, West London Institute, 1989-91; John Bennett Lecturer in Music, St Hilda's College, Oxford, 1992-2001; Member of Winchester Cathedral Choir, toured in USA, Brazil, Netherlands, France, Germany and Norway, 1991-2001; Administrative Head of Music, London College of Music & Media (Arts Faculty of Thames Valley University), 2001-02; Head of Research Development and Composition, London College of Music & Media, 2002-; freelance composer, piano recitalist and accompanist. Compositions: Organ: Mosaici di Ravenna [Gerald Finzi Trust Memorial Award], 1981; Empyrean [Lloyd's Bank National Composition Award, 1st and 2nd prizes], 1982; Passion Symphony, Christus, 1986-90, premiered Iain Simcock, 1991,

Dictionary of International Biography

Westminster Cathedral (widely performed in UK, USA and Germany); Toccata, 1991; Introduction, Toccata & Fugue, 2001; Many sacred choral works, widely published and recorded; Other: many solo piano works, including The Song of Amergin [after 'The White Goddess' by Robert Graves; Barclaycard National Composition Award, 1983] and Toccata [First Prize, SS Prokofiev International Composing Competition, Moscow, 1997]; Piano Quintet, premiered Smithsonian Institute, Washington, DC, 1993; Sonata for 'cello and piano, premiered Wigmore Hall, London, 1996; Sonata for violin and piano, premiered Jacqueline du Pré Building, Oxford, 1999; Oratorio, A Song on the End of the World (texts by Czeslaw Milosz and others) for soloists, chorus, organ and orchestra, 1999 Elgar Commission, Three Choirs Festival, premiered Worcester Cathedral, 26 August 1999. Works broadcast in UK, USA, Czech Republic, performed UK, USA, Canada, Australia, Scandinavia, Germany, France, Italy, Greece, Austria, Madeira, Czech Republic, Russia. CD Recordings: Christus, Iain Simcock, 1992 and Jeremy Filsell, 2004; 'Cello Sonata, David Watkin, Howard Moody, 1997; Solo piano works, the composer, 1997; Sacred choral works (Schola Cantorum/Mark Shepherd), 1998 and (Tenebrae/Nigel Short), 2003. Publications: Empyrean, 1989; Christus, 3 volumes, 1994-99; Introduction, Toccata & Fugue, 2004, UMP; Toccata for Organ, 2001, Fand Press; 'Cello Sonata, Fand Press, 2004; Solo piano works, Fand; Sacred choral works, OUP, Ricordi UK, Novello & Co. Scholarly work in progress: "Forgotten Melodies"?, The Music of Nikolai Medtner, extended critical study, for publication 2006-07. Memberships: Board of Governors, Thomas Coram Foundation, London, 1984-94; Liveryman, Worshipful Company of Grocers, City of London; Freeman of the City of London. Address: Thurlows, Main Road, Littleton, Winchester, Hampshire SO22 6PS, England. Website: www.britishacademy.com/members/pott.htm

POTTERS Louis, b. 5 October 1959, New Jersey, USA. Physician; Radiation Oncologist. m. Lenore Brancato, 3 sons. Education: BS, Biology, Emory University, Atlanta, Georgia, USA, 1977-81; MD, New Jersey Medical School, Newark, New Jersey, USA, 1981-85; Internship, 1985-86, Resident, 1986-88, Department of Internal Medicine, Beth Israel Medical Center, New York, New York, USA; Resident, 1988-90, Chief Resident, 1990-91, Department of Radiation Oncology, State University of New York Science Center at Brooklyn, USA. Appointments Include: Physician-in-Charge, 1992-94, Brachytherapy Section, Division of Radiation Oncology, North Shore University Hospital, Manhasset, New York, USA; Consultant, Radiation Oncology, LaGuardia Hospital, Queens, New York, USA, 1991-94; Chairman, Department of Radiation Oncology, Mercy Medical Center, Rockville Center, New York, USA, 1994-97; Chief and Associate Attending, Department of Radiation Oncology, Memorial Sloan-Kettering Cancer Center at Mercy Medical Center, 1997-2003; Co-Director, Mercy Medical Center Gamma-Knife Program, 2002-2003; Associate Director, Department of Radiation Oncology, 2003-, Medical Director, New York Prostate Institute, 2003- South Nassau Communities Hospital, Oceanside, New York, USA; Academic Appointments include: Assistant Professor, Cornell University Medical School, New York, New York, 1991-94; Clinical Associate Member, 1997-2002, Associate Member, 2003, Memorial Sloan-Kettering Cancer Center. Publications: Over 35 peer reviewed articles in medical journals as co-author include most recently: A Comprehensive and Novel Predictive Modeling Technique Using Detailed Pathology Factors in Men with Localized Prostate Cancer, 2002; Prognostic Significance of Gleason Grade in Patients Treated with Permanent Prostate Brachytherapy, 2003; The Importance of Implant Dosimetry for Patients undergoing Prostate Brachytherapy, 2003 (in press); 14 book chapters, reviews, editorials and letters; Numerous invited talks and lectures. Honours: Alpha Omega Alpha, 1990; Fellowship, American College of Radiology. Memberships include: American College of Radiology;

American Brachytherapy Society; American Medical Association; American Radium Society; American Society of Clinical Oncology; New York Metropolitan Breast Cancer Group. Address: Department of Radiation Oncology, South Nassau Communities Hospital, One Health Way, Oceanside, NY 11572, USA. E-mail: PottersL@yahoo.com

POVER Lesley, b. 1 April 1950, Plymouth, Devon, England. Sculptress. 2 sons. Education: New College, London; Training in Sculpture, 1981-84. Career: Designed and helped to produce costumes and props for the Torch Theatre, Milford Haven, 1979-81; Designed and installed a gallery for the first Hampton Court Flower Show, 1990; Artist-in-Residence, Colfes Independent School, 1991; Artist-in-Residence, Eltham College, London, 1995; Exhibitions: Group exhibitions: The Woodlands Gallery, Blackheath, London, 1991; Royal Academy Summer Exhibitions, 1992, 1993; Royal Society of British Artists Annual Exhibition, Mall Galleries, London, 1993, 1994, 1996; Royal Society of Marine Artists Annual Exhibition, The Mall Galleries, London, 1993; The Discerning Eye Exhibition, London, 1995; Sculpture Exhibition at the Henley Regatta, 1995; The Society of Portrait Sculptors, Cork Street, 1997; Solo exhibitions: Colfes Independent School, 1991; Rob Whittle Fine Arts, Islington Art Fair, 1994, 1995; Artspace, Henley, 1995; Commissions and other works include: Life size bronze of Mother and Child, Archbishop Runcie for Lambeth Palace Gardens, 1986; Bronze figure of Eric Liddell for the Eric Liddell Sports Centre, London, 1995; 25 ft Angel for a Church in Central London, 1997; Bronze bust of Admiral Lord Nelson, Royal Naval College, Greenwich, 1997; Life size memorial bust of Princess Diana, 1999; Life size White Hart, 2001; Bronze life size statue of Admiral Lord Nelson for Greenwich, London, 2004. Publication: Wildlife in Art. Honour: Elected Sculpture Selector for the Royal Society of British Artists, 1997. Memberships: Royal Society of British Artists; Equity. Address: 78B Inverine Road, Charlton, London SE7 7NL, England. E-mail: lesleypover@lesleypover.com

POWELL Geoffrey Stewart, (Tom Angus), b. 25 December 1914, Scarborough, Yorkshire, England. Soldier; Bookseller; Writer. m. Felicity Wadsworth, 15 July 1944, 1 son, 1 daughter. Education: Scarborough College, 1923-31; Army Staff College, 1945-46; United States Command and General Staff College, 1950-51; Joint Services Staff College, 1953-54; BA, Open University, 1981. Publications: The Green Howards, 1968; The Kandyan Wars, 1973; Men at Arnhem, 1978; Suez: The Double War (with Roy Fullick), 1979; The Book of Campden, 1982; The Devil's Birthday: The Bridges to Arnhem, 1984; Plumer: The Soldier's General, 1990; The Green Howards: 300 Years of Service, 1992; Buller: A Scapegoat: A Life of General Sir Redvers Buller, VC, 1994; The Green Howards (with John Powell), revised edition, 2002. Contributions to: Journals and magazines. Honour: Fellow, Royal Historical Society, 1989. Address: Chipping Campden, Gloucestershire GL55 6AE, England.

POWELL Robert, b. 1 June 1944, Salford, Lancashire, England. Actor. m. Barbara Lord, 1975, 1 son, 1 daughter. Career: TV roles include: Doomwatch, 1970; Jude the Obscure, 1971; Jesus of Nazareth, 1977; Pygmalion, 1981; Frankenstein, 1984; Hannay (series), 1988; The Sign of Command, 1989; The First Circle, 1990; The Golden Years, 1992; The Detectives, 1992-97; Theatre roles include: Hamlet, 1971; Travesties (RSC), 1975; Terra Nova, 1982; Private Dick, 1982; Tovarich, 1991; Sherlock Holmes, 1992; Kind Hearts and Coronets, 1998; Film include: Mahler, 1974; Beyond Good and Evil, 1976; Thirty Nine Steps, 1978; Imperative, 1981; Jigsaw Man, 1982; Shaka Zulu, 1985; D'Annunzio, 1987; The Mystery of Edwin Drood, 1993; The Sign of Command; Once on Chunuk Bar. Honours: Best Actor, Paris Film Festival, 1980;

Dictionary of International Biography

Venice Film Festival, 1982; Hon MA, 1990, Hon DLitt (Salford), 2000. Address: c/o Jonathan Altans Associates Ltd, 13 Shorts Gardens, London, WC2H 9AT, England.

POWELL Sandy, b. 7 April 1960. Costume and Set Designer. Education: St Martin's College of Art and Design, Central School of Art, London. Career: Costume designer for Mick Jagger on Rolling Stones European Urban Jungle tour, 1990, all shows by The Cholmondoleys and the Featherstonehaughs; Stage sets include: Edward II (RSC); Rigoletto (Netherlands Opera); Dr Ox's Experiment (ENO); Costumes for films include: Cobachan; The Last Of England; Stormy Monday; The Pope Must Die; Edward II; Caraveggio; Venus Peter; The Miracle; The Crying Game; Orlando; Being Human; Interview with a Vampire; Rob Roy; Michael Collins; The Butcher Boy; The Wings of the Dove; Felicia's Journey; Shakespeare in Love; Velvet Goldmine; Hilary and Jackie; The End of the Affair; Miss Julie; Gangs of New York; Far From Heaven. Honours: Best Technical Achievement Award, Evening Standard Awards, 1994; Academy Award, 1998; BAFTA Award, 1998. Address: c/o PFD, Drury House, 34-43 Russell Street, London, WC2B 5HA. E-mail: lmamy@pfd.co.uk

POWNALL Henry Charles, b. 25 February 1927, London, England. Barrister; Judge. m. Sarah Deverell, 1 son, 2 daughters, 1 deceased. Education: Trinity College, Cambridge, 1948-51. Appointments: Served in Royal Navy, 1945-48; Called to the Bar, 1954, Bencher, 1976; Junior Prosecuting Counsel, Central Criminal Court, 1964-76; Senior, later 2nd Senior, Prosecuting Counsel, Central Criminal Court, 1976-79; Judge of Courts of Appeal, Jersey and Guernsey, 1980-86; Circuit Judge, Knightsbridge Crown Court, 1984-88; Senior Circuit Judge, Central Criminal Court, 1988-99. Publications: Royal Service, Volume I, jointly 1996; Royal Service, Volumes II and III, jointly 2001. Honours: MA, LLB, 1951; QC, 1979; Officer of Order of St John, 1996. Memberships: Orders and Medals Research Society; Freeman, City of London, 1989; Liveryman, Worshipful Company of Fruiterers, 2000; Pratt's; Hurlingham; Ebury Court. Address: c/o Coutts and Co; 448 Strand, London WC2R 0QS, England. E-mail: henrypownall@aol.com

POYEN Vincent, b. 21 January 1958, Paris, France. Interventional Cardiologist. m. Florence Vignoles, 2 sons, 1 daughter. Education: Graduate, 1976; Medical Studies, Medical University of Marseilles, 1977-84. Appointments: Intern, St Joseph's Hospital, 1984; Officer, Health Cardiology Department, French Army, 1986; Specialist in Cardiology, 1986; Doctor in Medicine, 1987; Fellow, Department of Cardiology, 1984-89; Investigator, 2001-04. Publications: Direct angioplasty and systematic stenting of the culprit vessel during setting of acute myocardial infarction, 2001; Indications of coronary angioplasty and stenting, 2003; What is left to surgery? 2003; The French Registry on Renal Stenting, poster, 2003; Complete single session percutaneous revascularization of multi vessel disease in the setting of an acute myocardial infarction, 2003. Honours: Speaker at 5 international congresses, Phoenix, Arizona, USA, 1991-2000; Speaker, intra operative trainer, live case operator, Shanghai International Congress, 1995, 1996, 2002; Speaker, Cardiologia Interventistica, Rome, 2002; Speaker, Live Case Operator, Update in Cardio Vascular Medicine, Romania, 2002. Memberships: Associated Member, International Society for Endovascular Surgery, 1993; Intra Operative Trainer for Chinese interventional cardiologists in Marseilles, Sino-French Medical Association, Shanghai, 1995; Associated Member, Haemodynamics and interventional cardiology group, French Cardiology Society, 1997; Intra Operative Trainer, Romanian-French Association for Interventional

Cardiology, 1999. Address: Cardio-Vascular Unit (UCV), 24 avenue Viton, 13009 Marseilles, France. E-mail: vpoyen@hotmail.com

PRAGAY Desider A, b. 12 August 1921, Clausenburg-Kolozsvar. Scientist, Professor. m. Eva Bakay. Education: Agricultural Academy, Hungary, 1945; BS, University Clausenburg Political Economy, 1947; Chemistry University Budapest, 1950; MS, Biochemistry Budapest-Washington, 1961; PhD, Certified Clinical Chemist, 1969; New York State Special License for Laboratory Directors, 1972. Appointments: Student Leader during Hungarian Revolution, 1956; Assistant Professor, University Budapest; Instructor, Assistant Professor, University of Utrecht, 1956-60; Research Associate, Buffalo, New York, 1960-63; Postdoctoral Fellow, Massachusetts General Hospital, 1964-66; Assistant Professor, State University of New York, Buffalo, 1966-70; Secretary, International Congress of Clinical Chemistry; Associate Professor, Biochemistry and Pathology State University of New York Medical School, Buffalo, 1970-86; Professor, Chemistry, d'Youville College, 1975-86; Director, Chemistry Laboratory, University Hospital Buffalo Medical School, 1970-86; Emeritus Professor, Buffalo, Emeritus, Academy Clinical Laboratory Physicians and Scientists; Emeritus, Clinical Chemists; Emeritus, American Chemical Society; Emeritus, Sigma Xi. Publications: Numerous articles on the field; Co-author, author, 4 books on Clinical Chemistry; Author: 12 books on History, History of Science and Geography; Creator of S I Laboratory Values Converter, 1982. Honours: 2 postdoctoral fellowships; NIH Teaching Grant of $1.5 million; Certificate of Merit, International Biographical Centre, 1972; Visiting Professor, China, Korea, Thailand, Kuwait, Caribbean, South America, 1975-83; Bausch & Lomb Award for Teaching, 1975; Fisher Science Award, 1975; American Clinical Chemistry Award, 1985; Somogyi Award, 1984-; Sigma Xi; Several Cultural Awards in Hungary, 1990-99. Memberships: American Chemical Society; American Association of Clinical Chemistry, Committee President for Laboratory Safety and Introduction of Laboratory Pollution Control, 1973-75; Canadian Society Clinical Chemistry; Life Fellow, American Institute of Chemistry; Member, American Public Health Association; New York Academy of Sciences; Charter Member, Academy of Clinical Laboratory Science. Address: C/o Dr G Roland Hauzenberger str 13, D 80687, Munchen, Germany.

PRAKASH Om, b. 18 August 1927, Lucknow, UP, India. Senior University Professor; Vice-Chancellor. m. Sushil Kumari Mathur. Education: BCom, 1st Class 1st, 1945, MCom, 1st Class 1st, 1947, PhD, Foreign Trade, 1951, Doctor of Letters, Public Enterprise, 1961, University of Allahabad. Appointments: Assistant Professor, Commerce, Economics, Management, University of Allahabad, 1947-62; Professor and Head, Commerce and Business Management, Panjab University, Chandigarh, 1962-63; Senior Professor, Head, Director, Dean, Vice-Chancellor, University of Rajasthan, Jaipur, 1963-87; Vice-Chancellor, Bundelkhand University, Jhansi; Emeritus Fellow, University of Rajasthan; Visiting Professor, National Institute of Training in Industrial Engineering, Mumbai, National Academy of Direct Taxes, Nagpur, Kanpur University, 1988-; Principal Investigator, UGC Major Research Project, 1995-99; Professor Emeritus, Institute of Management Studies, Roorkee, 2000-; Honorary Distinguished Professor, Jaipur Institute for Integrated Learning in Management, 2000-; Professor Emeritus, International University for Human Transformation, 2004-; Promoter, Director of several management institutes. Publications: Over 20 books include: Commerce and Government, 1997; Great Thoughts of Commercists, 1997; Thoughts on Education, 2001; Multinational Sway over Indian Economy, 2002; Economic Environment and 21st Century Management, 2003; Over 300 articles and papers. Honours include: Only Indian to win CED International Award, Committee for

Economic Development, New York, 1958; First National Fellow in Commerce, University Grants Commission, New Delhi, 1978; Outstanding Researcher in Commerce, University of Bombay, 1996, 2002; Institute of Public Enterprise Citation, Allahabad, 1999. Memberships: President, Indian Commerce Association, 1978; Founder President, Mathur Society, 1995-; Economic Council of Britain in Europe, 2002-; Life Member, Indian Institute of Public Administration, New Delhi; Royal Economic Society, UK, 2004. Address: 1/245 SFS, Mansarovar, Jaipur 302020, Rajasthan, India.

PRASAD Raj (Raghubir), b. 5 July 1936, Allahabad, India. Scientist; Professor. m. Shashi Prabha Prasad, 2 sons, 1 daughter. Education: BSc, Agriculture, 1954, MSc, Agricultural Botany, 1956, University of Allahabad, India; PhD, University of Oxford, Oxford, England, 1961; PDF, University of California, Berkeley and Davis, USA, 1961-63. Appointments: Research Biochemist, University of California Berkeley, USA, 1963-65; Professor, Faculty of Agriculture, University of Ibadan, Nigeria, West Africa, 1965-67; FAO Agricultural Officer, Kenya, East Africa, 1967-68; Senior Research Scientist, Integrated Pest Management, Exotic-Invasive Weeds, Canadian Forest Service, 1968-. Publications: Over 300 including: Co-author, Herbicide Handbook, 1989; Numerous articles in scientific journals, book chapters, proceedings, extension (technology transfer), invited speaker at international conferences. Honours: Co-inventor of patent on Bioherbicide; Fellow, Weed Science Society of America; Fellow Indian Weed Science Society, India. Memberships: International Weed Science Society; Oxford Society, UK; Institute of Biology, UK, 1993-95. Address: Canadian Forestry Service, 506 W Burnside Road, Victoria V8Z 1M5, British Columbia, Canada.

PRASHAR Usha Kumari (Baroness of Runnymede), b. 29 June 1948, Nairobi, Kenya. First Civil Service Commissioner; Member of the House of Lords. m. Vijay Swarma. Education: BA, Honours, University of Leeds, 1967-70; Dip Soc, University of Glasgow, 1970-71. Appointments include: Conciliation Officer, Race Relations Board, 1971-76; Director, Runnymede Trust, 1976-84; Fellow, Policy Studies Institute, 1984-86; Director, National Council for Voluntary Organisations, 1986-91; Numerous activities from 1992-96 include: Membership of the Royal Commission on Criminal Justice, Lord Chancellors Advisory Committee on Legal Education and Conduct; The Arts Council; Chairman Parole Board of England and Wales, 1997-2000; First Civil Service Commissioner, 2000-; Chairman, National Literacy Trust, 2001-; Chancellor, De Montfort University; Chairman, Royal Commonwealth Society; Board Member, Salzburg Seminar. Publications include: Contributed to: Britain's Black Population, 1980; The System: a study of Lambeth Borough Council's race relations unit, 1981; Scarman and After, 1984; Sickle Cell Anaemia, Who Cares? A survey of screening, counselling, training and educational facilities in England, 1985; Acheson and After: primary health care in the innercity, 1986. Honours: CBE 1994; Peerage, 1999; Honorary LLD: De Montdort, 1994; South Bank University, 1994; Greenwich, 1999; Leeds Metropolitan, 1999; Ulster, 2000; Oxford Brookes, 2000. Address: House of Lords, London SW1A 0PW, England. E-mail: prasharu@parliament.uk

PRATCHETT Terry, b. 28 April 1948, Beaconsfield, Buckinghamshire, England. Author. m. Lyn Marian Purves, 1 daughter. Appointments: Journalist; Writer. Publications: The Carpet People, 1971, revised 1992; The Dark Side of the Sun, 1976; Strata, 1981; The Colour of Magic, 1983; The Light Fantastic, 1986; Equal Rites, 1987; Mort, 1987; Sourcery, 1988; Wyrd Sisters, 1988; Pyramids, 1989; Eric, 1989; The Unadulterated Cat, 1989; Co-author, Good Omens: The Nice and Accurate Predictions of Agnes Nutter, 1989; Truckers, 1989;

Guards! Guards!, 1989; Moving Pictures, 1990; Diggers, 1990; Wings, 1990; Reaper Man, 1991; Witches Abroad, 1991; Small Gods, 1992; Only You Can Save Mankind, 1992; Johnny and the Dead, 1993; Lords and Ladies, 1993; Men at Arms, 1993; Co-author, The Streets of Ankh-Morpork, 1993; Soul Music, 1994; Co-author, Interesting Times, 1994; The Discworld Companion, 1994; Maskerade, 1995; Co-author, The Discworld Map, 1995; Johnny and the Bomb, 1996; Feet of Clay, 1996; Hogfather, 1996; The Pratchett Portfolio, 1996; Jingo, 1997; The Last Continent, 1998; Co-author, A Tourist Guide to Loncre, 1998; Carpe Jugulum, 1998; Co-author, Death's Domain, 1999; Co-author, The Science of Discworld, 1999; The Fifth Elephant, 1999; Co-author, Nanny Ogg's Cookbook, 1999; The Truth, 2000; Thief of Time, 2001; The Amazing Maurice and His Educated Parents, 2002; Night Watch, 2002. Honours: OBE, 1998; Hon DLitt, (Warwick), 1999; Carnegie Medal. Address: c/o Colin Smythe, PO Box 6, Gerrards Cross, Buckinghamshire SL9 8XA, England.

PREBBLE Richard, b. 7 February 1948, Kent, England. Leader and List Member of Parliament, ACT New Zealand Party. m. (1) Nancy Prebble, 1970, (2) Doreen Prebble, 1991. Education: BA, LLB honours, Legal-economic problems, Auckland University; Lizzie Rathbone Scholar, 1967-70. Appointments: Admitted to Supreme Court as Barrister and Solicitor, 1971; Admitted to the Fiji Supreme Court Bar, 1973; Chair, Cabinet Committee, 1983-84; Headed privatisation programme; Key Minister, Labour Government, 1984-87; Elected Member of Parliament, Auckland Central, 1975-90; Professional Company Director, Works and Development Corporation, 1994-96; Elected Member of Parliament, Wellington Central, 1996-99; Leader and List Member of Parliament for ACT New Zealand Party, 1996-; Speaker and Advisor on regulatory, public sector, labour market, communications and transport reform; Speaking engagements in Europe, UK, USA, Indonesia, Australia and South America. Publications: I've Been Thinking, 1996; What Happens Next, 1997; I've Been Writing. Address: Parliament Buildings, Wellington 1, New Zealand. E-mail: richard.prebble@parliament.govt.nz

PREDA Dumitru, b. 17 June 1951, Bucharest, Romania. Diplomat; Delegate to UNESCO. m. Maria Preda, 1 son, 2 daughters. Education: Faculty of History, Bucharest; Doctorate, History of International Relations, University of Bucharest; Fulbright Alumn. Appointments: Principal Archivist, Scientific Researcher, Principal Scientific Researcher, Center of Studies and Researches of History and Military Theory, Institute of History and Military Theory, Bucharest, 1974-97; Chief, Historical Office, Romanian Diplomatic Archives, 1997-98; Diplomat; Director, Direction of Diplomatic Archives, Bucharest, Ministry of Foreign Affairs, 1999-2002; Member, Bureau of the Romanian Commission of Military History; Vice President, Romanian Committee of Military Archives; Vice President of European Committee of History and Strategy of the Balkans; Member, Committee of Bibliography and the Committee of Military Archives of the International Commission of Military History (ICMH); Member, Commission of the History of International Relations (Milan); former invited Professor, The Military Academy, Bucharest; Professor, University of Banat, Timisoara; Conferences in various European countries and USA; Congresses and international conferences on history in over 20 countries; Minister-Counsellor, Deputy Permanent Delegate to UNESCO. Publications: Over 35 books and manuals of history; Over 150 studies and articles in Romania and abroad. Honours: Romanian Academy Prize, 1994; 3 times winner of the Grand Prix of the Romanian Review of Military History. Address: MAE-Direction des Archives Diplomatiques, No 14, Aleea Modrogan, Sector 1, Bucharest, Romania.

Dictionary of International Biography

PREISIG Hans Rudolf, b. 20 May 1949, Winterthur, Switzerland. Biologist. m. Esther Ursula Huber, 12 July 1985, 3 sons. Education: Diploma, Botany, University of Zurich, 1973; PhD, 1979; University Lecturer, 1984; Professor in Botany. Appointments: Associate Editor, European Journal of Phycology, 1993-; Editor, Nova Hedwigia, 1993-; Professor in Botany, University of Zurich, 1995-; Member, Editorial Board of Systematics and Geography of Plants, 1999-. Publications: The Biology of Free-Living Flagellates, 1991; The Protistan Cell Surface, 1994; Microalgae - Aspects of Diversity and Systematics, 1997; Progress in Botany, 1999; Freshwater algae: Taxonomy, biogeography and conservation, 2000; Encyclopedia of chrysophyte genera, 2001; Culture Collections of Algae: Increasing Accessability and Exploring Algal Biodiversity, 2004. Honours: Listed in national and international biographical dictionaries. Memberships: British Phycology Society; International Society of Evolutionary Protistology; International Phycological Society; Phycological Society of America. Address: Bungertweg 6, CH-8404 Winterthur, Switzerland.

PRESCOTT John Leslie, b. 31 May 1938, Prestatyn, Wales. Politician; Trade Unionist. m. Pauline Tilston, 1961, 2 sons. Education: Ruskin College, Oxford; Hull University. Appointments: Trainee Chef, 1953-55; Steward, Merchant Navy, 1955-63; Recruitment Officer, General and Municipal Workers Union, 1965; Contested Southport for Labour, 1966; Full-time officer, National Union of Seamen, 1968-70; Member of Parliament, Kingston upon Hull East, 1970-83, Hull East, 1983-97, Kingston upon Hull East, 1997-; Member Select Committee, Nationalised Industries, 1973-79, Council of Europe, 1972-75, European Parliament, 1975-79; Personal Private Secretary to Secretary of State for Trade, 1974-76; Opposition Spokesman on Transport, 1979-81, Regional Affairs and Devolution, 1981-83, on Transport, 1988-89, on Employment, 1993-94; Member, Shadow Cabinet, 1983-97; Member, National Executive Deputy Council, 1989-; Deputy Leader, Labour Party, 1994-; Deputy Prime Minister and Secretary of State for the Environment, Transport and the Regions, May 1997-2001; Deputy Prime Minister and First Secretary of State, 2001-. Publications: Not Wanted on Voyage: report of 1966 seamen's strike, 1966; Alternative Regional Strategy: A framework for discussion, 1982; Planning for Full Employment, 1985; Real Needs - Local Jobs, 1987; Moving Britain into the 1990s, 1989; Moving Britain into Europe, 1991; Full Steam Ahead, 1993; Financing Infrastructure Investment, 1994; Jobs and Social Justice, 1994. Address: House of Commons, London, SW1A 0AA, England.

PRESCOTT Richard Chambers, b. 1 April 1952, Houston, Texas, USA. Poet; Writer. m. Sarah Elisabeth Grace. Education: Self-taught. Publications: The Sage, 1975; Moonstar, 1975; Neuf Songes (Nine Dreams), 1976, 2nd edition, 1991; The Carouse of Soma, 1977; Lions and Kings, 1977; Allah Wake Up, 1978, 2nd edition, 1994; Night Reaper, 1979; Dragon Tales, 1983; Dragon Dreams, 1986, 2nd edition, 1990; Dragon Prayers, 1988, 2nd edition, 1990; Dragon Songs, 1988, 2nd edition, 1990; Dragon Maker, 1989, 2nd edition, 1990; Dragon Thoughts, 1990; Tales of Recognition, 1991; Kings and Sages, 1991; Dragon Sight: A Cremation Poem, 1992; Three Waves, 1992; Years of Wonder, 1992; Dream Appearances, 1992; Remembrance Recognition and Return, 1992; Spare Advice, 1992; The Imperishable, 1993; The Dark Deitess, 1993; Disturbing Delights: Waves of the Great Goddess, 1993; The Immortal: Racopa and the Rooms of Light, 1993; Hanging Baskets, 1993; Writer's Block and Other Gray Matters, 1993; The Resurrection of Quantum Joe, 1993; The Horse and The Carriage, 1993; Kalee Bhava: The Goddess and Her Moods, 1995; Because of Atma, 1995; The Skills of Kalee, 1995; Measuring Sky Without Ground, 1996; Kalee: The Allayer of Sorrows, 1996; The Goddess and the God Man, 1996; Living Sakti:

Attempting Quick Knowing in Perpetual Perception and Continuous Becoming, 1997; The Mirage and the Mirror, 1998; Inherent Solutions to Spiritual Obscurations, 1999; The Ancient Method, 1999; Quantum Kamakala, 2000. Contributions to: Articles and essays to professional publications. Address: 8617 188th Street South West, Edmonds, WA 98026, USA.

PRESNIAKOV Alexander, b. 28 June 1963, San Francisco. Painter; Sculptor; Inventor; Author. Education: Academy of Arts College, San Francisco, 1979-82. Appointments: Curator, General Services Administration, 1983; Artist in Residence, 1984-85; Songwriter, Premier Melodies, 1996-. Civic Activities: Memorial Fund of Archbishop John. Honours: Distinguished Hall of Fame, International Society of Poets; Literary Excellence Award, Iliad Press. Memberships: Republican Party; Arts Accademia Internazionale, Italy. Creative Works: Artistic Ideal; Ultra Fictorilization used by US Government; Life Size Portraits of Prince Charles, Princess Diana, Miss Dame Barbara Cartland; President Reagan. Address: 3928 Cabrillo Street, San Francisco, California 94121, USA.

PRESS John Bryant, b. 11 January 1920, Norwich, England. Retired Officer of the British Council; Writer. m. Janet Crompton, 20 December 1947, 1 son, 1 daughter. Education: Corpus Christi College, Cambridge, England. Publications: The Fire and the Fountain, 1955; The Chequer'd Shade, 1958; A Map of Modern English Verse, 1969; The Lengthening Shadows, 1971; John Betjeman, 1974; Poets of World War ll, 1984; A Girl with Beehive Hair, 1986. Contributions to: Encounter; Southern Review; Art International. Honours: Royal Society of Literature Heinemann Award, 1959; 1st Prize, Cheltenham Poetry Festival, 1959. Membership: Royal Society of Literature, Fellow. Address: 5 South Parade, Frome, Somerset BA11 1EJ, England.

PRESS Vello, b. 13 October 1934, Tallinn, Estonia. Scientific Worker. m. Lubomira Maria Broniarz. Education: Graduate Engineer, Technical University of Tallinn, 1957; PhD, Academy of Sciences of Estonia 1970; Diploma of Senior Researcher, 1974. Appointments: Heat Power Engineer, The Shipyard and the Factory Building Materials, Tallinn, 1957-60; Junior Researcher, Institute of Thermal Physics and Electrophysics, 1960-70; Senior Researcher, 1970-93; Senior Lecturer, Poznan University of Technology, 1994-. Publications: About 50 papers and reports, field of combustion of fuels and the mass transport in multicomponent media. Honours: Medal of Honour 2000 Millennium, American Biographical Institute. Memberships: Board of Advisors, American Biographical Institute. Address: Brzoskwiniowa Str 4, PL 62-031, Lubon, Poland.

PRETORIUS Jacobus Willem Francois, b. 5 September 1935, Swakopmund, Namibia. m. Drix Potgieter, 1 son, 3 daughters. Education: Otjiwarongo; BA, Orange Free State; MA, Political Science Orange Free State. Appointments: Organising Secretary, Afrikaanse Studentebond, 1957-58; Farmer, 1959-; Assistant Secretary, 1960-61, Chief Secretary, 1961-69, NP/SWA; Member, Federal Council, 1968-78, National Party of South Africa; Director, Die Suidwes-Drukkery, 1965-; Chairman, Board of Directors SWD, 1981-; Deputy Chair, National Party of South West Africa, 1977-81; Minister of Water Affairs and Post and Telecommunication of SWA/Namibia, 1988-89; Leader, National Party/South West Africa (changed to an opinion forming pressure group called Monitor Action Group), 1981-91; Leader MAG, 1991-; Member, Legislative Assembly for Gobabis Constituency, 1962-89; Executive Committee, SWA, 1969-88; Chairman, Executive Committee, SWA, 1981-88; Member, Constituent Assembly for Namibia, 1989-90; Member representing Action Christian National in National Assembly of Namibia, 1990-95; Member representing, Monitor Action Group of National Assembly

Dictionary of International Biography

of Namibia, 1995-. Publications: Editor "Monitor" Magazine for 9 years; Columnist for newspapers on political and constitutional issues; Articles include: Namibia/South West Africa – Room for Both, 1983. Honours: 21st Century Award for Achievement, IBC, 2003; Year 2003 Universal Award of Accomplishment, ABI. Memberships: Founder Member and First Chair, Junior Rapportryers, Windhoek; Church Councillor, 1960-81, 1997-2002. Address: PO Box 80208 Olympia, Windhoek, Namibia, SW Africa.

PREVIN André George, b. 6 April 1929, Berlin, Germany. Conductor; Pianist; Composer. m. (1) Betty Bennett, divorced, 2 daughters, (2) Dory Langan, 1959, divorced 1970, (3) Mia Farrow, 1970, divorced 1979, 3 sons, 3 daughters, (4) Heather Hales, 1982, 1 son; (5) Anne-Sophie Mutter, 2003. Education: Berlin and Paris Conservatories. Appointments: Music Director, Houston Symphony, USA, 1967-69; Music Director, Principal Conductor, London Symphony Orchestra, 1968-79, Conductor Emeritus, 1979-; Composer, conductor, approximately 50 film scores; Guest Conductor, Guest Conductor most major world orchestras also, Royal Opera House, Covent Garden, Salzburg, Edinburgh, Osaka, Flanders Festival; Music Director, London South Bank Music Festival, 1972-74; Pittsburgh Symphony Orchestra, 1976-84; Los Angeles Philharmonic Orchestra, 1984-89; Music Director, Royal Philharmonic Orchestra, 1985-86, Principal Conductor, 1987-92; Conductor Laureate, London Symphony Orchestra, 1992-; Series of TV specials for BBC and American Public Broadcasting Service. Publications: Compositions, major works include: Every Good Boy Deserves a Favour (text by Tom Stoppard), 1977; Pages from the Calendar, 1977; Peaches, 1978; Principals, 1980; Outings, 1980; Reflections, 1981; Piano Concerto, 1984; Triolet for Brass, 1987; Variations for Solo Piano, 1991; Six Songs for Soprano and Orchestra, 1991; Sonata for Cello and Piano, 1992; The Magic Number, 1995; Trio for Bassoon, Oboe and Piano, 1994; Sonata for Violin, 1996; Sonata for Bassoon and Piano, 1997; Streetcar Named Desire (opera), 1998; Books: Music Face to Face, 1971; Orchestra (editor), 1977; Guide to Music, 1983; No Minor Chords: My Days in Hollywood, 1991. Honours include: TV Critics Award, 1972; Academy Awards for Best Film Score, 1959, 1960, 1964, 1965; Honorary KBE, 1995. Address: c/o Columbia Artists, 165 W 57th Street, New York, NY 10019, USA.

PRICE (Alan) Anthony, b. 16 August 1928, Hertfordshire, England. Author; Journalist; Editor. m. (Yvonne) Ann Stone, 1953, 2 sons, 1 daughter. Education: Exhibitioner, MA, Merton College, Oxford, 1952. Appointment: Editor, The Oxford Times, 1972-88. Publications: The Labyrinth Makers, 1970; The Alamut Ambush, 1971; Colonel Butler's Wolf, 1972; October Men, 1973; Other Paths to Glory, 1974; Our Man in Camelot, 1975; War Game, 1976; The '44 Vintage, 1978; Tomorrow's Ghost, 1979; The Hour of the Donkey, 1980; Soldier No More, 1981; The Old Vengeful, 1982; Gunner Kelly, 1983; Sion Crossing, 1984; Here Be Monsters, 1985; For the Good of the State, 1986; A New Kind of War, 1987; A Prospect of Vengeance, 1988; The Memory Trap, 1989; The Eyes of the Fleet, 1990. Honours: Silver Dagger, 1970, Gold Dagger, 1974, Crime Writers Association; Swedish Academy of Detection Prize, 1978. Address: Wayside Cottage, Horton cum Studley, Oxford OX33 1AW, England.

PRICE Margaret (Berenice) (Dame), b. 13 April 1941, Tredegar, Wales. Singer (Soprano). Education: Trinity College of Music, London. Debut: Operatic debut with Welsh National Opera in Marriage of Figaro, 1963. Career: Renowned for Mozart Operatic Roles; Has sung in world's leading opera houses and festivals; Many radio broadcasts and television appearances; Major roles include: Countess in Marriage of Figaro, Pamina in The Magic Flute, Fiordiligi in Così fan tutte, Donna Anna in Don Giovanni, Constanze in Die Entführung, Amelia in Simon Boccanegra, Agathe in Freischütz, Desdemona in Otello, Elisabetta in Don Carlo, Aida

and Norma; Sang: Norma at Covent Garden, 1987, Adriana Lecouvreur at Bonn, 1989, Elisabeth de Valois at the Orange Festival; Sang Amelia Grimaldi in a concert performance of Simon Boccanegra at the Festival Hall, 1990; Season 1993-94 in Ariadne auf Naxos at Opera de Lyon and Staatsoper Berlin. Recordings: Many recordings of opera, oratorio, concert works and recitals including, Tristan und Isolde, Le nozze di Figaro, Elgar's The Kingdom, Don Giovanni, Così fan tutte, Judas Maccabeus, Berg's Altenberglieder, Mozart's Requiem and Die Zauberflöte; Jury Member, Wigmore Hall International Song Competition, 1997. Honours: CBE; DBE, 1993. Memberships: Fellow of The College of Wales, 1991; Fellow of The College of Music and Drama of Wales, 1993. Address: c/o Stefan Hahn, Artist Management HRA, Sebastianplatz 3, 80331 Munich, Germany.

PRICE Nick, b. 28 January 1957, Durban, South Africa. Professional Golfer. m. Sue, 1 son, 1 daughter. Career: Professional Golfer, 1977-; Winner, PGA Championship, 1992, 1994, British Open, 1994, 3rd PGA Tour Money Leader, 1992; PGA Tour Money Leader, 1993; Zimbabwe Open, 1995; MCI Classic, 1997; Suntory Open, 1999; CVS Charity Classic, 2001; Mastercard Colonial, 2002; Founder, Nick Price golf course design, 2001; 10 US PGA victories, 25 world-wide victories. Honours: Vardon Trophy, 1993; Named Player of the Year, 1993. Address: c/o PGA Tour, 100 Avenue of the Champions, Palm Beach, FL 33410, USA.

PRICE Roger (David), b. 7 January 1944, Port Talbot, Wales. Professor of Modern History; Writer. Education: BA, University of Wales, University College of Swansea, 1965. Appointments: Lecturer, 1968-82, Senior Lecturer, 1982-83, Reader in Social History, 1984-91, Professor, European History, 1991-94, University of East Anglia; Professor of Modern History, University of Wales, Aberystwyth, 1993-. Publications: The French Second Republic: A Social History, 1972; The Economic Modernization of France, 1975; Revolution and Reaction: 1848 and The Second French Republic (editor and contributor), 1975; 1848 in France, 1975; An Economic History of Modern France, 1981; The Modernization of Rural France: Communications Networks and Agricultural Market Structures in 19th Century France, 1983; A Social History of 19th Century France, 1987; The Revolutions of 1848, 1989; A Concise History of France, 1993; Documents on the French Revolution of 1848, 1996; Napoleon III and the French Second Empire, 1997; The French Second Empire: an Anatomy of Political Power, 2001; People and Politics in France, 1848-1870, 2004. Contributions to: Numerous Magazines and journals. Honour: DLitt, University of East Anglia, 1985. Membership: Fellow, Royal Historical Society, 1983. Address: Department of History and Welsh History, University of Wales, Aberystwyth, Ceredigion SY23 3DY, Wales.

PRIEST Graham George, b. 14 November 1948, London, England. Philosopher. m. Anne Catherine Priest, divorced 2001, 1 son, 1 daughter. Education: BA, 1970, MA, 1974, St John's College, Cambridge University; MSc with distinction, Mathematical Logic, Bedford College, London University, 1971; PhD, Mathematics, London School of Economics, 1971-74; LittD, University of Melbourne, 2002. Appointments: Lecturer, Department of Logic and Metaphysics, University of St Andrews, Scotland, 1974-76; Lecturer, 1976-79, Senior Lecturer, 1979-87, Associate Professor, 1987-88, Department of Philosophy, University of Western Australia; Professor, Department of Philosophy, University of Queensland, 1988-2000; Visiting Professorial Fellow, University of St Andrews, Scotland, 2000-; Boyce Gibson Professor of Philosophy, University of Melbourne, 2001-. Publications: Over 100 papers; Books include: In Contradiction: a study of the transconsistent, 1987; Beyond the

Dictionary of International Biography

Limits of Thought, 1995; Introduction to Non-Classical Logic, 2001; Editor, 6 works; 26 reviews; Numerous papers at conferences and learned societies. Honours: President, Australasian Association for Logic, 1988; President, Australasian Association of Philosophy; Elected Life Member, Clare Hall, Cambridge, 1991; Elected Fellow, Australian Academy of Humanities, 1995; Chair of the Council, Australasian Association of Philosophy; 1st Vice-President, International Union for Logic, Methodology and Philosophy of Science, 1998-2003. Memberships: Australian Association of Philosophy; Australasian Association for Logic. Address: Department of Philosophy, University of Melbourne, Australia 3010.

PRIEST Jean Hirsch, b. 5 April 1928, Chicago, Illinois, USA. Professor Emeritus. m. Robert Eugene, deceased, 1 son, 2 daughters. Education includes: PhB Hons, 1947, BS, 1950, MD Hons, 1953, University of Chicago; MD, Illinois, 1957-1970; MD, Washington, 1959-1965; MD, Georgia, 1971-; MD, Montana, 1991-97. Appointments include: Clinical Instructor, Department of Pediatrics, Epidemiologist, Laboratory Bacteriologist, 1957-58, University of Illinois, Chicago, Illinois; Staff Physician, Respiratory Center, Columbus Hospital, Chicago Illinois, 1957-58; Clinical Instructor, Department of Pediatrics, University of Washington, Seattle, 1960-62; Instructor, Department of Pediatrics, 1963-65, Director, Birth Defects Clinic, 1964-67, Assistant Professor, Department of Pediatrics and Pathology, 1965-71, University of Colorado Medical Center, Denver, Colorado; Visiting Member of staff, Department of Zoology, University of St Andrews, Scotland, 1969-70; Visiting Professor, Department of Community Health, Research Cytogenecist, University of Auckland, New Zealand, 1980-81; Director, Prenatal Diagnosis Program, 1973-90, Professor Emeritus, 1990-, Emory University, Atlanta, Georgia; Director, Genetics Laboratory, Physician, Shodair Hospital, Helena, MT, 1990-95; Professor Emeritus, Faculdade de Medicina de Marilla, SP, Brasil, 2000-. Publications: 3 books; 7 book chapters; 7 book reviews; 26 abstracts; 86 refereed. Memberships: American Society for Cell Biology; Chair, Social Issues Committee, 1976-80, American Society of Human Genetics; American Board of Medical Genetics; Tissue Culture Association; Vice-President, 1977-81, American Dermatoglyphics Society; International Dermatoglyphics Society; Association of Cytogenetic Technologists; Sigma Xi; American Medical Association. Address: 843 Barton Woods Road NE, Atlanta, GA 30307, USA. E-mail: jpriest517@aol.com

PRIESTLEY John Christopher, b. 23 May 1939, Prestwich, Manchester, England. Anglican Priest. m. Margaret, 1 son, 1 daughter. Education: BA, 1960 MA, 1984, Trinity College, Oxford; Wells Theological College, 1960-61; MMin Th, Sheffield University, 1994; MTh, Westminster College, Oxford, 1998. Appointments: Teacher, St James' School, Clitheroe, 1962-64; Deputy Headmaster, The Green School, Padiham, 1964-70; Curate of Padiham-with-Higham, 1970-75; Vicar of Christ Church, Colne, 1975-2002; Warden of Pastoral Auxiliaries, Diocese of Blackburn, 1986-90; Chaplain to Her Majesty the Queen, 1990-; Rural Dean of Pendle, 1991-96; Director of Post-Ordination Training, Diocese of Blackburn, 1996-2000; Honorary Canon of Blackburn Cathedral, 2000-. Publications: Regular articles in the Church Times and Church of England Newspaper, 1978-90. Memberships: Colne Royal British Legion, 1975-; Colne Rotary Club, 1976-86; Movement for the Ordination of Women, 1983-93, Central Committee Member, 1984-89; Colne Orpheus Choir, 1995-; Westair Flying Club, Blackpool, 1995-2000. Address: 11 Chapman Court, Barnoldswich, Lancashire, BB18 5EE, England.

PRIMDAHL Soren, b. 16 July 1967, Skanderborg, Denmark. Chemical Engineer. 1 son, 1 daughter. Education: MSc, Chemical Engineering, Technical University of Denmark, 1993; PhD,

University of Twente, The Netherlands, 1999. Appointments: Research Scientist, 1993-98, Senior Research Scientist, 1998-2001, Risoe National Laboratory, Denmark; Development Engineer, OFS Fitel Denmark, 2001-04; Project Leader, Rockwool International A/S, 2004;. Publications: Patents and several articles in professional scientific journals. Address: Straedet 7, DK-3550 Slangerup, Denmark. E-mail: soeren.primdahl@rockwool.com

PRIMOST Norman Basil, b. 25 June 1933, London, England. Barrister. m. Debbie Doris Ferster, 3 sons, 1 daughter. Education: LLB (Hons), London School of Economics, University of London, 1950-53; Research on Comparative Law of Agency, Trinity Hall, Cambridge, 1953-54. Appointments: National Service, Censoring Mail RASC, Military Corrective Establishment, Colchester, 1954-56; Called to the Bar, Middle Temple, 1954; Pupillage with Montague Waters QC, 1956-57; General Common Law Practice specialising in property law with particular emphasis on landlord and tenant law, 1957-; Head of Chambers, Temple Gardens Temple, 1986-94. Publications: Legal Correspondent, Stock Exchange Journal, 1967-69; Editor, Restrictive Practices Reports, 1969-71. Memberships: Wig and Pen Club; King's Head Theatre; Hampstead Theatre. Address: Grande Vue, 98 West Heath Road, London NW3 7TU, England. E-mail: sprimost@hotmail.com

PRINCE (Prince Rogers Nelson), b. 7 June 1958, Minneapolis, Minnesota, USA. Singer; Songwriter; Producer. m. Mayté Garcia, 1996, 1 son (deceased). Appointments: Leader, Prince and The Revolution; Singer, New Power Generation, 1991-; Numerous tours and concerts. Creative Works: Singles: 1999; Alphabet Street; Controversy; I Could Never Take The Place; If I Was Your Girlfriend; Let's Go Crazy; Little Red Corvette; Purple Rain; Raspberry Beret; Sign O' The Times; U Got The Look; When Doves Cry; Cream; Gold. Albums: For You, 1978; Dirty Mind, 1979; Controversy, 1979; Prince, 1979; 1999, 1983; Purple Rain, 1984; Around the World in a Day, 1985; Parade, 1986; Sign of the Times, 1987; Lovesexy, 1988; Batman, 1989; Graffiti Bridge, 1990; Diamond and Pearls, 1991; Come, 1995; The Gold Experience, 1995; The Rainbow Children, 2002; One Nite Alone – Live! 2002; Musicology, 2004. Honours: Academy Award, Best Original Score, 1984; 3 Grammy Awards, 1985; Brit Awards, 1992, 1993, 1995; Q Award, Best Songwriter, 1990. Address: Warner Bros Records, 75 Rockefeller Plaza, New York, NY 10019, USA.

PRINCE Anna Lou, b. Isabella, Tennessee, USA. Composer; Music Publisher; Construction Company Executive. 3 children. Education: Diploma, Carolina School Broadcasting, 1966; Zion Diploma, Israel Bible School, Jerusalem, 1970; Diploma, SW Technical College, 1970; Student, United Christian Association, 1976; MusD, London Institute Applied Research, 1991; Diplomatic Diploma, Academy of Argentina de Diplomacia, 1993; PhD (Honours), Australian Institute of Co-ordinated Research, Victoria; Diploma of Honours of International Affairs, Institut des Affaires Internationales, Paris, 1994; Licenced Bible Teacher, United Christian Academy. Appointments: Songwriter, Hank Locklin Music Company, Nashville, 1963-70; Appeared Grand Ole Opry, 1970; Entertainer, 1982 World's Fair, Knoxville, Tennessee, 1982; Partner, owner, Prince Wholesale Bait Co, Canton, North Carolina, 1976-82; Grad Builders, Canton, 1982-86; Prince TV Co, 1986-; Music Publisher, Broadcast Music Inc, Nashville, 1982-; Member of production staff, talent co-ordinator (TV series) Down Home, Down Under, 1989-90; Executive producer, host, TV talk show, Real Heroes of Country Music, 1989-; Creative Works: Songs recorded: I Feel A Cry Coming On (#1 in England), 1965; Best Part of Loving You (#1 in England), Anna, 1969 (#1 New Zealand); Singer, composer: I'm In Love With You, 1995; Over 20 songs recorded. Honours include: Nominated Distinguished Women North Carolina, NC Council on Status of Women, 1984; Jefferson Award WYFF TV and American Institute for Public Service,

Dictionary of International Biography

Outstanding Business Woman, Small Business Administration, 1984; Emmy nomination for TV talk show, 1997. Address: 1447 Cane Creek Mountain Road, Bostic, NC 28018-8628, USA.

PRIOR Allan, b. 13 January 1922, Newcastle upon Tyne, England. Author. Education: Newcastle upon Tyne; Blackpool. Publications: A Flame in the Air, 1951; The Joy Ride, 1952; The One-Eyed Monster, 1958; One Away, 1961; The Interrogators, 1965; The Operators, 1966; The Loving Cup, 1968; The Contract, 1970; Paradiso, 1972; Affair, 1976; Never Been Kissed in the Same Place Twice, 1978; Theatre, 1981; A Cast of Stars, 1983; The Big March, 1983; Her Majesty's Hit Man, 1986; Führer - the Novel, 1991; The Old Man and Me, 1994; The Old Man and Me Again, 1996. Address: 11 Cokers Lane, Croxted Road, London SE21 8NF, England

PRITCHARD R(obert) John, b. 30 November 1945, Los Angeles, California, USA. Freelance Writer and Broadcaster. m. (1) Sonia Magbanna Zaide, 15 August 1969, divorced 1984, 1 son, 1 daughter, (2) Lady Elayne Antonia Lodge, 20 December 1989. Education: AB, University of California, 1967; MA, 1968, PhD, 1980, London School of Economics; LLB, University of Kent at Canterbury, 1996; Bar Vocational Course, Inns of Court School of Law, 1996-97, London. Appointments: Lecturer in History, University of Kent, 1990-93; Fellow in War Studies, King's College, London, 1990-93; Simon Senior Research Fellow in History, University of Manchester, 1993-94; Director, Historical Enterprises, 1993-; Director, Robert M Kempner Collegium, 1996-2000; Head of Law, Stafford House College, 2000-. Publications: The Reichstag Fire: Ashes of Democracy, 1972; Cry Sabotage, 1972; The Tokyo War Crimes Trial: An International Symposium (co-author), 1984, 2nd edition, 1986; Far Eastern Influences on British Strategy Towards the Great Powers 1937-39, 1987; Overview of the Historical Importance of the Tokyo War Trial, 1987; Total War (co-author), 1989, 2nd edition, 1995; Japan and the Second World War (with Lady Toshiko Marks), 1989; From Pearl Harbour to Hiroshima (co-author), 1993; La Déportation: La Système Concentrationnaire Nazi (co-author), 1995; Wada umi no Koe wo Kiku: senso sekinin to Ningen no Tsumi; to no Ma (Harken to the Cries at Our Birth: The Intervals Separating War Responsibility and Crimes of Humanity (co-author), 1996; The Tokyo Major War Crimes Trial: The Records of the International Military Tribunal for the Far East with an Authoritative Commentary and Comprehensive Guide, 1998-; World War II in Asia and the Pacific and the War's Aftermath, with General Themes: A Handbook of Literature and Research (co-author), 1998; Showa Japan: Political, Economic and Social History, 1926-1989, II: 1941-1952 (co-author), 1999; 1945: War and Peace in the Pacific, Selected Essays (co-author), 1999; The Penguin History of the Second World War, 1999, 2000; A History of Anglo-Japanese Relations, V: The Military Dimension (co-author), 2003; International Humanitarian Law: Origins, Challenges and Prospects (co-author), 3 volumes, 2003; Hostilities without Declaration of War, An Historical Abstract of the Cases in which Hostilities have Occurred between Civilised Powers without Prior Declaration or Warning from 1700-2000 (with Sir John Frederic Maurice), 2005. Honours: Many grants and fellowships. Memberships: Middle Temple, 1995-; Royal Historical Society, fellow, 1987-. Address: 11 Charlotte Square, Margate, Kent, CT9 1LR, England.

PRIVARNIKOV Arkadij Konstantinovich, b. 24 January 1937, Dnepropetrovsk, Ukraine. Professor of Mechanics. m. Natalja Georgievna Romanovich, 22 February 1964, 1 daughter. Education: Diploma Higher Education, Mechanics, Dnepropetrovsk University, 1959; Candidate of Science, Physics, Mathematics, Institute of Mechanics, Academy of Science, Kiev, 1963; Doctorate, Physics, Mathematics, Moscow State University, 1982. Appointments: Assistant, Theoretical Mechanics Chair, 1962-65,

Principal Lecturer, Theoretical Mechanics Chair, 1965-70, Senior Research Worker, 1970-72, Professor, Theoretical Mechanics Chair, 1973-87, University of Dnepropetrovsk; Professor, Chairman, Algebra and Geometry Chair, Zaporozhye State University, 1987. Publications: On contact of the layer with the elastic semispace, 1972; On character of die and elastic multilayer base interaction, 1975; The influence of the moving load on the visco-elastic base, 1981; Monographs: Elastic Multilayer Bases, 1985; The Definitions of the Strains and Stresses in the Elastic Multilayer Base with a Great Number of Layers, 1993. Honours: Silver Medal, Certificate of Secondary Education, 1954; Honorary Award, USSR Ministry of Higher Education, 1964; Honorary Diplomas, Pedagogical Activity, University of Dnepropetrovsk, 1965, 1973, 1985. Memberships: Directors Board, University of Dnepropetrovsk, 1990; National Committee Theoretical and Applied Mechanics, 1993; International Higher Education Academy of Sciences, St Petersburg Department, 2000. Address: 88b-43 Ul Gryasnova, 69068 Zaporozhye, Ukraine.

PROCHAZKA Ales, b. 27 February 1948, Prague, Czech Republic. Professor. Education: MSc, Czech Technical University, 1971; PhD, 1983, Associate Professor, 1990, Institute of Chemical Technology; Professor, Czech Technical University, 2000. Appointments: Lecturer, 1971-74, Senior Lecturer, 1974-90, Associate Professor, 1990-2000, Professor, 2000-, Institute Of Chemical Technology; Vice Dean of the Faculty of Chemical Engineering, 1997; Head of the Department of Computing and Control Engineering, 1997-. Publications: Neural Networks and Seasonal Time Series Prediction; Wavelet Use for Noise Rejection and Signal Modelling; Signal Segmentation Using Time Scale Signal Analysis. Honours: Rectors Award, 1988. Memberships: IEEE; Signal Processing Society; Computer Society; EURASIP; National Geographic Society. Address: Institute of Chemical Technology, Department of Computing and Control Engineering, Technicka 1905, 166 28 Prague 6, Czech Republic.

PROKOPOVIČ Pavel, b. 14 May 1939, Prešov, Slovakia. Engineer. m. Eva Prokopovičova, 1 son, 2 daughters. Education: Faculty of Electrical Engineering, Slovak Technical University, Bratislava. Appointments: Technician, West-Slovakian energetika enterprises; Designer, Orgrez, Bratislava; Teacher, Technical University, Košice; Chief, Slovak UNESCO-UNISPAR Working Group; Chief co-ordinator, CEEPUS No SK 01; Slovakian Chief, Project ERASMUS; Local Co-ordinator, TEMPUS SJEP 11011; Expert, PHARE Project; Pioneer in building a technical education system of a non-university type in Slovakia; Member of Organising Committees for Establishing International Faculty of Engineering, Poland, English Faculty Ukraine and of many domestic and international conferences in countries including: USA, Australia, Sweden, Norway, German and Poland; Expert on the Slovak Republic joining the European Union. Publications: More than 50 scientific articles published abroad in English, Russian, Polish and Czech; Publisher, Engineering education journal, Sensor; Specialist in sensors and sensor systems and applying signal processing, small electrical drive and machines and robotics. Honours: UNESCO International certificate for Engineering Education in Australia; Silver Badge of Honour for distinguished contributions to engineering education, outstanding achievements in the globalisation of engineering education. Memberships: ILG-EE; IGIP; EAIE; UNESCO-UNISPAR; UNESCO-CEE. Address: Smetanova 41, 08 005 Prešov, Slovakia. E-mail: prokopovic.p@post.sk

PROKUDINA Nina Alexandrovna, b. 2 June 1955, Novosibirsk, Russia. Chemist. m. Evgeny Shishchenko. Education: MS, Novosibirsk State University, Novosibirsk, Russia, 1977; PhD, Boreskov Institute of Catalysis, Novosibirsk, Russia, 1993.

Appointments: Probationer, Junior Researcher, Institute of Inorganic Chemistry, Novosibirsk, Russia, 1977-80; Senior Engineer, Technological Institute of Monocrystals, Novosibirsk, Russia, 1980-85; Senior Engineer, Junior Researcher, Researcher, Boreskov Institute of Catalysis, 1985-98; Postdoctoral Researcher, Korea Institute of Energy Research, Taejon, Korea, 1996-97; Visiting Researcher, Shizuoka University, Hamamatsu, Japan, 1997-98; Visiting Scientist, Korea Institute of Science and Technology, Seoul, Korea, 1998-2002; Researcher, Dong Won Speciality Chemical Co, Pyongtaek, Korea, 2002-2003. Publications: 17 papers; 20 communications at scientific meetings; 14 patents. Honours: Bronze Medal of the Exhibition of Achievements of the National Economy of the USSR, 1984; Veteran of Work, 2002. Address: #70 av. Akademika Anokhina, 44, Moscow 117602, Russia. E-mail: nprokudina@yandex.ru

PROSPERI Louis A, b. Altoona, Pennsylvania, USA. Attorney. m. Susan Irwin Prosperi, 1 daughter. Education: BS, Business Administration, Accounting Major, summa cum laude, Georgetown University, 1975; JD, cum laude, Harvard Law School, 1978. Appointments: Admitted to the Bar: Pennsylvania, 1978; US District Court for the Western District of Pennsylvania, 1978; US Tax Court, 1979; US Court of Appeals for the Federal Circuit, 1985; US Court of Federal Claims, 1985; Associate, 1978-85, Partner, 1986-94, Member of Business and Finance Department and Tax Group, Reed Smith Shaw & McClay (now Reed Smith LLP), Pittsburgh, Pennsylvania, USA; Founder and Owner, Law Office of Louis A Prosperi, Pittsburgh, Pennsylvania, 1994-. Publications: Commentary on the Proposed Fringe Benefit Regulations, 1986; Service Opposes Tax-Free Use of Parent Stock by Subsidiary's Rabbi Trust, 1997; Numerous lectures on Federal income tax measures to groups including: Pennsylvania Institute of Certified Public Accountants, Allegheny County Bar Association and the Pittsburgh Tax Club. Memberships: Council Member, Allegheny County Bar Association Tax Section; Pittsburgh Tax Club; National Registry of Who's Who. Address: Ste 3601, Grant Building, Pittsburgh, PA 15219, USA. E-mail: laprosperi@acba.org

PROST Alain Marie Pascal, b. 24 February 1955, Lorette, France. Motor Racing Team Owner; Former Racing Driver. 2 sons. Education: College Sainte-Marie, Saint-Chamond. Career: French and European Champion, Go-Kart racing, 1973; French Champion, 1974-75; French and European Champion, Formula Three Racing, 1979; Joined Marlboro MacLaren Group, 1980; Winner, French, Netherlands and Italian Grand prix, 1981; World Champion, 1985, 1986, 1989, 1993; Winner, Brazilian, French, Mexican, Spanish and British Grand Prix, 1990; South African, San Marino, Spanish, European, Canadian, French, British, German Grand Prix, 1993; Silverstone Grand Prix, 1993; Estoril Grand Prix; 51 Grand Prix wins; Technical consultant to McLaren Mercedes, 1995; Founder and President, Prost Grand Prix, -. Publication: Vive ma vie, 1993. Honours: Officer, Legion d'honneur; Honorary OBE, 1994. Address: Prost Grand Prix, 7 avenue Eugène Freyssinet, 78286 Guyancourt Cedex, France.

PROTASEVICH E T, b. 11 August 1943, Tomsk, Siberia. Physicist. m. Grigoryeva N M, 2 sons. Education: PhD, Tomsk Polytechnical University, 1973; DSc, Institute of Thermo-Physics, Russian Academy of Sciences, Novosibirsk, 1991. Appointments: Student, Institute of Radioelectronics, 1961-67; Postgraduate, 1970-73, Senior Scientist, 1973-76, 1982-, Professor of Ecology, 1993-, Tomsk Polytechnical University; Masaryk University, Czech Republic, 1976-77; Institute of High Current Electronics, Russian Academy of Sciences, 1978-82. Publications: Cold Nonequilibrium Plasma; Electromagnetic Waves; Electromagnetic Emission and Plasma Applied to Ecology; Natural electromagnetic background and long-lived glowing phenomena in the atmosphere; Effect of intensive laser and RF-radiation on air medium; Optical diagnostics of special types HF discharges; Propagation of the electromagnetic waves flow through the atmosphere; Plasma formation inside the energy active zones; Geophysical background objects and phenomena; Ball lightning; Electrical discharge photography; Natural electromagnetic radiation and localisation; Radiative transport of energy in SFG arc plasma; Spectral and equidensitometry diagnostic of electric arc plasma; Some words about science and myself. Memberships: New York Academy of Sciences; Academy of Creative Endeavors; International Academy of Ecology; Life Protection Society. Address: PO Box 763, Tomsk 50, Russia 634050.

PROULX E(dna) Annie, b. 22 August 1935, Norwich, Connecticut, USA. Writer. m. James Hamilton Lang, 22 June 1969, divorced 1990, 3 sons, 1 daughter. Education: BA, University of Vermont, 1969; MA, Sir George Williams University, Montreal, 1973. Publications: Heart Songs and Other Stories, 1988; Postcards, 1992; The Shipping News, 1993; Accordion Crimes, 1996; Brokeback Mountain, 1998; Close Range: Wyoming Stories, 1999; That Old Ace in the Hole, 2002. Contributions to: Periodicals. Honours: Guggenheim Fellowship, 1992; PEN/ Faulkner Award, 1993; National Book Award for Fiction, 1993; Chicago Tribune Heartland Award, 1993; Irish Times International Fiction Award, 1993; Pulitzer Prize in Fiction, 1994; Alumni Achievement Award, University of Vermont, 1994; New York Public Library Literary Lion, 1994; Dos Passos Prize for Literature, 1996; American Academy of Achievement Award, 1998; Book Award, The New Yorker, 2000; Ambassador Book Award, English Speaking Union, 2000. Memberships: Phi Alpha Theta; Phi Beta Kappa; PEN American Centre. Address: PO Box 230, Centennial, WY 82055, USA.

PROZOROV-BASTIANS Felix, b. 5 September 1969, Kirov, Russia. Lawyer. m. Doris Bastians, 2 sons, 1 daughter. Education: Diploma in Law, Lomonosov University, Moscow, Russia, 1995; State Exam in Law, Frankfurt, Germany, 1998. Appointment: Partner, Rossbach & Fischer, Frankfurt, Germany, 2000-. Publication: Co-editor, German Tax and Business Law Guide (loose-leaf edition). Address: Rossbach & Fischer, Schaumainkai, D-60596 Frankfurt an Main, Germany. E-mail: prozorov@rolaw.de Website: www.rolaw.de

PRUSINSKI Antoni, b. 23 June 1925, Czestochowa, Poland. Physician; Professor of Neurology. m. Maria Bryniarska, 2 daughters. Education: MD, Medical Faculty, Medical University of Lodz, Poland, 1947-52; Specialist in Neurology, 1956; PhD, Medical University of Lodz, 1960; DSc, Medical University of Lodz, 1962. Appointments: Assistant and Senior Assistant, Department of Neurology, Medical University of Lodz, 1952-63; Assistant Professor (docent), 1962-74; Extraordinary Professor of Neurology, 1974-83; Ordinary Professor of Neurology, 1984; Chairman, Head of the Chair and Department of Neurology, Medical University of Lodz, 1963-95; Retired, 1995. Publications: 400 articles and communications in field of clinical neurology and headache in various journals (mainly in Polish); 42 books (author, co-author or editor) include: Migrena (Migraine), 2 editions, 1976-82 (Russian and Czech translations); Principles of clinical neurology (in Polish), 5 editions, 1970-89. Honours: 1st degree award of Ministry of Health, 4 times, 1973-90; Honorary member, Polish Neurological Society, 1996; Copernicus Medal, Polish Academy of Sciences, 1996; Doctor honoris causa, Medical University of Lodz, 1997; Listed in several biographical dictionaries. Memberships: International Headache Society, Board Member, 1980-96; European Headache Federation, Board Member, 1990-97; Polish Neurological Society, President, 1991-97; Polish Headache Society, President, 1997-99. Address: 41 Bracka Street 91-709, Lodz, Poland.

PRYBYLA Jan S, b. 21 October 1927, Poland. Professor Emeritus. m. Jacqueline Meyer, 1 son, 1 daughter. Education: BComm, 1949; MEconSc, 1950; PhD, 1953. Appointments: Professor of Economics, Pennsylvania State University, 1958-95; Visiting Professor of Economics, Nankai University, Tianjin, China, 1987-88; Visiting Scholar, Institute of International Relations, National Chengchi University, Taipei, Taiwan. Publications: Co-author, Russia and China on the Eve of a New Millennium, 1997; Contributor, The Chinese Communist State in Comparative Perspective, 2000. Honours: Lindback Award for Distinguished Teaching, Pennsylvania State University, 1971; Distinction in the Social Sciences Award, Pennsylvania State University, 1979; Adjunct Faculty, US Department of State, Foreign Service Institute, Washington, DC, USA. Memberships: President, Conference on European Problems; Member, American Association for Chinese Studies; Member, Association for Comparative Economic Studies. Address: 5197 N Spring Pointe Pl, Tucson, AZ 85749, USA. E-mail: jprybyla@prodigy.net

PRYCE Jonathan, b. 1 June 1947, North Wales. Actor. Partner, Kate Fahy, 2 sons, 1 daughter. Education: Royal Academy of Dramatic Art. Career: Stage appearances include: The Comedians, 1975, 1976; Hamlet, Royal Court, London, 1980; The Caretaker, National Theatre, 1981; Accidental Death of an Anarchist, Broadway, 1984; The Seagull, Queen's Theatre, 1985; Macbeth, RSC, 1986; Uncle Vanya, 1988; Miss Saigon, Drury Lane, 1989; Oliver!, London Palladium, 1994; My Fair Lady, 2001; TV appearances include: Roger Doesn't Live Here Anymore (series), 1981; Timon of Athens, 1981; Martin Luther, 1983; Praying Mantis, 1983; Whose Line is it Anyway?, 1988; The Man from the Pru, 1990; Selling Hitler, 1991; Mr Wroe's Virgins, 1993; Thicker Than Water, 1993; Films include: Something Wicked This Way Comes, 1982; The Ploughman's Lunch, 1983; Brazil, 1985; The Doctor and the Devils, 1986; Haunted Honeymoon, 1986; Jumpin' Jack Flash, 1987; Consuming Passions, 1988; The Adventures of Baron Munchausen, 1988; The Rachel Papers, 1989; Glen Garry Glen Ross, 1992; The Age of Innocence, 1993; A Business Affair, 1993; Deadly Advice, 1994; Carrington, 1995; Evita, 1996; Tomorrow Never Dies, 1997; Regeneration, 1997; Ronin, 1998; Stigmata, 1999; Very Annie Mary, 2001; Unconditional Love, 2001; The Affair of the Necklace, 2001; Bride of the Wind, 2001; Recordings: Miss Saigon, 1989; Nine-The Concert, 1992; Under Milkwood, 1992; Cabaret, 1994; Oliver!, 1995; Hey! Mr Producer, 1998; My Fair Lady, 2001. Honours: Tony Award, 1976; Oliver and Variety Club Awards, 1991; Tony and Drama Desk Awards, 1994; Best Actor, Cannes Film Festival, 1995; Best Actor, Evening Standard Film Awards, 1996. Address: c/o Julian Belfrage Associates, 46 Albemarle Street, London W1X 4PP, England.

PRYCE-JONES David, b. 15 February 1936, Vienna, Austria. Writer. m. 29 July 1959, 1 son, 2 daughters. Education: BA, MA, Magdalen College, Oxford, 1956-59. Appointments: Literary Editor, Time & Tide, 1961, Spectator, 1964; Senior Editor, National Review, New York, 1999. Publications: Owls & Satyrs, 1961; The Sands of Summer, 1963; Next Generation, 1964; Quondam, 1965; The Stranger's View, 1967; The Hungarian Revolution, 1969; Running Away, 1969; The Face of Defeat, 1971; The England Commune, 1973; Unity Mitford, 1976; Vienna, 1978; Shirley's Guild, 1981; Paris in the Third Reich, 1983; Cyril Connolly, 1984; The Afternoon Sun, 1986; The Closed Circle, 1989; Inheritance, 1992; You Can't Be Too Careful, 1993; The War That Never Was, 1995. Contributions to: Numerous journals and magazines. Honours: Wingate Prize, 1986; Sunlight Literary Prize, 1989. Membership: Royal Society of Literature. Address: Lower Pentwyn, Gwenddwr, Powys LD2 3LQ, Wales.

PUCKETT Richard Edward, b. 9 September 1932, Klamath Falls, Oregon, USA. Artist; Consultant; Retired Recreation Executive. m. Velma Faye Hamrick, 14 April 1957 (deceased 1985), 1 son, 3 daughters. Education: Southern Oregon College of Education, 1951-56; Lake Forest College, Illinois, 1957-58; Hartnell Junior College, Salinas; College Major, Fine Arts and Education; San Jose State University, California, 1973; BA, Public Service, University San Francisco, 1978. Appointments: Acting Arts and Crafts Director, Ft Leonard Wood, Missouri, 1956-57; Arts and Crafts Director; Assistant Special Services Officer (designed and opened 1st Ft Sheridan Army Museum), Ft Sheridan, Illinois, 1957-59; Arts and Crafts Director, Ft Irwin, California, 1959-60; Arts and Crafts Director, Ft. Ord, California (directed and opened 1st Presidio of Monterey, California, Army Museum), 1960-; Artist, Consultant, Retired Recreation Executive, Ft Ord, California, 1986; Directed and built the largest and most complex arts and craft program in the Department of Defense; Had the model program for the army; Taught painting classes and workshops for 30 years. Creative Works: Exhibitions: One-Man Shows at Seaside City Hall, 1967-86, 2002, Ft Ord Arts and Crafts Centre Gallery, 6 times, 1967-86, Presidio of Monterey Art Gallery, Del Messa Gallery, Carmel, California, 1998; Southern Oregon Art Gallery, Medford, 2000, Country Rose Gallery, Hollister, California, 2001-03, Walter Avery Gallery Seaside City Hall, 2002; Sasoontsi Gallery, 2004; Works in private collections in USA, Canada and Europe; Designed and opened first Ft Sheridan Army Museum, Presidio of Monterey Museum, exhibited in group shows at Salinas Valley Art Gallery, Del Messa Gallery, 2001-03, 2001-04; Glass on Holiday, Gatlinburg, Tennessee, 1981-82. Donated over 4,000 photo slides and scrapbooks, etc to University of Monterey Bay, Ft Ord; Donated photo collection, Hartnell Junior College. Honours: 1st Place, Department of Army Programming Award, 6 times, 1975-84; 5 USA Army Forces Command 1st Place Awards for Programming and Publicity, 1979-84; 1st and 3rd Place, Modern Sculpture, Monterey, California Fair, Fine Arts Exhibition, 1979; 19 Awards for Outstanding Performance; Commanders Award Medal, 1987. Memberships: Salinas Fine Arts Association; Monterey Peninsula Art Association; Southern Oregon Art Association; President, Salinas Valley Art Association; Ford Ord Alumni Association; IBA; ABA; Listed in various Biographical Dictionaries including: Life Fellow, Institute of Biographical Association; Who's Who in America; Who's Who in the World. Address: 210 San Miguel Ave, Salinas, CA 93901, USA.

PUGH Richard Henry, b. 9 September 1927, Buxton, UK. Chartered Accountant. m. Ann Swales, 1 son, 1 daughter. Education: LLB, London University. Appointments: Deputy Chairman, GUS Plc, retired 1997; Chairman, Great Universal Home Shopping Plc; Chairman, Whiteaway Laidlaw Bank Ltd. Honours: DL, Worcestershire; Officer, Sovereign Order of St John. Memberships: LLB, London; FCA; FCIS; AICMA; FRGS. Address: 6/85 Gloucester Terrace, London, W2 3HB, UK.

PUGH Roberta Ann, b. 7 April 1953, Houston, Texas, USA. Research Associate. Widowed, 2 sons. Education: BSc, Biomedical Science, 1975, MSc, Veterinary Immunology, 1979, Texas A&M University; Certified NOVA trainer of prospective foster parents; Numerous leadership and other training courses, Boy Scouts of America. Appointments: Research Associate, Department of Veterinary Pathology, Texas A&M University, College Station, Texas USA, 1978-; Numerous leadership positions with Boy Scouts of America; Community activities with Boy Scouts of America include: Special Olympics, 1999-2002; Work on Nature Trail for Bryan Lake, 2001; Several projects with Brazos County Sheriff's Office, 2001-2001. Publications: Articles in scientific journals as co-author: Experimental induction of hemorrhagic-aplastic anemia in chickens II. Serum protein changes, 1978; Expression of viral arthritis-tenosynovitis infection in immunosuppressed chickens, 1984; Immunochemical and partial chemical characterization of fractions of membrane-bound smooth lipopolysaccharide-protein complex from Brucella abortus, 1987; Structural and immunochemical aspects of Brucella abortus endotoxins, 1988; The myth of Brucella L-forms and possible involvement of Brucella penicillin binding proteins (PBPs) in pathogenicity, 2002. Honours: Phi Kappa Phi; Phi Sigma; Numerous awards, Boy Scouts of America include most recently: Sam Houston Area Council District Award of Merit, 2000; Religious Emblem Award, 2000, Order of the Arrow Brotherhood, 2001; Venturing Leader Award, 2003; Sam Houston Area Council Venturing Leadership Award, 2003. Memberships: Boy Scouts of America positions include: District Training Chairman, 1997-2003; Youth Protection Training Staff, 1997-2003; Assistant District Commissioner for Venturing, 2003; Venturing Round Table Commissioner, 2002-2003; Coach and Board Member, Bryan Little League West, 1989-2001; Daughters of the American Revolution, 1999-2003. Address: Department of Veterinary Pathology, Texas A&M University, College Station, TX 77843-4467, USA. E-mail: rpugh@cvm.tamu.edu

PUIU Alexandru, b. 1 October 1933, Fāge?el, Olt District, Romania. University Professor. m. Vasilica Puiu, 1 son. Education: Student, Academy of Economic Studies, Bucharest; PhD, Economics. Appointments: Scientific Researcher, Romanian Academy; Professor, Dean, Pro-Rector, Rector, Academy of Economic studies, Bucharest; Rector and Founder, Constantin Brâncoveanu University, Pitesti, Romania; Conferences held in Romania, Germany, Belgium, France, Russia, Bulgaria, Norway and Great Britain. Publications: More than 40 books and treatise; More than 500 articles, papers and studies in the field of management and international economic relations and Romania's economy. Honours: PhD in Economics; Laureate of the Romanian Academy with PS Aurelian Prize; Citizen of Honour of the cities of Brăila, Pitesti and Rammicu Valcea, Medals and Diplomas of Excellency, Episcopal Church of R?mnic and Low Danube; Man of the Year 2003, American Biographical Institute, Institute of International Research. Memberships: National General Association of Romanian Economists; International Association for Conservation of Natural Resources and Energy; New York Academy of Sciences; National Council of Romanian Foreign Trade; National Council of Attestation for the University Titles, Diplomas and Certificates. Address: Universitatea "Constantin Brâncoveanu", Calea Bascov No 2A, Pitesti, Arges, Romania. E-mail: ucb_rectorat@cyber.ro. Website: www.univcb.ro

PULLMAN Bill, b. 1955, Hornell, New York, USA. Actor. Education: University of Massachusetts. m. Tamara, 3 children. Appointments: Former drama teacher, building contractor, director of theatre group; Started acting in fringe theatres, New York; Moved to Los Angeles; Films include: Ruthless People; A League of Their Own; Sommersby; Sleepless in Seattle; While You Were Sleeping; Caspar; Independence Day; Lost Highway, 1997; The End of Violence, 1997; The Thin Red Line, 1998; Brokedown Palace, 1998; Zero Effect, 1998; A Man is Mostly Water, 1999; History is Made at Night, 1999; The Guilt, 1999; Lake Placid, 1999; Coming to Light: Edward S Curtis and the North American Indians (voice), 2000; Titan AE, 2000; Numbers, 2000; Ignition, 2001; Igby Goes Down, 2002; 29 Palms, 2002; Rick, 2003. Address: c/o J J Harris, 9560 Wilshire Boulevard, Suite 50, Beverly Hills, CA 90212, USA.

PULLMAN Philip, b. 19 October 1946, Norwich, England. Author. m. Jude Speller, 15 August 1970, 2 sons. Education: BA, Oxford University, 1968. Appointments: Teacher, Middle School, 1972-86; Lecturer, Westminster College, Oxford, England, 1986-96. Publications: The Ruby in the Smoke, 1986; The Shadow in the North, 1987; The Tiger in the Well, 1990; The Broken Bride, 1992; The White Mercedes, 1992; The Tin Princess, 1994;

Northern Lights, 1995; The Golden Compass, 1996; Spring-Heeled Jack, 1997; Puss in Boots, 1997; The Subtle Knife, 1997; Count Karlstein, 1998; Clockwork, 1998; I Was a Rat! 2000; The Amber Spyglass, 2000; Lyra's Oxford, 2003. Contributions to: Reviews in Times Educational Supplement; The Guardian. Honours: Carnegie Medal, 1996; Guardian Children's Fiction Award, 1996; British Book Awards Children's' Book of the Year, 1996; British Book Awards WH Smith Children's Book of the Year, 2000; Whitbread Children's Book of the Year Prize, 2001; Whitbread Book of the Year Award, 2001; BA/Book Data Author of the Year Award, 2001; Booksellers' Association Author of the Year, 2001, 2002; British Book Awards Author of the Year Award, 2002; Whitbread Book of the Year Award, 2002. Address: c/o A P Watt Ltd, 20 John Street, London, WC1N 2DR, England.

PUNTER David Godfrey, b. 19 November 1949, London, England. Professor of English; Writer; Poet. m. Caroline Case, 5 December 1988, 1 son, 2 daughters. Education: BA, 1970, MA, 1974, PhD, 1984, University of Cambridge. Appointments: Lecturer in English, University of East Anglia, 1973-86; Professor and Head of Department, Chinese University of Hong Kong, 1986-88; Professor of English, University of Stirling, 1988-2000; Professor of English, University of Bristol, 2000-. Publications: The Literature of Terror, 1980; Blake Hagel and Dialectic, 1981; Romanticism and Ideology, 1982; China and Class, 1985; The Hidden Script, 1985; Introduction to Contemporary Cultural Studies (editor), 1986; Lost in the Supermarket, 1987; Blake: Selected Poetry and Prose (editor), 1988; The Romantic Unconscious, 1989; Selected Poems of Philip Larkin (editor), 1991; Asleep at the Wheel, 1997; Gothic Pathologies, 1998; Spectral Readings (editor), 1999; Selected Short Stories, 1999; Companion to the Gothic (editor), 2000; Writing the Passions, 2000; Postcolonial Imaginings, 2000. Contributions to: Hundreds of articles, essays, and poems in various publications. Honours: Fellow, Royal Society of Arts; Fellow, Society of Antiquaries (Scotland); Scottish Arts Council Award; Founding Fellow, Institute of Contemporary Scotland; DLitt, University of Stirling. Address: Department of English, University of Bristol, Bristol BS8 1TB, England.

PURBRICK Alister John, b. 25 May 1954, Deniliquin, New South Wales. Winemaker. m. Rosa, 1 son, 1 daughter. Education: Diploma of Oenology, Roseworthy Agricultural College, 1975. Appointments: Winemaker, Mildara Wines, 1976-77; Winemaker, Production Manager to General Manager, 1978-79, Winemaker, Managing Director, 1980-, Tahbilk Pty Ltd; Managing Director, East Coast Cellars Pty Ltd, 1987-; Managing Director, AHN Pty Ltd, 1989-; Dalfarras Pty Ltd, 1991-; Pogue Vineyards Pty Ltd, 1996-; Sinclair Vineyards Pty Ltd, 1998-; Chairman: Geoff Merrill Wines Pty Ltd, 1992-; McPherson Wines Pty Ltd, 1993-; Managing Director, Australian Vineyard Company Pty Ltd, 1998-. Memberships: Board member: Australian Regional Winemakers Forum, 1984-99, 2001-03; Winemakers Federation of Australia, 1990-2002; Australian Wine Export Council, 1993-; Selection Committee, Australian Wine and Brandy Corporation, 1989-; Vice President, Winemakers Federation of Australia, 1994-99; President, Winemakers Federation of Australia, 1999-2001; President, Australian Regional Winemakers Forum, 1989-92, 1994-96; Melbourne Cricket Club; Melbourne Club; Viticultural Wine Society of Victoria. Address: Tahbilk Pty Ltd, Tahbilk Winery, Tabilk, Victoria, Australia.

PURCELL Robert Harry, b. 19 December 1935, Keokuk, Iowa, USA. Virologist; Researcher. m. Carol Joan Moody, 2 sons. Education: BA, Chemistry, Oklahoma State University, 1957; MS, Biochemistry, Baylor University, 1960; MD, Duke University, 1962. Appointments: Intern, Paediatrics, Duke University Hospital, Durham, North Carolina, 1962-63; Officer, USPHS, 1963; with

Epidemic Intelligence Service, Communicable Diseases Centre; assigned to vaccine branch, 1965-69, Medical Officer, 1969-72, Medical Director, 1972-74, Head of Hepatitis Viruses Section, 1974-2001, Co-Chief, 2001-, National Institute Allergy and Infectious Diseases, NIH. Publications: Reviewer of numerous scientific journals; Contributor of 600 articles to professional journals, chapters to books; 20 patents in field. Honours: Superior Service Award, USPHS, 1972; Meritorious Service Medal, USPHS, 1974; Gorgas Medal, 1977; Distinguished Service Medal, USPHS, 1978; Distinguished Alumni Award, Duke University School of Medicine, 1978; Eppinger Prize, 5th International FALK Symposium on Virus and Liver, Switzerland, 1979; Medal of City of Turin, Italy, 1983; Gold Medal, Canada Liver Foundation, 1984; King Faisal International Prize for Medicine, 1998; Research Science Award, Hepatitis Foundation Internationals, 1999; Alumni Hall of Fame, East Oklahoma State College, 1996. Memberships: Fellow, AAAS; Washington Academy of Sciences; American Academy of Microbiology; Molecular Medicine Society; American Epidemiology Society; American Society of Microbiology; American Society of Virology; Society of Epidemiological Research; Infectious Diseases Society of America (Squibb Award, 1980); New York Academy of Sciences; American Society of Clinical Investigation; Association of American Physicians; American College of Epidemiology; American Association of Study and Prevention of Virus Associated Cancers; International Association of Biological Standardization; International Association of the Study of the Liver; Society of Experimental Biology and Medicine (Distinguished Scientist Award, 1986); National Academy of Sciences (Washington chapter). Address: NIH Laboratory of Infectious Diseases, 50 S Dr Msc 8009, Rm 6523, Bethesda, MD 20892-0001, USA. E-mail: rpurcell@niaid.nih.gov

PURI Sanjay, b. 23 November 1961, Rampur, India. Physicist. m. Bindu Puri, 2 sons. Education: MS Physics, IIT Delhi, India, 1982; PhD, Physics, University of Illinois at Urbana-Champaign, USA, 1987. Appointments: Assistant Professor, 1987-93, Associate Professor, 1993-2001, Professor, 2001-, Jawaharlal Nehru University (JNU), New Delhi. Publications: Approximately 115 papers and books on statistical physics and nonlinear dynamics. Honours: Young Scientist Medal, Indian National Science Academy, 1993; Satyamurthy Medal, Indian Physics Association, 1995; Birla Science Award, Birla Science Centre, 2001; Homi Bhabha Fellowship, Bhabha Fellowships Council, 2003. Address: School of Physical Sciences, Jawaharlal Nehru University, New Delhi 110067, India. E-mail: puri@mail.jnu.ac.in

PURSER Philip John, b. 28 August 1925, Letchworth, England. Journalist; Author. m. Ann Elizabeth Goodman, 18 May 1957, 1 son, 2 daughters. Education: MA, St Andrews University, 1950. Appointments: Staff, Daily Mail, 1951-57; Television Critic, Sunday Telegraph, 1961-87. Publications: Peregrination 22, 1962; Four Days to the Fireworks, 1964; The Twentymen, 1967; Night of Glass, 1968; The Holy Father's Navy, 1971; The Last Great Tram Race, 1974; Where is He Now?, 1978; A Small Explosion, 1979; The One and Only Phyllis Dixey, 1978; Halliwell's Television Companion (with Leslie Halliwell), 1982, 2nd edition, 1986; Shooting the Hero, 1990; Poeted: The Final Quest of Edward James, 1991; Done Viewing, 1992. Contributions to: Numerous magazines and journals. Memberships: Writers Guild of Great Britain; British Academy of Film and Television Arts. Address: 10 The Green, Blakesley, Towcester, Northamptonshire NN12 8RD, England.

PUSHKARYOV Sergei Valerievich, b. 14 January 1968, Dzerzhinsk, Gor'kovskaya oblast, Russia. Biogeographer; Consultant. Education: MS, Zoology and Botany, Biological

Faculty, Moscow State University, 1986-91; Postgraduate Course on Biogeography, Institute of Geography, Russian Academy of Sciences, 1991-94; Some courses, Faculty of Computational Mathematics and Cybernetics, Moscow State University, 1990-93; Training on Geographical Information Systems, 1993-98. Appointments: Expert, Biodiversity Conservation Centre, 1993-; Junior Researcher, Department of Biogeography, Institute of Geography, Russian Academy of Science, 1995-. Publications: Articles in professional journals and presented at conferences as author and co-author include: Geography of mammal diversity and searching for ways to predict global changes in biodiversity, 1995; Geography of species richness of mammal of North Eurasia, 1996; How to determine your own life goal. Algorithm, 2000; Creation of electronic grid maps of ranges (on material of amphibians of the Former Soviet Union), 2001; Algorithm of happiness, 2001; Algorithm of research, 2001; On tricks, discoveries and tricks of discoveries, 2002; Outline of "periodical system" of biogeography: current state, 2003; Outline of "periodical system" of biogeography: prospects, 2003. Address: ul Gor'kogo 4-39, Korolyov, 131080 Russia. E-mail: pushkaryov@newmail.ru Website: http://pushkaryov.newmail.ru

PUTIN Vladimir Vladimirovich, b. 7 October 1952, Leningrad, USSR. Lawyer. m. Ludmila A Putina, 2 daughters. Education: Graduate, Faculty of Law, Leningrad State University, 1975. Appointments: Soviet State Security Service, 1975-90; Assistant Rector, International Affairs, Leningrad State University, Adviser to Chairman, Leningrad City Council, 1990; Head, International Committee, St Petersburg Mayor's Office, 1991-96, concurrently, First Deputy Chairman of the Government of St Petersburg, 1994-96; Deputy Property Manager, under President Yeltsin, Moscow, 1996; Deputy Chief of Staff, Main Control Department of the Administration of the Russian Federation, 1997; First Deputy Chief of Staff in Charge of Russian Regions and Territories, 1998; Director, Russian Federal Security Service, 1998; Secretary, Russian Security Council, 1999; Prime Minister of the Russian Federation, 1999; Acting President, 1999, President of the Russian Federation, 2000-. Honours: Master of Sports in sambo wrestling, 1973; Master of Sports in judo, 1975; Won sambo championships in St Petersburg many times; Candidate of Economic Sciences. Address: The Kremlin, Moscow, Russia. E-mail: president@kremlin.ru

PUTTNAM David Terence (Baron), b. 25 February 1941, London, England. Film Producer. m. Patricia Mary Jones, 1 son, 1 daughter. Appointments: Advertising, 1958-66; Photography, 1966-68; Film production, 1968-; Chairman, Enigma Productions Ltd, 1978-, Spectrum Strategy Ltd, 1999-; Director, National Film Finance Corporation, 1980-85, Anglia TV Group, 1982-99, Village Roadshow Corporation, 1989-99, Survival Anglia, 1989-, Chrysalis Group, 1993-96; Chairman, CEO, Columbia Pictures, USA, 1986-88; President, Council for Protection of Rural England, 1985-92; Visiting Lecturer, Bristol University, 1984-86; Visiting Industrial Professor, 1986-96; Governor, Lecturer, LSE, 1997-; Governor, 1974-, Chair, 1988-96, National Film and TV School; Chair, Teaching Council, 2000-02; Productions include: That'll Be the Day; Mahler; Bugsy Malone; The Duellists; Midnight Express; Chariots of Fire; Local Hero; The Killing Fields; Cal; Defence of the Realm; Forever Young, 1984; The Mission, 1985; Mr Love, 1986; Memphis Belle, 1989; Meeting Venus, 1990; Being Human, 1993; War of the Buttons, 1993; Le Confessional, 1995; My Life So Far, 2000. Publications: Rural England: Our Countryside at the Crossroads, 1988; Undeclared War: The Struggle to Control the World's Film Industry, 1997; My Life So Far, 1999. Honours: Honorary FCSD; Honorary degrees (Bristol, Leicester, Manchester, Leeds, Bradford, Westminster, Humberside, Sunderland, Cheltenham and Gloucester, Kent, London Guildhall Universities, Royal Scottish Academy, Imperial College London;

Special Jury prize for the Duellist, Cannes, 1977; 2 Academy Awards, 4 BAFTA Awards for Midnight Express, 1978; 4 Academy Awards, 3 BAFTA Awards for Chariots of Fire, 1981; 3 Academy Awards and 9 BAFTA Awards for The Killing Fields, 1985; Michael Balcon Award, BAFTA, 1982; Palme d'Or, Cannes, 1 Academy Award, 3 BAFTA Awards for The Mission, 1987; Officier, Ordre des Arts et des Lettres, 1986. Memberships include: Vice President, BAFTA; Chancellor, University of Sunderland; Chairman, National Endowment for Science, Technology and the Arts, National Museum of Photography, Film and TV; Education Standards Task Force, 1997-2000. Address: Enigma Productions, 29A Tufton Street, London, SW1P 3QL, England.

PYBUS Rodney, b. 5 June 1938, Newcastle upon Tyne, England. Writer; Poet. m. Ellen Johnson, 24 June 1961, 2 sons. Education: BA, Honours, Classics, English, MA, 1965, Gonville and Caius College, Cambridge. Appointments: Journalist, TV producer, 1962-76; Lecturer, Macquarie University, Australia, 1976-79; Literature Officer, Cumbria, 1979-81; Co-editor, Stand, 1993-98. Publications: In Memoriam Milena, 1973; Bridging Loans, 1976; At the Stone Junction, 1978; The Loveless Letters, 1981; Talitha Cumi, 1985; Cicadas in Their Summers: New and Selected Poems, 1988; Flying Blues, 1994. Contributions to: London Review of Books; New Statesman; London Magazine; Kenyon Review; Ambit; Iowa Review; Sydney Morning Herald; Equivalencias; Poetry Review; Stand; Times Literary Supplement; Critical Survey; Guardian; Independent; Rialto. Honours: Alice Hunt Bartlett Award, Poetry Society, 1974; Arts Council Writer's Fellowships, 1982-85; National Poetry Competition Awards, 1984, 1985, 1988; 1st Prize Peterloo Poetry Competition, 1989; Hawthornden Fellowship, 1988. Memberships: Society of Authors; Poetry Society. Address: 21 Plough Lane, Sudbury, Suffolk CO10 2AU, England.

Dictionary of International Biography

Q

QIN Xi-Xuan, b. 16 January 1922, Hang-Zhou, China. Professional Composer; Senior Editor. m. Guangfen Tan, 2 sons, 1 daughter. Education: Bachelor Degree, Mathematics, Peking Yangjing University and Catholic University, 1940-44; Diploma, Department of Composition, Shanghai Conservatory of Music, 1944-49. Appointments: Professional Composer in Art Ensemble, People's Liberation Army, China, 1949-76; Senior Editor, People's Music Publishing House, China, 1976-88; Retired, 1988. Publications: Fundamental Theory of Music; Primary Technique of Music Composition; Secrets of Music; Practical Usage of Hindsmith's Harmonic Theory. Honour: Prize for Songs, People's Liberation Army, 1960. Membership: Chinese Musicians Association. Address: 4-4-101 Yu-Lang Yuan, Cui-Hua Street, 100034 Beijing, China.

QUAID Dennis, b. 9 April 1954, Houston, Texas, USA. Actor. m. (2) Meg Ryan, 1991, divorced, 1 son. Education: University of Houston. Career: Stage appearances in Houston and New York; Performances with rock band The Electrics; Songwriter for films: The Night the Lights Went Out in Georgia; Tough Enough; The Big Easy; TV appearances: Bill: On His Own; Johnny Belinda; Amateur Night at the Dixie Bar and Grill; Everything That Rises; Films: September 30 1955, 1978; Crazy Mama; Our Winning Season; Seniors; Breaking Away; I Never Promised You a Rose Garden; Gorp; The Long Riders; All Night Long; Caveman; The Night the Lights Went Out in Georgia; Tough Enough; Jaws 3-D; The Right Stuff; Dreamscape; Enemy Mine; The Big Easy; Innerspace; Suspect; DOA; Everyone's All-American; Great Balls of Fire; Lie Down With Lions; Postcards from the Edge; Come and See the Paradise; A 22 Cent Romance; Wilder Napalu; Flesh and Bone; Wyatt Earp; Something To Talk About, 1995; Dragonheart, 1996; Criminal Element, 1997; Going West, 1997; Gang Related, 1997; Savior, 1997; Switchback, 1997; The Parent Trap, 1998; On Any Given Sunday, 1999; Frequency, 2000; Traffic, 2000; The Rookie, 2002; Far From Heaven, 2002; Cold Creek Manor, 2003; The Alamo, 2004; The Day After Tomorrow, 2004.

QUANT Mary, b. 11 February 1934, London, England. Fashion, Cosmetic and Textile Designer. m. Alexander Plunket Greene, 1957, deceased 1990, 1 son. Education: Goldsmith's College of Art, London, England. Career: Started in Chelsea, London, 1954; Director, Mary Quant Group of Companies, 1955-; Joint Chair, Mary Quant Ltd; Design Council, 1971-74; UK-USA Bicentennial Liaison Committee, 1973; Retrospective exhibition of 1960s fashion, London Museum, 1974; Victoria and Albert Museum Advisory Council, 1976-78; Senior Fellow, Royal College of Art, 1991; Director (non-executive), House of Fraser, 1997-. Publications: Quant by Quant, 1966; Colour by Quant, 1984; Quant on Make-up, 1986; Mary Quant Classic Make-up and Beauty Book, 1996. Honours: Honorary Fellow, Goldsmiths College, University of London, 1993; Honorary FRSA, 1995; Sunday Times International Fashion Award, Rex Award, USA, Annual Design Medal, Society of Industrial Artists and Designers, Piavolo d'Oro, Italy, Royal Designer for Industry, Hall of Fame Award, British Fashion Council (for outstanding contribution to British fashion), 1990; Dr hc, Winchester College of Art, 2000. Address: Mary Quant Ltd, 3 Ives Street, London SW3 2NE, England.

QUIBEL Robert Henri Maurice, b. 12 October 1930, Le Havre, France. Musician (double bass); Arranger; Director. m. Madeleine Saumon, 23 March 1955, 1 son, 1 daughter. Musical Education: Petit Séminaire de Rouen. Career: Bass player with Berny Bennett; Jacques Helian; Claude Bolling, 1961-63; Backing for various French artistes including: Maurice Fanon; Jacques Martin; Musical director, director of house band on Dimanche-Matin, weekly

French TV programme (France 2), 1980-. Recordings: The Flight Of The Ox-Pecker, Claude Bolling, 1963; Various recordings for children include: Le Petit Ménestral, Lucien AdÈs; Various title songs and jingles for Dimanche-Matin. Honours: Grand Prix de la Chanson Comique, Les Cuisses de Grenouille by Fernand Raynaud, 1965. Memberships: SACEM; SDRM; SACD. Hobbies: Chess; Bridge; Travel. Address: 2 Rue Ronsard, 95560 Baillet-En-France, France.

QUIGLEY Stephen Howard, b. 29 May 1951, Boston, Massachusetts, USA. Executive Editor. m Suzanne Elizabeth Daley, 2 sons, 1 daughter. Education: BA, French and International Relations, Dartmouth College, Hanover, New Hampshire, 1973. Appointments: College Sales Representative, Acquisitions Editor, Regional Sales Manager, Addison-Wesley Publishing Co Inc, Boston, Chicago and DC, 1973-84; Acquisitions Editor, Scott, Foresman and Company, Chicago, 1985-88; Senior Mathematics Editor, PWS Publishing Company, Boston, 1988-95; Executive Editor, John Wiley & Sons Inc, Hoboken, New Jersey and Marblehead, 1995-. Honours: Editor of the Year, 1990; Man of Achievement Award, 2002; Listed in Who's Who publications and biographical dictionaries; Dartmouth Club of the Year, 1990; Association of American Publishers Professional/Scholarly Publications Book of the Year, 2001 and 2002. Memberships include: American Mathematical Society; MAA; National Council of Teachers of Mathematics; American Statistical Association; Association for Supervision and Curriculum Development; Geological Society of America; Massachusetts Bar Association; Boston Rotary International; American Red Cross; Boy Scouts of America. Address: John Wiley & Sons Inc, Two Hooper Street, Marblehead, MA 01945, USA. E-mail: squigley@wiley.com

QUINN Aiden, b. 8 March 1959, Chicago, USA. Actor. m. Elizabeth Bracco, 1987, 2 daughters. Career: Worked with various theatre groups, Chicago; Off-Broadway appearances in Sam Shepard plays: Fool for Love; A Lie of the Mind; Hamlet, Chicago; TV film: An Early Frost; Films: Reckless, 1984; The Mission; All My Sons; Stakeout; Desperately Seeking Susan; Crusoe; The Handmaid's Tale; At Play in the Fields of the Lord; Avalon; Legends of the Fall; Mary Shelley's Frankenstein, 1994; The Stars Fell on Henrietta, 1994; Haunted, 1994; Michael Collins, 1996; Looking for Richard, 1996; Commandants, 1996; The Assignment, 1997; Wings Against the Wind, 1998; This is My Father, 1998; Practical Magic, 1998; Blue Vision, 1998; The Imposters, 1998; 50 Violins, 1999; In Dreams, 1999; Two of Us, 2000; See You In My Dreams, 2000; Evelyn, 2002; A Song for a Raggy Boy, 2003; Bobby Jones: Stroke of Genius, 2004. Address: CAA, 930 Wilshire Boulevard, Beverly Hills, CA 90212, USA.

QUINN Sheila Margaret (Dame Sheila Quinn), b. 16 September 1920, Blackpool, Lancashire, England. Nurse. Education: SRN, Lancaster Royal Infirmary, Lancaster, 1943-47; SCM, Lordswood Maternity Hospital, Birmingham, 1948-49; Nurse Tutor Diploma, London University and Royal College of Nursing, 1955-57; BSc (Hons) Economics, London University, 1960-63; Henley Management College, 1968. Appointments: Various Hospital Posts, 1949-57; Principal Nurse Tutor, Prince of Wales Hospital, London, 1957-61; Director, Social and Economic Welfare Division, 1961-66, Executive Director, International Council of Nurses, Geneva, 1966-70; Chief Nurse, Southampton University Hospitals, 1970-74; Chief Area Nurse, Hampshire, 1974-78; Chief Regional Nurse, Wessex, 1978-83; Chief Nursing Advisor, British Red Cross, 1983-89; International Nursing Consultant, 1989-; Advisory Committee on Nursing of European Union, 1979-87, President, 1979-82; Standing Committee of Nurses of the European Union, 1975-89, President, 1983-89. Publications: Nursing in the European Community, 1980; Caring for the Carers, 1981; ICN Past and Present, 1993; Nursing, The European Dimension, 1993; Numerous articles in national and international nursing journals. Honours: Fellow Royal College of Nursing, 1977; CBE, 1978; Hon DSc (Soc Sc), Southampton University, 1986; DBE, 1987; Christiane Reemann International Award for Nursing, 1993. Memberships: Life Vice President and Fellow Royal College of Nursing; Fellow, Royal Society of Medicine; Vice Chair, Brendon Care Foundation for the Total Care of Elderly, Winchester; Trustee and Former Chair, SCA Community Care Service, Southampton. Address: 23 Albany Park Court, Winn Rd, Southampton SO17 1EN, England. E-mail: damesheilaquinn@tesco.net

QUINSEY Vernon Lewis, b. 10 October 1944, Flin Flon, Manitoba, Canada. Professor of Psychology. m. Jill L Atkinson, 4 sons, 1 daughter. Education: BSc, University of North Dakota at Grand Forks, 1966; MSc, 1969, PhD 1970, University of Massachusetts at Amherst. Appointments: Director of Research, Penetanguishene Mental Health Centre, 1976-84 and 1986-88; Visiting Scientist, Institut Philippe Pinel, 1984-86; Professor of Psychology, 1988-, Psychiatry, 1994-, Queen's University, Kingston, Ontario, Canada. Publications: 6 books; Over 100 articles and chapters. Honours: Senior Research Fellowship, Ontario Mental Health Foundation, 1997-2001. Memberships: Human Behavior and Evolution Society; Association for the Treatment of Sexual Abusers; International Academy of Sex Research; Fellow, Canadian Psychological Association. Address: Psychology Department, Queen's University, Kingston, Ontario, Canada, K7L 3N6.

QUINTANAR ROJAS Luis, b. 21 June 1953, Mexico D.F. Neuropsychologist. m. Yulia Solovieva, 1 daughter. Education: Graduate, Psychology, 1985, Masters Degree, Psychobiology, 1989, National Autonomous University of Mexico; PhD, Neuropsychology, Moscow State University, Russia, 1992. Appointments: Professor-Researcher and Director of Masters in Neuropsychology, Faculty of Psychology, University of Puebla, 1994-; Professor, University of Tlaxcala, 1995-. Publications: 13 books in Spanish; 51 articles and chapters in books in Spanish, English, Russian and Romanian. Honours: National System of Researchers of Mexico Level 1, 1999-2002, Level 2 (since 2002). Memberships: Member-Founder, Mexican Society of Neuropsychology; Secretary, Latino-American Society of Neuropsychology; Member, Board of Governors, International Brain Injury Association. Address: 3 Oriente 403, Centro, Puebla, 72000, Mexico.

QUIRK Sir Randolph (Baron Quirk of Bloomsbury), b. 12 July 1920, Isle of Man, England. Emeritus Professor of English Language and Literature; Writer. m. (1) Jean Williams, 1946, divorced 1979, 2 sons, (2) Gabriele Stein, 1984. Education: BA, 1947, MA, 1949, PhD, 1951, DLitt, 1961, University College, London. Appointments: Lecturer in English, 1947-54, Professor of English Language, 1960-68, Quain Professor of English Language and Literature, 1968-81, University College, London; Commonwealth Fund Fellow, Yale University and University of Michigan, 1951-52; Reader in English Language and Literature, 1954-58, Professor of English Language, 1958-60, University of Durham; Vice Chancellor, 1981-85, University of London; President, British Academy; Independent Peer, House of Lords. Publications: The Concessive Relation in Old English Poetry, 1954; Studies in Communication (with A J Ayer and others), 1955; An Old English Grammar (with C L Wrenn), 1955, enlarged edition (with S E Deskis), 1994; Charles Dickens and Appropriate Language, 1959; The Teaching of English (with A H Smith), 1959, revised edition, 1964; The Study of the Mother-Tongue, 1961; The Use of English, 1962, enlarged edition, 1968; Prosodic and

Paralinguistic Features in English (with D Crystal), 1964; A Common Language (with A H Marckwardt), 1964; Investigating Linguistic Acceptability (with J Svartvik), 1966; Essays on the English Language: Mediaeval and Modern, 1968; Elicitation Experiments in English (with S Greenbaum), 1970; A Grammar of Contemporary English (with S Greenbaum, G Leech, and J Svartvik), 1972; The English Language and Images of Matter, 1972; A University Grammar in English (with S Greenbaum), 1973; The Linguist and the English Language, 1974; Old English Literature: A Practical Introduction (with V Adams and D Davy), 1975; A Corpus of English Conversation (with J Svartvik), 1980; Style and Communication in the English Language, 1982, revised edition, 1984; A Comprehensive Grammar of the English Language (with S Greenbaum, G Leech and J Svartvik), 1985; English in the World (with H Widdowson), 1985; Words at Work: Lectures on Textual Structure, 1986; English in Use (with G Stein), 1990; A Student's Grammar of the English Language (with S Greenbaum), 1990, revised edition 1997; An Introduction to Standard English (with G Stein), 1993; Grammatical and Lexical Variance in English, 1995. Contributions to: Scholarly books and journals. Honours: Commander of the Order of the British Empire, 1976; Knighted, 1985; Life Peerage, 1994; Numerous honorary doctorates; Various fellowships. Memberships: Academia Europaea; American Academy of Arts and Sciences; British Academy, President, 1985-89. Address: University College London, Gower Street, London WC1E 6BT, England.

Dictionary of International Biography

R

RACINE Michel Marie Georges, b. 17 January 1942, Rabat, Morocco. Landscape Artist. m. Emmanuelle Faure, 2 sons, 2 daughters. Education: Architect DPLG, 1969. Appointments: Architect, Town Planner, Ministry of Housing and Environment; Director, Department of Permanent Education, National School of Landscape of Versailles, France. Publications: Many articles in newspapers; Collective works; Several books. Honours: 1st prize, Jardin des Arcenaulx, Marseilles; 1st prize, Prix de l'initiative touristique, Jardin du Gros-Morne, Martinique. Memberships: Founder member, Association for the Art of Landscapes and Gardens, 1983-; Organiser, National Campaign Visitez un Jardin en France, 1987, 1988; Corresponding Member, International Committee of Historic Gardens and Landscapes. Address: 970 Chemin du Puy du Roy, 13090 Aix-en-Provence, France. E-mail: m.racine@versaille.ecole-paysage.fr

RACZKA Tony, b. 16 January 1957, Pottsville, Pennsylvania. Artist; Educator. m. Patricia G Martinez, 1 daughter, 1 step-daughter. Education: BFA, Northern Arizona University, Flagstaff, USA, 1978; MFA, Northern Illinois University DeKalb, USA, 1980; Postgraduate Studies, University of California, San Diego, USA, 1991-92. Appointments: Instructor of Art, Southwestern College, Chula Vista, California, 1981-84; Instructor of Art, Northern Arizona University, Flagstaff, Arizona, 1983; Registrar, Mingei International Museum of Folk Art, San Diego California, 1985-86; Instructor of Art, San Diego State University, 1987; Senior Museum Preparator, University Art Gallery, University of California, San Diego, California, 1989-95. Publications: To Consociate and Foster the Self, 2000; Words of Wonder, Wit, and Well?....Well Being! 2000; The Blending of Natures and the Perception of the Real, 2000. Honours: Exhibitions at commercial galleries: Quint Gallery, La Jolla, 1982, San Diego, 1983; Printworks, Chicago, 1982, 1984; One-Person Show: Queens College Art Center, CUNY, Flushing, New York, 1999-; Recipient, Pollock-Krasner Foundation Award, 2001. Memberships: International Society of Phenomenology and the Sciences of Life; San Diego Museum of Art. Address: 4430 42nd Street #2, San Diego, CA 92116, USA. E-mail: raczkatony@aol.com

RADMANN Michael Wolfdieter, b. 26 May 1964, Mexico City, Mexico. International Business Executive. m. Virginia Gregoris, 1 daughter. Education: Bachelor of Science in Geology, Texas A & M University at College Station, Texas, USA, 1986; Master of Business Administration in International Management, Thunderbird at Glendale, Arizona, 1991. Appointments: United States Peace Corps: Assistant Project Manager working in conjunction with the Canadian International Development Agency in Swaziland, Southern Africa, 1987-89; United States Agency for International Development: Diplomat/Programme Officer in Albania, 1997-99, Diplomat/Project Development Officer in El Salvador, Central America, 1992-96, Diplomat/International Development Track, Washington DC State Department, 1992; International Business Analyst, Silver and Baryte Ores Mining Company, 2000-2002; Programming and Training Officer, Diplomat/US Peace Corps, 2004-. Publications: Congressional presentations and reports for Albania, US State Department, 1997-99. Honours: Superior Honor Award for Foreign Service in Albania, US State Department; Listed in several biographical dictionaries. Memberships: American Foreign Service Association; American Association of Petroleum Geologists; Society for International Development; National Peace Corps Association; UN Association of US. Address: Imittou #45, 15561 Holargos, Athens, Greece. E-mail: m_radmann@hotmail.com

RADONS Jürgen, b. 21 February 1960, Lünen, Germany. Biologist. m. Vera Beatrix Langhammer, 9 September 1999. Education: Diploma, Biology, 1985; PhD, Biochemistry, 1991. Appointments: Postgraduate Fellow, Cellular and Molecular Immunology, Biochemistry, 1986-91; Postdoctoral Fellow, Immunology and Biochemistry, 1991-92, Diabetology, 1992-96; Research Fellow, Rheumatology, 1996-98, Molecular Immunology, 1998-. Publications: Several articles in professional journals. Honours: International Scientist of the Year 2001; Leader of Science, Technology and Engineering, 2001; Great Minds of the 21st Century; One of 500 Leaders of Influence; Outstanding Scientist of the 20th Century; Outstanding Scientist of the 21st Century. Membership: The American Biographical Institute, Research Board of Advisors. Address: Arnulf-Enders-Strasse 5, D-93059 Regensburg, Germany.

RADUJKOVIC Branko M, b. 25 July 1945, Secanj, Serbia and Montenegro. University Professor. m. Vera, 1 son, 1 daughter. Education: Biology, Faculty of Sciences, Belgrade, 1970; Master Degree, 1980, Doctor of Science Degree, 1986, Faculty of Veterinary Medicine, Belgrade; Postgraduate studies in France, 1976-77, Canada, 1981. Appointments: Assistant, 1971, Senior Assistant, 1974, Responsible for the Laboratory of Parasitology, 1978, Head, Laboratory of General Biology and Mariculture, 1987, Assistant Professor, Research, 1987, Associate Professor, Research, 1990, Professor, Research, 1995, Institute of Marine Biology, Kotor, Serbia and Montenegro; Associate Professor, Vertebrates Anatomy and Taxonomy, 1991, Professor, Vertebrates, Environmental Protection, Philosophy and History of Biology, 1996-, University of Montenegro; Participant in numerous scientific missions to France, Germany, Italy and Poland, 1979-2002. Publications: Co-editor: Faune des parasites de poissons marins des cotes du Montenegro, 1989; 108 papers in scientific journals and presented at symposia. Honours: Nominated FAO, Expert for Ichthyopathology in Aquaculture, 1987; Yugoslav Expert for Evaluation of Scientific Projects, 1988; Correspondent Member, Academy of Sciences, Montpellier, France, 1999; Visiting Professor, Universita "La Sapienza" Rome, 1987, University of Gdansk, Poland, 1989. Memberships: Member of Federal Presidency, Yugoslav Association of Ichthyologists; Yugoslav Association of Biologists, Yugoslav Association of Ecologists, Yugoslav Association of Biotaxonomists, Yugoslav Association of Parasitologists; European Association of Fish Pathologists; European Ichthyological Union; Comite Scientifique d'Etangs sales et Lagunes, Comite Scientifique de Vertebres Marins et Cephalopodes, Commission Internationale pour L'Exploration Scientifique de la Mer Mediterranee; Committee for Flore and Fauna and Committee for Encyclopaedia Montenegrina, Montenegrin Academy of Sciences; National Committee for Biological Safety, Federal Government. Address: University of Montenegro, Faculty of Sciences, Department of Biology, Cetinjski put bb, PO Box 211, 81000 Podgorica, Serbia and Montenegro. E-mail: brradujkovic@yahoo.com

RAE John Malcolm, b. 20 March 1931, London, England. Writer; Educationist. Education: MA, Sidney Sussex College, Cambridge, 1955; PhD, King's College, London. Appointment: Headmaster, Westminster School, London, 1970-86. Publications: The Custard Boys, 1960; Conscience and Politics, 1970; The Golden Crucifix, 1974; The Treasure of Westminster Abbey, 1975; Christmas is Coming, 1976; Return to the Winter Place, 1979; The Third Twin: A Ghost Story, 1980; The Public School Revolution, 1981; Letters from School, 1987; Too Little, Too Late?, 1989; Delusions of Grandeur, 1993; Letters to Parents, 1998; Sister Genefieve, 2001. Contributions to: Encounter; Times Literary Supplement; Times Educational Supplement; Times; Sunday Telegraph. Honour: United Nations Award for Film Script, 1962. Address: 25 Cedar Lodge, Lythe Hill Park, Haslemere, Surrey GU27 3TD, England.

Dictionary of International Biography

RAEZ Luis E, b. 29 June 1967, Lima, Peru. Physician. m. Aida Chaparro, 2 sons. Education: Physician, 1984-92; Internal Medicine Residency, University of Miami, Florida, USA, 1993-96; Haematology Fellowship, 1996-99; Fellow, American College of Physicians, 2002. Appointments: Assistant Professor of Medicine, Epidemiology and Public Health, 2001-, Co-Chair, Thoracic Oncology Group, 2001, Director, Haemotherapy Unit, Sylvester Cancer Center, 2003-, Member, Thoracic Committee, 2003-, University of Miami, Florida, USA. Publications: More than 20 peer-reviewed articles in medical journals and more than 40 abstracts and presentations on cancer research in national and international meetings. Honours: Research Career Development Award, American Society of Clinical Oncology, 2002; Stanley Glasser Research Award, University of Miami, 2003. Memberships: American Society of Clinical Oncology; American Society of Hematology; American College of Physicians; Eastern Oncology Co-operative Group. Address: 1475 NW 12 Avenue #3510, Miami, FL 33136, USA.

RAFTIS Antonios Costa, b. 17 January 1955, Vasilia, Cyprus. Psychological Counsellor; Specialist in Diatetics. m. Rebecca, 1 son, 1 daughter. Education: AA, Sociology, 1980, AA, Psychology, 1981, BA, Psychology, 1984, University of Alaska, USA; American College of Nutrition, 1997; University of Minnesota, 1998; Maternal Nutrition, Southwestern School of Hypnotherapy, 1984; Clinical Hypnosis, American Council of Hypnotist Examiners, 2000; Certified Hypnotherapist. Appointments: Private Practice, 1984-; Counsellor of Social Psychological Problems; Specialist in Eating Disorders and Diatetics; Certified Clinical Hypnotherapist dealing with weight loss, stopping smoking, adolescents, marriage and personal problems. Publications: Many articles published in newspapers and magazines in the field of problems with weight loss, eating disorders, nutrition, adolescence, social problems, clinical hypnotherapy; Guest speaker on television, radio and at various associations. Honours: Certificates of appreciation from many associations; Honour Certificates, Lioness Club, 1989, Lions International, 1993. Memberships: American College of Nutrition; American Psychological Association; American Sociological Association; International Association of Counsellors and Therapists; International Medical Dental Hypnotherapy Association; American Council of Hypnotist Examiners. Address: 10 Stasandrou Street, Apt 202, Nicosia, Cyprus 1060. E-mail: antonisraftis@yahoo.com

RAGHU Rengachari, b. 22 March 1943, Amoor, India. Professor; Scientist; Businessman. m. Kamala, 2 sons. Education: MD, 1963; MS, 1965, MBA, 1973; PhD, 1974. Appointments: Senior Scientific Officer, Atomic Research Centre, Trombay, Mumbai, India; Chief of Clinical Biochemistry, Apollo Hospitals, Chennai, India; Director, Division of Research, Department of Obstetrics and Gynaecology, Medical School, Nashville, Tennessee, USA; Chairman, Nutrition and Biochemistry, Medical School, Chicago, Illinois, USA; International High Technology Transfer President, Nashville, Tennessee, USA. Publications: More than 100 publications in many international journals. Honours: Merit Scholarship, Bachelor and Masters Degrees; Best PhD Thesis Award; Best teaching and Management Award. Memberships: Life Member, Indian Phytopathological Society; Society of Biological Chemists; Nutritional Society; Pharmacological Society. Address: 833 Kendall Drive, Nashville, TN 37209-4512, USA. E-mail: arraghu@hotmail.com Website: www.raghus-resources.com

RAHMAN Mustafizur, b. 1 August 1942, Mitrapur, India. Hospital Doctor; Consultant. m. Sultana Rahman, 2 daughters. Education: MBBS, Dhaka University Medical School, Bangladesh, 1967; D. Bact, London University, 1972; MRCPATH, Royal College of Pathologists, London, 1975; FRCPATH, Royal College

of Pathologists, London, 1987. Appointments: Registrar, Lecturer, Pathology, Mymensingh Medical College, Bangladesh, 1968-70; Registrar, Pathology, Bart's Hospital, London, 1970-71; Senior Registrar in Microbiology, St Mary's and St George's Hospitals, London, 1972-77; Consultant Medical Microbiologist, King's Mill Hospital, Near Mansfield, Nottinghamshire and Honorary Clinical Teacher, Nottingham University Medical School, 1977-. Publications: 20 main papers and 17 short reports in various peer-reviewed professional journals (related to diagnosis, treatment or control of infections). Honour: Consultant's "C" Merit Award, 1992. Memberships: British Medical Association; British Infection Society; British Society for Antimicrobial Chemotherapy; Fellow, Royal College of Pathologists; Association of Medical Microbiologists; International Society of Infectious Diseases; European Society of Clinical Microbiology and Infectious Diseases. Address: 2 Chartwell Grove, Mapperley Plains, Nottingham NG3 5RD, England.

RAHR Tammy, b. 20 December 1958, Rochester, New York, USA. Artist; Educator. 1 son. Education: AFA, Museum Studies, Institute of American Indian Arts, 1987. Appointments: Co-ordinator, Ethnobotanical Trail, Wheelwright Museum of the American Indian, Santa Fe, 1992; Curator, Museum of Indian Arts and Culture, Santa Fe, 1994-97; Self-employed Artist, 1997-; Curator, Animals of the Heart, Governor's Galley, Capitol Building, Santa Fe, 1999-. Civic Activities: Children's Powwow Committee, Santa Fe Opera; Pueblo Opera Program, Visiting Artist and Artist in Residence in Public Schools and Museums, Wheelwright Museum of the American Indian. Publications: Native American Folk Art, Under the Influence of Gender, Ethnicity and Art, Cincinnati Art Museum, 1992; Wisdom Keepers, Audio Book on Cassette. Awards: Southwestern Association of Indian Arts, Indian Market, 1987; Inter-tribal Indian Ceremonial Gallup, New Mexico, 1992; Alumni Triennial, Institute of American Indian Arts Museum, 1993. Creative Works: Solo exhibition – Beads on the Edge of Cayuga Traditions, Smithsonian Institution, National Museum of the American Indian, 1991-92; Public collections include Museum of Natural History, Cincinnati, Ohio; Seneca Iroquois National Museum, Salamanca, New York; Museum of Indian Arts and Culture, Santa Fe, New Mexico; Institute of American Indian Arts, Santa Fe, New Mexico; Wheelwright Museum of the American Indian, Santa Fe, New Mexico; Armond Lara Beadwork. Memberships: Tribal Member, Cayuga Nation of Indians of New York State; Institute of American Indian Arts Alumni Association. Address: PO Box 15201, Santa Fe, NM 87592, USA.

RAINE Craig (Anthony), b. 3 December 1944, Shildon, County Durham, England. Poet; Writer. m. Ann Pasternak Slater, 27 April 1972, 3 sons, 1 daughter. Education: Honours Degree in English Language and Literature, 1966, BPhil, 1968, Exeter College, Oxford. Appointments: Lecturer, Exeter College, Oxford, 1971-72, Lincoln College, Oxford, 1974-75, Christ Church, Oxford, 1976-79; Books Editor, New Review, London, 1977-78; Editor, Quarto, London, 1979-80; Poetry Editor, New Statesman, London, 1981, Faber & Faber, London, 1981-91; Fellow, New College, Oxford, 1991-. Publications: Poetry: The Onion, Memory, 1978; A Journey to Greece, 1979; A Martian Sends a Postcard Home, 1979; A Free Translation, 1981; Rich, 1984, 1953: A Version of Racine's Andromaque, 1990; History: The Home Movie, 1994; Clay. Whereabouts Unknown, 1996; A la recherche du temps perdu, 2000; Collected Poems 1978-99, 2000. Other: The Electrification of the Soviet Union (libretto), 1986; A Choice of Kipling's Prose (editor), 1987; Haydn and the Valve Trumpet (essays), 1990; In Defence of T S Eliot (essays), 2000; Collected Poems 1978-1999, 2000; Rudyard Kipling: The Wish House and Other Stories (editor), 2002. Contributions to: Periodicals. Honours: 1st Prizes, Cheltenham Festival Poetry Competition,

Dictionary of International Biography

1977, 1978; 2nd Prize, National Poetry Competition, 1978; Prudence Farmer Awards, New Statesman, 1979, 1980; Cholmondeley Poetry Award, 1983. Memberships: PEN; Royal Society of Literature. Address: c/o New College, Oxford OX1 3BN, England.

RAINIER III His Serene Highness Prince Louis Henri Maxence Bertrand, b. 31 May 1923. Prince of Monaco. m. Grace Patricia Kelly, 1956, deceased, 1982, 1 son, 2 daughters. Education: Montpellier University; Ecole Libre des Sciences Politiques, Paris. Career: Lieutenant and Colonel, French Army, 1944-45; Hereditary Prince of Monaco, 1944; Succeeded grandfather Prince Louis II, 1949; Founded, Monaco Red Cross, 1948, American Friends of Monaco, 1952, Prix Rainier, 1955, Grand Master, Ordre de St Charles de Monaco, Grand Croix, Légion d'honneur, Belgian, Swedish, Greek, Lebanese, Italian, Netherlands and San Marino orders. Address: Palais princier, BP 518, MC 98015, Monaco cedex.

RAITT Bonnie, b. 8 November 1949, Burbank, California, USA. Musician (guitar, piano). Education: Radcliffe College. Career: Performer, blues clubs, US East Coast; Concerts include: MUSE concert, Madison Square Garden with Bruce Springsteen, Jackson Browne, Carly Simon, The Doobie Brothers, 1979; Roy Orbison Tribute Concert with artists including: Whoopi Goldberg; kd lang; Bob Dylan; B B King, 1990; Performances with artists including: Stevie Wonder, Bruce Springsteen, Aretha Franklin, Willie Nelson, Elton John. Recordings: Albums include: Bonnie Raitt, 1971; Give It Up, 1972; Takin' My Time, 1973; Streetlights, 1974; Home Plate, 1975; Sweet Forgiveness, 1977; The Glow, 1979; Green Light, 1982; Nine Lives, 1986; Nick Of Time, 1989; The Bonnie Raitt Collection, 1990; Luck Of The Draw, 1991; Road Tested, 1995; Fundamental, 1998; Singles include: Something to Talk About, 1991; Not the Only One, 1992; Burning Down the House, 1996. Honours include: 4 Grammy Awards: Album of Year; Best Rock Vocal Performance; Best Female Pop Vocal Performance; Best Traditional Blues Performance (with John Lee Hooker), and numerous nominations. Address: PO Box 626, Los Angeles, CA 90078, USA.

RAJ Mariapragasam Arputha, b. 24 May 1944, Mullanvilai, Tamil Nadu. Worker in vineyard of Jesus. m. Boomadevi Maria Packiam, 3 sons, 1 daughter. Education: Diploma in Company Law; Diploma in Labour Law and Administrative Law; Diploma in Taxation Laws; Diploma in Theology; Diploma in D T P; P G Diploma in Personnel Management and Industrial Relations; BA; Bachelor of General Law; Bachelor of Law; Graduate in Theology; Master of Biblical Studies; Master of Religious Education; Doctor of Divinity; Doctor of Ministry; LLD; PhD; D.Litt. Appointments: Catechist, Itinerant Evangelist; Cup-bearer in C.S.I; Sunday Class Teacher; Vacation Bible School Teacher, Director; Preacher, Bible Teacher; Youth Leader; Christian Leader; Tracts and Bibles Distributor; Prayer Partner; Bible Hymns and Lyrics Composer; Writer in Christian Journals; Director of Bible Institute and Library. Publications: Biblical Essays; Christian Songs; Sermons; Biblical Poems; Publisher in many Christian journals. Honours: Divine Dazzle; Philanthropic Devotee; Man of Religious Education; Awards from Christian Arts and Literature League; Biblical Leader Award, Call Christian Society, Madras. Memberships: Association of Theologians; Amen Prayer Army; Indian Prayer Force; Prayer Partner of Evangelical Literature Service; Research Board of Advisors, American Biographical Institute. Address: Director of Miracle Centre Bible Institute and Universal Christian Unit, Devakottai Extension, PO 630303 Tamil Nadu State, South India.

RAJENDRAM Guy de Fontgalland, b. 11 November 1934, Sri Lanka. Clergyman; Professor of Zoology. Education: BA, Philosophy, Madurai, India, 1958; MA, Theology, St Louis

University, USA, 1964; MS, Biology, Fordham University, USA, 1967; PhD, Entomology, California University, Berkeley, USA, 1974. Appointments: Ordained Priest in the Society of Jesus, 1963; Lecturer in Zoology, University of Peradeniya, Sri Lanka, 1975; Senior Lecturer in Zoology, 1981, Professor of Zoology, 1989, University of Jaffna, Sri Lanka; Vice-Chancellor, Eastern University, Sri Lanka, 1995-98. Publications: Articles in scientific journals. Honours: Listed in Who's Who publications and biographical dictionaries. Memberships: Sri Lanka Association for the Advancement of Science; Royal Entomological Society of London. Address: No 1 Jesuit Street, Batticaloa, Sri Lanka. E-mail: gfrajendram@yahoo.com

RALPH Richard Peter, b. 27 April 1946, London, England. Diplomat. (1) Margaret Elizabeth Coulthurst, 1970, divorced 2001, 1 son, 1 daughter. (2) Jemma Victoria Elizabeth Marlor, 2002. Education: Honours Degree, Politics, Edinburgh University, Scotland. Appointments: Joined, HM Diplomatic Service, 1969; Third Secretary, Foreign and Commonwealth Office (FCO), 1969-70; Third, then Second, Secretary, Laos, 1970-74; Second, then First, Secretary, Portugal, 1974-77; First Secretary, FCO, 1977-81; First Secretary and Head of Chancery, Zimbabwe, 1981-85; First Secretary, then Counsellor, FCO, 1985-89; Counsellor, Washington, USA, 1989-93; Ambassador, Latvia, 1993-95; Governor, Falkland Islands, Commissioner for South Georgia and the South Sandwich Islands, 1996-99; Ambassador, Romania (also accredited to Moldova), 1999-2002; Ambassador to Peru, 2003-. Honours: Companion of the Order of St Michael and St George (CMG); Commander of the Royal Victorian Order(CVO). E-mail: richard.ralph@fco.gov.uk

RAMAKRISHNAN Angarai G, b. 14 February 1958, Bangalore, India. Associate Professor. m. Gowri, 3 sons. Education: BE, honours, Electronics and Communication Engineering, University of Madras, 1980; MTech, Electrical Engineering, Madras, 1982; PhD, Biomedical Engineering, Madras, 1989. Appointments: Senior Project Officer, IIT, Madras, 1985-88; R&D Engineer, BPL India Ltd, 1989-90; Postdoctoral Fellow, USA, 1990-91; Research Associate, Bangalore, 1992-94; Assistant Professor of Electrical Engineering, Indian Institute of Science, 1994-2001; Associate Professor, 2002-; Principal Research Scientist, Language Technology Research, HP Laboratories, India, 2002-03. Publications: Several articles in professional journals including: Fetal lung maturity analysis using ultrasound image features. Honours: Young Scientist Award, Department of Science and Technology, Government of India, 1994; President, Biomedical Engineering Society of India; Chair, International Conference on Biomedical Engineering; Listed in Who's Who publications. Memberships: IEEE; Biomedical Engineering Society of India; Indian Association of Biomedical Scientists; Institution of Engineers, India; Institution of Electronics and Telecommunication Engineers; Computer Society of India; International Federation for information Technology in Tamil. Address: Department of Electrical Engineering, Indian Institute of Science, Bangalore 560 012, India.

RAMESH Dasari Jai, b. 22 May 1946, India. Businessman; Philanthropist. Education: M Tech (Electrical). Appointments: Entrepreneur; Chairman and Managing Director, Vijai Electrical Limited, 1973-; Introduced Completely Self Protected Transformers Single Phase and Three Phase for first time in India; Manufacturer of Single Phase and Three Phase Dry Type Cast Resin Transformers; Built most modern facilities in India for the manufacture of Single Phase and Three Phase Transformers, 1996; Company given Export House Status, 1994 and then Trading House Status by Indian Government, 1997; Company Achieved ISO-9001 Certification, 1994; Won largest ever single export order for

Dictionary of International Biography

transformers to the Philippines, 1995; Instrumental in popularising the concept of energy saving and cost effective Amorphous Metal Transformers in India by the State Electricity Boards; Created awareness and impact among State Electricity Boards for the reduction of transmission and distribution losses by adoption of LT Less – High Voltage Distribution System; Funded several community projects in neighbouring villages to the factory; Several welfare schemes for the poor in 70 neighbouring villages through a charitable trust; Gives financial aid to poor students and donations to educational institutions and community projects. Publication: US Patent: The Continuous Magnetic Annealing Furnace. Honours: Udyog Patra Award, Vice President of India, 1982; Udyog Ratna Award, Union Industries Minister, 1987; National Citizens Award, Honourable Chairman, United Nations Human Rights Commission, 2000; Best Export Awards and Trophies for the Company, EEPC, CII, Government of India; Quality Excellence Award, Union Minister for Rural Development, 2002. Memberships: Central Board of Irrigation and Power, Advisory Committee on Distribution; Development Council for Heavy Electricals and Allied Industries, Government of India; Standing Committee on Research and Development in the Indian Power Sector, Ministry of Power, Government of India.

RAMOS-ZUNIGA Rodrigo, b. 13 July 1962, Autlan, Jalisco, Mexico. Neurosurgeon; Professor. Education: Medical Degree, University of Guadalajara, Mexico; Certified Neurosurgeon; Master in Sciences and PhD, Neurosciences, University of Guadalajara, Mexico. Appointments: Chairman, Laboratory of Neurosciences, University of Guadalajara; Professor of Neurosurgery, Issste Hospital; Professor and Investigator, Neurosciences Department, University of Guadalajara. Publications: Articles on neuropharmacology, neurosciences, bioethics and cerebrovascular disease, and microsurgical treatments of brain aneurysms published in Mexican journals including Minimally Invasive Neurosurgery and Neurosurgery. Honours: National Youth Award in Academic Research, 1997; Chief Resident, Department of Neurosurgery, University Hospital; Advisor in the Mexican Council in Neurological Surgery. Memberships: West Neurosurgical Society of Mexico; Chief, Cerebro-vascular Section, Mexican Neurological Surgeons Society; President, Mexican Society of Experimental Surgery. Address: Victoria 1531, Providencia CP 44630, Guadalajara, Jalisco, Mexico. E-mail: rodrigor@cencar.udg.mx

RAMOS-SOBRADOS Juan I, b. 28 January 1953, Bernardos, Segovia, Spain. Professor of Mechanical Engineering. m. Mercedes Naveiro, 2 sons. Education: B Aeronautical Engineering, 1975, Dr Engineering, 1983, Madrid Polytechnic University, Spain, 1975; MA, Mechanical and Aerospace Engineering, 1979, PhD, Mechanical and Aerospace Engineering, 1980, Princeton University, USA. Appointments: Research Engineer, Helicopter Design, Madrid, 1976-77; Research Assistant, 1977-78, Teaching Assistant, 1979, Department of Mechanical and Aerospace Engineering, Princeton, New Jersey, USA; Instructor, 1979-80, Assistant Professor, 1980-85, Faculty Member of Center for Energy and Environmental Studies, 1980-91, 1991-93, Associate Professor, 1985-89, Professor, 1989-93, Department of Mechanical Engineering, Carnegie Mellon University, Pittsburgh, Pennsylvania; Visiting Professor, Universita degli Studi di Roma Tor Vergata, Rome, 1988-89; Visiting Professor, 1990-91, Professor, 1992- E T S Ingenieros Industriales, Universidad de Malaga, Spain. Publications: Book: Internal Combustion Engine Modelling, 1989; Over 200 papers in journals, proceedings of international conferences on fluid mechanics, combustion and applied mathematics. Honours: Prize Francisco Arranz, Association of Aeronautical Engineers, Madrid, 1975; Aeronautical Engineering Medal, Ministry of Education and Science, Madrid, 1977; National

Award in Aeronautical Engineering, King Juan Carlos I of Spain, 1977; Daniel and Florence Guggenheim Fellow, Princeton University September 1977 - January 1978, honorary May to August, 1978; George Van Ness Lothrop Fellowship in Engineering, Princeton, 1979-80; Ralph R Teetor Award, Society of Automotive Engineers, 1981. Address: ETS Ingenieros Industriales, Universidad de Malaga, Plaza El Ejido s/n, 29013 Malaga, Spain.

RAMPLING Charlotte, b. 5 February 1946, London, England. Actress. m. (2) Jean Michel Jarre, 1978, 2 sons, 1 step daughter (1 son from previous marriage). Career: Films include: The Knack, 1963; Rotten to the Core, Georgy Girl, The Long Duel, Kidnapping, Three, The Damned, 1969; Skibum, Corky, 1970; 'Tis Pity She's a Whore, Henry VIII and His Six Wives, 1971; Asylum, 1972; The Night Porter; Giordano Bruno, Zardoz, Caravan to Vaccares, 1973; The Flesh of the Orchid, Yuppi Du, 1974-75; Farewell My Lovely, Foxtrot, 1975; Sherlock Holmes in New York, Orca - The Killer Whale, The Purple Taxi, 1976; Stardust Memories, 1980; The Verdict, 1983; Viva la Vie, 1983; Beauty and Sadness, 1984; He Died with His Eyes Open, 1985, Max mon Amour, Max My Love, 1985; Angel Heart, 1987; Paris by Night, 1988; Dead on Arrival, 1989; Helmut Newton, Frames from the Edge, Hammers Over the Anvil, 1991; Time is Money, 1992; La marche de Radetsky, TV Film, 1994; Asphalt Tango, 1995; Wings of a Dove, 1996; The Cherry Orchard, 1998; Signs and Wonders, 1999; Aberdeen, 1999; Fourth Angel, Under the Sand, Superstition, 2000; See How They Run, 2002; TV: numerous appearances. Honours: Chevalier Ordre des Arts et des Lettres, 1986; Cesar d'honneur, 2001; Chevalier, Legion d'honneur, 2002. Address: c/o Artmédia, 20 avenue Rapp, 75007 Paris, France.

RAMSEYER J Mark, b. 19 March 1954, Chicago, Illinois, USA. Professor. m. Norma E Wyse, 1 son, 1 daughter. Education: BA, Goshen College, 1976; AM, University of Michigan, 1978; JD magna cum laude, Harvard University, 1982. Appointments: UCLA School of Law, 1986-92; University of Chicago Law School, 1992-98; Harvard University, Mitsubishi Professor of Japanese Legal Studies, 1998-. Address: Harvard Law School, Cambridge, MA 02138, USA.

RAMSING Jens, b. 4 February 1955, Svendborg, Denmark. Musician (Piano, Church Organ); Composer. Education: Piano Diploma, 1980, Organ Diploma, 1986, Royal Danish Conservatory. Career: Piano Debut, Royal Danish Conservatory, 1983; Soloist, Tivoli Symfoni Orchestra; Numerous appearances on Danish Radio. Compositions: Dodecagono (organ); Songs (soprano and piano); Organ chorales; Motets (SATB, a cappella). Recordings: Copenhagen Metope, 1997; Twining, 1999; 45 Pianopieces, 1999; Liszt: Legends, Weinen, Klagend-variations and other piano works from his years in Rome, 2000; Danish Church Music, 2001; 45 Danish Pianopieces, 2002; Organ Classics, 2003. Publications: Songs, 1992; Choralpartita, 1993; Motets, 1998. Honours: Queen Ingrid Foundation, 1977, 1978. Memberships: Danish Soloists Society; Danish Organ Society. Address: Husumvej 97, DK-2700, Bronshoj, Denmark.

RANA Shree Ram Singh, b. 8 May 1949, Chamoli, Uttaranchal, India. Children's Physician. m. Sarojini Devi, 2 sons. Education: MBBS, 1974; DCH, 1991. Appointments: Chief Medical Officer, Principal Regional Health and Family Welfare Training Centre and Joint Director Medical Care and Training, Directorate of Medical and Health Department, Uttaranchal; Currently, Senior Specialist in Child Health. Publication: Article in Health for All in local language: ARI Incidence in Tehri Garhwal. Honours: Award for Family Welfare Work; Award for Earth Quake Disaster Management. Memberships: Indian Academy of Paediatrics; health and Population Perspectives and Issues. Address: 172 South Van asthali, Mandir Lane, Ballupur, Dehradun, Uttaranchal, India 248001.

RANASINGHE Anne (Anneliese Henriette), b. 2 October 1925, Essen, Germany. Nurse; Writer. m. D A Ranasinghe, 3 sons, 4 daughters. Publications: And a Sun That Sucks The Earth to Dry, poems, 1971; With Words We Write Our Lives, stories and poems, 1972; Plead Mercy, poems, 1975; Love, Sex and Parenthood, 1978; Of Charred Wood Midnight Fear, poems, 1983; Against Eternity and Darkness, poems, 1985; Not Even Shadows, poems, 1991; At What Dark Point, essays and poems, 1991; The Letter, short stories, 1994; You Ask Me Why I Write Poems, 1994; Desire and Other Stories, 1994; Mascot and Symbol, poems, short stories and translations, 1997; work published in many anthologies and journals. Honours: Sri Lanka Annual Arts Council Prize for Poetry, 1985, 1992; Sri Lanka Arts Council Prize for Non Fiction, 1987; Sri Lanka State Award for Best Collection of Short Stories, 1994; numerous other prizes. Address: 82 Rosmead Place, Colombo 7, Sri Lanka.

RANDALL-PAGE Peter, b. 2 July 1954, Rochford, Essex. Sculptor. m. Charlotte, 1 son, 1 daughter. Education: Eastbourne College; BA, Bath Academy of Arts. Career: Research Fellow, Visual and Performance Arts, Dartington College of Arts, 1999-2000, 2002-2003, 2003-2004; Member, Design Team, Education Resource Centre, Eden Project, 2002-2004; Invited Artist, Gwangju Biennale, South Korea, 2004; Solo exhibitions include: Sculpture and Drawings, Leeds City Art Galleries, Yorkshire Sculpture Park, Royal Botanic Garden Edinburgh, Arnolfi Gallery, Bristol, organised by the Henry Moore Centre, Leeds, 1980-92; Boulders and Banners, Wenlock Priory, Shropshire and Reed's Wharf Gallery, London, 1994; In Mind of Botany, Royal Botanic Gardens, Kew and Atkinson Galleries, Millfield, 1996; Whistling in the Dark, Ljubljana, Slovenia and Gouda, The Netherlands, 1998; Nature of the Beast, Djanogly Gallery, Nottingham, Graves Gallery, Sheffield, Tower Gallery, Eastbourne, 2001; Sculpture and Drawings, Natural History Museum, London, 2003; Commissions include: National Trust, Dewentwater, 1995; LDDC Butlers Wharf, London, 1996; Manchester City Council, St Ann's Square, 1996; Lothian Regional Council and others, Hunter's Square, Edinburgh, 1996; BUPA House, London, 1996; Nuffield College, Oxford, 1999; Royal Botanic Gardens, Wakehurst Place, Sussex, 2000; Sculpture at Goodwood, 2000 and 2003. Works in collections including: Tate Gallery, British Museum. Publications: In Conversation with Tessa Jackson, 1995; Sculpture and Drawings, 1977-92; Boulders and Banners, 1994; In Mind of Botany, 1996; Whistling in the Dark, 1998; Granite Song, 1999; Nature of the Beast, 2001. Honour: Honorary Doctorate of Arts, University of Plymouth, 1999. Memberships: Fellow, Royal Society of Arts; Royal Society of British Sculptors; Royal West of England Academy. Address: PO Box 5, Drewsteignton, Devon EX6 9QN, England.

RANDLE CLINTON Dorothy Louise, b. 4 June 1925, Des Moines, Iowa, USA. Writer. m. Moses Clinton, 1 son. Education: Bachelor of Fine Arts, Drake University, 1949. Appointments: Bookkeeper; Recreation Leader; Teacher; Government Worker. Publications: Numerous; Poems include: Masks in a Strange Wind; Without the Bubbling; Parting Thoughts; It's Not Always Red; Arrant Bullet; The Look and the See; Bizarre Responses; Temporary Symphony; Then and Now; Memory Lapse; A Human Viper; The Comics Double Mouth; A Cruise. Honours: Inducted into International Poetry Hall of Fame; Several Editor's Choice Awards; Two Editor's Preference Awards of Excellence. Membership: International Society of Poets. Address: 1530 Maple, Des Moines, IA 50316, USA.

RANE Ganesh P, b. 5 July 1943, Karwar, India. Businessman; UN Consultant. m. Suchita, 1 daughter. Education: ADV DME, 1964; Graduate, Adv Engg, 1965; PGDIM (Bom), 1974; DOM, (Bom), 1975; EDP-Prof Mgt (USA), 1976; EDP-Prod Mgt (Bom), 1975; PhD (California, USA), 1995. Appointments: Design and Development Engineer, 1865-76; Production Manager, 1976-80; Management Educator, Entrepreneurship Trainer to Management Institutes in Mumbai and overseas, 1976-82; Chief Chartered Engineer and Management Consultant in Somalia, 1980-82; UNIDO Chief Technical Advisor to PDR Yemen, 1982-88; UNIDO Consultant, Somalia, 1986; UNIDO Consultant to Syrian Arab Republic, 1990-91; ILO Consultant to LDC Programme, 1990-91; UNDP/UNIDO Chief Technical Advisor (CTA) to Vietnam, 1990-94; Chief Executive Director, President, Entrepreneur, RRR Industries, 1987-; RANE Consultancy Services Pvt Ltd, 1988-; ULTRA-EDM Tools and Components Co Pvt Ltd, 1994-; MITSUCHI EDM Technologies Pvt Ltd, 1996-. Publications: Papers presented at international and national conferences and in journals. Honours: Presidents Honour, Somalia, 1982; Honour of Merit, Ministry of Industry and Trade of Government, Yemen, 1988; Vijaya Shree Award, Enriching Human Life and Outstanding International Achievement, 1994; The Best Citizens of India Award, 1999; District Chairman, Rotary UNAIDS Co-operation Programme on HIV/AIDS, Rotary International District 3140, 1998-; RRR Industries, a SMI leader of business initiative to "Break the Silence", active on care economy at the world of work, workplace awareness to unorganised and SMI Sector, 1998-; Numerous Rotary International Awards include: RI Presidential Citation Award, 1997, 1998, 1999. Memberships: Licensed Professional Engineer, ASME International (USA), 1974-; Licensed Industrial Engineer, European Institute of Industrial Engineers, 1974-; Institute of Management Services, UK; Institute of Mechanical Engineers, UK; International Golfing Fellowship of Rotary. Address: RR Industries, A/109 Ansa Industrial Estate, Saki-Vimar Road, Mumbai 400072, India.

RANTZEN Esther, b. 22 June 1940. Television Presenter. m. Desmond Wilcox, 1977, deceased 2000, 1 son, 2 daughters. Education: MA, Somerville College, Oxford. Appointments: Studio manager, making dramatic sound effects, BBC Radio, 1963; Presenter, That's Life, BBC TV 1973-94; Scriptwriter, 1976-94; Producer, The Big Time (documentary series), 1976; Presenter: Esther Interviews..., 1988; Hearts of Gold, 1988, 1996; Drugwatch; Childwatch; The Lost Babies (also producer); Esther (talk show), 1994-; The Rantzen Report, 1996-. Publications: Kill the Chocolate Biscuit (with D Wilcox), 1981; Baby Love, 1985; The Story of Ben Hardwick (with S Woodward), 1985; Once Upon a Christmas, 1996; Esther: The Autobiography, 2000; A Secret Life, 2003. Honours include: BBC TV Personality of 1975, Variety Club of Great Britain; Richard Dimbleby Award, BAFTA, 1988; Snowdon Award for Services to Disabled People, 1996; Royal TV Society Hall of Fame Award, 1998; Champion, Community Legal Service, 2000; Hon DLitt, South Bank University, 2000. Memberships: National Consumer Council, 1981-90; Health Education Authority, 1989-95; Chairman, Childline. Address: BBC TV, White City, 201 Wood Lane, London, W12 7RJ, England.

RAO D S Prakash, b. 17 June 1947, Hyderabad, India. Engineer (Civil). m. Roopa Rao, 1 daughter. Education: BEng, Civil Engineering (1st Class with distinction), Osmania University, Hyderabad, 1968; MEng, Structural Engineering (1st Class with distinction), Indian Institute of Science, Bangalore, 1968-70; PhD, University of Melbourne, 1988. Appointments: Scientist, Structural Engineering Research Centre, Roorkee, India, 1971-84; DAAD Fellow, Institut fuer Massivbau, University of Stuttgart, Germany, 1977-79; Tutor, University of Melbourne, 1984-88; Professor, Birla Institute of Technology and Science, Pilani, India, 1988-90;

Professor and Head, V R Siddhartha Engineering College, Vijayawada, India, 1991-92; Professor and Head, CBIT, Hyderabad, India, 1992-97; Professor, University College of Engineering, Hyderabad, 1997-. Publications: 1 handbook, 2 professional books, 4 textbooks; Over 200 papers; Over 200 reports; Lecture notes, discussions on papers, computer manuals. Honours: Scholarships, fellowships; ACCE - Nagadi Award, Association of Consulting Civil Engineers, India, 1997; Bharat Ratna Sir Mokshagundam Visvesvaraya Award, Government of Andhra Pradesh and Institution of Engineers (India), 1998; ISTE National Award, Indian Society for Technical Education, 1999; Man of the Year, ABI, 1999. Memberships: Fellow, Institution of Engineers (India); Fellow, Indian Institution of Bridge Engineers; Chartered Engineer, India; Professional Engineer, India; Member, Indian Concrete Institute; Indian Society for Technical Education; Eye Bank of India. Address: Department of Civil Engineering, University College of Engineering, Hyderabad 500 007, India. E-mail: prao5555@yahoo.com

RAO Kakarala Janardhana, b. 11 June 1933, Eluru, India. Physician. m. Lakshmi Vasundharadev, 1 son, 2 daughters. Education: GCIM, Government College of Integrated Medicine, Madras, India, 1959; DM & S, Kilpauk Medical College, Madras, India, 1964; MBBS, Chingleput Medical College, Madras, India, 1966; MD, Guntur Medical College, Andhra, India, 1970; Master's Degree in Community Health, University of Kansas, USA, 1992. Appointments include: Tutor, Physiology, Madurai Medical College, Tamil Nadu, India, 1965-66; Chief Endocrinology, VA Medical Center, Leavenworth, Kansas, USA, 1975-89; Staff Physician, VA Medical Center, Chillicothe, Ohio, USA, 1989-; Flight Surgeon, US Airforce Reserves, 1982-89, Air National Guard, 1989-95. Publications: Articles in professional medical journals include: Parathyroid hormone deficiency with Albrights osteodystrophy, 1974; Dissociation of calcium and sodium clearances in patients with hypoparathyroidism by infusion of chlorothiazide, 1975; Smoking Cessation and Theophylline Toxicity in Elderly Patients with Emphysema, in press. Honours: Employee of the Month, March 1990, VAMC, Chillicothe, Ohio, USA; Outstanding Achievement Award for duty in Saudi Arabia during Operation Desert Shield and Desert Storm, US Air Force, 1991. Memberships: Life Member: Association of Physicians of India, Association of Military Surgeons of US, Aerospace Medical Association, National Guard Flight Surgeons Association, Ohio National Guard Association, US National Guard Association, Reserve Officers Association, Sierra Club, National Geographic Society and American Medical Association. Address: VA Medical Center, Chillicothe, OH 45601, USA.

RAO M V M Satyanarayana, b. 22 January 1946, Ramachandrapuram, India. Geophysicist. m. Meenakshi, 1 son, 1 daughter. Education: BSc, 1963, MS, Physics, 1965, PhD, Geophysics, 1974, Osmania University. Appointments: Scientific Assistant, DLRL, 1965-66; Scientific Assistant, 1966-71, Scientist, 1971-92, NGRI; Deputy Director, NIRM, 1992-95, NGRI, 1995-. Publications: 90 research publications. Honours include: DAAD Fellowship, 1976; AP Akademi Young Scientist Award, 1981; US Fulbright Fellowship, 1987; Japan STA Fellowship, 1990; AEWG Gold Medal, 1997; ISNT National Award for Best Technical Paper in Research and Development in NDT, 1999; Listed in Who's Who publications and biographical dictionaries. Memberships: AEWG India; International Society of Rock Mechanics; AP Akademi of Sciences; Indian Geophysical Union; ISNT, India; Life Fellow, Ultrasonic Society of India; Fellow, Geological Society of India. Address: National Geophysical Research Institute (CSIR), Uppal Road, Hyderabad 500 007, India.

RAO Srikantam S P, b. 2 July 1942, Nellore. Professor. m. Rajeswari, 1 son, 1 daughter. Education: BSc, Maths, DMIT, Electronics; MTech, Applied Electronics; PhD, Computer Science. Appointments: Lecturer, E E Dept, I I T, Bombay, 1969-74; Assistant Professor, CSE Department, I I T, Bombay, 1974-83; Professor, CSE Department, IIT, Bombay, 1983-. Publications: 46 Conference Papers; 18 Journal Publications. Memberships: IEEE Computer Society; Computer Society of India; Vlsi Society of India; Institution of Electrical and Electronic Engineers. Address: Department of Computer Science and Engineering, Indian Institute of Technology, Powai, Bombay 400 076, India.

RAO Talasila Prasada, b. 2 June 1955, Munipalle, India. Scientist; Deputy Director and Head. m. Sarada, 1 son, 1 daughter. Education: BSc, Chemistry, 1971-74, MSc, Chemistry, 1974-76, Andhra University; PhD, Indian Institute of Technology, Madras, 1977-81. Appointments: Manager, R&D, Purex Laboratories, Bangalore, 1981-82; Scientist B, IICT, Hyderabad, 1982-83; Scientist B, CECRI, Karakudi, 1983-86; Scientist C, 1986-89; Scientist E_1, 1989-94, Scientist E_2, 1994-99, Scientist F, 1999-, Regional Research Laboratory, Trivandrum. Publications: 1 book; 18 reviews; 125 research papers; 4 patents; PhDs awarded under supervision: 5. Honours: Professor T L Ramachar Award for Best Paper in Electrochemical Science, 1987; Andhra University Medal in the field of Chemistry, 1994. Memberships: Kerala Academy of Sciences (KAS), Trivandrum; Society for the Advancement of Electrochemical Science and technology (SAEST), Karaikudi; Chemical Research Society of India (CRSI), Bangalore; Indian Society of Analytical Scientists, Mumbai; Indian Society for Electroanalytical Chemistry (ISEAC), Mumbai; ABI's Research Board of Advisors; New York Academy of Sciences. Address: Inorganic and Analytical Chemistry Group, Regional Research Laboratory (CSIR), Trivandrum-695019, India.

RAPHAEL Frederic Michael, b. 14 August 1931, Chicago, Illinois, USA. Writer. m. 17 January 1955, 2 sons, 1 daughter, deceased 2001. Education: St John's College, Cambridge, England. Publications: Obbligato, 1956; The Earlsdon Way, 1958; The Limits of Love, 1960; The Trouble With England, 1962; The Graduate Wife, 1962; Lindmann, 1963; Darling, 1965; Orchestra and Beginners, 1967; Two for the Road (film script with preface), 1968; Like Men Betrayed, 1970; Who Were You With Last Night?, 1971; April, June and November, 1972; Richard's Things, 1973; California Time, 1975; The Glittering Prizes, 1976; Somerset Maugham (biography), 1977; Sleeps Six (short stories), 1979; Cracks in the Ice: Views and Reviews, 1979; Oxbridge Blues (short stories), 1980; Byron (biography), 1982; Heaven and Earth, 1985; Think of England I, 1990; A Double Life, 1993; Of Gods and Men (Greek mythology revisited), 1993; The Latin Lover (short stories), 1994; Old Scores, 1995. Translations (with Kenneth McLeish): The Poems of Catullus, 1978; The Plays of Aeschylus, 2 volumes, 1991; Euripides: Bacchae, Medea; Sophocles, Ajax , 1992, 1993, 1996; Coast to Coast, 1998; All his Sons (short stories, 1999; Eyes Wide Open (A Memoir), 1999; Personal Terms, 2001; Petronius: Satyricon (translation), 2001; The Benefits of Doubt (essays), 2002; A Spoilt Boy, 2003. Contributions to: Sunday Times; Times Literary Supplement; Spectator; Poetry Nation Review; Areté. Honours: Lippincott Prize, 1961; Writers' Guild, 1965, 1966; USA Academy Award, 1966; British Academy Award, 1966; Royal TV Society Award, 1976; ACE (US Cable TV) Awards, 1985, 1991; Prix Génevois, 2000. Membership: Royal Society of Literature, fellow. Address: c/o Deborah Rogers, Rogers, Coleridge and White, 20 Powis Mews, London W11 1JN, England.

RAPOPORT Amos, b. 28 March 1929, Warsaw, Poland. Architecture Educator. m. Dorothy Hassin, deceased, 1 son. Education: BArch, University of Melbourne, 1955; MA, Rice

University, 1957; Dip TRP, University of Melbourne, 1966. Appointments: Registered Architect, Victoria, New South Wales, 1962; Lecturer, University of Melbourne, 1962; Assistant Professor, Assistant Research Architect, University of California, 1963-67; Lecturer, University College, London, 1967-69; Senior Lecturer, University of Sydney, 1969-72; Associate Professor, Architecture and Anthrology, University of Wisconsin, 1972-74; Professor, 1974-79, Distinguished Professor, 1979-2001; Distinguished Professor Emeritus, 2001-. Publications: 6 books; Editor or co-editor, 4 books; Over 200 articles to professional journals. Memberships: Royal Australian Institute of Architects; Institute for Human Ecology; Royal Institute of British Architects; Environmental Design Research Association. Address: 2925 N Summit Avenue, Milwaukee, WI 53211, USA.

RASHBROOK Albert Johann (Hans), b. 5 June 1964, Morden, Surrey, England. Freelance Illustrator. Education: BTEC National Diploma in Graphic Design, 1985, BTEC Higher National Diploma in Graphic Design, Archaeological Illustration Specialism, 1987, School of Art and Design, Swindon College, England. Appointments: Temporary Archaeological Illustrator, Trust for Wessex Archaeology, Salisbury, Wiltshire, 1987-88; Graphics Officer, Department of Medieval and Later Antiquities, 1988-90, Curator 'G' (Museum Assistant), Department of Ethnography, 1990-2000, British Museum, London, England; Freelance Illustrator including commissions received from: Priory Records, Leighton Buzzard, 2000-; British Museum Ethnography Department, 2000-; Victoria and Albert Museum, 2001; British Museum Education Department, 2002; St Paul's Cathedral, London, 2003; Various private commissions, 2000-. Publications: Aztecs, British Museum Colouring Books (illustrations and text), 1996; Illustrations and graphic work for various other British Museum publications, 1990-; Cover illustrations for CD series: Complete Morning and Evening Canticles of Herbert Howells, Vols 1-5, (Priory), 2000-; Complete Organ Works of Basil Harwood, Vols 1-4, (Priory), 2001-; Illustration series for digital resources on Victoria and Albert Museum website, 2001; Fleeting Views (greetings card illustration series), (Cornflower Press), 2002-; St Paul's Cathedral Celebrity Organ Recital Series (poster and programme cover illustration), 2003. Memberships: Licentiate Membership, Association of Archaeological Illustrators and Surveyors, 1987-; Earthwatch, 1991-; The National Trust, 1987-2001, 2003-; Tall Persons Club, GB and Ireland, 1998-. Address: 180 Regents Park Road, Finchley, London N3 3HR, England. E-mail: hans@rashbrook.fsnet.co.uk

RASHEED Hayder A, b. 3 September 1965, Baghdad, Iraq. Structural Engineer. m. Fatma A Radhi, 1 son, 1 daughter. Education: BSc, Civil Engineering, 1987, MSc, Structural and Civil Engineering, 1990 University of Baghdad, Iraq; PhD, Structural and Civil Engineering, The University of Texas at Austin, Texas, USA. Appointments: Research Assistant, Offshore Technology Research Center, The University of Texas at Austin, 1994-96; Senior Structural Engineer, Zentech Inc – USA, Houston, Texas, 1996-97; Assistant Professor of Civil Engineering, Bradley University, Illinois, USA, 1997-2000; Assistant Professor of Civil Engineering, Kansas State University, 2001-. Publications: Articles in professional journals include: Collapse of Composite Rings due to Delamination Buckling under External Pressure; Buckling of thin laminated orthotropic rings/long cylinders under external pressure, 2001; Bond slip analysis of FRP strengthened beams, 2002. Honours: Tau Beta Pi, National Engineering Honor Society, 1994; NSF Engineering Education Scholar, 1995; Chi Epsilon, National Civil Engineering Honor Society; 2003 Man of the Year Award, American Biographical Institute; Listed in Who's Who publications and biographical dictionaries. Memberships: American Society of Civil Engineers; American Concrete Institute; Structural

Engineering Institute. Address: Department of Civil Engineering, Kansas State University, 2118 Fiedler Hall, Manhattan, KS 66506, USA. E-mail: hayder@ksu.edu Website: www.engg.ksu.edu/CEDEPT/home.html

RATCH Jerry, b. 9 August 1944, Chicago, Illinois, USA. Writer; Poet. m. Sherry Karver, 18 March 1990. Education: BA, English, 1967; MFA, Creative Writing, 1970. Publications: Puppet X, 1973; Clown Birth, 1975; Osiris, 1977; Chaucer Marginalia, 1979; Hot Weather, 1982; Helen, 1985; Lenin's Paintings, 1987; Light, 1989. Contributions to: Avec; Ironwood; Sonoma Madala; Carolina Quarterly; Washington Review; Contact II; Northeast Journal. Address: 6065 Chabot Road, Oakland, CA 94618, USA.

RATHBONE Belinda, b. 30 October 1950, St Louis, Missouri, USA. Writer. m. John Ouchterlony, 1 son. Education: AA Liberal Arts, Simon's Rock of Bard College, 1970; MA, Photography, Goddard College, 1976. Appointments: Artists Liaison, Polaroid Corporation, 1977-79; Curatorial Intern, Museum of Modern Art, New York, 1979-80; Consultant, Spanish Ministry of Culture, Magnum Photographers Inc, Polaroid Corporation, Dai Nippon, Tokyo Publishing, 1980-90. Publications: American Dreams: a Survey of American Photography, 1987; Walker Evans: a Biography, 1995, 2000; Essays in: Two Lives: Georgia O'Keeffe and Alfred Stieglitz, 1992; Paul Strand: Essays on his Life and Work, 1990; Walker Evans: The Lost Work, 2000. Honour: 21st Century Award for Achievement, International Biographical Centre, Cambridge, England. Memberships: Collections Committee, Harvard University Art Museums; Angus Regional Committee, National Art Collections Fund. Address: 11A Walnut Avenue, Cambridge, MA 02140, USA.

RATHER Dan, b. 31 October 1931, Wharton, Texas, USA. Broadcaster; Journalist. m. Jean Goebel, 1 son, 1 daughter. Education: BA, Journalism, Sam Houston State College, Huntsville, Texas, 1953; University of Houston; South Texas School of Law. Appointments: Staff, United Press International, Houston Chronicle, KTRH Radio, Houston, KHOU-TV, Houston; White House Correspondent, 1964-65, 1966-74, Chief, London Bureau, 1965-66, CBS-TV; Anchorman-Correspondent, CBS Reports, 1974-75; Co-Editor, 60 Minutes, CBS-TV, 1975-81; Anchorman, Dan Rather Reporting, CBS Radio, 1977-; Anchorman and Managing Editor, CBS Evening News with Dan Rather, 1981-; CBS News special programmes. Publications: The Palace Guard (with Gary Gates), 1974; The Camera Never Blinks Twice (with Mickey Herskowitz), 1977; Memoirs: I Remember (with Peter Wyden), 1991; The Camera Never Blinks Twice: The Further Adventures of a Television Journalist, 1994; Deadlines and Datelines: Essays at the Turn of the Century, 1999. Honours: Many Emmy Awards; Dan Rather Communications Building named in his honour, Sam Houston State University, Huntsville, Texas. Address: c/o CBS News, 524 West 57th Street, New York, NY 10019, USA.

RATTLE Sir Simon, b. 19 January 1955, Liverpool, England. Conductor. m. (1) Elise Ross, 2 sons, (2) Candace Allen, 1996. Education: Royal Academy of Music. Career: Has conducted orchestras including: Bournemouth Symphony, Northern Sinfonia, London Philharmonic, London Sinfonietta, Berlin Philharmonic, Los Angeles Philharmonic, Stockholm Philharmonic, Vienna Philharmonic, Philadelphia Orchestra, Boston Symphony; Début: Queen Elizabeth Hall, 1974, Royal Festival Hall, 1976, Royal Albert Hall, 1976, Assistant Conductor, BBC Symphony Orchestra, 1977; Associate Conductor, Royal Liverpool Philharmonic Society, 1977-80; Glyndebourne début, 1977, Royal Opera, Covent Garden, 1990; Artistic Director London Choral Society, 1979-84; Principal Conductor and Artistic Advisor, City of Birmingham

Symphony Orchestra (CBSO), 1980-90, Music Director, 1990-98; Artistic Director, South Bank Summer Music, 1981-83; Joint Artistic Director, Aldeburgh Festival, 1982-93; Principal Guest Conductor, Los Angeles Philharmonic, 1981-94, Rotterdam Philharmonic, 1981-84; Principal Guest Conductor, Orchestra of the Age of Enlightenment, 1992-; Chief Conductor and Artistic Director, Berlin Philharmonic Orchestra, 2002-. Publications: Over 30 recordings with CBSO. Honours: Edison Award, 1987; Grand Prix du Disque, 1988; Grand Prix Caecilia, 1988; Gramophone Record of the Year Award, 1988; Gramophone Opera Award, 1989; International Record Critics' Award, 1990; Grand Prix de l'Academy Charles Cros, 1990; Gramophone Artist of Year, 1993; Montblanc de la Culture Award, 1993; Toepfer Foundation Shakespeare Prize, 1996; Gramophone Award for Best Concerto recording, Albert Medal (RSA), 1997; Choc de l'Année Award, 1998; Gramophone Award for Best Opera Recording, 2000; Gramophone Awards for Best Orchestral Recording and Record of the Year, 2000; Officier des Arts et des Lettres, 1995. Address: c/o Askonas Holt Ltd, Lonsdale Chambers, 27 Chancery Lane, London, WC2A 1PF, England.

RAU Magda, b. 31 August 1952, Zlin, Czech Republic. Ophthalmologist. m. Hans Pfeiffer, 1 son. Education: Graduate, College, Frydlant, Czech Republic, 1970; Medical Diploma, Palacky University, Olomouc, 1976; Ophthalmologist Diploma, Prague, Czech Republic; Ophthalmologist Diploma, Munich, Germany, 1984. Appointments: Intern Residency, Hospital Frydek-Mistek, Czech Republic, 1976-82; Ophthalmologist, Eye Department, Amberg, Germany, 1983-85; Practice Owner, Furth im Wald, 1985-; Day Clinic Owner, Tagesklinik, Cham, Germany, 1995-; Chief Ophthalmologist, Hospital, Cham, Germany, 1995-; Private Clinic Owner, Privatklinik Rau, Cham, Germany, 2000-. Publications: Managing of complications of foldable acrylic lenses, 1998; Acrylic multifocal working well at near and distance, 2001; LASEK effective for correction of myopia, 2002; Intrastromal corneal ring implantation for the correction of myopia, 2003; Erste Ergebnisse nach Implantationder multifokalen Linse MF4, 2003; ICR-Ring effective for the correction of myopia; CD Rom: Highlights of the ESCRS Vienna-ICR Ring, 1999. Honours: Listed in Who's Who publications and biographical dictionaries. Memberships: American and European Society of Cararact and Refractive Surgery; International Society of Refractive Surgery; Deutsche Ophthalmologische Gesellschaft. Address: Von Mueller Strasse 12, 93437 Furth im Wald, Germany. E-mail: info@privatklinik-dr-rau.de Website: www.privatklinik-dr-rau.de

RAVERTY Aaron (Thomas Donald), b. 13 March 1950, Stillwater, Minnesota, USA. Benedictine Monk; Anthropologist; Editor. Education: BA, Anthropology, 1972, MA, Anthropology, 1979, PhD, Sociocultural Anthropology, 1990, University of Minnesota, Minneapolis; MA, Systematic Theology, St John's University, Collegeville, Minnesota, 1979. Appointments: Preparatory School Instructor, St John's Preparatory School, Collegeville, Minnesota, 1975-76; University Instructor, St John's University, Collegeville, 1975-90; Editor, The Liturgical Press, Collegeville, 1991-; General Editor, Worship Magazine, 1993-94; Book Review Editor, The Bulletin of Monastic Interreligious Dialogue. Publications: Contributions to newsletters and journals; Editor, The Modern Catholic Encyclopedia, 1994, 2004; The Encyclopedia of American Catholic History, 1997. Honours: Certificate of Merit, St John's University, 1987; Fellowship Status in the American Anthropological Association, 1993; Choice Editorial Award, The Encyclopedia of American Catholic History, 1998. Memberships: American Benedictine Academy; American Association of Physical Anthropologists, 1972-79; Fellow, American Anthropological Association, 1980-; Board Member, Monastic Interreligious Dialogue; Secretary of the Board of

Monastic Interreligious Dialogue, 1994-99; International Graphoanalysis Society, 1996-; Communications Committee Member, St John's University Alumni Board of Directors, 1999-2003; Member, St John's Abbey Spiritual Life Program Board of Advisors, 2002-04. Address: PO Box 2015, St John's Abbey, Collegeville, MN 56321-2015, USA.

RAWNSLEY Andrew Nicholas James, FRSA (Fellow of the Royal Society of Arts) b. 5 January 1962, Leeds, England. Journalist; Broadcaster; Author. m. Jane Hall, 1990, 3 daughters. Education: Sidney Sussex College, Cambridge; MA, History, Cambridge. Appointments: BBC, 1983-85; Reporter, Feature Writer, 1985-87, Political Columnist, 1987-93, The Guardian; Writer, Presenter, A Week in Politics, 1989-97, Bye Bye Blues, 1997, Blair's Year, 1998, Channel 4 series; Associate Editor, Chief Political Commentator, The Observer, 1993-; Writer, Presenter, The Agenda, ITV series, 1996, The Westminster Hour, Radio 4 series, 1998-; The Unauthorised Biography of the United Kingdom, 1999. Publication: Servants of the People: The Inside Story of New Labour, 2000. Honours: Student Journalist of the Year, 1983; Young Journalist of the Year, 1987; Columnist of the Year, What the Papers Say Awards, 2000; Book of the Year, Channel 4/House Magazine Political Awards, 2001; Jounalist of the year, Channel 4 Awards, 2003. Address: The Observer, 119 Farringdon Road, London EC1R 3ER, England. E-mail: andrew.rawnsley@observer.co.uk

RAY Asim Kumar, b. 6 October 1937. Teacher; Researcher. m. Parul Basu, 1 daughter. Education: BSc (honours), Physics, University of Calcutta, 1956; MSc, Physics, University of Calcutta; PhD, Particle Physics, Carnegie Mellon University, 1969. Appointments: Trainee, Atomic Energy Establishment, Trombay, Bombay, 1959-60; Research Associate, Tata Institute of Fundamental Research, Bombay, 1960-63; Lecturer, 1969-76, Reader, 1976-84, Professor, 1984-, Head of Department of Physics, 1981-87, Dean of Faculty of Science, 1990-92, Professor in Charge, Computer Centre, 1991-97, Registrar, 1992-93, Retired, 2002, Visva-Bharati University, India; Visiting Scientist, USA, Japan, Italy, India, 1980-97. Publications: Editor and co-editor, Dirac and Feynman, Pioneers in Quantum Mechanics; Editor and co-editor, Proceedings of XI DAE Symposium on High Energy Physics; Over 40 professional research papers. Honours: Fulbright Scholar. Memberships: Indian Physics Association; Indian Physical Society; Indian Association of Cultivation Science; Indian Association of General Relativity and Gravitation. Address: Uttaran, Purva Palli (North), Santiniketan 731235, India. E-mail: asimkray@yahoo.co.in

RAYNER Colin Robert, b. 28 October 1938, London, England. Plastic Surgeon. m. Ruth Louise Lester, 2 sons, 2 daughters. Education: St George's College, Weybridge, Surrey; The Middlesex Hospital Medical School, London, 1957-64; MBBS, University of London, 1964; FRCS, England, 1969; Master of Surgery, University of London, 1977. Appointments: Consultant Plastic Surgeon, Aberdeen, 1978-91; Surgeon in Charge, Burns and Plastic Surgery Unit, Aberdeen Royal Infirmary, Scotland, 1986-91; Clinical Director, Co-ordinator, Burns and Plastic Surgery, University of Birmingham, NHS Trust, 1991-98; Consultant Plastic Surgeon, BUPA Hospital, Solihull, 1998-; Consultant Plastic Surgeon, BUPA Southbank Hospital, Worcester, 1998-; Visiting Professor, Oblast Oncology Centre and Postgraduate Institute, Chelyabinsk, South Urals, Russia, 1998-. Publications: Over 40 scientific peer-reviewed articles and chapters relating to burns, reconstructive plastic surgery, prosthetic implants, wound healing, Piper Alpha disaster and Urals train disaster; Approximately 20 radio broadcasts and several TV programmes. Honours: Surrey County Junior Exhibition, 1954-57; Surrey County

Exhibition, 1957-59; Surrey County Major Award, 1959-64; John Lawson Fellow, Westminster Hospital; Ethicon Research Scholar; Pulvertaft Prize Winner, Hand Surgery; Special Award for Education, Association of Surgeons of Great Britain; Fellow, Royal College of Surgeons of Edinburgh, 1980. Memberships: British Association of Plastic Surgeons; British Association of Aesthetic Plastic Surgeons. Address: 64 Wellington Road, Edgbaston, Birmingham, B15 2ET, England.

RE Edward Domenic, b. 14 October 1920, Santa Marina, Salina, Italy. Retired Federal Judge. m. Margaret A Corcoran, 5 sons, 7 daughters. Education: BS, 1940, LLB, 1943, St John's University; JSD, New York University Law School, 1950. Appointments: Colonel (retired), US Air Force; Judge Advocate General's Department; Distinguished Professor of Law, St John's University School of Law; Chairman, Foreign Claims Settlement Commission of the US, by appointments of President John F Kennedy and President Lyndon B Johnson; Assistant Secretary of State for educational and Cultural Affairs by appointment of president Lyndon B Johnson; Judge, United States Customs Court, by President Lyndon B Johnson; Chief Judge, United States Customs Court, by President Jimmy Carter; First Chief Judge of the United States Court of International Trade; Member, Judicial Conference of the United States; Member of the Executive Committee of the Judicial Conference of the United States. Publications: Books include: Foreign Confiscations in Anglo-American Law, 1951; Brief Writing and Oral Argument, 8th edition, 2000; Cases and Materials on the Law of Remedies, 5th edition, 2000; Selected essays on Equity, 1955; Freedom's Prophet (Writings of Zechariah Chafee, Jr), 1981; Numerous articles on international law, human rights, legal education, the judiciary and the legal profession. Honours: US Air Force Commendation Medal; Distinguished Service Award; First recipient "Pro Patria" Award, US Junior Chamber of Commerce; LI General Assembly, Knights of Columbus; Liberty Medal of City of New York, Mayor Koch; Highest Rank(Cavaliere Gran Croce) Legion of Merit, Republic of Italy; Trinacria Award, British-Italian Law Association, London, UK. Memberships: American Bar Association; International president, International Association of Jurist, Italy-USA; American Society for Legions of Merit of the Republic of Italy; Representative at the United Nations for International Association of Judges (NGO). Address: 305 Beach 147 Street, Neponsit, NY 11694, USA.

READ Anthony, b. 21 April 1935, Staffordshire, England. Writer; Dramatist. m. Rosemary E Kirby, 29 March 1958, 2 daughters. Education: Central School of Speech and Drama, London, 1952-54. Publications: The Theatre, 1964; Operation Lucy (with David Fisher), 1980; Colonel Z (with David Fisher), 1984; The Deadly Embrace (with David Fisher), 1988; Kristallnacht (with David Fisher), 1989; Conspirator (with Ray Bearse), 1991; The Fall of Berlin (with David Fisher), 1992; Berlin: The Biography of a City (with David Fisher), 1994; The Proudest Day: India's Long Road to Indendence (with David Fisher), 1997; The Devil's Disciples, 2003. Other: Over 200 television films, plays, series and serials. Honours: Pye Colour TV Award, 1983; Wingate Literary Prize, 1989. Membership: Trustee, Past Chairman, Writers Guild of Great Britain; Authors' Licensing and Collecting Society, vice-chairman. Address: 7 Cedar Chase, Taplow, Buckinghamshire, England.

READ John Emms (Sir), b. 29 March 1918, Brighton, England. Chartered Accountant. m. Dorothy Millicent Berry, 2 sons. Education: Administrative Staff College, Henley. Appointments: Commander (S), Royal Navy, 1939-46; Ford Motor Company Ltd, 1946-64, Director of Sales, 1961-64; Director, EMI Ltd, 1965-80; Joint Managing Director, 1967, Chief Executive, 1969-79, Deputy Chairman, 1973-74, Chairman, 1974-79, EMI Ltd; Deputy

Chairman, 1979-81, Director, 1981-87, Thorn-EMI; Director, 1973-88, Deputy Chairman, 1981-88, Thames Television; Director, Capital Industries-EMI Inc, 1970-83; Chairman, TSB Holdings, 1980-88; Chairman, Central Board, TSB Ltd, 1980-88; Chairman, TSB Group plc, 1986-88; Chairman, United Dominions Trust, 1981-85; Director, FI Group plc, 1989-93; Director, Cafman Ltd, 1991-2000; Director, NCVO Ltd, 1991-94; Partner, Cadmus Investment Management, 1993-99; Armed Forces Pay Review Board, 1976-83. Honours: Knighted, 1976; Honorary Doctorate, University of Surrey, 1989; Honorary Doctorate, International Management Centre, Buckingham, 1990; Honorary Fellow, Administrative Staff College, Henley, 1993; Honorary Fellow, University College London, 1999. Memberships: Fellow, Institute of Chartered Accountants, 1947-; Companion, Institute of Chartered Management, 1974-; Chairman, Council of Management, Institute of Neurology, 1982-99; Brain Research Trust, 1986-2001; Trustee: Westminster Abbey Trust, 1979-86, Community Action Trust (now Crimestoppers Trust), 1985-2000, United Westminster Almshouses, 1985 and other charities; Member, Governing Body, British Postgraduate Medical Federation, 1982-96, Deputy Chairman, 1987-96; Trustee, Charity Aid Foundation, 1985-98, Chairman of Trustees, 1990-94, President, 1994-98; National Theatre Development Council, 1987-90; Court, Surrey University; 1986-96 Royal Overseas League; MCC. Address: Flat 68, 15 Portman Square, London W1H 6LL, England.

READ Piers Paul, b. 7 March 1941, Beaconsfield, England. Writer. m. Emily Albertine Boothby, 29 July 1967, 2 sons, 2 daughters. Education: MA, St John's College, Cambridge. Publications: Game in Heaven with Tussy Marx, 1966; The Junkers, 1968; Monk Dawson, 1969; The Professor's Daughter, 1971; The Upstart, 1973; Polonaise, 1976; A Married Man, 1979; The Villa Golitsyn, 1981; The Free Frenchman, 1986; A Season in the West, 1988; On the Third Day, 1990; A Patriot in Berlin, 1995; Knights of the Cross, 1997; Alice in Exile, 2001. Non-Fiction: Alive, 1974; The Train Robbers, 1978; Quo Vadis?: The Subversion of the Catholic Church, 1991; Ablaze, 1993; The Templars, 1999; Alec Guinness: The Authorised Biography, 2003. Contributions to: Spectator; Tablet. Honours: Sir Geoffrey Faber Memorial Prize, 1968; Hawthornden Prize, 1969; Somerset Maugham Award, 1969; Thomas More Award, 1976; James Tait Black Memorial Prize, 1988. Memberships: Society of Authors; Royal Society of Literature, fellow. Address: 50 Portland Road, London W11 4LG, England.

REAGAN Nancy Davis (Anne Francis Robbins), b. 6 July 1921, New York, USA. Former American First Lady. m. Ronald Reagan, 1952, deceased 2004, 1 son, 1 daughter, 1 step-son, 1 step-daughter. Education: BA, Smith College, Massachusetts, USA. Appointments: Contract actress, Metro-Goldwyn-Mayer, 1949-56; Former author, syndicated column on prisoners-of-war and soldiers missing in action; Civic worker active on behalf of Vietnam War veterans, senior citizens, disabled children and drug victims; Member, Board of Directors, Revlon Group Inc, 1989-; Honorary National Chairman, Aid to Adoption of Special Kids, 1977; Actress in films including: The Next Voice You Hear, 1950; Donovan's Brain, 1953; Hellcats of the Navy, 1957. Publications: Nancy, 1980; To Love a Child (with Jane Wilkie); My Turn (memoirs), 1989. Honours: One of Ten Most Admired American Women, Good Housekeeping Magazine, 1977; Woman of Year, Los Angeles Times, 1977; Permanent member, Hall of Fame of Ten Best Dressed Women in US, Lifetime Achievement Award, Council of Fashion Designers of USA, 1988. Address: 2121 Avenue of the Stars, 34th Floor, Los Angeles, CA 90067, USA.

Dictionary of International Biography

REARDON Jeannine Renée McNaught, b. 19 April 1971, Melrose, Massachusetts, USA. Attorney. m. David M Reardon. Education: BS, summa cum laude, Suffolk University, Boston, Massachusetts, USA, 1993; JD, Suffolk University Law School, Boston Massachusetts, USA, 1996. Appointments: Attorney, 1996-; Admitted to Massachusetts Bar, 1996; Admitted to Federal District Court 1st Circuit, 1997; Admitted to Federal Court of Appeals 1st Circuit, 1997; Admitted Supreme Court of the United States, 2000; Admitted District of Columbia Court of Appeals, 2002; Assistant Professor, Suffolk University Law School, 1997-2003; Adjunct Faculty Member, MCLE, taking depositions workshops, 2001-2003. Honours: Hugh O'Brien Youth Leadership Foundation Representative; 1st Place Speaker in Law Day Essay Speech Contest, 1988; Commendation by 3rd Middlesex District Court Bar Association at Law Day, 1989; Top Speaker, University of Rhode Island Debate Tournament, 1991. Honours: Suffolk University Debate team, 1989-91; 4th Middlesex District Court Bar Association, Treasurer, 2002-2002, Vice-President, 2002-2003, President, 2003; Middlesex County Bar Association, Councilman, 2001-2003; Boston Inn of Court, 1997-2003; Essex Bar Association, 1996-2003; Massachusetts Bar Association, 1996-2003; Boston Bar Association; Phi Delta Phi, 1996-2003; Massachusetts Academy of Trial Attorneys, 1996-2000. Address: 8132 Casey Court, Elkridge, MD 21075, USA.

REARDON Raymond (Ray), b. 8 October 1932, Tredegar, Wales. Snooker Player. m. (1) Susan Carter, divorced, 1 son, 1 daughter. (2) Carol Lovington, 1987. Career: Welsh Amateur Champion, 1950-55; English Amateur Champion, 1965; Turned professional, 1967; Six times World Snooker Champion, 1970-78; Benson & Hedges Masters Champion, 1976; Welsh Champion, 1977, 1981, 1983; Professional Players Champion, 1982; Retired, 1992; Active in running World Professional Billiards and Snooker Association; Occasional TV appearances. Publications: Classic Snooker, 1974; Ray Reardon (autobiography), 1982. Honour: MBE.

RECHTIN Eberhardt, b. 16 January 1926, Orange, New Jersey, USA. Chief Executive; Professor; Engineer; Author. m. Dorothy Denebrink, 1 son, 4 daughters. Education: BS Electrical Engineering, 1946, PhD cum laude, 1950, California Institute of Technology. Appointments: Ensign to Lt, USNR, 1946-58; Assistant Director, NASA-California Institute of Technology Jet Propulsion Laboratory, 1956; Director, Chief Architect, NASA-California Institute of Technology Jet Propulsion Laboratory Deep Space Network, 1959; Director, Advanced Research Projects Agency, US Department of Defense, 1969; Deputy Director, Department of Defense Research and Engineering, Department of Defense, 1972; Assistant Secretary of Defence for Telecommunications, 1972; Chief Engineer, Hewlett Packard, 1973; CEO and President, Aerospace Corporation, 1977-89; Retired Emeritus CEO; Professor, Engineering, Aerospace Engineering, University of Southern California, 1988; Founder, University of Southern California Master's Program in Systems Architecture and Engineering, 1989; Retired Emeritus, 1994. Publications: About 75 in professional peer-reviewed journals; 3 books on systems architecture, 1991, 1997, 2000. Honours: IRE Electronic Achievement Award, 1960; NASA Space Act Award, 1961; NATO Service Award, 1962; Fellow, Institute of Radio Engineers, now Institute of Electrical and Electronics Engineers, 1963; Fellow, American Rocket Society, now American Institute of Aeronautical and Astronautical Engineers, 1963; Academician, International Astronautics Academy, 1965; Elected, National Academy of Engineering, 1968; American Institute of Aeronautics and Astronautics Aerospace Communications Award, 1969; Department of Defense Distinguished Public Service Award, 1973; Institute of Electrical and Electronics Engineers Graham Bell

Award, 1977; US Navy Distinguished Public Service Award, 1983; California Institute of Technology Distinguished Alumni Award, 1984; Gold Medal, Armed Forces Communications and Electronics Association, 1984; American Institute of Aeronautics and Astronautics von Karman Lecture, 1985; Honorary Fellow, Institute of Environmental Sciences, 1987; Air Force Exceptional Service Award, 1987; American Institute of Aeronautics and Astronautics Robert H Goddard Astronautics Award, 1991; C and C Prize, Japan, 1992; Fellow, American Association for the Advancement of Science, 1993; INCOSE Pioneer Award, 1999; Many more. Memberships: Fellow, Institute of Electrical and Electronics Engineers; Fellow, American Institute of Aeronautics and Astronautics; Tau Beta Pi, 1946; Fellow, INCOSE, 2000; Eminent Member, Eta Kappa Nu, 2002. Address: 8 Aurora Drive, Rolling Hills Estate, CA 90274, USA. E-mail: ebrechtin@earthlink.net

REDDY Pannala Venkat Ram, b. 2 January 1947, Anajpur, Andhra Pradesh, India. Structural Engineer. m. P Subhashini, 2 daughters. Education: BTECH, Civil Engineering, MTECH, Structural Engineering, JNTU, Hyderabad; PhD, registered in OU, Hyderabad, 1991. Appointments: Sriramsagar Project, State Government; Andhra Pradesh Housing Board, 5 years; Designs Organisation, 4 years; Founder, own business, Shilpi Estates, 1989; Established Shilpi Construction and Siddhartha Estates, 1991; Established Shilpi Builders, 1992; Established Bhavana Estates, 1993; Established Shilpi Constructions and Venkateshwara Constructions, 1993; Established Sai Constructions, 1997; Established Shiva Sai Builders, 2000. Honours: Rashtriya Ekta Award, 1999; Industrial Excellence Award, 1999; Jewel of India Award, 1999; Business Initiative Development Award for Excellence, 1999; Great Achiever of India Award, 1999; Gem of India Award, 1999; Lifetime Achievement Award, 1999; Outstanding Achievement Award, 1999; Business Excellence Award, 2000; Gem of New Millennium Award, 2000; International Gold Star Millennium, 2001. Memberships: Indian Concrete Institute; Institute of Engineers of India; Indian Society for Technical Education; Chartered Engineer, Institute of Engineers; Indian Water Resource Society; Indian Geotechnical Society. Address: Shilpi Groups, #1-2-384/1, Domalguda, Hyderabad 500 029, Andhra Pradesh, India. E-mail: shilpigroups_pvrreddy @yahoo.com

REDFORD Robert, b. 18 August 1937, Santa Monica, California, USA. American Actor. m. Lola Van Wegenen, divorced, 3 children. Education: University of Colorado. Creative Works: Films include, War Hunt, 1961; Situation Hopeless But Not Serious, 1965; Inside Daisy Clover, 1965; The Chase, 1965; This Property is Condemned, 1966; Barefoot in the Park, 1967; Tell Them Willie Boy is Here, 1969; Butch Cassidy and the Sundance Kid, 1969; Downhill Racer, 1969; Little Fauss and Big Halsy, 1970; Jeremiah Johnson, 1972; The Candidate, 1972; How to Seal a Diamond in Four Uneasy Lessons, 1972; The Way We Were, 1973; The Sting, 1973; The Great Gatsby, 1974; The Great Waldo Pepper, 1974; Three Days of the Condor, 1975; All the President's Men, 1976; A Bridge Too Far, 1977; The Electric Horseman, 1980; Brubaker, 1980; The Natural, 1984; Out of Africa, 1985; Legal Eagles, 1986; Havana, 1991; Indecent Proposal, 1993; The Clearing, Sacred Planet, 2004, Director, Ordinary People, 1980; Milagro Beanfield War (also producer), 1988; Promised Land (executive producer), 1988; Sneakers, 1992; A River Runs Through it (also director), 1992; Quiz Show (director), 1994; The River Wild, 1995; Up Close and Personal, 1996; The Horse Whisperer, 1997; The Legend of Bagger Vance, (also director, producer), How to Kill Your Neighbour's Dog (executive producer), 2000; The Last Castle, 2001; Spy Game, 2001. Honours: Academy Award, Golden Globe Award, Best Director, 1981; Audubon Medal, 1989; Dartmouth Film Society Award, 1990; Screen Actors' Guild Award for

Lifetime Achievement, 1996; Honorary Academy Award, 2002. Address: c/o Creative Artists Agency, 9830 Wilshire Boulevard, Beverly Hills, CA 90212, USA.

REDGRAVE Lynn, b. 8 March 1943. Actress; Playwright. m. John Clark, 1967, 1 son, 2 daughters. Education: Central School of Speech and Drama. Career: Films include: Girl With The Green Eyes; Tom Jones; Georgy Girl; Smashing Time; The Virgin Soldiers; The Deadly Affair; The National Health; Every Little Crook and Nanny; The Happy Hooker; Sunday Lovers; Getting It Right; Morgan Stewart's Coming Home; Everything You Always Wanted to Know About Sex; The Big Bus; Midnight; Shine; Strike; The Simian Line; Touched; The Annihilation of Fish; The Next Best Thing, 2000; My Kingdom, 2001; Unconditional Love, 2001; TV includes: Pygmalion; Egg on the Face of the Tiger; The Bad Seed; Whatever Happened to Baby Jane; Gauguin the Savage; White Lies; Gods and Monsters; Rude Awakening; Stage work includes: Hamlet; Much Ado About Nothing; Andorra; Hay Fever; Slag; My Fat Friend; Shakespeare for My Father; California Suite; Saint Joan; Les Liaisons Dangereuses; The Cherry Orchard; Mrs Warren's Profession; Don Juan in Hell; Notebook of Trigorin; Moon Over Buffalo, 1996; The Mandrake Root, 2001; Noises Off, 2001; Radio includes: As You Like It; Vile Bodies; Tales for Halloween. Honours include: Sarah Siddons, Chicago and Jefferson Awards (Misalliance). Publications: This is Living, 1991; Named President of the Players, 1994. Address: c/o John Clark, PO Box 1207, Topanga, CA 90290, USA,

REDGRAVE Steve, b. 23 March 1962, Marlow, England. Oarsman. m. Ann, 1 son, 2 daughters. Education: Doctor Civil Law, honoris causa. Appointments: Represented, UK at Junior World Championships, 1979; Silver medal, 1980; Stroke, British Coxed 4, Gold Medal Winners, Los Angeles Olympic Games, 1984; Gold Medals, Single Scull, Coxless Pair (with Andy Holmes) and Coxed 4, Commonwealth Games, 1986; Coxed Pair (with Holmes), World Championships, 1986; Coxless Pair Gold Medal and Coxed Pair Silver Medal (with Holmes), World Championships, 1987; Gold Medal (with Holmes), Coxless Pair and Bronze Medal, Coxed Pair, Olympic Games, Seoul, 1988; Silver Medal (with Simon Berrisford), Coxless Pairs, World Championships, 1989; Bronze Medal, Coxless Pair (with Matthew Pinsent), World Championships, Tasmania, 1990; Gold Medal, Coxless Pair (with Pinsent), World Championships, Vienna, 1991; Gold Medal, Olympic Games, Barcelona, 1992; Gold Medals at World Championships, Czech Republic, 1993, USA, 1994, Finland, 1995; Gold Medal, Olympic Games, Atlanta, 1996; Winners of World Cup, Gold Medal, Coxless 4, France, (with Pinsent, Foster, Cracknell), 1997; Gold Medal Winners, Coxless 4, World Championships, Cologne, 1998; Gold Medal Winners, Coxless 4, St Catherines (with Pinsent, Coode, Cracknell), 1999; Gold Medal, Olympic Games, Sydney, 2000. Publications: Steven Redgrave's Complete Book of Rowing, 1992; A Golden Age (autobiography), 2000. Honours: Sports Personality of the Year, 2000; British Sports Writers; Association Sportsman of the Year, 2000; Laurens Lifetime Achievement Award, 2001; Honorary DSc (Buckingham, Hull), 2001. Address: c/o British International Rowing Office, 6 Lower Mall, London W6 9DJ, England.

REDGRAVE Vanessa, b. 30 January 1937, England. Actress. m. Tony Richardson, 1962, divorced 1967, deceased 1991, 2 daughters, 1 son by Franco Reio. Education: Central School of Speech and Drama. Career: Films include: Morgan – A Suitable Case for Treatment; Sailor from Gibraltar, 1965; Charge of the Light Brigade; The Seagull; Isadora Duncan, 1968; The Devils, 1970; Mary Queen of Scots, 1971; Murder on the Orient Express, 1974; Julia, 1977; Playing for Time, 1980; Wetherby, 1984; Howard's End, 1992; Breath of Life, The Wall, Sparrow, They,

The House of the Spirits, Crime and Punishment, Mother's Boys, Little Odessa, A Month by the Lake, 1996; Mission Impossible, 1996; Looking for Richard, 1997; Wilde, 1997; Mrs Dalloway, 1997; Bella Mafia (TV), 1997; Deep Impact, 1998; Cradle Will Rock, 2000; The House of the Spirits; Crime and Punishment; Little Odessa; Produced and narrated documentary film The Palestinians, 1977; Theatre includes: A Midsummer Night's Dream, 1959; The Prime of Miss Jean Brodie, 1966; Cato Street, 1971; Threepenny Opera, 1972; Macbeth, 1975; Ghosts, 1986; A Madhouse in Goa, 1989; Heartbreak House, 1992; Antony and Cleopatra, Houston, Texas (also directed), 1996; John Gabriel Borkman, 1996; Song at Twilight, 1999; The Cherry Orchard, 2000; The Tempest, 2000; Lady Windermere's Fan, 2002. Publications include: An Autobiography, 1991. Honours: Variety Club Award; Evening Standard Award for Best Actress, 1961; Cannes Film Festival Best Actress (Morgan-A Suitable Case for Treatment, 1966); UK Film Critic's Guild and National Society of Film Critics Leading Actress Award (Isadora Duncan,) 1969; Academy Award Best Supporting Actress (Julia, 1978); TV Award for Best Actress (Playing for Time, 1981); Laurence Olivier Award, 1984; Dr hc, Massachusetts, 1990. Memberships: Co-Founder Moving Theatre, 1974; Workers' Revolutionary Party (Candidate for Moss Side, 1979); Fellow, BFI, 1988. Address: c/o Gavin Barker Associates, 45 South Molton Street, London, W1Y 1HD, England.

REDL Wolfgang, b. 24 July 1957, Vienna, Austria. Metallurgical and Ceramic Engineer. m. Astrid, 2 sons, 1 daughter. Education: BSc, Foundry Engineering, 1976; MSc, Ceramics, Construction Materials, Glass, 1983; Bachelor of Business Administration, 1991. Appointments: Director, Technical ceramics, Dr C Otto Feuerfest, Germany, 1989-91; General Manager Germany, Minerals Technologies (USA), 1991-94; Sales Manager, Europe, A P Green Industries (USA), 1995-98; Different positions in headquarters and in group companies, Holcim Ltd (Switzerland), 1998-. Membership: VDST Leoben. Address: Am Hagelholz 13, D-37217 Witzenhausen, Germany.

REDTENBACHER Andreas Gottlieb, b. 8 May 1953, Vienna, Austria. Roman Catholic Priest. Education: Mag. Theol., University of Vienna, Austria, 1977; Lic. Theol., 1979, Dr. Theol., 1983, Gregorian University, Rome; Postgraduate Student for Habilitation, University of Trier, Germany, 2002-. Appointments: Ordained Priest, 1978; Religions Professor and Rector for Students, 1979; University Assistant in Liturgy and Lecturer in Liturgy, University of Vienna, Austria, 1981; Parish Priest in St Vitus, 1990; Nominated President, Committee for Liturgy in the Episcopal-Vikariat of the City of Vienna, Austria, 1981; Nominated President of the Conference of Liturgists in the Austrian Roman Catholic Church, 1995. Publications: Presbyter und Presbytorium, 1980; Zukunft aus den Erbe, 1983, second edition, 2003: Wo Sich Wege Kreuzen, 1985; Liturgie und Leben, 2002; Many published articles. Honour: Archiepiscopal Konsistorialrat. Memberships: International Societas Liturgica; Editorial Board, Heiliger Dienst; Corresponding Member, Editorial Board, Bibel und Liturgie. Address: Stiftplatz 1, A-3400 Klosterneuburg, Austria. E-mail: a.redtenbacher@stift-klosterneuburg.at

REDWOOD John Alan (Rt Hon), b. 15 June 1951, Dover, England. Member of Parliament. m. Gail Chippington, 14 June 1974, 1 son, 1 daughter. Education: BA, Honours 1971, MA, DPhil, 1975, Oxford University. Appointments: Manager, then Director, NM Rothschild & Sons, 1977-89; Chairman Norcros Plc, 1987-89; MP for Wokingham, 1987-; Minister, UK Government, 1989-95; Shadow President, Board of Trade, 1997-99; Shadow Front Bench Spokesman on the Environment, 1999-2000; Chair, Murray Financial Corporation, 2002-. Publications: Reason, Ridicule and

Dictionary of International Biography

Religion, 1976; Public Enterprise in Crisis, 1980; Co-author, Value for Money Audits, 1981; Co-author, Controlling Public Industries, 1982; Going for Broke, 1984; Equity for Everyman, 1986; Popular Capitalism, 1989; Global Marketplace, 1994; The Single European Currency, with others, 1996; Our Currency, Our Country, 1997; The Death of Britain? 1999; Stars and Strife, 2001; Just Say No, 2001; Third Way – Which Way, 2002. Honours: Parliamentarian of the Year Awards, 1987, 1995, 1997. Address: House of Commons, London, SW1A 0AA, England.

REED Lou, b. 2 March 1942, Brooklyn, New York, USA. Musician. m. Sylvia Morales, 1980. Education: BA, Syracuse University. Songwriter and recording artist, 1965-; Founder member, Velvet Underground band, 1966-70; Toured with Andy Warhol's The Exploding Plastic Inevitable; Poet; Film actor. Publications: Recordings, solo albums include: Lou Reed, 1972; Rock'n'Roll Animal, 1972; Berlin, 1973; Sally Can't Dance, 1974; Metal Machine Music, 1975; Lou Reed Live, 1975; Coney Island Baby, 1976; Walk on the Wild Side; Street Hassle, 1978; Live, Take No Prisoners, 1978; Vicious, 1979; The Bells, 1979; Growing Up in Public, 1980; Rock 'n' Roll Diary, 1967-80; Blue Mask, Legendary Hearts, 1983; New York, 1989; Songs for Drella (with John Cale), 1990; Magic and Loss, 1992; Set the Twilight Reeling, 1996; Perfect Night Live in London, 1998; Ecstasy, 2000; Several albums with Velvet Underground. Publication: Between Thought and Expression (selected lyrics), 1991; Pass Thru Fire, 2000. Honour: Rock and Roll Hall of Fame, 1996. Address: c/o Sister Ray Enterprises, 584 Broadway, Room 609, New York, NY 10012, USA.

REES David William Alan, b. 12 March 1947, Ruislip, Middlesex, England. Engineering Educator and Researcher. Education: Student Apprentice, Black & Decker Ltd, Harmondsworth, Middlesex, National Diploma, Southall Technical College, Middlesex, 1963-68; Postgraduate Student, Applied Mechanics, Imperial College, London, 1969-70; PhD, Research, Kingston University, 1973-76. Appointments: Engineering Apprentice, 1963-68, Engineering Designer, 1968-69, Black & Decker Ltd; Postgraduate Student, 1969-70, Experimental Officer, 1970-71, Imperial College, London; Research Assistant, 1971-72, Lecturer, 1972-77, Kingston University; Lecturer, Trinity College, Dublin, 1977-84; Lecturer, Surrey University, 1984-85, Lecturer, 1985-95, Senior Lecturer, 1995-2004, Brunel University; Visiting Fellow, Joint Research Centre, Petten, 1982; National Physical Laboratory, 1983, 1985. Publications: Books: The Mechanics of Solids and Structures, 1990; Basic Solid Mechanics, 1997, Mechanics of Solids & Structures, 2000; Recent articles: Rim and Pole Failures from Elliptical Bulging, 2000; Influences of Rolling Reduction upon Sheet Metal Formability, 2001; Nutting Creep in Mono and Bi-layer Polymers, 2002; Nutting Creep in Polymer Composites, 2003; Anisotropy in Thin Canning Sheets, 2003. Honours: National Diploma Prize, 1968; MSc/DIC, Imperial College, 1970; PhD, Kingston University, 1976; Honorary MA, Trinity College, Dublin, 1981; Best Paper, Fylde Prize, "Strain", 1993; Best Paper, CEGB Prize "Journal of Strain Analysis", 1998; DSc, Brunel University, 2003. Memberships: Institution of Mechanical Engineers; Council of Engineering Institutions; Editorial Board, International Journal of Plasticity, 1985-91, Journal of Strain Analysis for Engineering Design, 1994-. Address: Brunel University, Kingston Lane, Uxbridge, Middlesex UB8 3PH, England. E-mail: david.rees@brunel.ac.uk

REES Peter Wynford Innes (Baron of Goytre in the County of Gwent), b. 9 December 1926. Life Peer; Barrister; Politician. m. Anthea Peronelle Wendell. Education: Christ Church, Oxford. Appointments: Served in Scots Guards, 1945-48; Called to the Bar, Inner Temple, 1953; Bencher; Practised Oxford circuit;

Contested, as a Conservative, Abertillery, 1964, 1965, Liverpool, West Derby, 1966; Elected MP (Conservative), Dover, 1970-74, Dover and Deal, 1974-83, Dover, 1983-87; PPS to Solicitor General, 1972; Minister of State, HM Treasury, 1979-81; Minister of Trade, 1981-83; Chief Secretary to the Treasury and Member of Cabinet, 1983-85. Honours: QC, 1969; PC, 1983. Memberships: Former Member, Court and Council, Museum of Wales, Museum and Galleries Commission; Liveryman, Worshipful Company of Clockmakers. Address: Goytre Hall, Abergavenny, Monmouthshire NP7 9DL, Wales.

REES-MOGG Lord William, Baron Rees-Mogg of Hinton Blewitt, b. 14 July 1928, Bristol, England; Journalist; Writer. m. Gillian Shakespeare Morris, 1962, 2 sons, 3 daughters. Education: Balliol College, Oxford. Appointments: Staff, The Financial Times, 1952-60; City Editor, 1960-61, Political and Economic Editor, 1961-63, Deputy Editor, 1964-67, The Sunday Times; Editor, 1967-81, Columnist, 1992-, The Times; Director, The Times Ltd, 1968-81, GEC, 1981-97, EFG Private Bank, 1993-, Value Realisation Trust, 1996-99; Vice-Chairman, Board of Governors, BBC, 1981-86; Chairman, Arts Council of Great Britain, 1982-89, Pickering and Chatto Ltd, 1983-, Sidgwick and Jackson, 1985-89, Broadcasting Standards Council, 1988-93, International Business Communications plc, 1994-98. Publications: The Reigning Error: The Crisis of World Inflation, 1974; An Humbler Heaven, 1977; How to Buy Rare Books, 1985; Blood in the Streets (with James Dale Davidson), 1988; The Great Reckoning (with James Dale Davidson), 1991; Picnics on Vesuvius: Steps Toward the Millennium, 1992; The Sovereign Individual: How to Survive and Thrive During the Collapse of the Welfare State (with James Dale Davidson), 1997. Honours: Honorary LLD, University of Bath, 1977; Knighted, 1981; Life Peerage, 1988. Address: 17 Pall Mall, London SW1Y 5NB, England.

REEVE Christopher, b. 25 September 1952, New York, USA. Actor. m. (1) 1 son, 1 daughter, (2) Dana Morosini, 1 son, 1 daughter. Education: Cornell University. Career: Actor, films include: Somewhere in Time, Superman, 1985; Superman 2, Deathtrap, Monsignor, Superman 3, The Bostonians, The Aviator, Superman 4, Street Smart, 1988; Switching Channels, 1988; Noises Off, 1992; The Remains of the Day, 1993; Morning Glory, 1993; Speechless, 1994; The Rhinehart Theory, 1994; Village of the Damned, 1995; A Step Toward Tomorrow, 1996; Rear Window, 1998; TV appearances include: Anna Karenina, 1985; The Great Escape, 1988; Theatre includes: Street Smart, 1986; The Winter's Tale, 1989; More than 110 stage productions in USA and England. Address: c/o Scott Henderson, William Morris Agency, 151 El Camino Drive, Beverly Hills, CA 90212, USA.

REEVE Marion José, b. 26 September 1926, Watford, England. Artist. m. Albert Edward Butcher, 6 November 1968, deceased. Education: St Joan of Arc School, Rickmansworth, England, 1937-44; Intermediate Examination, Art and Crafts, 1950; National Diploma, Design, 1953. Career: Landscape Painter and Sculptor. Honour: Stations of the Cross, St Michael and All Angles Church West Watford, England. Address: 10 Kelmscott Crescent, Watford, Hertfordshire, WD18 0NG, England.

REEVES Keanu, b. 2 September 1964, Beirut, Lebanon. Actor. Education: Toronto High School for Performing Arts; Training at Second City Workshop. Career: Stage appearances include: Wolf Boy; For Adults Only; Romeo and Juliet; with rock band Dogstar, 1996-; TV films: Letting Go, 1985; Act of Vengeance, 1986; Babes in Toyland, 1986; Under the Influence, 1986; Brotherhood of Justice, 1986; Save the Planet (TV special), 1990; Films: Prodigal, Flying, 1986; Youngblood, 1986; River's Edge, 1987; Permanent Record, 1988; The Night Before, 1988; The Prince of Pennsylvania,

1988; Dangerous Liaisons, 1988; I Love You to Death, 1990; Tune in Tomorrow, 1990; Bill and Ted's Bogus Journey, 1991; Point Break, 1991; My Own Private Idaho, 1991; Bram Stoker's Dracula, 1992; Much Ado About Nothing, 1993; Even Cowgirls Get the Blues, Little Buddha, 1993; Speed, 1994; Johnny Mnemonic, 1995; A Walk in the Clouds, 1995; Chain Reaction, Feeling Minnesota, The Devil's Advocate, 1996; The Last Time I Committed Suicide, 1997; The Matrix, 1998; The Replacements, 2000; The Watcher, 2000; The Gift, 2000; Sweet November, 2001; The Matrix: Reloaded, 2003; The Matrix: Revolutions, 2003; Something's Gotta Give, 2003. Address: c/o Kevin Houvane, 9830 Wilshire Boulevard, Beverly Hills, CA 90212, USA.

REGIS John, b. 13 October 1966, Lewisham, London, England. Athlete. Career: Winner, UK 200m (tie), 1985; 100m, 1988, Amateur Athletics Association 200m, 1986-87; UK record for 200m, Silver Medal, Olympic Games Seoul, 1988; 300m indoor record holder Commonwealth Games, 1990; Silver Medal 200m, 1991; Gold medal 4 x 100m relay, 1991; Gold Medal 200m 4 x 400m relay, 4 x 400m relay, 1993; Gold Medal World Cup, 1994; Member, British team Olympic Games, Atlanta, 1996; Retired, 2000; Member, Great Britain bobsleigh training team, 2000-; Founder, Stellar Athletes Ltd, 2001; Coach, UK Athletics sprint relay team, 2001-. Address: c/o Belgrave Harriers Athletic Club, Batley Croft, 58 Harvest Road, Englefield Green, Surrey, England.

REGNARD Thomy Maxime Christian, b. 7 October 1958, Curepipe, Mauritius. Company Managing Director. m. M A Alexandra Pitot, 3 sons. Education: SC; HSC. Appointments: Marketing Manager, Ferney Textiles, 1983-89; Managing Director, Associated Textiles, 1989-. Honours: Certificate of Award Department Management, 1980; Certificate of Merit, 1980; Certificate in Marketing Management, 1980; Diploma in Marketing Management, 1981. Memberships: Mauritius Turf Club; Dodo Club; Institute of Marketing Management, South Africa. Address: Bois Cheri Road, Moka, Mauritius. E-mail: tichris@intnet.mu

REICHMANN Susan Helene, b. 30 May 1959, Los Angeles, USA. Psychotherapist. m. Michael Dennis Lee, 1999, 2 sons. Education: Student, California Institute of Arts, 1983-84; Museum of Fine Arts, Boston, 1983-84; BA, Psychology, BA, French Literature, University of California at Berkeley, 1984; MA, Marital and Family Therapy, Loyola Marymount University, 1992; Licensed Marriage and Family Therapist, California; Registered Art Therapist, American Art Therapy Association. Appointments: Associate Producer, film, The Golem, 1994; Director, HIV-AIDS project Open Paths Counseling Centre, Los Angeles, 1995-98; Private Practice, Santa Monica, 1996-; Art Therapist, Haven House Shelter, Pasadena, California, 1997-98; Art Therapy Consultant: Helping Our Mobile Elderly, Venice, California, 1997-98; Continuing Education Lecturer, Campion Counseling Center, Ocean Park Community Center, Santa Monica, 1998-; Children's Hospital of Los Angeles, Hollywood, 1999; Media Spokesperson, Here2listen.com, San Mateo, 1999-2002; Sponsored Artist, A Community of Angeles, Los Angeles, 2001; Freelance writer and poet; Clinical Supervisor, Project Co-ordinator, Youth and Family Violence Project. Honours: Scholar, Squaw Valley, California, Community of Writers, 1998. Memberships: American Art Therapy Association; California Association of Marriage and Family Therapists; South California Art Therapy Association; Loyola Marymount Graduate Art Therapy Association; Psi Chi. Address: 3331 Ocean Park Blvd #103, Santa Monica, CA 90405, USA. E-mail: artpsych@aol.com

REID Dolores Born, b. Pickens, Mississippi, USA. Social Worker. m. Walter F Reid, 1 son, 1 daughter. Education: BS, Sociology, Psychology, Loyola University, Chicago, Illinois, 1954; MSW,

Boston University, Massachusetts, 1961; Postgraduate Study in Financial Management, 1979; Wharton School of Business, Philadelphia, Pennsylvania; PhD, Public Administration, Union Institute, Cincinnati, Ohio, 1985. Appointments include: Deputy Director, Illinois Department of Children and Family Services, 1972-78; Executive Director, Montgomery County Children Services, Montgomery, Co Dayton, Ohio, 1978-86; Executive Director, Allen County Children's Services, Lima Ohio, 1987-88; Director, Child Welfare Service, Montgomery County Department of Social Services, Rockville, Maryland, 1988-89, Chief of Assessment and Monitoring Programmes, Department of Addiction, Victim and Mental Health Services, 1989-93, Chief, Family Preservation Services, Department of Addiction, Victim and Mental Health Services, 1993-94; Executive Consultant, Metropolitan Washington Council of Government, 1994-95; Chief, Bureau of Children Services, Office of Child Care and Family Services, Ohio Department of Human Services, 1995-98; Programme Administrator Consultant, Technical Assistant, Ohio counties implementing ASFA, 1998-99; Deputy Assistant Director, Arizona Department of Economic Security, Division of Children, Youth and Families, 2000-; Numerous Professorships in Social Work. Publications: Numerous articles in professional journals; several presentations. Honour: NIMH Fellow, Social Worker of the Year, Moline, Illinois and Dayton, Ohio. Memberships: Black Administrators in Child Welfare; American Humane Society; National Network for Social Work Managers; National Association of Social Workers. Address: 13315 W Coronado Rd, Goodyear, AZ 85338, USA. E-mail: dbreid120193@aol.com

REID Susan Lee, b. 4 April 1958, Charlottesville, Virginia, USA. Conductor. Education: Royal College of Church Music, England, 1980; BMus, Westminster Choir College, England, 1980; MSc, Oklahoma State University, USA, 1987; MMus, University of Surrey, England, 1990; DMA, Arizona State University, USA, 1995. Appointments: Assistant Conductor, University Chorus and Orchestra, Instructor, Music Director, Principal Conductor, University Symphonic Wind Band, University of Surrey, 1989-90; Teaching Assistant, 1992-94, Faculty Associate, 1994-95, Arizona State University, School of Music, Tempe; Assistant Professor, Director of Choral Activities, South Dakota School of Mines and Technology, Rapid City, South Dakota, 1995-2000; Artistic Director, Dakota Choral Union, 1998-2000; Associate Professor, Director of Choral Activities, James Madison University, Harrisonburg, Virginia, 2000-. Publications: 7 journal publications; 4 copyright and non-copyright musical compositions. Honours: Rotary International Fellow; Regents Academic Scholar; YWCA Woman of Tomorrow; Guest Conductor, Austria, England, USA, 1980-; Nominated for Outstanding Professor of the Year, South Dakota School of Mines and Technology, 1999; Listed in national and international biographical dictionaries. Memberships: Lifetime Member, American Choral Directors Association; Member, College Music Society; Board of Directors, Conductors' Guild; Member, Music Educators National Conference; Member, Virginia Music Educators National Conference; MENSA; Phi Kappa Lambda; Phi Kappa Phi. Address: James Madison University, School of Music, Harrisonburg, VA 22807, USA. E-mail: reidsl@jmu.edu

REIF Stefan Clive, b. 21 January 1944, Edinburgh, Scotland. Professor; Writer. m. Shulamit Stekel, 19 September 1967, 1 son, 1 daughter. Education: BA, Honours, 1964, PhD, 1969, University of London; MA, 1976, LittD, 2002, University of Cambridge, England. Appointments: Professor of Medieval Hebrew Studies and Director of Genizah Research, University of Cambridge; Editor, Cambridge University Library's Genizah Series, 1978-. Publications: Shabbethai Sofer and his Prayer-book, 1979; Interpreting the Hebrew Bible, 1981; Published Material from the

Cambridge Genizah Collections, 1988; Genizah Research after Ninety Years, 1992; Judaism and Hebrew Prayer, 1993; Hebrew Manuscripts at Cambridge University Library, 1997; A Jewish Archive from Old Cairo, 2000; Why Medieval Hebrew Studies, 2001; The Cambridge Genizah Collections, 2002. Contributions to: Over 240 articles in Hebrew and Jewish studies. Memberships: Fellow, Royal Asiatic Society; Council, Jewish Historical Society of England; Fellow, Mekize Nirdamim Society, Jerusalem; British Association for Jewish Studies; Society for Old Testament Study. Address: Taylor-Schechter Genizah Research Unit, Cambridge University Library, West Road, Cambridge CB3 9DR, England.

REIFFEL Robert S, b. 1 June 1946, New York, New York. Plastic Surgeon. m. Suzanne T Reiffel, 2 daughters. Education: BA, Yale University, 1968; MD, Columbia University, 1972; Internship and Residency, General Surgery, The Roosevelt Hospital, New York City, 1972-77; Plastic Surgery Residency, 1977-78, Hand Surgery Fellowship, 1978-80, New York University Medical Center. Appointments: Private Practice, Plastic and Hand Surgery, White Plains, New York, 1980-; Chief, Plastic Surgery Section, Department of Surgery, White Plains Hospital, New York, 1998-2002. Publications: Articles in medical journals include most recently as co-author: Prevention of hypertrophic scars by long-term paper tape application, 1995; Periungual Myxoid Neruofibroma, 2002. Honours: First Prize, Resident's Night, Section of Plastic Surgery of the New York Academy of Medicine and the New York Regional Society of Plastic and Reconstructive Surgeons, 1979; First Prize, Senior Classification, Scholarship Contest of the Educational Foundation, American Society of Plastic and Reconstructive Surgeons, 1980. Memberships: American Burn Association; American Society for Aesthetic Plastic Surgery; American Society for Surgery of the Hand; American Society of Plastic Surgeons; Medical Society, State of New York; New York Regional Society of Plastic and Reconstructive Surgery; New York Society for Surgery of the Hand; Westchester County Medical Society; Fellow, American College of Surgeons. Address: 12 Greenridge Avenue, White Plains, NY 10605, USA. E-mail: r.reiffel@verizon.net Websites: www.plasticsurgery.org/md/rsreiffel.htm www.the bestplasticsurgeon.medem.com

REILLY-DEAS Anne, b. 28 November 1950, Mullingar, Ireland. Artist; Poet; Accounting Executive. m. Arthur Deas, divorced. Education: Loreto College; Bloomfield College; Business Studies, Rosse Business College and Christie Business College. Career: Accounting Executive in the private and public sectors, 1967-83; Volunteer work, campaign work, 1983-86; Artist, 1986-; Exhibitions: Invited to exhibit: Tullynally Castle, 1986; Caley House, 1988; Granard Library, 1989; Longford Library, 1989; Mullingar Library, 1989; Cheltenham Show, 1990; Irish Council Against Blood Sports Art Exhibition, 1990; ArtUs, Mullingar Arts Resource Centre, 1992; Art Horizons, New York, USA, 1992; Art 54 Gallery, New York, 1993; International Lions Club Art Auction, 1993; Townley Hall, Drogheda, 1996; Allen Manor, 1997-98; Mullingar Arts Centre, 1999; Christie Wild International, Florida and Harrogate, 2000; DFN Gallery, New York, 2000; International ArtExpo, New York, 1997-2001; International ArtExpo, San Francisco, 2000-2001; Special Olympic Games Art Exhibition, 2003; Orchard House, 2002-2004; Greenville, 1989-92, 1991-2004. Publications: Features in: Westmeath Examiner Newspaper; Longford Leader Newspaper; Modern Woman Magazine; Events Programme Alliance Française; Brochures; Catalogues; Poems published in newspapers and magazines. Honours: Prize Winner, Athlone Agricultural Show Art Section, 1986; Selected, Royal Hibernian Academy Summer Exhibition, Dublin, 1992; Selected/Commended Certificate National Irish Bank Exhibition, Dublin, 1994; Sponsored/Selected Solo Exhibition "Through Time," Alliance Française, Dublin, presented

with a book "Art Contemporain En France," 1996; Invited/Selected New York Prestige Artists Debut, 2000; Listed in Who's Who publications and biographical dictionaries. Membership: Qualified for Mensa Membership. Address: Greenville, Dublin Road, Castlepollard, Co. Westmeath, Ireland.

REINER Rob, b. 6 March 1947, New York, USA. Actor; Writer; Director. (1) Penny Marshall, 1971, divorced, (2) Michele Singer, 1989. Education; University of California at Los Angeles. Career: Appeared with comic improvisation groups: The Session; The Committee; Scriptwriter for Enter Laughing, 1967; Halls of Anger, 1970; Where's Poppa, 1970; Summertree, 1971; Fire Sale, 1977; How Come Nobody's on Our Side, 1977; TV appearances: All in the Family, 1971-78; Free Country, 1978; Thursday's Game, 1974; More Than Friends, 1978; Million Dollar Infield, 1972; Director, This is Spinal Tap, 1984; The Sure Thing, 1985; Stand By Me, 1986; The Princess Bride, 1987; Misery, 1990; Co-producer, director, When Harry Met Sally, 1989; A Few Good Men, 1992; North, The American President, 1995; Ghosts of the Mississippi, 1996; The Story of Us, 1999. Address: c/o Castle Rock Entertainment, 335 North Maple Drive, Suite 135, Beverly Hills, CA 90212, USA.

REINHARDT Heinrich, b. 14 March 1947, Freising, Germany. Professor of Philosophy. Education: Dr. Phil., Philosophy, 1972, Dipl. Theol., Catholic Theology, 1978, University of Munich, Germany; Ordained Priest, Cathedral of Chur, Switzerland, 1992. Appointments: Professor of Philosophy and Latin Conversation, International Seminary of St Petrus, Wigratzbad, Germany, 1989-91; Studies Director, Propedeutic Seminary "Lauretanum", Zizers, Switzerland, 1992-96; Professor of Philosophy, Theology Faculty of Chur, Switzerland, 1995-. Publications: 7 monographs about the philosophy of language; 8 volumes about Christian spirituality; 1 monograph about Renaissance research; 1 monograph about philosophy of state; 4 books of Latin poems; 3 books of German haiku; 106 other publications in Latin or German; 1500 lemmata in the Vatican Dictionary of Modern Latin (Lexicon Recentis Latinitatis, 2 volumes 1992-97). Honour: Gold Cross of Merit of the Grand Priory of Switzerland of the Military and Hospitaller Order of St Lazarus. Memberships: Görresgesellschaft; Gesellschaft für Antike Philosophie; Societas Latina; Churer Initiative Sprachphilosophie; The Military and Hospitaller Order of St Lazarus. Address: Blumenweg 6, CH-7205 Zizers, Switzerland.

REITMAN Ivan, b. 27 October 1946, Komarno, Czechoslovakia. Film Director and Producer. m. Genevieve Robert, 1 son, 2 daughter. Education: MusB, McMaster University. Career: Producer, stage shows: The Magic Show, 1974; The National Lampoon Show, 1975; Merlin (also director), 1983; Director and Executive Producer, films: Cannibal Girls, 1973; They Came From Within, 1975; Death Weekend, 1977; Blackout, 1978; National Lampoon's Animal House, 1978; Heavy Metal, 1981; Stop! Or My Mom Will Shoot, 1992; Space Jam, 1996; Private Parts, 1996; Producer and Director: Foxy Lady, 1971; Meatballs, 1979; Stripes, 1981; Ghostbusters, 1984; Legal Eagles, 1986; Twins, 1988; Ghostbusters II, 1989; Kindergarten Cop, 1990; Dave, 1993; Junior, 1994; Executive Producer: Rabid, 1976; Spacehunter: Adventures in the Forbidden Zone, 1983; Big Shots, 1987; Casual Sex?, 1988; Feds, 1988; Beethoven, 1992; Beethoven's 2nd, 1993; Commandments, 1996; Road Trip, 2000; Producer and director, TV series: The Late Shift, 1996; Father's Day, 1997. Membership: Director's Guild of America. Address: c/o CAA, 9830 Wilshire Boulevard, Beverly Hills, CA 90212, USA.

REMNICK David J, b. 29 October 1958, Hackensack, New Jersey, USA. Journalist; Writer. m. Esther B Fein, 2 sons, 1 daughter. Education: AB, Princeton University, 1981.

Dictionary of International Biography

Appointments: Reporter, Washington Post, 1982-91; Staff writer, 1992-, Editor-in-Chief, 1998-, The New Yorker. Publications: Lenin's Tomb: The Last Days of the Soviet Empire, 1993; The Devil Problem (and Other True Stories), 1996; Resurrection: The Struggle for a New Russia, 1997; King of the World: Muhammad Ali and the Rise of an American Hero, 1998; Life Stories: Profiles from The New Yorker (editor), 1999; Wonderful Town: Stories from The New Yorker (editor), 1999. Contributions to: Newspapers and periodicals. Honours: Livingston Award, 1991; Pulitzer Prize for General Non-Fiction, 1993; Helen Bernstein Award, New York Public Library, 1994; George Polk Award, 1994. Address: The New Yorker, Four Times Square, New York, NY 10036, USA.

REMOVILLE Jacques Robert Philippe, b. 17 December 1934, Hanoï, Vietnam. Chemical Engineer. m. Nicole Dramas, 1 son, 2 daughters. Education: Ingenieur, Ecole Centrale des Arts et Manufactures de Paris, 1959. Appointments: Scientific Officer, then Acting Head of Unit, Post-Irradiation Service, Joint Research Centre, Karlsruhe and Petten, 1962-68; Research Coordinator, Luxatom, 1969-84; Scientific Officer, Torus Remote Operations, Joint European Torus, Culham, UK, 1984-89; Senior Administrative Officer, Commission of the European Communities, DG Research, Brussels, 1990-99. Publications: 33 international presentations or publications, including 16 nuclear, 2 solar and 15 on science policy; 29 EC reports. Honour: Médaille de Reconnaissance, FLSG, 1985. Memberships: Association des Centraliens. Address: 1157 Avenue du Golf, La Tour de Mare, F 83600, Fréjus, France.

REN Yulong, b. 23 June 1944, Chong Qing, China. Professor. m. Jihui Yu, 1 son, 1 daughter. Education: Bachelor of Electric System Automation, 1962; Master of Electric Engineering: Theory and New Technology; Research on Energy Economics, Management School, Moscow State University, 1993-94. Appointments: Engineer, Petro-Planning Research Institute, Qinghai, China; Lecturer, Senior Lecturer, Dean, Management Faculty, Chongqing University, 1983-; One of the Academic Leaders in the national project, Technical Economy and Management; In charge of the 211 Key national Construction development Programme, Electric Technical Economy. Publications: Statistics Theory on Electric Engineering, 1995; Technical Economics, 1998; Research on Template Algorithm in Intellective Budget System of Construction Engineering; A Study on the Life Cycle Assessment of Venture Capital Investment. Honour: Innovative Woman conferred by Chingqing Municipality to first top ten women with prominent achievements. Memberships: China Electric and Mechanic Institute; AACE. Address: College of Economics and Business Administration, Chongqing University, Shapingba District, Chong Qing, PR China. E-mail: yujihui@cta.cq.cn

RENDELL Ruth Barbara (Baroness Rendell of Babergh), (Barbara Vine), b. 17 February 1930, England. Writer. m. Donald Rendell, 1950, divorced 1975, 1 son, remarried Donald Rendell, 1977, deceased 1999. Publications: From Doon with Death, 1964; To Fear a Painted Devil, 1965; Vanity Dies Hard, 1966; A New Lease of Death, 1967; Wolf to the Slaughter, 1967 (televised 1987); The Secret House of Death, 1968; The Best Man to Die, 1969; A Guilty Thing Surprised, 1970; One Across Two Down, 1971; No More Dying Then, 1971; Murder Being Once Done, 1972; Some Lie and Some Die, 1973; The Face of Trespass, 1974 (televised as An Affair in Mind, 1988); Shake Hands for Ever, 1975; A Demon in My View, 1976 (film 1991); A Judgement in Stone, 1977; A Sleeping Life, 1978; Make Death Love Me, 1979; The Lake of Darkness, 1980 (televised as Dead Lucky, 1988); Put on by Cunning, 1981; Master of the Moor, 1982 (televised 1994); The Speaker of Mandarin, 1983; The Killing Doll, 1984; The Tree of Hands, 1984 (film 1989); An Unkindness of Ravens, 1985;

Live Flesh, 1986; Heartstones, 1987; Talking to Strange Men, 1987; A Warning to the Curious: The Ghost Stories of M R James (editor), 1987; The Veiled One, 1988 (televised 1989); The Bridesmaid, 1989; Ruth Rendell's Suffolk, 1989; Undermining the Central Line (with Colin Ward), 1989; Going Wrong, 1990; Kissing the Gunner's Daughter, 1992; The Crocodile Bird, 1993; Simisola, 1994; The Reason Why (editor), 1995; The Keys to the Street, 1997; Road Rage, 1997; The Chimney Sweeper's Boy, 1998; A Sight for Sore Eyes, 1999; Harm Done, 1999; The Babes in the Wood, 2002; As Barbara Vine: A Dark-Adapted Eye, 1986 (televised 1994); A Fatal Inversion, 1987 (televised 1992); The House of Stairs, 1988; Gallowglass, 1990; King Solomon's Carpet, 1981; Asta's Book, 1993; No Night is Too Long, 1994; The Brimstone Wedding, 1996; Grasshopper, 2000; Piranha to Scurfy and Other Stories, 2000; Short Stories: The Fallen Curtain, 1976; Means of Evil, 1979; The Fever Tree, 1982; The New Girl Friend, 1985; Collected Short Stories, 1987; The Copper Peacock, 1991; Blood Linen, 1995. Honours: Arts Council National Book Award for Genre Fiction, 1981; Royal Society of Literature, Fellow, 1988; Sunday Times Award for Literary Excellence, 1990; Cartier Diamond Dagger Award, Crime Writers Association, 1991; Commander of the Order of the British Empire, 1996; Life Peerage, 1997. Memberships: Royal Society of Literature, Fellow. Address: 26 Cornwall Terrace Mews, London, NW1 5LL, England.

RENÉE, (Renée Gertrude Taylor), b. 19 July 1929, Napier, New Zealand. Playwright; Writer. Education: BA, University of Auckland, 1979. Appointments: Member of women's writers collective groups, 1979-84; Director and actress, Napier Repertory Players; Robert Burns Fellowship, University of Otago, 1989; Writers Fellowship, University of Waikato and Creative, New Zealand, 1995. Publications: Secrets: Two One-Woman Plays, 1982; Breaking Out, 1982; Setting the Table, 1982; What Did You Do in the War, Mummy?, 1982; Asking For It, 1983; Dancing, 1984; Wednesday to Come, 1984; Groundwork, 1985; Pass It On, 1986; Born to Clean, 1987; Jeannie Once, 1990; Touch of the Sun, 1991; Missionary Position, 1991; The Glass Box, 1992; Tiggy Tiggy Touchwood, 1992; Willy Nilly (novel), 1990; Daisy and Lily, 1993; Does This Make Sense To You?, 1995; The Snowball Waltz (novel), 1997; Let's Write Plays(textbook for schools), 1998; Yin and Tonic (humour), 1998; The Skeleton Woman, 2002. Other: Television plays and short stories. Honours: Queen Elizabeth II Arts Council Grant and Award; Project Grant, 1991; Queen Elizabeth II Arts Council Scholarship in Letters, 1993; Others. Literary Agent: (Plays) Playmarket, PO Box 9767, Wellington, New Zealand. Address: PO Box 31033, Lower Hutt, New Zealand.

RENFREW (Andrew) Colin (Baron Renfrew of Kaimsthorn), b. 25 July 1937, Stockton-on-Tees, England. Educator; Archaeologist; Author. m. Jane M Ewbank, 1965, 2 sons, 1 daughter. Education: St John's College, Cambridge; BA Honours, 1962, MA, 1964, PhD, 1965, ScD, 1976, Cambridge University; British School of Archaeology, Athens. Appointments: Lecturer, 1965-70, Senior Lecturer in Prehistory and Archaeology, 1970-72, Reader, 1972, University of Sheffield; Head of Department, Professor of Archaeology, University of Southampton, 1972-81; Head of Department, Disney Professor of Archaeology, University of Cambridge, 1981-; Master, Jesus College, Cambridge, 1986-97; Director, McDonald Institute for Archaeological Research, 1990-; Guest Lecturer, universities, colleges; Narrator, television films, radio programmes, British Broadcasting Corporation. Publications include: The Emergence of Civilisation: The Cyclades and the Aegean in the Third Millennium B.C., 1972; Before Civilisation: The Radiocarbon Revolution and Prehistoric Europe, 1973; Problems in European Prehistory, 1979; Approaches to Social Archaeology, 1984; The Archaeology of Cult: The Sanctuary at Phylakopi, 1985; Archaeology and Language: The Puzzle of

Indo-European Origins, 1988; The Idea of Prehistory, co-author, 1988; Archaeology: Theories, Methods, and Practice, co-author, 1991, 2nd edition, 1996; The Cycladic Spirit: Masterpieces from the Nicholas P Goulandris Collection, 1991; The Ancient Mind: Elements of Cognitive Archaeology, co-editor, 1994; Loot, Legitimacy and Ownership, 2000; Archaeogenetics (editor), 2000; Contributor to: Journals including Archaeology; Scientific American. Honours: Rivers Memorial Medal, Royal Anthropological Institute, 1979; Fellow, St John's College, Cambridge, 1981-86; Sir Joseph Larmor Award, 1981; DLitt, Sheffield University, 1987; Huxley Memorial Medal and Life Peerage, 1991; Honorary Degree, University of Athens, 1991; DLitt, University of Southampton, 1995; Foreign Associate, National Academy of Sciences, USA, 1997; Fyssen Prize, 1997. Memberships include: Fellow, British Academy; Ancient Monuments Board for England, 1974-84; Royal Commission on Historical Monuments, 1977-87; Historic Buildings and Monuments Commission for England, 1984-86; Ancient Monuments Advisory Committee, 1984-; British National Commission for UNESCO, 1984-86; Trustee, British Museum, 1991-. Address: McDonald Institute for Archaeological Research, Downing Street, Cambridge, CB2 3ER, England.

RENO Janet, b. 21 July 1938, Miami, Florida, USA. Lawyer. Education: BA, Cornell University; LLB, Harvard University. Appointments: Florida Bar, 1963; Associate, Brigham & Brigham, 1963-67; Partner, Lewis & Reno, 1971-72; Administrative Assistant State Attorney, 11th Judicial Circuit Florida, Miami, 1973-76, State Attorney, 1978-93; Partner, Steel, Hector & Davis, Miami, 1976-78; US Attorney-General, 1993-2001. Memberships: American Bar Association; American Law Institute; American Judicature Society. Honours: Women First Award, YWCA, 1993; National Women's Hall of Fame, 2000. Address: Department of Justice, 10th Street and Constitution Avenue, NW Washington, DC 20530, USA.

RENO Jean, b. 30 July 1948, Casablanca, Morocco. Actor. m. (1) divorced, 1 son, 1 daughter, (2) Nathalie Dyszkiewicz, 1996, 1 son, 1 daughter. Career: Films: Clair de Femme, 1979; Le Dernier Combat, 1983; Signes Extérieurs de Richesse, 1983; Notre Histoire, 1984; Subway, 1985; I Love You, 1986; The Big Blue, 1988; L'Homme au Masque d'Or, 1990; La Femme Nikita, 1991; L'Operation Corned Beef, 1991; Loulou Graffitti, 1991; The Visitors (also wrote screenplay), 1993; Leon, 1994; French Kiss, 1995; Roseanna's Grave, 1997; Les Couloirs du Temps, 1998; Godzilla, 1998; Les Rivieres pourpres, 2000; Just Visiting, 2001; Wasabi, 2001; Decalage horaire, 2002; Rollerball, 2002; Tais-toi, 2003; Les Rivieres pourpres – Les anges de l'apocalypse, 2004; Onimusha 3, 2004. Address: Chez Les Films du Dauphin, 25 rue Yves-Toudic, 75010 Paris, France.

REPLANSKY Naomi, b. 23 May 1918, Bronx, New York, USA. Poet. Education: BA, University of California, Los Angeles, 1956. Appointment: Poet-in-Residence, Pitzer College, Claremont, California, 1981. Publications: Ring Song, 1952; Twenty-One Poems, Old and New, 1988; The Dangerous World, New and Selected Poems, 1994. Contributions to: Ploughshares; Missouri Review; Nation; Feminist Studies. Honour: Nominated for National Book Award, 1952. Memberships: PEN American Center; Poetry Society of America. Address: 711 Amsterdam Avenue, No 8E, New York, NY 10025, USA.

REPPERT James E, b. 24 September 1958, Paxton, Illinois, USA. Mass Communication Educator. Education: Certificate, 1st Class Licence, FCC, Brown College, 1977; B University Studies, ND State University, 1981; MA, University of Nevada, Las Vegas, 1985. Appointments: Teaching Assistant, Associate Director,

Forensics, University of Nevada, Las Vegas, 1983-85; Visiting Instructor, Purdue University Calumet, Hammond, Indiana, 1985-86; Instructor, Southeastern Louisiana University, Hammond, Louisiana, 1986-87; Instructor, Southern Arkansas University, Magnolia, 1987-93; Director, Broadcast Journalism, 1987-; Executive Producer, Radio and Television Programmes, 1987-; Assistant Professor, 1993-2001; Associate Professor, 2001-; Audio Webcasts, 1999-; Faculty Senator, 2000-03. Publications: Contributing Author, Video Rating Guide for Libraries; C-Span Campaign '96; A Resource Guide for Professors; The Encyclopedia of Television News. Honours: Academy of Television Arts and Sciences Faculty Seminar; International Emmy Nominee Festival Faculty Fellow; C-Span in the Classroom Faculty Seminars; International Radio-TV Society Foundation Faculty/ Industry Seminars; Radio and Television News Directors Foundation Faculty Fellow; National Association of Television Programme Executives Faculty Fellow; Landmark Award; Scholar of the Year; Teacher of the Year; Stephen H Coltrin Award for Excellence in Communications Education, International Radio-TV Society Foundation. Memberships: National Association of Television Program Executives; Southern States Communication Association; Ark State Communications Association; Kentucky Communication Association; Arkansas Broadcast Education Association; International Radio-TV Society Foundation. Address: Department of Theatre and Mass Communication, Southern Arkansas University, PO Box 9229, Magnolia, Arkansas 71754-9229, USA.

RETNEV Vladimir Mikhailovich, b. 4 May 1926, Yaroslavl, Russia. Professor, Occupational Medicine. m. Retneva Elena Nickolaevna, 1 son, 1 daughter. Education: Doctor of Medicine, 1965. Appointments: Doctor, Occupational Medicine, 1950-51; Postgraduate Course, 1951-54; Assistant, 1954-59, Lecturer, 1963-68, Professor, 1968-74, Head, 1974-94, Professor, 1994-, Occupational Health Department, Saint Petersburg Medical Academy of Postgraduate Education; Deputy Director of Research, Scientific Research Institute of Industrial Hygiene and Occupational Diseases, 1959-63; St Petersburg Medical Academy of Postgraduate Studies, 1965-76. Publications: About 600 articles, including 18 monographs and guidelines. Honours: Professor; Honoured Scientist; Numerous orders and medals of Russia. Memberships: Academician, International Academy of Sciences in Ecology and Safe Lifestyle; Academician, Russian Academy of Natural Sciences. Address: 195027, PO Box N10, Saint Petersburg, Russia.

REUL George John, b. 19 April 1937, Milwaukee, Wisconsin, USA. Cardiovascular Surgeon. m. Susan K Reul, 6 sons. Education: BS, Marquette University, Milwaukee, Wisconsin, 1958; MD, 1962, MS, 1966, Marquette School of Medicine, Milwaukee, Wisconsin. Appointments: Military service: US Army Captain, 1966-68; 93rd and 24th Evacuation Hospitals, Vietnam, 1966-67; Wound Ballistics Research, Edgewood Arsenal, 1967-68; Hospital appointments: Deputy Chief of Surgery, Ben Taub Hospital 1971-73; Consultant in Cardiovascular Surgery, 1973-, Director, Peripheral Vascular Laboratory, 1981-, St Luke's Episcopal Hospital; Consultant in Cardiovascular Surgery, Texas Children's Hospital, 1973-; Associate Chief of Surgery, Texas Heart Institute, 1983-; Academic appointments: Clinical Instructor, Marquette School of Medicine, Department of Surgery, 1963-69; Instructor, 1971-72, Assistant Professor, 1972-73, Clinical Professor, 1994-, Baylor College of Medicine, Department of Surgery; Clinical Associate Professor, 1977-87, Clinical Professor, 1987-, The University of Texas Medical School at Houston, Department of Surgery, Division of Thoracic and Cardiac Surgery. Publications: More than 190 articles in scientific journals and book chapters as author and co-author which include most recently:

Hypercoaguable state leading to paraplegia in a middle-aged man, 2002; Perioperative Care of the Adult with Congenital Heart Disease in a Free-Standing Teriary Pediatric Facility, 2002; Coronary obstruction by a calcific pericardial ring, 2002. Honours: Fellow, National Institute of Health, 1960; Fellow, Allen Bradley Research Laboratory, 1965-66; Fellow, American Cancer Society, 1966; Fellow, National Tobacco Institute, 1969; Honorary Consulting Professor of Thoracic Surgery, Shanghai Second Medical College, Shanghai, China, 1985; Alumnus of the Year, Medical College of Wisconsin, 2002. Memberships include: American Medical Association; Texas Medical Association; Fellow, American Heart Association; American College of Chest Physicians; American Association for Vascular Surgery; American College of Surgeons; American Association for Thoracic Surgery; Past President, Denton A Cooley Cardiovascular Surgical Society. Address: 1101 Bates Street P514, Houston TX 77030, USA. E-mail: greul@heart.thi.tmc.edu

REYNOLDS Albert, b. 3 November 1935, Rooskey, County Roscommon, Ireland. Politician; Company Director. m. Kathleen Coén, 2 sons, 5 daughters. Education: Notre Dame University; Stoney Hill College, Boston; National University of Ireland; University of Philadelphia, Jesuits; University of Melbourne; University of Aberdeen. Appointments include: Company Director, own family business: C&D Foods, Edgeworthstown, Co Longford, Ireland; Director, many Irish and international companies; Political Career: Entered national politics, 1977, Elected to Dáil; Minister for Posts and Telegraphs and Transport, 1979-81; Minister for Industry and Energy, 1982; Minister for Industry and Commerce, 1987-88; Minister for Finance and Public Service, 1988-89; Minister of Finance, 1989-91; Vice-President, 1983-92, President, 1992-94, Fianna Fáil Party; Elected Taoiseach (PM), 1992-94; Chair, Bula Resources, 1999-2002; Longford Recreational Devt Centre. Memberships: Board of Governors: European Investment Bank; World Bank International Monetary Fund. Honour: Hon LLD (University College, Dublin), 1995. Address: Leinster House, Dáil Éirann, Kildare Street, Dublin 2, Ireland.

REYNOLDS Elbert Brunner, b. 17 September 1924, Bryan, Texas, USA. Associate Professor. m. Louise K Reynolds, 1 son, 1 daughter. Education: BS, Mechanical Engineering, 1947; MS, Mechanical Engineering, 1948; PhD, Mechanical Engineering, 1957. Appointments: Instructor, Mechanical Engineering, 1948-52, Assistant Professor, 1952-53, Pennsylvania State University; Part-time Instructor, Mechanical Engineering, University of Wisconsin, 1954-55; Service Engineer, E I, Du Pont de Nemours and Company, 1957-61; Associate Professor of Mechanical Engineering, University of Virginia, 1961-64; Consultant, US Naval Weapons Laboratory, 1963-64; Associate Professor of Mechanical Engineering, 1967-69, Coordinator of Mechanical Engineering Technology, 1979-90, of Mechanical Engineering Technology, 1983-90, Texas Technical University. Publications include: The Influence of Method of Junction Formation and Heat Treatment on the Electromotive Force, 1957; Compressible Fluid Flow, 1963; Heat Transfer and Thermodynamics, 1964. Memberships: American Society of Mechanical Engineers; Society of Automotive Engineers; American Society of Engineering Education; Sigma Xi; Phi Kappa Phi; Pi Tau Sigma. Address: 5437 8th Street, Lubbock, TX 79416, USA.

REYNOLDS Graham b. 10 January 1914, Highgate, London, England. Writer; Art Historian. Education: BA, Honours, Queens' College, Cambridge. Publications: Nicholas Hilliard and Isaac Oliver, 1947, 2nd edition, 1971; English Portrait Miniatures, 1952, revised edition, 1988; Painters of the Victorian Scene, 1953; Catalogue of the Constable Collection, Victoria and Albert Museum, 1960, revised edition, 1973; Constable, The Natural

Painter, 1965; Victorian Painting, 1966, revised edition, 1987; Turner, 1969; Concise History of Watercolour Painting, 1972; Catalogue of Portrait Miniatures, Wallace Collection, 1980; The Later Paintings and Drawings of John Constable, 2 volumes, 1984; English Watercolours, 1988; The Earlier Paintings of John Constable, 2 volumes, 1996; Catalogue of European Portrait Minatures, Metropolitan Museum of Art, New York, 1996; The Miniatures in the Collection of H.M. the Queen, The Sixteenth and Seventeenth Centuries, 1999. Contributions to: Times Literary Supplement; Burlington Magazine; Apollo; New Departures. Honours: Mitchell Prize, 1984; Officer of the Order of the British Empire, 1984; Commander of the Victorian Order, 2000; British Academy, fellow, 1993; Honorary Keeper of Minatures, Fitzwilliam Museum, Cambridge, 1994. Address: The Old Manse, Bradfield St George, Bury St Edmunds, Suffolk IP30 0AZ, England.

REYNOLDS Keith Ronald, (Kev Reynolds), b. 7 December 1943, Ingatestone, Essex, England. Author; Photojournalist; Lecturer. m. Linda Sylvia Dodsworth, 23 September 1967, 2 daughters. Publications: Walks and Climbs in the Pyrenees, 1978, 3rd edition, 1993; Mountains of the Pyrenees, 1982; The Weald Way and Vanguard Way, 1987; Walks in the Engadine, 1988; The Valais, 1988; Walking in Kent, 1988; Classic Walks in the Pyrenees, 1989; Classic Walks in Southern England, 1989; The Jura, 1989; South Downs Way, 1989; Eye on the Hurricane, 1989; The Mountains of Europe, 1990; Visitors Guide to Kent, 1990; The Cotswold Way, 1990; Alpine Pass Route, 1990; Classic Walks in the Alps, 1991; Chamonix to Zermatt, 1991; The Bernese Alps, 1992; Walking in Ticino, 1992; Central Switzerland, 1993; Annapurna, A Trekkers' Guide, 1993; Walking in Kent, Vol II, 1994; Everest, A Trekkers' Guide, 1995; Langtang: A Trekkers Guide, 1996; Tour of the Vanoise, 1996; Walking in the Alps, 1998; Kangchenjunga: A Trekkers' Guide, 1999; Walking in Sussex, 2000; 100 Hut Walks in the Alps, 2000; Manaslu: A Trekkers' Guide, 2000; Tour of Mont Blanc, 2002. Contributions to: The Great Outdoors; Climber and Hill Walker; Environment Now; Trail Walker; Country Walking; High. Membership: Outdoor Writers' Guild. Address: Little Court Cottage, Froghole, Crockham Hill, Edenbridge, Kent TN8 6TD, England.

REYNOLDS Vernon, b. 14 December 1935, Berlin, Germany. Professor Emeritus, Oxford University. m. Frances Glover, 5 November 1960, 1 son, 1 daughter. Education: BA, PhD, London University; MA, Oxford University. Publications: Budongo: A Forest and its Chimpanzees, 1965; The Apes, 1967; The Biology of Human Action, 1976, 2nd edition, 1980; The Biology of Religion (with R Tanner), 1983; Primate Behaviour: Information, Social Knowledge and the Evolution of Culture (with D Quiatt), 1993. Memberships: Fellow, Royal Anthropological Institute; Chairman, Biosocial Society; Primate Society of Great Britain; Society for the Study of Human Biology. Address: School of Anthropology, Oxford University, 51 Banbury Road, Oxford OX2 6PE, England.

RHODES Richard (Lee), b. 4 July 1937, Kansas City, Kansas, USA. Writer. m. Ginger Untrif, 1993, 2 children by previous marriage. Education: BA, cum laude, Yale University, 1959. Publications: Non-Fiction: The Inland Ground, 1970; The Ozarks, 1974; Looking for America, 1979; The Making of the Atomic Bomb, 1988; A Hole in the World, 1990; Making Love, 1992; Dark Sun, 1995; How to Write, 1995; Deadly Feasts, 1997; Trying to get some Dignity (with Ginger Rhodes), 1996; Visions of Technology, 1999; Why They Kill, 1999; Masters of Death, 2001; Fiction: The Ungodly, 1973; Holy Secrets, 1978; The Last Safari, 1980; Sons of Earth, 1981. Contributions to: Numerous journals and magazines. Honours: National Book Award in Non-Fiction, 1987; National Book Critics Circle Award in Non-Fiction, 1987;

Pulitzer Prize in Non-Fiction, 1988. Membership: Authors Guild. Address: c/o Janklow and Nesbit Associates, 455 Park Avenue, New York, NY10021, USA.

RHODES Zandra Lindsey, b. 19 September 1940. Fashion Designer. Education: Royal College of Art. Career: Designer (textile, 1964-); Print Factory/Studio with A McIntyre, 1965; Fashion Industry, 1966-; Produced dresses from own prints in partnership with S Ayton, shop on Fulham Rd, 1967-68; US solo collection, 1969; annual fantasy shows in US, founded Zandra Rhodes (UK) Ltd; with A Knight & R Stirling, 1975-86; now world-wide, currently works in: interior furnishings, fine art with various collections in US and England, Speaker. Honours include: English Designer of the Year, 1972; Emmy for Best Costume (Romeo and Juliet, US, 1984); Lifetime Achievement at the British Fashion Awards, 1995. Publication: The Art of Zandra Rhodes, 1984; The Zandra Rhodes Collection by Brother, 1988. Address: 79-85 Bermondsey Street, London, SE1 3XF, England.

RHOTEN Kenneth, b. 28 December 1950, Hammond, Indiana, USA. Author; Composer; Inventor; Artist. m. (1) Virginia Haynie, 1974, divorced 1977, (2) Robin Damron, December 1984, divorced 1985, (3) Josephine Meese, 1986, deceased, 2000. Appointments: Various, including Draftsman, Graphic Artist, Designer, Inventor; Patentholder; Winemaker. Publications include: Flying Saucer Man, album, 1977; A Brief Essay On The History Of Creativity; Your Tree; The Diamond; The Price of Paradise; Dark Twist Of Fate (novel), 1995; Dark Twist Of Fate and Other Works, 1999; Dark Twist of Fate, 3rd edition, 2003; A Voice From Beyond (short story). Songs include: Mornin' Daytime Dreamin'; All Night Long; Stretch Me A Road; Reflection In Your Eyes; Make A Dream Come True; Pages in a Book of Love; Fade Away; Let It Rain On Me. Honours: Winner, local Writer's Contest, 1984. Membership: American Society of Composers, Authors and Publishers, 1975-93. Address: Box 225, 9981 Firebaugh, Stoy, IL 62464, USA.

RIACHI Antoine Ayoub, b. 11 November 1933, Zahlé, Lebanon. Socio-economist. m. Sabah Adib Moawad, 3 children. Education: Oriental College, Zahlé, Lebanon; Collège des Apôtres, Jounieh, Lebanon; DEA, Ecole Practique des Hautes Etudes, Paris, France; PhD, Social Economics, University of Paris, France. Appointments: Analyst, Statistician, Ministry of Social Affairs, Lebanon; Journalist, Arabic Programmes at ORTF, Paris; Researcher, Expert for Middle East and African Affairs, Arnold Bergstrasse Institute, Freiburg, Germany; Expert, Committee Delegate to Congo, Africa; Director, Economics Research Group, Lebanon; Lecturer, Lebanese Civic Council; Director, ECOGROUP FRANCE, Paris; Editor-in-Chief, Eco Press Review and various socio-economic studies; Chairman, Société d'études, recherches et dévloppement industriels. Publications: Author: Disparity of Social Classes in Lebanon; Social Structure of Confessions in Lebanon; The New Trend of Socialism in the World; Security in the Gulf; A Conflict of Antagonism: nationalism and globalisation; Metaphysics of Social Ages. Address: ECOGROUP, 23 rue Washington, Paris 75008, France. E-mail: ecof@animail.net

RIBAROVA Fany, b. 17 March 1943, Vaksevo, Bulgaria. Biochemist. m. S Ribarov, 1 son. Education: Graduated, Biochemistry, 1967; Magister, 1968; PhD, 1977; Associate Professor, 1990; Key Qualifications: Food Composition Analysis; Food Quality and Safety; Total Diet Study – Risk Assessment and Risk Management; Nutritional Biochemistry. Appointments: Head of Department, Food Chemistry, National Centre of Hygiene, Medical Ecology and Nutrition, 1998-2001; Lecturer and Educator, Post-Graduate Courses on Food Chemistry and Nutritional Biochemistry; Coordinator, CEECFOODS, 2004, 2005. Publications: Over 90 publications in scientific journals; 2 monographs; Author, first Bulgarian table of amino acids content in foodstuffs. Honour: Medal of Balkan Medical Union. Memberships: Bulgarian Academy of Nutritional Sciences; Balkan Medical Union; European Academy of Nutritional Sciences; International Medical Association for the Study of Living Conditions; The National Civic Forum, BULGARKA; Member, editorial boards of: Archives of the Balkan Medical Union; Actual Lipidology; Bulgarian Journal of Osteoporosis. Address: National Centre of Hygiene, Medical Ecology and Nutrition, D Nesterov str 15, Sofia 1431, Bulgaria. E-mail: f.ribarova@nchmen.government.bg

RICCI Cristina, b. 12 February 1980, Santa Monica, California, USA. Film Actress. Career: Actor in commercials then in films: Mermaids, 1990; The Hard Way, 1991; The Addams Family, 1991; The Cemetery Club, 1993; Addams Family Values, 1993; Casper, 1995; Now and Then, 1995; Gold Diggers: The Secret of Bear Mountain, 1995; That Darn Cat, 1996; Last of the High Kings, 1996; Bastard Out of Carolina, 1996; Ice Storm, 1997; Little Red Riding Hood, 1997; Fear and Loathing in Las Vegas, 1998; Desert Blue, 1998; Buffalo 66, 1998; The Opposite Sex, 1998; Small Soldiers, 1998; Pecker, 1999; 200 Cigarettes, 1999; Sleepy Hollow, 1999; The Man Who Cried, 2000: Monster,2003: Address: c/o ICM, 8942 Wilshire Boulevard, Beverly Hills, CA 90211, USA.

RICE Stuart Glen, b. 15 February 1960, Seattle, Washington, USA. Physician; Neurosurgeon. M. Pam A Rice. Education: Bachelor of Science, Biology, 1983; Doctor of Medicine, 1987. Appointments: Staff Neurosurgeon, Altru Health System, Grand Forks, North Dakota, USA, 1993-2000; Neurosurgical Associates, Rapid City, South Dakota, 2000-. Publication: Fragile X (novel), 2000. Honours: International Peace Prize, United Cultural Convention, 2003; Man of the Year, American Biographical Institute; Listed in Who's Who publications and biographical dictionaries. Memberships: American Medical Association; American Association of Neurological Surgeons; Congress of Neurological Surgeons; Fellow, American College of Surgeons. Address: 4141 5th Street, Rapid City, SD 57701, USA. E-mail: neurotron1@aol.com Website: www.stuartrice.com

RICE Tim (Sir) (Miles Bindon), b. 10 November 1944, Amersham, Buckinghamshire, England. Songwriter; Broadcaster. m. Jane Artereta McIntosh, 1974, deceased 1990, 1 son, 1 daughter. Education: Lancing College. Career: EMI Records, 1966-68; Norrie Paramor Organisation, 1968-69; Founder, Director, GRRR Books Ltd, 1978-, Pavilion Books Ltd, 1981-97. Appearances on TV and radio including Just A Minute, Radio 4; Creative Works: Lyrics for stage musicals (with Andrew Lloyd Webber): Joseph and the Amazing Technicolor Dreamcoat, 1968; Jesus Christ Superstar, 1970; Evita, 1976; Cricket, 1986; Other musicals: Blondel, with Stephen Oliver, 1983; Chess, with Benny Andersson and Bjorn Ulvaeus, 1984; Tycoon, with Michel Berger, 1992; Selection of songs, Beauty and the Beast, with Alan Menken, 1994; Heathcliff, with John Farrar, 1996; King David, with Alan Menken 1997; Aida, with Elton John, 1998; Lyrics for musical films: Aladdin, with Alan Menken, 1992; The Lion King, with Elton John, 1994, theatre version, 1997; Aida, with Elton John, 1998; El Dorado, with Elton John, 1999; Lyrics for songs with other composers including Paul McCartney, Mike Batt, Freddie Mercury, Graham Gouldman, Marvin Hamlisch, Rick Wakeman, John Barry. Publications: Songbooks from musicals; Co-author of over 20 books in the series Guinness Book of British Hit Singles, Albums, etc; Fill Your Soul, 1994; Cricket Writer, National Newspapers and Cricket Magazines; Treasures of Lords, 1989; Oh, What a Circus, autobiography, 1995. Honours: Oscar, Golden Globe, Best New Song, A Whole New World, 1992, for Can You Feel The Love Tonight, with Elton John, 1994, and for You Must Love Me with Andrew Lloyd Webber, 1996; Gold and platinum records in

Dictionary of International Biography

numerous countries; 11 Ivor Novello Awards; 2 Tony Awards; 5 Grammy Awards; Kt, 1994. Memberships: Chairman, Stars Organisation for Spastics, 1983-85; Shaftesbury Avenue Centenary Committee, 1984-86; President, Lords Taverners, 1988-90; Dramatists' Saints and Sinners, Chairman, 1990; Cricket Writers; Foundation for Sport and the Arts, 1991-; Garrick Club; Groucho Club; Main Committee, 1992-94, 1995-, President, 2002-03, MCC. Address: c/o Lewis & Golden, 40 Queen Anne Street, London, W1M 0EL, England.

RICH Adrienne (Cecile), b. 16 May 1929, Baltimore, Maryland, USA. Professor of English and Feminist Studies; Poet; Writer. m. Alfred H Conrad, 1953, deceased 1970, 3 sons. Education: AB, Radcliffe College, 1951. Appointments: Visiting Poet, Swarthmore College, 1966-68; Adjunct Professor, Columbia University, 1967-69; Lecturer, 1968-70, Instructor, 1970-71, Assistant Professor, 1971-72, Professor, 1974-75, City College of New York; Fannie Hurst Visiting Professor, Brandeis University, 1972-73; Professor of English, Douglass College, New Brunswick, New Jersey, 1976-78; A D White Professor-at-Large, Cornell University, 1981-85; Clark Lecturer and Distinguished Visiting Professor, Scripps College, Claremont, California, 1983; Visiting Professor, San Jose State University, California, 1985-86; Burgess Lecturer, Pacific Oaks College, Pasadena, California, 1986; Professor of English and Feminist Studies, Stanford University, 1986-; Board of Chancellors, Academy of American Poets, 1999-; Clark Lecturer, Trinity College, Cambridge, 2002. Publications: Poetry: A Change of World, 1951; (Poems), 1952; The Diamond Cutters and Other Poems, 1955; Snapshots of a Daughter-in-Law: Poems 1954-1962, 1963; Necessities of Life: Poems 1962-1965, 1966; Selected Poems, 1967; Leaflets: Poems 1965-1968, 1969; The Will to Change: Poems 1968-1970, 1971; Diving into the Wreck: Poems 1971-1972, 1973; Poems Selected and New, 1975; Twenty-One Love Poems, 1976; The Dream of a Common Language: Poems 1974-1977, 1978; A Wild Patience Has Taken Me This Far: Poems 1978-1981, 1981; Sources, 1983; The Fact of a Doorframe: Poems Selected and New 1950-1984, 1984; Your Native Land, Your Life, 1986; Time's Power: Poems 1985-1988, 1989; An Atlas of the Difficult World: Poems 1988-1991, 1991; Collected Early Poems 1950-1970, 1993; Dark Fields of the Republic: Poems 1991-95, 1995; Midnight Salvage: Poems 1995-1998, 1999; Arts of the Possible: Essays and Conversations, 2001; Fox: Poems 1998-2000, 2001; The Fact of a Doorframe: Poems 1950-2000, 2002; Other: Of Woman Born: Motherhood as Experience and Institution, 1976; Women and Honor: Some Notes on Lying, 1977; On Lies, Secrets and Silence: Selected Prose 1966-1978, 1979; Compulsory Heterosexuality and Lesbian Existence, 1980; Blood, Bread and Poetry: Selected Prose 1979-1985, 1986; What Is Found There: Notebooks on Poetry and Politics, 1993. Honours: Yale Series of Younger Poets Award, 1951; Guggenheim Fellowships, 1952, 1961; American Academy of Arts and Letters Award, 1961; Bess Hokin Prize, 1963; Eunice Tietjens Memorial Prize, 1968; National Endowment for the Arts Grant, 1970; Shelley Memorial Award, 1971; Ingram Merrill Foundation Grant, 1973; National Book Award, 1974; Fund for Human Dignity Award, 1981; Ruth Lilly Prize, 1986; Brandeis University Creative Arts Award, 1987; Elmer Holmes Bobst Award, 1989; Commonwealth Award in Literature, 1991; Frost Silver Medal, Poetry Society of America, 1992; Los Angeles Times Book Award, 1992; Lenore Marshall/Nation Award, 1992; William Whitehead Award, 1992; Lambda Book Award, 1992; Harriet Monroe Prize, 1994; John D and Catharine T MacArthur Foundation Fellowship, 1994; Academy of American Poets Dorothea Tanning Award, 1996; Lannan Foundation Lifetime Achievement Award, 1999; Bollingen Prize for Poetry, 2003; Honorary doctorates. Address: c/o W W Norton & Co, 500 Fifth Avenue, New York, NY 10110, USA.

RICH Frank Hart, b. 2 June 1949, Washington, District of Columbia, USA. Journalist. m. (1) Gail Winston, 1976, 2 sons, (2) Alexandra Rachelle Witchel, 1991. Education: BA, Harvard University, 1971. Appointments: Co-Editor, Richmond Mercury, Virginia, 1972-73; Senior Editor and Film Critic, New York Times Magazine, 1973-75; Film Critic, New York Post, 1975-77; Film and Television Critic, Time Magazine, 1977-80; Chief Drama Critic, 1980-93, Op-Ed Columnist, 1994-, New York Times; Columnist, New York Times Sunday Magazine, 1993. Publications: The Theatre Art of Boris Aronson (with others), 1987; Hot Seat: Theater Criticism for the New York Times 1980-93, 1998; Ghost Light, 2000. Contributions to: Newspapers and periodicals. Address: c/o The New York Times, 229 West 43rd Street, New York, NY 10036, USA.

RICHARD Cliff (Harry Webb) (Sir), b. 14 October 1940, Lucknow, India. Singer. Appointments: Leader, Cliff Richard and The Shadows; Solo Artist; International Concert Tours, 1958-; Own TV Show; Numerous TV and radio appearances. Creative Works: Films: The Young Ones; Expresso Bongo; Summer Holiday; Wonderful Life; Musicals: Time, 1986-87; Heathcliff, 1996-97; Albums include: 21 Today, 1961; The Young Ones, 1961; Summer Holiday, 1963; 40 Golden Greats, 1977; Love Songs, 1981; Private Collection, 1988; The Album, 1993; Real as I Wanna Be; Over 120 singles. Publications: Questions, 1970; The Way I See It, 1972; The Way I See It Now, 1975; Which One's Cliff, 1977; Happy Christmas from Cliff, 1980; You, Me and Jesus, 1983; Mine to Share, 1984; Jesus, Me and You, 1985; Single-Minded, 1988; Mine Forever, 1989; My Story: A Celebration of 40 Years in Showbusiness, 1998. Honours: OBE, 1980; Knighted, 1995; Numerous music awards. Membership: Equity. Address: c/o PO Box 46C, Esher, Surrey KT10 0RB, England.

RICHARD-BRUCE Stella Omobolanle, b. 19 September 1967, Ekiti State, Nigeria. Public Relations. m. Nifemi Richard-Bruce, 2 sons. Education: Bachelors Degree, Education, 1988; Postgraduate Diploma, Public Relations, 1994. Appointments: Public Relations Manager, Toyota Nigeria Ltd, 2000-02; Vice Chair, Nigerian Institute of Public Relations, Lagos State Chapter, 2002-. Publications: Regular columnist, Brandfaces and Agoo, Nigeria and Ghana. Honours: Senior Prefect Girl, Ekiti Baptist High School, 1984. Memberships: Nigerian Institute of Public Relations; Nigerian Institute of Management; Nigerian Institute of Marketing. Address: Aeriel-Link Communications, 127 Ikorodu Road, Fade-11, Lagos, Nigeria. E-mail: tak46@yahoo.com

RICHARDS Denby, b. 7 November 1924, London, England. Music Critic; Author; Lecturer. m. Rhondda Gillespie, 29 May 1973. Education: Regent Street Polytechnic, London; Education: Self-taught Piano and 50 years attending concerts and studying scores. Career: Early writing on Kensington News, then Music Critic to Hampstead and Highgate Express for 30 years; Contributor to Music and Musicians from first issue, 1952; Editor, 1981-84; Opera Editor, 1984-; Editor, Musical Opinion, 1987-; Many radio and TV appearances in UK, USA, Scandinavia, Australia; Lecturer including Seminar Course on History and Function of Western Musical Criticism at Yale University, USA; Programme Notes and Record Sleeves. Publication: The Music of Finland, 1966. Contributions to: Music and Musicians; Records and Recording; Musical Opinion; New Film Review; Parade; Other journals in UK and internationally. Memberships: The Critics' Circle; Royal Overseas League; Zoological Society of London. Address: 2 Princes Road, St Leonards-on-Sea, East Sussex TN37 6EL, England.

RICHARDS Hubert John, b. 25 December 1921, Weilderstadt, Germany. Lecturer; Writer. m. 22 December 1975, 1 son, 1 daughter. Education: STL (Licence in Theology), Gregorian

University, Rome; LSS (Licence in Scripture), Biblical Institute, Rome. Publications: The First Christmas: What Really Happened?, 1973; The Miracles of Jesus: What Really Happened?, 1975; The First Easter: What Really Happened?, 1977; Death and After: What Will Really Happen?, 1979; What Happens When You Pray?, 1980; Pilgrim to the Holy Land, 1985; Focus on the Bible, 1990; The Gospel According to St Paul, 1990; God's Diary, 1991; Pilgrim to Rome, 1994; Quips and Quotes, 1997; Anthology for the Church Year, 1998; Philosophy of Religion, 1998, 2nd edition, 2000; The Bible: What Does It Really Say?, 1999; Who's Who and What's What in the Bible, 1999; More Quips and Quotes, 2000; Jesus, Who Did He Think He Was?, 2000; Plain English Bible: 160 Readings, 2001; 1600 Quips and Quotes, 2003. Contributions to: Regular articles and reviews in various publications. Membership: Norfolk Theological Society. Address: 59 Park Lane, Norwich, Norfolk NR2 3EF, England.

RICHARDS Isaac Vivian Alexander (Sir) (Viv), b. 7 March 1952, St John's, Antigua. Cricketer. m. Miriam Lewis, 1 son, 1 daughter. Career: Right-hand batsman, off-break bowler; Played for Leeward Islands, 1971-91 (Captain 1981-91), Somerset, 1974-86, Queensland, 1976-77, Glamorgan, 1990-93; 121 tests for West Indies, 1974-91, 50 as Captain, scoring 8,540 runs (average 50.2) including 24 hundreds and holding 122 catches; Scored 36, 212 first-class runs (114 hundreds, only West Indian to score 100 hundreds); Toured England, 1976, 1979 (World Cup), 1980, 1983 (World Cup), 1984, 1988 (as Captain), 1991 (as Captain); 187 limited-overs internationals scoring 6, 721 runs (11 hundreds including then record 189 not out v England at Old Trafford, 1984; Chair, Selectors, West Indies Cricket Board, 2002-. Publication: Co-author, Viv Richards (autobiography); Hitting Across the Line (autobiography), 1991; Sir Vivian, 2000. Honour: Wisden Cricketer of the Year, 1977; One of Wisden's Five Cricketers of the Century, 2000; Cricket Hall of Fame, 2001; Dr hc (Exeter), 1986. Address: West Indies Cricket Board, PO Box 616, St John's, Antigua.

RICHARDS Keith, (Keith Richard), b. 18 December 1943, Dartford, Kent, England. Musician; Vocalist; Songwriter. m. (1) Anita Pallenberg, 1 son, 1 daughter, (2) Patti Hansen, 1983, 2 daughters. Education: Sidcup Art School. Career: Member, The Rolling Stones, 1962-; Co-Writer (with Mick Jagger) numerous songs and albums, 1964-. Creative Works: Albums: The Rolling Stones, 1964; The Rolling Stones No 2, 1965; Out of Our Heads, 1965; Aftermath, 1966; Between the Buttons, 1967; Their Satanic Majesties Request, 1967; Beggar's Banquet, 1968; Let it Bleed, 1969; Get Yer Ya-Ya's Out, 1969; Sticky Fingers, 1971; Exile on Main Street, 1972; Goat's Head Soup, 1973; It's Only Rock'n'Roll, 1974; Black and Blue, 1976; Some Girls, 1978; Emotional Rescue, 1980; Still Life, 1982; Steel Wheels, 1989; Flashpoint, 1991; Voodoo Lounge, 1994; Stripped, 1995; Bridges to Babylon, 1997; No Security, 1999. Singles: It's All Over Now; Little Red Rooster; (I Can't Get No) Satisfaction; Jumping Jack Flash; Honky Tonk Women; Harlem Shuffle; Start Me Up; Paint It Black; Angie; Going to a Go-Go; It's Only Rock'n'Roll; Let's Spend the Night Together; Brown Sugar; Miss You; Emotional Rescue; She's So Cold; Undercover of the Night. Films: Sympathy for the Devil, 1970; Gimme Shelter, 1970; Ladies and Gentlemen, the Rolling Stones, 1974; Let's Spend the Night Together, 1983; Hail Hail Rock'n'Roll, 1987; Flashpoint, 1991. Honours: Grammy, Lifetime Achievement Award, 1986; Rock'n'Roll Hall of Fame, 1989; Q Award, Best Live Act, 1990; Ivor Novello Award, Outstanding Contribution to British Music, 1991; Songwriters Hall of Fame, 1993. Address: c/o Jane Rose, Raindrop Services, 1776 Broadway, Suite 507, New York, NY 10019, USA.

RICHARDS Rex Edward (Sir), b. 28 October 1922, Colyton, Devon, England. Academic. m. Eva Vago, 2 daughters. Education: BA (Oxon), 1945; FRS, 1959, DSc (Oxon), 1970; FRIC, 1970;

FRSC, FBA (Hon), 1990; Hon FRCP, 1987; Hon FRAM 1991. Appointments: Fellow of Lincoln College, Oxford, 1947-1964; Dr Lee's Professor of Chemistry, Oxford, 1964-70; Warden of Merton College, Oxford, 1969-84; Vice-Chancellor, Oxford University, 1977-81; Chairman, Oxford Enzyme Group, 1969-1983; Chancellor, University of Exeter, 1982-98; Commissioner, Royal Commission for Exhibition of 1851, 1984-1997; Director, The Leverhulme Trust, 1984-94; Chairman, British Postgraduate Medical Federation, 1986-93; President, Royal Society of Chemistry, 1990-92; Retired, 1994. Publications: Numerous in scientific journals. Honours: Corday-Morgan, Chemical Society, 1954; Fellow of the Royal Society, 1959; Tilden Lecturer, Chemical Society, 1962; Davy Medal, The Royal Society, 1976; Theoretical Chemistry and Spectroscopy, Chemical Society, 1977; Knight Bachelor, 1977; EPIC, 1982; Medal of Honour, University of Bonn, 1983; Royal Medal, The Royal Society, 1986; President's Medal, Society of Chemical Industry, 1991; Associé étranger, Académie des Sciences, Institut de France, 1995; Honorary degrees: East Anglia, 1971; Exeter, 1975; Dundee, 1977; Leicester, 1978; Salford, 1979; Edinburgh, 1981; Leeds, 1984; Kent, 1987; Cambridge, 1987; Thames Polytechnic (University of Greenwich) Centenary Fellow, 1990; Birmingham, 1993; London, 1994; Oxford Brookes, 1998; Warwick, 1999. Memberships: Trustee: National Heritage Memorial Fund, 1980-84, Tate Gallery, 1982-88, 1991-93, National Gallery, 1982-88, 1989-93; National Gallery Trust, 1996-, Chairman, 1996-99; National Gallery Trust Foundation, 1997-, (Chairman, 1997-1999); Henry Moore Foundation 1989-, (Chairman, 1994-2001). Address: 13 Woodstock Close, Oxford, OX2 8DB, England. E-mail: rex.richards@merton.oxford.ac.uk

RICHARDSON Donald MacCuaig, b. 2 December 1923, Portland, Oregon, USA. Retired Intelligence Officer; Translator. m. Patricia Ann Johnson Richardson, 2 sons, 1 deceased, 1 daughter. Education: Oriental Languages, University of California at Berkeley, 1941-43; Army Intensive Japanese Language School, University of Michigan, 1943-44; Military Intelligence Officers' Candidate School, Fort Snelling Minnesota, 1944-45; BA, 1951, MA, 1953, Oriental Languages, University of California at Berkeley. Appointment: Central Intelligence Agency, 1954-74. Publications: Numerous translations from the Japanese include: Prose: Nise Murasaki Inaka Genji (The Rustic Genji, by a Bogus Murasaki) by Ryutei Tanehiko, translated with Teruo Tanonaka; Udonge Monogatari (Tale of the Three Thousand Year Flower) by Santo Kyoden; Verse: Senzai Waka Shu (The Anthology of a Thousand Years of Japanese Poetry), compiled by Fujiwara Shunzei; Shu'i Waka Shu (A Collection of Rescued Japanese Poetry); Other: A Literary Translator's Japanese-English Dictionary. Honours: University of California Graduate Scholarship, 1953-54; Chairman, Phi Theta Honor Society, Department of Oriental Languages, University of California, 1954; Fellow, American Council of Learned Societies, 1953-54. Address: Huntingtower, 273 North Drive, Winchester, VA 22603, USA.

RICHARDSON Ian William, b. 7 April 1934, Edinburgh, Scotland. Actor. m. Maroussia Frank, 2 sons. Education: Edinburgh, Royal Scottish Academy of Music and Drama; Glasgow University. Career: Stage appearances in major roles, especially in Shakespeare, including: Proteus, Two Gentlemen of Verona, 1970; Prospero, The Tempest, 1970; Tom Wrench (Trelawny), Sadlers Wells, 1971-72; Richard II/Bolingbroke, 1973; Berowne, Love's Labours Lost, 1973; Iachimo, Cymbeline, 1974; Shalimov, Summer Folk, 1974; Henry Higgins, My Fair Lady, Broadway, 1974; Ford, Merry Wives of Windsor, 1975; Richard III, 1975; Jack Tanner (Man and Superman), Shaw Festival Theatre, Niagara-on-the-Lake, Canada, The Government Inspector, Romeo and Juliet, Old Vic, 1979; Lolita, New York, 1981; The Miser,

Dictionary of International Biography

Chichester, 1995; The Magistrate, Chichester and London, 1997; The Seven Ages of Man, Guildford, 1999. Film appearances include: The Darwin Adventure, 1971; Man of La Mancha, 1972; Marat/Sade, Hound of the Baskervilles, 1982; The Sign of Four, 1982; Whoops Apocalypse, 1986; The Fourth Protocol, 1986; Asking For Trouble, 1986; Burning Secret, 1988; Rosencrantz and Guildenstern are Dead, 1990; The Year of the Comet, 1991; Words Upon a Window Pane, 1993; Baps, 1996; Dark City, 1996; From Hell, 2002; TV includes: The Gravy Train Goes East, 1991; House of Cards, 1991; An Ungentlemanly Act, 1992; To Play the King, 1993; Remember (USA), 1993; Catherine the Great, 1994; Savage Play, 1994; The Final Cut, 1995; The Canterville Ghost, 1997; The Magicians House, 1999; Murder Rooms, 2000; Gormenghast, 2000; Murder Rooms II, 2001. Publications: Preface to Cymbeline, 1976; Preface to the Merry Wives of Windsor, 1988. Honours: James Bridies Gold Medal, RSAMD; Tony nomination, New York; Drama Desk Award, New York, Royal TV Society Award, 1981-82, 1991; Broadcasting Press Guild Award, 1990; BAFTA Award, 1991. Address: c/o London Management, 2-4 Noel Street, London, W1V 3RB, England.

RICHARDSON Joanna, b. London, England. Biographer. Education: MA, St Anne's College, Oxford. Publications: Fanny Brawne, 1952; Théophile Gautier: His Life and Times, 1958; The Pre-Eminent Victorian: A Study of Tennyson, 1962; The Everlasting Spell: A Study of Keats and His Friends, 1963; Essays by Divers Hands (editor), 1963; Introduction to Victor Hugo: Choses Vues, 1964; Edward Lear, 1965; George IV: A Portrait, 1966; Creevey and Greville, 1967; Princess Mathilde, 1969; Verlaine, 1971; Enid Starkie, 1973; Verlaine (translator, poems), 1974; Baudelaire (translator, poems), 1975; Victor Hugo, 1976; Zola, 1978; Keats and His Circle: An Album of Portraits, 1980; Paris Under Siege, 1982; Colette, 1983; The Brownings, 1986; Judith Gautier, 1987; Portrait of a Bonaparte, 1987; Baudelaire, 1994. Honours: Chevalier de l'Ordre des Arts et des Lettres, 1987; Prix Goncourt de la biographie, 1989. Membership: Royal Society of Literature, fellow. Address: c/o Curtis Brown Ltd, Haymarket House, 28-29 Haymarket, London SW1Y 4SP, England.

RICHARDSON Joely, b. 1958, Lancashire, England. Actress. m. Tim Bevan, divorced, 1 daughter. Education: The Thacher School, Ojai, California; Royal Academy of Dramatic Art. Career: London stage debut in Steel Magnolias, 1989; TV appearances include: Body Contact, Behaving Badly, 1989; Heading Home, Lady Chatterly's Lover, 1993; The Tribe, Echo; Films: Wetherby, 1985; Drowning by Numbers, 1988; Shining Through, 1991; Rebecca's Daughters, 1992; Lochness, 1994; Sister, My Sister, 1995; 101 Dalmatians, 1995; Believe Me, 1995; Hollow Reed, 1996; Event Horizon, 1996; Wrestling with Alligators, Under Heaven, The Patriot, Maybe Baby, Return to Me, 2000; The Affair of the Necklace, 2001; Shoreditch, 2003: Address: c/o ICM, Oxford House, 76 Oxford Street, London, W1N 0AX, England.

RICHARDSON Miranda, b. 3 March 1958, Southport, England. Actress. Education: Old Vic Theatre School, Bristol. Career: Theatre appearances include: Moving, 1980-81; All My Sons; Who's Afraid of Virginia Woolf?; The Life of Einstein; A Lie of the Mind, 1987; The Changeling; Mountain Language, 1988;Etta Jenks; The Designated Mourner, 1996; Aunt Dan and Lemon, 1999; Film appearances: Dance With a Stranger, 1985; The Innocent; Empire of the Sun; The Mad Monkey; Eat the Rich; Twisted Obsession; The Bachelor, 1992; Enchanted April, 1992; The Crying Game, 1992; Damage, 1993; Tom and Viv, 1994; La Nuit et Le Moment, 1994; Kansas City; Swann, 1995; Evening Star, 1996; The Designated Mourner, 1996; Apostle, 1996; All for Love; Jacob Two Two and the Hooded Fang; The Big Brass Ring, 1998; Sleepy Hollow, 1998-99; Get Carter, 1999; Snow

White, 2001; The Hours, 2001; Spider, 2001; Rage on Placid Lake, 2001; The Actors, 2002; Falling Angels, 2002; TV appearances include: The Hard Word; Sorrel and Son; A Woman of Substance; After Pilkington; Underworld; Death of the Heart; Blackadder II and III; Die Kinder (mini series), 1990; Sweet as You Are; Fatherland; Saint X, 1995; Magic Animals; Dance to the Music of Time, 1997; The Scold's Bridle; Merlin, 1997; Alice, 1998; Ted and Ralph, 1998. Honours: Golden Globe Award for Best Comedy Actress, 1993; BAFTA Award for Best Supporting Actress, 1993; Golden Globe Award, 1995; Royal TV Society's Best Actress. Address: c/o ICM, 76 Oxford Street, London, W1N 0AX, England.

RICHARDSON Natasha Jane, b. 11 May 1963. Actress. (1) Robert Fox, 1990, divorced, 1994, (2) Liam Neeson, 1994, 2 sons. Education: Central School of Speech and Drama. Career: Theatre includes: A Midsummer Night's Dream; Hamlet; The Seagull, 1985; China, 1986; High Society, 1986; Anna Christie, 1990, 1992; Cabaret, 1998; Closer, 1999; The Lady from the Sea, 2003; Film appearances include: Every Picture Tells a Story, 1985; Gothic, 1987; A Month in the Country, 1987; Patty Hearst, 1988; Fat Man and a Little Boy, 1989; The Handmaid's Tale, 1990; The Comfort of Strangers, 1990; The Favour, The Watch and the Very Big Fish, 1992; Past Midnight, 1994; Widows Peak, 1994; Nell, 1994; The Parent Trap, 1998; Blow Dry, 2000; Waking up in Reno, 2000; Maid in Manhattan, 2003; TV includes: In a Secret State, 1985; Ghosts, 1986; Hostages, 1992; Suddenly Last Summer, 1993; Zelda, 1993; Tales From the Crypt, 1996; Haven, 2000. Honours: Most Promising Newcomer Award, 1986; Plays and Players Award, 1986, 1990; Best Actress, Evening Stand Film Awards, 1990; London Theatre Critics Award, 1990; Tony Award, 1998. Address: ICM Limited, Oxford House, 76 Oxford Street, London, W1N 0AX, England.

RICHTER Vladimir, b. 14 July 1925, Chrlice, near Brno, Czechoslovakia. Emeritus Professor. Education: Dr rer Nat, University of Brno, 1949; Theology, University of Innsbruck. Appointments: Docent, 1964, Professor, 1969, Ordinary Professor, Christliche Philosophie, 1974, Emeritus Professor, 1993, University of Innsbruck. Publications: Guillelmi de Ockham Opera Philosophica IV, 1985; Studien zum literarischen Werk von Johannes Duns Scotus, 1988; Unterwegs zum historischen Ockham, 1998; Johannes Duns Scotus Über die Erkennbarkeit Gottes, 2000; Studia Minora Fac. Philos. Universitatis Brunensis B50, Autobiography, 2003. Honour: American Biographical Institute, Man of the Year, 2004. Memberships: Société International pour l'Étude de la Philosophie Médiévale, Leuven. Address; Sillgasse 6, Postfach 569, A-6021 Innsbruck, Austria.

RICKMAN Alan, Actor. Education: Chelsea College of Art; Royal College of Art; Royal Academy of Dramatic Art (RADA). Career: 2 seasons with Royal Shakespeare Company, Stratford; Stage Appearances include: Bush Theatre, Hampstead and Royal Court Theatre; Les Liasons Dangereuses (RSC, Stratford, London and Broadway); The Lucky Chance, The Seagull, (Royal Court); Tango at the End of Winter (Edinburgh Festival and Piccadilly), 1991; Hamlet, 1992; Antony and Cleopatra (National Theatre), 1998; TV appearances include: Obadiah Slope, The Barchester Chronicles, 1982; Pity in History, 1984; Revolutionary Witness, Spirit of Man, 1989; Rasputin (USA), 1995; Private Lives, 2001-02; Films include: The January Man; Close My Eyes; Truly Madly Deeply; Die Hard; Robin Hood: Prince of Thieves; Bob Roberts, 1992; Mesmer, 1993; An Awfully Big Adventure, 1994; Sense and Sensibility, 1995; Michael Collins, 1996; Rasputin, 1996; Mesmer; Dark Harbour, 1997; The Judas Kiss, 1997; Dogma, 1998; Galaxy Quest, 1999; Blow Dry, 1999; Play, 2000; The Search for John Gissing, 2000; Harry Potter and the Philosopher's Stone, 2001; Harry Potter and the Chamber of Secrets, 2002; Love

Actually, 2003; Harry Potter and the Prisoner of Azkaban, 2004; Director, The Winter Guest, 1997. Honours: Time Out Award, 1991; Evening Standard Film Actor of the Year, 1991; BAFTA Award, 1991; Golden Globe Award, 1996; Emmy Award, 1996; Variety Club Award, 2002. Address: c/o ICM, Oxford House, 76 Oxford Street, London, W1N 0AX, England.

RICKS Christopher (Bruce), b. 18 September 1933, London, England. Professor of the Humanities; Writer; Editor. m. (1) Kirsten Jensen, 1956, divorced 1975, 2 sons, 2 daughters, (2) Judith Aronson, 1977, 1 son, 2 daughters. Education: BA, 1956, BLitt, 1958, MA, 1960, Balliol College, Oxford. Appointments: Lecturer, University of Oxford, 1958-68; Visiting Professor, Stanford University, 1965, University of California at Berkeley, 1965, Smith College, 1967, Harvard University, 1971, Wesleyan University, 1974, Brandeis University, 1977, 1981, 1984; Professor of English, University of Bristol, 1968-75, University of Cambridge, 1975-86; Professor of the Humanities, Boston University, 1986-; Co-Director, Editorial Institute, 1999-. Publications: Milton's Grand Style, 1963; Tennyson, 1972, revised edition, 1987; Keats and Embarrassment, 1974; The Force of Poetry, 1984; Eliot and Prejudice, 1988; Beckett's Dying Words, 1993; Essays in Appreciation, 1996. Editor: Poems and Critics: An Anthology of Poetry and Criticism from Shakespeare to Hardy, 1966; A E Housman: A Collection of Critical Essays, 1968; Alfred Tennyson: Poems, 1842, 1968; John Milton: Paradise Lost and Paradise Regained, 1968; The Poems of Tennyson, 1969, revised edition, 1987; The Brownings: Letters and Poetry, 1970; English Poetry and Prose, 1540-1674, 1970; English Drama to 1710, 1971; Selected Criticism of Matthew Arnold, 1972; The State of the Language (with Leonard Michaels), 1980, new edition, 1990; The New Oxford Book of Victorian Verse, 1987; Inventions of the March Hare: Poems 1909-1917 by T S Eliot, 1996; Oxford Book of English Verse, 1999; Reviewery, 2002; Selected Poems of James Henry (editor), 2002; Allusion to the Poets, 2002. Contributions to: Professional journals. Honour: Honorary DLitt, Oxford, 1998. Memberships: American Academy of Arts and Sciences, fellow; British Academy, fellow; Tennyson Society, vice-president. Address: 39 Martin Street, Cambridge, MA 02138, USA.

RICKS David Trulock, b. 28 June 1936, London, England. Retired British Council Officer. m. Nicole Estelle Aimée Chupeau, 2 sons. Education: BA, MA, Merton College, Oxford, 1958; PGCE, University of London, Institute of Education, 1960; Licence-es-Lettres, University of Lille, 1967; MA, University of Essex, 1971. Appointments: Teacher, Lecturer, London, 1960-67; British Council, Rabat, Morocco, 1967-70, Jaipur, India, 1971-74, Dar Es Salaam, Tanzania, 1974-76; Deputy Director, Iran, 1976-79; Director, Iran, Cultural Attache, British Embassy, Tehran, 1979-80, London, 1980-85; Director, Italy, Cultural Counsellor, British Embassy, Rome, 1985-90; Director, France, Cultural Counsellor, British Embassy, Paris, 1990-96. Publications: Joint Editor, Penguin French Reader, 1967, New Penguin French Reader, 1992. Honours: OBE, 1981; CMG, 1997. Address: Saint Jean, Bd Raoul Dufy, 04300 Forcalquier, France.

RIDPATH Ian (William), b. 1 May 1947, Ilford, Essex, England. Writer; Broadcaster. Publications: Over 30 books, including: Worlds Beyond, 1975; Encyclopedia of Astronomy and Space (editor), 1976; Messages From the Stars, 1978; Stars and Planets, 1978; Young Astronomer's Handbook, 1981; Hamlyn Encyclopedia of Space, 1981; Life Off Earth, 1983; Collins Guide to Stars and Planets, 1984; Gem Guide to the Night Sky, 1985; Secrets of the Sky, 1985; A Comet Called Halley, 1985; Longman Illustrated Dictionary of Astronomy and Astronautics, 1987; Monthly Sky Guide, 1987; Star Tales, 1989; Norton's Star Atlas (editor), 1989; Book of the Universe, 1991; Atlas of Stars and

Planets, 1992; Oxford Dictionary of Astronomy (editor), 1997; Eyewitness Handbook of Stars and Planets, 1998; Gem Stars, 1999; Time Space, 2002; Times Universe, 2004. Membership: Fellow, Royal Astronomical Society. Address: 48 Otho Court, Brentford Dock, Brentford, Middlesex TW8 8PY, England.

RIDRUEJO-ALONSO Pedro, b. 26 February 1931, Soria, Spain. Professor. Education: Bachelor of Psychology; Bachelor of Biological Sciences; Bachelor of Pharmacy; Doctor of Law; Doctor of Political and Economical Sciences; Doctor of Philosophy; Doctor of Medicine. Appointments: Dean, School of Philosophy, 1980-1981, Chairman Department of Psychiatry, 1995-2001. Publications: Medicine Psychology, 1996; Articles on subjects including: ecopsychiatry; geriatric psychiatry, additions, psychosomatic, promotion of mental health. Honours: 4 extraordinary mentions in Bachelor and Doctoral Degrees; Cross of Isabel la Catolica, Bronze Victor. Memberships: American Psychiatric Association; Spanish Society of Psychiatry; Société Francophone d'Éthique Medicale. Address: Vegafria 1, Madrid 28035, Spain. E-mail: pedro.ridruejo@uam.es

RIEDER Milan, b. 5 May 1940, Prague, Czech Republic. Mineralogist; Educator. 1 son, 1 daughter. Education: Graduate, Geology, Charles University, 1962; PhD, Johns Hopkins University, 1968. Appointments: Geologist, Geology Survey, Prague, Czech Republic, 1962-69; Researching Geologist, Professor, Mineralogy, Faculty of Science, Charles University, 1969-. Publications: About 90 papers in scientific periodicals, 1 book. Membership: Editorial Board, Physics and Chemistry of Minerals, 1997-. Address: Faculty of Science, Charles University, Albertov 6, Prague 2 128 43, Czech Republic.

RIEGER Gebhard, b. 10 March 1940, Vienna, Austria. Researcher; Medical Educator. m. Irmgard Strasser, 3 sons, 1 daughter. Education: Degree, Secondary School in Linz, 1959; Med Dr, Medical School University, Vienna, 1966; Assistant, I U Eye Clinic, Vienna, 1966-72; Eye Specialist, 1972. Appointments: Head, Department of Ophthalmology, Paracelsus Institute, Bad Hall, Austria, 1972; Lecturer, University Eye Clinic, Innsbruck, Austria, 1998. Publications: Over 70 papers on dry eye syndrome and balneological themes. Honours: Grantee, Dr Heinz and Helen Adam, Frankfurt, 1990. Memberships: Austrian Ophthalmology Society; Vienna Ophthalmology Society; German Ophthalmology Society; New York Academy of Sciences; Society of Free Radical Research; Austrian Society of Balneology and Medical Climatology; Association of Austria Cure Physicians; Paracelsus Society of Balneology and Iodine Research; Medical Society of Upper Austria; Van Swieten Society, Vienna. Address: Paracelsus Institute, Eye Department, Dr Karl Renner Strasse 6, A-4540 Bad Hall, Upper Austria.

RIES Martin, b. 26 December 1926, Washington DC, USA. Artist; Art Historian. m. Dianys Frobisher, 1 son, 3 daughters. Education: BFA, American University, 1950; MA, Art History, 1967, Postgraduate, Museum Administration, 1968, Hunter College. Appointments: Assistant Director, Hudson River Museum, New York, 1957-67; Professor of Art and Art History, Long Island University, 1968-95; Juror, Fulbright Scholarships, International Education, United Nations, 1998-2001; Exhibitions: Museum of Modern Art, New York, 1956; Paul Gallery, Tokyo, Japan, 1968; Atelier Terre D'Ocre, France, 1973; Institute of Contemporary Art, London, 1988. Publications: Picasso and Myth of Minotaur, 1973, excerpt reprinted in Picasso in Perspective, 1991; Articles on Carl Andre, Salvador Dali, Franz Kline; Braque's Ateliers and Symbolic Bird, 1995; L'estasi del Disagio (The Ecstasy of Discontent), 2002. Honours: Fellowship to Yaddo Art Colony, Saratoga Springs, New York, 1954; Series of grants form Long

Island University for independent artwork and scholarly research, 1988-94. Memberships: Association Internationale des Critiques d'Art; Artists Equity Association; Katonah Museum Art Association. Address: 36 Livingston Road, Scarsdale, NY 10583-6845. USA. Website: www.martinries.com

RIGBY Alfred, b.18 June 1934, Lytham, England. Architect and Planner. m. (1) Ann Patricia, deceased 1998, 1 son, 1 daughter, (2) Shirley Ann. Education: BA, Class I Honours, Architecture, BA, Class I, Town and Country Planning, MA, Manchester University, 1952-57; Diploma in Town Planning, London University; Rome Scholar, British Academy Rome, 1958-60; Management Course, sponsored by Government, Oxford University. Appointments: Lecturer, Manchester University, 1957-58; Department Architect, NWMRHB, 1960-63; City Architect, Westminster, 1963-73; Director of Architecture, London Borough of Camden, 1973-79; Chief Architect W H Smith, 1979-81; Consultant, YRM, 1982-86; Senior Partner, John R Harris Partnership, 1986-93; Senior Partner, Rigby Culpin, 1994-98; Chairman and Chief Executive, Metropolitan and Country Development Co, 2001-. Publication: Contributor and Assistant Editor, Sir Bannister Fletcher: A History of Architecture on the Comparative Method, 16th edition. Honours: Prix de Rome in Architecture (Prize open to any graduate of a recognised university in the British Commonwealth and Empire up to the age of 35), 1958; 10 Civic Trust Awards; 21 Commendations. Memberships: Fellow Royal Institution of British Architects; Fellow British Institute of Management; Fellow Royal Society of Arts; Chairman, Committee for the Fine Arts, British Academy Rome, 1985-90; Member, Athenaeum; Life Member, MCC and LCCC, Patron, Bath RFC. Address: 1 West Court, Burley-on-the-Hill, Oakham, Rutland LE15 7TE, England.

RIGG (Enid) Diana (Elizabeth) (Dame), b. 20 July 1938, Doncaster, England. Actress. m. (1) Manahem Gueffen, 1973, divorced 1976, (2) Archibald Hugh Stirling, 1982, divorced 1993, 1 daughter. Education: RADA. Career: Professional début as Natella Abashwilli, The Caucasian Chalk Circle, York Festival, 1957; Repertory Chesterfield and Scarborough 1958; Films include: A Midsummer Night's Dream, 1969; On Her Majesty's Secret Service, 1969; Julius Caesar, 1970; The Hospital, 1971; Theatre of Blood, 1973; A Little Night Music, 1977; The Great Muppet Caper, 1981; Evil Under the Sun, 1982; A Good Man in Africa, 1993; TV appearances include: Emma Peel in the Avengers, 1965-67; Women Beware Women, 1965; Married Alive, 1970; Diana (USA), 1973; In This House of Brede, 1975; Three Piece Suite, 1977; Clytemnestra in The Serpent Son, 1979; The Marquise, 1980; Hedda Gabler, 1981; Rita Allmers in Little Eyolf, 1982; Reagan in King Lear, 1983; Witness for the Prosecution, 1983; Bleak House, 1984; Host Held in Trust, A Hazard of Hearts, 1987; Worst Witch, 1987; Unexplained Laughter, 1989; Mother Love, 1989; Host Mystery! (USA), 1989; Zoya, 1995; Rebecca, 1996; Many leading roles with RSC and with theatres in UK and USA. Publications: No Turn Unstoned, 1982; So To The Land, 1994; Honours include: Plays and Players Award for Best Actress, 1975, 1978; Honorary doctorates, Stirling University, 1988; Leeds, 1991, South Bank, 1996; BAFTA Award, Best Actress, 1990; Evening Stand Award, 1993, 1996, 1996; Tony Award, Best Actress, 1994; Emmy, Best Supporting Actress, 1997; BAFTA, 2000. Memberships include: Vice-President, Baby Life Support Systems (BLISS), 1984-; Chancellor, University of Stirling, 1997-. Address: c/o Duncan Heath, ICM, Oxford House, 76 Oxford Street, London, W1N 0AX, England.

RIKE Susan, b. 29 August 1952, New York City, USA. Publicist. Education: BA, cum laude, Art History, Brooklyn College. Appointments: Co-Owner, Say Cheese, Brooklyn, 1977-82;

Accountant Secretary, Robert Marston & Associates, New York, 1983-84; Assistant Account Executive, Marketshare, New York, 1984; Account Executive, Doremus Public Relations, New York, 1984-86; President, Susan Rike Public Relations, Brooklyn, 1986-. Honour: Certification of Appreciation, Days of Taste, Childrens Program, New York City Technical College and American Institute of Wine and Food. Memberships: James Beard Foundation; Women Chefs and Restaurateurs; National Association of Female Executives. Address: 335 State Street, Suite 3C, Brooklyn, NY 11217, USA.

RING Johannes, b. 3 June 1945, Bad Woerishofen, Germany. University Professor. Education: MD, 1970; PhD, 1976; Dr Phil, 1979; Professor, 1983. Appointments: Institute of Surgical Research, LMU, Munich, Germany, 1971-76; Scripps Clinic Research Foundation, La Jolla, California, USA, 1977-78; Department of Dermatology, LMU, Munich, Germany, 1978-90; Director, Department of Dermatology, University Hospital, Hamburg, Germany, 1990-95; Director and Chairman, Department of Dermatology and Allergy, Biederstein Technical University, Munich, 1995-. Publications: New Trends in Allergy I – V, 1981-2002; Handbook of Atopic Eczema; Allergy in Practice. Memberships: Collegium Internationale Allergologicum, President; European Academy of Dermato-venerology, President Elect. Address: Department of Dermatology and Allergy, Biederstein Technical University, Munich 80802, Germany.

RINK Thomas, b. 20 May 1963, Hanau, Germany. Physician. Education: State Medical Exam, 1989; Doctor, 1989; Specialist in Nuclear Medicine, 1996. Appointments: Training, Department of Nuclear Medicine, Municipal Hospital, Hanau, 1989-90; Assistant Physician, Department of Nuclear Medicine, Municipal Hospital, Wiesbaden, 1991-93; Assistant Physician, Department of Surgery, St Vincenz Hospital, Hanau, 1993-94; Assistant Physician, Department of Nuclear Medicine, Municipal Hospital, Hanau, 1994-95; Assistant Physician, Department of Nuclear Medicine, University Medical Centre, Frankfurt, 1995-96; Chief, Department Nuclear Medicine, Municipal Hospital, Hanau, 1996-; Teacher, University Medical Centre, Frankfurt, 1996-. Publications: 32 publications in professional journals. Memberships: European Association of Nuclear Medicine; Society of Nuclear Medicine; Deutsche Gesellschaft für Nuclear Medicine; New York Academy of Science; American Association for the Advancement of Science; Rotary International. Address: Röntgenstr 36, 63454 Hanau, Germany. E-mail: rink@em.uni-frankfurt.de

RIPPON Angela, b. 12 October 1944, Plymouth, Devon, England. Television and Radio Presenter; Writer. m. Christopher Dare, 1967, divorced. Education: Grammar School, Plymouth, England. Appointments: Presenter, Reporter, BBC TV Plymouth, 1966-69; Editor, Presenter, Producer, Westward Television, 1967-73; Reporter, BBC TV National News, 1973-75, Newsreader, 1975-81; Founder, Presenter, TV-am, 1983; Arts Correspondent, WNETV (CBS), Boston, 1983; Reporter, Presenter, BBC and ITV, 1984; TV appearances: Angela Rippon Meets...; Antiques Roadshow; In the Country; Compere, Eurovision Song Contest, 1976; The Morecombe and Wise Christmas Show, 1976, 1977; Royal Wedding, 1981; Masterteam, 1985, 1986, 1987; Come Dancing, 1988-; What's My Line? 1988-; Healthcheck; Holiday Programme; Simply Money, 2001-; Channel 5 News, 2003-; Radio: Angela Rippon's Morning Report for LBC, 1992; Angela Rippon's Drive Time Show, LBC, 1993; The Health Show, BBC Radio 4; Friday Night with Angela Rippon, BBC Radio 2; LBC Arts Programme, 2003-. Publications: Riding, 1980; In the Country, 1980; Mark Phillips: The Man and His Horses, 1982; Angela Rippon's West Country, 1982; Victoria Plum, 1983; Badminton: A Celebration, 1987; Many recordings. Honours: Dr hc, American

International University, 1994; New York Film Festival Silver Medal, 1973; Newsreader of the Year, Radio and Television Industries Awards, 1976, 1977, 1978; Television Personality of the Year, 1977; Emmy Award, 1984; Sony Radio Award, 1990; New York Radio Silver Medal, 1992; Royal TV Society Hall of Fame, 1996; European Woman of Achievement, 2002. Memberships: Vice-President, International Club for Women in Television; British Red Cross; NCH Action for Children; Riding for the Disabled Association; Director, Nirex, 1986-; Chair, English National Ballet, 2000-. Address: Knight Ayton, 114 St Martin's Lane, London, WC2N 4AZ, England.

RITCHIE Lewis Duthie, b. 26 June 1952, Fraserburgh, Scotland. Academic General Practitioner. m. Heather Skelton. Education: BSc, Chemistry, 1978, MBChB, Commendation, 1978, University of Aberdeen; MSc, Community Medicine, University of Edinburgh, 1982; MD, University of Aberdeen, 1993; Vocational Training in General Practice, 1979-82; Specialist Training in Public Health Medicine, 1982-87. Appointments: General Practice Principal, Peterhead Health Centre, 1984-; Consultant in Public Health Medicine, Grampian Health Board, 1987-92; Honorary Consultant in Public Health Medicine, Grampian Health Board, 1993-; Sir James Mackenzie Professor of General Practice, University of Aberdeen, 1993-; Membership of a number of national medical advisory committees on behalf of the Scottish Executive Health Department and the Department of Health England, 1989-. Publications: Book: Computers in Primary Care, 1986; Over 100 publications on computing, cardiovascular prevention, lipids, hypertension, immunisation, oncology, intermediate care, community hospitals, and fishermen's health. Honours: Munday and Venn Prize, University of Aberdeen, 1977; John Watt Prize, University of Aberdeen, 1977; Kincardine Prize, North East Faculty, Royal College of General Practitioners, 1978; John Perry Prize, British Computer Society, 1991; Ian Stokoe Memorial Award, Royal College of General Practitioners, 1992; Blackwell Prize, University of Aberdeen, 1995; OBE, 2001. Memberships: Diploma of the Royal College of Obstetricians and Gynaecologists, 1980; British Computer Society, 1985; Fellow, Royal Society of Medicine, 1987; Member Royal Environmental Health Institute for Scotland, 1991; Fellow, Faculty of Public Health Medicine, 1993; Fellow Royal College of General Practitioners, 1994; Fellow, Royal College of Physicians of Edinburgh,1995; Chartered Computer Engineer, 1993; Fellow, Royal Society of the Arts, 2001; Founding Fellow of the Institute of Contemporary Scotland, 2001. Address: Department of General Practice and Primary Care, University of Aberdeen, Foresterhill Health Centre, Westburn Road, Aberdeen AB25 2AY, Scotland. E-mail: l.d.ritchie@abdn.ac.uk

RITCHLEY Martin Howard, b. 1 July 1946, Oxford, England. Chartered Accountant; Chief Executive. m. Elizabeth, 1 son, 2 daughters. Education: City of London School, 1957-64; Qualified Chartered Accountant, 1969. Appointments: Trainee Accountant, Barton Mayhew & Co (London) Chartered Accountants, 1964-70; Chief Accountant, 1970-76, Secretary, 1976-83, Coventry Economic Building Society; Secretary, 1983-85, Coventry Building Society (following merger of Coventry Economic and Coventry Provident Building Societies); Secretary and Director, 1985-89, Deputy Chief Executive and Director, 1989-90, Chief Executive and Director, 1990-, Coventry Building Society; Chairman, Building Societies Association, 2001-2002; Member, Executive Committee, Council of Mortgage Lenders, 2001-2002; Director, Building Societies Ombudsman Company, 1997-2002; Governor, Coventry University, 1998-2001; Chairman, CV One Limited (the Company established to assume the combined responsibility of the City Centre Company and Coventry and Warwickshire Promotions), 2001-; Director, NFU Mutual Insurance Society Ltd,

2003-; Director, Coventry Housing Action Partnership, 1996-2003; Director, Belgrade Theatre Trust (Coventry) Ltd, 2002-. Honours: Mortgage Finance Gazette Ambassador Award, 2001; Honorary DBA, Coventry University, 2002. Memberships: Fellow, Institute of Chartered Accountants; Fellow, Chartered Institute of Bankers. Address: The Beeches, 1 Abberton Way, Coventry CV4 7HF, England. E-mail: martin.ritchley@coventrybuildingsociety.co.uk

RITTNER Leona Phyllis, b. USA. Independent Scholar of Comparative Literature. Education: Hunter College; Queens College; Brooklyn College; BA, French, CCNY, 1973; MA Equivalent, French, CCNY, 1982; CUNY Graduate Center; University of Valencia, Spain. Appointments: Graduate Assistantship, Department of Romance Languages, CCNY, 1973; Executive Committee, Romance Literary Relations, 1987-91; Executive Committee, Women in French, 1988-90. Publications include: Libraries and Independent Scholars, 1996; Compte-rendu of The World of the Paris Café: Sociability among the French Working Class, 1789-1914, 1997; Compte-rendu of Paris Was a Woman: Portraits From the Left Bank, 1997; A Golden Age of Jewish Intellectuals, 1998. Honours include: 2 Baruch Scholarships, City College, 1972; Graduate Assistantship, City College, 1973; George D McDonald Scholarship, City College, 1985; Women's Caucus for Modern Languages Travel Grant, 1990; NE Modern Language Association Graduate Student Travel Grant, 1993; Listed in Who's Who publications. Memberships include: Modern Language Association of America; South Atlantic Modern Language Association; Women's Caucus for Modern Languages; Women in French; Friends of the NYU Bobst Library; International Association for Philosophy and Literature; International Simone de Beauvoir Society; Simone de Beauvoir Circle; Société Americaine de Philosophie de Langue Française; W B Yeats Society of New York; Bernard Shaw Society; Sartre Society of North America; Association of French and Francophone Teachers of America; American Association of University Professors; National Coalition of Independent Scholars; Society for Phenomenology and Existential Philosophy; Society for Critical Exchange; Société des Amis de la Maison Française de Columbia University. Address: 120 Kenilworth Place 1J, Brooklyn, NY 11210-2407, USA.

RIVA-SANSEVERINO Eugenio, b. 23 December 1934, Palermo, Italy. Professor of Human Physiology. m. Patrizia Castellacci, 5 sons, 3 daughters. Education: Degree, Medicine, 1959; PhD, 1965; MD, Johns Hopkins University, USA, 1968; Diplomas: Physiotherapy, 1978, Homotoxicology, 1986; Chair, Human Physiology, 1976. Appointments: Assistant Professor, Catania University, Italy, 1959-63; Fellow, Johns Hopkins University Medical School, USA, 1966-68; Professor, Bologna, Italy, 1976-2002; Rector, Department of Science and Technology, Libera University, Lugano, Switzerland, 2002- Publications: Many publications in neurophysiology, oxygen-ozone therapy, homotoxicology, magnetic field therapy. Memberships: New York Academy of Sciences; Italian Physiological Society. Address: Via Besso 66, 6900 Lugano (CH), Switzerland. E-mail: riva@uniludes.ch

RIVAS-RAMIS Carlos A, b. 29 April 1863, San Juan, Puerto Rico. Physician. m. Tamara Lynn, 3 sons, 3 daughters. Education: Paramedic, Naval Laboratory Technician, US Navy, Great Lakes Naval Hospital, 1984-87; Graduate, US Navy Corpsman School, 1985; Medical Doctor, Kirksville College of Osteopathic Medicine, Missouri, 1989-91; Medical Doctor, Universidad Central del Caribe, Bayamon, Purto Rico, 1991-93; Family Practice Residency, University of Puerto Rico, Medical Sciences Campus, 1993; Family Practice Residency, Allegheny Family Physicians of Altoona, Pennsylvania, 1994-95; Family Practice Residency, E A Conway

Medical Center, Louisiana State University, Louisiana, 1995-96. Appointments: Williamson General Practice, Williamson, West Virginia, 1996-2003; Co-Chairman, Department of Medicine, 1998-99, Williamson Memorial Hospital, Williamson, West Virginia, 1996-2003; Medical Director, Southern West Virginia EMS, 1998-2001; Medical Director, Mingo Manor Nursing Home, Williamson, West Virginia, 1998-2001, Clinical Professor of Family Practice, Pikeville College, School of Osteopathic Medicine, 1999-; Medical Director, Stat EMS, Gilbert, West Virginia, 2000-2003; Staff Physician, Logan-Mingo Area Mental Health, Logan, West Virginia, 2001-2003; Pinnacle Physicians Group, Malvern, Arkansas, 2003-; Vice-Chief of Staff, Hot Spring County Medical Center, Malvern, Arkansas, 2003-. Honours: Graduate with Distinction, US Navy Hospital Corpsman School, 1985; Navy Achievement Medal, Great Lakes Naval Hospital, 1987; Cum Laude Graduate, Universidad Central del Caribe, 1993; Alpha Omega Alpha Medical Honor Society; West Virginia State Chairman, Physician's Advisory Board; US Veterans Administration Scholarship; Listed in Who's Who publications and biographical dictionaries. Memberships: Tug Valley Medical Society; American medical Society; American Academy of Family Physicians; Puerto Rican Medical Society; Association of Military Physicians and Surgeons; National Hispanic Medical Recruitment Network. Address: 1002 Schneider Drive, STE 105, Malvern, AR 72104, USA. E-mail: drrivas@pinnacledocs.net

RIVERS Ann, b. 26 January 1939, Texas, USA. Poet. Education: BA, 1959. Appointments: Editor-Publisher, SHY, 1974-79; Guest Editor, As-Sharq, 1979; Contributing Editor, Ocarina, 1979-82. Publication: Samos Wine, 1987; A World of Difference, 1995; Pilgrimage and Early Poems, 2000; Pluto Probe, 2003. Contributions to: Ore; Iotà; Orbis; Poetry Nottingham; Pennine Platform. Address: Hydra, GR 180 40 Greece.

RIVERSO Emanuele, b. 23 December 1928, Naples, Italy. University Professor. m. Mariagrazia Mancassola, 2 daughters. Education: Theology degree, 1952; Philosophy degree, 1956; Privatdozent, Philosophy, 1958. Appointments: Lecturer, 1961-79, Full Professor, 1987-2001, University of Salerne; Lecturer, 1970-81, Privatdozent, 1959-63, University of Naples; Privatdozent, University of Rome, 1964-66; Associate Professor, University of Naples, 1982-87. Publications: 39 books, including: The Process of Representation and Symbolism, 1995; Globalization and Plurality of Cultures, 1999; Understanding Islam, 2003. Honours: Nations Prize, Tetradramma d'Oro, Rome, Italy, 1966; New Century Award, The Europe 500. Memberships: Academy of Abbruzzi of Sciences and Arts, 1961-; Accademia Tiberina, 1966-; Roman Academy of 500, 1966-; Internationales Institut fur Kunstwissenschaften, Zurich, 1967-; American Association for the Advancement of Science, 1996-; New York Academy of Sciences, 1998-; The Planetary Society, 1999-. Address: Viale delle Mimose 12, 80131 Napoli, Italy. E-mail: emanuele.riverso@email.it Website: http://eriverso.altervista.org

RIVETTI BARBÒ Francesca, b. 28 March 1922, Milan, Italy. Professor of Philosophy; Researcher. m. Stefano Rivetti, deceased, 2 sons, 4 daughters. Education: Doctor in Philosophy, Catholic University of the Sacred Heart, Milan, Italy, 1950; Postdoctoral Lecturing Qualification, 1964. Appointments: Assistant Professor, Catholic University of the Sacred Heart, Milan, Italy, 1957-65; Associate Professor, University of Perugia, Italy, 1965-73; Associate Professor, University of Calabria, Cosenza, Italy, 1973-75; Professor, University of Macerata, Italy, 1975-77; Professor, University of Trieste, Italy, 1977-82; Professor, University of Tor Vergata, Rome, Italy, 1982-96; Retired, 1996. Publications: About 100 articles; 10 books include: The "Liar" Antimony. From Pierce to Tarski, 1986; Philosophy of Being, Foundation of Freedom,

1990; Philosophy of Man: an Outline, Italian, 1994, English, 2001; Philosophy of God: an Outline, Italian, 1994, English, forthcoming. Honours: 2 Italian Books: Discourse and Truth. Contributions in Honour of Francesca Rivetti Barbò, 1995; The Boldness of Reason. Reflections on the Philosophical Theology of Francesca Rivetti Barbò, 2000. Memberships: Italian Philosophical Society; Italian Society for Logic and Philosophy of Science; International Society for Metaphysics. Address: Via Frascati Antica 24/C, I-00040 Monte Porzio Catone (Rm), Italy. E-mail: barbof@virgilio.it

RO Hee-Myong, b. 10 March 1958, Seoul, Korea. Professor. m. Young-Mi Kim, 2 sons. Education: BS, 1980, MSc, 1982, PhD, 1989, Seoul National University, Korea. Appointments: Instructor, Seoul National University, Korea, 1985-90; Postdoctoral Studies, University of Manitoba, Canada, 1990-92; Senior Research Soil Scientist, RDA, Korea, 1992-2001; Assistant Professor, Seoul National University, Korea, 2001-. Publications: Numerous articles in scientific journals include most recently as corresponding author: Corn uptake and microbial immobilization of 15N-labeled urea-N soil as affected by composted pig manure, 2001; Differentiation in isotopic fractionation of nitrogen in water-saturated and unsaturated soils, 2003; Degradation of ethprophos in three physiochemically different soils treated with composted manure and chemical fertilizer, 2003. Honour: Outstanding Academic Achievement Award from the Korean Society of Soil Science and Fertilizer, 2000. Memberships: Korean Society of Soil Science and Fertilizer; American Society of Soil Science; Korean Society of Horticultural Science; Korean Society of Ecology. Address: Soil Science Laboratory, School of Agricultural Biotechnology, College of Agriculture and Life Sciences, Seoul National University, San 56-1, Sillim-dong, Gwanak-gu, Seoul, Korea 151-742. E-mail: hmro@snu.ac.kr

ROBB Graham Macdonald, b. 2 June 1958, Manchester, England. Writer. m. Margaret Hambrick, 2 May 1986. Education: BA, 1st Class Honours, Oxford, 1981; PGCE, Goldsmiths College, London, 1982; PhD, Vanderbilt University, Nashville, Tennessee, 1986. Publications: Le Corsaire - Satan en Silhouette, 1985; Baudelaire Lecteur de Balzac, 1988; Scenes de La Vie de Bohème (editor), 1988; Baudelaire, (translation), 1989; La Poésie de Baudelaire et La Poésie Française, 1993; Balzac, 1994; Unlocking Mallarmé, 1996; Victor Hugo: A Biography, 1998; Rimbaud, 2000; Strangers: Homosexual Love in the 19th Century, 2003. Contributions to: Times Literary Supplement; London Review of Books; New York Times. Honours: Postdoctoral Research Fellow; British Academy Fellowship, 1987-90; Whitbread Biography of the Year Award, 1997; Royal Society of Literature Heinemann Award, 1998. Memberships: Society of Authors; Fellow, Royal Society of Literature. Address: 139 Hollow Way, Oxford OX4 2NE, England.

ROBBERSTAD Magnus, b. 20 May 1932, Oslo, Norway. Neurology Consultant. m. Aslaug Goderstad, 3 daughters. Education: Dr Med, Oslo University, 1956; Examinee Government Health Administration School, 1964; Specialist, Physical Medicine and Rehabilitation, 1975; Specialist, Neurology, 1978; Specialist Society Administration. Appointments: Intern, Porsgrunn Hospital Group, 1957-58; Federal Health Officer, 1959-69; Staff Member Oslo Municipal Hospital Group, 1969-73; Staff Member Oslo University Hospital, 1973-80; Staff Member, Tromsoe University Hospital, 1981; Medical Consultant in Neurology to the National Insurance Administration, Norway, 1982-83; Chief Medical Consultant, 1983-2002, Senior Medical Consultant, 2002-; Member, Leirfjord County Parliament, 1963-69; Member, Nesodden County Parliament, 1969-73; Member and Vice-Chairman Board of Energy, Nesodden County. Publications: Author 3 textbooks; Articles to many journals. Honours: Storebrand Grantee, University of Vienna, 1972; Elected into the Academy of Norwegian Language, Norsk Maldyrkingslag 1979. Memberships: Medisinsk Mallag; Norwegian Society of Neurology; Norwegian Society of Physical Medicine and Rehabilitation. Address: Bjornemyr Terrace 12, N 1453 Bjornemyr, Norway. E-mail: magnuskr@online.no

ROBBINS Norman Nelson, b. 27 September 1919, Detroit, Michigan, USA. Lawyer. m. Pamela Eldred Robbins, 2 daughters. Education: JD, Wayne State University Law School, 1943. Appointments: Chairman, State Board of Marriage Counselors; Chairman, State Board Veterans Trust Fund. Publications: Co-editor, Law on Marriage (2 volume family law work); Over 350 articles in Michigan Family Law Journal; Numerous article in The Family Coordinator, American Bar Family Law Magazine, The Family Advocate; Senior Editor, The Family Advocate; Editor, Michigan Family Law Journal, 30 years. Honours include: Lifetime Achievement, Michigan Bar Family Law; Outstanding Contribution to Marriage Counseling; Dedicated Service Award (MIA); Michigan Governor's Award (Minuteman); Life Award, Michigan Cancer; Other civic and professional awards. Memberships: American Bar Association; Michigan Bar Association; American Academy of Matrimonial Lawyers; Michigan Interprofessional Association; Distinguished Affiliate, American Association of Marriage and Family Counseling. Address: 5543 Tadworth Place, West Bloomfield, MI 48322-4016, USA.

ROBBINS Thomas, b. 4 April 1955, Idaho, USA. Chief Executive Officer. m. Mary Robbins, 3 sons, 1 daughter. Education: Associate, Accounting, Ricks College, 1977; Bachelors Degree, Finance, Brigham Young University, 1979; Masters of Business Administration, Golden Gate University, 1989; PhD, Economics, Columbus University, 2003. Appointments: Chief Executive Officer, TEK Corporation; Chief Executive Officer, TEK Foundation which incorporate: TEK Corporation: TEK Foundation (USA); Venture TEK (USA); Utek AG (Liechtenstein); SMG Holdings AG (Liechtenstein); Mashy Establishment (Liechtenstein); Land Development Corporation (USA); TEK United Holdings, Inc (Australia); TEK Euro Holdings, (Ireland); TEK Corp Ltd (Guernsey); Bonam Holdings International, Inc (USA); Protec Industries Inc (USA); 13 other Oil and Gas Companies; Real Estate Investment; Oil and Gas Exploration; Drilling Operations; Education Resource Centres; 50,000 world-wide network being built to connect 6 billion people to Internet based schools. Publications: Speech to UN World Summit, Geneva: Globally Based Computerized and Electronic Education, Infrastructure Network of 50,00 Education Resource Centres in Every Country of the World. Honours: Great Minds of the 21st Century, ABI. Memberships: International Research Foundation for Development; Consultant to United Nations; TEK Foundation Member. Address: 5 Sonnblick Strasse, FL-9490 Vaduz, Liechtenstein. E-mail: t.robbins@utek.li

ROBBINS Tim, b. 16 October 1958, New York, USA. Actor; Director; Screen Writer. 2 sons with Susan Sarandon. Education: University College of Los Angeles. Career: Member, Theatre for the New City; Founder, Artistic Director, The Actor's Gang; Theatre includes: Ubu Roi, 1981; Director, A Midsummer Night's Dream, 1984; The Good Woman of Setzuan, 1990; Co-writer with Adam Simon: Alagazam, After the Dog Wars, Violence; The Misadventures of Spike Spangle; Farmer; Carnage – A Comedy (Represented USA at Edinburgh International Festival, Scotland); Films: Bull Durham, 1988; Cadillac Man; Jacob's Ladder; Five Corners; Tapeheads; Miss Firecracker; Eric the Viking; Jungle Fever; The Player; The Shawshank Redemption; Short Cuts; The Hudsucker Proxy; IQ; Actor, writer, director, Bob Roberts; Dead Man Walking; Writer, director, Nothing to Lose; Director, actor, The Moviegoer, Arlington Road, The Cradle Will Rock, 1999; Austin Powers: The Spy Who Shagged Me, 1999; Mission to Mars,

2000; High Fidelity, 2000; The Truth About Charlie, 2002; Mystic River, 2003; Code 46, 2003. Honours: Best Supporting Actor Oscar for Mystic River, 2004. Address: c/o ICM, 8942 Wilshire Blvd, Beverly Hills, CA 90211, USA.

ROBERSON John Royster, b. 7 March 1930, Roanoke, Virginia, USA. Editor; Writer. m. Charlene Grace Hale, 17 September 1966, 1 son, 1 daughter. Education: BA, 1950, MA, 1953, University of Virginia; Certificates of French Studies, 1st and 2nd Degrees, University of Grenoble, France, 1952; Diploma in Mandarin Chinese, US Army Language School, Monterey, California, 1956. Appointments: Assistant to Senior Editor, Holiday, 1959-70; Copywriter, N W Ayer Advertising, 1971-76; Associate to Senior Staff Editor, Reader's Digest Condensed Books, 1976-95. Publications: China from Manchu to Mao 1699-1976, 1980; Japan from Shogun to Sony 1543-1984, 1985; Transforming Russia 1692-1991, 1992; Japan Meets the West, 1998. Contributions to: Atlantic; Holiday; Reader's Digest; Studies in Bibliography; Virginia Magazine of History and Biography. Honours: Raven Society, University of Virginia, 1950; Rotary International Fellowship, University of Grenoble, 1951-52. Memberships: International House of Japan; US China People's Friendship Association; Board of Directors, Science Education Centre, Fairfield County, Connecticut. Address: 16 Hassake Road, Old Greenwich, CT 06870, USA.

ROBERT Leslie (Ladislas), b. 24 October 1924, Budapest, Hungary. Biochemist. m. Jacqueline Labat, 3 daughters. Education: MD, Paris, 1953; PhD, Lille, 1977; Postdoctoral Training, Department of Biochemistry, University of Illinois, Chicago; Columbia University, New York; Honorary Research Director, French National Research Center (CNRS), 1994-. Appointment: Research Director, Department of Ophthalmic Research, Hotel Dieu Hospital, Paris, France. Publications: 6 books on ageing biology; 1 book on time-regulations in biology; 12 books on connective tissues; 900 publications in international journals. Honours: Honorary doctorate, Semmelweis Medical University, Budapest, 1972; Verzar Medal for Gerontology Research, University of Vienna, 1994; Novartis Prize, International Gerontological Association, 1997. Memberships: Academy of Sciences of Hungary and Germany (Nordrheim-Westfalie); French and International Biochemical Societies; Past president, French Society for Connective Tissue Research; Past president, French Society of Atherosclerosis. Address: 7 Rue J B Lully, 94440 Santeny, France. E-mail: lrobert5@wonadoo.fr

ROBERTS Brian, b. 19 March 1930, London, England. Writer. Education: Teacher's Certificate, St Mary's College, Twickenham, 1955; Diploma in Sociology, University of London, 1958. Appointments: Teacher of English and History, 1955-65. Publications: Ladies in the Veld, 1965; Cecil Rhodes and the Princess, 1969; Churchills in Africa, 1970; The Diamond Magnates, 1972; The Zulu Kings, 1974; Kimberley: Turbulent City, 1976; The Mad Bad Line: The Family of Lord Alfred Douglas, 1981; Randolph: A Study of Churchill's Son, 1984; Cecil Rhodes: Flawed Colossus, 1987; Those Bloody Women: Three Heroines of the Boer War, 1991. Address: 7 The Blue House, Market Place, Frome BA11 1AP, Somerset, England.

ROBERTS Dorothy (Elizabeth), b. Brisbane, Queensland, Australia. Concert Pianist; Abstract Artist. Divorced, 1 son. Education: Studies at Sydney Conservatorium of Music, including Piano, Harmony, History of Music, Form of Music, Chamber Music; Clara Schumann technique with Adelina de Lara, London. Career: Music concerts at Balliol College, Oxford, Purcell Room, South Bank, London; Performed Liszt's Piano Concerto in E Flat with London Symphony Orchestra at Royal Albert Hall, London;

Other concerto performances with the Hallé Orchestra, Northern Sinfonia Orchestra and London Bach Players; Recitals in London, UK provinces, Glasgow, Germany, Australia, France, Netherlands, Canada; TV appearance with the Hallé Orchestra; Other TV appearances with Richard Bonynge, 2 pianos, including playing with the BBC Orchestra; Many one man shows as abstract painter including London, Provinces, New York; Works in collections in UK, Europe, Canada, USA and Australia as Dorothy Lee Roberts. Honours: AMusA; LMus; Honorary DLit, Bradford University, 1995; Recently confirmed as the only Grand Pupil of the Clara Schumann piano-playing tradition; Winner, 95 Art International, New York. Address: Alveley House, 17 Lindum Road, Lincoln LN2 1NS, England.

ROBERTS (Priscilla) Jane (Stephanie) (Hon Lady Roberts), b. 4 September 1949. Curator. m. Hugh Ashley Roberts, 2 daughters. Education: BA (Hons),Westfield College, University of London; MA, Courtauld Institute of Art, University of London. Appointments: Curator of the Print Room, Royal Library, Windsor Castle, Berkshire, England, 1975-. Publications: Holbein, 1979; Leonardo: a Codex Hammer, 1981; Royal Artists, 1987; A Dictionary of Michaelangelo's Watermarks, 1988; Master Drawings in the Royal Collection, 1985; Leonardo da Vinci (joint author), 1989; A Souvenir Album of Sandby Views of Windsor, 1988; A King's Purchase: King George III and the Collection of Consul Smith, 1993; Holbein and the Court of Henry VIII, 1993; Views of Windsor: Watercolours by Thomas and Paul Sandby, 1995; Royal Landscape: the Gardens and Parks of Windsor, 1997; Ten Religious Masterpieces: a Millennium Celebration, 2000; Articles in Burlington Magazine; Report of the Society of Friends of St George's. Address: Adelaide Cottage, Home Park, Windsor, Berkshire SL4 2QJ, England.

ROBERTS Julia, b. 28 October 1967, Georgia, USA. Actress. m. (1) L Lovett, 1993, divorced 1995, (2) Daniel Moder, 2002. Career: Films include: Blood Red; Mystic Pizza; Steel Magnolias; Flatliners; Sleeping with the Enemy; Pretty Woman; Hook; Batman; The Pelican Brief, 1993; Pret á Porter; I Love Trouble, 1994; Something to Talk About, 1996; Michael Collins, 1996; Everyone Says I Love You, 1996; My Best Friends Wedding, 1997; Conspiracy Theory, 1997; Notting Hill, 1998; Stepmom, 1998; Runaway Bride, 1999; Erin Brockovich, 2000; The Mexican, 2001; America's Sweethearts, 2001; Ocean's Eleven, 2001; Full Frontal, 2002; Confessions of a Dangerous Mind, 2003; Mona Lisa Smile, 2003; UNICEF Goodwill Ambassador, 1995. Honour: Golden Globe (Steel Magnolias, 1990). Address: ICM, 8942 Wilshire Boulevard, Beverly Hills, CA 90211, USA.

ROBERTS Michael Victor, b. 23 September 1941, High Wycombe, England. Librarian. m. Jane Margaret, deceased, 1 son, 1 daughter. Education: Bachelor of Arts, Clare College, Cambridge, 1960-63; Loughborough Technical College, 1963-64; Master of Arts, 1966. Appointments: Various junior professional posts in Loughborough, Leeds and City of London, 1964-70; Principal Cataloguer, 1970-73, Keeper of Enquiry Services, 1973-82, Guildhall Library, City of London; Deputy Director, City of London Libraries and Art Galleries, 1982-95. Publications: Numerous articles in professional and academic journals; Editor, Guildhall Studies in London History, 1973-82; Editor, Branch Journal of the Library Association Local Studies Group, 1996-98; Editor, Archives and the Metropolis, 1998; Editor, Framlingham Historical Society, 1997-. Honours: Associate of the Library Association, 1967; Chartered Librarian, 1967; Member, Chartered Institute of Library and Information Professionals, 2002. Memberships: Governor, Bishopsgate Foundation, 1996-; Deputy Chairman, Bishopsgate Foundation, 1999-2002; Chairman, Bishopsgate Foundation, 2002-; Member, Council of British Records

Association, 1987-; Member, East of England Regional Archives Council, 1999-; Member, Shadow East of England Museums, Libraries and Archives Council, 2001-02; Trustee, Housing the Homeless Central Fund, 1997-; Officer/Trustee of various local societies and charities. Address: 43 College Road, Framlingham, Suffolk IP13 9ER, England.

ROBERTS Owen Trevor, b. 31 March 1915, Llan Ffestiniog, Wales. Merchant Navy Officer; Laboratory Manager. m. (1) Elizabeth W Jones (2) Mair Jones. 2 daughters. Education: Part-time evening classes in Science and Technology, Liverpool Technical College and Newton Heath Technical College, Manchester; L P R I Diploma; L R I C Diploma. Appointments: Merchant Navy, 1931-41, served as 4th, 3rd, 2nd Officer on the Clan Line; Passed First Mate Certificate, 1940; Torpedoed on Clan Ogilvy and spent, with others, 16 days in an open boat, 1941; Discharged from Merchant Navy as physically unfit for further service at sea, 1943; Worked for Hydrographic Department of the Admiralty, Liverpool, 1943-45; Joined Dunlop Footwear Ltd, Liverpool, 1945; Taught Rubber Science and Rubber and Plastic Technology at evening classes at Liverpool Technical College (now John Moores University); Retired as Laboratory Manager, Dunlop Footwear, Liverpool, 1980. Publications: 7 books written in Welsh; Autobiography, Not Plain Sailing, 1997; Many articles for various magazines including: Maritime Wales; Liverpool Journal; Yr Enfys (a bilingual publication of the Welsh people outside Wales); Barddas (Welsh poetry magazine); Articles and book reviews in Y Faner (Welsh periodical). Honours: Holder of the 1939-45 Star; Atlantic Star, 1939-45, War Medal with Oak Leaf; King's Commendation for Brave Conduct, 1943; 9 Bardic Chairs for Poetry; 4 times winner at the Royal National Eisteddfod of Wales; Adjudicator at the Royal National Eisteddfod of Wales. Membership: Member of the Gorsedd of Bards of the Royal National Eisteddfod of Wales (Bardic Name Llanowain). Address: Maes y Delyn, 15 Y Parc, Ruthin, Denbighshire LL15 1PW, Wales.

ROBERTSON George Islay McNeill (Lord Robertson of Port Ellen), b. 12 April 1946. Politician. m. Sandra Wallace, 1970, 2 sons, 1 daughter. Education: MA honours, Economics, University of Dundee, 1968. Appointments: Research Assistant Tayside Study, 1968-69; Scottish Organiser, General and Municipal Workers Union, 1969-78; MP for Hamilton, 1978-97, for Hamilton South, 1997-99; Parliamentary Private Secretary to Secretary of State for Social Services, 1979; Opposition Spokesman on Scottish Affairs, 1979-80, on Defence, 1980-81, On Foreign and Commonwealth Affairs, 1981; Principal Spokesman for Scotland, 1994-97; Secretary of State for Defence, 1997-99; Secretary General, NATO, 1999-. Honours: Commander's Cross; Order of Merit (Germany); Joint Parliamentarian of the Year, 1993; Received life peerage, 1999; Grand Cross of the Order of the Star of Romania, 2000; Honorary Regimental Colonel of the London Scottish Volunteers; Honorary Doctorates: University of Dundee; University of Bradford; Cranfield University-Royal Military College of Science; Baku State University, Azerbaijan. Memberships: Vice-Chairman, Board British Council, 1985-94; Governor, Ditchley Foundation, 1989-; Member, Her Majesty's Privy Council, 1997; President, Royal Institute of International Affairs, 2001-; Elder Brother, Trinity House, 2002-; President, Burns Club, 2002-. Address: House of Lords, London, SW1A, England.

ROBERTSON Thomas John McMeel, b. 10 January 1928, Nagpur, India. Chartered Engineer. m. Maureen Enca, 12 June 1954, 2 sons. Education: BSc, Mechanical Engineering, Glasgow University, 1952; Member, Institute of Mechanical Engineers, 1961; European Engineer, 1988; Member, Institute of Patentees & Inventors, 1988. Appointments: Royal Air Force, Engineering

Dictionary of International Biography

Officer, English Electric Test & Design Engineer; Cowley Concrete - Works Manager, Sir W G Armstrong Whitworth Equipment Co, Development Engineer, UKAEA, Reactor Operations & Project Engineer. Publications: Anthologies: Crime Against the Planet, 1994; To You With Love, 1997; A Variety of Verse, 1997; Timeless Exposures, 1998; Isis Valley Verses, 1999; National Poetry Anthology, 2002; National Poetry Anthology, 2003. Contribution to: Creative Writing (Pamphlet), 1996. Membership: Sinodun Writing Group. Address: The Popars, School Lane, Milton, Abingdon, Oxon OX14 4EH, England.

ROBINSON (Alfred) Christopher, b. 18 November 1930, York, England. Soldier; Charity Worker. m. Amanda Boggis-Rolfe, dissolved, 2 sons, 2 daughters. Education: Royal Military Academy, Sandhurst. Appointments: Major, 16th/5th The Queen's Royal Lancers, 1951-65; Trade Indemnity Company Ltd. 1066-70; Glanvill Enthoren Ltd, 1970-73; The Spastic's Society, now Scope, 1973-91; Ferriers Barn Centre for Young Disabled People, 1973-, President, 1987; The Little Foundation, 199-, Chairman, 1996; The Mother & Child Foundation, 1994-, Chairman, 2001. Memberships: Institute of Fundraising, Welfare Committee Chairman, Royal British Legion, Bures Branch; Executive Committee, Dedham Vale Society; Vice-Chairman, Colne Stow Countryside Association; Fundraising Committee Chairman, British Red Cross, Suffolk Branch; Lay Chairman, Sudbury Deanery Synod; Member, St Edmundsbury and Ipswich Diocesan Synod. Address: Water Lane Cottage, Bures, Suffolk CO8 4DE, England.

ROBINSON David Milton, b. 22 November 1935, Ohio, USA. Microbiologist. m. Linda Hoy, 1 son, 2 daughters. Education: DVM, Ohio State University, Columbus, Ohio, USA, 1959; MD, MS, 1965, PhD, 1968, University of Maryland, College Park, Maryland, USA. Appointments include: Director of Military Disease Hazards, US Army Medical Research and Material Command, Ft Detrick, Maryland, USA, 1987-92; Deputy Director, Walter Reed Army Institute of Research, Washington DC, USA, 1992-93; Vice-President, Battelle Memorial Institute, Columbus, Ohio, USA, 1993-. Publications: Author of over 35 articles in microbiology scientific literature. Honours: Diplomate, American College of Veterinary Microbiology; Distinguished Service Medal US Army; Fellow, American Academy of Microbiology. Memberships: New York Academy of Sciences; American Academy of Microbiology; Royal Society of Tropical Medicine and Hygiene; Sigma Xi. Address: Battelle Memorial Institute, 505 King Avenue, Columbus, OH 43201-2693, USA. E-mail: robinsod@battelle.org

ROBINSON Derek, (Dirk Robson), b. 12 April 1932, Bristol, England. Writer. m. Sheila Collins, 29 April 1968. Education: MA, Downing College, Cambridge, England. Publications: Goshawk Squadron, 1971; Rotten With Honour, 1973; Kramer's War, 1977; The Eldorado Network, 1979; Piece of Cake, 1983; War Story, 1987; Artillery of Lies, 1991; A Good Clean Fight, 1993; Hornet's Sting, 1999; Kentucky Blues, 2002; Damned Good Show, 2002. Honour: Shortlisted for Booker Prize, 1971. Address: Shapland House, Somerset Street, Kingsdown, Bristol BS2 8LZ, England.

ROBINSON Derek Hugh, b. 5 June 1929, Derby, England. Civil and Structural Engineer. m. Heather Margaret Anne, 2 sons, 1 daughter. Education: University College, Southampton, 1947-49; BScEng, 1st class honours, University College, London, 1949. Appointments: Site Engineer, John Laing and Son Ltd, London, 1950-52; Bridge Design Engineer, Ontario Department of Highways, Canada, 1952-54; Engineer Officer, US Army Corps of Engineers, Labrador, Canada, 1954; Engineer, Turriff Construction Corporation, Warwick, 1954-55; Engineer, E W H

Gifford and Partners, Southampton, 1957-63; Principal, D H Robinson Associates private practice, Winchester, 1963-87; Employed by Allott and Lomax, Manchester, 1987-95; Retired, 1995-. Publications: Numerous articles in professional and popular journals. Memberships: Fellowships: Institution of Civil Engineers; Institution of Structural Engineers; Association of Consulting Engineers; Chartered Engineer, retired 1995. Address: 6 Palmerston Court, Barnes Close, Winchester SO23 9TS, England.

ROBINSON Ivor, b. 28 October 1924, Bournemouth, England. Artist-Bookbinder. m. Olive Trask, 14 April 1952, 1 son, 1 daughter. Education: Southern College of Art, Bournemouth 1939-42. Appointments: Royal Navy, 1942-45; Lecturer, Bookbinding, Salisbury School of Art, 1946-53; Lecturer, Bookbinding, London School of Printing and Graphic Arts, 1953-58; Lecturer, Bookbinding, Bookworks and Visual Studies, Oxford Polytechnic, 1959-89; External Examiner, Ecole National Superieur D'Architecture et des Arts Visuels, Brussels, 1979; Adviser, Banbury School of Art, 1995-96. Publications: Introducing Bookbinding, 1st edition, 1969, 2nd edition, 1984; Regular Contributor to the annual publication The New Bookbinder, 1981-. Creative Works: One-Man Exhibitions: Hantverket, Stockholm, Sweden, 1963; Galleria Del Bel Libro, Ascona, Switzerland, 1969; The Prescote Gallery, Cropredy, Oxfordshire, 1981; Contributor to 100 group exhibitions, 1951-2002' Work represented in collections of: The British Library; The Victoria & Albert Museum; The Bodleian Library, Oxford; Crafts Council Collection; The Keatley Trust; The Rhösska Museum, Gothenburg, Sweden; The Royal Library, Copenhagen, Denmark; The Royal Library, Stockholm, Sweden; The Royal Library, The Hague; British Royal Collections and major public and private collections in Great Britain and overseas. Honours: MBE; Honorary Fellow, Oxford Brookes University; Honorary Fellow, Designer Bookbinders; Honorary Fellow Meister Der Einbandkunst, Germany; Triple Medallist, Priz Paul Bonet, Ascona, Switzerland, 1971. Membership: Fellow, Designer Bookbinders, 1955-2003, President, 1968-73. Address: Trindles, Holton, Oxford, OX33 1PZ, England.

ROBINSON Karen, b. 15 August 1958, New Brunswick, New Jersey, USA. Dietician. m. Richard A Robinson. Education: BS, Home Economics, Montclair State College, New Jersey, 1980; Certified Food Services Sanitation Manager, New Jersey, 1984; Dietetic Internship, Veterans Affairs Medical Center, Virginia, 1991; Masters Degree, Health Sciences, Dietetics, James Madison University, Virginia, 1992. Appointments: Temporary Sales Secretary, Banquet preparation Staff, Boar's Head Inn, Charlottesville, Virginia, 1986-88; Head Diet Counsellor, Diet Center, Charlottesville, Virginia, 1986-90; Public Health Nutritionist, Central Shenandoah Health District, Waynesboro, Virginia, Health Department, 1993-97; Dietetic Intern Mentor, 1993-97; Consulting Dietician, Hebrew Hospital Home, Bronx, New York, 1998; Food Service Manager, Sodexho Marriot Services, Morningside House Nursing Home, Bronx, New York, 1998-99; Clinical Dietician, Yonkers General Hospital, Yonkers New York, 1999-2001; Community Services Instructor, Westchester Community College, Valhalla, New York, 2001; Inpatient/Outpatient Dietician, Park Care Pavilion (formerly Yonkers General Hospital, 2001-); Clinical Dietician, St John's Riverside Hospital, Yonkers, New York, 2002-. Publications: Abstract as co-author: The psychological predictors of successful weight loss, 1992; Contributed articles to local newspapers and journals. Honours: Recipient, New York State Dietetic Association Grant. Listed in Who's Who publications and biographical dictionaries. Memberships: American Dietetics Association; Dieticians in Nutrition Support; Gerontological Nutritionists Practice Group; Consulting Dieticians in Health Care Facilities; American Association Family and Consumer Sciences; Westchester

Rockland Dietetic Association; Virginia Dietetics Association, 1993-97; Virginia Public Health Association, 1995-97. Address: 10-02 Hunter Lane, Ossining, NY 10562, USA.

ROBINSON Kenneth (Ken), b. 4 March 1950, Liverpool, England. Educator. m. Marie Thérése, 1 son, 1 daughter. Education: B Ed (with Honours), English and Drama, University of Leeds, 1972; Certificate of Education (with Distinction); Doctor of Philosophy, University of London, 1980. Appointments: Co-ordinator, Drama 10-16, National Development Project, Schools Council of England and Wales, 1974-77; Freelance lecturer, writer, 1977-79; Director, Calouste Gulbenkian Foundation National Committee of Inquiry on The Arts in Schools, 1979-81; Director, Gulbenkian Foundation/Leverhulme Inquiry: The Arts and Higher Education, 1981-82; Director, Calouste Gulbenkian Foundation, Arts Education Development Programme, 1981-83; Publisher, Managing Editor, Arts Express, national monthly magazine, 1983-85; Director, National Curriculum Council's, Arts in Schools Project, 1985-89; Professor of Arts Education, 1989-2001, Professor Emeritus, 2001-, University of Warwick; Currently, Senior Adviser, J Paul Getty Trust, Los Angeles, California, USA. Publications: 18 books and monographs; 17 book chapters and journal papers; Numerous newspaper features and interviews and appearances on radio and television. Honours: Knighted for services to the arts, June 2003. Memberships include: Member of Board and Chairman, Education Committee, Birmingham Royal Ballet; Education Adviser, Chairman Education Policy Group, Arts Council of Great Britain; Education Advisory Council, Independent Television Commission; Director, British Theatre Institute; Adviser to Outreach Programme, The Royal Academy. Address: J Paul Getty Trust, 1200 Getty Center Drive, Los Angeles, 90049, USA.

ROBINSON Mary, b. 21 May 1944, Ballina, County Mayo, Ireland. International Civil Servant; Former Head of State. m. Nicholas Robinson, 1970, 2 sons, 1 daughter. Education: Trinity College, Dublin; King's Inns, Dublin; Harvard University, USA. Appointments: Barrister, 1967, Senior Counsel, 1980; Called to English Bar (Middle Temple), 1973; Reid Professor of Constitutional and Criminal Law, Trinity College, Dublin, 1969-75, Lecturer, European Community Law, 1975-90; Founder, Director, Irish Centre for European Law, 1988-90; Senator, 1969-89; President, Ireland, 1990-97; UN High Commissioner for Human Rights, 1997-. Honours include: LLD honoris causa (National University of Ireland; Cambridge; Brown; Liverpool; Dublin; Montpellier; St Andrews; Melbourne; Columbia; National University of Wales; Poznan; Toronto; Fordham; Queens University, Belfast); Dr honoris causa Public Services (Northeastern University); Honorary Docteur en Sciences Humaines (Rennes), 1996; Honorary LLD (Coventry), 1996; Berkeley Medal, University of California; Medal of Honour, University of Coimbra; Medal of Honour, Ordem dos Advogados, Portugal; Gold Medal of Honour, University of Salamanca; Andrés Bello Medal, University of Chile; New Zealand Suffrage Centennial Medal; Freedom Prize, Max Schmidheiny Foundation (Switzerland); UNIFEM Award, Noel Foundation, Los Angeles; Marisa Bellisario Prize, Italy, 1991; European Media Prize, The Netherlands, 1991; Special Humanitarian Award, CARE, Washington DC, 1993; International Human Rights Award, International League of Human Rights, New York, 1993; Liberal International Prize for Freedom, 1993; Stephen P Duggan Award (USA), 1994; Freedom of the City of Cork; Honorary AO; Council of Europe North South Prize, Portugal, 1997; Collar of Hussein Bin Ali, Jordan, 1997; F D Roosevelt Four Freedoms Medal, 1998; Erasmus Prize, Netherlands, 1999; Fulbright Prize, USA, 1999; Garrigues Walker Prize, Spain, 2000; William Butler Prize, USA, 2000; Indira Gandhi Peace Prize, India, 2000; Sydney Peace Prize.

Memberships include: Royal Irish Academy; Honorary Bencher Kings Inns, Dublin, Middle Temple, London. Address: Palais des Nations, United Nations, 1211 Geneva 10, Switzerland.

ROBINSON Robert Henry, b. 17 December 1927, Liverpool, England. Writer; Broadcaster. m. Josephine Mary Richard, 1958, 1 son, 2 daughters. Education: MA, Exeter College, Oxford. Publications: Landscape With Dead Dons, 1956; Inside Robert Robinson, 1965; The Conspiracy, 1968; The Dog Chairman, 1982; Everyman Book of Light Verse (editor), 1984; Bad Dreams, 1989; Prescriptions of a Pox Doctor's Clerk, 1991; Skip All That: Memoirs, 1996; The Club, 2000. Contributions to: Newspapers, radio and television. Address: 16 Cheyne Row, London SW3, England.

ROBINSON Scott, b. 2 February 1950, Denver, Colorado, USA. Attorney. m. Janice, 2 daughters. Education: BA, Phi Beta Kappa, University of Denver, 1972; Order of the Coif and Law Review Editor, University of Colorado School of Law, 1965. Appointments: Trial and Appeal Attorney, 1975-; Media Legal Analyst and Newspaper Columnist, ABC, BBC, NBC, CNN, Court TV, People Magazine, KOA Radio, The Rocky Mountain News. Publications: Author Rules vs. Approaches: Choosing A Choice of Law Principle for Colorado; Eyewitness Identification: Suggested Procedures in The Wake of Wade. Honours: Phi Beta Kappa; Order of the Coif, Law Review Editor. Memberships: Colorado and Denver Bar Associations; American Trial Lawyers Association; American Bar Association. Email: scottlaw@eazy.net

ROBSON Bryan, b. 11 January 1957, Chester-le-Street, England. Footballer. m. Denise Robson, 1979, 1 son, 2 daughters. Career: Professional footballer with Manchester United, FA Cup winners, 1983, 1985, 1990; European Cup Winners' Cup, 1991; Player, Manager, Middlesborough Football Club, 1994-; Assistant Coach English National Team, 1994-; Winner, League Championship, 1992-93, 1993-94; 90 caps (65 as captain), scoring 26 international goals. Honours: OBE; Hon MA (Salford), 1992, (Manchester), 1992.

ROCCA Costantino, b. 4 December 1956, Bergamo, Italy. Golfer. m. 1 son, 1 daughter. Career: Former factory worker and caddie; Turned professional, 1981; Qualified for PGA European Tour through 1989 Challenge Tour; Won Open V33 Da Grand Lyon and Peugeot Open de France; First Italian Golfer to be member European Ryder Cup team, 1993; Member, winning European Ryder Cup team, 1995.

RODDICK Anita Lucia, b. 23 October 1942, Littlehampton, England. Business Executive. m. Gordon Roddick, 1970, 2 daughters. Education: Newton Park College of Education, Bath. Appointments: Teacher, English and History; Worked in library of International Herald Tribune, Paris and Women's Rights Department of ILO, based at UN, Geneva; Owner, Manager, restaurant and hotel; Opened first branch of the Body Shop, Brighton, Sussex, 1976; The Body Shop International floated on Unlisted Securities Market, 1984; Group Manager, Director, -1994, Chief Executive Officer, 1994-98, Joint Chairman, 1998-2002, Director (non-executive), internal consultant, 2002-, The Body Shop International PLC; Trustee of the Body Shop Foundation, 1990-, New Academy of Business, 1996; Patron of various organisations. Publications: Body and Soul (autobiography), 1994; Business as Unusual, 2000. Honours: Veuve Cliquot Businesswoman of Year, 1984; British Association of Industrial Editors Communicator of Year, 1988; Co NatWest Retailer of Year Award, 1988; Hon D University (Sussex), 1989, (Open University), 1995; Global 55 Environment Award, 1989; Hon LLD (Nottingham), 1990, (New England College), 1991, (Victoria,

Dictionary of International Biography

Canada), 1995; Business Leader of Year, National Association of Women Business Owners (USA), 1992; Botwinick Prize in Business Ethics, 1994; Business Leadership Award, University of Michigan, 1994; 1st Annual Womanpower Award, Women's Business Development Centre, 1995; USA Women's Center Leadership Award, 1996; American Dream Award, Hunter College, 1996; Philanthropist of Year, Institute of Fundraising Managers, 1996. Address: The Body Shop International, Watersmead, Littlehampton, West Sussex, BN17 6LS, England.

RODES Toby Edward, b. 25 October 1919, Frankfurt. Consultant. m. W E Rodes-Bauer. Education: London School of Economics, 1937; Thesis, Columbia University-American Institute of Banking, 1938; NYU Law School, 1939-42. Appointments: Vice President, Anec Trading Company, NY, Paris, Zurich, Geneva, Oran, Casablanca, 1940-42, 1946-50; Information Officer, US Marshall Plan operations, Germany, 1950-55; Chairman, Chief Executive Officer, Vice President, various companies of Knoll International Group, 1955-66; Chairman, Toby E Rodes Consultants AG, Basel, Switzerland, 1966-2002. Publications: Numerous articles on interior design subjects in USA, United Kingdom, France, Italy, Germany, Switzerland, United Arab Emirates; Lecturer and Author on PR and communication. Honours: Various medals and citations. Memberships: Fellow RSA; PRSA; SPRG; IPRA; Swiss Federation of journalists; Cercle Républicain pour l'industrie; various Chambers of Commerce. Address: Toby E Rodes Consultants, St Alban-Anlage 25, CH-4052 Basel. E-mail: toby.rodes@terag.com

RODMAN Dennis Keith, b. 13 May 1961, Trenton, New Jersey, USA. Basketball Player. Education: Cooke County Junior College; Southeastern Oklahoma State University. Career: West Detroit Pistons, 1986-93; Forward San Antonio Spurs, 1993-95, Chicago Bulls, 1995-99; L A Lakers, 1999; NBA Defensive Player of Year, 1990, 1991; NBA Championship Team, 1989-90, 1996; All-Defensive First Team, 1989-93, All-Defense Second Team, 1994; All Star Team, 1990, 1992. Film appearances: Cutaway; Simon Sez; Double Team. Publications: Bad as I Wanna Be, 1997; Walk on the Wild Side, 1997; Words from the Worm: An Unauthorised Trip Through the Mind of Dennis Rodman, 1997. Address: L A Lakers, 3900 West Manchester Boulevard, Inglewood, CA 90306, USA.

ROGERS Howard Dennis, b. 20 March 1948, Miami, Florida, USA. Attorney. m. Mary Kathleen Rogers, 1 son, 1 daughter. Education: BA with Honors, Florida State University, 1970; JD, University of Florida, 1979. Appointments: Blake & Associates P.A., 1981-84; Jacobs, Robbins, Gaynor et al. P.A., 1984-86; Foley & Lardner P.A., 1986-93; Carey & Florin, P.A., 1993-96; Mitchell & Rogers P.A., 1996; Florin, Roebig, Walker Huddlestun & Rogers, 1996-2000; H Dennis Rogers, P.A., 2000-. Honours: The Bar Register of Pre-eminent Lawyers; Listed in Who's Who publications and biographical dictionaries. Memberships: National Lawyer Honor Society; Million Dollar Advocates Forum; American Mensa Society, 1971-80; Florida Bar; Association of Trial Lawyers of America; Academy of Florida Trial Lawyers; Clearwater Bar Association. Address: 28163 US Hwy 19 North, Suite 200, Clearwater, FL 33761-2696, USA.

ROGOZEA Radu, b. 21 June 1931, Cluj, Romania. Doctor; Senior Researcher. m. 24 October 1960. Education: MD, honours, University of Cluj, 1956; PhD, honours, Neurophysiology, Institute of Neurology, Bucharest, 1972. Appointments: Chief Senior Researcher, 1980-89, Head, Neurology and EEG Department, 1989, Science Director, Institute of Neurology, 1990-95; President, Romanian Society Against Epilepsy, 1993-; Head, National Centre Against Epilepsy, 1995-. Publications include: Handbook of

Neurology, 1979; Negative Learning: Habituation, 1982; Actualities in Epilepsy, 1999; Epilepsy – Diagnosis and treatment, 2000. Honours include: Gh Marinescu Award of Romanian Academy, 1978; Golden Star Award, IBC, 1999; Listed in several biographical publications. Memberships: British Brain Research Association; European Brain & Behavior Society; Fellow, America EEG Society; America Academy of Neurology. Address: et 4 ap 12 sector 5, Str Calea Plevnei no 1 sc A, 75622 Bucharest, Romania.

ROH Hyung-Keun, b. 24 June 1956, Seoul, South Korea. Clinical Toxicology Physician; Clinical Pharmacologist. m. Mikyung Roh, 2 daughters. Education: MD, Yonsei University Medical School, 1976-82; MSc, Yonsei University Graduate School, Seoul, South Korea, 1985-87; PhD, Karolinska Institutet, Stockholm, Sweden, 1995-2002. Appointments: Chief, Division of Clinical Pharmacology, Department of Internal Medicine, Inha University Hospital, Incheon, Korea, 1999-; Director, Inha Poison Centre, Incheon, Korea, 1999-; Chairman, Scientific Committee, Korean Society for Clinical Pharmacology and Therapeutics, 2000-; Chairman, Scientific Committee, The Korean Society of Clinical Toxicology, 2003-. Publications: Articles in scientific journals include: Debrisoquine and S-mephenytoin hydroxylation phenotypes and genotypes in a Korean population, 1996; CYP2C19 genotype and phenotype determined by omeprazole in a Korean population, 1996; Plasma concentrations of haloperidol are related to CYP206 genotype at low but not high doses of haloperidol in Korean schizophrenic patients, 2001. Memberships: Advisory Committee, Korea Food and Drug Administration. Address: Department of Internal Medicine, Inha University Hospital, 7-206, 3-Ga, Shinheung-Dong, Jung-Gu, Incheon, 400-711, South Korea. E-mail: keunroh@inha.ac.kr

ROH Moo-hyun, b. 6 August 1946, Gimhae, Gyeongsangnam-do, Korea. President of the Republic of Korea. m. Yong-sook Kwon, 1 son, 1 daughter. Education: Graduate, Busan Commercial High School, 1966; Passed 17th National Bar Examination, 1975. Appointments: Judge, Daejon District Court, 1977; Practising Attorney, 1978-; Human Rights Lawyer, 1981-; Chairman and Director, Busan Headquarters, Citizens' Movement for a Democratic Constitution, 1987; One of Leaders of June Democratisation Struggles, 1987; Elected to 13th National Assembly in Busan's Eastern District, 1988; Member, Special Committee to Investigate Political Corruption during the Fifth Republic, 1988; Spokesman, 1991, Senior Member, Central Committee, 1993, United Democratic Party; Director, Research Centre for Local Autonomy, 1993; Standing Committee Member, Committee for the Promotion of National Conciliation and Unity, 1996; Vice-President, National Congress for New Politics, 1997; Elected to 15th National Assembly, 1998; Minister of Maritime Affairs and Fisheries, 2000-2001; Advisor and Senior Member, Central Committee, Millennium Democratic Party, 2000; Elected President of the Republic of Korea, 2002; Sworn in as President for a 5 year term of office, 2003. Publications: Honey, Please Help Me! 1994; Roh Mo-hyun Meets Lincoln, 2001; Thoughts on Leadership, 2002.

ROHEKAR Joel Ezekiel, b. 5 October 1942, Nadiad, Gujarat State. Teacher. m. Sudha. Education: BA, 1966; BEd, 1970; MA, 1974; IWA (Honorary USA). Appointments: Teacher and Lecturer in English. Publication: Gomatesham Panamami: A Life Sketch of Lord Bahubali (A Jain Saint) (in English). Honours: Distinguished Leadership Award, American Biographical Institute; Appointed to Research Board of Advisors, American Biographical Institute. Membership: Life Member, International Writers and Artists Association, Bluffton, Ohio, USA. Address: c/o Mrs Shaila B Bakare, "Citadel", Flat No F-35, B T Kawade Road, Sopan Baug Extension, Ghorpadi, Pune – 411001, Mah States, India.

Dictionary of International Biography

ROHEN Edward, (Bruton Connors), b. 10 February 1931, Dowlais, South Wales. Poet; Writer; Artist. m. Elizabeth Jarrett, 4 April 1961, 1 daughter. Education: ATD, Cardiff College of Art, 1952. Appointments: Art Teacher, Ladysmith High, British Columbia, Canada, 1956-57; Head of Art, St Bonaventures, London, 1958-73; Ilford County High for Boys, Essex, 1973-82. Publications: Nightpriest, 1965; Bruised Concourse, 1973; Old Drunk Eyes Haiku, 1974; Scorpio Broadside 15, 1975; Poems/ Poemas, 1976; A 109 Haiku and One Seppuku for Maria, 1987; Sonnets for Maria Marriage, 1988; Sonnets: Second Sequence for Maria, 1989. Contributions to: Poetry Wales; Anglo-Welsh Review; Irish Press; Mabon; Tribune; Argot; Edge; Little Word Machine; Second Aeon; Planet; Carcanet; Poetry Nippon; Riverside Quarterly; Littack; Wormwood Review; Twentieth Century Magazine. Memberships: Korean War Veterans Writers and Arts Society; Academician, Centro Cultural Literario e Artistico de o Jornal de Felgeiras, Portugal; Welsh Academy. Address: 57 Kinfauns Road, Goodmayes, Ilford, Essex IG3 9QH, England.

RÖHLING Horst Rudolf, b. 28 October 1929, Zwickau/Sa, Germany. Retired Librarian; Lecturer in Eastern Churches History. Education: University final examination, 1953; Doctor's Degree, 1956; Librarian Examination, 1963. Appointments: University Assistant, 1955-58; Collaborator in University and Library, 1958-61; Librarian, 1963-94. Publications: Studien zur Geschichte der balkanslavischen Volkspoesie, 1975; Slavica-Bibliotheca-Ecclesia Orientalis, 1981; Drei Bulgaro-Germanica, 1983; Publikationsformen als verbindendes Element, 1992; Numerous publications on slavistics, eastern churches and library science. Memberships: Wolfenbüttler Arbeitkreis für Bibliotheks, Buch und Mediengeschichte; Deutsche Gesellschaft für die Erforschung des 18 Jahrhunderts; Study Group on 18th Century Russia; Südosteuropa-Gesellschaft; ABDOS; 4C's Club; Deutsch-Bulgarische Gesellschaft; Verein der Freunde der Ratsschulbibliothek Zwickau; Gesellschaft der Freunde und Förderer der Sächsischen Landesbiliothek Dresden. Address: Unterkrone 37, D-58455 Witten, Germany.

ROHRBACH Peter Thomas, (James Cody), b. 27 February 1926, New York, New York, USA. Writer. m. Sheila Sheehan, 21 September 1970, 1 daughter. Education: BA, MA, Catholic University of America. Publications: 17 books, including: Conversation with Christ, 1981; Stagecoach East, 1983; American Issue, 1985; The Largest Event: World War II, 1993; National Issue, 1994. Contributions to: Encyclopedias and periodicals. Memberships: Authors Guild of America; Poets, Playwrights, Editors, Essayists and Novelists; Washington Independent Writers. Address: 9609 Barkston Court, Potomac, MD 20850, USA.

ROMANENKO Vassily Yakovlevich, b. 15 January 1931, Bryansk region in Tolvinka. m. Galina Gregorevna, 5 sons, 2 daughters. Education: Secondary Technical Education, College, 1946-48; Courses for Pastors, 1976-79. Appointments: Worker, at the enterprises of the engine and wagon building industry, Bryansk Novocherkarsk, 1946-94; Military service in the Soviet Army, 1951-54; Member of Church Council, 1964-74; Deacon, 1974-79; Pastor, 1979-2003; Prisoners Bible Service, 1989-2003. Honour: Labour Veteran (medal). Membership: Evangelist Union of Christians (Baptists); Member, Priest Council of Rostov Region, 1979-2003. Address: Rostov region, Novocherkarsk, Clestchova Street, 1, ap 1, Russia.

ROMBACH Louis H, b. 4 April 1926, Cincinnati, Ohio, USA. Chemist; Lawyer. m. Ann M O'Brien, 4 sons, 1 daughter. Education: BS Chemistry, 1948; MS Chemistry, 1949; PhD Chemistry, 1953; JD Law, 1964. Appointments: Research Chemist, 1953-64; Senior Counsel, 1965-91; Admitted to the Bars of

Delaware and District of Columbia; Admitted to Practice US Federal Courts and US Patent and Trademark Office. Publications: US and Foreign Patents in Polymer Chemistry; Articles in Journal of Chemical Documentation and Encyclopaedia of Polymers and Plastics. Honours: BS, magna cum laude; Cancer Research Fellow National Institute of Health, 1951-53. Memberships: Royal Society of Chemistry; American Chemical Society; American Institute of Chemists; Scientific Research Society of America; Alpha Chi Sigma; Phi Lambda Upsilon; Phi Alpha Delta. Address: 201 North Pembrey Drive, Wilmington, DE 19803-2005, USA.

RONAN Frank, b. 6 May 1963, New Ross, Ireland. Novelist. Publications: The Men Who Loved Evelyn Cotton, 1989; A Picnic in Eden, 1991; The Better Angel, 1992; Dixie Chicken, 1994; Handsome Men are Slightly Sunburnt (collected stories), 1996; Lovely, 1996; Home, 2002. Honours: Irish Times/Aerlingus Irish Literature Prize, 1989. Address: c/o Rogers Coleridge & White, 20 Powis Mews, London W11 1SN, England.

RONAY Egon, b. Pozony, Hungary (UK citizen). Publisher; Journalist. m. (1) 2 daughters, (2) Barbara Greenslade, 1967, 1 son. Education: University of Budapest; Academy of Commerce, Budapest; Trained in kitchens of family catering firm and abroad. Appointments: Manager, 5 restaurants within family firm; Emigrated from Hungary, 1946; General Manager, 2 restaurant complexes in London before opening The Marquee Restaurant, 1952-55; Founder, The Egon Ronay Guides, 1957, Publisher, 1957-85; Gastronomic and good living columnist, Sunday Times, 1986-91, Sunday Express, 1991. Publications: The Unforgettable Dishes of My Life, 1989; Weekly columnist on eating out, food, wine and tourism, Daily Telegraph and later Sunday Telegraph, 1954-60; Weekly column, the Evening News, 1968-74; Editor-in-Chief, Egon Ronay Recommends (Heathrow Airport Magazine), 1992-94. Honours: Médaille de la Ville de Paris, 1983; Chevalier de l'Ordre du Mérite Agricole, 1987. Memberships: Academy des Gastronomes (France), 1979 Founding Vice-President, International Academy of Gastronomy; Founder, President, British Academy of Gastronomes. Address: 37 Walton Street, London SW3 2HT, England. 1.

ROONEY Mickey (Joe Yule Jr), b. 23 September 1920, Brooklyn, USA. Actor. m. (1) Ava Gardner, (2) Betty J Rase, 2 sons, (3) Martha Vickers, (4) Elaine Mahnken, (5) Barbara Thomason, 4 children, (6) Margie Lang, (7) Carolyn Hockett, 2 sons, (8) Jan Chamberlin, 2 stepsons. Education: Pacific Military Academy. Career: Served AUS, World War II; TV programmes including series: The Mickey Rooney Show; Films include: Judge Hardy's Children; Hold That Kiss; Lord Jeff; Love Finds Andy Hardy; Boys Town; Stablemates; Out West With the Hardys; Huckleberry Finn; Andy Hardy Gets Spring Fever; Babes in Arms; Young Tom Edison; Judge Hardy and Son; Andy Hardy Meets Debutante; Strike up the Band; Andy Hardy's Private Secretary; Men of Boystown; Life Begins for Andy Hardy; Babes on Broadway; A Yank at Eton; The Human Comedy; Andy Hardy's Blonde Trouble; Girl Crazy; Thousands Cheer; National Velvet; Ziegfeld Follies; The Strip; Sound Off; Off Limits; All Ashore; Light Case of Larceny; Drive a Crooked Road; Bridges at Toko-Ri; The Bold and the Brave; Eddie; Private Lives of Adam and Eve; Comedian; The Grabbers; St Joseph Plays the Horses; Breakfast at Tiffany's; Somebody's Waiting; Requiem for a Heavyweight; Pulp; It's a Mad Mad Mad Mad World; Everything's Ducky; The Secret Invasion; The Extraordinary Invasion; The Comic; The Cockeyed Cowboys of Calico Country; Skidoo; BJ Presents; That's Entertainment; The Domino Principle; Pete's Dragon; The Magic of Lassie; Black Stallion; Arabian Adventure; Erik the Viking; My Heroes Have Always Been Cowboys, 1991; Little Nimo: Adventures in Slumberland (Voice),

1992; Silent Deadly Night 5; The Toymaker; The Milky Life; Revenge of the Baron; That's Entertainment II; The Legend of OB Taggart, 1995; Kings of the Court, 1997; Killing Midnight, 1997; Boys Will Be Boys, 1997; Animals, 1997; Sinbad: The Battle of the Dark Knights, 1998; Babe: Pig in the City, 1998; The Face on the Barroom Floor, 1998; The First of May, 1998; Holy Hollywood, 1999; Internet Love, 2000; Lady and the Tramp II: Scamp's Adventure, 2001; Topa Topa Bluffs, 2002; Paradise, 2003; Strike the Tent, 2004; A Christmas Too Many, 2004. Address: PO Box 3186, Thousand Oaks, CA 91359, USA.

ROONEY Patrick Joseph, b. 8 December 1943, Coatbridge, Scotland. Physician. M. Katherine Boyle, 3 sons, 1 daughter. Education: MB, ChB, 1966, Doctor of Medicine, 1976, Glasgow University; Member, Royal College of Physicians, UK, 1970; Fellow, Royal College of Physicians and Surgeons of Glasgow, 1979; Fellow, Royal College of Physicians of Edinburgh, 1983; Licentiate, Medical College of Canada, 1986. Appointments: Senior House Officer and Registrar in Medicine, Southern General Hospital, Glasgow, Scotland, 1967-70; Registrar of Medicine, Royal Infirmary of Edinburgh, Scotland, 1970-72; Associate Clinical Fellow, National Institute of Arthritis, Metabolism and Digestive Diseases, National Institutes of Health, Bethesda, Maryland, USA, 1975-67; Senior Registrar in Medicine, Centre for Rheumatic Disease and University Department of Medicine, Royal Infirmary, Glasgow, 1973-77; Consultant Physician and Honorary Clinical Lecturer, Western District Teaching Hospitals, Glasgow, Scotland, 1977-81; Director, Rheumatic Diseases Unit, Chedoke Division of Chedoke-McMaster Hospitals; Director of Medical-Surgical Service, Hamilton Psychiatric Hospital, 1986-91; Director, Standardized Patient Program, McMaster University, 1989-91; Professor and Head, Centre for Medical Sciences Education, The University of the West Indies, Trinidad, 1991-93; Professor of Medicine, McMaster University, Hamilton, Ontario, 1981-94; Professor of Medicine, St George's University School of Medicine, Grenada, West Indies, 1994-. Publications: Over 40 publications of original research; Major collaborative or directive role in over 50 articles; Numerous editorial and review articles, communications, chapters in books and monographs. Honours: Awarded Copeman Fellowship, Arthritis and Rheumatism Council of Great Britain, 1975; Schering Travelling Award, Canadian Society for Clinical Investigation, 1989. Memberships: British Society of Rheumatology; Canadian Rheumatism Association; European Society for Clinical Investigation; Canadian Society for Clinical Investigation; International Back Pain Society; American College of Rheumatology; New York Academy of Sciences, Caribbean Academy of Sciences; Founding fellow, American Rheumatism Association. Address: Department of Educational Services, St George's University, School of Medicine, PO Box 7, St George's, Grenada, West Indies.

ROOSENDAAL Eddy Maria Cyrille, b. 1 April 1931, Antwerp, Belgium. Corporate Lawyer, retired. m. Josée Vandommele, 1 daughter. Education: Degree in Classical Humanities, Royal Atheneum Berchem, Antwerp, Belgium, 1950; BA, Philosophy and Literature, Free University Brussels, Belgium, 1952; LLD, Free University Brussels, Belgium, 1955; Barrister, Law Firm Calewaert, Dijck and Van Goethem, Antwerp, 1955-58. Appointments: Legal Counsel, Chartered Accountants Office Celis, Antwerp, 1958-61; Director, Insurance Brokers Lacroix-Baartmans and Van Tichelen, Antwerp, 1961-65; Business Administrator, Bell Telephone Manufacturing Company, Antwerp, 1965-68; Assistant Secretary, GTE Information Systems International Incorporated, Delaware, USA, 1975-81; Chairman and Managing Director, GTE Information Systems Europe NV, Herentals, Belgium, 1978-80; General Counsel, Director Legal Department, Siemens-Atea NV, Herentals, Belgium, 1968-96; Retired, 1996. Publications: many

articles to professional journals. Honours: Medal of Merit, Boy-Scouts of Belgium; Wood Badge, World Federation of Scouting; Knight in the Order of the Crown; Knight in the Order of Leopold; Officer in the Order of the Crown. Memberships: Federation of Open Scouting; Reconnaissance Armoured Cavalry Troops, Belgian Army; Belgian Institute of Corporate Lawyers; Flemish Association of Lawyers; Licensing Executives Society; Belgo-Chinese Lawyers Association; Benelux Association of Marks and Models Counsels; Belgian Association for Informatics Law; Alumni of Vlerick's Management School; Former Students of Free University Brussels. Address: Rucaplein 36, B-2610 Wilrijk-Antwerp, Belgium.

ROSARIO Luis Bras, b. 21 November 1964, Lisbon, Portugal. Physician. Education: Medical degree, University of Lisbon, 1988. Appointments: Resident, 1989-90, Cardiology Fellow, 1991-95, Hospital Santa Marta, Lisbon; Clinical and Research Fellow, Visiting Physician, Brigham and Women's Hospital, Harvard Medical School, Boston; Cardiologist, Head, Heart Failure Unit, 1999-, Hospital Garcia de Orta, Lisbon; Physiology Research Fellow, University College, London; Assistant, Physiology Department, University of Lisbon; Research Fellow, Institute of Molecular Medicine, Lisbon. Publications: Articles in professional journals. Honours: Research Award on Heart Failure; Portuguese Health Ministry; European Society Fellowship for Intervention Cardiology; Listed in national and international biographical dictionaries. Memberships: Portuguese Society Biology; Secretary to the Board, 2001-03, Portuguese Society of Cardiology; American Society Echocardiography; American Society Nuclear Cardiology; Fellow of European Society of Cardiology. Address: R Quinta Grande, 8 r/c 2780-186, Oeiras, Portugal.

ROSE Helen Carlotta, b. 14 June 1920, New York City, New York, USA. Retired. Widowed, 1 son, 1 daughter. Education: AB, MA, 1955, LHD, 1978, Emerson College, Boston, Massachusetts, USA. Appointments: Founder, Robbins Speech and Hearing Clinic, 1953; Founder, Speech and Hearing Foundation of Massachusetts, 1961; Founder, Friends of The Cuther Majestic Theatre of Emerson College, 1991; Trustee, Emerson College, Boston, Massachusetts, 1952-2000, Trustee Emeritus, 2000-. Honours: MA, Emerson College; LHD, Emerson College; Helen Rose Day, City of Boston, June 7 1976; President's Medal, Emerson College, 1994. Memberships: Mar-a-lago Club, Palm Beach; Governor's Club, Palm Beach; Le Club Intercontinental, Palm Beach; The International Society of Palm Beach; Order of St George. Address: 150 Bradley Place, Palm Beach, FL 33480, USA.

ROSEANNE (Roseanne Barr), b. 3 November 1952, Salt Lake City, USA. Actress. m. (1) Bill Pentland, (2) Tom Arnold, divorced 1994, 3 children from previous marriage, (3) Ben Thomas, 1994, 1 son. Appointments: Former window dresser, cocktail waitress; Comic in bars and church coffee-house, Denver; Producer, Performer for women performers Take Back the Mike, University of Boulder, Colorado; Performer, The Comedy Store, Los Angeles; Featured, TV special Funny and The Tonight Show; TV special, On Location: The Roseanne Barr Show, 1987; Star, TV series, Roseanne ABC, 1988-97; Host, Roseanne Show, 1998-; Actress in films: She Devil, 1989; Freddy's Dead, 1991; Even Cowgirls Get the Blues, 1994; Blue in the Face, 1995; Unzipped, 1995; Meet Wally Sparks, 1997. Publications: My Life as a Woman, 1989; Roseanne: My Lives, 1994. Honours: Emmy Award, Outstanding Actress in a Comedy Series, 1993.

ROSEMONT David John, b. 26 August 1945, Birmingham, England. Architect. m. 2 sons, 3 step-daughters. Education: Architectural Association, 1963-69; Common Purpose, 1992. Appointments: Tripe and Wakeham, 1969-70; Watkins Gray

Woodgate International, 1970; Thomas Saunders Partnership, 1970-71; Private Practice, 1971-75; Associate, Fairhursts, 1975-77; Associate, SKA, 1977-81; Director, Rosemont Holdings Ltd Group, 1981-; Chairman, Wandsworth Challenge Partnership, 1994-; Member, Wandsworth Strategic Partnership, 2001-. Honours: Design Awards, Kingston, Richmond and Lambeth; Competition Winner, Bath Spa Competition, 1988. Memberships: Royal Institute of British Architects; Architectural Association; The Academy of Experts; The Association of Consultant Architects; The Carlton Club, London; Berkshire Automobile Club; The Wandsworth Society; The Putney Society; The River Thames Society; The Victorian Society; SAVE; Wandsworth Chamber of Commerce. Address: 11 Prospect Place, Newbury, Berkshire RG14 7PZ, England. E-mail: admin@rosemont.co.uk

ROSEN Norma, b. 11 August 1925, New York, New York, USA. Writer; Teacher. m. Robert S Rosen, 1960, 1 son, 1 daughter. Education: BA, Mt Holyoke College, 1946; MA, Columbia University, 1953. Appointments: Teacher, Creative Writing, New School for Social Research, New York City, 1965-69, University of Pennsylvania, 1969, Harvard University, 1971, Yale University, 1984, New York University, 1987-95. Publications: Joy to Levine!, 1962; Green, 1967; Touching Evil, 1969; At the Center, 1982; John and Anzia: An American Romance, 1989; Accidents of Influence: Writing as a Woman and a Jew in America (essays), 1992; Biblical Women Unbound: Counter-Tales (narratives), 1996. Contributions to: Anthologies and other publications. Honours: Saxton, 1960; CAPS, 1976; Bunting Institute 1971-73. Memberships: PEN; Authors Guild; Phi Beta Kappa. Address: 133 East 35th Street, New York, NY 10016, USA.

ROSENKNOP John, b. 28 December 1929, Moscow. Mathematician. Education: Diploma, Moscow University, 1952; Scientific degree, equivalent to DSc, Kazan University, 1962. Appointments: Lecturer, Moscow Regional Pedagogical Institute, 1953-77; Free scientific associate (translations, reviewing), Zentralblatt fur Mathematik, 1980-99; Independent researcher and publisher, 1998-. Publications: Over 30 articles and a book in mathematics; Short communications on several international mathematical congresses. Honours: Several awards at student and pre-student time, 1945-52; Special Gröbner bases co-inventor Award, 1998. Memberships: Moscow Mathematical Society, -1977; American Mathematical Society. E-mail: Rosenknop2002@yahoo.de

ROSENSTOCK Gabriel Stefan, b. 29 September 1949, County Limerick, Ireland. Poet; Editor; Broadcaster; Translator. m. Eithne Ní Chléirigh, 1 son, 3 daughters. Appointment: Former Chairman, Poetry Ireland. Publications: Portrait of The Artist as an Abominable Snowman, 1989; Oráistí, 1991; The Confessions of Henry Hooter the Third, 1992; Hymn to the Earth, 2004. Contributions to: Poetry Ireland Review; Cyphers; Innti; Comhar; Celtic Dawn; Poetry USA; Irish Times; Ireland Journal; Die Andere; Krino; Poetry (Chicago); Tratti; Sirena; Neue Zürcher Zeitung; Akzente; Éire-Ireland; The Literary Review; Cinnamon Review; Author, Translator of over 100 books. Honours: Arts Council Bursary, 1988; Irish-American Cultural Foundation Award, 1989; Various Oireachtas prizes; Member Aosdana, Irish Academy of Arts and Letters. Memberships: Irish Writer's Union; Irish Translators' Association; British Haiku Society; Haiku Society of America; World Haiku Club; World Haiku Association. Address: 37 Arnold Grove, Glenageary, Co Dublin, Ireland. E-mail: grosenstock@forasnagaeilge.ie

ROSENTHAL Barbara, b. 17 August 1948, The Bronx, New York City. Photographer; Conceptual Artist; Video Artist; Artist. 2 daughters. Education: BFA Painting, Carnegie-Mellon University,

Pittsburgh, Pennsylvania, 1970; MFA, Painting, Queens College, City University of New York, 1973. Appointments: Parsons School of Design, New School University; CUNY; College of Staten Island; Nassau Community College; University of Bridgeport; Jersey City State College; School of Visual Arts; Stephens College. Civic Activities: Co-Director, eMediaLoft (helping artists to realize their projects). Publications: Soul & Psyche; Homo Futurus; Sensations; Clues to Myself. Commissions and Creative Works: Collections: Museum of Modern Art; Whitney Museum of American Art. Gallery: Monique Goldstrom Gallery, NYC. Honours: CAPS Grant; Experimental Video Center Finishing Funds; Harvest Works Finishing Fund; Visual Studies Workshop Artist-in-Residence Media Access; Adapters Creative Projects Grant. Address: 463 West St, #A-628, New York, NY 10014-2035, USA.

ROSHCHINA Valentina D, b. 7 April 1922, Bryansk, Russia. Plant Physiologist. m. Vladimir P Roshchin, 1 daughter. Education: Student, Biology Faculty of Moscow State University, 1940-46; Postgraduate Student, Lesgaft Natural Scientific Institute, 1947-49; PhD, 1951; DSc, Institute of Plant Physiology of the Ukrainian Academy of Science, Kiev, 1974. Appointments: Lecturer, Vozonezh Forest State Institute and Vozonezh State Pedagogical Institute, Professor, 1974-81; Honorary Professor, Cell Biophysics Institute, Pushchino, Moscow, 1981-. Publications: Monograph: The excretory function of higher plants, 1989; English variant, 1993; Ozone and Plant Cell, 2003; Papers in scientific journals. Address: Institute of Cell Biophysics, Pushchino, Moscow Region, 142292, Russia.

ROSS Diana, b. 26 March 1944, Detroit, Michigan, USA. Singer; Entertainer; Actress; Fashion Designer. m. (1) Robert Ellis Silberstein, 1971, 3 daughters; (2) Arne Ness, 23 October 1985, 1 son. Career: Backing singer, the Temptations, Marvin Gaye, Mary Wells; Lead singer, Diana Ross and The Supremes; Solo artiste, 1969-; Appearances include: Opening ceremonies, Football World Cup, USA, 1994; Rugby World Cup, South Africa, 1995; Film appearances: Lady Sings The Blues, 1972; Mahogany, 1975; The Wiz, 1978; Television specials: An Evening With Diana Ross, 1977; Diana, 1980; Christmas In Vienna, 1992; Business ventures: Diana Ross Enterprises Inc; Anaid Film Productions; RTM Management Corp; Chondee Inc. Recordings: Albums include: Diana Ross, 1970; Lady Sings The Blues, 1972; Touch Me In The Morning, 1973; The Boss, 1979; Why Do Fools Fall In Love?, 1981; Eaten Alive, 1984; Silk Electric, 1982; Chain Reaction, 1986; Ain't No Mountain High Enough, 1989; The Force Behind The Power, 1991; Motown's Greatest Hits, 1992; Live...Stolen Moments, 1993; One Woman - The Ultimate Collection, 1993; The Remixes, 1994; Take Me Higher, 1995; Very Special Christmas, 1998; Every Day is a New Day, 1999. Publication: Secrets Of A Sparrow (autobiography), 1993. Honours include: Citations: Vice-President Humphrey; Mrs Martin Luther King, Rev Abernathy; Billboard award: Record World award, World's Outstanding Singer; Grammy Award, 1970; Female Entertainer Of The Year, NAACP, 1970; Golden Globe, 1972; Antoinette Perry Award, 1977; Nominated Rock and Roll Hall Of Fame, 1988. Address: RTC Management, PO Box 1683, New York, NY 10185, USA.

ROSS James Magnus, b. 3 March 1972, United Kingdom. Orchestra Conductor. Education: MA, History, 1993, MST, Music, 1994, D Phil, Music, 1998, Christ Church, Oxford University. Appointments: Music Director: Christ Church Festival Orchestra, 1993-, Chorus and Orchestra, Royal College of Paediatricians, 1994-, Northampton University Orchestra, 2001-, Welwyn Garden City Music Society, 2000-, St Albans Symphony Orchestra, 2001-; Guest Conductor: Sarajevo Philharmonic Orchestra, Bosnia, 1998, 1999,

Dictionary of International Biography

Oxford University PhilharmoniA, UK, 1999, Camden Chamber Orchestra, UK, 1999, Oxford Opera Society, UK, 1999; Bologna University Chamber Choir, Italy, 2002, Harbin Symphony Orchestra, China, 2002; Nis Symphony Orchestra, Serbia, 2002, Symphony Orchestra of Sri Lanka, Sri Lanka, 2001, 2003. Publications: Book chapters: Music in the French Salon in French Music since Berlioz (eds. C Potter and R Langham Smith, 2004; Republican Patriotism in the Third Republic Opera in Nationalism and Identity in Third Republic France (ed. B Kelly), 2004; Vincent d'Indy l'interpreté in Vincent d'Indy et son temps, 2004; Articles and reviews in professional journals include: D'Indy's Fervaal: Reconstructing French Identity at the Fin de Siècle, 2003. Honours include: British Academy Studentship, 1993-97; Osgood Award, 1996; Sir Donald Tovey Memorial Prize, 1998. Memberships: Performers and Composers Section, Incorporated Society of Musicians, UK; Conductors Guild, USA. E-mail: conductor@saso.org.uk Website: www.james-ross.com

ROSS Nicholas David (Nick), b. 7 August 1947, London, England. Broadcaster. m. Sarah Patricia Ann Caplin, 3 sons. Education: BA (Hons), Psychology, Queen's University Belfast. Appointments: Broadcaster and Moderator; Freelance 1971-; Television: Northern Ireland's main news, 1971-72; Man Alive, BBC2, 1976-83; Out of Court, BBC2, 1981-84; Breakfast Time & Sixty Minutes, BBC1, 1983-85; Crimewatch UK, BBC1 1984-; A Week in Politics, Channel 4, 1985; Star Memories, BBC1, 1985; Crimewatch File, BBC1, 1986-; Watchdog, Presenter, BBC1, 1985-86; Crime Limited, BBC1, 1992-95; Westminster with Nick Ross, BBC2, 1994-97; Party Conferences live coverage, BBC2, 1997; Election Campaign, BBC2, 1997; Trail of Guilt, BBC1, 1999; Nick Ross, BBC2, 1999; Destination Nightmares, BBC1, 1999-2000; Storm Alert, BBC1, 1999; The Syndicate, BBC1, 2000; The Search, BBC1, 1999-2000; British Bravery Awards, BBC1, 2000; So You Think You Know How to Drive, BBC1, 1999-2002; Radio: Call Nick Ross, 1986-97; The Commission, 1998-. Publications: Various newspaper and magazine articles. Honours: Radio Broadcaster of the Year, Broadcasting Press Guild Awards, 1996; Winner, Best TV Documentary, Celtic Film Festival, 1999; Winner, Best Factual Programme, TV Quick Awards, 2001; Honorary Doctorate, Queen's University, Belfast. Memberships: Fellow, Royal Society of Arts, Fellow Royal Society of Medicine; Ambassador World Wildlife Fund; Chairman, Jill Dando Institute of Crime Science, University College London; Nuffield Council of Bioethics; President, Healthwatch; Advisory Board, Victim Support; Director, Health Quality Service; Patron: Saneline, National Missing Persons Helpline, Apex Trust, National Depression Campaign, Prisoners Abroad, Simon Community Northern Ireland. Address: PO Box 999, London W2 4XT, England. E-mail: nickross@lineone.net

ROSS Pamela Angela, b. 9 December 1964, Nashville, Tennessee, USA. Emergency Medicine Physician. Education: BA, Chemistry, University of Tennessee, Chatanooga, USA, 1987; MD, Emory University School of Medicine, 1991. Appointment: Emergency Medicine Physician, Virginia College of Emergency Physicians, University of Virginia, USA. Honours: Listed in Who's Who publications and biographical dictionaries. Address: 133 Woodlake Drive, Charlottesville, VA 22901, USA.

ROSS Tony, b. 10 August 1938, London, England. Writer; Illustrator. m. Zoe, 3 daughters. Education: Liverpool Regional College of Art. Career: Freelance Writer, Illustrator, Filmmaker; Lecturer in Graphic Design, Manchester Polytechnic; Art Director, Advertising Agency; Graphic Designer for various companies; Cartoonist. Publications: Author of approximately 80 children's books; Illustrator of approximately 700 children's books including: I Want My Potty (series); Dr Xargle (series); Little Wolf (series);

Horrid Henry (series); Just William (series); I'm Coming to Get You; Don't Do That; Super Dooper Jezebel; Alice in Wonderland; Worzel Gummidge; Pippi Longstocking; Towser; Figgie Hobbin. Honours: Deutschen Jugend Literatur Preis; Silveren Penseel; Silveren Griffel; National Art Library Award; Awards and exhibitions in England, America, Mexico, Japan, Holland, Germany, France. Membership: Chelsea Arts Club. Address: Andersen Press, 20 Vauxhall Bridge Road, London SW1V 2SA, England.

ROSS Wayne Bruce, b. 25 August 1950, Sacramento, California, USA. Toxicologist. m. Michele, 2 sons, 1 daughter. Education: BSc, Biological Science, concentration in Medical Laboratory Science, California State Polytechnic University, 1973; MSc, Clinical Laboratory Science, concentration in Clinical Chemistry and Analytical Toxicology, University of California, San Francisco, 1986. Appointments: Clinical Laboratory Scientist License, State of California Department of Health; Fellow, National Academy of Clinical Biochemistry; Diplomate, American Board of Forensic Examiners; Medical Technologist, American Association of Bioanalysts' Board of Registry. Publications: Specimen Collection for Drugs of Abuse Testing, 1992; Detection of Drug Abuse by Health Professionals (co-author), 2002. Memberships: American Association of Clinical Chemistry; American Academy of Forensic Sciences; California Association of Toxicologists; American College of Forensic Examiners; American Association of Bioanalysts. Address: 1377 Wikiup Drive, Santa Rosa, CA 95403, USA. E-mail: wayne@redwoodtoxicology.com

ROSS-MACDONALD M(alcolm) J(ohn), (Malcolm Macdonald, Malcolm Ross, M R O'Donnell), b. 29 February 1932, Chipping, Sodbury, Gloucestershire, England. Freelance Writer; Editor; Designer. m. Ingrid Giehr, 2 daughters. Education: Falmouth School of Art, 1950-54; Slade Diploma, University College, London, 1958. Appointments: Lektor, Folk University, Sweden, 1959-61; Executive Editor, Aldus Books, 1962-65; Visiting Lecturer, Hornsey College of Art, 1965-69. Publications: The Big Waves, 1962; Macdonald Illustrated Encyclopaedia (executive editor), 10 volumes, 1962-65; Spare Part Surgery (co-author), 1968; Machines in Medicine, 1969; The Human Heart, 1970; World Wildlife Guide, 1971; Beyond the Horizon, 1971; Every Living Thing, 1973; World from Rough Stones, 1974; Origin of Johnny, 1975; Life in the Future, 1976; The Rich Are With You Always, 1976; Sons of Fortune, 1978; Abigail, 1979; Goldeneye, 1981; The Dukes, 1982; Tessa'd'Arblay, 1983; In Love and War, 1984; Mistress of Pallas, 1986; Silver Highways, 1987; The Sky with Diamonds, 1988; A Notorious Woman, 1988; His Father's Son, 1989; An Innocent Woman, 1989; Hell Hath No Fury, 1990; A Woman Alone, 1990; The Captain's Wives, 1991; A Woman Scorned, 1991; A Woman Possessed, 1992; All Desires Known, 1993; To the End of Her Days, 1993; Dancing on Snowflakes, 1994; For I Have Sinned, 1994; Kernow and Daughter, 1994; Crissy's Family, 1995; Tomorrow's Tide, 1996; The Carringtons of Helston, 1997; Like a Diamond, 1998; Tamsin Harte, 2000; Rose of Nancemellin, 2001. Contributions to: Sunday Times; New Scientist; Science Journal; Month; Jefferson Encyclopaedia. Memberships: Authors Guild; Society of Authors. Address: c/o David Higham Ltd, 5-8 Lower John Street, London W1R 4HA, England.

ROSSELLINI Isabella, b. 18 June 1956, Rome, Italy (US citizen). Actress; Model. m. (1) M Scorsese, 1979, divorced 1982, (2) J Wiedemann, divorced, 1 daughter. Education: Rome Academy of Fashion and Costume; New York School for Social Research. Career: Costume Designer for Roberto Rossellini (father), New York, 1972; Journalist for Italian TV; Vogue Cover Girl, 1980; Contracted to Lancome Cosmetics, 1982-95; Vice President,

Dictionary of International Biography

Marketing Department, Lancaster Cosmetics GPs, 1995-; As Actress: Films include: A Matter of Time, 1976; Blue Velvet, 1986; Cousins, 1989; Wild at Heart, 1990; Death Becomes Her, 1994; Immortal Beloved, 1994; Wyatt Earp, 1994; The Innocent, 1995; The Funeral, 1996; Big Night, 1996; Crime of the Century, 1996; Left Luggage, 1998; The Imposters, 1998; The Real Blonde, 1998; Don Quixote, 2000; Il Cielo cade, 2000; Empire, 2002; Roger Dodger, 2002; The Tulse Luper Suitcases: The Moab Story, 2003; The Saddest Music in the World, 2003; The Tulse Luper Suitcases, Episode 3, Antwerp, 2003. Address: c/o United Talent Agency, 9560 Wilshire Boulevard, Floor 5, Beverly Hill, CA 90212, USA.

ROSSOR Martin Neil, b. 24 April 1950, London, England. Physician. m. Eve, 2 sons, 1 daughter. Education: Jesus College Cambridge, 1968-71; Kings College Hospital Medical School, London, 1971-74; MB BChir, 1974; MA, 1975; MD, 1986; FRCP, 1990. Appointments: Consultant Neurologist to National Hospital for Neurology and St Mary's Hospital, London; Professor of Clinical Neurology (Personal Chair), Imperial College, London, 2000-; Professor of Neurology, Institute of Neurology, University College London, 2002-. Publications: Articles on neurology and dementia; Editor-in-Chief, Journal of Neurology, Neurosurgery and Psychiatry, 2004-; Author, Unusual Dementias, 1992; Co-author, The Dementias, 1998; Co-author, Dementia Handbook, 1999. Memberships: Court Assistant, Society of Apothecaries, London, 1999-; Member of Council, Association of British Neurologists, 2004-. Address: National Hospital for Neurology and Neurosurgery, Queen Square, London, WC1N 3BG, England.

ROSSWICK Robert Paul, b. 1 June 1932. Consultant, General and Endocrine Surgery. Education: MB BS (Lond), The London Hospital Medical College, 1955; D Obst, RCOG, 1957; FRCS (Eng), 1961; MS (Surgery), Illinois, 1963; MAE, 1997. Appointments: House Surgeon, Poplar Hospital, London, England, 1955-1956; House Physician, Swindon Hospital, Wiltshire, 1956; Obstetric SHO, Greenwich Hospital, London, 1957; Lecturer in Anatomy, Kings College, London, 1957-59; Surgical SHO, 1959-1960, Locum SHO, 1963, The London Hospital; Surgical Registrar, St Andrew's, Bow, London, 1961-62; Surgical Registrar, Harold Wood Hospital, Essex, 1963-64; Surgical Registrar, 1964-66; Senior Registrar, 1966-70, St George's Hospital, London; Senior Registrar, Winchester and Royal Marsden Hospital, 1966-1970; Consultant-in-Charge, Accident and Emergency Department, 1970-74, Consultant Surgeon, 1970-93, Honorary Senior Lecturer in Surgery, St George's Hospital Medical School, 1970-93, St George's Hospital, London; Surgeon, The Royal Masonic Hospital, 1975-1993; Examiner in Surgery: The University of London; The Society of Apothecaries; PLAB. Publications: Numerous papers on abdominal surgery, thyroid surgery; Letters in medical journals; Addresses to medical societies; Presidential address, The Medical Society of London, a review of 1000 thyroidectomies, 1990. Honours: Robertson-Exchange Fellow in Surgery, Rush-Presbyterian-St Luke's Hospital, Chicago, USA, 1962-63; Past member of Council, Section of Surgery, Royal Society of Medicine; Chairman, Wandsworth Division, 1984-87, Delgate, ARM, etc, British Medical Association; Councillor, Hunterian Society, 1987-1995; Editor, 1984-1989, President, 1990-1991, Treasurer and Trustee, 1994-, The Medical Society of London. Memberships: Fellow: The Association of Surgeons; The British Association of Endocrine Surgeons; The CRC Multiple Endocrine Neoplasia Group; The British Society of Gastroenterology; The Collegium Internationale of Chirurgicae Digestiva; The Chelsea Clinical Society; Liveryman: The Worshipful Society of Apothecaries; Treasurer, Livery Committee, 1992-96; Member: Independent Doctors Forum; Medical Appeals Tribunals, Independent Tribunal Service; The Academy of Experts; UK Register of Expert Witnesses. Address: 110 Lorian Close, Holden Road, London N12 7DZ, England.

ROTBLAT Joseph (Sir), b. 4 November 1908, Warsaw, Poland. Professor Emeritus; Writer. Education: MA, University of Warsaw; PhD, University of Liverpool. Appointments: Professor, 1950-76, Professor Emeritus, 1976-, Medical College of St Batholomew's Hospital, University of London; Editor, Physics in Medicine and Biology, 1960-73; President, Pugwash Conferences on Science and World Affairs, 1988-; Emeritus, 1997. Publications: Radioactivity and Radioactive Substances (with Sir James Chadwick), 1961; Science and World Affairs, 1962; The Uses and Effects of Nuclear Energy (co-author), 1964; Aspects of Medical Physics (editor), 1966; Pugwash: The First Ten Years, 1967; Scientists in the Quest for Peace: A History of the Pugwash Conferences, 1972; Nuclear Reactors: To Breed or Not to Breed, 1977; Nuclear Energy and Nuclear Weapon Proliferation, 1979; Nuclear Radiation in Warfare, 1981; Scientists, the Arms Race and Disarmament, 1982; The Arms Race at a Time of Decision, 1984; Nuclear Strategy and World Security, 1985; World Peace and the Developing Countries, 1986; Strategic Defence and the Future of the Arms Race, 1987; Co-existence, Co-operation and Common Security, 1988; Verification of Arms Reductions, 1989; Global Problems and Common Security, 1989; Nuclear Proliferation: Technical and Economic Aspects, 1990; Global Security Through Co-Operation, 1990; Towards a Secure World in the 21st Century, 1991; Striving for Peace, Security and Development in the World, 1992; A Nuclear-Weapon-Free World: Desirable? Feasible?, 1993; World Citizenship: Allegiance to Humanity, 1997; Nuclear Weapons: The Road to Zero, 1998. Honours: Commander of the Order of the British Empire, 1965; Albert Einstein Peace Prize, 1992; Fellow, Royal Society, 1995; Nobel Prize for Peace, 1995; Knight Commander of the Order of St. Michael and St. George, 1998. Address: 8 Asmara Road, London NW2 3ST, England.

ROTENBERG Vadim, b. 5 August 1941, Kirov, USSR. Physician; Scientist. m. Samarovich Nataly, 2 daughters. Education: MD, 1st Moscow Medical Institute, 1964; Postgraduate Student, Academy of Sciences, USSR, 1966-69; PhD, 1970; DSc, 1979. Appointments: Junior Doctor, City Hospital, Moscow, 1964-66; Junior Scientist, 1st Moscow Medical Institute, 1969-78, Senior Scientist, 1978-88, Head of Laboratory, 1988-90; Emigration to Israel, 1990; Head Laboratory Abarbanel Mental Health Centre Bat-Iam, Israel, 1992-2001; Senior Lecturer, Tel Aviv University, 1995-; Head Psychologic Project Zionist Forum, 1996-2002. Publications: Over 150 scientific articles in professional journals; Books: The Adaptive Function of Sleep, 1982; Search Activity and Adaption, 1984; Self Image and Behaviour, 2001; Dreams, Hypnosis and Brain Activity, 2001. Honours: Best Annual Science Publication, Moscow Medical Institute, 1982, 1984; Wolfsson Grant for Outstanding Scientists, Tel-Aviv, 1992; Listed in Who's Who publications. Memberships: European Society Sleep Research; International Psychophysiological Society; New York Academy of Sciences. Address: Abarbanel Mental Health Centre, Keren Kayemet 15, Bat-Yam, Israel.

ROTH Andrew, b. 23 April 1919, New York, New York, USA. Political Correspondent. m. Mathilda Anna Friederich, 1949, divorced 1984, 1 son, 1 daughter. Education: BSS, City College of New York, 1939; MA, Columbia University, 1940; Harvard University. Appointments: Reader, City College, 1939; Research Associate, Institute of Pacific Relations, 1940; Editorial Writer, The Nation, 1945-46; Foreign Correspondent, Toronto Star Weekly, 1946-50; London Correspondent, France Observateur, Sekai, Singapore Standard, 1950-60; Director, Parliamentary Profiles, 1955-; Political Correspondent, Manchester Evening News, 1972-84; New Statesman, 1984-96. Publications: Japan Strikes South, 1941; French Interests and Policies in the Far East, 1942; Dilemma in Japan, 1945; The Business Background of MPs,

Dictionary of International Biography

1959, 7th edition, 1980; The MPs Chart, 1967, 6th edition, 1987; Enoch Powell: Tory Tribune, 1970; Can Parliament Decide..., 1971; Heath and the Heathmen, 1972; Lord on the Board, 1972; Sir Harold Wilson: Yorkshire Walter Mitty, 1977; Parliamentary Profiles, Vols I-IV, 1984-85, 2nd edition, 1988-90; 4th edition, 1998; New MPs of '92, 1992; Mr Nice Guy and His Chums, 1993; New MPs of '97, 1997. Address: 34 Somali Road, London NW2 3RL, England.

ROTH Tim, b. 1961, Dulwich, England. Actor. Education: Brixton and Camberwell College of Art. m. Nikki Butler, 1993, 2 sons (1 son from previous relationship). Career: Fringe groups including: Glasgow Citizens Theatre, The Oval House and the Royal Court; Appeared on London stage in Metamorphis; Numerous TV appearances; Films: The Hit; A World Apart; The Cook, The Thief, His Wife and Her Lover; Vincent and Theo; Rosencrantz and Guildenstern are Dead; Jumpin at the Boneyard; Resevoir Dogs; Bodies Rest and Motion; Pulp Fiction; Little Odessa; Rob Roy; Captives; Four Rooms; Hoodlums; Everyone Says I Love You; Liar; The War Zone (director); The Legend of 1900, Vatel; Lucky Numbers; Planet of the Apes; Invincible; The Musketeer; Emmett's Mark; Whatever We Do; To Kill A King; With It. Address: Ilene Feldman Agency, 8730 West Sunset Boulevard, Suite 490, Los Angeles, CA 90069, USA.

ROTHSCHILD Evelyn de (Sir), b. 29 August 1931. Banker. m. (1) Victoria Schott, 1972, dissolved 2000, 2 sons, 1 daughter, (2) Lynn Forester, 2000. Education: Trinity College, Cambridge. Appointments: Chairman, Economist Newspaper, 1972-89, United Racecourses Ltd, 1977-94, British Merchant Banking and Securities Houses Association (formerly Accepting Houses Committee), 1985-89; Chairman, N M Rothschild and Sons Ltd, 1976-. Address: N M Rothschild & Sons Ltd, New Court, St Swithin's Lane, London, EC 4, England.

RÖTTSCHER Peter, b. 10 October 1946, Göttingen, Germany. Chief Information Officer. Divorced, 1 son, 1 daughter. Education: Diploma, French Language and Civilisation, University of Lyon, Lyon, France, 1969-70; MA, Ludwig Maximilian University, Munich, Germany, 1970-73; Librarian Diploma VSB, Swiss Librarians' Association, Bern, Switzerland, 1976-80. Appointments: Chief Information Officer, Motor-Columbus Consulting Engineers, Baden, Switzerland, 1973-77; Chief Information Officer, Migros-Genossenschafts-Bund, Zürich, Switzerland, 1978-; Consultant, Institut für Empirische Wirtschaftsforschung, Zürich, Switzerland, 2001-2003. Publications: Books: Fünf Bemerkungen zur Bildsprache Lautréamont's, 1972; Terminologie der Dokumentation D/E/F/I/S, 1977; Librarium Register 1958-79, 1980; Postkarten für Bücherfreunde (editor), 1989. Honours: Ehrenpreis der Stadt Hildesheim, Germany, 1964; Deutsche Bestennadel, Deutscher Leichtathletik-Verband, 1964. Memberships: Association Internationale de Bibliophilie; Everly Brothers International; Deutsche Ludwig Wittgenstein-Gesellschaft; Deutsche Schiller-Gesellschaft; Lichtenberg-Gesellschaft; International Society for Contemporary Legend Research. Address: Frohbühlstrasse 7, CH-8052 Zürich, Switzerland. E-mail: peter.roettscher@mgb.ch

ROULSTON John Frank Clement, b. 12 August 1941, Brisbane, Australia. Association Executive Director. m. Lynette Catherine Burgess, 1 son, 1 daughter. Education: Cert. Teach., Kelvin Grove Teachers College, 1960; B. Ed., University of Queensland, 1967; M. Litt., 1972, M. Ed. Admin., 1975, University of New England; PhD, University of Idaho, USA, 1976. Appointments: Teacher, Subject Master, Deputy Principal, Principal of State Primary and Secondary Schools in Queensland, Australia, 1960-73; Principal, Cromwell College, University of Queensland, 1973-75; Senior

Lecturer, Education, Brisbane College of Advanced Education, 1977-84; Director, Education and Communication, The Uniting Church in Australia, 1985-95; Moderator Queensland Synod, Uniting Church in Australia, 1990-91; Executive Director, Association of Independent Schools, Queensland, Australia, 1995-. Publications: Numerous articles in educational journals, magazines and professional speakers publications; Co-author, published research reports on education and social policy issues; Numerous keynote addresses to a variety of audiences in Australia and internationally. Honours: National Travel Scholar, Australian Council for Educational Administration, 1988; Nganakarrawa Award in Educational Leadership, 1997; Walter Dickman National Award, National Speakers Association of Australia, 2002; Centenary of Federation Medal of Australian Government for Services to Education, 2003. Memberships: Fellow and Life Member, Australian College of Educators; Fellow, Australian Institute of Management; Fellow Queensland Institute of Educational Administration; Fellow Australian Institute of Educational Leaders; Phi Delta Kappa, USA. Address: 20 Noreen Street, Chapel Hill, Queensland 4069, Australia. E-mail: jroulston@aisq.qld.edu.au Website: www.aisq.qld.edu.au

ROURKE Mickey Philip Andre, b. 1956, New York, USA. Actor; Boxer. m. (1) Debra Fuer, (2) Carre Otis, divorced. Education: Actor's Studio, New York, USA. Career: Film appearances include: Fade to Black, 1941, 1979; Heaven's Gate, 1980; Body Heat, 1981; Diner, 1982; Eureka, 1983; Rumblefish, 1983; Rusty James, 1983; The Pope of Greenwich Village, 1984; 9½ Weeks, 1984; Year of the Dragon, 1985; Angel Heart, 1986; A Prayer for the Dying, 1986; Barfly, 1987; Johnny Handsome, 1989; Homeboy, 1989; Francesco, 1989; The Crew, 1989; The Desperate Hours, 1990; Wild Orchid, 1990; On the Sport, 1990; Harley Davidson and the Marlboro Man, 1991; White Sands, 1992; FTW; Fall Time; Double Time; Another 9½ Weeks; The Rainmaker, 1997; Love in Paris, 1997; Double Team, 1997; Buffalo '66, 1997; Thursday, 1998; Shergar, 1999; Shades, 1999; Out in Fifty, 1999; The Animal Factory, 2000; Get Carter, 2000; The Pledge, 2001; The Hire: Follow, 2001; Picture Claire, 2001; They Crawl, 2001; Spun, 2002; Masked and Anonymous, 2003; Once Upon A Time in Mexico, 2003; Driv3r (voice), 2004; Man on Fire, 2004.

ROUSE Prudence Alison, b. 8 August 1944, Epsom, Surrey, UK. Linguist. m. Grahame T Rouse, deceased 1998, 2 sons. Education: English and Spanish, Mrs Hoster's Secretarial College, London, 1962-63; Silver Medal in Spanish, London Chamber of Commerce, 1963; Diploma in French, Institute of Linguists, 1987; Honours Degree, Spanish, Institute of Linguists, London, 1987. Appointments: Executive Director, Sigma Security Services Ltd, Fiji Islands, 1998-2003; Vice President, Women in Business, Fiji Islands, 1998-2001; Fiji Government Planning Committee for Law & Order, 2003-04; Chairperson, Western Fiji Crimestoppers' Board, 2004-05; Delegate, Soroptimist International Pacific Region Conference, New Zealand, 2004. Memberships: Vice President, Fiji Committee of the Royal Commonwealth Society, 1998-2004; Associate Member, Fiji Hotel Association; The Royal Overseas League, London; Royal Commonwealth Society of Fiji and Great Britain; Human Rights Convenor, 2004-05; Nadi Soroptimists, Human Rights Convenor and Womens' Status; Chair, Vuda Pour Police Post, 1999-2004. Honour: Silver Medal in Spanish, London Chamber of Commerce, 1963. Address: PO Box 10051, Nadi Airport, Fiji Islands. E-mail: rousesigma@connect.com.fj

ROUX Albert Henri, b. 8 October 1935, Smur-en-Broinnais, France. Chef; Restaurateur. m. Monique Merle, 1959, 1 son, 1 daughter. Appointments: Military service, Algeria; Founder (with brother Michel Roux), Le Gavroche Restaurant, London (now co-owner with son Michel J), 1967-; The Waterside Inn, Bray (now sole owner), 1972-; Opened 47 Park Street Hotel, 1981; Opened Le Poulbot, le gamin, Gavvers, Les Trois Plats and Rouxl Britannia (all as part of Roux Restaurants Ltd), 1969-87; Began consultant practice, 1989. Publications: (with Michel Roux) New Classic Cuisine, 1983; The Roux Brothers on Pâtisserie, 1986; The Roux Brothers on French Country Cooking, 1989; Cooking for Two, 1991. Honours: Maître Cuisinier de France, 1968; Honorary Professor, Bournemouth University, 1995-; Chevalier du Mérite Agricole; Honorary DSc (Council for National Academic Awards), 1987. Memberships: Founder Member, Academy Culinaire de Grande Bretagne. Address: Le Gavroche, 43 Upper Brook Street, London, W1Y 1PF, England.

ROUX Michel André, b. 19 April 1941. Chef; Restaurateur. m. (1) Francoise Marcelle Becquet, divorced 1979, 1 son, 2 daughters. (2) Robyn Margaret Joyce, 1984. Appointments: Commis Patissier and Cuisinier, British Embassy, Paris, 1955-57; Commis Cook to Cécile de Rothschild, 1957-59, Chef, 1962-67; Military Service, 1960-62; Proprietor: Le Gavroche, 1967, The Waterside Inn, 1972, Le Gavroche, Mayfair, 1981. Publications: New Classic Cuisine, 1983; Roux Brothers on Patisserie, 1986; At Home With the Roux Brothers, 1987; French Country Cooking, 1989; Cooking for Two, 1991; Desserts, A Lifelong Passion, 1994; Sauces, 1996; Life is a Menu, autobiography, 2000; Only the Best, 2002. Honours: Numerous Culinary Awards including: Gold Medal, Cuisiniers Français, Paris, 1972; Laureate Restaurateur of the Year, 1985; Chevalier, Ordre National du Mérite, 1987; Ordre des Arts et des Lettres, 1990; Honorary OBE, 2002; Numerous other awards and decorations. Memberships: Academician, Culinaire de France, English Branch; Association Relais et Desserts; Association Relais et Chateaux. Address: The Waterside Inn, Ferry Road, Berkshire SL6 2AT, England.

ROWE John Richard, b. 1 August 1942, Woodford, Essex. Film and Television Producer and Director. m. Rosa Mary Balls. Education: Royal Society of the Arts Education Certificate in English Literature. Appointments: Cutting Rooms and Film Library, 20th Century Fox, 1958-61; Film Researcher, Associated Redifusion, 1962-65; Film Researcher first major ITV documentary series, The Life and Times of Lord Mountbatten, 1965-69; Film Researcher, Thames television, 1965-69; Principal Film Researcher, The World at War, 1971-74; Head of Production Research, Thames Television, 1972-82; Head of Programming, Sky Television, 1982-84; Head of Production, British Sky Broadcasting, 1984-93; Executive Producer and set up television side of QVC, The Shopping Channel, 1993-95; Producer and Director TV commercials for various clients, 1995-96; Producer, Director for Screeners, 13 half hour shows on the cinema, 1997; Producer, Director, children's series, Blue's Clues, 1997-2002; Producer, Director, children's comedy show, Havakazoo, 65 half hour shows, 2001; Director, Documentary on Anthony Quinn, Reflections in the Eye, 2001; Director, Monkey Makes, 2003; Currently, Chief Executive John Rowe Productions. Publications: In depth interview, Televisual, 1983; Contributor to: Satellite Wars, Channel 4, 1993. Honour: Part of the Emmy Award winning team for The World at War. Address: 24 Long Hill, Mere, Warminster, Wiltshire, BA12 6LR, England.

ROWLAND-ENTWISTLE (Arthur) Theodore (Henry), b. 30 July 1925, Clayton-le-Moors, Lancashire, England. Writer. Education: BA Honours, BSc, Open University. Publications: Famous Composers (with J Cooke), 1974; Animal Worlds (with J Cooke), 1975; Famous Explorers (with J Cooke), 1975; Facts and Records Book of Animals, 1975; Famous Kings and Emperors (with J Cooke), 1977; The World You Never See: Insect Life, 1976; Our Earth, 1977; The Restless Earth, 1977; Exploring

Animal Homes, 1978; Seashore Life (as T E Henry), 1983; Fishes (as James Hall-Clarke), 1983; Fact Book of British History (with J Cooke), 1984; Heraldry, 1984; Houses, 1985; World of Speed, 1985; Confucius, 1986; Stamps, 1986; Nebuchadnezzar, 1986; Rivers and Lakes, 1986; Focus on Rubber, 1986; Great British Architects, 1986; Great British Inventors, 1986; Great British Kings and Queens, 1986; Great British Reformers, 1986; Focus on Coal, 1987; The Royal Marines, 1987; The Secret Service, 1987; The Special Air Service, 1987; Jungles and Rainforests, 1987; Three-Dimensional Atlas of the World, 1988; Flags, 1988; Guns, 1988; Focus on Silk, 1989; Weather and Climate, 1991; Funfax History of Britain, 1993; Question and Answer Quiz Book (with A Kramer), 1995; World Events and Dates, 1995; Paras, 1997. Contributions to: Various encyclopaedias and periodicals. Memberships: Royal Geographical Society, fellow. Ltd. Address: West Dene, Stonestile Lane, Hastings, Sussex TN35 4PE, England.

ROWLANDS Robert Trevor, b. 15 September 1949, London, England. Scientific Consultant. Education: BSc (Honours), Biological Science, University of Leicester, England, 1971; PhD, Microbial Genetics, University of Bristol, England, 1974. Appointments: Beit Memorial Medical Research Fellow, University of London, England, post held at Department of Bacteriology, University of Bristol Medical School, 1974-77; Section Head, Genetics and Screening Sections, Glaxo Operations, Ulverston, Cumbria, England, 1977-81; Senior Section Head, Strain Improvement Section, Beecham Pharmaceuticals, Worthing, England, 1981-84; Director, Biotechnology Services, Panlabs, Inc., Cardiff, Wales, 1984-98; Self-employed Consultant under the name of Dragon Associates, 1998-. Publications: Over 30 publications in scientific journals and presented at conferences as author and co-author include most recently: The future of the fermentation industry. The shift to developing economic areas of the world, 1999; Rapid and sensitive quantitation of antibiotics in fermentations by electrospray mass spectrometry, 2001; Fermentation yield improvement – Part I. Strain improvement by traditional methods, Part II. Strain improvement by rational screening, Part III. Scale up for selected mutant strains, 2003. Honour; Honorary Lecturer in Applied Microbiology, University of Wales, Cardiff, 1996-2006. Membership: Society for General Microbiology. Address: 22 Adventurers Quay, Cardiff, CF10 4NP. E-mail: bobrowlands@compuserve.com

ROWLEY Rosemarie (Rosemary) Teresa, b. 7 October 1942, Dublin, Ireland. Writer; Poet; Essayist. 1 son. Education: BA, 1969, MLitt, 1984, Trinity College, Dublin, Ireland; Dip Psych, National University of Ireland, 1996. Career: Co-ordinator, Irish Green Party, 1983-87; Poet and Essayist. Publications: The Broken Pledge, 1985; The Sea of Affliction, 1987; Freedom & Censorship – why not have both?, 1987, reprinted 1996; Flight into Reality, 1989, issued on cassette tape, 1996; Hot Cinquefoil Star, 2002; In Memory of Her, forthcoming; Co-editor, Seeing the Wood and the Trees, 2003. Honours: Image/Maxwell House Award, 1988; Scottish International Open Poetry Competition, Long Poem Award, 1996, 1997, 2001, 2004. Memberships: MENSA, UK and Ireland; Irish Byron Society and Shaw Society at United Arts Club; Trinity College Dublin Alumni; Long Poem Group, UK. Address: Booterstown, Co Dublin, Ireland. E-mail: rosemarierowley@yahoo.co.uk

ROWLING J(oanne) K(athleen), b. 1965, Bristol, England. Writer. (1) divorced, 1 daughter, (2) Neil Murray, 2001, 1 son. Education: Graduated, University of Exeter, 1986. Publications: Harry Potter and the Philosopher's Stone, 1997; Harry Potter and the Chamber of Secrets, 1998; Harry Potter and the Prisoner of Azkaban, 1999; Harry Potter and the Goblet of Fire, 2000; Quidditch Through the Ages, 2001; Fantastic Beasts and Where to Find Them, 2001; Harry Potter and the Order of the Phoenix, 2003. Honours: British Book Award Children's Book of the Year, 1997; Rowntree Nestle Smarties Prizes, 1997, 1998; Officer of the Order of the British Empire, 2000. Address: c/o Christopher Little Literary Agency, Ten Eel Brook Studios, 125 Moore Park Road, London SW6 4PS, England. Website: www.jkrowling.com

ROXMAN (Pia) Susanna (Ellinor), b. 29 August 1946, Stockholm, Sweden. Writer; Poet; Literary Scholar. Education: King's College, London University; BA, hons, Comparative Literature, Philosophy, Lund University, Sweden, 1973; PhD, hons, Comparative Literature, Gothenburg University, Sweden, 1984. Appointments: Visiting Lecturer, Lund University and elsewhere, 1976-; Critic on Swedish National Newspapers, 1977-; Head, Centre of Classical Mythology, Lund University, 1996-; Lecturer, Classical Mythology, Department of Classics, Lund University, 2003-. Publications: Written in English: Guilt and Glory: Studies in Margaret Drabble's Novels 1963-80, 1984; Goodbye to the Berlin Wall, 1991; Broken Angels, 1996; Emblems of Classical Deities in Ancient and Modern Pictorial Arts, 2003; Several books written in Swedish; Numerous English poems in Cimarron Review, USA, Crab Orchard Review, USA, The Fiddlehead, Canada, Orbis, UK, Pembroke Magazine, USA, The Spoon River Poetry Review, USA, Staple, UK, Wascana Review, Canada, and many other magazines world-wide; Also more than a couple of thousand arts articles world-wide and scholarly contributions to academic journals, anthologies and encyclopaedias. Honours: Arts Award, County Council of Malmo, Sweden, 1984; Swedish Balzac Prize, 1990; Editor's Choice Prize, Marjorie Lees Linn Poetry Award, USA, 1994, 1995; Arts Award, City of Lund, for Broken Angels, 1996; Whitbread nomination, UK, for Broken Angels, 1997; Second Prize, for short story, Vigil in Berlin, New Fiction Award Contest, New York, 2001; Susanna Roxman is one of the internationally best known Scandinavian poets. Memberships: Authors' Centre South, Sweden; Conservatory of American Letters. Address: Lagerbrings Vag 5B, SE-224 60 Lund, Sweden. E-mail: susanna.roxman@telia.com

ROY Archie William Newton, b. 6 May 1961, Glasgow, Scotland. Education Advisor; Researcher. Education: BA (Hons), Psychology, 1982, PhD, Social-Developmental Psychology, 1987, MSc, Advanced Professional Studies in Education, 2000, University of Strathclyde, Scotland; SVQ Level 4, Guidance, Scottish National Qualifications Board, 2000. Appointments: Tutor in Psychology, University of Strathclyde, 1984-87; Guidance Officer, Centre for Training and Employment, Glasgow, 1988-89; Student Adviser, RNIB, London, 1989-2000; Specialist Visiting Lecturer, Glasgow Caledonian University, 1994-98; Post-16 Education Officer, RNIB, Scotland, 2000-2003; Evaluation Consultant, Real Choices Social Inclusion Consultancy, Nottingham, 2003; Careers Adviser, Universities of Strathclyde and Glasgow, 2003-. Publications: Many books, book chapters and articles in international journals including: Nature, European Journal of Social Psychology, Journal of Visual Impairment and Blindness; Books: Co-editor: Standards in Vocational Guidance for People with a Visual Impairment. A Guide for Practitioners; Author: Student Perspectives: Discussions with Visually Impaired Students on the Effects of Serious Sight Loss on Themselves, Their Families and Friends, 2001; Co-author: Shaping the Future: The Educational Experiences of Blind and Partially Sighted Young People Aged 16 to 25, 2001; Co-author: Equal Access to Technology Training: The IT Needs of People with Vision Impairments and the Related Needs of Training Service Providers, 2003. Honours: Grantee, Charity Know How, Poland, 1991, 1994; Leonardo da Vinci Grant, European Union, 1997; Listed in Who's Who publications and biographical dictionaries. Membership:

National Bureau for Students with Disabilities, London. Address: Flat 3/2, 96 Novar Drive, Glasgow G12 9ST, Scotland. E-mail: archie.roy@btopenworld.com

ROY Arundhati, b. 1961, Bengal, India. Writer. m. (1) Gerard da Cunha, divorced, (2) Pradeep Krishen. Education: Delhi School of Architecture. Appointments: Artist; Actress; Film and Television Writer. Publication: The God of Small Things, 1997; The End of Imagination, essay, 1998; The Great Common Good, essay, 1999; The Cost of Living, collected essays, 2002; The Algebra of Infinite Justice, collected essays, 2002; Screenplays: In Which Annie Gives It Those Ones; Electric Moon. Contributions to: Periodicals. Honour: Booker Prize, 1997. Address: c/o India Ink Publishing Co Pvt Ltd, C-1, Soami Nagar, New Delhi 110 017, India.

ROY Bimalendu Narayan. Professor. m. Manju Rani, 1 son. Education: BSc, Physics, 1958-61, BA, English and Bengali, 1961-63, LLB, Law, 1963-66, University of Calcutta, India; Postgraduate Diploma, Ceramic Diploma, University of Leeds, 1967-68; PhD, Crystal Growth, University of London, 1968-72. Appointments: Lecturer, Universiti Sains Malaysia, Penang, 1973-76; Scientific Officer, Central Glass & Ceramic Research Institute, India, 1977-78; Senior Lecturer, University of Science and Technology, Ghana, 1978-80; Visiting Professor, Montana and Arizona State Universities, USA, 1981-84; Senior Research Fellow, University of Northumbria, UK, 1984-85; Chief Research Officer, University of Essex, UK, 1986-89; Senior Lecturer, Sheffield Hallam University, UK, 1990-91; Senior Lecturer, University of Brunei Darussalam, Brunei, 1993-97; Visiting Scientist, University of Cambridge, UK, 1994, 1995; Senior Research Fellow and Lecturer, Brunel University, UK, 1997-99; Professor and Vice-Rector (Academic Affairs & Research), Polytechnic of Namibia, 2001-02; Professor, Department of Applied Sciences, Papua New Guinea University of Technology, Lae, Papua New Guinea. Publications: Sole author: Crystal Growth From Melts, 1991; Principles of Modern Thermodynamics, 1995; Fundamentals of Classical and Statistical Thermodynamics, 2002; 100 research papers and popular scientific articles. Honours: First Literary Prizes: Belur Higher Secondary School, India, 1951-54; Rotary International, India, 1955; Jawaharlal Nehru Birth Day Celebration Committee, 1955; Central Calcutta College, India, 1960, 1961; Second Literary Prizes: Bally Cultural and Literature Society, Bally, India, 1961; Youth Festival Committee, West Bengal, India, 1964; ABI Gold Medal, USA, 1997. Memberships: Fellow, Chartered Physicist, Institute of Physics, UK; Member, Chartered Chemist, Royal Society of Chemistry, UK; General Secretary, 1985-86, Vice President, 1988-92, community organisation, London; Treasurer, community organisation, Arizona, USA, 1983; Governor and Chairman of Curriculum Committee, Stockwell Park School, London, 1998-2001.

ROY Jagat Kumar, b. 9 October 1957, Kolkata, India. Teacher; Researcher. m. Smriti Roy, 1 son, 1 daughter. Education: BSc, 1976; MSc, 1978; PhD, 1983. Appointments: Scientist 'B' Centre for Cellular and Molecular Biology, Hyderabad, India, 1984-87; Lecturer, 1987-2003, Professor, 2003, Banaras Hindu University, Varanasi, India. Publications: 14 in professional journals, 1979-2000. Honour: Department of Science and Technology, Government of India, Boyscast Fellowship to visit USA, 1990; Department of Biotechnology, Government of India, Associateship to visit Germany, 1999. Memberships: Life Member, Indian Society of Cell Biology; Indian Society of Developmental Biology. Address: B 13/180A, Sonarpura, Varanasi 221001, India.

ROZBRUCH S Robert, 2 September 1965, Brooklyn, New York. Physician; Orthopaedic Surgeon. m. Yonina Jacobs, 1 son, 1 daughter. Education: BA Magna Cum Laude, University of

Dictionary of International Biography

Pennsylvania, 1985; MD Honours in Research, Weill Medical College, Cornell University, 1990; Internship, General Surgery, North Shore University Hospital, Manhasset, New York, 1990-91; Residency in Orthopaedic Surgery, Hospital for Special Surgery, Cornell University, New York, 1991-95. Appointments: Academic Appointments: Clinical Instructor of Orthopaedic Surgery, 1996-2001, Assistant Professor of Orthopaedic Surgery, 2001-, Weill Medical College, Cornell University; Hospital Appointments: Assistant Attending, Department of Orthopaedic Surgery, New York Presbyterian Hospital, Cornell Medical Center, 1996-; Assistant Attending, Co-chief Limb Lengthening Service, 1995-, Director, Institute for Limb Lengthening and Reconstruction, 2002-, Hospital for Special Surgery, New York, New York; Private Practice in Orthopaedic Surgery, 1999-. Publications: Articles in medical journals and chapters in books as author and co-author include most recently: Fractures of the Knee, 1999; Distraction of Hypertrophic Nonunion of Tibia with Deformity Using Ilizarov/Taylor Spatial Frame, 2002; Correction of Large Bilateral Tibia Vara with the Ilizarov Method, 2003. Honours include: Neer Award, American Shoulder and Elbow Surgeons, 1989; Professor Jorge Miniero Award, Lisbon, 1989; Harold Lamport Biomedical Research Prize, 1989; Editorial Board, Journal of Orthopaedic Trauma, 2002-. Memberships include: Fellow, American Academy of Orthopaedic Surgeons,; Limb Lengthening and Reconstruction Society; American College of Surgeons; American Medical Association; AO Alumni Association; Weill Medical College of Cornell University Alumni Association; University of Pennsylvania Alumni Association. Address: Hospital for Special Surgery, 535 East 70th Street, New York, NY 10021, USA. E-mail: rozbruchsr@hss.edu Website: www.limblengthening.com

ROZELL Kim Laine, b. 28 January 1959, Tyler, Texas, USA. Computer Consultant. Education: BS, Organisational Management, BA, Business Administration, Texas College; Degree, Micro Computer Science, 1997. Appointments: Micro Graphics and Document Imaging Specialist, Eastman Kodak, Rochester, New York, 1980; Software Author, 1996-; Computer Consultant for TekSystems Inc, 1997; Computer Consultant and Network Engineer on the Texaco Account, IBM Global Service; Own Computer and Telecom Consulting Service, Kimware Software and Consulting. Publications: Software: Pack-It-Up file compression and encryption, 1996. Honours: Member, Software Engineering Institute, Carnegie Mellon University; Certificate of Distinction Certification with SCO, as a SCO UnixWare and SCO Open Server Administrator; Listen in Who's Who publications and biographical dictionaries. Memberships: IEEE; Association for Computing Machinery; Software Engineering Institute. Address: 14786 – CR 1148, Tyler, TX 75704-5602, USA. Website: www.its.unimeb.edu.au//infosheets/159

ROZGONYI Ferenc, b. 21 September 1938, Tarcal, Hungary. MD; Specialist for Medical Microbiology. m (1) Gertrúd Maria Szécsi (deceased), (2) Katalin Szitha. Education: Student, Medical University of Debrecen, 1957-63; Medical Doctor, summa cum laude, 1963; Specialist for Laboratory Medicine, diploma, 1967; Specialist for Medical Microbiology, diploma, 1979. Appointments: PhD, 1978; Dr Med Sciences, 1988; Dr Med/Habil, Debrecen, 1995; University Professor in Debrecen, 1995; Director, Chairman, Institute of Medical Microbiology, Semmelweis University, Budapest, 1996-2003 (retired from this position); University Professor, 2003-. Publications: Over 140 articles and other publications on antibiotic resistance and pathogenicity of bacteria; About 350 lectures and posters presented in national and international conferences; Author: (manual) Rapid Microbiology Diagnostic Methods for General Practitioner. Honours: Doubly awarded by Hungarian Academy of Sciences, 1972, 1985; Honoured twice for excellent teaching, Ministry of Public Health, 1980, Ministry of Welfare, 1991; L Batthyány – Strattmann Award,

Minister of Public Health, Welfare and Family Affairs of Hungary, 2003, in recognition of his outstanding professional activity and achievement of several decades; Recipient, Doctoral School Medal, Semmelweis University, 2000; Honourable Certification, Hungarian Association for Innovation, 2003; Gold Seal-Ring, Ignác Semmelweis plaquette, Semmelweis University, 2003; Rezso Manninger plaquette, Hungarian Society for Microbiology, 2003. Memberships: Chairman, Curators Board for the Foundation of Struggle for Health, Hungary, 1990-; Executive Board: Hungarian Society of Chemotherapy, 1991-, Hungaria Helvetia Association, Debrecen, 1991-; Editorial Boards: Acta Microbiologica et Immunologica Hungarica, 1996-; Hungarian Venerology Archive, 1998-; Board of Advisors, Focus Medicinae, 1999-; Member, Hungarian Medical Chamber, 1992-; European Society for Clinical Microbiology and Infectious Diseases, 1992-, Hungarian Representative at its European Council, 2001-; World-wide Hungarian Medical Academy, 1999-. Address: Institute of Medical Microbiology, Faculty of Medicine, Semmelweis University, Nagyvárad tér 4, Budapest, H-1089, Hungary.

ROZSÍVAL Pavel, b. 27 September 1950, Cheb, Czech Republic. Ophthalmologist; Surgeon; Educator. m. Iva Fišerová, 1 son, 1 daughter. Education: MD, Charles University, Prague, 1974; Diploma in Nuclear Chemistry, Czech Technical University, 1977; PhD, 1979; Board Certified, 1981; Associate Professor, 1991; Professor, 1996. Appointments: Scientific Worker, Charles University, Hradec Králové, 1979-84; Head, District Department, Ophthalmology, Teplice, 1984-86; Head of Regional Department, Ophthalmology, Ústí nad Labem, 1986-93; Head of Department, Ophthalmology, Charles University, 1993-; Consultant, National Medical Library, Prague, 1978-92. Publications: Over 200 articles in professional journals; Over 500 lectures; Ophthalmology for Family Physicians; Modern Cataract Surgery; Diabetic Macro and Microangiopathy Eye Infections. Honour: Medal, 650th Anniversary of Charles University. Memberships: Czech Ophthalmological Society, President, 1997-; Scientific Advisory Board, Czech Ministry of Health, 1998-; Czech Glaucoma Society; Czech Society for Cataract and Refractive Surgery; American Academy of Ophthalmology; American Society of Cataract and Refractive Surgery; International Society for Cataract Surgery (Binkhorst Society); Deutschesprachigen Gesellschaft für Intraokularlinsenimplantationen; New York Academy of Sciences. Address: Department of Ophthalmology, Charles University, 500 05 Hradec Králové, Czech Republic.

RUBENS Bernice Ruth, b. 26 July 1923, Cardiff, Wales. Author. m. Rudi Nassauer, 1947, 2 daughters. Education: BA, University of Wales, 1944. Appointments: Author, Director, documentary films on Third World subjects. Publications: Novels: Set on Edge, 1960; Madame Sontsatzka, 1962; Mate in Three, 1964; The Elected Member, 1968; Sunday Best, 1970; Go Tell the Lemming, 1972; I Sent a Letter to My Love, 1974; Ponsonby Post, 1976; A Five-year Sentence, 1978; Spring Sonata, 1979; Birds of Passage, 1980; Brothers, 1982; Mr Wakefield's Crusade, 1985; Our Father, 1987; Kingdom Come: A Solitary Grief, 1991; Mother Russia, 1992; Autobiopsy, 1993; Yesterday in the Back Lane, 1995; The Waiting Game, 1997; I, Dreyfus, 1999; Milwaukee, 2001; Nine Lives, 2002; The Sergeant's Tale, 2003. Honours: Booker Prize, 1970; American Blue Ribbon, for Documentary film, 1972; Honorary DLitt, University of Wales. Membership: Fellow, University College, Cardiff. Address: 213A Goldhurst Terrace, London NW6 2ER, England.

RUBENSTEIN Leonard, b. 22 September 1918, Rochester, New York, USA. Mass Communicator. m. Ann Cox, 2 sons, 1 daughter. Education: BFA (cum laude and department honours), Alfred University, New York, 1939; Additional studies at University of

Dictionary of International Biography

Rochester (extension) and Cleveland School of Art. Appointments: Creative Director, Henry Hempstead Advertising Agency, Chicago, 1949-55; Vice President and Executive Art Director of the Clinton E Frank Advertising Agency, Chicago, Illinois, 1955-63; Vice President and Corporate Creative Consultant of Metromedia Inc (retired). Publications: Articles on graphics in international magazines; Co-author: Outdoor Advertising; Articles on ceramics in professional magazines; Educational videos on ceramics. Honours: Special award from the Art Directors Club of Chicago; Miscellaneous awards for creative projects; One-man exhibition, California Museum of Art and Science, 1970; Ceramic porcelains in permanent museum collections including the Smithsonian Renwick Gallery, 1999. Memberships: Art Directors Club of Chicago; American Ceramic Society. Address: 30616 Ganado Drive, Rancho Palos Verdes, CA 90275-6223, USA.

RUBIN Alfred Peter, b. 13 October 1931, New York, USA. Lawyer: Academic. m. Susanne Frowein, 1 son, 2 daughters. Education: BA, 1952, LLB, 1957, Columbia University; MLitt, University of Cambridge, United Kingdom, 1963. Appointments: Officer, US Navy, 1952-55; Tutor, International Law, Cambridge Colleges, 1958-60; Attorney Advisor, Office of the Assistant General Counsel, International Affairs, Department of Defense, 1961-66; Director, Directorate of Trade Control, Office of the Assistant Secretary of Defense, International Security Affairs, 1966-67; Associate Professor, Professor of Law, University of Oregon School of Law, 1967-73; Consultant, US Department of State in International Aviation Law, 1967-73, International Terrorism, 1979; Professor, Distinguished Professor of International Law, The Fletcher School of Law and Diplomacy, Tufts University, 1973-2002; Emeritus Professor of International Law, 2002-. Publications include: Four books sole author; 1 book editor; 105 articles and notes in learned journals; 114 book reviews in learned journals; 180 ephemeral pieces. Memberships: Grotian Society, 1974-76; International Association of Penal Law, 1992-97; State Department Advisory Council on Public International Law, 1994-2000; American Society of International Law, 1960-; President, 1994-2000, Chairman, Executive Committee, 2000-, American Branch, International Law Association. Address: 228 Slade Street, Belmont, MA 02478, USA. E-mail: arubin@tufts.edu

RUBIN Diana Kwiatkowski, b. 30 December 1958, New York, New York, USA. Poet; Writer. m. Paul Rubin, 4 January 1986, 1 son, 2 daughters. Education: AOS, The Wood School, 1982; BA, Marymount Manhattan College, 1988; MA, New York University, 1994. Publications: Spirits in Exile, 1990; Visions of Enchantment, 1991; Dinosauria, 1995. Contributions to: Poet; Amelia; Wind; Quest; Fox Cry; Voices International. Honours: 1st Prize, 1998; Sparrowgrass Poetry Forum Awards. Membership: Academy of American Poets. Address: PO Box 398, Piscataway, NJ 08855, USA.

RUBIN STUART Nancy (Zimman Stetson), 25 November 1944, Boston, Massachusetts, USA. Author; Journalist; Writer-Producer. m. William Stetson, 2 daughters. Education: BA, Jackson College, Tufts University; MAT, Brown University Graduate School; PhD (honorary), Mount Vernon College. Appointments: Writer-Producer, Restore America Series, Home & Garden TV Network, 1999-2001. Publications: Books: The New Suburban Woman: Beyond Myth and Motherhood, 1982; The Mother Mirror: How a Generation of Women is Changing Motherhood in America, 1984; Isabella of Castile: The First Renaissance Queen, 1992; American Empress: The Life and Times of Marjorie Merriweather Post, 1995; The Reluctant Spiritualist: A Life of Margaret Fox (in press); Screenwriter: The Grand Tour Series, 1997; America's Castles Series, Telly Award, Excellence in Writing, Communicator Award, 1998; The Gloria Vanderbilt Story, Crime Stories Series,

1999. Contributing Editor, several magazines, 1994-97; Theatre reviews in 4 publications including New York Times, Biography and Source Studies series in American Imago, 1995-97; Contributor: The New York Times; A & E Monthly Magazine; Business Week's Careers; Child; Family Circle; Ladies' Home Journal; McCall's; Newsday, Travel and Leisure; Savvy; Stamford Advocate (theatre reviews), 1986-. Honours: Fellow, MacDowell Colony, New Hampshire, 1981; Author of Year 1992, Excellence in Writing Award, American Society of Journalists and Authors, 1992; Washington Irving Book Award, Westchester Library Association, 1993; Editorial Judge, Benjamin Franklin Awards, Publishing Marketing Association for American Book Association Convention, 1994; Finalist, National Magazine Awards, 1995. Memberships: American PEN Center; American Society of Journalists and Authors; The Authors Guild Inc; National Arts Club. Address: c/o Patty Moosbrugger Literary Agency, 165 Bennett Avenue #6m, New York, NY 10040, USA.

RUBINSTEIN Julius B, b. 10 October 1940, Kiev, USSR. Metallurgical Engineer. m. Eugenia Ilyinichna Feldman, 1 daughter. Education: BS, MS, Metallurgical Engineering, Institute of Steels and Alloys, Moscow, 1957-62; PhD, Mineral Processing Research and Design, Mining Institute, Moscow, 1967; Doctor of Science, 1982; Professor of Science, 1985; Academician of the Russian Academy of Mining Science, 1995. Appointments: Scientist, 1862-68, Chief Scientist, 1968-70, Research and Design Mining Institute, Moscow; Chief Scientist, 1970-83, Head of Department, Flotation Equipment and Technological Processes Optimisation, 1983-99, Head of Department of Mineral Processing Processes and Apparatus, 1999-, Research and Design Institute of Solid Fossil Fuels Preparation, Moscow; Consulting assignments with Israeli, German and American companies, 1992-; Visiting Professor, Wuxan University, Wuxan, China, 1992; Principal Collaborating Scientist of the Research Project and Visiting Scholar, Nottingham University, England, 1994-98. Publications: 9 books; 10 brochures; 59 patents; More than 140 articles in scholarly journals; 20 papers at international conferences and congresses. Honours: 2 Awards, Russian Complex of National Achievements, 1977, 1984; Award, Russian Society of Authors and Inventors, 1989; Award, Russian Ministry of Energy for Outstanding Achievements in the Field, 2002. Memberships: President, Science Committee, Institute of Solid Fossil Fuels Preparation , Moscow; Member, Science Committee, Russian Academy of Sciences, Moscow; Russian Academy of Mining Science, Moscow, Russia. Address: Sireneviy Bulvar 36 Apt 20 Moscow, Russia 105077. E-mail: rubin@ekort.ru

RUBOMBORAS Grania Rosette, b. 25 July 1955, Kinoni, Uganda. Electrical Engineer. m. Michael Rubomboras, 1 son, 1 daughter. Education: BSc, Electrical Engineering; MBA, in progress. Appointments: Managing Director, Uganda Electricity Board; Director, Civil Aviation Authority of Uganda; Board Member, Rural Communications Development Fund, Uganda Communications Commission. Honours: Woman of the Year, ABI, 2004. Memberships: Uganda Institution of Professional Engineers; Institute of Electrical and Electronics Engineers. Address: PO Box 4297, Kampala, Uganda. E-mail: rubomboras@ueb.co.ug

RUCKMAN Robert Julian Stanley, b. 11 May 1939, Uxbridge, Middlesex, England. Chartered Engineer; Civil Servant. m. Josephine Margaret Trentham, 1 son, 1 daughter. Education: ONC, Electrical Engineering, 1957-60, HNC, Electrical and Electronic Engineering, 1960-62; IERE Endorsements, 1963, Harrow Technical College; MSc Transport Studies, Cranfield Institute of Technology, 1974-75. Appointments: Computer Testing and Commissioning, Elliott Bros Ltd, Borehamwood, Hertfordshire, 1961-64; Logic and Systems Designer, Serck Controls, Leamington Spa, Warwickshire, 1964-66; Technical Staff, System Sciences Corporation, Falls Church, USA, 1966-67; Transitron Electronic

Dictionary of International Biography

Corporation, Boston, USA, 1967-68; J Langham Thompson Ltd, Luton, Bedfordshire, 1968-70; Ministry of Transport, 1970-74; Birmingham Regional Office, Department of Transport, 1975-78; Cost Benefit Analyst, Computer Analyst, Department of Transport Road construction Unit, 1978-87; Computer Manager (Senior Professional Technical Officer), Department of Transport, West Midlands Region, Birmingham, 1987-95; Assessor, British Computer Society Professional Review Panel. Publications: Articles in scientific journals include: A Data Logger Scaler and Alarm Limit Comparator, 1967; Alarm Detection Using Delay Line Storage, 1966; Integral Alarms for Data Loggers, 1967; The Effects of Trip Characteristics on Interurban Model Choice, 1975; Guide for WMRO Geographical Information System, 1991. Honour: Department of Transport Award in recognition of work for development of Accident Analysis Geographical Information System, 1991. Memberships: Member of the Institution of Electrical Engineers; Member of The British Computer Society; Fellow, Institution of Analysts and Programmers; Member, Institute of Logistics and Transport; Chartered Engineer (C.Eng); European Engineer (Eur-Ing); Cranfield Society. Address: 'Flamingo', 13 Alexander Avenue, Droitwich Spa, Worcestershire WR9 8NH, England. E-mail: robert_ruckman@tinyworld.co.uk

RUDKIN James David, b. 29 June 1936, London, England. Dramatist. m. Alexandra Margaret Thompson, 3 May 1967, 2 sons, 1 deceased, 2 daughters. Education: MA, St Catherine's College, Oxford, 1957-61. Appointment: Judith E Wilson Fellow, University of Cambridge, 1984. Publications: Afore Night Come (stage play), 1964; Schoenberg's Moses und Aron (translation for Royal Opera), 1965; Ashes (stage play), 1974; Cries From Casement as His Bones are Brought to Dublin (radio play), 1974; Penda's Fen (TV film), 1975; Hippolytus (translation from Euripides), 1980; The Sons of Light (stage play), 1981; The Triumph of Death (stage play), 1981; Peer Gynt (translation from Ibsen), 1983; The Saxon Shore (stage play), 1986; Rosmersholm (translation from Ibsen), 1990; When We Dead Waken (translation from Ibsen), 1990. Opera Libretti: The Grace of Todd, music by Gordon Crosse, 1969; Inquest of Love, music by Jonathan Harvey, 1993; Broken Strings, music by Param Vir, 1994. Contributions to: Drama; Tempo; Encounter; Theatre Research Journal. Honours: Evening Standard Most Promising Dramatist Award, 1962; John Whiting Drama Award, 1974; Obie Award, New York, 1977; New York Film Festival Gold Medal for Screenplay, 1987; European Film Festival Special Award, 1989; Sony Silver Radio Drama Award, 1994. Memberships: Hellenic Society. Address: c/o Casarotto Ramsay Ltd, National House, 60-66 Wardour Street, London W1V 4ND England.

RUDRAIAH Nanjundappa, b. 18 August 1932, Bellave, Tumkur District, Bangalore. Senior Scientist. m. Mananmani, 1 son. Education: BsC, 1955, MSc, 1957, Mysore University; MA, University of Toronto, Canada, 1960; PhD, University of Western Ontario, Canada, 1964. Appointments: Lecturer of Mathematics, 1956-59, 1964-65, Principal, 1983-90, Central College; Reader of Mathematics, Mysore University, 1965-66; Professor of Mathematics, 1967-90, Dean, Faculty of Science, 1985-87, INSA Senior Scientists, 1996, Honorary Professor, 1996-, Bangalore University; Vice Chancellor, Gulbarga University, 1990-96. Publications include: Over 200 research papers in refereed journals. Honours: UGC National Lectureship in Mathematics, 1974-75; FICCI Gold Medal for outstanding contribution to science and technology, 1979; Karnataka State Rajyothsava Award in the field of education, 1986; KIT International Award of Foreign Researcher, 1990; Professor Vishnu Vasudeva Narlikar Memorial Lecture Award for outstanding contribution in the field of applied mathematics, 2000; William Mong International Award, University of Hong Kong, 2003. Memberships: International Society for the

interaction of Mechanics and Mathematics, Poland, 1982-; Indian Mathematical Society; Indian Society of Theoretical and Applied Mechanics; Indian Plasma Physics Society; Indian Science Congress Association; Indian National Science Academy; Indian Academy of Sciences; National Academy of Sciences; Indian Society of Biomechanics; UGC Mathematical Panel; UGC Standing Committee for SPA, Engineering and Technology; ISRO Standing Working Group; New York Academy of Sciences; National Book Trust. Address: National Research Institute for Applied Mathematics, 7th Cross, 7th Block West, Jayanagar, 560 082, Bangalore. E-mail: nrudraiah@hotmail.com

RUDSTRØM Erik Yngvar, b. 13 March 1920, Fredrikstad. Engineer. m. Gertie Verburg, 1 son, 1 daughter. Education: Student, Fredrikstad, 1939; Practice at Tandbergs Radiofabrikk A/S, Oslo, 1939-42; Economy, University of Oslo, 1950-52. Appointments: Started own factory making electrical appliances, 1942; Established factory making Air Humidifiers, Hamburg, Germany, 1978; Member, (SVO) government office supporting inventors, 1987-93; 10 years service as seaplane pilot in Royal Norwegian Air Force. Publications: How Inflationary Politics Brought Industry Into Trouble, article, 1982; 3 patents for Air Humidifiers, 1965. Honours: Winner, Scandinavian Championship, Finn Class, Olympic single-handed dinghy, 1963; Winner, Scandinavian Championship for small aircraft, SAABs airfield, Linkoping, Sweden, 1966. Memberships: Participant in sailing expeditions, 1974; Skipper: Hjemkomst Gogstad Vikingship copy from Duluth, MN, USA to Oslo, Norway, 1982; Crew member, Saga Siglar, 1984; Skipper: Gogstad-copy Havorn, 1990; Havorn i Osterled, from Oslo to Kopenhagen, Stockholm, Leningrad, Helsingfors, Tallinn, via Kiev, Black Sea, to Istanbul, Turkey, 1991. Chairman Norwegian Society of Inventors, 1987-91. Address: Lyngasvn 12, 1450 Nesoddtangen, Norway.

RUDY Dorothy L, b. 27 June 1924, Ohio, USA. Professor of English and Creative Writing; Poet. m. Willis Rudy, 31 January 1948, 1 son, 2 daughters. Education: BA, Queens College, 1945; MA, Philosophy, Columbia University, 1948. Appointments: Professor of English and Creative Writing, Montclair State University, 1964-88; Lecturer, Fairleigh Dickinson University, 1988-90, 1996-98, Bergen Community College, 1991-96, YMHA Wayne, Humanities Scholar of the Arts, 1993-. Publications: Quality of Small and Other Poems, 1971; Psyche Afoot and Other Poems, 1978; Grace Notes to the Measure of the Heart, 1979; Voices Through Time and Distant Places, 1993. Contributions to: Passaic Herald News; Letters; Poem; Laurel Review; Just Pulp; Composers; Authors and Artists Quarterly; Scimiter and Song; Bitterroot; Cellar Door; Pet Gazette; Black Buzzard Press. Honour: American Poets Fellowship, 1971; New Jersey Literary Society Hall of Fame, 1994; Certificate of Achievement in the Arts, Literature, Contemporary Women's Club of Bergenfield, 1997. Memberships: Composers; Authors and Artists of America; PEN Women; Bergen Poets; New York Poetry Forum; Browning Society; New England Small Press Association, Women's Board; Scambi International. Address: 161 West Clinton Avenue, Tenafly, NJ 07670, USA.

RUIZ Alfredo, b. 13 November 1938, Santiago, Chile. Psychotherapist. m. Ida Rudolph, 4 sons. Education: Psychologist, Pontifical Catholic University of Chile, 1969. Appointments: Psychotherapist, National Health Service of Chile, 1970-79; Private Practice, Psychotherapy, Santiago, 1979; Professor: Psychotherapy Cognitive Therapy Institute, Santiago, 1991; University of Chile, Santiago, 1992; Centre of Cognitive Therapists, Buenos Aires, Argentina, 1993-95; Catholic University of Portugal, Brag, Portugal, 2001; Director: Cognitive Therapy Institute, Santiago, 1991; Cognitive Post-Rationalist Institute, Santiago, 1997;

Advisory Human Science, Texas, USA, 1998. Publications: Qué nos Pasa Cuando Estamos Deprimidos, 1991; Tus Problemas el Psicólogo Responde, 1986; Cómo Ayudarse a uno Miso, 1991; Article: The contribution of Humberto Maturana to the Science of Complexity and Psychology. Honours: Awards, Colegio de Psicólogos de Chile. Memberships: American Psychological Association; College of Psychologists of Chile; Past President, Chilean Society of Clinical Psychology. Address: Providencia 2653 of. 406 Metropolitana, Santiago, Chile. E-mail: aruiz@inteco.cl Website: www.inteco.cl

RUKIEH Mohamad, b. 1 June 1951, Tartous, Syria. Geologist; Director General. m. Amal Ibrahim, 2 sons, 3 daughters. Education: Bachelor, Geological Sciences, Damascus University, 1973; Diploma, Mining Geological Engineering, 1977; PhD, Geology and Mineralogy, Moscow Geological Prospecting Institute. Appointments: Director of Prospecting, General Establishment of Geology and Mineral Resources, Ministry of Petroleum, 1980-86; General Supervisor of Marble Quarries, Marble Company; Director of Field Studies, 1986-, Director General, 2002-, General Organisation of Remote Sensing. Publications: Articles in professional technical journals include most recently: Tectonics of Lebanon and Western Part of Syria Using Space Imagery Interpretation, 1997; Annular Structures in the Space Images: Kinds, Distribution, Study Method and their Economic Importance, 2000; The Annular Structures in Lebanon and the Western Part of Syria, 2001. Honour: Man of the Year, 2002, American Biographical Institute, 2002. Memberships include: Academy of Engineering Sciences of the Russian Federation; National Committee, International Geological Project; Syrian geological Society; Arab Geologist Union; Editorial Board, Syrian Geological Magazine; Syrian Scientific Society of Information. Address: General Organisation of Remote Sensing, PO Box 12586, Damascus, Syria. E-mail: gors@mil-sy. Website: www.gors-sy.r.org

RULE Jane, b. 28 March 1931, Plainfield, New Jersey, USA. Writer; Teacher. Education: Mills College, Oakland, California. Appointments: Teacher of English, Concord Academy, Massachusetts, 1954-56; Assistant Director, International House, 1958-59; Intermittent Lecturer in English, 1959-70; Visiting Lecturer in Creative Writing, University of British Columbia, Vancouver, 1972-73. Publications: The Desert of the Heart, 1964; This Is Not You, 1970; Against the Season, 1971; Lesbian Images, 1975; Themes for Diverse Instruments, 1975; The Young in One Another's Arms, 1977; Contract With the World, 1980; Outlander, 1981; Inland Passage, A Hot-Eyed Moderate, 1985; Memory Board, 1987; After the Fire, 1989. Honours: Canadian Author's Association Best Novel of the Year, 1978, Best Story of the Year, 1978; US Gay Academic Union Literature Award, 1978; Fund for Human Dignity Award of Merit, 1983; Honorary Doctor of Letters, University of British Columbia, 1994; Order of British Columbia, 1998. Memberships: Writers' Union of Canada; PEN. Address: The Fork, Rte 1, S19 C 17, Galiano, British Columbia V0N 1P0, Canada.

RUMANE Abdul Razzak, b. 8 June 1948, Chandve, India. Electrical Engineer Consultant. m. Noor Jehan, 1 son, 1 daughter. Education: BE, Electrical Engineering, Government Engineering College, Marathwada University, Aurangabad, India, 1972; Diploma in Modern Management, British Career Training College, 1981; Diploma in International Trade, British Management Association, 1982; MS, General Engineering, Kennedy Western University, USA, 2002; Presently working towards PhD. Appointments include: Senior Electrical Engineer, Pan Arab Consulting Engineers, Kuwait, 1991-99; Senior Electrical Engineer, Dar Al Handsasah, (Shair and Partners), Kuwait, 1999-. Honours:

Twentieth Century Achievements Award, ABI; Global Award of Accomplishment, Who's Who Institute; International Order of Merit, IBC; The World Order of Science-Education-Culture, European Academy of Informatisation. Memberships: Kuwait Society of Engineers; Fellow, The Institution of Engineers (India); Senior Member, IEEE, USA; Associate Member, American Society of Civil Engineers; MEW (Kuwait) Registration (Supervisor First Class); London Diplomatic Academy. Address: At & PO Chandve, Talk – Mahad, Dist. Raigad, Maharashtra, India 402301. E-mail: rarazak@yahoo.com

RUPPEL Hartmut F E, b. 4 May 1954, Hannover, Germany. Lawyer. m. Daniela, 1 son, 1 daughter. Education: BA, LLB (Stell). Appointments: Member, Constituent Assembly, 1989-; Attorney General, Member of Cabinet, 1990-95; Member of Parliament, 1990-2000; Member of Executive of SWAPO Party, 1990-; Legal Practitioner, Partner, Lorentz & Bone. Honours: The Most Excellent Order of the Eagle, 2nd class, 2002. Memberships: Law Society of Namibia; SWAPO Party; Rotary International; Transparency International. Address: 12th Floor, Frans Indongo Gardens, Frans Indongo Street, Windhoek, Namibia. E-mail: hfr@lorentz.com.na

RUSH Alan de Lacy, b. 16 July 1936, Esher, England. Writer; Research Historian. Education: MA, University of Glasgow, Scotland, 1971; MA, University of Essex, England, 1973. Appointments: Lecturer, Riyadh University, Saudi Arabia, 1971-72; King Abdul-Aziz University, Jeddah, Saudi Arabia, 1973-75; Kuwait University, Kuwait, 1975-82. Publications: Al-Sabah, History and Genealogy of Kuwait's Ruling Family, 1987; Records of Kuwait, 1989; Ruling Families of Arabia, 1991; Records of the Hashemites, 1995; Records of Iraq, 2001. Contributions to: Burke's Royal Families of the World, 1982; Middle East Economic Digest; Financial Times; Arabic newspapers; Journal of Royal Society for Asian Affairs. Address: 8 Upper Addison Gardens, London W14 8AL, England.

RUSH Geoffrey, b. 6 July 1951, Toowoomba, Queensland, Australia. Actor. m. Jane Menelaus, 1988, 1 son, 1 daughter. Education: Jacques Lecoq of Mime, Paris. Career: Began with Queensland Theatre Company; Films include: The Wedding, 1980; Starstruck, 1982; Twelfth Night, 1986; Midday Crisis, 1994; Dad and Dave on our Selection, 1995; Shine; Children of the Revolution, 1996; Elizabeth, 1998; Shakespeare in Love, 1998; The Magic Pudding, 1999; Mystery Men, 1999; House on Haunted Hill, 1999; Quills, 1999; The Tailor of Panama, 2000; Lantana, 2001; Frida, 2002; Theatre includes: Hamlet; The Alchemist; The Marriage of Figaro; The Small Poppies; TV includes: Menotti, 1980-81; The Burning Piano, 1992; Mercury, 1995; Bonus Mileage, 1996. Honours: Academy and BAFTA Awards, Australian Film Institute Award, Golden Globe Award for Shine; BAFTA Award for Best Supporting Actor, for Shakespeare in Love. Address: C/o Shanahan Management, PO Box 478, Kings Cross, NSW 2011, Australia.

RUSHDIE (Ahmed) Salman, b. 19 June 1947, Bombay, India. Writer. m. (1) Clarissa Luard, 1976, dissolved 1987, died 1999, 1 son, (2) Marianne Wiggins, 1988, divorced 1993, 1 stepdaughter, (3) Elizabeth West, 1997, 1 son. Education: MA, King's College, Cambridge. Appointments: Actor, Fringe Theatre, London, 1968-69; Advertising Copywriter, 1969-73; Part-time Copywriter, 1976-80. Publications: Grimus, 1975; Midnight's Children, 1981; Shame, 1983; The Jaguar Smile: A Nicaraguan Journey, 1987; The Satanic Verses, 1988; Haroun and The Sea of Stories, 1990; Imaginary Homelands (essays), 1991; The Wizard of Oz, 1992; The Ground Beneath Her Feet, 1999; Fury, 2001; Step Across the Line: Collected Non-Fiction 1992-2002, 2002; TV Films: The Painter and The Pest, 1985; The Riddle of Midnight, 1988; Contributions to professional journals. Honours: Booker McConnell Prize for Fiction, 1981; Arts Council Literary Bursary, 1981; English Speaking Union Literary Award, 1981; James Tait Black Memorial Book Prize, 1981; Prix du Meilleur Livre Etranger, 1984; Nominated for Whitbread Prize, 1988; Booker Prize, 1993; Commander of the Order of Arts and Letters of France, 1999. Memberships: PEN; Production Board, British Film Institute; Advisory Board, Institute of Contemporary Arts; FRSL; Executive, Camden Committee for Community Relations, 1975-82. Address: c/o Aitken & Stone Ltd, 29 Fernshaw Road, London SW10 0TG, England.

RUŚKOWSKI Eugeniusz, b. 27 March 1951, Mława, Poland. Lawyer. m. Małgoizata Staręga-Ruśkowska, 1 son, 2 daughters. Education: Master's Degree in Law, 1972, Doctor's Degree in Law, 1976, Warsaw University, Poland; Professor, 1983; Titular Professor, 1995. Appointments: Vice-Director of the Institute and Vice-Dean, 1982-84; Vice-Rector, Warsaw University, Branch in Białystock, 1984-86; Judge of Supreme Administrative Court, 1994-98; Rector, The Siedlce High School of Finance and Management, 1999-. Publications: About 280 publications including 35 books among them 20 in foreign languages: French, English, Russian, German, Croatian and Serbian; Most of the publications concern: comparative problems of local finance, theory of public finance and financial control. Honours: Famous of the Suwalski Region, 1980; Science Award, Ministry of Finance, 1986; Famous of the Białystock Region, 1989; Rector's Science Awards, 1995, 1996, 1998. Memberships: Member of the Scientific Council, Revue Française de Finances Publiques; Association of Professors of Tax Law, Amsterdam; Institute of Public Finance. Address: Lewickie 2/2, Juchnowiec Koscielny 16-061, Poland. E-mail: eugen@list.pl

RUSSELL Colin Archibald, b. 9 July 1928, UK. Emeritus Professor of History of Science and Technology. Education: BSc (London), Special Chemistry, 1949; Postgraduate Certificate of Education, University College, Hull, 1950; MSc, 1958, PhD, 1962, DSc, History and Philosophy of Science, University College London; ARIC by examination, 1953; FRIC by election, 1962; Chartered Chemist, FRSC Appointments: Assistant Lecturer in Chemistry, Kingston Technical College (now University), 1950-59; Lecturer, Senior Lecturer, Principal Lecturer, Organic Chemistry, Director of Research, Chemistry Department, 1967-70, Harris College, Preston (now University of Central Lancashire), 1959-70; Senior Lecturer, 1970-72, Reader and Head of Department, 1972-81, Professor of History of Science and Technology and Head of Department, 1981-93, Emeritus Professor of History and Science of Technology, 1995- The Open University; Visiting Research Professor, Open University, Head of History of Chemistry Research Group, Part-time Consultant for the media, 1993-2001; Consultant, The Open University, 2001-. Publications: Author, co-author and editor of 19 books including: The Earth, Humanity and God, 1994; Edward Frankland: chemistry, controversy and conspiracy in Victorian England, 1996, paperback, 2003; Chemistry, society and environment: a new history of the British Chemical Industry, (editor) 2000; Michael Faraday: physics and faith, 2000; 8 research papers in organic chemistry; 60 research papers and book chapters in the history of science; 120 short articles; 120 reviews. Honours include: Visiting Fellow, Wolfson College, Cambridge, 1984-85; President, British Society for the History of Science, 1986-88; Dexter Award, American Chemical Society, 1990; David Mellor Medal, University of New South Wales, 1995. Memberships: Fellow, Chemical Society; Fellow, Royal Institute of Chemistry; Fellow, Royal Society of Chemistry; British Society for the History of Science; Society for the History of Alchemy and Chemistry; Vice President and Past President,

Christians in Science; Trustee and Director, John Ray Initiative. Address: 64 Putnoe Lane, Bedford, MK41 9AF, England. E-mail: colin.russell@open.ac.uk

RUSSELL John, b. 22 Jan 1919, Fleet, England. Art Critic; Writer. Education: MA, Magdalen College, Oxford, 1940. Appointments: Honorary Attaché, Tate Gallery, 1940-41; Staff, Ministry of Information, 1941-43, Naval Intelligence Division, Admiralty, London, 1943-46; Contributor, 1945-49, Art Critic, 1949-74, The Sunday Times; Art Critic, 1974-82, Chief Art Critic, 1982-91, The New York Times. Publications: Shakespeare's Country, 1942; British Portrait Painters, 1945; Switzerland, 1950; Logan Pearsall Smith, 1950; Erich Kleiber, 1956; Paris, 1960, 2nd edition, 1983; Seurat, Private View (with Bryan Robertson and Lord Snowdon), 1965; Max Ernst, 1967; Henry Moore, 1968; Ben Nicholson, 1969; Pop Art Redefined (with Suzi Gablik), 1969; The World of Matisse, 1970; Francis Bacon, 1971; Édouard Vuillard, 1971; The Meanings of Modern Art, 1981, new and enlarged edition, 1990; Reading Russell, 1989; London, 1994; Matisse: Father and Son, 1999. Contributions to: Various publications including New York Review of Books, 1999-2000. Honour: Honorary Member, Century Association, New York, 2000. Membership: American Academy of Arts and Letters, 1966; Guggenheim Fellow, 2000-2001. Address: 166 East 61st Street, New York, NY 10021, USA.

RUSSELL John McRae, b. 18 June 1949. Specialist Urologist. m. Lorraine, 2 sons, 1 daughter. Education: MBBS, Melbourne University; FRACS (Urology); FACS. Appointments: Senior Urologist, Albury Base Hospital, 1981-; Senior Urologist, Wodonga District Hospital, 1981-; Urologist, Albury Wodonga Private Hospital, 1981-; Austin Repatriation Medical Centre, 1996-; Deniliquin Hospital, 1998-; Conjoint Senior Lecturer, University of New South Wales Medical School, 2001-. Publications: Articles in professional journals. Memberships: AMA; Australian Urology Association; Victoria Executive AUA, 1997-, Chairman, Victoria Section, 2002-; European Urological Society; American Urology Society; Société International Urologie (SIU). Address: Murray Valley Urology, PO Box 1058, Albury, NSW, Australia 2640.

RUSSELL Ken, b. 3 July 1927, Southampton, England. Film Director. m. (1) Shirley Russell, 4 sons, 1 daughter, (2) Vivian Jolly, 1 son, 1 daughter, (3) Hetty Baines, 1992, 1 son. Education: Nautical College, Pangbourne, England. Career: Former actor, freelance magazine photographer; Director, numerous TV documentaries for BBC, shown all over world; Documentaries include: Elgar; Bartok; Debussy; Hebri Rousseau; Isadora Duncan; Delius; Richard Strauss; Clouds of Glory; The Mystery of Dr Martini; The Secret Life of Arnold Bax; TV series: Lady Chatterly's Lover; Director, films: French Dressing, 1964; Billion Dollar Brain, 1967; Women in Love, 1969; The Music Lovers, 1970; The Devils, 1971; The Boyfriend, 1971; Savage Messiah, 1972; Mahler, 1973; Tommy, 1974; Lisztomania, 1975; Valentino, 1977; Altered States, 1981; Gothic, 1986; Aria (segment), 1987; Salome's Last Dance, 1988; The Lair of the White Worm, 1988; The Rainbow, 189; Whore, 1990; Prisoners of Honour, 1991; Lion's Mouth, 2002; Actor, film: The Russia House, 1990; The Rake's Progress (Stravinsky), 1982; Die Soldaten (Zimmerman), 1983; Opera: Princess Ida, 1992; Salome, Bonn, 1993. Publications: A British Picture: An Autobiography, 1989; Altered States: The Autobiography of Ken Russell, 1991; Fire Over England, 1993. Address: c/o Peter Rawley, ICM, 8942 Wilshire Boulevard, Beverly Hills, CA 90021, USA.

RUSSELL Kurt von Vogel, b. 17 March 1951, Springfield, Massachusetts, USA. Actor. m. Season Hubley, 1979, divorced, 1 son, 1 son with Goldie Hawn. Career: Child actor, Disney shows and films; Professional baseball player, 1971-73; Films include: It

Happened at the World's Fair, 1963; Unlawful Entry, 1992; Captain Ron, 1992; Tombstone, 1993; Stargate, 1994; Executive Decision, 1996; Escape from LA, 1996; Breakdown, 1997; Soldier, 1998; Vanilla Sky, 2001; Interstate 60, 2002; Dark Blue, 2002; Miracle, 2004; TV series include: lead role in Travels With Jamie McPheeters, 1963-64; The New Land, 1974; The Quest, 1976; TV films include: Search For the Gods, 1975; The Deadly Tower, 1975; Christmas Miracle in Caulfield USA, 1977; Elvis, 1979; Amber Waves, 1988; Numerous guest appearances. Honours: 5 acting awards; 10 baseball awards; 1 golf championship. Memberships: Professional Baseball Players' Association; Stuntman's Association. Address: Creative Artists' Agency, 9830 Wilshire Boulevard, Beverly Hills, CA 90212-1825, USA.

RUSSELL Martin James, b. 25 September 1934, Bromley, Kent, England. Writer. Publications: No Through Road, 1965; The Client, 1975; Mr T, 1977; Death Fuse, 1980; Backlash, 1981; The Search for Sara, 1983; A Domestic Affair, 1984; The Darker Side of Death, 1985; Prime Target, 1985; Dead Heat, 1986; The Second Time is Easy, 1987; House Arrest, 1988; Dummy Run, 1989; Mystery Lady, 1992; Leisure Pursuit, 1993. Memberships: Crime Writers' Association; Detection Club. Address: 15 Breckonmead, Wanstead Road, Bromley, Kent BR1 3BW, England.

RUSSELL Norman Atkinson, b. 7 August 1943, Belfast, Northern Ireland. Anglican Priest. m. Victoria Christine Jasinska, 2 sons. Education: MA, Churchill College, Cambridge; BD, London. Appointments: Articled Clerk, Cooper Brothers & Company, London, 1966-67; Curate, Christ Church with Emmanuel, Clifton, Bristol, 1970-74; Curate, Christ Church, Cockfosters, London and Anglican Chaplain, Middlesex Polytechnic, 1974-77; Rector of Harwell with Chilton, 1977-84; Priest in Charge of Gerrrards Cross, 1984-88 and Fulmer, 1985-88; Rector of Gerrards Cross and Fulmer, 1988-98; Archdeacon of Berkshire, 1998-. Honour: Honorary Canon, Christ Church, Oxford, 1995-98. Address: Foxglove House, Love Lane, Donnington, Newbury, Berkshire RG14 2JG, England. E-mail: archdber@oxford.anglican.org

RUSSELL Willy, (William Martin Russell), b. 23 August 1947, Liverpool, England. Dramatist; Writer. m. Ann Seagroatt, 1969, 1 son, 2 daughters. Education: Certificate of Education, St Katherine's College of Education, Liverpool. Appointments: Teacher, 1973-74; Fellow, Creative Writing, Manchester Polytechnic, 1977-78. Publications: Theatre: Blind Scouse, 1971-72; When the Reds (adaptation), 1972; John, Paul, George, Ringo and Bert (musical), 1974; Breezeblock Park, 1975; One for the Road, 1976; Stags and Hens, 1978; Educating Rita, 1979; Blood Brothers (musical), 1983; Our Day Out (musical), 1983; Shirley Valentine, 1986; The Wrong Boy (novel), 2000; Songs and poetry. Television Plays: King of the Castle, 1972; Death of a Young Young Man, 1972; Break In (for schools), 1974; Our Day Out, 1976; Lies (for schools), 1977; Daughter of Albion, 1978; Boy With Transistor Radio (for schools), 1979; One Summer (series), 1980. Radio Play: I Read the News Today (for schools), 1979. Screenplays: Band on the Run, 1979; Educating Rita, 1981. Honours: Honorary MA, Open University; Honorary Director, Liverpool Playhouse. Address: c/o Margaret Ramsay Ltd, 14A Goodwin's Court, St Martin's Lane, London WC2, England.

RUSSELL William Moy Stratten, b. 26 March 1925, Plymouth, Devon, England. Biologist; Historian; Folklorist. m. Claire Hillel, deceased. Education: Marlborough College, 1938-43; BA, Natural Science , Zoology, 1948, MA, 1950, DPhil, 1952, University of Oxford; Chartered Biologist, Institute of Biology. Appointments: War Service: 2nd Motor Training Battalion, The Rifle Brigade, 1943-44; Active Service, 12th Battalion, The King's Royal Rifle

Corps, 1944-45; Christopher Welch Research Scholar, Department of Zoology and Comparative Anatomy University of Oxford, 1948-51; Junior Agricultural Research Fellow, 1951-54; Research Fellow, Universities Federation for Animal Welfare, London, 1954-59; Scientific Information Officer, Commonwealth Bureau of Pastures and Field Crops, Hurley, England, 1964-66; Lecturer, Department of Sociology, 1966-71, Reader, 1971-86, Professor, 1986-90, Professor Emeritus, 1990-, University of Reading; External Examiner, University of London Institute of Education, 1970-80. Publications: Co-author: The Principles of Humane Experimental Technique (with R L Burch), 1959; Human Behaviour: a New Approach (with Claire Russell), 1961; Violence, Monkeys and Man, 1968 (also Dutch, Swedish and German editions), 1968; Population Crises and Population Cycles, 1999; Author: Man, Nature and History (also Italian Edition), 1967; The Barber of Aldebaran, 1995; Editor: Animals in Folklore (with J R Porter), 1978; The Folklore of Ghosts (with H R E Davidson), 1981; Contributed over 200 articles to professional journals; Contributed to 40 books. Honours: Ella Stevens Greek Scholar, 1942, Classics and English Literature Scholar, New College Oxford, 1945; Award named in his honour (Russell and Burch) by Humane Society of the United States, 1990; Smith-Kline Beecham Prize for Laboratory Animal Welfare, Research Defence Society, London, 1994; Bronze Medal, Charles University Faculty of Medicine, Czech Republic, 1997; Silver Seal, University of Bologna, Italy, 1999. Memberships: Life Fellow, Institute of Biology; Life Fellow, Royal Society of Medicine; The Galton Institute; President, Pendragon Society; Honorary Member, Universities Federation for Animal Welfare; Honorary Librarian, 1977-79, President, 1979-82, Vice President, 1983-90, Folklore Society. Address: Department of Sociology, University of Reading, Whiteknights, PO Box 218, Reading, Berkshire RG6 6AA, England.

RUSSO Carlo Ferdinando, b. 15 May 1922, Naples, Italy. University Professor. m. Adele Plotkin. Education: Degree in Filologia antica, University of Pisa, 1943; Diploma, Scuola Normale, Pisa, 1945. Appointments: Assistant Editor, 1946-62, Managing Editor, 1962-, Belfagor journal; Instructor, University of Florence, Italy, 1946-48; Instructor, University of Cologne, Germany, 1948-50; Libero Docente, Greek and Latin Philology, Rome, 1951; Professor, University Bari, Italy, 1950-62; Professor tenure, 1962-97; Professor Emeritus, 1999. Publications: Senecae, Apocolocyntosis, 1948, 6th edition, 1985; Hesiodi, Scutum, 1950, 3rd edition, 1968; La Coppa di Nestore di Pitecusa-Ischia, (Monumenti Antichi, Accademia dei Lincei), 1955-92; Aristofane Autore di teatro, 1962, 3rd edition, 1992, English edition, 1994, paperback, 1997; Die Gestalt einer archaischen Handschrift und einer kyklischen Ilias, 1983; Omero e il Disco di Festo, 1995; Omero nasce con le Olimpiadi (Olimpiade seconda), 1999; L'anno poetico XXXVI, i dolori di Omero omicida, 2004; Curator of works by H Fränkel, G Pasquali and E Fraenkel, 1969-83, 1992, 1994. Address: Casa ed Olschki, Casella post 66, 50100 Florence, Italy. E-mail: cf.russo@lgxserve.ciseca.uniba.it

RUSSO René, b. 1955, California, USA. Actress. m. Dan Gilroy, 1992, 1 daughter. Career: Formerly model Eileen Ford Agency; Film appearances include: Major League, 1989; Mr Destiny; One Good Cop; Freejack; Lethal Weapon 3; In the Line of Fire; Outbreak; Get Shorty; Tin Cup; Ransom; Buddy; Lethal Weapon 4, 1998; The Adventures of Rocky and Bullwinkle, 1999; The Thomas Crown Affair, 1999; Showtime, 2002; Big Trouble, 2002; TV appearance: Sable (series). Address: c/o Progressive Artists Agency, 400 South Beverly Drive, Suite 216, Beverly Hills, CA 90212, USA.

RUST Graham Redgrave, b. 17 February 1942, England. Painter. Education: Polytechnic School of Art, Regent Street, London, 1958-60; Central School of Arts and Crafts, 1960-61; National Academy of Art, New York, USA, 1962. Career: Artist in Residence, Woodberry Forest School, Virginia, USA, 1967-68; Mural Paintings including the South Staircase, Ragley Hall, Warwickshire, 1969-83; 25 One-man Exhibitions including 4 in aid of the Royal Commonwealth Society for the Blind. Publications: The Painted House, 1988; Decorative Designs, 1996; Needlepoint Designs, 1998; The Painted Ceiling, 2001; Illustrations for: Fruits of the Earth, 1986; The Secret Garden, 1986; A Little Princess, 1989; The Secret Garden Notebook, 1991; Little Lord Fauntleroy, 1993; Some Flowers by Vita Sackville West, 1993; The Fine Art of Dining, 1994; Claro en la Selva, 2001. Membership: The Art Workers Guild; Brooks's. Address: The Old Rectory, Somerton, Suffolk IP29 4ND, England.

RUSTAGI Urmila, b. 1 May 1945, Chhainsa, Haryana, India. Teacher. m. Tulsi Ram, 3 sons. Education: Certificate Course in German, 1965; MA, Sanskrit, 1966; PhD, 1973. Appointments: Assistant Lecturer, Miranda House, University of Delhi, 1967-69; Lecturer, 1969-85; Reader, 1986-; Staff Council Secretary, 1994; Finance Advisor, 1995-97; Vice Principal, 2000, Acting Principal, 2000-2002, Miranda House, University of Delhi. Publications: Veda and Environment; Manu/Manusmriti – An Appraisal and 7 other books; 20 articles; 1 research study, in progress. Honours: Rahim Khankhana Award for Literary Publication; Awarded twice by Delhi Sanskrit Academy; Bharati-Mishra award by Rajasthan Sanskrit Academy and a literary award by Utter Pradesh Sanskrit Institution; Sanskrit Teacher Award (twice); Indira Gandhi Priyadarshini Award, 2002. Memberships: WSC; AIOC. Address: SD 84, Tower Apartments, Pitampura, Delhi 110088, India.

RUTBERG Philip Grigorievich, b. 22 September 1931, Vinnitca. Scientist. m. Klara Leonidovna Emelianova, 1 son. Education: State University, St Petersburg, 1954; Polytechnical Institute, 1961; Doctor (Professor), 1981; Member Correspondent, 1990, Member, 2000, Russian Academy of Sciences, 2000. Appointments: Teacher, college, 1954-60; Junior Researcher, Physical Technical Institute of Ioffe, 1961-63; Senior Researcher, Chief of Laboratory Vice Director, Institute of Electromechanics, RAS, 1963-91; Director, Institute of Problems of Electrophysics of RAS, 1992. Publications: 4 books; 300 papers. Honour: State Reward of USSR, 1982. Memberships: AIAA; IEEE; International Engineering Academy; Russian Academy of Sciences. Address: Institute for Problems of Electrophysics, Russian Academy of Sciences, 18 Dvortsvaaya Naberezhnaya, St Petersburg 191186, Russia. E-mail: rutberg@iperas.spb.su

RUTKIN Seymour Sy, b. 22 October 1921, Weehawken, New Jersey, USA. Architect. m. Anne Rochelle Teicher. Education: Associate Degree, Architecture, Cooper Union for Advancement of Science and Art, New York City, New York, 1946; Bachelor of Science and Urban Planning, Illinois Institute of Technology, Chicago, 1949. Appointments: Designer, H K Ferguson Co, New York City, 1954-56; Senior Consultant on Design, Ebasco Services Inc, New York City, 1957; Design Consultant and Architect, 1958-61; Senior Architect, Headquarters, Army and Air Force Exchange Service, New York City, 1964-66; Project Senior Designer, Ferrenz & Taylor Architects, New York City; Architect, Designer, Consultant, 1967-82; University Architect III, City University, New York City, 1983-2003; Architect, Consultant, 2004-. Publications: Articles in professional journals and papers presented at conferences include: "A shell of variable thickness with a middle surface not expressible analytically", published by National Academy of Sciences, USA in book, "World Conference on Shell

Structures 1964", publication no.1187; "New freedom of shape in new shell forms – freeform shells", presented in Mexico City, published by IASS, 1957; "Shell structure – future design development – new families of new shell surfaces defined by mathematics/computers", presented in Madrid, Spain, published by IASS, 1959. Honours: Top Architecture Student and Schweinberg Scholarship, Cooper Union, 1946; New Talent USA Award, Art in America, 1959; House of the Month, www.archrecord.com, January 2004; Water Color Award; Listed in Who's Who publications and biographical dictionaries. Memberships: International Association of Shell and Spacial Structures (IASS), Madrid, Spain, Past Associate Member, 1962-71; District Council 37 New York City, 1983-2003; Local 375 Architects and Engineers, City University of New York Ch 36, President, 1999-2003. Address: 445 East 65th St, Apt 2B, New York, NY 10021, USA. E-mail: syandanne@earthlink.net

RUTSALA Vern, b. 5 February 1934, McCall, Idaho, USA. Writer; Teacher. m. Joan Colby, 1957, 2 sons, 1 daughter. Education: BA, Reed College, 1956; MFA, University of Iowa, 1960. Publications: The Window, 1964; Small Songs, 1969; The Harmful State, 1971; Laments, 1975; The Journey Begins, 1976; Paragraphs, 1978; The New Life, 1978; Walking Home from the Icehouse, 1981; Backtracking, 1985; The Mystery of Lost Shoes, 1985; Ruined Cities, 1987; Selected Poems, 1991; Little-Known Sports, 1994; Greatest Hits: 1964-2002, 2002. Contributions to: New Yorker; Esquire; Poetry; Hudson Review; Harper's; Atlantic; American Poetry Review; Paris Review. Honours: National Endowment for the Arts Fellowships, 1974, 1979; Northwest Poetry Prize, 1976; Guggenheim Fellowship, 1982; Carolyn Kizer Poetry Prize, 1988, 1997; Masters, Fellowship, Oregon Arts Commission, 1990; Hazel Hall Award, 1992; Juniper Prize, 1993; Duncan Lawrie Prize, Arvon Foundation, 1994. Memberships: PEN; Poetry Society of America; Associated Writing Programs. Address: 2404 North East 24th Avenue, Portland, OR 97212, USA.

RUTTER Michael Llewellyn, b. 15 August 1933, Brummanna, Lebanon. Professor of Developmental Psychiatry; Writer. m. Marjorie Heys, 27 December 1958, 1 son, 2 daughters. Education: MB ChB, 1950-55, MD, 1963, University of Birmingham; DPM, University of London, 1961. Appointments: Professor of Developmental Psychopathology, University of London; Social, Genetic and Developmental Psychiatry Research Centre. Publications: Depression in Young People: Development and Clinical Perspectives (co-editor), 1986; Language Development and Disorders (co-editor), 1987; Treatment of Autistic Children (co-editor), 1987; Parenting Breakdown: The Making and Breaking of Intergenerational Links (co-author), 1988; Assessment and Diagnosis in Child Psychopathology, 1988; Straight and Devious Pathways From Childhood to Adulthood, 1990; Biological Risk Factors for Psychosocial Disorders, 1991; Developing Minds: Challenge and Continuity Across the Lifespan, 1993; Stress, Risk and Resilience in Children and Adolescents, Processes, Mechanisms and Interventions (co-editor), 1994; Child and Adolescent Psychiatry: Modern Approaches (co-editor), 3rd edition, 1994; Development Through Life: A Handbook for Clinicians (co-editor), 1994; Psychosocial Disorders in Young People: Time Trends and their Causes (co-editor), 1995; Behavioural Genetics (co-author), 3rd edition, 1997; Antisocial Behaviour by Young People (co-author), 1998. Contributions to: Numerous professional journals. Honours: 10 honorary doctorates; Knight Baronet, 1992; American Psychological Association Distinguished Scientific Contribution Award, 1995; Castilla del Pino Prize for Achievement in Psychiatry, Cordoba, Spain, 1995; Royal Society of Medicine, honorary fellow, 1996; Royal College of Paediatrics and Child Health, honorary founding fellow, 1996; Society for Research in Child Development, president elect, 1997.

Memberships: American Academy of Arts and Sciences, honorary foreign member; Royal College of Psychiatrists, fellow; Royal College of Physicians, fellow; Fellow, Royal Society, 1997-; President, Society for Research into Child Development, 1999-. Address: SGDP Research Centre, Institute of Psychiatry, De Crespigny Park, Denmark Hill, London SE5 8AF, England.

RYABOV Yuri, b. 15 June 1923, Charkov City, Ukraine. Scientist; Teacher. m. Alla, 1 son, 2 daughters. Education: Graduated, 1950, Postgraduate, 1950-53, Candidate of Science, Physics and Mathematics, 1953, DrSc, 1963, Professor, 1965, Department of Celestial Mechanics, Moscow University. Appointments: Junior Researcher, Astronomy Institute, Moscow University, 1953-55; Docent, Moscow Energetic Institute (by correspondence), 1955-60; Docent, Department of Celestial Mechanics, Moscow University, 1960-65; Head, Department of Numerical Methods, Moscow Patric Lumumba University, 1965-71; Head, Department of Mathematics, 1971-93, Professor, 1993-, Moscow State Auto and Highway Construction University. Publications: Over 140 articles, monographs, science-for-laymen articles, books and scholarly texts on theory and applications of differential equations, nonlinear oscillations, numerical methods, celestial mechanics and astronomy. Honours: Honoured Scientist of Russia, 1992; Order of Patriotic War and other awards as participant of World War II; Twentieth Century Award for Achievement, IBC, 1993; Distinguished Leadership Award, ABI. Memberships: International Astronomical Union; European Astronomical Society; Editorial Board, Earth and Universe magazine. Address: Chernyachovsky str 12-81, Moscow 125319, Russia. Email: ryabov@vmat.madi.ru

RYAN Meg, b. 19 November 1961, Fairfield, Connecticut, USA. Actress. m. Dennis Quaid, 1991, divorced, 1 son. Education: New York University. Career: Formerly in TV commercials; TV appearances: As The World Turns; One of the Boys; Amy and the Angel; The Wild Side; Charles in Charge; Owner, Prufrock Pictures; Films: Rich and Famous, 1981; Amytyville III-D; Top Gun; Armed and Dangerous; Innerspace; DOA; Promised Land; The Presidio; When Harry Met Sally; Joe Versus the Volcano; The Doors; Prelude to a Kiss; Sleepless in Seattle; Flesh and Bone; Significant Other; When a Man Loves a Woman; IQ; Paris Match; Restoration; French Kiss, 1995; Two for the Road, 1996; Courage Under Fire, 1996; Addicted to Love, 1997; City of Angels, 1998; You've Got Mail, 1998; Hanging Up, 1999; Lost Souls, 1999; Proof of Live, 2000; Kate & Leopold, 2001; In the Cut, 2003; Against the Ropes, 2004. Address: c/o ICM, 8942 Wilshire Boulevard, Beverly Hills, CA 90211, USA.

RYASHENTSEVA Margarita Alexsandrovna, b. 21 February 1927, Moscow, Russia. Chemist. m. Volkenstein Yuri B, 6 January 1949, 1 son. Education: Chemical Engineer, MV Lomonosov Institute of Fine Chemical Technology, 1950; Candidate of Chemical Science, 1958; Doctor of Chemical Science, 1974. Appointments: Leading Researcher, 1985-, Professor, 1991-, ND Zelinsky Institute of Organic Chemistry, Russian Academy of Sciences, Moscow. Publications include: Rhenium and its compounds in heterogenous catalysis, 1983. Honour: Honoured Scientist of the Russian Federation, 1999. Memberships: Foreign Corresponding Member, Academy of Sciences, Bologna, Italy; New York Academy of Sciences; ICMCC. Address: Profsojuznaya 101, bl 3, Flat 220, 117279 Moscow, Russia. E-mail: khutor@ioc.ac.ru

RYCHLAK Joseph Frank, b. 17 December 1928, Cudahy, Wisconsin. Professor. m. Lenora Smith, 1 son, 1 daughter. Education: BA, University of Wisconsin, 1949-53; MA, 1954, PhD Clinical Psychology, 1957, Ohio State University. Appointments: Assistant Professor, Psychology, Florida State University, 1957-58; Assistant Professor, Psychology, Washington State University, 1958-61; Associate and Full Professor, Psychology, St Louis University, 1961-69; Professor, Psychology, Purdue University, 1969-83; Maude C Clarke Professor of Psychology, 1983-99, Emeritus Professor, Loyola University of Chicago. Publications: Psychology of Rigorous Humanism, 1988; Artificial Intelligence and Human Reason, 1991; Logical Learning Theory, 1994; In Defence of Human Consciousness, 1997; The Human Image in Postmodern America, 2003. Honours: President, American Psychological Association, (Division 24), 1977-78, 1986-87. Memberships: Fellow, American Psychological Association; Fellow, American Psychological Society; Fellow, Society for Personality Assessment. Address: 12974 Abraham Run, Carmel, IN 46033, USA.

RYDER Winona, b. 29 October 1971, Minnesota, USA. Actress. Education: American Conservatory Theatre, San Francisco. Career: Films include: Lucas, 1986; Beetlejuice, 1988; Great Balls of Fire; Heathers, 1989; Edward Scissorhands, 1990; Bram Stoker's Dracula, 1992; Age of Innocence, 1993; Little Women; How to Make an American Quilt; The Crucible; Looking for Richard; Boys; Alien Resurrection; Girl Interrupted, 1999; Lost Souls, 1999; Autumn in New York, 1999; Mr Deeds, 2002; S1m0ne, 2002; The Day My God Died, voice, 2003. Honours: Golden Globe Best Supporting Actress, 1994. Address: 10345 W Olympic Boulevard, Los Angeles, CA 90064, USA.

RYDYGIER Edward, b. 17 November 1953, Warsaw, Poland. Physicist; Financial Analyst; Teacher. m. Hanna Rydygier. Education: Master of Science in Physics, Warsaw University, 1978; Postgraduate Studies, Statistical Methods Diploma, 1992, Computer Science Diploma, Polish Academy of Sciences, Mathematical Institute, 1992; PhD, Technical Science, 2001; Postgraduate Studies, Insurance and Banking Diploma, 2001, Warsaw Technical University. Appointments: Physicist, Institute of Nuclear Research, Otwock, Poland, 1978-82; Adjunct Lecturer, Institute for Nuclear Studies, Otwock, Poland, 1983-99; Inspector Warsaw District Labour Office, Warsaw, Poland, 2000; Consultant of the World Bank with the Ministry of the State Treasury, Warsaw, Poland, 2000; Lecturer, Education Centre, Vocational Studies of Business and Economics, Warsaw, Poland, 2001-; Inspector, City Office of Warsaw, 2002-; Lecturer, High School of Economics and Technology in Legionowo, Poland, 2004-. Publications: 80 scientific publications including 50 conference articles presented at international scientific conferences and workshops, Honours: European Vocational Title, European Physicist, conferred by President of European Physical Society, 1997; Member, Research Board of Advisors of the American Biographical Institute, 2001-. Memberships: Polish Physical Society; Founder Member, Polish Nuclear Society; Member General Revision Committee Polish Society of Universalism. Address: ul Narbutta 60 m. 8, 02-541 Warsaw, Poland. E-mail: erydygier@targowek.waw.pl

RYGERT Göran T, b. 1 May 1935, Tranås, Sweden. m. (1) 2 sons, (2) Janet A Rybka, 19 September 1997. Education: Master of Architecture, Chalmers University of Technology, Göteborg, Sweden; Private, with Torsten Rygert (father), Music Director and Composer. Career: Arranger and Composer, field of song - ballad and folk music; String Bass Musician, Swedish song - ballad artists, in many folk music orchestras, Sweden and USA; Appearances in Swedish, American and Russian Radio and TV; many song festivals; Producer, many song books, Freelance Editor, Warner/ Chappell Music Scandinavia AB, Sweden. Compositions: A number of songs with words by Swedish Poets and Writers; CD, Visituder, 2004. Publications: Ölands Folkliga Visor och Melodier Genom Tiderna, 1987; Visor Kring Bordet, 1993; Festvisor, 1994; many other song-books, 1994-2003. Honours: Royal Gustav

Adolf's Academy Prize, 1991; Kalmar County Council Cultural Award, 1997. Memberships: Honorary Member, Visans Vänner; Swedish Composers of Popular Music; Balalaika and Domra Association of America. Current Management: Composing and arranging. Address: 4390 Ivywood NE, Marietta, GA 30062, USA.

RYLE-HODGES Carolyn, b. 10 June 1961, London, England. Art Dealer. m. Rupert, 1 son, 1 daughter. Education: BA, Courtauld Institute of Art; History of Art, London University. Career: Partner, Long and Ryle Art Gallery, 1988-; Monthly exhibitions of mainly figurative work by contemporary artists from Europe and USA; Long and Ryle Corporate Art Consultancy Service, providing artworks to major banks and companies such as Morgan Grenfell, Lloyd Thompson, Societe Generale, Mitsubishi Corp plc, HM Customs and Excise, London Underground Ltd; Canary Wharf, Kreditbank, Paribas, Barclays Bank, Bank of America in Jersey, Capsticks Solicitors, Cazenove and Co; Long and Ryle Private Client Advisory Service, specialising in Modern British painting and contemporary art. Memberships: Worshipful Company of Carpenters; Friends of the Tate; Friends of the Royal Academy; Life Member, National Art Fund Collection; Member, National Trust. Address: Long & Ryle, 4 John Islip Street, London SW1P 4PX, England. E-mail: caryolynryle@long-and-ryle.demon.co.uk

RYOU Hong Sun, b. 28 December 1955, Choong Ju, Korea. Professor. m. Chin Ok Ryou, 1 son. Education: BS, 1977, MS, 1979, Seoul National University, Seoul, Korea; PhD, 1988, Diploma, 1988, University of London, Imperial College, London, England. Appointments: Lecturer, 1981-82, Assistant Professor, 1983-90, Associate Professor, 1991-95, Professor, 1996-, Chung Ang University, Seoul, Korea; Developer, GEC Turbine Ltd, Manchester, England, 1986-87; Research Assistant, Imperial College, London, 1987-88; Visiting Professor, Stanford University, 1993-94. Publications: Articles in scientific journals include: Development of a new spray/wall interaction model; Development and assessment of a hybrid droplet collision model for two impinging sprays; An experimental and numerical study on fine suppression using a water mist in enclosure. Memberships: Senior Member, AIAA; KSME; KSAE. Address: 203-1704 LG Village Apt, 90 Seong Bok Dong, Sujieup, Yong In Si, Kyoung Ki Do, 449-981 Korea. E-mail: cfdmec@cau.ac.kr

RYZHIKOV Gennady A, b. 26 February 1945, Pskov, Russia. Geophysicist. m. Marina S Biryulina, 4 sons. Education: BSc, Nuclear Physics, 1967, MSc, Theoretical Physics, 1974, PhD, Geophysics, 1989, University of St Petersburg, Russia. Appointments: Senior Researcher, St Petersburg University, Russia, 1971-; Senior Researcher, Physics Department, University of Bergen, 1993-; Consultant, Geminali AS, Oslo, Norway, 1997-. Publications include: Tomography and Remote Sensing Inverse Problems; Articles in professional books and journals. Address: University of Bergen, Department of Physics, Allégaten 55, Bergen 5007, Norway. Email: gennady.ryzhikov@fi.uib.no

Dictionary of International Biography

S

SAAIMAN Nolan, b. 21 December 1960, Pretoria, South Africa. Internal Auditor. m. Anita, 2 sons. Education: B Comm, Accounting Sciences, 1982; B Comm, Honours, Accounting, 1988; Diploma, Datametrics, 1992; Certified Information Systems Auditor, 1992; Certified Financial Services Auditor, 1996; Computer Professional Qualifying Examination of the Computer Society of South Africa, 1996; Certified Internal Auditor, 1998; Certified Financial Consultant, 2001; Certified Business Manager, 2001. Appointments: Senior Internal Auditor, South African Post Office, 1985-88; Accountant Van Wyk and Louw, 1988-89; Manager's Assistant, Information Systems Audit Department, First National Bank, 1990-92; Manager, Computer Audit Services, SA Eagle, 1992-94; IT Audit Manager, SA Housing Trust, 1995-97; Audit Manager, Senior Auditor, Daimler Chrysler, South Africa, 1997-. Publications: Articles about computer audit, membership matters and internal audit, in Newsletter of the Institute of Internal Auditors, South Africa, 1995-96; Article on internal audit in Institute of Directors Directorship Magazine, 1997. Honours: Completed Comrades Marathon (90kms), 1984, 1986; Served on Board of Institute of Internal Auditors, South Africa, 1996-97; 21st Century Award for Achievement, IBC, 2001; Listed in Who's Who Publications and biographical dictionaries. Memberships: Information Systems Audit and Control Association; Institute of Directors; Institute of Internal Auditors; Computer Society of South Africa; Institute of Financial Consultants, The Association of Professionals in Business Management, USA; Who's Who Historical Society. Address: 26 Retha Court, Veglaer Street, Pierre Van Ryneveld Park, 0157 South Africa. E-mail: nolan.saaiman@daimlerchrysler.com

SAATCHI Charles, b. 9 June 1943. Advertising Executive. m. (1) Doris Lockhart, (2) Kay, 1990, divorced 2001, 1 daughter. Education: Christ's College, Finchley, London, England. Appointments: Former junior copywriter, Benton and Bowles (US advertising agency), London; Associate Director, Collett Dickinson Pearce, 1966-68; with Ross Cramer formed freelance consultancy, Cramer Saatchi, Director, 1968-70; Co-founder (with Maurice Saatchi) of Saatchi and Saatchi (advertising agency), 1970, Saatchi & Saatchi PLC, 1984, Director, 1970-93, President, 1993-95; Co-founder, Partner, M&C Saatchi Agency, 1995-; Founder, The Saatchi Gallery, 2003-. Address: 36 Golden Square, London, W1R 4EE, England.

SAATCHI Baron (Life Peer) Maurice, b. 21 June 1946. Advertising Executive. m. Josephine Hart, 1984, 1 son, 1 stepson. Education: BSc, London School of Economics. Appointments: Co-Founder, Saatchi & Saatchi Company, 1970; Chairman, Saatchi & Saatchi Company PLC, 1984-94, Director, 1994; Co-founder, Partner, M&C Saatchi Agency, 1995-; Chairman, Megalomedia PLC, 1995-; Director (non-executive) Loot, 1998-; Shadow Cabinet Office Minister, 2001-. Publications: The Science of Politics, 2001. Memberships: Governor, LSE; Council, Royal College of Art, 1997-; Trustee, Victoria & Albert Museum, 1988-. Address: 36 Golden Square, London, W1R 4EE, England.

SABATINO Dominick, b. 10 February 1939, Brooklyn, USA. Physician. Education: BS, Brooklyn College, USA, 1961; MD, Bologna University, 1968; Board Certified in Pediatrics, 1975; Board Certified in Pediatric Hematology-Oncology, 1982. Appointments: Attending Physician, Pediatrics and Pediatric Hematology-Oncology, Long Island College Hospital, Brooklyn, 1975-88; Assistant Professor, Clinical Pediatrics, Chief, Pediatric Hematology-Oncology, Nassau University Medical Center; Associate Professor, Clinical Pediatrics, 1988-. Publications: 7 books; 9 articles in journals; 8 abstracts. Honours: Humanitarian Award, Cooley's Anaemia Foundation Inc; Lifetime Achievement Award for work with Cooley's Anaemia; Clinical Pioneer Award, Sickle-Thalassemia Patients Network; Avron Ross Faculty Teaching Award; Nassau University Medical Center. Memberships: American Academy of Pediatrics; Cooley's Anemia Foundation; NYS Genetic Sickle Cell Network for Screening; Pediatric Hematology-Oncology. Address: Nassau University Medical Center, Department Pediatrics, 2201 Hempstead Tpke, East Meadow, NY 11554, USA. E-mail: dsabatin.numc.educ

SABIT Ahmed Shaher, b. 10 January 1939, Cairo, Egypt. Professor. m. Mavis, 1 son, 1 daughter. Education: BSc, Faculty of Engineering, Alexandria University, Egypt, 1961; PhD, Department of Naval Architecture, University of Newcastle upon Tyne, England, 1966. Appointments: Lecturer, 1967-71, Assistant Professor, 1971-76, Professor, 1976-91, Head of Department, 1991-94, Professor, 1994-98, Head of Department, 1998-99, Visiting Professor, 1999-, Department of Naval Architecture and Marine Engineering, Alexandria University, Egypt; Supervisor of 13 awarded MSc's and 3 awarded PhD's. Publications: 46 international research papers on ship hydrodynamics and design; 2 Arabic books on ships; University textbooks for undergraduates and postgraduates; Several designs for marine and Nile units including some 33 floating hotels and restaurants for the Nile, some 64 tugs, service boats, floating pumping stations, floating cranes and split barges. Honours: State Prize of Science and Technology, 1973, Decoration of First Class in Science, 1975; Honorary Prize, Alexandria University, 1999; Alexandria University Gold Medal, 1999. Memberships: American Bureau of Shipping; Society of Shipbuilders, Egypt; Marine Engineers Society, Egypt. Address: Department of Naval Architecture and Marine Engineering, Faculty of Engineering, Alexandria University, Alexandria, Egypt.

SABOLIC Ivan, b. 15 January 1950, Kljuc. Scientific Adviser. m. Branka Sabolic, 2 daughters. Education: MD, School of Medicine, 1973, MSc, Biomedicine, 1976, PhD, Biomedicine, 1980, University of Zagreb, Zagreb, Croatia. Appointments: Assistant, 1973-84; Assistant Professor, 1984-87; Professor, 1987-91, Department of Physiology, School of Medicine, University of Zagreb, Croatia; Research Fellow, Massachusetts General Hospital/Harvard Medical School, Boston, USA, 1991-93; Scientific Adviser, Institute for Medical Research and Occupational Health, Zagreb, Croatia, 1994-. Publications: 185 Research articles in international and national scientific journals; 1600 citations. Honours: Fogarty International Research Collaborative Award, 1995 and 1999; Croatian State Award for Science, 1999. Memberships: The Croatian Biochemical Society; The Croatian Physiological Society; The American Physiological Society; The German Physiological Society. Address: Institute for Medical Research and Occupational Health, Ksaverska cesta 2, HR 10001 Zagreb, Croatia. E-mail: sabolic@imi.hr

SACHS Leo, b. 14 October 1924, Leipzig, Germany. Scientist. m. Pnina Salkind, 1 son, 3 daughters. Education: BSc, University of Wales, Bangor, 1948; PhD, Trinity College, Cambridge University, England, 1951. Appointments: Research Scientist, Genetics, John Innes Institute, England, 1951-52; Research Scientist, 1952-, Founder, Department of Genetics and Virology, 1960, Professor, 1962, Head, Department of Genetics, 1962-89, Dean, Faculty of Biology, 1974-79, Otto Meyerhof Professor of Biology, Weizmann Institute of Science, Rehovot, Israel. Publications: Science papers in professional journals. Honours: Israel Prize, Natural Sciences, 1972; Fogarty International Scholar, National Institutes of Health, Bethesda, 1972; Harvey Lecture, Rockefeller University, New York, 1972; Rothschild Prize, Biological Sciences, 1977; Wolf Prize, Medicine, 1980; Bristol-

Myers Award, Distinguished Achievement in Cancer Research, New York, 1983; Doctor Honoris Causa, Bordeaux University, France, 1985; Royal Society Wellcome Foundation Prize, London, 1986; Alfred P Sloan Prize, General Motors Cancer Research Foundation, New York, 1989; Warren Alpert Foundation Prize, Harvard Medical School, Boston, 1997; Doctor of Medicine Honoris Causa, Lund University, Sweden, 1997; Honorary Fellow, University of Wales, Bangor, 1999; Emet Prize for Life Sciences, 2002. Memberships: European Molecular Biology Organization; Israel Academy of Sciences and Humanities; Foreign Associate USA National Academy of Sciences; Fellow, Royal Society, London; Foreign Member, Academia Europaea; Honorary Life Member, International Cytokine Society. Address: Weizmann Institute of Science, Department of Molecular Genetics, Rehovot, Israel.

SACHS Murray, b. 10 April 1924, Toronto, Canada. Teacher; Scholar. m. Miriam Blank Sachs, 1 son, 1 daughter. Education: BA, 1st class honours, Modern Languages, University of Toronto, 1946; MA, French & Romance Philology, Columbia University, 1947; PhD, French & Romance Philology, 1953. Appointments: Instructor, Columbia School of General Studies, 1946-48; Lecturer, University of California, Berkeley, 1948-50, University of Detroit, 1951-52; Assistant Professor, Williams College, Williamstown, 1954-60; Assistant Professor, 1960-61; Associate Professor, 1961-66, Professor, 1966-96, Professor Emeritus, 1996-, Brandeis University. Publications include: The Career of Alphonse Daudet, 1965; The French Short Story in the 19th Century, 1969; Anatole France: The Short Stories, 1974; Émile Zola's Last Word: Vérité and the Dreyfus Affair, 1998. Honours: Governor-General's Silver Medal, University of Toronto, 1946; Henry Alfred Todd Fellowship, Columbia University, 1946-48; Palmes Académiques, French Government, 1971. Memberships: Modern Language Association; Modern Humanities Research Association; American Association of Teachers of French; American Comparative Literature Association. Address: Department of Romance and Comparative Literature, Mailstop 024, Brandeis University, Waltham, MA 02454-9110, USA.

SACKS Jonathan Henry, b. 8 March 1948, London, England. Rabbi. m. Elaine Taylor, 1970, 1 son, 2 daughters. Education: Christ's College, Finchley; Gonville and Caius College, Cambridge; New College, Oxford; London University; Jews' College, London; Yeshivat Etz Hayyim, London. Appointments: Lecturer, Middlesex Polytechnic, 1971-73; Jew's College, London, 1973-76, 1976-82; Rabbi, Golders Green Synagogue, London, 1978-82, Marble Arch Synagogue, London, 1983-90; Chief Rabbi Lord Jakobvits Professor (1st incumbent), Modern Jewish Thought, 1982-; Director, Rabbinic Faculty, 1983-90, Principal, 1984-90, Chief Rabbi, 1991-, United Hebrew Congregations of the Commonwealth; Editor, Le'ela (journal), 1985-90; Presentation Fellow, King's College, London, 1993; Association President, Conference of European Rabbis, 2000-; Visiting Professor of Philosophy, Hebrew University, Jerusalem and of Theology and Religious Studies, King's College, London. Publications: Torah Studies, 1986; Tradition and Transition, 1986; Traditional Alternatives, 1989; Traditional in an Untraditional Age, 1990; The Persistence of Faith, 1991; Orthodoxy Confronts Modernity (Editor), 1991; Crisis and Covenant, 1992; One People? Tradition, Modernity and Jewish Unity, 1993; Will We Have Jewish Grandchildren? 1994; Faith in the Future, 1995; Community of Faith, 1995; The Politics of Hope, 1997; Morals and Markets, 1999; Celebrating Life, 2000; Radical Then Radical Now, 2001; The Dignity of Difference: How To Avoid the Clash of Civilizations, 2002; The Chief Rabbi's Hagadah, 2003. Honours: Honorary degrees: Cambridge, Middlesex University, Haifa University, Yeshiva University, St Andrews University, University

of Liverpool; Honorary Fellow, Gonville and Caius College, Cambridge, 1993; Jerusalem Prize, 1995. Memberships: Member, CRAC. Address: 735 High Road, London, N12 0US, England.

SADDAM HUSSEIN, b. 1937, Tikrit, Baghdad, Iraq. Military Dictator. m. Sajida Khairalla, 1963, 2 sons, deceased, 2 daughters. Education: Cairo University; Mustanseriya University, Baghdad, Iraq. Appointments: Member, Arab Baath Socialist Party, 1957; Death Sentence for attempted Execution of General Abdul Karim Qassim, 1959; Joined leadership, Cairo branch, Baath Party, 1962; Returned to Iraq, 1963; Member, 4th Regional and 6th National Congress of Baath Party, 1963; Member, Regional Leadership, Baath Party, Iraq, 1963; Member, 7th National Congress, Syria, 1964; Arrested for plotting overthrow, Abdul Salam Aref, 1964; Deputy Secretary, Regional Leader, Baath Party, 1966-79, Secretary, 1979-; Prominent in July Revolution, 1968; Acting Deputy Chairman, Revolutionary Command Council, 1968-69, Deputy Chairman, 1969-79, Chairman, 1979-; Prime Minister, 1994-; Deputy Secretary Regional Leadership, 7th Regional Congress, 1968; Member, National Leadership of Party, 10th National Congress, 1970; Rank of General, 1976; Forces invaded Iran, 1980, 1980-88 Iran-Iraq War; Illegally invaded and annexed Kuwait, 1990; Forces defeated and forced to withdraw by UN-backed Allied Force, 1991; USA led coalition forces in invasion of Iraq, March-April 2003, Baath Party leadership overthrown, Saddam Hussein captured December 2003 and awaiting trial. Publication: Zazibah and the King; One Trench or Two; The Impregnable Fortress, 2002. Honour: Order of Rafidain, 1st Class, 1976.

SADDLEMYER (Eleanor) Ann, b. 28 November 1932, Prince Albert, Saskatchewan, Canada. Critic; Theatre Historian; Educator. Education: BA, 1953, Honours English Diploma, 1955, University of Saskatchewan; MA, Queen's University, 1956; PhD, Bedford College, University of London, England, 1961. Appointments: Faculty, University of Victoria, British Columbia, 1960-71; Faculty, Victoria College, 1971-, Director, Graduate Centre for the Study of Drama, 1972-77, 1985-89, Master, Massey College, 1988-95, Professor and Master Emeritus, 1995, University of Toronto; Berg Chair, New York University, 1975; Adjunct Professor, University of Victoria, British Columbia, 1996-. Publications: The World of W B Yeats, 1965; In Defence of Lady Gregory, Playwright, 1966; J M Synge Plays, Books I and II, 1968; Synge and Modern Comedy, 1968; Letters to Molly: J M Synge to Maire O'Neill, 1971; Lady Gregory Plays, 4 volumes, 1971; Theatre Business, 1982; The Collected Letters of J M Synge, 2 volumes, 1983-84; Lady Gregory Fifty Years After, 1987; Early Stages: Essays on the Theatre in Ontario 1800-1914, 1990; Synge's Playboy of the Western World and other Plays, 1995; Later Stages: Essays on the Theatre in Ontario, World War I to the 1950's, 1997; Becoming George: The Life of Mrs W B Yeats, 2002. Contributions to: Professional journals. Honours: Royal Society of Canada, 1977; Honorary doctorates, Queen's, 1977, Victoria, 1989, McGill, 1989, Windsor, 1990, Saskatchewan, 1991, Toronto, 1999, Concordia, 2000, universities; British Academy Rosemary Crawshay Award, 1986; Fellow, Royal Society of Arts, 1987; Alumni Award of Excellence, University of Toronto, 1991; Woman of Distinction, 1994; Officer of the Order of Canada, 1995; M L Rosenthal Award, Yeats Society of New York, 2001. Memberships: Past Chair, International Association for Study of Anglo-Irish Literature; Association for Canadian Theatre Research, founding president; Colin Smythe Publishing, board of directors; Canadian Theatre Museums Association, board; Fellow, Royal Society of Canada; Fellow, Royal Society of Arts. Address: 10876 Madrona Drive, Sidney, British Columbia V8L 5N9, Canada.

SADGROVE Sidney Henry, (Lee Torrance), b. 1920, England. Artist; Teacher; Writer. Publications: You've Got To Do Something, 1967; A Touch of the Rabbits, 1968; The Suitability Factor, 1968; Stanislaus and the Princess, 1969; A Few Crumbs, 1971; Stanislaus and the Frog, 1972; Paradis Enow, 1972; Stanislaus and the Witch, 1973; The Link, 1975; The Bag, 1977; Half Sick of Shadows, 1977; Bleep, 1977; All in the Mind, 1977; Icary Dicary Doc, 1978, Angel, 1978; Filling, 1979; First Night, 1980; Only on Friday, 1980; Hoodunnit, 1984; Pawn en Prise, 1985; Just for Comfort, 1986; Tiger, 1987; State of Play, 1988; Warren, 1989; Dear Mrs Comfett, 1990. Membership: Writers Guild of Great Britain. Address: Pimp Barn, Withyham, Hartfield, Sussex, TN7 4BB, England.

SADIE Stanley (John), b. 30 October 1930, Wembley, Middlesex, England. Musicologist; Lexicographer; Writer. m. (1) Adèle Bloom, 10 December 1953, deceased 1978, 2 sons, 1 daughter, (2) Julie Anne McCornack, 18 July 1978, 1 son, 1 daughter. Education: BA, 1953, Mus B, 1953, MA, 1957, PhD, 1958, University of Cambridge. Appointments: Faculty, Trinity College of Music, London, 1957-65; Music Critic, The Times of London, 1964-81; Editor, The Musical Times, 1967-87. Publications: Handel, 1962; The Pan Book of Opera (with Arthur Jacobs), 1964, 3rd edition, 1984; Mozart, 1966; Beethoven, 1967, 2nd edition, 1974; Handel, 1968; Handel Concertos, 1972; The New Grove Dictionary of Music and Musicians (editor), 20 volumes, 1980, revised edition, 29 volumes, 2001; The New Grove Dictionary of Musical Instruments (editor), 1984; The Cambridge Music Guide (with Alison Latham), 1985; The New Grove Dictionary of American Music (editor with H Wiley Hitchcock), 4 volumes, 1986; Mozart Symphonies, 1986; The Grove Concise Dictionary of Music (editor), 1988; Handel Tercentenary Collection (editor with A Hicks), 1988; History of Opera (editor), 1989; Performance Practice (editor with Howard M Brown), 2 volumes, 1989; Man and Music (general editor), 8 volumes, 1989-93; Music Printing and Publishing (co-editor), 1990; The New Grove Dictionary of Opera (editor), 4 volumes, 1992; Wolfgang Amadè Mozart: Essays on His Life and Music (editor), 1995; New Grove Book of Opera (editor), 1996. Contributions to: Professional journals and general publications. Honours: Commander of the Order of the British Empire, 1982; Honorary LittD, 1982. Memberships: Critics Circle; International Musicological Society, president, 1992-97; Royal College of Music, fellow; Royal Academy of Music, honorary; Royal Musical Association, president, 1989-94; American Musicological Society. Address: The Manor, Cossington, Somerset TA7 8JR, England.

SAEDEN Erik, b. 3 September 1924, Vanersborg, Sweden. Singer (Baritone). m. Elisabeth Murgard. Education: Studied at the Royal College of Music, Stockholm and at the Royal Opera School; Private studies with Arne Sunnegardh, Martin Ohman and W Freund. Career: Royal Opera Stockholm from 1952 as Mozart's Figaro and Count, Wagner's Sachs, Beckmesser, Pogner, Dutchman and Wolfram, Verdi's Iago, Renato, Macbeth, Germont, Ford and Nabucco; Berg's Wozzeck, Stravinsky's Nick Shadow, Tchaikovsky's Eugene Onegin, Busoni's Faust and the title role in Dallapiccola's Il Prigionierlo; created leading roles in Blomdahl's Aniara, Werle's Drommen om Therese, Berwald's Drottningen av Golconda, Dallapiccola's Ulisse, Rosenberg's Hus med Dubbel Ingang and Ligeti's Le Grand Macabre; Guest Appearances at Bayreuth, Edinburgh, Covent Garden, Montreal; Also Savonlinna as Father Henrik in Singoalla; recorded the role in complete recording of Singoalla. Recordings include: The Speaker in Bergman film version of Die Zauberflöte; Swedish Romances, Schubert's Winterreise. Honours: Swedish Court Singer; Order Litteris et Artibus. Memberships: Stockholm Academy of Music. Address: Höglidsv 17 A, 182 47 Enebyberg, Sweden.

SAFARGALEEV Irek, b. 11 June 1973, Ufa, Russia. Artist. Education: St Petersburg State Pedagogical University. Career: Artist; Participated in many collective and private exhibitions; Russian State Museum organised and supported project "Abstraction of the 21st Century"; Works belong to many private and corporate collections in many countries; Founder, Institute of Futuristic Research to investigate the philosophy of futurism; Businessman, Joint Stock Enterprise. Publications: Kandinski, Malevich, Filonov: What next?; Art in the XXth Century; Aesthetic Principles of Futurism; The East & the West: aesthetic parallels, (all articles are represented in the virtual annals of universalism). Honours: The Safe Conduct from International School of Universal Art for distinguished contribution to the development of object-abstract suprematism; Honoured with Rank of "Grand Master of Futurism". Membership: Chairman, Scientific Council, Institute of Futuristic Research. Address: Dolgoozyornaya Street 5, corpus 1, flat 446, St Petersburg 197373, Russia. E-mail: safarghali@mail.ru

SAFAROV Mahmadali Mahmadievich, b. 5 May 1952, Nurek, Tajikistan. Professor. m. Safarova Mohira, 5 sons, 3 daughters. Appointments: Teacher, Physics and Mathematics, 1974; Master of Technical Sciences, 1986 ; Docent, Molecular Physics Chair, 1991; Doctor of Technical Science, 1994; Professor, Experimental Physics Department, 1997; Research into the thermophysical, thermodynamics and electrophysical properties of liquids, solutions, gases, crystals, liquid crystals, electrolytes, plasms, alloys and materials. Publications: More than 350 works including 2 monographs, one reference book twenty methodical developments and manuals, seven inventions; More than 60 works published in the foreign press in English. Honour: Excellent Pupil, Republic of Tajikistan; Excellent Teacher of National Education of Tajikistan; The Best Inventor in the Republic of Tajikistan. Memberships: Engineering Academy of Republic of Tajikistan, 1999; New York Academy of Sciences, 1996; TPAC, 1997; ASTM. Address: Dushanbe, S Nosirov st 29/20, Tajikistan. E-mail: mahmad@cada.tajik.net

SAFIRE William, b. 17 December 1929, New York, New York, USA. Columnist; Writer. m. Helene Belmar Julius, 16 December 1962, 1 son, 1 daughter. Education: Syracuse University, 1947-49. Appointments: Reporter, New York Herald-Tribune Syndicate, 1949-51; Correspondent, Europe and the Middle East, WNBC-WNBT, 1951; Radio-TV Producer, WMBC, New York City, 1954-55; Vice-President, Tex McCrary Inc, 1955-60; President, Safire Public Relations, 1960-68; Special Assistant to President Richard M Nixon, 1969-73; Columnist, The New York Times, 1973-. Publications: The Relations Explosion, 1963; Plunging into Politics, 1964; Safire's Political Dictionary, 1968, 3rd edition, 1978, new edition as Safire's New Political Dictionary, 1993; Before the Fall, 1975; Full Disclosure, 1977; Safire's Washington, 1980; On Language, 1980; What's the Good Word?, 1982; Good Advice on Writing (with Leonard Safire), 1982, new edition, 1992; I Stand Corrected, 1984; Take My Word for It, 1986; You Could Look It Up, 1988; Language Maven Strikes Again, 1990; Leadership (with Leonard Safire), 1990; Fumblerules, 1990; The First Dissident, 1992; Lend Me Your Ears, 1992; Quoth the Maven, 1993; In Love with Norma Loquendi, 1994; Sleeper Spy, 1995; Watching My Language, 1997; Spread the Word, 1999; Scandalmonger, 2000; Let A Smile Be Your Umbrella, 2002. Contributions to: Newspapers and magazines. Honour: Pulitzer Prize for Distinguished Commentary, 1978. Membership: Pulitzer, Board, 1995-; Chairman, The Charles A Dana Foundation. Address: c/o The New York Times, 1627 Eye Street North West, Washington, DC 20006, USA.

Dictionary of International Biography

SAFRONOV Alexander Yu, b. 7 December 1955, Irkutsk, Russia. Chemist. m. L L Sintsova, 1 daughter. Education: MSc, Chemistry, 1978; PhD, Chemistry, 1983; C Chem, FRSC, 1997; DSc, Chemistry, 1995; Professor, 1997. Appointments: Engineer, Inorganic Chemistry Chair, 1978-79; Research Worker, 1979-90; Head of General and Inorganic Chemistry Chair, 1990; Professor, 1995; Dean of Chemical Department, 1998. Publications: Contributions to 3 books. Honours: Honourable Deed of Russian Ministry of Science and Education, 1998. Membership: Fellow, Royal Society of Chemistry, 1997. Address: Irkutsk State University, Chemical Department, 1 K Marx Str, 664003 Irkutsk, Russia. E-mail: dekan@chem.isu.ru

SAFRONOV Nikas (Nikolay), b. 8 April 1955 Ulyanovsk, USSR. Artist; Painter. 3 sons. Education: Rostov Art School, 1972-74; Vilnius Academy of Fine Arts, 1979-82. Career: Free Lance Painter of portraits, landscapes, using various techniques and their combinations, experiments with them and works with texture and classical painting; Professor, Ulyanovsk University. Publications: 5 art albums in the last 5 years; Numerous articles in newspapers and journals. Honours: International Order of St Konstantin the Great; Order of St Stanislav; Order of St Anna; Knight of Science and Fine Arts, Russian Academy of Natural Sciences; Title of Prince Awarded by the Russian Assembly of Nobility; Gold Watch from Vladimir Putin, President of Russia; Honourable Citizen of Ulyanovsk and Saratov; Honourable Citizen of Baku, Republic of Azerbaijan; Honorary Doctor, Azerbaijan State Art and Culture University; Listed in Who's Who publications and biographical dictionaries. Memberships: Academician, International Art Academy; Russian Professional Union of Artists, Moscow. Address: Flat 2, House 17, Brusov Side-Street, Moscow 125009, Russia.

SAGGS Henry William Frederick, b. 2 December 1920, Weeley, Essex, England. Retired Professor of Semitic Languages. m. Joan Butterworth, 21 September 1946, 4 daughters. Education: King's College, London, 1939-42, 1946-48; School of Oriental and African Studies, London, 1949-52; BD, 1942; MTh, 1948; MA, 1950; PhD, 1953. Appointments: Lecturer, then Reader in Akkadian, School of Oriental and African Studies, London, 1953-66; Professor of Semitic Languages, University College Cardiff, University of Wales, 1966-83. Publications: The Greatness That Was Babylon, 1962, revised edition, 1987; Everyday Life in Babylon and Assyria, 1965, 2nd edition, 1987; The Encounter With the Divine in Mesopotamia and Israel, 1978; The Might That Was Assyria, 1984, 2nd edition, 1990; Civilization Before Greece and Rome, 1989; Babylonians, 1995; Au Temps de Babylone, 1998. Contributions to: Iraq; Sumer; Journal of Cuneiform Studies; Journal of Theological Studies; Archiv für Orientforschung; Revue d'Assyriologie; Journal of Semitic Studies; Bibliotheca Orientalis. Memberships: Society of Authors; Society of Antiquaries; British School of Archaeology in Iraq, council member; Savage Club; Royal Asiatic Society. Address: Eastwood, Bull Lane, Long Melford, Suffolk CO10 9EA, England.

SAH Bindeshwar Prasad, b. 3 September 1946, Chak Kusiyari, Bidupur R.S., Bihar, India. Lecturer; Teacher. m. Smt Sumitra, 3 sons. Education: BA, Honours, English, 1967; MA, English, 1969; LLB, 1971; MA, Hindi, Gold Medal; Bachelor of Teaching (BT); Master of Education (M.Ed); Diploma in Distance Education from IGNOU; PhD, English, English and Hindi Drama. Appointments: Postgraduate Teacher, 1972; Lecturer in English, 1981; Counsellor and Assistant Co-ordinator, IGNOU, 1987-94; Senior Lecturer in English, 1986; Reader in English, 1994; Guest Lecturer, Arunachal University, 1999. Publications: Poems in English and Hindi, 1962-; Articles in English and Hindi; Editor, 12 books; Institutional magazines; Presented research papers in professional seminars and

workshops. Honours: Nehru Academic Award, 1964; National Merit Scholarship, 1964; University Topper in English Honours Exam, 1967; International Man of the Year, IBC, 1999-2000; Man of the Year, ABI, 1999; International Distinguished Leadership Award, ABI, 2000. Memberships: Life Member, ASRC, Hyderabad; The Quest, Ranchi; Board of Studies, English, of Arunachal Varsity; Secretary, Ar Pr College Teachers' Association; Fellow of the United Writers' Association of India, Chennai; Member, Research Board of Advisers, American Biographical Institute, 2000-; Deputy Governor, ABI; Deputy Director General, International Biographical Centre, England. Address: Head, Department of English, Government College, Itanagar 791113, Arunachal Pradesh, India.

SAHA Manoranjan, b. 8 January 1952, Manikganj, Dhaka, Bangladesh. Professor of Applied Chemistry and Chemical Technology. m. Kabita, 1 son, 1 daughter. Education: BS (Hons), Chemistry, Dhaka University, 1974; MS, Chemical Engineering, Azerbaijan Institute of Petroleum and Chemistry, Baku, USSR, 1977; PhD, Petroleum and Petrochemicals, 1982; Postdoctoral Studies, Indian Institute of Science, Bangalore, 1995; Indian Institute of Petroleum, Dehradun, 1996. Appointments: Assistant Professor, 1983-90, Associate Professor, 1990-94, Professor, 1994-, Chairman, Department of Applied Chemistry and Chemical Technology, 1998-2001, Dhaka University, Dhaka, Bangladesh. Publications: 125 publications in national and international journals. Honours: Listed in Who's Who publications and biographical dictionaries. Memberships: Asiatic Society Bangladesh; Bangladesh Association for the Advancement of Science; Bangladesh Chemical Society; Bangladesh Association of Scientists and Scientific Professions. Address: Department of Applied Chemistry and Chemical Technology, University of Dhaka, Dhaka-1000, Bangladesh. E-mail: msaha@udhaka.net

SAHA Uttam Kumar, b. 30 September 1961, Pabna, Bangladesh. Researcher. m. Rupa Rani Saha, 1 son. Education: BSc Ag (with first class honours), MSc, Soil Science, Bangladesh Agricultural University; PhD, Environmental Soil Chemistry, Iwate University, Japan. Appointments: Assistant Professor, BSMRAU, Bangladesh, 1993-99; Postdoctoral Research Fellow, Japan Society for the Promotion of Science, 1999-2001; Postdoctoral Research Fellow, University of Saskatchewan, Canada, 2001-2003; Visiting Fellow, NSERC, Canada, 2003-. Publications: More than 45 original research articles published in peer refereed journals in the field of environmental and agricultural sciences for human welfare. Honours: Awardee, JSPS Postdoctoral Fellowship, Japan; Awardee, Alexander-von-Humboldt Fellowship, Germany. Memberships: Life Member, Bangladesh Society of Soil Science; ASA, CSSA, SSSA, USA; International Union of Soil Scientists. Address: NSERC Visiting Fellow, Agriculture and Agri-Food Canada, GPCRC, 2585 County Road 20, Harrow, ON, Canada N0R 1G0. E-mail: sahau@agr.gc.ca

SAID Edward, b. 1 November 1935, Jerusalem, Palestine. Professor; Writer. m. Mariam Cortas, 14 December 1970, 2 children. Education: AB, Princeton University, 1957; AM, 1960, PhD, 1964, Harvard University. Appointments: Instructor, 1963-65, Assistant Professor, 1965-67, Associate Professor, 1967-70, Professor, 1970-77, Parr Professor of English and Comparative Literature, 1977-89, Old Dominion Foundation Professor of Humanities, 1989-, University Professor, 1992-, Columbia University; Visiting Professor, Harvard University, 1974, Johns Hopkins University, 1979, Yale University, 1985; Fellow, Center for Advanced Study in the Behavioural Sciences, Palo Alto, California, 1975-76; Christian Gauss Lecturer in Criticism, Princeton University, 1977; Carpenter Professor, University of Chicago, 1983; T S Eliot Lecturer, University of Kent, Canterbury,

Dictionary of International Biography

1985; Northrop Frye Chair, University of Toronto, 1986; Messenger Lecturer, Cornell University, 1986; Wilson Lecturer, Wellesley College, 1991; Amnesty Lecturer, University of Oxford, 1992; Lord Northcliffe Lecturer, University College, London, 1993; Reith Lecturer, BBC, London, 1993. Publications: Joseph Conrad and the Fiction of Autobiography, 1966; Beginnings: Intention and Method, 1975; Orientalism, 1978; The Question of Palestine, 1979; Literature and Society, 1979; Covering Islam, 1981; The World, the Text and the Critic, 1983; After the Last Sky, 1986; Blaming the Victims, 1988; Muscial Elaborations, 1991; Culture and Imperialism, 1993; Representations of the Intellectual, 1994; The Politics of Dispossession, 1994; Ghazzah-Arihah: Salam Amriki, 1994; Out of Place: A Memoir, 1999; The End of the Peace Process: Oslo and After, 2000; Reflections on Exile, essays, 2001. Contributions to: Professional journals and other publications. Honours: Guggenheim Fellowship, 1972-73; Social Science Research Fellow, 1975; Lionel Trilling Awards, Columbia University, 1976, 1994; René Wellek Award, American Comparative Literature Association, 1985; Spinoza Prize, 1999; Morton Dauwen Zabel Award, 2000. Memberships: American Academy of Arts and Sciences; American Comparative Literature Association; Association of Arab-American University Graduates; Council on Foreign Relations; Modern Language Association; PEN, executive board, 1989-. Address: c/o Department of English, Columbia University, New York, NY 10027, USA.

SAIKIA Prayag, b. 7 October 1959, Nagaon (Assam), India. Medical Practitioner; Poet. m. Rasna Hiloidari, 24 November 1990. Education: MBBS, 1985; Fellow, Society for Advanced Studies in Medical Science (FSASMS), 1993. Appointment: Private medical practitioner. Publications: Prithivi Preosy, 1987; Baushit Dukhan Deuka, 1990; Amitabha Phule, 1993; Edin Vivekar Prithivit, novel, 1996; Yearning For Dawn, poetry collection, 2000; Patmadoi pakhir jangam, poetry, 2000; Easelor Elegy Aru Anyanya, poetry, 2003; Keikhanman Nadir Kathare, collection of short stories in assamese, 2003. Contributions to: Assamese gariyashi; Prantik; Siralu; Prakash; Nabadut; Ajir Batari; Natun Dainik; Bengali-Jatinga; Ma-Nishad; Durer Kheya; English Poet; World Poetry '96; Poems '96; Sentinal; Indian Literature; Chandrabhaga; Festival, The Statesman, 2001; Chicago poetry online anthology. Memberships: Assam Sahitya Sabha; Kallol Sansritik Gusthi; Advisor of Nagaon Cultural Troup. Address: B Bora Road, Fauzdaripatty, Nagaon - 1, PIN: 782001, Assam, India.

SAINT Dora Jessie, (Miss Read), b. 17 April 1913, Surrey, England. Novelist; Short Story and Children's Fiction Writer. Education: Homerton College, 1931-33. Publications: Village School, 1955; Village Diary, 1957; Storm in the Village, 1958; Hobby Horse Cottage, 1958; Thrush Green, 1959; Fresh From the Country, 1960; Winter in Thrush Green, 1961; Miss Clare Remembers, 1962; The Market Square, 1966; The Howards of Caxley, 1967; Country Cooking, 1969; News from Thrush Green, 1970; Tyler's Row, 1972; Christmas Mouse, 1973; Battles at Thrush Green, 1975; No Holly for Miss Quinn, 1976; Village Affairs, 1977; Return to Thrush Green, 1978; The White Robin, 1979; Village Centenary, 1980; Gossip From Thrush Green, 1981; A Fortunate Grandchild, 1982; Affairs at Thrush Green, 1983; Summer at Fairacre, 1984; At Home in Thrush Green, 1985; Time Remembered, 1986; The School at Thrush Green, 1987; The World at Thrush Green, 1988; Mrs Pringle, 1989; Friends at Thrush Green, 1990; Changes at Fairacre, 1991; Celebrations at Thrush Green, 1992; Farewell to Fairacre, 1993; Tales From a Village School, 1994; The Year at Thrush Green, 1995; A Peaceful Retirement, 1996. Honour: Member of the Order of the British Empire, 1998. Membership: Society of Authors. Address: c/o Michael Joseph, 27 Wrights Lane, London W8 5TZ England.

SAINT LAURENT Yves (Henri Donat), b. 1 August 1936, Oran, Algeria. Couturier. Appointments: With Christian Dior, 1954-57, successor to Christian Dior, 1957-60; Shareholder Société Yves Saint Laurent, 1962-; Consultant to Chinese government, 1987-; Announced retirement, 2002; Designer, costumes for ballets: Cyrano de Bergerac, 1959; Adage et Variations, Notre-Dame de Paris, 1965; Sheherezade, 1973; Delicate Balance, 1967; Films: The Pink Panther, 1962; Belle de Jour, 1967; La Chamade, 1968; La Sirène du Mississippi, 1969; L'Affaire Stavisky, 1974; Designer, stage sets and costumes for Les Chants de Maldoror, 1962; Spectacle Zizi Jeanmaire, 1961, 1963, 1968; Exhibitions: Metropolitan Museum of Art, NY, 1983; Beijing Museum of Fine Arts, 1985; Musée des Arts de la Mode, Paris, 1986; House of Painters of USSR, 1986; Hermitage Museum, Leningrad, 1987; Art Gallery of NSW, Sydney, 1987; Sezon Museum, Tokyo, 1990; Espace Mode Méditerranée, Marseilles, 1993. Publication: La Vilaine Lulu, 1967. Honours: International Award of Council of Fashion Designers of America, 1982; Best Fashion Designer Oscar, 1985; Chevalier Légion d'honneur. Address: 5 avenue Marceau, 75116 Paris, France.

SAITO Keiichi, b. 24 February 1958, Sendai, Japan. Dentist. m. Megumi Ishida, 1 son. Education: Graduate, Tohoku University School of Dentistry, 1985; PhD (DDS), 1997. Appointment: Lecturer, Tohoku University School of Dentistry, 1985-. Publications: Articles in scientific journals include: Journal of Periodontal Research, 1996; Journal of Periodontology, 1999, 2000; Journal of Oral Pathological Medicine, 2000. Honours: Lion Award, 2001; Listed in Who's Who publications and biographical dictionaries. Memberships: International Association of Dental Research, 1996-; New York Academy of Science, 1999-2001; American Association for the Advancement of Science, 2002. Address: Department of Preventive Dentistry, Tohoku University School of Dentistry, 4-1 Seiryo-machi, Aoba-ku, Sendai 980-8575 Japan. E-mail: upup@mail.tains.tohoku.ac.jp

SAITO Makoto, b. 30 August 1940, Japan. Professor of Economics. Education: BA, Commerce, Waseda University, Tokyo, 1967; MA, Economics, 1972; ABD, Economics, Keio University, Tokyo, 1976. Appointments: Lecturer, Daito Bunka University, Tokyo, 1977-81; Associate Professor, 1981-90; Professor, Economics, 1990-. Publications: A Unification of European Currencies and Development; Adjustment of Incomes and Prices in the Process of General Equilibrium, 1999. Honours: Visiting Scholar, University of Cambridge, England. Memberships: Japan Association of Monetary Economics. Address: 3-27-A-1202 Nakadai, Itabashi-Ku, Tokyo, Japan.

SAITO Seiichi, b. 6 April 1956, Rubeshibe, Hokkaido, Japan. Medical Doctor; Urologist. m. Ryuko Sakuraba, 1 son, 2 daughters. Education: MD, 1982, PhD, 1986, Sapporo Medical Hospital. Appointments: Instructor, Sapporo Medical Hospital, 1987-87; Research Fellow, Mayo Clinic, 1987-89; Senior Research Fellow, 1989; Director, Art Park Urology Hospital, Sapporo, Japan, 1991-; Sex-check Chief, Asian Olympic Games, 1990 and Universtade, 1991; Secretary, Hokkaido Hemodialysis Association; Academic Instructor, Sapporo Medical Association. Publications: Transuretheral en bloc resection of bladder tumors, 2001; Radical Perineal Prostatectomy: Novel approach for lymphadenectomy from perineal incision, 2003; Evaluation of the cases where the right kidney is higher than the left kidney, 2003. Honour: Diploma for the Chief of Sex-check at Asian Winter Olympic Games, 1990 and Winter Universtade, 1991. Memberships: American Urological Association; Entourological Society; American Society of Andrology; American Fertility Society; Société Internationale d'Urologie. Address: Art Park Urology Hospital & Clinic, Ishiyama-Higashi 3-1-31, Sapporo, 005-0850 Japan. E-mail: apu@mb.infosnow.ne.jp

SAJIN Tudor, b. 10 June 1951, Mihaileni, Moldova. Professor. Divorced. 1 son. Education: Diploma, Engineer in Thermotechnics, Faculty of Mechanical Engineering, 1968-73, Diploma, Engineer in Inventions, Faculty of Inventions, 1975-77, Kishinev; Doctor Engineer in Thermophysics and Molecular Physics, Moscow Energetic Institute, 1989. Appointments: Scientific Researcher, Technical University, Kishinev, 1975-77; Engineer, 1978, Senior Engineer, 1979-82, Junior Researcher, 1983-89, Senior Researcher, 1990-94, Leading Scientific Researcher, 1995-, Institute of Applied Physics, Moldavian Academy of Science, Kishinev; Engineer in Inventions, Medicine State University, Kishinev, 1979-81, 1990-91; Senior Lecturer, 1990-97, Docent, 1997-98, Technical University, Kishinev; Docent, State Agricultural University, Kishinev, 1997-98; Docent and Professor, University of Bacau, Faculty of Engineering, Department of Energetics, Bacau, 1998-. Publications: 158 scientific papers; 62 patents; 14 books; 2 teaching aids. Honours: Inventor of USSR, 1982; Excellent Pupil in Invention and Rationalization, 1983; Support in NATO Advanced Study Institute, 1998; Diploma of Honour, Exhibitions Centre, Bucharest, 1998; Diploma of Second Degree, Exhibitions Centre, Kishinev, 2000; Diploma and Bronze Medal, Exhibitions Centre, Kishinev, 2002; Diplomas and Bronze Medals, Salon ECOINVENT, Iasi, 2003; Diploma and Gold Medal, Exhibitions Centre, Kishinev, 2003; Diploma and Argent Medal, XIV-th International Salon of Rationalizations and Investments, Moscow, 2004. Memberships: Romanian Society of Thermotechnical Engineers; Institute of Applied Physics of Moldavian Academy of Science; International Committee of Community of Independent States in Drying Problems, Kiev. Address: University of Bacau, Faculty of Engineering, Department of Energetics, 157 Calea Marasesti str, RO-600115, Bacau, Romania. E-mail: sajin@ub.ro

SAKA Mehmet Polat, b. 17 January 1947, Trabzon, Turkey. Professor. m. Gulten, 3 daughters. Education: BSc, MSc, Istanbul Technical University, Turkey; PhD, University of Aston, Birmingham, England, 1975. Appointments: Assistant Professor, 1975-82, Associate Professor, 1982-92, Professor, 1992-. Publications: Over 75 papers in international journals and conferences. Memberships include: ASCE; Asian Center for Engineering Computation; International Association for Bridge and Structural Engineers. Address: University of Bahrain, Department of Civil Engineering, PO Box 32038, Isa Town, Bahrain.

SAKAKIBARA Kuniki, b. 17 August, 1944, Nagoya, Japan. Professor. m. Kunie Matsumoto, 1 son, 1 daughter. Education: Master of Education, 1970, PhD, 2003, Nagoya University, Japan. Appointments: Sectional Chief, Nippon Recruit Centre Co Inc, Tokyo, 1976-83; Assistant Professor, 1983-88, Professor, 1988-81, Toyohashi Junior College; Professor, Aichi Shukutoku Junior College, 1991-96; Professor, Aichi Shukutoku University, Aichi Gun, 1996-. Publications: Author, Psychology of People and Organizations, 1999; Co-author: Organizational Psychology, 1988; Nagoya Towards the 21st Century, 1998; Handbook of Personnel Assessment, 2000. Memberships: Academy of Management; Japanese Association of Industrial and Organizational Psychology; Japanese Psychology Association. Address: 6-12-6 Oshizawadai Kasugai, Aichi Pref, 487-0005 Japan. E-mail: saki@asu.aasa.ac.jp

SALIMONU Lekan Samusa, b. 31 March 1939, Ibadan, Nigeria. University Professor. m. Sikirat Idowu Adelaja, 1 son, 2 daughters. Education: Associate, 1964, Fellow, 1966, Institute of Medical Laboratories; Master of Science, 1974; PhD, 1980. Appointments: Research Fellow, 1974-76, Lecturer I, 1976-78, Senior Lecturer, 1978-80, Associate Professor, 1980-83, Professor, 1990-, College of Medicine, University of Ibadan, Nigeria. Publications: Over 80 scientific publications in reputable national and international journals on immunology of protein energy malnutrition and related topics. Honours: Temporary Advisor, Consultant, WHO, 1973; Visiting Scientist, Immunogenetics Laboratory, Amsterdam; WHO Fellow; CIDA Fellow. Memberships: Treasurer, Nigerian Society for Immunology; Deputy Chairman, International UNS Commission on Nutrition and Immunity; CS for Immunology. Address: Via Bodija, 5 Salimonu Street, Kongi Layout, Ibadan, Nigeria.

SALINGER J(erome) D(avid), b. 1 January 1919, New York, USA. Author. m. Claire Douglas, divorced, 1 son, 1 daughter. Education: Military college. Career: Travelled in Europe, 1937-38; Army service with 4th Infantry Division (Staff Sergeant), 1942-46. Publications include: Novels: The Catcher in the Rye, 1951; Franny and Zooey; Raise High the Roof Beam; Carpenter and Seymour - An Introduction, 1963; Stories: For Esme with Love and Squalor, 1953; Numerous stories, mostly in the New Yorker, 1948-; Hapworth 16, 1924, 1997. Address: c/o Harold Ober Associates Inc, 425 Madison Avenue, New York, NY 10017, USA.

SALISBURY-JONES Raymond Arthur, b. 31 July 1933, Camberley, England. Director of Music. Education: MA (Hons), Modern History, Christ Church, Oxford, 1953-56. Appointments: Executive, Rolls Royce Ltd/Rolls Royce Motors Ltd, 1956-75; Director, Rolls Royce Motors International, 1973-75; Chairman, Hambledon Vineyards Ltd, 1974-85; Managing Director, RSJA Aviation International Ltd, 1976-91; Non-executive Director Daniel Thwaites plc, 1974-98; Senior Consultant, Middle east Consultants Ltd, 1995-98; Consultant to mi2g Ltd (Internet Security Specialists), 1997-2000; Organist and Director of Music at 3 churches in London, St Andrew, Holborn, Most Holy Redeemer, Clerkenwell, St Mark's, Islington, 2002-. Honours: Rowe Piano Competition, 1948; Harford Lloyd Organ Prize, 1950; MA (Hons), Oxon. Memberships: Air League; Royal College of Organists; Pratt's Club. Address: 6A Bristol Gardens, London W9 2JG, England. E-mail: rsj100@talk21.com

SALLAKU Agim, b. 5 February 1956, Tirana, Albania. Physician. m. Laureta, 2 daughters. Education: GP Diploma, Faculty of Medicine, 1980; Radiotherapy Physician, Institute of Oncology, 1981-89; Doctor of Science, 1997. Appointments: Head of Radio Therapy Department, 1997-, Director of Oncology Service, 2003, University Hospital Centre "Mother Teresa", Tirana, Albania. Honour: Doctor of Science Award on Larynx Cancer and Its Treatment, 1997. Publications: Home Palliative Care in Developing Countries, 1995; Pre-operative Chemotherapy and Radiotherapy in Locally Advanced Cancer, 1998; The role of radiotherapy with or without adjuvant chemotherapy in the context of breast cancer, 2003. Memberships: ESTRO; ASTRO; BUON. Address: University Hospital Centre, Mother Teresa OSUT, Tirana, Albania. E-mail: agimsallaku@hotmail.com

SALTER Arthur Thomas John Alexis, b. 22 November 1934, Tong-Norton Farm, Shropshire, England. Priest. Education: King's College, University of London, 1957-60; A.K.C. 1960, St Boniface's Theological College, Warminster, 1960-61. Appointments: Curate, St Peter, Mount Park, Ealing, London, 1961-65; Curate, St Stephen-with-St Thomas the Apostle, Shepherd's Bush, London, 1965-66; Curate, St Alban the Martyr, Holborn, London with St Peter, Saffron Hill, 1966-70; Priest-in-charge of St Michael the Archangel, Islington, London, 1970-1979; Priest-in-charge of St Clement of Rome, Barnsbury, London, 1970-79; Vicar of St Silas-with All Saints and St James, Pentonville, London, 1970-2000; Chairman, Anglican and Eastern Churches' Association, 1975-2001; Guild Vicar of St Dunstan-in-the-West with St Thomas of Canterbury-within-the-Liberty of the Rolls, 1979-1999; Chairman, Pontifical Society of St John Chrysostom, 2002. Publications: Anglicans and the Holy See; Should I Receive

Unction?; Numerous articles in church journals. Honours: Chaplain to Her Majesty's Territorial Army, Royal Army Chaplains' Department, 1975-94, with rank of Major; Territorial Decoration (TD), 1988; Chaplain to the survivors of HMTS Lancastria, 1996-; Chaplain of Justice Sacred Military Order of St Lazarus of Jerusalem; Honorary Knight of Justice, Order of St Michael of the Wing (Royal House of Portugal); Order of Orthodox Hospitallers; Ethnarchy of Cyprus; Archimandrite's Cross, Byelorussian Autocephatic Orthodox Church; Archpriest's Cross, Ethiopian Catholic Uniate Eparchy of Eritrea; Archpriest's Cross, Coptic Patriarchate of Alexandria; Locum Tenens Apocrisarios to His All Holiness the Ecumenical Patriarch and to His Sacred Beatitude the Armenian Patriarch of Constantinople and Chaplain to Her Majesty's Consul General, Istanbul, 1975. Memberships: Member, Descendants of the Knights of the Garter, Windsor Castle; Fellow, Sion College; Member, Committee of the Nikaean Club, Lambeth Palace, 1999-2001; Regular Army Reserve of Officers, 1994-96; Served, Intelligence Corps and Royal Army Medical Corps, 1954-56; A co-heir, Barony of Umfraville and Earldom of Angus; Member, Centro Coptico, Venice; Athenaeum Club, Pall Mall, London W1; Freeman of the City of London, 1990; Priest of the Melkite Greek Patriarchate of Antioch and All the East, of Alexandria and of Jerusalem, 2000; Counsellor for Foreign Relations to His Sacred Beatitude Gregory III, Patriarch of the Melkite Greek Catholic Church; Member, Friends of the Holy Father. Address: 1 St James's Close, Bishop Street, Islington, London N1 8PH, England.

SALTER James, b. 10 June 1925, New York New York, USA. Writer. m. Ann Altemus, 5 June 1951, divorced 1976, 2 sons, 3 daughters. M. Kaya Eldredge 22 April 1998. Publications: The Hunters, 1957; The Arm of Flesh, 1960-; A Sport and a Pastime, 1967; Light Years, 1976; Solo Faces, 1980; Dusk and Other Stories, 1989; Burning the Days, 1997; Cassada, 2000. Contributions to: Paris Review; Antaeus; Grand Street; Vogue; Esquire. Honours: American Academy of Arts and Letters, Grant, 1982; PEN-Faulkner Award, 1989. Membership: American Academy of Arts and Letters: PEN USA. Address: Box 765, Bridgehampton, NY 11932, USA.

SAMANTARAY Pyari Mohan, b. 5 February 1918, Orissa, India. Officer, Indian Administrative Service. m. Pramila, 8 sons. Education: BSc with honours, Patna University, 1939; MSc, Calcutta University (interrupted by World War II). Appointments: Orissa State Administrative Service, 1942; Promoted to Indian Administrative Service; Many important posts held under the State Government of Orissa, including: Collector and District Magistrate; Secretary, Board of Revenue; Director of Community Development and Panchayat Raj. Publications: Author of the book, Antah Swarara Ragini (Song of the Soul), selected for the degree course at Utkal University; Editor and writer, fortnightly newspaper, Digbijayee; Composer of songs and poems. Honours: Bhima Bhoi Award for social and literary work, All Orissa Tribal Cultural Organisation; Bira Gaurab (Glory of Heroes), The Kshatriza Mahasabha, organisation for the advancement of the largest population of Orissa. Memberships: Permanent Member, Utkal Sahitza Samaj, premier literary institution in Orissa; President, Kshatriza Mahasabha; President, Bira Oriza Party, Political Party; Title of Orissa-Ra-Garba (Pride of Orissa) conferred by Small and Medium Newspaper Federation of India (Orissa Branch); Known as Eminent Scientist of the World for invention of "Photo-Periodism in Paddy" theory. Address: At PO Madhupatna, Cuttack 10, Orissa, India.

SAMARTSEV Vitaly V, b. 29 October 1939, Kazan, Russia. Physics (Optics). m. V A Samartseva. Education: Kazan State University, 1960-66; Candidate of Sciences, 1970; Doctor of Phys-

Math Sciences, 1981; Professor, 1990; Correspondent Member of Russian Academy of Natural Sciences, 1995. Appointments: Army, 1958-60; Kazan State University, 1960-66; Kazan Phys Tech Institute RAS-Aspirantura, 1966-69; Researcher, 1969-73; Senior Researcher, 1973-86, Main Researcher, 1986-91, Chief of Laboratory, 1991-2003, Kazan Phys-Tech Institute RAS. Publications: 348 articles in Russian and international journals on problems of coherent and quantum optics; 9 books on coherent optics, laser spectroscopy, optical processing, laser cooling. Honour: Prize of MAIK/NAUKA for investigation in laser physics and laser cooling of solids, 1998. Memberships: Correspondent member, Russian Academy of Natural Sciences; Actual member, Russian Optical Society. Address: Uliavovs Street 57, apt 43, Kazan 12, Tatarstan 420012, Russia.

SAMATA Mitsuo, b. 1 January 1949, Kawasaki, Japan. Chemical Engineer. m. Fumiyo, 2 daughters. Education: Graduate, Tokyo Science University, Japan, 1971; Doctor of Engineering, Kanazawa University, Japan, 1998. Appointment: Chief Researcher, Yokohama Environmental Research Institute, Japan, 1973-. Publication: A Statistical Estimation of Precision in Sampling of Aerosol Particles with Monte Carlo Method, Kagakukougaku Ronbunshu, Japan, Vol 27, No 5, 2001. Honours: Da Vinci Diamond, IBC; Outstanding Scientists of the 21st Century, IBC. Memberships: LFIBA; MOIF. Address: Yokohama Environmental Research Institute, 1-2-15 Takigashira, Isogo-ku, Yokohama 235-0012, Japan. E-mail: mi00-samata@city.yokohama.jp

SAMBROOK Richard, b. 24 April 1956, Canterbury, England. Broadcasting Executive. m. Susan Jane Fisher, 1 son, 1 daughter. Education: BA (Hons) Reading University; MSc, London University. Appointments: Thomson Regional Papers, 1977-80; BBC Radio News, 1980-84; News Editor, Department Editor, 9 O'clock News; Head of Newsgathering, 1996-2000; Deputy Director, BBC News, 2000-2001; Director, BBC News, 2001-. Honours: Fellow, RTS; Fellow, RSA. Address: BBC TV Centre, Wood Lane, London W12 7RJ, England.

SAMDANI Attique, b. 2 November 1966, Pakistan. Physician. Education: MBBS, Khyber Medical College, Peshawar, Pakistan, 1990. Appointments: Arizona Cancer Center, USA, 1993-95; Internal Medicine, University of Arizona, USA, 1995-98; Haematology and Oncology, University of Virginia, USA, 1998-2001; Virginia Cancer Institute, 2001-. Publication: Article in Leukaemia Research Journal, 1996. Honours: First Prize and Certificate of Merit with Distinction, American College of Physicians Poster Presentation Competition, Arizona, 1996; Listed in Who's Who publications and biographical dictionaries. Memberships: American Society of Clinical Oncology; American Society of Hematology. Address: 12900 Scrimshaw Circles, Chester, VA 23836, USA. E-mail: attique_samdani@hotmail.com

SAMPRAS Pete, b. 12 August 1971, Washington DC, USA. Tennis Player. m. Brigette Wilson, 1 son. Career: US Open Champion, 1990, 1993, 1995, 1996; Grand Slam Cup Winner, 1990; IBM/ATP Tour World Championship - Frankfurt Winner, 1991; Member, US Davis Cup Team, 1991, 1995; US Pro-Indoor Winner, 1992; Wimbledon Singles Champion, 1993, 1994, 1995, 1997, 1998, 1999, 2000; European Community Championships Winner, 1993, 1994; Ranked No 1, 1993; Winner, Australian Open, 1994; RCA Championships, 1996, ATP Tour World Championships, 1996, Australian Open, 1997; Winner, San José Open, 1997; Philadelphia Open, 1997; Cincinnati Open, 1997; Munich Open, 1997; Paris Open, 1997; Hanover Open, 1997; Advanta Championship, 1998; Winner of 63 WTA Tour singles titles and 2 doubles. Address: ATP Tour, 420 West 45th Street, New York, NY 10036, USA. Website: www.petesampras.com

Dictionary of International Biography

SAMUELS Russell Henry Ashleigh, b. 13 July 1951, Mombasa, Kenya. Consultant Orthodontist. m. Therese Anne, 2 sons. Education: Liverpool University; University of Wales, College of Medicine. Appointments: House Officer, Senior House Officer, Registrar, 1983-87, Registrar, Orthodontics, 1987-90, Liverpool University Dental Hospital, Liverpool; Senior Registrar, Cardiff Dental Hospital, University of Wales, College of Medicine, 1990-96; Consultant Orthodontist, Genfield Hospital, University Hospitals of Leicester, 1996-. Publications: 34 articles in international journals; Designer/Inventor of: The Nitom Locking Facebow; The TN3 Bracket Positioning Instrument; The U-Flex Bracket. Honours: Fellowship, Institute of Medical Laboratory Sciences, 1976; BDS (Honours), 1982; Fellowship in Dental Surgery, Royal College of Physicians and Surgeons, Glasgow, 1986; Diploma in Orthodontics, Royal College of Surgeons, Edinburgh and England, 1989; Master in Dental Science, Liverpool, 1990; Membership in Orthodontics, Royal College of Surgeons, Edinburgh, 1990. Memberships: British Dental Association; British Orthodontic Society; European Orthodontic Society; American Association of Orthodontics; World Federation of Orthodontics. Address: Department of Orthodontics, Glenfield Hospital, University Hospitals of Leicester, Groby Road, Leicester LE3 9QP, England.

SANCHEZ ARELLANO Elpidio, b. 3 April 1934, Mazatlan, Sinaloa, Mexico. Physician; Surgeon. m. Lydia A Mora. 3 sons. Education: University, 1955-60; General Practitioner, Neurology and Neurosurgery Training, 1963-68; Physician, Surgeon Examination, 1963. Appointments: Private Practice, 1960-; Professor of Neurology, National Autonomous University of Mexico (UNAM); National Institute of Cardiology-Neurology, 1969-78; National Institute of Orthopedy-Neurosurgery, 1971-86; General Hospital Atizapan, 1986-91; Xoco General Hospital, Neurosurgery, 1988-91; Retired, 1991. Publications: Articles in professional journals include: Bolatin de Ciencias Neurologices, 1968; Various issues of Rev. Med. Hosp. Grad. Mex; Trauma; Diverse abstracts. Honours: Honourable Diplomas awarded by: City Council of Pueblo Puella, Mexico; Tlaxcala, Mexico; Hidalgo, Mexico and others in the USA. Memberships: International College of Surgeons, 1973; New York Academy of Sciences, 1997; American Chemical Society, 1999-. Address: Colina de Hernan 34, 53140 Boulevares, Mexico.

SANCHEZ-IBARRA Antonio, b. 30 August 1955, Mexicali, BC, Mexico. Astronomer. m. Marcela Barraza-Paredes, 1 son. Education: Self-taught Astronomy studies; Teacher Degree, Autonomous University of Guerrero, 1979; Graduate and Master Degree, Swinburne University of Australia. Publications: 4 books; 23 research articles; More than 200 articles in magazines and newspapers; Production and direction of programmes for radio, TV and internet. Honours: Mexican National Prize in Public Outreach of Science, 2000; Distinguished Citizen of Hermosillo, 2000, 2001; Listed in Who's Who publications and biographical dictionaries. Memberships: Solar Physics Division, AAS; SOMEDICYT; LIADA. Address: Lopez del Castilo 33, Col Olivares, Hermosillo Sonora 83180, Mexico. E-mail: asanchez@cosmos.astro.uson.mx Website: http://cosmos.astro.uson.mx/asi.htm

SANCHEZ-VICARIO Arantxa, b. 18 December 1971, Barcelona, Spain. Tennis Player. Career: Coached Juan Nunez; Winner, 1st professional title at Brussels, 1988; Winner, French Open Women's title, 1989, 1994, 1998; International Championships of Spain, 1989, 1990, Virginia Slims Tournaments, Newport, 1991, Washington, 1991; Winner, Canadian Open, 1992, Australian Open, 1992, 1993, US Open, 1994, named International Tennis Federation World Champion, 1994; Silver Medal, doubles,

Bronze Medal, singles, Olympics, 1992; Silver Medal, singles, Bronze Medal, doubles, Olympics, 1996; Spanish Federal Cup team, 1986-98, 2000-01; winner of 14 Grand Slam titles, 96 WTA Tour titles and over 16 million dollars in prize money at retirement November 2002. Honours: Infiniti Commitment to Excellence Award, 1992; Tennis Magazine Comeback Player of the Year, 1998; Principe de Asturias Award, Spain, 1998; International Tennis Federation Award of Excellence, 2001. Memberships: Spanish Olympic Committee, 2001. Addresss: International Management Group, 1 Erieview Plaza, Suite 1300, Cleveland, OH 4414, USA.

SANCTUARY Gerald P, b. 22 November 1930, Bridport, Dorset, England. Solicitor. Divorced, 3 sons, 2 daughters. Education: Law Society's School of Law London, 1949-53; Royal Air Force, qualified as pilot on jets (Vampire Mark V), awarded Wings, 1955. Appointments: Assistant Solicitor, Sherrards, Kingston-on - Thames, 1955-57; Partner, Hasties Solicitors, Lincoln's Inn Fields, London, 1957-63; Field Secretary, National Marriage Guidance Council, 1963-65; National Secretary, National Marriage Guidance Council, 1965-68; Executive Director, Sex Information and Education Council of the United States (SIECUS), 1969-71; Secretary, Professional and Public Relations, The Law Society, 1971-78; Executive Director, International Bar Association, London, 1978-79; Legal Adviser and Senior HQ Co-ordinator for regional and Local Affairs, MENCAP (Royal Society for Mentally Handicapped Children and Adults), London, 1979-84; Secretary, NUJ Provident Fund, London, 1985-95; Retired, 1995. Publications: Marriage Under Stress, 1968; Divorce - and After, 1970; Before You See a Solicitor, 1973; After I'm Gone - What Will Happen to my Handicapped Child? 1984, second edition, 1991; The Romans in St Albans, The Monastery at St Albans, Tudor St Albans, Fishpool Street St Albans, historical booklets, 1984, 1985, 1986; Shakespeare's Globe Theatre, 1992; Running a Marriage Guidance Council; Local Society Handbook; Editor, 12 titles in the series: It's Your Law, 1973-78; Numerous articles in professional journals and newspapers and magazines. Memberships: The Law Society; The Guild of Air Pilots and Air Navigators of the City of London, Past Honorary Treasurer; The Institute of Public Relations. Address: 99 Beechwood Avenue, St Albans, Hertfordshire AL1 4XU, England.

SANDBACH Richard Stainton Edward, b. 13 June 1915, Sale, Cheshire, England. Solicitor. m. Brenda Mary (Wendy) Cleminson, 2 sons. Education: MA, LLM, Macmahon Law Student, St John's College, Cambridge; Final examination (distinction), Law Society, 1978. Appointments: Articled clerk, Slater Heelis, Manchester, 1937; Army Service, 1939-47; Solicitor, 1950-79, Partner, 1951, Senior Partner, 1970, Greenwoods, Peterborough; Chairman, Peterborough Diocesan Board of Finance, 1974-84; Solicitor, Horwood and James, Aylesbury, 1979; Chairman, 1985-96, Director, 1988-96, Paten and Co Ltd; Director, Gibbons (Holdings) Ltd, Arcade Properties (Peterborough) Ltd. Publications: Introduction, Book of the Lodge, 1986; Priest and Freemason, 1988; Peterborough Booklets 1-5, 1990-92; Notes for a Candidate for Freemasonry, 1991; Understanding the Royal Arch, 1992; History of The Fitzwilliam Lodge 2533, 1994; Letter to a Master Elect, 1994; Talks for Lodge and Chapter, 1996; History of Clerestory Lodge 6551, 1998; Square Pomes, 1998; Articles in Ars Quatuor Coronatorum. Memberships: Oxford and Cambridge; Victory Services; Royal Commonwealth Society; Burgh Society; Freemasonry: Provincial Grand Master, Northants and Hunts, 1984-90; Grand Superintendent, 1978-90; Member, Supreme Council, Ancient and Accepted Rite, 1989-; Sovereign Grand Commander, 2002-. Address: 91 Lincoln Road, Peterborough, PE1 2SH, England. E-mail: rsandbach@lineone.net

Dictionary of International Biography

SANDER Louis Wilson, b. 31 July 1918. San Francisco, California, USA. Professor of Psychiatry. m. Betty Thorpe, 2 sons, 1 daughter. Education: AB, 1939, MD, Medical School, 1942, University of California; Intern, University of California Hospital, 1942-43. Appointments: 2nd Lieutenant to Major, USAAF Medical Corps, 1943-46; Resident in Psychiatry to Professor of Psychiatry, School of Medicine, 1947-68; Principal Investigator, Longitudinal Study in Early Personality Development, 1963-87, Professor of Psychiatry, School of Medicine, 1968-78, Boston University; Professor of Psychiatry, Senior Scholar, School of Medicine, University of Colorado, 1978-87. Publications: Contributor, over 50 articles, book chapters; reviews to professional publications, 1962-2002. Honours: Recipient, Research Career Development Award, US Public Health Service, 1963-68; Research Scientist Awards, US Public Health Service, 1968-78; Research Grantee, US Public Health Service, March of Dimes, W Grant Foundation; MacArthur Foundation, Spencer Foundation, National Council on Alcoholism; other organisations; Honorary Membership Award, American Psychoanalytic Association, 2001. Memberships: American Medical Association; American Psychiatric Association; American College of Psychoanalysts; Boston Psychoanalytic Society; American Association for the Advancement of Science; Society for Research in Child Development; American Academy of Child Psychiatry; World Association for Infant Mental Health; Boston Change Process Study Group, 1995-; San Francisco Psychoanalytic Society and Institute. Address: 2525 Madrona Ave, St Helena, CA 94574-2300, USA.

SANDERS Alan J K, b. 22 July 1937. London, England. Mongolist. m. (1) Nora, 2 sons (2) Tina. Education: Joint Services School for Linguists, 1956-58; Civil Service Interpretership, Russian, 1958; Fellowship, Russian, Institute of Linguists, London, 1968. Appointments: Royal Air Force, 1956-60; Russian Monitor, Editorial Report Writer, Editor, BBC Monitoring Service, 1961-90 including: Manager, BBC Monitoring Service, Hong Kong, 1971-75; Lecturer in Mongolian Studies, School of Oriental and African Studies, University of London, 1991-95; Freelance Mongolist, 1996-. Publications: 4 reference books about Mongolia, 2 language books, 1968-2003; Numerous yearbook chapters, book chapters and papers mostly about Mongolia. Honour: British Council Scholarship to Mongolian State University, Ulaanbaatar, 1968-69. Memberships include: At various times: Officer, Anglo-Mongolian Society; Member, Royal Institute of International Affairs; Member, Royal Society for Asian Affairs. Address: 29 Cardinal Close, Reading, RG4 8BZ, England.

SANDERSON Anne Hilary, b. 13 January 1944, Brighton, England. University Lecturer (retired). m. Michael Sanderson, 25 September 1976. Education: BA, 1966, MA, 1970, MLitt, 1978, St Anne's College, Oxford, England. Appointments: English Lectrice, Ecole Normale Supérieure De Jeunes Filles, University of Paris, 1969-71; Lecturer in European Literature, University of East Anglia, 1972-98. Publications: Poetry and short stories in small press anthologies and magazines. Contributions to: Poems in Poetry Now; Peace & Freedom; Purple Patch; The Poetry Church, Advance!, Isthmus Triumph Herald; Reflections; Tree Spirit; The Firing Squad; All Year Round; Articles in Studies on Voltaire & The 18th Century; Jeunesse De Racine; Norwich Papers. Honours: Prix Racine, 1969; 3rd Prize, Hilton House National Open Poetry Awards for Collections, 1998, 1999; 1st Prize for Free Verse, Country Writers' Guild Competition. Memberships: Norwich Writers' Circle, Open Poetry Competition Secretary, 1998-2003; Norwich Poetry Group; Playwrights East; Association of Christian Writers.

SANDERSON Teresa (Tessa) Ione, b. 14 March 1956. Athlete. Career: Represented Britain in javelin, 1974-; Commonwealth Games Gold Medallist, 1978, 1986, 1990; European Championship Gold Medallist, 1978; Olympic Games Gold Medallist, Olympic Record, 1984; World Cup Gold Medallist, 1992; Other achievements: Fourth Place at Barcelona Olympics, 1992; Several records including: UK Javelin record, 1976; Presenter, Sky News Sports, 1989-92; Involvement with various charities. Publications: My Life in Athletics, 1985. Honours: British Athletics Writers Association Female Athlete of the Year, 1977, 1978, 1984; Honorary BSc University of Birmingham; OBE; MBE. Memberships: Board member, English Sports Council, 1998-. Address: c/o Derek Evans, 68 Meadowbank Road, Kingsbury, London NW9, England. E-mail: tessa@tprmplus.freeserve.co.uk

SANDLER Adam, b. 9 September 1966, Brooklyn, New York, USA. Actor; Screenwriter. m. Jackie Titone, 2003. Education: New York University. Career: Actor, films include: Shakes the Clown; Coneheads; Mixed Nuts; Airheads; Billy Madison; Happy Gilmore; Bullet Proof; Guy Gets Kid, 1998; The Wedding Singer, 1998; The Water Boy, 1998; Big Daddy, 1999; Little Nicky, 2000; Punch-Drunk Love, 2002; Mr Deeds, 2002; Anger Management, 2003; Fifty First Dates, 2004; Actor, writer, Saturday Night Live; TV appearances include: Saturday Night Live Mother's Day Special, 1992; MTV Music Video Awards, 1994; Saturday Night Live Presents President Bill Clinton's All-Time Favourites, 1994; 37th Annual Grammy Awards, 1995; ESPY Awards, 1996. Publications: Co-writer: Billy Madison; Happy Gilmore; The Water Boy; Recordings: Album: Stan and Judy's Kid; They're All Gonna Laugh at You! 1993. Honours: Peoples Choice Award, 2000. Address: c/o Ballstein-Grey, 9150 Wilshire Boulevard, Suite 350, Beverly Hills, CA 90212, USA.

SANDRAS Jean-Jacques, b. 20 October 1947, Paris, France. Writer. 1 daughter. Education: Various diplomas from IBM and Tandem Computers. Appointments: Data Base Administrator, Paris Stock Exchange, 1992-96; Currently Writer, 1996-. Publication: Novel, Le Chevalier a la Fleur (The Knight of the Flower), 2001. Address: 14 rue des Vignerons, 94300 Vincennes, France.

SANER Reg(inald Anthony), b. 30 December 1931, Jacksonville, Illinois, USA. Poet; Writer; Professor. m. Anne Costigan, 16 August 1958, 2 sons. Education: BA, St Norbert College, Wisconsin, 1950; MA, 1954, PhD, 1962, University of Illinois at Urbana; Università per Stranieri, Perugia, 1960-61; Università di Firenze, Florence, 1960-61. Appointments: Assistant Instructor, 1956-60, Instructor, in English 1961-62, University of Illinois at Urbana; Assistant Professor, 1962-67, Associate Professor, 1967-72, Professor of English, 1972-, University of Colorado at Boulder. Publications: Poetry: Climbing into the Roots, 1976; So This is the Map, 1981; Essay on Air, 1984; Red Letters, 1989. Non-Fiction: The Four-Cornered Falcon: Essays on the Interior West and the Natural Scene, 1993; Reaching Keet Seel: Ruin's Echo and the Anasazi, 1998. Contributions to: Poems and essays in numerous anthologies and other publications. Honours: Fulbright Scholar to Florence, Italy, 1960-61; Borestone Mountain Poetry Awards, 1972, 1973; Walt Whitman Award, 1975; National Endowment for the Arts Creative Writing Fellowship, 1976; Pushcart Prize II, 1977-78; Colorado Governor's Award for Excellence in the Arts, 1983; Quarterly Review of Literature Award, 1989; Rockefeller Foundation Resident Scholar, Bellagio, Italy, 1990; Hazel Barnes Award, University of Colorado, 1993; Wallace Stegner Award, 1998. Memberships: Dante Society; PEN; Renaissance Society; Shakespeare Association. Address: 1925 Vassar, Boulder, CO 80303, USA.

SANFORD Geraldine A Jones, b. 8 January 1928, Sioux Falls, South Dakota, USA. Poet; Teacher; Editorial Assistant. m. Dayton M Sanford, 28 August 1948, deceased 1993, 4 sons, 1 daughter. Education: BA, English and Psychology, Augustana College, 1971;

MA, English, University of South Dakota. Appointments: Editorial Assistant, South Dakota Review, 1973- Instructor and Lecturer in English, University of South Dakota, 1978, 1979; Instructor, University of Minnesota, 1979-82; Extension Instructor, University of South Dakota, 1991. Publication: Unverified Sightings From Dakota East. Contributions to: Real Dakota; Vermillion Literary Project; Longneck; Mankato Poetry Review; Prairie Winds; South Dakota Magazine; Yearnings; Poets Portfolio; Spirits from Clay; South Dakota Review; North Country; Rocky Mountain Creative Arts Journal; North Country Anvil; Aspect; Sunday Clothes. Honours: Graduate Student Poetry Award, Unversity of South Dakota, 1976; Gladys Haase Poetry Prize, 1977. Address: 306 West 36th Street, Apt 22, Sioux Falls, SD 57105, USA.

SANNER George Elwood, b. 30 August 1929, Rockwood, Pennsylvania, USA. Electrical Engineer. m. Marjorie, 1 son, 2 daughters. Education: BS, Engineering and Physics, University of Pittsburgh, 1951; Graduate, Physics and Mathematical Studies, Johns Hopkins University, 1956; PE (Registered Professional Engineer); Computing Technology Industry Association Certification: Computer Specialist A+, 2001; Microsoft Professional Network Certifications: MCP, 2000, MCP+I, 2001 and MCSE, 2001; Numerous professional certificates include: Network Administration, 1998; Microsoft Certified System Engineering, 1999, Mercer University, Atlanta, Georgia. Appointments: Radar/Electronics Officer, US Navy, 1951-59; Supervising Microwave and Radar Design and Development Engineer, Westinghouse Electric Corporation, Baltimore, 1952-58; Space Communications Programmes Director, Engineer Manager, Bendix Corporation Radio Division, 1958-64; Chief Scientist, Consulting Engineer, Advanced Electronic Systems, Westinghouse, 1964-71; President, Chief Engineer, Electronic Control Systems, Santron Corporation, Baltimore, 1971-80; Senior Project Engineer, Bendix NASA/JPL Voyager II Program, Field Engineering Corporation, 1980-81; Senior Engineering Specialist, Air Defence Systems, Litton Data Systems, New Orleans, 1981-83; Consultant, Eaton Corporation, AIL Division, 1983-87; Senior Principal Engineer, Advanced Avionic Systems, American Electronic Laboratories Inc, Pennsylvania, 1987-92; Engineering Consultant, George E Sanner Consultants, Georgia, 1992-. Publications: 17 US patents; Several research reports and lectures. Honours: Special Faculty Award Plaque, RETS Electronic Schools Inc, Baltimore, 1977; Eisenhower People-to-People Tour, European Crop Irrigation, 1978. Memberships: Life Member, IEEE; (CompTIA) Computing Technology Industry Association; Quarter Century Wireless Association; American Technical Education Association. Address: 2501 Hidden Hills Drive, Marietta, GA 30066, USA. E-mail: GESTE@MSN.com

SANTEE Dale William, b. 28 March 1953, Washington, USA. Lawyer; Air Force Officer. m. Junko Mori, 2 June 1992. Education: BA, Washington and Jefferson College, 1975; JD, University of Pitts, 1978; MA, Northern Arizona University, 1982. Appointments: Floor Manager, Commission Salesman, J C Penney Company, Washington, 1971-76; Assistant Manager, Rach Enterprises, Charleroi, Pennsylvania, 1977-78; Bar, Pennsylvania, 1978; US Court of Military Appeals, 1979, California, 1989; Legal Intern, Washington County Public Defender; Commissioned, 2nd Lieutenant, USAF, 1979, advanced through ranks to Colonel, 2001; Assistant Staff Judge Advocate to Area Defence Counsel, Luke Air Force Base, Arizona, 1979-81; Claims Officer 343 Combat Support Group/Judge Advocate, Eielson AFB, Alaska, 1981-83; Senior Staff Legal Advisor, Department of Veteran Affairs, Washington DC, 1983-89; Vice President, Neuer Enterprises, Nanjemoy, Maryland, 1983-89; Assistant Staff Judge Advocate Military Justice Division, Air Force Judge Advocate General's Department, Washington DC, 1986-89; Participant OPM

Management Development Seminar, 1988; 63CSG/Judge Advocate, Norton Air Force Base, California, 1989-91; Deputy Public Defender Juvenile Division, San Diego County, 1990-93; Deputy Staff Judge Advocate, 452 AMW/Judge Advocate, March Air Reserve Base, California, 1991-98; Department of Alternate Public Defender, 1993-98; Supervising Attorney, Alternate Public Defender, Conflict-Parent Child Office, San Diego, California, 1998-2001; Staff Judge Advocate, 452 AMW March Air Reserve Base, California, 1999-2001; Senior Individual Mobilization Augmentee, HQ 21AF/JA McGuire Air Force Base, New Jersey, 2001-03; Deputy Alternate Public Defender, San Diego, California, 2001-; Senior Individual Mobilization Augmentee, HQ ARPC/JA, Denver, CO, 2003-04; Senior Individual Mobilization Augmentee, HQ PACAF/JA, 2004-. Honours: Decorated, Air Force Commendation Medal, 1981, 1989; Air Force Meritorious Service Medal, 1991, 1996, 1999, 2001, 2003; Outstanding Young Man of America; Academic Scholar and Beta Scholar, Washington and Jefferson College; Juvenile Justice Commission Attorney of the Year, 1997; US Air Force Reserve Command Attorney of the Year, 1997; US Air Force, Fourth Air Force Attorney of the Year, 1997; American Bar Association and Legal Aid and Defender Association Clara Shortridge Foltz Award, 1999; The Judge Advocates Association Outstanding Career Armed Services Attorney Award, 2000; Air Force Achievement Medal, 2000. Memberships: Pennsylvania Bar Association; California Bar Association; San Diego County Bar Association; California Western School of Law McGill Center for Creative Problem Solving; Adjunct Teaching Staff, Air Force Judge Advocate School, Maxwell AirForce Base, Alabama; International Institute of Humanitarian Law, San Remo, Italy. Address: 8525 Gibbs Drive, Ste 201, San Diego, CA 92123, USA.

SANTER Jacques, b. 18 May 1937, Wasserbilig. Politician. m. Danièle Binot, 2 sons. Education: Athenée de Luxembourg; University of Paris; University of Strasbourg; Inst d'Etudes Politiques, Paris. Appointments: Advocate, Luxembourg Court of Appeal, 1961-65; Attaché, Officer of Minister of Labour and Social Security, 1963-65; Govt attaché, 1965-66; Parliament Secretary Parti Chrétien-Social, 1966-72, Secretary-General, 1972-74, President, 1974-82; Secretary of State for Cultural and Social Affairs, 1972-74; Member, Chamber of Deputies, 1974-79; Member, European Parliament, 1975-79, VP, 1975-77; Municipal Magistrate, City of Luxembourg, 1976-79; Minister of Finance of Labour and of Social Security, 1979-84; Prime Minister, Minister of State and Minister of Finance, 1984-89; Prime Minister, Minister of State, of Cultural Affairs and the Treasury and Financial Affairs, 1989-94; President, European Committee, 1994-99. Honour: Hon LLD (Wales), 1998. Address: 69 rue J-P Huberty, 1742 Luxembourg.

SANTIC Ante, b. 12 November 1928, Novi Sad, Serbia and Monte Negro. University Professor Emeritus. m. Nada Saks, 1 daughter. Education: Dipl. Ing., Electrical Engineering, 1953, Doctor of Science (DSc), 1966, Faculty of Electrical Engineering, University of Zagreb, Croatia. Appointments: Researcher, 1954-59, Head, Electronic Laboratory, 1959-69, Institute of Electrical Engineering; Associate professor, 1969-75, Full Professor, 1975-99, Professor Emeritus, 2000-, Vice-Dean, 1976-78, Dean, 1978-80, Faculty of Electrical Engineering, University of Zagreb, Croatia; Fulbright Fellow, 1975-76, Visiting Professor, 1982-84, Case Western Reserve University, Cleveland, Ohio, USA. Publications: More than 100 papers in journals and proceedings of conferences; 2 books: Electronic Instrumentation, 1982, 3rd edition 1993; Biomedical Electronics, 1995; Editor, Biomedical Engineering Dictionary; Chapter, Biotelemetry Systems in Webster's Encyclopaedia; 5 chapters in other encyclopaedias; 2 chapters in Electrical Engineering Manual; 2 patents. Honours: Nikola Tesla

Dictionary of International Biography

Award, Republic of Croatia, 1980; Academy of Science Award for "Biomedical Electronics", 1995; Award for Contribution to Engineering Sciences, Croatian Academy of Science, 1997; Award for Scientific Achievement, President of Croatia; State Award for Life Achievement in Engineering Science, 2000; EMBS Career Achievement Award, IEEE, 2003. Memberships: President, 1977-2000, Honorary President, 2000-, Croatian Biomedical Engineering Society; Senior Life Member, IEEE; IFMBE; Representative of IMEKO; Member of IEEE Societies: EMBS, EIMS; Society IFMBES; ESEM. Address: Faculty of Electrical Engineering and Computing, University of Zagreb, Unska Str 3, 10000 Zagreb, Croatia. E-mail: ante.santic@fer.hr

SANTOS Conrado R, b. 26 November 1934, Philippines. University Teacher. m. Emerita M, 2 sons, 1 daughter. Education: BA cum laude, 1958, BSJ cum laude, LLB, 1959, MPA, 1961, University of Philippines; LLM, Harvard Law School, 1962; PhD, University of Michigan, 1964. Appointments: Research Assistant, Institute of Public Administration, 1963, Teaching Fellow, Department of Political Science, 1964, University of Michigan; Assistant Professor, 1965, Associate Professor, 1967, Department of Political Studies, University of Manitoba; Member, Manitoba Legislative Assembly for Burrows, 1981; Member, Manitoba Legislative Assembly for Broadway, then Wellington, 1991-. Publications: The Use of Analytical Models in Comparative Study of Bureaucratic Organisations, 1965; The Political Neutrality of the Civil Service Re-Examined, 1969; Public Administration as Politics, 1969; Some Collective Characteristics of Delegates to the 1968 Liberal Party Leadership Convention, 1970; Public Administration: The Gap Between Theory and Practice, 1971; A Theory of Bureaucratic Authority, 1978. Honours: Harvard Tuition Fellowship, 1961-62; Johnson Wax Foundation Scholarship, 1961-62; Smith-Mundt/Fulbright Partial Scholarship, 1961-62. Memberships: Canadian Political Science Association; American Political Science Association; Institute of Public Administration of Canada; American Society for Public Administration. Address: 596 Townsend Ave, Winnipeg, Manitoba R3T 2V2, Canada.

SANTOSO Michelle Jo, b. 8 September 1968, Surabaya, Indonesia. Pianist; Piano Teacher. m. Peter Santoso, 1 son, 1 daughter. Education: Master of Arts, California State University, Los Angeles. Appointments: Director of Master Artists Piano Performing Studio; Piano Instructor; Performances: International Chamber Music Festival, Prague, Czech Republic; International Chamber Music Festival, Positano, Italy; Piano Concerto performance with Bratislava Chamber Orchestra, Austria; ASEAN Music Festival, Singapore. Honours: Prize Winner, Los Angeles Liszt Piano Competition; Prize Winner, Yamaha Piano Competition; The Inez Schubert Scholarship Awards; Dean's Awards; Hall of Fame. Memberships: Associated Board of Royal School of Music, England; American Pianists Association; American College of Musicians; California Association of Professional Music Teachers; Music Teachers Association of California; Music Teachers National Association; National Federation of Music Clubs; Southwestern Youth Music Festival. Address: 1475 Rubio Drive, San Marino, CA 91108, USA. E-mail: michellesantoso@hotmail.com

SAPOSNIK Ira, b. 16 December 1952, Chicago, Illinois, USA; Medical Doctor; Lawyer; Musician; Composer; Author; Researcher. Education: AB, summa cum laude, Loyola University, 1974; MS, Northeastern Illinois State University, 1977; MD, Honours, Loyola University Medical School, 1980; Internship, Northwestern University, Illinois, 1981; Residency in Ophthalmology, University of Pittsburgh, 1981-85; Fellowship, Glaucoma, University of Pittsburgh, 1985; JD, Nashville School of Law, 1997; PhD, magna cum laude, History, Imperial War

College, 2001. Appointments: Associate Professor of Ophthalmology, University of Virginia, 1985-88; Director, Chief of Ophthalmology, United States Veterans Administration Hospital, Salem, Virginia, 1986-88; Chief of Ophthalmology, Lewis-Gale Chair, 1986-88; Chief of Ophthalmology, Omega Healthcare, Knoxville, Tennessee, 1988-91; Chief of Ophthalmology, Omega Healthcare, Nashville, Tennessee, 1990-93; Clinical Instructor, Ophthalmology Vanderbilt University Medical School, 1993-2000. Publications: Argon Laser Tracheoplasty, 1988; Isotope Treatment in Multiple Sclerosis, 2002; Conspiracy in American History. Mexican War to Cuba, 2003. Honours include: Chicago City Medal 1987; New York City Medal, 2001; Musical Composition Award, 2003; Teaching Awards. Memberships: American Academy of Ophthalmology; American Civil War Recreator; Napoleonic Tactics. Address: 320 N Lauderdale, Nashville, TN 37205-1838, USA.

SARAMAGO José, b. 16 November 1922, Azinhaga, Portugal. Author; Poet; Dramatist. Education: Principally self-educated. Publications: Fiction: Manual de Pintura e Caligrafia, 1977, English translation as Manual of Painting and Calligraphy, 1994; Objecto Quase (short stories), 1978, English translation as Quasi Object, 1995; Levantado do Chao (Raised from the Ground), 1980; Memorial do Convento, 1982, English translation as Baltasar and Blimunda, 1987; A Jangada de Pedra, 1986, English translation as The Stone Raft, 1994; O Ano da Morte de Ricardo Reis, 1984, English translation as The Year of the Death of Ricardo Reis, 1991; Historia do Cerco de Lisboa (The History of the Siege of Lisbon), 1989; O Evangelho segundo Jesus Cristo, 1991, English translation as The Gospel According to Jesus Christ, 1994; Ensaio Sobre A Cegueira, 1996, English translation as Blindness; All the Names, 2000. Other: Poems, plays, diaries, etc. Contributions to: Various publications. Honours: Several literary awards and prizes, including the Nobel Prize for Literature, 1998. Address: c/o Harcourt Brace & Co, 6277 Sea Harbor Drive, Orlando, FL 32887, USA.

SARANDON Susan Abigail, b. 4 October 1946, New York, USA. Actress. m. Chris Sarandon, divorced, 1 daughter, 1 daughter with Franco Amurri, 2 sons with Tim Robbins. Education: Catholic University of America. Career: Stage appearances include: A Coupla of White Chicks Sittin' Around Talkin'; An Evening with Richard Nixon; A Stroll in the Air; Albert's Bridge; Private Ear, Public Eye; Extremities; numerous TV appearances; Actor, films include: Joe, 1970; Lady Liberty, 1971; The Rocky Horror Picture Show, 1974; Lovin' Molly, 1974; The Great Waldo Pepper, 1975; The Front Page, 1976; Dragon Fly, 1976; Walk Away Madden; The Other Side of Midnight, 1977; The Last of the Cowboys, 1977; Pretty Baby, 1978; King of the Gypsies, 1978; Loving Couples, 1980; Atlantic City, 1981; Tempest, 1982; The Hunger, 1983; Buddy System, 1984; Compromising Positions, 1985; The Witches of Eastwick, 1987; Bull Durham, 1988; Sweet Hearts Dance, 1988; Married to the Mob; A Dry White Season, 1989; The January Man, 1989; White Palace; Thelma and Louise, 1991; Light Sleeper, 1991; Lorenzo's Oil; The Client; Little Women, 1995; Safe Passage, 1995; Dead Man Walking, 1996; James and the Giant Peach, 1996; Illuminate, 1998; Twilight, 1998; Stepmom, 1999; Anywhere But Here, 1999; Cradle Will Rock, 1999; Rugrats in Paris, 2000; Joe Gould's Secret, 2000; Cats and Dogs, 2001; Igby Goes Down, 2002; The Banger Sisters, 2003. Honour: Academy Award for Best Actress, 1996. Address: c/o ICM, Martha Luttrell, 8942 Wilshire Boulevard, Beverly Hills, CA 90211, USA.

SARBU Ion, b. 17 September 1933, T Vladimirescu, district Galati, Romania. Researcher. m. Sarbu Maria, 1 son, 2 daughters. Education: Faculty of Biology, 1963; Doctor of Biology, 1978. Appointments: Teacher, 1963-67; Researcher, 1967-2003; Retired, 2003-. Publications: 112 articles; 9 books: Explanation to the vegetation map of the Romanian Danube Delta Biosphere Reserve, 1993; Vegetation of the Biosphere Reserve, Danube Delta, 2002; Flora lemnoasa spontana si cultivata din Romania, I, 1996, II, 2000, III, IV, 2004; Contributor to the Atlas Florae Europaeae, 12, 1999; Vascular Plants in the Eastern Part of Romania, I and II, 2001. Memberships: Romanian Society of Biology; Romanian Society of Phytocoenology. Address: Al I Cuza University of Iasi, Botanical Garden, Str Dumbrava Rosie 7-9, 6600 Iasi, Romania.

SARGENT John Richard, b. 22 March 1925, Birmingham, England. Economist. m. Hester, 1 son, 2 daughters. Education: BA, First Class, Christ Church, Oxford, 1948. Appointments: Fellow and Lecturer in Economics, Worcester College, Oxford, 1951-62; Economic Consultant, H M Treasury, 1963-65; Professor of Economics, Founder Member of Department of Economics, 1965-73, Pro-Vice-Chancellor, 1970-72, University of Warwick; Group Economic Advisor, Midland Bank, 1974-84; Houblon-Norman Research Fellow, Bank of England. Publications: Numerous articles in economic journals include most recently: Roads to Full Employment, 1995; Towards a New Economy? Recent Inflation and Unemployment in the UK, forthcoming; Book, British Transport Policy, 1958. Honours: Rockefeller Fellow, USA, 1959-60; Honorary Professor of Economics, University of Warwick, 1974-81; Visiting Professor, London School of Economics, 1981-82. Memberships: Reform Club, 1965-; Member of Council, Royal Economic Society, 1969-74; Member, Doctors and Dentists Pay Review Body, 1972-75; Member, Armed Forces Pay Review Body, 1972-85; Member, Economic and Social Research Council, 1980-85. Address: Trentham House, Fulbrook, Burford, Oxfordshire OX18 4BL, England.

SARGSYAN Tigran Edvard, b. 11 August 1978, Stepanavan Lory, Armenia. Economist. Education: BS, 1999, MS, 2000, State Institute of Economics, Yerevan, Armenia. Appointments: Manager, Tsovinar Scientific Manufacturing Company, Stepanavan, Lory Armenia, 1995-96; Computer Programmer, Macro Corporation, Yerevan, Armenia, 1996-97; Vice-President, Yoske Arevatsak, Yerevan, Armenia, 1996-98; Assistant to Mayor's Adviser, City Hall, Spitak, Armenia. 1997-99; Consultant, Sugar Corporation, Spitak, Armenia, 2000-2001; Operator of Information, Analytical Department, Base Metals, Armenia, 2003-2004; Founder, Salmon Fish Farming in Northern Armenia; Co-ordinator, Re-establishment of Armenian Sugar Industry; Author, Project for Rehabilitation of the Disaster Zone of Armenia; New Technology of Formation of Semiconductor Layers. Publications: Books: Development of Business in Armenia, 2000; Easy Steps to Become Rich by Fish Farming, 2001; Doing Business with Armenia, 2002; The Principals of Restoration of Armenian Economy, 2003; Doing Business with USA, 2003; Author of Invention's Disclosure: Formation of Semiconductor Layers, 2003. Honours: Club Aragats (Life 3rd prize 1996); Scholar, Ministry of Higher Education, 1996-2001; Distinguished Certificate, 1996; Silver Medal, Ministry of Education, 1996; Honours, Ministry of Defence, 2001, 2002; Business Initiative Medal, 2003; Military Rank: Senior Sergeant. Memberships: New York Academy of Sciences; Canadian Aquaculture Association; Asian Fisheries Association; US Trout Farmers Association; Congress of Lake and Pond Association, Pennsylvania, USA; Mamikonyan-Chilingaryan Folk, Yerevan; Spitak-Thousand Oaks Sister Cities, Spitak Armenia. Address: Apt 27, Bldg 7-2 Toumanyan Q, Avan 3-1, Yerevan 375101, Armenia.

SARMA Chandra Mohan, b. 1 February 1941, Kakaya (Nalbari), Assam, India. University Professor. m. Bhanu Devee, 2 sons, 1 daughter. Education: MSc, Botany, Gauhati University, 1962; PhD, Plant Tissue Culture, 1971. Appointments: Lecturer in Botany, Cotton College, Gauhati, 1963-64; Lecturer, Agri-Botany, 1964-

81, Reader, Biotechnology, 1981-88, Professor of Botany, 1988-2004, Gauhati University; 43 students obtained PhD and 16 students obtained M Phil degrees. Publications: 112 research articles in Indian and international journals; 64 research articles in Indian and international conferences; Author, 2 books; Co-author, 10 books; Over 362 articles in regional English languages on popular science. Honours: Gold Medal, First in First Class MSc (Botany); Gold Medal, Citation and cash award for Rohini Kanta Barua Award for outstanding contribution in Plant Tissue Culture, 1997; Fellow, Linnean Society, London (FLS); Fellow, Indian Society Plant Physiology (FISPP); Fellow, International Society for Conservation of Natural Resources (FNRS); Fellow, Botanical Society of India (FBS). Memberships: Life member: National Academy of Science, India; Assam Science Society; Botany Society, Assam; Botany Society of India; Society for Promotion of Plant Science Research; Orchid Society, India; Agricultural Society of India; Indian Society of Plant Physiology; Indian Science Congress Association; Academy of Plant Science; International Society for the Conservation of Natural Resources. Address: Department of Botany, Gauhati University, 53 GU Campus, Guwahati 781014, India. E-mail: cmsarma@siffy.com

SARMIN Nor Haniza, b. 8 September 1967, Pontian, Johor, Malaysia. Associate Professor. m. Yosman M Bain, 3 sons. Education: BSc (Hons), 1989; MA, Mathematics, 1990; PhD, Mathematics, 1998. Appointments: Lecturer, 1991-, Associate Professor, 2002, Mathematics Department, Universiti Teknologi Malaysia. Publications: Articles in professional journals as author and co-author include: Two-generator two-groups of class two and their nonabelian tensor squares, 1999; Infinite 2-generator groups of class two..., 2001. Honour: University Excellence Award, 1994. Memberships: MAA; AMS; PERSAMA. Address: Mathematics Department, Faculty of Science, Universiti Teknologi Malaysia, 81310 UTM Skudai, Johor, Malaysia. E-mail: nhs@mel2.fs.utm.my

SARNO Christopher Edward, b. 25 January 1932, New York, New York, USA. Published Writer. 1 son. Appointments: Enlisted United States Marine Corps, 1950; Served 4 years' combat operations during Korean War, 1950-55; Tank Commander A Company, 1st Tank Battalion, Anti-Tank Company, 7th Marine Regiment, 1st Marine Division, FLEET Marine Force; Attained rank of Staff Sergeant; Member, Medford Police Department, 1958-80. Publications: Contributing author: Tank Aces; Korean Vignettes: Faces of War and US Marine Corps in Korea, 1952; 101 Sea Stories; Red Dragon: The Second Round; Author of 17 copyright tales to military history publications; Author audio cassette books: You'll Be Sorree and R & R in Japan 1954. Honours: Medal of Valor, New England Chiefs of Police Association, 1972; Citizen of the Year, VFW Post #1012, Medford, 1972. Memberships: Lifetime Member, 1st Marine Division Association (Boston Chapter); USMC Tanker Association; Semper Fidelis Society, Boston; Medford Patrolman's Union; Medford Police Relief Association; Massachusetts Police Association. Address: 12 Butler Street, Medford, MA 02155-1856, USA.

SASAKI Tsuyoshi Samuel, b. 9 January 1944, Tokyo, Japan. Professor. m. Noriko. Education: Bachelor of Arts, Department of Languages, College of Arts and Sciences, International Christian University, Tokyo, Japan, 1963-67; Master of science, Linguistics, 1971, PhD, Theoretical Linguistics, 1975, Georgetown University. Appointments: Senior Fellow, 1966-67, Assistant, Teaching Japanese as a Foreign Language, 1967-69, Department of Languages, International Christian University; University Fellow, Teaching Japanese, 1969-73, Assistant, Japanese, 1973-74, School of Languages and Linguistics, Georgetown University; Assistant, 1974, Lecturer, 1974-83, Assistant Professor, 1983-98, Professor,

Dictionary of International Biography

1998-, Chair, 1999-, Department of American Studies and English, School of Foreign Studies, Nanzan University. Honour: Certificate of Commendation, for the improvement in the English abilities of postal clerks, Minister of Posts and Telecommunications. Memberships: Past Member, Linguistic Society of America; Society for Teaching Japanese as a Foreign Language; Japan Society of Information and Communication Research; Linguistic Society of Japan; Society of English Grammar and Usage; Japan Association for Language Teaching; New York Academy of Sciences; American Association for the Advancement of Science. Address: 33-14 Minami-Besso, Inuyama, Inuyama, 484-0081, Japan. E-mail: samsaski@nanzan-u.ac.jp

SASLAW Leonard David, b. 27 August 1927, Brooklyn, New York, USA. Chemist. Education: BS, CCNY, 1949; MSc, Biochemistry, George Washington University, 1954; PhD, Chemistry, Georgetown University, 1963. Appointments: Military service, seaman, US Navy Reserve, 1945-46; Chemist, National Cancer Institute, 1951-57; Biophysics Division, Sloan-Kettering Institute, 1957-58; Biochemistry Branch, Armed Forces Institute of Pathology, 1958-65; Director, Biochemical, Pharmacology Division of Cancer Chemotherapy Department, Microbiological Associates Inc, 1965-68; Senior Biochemist, National Drug Co, 1968-69; Chief, Laboratory of Cellular Biochemistry, Albert Einstein Medical Centre, 1969-70; Clinical Laboratory Director, Medical Diagnostic Centres Inc, 1970-71, Laboratory Director and Research Associate, Renal Laboratory, New York Medical College, 1971-73; Manager, Biochemistry, Bio/Dynamics Inc, New Jersey, 1973-74; Professional Associate, Smithsonian Science Information Exchange, 1975-77; Consultant, Burton Parsons Co Inc, Seat Pleasant, Maryland, 1977-78; Physiologist, Toxicology Branch of Division of Vet Medicine, FDA, Washington DC and Rockville, Maryland, 1978-92. Publications: 50 scientific articles in professional journals including: A sensitive colorimetric method for the estimation of 2-deoxy sugars with the use of the malonadehyde-thiobarbituric acid reaction, 1959; Sparing action of uridine on the activity of arabinosylcytosine with normal and leukaemic mice, 1968. Honours: Meritorious Achievement Award, Armed Forces Institute of Pathology. Memberships: American Society of Pharmacology and Experimental Therapeutics; American Association for Cancer Research. Address: 2939 Van Ness St NW, Apt 1237, Washington DC 20008-4616, USA.

SASSOON Vidal, b. 17 January 1928, London, England. Hair Stylist. m. divorced 1980, 2 sons, 2 daughters. Education: New York University. Career: Served with Palmach Israeli Army; Creator, hairdressing style based on Bahaus and geometric forms; Founder, Chairman, Vidal Sassoon Inc; President, Vidal Sassoon Foundation; Founder, Vidal Sassoon Centre for the Study of Anti-Semitism and Related Bigotries at Hebrew University, Jerusalem. Honours: Awards include: French Ministry of Culture Award; Award for services rendered, Harvard Business School; Intercoiffure Award, Cartier, London, 1978; Fellow, Hair Artists International.

SATO Kunitomo, b. 19 August 1954, Osaka, Japan. Medical Doctor. Education: Graduate, Medical Department, National University of Osaka, 1978; Doctor of Health and Sport, Doctor of Industry, Certificate of Lifetime Education, Japan Medical Society; Approved doctor to handicapped people, heart, kidneys and limbs; Specialist of Internal Medicine approved by the Japanese Internal Medical Society. Appointments: Cardiovascular Division of the Institute of Internal Medicine, National Osaka University Hospital, 1978-; Chief, Sakurabashi-Watanabe Hospital, 1979-; Head, Cardiovascular division of both the North-Osaka Hospital and General Kanoh Hospital, 1980-; Chairman, President General, Kunitomo Hospital Centre, 1986-; President, Trustee, New

Miyajima Hospital; Main doctor of Oono town; Cardiovascular Specialist, Japanese Circulation Society; President, Cardiac Transplantation Centre of Japan; Councillor, WSTSC-JC; Consul, American Heart Association, American Stroke Association. Publications: Over 500 medical articles including: Clinical Significance of Human Plasma ANP, BNP measurement – current and future prospectives; Numerous books including: Sudden Death Occurs to People Who are in the Prime of Life!; Your Life Depends on the Selection of a Cardiac Doctor; The Ultimate Strategies for Bland-White-Garland Syndrome; Histories of Surgeons; My Ultimate Therapies; Newspaper columnist on arts and sports. Honours: Distinguished Service Medal, 1998; Companion of Honour, 2001; Deputy Director General, IBC, 2001; Founder, The Scientific Faculty, 2001-02; Presidential Seal of Honor, 2001; Lifetime Achievement Award, 2002; Vice Consul to the IBC, 2002; International Honour Society, 2002; Deputy Governor, ABI, 2002; Key of Success, Notable Author; World Citizen of the Year, ABI, 2002; Life Senator, WNC; Leading Intellectuals of the World, 2003; World Peace and Diplomacy Forum, IBC, 2003; Man of the Year, IBC, 2003, 2004. Listed in: 2000 Outstanding Intellectuals of the 21st Century, IBC, 2003; Who's Who in the 21st Century, IBC, 2003; 500 Founders of the 21st Century, IBC, 2001; One Thousand Great Asians of the 21st Century, IBC, 2002; The Lifetime of Achievement 100, IBC, 2004. Memberships: Japan Medical Society; Japan Circulation Society; American Heart Association; World Society of Cardio-Thoracic Surgeons; Pan-Pacific Surgical Association; Japanese Heart Rehabilitation Society; Japanese International Medical Society, Order of International Fellowship, IBC, 2003. Address: 505 1-6 3-chome, Higashi-Tada, Kawanishi City, Hyogo pref, Japan 666-0122. E-mail: kunitomo-office2@mtf.biglobe.ne.jp

SATPATHY Sashi, b. 1 March 1956, Berhampur, India. Professor of Physics. m. Namita Satpathy, 2 sons, 1 daughter. Education: MSc, 1977; PhD, 1982. Appointments: Scientific Staff Member, Max-Planck Institute, Germany, 1982-86; Research Associate, Xerox, Palto Alto, California, 1986-87; Assistant Professor, 1987-93, Associate Professor, 1993-98; Professor, 1998-, University of Missouri. Publications: Over 70 papers in professional journals. Fellow of the American Physical Society. Address: University of Missouri, Department of Physics, Columbia, MO 65211, USA.

SATSIOS Kostas, b. 10 May 1971, Serres, Greece. Electrical Engineer. m. Maria Tsinari, 2 sons. Education: Diploma of Electrical Engineer, 1994, PhD, Electrical Engineering, 1999. Appointments: General Manager, NRG-ORION (An energy saving company); Consultant to Holy and Great Monastery of Vatopaidi, Mouth Athos. Publications: 17 articles in scientific journals and papers presented at international refereed conferences as co-author include most recently: The Influence of Nonhomogeneous Earth on the Inductive Interference Caused to Telecommunication Cables by Nearby AC Electric Traction Lines, 2000; A fuzzy logic system for calculation of the interference of overhead transmission lines on buried pipelines, 2001; Combined fuzzy logic and genetic algorithm techniques – application to an electromagnetic field, 2002. Honours: Listed in Who's Who publications and biographical dictionaries. Memberships: IEEE; Power Engineering Society; Magnetics Society. Address: Petrou Syndika 2, Thessaloniki, 54645 Greece. E-mail: drsatsios@nrg-orion.gr

SATUBALDIN Sagandyk, b. 5 May 1937, Republic of Kazakhstan. Accountant; Economist. m. Azhai Satulbaldina, 1 son, 2 daughters. Education: Diploma, Accountant and Economist, Kazakh State University "C M Kirov", 1960; Candidate of Economic Sciences, 1968, Doctor of Sciences in Economics, 1981, Department of Economics, Moscow State University "M V Lomonisov"; Assistant Professor, 1969, Professor, 1982,

Dictionary of International Biography

Department of Economic Analysis, Almaty Institute of National Economy. Appointments: Senior Lecturer, Department of Planning of National Economy and Accounting, Kazakh State University, 1962-63; Deputy Dean, 1963-65, Dean, 1968-79, Faculty of Accounting and Economics, Head of Department of Economic Analysis, 1970-77, 1979-83, Almaty Institute of National Economy; Rector, Ural Pedagogical Institute, 1985-89; First Deputy Chairman, Council for Productive Forces Research, 1983-85, First deputy Director, Institute of Economy, 1989-93, Deputy Vice-President, Department of Social Sciences, 1993, Director, International Centre for Training Higher Qualification Personnel, 1993, National Academy of Sciences of Khazakhstan; First Deputy of Executive Director, 1993-98, Acting Executive Director, 1998-2000, Senior Vice-President, 2000-2002, Senior Advisor to the President and Chairman of the Board of Trustees, 2002-, Kazakhstan Institute of Management, Economics and Strategic Research under the President of the Republic of Kazakhstan. Publications: Over 350 scientific works; Monographs include: "Dragons" and "Tigers" of Asia: would the Kazakh "Snow Leopard" be able to follow their paths? 1998; Asian crisis: reasons and lessons, 2000; Chronicles of future; Accounting Systems, 2003; Asian Economic Miracle, 2003. Honours include: Awards: For Active Work in the Komsomol; Excellent Worker of Enlightenment in the USSR; S I Vavilov Medal; Astana Anniversary Medal; Labour Veteran; Honoured Worker in Science and Technology, Republic of Kazakhstan; Laureate, International Prize of Eurasia, 2002; Laureate, State Prize, Republic of Kazakhstan, 2002. Memberships include: National Academy of Sciences; International Academy of Informatization; Kazakh Academy of Social Sciences. Address: 41 Kaldayakova str, apt 27, 480100 Almaty, Republic of Kazakhstan. E-mail: ssatubaldin@nursat.kz

SATYAMURTI Carole, b. 13 August 1939, Bromley, Kent, England. Poet; Writer; Lecturer. Education: BA, Honours, London University, 1960; Diploma in Social Work, University of Birmingham, 1965; MA, University of Illinois, 1967; PhD, University of London, 1979. Appointments: Lecturer, Principal Lecturer, University of East London, 1968-. Publications: Occupational Survival, 1981; Broken Moon (poems), 1987; Changing the Subject (poems), 1990; Striking Distance (poems), 1994; Selected Poems, 1998; Love and Variations (poems), 2000. Honours: 1st Prize, National Poetry Competition, 1986; Arts Council of Great Britain Writers Award, 1988; Cholmondeley Award, 2000. Address: 15 Gladwell Road, London N8 9AA, England.

SAUNDERS Sally Love, b. 15 January 1940, Bryn Mawr, Pennsylvania, USA. Poet; Poetry Therapist; Lecturer; Freelance Writer. Education: BS, George Williams College, Downers Grove, IL, 1965; Poetry Writing Course, The New School, 1968-69; Several other courses. Appointments: Poetry Therapist, Institute of Pennsylvania Hospital, Philadelphia, University of Louisville, Kentucky; Lectures, teaching at schools and other venues; Appearances on TV and radio; Numerous poetry writing workshops; Poetry readings. Publications: Past the Near Meadows, 1961; Pauses, 1978; Fresh Bread, 1982; Random Thoughts, 1992; Patchwork Quilt, 1993; Quiet Thoughts and Gentle Feelings, 1996; Word Pictures, 1998. Contributions to: Anthologies and journals. Honours: Honourable Mention, New American Poetry Contest, 1988; Silver Poet Award, World of Poetry, 1989; Nutmegger Book Award. Memberships: National Writers Club; Press Club of San Francisco; Poets and Writers Guild; Association for Poetry Therapy; Poetry Society of America; Ina Coolbirth Circle; Pen and Pencil Club, Philadelphia; Academy of American Poets; American Poetry Center. Address: 609 Rose Hill Road, Broomall, PA 19008, USA.

SAUNDERS WATSON Leslie Michael MacDonald, b. 9 October 1934, Rockingham Castle, Northamptonshire, England. Naval Officer; Landowner. m. Georgina Davis, 2 sons, 1 daughter. Education: Britannia Royal Naval College, Dartmouth, 1948-51. Appointments: Royal Navy (Commander), 1951-71; Owned and managed Rockingham Castle Estate, 1971-99; Public appointments include: President, Historic Houses Association, 1983-89; Trustee, Royal Botanical Gardens, Kew, 1983-92; National Heritage Memorial Fund, 1987-96; Chairman, National Curriculum History Working Group, 1989-91; Chairman, British Library Board, 1991-93; Chairman, Kettering General NHS Trust, District Hospital, 1993-96; Chairman, Friends of the British Library, 1996-2001. Honours: DL, 1979; Honorary DLitt, Warwick, 1992; CBE, 1993; Honorary DLitt, Leicester, 1996. Memberships: Fellow, Society of Antiquaries of London; Country Landowners Association; Historic Houses Association. Address: The Manor House, Ashley Road, Stoke Albany, Market Harborough, LE16 8TH, England.

SAVKOVIC-STEVANOVIC Jelenka, 21 January 1946, Markovica, Serbia. Professor of Chemical Engineering. m. Miroljub Stevanovic. Education: BS, Degree,1970; MSc, Degree, 1975, Department of Chemical Engineering, University of Belgrade; PhD, Degree, Institut für Thermodynamik und Anlegentechnik, Technische Universität, West Berlin, 1981. Appointments: Researcher, Department of Chemical Catalysis, Institute for Chemical Technology and Metallurgy, Belgrade; 1970; Assistant, 1972, Assistant Professor, 1982, Associate Professor, 1988, Full Professor, 1993, Department of Chemical Engineering Faculty of Technology and Metallurgy, University of Belgrade, Yugoslavia. Publications: Author and co-author: Books, Information Systems in the Process Techniques, 1987; Artificial Intelligence in Chemistry and Chemical Engineering, 1989, Process Modeling and Simulation, 1995; Process Engineering Intelligent Systems, 1999; Over 500 articles to professional journals, patentee in field. Honours: First Prize from Belgrade City for Bachelor of Science Thesis, 1970; DAAD Prize for Research Work, 1980; 2nd Prize TI, St Petersburg, 1989; The Gold Medal, Nikola Tesla, 1993. Address: Faculty of Technology and Metallurgy, University of Belgrade, Karnegijeva, 4, 11000 Belgrade, Yugoslavia.

SAVOY Douglas Eugene, (Gene Savoy), b. 11 May 1927, Bellingham, Washington, USA. Bishop; Writer; Educator; Explorer. 2 sons, 1 daughter. Publications: Antisuyo: The Search for the Lost Cities of the Amazon, 1970; Vilcabamba: Last City of the Incas, 1970; The Child Christ, 1973, Arabic edition, 1976, Japanese edition, 1981; The Decoded New Testament, 1974, Millennium edition, 1983; On the Trail of the Feathered Serpent, 1974; The Prophecies of Jamil, 7 volumes, 1976-83; The Secret Sayings of Jamil: The Image and the World, 7 volumes, 1976-87; The Essaei Document: Secrets of an Eternal Race, 1978, Project X: The Search for the Secrets of Immortality, 1977; The Lost Gospel of Jesus: Hidden Teachings of Christ, 1978, Millennium edition, 1983, Miracle of the Second Advent, 1984. Other: 39 texts, 400 audio tapes: Lectures on Religious Systems and Theology, 5 documentary videos. Contributions to: Various publications. Honours: Over 40 Flag Awards, Andean Explorers Foundation, Explorers Club, New York City, 1958-94; Silver Hummingbird Award, Ministry of Industry and Tourism of Peru, 1987; Explorer of the Century Trophy, Andean Explorers Foundation, 1988; Decorated Officer, Order of the Grand Cross, Republic of Peru, 1989; Medal of Merit Andres Reyes, 1989; Award, City of Ica, Peru, 1995. Memberships: Authors Guild; Explorers Club, New York City; Geographical Society, Lima, Peru; Andean Explorers Foundation; Ocean Sailing Club; World Council for Human Rights, Advocates for Religious Rights and Freedoms. Address: 2025 LaFond Drive, Reno, NV 89509, USA.

Dictionary of International Biography

SAWYER Roger Martyn, b. 15 December 1931, Stroud, England. Author. m. Diana Margaret Harte, 30 August 1952, 2 sons. Education: BA Honours, Diploma in Education, University of Wales, 1958; PhD, History, University of Southampton, 1979. Publications: Casement: The Flawed Hero, 1984; Slavery in the Twentieth Century, 1986; Children Enslaved, 1988; The Island from Within (editor), 1990; 'We are but Women': Women in Ireland's History, 1993; Roger Casement's Diaries 1910: The Black and The White (editor), 1997. Contributions to: Anti-Slavery Reporter; Immigrants and Minorities; South. Honour: Airey Neave Award, 1985. Memberships: Anti-Slavery International, council member, 1984-98; Bembridge Sailing Club; Old Wycliffian Society. Address: Ducie House, Darts Lane, Bembridge, Isle of Wight PO35 5YH, England.

SAYER Gerald Robert, b. 28 March 1937, Melrose Park, Illinois, USA. Management Consultant. m. Lorraine M Sayegh, 3 sons, 1 daughter. Education: BS, Mechanical Engineering, Texas Tech University, USA, 1959; MS, Aero Engineering, Oklahoma State University, USA, 1960; PhD, Mechanical Engineering and Astro Science, Northwestern University, USA, 1963. Appointments: Fellow, Von Karman Institute, Rhode Saint Genese, Belgium, 1963-64; Manger, Re-entry Physics, Litton Space Science Laboratory, 1964-68; Section Chief, McDonald Douglas Corporation, 1968-70; Chairman, Lear Astronics Corporation, 1987-93; President, Developmental Sciences, Inc., 1970-94; President, GL International, 1994-. Publications: Published and presented over 75 technical papers in aerospace sciences. Honours: Distinguished Engineer, 1978, Alumni, 1985, Texas Tech University; Gustus L Larson Memorial Award, ASME, 1979; Laurels for 1983, Aviation Week and Space Technology; Small Business Man of the Year for Southern California, SBA Award, 1983; Outstanding Contributor Award, AUVS, 1985; Who's Who in America, 1989-; American Men and Women in Science, 1969-; Registered Professional Engineers, California. Memberships: President, Association of Unmanned Vehicles; AIAA; ASME; APS; Industry Manufacturing Council. Address: 25481 Bootstrap Place, Laguna Hills, CA 92653, USA.

SCACCHI Greta, b. 18 February 1960, Milan, Italy. Actress. 1 son, 1 daughter. Education: Bristol Old Vic Drama School. Career: Films include: Second Sight; Heat and Dust; Defence of the Realm; The Cocoa-Cola Kid; A Man in Love; Good Morning Babylon; White Mischief; Paura e Amore (Three Sisters); La Donna dell Luna (Woman in the Moon); Schoolmates; Presumed Innocent; Shattered; Fires Within; Turtle Beach; Salt on Our Skins; The Browning Version; Jefferson in Paris, 1994; Country Life, 1995; Emma, 1996; Cosi; The Serpent's Kiss, 1997; The Red Violin, 1998; Cotton Mary, 1998; Ladies Room, 1999; The Manor, 1999; Tom's Midnight Garden, 2000; Looking for Anbrandi, 2000; One of the Hollywood Ten, 2000; Festival in Cannes, 2001; Baltic Storm, 2003; Il Ronzio delle mosche, 2003; Sotto falso nome, 2004; Theatre includes: Cider with Rosie; In Times Like These; Airbase; Uncle Vanya; The Guardsman; TV includes: The Ebony Tower; Dr Fischer of Geneva; Waterfront (series); Rasputin; The Odyssey (series), 1996; Macbeth, 1998; Christmas Glory, 2000; Jeffrey Archer: The Truth, 2002. Honours: Emmy Award, 1996. Address: Susan Smith Associates, 121 San Vincente Boulevard, Beverly Hills, CA 90211, USA.

SCALES Prunella M R West. Actress. m. Timothy West, 1963, 2 sons. Education: Old Vic Theatre School, London; Herbert Berghof Studio, New York, USA; Repertory in Bristol Old Vic, Oxford, Salisbury, England; Chichester and Stratford, 1967-68; London Theatre Appearances include: The Promise, 1967; The Wolf, 1975; An Evening with Queen Victoria, 1979-99; Quartermaine's Terms, 1981; When We Are Married, 1986; Single

Spies, National Theatre, 1988; School for Scandal, National Theatre, 1990; Long Day's Journey Into Night, National Theatre, 1991; At Leeds: Happy Days, 1993; The Birthday Party, 1999; The Cherry Orchard, 2000; The External, 2001; Too Far to Walk (King's Head), 2002; TV includes: Fawlty Towers, 1975, 1978; Mapp and Lucia (series), 1985-86; What the Butler Saw, 1987; After Henry, 1988-92; Signs and Wonders, 1995; Breaking the Code, 1997; Emma, 1997; Midsommer Murders, 1999; Silent Witness, 2000; Queen Victoria, 2003; Films: An Awfully Big Adventure, 1994; Stiff Upper Lips, 1997; An Ideal Husband, 1998; The Ghost of Greville Lodge, 1999 Numerous other areas of work including: Radio; Directing (Leeds, South Australia, National Theatre Studio, Nottingham Playhouse). Honours: CBE; Honorary DLitt, Bradford; Honorary DLitt, University of East Anglia. Address: c/o Conway Van Gelder, 18-21 Jermyn Street, London SW1Y 6HP, England.

SCALETCHI Florentin, b. 11 September 1954, Constanta, Romania. Professor; Doctor in Law. m. Monica, 1 daughter. Education: Doctor in Science, 2002. Appointment: The Symposium, Romania at World's Door – the Right to Free Circulation, held with the Border Police General Department, 2003. Publications: Articles in Human Rights Gazette, 1999-; The Human Rights Manual, 2001. Honour: Award, Romania 2000 for activity in the field of human rights defence. Membership: The Association of Former Political Detainees. Address: 4 Maior Bacila Street, Bloc 18, Parter, Sector 2, Bucharest, Romania. E-mail: oado@dial.kappa.ro Website: www.oado.ro

SCAPERLANDA Maria de Lourdes Ruiz, b. 13 August 1960, Pinar del Rio, Cuba. Freelance Writer and Author. m. Michael Anthony Scaperlanda, 1 son, 3 daughters. Education: Bachelor of Journalism, University of Texas, Austin, 1981; MA, Theology (not completed) St Mary's University, San Antonio Texas, attended 1982; MA, English, University of Oklahoma, Norman, Oklahoma, 1997. Appointments: Public Information Specialist, Austin Parks and Recreation Summer Neighborhood Park Program, 1980-81 Freelance Writer, 1981-; Media Co-ordinator, Catholic Diocese of Austin Religious Education Center, 1983-84; Managing Editor, The Forum Magazine (Official publication of Phi Sigma Iota, the Foreign Language National Honor Society), 1983-86; State Correspondent, Texas Catholic Press, 1990-94; Columnist "Webreview", Catholic Practice e-zine, PostoraLink Online Service, 1998-2000; Senior Correspondent, Our Sunday Visitor, 1997-2000; Columnist, Heartland, Catholic Parent Magazine, 1997-. Publications: Books: Their Faith Has Touched Us: the Legacies of Three Young Oklahoma City Bombing Victims, 1997; Edith Stein: St Teresa Benedicta of the Cross, 2002; The Seeker's Guide to Mary, 2002; The Journey: A Guide for the Modern Pilgrim, 2004; Cuba Perdida (novel) in progress; Numerous articles in in national and regional publications including: US Catholic Practice Magazine, St Anthony Messenger, Catholic Digest, Vision, New Covenant, Austin Magazine, The Daily Oklahoman, The Lutheran. Honours: Numerous awards for articles and features include most recently: Best Body of Work, Catholic Press Association, 1999, Second Place, Excellence in Public Service Journalism, Society of Professional Journalists, 2000, Best Regular Column, Catholic Press Association, 2001; Goldia D Cooksey Memorial Award, English Department University of Oklahoma, 1997; Book Award: Honourable Mention, History Biography, Catholic Press Association Annual Awards, 2002; Listed in Who's Who publications and biographical dictionaries. Memberships: American Society of Journalist and Authors; Society of Professional Journalists; International Women's Writing Guild; Catholic Press Association. Address: 3816 Waverley Court, Norman, OK 73072, USA. E-mail: mscaperlanda@cox.net

SCARFE Gerald A, b. 1 June 1936, London, England. Cartoonist. m. Jane Asher, 2 sons, 1 daughter. Career: Contributor, cartoons to Punch, 1960-, Private Eye, 1961-, Daily Mail, 1966-, Sunday Times, 1967-, Time, 1967-; Animator and film director, BBC, 1969-; Group exhibitions at Grosvenor Gallery, 1969, 1970, Pavilion d'Humour, Montreal, 1969, Expo, 1970, Osaka, 1970; Solo exhibitions: Waddell Gallery, New York, 1968, 1970, Vincent Price Gallery, Chicago, 1969, Grosvenor Gallery, 1969, National Portrait Gallery, 1971, Royal Festival Hall, 1983, Langton Gallery, 1986, Chris Beetles Gallery, 1989, National Portrait Gallery, 1989-99; Comic Art Gallery, Melbourne; Gerald Scarfe in Southwark, 2000; Consultant designer and character designer for film: Hercules, 1997; Theatre design: Ubu Roi, Traverse Theatre, 1957; What the Butler Saw, Oxford Playhouse, 1980; No End of Blame, Royal Court, London, 1981; Orpheus in the Underworld, English National Opera, Coliseum, 1985; Who's A Lucky Boy, Royal Exchange, Manchester, 1985; Born Again, 1990; The Magic Flute, Los Angeles Opera, 1992; An Absolute Turkey, 1993; Mind Millie for Me, Haymarket, 1996; Fantastic Mr Fox, Los Angeles Opera, 1998; Peter and the Wolf, Holiday on Ice, Paris and world tour; Television: Director and presenter: Scarfe on Art; Scarfe on Sex; Scarfe on Class; Scarfe in Paradise; Subject of Scarfe and His Work with Disney, South Bank Special. Publications: Gerald Scarfe's People, 1966; Indecent Exposure, 1973; Expletive Deleted: The Life and Times of Richard Nixon, 1974; Gerald Scarfe, 1982; Father Kissmas and Mother Claus, 1985; Scarfe by Scarfe (autobiography), 1986; Gerald Scarfe's Seven Deadly Sins, 1987; Line of Attack, 1988; Scarfeland, 1989; Scarfe on Stage, 1992; Scarfe Face, 1993; Hades: the truth at last, 1997. Honours: Zagreb Prize for BBC film, Long Drawn Out Trip, 1973. Address: c/o ICM, Oxford House, 76 Oxford Street, London W1N 0AX, England.

SCATENA Lorraine Borba, b. 18 February 1924, San Rafael, California, USA. Farmer-Rancher; Women's Rights Advocate. m. Louis G Scatena, 14 February 1960, deceased 1 November 1995, 1 son, 1 daughter. Education: BA, Dominican College, San Rafael, 1945; California Elementary Teacher Certificate, 1946; California School of Fine Arts, 1948; University California, Berkeley, 1956-57. Appointments: Teacher, Fairfax Elementary School, California, 1946-53; Assistant to Mayor Fairfax City Recreation, 1948-53; Teacher, Librarian, US Dependent Schools, Mainz am Rhine, Germany, 1953-56; Translator, Portugal Travel Tours, Lisbon, 1954; Bonding Secretary, American Fore Insurance Group, San Francisco, 1958-60; Rancher, Farmer, Yerington, Nevada, 1960-98; Member, Nevada State Legislative Commission, 1975; Co-ordinator, Nevadans for Equal Rights Amendment, 1975-78; Testifier, Nevada State Senate and Assembly, 1975, 1977; Member, Advisory Committee, Fleischmann College of Agriculture, University of Nevada, 1977-80, 1981-84; Speaker, Grants and Research Projects, Bishop, California, 1977, Choices for Tomorrow's Women, Fallon, Nevada, 1989; Trustee Wassuk College Hawthorne, Nevada, 1984-87; Travelled to AAUW South Pacific Conferences in Hawaii, to address women of Arizona, California, Hawaii and Nevada on women's study and action projects through networking and coalition, continued tour to Washington DC where she led discussion groups for AAUW presidents of North Dakota, Louisiana, Maine and Montana, states where women share the same problems of transportation, communication, employment and medical care, 1982; Attended and assisted with leadership meetings with AAUW elected officers from 16 states in Denver, Colorado, 1982. Honours include: AAUW Nevada State Humanities Award, 1975; Invitation to first all-women delegation to USA from People's Republic of China, US House of Representatives, 1979; AAUW branch travelship, Discovering Women in US History, Radcliffe College, 1981; NRTA State Outstanding Service Award, 1981; AAUW Future Fund National Award, 1983; Soroptimist International Women Helping Women Award, 1983; Fellow World Literary Academy, 1993; AAUW, Lorraine Scatena Endowment Gift named in her honour for significant contributions to AAUW National Educational Foundation, 1997. Memberships include: Marin Society of Artists, 1948-53; American Association of University Women, 1968-, Nevada State Convention General Chairman, 1976, 1987; Lyon County Museum Society, 1978-; Lyon County Retired Teachers' Association, Unit President, 1979-80, 1984-86; State Convention General Chairman, 1985; Participated in public panel with solo presentation, Shakespeare's Treatment of Women Characters, Nevada Theatre for the Arts hosting Ashland, Oregon Shakespearean actors local performance, 1987; Rural American Women Inc; AAUW, Branch President, 1972-74, 1974-76; President, AAUW, Nevada State, 1981-83; Nevada Representative for First White House Conference for Rural American Women, Washington, 1980; Italian Catholic Federation, Branch President, 1986-88; Charter Member, Eleanor Roosevelt Education Fund for Women and Girls, 1990, sustaining member, 1992-; Member, Nevada Women's History Project, University Nevada, 1996-; Poetry presenter, World Congress on Arts and Communication, Lisbon, Portugal, 1999; Washington, 2000; Cambridge University, St John's College, 2001; Vancouver, Canada, 2002; Dominican University of California, President's Circle, 1997-; American Association of University Women, Leaders Circle, 1998-; The National Museum of Women in the Arts, Washington DC, charter member, 1987, council member, 1999-; University of California, Berkeley, Bancroft, Librarian's Council, 2002. Address: PO Box 247, Yerington, NV 89447-0247, USA.

SCHALLER George B(eals), b. 26 May 1933, Berlin, Germany. Researcher; Writer. m. Kay Morgan, 26 August 1957, 2 sons. Education: BS, Zoology, BA, Anthropology, University of Alaska; MS, PhD, University of Wisconsin. Publications: The Mountain Gorilla, 1963; The Year of the Gorilla, 1964; The Deer and the Tiger, 1967; The Serengeti Lion, 1972; Golden Shadows, Flying Hooves, 1973; Mountain Monarchs: Wild Sheep and Goats of the Himalaya, 1977; Stones of Silence: Journeys in the Himalaya, 1980; The Giant Pandas of Wolong (co-author), 1985; The Last Panda, 1993; Tibet's Hidden Wilderness, 1997; Wildlife of the Tibetan Steppe, 1998. Contributions to: Zoological journals and popular periodicals. Honours: National Book Award, 1973; Cosmos Prize, Japan, 1996; Tyler Environmental Prize, 1997. Address: Wildlife Conservation Society, Bronx Park, NY 10460, USA.

SCHARF Bertram, b. 3 March 1931, New York, USA. Professor. m. Anna-Liisa Scharf, 1 son, 1 daughter. Education: BA, cum laude, City College of New York, 1953; Diploma, University de Paris, 1955; PhD, Harvard University, 1958. Appointments: Research Assistant, Psychoacoustics Laboratory, Harvard University, 1955-56; Assistant Professor, 1958-64, Associate Professor, 1964-69, Professor, 1969-94, Research Professor, 1994-, Department of Psychology, Northeastern University; Visiting Research Associate, Technische Hochschule, Stuttgart, Germany, 1962; Visiting Scientist, Laboratory of Sensory Communication, Syracuse University, 1966, Institute of Physiology, University of Helsinki Medical School and Laboratory of Acoustics, 1971-72; Professor, University de Provence and Laboratoire de Mécanique et d'Acoustique, CNRS, Marseille, 1978-79; Visiting Scientist, Research Laboratory of Electronics, Massachusetts Institute of Technology, 1979-82, Laboratoire de Mécanique et d'Acoustique, CNRS Marseille, 1982-83, 1990-91, 1993; Professor, Université d'Aix-Marseille, 1985-86, 1989, 1994-95. Publications: Numerous articles in professional journals. Honours include: Distinguished Service Award, Massachusetts Speech and Hearing Association, 1977; Exchange Award, NSF US-France Program, 1985-86; Fechner Medal, International Society for Psychophysics, 1995.

Memberships: International Society for Psychophysics; Acoustical Society of America; Psychonomic Society. Address: Northeastern University, 431NI, Boston, MA 02115-5096, USA.

SCHARLEMANN Robert Paul, b. 4 April 1929, Lake City, Minnesota, USA. University Professor; Clergyman. Education: BA, Northwestern College, Concordia College, 1952; BD, Concordia Seminary, 1955; MDiv, 1955; Dr theol, University of Heidelberg, Germany, 1957. Appointments: Instructor, Philosophy, Valparaiso University, 1957-59; Post-doctoral Research Fellow, Yale University, 1959-60; Lutheran Pastor, 1960-63; Assistant Professor, Associate Professor, University of Southern California, 1963-66; Associate Professor, Professor, University of Iowa, 1966-81; Commonwealth Professor, University of Virginia, 1981-97; Professor Emeritus, 1997-. Publications: The Scriptures and the Church; Home Grown Materialism; Shadow on the Tomb; Theology in Church and University; Concepts Symbols and Sentences; The Being of God; The Reason of Following; The Mystical Correlate of Symbolic Appearing, 2000. Honours: Fulbright Scholar; Fulbright Hays Senior Research Fellow. Memberships: American Academy of Religion; German Theological Society; Deutsche Paul-Tillich-Gesellschaft; Duodecim Theological Society; North American Paul Tillich Society; Société Européenne de Culture; Society for the Philosophy of Religion; Society for the Scientific Study of Religion. Address: 1529 Rutledge Avenue, Charlottesville, Virginia 22903-1417, USA.

SCHENK Richard Scott, b. 22 September 1958, New York, New York, USA. Orthopaedic Trauma Surgeon. m. Maria, 2 sons, 1 daughter. Education: BA, Biochemistry, Cornell University, USA, 1980; Doctor of Medicine, 1984, Internship, General Surgery, 1985, Orthopaedic Clinical Research Fellowship, 1986, Residency in Orthopaedic Surgery, 1990, University of Medicine and Dentistry of New Jersey, USA; Fellowship in Orthopaedic Trauma and Joint Reconstruction, University of Toronto, Canada, 1991. Appointments: Instructor, Department of Surgery Division of Orthopaedics, 1991; Assistant Professor, Department of Orthopaedics, University of Medicine and Dentistry of New Jersey, 1995; Currently, Attending Physician and Vice Chairman of Orthopaedics, Morristown Memorial Hospital; Consultant: Kessler Institute for Rehabilitation. Publications: Articles in scientific journals include: Follow-up of Achilles tendon repair with an absorbable polymer-carbon fiber composite, 1989; Bicondylar Tibial Plateau Fractures Treated with A Hybrid Ring External Fixator, 1994 Complications of femoral nailing, 1995; The Treatment of Pelvic Ring Disruption Associated with L-5 Burst Fracture – A Case Report, 1995; Femoral Nailing Without a Fracture Table: Safety and Efficacy, 1996; Hybrid External Fixation in the Treatment of Tibial Plafond Fractures, 1996; 4 book chapters. Honours: America's Top Surgeons, Consumers' Research Council of America; Recognition Award, Physician Recognition Award, American Medical Association; Listed in Who's Who publications and biographical dictionaries. Memberships include: American Academy of Orthopaedic Surgeons; American Board of Orthopaedic Surgery; Orthopaedic Trauma Association; American Medical Association; AO/ASIF North American Teaching Faculty; AO Alumni Association; AO North America; Medical Society of New Jersey; Morris County Medical Society; New Jersey Orthopaedic Society; Association for the Advancement of Automotive Medicine. Address: 556 Eagle Rock Avenue, Suite #5, Roseland, NJ 07068, USA.

SCHIFFER Claudia, b. 25 August 1970, Düsseldorf, Germany. Model. m. Matthew Vaughn, 2002, 1 son. Career: Worked for Karl Lagerfeld, 1990; Revlon Contract, 1992-; Appearances on magazine covers, calendars, TV; Released own exercise video; Appeared in films: Ritchie Rich; The Blackout, 1997; Desperate But Not Serious, 1999; The Sound of Claudia Schiffer, 2000; Black and White, 2000; Chain of Fools, 2000; In Pursuit, 2000; Life Without Dick, 2001; Love Actually, 2003; Retired from modelling, 1998; Owns share in Fashion Café. Publication: Memories. Memberships: US Committee, UNICEF, 1995-98. Address: c/o Elite Model Management, 40 Parker Street, London WC2B 5BH, England.

SCHILD Rudolph Ernst, b. 10 January 1940, Chicago, Illinois, USA. Astrophysicist. m. Jane Struss. Education: BS, 1962, MS, 1963, PhD, 1967, University of Chicago. Appointments: Research Fellow, Postdoctorate, California Institute of Technology, 1967-69; Scientist, Smithsonian Astrophysical Observatory, 1969-; Lecturer, Harvard University, 1977-82. Publications: Over 200 scientific papers in refereed journals; The Electronic Sky: Digital Images of the Cosmos, 1985; Voyage to the Stars, CD Rom, 1994; 2 patents. Honours: Discovered gravitational lens time delay, 1986; Discovered nature of missing mass, 1997. Memberships: American Astronomical Society, 1967-; International Astronomical Union, 1969-. Address: Centre for Astrophysics, 60 Garden Street, Cambridge, MA 02138, USA. E-mail: rschild@cfa.harvard.edu

SCHILLING (Karl Friedrich) Guenther, b. 16 August 1930, Leipzig, Germany. Agricultural Chemistry Educator. m. Gudrun Linschmann, 2 sons. Education: Studies in Agricultural Sciences and Chemistry, Friedrich-Schiller-University, Jena, Germany, 1951-56; Diploma in Agricultural Sciences, 1954, in Chemistry, 1956; Dr agr, 1957; Training in Radio Chemistry, Moscow, USSR, 1958; Dr agr habilitatus, 1960. Appointments: Lecturer, Plant Nutrition, 1960-61, Full Professor, Plant Nutrition and Soil Science, Director, Institute of Agricultural Chemistry, 1961-70, Friedrich-Schiller-University, Jena, Germany; Full Professor, Physiology and Nutrition of Crop Plants, Martin-Luther-University Halle-Wittenberg, Germany, 1970-95; Professor Emeritus, 1995; Dean of Agricultural Faculty, 1983-90; Rector of Martin-Luther-University Halle-Wittenberg, 1990-93; Vice President, Rector's Conference of the Federal Republic of Germany, 1991-95. Publications: 229 contributions to scientific journals and books; 1 monograph; Author and editor, Pflanzenernährung und Düngung, university textbook, revised edition, 2000. Honours include: Medal and Diploma, 8th International Fertiliser Congress, Moscow, 1976; National Prize for Science and Technology, Berlin, 1982; Dr Heinrich Baur Prize, Munich, 1994; Golden Sprengel-Liebig-Medal, Leipzig, 1997. Memberships: Deutsche Akademie der Naturforscher Leopoldina; Matica Srbska; Verband Deutscher Landwirtschaftlicher Untersuchungs-und Forschungsanstalten, Vice-President, 1993-96. Address: Institute for Soil Science and Plant Nutrition of the Martin-Luther-University Halle-Wittenberg, Julius-Kuehn-Str 31, 06112 Halle (Saale), Germany. E-mail: schilling@landw.uni-halle.de

SCHLEINKOFER Boris Dunne, b. 10 July 1971, San Francisco, California, USA. Artist; Entertainer. m. Mary C Izard, 23 March 1994. Education: School of Redundant Karma, ongoing. Publication: The Art of Arranging the Shadow. Address: 1607 Carolina Street #5, Bellingham, WA 98229, USA.

SCHLESINGER Arthur M(eier) Jr, b. 15 October 1917, Columbus, Ohio, USA. Historian; Retired Professor. m. (1) Marian Cannon, 1940, divorced 1970, 2 sons, 2 daughters, (2) Alexandra Emmet, 1971, 1 son. Education: AB, Harvard University, 1938; Honorary Fellow, University of Cambridge, 1938-39; Society of Fellows, Harvard University, 1939-42. Appointments: Associate Professor, 1946-54, Professor of History, 1954-61, Harvard University; Special Assistant to President John F Kennedy, 1961-63; Visiting Fellow, Institute for Advanced Study,

Princeton, New Jersey, 1966; Schweitzer Professor in Humanities, City University of New York, 1966-95. Publications: Orestes A Brownson: A Pilgrim's Progress, 1939; The Age of Jackson, 1945; The Vital Center, 1949; The General and the President (with R H Rovere), 1951; The Age of Roosevelt, Vol I, The Crisis of the Old Order 1919-1933, 1957, Vol II, The Coming of the New Deal, 1958, Vol III, The Politics of Upheaval, 1960; Kennedy or Nixon: Does It Make Any Difference?, 1960; The Politics of Hope, 1963; The National Experience (with John Blum), 1963; A Thousand Days: John F Kennedy in the White House, 1965; The Bitter Heritage: Vietnam and American Democracy 1941-66, 1967; The Crisis of Confidence, 1969; The Imperial Presidency, 1973; Robert Kennedy and His Times, 1978; The Cycles of American History, 1986; The Disuniting of America, 1991; A Life in the 20th Century: I. Innocent Beginnings, 2000. Editor: Paths to American Thought, 1963; The Promise of American Life, 1967; The Best and Last of Edwin O'Connor, 1970; The History of American Presidential Elections (with F L Israel), 1971, new edition, 1986; The Coming to Power, 1972; The Dynamics of World Power: A Documentary History of United States Foreign Policy 1945-1972, 1973; History of US Political Parties, 1973; Running for President, 1994. Contributions to: Professional journals. Honours: Francis Parkman Prize, Society of American Historians, 1957; Bancroft Prize, Columbia University, 1958; Pulitzer Prize in History, 1946, in Biography, 1966; National Book Awards, 1966, 1979; American Academy of Arts and Letters Gold Medal in History and Biography, 1967; Fregene Prize for Literature, Italy, 1983; National Humanities Medal, 1998; Grants, fellowships and honorary doctorates. Memberships: American Academy of Arts and Letters, president, 1981-84, chancellor, 1984-87; American Civil Liberties Union; American Historical Association; American Philosophical Society; Americans for Democratic Action, chairman, 1952-54; Massachusetts Historical Society; Council on Foreign Relations; Franklin and Eleanor Roosevelt Institute, co-chairman, 1983-; Society of American Historians; Phi Beta Kappa. Address: 455 East 51st Street, New York, NY 10022, USA.

SCHLEVOGT Kai-Alexander, b. 2 March 1971, Bonn, Germany. International Strategic Management Educator; Organisational Researcher; Political Economic Writer; Academic Entrepreneur; China Expert. m. Emily Schlevogt, 1 daughter. Education includes: BSc (Hons), Management, 1991-94, MSc, Management, 1994-95, London School of Economics, England; Degree, International Enterprise Management, Beijing University of International Business and Economics, China, 1993-94; PhD, Management Studies, University of Oxford, England, 1995-98; Postdoctoral Studies Harvard University, USA, 1998-99. Appointments include: Country Manager, Chief Representative, Colonia-Victoire Insurance, Moscow, Soviet Union, 1990-92; Assistant Producer, Strategic Advisor to Chief Executive Officer, Trans-World Television Production Corporation, Taipei, Taiwan, 1994-95; Associate, McKinsey & Company Inc, Shanghai, China, 1996-98; Visiting Scholar, Harvard University, 1998-99; Associate Professor, Peking University, Guanghua School of Management, China, 1999; Senior Consultant, China Marketing (Journal), 1999-; National Correspondent for China, European Group for Organisational Studies, 1999-; Senior Research Fellow, Professor, Peking University, China, 1999-; Visiting Professor, Australian Graduate School of Management, University of New South Wales and University of Sydney, 2000-2001; Founder, President and Managing Director, Schlevogt Business School, Germany, 2001-; Visiting Professor, Henley Management College, UK, 2001-. Publications: More than 100 publications include: Books: Power and control in Chinese private enterprises: Organisational design in the Taiwanese media industry, 1998; Inside Chinese organisations: An empirical study of business practices in China, 1999; The art of Chinese management: Theory, evidence and applications, 2002. Honours: ESRC Research Scholarship, 1996-98; Listed in Who's Who publications and biographical dictionaries. Memberships include: LSE Alumni Organisation; Oxford Union Society; McKinsey Alumni Organisation; Christ Church Association; Oxford Business Alumni; Oxford University Society; Academy of Management; Academy of International Business. Address: Schlevogt Business School, Parkschloss Schlevogt, Büro des Präsidenten, Parkstrasse 9, 17235 Neustrelitz bei Berlin, Germany. E-mail: schlevogt@schlevogt.de

SCHMEIDLER Felix, b. 20 October 1920, Leipzig, Germany. m. Marion Pampe, 1 son, 1 daughter. Education: Universität München, Studium der Astronomie, 1938-41; Dr rer nat, Universität München, 1941; Habilitation für Astronomie an Universität München, 1950. Appointments: Assistant der Universitätssternwarte München, 1943; Professor für Astronomie an Universität München, 1957; Assistant Director, Universitätssternwarte, München, 1979-86; University Observatory Cambridge, England, 1950-51; Mt Stromlo Observatory, Canberra, Australia, 1954-55. Publications: More than 100 articles in scientific journals; Books: Alte und moderne Kosmologie, 1961; Nikolaus Copernicus, Serie Große Naturforscher, 1970; Edition, Works of the Astronomers Hevelius, 1969, Regionmontanus, 1972; Kommentar zu "De revolutionibus, 1998. Honours: Silberne Medaille der Universität Helsinki, 1968; Kulturpreis der Landsmannschaft Westpreußen, Münster, 1973; Honorary Citizen der Stadt Königsberg in Bayern, 1982; Ehrenschild Deutschordensland der Ost- und Westpreußenstiftung in Bayern, 1997. Memberships: Royal Astronomical Society London, 1951; International Astronomical Union, 1955; Altpreußische Gesellschaft für Wissenschaft, Kunst und Literatur, 1981. Address: Mauerkircher Strasse 17, D81679 München, Germany.

SCHMID-SCHONBEIN G W, b. 1 January 1948, Albstadt, Germany. Professor. m. Renate Schmid-Schonbein, 3 sons. Education: PhD, University of California at San Diego, 1976. Appointments: Staff Associate, Columbia University, New York, 1976-79; Assistant Professor, 1979-84, Associate Professor, 1984-89, Professor of Bioengineering, 1989-, Department of Bioengineering, University of California at San Diego. Publications: Fundamental research articles in cardiovascular research and bioengineering. Honours: Honorary Professor of Chinese Academy of Science, 1997; Ratchow Gold Medal, 1999; Fellow, American Heart Association, 2001. Memberships: American Microcirculatory Society; European Microcirculatory Societies; Biomedical Engineering Society; American Physiological Society; American Heart Association; American Institute for Medical and Biological Engineering. Address: 9500 Gilman Drive, University of California at San Diego, La Jolla, CA 92093-0412, USA.

SCHMIDT Robert Milton, b. 7 May 1944, Milwaukee, Wisconsin, USA. Physician; Scientist; Educator. m. Jessie Knight, 2 sons. Education: AB, Northwestern University, 1966; MD, Columbia University College of Physicians and Surgeons, 1966-70; Further studies at University of California (San Diego); Centers for Disease Control, Atlanta; Master Public Health, Harvard, 1974-75; PhD studies including Law, Emory Institute Liberal Arts, 1975-76, 1981-82; MA, Health and Ageing, San Francisco State University, 1989-99. Appointments: Hematology Division, US Public Health Service, Centers for Disease Control, Atlanta, Georgia, 1971-79; Special Assistant to Director, State Laboratory Institute of Massachusetts, Boston, 1974-75; President, Founder, Medical Director, Component Centers, International Health Resource Center of Hawaii, 1979-82; Director of California Pacific Medical Center, Health Watch Medical Center and Health Watch International, Director, Center for Preventive Medicine and Health

Dictionary of International Biography

Research, Senior Scientist, Institute of Cancer Research, 1983-; Institute of Epidemiology and Behavioral Medicine, 1983-88; Professor, Biomedical Science, Hematology and Preventive Medicine, Director of Health Professions Programs, Chair of the Health Professions Advising Committee, member Gerontology Faculty Council, San Francisco State University, 1983-99; Author or co-author over 300 reviewed publications in professional journals and conference proceedings; 17 major books and 28 technical manuals. Memberships include: Fellow, American Association for the Advancement of Science; American College of Physicians; American Society of Clinical Pathologists; American College of Pathologists; American College of Preventive Medicine; American Medical Informatics Association; International Society of Hematology; The Royal Society of Medicine; American Geriatrics Society; Knight of Malta; Cosmos Club; Alumni Regent, Columbia University of Physicians and Surgeons; Harvard Clubs of New York City and Northern California; Northwestern University; Emory University Graduate School of Arts and Sciences; Circle Club; National Gallery of Art, Washington, DC; Many others. Address: Whaleship Plaza, 25 Hinckley Walk, San Francisco, CA 94111-2303, USA.

SCHMIED-KOWARZIK Wolfdietrich, 11 March 1939, Friedberg, Germany. University Professor of Philosophy. m. Iris von Gottberg, 2 sons, 1 daughter. Education: Study of Philosophy, Cultural Anthropology, Psychology in Vienna, Austria; Dr. Phil. Vienna, 1963; Habilitation, University of Bonn, Germany, 1970. Appointments: Wiss. Assistant, University of Bonn, 1964-71; Professor Philosophy, University Kassel, Germany, 1971-. Publications: 16 Books; 31 Editions; Articles in professional journals. Honours: Bundesverdienstkreuz given by the President of the Federal Republic of Germany; Ehrenkreuz für Wissenschaft und Kunst I.Kl, President of Austria; Kritik und Praxis – Festschrift zum 60 Geburtstag, 1999. Memberships include: President, Internationale Rosenzweig Gesellschaft; Director, Ulrich Sonnemann-Gesellschaft, Internationale Hegel Gesellschaft; Academia Scientiarum et artium Europaea, others. Address: Universität Kassel, Nora-Platiel-Str 1, 34109 Kassel, Germany. E-mail: schmiedk@uni-kassel.de

SCHNAGL Roger Dieter, b. 10 October 1944, Reitendorf, Austria. Microbiology Educator; Researcher in Virology. m. Heather York Syme. Education: BS (Hons), 1969, PhD, 1975, University of Melbourne. Appointments: Postdoctoral Research Fellow, University of Melbourne, 1975-78; Lecturer, 1979-86, Senior Lecturer, 1987-, Head of Department, 1993-95, 2000-, Deputy Head of Department, 1996-2000, Department of Microbiology, La Trobe University, Melbourne; Director, Advanced Electron Microscope Facility, La Trobe University, Melbourne, 2001-2002. Publications: Over 50 articles in numerous international science journals. Honours: Numerous research grants and awards, 1979-. Memberships: Fellow, Australian Society for Microbiology; New York Academy of Sciences. Address: Department of Microbiology, La Trobe University, Bundoora, Victoria 3083, Australia.

SCHNEIDER Kirk J, b. 27 July 1956. Psychologist. m. Jurate Raulinaitis. Education: BA, Psychology, Ohio State University, 1978; MA, Psychology, West Georgia College, 1979; PhD, Psychology, Saybrook Institute, 1984. Appointments: Adjunct Faculty Member, Saybrook Graduate School, California Institute of Integral Studies; President, Existential-Humanistic Institute, San Francisco, 1999-2003. Publications: Over 70 articles and chapters; 5 books including: The Paradoxical Self; Horror and the Holy; The Psychology of Existence, co-author; The Handbook of Humanistic Psychology, 2001; The Rediscovery of Awe, forthcoming 2004. Honours: Distinguished Saybrook Author, 1996.

Memberships: Fellow, 2002, American Psychological Association; American Association for the Advancement of Science; President, Existential Humanistic Institute. Address: Saybrook Graduate School, 450 Pacific Street, 3rd Floor, San Francisco, CA 94133, USA.

SCHOENHAGEN Paul, b. 27 January 1964, Koblenz, Germany. Physician; Cardiovascular Imaging Specialist. m. Noelle Schoenhagen, 2 sons, 1 daughter. Education: Medical School Marburg, Germany, 1985-91, Tuebingen, Germany, 1991-92; MD, 1992; Doctoral Thesis, Cardiovascular Medicine, Marburg, Germany, 1995. Appointments: Residency, Internal Medicine and Radiology, Stuttgart, Germany, 1992-96; Residency, Internal Medicine, 1996-99, Fellowship, Cardiovascular Medicine, 1999-2002; Fellowship, Cardiovascular Tomography, 2002-2003, Staff, Department of Diagnostic Radiology and Cardiovascular Medicine, 2003-, The Cleveland Clinic Foundation, Cleveland, Ohio, USA. Publications: Articles in scientific journals include most recently: Extent and Direction of Arterial Remodeling in Stable versus Unstable Coronary Syndromes: An Intravascular Ultrasound Study, 2002; Relation of matrix-metalloproteinase 3 found in coronary lesion samples retrieved by directional coronary atherectomy to intrvascular ultasound observations on coronary remodeling, 2002; Coronary Plaque Morphology and Frequency of Ulceration Distant from Culprit Lesions in Patients with Unstable and Stable Presentation, 2003. Honours: Postdoctoral Fellowship Grant, Ohio Valley, American Heart Association, 2001-2003; 2nd James E Muller Vulnerable Plaque Award, 2002. Memberships: European Society of Cardiology; Fellow American Heart Association; Radiologic Society of North America. Address: The Cleveland Clinic Foundation, Radiology H6-6, 9500 Euclid Avenue, Cleveland, OH 44195, USA. E-mail: shoenp1@ccf.org

SCHOLEY Arthur (Edward), b. 17 June 1932, Sheffield, England. Children's Writer; Playwright; Librettist; Lyric Writer. Publications: The Song of Caedmon (with Donald Swann), 1971; Christmas Plays and Ideas for Worship, 1973; The Discontented Dervishes, 1977; Sallinka and the Golden Bird, 1978; Twelve Tales for a Christmas Night, 1978; Wacky and His Fuddlejig (with Donald Swann), 1978; Singalive (with Donald Swann) 1978; Herod and the Rooster (with Ronald Chamberlain), 1979; The Dickens Christmas Carol Show, 1979; Baboushka (with Donald Swann) 1979; Candletree (with Donald Swann), 1981; Five Plays for Christmas, 1981; Four Plays About People, 1983; Martin the Cobbler, 1983; The Hosanna Kids, 1985; Make a Model Christmas Crib, 1988; Who'll Be Brother Donkey?, 1990; Brendan Ahoy!, (with Donald Swann), 1994; The Journey of the Christmas Creatures (with Karen Bradley), 1998; The Discontented Dervishes, 2002; The Panagon Parrot, 2002. Address: 10 Chiltern Court, Pages Hill, London N10 1EN, England. E-mail: scholey@arthurscholey.co.uk

SCHOLZ Roland Werner, b. 15 April 1950, Halle, Saale. University Professor. m. Maya Urbatzka, 2 sons. Education: Diploma in Mathematics, University of Marburg, 1976; PhD, Social Psychology, University of Marburg, 1979; PhD, Cognitive Psychology, Dr phil habil, University of Marburg, 1985. Appointments: Research Assistant, Center for Social and Economic Decision Research (SFB 24) University of Mannheim, 1976-78; Research Associate, Institute of Didactics of Mathematics, University of Bielefeld, 1978-93; Adjunct Professor, Psychology, University of Mannheim, 1987-95; Founder and Head, Gesellschaft für Organisation und Entscheidung (Bielefeld/Stuttgart/Zurich); 1988-; Full Professor, Environmental Sciences, Natural and Social Science Interface (ETH), Zurich, 1993-; Adjunct Professor, Psychology, University of Zurich, 1998-; Visiting Professor, MIT, 2002; King Carl XVI Gustaf's Professorship of Environmental

Dictionary of International Biography

Sciences, Chalmers University of Technology, Gothenburg, Sweden, 2002-03; Lecturer, Institute of Innovation and Environmental Management, Karl-Franzens-University of Graz, Austria; Lecturer, University of Natural Resources and Applied Life Sciences of Vienna, Austria; Lecturer, Centre for Sustainability Management (CSM), University of Lueneburg, Germany. Publications: 29 books include: (author) Cognitive Strategies in Stochastic Thinking, 1987; Qualitative Aspects of Decision Making, 1997; Embedded Case Study Methods: Integrating Quantitative and Quantitative Knowledge, 2002; Over 200 papers in Environmental Sciences, Decision Theory, Psychology, Mathematics Education. Memberships: APA; Verein für Socialpolitik. Address: ETH Zurich, Natural and Social Science Interface HAD, CH 8092 Zurich, Switzerland.

SCHOU Søren Thorkild, b. 21 December 1943, Copenhagen, Denmark. Associate Professor of Literature. m. Rigmor Bækholm, 1 daughter. Education: MA, Comparative Literature, University of Copenhagen, 1971; Lecturer, Senior Lecturer, Associate Professor, University of Roskilde, Denmark, 1972-. Publications: Heinrich Böll, 1972; Dansk Realisme, 1976; De Danske Østfront-Frivillige, 1981; Dansk Litteraturhistorie, 1985; Dansk Mediehistorie, 1997; Og Andre Forfattere, 2001; Gads Danske Forfatterleksikon, 2003. Honour: The Georg Brandes Prize of 2002. Membership: The Henrik Pontoppidan Society. Address: Fasanvej 5, 4000 Roskilde, Denmark. E-mail: sts@nuc.dk

SCHREINER Lothar, b. 25 November 1925, Hamburg, Germany. Professor of Theology. m. Lieselotte Wevelmeyer, 1 son, 2 daughters. Education: Theology, Universities of Tübingen and Münster, Germany; Scholarship to Mansfield College, Oxford, England, 1947; BA, 1949, MA (Oxon), 1956; 1st and 2nd Ministers Examinations, Evangelical Church of Westphalia, Bielefeld, Germany, 1950-52; Ordained Minister, 1953; Doctor of Theology, University of Zurich, Switzerland, 1953; Habilitation, Theology, University of Heidelberg, Germany, 1969. Appointments: Professor, New Testament, Theology Faculty, Nommensen University, Pematang Siantar, Sumatra, Republic of Indonesia, 1956-65; Secretary for Missionaries' Promotion, Rhenish Missionary Society, Wuppertal, Germany, 1968-78; Professor of History of Religions and Missiology, Barmen School of Theology, Wuppertal, Germany, 1972-91; Honorary Professor, Bergische University, Wuppertal, 1984-; Guest-Lectureships: MICT Insein, Myanmar, 1957; Otjimbingue, Namibia, 1974; Chinese Rhenish Church, Hongkong, 1980; Eden Theological Seminary, St Louis, USA, 1987; Wesley Theological Seminary, Washington DC, USA, 1996. Publications: J G Hamann's Chief Writings. Text a Commentary volumes 1-3 and 7 (co-editor with F Blanke), 1956-63; The Confession of Faith of the Batak Church rev. tr. Origin and Relevance, 1966, 2nd enlarged edition, 1984; Customary Law and the Gospel, the Relevance for Church and Mission with the Bataks, 1972, Indonesian translation edition, 1978, 3rd edition 1996; Nommensen According to his own Writings, 1996. Honours: Publication: Injil dan Tata Hidup/The Gospel and Life Order, Essays in honour of the 75th Birthday of The Rev Professor Dr Lothar Schreiner, 2001. Memberships: IAMS; IAHR; DGWM; Amnesty International. Address: Theodor-Heuss-Str 110, 42109 Wuppertal, Germany. E-mail: lignarius@t-online.de

SCHROEDER Klaus-Henning, b. 13 October 1932, Schwerin, Germany. University Professor. m. Renate Döhlemeyer. Education: Dr Phil, 1961, Habilitation, 1972, Professor of Romance Languages, 1972, Free University, Berlin, Germany. Appointments: Assistant, Institute of Balkan Languages, 1960; Professor of Romance Languages, Free University, Berlin, 1972. Publications: Einführung in das Studium des Rumänischen: Sprachwissenschaft und Literaturgeschichte, 1967; Geschichte van trojanischen Krieg

in der älteren rumänische Literatur, 1976; Die rumänische Version der "Historia Destructionis Troiae" des Guido delle colonne, 1977; David's Enkel, 1991; Geschichte der französischen Sprache im Überblick, 1997. Address: Johann-Sigismund-Str 16, D-10711 Berlin, Germany.

SCHUBERT Guenther Erich, b. 17 August 1930, Mosul, Iraq. Pathologist. Divorced, 2 sons, 1 daughter. Education: MD, University of Heidelberg, Germany, 1957; Private Docent, Pathology, University of Tuebingen, Germany, 1966; Professor, Pathology, 1972. Appointments: Assistant Medical Director, University of Tuebingen, Germany, 1966-76; Head, Institute of Pathology, Klinikum Wuppertal GmbH, 1966-76; Chief, Pathology, University of Witten, Herdecke, 1985-96. Publications: 4 books in English, German, Spanish; Textbook of Pathology; Pathologie; Coloratlas of Cytodiagnosis of the Prostate; Endoscopy of the Urinary Bladder. Memberships: Numerous. Address: Am Anschlag 71, D-42113, Wuppertal 1, Germany.

SCHULBERG Budd, b. 27 March 1914, New York, New York, USA. Author. m. (1) Virginia Ray, 23 July 1936, divorced 1942, 1 daughter, (2) Victoria Anderson, 17 February 1943, divorced 1964, 2 sons, (3) Geraldine Brooks, 12 July 1964, deceased 1977, (4) Betsy Anne Langman, 9 July 1979, 1 son, 1 daughter. Education: AB cum laude, Dartmouth College, 1936. Appointments: Founder-President, Schulberg Productions; Founder-Director, Watts Writers Workshop, Los Angeles, 1965-; Founder-Chairman, Frederick Douglass Creative Arts Center, New York City, 1971-. Publications: What Makes Sammy Run?, 1941; The Harder They Fall, 1947; The Disenchanted, 1950; Some Faces in the Crowd, 1953; Waterfront, 1955; Sanctuary V, 1969; The Four Seasons of Success, 1972; Loser and Still Champion: Muhammad Ali, 1972; Swan Watch, 1975; Everything That Moves, 1980; Moving Pictures: Memories of a Hollywood Prince, 1981; Love, Action, Laughter and Other Sad Tales, 1990; Sparring with Hemingway and Other Legends of the Fight Game, 1995. Editor: From the Ashes: Voices of Watts, 1967. Screenplays: Little Orphan Annie (with Samuel Ornitz), 1938; Winter Carnival (with F Scott Fitzgerald), 1939; Weekend for Three (with Dorothy Parker), 1941; City Without Men (with Martin Berkeley), 1943; Government Girl, 1943; On the Waterfront, 1954; A Face in the Crowd, 1957; Wind Across the Everglades, 1958. Contributions to: Leading magazines. Honours: Academy Award, 1954; New York Critics Circle Award, 1954; Screen Writers Guild Award, 1954; Venice Film Festival Award, 1954; Christopher Award, 1955; German Film Critics Award, 1957; B'hai Human Rights Award, 1968; Prix Literaire, Deauville Festival, 1989; Westhampton Writers Lifetime Achievement Award, 1989; World Boxing Association Living Legend Award, 1990; Southampton Cultural Center 1st Annual Literature Award, 1992. Memberships: American Civil Liberties Union; American Society of Composers, Authors and Publishers; Authors Guild; Dramatists Guild; Players' Club, founder member; PEN; Phi Beta Kappa; Writers Guild East. Address: c/o Miriam Altschuler Literary Agency, RR1, Box 5, Old Post Road, Red Hook, NY 12571, USA.

SCHULER Robert Jordan, b. 25 June 1939, California, USA. Professor of English; Poet. m. Carol Forbis, 7 September 1963, 2 sons, 1 daughter. Education: BA, Honours, Political Science, Stanford University, 1961; MA, Comparative Literature, University of California, Berkeley, 1965; PhD, English, University of Minnesota, 1989. Appointments: Instructor in English, Menlo College, 1965-67; Instructor in Humanities, Shimer College, 1967-77; Professor of English, University of Wisconsin, 1978-. Publications: Axle of the Oak, 1978; Seasonings, 1978; Where is Dancers' Hill?, 1979; Morning Raga, 1980; Red Cedar Scroll, 1981; Floating Out of Stone, 1982; Music for Monet, 1984; Grace:

Dictionary of International Biography

A Book of Days, 1995; Journeys Toward the Original Mind, 1995; Red Cedar Suite, 1999; In search of "Green Dolphin Street", 2004. Contributions to: Caliban; Northeast; Tar River Poetry; Longhouse; Dacotah Territory; Wisconsin Academy Review; Wisconsin Review; North Stone Review; Wisconsin Poetry 1991 Transactions; Hummingbird; Abraxas; Lake Street Review; Inheriting the Earth; Mississippi Valley Review; Coal City Review; Gypsy; Imagining Home, 1995. Honour: Wisconsin Arts Board Fellowship for Poetry, 1997; Awards from Wisconsin Humanities Council; Illinois Arts Council; NEA. Membership: Phi Kappa Phi. Address: E4549 479th Avenue, Menomonie, WI 54751, USA. E-mail: Schulerr@vw.stout.edu

SCHULLER Gunther (Alexander), b. 22 November 1925, New York, New York, USA. Composer; Conductor; Music Educator; Publisher. m. Marjorie Black, 8 June 1948, deceased 1992, 2 sons. Education: St Thomas Choir School, New York City, 1937-40. Appointments: Teacher, Manhattan School of Music, New York City, 1950-63; Teacher, 1963-84, Artistic Co-Director, 1969-74, Director, 1974-84, Berkshire Music Center, Tanglewood, Massachusetts; Co-Director, Smithson Jazz Masterworks Orchestra, 1991-1997; Faculty, Yale School of Music, 1964-67; President, New England Conservatory of Music, Boston, 1967-77; Music Publisher, 1975-99; Record Producer, GM Recordings, 1980-; Artistic Director, Festival at Sandpoint, 1985-98. Publications: Horn Technique, 1962, 2nd edition, 1992; Early Jazz: Its Roots and Musical Development, 1968; Musings, 1985; The Swing Era, 1988; The Compleat Conductor, 1997. Contributions to: Various publications. Honours: Guggenheim Fellowship, 1962-63; ASCAP-Deems Taylor Award, 1970; Rodgers and Hammerstein Award, 1971; William Schuman Award, Columbia University, 1989; John D and Catharine T MacArthur Foundation Fellowship, 1991; Pulitzer Prize in Music, 1994; Honorary doctorates. Memberships: American Academy of Arts and Sciences; American Academy of Arts and Letters. Address: 167 Dudley Road, Newton Centre, MA 02159, USA.

SCHULTZ Gwen M, b. 6 January 1923, Milwaukee, Wisconsin, USA. Professor Emerita of Geography; Writer; Cartographer. Education: Degrees in English and Geography, University of Wisconsin, Madison. Appointments: Geography Professor with several departments, University of Wisconsin, Madison, and with Wisconsin Geological and Natural History Survey. Publications: Books: Wisconsin's Foundations; Ice Age Lost; Glaciers and the Ice Age; Icebergs and their Voyages; Crest Colorprint World Atlas; The Blue Valentine; The Bucky Badger Story; and articles in scholarly journals in USA and abroad and in magazines, essays, reviews, fiction, poetry, maps; Contributions to others' books. Honours: Writing Awards: The National League of American Pen Women; Midwest Authors and Artists; The Wisconsin Historical Society; Council for Wisconsin Writers; Wisconsin Regional Writers' Association. Memberships: Association of American Geographers; American Quaternary Association; American Polar Society; Center for the Study of the First Americans; Ice Age Park and Trail Foundation; Authors Guild, Authors League of America; Wisconsin Academy of Sciences, Arts and Letters; National Geographic Society; Wisconsin Geographical Society. Address: 111 W Wilson Street, #201, Madison, WI 53703, USA.

SCHULZE Juergen H, b. 16 June 1939, Brockwitz, Germany. Businessman. m. Barbara, 2 sons. Education: BSME, Technical University, Stuttgart, Germany, 1963; MBA, Columbia University, New York, USA, 1972. Appointments: General Manager, Business Systems, Rank Xerox, Germany; Managing Director, Alu-Suisse-Lonza, Germany; Chairman of the Management Board, Deutz Motor Corporation, Germany; Chairman, Helmut Schulze GmbH,

Germany. Memberships: Columbia Alumni; Mensa Organisation; Golf Club, VDMA Germany; American Chamber of Commerce, Germany. Address: Habichtweg 2, 40670 Meerbusch, Germany.

SCHUMACHER Joel, b. 29 August 1939, New York, USA. Film Director. Education: Parson School of Design, New York. Appointments: Work in fashion industry aged 15; Owner boutique Paraphernalia; Costume designer, Revlon, 1970s; Set and production design; Writer, director for TV; Films include: The Incredible Shrinking Woman; DC Cab (also screenplay); St Elmo's Fire (also screenplay); The Lost Boys; Cousins; Flatliners; Dying Young; Falling Down; The Client; Batman Forever; A Time to Kill; Batman and Robin; Eight Millimeter; Flawless (also screenplay and producer); Gossip; Tigerland; Phone Booth; Bad Company. Publications: (screenplays) Sparkle; Car Wash; The Wiz. Address: Joel Schumacher Productions, 400 Warner Boulevard, Burbank, CA 91522, USA.

SCHUMACHER Michael, b. 3 January 1969. Motor Racing Driver. m. Corinna Betsch, 1995, 2 children. Appointments: Began Professional Career, 1983; 2nd Place, International German Formula 3 Championship, 1989; Driver for Mercedes, 1990; International German Champion Formula 3 Championship, 1990; European Formula 3 Champion, 1990; World Champion, Formula 3, Macau and Fiji, 1990; Formula 1 Contestant, 1991-; 1st Formula One Victory, Belgium, 1992; Other Grand Prix wins: Portuguese, 1993, Brazilian, 1994, 1995, 2000, 2002, Pacific, 1994, San Marino, 1994, 2000, 2002, Monaco, 1994, 1995, 1999, 2001, Canadian, 1994, 1998, 2000, French, 1994, 1995, Hungarian, 1994, 1998, 2001, European, 1994, 1995, 2000, 2001, Spanish, 1995, 2001, 2002, Italian, 1996, Japanese, 1997, Australian, 2000, 2001, 2002, Italian, 1996, 2000, American, 2000, Japanese, 1997, 2000, Malaysian, 2000, 2001, Austrian, 2002; Third Place, World Motor Racing Championship, 1992, Fourth Place, 1993; Formula One World Champion, 1994, 1995, 2000, 2001, 2002, 2003; Publication: Formula for Success (with Derick Allsop), 1996; Michael Schumacher (biography with Christopher Hilton), 2000. Address: c/o Weber Management GmbH, 70173 Stuttgart, Hirschstrasse 36, Germany. Website: www.mschumacher.com

SCHUR Peter, b. 9 May 1933, Vienna, Austria (US Citizen). Physician. m. Susan Dorfman, divorced, 2 daughters. Education: BSc, Yale University, 1955; MD, Harvard Medical School, 1958; Postdoctoral training at Bronx Municipal Hospital Center, 1958-62; Walter Reed Army Institute of Research and Walter Reed Army Medical Center, 1962-64; Fellow, Helen Hay Whitney Foundation, Rockefeller University, 1964-67. Appointments: Tutor in Medicine, Harvard College, 1973-; Consulting Staff: Beth Israel Hospital, Boston, New England Baptist Hospital, Boston, Massachusetts, 1973-, Professor of Medicine, Harvard Medical School, 1978-; Medical Director, Clinical Immunology Lab, 1980-, Senior, Physician, 1980-, Attending on Medicine, 1980-, Consultant in Rheumatology, 1980-, Director, Lupus Clinic, 1980-, Rheumatologist and Immunologist, 1981-, Physician in Medicine, 1981-, Brigham and Women's Hospital; Editor, Arthritis and Rheumatism, 1990-95; Editor, Up To Date in Rheumatology, 1995-. Publications: 190 in professional journals, 15 proceedings of meetings; 86 reviews, chapters and editorials; 3 books include: The Clinical Management of Systemic Lupus Erythematosus, 2nd edition (editor), 1996. Honours include: Visiting professorships at over 50 medical schools, 1970-; Lupus Foundation, President's award, 1987; American Lupus Society, Hall of Fame, 1990; Masters Award, ACR, 1998; Medal, University of Caracas, 1998. Memberships include: American Society for Clinical Investigation; Fellow, American College of Physicians; American Association of Immunologists; American Federation of Clinical Research; Association of American Physicians; Master, American College of Rheumatology. Address: Department of Medicine, Division of Rheumatology, Immunology, Allergy, 75 Francis Street, Boston, MA 02115, USA.

SCHWARZ Markus J, b. 16 April 1966, Ingolstadt, Germany. Research Assistant. Divorced, 1 daughter. Education: Military Service, 1986-87; Studies in Chemistry, Regensburg University, 1989-90; Studies in Human Medicine, Munich Ludwig Maximilian University, 1990-96. Appointments: Physician, Practical Training, 1996-97, Intern and Research Assistant, Department for Neurochemistry, 1997-, Psychiatric Hospital, Munich University; Doctorate, 1998. Publications: 43 research articles in international peer-reviewed journals; 10 book chapters; Approximately 50 abstracts. Honours: 1st Regional Prize Winner, Youth Research Programme in the field of Biology, 1986; Fellowship Award, World Psychiatric Association, 1999; Fellowship Award, European College of Neuropsychopharmacology, 1999; ECNP Poster Award, 1999; Fellowship Award, German Association of Neuropsychopharmacology and Pharmacopsychiatry, 1999; Fellowship Award, German Society of Biological Psychiatry, 2001; Fellowship Award, World Psychiatric Association, 2001; Fellowship Award, German Society for Biological Psychiatry, 2002; Numerous research grants, 1998-2005; Listed in national and international biographical publications. Memberships: Association of European Psychiatrists; German Association of Neuropsychopharmacology and Pharmacopsychiatry; American Psychiatric Association; European College of Neuropsychopharmacology; German Society of Immunology; International Society for Neuroimmunomodulation; Secretary of the Section 'Immunology and Psychiatry' of the World Psychiatric Association. Address: Psychiatrische Klinik-Neurochemische Abteilung, Ludwig-Maximilians-Universität, Nussbaumstrasse 7, D-80336 München, Germany. E-mail: markus.schwarz@med.uni-muenchen.de

SCHWARZENEGGER Arnold Alois, b. 30 July 1947, Graz, Austria (US citizen, 1963). Actor; Author; Businessman; Former Bodybuilder; US Governor of California. m. Maria Owings Shriver, 1985, 2 sons, 2 daughters. Education: University of Wisconsin-Superior. Appointment: Elected Governor of California, 2003. Career: Film appearances include: Stay Hungry, 1976; Pumping Iron, 1977; The Jayne Mansfield Story, 1980; Conan the Barbarian, 1982; The Destroyer, 1983; The Terminator, 1984; Commando, 1985; Raw Deal, 1986; Predator, 1987; Running Man, 1987; Red Heat, 1988; Twins, 1989; Total Recall, 1990; Kindergarten Cop, 1990; Terminator II, 1991; Last Action Hero, 1993; Dave (cameo), 1993; True Lies, 1994; Junior, 1994; Eraser, 1996; Single All the Way, 1996; Batman and Robin, 1997; With Wings with Eagles, 1997; End of Days, 1999; The Sixth Day, 2001; Collateral Damage, 2002; Terminator 3: Rise of the Machines, 2003; The Rundown, 2003; Around the World in 80 Days, 2004. Publications: Arnold: The Education of a Bodybuilder, 1977; Arnold's Bodyshaping for Women, 1979; Arnold's Bodybuilding for Men, 1981; Arnold's Encyclopedia of Modern Bodybuilding, 1985; Arnold's Fitness for Kids (jointly), 1993. Honours: National Weight Training Coach Special Olympics; Bodybuilding Champion, 1965-80; Junior Mr Europe, 1965; Best Built Man of Europe, 1966; Mr Europe, 1966; Mr International, 1968; Mr Universe (amateur), 1969. Memberships: Volunteer, prison rehabilitation programmes; Chairman, President's Council on Physical Fitness and Sport, 1990. Address: PMK, Suite 200, 955 South Carillo Drive, Los Angeles, CA 90048, USA.

SCHWARZKOPF Elisabeth (Dame), b. 9 December 1915, Jarocin, Poland. Singer (Soprano). m. Walter Legge 1953, deceased 1979. Education: High School of Music, Berlin studied with Maria Ivogün-Raucheisen, Lula Mysz-Gmeiner and Dr. Heinrich Egenolf.

Debut: Deutsches Opernhaus Berlin; appeared at Staatsoper Wien, Royal Opera House Covent Garden, London; La Scala Milan; San Francisco Opera; Reopening Bayreuth Festival, 1951; Salzburger Festspiele 1947-64; Film "Der Rosenkavalier", Salzburger Festspiele, 1960. Recordings: 16 complete Operas, various Symphonies; Songs and Arias with Orchestra, 6 complete Operettas, Leider with pianoforte: 21 LP's and 16 CD's. Publications: Editor, On and Off the Record: a memoire of Walter Legge. Honours: Recipient of numerous awards including: Cambridge MUsd; Lilli Lehmann Medal, Salzburg; MusD,(hc) University of Washington DC; Mozart Medal Frankfurt, Arts et Letters, Paris; Ehrensenatorin Hochschule für Musik Carl Maria von Weber, Dresden; DMus (hc) Glasgow. Address: Rebhusstrasse 29, CH 8126 Zumikon, Switzerland.

SCIRIHA AQUILINA Irene N M, b. 16 September 1949, Malta. Researcher; Lecturer. m. Joseph, 1 son, 1 daughter. Education: BSc, 1969; MSc, 1971; PhD, 1999; Fellow, Institute of Combinatories and its Applications. Appointments: Graduate Teacher, Physics, Government Secondary School, 1969; Head, Maths Department, De La Salle College, 1974; Lecturer, Maths Department, University of Malta, 1990-; Editor of two scientific journals; Chair of Boards of Examiners for Mathematics, 1996-; Referee, Mathematical Papers in Learned Journals, 1997-; Chair, European Women in Maths, 1999-; Malta representative to the Helsinki Group, European Commission, European Union, 2000-; Vice-Chair, European Mathematical Society, Women Scientific Committee, 2003-; Chair, Gender Issues Committee, University of Malta. Publications: On the construction of graphs of nullity one; Many others. Memberships: EWM; ICA; AMS. Address: Troika, G Montebello Street, Tarxien, PLA 12, Malta.

SCOFIELD Paul, b. 21 January 1922, Hurstpierpoint, Sussex, England. m. Joy Parker, 1943, 1 son, 1 daughter. Education: London Mask Theatre Drama School. Career: Actor, Member Birmingham Repertory Theatre, 1941, 1943-46, Stratford-upon-Avon, Shakespeare Memorial Theatre, 1946-48, Arts Theatre, 1946, Phoenix Theatre, 1947, W H M Tennent, 1949-56, Associate Director, National Theatre, 1970-71; Films include: The Train, 1963; A Man for All Seasons, 1967; King Lear, 1970; Scorpio, 1972; A Delicate Balance, 1972; 1919, Anna Karenina, 1984; When the Whales Came, 1988; Henry V, 1989; Hamlet, 1991; Quiz Show, 1993; The Little Riders, 1995; The Crucible, 1995; TV: The Ambassadors, 1977; The Potting Shed, 1981; If Winter Comes, 1981; Song at Twilight, 1982; Come into the Garden Maud, 1982; A Kind of Alaska, 1984; Summer Lightning, 1985; Only Yesterday, 1986; The Attic, 1988; Utz, 1991; Martin Chuzzlewit, 1994; Theatre appearances include: Hamlet (also in Moscow); A Man for All Seasons, London, 1962-63; King Lear (Eastern Europe, Helsinki, Moscow, New York), 1963, 1964; Timon of Athens, 1965; The Government Inspector, London, 1966; Staircase, 1967; Macbeth, 1968; Uncle Vanya, 1968; The Tempest, 1974; Amadeus, 1979; Othello, 1980. Honours: CBE; Honorary LLD, Glasgow University, Honorary D Lit, Kent, 1973, Sussex University, 1985; Shakespeare Prize, Hamburg, 1972; Danish Film Academy Award; Tony Award, Evening Standard Drama Award for John Gabriel Borkman, 1996. Address: The Gables, Balcombe, Sussex, RH17 6ND, England.

SCORSESE Martin, b. 17 November 1942, Flushing, New York, USA. American Film Director; Writer. m. (1) Laraine Marie Brennan, 1965, 1 daughter. (2) Julia Cameron, divorced, 1 daughter. (3) Isabella Rossellini, 1979, divorced 1983. (4) Barbara DeFina, 1985. Education: New York University. Appointments: Faculty Assistant, Instructor, Film Department, New York University, 1963-66; Instructor, 1968-70; Director, Writer of Films, including: What's a Nice Girl Like You Doing in a Place Like This?, 1963;

Dictionary of International Biography

It's Not Just You, Murray, 1964; Who's That Knocking At My Door?, 1968; The Big Shave, 1968; Director, Play, The Act, 1977-78; Director, Writer of Documentaries; Supervisor Editor, Assistant Director, Woodstock, 1970; Associate Producer, Post-Production Supervisor, Medicine Ball Caravan, 1971, Box Car Bertha, 1972; Director, Films: Mean Streets, 1973; Alice Doesn't Live Here Any More, 1974; Taxi Driver, 1976; New York, New York, 1977; King of Comedy, 1981; Actor, Director, The Last Waltz, 1978; Director, Raging Bull, 1980, After Hours, 1985, The Color of Money, 1986; Director, The Last Temptation of Christ, 1988, Goodfellas, 1989, Cape Fear, 1991, The Age of Innocence, 1993, Clockers, 1994, Casino, 1995; Kundun, 1997; Bringing Out the Dead, 1999; The Muse, 1999; The Gangs of New York, 2002; Executive Producer, The Crew, 1989; Producer, The Grifters, 1989; Co-Producer, Mad Dog and Glory, 1993. Publications: Scorsese on Scorsese, 1989; The Age of Innocence: The Shooting Script (with Jay Cocks), 1996; Casino (with Nicholas Pileggi), 1996; Kundun, 1997; Bringing Out the Dead, 1999; The Muse, 1999; Gangs of New York, 2002. Honours: Edward J Kingsley Foundation Award, 1963, 1964; 1st Prize, Rosenthal Foundation Awards of Society of Cinematologists, 1964; 1st Prize, Screen Producers Guild, 1965, Brown University Film Festival, 1965, Shared Rosellini Prize, 1990; Named Best Director, Cannes Film Festival, 1986; Courage in Filmmaking Award, Los Angeles Film Teachers Association, 1989; Award, American Museum of the Moving Image, 1996; Award for Preservation, International Federation of Film Wards, 2001; Golden Globe for Best Director, 2003. Address: c/o United Artists, 10202 West Washington Blvd, Culver City, CA 90230, USA.

SCOTT David Aubrey (Sir), b. 3 August 1919, London, England. Retired Diplomat. m. Vera Kathleen Ibbitson, 2 sons, 1 daughter. Education: Mining Engineering, Birmingham University, 1938-39 (Degree uncompleted because of war). Appointments: Royal Artillery, 1939-47; Chief Radar Adviser, Military Mission to Egypt, 1945-47; Entered Commonwealth Relations Office, 1948; Assistant Private Secretary to the Secretary of State, 1949; South Africa, 1951-53; Cabinet Office, 1954-56; Singapore, 1956-58; Secretary to Monckton Commission, 1960; Deputy High Commissioner to Rhodesia & Nyasaland, 1961-63; Imperial Defence College, 1964; Deputy High Commissioner to India, 1965-67; British High Commissioner to Uganda and Ambassador, non-resident, to Rwanda, 1967-70; Assistant Under Secretary of State with responsibility for Dependent Territories, 1970-72; British High Commissioner to New Zealand and Governor of Pitcairn Island, 1973-75; HM Ambassador to South Africa, 1976-79; Post Retirement: Director Barclays Bank International, 1979-85; Trustee then Chairman, John Ellerman Foundation, 1979-2001; Mitchell Cotts plc, 1980-86; Delta Metal Overseas Ltd, 1980-83; Chairman, Ellerman Lines plc, 1982-83; Nuclear Resources Ltd, 1984-88; Bradbury Wilkinson plc, 1984-86; Governor, Sadlers Wells Trust, 1984-89; Consultant, Thomas de la Rue plc, 1986-88. Publication: Ambassador in Black and White, 1981; Window into Downing Street, 2003. Honours: CMG, 1966; KCMG, 1974; GCMG, 1979. Memberships: Royal Overseas League, Chairman, 1981-86, Vice-President, 1986-98, President, 1998-2002; President, Uganda Society for Disabled Children, 1984-2000; Vice-President, UK-South Africa Trade Association, 1980-85; Freeman City of London, 1982; Liveryman Shipwrights Company, 1983. Address: 4 Birtley Mews, Birtley Road, Bramley, Surrey, GU5 0LB, England.

SCOTT Nancy L, b. 11 September 1962, Berwyn, Illinois, USA. Healthcare Consultant. Education: BS, Biology, College of Liberal Arts and Sciences, University of Illinois, Urbana, Illinois, 1983; MBA with honours, Finance and Economics, Graduate School of Business, University of Chicago, Illinois, USA, 1991. Appointments: Cytogenetics Technologist, Senior Cytogenetics Technologist, Supervisor, Cytogenetics Laboratory, Northwestern Memorial Hospital, Chicago, Illinois, 1983-86; Cytogenetics Research Technologist, University of Chicago, Illinois, 1986-88; Supervisor of Tissue Culture, Reproductive Genetics Institute, Chicago, Illinois, 1988-90; Healthcare Consultant, Logistics Management Corporation, Annapolis, Maryland, 1992; Implementation Representative, Implementation Specialist, Project Manager, Financial Product Manager, Enterprise Systems Inc, Wheeling, Illinois, 1993-1996; Senior Consultant, Manager, Ernst & Young LLP, Chicago Illinois, 1996-2000, Cap Gemini Ernst & Young US LLC, Chicago Illinois, 2000-2003; Account Executive, Technology, AHA Financial Solutions Inc, Chicago, Illinois, 2003-. Publications: Co-author: What's happening in automated karyotyping, 1985; Chorionic chromosome abnormalities and intrauterine growth retardation, 1990. Honours: Invited Delegate, People to People Ambassador Program to Russia and Estonia, 2000; Listed in Who's Who publications and biographical dictionaries. Memberships: American College of Healthcare Executives; Chicago Health Executive's Forum; Graduate School of Business Club; Health Information Management Systems Society; People to People International; Life Member, Riverside Branch, American Association of University Women; University of Chicago Women's Business Group. Address: 3238 Elm Avenue, Brookfield, IL 60513, USA. E-mail: nlscott@aol.com

SCOTT Paul Henderson, b. 7 November 1920, Edinburgh, Scotland. Essayist; Historian; Critic; Former Diplomat. Education: MA, MLitt, University of Edinburgh. Publications: 1707: The Union of Scotland and England, 1979; Walter Scott and Scotland, 1981; John Galt, 1985; Towards Independence: Essays on Scotland, 1991; Scotland in Europe, 1992; Andrew Fletcher and the Treaty of Union, 1992; Scotland: A Concise Cultural History (editor), 1993; Defoe in Edinburgh, 1994; Scotland: An Unwon Cause, 1997; Still in Bed with an Elephant, 1998; The Boasted Advantages, 1999; A Twentieth Century Life, 2002; Scotland Resurgent, 2003. Contributions to: Newspapers and journals. Honours: Andrew Fletcher Award, 1993; Oliver Award, 2000. Memberships: International PEN, president, Scottish Centre; Saltire Society; Advisory Council for the Arts in Scotland; Association for Scottish Literary Studies; Scottish National Party. Address: 33 Drumsheugh Gardens, Edinburgh EH3 7RN, Scotland.

SCOTT Ridley, b. 30 November 1937, South Shields, England. Film Director. Education: Royal College of Art. Career: Director, numerous award-winning TV commercials, 1970-; Début as feature film director with The Duellists, 1978; Other films include: Alien; Blade Runner; Legend; Someone to Watch Over Me; Black Rain; Thelma and Louise, 1942; Conquest of Paradise, 1992; White Squall, 1995; G I Jane, 1997; Gladiators, 1999; Hannibal, 2000; Black Hawk Down, 2001; The Gathering Storm, 2002; Co-Producer, The Browning Version, 1994. Honour: Honorary D Litt, Sunderland; TV Emmy for Best Made-for-TV Film, 2002. Address: Scott Free 42/44 Beak Street, London, W 1R, 3DA, England.

SCOTT Tony, b. 21 June 1944, Newcastle upon Tyne, England. Film Director. Education: Sunderland College of Art; Leeds College of Art; Royal College of Art Film and TV Department. Career: Assistant Director, Dream Weaver, 1967; The Movement Movement, 1967; Cameraman: The Visit; Untitled; Compromise; Milian; Fat Man; Worked for Derrick Knight & Alan King Associates; Visual Director and Cameraman, pop promotional films, Now Films Ltd; TV cameraman, Seven Sisters, 1968; Co-producer, actor, Don't Walk; Assistant Director, Gulliver; Writer, Director, Editor, Loving Memory, 1969-70; Visual Director, Cameraman, publicity film for Joe Egg; Director, One of the Missing, 1989; Other films include: Revenge; Top Gun; Beverly Hills Cop II; Days of Thunder; The Last Boy Scout; True Romance;

Crimson Tide; The Fan; Enemy of the State; Director, Scott Free Enterprises Ltd; Director, TV and cinema commercials for Ridley Scott and Associates. Honours: Grand Prix, Mar del Plata Festival, Argentina; Prix de la TV Suisse, Nyon; 2nd Prize, Esquire Film Festival, USA; Diploma of Merit, Melbourne. Address: Totem Productions, 8009 Santa Monica Boulevard, Los Angeles, CA 90046, USA.

SCOTT-THOMAS Kristin, b. Redruth, England. Actress. m. François Oliviennes, 1 son, 1 daughter. Education: Central School of Speech and Drama; Ecole National des Arts et Technique de Théâtre, Paris. Career: Resident in France from age of 18; Stage appearances include: La Terre Etrangère; Naive Hirondelles and Yves Peut-Etre; Appearances on TV in France, Germany, Australia, USA, Britain include: L'Ami d'Enfance de Maigret; Blockhaus; Chameleon La Tricheuse; Sentimental Journey; The Tenth Man; Endless Game; Framed; Titmuss Regained; Look at it This Way; Body and Soul; Actress in films: Djamel et Juliette; L'Agent Troubé; La Méridienne; Under the Cherry Moon; A Handful of Dust; Force Majeure; Bille en tête; The Bachelor; Bitter Moon; Four Weddings and a Funeral; Angels and Insects; Richard III; The English Patient; Amour et Confusions; The Horse Whisperer; Random Hearts; Up at the Villa; Gosford Park; Life As a House; Petites Coupures, 2003. Honours include: BAFTA Award; Evening Stand Film Award.

SCUDAMORE Peter, b. 13 June 1958, Hereford, England. Jockey. m. Marilyn, 1980, 2 sons. Career: Former point-to-point and amateur jockey; Estate agency; Professional National Hunt Jockey, 1979-93; 1,677 winners; 7 times champion National Hunt Jockey, record 221 winners, 1988-89; Retired as Jockey, 1993; Director, Chasing Promotions, 1989-; Racing Journalist, Daily Mail, 1993-; Partner with Trainer Nigel Twiston-Davis. Publications: A Share of Success (co-author), 1983; Scudamore on Steeplechasing (co-author); Scu: The Autobiography of a Champion, 1993. Membership; Joint President, Jockeys Association.

SCUPHAM John Peter, b. 24 February 1933, Liverpool, England Writer; Poet. m. Carola Nance Braunholtz, 6 August 1957, 3 sons, 1 daughter. Education: Honours Degree, English, Emmanuel College, Cambridge, 1957. Appointment: Founder-Publisher, The Mandeville Press. Publications: The Snowing Globe, 1972; Prehistories, 1975; The Hinterland, 1977; Summer Places, 1980; Winter Quarters, 1983; Out Late, 1986; The Air Show, 1989; Watching the Perseids, 1990; Selected Poems, 1990; The Ark, 1994; Night Watch, 1999; Collected Poems, 2002. Contributions to: Anthologies and magazines. Membership: Royal Society of Literature, fellow. Address: Old Hall, Norwich Road, South Burlingham, Norfolk NR13 4EY, England.

SEBALD Jama Lynn, b. 16 January 1949, Dayton, Ohio, USA. Academic Administrator. Education: Bachelor of Arts Cum Laude, Ohio University, Athens, Ohio, 1971; Master of Arts, 1973, Educational Specialist, 1975, University of Northern Colorado, Greeley, Colorado. Appointments: Graduate Assistant in Financial Aid, University of Northern Colorado, Greeley, Colorado, 1974-75; Assistant Director of Financial Aid, Medical College of Georgia, Augusta, Georgia, 1975-76; Student Financial Aid Advisor, University of Idaho, Moscow, Idaho, 1976-. Honours: Buckeye Girls State, 1966; Daughters of the American Revolution Medal, 1967; Eta Sigma Phi Honor Sociaty, Ohio University, 1968-71; Ohio University Upperclass Scholarship, 1968-71; Pi Gamma Mu Honor Society, Ohio University, 1970-71; Mortar Board President, Ohio University, 1970-71; Outstanding Young Woman of America Award, 1978; American Association of University Women Moscow Branch Named Gift to the American Association

of University Women Educational Foundation, 1991, 1995; Circle of Excellence Team Award, University of Idaho, 2001; Listed in Who's Who Publications and biographical dictionaries. Memberships: Current Memberships include: American Association of University Women, Member of Moscow Branch, 1977-2004 (holder of numerous executive offices, 1977-2000); National Association of Student Financial Aid Administrators, 1974-; Idaho Association of Student Financial Aid Administrators, 1976-, Secretary/ Treasurer, 1978-79, President, 1989-90; Athena (University of Idaho Professional Women's Organization); Past and Present Member of numerous committees, University of Idaho. Address: Student Financial Aid Services, University of Idaho, Moscow, ID 83844-4291, USA. E-mail: jama@uidaho.edu

SEBASTIAN Phylis Sue (Ingram), b. 24 January 1945, Childersburg, Alabama, USA. Real Estate Broker; Real Estate Appraiser; Fine Art Appraiser. m. (1) Robert E Martin, 1965, divorced 1978, 2 sons, 2 daughters, (2) Thomas Haskell Sebastian III, 1985, 1 step son, 3 step daughters. Education: BS, Accounting and Business Administration, 1988; Real Estate Broker, Career Education Systems, 1988; Real Estate Appraisal Certificate, PREA, CIMA, International College of Real Estate Appraisal, Nashville, Tennessee; Computer Specialist, 1999. Appointments: Hostess, radio show, St Louis, Missouri, 1970s; Numerous feature articles published in St Louis Globe Democrat and Post Dispatch Newspapers, 1970s; Owner, Astrology Consultants, 1970-2003; Licensed Real Estate Broker, Owner, Broker Phylis Sebastian Real Estate, Farmington, Missouri, 1989-2003; US Auto Sales, Park Hills, Missouri, 1993-97; Owner, Business & Legal Services, Park Hills, 1993-2003; Partner La Femme Fine Antique Auction Service, Ironton, Missouri, Arcadia Valley Auction Co Inc, 1997-2003; Ordained minister, Progressive Universal Life Church, 2002; Numerous appearances on TV, St Louis. Publications: 5 books including: Marriages in Madison County Missouri for 1848-1868, 1998; 1910 Census for Madison County Missouri, 1998; Published poet; Many articles in various newspapers. Memberships: 1st Treasurer, Co-founder, Astrological Association of St Louis, 1976-77; Co-founder, Missouri Mental Health Consumer Network, Mineral Area Chapter, 1989-93; Member, National Gardening Club; Library of Congress; Smithsonian; National Historic Society; Founder, Genealogy Society of Madison County Missouri. Address: Arcadia Valley Auction Co Inc & Real Estate, 315 West Russell Street, Ironton, Missouri 63650-1316, USA. E-mail: phylis@phylissebastian.com

SEDAGHATIAN Mohamad Reza, b. 11 February 1938, Shiraz, Iran. Consultant Neonatologist. m. Nezhat Khalili, 3 sons, 1 daughter. Education: MD, Shiraz medical School, Iran, 1964; American Board of Pediatrics, USA, 1972; American Sub-Board of Neonatal and Perinatal Medicine, 1991, 1998. Appointments: Professor of Paediatrics, Shiraz medical School, Shiraz, Iran, 1973-84; Senior Consultant, Head, Neonatal Department, 1985-, Acting Medical Director, 2003, Mafraq Hospital, Abu Dhabi, United Arab Emirates. Publications: More than 40 articles in different medical journals. Honour: Physician Recognition Award, American Medical Association, 1998-2000. Membership: President, Emirates Perinatal Society; Emirate Medical Association; American Academy of Pediatrics; American Academy of Perinatal Medicine. Address: PO Box 2851, Abu Dhabi, United Arab Emirates. E-mail: reza@sedaghatian.net

SEDAKA Neil, b. 13 March 1939. Singer; Songwriter. m. Leba Margaret Strassberg, 11 September 1962, 1 son, 1 daughter. Musical Education: Graduate, Juilliard School of Music. Career: Solo performer, worldwide, 1959-; Television appearances include: NBC-TV Special, 1976. Compositions include: Breaking Up Is Hard To Do; Stupid Cupid; Calendar Girl; Oh! Carol; Stairway

To Heaven; Happy Birthday Sweet Sixteen; Laughter In The Rain; Bad Blood; Love Will Keep Us Together; Solitaire; The Hungry Years; Lonely Night (Angel Face). Recordings: Albums include: In The Pocket; Sedaka's Back; The Hungry Years; Steppin' Out; A Song; All You Need Is The Music; Come See About Me; Greatest Hits, 1988; Oh! Carol And Other Hits, 1990; Timeless, 1992; Calendar Girl, 1993; Tuneweaver, 1995; The Immaculate, 1997; Tales Of Love, 1999. Honours: Songwriters' Hall Of Fame, 1980; Platinum album, Timeless, 1992; Numerous Gold records; Various industry awards. Memberships: AGVA; AFofM; AFTRA. Address: c/o Neil Sedaka Music, 201 East 66th Street, Suite 3N, New York, NY 10021, USA.

SEDKY Sherif Salah, b. 16 December 1969, Giza, Egypt. Professor. m. Marwa Sorour, 2 sons, 1 daughter. Education: BSc (Hons), Electronics and Communications, 1992; Masters degree, Engineering Physics, 1995; Masters Degree, Electrical Engineering, 1996; PhD, Engineering, 1998. Appointments: Assistant Professor, Cairo University, 1999-; Visiting Professor, Catholic University, Leuven, Belgium, 2000; Visiting Professor, University of California, Berkeley, USA, 2002; Visiting Professor, American University in Cairo, 2002-2003. Publications: Author of a chapter in Handbook of Computer Vision Applications; Author and co-author of more than 35 papers published in international conferences and journals; 3 patents for design, fabrication and monolithic integration of micro electro mechanical systems. Honours: Prestigious State Prize in Engineering Science, 2003; Listed in Who's Who publications and biographical dictionaries. Membership: Institute of Electrical and Electronics Engineers. Address: Physics Department, The American University in Cairo, 113 Kasr El Eini Street, PO Box 2511, Cairo 11511, Egypt. E-mail: sedky@aucegypt.edu

SEE Carolyn, (Monica Highland), b. 13 January 1934, Pasadena, California, USA. Writer. m. (1) Richard See, 18 February 1954, (2) Tom Sturak, 30 April 1960, 2 daughters. Education: PhD, University of California at Los Angeles, 1953. Appointment: Professor of English, University of California at Los Angeles. Publications: The Rest is Done with Mirrors, 1970; Blue Money, 1974; Mothers, Daughters, 1977; Rhine Maidens, 1980; Golden Days, 1985; When Knaves Meet, 1988; The Mirrored Hall in the Hollywood Dance Hall, 1991; Dreaming: Hard Luck and Good Times in America, 1995; The Handyman, 1999. As Monica Highland: Lotus Land, 1983; 1-10 Shanghai Road, 1985; Greetings From Southern California, 1987; Precious Cargo, 1990; Two Schools of Thought (with John Espey), 1991. Contributions to: Newspapers and magazines. Honours: Samuel Goldwyn Award, 1963; Sidney Hillman Award, 1969; National Endowment for the Arts Grant, 1974; Bread and Roses Award, National Womens Political Caucus, 1988; Vesta Award, 1989; Guggenheim Fellowship in Fiction, 1989; Lila Wallace Grant, 1993; Lifetime Achievement Award, PEN Center USA West, 1998. Membership: PEN Centre USA West, president, 1993-94. Address: 17339 Tramonto #303, Pacific Palisades, CA 90272, USA.

SEGAL Lore (Groszmann), b. 8 March 1928, Vienna, Austria. Writer. m. David I Segal, 3 November 1960, deceased, 1 son, 1 daughter. Education: BA, English, Bedford College, University of London, England, 1948. Appointments: Professor, Writing Division, School of Arts, Columbia University, Princeton University, Sarah Lawrence College, Bennington College; Professor of English, University of Illinois, Ohio State University. Publications: Novels: Other People's Houses, 1964; Lucinella, 1976; Her First American, 1985. Children's Books: Tell Me a Mitzi, 1977; The Story of Mrs Brubeck and How She Looked for Trouble and Where She Found Him, 1981; The Story of Mrs Lovewright and Purrless Her Cat, 1985. Translations: Gallows Songs (with W

D Snodgrass), 1968; The Juniper Tree and Other Tales from Grimm, 1973; The Book of Adam to Moses; The Story of King Soul and King David; Morris the Artist, 2003; Why Mole Shouted and Other Stories, 2004. Contributions to: Periodicals. Honours: Guggenheim Fellowship, 1965-66; National Endowment for the Arts Grant, 1982; National Endowment for the Humanities Grant, 1983; Academy of Arts and Letters Award, 1986; Grant, Ohio Arts Council, 1996. Address: 280 Riverside Drive, New York, NY 10025, USA.

SEGEL Joseph, b. 23 July 1930, Johannesburg, South Africa. Medical Practitioner. m. Adele Harrriet, 1 son, 2 daughters. Education: MBBCH, 1954; MFGP; American Board of Family Practice, 1979. Appointments: Internship, Medicine and Surgery, Johannesburg, South Africa, 1954-55; Senior Internship, Johannesburg Fever Hospital, Johannesburg Children's Hospital, 1955-56; Private Practice, Johannesburg, South Africa, 1956-77; Family Practice, Houston, Texas, USA, 1977-. Honours: Best Doctors in America; Best Doctors, Houston, Texas. Memberships: Harris County Medical Association; Texas Medical Association. Address: 1500 Dairy-Ashford #198, Houston, TX 77077, USA.

SEHERR-THOSS Hans Christoph, b. 13 October 1918, Potsdam, Nr Berlin. Mechanical Engineer; Historian. m. Therese Kunath. Appointments: Design Work, ZF Friedrichshafen, 1947-49; Librarian, German Automobile Club, 1954-83; Vice President, FIA Historical Commission, 1983-98; Consulting Engineer; Registrar; Author, Independence, 1984-. Publications: Die Entwicklung der Zahnradtechnik, 1965; Die deutsche Automobilindustrie, 1974, 1979; Automobile World Records, 1988; Oldtimer, 1965; 75 Years ADAC, 1978; FIA, Dictionary of Famous Personalities in the Automobile World, 2000, 2002; Co-author: Sport – Ueberblick, 1951; Forum der Technik, 1966; 50 Years of BMW, 1966, 1972; 160 Biographies in NDB; Raederwerk, 1989; Yearbook Presse u Sport, 1958; H Buessing, 1986; MAN Nutzfahrzeugbau, 1991; Universal Joints and Driveshafts, 1992; Editor: Zwei Maenner – ein Stern, 1984. Memberships: German Units: ADAC; German Archivists Association (VdW); FIA Historical Commission, 1983-, Chairman Personalities, 1988-. Address: Habichtstreet 39, Unterhaching Nr Munich, D-82008, Germany.

SEIBERT Peter, b. 13 April 1927, Munich, (Bavaria), Germany. University Professor. Education: Doctorate of the Faculty of Science (doctor rerum naturalium), University of Munich, 1950. Appointments include: Research Scientist, Research Institute for Advanced Studies, Baltimore, USA, 1958-63; Professor, National Polytechnic Institute, Mexico, 1966-71; Professor, University Simón Bolívar, Caracas, Venezuela, 1975-78; Professor, Autonomous Metropolitan University, México, 1987-. Publications include: On a problem of Mazurkiewicz, 1959; Co-author, Prolongations and stability in dynamic systems, 1964; Co-author, On the reduction to a subspace of stability properties, 1998; On bifurcations arising from unstable equilibria, 1998; Co-author, Types of change of Stability and corresponding types of bifurcations, 1999; Co-author, On the flow outside an unstable equilibrium point or invariant set, 2003. Honours: Appointed National Researcher, Level III (top) "for Outstanding Leadership in the Academic Community", 1999; Renewal of Doctoral Degree by the University of Munich "in Appreciation of Merit in the Research of Stability", 2000. Memberships: Mexican Academy of Sciences; New York Academy of Sciences; American Mathematical Society; Mexican Mathematical Society; International Federation of Non-linear Analysts. Address: Departamento de Matemáticas, Universidad Autónoma Metropolitana - Iztapalapa, San Rafael Atlixco 186, col. Vicentina, 09340, Mexico, D F, Mexico. E-mail: pskm@xanum.uam.mx

Dictionary of International Biography

SEIDOV Dan, b. 6 December 1948, Baku, USSR. Oceanographer. m. Maria Karpova Seidov. Education: Diploma in Physics, Moscow State University, 1972; PhD in Oceanology, 1975, DSc in Oceanography, 1982; Shirshov's Institute of Oceanology, Moscow; Professor of Oceanography, 1986. Appointments: Doctoral student, Researcher, Senior Researcher, Head of Ocean Climate Modelling Department, Shirshov's Institute of Oceanology, USSR Academy of Sciences, 1972-91; Guest Professor, Researcher, Kiel University, Germany, 1991-97; Senior Researcher, Earth System Science Center, Pennsylvania State University, USA, 1997-; Pioneer, application of methods of ocean circulation modelling to palaeocirculation problems. Publications: More than 150 scientific papers on modelling of geophysical systems; Author and co-author, 3 books on oceanography and palaeo-oceanography: Modelling of synoptic and climatic variability of oceans, 1985; Pioneer paper on palaeo-oceanographic modelling in Mesozoic and Cenozoic Oceans, 1986; Synergetics of ocean processes, 1989. Honours: Doctorate and Professorship in Oceanography, Moscow, 1982. Memberships: European Geophysical Society, 1993-97; American Geophysical Union, 1995-. Address: Pennsylvania State University, 2217 Earth-Engineering Science Bldg, University Park, PA 16802-6813, USA. E-mail: dseidov@psu.edu

SEINFELD Jerry, b. 29 April 1955, Brooklyn, USA. Comedian. Education: Queens College, New York. Career: Former Salesman; Stand-up Comedian, 1976-; Joke-writer, Benson (TV series), 1980; Actor, Seinfeld (TV series), 1989-97, also co-writer, producer; The Ratings Game, film, 1984; The Seinfeld Chronicles, 1990; I'm Telling You for the Last Time, 1999. Publication: Sein Language, 1993. Honours: 2 American Comedy Awards; Emmy Award for Outstanding Comedy Series (Seinfeld), 1993. Address: c/o Lori Jonas Public Relations, 417 South Beverly Drive, Suite 201, Beverly Hills, CA 90212, USA.

SEITAMAA-ORAVALA Pirkko Marjatta, b. 22 May 1941, Kemi, Finland. Professor emerita. m. Martti Oravala, deceased 1998. Education: Art Teacher, University of Industrial Art, Helsinki, Finland, 1965; BA, Education, University of Oulu, Finland; MA, Art Education, 1984, Licentiate of Art Education, 1990, University of Industrial Art, Helsinki. Appointments: Teacher Trainer, Normal Lyceum, Oulu, 1968-79; Lecturer in Art Education, University of Oulu, 1979-90; From Acting Professor, Dean, to Associate Professor, 1990-98, Professor of Art Education, 1998-2002, Professor Emerita, 2002-, University of Lapland. Publications: in Finnish, Come to Look At! 1984; Pictures Behind the Pictures, 1990; Articles in professional journals include: If snow is white, in University of Lapland, there lives art too; Romantic and Classical Paradigms in Art Education. Honours: White Rose Award, First Class, President of Finland, 2000; Listed in Who's Who publications and biographical dictionaries. Memberships: Team Member, National Board of Education, 1981-85; Helsinki Ministry of Education, 1991-93; Team Member, International Society of Education through Art. Address: Kirkkokatu 53 A1, 90100 Oulu, Finland. E-mail: pirkko.seitamaa-oravala@mail.suomi.net

SEKE Josip, b. 9 June 1949, Sombor, Yugoslavia. Professor. Education: PhD, Physics, Vienna Technical University, 1979; Postdoctoral Fellow, SUNY, Albany, 1981. Appointments: Visiting Member, Courant Institute, New York University, 1981-82; Research Physicist, Lecturer, Vienna Technical University, 1983-86, Docent, 1986-93; Professor, Theoretical Physics, Vienna Technical University, 1993-; Developed self-consistent projection-operator method; Formulated conceptually improved renormalisation method for the U-matrix in QED where the conventional on-shell renormalisation is inapplicable. Publications:

Contributor of over 140 articles to professional journals. Address: Institute of Theoretical Physics, Technical University, Wiedner Hauptstr 8-10/136, A-1040 Vienna, Austria.

SELEŠ Monica, b. 2 December 1973, Novi Sad, Yugoslavia (US Citizen, 1994). Tennis Player. Career: Winner of: Sport Goofy Singles, 1984; Singles and Doubles, 1985; French Open, 1990, 1991, 1992; Virginia Slims Championships, 1990, 1991, 1992; Australian Open, 1991, 1992, 1993, 1996; US Open, 1991, 1992; Canadian Open, 1995, 1996, 1997; Los Angeles Open, 1997; Tokyo Open, 1997; Semi-finalist at: French Open, 1989; Quarter-finalist at: Wimbledon, 1990; Member, winning US Federal Cup team, 1996, 1999, 2000; 59 WTA Tour titles, 9 Grand Slam titles and over $14 million in prize money, -2002. Publication: Monica: From Fear to Victory, 1996. Honours: Named youngest No 1 ranked player in tennis history for women and men, at 17 years, 3 months and 9 days; Ted Tinling Diamond Award, 1990; Associated Press Athlete of the Year 1990-91; Tennis Magazine Comeback Player of the Year, 1995; Flo Hyman Award, 2000. Address: IMG, 1 Erieview Plaza, Cleveland, OH 44114, USA.

SELEZOV Igor, b. 30 June 1930, Nevel, Pskov, Russia. Mechanics Educator; Researcher. m. Ludmila Selezova. Education: Engineer, Kharkov Aviation Institute, 1948-54; Candidate of Science, Institute of Mechanics, Ukrainian Academy of Sciences, 1957-60; DSc, 1971, Professor, 1979, Kiev University. Appointments: Engineer, Antonov Aviation Bureau, Kiev, 1954-57; Senior Research Associate, Institute of Mechanics, 1961-63, Institute of Cybernetics, 1963-72, Ukrainian Academy of Sciences; Head, Department of Wave Processes, Institute of Hydromechanics, National Academy of Science, Kiev, 1972-. Publications include: Waves in Magnetohydroelastic Media, 1975; Modelling of Wave and Diffraction Processes in Continuous Media, 1989; Nonstationary and Nonlinear Waves in Electrically Conducting Media, 1991. Honours: Grant, American Physical Society, 1993; Title, Soros Professor, International Soros Science Education Program, New York, 1994-96; Timoshenko Prize, National Academy of Science, Ukraine, 2002, Merited Science and Engineering Worker of Ukraine. Memberships: Gesellschaft fur Angewandte Mathematik und Mechanik; EUROMECH; International Society of Biorheology; International Society of Cardiovascular Medicine and Science; Ukrainian Physical Society; National Committee on Theoretical and Applied Mechanics of Ukraine. Address: 11 Dobrokhotov St Apt 37, 03142 Kiev, Ukraine.

SELF Will, b. 26 September 1961. Author; Cartoonist. m. (1) Katherine Sylvia Anthony Chancellor, 1989, divorced 1996, 1 son, 1 daughter, (2) Deborah Jane Orr, 1997, 1 son. Education: Christ's College; Exeter College, Oxford. Appointments: Cartoon illustrator, New Statesman, City Limits; Columnist: The Observer, 1995-97; The Times, 1997-; Independent on Sunday, 2000-. Publications: Collected cartoons, 1985; Short stories: Quantity Theory of Insanity, 1991; Grey Area, 1994; Tough Tough Toys and Tough Tough Boys, 1998; Novellas: Cock and Bull, 1992; The Sweet Smell of Psychosis, 1996; Novels: My Idea of Fun, 1993; Great Apes, 1997; How the Dead Live, 2000; Perfidious Man, 2000; Feeding Frenzy, 2001; Dorian, 2002; Junk Mail (selected journalism), 1995; Sore Sites, collected journalism, 2000. Address: c/o David Godwin, 14A Goodwins Court, London, WC2, England.

SELIN Shannon, b. 30 May 1963, Biggar, Saskatchewan, Canada. Policy Analyst. m. George Feaver, 1 son, 2 daughters. Education: BA, 1985; MA, 1986. Appointments: Research Assistant, Canadian Centre for Arms Control and Disarmament, 1986-87; Technical Writer, Newbridge Networks Corporation, 1988-89;

Public Liaison Officer, Arms Control and Disarmament Division, Department of Foreign Affairs and International Trade, Canada, 1989-92; Research Associate, Institute of International Relations, University of British Columbia, 1992-98; Policy Analyst, Provincial Blood Co-ordinating Office, British Columbia Ministry of Health Services, 1998-. Publications: Beyond Supply Side Controls and Verification? The Asia Pacific Case, 1995; Stability, Security and Economics in Asia Pacific, 1996; East Asian Arms Build-ups and Regional Security, 1997. Honours: Social Sciences and Humanities Research Council of Canada Special MA Scholarships, 1985; Copland Prize in Social Sciences, 1985. Memberships: Canadian Consortium on Asia Pacific Security; Asia Pacific Foundation of Canada Research Network; Society for Technical Communications. Address: 4776 7th Avenue West, Vancouver, BC, V6T 1C6 Canada.

SELKIN Michael Vasilievich, b. 30 August 1947, Vetka, Belarus. Mathematician. m. Ludmila Kalugina, 1 son. Education: Diploma of Teacher of Mathematics, 1969; Candidate of Science, Physics and Mathematics, 1977; Assistant Professor, 1981; Professor, 1991; Doctor of Science, Physics and Mathematics, 1998. Appointment: Rector, Fransisk Scorina Gomel State University, Gomel, Belarus. Publications: 80 publications; 3 scientific monographs. Honours: Honoured Worker of Education of the Republic of Belarus; Certificate of Honour of the National Assembly of the Republic of Belarus. Address: ul Artillerijskaya d 4, Kv 38, 246000 Gomel, Belarus. E-mail: selkin@gsu.unibel.by

SELLARS Doris Carrison, b. 11 February 1916, Adair, Illinois, USA. Illinois Farm Owner; Military Wife; Teacher; Psychologist. m. Charles W Sellars, deceased, 1 son, 1 daughter. Education: B Ed, Western Illinois University, 1938; Classes, University of Colorado (2 summer sessions), 1939; MS, University of Illinois, 1941; Teaching Certificate (Illinois), Michigan Civil Service. Appointments: Third Grade Teacher, Macomb, Illinois Public School; Assistant to Dr Heinz Werner, Wayne County Training School, Northville, Michigan; Psychologist, State Hospital, Kalamazoo, Michigan; Military Wife, 18 years; Manager of over 500 acres of Illinois farmland and 2 rental houses; Founder, Director, Nursery School, Guantanamo Bay, Cuba. Publications: Relation and Accuracy of Number Perception to Density of Simultaneous Visual Sense Impressions (MS Thesis), 1941; Co-author of articles in scientific journals and papers presented at conferences: Measurement and Development of the Finger Schema in Mentally Retarded Children: Relation of Arithmetic Achievement to Performance on the Finger Schema Test, 1942; Methods of Teaching Arithmetic to Mentally Deficient Children, 1943; Animistic Thinking in Brain-Injured Children, 1944; Author: John Carrison Jr: The History of Illinois Centennial Farms, 1986; Articles on the following families: Carrison, Allen, Miner, Holmes, Andrus, Humphrey and Manly; Article on the town of Shoo Fly, Fulton County Illinois Heritage, 1988; John Carrison Jr, McDonough County History, 1992. Honours: Presented to Admiral Mountbatton and Emperor Hailie Selassie in Malta where husband was in charge of the American unit associated with the British Halfar Station, 1955; Parties and gifts when locating to another assignment before and during military service; Plaque "in recognition of restoration and preservation efforts" of the John Carrison Barn c. 1885, McDonough County Historic Preservation Society, 2003; Listed in Who's Who publication and biographical dictionaries. Memberships: Undergraduate: French Club, English Club, Dramatic Club, Sigma Kappa Sorority; McDonough County Illinois Farm Bureau; Several genealogical societies; 3 military groups in Tucson; Presbyterian Church; The American Air Museum in Britain; Past Member, American Psychological Association; Michigan Psychological Society; Life Member, Western Museum, Macomb, Illinois. Address: 46 S, Bonanza Avenue, Tucson, AZ 85748, USA.

SELLECK Tom, b. 29 January 1945, Detroit, Michigan, USA, Actor. Education: University of Southern California. m. (1) Jackie Ray, 1 step son, (2) Julie Mack, 1 daughter. Career: Actor, films include: Myra Beckinridge; Midway; Coma; Seven Minutes; High Road to China; Runaway; Lassiter; Three Men and a Baby; Her Alibi, 1988; Quigley Down Under; An Innocent Man, 1989; Three Men and a Lady, 1991; Folks, 1991; Mr Baseball, 1991; Christopher Columbus: The Discovery, 1992; Folks!, 1992; Mr Baseball, In and Out; The Love Letter, 1999; Running Mates, 2000; TV includes: Returning Home; Bracken's World; The Young and the Restless; The Rockford Files; The Sacketts; Role of Thomas Magnum in Magnum PI; Divorce Wars; Countdown at the Super Bowl; Gypsy Warriors; Boston and Kilbride; The Concrete Cowboys; Murder She Wrote; The Silver Fox; The Closer (series), 1998; Last Stand at Saber River; Friends, 1996, 2000; Ruby Jean and Joe; Broken Trust, 1995; Washington Slept Here, 2000; Louis l'Amour's Crossroads Trail, 2000. Address: c/o Esme Chandlee, 2967 Hollyridge Drive, Los Angeles, CA 90068, USA.

SEN Amartya Kumar, b. 3 November 1933, Santiniketan, India. Professor of Economics and Philosophy; Writer. m. (1) Nabaneeta Dev, 1960, divorced 1974, 2 daughters, (2) Eva Colorni, 1977, deceased 1985, 1 son, 1 daughter, (3) Emma Rothschild, 1991. Education: BA, Presidency College, Calcutta, 1953; BA, 1955, MA, PhD, 1959, Trinity College, Cambridge. Appointments: Professor of Economics, Jadavpur University, Calcutta, 1956-58; Fellow, Trinity College, Cambridge, 1957-63, All Souls College, Oxford, 1980-88; Professor of Economics, Delhi University, 1963-71, London School of Economics and Political Science, 1971-77; Professor of Economics, 1977-80, Drummond Professor of Political Economy, 1980-88, University of Oxford; Andrew D White Professor at Large, Cornell University, 1978-85; Lamont University Professor and Professor of Economics and Philosophy, Harvard University, 1988-98; Master Trinity College, Cambridge, 1998-. Publications: Choice of Techniques, 1960; Collective Choice and Welfare, 1970; Guidelines for Project Evaluation (with P Dasgupta and Stephen Marglin), 1972; On Economic Inequality, 1973; Employment, Technology and Development, 1975; Poverty and Famines: An Essay on Entitlement and Deprivation, 1981; Choice, Welfare and Measurement, 1982; Resources, Values and Development, 1984; Commodities and Capabilities, 1985; On Ethics and Economics, 1987; The Standard of Living (with others), 1987; Hunger and Public Action (with Jean Dreze), 1989; Jibanayatra o arthaniti, 1990; The Political Economy of Hunger (editor with Jean Dreze), 3 volumes, 1990-91; Money and Value: On the Ethics and Economics of Finance/Denaro e valore: Etica ed economia della finanza, 1991; Inequality Reexamined, 1992; The Quality of Life (editor with Martha Nussbaum), 1993; Economic Development and Social Opportunity (with Jean Dreze), 1995; Development as Freedom, 1999. Contributions to: Professional journals. Honours: Mahalanobis Prize, 1976; Honorary Doctor of Literature, University of Saskatchewan, 1979; Nobel Prize in Economic Science, 1998; Honorary CH, 2000; Grand Cross, Order of Scientific Merit, Brazil, 2000. Memberships: American Academy of Arts and Sciences; American Economic Association, president, 1994-; British Academy, fellow; Development Studies Association; Econometric Society, fellow; Indian Economic Association; International Economic Association, president, 1986-88, honorary president, 1988-; Royal Economic Society. Address: c/o Trinity College, Cambridge CB2 1TQ, England.

SEN Luyi, b. 19 July 1958, Shanghai, China. Physician; Scientist. Education: Electrical Engineer, Shanghai Science and Technology University, 1975-77; BS, MD, Shanghai No 2 Medical University, China, 1982. Appointments: Professor of Medicine and Surgery, University of California, Los Angeles, Medical Center, David

Dictionary of International Biography

Geffen School of Medicine at University of California, Los Angeles, USA. Publications: 68 research papers in scientific medical journals include most recently as co-author: Localized immunosuppression in the cardiac allograft induced by a new liposome-mediated IL-10 gene therapy, 2002; Cause of artioventricular conduction block in patients after heart transplantation, 2003; Dual upregulation of surface Tas and mitichondia Bax promotes alloreactive T cell apoptosisi in interleukine10 gene targeting of cardiac allografts, 2003; Balancing expression of competing mitochondrial apoptosis regulatory proteins correlates with the long-term survival of cardiac allografts, 2003; Combinatorial cytokine gene therapy induces localized synergistic immunosuppression and cardiac allograft tolerance, 2003; 2 US Patents, 2 US Patents pending. Honours: National Scientific Award, China, 1984, 1987; American Heart Association Fellowship, University of California, Los Angeles, 1988; First Independent Research Award, NIH, 1996. Memberships: Fellow, Council of Clinical Cardiology, 1989-, Fellow, Council of Basic Science, 1989, American Heart Association; Biophysical Society, 1990-; New York Academy of Science, 1991-; International Society for Heart and Lung Transplantation, 1998-; Adviser, Federal Science Advisory Board, 1999-; Fellow, American College of Cardiology, 2002-. Address: UCLA Medical Center, David Geffen School of Medicine at UCLA, 47-123 CHS, 10833 Le Conte Avenue, Los Angeles, CA 90095-1679, USA. E-mail: lsen@mednet.ucla.edu

SEN Ranjit K, b. 19 January 1946, Bihar, India. Engineer. m. Sarmistha Sen, 1 daughter. Education: BSME, Mechanical Engineering, Bengal Engineering College, University of Calcutta, 1969. Appointments: Senior Engineer in nuclear power plant and other process plant design; Group Supervisor for design group; President, Chief Executive Officer, International Chemical Products Inc, Huntsville, Alabama, USA; Developed unique "Picklex®Process" for metal surface preparation and pre-treatment with zero waste disposal. Publications: Assisted USEPA publication on: "Picklex® Process" for metal pre-treatment before finishing (non-polluting metal surface preparation). Honour: National Award for most valuable pollution prevention award, National Pollution Prevention Round Table, 2001. Memberships: ASME; NACE. Address: 1209 Meadow Park Drive, Huntsville, AL 35803, USA. E-mail: rsen@icpi.net Website: www.picklex.com

SEN Tapas Kumar, b. 1 March 1933, Calcutta, India. Teacher; Manager. m. Sondra Kotzin Sen, 1 son, 1 daughter. Education; MSc, Applied Psychology, Calcutta University, 1954; PhD, Psychology, Johns Hopkins University, 1963. Appointments: Member, Technical Staff, Bell Laboratories, 1963-72; Human Resources Director, AT&T, 1973-96; Executive Director, Workforce Development, Rutgers University, New Brunswick, New Jersey, USA, 1999-; Executive Committee Member, Governor's State Employment and Training Commission, New Jersey, 2000-; Chair, Governance Committee, State Employment and Training Commission, 2004-. Publications: 15 papers in professional publications include: Building the Workplace of the Future in A Blueprint for Managing Change, A Conference Board Report; Advisory Editor, Work in America Encyclopedia, 2003. Honours: The Mayflower Group Leadership Award, 1985; Toastmasters International, Area Governor of the Year, public speaking, 1970. Memberships: Fellow, Human Factors and Ergonomics Society; American Psychological Association; The Dearborn Group. Address: 29 Arden Road, Mountain Lakes, NJ 07046, USA. Website: tsitsi@att.net

SENGENDO Kawesa Ahmad, b. 24 September 1958, Mbarara, Uganda. Educator. m. Fatuma and Zulaikh, 3 sons, 3 daughters. Education: BSc, Honours, 1982, Postgraduate Diploma in Education, First Class, 1983, Makerere University; MScEd, 1985, PhD, Education, 1987, University of Kansas, USA. Appointments: Teaching Assistant, Makerere University; Research Assistant, 1985-86, Graduate Teaching Assistant, 1986-87, University of Kansas; Lecturer, School of Education, Makerere University, 1987; Part-time Lecturer, University Secretary, Islamic University, Uganda, 1988-2000; Director, 2001-03, Kampala Campus, Vice Rector, 2003-04, Rector, 2004-, Islamic University in Uganda. Publications: Articles: The Amic University in Uganda; Educational Challenges in the New South Africa; Challenges of Inter-Faculty Cooperation and Coordination. Honour: AFGRAD Fellow, 1984-87. Memberships: Uganda National Council for Science and Technology; Board of Governors Gombe Secondary School and Kawempe Muslim Secondary School; Secretary Uganda Muslims' Scholarship Board; Uganda Muslims' Welfare Association; Patron, Uganda Muslims' Students' Association. Address: Islamic University in Uganda, PO Box 2555, Mbale, Uganda. E-mail: aksengendo@yahoo.com

SENNAROGLU Alphan, b. 10 November 1966, Nicosia, Cyprus. Physicist, Associate Professor. m. Figen Ecer Sennaroglu, 1 daughter. Education: BS, 1988, MS, 1990, PhD, 1994, Electrical Engineering, Cornell University, Ithaca, New York. Appointments: Assistant Professor, 1994-99; Associate Professor, 1999-, Koc University, Istanbul, Turkey. Publications: Over 50 journal and conference articles in the field of ultrashort lasers, nonlinear optics and spectroscopy. Honours: Several, including Werner Von Siemens Excellence Award, 2001; Distinguished Young Scientist Award, 2001, Turkish Academy of Science. Memberships: IEEE; OSA. Address: Department of Physics, Koc University, Rumelifeneri Yolu, Sariyer 80910 Istanbul, Turkey. E-mail: asennar@ku.edu.tr

SEO Ju Tae, b. 4 September 1961, Busan, Korea. Professor; Urologist. m. Hye Kyung Ahn, 2 daughters. Education: MD, Yonsei University, Seoul, Korea, 1986; Diplomate, Korean Board of Urology, PhD, Kyung Hee University, Seoul, Korea, 2003. Appointments: Director of Urology, Samsung Cheil Hospital, 1994-; Associate Professor, Sungkyungkwan University School of Medicine, 1997-. Publications: Male Aging and Androgen (co-author); Textbook of Andrology (co-author); Textbook of Voiding Dysfunction and Female Urology. Memberships: Korean Society of Continence, Board, Secretary General; Korean Society of Andrology, Board, Editor; International Urogynecology; American Society of Andrology. Address: Daerim Apt 1-503; Jamwon-dong, Seocho-gu, Seoul, Korea.

SEPPET Enn, b. 26 February 1950, Võõpste, Estonia. Professor of Pathophysiology. m. Elviira, 2 daughters. Education: MD, 1974, PhD, Physiology, 1991, University of Tartu; Cand Sci, Biochemistry, USSR National Centre for Cardiology, Moscow, 1980. Appointments: Junior, Senior Research Fellow, Laboratory of Muscle Research, University of Tartu, 1974-81; Head, Laboratory of Hormonal Regulation, Faculty of Medicine, 1981-92; Professor and Chairman, Department of Pathophysiology, Faculty of Medicine, University of Tartu, 1992-. Publications: Numerous articles in professional journals. Memberships: International Society for Heart Research; American Physiological Society; Federation of European Biochemical Societies; Finnish Physiological Society; Scandinavian Laboratory Animal Science Societies; Rotary International. Address: 19 Ravila Street, 50411 Tartu, Estonia. E-mail: enn@ut.ee

SERAFINI Eugenia, b. Tolfa, Rome, Italy. Professor of Drawing; Poet-Performer; Visual Poet. m. Nicolo G Brancato, 2 daughters. Education: Graduate, Classical Literatures; Specialised in Art History and Archaeology; Studied Graphic, Serigraphic Engraving and Painting. Career: Art Director, Artistic Editions, Grafic Arts Brancato, 1986-92; Journalist for Folium, 1994-, Corriere dell'Arte, 1997-; Poet-Performer; Art Director, Artecom Editions Rome, 2002; Professor of Drawing, University of Calabria; Professor, Academy of Illustration and Visual Illusion; Installationist; Visual Poet; Personal shows, installations and performances include: Planet Paper in the Third Millennium, National Museum of Arts and Popular Traditions, Rome Italy, 2001; Sky wave: Art wave-night wave, Trade Fair of Rimini, Italy, 2001; Performance-installation "Dreams Fisher", Biblioteca Judeteana, Craiova, Romania, 2002; Art-science biotechnologies, Rome, Ancona, Bari, Italy, 2002; Lessons and performances at the Universities of Bucharest, Craiova and Iasi, Romania, 2003; Histoire Gothique, Academy of Romany, Rome, Siracusa, Milan, Cosenza, Italy, 2003; Works in public collections including: International Museum of Marian Contemporary Art, Alessano, Italy; Museum of Contemporary Art, Blaj, Romania; University of Fine Arts, Luxor, Egypt; G Marconi School, New York, USA; Collection of the Popular Bank of Milan, Rome; Frank V De Bellis Collection, San Francisco State University, USA. Publications include: Epifania e parusia. The Installations of Eugenia Serafini: 12 projects, 1995; Les Oiseaux, 1996; I racconti del Laurentino 38, 1998; Silver Bird, 2000; Carillons of Wind, 2003; Monograph, Eugenia Serafini, production 1993-2003, 2003. Honours: Invitation for XXIV Prize Sulmona, Italy; XVI Prize, Italy for Visual Arts, Certaldo, Italy, 2001; Invitation for 54th Prize Michetti, Francavilla al Mare, Italy, 2003. Memberships: Academician, ARTECOM, Academy in Europe of High Studies, Rome Italy; Founder, Free Academy of Dreams and Clouds. Address: Via dei Campani 38, 00185 Rome, Italy. E-mail: mariposa.eu@tiscali.it

SEREBRIER José, b. 3 December 1938, Montevideo, Uruguay. Musician; Conductor. m. Carole Farley, 29 March 1969, 1 daughter. Education: Diploma, National Conservatory, Montevideo, 1956; Curtis Institute of Music, 1958; BA, University of Minnesota, 1960; Studied with Aaron Copland, Antal Dorati, Pierre Monteux. Career: Debut, Carnegie Hall; Independent Composer and Conductor, 1955-; Apprentice Conductor, Minnesota Orchestra, 1958-60; Associate Conductor, American Symphony Orchestra, New York, 1962-66; Musical Director, American Shakespeare Festival, 1966; Composer-in-Residence, Cleveland Orchestra, 1968-71; Artistic Director, International Festival of Americas, Miami, 1984-; Opera Conductor, United Kingdom, USA, Australia and Mexico; Guest Conductor, numerous orchestras; International tours in USA, Latin America, Australia and New Zealand. Compositions: Published over 100 works; Variations on a Theme from Childhood, for chamber orchestra; Symphony for Percussion; Concerto for Violin and Orchestra; Concerto for Harp and Orchestra; Symphonie Mystique, 2003; Orchestration and recording of George Gershwin's Three Piano Preludes and the Lullaby; Also works for chorus, voice, keyboard; Over 180 recordings for major labels with orchestras from United Kingdom, Germany, Oslo, Spain, Italy, Sicily, Belgium, Czechoslovakia and Australia. Honours: Ford Foundation Conductors Award; Alice M Ditson Award, 1976; Deutsche Schallplatten Critics Award; Music Retailers Association Award; Guggenheim Fellow, 1958-60; 2 Guggenheim awards; Rockfeller Foundation Grants; Commissions, National Endowment for the Arts and Harvard Musical Association; BMI Award; Koussevitzky Foundation Award; 8 Grammy Nominations, 1975-2004; Subject of book by Michel Faure, 2002. Memberships: American Symphony Orchestra League; American Music Center; American Federation of Musicians. Address: 270 Riverside Drive, New York, NY 10025, USA.

SEREGIN Artur Alexandrovich, b. 27 December 1941, Voronezh, USSR. Physicist. m. 1967, 2 daughters. Education: Physicist, University of Voronezh, 1964; Candidate of Physics-

maths Science, University of Moscow, 1970; Doctor of Physics-maths Science, JINR of Dubna, 1990. Appointments: Senior Laboratory Assistant IPPE, Obninsk, Russia, 1965-69; Junior Scientific Worker, 1969-73; Senior Scientific Worker, 1973-93; Chief Scientific Worker, 1993-. Publications: Author and co-author of 102 scientific works, articles, on nuclear physics and laser physics. Honours: Senior Scientific Worker. Address: Institute of Physics and Power Engineering, Bondarenko Sq 1, Obninsk 249 033, Russia. E-mail: seregin@ippe.obninsk.ru

SERNICKI Jan Kazimierz, b. 7 April 1943, Warsaw, Poland. Electronic Engineer - Nuclear Electronics. m. Krystyna Elzbieta Łysakowska-Sernicka. Education: Master's degree, 1969, Postgraduate training, 1971-75, Doctor of Engineering, 1976, Warsaw Technical University. Appointments: Electronic Engineer, 1969-71, Research Engineer, 1976-78, Institute of Nuclear Research, Świerk; Scientific Worker, Joint Institute of Nuclear Research, Dubna, Russia, 1978-81; Specialist, Department of Nuclear Spectroscopy and Technique, The Andrzej Soltan Institute for Nuclear Studies, Świerk, 1981-. Publications: Author, papers in Progress in Medical Physics, 2 in 1977, 3 in 1978; Co-author, paper in Nukleonika, 1981; Author, papers in Nuclear Instruments and Methods in Physics Research A, 1983, 2 in 1985, 1986, 2 in 1988, 1990, 1997, in Nukleonika, 1995, 2000. Address: Saska 99-4, 03-914 Warsaw, Poland.

SEROK Shraga, b. 10 April 1929, Poland. Psychotherapist. m. Fryda, 3 daughters. Education: Diploma in Social Work, 1959; MA, Psychology, Israel, 1970; PhD, School of Applied Social Science, Case Western Reserve University, Cleveland, Ohio, USA, 1975; Postgraduate Study, Gestalt Institute of Cleveland, 1975. Appointments: Lecturer, Psychopathology, Human Development and Gestalt Therapy; Founder, Faye Ratner Gestalt Programme; Director, Tel Aviv University, for 20 years; Professor, Ben Gurion University, Beer Sheva; Private practice, individual, couples, group, family psychotherapy; Professor Emeritus. Publications: 45 articles in English and Hebrew in various areas of human behaviour; Books: Human Fulfilment (Hebrew), 1984; Innovative Applications of Gestalt Therapy (English), 2000. Memberships: American Psychological Association, 1982-2000; Israel Psychotherapy Association; Israeli Association of S W; International Group Psychotherapy; Israeli Association of Family Therapy; Member of Board of Director of International Gestalt Therapy Association. Address: 8 Shimshon str, Rishon le Zion 75270, Israel.

SERRA-BROOKS Beverly, b. 27 July 1957, Azusa, USA. Concert Pianist. m. Education: AA degree, Santa Barbara City College; BFA Degree, California Institute of the Arts; MM Degree, California State University Northridge; American Conservatory at Fontainbleau, France; Scholarship Fellow, The Music Academy of the West, Santa Barbara, California; DMA, Claremont Graduate University, 2003; Major teachers: James Shearer in Pasadena, Reginald Stewart at the Music Academy of the West, Jorg Demus in Austria, Leonid Hambro at Cal-Arts, Michel Beroff in France and Jerome Lowenthal in the USA. Debut: Carnegie Hall, 1998. Career: Professor of Piano, Mount St Mary's College, Los Angeles, California; National Public Radio, Performance Today; Classic King Radio, Seattle; KUSC, Los Angeles; Guest artist, John Hopkins University special event series; Carmel Performing Arts series; Clara Schuman at the Piano, Starring as Clara in the One-Woman Histro-drama Broadway production; Recording Artist for EROICA Classical Recordings and CD's, 2000-; Recitals in Paris and Boston, San Diego Museum of Art, 2000-02. Recordings: From the Musical Tree: Music of Beethoven, Bach and Debussy, 2001; Romantic Variations; Music of Clara Schuman, Robert Schuman and Chopin. Honours: Winner, Artists International Competition, 1997; Gold medal, Music Arts Award; James Irvine

Dictionary of International Biography

Music Award, 1985-86; Pillsbury Foundation Music Award, 1983-86; Fellowships, International Institute for Chamber Music; California Association of Professional Music, 1998. Memberships: Teachers Board Member; The College Music Society and American College of Musicians. Address: 2805 Mataro St, Pasadena, CA 91107, USA.

SESÉ Luis M, b. 18 September 1955, Madrid, Spain. Chemistry Educator; Researcher. m. Mercedes Mejias, 1 son. Education: BS, University Complutense Madrid, 1976; MSc, honours, 1978; PhD, 1983. Appointments: Ayudante, 1978-80, Encargado, 1980-81, University Complutense; Encargado, 1981-82, Colaborador, 1982-84, Titular, 1985-87, Titular Numerario, 1987-, University National Educational Distance, Madrid. Publications: Research papers in professional journals; Books; Educational Video. Honours: Premio Extraordinario de Licenciatura, University Complutense, 1979; 3rd Prize, X Bienal Internacional de Cine y Video Cientifico, Spain, 2001; 2nd Prize, XXII Bienal Internacional de Cine Cientifico, Spain, 2002; 2nd Prize, Fisica en Acción 3 (RSEF), Spain, 2002. Memberships: New York Academy of Sciences; Planetary Society; Spanish Royal Society of Physics. Address: Facultad de Ciencias, University National Educational Distance, Senda del Rey 9, 28040 Madrid, Spain.

SESTAN Branko, b. 30 September 1961, Rijeka, Croatia. Orthopaedic Surgeon; Consultant. m. Loredana, 1 son, 1 daughter. Education: MD, Medical Faculty, Rijeka, Croatia; MS, 1986; DSc, 1992; Postgraduate, Oxford University, England, 1994; Specialist in Orthopaedic Surgery, 1996; Resident, Nuffield Orthopaedic Centre, Oxford University, 1991-92; Consultant in Orthopaedic Surgery, 1996. Appointments: Head of Hospital Department, 1997-, Assistant Professor, 1998-2003, Associate Professor, 2003-, Orthopaedic Clinical Hospital, Lovran, Croatia. Publications include: Kniest Dysplasia: Patients Growth Process and Development, Evolution of Abnormalities; Femoral Anteversion Related to Side Differences in Hip Rotation; Comparison in Regression of Femoral Neck Anteversion in Children with Normal Intoeing and Outtoeing Gait. Memberships Include: New York Academy of Sciences; Girdleston Orthopaedic Society; Croatian-Austrian Society; Croatian Orthopaedic Society; Croatian Society for Children's Orthopaedics. Address: Orthopaedic Clinical Hospital, 51415 Lovran, Croatia.

SETHI Kapil Dev, b. 19 June 1953, Sultanpur, India. Professor of Neurology. m. Ranjit, 3 children. Education: Undergraduate, DAV College, Jullundar, India, 1968-70; MBBS, Medical School, Christian Medical College, Ludhiana, India, 1970-75; Postdoctoral Training, India, UK and USA, 1975-85. Appointments: Director of Movements Disorder Clinic, 1985-, Assistant Professor of Neurology, 1985-91, Co-Director, Chemodenervation (Botox) Clinic, 1991-, Associate Professor of Neurology, 1991-98, Vice-Chairman, CME Committee, 1998-, Professor of Neurology, 1998-, Director, National Parkinson Foundation Center of Excellence, 2000-, Medical College of Georgia, Augusta; Staff Physician 3/8th Appointment, Veterans Administration Medical Center, 1985-; Teaching Director, 1988-93, Director, 1997, Neuro 500 Course for Medical Students; Director, Phase I Neuro Science Course, 1994-96; Consulting Physician, University Hospital, Augusta, 1996-2000. Publications: Numerous articles in professional journals, book reviews and editorial reviews. Honours: 1st Prize, Anatomy, 1971, 2nd Prize, Pathology, 1973, Christian Medical College, Ludhiana; Listed in America's Top Doctors, 1994, 1996, 1998, 2001, 2002; Neurology NS Clerkship Outstanding Teacher Award, 2000; Outstanding Award, AINA, 2002; Many invited lectures and visiting professorships. Memberships: American Neurological Association; Fellow, American Academy of Neurology; Movement Disorder Society; Fellow, Royal College of Physicians of London; American Association of Physician from India; Association of Indian Neurologists of North America; Parkinson's Study Group; Christian Medical College Alumni. Address: Medical College of Georgia, Department of Neurology (HB-2060), Augusta, GA 30912, USA. E-mail: ksethi@neuro.mcg.edu

SEWELL Rufus Frederick, b. 29 October 1967. Actor. m. Yasmin Abdallah, 1999, 1 son with Amy Gardner. Career: Actor; Films include: Twenty-One; Dirty Weekend; A Man of No Importance; Carrington; Victory; Hamlet; The Woodlanders; The Honest Courtesan; Martha Meet Frank; Daniel and Laurence; Illuminata; Dark City; Bless The Child; A Knight's Tale; The Extremists; Tristan and Isolde; TV appearances include: The Last Romantics; Gone To Seed; Middlemarch; Dirty Something; Citizen Locke; Cold Comfort Farm; Henry IV; Charles II: The Power and the Passion; Helen of Troy; Stage appearances include: Royal Hunt of the Sun; Comedians; The Last Domain; Peter and the Captain; Pride and Prejudice; The Government Inspector; The Seagull; As You Like It; Making it Better; Arcadia; Translations; Rat in the Skull; Macbeth; Luther; Taste. Address: c/o Julian Belfrage Associates, 46 Albermarle Street, London, W1X 4PP, England.

SEYMOUR David, b. 24 January 1951, Surrey, England. Lawyer. m. Elisabeth, 1 son, 2 daughters. Education: MA, Jurisprudence, The Queen's College, Oxford, 1969-72; LLB, Fitzwilliam College, Cambridge, 1973-74; Gray's Inn, Called to the Bar, 1975. Appointments: Law Clerk, Rosenfeld, Meyer & Susman (Attorneys), Beverly Hills, California, 1972-73; Legal Adviser's Branch, Home Office, 1975-97; Legal Secretary to the Attorney General, 1997-2000; Legal Adviser, Home Office, 2000-. Honours: Open Exhibition, The Queen's College, Oxford, 1969-72; Holt Scholar, Gray's Inn, 1974; Elected Bencher, Gray's Inn, 2001. Address: Home Office, 50 Queen Anne's Gate, London SW1H 9AT, England. E-mail: david.seymour@homeoffice.gov.uk

SHACHMUROVE Yochanan, b. 10 October 1951, Tel-Aviv, Israel. Professor of Economics. m. Mina, 3 sons. Education: BA, Economics, 1975, MBA, Finance and Operations Research, 1977, Tel Aviv University; MA, Economics, 1980, PhD, Economics, 1983, University of Minnesota. Appointments include: Research and Teaching Assistant, Tel Aviv University School of Business and Department of Economics, 1973-76; Teaching Associate II, University of Minnesota, 1977-82; Lecturer, 1982-83, Assistant Professor, 1984-85, Department of Economics, University of Indiana, USA; Graduate courses in International Trade and Finance, Advanced Macroeconomics, 1985-94; University of Pennsylvania, Department of Economics, Philadelphia, 1991-2004; Temple University, School of Business and Management, Department of Finance, Philadelphia, Pennsylvania, USA, Summers, 1992, 1993, 1995; Visiting Associate Professor, Harvard University, Cambridge, Massachusetts, summer, 1994; University of Pennsylvania, Center for Analytic Research in Economics and the Social Sciences, Summers, 1995-99; New Economic School, Moscow, Russia, Fall, 1996; National University "KIev-Mohyla Academy", Ukraine, Economics MA Program, Kiev, Summer, 1999; City College of New York, Department of Economics, New York, New York, 1997-2004. Publications: 58 in professional journals; Numerous working papers. Honours: Magna cum Laude Honours, BA, 1975, MBA, 1977, Tel Aviv University; MBA Fellowship, Tel Aviv University, 1976-77; Leadership and Service Award, University of Minnesota, 1977-78, 1979-80, 1980-81; Department of Economics Fellowship, University of Minnesota, 1978, 1979; Irving B Kravis Award for Distinction in Undergraduate Teaching, University of Pennsylvania, 1996. Address: 56 Trent Rd, Wynnewood, PA 19096, USA.

Dictionary of International Biography

SHACKLEY Michael Steven, b. 13 May 1949, San Diego, California, USA. Research Professor, Archaeology and Geology. m. Kathleen L Butler, 1 daughter. Education: AB, Anthropology and Geology, 1979, MA, Anthropology, 1981, San Diego University; PhD, Anthropology, Arizona State University, 1990. Appointments: Lecturer, Archaeology, Desert Studies, California University, Fullerton, 1987-91; Adjunct Assistant Professor, Department of Anthropology, San Diego University, 1989-90; Faculty Member, Archaeological Research Faculty, 1990-, Adjunct Assistant Professor, Department of Anthropology, 1994-95, Adjunct Associate Professor, Department of Anthropology, 1995-99, University of California, Berkeley; Adjunct Professor, Department of Anthropology, University of California, Berkeley; Research Archaeologist, Phoebe Hearst Museum of Anthropology, 1990-; Director, Archaeological XRF Lab, 1990-. Publications: Several books; Numerous articles in professional journals. Honours include: Re-Entry Mentor Award, University of California, Berkeley, 1994. Memberships: American Association for the Advancement of Science; Arizona Archaeological and Historical Society; Geological Society of America; International Association for Obsidian Studies; Phi Beta Kappa; Society for American Archaeology; Society for Archaeological Sciences; Society for California Archaeology; Society of Professional Archaeologists. Address: Phoebe Hearst Museum of Anthropology, 103 Kroeber Hall, University of California, Berkeley, CA 94720-3712, USA.

SHADBOLT Maurice (Francis Richard), b. 4 June 1932, Auckland, New Zealand. Novelist. m. Bridget Armstrong, 1978. Education: University of Auckland. Appointments: Journalist, New Zealand, 1952-54; Documentry Screenwriter, Director, New Zealand Film Unit, 1954-57; Full Time Writer, 1957-. Publications: Among the Cinders, 1965; This Summer's Dolphin, 1969; An Ear of the Dragon, 1971; Danger Zone, 1975; The Lovelock Version, 1980; Season of the Jew, 1986; Monday's Warrior, 1990; Dove on the Waters, 1997. Story Collections: The New Zealander: A Sequence of Stories, 1959; Summer Fires and Winter Country, 1963; The Presence of Music: Three Novellas; Figures in Light: Selected Stories. Play: Once on Chunk Bair, 1982. Guides and Histories of New Zealand. Honours: James Wattie Awards, 1973, 1991; New Zealand Book Award, 1981; Officer of the Order of the British Empire, 1989; Commander of the Order of the British Empire. Address: Box 60028 Titirangi, Auckland 7, New Zealand.

SHAFAEDDIN Mehdi, b. 21 July 1945, Iran. Economist. Educator. m. Shahnaz, 28 August 1970, 2 daughters. Education: BA, Economics, Tehran University, 1969; MA, Economics, Tehran University, 1971; DPhil, Economic Development, Oxford, 1980. Appointments: In charge of Macroeconomic and Development Polices Branch, UNCTAD; Senior Economist, Co-ordinator, Economic Co-operation Among Developing Countries; Chief, Enterprise Development Strategy; Chief, Policy Development; Senior Adviser, Trade Policy; Lecturer, Webster University, Geneva; Editor, UNCTAD Bulletin; Assistant Professor, University of Abureyhan, Tehran; Acting Chief, Industrial Research and Programmes, Institute of Standards and Industrial Research, Tehran. Publications: Fallacies in Trade and Industrial Policies, forthcoming and many articles in professional journals. Honours: Scholarship, British Counsel for B Lit, Oxford; Scholarship, Tehran University, D Phil and BA; Listed in National and International Biographical Who's Who Publications. Memberships: Development Study Association, UK. Address: United Nations, Geneva, Switzerland. E-mail: shafaeddin@bluewin.ch

SHAFER Sharon Guertin, b. 3 October 1943, Detroit, Michigan, USA. Professor. m. Robert, 1 son. Education: BA, Catholic University of America, 1965; MM, University of Maryland, 1970; DMA, University of Maryland, 1973. Career: Freelance singer,

pianist and composer, 1965-; Professor of Music, Full time faculty member, Chair of the Music and Fine Arts Program, Trinity College in Washington, DC, 1974-; New York debut, 1987; Concerts in France, Germany and US, 1975-; Original Composition: Butterflies and Bumblebees for voice and piano, 2004. Publications: 4 articles; 1 book. Honours: Outstanding Faculty Award, 1987; Young Artists Award in Vocal Performance, 1974; NDEA Title IV Fellowship, University of Maryland, 1970-73. Memberships: The College Music Society; The International Alliance of Women in Music; Friday Morning Music Club; Phi Beta Kappa; Washington Alumnae Chapter of Sigma Alpha Iota. Address: Trinity College Fine Arts Program, 125 Michigan Avenue, NE Washington, DC 20017, USA. E-mail: shafers@trinitydc.edu Website: www.trinitydc.edu/academics/faculty/shafers/~facinfo.html

SHAFFER (Sir) Peter (Levin), b. 15 May 1926, Liverpool, England. Dramatist. Education: BA, Trinity College, Cambridge, 1950. Appointments: Literary Critic, Truth, 1956-57; Music Critic, Time and Tide, 1961-62; Cameron Mackintosh Visiting Professor of Contemporary Theatre and Fellow, St Catherine's College, Oxford, 1994. Publications: Plays: Five Finger Exericse, 1958; The Private Ear and the Public Eye, 1962; The Merry Roosters Panto (with Joan Littlewood), 1963; The Royal Hunt of the Sun, 1964; Black Comedy, 1965; White Lies, 1967; The White Liars, 1968; The Battle of Shrivings, 1970; Equus, 1973; Amadeus, 1979; Yonadab, 1985; Lettice and Lovage, 1987; The Gift of the Gorgon, 1992. Contributions to: Radio and television. Honours: Evening Standard Drama Awards, 1958, 1979, 1988; New York Drama Critics Cricle Awards, 1959, 1976; London Theatre Critics Award, 1979; Plays and Players Award, 1979; Tony Awards, 1979, 1980; Drama Desk Award, 1980; Academy Award, 1985; Golden Globe Award, 1985; Los Angeles Film Critics Association Award, 1985; Premi David di Donatello, 1985; Commander of the Order of the British Empire, 1987; Shakespeare Prize, Hamburg, 1989; William Inge Award for Distinguished Achievement in the American Theatre, 1992. Membership: Royal Society of Literature, fellow. Address: c/o McNaughton-Lowe Representation, 200 Fulham Road, London SW10 9PN, England.

SHAFIK Ahmed, b. 10 May 1933, Shebin-el-Kom, Menoufia Governorate, Egypt. Surgeon. m. Olfat Elsibai, 2 sons. Education: Undergraduate studies, 1951-57, MD, 1962, Cairo University Faculty of Medicine. Appointments at Cairo University Faculty of Medicine, Kasr elAini Teaching Hospital: House Officer, 1957-58; Lecturer of Surgery, 1962-70; Assistant Professor of Surgery, 1970-75; Full Professor of Surgery, 1975; Head, Emergency Division, 1980-84; Head, Surgical Divisions 27 and 29, 1984-90; Chairman, Department of Surgery and Experimental Research, 1990-. Publications: Over 700 contributions to medical research, introducing new anatomical, physiological, pathological and therapeutical findings in coloproctology, gastroenterology, urology, andrology, gynaecology and others, describing amongst other entities over 80 hitherto unknown reflexes there by enhancing the understanding of mechanisms that regulate and co-ordinate anal and vesical continence and evacuation, or are responsible for deglutination or control genital functions and sexual performance including coitus in both sexes; Also created an (unconventional) immunostimulating antiviral drug, MM1, which has proved very successful in the combat of AIDS. Honours: State Award for Science and Arts, 1st Class, 1977; Nomination for Nobel Prize in Medicine, 1981. Memberships include: International Society of University Colon and Rectal Surgeons; The American Society of Colon and Rectal Surgeons; American Association of Anatomists; New York Academy of Sciences; Society of Experimental Biology and Medicine; Academy of Surgical Research; International Pelvic Floor Dysfunction Society; Mediterranean Society of Pelvic Floor Disorders; Mediterranean Society of Coloproctology. Address: 2 Talaat Harb Street, Cairo, Egypt. E-mail: shafik@ahmed-shafik.org

Dictionary of International Biography

SHAGIDULLIN Roal'd Rifgatovich, b. 5 August 1928, Tersy Village, Agriz Region of Tatarstan. Scientist. m. Bacirova Aida Zaudjiatovna, 1 son, 1 daughter. Education: Bachelor of Physicomathematical Sciences, University, Kazan, Soviet Union, 1967; Doctor, Professor Physical Chemistry, University, Arbuzov Institute, Kazan, Russia, 1996, 1997. Appointments: Seasonal Agricultural Worker, Tatarstan, 1942-45; Student, University Kazan, Tatarstan, 1945-50; Secretary, District Regional Komsomol Committees, Kazan, Tatarstan, 1950-1953; Laboratory Assistant, Aspirant, Physicotechnical Institute of Kazan Branch of Academic Sciences, Kazan, Tatarstan, 1953-56; Junior Scientist, Scientific Secretary, Chief of Laboratory, Chief Scientist, Arbuizov Institute of Academy of Science, Kazan, Tatarstan, 1956-; Scientific Chief, Spectroanalitical Centre, Academy of Science of Tatarstan and Institute, Kazan, Tatarstan, Russia, 1990. Publications include: Author and co-author of 4 books; Over 400 articles in scientific journals. Honours: Order, The Badge of Honour, Soviet Union, 1970; Medals, for Distinguished Public Service and Merits, Soviet Union, Russia, 1945, 1970, 1987, 1995, 2000, and others. Memberships: Many social and administrative committees, Scientific Soviets of Arbuzov Institute, University, Kazan, Tatarstan, Soviet Union, Russia, 1955-. Address: Iscra Street 9-19, 420045, Kazan – 45, Tatarstan, Russia. E-mail: arbuzov@iopc.knc.ru.

SHAH Kumar Chimanlal, b. 3 August 1937, Nadiad, Gujarat, India. Civil Engineer. m. Varsha Shah, 1 son, 1 daughter. Education: BE (Civil) University of Mysore, 1959; MSc (Civil) Case Institute of Technology, Cleveland, Ohio, USA, 1962. Appointments: Senior Engineer, Adache Associates Inc, Cleveland, Ohio, USA, 1962-64; Senior Engineer with Dorr-Oliver (India) Ltd (now Hindustan Dorr Oliver Ltd), 1964-94; Operations Manager, 1979; General Manager (Business Development), 1989; Technical Director, Shrinavas Plates and Structurals Co (pvt) Ltd, 1994-. Honours: Nominated for Bharat Gaurav Award, Industrial Economic Forum, New Delhi, 1998; Best Citizen of India Award, International Publishing House, 1998; Distinguished Leadership Award, ABI, 1998. Memberships: Institution of Engineers (India); American Society of Civil Engineers (USA). Address: 66, Mansha, 14B Road, Khar, Mumbai 400052, India.

SHAHJAHAN Munir, b. 23 July 1962, Dhaka, Bangladesh. Medical Researcher; Physician Scientist. m. Sabrina Sultana, 1 son, 1 daughter. Education: MBBS (MD), University of Dhaka, 1990; MPH (Master of Public Health), University of Texas, Houston, School of Public Health, 1996. Appointments: House Physician, Dhaka Medical College Hospital, Bangladesh, 1991-93; Lecturer and Medical Officer, Medical College for Women, Dhaka, Bangladesh, 1993-94; Research Assistant, University of Texas Houston, School of Public Health, USA, 1994-97; Research Assistant, AIDS Educational and Training Center for Texas and Oklahoma, 1997-98; Senior Research Assistant, Clinical Research Protocol Co-ordinator, Data Manager, Senior Data Analyst, M D Anderson Cancer Center, Houston, Texas, USA, 1998-. Publications: Co-author, Ethnic Differences in HIV Testing, 1999; Non-Adherence to Protease Inhibitors, 2000; Nonablative Stem Cell Transplantation for Older Patients with AM L/MDS, 2002. Honour: Recipient of Scholarship Award for Academic Excellence, Bangladesh Government, 1983-90; Travel Grant Award for best Abstract, American Society of Blood and Marrow Transplantation, 2004. Memberships: American Public Health Association; American Society of Blood and Marrow Transplantation; American Society of Clinical Oncology; American Society of Hematology; Association of Clinical Research Professionals. Address: 7900 Cambridge #9-2G, Houston, TX 77054, USA. E-mail: msjahan@hotmail.com

SHAIMIEV Mintimer Sharipovich, b. 20 January 1937, Anyakovo, Tatarstan, Russia. Politician. m. Sakina Shakirovna Shaimieva, 2 sons. Education: Mechanical Engineer, Kazan Institute of Agriculture, 1959. Appointments: Engineer, Chief Engineer, Service and Repair Station, Mouslyumovsky District, Tatar ASSR, 1959-62; Manager "Selkhoztechnika" District Association, Menzelinski District, Tatar ASSR, 1962-67; Instructor, Deputy Head, Department of Agriculture, Tatar Regional Committee of the CPSU, Kazan, 1967-69; Minister of Melioration and Water Resources, Kazan, 1969-83; First Deputy Chairman, Council of Ministers, Tatar ASSR, 1983; Secretary, Tatar Regional Committee of the CPSU, Kazan, 1983-85; Chairman, Council of Ministers, Tatar ASSR, Kazan, 1985-89; First Secretary, Tatar Regional Committee of the CPSU, Kazan, 1989-90; Chairman, Supreme Council, Tatar ASSR, 1990-91; President of the Republic of Tatarstan, 1991-. Honours: Koul-Gali International Prize of the Tatar People; Order of Lenin, 1966; Order of the October Revolution, 1976; Order of the Red Banner of Labour; Order of the Peoples Friendship; Order of the Service for the Fatherland, II Degree, 1997; 2 Medals; UNESCO Avitsenna Medal for great contribution in preservation of cultural and historic values, 2001. Memberships: Co-Chairman, Higher Council of the United Russia Party; Academician, Academy of Technological Sciences of the Russian Federation; Honorary Academician of the International Academy of Informatisation; Honorary Professor of Moscow State Institute of International Relations under the RF MFA; Honorary Member, Presidium of International Parliament of the World Knight Confederation under the auspices of the UN. Address: President's Office, Kremlin, Kazan 420014, Tatarstan, Russia. E-mail: dfa@kremlin.kazan.ru Website: www.tatar.ru/president

SHAKHOVSKY Larissa, b. 10 October 1943, Blagoveschinsk, Amur Region, Russia. Historian; Economist. m. Victor I Shakhovsky, 1 daughter. Education: Diploma with Distinction, Teacher of History, Regional Teachers' Training Institute, Moscow, Russia, 1967; Candidate of Sciences, Economics, State University, Rostov-on-Don, Russia, 1974; Doctor of Sciences, Economics, Financial Academy of the Russian Federation Government, 1995. Appointments: Associate Professor, Political Economy Department, 1977, Chair, Associate Professor, 1986, Chair, Professor, 1996, International Economics Department, State Technical University, Volgograd, Russia. Publications: 300 titles including the monographs: Motivation of Labor in Transitional Economics, 1995; The Motivation of Law of Human Activity & Stochastic Modeling of Human Capital, 1996. Honour: National Order of Friendship, 2000. Memberships: Academy of Humanities of the Russian Federation; Academy of Natural Sciences of the Russian Federation; Academy of Economic Sciences and Entrepreneurship of the Russian Federation. Address: State Technical University, Room # 333, Lenin Avenue 28, Volgograd, 400131, Russia. E-mail: econom@vstu.ru

SHALABY Samir Shafik, b. 9 October 1938, Cairo, Egypt. Professor of Surgery. m. Shadia Assaad. Education: MBB Ch, Faculty of Medicine, Cairo University, Egypt, 1961; Diploma, Surgery, 1964, MD, General Surgery, 1968, Cairo University. Appointments: Registrar, General Surgery, Cairo University Hospitals, 1963-65; Consultant Surgeon, Khazindare Hospital, Cairo; Head of Surgery Department, Kitchener Memorial Hospital, Cairo, 1969-79; Member of Staff, Lecturer, Assistant Professor, Professor, Currently Emeritus Professor, Cairo University Hospital and Faculty of Medicine. Publications: over 25 surgical publications, some single author others multi-author; Supervision of many MS thesis and essays in preparation for Master of Surgery degrees. Honours: Prize of Clinical Surgery in MBBCh Exams; Medal for Public Service, Al Jewfig Benevolent Society; Certificate of Appreciation from Faculty of Medicine and Medical Syndicate.

Memberships: Fellow, International College of Surgeons; Board Member, Al Jewfig Benevolent Society. Address: 9 Bani Tai Street, Qubba Palace, Cairo 11331, Egypt. E-mail: ssshalaby@link.net

SHAMI Charles Henry, b. 13 May 1936, Manchester, England. Dual Nationality, USA and UK. Professor of Economics. m. Kikuko Nakamura Shami. Education: BS, Economics, School of General Studies, 1961, MA, Economics, Department of Economics, 1964, PhD, Economics, Department of Economics, 1968, Columbia University, USA. Appointments: Manager, American Telephone and Telegraph Company, New York City, USA, 1969-78; Assistant Professor of Economics, Florida Atlantic University, Boca Raton, Florida, USA, 1968-69; Assistant Professor of Economics, Yeshiva University, New York City, USA, 1969-73; Economic Analyst, Congressional Research Service, US Library of Congress, Washington DC, USA, 1978-79; Senior Economist, Combustion Engineering Inc., Stamford, Connecticut, USA, 1979-84; Research Analyst, ABC TV network, 1984-86; Professor of Economics, Kanto Gakuen University, Gunma-Ken, Japan, 1989-96; Professor of Economics, Nihon University, Tokyo, Japan, 1996-. Publications: Regular contributor to Nihon University Economic Review, Japan including: Redefining the Elasticity of Substitution of Capital for Labor in Cobb-Douglas-Type and CES-type Production Functions: Correcting a Theoretical Error in Production Function Theory that has persisted for 68 Years, 2000; A Theoretical and Empirical Analysis of the Elasticity of the Aggregate Demand and Supply Curves: After Classical Macroeconomics and the Rational Expectations Theories of the 20th Century; Experimental Consumption Functions for the US in Real Disposable Income Space and in Real GDP Space, 1949:1-99:4, 2002; Consumption Functions for Japan in Real Household Disposable Income Space and in Real GDP Space, 1955:2-99:1, 2002; Empirical, Linear Quasi-Phillips Curves for the US Economy, 1962:1-2000:4, 2002; 3 bilingual textbooks in English and Japanese: Microeconomics, 1998; Macroeconomics, 2001; Elementary Economics, 2001. Membership: American Economic Association. Address: 3-14-1 Katase-Kaigan, Fujisawa-shi; 251-0035, Japan. E-mail: ch-shami@abox7.so-net.ne.jp

SHANGGUAN Dongkai, b. 12 December 1963, Henan Province, China. Materials Scientist. m. Guilian Gao, 2 sons. Education: BSc, Tsinghua University, China, 1984; DPhil, University of Oxford, England, 1989. Appointments: Postdoctoral Visiting Fellow, University of Cambridge, England, 1989; Postdoctoral Research Fellow, The University of Alabama, USA, 1989-91; Manufacturing Engineer, Technical Specialist, Senior Technical Specialist, Supervisor, Ford Motor Co, USA, 1991-2001; Director of Advanced Technology, Flextronics, 2001-. Publications: Book, "Cellular Growth of Crystals"; Over 100 technical papers; 19 US and international patents. Honours: St Edmund Hall Brockhues Graduate Awards, Oxford University, 1986, 1987; Outstanding Young Manufacturing Engineer Award, Society of Manufacturing Engineers, 1998; Soldertec Lead-Free Soldering Award, 2002. Memberships: Board of Review, Metallurgical and Materials Transactions; Board of Advisors, Association of Forming and Fabricating Technologies - Society of Manufacturing Engineers; SAE Transactions Review Committee; Senior Member, IEEE. E-mail: dshangguan@yahoo.com

SHANNON (The Right Honourable the Countess of, Baroness Carlton, Baroness of Castle Martyr), Almine de Villiers Barton Boyle, b. 25 October 1950, South Africa. Author; Lecturer; Business Owner. m. The Earl of Shannon. 2 daughters, 1 son. Education: Degree in Religious Studies; Licensed Minister; Associates Degree, Brigham Young University. Appointments: Patroness to several charitable organisations, including the Masonic Homes for the Aged: Shannon Court and James Terry Court;

Actively involved in many charitable events including: Friends of Belize; Armenian School Programmes; Established world-wide non-denominational ministry and charitable foundation: Bringing the Children Home Global Foundation; Director of non-profit organisation: Good Works on Earth; International Lecturer; Teacher of Cultural Refinement, Relief Society of Women, United States; Spokesperson for the Indigenous People of Hawaii; Representative for H R H The Prince d'Altavilla of Naples and Sicily; Author; Business Owner. Publications: Books: A Life of Miracles; Healers of the West Wind; Books produced for charities: Cooking with Class (co-authored with the Duchess of Valderano); Memoirs and Meals; Extensive tape library. Honours: Title: The Countess Palatine of the Norman Crown of Naples and Sicily bestowed by H R H The Prince d'Altavilla; Included in The Greatest American Contemporary Poets; Many Literary Awards; Writings read for over a year at Geneva Art Association, Switzerland; Many Theatrical Awards for stage acting; Published to 29 million readers; Honoured by Edgar Cayce Foundation, Indigenous Wisdom Conference; Named Top Speaker: Ohio Light Expo, Toronto Consumer Health Show, Canada. Memberships: Patroness, Friends of the Masonic Benevolent Society of Great Britain; Fellow of the Royal Society of Art. Address: 2114 NE Crestview Drive, Newport, Oregon, USA. Website: www.spiritualjourneys.com

SHAPOVAL Sergei, b. 27 December 1949, Dnepropetrovsk, USSR. Physicist. m. Elena Nosovo, 1 daughter. Education: Master Degree, Moscow Institute of Electronics, 1975; PhD, Institute of Physics and Technology, Russian Academy of Science, 1989. Appointments: Senior Engineer, Semi-conductor factory, Alexandrov, 1972-76; Vice-Director of Technology, R&D Corporation "Souz", Novosibirsk, 1977-86; Head of Laboratory, Institute of Microelectronics Technology, Russian Academy of Science, 1986-. Publications: Cubic boron nitride films deposited by ECR plasma, 1990; Conductance quantitisation of the nanocontacts at room temperature, 1995; Microfabricated adhesive mimicking gecko foot-hair, 2003. Honour: USONR Award for article, Passivation of the wide-band-gap transistors, 2001. Membership: Material Research Society. Address: School Blvd 20, Apt 57, Chernogolovka 141432, Moscow District, Russia. E-mail: shapoval@ipmt-hpm.ac.ru

SHARIF Omar (Michael Chalhoub), b. 10 April 1932, Cairo, Egypt. Actor. m. (1) Faten Hamama, 1 son, (2) 1973. Education: Victoria College, Cairo. Career: Salesman, lumber-import firm; 24 Egyptian films and 2 French co-production films; Films include: Lawrence of Arabia; The Fall of the Roman Empire; Behold a Pale Horse; Genghis Khan; The Yellow Rolls Royce; Doctor Zhivago; Night of the Generals; Mackenna's Gold; Funny Girl; Cinderella-Italian Style; Mayerling; The Appointment; Che; The Last Valley; The Horseman; The Burglars; The Island; The Tamarind Seed; Juggernaut; Funny Lady; Ace Up My Sleeve; Crime and Passion; Bloodline; Green Ice; Top Secret; Peter the Great (TV); The Possessed; Mountains of the Moon; Michaelangelo and Me; Drums of Fire; Le Guignol; The Puppet; The Rainbow Thief; 558 rue Paradis; Gulliver's Travels (TV); Heaven Before I Die; The 13th Warrior; The Parole Officer; Shaka Zulu: The Citadel (TV); Monsieur Ibrahim et les fleurs de Coran; Soyez prudents… (TV); Urban Myth Chillers (TV); Hidalgo; Theatre: The Sleeping Prince, England, 1983. Publications: The Eternal Male (autobiography), 1978. Address: c/o William Morris Agency, 151 El Camino Drive, Beverly Hills, CA 90212, USA.

SHARON Ariel, b. 1928. Politician; Army Officer - retired. m. 2 sons. Education: Studies at Hebrew University, 1952-53; Studies Staff College, Camberley UK, 1957-58. Appointments: Active in Hagana since early youth; Instructor Jewish Police units, 1947; Platoon Commander Alexandroni Brigade; Regimental Intelligence

Officer, 1948; Company Commander, 1949; Commander Brigade Reconnaissance Unit, 1949-50; Intelligence Officer Central Command and Northern Command, 1951-52; In charge of Unit 101 on numerous reprisal operations until 1957; Commander Paratroopers Brigade Sinai Campaign, 1956; Training Commander General Staff, 1958; Commander Infantry School, 1958-69; Commander Armoured Brigade, 1962; Head of Staff Northern Command, 1964; Head Training Department of Defence Forces, 1966; Head Brigade Group during Six-Day War, 1967; Resigned from Army, July 1973; Recalled as Commander Central Section of Sinai Front during Yom Kippur War, October1973; Forged bridgehead across Suez Canal; Adviser to Prime Minister, 1975-77; Minister of Agriculture in charge of Settlements, 1977-81; Minister of Defence, 1981-83; Minister without Portfolio, 1990-92; Minister of Trade and Industry, 1984-90; Minister of Construction and Housing, 1990-92; Minister of National Infrastructure, 1996-99; Chairman Cabinet Committee to oversee Jewish immigration from USSR, 1991-96; Prime Minister of Israel, 2001-. Publication: Warrior (autobiography), 1989. Memberships: Founder Member Likud Front, 1973; Member Knesset - Parliament - 1973-74, 1977-; Member Ministerial Defence Committee, 1990-92. Address: Ministry of National Infrastructure, P O Box 13106, 234 Jaffa Street, Jerusalem 91130, Israel.

SHAROUNI Youssef, b. 14 October 1924, Menuf. Writer. m. 1 son, 1 daughter. Education: BA, University of Cairo, 1945. Appointments: Teacher, French, Secondary Schools, Cairo and Sudan, 1945-56; Translator, News Section, Cairo Broadcasting Station, 1953-58; Affiliated, High Council for Arts, Letters and Social Sciences, 1956-; Permanent Member of Fiction Committee, 1965-85, 1992-; Lecturer, Spains Institute Hispano Arabe de Culture, 1978; Under Secretary, Ministry of Culture, 1978-83; Consultant, Kuwait's National Council for Culture and Arts, 1978-; Part time Professor, Cairo University, 1979-81; University of Amsterdam, University of Nijmegen, 1980; University of Leiden, 1980; 1981-82; St Anthony's College, Oxford, 1982; Ministry of Information, Muscat, Oman, Expert, Department of Publications, 1985-92; Lecturer, Department of Oriental Studies, Peking University, 1996; Head, Story Club, Cairo, 2001; Head Fiction Committee, 2003. Publications: Blood Feud; The Five Lovers; (Al-Ushag-al Khamsa); A Letter to a Woman (Risala ila Imra's); The Last Evening (Al Masa'al Akhir); Studies on Love (Dirasatfi Al Hubb); Many others. Honours: Egyptian State Prize, in short story, 1970, in literary studies, 1978; Estimation State Prize in literature, 2001; Fellow, German Academic Exchange Service, Free University of Berlin; Order of Science and Arts; Order of the Republic, Arab Republic of Egypt. Memberships: Egyptian Writers Union; Story Club, Cairo. Address: 12 El-sad El-Aali Street, El Maadi, Cairo, Egypt.

SHARPE Tom (Thomas Ridley), b. 30 March 1928, London, England. Novelist. m. Nancy Anne Looper, 1969, 3 daughters. Education: Pembroke College, University of Cambridge. Appointments: Social Worker, 1952; Teacher, 1952-56; Photographer, 1956-61; Lecturer in History at Cambridge College of Arts and Technology, 1963-71; Full-time novelist, 1971-. Publications: Riotous Assembly, 1971; Indecent Exposure, 1973; Porterhouse Blue, 1974; Blott on the Landscape, 1975; Wilt, 1976; The Great Pursuit, 1977; The Throwback, 1978; The Wilt Alternative, 1979; Ancestral Vices, 1980; Vintage Stuff, 1982; Wilt on High, 1984; Grantchester Grind, 1995; The Midden, 1996. Address: 38 Tunwells Lane, Great Shelford, Cambridge, CB2 5LJ, England.

SHATNER William, b. 22 March 1931, Montreal, Quebec, Canada. Actor. m. (1) Gloria Rand, 1956, divorced 1969, (2) Marcy Lafferty, 1973, divorced 1996, 3 daughters, (3) Nerine Kidd, 1997,

deceased 1999, (4) Elizabeth Martin, 2001. Education: BA, McGill University. Career: Appeared, Montreal Playhouse, 1952, 1953; Juvenile roles, Canadian Repertory Theatre, Ottawa, 1952-53, 1953-54; Shakespeare Festival, Stratford, Ontario, 1954-56; Broadway appearances include: Tamburlaine the Great, 1956; The World of Suzie Wong, 1958; A Shot in the Dark, 1961; Numerous TV appearances; Films include: The Brothers Karamazov, 1958, The Explosive Generation, 1961, Judgement at Nuremberg, 1961, The Intruder, 1962, The Outrage, 1964, Dead of Night, 1974, The Devil's Rain, 1975, Star Trek, 1979, The Kidnapping of the President, 1979, Star Trek: The Wrath of Khan, 1982, Star Trek III, The Search for Spock, 1984, Star Trek IV: The Voyage Home, 1986, Star Trek V: The Final Frontier, 1989, Star Trek VI: The Undiscovered Country, 1991, National Lampoon's Loaded Weapon, 1993; Star Trek: Generations, 1994; Ashes of Eden, 1995; Star Trek: Avenger, 1997; Tek Net, 1997; Free Enterprise, 1999; Miss Congeniality, 2000; Groom Lake (also director and co-writer), 2002. Publications: Ashes of Eden; Star Trek: Avenger, 1997; Step into Chaos, 1999; Get a Life, 1999; The Preserver, 2000; Spectre, 2000. Address: c/o Lemli Productions, 760 North La Cienega Boulevard, Los Angeles, CA 90069, USA.

SHAUGHNESSY Alfred James, b. 19 May 1916, London, England. Writer. m. Jean Lodge, 18 September 1948, 2 sons. Education: Eton College; Royal Military College, Sandhurst. Publications: Both Ends of the Candle (autobiography), 1978; Sarah - Letters and Diaries of a Courtier's Wife, 1906-1936, 1989; Dearest Enemy (novel), 1991; Hugo (novel), 1994; A Confession in Writing (memoir), 1997. Stage plays, including: Release; Holiday for Simon; The Heat of the Moment; Old Herbaceous; Double Cut; Love Affair (from the French). Honours: Nominated for US Television Emmy Award for Best Series Script, 1974, 1976; US Television Critics Circle Achievement in Writing Award, 1976-77; Address: The Grange, Yattendon, Thatcham, Berkshire RG18 0UE, England.

SHE Jin-Hua, b. 23 May 1963, Jinshi, Hunan, China. University Professor. m. Yoko Miyamoto. 1 son. Education: Masters Degree, 1990, PhD, 1993, Tokyo Institute of Technology, Japan. Appointments: Lecturer, 1993-2001, Associate Professor, 2001-, Tokyo University of Technology, Japan; Guest Lecturer, Toyota Techno Service Corporation, Japan, 2001-; Guest Professor, Central South University, China, 2002-. Publications: Articles in scientific journals including: Transactions of ASME; Control Engineering Practice; Engineering Application of Artificial Intelligence; IEE Proceedings. Honour: Prize Paper Award, International Federation of Automatic Control. Memberships: IEEE; Institute of Electrical Engineers of Japan; Society of Instrument and Control Engineers. Address: School of Bionics, Tokyo University of Technology, 1404-1 Katakura, Hachioji, Tokyo 192-0982, Japan. E-mail: she@cc.teu.ac.jp Website: www.teu.ac.jp/ikeoh/shehp/She.htm

SHEARER Alan, b. 1970, Gosforth, Newcastle upon Tyne. Footballer. Career: Coached as child at Wallsend Boys' Club; Striker; Played for Southampton, 1987-92, Blackburn Rovers, 1992-96; Signed by Newcastle United for world record transfer of £15 million (Captain), 1996; First played for England, 1992, Captain 1996-2000. Address: Newcastle United Football Club, St James Park, Newcastle Upon Tyne, NE1 4ST, England.

SHEDAKER Kathleen Edith, b. 2 May 1953, Boston, Massachusetts, USA. Publishing Executive. m. Jon Patterson Speller Sr, 1 son. Education: Associate in Business Administration, 2001, Bachelor in Business Management, 2003, Monroe College; Monroe College Co-operative Internship in International Law Research, 2001; Monroe College Co-operative Internship in

International Business Research, 2003. Appointments: Backster Research Foundation, San Diego, California, 1985; Associate Co-ordinator, Cleve Backster Lecture, Cosmos Club, Washington DC, 1985; Co-founder, Morning Star Chapel, 1986; Researcher, Press Office Saudi Arabia, New York City, 1986-96; Publisher, Morning Star Chapel and Press, New York City, 1986-; Researcher, Bosniac National Council of Sanjak Representative in the USA, 1996; Director, microgenepools.com, 2000-. Publications: Book, The American Dynasty, 1998; Research monograph, Micro Gene Pools, 2000; Article, Color and Race, 2003; Book, The Classic Seed, Money in Action, 2003. Honours: Morning Star Chapel, Interfaith Award, 1986; Honors Roll, Monroe College, 2000-2003; Recipient, Cold War Victory Medal, Anti-Communist International, 2000; Listed in Who's Who publications and biographical dictionaries. Membership: New York Genealogical and Biographical Society. Address: PO Box 1095, Grand Central Station, New York, NY 10163-1095, USA. E-mail: kshedaker@lycos.com

SHEEN Charlie, b. 3 September 1965, New York, USA. Actor. m. Donna Peele, 1995. Actor, TV films include: Silence of the Heart; The Boys Next Door; Films include: Apocalypse Now; Grizzly II; The Predator; The Red Dawn; Lucas; Platoon; The Wraith; Day Off; Young Guns; Wall Street; Eight Men Out; Major League; Backtrack; Men at Work; Courage Mountain; Navy Seals; The Rookie; Stockade (director); Secret Society; Hot Shots; Dead Fall; The Three Musketeers; The Chase; Major League II, 1994; Terminal Velocity, 1994; The Shadow Conspiracy, 1995; Shockwave, 1995; All Dogs Go to Heaven (voice), The Arrival, 1996; Money Talks, 1997; No Code of Conduct, 1998; Free Money, 1998; Letter From Death Row, 1998; Being John Malkovich, 1999; Cared X; Good Advice, 2000; Lisa Picard is Famous, 2001. Address: c/o Jeffrey Ballard Public Relations, 4814 Lemara Avenue, Sherman Oaks, CA 91403, USA.

SHEEN Martin (Ramon Estevez), b. 3 August 1940, Dayton, Ohio, USA. Actor. m. Janet Sheen, 1961, 3 sons, 1 daughter. Career: Actor, films include: The Incident; Catch 22; Rage; Badlands; Apocalypse Now; Enigma; Gandhi; The King of Prussia; The Championship Season; Man, Woman and Child; The Dead Zone; Final Countdown; Loophole; Wall Street; Night Beaker; Da, 1988; Personal Choice, 1989; Cadence (also director), 1990; Judgement in Berlin, 1990; Limited Time; The Maid, 1990; Cadence (also director), 1990; Hear No Evil; Hot Shots part Deux (cameo); Gettysburg, 1993; Trigger Fast; Hit!; Fortunes of War; Sacred Cargo; The Break; Dillinger and Capone; Captain Nuke and the Bomber Boys; Ghost Brigade; The Cradle Will Rock; Dead Presidents; Dorothy Day; Gospa; The American President; The War At Home; Spawn; Storm, Monument Avenue, Free Money; Lost & Found, 1999; Apocalypse New Redux, 2001; Catch Me If You Can, 2003; TV appearances include: The Defenders; East Side/West Side; My Three Sons; Mod Squad; Cannon; That Certain Summer; Missiles of October; The Last Survivors; Blind Ambition; Shattered Spirits; Nightbreaker; The Last POW?; Roswell; The West Wing; Stage appearances: The Connection (New York and European tours); Never Live Over A Pretzel Factory; The Subject was Roses; The Crucible. Honours include: Honorary Mayor of Malibu, 1989-; Golden Satellite Award, 2000; Golden Globe Award, 2000. Address: c/o Jeff Ballard, 4814 Lemara Avenue, Sherman Oaks, CA 91403, USA.

SHELDON Sidney, b. 11 February 1917, Chicago, Illinois, USA. Author. m. (1) Jorja Curtright, deceased 1985, 1 daughter (2) Alexandra Kostoff, 1989. Education: Northwestern University. Appointments: Served USAAF WWII; Former reader, Universal and 20th Century Fox Studios; Creator, writer and producer: Nancy; The Patty Duke Show; I Dream of Jeannie; Creator, Hart

to Hart (TV) show. Publications: Screenplays include: Billy Rose's Jumbo; The Bachelor and the Bobby Soxer, 1947; Easter Parade; Annie Get Your Gun; Dream Wife (also director); Buster Keaton Story (also director); Plays include: Roman Candle; Jackpot; Dream With Music; Alice in Arms; Redhead; Novels: The Naked Face, 1970; The Other Side of Midnight, 1975; A Stranger in the Mirror, 1976; Bloodline, 1977; Rage of Angels, 1980; Master of the Game, 1982; If Tomorrow Comes, 1985; Windmills of the Gods, 1987; Memories of Midnight, 1991; The Doomsday Conspiracy, 1991; The Stars Shine Down, 1992; Nothing Lasts Forever, 1994; Morning Moon and Night, 1995; The Best Laid Plans, 1997; Tell Me Your Dreams, 1998; The Sky is Falling, 2000. Honours: Academy Award for The Bachelor and the Bobby Soxer, 1947; Writers Guild of America Award for Easter Parade, 1948. Address: c/o William Morrow & Co, 1350 Avenue of the Americas, New York, NY 10019, USA.

SHELIHOVA Svetlana, b. 26 June 1971, Moscow, Russia. Illustrator. m. 1 son. Education: Graphics Faculty, Moscow Poligraph Institute, 1992-97. Appointment: Illustrator, TBWA advertising agency, 2001-. Publications: Participation in exhibitions of Russian women artists, Irida Art Association, 1997-2003; Personal doll exhibition, Shalyapins Museum, 2002. Honours: State Bakhrushins Museum Diploma for the "Doll Fantasy"; Vernacular Arts Fund Award for the work "Nomadic Theater"; Winner, art competition among Russian women artists, "Spring Salon", 1997, 1999. Address: Lyotnaya ul 34/2, 194 Mytischy, Moscow Region 141021, Russia. E-mail: sshelikhova@tbwa.ru

SHELLEY Clyde Burton, b. 21 March 1922, Murphy, Texas, USA. Artist. m. Rosamond Landry. Education: Ohio Wesleyan University, 1944-45; Art Center School, Los Angeles, 1957-58. Career: Apprentice Artist, art studio, Dallas; Artist, Interstate Theaters, Dallas; Served in US Navy, World War II; Art Editor, Cover Illustrator, Cartoonist, The Sky Ranger, Dallas Naval Air Station; Cartoonist, The Bulletin, Norfolk Receiving Station publication; Advertising syndicate, Dallas; Cartoonist, Oakite Products, New York, then Reddy Kilowatt Service; Freelance Cartoonist, various magazines and newspapers, companies, conventions; Cartoonist for Northrop Corporation and Douglas Aircraft Company, California, Created cartoon character Alfie Atom for security, safety and cost improvement posters, Holmes and Narver Inc, Atomic Energy Commission contractor; Cartoonist for The Breeze, Johnston Island, and Am-Chit-Sheet, Amchitka, Alaska; Developed editorial cartoons for Las Vegas Sun and Las Vegas Review-Journal; Most recently worked for The Houston Post. Publications include: Cartoons for American Magazine, Bluebrook Magazine, King Features Syndicate, AT and T, Las Vegas Sun and Las Vegas Review Journal, others; Comic strip in Pet Times; Caricatures; Paintings, mainly westerns and sports. Honours: Security Posters on display in Washington DC, featuring cartoon character Alfie Atom; Exhibit of western paintings, First City National Bank, Houston; 1985 and 1987 exhibits of paintings of well-known sports figures including Evander Holyfield, George Foreman and Rocky Marciano. Memberships: Member, Houston World Affairs Council, 1996-; Member, Houston Museum of Fine Arts; Member, American Legion. Address: 9443 Portal Drive, Houston, TX 77031-2212, USA.

SHELLEY John Philip Bernhard, b. 24 May 1932, London, England. Royal Photographer. m. Mary Elizabeth Lewis. Education: Scholarship to a Technical College; Trained as a Metallurgical and General Photographer, The Royal Military College of Science, Shrivenham University. Appointments: General Professional Photographer, 1948-; Photographer to Swindon Town Speedway, early 1950's; Royal Photographer, 1978-; Invited Manager, Leeds Cameras, Brunswick Centre, London, Mid 1970's-

80; Managing Director and Owner, J. S. Library International, London, 1978-; Managing Director and Owner, John Shelley Photographic Ltd, John Shelley Photography, John Shelley International, Library and Gallery International, Mayfair, London, 1980-81; Supplier of Photographic Services to Members of the Saudi Royal Family, 1970's; Private Photographer to Sir Lynden Pindling, Prime Minister of the Bahamas, 1980's; Many invited lectures, 1980-; Interviewed, photographed and prepared features on many authors and celebrities, 1990-; Exhibitions: First exhibited in 1952; Most recent exhibition: The Royal Jubilee Display, Foreign and Commonwealth Office, exhibited internationally in up to 180 countries world-wide, 2002. Publications: Numerous illustrations for books and magazines published throughout the world include: Books: The Man From Rome...The Pope in England, Scotland and Wales, 1982; Anne...The Working Princess, 1987; Down to Earth...His Royal Highness Prince Philip, 1988; Charles and Diana...A 10th Anniversary Celebration, 1991; Elizabeth by Sarah Bradford, cover and majority of colour photographs by John Shelley, 1996; Covers, features or photographs published in magazines including: Life Magazine, Time, Newsweek, Oggi, Paris Match, Figaro, Harpers, Tatler, Woman's Own, Woman, Woman's Realm, The London Illustrated News, Majesty, Royalty, Hello, Country Life, The Field, Radio Times; Posters, Calendars, Postcards, Diaries. Memberships: Swindon Town Young Conservatives, Chairman and Treasurer, early 1950's; NUPE, Local Branch, Swindon, Secretary, early 1950's; The Guards Polo Club, Windsor, 1981-; Association of Buckingham Palace Accredited Photographers, Invited Founder Member, Chairman and Secretary, early 1980's-.

SHEN Dingkun, b. 9 May 1935, Jiangsu, China. Professor. m. Zhou Shigui, 1 son, 1 daughter. Education: BS, Chemical Engineering, Lensoviet Institute of Chemical Technology, Russia, 1959; PhD, Material Science and Engineering, Institute of Chemical Technology, Prague, Czechoslovakia, 1965. Appointments: Assistant Professor, 1959-61, 1965-85, Associate Professor, 1985-90, Head of Department, 1987-, Professor, Chinese Academy of Sciences. Publications: 60 publications including: Sol-gel Process of PbO-B_2O_3-SiO_2, 1995. Honours: 1st Class Award, Ministry of Electronic Industry of China; 2nd Class Award, City of Shanghai. Membership: Chinese Ceramic Society. Address: 9-201 No 1661 Changning Road, Shanghai 200051, China. E-mail: sital@sh163.sta.net.cn

SHEN Jin, b. 25 February 1963, Zhejiang, China. Technology Manager. m. Pang Li, 1 son. Education: BSc, 1978-1982, MSc, 1982-1985, Department of Electrical Engineering, Zhejiang University, Hangzhou, China; Dr. Ing, Institute of Electrical Machines, Technical University of Berlin, Germany, 1988-1992. Appointments: Development Engineer, Zhejiang Household Motor Company, Huzhou, Zhejiang, China, 1982; Assistant, Department of Electrical Engineering, University of Zhejiang Hangzhou, China, 1985-88; Research Assistant, 1988-91, Research Associate, 1992-95, Institute of Electrical Machines, Technical University of Berlin, Germany; Project Leader, United Technologies Research Centre, UTC, East Hartford, CT, USA, 1992; R and D Engineer, Integrated Engineering Software, Winnipeg, Canada, 1995; Technical Staff, 1996, Project Leader, 1997-99, Senior Scientist/Referent, Group Manager, 2000-02, ABB Corporate Research, Ladenburg, Germany; Assistant Technology Manager, Business Unit Plant Automation, ABB Utility, Mannheim, Germany, 2002-. Publications: 20 Patents; 30 Scientific papers; 1 Technical Book. Memberships: IEEE; COMPUMAG Conference Editorial Board. Address: ABB Utility GmbH, Kallstadter Str 1, D-68309 Mannheim, Germany. E-mail: jin.shen@de.abb.com

SHENG Ching-Lai, b. 20 July 1919, Kahsing, Chekiang, China. Professor. m. Josephine Yu-Ying Chou, 2 sons, 3 daughters by 1st marriage. Education: BSc, National Chiao Tung University, Shanghai, 1941; PhD, University of Edinburgh, Scotland, 1948. Appointments: Professor, National Taiwan University, University of Ottawa, University of Windsor; President, National Chiao Tung University, Hsin-Chu, Taiwan; Chair Professor, Professor Emeritus, Tamkang University. Publications: Over 120 articles in professional journals; 8 monographs including: Threshold Logic, 1969; A New Approach to Utilitarianism, 1991; On the Regulation of Capital, 1995; A Utilitarian General Theory of Value, 1998; An Introduction to Unified Utilitarian Theory, 2000; A Defence of Utilitarianism, 2004. Honour: Sun Yat-Sen Cultural Foundation Prize for Scholarly Publication, 1972. Memberships: Philosophical Association of China, Canada, England, USA. Address: 8F 16 Lane 51, Pao-Shun Road, Yung-Ho, Taipei, Taiwan, 234, Republic of China.

SHENGELIA Ramaz, b. 28 September 1952, Tbilisi, Georgia. Physician. m. Nana Mosidze, 21 November 1982, 1 son. Education: Surgeon, Tbilisi State Medical University, 1975; Arts Faculty, Tbilisi State University, 1975; MD, PhD, 1984; DSc, Professor, 1997. Appointments: Senior Surgeon, 1984, Head, Chair of History of Medicine, Professor, 1991-, Tbilisi State Medical University. Publications: Several articles in professional medical journals; Collection of ghost stories. Honours: Medal for Unique Surgical Operation at 4000m above Sea Level, 1977; Medal, Zaza Phanaskerteli Tsitsishvili, 1994; Medal, Al Jazar, 1998; Listed in national and international biographical dictionaries. Memberships: Councillor of Administrative Council, International Society of History of Medicine; Georgian Academy of Medical Sciences; New York Academy of Sciences; Peter The Great Academy of Sciences and Art, Russia. Address: 11 Tamarashvili Street, 0162 Tbilisi, Georgia.

SHENK Carolyn, b. 10 February 1934, Valley View, Pennsylvania, USA. Nurse; International Service Worker. m. Ellis Shenk, 2 sons, 3 daughters. Education: Registered Nurse; Teacher of Stress Reduction, Omega University Course; Reiki Master; Personal education by experience in international situations. Appointments: Nurse, Washington DC, USA; Nurse, Midwife in rural Puerto Rico on 2 occasions; Refugee Resettlement Programme, Sardinia, Italy; Home School Teacher with World Vision, Bangladesh; Nurse In Ecuador; Nurse in USA; Student of esoteric wisdom and seeker of world understanding; Retired Volunteer; Reiki Master. Publications: Articles in various small publications. Memberships: Various groups and organisations. Address: 955H Hillswood Road, 9A, Bel Air, MD 21014, USA. E-mail: ellisshenk@spiritmail.com

SHEPARD Sam, (Samuel Shepard Rogers), b. 5 November 1943, Fort Sheridan, Illinois, USA. Dramatist; Actor. m. O-Lan Johnson Dark, 9 November 1969, divorced, 1 son; 1 son, 1 daughter with Jessica Lange. Education: Mount San Antonio Junior College, Walnut, California, 1961-62. Career: Plays: Cowboys, Rock Garden, 1964; 4-H Club, 1965; Up to Thursday, 1965; Rocking Chair, 1965; Chicago, 1965; Icarus's Mother, 1965; Fourteen Hundred Thousand, 1966; Red Cross, 1966; Melodrama Play, 1966; La Turista, 1967; Cowboys #2, 1967; Forensic and the Navigators, 1967; The Holy Ghostly, 1969; The Unseen Hand, 1969; Operation Sidewinder, 1970; Shaved Splits, 1970; Mad Dog Blues, 1971; Terminal, 1971; Cowboy Mouth (with Patti Smith), 1971; Black Bog Beast Bait, 1971; The Tooth of Crime, 1972; Blue Bitch, 1973; Nightwalk (with Megan Terry and Jean-Claude van Itallie), 1973; Geography of a Horse Dreamer, 1974; Little Ocean, 1974; Action, 1974; Killer's Head, 1974; Suicide in B-Flat, 1976; Angel City, 1976; Curse of the Starving Class, 1977; Buried Child, 1978; Tongues, 1979; Savage/Love, 1979; Seduced,

1979; True West, 1981; Fool for Love, 1983; Superstitions, 1983; The Sad Lament of Pecos Bill on the Eve of Killing his Wife, 1983; A Lie of the Mind, 1985; States of Shock, 1991; Simpatico, 1993; TV: Lily Dale, 1996; Purgatory, 1999; Hamlet, 2000; Films: Days of Heaven; Frances; The Right Stuff; Country; Crimes of the Heart; Baby Boom; Defenceless, 1989; Voyager; Thunderheart, 1992; The Pelican Brief, 1994; Safe Passage, 1995; The Good Old Boys, 1995; Curtain Call, 1997; The Only Thrill, 1997; Snow Falling on Cedars, 1999; One Kill, 2000; Shot in the Heart, 2001; Swordfish, 2001; The Pledge, 2001. Publications: A Murder of Crows, novel, 1996; Cruising Paradise, short stories, 1996. Honours: Obie Awards, 1966, 1966, 1966, 1968, 1973, 1975, 1977, 1979, 1984; Rockefeller Foundation Grant, 1967; Guggenheim Fellowships, 1968, 1971; National Institute and American Academy of Arts and Letters Award, 1974; Creative Arts Award, Brandeis University, 1975; Pulitzer Prize in Drama, 1979; New York Drama Critics' Circle Award, 1986. Memberships: American Academy of Arts and Letters; Theater Hall of Fame. Address: c/o International Creative Management, 8942 Wilshire Boulevard, Beverly Hills, CA 90211, USA.

SHEPHARD Gillian Patricia (Rt Hon), b. 22 January 1940, Great Britain. Politician. m. Thomas Shephard, 1975, 2 step sons. Education: St Hilda's College, Oxford. Appointments: Schools Inspector and Education Officer, 1963-75; Cambridge University Extra Mural Board Lecturer, 1965-87; Norfolk County Council, 1977-89; For Norfolk County Council: Chair of Social Services Committee, 1978-83; Education Committee, 1983-85; Chair, West Norfolk and Wisbech Health Authority, 1981-85; Norwich Health Authority, 1985-87; Conservative MP South West Norfolk, 1987-97, Norfolk South West, 1997-; Parliamentary Private Secretary to Economic Secretary to the Treasury, 1988-89; Parliamentary Under Secretary of State, Department of Social Security, 1989-90; Treasury Minister of State, 1990-92; Employment Secretary of State, 1992-93, for Agriculture, Fisheries and Food, 1993-94, For Education, 1995; For Education and Employment, July 1995; Women's National Commission Co-Chair, 1990-91. Publication: Shephard's Watch, 2000. Memberships: Council Member, University of Oxford, 2000-. Honour: Honorary Fellow, St Hilda's College, Oxford, 1991. Address: House of Commons, London SW1A 0AA, England.

SHEPPARD David (Stuart) (Lord Sheppard of Liverpool), b. 6 Mar 1929, Reigate, Surrey, England. Retired Bishop; Writer. m. Grace Isaac, 19 June 1957, 1 daughter. Education: MA, Trinity Hall, Cambridge. Appointments: Ridley Hall Theological College Assistant Curate, St Mary's, Islington, 1955-57; Warden, Mayflower Family Centre, Canning Town, 1957-69; Bishop Suffragan, Woolwich, 1969-75; Bishop of Liverpool, 1975-97; Chairman, Martin Luther King Foundation, 1970-75, General Synod Board for Social Responsibility, 1991-96; Chairman, Churches' Enquiry into Unemployment and the Future of Work, 1995-97; President, Sussex County Cricket Club, 2001-03. Publications: Parson's Pitch, 1964; Built as a City, 1974; Bias to the Poor, 1983; The Other Britain, 1984; Better Together (with D Worlock), 1988; With Christ in the Wilderness (with D Worlock), 1990; With Hope in Our Hearts (with D Worlock), 1994; Steps Along Hope Street, 2002. Honours: Honorary LLD, University of Liverpool, 1981; Honorary Fellow, Trinity Hall, Cambridge, 1983; Honorary DTech, Liverpool Polytechnic, 1987; Honorary DD, University of Cambridge, 1991; Honorary DD, University of Exeter, 1998; Freedom, City of Liverpool, 1995; Life Peerage, 1998; Honorary DUniv, Open University 1999; Honorary DD, University of Wales, 2000. Address: Ambledown, 11 Melloncroft Drive, West Kirby, Merseyside L48 2JA, England.

SHER Antony, b. 14 June 1949, Cape Town, South Africa. Actor; Artist; Author. Career: Films: Shadey; the Young Poisoner's Handbook; Alive and Kicking; Mrs Brown; Shakespeare in Love; TV appearances include: The History Man; Collision Course; The Land of Dreams; Genghis Cohn; The Moon Stone; Plays include: John, Paul, Ringo and Bert; Teeth n' Smiles; Cloud Nine; A Prayer for My Daughter; Goosepimples; King Lear; Tartuffe; Richard II; Merchant of Venice; The Revenger's Tragedy; Hello and Goodbye; Singer; Tamburlaine the Great; Travesties; Cyrano de Bergerac; The Winter's Tale; Torch Song Trilogy; True West; Arturo Ui; Uncle Vanya; Titus Andronicus; Stanley; Mahler's Conversion; ID, 2003; The Malcontent. Publications: Year of the King, 1986; Middlepost, 1988; Characters, 1989; Changing Steps (Screenplay), 1989; The Indoor Boy, 1991; Cheap Drives, 1995; Woza Shakespeare! (co-author), 1996; The Feast, 1998; Beside Myself (autobiography), 2001. Honours: Best Actor Awards, Drama Magazine, London Standard Awards, 1985; Olivier Award for Best Actor, Society of West End Theatres, 1985, 1997; Best Actor Award, Martini TMA Awards, 1996; Peter Sellers Evening Standard Film Award, 1998; Honorary D Litt (Liverpool), 1998. Address: c/o ICM, Oxford House, 76 Oxford Street, London W1N 0AX, England.

SHER Emmanuil Moiseyevich, b. 29 March 1929, Port Khorly, Ukraine. Physicist Researcher. m. Elena, 1 son. Education: BS, Moscow State University, 1951; Physicist, St Petersburg State University, 1952; PhD, Physical Electronics, 1967; DSc, Physics of Semiconductors and Dielectrics, 1983. Appointments: Senior Engineer, Vacuum Technology, 1952-59; Researcher, Senior Scientific Researcher, Leading Scientific Researcher, Physics of Thermoelectricity, Electron Emission, High Temperature Superconductors and Thin Solid Films, 1959-. Publications: 100 articles, 21 patents, scientific editor of 2 books. Honours: Bronze Medal, 1963, Silver Medal, 1983; Honorary Academician, International Academy of Refrigeration, 1999. Memberships: AF Ioffe Physico-Technical Institute, Russian Academy of Sciences, 1959-; International Thermoelectric Society, 1991; New York Academy of Sciences, 1996. Address: 20 Orbely Str, apt 73, 194223 St Petersburg, Russia. E-mail: em.sher@mail.ioffe.ru

SHERMAN William David, Poet; Writer. Education: MA, PhD, English, State University of New York at Buffalo. Appointments: Lecturer in American Studies, University of Hull, 1967-68; Lecturer, Department of English, UCW, Aberystwyth, 1969-72. Publications: The Horses of Gwyddno Garanhir, 1976; Tahitian Journals, 1990; From the South Seas, 1997. Contributions to: Exquisite Corpse; Fire; Spanner; Poetry Review; Branch Redd. Honour: Poetry Prize, Royal Albert Hall Reading, 1995. Address: 9300 Atlantic Avenue #218, Margate, NJ 08402, USA.

SHEROTSKY Priscilla Colleen Ekblad, b. 6 May 1943, Colorado, USA. Artist. m. George Demetrius Sherotsky, 12 July 1969, 1 son. Education: Freefall Writing in 1994 with Barbara Turner-Vesselago; Toronto based Cambridge PhD, 1994; Design Graduate, Cornish College of the Arts, 1962-65; Pacific Rim Cultures, Burke Museum, University of Washington, 1974; Scientific Illustration, University of Washington, 1977-78; Arts Management, Seattle University, 1980. Career: Designer, Walter Dorwin Teague Inc, 1966-68; Manager, Sun Valley Flower Shop, Idaho, 1968; Visual Merchandising/Display Art, 1968-; Docent, The Burke Museum, 1973-75; Designer, University of Washington, Medical Illustration and Learning Resources, 1977; Panaca/ Bellevue Art Museum Gallery, Bellevue, Washington, 1978-81; Self-employed, Scientific Illustration, Design, Graphics, Fine Art, and Research for marketing with academic and commercial Research Studies, 1979-; The Frye Museum "Northwest Annual", Seattle Washington, 1981; Tolles Gallery, Mercer Island,

Washington, 1980-83; Solo exhibit, Overlake Hospital, 1982-83; Lakeshore Gallery, Pelican Wharf, Kirkland, Washington, 1982-86; 100 Image Card Art and Distribution, 1993-95; Artifacts Gallery, San Juan Islands, Eastsound, Washington, 1997; The Museum Depot, juried in Anacortes, Washington, 1998; Anacortes Art Walk, The Keystone Design Centre, Anacortes, Washington, 1998; allsations Art Therapy emerged 1998; EAFA, juried for Meydenbauer Centre, Bellevue, Washington, 1999 and The Hyatt Winter Garden, Bellevue, Washington, 2000; Music and Art, Skagit Valley Youth Symphony, Sharyn Peterson, Conductor, 1999; Eastside Association of Fine Arts, 23rd Annual Exhibition, juried for the Issaqrah Gallery, Washington, 1999 and 24th Annual Exhibition at the Redmond Arts Centre, 2000; Puget Sound Sumi Artists, juried art at Mercer View Community Centre, MI, Washington, 2000; Artful Style Inc, juried art for Manhattan Beach, California internet site, 2000-02; Checkers Gallery presents the National League of American Pen Women at Poulsbo, 2002, collaborative art of poems, paintings and prose; Mixed-media painter with various exhibits most recently, Annie Wright School Exhibit, What is Sumi?, Tacoma, Washington, 2002; South Seattle Community College Campus Gallery, 2002; Sandpiper Gallery, Tacoma, Washington, 2002; Amy Burnett Gallery, Bremerton Washington, 2003; Karpeles Manuscript Museum, Tacoma, Washington, 2003; Hanford Gallery, Tacoma, Washington, 2002; Fisher Pavilion at the Seattle Center in Washington, 2003. Publications: Published paintings in art and poetry quarterly, Chiyo's Corner, 1999-2002; Published Art Cards/SIGDFA limited edition, 1993-95; Writer of articles published in New Age Times and Eastside Journal 1994-97; Author, Brusseled Sprouts and sulphur, Road Pressed Publishing, 1997. Honours: Frye Museum, Northwest Artists, 1981; Published Artist of the Year, Chiyo's Corner, 2001; Listed in national and international biographical dictionaries. Memberships: Elected, New York Academy of Science, 1989; Master Restoration Council Officer and Board Member, 1995-97; PTSA, Cultural Arts Chair, 1978-79; Co-Chaired Northwest Boychoir sponsored Painting Exhibition, 1979; PTSA Legislative Chair, 1987; Citizens' Advisory Council Board Officer at School District, 1983-985; Appointed to Legislative Coalition, 1986; 2001 Research and Development for the Arts at Lake Washington School District, 1984-86; Elected, EAFA Board Member, 2001; Elected PSSA Board Member, 2002; Newly elected Vice-President, Exhibits at Puget Sound Sumi Artists. Address: PO Box 2951, Kirkland, WA 98083, USA. E-mail: allsations@excite.com

SHERRIN Ned, (Edward George Sherrin), b. 18 February 1931, Low Ham, Somerset, England. Director; Producer; Writer. Education: MA, University of Oxford; Barrister-at-Law. Publications: Cindy-Ella (with Caryl Brahms), 1962; Rappel 1910 (with Caryl Brahms), 1964; Benbow Was His Name (with Caryl Brahms), 1967; Ooh La (with Caryl Brahms), 1973; After You Mr Feydeau (with Caryl Brahms), 1975; A Small Thing Like an Earthquake, 1983; Song by Song (with Caryl Brahms), 1984; Cutting Edge, 1984; 1956 and All That (with Neil Shand), 1984; The Metropolitan Mikado (with Alistair Beaton), 1985; Too Dirty for the Windmill (with Caryl Brahms), 1986; Loose Neds, 1990; Theatrical Anecdotes, 1991; Ned Sherrin in His Anecdotage, 1993; The Oxford Dictionary of Humorous Quotations, 1994; Sherrin's Year, diary, 1996; Scratch an Actor, novel, 1996. Honour: Commander of the Order of the British Empire. Address: 4 Cornwall Mansions, Ashburnham Road, London SW10 0PE, England.

SHERROD Philip Lawrence, b. 12 October 1935. Artist; Painter; Poet. Education: BS, Science, Zoology, 1957, BA, Art, Painting, 1959, Oklahoma State University; Art Students League, New York, Art, Painting, 1961-63. Appointments: Teacher, Life Class – oil,

Morristown Art Association, New Jersey, 1973-74; New Jersey Center for Visual Arts, 1977-; Art Students League, New York, 1984-; National Academy of Design, School of Fine Arts, New York City, 1993-. Creative Works: Museum Collections include: Phillips Exedir Academy, Exedir, New Hampshire; Tulane University Museum (Women's Branch), New Orleans, Louisiana; Hirshhorn Museum, Smithsonian Institute, Washington DC; Museum of Fine Art, Springfield, Massachusetts; Everhart Museum, Scranton, Pennsylvania; Rose Art Museum, Brandeis University, Massachusetts; AlmsFord House, Fine Arts Center, Anderson, Indiana; Herbert Johnson Museum, Cornell University, Ithaca, New York; Work in corporate collections: American Broadcasting (ABC); Paramount Pictures Production; INA Corporation; Customs Communications Systems Inc; Montgomery Securities, San Francisco, California, and New York; Also in private collections; Exhibitions include: Art Students League, 1980-; National Academy School of Design: School of Fine Arts (Instructors Exhibition) New York City, 1983-; National Academy of Design Museum, 174th Annual Exhibition, New York City, 1973-; American Academy of Arts & Letters (International Exhibitions), 1975, 1976, 1977, 1995, 1996; Federation of Modern Painters & Sculptors (Exhibitions), 1990, 1992, 1993, 1994, 1996, 1998, 2000, 2002, 2003; Street Painters, Cork Gallery, Lincoln Center, New York City, 1981-. Publications: 5 books of poetry and poems in 130 anthologies. Honours: Grants and scholarships including: American Academy of Arts and Letters (Childe Hassam Purchase Awards) 1967, 1969, 1974; Creative Public Service Grant, 1980; Adolph/Esther Gottlieb Foundation Grant, 1981, 1988, 1996; Academy in Rome (Prix de Roma) Fellowship, (New York City, Rome) 1985-86; The Pollack-Krasner Foundation Inc Grant, 1989. Address: 41 West 24th Street 4th Fl, New York, NY 10010-3210, USA.

SHETTIMA Saidu Abdulkadir, b. 10 February 1961, Bauchi, Nigeria. Academic. m. Hadiza Abdulkadir, 4 sons, 2 daughters. Education: BSc (Hons), Chemistry, 1984, Postgraduate Diploma in Education, 1991, Postgraduate Diploma in Public Administration, 1991, MSc, Chemistry, 1994, PhD, Pharmaceutical Chemistry, 2003, Ahmadu Bello University, Zaria, Nigeria. Appointments: Assistant Lecturer, 1985; Lecturer III, 1988; Lecturer II, 1991; Principal Planning Officer (Research), 1993; Senior Lecturer, 1995; Principal Lecturer, 1998; Chief Lecturer, 2002; Head, Department of Science Laboratory Technology, 1995-2001; Director School of Science Technology, 1999-2001; Deputy Rector, 2002-, Acting Rector, 2001, 2002, Federal Polytechnic, Damaturu, Nigeria. Publications: Textbooks: Essentials for Research Methodology, 2001; Introductory Practical Chemistry: Theory and Practice, in press; 10 national and international journal papers; 16 national and international conference and seminar papers. Honour: Award for the Best Academic Staff, Academic Staff Union of the Polytechnic, 2002; Memberships: Member, West African Society of Pharmacology; Council Member, Chemical Society of Nigeria; Associate Member, National Institute of Science and Technology; President, National Association of Allied Science and Technology; Full Member, Nigerian Institute of Management; Council Member, Nigerian Corrosion Association. Address: Federal Polytechnic Damaturu, PMB 1006, Damaturu, Yobe State, Nigeria. E-mail: saidu_shettima@yahoo.co.uk

SHI Feng, b. 1 July 1949, Tianjin, China. Linguistics. m. Meihua Tian, 1 son. Education: Harbin Normal University, 1979; MA, Chinese People University, Beijing, 1982; PhD, Nankai University, 1990. Appointments: Faculty, Tianjin Foreign Language College, 1982-85; Teacher, Nankai University, 1985, Professor, Chinese Linguistics and Phonetics, Nankai University, 1993; Professor, Beijing Language and Culture University, 1993; Research Fellow, City University of Hong Kong, 1995; Professor, Nagoya Gakuin University, Japan, 1998; Dean, International College of Chinese

Studies, Nankai University, 2001-. Publications: 8 books and over 60 articles in professional journals. Address: International College of Chinese Studies, Nankai University, Tianjin, China.

SHIBAMOTO Yuta, b. 13 December 1955, Kakogawa, Japan. Educator; Radiation Oncologist. m. Hiromi Yanagawa, 1 son, 2 daughters. Education: MD, 1980, DrMedSc, 1987, Kyoto University. Appointments: Assistant Professor, Lecturer, Associate Professor, Kyoto University; Professor, Chairman, Nagoya City University. Honour: Hanns-Langendorff Prize, 1992. Membership: Japanese Society for Therapeutic Radiology and Oncology. Address: Department of Radiology, Nagoya City University Graduate School of Medical Sciences, Japan.

SHIBAYAMA Hiroshi, b. 15 December 1919, Kyoto, Japan. Professor Emeritus. m. Chieko Kubo, 3 November 1949, deceased 27 January 1984. Education: BE, 1942, DEng, 1962, Electrical Engineering, Kyoto University, Japan. Appointments: Research Engineer, Mitsubishi Electric Corporation, Itami, Hyogo, Japan, 1942-46; Teacher, Rakuyo High School, Kyoto, 1946-50; Lecturer, 1950-56, Assistant Professor, 1956-62, Professor, 1962-90; Visiting Professor, 1990-92; Professor Emeritus, 1992-, Electrical Engineering, Osaka Institute of Technology. Publications: IRE Transactions on Circuit Theory, 1960; Proceedings of International Symposium of Nonlinear Oscillations, Kiev, 1963; Transactions of Institute of Electronics, Information and Communication Engineers, Japan, 1991. Honours: Commended in Public for Services to Industrial Education by the Minister of Education, Japan, 1984; Decorated, 4th Order of Sacred Treasure by the Emperor of Japan, 1993. Memberships: Institute of Electrical Engineers of Japan; Institute of Electronics, Information and Communications Engineers. Address: KouriMinamino-cho 28-24-806, Neyagawa, Osaka 572-0084, Japan.

SHIBUE Yasuhiro, b. 9 September 1955, Osaka, Japan. University Professor. m. Yumiko Yanai, 1 son, 1 daughter. Education: BSc, 1979, MSc, 1981, PhD, 1986, University of Tokyo. Appointments: Research Assistant, 1987-88, Assistant Professor, 1988-90, Associate Professor, 1990-99, Professor, 1999-, Hyogo University of Teacher Education. Publications: Mineralization and Transportation of Tungsten in Hydrothermal Solution: Some Studies on Several Japanese Tungsten Deposits; Cation Exchange Properties of Phillipsite: The Difference Between Si-rich and Si-poor Phillipsites. Memberships: The Geochemical Society; American Geophysical Union; The Japanese Association of Mineralogists, Petrologists and Economic Geologists. Address: Geoscience Institute, Hyogo University of Teacher Education, Yashiro, Kato-gun, Hyogo 673 1494 Japan. E-mail: yshibue@sci.hyogo-u.ac.jp

SHIEH Wung Yang, b. 22 September 1956, Taipei, Taiwan. Professor. m. Jiin Jiun Leu, 2 sons, 1 daughter. Education: Master's Degree, University of Tokyo, 1986; Doctor's Degree, 1989. Appointments: Associate Professor, 1989-94, Professor, 1994- Institute of Oceanography, National Taiwan University, Taipei. Publications: Contribution of articles to professional journals including International Journal of Systemic and Evolutionary Microbiology and Canadian Journal of Microbiology. Memberships: The Japanese Society of Microbial Ecology; The Chinese Society of Microbiology. Address: Institute of Oceanography, National Taiwan University, PO Box 23-13, Taipei, Taiwan. E-mail: winyang@ntu.edu.tw.

SHIEL Derek Alexander George, b. 18 April 1939, Dublin, Ireland. Painter; Writer; Sculptor; Landscape Designer; Lecturer; Curator; Psychotherapist. Education: Fettes College, Edinburgh; Edinburgh College of Art, 1956-61; Diploma of Art, 1960;

Travelling Scholarship to USA, 1961-62. Appointments: Art Tutor, Berkshire College of Art, 1963-65; Art Tutor, West Sussex College of Art, 1964-69; Lecturer in Art Appreciation and Art Tutor, The City Literary Institute, London, 1965-77. Landscape Gardener/Designer, 1978-98. Theatre: Writer and Director, 1980-2004; wrote stage adaptation of Gogol's The Overcoat; wrote and directed, Which One of Me?, performed in 5 European countries; wrote and directed, Landing Site; currently writing opera libretto for Composer Tazul Tajuddin; directed puppet play, The Way to St Bernard; co-directed improvised production of Bluebeard; Director and Actor/Puppeteer for Hilary Pepler Celebration, Ditchling Museum, East Sussex. Exhibitions: paintings, sound sculpture, works in theatre, landscape design, colour structures with living plants, held in Britain and Europe. Music: Originator/Percussionist with Nicky Heinen and Trevor Taylor in Shiel's trio, Sculpted Sound, performing at museums, art galleries, theatres, festivals; fourteen composers have so far written for Shiel's sound sculptures; Painter/Performer with Composer Julia Usher in their duo, SoundPaint, performances at art and music festivals, universities, conferences. Psychotherapist and participant in the Men's Movement; articles in magazines, Wingspan (USA), Achilles Heel (UK); Founder of the Men's Databank. Publications: essay in Fathers and Sons, 1995; Co-author, David Jones: The Maker Unmade, 1995 (2nd edition, 2003); Editor, David Jones: Ten Letters, 1996; essay in The Chesterton Review, David Jones Special Issue, 1997; essay in Diversity in Unity, 2000; essay in David Jones in Ditchling, 2003; Author, Arthur Giardelli, Paintings, Constructions, Relief Sculptures, Conversations with Derek Shiel, 2001. Curator of exhibitions: Arthur Giardelli, National Library of Wales, 2002; Co-curator, David Jones in Ditchling, Ditchling Museum, 2003. Lecturer: lectures at art galleries, museums, universities, on David Jones, Arthur Giardelli or Sound Sculptures. Honour: First Artist-in-Residence, Estorick Collection of Modern Italian Art, London, 2000. Membership: P.E.N. Address: 25 Randolph Crescent, London W9 1DP, England.

SHIH Frank Yeong-Chyang, b. 11 June 1957, Taiwan. Professor. m. An-Ling Huang, 1 son, 1 daughter. Education: BS, National Cheng-Kung University, Taiwan, 1980; MS, State University of New York, Stony Brook, 1984; PhD, Purdue University, 1987. Appointments: Systems Engineer, China Steel Incorporated, 1982-83; Research Assistant, Purdue University, 1984-87; Assistant Professor, 1988-93, Associate Professor, 1993-98, New Jersey Institute of Technology; Visiting Research Fellow, Air Force Rome Laboratory, New York, 1995; Guest Professor, Project Co-ordinator, National Taiwan University, 1995-96; Professor, New Jersey Institute of Technology, 1998-. Publications: Over 120 articles in professional journals and conferences. Honours include: Merit Awards, New Jersey Institute of Technology, 1988-98; Research Initiation Award, National Science Foundation, 1991. Membership: IEEE. Address: 153 Sun Valley Way, Morris Plains, NJ 07950-2017, USA.

SHIKITA Minoru, b. 13 February 1932, Japan. Lawyer; Executive of International Organisations. m. Hideko Shikita, 2 daughters. Education: Law degree, Kyushu University, Japan, 1954; Judicial Training Institute of Supreme Court of Japan, 1954-56; Graduate Study at Harvard Law School, 1957-58. Appointments: Appointed Public Prosecutor of Japan, 1956; Head, Crime Prevention and Criminal Justice Branch of UN Secretariat, 1982-86; Chairman, UN Committee on Crime Prevention and Control, 1987-89; Superintending Prosecutor, Nagoya High Public Prosecutors Office, 1993-95; President, Asia Crime Prevention Foundation, 1995-; Vice-President, International Association of Prosecutors, 1996-. Publications: Comparative Study of Traffic Offences Adjudication System, 1959; Crime and Criminal Policy in Japan, 1992; Prosecution in Asia, 1998; Numerous others in criminology and criminal policy. Honours: Testimonial from UN Secretary General for contribution to UN Crime Program, 1992; Honorary Professor, East China University of Law, Shanghai, 1999. Memberships: International Penal and Penitentiary Foundation, Vice-President; Asia Crime Prevention Foundation, president; International Association of Prosecutors, Vice President. Address: Apt 1102, 1-2-9 Katase Kaigan, Fujisawa, Kanagawa, Japan 251-0035.

SHILSON Wayne Stuart, b. 14 July 1943, Minnesota, USA. Artist; Art Teacher. m. Kathleen Shilson, 2 daughters. Education: BS, 1971, MFA, 1972, University of Minnesota. Appointments: Art Laboratory Assistant, University of Minnesota, 1970-71; Art Consultant, Designer, Impulse Art Gallery, 1971; Artist-Illustrator, Honeywell, Minnesota, 1974-96; Illustrator, Keyliner, Nokomis Newspaper, 1979-80; Illustrator, Artist, Red Bridge Inn, 1994-95; Graphic Artist, Bemidji Pioneer Newspaper, Minnesota, 1997-99; Illustrator, Layout, Weber Company, Wisconsin, 1995-96; Art Director, Top Dog Productions, 1996-97; Teacher-Art Teacher, Pine Point School, Ponsford, Minnesota, 1998-99. Civic Activities: Board Member, Judge, North Country Museum of Arts. Honours: Sky 1976 Merit for Painting; Art Centre of Minnesota Merit; STC 1983 First Place; Minnesota State Fair Merit, 1990; Second Place, Painting, Egan Rotary Club, 1990; STC 1991 Award of Excellence; STC 1992 Award of Achievement; Regent Two Arts Grant Recipient, Bemidji, Minnesota, 1998. Memberships: American Watercolor Society; American Wildlife Artists. Commissions and Creative Works: Collectors include many of americas large corporations and many fine private collections. Address: 17767 Emerald Island Circle, Park Rapids, MN 56470, USA. Wesite: geocities.com/shilsonart

SHIMADA Atsuyoshi, b. 12 February 1963, Tsuna County, Hyogo Prefecture, Japan. Neuropathologist; Researcher. m. Yoshie Hashimoto, 1 son. Education: MD, 1988, Doctor of Medical Science, 1992, Kyoto University, Japan; Physician's License, Japan, 1988; Education Commission for Foreign Medical Graduates Certificate, 1995; Neuropathology Clinical Fellowship Training Program, Columbia University, USA, 1995-97. Appointments: Postdoctoral Fellow, Japan Society for the Promotion of Science, Kyoto, Japan, 1992-93; Visiting Fellow, National Institute of Health, Baltimore, USA, 1993-95; Postdoctoral Residency Fellow, Columbia-Presbyterian Medical Center, New York, USA, 1995-97; Postdoctoral Research Scientist, Columbia University, New York, 1997; Research Associate, Nagasaki University, Nagasaki, Japan, 1998; Laboratory Director, Institute for Developmental Research, Aichi Human Service Center, Kasugai, Japan, 1998-. Publications: Book chapter in: Pathobiology of the Aging Mouse Vol 2, 1996; Articles in scientific journals including: Journal of Neuropathology and Experimental Neurology, 1992; Brain Research, 1993; Neuroscience, 1994; European Journal of Pharmacology, 1994; Neurobiology of Aging, 1997, 1999; Journal of Neuroscience, 1998; Acta Neuropathologica, 1999; Journal of Gerontology, 2002; Synapse, 2003. Honours: Listed in Marquis Who's Who publications and biographical dictionaries. Memberships: Trustee, Japan Society of Pathology; Trustee, Japanese Society of Neuropathology; Japan Society for Biomedical Gerontology; Society for Neuroscience; Japan Neuroscience Society; American Society for Investigative Pathology. Address: Institute for Developmental Research, Aichi Human Service Center, 713-8 Kamiya, Kasugai, Aichi 480-0392, Japan.

SHIN Ilsoon, b. 18 July 1939, South Korea. Educator. m. Kyecha Shin, 13 May 1971, 2 sons, 1 daughter. Education: PhD, Columbia Pacific University, 1987; EdD, University of Sarasota, 1999; PhD, Walden University, 1999. Appointments: Public School Teacher,

South Korea, 1957-71; Professor, Kunsan College, Korea, 1973-78; Professor, Defense Language Institute, Foreign Language Centre, 1985-99; Director, Korean Language Programme, Harvard University, 1998-99. Publications: Articles include: Classroom Observation; Sweeping the Darkness, 1998; Harvard Grammar Korean, 1999. Honours: Numerous honours and awards; DLIFLC. Memberships: Korean Language Professors Association; Harvard Facility Member. Address: 1101 David Ave, Pacific Grove, CA 93950, USA.

SHINAISHIN Mervat Abd El-Monem, b. 6 December 1945, Tala-Menofia, Egypt. Professor of Nuclear Engineering. Education: BSc, Nuclear Engineering Department, University of Alexandria, Egypt, 1968; MSc, Mechanical Nuclear Engineering Department, Ohio State University, USA, 1973; PhD, Nuclear Engineering Department, University of Arizona, Tucson, Arizona, USA, 1976. Appointments: Researcher, 1969-71, Assistant Professor, 1976-82, Associate Professor, 1982-89, Reactors Department, Atomic Energy Authority, Inshas, Egypt; Professor, National Centre for Nuclear Safety, Cairo, Egypt, 1989-. Publications include: Articles in scientific journals including: IEEE Nuclear Transactions; The Journal of Nuclear Safety; Nuclear Science and Engineering; Articles in proceedings of conferences held in Egypt, France, Japan, USA. Honours: Egypt State Award in Engineering; First Rank "Naut" of Distinction from the President of Egypt; Woman of the Year 2003, ABI, USA. Address: Building No 15B, Sarai El-Kobba St, Cairo, Egypt.

SHINAWATRA Thaksin, b. 26 July 1949, Chiangmai Province, Thailand. Prime Minister of Thailand. m. Khunying Potjaman Shinawatra, 1 son, 2 daughters. Education: Graduate, Police Academy, Thailand, 1973; Master Degree in Criminal Justice, Eastern Kentucky University, USA, 1975; Doctorate Degree in Criminal Justice, Sam Houston State University, USA, 1978. Appointments: Royal Thai Police Department, 1973-87; Founder, Shinawatra Computer and Communications Group, 1987-94; Founder, THAICOM Foundation, long distance satellite education programme, 1993; Established Thai Rak Thai Party and Leader of Thai Rak Tai Party, 1998-; 23rd Prime Minister of Thailand, 2001-. Honours: Royal Decorations: Knight Grand Cordon (Special Class) of the Most Noble Order of the Crown of Thailand, 1995; Knight Grand Cordon (Special Class), Most Exalted Order of the White Elephant, 1996; Knight Grand Cross (First Class), Most Admirable Order of the Direkgunabhorn, 2001; Knight Grand Commander, Most Illustrious Order of Chula Chom Klao, 2002; Foreign Decorations: The Royal Order of Sahametrei (Grand Cross), Kingdom of Cambodia, 2001; Ahmed Al Fateh, Kingdom of Bahrain, 2002; The Most Blessed Order of Setia Negara Brunei (First Class), Brunei Darussalam, 2002; Commander Grand Cross of the Royal Order of the Polar Star of the Kingdom of Sweden, 2003; Numerous other awards include: Honorary Doctorate, Thammasat University, 1994; Sam Houston Humanitarian Award, Sam Houston State University, USA, 2002; Honorary Doctorate, Tokyo Institute of Technology, Japan, 2003. Memberships: President, Northerners Association of Thailand, 1998-. Address: Office of the Prime Minister, Government House, Thanon Nakhon Pathem, Bangkok 10300, Thailand.

SHINDI Josiah Anongo, b. 15 March 1950, Gboko, Benue State, Nigeria. Psychologist. m. Agnes M Shindi, 2 sons, 3 daughters. Education: Diploma in Library Science, ABU, Zaria, Nigeria, 1970; Diploma in Guidance and Counselling, University of Reading, England, 1977; MEd, Education of Maladjusted Children, University of Manchester, England, 1978; PhD, Psychology, University of Manchester, England, 1981; Licentiate, Nigerian Association of Clinical Psychologists. Appointments: Library Officer, University of Ibadan, 1972-76; Lecturer, Professor of

Dictionary of International Biography

Psychology, University of Jos, 1980-92; Professor of Psychology, Director, Academic Planning, Benue State University, Makurdi, 1992-94; Currently Professor of Psychology and Dean, Faculty of Social Sciences, Benue State University, Makurdi, Nigeria; Visiting Professor of Psychology, University of Texas at Austin, 1987, City College, New York, 1988, Bar-Ilan, Israel, 1991; Consultant, United Nations. Publications; The Nigerian Child; Career in Psychology; Conflict Resolution in Sub-Saharan Africa; The Role of Perception in Conflicts in Nigeria. Honours: Manchester University PG Scholar, 1979; British Council Scholarship, 1980; Distinguished Member Association for Advancement of Science, 1980. Memberships: Nigerian Psychological Association; International Association of Applied Psychologists; New York Academy of Science; International Network for Conflict Resolution. Address: Benue State University, Makurdi, Nigeria. E-mail: josiahshindi@yahoo.co.uk

SHIPLEY Jenny, b. 1952, New Zealand. Politician. m. Burton, 1 son, 1 daughter. Appointments: Former School Teacher; Farmer, 1973-88; Joined National Party, 1975; Former Malvern County Councillor; MP for Ashburton (now Rakaia), 1987-; Minister of Social Welfare, 1990-93, Womens Affairs, 1990-98, Health, 1993-96, State Services, 1996-97, State Owned Enterprises, Transport, Accident Rehabilitation and Compensation Insurance; Minister Responsible for Radio New Zealand; Minister in Charge of New Zealand Security Intelligence Services, 1997-; Prime Minister of New Zealand, 1997-99; Leader of the Opposition, 2000-2001. Address: Parliament Buildings, Wellington, New Zealand. E-mail: hq@national.org.nz

SHIRAISHI Hiroyasu, b. 15 January 1937, Tokyo, Japan. Psychiatrist. m. Hiroko Kawamura, 2 sons. Education: Doctor of Medicine, 1961, Doctor of Philosophy, 1966, China University, Chiba, Japan. Appointments: Associate Professor, 1977-93, Professor, 1993-2000, Department of Psychiatry, Tsukuba University, Tsukuba, Japan; Director, Tsuchiura Mental Clinic, Tsuchiura, Japan, 2000-. Publications: Articles in scientific journals including: Experimental Brain Research, 1970; Brain Research, 1998; Journal of Clinical Psychopharmacology, 1999; American Journal of Medical Genetics, 1999; Journal of Psychosomatic Research, 2000. Memberships: The Japanese Society of Psychiatry and Neurology; International Brain Research Organisation. Address: 4-24-7 Kasuga, Tsukuba, Ibaraki 305-0821, Japan

SHIVAPRASAD Kodakkal, b. 4 July 1957, India. Social Worker. m. K S Nagarathna, 7 July 1989, 1 son, 1 daughter. Education: SSLC, (MA), Apprentice, All India Trade Test in Clerk/Bee-Keeping; MA Apprentice in Clerical, English and Kannada Typewriting, Delphi; General knowledge in Banking. Appointments: M/S Bharath Electronics Ltd, Bangalore and Indian Institute of Management, Bangalore; Officer, Canana Bank; Permanent Midday Meal Donor, Sri Sharada Devi Blind School, Shimoga; Donor, Regeneration of Hindu temples of Karnataka. Publications: Several articles and poems; Several disabled welfare articles. Honours: Best Handicapped Employee Award, Naseoh (K) Bangalore; Intelligent Man Award, Disabled Firm; Best Poetry Writer Award, Bangalore Police; Ex-State Vice President, Karnataka Federation Physically Handicapped, Shimoga; Chairman, Disabled Conference Reception Committee, Mangalore; Master Trainer, CBR Network South Asia, Bangalore; "Kodakkal Shivaprasad Nagarathna Award for Best investigation Reports" named in his honour by District Press Guild, Shimoga; Best Delphian Award, Canara Bank; Best Slogan Writer Award; Apprentice award, M/S Bharath Electronics, Bangalore; Blood Donor Award, Shimoga Midtown Rotary Charity; Best Handicapped Writer, Government of Karnataka; Award Scheme in his name to Media People. Memberships: Common Cause, New

Delhi; Association of Physical Handicapped, Bangalore; Akhila Havyaka Maha Shaba, Bangalore; Vishwa Hindu Parishad, New Delhi; General Secretary, Shimoga District Physically Handicapped Welfare Sangha (Regd); Canara Bank Officers Association, Mumbai; Indian Institute of Bankers, Chennai; Indian Red Cross Society, Shimoga; Canara Bank, Kannada Sangha, Bangalore; Fellow, United Writers' Association, Chennai; Administrative Member, Sri Bharathi Higher Primary School, Mudipu; Member, Sri Keshava Trust (Eye Care Unit), Bangalore; Several disabled firms and others. Address: Shivanag, No 45, 2nd Cross, 2nd Street, Malleswaranagar Exntn, Gundappa Shed, Shimoga - 577 201, Karnataka State, India.

SHKOLNIKOVA Nelli, b. 8 July 1928, Zolotonosha, Ukraine. Violinist. Education: Music studies, BMus, MMus, Moscow Conservatory, 1949-57; Honours degree in Violin. Career: Concert tours in USSR, Austria, Australia, Bulgaria, Czechoslovakia, France, Finland, Hungary, East Germany, Canada, USA, Norway, New Zealand, Japan, 1953-; Appeared with conductors such as Kondrashin, Rozhdestvensky, Munch, Cluytens, Sanderling, Masur, Ormandy; Currently Professor of Violin at Indiana University School of Music, USA. Recordings: Tchaikovsky - Concerto in D op 35; Mozart - Concerto No 4 in D K218; Mendelssohn - Concerto in E Minor; Beethoven - Sonata No 2 in A major op 12 No 2, Sonata No 8 in G major op 30 No 3; Copland - Sonata in G major; Handel - Sonata No 1 in A major, Sonata No 3; Pieces by Paganini, Prokofiev and others. Contributions to: Reviews in Le Figaro, New York Post, Berliner Morgenpost, Arbeiderbladet, Pravda, others. Honours: Grand Prix at Marguerite Long-Jacques Thibaud Competition, Paris, France, 1953; Honoured Artist of Russian Republic, 1978. Membership: American String Teachers' Association. Address: 2814 St Remy Circle, Bloomington, IN 47401, USA.

SHLYGIN Victor Victorovich, b. 30 June 1950, Smolensk, Russia. Biophysicist. m. Timoshina Valentina, 1 son, 1 daughter. Education: Graduate, Department of Automotive and Apparatus Building, Kharkov Polytechnic Institute, 1973; Doctor of Physico-Mathematics, Moscow State University, 1992. Appointments: Scientific Collaborator, Institute of Biophysics, Academy of Science, USSR, 1973-86; Scientific Collaborator, All Union Institute of Biotechnology, Moscow, 1986-88; Scientific Collaborator, Intersectional Research and Technology Complex, "Eye Microsurgery", 1988-2002; Director, Private Liceum, Moscow, 1993-94; Institute of Informatic Problems, Russian Academy of Science, 1999-2003. Publications: 20 patents; 65 articles include: Possible Change in the Blood Vessel on Electromagnetic Exposure; Identifiability of an Enzyme Network, 1990; Effect of Magnetic Field on the Excitation Transmission along Nerve Fibers Innervating a Blood Vessel, 2001. Honour: Award for Biophysics, 1975. Membership: New York Academy of Sciences. Address: Taininskaja 26, A 79, 129345 Moscow, Russia.

SHOKHIN Alexander Nikolayevich, b. 25 December 1951, Savinskoye Village, Arkhangelsk Region, Russia. Economist. Politician. m. Tatiana Shokhina, 1 son, 1 daughter. Education: Doctor of Economics, Economics Department, Moscow State University, 1974; Professor, President, Higher School of Economics, State University. Appointments: Economic Advisor to the Minister of Foreign Affairs, 1987-91; Deputy Prime Minister of the Russian Federation, 1991-94, 1998; Minister of Labour, Minister of Economics, Russian Governor at the IMF and the World Bank, 1991-94; Deputy of the State Duma, 1993-2003, Head of the Duma Committee on Credit Institutions and Capital Markets, 2000-02; 1st Vice-Chairman of the State Duma, 1996-97; Leader of the Duma Party Block "Our Home is Russia", 1997-98; Head of the Duma's Representation in the Parliamentary Assembly of the Council of Europe and Vice Speaker of the Assembly, 1996-98; Chairman of the Expert Council of the Federal Commission for Securities Market, 2002-04; Member of the Bureau of the Russian Union of Industrialists and Entrepreneurs; Member, National Council of Corporate Governance; Chairman of the Supervisory Board, Renaissance Capitor, 2002-. Publications: Several books and over 250 articles in major Russian and foreign magazines. Address: 22 Voznesensky per, Moscow 103009, Russia. E-mail: ashokhin@rencap.com Website: www.shokhin.ru

SHORT Clare (Rt Hon), b. 15 February 1946, Birmingham, England. Politician. m. (1) 1964, divorced 1974, (2) A Lyon, 1981, deceased 1993, 1 son. Education: BA Honours, Political Science, Universities of Leeds and Keele. Appointments: Civil Service, Home Office, 1970-75; Director, All Faith for One Race, 1976-78; Youthaid, 1979-83; Labour MP, Birmingham Ladywood, 1983-; Shadow Employment Spokesperson, 1985-89, Social Security Spokesperson, 1989-91, Environmental Protection Spokesperson, 1992-93, Spokesperson for Women, 1993-95; Shadow Secretary of State for Transport, 1995-96, for Overseas Development, 1996-97; Secretary of State for International Development, 1997-2003; Select Committee Home Affairs, 1983-85; Chair, All Party Group on Race Relations, 1985-86; NEC, 1988-98; Vice-President, Socialist International Women, 1992-96; Chair, Women's Committee National Executive Committee, 1993-97; Chair, NEC International Committee, 1996-98; Party Representative, Social International Congress, 1996. Membership: UNISON. Address: House of Commons, London SW1A 0AA, England.

SHORT Nigel, b. 1 June 1965, Leigh, Lancashire, England. Chess Player. m. Rea Karageorgiou, 1987, 1 daughter. Appointments: At age of 12 beat Jonathan Penrose in British Championships; International Master, 1980; Grand Master, 1984; British Champion, 1984, 1987; English Champion, 1991; President, Grand Masters Association, 1992; Defeated Anatoly Karpov, 1992; Defeated by Kasparov, 1993; Ranked 7th Player in World; Chess Columnist, The Daily Telegraph, 1991; Stripped of International Ratings by World Chess Foundation, 1993, reinstated, 1994; Resigned from FIDE and formed Professional Chess Association with Gary Kasparov, 1993, left PCA, 1995; Ranked 17th in the world by FIDE, January 2003. Publications: Learn Chess with Nigel Short, 1993. Honours: Honorary Fellow, Bolton Institute, 1994; Honorary MBE, 1999. Address: c/o The Daily Telegraph, 1 Canada Square, London, E14 5DT, England. E-mail: ndshort@hotmail.com

SHORTER John, b. 14 June 1926, Redhill, Surrey, England. Chemist. m. Mary Patricia Steer, 28 July 1951, 2 sons, 1 daughter. Education: BA, 1947, BSc, 1948, DPhil, 1950, Exeter College, Oxford. Appointments: Assistant Lecturer, 1950-52, Lecturer in Chemistry, 1952-54, University College, Hull; Lecturer in Chemistry, 1954-63, Senior Lecturer, 1963-72, Reader, Physical Organic Chemistry, 1972-82, Emeritus Reader in Chemistry, 1982-, University of Hull; RT French Visiting Professor, University Rochester, New York, USA, 1966-67. Publications include: Correlation Analysis in Organic Chemistry, 1973; Correlation Analysis of Organic Reactivity, 1982; Co-editor: Advances in Linear Free Energy Relationships, 1972; Correlation Analysis in Chemistry, 1978; Similarity Models in Organic Chemistry, Biochemistry and Related Fields, 1991. Honour: 75th Anniversary Medal, Polish Chemical Society, 2001. Memberships: Fellow, Royal Society of Chemistry; Secretary, International Group for Correlation Analysis in Chemistry (formerly organic chemistry); International Union of Pure and Applied Chemistry. Address: 29 Esk Terrace, Whitby, North Yorkshire YO21 1PA, England.

SHOWALTER David Scott, b. 23 May 1953, Harrisonburg, Virginia, USA. Accountant. m. Elizabeth K Allison, 1 June 1974, 2 sons, 1 daughter. Education: Associate Degree, 1973; BSc, Business Administration, 1975. Appointments: Assistant to National Director, Government Services,1981-84; Assistant to Vice Chair, Marketing and Specialized Industries, 1986-88; Partnership, 1986; Area Line of Business Partner in Charge, 1993-96; National Industry Director, Public Service, 1996-98; National Managing Partner, Assurance & Advisory Services Center, 1998-2002; Industry Sector Leader – Public Sector, 2002-. Publications: Newsletter Editor, Government Accounting & Auditing Update, 1997-. Honours include: Distinguished Eagle Scout, 1998; Silver Beaver, Boy Scouts of America, 1994; Kentucky Colonel, 1987; Top 100 Most Influential People in Accounting, Accounting Today, 2001. Memberships: American Institute of CPA's; Indianapolis Youth Hockey Association: Trustee, Orchard Park Presbyterian Church; Board Member, Three Fires Council, BSA. Address: KPMG LLP, 3 Chestnut Ridge Road, Montvale, NJ 07645, USA.

SHPANIN Vladimir, b. 16 May 1990, Azerbaijan. Artist. Career: International Children's Contest, Boys and Girls from All Over the World, Azerbaijan, work included in book for world-wide distribution, 1997; Contest Prize in Drawing Contest, The Young Reclaimer by Azerbaijan, Azerbaijan, 1997; 1st Solo Art Exhibition, Baku, Azerbaijan, 1997; Member of Art Exhibition, The Young Talents, Azerbaijan, 1998; 2nd Place and Diploma, Art Contest, NOVRUZ-98, Azerbaijan, 1998; 2nd Place and Diploma, Art Contest, Azerbaijan-90 Years!, Azerbaijan, 1998; 1st Place in Grade, Prize and Diploma, IV International Children's Art Contest, A S Pushkin – 200 Years!, Moscow Russia, 1999; 2nd and 3rd Solo Art Exhibitions, Salerno and Oliverto-Chitta, Italy, 1999; 1st Place, Children's Art Contest, What the Caspian Means to Me, 1999; 1st Place and Diploma, Art Contest, The 21st Century, Azerbaijan, 2000; 1st Place and Diploma, Art Contest, Freedom to Israel, Hadera, Israel, 2000; Minister of Transport Prize, 12 Yamaha Children's Seascape Painting Contest, Japan, 2000; 8 works included in Internet Art Gallery, Doodleshop, USA; 7 works in Internet Art Gallery, Artkids, USA; 5 works in Internet Art Website, The ArtGallery, Australia, 2001; 10 works on Internet Website, Cyberkids, USA; Art Finalist in Contest, River of Words, USA, 2001, 2002; 4th Solo Art Exhibition, Netania, Israel, 2001; Youngest Professional Artist to have works purchased and displayed, Guinness Book of Records, US, 2002; 5th Solo Exhibition, Ellicott City, Washington Post, USA, 2003; Art Exhibition, Art Gallery, Baku, Azerbaijan, 2003. Address: Kasum-Ismailova 5, Flat 26, Baku 37000, Azerbaijan. E-mail: stass@mail.az

SHTRAUSS Vairis, b. City Sabile, Latvia. Radio Engineer. m. Iveta Abolina, 1974, 2 sons. Education: Dipl Ing, Riga Polytechnical Institute, 1970; Dr Sc Ing, Institute of Polymer Mechanics, Riga, 1978; Dr Habil Sc Ing, Institute of Physical Energy, Riga, 1993. Appointments: Engineer, 1969-72, Junior researcher, Researcher, 1972-80, Senior Researcher, 1980-, Institute of Polymer Mechanics, Riga, Latvia. Publications: Author of more than 100 journal articles and conference papers in the fields of mechanics, signal processing, mechanics of composite materials. Honour: Gold Medal, International Leipzig Fair, 1988. Memberships: Head of Metrology, Latvian National Accreditation Bureau; Member of TCs (Legal Metrology NDT), Latvian National Standardisation Body. Address: Institute of Polymer Mechanics, 23 Aizkraukles Street, LV 1006 Riga, Latvia. E-mail: strauss@edi.lv

SHTYKHAU Heorhi, b. 14 July 1927, Staraya Belitsa, Comel Region, Belarus. Historian; Archaeologist. m. Vera Badrova, 1 daughter. Education: Doctor of History, 1983; Professor, 1989.

Appointments: Institute of Historical Sciences and Academy of Sciences Belarus, 1959-2003; Lecturer, Archaeology, Minsk Pedagogical University; Lecturer, History of Belarus, Polotsk State University. Publications: The Ancient Polotsk of the IX-XIIth Centuries, 1975; Towns of Polotsk Land (the IX-XII centuries), 1978; Archaeology of Belarus in 4 volumes, 2000. Honours: Laureate of the State Prize of Belarus for assistance with "Collection of Historical Monuments and Literary Heritage", 1990; Research Board of Advisors, 2003; Elected Chairman, National Committee, International Union on Slavic Archaeology. Membership: Byelorussian Association of Victims of the Political Repressions. Address: Institute of History, 1 Akademicheskaya Str, 220072 Minsk, Belarus.

SHU Peter H C, b. 2 June 1948, Nanjing, China. Business Development Manager. m. Chun Wan Liu Shu, 1 daughter. Education: BS, National Taiwan University, 1970; MS, The Ohio State University, USA, 1974; PhD, Rensselaer Polytechnic Institute, 1978; Post Doctoral Research Fellow, University of Massachusetts at Amherst, Massachusetts, 1978-79; MBA, State University of New York at Albany, 1982. Appointments: Project Leader, General Electric Corporation, Selkirk, New York, 1979-85; Materials Specialist, Bayer Corporation, Pittsburgh, Pennsylvania, 1985-90; Deputy Technical General Manager, Bayer Taiwan Co Ltd, 1990-99; Regional Technical Manager, Asia Pacific Region, Bayer Polymers Co Ltd, Hong Kong, 1999-2001; Manager, Business Development and Technical Service, NAFTA, Bayer Polymers LLC, Pittsburgh, USA, 2001-. Publications: 14 papers; 1 book chapter; 25 patents; 50 talks. Honours: Taiwan Ministry of Education, Merit Scholarship, 1966-70; Chinese Army Academy, Teaching Officer of the Year, 1971; General Electric Management Award, 1983. Memberships: ACS; SPE; SAE; Chairman, Chinese School Board, Pittsburgh, 1984; Board Member, Overseas Chinese Association, 1984. Address: 206 Doubletree Drive, Venetia, PA 15367, USA. E-mail: peter.shu@bayerpolymers.com

SHUBIK Martin, b. 24 March 1926, Manhattan, New York, USA. Economics Educator. m. Julia Kahn, 1 daughter. Education: BA, 1947, MA, 1949, University of Toronto, Canada; AM, Political Economy, 1951, PhD, 1953, Princeton University, New Jersey, USA. Appointments: Part-time Demonstrator, Physics, University of Toronto, 1948-49; Part-time Research Assistant, 1950-51, Research Assistant, 1951-53, Research Associate, 1953-55, Economics Research Project, Princeton University; Fellow, Center for Advanced Study in Behavioural Sciences, Palo Alto, California, 1955-56; Consultant, Management Consultation Services, General Electric Company, 1956-60; Adjunct Research Professor, Pennsylvania State University, 1957-59; Visiting Professor of Economics, Yale University, 1960-61; Staff, T J Watson Research Laboratories, IBM, 1961-63; Professor of Economics of Organization, Yale University, 1963-75; Visiting Professor, Escuela de Estudios Economicos, University of Chile, 1965; Institute for Advanced Studies, Vienna, Austria, 1970; Consultant, RAND Corporation, California, 1970-71; Visiting Professor, Department of Economics, University of Melbourne, Australia, 1973; Director, Cowles Foundation for Research in Economics, 1973-76, Seymour H Knox Professor of Mathematical Institutional Economics, 1975-, Yale University. Publications: Books include: Readings in Game Theory and Political Behaviour, 1954; Strategy and Market Structure, 1959; Editor, Essays in Mathematical Economics in Honour of Oskar Morgenstern, 1967; Uses and Methods of Gaming, 1975; The War Game, co-author, 1979; The Mathematics of Conflict, 1983; The Theory of Money and Financial Institutions, Volumes I and II, 1999; Numerous articles in professional journals. Honours: Lanchester Prize, 1984; Koopman Prize, Military Application Section, INFORMS, 1995; International Insurance Society Shin

Research Excellence Award, 1999; Numerous scholarships. Memberships include: Fellow, Center for Advanced Study in Behavioural Sciences, 1955; Fellow, Econometric Society, 1971; Fellow, World Academy of Arts and Sciences, 1975; Fellow, American Academy of Arts and Sciences, 1985; Fellow, Connecticut Academy of Arts and Sciences, 1993; Science Board, Santa Fe Institute, 1997-. Address: Cowles Foundation for Research in Economics, Yale University, PO Box 208281, New Haven, CT 06520, USA.

SHUCKBURGH Julian John Evelyn, b. 30 July 1940, Ottawa, Canada. Publisher. 2 sons, 3 daughters. Education: Law Tripos, Peterhouse, Cambridge, 1958-61. Appointments: Editor, Methuen & Co, 1961-65; Senior Editor, Weidenfeld & Nicolson Ltd, 1965-72; Editorial Director, W H Allen Ltd, 1972-75; Publishing Director and Managing Director, Pitkin Pictorials Ltd, Garrod & Lofthouse (Printers), 1975-78; Managing Director and Founder, Shuckburgh Reynolds Ltd, 1978-87; Publishing Director, Condé Nast Books, 1992-97; Associate Publisher, Ebury Press, 1992-2000; Managing Director, Barrie & Jenkins Ltd, 1987-2000. Publications: The Bedside Book, 1979; The Second Bedside Book, 1981; London Revealed, 2003. Memberships: The Garrick Club; The Bach Choir. Address: 22 Ellingham Road, London W12 9PR, England. E-mail: julianshuckburgh@22ellingham.com

SHUKMAN David Roderick, b. 30 May 1958, London, England. Journalist. m. Jessica Pryce-Jones, 2 sons, 1 daughter. Education: Durham University, 1977-80. Appointments: Coventry Evening Telegraph, 1980-83; News Trainee, 1983-85; Reporter, BBC Northern Ireland, 1985-87; Defence Correspondent, 1987-95; European Correspondent, 1995-99, World Affairs Correspondent, 1999-, BBC News. Publications: All Necessary Means: Inside the Gulf War (with Ben Brown), 1991; The Sorcerer's Challenge, 1995 (US edition, Tomorrow's War, 1996); Various newspapers and magazines. Memberships: Royal Institute for International Affairs; International Institute for Strategic Studies. Address: World Affairs Unit, BBC TV Centre, London W12 7RJ, England. E-mail: david.shukman@bbc.co.uk

SHUREY Richard, b. 22 September 1951, Wales. Factory Worker. m. Christine, 6 May 1972, 2 sons, 1 daughter. Publications: Jewels of the Imagination, 1997; By the Light of the Moon, 1997; On Reflection, 1997; Never Forget, 1998; From the Hand of a Poet, 1999; Open Minds, 1999. Contributions to: South Wales Echo; Celtic Press; Rhondda Leader. Honours: Editor's Choice Award for Outstanding Achievement in Poetry, International Library of Poetry, 1997. Memberships: Poetry Guild. Address: 107 Tylacelyn Road, Penygraig R.S., Tonypandy, Mid Glamorgan CF40 1JR, South Wales.

SIEBE Wilfried, b. 29 December 1946, Preussisch Oldendorf, Germany. Professor; Consultant. Education: Diploma in Mathematics, 1973, PhD in Mathematics, 1980, University of Münster; Habilitation in Economics, University of Bonn, 1991. Appointments: Research Associate, International Institute for Applied Systems Analysis, Laxenburg, Austria, and German National Science Foundation, 1988-92; Research Fellow, Centre for Operations Research and Econometrics, Catholic University of Louvain, Belgium, 1992-94; Professor of Economics, Rostock University; Co-founder, Principal, RISKVISION Ltd, Cologne. Publications: Author and Co-author, numerous articles published in professional journals. Memberships: European Finance Association; Fellow, Salzburg Seminar. Address: Chair of Microeconomics, Faculty of Business, Economics and Social Sciences, Rostock University, Ulmenstrasse 69, D-18051 Rostock, Germany. E-mail: wsiebe@t-online.de

SIEGEL Robert (Harold), b. 18 August 1939, Oak Park, Illinois, USA. Professor of English. m. Roberta Ann Hill, 19 August 1961, 3 daughters. Education: BA, Wheaton College, 1961; MA, Johns Hopkins University, 1962; PhD, Harvard University, 1968. Appointments: Assistant Professor, Dartmouth College, 1968-75; Visiting Lecturer in Creative Writing, Princeton University, 1975-76; Poet-in-Residence, McManes Visiting Professor, Wheaton College, 1976; Visiting Professor, J W v Goethe Universitat, Frankfurt, 1985; Coordinator, Graduate Program in Creative Writing, University of Wisconsin-Milwaukee, 1992-94; Professor of English, University of Wisconsin-Milwaukee, 1983-. Publications: Poetry: The Beasts and The Elders, 1973; In A Pig's Eye, 1980. Fiction: Alpha Centauri, 1980; Whalesong, 1981; The Kingdom of Wundle, 1982; White Whale, 1991; The Ice At the End of the World, 1994. Contributions to: Anthologies and journals. Honours: Honorable Mention, Merit Awards, Atlantic Monthly College Poetry Contest, 1960; Margaret O'Loughlin Foley Award, 1970; The Cliff Dwellers' Arts Foundation Award, 1974; Chicago Poetry Prize, Society of Midland Authors, 1974; Prairie Schooner Poetry Prize, 1977; Jacob Glatstein Memorial Prize, 1977; Merrill Ingram Award, 1979; National Endowment for the Arts Fellowship, 1980; ECPA Gold Medalion, 1981; Book of the Year Award, Campus Life Magazine, 1981; 1st Prize for Juvenile Fiction, Council for Wisconsin Writers, 1981; 1st Prize for Poetry, Society of Midland Authors, 1981; Matson Award, 1982; Golden Archer Award, 1986; Pushcart Prize Nominations, 1990, 1995; Milton Center Poetry Prize, 1994. Memberships: Author's Guild; Association of Scholars and Critics. Address: University of Wisconsin, PO Box 413, Milwaukee, WI 53201, USA.

SIEPMANN James Patrick, b. 16 January 1960, Rochester, Minnesota, USA. Physician; Executive Editor. m. Victoria L Siepmann, 2 sons, 4 daughters. Education: BA, Summa cum Laude, University of St Thomas, St Paul, Minnesota, 1982; MD, Mayo Medical School, Rochester, Minnesota, 1986; ABFP, Mayo Graduate School of Medicine, Rochester, Minnesota, 1989. Appointments: Family Medicine, Oshkosh, Wisconsin, 1989-2000; Founder, Chairman and CRO, LightTime (an optoelectronic R&D company), 2000-; Editor, The Journal of Theoretics (a peer reviewed journal), 1999-. Publications: Articles in scientific journals include: HTN-APT: Computer Aid in Hypertension Management, 1987; The Laws of Space and Observation, 1999; The Light Clock: A New Method for Measuring True Time, 1999; A New Method for Calculating Gravity, 1999. Honours: Catholic School Board President, 1991-93; Wisconsin Physician – Citizen of the Year 1994. Memberships: AMA; WISMS; IEEE; OSA; SPIE; LIA (Laser Institute of America); AAFP; AAAS. Address: 2941 Prairie Wood Drive, Oshkosh, WI 54904, USA. E-mail: siepmann@lightime.com

SIERRA Carlos Eduardo, b. 1 March 1963, Medellín, Antioquia, Colombia. Chemical Engineer; University Professor. Education: Academic Bachelor, Liceo Nacional Marco Fidel Suárez, Medellín, Colombia, 1980; Chemical Engineer, Universidad Nacional de Colombia, Medellín, Colombia, 1987; Magister in Education, Pontificia Universidad Javeriana, Bogotá, Colombia, 2001. Appointments: Teaching Assistant, 1986-87, Chair Occasional Teacher, 1988-89, Universidad Nacional de Colombia; Research and Development Assistant, Empresa de Refractarios Colombianos, 1987; Chair Assistant Teacher, 1989, Assistant Teacher, 1990-93, Universidad Pontificia Bolivariana; Associate Instructor, 1993-98, Assistant Teacher, 1998-2003, Associate Professor, 2003-, Universidad Nacional de Colombia. Publications: El enigma de la Formación integral en una era acientífica (ensayos); Al rescate del experimento recreativo en el contexto de la antropogogía de la termodinámica y la fisicoquimica; Articles in: The Newcomen Bulletin; Education Forum; Serrablo, Spain;

Ciencias Humanas, Colombia; Mensuario de la Sociedad Julio Garavito, Colombia; El Colombiano Dominical, Colombia; Kabai, Colombia and some additional publications. Honours: Honour degree, Chemical Engineering; Marco Fidel Suárez Prize, 1979, 1980; Assistant Fellow, Universidad Nacional de Colombia, 1986-87. Memberships: New York Academy of Sciences; History of Science Society; Society for the History of Technology; British Society for the History of Science; The Newcomen Society for the Study of the History of Engineering and Technology; Sociedad Julio Garavito para el Estudio de la Astronomia; International Committee for the History of Technology and History of Earth Sciences Society. Address: Apartado Aéreo 95485, Medellín, Colombia. E-mail: cesierra48@epm.net.co

SIFUNISO Monde Akokwa, b. 28 April 1944, Mongu, Zambia. Publisher. 1 son, 2 daughters. Education: Diploma, Education, University College of Rhodesia and Nyasaland, 1963-65; Certificate, Educational Broadcasting, ABC Training School, 1970; Diploma, Advanced Studies, Publishing, Oxford Brookes University, 1985-86. Appointments: Teacher, 1966-68; Scriptwriter/Producer, 1968-71; Public Relations Officer, 1971-76; Publisher, 1976-97. Publications include: Eavesdropping, 2001; Women of the East, 2002. Membership: Committee member, Zambia PEN. Address: Box 51378, Lusaka, Zambia.

SIGWART Ulrich, b. 9 March 1941. Cardiologist. 2 sons, 2 daughters. Education: Medical Degree, University of Munster, 1967; Dr med, magna cum laude, University of Freiburg, 1967; Dr med habil, 1978, Professor Dr med habil, 1985, University of Dusseldorf; Professor of Cardiology, University of Geneva, 2001. Appointments: Intern, Community Hospital Lorrach, 1967-68; Resident, Framingham Union Hospital, Boston, USA, 1968-71; Fellowship, Baylor College of Medicine, Houston, 1971-72; Training, University Hospital, Zurich, Switzerland, 1972-73; Chief of Cath Laboratory, Gollwitzer Meier Institute, Bad Oeynhausen, 1973-79; Medecin Associé, then Ajoint, University Hospital, Lausanne, 1979-89; Director, Department of Invasive Cardiology, Royal Brompton Hospital, London, 1989-2001; Chief of Cardiology, University of Geneva, current; Consultant Cardiologist to hospitals in UK, Switzerland and Monaco. Publications: 600 papers; 6 books. Honours: Gold Medal, European Society of Cardiology, 1996; Honorary Doctorate, University of Lausanne, 1998; Forssmann Prize, University of Bochum, 2000; Honorary Member, Polish Society of Cardiology; Sven Effert Prize, Germany Society of Cardiology, 2002; Honorary Member, Russian Society of Cardio-Angiology. Memberships: Fellow, Royal College of Physicians; Fellow, American College of Cardiology; Fellow, European Society of Cardiology. Address: Centre and Division of Cardiology, University Hospital, CH-1211 Geneva, Switzerland. E-mail: ulrich.sigwart@hcuge.ch

SIKI Bela, b. 21 February 1923, Budapest, Hungary. Pianist; Professor. m. Yolande Oltramare, 1 son, 1 daughter. Education: Franz Liszt Academy, Budapest, 1945; Prix De Virtuosite Avec Distinction, 1948. Appointments: Adjunct Professor, Geneve, 1951-53; Professor, University of Washington, Seattle, 1965-93; Professor, University of Cincinnati, 1980-85. Publications: Piano Repertoire, 1981; Worldwide concert tours, numerous recordings. Honour: Concours International D'Execution Musicale. Address: 5424 Elleray Lane NE, Seattle, WA 98105, USA.

SILLITOE Alan, b. 4 March 1928, Nottingham, England. Writer; Poet; Dramatist. m. Ruth Fainlight, 19 November 1959, 1 son, 1 daughter (adopted). Education: Principally self-taught. Appointments: Writer, 1948-. Publications: Without Beer or Bread (poems), 1957; Saturday Night and Sunday Morning (novel), 1958; The General (novel), 1960; The Rats and Other Poems, 1960;

Key to the Door (novel), 1961; Road to Volgograd (travel), 1964; A Falling Out of Love and Other Poems, 1964; The Death of William Posters (novel), 1965; A Tree on Fire (novel), 1967; A Start in Life (novel), 1967; Shaman and Other Poems, 1968; Love in the Environs of Voronezh and Other Poems, 1968; Travel in Nihilon (novel), 1971; Raw Material (memoir), 1972; The Flame of Life (novel), 1974; Storm and Other Poems, 1974; Barbarians and Other Poems, 1974; Mountains and Caverns: Selected Essays, 1975; The Widower's Son (novel), 1976; The Storyteller (novel), 1979; Snow on the North Side of Lucifer (poems), 1979; Her Victory (novel), 1982; The Lost Flying Boat (novel), 1983; Down from the Hill (novel), 1984; Sun Before Departure (poems), 1984; Life Goes On (novel), 1985; Tides and Stone Walls (poems), 1986; Out of the Whirlpool (novel), 1987; The Open Door (novel), 1989; Lost Loves (novel), 1990; Leonard's War, 1991; Snowstop, 1993; Collected Poems, 1994; Collected Stories, 1995; Leading the Blind (travel), 1995; Life Without Armour (autobiography), 1995; Alligator Playground (stories), 1997; Collected Stories, 1997; The Broken Chariot (novel) 1998; The German Numbers Woman (novel), 1999; Birthday, novel, 2001; Flight of Arrows, essays, 2003; A Man of His Time, novel, 2004. Other: Short stories; Plays. Honours: Author's Club Prize, 1958; Hawthornden Prize, 1960; Honorary Fellow, Manchester Polytechnic, 1977; Honorary Degrees, Nottingham Polytechnic, 1990, Nottingham University, 1994; Visiting Professor, Honorary Doctorate, 1998, De Montfort University, Leicester. Memberships: Royal Geographical Society, fellow; Society of Authors; Writers Action Group. Address: 14 Ladbroke Terrace, London W11 3PG, England.

SILMAN Roberta, b. 29 December 1934, Brooklyn, New York, USA. Writer. m. Robert Silman, 14 June 1956. Education: BA, English Literature, Cornell University, 1956; MFA, Writing, Sarah Lawrence College, 1975. Publications: Somebody Else's Child, 1976; Blood Relations, 1977; Boundaries, 1979; The Dream Dredger, 1986; Beginning the World Again, 1990. Contributions to: Numerous magazines in USA and UK. Honours: Child Study Association Award, Best Children's Book, 1976; Pen Hemingway Honorable Mention, 1978; Janet Kafka Prizes, 1978, 1980; Guggenheim Fellowship, 1979; National Endowment for the Arts, Fellowship, 1983; PEN Syndicated Fiction Project Awards, 1983, 1984. Memberships: PEN; Authors Guild; Poets and Writers; Phi Beta Kappa. Address: 18 Larchmont Street, Ardsley, NY 10502, USA.

SILVA Christopher P, 17 March 1960, Fortuna, California, USA. Electrical Engineer. Education: BSc, Electrical Engineering, 1982, MSc, 1985, PhD, 1993, University of California at Berkeley. Appointments: Researcher, Principal Investigator, 1989, Senior Member of the Technical Staff, 1995, Engineering Specialist, 1999, Senior Engineering Specialist, 2003-, The Aerospace Corporation, El Segundo, California. Publications: Scientific papers in professional journals and at conferences; numerous presentations at conferences, companies, society meetings, universities. Honours: B.S.E.E. with highest honors distinction, UC Alumni Scholar, National Science Foundation Fellowship; Lockheed Leadership Fellowship; Fellowship, Institute for Electrical and Electronic Engineers; Senior Membership, American Institute of Aeronautics and Astronautics; Electronic Systems Division Team Achievement and Individual Awards; Corporate President's Award; Listed in several Biographical Publications. Memberships include: American Association for the Advancement of Science, American Mathematical Society; Society of Industrial and Applied Mathematics; Eta Kappa Nu; Phi Beta Kappa; Tau Beta Pi. Address: 26766 Menominee Place, Rancho Palos Verdes, CA 90275, USA. E-mail: chris.p.silva@aero.org

SILVERSTONE Alicia, b. 4 October 1976, California, USA. Actress. Appointments: Stage Debut in Play, Carol's Eve, Metropolitan Theatre, Los Angeles; Stared in 3 Aerosmith Videos including: Cryin; Formed own production company, First Kiss Productions; Films: The Crush, 1993; The Babysitter, 1995; True Crime, 1995; Le Nouveau Monde, 1995; Hideaway, 1995; Clueless, 1995; Batman and Robin, 1997; Excess Baggage (also Producer), 1997; Free Money, 1998; Blast from the Past, 1999; Love's Labour Lost, 2000; Scorched, 2002; Global Heresy, 2002; Scooby Doo: Monsters Unleashed, 2004; TV: Torch Song, 1993; Shattered Dreams, 1993; The Cool and the Crazy, 1994; The Wonder Years, 1997. Address: c/o Premiere Artists Agency, Suite 510, 8899 Beverly Boulevard, Los Angeles, CA 90048, USA.

SIMIC Charles, b. 9 May 1938, Belgrade, Yugoslavia (US citizen, 1971). Associate Professor of English; Poet; Writer. m. Helen Dubin, 1964, 1 son, 1 daughter. Education: University of Chicago, 1956-59; BA, New York University, 1967. Appointments: Faculty, California State College, Hayward, 1970-73; Associate Professor of English, University of New Hampshire, 1973-. Publications: Poetry: What the Grass Says, 1967; Somewhere Among Us a Stone is Taking Notes, 1969; Dismantling the Silence, 1971; White, 1972, revised edition, 1980; Return to a Place Lit by a Glass of Milk, 1974; Biography and a Lament, 1976; Charon's Cosmology, 1977; Brooms: Selected Poems, 1978; School for Dark Thoughts, 1978; Classic Ballroom Dances, 1980; Shaving at Night, 1982; Austerities, 1982; Weather Forecast for Utopia and Vicinity: Poems: 1967-1982, 1983; The Chicken Without a Head, 1983; Selected Poems 1963-1983, 1985, revised edition, 1990; Unending Blues, 1986; The World Doesn't End: Prose Poems, 1989; In the Room We Share, 1990; The Book of Gods and Devils, 1990; Hotel Insomnia, 1992; A Wedding in Hell, 1994; Walking the Black Cat, 1996; Jackstraws, 1999. Other: The Uncertain Certainty: Interviews, Essays and Notes on Poetry, 1985; Wonderful Words, Silent Truth, 1990; Dimestore Alchemy, 1992; Unemployed Fortune Teller, 1994; Orphan Factory, 1998; A Fly in the Soup, 2000. Editor: Another Republic: 17 European and South American Writers (with Mark Strand), 1976; The Essential Campion, 1988. Translator: 12 books, 1970-92. Honours: PEN Awards, 1970, 1980; Guggenheim Fellowship, 1972; National Endowment for the Arts Fellowships, 1974, 1979; Edgar Allan Poe Award, 1975; American Academy of Arts and Letters Award, 1976; Harriet Monroe Poetry Award, 1980; Fulbright Fellowship, 1982; Ingram Merrill Foundation Fellowship, 1983; John D and Catharine T MacArthur Foundation Fellowship, 1984; Pulitzer Prize in Poetry, 1990; Academy of American Poets Fellowship, 1998. Address: c/ o Department of English, University of New Hampshire, Durham, NH 03824, USA.

SIMMONS Janet Bryant, b. 22 April 1925, Oakland, California, USA. Writer; Publisher. m. William Ellis Simmons, divorced, 1 son, 1 daughter. Education: BA, Social Work, San Jose State University, 1965; MA, Public Administration, University of San Francisco, 1979. Appointments: Social Worker, Santa Clara County Department of Social Services, 1965-91; Writer, Publisher, Enlightenment Press, 1994-. Publication: The Mystical Child, 1996. Memberships: AAUW; American Booksellers Association; Publishers Marketing Association; Bay Area Independent Publishers Association; Audubon Society. Address: Enlightenment Press, PO Box 3314 Santa Clara, CA 95055, USA.

SIMMONS Michael, b. 17 October 1935, Watford, England. Writer. m. Angela Thomson, 20 April 1963, 2 sons. Education: BA, Honours, Russian, Manchester University, 1960; Birkbeck College, 1998-. Appointments: Parliamentary Correspondent, Glasgow Herald, 1964-67; East Europe Correspondent, Financial Times, 1968-72; Deputy Editor, Society, East Europe

Correspondent, Third World Editor, The Guardian, 1977-97; Freelance Writer and Editor, 1997-. Publications: Berlin: The Dispossessed City, 1988; The Unloved Country; A Portrait of the GDR, 1989; The Reluctant President, A Life of Vaclav Havel, 1992; Landscapes of Poverty, 1997; On the Edge, 2001; Essays on: Church and Community, 2000; Getting a Life, 2002. Membership: Trinity Cricket Club. Address: 24 Rodney Road, New Malden, Surrey KT3 5AB, England. E-mail: micsimmo@compuserve.com

SIMMS Albert Leon, b. 21 January 1931, b. Claremont, West Virginia, USA. Clergyman. Education: Certificate in Religious Education; Diploma in Education; Diploma in Pastoral Ministries; Advance in Pastoral Ministries; 4 years of Graduate Study Internal Bible at ABC Bradley, West Virginia. Appointments: Assistant Directory of Hill Top Baptist Seminary, -1961; Historian for New River Valley Baptist Association; Past Historian of WVA Baptist State Convention, 1963; Chairman of Ordination Committee of New River Valley Baptist Association and WVA State Baptist Convention, past Treasurer of New River Valley Baptist Association. Honour: Award of Merit Profiles of a Christian, 1972. Memberships: Alumnus, AB College, Bradley, WVA; WVA Baptist State Convention; Past member, WVA Baptist State Ministers Conference; Cripple Children Division Association of WVA. Address: 216 Broadway Ave, Oak Hill, WV 25901, USA.

SIMMS Michael Arlin, (Michael Garcia-Simms), b. 6 April 1954, Houston, Texas, USA. Publisher, Poet. m. Eva Maria Spork, 29 September 1987, 1 son, 1 daughter. Education: Attended School of Irish Studies, 1974; BA, Southern Methodist University, 1976; MFA, University of Iowa, 1978. Appointments: Teaching Assistant, University of Iowa, 1976-78; Instructor of Rhetoric, Southern Methodist University, 1979-87; Instructor of Communication, CCAC, 1988-; Instructor of English, Duquesne University, 1995-2000; Contributing Editor, The Pittsburgh Quarterly, 1997-; Poet-in-Residence, Carnegie Mellon University, 1998; Executive Director, Autumn House Press, 1998-. Publications: Notes on Continuing Light, 1988; Migration, 1985; The Fire-Eater, 1988. Contributions to: Southwest Review; Mid-American Review; Blue Buildings; Intro 9; Poets of the West; Telescope; Pittsburgh Poets; Rhetoric Review; Black Warrior Review; West Branch; Pittsburgh Quarterly; Texas Observer; Pittsbugh Post-Gazette, Pittsburgh Tribune; 5 AM. Honours: Assistantship, University of Iowa, 1976-78; Yaddo Fellowships, 1979, 1980, 1987; National Endowment for the Humanities Fellowship, 1982; Beyond the Classroom Grants, CCAC, 1988, 1989; International Poetry Forum, 1993-2003. Address: 87 1/2 Westwood Street, Pittsburgh, PA 15211, USA.

SIMON Maurya, b. 7 December 1950, New York, USA. Poet. m. Robert Falk, 17 June 1973, 2 daughters. Education: BA, Pitzer College, 1980; MFA, University of California, Irvine, 1984. Appointment: University of California, Riverside, 1984-. Publications: The Enchanted Room, 1986; Days of Awe, 1989; Speaking in Tongues, 1990; The Golden Labyrinth, 1995. Contributions to: Los Angeles Times; Georgia Review; Grand Street; Hudson Review; Ironwood; Kenyon Review; Literary Review; Michigan Quarterly Review; Missouri Review; Pacific Review; Poetry; Poetry East. Honours: University Award, Academy of American Poets; 1st Prize, National Federation of State Poetry Societies, 1984; 1st Prize, SCCA International Poetry Competition, 1987; Georgia State Poetry Award, 1988; Fulbright, Indo-American Fellowship, 1990. Memberships: Academy of American Poets; Poetry Society of America; Poets and Writers; PEN USA West; Modern Language Association; Associated Writing Programs. Address: University of California, Riverside, Creative Writing Department, 900 University Avenue, Riverside, CA 92521, USA.

SIMON Neil, b. 4 July 1927, New York, USA. Playwright. m. (1) Joan Baim, 1953, deceased, 2 daughters, (2) Marsha Mason, 1973, divorced, (3) Diane Lander, 1987, 1 daughter. Education: New York University. Appointments: Wrote for various TV programmes including: The Tallulah Bankhead Show, 1951; The Phil Silvers Show, 1958-59; NBC Special; The Trouble with People, 1972; Plays: Come Blow your Horn, 1961; Little Me (musical), 1962; Barefoot in the Park, 1963; The Odd Couple, 1965; Sweet Charity (musical), 1966; The Star-Spangled Girl, 1966; Plaza Suite, 1968; Promises, Promises (musical), 1968; Last of the Red Hot Lovers, 1969; The Gingerbread Lady, 1970; The Prisoner of Second Avenue, 1971; The Sunshine Boys, 1972; The Good Doctor, 1973; God's Favourite, 1974; California Suite, 1976; Chapter Two, 1977; They're Playing Our Song, 1979; I Ought to be in Pictures, 1980; Fools, 1981; Little Me (revised version), 1982; Brighton Beach Memoirs, 1983; Biloxi Blues, 1985; The Odd Couple Female Version, 1985; Broadway Bound, 1986; Rumors, 1988; Lost in Yonkers, 1991; Jake's Women, 1992; The Goodbye Girl (musical), 1993; Laughter on the 23rd Floor, 1993; London Suite, 1995; Screenplays include: After the Fox, 1966; Barefoot in the Park, 1967; The Odd Couple, 1968; The Out of Towners, 1970; Plaza Suite, 1971; The Last of the Red Hot Lovers, 1972; The Heartbreak Kid, 1973; The Prisoner of Second Avenue, 1975; The Sunshine Boys, 1975; Murder by Death, 1976; The Goodbye Girl, 1977; The Cheap Detective, 1978; California Suite, 1978. Honours: Many awards and nominations include: Emmy Award; Antoinette Perry (Tony) Awards for The Odd Couple; Writers Guild Screen Award for the Odd Couple, 1969; American Comedy Award for Lifetime Achievement, 1989; Pulitzer Prize, 1991. Publication: Rewrites: A Memoir, 1996; Individual Plays. Address: c/o A DaSilva, 502 Park Avenue, New York, NY 10022, USA.

SIMON Norma, b. 24 December 1927, New York City, USA. Children's Book Author. m. Edward Simon, 7 June 1951, 1 son, 2 daughters. Education: BA, Economics, Brooklyn College, 1943-47; MA, Early Childhood Education, Bank St College of Education, 1968; Graduate Work, New School of Social Research. Appointments: Clerical Worker, Frances I duPont & Co, New York City, 1943-46; Teacher, Vassar Summer Institute, Poughkeepsie, New York, Department of Welfare, Brooklyn, New York, 1948-49, Downtown Community School, New York City, 1949-52; Thomas School, Rowayton, Connecticut, 1952-53; Founder, Director, Teacher, Norwalk Community Cooperative Nursery School, Rowayton, Connecticut, 1953-54; Teacher, Norwalk Public Schools, Connecticut, 1962-63; Group Therapist, Greater Bridgeport Child Guidance Center, Connecticut, 1965-67; Special Teacher, Mid-Fairfield Child Guidance Center, Connecticut, 1967-69; Consultant, Stamford Pre-School Program, Connecticut, 1965-69; Consultant, School Division, Macmillan Publishing Co, Inc, New York City, 1968-70; Consultant to Publishing Division, Bank Street College of Education, 1967-74, Follow-Through Program, 1971-72; Consultant, Davidson Films Inc, 1969-74, Aesop Films, 1975-79, San Francisco, California; Consultant, Children's Advertising, Dancer-Fitzgerald-Sampler Inc, New York City, 1969-79; Volunteer, Wellfleet Elementary School, 1972-2000; Consultant, Fisher-Price Toys, East Aurora, New York, 1978. Publications include: Firefighters, 1995; The Baby House, 1995; Wet World, 1995; The Story of Hanukkah, 1997; The Story of Passover, 1997; Looking Back at Wellfleet, 1997; All Kinds of Children, 1999; All Families are Special, 2003. Honours include: Jeremiah Cahir Friend of Education Award, Barnstable County Education Association, 1987; Parents' Council on Books Choice, 1998. Memberships: Authors Guild; Delta Kappa Gamma; AAUW. Address: PO Box 428, South Wellfleet, MA 02663-0428, USA.

Dictionary of International Biography

SIMON Paul, b. 13 October 1941, Newark, New Jersey, USA. Singer; Composer. m. (1) Peggy Harper (divorced), 1 son, (2) Carrie Fisher (divorced), (3) Edie Brickell, 30 May 1992, 2 sons, 1 daughter. Education: BA, Queens College; Postgraduate, Brooklyn Law School. Career: Duo, Simon And Garfunkel, with Art Garfunkel, 1964-71; Appearances with Garfunkel include: Monterey Festival, 1967; Royal Albert Hall, 1968; Reunion concerts: Central Park, New York, 1981; US, European tours; Solo artiste, 1972-; Apperances include: Anti-war Festival, Shea Stadium, New York, 1970; Farm Aid V, 1992; Hurricane Relief concert, Miami, 1992; Born At The Right Time Tour; Tour, Europe and Russia; Television includes: Paul Simon Special, 1977; Paul Simon's Graceland - The African Concert, 1987; Paul Simon - Born At The Right Time, 1992; Film appearances: Monterey Pop, 1968; Annie Hall, 1977; All You Need Is Cash, 1978; One Trick Pony, 1980; Steve Martin Live, 1985. Compositions include: The Sound Of Silence; Homeward Bound; I Am A Rock; Mrs Robinson; The Boxer; Bridge Over Troubled Water; Cecilia; Slip Slidin' Away; Late In The Evening; You Can Call Me Al; The Boy In The Bubble; Graceland; Paul Simon - Songs From The Capeman, 1997. Albums: with Art Garfunkel: Wednesday Morning 3AM, 1964; Sounds Of Silence, 1965; Parsley Sage Rosemary And Thyme, 1967; The Graduate (film soundtrack), 1967; Bookends, 1968; Bridge Over Troubled Water, 1970; Simon and Garfunkel's Greatest Hits, 1972; Breakaway, 1975; Watermark, 1978; Collected Works, 1981; The Concert In Central Park, 1982; Various compilation albums; Solo albums: Paul Simon, 1972; There Goes Rhymin' Simon, 1973; Live Rhymin': Paul Simon In Concert, 1974; Still Crazy After All These Years, 1975; Greatest Hits Etc, 1977; One-Trick Pony, 1980; Hearts And Bones, 1983; Graceland, 1986; Negotiations and Love Songs, 1988; Rhythm Of The Saints, 1990; Paul Simon's Concert In The Park, 1991; Paul Simon 1964-1993, 1993; Paul Simon - Songs From The Capeman, 1997; You're the One, 2000. Publications: The Songs of Paul Simon, 1972; New Songs, 1975; One-Trick Pony (screenplay), 1980; At The Zoo (for children), 1991. Honours include: Grammy awards: two for The Graduate soundtrack, 1968, six for Bridge Over Troubled Water, 1970, two for Still Crazy After All These Years, 1986, one for Graceland, 1987; Emmy Award, Paul Simon Special, NBC-TV, 1977; Inducted into Rock And Roll Hall Of Fame, with Art Garfunkel, 1990; Antoinette Perry Award, The Capeman, Best Original Score Written For The Theatre 1997-98; Honorary Doctorate of Music, Berkelee College of Music, 1986, Yale University, 1996, Queens College, 1997; Numerous Grammy Awards. Address: Paul Simon Music, 1619 Broadway, Suite 500, New York, NY 10019, USA.

SIMPSON Helen Elizabeth, b. 12 November 1968, Great Britain. Museum Curator; Exhibition Organiser. Education: BA (Hons), Egyptology and Ancient History, University College London, 1987-90; MA, Museum Studies (Museum Management and International Museum Studies), University of Leicester; Associateship of the Museums Association, 1998. Appointments: Publications Assistant, The British Museum, London, 1990-91; Curatorial Assistant, Royal Photographic Society, Bath, Somerset (work experience), 1992; Registrar, Southampton City Art Gallery, Southampton, Hampshire, 1994-98; Curator, New Art Centre Sculpture Park and Gallery, Roche Court, Wiltshire, 1998-2002; Exhibition Organiser, Hayward Gallery, London, 2002-2004. Address: 197 Nieuwpoortsesteenweg, 8400 Ostend, Belgium.

SIMPSON Jerry Howard Jr, b. 11 December 1925, Providence, Rhode Island, USA. Writer; Founder, President, Director of Bike Tour, France. m. Jane Coral Augustine Simpson, 4 September 1973, 1 son, 1 daughter. Education: BA, History/Languages, Moravian College for Men, University of North Carolina. Publications: Torn Land, 1970; Cycling France, 1992; Notes on the French Revolution,

1994; Paris in Winter, 1995; Pensées Impolies, 1996. Contributions to: Reader's Digest; American History Illustrated; Bicycling; Wall Street Journal; Bike World. Honour: 1st Place, Virginia Press Association, 1969-70. Membership: Comenian Literary Society. Address: 5523 Wedgewood Drive, Charlotte, NC 28210-2432, USA.

SIMPSON John (Cody Fidler), b. 9 August 1944, Cleveleys, England. Broadcaster; Writer. m. (1) Diane Jean Petteys, 1965, divorced 1995, 2 daughters, (2) Adèle Krüger, 1996. Education: MA, Magdalene College, Cambridge. Appointments: Various positions, BBC, 1966-82; BBC Diplomatic Editor, 1982-88; Foreign, later World Affairs Editor, 1988-; Associate Editor, The Spectator, 1991-95; Columnist, The Sunday Telegraph, 1995-. Publications: The Best of Granta (editor), 1966; Moscow Requiem, 1981; A Fine and Private Place, 1983; The Disappeared: Voices From a Secret War, 1985; Behind Iranian Lines, 1988; Despatches From the Barricades, 1990; From the House of War: Baghdad and the Gulf, 1991; The Darkness Crumbles: The Death of Communism, 1992; In the Forests of the Night: Drug-Running and Terrorism in Peru, 1993; The Oxford Book of Exile (editor), 1995; Lifting the Veil: Life in Revolutionary Iran, 1995; Strange Places, Questionable People (autobiography), 1998; A Mad World, My Masters, 2000; News from No Man's Land: Reporting the World, 2002. Honours: Fellow, Royal Geographical Society, 1990; Commander of the Order of the British Empire, 1991; BAFTA Reporter of the Year, 1991, 2001; RTS Richard Dimbleby Award, 1991; Columnist of the Year, National Magazine Awards, 1993; Honorary DLitt, De Montfort University, 1995; RTS Foreign Report Award, 1997; Peabody Award, USA, 1997; Dr hc, Nottingham, 2000. Address: c/o BBC Television Centre, Wood Lane, London W12 7RJ, England.

SIMPSON John Michael, b. 23 May 1937, Birmingham, England. Physician. m. Maria Rosa Baptista, 1 son, 1 daughter. Education: MRCS LRCP, 1961; MB, BS, London, 1962; Fellow, Faculty Anaesthesia, 1968; FRCA/Specialist Register, Europe, 1992. Appointments: House Appointments Guys Hospital, London, 1961-62; Senior House Officer, Neurosurgery, Whittington Hospital, London, 1963-64; Senior House Officer/Registrar, Anaesthesia, Dulwich/Kings College Hospital, 1965-67; Registrar, Anaesthesia, University of the West Indies, Jamaica, 1967-68; Senior Registrar, Anaesthesia, Poole General Hospital, Dorset/ National Heart Hospital, London, 1968-70; Consultant, Anaesthesia, General and Heart Surgery, Tilburg, Netherlands, 1971-80; Consultant, Anaesthesia, Armed Forces Hospital, Riyadh, Saudi Arabia, 1981-91; Bristol Royal Infirmary, Bristol, 1992-95; Hospital Particular Do Algarve, Algarve, Portugal, 1996-. Publications: Monograph: Infant Stress and Sleep Deprivation as Aetiological Basis for Sudden Infant Death Syndrome, 2001; Contributor of articles to professional journals; USA Patent for method for opening "Band-Aid" type dressing for use as a pressure plaster. Membership: Fellow, Royal Society of Medicine, London. Address: Quinta S. Miguel, Apartado 128, 8401-902 Lagoa, Algarve, Portugal. E-mail: NS335928@hotmail.com

SIMPSON N(orman) F(rederick), b. 29 January 1919, London, England. Author. Education: BA, University of London, 1954. Appointments: Teacher and Extramural Lecturer, Westminster College, London, 1946-62; Literary Manager, Royal Court Theatre, London, 1976-78. Publications: The Hole, 1958; One Way Pendulum, 1960; The Form, 1961; The Hole and Other Plays and Sketches, 1964; The Cresta Run, 1966; Some Tall Tinkles: Television Plays, 1968; Was He Anyone, 1973; Harry Bleachbaker (novel), 1974, US edition as Man Overboard, 1976; Inner Voices, 1983. Address: The Sea House, Townsend, Polruan, Cornwall PL23 1QH, England.

Dictionary of International Biography

SIMPSON O J (Orenthal James), b. 9 July 1947, San Francisco, USA. Former Professional Football Player; Actor; Sports Commentator. m. (1) Marguerite Whitley, 1967, divorced, 1 son, 1 daughter, (2) Nicole Brown, 1985, divorced 1992, deceased 1994, 2 sons. Education: University of Southern California; City College, San Francisco. Appointments: Member, World Record 440 yard relay team (38.6 sec), 1967; Downtown Athletic Club, 1968; Halfback, Buffalo Bills, 1969-75; San Francisco 49'ers, 1978-79; American Football League All-Star team, 1970; ProBowl Team, 1972-76; Sports Commentator, ABC Sports, 1979-86; Analyst, ABC Monday Night Football Broadcasts, 1984-85; co-host, NFL Live on NBC, 1990; Has appeared in several TV films; Acquitted of two charges of murder, 1995; Found responsible for the deaths of Nicole Brown Simpson and Ronald Goldman by civil jury, 1997; Films include: The Towering Inferno, 1974; Killer Force, 1976; The Cassandra Crossing, 1977; Capricorn One, 1978; Firepower, 1979; Hambone and Hillie, 1984; The Naked Gun, 1988; The Naked Gun 2 ½: The Smell of Fear, 1991; The Naked Gun 33 ½: The Final Insult. Publication: I Want to Tell You, 1995. Honours: Recipient of various football awards.

SINAGATULLIN Ilghiz Mirgalimovich, b. 13 July 1954, Belebey, Bashkortostan, Russia. Teacher; Educator. m. Zemfira Sinagatullina, 1 son. Education: Linguistics, Foreign Languages, Bashkir State University, Ufa, Bashkortostan, Russia, 1976; Candidate of Pedagogical Sciences, 1984, Doctor of Pedagogical Sciences, 1995, Moscow Pedagogical State University, Russia. Appointments: English Language Teacher, Secondary School No. 39, Ufa, Bashkortostan, Russia, 1976-77; English Language Assistant, Bashkir State Pedagogical Institute, Ufa, Bashkortostan, Russia, 1977-79; English Language Chair Assistant, Senior Teacher, Associate Professor, 1980-90, Department Chair of Foreign Languages, Associate Professor, 1990-95, Department Chair of Pedagogy and Elementary Education, Professor, 1995-, Birsk State Pedagogical Institute, Birsk, Bashkortostan, Russia. Publications: Over 80 publications include most recently: Diversity and multicultural education: A glance at the Russian front, 1998; Expectant times: rural education in Russia, 2001; In Russia: multicultural strategies of an elementary teacher, 2001; The impact of globalization on Russian Education, 2003; Constructing multicultural education in a diverse society, 2003. Honours include: Birsk Institute's Honourable Certificate for Professional Excellence, 1997; Bashkortostan's Honourable Certificate for Professional Excellence, 1999; Excellent Educator of Bashkortostan, 2001; Certificate of Recognition for Scholar in Residence, 2001, Certificate of Appreciation for Presentation, 2001, Kent State University, USA; Russian Federation's Honourable Certificate for Professional Excellence, 2003; Scholarships and Research Grants include: International Research and Exchange Open Competition Program Grant, USA, 1994; Fulbright Scholarship, USA, 1996-97; The Netherlands Management Program Scholarship, the Netherlands, 1999; Regional Scholar Exchange Program Scholarship, USA, 2001; Listed in Who's Who publications and biographical dictionaries. Memberships: Scientific Council, Birsk Pedagogical Institute, 1998-; Dissertational Council, Bashkir State Pedagogical University, 2003-. Address: Gagarina ul. 86-A, Apt 46, Birsk, Bashkortostan, Russia 452452. E-mail: ilghiz56@yahoo.com

SINCLAIR Andrew Annandale, b. 21 January 1935, Oxford, England. Writer; Historian. m. Sonia Melchett, 25 July 1984, 2 sons. Education: Major Scholar, BA, PhD, Trinity College, Cambridge, 1955-59; Harkness Fellow, Harvard University,1959-61; American Council of Learned Societies Fellow, Stanford University, 1964-65. Appointments: Founding Fellow, Churchill College, 1961-63; Lecturer, University College, London, 1966-68; Publisher, Lorrimer Publishing, 1968-89; Managing Director,

Timon Films Limited, 1968-2004. Publications: The Breaking of Bumbo, 1959; My Friend Judas, 1959; Prohibition: The Era of Excess, 1961; Gog, 1967; Magog, 1972; Jack: A Biography of Jack London, 1977; The Other Victoria, 1981; King Ludd, 1988; War Like a Wasp, 1989; The War Decade: An Anthology of the 1940's, 1989; The Need to Give, 1990; The Far Corners of the Earth, 1991; The Naked Savage, 1991; The Strength of the Hills, 1991; The Sword and the Grail, 1992; Francis Bacon: His Life and Violent Times, 1993; In Love and Anger, 1994; Jerusalem: The Endless Crusade, 1995; Arts and Cultures: The History of the 50 Years of the Arts Council of Great Britain, 1995; The Discovery of the Grail, 1998; Death by Fame: A Life of Elisabeth, Empress of Austria, 1998; Guevara, 1998; Dylan the Bard: A Life of Dylan Thomas, 1999; The Secret Scroll, 2001; Blood and Kin, 2002; An Anatomy of Terror, 2003. Contributions to: Sunday Times; Times; New York Times; Atlantic Monthly. Honours: Somerset Maugham Prize, 1967; Venice Film Festival Award, 1971. Memberships: Royal Literary Society, fellow, 1968; Society of American Historians, fellow 1970. Address: Flat 20, Millennium House, 132 Grosvenor Road, London SW1V 3JY, England.

SINCLAIR Nicholas Hilary, b. 28 January 1954, London, England. Photographer. Education: Fine Art, University of Newcastle-upon-Tyne, 1973-76. Career: Individual Exhibitions: Photography Centre of Athens, Greece, 1986; Brighton Museum and Art Gallery, 1995; Tom Blau Gallery, London, 1996; Brighton Museum and Art Gallery, 1997; Luciano Inga-Pin Gallery, Milan, Italy, 1999; Focus Gallery, London, 2000; Selected Group Exhibitions: National Portrait Gallery, London, 1998-99; Padiglione d'Art Contemporanea, Milan, Italy, 1999; Culturgest, Lisbon, Portugal, 1999; Caterina Gualco Gallery, Genova, Italy, 2000; Musée de l'Elysée, Lausanne, Switzerland, 2000; National Portrait Gallery, London, 2001; Public Collections: National Portrait Gallery, London; Victoria and Albert Museum, London; Staatsgalerie, Stuttgart, Germany; Folkwang Museum, Essen, Germany; Musée de l'Elysée, Lausanne, Switzerland. Publications: The Chameleon Body, 1996; Franko B, 1998; Portraits of Artists, 2000; Crossing the Water, 2002; Kyffin Williams – A Studio Monograph, 2004. Honours: Hasselblad Award, 1998; Arts Council of England Publishing Award, 1998; South East Arts Award, 1999, 2002; Year of the Artist Award, 2000; British Book Design and Production Award, 2001; Hasselblad Master, 2003. Address: 56 Denmark Villas, Hove, East Sussex, BN3 3TE, England. E-mail: nicholas.sinclair@virgin.net

SINCLAIR Sonia Elizabeth, (Sonia Graham, Sonia Melchett), b. 6 September 1928, Nainital, India. Writer. m. (1) Julian Mond (Lord Melchett), deceased June 1973, 1 son, 2 daughters, (2) Andrew Sinclair, 1984. Education: Queen's Secretarial College, Windsor, England. Appointments: Writer, Member of Board of Directors, English Stage Company. Publications: (as Sonia Graham) Tell Me Honestly (non-fiction), 1964; (as Sonia Melchett) Someone is Missing (non-fiction), 1987; (as Sonia Melchett) Passionate Quests - Five Contemporary Women Travellers, 1989; Sons and Mothers (edited by Matthew and Victoria Glendinning), 1996. Contributions to: Periodicals. Honour: Prizewinner, Short Story Competition, Raconteur Magazine. Address: Flat 20, Millennium House, 132 Grosvenor Road, London SW1V 3JY, England.

SINDEN Donald (Sir), b. 9 October 1923, Plymouth, Devon, England. Actor; Writer. m. Diana Mahony, 1948, 2 sons. Appointments: Professional Actor, 1942-; Films for the Rank Organisation, 1952-60; Associate Artist, Royal Shakespeare Company, 1967-. Publications: A Touch of the Memoirs, 1982; Laughter in the Second Act, 1985; Everyman Book of Theatrical Anecdotes (editor), 1987; The English Country Church, 1988; The

Dictionary of International Biography

Last Word (editor), 1994. Honour: Commander of the Order of the British Empire, 1979; Knighted, 1997. Memberships: Council of British Actors Equity, 1966-77, trustee, 1988-; Arts Council, Drama Panel, 1973-77, Advisory Board, 1982-86 Federation of Playgoers' Societies, president, 1968-93; Royal Theatrical Fund, president, 1983-; Royal Society of Arts, fellow, 1966-; Green Room Benevolent Fund, president, 1998-. Literary Agent: Vivien Green, Shiel Land, 43 Doughty Street, London WC1N 2LF. Address: Number One, NW11 6AY, England.

SINDLEROVA Eva, b. 5 January 1935, Brno, Czech Republic. Opthalmologist. m. Jiri Sindler, 2 daughters. Education: Medical Faculty, Masaryk University, Brno, 1959; Opthalmology, Karvina Hospital, 1968; II degree, 1978. Appointments: Leader of the Department of Opthalmology, Karvina Hospital, 1979-96; Private Opthalmologist, 1996-. Publications: 12 professional publications, 1970-87; Deyl's Honour, 1975; 97 professional lectures. Memberships: Czech Opthalmologic Society; Czech Society of Refractory Surgery; Czech Glaucoma Society; European Society of Cataract and Refractive Surgeons. Address: Bastlova 21, 704 00 Ostava Zabrech, Czech Republic.

SINGER Gali-Dana, (Adel Kilka, Gad Gresin), b. 23 April 1962, Leningrad, USSR. Education: State Institute of Theatre, Music & Cinematography, Leningrad, 1979-82. Appointments: Chief Editor, Literary Magazines: IO, Jerusalem, 1994-95; Dvojetochije (Colon), 1995-. Publications: Russian: Collection, 1992; Adel Kilka, From, 1993; Jerusalem beseiged, 2002; Hebrew: To Think River, 2000; Blind Poems, 2002. Contributions to: Russian: 22; Slog; Dvojetochije; Narod i Zemlja; Solnechnoe Spletenie; Arion; Kamera Chranenija; Targum; Scopus II; in Hebrew: Helicon; Dimui; Gag; Chadarim; Alpaim; Siach Meshorerim; Shwo; Carmel; 77; R'hov; The Poems, 4 International Poet's Festival, Jerusalem. Honour: Prizes, Minister of Absorbtion of Israel, 1996; Poetry-2000; Prime Minister, 2003. Memberships: The General Union of Writers in Israel. Address: Zipori st 33, Nachlaot, 94544 Jerusalem, Israel.

SINGER Jonathan Douglas, b. 15 May 1952, Bronx, New York, New York. Writer; Artist; Poet. Education: Oxford University BUNAC Programme, Mansfield College, England, Summer 1969; BA, History, 1970-74, MA, History, 1975-78, New York University, New York City, USA. Appointments: Press Aid, Office of Mayor, City Hall, New York City, USA, 1978; Library Assistant, Yale University Medical Library, New Haven, Connecticut, 1986-87; Library Assistant, Yale University School of Medicine, 2002-2003. Publications: Books: La Filière Égyptienne (chapter in French in Les Atlantes by Jacques Gossart), 1986; Lost Lands and Cities Beneath the Sea, 1997; Ireland's Mysterious Lands and Sunken Cities, 2000. Honours: High School Social Studies Award, 1970; New York University Undergraduate History Award, 1974. Memberships: Fellowship Club; Running Strong for American Indian Youth; Arts Council of Greater New Haven Artship Co-operative. Address: 305 Audubon Court, New Haven, CT 06510, USA.

SINGH Ashok Kumar, b. 29 June 1945, Bihar, India. Geologist; Geotech Engineer. m. Pushpalata, 3 daughters. Education: BSc (Hons), Applied Geology, 1964, MSc, AISM, Applied Geology, 1965, Indian School of Mines; MSc, DIC, Engineering Rock Mechanics, Imperial College, London, 1972. Appointments: Geologist, Head of Rock Mechanics, Hindustan Copper, India, 1966-79; Rock Mechanics Engineer, Chief Geologist, Zambia Consolidated Copper Mines Ltd, 1980-99; Mine Manager, Manager Mining Services, Mopani Copper Mines plc, Zambia, 2000-2001; Group Hydrogeological Engineer, Konkola Copper Mines plc, Zambia, 2002-. Publications: 12 technical papers in various symposia, seminars and technical magazines. Honours: Commonwealth Fellowship to Australia for research in the field of geomechanics, 1977. Memberships: The Institute of Materials, Minerals and Mining, UK; Chartered Engineer, Council of Engineers, UK; Engineering Institution of Zambia; Registered Engineer, Zambia. Address: 22 Spurwing Avenue, Post Box 210071, Chililabombwe, Zambia. E-mail: ashoks@zamtel.zm

SINGH Simon Lehna, b. 19 September 1964, Wellington, Somerset, England. Writer. Education: BSc, Imperial College; PhD, Cambridge University. Publication: Fermat's Last Theorem, 1997; The Code Book, 1999; The Science of Secrecy, 2000; Big Bang, 2004. Address: Conville and Walsh Ltd, 2 Ganton Street, London W1F 7QL, England.

SINGH Yudh Vir, b. 20 December 1952, Hamirpur (HP), India. Researcher. m. Sarita Singh, 1 son, 2 daughters. Education: Matric, 1968, Intermediate, 1971, BSc Ag (Honours) and AH, 1975; MScAg (Agron), 1977; PhD, 1990. Appointments: Joined ICAR services at CAZRI Jodhpur, 1978; Integrated Water and nutrient management with special reference to arid and semi-arid regions; Principal Scientist (Agronomy), National Research Centre for ground nut, Junagadh, 1999-2003; Head, Regional Research Station, CAZRI Pali, 2003-. Publications: 50 papers, popular articles in international and national journals; conferences. Honour: ICAR team Research Award for biennium, 1983-84. Membership: Arid Zone Association of India. Address: Regional Research Station, Central Arid Zone Research Institute, Pali 306401, India.

SINGLETON Valerie, b. 9 April 1937, England. Education: Arts Educational School London, RADA. Appointments: Broadcast Personality and Writer; Bromley Rep, 1956-57, subsequently, No 1 Tour, Cambridge Arts Theatre, Theatre work, TV appearances, Compact and Emergency Ward 10 and others, top voice over commentator for TV commercials and advertising magazines; BBC 1: Continuity Announcer, 1962-64, Presenter, Blue Peter, 1962-72, Nationwide, 1972-78, Val Meets the VIPs (3 series), Blue Peter Special Assignment (4 series), Blue Peter Royal Safari with HRH The Princess Anne, Tonight and Tonight in Town, 1978-79, Blue Peter Special Assignments Rivers Yukon and Niagara, 1980; BBC 2: Echoes of Holocaust, 1979, The Migrant Workers of Europe, 1980, The Money Programme, 1980-88; Radio 4: PM 1981-93, several appearances Midweek; Freelance Broadcaster and Travel Writer, 1993-; Channel 4: Presenter, Back-Date (daily quiz programme), 1996; Playback, History Channel, 1998, second series, 1999; Numerous appearances in TV advertising. Honour: OBE. Membership: Equity. Address: c/o Arlington Enterprises, 1-3 Charlotte Street, London W1, England.

SINHA Neeti, b. 29 June 1970, Lucknow, India. Scientist. m. Sandeep Kumar, 1 daughter. Education: PhD/DPhil, University of Oxford England; Post-doctoral Research, NCI, National Institutes of Health, USA, 1998-2003. Appointment: Associate Research Scientist, Johns Hopkins University, Baltimore, USA, 2003-. Publications: 14 research articles on protein thermodynamics and structure in top-rated scientific journals such as: PNAS, USA; Structure, Folding and Design; Biophysical Journal; Protein Engineering; and invited reviews. Honours: Felix Scholarship Award, Oxford; Radhakrishnan Bequest at Oxford; Post-doctoral Visiting Fellowship, NIH, USA; Outstanding Scientist Category in USA; JR Fellowship and Lecturership, CSIR, India. Memberships: American Association for the Advancement of Science; The Protein Society; International Society for Computational Biology. Address: Biocalorimetry Center, Biology Department, Johns Hopkins University, 3400 N Charles Street, Baltimore, MD 21218, USA. E-mail: nsinha@jhu.edu

Dictionary of International Biography

SINNADURAI Nihal, b. 25 September 1941, Colombo, Sri Lanka. Consultant. 1 son, 1 daughter. Education: BSc, Physics with Honours, 1966, MSc Semiconductor Physics, 1969, University of London; PhD, Reliability, Southampton, England, 1978. Appointments: Head of Section, Advanced Hardware Technologies, BT Labs, England, 1980-85; Senior Consultant, BPA, England, 1985-86; Head of CAE Strategy, Head of Intelligent Networks, British Telecommunications Plc, England, 1986-93; Professor and Head of Microelectronics Centre, Middlesex University, 1994-95; Corporate Director, Reliability and Quality, Bookham Technology, 2001-; Managing Director and Principal Consultant, Advanced Technology Transfer Associates, 1987-. Publications: Mechanisms and Modes of Failure in Semiconductor Devices, 1970; Handbook of Microelectronics Packing and Interconnection Technologies, 1985; More than 90 papers in refereed journals; Chapters into 3 NATO Advanced Technology Books; Inventions: Highly Accelerated Stress Test (HAST) for Reliability, 1968; Liquid Crystal Microthermography, 1974; Epic Microelectronics Package, 1981. Honours: Various Best Papers Awards, 1982-; Outstanding Technical Achievement Award, 1984; Daniel Hughes Jr Memorial Award for Outstanding Professional Achievement, IMAPS, North America, 2003. Memberships: Fellow, IEEE; Fellow, Institute of Physics; Chairman, IEEE CPMT and Reliability Society, 2001-; Chairman, IMPS Europe, 1987-89; Chairman, IMPS UK, 1986088, 1994-96, 2001-03.

SINNOTT Jan Dynda, b. 14 June 1942, Cleveland, Ohio. Psychologist. Life partner: Lynn Johnson, 2 sons, 2 daughters. Education: BS, St Louis University, 1964; MA, 1973, PhD, 1975, Catholic University of America. Appointments: Workshop Lecturer, 1971-; Social Rehabilitation Services Research Trainee, 1971-74; Research Assistant, 1971-72, Teaching Assistant, 1973, Catholic University of America; Research Associate, Human Sciences Research, Virginia, 1975; Lecturer, 1975-77, Research Associate, 1975-77, Catholic University of America; Founder and Director, Human Development Research, 1977-80; Principal Investigator, Centre on Ageing, University of Maryland, 1977-80; Guest Scientist, Gerontology Research Centre, National Institute on Ageing, NIH, 1980-89; Director, Centre for Study of Adult Development and Ageing, 1989-91, Associate Director, Institute for Cognition and Teaching, 2001-, Tenured Professor of Psychology, 1978-, Towson University, Maryland. Publications: The Development in Logic in Adulthood: Postformal Thought and Its Application; Plus numerous other reviews, books, articles, book chapters and papers. Honours: Towson University Faculty Excellence Award; Listed in Who's Who publications and biographical dictionaries. Memberships: Fellow, American Psychological Association; Fellow, Gerontological Society of America; Fellow, American Psychological Society; many others. Address: 9923 Cottrell Terrace, Silver Spring, Maryland 20903, USA. E-mail: jsinnott@towson.edu

SIO Jimmy Ong, b. 9 March 1954, Manila, Philippines. Education: BS, Biology, California State College in Bakersfield, California, USA, 1976; PhD, Cell Biology, University of Texas Health Science Center, Dallas, 1985; MD, Emory University School of Medicine, Atlanta, Georgia, 1985. Appointments: PGY-1 Resident in Anatomical Pathology, Emory University School of Medicine, 1985-86; Resident in Internal Medicine, Kern Medical Center, Bakersfield, 1990-93; Physician, Southern California Permanente Medical Group, Bakersfield, 1993-. Publications: Article for the book, Immunological Aspects of Infertility and Fertility Regulation, 1980; Article for the journal, Biology of Reproduction, 1982. Honours: Outstanding Physician of the Year 2002, Southern California Permanente Medical Group; Universal Award of Accomplishment 2003, ABI. Memberships: InterNet Associates; New York Academy of Sciences. Address: 8800 Ming Avenue, Bakersfield, CA 93311, USA.

SÎRBU Valeriu, b. 25 February 1950, Cladova, Romania. Archaeologist; Researcher. m. Livia Sîrbu, 2 sons. Education: History Studies, University of Bucharest, 1970-74; Doctors degree, University of Jassy, 1993. Appointments: Museologist, 1975-81, First Museologist, 1981-91, Department Chief, 1991-93, Manager Assistant, 1993-96, Senior Researcher, 1993-2004, Department Chief, 1996-99, Manager Assistant, 1999-2004, Museum of Brăila, Romania; Senior Researcher, Romanian Institute of Thracology, 1996-99; Professor, University "Constantin Brâncoveanu", Brăila, 2000-2002; Senior Researcher, Institute of Archaeology, Bucharest, 2003-04; Visiting Professor, Sorbonne University, 2004; Archaeological excavations in 14 settlements and necropolises, Bronze Age and Iron Age in Romania, 2 sites in Ukraine, other sites in the Republic of Moldavia. Publications: 9 books, 6 co-authored; 115 studies and articles, some co-authored in the field of history and archaeology of the Thracian world in Hallstatt and La Tène; Numerous lectures at international symposia and conferences. Honours: Prize "Nicolae Bălcescu", Romanian Academy, 1993. Memberships: National Commission of Archaeology, Romania; President, Funerary Archaeology Studies Association; President, XXXth Commission of the International Union of Prehistoric and Protohistoric Sciences. Address: Museum of Brăila, 3 Square Traian, 810135 Brăila, Romania. E-mail: valeriu_sirbu@yahoo.co.uk

SISK Fred Dean, b. 26 May 1940, Johnson City, Tennessee, USA. Retired Cartographer. m. Martha Lynn Robinson Sisk. Education: BS, Geography, East Tennessee State University, 1962; MS, Cartography, George Mason University, 1984. Appointments: Artillery Officer, United States Army Battery Commander, Fort Sill, Oklahoma, 1962-65; Cartographer, Army Map Service, US Army Topographic Command, Defense Mapping Agency, Washington DC, 1965-79; Senior Cartographer, Course Manager, Deputy Division Chief, Senior Instructor, Master Instructor, Defense Mapping School, Fort Belvoir, Virginia, 1979-88; Training Co-ordinator, 1988-89, Cartographer, Security Officer, 1989-95, Defense Mapping Agency, Reston, Virginia; Retired, 1995; Security Officer, Notary Public, State of Virginia, Officer of Election, City of Fredricksburg, 1996-2004. Honours: Sustained Superior Performance Award, US Army Topographic Command, 1971; Outstanding Performance Award, Defense Mapping School, 1985, 1986; Lifetime Achievement Award in Photography, International Freelance Photographers Organization, 2004; Listed in Who's Who publications and biographical dictionaries. Memberships: President, Fox Run Homeowners Association, Fredericksburg, Virginia, 1996-; Past Chairman, Memorial Advisory Commission, City of Fredericksburg, Virginia; Board of Directors, Fredericksburg Regional Transit System; Master Photographer, International Freelance Photographers Organization; Life Member, National Rifle Association, Washington DC; Civil War Round Table, Fredericksburg, Virginia; Republican National Committee, Washington DC; Republican Presidential Task Force, Washington DC; The Heritage Foundation, Washington DC. Address: 18 Devonshire Drive, Fredericksburg, VA 22401, USA

SISSON C(harles) H(ubert), b. 22 April 1914, Bristol, England. Poet; Writer; Translator; Editor; Retired Civil Servant. m. Nora Gilbertson, 19 August 1937, 2 daughters. Education: BA, 1st Class Honours, University of Bristol, 1934; Postgraduate studies, University of Berlin and Freiburg, 1934-35, Sorbonne, University of Paris, 1935-36. Appointments: Assistant Principal, 1936-42, Principal, 1945-53, Assistant Secretary, 1953-62, Undersecretary, 1962-68, Assistant Undersecretary of State, 1968-71, Director of Occupational Safety and Health, 1971-73, Ministry of Labour. Publications: Poetry: Poems, 1959; Twenty-One Poems, 1960; The London Zoo, 1961; Numbers, 1965; The Discarnation: Or, How the Flesh Became Word and Dwelt Among Us, 1967;

Metamorphoses, 1968; Roman Poems, 1968; In the Trojan Ditch: Collected Poems and Selected Translations, 1974; The Corridor, 1975; Anchises, 1976; Exactions, 1980; Selected Poems, 1981; Night Thoughts and Other Poems, 1983; Collected Poems, 1943-1983, 1984; God Bless Karl Marx!, 1987; Antidotes, 1991; Nine Sonnets, 1991; The Pattern, 1993; What and Who, 1994: Novels: An Asiatic Romance, 1953; Christopher Homm, 1965. Non-Fiction: The Spirit of British Administration and Some European Comparisons, 1959, 2nd edition, 1966; Art and Action (essays), 1965; Essays, 1967; English Poetry 1900-1950: An Assessment, 1971; The Case of Walter Baghot, 1972; David Hume, 1976; The English Sermon: An Anthology, Vol 2, 1976; The Avoidance of Literature: Collected Essays, 1978; Anglican Essays, 1983; The Poet and the Translator, 1985; On the Look-Out: A Partial Autobiography, 1989; In Two Minds: Guesses at Other Writers, 1990; English Perspectives: Essays on Liberty and Government, 1992; Is There a Church of England?, 1993. Translator: Versions and Perversions of Heine, 1955; The Poetry of Catullus, 1966; The Poetic Art: A Translation of Horace's "Ars Poetica", 1975; Lucretius: De Rerum Natura: The Poem on Nature, 1976; Jean de La Fontaine: Some Tales, 1979; Dante Alighieri: The Divine Comedy, 1981; The Song of Roland, 1983; Joachim du Bellay: The Regrets, 1984; Virgil: The Aeneid, 1986; Jean Racine: Britannicus, Phaedra, Athaliah, 1987. Editor: David Wright: South African Album, 1976; Jonathan Swift: Selected Poems, 1977; Thomas Hardy: Jude the Obscure, 1979; Philip Mairet: Autobiographical and Other Papers, 1981; Christina Rossetti: Selected Poems, 1984; Jeremy Taylor: Selected Writings, 1990; Collected Poems, 1998. Contributions to: Agenda; London Magazine; London Review of Books; New Criterion; New York Times Review of Books; Poetry Nation Review; Spectator; Times Literary Supplement. Honours: Senior Simon Research Fellow, University of Manchester; Fellow, Royal Society of London, 1975; Honorary DLitt, University of Bristol, 1980; Companion of Honour, 1993. Address: Moorfield Cottage, The Hill, Langport, Somerset TA10 9PU, England.

SISSONS Peter George, b. 17 July 1942. British Television Presenter. m. Sylvia Bennett, 1965, 2 sons, 1 daughter. Education: University College Oxford. Appointments: Graduate Trainee, 1964, General Reporter, 1967, Industrial Correspondent, 1970, Industrial Editor, 1972-78, Independent TV News; Presenter, News at One, 1978-82; Presenter, Channel 4 News, 1982-89; Presenter, BBC TV News (9 O'Clock News 1994-2000, 10 O'Clock News, 2000-), 1989-; Chair, BBC TV Question Time, 1989-93. Honours: Broadcasting Press Guild Award, 1984; Royal TV Society Judges' Award, 1988; Honorary Fellow, Liverpool John Moores University, 1997. Address: BBC Television Centre, Wood Lane, London, W12 7RJ, England.

SITSKY Larry, b. 10 September 1934, China (Australian Citizen). Education: Piano studies; Graduate, Piano and Composition, New South Wales State Conservatorium of Music, 1955; Studied with Egon Petri, San Francisco Conservatory, 1958-1961. Appointments: Piano teacher, Queensland State Conservatorium of Music, Guest lecturer, Queensland University, 1961-65; Head of Keyboard Studies, 1966-78, Head, Department of Composition and Electronic Music, 1978-81, Head, Department of Composition 1983, School of Music, Australian National University; Guest lecturer, Australian National University in Department of Extension and Continuing Studies, 1983-; Reader, 1993-94, Professor, 1994-; Resident Composer, International String School (Melbourne), 1996, 1997; Resident Composer, Australian Academy of Music, 1998; Invited to jury of Busoni piano competition, Bolzano, Italy, 1999. Creative Works: Compositions include: solo instrumental pieces to large orchestral works including the award-winning: Violin Concerto No 1, 1971, Clarinet Concerto, 1981, String

Quartet, 1968, Maherq, 1989, Secret Gates of the House of Osiris, 1989; Opera: The Golem, 3 CD set, ABC Classics, 1993; CD, sonatas of Australian composer Roy Agnew; 3 CDs of Australian Piano Music; Numerous commissions. Publications: Books: Busoni and the Piano; The Classical Reproducing Piano Roll; Music of the Repressed Russian Avant-garde 1900-1929; Anton Rubinstein, 1998; Music of the Twentieth Century avant-garde, 2003; Editor, Anthology of Australian Piano Music, 2001. Honours include: Prizes for compositions; Inaugural Australian Composer's Fellowship, 1984; Fulbright Award, 1988-89; Advance Australia Award, 1989; Professor (personal Chair) Australian National University; Higher Doctorate in Fine Arts, 1997; Order of Australia, 2000; Artist of the Year, 2001; Centenary Medal, 2003. Address: 29 Threlfall St, Chifley, ACT 2601, Australia.

SIU Wing Tai, b. 20 November 1964, Hong Kong. Surgeon. m. Bonita Ka Bo Law, 1 son. Education: MB, ChB, The Chinese University of Hong Kong, 1989. Appointments: Chief of Division of Upper Gastrointestinal and Vascular Surgery, Department of Surgery, 1996-, Co-director, Minimal Access Surgery Training Center, 2003-, Pamela Youde Nethersole Eastern Hospital, Hong Kong; Honorary Assistant Professor, Department of Surgery, Faculty of Medicine, Chinese University of Hong Kong, 1996-; Visiting Surgeon, General Surgery, Ruttonjee and Tang Shiu Kin Hospitals, 2002-; Honorary Clinical Supervisor, The Hong Kong College of Family Physicians, 2003-. Publications include: 48 articles and reports in medical and scientific journals including most recently: Laparoscopic repair for perforated ulcer: a randomized controlled trial, 2002; Laparoscopic repair of iatrogenic endoscopic perforated peptic ulcers, 2003; The role of laparoscopy in emergency peptic ulcer surgery, 2003; Therapeutic minilaparoscopy for perforated peptic ulcer, 2004; Routine use of laparoscopic repairs for perforated peptic ulcers, 2004. Honours include: Hong Kong Pathology Society Prize, 1987; 1st Prize, Health Medical Diagnostic Centre Prize in Morbid Anatomy, 1987; 2nd Prize, Wealth Physiology and Medical Laboratory Prizes in Chemical Pathology, 1987 ; B Y Lam Foundation Scholarship, 1988; City Lion Gold Medal Award, 1989; Young Clinican Program award, 11th World Congress of Gastroenterology, 1998; Best Original Paper Award, Annals of College of Surgeons of Hong Kong, 2001; Listed in several Who's Who and biographical publications. Memberships: Council Member, 1996-, Honorary Secretary, 1999-, Hong Kong Society of Minimal Access Surgery; Fellow, Royal College of Surgeons, Edinburgh, 1993-; Fellow, Hong Kong College of Surgeons, 1993-; Endolaparoscopic Surgeons of Asia, 1996-; Hong Kong Society of Digestive Endoscopy, 1994-; Hong Kong Chinese Medical Association, 1997-; Hong Kong Medical Association, 1989-; Medical Protection Society, 1990-; International Gastric Cancer Association, 2001-. Address: Flat A, 11/F, Block 28, Grand Dynasty View, Tai Po, New Territories, Hong Kong. E-mail: wtsiu@netvigator.com

SKAALVIK Einar Melgren, b. 11 April 1941, Norway. Educator; Professor. m. Sidsel, 1 daughter. Education: Teacher Certificate, Trondheim Teacher Training College, 1965; MA, Education, Magistergrad, University of Oslo, 1969; PhD, Education, University of Oslo, 1974. Appointments: Research Assistant, University of Trondheim, 1967-68; Scholarship, 1970-74; Visiting Professor, Pennsylvania State University, 1972-73; Associate Professor, 1974-81, Professor, 1981-, Norwegian University of Science and Technology; Courtesy Professor, University of Oregon, 1988-92; Part time Professor, Norwegian Institute, Adult Education, 1994-2002; Visiting Professor, California State University, 2003. Publications: 18 published books and research reports; 31 International articles; 34 conference papers; 23 articles in Norwegian books and journals. Memberships: AERA; EARLI; Phi Beta Delta; Self Research Centre. Address: Ranheimsveien 236, 7054 Ranheim, Norway.

SKÁRMETA Antonio, b. 7 November 1940, Antofagasta, Chile. Writer. Education: Graduated, University of Chile, 1963; MA, Columbia University, 1966. Appointments: Ambassador to Germany, 2000-01. Publications: El entusiasmo, 1967; Desnudo en el tejado, 1969; El ciclista del San Cristóbal, 1973; Tiro libre, 1973; Soñé que la nieve ardía, 1975, English translation as I Dreamt the Snow Was Burning, 1985; Novios y solitarios, 1975; La insurrección. 1980, English translation as The Insurrection, 1983; No pasó nada, 1980; Ardiente paciencia, 1985, English translation as Burning Patience, 1987; Match Ball, 1989; Watch Where the Wolf is Going, 1991. Contributions to: Periodicals. Honours: Premio Casa de las Américas, 1969; Guggenheim Fellowship, 1986; Academy Award Nomination, 1996. Address: Chilean Embassy, 53173 Bonn, Kronprinzenstr 20, Germany.

SKARSGÅRD J Stellan, b. 13 June 1951, Goteborg. Swedish Actor. m. My Gunther, 1976, 5 sons, 1 daughter. Appointments: With Royal Dramatic Theatre, Stockholm, 1972-87; Films Include: Simple Minded Murderer, 1982; Serpent's Way, 1986; Hip Hip Hurrah, 1987; The Unbearable Lightness of Being, 1988; Good Evening Mr Wallenberg, 1990; The Ox, 1992; Wind, 1992; The Slingshot, 1993; Zero Kelvin, 1994; Breaking the Waves, 1995; Insomnia, 1997; Amistad, 1997; Good Will Hunting, 1997; Ronin, 1998; Deep Blue Sea, 1998; Passion of Mind, 1999; For TV, Hamlet, 1984. Honours: Best Actor, Berlin Film Festival, 1982; Twice Best Film Actor in Sweden; Best Actor, Rouen Film Festival, 1988, 1992; Best Actor, Chicago Film Festival, 1991; Jury's Special Prize, San Sebastian Film Festival, 1995; European Film Award.

SKAU Michael, b. 6 January 1944, Illinois, USA. Professor of English; Poet. Education: BA, 1965, MA, 1967, PhD, 1973, University of Illinois. Appointments: Assistant Professor, 1973-78, Associate Professor, 1978-85, Professor of English, 1985-, University of Nebraska, Omaha; Jefferis Chair in History, 1997-200. Publication: Me and God Poems, 1990. Contributions to: Midland Review; Cumberland Poetry Review; Nothwest Review; Kentucky Poetry Review; Prophetic Voices; Sequoia; Paintbrush; Galley Sail Review; Carolina Quarterly; Great River Review; Illuminations; Passaic Review; Blue Unicorn; Minotaur. Membership: Modern Language Association. Address: Department of English, University of Nebraska, Omaha, NE 68182, USA.

SKINNER Richard, b. 15 July 1950, London, England. Writer; Poet; Counsellor. Education: MA, Natural Science, University of Cambridge, 1972; BPhil, CQSW, Social Work, University of Exeter, 1982. Appointments: Various posts. Publications: Leaping and Staggering, 1988; In The Stillness, 1990; Is The Clock Slow a Little Up, 1990; The Melting Woman, 1993; Still Staggering..., 1995; Echoes of Eckhart, 1998; The Logic of Whistling, 2002. Contributions to: Outposts; Orbit; Acumen; Westwords. Address: Little Bystock, Bystock Close, Exeter, Devon EX4 4JJ, England.

SKINNER Sandford Lloyd, b. 6 August 1933, Clare, South Australia. Physiologist. 1 son, 3 daughters. Education: Matriculation, 1951; MBBS, Adelaide, 1957; MD, Adelaide, 1962. Appointments: Reader, Physiology, University of Melbourne, 1968-98; Assistant Physician, Austin Hospital, Melbourne, Australia, 1977-2001; Principal Fellow, Department of Physiology, University of Melbourne, 1999-. Publications: Over 120 articles in professional medical journals. Honours: Travelling CJ Martin Research Fellowship, NH and MRC, 1962-64; Grant, Danish Government, 1973; Stipend, French Government, 1980. Memberships: Australian Physiological and Pharmacological Society; Australian Society of Endocrinology; International Society of Hypertension; Australasian Society of Nephrology; Fellow, Royal Australian College of Physicians. Address: 50 Molesworth Street, North Melbourne, Vic 3051, Australia.

SKNARIN Gennady Evseevich, b. 11 September 1938, Sochi, Russia. Teacher of Physics. m. Natalja Yurjevna Sknarina, 1 son, 2 daughters. Education: Physics Faculty, Odessa State University, 1958-63; Postgraduate Studentship, Philosophical Questions of Natural Physics, 1969-73. Appointment: Principal, Children's Proforientation Centre. Publications: 18 scientific works and textbooks; 20 computer programmes in the series: Euristic Stimulator; 10 databases for general professional training of teenagers; Systems for accelerating education by 10-15 times. Address: Cheltenham Avenue 48, Kvartal Kiparis, Sochi 354024, Russia. E-mail: sknarin@mail.ru Website: http://www.sochi.ru/school

SKOLNICK Judith A Colton, b. 31 January 1947, Washington, District of Columbia, USA. Artist. Divorced, 1 son, 1 daughter. Education: BA Honours, Studio Art, Art History, University of Maryland, 1972. Career includes: Technical Illustrator, Vitro Corporation, 1981-86; Art Consultant's Assistant, Capitol Arts, Washington DC, 1992-96; Artworks with juveniles, Northern Virginia Juvenile Detention Centre, 1993; Artist Associate to Mary Anne Reilly, 1995; Artist Guest Lecturer, Radford University, Virginia, 1996; Teaching, Very Special Arts Articulate Gallery School, Washington DC, 1998-99; Solo exhibitions: Artful Framer, Olney, MD, 1991, Kurz, Koch, Doland and Dembling, Washington DC, and Heartland Café, Washington DC, 1992, R St Gallery, Jackson School, Washington DC, 1993, Franklin Court Gallery, Washington DC, 1994, Parish Gallery, Washington DC, 1995, Flossie Martin Gallery, Radford University, Blacksburg, VA, 1996, Sunrise Gallery, Kilmarnock, Virginia, 1997, National Press Club Building, Washington DC, 1997-98, Art Mine, Internet, Agora Gallery, New York City, 1998, 1999, Guest Artist, Very Special Arts ONLINE GALL, Washington DC, 1999, Amsterdam Whitney Gallery, NYC, 2002, 2003; 9 Museum juried exhibitions, group exhibitions, numerous US venues, also Canada, Holland, Italy; Exhibitions, mail art, small works, numerous US venues, also Belgium, Germany, Argentina, Italy, Japan, England, Finland; France; Korea; Brazil. Creative Works: Oils; Acrylics; Collage; Miniature prints; Murals; Drawings. Publications: Gallery and Studio: The World of the Working Artist, 2000. Honours: 3rd Place, 1958, Honorary Mention, 1965, 2nd Place, Annual Art Show, St Christopher's Church, 1970, Montgomery County Art Association; 2nd Place, Corcoran School Art Exhibition, 1963; Professor-Student Award, Excellence in Printmaking, University of Maryland, 1971; Honorary Mention, Really Red Show, Capitol Hill Art League Gallery, 1992; Work on publication cover, WHO Aids Benefit publication cover, 1995; Artist Awards, Aidswalk Benefit, Embassy of Argentina, Washington DC, 1997; 20th Century Award for Achievement in Art, IBC; Listed in national and international biographical dictionaries. Memberships: Corcoran School Art Alumni Association; National Association Women Artists Inc; National Museum Women in Arts; International Order of Merit; Life Fellow, International Biographical Association. Address: 2301 E St NW #A1115, Washington, DC 20037, USA.

SKOLYSZEWSKI Jan, b. 27 January 1935, Krakow, Poland. Radiation Oncologist. m. Romana Machowska, 1 daughter. Education: Diploma in Medicine, School of Medicine, Krakow, 1958; MD, 1964; PhD, 1975; Diploma in Radiation Oncology, 1966. Appointments: Clinical Assistant, Centre of Oncology, Krakow, Poland, 1959-74; Head of Radiation Oncology Department, 1974-; Director, Centre of Oncology in Krakow, 1981-2001. Publications: About 170 articles in scientific journals; 3 manuals in the field of radiation oncology. Honours: Prize of Achievements of the Polish Ministry of Health, 1965; Prize of the Mayor of Krakow City, 1980; Hon M Sklodowska-Curie Medal of the Polish Society for Radiation Research, 1995. Memberships: Polish Society of Oncology, Secretary General, 1971-74; Polish

Dictionary of International Biography

Society of Radiation Oncology, President, 1997-2002; European Society for Therapeutic Radiology and Oncology; UK Radiotherapy Club. Address: Centre of Oncology, Garncarska 11, 31-115 Krakow, Poland.

SKOPINSKY Vadim Nikolaevich, b. 3 May 1946, Moscow. Higher School Professor. m. Elena, 2 sons. Education: Graduate, 1970; Post Graduate, 1970-73; Candidate of Technical Sciences, 1974; Doctor of Technical Sciences, Moscow Engineer Construction Institute, 1989. Appointments: Research Worker, 1973-76; Associate Professor, 1976-89; Professor, 1989-90; Head of Material Strength Chair, 1990-. Publications: Articles to professional journals and proceedings at conferences. Honours: Science Grantee, Academy of Transport Sciences, Moscow; Fundamental Research Grantee, Russian State Commission in Higher Education, 1996. Memberships: Member Academic Board; Member, Research Board of Advisors, ABI, USA; Member, Special Science Council, Institute of Technology and Mechanical Engineering; Member, Science Council, Moscow. Address: Alleya Zhemchugovoy 1-1-127, 111402 Moscow, Russia.

SKOROBOGATOV German, b. 10 January 1937, Datsan Cheata Region, Siberia. Physics-Chemistry Educator. m. Eugeniaja Nadeoshkeana, 3 daughters. Education: Magister, 1959, PhD, 1967, Department of Chemistry, Leningrad State University; Professor of Chemistry, St Petersburg State University, 1996. Appointments: Researcher, Institute of Silicate Chemistry, 1960-61; Researcher, Department of Physics, 1966-67, Chief of Photochemistry Laboratory, Department of Chemistry, 1968-2004, Professor, Department of Chemistry, 1984-2004, St Petersburg (Leningrad) State University. Publications: Radiochemistry and Chemistry of Nuclear Reactions, 1960; Orthodoxical and Paradoxical Chemistry, 1985; Co-author, book: Theoretical Chemistry, 2000; Take Care! Tap Water!, 2003; Foundations of Theoretical Chemistry, 2003; Articles in professional journals. Honours: Research Fellow, Coin, ABI, Bronze edition, 1993, Silver edition, 1996; Listed in national and international biographical dictionaries. Memberships: Mendeleev's Chemical Society (Moscow), 1975-2003; American Mathematical Society, 1988-98; Planetary Society, 1992-99. Address: Department of Chemistry, St Petersburg State University, Universitetskii prosp 26, 198504 St Petersburg, Russia. E-mail: gera.skor@pobox.spbu.ru

SKORTON David Jan, b. 22 November 1949, Milwaukee, Wisconsin, USA. Physician; Higher Education Administrator. 1 son. Education: BA, Psychology, Northwestern University at Evanston, 1970; MD, Northwestern University at Chicago, 1974; Medical Internship and Residency, 1974-77, Cardiology Fellowship, 1977-79, University of California at Los Angeles. Appointments: Adjunct Assistant Professor, Chief Resident, Department of Medicine, University of California at Los Angeles, 1978-79; Instructor, Assistant Professor, 1980-81, Associate Professor, 1984, Acting Director, 1985, Director, 1985-89, Division of General Internal Medicine, Associate Chair for Clinical Programs, 1989-92, Department of Internal Medicine, Assistant Professor, Department of Electrical and Computer Engineering, 1982, Director, Cardiovascular Research Center, 1982-96, Professor, Department of Internal Medicine, Electrical and Computer Engineering, and Biomedical Engineering, 1988, Vice President for Research, 1992-2002, Special Assistant to the President for the Health Sciences, 1996-97, Interim Vice President for External Relations, 2000-02, Vice President for Research and External Relations, 2002-03, President, 2003-, University of Iowa. Publications: Numerous papers, peer-reviewed investigations, reviews, editorials, reports and conference proceedings. Honours: Veterans Administration Research Associate Career Development Award, 1981-84; National Heart, Lung and Blood Institute

Research Career Development Award, 1984-89. Memberships: American Association for the Advancement of Science; American College of Cardiology; American College of Physicians; American Heart Association; American Physiological Society; Association of University Cardiologists. Address: The University of Iowa, 101 Jessup Hall, Iowa City, IA 52242-1316, USA. E-mail: david-skorton@uiowa.edu

SKOUTELIS Athanasios, b. 12 July 1954, Lamia, Greece. Professor of Medicine. m. Alexandra Filandrianu. 1 son, 1 daughter. Education: MD, Diploma, Athens University Medical School, 1978. Appointments: Lecturer, Medicine and Infectious Diseases, 1985-90, Assistant Professor, 1990-95, Associate Professor, 1995-2000, Professor of Medicine and Infectious Diseases, 2000-, Patras University Medical School, Greece. Publications: 100 papers in medicine and infectious diseases. Address: 32 Karaiskaki Str, Kifisia, Greece.

SKROMNE-KADLUBIK Gregorio, b. 9 April 1939, Mexico City. Nuclear Medicine Physician. m. Blanca Sofia Castillo, 1 son. Education: MD, National University, 1962; Nuclear Medicine, MD University of Sao Paulo, Brazil, 1968; MSc, National University, 1972. Appointments: Professor, Physiology, 1965; Head, Section, Nuclear Medicine, 1969-; Researcher, Faculty of Medicine, Mexico City, 1972; Coordinator, Nuclear Medicine, National Polytechnic Institute, 1978-88; Head, Nuclear Medicine, ISSSTF Mexico, 1974-88. Publications: 320 articles in nuclear medicine. Honours: Golden Medal, Sao Paulo, Brazil; G Soberan Medal, Health Society of Mexico. Memberships: AAAS; New York Academy of Sciences; International Brain Organisation. Address: Holbein 65 # 101, Mixcoac, DF, Mexico.

SKULJ Jola Jozica, b. 8 December 1947, Slovenia. Senior Research Fellow. m. Madzarevic Branko, 1 daughter. Education: Diploma, Comparative Literature, Literary Theory, 1980; MA, Comparative Literature, Literary Theory, 1991. Appointments: Free Lance Critic, several literary magazines, 1968-74; Students Assistant, Department of Comparative Literature, 1973-78; Part time Research Work, Institute of Literature, 1979-81; Research Assistant, 1981-91; Senior Research Fellow, 1991-96; Senior Specialist Adviser, 1996-. Publications: The Modern Novel, 1990; Dialogism as a non finalized concept of truth, 1997; Comparative Literature and Cultural Identity, 1999; Literature as Repository of Historical Consciousness: Reinterpreted Tales of Mnemosyne, 2000; Multilingualism as Strategy of Modern Dialogism, 2002; Modernism and the Crisis of Consciousness, 2003; others. Honour: Salzburg American Seminar Fellowship. Memberships: International Comparative Literature Association; Slovene Comparative Literature Association; ICLA Research Committee on Eastern and South-Eastern Europe, 2003-; Executive Board, European Network of Comparative Literary Studies, 2003-. Address: Tavcarjeva 1, 1000 Ljubljana, Slovenia.

SKYTTNER Lars, b. 20 August 1939, Gävle, Sweden. Education Educator; Army Air Force Pilot. m. Lisette Gustafsson, 2 sons, 1 daughter. Education: Commercial Pilot, Stockholm Flight School, Sweden, 1969; Military Officer, 5th Infantry Regiment, Östersund, 1974; PhD, Stockholm University, 1991. Appointments: Captain, Army Air Force, 1975; Assistant Professor, University of Stockholm, Sweden, 1998; Professor of Informatics, University of Gävle, 2001; Professor, Royal Swedish Military Academy, 1999-2003. Publications: Books: General Systems Theory: An Introduction, 1997; GST-Ideas and Applications, 2001; The Gateway of Knowledge, 2002. Honours: Military Medal, United Nations, 1992; Medal for Service Abroad, Swedish Defence Staff, 1994. Membership: Honorary Member, Society of Wireless Pioneers. Address: Helgeåkilen Törvallsgården, S-83070 Hammerdal, Sweden. E-mail: sky@hig.se

Dictionary of International Biography

SLAMA-CAZACU Tatiana, b. Bucharest, Romania. University Professor; Researcher; Writer. m. Boris Cazacu, deceased. Education: MA, Philosophy, Psychology, Pedagogy, 1942, MA, Modern Philology, 1943, Pedagogical Teachers Training, 1945-46, Romania; PhD, Psychology, 1966, Doctor in Sciences, 1969, Bucharest, Romania. Appointments: Teacher, Bucharest, 1948; Assistant Professor, University of Bucharest, 1949-52 (expelled for political reasons); From Researcher to Head of Laboratory of Psychology of Language and Head of Department of General Psychology, Institute of Psychology of Romanian Academy, 1954-68; Professor of Psycholinguistics and Applied Linguistics, University of Bucharest, 1968-80; Consulting Professor, 1980-; Nominated Visiting Professor, University of Paris, 1979-80. Publications: Over 40 books; 500 scientific articles in Romanian and other languages in psycholinguistics, psychology, linguistics. Honours: Prize of Romanian Academy, 1963; Woman of the Year, ABI, 1997, 2000, 2001, 2002, 2003; Various in IBC; Listed in Who's Who publications and biographical dictionaries. Memberships include: President, currently Honorary President, International Society of Applied Psycholinguistics; President; AILA founding member, Member, International Committee, Romanian Working Commission of Applied Linguistics; Editor-in-Chief, International Journal of Psycholinguistics. Address: Str. Moxa 10, Bucharest, Romania.

ŠLAPAL Josef, b. 21 December 1955, Brno, Czech Republic. Mathematician. m. Ivana Rybárová, 2 daughters. Education: MA Pure Mathematics, 1975-80, PhD Algebra, 1989-92, Masaryk University, Brno. Appointments: Lecturer, 1981-82, Senior Lecturer, 1982-86, Technical University of Ostrava; Senior Lecturer, 1986-94, Associate Professor, 1994-2000, Professor, 2000-, Technical University of Brno. Publications: Over 50 research papers in renowned mathematical journals. Honours: German Academy of Sciences Fellowship, 1994; DAAD Fellowship, Germany, 1998; Dr Jiri Nehnevajsa Memorial Award, University of Pittsburgh, 1999; NATO-CNR Outreach Fellowship, Italy, 2002. Memberships: American Mathematical Society; New York Academy of Sciences; Union of Czech Mathematicians and Physicists; National Geographic Society. Address: Department of Mathematics, Technical University of Brno, 616 69 Brno, Czech Republic. E-mail: slapal@um.fme.vutbr.cz Website: http://at.yorku.ca/h/a/a/a/10.htm

SLATER Edward Charles, b. 16 January 1917, Melbourne, Australia. Biochemist. m. Marion Winifred Hutley, 1 daughter. Education: MSc, University of Melbourne, 1935-39; PhD, DSc, Cambridge University, England, 1946-48. Appointments: Biochemist, Australian Institute of Anatomy, Canberra, Australia, 1939-46; Research Fellow, Molteno Institute, Cambridge University, 1946-55; Professor of Biochemistry, University of Amsterdam, 1955-85; Honorary Professor, Southampton University, 1985-90. Publications: About 400 articles in scientific journals and books; 1 monograph: The Story of a Biochemical Journal, 1986; Co-editor several publications. Honours include: Dixon Scholarship, Major James Cuming Memorial Scholarship in Chemistry, University of Melbourne, 1937; British Council Scholarship, 1946; Rockefeller Foundation Fellowship, 1949; University of Brussels Medal, 1956; Gold Medal, University of Bari, Italy, 1965; Medal of the Societe de Chimi Biologiqie, France, 1966; Keilin Medal, Biochemical Society, 1974; Knighthood in the Order of the Netherlands Lion, 1984; Honorary DSc, University of Southampton, 1993; Honorary D Biol. Sci., University of Bari, 1997. Memberships: Royal Netherlands Academy of Science, 1964; Dutch Company of Science, 1970; Corresponding Member, National Academy of science of Argentina, 1973; Honorary Member, Japanese Biochemical Society, 1973; Fellow of the Royal Society, 1975; Honorary Member, Biochemical Society, 1987;

Fellow World Innovation Foundation, 2001. Address: 9 Oaklands, Lymington, Hants SO41 3TH, England. E-mail: ecslater@btinternet.com

SLAVITT David R(ytman), (David Benjamin, Henry Lazarus, Lynn Meyer, Henry Sutton), b. 23 March 1935, White Plains, New York, USA. Novelist; Poet; Translator; Lecturer. m. (1) Lynn Nita Meyer, 27 August 1956, divorced 1977, 2 sons, 1 daughter, (2) Janet Lee Abrahm, 16 April 1978. Education: BA, magna cum laude, Yale University, 1956; MA, Columbia University, 1957. Appointments: Instructor in English, Georgia Institute of Technology, Atlanta, 1957-58; Staff, Newsweek magazine, 1958-65; Assistant Professor, University of Maryland, College Park, 1977; Associate Professor of English, Temple University, Philadelphia, 1978-80; Lecturer in English and Comparative Literature, Columbia University, 1985-86; Lecturer, Rutgers University, 1987-; Lecturer in English and Classics, University of Pennsylvania, 1991-97; Faculty Member, Bennington College, 2000-; Visiting Professorships; Many university and college poetry readings. Publications: Novels: Rochelle, or Virtue Rewarded, 1966; Anagrams, 1970; ABCD, 1972; The Outer Mongolian, 1973; The Killing of the King, 1974; King of Hearts, 1976; Jo Stern, 1978; Cold Comfort, 1980; Alice at 80, 1984; The Agent, 1986; The Hussar, 1987; Salazar Blinks, 1988; Lives of the Saints, 1989; Turkish Delights, 1993; The Cliff, 1994; Get Thee to a Nunnery: Two Divertimentos from Shakespeare, 1999. Henry Sutton: The Exhibitionist, 1967; The Voyeur, 1969; Vector, 1970; The Liberated, 1973; The Sacrifice: A Novel of the Occult, 1978; The Proposal, 1980. As Lynn Meyer: Paperback Thriller, 1975. As Henry Lazarus: That Golden Woman, 1976. As David Benjamin: The Idol, 1979. Non-Fiction: Understanding Social Life: An Introduction to Social Psychology (with Paul F Secord and Carl W Backman), 1976; Physicians Observed, 1987; Virgil, 1991; The Persians of Aeschylus, 1998; Three Amusements of Ausonius, 1998; Re-Verse: Essays on Poets and Poetry, forthcoming. Other: Editor: Adrien Stoutenburg: Land of Superior Mirages: New and Selected Poems, 1986; Short Stories Are Not Real Life: Short Fiction, 1991; Crossroads, 1994; A Gift, 1996; Epigram and Epic: Two Elizabethan Entertainments, 1997; A New Pleade: Seven American Poets, 1998. Translator: The Eclogues of Virgil, 1971; The Eclogues and the Georgics of Virgil, 1972; The Tristia of Ovid, 1985; Ovid's Poetry of Exile, 1990; Seneca: The Tragedies, 1992; The Fables of Avianus, 1993; The Metamorphoses of Ovid, 1994; The Twelve Minor Prophets, 1999; The Voyage of the Argo of Valerius Flaccus, 1999; Sonnets of Love and Death of Jean de Spande, 2001; The Elegies of Propertius, 2001. Contributions to: Various other books as well as periodicals. Honours: Pennsylvania Council on the Arts Award, 1985; National Endowment for the Arts Fellowship, 1988; American Academy and Institute of Arts and Letters Award, 1989; Rockefeller Foundation Artist's Residence, 1989. Address: 523 South 41st Street, Philadelphia, PA 19104, USA.

SLAWTER John David Jr, b. 11 May 1917, Winston-Salem, North Carolina, USA. Oil Company Executive. m. Joan Pirek Slawter, 2 daughters from a previous marriage. Education: Geology and Economics, University of North Carolina. Appointments: Chairman and Chief Executive Officer: Atlantic International Oil, Mid-Continent Oil, Coastal States Energy, OFG Corporation, HTS Corporation, EMTEC Inc, Activated Carbon Corporation of America, Interstate Hotels Inc. Publications: Oil Field Technology to Enhance Crude Oil Production and Simultaneously Increase Producible Reserves in Oil Fields; 47 US and International patents; 38 copyrights. Honours: Silver Star; Bronze Star with Oak Leaf Cluster; Purple Heart; Presidential Citation; 4 Battle Stars. Memberships: Republican National Committee, Washington;

World Peace Symposium, Geneva; IADC and AGC International. Address: PO Box 795273, Dallas, TX 75379, USA. E-mail: joslawter2@earthlink.com

SLECHTA Jiri, b. 26 April 1939, Havlikuv Brod, Czechoslovakia. Theoretical Physicist; Cyberneticist. 1 daughter. Education: RnDr, Charles University, Prague, Czechoslovakia, 1957-62. Appointments: Lecturer, 1964-65, Senior Lecturer, 1965-69, Department of Theoretical Physics, Charles University, Prague; Research Fellow, Department of Physics, University of Warwick, England, 1969-71; Senior Research Associate, School of Mathematics and Physics, University of East Anglia, England, 1971-74; Research Fellow, Physics Department, University of Leeds, England, 1976-77. Publications: Numerous article in professional scientific journals. Honours: Listed in national and international biographical dictionaries. Memberships: American Physical Society; Institute of Physics, London; European Physical Society; Institute of Mathematics and its Applications, UK; New York Academy of Sciences; British Cybernetic Society; Czechoslovak Mathematics and Physics Society; International Association of San Marino; TAKIS. Address: 5 Beckhill Chase, Leeds 7, LS7 2RQ, England. E-mail: jiri.slechta@amserve.net

SLEEP Wayne, b. 17 July 1948, Plymouth, England. Dancer; Actor; Choreographer. Education: Royal Ballet School (Leverhulme Scholar). Appointments: Joined Royal Ballet, 1966; Soloist, 1970; Principal, 1973; Roles in: Giselle; Dancers at a Gathering; The Nutcracker; Romeo and Juliet; The Grand Tour; Elite Syncopations; Swan Lake; The Four Seasons; Les Patineurs; Petroushka (title role); Cinderella; The Dream; Pineapple Poll; Mam'zelle Angot; 4th Symphony; La Fille Mal Gardee; A Month in the Country; A Good Night's Sleep; Coppelia; Also roles in operas: A Midsummer Nights Dream; Aida; Theatre Roles: Ariel in the Tempest; title role in Pinocchio; Genie in Aladdin; Soldier in The Soldiers Tale; Truffaldino in the Servant of Two Masters; Mr Mistoffelees in Cats; Choreography and lead role, The Point; co-starred in Song and Dance, 1982, 1990; Cabaret, 1986; formed own company, DASH, 1980; Dancer and Joint Choreographer, Bits and Pieces, 1989; Film: The Virgin Soldiers; The First Great Train Robbery; The Tales of Beatrix Potter; Numerous TV appearances include: Series, The Hot Summer Show, 1983, 1984. Publications: Variations on Wayne Sleep, 1983; Precious Little Sleep, 1996. Honours: Show Business Personality of the Year, 1983. Address: c/o Nick Thomas Artists, Event House, Queen Margaret's Road, Scarborough, YO11 2SA, England.

SLIMACEK Jan, b. 31 July 1939, Kelc, Czechoslovakia. Composer. m. Marie Chvatikova, 19 December 1964, 2 daughters. Education: Studied at Prague Conservatory. Debut: Symfonietta for Strings, Tape Recording Czech Radio. Career: Music Director, Radio, Plzen, 1967-93; 1994-; Sonatina for strings, Northern Music Festival, Ontario, 1988, Vassa, 1992; Divertimento for flute and piano, Inter Music Festival, Brno, 1989, Graz Wien, 1993; Quattro Intermezzi per Orchestra, Gera, 1983, Musical Festival Rostow Don, 1988; Concertino for accordion, electravox and orchestra, Gera, 1976, Nuremberg 1982, Bern, 1983; Dramatic Picture Szczecin, Weimar, 1979; Piano Quartet, Warsaw, 1977; Three Etudes for piano, Bristol, 1981; Professor of Music, Gymnasium Plzen, 1994-2000, 2000-. Compositions include: Piano Quartet; Sonatina for strings; Three Etudes for piano; Dramatic Picture; Songs for childrens choir and piano; Variations for strings and harpsichord. Recordings include: Quattro Intermezzi per orchestra; The Victory Overture for orchestra; Musica per orchestra; Three Miniatures for chamber orchestra; Music per ottoni. Honours: Audience Prize at Jihlava; Festival of Vocal Creation; Three first prizes at Olomouc Song Festival; Prize of Union of Czech

Composers and Concert Artists for 3 of his compositions, 1979. Membership: Association of Musicians and Musicologists. Address: Mohylová 109, Plzen 312 06, Czech Republic.

SLIWA Krzysztof, b. 5 July 1964, Poland. Professor of Spanish. 2 daughters. Education: Diploma, Department of Business, Liverpool Polytechnic, 1989; Diploma, Escola Universitaria de Traductores I d'Interpretes de la Universidad de Barcelona, 1989; BA, Universität von Hildesheim, 1993; MA, 1995, PhD, 1997, Florida State University. Appointments: Visiting Assistant Professor, University of Indiana, 2000; Visiting Assistant Professor, Idaho State University, 2001; Visiting Assistant Professor, Vanderbilt University, 2002; Assistant Professor, University of Utah, 2003-. Publications: Documentos de Miguel de Cervantes Saaveda, 1999; Documentos cervantinos: Nueva recopilacion; lista e indices, 2000; El licenciado Juan de Cervantes, 2001. Honours: Listed in Who's Who publications and biographical dictionaries. Memberships: American Association of Teachers of Spanish and Portuguese; Asociación de Cervantistos, Spain; Bulletin of Hispanic Studies, Liverpool. Address: 24 South 500 East #204, Salt Lake City, UT 84102. E-mail: chrissliwa@hotmail.com

SLOANE J P, b. 1942, Hollywood, California, USA. Biblical Scholar; Lecturer; Author. Education: Graduate of Oral Roberts Institute of Charismatic Studies, Tulsa, Oklahoma, 1985; Institute of Jewish-Christian Studies, Dallas, Texas, 1992; Moody Blue Institute, Chicago, Illinois, 1998; IBEX Campus, Abu Gosh, Israel, 2001; Graduate, BA, Summa Cum Laude, 2003, currently, Master in Nouthetic Counseling, The Masters College, Los Angeles, California; Studied: Religions of the Middle East, Jewish Thought and Culture, Physical Geography of Israel and Archeology. In addition to lectures around the USA, Christian TV appearances include The PTL Club; Lester Sumrall Today; Richard Roberts Live; The 700 Club; LeSea Broadcasting's World Harvest and Trinity Broadcasting's Praise The Lord. Author of children's series: Awesome Animal Adventures; Kingdom of the Butterflies; Do Our Pets Go To Heaven and Do Animals Go To Heaven? Contributor to Focus on the Family's; Adventures in Odyssey; Alexander Scourby's Dramatized Version of the Bible; Word, Inc. Featured in the 1998-99, 1999-2000 publications of The National Dean's List, representing only the top ½ of 1% of the United States college students. Appeared in the Smithsonian and Who's Who in the World, Millennium edition, also current editions of Who's Who in the World and Who's Who in America, Providence, New Jersey; Dictionary of International Biography, Cambridge, England; recipient of three international Angel awards; Medal of Merit, President Ronald Reagan; Keys to the Cities of New Orleans, Louisiana; Nashville, Tennessee; Monticello, Indiana. Governor's Commendation and appointment as Honorary Lieutenant Governor for the State of Indiana; Honorary Kentucky Colonel; Honorary Colonel and Aide-de-Camp of Governor Treen and Governor Edwards and , State of Louisiana; Honorary Sheriff of Los Angeles County; more. Address: Ste 407, 2219 East Thousand Oaks Blvd, Thousand Oaks, California 91362-2930, USA. Website: www.jpsloane.com

SLOMOVITZ Daniel, b. 25 May 1952, Montevideo, Uruguay. Electrical Engineer. m. Esther Joskowicz, 26 July 1975, 1 son, 1 daughter. Education: Electrical Engineer, Universidad de la Republica, Uruguay, 1978; Doctor in Engineering, Universidad de la Republica, 2000. Appointments: Assistant Engineer, 1977-78, Deputy Head, UTE Laboratory, 1978-79, Head, UTE Laboratory, 1979-, Professor, Electrical Measurements, 1999-, Universidad de la Republica. Publications: Over 70 articles in professional journals. Honours: Eminent Engineer, IEEE, 1994; Outstanding Engineer, IEEE, 1998. Memberships: IEEE; CIER; CIGRE. Address: E Lopez 4716/904, PO Box 19934, Montevideo, Uruguay. E-mail: d.slomovitz@ieee.org

SLYNKO Basil, b. 19 August 1951, Australia. Educator. Education: Diploma in Teaching; Bachelor of Educational Studies; MA. Appointments: Teacher, 1973-75, 1977-80; Lecturer, 1976; Head, Department, 1981-82, 1984-89, 1991-92, 1996-2001. Graduate Teaching Assistant, 1983-84; Education Officer, 1990-91, 1994-96. Publications include: Graphics 8, 1983, Teacher's Edition, 1983; Co-author, Technology Activity Book 1, 1986, 2nd Edition, 1994, Teacher's Edition, 1986, 2nd Teacher's Edition, 1994; Introducing Technology: A Text for Australian Secondary Schools, 1991; Co-author, Technology Activity Book 2, 1992, Teacher's Edition, 1992; Contributing author, Queensland Cement: Project and Activity Folder, 1995; Co-author, Graphics Booklets and Work Sheets, 1994-96. Honours: Postgraduate Scholarship, 1983-84; Epsilon Pi Tau, 1984; Laureate Citation, 2001. Memberships: International Technology Education Association, 1983-2000; Design in Education Council Australia, 1991-2000. Address: PO Box 4158, Robina Town Centre, Q 4230, Australia.

SMAGORINSKY, Peter, b. 24 October 1952, Princeton, New Jersey, USA. Professor of Education. m. Jane E Farrell, 1 son, 1 daughter. Education: BA, Kenyon College, 1974; MAT, 1977, PhD, 1989, University of Chicago. Appointments: English Teacher, Westmont High School, Illinois, 1977-78, Barrington High School, Illinois, 1978-85, Oak Park and River Forest High School, Illinois, 1985-90; Professor of English Education, University of Oklahoma, 1990-98, University of Georgia, 1998-. Publications: Vygotskian Perspectives on Literary Research; Standards in Practice 9-12; How English Teachers Get Taught; Speaking About Writing. Honours: Steve Cahir Award, Research in Writing, 1991; Raymond B Cattell Award, Distinguished Programmatic Research, 1999. Memberships: American Educational Research Association; National Council of Teachers of English. Address: University of Georgia, 125 Aderhold Hall, Athens, GA 30605, USA.

SMELLIE Jean McIldowie, b. 14 May 1927, Liverpool, England. Paediatrician. m. Ian Colin Stuart Normand, 1 son, 2 daughters. Education: St Hugh's College, Oxford; University College Hospital, London; Degrees and Diplomas: BA Hons Physiology Oxon, 1947; BM Oxon, 1950; DCH England, 1953; MRCP London, 1954; MA Oxon, 1957; FRCP London, 1975; DM Oxon, 1981. Appointments include: House appointments, 1951-54; Paediatric Registrar, 1955-56, Paediatric First Assistant, 1956-60, University College Hospital, London; Lecturer, Infant Nutrition and Dietetics, Queen Elizabeth College, University of London, 1957-60; Lecturer, Paediatrics, Nuffield Department of Medicine, Oxford, 1960-61; Fellow in Pathology, Johns Hopkins Hospital, Baltimore, USA, 1964-65; Locum Consultant Paediatrician, 1968-69, Honorary Consultant Paediatrician (part-time), 1970-93, University College Hospital, London; Part-time appointments: Senior Lecturer, Paediatrics, Department of Clinical Sciences, University College, London, 1976-93; Senior Clinical Medical Officer, Southampton and SW Hampshire District, 1977-92; Honorary Senior Clinical Lecturer, University of Southampton, 1987-93; Honorary Consultant Paediatric Nephrologist, Guy's Hospital, London, 1984-93, Honorary Consultant Paediatric Nephrologist, Hospital for Sick Children, Great Ormond Street, London, 1984-; Emeritus Consultant Paediatrician, University College Hospitals, 1993-; Scientific Adviser, International Reflux Study in Children (Europe and USA), 1974-; Member, Medical Advisory Committee, Sir Jules Thorn Charitable Trust, 1987-97. Publications: More than 120 original articles, approximately 56 in peer reviewed journals, on urinary tract infections, vesico-ureteric reflux, renal scarring, neonatal, general and metabolic paediatric conditions including most recently: Childhood reflux and urinary infection: a follow-up of 10-41 years in 226 adults, 1998; Medical versus surgical treatment in children with severe bilateral vesicoureteric reflux and bilateral nephropathy: a randomised trial, 2001; Outcome of 10 years of severe vesicoureteric reflux managed medically: Report of the International Reflux Study in Children, 2001; 10-12 book chapters. Honours: Open Scholarship, St Hugh's College, Oxford, 1944-48; Honorary Member: European Society for Paediatric Urology, 1993; British Paediatric Association, 1995; British Association for Paediatric Nephrology, 1995; American Urological Association, 1998; Honorary Fellow, Royal College of Paediatrics and Child Health, 1996. Memberships: European Society of Paediatric Nephrology; Renal Association; International Paediatric Nephrology Association; Founder Member: British Association for Paediatric Nephrology; Neonatal Society. Address: 23 St Thomas Street, Winchester, Hampshire SO23 9HJ, England.

SMENDZIANKA Regina, b. 9 October 1924, Toruń, Poland. Pianist; Teacher. Education: MA, (Diploma with Highest Distinction) Academy of Music in Cracow, Poland, 1948. Appointments: Concert-pianist debut with Cracow Philharmonic Orchestra, 1947; Numerous concert tours in Poland and 33 countries of Europe, Asia and the Americas as recitalist and as soloist with orchestras, 1947-; Numerous gramophone records in Poland, Japan, Holland, Italy, Germany; Numerous radio and TV records, films in Poland and abroad; Large repertoire from 16th century to contemporary music; Teacher, Cracow Academy of Music, 1964; Assistant Professor, 1967; Rector, 1972, 1973; Head of Chair of Piano, 1972-96, Professor, 1977-96, Honorary Member of Chair of Piano, 1996-, Honorary Professor, 1997-, Doctor honoris causa, 2002, F Chopin Academy of Music, Warsaw; Numerous courses of interpretation, lectures and concert lectures in Poland, Denmark, Germany, Finland, Japan, France, Venezuela and Mexico; Member of Piano Competition Juries in Poland, Japan, Russia, Finland, Germany, Italy and Sweden. Publications: Editor, music publications and records; Articles on music in Poland, USA and Japan; Papers on scientific issues of Warsaw F Chopin Academy of Music; Introductions and articles to concert-programmes; Book, How to Play Chopin – an attempt to answer, 2000. Honours include: Prize winner, IV International F Chopin Competition, Warsaw, 1949; Composers Association Medal, 1971; Badge of Merit Culture Worker, 1971 Minister of Culture Prizes, 1955 1959, 1965, 1977, 1987, 1994; Chevalier Cross, 1959, Officer Cross, 1964, Polonia Restituta Order; Tadj Order, Shah of Iran, 1968, Banner of the Labour Order II class, 1975, I class, 1985; Aguilla de Tlatelolco Medal of the Foreign Affaires Minister of Mexico, 1978; Minister of Culture Team Prize, 1979; Excellentia International Order of Merit, IBC Cambridge, 1990; Listed in numerous Who's Who publications and biographical dictionaries. Memberships include: F Chopin Society, Warsaw, 1947-; Polish Musicians Association (SPAM), 1958-; Member Correspondent, Mexico Institute of Culture, 1978-; Iberian Culture Society, Warsaw, 1978-; President of own Foundation (Regina Smendzianka Foundation) in support of Polish music culture and young Polish pianists, 1988-; Honorary Vice-President of EPTA Society (Polish section of European Pianist Teachers Association in London), 1991; Honorary Friend of PTNA (Piano Teachers National Association of Japan), 1999-. Address: 02-529 Warszawa, Narbutta 76/10, Poland.

ŠMÍDKOVÁ Kateřina, b. 24 December 1967, Prague. Economist. Education: MSc, Mathematics, 1988-92, PhD, Economics, 1995-96, Charles University; MA, Economics, Central European University, 1992-93. Appointments: Assistant Lecturer, Central European University, 1993-95; Researcher, Institute of Economics, 1995-97, Adviser to the Board, 1998-, Deputy Director, Economic Research, 2002-, Czech National Bank. Publications: Numerous chapters in books including 2 chapters in Book of the Year 2000, several articles in newspapers and more than 50 articles in economic journals. Honour: The CNB

Dictionary of International Biography

Governor's Annual Award, 1997. Memberships: European Economic Association; Czech Economic Society; Friends of National Gallery; Anina Club. Address: Czech National Bank, Na Prikope 28, 11503 Prague.

SMIRNOVA Olga Andreevna, b. 11 June 1946, Taganrog, Russia. Physicist. m. Nesterenko Vladimir, 1 son. Education: Diploma, 1970, Candidate of Physical and Mathematical Sciences, 1976, Doctor of Physical and Mathematical Sciences, 1992, Physical Department, Moscow State University. Appointments: Junior Scientific Researcher, Scientific Researcher, Institute for Biomedical Problems, 1976-90; Scientific Researcher, Senior Scientist, Leading Scientific Researcher, Research Center of Spacecraft Radiation Safety, 1990-. Publications: Author, 112 publications. Memberships: Member, Scientific Commission F, Committee on Space Research. Address: Research Center of Spacecraft Radiation Safety, 40 Shchukinskaya str, Moscow, 123182, Russia. E-mail: nestr@thsun1.jinr.ru

SMIRNYAGINA Nelly, b. 6 July 1946, Moscow Region. Artist (Painting, Graphics, Tapestry); Applied and Fine Arts. m. Juriy Smirnyagin, 1 daughter. Education: Studio of Fine Arts directed by Yuriy Smirnyagin, 1964-66; Diploma, Applied and Fine Arts, Higher School of Arts and Crafts named V I Muchina (St Petersburg), 1966-72; Painting, Cité Internationale des Arts, Paris, 1991-; International Summer Academy of Geteborg, 1994. Appointments: About 250 exhibitions in Russia, Poland, Germany, France, 1967; Petrushka for the Puppet Theatre, 1972; Member, Union of Artists of USSR, 1973; Exhibition, Distinguished Students Diploma Works in Prague, 5th Republican Exhibition, The Soviet Russia in Central Exhibition Hall, Moscow, 1975; All Russian Art Exhibition in Russia Central Exhibition Hall, Moscow, 1999. Publications: Magazines; Albums: Soviet Art Today; Soviet Russia; I sing praise to my Fatherland, my Republic, to you I sing; Nelly Smirnyagina, 1998. Honours: Honoured Artist of the Russian Federation; Laureate of the Prize, Mayor of Kaliningrad; Woman of Year, ABI, 1998; Laureate, Gold Pushkin Medal, 1999; Laureate of the Prize, Kaliningrad Region, Gubernator, 2001. Memberships: Union Artists of Russia. Address: ul Frunze 72-5, Kaliningrad 236016, Russia.

SMITH Chris(topher) Robert (Rt Hon), b. 24 July 1951. Politician. Education: Pembroke College, Cambridge; Harvard University (Kennedy Scholar 1975-76). Appointments: Development Secretary, Shaftesbury Society Housing Association, 1977-80; Development Co-ordinator, Society for Co-operative Dwellings, 1980-83; Councillor, London Borough of Islington, 1978-83; Chief Whip, 1978-79; Chair, Housing Committee, 1981-83; Labour, MP for Islington South and Finsbury, 1983-; Opposition Spokesman on Treasury and Economic Affairs, 1987-92; Principal Opposition Spokesman on Environmental Protection, 1992-94; National Heritage, 1994-95; Social Security, 1995-96; Health, 1996-97; Secretary of State for Culture, Media and Sport, 1997-2001; Chairman, Millenium Commission, 1997-2001; Currently: Member Wicks Committee on Standards in Public Life; Chairman, Classic FM Consumer Panel, 2001-; Senior Adviser to The Walt Disney Company Ltd on UK film and television work; Visiting Professor in Culture and Creative Industries, The London Institute, 2002-; Member of Board of Royal National Theatre and Donmar Warehouse; Chairman of Wordsworth Trust; Member of Advisory Council of London Symphony Orchestra; Senior Associate of Judge Institute in Management Studies, Cambridge University; Formerly: Chair, Labour Campaign for Criminal Justice, 1985-88; Tribune Group of MP's, 1988-89; President, Socialist Environmental and Resources Association, 1992-; Member, Executive of the Fabian Society, 1990-97 (Chair, 1996-97);

Member of the Board of Shelter, 1986-92; Has held positions in several other organisations. Publication: Creative Britian, 1998. Address: House of Commons, London, SW1A 0AA, England.

SMITH David John, b. 10 October 1948, Melbourne, Australia. Physicist; Educator. m. Gwenneth Bland, 1971, divorced 1992, 2 daughters. Education: BSc, Honours, University Melbourne, 1970; PhD, University Melbourne, 1978; DSc, University Melbourne, 1988. Appointments: Postdoctoral Scholar, University Cambridge, England, 1976-78; Senior Research Associate, 1979-84; Associate Professor, 1984-87, Arizona State University; Professor, 1987-, Regents' Professor, 2000-. Publications: Author, 12 book chapters, 350 professional journal articles; Editor, 15 conference proceedings. Honours: Fellow, Institute of Physics, England, 1981; Charles Vernon Boys Prize, Institute Physics, England, 1985; Faculty Achievement Award, Burlington Resources Foundation, 1990; Director, Cambridge University High Resolution Electron Microscope, 1979-84; NSF Center for High Resolution Electron Microscopy, 1991-96; Director, Center for Solid State Science, Arizona State University, 2001-; Fellow, American Physical Society, 2002. Memberships: American Physical Society; Microscopy Society of America; Material Research Society; Institute of Physics, UK. Address: Department of Physics and Astronomy, Arizona State University, Tempe, AZ 85287-1504, USA.

SMITH Delia, b. 18 June 1941. m. Michael Wynn Jones. Cookery Writer; Broadcaster. m. Michael Wynn Jones. Appointments: Several BBC TV Series; Cookery Writer, Evening Standard, (later Standard), 1972-85; Columnist, Radio Times; Consultant Food Editor, Sainsbury's Magazine; Director, Norwich City Football Club; Announced retirement from TV and book career, 2003. Publications: How to Cheat at Cooking, 1971; Country Fare, 1973; Recipes From Country Inns and Restaurants, 1973; Family Fare, book 1, 1973, book 2, 1974; Evening Standard Cook Book, 1974; Country Recipes From "Look East", 1975; More Country Recipes From "Look East", 1976; Frugal Food, 1976; Book of Cakes, 1977; Recipes From "Look East", 1977; Food For Our Times, 1978; Cookery Course, part 1, 1978, part 2, 1979, part 3, 1981; The Complete Cookery Course, 1982; A Feast For Lent, 1983; A Feast For Advent, 1983; One is Fun, 1985. Editor: Food Aid Cookery Book, 1986, A Journey into God, 1988, Delia Smith's Christmas, 1990, Delia Smith's Summer Collection, 1993; Delia Smith's Winter Collection, 1995; How to Cook, Book 1, 1998; How to Cook Book 2, 1999; How to Cook Book 3, 2001; Delia's Chocolate Collection, 2001; Delia's Vegetarian Collection, 2002. Honours: Special Award, Andre Simon Memorial Fund, 1994; OBE, 1995; Honorary Degree, Nottingham Univerity, 1996; Fellowship, Royal TV Society, 1996. Address: c/o Deborah Owen Ltd, 78 Narrow Street, London E14 8BP, England.

SMITH Francis Joseph, b. 22 May 1920, Ohio, USA. Priest; Professor; Poet. Education: Xavier University, Cincinnati, 1943; MA, Loyola University, Chicago, 1949; MA, University of Oxford, 1961. Appointments: Instructor, University of Detroit; Assistant Professor, Associate Professor, Professor, John Carroll University. Publications: First Prelude, 1981; All is a Prize, 1989; Haiku Yearbook, 1991. Contributions to: Aethlon; Chicago Poetry Review; New York Quarterly; Samizdat; Snowy Egret; Song; Spoon River Quarterly. Honour: 1st Place, Cuyahoga Writers Workshop. Memberships: Poetry Society of America; Poets and Writers. Address: John Carroll University, 2520 Miramar Boulevard, Schell House, University Heights, OH 44118, USA.

SMITH Hamilton Othanel, b. 23 August 1931, New York, New York, USA. Microbiologist. m. Elizabeth Anne Bolton, 1957, 4 sons, 1 daughter. Education: Graduated, Mathematics, University

Dictionary of International Biography

of California at Berkeley, 1952; MD, Johns Hopkins University, 1956. Appointments: Junior Resident Physician, Barnes Hospital, 1956-57; Lieutenant, USNR, Senior Medical Officer, 1957-59; Resident, Henry Ford Hospital, Detroit, 1959-62; Postdoctoral Fellow, Department of Human Genetics, 1962-64, Research Associate, 1964-67, University of Michigan; Assistant Professor, 1967-69, Associate Professor, 1969-73, Professor of Microbiology, 1973-81, Professor of Molecular Biology and Genetics, 1981-, Johns Hopkins University; Sabbatical year with Institut fur Molekular-Biologie, Zurich University, 1975-76. Honour: Guggenheim Fellow, 1975-76; Joint Winner, Nobel Prize for Physiology or Medicine, 1978. Memberships: NAS; AAAS. Address: Department of Molecular Biology, Johns Hopkins University School of Medicine, 720 Rutland Avenue, Baltimore, MD 21205, USA.

SMITH James Cuthbert, b. 31 December 1954, London, England. m. 3 children. Chairman; Professor. Education: First Class honours degree, Natural Sciences (Zoology), Christ's College, Cambridge, England, 1976; PhD, London University, 1979. Appointments: NATO Postdoctoral Fellow, Sidney Farber Cancer Institute and Harvard Medical School, 1979-1981; ICRF Postdoctoral Fellow, 1981-1984; National Institute for Medical Research, 1984-1990; Head, Laboratory of Developmental Biology, 1991, Head Genes and Cellular Controls Group, 1996, NIMR; Member of Zoology Department, Senior Group Leader and Chairman-designate, Wellcome/CRC Institute, Cambridge, 2000; Fellow, Christ's College, Cambridge, 2001; Chairman, Wellcome Trust/Cancer Research UK Institute, Cambridge, 2001-; Humphrey Plummer Professor of Developmental Biology, University of Cambridge, 2001-. Publications: 146 co-authored papers and articles to professional journals. Honours: Zoological Society's Scientific Medal, 1989; Otto Mangold Prize, German Society for Developmental Biology, 1991; Wellcome Visiting Professor, Basic Medical Sciences, 1991-1992; Elected member, European Molecular Biology Organisation, 1992; Howard Hughes Medical Institute International Research Scholar, 1993-98; Elected Fellow, Royal Society, 1993; EMBO Medal, 1993; Honorary Senior Research Fellow, Department of Anatomy and Developmental Biology, University College, London, 1994; Jenkinson Lecture, Oxford University, 1997; Marshal R Urist Lecture and Award, 1997; Elected Fellow, Institute of Biology, 1997; Visiting Professor, Queen Mary and Westfield College, University of London, 1997-; Founder Fellow, Academy of Medical Sciences, 1998; Feldberg Foundation Award, 2000; Member, Academia Europaea, 2000; William Bate Hardy Prize, 2001. Memberships: Numerous committees including: HFSPO Review Committee – Molecular Approaches, 1997-2000; Council, Royal Society, 1997-1999; Council, Academy of Medical Sciences; 1998-2001. Address: Wellcome Trust/Cancer Research UK Institute of Cancer and Developmental Biology, University of Cambridge, Tennis Court Road, Cambridge CB2 1QR, England.

SMITH Karen A, b. 3 January 1957, Honolulu, Hawaii, USA. Senior Crime Laboratory Analyst. 1 daughter. Education: AA, 1976; BA, 1978. Appointments: Deputy Sheriff, Escambia County, Florida, Sheriff's Department, 1982-87; Special Senior Agent, Florida Lottery, 1987-89; Senior Crime Laboratory Analyst, Florida Department of Law Enforcement, 1989-. Publications: Deciphering the Undecipherable – CRII Computer Printer Ribbon, 1990; The PC Based Typestyle Classification System – A Practical Application, 1994; Premeditated Handwriting, 1995; The Decipherment of Correction Fluid Using the HP Scanjet 4C Scanner, 1998; Image Recovery from the Brother Intellifax 1270, 2000. Honours: Outstanding Young Woman of America 1985; Davis Productivity Award, 2001, 2003. Memberships: American Academy of Forensic Sciences; Southeastern Association of Forensic Document Examiners; Association of Certified Fraud Examiners. Address: 1301 N Palafox Street, Pensacola, FL 32501, USA. E-mail: karensmith@fdle.state.fl.us Website: www.karenasmith.com

SMITH Maggie Natalie (Dame), b. 28 December 1934, Ilford, Essex, England. Actress. m. (1) Robert Stephens, 1967, divorced 1975, deceased 1995, 2 sons, (2) Beverley Cross, 1975, deceased 1998. Career: Theatre appearances include: With Old Vic Company, 1959-60; Rhinoceros, 1960; The Private Ear and the Public Eye, 1962; With the National Theatre played in The Recruiting Officer, 1963; Othello, 1964; Much Ado About Nothing 1965; The Beaux' Stratagem, 1970; Private Lives, 1972; 1976, 1977, 1978, 1980 seasons, Stratford Ontario Canada; Lettice and Lovage, London, 1987, New York, 1990; The Importance of Being Earnest, 1993; Three Tall Women, 1994-95; Talking Heads, 1996; The Lady in the Van, 1999; Films include: The VIP's 1963; The Pumpkin Eater, 1964; Young Cassidy, 1965; Othello, 1966; The Honey Pot, 1967; Hot Millions, 1968; The Prime of Miss Jean Brodie, 1969; Travels with My Aunt, 1972; Love and Pain and the Whole Damn Thing, 1973; Murder by Death, 1975; Death on the Nile, 1978; California Suite, 1978; Quartet, 1980; Clash of the Titans, 1981; Evil Under the Sun, 1982; The Missionary, 1982; A Private Function, 1984; A Room with a View, 1986; The Lonely Passion of Judith Hearn, 1987; Hook, 1991; The Secret Garden, 1993; Richard III, 1995; First Wives Club, 1996; Washington Square, 1998; Tea with Mussolini, 1999; The Last September, 2000; Harry Potter and the Philosopher's Stone, 2001; Gosford Park, 2002; Harry Potter and the Chamber of Secrets, 2002; Harry Potter and the Prisoner of Azkaban, 2004. Honours include: Honorary D Lit, St Andrew's and Leicester Universities, 1982, Cambridge, 1993; Evening Standard Best Actress Award, 1962, 1970, 1982, 1985, 1994; Best Actress Award, Film Critics' Guild, USA, 1969; BAFTA Award, Best Actress,1984, 1987, 1989; BAFTA Award for Lifetime Achievement, 1992; Tony Award, 1990. Address: c/o Write on Cue, 29 Whitcomb Street, London, WC2H 7EP, England.

SMITH Melvyn Lionel, b. 3 October 1962, Gloucestershire, UK. Engineer. m. Zsuzsa Karoly-Smith. Education: BEng (Hons), Mechanical Engineering, University of Bath, UK, 1987; MSc, Robotics and Automation, Cranfield, UK, 1988; PhD, Machine Vision, University of the West of England, 1997. Appointments: Project Engineer, Bensons International Systems Ltd, Gloucestershire, UK, 1979-88; Research Associate, School of Mechanical Engineering, University of Bristol, UK, 1988-91; Lecturer, Faculty of Engineering, 1991-95, Senior Lecturer, Faculty of Engineering, 1995-, Co-director, Machine Vision Group, Faculty of Computing, Engineering and Mathematical Sciences, 2000-, Co-director, Centre for Innovative Manufacturing and machine Vision Systems, 2002-, University of the West of England, UK. Publications: Book: Surface Inspection Techniques – Using the integration of innovative machine vision and graphical modelling techniques, 2000; Co-author 2 book chapters; Numerous articles in refereed journals and conference proceedings as author and co-author include most recently: Machine vision research and development for powder metallurgy, 2002; Advanced machine vision inspection of surfaces, 2003; Automatic machine vision calibration using statistical and neural network methods. Memberships: EPSCR Peer Review College; Editorial Board Member: Computers in Industry; Advanced Imaging; Refractory Metals. Address: 30 Lantern Close, Berkeley, Gloucestershire GL13 9DE, England. E-mail: melvyn.smith@uwe.ac.uk

SMITH Michael Robert, b. 24 August 1937, Tela Honduras. Engineer. m. 1 son, 2 daughters. Education: BME, Georgia Institute of Technology, 1959; MS Nuclear Engineering, 1961; PhD, Case Institute of Technology, 1965. Appointments: Member of Technical

Staff, Hughes Research Laboratories, Malibu, California, 1965-68; Vice President, Director of Research, Britt Corporation, Los Angeles, 1968-73; Senior Staff Engineer, Singer/Librascope division, Glendale, California, 1973-78; President, Exocor Technology, Newbury Park, California, 1978-95; Assistant Professor, Head of Physics Programme, California Lutheran University, Thousand Oaks, 1990-96; Design Leader, LIGO project, California Institute of Technology, Pasadena, 1996-. Publications: Articles to professional journals; 8 US patents; 9 foreign patents. Memberships: IEEE; Laser Electro-Optic Society; Sigma Xi; Pi Tau Sigma; Republican. Address: 1611 N Roosevelt Ave, Pasadena, CA 91104-1927, USA.

SMITH Sandra Lee, b. 28 June 1945, San Francisco, California, USA. Writer; Teacher. m. Edward Leroy Smith Jr, 4 March 1967. Education: BA, 1967; Masters Degree, Bilingual/Multicultural Education, 1980. Publications: Loves Miracles (fiction), 1988; Coping with Decision Making, 1989; Dream Song (fiction), 1990; Value of Self Control, 1990; Drug Abuse Prevention, 1995; Flower for Angela (fiction), 1999. Contributions to: Various publications. Honour: Silver Pen Award, 1990. Address: 5433 South Mill Avenue, Tempe, Arizona, USA.

SMITH Stanley Desmond, b. 3 March 1931, Bristol, England. Physicist. m. Gillian Anne Parish, 1 son, 1 daughter. Education: BSc, Physics Department, University of Bristol, 1949-52, PhD, Physics Department, University of Reading, 1952-56; DSc, University of Bristol, 1966. Appointments: Senior Scientific Officer, Royal Aircraft Establishment, Farnborough, 1956-58; Research Assistant, Department of Meteorology, Imperial College, 1958-59; Research Assistant, Lecturer, Reader, Physics Department, University of Reading, 1959-70; Professor of Physics, Head of Department, Dean of Science Faculty, Heriot-Watt University, Edinburgh, 1970-96; Chairman and Chief Executive Officer, Edinburgh Instruments Ltd, 1996- (previously part-time Chairman and Founder, Director, 1971-). Publications: Books: Infrared physics, 1966; Optoelectronic Devices, 1995; Some 215 scientific papers and review articles on semiconductors, IR spectroscopy, interference filters, tunable lasers, optical computing, satellite meteorology. Honours: C V Boys Prize, Institute of Physics, 1976; EPIC Award (Education in Partnership with Industry or Commerce) 1st Prize, 1982; TOBIE Award (Technical or Business Innovation in Electronics), Department of Trade and Industry, 1986; James Scott Prize, Royal Society of Edinburgh, 1987; OBE, 1998. Memberships: Fellow, Royal Society of Edinburgh, 1973; Fellow, Royal Society, 1976; Fellow, Institute of Physics, 1976; Advisory Council on Science and Technology, Cabinet Office, 1985-88; Defence Scientific Advisory Council, 1985-91. Address: Treetops, 29D Gillespie Road, Edinburgh EH13 0NW, Scotland. E-mail: des.smith@edinst.com

SMITH Steven Ross, b. 25 June 1945, Toronto, Canada. Writer; Poet; Fiction Writer; Sound Poet. m. J Jill Robinson, 1 son. Education: Diploma in Radio & Television Arts, Ryerson Polytechnic University. Appointments: Writer in Residence, Weyburn Public Library, Weyburn, SK, Canada, 1987-88; Writer in Residence, Saskatoon, SK, 1996-97. Publications: Ritual Murders, 1983; Blind Zone, 1985; Sleepwalkers, with Richard Truhlar, 1987; Transient Light, 1990; Reading My Father's Book, 1995; Fluttertongue: Book 1, The Book of Games, 1998; Fluttertongue, Book 2, The Book of Emmett, 1999; Ballet of the Speech Organs: Bob Cobbing on Bob Cobbing, 1998. Contributions to: Open Letter; The New Quarterly; Contemporary Verse 2; Prairie Fire. Memberships: The League of Canadian Poets; The Writers Union of Canada; Saskatchewan Writers Guild. Address: 920-9th Avenue North, Saskatoon, SK S7K 2Z4, Canada.

SMITH Troy Alvin, b. 4 July 1922, Sylvatus, Virginia. Aerospace Research Engineer. m. Grace Marie Peacock, 24 November 1990. Education: BCE degree, University of Virginia, 1948; MSE degree, University of Michigan, 1952; PhD degree, University of Michigan, 1970; Registered Professional Engineer, Virginia, Alabama. Appointments: US Navy Reserve, Pacific Theatre of Operations, 1942-46; Structural Engineer, Corps of Engineers, US Army, 1948-59; Chief Structural Engineer, Brown Engineering Company Inc, Huntsville, Alabama, 1959-60; Structural Research Engineer, US Army Missile Command, 1960-63; Aerospace Engineer, US Army Missile Command, 1963-80; Aerospace Research Engineer, US Army Missile Command, 1980-96; Aerospace Engineer Emeritus, US Army Aviation and Missile Command, 1996-. Publications: Numerical Solution for the Dynamic Response of Rotationally Symmetric Shells of Revolution under Transient Loadings, (doctoral dissertation, University of Michigan, 1970); Articles in AIAA Journal and Journal of Sound and Vibration on analysis of shells; 14 major US Army technical reports on analysis of shells and other structures. Honour: Awarded Secretary of the Army Research and Study Fellowship for Graduate Study at the University of Michigan, 1969. Memberships: Sigma Xi; New York Academy of Sciences; Association of US Army. Address: 2202 Yorkshire SE, Decatur, AL 35601-3470, USA.

SMITH Will, (Willard C Smith II), b. 25 September 1968, Philadelphia, Pennsylvania, USA. Singer; Rap Artist; Actor. m. (1) Sheree Zampino, 1 son, (2) Jada Pinkett, 1997, 1 son. Career: Formed duo, DJ Jazzy Jeff and the Fresh Prince; Star of TV sitcom, The Fresh Prince of Bel Air; Film appearances, Six Degrees of Separation, 1993, Bad Boys, 1995, Independence Day, 1996, Men in Black, 1997, Enemy of the State, 1998; Wild Wild West, 1999; Men in Black: Alien Attack, 2002; Legend of Bagger Vance, 2000; Ali, 2002. Recordings: With DJ Jazzy Jeff: Singles: Parents Just Don't Understand; I Think I Could Beat Mike Tyson; Summertime, 1991; Boom! Shake the Room, 1993; Albums: Rock the House, 1997; He's the DJ, I'm the Rapper, 1988; And In This Corner..., 1989; Homebase, 1991; Code Red, 1993; Greatest Hits, 1998; Solo: Singles: Just Cruisin', 1997; Men in Black, 1997; Gettin' Jiggy With It, 1998; Miami, 1998; Wild Wild West, 1999; Albums: Big Willie Style, 1997; Willennium. 1999. Honours: Grammy Awards, with DJ Jazzy Jeff, Best Rap Performance, 1988, 1991; Grammy Award, Best Rap Solo Performance, 1998; MTV Music Video Awards, Best Male Video, Best Rap Video, 1998; American Music Awards, Favorite Male Artist, Favorite Album, Favorite Male Soul/R&B Artist, 1999.

SMITH OF CLIFTON (Lord), Professor Sir Trevor Arthur Smith, b. 14 June 1937, London, England. Politician. m. Julia, 2 sons, 1 daughter. Education: London School of Economics, 1955-58. Appointments: Lecturer in Politics, University of Exeter, England, 1959-60; Lecturer in Politics, University of Hull, England, 1962-67; Lecturer, Senior Lecturer, Professor of Politics, 1967-91, Deputy Principal, 1985-90, Queen Mary, London; Vice-Chancellor, University of Ulster, 1991-99; Liberal Democrat Front Bench Spokesman on Northern Ireland, 2000-. Publications: The Fixers; The Politics of Corporate Economy; Anti-Politics; Direct Action & Representative Democracy; Town & County Hall; Town Councillors; Training Managers; Numerous articles. Honours: Knighted, 1996; Life Peer, 1997; Honorary LLD, Dublin, Hull, Belfast, National University of Ireland; Honorary DHL, Alabama; Honorary DLitt, Ulster; Honorary Fellow, Queen Mary, London. Memberships: Fellow Royal Historical Society; AcSS; Vice-President, Political Studies Association. Address: House of Lords, London SW1A 0PW, England. E-mail: smitht@parliament.uk

SNÆDAL Magnús, b. 17 April 1952, Akureyri, Iceland. Linguist; Philologist; Educator. 1 son. Education: BA, Icelandic Language and Literature, 1978, Cand. mag. Degree, Icelandic Linguistics,

1982, University of Iceland, Reykjavík. Appointments: Language Consultant for the Terminological Committee of the Icelandic Medical Association, 1984-96; Lecturer, General Linguistics, 1989-94, Associate Professor of General Linguistics, 1994-, University of Iceland, Reykjavík. Publications: Book: A Concordance to Biblical Gothic, Volumes I and II, 1998; 18 articles, 7 of them on the Gothic language written in English; Editor of 5 books/dictionaries in the field of Icelandic medical terminology. Address: Ránargata 35a, 101 Reykjavík, Iceland. E-mail: hreinn@hi.is

SNIPES Wesley, b. 31 July 1962, Orlando. Actor. 1 son. Education: High School for Performing Arts, New York; State University of New York. Appointments: Telephone Repair Man, New York; Broadway Appearances include Boys of Winter; Execution of Justice; Death and King's Horseman; Waterdance; Appeared in Martin Scorsese's video Bad, 1987; Films Include: Wildcats; Streets of Gold; Major League; Mo Better Blues, 1990; Jungle Fever, 1991; New Jack City; White Men Can't Jump; Demolition Man; Boiling Point; Sugar Hill; Drop Zone; To Wong Foo: Thanks for Everything, Julie Newmar, 1995; The Money Train; Waiting to Exhale; The Fan, 1996; One Night Stand; Murder at 1600; Blade, 1997; The Vampire Slayer, 1997; US Marshals, 1998; Down in the Delta, 1998; The Art of War, 2000; Blade 2, 2002; Co-Founder, Struttin Street Stuff Puppet Theatre, mid 1980's. Honours: ACE Award for Best Actor for Vietnam War Stories, 1989. Address: Amen RA Films, 9460 Wilshire Boulevard, Beverly Hills, CA 90212, USA.

SNODGRASS W D (S S Gardons, Will McConnell, Kozma Prutkov), b. 5 January 1926, Wilkinsburg, Pennsylvania, USA. Poet; Writer; Dramatist; m. (1) Lila Jean Hank, 6 June 1946, divorced December 1953, 1 daughter, (2) Janice Marie Ferguson Wilson, 19 March 1954, divorced August 1966, 1 son, (3) Camille Rykowski, 13 September 1967, divorced 1978, (4) Kathleen Ann Brown, 20 June 1985. Education: Geneva College, 1943-44, 1946-47; BA, 1949, MA, 1951, MFA, 1953, University of Iowa. Appointments: Instructor in English, Cornell University, 1955-57; Instructor, University of Rochester, New York, 1957-58; Assistant Professor of English, Wayne State University, Detroit, 1959-67; Professor of English and Speech, Syracuse University, New York, 1968-77; Visiting Professor, Old Dominion University, Norfolk, Virginia, 1978-79; Distinguished Professor, 1979-80, Distinguished Professor of Creative Writing and Contemporary Poetry, 1980-94, University of Delaware, Newark; Various lectures and poetry readings. Publications: Poetry: Heart's Needle, 1959; After Experience, 1967; As S S Gardons, Remains: A Sequence of Poems, 1970, revised edition, 1985; The Fuehrer Bunker, 1977; If Birds Build With Your Hair, 1979; D D Byrde Calling Jennie Wrenne, 1984; A Colored Poem, 1986; The House the Poet Built, 1986; A Locked House, 1986; The Kinder Capers, 1986; Selected Poems, 1957-87, 1987; W D's Midnight Carnival (with DeLoss McGraw), 1988; The Death of Cock Robin (with DeLoss McGraw), 1989; Each in His Season, 1994; The Fuehrer Bunker: The Complete Cycle, 1995. Essays: In Radical Pursuit, 1975; After-Images, 1999. Play: The Fuehrer Bunker, 1978. Other: Translations of songs; Selected Translations, 1998; Criticism: Del Compositions: 101 Good Poems Gone Wrong, 2001; To Sound Like Yourself: Essays on Poetry (criticism), 2002. Contributions to: Essays, reviews, poems to many periodicals. Honours: Ingram Merrill Foundation Award, 1958; Longview Foundation Literary Award, 1959; National Institute of Arts and Letters Grant, 1960; Pulitzer Prize in Poetry, 1960; Yaddo Resident Awards, 1960, 1961, 1965; Guinness Poetry Award, 1961; Ford Foundation Grant, 1963-64; National Endowment for the Arts Grant, 1966-67; Guggenheim Fellowship, 1972-73; Government of Romania Centennial Medal, 1977; Honorary Doctorate of Letters, Allegheny College, 1991;

Harold Morton Landon Translation Award, Academy of American Poets, 1999. Memberships: National Institute of Arts and Letters; Poetry Society of America; International PEN; Marin Sorescu Foundation. Address: 3061 Hughes Road, Erieville, NY 13061, USA.

SNOW Peter John, b. 20 April 1938, Dublin, Ireland. Television Presenter; Reporter; Author. m. (1) Alison Carter, 1964, divorced 1975, 1 son, 1 daughter, (2) Ann Macmillan, 1976, 1 son, 2 daughters. Education: Wellington College and Balliol College, Oxford. Appointments: 2nd Lieutenant, Somerset Light Infantry, 1956-58; Newscaster, Reporter, ITN, 1962-79; Diplomatic and Defence Correspondent, 1966-97; Presenter, BBC Newsnight, 1979-97; Tomorrows World, 1997-2001; BBC Election Programmes, 1983-; BBC Radio 4 Mastermind, 1998-2000; Radio 4 Random Edition, 1998-; Radio 4 Masterteam, 2001. Publications: Leila's Hijack War (co-author), 1970; Hussein: a biography, 1972. Honours: Judges Award, Royal TV Society, 1998. Address: c/o BBC TV Centre, Wood Lane, London W12 7RJ, England. E-mail: peter.snow@bbc.co.uk

SNOWDON Anthony Charles Robert Armstrong-Jones (1st Earl of) b. 7 March 1930, London, England. Photographer. m. (1) HRH The Princess Margaret, 1960, divorced 1978, deceased 2002, 1 son, 1 daughter, (2) Lucy Lindsay-Hogg, 1979, 1 daughter. Education: Jesus College, Cambridge. Appointments: Consultant, Council of Industrial Design, 1962-89; In charge of design of Investiture of HRH the Prince of Wales, Caernarfon, 1969; Editorial Adviser, Design Magazine, 1961-67; Artistic Adviser to The Sunday Times, Sunday Times Publications Ltd, 1962-90; Photographer, Telegraph Magazine, 1990-96; Constable of Caernarfon Castle, 1963-; President, Civic Trust for Wales, Contemporary Art Society for Wales, Welsh Theatre Company; Vice President, University of Bristol Photographic Society; Senior Fellow, Royal College of Art, 1986; Provost, 1995-; Fellow, Institute of British Photographers, British Institute of Professional Photographers; Chartered Society of Design; Royal Photographic Society; Royal Society of Arts; Manchester College of Art and Design; Member, Faculty Royal Designers for Industry; South Wales Institute of Architects; Chair Snowdon Report on Integrating the Disabled, 1972; Member, Council, National Fund for Research for the Crippled Child; Founder, Snowdon Award Scheme for Disabled Students, 1980; President, International Year of Disabled People, 1981; Patron, British Disabled Water Ski Association; Member, Prince of Wales Advisory Group on Disability, 1983; Metropolitan Union of YMCAs; British Water Skiing Federation; Welsh National Rowing Club; Circle of Guide Dog Owners. Publications: London, 1958; Malta, 1958; Private View, 1965; Assignments, 1972; A View of Venice, 1972; Photographs by Snowdon: A Retrospective, 2000; Many others. Honours include: Honorary Member, North Wales Society of Architects; Dr hc, Bradford, 1989; LLD, Bath, 1989; Dr hc, Portsmouth, 1993; Art Directors Club of New York Certificate of Merit, 1969; Society of Publication Designers Certificate of Merit, 1970; The Wilson Hicks Certificate of Merit for Photocommunication, 1971; Society of Publication Designers Award of Excellence, 1973; Designers and Art Directors Award, 1978; Royal Photographic Society Hood Award, 1979. Address: 22 Launceston Place, London, W8 5RL, England.

SNYDER Allan Whitenack. Director, Centre for the Mind; 150th Anniversary Chair of Science and the Mind, University of Sydney; Peter Karmel Chair, Australian National University. Education: BS, Pennsylvania State University; SM, Massachusetts Institute of Technology; MS, Harvard University; PhD, University College, London, England; DSc, London. Appointments: Greenland Icecap Communications Project, 1961; General Telecommunications and

Electronic Research Laboratory, 1963-67; Consultant to British Post office and Standard Telecommunications Laboratory, 1968-70; National Science Foundation Fellow, Yale University, 1970-71; Senior Research Fellow, Senior Fellow, Professorial Fellow, Australian National University, 1971-77; John Simon Guggenheim Fellow, Yale University Medical School, 1977-78; Professor of Optical Physics and Visual Sciences, 1978-, Head, Department of Applied Mathematics, Institute for Advanced Studies, 1980-83, Head Optical Sciences Centre, 1987-, Peter Karmel Professor of Science and Mind, 1998-, Australian National University; Royal Society Quest Research Fellow, Cambridge University, England, 1987; Founding Director, Australian Photonics Co-operative Research Centre, 1992-95. Publications: Photoreceptor Optics, 1975; Optical Waveguide Theory, 1983; Optical Waveguide Sciences, 1983; What Makes a Champion, 2002; Articles in international scientific journals. Honours: Research Medal, Royal Society, Victoria, 1974; Edgeworth David Medal, Royal Society, New South Wales, 1974; Thomas Rankin Lyle Medal, Australian Academy of Science, 1985; Royal Society London, 1990; Stuart Sutherland Memorial Medal, Australian Academy of Technological Science and Engineering, 1991; CSIRO External Medal for Research, 1995; A E Mills Memorial Orator, RACP, 1996; Australia Prize, 1997; Harrie Massey Prize and Lecturer, Institute of Physics, 1996; Inaugural Edwin Flack Lecturer, Australian Olympic Committee, 1998; Clifford Patterson Lecturer, Royal Society, 2001; Marconi International Prize, 2001. Memberships: Fellow Optical Society of America, 1980; Foundation Fellow, National Vision Research Institute of Australia, 1983; Fellow, Australian Academy of Science; FRS, 1990; FAA; FTS. Address: Centre for the Mind, Institute of Advanced Studies, Australian National University, Canberra, ACT 2601, Australia. E-mail: allan@centreforthemind.com Website: www.centreforthemind.com

SOCOTEANU Ion, b. 15 March 1944, Bucharest, Romania. Physician; Cardiac Surgeon; Professor. m. Eugenia Socoteanu, 5 daughters. Education: University of Medicine, Bucharest, 1968; General Surgeon, Emergency Hospital, Bucharest, 1975; Cardiovascular Surgeon, Fundeni Hospital, Bucharest, 1976; Professor, Cardiovascular Surgery, University of Medicine, Timişoara, Romania, 1997. Appointments: Chief of Paediatric Cardiac Surgery, Fundeni Hospital, Bucharest, 1982-97; Chief of Cardiovascular Diseases, Timişoara, Romania, 1997-. Publications: Co-author of 9 main handbooks of cardiology and cardiovascular surgery; Over 200 other publications. Honour: Diploma of Excellency, Academy of Sciences, Romania, 2001. Memberships include: European Society of Cardiovascular Surgery; Romanian Society of Cardiovascular Surgery. Address: 34 Viitorului Str, Bucharest 70266, Romania. E-mail: teosocoteanu@yahoo.com

SOCZKIEWICZ Eugeniusz Stanislaw, b. 26 October 1934, Poland. Associate Professor. Education: MS, University of Torun, 1956; Doctor Degree, Technical Sciences, Polish Academy of Sciences, Warsaw, 1973; DSc, Physics, University of Poznan, 1984. Appointments: Assistant Professor, Physicist, Institute of Physics, Silesian Technical University, Gliwice, 1986; Associate Professor, Physics, 1993. Publications: Several articles in professional journals. Honours: Gold Cross of Merit, 1980; Knight Cross Polonia Restitute; Gold Medal of Merit, Katowice Province; Medal of Merit, Silesian Technical University. Memberships: Polish Physical Society; Polish Acoustical Society; European Physical Society; European Acoustics Association; The Institute of Electrical and Electronics Engineers, New York. Address: Derkacza 6/25, 44-100 Gliwice Katowice, Poland.

SODERBERGH Steven, b. 14 January 1963, Atlanta, USA. Film Director. m. Elizabeth Jeanne Brantley, 1989, divorced 1994. Education: high school and animation course, Louisiana State University. Appointments: Aged 15 made short film Janitor; Briefly editor, Games People Play (TV show); Made short film Rapid Eye Movement while working as coin-changer in video arcade; Produced video for Showtime for their album 90125; Author, Screenplay for Sex, Lies and Videotape, 1989; Kafka, 1991; The Last Ship, 1991; King of the Hill, 1993; The Underneath, 1996; Schizopolis, 1996; Out of Sight, 1998; Executive Producer: Suture, 1994; The Daytrippers, 1996; Writer Mimic, 1997; Nightwatch, 1998; The Limey, 1999; Erin Brockovich, 1999; Traffic, 2000; Ocean's Eleven, 2001; Solaris, 2002. Honours: Academy Award for Best Director, Traffic, 2000. Address: P O Box 2000, Orange, VA 22960, USA.

SOEFFNER Rita Annette, b. 25 April 1962, Wadena, Minnesota, USA. Artist. m. Bruce Jon Soeffner. Education: Private lessons with Nasser Pirasteh, Clearwater, 1995-96, Mic Benson, St Cloud, 1996-. Civic Activities: Speaker at schools, family violence centres and self-help groups. Honours: Numerous art show awards and prizes. Memberships: Central Minnesota Watercolorists; Artists of Minnesota; Elk River Area Arts Council; Great River Arts Association, Little Falls; Very Special Arts, Minnesota. Commissions and Creative Works: The Oppression of the Innocent, 32-piece collection; 1999-Forging Ahead, Family Violence Crisis Centers, Deadwood, Wild Bills Gift Shop, Spearfish, Country Hearth Inn, Spearfish, South Dakota; Healing Through Awareness Conference, Understanding the Effects of Sexual Abuse in our Community, Atonement Lutheran Church, St Cloud; Pathway of West Central Minnesota, Montevideo, Displayed in 3 Counties, Chippewa, Lincoln & Yellow Medicine; Little Falls Government Center, Historic Courthouse, Little Falls; St Cloud Hospital; The Bam Theater, Willmar. Address: 7584 153rd Street NW, Clearwater, MN 55320, USA.

SOHN Ilseon, b. 6 June 1960, Seoul, Korea. Engineering Educator. m. Yeonyong Lee, 1 son, 1 daughter. Education: Bachelor of Mechanical Engineering, 1984, MS, 1986, PhD, 1999, Sungkyunkwan University, Korea. Appointments: Engineer, Daewoo Heavy Industry Co, Changwon, Korea, 1988-89; Senior Research Engineer, 1989-98, Manager, 2000-2001, Sangyong Motor Co, Pyungteak, Korea; Senior Research Engineer, Daewoo Motor Co., Incheon, Korea, 1998-2000; Professor, Department of Computer Applied Design Engineering, Osan College, Osan, Korea, 2001-. Publications: Articles as author and co-author in professional engineering journals including: KSME International Journal, 2000, 2001, 2004; FISITA, 2000; Key Engineering Material, 2000, 2004; JSME International Journal, 2002; Journal of Automobile Engineering, 2002; Welding Journal, 2003; International Journal of Modern Physics B, 2003. Memberships: Korean Society of Automotive Engineers; Korean Society of Mechanical Engineers; Korea Welding Society. Address: Department of Computer Applied Design Engineering, Osan College, #17 Chunghak-Dong, Osan, Kyunggi-Do, 447-749, Korea. E-mail: issohn@osan.ac.kr

SOHN Young Taek, b. 6 January 1955, Seoul, Korea. Professor. m. Ok Ha Choe, 1 son. Education: Bachelor of Science, 1977, Master of Science, 1981, Seoul National University, Korea; Dr rer. nat, Technical University of Braunschweig, Germany, 1986. Appointments: Assistant Professor, Associate Professor, Kangweon National University, College of Pharmacy, 1987-92; Professor, 1992-, Dean, College of Pharmacy, 2001-, DukSung Women's University. Publications: Articles in scientific journals include: Effect of Crystal Form on in vivo Topical Anti-inflammatory Activity of Corticosteroids, 2002; Characterization of physicochemical properties of Ferulic Acid, 2003. Honours: Best Publication Award, Korean Federation of Science and Technology, 1998; Academic Award, Korean Society of Pharmaceutics, 1999. Memberships: Vice-President, Korean

Society of Pharmaceutics; Director, Pharmaceutical Society of Korea. Address: Sk Bukhansan City Apt 144-1802, Mia-Dong 1353, Gangbuk-Gu, 142-777 Seoul, Korea. E-mail: ytsohn@duksung.ac.kr

SOKOLOV Kirill, b. 27 September 1930, Moscow, Russia. Artist. m. Avril Pyman, 1 daughter. Education: Moscow Secondary Art School, 1943-51; Surikov Art Institute, Moscow, 1951-57. Career: Artist and Book Illustrator, Moscow, 1957-74; Free-Lance Artist and Sculptor, Great Britain, 1974; Co-editor, 1976, Member of the Editorial Board, 1982 International Art Journal "Leonardo"; Exhibitions: Numerous group exhibitions Moscow and All-Union venues, various galleries in Great Britain, Art Expos, London, New York, Washington, Norway and Edinburgh Festival, 1957-; One-man exhibitions include: linocuts for Shakespeare's Hamlet, Literature Museum, Moscow, 1964; Retrospective of paintings and sculpture Gulbenkian Gallery, Newcastle, 1976; Illustrated books, University of Durham, 1977; Paintings and prints, The Arts Centre, Jersey, 1977; University of London, 1979; Paintings, Hellmann Gallery, Germany, 1980; Prints and collages, Bishopsgate Foundation, 1985; Series of prints for Goethe's Faust, Lyric Theatre, Hammersmith, London, 1988; Graphic works, Academy of Art, Riga, Latvia, 1990; "Ten Years Work", The House of the Artist, Krymskaya Naberezhnaya, Moscow, 1992; Works for the Theatre, Hatton Gallery, Newcastle, 1993; Paintings and graphic works, State Art Gallery Perm, Russia, 1998; New prints the Faust series, Manchester Cathedral, 1999; "Nashe nasledie", Moscow, 2003; New work, Perm State Art Gallery, Russia, 2004; Works in public collections include: Victoria and Albert Museum; Laing Art Gallery, Newcastle upon Tyne; Museum of Fine Art, Moscow; Museum of Fine Arts, Riga, Latvia; Dostoevsky Museum, St Petersburg, Russia; Russian State Archive of Literature and Art, Moscow. Publications: About 60 illustrated books published in Russian and England; Covers for Strand Magazine, 1970's; Engravings for "Requiem" by Anna Akhmatova, 2002; Engravings for "Selected Poems" by Fedor Tyutchev, 2003. Honours: Laureate of International Youth Festival, Moscow, 1957; 2 Prizes for Illustrated Books, USSR; Award for best produced and illustrated books for Pergamon Press, Bookseller Magazine, 1973. Memberships: Society of Fine Art Graphic Artists, 1980 (lapsed); Member of Group, True North, 1992-94. Address: 213 Gilesgate, Durham City, DK1 1QN, England. E-mail: pyman@sokolov.fsnet.co.uk

SOKOLOVA Natalia, b. 20 May 1945, St Petersburg, Russia. Biologist. m. A. Peshechonov, 1 son, 2 daughters. Education: Diploma with Excellence, Biology, Physiology, 1969; Candidate of Science, 1975; Docent, 1983. Appointments: Scientific Contributor, Physiology Institute, 1969, Assistant Professor, 1974, Docent, 1983-, Department of Higher Nervous Activity, Sub-Dean, Faculty of Biology, 1984, Headmistress, Academic Gymnasium, Docent, 1991-, St Petersburg State University. Publications: Co-author 4 books; Author of more than 70 articles. Honours: Medal of Veteran of Labour, 1990; Meritorious Teacher of Russia, Degree of President of Russia, 1999. Memberships: Academic Council, St Petersburg State University; Russian Federal Council of Development of Education, Education Ministry, Russian Federation. Address: St Petersburg State University, Sobstvenij pr, 1, St Petersburg, 198504, Russia. E-mail: sona_ag@mail.ru

SOLBRIG Ingeborg Hildegard, b. 31 July 1923, Weissenfels, Germany. (US Citizen). Professor Emerita. Education: Diploma, Chemist, University of Halle, Germany, 1948; BA, summa cum laude, German Studies, San Francisco State University, 1964; Graduate Studies, German Literature, University of California at Berkeley, 1964-65; MA, 1966, PhD, Humanities and German Studies, 1969; Stanford University. Appointments include:

Assistant Professor, University of Rhode Island, Kingston, 1969-70; Assistant Professor, University of Tennessee, Chattanooga, 1970-72; Assistant Professor, University of Kentucky, Lexington, 1972-75; Associate Professor, 1975-81, Professor, 1981-93, Professor Emerita, 1993-, University of Iowa, Iowa City. Publications: Books: Hammer-Purgstall and Goethe, 1973; Rilke Heute. Beziehungen und Wirkungen, 1975; Reinhard Goering. Seeschlacht/Seabattle, translator, editor, 1977; Momentaufnahmen, 2000; Essay: Orient-Rezeption, 1996, 2000; Numerous book chapters and scholarly articles in professional journals; Report, interviews, poems, observations, stories and travelogues published in various journals, magazines and newspapers, 1955-75. Honours: Fellow, Austrian Ministry of Education, 1968; Dissertation Fellow, Stanford University, 1968-69; Gold Medal "pro rebus orientalibus", 1974; Old Gold Fellow, University of Iowa, 1977; Grantee, American Council of Learned Societies and DAAD, 1980; Senior Faculty Research Fellow, University of Iowa, 1983; National Endowment for the Humanities Grantee, 1985; Fellow, May Brodbeck Faculty Research Grant, 1989; 2000 Millennium Medal of Honor; Listed in Who's Who publications and biographical dictionaries. Memberships: Life Member, Modern Language Association; Founding Member, Goethe Society of North America; Honorary Member, Egyptian Society for Literary Criticism; Member, Society for the History of Alchemy and Chemistry; Canadian and American Societies for Eighteenth Century Studies; Goethe Society of Weimar; Deutsche Schiller-Gesellschaft; Founding Member, International Herder Society. Address: 1126 Pine Street, Iowa City, IA 52240, USA.

SOLIMANDO Dominic A, Jr, b. 4 April, Brooklyn, New York, USA. Pharmacist; Medical Writer; Consultant. Education: BSc Pharmacy, Philadelphia College of Pharmacy and Science, 1976; AMEDD Officer Basic Course, US Army Academy of Health Sciences, Fort Sam, Houston, Texas, 1976; MA, Management and Supervision: Healthcare Administration, Central Michigan University, Mt Pleasant, 1980; AMEDD Officer, Advanced Course, US Army Academy of Health Sciences, Fort Sam, Houston, Texas, 1982; US Army Command and General Staff College, Fort Leavenworth, Kansas, 1985; PhD Candidate, Clinical Pharmacy, Purdue University, West Lafayette, Indiana, 1986-89. Appointments: Staff Pharmacist, Walter Reed Army Medical Centre, Washington, DC, 1977; Chief, Pharmacy Service, Andrew Rader Army Health Clinic, Fort Myer, Virginia, 1977-79; Clinical Pharmacist, Haematology-Oncology Service, Walter Reed Army Medical Centre, 1979-82; Clinical Preceptor, College of Pharmacy, Medical College of Virginia, Virginia Commonwealth University, 1982; Chief, Oncology Pharmacy Section, Tripler Army Medical Centre, Honolulu, Hawaii, 1983-86; Clinical Preceptor, 1983, Adjunct Professor, 1984-86, 1989-90, College of Pharmacy, University of the Pacific; Chief, Haematology-Oncology Pharmacy, Letterman Army Medical Centre, San Francisco, 1989-90, 1991-92; Clinical Preceptor, Oncology, ASHP Residency in Pharmacy Practice, Letterman Army Medical Centre, 1989-90; Chief, Pharmacy Service, Operation Desert Shield/Desert Storm, Saudi Arabia/Iraq, 1990-91; Chief, Haematology-Oncology Pharmacy Section, Walter Reed Army Medical Centre, 1992-96; Clinical Assistant Professor, School of Pharmacy, University of Maryland, 1992-96; Clinical Preceptor, School of Pharmacy and Pharmacal Sciences, Howard University, 1992-96; Clinical Preceptor, Oncology, ASHP Residency in Pharmacy Practice, Walter Reed Army Medical Centre, 1992-96; Programme Director, ASHP Speciality Residency in Oncology Pharmacy, Walter Reed Army Medical Centre, 1992-96, 2001-02; Clinical Associate Professor, School of Pharmacy, University of Arkansas, 1995, 2001; Oncology Pharmacist, Department of Pharmacy, Thomas Jefferson University Hospital, Philadelphia, 1996-98; Clinical Preceptor (Oncology), ASHP Residency in Pharmacy Practice, Thomas

Jefferson University Hospital, Philadelphia, 1996-98; Clinical Preceptor, College of Pharmacy, Temple University, 1998; Clinical Associate Professor, 1998, Clinical Preceptor, 1996-98, Philadelphia College of Pharmacy, University of the Sciences in Philadelphia; Oncology Pharmacy Manager, Lombardi Cancer Centre, Georgetown University Medical Centre, Washington, 1998-99; Director of Oncology Drug Information/Consultant, cancereducation.com, New York, 1999-2000; Oncology Pharmacy Consultant/Medical Writer, Arlington, Virginia, 1999-; Oncology Pharmacist, Department of Pharmacy, Walter Reed Army Medical Centre, 2000-; President, Oncology Pharmacy Services Inc, Arlington, Virginia, 2000-; Assistant Professor, School of Pharmacy, Howard University, Washington, DC, 2003-. Publications: Numerous articles in scientific journals; Drug Information Handbook for Oncology, 1999, 2000, 2003. Honours include: 'A' Proficiency Designator, Office of the Surgeon General, Department of the Army, 1994; WMSHP-Bayer Recognition Award, Washington Metropolitan Area Society of Health System Pharmacists, 2000; Board Certified Oncology Pharmacist, 2000-; Distinguished Achievement Award in Hospital and Institutional Practice, Academy of Pharmacy Practice and Management, American Pharmaceutical Association, 2001. Memberships: American College of Clinical Pharmacy; American Institute of the History of Pharmacy; American Medical Writers Association; American Pharmacists Association; American Society of Health-System Pharmacists; Federation Internationale de Pharmaceutique; International Society of Oncology Pharmacy Practitioners. Address: Oncology Pharmacy Services Inc., 4201 Wilson Boulevard # 110-545, Arlington, VA 22203, USA. E-mail: oncrxsvc@aol.com

SOLIVEN V Emeterio, b. 20 February 1939, Bangued, Abra, Philippines. Lawyer. m. Rosario Gapas Soliven, 6 sons, 5 daughters. Education: Bachelor of Laws, Philippine Law School, 1955; Seminars and Conferences on Intellectual Property Law, University of the Philippines, 1980. Appointments: Chief, Intellectual Property Law Department, Paredes and Poolador Law Offices, 1977-80; Established Emeterio V Soliven & Associates Law Office 1980-, Senior Partner, E V Soliven & Associates Law Offices 2000-; Member, 1984-, Chairman of the Board, 1995-97, Intellectual Property Association of the Philippines. Publication: Primer on Patents, Trademarks and Copyrights. Memberships: APAA; IPAP; INTA; AIPPI (WIPO). Address: G/F Soliven Building, 860 Sto Tomas St, Sampaloc, Manila, Philippines. E-mail: evsa@skyinet.net

SOLOMON Nathaniel, b. 20 November 1925, London, England. Company Director. m. Patricia Creak, 2 sons, 1 daughter. Education: MA (Cantab), Emmanuel College, Cambridge; Harvard Business School. Appointments: Unilever plc, 1949-72, Executive Director, United Africa Company Limited, 1964-72; Managing Director, Associated Leisure plc, 1974-84; Chairman, Pleasurama plc, 1974-84; Non-executive Director, Jeffries International Ltd, 1985-99; Deputy Chairman, The Grass Roots Group plc, 1986-; Non-executive Director, Bally Manufacturing Corporation, Chicago, 1989-91; Chairman, Deputy Chairman, 1991-92, currently Life Vice-president, Tottenham Hotspur plc; Chairman, Crown Leisure plc, 1993-99; Chairman, Gala Group Ltd, 1997-2000; Non-executive Director, Lexington Group Ltd, 2000-; Deputy Chairman, Berry Recruitment Group plc, 2000-; Chairman, RAL Holdings Ltd, 2000-2003; Leisure Industry Adviser, Livingstone Guarantee, 2003-. Honour: Companion of Chartered Management Institute. Memberships: Reform Club; MCC; The Wimbledon Club. Address: Livingstone Guarantee, 15 Adam Street, London WC2N 6RJ, England.

SOLOMON Robert Douglas, b. 28 August 1917, Delavan, Wisconsin, USA. Medical Scientist. m. Helen Fisher, 2 sons, 2 daughters. Education: MIT, Biochemistry, 1934-36; BS, Biochemistry, University of Chicago, 1936-38; MD, John Hopkins Medical School, 1938-42. Appointments: Fellowships, National Cancer Institute; Assistant Professor, University of Maryland, 1950-54; Associate Professor, USC, 1960-68; Professor, Pathology, University of Missouri, 1976-78; Professor, Pathology, SUNY, 1978-86; Adjunct Professor, University of North Carolina, 1986-. Publications: 45 articles, Cancer Chemotherapy; General pathology; Developer of fibre-optic arterial catheter, 1962; Discovery of reversibility atherosclerosis; others. Honours: Sigma Xi; Phi Beta Kappa; others. Memberships: American Chemical Society; Royal Society of Medicine; American College of Physicians; College of American Pathology. Address: 7715 Blue Heron Dr West, Wilmington, NC 28411, USA. E-mail: rdsolomon@aol.com

SOLTAN Mohamed Hashem, b. 27 January 1948, Assiut, Egypt. Professor of Obstetrics and Gynaecology. m. Wafaa Abdul Hamid, 3 sons, 1 daughter. Education: MBBCh, 1972; LM, 1975; DO, 1976; MRCOG, 1981; PhD, 1982; FRCOG, 1996. Appointments: Trainee, teaching hospitals and universities in UK, 1975-82, and Ireland, 1983-92; Assistant Professor, Associate Professor, Professor, Obstetrics and Gynaecology, King Saud University, Saudi Arabia, and El-Menya University, Egypt; Established weekly scientific meetings, Department of Obstetrics and Gynaecology, El-Menya Faculty of medicine, Egypt, 1998-. Publications: 49 publications in British, American, European, Middle Eastern and Egyptian journals in the fields of obstetrics and gynaecology; Many textbook references; Author: Basic Obstetrics for Undergraduates. Memberships: Royal College of Obstetrics and Gynaecology, London; Irish Society of Obstetrics and Gynaecology; Midland Society of Obstetrics and Gynaecology; Egyptian society for Fertility and Sterility; Saudi Society of Obstetrics and Gynaecology. Address: 13-TAHA Hussien St, El-Menya, Egypt. Email: mohamedsoltan552@hotmail.com

SOMER Ljiljana, b. 13 April 1947, Subotica, Yugoslavia. Professor of Histology and Embryology; Specialist in Pathology. m. Tibor Somer, 2 sons, 1 daughter. Education: MD, Faculty of Medicine, Novi Sad, Serbia and Montenegro, 1967-73; MSc, Faculty of Natural Sciences, Novi Sad, 1980; PhD, Faculty of Medicine, Novi Sad, 1984; Certified Pathologist, Clinical Centre, Novi Sad, 1993. Appointments: Assistant Researcher, Histology and Embryology, 1975-86, Assistant Professor, 1986-91, Associate Professor, 1991-96, Professor, 1996-, Head of the Institute of Histology and Embryology, 1998-, Faculty of Medicine, Novi Sad. Publications: 137 scientific papers and articles in domestic and international scientific journals; Master's thesis: Histophysiological Characteristics of the Pineal Gland in Experimental Diabetes, 1980; Doctoral thesis: Hypophysis under the Influence of Alcohol, 1984. Memberships: Association of Anatomists of Serbia and Montenegro; Association of Pathologists of Serbia and Montenegro. Address: Institute of Histology and Embryology, Faculty of Medicine, Hajduk Veljkova 3, 21000 Novi Sad, Serbia and Montenegro. E-mail: biblmf@uns.ns.ac.yu

SOMEYA Tsuneo, b. 1 January 1931, Chiba Prefecture, Japan. Professor Emeritus. m. Fusako Someya, 3 sons. Education: Bachelor of Engineering, University of Tokyo, Japan, 1955; Doktor-Ingenieur, Technische Hochschule, Karlsruhe, Germany, 1962; Doctor of Engineering, University of Tokyo, Japan, 1972. Appointments: Associate Professor, 1964-73, Professor, 1973-91, University of Tokyo, Japan; Retired from the University of Tokyo, 1991; Professor, Musashi Institute of Technology, Japan, 1991-2001. Publications: Journal-Bearing Databook, 1988; Articles in scientific journals include: Stabilität einer in zylindrischen Gleitlagern laufenden, unwuchtfreien Welle, 1963; Das dynamisch belastete Radial-Gleitlager beliebigen Querschnitts, 1963; Schwingungs- und Stabilitätsverhalten einer in zylindrischen Gleitlagern laufenden Welle mit Unwucht, 1965. Honours: Scholarship, German Academic Exchange Service, DAAD, 1955; Award for papers, The Japan Society of Mechanical Engineers, 1967, 1983; Research Award, A von Humboldt Foundation, 1990; Doctor, honoris causa, Technical University of Lodz, 2003. Address: Kohinata 2-30-5, Bunkyo-Ku, Tokyo, 112-0006 Japan. E-mail: t-someya@tcn-catv.ne.jp

SOMMARIVA Corrado, b. 5 April 1962, Genoa, Italy. Consultant. 1 son, 1 daughter. Education: PhD, Chemical Engineering, University of Genoa; Diploma in Management, University of Leicester; Ashridge Leadership Course. Appointments: Director of Water Projects, Ansaldo Energia; Research Director, Middle East Research Center; Head of Desalination Department, Mott MacDonald Ltd; Vice President, International Desalination Association. Publications: Numerous articles and papers published in professional scientific journals. Honours: High Quality Treatise Award, High Quality Essay Award, IDA, 1995; Best Paper Award, 2001, 2002, 2003, Technology Innovation Award, 2003, Mott MacDonald. Memberships: Board of Directors, IDA; Board of Directors, European Desalination Association; Powergen Advisory Board; Waste Water Europe. Address: Mott MacDonald Ltd, PGB, Victory House, Trafalgar Place, Brighton, East Sussex BN1 4FY, England.

SOMMERLATTE Tom (Werner Hermann Albert), b. 24 March 1938, Dessau, Germany. m. Christine, 4 sons, 7 daughters. Education: Master of Science, Radiation Chemistry, Technical University of Berlin, 1964; PhD, Chemical Engineering, University of Paris, 1965; Master of Business Administration, European Institute of Business Administration, INSEAD, Fontainebleau, France, 1970; Professorship, Systems Design, University of Kassel, 1999. Appointments: Member, European Directorate of Arthur D Little Inc, 1976; Vice President, 1979; Managing Director, Germany, 1983, and European 1990; Chairman, 1996-; Several advisory and supervisory boards. Publications: 15 books on management and technology issues including Innovation Premium; Discovering Needs; Technology Marketing; Numerous articles on innovation and research and development strategies in business magazines. Honours: Award, one of the best business books of 2000; Honorary Professorship, University of Kassel. Memberships: Association of Friends of the Arts. Address: Falkenweg 6, D-65527 Engenhahn-Wildpark, Germany. E-mail: tomsommerlatte@osiris-mic.com

SONDHEIM Stephen Joshua, b. 22 March 1930, New York, New York, USA. Composer; Lyricist. Education: BA, Williams College, 1950. Compositions: Incidental Music: The Girls of Summer, 1956; Invitation to a March, 1961; Twigs, 1971; Lyrics: West Side Story, 1957; Gypsy, 1959; Do I Hear A Waltz?, 1965; Candide, (additional lyrics) 1973; Music and Lyrics: A Funny Thing Happened on the Way to the Forum, 1962; Anyone Can Whistle, 1964; Evening Primrose, 1966; Company, 1970; Follies, 1971; A Little Night Music, 1973; The Frogs, 1974; Pacific Overtures, 1976; Sweeney Todd, 1979; Merrily We Roll Along, 1981, 1997; Sunday in the Park With George, 1984; Into the Woods, 1987; Assassins, 1991; Passion, 1994; Anthologies: Side by Side by Sondheim, 1976; Marry Me A Little, 1980; You're Gonna Love Tomorrow, 1983; Putting It Together, 1992; Company ...In Jazz, 1995; A Little Night Music, 1996. Film: Stavisky, 1974; Reds, 1981; Dick Tracy, 1990. Honours: Antoinette Perry Award, 1971, 1972, 1973, 1979; Drama Critics' Award, 1971, 1972, 1973, 1976, 1979; Evening Standard Drama Award, 1996; Grammy Award,

1984, 1986. Memberships: President, Dramatists Guild, 1973-81; American Academy and Institute of Arts and Letters. Address: c/o Flora Roberts, 157 West 57th Street, New York, NY 10019, USA.

SONDOCK Ruby Kless, b. 26 April 1926. Arbitrator; Mediator. m. Melvin Adolph Sondock, 2 daughters. Education: BS, Cum Laude, University of Houston, Texas; LLB, Valedictorian, University of Houston College of Law, Texas. Appointments: General Civil Trial Litigation, Houston, Texas, 1961-73; Judge, Harris County Court of Domestic Relations #5 (currently 312th District Court), Houston, Texas, 1973-77; Judge, 234th Judicial District Court, Houston, Texas, 1977-82; Justice, Supreme Court of Texas, Austin, Texas, 1982-83; Judge, 234th Judicial District Court, Houston, Texas, 1989-93; Solo Practice, Houston, Texas, 1993-; Participation in numerous CLE programmes as speaker, moderator or chairperson for State Bar of Texas, Houston Bar Association, University of Houston, South Texas College of Law; Member, Commission for Lawyer Discipline; Advisory Committee to Dean, University of Houston College of Law. Honours: Numerous honours and awards include: Outstanding Alumna, University of Texas, 1983; Ranked First, Civil Courts, Harris County, Houston Post Survey, 1988; Business Woman of the Year, United Cerebral Palsy of Greater Houston; 1990; Honorary Member, Order of the Coif, University of Houston Law Alumni Association; Helen Susman Award "Woman of Prominence", 1993; Listed in Who's Who publications and biographical dictionaries. Memberships: Fellow, American Bar Association; State Bar of Texas; Fellow Houston Bar Association; Association of Women Attorneys; Board Member, Galveston Historical Association; Phi Theta Kappa; Phi Kappa Phi; Order of the Barons; Alpha Epsilon Pi. Address: 550 Westcott, Suite 220, Houston, TX 77007, USA. E-mail: sondock@airmail.net

SONG Yeong Wook, b. 13 February 1956, Taejon, Korea. Physician. m. Hee Jeong Kwon, 20 December 1982, 1 son, 2 daughters. Education: MD, 1980, PhD, 1990, Seoul National University, 1980. Appointments: Intern, 1980-81, Resident, 1981-84, Seoul National University Hospital; Captain, Korean Army, 1984-87; Instructor, 1988-90, Assistant Professor of Medicine, 1992-95, Associate Professor of Medicine, 1995-2000, Professor, Chief of Division of Rheumatology, 2000-, Seoul National University; Clinical Fellow, Rheumatology, University of California Medical Center, Los Angeles, 1990-92. Publications: Abnormal Distribution of Fcg Receptor Type IIA Polymorphisms in Korean Patients with Systemic Lupus Erythematosus, 1998; Paclitaxel Reduces Anti-DNA Antibody Titer and BUN Prolonging Survival in Murine Lupus, 1998. Honour: Ellis Dressner Award, Southern California Chapter, Arthritis Foundation, 1992; Young Investigator Award, Seoul National University Hospital, 2000. Memberships: Fellow, American College of Rheumatology; Korean Association of Internal Medicine; Korean Rheumatism Association. Address: Seoul National University Hospital, Chongno-ku 28 Yongun-dong, Seoul 110-744, Korea.

SONNENFELD Barry, b. 1 April 1953, New York. Cinematographer; Film Director. Appointments: Cinematographer (Films): Blood Simple, 1984; Compromision Positions, 1985; Three O'Clock High, 1987; Raising Arizona, 1987; Throw Momma from the Train, 1987; Big, 1988; When Harry Met Sally..., 1989; Miller's Crossing, 1990; Misery, 1990; TV: Out of Step, 1984; Fantasy Island, 1998; Secret Agent Man, 2000; The Crew, 2000; Director (films): The Addams Family, 1991; Addams Family Values, 1993; Get Shorty, 1995; Men in Black, 1997; Wild Wild West, 1999; Chippendales, 2000; Director, Co-producer, For Love of Money, 1993. Honours: Emmy Award for best cinematography. Address: Gersh Agency, 232 North Canon Drive, Beverly Hills, CA 90210, USA.

Dictionary of International Biography

SONNTAG Philipp, b. 28 December 1938, Halle/Saale, Germany. Writer; Physicist. m. Mechthild Sonntag, 1 son from first marriage. Education: Physicist Diploma, University of Munich, Germany, 1964; Dr.rer.nat., Technical University, Hanover, Germany, 1969; Copywriter Diploma, Axel Andersson Academy, 1998. Appointments: Member of Staff, Max Planck Institute on the Conditions of Life, 1964-78; Active Member, Expert Committees of the Liberal Party (FDP), 1975-; Main political impact for avoiding nuclear armament and warfare until 1983; Science Centre, Berlin, 1979-86; Founding Member, Institute for Interdisciplinary and Alternative Technology Development, Styria, Austria; Shareholder and Innovation Manager of several technically oriented firms; Author, short stories, essays, science fiction. Publications: More than 200 publications in science, politics and literature include: Mathematical Analysis of the Impact of Nuclear Weapons, 1970; Stability and Deterrence regarding Nuclear Weapons (with H Afheldt), 1971; Verhinderung und Linderung atomarer Katastophen, 1981; Wege in die Informationsgesellschaft (co-author Peter Otto), 1985; Key Technologies, 1988; The Role of Technology Transfer Agencies for Establishing European Co-operation, 1995. Honours: Publicist Award on "Town Ecology" Banking Consortium, 1978; Award as Human Rights Promoter, German Group of Citizens Commission on Human Rights. Memberships: Association of German Scientists; Association of Technical Communication; New Society for Literature, Berlin; Liberal Party, Germany; Institute for Interdisciplinary and Alternative Technology Development, Styria, Austria; Society for Wood Research; Jewish Culture Association; Lichtblick (support of prisoners' journalism); Activism for deletion of mines; Network Future; c-base (unification of media artists). Address: Lepsiusstr. 45, D-12163 Berlin, Germany. E-mail: phil.sonntag@t-online.de Website: www.philipp-sonntag.de

SOOMRO Shaukat Qadir, b. 12 March 1947, Shikarpur Sindh, 2 sons, 1 daughter. Education: Bachelor's degree, 1967, Master of Economics, 1971, University of Sindh; Central Superior Service of Pakistan, 1976. Appointment: Commissioner, Income Tax and Wealth Tax, Karachi, Pakistan. Honours: Numerous awards for meritorious service, 1979-80, 1990-91, 1991-92, 1994-95, 1995-96, 1997-98, 1998-99, 2002-03. Memberships: Pakistan Taxation Club, Karachi, Pakistan. Address: C6/B3, Street No 2, Bath Island, Clifton, Karachi, Pakistan.

SOPENA-BALORDI A Emma, b. 9 May 1954, Valencia, Spain. University Professor. Divorced, 1 son. Education: BA, French Philology, 1977, Outstanding Graduate Thesis, 1979, Doctoral Thesis, Highest Honours, 1983, University of Barcelona. Appointments: Professor, University of Valencia, 1977-; Full Professor, Department of French and Italian Philology, 1985; Responsibility for core courses in French Language, doctoral courses in pragmatics, cognitive, social and psycholinguistics; Speciality, Scientific and Literary Translation. Publications: Papers on linguistics in national and international professional journals including: Contrastes, Paris; Meta, Montreal, Langues Modernes, Paris; Equivalences, Brussels; Humoresques, Paris, 1993-. Honours: Research Grants, 1982-87, 1989-96, 1997-2002; Researcher for Ministry of Education Projects, Comparative French-Spanish Linguistics 1998-. Memberships: Member, Scientific Committee of Humoresques, University of Paris VIII; Member, Orfeón Universitario (Official choir, Universitat de Valencia). Address: C/101, n3 46182 La Canyada, Valencia, Spain. E-mail: emmasopena@yahoo.es

SOPHOCLEOUS Sophocles, b. 8 October 1958, Lefkosia (Nicosia), Cyprus. Director. Divorced, 1 son. Education: National Service, 1976-78; Diplôme Supérieur d'Études Françaises, Université des Sciences Humaines de Strasbourg, 1978-79; Licence d'Histoire de l'Art et d'Archéologie, Maîtrise d'Histoire de l'Art et d'Archéologie, Université des Sciences Humaines de Strasbourg, 1979-82; Diplôme d'Études Approfondies, Université de Paris X, Nanterre, France, 1982-83; Certificate, German as a Foreign Language, Goethe Institute of Nicosia, 1984-86; Diplôme de Docteur, PhD, Sciences de l'Antiquité, Université des Sciences Humaines de Strasbourg, 1990. Appointments: Monitor, Institute of Archaeology Library, University of Strasbourg, 1981-82; Founder, First President, Association of Cypriot Archaeologists, 1983-; Participated, American Archaeologists excavation, Kalavasos, 1983; Temporary Official, Department of Antiquities of Cyprus, 1983; Part-time teacher of French, 1983-86; Work with Cypriot radio and television, 1985-; Establishment of the inventory of the Ecclesiastical Heritage of the Diocese of Limassol and creation of the Koilani Ecclesiastical Museum, Limassol, 1986-90; Organiser, Post-Byzantine Icons and Contemporaries of Limassol exhibition, 1990; Organiser, Byzantine Icons of Cyprus exhibition at the Council of Europe, 1991; Paphos District Archaeological Officer, Department of Antiquities, Cyprus, 1991; Founder, Director, Centre of Cultural Heritage a non-governmental organisation, 1991-; Organiser, The Image of God: Byzantine Icons of Cyprus, exhibition at Strasbourg and Mulhouse, 1994; Founder, Ecclesiastical Museum, Kyperounta, 1994-95; Visiting Professor, Ecole Pratique des Hautes Etudes, Sorbonne, Paris, 1996-97; Founder, Museum of the Byzantine Heritage of Palaichori, 1996-98; Founder, Ecclesiastical Museums in Prodromos, Lemithou and Pelendri, 1998-2001; Curator, Cyprus the Holy Island: Icons Through the Centuries, 10th-20th Century exhibition, London, Hellenic Centre, 2000; President, Community of Rogiatiko placed in the intra muros city of Lefkosia, (Nicosia), 1998-. Publications: 2 collections of poems, 1978, 2002; 11 books, 1985-; Numerous articles and contributions to publications; Papers presented at congress; Articles in professional journals and popular newspapers and magazines. Honours: Bursary for PhD thesis, French Government, 1986-89; Honoured by community of Palaichori for contribution to safeguarding, conservation and protection of Palaichori's cultural heritage; 21st Century Award for Achievement, IBC, 2001; 500 Founders of the 21st Century, IBC, 2001; 2000 Outstanding Intellectuals of the 21st Century, IBC, 2001; 2000 Outstanding Europeans, IBC, 2002; Great Minds of the 21st Century, ABI, 2001; Lectured and presented papers at different congresses across Cyprus, Greece, France, Switzerland, England, Slovenia, Russia, Italy, Lebanon, Malta and Germany. Memberships: Member, Society of Cypriot Studies; Member, International Council of Museums, Paris, 1987-; Member, Departmental Committee of Antiquities of Limassol, 1989-95; Committee Member, Work Group Icons, International Council of Museums, 1992-. Address: Corner of Alexander the Great, No 10 and Alexios Comnenos, 1010 Nicosia, PO Box 20119, 1601 Nicosia, Cyprus. E-mail: contact@heritage.org.cy Website: www.heritage.org.cy

ŞORA Gheorghe, b. 16 September 1927, Grăniceri, Arad, România. Teacher. Education: Bachelors Degree, 1959; Masters Degree, History, 1964; Doctorate in Philosophy. Appointments: Lecturer, 1961, Professor, 1964, Timisoara. Publications: 14 academic books in Romanian include: Vasile Goldiş, Corespondenţă, volume I (1880-1934), 1992; Biografia unui mare lupător, 1994; Cuvântarea istorică a lui Vasile Goldiş din 1 decembrie 1918 la Alba Iulia, 2000; Co-author 11 books; Author 50 brochures and over 100 articles in academic journals. Honours: Honoured Citizen of Grăniceri, Beliu; Arad City, Academy Prize, 1993; Congratulated by Keith Hitchins from Illinois University, USA; Nominated for the Academic Title: The Biography of Vasile Goldiş. Membership: ASTRA. Address: B-dul Revolutiei Nr 26, Sc F et 2, Apt 4, Arad 2900, România.

Dictionary of International Biography

SOROKOUMOVSKAJA Maria, b. 29 January 1938, Moscow, Russia. Musician; Harpist. m. Jaroslav Kounakov. Education: Graduate, Gnessin Special School, 1957; Diploma with honours, Moscow State Conservatory, 1963. Appointments: Harpist-soloist, Moscow State Academic Philharmonic Society, 1963-. Publications: Enthusiastic concert reviews in newspapers, magazines and online media; Subject of a chapter in V L Raikov's book, "Art and Mind", 2000. Honours: Diplom, Moscow State Academic Philharmonic Society, 1988; Honoured Artist of Russia, Decree of Russian President, 1994; Government Medal, 1997. Memberships: Union of Moscow Musicians; Russian Harpist Society; Committee member, International Order "Glory of Russia". Address: ul Kuusinena dom 15, kv 6, 125252 Moscow, Russia.

SORVINO Mira, b. 28 September 1968. Actress. Education: Harvard University. Career: Film appearances include: Amongst Friends, 1993; The Second Greatest Story Ever Told, 1993; Quiz Show, 1994; Parallel Lives, 1994; Barcelona, 1994; Tarantella, 1995; Sweet Nothing, 1995; Mighty Aphrodite, 1995; The Dutch Master, 1995; Blue in the Face, 1995; Beautiful Girls, 1996; Norma Jean and Marilyn, 1996; Jake's Women, 1996; Romy and Michele's High School Reunion, 1997; The Replacement Killers, 1997; Mimic, 1997; Summer of Sam, 1999; At First Sight, 1999; Joan of Arc: The Virgin Warrior, 2000; Television: The Great Gatsby, 2000. Honours: Academy Award, Best Supporting Actress, Mighty Aphrodite. Address: The William Morris Agency, 1325 Avenue of the Americas, New York, NY 10019, USA.

SOUCY Robert Joseph, b. 25 June 1933, Topeka, Kansas, USA. Historian. m. Sharon Soucy, 2 daughters. Education: BA, Washburn University, 1955; MA, Kansas University, 1957; Université de Dijon, France, 1956-57; PhD, University of Wisconsin, 1963. Appointments: US Air Force, 1957-60; Teaching Assistant, University of Wisconsin, 1961-63; Instructor, Harvard University, 1963-64; Assistant Professor, Kent State University, 1964-65; Professor, Oberlin College, 1966-98; Retired, 1998. Publications: Books: Fascism in France: The Case of Maurice Barrès, 1972; Fascist Intellectual: Drieu La Rochelle, 1979; French Fascism: The First Wave, 1924-1933, 1986; French Fascism: The Second Wave 1933-1939, 1995; Fascismes Français? 2004. Memberships: American Historical Association; Society for French Historical Studies. Address: 143 E College St, Apt 402, Oberlin, OH 44074, USA.

SOUDAN Jean Pol, (Soudan Lord John's) b. 2 July 1953, Louise-Marie, Belgium. Flemish Artist; Painter. Divorced, 1 son. Education: Academy of Tournai, 1968-70; Academy of London, 1972-73; Academy of Lille, 1973-74; Academy of Brussels, 1974-76. Career to date: Painter, originally inspired by the Ardennes countryside and the North Sea; Later work in more fantastic and symbolic style, oriented towards an austral painting looking for high colours; Puts finishing touches to his paintings by scraping with a palette knife, which is an expression of excellence; Represented in many different museums in Belgium and several other countries; Architect, Industrial Design Draughtsman, concentrated on making projects concerning various ancient and new villas styles or luxury buildings; Involved with projects on Belgian power stations, Brussels Underground system and many building companies in Brussels; Signs paintings under the name of Lord John's. Publications: Featured in many reference publications and other books. Memberships: Royal Association and Royal Foundation of the Professional Belgian Artists Painters; Royal Association and Royal Foundation, Sabam of Belgium; Authors Rights Copyright and Preservations for the Belgian Artists; Member, Accadémia del Verbano. Address: 95 rue de la Lorette, The Old Memphis, Renaix 9600, Belgium. Website: www.artpartnerscenter.com

SOUSA Fernando Alberto Pereira de, b. 1 October 1942, Santa Marinha, Vila Nova de Gaia, Portugal. Cathedratic Professor. m. Ana Cristina Lacerda Almas de Sousa, 1 son. Education: Course in Pedagogical Sciences, 1971, Degree in History, 1973, PhD in History, 1980, Oporto University, Portugal. Appointments: Cathedratic Professor, Economic and Social History, Faculty of Arts, Oporto University, Portugal, 1984-; Director, International Relations Department, Lusíada University, Oporto, Portugal, 1996-; Chairman, Population, Economy and Society Study Centre; Director of the Journal, População e Sociedade; Member, Portuguese Parliament; Member NATO General Assembly. Publications: Numerous publications include: História da Estatística em Portugal, 1995; Banco Borges e Irmão. Uma Instituição Centenária, 1984; A Associação Industrial Portuguesa, 1997; Os Transportes Colectivos do Porto, 2001. Honours: Cross of War; New Orleans International Honorary Citizen; Houston Honorary Citizen and Goodwill Ambassador. Memberships: Portuguese Economic History Association; Société de Demographie Historique; Centro de Estudos Norte de Portugal – Aquitania. Address: Centro de Estudos da População, Economia e Sociedade, Rua do Campo Alegre 1055, 4169-004 Porto, Portugal. E-mail: cepese@cepese.pt Website: www.cepese.pt

SOUTET Olivier, b. 1 November 1951, Paris, France. Professor. m. Josette Quillard, 1 son, 1 daughter. Education: Ecole Normale Supériure, 1971-74; Agrégation, 1978; Doctorate, French Linguistics, 1986. Appointments: Assistant Professor, Sorbonne, Paris, 1974-88; Professor, University of Dijon, 1988-94; Professor, University of Paris-Sorbonne, 1994-. Publications: Syntax in French, 3rd edition, 1994; Linguistics, 2nd edition, 1997; Studies in Ancient and Middle French, 1992; The Concession in French, 1990. Honours: Director of Research Team, Sens et Texte, Sorbonne; Director of Collection, Editions Champion, Paris, Geneva. Address: 34 rue Bezout, 75014 Paris, France. E-mail: osoutet@freesurf.fr

SOUZA DOS SANTOS Paulo Afonso, b. 4 September 1943, Rio de Janeiro, Brazil. Diplomat. Education: Scientific Studies, 1959-61; Museology, 1964; Institute of Rio Branco, 1966-67. Appointments: Second Secretary and Chargé d'Affaires, Ivory Coast, Sweden, Iran; Provisional Service in Finland and Norway, 1969-75; Commercial Attaché, Stockholm Sweden, 1972-74. Publications: Newspaper and cultural articles; poetry, 1979, 1980. Honours: Premio Walmap, 1968; Order of the Polar Star, Stockholm, 1974. Address: Rua Santo Amaro 36/401, Catete, Rio de Janeiro, Brazil.

SOWERS Miriam R, b. 4 October 1922, Buffton, Ohio, USA. Artist. 2 sons. Education: BFA, Miami University; Chicago Art Institute; University of New Mexico. Appointments: WWII Army Map Service; Owner, Art Studio, 1946-; Owner, Public Art Gallery, 1961-80. Publications: Books: Parables from Paradise; The Suns of Man Commissions and Creative Works: One Man Shows include: Aliso Gallery, Albuquerque, 1986; Statesman Club, Albuquerque; Arts International Gallery, Findlay, Ohio; Findlay College; Springfield Museum of Art, Ohio; Alcove Show, Museum of Santa Fe; Fairmont Hotel, San Francisco; Albuquerque Convention Center; Goldwaters Department Store; Provenance Gallery, Lahaina, Hawaii; St Johns College, Santa Fe; King Kamehameha Hotel, Hawaii; Kona Surf Resort, Hawaii; Foxfire Gallery; Blankley Gallery; Southwest Cornerhouse; Numerous museum and group exhibitions. Address: c/o Symbolic Art Studio, 4833 Brenda NE, Albuquerque, NM 87109, USA.

SPACEY Kevin, b. 26 July 1959, South Orange, New Jersey, USA. Actor. Education: Juilliard Drama School, New York. Career: Stage debut in Henry IV, Part 1; Broadway debut in Ghosts, 1982;

Dictionary of International Biography

Other theatre appearances include: Hurlyburly, 1985; Long Day's Journey into Night, London, 1986; Yonkers, New York; The Iceman Cometh, London, 1998; Films: Working Girl, 1988; See No Evil, Hear No Evil, 1989; Dad, 1989; Henry and June, 1990; Glengarry Glen Ross, 1992; Consenting Adults, 1992; Hostile Hostages, 1994; Outbreak, 1995; The Usual Suspects, 1995; Seven, 1995; Looking for Richard, 1996; A Time to Kill, 1996; LA Confidential, 1997; Midnight in the Garden of Good and Evil, 1997; American Beauty, 1999; Ordinary Decent Criminal, 2000; Pay It Forward, 2000; The Shipping News, 2001; The Life of David Gale, 2003; Director, Albino Alligator, 1997. Honours Tony Award, 1986; Academy Award for Best Actor, 1999. Address: William Morris Agency, 151 South El Camino Drive, Beverly Hills, CA 90212, USA.

SPAHIU Dritan, b. 12 June 1938, Kukes, Albania. Physicist. m. Sabahet Spahiu, 2 daughters. Education: Physicist Diploma, University of Tirana, 1961; Lecturer, General Physics University of Tirana, 1962-66; DSc, 1994; Professor, 1995. Appointments: Head of Section, Nuclear Magnetic Resonance, University of Tirana, 1973, Head of Section, Physics, Geophysical Institute, Tirana, 1986; Head of Department of Physics, 1992, Dean of Faculty of Natural Sciences, 1993-97, Head of Section of Experimental Physics, 1997, University of Tirana. Publications: Laboratory Exercises (textbook), 1969; Classical Electrodynamics (textbook), 1972; Russian-Albanian Dictionary, 1974; Graduate Problems in Electrodynamics, 1975; Preparation of ferromagnetic thin films for measurements of weak magnetic fields, 1994; 11 papers on Physics in Albanian journals. Membership: Albanian Society of Physicists. Address: Rr D Hima Nr 15, Tirana, Albania.

SPALLONE Jeanne Field, b. 18 January 1928, New York, New York, USA. Retired Probate Judge; Freelance Writer. m. Daniel F Spallone, 2 sons, 1 daughter. Education: BSc, University of Connecticut, Storrs, Connecticut, USA, 1950. Appointments: Reporter, News and Feature Writer, Middletown Press, Middletown, Connecticut, 1952-53, 1959-65; Administrative Assistant to former Connecticut Governor and former Ambassador to India, Honorable Chester Bowles, Essex, Connecticut, 1953-56; State Representative, District of Deep River, Connecticut State Legislature. 1959-61; Judge of Probate, District of Deep River, Connecticut in the Probate Court System, State of Connecticut, USA, 1979-95; Monthly Op-Ed Columnist, 1993-96; Currently Freelance Writer. Publications: A Watch to Keep, 1976; The Encyclopedia of New York City edited by Professor Kenneth Jackson, 1995; Chapter in Images of America –Deep River and Ivoryton, 2002; The Winter Toys (children's book), 2003; Numerous articles in newspapers and magazines. Honour: Third Prize, Poetry Competition, Friends of the Action Library of Old Saybrook, Connecticut and the Connecticut Poetry Society, 1998. Memberships: Connecticut Order of Women Legislators; Trustee/ Historian, Deep River Historical Society, 1976-94; Chairman, Board of Directors, Winthrop Cemetery Association, 1978-; President, Block Island Club, 1982-84; Essex Corinthian Yacht Club. Address: 6 Westbrook Road, Deep River, CT 06417-1504, USA.

SPÄNKUCH Dietrich Hartwin, b. 17 February 1936, Würzburg. Meteorologist. m. Sieglinde, 1 son. Education: Diploma, 1959; Dr rer nat, 1965; DSc, 1973. Appointments: Assistant, Head of Department, Institute of Optics and Spectroscopy, Academy of Sciences, Germany, 1959-65; Director, Senior Scientist, Meteorological Observatory, 1965-2001; Visiting Scientist, University Pierre et Marie Curie, Paris VI, 1999. Publications: Over 180 in scientific journals. Honour: Suering Silver Medal, 1986. Memberships: Intercosmos, permanent WG Cosmic Meteorology, National Principal Investigator for Remote Sensing

of the Atmosphere, 1970-89; Radiation Commission, International Association of Meteorology and Atmospheric Physics, 1971-92; Academy of Sciences of the GDR, member of the Scientific Council of the Scientific Panel on Solar-Terrestrial Physics, 1976-89; Committee on Space Research, Member Sub –Commission A1, 1979-84, Commission A, 1984-88; Joint Scientific Committee of ICSU/WMO, World Climate Research Programme, Expert on Aerosols and Climate, 1980; WMO Commission of Atmospheric Sciences, invited expert for CAS Global Climate Group, 1981; Ad Hoc Interdisciplinary Group of Remote Sensing for Global Change, 1985-86; Deutsche Meteorologische Gesellschaft, Deputy Chair, Berlin-Brandenburg Branch, 1990-98; EUMETSAT Sounder Science Working Group, Member, 1991-94; Leibniz-Sozietaet ev, Berlin, 1994-; Member of several editorial boards. Address: Schmerberger Weg 72, D-14548 Schwielowsee, OT Caputh, Germany.

SPARK Muriel (Sarah) (Dame), b. 1 February 1918, Edinburgh, Scotland. Author; Poet. m. S O Spark, 1937, dissolved, 1 son. Education: Heriot Watt College, Edinburgh. Appointments: Political Intelligence Department, British Foreign Office, 1944-45; General Secretary, Poetry Society, 1947-49; Editor, The Poetry Review, 1947-49; Founder, Forum literary magazine. Publications: Fiction: The Comforters, 1957; Robinson, 1958; The Go-Away Bird and Other Stories, 1958; Memento Mori, 1959; The Ballad of Peckham Rye, 1960; The Bachelors, 1960; Voices at Play, 1961; The Prime of Miss Jean Brodie, 1961; The Girls of Slender Means, 1963; The Mandelbaum Gate, 1965; Collected Stories I, 1967; The Public Image, 1968; The Very Fine Clock (for children), 1969; The Driver's Seat, 1970; Not to Disturb, 1971; The Hothouse by the East River, 1973; The Abbess of Crewe, 1974; The Takeover, 1976; Territorial Rights, 1979; Loitering with Intent, 1981; Bang-Bang You're Dead and Other Stories, 1982; The Only Problem, 1984; The Stories of Muriel Spark, 1985; A Far Cry from Kensington, 1988; Symposium, 1990; The French Window and the Small Telephone (for children), 1993; Omnibus I, 1993; Omnibus II, 1994; Reality and Dreams, 1996; Omnibus III, 1996; Omnibus IV, 1997; Aiding and Abetting, 2000; The Complete Short Stories, 2002. Poetry: The Fanfarlo and Other Verse, 1952; Collected Poems I, 1967; Going Up to Sotheby's and Other Poems, 1982. Play: Doctors of Philosophy, 1962. Non-Fiction: Child of Light: A Reassessment of Mary Wollstonecraft Shelley, 1951, revised edition as Mary Shelley, 1987; John Masefield, 1953, revised 1992; Curriculum Vitae (autobiography), 1992; The Essence of the Brontës, 1993. Editor: 1950; Selected Poems of Emily Brontë, 1952; The Brontë Letters, 1954. Honours: Prix Italia, 1962; FRSL, 1963; Yorkshire Post Book of the Year Award, 1965; James Tait Black Memorial Prize, 1966; Hon DLitt, Strathclyde, 1971, Edinburgh, 1989, Aberdeen, 1995, St Andrews, 1998, D University, Heriot Watt University, DLitt, University of Oxford, 1999; Honorary Member, American Academy of Arts and Letters, 1978; 1st Prize, FNAC La Meilleur Recueil des Nouvelles Etrangères, 1987; Saltire Scottish Book of the Year Award, 1987; CLit, 1991; Ingersoll Foundation T S Eliot Award, 1992; Honorary Member, FRSE, 1995; Dame Commander of the Order of the British Empire, 1993; Commandeur de l'Ordre des Arts et des Lettres, France, 1996; David Cohen British Literature Prize, 1997; International PEN Gold Pen Award, 1998. Address: c/o David Higham Associates Ltd, 5-8 Lower John Street, Golden Square, London W1R 4HA, England.

SPEAR Walter Eric, b. 20 January 1921. Physicist. m. Hilda Doris King, 2 daughters. Education: BSc, PhD, DSc, University of London. Appointments: Lecturer then Reader, Physics, University of Leicester, 1953-68; Harris Professor of Physics, 1968-91, Professor Emeritus, 1991-, University of Dundee. Publications: Author of numerous research papers on electronic

Dictionary of International Biography

and transport properties in crystalline solids, liquids and amorphous semi-conductors. Honours: Europhysics Prize, European Physical Society, 1977; Max Born Medal and Prize, Institute of Physics and German Physical Society, 1977; Makdougall-Brisbane Medal, Royal Society of Edinburgh, 1981; Maxwell Premium, Institute of Electrical Engineers, 1981, 1982; Rank Prize for Optoelectronics, 1988; Mott Award, 1989; Rumford Medal, Royal Society, 1990. Memberships: FInstP, 1962; Fellow of the Royal Society of Edinburgh, 1972; Fellow of the Royal Society, 1980. Address: 20 Kelso Place, Dundee DD2 1SL, Scotland.

SPEARMAN Richard Ian Campbell, b. 14 August 1926, Ealing, London, England. Chartered Biologist. Education: BSc, Birkbeck College, University of London, England; PhD, DSc, University College London. Appointments: Infestation Control Division, Ministry of Agriculture, Food and Fisheries, 1949-52; National Institute for Medical Research, 1952-54; Genetics Department, UCL, 1954-57; Research Staff, Medical Research Council, 1957-70; Honorary Senior Lecturer, UCL, 1970; Research Consultant, 1970-86. Publications: Over 90 research papers, definitive chapters, reviews, articles, books and edited symposia. Memberships: Universities Federation for Animal Welfare; British Ecological Society; Society for Experimental Biology; Scientific Fellow, Zoological Society of London; Past Vice President, Linnean Society of London; Royal Society and Institute of Biology, Joint Committee on Biological Education, 1980-86; President, European Society for Comparative Skin Biology, 1978-82; Fellow, Institute of Biology. Address: 70 Hatherley Road, Winchester, Hampshire SO22 6RR, England.

SPEARS Michael Eugene, b. 21 June 1949, Columbia, South Carolina, USA. Attorney. m. Eileen L Spears, 1 son, 1 daughter. Education: Bachelor of Science, Biology, 1972, Doctor of Laws, 1977, University of South Carolina, USA; Education for Ministry Diploma, The University of the South, Sewanee, USA. Appointments: Assistant Public Defender, Spartanburg, South Carolina, USA, 1977-78; Partner, Swofford, Turnipseed, Allen & Smith, 1978-79; Partner, Swofford & Spears, 1979-81; Sole Practitioner, Michael E Spears PA, 1981-. Publication: Investigation, Discovery & Pre-trial Motions, The South Carolina Practice Manual, 2003. Honours: Best Lawyers in America, 1999-2004; Bar Register of Pre-eminent Lawyers, 85th and 86th editions; Listed in Who's Who publications and biographical dictionaries. Memberships: American Bar Association; American Trial Lawyers Association; South Carolina Bar Association; South Carolina Trial Lawyers Association. Address: PO Box 5806, Spartanburg, South Carolina 29304, USA. E-mail: attyspears@charter.net.

SPEISER Phyllis W, b. 20 October 1953, Newark, New Jersey, USA. Physician. m. Mark A Speiser, 2 sons, 1 daughter. Education: BA, Brandeis University, 1971-75; MD, Columbia University College of Physicians and Surgeons, 1975-79. Appointments: Director, Paediatric Endocrinology, Schneider Children's Hospital, New Hyde Park, New York; Professor of Paediatrics, New York University School of Medicine, New York. Publications: Over 100 publications in a variety of medial journals including: The New England Journal of Medicine; Journal of Clinical Investigation; Journal of Clinical Endocrinology and Metabolism. Honours: Fellow, American College of Endocrinology; Listed among Best Doctors, Castle Connolly Center for the Study of Services; Best Doctors.com; Top Pediatricians in America. Memberships: The Endocrine Society; The Lawson Wilkins Pediatric Endocrine Society; The Society for Pediatric Research; The American Association of Clinical Endocrinologists. Address: Schneider Children's Hospital, Rm 139, 269-01 76th Avenue, New Hyde Park, NY 11040, USA.

SPELLING Aaron, b. 22 April 1923, Dallas, Texas, USA. Television Producer; Writer. m. Carole Gene Marer, 1968, 1 son, 1 daughter. Education: University of Paris, Sorbonne; Southern Methodist University. Appointments: Served, USAAF, 1942-45; Co-owner, Thomas-Spelling Productions, 1969-72; Co-President, Spelling-Goldberg Productions, 1972-76; President, Aaron Spelling Productions Inc, Los Angeles, 1977-86; Chairman and Chief Executive Officer, 1986-; Producer, numerous TV programmes including: Dynasty; The Colbys; Love Boat; Hotel; Beverly Hills 90210; Melrose Place; Sunset Beach; Pacific Palisades; Over 110 Movies of the Week for American Broadcasting Corporation; Films produced include: Mr Mom; 'Night; Mother; Surrender; Cross My Heart; Soapdish. Publications: Author of numerous TV plays and films; Aaron Spelling: A Prime Time Life, 1996. Honours: Bronze Star Medal; Purple Heart with Oak Leaf Cluster; Eugene O'Neil Award, 1947, 1948; National Association for Advancement of Colored People Image Award, 1970, 1971, 1973, 1975; Man of the Year Award, Publicists' Guild of America, 1971; B'nai B'rith Man of the Year Award, 1985; NAACP Humanitarian of the Year, 1983. Memberships: Board of Directors, American Film Institute; Writer's Guild of America; Producers Guild of America; The Caucus, Hollywood Radio and TV Society; Hollywood TV Academy of Arts and Science. Address: Spelling Entertainment Group, 5700 Wilshire Boulevard, Floor 5, Los Angeles, CA 90036, USA.

SPENCER David A, b. 7 November 1963, Stepney, London, England. Geologist. Education: BSc (Honours), Geology, University of Exeter, UK, 1983-86; Diploma of Imperial College, Structural Geology and Rock Mechanics, Royal School of Mines, Imperial College of Science and Technology, University of London, 1987-88; MSc, Structural Geology and Rock Mechanics, Royal School of Mines, London, 1987-88; Doctor of Natural Sciences, Swiss Federal Institute of Technology (ETH), Zurich, 1989-93. Appointments include: Hydrological Consultant, Partnerscaft Pro Aliminos, Philippines, 1992-94; Accepted as Senior Post-Doctoral Research Fellow (SNSF) at Universities of: Cambridge (UK), Stanford (USA), California (Santa Barbara), Maine (USA), Punjab (Pakistan), Tokyo Institute of Technology, MIT, Boston, USA, 1997-99; Research Assistant Professor, Lecturer in Structural Geology, University of Maine, Orono, USA, 1997-98; Staff Geologist - Structural Geologist, Project Manager, Saga Petroleum ASA, Oslo, Norway, 1998-2000; Senior Reservoir Geologist, Roxar Software Solutions, London, 2003-. Publications: 24 scientific publications, 46 articles, 81 abstracts, 4 theses, 1 consultant report, 22 research reports, 6 expedition reports. Honours: Many scholarships and awards, also many athletic awards in a variety of sports. Memberships include: Fellow, Royal Geographic Society (with Institute of British Geographers); Fellow, Royal Astronomical Society; Fellow, American Geographical Society; Fellow, Geological Society; Fellow, Geological Association of Canada; Fellow, Geological Society of India; Fellow, Royal Society of Arts; Fellow, Linnean Society of London. Address: PO Box 30692, London E1 0TH, Great Britain. E-mail: DSpencer@online.no

SPENCER Elizabeth, b. 19 July 1921, Carrollton, Mississippi, USA. Writer. m. John Arthur Rusher, 29 September 1956. Education: AB, cum laude, Belhaven College, 1942; MA, Vanderbilt University, 1943. Appointments: Writer-in-Residence, Adjunct Professor, 1977-86, Concordia University, Montreal; Visiting Professor, University of North Carolina at Chapel Hill, 1986-92. Publications: Fire in the Morning, 1948; This Crooked Way, 1952; The Voice at the Back Door, 1956; The Light in the Piazza, 1960; Knights and Dragons, 1965; No Place for an Angel, 1967; Ship Island and Other Stories, 1968; The Snare, 1972; The

Dictionary of International Biography

Stories of Elizabeth Spencer, 1981; The Salt Line, 1984; Jack of Diamonds, 1988; For Lease or Sale (drama), 1989; The Night Travellers, 1991; Landscapes of the Heart (memoir), 1998. Contributions to: New Yorker; Atlantic; Southern Review; Kenyon Review. Address: 402 Longleaf Drive, Chapel Hill, NC 27514, USA.

SPEVAKOVSKY Alexander, b. 20 February 1947, Leningrad, now St Petersburg, USSR. Historian-Ethnologist. m. Marina, 1 son. Education: MD, Graduate, Leningrad State University, 1974; PhD, History, Institute of Ethnography, Leningrad, 1981; Doctor of Historical Sciences, Institute of Ethnography, St Petersburg, 1993. Appointments: Research Fellow, 1974, Scientific Secretary, 1983, Institute of Ethnography, Leningrad, Academy of Sciences of the USSR; Docent, Historical Faculty, Leningrad State University, part-time, 1983; Associate Professor, Centre for Language Studies, Otaru, University of Commerce, Japan, 1992-2000. Publications: Samurai – Military Class of Japan, Moscow, 1981; Shinto and Wars, Leningrad, 1987; Spirit, Werewolves, Demons and Gods of Ainu, Moscow, 1988; Samurai, Warsaw, 1989; History and Culture of the Evens, St Petersburg, 1997. Address: Shukutsu 1-3-328, Otaru, 047-0047, Japan.

ŠPIČÁK Julius, b. 10 June 1952, Prague, Czech Republic. Medical Doctor. 2 daughters. Education: Doctor of Medicine, Charles University, Prague, Czech Republic, 1976; Specialist in Internal Medicine, 1st Degree, 1980, 2nd Degree, 1983; Specialist in Gastroenterology, 1992; Assistant Professor, Internal medicine, 1983; PhD, 1992; Habilitation, 1994. Appointments: Head of the Clinic of Hepatogastroenterology, Institute of Clinical and Experimental Medicine, Prague, Czech Republic; President, Czech Society of Gastroenterology. Publications: About 200 papers on digestive endoscopy, pancreatology, liver transplantation; Chapters in monographs, textbooks and manuals as co-author: The alcohol related diseases of liver, pancreas and gastrointestinal tube, 1996; Gastrointestinal Endoscopy: the basis, 1996; Clinical gastroenterology, 1999; Advanced gastrointestinal endoscopy, 2000; Diseases of the stomach and duodenum, 2000; Diseases of the pancreas, 2000; Antioxidants and ROS in health and diseases. Memberships: Czech Society of Gastroenterology; Czech Society of Internal Medicine; Czech Society of Hepatology; International Gastro-Surgical Club; American Society of Gastrointestinal Endoscopy; Board Member, European Society of Gastrointestinal Endoscopy; Corresponding Member, German Society of Gastroenterology. Address: Institute for Clinical and Experimental Medicine, Videnská 1958/9 Prague 4, 140 21 Czech Republic.

SPICER Kevin Paul, b. 22 May 1965, Washington, DC, USA. Professor; Priest. Education: BA, Stonehill College, 1987; MDiv, University of St Michael's College, Toronto, 1991; MA, 1996, PhD, 2000, Boston College. Appointments: Assistant Professor, Stonehill College, 2000-. Publications: Discovering the Foundation of the Sacrament of Marriage: The Trinitarian Formula of Love, 1994; Selective Resistance: The German Catholic Church's Response to National Socialism, 1998; The Provost from St Hedwig: Bernhard Lichtenberg as a Paradigm for Resistance, 2000; To Serve God or Hitler: Nazi Priests, a Preliminary Discussion, 2000; Last Years of a Resister in the Diocese of Berlin: Bernhard Lichtenberg's Conflict with Karl Adam and his Fateful Imprisonment, 2001. Honour: Holocaust Educational Foundation Research Fellowship, 2001-2002. Memberships: Church Relations Committee of the Center for Advanced Holocaust Studies, US Memorial Holocaust Museum, 2000-; American Catholic Historical Association; American Historical Association; German Studies Association. Address: Stonehill College, 320 Washington Street, Easton, MA 02357, USA. E-mail: kspicer@stonehill.edu

SPIELBERG Steven, b. 18 December 1947, Cincinnati, Ohio, USA. Film Director; Producer. m. (1) Amy Irving, 1985, divorced 1989, 2 sons, (2) Kate Capshaw, 1 daughter, 1 adopted daughter. Education: California State College, Long Beach. Career: Film Director, Universal Pictures; Founder, Amblin Entertainment; Co-founder, Dreamworks SKG Inc, 1995-; Founder, Starbright Foundation. Creative Works: As Film Director: Duel (for TV), 1971; Something Evil (for TV), 1972; The Sugarland Express, 1974; Jaws, 1975; Close Encounters of the Third Kind, 1977; 1941, 1979; Raiders of the Lost Ark, 1981; E.T. (The Extra Terrestrial), 1982; Twilight Zone - The Movie, 1983; Indiana Jones and the Temple of Doom, 1984; The Color Purple (also producer), 1985; Empire of the Sun, 1988; Always, 1989; Hook, 1991; Jurassic Park, 1992; Schindler's List, 1993; Some Mother's Son, 1996; The Lost World, 1997; As Producer: I Wanna Hold Your Hand, 1978; Poltergeist (also co-writer), 1982; Gremlins, 1984; Young Sherlock Holmes (executive producer), 1985; Back to the Future (co-executive producer), 1986; The Goonies (writer, executive producer), 1986; Batteries Not Included (executive producer), 1986; The Money Pit (co-producer), 1986; An American Tail (co-executive producer), 1986; Who Framed Roger Rabbit, 1988; Gremlins II (executive producer), 1991; Joe Versus the Volcano (executive producer), 1991; Dad (executive producer) 1991; Cape Fear (co-executive producer), 1992; The Flintstones, 1994; Casper, 1995; Twister (executive producer), 1996; Men in Black, 1997; The Lost World: Jurassic Park, 1997; Amistad, 1997; Deep Impact, 1998; Saving Private Ryan, 1998; The Last Days (documentary), 1999; AI; Artificial Intelligence, 2001; Minority Report, 2002; Catch Me If You Can, 2002; Director, TV episodes, including Columbo; E.R; Band of Brothers, 2000; Semper Fi, 2000; Taken, 2002. Publication: Close Encounters of the Third Kind (with Patrick Mann). Honours include: Directors Guild of America Award Fellowship, 1986; BAFTA Awards; Irving G Thalberg Award, 1987; Golden Lion Award, Venice Film Festival, 1993; Academy Awards; John Huston Award, 1995; Dr hc, University of Southern California, 1994; Lifetime Achievement Award, Directors' Guild of America, 1999; Britannia Award, 2000; Grosses Bundesverdienstkreuz, 1998; Hon KBE. Address: CAA, 9830 Wilshire Boulevard, Beverly Hills, CA 90212, USA.

SPIES Stephen Bruce, b. 13 February 1950, New York City, New York, USA. Forensic Scientist. m. Audrey C Spies. Education: BA, Economics; MS, Criminology; PhD, Psychology (Clinical) summa cum laude. Appointments: Special Agent, US Department of the Treasury; Director, Scientific and Forensic Applications of Explosives Engineering Technologies; Judge Emeritus, City of Sachse, Texas; Captain United States Army; Certified Fire Investigator; Certified Explosives Specialist; Polygraph Examiner. Publications: Treatise on the Behavior of Structural Metals in the Elevated Temperature Environment; US v. Winchester: An Analytical Treatise on the Failure of Munitions Control Regulations; Analysis of Military Aircraft Fires and Explosions. Honours: Alpha Phi Sigma, National Criminal Justice Honor Society; Bronze Star Medal; Air Medal; Vietnam Civil Actions Medal; PhD, summa cum laude; Master Army Aviator. Memberships: International Society of Explosives Engineers; International Association of Bomb Technicians and Investigators; International Association of Arson Investigators. E-mail: leasprog@aol.com

SPILLER Andres, b. 24 December 1946, Buenos Aires, Argentina. Oboist; Conductor. m. Marcela Magin, 2 sons, 1 daughter. Education: Conservatorio Nacional; Private studies, Hochschule für Musik Köln, Germany; Summer courses with Heinz Holliger, Bruno Maderna, Franco Ferrara, Michael Gielen, Volker Wangenheim. Career: Assistant Conductor, National Symphony Orchestra and Oboe Soloist; Oboe Soloist, Camerata Bariloche and Soloist of Bach Academy, Buenos Aires; Conductor, La Plata

Dictionary of International Biography

Chamber Orchestra; Performed with Koeckert Quartet in Munich; Other European appearances include Madrid, Rome and Radio Zürich; Toured America and Europe with Camerata Bariloche; Professor of Oboe and Chamber Music. Recordings: Death of an Angel; Tango. Honours: DAAD Fellowship for study in Germany; Sociedad Hebraica Prize; 2nd Prize, Promaciones Musicales; Premio Konex, 1989, 1999. Address: Medrano 47, 5øA, 1178 Buenos Aires, Argentina.

SPLENDIANI Georgio, b. 26 July 1934, Macerata, Marche, Italy. Nephrology Educator. m. Maria Sofia Giordano, 2 sons, 3 daughters. Education: MD, University of Rome, Italy, 1958; Medical Assistant, Governative Hospital, Tripoli, Libya, 1960-61, Civil Hospital L'Aquila, Italy, 1962-65; Medical Aivto, 1965-70, Director, Nephrology Department, 1971-86, Associate Professor of Nephrology, 1986-, University of Rome, Italy. Publications: Editor: Artificial Support in Severe Organ Failure (conference proceedings), 1984; Hemoperfusion Adsorbendo Immobilist Bioreactants, 1992; Bionics in the Third Millennium, 2003. Memberships: International Society of Nephrology; International Society of Artificial Organs; American Society of Nephrology; American Society of Artificial Organs; Past President, Rotary Club. Address: University Tor Vergata Roma, viale Oxford 81, 00136 Rome Italy. E-mail: splendiani@med.uniroma2.it

SPURWAY Marcus John, b. 28 October 1938, Surrey, England. Retired Insurance Broker and Director. m. Christine Kate, 2 sons. Appointments: National Service, 4 Regiment, Royal Horse Artillery; Insurance Broker, Director, Morgan Reid & Sharman, Ltd (Lloyd's Brokers, formerly B&C Aviation Insurance Brokers); Specialist in Aviation Insurance; Retired 1999. Publications: Aviation Insurance Abbreviations, Organisations and Institutions, 1983; Aviation Insurance. The Market and Underwriting Practice, 1991; Aviation Law and Claims, 1992. Address: Lomeer, Common Road, Sissinghurst, Kent TN17 2JR, England.

SQUIRE Margaret Louise, b. 12 February 1932, London, Ontario, Canada. Artist. m. C Donald Squire, 4 daughters. Education: BA, University of Western Ontario, 1953; London Teachers College, 1954. Appointments: Teacher, 1967-82; Freelance Artist, 1982-. Civic Activities: President, Canadian Society of Painters in Watercolour, 1995, 1996. Honours: Several. Memberships: Canadian Society of Painters in Watercolour; Colour and Form Society. Commissions and Creative Works: Collections: Harbour Castle Westin; Pellow Architect Inc; Peel County Board of Education; Bank of Montreal; Canadian Society of Painters in Watercolour; Diamond Jubilee Collection presented to Her Majesty Queen Elizabeth II for the Royal Collection of Drawings and Watercolours, Windsor Castle; Bruce County Offices, Walkerton, Ontario; Family Services Clinic, Mississauga, Ontario; Numerous group and solo exhibitions. Address: 39 Suburban Drive, Mississauga, Ontario L5N 1G8, Canada.

SQUIRES Digby Peter (Leighton-), b. 9 November 1953, Wolverhampton, England. Businessman. m. Ame-Mary-Love Akré-Loba. Education: University of Dundee, -1973; BSc (Econ), Queen Mary College London, 1978. Appointments: Articled Clerk, KPMG Peat Marwick, 1978-81; Insolvency Manager, KPMG, 1981-83; Divisional Finance Officer, Mitsubishi Electric UK, London, 1983-85; Director, Leighton Properties Ltd, London, 1985-97; Principal, Squires Consulting, London and Madrid, 1989-99; Founding Trustee, Delfina Studio Trust, 1987-; Director Delfina Studio Café Ltd, 1995-. Memberships: Honorary Member, Chelsea Arts Club; Bentley Drivers Association. Address: Delfina, 50 Bermondsey Street, London SE1 3UD, England. E-mail: digby.squires@delfina.org.uk

SRINIVASA Arehalli Muniswariah, b. 17 November 1946, Bangalore, India. Medical Practitioner. m. Malathi Srinivasa, 1 son, 1 daughter. Education: MBBS, Bangalore Medical College, India, 1970; FRCS (Edinburgh), 1974; FACS (USA), 1992; FRACGP (Australia), 1996. Appointments: Senior House Officer, Surgery, Victoria Hospital, Bangalore, India, 1970-71; Lecturer, Anatomy, Bellary Medical College, India, 1971; Senior House Officer, Trauma and Orthopaedics, Neath General Hospital, UK, 1971-72; Rotating House Officer, Surgery, Lewisham Hospital, London, 1972-74; Registrar, General Surgery, Neath General Hospital, UK, 1974-77; Specialist Medical Officer, Papua New Guinea, 1978-90; Medical Officer, Family Medicine Practice Rotation, Queen Elizabeth II Jubilee Hospital, Brisbane, Australia, 1991; Senior Medical Officer, Emergency Department, Logan Hospital, Queensland, Australia, 1992-94; Principal Partner, Ormeau Medical Centre, Ormeau, Queensland, Australia, 1994-. Publications: Ruptured Spleen in Adults – Account of 205 cases with reference to conservative management, 1987; Tropical Ulcers in East Sepik Province of PNG – diagnosis and management, 1989; Oral Cavity cancers – current status and its relevance to PNG, 1990; Case Report on Gastric Stenosis following ingestion of battery acid, 1991. Memberships: Associate Member International Federation of Surgical Colleges; Fellow, American College of Surgeons; Surgical Society of Papua New Guinea, Part Vice-President and President. Address: 38 Vaughan Drive, Ormeau, Queensland 4208, Australia. E-mail: Srini@austonnet.com.au

SRIVASTAVA Radhey Shyam, b. 7 June 1931, Bahadurganj (UP), India. Scientist. m. Vijay Laxmi, 1 son, 2 daughters. Education: BSc, 1951, MSc, 1953, PhD, 1963, Lucknow University; Certificate in Proficiency in French, 1957. Appointments: Research Fellow, Lecturer, 1954-58, Lucknow University; Junior Scientific Officer, 1958-61, Senior Scientific Officer, 1961-71, Principal Scientific Officer, 1971-80, Deputy Chief Scientific Officer, 1980-91, Defence Science Centre, New Delhi, India; Publications: Books: Turbulence (pipe Flows), 1977; Interaction of Shock Waves, 1994; Research papers and reports. Honours: Postdoctoral Royal Society Research Fellow, Imperial College of Science and Technology, London, 1965-67; Visiting Scientist: Institute for Aerospace Studies, University of Toronto, 1980-81; Materials Research Laboratories, Melbourne, 1983; Chiba University, Japan, 1991; Visiting Professor, Ernst Mach Institute, Freiburg, Germany, 1995; Visiting Professor, Chiba University, Japan 2000; Visiting Professor, Tohoku University, Japan, 2000; Visiting Professor, Tokyo Denki University, Japan, 2001; Visiting Professor, Aachen University, Germany, 2002; 2000 Millennium Medal of Honor, ABI, USA, 2000; 20th Century Award for Achievement, 1998. Memberships: Fellow, National Academy of Science, India; Life Member, Bharat Ganita Parishad, India; Indian Science Congress; Kothari Centre for Science, Ethics and Education (KCSEE); Fellow, United Writers' Association of India. Address: A-3/260, Janakpuri, New Delhi 110058, India.

SRUOGA Aniolas, b. 20 November 1936, Baibokai, Lithuania. Genetics. m. Aldona, 1961, 2 sons, 1 daughter. Education: 4th Lithuanian Veterinary Academy, 1956-61; Vilnius University, 1964-67; Postgraduate, Institute of Cytology and Genetics, Siberian Academy of Sciences, 1967-70; Dr habil, 1995. Appointments: Junior Researcher, 1971-75, Senior Researcher, 1975-83, Institute of Zoology and Parasitology, Academy of Sciences, Lithuania; Head, Laboratory of Innumogenetics, 1983-, Deputy Director, Scientific Affairs, 1984-87, Institute of Ecology, Lithuanian Academy of Sciences; Visiting Professor, 1995-, Professor, 2001-, Department of Biology, Vyfaufas Magnus University, 1995-. Publications: Over 170 articles in professional science journals. Honours: Several grants and doctoral degrees. Memberships:

Secretary, Lithuanian Society of Selectors and Geneticists; Head, Sector of Animal Genetics, Baltic Genetic Federation. Address: str Architektics 178-21, Vilnius 20049, Lithuania.

ST CLAIR Frank Creel, b. 17 November 1936, Jacksonville, Texas, USA. Publisher; Writer; Recording Artist; Musician (Guitar). m. Barbara Mae Young, 29 October 1963, 4 sons, 3 daughters. Education: Fine Arts, Kilgore College, 1968-70; Graphic Arts, Texas State Technical Institute, Waco, 1970-72; Commercial Art, Tyler College, 1978-80; Understudied with Jack Rhodes, Curly Putman and others. Career: 3rd Army Special Services, Touring Southeast US; KLTV, Tyler, Texas; WFLB TV, Fayetteville, North Carolina; Major TV Stations in Deep South, 1955-70; Performed as singer in night clubs and stage shows throughout Texas, 1957-; Formed Rosebud Publishing Company Inc, 1969; Started Country Crossroad Music Show, Henderson, Texas, 1998; Formed road band, Frank St Clair and The Good Timers, 1998. Compositions: My Heart and Mind are at War, 1964; Portrait of a Fool, 1964; Guitar Bum, 1966; Mr Blues, 1966; Night Bird, 1969; This Is Life, 1969; I Hope My Guilty Don't Show, 1970; Pollution of the Mind, 1980; Good Times Are Fleeting Things, 1982. Memberships: BMI; Country Music Association; MCPS, London. Address: Rr 5 Box 1635, Henderson, TX 75652, USA.

ST CLEMENT Pamela, b. 11 May 1942. Actress; Presenter. m. Andrew Louis Gordon, 1970, divorced 1979. Education: The Warren, Worthing; Rolle College, Devon; Rose Bruford College of Drama, Kent. Career: Television appearances include: Wild at Heart; BBC Animal Awards: Zoo Chronicles; Adopt-a-Wild-Animal; BBC Eastenders, 1986-; Whipsnade, (2, 13 part wildlife series); Not for the Likes of Us (Play for Today); The Tripods; Cats Eyes; Partners in Crime; Shoestring; Emmerdale Farm; Horseman Riding By (BBC series); Shall I See You Now (BBC play); Within these Walls (2 series); Theatre includes: Joan Littlewood's Theatre Royal, Stratford; Royal Shakespeare Company; Prospect Theatre Company (Strindberg and Chekov); Thorndike Theatre (Macbeth); Yvonne Arnaud Theatre (I am a Camera); Leeds Playhouse (Once a Catholic); Victoria Theatre/Dome Brighton (The Music from Chicago); Films include: Hedda; Dangerous Davies; The Bunker; Scrubbers. Honour: Presented Duke of Edinburgh Awards, St James' Palace, 2000. Memberships: President, West Herts RSPCA; Vice-President, Scottish Terrier Emergency Care Scheme; Patron: London Animal Day; Tusk Trust; Africat (UK); Pets as Therapy; Leicester Animal Aid Association; Ridgeway Trust for Endangered Cats; Pro-Dogs; Other charities involved with: PDSA; Blue Cross; National Animal Welfare Trust; Battersea Dogs Home; Environmental Investigation Agency; Hearing Dogs for Deaf People; International League for the Protection of Horses; Kennel Club Good Citizens Dog Scheme; Project Life Line; Earth Kind; WSPA; Humane Education Trust; Member, Institute of Advanced Motorists. Address: c/o Saraband Associates, 265 Liverpool Road, London N1 1LX, England.

ST JOHN Katherine Marie, b. 13 March 1953, Detroit, Michigan, USA. Philosophy, Theology, Psychology Instructor. Education: BA, Philosophy, California State University, 1974; MA, Philosophy, San Diego State University, 1977; MDiv, Theology, Pacific School of Religion, 1982; Certificate, Substance Abuse, Pacific School of Religion, 1982; PhD, Psychology, United States International University, 1993; Certificate, English/Creative Writing, Grossmont College, 2001. Appointments: Instructor, Philosophy, Theology and Humanities, Grossmont College; Psychology Instructor, Cuyamaca College; Administrator of Pastoral Services, Deaconess Hospital of Cleveland, Ohio; Chaplain, Clinical Instructor, Baptist Memorial Hospital, San Antonio; Chaplain, Good Samaritan Hospital, Phoenix; Chaplain, Finan Psychiatric Hospital/Memorial Hospital, Cumberland,

Maryland; Chaplain, Austin State Hospital, Austin, Texas; Consultant to Chaplaincy, Department of Military Chaplain Training, Brooke Army Medical Center, San Antonio; Marriage and Family Therapy Intern, Baptist Memorial Hospital, San Antonio. Honours: Numerous scholarships; Formal recognition by the American Psychological Association, for counselling of victims of the Oklahoma Bombing, 1995; Phi Theta Kappa; Psi Chi; The National Deans List, 1999-2000; Listed in several Who's Who and biographical publications. Membership: Life Member, American Psychological Association. Address: 853 Ronda Mendoza Unit "N", Laguna Woods, CA 92653, USA.

STACK Steven, b. 20 December 1947, Providence, Rhode Island, USA. College Professor. 3 sons. Education: Assistant Professor of Sociology, Alma College, 1976-79; Assistant Professor of Sociology, Indiana University, 1979-81; Associate Professor of Sociology, Penn State University, 1981-85; Associate, Full Professor, Sociology, Auburn University, 1985-90; Full Professor of Criminal Justice, Wayne State University, 1990-. Publications include: 175 articles in professional journals; 33 book chapters; 249 papers read in professional meetings. Honours: Grant, National Institute of Mental Health; grants, Henry Frank Guggenheim Foundation; Edwin Shasidman Award, American Association of Suicidology; Louis Dublin Award, American Association of Suicidology. Memberships: American Association of Suicidology; American Sociological Association; National Council on Family Relations; American Society of Criminology; Academy of Criminal Justice Sciences. Address: Department of Criminal Justice, Wayne State University, Detroit, MI 48292, USA. E-mail: aa1051@wayne.edu

STAFFORD C Carolyn, b. 9 August 1935, Bolton, England. Painter in Oil and Watercolour; Printmaker. m. Gordon Clough, deceased, 1 son, 3 daughters. Education: Bolton School of Art; Manchester College of Art, under Ralph Downing, Ian Grant, 1955; Diploma of Fine Art, Slade School of Fine Art, under William Coldstream, Claude Rogers, Anthony Gross, 1957; Esmond Scholar, British Institute in Paris, etching with S W Hayter, 1957-58. Career: Painter, Oils and Watercolour, Printmaker. Exhibitions: John Moores, Liverpool; Royal Academy; Bankside Open Prints; London Group; Arts Council Tours; R I; RBA; Print Makers Council; Malta; US/UK Art Olympia, 1990-93; Pump House, 1993; Contemporary Portrait Society; Northern School (Pelter-Sands and touring exhibition); Lvov, 1991; New Academy Gallery, 1991; Paris 1994, 1996; Universities of Bristol, Cambridge, London, Oxford, Surrey, 1980-90; Ben Uri Gallery, Tel Aviv; Curwen; FPS; Munich 1997; North-South Printmakers, Barbican, 1999; Yehudi Menuhin School; Work in collections: Slade School; DOE; Bolton School, Girls Division; Bolton Art Gallery; Lvov Art Gallery; Landau Art Gallery; Scarborough Art Gallery. Publications: Art Review; A Northern School (Peter Davies). Memberships: Art Societies; CPS; SGFA; PMC; NS; AVA; FPS. Address: 52 Ellerton Road, London SW 18 3NN, England.

STAFFORD Francis Melfort William Fitzherbert (Lord), b. 13 March 1954, Rhynie, Scotland. Landowner. m. Katharine, 2 sons, 2 daughters. Education: Reading University, England; RAC, Cirencester, England. Appointments: Non Executive Director, Tarmac Industrial Products, 1985-94; Chair, Governor, Swynnerton School, 1986-; Non Executive Director, NHS Foundation Trust, 1990-99; Vice Chairman, Harper Adams University College, 1990-; Vice Chairman, Hanley Economic Building Society, 1993-; Pro Chancellor, Keele University, 1993-; Landowner. Honours: Deputy Lieutenant, 1994-. Memberships: Army and Navy Club; Lord's Taverners; Sunningdale Golf Club; Patron and President various organisations mainly in Staffordshire. Address: Swynnerton Park, Stone, Staffordshire, ST15 0QE, England. E-mail: ls@lordstafford.demon.co.uk

Dictionary of International Biography

STAFFORD-CLARK Max, b. 17 March 1941. Theatre Director. m. (1) Carole Hayman, 1971, (2) Ann Pennington, 1981, 1 daughter. Education: Trinity College, Dublin. Appointments: Artistic Director, Traverse Theatre, Edinburgh, 1968-70; Director, Traverse Workshop Company, 1970-74; Artistic Director, Joint Stock, 1974-79; English Stage Company, Royal Court Theatre, 1979-93; Out of Joint, 1993-; Visiting Professor, Royal Holloway and Bedford College, University of London, 1993-94; Maisie Glass Professor, University of Sheffield, 1995-96; Visiting Professor, University of Hertfordshires, 1999-; Principal Productions: Fanshen; Top Girls; Tom and Viv; Rat in the Skull; Serious Money; Our Country's Good; The Libertine; The Steward of Christendom; Shopping and Fucking; Blue Heart; Drummers; Some Explicit Polaroids; Rita, Sue and Bob Too/A State Affair; A Laughing Matter. Publication: Letters to George 1989. Honours: Hon Fellow, Rose Bruford College, 1996; Hon DLitt, Oxford Brookes, 2000; Hon DLitt, Hertfordshire, 2000. Address: 7 Gloucester Crescent, London, NW1 7DS, England.

STAGNARO Sergio, b. 7 December 1931, Sestri Levante, Genoa. Medical Doctor. m. Marina Neri, 1 son, 1 daughter. Education: MD, Genoa University, 1956; Haematology, Gastroenterology, Metabolic Diseases, Pavia University. Appointments: Retired General Practitioner; Researcher in Physical Semiotics; Founder, Biophysical Semeiotics. Publications: 150 articles on Biophysical Semeiotics; Book: Introduzione Alla Semeiotica Biofisica Terreno Oncologico; Nuovi Aspetti e Fondamentali Sviluppi di un Importante Metodo Diagnostico Clinica. Membership: Active member, New York Academy of Sciences. Address: Via E Piaggio 23/8, 16037 Riva Trigoso, Genoa, Italy. E-mail: dottsergio@semeioticabiofisica.it

STAHL Alexander Hans Joachim, b. 27 April 1938, Netzschkau, Vogtland. Official. m. Bärbel Schultheis, 2 sons. Education: Diploma in Politics, Free University, Berlin, 1965. Appointments: Adviser in informal education for the young at the Arbeitskreis deutscher Bildungsstätten, Bonn, 1965-67; Lecturer, Political Education, Jugenhof Vlotho, 1967-69; Youth Officer, Land Youth Office Westfalen-Lippe, Landschaftsverband Westfalen-Lippe, 1972-; Deputy-in-Chief, board of film censors, (Freiwillige Selbstkontrolle der Filmwirtschaft) Wiesbaden, 1989-. Publications: Editor, journal: Mitteilungen des Landesjugendamtes Westfalen-Lippe, Landschaftsverband Westfalen-Lippe, Landeshaus Münster, 1969-; Honour: Councillor, Stadt Münster, 1975-79; Honorary Member, Bavarian Association of Youth Officers. Address: Von-Humboldt-Str 33, D48159 Münster, Germany.

STAHL Douglas R, b. 24 October 1950, Sandwich, Illinois, USA. Building Contractor. Education: Associate Degree, Fire Science, 1974; Associate Degree, Business Administration, 1974; Bachelor Degree, Fire Science Safety, 1977. Appointments: Family Building Business, 1968-; Volunteer Fire Fighter, 1970-; Superintendent, Open Beef Show, Sandwich Fair, Sandwich, Illinois, 1976-. Honours: 2000 Fire Fighter of the Year, Sandwich Community Fire Protection District, Sandwich, Illinois; Featured in June 1990 Builder Dealer Magazine; Listed in Who's Who publications and biographical dictionaries. Membership: International Association of Arson Investigators. Address: 15626 N, Memory Lane, Sandwich, Illinois, 60548-4070, USA.

STALLONE Sylvester Enzio, b. 6 July 1946, New York, USA. Actor; Film Director. m. (1) Sasha Czach, 1974, divorced, 2 sons, (2) Brigitte Nielsen, 1985, divorced 1987, (3) Jennifer Flavin, 1997, 2 daughters. Education: American College of Switzerland; University of Miami. Appointments: Has had many jobs including: Usher; Bouncer; Horse Trainer; Store Detective; Physical

Education Teacher; Now Actor, Producer, Director of own films; Founder, White Eagle Company; Director, Carolco Pictures Inc, 1987-; Film appearances include: Lords of Flatbush, 1973; Capone, 1974; Rocky, 1976; FIST, 1978; Paradise Alley, 1978; Rocky II, 1979; Nighthawks, 1980; Escape to Victory, 1980; Rocky III, 1981; First Blood; Rambo, 1984; Rocky IV, 1985; Cobra, 1986; Over the Top, 1986; Rambo II, 1986; Rambo III, 1988; Set Up, 1990; Tango and Cash, 1990; Rocky V, 1990; Isobar, 1991; Stop or My Mom Will Shot, 1991; Oscar, 1991; Cliffhanger, 1992; Demolition Man, 1993; Judge Dredd, 1994; The Specialist, 1994; Assassins, 1995; Firestorm, 1996; Daylight, 1996; Cop Land, 1997; An Alan Smithee Film: Burn Hollywood Burn, 1998; Get Carter, 2000; Producer, Director, Staying Alive, 1983. Publications: Paradise Alley, 1977; The Rocky Scrapbook, 1997. Honours: Oscar for best film, 1976; Golden Circle Award for best film, 1976; Donatello Award, 1976; Christopher Religious Award, 1976; Honorary Member, Stuntmans' Association; Officier Ordre des Arts et des Lettres. Memberships: Screen Actors' Guild; Writers' Guild; Directors' Guild. Address: William Morris Agency, 151 El Camino Drive, Beverly Hills, CA 90212, USA.

STALTER Richard, b. 16 January 1942, Montvale, New Jersey, USA. Professor of Biology. 1 daughter. Education: BSc, Biology, Rutgers University, New Brunswick, 1963; PhD, Biology, University of South Carolina, Columbia, South Carolina, 1968. Appointments: Professor of Biology, St Johns University, Jamaica, New York (USA), 1971-. Publications: Over 300 publications including 4 books, book chapters, refereed articles, abstracts, book reviews and field trip reports. Honours: Phi Sigma, Sigma Xi; Skull and Circle. Memberships: Torrey Botanical Society; Long Island Botanical Society; Southern Appalachian Botanical Club; Philadelphia Botanical Society; South Carolina Academy of Science. Address: Department of Biology, St John's University, Jamaica, NY 11439, USA.

STAMFORD Newton Pereira, b. 28 May 1942, Recife, Pernambuco, Brazil. Engineer; Agronomist. m. Tânia Lúcia Montenegro Stamford, 1 son, 3 daughters. Education: Graduate, Agronomy, University Federal Rural of Pernambuco, Brazil, 1966; MSc, University Federal Rural of Rio de Janeiro, Brazil, 1970; PhD, Plant and Soil Science, USP, Piracicaba, Brazil, 1978; Postdoctoral, CIDA, Seville, Spain, 1998. Appointments: Auxiliary Professor, 1970-73, Assistant Professor, 1973-78, Adjunct Professor, 1978-91, Titular Professor, 1991-1996. Department of Agronomy, Pro-Rector, 1996, University Federal Rural of Pernambuco, Brazil. Publications: More than 60 scientific articles published in professional journals which include: Bioresource Technology; Journal of Agricultural Science, Cambridge University; Tropical Grasslands; Journal of Plant Physiology; Soil Biology Biochemistry; Revista Brasileira de Ciência do Solo; Scientia Agricola; Acta Scientarium; Ecossistema; Agropecuária Téchnica. Honour: Honour Professor, Department of Agronomy, 1978. Memberships: Brazilian Society of Soil Science; Brazilian Society of Microbiology. Address: Rua Jader de Andrade, 335 Casa Forte 52061-060 Recife, Pernambuco, Brazil. E-mail: newtonps@fastmodem.com.br

STAMP Terence, b. 22 July 1938, London. Actor. Career: Theatre work before film debut in Billy Budd, 1962; Other films include: Term of Trial, 1962; The Collector, 1965; Modesty Blaise, 1966; Far From the Madding Crowd, 1967; Poor Cow, 1967; Blue, 1968; Theorem, 1968; Tales of Mystery, 1968; The Mind of Mr Soames, 1969; A Season in Hell, 1971; Hu-man, 1975; The Divine Creature, 1976; Striptease, 1977; Meetings With Remarkable Men, 1978; Superman, 1978; Superman II, 1979; Death in the Vatican, 1980; The Bloody Chamber, 1982; The Hit, 1984; Link, 1985; Legal Eagles, 1986; The Sicilian, 1986; Wall Street, 1988; Alien Nation,

1988; Young Guns, 1988; Prince of Shadows, 1991; The Real McCoy, 1992; The Adventures of Priscilla Queen of the Desert, 1994; Bliss, 1995; Limited Edition, 1995; Mindbender; Love Walked In, 1996; Kiss the Sky, 1997; The Limey, 1999; Bow Finger, 1999; Red Planet, 2000; Theatre: Dracula; The Lady from the Sea. Publications: Stamp Album, 1988; Coming Attractions, 1988; Double Feature, 1989; The Night, 1992; Stamp Collection, 1997. Honours: Hon Dr of Arts, University of East London, 1993. Address: c/o Markham and Froggatt, 4 Windmill Street, London, W1P 1HF, England.

STANCEVIČIUS Antanas, b. 8 January 1920, Lomiai village, Taurage region, Lithuania. Agronomist. Widower, 1 son, 2 daughters. Education: Diploma of Agronomist, Lithuanian Academy of Agriculture, Dotnuva, 1943; Doctor Degree, 1958. Appointments: Assistant, Dotnuva Plant Protection Station, 1942-43; Head, Agronomy Department, Kaunas Tobacco Cultivation Centre, 1943-44; Director, Aniškis State Farm, Alytus region, 1944-46; Assistant, Lithuanian Academy of Agriculture, 1947-52, Senior Instructor, 1952-60, Associate Professor, 1961-62, Chairman of Agriculture Department, 1962-92, Lithuanian Academy of Agriculture; Associate Professor, 1961-89, Professor, 1990-, Council Chairman, 1989-92, Lithuanian Academy of Agriculture; Chairman, 1991-2000, Honorary Chairman, 2000-, Lithuanian Chamber of Agriculture. Publications: Co-author, Flora in Lithuania, volumes 2-6, 1961-80; Soils in Lithuania, 1965; Reference of Grain Crops and Leguminous Forage Plants, 1970; Methods of Date Evaluation of Field Tests, 1981; Field and Pasture Forage Plants, 1982; Flora of Baltic Countries, in Russian and English, Vol 1, 1993, Vol 2, 1996; Author: Development of Agricultural Systems and Specificity of Lithuanian Agricultural Systems, 1982; Compiling of Cartograms of Field and Crops Weeds, 1988; Over 180 scientific articles. Honours: Lithuanian Grand Duke Gediminas 5th Degree Order; Honorary Doctor/ Professor of Lithuanian University of Agriculture; Academician, International Informatization Academy, 2002; Honorary Chairman, Lithuanian Chamber of Agriculture; Lithuanian Merited Agronomist, 1965; State Award Laureate, 1966. Memberships: Lithuanian Science Council, 1991-95, 2003; Lithuanian National Union Experts Council, 1995; Lithuanian Botanists Society; Board, Lithuanian Agronomists Union; European Weed Research Society; International Soil Tillage Research Organisation; Chairman, Lithuanian Weed Research Society; Vice Chairman, Lithuanian Agricultural Science Council; Honorary member and Chairman of Honorary Court, Lithuanian National Union. Address: Kęstučio 27a-5, LT-3000 Kaunas, Lithuania.

STANDER Ilse Anna, b. 9 September 1964, George, South Africa. Medical Statistician. m. Marthinus Stander, 2 sons. Education: BSc, 1985, BSc (Hons), 1986, MSc, Mathematical Statistics, 1992, University of Stellenbosch, South Africa. Appointments: Medical Research Council of South Africa, 1987-2001; Part-time Lecturer, University of Stellenbosch Dental School, 1990-96. Publications: 30 scientific articles. Honour: Fellow, South African Statistical Association. Membership: South African Statistical Association. Address: 16 Ronalds Road, Kloof 3610, South Africa. E-mail: ilsestander@absamail.co.za

STANDISH Norman Weston, b. 4 April 1930, Marion, Iowa, USA. Chemist; Chemical Engineer. m. Ingrid C J Jueschke, 1 son, 2 daughters. Education: BS, Beloit College, Beloit, Wisconsin, 1952; MS, 1958, PhD, 1960, Purdue University, Lafayette, Indiana. Appointments: Research Chemist, 1961-68, Manager, Technical Services, 1968-82, Standard Oil, Ohio; Laboratory Director, Exploration and Production, Sohio-BP American Inc, 1982-85; Manager, Strategic Planning, BP Exploration and Production Company, 1985-88; Executive Director, EPIC Polymer Lifecycle

Center, 1992-94; International Business Consultant, 1995-; Currently President, Standish House Inc and Standish House Consulting Inc. Publications: Reinforced Plastics, chapter in Tool and Manufacturing Engineers Handbook; 24 US patents; 37 published papers; 87 technical presentations; 15 invited papers. Honours include: Commercial Solvents Fellowship; Science Advisory Board, Texas A and M University, 1985-; DAR Citizenship Award, 2004; Listed in national and international biographical dictionaries. Memberships: American Men and Women of Science, Advisory Board, Holyoke Community College, 1965-67; Lt Governor, Cleveland Mayflower Society, 1979; American Chemical Society, Career Consultant, 2000-, Chair, Employment Services Advisory Board, 1997, committees including Committee on Economic and Professional Affairs, 1997-, Chair, Sub-Committee on Employment Services, also regional and divisional offices; Society of Manufacturing Engineers; Society of Petroleum Engineers; Society of Plastic Engineers, Plastic Recycling Committee; Past Chair, Cleveland Technical Societies Council; President, North American Manx Association, 2003-04; President, Soule Kindred in America, 2003-04. Address: PO Box 105, 540 West Carroll Street, Lanark, IL 61046-0105. E-mail: nstandish@aeroinc.net

STANFORD Adrian Timothy James, b. 19 July 1935, Stratford-on-Avon, England. Merchant Banker. Education: MA, Merton College, Oxford. Appointments: 2nd Lieutenant, The Sherwood Foresters, 1954-55; Samuel Montagu & Co Ltd, Merchant Bankers, 1958-95, Director, 1972-95; Adviser, Royal Fine Art Commission Trust, 1995-; Member, Executive Committee, 1996-, Treasurer, 1996-2001, The Georgian Group; Chairman, Louis Franck Insead Scholarship Fund; Trustee, Old Broad Street Charity Trust. Memberships: Boodle's; Brooks's. Address: The Old Rectory, Preston Capes, near Daventry, Northamptonshire, NN11 3TE, England.

STANFORD Henry King, b. 22 April 1916, Atlanta, Georgia, USA. Higher Education Administrator. m. Ruth King Stanford, 3 sons, 1 daughter. Education: AB, Emory University, 1936; Certificate, University of Heidelberg, Germany, 1937; MA, Emory University, 1940; MS in Government Management, University of Denver, 1943; PhD, New York University, 1948. Appointments: Instructor, Emory Junior College, 1937-39; Instructor, Emory University, 1939-40; Assistant Professor, Georgia Institute of Technology, 1940-41; Alfred P Sloan Foundation Fellow, University of Denver, 1941-43; Research Assistant, Tax Foundation, New York City, 1943-44; Administrative Assistant, National Association of Manufacturers, New York City, 1944-46; Professor and Director, School of Public Administration, University of Denver, 1946-48; President, Georgia Southwestern College, 1948-50; Director, University Centre in Georgia, 1950-52; Assistant Chancellor, University System of Georgia, 1952-53; President, Georgia College and State University, 1953-56; Chief of Party, New York University-International Co-operation Administration Mission to Ankara, Turkey, 1956-57; President, Birmingham-Southern College, 1957-62; President, 1962-81, President Emeritus, 1981-, University of Miami; Interim President, 1986-87, President Emeritus, 1987-, University of Georgia. Honours include: Emory Medal, 1991; Adrian Dominican Educational Leadership Award, 1991; Atlanta Boys' High School Alumni Association Distinguished Alumnus Award, 1992; Troy Westmeyer Public Service Award, New York University, 1993; Honorary Alumnus, Georgia College and State University, 1996; Elbert Head Distinguished Service Award, 1999. Memberships: Phi Beta Kappa; Omicron Delta Kappa; Rotary Club; Orange Bowl Committee; First United Methodist Church, Americus. Address: PO Box 1065, Americus, GA 31709-1065, USA. E-mail: hksumuga@sowega.net

STANOMIR Dumitru G, b. 12 September 1930, Bucharest, Romania. Electronic Engineer; Professor. m. Mihaela, 1 son. Education: Electronic Engineer, Faculty of Electronics, Polytechnic Institute of Bucharest (now Polytechnica University of Bucharest, UPB), 1949-54; PhD, UPB, 1973. Appointments: Assistant, 1954-61, Lecturer, 1961-74, Associate Professor, 1974-90, Professor, 1990-, UPB; Conducting doctoral activity in Radiotechnics and Radiocommunications; Reviewer, Zentralblatt für Mathematik and Mathematical Reviews, referee (anonymous) Signal Processing. Publications: 20 books include: Mathematical Methods in Signal Theory, 1980; The Physical Theory of Electromechanical Systems, 1982; The Theory of Electroacoustical Systems, 1984; Discrete Signals and Systems, 1997; 140 numerous papers. Honours: Romanian Academy Prize, 1995; Member, Technical Science Academy in Romania, 1999; Man of the Year, American Biographical Centre, 1999. Memberships: Senior Member, IEEE; Audio Engineering Society (AES); American Mathematical Society, Acustica, Rumania; Corresponding Member, American Romanian Academy of Arts and Sciences. Address: PO Box 53-104 Bucharest, Romania. E-mail: dumitru.stanomir@elcom.pub.ro

STANWITT Pauline Eugenia, b. 12 November 1917, Riverside, Michigan, USA. Educator. m. Walter Stanwitt, deceased. Education: BS, Milwaukee State Teachers College, 1938; MA, University of Wisconsin, Madison, 1959; Post Graduate Studies, Marquette University and University of Wisconsin, Madison, 1959-84. Appointments: Substitute Teacher, Milwaukee Public Schools, 1938-42; Upper Elementary teacher, Trowbridge School, Milwaukee, 1942-51; English and Social Studies Teacher, 1951-55, Speech teacher, 1955-62, Director of Drama and Forensics, 1955-62, Guidance Counselor, 1962-77, Guidance Director, 1977-94, College Counselor, 1977-94, Pulaski High School, Milwaukee, Wisconsin; Currently establishing organisation called: Society of Distinguished Italian American Teachers in Metropolitan Milwaukee. Publications: Author: Developing Adolescent Personalities with Dramatics Activities, 1959; Contributing Author: Milwaukee Public Schools Speech Curriculum Guide, 1960; The Speech Arts, 1966; The Guidance Manual for Milwaukee Public Schools, 1984. Honours include: Distinguished Alumni Award in Speech Education, Marquette University, Milwaukee, 1965; Educator Recognition Award, Milwaukee Chapter, UNICO National, 1982; Distinguished Italian-American Woman, Festa Italiana, 1983; Career Guidance Award, Wisconsin Society of Women Engineers, 1983; Milwaukee Teacher of the Year Award, 1987; Teacher Recognition Award, Wisconsin Bell/Ameritech Foundation, 1990; Teacher Award Program, Greater Milwaukee Education Trust, 1990, 1991; Educational Foundation Achievement Award, US Senator Herb Kohl, 1992; National Older Workers Association Award, 1992; Special Services Teacher of the Year Award, Milwaukee, 1993; Wisconsin Secondary School Counselor of the Year Award, 1993; Milwaukee Common Council Recognition Award for 55 Years of Service, 1994; The National Italian American Foundation, Washington DC, 2000; Great Minds of the 21st Century, 2002; Outstanding Female Executive Award in Education, 2002; 2000 Outstanding Scholars of the 21st Century, 2002; Listed in national and international biographical dictionaries. Memberships include: Milwaukee Guidance Counselors Association; Milwaukee Teacher Association; Milwaukee Federation of Teachers; Sigma Omicron Phi Sorority; Marquette University Alumni Association; University of Wisconsin, Madison Alumni Association; University of Wisconsin, Milwaukee, Alumni Association; Wisconsin Education Association; Wisconsin School Counselor Association; National Education Association. Address: 3350 West Edgerton Avenue, Greenfield, WI 53221, USA.

STARITSKY Yuri Grigorievich, b. 28 October 1913, St Petersburg, Russia. Geologist. m. Staritskaya (Morozova) M, 2 daughters. Education: Engineer Geologist, Mining Institute, St Petersburg, 1947; Candidate of Science, 1951; DSc, 1969. Appointments: Senior Researcher, 1946-51, Head of Department, 1955-73, Leading Researcher, 1973-, All Russian Geological Research Institute, St Petersburg; Assistant Professor, Mining Institute, Krivoi Rog, Ukraine, 1951-53; Researcher, Academy of Sciences, St Petersburg, 1953-55; Head of Regional Department of West Russia; Leading Research, 1975-. Publications: Minerageny of the Siberian Platform Cover, 1970; History of Development and Minerageny of the Russian Platform Cover, 1987; Metallogenic Map of the Russian Platform Cover, 1985; Metallogenic Map of the West-Siberian Platform Cover, 1985; Life of the Expanding Earth, 1998; Map of Ore-Bearing Formations and Ore Zones of the East-European Platform Cover, 2000; Mineral deposits of the European Russia, 2003; Co-author, Russian Metallogenic Dictionary; More than 200 articles in professional journals; Member, editorial boards of all metallogenic maps of the former USSR and Russian Federation. Honours: Order of Great Patriotic War, President of Supreme Soviet of Russian Federation, 1990; Scholar Emeritus of Russian Federation, 1990. Memberships: Russian Mineralogy Society; St Petersburg Scientists Club. Address: Apt 54, 82/11 Moika Embankment, 190000 St Petersburg, Russia. E-mail:dashak@mail.line.ru

STARKEY Lawrence Harry, b. 10 July 1919, Minneapolis, Minnesota, USA. Synoptic Philosopher. m. (1) 1 son, 2 daughters, (2) Hallie Jean Hughes. Education: BA, honours, University of Louisville, 1942; MDiv, Southern Baptist Theological Seminary, 1945; MA, 1951, PhD, 1960, University of Southern California. Appointments: Engineering Draftsman, Electromotive Division, General Motors, 1937-39; Instructor, Assistant Professor, Registrar, Los Angeles Baptist College and Seminary, 1945-51; Science Film Writer, Moody Institute of Science, 1955-57; Associate Professor, Bethel College, St Paul, 1958-62; Associate Professor, Department Chair, Linfield College, 1962-63; Engineering Writer, Convair Division, General Dynamics, 1963-66; Associate Professor, Alma College, 1966-68; Associate Editor, Principal Editor, Philosophy, Encyclopaedia Britannica, 1968-72; Associate Professor, Department Chair, Jamestown College, 1973-75; Part-time Lecturer, Program Co-ordinator, Television Producer, North Dakota State University, 1976-79; Draftsman, Designer, Concord Inc, North Dakota, 1977-85; Instructor, Moorhead State University, 1985-86; Lecturer, University of Missouri, Rolla, 1986-88. Publications: Red River of Life (film); Several articles in professional journals, a children's encyclopaedia, the World Congress of Philosophy Web site; Abstracts of the Particles Conference, Sweden; The Vorträge of the Leibniz-Kongress. Honours: Speed Junior Scholarship; University Graduate Scholarship; Citizen Ambassador to Russia, Hungary. Memberships include: American Philosophical Association; Section President, American Scientific Affiliation, 1954, 1970, 1971; Metaphysical Society of America. Address: 1325 North 63rd Street, Wauwatosa, WI 53213-2919, USA.

STARR Kenneth Winston, b. 21 July 1946, Vernon, Texas, USA. Lawyer. m. Alice J Mendell, 1970, 1 son, 2 daughters. Education: George Washington University; Brown University; Duke University. Appointments: Law Clerk, Court of Appeals, Miami, 1973-74; Supreme Court, 1975-77; Associate, Gibson, Dunn and Crutcher, Los Angeles, 1974-75; Associate Partner, 1977-81; Counsellor to Attorney General, Justice Department, Washington, DC, 1981-83; Solicitor General, 1989-93; Judge, Court of Appeals, 1983; Partner, Kirkland and Ellis, Washington, DC, 1993-94; Independent Counsel for Whitewater Investigations as well as any collateral matters arising out of any investigation of such matters including obstruction of justice or false statements, 1994-. Publications: Contributor, articles to legal journals. Memberships: Several law organisations. Address: Kirkland and Ellis, 655 15th Street, Suite 1200, Washington, DC 2005, USA.

Dictionary of International Biography

STARR Ringo (Richard Starkey), b. 7 July 1940, Dingle, Liverpool, England. Musician. m. (1) Maureen Cox, 1965, divorced, 2 sons, 1 daughter, (2) Barbara Bach, 1981. Career: Member, Rory Storm and The Hurricanes; Member, The Beatles, 1962-70; Worldwide tours, 1963-; Attended Transcendental Meditation Course, Maharishi's Academy, Rishkesh, India, 1968; Co-Founder, Apple Corps Ltd, 1968; Solo Artiste, 1969-; Narrator, Thomas The Tank Engine, (children's TV). Creative Works: Recordings by the Beatles include: Please, Please Me, 1963; With the Beatles, 1963; A Hard Day's Night, 1964; Beatles for Sale, 1965; Help!, 1965; Rubber Soul, 1966; Revolver, 1966; Sergeant Pepper's Lonely Hearts Club Band, 1967; The Beatles (White Album), 1968; Yellow Submarine, 1969; Abbey Road, 1969; Let it Be, 1970; Films by the Beatles: A Hard Day's Night, 1964; Help!, 1965; Yellow Submarine (animated colour cartoon film), 1968; Let it Be, 1970; Individual appearance in films: Candy, 1968; The Magic Christian, 1969; 200 Motels, 1971; Blindman, 1971; That'll Be the Day, 1973; Born to Boogie (also directed and produced), 1974; Son of Dracula (also produced), 1975; Lisztomania, 1975; Ringo Stars, 1976; Caveman, 1981; The Cooler, 1982; Give My Regards to Broad Street, 1984; Singles as solo artist: It Don't Come Easy; Back Off Boogaloo; Photograph; You're Sixteen; Oh My My; Snookeroo; Only You. Honours: BPI Awards; Rock'n'Roll Hall of Fame, 1988. Address: c/o Mercury Records, 825 8th Avenue, New York, NY 10019, USA.

STARY Frank E, b. 3 January 1941, St Paul, Minnesota, USA. Professor. m. Education: Bchem, University of Minnesota, 1963; PhD, Inorganic Chemistry, University of Cincinnati, 1969; Appointments: Undergraduate Research, University of Minnesota, 1960-63; Graduate Research, University of Cincinnati, 1964-68; Postdoctoral Research, University of California Irvine, 1968-72; Research Associate, University of Missouri-St Louis, 1972-74; Assistant Professor, Professor, Maryville University-St Louis, Missouri, 1974-. Publications: 15 articles. Honours: Distinguished Teaching Award, 1981. Memberships: American Chemical Society; Phi Lambda Upsilon, Sigma Xi. Address: Maryville University, 13550 Conway Road, St Louis, MO 63141-7299, USA. E-mail: fstary@maryville.edu

STAUB August William, b. 9 October 1931, New Orleans, Louisiana, USA. University Professor; Theatre Director. m. Patricia Kay Gebhart, 1 daughter. Education: BA, English, 1952, MA, Theatre, 1956, PhD, Theatre, 1960, Louisiana State University. Appointments: Instructor, Eastern Michigan University, 1956-58; Instructor, Louisiana State University, 1959-60; Assistant Professor, University of Florida, 1960-64; Associate Professor, Director of Theatre, 1964-65, Chairman, Department of Drama, 1965-68, Professor and Chairman, 1968-76, University of New Orleans; Professor, Head of Drama, 1976-95, Professor, 1995-97, Professor Emeritus, 1997-, University of Georgia; Producer, several theatre works and seasonal festivals; Staff Director, Theatre in the Square, Atlanta, 1997-; Directed over 150 professional and amateur productions and 2 films; Designed sets and costumes; Wrote 5 produced plays; Acted professionally in several productions. Publications: Introduction to Theatrical Arts, 1972; Creating Theatre: The Art of Theatrical Directing, 1973; Varieties of Theatrical Art, 1980; Several book chapters; Numerous articles in professional journals. Honours: Numerous grants awarded; Distinguished Faculty Fellow, Louisiana State University; Creativity in Research Medal, University of Georgia; College of Fellows of American Theatre. Memberships include: President, American Theatre Association, 1986-87; President, National Association of Schools of Theatre, 1979-81; President, Southwest Theatre Association, 1972-73; Board of Directors, College of Fellows of the American Theatre, 1999-2001; Board of Directors, Georgia Theatre Conference, 1977-78. Address: 190 Ravenwood Court, Athens, GA 30605, USA.

STAUBUS George Joseph, b. 26 April 1926, Brunswick, Missouri, USA. Accounting Educator. m. Sarah Mayer, 2 sons, 2 daughters. Education: BS, University of Missouri, 1947; MBA, 1949, PhD, 1954, University of Chicago; Certified Public Accountant, Illinois, 1950. Appointments: Instructor of Accounting, University of Buffalo, 1947-49; Instructor of Accounting, University of Chicago, 1949-52; Assistant Professor, Associate Professor, Professor of Business Administration, University of California, Berkeley, 1952-91; Director of Research, Financial Accounting Standards Board, 1976-78. Publications: 8 books on accounting. Honours: Distinguished Professor Award, California Society of CPAs, 1981; Distinguished International Lecturer, American Accounting Association, 1982. Memberships: American Accounting Association; American Institute of Certified Public Accountants; Financial Executives Institute.

STAUNTON Imelda Mary Philomena Bernadette, b. 9 January 1956. Actress. m. Jim Carter, 1983, 1 daughter. Appointments: Repertory Exeter, Nottingham, York, 1976-81; Stage appearances include: Guys and Dolls, 1982, 1996; Beggar's Opera, 1985; She Stoops to Conquer; Chorus of Disapproval, 1985; The Corn is Green, 1985; Fair Maid of the West, 1986; Wizard of Oz, 1986; Comrades, 1987; Uncle Vanya, 1988; Into the Woods, 1990; Phoenix, 1990; Life x 3, 2000; TV appearances include: The Singing Detective, 1986; Yellowbacks, 1990; Sleeping Life, Roots, Up the Garden Path, 1990; Antonia and Jane; David Copperfield, 1999; Victoria Wood Xmas Special, 2000; Murder, 2001; Cambridge Spies, 2002; Strange, 2002; Film appearances include: Peter's Friends, 1992; Much Ado About Nothing, 1993; Deadly Advice, 1994; Sense and Sensibility; Twelfth Night; Remember Me, 1996; Shakespeare in Love, 1998; Another Life, 1999; Rat, 1999; Crush, 2000; Bright Young Things, 2002; Virgin of Liverpool, 2002; Blackball, 2002; Family Business, 2002. Honours: Oliver Award, Best Supporting Actress; Oliver Award, Best Actress in a Musical. Address: c/o ARG, 4 Great Portland Street, London, W1W 4PA, England.

STEAD C(hristian) K(arlson), b. 17 October 1932, Auckland, New Zealand. Poet; Writer; Critic; Editor; Professor of English Emeritus. m. Kathleen Elizabeth Roberts, 8 January 1955, 1 son, 3 daughters. Education: BA, 1954, MA, 1955, University of New Zealand; PhD, University of Bristol, 1961; DLitt, University of Auckland, 1982. Appointments: Lecturer in English, University of New England, Australia, 1956-57; Lecturer, 1960-61, Senior Lecturer, 1962-64, Associate Professor, 1964-67, Professor of English, 1967-86, Professor Emeritus, 1986-, University of Auckland; Chairman, New Zealand Literary Fund Advisory Committee, 1972-75, New Zealand Authors' Fund Committee, 1989-91. Publications: Poetry: Whether the Will is Free, 1964; Crossing the Bar, 1972; Quesada: Poems 1972-74, 1975; Walking Westward, 1979; Geographies, 1982; Poems of a Decade, 1983; Paris, 1984; Between, 1988; Voices, 1990; Straw Into Gold: Poems New and Selected, 1997; The Right Thing, 2000; Dog: Poems, 2002. Fiction: Smith's Dream, 1971; Five for the Symbol, 1981; All Visitors Ashore, 1984; The Death of the Body, 1986; Sister Hollywood, 1989; The End of the Century at the End of the World, 1992; The Singing Whakapapa, 1994; Villa Vittoria, 1997; The Blind Blonde with Candles in her Hair (stories), 1998; Talking about O'Dwyer, 2000; Non-fiction: The New Poetic: Yeats to Eliot, 1964, revised edition, 1987; In the Glass Case: Essays on New Zealand Literature, 1981; Pound, Yeats, Eliot and the Modernist Movement, 1986; Answering to the Language: Essays on Modern Writers, 1990; Werner Forman's New Zealand, 1994; Kin of Place: Essays on Twenty New Zealand Writers, 2002; The Secret History of Modernism, 2002. Editor: World's Classics: New Zealand Short Stories, 1966, 3rd edition, 1975; Measure for Measure: A Casebook, 1971, revised edition, 1973; Letters and Journals of

Dictionary of International Biography

Katherine Mansfield, 1977; Collected Stories of Maurice Duggan, 1981; The New Gramophone Room: Poetry and Fiction (with Elizabeth Smither and Kendrick Smithyman), 1985; The Faber Book of Contemporary South Pacific Stories, 1994. Contributions to: Poetry, fiction and criticism to various anthologies and periodicals. Honours: Katherine Mansfield Prize, 1960; Nuffield Travelling Fellowship, 1965; Katherine Mansfield Menton Fellowship, 1972; Jessie Mackay Award for Poetry, 1972; New Zealand Book Award for Poetry, 1975; Honorary Research Fellow, University College, London, 1977; Commander of the Order of the British Empire, 1984; Queen Elizabeth II Arts Council Scholarship in Letters, 1988-89; Queen's Medal for services to New Zealand literature, 1990; Fellow, Royal Society of Literature, 1995; Senior Visiting Fellow, St John's College, Oxford, 1996-97; Creative New Zealand, member, 1999. Membership: New Zealand PEN, chairman, Auckland branch, 1986-89, national vice president, 1988-90. Address: 37 Tohunga Crescent, Auckland 1, New Zealand.

STEADMAN Alison, b. 26 August 1946, Liverpool, England. Actress. m. Mike Leigh, 2 sons. Education: Drama School, Loughton, Essex. Appointments: Began career in repertory theatre, Lincoln, Bolton, Liverpool Worcester and Nottingham; Stage appearances include: Sandy in the Prime of Miss Jean Brodie; Beverley in Abigail's Party; Mae-Sister Woman in Cat on a Hot Tin Roof, National Theatre; Mari Hoff in The Rise and Fall of Little Voice; David Edgar's Maydays, Royal Shakespeare Company, Joking Apart; Kafka's Dick, Royal Court; Marvin's Room, 1993; The Plotters of Cabbage Patch Corner; The Provoked Wife, Old Vic, 1997; When We Are Married; The Memory of Water; Entertaining Mr Sloane; Bette in Cousin Bette; TV Appearances: Z Cars; Hard Labour; Abigail's Party; Nuts in May; The Singing Detective; Virtuoso; Newshounds; The Short and Curlies; Gone to Seed; Selling Hitler; Pride and Prejudice; The Wimbledon Poisoner; Karaoke; No Bananas; The Missing Postman; Let Them Eat Cake; Fat Friends; The Cappuccino Years; Films: Champions; Wilt; Shirley Valentine; Life is Sweet; Blame it on the Bellboy; Topsy Turvy; Happy Now. Honours: Honorary MA, University of East London; Evening Standard Best Actress Award, 1977; Olivier Award for Best Actress, 1993. Address: Peters, Fraser and Dunlop, The Chambers, Chelsea, London, SW10 0XF, England.

STEADMAN Stephen Geoffrey, b. 28 June 1942, Rochester, New York, USA. Physicist. m. Brigitte M Kreuzer, 2 sons, 1 daughter. Education: BS, University of Rochester, 1964; MS, Rutgers University, 1966; PhD, 1969. Appointments: Visiting Scientist, University of Erlangen-Nürnberg, Erlangen, Germany 1969-71; Assistant, University of Freiburg, Germany, 1971-72; Senior Research Associate, 1972-74, Assistant Professor, 1975-79, Associate Professor, 1979-82, Senior Research Scientist, 1982-98, Massachusetts Institute of Technology, Cambridge, Massachusetts, USA; Guest Scientist, Max Planck Institute, Heidelberg, Germany, 1974-75; Program Director, Nuclear Physics, NSF, Arlington, Virginia, USA, 1994-97; Program Manager, US Department of Energy, Germantown, Maryland, 1998-2001; Senior Nuclear Physics Advisor, 2001-; E866 Co-spokesman, Brookhaven National Laboratory, Upton, New York, 1992-98. Publications: Contributor of articles to professional journals. Honours: Listed in Who's Who publications and biographical dictionaries. Membership: Watertown Provincial Guard, 1998-; American Association for the Advancement of Science; American Physical Society. Address: US Department of Energy, SC-90, Germantown Building, 1000 Independence Avenue SW, Washington DC, 20585-1290, USA. E-mail: stephen.steadman@science.doe.gov

STEEL Danielle, b. 14 August 1950, New York. Writer. m. (2) Bill Toth, 1977; (3) John A Traina Jr, 4 sons, 5 daughters. Education: Lycee Francais; Parsons School of Design, New York; University of New York. Appointments: Public Relations and, Advertising Executive, Manhattan, New York; Published first novel, 1973, then wrote advertising copy and poems for women's magazines; Wrote first bestseller, The Promise, 1979. Publications: Going Home, 1973; Passion's Promise, 1977; Now and Forever, 1978; Seasons of Passion, 1978; The Promise, 1979; Summer's End, 1980; The Love Again, 1981; Palomino, 1981; Loving, 1981; Rememberance, 1981; A Perfect Stranger, 1982; Once in a Lifetime, 1982; Crossings, 1982; Thurston House, 1983; Full Circle, 1984; Having a Baby, 1984; Family Album, 1985; Wanderlust, 1986; Fine Things, 1987; Kaleidoscope, 1987; Zoya, 1988; Star, 1989; Daddy, 1989; Heartbeat, 1991; Message from Nam, 1991; No Greater Love, 1991; Jewels, 1992; Mixed Blessings, 1992; Vanished, 1993; Accident, 1994; The Gift, 1994; Wings, 1995; Lightning, 1995; Five Days in Paris, 1995; Malice, 1995; Silent Honor, 1996; The Ranch, 1996; The Ghost, 1997; Special Delivery, 1997; The Ranch, 1998; The Long Road Home, 1998; The Klone and I, 1998; Mirror Image, 1998; Bittersweet, 1999; The Wedding, 2000; The House on Hope Street, 2000; Journey, 2000; Lone Eagle, 2001; Answered Prayers, 2002; Dating Game, 2003; Eight Childrens Books; One Book of Poetry. Address: c/o Dell Publishing, 1540 Broadway, New York, NY 10036, USA.

STEEL OF AIKWOOD David Martin Scott Steel (Baron) (Life Peer), b. 31 March 1938, Kirkcaldy, Scotland. Politician; Journalist; Broadcaster. m. Judith Mary MacGregor, 1962, 2 sons, 1 daughter. Education: Prince of Wales School, Nairobi, Kenya; George Watson's College; Edinburgh University. Appointments: President, Edinburgh University, Liberals, 1959; Member, Students Representative Council, 1960; Assistant Secretary, Scottish Liberal Party, 1962-64; Member of Parliament for Roxburgh, Selkirk and Peebles, 1965-83; for Tweeddale, Ettrick and Lauderdale, 1983-97; Scottish Liberal Whip, 1967-70; Liberal Chief Whip, 1970-75; Leader, Liberal Party, 1976-88; Co-Founder Social and Liberal Democrats, 1988; Vice President, Liberal International, 1978-93; President, 1994-96; Member of Parliament delegate to UN General Assistant, 1967; Former Liberal Spokesman on Commonwealth Affairs: Sponsor, Private Member's Bill to Reform law on abortion, 1966-67; President, Anti-Apartheid Movement of UK, 1966-69; Chair, Shelter, Scotland, 1969-73; Countryside Movement, 1995-97; BBC TV Interviewer in Scotland, 1964-65; Presenter of Weekly Religious Programmes for Scottish TV, 1966-67; for Granada, 1969; for BBC, 1971-76; Director, Border TV, 1991-; Rector, University of Edinburgh, 1982-85; Chubb Fellow, Yale University, USA, 1987; D L Ettrick and Launderdale and Roxburghshire. Publications: Boost for the Borders, 1964; No Entry, 1969; A House Divided, 1980; Border Country, 1985; Partners in One Nation, 1985; The Time Has Come, 1987; Mary Stuart's Scotland, 1987; Against Goliath, 1989. Honours: Freedom of Tweeddale, 1989; Ettrick and Launderdale, 1990; Hon Dr, Stirling, 1991; Hon D Litt, Buckinghamshire, 1994; Heriot Watt, 1996; Hon LLD, Edinburgh, 1997, Strathclyde, 2000, Aberdeen, 2001; Bronze Medal London-Cape Town Rally, 1998. Address: House of Lords, London, SW1A 0PW, England.

STEELE Tommy (Thomas Hicks), b. 17 December 1936, Bermondsey, London, England. Actor; Singer. m. Ann Donoghue, 1960, 1 daughter. Career: First stage appearance, Empire Theatre, Sunderland, 1956; First London appearance, Dominion Theatre, 1957; Major roles include: Buttons, Rodgers and Hammerstein's Cinderella, Coliseum, 1958; Tony Lumpkin, She Stoops To Conquer, Old Vic, 1960; Arthur Kipps, Half A Sixpence, Cambridge Theatre, 1963-64; The same, Broadhurst Theatre, New York, 1965; Truffaldino, The Servant Of Two Masters, Queen's,

1969; Dick Whittington, London Palladium, 1969; Meet Me In London, Adelphi, 1971; Jack Point, The Yeoman Of The Guard, City Of London Festival, 1978; The Tommy Steele Show, London Palladium, 1973; Hans Andersen, 1974, 1977; One-man show, Prince of Wales, 1979; Singing In The Rain (also director), 1983; Some Like It Hot, 1992; What A Show, Prince of Wales Theatre, 1995; Film appearances: Kill Me Tomorrow, 1956; The Tommy Steele Story; The Duke Wore Jeans; Tommy The Toreador; Light Up The Sky; It's All Happening; The Happiest Millionaire; Half A Sixpence; Finian's Rainbow; Where's Jack?; Television: Writer, actor, Quincy's Quest, 1979. Compositions; Composed, recorded, My Life My Song, 1974; A Portrait Of Pablo, 1985; Publications: Quincy, 1981; The Final Run, 1983; Rock Suite - An Elderly Person's Guide To Rock, 1987. Honour: OBE, 1979. Current Management: James Kelly, International Artistes Ltd, 235 Regent Street, London W1R 8AX, England.

STEENBURGEN Mary, b. 8 February 1953, Newport, Arizona, USA. Film Actress. m. (1) Malcolm McDowell, 1980, divorced, 1 son, 1 daughter, (2) Ted Danson, 1995. Education: Neighborhood Playhouse. Appointments: Films include: Goin' South, 1978; Time After Time, 1979; Melvin and Howard, 1980; Ragtime, 1981; A Midsummers Night's Sex Comedy, 1982; Romantic Comedy, 1983; Cross Creek, 1983; Sanford Meidner - Theatre's Best Kept Secret, 1984; One Magic Christmas, 1985; Dead of Winter, 1987; End of the Line, 1987; The Whales of August, 1987; The Attic: The Hiding of Anne Frank, 1988; Parenthood, 1989; Back to the Future Part III, 1989; Miss Firecracker, 1989; The Long Walk Home, 1990; The Butcher's Wife, 1991; What's Eating Gilbert Grape, 1993; Philadelphia, 1993; Pontiac Moon, 1994; Clifford, 1994; It Runs in the Family, 1994; Pontiac Moon; My Family; Powder; The Grass Harp; Nixon; About Sarah, 1995; Trumpet of the Swan, 1999; Picnic (TV), 2000 Theatre appearances include: Holiday, 1987; Candida, 1993. Address: c/o Ames Cushing, William Morris Agency Inc, 151 El Camino Drive, Beverly Hills, CA 90212, USA.

STEFAN-NICOLIN Mihail, b. 9 May 1953, Craiova, Romania. Director, Military Museum. m. Rosaura-Mariana, 2 daughters. Education: Infantry Specialisation, "Nicolae Balcesco" Military School for Officers, Sibiu, Romania, 1972-75; Faculty of Political and Military Sciences, 1985-87, Faculty of Military Sciences, 1992-94, Military Academy, Bucharest, Romania; Post University Course in PSYOPS, College of Command and General Staff, Bucharest, Romania, 1999. Appointments: Officer, Sub-Unit Commanding Officer, Ministry of Defence, 1975-84; Deputy, Information Centre, Civil Protection Command, 1984-85; Officer and Head Clerk, Inspectorate of Education and Culture, the Cultural Department and Public Relations Department, Director, National Military Museum, Bucharest, Romania, 2000-. Publications: Author, 3 books; Publicity and literary works in magazines and journals including: Luceafarul; Contemporanul; Romania Literara; Observatorul militar; La Datorie; Viata armatei; Revista de istorie militara. Honours: Award, Viata armatei Magazine; Military Merit Medal, 2nd class, 1980, 1st class, 1998; Military merit Order, 3rd class, 1990, 2nd class, 1995, 1st class, 1998; Other Romanian Military Orders and Civilian Cultural Distinctions. Membership: International Committee of Museums of Arms and Military History. Address: National Military Museum, Mircea Vulcanescu Street No 125-127, Bucharest, Romania. E-mail: director@muzeulmilitar.ro

STEFANILE Felix Neil, b. 13 April 1920, New York, New York, USA. Retired Professor; Poet. m. Selma Epstein, 17 January 1953. Education: BA, City University of New York, 1944. Appointments: Visiting Poet, Lecturer, 1961-62, Assistant Professor, 1962-64, Associate Professor, 1964-69, Professor, 1969-87, Purdue University; Chairman, Editorial Board, Purdue University Press,

1964-69; Editor, Publisher, Sparrow Press, 1954-89. Publications: If I Were Fire; In That Far Country; The Blue Moustache; Umberto Saba; East River Nocturne; A Fig Tree in America; The Dance at St Gabriel's, 1995; The Country of Absence, 2000. Contributions to: New York Sunday Times Book Review; Sewanne Review; Virginia Quarterly Review; Poetry; Parnassus; TriQuarterly; Hudson Review; New York Times. Honours: Pushcart Press Prize; Standard Oil of Indiana Foundation Award; Virginia Quarterly Review Emily Clark Balch Award; Nathan Haskell Dole Prize; National Endowment for the Arts Prize; John Ciardi Award for Lifetime Achievement in Poetry, 1997. Memberships: Poetry Society of America; American Literary Translators Association. Address: 103 Waldron Street, West Lafayette, IN 47906, USA.

STEFANOV Stefan Minev, b. 8 August 1964, Sevlievo, Bulgaria. Professor of Mathematics. Education: BA, 1986; BSc, 1988; MS, 1989; MEd, 1989; PhD, 1991; DSc, 1996. Appointments: Assistant Professor, 1991-96; Associate Professor, 1996-97; Professor, 1997-. Publications: Books: Mathematical Programming; Operations Research; Numerical Analysis; Quantitative Methods of Management; Separable Programming; Numerous papers in professional journals. Honours: Medal, Ministry of Education, Republic of Bulgaria, 1982; Awards for Contributions to Mathematics and Science, 1996, 1998; First Prize for Contribution to Science Engineering and Computer Science for the Monograph, Separable Programming, Open Society Fund, 2001. Memberships: Union of Bulgarian Mathematicians, 1989; Union of Bulgarian Scientists, 1995; American Math Society, 1995; Math Programming Society, USA, 1995; Society for Industrial and Applied Mathematics, USA, 1996, SIAM Activity Group on Optimization, 1996; London Mathematical Society, 1997; European Mathematical Society, 1997; Canadian Mathematical Society, 1998; Canadian Applied and Industrial Mathematics Society, 1999; Research Group in Mathematical Inequalities and Applications, 1999; National Geographic Society, 2000; Fellow, National Academy of Sciences; International Biographical Association. Address: 4 Ilio Vlaev Str, 5400 Sevlievo, Bulgaria.

STEIN Clarissa Ingeborg, b. 3 September 1948, Munich, Germany. Editor; Poet. m. Herbert Stein, 26 May 1981, 1 daughter. Education: Diploma, Beamtenfachhochschule, Herrsching, Bavaria, 1975. Appointment: Editor, Papyrus Publishing, 1991-. Publications: New Melodies, Neue Melodien, 1992; Notes From My Land, 1993; Billy Tea and Sand Ballet, 1996; In Meinem Land, 1997. Contributions to: Journals and magazines in Australia and overseas. Memberships: Deakin Literary Society, Deakin University; Ballarat Regional Multicultural Council; Foundation for Australian Literary Studies. Address: C/- Post Office Scarsdale, Vic 3351, Australia. E-mail: editor@papyrus.com.au

STEIN Robert A, b. 5 August 1933, Duluth, Minnesota, USA. Writer; Educator. m. Betty L Pavlik, 1955, 3 sons. Education: MA, Writing, 1986, MA, Counselling/Education, 1968, BSc, Industrial Management, 1956, University of Iowa; Permanent Professional Counselling/Teaching Certificate, Iowa Board of Public Instruction, 1968; US Air Force Squadron Officers' School, 1960; US Air Force Command and Staff College, 1966; Air Force Academic Instructor School, with Honors, 1966; Industrial College of the Armed Forces, with Honors, 1973. Appointments: Officer and Pilot, USAF, 1956-77, Retired as Colonel; Assistant Professor of Aerospace Studies, 1964-66, University of Iowa; Associate Professor, 1966-68; Professor, 1975-77; Member, Faculty Division of Writing, Kirkwood Community College, Iowa City and Cedar Rapids, Iowa, 1984-89; Instructor, Creative Writing Program, Iowa City/Johnson County Senior Center, 1994-. Publications: Novels: Apollyon: A Novel, 1985; The Chase, 1988; The Black Samaritan, 1997, 2nd edition, 2000; The Vengeance Equation, 2000, 2nd edition, 2001, Screenplay, 2001; Fiction: Death Defied, 1988; Non-Fiction: Statistical Correlations, 1967; Engineers Vs. Other Students: Is There A Difference?, 1967; WhatEVER Happened to Moe Bushkin?, 1967; Quest for Viability: One Way!, 1976; Threat of Emergency, 1988. Honours: 5 Wartime Decorations, 9 Merit Awards; All-American Swimming, 1950; Outstanding Faculty Award, University of Iowa, 1967-68; Iowa Authors' Collection, 1985; Minnesota Authors' Collection, 1987; International Literary Award, 1988; Lifetime Achievement Award, University of Iowa, 1999; Entered in Iowa Athletics Hall of Fame, 2002. Memberships: The Authors Guild; The Authors League of America.

STEINEM Gloria, b. 25 March 1934, Toledo, Ohio, USA. Feminist; Political Activist; Lecturer; Editor; Writer. Education: BA, Smith College, 1956; Chester Bowles Asian Fellow, India, 1957-58. Appointments: Contributing Editor, Glamour Magazine, 1962-69; Co-Founder and Contributing Editor, New York Magazine, 1968-72; Co-Founder and Member of the Board of Directors, Women's Action Alliance, 1970-; Co-Founder and Editor, 1971-87, Columnist, 1980-87, Consulting Editor, 1987-, Ms Magazine; Convenor and Member of the National Advisory Committee, Women's Political Caucus, 1971-; Co-Founder and President of the Board of Directors, Ms Foundation for Women, 1972-; President, Voters for Choice, 1979-. Publications: The Thousand Indias, 1957; The Beach Book, 1963; Wonder Woman, 1972; Outrageous Acts and Everyday Rebellions, 1983; Marilyn: Norma Jeane, 1986; Revolution from Within: A Book of Self-Esteem, 1992; Moving Beyond Words, 1994. Contributions to: Anthologies and magazines. Honours: Penney-Missouri Journalism Award, 1970; Ohio Governor's Award for Journalism, 1972; Woman of the Year, McCall's Magazine, 1972; D Human Justice, Simmons College, 1973; Bill of Rights Award, American Civil Liberties Union of Southern California, 1975; Woodrow Wilson International Center for Scholars Fellow, 1977; National Woman's Hall of Fame, 1993. Memberships: American Foundation of Television and Radio Artists; Authors Guild; National Organization for Women; National Press Club; Phi Beta Kappa; Society of Magazine Writers. Address: c/o Ms Magazine, 230 Park Avenue, 7th Floor, New York, NY 10169, USA.

STEINER Andreas Konrad, b. 29 January 1937, Zurich, Switzerland. Surgeon; Writer. m. Tshabu Cécile Mbombo, 12 May 1995, 3 sons, 2 daughters. Education: MD, Zurich University, 1961; Surgeon, FMH, 1971; Master of Philosophy, Zurich University, 2003. Appointments: Medical Officer, ICRC, Yemen, 1964; Head Surgeon, Mannedorf, Zurich, 1973-76; Medical Superintendent, Albert Schweitzer Hospital, Peru, 1976-80; Project Director, Hospital del Alto Chicama, Peru, 1980-84; Project Director, health project, Zaire, 1984-91; Associated Professor, University of Addis Ababa, Ethiopia, Consultant, various medical projects, 1991-95; Relief work, Rwanda, 1995; Evaluation, medical project, Senegal, 1995; Consultant for Surgery, Mauretania, 1995; Evaluation, health project, Zaire, 1996. Publications: Arzt im Busch, eine Herausforderung, 1990; Geschichten im Busch, Begegnungen eines Arztes in Afrika, 1993; Afrika und Wir. Über unser Eingreifen in Afrika, Bilanz nach 15 Jahren als Arzt in Afrika, 1996; Wir in Afrika, Drei Theaterstücke, 1997; Flammenzeichen, 2001; About 25 articles in medical journals on developments in health, tropical medicine and surgery. Membership: Swiss Medical Association; Swiss Society of Surgery; German Society for Tropical Surgery; Authors of Switzerland. Address: Hanfroosenweg 13, CH-8615 Wermatswil, Switzerland.

STEINWACHS Matthias Reinhard, b. 13 June 1958, Tübingen, Germany. Physician; Orthopaedic Surgeon. m. Ute Guhlke-Steinwachs, 1 daughter. Education: Study of Law, University of Konstanz, Germany, 1980-83; Medical Studies, Universities of Heidelberg and Göttingen, 1983-90; Examination for MD, 1990; Department of Trauma Surgery, Hildesheim, Germany, 1991-92; Doctorate, University of Göttingen, 1992; Specialist Education, Department of Orthopaedic Surgery, University of Freiburg, Germany, 1992-97; Specialist Examination for Orthopaedic Surgery, 1997; Habilitation (PhD) in progress, 2003. Appointments: Scientific Work on biochemistry, intracellurar metabolism, cell culture, animal studies, drug monitoring, oxidative stress, HPLC, DC and tracer analytic, Department of Pharmacology and Toxicology, 1987-92; Scientific Work, on tissue engineering, cultivation of human chondrocytes, meniscal cells, disc cells, collagen carrier, autologous chondrocyte transplantation, Department of Orthopaedic Surgery, Assistant Professor, Senior Physician, Specialist for Cartilage Repair and Tissue Engineering, 1997-, Head of Cartilage Research Group, Member of Steering Committee, Valley Tissue Engineering Centre, 1998-, University of Freiburg, Germany; Project Leader, Cartilage Engineering Group, Ministry of Science, 1998-2001. Publications: Articles in scientific medical journals and book chapters as first author include: Clinical and cellbiological aspects of the autologous chondrocyte transplantation, 1999; Die Autologe Chondrozytentransplantation, 2003; Clinical results of ACT using a collagen membrane instead of periost, 2003. Memberships: Financial Committee, International Cartilage Repair Society; Osteoarthritic Research Society; DGOOC; TES; ETES; DVOST. Address: Department of Orthopaedic and Trauma Surgery, University Hospital Freiburg, Hugstetter Strasse 55, D-79106 Freiburg, Germany. E-mail: steinwa@ch11.ukl.uni-freiburg.de Website: dr-steinwachs.com

STENGAARD Erik, b. 18 June 1947, Skive, Denmark. Headmaster. m. Sonja Stengaard, 1 daughter. Education: Cand mag (Master's Degree), History and English, Copenhagen University, 1975. Appointments: Teacher, Rosborg Gymnasium and HF, 1975-84; Vice-President, Member of Executive Committee, in charge of salary negotiations and educational affairs, Trade Union for Danish Teachers at Upper Secondary Level (GL), 1979-84; Headmaster, Haslev Gymnasium and HF, Upper Secondary School, Grammar, Sixth Form, 1985-86, 1988-; President, Trade Union Centre for the Academic Professions in Denmark (AC), 1986-87; Chairman, Educational Committee within Radical Left Party in Denmark (liberal-social), 1989-. Publications: Co-author, History of Haslev Gymnasium, 1989; The Mural Paintings of Queen Agnes in the Church of Sct Bendts, 1995; A Fair Salary Policy, contribution to the History of The Trade Union Centre for the Academic Professions in Denmark, 1997. Honour: Knight of the Order of Dannebrog. Membership: The Sandbjerg Group of Danish Headmasters Address: Tofteagervej 20, DK 4690 Haslev, Denmark. E-mail: 302es@vestamt.dk

STEPHENS Jack, b. 1 December 1936, Huntington Park, California, USA. Writer; Photographer. m. Kristi Kellogg Stephens. Education: BA, Journalism, Washington State University, 1962. Appointments: Editor-Reporter, Ferndale Record, 1961; Reporter Maui News, 1963-67; Reporter, Pacific Business News, 1969-72; Journalism Instructor, Maunaolu College, 1967-73; Owner, Aquarius Enterprises, 1968-. Publications: Contributions to a variety of magazines. Honours: Bay League Long Jump Champion, 1953-54; Southern California Long Jump Champion, 1954; Martin Relays Long Jump Champion, 1960. Memberships: Society of Professional Journalists, 1959-; Maui's Maunaolu College Journalism Instructor and Publications Director, 1967-73. Address: 3-3400 Kuhio Highway A-103, Lihue, HI 96766-1051, USA.

STETTLER Simon (Simon de Beauvalleé), b. 2 June 1944, Arni, Switzerland. Writer. m. Brunhilde Tritten, 1 son, 1 daughter. Education: Vocational School; Master Course; Pilotenbrevet. Appointments: Self-employed writer; Freelance journalist, Radio

DRS. Publications: Poetry: Geistesblitze, 1981; Literarische Wirtinnenverse, 1997; Last-Minute-Gedichte, 1999; Thousands of letters to the editor and newspaper articles; Iron Sculptures, including at Thun station. Memberships: Schweiz Schriftstellerverein; Bernischer Schriftstellerverein; ProLitteris. Address: Bahnhofstrasse 2, CH 3507 Biglen, Switzerland. E-mail: simon.stettler@bluewin.ch

STEVEN Stewart Gustav, b. 30 October 1935, Hamburg, Germany. Journalist. m. Inka Sobieniewska, 1 son. Education: Mayfield College, Sussex. Appointments: Political Reporter, Central Press Features, 1961-63; Political Correspondent, Western Daily Press, 1963-64; Political Reporter, 1964-65, Diplomatic Correspondent, 1965-67, Foreign Editor, 1967-72, Daily Express; Assistant Editor, 1972-74, Associate Editor, 1974-82, Daily Mail; Editor, 1982-92, Columnist, 1996-, Mail on Sunday; Director, Associated Newspapers Holdings Ltd, 1989-95; Editor, Evening Standard, 1992-95. Publications: Operation Splinter Factor, 1974; The Spymasters of Israel, 1976; The Poles, 1982. Memberships: Chair, Liberty Publishing and Media Ltd, 1996-97; Chair, Equity Theatre Commission, 1995-96; National Campaign for the Arts, 1996-; Member, Board for Better English Campaign, 1995-97; Thames Advisory Group, 1995-97; London Film Commission, 1996-; Honorary Perpetual Student, Bart's Hospital, 1993. Address: 29 Priory Avenue, Chiswick, London, W4 1TZ, England.

STEVENS Barbara Christine, b. 4 September 1939, Guildford, Surrey, England. Clinical Psychologist. m. John Ridsdale, 1974, deceased. Education: BA Honours, Sociology, London School of Economics, 1961; BA Honours, Psychology, University College London, 1962; PhD, Institute of Psychiatry, London, 1967; Academic Postgraduate Diploma, Clinical Psychology, British Psychology Society, 1982. Appointments: Medical Research Council Social Psychiatry Unit, 1962-72; Research Staff, Institute Psychiatry, 1972-77; Senior Psychologist, HM Prison Service, 1977-83; Senior Psychologist, 1983-85, Consultant Forensic Psychologist, 1985-2002, Runwell Hospital, Wickford, Essex. Publications: Marriage and Fertility of Women Suffering from Schizophrenia and Affective Disorders, 1969; Dependence of Schizophrenic Patients on Elderly Relatives, 1972; The Role of Fluphenazine Decanoate in Lessening the Burden of Chronic Schizophrenics in the Community, 1973; Numerous other scientific papers. Honours: Mapother Research Fellowship, 1962-66; Member, Medical Research Council Scientific Staff, 1962-72. Memberships: Associate Fellow, British Psychology Society, Member Criminological and Clinical Divisions, 1982; Elected, Academy of Experts, Grays Inn, London, 1996; Member of Royal Society for the Prevention of Cruelty to Animals, National Canine Defence League, Peoples Dispensary for Sick Animals, World Wildlife Fund; World Society for Protection of Animals. Address: 14 Devonshire Place, London W1G 6HX, England.

STEVENS Jocelyn Edward Greville (Sir), b. 14 February 1932, London, England. Publisher. m. Jane Armyne Sheffield, 1956, dissolved 1979, 1 son, deceased, 2 daughters. Education: Cambridge University. Appointments: Military Service, Rifle Brigade, 1950-52; Journalist, Hulton Press, 1955-56; Chair and Managing Director, Stevens Press Ltd, Editor, Queen Magazine, 1957-58; Personal Assistant to Chair, 1968, Director, 1971-81, Managing Director, 1974-77, Beaverbrook Newspapers; Managing Director, Evening Standard Co Ltd, 1969-72; Managing Director, Daily Express, 1972-74; Deputy Chair and Managing Director, Express Newspapers, 1974-81; Editor and Publisher, The Magazine, 1982-84; Director, Centaur Communications, 1982-84; Governor, Imperial College of Science, Technology and Medicine, 1985-92; Governor, Winchester School of Art, 1986-89; Rector and Vice Provost, RCA, 1984-92; Chair, The Silver

Trust, 1990-93; English Heritage, 1992-2000; Deputy Chair, Independent TV Commission, 1991-96; Non Executive Director, The TV Corporation, 1996, Asprey & Co, 2002, Garrad & Co, 2002; President, The Cheyne Walk Trust, 1989-93; Trustee, Eureka! Children's Museum, 1990-2000; Chair, The Phoenix Trust; Director, The Prince's Foundation, 2000. Honours: Hon D Litt, Loughborough, 1989, Buckingham, 1998; Hon FCSD, 1990; Senior Fellow, RCA, 1990. Address: 14 Cheyne Walk, London, SW3 5RA, England.

STEVENSON Juliet, b. 30 October 1956, England. Actress. 1 son, 1 daughter, 2 stepsons. Education: Hurst Lodge School, Berkshire; St Catherine's School, Surrey; Royal Academy of Dramatic Arts. Appointments: Plays include: Midsummer Night's Dream; Measure for Measure; As You Like It; Troilus and Cressida; Les Liaisons Dangerouses; Caucasian Chalk Circle; No I; Footfalls; Other Worlds; Yerma; Hedda Gabler; Death and the Maiden; Duchess of Malfi; Films include: Drowning by Numbers; Ladder of Swords; Truly Madly Deeply; The Trial; The Secret Rapture; Emma; The Search for John Gissing; Who Dealt?; Beckett's Play; Bend It Like Beckham; Food of Love; Several TV roles include: The Politician's Wife; Cider with Rosie; The Politician's Wife; A Doll's House; Life Story; Antigone; The March; Maybury; Thomas and Ruth; Aimée; The Mallens; Living With Dinosaurs; Wrote and fronted BBC documentary Great Journeys; Radio includes: To the Lighthouse; Volcano; Albertina; House of Correction; Hang Up; Cigarettes and Chocolate; A Little Like Drowning; Victory. Publications: Clamourous Voices, 1988; Shall I See You Again?; Players of Shakespeare. Honours: Bancroft Gold Medal, Royal Academy of Dramatic Arts, 1977; Time Out Award for Best Actress, 1991; Evening Standard Film Award for Best Actress, 1992; Lawrence Olivier Theatre Award for Best Actress, 1992. Address: c/o Markham and Froggatt Ltd, Julian House, 4 Windmill Street, London, W1P 1HF, England.

STEWART Alec James, b. 8 April 1963, Merton, London, England. Cricketer. m. Lynn, 1 son, 1 daughter. Education: Tiffin Boys' School, Kingston Upon Thames. Appointments: Right-hand opening Batsman; Wicket Keeper; Surrey, 1981- (Captain 1992-97); 126 Tests for England, 1989-90 to 2 Jan 2003, 14 as Captain, scoring 8187 runs (average 40.13) including 15 hundreds; Scored 25,438 first class runs (48 hundreds) to end of 2002; Held 11 catches, equaling world first-class record, for Surrey v Leicestershire, Leicester, 19-22 August, 1989; Toured Australia, 1990-91, 1994-95 and 1998-99 (captain); 161 limited-overs internationals to 7 January 2003; Overtook record (118) of Graham Gooch to become England's most-capped cricketer, Lords July 2002. Publications: Alec Stewart: A Captain's Diary, 1999. Honour: Wisden Cricketer of the Year, 1993. Address: c/o Surrey Cricket Club, Kennington Oval, London, SE11 5SS, England.

STEWART Bruce Edmund, b. 9 November 1930, Minneapolis, USA. Writer; Former Mechanical Draftsman. m. Mary Incornata, 2 sons. Education: AA, University of Minnesota; Analyst, Army Security Agency, Famous Writers School. Appointment: Retired Design Mechanical Draftsman. Publications: 45 books, 10 US patents. Memberships: Moose Lodge; Inventor's Network; American Legion; Minnesota Korean War Veterans Chapter #1. Address: 771 Belland Avenue, Saint Paul, MN 55127-5038, USA.

STEWART Dave, b. 9 September 1952, Sunderland, Tyne and Wear, England. Musician (guitar, keyboards); Songwriter; Composer. m. Siobhan Fahey, 1 August 1987, divorced, 1 son. Career: Musician, Harrison and Stewart (with Brian Harrison); Longdancer; The Catch, 1977; Renamed The Tourists, 1979-80; Formed Eurythmics with Annie Lennox, 1980-89; Worldwide concerts include Nelson Mandela's 70th Birthday Tribute,

Wembley, 1988; As solo artiste: Nelson Mandela Tribute concert, Wembley, 1990; Amnesty International Big 30 concert, 1991; Founder, Spiritual Cowboys, 1990-92; Vegas, with Terry Hall, 1992-93; Founder, own record label Anxious Records, 1988; Owner, The Church recording studio, 1992; Producer, session musician, for artistes including Bob Dylan; Mick Jagger; Tom Petty; Daryl Hall; Bob Geldof; Boris Grebenshikov. Compositions: All Eurythmics songs co-written with Lennox; Theme for Jute City, BBC1; Co-writer, film score Motorcycle Mystics; Co-writer with Gerry Anderson, music for children's series GFI, 1992. Recordings: Albums: with The Tourists: The Tourists; Reality Affect; Luminous Basement; with Eurythmics: In The Garden, 1982; Sweet Dreams (Are Made Of This), 1983; Touch (Number 1, UK), 1984; 1984 (For The Love Of Big Brother), film soundtrack, 1984; Be Yourself Tonight, 1985; Revenge, 1986; Savage, 1988; We Too Are One (Number 1, UK), 1989; Eurythmics Greatest Hits (Number 1, UK), 1991; Eurythmics Live 1983-89, 1992; with the Spiritual Cowboys: Dave Stewart And The Spiritual Cowboys, 1990; with Vegas: Vegas, 1992; Solo: Greetings From The Gutter, 1994; Film directed: Honest, 2000; Film soundtrack: De Kassiere, with Candy Dulfer, 1990; Hit singles include: with the Tourists: I Only Want To Be With You, 1979; So Good To Be Back Home, 1979; with Eurythmics: Sweet Dreams (Are Made Of This) (Number 1, US), 1983; Love Is A Stranger, 1983; Who's That Girl?, 1983; Right By Your Side, 1983; Here Comes The Rain Again, 1984; Sex Crime (1984), 1984; Would I Lie To You?, 1985; There Must Be An Angel (Playing With My Heart), 1985; It's Alright (Baby's Coming Back), 1986; When Tomorrow Comes, 1986; Thorn In My Side, 1986; Missionary Man, 1986; You Have Placed A Chill In My Heart, 1988; Love Is a Stranger, 1991; Sweet Dreams, 1991; I Saved the World, 1999; 17 Again, 1999; Solo: Lily Was Here, with Candy Dulfer, 1990; Contributor, Rock The World, 1990; Give Peace A Chance, Peace Choir, 1991; Videos: Eurythmics Live; Sweet Dreams; Savage. Honours: MTV Music Awards, Best New Artist Video, Sweet Dreams, 1984; BRIT Awards: Best Producer, 1986, 1987, 1990; Grammy, Best Rock Performance, Missionary Man, 1987; Ivor Novello Awards: Songwriters of the Year (with Annie Lennox), 1984, 1987; Best Song, It's Alright, 1987. Current Management: Miss Management, 16101 Ventura Blvd, Suite 301, Encino, CA 91436, USA. Address: c/o East West Records, Electric Lighting Station, 46 Kensington Court, London W8 5DP, England.

STEWART Gordon Thallon, b. 5 February 1919, Paisley, Scotland. Physician; University Professor. m. (1) Joan Kego, deceased (2) Georgina Walker, 2 sons, 2 daughters. Education: BSc, 1939, MB,ChB, 1942., MD 1949, University of Glasgow; DTM and H, University of Liverpool, 1947. Appointments: House Surgeon then House Physician, Glasgow, Scotland, 1942-43; Medical Officer, Royal Navy (Surgeon Lieutenant, RNVR), 1943-46; Hospital and research appointments in UK (Aberdeen, Liverpool, London), 1947-63; Professor of Epidemiology, Schools of Medicine and Public Health, University of North Carolina at Chapel Hill, USA, 1963-68; Watkins Professor and Head, Department of Epidemiology and Professor of Medicine, Tulane University, New Orleans Louisiana, USA, 1968-72; Consultant Physician, Epidemiology and Preventive Medicine, National Health Service, UK and Mechan Professor of Public Health, University of Glasgow, 1972-84; Emeritus Professor, 1984-. Publications: Books: Chemotherapy of Fungal Infection (with R W Riddell), 1955; Penicillin Group of Drugs, 1965; Penicillin Allergy (with J McGovern), 1970; Editor: Trends in Epidemiology, 1972; Chapters on epidemiology, control of infectious diseases and education in other books; Articles on same and on drug abuse and public health subjects in mainline medical journals, articles on liquid crystals and ordered structures in biology and medicine. Honours: High Commendation for MD Thesis, University of Glasgow, 1949;

WHO Visiting Professor, Dow Medical College, Karachi, Pakistan, 1953; Senior Visiting Foreign Fellow, US National Science Foundation, 1963-64; Visiting Professor, Cornell University Medical College, New York, USA, 1971; Emeritus Fellow, Infectious Diseases Society of America; Visiting Lecturer and Consultant at various hospitals and colleges in Europe, Canada, America, India, Pakistan, Middle East, Africa; Consultant WHO; New York City Health Department; US Navy (Camp Lejeune, North Carolina). Memberships: Fellow: Royal College of Physicians, Glasgow; Royal College of Pathology, London; Faculty of Public Health of the Royal College of Physicians; Royal Statistical Society; Medical Society of London; Royal Society of Medicine; Member, British Medical Association. 29/9 Inverleith Place, Edinburgh EH3 5QD, Scotland.

STEWART Ian, b. 28 August 1950, Blantyre, Scotland. Member of Parliament. m. 2 sons, 1 daughter. Education: Stretchford Technical College; Manchester Metropolitan University. Appointments: Regional Office, Transport and General Workers Union, 1978-97; Fellow, Industry and Parliament Trust; Member of Parliament for Eccles, 1997-; Member, Deregulation Select Committee, 1998-2001; Member, Information Select Committee, 1998-2001; Backbench PLP Groups: Education and Employment, 1997-, Trade and Industry, 1997-, Foreign Affairs, 1997-2001; Treasury, 2001-; All Party Groups: Chemical Industry Group, Retail Industry Group, Regeneration Group. Occupational Health & Safety Group, Parliamentary Information Technology Committee; United Nations Association, Commonwealth Parliamentary Association, Vice-Chair, All Party China Group; Chair, Group for Vaccine Damaged Children, Chair, All Party Community Media Group; Parliamentary Private Secretary to Brian Wilson MP, Minister for Industry and Energy, 2001-. Address: London Parliamentary Office, House of Commons, London SW1A 0AA, England. E-mail: ianstewartmp@parliament.uk

STEWART Jack, b. 27 January 1926, Atlanta, Georgia, USA. Painter; Muralist. m. (1) Margot Stewart, 1 son, (2) Regina S Stewart. Education: BFA, Yale University, 1951; Columbia University School of Architecture, 1951-53; MA, PhD, New York University, 1975, 1989. Appointments: Columbia Graduate School of Arts, 1965-75; Cooper Union Art School, 1960-74; Chairman Art Department, 1971-74; Provost and Vice President, Rhode Island School Design, 1976-77; President, New York Artists Equity Association, 1985-87; President, National Society of Mural Painters, 1996-2000. Publications include: Spraycan Art of the Ludwig Collection, Rome, Italy, 1997. Honours: Elected Academician, National Academy of Design, 1995; Director and President, Board of Fine Arts Federation of New York; Advisory Board of Steffen Thomas Museum and Archives, Georgia. Commissions and Creative Works: 12 solo shows, 1950-; 28 group shows; 26 murals throughout USA; Public School 28, New York City, 2 mosaics, 1958; Robin International, stained glass, 1960; Cluett Peabody Museum, mixed media, 1990; Mosaic murals: The Facade of the Versailles Hotel, Miami Beach, Florida, 1955; 11 on S S Santa Paula, 1958; Aruba Caribbean Hotel, Aruba Neth Ant. Address: 31 East 7th, New York, NY 10003, USA.

STEWART M Dee, b. 8 October 1935, Indianapolis. Musician (trombonist); Professor. m. Rozella, 1 son, 1 daughter. Education: BS, Music Education, Ball State University, 1957; MM Music Education, 1962, Northwestern University. Appointments: Philadelphia Orchestra, 1962-80; Indiana University, 1980-. Publications: Books: Arnold Jacobs: Legacy of a Master; Philip Farker: Legacy of a Master; CDs: Trombone Under a Tree; Stewart Sounds. Honours: Neill Humfeld Award for Excellence in Teaching, 1998; Teaching Excellence Award, Indiana University.

Memberships: International Trombone Association; American Federation of Musicians. Address: School of Music, Indiana University, Bloomington, IN 47405, USA.

STEWART Paul, b. 4 June 1955, London, England. Author. m. Julie, 1 son, 1 daughter. Education: English, 1st class honours, Lancaster University, 1974-77; Creative Writing with Malcolm Bradbury, UEA, 1978-79; German, University of Heidelberg, 1980-82. Appointments: EFL Teacher, Greece, 1978; EFL Teacher, Germany, 1980-82; EFL Teacher, Sri Lanka, 1982-83; EFL Teacher, Brighton, 1984-90; Writer, Child Carer (of own children), 1990-. Publications include: Stormchaser, 1999; The Birthday Presents, 1999; An Elephant Never Forgets, 2000; The Blobheads, series of 8 books, 2000; Football Mad IV – Teamwork, 2000; Midnight Over Sanctaphrax, 2000; Rabbit's Wish, 2001; The Curse of the Gloamglozer, 2001; The Were-pig, 2001; Muddle Earth, 2003, VOX, 2003.

STEWART Robert Arthur Churchill, b. 1 November 1939, Wellington, New Zealand. Scientific Journal Publisher and Editor. m. Mary Cornelia Jones, 2 sons. Education: BA, Victoria University of Wellington, New Zealand, 1959-61; MEd, Harvard University, Cambridge, Massachusetts, USA, 1965; PhD, Massey University, New Zealand, 1971. Appointments: Lecturer in Psychology, Carleton University, Ottawa, Canada, 1965-66; Lecturer, Senior Lecturer, Education. Massey University, 1968-74; Founding Editor, Social Behavior and Personality: An International Journal, 1973-; Associate Professor, Psychology, Laurentian University, Sudbury, Canada, 1975-78; Reader, Professor of Human Development, University of South Pacific, Suva, Fiji, 1978-89; Sometime Head, School of Education, Pro-Vice-Chancellor, Deputy Vice-Chancellor, Head of School of Humanities, University of South Pacific, Suva, 1982-88. Publications: Cultural Dimensions: Factor Analysis of Textor's A Cross Cultural Summary, 1972; Adolescence in New Zealand: A Book of Readings (2 vols), 1976; From the South Pacific: Profiles in Human Experience, 1980; Pacific Profiles: Personal Experiences of 100 South Pacific Islanders, 1982; Towards a World of Peace: People Create Alternatives, 1986; 61 chapters in books, articles in professional journals. Honours: American Field Service scholarship to the Wisconsin, 1957-58; Selected, Rotary Peace Forum International Committee, 1988-89; Ken Scheller Rotary Award for Writing Excellence, Sydney, Australia, 1990. Address: 30 Summerhill Drive, PO Box 1539, Palmerston North 5331, New Zealand.

STEWART Rod (Roderick David), b. 10 January 1945, Highgate, North London, England. Singer. m. (1) Alana Collins, 1 son, 1 daughter, 1 daughter with Kelly Emberg, (2) Rachel Hunter, 1990, 1 son, 1 daughter. Career: Singer with: Steampacket; Shotgun Express; Jeff Beck Group, 1967-69; Concerts include: UK tour with Roy Orbison, 1967; US tours, 1967, 1968; The Faces, 1969-75; Appearances include: Reading Festival, 1972; UK, US tours, 1972; Solo artiste, 1971-; Solo appearances include: Rock In Rio, Brazil, 1985; Vagabond Heart Tour, 1991-92. Recordings: Singles include: Reason To Believe; Maggie May; (I Know) I'm Losing You; Handbags And Gladrags; You Wear It Well; Angel; Farewell; Sailing; This Old Heart Of Mine; Tonight's The Night (Gonna Be All Right); The Killing Of Georgie (Parts 1 and 2); Get Back; The First Cut Is The Deepest; I Don't Want To Talk About It; You're In My Heart; Hot Legs; D'Ya Think I'm Sexy?; Passion; Young Turks; Tonight I'm Yours; Baby Jane; What Am I Gonna Do; Infatuation; Some Guys Have All The Luck; Love Touch; Every Beat Of My Heart; Downtown Train; Rhythm Of My Heart; This Old Heart Of Mine; Have I Told You Lately; Reason To Believe; Ruby Tuesday; You're The Star; Albums include: 2 with Jeff Beck; 4 with the Faces; Solo albums: Every Picture Tells A Story, 1971; Never A Dull Moment, 1972; Atlantic Crossing, 1975; A Night

On The Town, 1976; Foot Loose And Fancy Free, 1977; Blondes Have More Fun, 1978; Foolish Behaviour, 1980; Tonight I'm Yours, 1981; Camouflage, 1984; Love Touch, 1986; Out Of Order, 1988; The Best Of, 1989; Downtown Train, 1990; Vagabond Heart, 1991; Lead Vocalist, 1992; Unplugged... And Seated, 1993; A Spanner In The Works, 1995; When We Were the New Boys, 1998; It Had To Be You: The Great American Songbook, 2002; Numerous compilations. Honours include: BRIT Awards, Lifetime Achievement Award, 1993; First artist to top US and UK singles and album charts simultaneously, 1971. Address: c/o Warner Music, 28 Kensington Church Street, London, W8 4EP, England.

STEWART William Gladstone, b. 15 July 1933, Lancaster, England. Television Producer; Presenter; Writer. m. Laura Calland Stewart, 2 daughters, 3 other children. Education: Shooters Hill Grammar School, London, 1945-52; Woolwich Polytechnic, 1951-52. Appointments: Royal Army Educational Corps, 1952-55; Served with Kings African Rifles in Kenya; Worked with BBC, 1958-67; Independent and Freelance, Producer, Director, 1967-; Productions include: Eric Sykes, Bless this House with Sid James; Father Dear Father with Patrick Cargill; Entertainment Series and one off "specials" with Max Bygraves, Tommy Cooper, Frankie Howerd, Bruce Forsyth; Major long-running series with David Frost, The Frost Programme, David Frost Live from London; With Johnny Speight, Lady is a Tramp, 'Till Death, The 19th Hole; Major drama series for Channel 4, Tickets for the Titanic; Co-Founder (with Colin Frewin), Sunset and Vine Productions, 1976; Founder, Regent Productions, 1980-; Currently, Presenter Channel 4 programme, Fifteen-to-One, 1988-. Publications: Regular contributor of articles on media matters to national newspapers and journals including, Independent, RTS Journal, Broadcast, The Listener, The Producer, Televisual, Evening Standard, Impact; Lectures on the return of cultural artefacts, especially the Parthenon Marbles to Athens, at The European Parliament in Strasbourg, UNESCO in Paris, The Smithsonian in Washington, in Athens, London and New York; Institute of Art and Law Annual Lecture, 2000; 5 city lecture tour across USA and Canada, 2003. Memberships: Fellow, Royal Television Society; British Academy Film and Television Arts; Royal Horticultural Society; Hall of Fame of the Royal Television Society. Address: 6 Putney Common, London SW15 1HL, England. E-mail: haybohan@aol.com

STICH Michael, b. 18 October 1968, Pinneberg, Germany. Tennis Player. m. Jessica Stockmann, 1992. Appointments: National Junior Champion, 1986; Turned professional, 1988; Semi-finalist, French Open, 1990; Member, West German Davis Cup Team, 1990; Won first professional title, Memphis, 1990; Winner, Men's Singles Championship, Wimbledon, 1991; Men's Doubles (with John McEnroe), 1992; Won ATP World Championship, 1993; Retired, 1997; Won 28 professional titles; UN Ambassador, 1999-; German Davis Cup team Captain, 2001-2002. Address: Ernst-Barlach-Strasse 44, 2200 Elmshorn, Germany.

STIEGLER Drago, b. 24 October 1919, Zagreb, Croatia. Mathematician. m. Hildegard Sarko, 1 daughter. Education: Study of mathematics and theoretical physics, University of Zagreb, 1938-46; Study of philosophy, 1946-49; UNESCO Research Fellow, Institut Henri Poincaré, Paris, 1954-55; Active Participant in Séminaire de Recherches Louis de Broglie, Paris 1954-55 and Séminaire Bourbaki; Research Scholarship, Balokovich Foundation, Harvard University, USA, 1961-63; PhD, Relativity, 1963. Appointments: Professor of Mathematics, School of Engineering, Zagreb, 1946-50; Researcher in Optics, Ghetaldus, Optical Industry Zagreb, 1950-59; Constructed all sorts of eyeglasses for correction of Myopia, Hypermetropia and Astigmatismus, produced since 1957 in Ghetaldus and exhibited at the International Trade Exhibition for Ophthalmic Optics in

Cologne, 1984; AGFA, Optics, Munich, 1960; T University Munich, 1964-84. Publications: Research in Relativity; Quantum Theory; Cosmology; Optics; History and Philosophy of Mathematical Sciences including: Proof that the velocity of light is equal in all galilean systems of reference, 1952, 1953, 1958; Correspondence with Albert Einstein concerning the Axiomatic Foundations of Special Theory of Relativity, 1951 (Einstein Archives, Boston, Jerusalem, Collected Papers of Albert Einstein) Discovered: the law of anomalous (differential) rotation of spherical cosmical bodies with application to the Sun, Jupiter and Saturn, communicated at the International Congress of Mathematicians, Nizza, 1970, published in Academy of Sciences, Paris, 1971, 1972; Right and Left in the electrodynamics of moving bodies are physically no equivalent, 1972, 1978; Showed that the velocity of expanding matter in Einstein Friedmann theory in the case of the model of the universe with constant negative curvature is in the neighbourhood of the beginning greater than the velocity of light in vacuo, 1967; Honours: DMathSci, honoris causa; Twentieth Century Award for Outstanding Achievement in Physics and Cosmology. Memberships: Different academies of sciences; Fellow, Royal Astronomical Society, London.

STIGWOOD Robert Colin, b. 16 April 1934, Adelaide, Australia. Business Executive. Education: Sacred Heart College, Adelaide. Appointments: Established Robert Stigwood Organisation (RSO), 1967; Formed RSO Records, 1973; Founder, Music for UNICEF; Producer of films: Jesus Christ Superstar; Bugsy Malone; Gallipoli; Tommy; Saturday Night Fever; Grease; Sergeant Pepper's Lonely Hearts Club Band; Moment by Moment; Times Square; The Fan; Grease 2; Staying Alive; Evita; Gallipoli; Producer of stage musicals: Hair; Oh! Calcutta; The Dirtiest Show in Town; Pippin; Jesus Christ Superstar; Evita; Grease, 1993; Saturday Night Fever; TV producer in England and USA: The Entertainer; The Prime of Miss Jean Brodie; Chair of Board, Stigwood Group of Companies. Honours: Key to City of Los Angeles; Tony Award, 1980, for Evita; International Producer of the Year, ABC Interstate Inc. Address: c/o Robert Stigwood Organization, Barton Manor, Wippingham, East Cowes, Isle of Wight, PO32 6LB, England.

STILES Lindley Joseph, b. 1 July 1913, Tatum, New Mexico, USA. Teacher. m. Marguerite Croonenberghs, 2 daughters. Education: BA, 1935, MA, 1939, EdD, 1945, University of Colorado; Stanford University, 1940. Appointments: Teacher of English, Colorado Public Schools, 1935-45; Associate Professor, College of William and Mary, 1945-46; Associate Professor, University of Illinois, 1946-47; Associate Professor, Ohio State University, 1947-49; Dean, School of Education, University of Virginia, 1949-55; Dean, School of Education, University of Wisconsin, 1955-65; Professor of Education for Interdisciplinary Studies, 1966-79; Consultant, 1979-. Publications: Author and Editor of over 60 books on aspects of teacher education, educational policy, theory of teaching; Over 400 papers and articles for professional journals. Honours: Vandenbergh Trophy, US Airforce Association, 1966; Honorary Doctor's Degrees, Rider College, 1966, McKendree College, 1967, College of William and Mary, 1978; Alumnus of the Fort Lewis College; 20th century's leading teacher educator. Conceptualised and advocated world-wide the social wisdom, The Best Should Teach. Listed in numerous biographical dictionaries. Memberships: American Association of University Professors; National Education Association; John Dewewy Society; Phi Delta Kappa; Kappa Delta Pi; Phi Sigma Mu; Phi Eta Sigma; Phi Eta Omega. Address: 4595 Laguna Place, Apartment 345, Boulder, CO 80303, USA. E-mail: lindleystiles@webtv.net

STILLER Robert Reuven, b. 25 January 1928, Warsaw, Poland. Writer; Translator; Philologist; Essayist. m. Nina Gajewska. Education: Polish, Slavic and Indian Philologies, University of Warsaw, 1947-63; Old Norse Philology, University of Iceland, 1974-75. Publications: over 200 books, original and translated. Honour: Fellow in Writing, University of Iowa, 1981; Order of Polonia Restituta, 2003. Memberships: Malaysian Branch, Royal Asiatic Society, Singapore; Association Jean Hans Arp, Strassburg; President, Jewish Reform Community, Warsaw; President, Jewish Cultural Association "Kesher", Warsaw. Address: Aleja Wojska Polskiego 38 apt 9, 01-554 Warsaw, Poland.

STINES Betty Irene (Parham), b. 3 May 1918, Stinesville, Indiana, USA. Professional Artist. m (1) Willard Russell Elliot, deceased, 1 son, 2 daughters, (2) Edmond Glen Stines. Career: Leader, Brownie Scouts, Ellettsville, 1943-47; Sunday School Teacher, First Baptist Church, Ellettsville, 1950's; Floral Designer, Unique Florist Shoppe, 1963-69; Chairman and Co-chairman, Art Exhibits, Monroe County Fall Festival, Ellettsville, Indiana, 1950's-60's; Organiser and Member, Hoosier Hills Art Guild, 1964-80; Recording Secretary, 1964-67, Organiser, Annual Student Art Exhibit, 1964-73, Board of Directors, 1964-80, Hoosier Hills Art Guild, Bloomington, Indiana; Numerous art exhibitions, 1952-2002 include: Indiana University; Manchester College; Hoosier Hills Art Gallery, Bloomington, Indiana; Owen County Art Guild, Spencer, Indiana; Swope Art Gallery, Terre Haute, Indiana. Publications: Numerous photographs and articles about exhibitions and paintings include: Mural, First Baptist Church, Ellettsville, Indiana, Bloomington Herald Telephone Newspaper, 1949; Opening of First Fall Festival Art Show, Ellettsville Journal; Photograph and article of Officers and Directors of Hoosier Hills Art Guild planning for the Grand Opening of the new Art Gallery, Bloomington Herald Telephone, 1964; Photographs of Painting in Indiana State House Art Salon, Painting in Hoosier Hills Art Gallery, 1964, 1967; Photo and article of presentation of painting to Indiana Gas and Water Company by Ellettsville Chamber of Commerce, Ellettsville Journal. Honours: Certificate of Award as Exhibitor of Fine Arts, Indiana, State House Salon, Indianapolis, 1967; Painting purchased by Ellettsville, Indiana Chamber of Commerce and presented to Indiana Gas and Water Company; Many First Prizes in Juried Art Shows; Best of Show and Champion Exhibitor Awards; Listed in Who's Who publications and biographical dictionaries. Memberships: First Baptist Church, Ellettsville, Indiana; National Museum of Women in the Arts, Washington DC. Address: 7935 W Ratliff Road, Bloomington, IN 49404-9685, USA.

STING (Gordon Matthew Sumner), 2 October 1951, Wallsend, Newcastle-Upon-Tyne, England. Singer; Musician (bass); Actor. m. (1) Frances Tomelty, 1 May 1976, divorced 1984, 1 son, 1 daughter; (2) Trudie Styler, 20 August 1992, 2 sons, 2 daughters. Career: School teacher, Newcastle, 1975-77; Singer, songwriter, bass player, The Police, 1977-86; Solo artiste, 1985-; Numerous worldwide tours, television and radio, with the Police and solo; actor in films: Quadrophenia, 1980; Secret Policeman's Other Ball, 1982; Brimstone And Treacle, 1982; Dune, 1984; The Bride, 1985; Plenty, 1985; Julia And Julia, 1988; Stormy Monday, 1988; The Adventures Of Baron Munchausen, 1989; Stormy Monday, 1989; Rosencrantz and Guildenstern are Dead; Resident Alien; The Music Tells You; The Grotesque; Mercury Falling, 1996; Broadway Performance, Threepenny Opera, 1989. Recordings: Hit singles include: Walking On The Moon; Message In A Bottle; So Lonely; Roxanne; De Do Do Do, De Da Da Da; Every Little Thing She Does; Every Breath You Take; Invisible Sun; Can't Stand Losing You; Don't Stand So Close To Me; If You Love Somebody; Englishman In New York; If I Ever Lose My Faith In You; Fields Of Gold; Love Is Stronger Than Justice; Cowboy Song (with Pato

Banton); Let The Soul Be Your Pilot; Roxanne 97; Brand New Day; After the Rain has Gone, 2000; Albums: with the Police: Outlandos D'Armour, 1977; Regatta De Blanc, 1979; Zenyatta Mondatta, 1980; Ghost In The Machine, 1981; Synchronisity, 1983; Bring On The Night, 1986; Solo albums: The Dream Of The Blue Turtles, 1985; Nothing Like The Sun, 1987; The Soul Cages, 1991; Ten Summer's Tales, 1994; Mercury Falling, 1996; Brand New Day, 1999; After the Rain has Gone, 2000; Contributor, Tower Of Song (Leonard Cohen tribute), 1995. Publications: Jungle Stories: The Fight for the Amazon, 1989. Honours include: 10 Grammy Awards (with Police and solo); Ivor Novello Award for Best Song They Dance Alone, 1989; Q Award, Best Album, 1994; BRIT Award, Best Male Artist, 1994; 4 songwriting awards (BMI) 1998; Brit Award for Outstanding Contribution to Music, 2002; Emmy Award for Best Performance (Sting in Tuscany.... All This Time), 2002. Membership: PRS. Current Management: Firstars, 1 Water Lane, Camden Town, London NW1 8NZ, England.

STIPE Michael, b. 1960, Decatur, Georgia, USA. Rock Musician. Education: University of Georgia. Appointments: Lead singer and song writer with REM band, 1980-; Owner OO (film co). Albums include: (for IRS): Murmur, 1982-83; Document; (for Warner): Green, 1988; Out of Time, 1991; Automatic for the People, 1992; Monster, 1994; New Adventures in Hi-Fi, 1996; Up, 1998. Address: c/o Warner Bros Records, 3300 Warner Boulevard, Burbank, CA 91505, USA.

STIRES Midge, b. 5 April 1943, Orange, New Jersey, USA. Painter. m. Peter D Schnore, 2 sons. Education: Bachelor of Fine Art, Syracuse University, USA. Honours: Pollock and Krasner Foundation Grant; Elizabeth Foundation for the Arts Grant; Artists for the Environment Residency Grant. Publications: Painting Panoramas, The Artists Magazine, 1990. Memberships: National Association of Painters in Casein and Acrylic. Address: 144 Red Oak Dr, Boyertown, PA 19512 8963, USA.

STOCKTON William M Jr, b. 22 March 1956, McKeesport, Pennsylvania, USA. Cosmetic Dentist. Education: BS, Howard University, 1983; DDS, Howard University College of Dentistry, 1988. Appointments: Staff Dentist, Syracuse Community Health Center, 1989-90; Private Practice focusing on cosmetic dentistry, 1990-. Honours: Congressional Businessman's Advisory Council, 1998, Honorary Chairman, 2000; Gold Medal for Community Service and Mentoring, US Congress, 2001; Congressional Business Advisory Council Businessman of the Year, State of New York, 1999, 2000, 2001; Named as One of the Top Cosmetic Dentists in North America, 2000-; Listed in Who's Who publications and biographical dictionaries. Memberships: American Dental Association; Congressional Businessman's Advisory Council; Life member, Republican National Committee; President's Inner Circle Club. Address: 2323 Main Street, Buffalo, NY 14214, USA.

STODDART James Fraser, b. 24 May 1942, Edinburgh, Scotland. Professor of Chemistry. m. Norma, 2 daughters. Education: BSc, 1964, PhD, 1966, DSc, 1980, University of Edinburgh. Appointments: Lecturer, Chemistry, Sheffield University, UK, 1970-78; Secondment to ICI, 1978-81; Reader in Chemistry, Sheffield University, 1981-90; Professor of Chemistry, 1990-97, Head of School of Chemistry, 1993-97, Birmingham University, UK; Winstein Chair of Chemistry, University of California, Los Angeles, 1997-2003; Director, California Nano Systems Institute and Fred Kavli Chair, Nano Systems Sciences, 2003-. Publications: 640 publications. Honours include: Fellow of the Royal Society (FRS), 1995; Humboldt Fellowship, 1998; Cope Scholar Award, American Chemical Society, 1999; Nagoya Gold Medal, Organic Chemistry, 2004. Memberships include: FRS;

Royal Society of Chemistry; American Chemical Society. Address: Department of Chemistry and Biochemistry, University of California, Los Angeles, 405 Hilgard Avenue, Los Angeles, CA 90095-1569, USA.

STOKER Gill, b. 17 April 1954, Derby, England. Actress; Tutor. m. Richard Stoker. Education: Rose Bruford College, Sidcup, Kent; The Actors Centre; BA (Hons), MA, PhD, Birkbeck College, Kings College, University of London; Blackheath Conservatoire of Music. Career: Theatre includes: Rose Theatre, Sidcup: King Lear, Othello, The Winter's Tale, King John, Top Girls, Vinegar Tom, The Way of the World, Medea, The Old Ones, Mistress of Many, Female Pipings in Eden; Greenwood Theatre, London: Kasimir and Karoline; Zecora Ura Theatre, Sidcup: Publish and be Damned; Opera/Operetta: South London Opera: Iphigénie en Tauride, English Eccentrics, Medea; Blackheath Opera: La Vie Parisienne, La Belle Hélène; The Gypsy Baron; King Arthur; The Marriage of Figaro; The Daughter of the Regiment; TV/Radio: BBC: The Much Loved Music Show; The Proms; Test the Nation; Brain of Britain; LWT: The London Palladium, Christmas Charity Gala; Open University Tutor, Arts Faculty, 1990-. Publications: Various book reviews on First Monday (Science and Technology Website); Various theatre reviews on British Theatre Guide Website; Articles: Sir John Tenniel and the Pre-Raphaelites, 1995; William Holman Hunt: from Literature to Art, 1997. Memberships: Blackheath Poetry Society; Association of University Teachers; Equity.

STOKER Richard, b. 8 November 1938, Castleford, Yorkshire, England. Composer; Conductor; Artist; Writer. m. Gillian Patricia Watson, 10 July 1986. Education: Huddersfield School of Art with Reginald Napier, Sugden: Huddersfield School of Music, with Harold Truscott, 1953-58; Royal Academy of Music, with Sir Lennox Berkeley, 1958-62; Composition with Nadia Boulanger, on Mendelssohn Scholarship, Paris, 1962-63. Career: Assistant Librarian, LSO, 1962-63; Professor, Royal Academy of Music, 1963-87; Tutor, Royal Academy of Music, 1970-81; Teacher of Composition, St Paul' School, 1972-74; Magdalen College, Cambridge, 1974-76; Lecturer, U3A, 1996-98; 1957 Society, 2001. Civic Activities: Member, Treasurer, Stearing Committee, Lewisham Visual Arts Festivals, 1990, 1992; MIND, 1990-91; Samaritan, 1991-94; Founder member, Atlantic Council, 1993; Founder member, Treasurer, RAM Guild, 1994; International Promotions Committee, APC, 1995-97; Magistrate (Inner London), 1995-2003, Crown Court, 1998-2003. Publications: Portrait of a Town, 1974; Words Without Music, 1974; Strolling Players, 1978; Open Window-Open Door, 1985; Tanglewood, 1990; Diva, 1992; Collected Short Stories, 1993; Over 36 anthologies; Advisor, 2003-, 8 commissioned entries, 2004, Oxford Dictionary of National Biography. Honours: Mendelssohn Scholarship, 1962; Numerous awards, 1962-65, 1972-; ARCM, 1962; ARAM, 1971; FRAM, 1978; Twice winner, Editors Choice Award, National Library of Poetry, USA, 1995, 1997; Man of the Year, American Biographical Institute, 1996. Memberships: PEN International and English PEN; RSL; British Academy, 1998-, Committee member, 1999-; PRS; MCPS; Blackheath Art Society; Lewisham Society of Art; Magistrates Association, 1995; Founder Member, Atlantic Council, 1994; European Atlantic Group, 1995. Commissions and Creative Works: Lewisham Society of Arts, 1990; Summer exhibitions, 1992; Blackheath Art Society, 1988; Tudor Barn Eltham, 1989; Laurence House (One man shows), 1992-93; Editor, Composer magazine, 1969-80; Composed over 200 works; Frequent broadcasts, appeared on BBC TV, Channel 4, BBC Radio 3 and 4; Adjudicated numerous awards including Cyprus 2002 Orchestra Composer Award; BBC Brit Composer Awards; Royal Philharmonic Society Awards; Designed many CD covers; Works in private collections; Painted in oils by John Bratby, 1983.

Dictionary of International Biography

Address: c/o Ricordi, 210 New Kings Road, London SW6 4NZ, England. E-mail: gps5@tutor.open.ac.uk Website: www.boosey.com/publishing/pages/catalogue

STOKES Daniel Patrick, b. 7 September 1945, Dublin, Ireland. Writer; Poet. Education: MA, English and Philosophy, Trinity College, Dublin, 1968; HDipEd, National University of Ireland, 1969. Appointments: Teacher, 1969-78; Vice Principal, St Patrick's Cathedral School, 1976-80; Full-time Writer, 1980-. Publications: Keepsake Poems, 1977; Poems for Christmas, 1981; Interest and Other Poems, 1982. Contributions to: New Poetry; Lines Review; Poetry Ireland Review; Sunday Tribune; Journal of Irish Literature; Irish Times; Ariel; Atlantic Review; Dekalb Literary Arts Journal; Studies; Cyphers; Ulster Tatler; Cork Examiner; Connacht Tribune; Prism International. Honours: Yorkshire Poets Award, 1977; New Poetry Competition, 1978; Poetry Athlone Award, 1980; Edinburgh Fringe First Award, 1982. Address: 4 New Bridge Drive, Sandymount, Dublin 4, Ireland.

STOKES John Gerard, b. 15 October 1923, Perth, Australia. Inventor; Engineer. m. Inge Stokes, 3 sons, 4 daughters. Education: B Science, University of Western Australia 1943; Graduate School of Military Engineering Course 1244 Casula, New South Wales. Appointments: Chairman, Information Radio; Chairman, Museum of Contemporary Science and Technology; Governor, Foundation for International Training, Toronto, Canada; National President, Royal Guide Dogs for the Blind, Australia; Board Member, various companies. Publications: Numerous in field. Honour: Order of Australia. Membership: Club of Rome, 1974-2002; Post World President, The World Council of Young Men's Service Clubs. Address: 16 Grant Street, North Cottesloe 6011, Western Australia, Australia.

STONE Carole, b. 30 May 1942, Maidstone, Kent, England. Media Consultant; Journalist. m. Richard Lindley, 1999. Education: Southampton Technical College. Appointments: Secretary, for a firm of architects, Southampton, 1961; Copy-Typist then Secretary, BBC South, 1963; Station Assistant, BBC Radio Brighton, 1967; Regional News Producer, BBC Bristol, 1970; Network Radio Talks Producer, producing regular editions of Radio 4's Woman's Hour, Down Your Way, You and Yours, BBC, based Bristol, 1972; Editor, BBC Radio 4's current affairs series, Any Questions and Any Answers, 1977-1989; Department Editor, BBC1 Topical Features, 1989; Originated and Presented, Mother of Mine for BBC 1, 1990; Reporter, BBC 1, Bite Back, 1991-93; Host of Carole Stone and Company, Viva! 963 am, 1996-96; Mental health manager, Camden and Islington Community Health Services, 1995-98; Currently: Media Consultant to Chairs and Chief Executives of public companies; Journalist, Author, television and radio Producer/ Presenter; Director, Lindley Stone Ltd, independent television production company. Publications: Networking – the Art of Making Friends, 2001; Articles published in the national press magazines and specialist business publications. Honours: Judge, Women of Tomorrow Awards; Award Winner, London Businesswomen's Network Achievers Awards, 1983; President's Award, European Federation of Black Women Business Owners. Memberships include: Life Member, Bristol Business Ladies Club; Fellow, Royal Society of Arts; Council Member, Royal Television Society, 1991-94; Board, London Press Club; Council, Women in Journalism; President, The Media Society, 1997-99; Vice Patron, National Missing Persons' Helpline; Patron SANE; Patron, Triumph Over Phobia; Council Member, Central Council for Education and Training in Social Work , 1996-99; Trustee, Facial Surgery Research Foundation; Trustee, The Wallace Collection. Address: Flat 1, 19 Henrietta Street, London WC2E 8QH, England. E-mail: carole@carolestone.com

STONE Ingeborg Eda, b. 15 June 1923, Hamburg, Germany. Choreographer; Professional Ice Skater. m. Gregory, 2 daughters. Education: Graduate, University of California, Berkeley, 1944; Post Graduate, 1944-45. Appointments: Professional Ice Skater, Shipstad and Johnson Ice Follies, 1945-47; Choreographer, Hielo y Estrellas, South America, 1947-48; Educator, City of Los Angeles School System, 1954-68; Washoe County, NV Schools, Reno, 1968-83; Co-Founder, Reno Philharmonic Symphony Orchestra, 1969; Board of Directors, 1969-82; President, Credo Music Company, Impromptu Records, Spain, 1991; Director, Gregory Stone Music Library, Mijas, 1991-. Publications: Operetta Liebestraum; Music Has No Frontiers; CD, My Grisha's Gypsy Soul; Currently preparing exhibition: International Dance (medium:paper); Exhibition, Photography: That Dog, Boo. Honours: Delta Kappa Gamma; Admission Knights Templar, 1985; Association Amigos Orquesta Ciuded de Malaga, 1999; Commemorative Plaque from the Provincial Sinfonia Orchestra of Malaga, Spain, 2000; Inclusion into various Who's Who publications; The Europe 500. Memberships: Delta Kappa Gamma; Knights Templar; Association Amigos Orquesta Ciudad de Malaga. Address: Urbanizacion El Coto, Calle Los Zorzales 49, 26949 Mijas Malaga, Spain.

STONE Oliver William, b. 15 September 1946, New York, USA. Screenwriter; Director. Education: BFA, Yale University; New York University Film School. Appointments include: Teacher, Cholon, Vietnam, 1965-66; US Merchant Marine, 1966; Served, US Army, Vietnam, 1967-68; Taxi Driver, New York City, 1971; Screenwriter, Seizure, 1973, Midnight Express, 1978, The Hand, 1981, Conan the Barbarian, with J Milius, 1982, Scarface, 1983, Year of the Dragon, with M Cimino, 1985, 8 Million Ways to Die, with D L Henry, 1986, Salvador, with R Boyle, 1986; Writer, Director, Platoon, 1986; Co-writer and Director: Wall Street, 1987; Talk Radio, 1988; The Doors, 1991; Screenwriter, Producer and Director: Born on the Fourth of July, 1989; JFK, 1991; Heaven and Earth, 1993; Natural Born Killers, 1994; Nixon, 1995; Director, U-Turn, 1997; Co-Writer, Evita, 1996; Producer: South Central, 1992; Zebrahead, 1992; The Joy Luck Club, 1993; New Age, 1994; Wild Palms, TV mini-series, 1993; Freeway, 1995; The People vs Larry Flynt, 1996; Any Given Sunday, 2000; Comandante (documentary), 2003; Executive Producer: Killer: A Journal of Murder, 1995; (HBO)Indictment: The McMartin Preschool, 1995. Honours: Winner of numerous awards including: 2 Academy Awards for Platoon and Born of the Fourth of July; BAFTA Award, Directors Guild of America Award, for Platoon; Purple Heart with Oak Leaf Cluster; Bronze Star. Memberships: Writers' Guild of America; Directors' Guild of America; Academy Motion Pictures Arts and Sciences. Address: Ixtlan, 201 Santa Monica Boulevard, 6th Floor, Santa Monica, CA 90401, USA.

STONE Sharon, b. 10 March 1958, Meadville, USA. Actress. m. (1) Michael Greenburg, 1984, divorced 1987, (2) Phil Bronstein, 1998, 1 adopted son. Education: Edinboro College. Career: Films include: Star Dust Memories (debut); Above the Law; Action Jackson; King Solomon's Mines; Allan Quatermain and the Lost City of Gold; Irreconcilable Differences; Deadly Blessing; Personal Choice; Basic Instinct; Dairy of a hit Man; Where Sleeping Dogs Lie; Sliver; Intersection; The Specialist; The Quick and the Dead; Casino; Last Dance; Diabolique, 1996; Sphere; The Might, 1999; The Muse, 1999; Simpatico, 1999; TV includes: Tears in the Rain; War and Remembrance; Calendar Girl Murders; The Vegas Strip Wars. Honour: Chevalier, Ordre des Arts et des Lettres. Address: c/o Guy McElwaine, PO Box 7304, North Hollywood, CA 91603, USA.

STOPPARD Tom (Sir), (Thomas Straussler), b. 3 July 1937, Zin, Czechoslovakia (British citizen). Dramatist; Screenwriter. m. (1) Jose Ingle, 1965, divorced 1972, 2 sons, (2) Dr Miriam Moore-

Robinson, 1972, divorced 1992, 2 sons. Publications: Plays: Rosencrantz and Guildenstern are Dead, 1967; The Real Inspector Hound, 1968; Albert's Bridge, 1968; Enter a Free Man, 1968; After Magritte, 1971; Jumpers, 1972; Artists Descending a Staircase, and, Where Are They Now?, 1973; Travesties, 1975; Dirty Linen, and New-Found-Land, 1976; Every Good Boy Deserves Favour, 1978; Professional Foul, 1978; Night and Day, 1978; Undiscovered Country, 1980; Dogg's Hamlet, Cahoot's Macbeth, 1980; On the Razzle, 1982; The Real Thing, 1983; The Dog It Was That Died, 1983; Squaring the Circle, 1984; Four Plays for Radio, 1984; Rough Crossing, 1984; Dalliance and Undiscovered Country, 1986; Largo Desolato, by Vaclav Havel (translator), 1987; Hapgood, 1988; In the Native State, 1991; Arcadia, 1993; Indian Ink, 1995; The Invention of Love, 1997; The Seagul, 1997; The Coast of Utopia: Ttrilogy: Part One: Voyage, Part Two: Shipwreck, Part Three: Salvage, 2002; The Television Plays 1965-1984, 1993. Fiction: Introduction 2, 1964; Lord Malquist and Mr Moon, 1965. Other: 8 screenplays; Various unpublished state, radio, and television plays. Honours: John Whiting Award, Arts Council, 1967; New York Drama Critics Award, 1968; Italia Prize, 1968; Tony Awards, 1968, 1976, 1984; Evening Standard Awards, 1968, 1972, 1974, 1978, 1993, 1997; Olivier Award, 1993; Knighted, 1997; Order of Merit, 2000. Address: c/o The Peters, Fraser and Dunlop Group Ltd, Drury House, 34-43 Russell Street, London WC2B 5HA, England.

STOREY David (Malcolm), b. 13 July 1933, Wakefield, England. Writer; Dramatist; Screenwriter; Poet. m. Barbara Rudd Hamilton, 1956, 2 sons, 2 daughters. Education: Diploma, Slade School of Art, 1956. Publications: This Sporting Life, 1960; Flight into Camden, 1960; Radcliffe, 1963; Pasmore, 1972; A Temporary Life, 1973; Edward, 1973; Saville, 1976; A Prodigal Child, 1982; Present Times, 1984; Storey's Lives: Poems 1951-1991, 1992; A Serious Man, 1998. Honours: Macmillan Fiction Award, 1960; John Llewellyn Memorial Prize, 1960; Somerset Maugham Award, 1960; Evening Standard Awards, 1967, 1970; Los Angeles Drama Critics Award, 1969; Writer of the Year Award, Variety Club of Great Britain, 1969; New York Drama Critics Award, 1969, 1970, 1971; Geoffrey Faber Memorial Prize, 1973; Fellow, University College, London, 1974; Booker Prize, 1976. Address: c/o Jonathan Cape Ltd, Random Century House, 20 Vauxhall Bridge Road, London SW1V 2SA, England.

STORME Marcel Leon Victor, b. 3 August 1930, Gent, Flanders, Belgium. Barrister; Educator. m. Godelieve de Schrijver, 1 son. Education: JD, State University of Gent, Belgium, 1952; Lic. Economy, 1955; Barrister, Bar of Gent, 1952-. Appointments: Private Practice, Gent, 1952-; Professor of Law, University of Antwerp, 1958-91, University of Gent, 1961-95, Queen Mary College, London, 1985-86, Vlaamse Leergangen, Leuven, Belgium, 1986-87, University of Leiden, 1987-88; Dean, Law Faculty, University of Gent, 1982-84; Chair, Leverhulme, London, 1991-92; Editor: Tijdschrift Privaatrecht, 1964, Procedural Reporter, 1983-, European Private Law Review, 1992-. Publications: The Burden of Proof, 1962; European Caselaw, 1973, 1984 and the Law, 1984; International Arbitration, 1989. Honours: Professor honoris causa, China University, Beijing, China, 1988; Dr honoris causa, Curie University, Lublin, 1994; Commander, Order Orange Nassau; Premio Enrico Redenti. Memberships include: Provincial Council, Gent, 1958-77; Young Barristers Association, president, 1967-69; Vice-President of the Board, Belgian Radio and TV, Brussels, 1968-77; Senator, Belgian Senate, Brussels, 1977-81; Centre Arbitration Brussels, vice-president, 1980; Flemish Lawyers Association, president, 1983; Comparative Law Society, president, 1988; International Association of Procedural Law, secretary general 1983-85, President, 1995; Belgian Centre for Procedural Law, president, 1991; Royal Academy of Sciences, president, 1997-98; Academia Europaea; De Prince Club; Anglo Belgian Club, London. Address: Coupure 3, 9000 Gent, Belgium. E-mail: m.storme@storme-law.be

STRANGE Curtis, b. 30 January 1955, Norfolk, Virginia, USA. Professional Golfer. m. Sarah Jones, 2 sons. Education: Wake Forest University. Career: Professional, 1976-; First joined PGA tour, 1977; Won Pensacola Open, 1979; Won Sammy Davis Jr Greater Hartford Open, 1983; Won LaJel Classic, 1984; Won Honda Classic, Panasonic-Las Vegas International, 1985; Won Canadian Open, 1985; Won Houston Open, 1986; Won Canadian Open, Federal Express – St Jude Classic, NEC Series of Golf, 1987; Won Sandway Cove Classic, Australia, 1988; Won Industry Insurance Agent Open, Memorial Tournament, US Open, Nabisco Championships, 1988; Won US Open, Palm Meadows Cup, Australia, 1989; Won Holden Classic, Australia, 1993. Memberships: Member, PGA Tour Charity Team, Michelob Championship, Kingsmill, 1996. Honours: Captain US Ryder Cup Team after playing on five Ryder Cup Teams, 2002; Golf Analyst, ABC Sports, 1997-; Golfer of the Year, 1986, 1987. Address: c/o IMG, 1 Erieview Plaza, Suite 1300, Cleveland, OH 44114, USA.

STRANGE John, b. 20 July 1934, Gentofte, Copenhagen, Denmark. Biblical Archaeologist. m. Lisbeth Bundgaard, 3 sons, 2 daughters. Education: Master of Divinity, University of Copenhagen, 1962; Theological College of Education, 1962; Student of Archaeology, Copenhagen, Jerusalem, 1962-67; Doctor of Divinity, 1980. Appointments: Research Fellow, 1962-64, Senior Research fellow, 1964-67, Assistant Professor, 1967, Associate Professor, 1972, Reader, 1989, Biblical Archaeology, Director, Department of Biblical Exegesis, 1982-84, 1999, Dean of the Faculty of Theology, 1984-91, 1999-2002, Pro-Rector, 1991-94, University of Copenhagen; Retired, 2002; Archaeological studies, Jerusalem, Damascus and Cairo, 1963-64, 1976, London, 1995-96, Paris, 1999; Assistant in excavations, Hazor, 1958, Ashdod, 1963; Site Supervisor, Jerusalem, Jordan, 1964 and 1967 (Kathleen Kenyon's Jerusalem Excavations); Site Supervisor, Umm Qes, Jordan, 1978, 1981, 1983 (Svend Holm-Nielsen's excavations); Director of excavations at Tell el-Fukhar, Jordan, 1990-93, 2002 and director of publication; Nonstipendary Curate, 1979-; Army Chaplain, 1984-94. Publications: Member of the committee for a new translation of the Bible into Danish, 1978-90; Captor/Keftiu, doctoral thesis, 1980; Bible Atlas, translated into 17 languages, 1988; Editor, The National Encyclopaedia of Denmark (Archaeology and history of the Levant until 622 AD), 1992-2001; Editor, Danish Bible Lexicon (Archaeology, geography and history), 1992-98. Memberships: National Advisory Group for the Minister of Education, 1986-90; Liaison Committee, Task Force for Quality Assessment under European Rectors' Conference, Brussels, 1992-97; Danish Society for the Study of the Bible (Collegium Biblicum), 1975, Chairman, 1998-2001. Address: Trondhjemsgade 5 II, DK-2100 Copenhagen Ø, Denmark. E-mail strange@teol.ku.dk

STRAUB Peter Francis, b. 2 March 1943, Milwaukee, Wisconsin, USA. Writer. m. 27 August 1966. Education: BA, University of Wisconsin, 1965; MA, Columbia University, 1966. Publications: Open Air (poems), 1972; Marriage, 1973; Julia, 1975; If You Could See Me New, 1977; Ghost Story, 1979; Shadowland, 1980; Floating Dragon, 1983; The Talisman (with Stephen King), 1984; Koko, 1988; Mystery, 1989; Houses Without Doors, 1990; The Throat, 1993; The Hellfire Club, 1996; Mr X, 1999; Magic Terror, 2000; Black House (with Stephen King), 2001; Lost Boy Lost Girl, 2003. Contributions to: Times Literary Supplement; New Statesman; Washington Post. Honours: British Fantasy Award, 1983; August Derleth Award , 1983; World Fantasy Best Novel Awards, 1988, 1993; Bram Stoker Award for Best Novel, 1993,

1998, 2000. Memberships: Mystery Writers of America; Horror Writers of America; PEN. Address: 53 West 85th Street, New York, NY 10024, USA.

STRAUER Bodo-Eckehard, b. 16 January 1943, Babelsberg, Germany. Physician; Professor of Medicine. m. Elisabeth, 2 sons, 1 daughter. Education: Medical Studies, Universities of Goettingen and Munich, 1961-66; Medical Examination 1966; Promotion MD, 1966; Assistant Professor of Medicine, 1974; Associate Professor of Medicine, 1980. Appointments: Chief Professor of Cardiology, University of Marburg, 1984; Chief and Professor of Cardiology, University of Duesseldorf, 1987-. Publication: Hypertensive Heart Disease, 1991. Honour: Frerichs Award, German Society of Internal Medicine. Memberships: Fellow, American College of Cardiology; Fellow, European Society of Cardiology; Fellow, Royal College of Physicians. Address: University Clinic of Duesseldorf, Mooren Street, 40225 Duesseldorf, Germany.

STRAUSS Botho, b. 2 December 1944, Naumberg-an-der-Saale, Germany. Author; Poet; Dramatist. Education: German Language and Literature, Drama, Sociology, Cologne and Munich. Publications: Bekannte Gesichter, gemischte Gefühle (with T Bernhard and F Kroetz), 1974; Trilogie des Wiedersehens, 1976; Gross und Klein, 1978; Rumor, 1980; Kalldeway Farce, 1981; Paare, Passanten, 1981; Der Park, 1983; Der junge Mann, 1984; Diese Erinnerung an einen, der nur einen Tag zu Gast War, 1985; Die Fremdenführerin, 1986; Niemand anderes, 1987; Besucher, 1988; Kongress: Die Kette der Demütigungen, 1989; Theaterstücke in zwei Banden, 1994; Wohnen Dammern Lügen, 1994. Honours: Dramatists' Prize, Hannover, 1975; Schiller Prize, Baden-Württemberg, 1977; Literary Prize, Bavarian Academy of Fine Arts, Munich, 1981; Jean Paul Prize, 1987; Georg Büchner Prize, 1989. Membership: PEN. Address: Keithstrasse 8, D-17877, Berlin, Germany.

STRAW Jack (John Whitaker Straw) (Rt Hon), b. 3 August 1946, Buckhurst Hill, Essex, England. Politician; Lawyer. m. (1) Anthea L Watson, 1968, divorced 1978, 1 daughter, deceased, (2) Alice E Perkins, 1978, 1 son, 1 daughter. Education: University of Leeds. Appointments: President, National Union of Students, 1969-71; Member, Islington Borough Council, 1971-78; Inner London Education Authority, 1971-74; Deputy Leader, 1973-74; Called to bar, Inner Temple, 1972; Bencher, 1997; Practised as Bar, 1972-74; Special Adviser to Secretary of State for Social Services, 1974-76; To Secretary of State for Environment, 1976-77; On Staff of Granada TV (World in Action), 1977-79; Member of Parliament for Blackburn, 1979-; Opposition Treasury Spokesman, 1980-83; Local Government Spokesman, 1982-87; Member of Parliament, Committee of Labour Party (Shadow Cabinet), 1987-97; Shadow Secretary of State for Education, 1987-92; For the Environment (Local Government), 1992-94; Shadow Home Secretary, 1994-97; Home Secretary, 1997-2001; Secretary of State for Foreign and Commonweath Affairs, 2001-; Member, Council Institute for Fiscal Studies, 1983-2000; Lancaster University, 1988-92; Vice President, Association of District Councils; Visiting Fellow, Nuffield College, Oxford, 1990-98; Governor, Blackburn College, 1990-; Pimlico School, 1994-2000 (Chair 1995-98); Fellow, Royal Statistics Society, 1995-; Labour; Hon LLD, 1999; Labour Publications: Contributions to pamphlets, newspaper articles, Policy and Ideology, 1993. Address: House of Commons, London, SW1A 0AA, England.

STRAWSON Peter (Frederick) (Sir), b. 23 November 1919, London, England. Retired Professor of Metaphysical Philosophy; Author. m. Grace Hall Martin, 1945, 2 sons, 2 daughters. Education: Christ's College, Finchley; St John's College, Oxford. Appointments: Assistant Lecturer in Philosophy, University College

of North Wales, 1946; John Locke Scholar, 1946, Reader, 1966-68, Waynflete Professor of Metaphysical Philosophy, 1968-87, University of Oxford; Lecturer in Philosophy, 1947, Fellow and Praelector, 1948, Fellow, 1948-68, Honorary Fellow, 1979-, University College, Oxford; Visiting Professor, Duke University, 1955-56; Fellow of the Humanities Council and Visiting Associate Professor, 1960-61, Visiting Professor, 1972, Princeton University; Fellow, 1968-87, Honorary Fellow, 1989, Magdelen College, Oxford; Woodbridge Lecturer, Columbia University, 1983; Immanuel Kant Lecturer, University of Munich, 1985; Visiting Professor, Collège de France, 1985. Publications: Introduction to Logical Theory, 1952; Individuals, 1959; The Bounds of Sense, 1966; Philosophical Logic (editor), 1966; Studies in the Philosophy of Thought and Action (editor), 1968; Logico-Linguistic Papers, 1971; Freedom and Resentment, 1974; Subject and Predicate in Logic and Grammar, 1974; Scepticism and Naturalism: Some Varieties, 1985; Analyse and Métaphysique, 1985, English translation as Analysis and Metaphysics, 1992; Entity and Identity, 1997. Contributions to: Scholarly journals. Honours: Knighted 1977; Honorary Doctorate, Munich, 1998. Memberships: Academia Europaea; American Academy of Arts and Sciences, honorary member; British Academy, fellow. Address: Magdalen College, Oxford, OX1 4AU, England.

STREEP Meryl (Mary Louise), b. 22 June 1949, Summit, New Jersey, USA. Actress. m. Donald Gummer, 1978, 1 son, 3 daughters. Education: Singing Studies with Estelle Liebling; Studied Drama, Vassar; Yale School of Drama. Appointments: Stage debut, New York, Trelawny of the Wells; 27 Wagons Full of Cotton, New York; New York Shakespeare Festival, 1976 in Henry V and Measure for Measure; Also in Happy End (musical); The Taming of the Shrew; Wonderland (musical); Taken in Marriage; Numerous other plays; Films include: Julia, 1976; The Deer Hunter, 1978; Manhattan, 1979; The Seduction of Joe Tynan, 1979; The Senator, 1979; Kramer vs Kramer, 1979; Still of the Night, 1982; Silkwood, 1983; Plenty, 1984; Falling in Love, 1984; Ironweed, 1987; A Cry in the Dark, 1988; The Lives and Loves of a She Devil, 1989; Hollywood and Me, 1989; Postcards from the Edge, 1991; Defending Your Life, 1991; Death Becomes Her, 1992; The House of the Spirits; The River Wild, 1994; The Bridges of Madison County, 1995; Before and After; Marvin's Room; One True Thing, 1998; Dancing at Lughnasa, 1999; Music of the Heart, 1999; The Hours, 2002; Adaptation, 2003; Many others; TV appearances include: The Deadliest Season; Uncommon Women; Holocaust; Velveteen Rabbit; First Do No Harm, 1997; Many others. Honours: Academy Award for Best Supporting Actress for Kramer vs Kramer, 1980; Best Supporting Actress Awards from National Society of Film Critics for the Deer Hunter; New York Film Critics Circle for Kramer vs Kramer, The Seduction of Joe Tynan and Sophie's Choice; Emmy Award for Holocaust; British Academy Award, 1982; Academy Award for Best Actress for Sophie's Choice, 1982; Hon Dr, Yale, 1983; Dartmouth, 1981; Lafayette, 1985; Bette Davis Lifetime Achievement Award, 1998; Special Award Berlin International Film Festival, 1999; Golden Globe for Best Supporting Actress, Adaptation, 2003. Address: c/o Creative Artists Agency, 9830 Wilshire Boulevard, Beverly Hills, CA 90212, USA.

STREET-PORTER Janet, b. 27 December 1946, England. Journalist; TV Presenter; Producer; Editor. m. (1) Tim Street-Porter, 1967, divorced 1975, (2) A M M Elliot, 1976, divorced 1978, (3) Frank Cvitanovich, divorced 1988, deceased 1995, (4) David Sorkin, 1996, divorced. Education: Architectural Association. Career: Petticoat Magazine Fashion Writer and Columnist, 1968; Daily Mail, 1969-71; Evening Standard, 1971-73; Own Show, LBC Radio Programme, 1973; Presenter, London Weekend Show, London Weekend Television (LWT), 1975; Producer, presenter,

Dictionary of International Biography

Saturday Night People (with Clive James and Russell Harty), The Six O'Clock Show (with Michael Aspel), Around Midnight, 1975-85; Network 7 and 4, 1986-87; BBC Youth and Entertainment Features Head, 1988-94; Head, Industry Production for Entertainment, 1994; Mirror Group plc, 1994-95; TV Presenter, Design Awards, Travels with Pevsner, Coast to Coast, The Midnight Hour, 1996-98, As the Crow Flies (series), 1999; Cathedral Calls, 2000; J'Accuse, Internet 1996; Editor, The Independent on Sunday, 1999-2001; Editor-at-Large, 2001-. Publications: Scandal, 1980; The British Teapot, 1981; Coast to Coast, 1998; As the Crow Flies, 1999. Honours: Italia for the Vampyr, 1992; BAFTA award for originality for Network 7, 1998. Memberships: Ramblers' Association, Vice President; Globetrotters Club, 2003-. Address: c/o Bob Storer, Harbottle & Lewis, 14 Hanover Square, London W1R 0BE, England.

STREETEN Paul Patrick, b. 18 July 1917, Vienna, Austria. Retired Professor. m. Ann H Higgins, 9 June 1951, 1 stepson, 2 daughters. Education: MA, University of Aberdeen, 1944; BA, 1947 MA, 1952, Oxon; DLitt, 1976. Appointment: Chairman of the Board of World Development, 1972-2003. Publications: Economic Integration, 1961, 2nd edition, 1964; Frontiers of Development Studies, 1972; Development Perspectives, 1981; First Things First, 1981; What Price Food?, 1987; Mobilizing Human Potential, 1989; Thinking About Development, 1995, paperback, 1997. Contributions to: Magazines, journals and books. Honours: Honorary Fellow, Institute of Development Studies, 1980; Honorary Fellow, Balliol College, 1986; Essays in Honour of Paul Streeten: Theory and Reality in Development, (edited by Sanjaya Lall and Frances Stewart), 1986; Development Prize, Justus Liebig University, 1987; Honorary LLD, University of Aberdeen, 1988; Honorary DLitt, University of Malta, 1992; Silver Sign of Honour for Services to the Land of Vienna; Wassily Leontief Award, Tufts University. Memberships: Royal Economic Society; American Economic Association; Society for International Development Address: Box 92, Spencertown, NY 12165, USA.

STREISAND Barbra Joan, b. 24 April 1942, Brooklyn, New York, USA. Singer; Actress; Director; Producer; Writer; Composer; Philanthropist. m. (1) Elliott Gould, 1963, divorced 1971, 1 son, (2) James Brolin, 1998. Education: Erasmus Hall High School. Career: Began recording career with Columbia records, 1963; Appeared in musical play Funny Girl, New York, 1964, London, 1966; TV programme My Name is Barbra shown in England, Holland, Australia, Sweden, Bermuda and the Philippines; Films: Funny Girl, 1968; Hello Dolly, 1969; On a Clear Day You Can See Forever, 1969; The Owl and the Pussycat, 1971; What's Up Doc?, 1972; Up the Sandbox, 1973; The Way We Were, 1973; For Pete's Sake, 1974; Funny Lady, 1975; A Star is Born, 1977; The Main Event, 1979; All Night Long, 1981; Yentl, 1934; Nuts, 1987; Sing 1989; The Prince of Tides, 1990; The Mirror Has Two Faces, 1996; Numerous albums, singles, TV and concert appearances. Honours: New York Critics Best Supporting Actress Award, 1962; Grammy Awards for Best Female Pop Vocalist, 1963, 64, 65, 77, 86; GB Variety Poll Award, Best For Actress, 1966; Golden Globe Academy Award, 1968; Special Tony Award, 1970; Golden Globe, Best Picture, Best Director, 1984; 5 Emmy Awards; Peabody Award; 3 Cable Ace Awards; 37 Gold and 21 Platinum Albums. Address: c/o Jeff Berg, ICM, 8942 Wilshire Boulevard, Beverly Hills, CA 90211, USA.

STRELNIKER Yakov M, b. 23 May 1956, Hnivan, Vinnitsa Region, USSR. Physicist; Researcher. Education: MSc, Perm University, USSR, 1978; PhD, 1989. Appointments: Senior Research Scientist, Vinnitsa Medical University, 1987-90; Postdoctoral Research Associate, Tel Aviv University, 1991-94; Research Scientist, 1994-2000; Gileadi Fellow, 1996-2000; Senior

Research Scientist, KAMEA programme, Bar-Ilan University, 2000-. Publications: Many publications. Memberships: Israel Physical Society. Address: Minerva Centre and Department of Physics, Bar-Ilan University, Ramat-Gan 52900, Israel.

STROJNIK Marija, b. 13 July 1950, Ljubljana, Slovenia. Scientist. 3 daughters. Education: BS, Physics, 1972; MS, Physics, 1974; MS, Optical Sciences, 1977; PhD, Optical Sciences, 1979; MS, Engineering, 1981. Appointments: Manager, Optics Technology, Rockwell International, 1978-81; Staff Scientist, Honeywell Technology Center, 1981-87; Senior Optical Scientist, California Institute of Technology, 1987-93; Professor, Centro de Inv en Optica, Mexico, 1994-. Honours: Fellow, International Society for Optical Engineering, 1994; Infrared Physics and Technology Editorial Board, 1994-; George W Goddard Award, SPIE, 1996. Memberships: Fellow, Optical Society of America, 1999; Fellow, International Society for Optical Engineering, 1994; Member, Sigma Xi; Member, AAAS. Address: Centro de Inv en Optica, Apdo Postal 1-948, CP 37000 Leon, Mexico.

STRONG Roy (Colin) (Sir), b. 23 August 1935, London, England. Art Historian; Writer; Lecturer. m. Julia Trevelyan Oman. Education: Queen Mary College, London; Warburg Institute, London. Appointments: Assistant Keeper, 1959, Director, Keeper and Secretary, 1967-73, National Portrait Gallery, London; Ferens Professor of Fine Art, University of Hull, 1972; Walls Lecturer, J Pierpoint Morgan Library, New York, 1974; Director, Victoria and Albert Museum, London, 1974-87; Director, Oman Publications Ltd; Andrew Carnduff Ritchie Lecturer, University of Yale, 1999. Publications: Portraits of Queen Elizabeth I, 1963; Holbein and Henry the VIII, 1967; The English Icon: Elizabethan and Jacobean Portraiture, 1969; Tudor and Jacobean Portraits, 1969; Van Dyck: Charles I on Horseback, 1972; Splendour at Court: Renaissance Spectacle and the Theatre of Power, 1973; Nicholas Hilliard, 1975; The Renaissance Garden in England, 1979; Britannia Triumphans: Inigo Jones, Rubens and Whitehall Palace, 1980; Henry, Prince of Wales and England's Lost Renaissance, 1986; Creating Small Gardens, 1986; Gloriana: Portraits of Queen Elizabeth I, 1987; A Small Garden Designer's Handbook, 1987; Cecil Beaton: The Royal Portraits, 1988; Creating Small Formal Gardens, 1989; Lost Treasures of Britain, 1990; A Celebration of Gardens (editor), 1991; The Garden Trellis, 1991; Small Period Gardens, 1992; Royal Gardens, 1992; A Country Life, 1994; Successful Small Gardens, 1994; William Larkin: Vanitù giacobite, Italy, 1994; The Tudor and Stuart Monarchy, 2 volumes, 1994-95; The English Vision: Country Life 1897-1997; The Story of Britain, 1996; The Tudor and Stuart Monarchy, 3 volumes, 1995-97; The Story of Britain, 1996; The English Vision: Country Life 1897-1997, 1997; The Roy Strong Diaries 1967-1987, 1997; The Spirit of Britain. A Narrative History of the Arts, 1999; Garden Party, 2000; The Artist and the Garden, 2000; Ornament in the Small Garden, 2001; Feast – A History of Grand Eating, 2002; The Laskett – The Story of a Garden, 2003. Co-Author: Leicester's Triumph, 1964; Elizabeth R, 1971; Mary Queen of Scots, 1972; Inigo Jones: The Theatre of the Stuart Court, 1973; An Early Victorian Album: The Hill-Adamson Collection, 1974; The English Miniature, 1981; The English Year, 1982; Artists of the Tudor Court, 1983. Memberships: Fellow, Queen Mary College, 1976; Knighted, 1982; Senior Fellow, Royal College of Arts, 1983; Fellow, Royal Society of Literature, 1999; High Bailiff and Searcher of the Sanctuary of Westminster Abbey, 2000; Honorary doctorates: Leeds 1983; Keele, 1984. Memberships: Arts Council of Great Britain, chairman, arts panel, 1983-87; British Council, Fine Arts Advisory Committee, 1974-87; Royal College of Arts Council, 1979-87; Westminster Abbey Architectural Panel, 1975-89; President, Garden History Society, 2000-. Address: The Laskett, Much Birch, Herefordshire HR2 8HZ, England.

Dictionary of International Biography

STRONG-BOAG Veronica Jane, b. 1947, Prestwick, Scotland. Historian. 3 sons. Education: BA (Hons), Toronto, Canada, 1970; MA, Carleton, 1971; PhD, Toronto, 1975. Appointments: Assistant Professor of History, Trent University, Ontario, Canada, 1974-76; Assistant Professor of History, Concordia University, Quebec, Canada, 1976-80; Professor, History and Women's Studies, Simon Fraser University, British Columbia, Canada, 1980-90; Director, Centre for Women's Studies and Gender Relations, 1990-96, Professor, Women's Studies and Educational Studies, 1997-, University of British Columbia, Canada. Publications: Books include: The New Day Recalled. Lives of Girls and Women in English Canada 1919-39, 1988; Rethinking Canada. The Promise of Women's History, 1986, 1992, 1997, 2000; Paddling Her Own Canoe. The Times and Texts of E Pauline Johnson Tekahionwake, 2000. Honours: President, Canadian Historical Association, 1994; Fellow, Royal Society of Canada, 2000-. Memberships: Canadian Women's Studies Association; Canadian Historical Association. Address: Centre for Research in Women's Studies and Gender Relations, University of British Columbia, Vancouver, Canada V6T 1Z1. E-mail: veronica.strong-boag@ubc.ca

STRYDOM Irene, b. 9 November 1956, Cape Town, South Africa. Psychologist; Lecturer. widow, 1 son, 3 daughters. Education: Diploma Remedial Education; Initial B Prim Ed Degree; 2 Master's Degrees; D Ed, 1995. Appointments: Lecturer, 1986-2004; Psychologist developing a new spontaneous healing therapeutic treatment model in children, 2000-; Board Member of the SHIP® Foundation. Publications: National lectures and publications on spontaneous healing in children; Trademarked SHIPIC™, Spontaneous Healing Intrasystemic Process in Children. Honours: 2 awards for further doctoral studies. Memberships: Psychological Society of South Africa; Member, SHIP® (Spontaneous healing intrasystemic process) Foundation. Address: Department of Educational Studies, AJH 6-110, UNISA, PO Box 392, Pretoria 0003, South Africa. E-mail: irenes@mweb.co.za

STUART Jessica Jane, b. 20 August 1942, Ashland, Kentucky, USA. Retired; Teacher; Poet; Writer. Divorced, 2 sons. Education: AB, Western Reserve University, Cleveland, Ohio, 1964; MA, 1967, MA, 1969, PhD, 1971, Indiana University, Bloomington, Indiana. Appointments: Teaching, University of Florida, 1986-88; Santa Fe Community College, Gainesville, Florida, 1986-88; Flagler College and St Johns River Community College, St Augustine, Florida, 1989-90. Publications: Eyes of the Mole, 1968; White Barn, 1971; A Year's Harvest, 1956; Transparencies (with prose), 1986; Novels: Yellowhank, 1973; Passerman's Hollow, 1974; Land of the Fox, 1975; A Peaceful Evening Wind, 2002; Short stories: Gideon's Children, 1976; Chapbooks: Finding Tents, 2002; Celestial Moon, 2003; Spanish Moss, 2003; Mardi Gras, 2004. Honours: Grand Prix, KSPS Kentucky State Poetry Society, 1993; Cameo Chapbook Contest Award (Poetry), 1998; State Poetry Contests Award; Mississippi Poetry Society First Place, 2002. Memberships: MPS (Mississippi); OSPS (Oregon). Address: 1000 W-Hollow Road, Greenup, KY 41144, USA.

STUBBS Imogen Mary, b. 20 February 1961, Rothbury, England. Actress. m. Trevor Nunn, 1994, 1 son, 1 daughter. Education: Exeter College, Oxford; Royal Academy of Dramatic Arts. Appointments: Appeared with RSC in The Rover; Two Noble Kinsmen; Richard II, 1987-88; Othello, 1991; Heartbreak House, 1992; St Joan, 1994; Twelfth Night, 1996; Blast from the Past, 1998; Betrayal, 1998; The Relapse, 2001; TV appearances include: The Rainbow; Anna Lee; After the Dance; Films include: Nanou; A Summer Story; Erik the Viking; True Colours; A Pin for the Butterfly; Fellow Traveller; Sandra c'est la vie; Jack and Sarah;

Sense and Sensibility, 1995; Twelfth Night, 1996. Honours: Gold Medal, Chicago Film Festival. Address: c/o Michael Foster, ICM, Oxford House, 76 Oxford Street, London, W1N 0AX, England.

STUBBS Jean, b. 23 October 1926, Denton, Lancashire, England. Author. m.(1) Peter Stubbs, 1 May 1948, 1 son, 1 daughter, (2) Roy Oliver, 5 August, 1980. Education: Manchester School of Art, 1944-47; Diploma, Loreburn Secretarial College, Manchester, 1947. Appointments: Copywriter, Henry Melland, 1964-66; Reviewer, Books and Bookmen, 1965-76; Writer-in-Residence for Avon, 1984. Publications: The Rose Grower, 1962; The Travellers, 1963; Hanrahan's Colony, 1964; The Straw Crown, 1966; My Grand Enemy, 1967; The Passing Star, 1970; The Case of Kitty Ogilvie, 1970; An Unknown Welshman, 1972; Dear Laura, 1973; The Painted Face, 1974; The Golden Crucible, 1976; Kit's Hill, 1979; The Ironmaster, 1981; The Vivian Inheritance, 1982; The Northern Correspondent, 1984; 100 Years Around the Lizard, 1985; Great Houses of Cornwall, 1987; A Lasting Spring, 1987; Like We Used To Be, 1989; Summer Secrets, 1990; Kelly Park, 1992; Charades, 1994; The Witching Time, 1998. Contributions to: Anthologies and magazines. Honours: Tom Gallon Trust Award, 1964; Daughter of Mark Twain, 1973. Memberships: PEN; Society of Women Writers and Journalists; Detection Club; Lancashire Writers Association; West Country Writers; Society of Authors. Address: Trewin, Nancegollan, Helston, Cornwall TR13 0AJ, England.

STUDER Gerald C, b. 31 January 1927, Smithville, Ohio, USA. Christian Minister. m. Marilyn Ruth Kreider, 2 daughters. Education: BA, Goshen College, 1947; ThB, Goshen Biblical Seminary, 1949; BD GBS, 1957, MDiv, GBS, 1971. Appointments: Pastor, Smithville (Ohio) Mennonite Church, 1947-61; Scottdale (PA) Mennonite Church, 1961-73; Plains Mennonite Church, Lansdale, Pennsylvania, 1973-90; Conference Minister, Atlantic Coast Mennonite Conference, 1990-94. Publications: Numerous articles in magazines; Books: Christopher Dock: Colonial Schoolmaster, 1967; After Death, What?, 1976. Memberships: First President of the North American Mennonite Youth Fellowship, 1947-50; Mennonite Publication Board, 1956-59, 1965-68, 1993-01; General Mennonite Board, 1971-73; Mennonite Historical and Research Committee, 1960-71; International Society of Bible Collectors, 1965-, President, 1988-2002. Address: 1260 Orchard Lane, Lansdale, PA 19446, USA.

STULTING Andries Andriessen, b. 29 August 1948, Cape Town, South Africa. Ophthalmologist. m. Lemainé, 2 daughters. Education: MB ChB (Pret), 1973; MMed (Ophth) (Pret), 1981; FRCOphth, 1989; FCS (SA) (Ophth), 1993; FACS, 1995; FICS, 1996. Appointments: Professor and Chairman, Department of Ophthalmology, Faculty of Health Sciences, University of the Free State, South Africa, 1982-. Publications: 300 presentations at congresses; 50 articles. Honours: President, Ophthalmological Society of South Africa, 1989-91, 1997-99; President, Free State Branch, South African Medical Association, 1995, 2001, 2003; Best Clinical Lecturer at the Faculty of Medicine, University of the Orange Free State, 1982, 1985, 1989, 1991, 1993, 1996; Frik Scott Memorial Lecturer, 1989; D J Wood Memorial Lecturer, 1993; Bloemfonteiner of the Year, 1996; Vice-President, The Colleges of Medicine of South Africa, 1998-; Seven Star Merit Award, National Council of the Blind, 1999; President, College of Ophthalmologists, 2000-; Eddy Epstein Lecturer, 2001; Giel Kritzinger Safari Award Lecturer, 2001; Hennie Meyer Lecturer, 2001. Memberships: Vice Chairperson, South African Medical Association; Health Professions Council; Medical and Dental Professions Board; Past President, Honorary Secretary, Ophthalmological Society of South Africa; American Academy of Ophthalmology; Fellow, Royal College of Ophthalmologists;

Dictionary of International Biography

International Intraocular Implant Club; Southern African Cataract and Refractive Society; Past President, Vitreoretinal Association. Address: 50 Gascony Crescent, Bayswater, Bloemfontein 9301, Republic of South Africa. E-mail: stulting@doh.ofs.gov.za

STUMMER Peter Olaf, b. 1 June 1942, Jauernig, Czech Republic. Senior Lecturer. m. Anne Stummer-Schwegmann. Education: English, Romance Philology, Philosophy, 1961-66; Teacher's Diploma, 1966; PhD, 1969; 2nd Teacher's Diploma, 1970. Appointments: Tutor Students' Hall of Residence, 1965-70; Tutor, English Department, Munich, 1967-69; Secondary School Teacher and University Lectureship, 1979-71; Assistant Professor, University of Cologne, 1971-74; Assistant Professor, 1974-78, Lecturer (tenured), 1978-, Senior Lecturer, Literatures Written in English, 1980-, University of Munich. Publications: Author and editor of several books; Author of over 30 articles on various aspects of diverse literatures written in English, especially from Africa, India and Australia; Conference Convenor; Originator of Postgraduate Programme on English Speaking Countries. Honours: German Studies Association, University of Aberdeen; Visiting Professor, University of Trento; Lectureship, University of Passau. Memberships: One-time Vice President, ASNEL; EACLALS; ACLALS; EASA; ASAL; BASA; German Association for Australian Studies. Address: Edelweiss-strasse 115, D-82178 Puchheim, Germany. E-mail: peter.stummer@lmu.de

STURT Richard Harry Brooke, b. 14 November 1939, Bath, England. Solicitor. m. Ann, 4 sons. Education: BA, 1961, MA, 1964, Peterhouse, Cambridge, England. Appointments: Solicitor, Dover Harbour Board, 1979-2001; Senior Partner, Mowll and Mowll, 1984-2001; Her Majesty's Coroner for East Kent, 1979-2001, conducted inquests into: Capsize of the Herald of Free Enterprise, Deal Bombing, M2 Coach Crash; investigated deaths of 58 Chinese immigrants at Dover, 1979-2001; Chairman, Invicta Sound plc, 1984-91; Board Member, Civil Aviation Authority, 1990-96; Chairman AIRPROX Review, 1997-98; Lecturer, Bramshill Police Staff College, 1990-97; Chairman of the Governors, Northbourne Park School; Chairman of the Trustees, East Kent Holiday Music Trust; Governor, Canterbury Christ Church University College and The King's School Canterbury; Director, East Kent Hospitals NHS Trust; Director, Canterbury Theatre and Festival Trust; Member, Ofwat WaterVoice National Council; Chairman, Ofwat WaterVoice Southern Customer Committee; Registrar, Diocese of Canterbury and Legal Secretary to the Bishop in Canterbury. Publications: Fishery Prosecution and Foreign Fishing Boats, 1973; Halsbury's Laws of England, 4th edition, Fisheries; Halsbury's Laws of England, 4th edition, Ports and Harbours; Halsbury's Laws of England, 4th edition, European Fisheries; Vaughan on European Law, Title, Fisheries; The Collision Regulations, 1979, 1983, 1990; The Role of the Coroner in Major Disasters, 1988. Honour: Honorary DCL, University of Kent, 2001. Memberships: Honorary Senior Member, Rutherford College, University of Kent; Fellow, Royal Society of Arts, Manufactures and Commerce; Member Athenaeum Club; Flyfishers' Club; Marylebone Cricket Club; Kent County Cricket Club. Address: Kent Cottage, 7 Granville Road, Walmer, Deal, Kent CT14 7LU, England. E-mail: richard.sturt@mowll.co.uk

SU Xiao-Ping Susan, b. 27 April 1970, China. Scientist. m. Henry S Yang, 2 daughters. Education: BSc, Tsinghua University, China, 1991; MSc, Mechanical Engineering, University of California, Davis, 1996; PhD, Mechanical Engineering, University of California, Berkeley. Appointments: Graduate Researcher, Integrated Engineering Laboratory, Department of Mechanical and Aeronautical Engineering, UC Davis, 1994-96; Graduate Researcher, Berkeley Sensor and Actuator Center, UC Berkeley, 1996-98; Graduate Researcher, Microscale Heat Transfer Laboratory Engineering Department, UC Berkeley, 1998-99; Researcher, Building Technologies Department, Energy Environmental Technology Division, Lawrence Berkeley National Laboratory, 1999-. Publications: Analysis of Diametral Strain in Uniaxial Tensile and Compression Testing of Anisotropic Materials; Design of Microleverage Mechanism. Honours: National Science Foundation Graduate Research Fellowship; American Association of University Women Selected Professional Fellowship; International Cultural Diploma of Honour. Memberships: American Association of University Women; American Society of University Women. Address: MS 2-300 Lawrence Berkeley National Laboratory, One Cyclotron Road, Berkeley, CA 94720, USA.

SUCHET David Courtney, b. 2 May 1946, London, England. Actor. m. Sheila Ferris, June 1976, 1 son, 1 daughter. Appointments: Former Member, National Youth Theatre, Chester Repertory Company; RSC, 1973, Associate Artist. Creative Works: Roles includes: Tybalt in Romeo and Juliet, 1973, Orlando in As You Like It, 1973, Tranio in Taming of the Shrew, 1973, Zamislov in Summerfolk, 1974, 1975, Wilmer in Comrades, 1974, The Fool in King Lear, 1974, 1975, Pisanio in Cymbeline, 1974, Hubert in King John, Ferdinand King of Navarre in Love's Labour's Lost, 1975, Shylock in The Merchant of Venice, 1978, Gruio in Taming of the Shrew, 1978, Sir Nathaniel in Love's Labour's Lost, 1978, Glougauer in Once in a Lifetime, 1978, Caliban in The Tempest, 1978, Shylock in The Merchant of Venice, 1978, Sextus Pompey in Antony and Cleopatra, 1978, Angelo in Measure for Measure, 1979; Oleanna, 1993; What a Performance, 1994; Who's Afraid of Virginia Woolf?, 1997; Saturday, Sunday and Monday, 1998; Amadeus, 1998-2000. Films include: Big Foot & The Hendersons, 1986; Crime of Honour, 1987; The Last Innocent Man, 1987; A World Apart, 1988; To Kill a Priest (also known as Popielusko), 1988; The Lucona Affair, When the Whales Came, 1990; Executive Decision, 1995; Deadly Voyage, 1995; Sunday, 1996; A Perfect Murder, 1998; Wing Commander, 1998; RKO, 1999; Sabotage, 1999; Live From Baghdad, 2002; The Wedding Party, 2002; Foolproof, 2002; Numerous TV appearances including: Master of the Game, 1984; Reilly – Ace of Spies, 1984; Mussolini: The Untold Story, 1985; The Life of Agatha Christie, 1990; Hercule Poirot in Agatha Christie's Poirot, 7 Series including 100th Anniversary Special: The Mysterious Affair at Styles, 1990; Days of Majesty, 1994; The Cruel Train, Moses, 1995; Solomon, 1997; Seesaw, 1997; The Way We Live Now, 2001; National Crime Squad, 2001-02; Maggie, 2003; Several radio drama roles, audio recordings and voice overs. Publications: Author of essays in Players of Shakespeare, 1985. Honours: Brown Belt in Aikido; 1st Master of Japanese Samurai; Best Radio Actor of the Year for The Kreutzer Sonata (one-man show), 1979; Best Actor for Beria in Red Monarch, Marseilles Film Festival, 1983; Best Actor for Stress, British Industry/Science Film Association, 1986; Best Actor for Song for Europe, Freud, Blott on the Landscape, Royal TV Society Performance Awards, 1986; Best Actor, Variety Club Award for John in Oleanna and Salieri in Amadeus, 1998; 1994; Several BAFTA, SWET, Oliver and other nominations; Critics' Circle Award for Best Actor as George in Who's Afraid of Virginia Woolf?, 1997; Best Actor for Salieri in Amadeus, Backstage Theatre Award, LA, 2000; Best Actor for Melmotte in The Way We live Now, TV, Radio and Industry, Royal Television Society, Broadcasting Press Guild, 2002. Memberships: Fight Dirs Association; Garrick Club, London; St James's Club, London. Address: c/o Ken McReddie, 91 Regent Street, London W1R 7TB, England.

SUDDABY Arthur, b. 26 February 1919, Hull, East Yorkshire, England. Retired Polytechnic Director; Retired Scientific Consultant; Author. m. Elizabeth Bullin Vyse, 1944, deceased 1965,

2 sons. Education: BSc in Chemistry, Hull Technical College; BSc in Mathematics, MSc in Mathematical Physics, Chelsea College, London; PhD in Theoretical Physics, Queen Mary College, London; Professional Qualifications, CChem, FRSC, CEng MIChemE. Appointments: Organic chemist and biochemist in various industrial posts in pharmaceuticals, solvent manufacture, edible oil refining and research on therapeutic drug intermediates, 1937-47; Lecturer in Physical Chemistry and Chemical Engineering, West Ham College of Technology, 1947-50; Senior Lecturer in Physics, 1950-61, Head, Department of Physics, 1961-66, Principal, 1966-70, Sir John Cass College, London; Provost of the City of London Polytechnic, now London Metropolitan University, 1970-81; Retired, 1981-; Scientific Consultant on the carriage of goods by sea, 1981-90. Publications: Scientific research and review papers in various scientific journals; Contributions on educational matters; Articles in the press on educational matters. Honour: CBE, 1980. Memberships: Member, Education Committee of the Institute of Chemical Engineers, 1948-51; Member, various CNAA committees, 1969-81; Member, London and Home Counties Regional Advisory Council on Higher Education, 1971-81; Member, Court of the City University, 1967-81; Member, Oakes Committee on Management of Public Sector Higher Education, 1977-78; Member, Visiting Committee, Cranfield Institute of Technology; Chairman, Committee of Directors of Polytechnics, 1976-78; Chairman, Association of Navigation Schools, 1972; Member, Athenaeum. Address: Castle Hill House, Godshill Wood, Fordingbridge, Hampshire, SP6 2LU, England.

SUDMEYER Alice Jean, b. 17 February 1946, Goldbeach, Oregon, USA. Retired Soldier; Full Time Artist and Poet. m. Larry Everett Sudmeyer, 1 son, 1 daughter. Education: Florida Junior College, Jacksonville, Florida, USA, 1973-76; AA Degrees, Mt Hood Community College, Gresham, Oregon, USA, 1974-77; University of New Mexico, Albuquerque, New Mexico, USA, 1981-82. Career: US Women's Army Corps, White Sands Missile Range, New Mexico, 1967-70; Homemaker, 1970-88; US Army Reserve, College Student, 1975-95; Served in Operation Desert Storm Combat, Persian Gulf, 1991; Full Time Artist, Poet, Photographer, Owner of Studio/Gallery, Fredericktown, Missouri, USA, 1995-. Publications: Self-published limited editions: Soul Search, 1987-91; Winter Chill, 1988; Silent Struggle, 1989; Soul's Child, 1991, 2003; Into the Ordinary, 2001; Others: Questions Book Veterans Voices vol 48 No 1, 2000; A Thoughtful Invitation, 2001. Honours: Numerous varied artist's awards; Army Commendation Medal with oak leaf; Liberation of Kuwait Medal, Arab Government; Southwest Asia Medal; Army Achievement Medal with 2 oak leaves; Expert Rifle Badge. Memberships: Poplar Bluff Artists Guild, Poplar Bluff, Missouri; Past Administrative Director, Arts OK! An art group of muralists, San Diego, California; Life Member, Veterans of Foreign Wars; Life Member, Disabled American Veterans; Life Member, American Legion. Address: 715 South Wood Avenue, Fredericktown, MO 63645-7923, USA. E-mail: 2suds4u7074@sbcglobal.net

SUEIRO RODRIGUEZ Victoria Maria, b. 16 May 1959, Cienfuegos, Cuba. Professor. 1 son. Education: MA Philology; Doctor in Historical Sciences; Graduated in Russian Languages; Graduated in Scientific and Technical Information and Bibliotechnology. Appointments: Doctor in Historical Science, University of Havana. Publications: 12 articles in professional journals. Honours: National Reward, Bicentenary of Simon Bolivar's Birth, 1983; National Reward, XX Seminary of Marti's Studies, 1992; Friend of the Library Distinction, 1993; Collective Reward, 1st version of the Cienfuegos Local Story, Sciences Academy of Cuba; National Reward, Red Majagua Contest of Reference Works, 1996; Best Result of Research on Social Science,

Cienfuegos Sciences Academy, 1996; Greatest Relevancy in Social Sciences, Rector of Cienfuegos University, 1996; National Vanguard, Science Trade Union, 1996; Honorary Client Distinction, Cienfuegos Provincial Library, 2000. Memberships: Union of Cuban Historians; Spanish Association of Literary Spanish American Studies; Spanish Association for the Study of Exiles and Iberian Contemporary Migrations; Caribbean Studies Association; Centre of Investigation studies about Iberian Migrations; Center of Senderianos Studies, Institute of Altoaragoneses Studies. E-mail: aemic@iponet.es

SUGA Kazuhiko, b. 11 October 1959, Aichi, Japan. Researcher; Mechanical Engineer. m. Yoko Kanazawa, 1 son, 1 daughter. Education: BSc, Mechanical Engineering, 1983, MSc, Mechanical Engineering, 1985, Kyoto University, Japan; PhD, Mechanical Engineering, UMIST, England, 1996. Appointments: Senior Researcher, Toyota Central R&D Laboratories, 1985-; Part-time Lecturer, Kyoto University, 2002; Part-time Lecturer, Osaka Prefecture University, 2003-. Publications: Scientific papers in journals on turbulence, heat transfer, fluids engineering and mechanical engineering. Honours: Award, Japan Society of Mechanical Engineers Tokai Branch for Outstanding Research, 1999; Japan Society of Mechanical Engineers Thermal Engineering Contribution Award, 1999. Memberships: Japan Society of Mechanical Engineers; Heat Transfer Society, Japan; Ilass Europe; Academic Alpine Club of Kyoto. Address: Spray and Combustion Laboratory, Toyota Central R&D Laboratories, 41-1, Yokomichi, Nagakute Aichi, Japan. E-mail: k-suga@mosk.tytlabs.co.jp

SUGISHITA Morihiro, b. 6 March 1943, Tokyo, Japan. Psychologist; Neuroscientist. m. Chieko Mori, 2 sons. Education: BA, Psychology, 1968, MA, Psychology, 1970, Waseda University, Tokyo, Japan; Doctor of Health Science, 1973, Doctor of Medical Science, 1981, University of Tokyo, Japan. Appointments: Research Associate, Department of Neurology, University of Tokyo, 1978-81; Director, Department of Rehabilitation, Tokyo Metropolitan Institute for Neuroscience, 1981-93; Professor, Department of Cognitive Neuroscience, Graduate School and Faculty of Medicine, University of Tokyo, 1993-2003; Professor, Department of Clinical Psychology, Graduate School, Tokyo University of Social Sciences, 2003-2004. Publications: Articles in scientific journals include: Electropalatographic analysis of apraxia of speech in a left hander and in a right hander, 1987; A critical appraisal of neuropsychological correlates of Japanese ideogram (Kanji) and phonogram (Kana) reading, 1992; Dichotic listening in patients with partial section of the corpus callosum, 1995; Functional magnetic resonance imaging (FMRI) during mental writing with phonograms, 1996; Learning Chinese characters may improve visual recall, 2001. Memberships: Japanese Society of Cognitive Neuroscience; Neurophysiology Association of Japan. Address: 1-8-6 Nishiazabu, Minato-ku, Tokyo, Japan 106-0032. E-mail: morihiro_sugi@ybb.ne.jp

SUGIURA Takeyuki, b. 20 October 1960, Kaizuka, Osaka, Japan. Pharmacist; Researcher; Research Manager. Education: BS, 1979-83, MS, 1983-85, PhD, Faculty of Pharmaceutical Science, 1992, University of Tokyo; Visiting Scientist, Molecular Biology Department, Harvard Medical School, Massachusetts General Hospital, 1994-96. Appointments: Research Scientist, Banyu Pharmaceutical, 1985-86; Project Leader, Hoechst Japan, 1987-98; Senior Research Scientist, Daiichi Pharmaceutical, 1999-. Publications: Articles in scientific journals including: Biotechnical Letters, 1990; Cytotechnology, 1991; Journal of Biotechnology, 1992, 2003; Biotechnology Bioengineering, 1992, 1996; Protein Expression and Purification, 1995; Enzyme and Microbial Technology, 1998; Biochemical Journal, 1999; Biochemical and Biophysical Research Communications, 1999; Bone, 2001.

Dictionary of International Biography

Address: Daiichi Pharmaceutical Co Ltd, 16-13 Kitakasai 1-chome, Edogawa-ku, Tokyo 134-8630, Japan. E-mail: sugiuy79@daiichipharm.co.jp

SUH Dong Jin, b. 12 June 1958, Taegu, Korea. Chemical Engineer. m. Sun-Ae Kim, 2 daughters. Education: BS, Seoul National University, 1982; MS, 1984, PhD, 1991, Korea Advanced Institute of Science and Technology. Appointments: Research Engineer, Senior Research Engineer, Principal Research Engineer, Korea Institute of Science and Technology, 1984-; Visiting Research Scholar, Carnegie Mellon University, 1992-93; Research Fellow, University of Tokyo, 1995-96; Visiting Research Scholar, University of Notre Dame, 2003-04. Publications: 30 articles in professional journals. Memberships: AIChE; KIChE. Address: Korea Institute of Science and Technology, PO Box 131, Cheongyang 136 791, Seoul, Korea.

SUH Ok-Shik, b. 13 May 1944, Kwangyang, Republic of Korea. Special Advisor for Political Party; Research Fellow; Editor. m. Kyung-Ja Lee, 1 son, 1 daughter. Education: BA, Seoul National University, 1973; Master of Political Science, 2002, PhD Candidate, 2003, Kyonggi University. Appointments: Foreign News Editor, 1993-94, Correspondent in Bangkok, 1994-97, Acting Director and North Korea Editor, 1997-98, Managing Editor, 1998-2000, Senior Editor, 2000, Senior News Analysis Editor, 2001-2002, Deputy Executive Director, 2002, Yonhap News Agency; Policy Advisor, Advisory Council on Democratic and Peaceful Unification, 1999-2001; Editor, Seoul National University Alumni News, 1999-; Special Advisor, HANARO National Union, 2002-; Visiting Research Fellow, Institute for Far Eastern Studies, Kyungnam University, 2003-. Publication: A Comparative Study on the Unification Policies and Formulas of South and North Korea (research thesis), 2002. Honour: First Prize for Academic Achievement, Kyonggi University, 2003. Membership: Korea News Editors' Association, Executive Committeeman, 1999-2000. Address: 115-1101 Useong Apartment 615, Ilwong-dong, Kangnam-ku, Seoul 135-946, Korea.

SULEIMAN Michael Wadie, b. 26 February 1934, Tiberias, Palestine. University Professor. m. Penelope Ann Powers, 1 son, 1 daughter. Education: BA, Bradley University, 1960; MSc, 1962, PhD, 1965, University of Wisconsin-Madison, Wisconsin. Appointments: Assistant Professor, 1965-68, Associate Professor, 1968-72, Professor, 1972-90, University Distinguished Professor, 1990-, Kansas State University. Publications: Books, monographs and edited works include: Political Parties in Lebanon: The Challenge of a Fragmented Political Culture, 1967; American Images of Middle East Peoples: Impact of the High School, 1977; The Arabs in the Mind of America, 1988; Arab Americans: Continuity and Change (Co-editor, co-author), 1989; US Policy on Palestine from Wilson to Clinton, (editor and co-author), 1995; (Arabic translation) US Policy on Palestine from Wilson to Clinton, 1996; Arabs in America: Building a New Future (editor and co-author), 1999; Numerous journal articles, essays, papers. Honours: Ford Faculty Research Fellowship, 1969-70; American Research Centre in Egypt Fellowship, 1972-73; Center for International Exchange of Scholars (CIES) Islamic Civilization Grant, 1985; National Endowment for the Humanities (NEH) Grant, 1989-91; University Distinguished Professor, Kansas State University, 1990-; Faculty Research Abroad Program (Fulbright-Hayes) Fellowship, 1983-84, summers, 1991, 1993, 1994; Institute for Advanced Study Fellowship, Princeton, NJ, 1994-95. Address: Department of Political Science, Kansas State University, Manhattan, KS 66506-4030, USA. E-mail: suleiman@ksu.edu

SULEJMANI Fadil, b. 5 December 1940, Bozovca, Tetova, Macedonia. Professor. m. Haxhere Voca-Sulejmani, 1 son, 3 daughters. Education: Albanian Language, Faculty of Philosophy, University of Prishtina, Kosova; MSc, Albanian Langugage, Belgrade, Yugoslavia; PhD, Albanology, Prishtina University. Appointments: Professor of Albanian Language, Morphology, Phonetics and Syntax, Faculty of Philology, University of Prishtina, 1971-94; Professor of Albanian Language, Faculty of Philology, Chair of the Board, 1994-95, Rector, 1994-2003, University of Tetova. Publications: Numerous scientific and professional works in the field of Albanian Language, Dialectology, Albanian Ethnography, German Language, etc. Honours: Gold Medal, Rector of Honour, University of Tetova 2002. Memberships: Albanian Cultural Society of FYROM; Alexander Humboldt Foundation, Germany. Address: Str Radovan Conic 43A, Tetova, Macedonia. E-mail: fadilsulejmani@yahoo.com

SULIVAN Elizabeth, b. 4 August 1916, Naini Tal, India. Map Dowser. Widowed, 2 sons. Education: Illustration, Chelsea Polytechnic; Dress Design, Central School of Arts and Crafts; Cipher Officer Training, RAF Training Command, Oxford. Appointments: Cipher Officer, working at a secret location, WWII; Army Officer's wife living in Germany, France and Egypt; Self taught in the art of Map Dowsing; Planned and constructed a labyrinth by pendulum on the lower ward of Benton Castle, Pembrokeshire which turned out to be an exact copy of the labyrinth at Chartres Cathedral in France; Research results include: Gravity inside the labyrinth circle is different to that outside it and it activates the right side of the brain; Labyrinth aligned to the Winter Solstice and attracts ley lines; Researchers believe that a Frensel lens in stone may have been constructed which collects energy which is neither electrical nor magnetic. Honour: Pogram Silver Goblet Award, British Society of Dowsers, 2002. Membership: British Society of Dowsers. Address: Benton Castle, Milford Haven, Pembrokeshire, SA73 1PE, England.

SULJAGIC Strahinja-Straja, b. 16 January 1941, Belgrade, Serbia. Dramatist; Translator. 1 son. Education: High Journalist School; German Language. Career: Dramatist for theatre, radio and TV; Translator. Creative Works include: A Slow Steamboat for Shanghai; From the Old Days; Please Hold My Hand; Sister Helen; Rose Carli (drama for Rose and Patrick Carli); Love Letter of a Big Tragedy Actress, Mary Jaszai to her Young Lover Dr Janos Plese; Good-By Abazia (Comedy); Autumn Passions (drama for two); England's Spring and Citizens of Calais; The Rockfellers Violin; Jelena Dimitriewna; Zinocka; Scream of Bird Turaku; 3 books. Honours: Many awards for translations of Jewish poetry and prose. Memberships: NUNS (Free Journalists); Dramatists Alliance; Blood Donor. Address: Karadordeva St 49, 111 Entr., Apr 18/IX Floor, 11000 Belgrade, Serbia.

SULTAN (Ashkenazi) Esther, b. 24 January 1951, Izmir, Turkey. Director of Statistics. m. Rafael Amram, 1 son, 2 daughters. Education: BSc, Mathematics and Statistics, Hebrew University in Jerusalem, 1974; MBA, Business Administration, University of Lincolnshire and Humberside, 1998. Appointments: Demographic Section, Central Bureau of Statistics, 1973-78; Statistician/Economist, 1978-85, Director, Statistics Branch, 1986-91, Director of Statistics Division, 1992-94, Director of Statistics and Databases, 1994-, Ministry of Tourism, Jerusalem, Israel. Publications: The Economic Impact of Tourism in Israel, in Tourism Economics, 1997; Israel-Country Reports, TTI, 2000. Honour: Award of Excellent Worker in the Ministry of Tourism, 1989. Memberships: AIOS; AIEST; TTRA; Management of the Dead Sea Medical Research Center; Public Committee of Statistics in Israel; Committee for tenders in researches and surveys, Ministry of Tourism. Address: Moshe Shareth 25/49, Jerusalem 96920, Israel. E-mail: esthers@tourism.gov.il

Dictionary of International Biography

SULTANOVA Razia R, b. Vladivostok, Russia. Musicologist; Ethnomusicologist; Musician. m. Hamid Ismailov, 1 son, 1 daughter. Education: BA, MMus, Uzbek State Conservatory; PhD, Moscow State Conservatory. Appointments: Teacher, Uzbek State Conservatory, 1979-84; Research Fellow, Goldsmiths College, University of London, 1997-; Visiting Professor, Moscow State Conservatory, 2000-; Research Fellow, SOAS, 2004-; Public lectures and academic courses on Central Asian Music in France, Germany, England and Northern Ireland; Solo performances (dutar and singing) in Belgium, Germany, France, England and USA. Publications: 3 books, 2 forthcoming; 5 CD productions; Articles in English, French and German. Honours: Numerous scholarships; Award, London Sinfonietta and Royal Academy of Drama and Music, 2003; Award, Committee for Central and Inner Asia, Cambridge University, 2003; Small Award, British Academy, 2003; 3 year scholarship, Arts and Humanities Research Board, 2004. Memberships: The International Council for Traditional Music; Society for Ethnomusicology; European Seminar of Ethnomusicology; British Forum for Ethnomusicology; French Association of Ethnomusicology; British-Uzbek Society; National Geographic Society. Address: Goldsmiths College, Music Department, University of London, New Cross, London SE14 6NW, England.

SUMMER Donna, b. 31 December 1948, Boston, USA. Singer; Actress. m. (1) Helmut Sommer, divorced, 1 daughter, (2) Bruce Sudano, 1 son, 1 daughter. Appointments: Singer, 1967-; Appeared in German stage production, Hair, in Europe, 1967-75; Appearing in Vienna Folk productions of Porgy and Bess; German production of The Me Nobody Knows; Has sold over 20 million records; Albums: The Wanderer; Star Collection; Love to Love You Baby; Love Trilogy; Four Seasons of Love; I Remember Yesterday; The Deep; Shut Out; Once Upon a Time; Bad Girls; On the radio; Walk Away; She Works Hard for the Money; Cats without Claws; All Systems Go, 1988; Another Time and Place, 1989; Mistaken Identity, 1991; Endless Summer, 1994; I'm a Rainbow, 1996; Live & More Encore, 1999. Honours: Best Rhythm and Blues Female Vocalist, National Academy of Recording Arts and Sciences, 1978; Best Female Vocalist, 1879; Favourite Female Pop Vocalist, American Music Awards, 1979; Favourite Female Vocalist of Soul Music, 1979; Ampex Golden Reel Award for single and album On the radio, 1979; Album Bad Girls, Soul Artist of Year, Rolling Stone Magazine, 1979; Best Rock Performance; Best of Las Vegas Jimmy Award, 1980; Grammy Award for Best Inspirational Performance, 1984; Several Awards for Best Selling Records. Address: 2401 Main Street, Santa Monica, CA 90405, USA.

SUMNER Humphrey Louis, b. 15 April 1946, Harrow, Middlesex, England. Research Immunologist in Ophthalmology. Education: Bachelor of Arts, Biology, 1969; Master of Science, Immunology, 1977; California State University at Fullerton, USA; US Army Training, 1969-73; Certified Cytotechnologist, ASCP. Appointments: Research Immunologist, Newport Pharmaceuticals, Inc, Newport Beach, California, USA, 1976-77; Ophthalmic Immunologist, 1978-97; Director, Microsurgery Laboratory and Supervisor, Core Research Equipment, 1997-, Jules Stein Eye Institute, University of California, Los Angeles, USA. Publications: 17 publications in scientific journals include: In vitro studies on cell-mediated immunity in patients treated with Inosiplex for herpes virus infection, 1977; Experimental retinal autoimmunity (ERA) in strain 13 guinea pigs: Induction of ERA-retinopathy with rhodopsin, 1983; Complement-derived anaphylatoxins in human donor corneas treated with excimer laser, 1995; Mitigation of neutrophil infiltration in rat model of early Staphylococcus aureus endophthalmitis, 2003. Honours: Bausch and Lomb Science Award, 1964; Listed in Who's Who publications and biographical dictionaries. Memberships: American Society of Clinical Pathologists, 1972-77; Los Angeles Parks and Recreation Softball League, 1979-. Address: Jules Stein Eye Institute, 100 Stein Plaza, Room BH-731, Los Angeles, CA 90095, USA. E-mail: sumner@jsei.ucla.edu

SUN Andy, b. 23 November 1953, Taiwan, Republic of China. Doctor; Professor. m. Hsiung Shu-Yun, 1 son, 1 daughter. Education: DDS, School of Dentistry, Medical College, National Taiwan University; PhD, Immunology, Medical College, National Taiwan University, 1992. Appointments: Attending Physician, National Taiwan University Hospital, 1989-; Associate Professor, Fu-Jen Catholic University, 1993-94; Associate Professor, 1996-2003, Professor, 2003-, The Shih Hsin University; Visiting Professor, Tianjin Medical University, 1999-; Visiting Professor, Hu-Bei Traditional Chinese Medical College, 1999-2004; Visiting Associate Professor, Shanghai Traditional Chinese Medical University, 1999-2003; Visiting Professor, Shanghai Traditional Chinese Medical University. Publications: Articles in professional journals. Honours: Outstanding Immunology Research, Graduate of Medical College, 1987; Awards for papers, National Science Council, 1988-96, 1998, 2000. Memberships: Central Committee, 14th Plenary Session, KMT; President, University and College Lecturers Association; New York Science Council; President, Straits Academic and Cultural Exchange Association; President, Chinese Health and Spirit Research and Development Association; Chinese Society of Immunology. Address: National Taiwan University Hospital, Taipei, Taiwan, ROC.

SUN Minghua, b. March 1934, Shanghai, China. Professor of Arts. Education: Academy of Fine Arts of China, 1956-61. Appointments: Arts Teacher, Suzhou Industrial Art Training School, 1961-63; Creative Design, Suzhou Embroidering Research Institute, 1964-82; Art Educator, East of China Ship-building Industry University, 1983-94; Traditional Chinese Painting Creation and Art Guidance, 1995-. Creative Works include: Happiness of a Poultry Raiser, China Art Gallery; A Joyous Morning, Nanchang Revolutionary Museum; Picture of a Shepherd Boy, Xu Beihong Museum; A Scene of the Countryside, Mao Dun Museum; A Summer Day, Municipal Hall, Auckland, New Zealand. Publications: Paintings included in several books and collections of artistic works. Honours: Honorary Award of International Exchanges; Honorary Gold Medal, China and Thailand Artists; Golden Dragon Award, Singapore Shenzou Art Gallery; Honorary Title of the World Most Famous Artists. Memberships: Chinese Artists Association; Art Education of Chinese High Learning Research Society; Chinese Holy Sword Literature and Art Institute; Honorary Adviser, Shengzhou Art Institute, Singapore; Specially Engaged Painter of Chinese Painting Institute in Thailand. Address: 302-15 67 Xue Fu Road, Zhen Jiangsu, China Post Box 212003.

SUN Ron, b. 8 October 1960, Shanghai, China. Computer Scientist; Cognitive Scientist. Education: BSc in Computer Information Science, Fudan University, 1983; MSc in Mathematics and Computer Science, Clarkson University, USA, 1986; PhD in Computer Science, Brandeis University, 1991. Appointments: Assistant Professor of Computer Science and Psychology, 1992-98, Associate Professor of Computer Science and Psychology, 1998-99, Departments of Computer Science and Psychology, University of Alabama at Tuscaloosa; Adjunct Professor of Psychology, University of Alabama at Birmingham, 1998-2000; Visiting Scientist, NEC Research Institute, Princeton, New Jersey, 1998-2003; Associate Professor of Computer Engineering and Computer Science, Department of Computer Engineering and Computer Science, University of Missouri-Columbia, Columbia, 1999-2002; Full Professor and James C Dowell Endowed Professor of CECS, Department of CECS, University of Missouri, Columbia, 2002-2003; Full Professor, Department of Cognitive Science, Rensselaer Polytechnic Institute, 2003-. Publications: Author, Integrating Rules and Connectionism for Robust Commonsense Reasoning, 1994; Duality of the Mind, 2002; Co-editor: Computational Architectures Integrating Neural and Symbolic Processes, 1994; Connectionist Symbolic Integration, 1997; Hybrid Neural Systems, 2000; Sequence Learning: Paradigms, Algorithms, and Applications, 2001; Numerous book chapters, papers and articles in the field, especially in human and machine learning, reasoning and representation in neural networks, hybrid models, autonomous agents and multi-agent systems. Honours include: Graduate Fellowship and Scholarship in Computer Science, Brandeis University, 1988-91; David Marr Award in Cognitive Science, Cognitive Science Society, 1991; Senior Member, Institute of Electrical and Electronics Engineers, 1998; Member, European Academy of Science, 2002. Memberships: Institute of Electrical and Electronics Engineers; Cognitive Science Society; Life Member, American Association for Artificial Intelligence; International Neural Network Society; Upsilon Pi Epsilon. Address: Cognitive Science Department, Rensselaer Polytechnic Institute, 110 8th Street, Troy, NY 12180, USA.

SUN Shi-Ying, b. 11 March 1933, Shanghai, China. Professor in Microwave and Communication. m. Zhang Han-Yang, 1 daughter. Education: Graduate, Electronic Engineering, Shanghai Jiao Tong University, 1953; Graduate, Russian, Harbin Foreign Language Institute, 1955; Graduate Student, Microwave Devices and Techniques, University of Electronic Science and Technology, China, Chengdu, 1956-58. Appointments: Lecturer, Microwave Devices and Techniques, UESTC, 1961-; Joined, 1978-, Associate Professor, 1982-88, Full Professor, 1988-, Microwave Theory and Techniques, Shanghai Jiao Tong University; Co-chairman, MMIC session APMC'88, 1988; Director, 5 research projects sponsored by National Natural Science Foundation of China, 1983-; Director, research project sponsored by Electronic Scientific Academy of Electronic Industrial Ministry, 1988-89; Director, Research Project, Multimedia Visible Telephone Compression Coder Including ITU-T G723.1-Dual Rate Speech Coder for Multimedia Communication Transmitting at 5.3 & 6.3 kbps, 1997-2001; Director, Research Project, Video Compression Coder, 1999-2002; Co-director, Research Project, MPEG-4 Real Time Compression Encoder/Decoder and Real Time Video Transmission over IP Networks, 2002-04. Publications include: Over 50 scientific papers including: CAD and Performance of the Ultra Wide Band GaAs FET Amplifiers; Multiplier Method and Performance of the Developed Broadband Low Noise GaAs FET Amplifiers; A Variation Method of Predicting Resonant Frequency of Cylindrical Dielectric Resonator; Books: Author, Measurement of Microwave Devices; Co-author, Microwave Techniques, Microwave Electronic Devices, volumes I and II. Honours include: Award, State Council and Education Committee, China, 1960; 1st Class Prize, Excellent Advisor to Graduate Students, Shanghai Jiaotong University, 1986; World Lifetime Achievement Award, Gold Statue, American Biographical Institute, 1997; 3rd Prize and Diploma for Microwave Achievement, Pei-yuan Zhou Foundation, 1998; The Who's Who New Century Medal – Leaders for the New Century, Baron's Who's Who, USA, 2001; Listed in numerous Who's Who publications and biographical dictionaries. Memberships: Senior Member, IEEE; Senior Member, Chinese Institute of Electronics; Board Member, Microwave Board of Shanghai Institute of Electronics, 1990-2002. Address: Department of Electronic Engineering, Shanghai Jiaotong University, No 1954 Hua Shan Road, Shanghai 200030, China.

SUN Teresa Chi-Ching, b. 24 December 1935, China. Teacher. m. Terry Tseng-Yao Sun, 1 son, 1 daughter. Education: BA, Chinese Literature, Taiwan Normal University, 1957; MA, Education, University of California, Los Angeles, 1964; Doctorate Candidate, East Asian Language and Literature, University of California, Los Angeles, 1972-76, Claremont Graduate School of Education, 1978; Graduate Courses, 1980, 1986; Doctorate in Higher Education and Human Services, Seton Hall University, New Jersey, 1995. Appointments: Lecturer, Mandarin Training Center for Foreign Scholars, Taiwan Normal University, 1956-57; Teacher, Chinese Literature, Taipei First Girls High School, 1957-58, Subordinate High School, Taiwan Normal University, 1958-59; Teaching Assistant, Department of East Asian Studies, University of Southern California, 1962-64; Instructor, Department of Foreign Languages, Evening Division, Los Angeles City College, 1965-67; Instructor, Assistant Professor, Department of Foreign Languages and Literature, California State University, Los Angeles, 1967-78; Visiting Lecturer, Adjunct Assistant Professor, Department of Foreign Language, Whittier College, 1991-97; Lecturer, California State University at Long Beach, 1999-2003; Lecturer, East Asian Language and Literature, University of California, Irvine, California, 2004. Publications: The Admissions Dispute: Asian Americans Versus University of California at Berkeley (book), 1997; Several articles in professional journals. Honours include: Honorary Citizen, City of Albuquerque, 1976, Austin, 1977; Certificate, Personalities of America, 1978-79. Memberships include: American Association on Asian Studies. Address: 28717 Trailriders Drive, Rancho Palos Verdes, CA 90275, USA.

SUN Xue-Zhi, b. 3 September 1963, Jilin Province, China. Researcher; Medical Doctor. m. Zhang Rui, 1 son. Education: BMed, Medical Diploma, Norman Bethune University of Medical Sciences, Changchun, China 1985; PhD, School of Medicine, Nagoya University, Nagoya, Japan 1996. Appointments: Researcher, Doctor, Laboratory of Industry Hygiene, Ministry of Public Health, China, Beijing, China, 1985-91; Professor Assistant, School of Medicine, Tokushima University, Tokushima, Japan, 1996-97; Researcher, National Institute of Radiological Sciences, Chiba, Japan, 1997-; Visiting Professor, Nagoya University, Nagoya, Japan, 2000-; Research Adviser, National Institute of Radiological Sciences, Chiba, Japan, 2001-. Publications: Author, The World of Human Being; Contributor of articles to professional Journals. Honours: Recipient of numerous awards including: Academic Awards of the Japanese Teratology Society; Certificate of Recognition of Who's Who, 2000; Academic Awards of the Medical Society of China; Academic Awards of The Japan Radiation Research Society, 2002. Memberships: Japanese Teratology Society; Japanese Association of Anatomists; Japan Radiation Research Society; Medical Society of China; American Association for the Advancement of Science; New York Academy of Sciences; Japan Neuroscience Society. Address: National Institute of Radiological Sciences, 4-9-1 Anagawa, Inage-ku, Chiba-shi, Chiba 263-8555, Japan. E-mail: sun_s@nirs.go.jp

SUN Ying, b. 3 June 1956, Jilin, China. Asthma, Allergy and Lung Pathologist. m. Meng Qiu, 1 daughter. Education: MD, Faculty of Jilin Medical College, China, 1981; MSc, Molecular Immunology, Beijing Medical University, China, 1988; PhD, Allergy and Clinical Immunology, National Heart and Lung Institute, London, UK, 1994. Appointments: Assistant Professor, Department of Microbiology and Immunology, Jilin Medical College, China, 1981-84; Lecturer, Department of Immunology, Beijing Medical University, China, 1988-89; Research Fellow, 1989-94, Postdoctoral Research Fellow, 1994-95, Lecturer, 1996-, Department of Allergy and Clinical Immunology, Faculty of Medicine, Imperial College School, National Heart and Lung Institute, London, UK; Principal Investigator and Head of Immunology, TaiGen Biotech, Taiwan, 2002-2003; Senior Lecturer, Division of Asthma, Allergy and Lung Biology, Guy's, King's and

Dictionary of International Biography

St Thomas' Medical School, London, UK, 2003-. Publications: 3 book chapters; More than 65 articles in international scientific journals include most recently as first author and co-author: The relationship between allergen-induced tissue eosinophilia and markers of Repair and remodeling in human atopic skin, 2002; Allergen-induced fluctuation in CC chomokine receptor 3 expression on bone marrow CD34+ cells from asthmatic subjects: significance for mobilization of haemopoietic progenor cells in allergic inflammation, 2003; Inhibition of Late Asthmatic Reactions by Cyclosporin A is Associated with Enhanced Apoptosis of Bronchoalveolar Lavage T Cells together with Decreases in the Expression of Bcl-2 and IL-4, 2003; 6 articles in Chinese journals. Honours: International Travel Fellowship, American Academy of Allergy, 1993, 1994, 1995; Fellowship, Pharmacia Allergy Research Foundation, 1995; Honorary Research Professor, Norman Bethune University of Medical Sciences, PR China, 1997-; The Royal Society International Travel Fellowship, 1999. Membership: British Society of Allergy and Clinical Immunology. Address: Guy's, King's & St Thomas' School of Medicine, Department of Asthma, Allergy & Respiratory Science, 5th Floor Thomas Guy House, Guy's Hospital, London SE1 9RT, England. E-mail: ying.sun@kcl.ac.uk

SUNDARALINGAM Kandiah, b. 15 January 1942, Jaffna, Sri Lanka. University Academic. m. Sivamalar Sundaralingam, 2 sons. Education: BSc Honours, University of Ceylon, Colombo, 1965; PhD, University of Durham, England, 1971; Advanced Certificate in Microcomputer Technology, CPTI, Melbourne, Australia, 1994. Appointments: Physics Staff, University of Sri Lanka, 1965-75; Physics Staff, University of Technology, Lae, Papua New Guinea, 1975-82; Physics Staff, University of the South Pacific, Fiji, 1982-90; Sessional Staff, Monash and Swinburne Universities, Australia, 1991-; Member, International Lithospheric Program, University of California, Los Angeles. Publications: Crust and uppermost mantle structure of the arc regions of South West Pacific Islands, 1990; Shear velocity structure beneath the Western Australian region, 1997. Honours: Postdoctoral Fellow, University of California at Los Angeles; Associate, ICTP, Trieste, Italy; Research Scientist, BMR, Canberra, Australia. Memberships: Former Fellow, Royal Geological Society, London; AIP; ACS; ASEG. Address: 77 Camelot Drive, Glen Waverley, Victoria 3150, Australia. E-mail: sundak@hotmail.com

SUNKLODAS Jonas Kazys, b. 28 September 1945, Užpaliai Town, Utena District, Lithuania. Mathematician. m. Janina Survilaitė, 1 son, 3 daughters. Education: Mathematics major, Vilnius University, 1963-68; Postgraduate studies, Institute of Physics and Mathematics, Lithuanian Academy of Sciences, 1972-74; Doctors degree, Mathematics, Vilnius University, 1979; Habilitated Doctors degree of Physical Sciences, Mathematics, Institute of Mathematics and Informatics, 1999; Title of Professor, Vilnius Gediminas Technical University, 2004. Appointments: Junior Research Fellow, Institute of Physics and Mathematics, Lithuanian Academy of Sciences, 1970-71; Instructor, Faculty of Mathematics and Mechanics, Vilnius University, 1973-78; Junior Research Fellow, 1975-81, Senior Research Fellow, 1982-2002, Chief Research Fellow, 2003-, Institute of Mathematics and Informatics, Lithuanian Academy of Sciences; Associate Professor, 1997-99, Professor, 1999-, Faculty of Fundamental Sciences, Vilnius Gediminas Technical University. Publications: Articles in science publications on probability theory; Author, over 50 scientific publications. Memberships: Lithuanian Mathematicians' Society. Address: Institute of Mathematics and Informatics, Akademijos 4, 220 cab, LT-08663 Vilnius, Lithuania.

SUPPES Christine Johnson, b. 3 March 1953, Los Angeles, California, USA. Publishing Executive. m. Patrick Suppes, 1 son, 1 daughter. Appointments: Copy Girl, Editorial Assistant, San

Francisco Examiner, San Francisco, USA, 1972-73; President, Gravure at Home, Stanford, California, USA, 1997-2001; Publisher, Editor-in-Chief, www.Fashionlines.com, Stanford California, 1999-; Chief Jewellery Designer, www.jewelsbychristine.com, Stanford, California, 2003-; Chief Site Designer, www.Gravureathome.com, www.Fashionlines.com, www.Jewelsbychristine.com. Publications: Amanda Prescott, 1984, Clinic, 1985 (published under maiden name of Christine Johnson). Honour: Angel of Fashion Award, New York City, 1999-; Memberships: Organiser, Teacher's Fund, Bing School, Stanford, California, 1995-; Peninsula Chapter, NARAL, 1997-2001; Supporter, American Red Cross, 2001-; Fashion Group International; Camera Nazionale della Moda Italiana; Federation Française de la Couture. Address: 678 Mirada Avenue, Stanford, CA 94305, USA. E-mail: suppes@fashionlines.com

SURANYI György, b. 3 January 1954, Budapest, Hungary. Economist; Professor of Finance. m. Judit Marmoly, 1 son, 1 daughter. Education: MA, 1977, Doctor of Economics, 1979, Dr Habil., 1996, University of Economics, Budapest, Hungary; PhD, Hungarian Academy of Sciences, Budapest, 1986. Appointments: Research Fellow, Financial Research Institute, Budapest, 1977-86; Consultant, World Bank, Washington, DC, USA, 1986-87; Counsellor to Deputy Prime Minister, Hungary, 1988-89; State Secretary, National Planning Office, Hungary, 1989-90; Governor, Hungarian Central Bank, 1990-91; Co-Chief Executive Officer, CIB Bank Ltd, Hungary, 1992-95; Governor of the Central Bank, Hungary, 1995-2001; Head of Foreign Division for Central Europe, Banca Intesa, Italy, 2001-. Publications: Author of several articles and books on monetary and financial policies. Honours: Awards for Central Bankers, Euromoney, Global Finance Magazine, 1996, 1997, 1998, 1999; Decoration of Commander's Cross with Star – Order of Merit of the Republic of Hungary, 2002. Address: CIB Bank Ltd, Medve utca 4-14, H-1027, Budapest, Hungary. E-mail: gsuranyi@cib.hu

SURJIT SINGH (Surjit Singh Jeet), b. 1 June 1946, Jallandhar, India. Research Fellow. m. Avtarkaur Saggu, 2 sons, 2 daughters. Education: MABA, Honours; MA (RS); MA, Imperialism and Culture; Diploma in Astrology, Palmistry and Numerology; Diploma in Spiritual Healing. Appointments: Royal Mail Parcel Force International, London; Friend, Royal Institute of Historical Research, University of London. Publications: In Punjabi: Articles in daily and monthly papers; Short stories and articles on Punjabi History; In English: Editor of 2 books: Maharaja Duleep Singh and the British Government; The Namdhari Sikhs; Numerous articles in papers. Honours: BA Hons; Ashirwad Purskar ; All India Namdhari; Vidyak Jatha; Ambassador of Peace; Speaker of the Year, W.C.F. Memberships: Vegetarian Society UK; The Historical Association, UK; The Labour Party; The Fabian Society; Progress; Institute of Historical Research; Friends Society of the British Library; Friends Society of the Victoria & Albert Museum. Address: "The Sutlej", 36 Margery Park Road, Forest Gate, London E7 9JY, England. E-mail: surgjtsinghjeet@btinternet.com

SURYAVANSHI Arvind Krishnajirao, b. 13 October 1957, Sirsi, Karnataka, India. Teaching; Researcher. m. Vani A Suryavanshi, 1 son, 1 daughter. Education: PhD, UMIST, England, 1991-94; MTech, IIT, Mumbai, 1986-88; BEng, Karnataka, India, 1974-79. Appointments include: Scientists-C, National Institute of Oceanography, (NIO), Goa, India, 1982-91; Research Associate, University of Sheffield, UK, 1995-97; Manager, Concrete Consultancy, The Associated Cement Company Ltd, India, 1997; Research Fellow, National University of Singapore, Singapore, 1997-99; Senior Engineer, Poh Cheong Concrete Products Pte Ltd, 1999-2001; Teaching Fellow, Nanyang Technological University (NTU), Singapore. 2001-2003; Senior Engineer, Setsco Pte Ltd,

Singapore, 2003-. Publications: 24 technical papers published in International Journals and International Conference proceedings related to Civil Engineering. Honours: Commonwealth Fellow, 1991-94. Listed in: Biographical Publication. Address: Blk116, #03-619, Yishun Ring Road, Singapore 760116.

SUSANTO Ken, b. 1972, Indonesia. Researcher. Education: BSc, Mathematics and Applied Sciences, University of California, Los Angeles, USA, 1995; MSc, Mechanical Engineering, MSc, Electrical Engineering, 1999, PhD, Mechanical Engineering, 2004, University of Southern California, USA. Appointments: Control Systems Engineer, Honeywell Inc, 1998-99; Researcher, University of Southern California, 1999-. Publications: Design News Magazine: High-Tech Forceps Grab Award, 2003; ASME: Static Deflection Behavior of a Piezoelectric Forceps, 2003; US Patent Pending: Miniature Piezoelectric Forceps Integrated with Fibre Optics Camera. Honours: NAFSA and US Information Agency Scholarship Award, 1998; IEEE Biomedical Device Application Award, 2002; Design News Award, 2003. Memberships: IEEE; ASME; SME; AIAA. Address: E-mail: kensusanto@hotmail.com

SUSHANSKAYA Rimma, b. 1950, Leningrad, Russia. Concert Violinist. Education: Studied at Leningrad and Moscow Conservatoires with David Oistrakh; PhD. Career: Emigrated to America in 1977 and has given many concerts there, in South America, throughout Russia and in Europe; Orchestras include Czech Philharmonic, Moscow Philharmonic, Leningrad Philharmonic Orchestras and Prague Radio Symphony Orchestra; Orchestral and recital tours of Russia, Finland and Czechoslovakia; London recital debut in 1987 at the Wigmore Hall, followed by Tchaikovsky's Concerto with the Royal Liverpool Philharmonic Orchestra and the City of Birmingham Symphony Orchestra; Based in Britain, residing in London, Stratford and New York. Honours include: First Prize, Prague International Competition; Ysaye Medal. Address: 9 Central Chambers, Wood Street, Stratford-upon-Avon, Warwickshire CV37 6JQ, England.

SUSSO Alhaji Papa, b. 29 September 1947, Sotuma Sere, The Gambia. Musician; Historian. m. Mariatu, 6 sons, 5 daughters. Education: Bachelors Degree in Business Administration, 1966-69. Appointments: Agricultural Assistant, 1957-58; Secretary, The Bayo Company, Monrovia, Liberia, 1965-67; Liaison Officer, Gambia Embassy, Freetown, Sierra Leone, with concurrent accreditation to the Republics of Liberia, Guinea and the Ivory Coast, 1967-; Senior Accountant, Ministry of Works and Communication, The Gambia; International Griot and Oral Historian. Publications: Mentioned in: Scribe, Griot and Novelist, by Thomas A Hale, Griots and Griottes, by Thomas A Hale, Pennsylvania State University. Memberships: African Studies Association; African Literatures Association; Society for Ethnomusicology; Member, United Nations Development Programmes; Committee on Eradication of Poverty. Address: 18 Samuel Forster Street, Old Jeshwng, The Gambia. Email: papasusso@hotmail.com Website: http://tcd.freehosting.net/papasusso.htm

SUTHANTHIRAN Manikkam, b. 15 August 1947, India. Doctor of Medicine. m. Phyllis August. Education: Doctor of Medicine, 1970; American Board of Internal Medicine, 1976; American Board of Nephrology, 1976. Appointments: Professor of Medicine, 1989; Chief of Nephrology, 1994; Chief of Transplantation, 1994. Publications: 173 Original Articles; 56 Chapters/Reviews; 366 Abstracts. Honours: Stanton Griffis Distinguished Professor of Medicine; Roche Distinguished Achievement Award; Established Investigator Award; President, American Society of Transplant Physicians, 1993-94. Memberships: American Society for Clinical Investigation; American Society for Transplant Physicians. Address: 6 Uxbridge Road, Scarsdale, NY 10583, USA. E-mail: msuthan@med.cornell.edu

SUTHERLAND David Hollinworth, b. 18 June 1923, Taming, China. Paediatric Orthopaedic Surgeon. m. Mildred June Sutherland, 4 sons, 2 daughters. Education: BS, University of Washington, 1944; MD, Marquette University, 1946; Internship, St Louis City Hospital, 1947-48; Residencies: General Surgery, Welborn Hospital Clinic, 1948-49; Orthopaedic Surgery, VA Hospital San Francisco, 1952-55; Children's Hospital San Francisco, 1953; Shriners Hospital, San Francisco, 1954. Appointments: Associate Professor, 1972-84, Professor of Surgery, Orthopaedics and Rehabilitation, 1984-, Currently Professor Emeritus, University of California San Diego School of Medicine; Director of Paediatric Orthopaedics, 1972-90, Medical Director, 1974-99, Senior Consultant, 1999-, Motion Analysis Laboratory, Children's Hospital San Diego. Publications: Books: Author: Gait Disorders in Childhood and Adolescence, 1984; Co-author , The Development of Mature Walking, 1988; Over 30 articles in professional medical journals and presented at conferences as author and co-author include most recently: Double-Blind study of Botulinum A Toxin Injections into the Gastrocnemius muscle in patients with cerebral palsy. 1999; The Evolution of Clinical Gait Analysis: Part I – Kinesiological EMG, 2001, Part II – Kinematics, 2002; 10 book chapters. Honours: Weinstein-Goldenson Award, United Cerebral Palsy Association, 1988; Annual Paediatric Orthopaedic Visiting Professorship UCSD & Children's Hospital Health Center, renamed David H Sutherland Pediatric Orthopaedic Visiting Professorship, 1990; Pioneer Award, Pediatric Orthopaedic Society of North America, 1993; Lifetime Achievement Award "Fifty Years of Caring", 1998; GCMA Best Paper Award, 1999; Lifetime Achievement Award, The Gait and Movement Analysis Society, 2002. Memberships: American Academy for Cerebral Palsy and Developmental Medicine; American Academy of Orthopaedic Surgeons; American Academy of Pediatrics; American Medical Association; American Orthopaedic Association; Pediatric Orthopaedic Association of North America; Western Orthopedic Association. Address: Children's Hospital San Diego, Motion Analysis Laboratory MC 5054, 3020 Children's Way, San Diego, CA 92123-4282, USA. E-mail: dsutherland@chsd.org Website: www.sandiegogaitlab.com

SUTHERLAND Donald McNichol, b. 17 July 1935, St John, Canada. Actor. m. (1) Lois May Hardwick, 1959; m. (2) Shirley Jean Douglas, 1966, divorced, 1 son, 1 daughter, (3) Francine Racette, 1971, 3 sons. Education: University of Toronto. Appointments: Appeared on TV (BBC and ITV) in Hamlet; Man in the Suitcase; The Saint; Gideon's Way; The Avengers; Flight into Danger; Rose Tattoo; March to the Sea; Lee Harvey Oswald; Court Martial; Death of Bessie Smith; Max Dugan Returns; Crackers; Louis Malle; The Disappearance; Films include: The World Ten Times Over, 1963; Castle of the Living Dead, 1964; Dr Terror's House of Horrors; Fanatic, 1965; Act of the Heart, 1970; M*A*S*H*, 1970; Kelly's Heroes, 1970; Little Murders, 1970; Don't Look Now, 1973; The Day of the Locust, 1975; 1900, 1976; The Eagle Has Landed, 1977; The Great Train Robbery, 1978; Lock Up, 1989; Apprentice to Murder, 1989; Los Angeles, 1989; The Railway Station Man, 1991; Scream from Stone, 1991; Faithful, 1991; JFK, 1991; Backdraft; Agaguk; Buffy the Vampire Slayer; Shadow of the Wolf, 1993; Benefit of the Doubt; Younger and Younger, 1993; Six Degrees of Separation, 1993; The Puppet Masters; Disclosure; Outbreak; Hollow Point; The Shadow Conspiracy; A Time To Kill; Virus, 1999; Instinct, 1999; Toscano, 1999; The Art of War, 2000; Panic, 2000; Space Cowboys, 2000; Uprising, 2001; The Big Herst, 2001; Final Fantasy: The Spirits Within, 2001; Plays: Lolita, 1981; Enigmatic Variations, 2000;

President, McNichol Pictures Inc. Honours: TV Hallmark Hall of Fame; Officer, Ordre des Lettres; Order of Canada; Hon PhD; Golden Globe for Best Supporting Actor in a TV series or TV Movie, 2003. Address: 760 N La Cienega Boulevard, Los Angeles, CA 90069, USA.

SUZMAN Janet, b. 9 February 1939, Johannesburg, South Africa. Actress; Director. m. Trevor Nunn, 1969, divorced 1986, 1 son. Education: BA, University of Wittwatersrand; Graduate, London Academy of Music and Dramatic Arts, 1962. Career: For the RSC: The Wars of the Roses; Portia, Ophelia, Celia, Rosalind, Katherina; The Relapse; The Greeks, 1980; London Theatre includes: The Birthday Party; Three Sisters; Hedda Gabler; The Duchess of Malfi; Andromache; The Retreat from Moscow; Television includes: The Family Reunion; St Joan; Macbeth; Twelfth Night, Hedda Gabler; Three Men in a Boat; Clayhanger (serial), 1975-76; Mountbatten-Last Viceroy of India, 1985; The Singing Detective, 1986; The Miser, 1987; Revolutionary Witness, 1989; Masterclass on Shakespearean Comedy, 1990; Masterclass from Haymarket Theatre (Sky TV), 2001; White Clouds (BBC), 2002; Films include: A Day in the Death of Joe Egg, 1970; Nicholas & Alexandra, 1971; Nijinsky, 1978; The House on Garibaldi Street; The Priest of Love, 1981; The Black Windmill; Nuns on the Run, 1990; Leon the pig-Farmer, 1992; Max, 2001; Fairy Story, 2002; Numerous performances in South Africa; Wrote and Directed The Free State – a South African response to the Cherry Orchard, performed at the Birmingham Repertory Theatre, 1997 (revived for UK tour, 2000); Lectures include: The Spencer Memorial Lecture, Harvard University, USA, 1987; The Tanner Lectures, Brasenose College, Oxford, 1995; The Judith E Wilson Annual Lecture, Trinity Hall, Cambridge, 1996; The Draper's Lecture, Queen Mary and Westfield College, University of London. 1997. Publications: Hedda Gabler: The Play in Performance, 1980; Acting with Shakespeare – Three Comedies, 1996; The Free State, 2000; A Textual Commentary on Anthony and Cleopatra, 2001. Honours: Honorary Degrees: MA, Open University; D Lit, Warwick University; D Lit, Leicester University; D Lit, Queen Mary and Westfield College, London University; D Lit, University of Southampton, 2002; Vice-President of London Academy of Music and Dramatic Arts. Address: c/o Steve Kenis & Co, Royalty House, 72-74 Dean Street, London W1D 3SG, England. E-mail: sk@sknco.com

SUZUKI Hironori, b. 18 November 1957, Hanawa, Fukushima, Japan. English Language Educator. m. Sanae Terashima, 1 son. Education: BA, Waseda University, Tokyo, Japan, 1982; MA, International Christian University, Tokyo, 1992. Appointments: English Teacher, Aizu Norin High School, Aizubange, 1982-84; Tanagura High School, 1984-90; Lecturer, 1993-2002, Associate Professor, 2002-03, Department of English, Ohu University, Koriyama, Japan; Associate Professor, Department of Communication and Information Science, Fukushima National College of Technology, Japan, 2003-. Publication: Contributor, Aspects of Modern English: 10th Anniversary of Kindai Eigo Kyokai. Honour: Grantee, Ministry of Education, 1994. Memberships: English Linguistic Society of Japan; International Conference on English Historical Linguistics; Japan Society for Medieval English Studies; The Society for the History of the English Language and Linguistics. Address: 1-6-3-407 Fukazawa, Koriyama-shi, Fukushima 963-8874, Japan. E-mail: suzuki@h.biglobe.ne.jp

SUZUKI Isao, b. 6 January 1945, Akiruno, Tokyo. Scientist. m. Chikako, 21 May 1972, 3 daughters. Education: MSc, 1970, DSc, 1977, University of Tokyo. Appointments: Researcher, 1970, Senior Researcher, 1977, Section Chief, 1990, Electrotechnical Laboratory; Manager, Division of National Metrology Institute of Japan, National Institute of Advanced Industrial Science and Technology, 2001. Publications: Synchrotron Radiation Technique (book), 1990; Scientific papers in professional journals. Honours: Research Award, Electrotechnical Laboratory, 1989; Award, Outstanding Invention, Minister of STA, 1998. Memberships: Chemical Society, Japan; Physical Society, Japan; Japan Society of Applied Physics. Address: Umezono, Tsukuba, Ibaraki 305-8568, Japan.

SUZUKI Toru, b. 12 May 1967, Kamakura, Kanagawa, Japan. Cardiologist; Educator. m. Mitsuko Suzuki. Education: MD, University of Tokyo School of Medicine, Japan, 1992; PhD, University of Tokyo Graduate School of Medicine, Japan, 1998. Appointment: Faculty, Department of Clinical Bioinformatics, University of Tokyo, Japan, 2002-. Publications: Over 80 publications in scientific journals. Honours: Finalist, Samuel Levine Young Investigator Award, American Heart Association, 1995; IFCC/AVL Award, International Federation of Clinical Chemistry, 1996. Address: Department of Clinical Bioinformatics, Graduate School of Medicine, The University of Tokyo, 7-3-1 Hongo, Bunkyo-ku, Tokyo 113-8655, Japan.

SVARC-GRENDA Ivana, b. 17 February 1970. Pianist. Education: Music Academy in Zagreb; Peabody Conservatory of Music, Baltimore; Hochschule der Kunste, Berlin; Mozarteum, Salzburg. Career: Winner of the Kosciuszko Chopin Competition, New York; Winner Croatian National Artists Competition; Solo appearances at Carnegie Recital Hall; Lincoln Center Library, New York; Kennedy Center, Washington DC; Philharmonie Berlin; Alte Oper Frankfurt; Chamber Music appearances, Salle Cortot, Paris; Philharmonie Berlin; Schauspielhaus Berlin; Glinka Hall, St Petersburg; Orchestra appearances with Zagreb Philharmonic; Soloisti di Zagreb Croatian Chamber orchestra; Symphonie orchester Berlin; Gives master courses at International Summer school, Hvar, Croatia. Recordings: Cello-piano duo with Monika Leskovar. Honours: Milka Trnina prize for the best Croatian Musician, 1996; Porin award for the best Croatian recording, 1996. Address: Eigerstr 19, 81825 Munchen, Germany.

SVARDSUDD Kurt Folke, b. 7 September 1942, Pitea, Sweden. Medical Doctor. m. Katharina, 2 sons, 1 daughter. Education: Graduate, Medical School Gothenburg and Umea University, 1968; Postgraduate Education in Boden and Gothenburg; PhD, Gothenburg University, 1978. Appointments: Lecturer, Gothenburg, 1978-80; Research Associate, University of Minnesota, USA, 1980-81; Associate Professor, Gothenburg University, 1982-88; Associate Professor, 1988-90, Professor of Epidemiology, 1990-95, Professor of Family Medicine, 1995-, Chairman of Department of Public Health and Caring Sciences, 1998-2002, Uppsala University. Publications: More than 300 scientific publications in international scientific journals. Honour: First Prize, Scientific Manuscript Contest, Radio Sweden, 1978. Memberships: Swedish Medical Association; Swedish Epidemiology Association; Swedish Family Medicine Association; European Society of Cardiology; International Society and Federation of Cardiology. Address: Department of Public Health and Caring Sciences, Family Medicine and Clinical Epidemiology Section, Uppsala Science Park, SE-75185 Uppsala, Sweden. E-mail: kurt.svardsudd@pubcare.uu.se

SVENSÉN Bo L, b. 4 February 1941, Stockholm, Sweden. Lexicographer; Terminologist; Philologist. m. Margareta Svensén. Education: BA, Latin, Greek, French, 1963; Licentiate's Degree, Latin, 1967, Stockholm University, Stockholm, Sweden. Appointments: Editor of university textbooks in various publishing houses, 1967-76; Managing Editor, Esselte Studium Dictionary Department, 1976-83; Terminologist, Swedish Centre for Technical

Terminology, 1983-88; Private Secretary to the Permanent Secretary, Swedish Academy, 1988-. Publications: Handbok i lexikografi (Manual of Lexicography), 1987, English translation: Practical Lexicography. Principles and methods of dictionary making, 1993; Co-author of several dictionaries, notably Stora engelsk-svenska ordboken (A Comprehensive English-Swedish Dictionary), 1980; Nordisk leksikografisk ordbok (Nordic Dictionary of Lexicography), 1997; Books on the Swedish Academy and editions of documents from the Academy's archives; Articles on lexicographic topics in journals and conference proceedings. Honour: Doctor of Philosophy Honoris Causa, Stockholm University, 1998. Memberships: Nordic Association for Lexicography; European Association for Lexicography; Dictionary Society of North America; Royal Swedish Society for the Publication of Manuscripts concerning the History of Scandinavia. Address: Tantogatan 43, SE-118 42 Stockholm, Sweden. E-mail: bo.svensen@telia.com

SVENSSON Charles Robert Vilhelm, b. 11 September 1947, Göteburg. Associate Professor; Scientist. Education: Associates Degree, Electronics, 1969; BSc, Physics, 1983, MSc, Physics, 1991, PhD, Thermionic Energy Converter Concept, 1994, Göteburg University. Appointments: Design Engineer, electronic temperature meters and heart beat monitors, -1981; Part-time teacher, 1981-83, Full-time Teacher, 1983-87, College of Applied Engineering and Maritime Studies, Chalmers University of Technology; Graduate Student, Department of Physical Chemistry, Göteburg University and Chalmers University of Technology, 1987-94; Assistant Professor, Chalmers University of Technology, 1995-96; Associate Professor, Chalmers University of Technology, 1996-. Publications: Numerous articles and papers; 2 patents. Memberships: Society of Automotive Engineers; American Society of Mechanical Engineers. Address: Dörravägen 1, SE-43893 Landvetter, Sweden. E-mail: term@chl.chalmers.sc Website: www.chl.chalmers.se/~term

SVIRIDOV Andrei Valentinovitsh, b. 22 December 1946, Moscow, Russia. Entomologist. Education: Moscow Lomonosov State University, 1965-70. Appointments: Senior Laboratory Assistant, 1970-71, Junior Researcher, 1971-86, Researcher, 1987-92, Senior Researcher, 1992-, Moscow Lomonosov State University; Scientific degree, Candidate of Biological Sciences (Dr), 1984; Academic Studies, Senior Researcher, 1995. Publications: 300 scientific publications, 1970-, include books: Types of the Biodiagnostic Keys and Their Applications, 1994; Biodiagnostical Keys: Theory and Practice, 1994; Key to the insects of Russian Far East, Vol 5, Part 4, 2003. Memberships: Russian Entomological Society; Moscow Society Naturalists; Society Europea Lepidopterology; Systematic Zoology/Biology; Hist-Genealogy Society, Moscow; Descendents Council of the Great War of 1812-1814 Vets; Commission of Red Book of Russia; Commission of Red Book of CIS. Address: Dr A V Sviridov, Zoological Museum, Moscow State Lomonosov University, Bolshaya Nikitskaya St 6, 125009 Moscow, Russia.

SVYAZHIN Anatoly, b. 11 October 1934, Verkhnaya Tura, Russia. Metallurgy Educator; Researcher. 1 son. Education: Diploma in Engineering, Moscow Steel and Alloys Institute, 1962; PhD, 1966; DSc, 1987; Professor, Moscow Steel and Alloys, 1989. Appointments: Graduate Student, Moscow Steel and Alloys Institute, 1962-66; Senior Research Scientist, 1967-71; Head, Steelmaking Division Research Laboratory, 1972-76; Head, Research Laboratory of Metals and Alloys, 1977-; Visiting Professor, Technical University of Czestoshwa, Poland, 1994-99; Adviser, Eko Stahl GmbH, Germany. Publications: Over 300 articles to scientific journals and conference proceedings; 17 inventions and patents. Honours: Recipient of Prize of Board of

Ministers of USSR, 1987; Awards of Minister of Education and Ferrous Metallurgy, 1980-95. Memberships: Science Committee, High Nitrogen Steels of Russian Federation, 1990-; Science Committee for Resources and Ecology, Ministry of Science and Technology of Russian Federation, 1996-; Association Steelmakers and International Metallurgist Union of Commonwealth Independent States; International Biographical Association. Address: Steel and Alloys Institute Tech University, Leninsky Prospect 4, 119049 Moscow, Russia.

SWAIM Mark W, b. 4 December 1960, Winston-Salem, North Carolina, USA. Hepatologist; Gastroenterologist; Academic Physician. Education: BA, summa cum laude, University of North Carolina, 1983; PhD, honours, 1990, MD, Duke University, 1990; Fellow, American College of Physicians, 2002 Diplomate, Internal medicine, 1993, Gastroenterology, 1998. Appointments: Attending Physician, Duke University Medical Center, 1998-2000; Associate, Department of Medicine, Duke University, 1998-2000; Physician, Durham Veterans Administration Medical Center, 1998-2000; MD, Anderson Cancer Center, University of Texas, 2000-; Founder, Southeastern Liver Institute, Jackson Tennessee, 2002-; Medical Director and Principal Investigator, Regional Research Institute, Jackson Tennessee, 2002-. Publications include: Rethinking the Art of Medicine, 1996; numerous publications in professional journals. Honours: Alpha Omega Alpha; Phi Beta Kappa; Phi Lambda Upsilon, Student Excellence Award, 1982; Hewlett-Packard Award, Clinical Excellence; First Walter A Puterbaugh Memorial Award, 1983; Conoco Chemicals Research Fellowship, 1983. Memberships: American College of Physicians; Alpha Omega Alpha; Sigma Xi; Reticuloendothelial Society; American Society for Gastrointestinal Endoscopy; American Association for the Study of Liver Diseases; American College of Forensic Examiners; American Gastroenterology Association. Address: 61 Valley Oak Loop, Jackson, TN38305, USA.

SWAMINATHAN Monkombu Sambasivan, b. 7 August 1925, Tamil Nadu, India. Director. Education: BSc, Travancore University, 1944; BSc, Agriculture, Coimbatore Agricultural College, Madras University, 1947; Associateship, Indian Agricultural Research Institute, New Delhi, 1949; UNESCO Fellow, Agricultural University, Wageningen, The Netherlands, 1949-50; PhD, School of Agriculture, University of Cambridge, England, 1952; Research Associate, Genetics, University of Wisconsin, USA, 1952-53. Appointments: Teacher, Researcher, Research Administrator, Central Rice Research Institute, Cuttack, Indian Agricultural Research Institute, New Delhi, 1954-72; Director General, Indian Council of Agricultural Research, Secretary, Government of India, Department of Agricultural Research and Education, 1972-80; Secretary, Government of India, Ministry of Agriculture and Irrigation, 1979-80; Acting Deputy Chairman, Planning Commission, Government of India, 1980; Member, Planning Commission, Government of India, 1980-82; Director General, International Rice Research Institute, Los Banos, Philippines, 1982-88; Honorary Director, Centre for Research on Sustainable Agricultural and Rural Development, Madras, 1989-; UNESCO Chair in Ecotechnology and President, Pugwash Conferences on Science and World Affairs. Publications: Numerous articles in professional journals. Honours include: 1st World Food Prize laureate, 1987; Tyler Prize, 1992; UNEP-Saskawa Environment Prize, 1994; V Gangadharan Award, Outstanding Contributions to National Development, 1997; BP Pal Memorial Award, Indian Science Congress Association, 1998; Volvo Environment Prize, 1999; UNESCO Gandhi Gold Medal, 1999; Franklin D Roosevelt Four Freedoms Award, 2000; Plant and Humanity Medal, 2000; Indira Gandhi Prize for Peace, Disarmament and Development, 2000; Millennium Alumnus Award, Tamil Nadu Agricultural University, 2000; Millennium

Dictionary of International Biography

Scientist Award, Indian Science Congress Association, 2001; 45 honorary doctorates from numerous universities world wide. Address: M S Swaminathan Research Foundation, 3rd Cross Street, Taramani Institutional Area, Chennai (Madras) 600 113, India.

SWAN Susan, b. 31 May 1943, Everett, USA. World History Professor. 1 daughter. Education: BA, English Composition, 1965; BA, History, 1965; MA, History, 1969; PhD, History, 1976. Appointments: Professor, History, Washington State University, 1977-82; Instructor, English, 1983-84; Student Affairs Officer, 1984-95; Mexico Research Associate, 1991-92; Professor, General Education Program, 1993-. Publications: Mexico, Breve Historia de la Sequias en Mexico, 1995; Reading About the World; Study Guide, 2002; Professional Journal Articles. Honours: Phi Alpha Theta; Phi Kappa Phi. Memberships: World History Association; American Association for the Advancement of Science; National Museum of Women in the Arts; WSU- Association of Faculty Women. Address: PO Box 2728, C S Pullman, WA 99165, USA.

SWANGER David, b. 1 August 1940, New Jersey, USA. Professor; Poet. m. Lynn Lundstrom, 5 April 1969, 1 son, 2 daughters. Education: BA, Swarthmore College, 1963; MAT, 1964, EdD, 1970, Harvard University. Appointments: Assistant Professor, Harvard University, 1970-71; Associate Professor, 1976-85, Professor 1985-, University of California, Santa Cruz. Publications: The Poem as Process, 1971; Lemming Song, 1976; The Shape of Waters, 1978; Inside the Horse, 1981; Essays in Aesthetic Education, 1991; Family, 1994; The Evolution of Education, 1995; This Waking Unafraid, 1995. Contributions to: Georgia Review; Malahat Review; Poetry Northwest; Chariton Review; America Post and Critic; Quarry West; New Letters; Mother Earth News; Negative Capability; Whetstone; Nimrod; Minnesota Review; Cutbank; Tendril; America; Reaper. Honours: National Endowment for the Arts Poetry Award, 1989; Foley Award, 1991. Memberships: Academy of American Poets; Poets and Writers. Address: Porter College, University of California, Santa Cruz, CA 95064, USA.

SWAYZE Patrick, b. 18 August 1954. Actor; Dancer. m. Lisa Niemi, 1976. Education: Harkness and Joffrey Ballet Schools. Appointments: Began as dancer in Disney on Parade on tour as Prince Charming; Appeared on Broadway as dancer in Goodtime Charley Grease; TV appearances in North and South: Books I and II; The New Season; Pigs vs Freaks; The Comeback Kid; The Return of the Rebels; The Renegades. Films include: Skatetown USA, 1979; The Outsiders; Uncommon Valor; Red Dawn; Grandview USA - also choreographer; Dirty Dancing - co-wrote song and sings She's Like the Wind; Steel Dawn; Tiger Warsaw; Road House; Next of Kin; Ghost; Point Break; City of Joy; Father Hood; Tall Tales; To Wong Foo - Thanks for Everything - Julie Newmar; Three Wishes; Letters from a Killer, 1997; Vanished, 1998; Black Dog, 1998; Without a Word, 1999; The Winddrinker, 2000; Wakin'Up In Reno, 2000; Forever Lulu, 2000; Donnie Darko, 2001. Address: c/o William Morris Agency, 151 South El Camino, Beverly Hills, CA 90212, USA.

SWE Nyein (Gary), b. 10 September 1946, Taikyi, Yangon, Burma. Physician. m. May Kyi, 2 sons. Education: MBBS, Yangon, 1971; Master of Medical Sciences, Internal Medicine, Yangon, 1981. Appointments: First Assistant, Medical Unit, Mawlamyine General Hospital, 1981; Consultant Physician, Chin State, Falam Township; Lecturer, Consultant Physician, Bago General Hospital, Bago Division; Lecturer, Consultant Physician, Mawlamyine General Hospital, Mon State, Myanmar. Publications: Comparative Drugs Trial on Falciparum Malaria, 1981-82; Incidence, Prevalence and Type of Diabetes in Mon State, 1992-93; Incidence and Mortality of Viper Bite in Mon State, 2000-

2001. Honour: Best Golf Player in Ministry of Health for 3 successive years, 1981-83. Membership: Member and Academic Chairman of Myanmar Medical Association, Mawlamyine Branch, Mon State. Address: No 37 (A), W Zina Pagoda Road, Papedan Drive, Mawlamyine, Mon State, Myanmar.

SWENSON Ulf, b. 11 June 1959, Berga, Ljungby, Sweden. Plant Systematist; Biographer. m. Karin Martinsson. Education: BSc, 1991, PhD, 1995, Uppsala University; Associate Professor (Docent), Lund University, 1999. Appointments: Research Fellow, Department of Systematic Botany, 1996-97, Lecturer, Biology Education Centre, 1997-98, Uppsala University; Research Fellow, Department of Systematic Botany, Lund University, 1998-99; Associate Professor, Department of Botany, Stockholm University, 1999-2002; Senior Curator, Swedish Museum of Natural History, 2002-. Publications: Several articles in professional journals. Memberships: International Association for Plant Taxonomy; Society of Systematic Biologists; American Society of Plant Taxonomists. Address: Swedish Museum of Natural History, Phanerogam Section, Box 50007, 10405 Stockholm, Sweden.

SWENSSON Evelyn Dickenson, b. 18 September 1928, Woodstock, Virginia, USA. Conductor; Composer. m. Sigurd Simcox Swensson, 9 June 1949, 2 sons, 2 daughters. Education: MusM, West Chester University, 1972. Career: Conductor: Aldersgate Methodist Church, Wilmington, Delaware, 1969-; Brandywiners Ltd, Kennett Square, Pennsylvania, 1973-2004; Conductor and Director of Education, Opera Delaware, Wilmington, 1974-; Conductor: Bi-Centennial Chorus, Wilmington, 1976; Northern Delaware Choral Society, Wilmington, 1977; Guest Conductor, Delaware Symphony Orchestra, Wilmington, 1977; Conductor: Ardensingers, Wilmington, 1978-80; Methodist Bi-Centennial in America, 1984; First State Chorus, Wilmington, 1987; Vice-President. Opera for Youth Inc; Conductor, over 50 operas including US premieres of Sleeping Beauty (Respighi), 1977, The Zoo (Sullivan and Rowe), 1980, The Lion, the Witch and the Wardrobe (McCabe), 1990, and world premieres of The Boy Who Grew Too Fast (Menotti), 1982, Charlotte's Web (Strouse), 1989, A Wrinkle in Time (Libby Larsen), 1992; The Phantom Tollbooth (Harnick/Black), 1995; Conductor of inaugural concert for Governor P S duPont IV, Wilmington, 1977; Conductor of world premieres of own compositions, The Enormous Egg, 1993, The Adventures of Beatrix Potter, 1994; The Jungle Book, 1995, Anne of Green Gables, 1996; The Homecoming, 1997, The Legend of Redwall Abbey, 1998, All Through the Night, 1999, The Trumpet of the Swan, 2000; From the Mixed Up Files of Mrs Basil E. Frankweiler, 2002, The Secret of Nimh, 2004. Honours: W W Laird Music Award, 1987; International Reading Council Literacy Award, 1989; Distinguished Alumna Award West Chester University, 1989; National League of American Pen Women, 5 composer awards, 2000. Address: 166 Heyburn Rd, Chadds Ford, PA 19317, USA.

SWERDLOW Steven Howard, b. 1 September 1950, Chicago, Illinois, USA. Haematopathologist. m. Jennifer, 2 daughters. Education: AB Summa cum laude, Brandeis University, USA, 1971; MD, Harvard Medical School, USA, 1975. Appointments: Director, Division of Haematopathology, 1992-, Professor (with tenure), 1997, University of Pittsburgh Medical Center-Presbyterian; Medical Staff Member, University of Pittsburgh Medical Center Shadyside Hospital, 1998-; Medical Staff Member, Children's Hospital of Pittsburgh, 1999-. Publications: Author or co-author of 130 publications, including 89 peer-reviewed reports. Honours: Listed in numerous Who's Who publications and biographical dictionaries. Memberships: AISP; Executive Committee, EAHP; Vice-President, President Elect, Society for Haematopathology; Council, United States and Canadian Academy of Pathology. Address: UPMC-Presbyterian, Pathology Department, Sixth Floor, C606, 200 Lothrop Street, Pittsburgh, PA 15213, USA.

SWETCHARNIK Sara Morris, b. 21 May 1955, Shelby, NC, USA. Artist; Sculptor; Painter; Writer. m. Norton Swetcharnik, 2 August 1981. Education: The Art Students League of New York, 1979-81; Postgraduate, Schuler School of Fine Art, Baltimore, Maryland, 1973-78; Private Study, Melvin Gerhold Studio, Frederick, Maryland, 1970-73. Appointments: Instructor, Frederick Academy for the Arts, Frederick, Maryland, 1981-82; Workshop Instructor, Landon School, Washington DC, 1991-96; Invitational Lecturer, Arts Task Force, Fulbright Conference, 2000, 2001; Guest Lecturer, The Institute, Mount Saint Mary's College, Emmitsburg, Maryland, 2001; Juror at several national and international exhibitions. Creative Works: Solo Exhibitions including: Catepetl Gallery, Frederick, Maryland, 1977; Holly Hills Country Club, Frederick, Maryland, 1991; Landon School Gallery, Washington DC, 1992; Frederick Community College Art Gallery, Maryland, 1993; Showcase of Terra-cotta Animal Sculpture, Weinberg Center for the Arts, Frederick, Maryland, 1994; Komodo Dragon Yearling and other Animal Sculptures, Reptile Discovery Center, National Zoological Park, Washington DC, 1995-2001; Jungle Tails: Narratives and Sculptures of Animals, http://www.marrder.com/htw/special/jungletails; Several group and two person exhibitions; Publications include: Glass Lizard, 1998; Marked for Life, 1998; Birthday Burro, 1998; Alfredo's Tigrillo, 1998. Honours include: IIE Fulbright Fellowship, Sculpture, Spain, 1987-88, 1988-89; Artist in Residence Fellowship, American Numismatic Association Conference, 1994; Fellowship, Virginia Center for the Creative Arts. Memberships: Delaplaine Visual Art Centre, Frederick, Maryland; Fulbright Association. Address: National Capitol Post Office Station, PO Box 77794, Washington, DC 20013, USA. E-mail: saraswetcharnik@fulbrightweb.org

SWETCHARNIK William Norton, b. 18 October 1951, Philadelphia, Pennsylvania, USA. Artist; Painter; Writer. m. Sara Morris Swetcharnik, 2 August 1981. Education: Rhode Island School of Design, 1969-71; University of California, San Diego, 1972-75; Schuler School of Fine Art, 1975-76; BS, Towson State University, Baltimore, Maryland, 1977; Art Students League, NYC, 1980. Career: Solo and Group Exhibitions include: Chrysler Museum, Norfolk, Virginia, 1992; Peninsula Fine Arts Centre, Newport News, Virginia, 1992; Gordon College, Wenham, Massachusetts, 1993; Washington County Museum of Fine Arts, Hagerstown, Maryland, 1993; Hood College, Frederick, Maryland, 1991, 1995. Honours: Several grants, residencies and fellowships. Memberships: Delaplaine Visual Art Centre, Frederick, Maryland; Fulbright Association. Address: 7044 Woodville Road, Mt Airy, MD 21771, USA. E-mail: swetcharnik@hood.edu

SWIEBODA Jozef, b. 25 November 1935, Lukawiec, Poland. Historian. m. Jozefa Kruczek, 1 son. Education: MA, History, Jagiellonian University; Doctor of Humanistic Science. Appointments: Teacher, High School, 1967-98; Lecturer, Supervisor of Teacher Trainees, High Pedagogical School, Rzeszow. Publications: 8 books, 60 papers in professional journals. Honours: Prizes, Polish Academy of Science, 1976, Ministry of Education, 1990; Prizes, Prime Minister of Poland, 1995. Memberships: Polish Historical Society; Historical Schools Association; New York Academy of Sciences. Address: Puszkina 6, 35-328 Rzeszow, Poland.

SWIFT Graham Colin, b. 4 May 1949, London, England. Writer. Education: Dulwich College; Queens' College, Cambridge; University of York. Publications: The Sweet Shop Owner, 1980; Shuttlecock, 1981; Waterland, 1983; Out of This World, 1988;

Ever After, 1992; Last Orders, 1996; The Light of Day, 2003; Short Stories: Learning to Swim and Other Stories, 1982; The Magic Wheel, 1986. Honours: Geoffrey Fabor Memorial Prize; Guardian Fiction Prize; Royal Society of Literature Winifred Holtby Award, 1983; Premio Grinzane Cavour, Italy, 1987; Prix du Meilleur livre etranger, France, 1994; Booker Prize, James Tait Black Memorial Prize, 1996; Hon LittD, East Anglia, 1998; Hon DUniv, York, 1998. Address: c/o A P Watt, 20 John Street, London, WC1N 2DR, England.

SYBRANDI Cornelis Pieter, b. 27 July 1938, Dokkum, The Netherlands. Minister; Clergyman. m. Pieternella Huiser, 2 sons. Education: Academic, Social and Cultural Work, 1961; Theological University, 1973. Publications: Magnetism as Healing Method, 1971; Ten Awesome Days, 1999; Got Even With The Past? 1999. Membership: Christian Union; Evangelical Reformed Church. Address: Tjalk 41-40, 8232 MX Lelystad, The Netherlands. E-mail: sybrandi@solcon.nl

SYDDALL Thomas Harold, b. 23 December 1938, Auckland, New Zealand. Patent Attorney. m. Ann Antrobus. Education: BSc, University of New Zealand, 1960; LLB, Victoria University of Wellington, 1966. Appointments: Registered Patent Attorney, 1963; Bar and Solicitor, High Court of New Zealand, 1966; Partner, A J Park (formerly A J Park & Son), Intellectual Property Lawyers, 1966-; Notary Public, 1995. Publications: Contributor to professional journals; New Zealand chapter in Katzarov's Manual on Industrial Property all over the World. Honour: International Order of Merit, 1997. Memberships: Fellow, New Zealand Institute of Patent Attorneys, President, 1980-82, Exam Board, 1991-; Wellington District Law Society; New Zealand Group, Asian Patent Attorneys Association, Executive, 1985-; New Zealand Institute of Chemistry; New Zealand Association of Scientists, Council Member, 1992-; New Zealand Group, International Association for the Protection of Industrial Property; New Zealand Section, International Federation of Industrial Property Attorneys; British Overseas Member, Chartered Institute of Patent Agents. Address: A J Park, Huddart Parker Building, Post Office Square, Wellington, New Zealand.

SYKES Eric, b. 4 May 1923, England. Actor; Writer; Director. m. Edith Eleanor Milbradt, 1 son, 3 daughters. Education: Ward St School, Oldham. Appointments: Long running TV comedy show Sykes (with Hattie Jacques); Many other TV appearances; Films include: actor: Orders are Orders; Watch Your Stern; Very Important Person; Heavens Above; Shalako; Those Magnificent Men in Their Flying Machines; Monte Carlo or Bust!; The Boys in Blue; Absolute Beginners; The Others, 2000; Plays include: Big Bad Mouse, 1977-78; A Hatful of Sykes, 1977-78; Run for your Wife, 1992; The 19th Hole, 1992; Two of a Kind, 1995; Fools Rush In, 1996; The School for Wives, 1997; Kafka's Dick, 1998-99; Caught in the Wet, 2001-02; Radio includes: (as writer) Educating Archie; The Goon Show, Co-wrote 24 episodes with Spike Milligan including 2 specials; The Frankie Howerd Show. Publications: The Great Crime of Grapplewick, 1996; UFO's Are Coming Wednesday, 1995; Smelling of Roses, 1997; Sykes of Sebastopol Terrace, 2000. Honours: Freeman City of London, 1988; Lifetime Achievement Award, Writer's Guild, 1992. Address: 9 Orme Court, London, W2 4RL, England.

SYKULSKI Jan Kazimierz, b. 28 March 1951, Lodz, Poland. University Professor. m. Elizabeta Sykulska, 1 son, 1 daughter. Education: MSc (with distinction), 1973, PhD, 1978, Electrical Engineering Technical University of Lodz, Poland. Appointments: Lecturer, Senior Lecturer, Technical University of Lodz, Poland, 1973-84; Lecturer, 1984-94, Senior Lecturer, 1994-95, Royal Academy of Engineering Professor of Distribution Engineering,

Dictionary of International Biography

1995-2000, Professor of Applied Electromagnetics and Head of Electrical Power Engineering Research Group, 2000-, University of Southampton, England. Publications: 168 articles. Honours: Fellow, Institution of Electrical Engineers; Fellow, Institute of Physics. Memberships: Chartered Engineer, UK; Senior Member, Institute of Electrical and Electronics Engineers, USA. Address: Electrical Power Engineering Research Group, Department of Electronics and Computer Science, University of Southampton, Highfield, Southampton SO17 1BJ, England. E-mail: jks@soton.ac.uk

SYMS Sylvia, b. 6 January 1934, London, England. Actress; Director. m. Alan Edney, 1957, divorced 1989, 1 son, 1 daughter. Education: Royal Academy of Dramatic Art. Appointments: Founder Member, Artistic Director, Arbela Production Company; Numerous lectures include: Dodo White McLarty Memorial Lecture, 1986; Member, The Actors' Centre, 1986-91; Films include: Ice Cold in Alex, 1953; The Birthday Present, 1956; The World of Suzie Wong, 1961; Run Wild Run Free, 1969; The Tamarind Seed, 1974; Chorus of Disapproval, 1988; Shirley Valentine, 1989; Shining Through, 1991; Dirty Weekend, 1992; Staggered, 1994; Food for Love, 1996; Mavis and the Mermaid, 1999; TV includes: Love Story, 1964; The Saint, 1967; My Good Woman, 1972-73; Nancy Astor, 1982; Ruth Rendell Mysteries, 1989; Dr Who, 1989-90; May to December, 1989-90; The Last Days of Margaret Thatcher, 1991; Natural Lies: Mulberry; Peak Practice; Ruth Rendell Mysteries, 1993, 1997-98; Ghost Hour, 1995; Heartbeat, 1998; At Home with the Braithwaites, 2000, 2001; Theatre includes: Dance of Death; Much Ado About Nothing; An Ideal Husband; Ghosts; Entertaining Mr Sloane, 1985; Who's Afraid of Virginia Woolf?, 1989; The Floating Lightbulb, 1990; Antony and Cleopatra, 1991; For Services Rendered, 1993; Funny Money,1996; Ugly Rumours, 1998; Radio includes: Little Dorrit; Danger in the Village; Post Mortems; Joe Orton; Love Story; The Change, 2001; Plays and TV Director: Better in My Dreams, 1988; The Price, 1991; Natural Lies, 1991-92. Honours: Variety Club Best Actress in Films Award, 1958; Ondas Award for Most Popular Foreign Actress, Spain, 1966. Address: c/o Barry Brown and Partners, 47 West Square, London, SE11 4SP, England.

SYNEK Jiri (George), (Frantisek Listopad), b. 26 November 1921, Prague, Czechoslovakia. University Teacher; Poet; Writer. 1 son, 5 daughters. Education: Dr Phil. Publications: Malelasky, 1945; Slava urknuti, 1945; Vzduch, 1946; Prvni veta, 1946; BojoVenezuel, 1947; Jarmark, 1947; Svoboda a jine ovoce, 1960; Tristao ou a Traiçao de um Intelectual, 1960; Cerny bily nevim, 1973; Contos Carcomidos, 1974; Secos & Molhados, 1982; Estreitamento Progressivo, 1983; Primeiro Testamento, 1985; Mar-Seco-Gelado-Quente, 1986; Os Novos Territórios, 1986; Album de Família, 1988; Outubro Oriente, 1992; Biografia de Cristal, 1992; Nastroje Pameti, 1992; Final Rondi, 1992; Blizko Daleko, 1993; Meio Conto, 1993; Oprava houslí a kytar, 1996; Prvni vety, 1997; Tristan z mesta do mesta, 1998; Krles, 1998; Milostná stehování, 2001; Prísti poezie; Em Chinatown com a Rosa, 2001; Chinatown S Rózou, 2001; Fruta tocada por falta de jardiniero, 2003; O jardim fecha as 18:30, 2004. Contributions to: Czech, Portuguese, American and French newspapers and reviews. Honours: Academy of Fine Arts, Prague, 1948; Swedish Academy, Lund, 1949; Christian Academy, Rome, 1950; Prize, Radio Free Europe, 1952; Critic's Prizes, Lisbon, 1968, 1970, 1980; Doctor honoris causa, CSFR, 1992; Franz Kafka Prize and Medal, 2000; Medal of Merit for Extraordinary Artistic Achievement, Prague, 2001; Prize Gracias Agit, Prague, 2004. Memberships: PEN Club International; Society of Portuguese Writers. Address: Rua Joao Dias 15, Lisbon 1400, Portugal.

SYRISTOVA Eva, b. 7 November 1928, Prague. Professor Emeritus of Psychopathology and Psychotherapy. m. Syriste Jaroslav MD, 1 son. Education: PhD, 1951, C Scientiarum in Psychopathology and Psychotherapy, Charles University, 1962. Appointments: Editor, SPN Publications, Prague, 1951-53; Clinical Psychologist, Institute of Psychiatry, Prague, 1953-57; Lecturer, 1957-67, Professor 1967-94, Prodean for Scientific Research, 1992-94, Professor Emeritus, 1994-, Psychopathology, Psychotherapy, Charles University, Prague; Pioneer of psychotherapy and art-therapy of schizophrenic psychosis in the Czech Republic. Publications: The Possibilities and Limitations of the Psychotherapy of Schizophrenic Diseases, 1965; The Imaginary World, 1973; Normality of the Personality, 1973; The Cracked Time, 1988; The Group Psychotherapy of Psychoses, 1989; Man in Crisis, 1994; The Poem as a Home in the Homelessness of Paul Celan, 1994. Honours: Honorary Appreciation Czech Medical Society for contribution to Czech Sciences, 1978; Honorary Prize for Translation of Celan's Poetry, 1983. Memberships: IAAP; IBRO; World Phenomenology Institute, International Association of Phenomenology and Sciences of Life; New York Academy of Sciences; Czech Medical, Psychiatric and Artistic Association; Director, White Rawen for Non-professional Art in Prague. Address: Sluknovska 316, 190 00 Prague 9, Czech Republic.

SYRKIN Alexander, b. 16 August 1930, Ivanovo, USSR. Philologist; Professor Emeritus. Education: Graduate (MA), Moscow State University, 1953; Candidate of History (PhD), 1962; Doctor of Philology, 1971. Appointments: Junior Research Associate, Institute of History, Academy of Science of USSR, Moscow, 1955-61; Junior Research Associate, 1961-71, Senior Research Associate, 1971-77, Institute of Oriental Studies, Academy of Science of USSR, Moscow; Research Fellow, Associate Professor, Institute of Asian and African Studies, 1978-98, Professor Emeritus, 1998-, Hebrew University, Jerusalem. Publications: Books, articles, commented translations of classical texts, essays on subjects including: Indology, Byzantine Studies, Russian Literature, etc; Examples include: Poem about Digenes Akritas, Moscow, 1964; Certain Problems Regarding the Study of the Upanishads, Moscow, 1971; To Descend in Order to Rise, Jerusalem, 1993. Former Memberships include: FRAS of Great Britain and Ireland; International Association of Buddhist Studies; International Association of Semiotic Studies. Address: Dov Gruner Str 236, Apt 17, Talpiot Mizrah, Jerusalem 91291 (POB 29278), Israel.

SYSE Aslak, b. Oslo, Norway. Professor of Public and International Law. m. Karin B Theodorsen, 2 daughters. Education: MD, 1972, Degree in Law, 1988, JD, 1996, University of Oslo, Norway. Appointments: Medical Doctor in various posts, Finmark, Norway, 1972-81; Medical Superintendent for Mentally Retarded, 1982-90; District Medical Officer, Mtoko, Zimbabwe, 1984-85; Assistant Professor of Public and International Law, 1989-96, Professor of Public and International Law, 1997-, University of Oslo, Norway; Visiting Scholar, Wolfson College, Oxford, England, 2001. Publications: Health Law, 1994; Welfare Law I, 1997, 2001; Welfare Law II, 1999, 2003; Welfare Law III, 2001, 2003; Patients Rights, 2001, 2004; Medical Faults, 2000. Membership: Centre for Socio-Legal Studies, Oxford, 2001. Address: University of Oslo, Department of Public and International Law, PO Box 6706, St Olav's Plass, NO-0130 Oslo, Norway.

SZABO Miklos, b. 14 March 1942, Tiszadorogma, Hungary. Military Historian. m. Vörös Márta, 1 son, 1 daughter. Education: Bachelor's Degree, Joint Military Academy, 1964; Army Staff College, 1972; Master's Degree, 1976; PhD, 1981, DSc, 1987,

Dictionary of International Biography

Hungarian Science Academy; Corresponding Member, Hungarian Academy of Sciences, 2001-. Appointments: 2nd Lieutenant, Army (Mechanised Infantry), 1964; First Lieutenant, 1967; Captain, 1972, Major, 1977; Teacher, 1972-77, Deputy Head, 1977-81, Head, 1981-84, Department of Art of War; Lieutenant Colonel, 1981, Colonel, 1984, Deputy Commandant, Joint Staff College, 1984-89; Commandant of Military Technical College, 1989-91; Major-General, 1990; President, Hungarian National Defence University, 1991-. Publications: 14 scientific books; 4 university books and lecture notes; 99 domestic and 16 international articles; 1048 national and 121 international references to scientific and public activity; 32 domestic and 23 international scientific presentations. Honours: Order of Merit, Hungarian Republic, Medium Cross; Grand Order of the Austrian Republic; Order for Law Enforcement History; 12 governmental honours; Miklos Zrinyi Award. Memberships: Committee of Military Sciences, National Postgraduate Degree Granting Board, 1991-96; Council of Higher Education and Sciences, Ministry of Defence, 1992-2001; Member, Scientific Council, Governmental Co-ordination Committee, 2001-; General Assembly of Deputies of Hungarian Science Academy, 1994-2001; President, Committee of Military Science, Hungarian Science Academy, 1994-2002; Corresponding Member, Hungarian Academy of Sciences, 2001-. Address: Budapest 146, Pf 15, H-1581, Hungary.

SZAKALY Agnes, b. 14 March 1951, Budapest, Hungary. Cimbalom Artist; Professor. m. Gabor Baross, 23 August 1975. Education: Cimbalom Faculty, Ferenc Liszt Academy of Music, Budapest, 1974; Faculty of Pedagogy, Eotvos Lorand University, 1983. Debut: Royal Opera House, Norway, Oslo, 1973. Career: Soloist, Concerts in Austria, England, Germany, Italy, Japan, Mexico, South Korea, Spain, Russia. Recordings: Bach, French Suites, 1982; Folk Arrangements, 1984; All That Music, 1986; Solo CD, Preludio, 1993; Music of 300 Years of Cimbalom, 1994; Works for Cimbalom, 1997; J S Bach, Goldberg Variations, 1998; Parallel Monologues, 2001. Honours: Artisjus Prize, 1983, 1985, 1986, 1988, 1992, 1996, 1999, 2001, 2003; Ferenc Liszt Prize, 1993; László Németh Prize, 1997. Memberships: Cimbalist Friendship Association, President; Hungarian Music Council. Current Management: A-G HA'P Bt, Baross u 148, 1161 Budapest, Hungary. Address: Baross u 148, H-1161 Budapest, Hungary.

SZASZ Andras, b. 4 November 1947, Budapest, Hungary. Physicist. m. Susan Szasz, 1 son, 1 daughter. Education: MSc, 1972, PhD, 1974, Budapest University; Cand Sci, St Petersburg University, 1982; CandSci Hungarian Academy Science, 1983; Habilitation Godollo University, 1996. Appointments: Assistant Professor, 1974, Associate Professor, 1984, Budapest ELTE University; Professor, 1996, Head, Biotechnics Department, 2003, St Istvan University, Godollo. Publications: 282; 25 patents. Memberships: European Physical Society; New York Academy of Science; European Hyperthermia Society; American Institute of Physics; IEEE. Address: 20 Szent Istvan Krt, H-1137 Budapest, Hungary.

SZLAZAK Anita Christina, b. 1 January 1943, Fulmer, England. Retired Public Servant. Education: BA (Economics), University of Toronto, 1963; Bruges, Certificate, Advanced European Studies (Economics) College of Europe, 1964; Boston, Advanced Management Program, Harvard Graduate School of Business Administration, 1981. Appointments: Research Economist, Development Centre, Organisation for Economic Co-operation and Development, Paris, 1964-67; Foreign Service Officer, Department of External Affairs, Ottawa, 1967-72; Deputy Director General, International Telecommunications, 1972-73; Director General, 1973-76, Department of Communications, Ottawa; Commissioner, Public Service Commission of Canada, 1976-82; Executive

Director, Government of Canada Office for the 1988 Olympic Winter Games, 1982-84; Special Advisor, Department of External Affairs, 1984-86; Senior Policy Advisor, Treasury Board of Canada, 1986-88; Special Advisor, International Relations, Canada Mortgage and Housing Corp, 1988-90; Director General, Program Management, Canadian Parks Service, Environment Canada, 1990-92; Director General, Special Projects, Atmospheric Environment Service, Environment Canada, 1992-94; Member, Canadian International Trade Tribunal, 1995-99; Member, United Nations International Civil Service Commission, New York, 2003-. Honour: HRH Queen Elizabeth II Silver Jubilee Medal, 1977. Memberships: Former Member, Institute of Public Administration of Canada, National Executive Committee, 1976-80; International Institute of Administrative Sciences, Brussels, Executive Committee, 1983-89, Vice President for North America, 1986-89; National Capital Harvard Business School Alumni Club, Vice President, 1990-92, 1995-2001. Address: 60 Belvedere Crescent, Ottawa, Ontario, K1M 2G4, Canada.

SZULMAN Aron E, b. 3 May 1920, Poland. Physician; Pathologist. m. Irene Gulder, 1 son, 1 daughter. Education: MB, ChB, School of Medicine, University of Birmingham, UK; Fellow Royal College of Pathology, London, 1984. Appointments: Instructor to Clinical Associate, Harvard Medical School, 1951-64; Associate Professor and Professor, School of Medicine, University of Pittsburgh, USA, 1964-90; Professor Emeritus (active), 1990-; Annual Szulman Lectureship, 1990-. Publications: Many papers and articles in professional medical journals and textbooks; Co-editor of textbook. Address: Department of Pathology, Magee Women's Hospital, Forbes Avenue and Halket Street, Pittsburgh, PA 15213, USA.

Dictionary of International Biography

T

TABOR David, b. 23 October 1913, London, England. m. Hannalene Stillschweig, 2 sons. Physicist. Education: BSc, Physics, Royal College of Science, London, 1934; Researched with George Thomson, 1934-36, Frank Bowden, 1936-39; PhD, 1939. Appointments: Division of the Commonwealth Scientific Research Organisation, Melbourne, 1940-46; Assistant Director of Research, 1946-61, Lecturer in Physics, 1961-64, Reader in Physics, 1964-73, Professor of Physics, 1973-81, Emeritus Professor of Physics, 1981-, Physics and Chemistry of Solids, Cavendish Laboratory, Cambridge Studied the effects between solid surfaces (tribology). Publications: Hardness of Metals, 1951; Gases, Liquids and Solids, 1969; Friction and Lubrication of Solids, Part I, 1959, 1986, Part II, 1964; Friction – An Introduction to Tribology, 1973; Contributions to learned journals on friction and adhesion. Honours include: Guthrie Medal, Institute of Physics, 1974; Royal Medal, Royal Society, 1992. Address: Cavendish Laboratory, Madingley Road, Cambridge, CB3 0HE, England.

TABORSKY Roger Emil, b. 21 January 1949, Baltimore, Maryland, USA. Electronics Engineer; Gymnast. Education: BS, Engineering, University of Maryland, USA, 1972; ASEP Coaching Principles Course; PDP Level One and Level Two Coaching Accreditation Three times National Safety Certified; 18 Certifications in Oceanography including: Master Scuba Diver Instructor; Rescue, Search and Recovery; Medic First Aid; Underwater Photographer; Certified Rifle and Pistol Instructor, National Rifle Association. Appointments: Currently, Electronic Engineer, Gramophone, Towson, Maryland, USA; Level II USA Gymnastics Coach; Gymnastics Career: State Champion, Men's Class I, 1971; Retired from competitive gymnastics, 1972; Member, American Sokol Organization, 1984-97; Team Coach, Sokol Baltimore Gymnastics, 1988-97; Member, Board of Appeals for National Competitions (American Sokol); Head Judge for National Competitions (American Sokol), 1992-97; Director Sokol Baltimore Gymnastics, 1992-97; Eastern District Director, American Sokol Organization, 1992-97; Team Gymnastics Coach for White Marsh Gymnastics, 1994-98; Professional Member, Athlete Member, USA Gymnastics; United States Elite Coaches Association for Women's Gymnastics; Team Gymnastics Coach, Baltimore County Gymnastics; Gymnastics Judge, USA Gymnastics, 1994-99; USA Gymnastics Course Administrator; Skill Evaluator for USA Gymnastics; Licensed with the Federal Communications Commission to operate a radio station. Honours: 1000 Logged Dives Underwater Award, Professional Association of Diving Instructors; Distinguished Expert, Small Bore Rifle Marksmanship Target Shooting. Memberships: United States Elite Gym Coaches Association; Professional Association of Diving Instructors; National Association of Diving Instructors; Life Time Endowment Member, National Rifle Association; Planetary Society; Amateur Radio Relay League. Address: Gramophone, 708 Saylor Court, Towson, MD 21286, USA. E-mail: r.taborsky@erols.com

TADA Takashi, b. 25 March 1961, Noshiro-Shi, Akita-Ken, Japan. Assistant Professor. m. Masako Tada, 1 son, 1 daughter. Education: PhD, Hokkaido University, Sapporo, Japan, 1993. Appointment: Research Associate, Wellcome/CRC Institute, University of Cambridge, England, 1994-97; Assistant Professor, National Institute of Genetics, Mishima, Japan, 1998-2000; Assistant Professor, Kyoto University, Kyoto, Japan, 2000-. Address: Kyoto University, 53 Kawahara-Cho, Shogoin, Sakyo-Ku, Kyoto 606-8507, Japan. E-mail: ttada@frontier.kyoto-u.ac.jp

TAFTI Hussein Arbab, b. 22 November 1958, Iran. Scientist; Engineer. m. Fatima N Farkhrooz, 2 sons. Education: PhD, Electrical Engineering. Appointments: Researcher into design of fibre optics telecom networks for Long-haul and Metro; Development of OC-192 ultra long-haul transmitters and receivers. Publications: More than 30 research papers in the area of semiconductor laser and fibre optics communications in international journals and conference proceedings. Address: 6908 Timber Creek Court, Clarksville, MD 21029, USA.

TAGHIPOUR Jahangir, b. 31 May 1950, Dehe Goroo (Shadegan), Iran. Physician; Medical Doctor. m. Golnaz Taheri, 2 sons. Education: MD, Gundi Shapour University, Ahwaz, Iran, 1979; Diploma in Thoracic Medicine, London University, England, 1987; Diploma, Royal College of Obstetricians and Gynaecologists, 1996; Diploma of Family Planning and Reproductive Health Care, 1995. Appointments: Member, Surgical Team, Royal Postgraduate Medical School (Hammersmith Hospital), London, 1982-84; Member, Thoracic Team, Royal Brompton and London Chest Hospitals, 1985-87; With University College Hospital and Middlesex Hospital, 1987-90; Member, Surgical Team, Crawley Hospital, England, 1990-91; Surgeon, Accident and Emergency Medicine, Mayday University Hospital, Greater London, 1992-93; Good Hope Hospital, Birmingham, England, 1993-94; Accident and Emergency Medicine and Surgery, Northwick Park Hospital, London, 1994-95; Barnet and Edgeware Hospitals, Greater London, 1996-97; Kingston and St George's Hospitals, London, 1998-99; Physician, Surgeon, Medical Co-ordinator, DF Medical Centre, West London, 2000-. Publication: Effects of Prolonged War and Repression on a Country's Health Status and Medical Services: Some Evidence from Iran, 1979-90 (co-author), 1992. Memberships: Expert, Medico-legal panels, various organisations; Fellow Royal College of Surgeons of Edinburgh; Member Royal College of Surgeons of England. Address: DF Medical Centre, 110 Marsh Road, Pinner, Middlesex, HA5 5NA, England. E-mail: drtaghipour@df-medical.com

TAHERZADEH Mohammad J, b. 22 March 1965, Isfahan, Iran. Biotechnologist. m. Arezoo Keivandarian, 2 sons. Education: BSc, Chemical Engineering, 1989; MSc, Chemical Engineering, 1991; PhD, Biochemical Engineering, 1999. Appointments: Vice Director, Jahad Daneshgahi, Isfahan University of Technology, Iran, 1988-91; Lecturer, Chemical Engineering, Isfahan University of Technology, 1992-94; Assistant Professor, Chemical Reaction Engineering, Chalmers University of Technology, Sweden, 1999-2001; Assistant Professor, Chemical Engineering, Lund University of Technology, Sweden, 1999-2001; Associate Professor, Chemical Reaction Engineering, Sweden, 2002-. Honours: Prize for the Excellent Rank among the Graduated MSc students by Iran's President; Listed in biographical publications. Address: Chemical Reaction Engineer, Chalmers University Technology, Kemivagen 10, 412-96 Göteborg, Sweden.

TAHMIZYAN Nikoghos, b. 9 May 1926, Athens. Musicologist. m. Svetlana, 2 sons. Education: MSc, 1962; DSc, 1980. Appointments: Professor of the Department of History of Music, 1987-. Publications: Over 150 scientific articles; 6 books including: Komitas and the Musical Legacy of the Armenian Nation, 1994; Sayat-Nova and the Armenian Minstrel Tradition, 1995; Tigran Tchoukhajian, His Life and Work, 1999. Honours: Doctor of Science diploma, 1980; Honoured Art Worker of the Armenian Republic, 1984. Memberships: Union of Composers of the USSR. Address: 275 Cordova St, #603, Pasadena, CA 91101, USA. E-mail: soundappeal@altrionet.com

TAKAYAMA Kiyoshige, b. 27 October 1948, Isesaki, Japan. Neurophysiologist. Education: Bachelor's Degree, 1971; Master's Degree, 1973, PhD, 1977, Gunma University, Japan.

Appointments: Assistant, 1980, Assistant Professor, 1980-91, Associate Professor, 1991-97, Professor, 1997-, Gunma University School of Health Sciences, Gunma, Japan. Publications: Articles in scientific journals including: Tetrahedron, 1973; Journal of the American Chemical Society, 1976; Biochemistry, 1976; Journal of Organic Chemistry, 1980; Japanese Journal of Physiology, 1981; Journal of Autonomic Nervous System, 1982, 1998; Brain Research, 1993; Neuroscience Letters, 1994, 2001. Memberships: Japanese Neuroscience Society; The Physiological Society, Japan. Address: Gunma University School of Health Sciences, 3-39-15 Showa, Maebashi, Gunma, 371-8514, Japan.

TAKEDA Kaoru, b. 28 September 1953, Okayama, Japan. Art Educator's Educator. m. Chiemi Kosuna, 2 daughters. Education: B E, Osaka Kyoiku University, 1978; M Ad, 1980. Education: Teacher, Osaka Kyoiku University Tennousi Junior High School, Japan, 1980-91; Associate Professor, 1991-97, Professor, 1997-2003, Hokkaido Kyoiku University, Asahikawa, Japan. Publications: The Journal for Society of Art Education in University (six thesis volumes); The Journal for the Society of Art Education (three thesis volumes). Memberships: Society for Art Education, Japan, Board of Directors, 1994-99; Society for Art Education in University, Regional Board, 1997-98, 2002-2003. Address: 2-30 5-jo 1-chome, Midori ga Oka, Asahikawa, Hokkaidou, Japan 078-8305.

TAKEI Noriyoshi, b. 3 August 1955, Tochigi prefecture, Japan. Epidemiologist; Psychiatrist. m. Atsuko, 2 sons. Education: MD, Iwate Medical College, Japan, 1982; Seishin-Eisei-Kanteii, 1988; MSc Epidemiology, London School of Hygiene and Tropical Medicine, University of London, 1994; PhD Medicine, University of Tokyo, 1997. Appointments: Trainee Psychiatrist, Tokyo Women's Medical College, 1982-84; Clinical Psychiatrist, Tokyo Kousei-Nenkin Hospital, 1984-85; Assistant, Tokyo Women's Medical College, 1985-91; Visiting Research Psychiatrist, 1989-91, Research Psychiatrist, 1991-, Honorary Lecturer, 1993-, Senior Lecturer, 1995-, Honorary Senior Lecturer, 1998-, Visiting Professor, 2002-, Institute of Psychiatry, London; Assistant Professor, 1998-, Associate Professor, 2000-, Hamamatsu University School of Medicine, Japan. Publications: Over 100 articles in international peer-reviewed journals; Over 70 published abstracts; 4 book chapters; Numerous conference presentations. Honours: Scholarship, Institute of Psychiatry, 1991; Travel Grant, Wellcome Trust, 1992; Wellcome Training Fellowship Grant, 1993-94; Young Scientist's Award, 1992; New Research Award, 1992; Stanley Foundation Fellowship, 1994-98; Stanley Foundation Research Center, Japan, 1999-. Address: Hamamatsu University School of Medicine, Department of Psychiatry and Neurology, 1-20-1 Handayama, Hamamatsu 431-3192, Japan. E-mail: ntakei@hama-med.ac.jp

TAKESHITA Toru, b. 16 December 1931, Nishinomiya City, Japan. Computer Software Researcher. m. Yumiko Taniguchi, 1 son, 1 daughter. Education: BA, Science, University of Kyoto, Japan, 1957; PhD, Computer Science, University of Beverley Hills, USA, 1983. Appointments: With IBM Japan Ltd, 1957-91: Senior Programmer IBM Data Systems Division, 1960-62; Systems and Programming Manager, IBM, Tokyo Olympic System, 1962-68; Production Manager, IBM WTC Advanced Systems, 1972-75; Consultant Software Technology, IBM CHQ, 1983-87; IBM Tokyo Research Laboratory, 1987-91; Professor, Chubu University, 1991-. Publications: 30 books related to computer programming; Numerous articles in professional journals. Honours: Yamanouchi Outstanding Achievement Award, Information Processing Society of Japan, 1988; IEEE Software Senior Referee Award, 1989.

Memberships: Information Processing Society of Japan; IEEE Computer Society; ACM. Address: 3-11-1-410, Soshigaya, Setagaya-ku, Tokyo 157-0072, Japan.

TALAIE Farhad, b. 24 August 1964, Tehran, Iran. Academic. Education: LLB, Iran, 1988; BSc, Applied Chemistry, Iran, 1991; LLM, International Law, Iran, 1992; PhD, International Law, Australia, 1998. Appointments: English Teacher, University Teacher, Researcher, International Law. Publications: Applied International Law (in Persian); UN Treaties on Outer Space (translation into Persian); Several papers in professional journals and proceedings of international conferences. Honours: Scholarship, Iranian Ministry of Culture and Higher Education, 1989, 1992. Memberships: Australian Branch, International Law Association; Australian Institute of International Affairs; Knowledge Society, England. Address: Faculty of Law and Political Sciences, Shiraz University, Pardiceh Eram, Shiraz 71945, Iran. E-mail: talaie@shirazu.ac.ir

TALAMO Maurizio, b. 11 May 1954, Rome, Italy. Professor. 1 son, 1 daughter. Education: PhD, Electronic Engineering, 1981; Full Professor, University of Rome, 1990. Appointments: Chief Executive of Projects, The Authority for IT in the Public Administration, 1995-2001; President of Nestor, University of Rome "Tor Vergata" Research Centre for e-government services with projects involving 8000 municipalities, 2001-; Supervisor of the Electronic Identity Card Project, Interior Ministry. Publications: Numerous articles as co-author include: A Reference Architecture for the Certification of E-Services in Digital Government Infrastructure. Distributed and Parallel Databases; An Efficient Data Structure for Lattice Operations; The Set Union Problem with Unlimited Backtracking; Esprit Project EP 6881 Amusing. Honours: Italian Interior Ministry Award for INA Project; UNCEM Honour for SIM Project. Address: via Emanuele Filiberto 233, 00185 Rome, Italy. E-mail: talamo@nestor.uniroma2.it

TALONEN Jouko Juhani, b. 11 April 1953, Vähäkyrö, Finland. Church Historian. Education: Master in Political Science, University of Turku, Finland, 1985; ThD, University of Helsinki, Finland, 1989; PhD. University of Oulu, Finland, 1997. Appointments: Pastor, Helsinki Diocese, Finnish Evangelical Lutheran Church, 1981, 1985; Acting Junior Assistant and Researcher, University of Helsinki, 1981-91; Docent, Political History, University of Turku, 1991-; Docent, Church History, University of Helsinki, 1993-, University of Oulu, 1993-; Researcher, Church History, Finnish Academy, 1992-2003; Visiting Scholar, Lutheran School of Theology, Chicago, Illinois, 1999; Lecturer, Church History, University of Joensuu, 2003-. Publications: Pohjois-Suomen lestadiolaisuuden poliittis-yhteiskunnallinen profiili 1905-1929, 1988; Viron lestadiolaisuus 1886-1953, 1989; Church under the Pressure of Stalinism: The development of the status and activities of the Soviet Latvian Evangelical Lutheran Church in 1944-50, 1997; Contributor of over 500 articles to professional and scientific journals and newspapers. Honours: Grantee, University of Helsinki, 1986-97; Exchange Grant, Latvian Government, 1996-98. Memberships: Research Member, Finnish Historical Society; Board of Directors, 2001-, Finnish Theological Institute; Board of Directors, 1996-96, Finnish Society for Local History. Address: Karjopolku 11B 33, 01360 Vantaa 36 Finland.

TALVET Jüri, b. 17 December 1945, Pärnu, Estonia. Professor of Literature. m. Margit Oja, 1 son, 2 daughters. Education: MA, University of Tartu, Estonia, 1972; PhD, University of St Petersburg, Russia, 1981. Appointments: Lecturer of Western Literature, 1974-86, Associate Professor of Western Literature, 1986-91, Chair of Comparative Literature, 1992-, Tartu University,

Estonia. Editor, Interlitterataria, annual international journal of comparative literature of the Estonia Association of Comparative Literature. Publications: In Estonian: Awakenings (poetry), 1981; A Travel to Spain, 1986; The Archer and the Cry (poetry), 1986; Soul's Progress and Surprises of Climate (poetry), 1990; From Spain to America (essays about Spain, Mexico, Cuba and Nicaragua), 1993; The Spanish Spirit (a collection of articles on Spanish and Catalan literature), 1995; Estonian Elegy and Other Poems, 1997, Spanish translation, 2002; American Notes or Contemplations of Estonia (essays), 2000; Do You Also Have Grapes? (poetry), 2001. Honours: Prize of Estonian Literature for essay genre, 1986; Order of Isabel the Catholic of Spain, 1992; Order of White Star of 4th Class of the Republic of Estonia, 2001. Memberships: Estonian Writers Union, 1984; Chairman, Estonian Association of Comparative Literature, 1994-; International Comparative Literature Association, 1994-, Member of Executive Committee, 2000-2003. Address: Pikk 100-12, 50606, Tartu, Estonia. E-mail: talvet@ut.ee

TAMARI Shmuel, b. 16 June 1937, Jerusalem, Israel. Iconotextologist. m. Miryam, 1 son. Education: BA, Institutes of Archaeology and Asian and African Studies, 1960; MG Environmental Studies, Muslim Medieval Urbanisation, Faculty of Architecture and Urbanism, Technion, Haifa, Israel, 1962; PhD, Oriental School, Rome University, 1966; Postdoctoral specialisation in restoration and preservation of historical monuments, Faculty of Architecture, Rome University. Appointments: Lecturer, 1968-72, Senior Lecturer, 1972-76, Professor, 1976-2000, Professor Editor, 2000-, Director department of Arabic, 1972-80, Bar-Ilan University, Ramat-Gan, Israel; Lecturer, 1968-72, Senior Lecturer, 1972-76, Tel Aviv University, Israel; Directorship, Israeli Oriental Society, 1972-86. Publications: Numerous articles and books including the following in English: Qala?at al-T?īna in Sinai: a historical and architectural analysis; Darb al-h?ajj in Sinai: an archaeological and historical study; Topological studies in the "Masālik al abs?ār fī mamālik al-ams?ār" of Ibn Fad?lallāh al-?Umarī; Iconotextual studies in mid-eastern Islamic religious architecture and urbanism in the early Middle Ages; Iconotextual studies in the Muslim ideology of Umayyad architecture and urbanism; Iconotextual studies in the Muslim vision of paradise; A comprehensively annotative edition of Kitāb ?Ajā'ib al-malakūt of Abū Ja?far Muh?ammad b. ?Abīdallāh al-Kis'ā'ī. Membership: The International Centre for the Study of Preservation and Restoration of Cultural Property. Address: 15 Nordau Street, Ramat Gan 52464, Israel.

TAMAS Christian, b. 13 November 1964, Letca-Salaj, Romania. Writer. m. Brandusa Bardas, 24 March 1993. Education: Foreign Languages, University of Bucharest. Appointments: Lecturer, University of Kishinev, Moldavia; Editor, Junimea Publishing House, Iasi; Editor in Chief, Graphix Publishing House, Iasi; President, ARS Longa Publishing House, Iasi; Translator, 7 languages; Lecturer, University of Perous, Italy. Publications include: Novels: The Black Knight, 1992; The Curse of the Cathars, 1993; Labyrinth, 1995; Studies of Comparative Religion: Awakening to Immortality, 1997.Honour: Listed in several biographical publications. Memberships: ASPRO; Liter Art XXI, USA. Address: Str Elena-Doamna, Nr 2, 6600 Iasi, Romania.

TAMAS Viorica, b. 19 November 1932, Ocna-Dej, Cluj, Romania. Doctor of Chemistry. m. Sergiu Tamas, 1 daughter. Education: Chemical Diploma, University of Bucharest, 1957; Dr of Chemistry, 1976; Researcher, Junior to Senior, National Institute for Chemical and Pharmaceutical Research, 1957-90. Appointments: Scientific Investigator, 1957-60, Junior Researcher - Senior Researcher, 1960-90; Head of Analytical Laboratory, Head of Analytical Department, 1965-85, Scientific Director, 1985-91;

Director of Research and Development, Biotehnos Research Institute, Bucharest, 1991-2000; Director of Research, S. C. Hofigal S. A. Bucharest, 2000-; Professional activity focused exclusively in the field of drugs research. Publications: Thin Layer Chromatography, 1972; 205 scientific papers in Romanian and foreign journals; 64 patents. Honours: Two Medals for Scientific Skill; Six Gold Medals in Romania, Geneva, Budapest and Brussels; Several Silver Medals and Diplomas for Patents; Diplomas: International Woman of the Year 2000-2001 for contribution to drugs research; 2000 Outstanding Intellectuals of the 20th Century; International Scientist of the Year 2002, International Biographical Centre, Cambridge, England; Citizen of Honour, Dej City, Romania. Memberships: Analytical Chemistry Society of Romania; General Association of Engineers from Romania. Address: str Dimitrie Grecescu nr 5, Sector 5, 76221 Bucharest, Romania.

TAMBS Lewis Arthur, b. 7 July 1927, San Diego, California, USA. Professor Emeritus. m. Phyllis Greer Tambs, 1 son, 6 daughters. Education: BS, University of California, Berkeley, 1953; MA, 1962, PhD, 1967, University of California, Santa Barbara. Appointments: US Army, 1945-47, 1950-51; Engineer, Venezuela, 1954-59; Assistant Professor, Creighton University, 1965-69; Professor of History, Arizona State University, 1969-2002; Consultant, NSC, 1982-83; Ambassador to Colombia, 1983-85, Costa Rica, 1985-87. Publications: over 100 books and articles. Honours: DEA, 1985; University of California, Santa Barbara Alumni Award, 1986. Memberships: Rotary International; Knights of Colombus. Address: 1041 E Sandpiper Dr, Tempe, AZ 85283-2020, USA.

TAMULEVICIUS Sigitas, b. 2 December 1955, Lithuania. Physicist. m. Egle, 1 son, 1 daughter. Education: Engineer, Moscow Engineering Institute of Physics, 1979; PhD, 1984; DSc, 1994. Appointments: Assistant Professor, 1979-89, Associate Professor, Institute of Technology, 1989, Professor, Physics Department, 1996, Kaunas University of Technology. Publications: Several articles in professional journals. Honours: Fulbright Scholarship, 1994; American Physical Society Scholarship, 1993; Winner. National Award for Science, 2001-. Membership: European Materials Research Society; Member, Lithuanian Academy of Sciences, 2002. Address: Vyduno Aleja 57-1, Kaunas 3028, Lithuania.

TAN Amy, b. 19 February 1952, Oakland, California, USA. Writer. m. Lou DeMattei, 6 April 1974. Education; BA, 1973, MA, 1974, San Jose State College; Postgraduate studies, University of California at Berkeley, 1974-76. Publications: The Joy Luck Club, novel, 1989, film, 1993; The Kitchen God's Wife, novel, 1992; The Moon Lady, children's book, 1992; The Chinese Siamese Cat, children's book, 1994; The Hundred Secret Senses, novel, 1995; The Bonesetter's Daughter, 2000; Numerous short stories and essays. Contributions to: Various periodicals. Honours: Commonwealth Club Gold Award for Fiction, San Francisco, 1989; Booklist Editor's Choice, 1991; Marian McFadden Memorial Lecturer, Indianapolis-Marion County Public Library, 1996. Address: c/o Ballantine Publications Publicity, 201 East 50th Street, New York, NY 10022, USA.

TAN Boen Hie, b. 14 December 1926, Padangan, Java, Indonesia. Analytical Chemist; Biomedical Scientist. Education: BS, 1952, MS, 1955, ScD, 1962, University of Leyden, Netherlands; Nuclear Medicine Specialist. Appointments: Fellow, Assistant Professor, University of Leyden, 1953-55, 1962-64; Fellow, Research Associate, Max Planck Institute, Göttingen, Germany, 1961-62, University of Minneapolis, Minnesota, USA, 1955-61, 1964-68, 1971-72; Research Associate, New York Hospital, Cornell Medical

Center, New York City, 1968-72; Research Associate, University of Groningen, Maastricht, Netherlands, 1973-81; Research Associate, University of Alabama, Mobile, USA, 1982-92; Analytical Chemist, Alabama State Environmental Management, Montgomery, 1992-. Publications: Over 55 articles in professional journals, including research on sulfhydryl, disulphide groups in denatured and renatured proteins; purification, QA/QC analyses of environmental pollutants, pharmacokinetic, pharmacological activities of new drugs; alpha-1-antitrypsin, plasma proteins, enzymes, inhibitors, fibrin formation and lysis; vanadate-sulfhydryl complexes and PDE activities; diabetes and the heart; DNA damage and repair. Honours: Research Fellow, University of Minnesota, 1955-61, 1964-65, 1972; Research Fellow, Max Planck Institute of Biophysical Chemistry, 1961. Memberships: American Association for the Advancement of Science; American Chemical Society; American Association for Clinical Chemistry, Nederlandse Vereniging voor Nucleaire Geneeskunde; New York Academy of Sciences; Alabama Academy of Science. Address: PO Box 230451, Montgomery, AL 36123, USA.

TAN Lihua, b. 22 October 1955, Jiangsu, China. Conductor. m. Lumin Qiao, October 1980, 1 daughter. Education: Graduated, Shanghai Conservatory of Music. Debut: Conducting Bruch's Violin Concerto and Dvořák Symphony No 9, Wuhan Orchestra, China. Career: Conductor, Chinese Ballet, 1990-96; Conductor, China Central Philharmonic Symphony Orchestra, 1993-; Music Director, Principal Conductor, Beijing Symphony Orchestra; Guest Conductor, Russian State Academic Symphony Orchestra, 2000-2001; Chinese premieres include: Pines of Rome, Dvořák Symphony No 7, Prokofiev Symphony No 5; Tchaikovsky Manfred Symphony; Guest conducting appearances include: New York Youth Symphony, Seattle Federal Way Symphony, Russian National Symphony, China Philharmonic Orchestra, Novosibirsk, Symphony Orchestra, London Philharmonic Orchestra, Britain Royal Philharmonic Orchestra, Trier Opera House, Germany, International Philharmonic, Germany, Australian Youth Symphony Orchestra, Australian Tasmania Symphony Orchestra; Israel Symphony Orchestra, Panama State Symphony Orchestra, Bogota Philharmonic Orchestra, Seoul Symphony Orchestra; Venues include New York City's Avery Fisher Hall, Lincoln Center; Moscow's Tchaikovsky Conservatory of Music; Sydney Town Hall, Beijing Forbidden City Concert Hall, Munich Philharmonic Concert Hall, Lisinski Concert Hall, Congress Centre Villach. Recordings: Beethoven Symphony No 5; Brahms Symphony No 4, with Beijing Symphony Orchestra; Dvořák Symphony Nos 8 and 9; Haydn Symphony No 94; Mendelssohn, Saint-Saëns and Tchaikovsky's Violin Concertos, China Central Philharmonic Symphony Orchestra. Publication: Article, Conducting Technique and Instrumental Performance, 1988. Honour: Professor Laureate, Tianjin Conservatory of Music. Memberships: Chairman, Beijing Musicians' Association; Director, China Musicians' Association; Standing Committee, China Symphony Development. Address: Beijing Symphony Orchestra, No A-1 Eight Poplar, Shuang Jing, Chao-Yang District, Beijing 100022, China.

TAN Robert See-Hoong, b. 5 November 1959, Singapore. Physician. m. Grace, 1 son, 1 daughter. Education: MD, Singapore, 1983; FRACGP, Australia, 1988; DGM, London, 1989; ABFP, USA, 1994; CAQ Geriatrics, USA, 1996; CMD, USA, 1998; MBA, California, USA, 1998; CPE, USA, 1999. Appointments: Assistant Professor, Associate Chief of Staff, 1995-99; Associate Professor, 1999-, Clinical Director, Geriatrics, VA Medical Center, 2003-, University of Texas, Houston, Texas, USA. Publications: Book: Aging Men's Health; The Andropause Mystery; More than 80 publications on various aspects of men's health, gerontology, entrepreneurship. Honours: Best Doctors in America; Listed in Who's Who publications and biographical dictionaries.

Membership: Fellow, American Geriatrics Society. Address: University of Texas, 6431 Fannin JJL Suite 308, Houston, TX 77030, USA. E-mail: robert.s.tan@uth.tmc.edu

TAN Xuehou, b. 19 March 1962, Jiangsu Province, China. Computer Scientist. m. Jie Cheng, 2 sons. Education: Bachelor, 1982, Master, 1985, Nanking University, China. Doctor, Nagoya University, Japan, 1992. Appointments: Research Associate, Nanking University, China, 1985-87; Postdoctoral Fellow, University of Montreal, Canada, 1992-93; Assistant Professor, 1993-2000, Associate Professor, 2000-, Tokai University. Publications: Book: An Introduction to Computational Geometry, 2001; Articles: Approximation algorithms for the watchman route and zookeeper's problem; Finding shortest safari routes in simple polygons; Finding an optimal bridge between two polygons. Memberships: Institute of Electronics Information and Communications Engineers; Information Processing Society of Japan. Address: Tokai University, 317 Nishino, Numazu 410-0395, Japan. E-mail: tan@wing.ncc.u-tokai.ac.jp

TANAKA-AZUMA Yukimasa, b. 7 March 1964, Sakai, Japan. Pharmacologist; Biochemist; Researcher. m. Hiromi Tanaka, 1 son, 1 daughter. Education: BSc, Biology, 1982-86, MSc, Biology, 1986-88, Konan University, Kobe, Japan; PhD, Pharmacology, Okayama University, Okayama, Japan, 2000. Appointments: Central Research Institute, Nissin Food Products Co, Ltd, 1988-2002; Research Student, Japan Collection of Micro-organisms, RIKEN, Wako, Japan, 1999-2000; Food Safety Research Institute, Nissin Food Products Co Ltd, 2002-. Publications: 19 papers in scientific journals include: Cholesterol-lowering effects of NTE-122, a novel acyl-CoA:cholesterol acyltransferase (ACAT) inhibitor, on cholesterol diet-fed rats and rabbits, 1998; Lactobacillus casei NY1301 increases the adhesion of Lactobacillus gasseri NY0509 to human intestinal Caco-2 cells, 2001. Honours: Listed in Who's Who publications and biographical dictionaries. Memberships: Member, Scientific Council, Japanese Pharmacological Society; Japanese Society for Food Science and Technology. Address: Food Safety Research Institute, Nissin Food Products Co Ltd, 2247 Noji, Kusatsu, Shiga 525-0055, Japan. E-mail: y-azuma@mb1.nissinfoods.co.jp

TANIGUCHI Makoto, b. 31 March 1930, Osaka, Japan. Diplomat; Professor. m. Hiroko Kanari, 1 son. Education: BA, 1954, MA, 1956, Hitotsubashi University; Tripos, BA, 1958, MA, 1960, St John's College, Cambridge University, England.. Appointments: Ambassador of Japan to The United Nations, 1986-89; Deputy Secretary-General of Organisation for Economic Co-operation and Development, 1990-96; Professor, Graduate School of Asia-Pacific Studies, Waseda University, 1997-2000; Visiting Professor, International Christian University, 1998-2000; Director, Research Institute on Current Chinese Affairs, Waseda University, 2000-; Visiting Professor, Toyo Eiwa Women's University, 1997-; External Auditor, Hitachi Metals, 1994-2003. Publications: North-South Issues - A Path to Global Solutions, 1993; The World in 2020 - Towards a New Global Age, 1997; North South Issues in the 21st Century – A Challenge of Globalisation, 2001. Honour: The Second Order of Merit, 2000. Membership: The Tokyo Club. Address: 901 Azabu House, 1-7-13 Roppengi, Minato-Ku, Tokyo 106-0032, Japan.

TANIGUCHI Tomoyo, b. 12 March 1965, Nagoya, Japan. Seismic Engineer; Offshore Engineer. m. Mariko Taniguchi, 2 daughters. Education: Bachelor of Engineering, Ocean-Civil Engineering, Kagoshima University, 1987; Master of Engineering, Civil Engineering, Tokyo University, 1989; Doctor of Philosophy, Ocean-Civil Engineering, Kagoshima University, 1998. Appointments: Designer, 1989, Deputy Manager, 1997, Kawasaki

Heavy Industries Ltd; Associate Professor, Tottori University, 2001-. Publications: Articles in scientific journals include: Non-linear response analysis of rectangular rigid bodies subjected to horizontal and vertical ground motion, 2002; Rocking behaviour of unanchored flat-bottom cylindrical shell tanks under action of horizontal base excitation, 2004. Memberships: Department of Civil Engineering, Tottori University, 4-101 Koyama-Minami, Tottori, 680-8552 Japan. E-mail: t_tomoyo@cv.tottori-u.ac.jp

TANIMURA Makoto, b. 24 October 1966, Kunitachi, Tokyo, Japan. Solid-State Physicist. m. Fumika Ayakoji, 1 son. Education: Bachelor of Engineering, 1990, Master of Engineering, 1992, PhD, Engineering, 1998, Waseda University, Japan. Appointments: Senior Researcher, NISSAN ARC, LTD, 1992-; Visiting Researcher, Yokohama City University, 2000-; Part-time Teacher, Waseda University, 2003-. Publications: Articles in scientific journals including: Physical Review, 1995, 1996, 1997, 2003; Journal of Chemical Society Faraday Transaction, 1998; Applied Physics Letters, 2001; Journal of Physics Condensed Matter, 2002. Honour: Best Poster Award, Japan Institute of Metals, 2003. Memberships: Physical Society of Japan; Japan Institute of Metals. Address: Research Department, NISSAN ARC LTD, 1 Natsushima-cho, Yokosuka, Kanagawa 237-0061, Japan. E-mail: tanimura@nissan-arc.co.jp

TANNER Dee Boshard, b. 16 January 1913, Provo, Utah, USA. Lawyer. m. Jane. 1 son, 1 daughter. Education: BA, Utah University, 1935; Postgraduate Studies, Harvard Law School, 1936, Loyola University, 1937; Bachelor of Law, Pacific Coast University, 1940. Appointments: Admitted to Practice, California Supreme Court, 1943; US District Court, Southern District California, 1944; US Court of Appeals, 9th Circuit, 1947; US District Court, Eastern District California, 1969; US Supreme Court, 1971; Associate, Spray, Davis & Gould, 1943-44; Private Practice, 1944; Associate, Tanner & Sievers, 1944-47, Tanner and Thornton, Los Angeles, 1947-54, Tanner, Hanson, Myers, Los Angeles, 1954-64; Partner, Tanner & Van Dyke, 1964-65; Gallagher & Tanner, Los Angeles, 1965-70; Private Practice, Pasadena, California, 1970-95; Retired 1995. Honours: Republican Gold Medal, 2003; Listed in Who's Who publications and biographical dictionaries. Memberships: Former Member, Los Angeles Bar Association; World Affairs Association; Harvard Law School Association; Lawyer's Club Los Angeles. Address: 1720 Lombardy Road, Pasadena, CA 91106, USA.

TANNINEN Seppo Johannes, b. 9 June 1948, Alavus. Painter; Poet; Critic. 1 son, 1 daughter. Education: Finnish Art Academy, 1968-70. Appointments: Artists Association of Finland; Seinajoki Art Museum Association. Creative Works: Amos Anderson Museum; Vaino Aaltonen Museum; Nelimarkka Museum; Collection of the State of Finland; Merita Collections; Collections of the Finnish Post and Tele; Pohjola Collections; K H Renlund Museum; Ostrobothnian Museum. Publications: Krunoja, Visual Poems, WSOY, 1977; Italy Diary, poems, 1983; Articles and Art Critics. Honours: 3 Years Artist Scholarship, State of Finland, 1989; 5 years Artist Scholarship, State of Finland, 1993. Memberships: Finnish Painters Union; Ostrobothnian Artists Association; Seinajoki Artists Association; Non Art Group; Union of Finnish Critics; International Association of Art Critics. Address: Villenraitti 8, 60200 Seinajoki, Finland.

TANTRA Muljadi, b. 1 July 1971, Selatpanjang, Indonesia. Director of Corporate Marketing. m. Vivi Effendy, 1 son, 1 daughter. Education: BS, Aerospace Engineering, Iowa State University, USA, 1992; MBA, San Diego State University, USA, 1996. Appointments: APC Software Business Development Manager, Marketing Analysis Manager, Cymer Inc; Director of Business Development, North America, currently Director of Corporate Marketing, Lam Research. Publications: Article: Analyzing Technological Solution Process with Ecological Model, 1997; Other articles in non-peer reviewed journals. Honours: Two US Patents; Phi Beta Delta (Honor Society for International Scholars); Beta Gamma Sigma (Business Honor Society); Sigma Xi (Scientific Research Society). Address: 2667 Torrey Court, Pleasanton, CA 94588, USA. E-mail: muljadi.tantra@lamrc.com

TAOOKA Yasuyuki, b. 13 September1963, Hiroshima, Japan. Pulmonologist; Researcher. m. Megumi Taooka, 2 sons. Education: MD, Tokushima University School of Medicine, 1989; PhD, Hiroshima University School of Medicine, 1998; Diplomate, Japanese Board of Respiratory Disease, 2001; Fellow of the Japanese Society of Internal Medicine, 2003. Appointments: Resident, Hiroshima University Hospital, 1989-91; Medical Staff, Saijo Central Hospital, Hiroshima, 1991-94; Postdoctoral Fellow, University of California San Francisco, USA, 1998-2000; Medical Staff, Hiroshima Red Cross Hospital, 2001-2002; Research Associate (Faculty), Research Institute for Radiation Biology and Medicine, Hiroshima University, 2002-; Lecturer, Nurses Teaching School, Hiroshima Medical Association, 1995; Medical Staff Expert, Japan International Co-operation Agency, 2002. Publications: Original articles in scientific journals including: American Journal of Respiratory Critical Care, 1997, 2000; Journal of Cell Biology, 1999; Journal of Biological Chemistry, 2000; Molecular Cellular Biology, 2001; Books: Integrated Handbook of Internal Medicine, volume 74, 1995; Keyword Pulmonary Diseases 1996-97, 1996, 1998-99. Honours: Scholarship for Young Doctors, Organization of Health and Aging, 1998; Listed in Who's Who publications and biographical dictionaries. Memberships: Japanese Society of Internal Medicine; Japanese Respiratory Society; American Society for Cell Biology; American Thoracic Society; American College of Chest Physicians. Address: 1-2-3 Kasumi, Minami-ku, Hiroshima, 734-8553, Japan.

TAPLIN Ruth, b. 12 January 1963, San Francisco, California, USA. Company Director; Author; Writer; University Researcher. 1 son. Education: PhD, London School of Economics, 1985. Appointments: Centre for Management Studies, University of Exeter; Westminster University; The Open University; Research Fellow, University of Durham, 1997-2000; Research Fellow, Birkbeck College University of London and the Management Centre, University of Leicester, 2002-; Commentator on East Asia on radio and television such as Newsnight, BBC Radio 4, Australian and Hong Kong television; Consultant, Federation of Electronics Industry, 9 years; Editor, Journal of Interdisciplinary Economics, 9 years; Writer, Times Newspaper, 9 years; Feature Writer and East Asian Editor, CBI News, 6 years; UK Government Representative, Asian Economic Business Forum, 1999-2001; Currently, Director, Centre for Japanese and East Asian Studies. Publications: 9 books include: Decision Making and Japan, 1995; UK Australia Trade (co-author), 2001; Exploiting Patent Rights and a New Climate for Innovation in Japan (editor and contributor), 2003; Valuing Intellectual Property Japan Britain and the USA, 2004; Articles in professional magazines including: Mobile Asia Pacific; BioPeople; The IEE Review. Honour: Named Exporter of the Year 2000, Partnership in Trading/Pathfinder, Export Times, British Exporters Association and BTI. Address: Centre for Japanese and East Asian Studies, PO Box 427, Pinner HA5 3FX, England. E-mail: ruth.taplin@btinternet.com

TARANTINO Quentin, b. 1963, Los Angeles, USA. Film Director. Appointments: Worked in Video Archives, Manhattan Beach; Actor; Producer: Killing Zoe; Red Rain, 1995; Four Rooms, 1995; From Dusk Till Dawn, 1996; Curdled, 1996; Ying xiong, 2002; Director: Reservoir Dogs; Pulp Fiction, 1994; Jackie Brown,

1997; 40 Lashes (also writer), 2000; Kill Bill: Vol 1 (also writer), 2003; Kill Bill: Vol 2 (also writer), 2004 Appearances include: Sleep With Me, 1994; Destiny Tunes on the Radio, 1995; Desperado, 1995; Girl 6, 1996; From Dusk Till Dawn, 1996; Little Nicky, 2000. Publications: Screenplays: True Romance, 1995; Natural Born Killers, 1995; Jackie Brown, 1998; Kill Bill (novel), 2003. Honours: Golden Palm, Cannes Film Festival, 1994. Address: WMA, 151 El Camino Drive, Beverly Hills, CA 90212, USA.

TARNANAS Ioannis, b. 21 November 1974, Thessaloniki, Greece. Mathematician. Education: Psychology degree, 1998; MSc, Human-Computer Interaction, 1999. Career: PhD Candidate in Affective Computing, Human-Computer Interaction; EU funding projects researcher; Owner, HCI-Informatics Company; TV show host on Human-Computer Interaction and CyberPsychology matters. Publications: Book: Human Factors for Mobile Learning; Articles in professional scientific journals. Honours: Electralis project selection award, 2001; Archimedes Award, 2001. Memberships: Psychophysiology in Ergonomics Society; International Association for Applied Psychology; Socrates EU Experts. Address: 1st Emm Papa Street, Thessaloniki 55236, Greece. E-mail: ioannist@psy.auth.gr

TAY Richard Soon-Teck, b. 16 July 1959, Singapore. Professor. m. Sherry Tay, 2 daughters. Education: BS, Electrical Engineering, Texas Technical University, USA; MS, Engineering Economics, Stanford University, USA; PhD, Economics, Purdue University, USA. Appointments: Assistant Professor in Applied Economics, Nayang Technical University; Visiting Scholar, Sloan School of Management, Massachusetts Institute of Technology, USA; Assistant Professor, Managerial Economics, Chinese University of Hong Kong; Associate Professor, Road Safety, Queensland University of Technology, Australia. Honour: Listed in Who's Who publications and biographical dictionaries. Address: Carrs-Q, Queensland University of Technology, Carseldine, Queensland 4034, Australia. E-mail: r.tay@qut.edu.au

TAYLOR Alison, b. 20 April 1944, Stockport, Cheshire, England. Author; Journalist. 1 son, 1 daughter. Education: Certificate of Qualification in Social Work; Diploma in Social Work. Appointments: Psychiatric social work and probation; Senior childcare posts, Gwynedd County Council, 1976-86; Claim for unfair dismissal settled, 1989; Author; Journalist; Conference guest speaker. Publications: 5 novels: Simeon's Bride; In Guilty Night; The House of Women; Unsafe Convictions; Child's Play; Papers on child care, ethics and social issues; Lectured and written on 18th and 19th century Welsh and German literature, music and poetry. Honours: Community Care Readers Award, 1996; Campaign for Freedom of Information Award, 1996; Pride of Britain Award, 2000. Memberships: Elected, Welsh Academy, 2001; Member, American Beethoven Society. Address: c/o Sara Fisher, A M Heath and Co, 79 St Martins Lane, London WC2N 4AA, England.

TAYLOR Eldon, b. 27 January 1945, Anchorage, Utah, USA. Research Psychologist; Author. m. Ravinder Kaur, 4 sons, 3 daughters. Education: Political Science, Philosophy, Weber State University, Ogden, Utah, 1971-74; Metaphysics Bachelor, University of Metaphysics, Los Angeles, 1982-83; Metaphysics Masters, 1983; Doctorate, Metaphysical Science, 1984; Doctorate Divinity, Un College Seminary, 1985; Doctorate, Pastoral Psychology, 1986; Doctorate, Philosophy of Hypnotherapy, American Institute of Hypnotherapy, 1986; Doctorate, Philosophy of Clinical Psychology, St John's University, Springfield, 1990. Appointments: Self Employed, Intelligence and Counterintelligence, 1977-87; Pastoral Counsellor, International

Metaphysical Ministry, 1984-87; Counsellor, Utah State Prison, Unpaid Staff, Maximum Security Clearance, 1985-88; Spiritual Advisor, Intermountain Hospice Center, 1986-88; Director, Progressive Awareness Research, 1987-. Publications: Self Power; Thinking Without Thinking; Simple Things and Simple Thoughts; Subliminal Technology; Subliminal Learning; Many others. Honours: Pen and Quill Award; Golden Palms Award; Cultural Doctorate in Pastoral Psychology; Golden Poet Award; Honorary Doctor of Humanities; Inclusion into many Who's Who publications. Memberships: Diplomat, The American Psychotherapy Association; United States National Judo Association; American Psychological Practitioners Association; International Academy of Criminology; American Law Enforcement Officers Association; The National Society of Hypnotherapists; The American Association of Behavioural Therapists; Many others. Address: Progressive Awareness Research, P O Box 1139, Medical Lake, WA 99022, USA.

TAYLOR Harris C, b. 30 April 1940, Brooklyn, New York, USA. Physician; Endocrinologist. m. Diana Kahn Taylor, 1 son, 1 daughter. Education: BS, Queens College, City University of New York, 1961; MD, University of Chicago School of Medicine, 1965. Appointments: Director, Endocrinology Laboratory, 1978-96; Director, Internal Medicine Residency, 1985-94, Lutheran Hospital, Cleveland, Ohio; Currently Clinical Professor of Medicine-Endocrinology, Case Western Reserve University School of Medicine, Cleveland. Publications: 30 papers in peer reviewed journals; 2 book chapters. Honours include: Phi Beta Kappa; Best Doctors in America, 1998, 2001-02, 2003-04; Master Teacher Award, American College of Physicians, 2001. Memberships: Fellow, American College of Physicians; Fellow, American College of Endocrinology; Endocrine Society; President, Diabetes Association of Cleveland, 1982-84. Address: 3166 Huntington Road, Shaker Heights, OH 44120, USA.

TAYLOR John C, b. 22 July 1914. Dentist; Missionary; Teacher; Writer; Political Advisor and Counsellor. m. Adah, 2 sons, 5 daughters. Education: BS, Muskingum College, 1937; BD Reformed Presbyterian Seminary, Ordained 1939; Certificate, Landour Language School, India, 1941, Hindi; Certificate, Henry Martin School of Islamics, India, 1941, Urdu; Medical College of Virginia School of Dentistry, 1945-46; DDS, University of Pittsburgh School of Dentistry, 1949; Diploma, Northwestern School of Taxidermy, 1952; Diploma, Academy of General Dentistry, 1975. Career includes: Pastor, 5 Churches in Pennsylvania; Appointed Missionary (serving under several denominational boards and authorities); Teacher/Lecturer/Clinical, Schools, Clubs, Churches, Seminars; Registered General Dentist, 7 Different Practices; Artist/Photographer, Superintendent, Presbyterian Home Mission Board, 1947-52; Director of Dental Clinic, Methodist Mission Hospital, Bariely, India, 1954-55; Founder and Director, Landour Community Hospital Dental Department 1955-59. Publications: Books: Wildlife in India's Tiger Kingdom; Face the Devil's Roar; God's Kingdom Helps Animal Kingdoms. Honours: Athlete of the Year Award, Woodstock High School, 1931; 4-Letter Man, Muskingum College, 1933-37; Past President, Diamond-Studded Medallion, Mt. Union Rotary Club, 1965; Lecturer's Award for Serving 7th District Rotary Club; Listed in: Who's Who in the East; Who's Who in North America; Dictionary of International Biography; Men of Achievement; International Who's Who of Intellectuals; Personalities of America; International Register of Profiles; Two Thousand Notable Americans; Five Thousand Personalities of the World; Marquis Who's Who in the World, 2001; Marquis Who's Who in Medicine and Healthcare, 2002-2003; Memberships: American Dental Association; Academy of General Dentistry; Rotary Club; Lions

Club; Sportsmen's Club; Life Fellow, International Biographical Association; Global Outreach Mission. Address: 110 Highland Avenue, Herminie, PA 15637, USA.

TAYLOR Judy, (Julia Marie Hough), b. 12 August 1932, Murton, Swansea, Wales. Writer. m. Richard Hough, 1980. Appointments: Bodley Head Publishers, 1951-81; Director, Bodley Head Ltd, 1967-84, Chatto, Bodley Head and Jonathan Cape Ltd, 1973-80, Chatto, Bodley Head & Jonathan Cape Australia Pty Ltd, 1977-80; Consultant to Penguin, Beatrix Potter, 1981-87, 1989-92. Publications: Sophie and Jack, 1982; My First Year: A Beatrix Potter Baby Book, 1983; Sophie and Jack in the Snow, 1984; Dudley and the Monster, 1986; Dudley Goes Flying, 1986; Dudley in a Jam, 1986; Dudley and the Strawberry Shake, 1986; That Naughty Rabbit: Beatrix Potter and Peter Rabbit, 1987; Beatrix Potter 1866-1943, 1989; Beatrix Potter's Letters: A Selection, 1989; So I Shall Tell You a Story, 1993. Play: Beatrix (with Patrick Garland), 1996; Edward Ardizzone's Sketches for Friends: A Selection, 2000. Contributions to: Numerous professional journals. Honour: Member of the Order of the British Empire, 1971. Memberships: Publishers Association Council; Book Development Council; UNICEF International Art Committee; UK UNICEF Greetings Card Committee; Beatrix Potter Society; Royal Society of Arts, fellow. Address: 31 Meadowbank, Primrose Hill Road, London NW3 3AY, England.

TAYLOR Kent, b. 8 November 1940, New Castle, Pennsylvania, USA. Writer; Poet. Widower, 1 son. Education: BA, Ohio Wesleyan University, 1962. Appointment: Medical Research Associate. Publications: Rabbits Have Fled; Late Show at the Starlight Laundry; Driving Like the Sun; Empty Ground; Shit Outside When Eating Berries; Cleveland Dreams; Torn Birds; Late Stations; Fortuitons Mother Fucker; Aleatory Letters; Selected Poems. Contributions to: Many reviews, quarterlies, and magazines. Address: 1450 10th Avenue, San Francisco, CA 94122, USA.

TAYLOR Percy Ronald, b. 4 April 1918, Sheffield, Yorkshire, England. Metallurgist. Ruth Wilmot, 1 son. Education: Studies for Civil Service Examination (Post Office Engineering); City and Guilds of London Institute Course on Principles and Practice of Metallurgical Operations and Principles of Physical Metallurgy, Rotherham College of Technology, 1943; Course on Statistical Methods for Industry, Sheffield University; Course on Ceramic/Metal Mixtures, Imperial College of Science and Technology. Appointments: Member of Staff, Research Department, Wm. Jessop & Sons Ltd, Sheffield, England, 1940-47; Research Metallurgist, Head of Precision Casting Pilot Plant, Birmingham Small Arms Group Research Centre, 1947-52; Production Manager, Lost-Wax Casting Foundry, Firth-Vickers Stainless Steels Ltd, Sheffield, 1952-63; Senior Foundry Technologist, Marketing Technical Service Department, Monsanto Chemicals (UK), South Wales, 1964-73; Monsanto-Europe International Technical Centre, Brussels, Belgium, 1973-83; Retired, 1983; Free-lance Consultant, 1983-. Publications: Over 25 published articles and papers presented at conferences include: Lost Wax casting – A Short Illustrated Review, 1986; Quantum Leaps in the Development of Lost Wax Casting; To Use of Robots. What Comes Next? 1988; Robot Molding – New Dimensions in Lost Wax, 1989; Lost Wax Castings in Your Life from before Birth to after Death, 1990. Honours: International Award Diploma, European Investment Casting Conference, Paris, France, 1958; The Douglas Armitage Award; Award for Outstanding Contributions to the British Institute for Lost-Wax Casting and Trade Association and the Industry, British Investment Casting and Trade Association, 1983; Assigned to Employers 18 patents relating to lost wax casting production.

Memberships: Fellow, Institute of British Foundrymen; Fellow, Institute of Cast Metals Engineers. Address: 18 Snowdon Drive, Wrexham LL11 2UY, Wales.

TAYLOR Theodore Langhans, b. 23 June 1921, Statesville, North Carolina, USA. Writer. m. (1) Gwen Goodwin, 25 October 1946, 2 sons, 1 daughter, (2) Flora Gray, 18 April 1982. Publications: The Magnificent Mitscher, 1954; Fire on the Beaches, 1957; The Cay, 1968; The Children's War, 1971; The Maldonado Miracle, 1973; Teetoncey, 1974; Jule, 1979; The Trouble with Tuck, 1981; Battle of the Midway Island, 1982; HMS Hood vs Bismarck, 1983; Battle in the English Channel, 1984; Sweet Friday Island, 1984; The Cats of Shambala, 1985; Walking Up a Rainbow, 1986; The Stalker, 1987; The Hostage, 1988; Sniper, Monocolo, 1989; Tuck Triumphant, 1990; The Weirdo, 1991; Maria, 1992; To Kill a Leopard, 1993; Timothy of the Clay, 1993; The Bomb, 1996; Rogue Wave, 1996; The Flight of Jesse Leroy Brown; A Sailor Returns, 2001. Contributions to: Saturday Evening Post; McCall's; Ladies Home Journal; Saturday Review of Literature; Argosy. Honours: Lewis Carroll Shelf Award; Jane Addams Peace and Freedom Foundation Award; Western Writers of America Award; George G Stone Center Award; Edgar Allan Poe Award; International Association of School Librarians Award; Best Books, American Library Association, 1993, 1995; Scott O'Dell Historical Novel. Address: 1856 Catalina Street, Laguna Beach, CA 92651, USA.

TAYLOR Wendy Ann, b. 29 July 1945, Stamford, Lincolnshire, England. Artist; Sculptor. m. Bruce Robertson, 1 son. Education: St Martin's School of Art, London. Career includes: Sculptor; Member, CNAA Fine Art Board, 1980-85; Member, Royal Fine Art Commission, 1981-99; External Assessor, London University, 1982-84; Member, Court of the Royal College, 1982-; Member, Morley College Council, 1984-88; Design Consultant, Basildon Development Corporation; 1985-88; Specialist Adviser, CNAA, 1985-93; Committee for Art and Design, CNAA, 1987-91; Design Consultant Commission for the New Towns, 1986-88; Design Consultant, London Borough of Barking and Dagenham, 1989-93, 1997-; London Docklands Advisory Panel, 1989-98; Trustee, LAMA, 1993-; Member, Council, Royal Society of British Sculptors, 1999-2000; Represented in collections world-wide; Over 60 commissioned sculptures since the early 1970's which include: Timepiece, The Tower Hotel, St Katherine's Dock, London, 1972-73; Octo, Milton Keynes Development Corporation, 1979-80; Sentinel, Redland House, Reigate, Surrey, 1980-81; Equatorial Sundial, Telephone Rentals Limited, Bletchley, 1981-82; Essence, Milton Keynes Development Corporation, 1982; Gazebo, Golder's Hill Park, London, 1983; Pharos, East Kilbride Development Corporation, Scotland, 1986; Spirit of Enterprise, London Docklands Development Corporation, Isle of Dogs, London, 1987; Globe Sundial, Swansea Maritime Quarter, South Wales, 1987; Pilot Kites, Norwich Airport, 1988; Phoenix, Kelvin Industrial Estate, East Kilbride Development Corporation, Scotland, 1989-90; Sundial, Memorial to Harry Breadley, East End Park, Sheffield, 1991; Anchorage, Salford Quays, Manchester; Jester, Emmanuel College, Cambridge, 1994; Equilibrium, Coopers & Lybrand, London, 1995; Spirit of Barrow, The Dock Museum, Barrow-in-Furness, Cumbria, 1997; Waves, The Osborne Group, London, 1998; Dancer, Chelsea and Westminster Hospital, London, 1999; Dung Beetles, Millennium Conservation Building, Zoological Society, Regent's Park, London, 1999; Mariner's Astrolabe, Virginia Settlers Memorial, Brunswick Quay, London, 1999; Globe View, Blackfriars, London, 2000; Tortoises with Triangle and Time, Holland Park, London, 2000; Millennium Fountain, New River Loop, Chase Green, Enfield, Middlesex, 2000; Voyager, Cinnibar Wharf, London, 2001; Three Reclining Rope Figures, Glaxo SmithKline, Brentford, Middlesex, 2001;

Through the Loop, Pacific Place, Hong Kong, 2002; Around the Square, Pacific Place, Hong Kong, 2002; Chain Piece, Hunters Square, Warren, Ohio, USA, 2002; Knowledge, Library Square, Queen Mary University of London, 2003. Publication: Wendy Taylor, by Edward Lucie-Smith, 1992. Honours: Walter Neurath Award, 1964; Pratt Award, 1965; Arts Council Award, 1977; CBE, 1988; Fellow, Zoological Society, 1989; Fellow, Queen Mary and Westfield College, London University, 1993; Fellow, Royal Society of British Sculptors, 1994. Address: 73 Bow Road, Bow, London E3 2AN, England. Website: www.wendytaylorsculpture.com

TE KANAWA Kiri Jeanette Claire (Dame), b. 6 March 1944, Gisborne, New Zealand. Singer (Soprano). m. Desmond Park, 1967, divorced, 1997, 1 son, 1 daughter. Education: St Mary's College, Auckland; London Opera Centre. Appointments: Debut, Royal Opera Covent Garden, 1970; La Scala, Milan, debut 1978; Sang at Salzburg Festival in 1979, with San Francisco Opera Company in 1980, and at Edinburgh and Helsinki Festivals, 1980; Operas include: Boris Godunov; Parsifal; The Marriage of Figaro; Otello; Simon Boccanegra; Carmen; Don Giovanni (also film version 1979); Faust; The Magic Flute; La Bohème (5 times); Eugene Onegin; Cosi Fan Tutte; Arabella; Die Fledermaus; La Traviata; Der Rosenkavalier; Manon Lescaut; Sang at the wedding of HRH The Prince of Wales, London, 1981; Sang the Countess in Capriccio at San Francisco, 1990, and Covent Garden; Sang the premiere of Paul McCartney's Liverpool Oratorio, at Liverpool Cathedral and in London, 1991; Sang Amelia in new production of Simon Boccanegra at Covent Garden, 1991; Season 1992 with Mozart's Countess at Metropolitan Opera, and Desdemona at Covent Garden; Appeared on 2000 Today from Gisborne, New Zealand, 1 January 2000; Sang at Queen's Jubilee Prom, 2002. Creative works: Recordings include: Elvira in Don Giovanni; Fiordiligi in Cosi Fan Tutte; Otello; Micaela in Carmen; Mozart Vespers and C Minor Mass; Pamina in The Magic Flute; The Marriage of Figaro; Hansel and Gretel; Strauss' Songs with Orchestra; Die Fledermaus; Woodbird in Siegfried; Recitals records. Publications: Land of the Long White Cloud, 1989; Opera for Lovers, 1997. Honours: OBE; DBE; ONZ, 1995; Honorary Degrees, Oxford, Cambridge, Dundee, Nottingham, Auckland, Durham; Sunderland, Chicago, Waikato Universities and Post University in USA. Address: c/o Nick Grove Management, Ltd, 69 Sheen Road, Richmond, Surrey TW9 1YJ, England.

TEAGUE Abner Franklin, b. 25 May 1919, Gainesville, Texas, USA. Specialist in Engineering and Management. m. (1) Doris New, deceased, (2) Nora Katharine Henderson, 1 son, 1 stepson, 2 daughters. Education: BS, Chemical Engineering, Texas Tech University, Lubbock, 1943; Nuclear Reactor Materials, University of California, Los Angeles, 1959; MS, Aerospace Management, University of Southern California, Los Angeles, 1967. Appointments: Engineer-Chemist, research on plastic explosives and propellant processing, Inyokern, California; Project Manager, Engineer, TRW, Redondo Beach, California; Engineer, Naval Weapons Support System, Washington DC; Head, Mechanical System Branch, Joint Cruise Missile Project Office, Washington DC; President, A Teague Associates, engineering and management consulting firm, Hamilton, TX; Retired. Publications: Various articles on plastic explosives research, logistic support plans for major satellite development; Classified paper presented to Solid Propellant Industry on Advanced Rocket Motor for Tomahawk Cruise Missile. Honours: Patent on propellant grain design; Panel Chairman, Session on Space Systems, 61st National Meeting of American Institute of Chemical Engineers. Memberships: Masonic bodies, Master Mason, Chapter, Council, Commendry; Lions Club International; Member, Executive Council, Episcopal Diocese of Fort Worth; Warden and Vestry man, St Mary's Episcopal Church,

Hamilton; Director and Vice President, Hamilton County Cemetery Association; Member, Texas Silver Hair Legislature. Address: 905 East Henry Street, PO Box 626, Hamilton, TX 76531-0626, USA.

TEBBIT Baron of Chingford (Norman Beresford Tebbit), b. 29 March 1931, Enfield, England. Politician. m. Margaret Elizabeth Daines, 1956, 2 sons, 1 daughter. Education: Edmonton County Grammar School. Appointments: RAF Officer, 1949-51; Commercial Pilot and holder of various posts, British Air Line Pilots' Association, 1953-70; Member of Parliament for Epping, 1970-74; Chingford, 1974-92; Parliamentary Private Secretary, Department of Employment, 1972-73; Under Secretary of State, Department of Trade, 1979-81; Ministry of State, Department of Industry, 1981; Secretary of State for Employment, 1981-83; Trade and Industry, 1983-85; Chancellor of the Duchy of Lancaster, 1985-87; Chair, Conservative Party, 1985-87; Director, BET Plc, 1987-96; British Telecom Plc, 1987-96; Sears PLC; Spectator Ltd; Advisor, JCB Excavators, 1991-; Co-Presenter, Target, Sky TV, 1989-97; Columnist, The Sun, 1995-97; Columnist, Mail on Sunday, 1997-2001. Publications: Upwardly Mobile, 1988; Unfinished Business, 1991; Weekly Columnist, The Sun, 1995-97 and The Mail on Sunday, 1997-2001; Numerous political booklets, newspapers and magazine articles. Honours: Life Peer, Baron Tebbit of Chingford; Companion of Honour. Memberships: Association of Conservative Peers; Liveryman of the Guild of Air Pilots and Navigators; Council Member of the Air League; Companion of the Royal Aeronautical Society; Chairman Nuffield Orthopaedic Centre Appeal. Address: House of Lords, Westminster, London, SW1A 0PW, England.

TEITELL Charles M, b. 1 July 1933, New York City, New York, USA. Certified Public Accountant. m. (1) Lillian, (2) Edith, 2 sons, 1 daughter. Education: Bachelor of Arts, Cornell University, 1957; Master of Business Administration, New York University, 1959; Certified Public Accountant, California, 1961; Certified Public Accountant, New York, 1971; Certified Public Accountant, Michigan, 1982. Appointments: Senior Accountant, Arthur Young & Co, 1959-62; Assistant Controller, Oil/Natural Gas and Real Estate, Sunset International Petroleum, 1962-64; Divisional Controller, Apparel/Textiles, Jonathan Logan, Inc, 1975-77; Management Consultant, Energy, Auto and Construction Industries, 1978-; Adjunct Professor, Marymount College and Bramson Ort, New York City, 1990-91; Internal Revenue Service Volunteer; Registered Investment Advisor. Publications: Restaurant Guide: Experience Gastronomique; Tanya- A Russian Immigrant. Memberships: American Institute of Certified Accountants; Cornell Club, New York City. Address: 110 Culver Blvd, Playadel Reg, CA 90293, USA.

TEKAVČIĆ Pavao, b. 23 August 1931, Zagreb, Croatia. University Professor. m. Zorica Živković-Tekavčić. Education: Graduate, Romance Linguistics, 1954, PhD, Istro Romance Linguistics, 1963, Zagreb University. Appointments: Assistant Professor of Italian Linguistics, 1957; Ordinary Professor of Italian Linguistics, 1973; Retired, 1983. Publications: 3 books; 349 articles including scientific papers and review articles. Honours: Award, Italian Government, 1979; Award, Italian Institute in Zagreb, 2001; Commendatore dell'Ordine della Stella della Solidarietà Italiana Award, Italian Government, 2004. Memberships: Society of Romance Linguistics; Society of Italian Linguistics. Address: Berislaviceva 12, 10000 Zagreb, Croatia.

TELLO ROLDAN Enrique Daniel Nicolás, b. 8 October 1946, Villa Santa Rita de Catuna, Provincia de la Rioja, Argentina. Lawyer; Professor. m. Miriam Leonor Yunes, 2 sons, 2 daughters. Education: School Teacher, Pedro de Castro Barros Superior Teachers School, 1964; Lawyer, 1971, Law Procurator, 1971,

Dictionary of International Biography

Faculty of Law, National University of Córdoba, Argentina. Appointments: College Professor, teaching: Regional Present day Activities at the UPLR, History of Political Ideas, Universal History of Education, History of Argentine Education, 1975-; Chair, Provincial Council of Education of La Rioja, 1974-75; Academic Secretary of the Provincial University of La Rioja; Judge, Superior Court of Justice, La Rioja, 1983-85; Rector, Provincial University of La Rioja, 1992-94; Rector of the National University of La Rioja, 1994-95, 1995-98, 1998-2001, 2001-2004-. Publications: Handbook on the History of Education and Pedagogy, 2000; The Development of Higher Education in Latin America, 2001; The Technology Innovation and the Education of Paradigms of the New World Society, in press 2003. Honours: Award, International Association of University Presidents, 1996-97; Award, Jacksonville University, Florida, USA for work on Innovative Excellence in Teaching, Learning and Technology, 1998; Balseiro Diploma of Honour, Ministry of Culture and Education; Prize for book: The Academic Vocation, Book Foundation of the International Book Fair in Buenos Aires, 2001. Memberships include: International Association of University Presidents; Organización Universitaria Interamericana; Ibero-American Group of La Rábida University; Ibero-American Group, International University of Andalucía, Spain. Address: Copiapó 660, La Rioja 5300, Argentina. E-mail: rector@unlar.edu.ar Website: www.unlar.edu.ar

TERASHIMA Takeshi, b. 13 October 1963, Japan. Internist; Educator. m. Sanae, 1 son, 1 daughter. Education: Diplomate, School of Medicine, 1988, Resident, Department of Internal Medicine, 1988-95, Keio University, Tokyo, Japan; Postdoctoral Fellow, University of British Columbia, Vancouver, Canada, 1995-97. Appointments: Assistant Professor, Tokyo Dental College, Ichikawa General Hospital, Japan, 1999-. Publications: Papers in scientific journals including: Chest; American Journal of Respiratory and Critical Medicine. Honours: Grantee, Pfizer Health Research Foundation, 1995; Grantee, Japanese Ministry of Education, Science and Culture, 2001. Memberships: Japanese Society of Internal Medicine; Japanese Respiratory Society; American Thoracic Society. Address: Tokyo Dental College, Ichikawa General Hospital, 5-11-13 Sugano, Ichikawa, Chiba 272-0824, Japan. E-mail: terashima@1988.jukuin.keio.ac.jp

TETSUO Sakai, b. 9 December 1951, Yame City, Japan. Physician; Neurologist. m. Mitsuko, 2 sons, 1 daughter. Education: MD, Kurume University School of Medicine, 1977; Degrees of Medical Science, Kyushu University, 1982. Appointments: Medical Staff, Department of Neurology, Faculty of Medicine, Kyushu University, 1980-81; Medical Staff, 1981-85, Chief of Department, 1985-2002, Department of Neurology, National Chikugo Hospital; Director, Neuro-Incurable Diseases Centre, Yanagawa Rehabilitation Hospital, 2002-. Publications: Articles as author and co-author in medical journals include: Joseph disease in a non-Portuguese family, 1983; Chorea-Acanthocytosis: Abnormal composition of covalently bound fatty acids of erythrocyte membrane proteins, 1991; Effects of tetrahydrobiopterin on ataxia in Machado-Joseph disease may be based upon the theory of "cerebellar long-term depression", 2001. Memberships: Council Member, Japanese Society of Neurology; Japanese Society of Neurotherapeutics. Address: 113-2 Kamimiyanaga-machi, Yanagawa City 832-0058, Fukuoka Prefecture, Japan. E-mail: sakai-t@kouhoukai.org

THALDEN Barry, b. 5 July 1942, Chicago, USA. Architect. m. Kathryn McKnight, 3 daughters. Education: BArch, University of Illinois, 1965; Masters Degree, Land Architecture, University of Michigan, 1969. Appointments: Landscape Architect, Hellmuth, Obata, Kassebaum, St Louis, 1969-70; Director, Landscape Architecture, PGAV Architects, St Louis, 1970-71; Chairman,

Thalden Corporation Architects, Las Vegas/St Louis, 1971-; Partner, Thalden Boyd Architects, Las Vegas/St Louis/Tulsa, 1998-. Principal Works: Rock Hill Park, Missouri (St Louis AIA Award); Wilson Residence, St Louis (St Louis AIA Award); St Louis University Campus Mall (St Louis ASLA Award); Crown Plaza Hotel, St Louis; National Bowling Hall of Fame and Museum, St Louis; Plaza of Champions, Busch Stadium, St Louis (St Louis ASLA Award); Palace Casino and Resort, Biloxi, Mississippi; Ho Chunk Casino, Wisconsin Dells (ABC Award, Best Building in Wisconsin); Potowatomi Casino, Milwaukee; Chumash Casino Resort, Santa Ynez, California. Honours: Board of Directors, Open Space Council of St Louis, 1973-83; National Vice-President, American Society of Landscape Architects, 1989-81; President, World Future Society, St Louis Chapter, 1984-94; Architect of the Year, Builder Architect Magazine, 1986; Fellow, American Society of Landscape Architects, 1988; State Council, Missouri Landscape Architects, 1990-94; Arts and Education Council, Board of Directors, St Louis, 1995-2001; Board of Trustees, Las Vegas Art Museum, 2000-; Listed in Who's Who publications and biographical dictionaries. Memberships: American Institute of Architects; American Society of Landscape Architects; National Council of Architectural Registration Boards. Address: 931 American Pacific Drive #108; Las Vegas, NV 89014, USA. Website: www.thaldenboyd.com

THAM-GOLDBERG Hilary, (Hilary Tham), b. 20 August 1946, Kelang, Malaysia. Writer. m. Joseph R Goldberg, 16 February 1971, 3 daughters. Education: BA, Honours in English Literature, University of Malaya. Appointments: Chair, Coalition for Resettlement of Vietnamese Refugees, 1979-80; Editor-in-Chief, Word Works; Poetry Editor, Potomac Review, 1992-. Publications: No Gods Today, 1969; Paper Boats, 1987; Bad Names for Women, 1989; Tigerbone Wine, 1992; Men and Other Strange Myths, 1994; Lane With No Name: Memoirs and Poems of a Malaysian-Chinese Girlhood, 1997; Counting, 2000; Reality Check and other Travel Poems, 2001; The Tao of Mrs Wei, 2003. Contributions to: Antietam Review; International Quarterly; Double Take; Palo Alto Review; Excursus; Waterways; Encodings; Delhi-London Quarterly; Poet Lore; Wind; Maryland Poetry Review; Gargoyle; Phoebe; Minimus; Pig Iron. Honours: 2nd Prize, Virginia Poetry, 1978; 3rd Prize, Paterson Poetry, 1989; Virginia Fellowship Award for Poetry, 2002. Membership: New Room Poets, chair and founder, 1982-. Address: 2600 North Upshur Street, Arlington, VA 22207, USA.

THAMBIRATNAM David Pathmaseelan, b. 12 August 1943, Sri Lanka. Professor of Structural Engineering. m. Sulogini Vethanayagam, 2 sons, 1 daughter. Education: BSc (Engin) First Class Honours, 1968; MSc (Struct), 1975; PhD (Struct), 1978. Appointments include: District, Construction Engineer, Department of Buildings and PWD, Government of Sri Lanka, 1968-73; Chief Construction Engineer, (Colombo South) Department of Buildings, Government of Sri-Lanka, 1978-79; Senior Structural Engineer, Department of Buildings, Government of Sri Lanka, 1979-80; Lecturer, 1980-81, Senior Lecturer 1981-87, 1988-90; Department of Civil Engineering, National University of Singapore; Lecturer, 1990-91, Senior Lecturer, 1991-93, Associate Professor, 1993-96, Professor, 1996-, Structural Engineering, School of Civil Engineering, Queensland University of Technology. Publications: 150 articles in international journals and conference proceedings. Honours: Canadian Commonwealth Scholarship, 1973-78; Graduate Fellowship, University of Manitoba, 1975-78; Commendation by Prime Minister of Sri Lanka, 1979. Memberships: Fellow, American Society of Civil Engineers; Fellow, Institution of Engineers, Australia, Fellow, Institution of Civil Engineers, UK. Address: School of Civil Engineering, Queensland University of Technology, GPO Box 2434, Brisbane, QLD 4001, Australia.

THAMILSERAN Sabaratnan, b. 19 May 1962, Sri Lanka. Engineer; Researcher. m. Krishnakumary, 1 daughter. Education: B Eng, University of Peradeniya, 1985; M Eng, Asian Institute of Technology, 1989; PhD, Texas A&M University, Texas, USA, 1999. Appointments: Postgraduate Research, Energy Systems Laboratory, Texas A&M University, 1993-97; Mechanical Engineer (Research), ADM Associates Inc., Sacramento, California, USA, 1997-. Publications: 5 publications in: ASHRAE, ASME, ASHRAE Transactions, ASHRAE Journal; Papers in: Hot and Humid Conference and International ASME/SSME Conferences. Honours: Awards for projects completed for Local Energy Assistance Program; Listed in Who's Who publications and biographical dictionaries. Memberships: ASHRAE; AEE; EEMI of AEE. Address: ADM Associates Inc., 3239 Ramos Circle, Sacramento, CA 95826, USA. E-mail: seran@adm-energy.com Website: http://www.adm-energy.com/

THATCHER Rt Hon Baroness Margaret Hilda, b. 13 October 1925, Grantham, England. Barrister; Politician; Former Prime Minister. m. Dennis Thatcher, 1951, deceased 2003, 1 son, 1 daughter. Education: Somerville College, Oxford. Appointments: Research Chemist, 1947-51; Entered Bar, Lincoln's Inn, 1953; Conservative Member of Parliament, Barnet, Finchley, 1959-92; Minister of Pensions and National Insurance parliamentary secretary, 1961-64; Opposition Spokesperson for Education, 1969-70; Secretary of State for Education and Science, 1970-74; Leader of Her Majesty's Opposition, 1975-79; First Lord of the Treasury and Minister for Civil Service, 1979-90; Conservative Party Leader, 1975-90; Prime Minister, 1979-90; Retired from public life, 2002. Publications: In Defence of Freedom, 1986; The Downing Street Years, 1979-90, 1993; The Path to Power, 1995; The Collected Speeches of Margaret Thatcher, 1997; Statecraft, 2002. Honours: Honorary Fellow, Royal Institute of Chemistry, Freedom of the Royal Borough of Kensington and Chelsea, 1979; Freedom of the London Borough of Barnet, 1980; Freedom of the Falkland Islands, Honorary Master of the Bench at Gray's Inn, 1983; Freedom of the City of London, 1989; Freedom of The City of Westminster, 1990; Hon LLD, Buckingham, 1986; Dr hc, Rand Afrikaans, 1991; Presidential Medal of Freedom, US, 1991; Order of Good Hope, South Africa, 1991; Dr hc, Weizman Institute of Science, 1992; MacArthur Foundation Fellowship, 1992; Hon Citizen of Gorasde, 1993; Dr hc, Mendeleyev, 1993; Hilal-i-Imitaz, 1996; LG; OM; PC; FRS; Life Peer, created 1992. Memberships: Honorary Bencher, Gray's Inn, 1975; No Turning Back Group President, 1990-; Bruges Group Honorary President, 1991-; International Advisory Board, British American Chamber of Commerce; Worshipful Company of Glovers (Member); Chancellor, University of Buckingham, 1993-; Advisory Board Chair University of London Institute of US Studies, 1994-; Royal Society of St George Vice President, 1999-; Conservative Companion of Guild of Cambridge Benefactors, 1999-. Address: The House of Lords, Westminster, London SW1A 0PW, England.

THAYER Carlyle Alan, b. 5 November 1945, Nevada City, California, USA. Professor. Appointments: Teacher, International Voluntary Services, Vietnam, 1967-68; Teacher, Swaneng Hill School, Botswana, 1968-69; Tutor, Department of Asian Civilisations, Australian National University, 1973; Lecturer, Bendigo College of Advanced Education, 1975-78; Lecturer, 1979-83, Senior Lecturer, 1983-85, Royal Military College, Duntroon; Senior Lecturer, 1986-89, Associate Professor, 1990-97, Professor, 1998-, School of Politics, Australian Defence Force Academy; Visiting Fellow on Secondment, Research School of Pacific and Asian Studies, Australian National University 1991-94; Research Associate, International Institute for Strategic Studies, London, 1993; Head, Department of Politics, Australian Defence Force Academy, 1995-97; Visiting Fellow, Strategic and Defence Studies

Centre, The Australian National University 1998; Professor and Deputy Chair, Department of Regional Studies, Asia-Pacific Center for Security Studies, Hawaii, 1999-2001; Deakin's University's On Site Academic Co-ordinator, Center for Defence and Strategic Studies, Australian Defence College, Canberra, 2002-03. Publications: War By Other Means: National Liberation and Revolution in Vietnam, 1954-1960, 1989; Soviet Relations with India and Vietnam, 1992; Vietnam, 1992; Soviet Relations with India and Vietnam, 1945-1992, 1993; The Vietnam People's Army Under Doi Moi, 1994; Beyond Indochina, 1995; Numerous other professional publications. Honours: US National Defence For Language Fellowship, Yale University 1969-71; Cornell University 1970; Centre for Vietnamese Studies Fellowship, Southern Illinois University, USA, 1971; PhD Research Scholar, Australian National University 1971-74; Australian Research Council Research Award, 1990; Listed in national and international biographical dictionaries. Memberships: National Secretary, Australian Soccer Referees Federation, 1989-95; National Secretary, Vietnam Studies Association of Australia, 1994-98; Life Member, Bendigo CAE Soccer Club, Australian Soccer Referees Federation (ACT Division); National Secretary, Asian Studies Association of Australia, 1996-98. Address: 11 Ambara Place, Aranda, ACT 2614, Australia.

THEIS Jacques, b. 21 January 1957, Charleroi, Belgium. Cardiologist. Life Partner, Dominique Donati, 2 sons, 1 daughter. Education: Cardiology Specialist, Free University of Brussels, Belgium, 1989. Appointments: General Practice Physician, 1981-84; Cardiologist, 1984-89; General Cardiology, Avesnes sur Helpe, France, 1989-. Honours: Listed in Who's Who publications and biographical dictionaries. Membership: Belgian Working Group in Pacing and Electrophysiology. Address: 22 Route D'Etroeungt, 59440 Avesnelles, Nord France.

THEISEN Rolf John, b. 4 October 1936, Durban, South Africa. Researcher and Writer. m. Wendy Florence, 1 son. Education: Diploma in Agriculture, Gwebi Agricultural College; BA, Psychology and Sociology University of South Africa. Appointments: Land Development Officer, 1955-58, Research Officer, Agricultural Officer, Extension Officer, 1959-73, Rhodesian Government; Research Fellow and Head of Rural Development Research Unit (Secondment), Faculty of Social Studies, University of Rhodesia, 1973-79; Margate Art Museum Curator and Author, 1980-2002. Publications: Numerous articles in journals and papers presented at 3rd Rhodesian Science Congress and at conferences and seminars including: Variables of population growth, 1973; Agro-economic factors influencing the health and academic achievement of rural school children, 1973; Development in rural communities, 1975-76; Supplementary feeding of school children in a tribal land of Rhodesia, 1976; Limitations to progress in African agriculture; Socio-economic Factors Involved in the Profitable Cropping of Worked Out Granite Soils in Tribal Communities. Honours: Several minor awards. Memberships include: Natal Arts Trust; Wild Life Society. Address: PO Box 391, Margate 4275, Kwazulu Natal, Republic of South Africa.

THEO Milton Costa, b. 9 June 1945, Johannesburg, South Africa. Attorney. 2 sons, 3 daughters. Education: Bachelor of Commerce, 1967; Bachelor of Laws (with honours), 1969. Appointments: Partner, Surgey, Pittman & Kerswell, Harare, Zimbabwe, 1969-76; Assistant Group Legal Advisor, Ace (Liberia) Inc, Athens, Greece, 1978-80; Associate with Dr M H Hoshaw, Riyadh, Saudi Arabia, 1980-84; Private Practice, Athens, Greece, 1984-.

THEODOROU Stavroula, b. 6 March 1973, Ioannina, Greece. Physician; Radiologist. Education: MD, University of Ioannina School of Medicine, Ioannina, Greece, 1997; Speciality in

Radiology, University of Ioannina Medical Centre, 1998-2003; Clinical duties and research in Musculoskeletal Imaging and Quantitative Bone Densitometry, University of California San Diego Medical Center, San Diego, California, USA, 1999, 2000-2001. Appointments: Department of Radiology, University of Ioannina Medical Centre, Ioannina, Greece, 1998-2003; Department of Radiology, University of California, San Diego, California, USA, 1999, 2000-2001; Department of Radiology, Thornton Hospital, University of California San Diego, California, USA, 1999. Publications: 23 original articles; Co-author, 5 books. Honours: Award of Excellence in University Studies, Greek National Scholarship Foundation, 1992, 1994; Award of Excellence in Pathology, University of Ioannina Medical Centre, 1996; Support in Research, Veterans Affairs, San Diego Medical Center Grant, California, USA; Certificate of Merit for Educational Exhibit, Radiological Society of North America, 1999, 2000; Certificate of Merit for Educational Exhibit, American Roentgen Ray Society, Washington DC, 2000; Best Scientific Exhibit, American Society of Spine Radiology, Florida, 2001. Memberships: American College of Radiology, Radiological Society of North America; Society for Clinical Densitometry; American Society for Bone Mineral Research; Los Angeles Radiological Society; National Osteoporosis Foundation. Address: 13 Papadopoulos Street, Ioannina 45444, Greece. E-mail: rjtheodorou@hotmail.com

THEODORU Pavlos, b. 4 March 1970, Trikala, Greece. Lecturer. Education: B Eng, Electronic Engineering, Technological Educational Institute of Thessaloniki, Greece; MSc, Optoelectronics and Communications Systems, University of Northumbria, Newcastle upon Tyne, England, 1996; PhD, ATM Optical Wireless Networks, 1999. Appointments: Communications Engineer, Greek Army, 1991-99; Part-time Lecturer, University of Northumbria, Newcastle upon Tyne, England, 1996-99; Lecturer, University of the Aegean, Greece, 1999-2002; Lecturer, University of Crete, Greece, 2003-. Publications: Translator and proof reader, Greek edition of the book, Data and Computer Communications by W Stallings, 2002; More than 10 scientific publications in international recognised journals, magazine and conferences. Honours: Prize, Greek Institution of National Scholarships, 1987; PhD Studentship, 1996; IEEE Grant, 1997. Membership: Associate Member, IEEE. Address: Trikala, Petroto 49300, Greece. E-mail: pavlos@aegean.gr

THEODORU Stefan Gheorghe, b. 11 June 1921, Braila, Romania. Civil Engineer; Writer; Editor. m. Nina Bogos, 2 sons. Education: MS, Civil Engineering, Politechnic Institute of Bucharest, Romania, 1947. Appointments: Civil Engineer, Bucharest, Vienna, New York; Inventor, Writer, Editor, New York and Bucharest; Co-inventor, Pattern Recognition System. Publications include: Poetry: Versuri Vol I, 1973; Versuri Vol II, 1988; La Lumina, 1993; Odiseea Unui Cuget, 1993; Meeting in Twilight, 1994; The Bag of Stars, 1995; Centum, 1997; The Whispers of the Old Walnut Tree, 2001; Drama: Un Drac de Fata, 1952; Ciclu, 1954; Teatru, 1993; Doamna, 1995; Duminica la Ora Sase, 1997; Cersetorul, 1998; TATI, 2002; Prose: Fata Fara Glas, 1993; Un Milionar Nebun, 1996; Genius, 1996; Nascuta in Castelul lui Dracula, 1997; Adam si Sotiile Sale, 1998; Iac'asa, 1999; Marul din Poveste, 1998; Refugiatii, 2002; History: Lupta de la Nicopole, 1975; A Wallachian Flag, 1977; Transylvania, 1995; Drapelul de Margine, 1999; Contributions to numerous anthologies; Numerous articles in magazines and newspapers. Honours: Poetry: Daily Yomiuri Award, Tokyo, 1995; Pantheon Publishing House Semn Award, 1997; Romanian-Japanese Magazine Award, 1997; Orion Award, 1997; International Ashiya Haiku Festa Award, Hyogo, Japan, 2000; The British H S J W Hackett International Haiku Award, 2000; Prose: Tempus Foundation Award, Best Novel of the Year, 1998; Literary Circle V Carlova Award, 1995-98; Drama:

Romanian Cinematography Award, 1952; Dacoromanian Academy Award, Best Theatre Play, 1998, 1999. Memberships include: Engineering Association of Romania, 1948; Romanian Academic Society, Münich, 1966; Society of American Inventors, 1981; New York Academy of Sciences; Union of Romanian Journalists; Haiku Society of America; International Association of Romanian Writers and Artists, Georgia; American Legion; Romanian Vexilologic Society. Address: 28-18 29th St, Long Island City, NY 11102, USA.

THERON Charlize, b. 7 August 1975, South Africa. Actress. Education: Trained as a ballet dancer. Appointments: Model, Milan, 1991; Actress, Los Angeles, 1992-; Films include: Children of the Corn III, 1994; Two Days in the Valley, 1996; That Thing You Do! 1996; Trial and Error, 1997; Hollywood Confidential, 1997; Devil's Advocate, 1997; Cop Lane/The Yards, 1997; Might Joe Young, 1998; Celebrity, 1998; The Cider House Rules, 1999; The Astronaut's Wife, 1999; The Yards, 2000; Reindeer Games, 2000; Men of Honour, 2000; The Legend of Bagger Vance, 2000; Navy Diver, 2000; Sweet November, 20001; The Curse of the Jade Scorpion, 2001; 15 Minutes, 2001; The Yards/Nightwatch, 2002; Waking Up in Reno, 2002; Trapped, 2002; 24 Hours, 2002; Executive Producer, Sweet Home Alabama, 2002; The Italian Job, 2003; Monster, 2003. Honours: Best Actress Oscar for Monster, 2004. Address: c/o Spanky Taylor, 3727 West Magnolia, Burbank, CA 91505, USA.

THEROUX Paul Edward, b. 10 April 1941, Medford, Massachusetts, USA. Writer. m. (1) Anne Castle, 4 December 1967, divorced 1993, 2 sons, (2) Sheila Donnelly, 18 November 1995. Education: BA, University of Massachusetts. Appointments: Lecturer, University of Urbino, Italy, 1963, Soche Hill College, Malawi, 1963-65; Faculty, Department of English, Makerere University, Uganda, 1965-68; University of Singapore, 1968-71; Visiting Lecturer, University of Virginia, 1972-73. Publications: Fiction: Waldo, 1967; Fong and the Indians, 1968; Girls at Play, 1969; Murder in Mount Holly, 1969; Jungle Lovers, 1971; Sinning with Annie, 1972; Saint Jack, 1973; The Black House, 1974; The Family Arsenal, 1976; The Consul's File, 1977; Picture Palace, 1978; A Christmas Card, 1978; London Snow, 1980; World's End, 1980; The Mosquito Coast, 1981; The London Embassy, 1982; Half Moon Street, 1984; O-Zone, 1986; My Secret History, 1988; Chicago Loop, 1990; Millroy the Magician, 1993; My Other Life, 1996; Kowloon Tong, 1997; Collected Stories, 1997; Fresh-Air Fiend, 1999; Hotel Honolulu, 2000; Dark Star Safari: Overland from Cairo to Cape Town, 2002; Non-Fiction: V S Naipaul, 1973; The Great Patagonian Express, 1979; The Kingdom by the Sea, 1983; Sailing Through China, 1983; Sunrise with Sea Monsters, 1985; The White Man's Burden, 1987; Riding the Iron Rooster, 1988; The Happy Isles of Oceania, 1992; The Pillars of Hercules, 1995; Sir Vidia's Shadow: A Friendship Across Five Continents, 1998. Honours: Editorial Awards, Playboy magazine, 1972, 1976, 1977, 1979; Whitbread Award, 1978; James Tait Black Award, 1982; Yorkshire Post Best Novel Award, 1982; Thomas Cook Travel Prize, 1989; Honorary doctorates. Memberships: Royal Geographical Society; Royal Society of Literature, fellow; American Academy of Arts and Letters. Address: The Wylie Agency, 250 West 57th Street, New York, NY 10107, USA.

THETFORD Frances, b. 9 June 1943, Marlow, Oklahoma, USA. Retired Executive. m. Billy Thetford Sr, deceased, 1 son, 1 daughter. Education: BSBA, Business Administration, Southern Illinois University. Appointments: Marine Electronics Business, 15 years; Home Improvement Business, 10 years; Salvation Army Business Director, Retired 2002. Publications: America the Deathful, Archdiocese of St Louis; ISP Anthologies: The Old Man, Remembering Ryan, Israel's Gold; Nobel House Anthology;

Dictionary of International Biography

Famous Poets Anthology. Honours: Nominated for International Poet of the Year, 2002, 2003; International Lions' Club Award of Merit. Memberships: Secretary, Regional Secular Franciscans; Past-President, St Louis Hampton Lions Club; Past Governor's Council St Louis Lions' Clubs. Address: 12160 Plainsman Drive, St Louis, MO 62146-4837, USA. E-mail: fthe78@aol.com

THEVOZ Jacqueline Adelheid, b. 29 April 1926, Estavayer-le-Lac, Switzerland. Author; Journalist; Choreographer; Composer; Writer. m. Jacques Congnard, 2 daughters. Education: Political Sciences, Catholic Institute, Conservatory of Music, University of Lausanne; Conservatory of Ballet Lausanne, Paris; Numerous professors and teachers, Lausanne, Vevey, Fribourg and Geneva. Appointments: Teacher, Ballet, Eurhytmics and Music, Pensionnat La Chassotte, Fribourg; Cooperatives, Lausanne; Official Schools, Lausanne; Renens; Romanel-Cheseaux; Founder, Studio of Zaehringen; Studio du Theatre of Fribourg; Centre de Choregraphie Musicale; Ballet Presence Humaine; Journalist, La Suisse Tribune. Publications: 24 books published; Numerous musical opus; Numerous articles. Honours: Knight (silverstar) Internationale des Arts; Academical Knight, Order Greci-Marino; Gold and Silver Medals, Academie Internationale de Lutece; Academie Arts, Sciences, Letters; Many others. Memberships: Societe Suisse des Ecrivains; Societe Fribourgeoise des Ecrivains; Societe Genevoise des Ecrivains; Swiss Delegate, International Academy of Lutece; Societe de Pedagogie Musicale. Address: Hermone, Verossier Haut, F-74500 Larringes-sur-Evian, France.

THIAN Robert Peter, b. 1 August 1943, South Africa. Chief Executive Officer; Chairman. m. Liselotte Von Borges, 2 daughters. Education: Licence en Droit, Geneva, Switzerland, 1962-67; Barrister, Gray's Inn, London, 1968-71. Appointments: Legal Advisor, Glaxo Group Ltd, Project Development Executive, Glaxo-Allenburys Export Ltd, Managing Director, Glaxo Farmaceutica Lda, 1968-80; European Business Development Director, Abbot International, European Regional Director, Abbot Laboratories, 1980-87; Vice president, International Operations, Novo Industri A/S, 1987-89; Group Chief Executive, North West Water Group plc, 1990-93; Director, Celltech Group plc, 1992-99; Founder and Chief Executive, Renex Ltd, 1993-95; Director, Medeval Ltd, 1995-98; Group Chief Executive, The Stationery Office Group, ex HMSO, 1996-99; Chairman, Imo Group Ltd, 1999-2000; President du Conseil de Surveillance, Expand Sante, Paris, 1999-2001; Chairman, Tactica Solutions Ltd, 1999-2001; Chairman, Astron Group Ltd, 2001-; Chairman, Orion Group Ltd, 2001-; Chairman, Whatman Plc, 2002-; Chairman, Southern Water Services Ltd, 2003-. Memberships: Le Club de Golf de Chantilly; Lansdowne Club. Address: 16 Princes Gate Mews, London SW7 2PS, England. E-mail: bob@thian.net

THIELE Albert Neville, b. 4 December 1920, Brisbane, Queensland, Australia. Engineer. m. Lexie Elizabeth Anderson, 1 son, 1 daughter. Education: Queensland University, 1938-41; Sydney University, 1947-51; BE (Mechanical and Electrical), 1952. Appointments: Australian Army, 1941-46; EMI (Australia), 1952-61; Advanced Development Engineer, 1957-61; Australian Broadcasting Corporation, 1962-85, Director, Engineering Development, 1980-85; Consulting Engineer, 1986-; Honorary Visiting Fellow, University of New South Wales, 1991-93; Honorary Associate, Sydney University, 1995-. Publications: 38 peer reviewed papers to professional journals including: Origination of Thiele - Small parameters for measuring and designing loudspeakers, 1961; Total difference frequency distortion method of testing transmission channels, 1975. Honours: Norman W V Hayes Award, IREE, 1968, 1992; Silver Medal, AES, 1994; Masaru Ibuka Award, IEEE, 2003; Order of Australia Medal (OAM), 2003. Memberships: Fellow, Institution of Radio and

Electronics Engineers, Australia, President, 1986-88; Fellow, Institution of Engineers, Australia; Fellow, Audio Engineering Society, Vice-President International Region, 1991-93 and 2001-2003; Society of Motion Picture and Television Engineers; Australasian Sound Recordings Association. Address: 10 Wycombe Street, Epping, NSW 2121, Australia.

THIENE Gaetano, b. 1 July 1947, Longara (VI), Italy. Medical Doctor; Professor. m. Marialuisa Valente, 2 sons, 1 daughter. Education: Medical Degree, 1972; ECEMG, 1972; Postgraduate Diploma, Cardiology, 1975; Postgraduate Diploma, Pathological Anatomy, 1978. Appointments: Assistant Professor, 1972-77, Assistant Professor-Chief Resident, 1977-80, Associate Professor in Cardiovascular Pathology, 1980-90, Professor in Cardiovascular Pathology, 1990-, Director, PhD Course on Cardiosciences, 1991-, Director, Institute of Pathological Anatomy, 1998-, University of Padua Medical School, Padua, Italy; President, Society for Cardiovascular Pathology, USA and Canadian Academy of Pathology, 2003-. Publications: 614 (448 Index Medicus); 627 abstracts; 614 papers at congresses and lectures; 12 monographs. Honours: Giovanni e Silvio Cagnetto, 1972; NATO Jr CNR, 1977; Giacomo Binda, 1980; Furio Cicogna, 1981; Mannheim Lecture, 1985. Memberships: AECVP; AEPC; EACTS; ESC; IAP; SCVP; SHVD; SIC; SICP. Address: University of Padua Medical School, Institute of Pathological Anatomy, Via A Gabelli N 61, 35121 Padua, Italy. E-mail: cardpath@unipd.it

THILL Georges Emile André, b. 30 November 1935, Bullange, Belgium. University Emeritus Professor. Education: Mathematics, Belgian Licence and Agregation enseignement secondaire, University of Louvain, Philosophy, BA; Doctorate, Theological Sciences, Paris; Postgraduate Studies, High Energy Physics. Appointments: Researcher, Laboratoire de Physique Nucléaire, Collège de France, Paris, 1966-67 and Institut Interuniversitaire belge des sciences nucléaires, Laboratoire des Hautes Energies, Brussels, 1962-73; Scholar, University of Namur, Belgium, 1973-2001; Director of the interdisciplinary Department for Sciences, Philosophies, Societies, Faculty of Natural Science, Namur, 1976-88; Member of the Executive Committee, Course Director in the Field, Science Technology Society, Inter-University Centre of Postgraduate Studies, Dubrovnik, 1986-94; Senior Fellow, EC Programme Monitor/FAST, Science Research Development, Brussels, 1991-94; Chair Professor, Professeur Ordinaire, 1986-2001, Emeritus Professor, University of Namur, 2001-; Emeritus Professor, Faculty of Human Sciences, State University of Haiti, Port-au-Prince, Haiti, 2002-; Visiting or Invited Professor in different universities: Dakar, Louvain, Brussels, Copenhagen, Donetsk National Technical University and others; Director of the Scientific Co-ordination, PRELUDE, International Networking Programme of Research and Liaison between Universities for Development, Research and Educational Network for sustainable co-development, NGO of UNESCO Collective Consultation on Higher Education implemented on the five continents (72 countries), 1985-; Responsible for the UNESCO-PRELUDE Chair of Sustainable Development, 2001-. Publications: 26 books including: La fête scientifique, 1973; Technologies et sociétés, 1980; Plaidoyer pour des universités citoyennes et responsables, 1998; Le dialogue des savoirs, 2001; L'eau, patrimoine commun mondial, 2002; Femmes, Savoirs, Sciences et Développement Durable, 2004. Over 100 scientific articles. Honours: Director of the Scientific Co-ordination of PRELUDE; Scientific Director, UNESCO Unitwin-PRELUDE Chair; President, Institut Interuniversitaire Belge de la Vie, Sciences et Qualité de Vie, Brussels; 2003 International Peace Prize, United Cultural Convention, USA. Memberships: Notably Scientific Society of Brussels; Steering Committee, International Network on the Role of the Universities for Developing Areas; Deontological

Dictionary of International Biography

Committee, Service Public Federal (SPF) de Belgique, Sante Publique, Sécurité del la Chaîne Alimentaire et Enviroment Division Bien-Être Animal et CITES; Joint Committee of Bioéthics of the Centre d'etudes et de recherches vétérinaires et agronomiques (CERVA), Institut Pasteur, Institut Scientifique de Santé Publique (ISP), Brussels; Editing Board, La Revue Nouvelle, PRELUDE Review and Newsletter. Address: 65, Rue Saint-Quentin, B-1000, Brussels, Belgium.

THOEN Hugo Florent, b. 30 January 1941, Vrasene, East Flanders, Belgium. Retired Archaeologist. m. Anne Mary Weissenborn, 1 son. Education: Degree in History, 1964, PhD Archaeology, 1973, University of Ghent, Belgium. Appointments: Scientific Collaborator, National Centre for Archaeological Research in Belgium, Brussels, Belgium, 1964-66; From Assistant to Professor, 1966-91, Professor, 1991-2002, Retired, 2002, University of Ghent, Belgium; Member of the Committee, Archaeological Museum of Velzeke, East Flanders, Belgium; Research into excavations in Belgium (Roman sites), Italy, Alba Fucens and Pessinus in Turkey. Publications: Editor (exhibition and publication): The Belgian Coastal Plain in Roman Times, 1987, Temse and the River Scheldt, 1989; Co-editor (with K Sas): (exhibition and publication) Roman Jewellery in the Northern Provinces, 2002; Editorial board: Monographs on Antiquity, 2002; Contributor of articles to professional journals. Honours: History Award, County of East Flanders, 1964; Laureate Award, Royal Flemish Academy of Sciences, 1975; Officer, Leopold II Order, Belgian Government, 1988; First Class Civil Medal, Belgian Government, 1990; First Class Civil Cross, Belgian Government, 2001; Achievement Award, Marquis Who's Who Publications Board, New Providence, New Jersey, USA. Memberships: Archaeological Inventory of Flanders; Flemish Archaeological Council; Rei Cretariae Romanae Fautores. Address: Erfgoedlaan 7, East-Flanders, Deinze B 9800, Belgium. E-mail: hugo.thoen@pandora.be

THOM James Alexander, b. 28 May 1933, Gosport, Indiana, USA. Novelist. m. Dark Rain, 20 May 1990. Education: AB, Butler University, Indianapolis, 1961. Appointments: Reporter and Columnist, The Indianapolis Star, 1961-67; Lecturer in Journalism, Indiana University, 1978-80. Publications: Spectator Sport, 1978; Long Knife, 1979; Follow the River, 1981; From Sea to Shining Sea, 1984; Staying Out of Hell, 1985; Panther in the Sky, 1989; The Children of First Man, 1994; The Spirit of the Place, 1995; Indiana II, 1996; The Red Heart, 1997; Sign-Talker, 2000. Warrior Woman (co-author Dark Rain), 2003. Contributions to: Magazines. Honour: Honorary DHL, Butler University, 1995. Membership: Authors Guild; Address: 6276 West Stogsdill Road, Bloomington, IN 47404, USA.

THOMAS Donald Michael, b. 27 January 1935, Redruth, Cornwall, England. Poet; Writer; Translator. 2 sons, 1 daughter. Education: BA, 1st Class Honours, English, MA, New College, Oxford. Appointment: English teacher, Teignmouth, Devon, 1959-63; Lecturer, Hereford College of Education, 1963-78; Full-time author, 1978-. Publications: Poetry: Penguin Modern Poets 11, 1968; Two Voices, 1968; Logan Stone, 1971; Love and Other Deaths, 1975; The Honeymoon Voyage, 1978; Dreaming in Bronze, 1981; Selected Poems, 1983; Puberty Tree, 1992. Fiction: The Flute Player, 1979; Birthstone, 1980; The White Hotel, 1981; Ararat, 1983; Swallow, 1984; Sphinx, 1986; Summit, 1987; Lying Together, 1990; Flying into Love, 1992; Pictures at an Exhibition, 1993; Eating Pavlova, 1994; Lady With a Laptop, 1996; Alexander Solzhenitsyn, 1998; Charlotte, 2000. Translator: Requiem, and Poem Without a Hero, by Akhmatova, 1976; Way of All the Earth, by Akhmatova, 1979; The Bronze Horseman, by Pushkin, 1982. Honours: Gollancz/Pan Fantasy Prize; Pen Fiction Prize;

Cheltenham Prize; Los Angeles Times Fiction Prize. Address: The Coach House, Rashleigh Vale, Tregolis Road, Truro TR1 1TJ, England. E-mail: dmthomas@btconnect.com

THOMAS Gregory, b. 28 June 1949, Albany, New York, USA. Designer; Brand Strategist. m. Sosse Thomas, 1 son. Education: BFA, Graphic Design, Kansas City Art Institute, 1967; MFA, Design, California Institute of the Arts, 1971; MFA, Graphic Design, Yale University, 1974. Appointments: Graphic Designer, IBM Corporation, IBM Design Center, San Jose, California, 1967-74; Graphic Designer in charge of exhibition design, Office of Charles and Ray Eames, 1974; Graphic Designer, Saul Bass & Associates; Art Director Sussman/Prejza Company, 1975-76; Teacher, California Institute of the Arts, 1974-78; Owner and Principal of Design Consultancy, Gregory Thomas Associates, 1978-; Design Consultant CBS Television Network, 4 years; Design Consultant, Avery/Dennison Corporation; Associate Chair, Graphic Design Department, 1996-97, Acting Chair, 1997-2000, Art Center College of Design; Adjunct Professor, School of Fine Arts and Annenberg School for Communication, Lecturer Marshall School of Business, University of Southern California. Publications: Author, How to Design Logos, Symbols and Icons; Numerous international articles on branding and brand strategy; Guest writer for Designer Magazine, publication of the University and College Design Society. Honours: First Recipient of the "Teaching Has No Boundaries Award", University of Southern California; Recipient, 2 University of Southern California Arts Initiative Grants; Recipient, Sappi International Papers Grant. Memberships: Yale Club of Southern California; Advisor, University and College Designers Association; American Institute of Graphic Arts, Los Angeles; American Institute of Graphic Arts; American Center for Design; International Institute for Information Design, Vienna; Design Management Institute, Boston; University of Southern California Norris Cancer Center Advisory Council; John Wayne Cancer Institute, St John's Hospital. Address: 2812 Santa Monica Blvd, Suite 201, Santa Monica, CA 90404, USA. E-mail: gregory@gtabrands.com Website: www.gtabrands.com

THOMAS Iwan, b. 5 January 1974, Farnborough, Hampshire. Athlete. Education: Brunel University. Appointments: Fourth-ranked BMX rider, Europe, 1988; Fifth Olympic Games 400m, 1996; Silver Medal, 4 x 400m relay; Gold Medal Amateur Athletics Association, Championships 400m, 1997, British records, 44.36 seconds, 1998; Silver Medal World Championships 4 x 400m relay, 1997; Gold Medal European Championships 400m, 1998; Gold Medal, World Cup 400m, 1998; Gold Medal Commonwealth Games 400m, 1998. Honours: British Athletics Writers Male Athlete of the Year, 1998; Patron Norwich Union Startract Scheme. Address: c/o UK Athletics, Athletics House, 10 Harbourne Road, Edgbaston, Birmingham, B15 3AA, England. Website: www.iwanthomas.com

THOMAS Richard Stephen, b. 13 June 1943, London, England. National Health Service Confederation Director. m. Sandra Thomas, 1 son, 1 daughter. Education: University of Wales Institute of Science and Technology; Member of the Institute of Health Service Management. Appointments: Various NHS Management Posts in Wales, 1961-78; Area Personnel Officer, Dyfed Health Authority, Wales, 1978-86; Assistant General Manager, East Dyfed Health Authority, 1986-93; Chief Executive, Carmarthen NHS Trust, 1993-97; Chief Executive, Morriston Hospital NHS Trust, 1997-99; Director, The Welsh NHS Confederation, 1999-. Memberships: Past Chairman, South West Branch, Institute of Health Service Management; Former Honorary Secretary, Welsh Association of Health Authorities; Non-Executive Director, College of Sir Gar Carmarthen; Past Chairman and Past President, Carmarthen Round Table; Past Chairman, Carmarthen Ex-Round

Dictionary of International Biography

Tablers Club; Member and Past Chairman, Carmarthen Tywi Rotary Club. Address: Underhill, 7 Llygad-yr-Haul, Llangunnor, Carmarthen SA31 2LB, Wales. E-mail: richard.thomas@confed.wales.nhs.uk

THOMAS Rosamund Margaret, b. 19 May 1940, Paignton, Devon. Director, Educational Charitable Trust (Centre for Business and Public Sector Ethics); Academic; Ethicist. Education: Undergraduate, Sorbonne, University of Paris, France, 1959-60; Post Graduate Diploma, Social Administration, University of Southampton, England 1969-70; Master's Degree in Public Administration, University of Birmingham, England, 1970-71; Fulbright Research Scholar, Department of Government, Harvard University, USA, 1972-73; PhD, Institute of Local Government Studies, University of Birmingham, England, 1971-72, 1973-75; Postdoctoral Research Fellow, John Kennedy School of Government, Harvard University, USA, 1977-78; MA by research, University of Cambridge, England, 1996. Appointments: Earlier career as an Executive, French Government; British Manufacturing Industry and Bank of England, 1963-69; Lecturer, Public and Social Administration, London School of Hygiene and Tropical Medicine, 1975-77; Lecturer, Public Administration, London School of Economics and Political Science, 1978-83; Fellow, Wolfson College, Cambridge, 1983-87; Member, Faculty of Law, University of Cambridge, 1983-91; Founding Trustee and Director, Centre for Business and Public Sector Ethics, Cambridge, 1988-. Publications: Books: The British Philosophy of Administration, 1978, paperback editions, 1993, 1996; Espionage and Secrecy, 1991, paperback 1996; Government Ethics (editor), 1993, reprinted 1996; Environmental Ethics (editor), 1996; Numerous articles in professional journals include: Public Trust, Integrity and Privatization, 2001; A Greater Understanding of Environmental Ethics, 2002. Honours: Fulbright Scholar to Harvard, 1972-73; American Association for the Advancement of Science Research Grant, 1973; American Association of American University Women International Fellowship, 1977-78; Leverhulme Research Grant held at Wolfson College, Cambridge, 1983-85; Foreign Book Award, US National Intelligence Center, Washington DC, 1992; Evidence given to distinguished bodies including: UK Nolan and Neill Committees on Standards of Conduct in Public Life; UK Law Commission; UK House of Lords and House of Commons; US President's Ethics Law Commission; Government of the People's Republic of China. Memberships: Fellow Royal Society of Arts; Publishers Association of Great Britain; Wolfson College, Cambridge. Address: St Andrew's Castle, St Andrew's Street South, Bury St Edmunds IP33 3PH, England. E-mail: info@ethicscentre.org Website: www.ethicscentre.org

THOMEY Tedd, b. 19 July 1920, Butte, Montana, USA. Journalist; Author. m. Patricia Natalie Bennett, 11 December 1943, 1 daughter. Education: BA, University of California, 1943. Appointments: Publicity Director, San Diego State College, 1941-42; Reporter, San Diego Union-Tribune, 1942; Reporter, Assistant Editorial Promotion Manager, San Francisco Chronicle, 1942-43, 1945-48; News Editor, Columnist, Long Beach Press Telegram, 1950-; Creative Writing Instructor, Long Beach City College; Guest Lecturer, University of Southern California; Consultant, 20th Century Fox Studios. Publications: And Dream of Evil, 1954; Jet Pilot, 1955; Killer in White, 1956; Jet Ace, 1958; I Want Out, 1959; Flight to Takla-Ma, 1961; The Loves of Errol Flynn, 1961; The Sadist, 1961; Doris Day (biography), 1962; All the Way, 1964; Hollywood Uncensored, 1965; Hollywood Confidential, 1967; The Comedians, 1970; The Glorious Decade, 1971; The Big Love (co-author), 1986; The Prodigy Plot, 1987. Plays: The Big Love (co-author), 1991; Immortal Images, 1996. Contributions to: Many magazines. Honours: 1st Place, Distinguished Newspaper Feature

Writing, Theta Sigma Phi Journalism Society, 1952; Award, Best Front Page, California Newspaper Publishers. Address: 7228 Rosebay Street, Long Beach, CA 90808-4363, USA.

THOMPSON Daley, b. 30 July 1958, Notting Hill, London, England. Athlete. m. Tisha Quinlan, 1987, 1 child. Appointments: Sussex Schools 200m title, 1974; First competitive decathlon, Welsh Open Championship, 1975; European Junior Decathlon Champion, 1977; European Decathlon Silver Medallist, 1978; Gold Medallist, 1982, 1986; Commonwealth Decathlon Gold Medallist, 1978, 1982, 1986; Olympic Decathlon Gold Medallist, Moscow, 1980, LA, 1984; World Decathlon Champion, 1983; Established new world record for decathlon (at Olympic games, LA); Set four world records and was undefeated between 1978 and 1987; Retired, July 1992; Invited to run leg of the Olympic Torch relay at the opening of Sydney Olympic Games, 2000. Publications: Going for Gold, 1987; The Greatest, 1996. Address: Church Row, Wandsworth Plain, London, SW18, England.

THOMPSON Emma, b. 15 April 1959, England. Actress. m. (1) Kenneth Brannagh, 1989, divorced, (2) Greg Wise, 1 daughter. Education: Newnham College, Cambridge, England. Career: Cambridge Footlights while at University; Films include: Henry V, 1989; Howards End, Dead Again, 1991; Cheers, 1992; Peter's Friends, 1992; Much Ado About Nothing; In the Name of the Father, Remains of the Day, 1993; My Father the Hero, 1994; Junior, 1994; Sense and Sensibility, wrote screenplay and acted, 1996; The Winter Guest, 1997; Primary Colors, 1997; Judas Kiss, 1997; Imagining Argentina, 2002; Love Actually, 2003; Harry Potter and the Prisoner of Azkaban, 2004; Nanny McPhee, in progress; TV includes: Carrott's Lib; Saturday Night Live; Tutti Frutti; Fortunes of War; Thompson; Knuckle; The Winslow Boy; Look Back in Anger; Blue Boy; Ellen; Wit; Angels in America, 2002; Stage appearances include: Me and My Girl, 1984-85; Look Back in Anger, 1989; A Midsummer Night's Dream, 1990; King Lea, 1990. Honours: Best TV Actress Awards: Tutti Frutti and Fortunes of War; Evening Standard Awards: Howards End, 1992; Remains of the Day, 1994; Academy Awards: Howards End, 1994; Sense and Sensibility (for Best Screenplay Adaptation, 1996); BAFTA Award: Howards End, 1994. Address: Hamilton Hodell Ltd, 1st Floor, 24 Hanway Street, London W1T 1UH, England.

THOMPSON Ernest Victor, b. 14 July 1931, London, England. Author. m. Celia Carole Burton, 11 September 1972, 2 sons. Publications: Chase the Wind, 1977; Harvest of the Sun, 1978; The Music Makers, 1979; Ben Retallick, 1980; The Dream Traders, 1981; Singing Spears, 1982; The Restless Sea, 1983; Cry Once Alone, 1984; Polrudden, 1985; The Stricken Land, 1986; Becky, 1988; God's Highlander, 1988; Lottie Trago, 1989; Cassie, 1990; Wychwood, 1991; Blue Dress Girl, 1992; Mistress of Polrudden, 1993; The Tolpuddle Woman, 1994; Ruddlemoor, 1995; Moontide, 1996; Cast no Shadows, 1997; Mud Huts and Missionaries, 1997; Fires of Evening, 1998; Somewhere a Bird is Singing, 1999; Here, There and yesterday, 1999; Winds of Fortune, 2000; Seek a New Dawn, 2001; The Lost Years, 2002; Paths of Destiny, 2003. Various books on Cornish and West Country subjects. Contributions to: Approximately 200 short stories to magazines. Honour: Best Historical Novel, 1976. Memberships: Society of Authors; West Country Writers Club, vice president; Mevagissey Male Choir, vice patron; Royal Society of Literature; Cornish Literary Guild, president, 1998. Address: Parc Franton, Pentewan, St Austell, Cornwall, England.

THOMPSON Terence, b. 19 January 1928, Staffordshire, England. Composer; Teacher; Clarinettist; Saxophonist. Education: ABSM, performer and teacher; ABSM, (T T D), Birmingham School of Music, after Military Service in the South Staffordshire

Regiment. Career: Music Master, West Bromwich Technical High School, 1950-59; Part-Time Clarinet Tutor, Birmingham School of Music, 1954-55; Head of Music, March End School, Wednesfield, 1960-66; Part-Time Lecturer, West Midlands College of Higher Education, 1965-89; Senior Teacher, Wolverhampton Music School, 1968-93. Compositions: Boogie and Blues; Suite Chalumeau Swing; Suite City Scenes; Back to Bach; Two syncopated dances; Something Blue; 36 other arranged works published; 17 other compositions self published; 37 other arranged works self published. Recordings: London Saxophone Quartet in digital; Two Light Pieces, 1999; A Cumbrian Voluntary, 2000 Music for a While; Music for the New Millennium; Variations on The Young May Moon. Memberships: Performing Right Society; British Academy of Composers and Songwriters; The Light Music Society; National Union of Teachers; Mechanical-Copyright Protection Society; Birmingham Conservatoire Association. Address: 58 Willenhall Road, Bilston, West Midlands WV14 6NW, England.

THOMPSON-CAGER-STRAND Chezia Brenda. Poet; Director; Artist; Educator. Education: BA, 1973, MA, 1975, Washington University; Doctorate of Arts, Carnegie-Mellon University, 1984. Appointments: Assistant Professor of English, Clarion State College, 1980-82; Site Reviewer, National Endowment for the Arts Expansion Arts Program, 1984; Assistant Professor, Afro-American Studies, University of Maryland, Baltimore, 1982-85; Associate Professor, Theater/African – American Studies, Mendenhall Center for the Performing Arts, Smith College, 1985-88; Artist in Residence, Theater Department, University of Pennsylvania; Consultant, African American Newspaper Archives and Research Center, 1989-92; Artist in Residence, Albany (Georgia) State College, 1994; Consultant, Baltimore City Public Schools Multicultural Initiative, 1992-94; Professor of Language and Literature, 1994-, Director, Spectrum of Poetic Fire Reading Series, 1999-, Maryland Institute College of Art. Publications: 2 books; 3 poetry chapbooks; Teaching Jean Toomer's 1923 Cane, 2004; When Divas Dance, poetry, 2004; Regional Poetry CD, The Road Less Taken: The Saint Valentine Sunday Poetry Marathon, 2001; Contributor of poems, reviews and articles in professional and public journals. Honours include: Distinguished Black Marylander Award in the Arts, Towson University, 2000; Maryland State Arts Council Individual Artist Award in Poetry, 1999, 2001; Lucus Grant in Teaching, MICA, 2001; Associate Fellowship in Poetry, Atlantic Center for the Arts, 2002; Tuition Grant in Poetry, Bread Loaf, 2002; Finalist in 2002 Naomi Madgett Long Poetry Competition for Lotus Press. Memberships: Board of Directors, LINK: A Journal of the Arts in Baltimore and the World; Modern Language Association; Poetry Society of America; Academy of American Poets; National Council of Teachers of English. Address: 1300 Mount Royal Avenue, Baltimore, MD 21217, USA. E-mail: spectrum@mica.edu Website: www.spectrumofpoeticfire.com.

THORLEY Simon Joe, b. 22 May 1950, Staffordshire, England. Queens Counsel. m. Jane Elizabeth Cockcroft, 2 sons, 1 daughter. Education: MA Jurisprudence, Keble College, Oxford, 1968-71; Called to Bar, Inner Temple, 1972. Appointments: Barrister specialising in intellectual property law, 1972-; Queens Counsel, 1989-; Chairman, IP Bar Association, Member, Bar Council, 1995-99; Lord Chancellors appointed person to hear trade mark appeals, 1995-2003; Deputy Chairman, Copyright Tribunal, 1998-; Deputy High Court Judge, 1998-. Publications: Joint Editor, Terrell on the Law of Patents. Honours: Queens Counsel, 1989; Master of the Bench, Inner Temple, 1999. Address: 3 New Square, Lincoln's Inn, London, WC2A 3RS, England. Email: thorley@3newsquare.co.uk

THORNTON Billy Bob, b. 4 August 1955, Hot Springs, Arizona, USA. Actor. m. Angelina Jolie, 2000, 1 adopted son. Appointments: Films include: Sling Blade, 1996; U-Turn, 1997; A Thousand Miles, 1997; The Apostle, 1997; A Gun a Car a Blonde, 1997; Primary Colours, 1997; Homegrown, 1998; Armageddon, 1998; A Simple Plan, 1998; Pushing Tin, 1998; The Man Who Wasn't There, 2001; Bandits, 2001; TV: The 1000 Chains; Don't Look Back; The Outsiders; Hearts Afire. Honours: Academy Award for Best Actor, Independent Spirit Awards. Address: c/o Miramax, 7966 Beverly Boulevard, Los Angeles, CA 90048, USA.

THORNTON Caroline Rouse, b. 29 October 1937, New South Wales, Australia. Freelance writer; Teacher. m. E B C Thornton. Education: BA (UNE), 1970; MEd (UWA), 1982; FTCL, 1962; PGCE (Southampton), 1972. Appointments: Teacher, English, History, Theatre, Drama, Speech including English as a Foreign Language (9-18 age range). Publications: Rouse Hill House and the Rouses, 1988; Buchanans in Australia, 2003. Memberships: Past President, Graduate Dramatic Society; Past President, University of Western Australia Choral Society; Royal Australian Historical Society; Karrakatta Club; President, Shakespeare Club, Perth. Address: 18 Doonan Road, Nedlands 6009, Western Australia.

THORNTON Frank (Frank Thornton Ball), b. 15 January 1921, Dulwich, London. Actor. m. Beryl Jane Margaret Evans. 1 daughter. Education: London School of Dramatic Art, Scholarship, 1938-39; Qualified as Navigator, RAFVR, 1944; Demobbed as Flying Officer, 1947. Appointments: Council Actors' Benevolent Fund, Vice-President, 1982-90; Actor; Theatre includes: Laertes, Bassanio, Lysander, Catesby, Bardolph, Mosca in Jonson's Volpone, Donald Wolfit's Shakespeare Company, Strand and St James's Theatres, 1941-42; John Gielgud's Macbeth, Piccadilly Theatre, 1942; Flare Path, Apollo Theatre, 1942-43; Post-war several tours and repertory; Meals on Wheels, Royal Court, 1965; Alibi for a Judge, Savoy, 1966-67; The Young Visiters, Piccadilly, 1969; When We are Married, Strand, 1970; Eeyore in Winnie-the-Pooh, Phoenix, 1971-72; Aguecheek in Twelfth Night, Duncan in Macbeth, RSC, Stratford and Aldwych, 1974-75; Sir Patrick Cullen in The Doctor's Dilemma, Mermaid; The Chairs, Royal Exchange, Manchester, 1980; Sir John Tremayne in Me and My Girl, Adelphi, 1984-85; John of Gaunt in Richard II, Ludlow Festival, 1987; The Tutor, Old Vic, 1988; Ivanov and Much Ado About Nothing, Strand, 1989; George Bernard Shaw in The Best of Friends, 1990 and 1991; The Major General in The Pirates of Penzance, London Palladium, 1990; It Runs in the Family, Playhouse, 1993; Harvey, Shaftesbury, 1995; Hobson in Hobson's Choice, Lyric, 1995-96; Cash on Delivery, Whitehall, 1996-97; The Jermyn Street Revue, J S Theatre, 2000; Television: Many dramas and situation comedies include: It's a Square World; The World of Beachcomber; HMS Paradise; Scott on....; The Taming of the Shrew; Captain Peacock in Are You Being Served?, 1972-84; Truly in Last of the Summer Wine, 1997-; Films include: The Bed-Sitting Room; A Funny Thing Happened on the Way to the Forum; A Flea in her Ear; Great Expectations; The Old Curiosity Shop; Gosford Park; Radio includes: Propaganda broadcasts, 1942-43; The Embassy Lark; The Big Business Lark; Mind Your Own Business. Membership: The Garrick Club. Address: c/o David Daly Associates, 586A King's Road, London SW6 2DX, England.

THRUSH Brian Arthur, b. 23 July 1928, Hendon, England. Retired University Professor. m. Rosemary Catherine Terry, 1 son, 1 daughter. Education: BA, MA, PhD, ScD, Emmanuel College, Cambridge. Appointments: Lecturer, Assistant Director of Research, Demonstrator in Physical Chemistry, 1953-69, Reader in Physical Chemistry, 1969-78, Professor of Physical Chemistry,

1978-95, Professor Emeritus, 1995-, University of Cambridge; Fellow, 1960, Vice Master, 1986-90, Emmanuel College, Cambridge; Visiting Professor of Chinese Academy of Sciences, 1980-90. Publications: Many original papers in learned scientific journals. Honours: Tibler Lecturer, Chemical Society , 1965; Michael Polanyi Medallist, Royal Society of Chemistry, 1986; Raule Prize for Opto-Electronics, 1992. Memberships: Fellow Royal Society, 1976, Council Member, 1990-92; Fellow, Royal Society of Chemistry, 1977; Lawes Trust Committee, 1979-89; National Environment Research Council, 1985-90; Member, Academia Europaea, 1990, Council Member, 1992-98. Address: Brook Cottage, Pemberton Terrace, Cambridge, CB2 1JA, England. E-mail: bat@hermes.com.ac.uk

THURGOOD Nevil (a.k.a. Walter Plinge), b. 29 December 1919, Stansted Mount Fitchett, Essex, England. Freelance Actor; Director; Writer. m. Eva Mary Hopper, 23 August 1941, 4 sons. Education: National Certificate Mechanical Engineering, Technical College, 1934-36. Appointments: President Actors Equity, Victoria Division, 1966-84; Now retired; Writer; Director; Performer; Plinge's Famous Music Hall. Publications: Two Magnificent Melodramas; Good Evening Ladies and Gentlemen; Sleeping Beauty; Mr Plinge's Magnificent Melodramas and Charismatic Comicalities; "Thurgood"- A Family History from 15th Century. Honours: Man of the Year, 1994; Citation of Meritorious Achievement to Theatrical Profession. Memberships: Actors Equity - Life Member, Ex President Victoria Division; President, Gisborne Genealogical Group; Life Member, Severn Valley Railway; British Music Hall Society; Australian Writers Guild. Address: The Croft, 674 Mount Macedon Road, Mount Macedon, Vic 3441, Australia.

THURSBY Peter Lionel, b. 23 December 1930, Salisbury, Wiltshire. Sculptor. m. Maureen Aspden. Education: West of England College of Art; Exeter College of Art; ATD, Bristol University. Appointments: Head of Art, Hele's Grammar School, Exeter, 1960-71; Head of School of Art and Design, Exeter College, 1971-89. Publications: Art Education for New Society, 1968; Turning Bronzes, 1975; Painting and Sculpture in Britain, 1976; Open Air Sculpture in Britain, 1984. Honours: Silver Medal, Royal Society of British Sculptors, 1986; Hon D'Art, University of the West of England, Bristol, 1995; President, Royal West of England Academy, Bristol, 1995-2000; Honorary Member, Royal Academy, 2004. Memberships: Royal West of England Academy; Fellow, Royal Society of British Sculptors; Fellow, Royal Society of Arts; Member, Art and Architecture Association; Chelsea Arts Club. Address: Oakley House, 28 Oakley Close, Pinhoe, Exeter EX1 3SB, England. E-mail: thursby.sculpture@virgin.net

THWAITE Ann, b. 4 October 1932, London, England. Writer. m. Anthony Thwaite, 4 August 1955, 4 daughters. Education: MA, Dlitt, Oxford University (St Hilda's College). Appointments: Visiting Professor, Tokyo Women's University; Contributing Editor, Editorial Board, Cricket Magazine (US). Publications: Waiting for the Party: A Life of Frances Hodgson Burnett; Edmund Gosse: A Literary Landscape; A A Milne: His Life; Emily Tennyson: The Poet's Wife; Glimpses of the Wonderfull, The Life of Philip Henry Gosse. Honours: Duff Cooper Prize, 1985; Whitbread Biography Award, 1990. Memberships: Fellow, Royal Society of Literature; Society of Authors; PEN. Address The Mill House, Low Tharston, Norwich NR15 2YN, England.

THWAITE Anthony Simon, b. 23 June 1930, Chester, Cheshire, England. Poet; Critic; Writer; Editor. m. Ann Barbara Harrop, 4 August 1955, 4 daughters. Education: BA, 1955, MA, 1959, Christ Church, Oxford. Appointments: Visiting Lecturer in English, 1955-57, Japan Foundation Fellow, 1985-86, University of Tokyo; Producer, BBC, 1957-62; Literary Editor, The Listener, 1962-65,

New Statesman, 1968-72; Assistant Professor of English, University of Libya, 1965-67; Henfield Writing Fellow, University of East Anglia, 1972; Co-Editor, Encounter, 1973-85; Visiting Professor, Kuwait University, 1974, Chairman of the Judges, Booker Prize, 1986; Director, 1986-92, Editorial Consultant, 1992-95, André Deutsch, Ltd; Poet-in-Residence, Vanderbilt University, 1992. Publications: Poetry: Home Truths, 1957; The Owl in the Tree, 1963; The Stones of Emptiness, 1967; Inscriptions, 1973; New Confessions, 1974; A Portion for Foxes, 1977; Victorian Voices, 1980; Poems 1953-1983, 1984, enlarged edition as Poems 1953-1988, 1989; Letter from Tokyo, 1987; The Dust of the World, 1994; Selected Poems, 1956-1996, 1997; A Different Country, 2000. Other: Contemporary English Poetry, 1959; Japan (with Roloff Beny), 1968; The Deserts of Hesperides, 1969; Poetry Today, 1973, 3rd edition, revised and expanded, 1996; In Italy (with Roloff Beny and Peter Porter), 1974; Twentieth Century English Poetry, 1978; Odyssey: Mirror of the Mediterranean (with Roloff Beny), 1981; Six Centuries of Verse, 1984. Editor: The Penguin Book of Japanese Verse (with Geoffrey Bownas), 1964 revised and expanded, 1998; The English Poets (with Peter Porter), 1974; New Poetry 4 (with Fleur Adcock), 1978; Larkin at Sixty, 1982; Poetry 1945 to 1980 (with John Mole), 1983; Collected Poems of Philip Larkin, 1988; Selected Letters of Philip Larkin, 1992; Further requirements: Philip Larkin, 2001; A Move in the Weather, 2003. Honours: Richard Hillary Memorial Prize, 1968; Fellow, Royal Society of Literature, 1978; Cholmondeley Prize, 1983; Officer of the Order of the British Empire, 1990. Address: The Mill House, Low Tharston, Norfolk NR15 2YN, England.

TIBBS Martha Jane Pullen, b. 12 February 1932, Memphis, Tennessee, USA. Teacher; Volunteer; Genealogist. m. Eugene Edward Tibbs, 1 son, 1 daughter. Education: Stephens College and Rhodes (Southwestern) University, Memphis, Tennessee, 1948-52; BS, Business Administration, University of Tennessee, 1953; MA, Education, University of Memphis, 1958. Appointments: Teacher, Lausanne School, 1954-55; Teacher, Millington High School, 1955-56; Teacher, Presbyterian Day School, 1956-57; Teacher, St Mary's School, 1958-60; Tennessee Social Worker, 1962-63; Memphis Volunteer Service Board, 1963-64; Shelby County Historical Commission, Member, 1883-97, Commissioner, 1983-; Block Worker, Cancer, Kidney and Heart Fund, Memphis, 1984-; Author of genealogical works. Publications: Genealogical Sketches, Early Settlers of Shelby County; Biography of Mayor James McDonald Coleman for Coleman Room, Raleigh, Tennessee; 19th Century Club Newsletter Editor; Articles in national genealogy newsletters and magazines and commercial newspapers. Honours: Numerous official positions in clubs and societies; Listed in Who's Who publications and biographical dictionaries. Memberships include: DAR; AAUW; NEA; Tennessee Genealogical Society; Tennessee Teachers Association; Plantagenet Society; Sovereign Colonial Society; American of Royal Descent; Tennessee State Dames of Court of Honor; Colonial Dames of America; West Tennessee Historical Society; National Registrar, Daughters of Founders and Patriots of America; Tennessee State Registrar, Founders and Patriots; National Society of Colonial Dames of the XVII Century; National Society of Southern Dames of America; Colonial Order of Crown; Society of Descendants of Knights of the Most Noble Order of the Garter; American Clan Gregor Society; Family of Bruce Society; Memphis Scottish Society; American Clan Donald Society; National Society of Magna Carta Dames and Barons; Cleveland Garden Club; University Club, Memphis; Nineteenth Century Club; Racquet Club; Cleveland Women's Club; Alpha Omega Pi. Address: 2008 Massey Road, Memphis, TN 38119-6404, USA.

Dictionary of International Biography

TIBREWAL Sheo Bhagwan, b. Mahagama, Bihar, India. Consultant Orthopaedic Surgeon. m. Kusum Tibrewal, 3 children. Education: MB BS, Ranchi Medical College, India, 1966-72; FRCS (England), 1980; FICS, 1991; FLLA, 1995. Appointments include: Senior Registrar, Orthopaedic Surgery, St Bartholomew's and Homerton Hospitals, London; Clinical Lecturer (Honorary Senior Registrar) Orthopaedic and Accident Surgery, Royal Victoria Infirmary and Freeman Hospital, University of Newcastle upon Tyne; Locum Senior Registrar, Orthopaedic Surgery, The Royal London Hospital; Honorary Research Fellow, Orthopaedic Surgery, Bone and Joint Research Unit, The Royal London Hospital; Registrar, Orthopaedic Surgery, Nuffield Orthopaedic Centre, Oxford; Registrar, Accident Services, John Radcliffe Hospital, Oxford; Oxford Registrar Rotation, Orthopaedic Surgery, Stoke Mendeville Hospital, Aylesbury/Nuffield Orthopaedic Centre, Oxford, Royal Berkshire Hospital, Reading; Research Fellow, Orthopaedic Biomechanics, Oxford Orthopaedic Engineering Centre, Nuffield Orthopaedic Centre, University of Oxford; Registrar in Trauma and Orthopaedic Surgery, Hackney Hospital, London; Current appointments: Consultant Orthopaedic Surgeon, Queen Elizabeth Hospital NHS Trust, London, 1992-; Independent Professional Advisor, NHS Executive, London, 1998-; Honorary Senior Lecturer, Guy's King's and St Thomas' School of Medicine, London, 2001-; Court of Examiners, Royal College of Surgeons of England; Court of Examiners, Inter-Collegiate Board in Orthopaedics, Royal Colleges of Edinburgh, Glasgow, London and Dublin. Publications: More than 30 articles published in peer-reviewed medical journals. Honours: British Orthopaedic Association Travel Scholarship, British and European Orthopaedic Associations, Cocomac Fellow, Denmark, 1990; Honorary Fellow, Indian Orthopaedic Association, 1997, Overseas Co-ordinator, 1997. Memberships: American Academy of Orthopaedic Surgeons; Fellow, International College of Surgeons; Fellow, Royal College of Surgeons; Fellow, British Orthopaedic Association; Fellow, Royal Society of Medicine; Hunterian Society; Fellow, Licentiate Law Association; Member, British Orthopaedic Sports Trauma Association; Member, British, European and American Foot and Ankle Society. Address: Queen Elizabeth Hospital NHS Trust, Stadium Road, Woolwich, London SE18 4QH, England.

TIDMARSH James Napier, b. 15 September 1932, Bristol, England. Lord Lieutenant of the County of Bristol. m. Virginia, 2 sons. Education: Taunton School, Taunton, Somerset, England, 1941-49. Appointments: National Service, commissioned First Battalion Duke of Cornwall's Light Infantry, served Germany, Jamaica, and British Honduras, 1952-54; Factory Manager, Director, Managing Director, footwear industry, United Kingdom and Australasia, 1952-72; Managing Director, Dycem Ltd, 1972-96; Founder Director, GWR Radio plc, 1985-89; Director, Bristol Chamber of Commerce, 1992-; President, Avon Bristol Federation of Clubs for Young People, 1994-98; High Sheriff for Avon, 1995-96. Honours: MBE, 1989; Honorary Colonel, Royal Marine Reserve, West of England, 1998-; FRSA, 2000; KStJ, 1997; Hon LLD, University of Bristol, 2002; Hon LLD, University of West England, 2003. Memberships: Vice Chairman, National Association of Prison Visitors, 1966-69; Member, Council of the University of Bristol, 1994-2000; Trustee, Bristol Benevolent Institution, 1974-; Numerous other charities. Address: Leigh Court, Abbots Leigh, Bristol BS8 3RA, England.

TIGHE Margaret Mary, b. 16 January 1932, Melbourne, Australia. Retired Pharmacist; Full-Time Volunteer. m. Ronald James Tighe, 3 sons, 1 daughter. Education: Graduated as Pharmaceutical Chemist, Victorian College of Pharmacy, 1954. Appointments: Pharmacist in hospitals in Australia and UK; Volunteer, 1969-, currently, President, Right to Life Australia; Well known commentator of life issues. Publications: Occasional articles in leading newspapers in Australia; Featured in books including: Women in Australian Politics by Clarke and White 1983; Protesters, Gloria Frydman, 1987. Address: 29 Kalimna Street, Essendon, 3040 Victoria, Australia. E-mail: rtl@rtlaust.com

TIRIMO Martino, b. 19 December 1942, Larnaca, Cyprus. Concert Pianist; Conductor. m. Mione J Teakle, 1973, 1 son, 1 daughter. Education: Royal Academy of Music, London; Vienna State Academy. Debut: Recital, Cyprus, 1949. Career: Conducted La Traviata 7 times at Italian Opera Festival, Cyprus, 1955; London debut, 1965; Concerto performances with most major orchestras, and recitals, TV and radio appearances in Britain, Europe, USA, Canada, South Africa and the Far East from 1965; Gave public premiére of complete Schubert Sonatas, London, 1975, 1985; Public premiére of Beethoven concertos directing from the keyboard, Dresden and London, 1985, 1986; Gave several premiéres of Tippett Piano concerto since 1986; Performed as special Athens Festival during Olympic period with Vienna Philharmonic in 2004. Compositions include: film score for the Odyssey in 8 episodes for Channel 4 TV, 1998. Recordings: Brahms Piano Concertos; Chopin Concertos; Tippett Piano Concerto (with composer conducting); Rachmaninov Concertos; Complete Debussy piano works; Complete Schubert Piano Sonatas; Various other solo recordings with mixed repertoire. Publications: Schubert: The Complete Piano Sonatas, 3 volumes, edited for Wiener Unitext Edition (with own completions to the unfinished movements), 1997-99. Honours: Gold Medal, Associated Board of the Royal Schools of Music; Liszt Scholarship, Royal Academy of Music; 11 other Prizes at Royal Academy of Music including Macfarren Medal; Boise Foundation Scholarship, 1965; Gulbenkian Foundation Scholarship, 1967-69; Joint Winner, Munich International Competition, 1971; Winner, Geneva International Competition, 1972; ARAM, 1968; FRAM, 1979; Silver Disc, 1988; Gold Disc, 1994. Address: 1 Romeyn Road, London SW16 2NU, England.

TITIUS Ruth Latitia Dorothea, b. 9 May 1922, Hamburg-Wilhelmsburg, Germany. Painter; Writer. Education: 2 Certificates of Chamber of Commerce, Commercial School, 1939; Graduation, 1943; Experience as Interpreter, French, German, 1945; Phil Fac, Universities of Hamburg and Heidelberg, 1944, 1946-49; 15 Certificates as Guest Student, Humanities, political science, sociology, philosophy, letters, University of Hamburg, 1989-95. Appointments: Secretary in commerce, industry, cultural offices, diplomatic offices in Kassel, Damascus, Beirut, Hamburg and Bad Godesberg, 1940 and 1952-79; Concurrently, Painter, Writer, literary and scientific; Student of parapsychology, telepathy, tantra and astrology. Creative Works: More than 400 pictures, drafts, oil paintings, drawings in pencil and pen and ink, experimental works such as entouring and gummed patterns; 12 exhibitions in Germany and abroad. Publications: Numerous works several published include: Man kann doch alles haben, Aspects of Lebanon; Vom New-Look der Pharonen zum Reissverschluss; Die Überfahrt, Crossing the River; Das Leben eine Pause in der Ewigkeit? (Life is a pause in eternity), 2003; Translation of van Lier's Le Nouvel Age, unpublished. Honours: Several awards, including gold medals, diplomas and certificates for paintings and expositions. Memberships: Deutsch-Französisches Gesellschaft, Cluny; Kunstverein, Hamburg; International Gesellschaft für Menschenrechte; Europäischer Kulturkreis Baden-Baden; Deutsches Rotes Kreuz; Accademia Italia delle Arti e del Lavoro, Parma, 1979-80. Address: Baurvereinsweg, 5 II, 21 107 Hamburg, Germany.

TLÁSKAL Tomáš, b. 2 April 1950, Prague, Czech Republic. Paediatric Cardiac Surgeon. m. Květa Laurinová, 1 daughter. Education: MD, Charles University, Prague, 1974; General Surgery

Diploma, 1978, Cardiac Surgery Diploma, 1984, Institute for Postgraduate Medical Education, Prague; CSc, PhD, Medicine, 1991, Associated Professor of Surgery Diploma, 1997, Charles University, Prague; Fellow, European Board of Thoracic and Cardiovascular Surgery Diploma, 1998. Appointments: Senior House Officer, Hospital Novy Bydzov, 1974-76; Senior House Officer, 1976-1978, Senior Registrar, 1979-84, Staff Cardiac Surgeon, 1985-90, Consultant Paediatric Cardiac Surgeon and Deputy Chief, 1991-2004, Chief of Division of Cardiac Surgery, 2004-, Kardiocentrum, University Hospital Motol, Prague; Consultant Paediatric Cardiac Surgeon, Cardiocentro, Hospital W Soller, Habana, Cuba, 1987-88; Teacher, 2nd School of Medicine, Charles University, 1992-; Associate Professor of Surgery, Charles University, Prague, 1997-; Associate Professor of Surgery, Institute of Postgraduate Education in Medicine, 1999-; Consultant, Institute for Mother and Child Care, 1999-. Publications: Over 100 articles published in professional journals. Memberships: Association for European Paediatric Cardiology; European Association for Cardio-Thoracic Surgery; Czech Medical Society; Czech Society of Cardiology; Czech Society of Cardiovascular Surgery; International Society of Cardio-Thoracic Surgeons; CTS Net. Address: Nad Palatou 3, 150 00 Prague 5, Czech Republic. E-mail: tomas.tlaskal@lfmotol.cuni.cz Website: www.ctsnet.org/home/ttlaskal

TOBIAS Phillip Vallentine, b. 14 October 1925, Durban, Natal, South Africa. Retired University Professor. Education: BSc, 1946, BSc Hons, 1947, MBBCh, 1950, PhD, 1953, DSc, 1967, University of Witwatersrand, Johannesburg. Appointments: Lecturer, 1951-52, Senior Lecturer, 1953-58, Professor, 1959-93, Head of Department, 1959-90, Dean of Faculty of Medicine, 1980-82, Member of Council, 1971-74, 1975-84, Professor Emeritus, 1994-; Honorary Professorial Research Fellow, 1994-, School of Anatomical Sciences, University of Witwatersrand; Chairman, Kalahari Research Committee; Past Director, Palaeo-Anthropology Research Unit; Director, Sterkfontein Research Unit; Past President, International Association of Human Biologists; Former President, Royal Society of South Africa; Founder and Sometime President, Institute for the Study of Mankind in Africa, Anatomical Society of Southern Africa, South African Society for Quaternary Research; Former President, South African Science Writers Association. Publications: Over 1100 including 40 books, 90 chapters in books; Notable works Chromosomes, sex cells and evolution in a mammal, 1956; Australopithecus boisei, 1967; The Bushmen, San Hunters and Herders of the Kalahari, 1978; Hominid Evolution Past Present and Future, 1985; The Brain in Hominid Evolution, 1971; Man's Anatomy, 1963-88; The Meaning of Race, 1961-72; Homo habilis, 1991; Humanity from African Naissance to Coming Millennia, 2001. Honours: Rivers Memorial Medal, 1978; Balzan Prize, 1987; LSB Leakey Prize, 1991; Carmel Award of Merit, 1992; Order of Meritorious Service of South Africa, 1992; Fellow of the Royal Society London, 1996; Charles Darwin Lifetime Achievement Award, 1997; Commander of the National Order of Merit of France, 1998; Order of the Southern Cross of South Africa, 1999; Hrdlicka Medal, 1999; Commander of the Order of Merit of Italy, 2000; UNESCO Medal, 2001; ISMS Medal, 2001; Honorary Cross for Science and Arts, First Class, Austrian Federal Government, 2002. Memberships: Academy of Science of South Africa; Royal Society, London; Royal Society of South Africa; South African Medical Association; South African Archaeological Society; American Association of Physical Anthropologists; National Academy of Sciences, USA; American Philosophical Society; American Academy of Arts and Sciences; American Anthropological Association; Royal Anthropological Institute of Great Britain and Ireland; Royal College of Physicians, London; Linnean Society, London; South African Institute of Race Relations; Anatomical Society of Southern Africa; Anatomical

Societies (hon) of USA, Great Britain and Ireland, Canada, Israel. Address: School of Anatomical Sciences, University of the Witwatersrand Medical School, 7 York Road, Parktown, Johannesburg 2193, South Africa. E-mail: tobiaspv@anatomy.wits.ac.za

TODD Mary King, b. 6 July 1942, Northern Ireland. Educator. m. John Todd. Education: BA, Arts, 1964, Dip Ed, 1965, The Queen's University of Belfast, Northern Ireland; DASE, 1974, MA, Education, 1979, DPhil, Education, 1990, The University of Ulster, Coleraine, Northern Ireland. Appointments: Lecturer, Modern Languages, 1965-75, Adult Basic Education Organiser, 1976-89, Head of Adult Education, 1989-94, Ballymena College, Northern Ireland; Occasional Lecturer, Adult Education, DENI/NEELB, 1976-90; Trainer, ABE Tutors, Ireland, 1976-90; Information Officer, Irish Christian Endeavour, 1991-; Director, Modern Languages Research Project, NEELB, 1992-93; Course Tutor (Higher Degrees), Open University, 1995-2000; Writer of teaching materials for Go Teach Publications, 2000-; Director, Christian Endeavour Union of Great Britain and Ireland (incorporated), 2002-. Publications: Articles in: International Reading Association, 1987, Modern Management, 1988, ALO Magazines, Go Teach, 2001-; Editor, The Irish Endeavour, 1986-; Editor, Focus Magazine, 1997-2000. Honours: President, Irish Christian Endeavour Union, 1990-91; President, Christian Endeavour Union of Great Britain and Ireland, 1998-99. Memberships: Department of Education (NI) Adult Literacy/Basic Education Committee, 1976-89; Irish CE Executive, 1986-; Training and Advisory Panel, NICOD (Belfast), 1994-98; Executive of Christian Endeavour Union of Great Britain and Ireland, 1996-; Council of Leprosy Mission (NI), 1999-. Address: 4 Chapeltown Road, Antrim BT41 2LD, Northern Ireland. E-mail: maryktodd@btinternet.com

TODRES Zory Vlad, b. 8 August 1933, Moscow, Russia. Chemist. m. Irina, 1 son, 1 daughter. Education: BA, Leningrad Institute of Technology, 1954; MS, Leningrad Institute of Technology, 1956; PhD, Industrial Organic Chemistry, Moscow Institute of Fine Chemical Technology, 1962; DSc, Physical Organic Chemistry, Russian Academy of Sciences, 1978. Appointments: Science Analyst, Chemical Abstracts Services, USA; Senior Researcher, Detrex/ELCO Co, USA; Senior Technologist, Cleveland Clinic Foundation, USA; Leading Scientist, Science Academy, Russia; Professor, Moscow Pedagogical School, Ufa Oil Institute; Visiting Professor, Universities in Italy, Portugal and Denmark. Publications: Patents; Articles; Reviews; Books, including: Organic Ion Radicals, 2003. Honours: Mendleleev Society Prize in Organic Chemistry; Russian Medal for Inventions; Invited to be Main Lecturer, International Union of Pure and Applied Chemistry. Memberships: American Chemical Society; Russian Mendeleev Society; USSR Science Academy's Chemical Kinetics Counsel. Address: The Chemical Abstracts Services D58, PO Box 3012, 2450 Olentangy River Road, Columbus, OH 43210-0012, USA. Website: www.dekker.com/servlet/product/productid/0810-5

TOENNESSEN Finn Egil, b. 22 April 1952, Arendal, Norway. Professor. m. Anne Liv, 2 sons. Education: PhD, Philosophy, Logic, University of Oslo, 1979; PhD, Psychology, University of Bergen, 1993. Appointments: Teacher, High School, Norway, 1972-74; Lecturer, University of Oslo, 1979-82; Associate Professor, Teacher's College, Stavanger, Norway, 1982-94; Professor, Assistant Director, Centre for Reading Research, Stavanger, Norway, 1994-; National Research Co-ordinator, International Reading Literacy Study, 1989-92. Publications: 10 books include: Educational Philosophy in Schools and Kindergartens (in Norwegian), 1983; Humanism and Christianity (in Norwegian),

1985; The Etiology of Dyslexia, 1993; In Norwegian: Reading Pleasures and Reading Matters, 1995; Reading and Learning, 1996; Lines in Children's Reading, 1996; Vision and Reading, 1996; Hundreds of articles in journals and newspapers. Honours: Completed university studies/exams in history, history of ideas, maths, medicine, pedagogics, philosophy, psychology, sociology, theology in 5 years, 1975-80, declared to be a national record by Norwegian newspapers. Address: Centre for Reading Research, Box 2504 Ullandhaug, Stavanger N-4004, Norway.

TOKEDE Michael Segun, b. 8 December 1952, Otan-Aiyegbaju, Nigeria. Physician. m. Stella Boluwade, 2 sons, 2 daughters. Education: MBBS, College of Medicine, University of Ibadan, 1973-79; FMCP, National Postgraduate Medical College Nigeria, 1981-90. Appointments: House Officer, Lagos University Teaching Hospital, 1979-80; General Hospital Isheagu, Delta State, Nigeria, 1980-81; Resident Intern, Lagos University Teaching Hospital, 1981-85; Consultant Neurophysician, Segun Alayo Medical Centre, Lagos, 1985-99; Medical Director, Miset Specialist Hospital, Ipaja-Lagos, 1999-. Publication: Phenytoin Induced Immunopathy in Nigerian Africans (Dissertation). Honour: Uzodike Award, Best Final Result, National Postgraduate Medical College in Internal Medicine, 1990. Memberships: New York Academy of Sciences, 1992; Nigerian Institute of Management. Address: 12/14 Segun Tokede Street, Baruwa-Ipaja, PO Box 1491, Oshodi, Lagos, Nigeria. E-mail: misetspecialisthospital@yahoo.com

TOMALIN Claire, b. 20 June 1933, London, England. Author. m. (1) Nicholas Osborne Tomalin, deceased 1973, 2 sons (1 deceased), 3 daughters (1 deceased), (2) Michael Frayn, 1993. Education: MA, Newnham College, Cambridge, 1954. Appointment: Literary Editor, New Statesman, 1974-77; Literary Editor, The Sunday Times, London, 1979-86. Publications: The Life and Death of Mary Wollstonecroft, 1974; Shelley and His World, 1980; Parents and Children, 1981; Katherine Mansfield: A Secret Life, 1987; The Invisible Woman: The Story of Nelly Teran and Charles Dickens, 1990; The Winter Wife, 1991; Mrs Jordan's Professions, 1994; Jane Austin: A Life, 1997; Maurice by Mary Shelley, 1998; Several Strangers: writing from three decades, 1999; Samuel Pepys: The Unequalled Self, 2002; Exhibitions: Mrs Jordan, English Heritage Kenwood, 1995; Hyenas in Petticoats: Mary Wollstonecraft and Mary Shelley, Wordsworth Trust and National Portrait Gallery, 1997-98; Play: The Winter Wife, 1991. Honours: Whitbread First Book Prize, 1974; James Tait Black Memorial Prize, 1990; Hawthornden Prize, 1991; NCR Prize, 1991; Trustee, National Portrait Gallery, 1992-; Theatre Literary Award, New York 1995; Whitbread Awards for Book of the Year and Best Biography. Membership: PEN, Vice-president, 1998; Member, London Library Committee, 1997-2000; Advisory Committee for the Arts, Humanities and Social Sciences, British Library, 1997-; Council, Royal Society of Literature, 1997-2000. Address: 57 Gloucester Crescent, London NW1 7EG, England. E-mail: clairetomalin@dial.pipex.com

TOMASELLI Keyan Gray, b. 31 August 1948, Johannesburg, South Africa. Director; Professor. m. Ruth Teer-Tomaselli, 1 son, 1 daughter. Education: BA, honours; MA, Dramatic Art; PhD. Appointments include: Demonstrator in Geography, 1972; Instructor, Sussex Study and Speed Reading Course, Educational Technology Unit, 1973, Tutor, School of Dramatic Art, 1978-79, Senior Tutor, 1981, University of Witwatersrand; Lecturer, Department of Journalism and Media Studies, Rhodes University, 1981-84; Professor, Director, Cultural and Media Studies, University of Natal, Durban, 1985-. Publications include: Action Research, Participatory Communication: Why Governments Don't Listen, 1997; Cultural Studies and Theoretical Impoverishment,

1998; Die volgen der apartheid und ihre Uberwindung durch Zeichenanaluse Semiotik Sudafrika, 1998; Cultural Studies in Africa, 1998. Honours: Nominated, International Journalism Scholarship Award, Rotary South Africa, 1984; Honorary Member, South Africa Film and Television Technicians' Association, 1988; Africa Network's (Chicago) KW ANZAA Award, 1988; Fellow, University of Natal, 1995. Memberships include: International Visual Sociology Association; International Association for Media Communication Research. Address: University of Kwazulu-Natal, King George V Avenue, Durban 4041, South Africa.

TOMITA Ken-ichi, b. 5 June 1928, Nagasaki, Japan. Professor Emeritus. m. Namie Tokuhisa, 1 son, 1 daughter. Education: BSc, Hiroshima University, 1953; DSc, Osaka University, 1959. Appointments: Research Associate, Massachusetts Institute of Technology, 1959-64; Research Associate, Institute of Protein Research, 1964-65, Professor, Faculty of Pharmaceutical Science, 1965-92, Osaka University. Publications include: Nucleic Acid Structure. Honour: Scientific Award, Pharmaceutical Society of Japan, 1989. Memberships: Crystallographic Society of Japan; Pharmaceutical Society of Japan. Address: 1-82 Hagiwaradai Higashi, Kawanishi 666-0005, Japan.

TOMLINSON Gerald (Arthur), b. 24 January 1933, Elmira, New York, USA. Writer; Editor; Publisher. m. (Mary) Alexis Usakowski, 13 March 1967, 2 sons. Education: BA, Marietta College, Ohio, 1955; Columbia Law School, New York City, 1959-60. Appointments: Associate Editor, Business and Professional Books, Prentice Hall, 1960-63, School Department, Harcourt Brace Jovanovich, 1963-66; Senior Editor, English Department, Holt, Rinehart and Winston, 1966-69; Executive Editor, K-12 English, Silver Burdett and Ginn, 1969-82; Publisher, Home Run Press, 1985-. Publications: On a Field of Black (novel), 1980; School Administrator's Complete Letter Book, 1984, 2003; Speaker's Treasury of Sports Anecdotes, Stories and Humor, 1990; Encyclopedia of Religious Quotations, 1991; The New Jersey Book of Lists (co-author), 1992; Murdered in Jersey, 1994, 1997; Fatal Tryst, 1999; How to do Baseball Research (general editor), 2000; Seven Jersey Murders, 2003. Contributions to: Magazines and journals. Honours: Best Detective Stories of the Year, E.P. Dutton, 1976; Mystery Writers of America Annual Anthologies, 5 appearances, 1977-87. Memberships: Authors Guild; Mystery Writers of America; Society for American Baseball Research. Address: 19 Harbor Drive, Lake Hopatcong, NJ 07849, USA.

TOMLINSON Stephen Miles (Sir), b. 29 March 1952, Wolverhampton, England. Justice of the High Court. m. Joanna Greig, 1 son, 1 daughter. Education: Scholar, Worcester College, Oxford; Eldon Law Scholar, MA; Called to the Bar, Inner Temple, 1974. Appointments: Barrister in practice, 1975-2000; QC, 1988; A Recorder of the Crown Court, 1995-2000; Judge of the High Court of Justice, 2000. Honour: Knighted, 2000. Address: Royal Courts of Justice, Strand, London WC1A 2LL, England.

TOMOVA Malina, b. 21 January 1950, Plovdiv, Bulgaria. Poet; Script Writer. m. Ivan Tzanev, 3 daughters. Education: Russian Language and Literature, Slavic Languages Department, Sofia University "St Clement Ohridsky", 1976. Appointments: Editor, Narodna Mladezh Newspaper, 1976-78; Free-lance Translator, 1978-80; Editor, Yantra Literary Magazine, 1980-89; Editor, Literary Newspaper, 1989-2003; Editor-in-Chief, Romano Ilo Newspaper, 1994-99; Director and Editor, Stigmati Publishing House, 1996-2003. Publications: Books: Poetry: Dusha, 1978; Ezheliubov, 1987; Stigmati, 1994; Translations: 14 books by Russian authors; Films: Burn, burn, little flame, 1994; Vasilitsa (documentary), 1996; The Story of a Hat, 2003. Honours: The Critics' Award at the Varna Film Festival "Golden Rose" for humanitarian ideas for film Burn, burn, little flame, 1994; Award for Creative Works, Ministry of Culture of Bulgaria, 2002. Memberships: Union of Bulgarian Writers, 1986-95; Association of Bulgarian Writers, 1995-; Association of Bulgarian Film Makers, 1996-. Address: 41 Skobelev Blvd, Sofia 1606, Bulgaria. E-mail: stigmati@abv.bg

TOOLE James Francis, b. 22 March 1925, Atlanta, Georgia, USA. Neurologist. m. Patricia Wooldridge Toole, 3 sons, 1 daughter. Education: BA, Princeton University, New Jersey, 1947; MD, Cornell University Medical College, New York, 1949; LLB, LaSalle Extension University, Chicago, Illinois, 1963. Publications: Over 600 focusing on cerebrovascular disease, medical ethics and medical history. Honours: Combat Medical Badge, 1952; Bronze Star with V, 1952; Best Doctors in America, 1996; Who's Who in the World, 1997. Memberships: President, American Neurological Association, 1985; President, American Society of Neuroimaging, 1992-94; Editor-in-Chief, Journal of Neurological Sciences, 1989-97; President, International Stroke Society, 2000-04; President, World Federation of Neurology, 1998-2001. Address: Stroke Research Center, Wake Forest University School of Medicine, Medical Center Boulevard, Winston-Salem, NC 27157-1068, USA.

TOOTHE Karen Lee, b. 13 December 1957, Seattle, Washington, USA. Educator. m. Edward Frank Toothe, 1 daughter. Education: BA, Psychology, High Honours, University Florida, 1977; MEd, Emotional Handicaps and Learning Disabilities, 1979; Certificate, Behaviour Analysis, Florida Department of Professional Regulation, 1993; National Board Certificate, Behaviour Analysis, 1999. Appointments include: Resource Compliance Specialist, Program Specialist for Mentally Handicapped, Physically Impaired, Occupational and Physical Therapy Programs, St Cloud, Florida, Middle School, 1993-96; Local Augmentative/Assistive Technology Specialist, Resource Compliance Specialist for Hickory Tree Elementary School and Program Specialist for Physically Impaired, Occupational and Physical Therapy, 1996-97; District Assistive Technology Program Specialist and Program Specialist for Physically Impaired, Occupational and Physical Therapy, 1997-; 99 District Assistive Technology Program Specialist, 1999-. Publications: Diagnostic Testing in Mathematics: An Extension of the Piat?; Teaching Exceptional Children, 1980; Contributions to: A Structured Approach to the Teaching of Mathematics for Children with Specific Learning Difficulties: A Teacher's Manual, Dyslexia Institute, 1990; Computing in Fairley House School Educational Computing. Honours: Phi Beta Kappa; Osceola Chapter of Council for Exceptional Children, Middle School Professional of Year, 1995, 1996; Disney's Teacherrific Special Judges Award, 1997; Awarded Board Certified Behaviour Analysis by National Behaviour Analyst Certification Board, 2000; Outstanding Services to CEC Award, 2002, 2003; CEC Outstanding Related Services Teacher of the Year, 2003; CEC Outstanding Support Services Award, 2003. Memberships: Children's Advocacy Network Rep, CEC, 1997-99, President Elect CEC, 1999-2000; Florida Society for Augmentative and Alternative Communication; Board Member of Center for Independent Living Assistive Technology; President, CEC, 2000-2001; Past President CEC, 2001-2002. Address: 2175 James Drive, St Cloud, FL 34771-8830, USA.

TOPLITT Gloria Hamilton, b. 22 May 1925, St Louis, USA. Singer; Actress; Voice Coach. m. (1) James Parnell, divorced, (2) Abraham Toplitt, 1 son. Education: Graduated, Guy Bates Academy, Dramatic Arts, Los Angeles. Appointments: Has appeared in numerous New York stage musical productions as a leading lady, including Oklahoma, Chocolate Soldier, Three Musketeers, Show Boat, Lend an Ear and Brigadoon; Stage

Performer, New York City, 1944-59; Director of Entertainment, Holland American Lines, 1959-61; Teacher of Voice North Hollywood Conservatory, California, 1965-67; Voice Teacher, Coach for Impaired Voices, North Hollywood, 1968-; Music Specialist, Outreach Program, NASA Space Science and Technology Institute, 1997-. Publications: Parade of Planets, 1998, Space Challenge, 1999, author, composer. Memberships: Election Board, Office of the Voter Registrar, North Hollywood; Vice President, National Association for Singing; Vice President, Music Teachers Association, 1970-80. Address: 4405 Carpenter Ave, North Hollywood, CA 91607-4110, USA.

TORINA Philip, b. 25 July 1977, New York City, USA. Plastic Surgery Resident. Education: Bachelors Degree, University of Delaware, 1999; MD, cum laude, Jefferson Medical College, 2003. Appointments: Plastic Surgery Resident, Mt Sinai, New York City, USA. Publications: Co-author, Early vs late surgical decompression in the setting of cervical spine injury. Honours: Most Outstanding Senior Man, University of Delaware, 1999. Memberships: Alpha Omega Alpha. Address: 130 Kingsbury Road, New Rochelle, NY 10804, USA.

TORMALA Pertti Olavi, b. 26 November 1945, Tampere, Finland. Academy Professor. m. Mirja Tormala, 2 daughters. Education: BS, Medicine, 1973; PhD, Polymer Science, 1974. Appointments: Professor of Textile, 1983-85; Research Professor, Academy of Finland, 1986-91; Professor of Plastics Technology, 1985-99; Executive Vice-President R&D, Board Member, Bionx Implants Inc, 1996; Professor of Biomaterial Technology, Tampere University of Technology, Finland, 1999-. Publications: 200 refereed papers; 700 abstracts and other scientific papers; 150 patents. Address: Saarenkarjenkuja 5A2, FIN-33300 Tampere, Finland.

TORNARITIS George Criton, b. 2 January 1936, Cyprus. Lawyer. 3 sons, 1 daughter. Education: MA, LLB (Cantab), Trinity College, University of Cambridge, England. Barrister-at Law, Gray's Inn, London. Appointments: Member, Educational Committee, Cyprus, 1960-65; Practised Law in Cyprus defending most of the cause celebres of his time. Publications: Books: Mediterranean Sea Shells Cyprus; Art and Shells; My Cyprus Cats; The Fish; Articles in magazines and newspapers in Cyprus and Greece on natural history. Honours: President, Tonaritis-Pierides Marine Life Foundation; Founder, President, Tornaritis-Pierides Paleontology Museum, Larnaca, Cyprus; Founder, President, Tornaritis-Pierides Marine Life Museum, Agia Napa, Cyprus; First Prize for Underwater Photography. Membership: Nautical Club, Greece. Address: Telos Varnali, Latsia, Cyprus.

TÖRÖK Tamás László, b. 23 January 1944, Budapest, Pharmacist. m. Melinda Kontsek, 2 daughters. Education: Diploma, Pharmaceutical Faculty of Semmelweis University, Budapest, 1968; Doctor Degree, 1972; PhD degree, Hungarian Academy of Sciences, 1981; ScD degree, Hungarian Academy of Sciences, 1991. Appointments: Scientific co-worker, Department of Pharmacology, Semmelweis University of Medicine, 1970; British Council Student at the Pharmacology Department of Oxford University, 1978-79; Assistant Professor, 1981-, Associate Professor, 1989, Professor, 1994, Head, 1998, Department of Pharmacodynamics of Semmelweis University. Publications: 28 Scientific Papers; 237 Citations. Honours: Award for Outstanding Work, 1985; Outstanding Teacher Award 1st Degree, 1995; Szechenyi Professorship, 1998. Memberships: Union of Pharmacology, IUPHAR; European Society for Neurochemistry, ESN. Address: Department of Pharmacodynamics, Semmelweis University of Medicine, H 1445 Budapest, Hungary.

TORRANCE Sam, b. 24 August 1953, Largs, Scotland. Golfer. m. Suzanne, 1 son, 2 daughters. Appointments: Professional Golfer, 1970-; Has played in 8 Ryder Cups and represented Scotland on numerous occasions; Winner, Scottish PGA Championship, 1978, 1980, 1985, 1991, 1993; Member, Dunhill Cup Team (8 times); World Cup Team (11 times); Hennessy Cognac Cup Team (5 times); Double Diamond Team (3 times); Captain, European Team in Ashai Glass Four Tours Championships, Adelaide, 1991; Captain, Ryder Cup Team, 2001; Winner of 28 tournaments world-wide since 1972 including: Italian Open, 1987; Germany Masters, 1990; Hersey Open, 1991; Kronenbourg Open, 1993; Catalan Open, 1993; Honda Open, 1993; Hamburg Open, 1993; British Masters, 1995; French Open, 1998. Address: c/o Katrina Johnston, Carnegie Sports International, The Glassmill, 1 Battersea Bridge Road, London, SW11 3BZ, England.

TORRANCE Thomas F(orsyth), b. 30 August 1913, Chengdu, China. Minister of Religion; Professor of Theology. m. Margaret Edith Spear, 2 October 1946, 2 sons, 1 daughter. Education: MA, 1934; BD, 1937; DrTheol, 1946; DLitt, 1971. Appointments: Founder-Editor, Scottish Journal of Theology, 1948-88; Moderator, General Assembly, Church of Scotland, 1976-77. Publications: The Doctrine of Grace, 1949; Calvin's Doctrine of Man, 1949; Kingdom and Church, 1956; Conflict and Agreement in the Church, 2 volumes, 1959-60; Theology in Reconstruction, 1965; Theological Science, 1969; God and Rationality, 1971; Theology in Reconciliation, 1975; Space, Time and Resurrection, 1976; Space, Time and Incarnation, 1979; The Ground and Grammar of Theology, 1980; Christian Theology and Scientific Culture, 1980; Divine and Contingent Order, 1981; Reality and Scientific Theology, 1984; The Hermeneuntics of John Calvin, 1987; The Trinitarian Faith, 1988; The Christian Frame of Mind, Reason, Order and Openness in Theology and Natural Science, 1989; Karl Barth, Biblical and Evangelical Theological Theologian, 1990; Senso del divino e scienza mnoderna, 1992; Theological Dialogue between Orthodox and Reformed Churches (editor), 1993; Royal Priesthood, 1993; Divine Meaning: Studies in Patristic Hermeneutics, 1994; Trinitarian Perspectives: Toward Doctrinal Agreement, 1994; The Christian Doctrine of God, One Being Three Persons, 1996; Scottish Theology: From John Knox to John McLeod Campbell, 1996. Contributions to: Numerous publications. Honours: Honorary doctorates; Honorary DD, Edinburgh, 1996. Memberships: British Academy; International Academy of Religious Sciences, president, 1972-81; International Academy of the Philosophy of Sciences; Center of Theological Inquiry, Princeton, New Jersey; Royal Society of Edinburgh. Address: 37 Braid Farm Road, Edinburgh EH10 6LE, Scotland. E-mail: ttorr@globalnet.co.uk

TORVILL Jayne, b. 7 October 1957, England. Ice Skater. m. Philip Christensen, 1990. Career: British Pair Skating Champion with M Hutchinson, 1971; Insurance Clerk, 1974-80; With Christopher Dean: British Ice Dance Champion, 1978-83, 1994; European Ice Dance Champion, 1981-82, 1984, 1994; World Ice Dance Champion, 1981-84; World Professional Ice Dance Champion, 1984, 1985, 1990, 1995, 1996; Olympic Ice Dance Champion, 1984; Olympic Ice Dance Bronze Medal, 1994; Tours include: Australia and New Zealand, 1984; Royal Variety Performance, London, 1984; World tour with own company of international skaters, 1985; Guest artists with IceCapades, 1987; World tour with company of skaters from Soviet Union, 1988; Guest of South Australian Government, 1991; Great Britain tour with company of Ukraine skaters, 1992; Torvill & Dean, Face the Music, World Tour, UK, Australia and North America, 1994; Stars on Ice Tour, USA and Canada, 1997-98; Torvill and Dean Ice Adventures, UK, 1997-98; Television: Path of Perfection, 1984; Fire & Ice, 1986; World Tour (video), 1988; Bladerunners

(documentary), 1991; Great Britain Tour (TV special and video), 1992; The Artistry of Torvill and Dean, 1994; Face the Music (video), 1995; Torvill and Dean: The Story So Far (video), 1996; Bach Cello Suite (with Yo-Yo Ma), 1996. Publications: with Christopher Dean: Torvill and Dean: Autobiography, 1984; Torvill and Dean: Facing the Music, 1995. Honours: MBE, 1981; BBC Sports Personality of the Year with Christopher Dean, 1983-84; Olympic Ice Dance Gold Medal, 1984; Figure Skating Hall of Fame with Christopher Dean, 1989; Olympic Ice Dance Bronze Medal, 1994; Hon MA, Nottingham Trent University, 1994; OBE, 2000. Address: c/o Sue Young, PO Box 32, Heathfield, East Sussex TN21 0BW, England.

TOSSETT Gloria Vay, b. 31 January 1926, Hamar, North Dakota, USA. Education Administrator. m. A A Borstad, deceased, 1 son, 1 daughter. Education: BS, Concordia College, 1968; MS, North Dakota State University, 1972; BA, Jamestown College, 1983; Graduate Study Credits, University of North Dakota; University of Montana, University of Minnesota. Appointments: School Co-ordinator for fifteen schools, Harding County, South Dakota, 1972-73; School Superintendent, School Principal, Balfour, Flaxton and Buchanan Public Schools, 1973-86; College Teacher, Little Hoop Community College, 1984-85; Title Seven Administrator, Bilingual Co-ordinator, Music and Art Instructor, Trenton, North Dakota, 1986-89; Rancher, 1989-2002. Publications: Twuddleville Mouse; Angel Album. Honours: North Dakota Candidate for State Superintendent of Public Instruction; North Dakota Centennial Commission Recognition. Memberships: Pioneer Daughters of North Dakota; American Association of Retired Persons; Member, Sons of Norway Lodge; Order Eastern Star, North Dakota Council on the Arts, 2000. Address: PO Box 115, 321 Riverside Avenue, Sheyenne, North Dakota 58374, USA.

TOURNAS Kostas, b. 23 September 1949, Tripolis, Greece. Musician (guitar); Singer; Composer; Lyricist; Producer; Recording Studio Owner. m. Maria, 4 December 1977. Musical Education: Harmony; Synthesis; Guitar. Career: many tours, Greece, Cyprus, Europe and USA; Club appearances; Host or guest, radio and television talk shows; Owner, City Studios, Athens. Compositions: More than 700 titles released since 1971. Recordings: Aperanta Horafia (Endless Fields); Kiries Kai Kirioi (Ladies and Gentlemen) Duets; Poll/Anthrope (Man). Publications: Kostas Tournas' Songs (sheet music and lyrics of his best). Honours: Gold, Platinum records; Lyric awards; Forhis offer in Music Award. Memberships: AEPI Greece; ETE Greece; FIA. Address: 133 Kafkassou Street, Kipseli, Athens, 11364, Greece.

TOURNOIS Nadine-Françoise, b. 3 May 1954, Nice, France. University Professor. 2 daughters. Education: Doctorate, 3ème cycle, Management Science, 1981; State Doctorate, Management Science, 1984. Appointments: Financial Analyst, Texas Instruments, 1977-79; Technical-Commercial Engineer, IBM, 1979-81; University Professor, 1984-2002, Dean of the Business School, 2002-, University of Nice, France. Publications: Book chapter: L'èthique et TIC in L'impossible èthique des Enterprises, 2002; Editor, le marketing bancaire face aux nouvelles technologies, 2 volumes, 2003; European Marketing: the case of banking, 2003. Honours: Doctor Honoris Causa, University of Timisoara, 2003; Listed in Who's Who publications and biographical dictionaries. Address: 3 rue de Rivoli, 06000 Nice, France. E-mail: nadinetournois@aol.com

TOWNES Charles Hard, b. 28 July 1915, Greenville, South Carolina, USA. Physicist. m. Frances Brown, 4 daughters. Education: BA, BS, Furman University, 1935; MA, Duke University, 1937; PhD, California Institute of Technology, 1939. Appointments: Bell Telephone Laboratories, 1939-47; Associate

Professor, 1948-50, Professor, 1950-61, Chairman, Department of Physics, 1952-55, Columbia University; Executive Director, Columbia Radiation Laboratory, 1950-52; Vice-President, Director of Research, Institute for Defense Analyses, 1959-61; Provost, Professor of Physics, 1961-66, Institute Professor, 1966-67, Massachusetts Institute of Technology; University Professor, 1967-86, Emeritus Professor, 1986-94, Professor, Graduate School, 1994-, University of California, Berkeley. Publications: Books: Microwave Spectroscopy, 1955; Making Waves, 1995; How the Laser Happened. Adventures of a Scientist, 1999. Honours: Thomas Young Medal and Prize, Institute of Physics and The Physical Society, England, 1963; Nobel Prize for Physics, 1964; Medal of Honour, Institute of Electrical and Electronics Engineers, 1966; Wilhelm Exner Award, Austria, 1970; Niels Bohr International Gold Medal, 1979; Officier de la Légion d'Honneur, France, 1990; Rabindranath Tagore Birth Centenary Plaque of the Asiatic Society, 1999; Founders Award of the National Academy of Engineering, 2000; Lomonosov Gold Medal of the Russian Academy of Science, 2001; 25 honorary doctorates, US and abroad; Numerous prizes, awards, lectureships, other honours. Memberships: Fellow, American Physical Society, Council, 1959-62, 1965-71, President, 1967; Life Fellow, Institute of Electrical and Electronics Engineers; National Academy of Sciences; American Philosophical Society; Royal Society of London; National Academy of Engineering; Many more. Address: Department of Physics, University of California, Berkeley, CA 94720, USA. E-mail: cht@ssl.berkeley.edu

TOWNSEND Sue, b. 2 April 1946, Leicester, England. Author. Publications: The Secret Diary of Adrian Mole Aged Thirteen and Three-Quarters, 1982; The Growing Pains of Adrian Mole, 1984; The Diaries of Adrian Mole, 1986; Bazaar and Rummage, Groping for Words, Womberang: Three Plays, 1984; True Confessions of Adrian Albert Mole; Mr Bevan's Dream, 1989; Ten Tiny Fingers, Nine Tiny Toes, play, 1989; Adrian Mole From Minor to Major, 1991; The Queen and I, 1992; Adrian Mole – The Wilderness Years, 1993; Plays, 1996; Ghost Children, 1997; Adrian Mole: The Cappuccino Years, 1999; Number Ten, 2002. Memberships: Writers Guild; PEN. Address: Reed Books, Michelin House, 81 Fulham Road, London, SW3 6RB, England.

TOWNSHEND Peter Dennis Blandford, b. 19 May 1945, Isleworth, London. British Composer; Performer of Rock Music; Author. m. Karen Astley, 1968, 1 son, 2 daughter. Education: Acton County Grammar School; Ealing Art College. Appointments: Contracted as member of The Who to Fontana Records, 1964; MCA Records, 1965; WEA Records, 1979; Retired from the Who, 1984; Contracted as solo artist to Atco Records, USA, 1979; To Virgin Records, 1986; Owner, Eel Pie Recording Ltd, 1972-83; Established, Eel Pie (bookshops and publishing co), 1976-83; Established Meher Baba Oceanic (UK archival library), 1976-81; Editor, Faber and Faber (publishers), 1983; Final tour with The Who, 1989; Recordings include: with The Who, I Can't Explain, 1965; My Generation; Tommy (rock opera); Quadrophenia (rock opera); The Iron Man, 1989; Solo, Empty Glass, 1980; Chinese Eyes, 1982; White City, 1985; Iron Man, 1989. Publications: The Story of Tommy (with Richard Barnes); Horse's Neck, 1985; Tommy: The Musical, 1995; London, 1996. Honours: Ivor Novello Award, 1981; British Phonographic Industry Award, 1983; Rock and Roll Hall of Fame, 1990; Oliver Award, 1997; Ivor Novello Lifetime Achievement Award, 2001. Address: c/o Trinifold Management, 12 Oval Road, London, NW1 7DH.

TRAJKOVSKI Boris, b. 25 June 1956, Strumica, Macedonia. President of the Republic of Macedonia. m. Vilma, 1 son, 1 daughter. Education: Law Degree, Faculty of Law, University of St Cyril and Methodius, Skopje, Macedonia; Specialised in

Commercial Law and Employment Law; Several study visits to the USA. Appointments: Head of the Legal Department of the construction company "Sloboda", Skopje, -1997; Chief of the Cabinet of the Mayor of the municipality Kisela Voda, Skopje, 1997-97; Deputy Minister of Foreign Affairs, Republic of Macedonia, 1998-; President, Republic of Macedonia, 1999-. Honours: Knight Grand Cross of the Order of St Michael and St George, Buckingham Palace, London, England, 2000; Insignia of the Collar of the Order of Merit "Pro Merito Melitense", Sovereign Order of Malta, 2000; 2002 World Methodist Peace Award, Oslo, Norway, 2002. Address: Office of the President of the Republic of Macedonia, 11 Octomvri bb, 1000 Skopje, Republic of Macedonia. E-mail: rmpretsedatel@president.gov.mk

TRAPPE Paul, b. 12 December 1931, Trier/Moselle, Germany. Professor of Sociology. 2 sons, 1 daughter. Education: Prom. Dr. Phil, Mainz University, Germany, 1959; Habilitation, Bern University Switzerland, 1964; Language Examinations: Italian, Perugia, Italy; English, London, England; Spanish, Madrid, Spain, French, Frankfurt, Germany; Government Consultant, Field Research in Mediterranean and African countries. Appointments: Assistant, Law Faculty, Mainz, Germany, 1959-61; Assistant, Law and Economics Faculty, Bern, Switzerland, 1961-64; Docent for Sociology, Bern University, Switzerland, 1964-66; Ordinary Professor and Director, Institute for Sociology, Kiel University, Germany, 1966-69; Ordinary Professor and Director, Institute for Sociology, Basle University, Switzerland, 1968-2002; President, European Faculty for Land Use and Development, Strassburg, 1999-; Editor, Social Strategies, 1975-. Publications: Several books on sociology of law and socio-economic development; About 200 articles in professional journals. Honours: Triennial Jubilee Prize, International Co-operative Alliance, London, 1970; Festschrift in Honour of P Trappe: Social Strategies, vol 35, Peter Lang AG, Bern, 2002. Memberships: International Association for Philosophy and Social Philosophy, President, 1979-83; International Sociological Association, 1964-; The Communitarian Network (SASE), Washington DC, 1990; AAAS, Washington DC, USA; New York Academy of Sciences, New York, USA. Address: PO Box 63, CH-3127, Mühlethurnen, Switzerland. E-mail: p.trappe@bluewin.ch

TRATTNER Egon, b. 8 September 1923, Brasov, Romania. Economist. m. Carola Klekner, 1 son. Education: MSc, Economic, Financial and Social Studies, Academy of High Commercial and Industrial Studies, Cluj-Brasov, Romania, 1948; PhD, Economic Sciences, Academy of Economic Studies, Bucharest, Romania, 1962. Appointments: Laboratory Worker, Vacuum Oil Co, Oil Refinery, Brasov Romania, 1940-41; Forced Labourer, Romanian Army, Romania, 1941-44; Secretary, Indumin Sugar Factories, Tg-Mures & Bod, Romania, 1945-49; Section Chief, Ministry of Food Industry, Bucharest, 1950-51; Economist, Institute for Food Industry Projects, Bucharest, 1951-52; Planning Co-ordinator, Department Chief, Ministry of Consumer Goods Industry, Bucharest, 1952-1956; Head Economic Research Division, Food Technological Research Institute, Bucharest, 1956-72; Expert Instructor, Food Industry Postgraduate Study Centre, 1972-73; Senior Research Fellow, Tel-Aviv University Centre for Interdisciplinary Forecasting, Tel-Aviv, Israel, 1974-76; Project Leader, Israeli Productivity Institute, Tel-Aviv, 1976-79; Senior Researcher, Institute for Development Studies, Rechovot, Israel, 1979-88. Publications: Over 100 articles published internationally on forecasting and planning, siting and sizing industrial units, measurement of labour productivity, economics of the food industry, philosophy of science. Honour: Medal of Labour, 1953. Memberships: Israeli Association of Graduates in the Social Sciences and Humanities, Israel; Israel's Economic Association;

New York Academy of Sciences; World Future Studies Federation. Address: 52 Eilat St, Holon 58364, Israel. E-mail: trattner@POBoxes.com

TRAVERS Desmond Benedict, b. 28 August 1924, Sydney, New South Wales. Medical Practitioner. m. Yvonne Gloria Terry, 2 sons, 3 daughters. Education: MBBS, University of Sydney, 1954; DPH, 1967; FRSH, 1976. Appointments: RMO, Royal Prince Alfred Hospital, Sydney, 1954; General Practitioner, Bombala, New South Wales, 1955-63; MO, Commonwealth Department of Health, 1963-67; Director, National Poisons Service, 1968-70; Assistant Director General, Public Health, 1970-72; Director, N T Medical Services, 1973-74; Director, Queensland, 1974; First Assistant Director General, Australian Director of Tuberculosis, 1975-84; Member, Adinin Appeals Tribunal, 1985-94. Publications: Numerous on Public Health. Memberships: AIF, 1942-46; Royal Society of Health; N T Legislative Assembly. Address: 5 Rosson Place, Isaacs, ACT 2607, Australia.

TRAVOLTA John, b. 18 February 1954, Englewood, New Jersey, USA. Actor. m. Kelly Preston, 1991, 1 son. Appointments: Films: Carrie, 1976; The Boy in the Plastic Bubble (for TV), 1976; Saturday Night Fever, 1977; Grease, 1978; Moment by Moment, 1978; Urban Cowboy, 1980; Blow Out, 1981; Staying Alive, 1983; Two of a Kind, 1983; Perfect, 1985; The Experts, 1988; Chains of Gold, 1989; Look Who's Talking, 1989; Look Who's Talking Now, 1990; The Tender, 1991; All Shook Up, 1991; Look Who's Talking 3, 1994; Pulp Fiction, 1994; White Man's Burden, 1995; Get Shorty, 1995; Broken Arrow, 1996; Phenomenon, 1996; Michael, 1997; Face Off, 1997; She's So Lovely, 1997; Primary Colors, 1998; A Civil Action, 1998; The General's Daughter, 1999; Battlefield Earth, 2000; Lucky Numbers, 2000; Swordfish, 2001; Domestic Disturbance, 2001; TV Series: Welcome Back Kotter, 1975-77; l.p. records, 1976, 1977. Publication: Staying Fit, 1984. Honours: Billboard Magazine Best New Male Vocalist Award, 1976; Best Actor Award, National Board of Review, 1978; Male Star of the Year, National Association of Theatre Owners, 1983; Alan J Pakula Prize, 1998.

TREGLOWN Jeremy Dickinson, b. 24 May 1946, Anglesey, North Wales. Professor of English; Biographer; Editor; Critic. m. (1) Rona Bower, 1970, divorced,1982, 1 son, 2 daughters, (2) Holly Urquhart Eley, 1984. Education: BLitt, MA, Oxon; PhD, London. Appointments: Lecturer in English, Lincoln College, Oxford, 1974-77; University College, London, 1977-80; Assistant Editor, 1980-82, Editor, 1982-90, Times Literary Supplement; Chairman of Judges, Booker Prize, 1991; Ferris Professor of Journalism, Princeton University, USA, 1992; Professor of English, University of Warwick, England, 1993-; Chairman of the Judges, Whitbread Book of the Year Award, 1998; Leverhulme Research Fellow, 2001-03. Publications: Letters of John Wilmot, Earl of Rochester (editor), 1980; Spirit of Wit: Reconsiderations of Rochester (editor), 1982; Introduction, R L Stevenson, In the South Seas, 1986; Selection, and Introduction, The Lantern Bearers: Essays by Robert Louis Stevenson, 1987; Introductions to reprints of complete novels of Henry Green, 1991-98; Roald Dahl: A Biography, 1994; Grub Street and the Ivory Tower: Literary Journalism, and Literary Scholarship from Fielding to the Internet, (editor with Bridget Bennett), 1998; Romancing: The Life and Work of Henry Green, 2000. Contributions to: Numerous magazines and journals. Membership: Fellow, Royal Society of Literature. Address: Gardens Cottage, Ditchley Park, Enstone, Nr Chipping Norton, Oxford OX7 4EP, England.

TREITLER Byron M, b. 21 April 1931, New York City, New York, USA. Physician. m. Rhoda C Treitler, 1 son, 1 daughter. Education: BA, New York University, 1951; MD, State University

of New York, 1955; American Board of Surgery Inc Certified, 1961. Appointments: Deputy Commander and Chief of Surgery, 3565 USAF Hospital, J Conally Airforce Base, Texas, USA; Chief of Surgery, Hampstead Hospital, Hampstead, New York; Police Surgeon, Nassau County, New York. Publications: Chemical and Metabolic Studies in Wound Healing; Chemical, Metabolic and Histologic Studies in Wound Healing. Memberships: Fellow, American College of Surgeons; Nassau Surgical Society. Address: 81 Finch Drive, Roslyn, NY 11576, USA. E-mail: treitlermd@hotmail.com

TREVELYAN (Walter) Raleigh, b. 6 July 1923, Port Blair, Andaman Islands. Author. Appointment: Publisher, 1948-88. Publications: The Fortress, 1956; A Hermit Disclosed, 1960; Italian Short Stories: Penguin Parallel Texts (editor), 1965; The Big Tomato, 1966; Princes Under the Volcano, 1972; The Shadow of Vesuvius, 1976; A Pre-Raphaelite Circle, 1978; Rome '44, 1982; Shades of the Alhambra, 1984; The Golden Oriole, 1987; La Storia dei Whitaker, 1989; Grand Dukes and Diamonds, 1991; A Clear Premonition, 1995; The Companion Guide to Sicily, 1996' Sir Walter Raleigh, 2002. Contributions to: Newspapers and journals. Honours: John Florio Prize for Translation, 1967. Memberships: Anglo-Italian Society for the Protection of Animals, chairman; PEN, a vice-president; Royal Society of Literature, fellow. Address: 18 Hertford Street, London W1J 7RT, England.

TRIBHUWAN Robin David, b. 8 October 1964, Manmad, India. Anthropologist. m. Preeti, 1 son, 1 daughter. Education: MA, Sociology; MSc Anthropology; Postgraduate Diploma, Indology and Museology; PhD, Anthropology. Appointments: Worked for research projects funded by WHO, UNICEF, UNESCO and several national and international organisations; Scientific Advisor on 2 documentary films for S R Films, Heidelberg, Germany; Advisor to other well known film makers; Associated as a resource person with several NGO's research organisations and universities; Currently working in Tribal Research and Training Institute, Pune, India. Publications: 23 books; 150 research papers and articles. Honour: Best Social Worker Award in recognition of services to slum dwellers, tribal and rural inhabitants; Mayor of Pune City, 1992. Address: 9 Krishna Kunj, Vikas Nagar, Wanawadi, Pune, India. E-mail: drtribhuwan@hotmail.com

TRICKER Brian John Kingsbury, b. 11 May 1937, Manchester, England. School Master. Education: BA, 1959, MA, 1962, Natural Sciences, Diploma Ed, 1960, Corpus Christi College, Cambridge. Appointments: Assistant Master, Eton College, 1960-67; Team Leader, Nuffield A Level Biology, 1966-68; Head of Science, Vice Principal, Victoria College, Jersey, Channel Isles, 1968-73; Head, Underschool Science, Proprietor of School Farm, Charterhouse School, 1974-79; Honorary Secretary, International Association of Science Clubs, 1982-. Publications include: The Science of Movement, 1967; Exploration for Young Scientists: Students' Text and Teachers' Guide, 1976; Editor, A Science of Relative Peace, IASC's journal. Honour: Open Exhibition, Corpus Christi College, Cambridge. Memberships: International Council of Associations for Science Education; International Association of Science Clubs. Address: IASC HQ, The Firs, Southdown Road, Freshwater Bay, Isle of Wight PO40 9UA, England.

TRIFONOV Nikolai Yurievich, b. 27 June 1948, Voronezh, Russia. Civil Servant; Valuer. m. Evgeniia Trifonova, 2 sons. Belarusian State University, Physics Faculty, Minsk, 1966-71; Honorary Diploma, Belarusian State University, Special Faculty Applied Mathematics, Minsk, 1972-75; Candidate of Science, Institute of Physics, Belarusian Academy of Science, Minsk, 1987; Centre Formation Realites Internationales, Paris, France, 1992. Appointments: Held posts in Ukrainian Academy of Science,

Kharkov, Belarusian Academy of Science, Minsk, 1973-81; Posts in Belarusian Polytech Institute, Minsk, 1981-91; Council Co-Chairman, Minsk Exchange, Belarus, 1991; Vice President, Western Real Estate Exchange, Minsk, Belarus, 1991-94; Council Member, Belarusbank, Minsk, 1993-95; President, Belarusian Real Estate Guild, Minsk, 1994-; President, Belarusian Society Valuers, Minsk, 1996-; Director East And Central European Relations, European Real Estate Society, 1998-; Managing Director, Council of Valuers' Associations of CIS, Minsk, 2003-. Publications: Over 200 on economics, law, mathematics, physics, chemistry in Russian and English including Valuation in Transition Economies, 1999. Honours: Honorary Member, Osteropaische Sachverstandige Verein, OSV, 1995; Honorary Member, Associasao Portugesa Avaliadores Activos Fixos, AAPOR, 1996; Union Kyrgyz Appraiser, OKO, 2000. Memberships: Belarusian Real Estate Guild, BREG, 1994; Osteropaische Sachversatndige Verein, OSV, 1995; European Real Estate Society, ERES, 1995; Belarusian Society of Valuers, BSV, 1996; International Club Directors, ICD, 2001; Fellow, Royal Institution of Chartered Surveyors, FRICS, 2003. Address: Belarusian Society of Valuers, 17A Kalvaryiskaya Street, Minsk 220004, Belarus.

TRIMBLE W David, b. 15 October 1944. Politician. m. (1) Heather McComb, divorced, (2) Daphne Elizabeth Orr, 1978, 2 sons, 2 daughters. Education: LLB, 1st class, Queens University, 1968. Appointments: Bar at Law, 1969, Lecturer, Law, Senior Lecturer, 1977, Head of Department, Commercial and Property Law, 1981-89; Convention Member, South Belfast, 1975-76; Joined Ulster Unionist Party, 1977; Vice Chairman, Lagan Valley Unionist Association, 1983-85; Chairman, 1985, 1990-96, Honorary Secretary, Ulster Unionist Council; Chairman, UUP Legal Committee, 1989-95; Member of Parliament, Upper Bann, 1990-; Chairman, UUP Constitutional Development Committee, 1995-; Leader, Ulster Unionist Party, 1995-; Member of the New Northern Ireland Assembly, Upper Bann Constituency, 1998-; First Minister Designate. Honours: Shared Nobel Peace Prize, 1998; Hon LLD, Queen's, 1999, New Brunswick, 2000, Wales, 2002. Memberships: Devolution Group, 1979-84; Founder, Chairman, Ulster Society, 1985-90; Chairman, Lisburn Ulster Club, 1985-86. Address: 2 Queen Street, Lurgan, County Armagh, BT66 8BQ, Northern Ireland. E-mail: uup@uup.org

TROFIMIUK Zoja, b. 17 February 1952, Prague, Czech Republic. Sculptor; Printmaker. m. Jurek Trofimiuk, 1 son. Education: Diploma in Fine Art, Academy of Fine Art, Cracow, Poland, 1977; Master of Fine Art, RMIT, Melbourne, Australia, 1991. Career: Solo Exhibitions: Hugo Gallery, Canberra, 1991; George Gallery, Melbourne, 1996; Adam Galleries, Melbourne, 1999; Group Exhibitions: Association of Sculptors of Victoria, 1985; Spirit of Our Time, 1988; Small Forms, Castellanza, Italy, 1990; Sculpture, Robin Gibson Gallery, Sydney, 1995, 1996; Group Exhibition: Women on the Move, Adams Galleries, 2000; Axia Modern Art Gallery, Melbourne, 2003. Honours: Honorary Award, Dante's Biennale, Ravenna, Italy, 1981, 1990; Member, Print Commission, Print Council of Australia, 1999; Listed in a Dictionary of Women Artists of Australia. Memberships: Glass Artists of Australia; New Group of Prague Artists. Commissions and Creative Works: Lyceum Club, Melbourne; Germany Embassy, Prague; New South Wales Art Gallery; 2nd Annual International Exchange Print Portfolio, 1999. Address: Factory 6, Coora Rd 6, Huntingdale, Victoria 3166, Australia. E-mail: airx@bigpond.com

TROITSKI Yuri Vladimirovich, b. 10 July 1928, Semipalatinsk, USSR. Researcher; Physicist. m. Galina S Rodyukova, 2 sons. Education: MS, University of Nizhni Novgorod, 1952; PhD, Tomsk Polytechnic Institute, 1960; DSc, 1972, Professor, 1990, Siberian Division of the USSR Academy of Sciences, Novosibirsk.

Appointments: Researcher, Siberian Division of USSR Academy of Sciences, 1955-62, 1967-72; Head of Laboratory, Institute of Semiconductor Physics, 1963-66; Head of Laboratory, 1973-98, Chief Scientist, 1999-, Institute of Automation and Electrometry, Siberian Division of the Russian Academy of Sciences, Novosibirsk. Publications: Books: Single-frequency gas lasers, 1975; Reflection multiple-beam interferometers, 1985; Author and co-author of 200 published papers in microwave electronics, optics, lasers, interferometry, gravitational wave detectors; 14 registered inventions. Memberships: SPIE, 1993; OSA, 1995; New York Academy of Sciences, 1996; Honoured Scientist of the Russian Federation, 2002. Address: Institute of Automation and Electrometry, Academician Koptyug Avenue 1, Novosibirsk, 630090, Russia. E-mail: troitski@iae.nsk.su

TROLLOPE Joanna, b. 9 December 1943. Author. m. (1) David Potter, 1966, 2 daughters, (2) Ian Curteis, 1985, separated 1998, 2 step-sons. Education: St Hugh's College, Oxford. Appointments: Information and Research Department, Foreign Office, 1965-67; Various teaching posts, 1967-79; Chair, Advisory Committee on National Reading Initiative, Department of National Heritage, 1996; Member, Advisory Committee on National Year of Reading, Department of Education, 1998; Vice President, Trollope Society: Trustee Joanna Trollope Charitable Trust, 1995-; Patron County of Gloucestershire Community Foundation, 1994. Publications: Eliza Stanhope, 1978; Parson Harding's Daughter, 1979; Leaves from the Valley, 1980; The City of Gems, 1981; The Steps of the Sun, 1983; Britannia's Daughter: A Study of Women in the British Empire, 1983; The Taverner's Place, 1986; The Choir, 1988; A Village Affair, 1989; A Passionate Man, 1990; The Rector's Wife, 1991; The Men and the Girls, 1992; A Spanish Lover, 1993; The Country Habit, 1993; The Best of Friends, 1995; Next of Kin, 1996; Faith, 1996; Other People's Children, 1998; Marrying the Mistress, 2000; Girl From the South, 2002; as Caroline Harvey: Legacy of Love, 1992; A Second Legacy, 1993; A Castle in Italy, 1993; The Brass Dolphin, 1997; Contributions to newspapers and magazines. Address: c/o Peters Fraser and Dunlop, Drury House, 34-43 Russell Street, London, WC2B 5HA, England.

TROWELL Jonathan Ernest Laverick, b. 30 December 1938, Easington, Co. Durham, England. Artist. Education: Sunderland College of Art; Scholarship to Royal Academy Schools. Career: One Man Shows: Brod Gallery, London; The Osborne Studio Gallery, London; Culham College, Oxford; Century Gallery, Henley; Zillah Bell Gallery, Thirsk; Stern Gallery, Sydney, Australia; Richard Stone Reeve, New York; Mixed Shows: W H Patterson, London; Alpine Gallery, London; Leighton House, London; Messums, London; The Royal Academy; Young Contemporaries; Royal Society of British Artists; Royal Society of Portrait Painters; New English Arts Club; Sothebys; Christies; National Racing Museum, Newmarket; Castle Museum, Norwich; Woodgate Gallery, Suffolk; Langham Fine Art, Suffolk; Falle Fine Art, Jersey; John Moores; New Bauhaus, Cologne, Germany; Bilan de l'Art Contemporain, Paris, France; Lee Nordness, New York, USA; Zillah Bell Gallery, Thirsk. Works in Public Collections: Bank of Japan; Culham College, Oxford; de Beers Diamond Co; Oriental Diamond Co; Ciba Geigy; British Petroleum; Cable Co; Newnham College, Cambridge; Imperial College; Royal College of Art; Harlands of Hull; University of East Anglia; University of Kent; Martell Grand National Collection; Works in Private Collections: HRH The Prince of Wales; Sir Charles Wheeler PPRA; John Alston CBE; Sir Robert Horton; Sir C Mott-Radclyffe; The Rt Hon Gillian Shephard; Count Konrad Goess-Sauran; Baroness Brigstocke; Professor A U Ubbelhode; Matthew Prichard; Lord Tavistock; Lord Wolverton. Honours: Landseer Silver Medal for Painting, Bronze Medal for Drawing, Royal Academy Schools;

Sir James Knott Travelling Scholarship, Royal College of Art, painted in Spain and North Africa; Agnew Prize, 1991. Address: Carr Farm, Old Buckenham, Norfolk NR17 1NN, England.

TRUBKO Sergey, b. 26 September 1948, St Petersburg, Russia. Optical Designer; Scientist. m. Liza Trubko, 1 son, 1 daughter. Education: BS, University of Fine Mechanics and Optics, St Petersburg, 1971; MS, Honours, 1973; PhD, 1977. Appointments: Scientist, to Senior Scientist, D I Mendeleev Metrology Institute, S I Vavilov State Optical Institute, St Petersburg, 1977-94; Senior Optical Engineer, Symbol Tech, Holtsville, New York, USA, 1996-98; Senior Scientist, CycloVision Tech, New York, 1998-99; Vice President, Chief Scientist, RemoteReality, Westborough, Massachusetts, 2000-. Publications: Design of Cemented Doublets, 1984; numerous articles in professional journals; 9 patents. Honours: Silver Medal, high school; Inventor and Rationalizer Medal. Membership: International Society of Optical Engineering. Address: RemoteReality 4 Technology Drive, Westborough, MA 01581, USA. E-mail: strubko@remotereality.com

TRUMP Donald John, b. 14 June 1946, New York, USA. Property Developer. m. (1) Ivana Zelnicek, 1977, divorced 1991, 2 sons, 1 daughter, (2) Marla Maples, 1993, 1 daughter. Education: Fordham University; University of Pennsylvania. Appointments: President, Trump Organisation; Board of Directors, Police Athletic League; Advisory Board, Lenox Hill Hospital and United Cerebral Palsy; Director, Fred C Trump Foundation; Founder Member, Committee to complete construction of Cathedral of St John the Divine and Wharton Real Estate Centre; Former Co-Chair, New York Vietnam Veterans Memorial Fund. Publications: Trump: The Art of the Deal, 1987; Trump: Surviving at the Top, 1990; the Art of the Comeback, 1997. Address: Trump Organization, 725 Fifth Avenue, New York, NY 10022, USA.

TRUNIN Ryurik Fedorovich, b. 2 March 1933, Tuma Village, Ryazan Region, Russia. Physicist. m. Nina Pavlova Trunina, 3 sons. Education: Graduated with Diploma, Moscow Engineering-Physics Institute, 1957; PhD, Physics, Mathematics, 1971; Certificate as Senior Research Associate, 1973; DSc, Physics, Mathematics, 1983. Appointments: Engineer, 1957-60; Senior Engineer, 1960-66; Deputy Head of Department, 1966; Head of Laboratory, 1966-70; Head of Department, 1970-97; Principal Research Associate, All Russian Institute for Experimental Research, Sarov, 1997-. Publications: More than 100 in various leading scientific and technical journals; 5 books. Honours: Winner, 2 State Prizes for Best Publications, 1968, 1989; Russian Government Prize Winner, 1999; Winner, MARIVD Principal Prize. Address: Mira ave 37, 607190 Sarov, Nizhni Novgorod Region, Russia.

TRUTER Ilse, b. 5 May 1964, Port Elizabeth, South Africa. Pharmacist; University Professor. Education: BCom, 1985, BCom Hons, 1987, MCom, 1988, DCom, 1993, BPharm, 1993, MSc, 1994, University of Port Elizabeth; PhD, Potchefstroom University for Christian Higher Education, 2000. Appointments: Temporary Lecturer, Department of Business Economics, University of Port Elizabeth, 1988; Pharmacist Intern, Westway Pharmacy, Port Elizabeth, 1993-94; Temporary Lecturer, Pharmacy Practice, Department of Pharmacy, 1993, Temporary part-time Lecturer, Pharmacy Practice, Department of Pharmacy, 1994-95, Researcher, Drug Utilisation Research Unit, 1994-, Permanent full-time Lecturer, Pharmacy Practice, Department of Pharmacy, 1995-97, Permanent full-time Senior Lecturer, Department of Pharmacy, 1998-2000. Associate Professor, Department of Pharmacy, 2001-, University of Port Elizabeth. Publications: Author, over 140 research publications; Author and co-author, 139 presentations at conferences and symposia; Author, 18 radio talks. Honours:

Runner-up, 1985, Winner, 1986; AIESEC-Barclays National Essay Competition; Alfred Radis Memorial Award and Medal, 1990; Gencor S_2A_3 Bronze Medal, Best Masters study, 1994; Pharmacia and Upjohn Achievement Award winner, 1996, 1997; Euro Durg EACPT Poster Prize, Germany, 1998; ISPE Poster Prize, USA, 1999; Recipient of the Roche Best Publication Award, in conjunction with The Academy of Pharmaceutical Sciences in 2001 for the best publication in Pharmacy Practice in South Africa in 2000; Wellness Excellence Award, South African National Wellness Conference, University of Port Elizabeth, 2003; Pharmacy Teacher of the Year Award, South Africa, 2003; Listed in national and international biographical publications. Memberships: South African Pharmacy Council; Pharmaceutical Society of South Africa; South African Academy of Pharmaceutical Sciences; South African Association of Hospital and Institutional Pharmacists; International Society for Pharmacoepidemiology; Pharmacological Society of South Africa; Public Health Association of South Africa; Southern African Institute for Management Scientists. Address: Department of Pharmacy, University of Port Elizabeth, PO Box 1600, Port Elizabeth 6000, South Africa. E-mail: ilse.truter@upe.ac.za

TSANG Hector W H, b. 9 July 1962, Hong Kong. Professor. m. Wai Ming Cheung, 1 son. Education: Doctor of Philosophy. Appointment: Associate Professor, Department of Rehabilitation Sciences, The Hong Kong Polytechnic University. Publications: Articles in scientific journals include most recently as co-author and first author: Social skills training for finding and keeping a job with the mentally ill, 2001; Requirements for multidisciplinary teamwork in psychiatric rehabilitation, 2001; Family needs and burdens of the mentally ill offenders, 2002; An end user survey on the development of an on-line job information system for people with schizophrenia in Hong Kong, 2002; Job profiles of people with schizophrenia. Implications for rehabilitation, 2002; Qigong as a psychosocial intervention for depressed elderly with chronic physical illnesses, 2002; The effect of Qigong on general and psychosocial health of elderly with chronic physical illnesses: a randomized clinical trial, 2003; Stigmatizing attitudes towards individuals with mental illness in Hong Kong: Implications of their recovery, 2003; Sources of family burden of individuals with mental illness. Honours: Best Case Study Award, International Forum for Social Sciences in Health, 1996; Listed in Who's Who publications and biographical dictionaries. Memberships: American Psychological Society; American Occupational Therapy Association; World Association for Psychosocial Rehabilitation. Address: Department of Rehabilitation Sciences, The Hong Kong Polytechnic University, Hunghom, Hong Kong. E-mail: rshtsang@polyu.edu.hk

TSAO Vivian J Y, b. 24 April 1950, Taipei, Taiwan (American Citizen). Artist; Art Professor; Author. m. Raymond Clyde Coreil. Education: BA, Fine Arts, National Taiwan Normal University, Taiwan, 1973; Master of Fine Arts in Painting, Carnegie Mellon University, Pittsburgh, Pennsylvania, USA, 1976. Appointments: Assistant Editor, Children's Art Page, Central Daily News, Taiwan, 1971-74; Art Instructor, National Taipei Teachers College, Taiwan, 1972-74; Worked on consignments for: Kingpitcher Gallery, Pittsburgh, Pennsylvania, USA, 1976-77; Nardin Galleries, New York City, USA, 1979-80; The Art Collaborative, New York City, USA, 1985-87; Correspondent, Hsiung Shih Art Monthly, Taiwan, 1980-96; Programme Auditor, Free-lance Reviewer of Exhibitions, 1990-96; Juror on Panel, 1996-99, New York State Council on the Arts, New York City; Adjunct Assistant Professor of Drawing and Design, Department of Fine Arts, Pace University, New York City, 1990-; Contributing writer in the USA, United Daily News, Literary Page, Taiwan; 13 solo and 47 group exhibitions include: American Academy of Arts and Letters; The Brooklyn Museum;

Taipei Fine Arts Museum; Ceres Gallery; Biddington's Internet Gallery. Publications: Book: The Mark of Time: Dialogues with Vivian Tsao on Art in New York, 2003; Article: A Holistic Approach to Art Criticism: An Interview with Art Critic Michael Brenson, 1988; Black Velvet at Dusk (essay), 2000. Honours: Artist-in-Residence, New York State Council on the Arts; Certificate of Merit, Pastel Society of America; Scholarship Grant, Carnegie Mellon University. Memberships: Inducted Fellow, Society of Fellows, Dyson College, Pace University; Elected Full Member, Pastel Society of America; College Art Association of America. Address: 17 Fuller Place, Brooklyn, NY 11215-6006, USA. E-mail: viviantsao@earthlink.net

TSARFIN Mikhail, b. 8 April 1957, Vladimir City, Russia. Chemical Engineer. m. Irina Tsarfina, 1 son, 1 daughter. Education: Engineering Diploma, Polytechnical University, Vladimir, Russia, 1979; Post Graduate Course, Polymerintez Co, Vladimir; Post Graduate degree received in Kargin Polymer Research Institute, Dzerzhinsk; PhD 1991. Appointments: Project Associate, 1979-86, Senior Project Associate, 1986-91, Polymersintez Co, Vladimir; General Manager, Blockform Co, Vladimir, 1994-96; General Manager, Izolan Co, Vladimir, 1996-. Publications: 20 including: The impact of the balance of basic reactions on the chemical structure of polyurethane-isocyanurate foams; Kinetics of simultaneous of isocyanate cyclomerization reactions and urethane formation. Membership: Association of Producers and Consumers of Pipelines with Industrial Polymeric Isolation; Noncommercial Partnership, Energyresources Saving. Address: P O Box 19, 81 Bolshaya Nizhegorodskaya St, Vladimir, 600016 Russia. E-mail: root@izolan.elcom.ru

TSE Kui Yin, b. 14 January 1943, Meizhou, China. Artist. m. Leung Lai-kuen, 2 sons. Career: Artist; Solo Painting Exhibitions, by invitation, Chinese Traditional Painting Research Institute, Beijing, China, 1988, 1991, 1995; Individual Painting Exhibition, Bangkok, Thailand jointly presented by Thailand Chinese Artists Association and Landmark Hotel, 1989, 1992; Visions of the Master Exhibition, Balai Seni, Mernala May Bank Malaysia, presented by Thong Dia Sdn Bhd and Malayan Banking Berhad, 1992; Individual Painting Exhibition, Singapore, presented by Singapore Cultural Studies Society and Thong Sia Co (S) PRE Ltd, 1992. Publications: Painting Album of Flowers and Fruits, 1985; Painting by Tse Kui Yin, albums I and II, 1987, 1996; Painting series of figures by Tse Kui Yin, 2001; Over 200 articles on fine art critics, poems and prose in journals magazines and newspapers, 1975-. Honours: Certificate of World Artist, Central Television Broadcasting of China and the Community of Famous Artists in the World et al., 1993; Certificate of Gold Award, China Hainan International Phoenix Cup Art Exhibition, 1994; Certificate of Honour, Famous Figures Works Exhibition, Arts Circles in China, 1994; Award of Excellence, Forte Cup Twentieth Century Asian Pacific Art Competition, Asian Pacific Art Institute of America, Forte International Inc and People's Daily Overseas Edition, 1999; Twentieth Century Award for Art Accomplishment, Asian Pacific Institute of America, 1999; Gold Prize for the Artwork, Night Scene in City, Global International Arts Contribution Prize, 2003; Outstanding Achievement and Contribution in Art, Chinese Realm of Art and Literature Outstanding Achievement Gold-Portrait Medal, 2003; Biography featured in several reference and art books. Memberships: Founder and President, Hong Kong Prima Club, 1979; Adviser, Hong Kong Calligraphers Association; Art Consultant, Chinese Art Association of Thailand, Honourable Director, Huaihai Chinese Painting and Calligraphy Institute; Honourable Advisor, Asian Art Association. Address: 6C Broadway 5/F, Mei Foo Sun Chuen, Hong Kong.

TSEMEKHMAN Lev, b. 21 July 1934, Leningrad, USSR. Metallurgist. m. Marina Veizager, 2 sons. Education: Graduate, Leningrad Mining Institute, 1958; Candidate of Sciences Degree in Engineering, 1965; Doctorate of Sciences in Engineering, 1972; Title of Professor, 1979. Appointments: Engineer, 1959, Junior Scientific Staff Member, 1960, Chief Assistant, 1962, Head of a Section, 1972, Head of a Laboratory, 1976, Head of the Pyrometallurgical Department of the Institute Gipronickel, JS, 1989-. Publications: More than 600 published works including 6 monographs, 90 patents and author's certificates. Honours: Academic Konstantinov Experimental Physics Prize, Academy of Sciences of the USSR, 1983; Distinguished Scientist of Russian Federation, 1994. Membership: Full Member of Russian Academy of Natural Sciences, 1993. Address: Inst. Gipronickel, JS, 11 Grazhdansky Pr. St Petersburg, 195220 Russia. E-mail: lst@nikel.spb.su

TSENG King-Jet, b. 26 March 1963, Singapore. Professor. m. Mona Chew, 1 son, 1 daughter. Education: BEng, 1st class honours, 1984-88, MEng, 1988-89, National University of Singapore; PhD, Cambridge University, England, 1990-93. Appointments: Associate Professor, Power Electronics and Drives Division of Power Engineering, Director, Power Electronics and Drives Laboratory, Chairman, EEE IHPT Committee, Nanyang Technological University. Publications include: Using power diode models for circuit simulations - a comprehensive review; Analysis of flux distribution and core losses in interior permanent magnet motor; A new structure transcutaneous transformer for totally implantable artificial heart system. Honours: Cambridge Commonwealth Trust Shell Scholarship, 1990-93; Overseas Research Students Award, Committee of Vice Chancellors and Principals of the Universities of the United Kingdom, 1990-93; IEE Swan Premium, 1996; Tan Chin Tuan Exchange Fellowship Award, 1998; IEEE, Millennium Medal, 2000. Memberships: IEEE; Institute of Engineers, Singapore; Life Fellow, Cambridge Commonwealth Society, Cambridge Philosophical Society; Institution of Electrical Engineers, England. Address: School of Electrical and Electronic Engineering, Nanyang Technological University, Blk S2, Nanyang Avenue, Singapore 639798, Singapore.

TSEU Lawrence K W, b. 23 June 1932, Hong Kong. Dentist. m. Bo Hing Chan, 2 sons, 4 daughters. Education: BSc, Brigham Young University, 1958; DDS, North Western University Dental School, 1962; PhD, Olympian International Sports Medicine College, 1991; Served in the US Airforce 1951. Appointments: Board of Regents, Oxford University, England; East-West Center International Foundation Board; Bishop Museum of Hawaii; University of Hawaii Culinary Board; Hawaii Theatre Center; Asian-Pacific Center Foundation; President of Jackie Chan Foundation, USA. Honours: America's Top Dentist; Alumni Merit Award, Northwestern University; Omicron Kappa Upsilon, Honorary Dental Society, Northwestern University Dental School; Listed in Who's Who publications and biographical dictionaries. Memberships: Fellow: International College of Dentist; American College of Dentist; Academy of General Dentistry; Academy of Dentistry International; Member: Academy of Implant Dentistry; International Congress of Oral Implantology; Academy of Forensic Examiners; American Academy of Forensics Science; Academy of Cosmetic Dentistry; American Dental Association; Hawaii State Board of Dental Examiners; USA Nationally Certified Bodybuilding Judge; Private Clubs: The Royal Hong Kong Jockey Club; Waialae Country Club; Oahu Country Club; Outrigger Canoe Club. Address: 1441 Kapiolani Blvd, Suite #708, Ala Moana Building, Honolulu, HI 96814, USA.

TSIBOUKLIS John, b. 6 November 1959, Thassos, Greece. m. Cornelia Anne, 1 son, 3 daughters. Education: BSc, Chemistry, North London Polytechnic, England, 1984; MSc, Analytical Chemistry, London University, England, 1985; PhD, Polymer Chemistry, Napier University of Edinburgh, 1988. Appointments: Research Fellow, University of Durham, England, 1988-94; Senior Lecturer, Chemistry, 1994-99, Reader, Polymer Science, 1999-, University of Portsmouth, England. Publications: 62 research papers; 8 book chapters; 17 conference proceedings; 2 book reviews; 6 patents; Numerous science communication activities. Honours: Fellowship of the Royal Society of Chemistry, 1999; Greek Pharmaceutical Laboratories Award for Contribution to the Advancement of the Pharmaceutical Sciences, 2001; S C Johnson Silver Dollar Award, 2001, 2002; Visiting Professor, Chulalongkorn University, Thailand, 2002. Memberships: Analytical Division, Royal Society of Chemistry; Faraday Division, Royal Society of Chemistry. Address: School of Pharmacy, White Swan Road, University of Portsmouth, Portsmouth, Hampshire PO1 2DT, England. E-mail: john.tsibouklis@port.ac.uk

TSITVERBLIT Naftali Anatol, b. 29 October 1963, Kiev, Ukraine. Researcher. Education: MSc, Faculty of Mechanical and Power Engineering, Kiev Polytechnic Institute, 1987; PhD, Faculty of Mechanical Engineering, Tel-Aviv University, 1995. Appointments: Engineer, Scientific Research Institute of Robotics, Kiev, USSR, 1985-87; Teaching Assistant, Instructor, Tel-Aviv University, 1988-94; Visiting Scientist, Cornell University, 1994; Postdoctoral Research Fellow, Lamont-Doherty Earth Observatory of Columbia University, 1995-97; Postdoctoral Fellow, Geophysical Fluid Dynamics Summer Program, Woods Hole Oceanographic Institution, 1996; Visiting Scientist, Department of Fluid Mechanics and Heat Transfer of Tel-Aviv University, 1997-. Publications: In scientific journals, books and conference proceedings; Finite-Amplitude double-component convection due to different boundary conditions for two compensating horizontal gradients, 2000; Mechanism of finite-amplitude double-component convection due to different boundary conditions, 2001(submitted). Memberships: American Physical Society; American Geophysical Union; New York Academy of Science; American Association for the Advancement of Science. Address: 1 Yanosh Korchak Street, Apt 6, Kiryat Nordau, Netanya 42495, Israel. E-mail: naftali@eng.tau.ac.il

TSUCHIYA Masahiko, b. 18 October 1958, Kofu, Yamanashi, Japan. Biochemist; Anaesthesiologist. m. Hisaka Higashi, 2 sons, 2 daughters. Education: MD, 1984, PhD, 1988, Kochi Medical School, Japan. Appointments: Postdoctoral Fellow, University of California, Berkeley, USA, 1990; Associate Professor, Kochi Medical School, Japan, 1994; Head Physician, National Hospital Tokyo Disaster Medical Centre, Japan, 1995; Associate Professor, Osaka City University Medical School, Japan, 2000. Publications: Articles as co-author: Antioxidant protection of propofol and its recycling in erythrocyte membranes, 2002; Smoking a single cigarette rapidly reduces combines concentrations of nitrate and nitrite and concentrations of antioxidant in plasma, 2002. Memberships: Japanese Biochemical Society; Japanese Society of Anaesthesiology. Address: 5-6-16-304 Dido, Tennoji-ku, Osaka 543-0052, Japan. E-mail: oxymasa@ea.mbn.or.jp

TSUIKI Takahide, b. 13 July 1939, Hiroshima, Japan. University Professor. m. Katsuko Uchiyama, 2 sons. Education: BA, 1962, MA, 1964, Doctoral course, 1964-67, Hitotsubashi University. Appointments: Lecturer, 1967, Assistant Professor, 1970, Full Professor, 1976, Seikei University, Tokyo. Publications: Books: Modern Business Administrators, 1978; Social Responsibilities and Corporate Structure, 1979; A Scheme of Management as a Force, 1982. Honours: Management Science Literature Award,

Foundation to Promote Management Science, Tokyo. Memberships: Japan Society of Business Administration; Academy of Management; Academy of International Business. Address: 158-43 Arahata, Tokorozawa-shi, Saitama 359-1133, Japan.

TSUJI Yoshiro, b. 10 May 1956, Kyoto, Japan. Orthopaedic Surgeon. m. Ayano Ohashi, 1 son, 1 daughter. Education: Doctor, Kyoto Prefectural University of Medicine; MD, Graduate School of Medical Science, Kyoto Prefectural University of Medicine, 1990. Appointments: Vice-President, Mizuta Orthopaedic Hospital, Kyoto, Japan, 199-92; Research Fellow, Istituti Ortopedici Rizzoli, Bologna, Italy, 1992-94; Orthopaedist, Kyoto 2nd Red Cross Hospital, 1994-96; Chief of the Department, Yokaichi National Hospital, Shiga, Japan, 1996-2000; Chief of Department, Seika National Health Insurance Hospital, Kyoto, Japan, 2000-2002; Vice-President, Nishijin Hospital, Kyoto, Japan, 2003-. Publications: Articles in medical journals include: Cell proliferation and differentiation of cultured chondrocytes isolated from growth plate cartilage of rat rib, 1995; Retinoblastoma susceptibility gene product retrieval in formalin-fixed, paraffin-embedded tissue, 1998; Calcaneal Osteosarcoma associated with Werner syndrome, 2000. Honour: Award, Japan Cytochemistry and Histochemistry Association, 1986. Memberships: Japan Orthopaedic Association; Japan Cytochemistry and Histochemistry Association; Japan Fracture Society; Japan Arthroscopy Society; Japan Rehabilitation Medicine. Address: Department of Orthopaedic Surgery, Nishijin Hospital, 1035 Minami-Mizomae-cho, Hichihonmatsu Street, Kamigyo-ku, Kyoto 602-8319, Japan. E-mail: yo.tsuji@nisijin.net

TSUTSUI Toshinori, b. 14 March 1952, Shiota, Saga, Japan. Anaesthesiologist. m. Kimiko Takeda. Education: Master of Science, 1978, Doctor of Medicine, 1986, Yamaguchi University, Japan. Appointments: Assistant Lecturer, Yamaguchi University, 1980-84; Senior Lecturer, Osaka City University, 1986-88; Chief Anaesthesiologist, Shimonoseki Welfare Hospital, 1988-96; Chief Anaesthesiologist, Saga National Hospital, 1996-2004. Memberships: Fellow, Japanese Society of Anaesthesiologists, 1978-; Fellow, Biomedical Fuzzy Systems Association, 1988-. Address: Department of Anaesthesiology, Saga National Hospital, 1-20-1, Hinode, Saga, Saga 849-8577 Japan. E-mail: ksikyoku@vega.ocn.ne.jp

TSUTSUMI Yutaka, b. 9 September 1951, Yokohama, Japan. Physician; Pathologist. m. Yoko Tsutsumi, 3 daughters. Education: MD, Keio University School of Medicine, Tokyo, 1976; PhD, Pathology, Postgraduate School, Keio University, 1980. Appointments: Instructor, 1980, Assistant Professor, 1986, Associate Professor, 1992, Tokai University School of Medicine, Isehara; Professor, Fujita Health University School of Medicine, Toyoake, 2001. Publications: Practical Manual of Universal Precautions, 1998; Easy Access to Pathology Images, 1998; Atlas of Infectious Disease Pathology; 2000; Enzyme-labelled Antibody Methods, 4th edition, 2002; Pathology of Infectious Diseases. http://www.yamagiku.co.jp/pathology/index.htm; About 200 articles in English. Memberships: Japan Society of Pathology; Japan Association of Cancer Research; Japan Society of Clinical Cytology; Japan Society of Histochemistry and Cytochemistry; Japan Society of Gastric Cancer. Address: Department of Pathology, Fujita Health University School of Medicine, Toyoake, Aichi 470-1192, Japan. E-mail: tsutsumi@fujita-hu.ac.jp

TUCKER Helen, b. 1 November 1926, Raleigh, North Carolina, USA. Writer. m. William Beckwith. Education: BA, Wake Forest University, 1946; Graduate Studies, Columbia University, 1957-58. Publications: The Sound of Summer Voices, 1969; The Guilt of August Fielding, 1972; No Need of Glory, 1973; The Virgin of Lontano, 1974; A Strange and Ill-Starred Marriage, 1978; A

Reason for Rivalry, 1979; A Mistress to the Regent: An Infamous Attachment, 1980; The Halverton Scandal, 1980; A Wedding Day Deception, 1981; The Double Dealers, 1982; Season of Dishonor, 1982; Ardent Vows, 1983; Bound by Honor, 1984; The Lady's Fancy, 1991; Bold Impostor, 1991. Contributions to: Lady's Circle; Ellery Queen Mystery Magazine; Alfred Hitchcock Mystery Magazine; Ladies Home Journal; Crecent Review; Montevallo Review; Redbook Magazine. Honours: Distinguished Alumni Award, Wake Forest University, 1971; Franklin County Artist of the Year Award, 1992. Address: 2930 Hostetler Street, Raleigh, NC 27609, USA.

TUDAWE Ajith Erandan, b. 9 June 1953, Colombo, Sri Lanka. Chartered Accountant. m. Rohini Lasitha Fernando, 2 sons. Education: Bachelor of Arts, Accounting, Bachelors Degree programme in Accounting (CNAA) (formerly PNL), London Metropolitan University, England. Appointments: Tudawe Brothers Limited, 1982-83, Tudawe Trading Company Limited, 1982-83; Group Financial Director, Tudawe Brothers Limited, 1984-, Tudawe Trading Company Limited, 1984-, Tudawe Property Development Company (Pvt) Limited, 1984-, Universal Interiors (Pvt) Limited, 1995-; Director Consultant, Ceylon Hospital Limited, Durdans Hospital, 1987-89; Chairman, Chief Executive Director, Ceylon Hospitals Limited, Durdans Hospital, 1989-, Durdans Heart Surgical Centre (Pvt) Limited, 2000-. Publications: Accounting and management articles. Memberships: Institute of Chartered Accountants of New Zealand; Fellow, CPA Australia; Fellow, Association of Chartered Certified Accountants of the UK; Fellow, Chartered Institute of Marketing in the UK; Fellow, Institute of Chartered Secretaries in the UK. Address: 175/2 Havelock Road, Colombo 5, Sri Lanka. E-mail: aetudawe@sri.lanka.net

TUDEV Lodongiyn, b. 8 February 1935. m. Naidangiin Tsagaach, 17 October 1960, 1 son, 2 daughters. Education: BS, Pedagogical Institute, Ulan Bator, Mongolia, 1956; MS, Linguistics, Academy of Social Sciences, Moscow, 1967; DrSc, Linguistics, 1984. Appointments: Teacher, Second School, Altai, Mongolia, 1956-59; Methodist Teachers Institute, Ulan Bator, 1959-60; Literary Secretary, Unen, Ulan Bator, 1960-63; Editor-in-Chief, 1984-; Editor-in-Chief, Soyol Utga Zohiol, 1963-64; Vice Chairman, Chairman, Mongolian Writers Union, 1969-75; General Secretary, Mongolian Youth Union, 1975-84; Professor, 1996-; Founder, Owner, Editor-in-Chief, Scapula, newspaper, 1996-. Publications: Mountain Stream, 1960; Nomadism and Urbanism, 1964; First Year of Republic, 1981; Roofless Temple, 1985; Spiral, 1988; Problem, 1990; Blue Sky Above, Brown Earth Below, 1994; Three Doors to Sin, 1996; Klôn, 2000; Printed 25 Volumes of selected works, 2002. Honours include: Orders of Sukhhaatar, 1981, 1998; Order of People's Friendship, Government of Russia, 1979; Order of Kirill and Mephodil, Government of Bulgaria, 1980; Honored Culture Worker, Government of Ulaan Baatar, 1989; Listed in Who's Who in Asia and the Pacific Nations; Labor Hero of Mongolia, Highest Honour of Mongolia, by decree of the President of Mongolia, 1998. Memberships include: MP, People's Great Khural, 1963-91; Head, Parliamentary Union, 1984-90; Head, Peace Commission, 1973-76; Candidate for President of Mongolia, 1993; Chairman, Journalists Union. Address: Central Post Office, CPO Box 5, Ulan Bator, Mongolia.

TUITE Kathleen, b. 28 March 1956, Ottawa, Illinois, USA. Controller. Education: BS in Journalism, Ball State University; MBA, Keller Graduate School, Tampa, Florida, in progress. Appointments: Account Executive, WWBA, Tampa, Florida; Tampa Regional Manager, WSSP Radio, Orlando, Florida; District Sales Manager, State of North Carolina; Controller, Brandon Construction. Honours: Listed in national biographical dictionaries.

Memberships: NAFE; Institute of Management Accountants. Address: 3366 Mermoor Drive, #201, Palm Harbor, FL 34685, USA. E-mail: kay@brandonconstruction.net

TUKE Diana Rosemary, b. 5 July 1932, Weymouth, Dorset, England. Lecturer; Freelance Journalist; Writer; Author. Education: British Horse Society Preliminary Instructor's Certificate, Porlock Vale Riding School, 1954. Appointments: Picture Editor, The Encyclopaedia of the Horse, 1973; Lectured, updated Equine Feeding Section of Instruction Manual, Metropolitan Police, 1986. Publications: A Long Road to Harringay, 1960; Bit-by-Bit, 1965; Riding Cavalcade, contributor, 1967; Tomorrow, short story, 1968; Stitch-by-Stitch, 1970; Horse-by-Horse, 1973; The Complete Book of the Horse (contributor), 1973; The Encyclopaedia of the Horse (contributor), 1973; Getting Your Horse Fit, 1977; The Rider's Handbook, 1977; Feeding Your Horse, 1980; Cottage Craft Guide to Aintree Bits, 1982; Horse Tack - The Complete Equipment Guide for Riding and Driving (contributor), 1982; The Country Life Book of Saddlery and Equipment (contributor), 1982; Clipping Your Horse, 1984; Feeding Your Horse and Pony, 2nd edition, 1988; Horse Trials Review No 2 - Feeding for Fitness, video, 1990; Clipping, Trimming and Plaiting Your Horse, 2nd edition, 1992; Nursing Your Horse, 1999, 2nd edition, 2002; Novels: Ravensworth, 2000; When the Rivers Roared, 2000; Away in the Mountains, 2001; The Lonely Shore, 2001; The Old Mill, in progress; Contributions to: Riding; Horse and Hound; The Daily Telegraph; The Field; The Cronical of the Horse, USA; Others. Honours: Trophies for sale of books: Bit-by-Bit, 25,000 copies, 1995; Getting Your Horse Fit, 25,000 copies, 1995; Clipping, Trimming and Plaiting Your Horse, 10,000 copies, 1998. Membership: British Equestrian Writer's Association. Address: Gallery House, Duddenhoe End, Saffron Walden, Essex CB11 4UU, England.

TULEEV Aman Gumirovich, b. 13 May 1944, Krasnovodsk, Turkmenian Republic. Politician. m. Elvira Solovyeva, 2 sons, 1 deceased. Education: Novosibirsk Institute of Railway Engineering, 1973; Academy of Social Studies, 1989. Appointments: Assistant Station Master, 1964-69, Station Master, 1969-73, Railway Station, Moundebash; Station Master, Railway Station, Mezhdurechensk, 1973-78; Head, Novokuznetsk Line, Kemerovo Railway, 1978-85; Head, Transport Department, Kemorovo's Regional Committee of the CPSU, 1985-88; Head, Kemerovo Railway, 1988-90; Chairman. Kemerovo's Regional Council of People's Deputies, People's Deputy of RSFSR, 1990-93; Candidate for Presidency, 1991, 1996, 2000; Chairman, Legislative Assembly of Kemerovo Region, Member of the Council of Federations of the Federal Assembly of the Russian Federation, 1994-96; Minister, Russian Federation for collaboration with the States, Members of CIS, 1996-97; Governor, Kemerovo Region, 1997-. Publications: Author of more than 100 articles and books including: Power in hands of a man and man in hands of the power, 1993; State power in region: personal factor, social contacts, 1998; To remain yourself, 1999; Political leader and political leadership in regional conflicts, 1999; We have the only Russia, 1999; Political leadership in modern Russia, 2000. Honours: The Order of Honor, the highest award of Mongolia; The Order of the North Star. Memberships: Honorary Railwayman; Freeman of Kemerovo and Novokuznetsk; Honorary Doctor of Sciences, Ulan-Bator University of Mongolian Academy of Sciences; Full Member, International Academy of Informatization; Full Member, International Engineering Academy. Address: pr Sovetskiy, 62, 650099 Kemerovo, Russia. Website: www.mediakuzbass.ru

TULLOCH Clive William, b. 21 June 1948, Richmond, Surrey, England. Chartered Accountant. m. Tessa Celia Geraldine Trewman, 1 son, 1 daughter. Appointments: Coopers & Lybrand,

Dictionary of International Biography

1967-79; Morison Stoneham & Co, 1979-81, Partner, 1980-81; Pricewaterhouse Coopers, 1981-, Partner, 1983-, with responsibility for risk management in UK tax and human resource consulting practice, 2001-; London Chamber of Commerce Taxation Committee, 1987-2001, Chairman, 1994-97, Council, 1994-2001; Member of Working Party on Practice Assurance for Tax, Institute of Chartered Accountants in England and Wales, 2002. Publications: Books: Author, Car or Cash? 2nd Edition 1994; Editor and Joint Author, The CCH Company Car Tax Guide, 1999/2000; Joint Author, Employee Share Schemes in Practice. Memberships: ACA, 1971; FCA, 1976; CTA (Fellow), 1994; Governor, St Nicholas Primary School, Chislehurst, England, 1989-95; Company of Tax Advisers, Member of Court of Assistants, 1998-, Middle Warden, 2003-; Honorary Treasurer, The Bach Choir, 1997-, Member, 1969-. Address: Pricewaterhouse Coopers, 1 Embankment Place, London WC2N 6RH, England. E-mail: clive.w.tulloch@uk.pwc.com

TULLY (William) Mark, b. 24 October 1935, Calcutta, India. Journalist; Broadcaster. m. Margaret Frances Butler, 13 August 1960, 2 sons, 2 daughters. Education: Marlborough College; MA, Trinity Hall, Cambridge, 1959. Appointments: Regional Director, Abbeyfield Society, 1960-64; Assistant, Appointments Department, 1964-65, Assistant, later Acting Representative, New Delhi, 1955-69; Programme Organiser and Talks Writer, Eastern Service, 1969-71; Chief of Bureau, Delhi, 1972-93; South Asia Correspondent, 1993-94, BBC; Freelance writer, broadcaster, journalist, 1994-. Publications: Amritsar: Mrs Gandhi's Last Battle (with Satish Jacob), 1985; From Raj to Rajiv (with Z Masani), 1988; No Full Stops in India, 1991; The Heart of India, 1995; The Lives of Jesus, 1996; India in Slow Motion (with Gillian Wright), 2002. Honours: Officer of the Order of the British Empire, 1985; Padma Shri, India, 1992; Honorary Fellow, Trinity Hall, Cambridge, 1994; Honorary Doctor of Letters, University of Strathclyde, 1997. Address: 1 Nizamuddin East, New Delhi 110 013, India. E-mail: tulwri@ndf.vsnl.net.in

TURBATU Dumitru, b. 21 May 1937, Rotunda Olt, Romania. Senior Surgeon. m. Marina Gabriela, 1 daughter. Education: Graduate, Faculty of Medicine, Bucharest, 1961; MD, 1972; Perfection in Surgery, Endoscopy and Laser Surgery, 1986; Studies in USA, 1976, Germany, 1980 and Japan, 1985. Appointments: Scholarship to Beth Israel Hospital, New York; University of California at Los Angeles; St Luke's Hospital, New York; Cornell University, New York; Goethe University, Germany; Eppendorf University, Hamburg Germany; Cancer Institute Hospital, Tokyo, Japan; Hospital of the Tokyo Women's Medical College; Aichi Cancer Center Hospital, Nagoya, Japan. Publications: Biliopancreatic Endoscopy, 1997; Editura Tehnica and CD ROM, 1997. Honours: Medical Merited, 1980; Listed in Who's Who publications. Memberships: International Gastro-Surgical Club; Romanian Surgical Society. Address: 7 Constantin Nacu Street, Bucharest 2, Romania 020995

TURCOTTE Paul-André Gaétan, b. 10 July 1943, Saint-Cuthbert, Canada. Professor; Researcher. Education: Baccalaureate of Arts, Collège de Joliette, 1964; Baccalaureate in Education, Laval University, Quebec, 1970; Licence and Master in Theology, University of Montreal, 1970; Doctorate in Sociology, École des Hautes Études en Sciences Sociales, 1979; Doctorate in Theology, Institut Catholique de Paris, 1987. Appointments: Professor, University of Haiti, 1971-75; Associate Researcher, French National Research Centre, 1977-; Professor, Saint-Paul's University, Ottawa, 1980-98; Professor, University of Montreal, 1984; Fellow, School of Graduate Studies and Research, University of Ottawa, 1987-98; Professor of Sociology, Institut Catholique de Paris, 1993-; Visiting Professor, UCAC, Yaoundé, Cameroon,

2000-2003. Publications: Réconciliation et Libération, 1972; L'éclatement d'un monde, 1981; Les chemins de la différence, 1982; L'enseignement secondaire public des frères éducateurs, 1988; Intransigeance et compromis, 1994; Le phénomène des sectes, 2002; Handbook of Early Christianity, 2002; Editor of 5 collective works and 12 issues of Social Compass and Claretianum; Over 100 articles in 15 different journals or chapters of collective works. Honours: Prize of the Provincial Bank, Faculty of Theology, University of Montreal, 1970; Cafe-Best Publication, Canadian Society for the Study of Education, 1989. Memberships: Confrontations, Paris, 1994-; International Council of Museums, UNESCO, 1998-; Association of Canadian Studies, 1998-. Address: 170 Blvd du Montparnasse, 75014 Paris, France.

TURK Austin Theodore, b. 28 May 1934, Gainesville, Georgia. USA. Sociologist; Criminologist. m. Ruth-Ellen Marie Grimes. Education: BA, cum laude, University of Georgia, 1956; MA, University of Kentucky, 1959; PhD, University of Wisconsin, 1962. Appointments: Instructor, to Professor, Indiana University, 1962-74; Professor of Sociology, University of Toronto, 1974-88; Professor of Sociology, 1988-, Chair, 1989-94, University of California at Riverside. Publications: Criminality and Legal Order, 1969; Political Criminality: The Defiance and Defense of Authority, 1982. Honours: President, American Society of Criminology, 1984-85; Fellow, American Society of Criminology, 1978. Memberships: American Society of Criminology; American Sociological Association; Academy of Criminal Justice Sciences; Law and Society Association. Address: Department of Sociology, University of California, Riverside, CA 92521, USA.

TURK Elizabeth Ann, b. 10 July 1957, New York City, New York, USA. Musician; Teacher. Education: BA, History and Music, Dowling College, New York; MA, German Language and Literature, Hofstra University; MA, German Military History (72 credits towards PhD), SUNY, Stony Brook; MA, Music and Public Library Studies, Columbia University. Appointments: History Lecturer, SUNY, Stony Brook, 1985-87; Music Lecturer, Dowling College, 1986-90; Music Administrative Assistant, Columbia University, 1989-90; Librarian, Amityville Public Library, 1986-92; Music Teacher, Miller Place Schools, 1987-89; Music Teacher Amityville Public Schools, 1991-. Publication: Fiction book submitted to publishers, 2003. Honours: Various Awards, Suffolk County Wrestling Coach's Association; Hearald Awards, Choreography, Music Director; Private Award to continue study and training, Metropolitan Opera House; Study Award, Minnesota Opera; Travel and Performing Grant, Rome Opera Festival; Study Grant, New Jersey Opera. Listed in numerous Who's Who publications and biographical dictionaries. Memberships: Music Educators National Conference; Suffolk County Music Educators Association; American Library Association; Masonic Order of the Eastern Star; Masonic Triangle; Music Library Association; Suffolk County Wrestling Coach's Association. Address: 90 Clock Blvd, Massapequa, NY 11758, USA.

TURNBULL Gael Lundin, b. 7 April 1928, Edinburgh, Scotland. Poet; Former Medical Practitioner. m. (1) Jonnie May Draper, 1952, 3 daughters, (2) Pamela Jill Iles, 1983. Education: BA, University of Cambridge, 1948; MD, University of Pennsylvania, 1951. Publications: A Trampoline, 1968; Scantlings, 1970; A Gathering of Poems, 1950-80, 1983; A Year and a Day, 1985; A Winter Journey, 1987; While Breath Persist, 1992; For Whose Delight, 1995; A Rattle of Scree, 1997; Transmutations, 1997; Might a Shape of Words, 2000. Contributions to: Numerous journals and magazines. Honour: Alice Hunt Bartlett Award, 1969. Address: 12 Strathearn Place, Edinburgh EH9 2AL, Scotland.

Dictionary of International Biography

TURNER Amédée Edward, b. 26 March 1929, London, England. Queens Counsel. m. Deborah Dudley Owen, 1 son, 1 daughter. Education: BA, 1951, MA, 1953, Christchurch College, Oxford. Appointments: Practised at Patent Bar, Inner Temple, London, 1954-57; Counsel at Kenyon & Kenyon (Patent Attorneys) New York, USA, 1957-60; Practice at Patent Bar, London, 1960-; Contested General Elections (Conservative) Norwich North, 1964, 1966, 1970; Appointed Queens Counsel, 1976-; Elected to European Parliament for Suffolk and Harwich and Suffolk and Cambridgeshire (Conservative), European Democratic Group, European People's Party, 1979-94; Counsel, Oppenheimer Wolff & Donnelly, Brussels, 1994-; Senior Counsel, Apco Europe, 1995-98; Member Executive Committee European League for Economic Co-operation, 1996-; Director, CJA Consultants, 2001-; Phare Advisor to Macedonian Parliament on approximation of EU legislation, 2001-2002; Member, Advisory Council to the Anglican Observer to UN, 2002. Publications: The Law of Trade Secrets, 1964; The Law of the New European Patent, 1979; Reports for the European Commission including Intellectual Property Law and the Single Market, 1997; Numerous political articles on behalf of the Conservative Party. Honours: Queens Counsel, 1976; Honorary Member of the European Parliament, 1994. Memberships: Carlton Club; The European Network; Conservative Group for Europe; Tory Reform Group; Kenya Society; African Society; International Association for the Protection of Industrial Property; Bar Association for Commerce and Industry. Address: Penthouse 7, Bickenhall Mansions, London W1U 6BS, England. E-mail: amedee.turner@btinternet.com

TURNER Cyril Boyland, b. 10 September 1929, Aldeby, Norfolk, England. Fine Art Miniaturist. Career: National Service, RAF, 1947-49; Merchant Navy Radio Officer, 1954-69; Fine Art Miniaturist, 1970-; Introduced "Cold Enamel" as a painting medium for miniature paintings; Inventor of Lumitex, the only known archival quality substitute for natural ivory, used as a base material for fine art miniature paintings; The Turner Travelling Exhibition of original fine art miniature paintings. Publications: Painting Miniatures in Acrylics, 1990; The Miniature Section of Painting in Acrylics, 1991; Painting Original Fine Art Miniatures, Informative Series Books #1-13, 1993-99; Miniature Books (less than 3" x 3"); Original Fine Art Miniature Paintings by Cyril B Turner, Books I and II, 1997; Collecting Contemporary Original Fine Art Miniature Paintings, 1997; Miniature Artists of America Turner 2000, 2000; Tasmania 2000 Painting Original Fine Art Miniatures, 2000; Clearwater Florida 2001 Turner Miniature Collections, 2001; Original Fine Art Miniature Paintings with Words 2002, 2002; The Turner School of Miniature Painting Stamp Collection, 2002; Old English Apples The Turner Brothers Aldeby Norfolk, 2003; Collections of Original Fine Art Miniature Paintings 2004, 2004; East Norfolk and East Suffolk Old English Apples, 2004. Honours: First non-American to be elected as a Signature Member of the Miniature Artists of America, 1988; Elected Fellow of Fine Art, International Guild of Miniature Artisans, 1994; Stamp Vignettes of original miniature painting Haddiscoe Norfolk issued by the Swiss publishers of Who's Who in International Art, 1996; First non-American to be elected as a signature member of the Cider Painters of America; 118 original fine art miniature paintings have won awards. Memberships: Miniature Painters Sculptors and Gravers Society, Washington DC, USA; Miniature Art Society of Florida, USA; Signature Member, Miniature Artists of America; Signature Member, Cider Painters of America; Founder Member, Hilliard Society of Miniaturists; Independent Member, World Federation of Miniaturists; Australian Society of Miniature Art; Miniature Book Society. Address: 6 Gablehurst Court, Long Lane, Bradwell, Great Yarmouth, Norfolk NR31 7DS. E-mail: miniatures@cyril.turner.britishlibrary.net Websites: http://miniaturepaintings.mysite.wanadoo-members.co.uk

TURNER Frederick, b. 19 November 1943, East Haddon, Northamptonshire, England. Professor of Arts and Humanities; Writer; Poet. m. Mei Lin Chang, 25 June 1966, 2 sons. Education: BA, 1965, MA, 1967, BLitt, 1967, English Language and Literature, University of Oxford. Appointments: Assistant Professor of English, University of California, Santa Barbara, USA, 1967-72; Associate Professor of English, Kenyon College, 1972-85; Editor, Kenyon Review, 1978-83; Visiting Professor of English, University of Exeter, 1984-85; Founders Professor of Arts and Humanities, University of Texas at Dallas, Richardson, 1985-. Publications: Shakespeare and the Nature of Time, 1971; Between Two Lives, 1972; The Return, 1979; The New World, 1985; The Garden, 1985; Natural Classicism, 1986; Genesis: An Epic Poem, 1988; Rebirth of Value, 1991; Tempest, Flute and Oz, 1991; April Wind, 1991; Beauty, 1991; Foamy Sky: The Major Poems of Miklos Radnoti (translator with Zsuzanna Ozsváth), 1992; The Culture of Hope, 1995; The Ballad of the Good Cowboy, 1997; Hadean Eclogues, 1999; Shakespeare's Twenty-First Century Economics: The Morality of Love and Money, 1999; The Iron-Blue Vault: Selected Poems of Attila József (translations with Zsuzsanna Ozsváth), 1999. Contributions to: Journals and periodicals. Honours: Ohioana Prize for Editorial Excellence, 1980; Djerassi Foundation Grant and Residency, 1981; Levinson Poetry Prize, 1983; Missouri Review Essay Prize, 1986; PEN Golden Pen Award, 1992; Milan Fust Prize (Hungary's highest literary honour), 1996. Membership: PEN. Address: 2668 Aster Drive, Richardson, TX 75082, USA.

TURNER Martin Vernon Lawrence, b. 9 February 1948, London, England. Educational Psychologist; Poet. m. Farah, 9 August 1981, 2 daughters. Education: BA, University of Exeter, 1975; PGCE, St Lukes College, Exeter, 1976; MSc, University of Strathclyde, 1978; MA, University of Kent, 1988. Appointment: Educational Psychologist, Motherwell, Lawarkshire, 1978-79, Newham, 1979-84; Senior Educational Psychologist, Croydon, 1984-91; Head of Psychology, Dyslexia Institute, Staines, 1991-2003. Publication: Trespasses. Contributions to: Ashes; Litmus; Poetry Durham; Wasafiri; Other Poetry; Poetry Book Society Anthology; Sepia; Poetry World; Comparative Criticism. Honour: Kent Literature Festival National Poetry Competition. Membership: Poetry Society. Address: Brocksett Cottage, Kennel Lane, Windlesham, Surrey, England GU20 6AA.

TURNER Neil Clifford, b. 13 March 1940, Preston, England. Research Scientist. m. Jennifer Gibson, 3 sons. Education: BS (Hons), 1962; PhD, 1968; DSc, 1983. Appointments: Plant Physiologist, CT Agricultural Experimental Station, New Haven, USA, 1967-74; Senior Research Scientist, 1974-84, Research Leader, 1984-93, Chief Research Scientist, 1993-, CSIRO Plant Industry, Canberra and Perth, Australia; Adjunct Professor, University of Western Australia, Perth, Australia, 1998-. Publications: Adaption of Plants to Water and High Temperature Stress, 1980; Plant Growth, Drought and Salinity, 1986; Crop Production on Duplex Soils, 1992; The Role of Agroforestry and Perennial Pasture in Mitigating Waterlogging and Secondary Salinity, Special Issue, Agricultural Water Management, 2002. Honours: Fellow, American Society of Agronomy, 1982; Fellow, Crop Science Society of America, 1985; Fellow, Australian Academy of Technology Science and Engineering, 1992; Medallist, 1993, Fellow, 1995, Australian Institute of Agricultural Science and Technology; Institute for Scientific Information Australian Citation Laureate, 2001; Fellow, Indian Academy of Agricultural Sciences, 2003; Centenary Medal, Australia, 2003. Memberships: Australian Academy of Technology Science and Engineering; Australian Institute of Agricultural Science and Technology, ACT President, 1978-79. Address: CSIRO Plant Industry, Private Bag PO 5, Wembley (Perth), Western Australia 6913 Australia.

Dictionary of International Biography

TURNER Peter John, b. 8 April 1959, Leicester, England. Professional and Technology Officer; Civil Servant; Naval Architect. Education: ONC, Naval Architecture, 1979, HNC, Naval Architecture, 1981, Bath technical College; BSc, Southampton University, 1985. Appointments: Technical Apprenticeship, Mod(n), 1977-81; Sponsored Undergraduate, Southampton University, 1981-85; Goddess Computer Section, 1981-85; Professional Technology Officer, Grade IV, Naval Architecture, Constructive, 1981-86; Professional Technology Officer, 1986-; Logistic Support Section, 1985-91; Goddess Computer Section, 1991-93; Drawing Office Control Section, 1993-97; Technical Publication Section, 1997-98; General Engineering Section, 1998-2002; Frigate Integrated Project Team, 2002-. Publications: Articles in professional journals and newsletters; Front Cover, Wotton-under-Edge Branch of Bellringers Newsletter; Front Cover Drawing for Centenary, Ringing World, 1978. Honours: Selected to attend the 14th World Scout Jamboree, Norway, 1975; Technician Apprentice of the Year, D G Ships, 1981; 156 certificates for various achievements. Memberships: Graduate Member, Royal Institution of Naval Architects; Member, Society of Naval Architecture and Marine Engineers; Life Governor, Royal National Lifeboat Institution; Fellow, Institute of Diagnostic Engineers; Associate Member, Chartered Institute of Management. Address: 8 Stanthill Drive, Dursley, Gloucestershire GL11 4PP, England.

TURNER Ted (Robert Edward II), b. 19 November 1938. American Broadcasting Executive; Yachtsman. m. (1) Judy Nye, divorced, 1 son, 1 daughter, m. (2) Jane S Smith, 1965, divorced 1988, 1 son, 2 daughters, (3) Jane Fonda, 1991, separated, 1999. Education: Brown University. Appointments: General Manager, Turner Advertising, Macon GA, 1960-63; President, CEO, Various Turner Companies, Atlanta, 1963-70; Chair of Board, President, Turner Broadcasting System Inc (merged with Time Warner to form Time Warner Inc), 1970-96; Vice Chair, Time Warner Inc, 1996; President, Atlanta Vraves, 1976; Now Owner; Chair of Board, Atlantic Hawks, 1977; Better World Society, WA, 1985-90; Founder and Chair, UN Foundation; Director, Martin Luther King Center, Atlanta; Acquired New Line Cinema Corporation, 1993; Sponsor, Creator, The Goodwill Games, Moscow, 1986; Winner, 1977 America's Cup in yacht Courageous. Publication: The Racing Edge, 1979. Honours: Named Yachtsman of the Year 4 times; Numerous Awards. Address: Turner Broadcasting System Inc, One CNN Centre, Box 105336, Atlanta, CA 30348, USA.

TURNER Tina (Annie Mae Bullock), b. 26 November 1939, Brownsville, Tennessee, USA. Singer; Songwriter. m. Ike Turner, 1958, divorced 1978, 4 sons. Appointments: Member, Ike and Tina Turner, 1958-78; Numerous TV, films and concert appearances world-wide. Creative Works: Solo Recordings: Let's Stay Together, 1983; What's Love Got To Do With It?, 1984; Better Be Good To Me, 1984; Private Dancer, 1984; We Don't Need Another Hero, 1985; One of the Living, 1985; It's Only Love, 1985; Typical Mae, 1986; The Best, 1989; I Don't Wanna Lose You, 1989; Be Tender With Me Baby, 1990; It Takes Two, 1990; Way of the World, 1991; I Don't Wanna Fight, 1993; Goldeneye, 1995; Wildest Dreams, 1996; Films: Gimme Shelter, 1970; Soul to Soul, 1971; Tommy, 1975; Mad Max Beyond the Thunderdome, 1985; What's Love Got to Do with It , vocals, 1993; Last Action Hero, 1993. Publication: I, Tina (autobiography), 1985. Honours: Grammy Awards; Record of the Year; Song of the Year; Best Female Vocal Performance; Best Female Rock Vocal, 1985; Favourite Soul/R&B Female Artist & Video Artist, 1985; Best Female Pop/Rock Artist, 1986; MTV Music Video Award, 1985; Star on Hollywood Walk of Fame, 1986; Rock'n'Roll Hall of Fame (with Ike Turner), 1991; World Music Award, Outstanding Contribution to The Music Industry, 1993. Address: c/o CAA, 9830 Wilshire Boulevard, Beverly Hills, CA 90212, USA.

TURNOVSKY Stephen John, b. 5 April 1941, Professor. m. Michelle Henriette Louise, 1 son, 1 daughter. Education: BA, 1962, MA, 1st class honours, 1963, Victoria University of Wellington, New Zealand; PhD, Harvard University, 1968. Appointments: Assistant Professor, University of Pennsylvania, 1968-71; Associate Professor, University of Toronto, 1971-72; Professor of Economics, Australian National University, 1972-82; IBE Distinguished Professor of Economics, University of Illinois, 1982-87; Professor of Economics, University of Washington, 1988-. Publications: 3 books. Honours: Fellow, Econometric Society. Memberships: Royal Economic Society; American Economic Association. Address: Department of Economics, University of Washington, Box 353330, Seattle, WA 98195, USA. E-mail: sturn@u.washington.edu

TURPIN David Howard, b. 14 July 1956, Duncan, British Columbia, Canada. Professor of Biology; President and Vice-Chancellor. m. S Laurene Clark, 1 son, 1 daughter. Education: BSc, Cell Biology, 1977, PhD, Botany and Oceanography, 1980, University of British Columbia. Appointments: Research Associate, Simon Fraser University, 1980; Vice President, Sigma Resource Consultants, Vancouver, 1980-81; Assistant Professor, 1981-85, Associate Professor, 1985-90, Professor, 1990-2000, Dean, Faculty of Arts and Science, 1993-95, Vice Principal, 1995-2000, Queen's University; Professor, Head, Department of Botany, University of British Columbia, 1991-93; President and Vice-Chancellor, University of Victoria, 2000-. Publications: Over 100 articles, books and book chapters. Honours include: Queen's Alumni Award, Excellence in Teaching, 1989; Steacie Fellowship, Natural Sciences and Engineering Research Council of Canada, 1989; C D Nelson Award, Canadian Society of Plant Physiologists, 1989; Award of Merit, UBC Alumni Association, 1990; Darbaker Prize, Phycology, American Botanical Association, 1991; Queen's Golden Jubilee Medal, 2002; Fellow of the Royal Society of Canada. Address: University of Victoria, Business and Economics Building, Room 454, Victoria, British Columbia V8W 2Y2, Canada

TUTT Leslie William Godfrey, b. London, England. Mathematical Statistician and Actuary. Education: MSc, PhD, London University. Appointments: Lecturer on financial, business statistical and actuarial topics to professional bodies and universities in UK, USA and throughout central and eastern Europe, 1970-; Joint Senior Director, Clems Associates Business Advisers, Consultant to a number of British companies, 1981-. Publications: Many research papers and technical articles on finance, pensions and insurance, modelling of mortality and morbidity trends, application of stochastic simulation to decision making, social policy issues associated with genetics, for UK and overseas actuarial, statistical and financial journals; Author, joint author of 16 books including: Private Pension Scheme Finance, 1970; Pension Scheme Investment, Communications and Overseas Aspects, 1977; Financial Advisers Competence Test, 1985; Financial Services Marketing and Investor Protection, 1988; Taxation and Trusts, 1989; Private Investment Planning, Corporate Investment Planning, 1990; Pensions and Insurance Administration, 1992; Personal Financial Planning, 1995; Pension Law and Taxation, 2002. Honour: Lectureship Diploma, Department of Mathematics, Moscow State University, Russia, 1995. Memberships: Fellow, Institute of Statisticians of Royal Statistical Society, Member of Council 1975-81, Vice-Chairman, 1981-84, Chairman, 1984-87, Vice-President, 1987-93; Fellow, Faculty of Actuaries, Member of Council, 1975-78, Board of Examiners,

1980-90; Associate, Society of Actuaries, USA, Fellow Society of Actuaries of Ireland, 1977; Chartered Insurance Institute, Examinations Assessor, 1980-2000; Fellow, Pensions Management Institute, 1976; Founder Member, Pensions Research Accountants Group, Member of Executive Committee, 1976-85; National Association of Pension Funds, Member of Council, 1979-83. Address: 21 Sandilands, Croydon, Surrey CR0 5DF, England.

TUTT Sylvia Irene Maud, b. London, England. Chartered Secretary and Administrator. Appointments: Chartered Secretary and Administrator in private practice; Writer. Publications: Author of numerous articles in professional and financial journals; Author or joint author of the following books: Private Pension Scheme Finance, 1970; Pensions and Employee Benefits, 1973; Pension Law and Taxation, 1981; Financial Aspects of Pension Business, 1985; Financial Aspects of Life Business, 1987; A Mastership of a Livery Company, 1988; Financial Aspect of Long Term Business, 1991; Pension Law and Taxation, 2002. Memberships: Fellow and Past member of Council, Institute of Chartered Secretaries and Administrators; Fellow Royal Statistical Society; Fellow Royal Society of Arts; Examiner, Society of Financial Advisers; Senior Examiner, Chartered Insurance Institute; Member of Court of City University London; Past President, Soroptimist International of Central London; President, City Livery Club, 2001-2002; Court Assistant, The Scriveners Company; Master, 1983-84, Worshipful Company of Chartered Secretaries and Administrators, Managing Trustee of its Charitable Trust, 1978-. Address: 21 Sandilands, Croydon, Surrey CR0 5DF, England.

TUTU Desmond Mpilo, (Most Rev), b. 7 October 1931, Klerksdorp, South Africa. m. Leah Nomalizo Tutu, 1955, 1 son, 3 daughters. Education: Bantu Normal College; University of South Africa; St Peter's Theological College, Rosettenville; King's College, University of London; LTh; MTh. Appointments: Schoolmaster, 1954-57; Parish priest, 1960-; Theology Seminary Lecturer, 1967-69; University Lecturer, 1970-71; Associate Director, Theology Education Fund, World Council of Churches, 1972-75; Dean of Johannesburg, 1975-76; Bishop of Lesotho, 1977-78; Bishop of Johannesburg, 1984-86; Archbishop of Cape Town, Metropolitan of the Church of the Province of Southern Africa, 1986-96; Chancellor, University of Western Cape, 1988-; President, All Africa Conference of Churches, 1987-; Secretary-General, South Africa Council of Churches, 1979-84; Visiting Professor, Anglican Studies, New York General Theology Seminary, 1984; Elected to Harvard University Board of Overseers, 1989; Director, Coca Cola, 1986-; Visiting Professor, Emory University, Atlanta, 1996-; Leader, Truth and Reconciliation Commission, 1995-; Archbishop Emeritus, Cape Town, 1996-; Robert R Woodruff Visiting Distinguished Professor, Candler School of Theology, 1998-99; William R Cannon Distinguished Visiting Professor, Emory University, 1999-2000. Publications: Crying in the Wilderness, 1982; Hope and Suffering, 1983; The Rainbow People of God, 1994; An African Prayer Book, 1996; The Essential Desmond Tutu, 1997; No Future without Forgiveness, 1999. Honours include: Numerous Honorary Degrees; Nobel Peace Prize, 1984; Carter-Menil; Human Rights Prize, 1986; Martin Luther King Junior Peace Award, 1986; Third World Prize, 1989; Order of Jamaica; Freedom of Borough of Merthyr Tydfil, Wales; Order of Meritorious Service, South Africa, 1996; Order of Grand Cross, Germany; Nelson Mandela Award for Health and Human Rights, Florida, USA, 1998; Monismanien Prize, Uppsala University Sweden, 1999; MESB Service Award, Medical Education for South African Blacks, 1999; Athenagoras Award for Human Rights, 2000. Memberships: Third Order of Society of St Francis; President, All Africa Conference of Churches; Council for National Orders, Republic of South Africa. Address: c/o Truth and Reconciliation Commission, PO Box 3162, Cape Town 8000, South Africa.

TWAIN Shania, b. 28 August 1965, Windsor, Toronto, Canada. Country Singer; Songwriter. m. Robert John Lange, 1 son. Appointments: Several TV performances on CMT & TNN; Songwriter with husband. Creative Works: Albums: Shania Twain: The Woman in Me; Come On Over; Up! 2002; Singles: Any Man of Mine; From This Moment On; That Don't Impress Me Much; Man! I Feel Like A Woman; Don't Be Stupid (You Know I Love You); I'm Gonna Get You Good, 2002; Up! 2003; Ka-Ching! 2003. Honour: CMT European Rising Video Star of the Year, 1993; Favourite New Country Artist, American Music Award, 1995; Female Vocalist Award, Canadian Country Music Awards, 1995; Female Artist of the Year; Country Music TV/Europe, 1996; numerous other awards. Address: Mercury Nashville, 54 Music Square E, Nashville, TN 37203, USA. Website: www.shaniatwain.com

TYLER Anne, b. 25 October 1941, Minneapolis, Minnesota, USA. Writer. m. Taghi M Modaressi, 3 May 1963, 2 children. Education: BA, Duke University, 1961; Postgraduate Studies, Columbia University, 1962. Publications: If Morning Ever Comes, 1964; The Tin Can Tree, 1965; A Slipping Down Life, 1970; The Clock Winder, 1972; Celestial Navigation, 1974; Searching for Caleb, 1976; Earthly Possessions, 1977; Morgan's Passing, 1980; Dinner at the Homesick Restaurant, 1982; The Best American Short Stories, 1983 (editor with Shannon Ravenel); 1983; The Accidental Tourist, 1985; Breathing Lessons, 1988; Saint Maybe, 1991; Tumble Tower (juvenile), 1993; Ladder of Years, 1995; A Patchwork Planet, 1998; Back When We Were Grown-ups, 2001; Short stories in magazines. Honours: National Book Critics Circle Award for Fiction, 1985; Pulitzer Prize for Fiction, 1989. Memberships: American Academy of Arts and Letters; American Academy of Arts and Sciences. Address: 222 Tunbridge Road, Baltimore, MD 21212, USA. E-mail: atmBaltimore@aol.com

TYLER Liv, b. 1 July 1977, Portland, Maine, USA. Actress. m. Royston Langdon, 2003. Career: Film appearances include: Silent Fall; Empire Records; Heavy; Stealing Beauty; That Thing You Do!; Inventing the Abbotts; Plunkett and Macleane, 1999; Armageddon, 1998; Cookie's Fortune, 1999; Onegin, 1999; The Little Black Book, 1999; Dr T and the Women, 2000; The Lord of the Rings: The Fellowship of the Ring, 2001; One Night at McCool's, 2001; The Lord of the Rings: The Two Towers, 2002; The Lord of the Rings: The Return of the King, 2003; Jersey Girl, 2004; Lonesome Jim, 2004. Address: c/o CAA, 9830 Wilshire Boulevard, Beverly Hills, CA 90212, USA.

TYLEVICH Alexander, b. 12 September 1947, Minsk, Belarus. Sculptor; Architect; Educator. m. Poline M Dvorkin, 1 son, 1 daughter. Education: BA, Minsk Architectural Institute, 1965; MA, Byelorussian Politechnical Institute, 1971. Appointments: Principal, Senior Architect, Minskprojekt, 1971-84; Artist, Architect, Fine Arts Foundation, 1980-89; Sculptor, Architect, Alexander Tylevich Arts, 1989-; Selected Public Art Works include: Master plan for the centre of Minsk; Minsk historical district; Vincentian Letter, DePaul University Plaza, Chicago, Illinois; Letters of Creation, Wayzata, Minnesota; Blue Springs.Net, Blue Springs, Missouri; St Thomas More Chapel, University of St Thomas, Minneapolis; Letterdance, Minnesota State University, Mankato; Madonna and Child, The Church of St Mary, Alexandria, Minnesota; Resurrection, Church of St Stephen, Anoka, Minnesota; Zenon Possis, North Memorial Hospital, Minneapolis, Minnesota; Gateway to Belief, St Mary's University, Winona, Minnesota; The Process of Becoming Airborne, sculptural ensemble including a 30 foot high triumphal arch, a bronze sculpture of Charles Lindbergh and a ceremonial table, Winona Technical College Aviation Facility, Winona, Minnesota; North Shore Synagogue, Syosset, New York; Mount Zion Temple, St Paul, Minnesota; Saint

Benedict, Louisiana; Many other works in private collections in USA, Russia, Belarus, Poland, Israel and England. Publications include: the Best of Soviet Architecture; Encyclopedia of Historical and Cultural Monuments of Byelorussia; Progressive Architecture 1991; Architecture Minnesota, 1998. Honours include: Gold Medal and First Prizes, Many Byelorussian and National USSR Competitions; Listed in numerous biographical publications. Memberships: Architects Association of the USSR. Address: 1937 Highland Parkway, St Paul, MN 55116. USA.

TYSON Mike G, b. 30 June 1966, New York, USA. Boxer. m. Robin Givens, 1988, divorced 1989. Appointments: Defeated Trevor Berbick to win WBC Heavyweight Title, 1986; Winner WBA Heavyweight Title, 1987; IBF Heavyweight Title, 1987; Former Undefeated World Champion, winner all 32 bouts, lost to James Buster Douglas, 1990; Defeated Donovan Ruddock, 1991; Sentenced to 6 years imprisonment for rape and two counts of deviant sexual practice, 1992; Appealed against sentence; Appeal rejected by US Supreme Court, 1994; released, 1995; Regained title of Heavyweight World Champion after defeating Frank Bruno, 1996; Lost to Evander Holyfield, 1996; License revoked by Nevada State Athletics Commission after disqualification from rematch against Holyfield, 1996; reinstated on appeal 1998; Sentenced to a years imprisonment for assault, 1999; released on probation, 1999; Fought Lennox Lewis, 2002 for the WBC and IBF titles, knocked out in eighth round. Honours: Honorary Chair Cystic Fibrosis Association, 1987; Young Adult Institute, 1987. Address: Don King Productions, 501 Fairway Drive, Deerfield Beach, FL 33441, USA.

TZANEV Ivan, b. 30 November 1941, Ostritza, Bulgaria. Poet. m. Malina Tomova, 3 daughters. Education: Slavic Languages Department, Sofia University "St Clement Ohridsky", 1968. Appointments: Editor, Studentska Tribuna Newspaper, 1967-69; Editor, Rodna Rech Literary Magazine, 1969-72; Editor, Plamak Literary Magazine, 1973-81; Editor, Bulgarian Artist Publishing House, 1981-82; Editor, Bulgarian Writer Publishing House, 1982-91; Editor-in-Chief, Children's Literary Supplement, Alf, of Literary Forum Newspaper, 1991-92; Free-lance Poet, 1992-99; Editor, Rodna Rech Literary Magazine, 1999-2000; Free-lance Poet, 2000-. Publications: 8 books of poetry; 14 books of poetry for children. Honours: National Literary Award "P R Slavejkov for contribution to development of literature for children, 1994; National Literary Award, "Ivan Nikolov", 1997; Andrersen's Author Diploma, 1998; Award, International Art Academy, Paris, 1998; National Award "Hr G Danov" for the Best Children's Book, 2000; National Award, "Furnadjiev", 2000; National Award, Yavorov, 2001; National Award, Penjo Penev, 2002. Memberships: Union of Bulgarian Writers, 1972-95; Association of Bulgarian Writers, 1995-; International Art Academy, Sofia-Paris, 1998-. Address: 41 Skobelev Blvd, Sofia 1606, Bulgaria. E-mail: stigmati@abv.bg

Dictionary of International Biography

U

UDEANI Uchenna Nkiruka, b. 3 February 1956, Nigeria. University Lecturer. m. Ugwu Udeani, 1 son, 1 daughter. Education: BSc, Zoology, 1978; Postgraduate Diploma in Education, 1980; Master of Educational Measurement and Evaluation, 1981; PhD, Science Education, 1992. Appointment: University Lecturer, involved in Teaching and Research, 1982-. Publications: Over 35 articles in national and international professional journals. Memberships: Third World Organisation for Women in Science; Girls and Science and Technology; National Association for Research in Science Teaching. Address: Department of Curriculum Studies, University of Lagos, Lagos, Nigeria. E-mail: ucheudeani@yahoo.co.uk

UEDA Isao, b. 18 March 1955, Toyonaka, Japan. Professor. m. Yuko Ueda. Education: BA, Arabic language, 1976, BA, English Language, 1983, MA, English Linguistics, 1985, Osaka University of Foreign Studies. Appointments: Lecturer, 1985, Assistant Professor, 1986, Osaka Gakuin University; Associate Professor, Shizuoka University, 1990; Associate Professor, Osaka University of Foreign Studies, 1995-; Visiting Scientist, Indiana University, USA, 1997-98. Publications: On the phonology of Japanese Kappacism, 1998; Segmental acquisition and feature specification in Japanese, 1998; Promotion and demotion of phonological constraints in the acquisition of the Japanese liquid, 2001. Memberships: Clinical Linguistics and Phonetics Association; Linguistic Society of Japan; Phonetic Society of Japan. Address: Osaka University of Foreign Studies, 8-1-1 Aomatani-Higashi, Minoo-shi, Osaka, 562-8558 Japan. E-mail: uedais@osaka-gaidai.ac.jp

UENO Haruki, b. 28 May 1941, Kogoshima, Japan. Professor. m. Hisako Ueno, 1 son, 1 daughter. Education: Bachelor in Engineering, National Defence Academy of Japan, 1964; Master in Engineering, 1968, PhD in Engineering, 1971, Tokyo Denki University. Appointments: Lecturer, Aoyama Gakuin University, Japan, 1971-76; Associate Professor, 1977-80, Professor, 1981-97, Tokyo Denki University; Professor, National Center for Science Information Systems, Japan, 1998-99; Professor and Director of Intelligence Systems Research Division, National Institute of Informatics, Japan, 2000-; Professor, The University of Tokyo Graduate school of Information Science and Technology, Computer Science, Japan, 2001-; Professor, The Graduate University for Advanced Studies, Japan, 2002-. Publications: Articles in professional journals including: IOS Press (volume 55), 1999; Proceedings 10th EJC, 2000; NII Journal (volume 3), 2001; IEICE Transactions on Information Systems (volume E-85-D), 2002. Honours: Science and Technology Award, Nikkan Kogyo Shimbun, Tokyo, 1985; Standardisation Reference Award, Japanese Standards Association, Tokyo, 1987; Distinguished Service Award, Japanese Society for Artificial Intelligence, Tokyo, 1996. Memberships: Fellow, Institute of Electronics, Information and Communication Engineers; New York Academy of Science, 1996; The Institute of Electrical and Electronics Engineers, USA, 2000. Address: National Institute of Informatics, National Center of Sciences Building, 101-8430, 2-1-2 Hitotsubashi, Chiyoda-ku, Tokyo, Japan. E-mail: ueno@nii.ac.jp

UENO Makato, b. 2 December 1969, Matsue, Japan. Paediatrician; Neurologist. m. Noriko. Education: MD, 1995, PhD, 2003, Tottori University, Yonago, Japan. Appointments: Physician, Division of Child Neurology, Institute of Neurological Sciences, Faculty of Medicine, Tottori University, Yonago, Japan, 1995-96, 1997-2004; Physician, Department of Paediatrics, Faculty of Medicine, Kyushu University, Fukuoka, Japan, 1996-97.

Publications: Books: Neural tube defect, congenital malformation of the brain, 2001; Congenital disorders of glycosylation, 2003; 7 articles in medical journals include most recently: High-dose ethosuximide for epilepsy in Angelman syndrome: implication of GABA (A) receptor subunit, 2001; Unilateral occlusion of the middle cerebral artery after varicella-zoster virus infection, 2002; Photosensitivity in electroencephalogram of child with 45, X/46, X, mar (X) Turner Syndrome, 2003. Memberships: Japan Paediatric Society; Japan Society of Human Genetics; Japan Society of Child Neurology; Japan Epilepsy Society. Address: Division of Child neurology, Institute of Neurological Sciences, Faculty of Medicine, Tottori University, 36-1 Nishi-Machi, Yonago 683-8504, Japan.

UHLIG Harald Friedrich Hans Volker Sigmar, b. 26 April 1961, Bonn, Germany. Professor of Economics. Education: Vordiplom, Mathematics, 1982, Vordiplom, Economics, 1983, Diplom, Mathematics, 1985, Technical University, Berlin; PhD, Economics, University of Minnesota, USA, 1990. Appointments: Student Teaching Assistant, Technical University, Berlin, 1982-85; Teaching Assistant, University of Minnesota, 1987; Research Assistant, Federal Reserve Bank of Minneapolis and Institute for Empirical Macroeconomics, 1986-89; Assistant Professor, Department of Economics, Princeton University, 1990-94; Visiting Assistant Professor, Munich, Bonn and Chicago, 1992-93; Guest Lecturer, University of Bonn, Germany, 1993, 1994; Research Professor for Macroeconomics, Tilburg University, The Netherlands, 1994-2000; Visiting Professor, Department of Economics, Stanford University, 1999-2000; Professor of Economics, Humboldt University, Berlin, 2000-. Honours: Numerous research and study grants. Memberships: Econometric Society; American Economic Association; European Economic Association; CEPR Research Fellow. Address: School of Busines Administration and Economics, Institute for Economic Policy, Humboldt University, Spandauer Str 1, 10178 Berlin, Germany. E-mail: uhlig@wiwi.hu-berlin.de Website: www.wiwi.hu-berlin.de/wpol/html/uhlig/uhlig.html

UKAEGBU David Okwukanmanihu, b. 28 January 1939, Umuahia, Nigeria. Professional Accountant; MGT Scientist. Education: General Certificate of Education, Wolsey Hall, Oxford, Kings College, University College, London, 1958-66; Taxation, Foulks Lynch & Co Ltd, London; Chartered Secretary and Administration, Metropolitan College, St Albans and Manchester College, England, 1962-70; Doctorate thesis, at Harvard University, Massachusetts Institute of Technology and Alexander Hamilton Institute Inc, through the Institute for International Research, London and New York, 1975-79; Degree in Management Sciences, MBIM, from the Institute of Management, UK and American Management Association, USA; BSc/MBA, Business Administration, California Coast University, Santa Ana, USA, 1982; Diploma, Kings College, Cambridge, 2000-01; Graduated with honours, Crossroads Bible Institute, USA, 2003. Appointments: Chief Audit Clerk, 1958-60, Assistant Audit Manager, 1961-64, Audit Manager, 1964-66, Articled Clerk, 1967-70, Firms of Chartered Accountants; Professional Accountant, MGT Consultant, Charter House, 1971-2001; Chief Accountant, Consultant, Silver Shoes Manufacturing Company Ltd, 1974-99; Honorary Treasurer, Employers Association of Leather Footwear and Rubber Industries of Nigeria, 1990-94. Publications: Unpublished work in investment financing, 1986; Articles in professional financial journals. Honours: IBC Outstanding Speaker Award; ABI World Laureate; Recommended as Decision Maker in International Finance, Currencies and Foreign Exchange, International Reports, London; 2000 Scholars of the 20th Century; 2000 Scholars of the 21st Century; ABI International Peace Prize, 2003; 1000 Leaders of World Influence, Ambassador of Grand

Dictionary of International Biography

Eminence, Leading Intellectuals of the World, ABI; The Da Vinci Diamond for Inspirational Excellence, IBC; Certificate of Achievement, Crossroads Bible Institute, 2003. Memberships: New York Academy of Sciences; American Association for the Advancement of Science; Planetary Society; British Institute of Securities Laws; FFA; FCEA; AIPA, Dublin, Ireland. Address: Charter House Auditors, PO Box 998, Umuahia Abia State, Nigeria.

UKAEGBU James Udogu, b. 18 October 1941, Bende, Abia State, Nigeria. Presbyterian Minister; Counsellor. m. Abigail Chimezie, 4 children. Education: Bachelor of Divinity, 1983, Master of Theology, 1985, Doctorate in Pastoral Counselling and Psychology, 1990; Doctor of Divinity, Ephraim Moore Seminary and Theological College and Honolulu University, Hawaii, USA; Diplomas: Theology, 1968, Biblical Studies, 1960-63, Journalism, Radio and TV, 1975; Public Administration and Personnel Management, 1975, Certificate on Leadership and Management, 1999. Appointments include: Rector, Goldie/Lay Theological College, Arochukwu, Nigeria, 1975-76; Minister, Owerri Presbyterian Church, 1977-85; Commissioner, Local Government Service Commission, 1977-83; Minister, Lagos Presbyterian Church, Yaba and adjoining congregations, 1985-89; Served as First and Second Moderator of the General Assembly of the Presbyterian Church of Nigeria, 1986-89; Minister, Duke Town Presbyterian Church, Calabar, 1990-93; Minister, St Stephen's Presbyterian Church, Aba East Parish, 1994-97; Minister, St Peter's Presbyterian Church, Umuahia, 1998-2001; Retired 2001; Currently, Counsellor and Chairman, The Total Response Network International (TRENET) an NGO to foster human, women's and children's rights, and ethics; Manager, The Total Response Network International Resource Centre; Head, National Directorate for Missions in the PCN; Frequent Speaker on TV and radio. Publications: Autobiography, This is My Story; Books in publication: The Grace of Marriage; Nigeria in the Valley of Decision; Possessing our Possessions; The Comforter Has Come; The Complete Disciple; Numerous articles in Christian magazines and newspapers. Honours: Best Preacher, Nigerian Newspapers, 1989; Fellowship, Trinity College of Ministerial Arts, Honolulu University, Hawaii, USA, 2002; Merit Award, Nigeria Directorate of West African Council in collaboration with United National Millennium Award of Excellence, 2002; Man of the Year 2003, American Biographical Institute; IBC Man of the Year, 2004; Deputy Director General, IBC; American Medal of Honor, ABI; 2000 Outstanding Intellectuals of the 21st Century Award. Memberships include: Member, Chartered Nigerian Institute of Management; Nigerian Institute of Public Relations; Chairman and Trustee, Ministers Prayer Network; Trustee, Presbyterian Church of Nigeria; Egwuatu Age Grade Igbere; Research Board of Advisors, American Biographical Institute, 2003. Address: 29A Macaulay Street, PO Box 2660 (44001) Umuahia, Abia State, Nigeria. E-mail: udogujammy@yahoo.com

ULLMAN Susanne, b. 15 May 1938, Copenhagen, Denmark. Physician; Professor of Dermatology; Doctor of Medical Science. Education: Medical Degree, University of Copenhagen, 1965; Postgraduate Training in Dermatology, Rigshospital, University of Copenhagen. Appointments: Visiting Professor, University of Minnesota, Minneapolis, USA, 1974-76; Professor of Dermatology, Rigshospital, University of Copenhagen, 1979; Visiting Professor, King Faisal University, Dahran, Saudi Arabia, 1981; Visiting Professor, Hunan Medical University, Changsa, Hunan, China, 1989; Professor of Dermatology, Bispebjerg Hospital and Rigshospital, University of Copenhagen, 1996; Co-ordinator, Education of Dermatologists in Denmark, 1983-90; Member, National Board of Health's Advisory Group on AIDS, 1984-89; Member, National Board of Health's Advisory Group

on Sexually Transmitted Diseases, 1987-; Member, Committee for The Robert J Gorlin Conference on Dysmorphology, Minneapolis, 1996-. Publications: Author and Co-author, 90 publications in international and Danish journals. Address: Bispebjerg Hospital, Department of Dermatology, DK 2400, Copenhagen, Denmark.

UNBEHAUEN Heinz Dietrich, b. 7 October 1935, Stuttgart, Germany. Emeritus Professor. m. Elke Erbele, 2 sons, 1 daughter. Education: Dipl Ing (ME), 1961, Dr-Ing (PhD), 1964, Dr-Ing habil, 1969, University of Stuttgart. Appointments: Scientific Research Fellow, 1961-64, Scientific Assistant and Lecturer (Assistant Professor), 1964-69, Dozent (Associate Professor), 1969-71, Professor of Control Engineering, 1971-75, University of Stuttgart; Professor, Chair and Head of Control, Engineering Department, 1975, Dean, 1978-79, Emeritus Professor, 2001-, Ruhr-University, Bochum; Consultant, UNESCO and several international governmental organisations; Consultant, industrial companies including Siemens, Bayer, and others. Publications: Over 430 articles to professional journals and congress proceedings; 9 books. Honours: Recipient, IEEE-Heaviside Premium; Fellow, IEEE; Honorary Professor, Tongji-University, Shanghai; Fellow, Japanese Society for Promotion of Science; Fellow, VW-Foundation. Memberships: Verein Deutscher Electrotechniker; Institute of Electrical and Electronics Engineers. Address: Faculty of Electrical Engineering and Information Science IC-3, Ruhr-University, 44780 Bochum, Germany.

UNCUŢA Cornelia, b. 10 December 1944, Com Macedonia, Romania. Chemical Engineer. Education: Diploma, Engineer, 1966, PhD, 1982, Polytechnical Institute, Bucharest, Romania. Appointments: Researcher, Institute of Atomic Physics, Bucharest, 1966-77; Senior Researcher, Centre of Organic Chemistry C D Nenitzescu, Romanian Academy, Bucharest, 1977-. Publications: Scientific papers on heterocyclic chemistry. Honour: Gh Spacu Award, Romanian Academy, 1988. Membership: Romanian Chemical Society. Address: Centre of Organic Chemistry C D Nenitzescu, 71141 Bucharest, 15-254 Romania. E-mail: cuncuta@cco.ro

UNDE Madhavji (Mark), b. 28 June 1934, Pune, India. Welding Scientist; Engineer. 1 son, 2 daughters (adopted). Education: MS, Welding Engineering, The Ohio State University, Columbus, Ohio, USA, 1978. Appointments: Senior Scientific Officer (1), Defence R&D, Government of India, 1965-74; Division Welding Engineer, Fruehauf Corporation; Tool Design Engineer, Danly Machines/Ingersol Milling Machines Inc; Mechanical Engineer, Sacramento Army Depot, Sacramento, California, USA; President, California Consulting Engineers. Publications include: Effect of back-up on Welding of Thin Sections of Aluminium Alloy; Mathematical Theory of Heat Diffusion, 1994; A Brief on IPSR technology for weld-joints, 2nd revision, 2003; Several other professional articles; Patented processes in casting, non-destructive testing, mechanisms and welding; IPSR, the in process stress relief of welds (US patent 1983); EHS the equivalent heat sink process for in process production of welds without defects and reduced residual stress (US patent 1991); US Patents: Covered Trailing Edge of Weld, 2000; Trailing Edge Stress Relief, 2001; Total of 4 processes in IPSR technology to produce a metal joint without defect and known value residual stress during welding; IPSR technology eliminates 70% of the welding labour. Honour: Presidential Award, ARPA, for development of IPSR process. Memberships: Chartered Engineer, UK; MIProdE, London; MIE, India; AWS; ASM International. Address: California Consulting Engineers, 1980 Watt Avenue, Sacramento, CA 98825-2151, USA.

Dictionary of International Biography

UNGARO Mario, b. Lima, Peru. Medical Doctor; Pathologist; Educator. Education: Bachelor of Medicine and Medical Surgeon, National University of San Marcos, Lima, Peru, 1954; Doctor in Medicine; MD. Appointments: Intern, Marymount Hospital, Gasfield Heights, Ohio, USA, 1954-55; Resident in Pathology, St Vincent Charity Hospital, Cleveland, Ohio, USA, 1955-57; Forensic Pathology, Frank E Bunts, Educational Institute, Cleveland, Ohio, USA, 1957-58; Resident in Pathology, ABG Hospital, New Britain, Connecticut, USA, 1958-59; Resident in Pathology, P Rowell Park Memorial Institute, Buffalo, USA, 1959-60; Diplomate, American Board of Pathology, 1960; Assistant Pathologist, Mercy Hospital, Buffalo, New York, USA, 1960-61; Professor of Pathology, National University of Trujillo, 1961-87; Chief of Pathology, Hospital Regional, 1963-87; Emeritus Professor, National University of Trujillo, Peru, 1993. Membership: Peruvian Society of Pathologists. Address: C-2 Parque del Reservorio, Monservete, Trujillo, Peru.

UNSWORTH Barry (Forster), b. 10 August 1930, Durham, England. Novelist. m. (1) Valerie Moor, 15 May 1959, divorced, 1991, 3 daughters, (2) Aira Pohjanvaara-Buffa, 1992. Education: BA, University of Manchester, 1951. Appointments: Lectureships in English; Writer-in-Residence, University of Liverpool, 1984-85, University of Lund, Sweden, 1988. Publications: The Partnership, 1966; The Greeks Have a Word for It, 1967; The Hide, 1970; Mooncrankers Gift, 1973; The Big Day, 1976; Pascalis Island, 1980, US edition as The Idol Hunter, 1980; The Rage of the Vulture, 1982; Stone Virgin, 1985; Sugar and Rum, 1988; Sacred Hunger, 1992; Morality Play, 1995; After Hannibal, 1996; Losing Nelson, 1999; The Songs of the Kings, 2002. Honours: Heinemann Award, Royal Society of Literature, 1974; Arts Council Creative Writing Fellowship, 1978-79; Literary Fellow, University of Durham and University of Newcastle upon Tyne, 1983-84; Co-Winner, Booker Prize, 1992; Hon LittD, Manchester, 1998. Address: c/o Hamish Hamilton, 22 Wrights Lane, London W8 5TZ, England.

UOTILA Jari V J, b. 9 November 1953, Akaa, Finland. Manager, Public Funding. m. Irma Uotila, 3 sons. Education: MSc (Engineering), 1980. Appointments: Research Engineer, 1980-82, Technical Service Engineer, 1982-84, Oy Lohja Ab Minerals; Technical Service Engineer, 1985-88, Technical Service Manager, 1989-95, Technical Sales Manager, 1996-97, ECC International Oy; Marketing Manager, 1997-2001, Manager, Public Funding, 2002-, Oy Keskuslaboratorio, KCL, 1997-. Memberships: Suomen Paperi-insinöörien yhdistys, 1985; Vuorimiesyhdistys, 1980; Suomen Partikkeliseura, 1990. Address: PL70, Fin 02151 Espoo, Finland.

UPDIKE John (Hoyer), b. 18 March 1932, Shillington, Pennsylvania, USA. Author; Poet. m. (1) Mary Entwistle Pennington, 26 June 1953, divorced 1977, 2 sons, 2 daughters, (2) Martha Ruggles Bernhard, 30 September 1977, 3 stepchildren. Education: AB, Harvard University, 1954; Ruskin School of Drawing and Fine Art, Oxford, 1954-55. Publications: Fiction: The Poorhouse Affair, 1959; The Same Door, 1959; Rabbit, Run, 1960; Pigeon Feathers and Other Stories, 1962; The Centaur, 1963; Of the Farm, 1965; The Music School, 1966; Couples, 1968; Bech: A Book, 1970; Rabbit Redux, 1971; Museums and Women and Other Stories, 1972; A Month of Sundays, 1975; Marry Me: A Romance, 1976; The Coup, 1979; Too Far to Go: The Maples Stories, 1979; Problems and Other Stories, 1979; Your Lover Just Called: Stories of Joan and Richard Maple, 1980; Rabbit is Rich, 1981; Bech is Back, 1982; The Witches of Eastwick, 1984; Roger's Version, 1986; Trust Me: Short Stories, 1987; S, 1988; Rabbit at Rest, 1990; Memories of the Ford Administration, 1992; Brazil, 1994; The Afterlife and Other Stories, 1994; Toward the End of

Time, 1997; Bech at Bay, 1998; More Matter: Essays and Criticism, 1999; Gertrude and Claudius (novel), 2000; Licks of Love, 2001. Poetry: The Carpenter Hen and Other Tame Creatures, 1958; Telephone Poles and Other Poems, 1963; Midpoint and Other Poems, 1969; Seventy Poems, 1972; Tossing and Turning, 1977; Sixteen Sonnets, 1979; Jester's Dozen, 1984; Facing Nature, 1985; Collected Poems, 1953-1993, 1993. Non-Fiction: Picked Up Pieces, 1975; Hugging the Shore: Essays and Criticism, 1983; Just Looking: Essays on Art, 1989; Self-Consciousness: Memoirs, 1989; Odd Jobs, 1991; A Century of Arts and Letters (editor), 1998. Play: Buchanan Dying, 1974. Contributions to: Many publications. Honours: Guggenheim Fellowship, 1959; National Book Award for Fiction, 1966; Prix Medicis Etranger, 1966; O Henry Awards for Fiction, 1966, 1991; MacDowell Medal for Literature, 1981; Pulitzer Prizes in Fiction, 1982, 1991; National Book Critics Circle Awards for Fiction, 1982, 1991, and for Criticism, 1984; PEN/Malamud Memorial Prize, 1988; National Medal of Arts, 1989. Memberships: American Academy of Arts and Letters; American Academy of Arts and Sciences. Address: Beverly Farms, MA 01915, USA.

UPHILL Eric Parrington, b. 15 September 1929, Croydon, Surrey, England. Egyptologist. m. Patricia Ann Read, 1980. Education: BA, Emmanuel College, Cambridge, England, 1954; MA, 1957. Appointments: Lecturer, Archaeology and Egyptology Centre for Extra-Mural Studies Faculty of Continuing Education, Birbeck College, University of London, 1960-; Member, Institute of Archaeology London, 1952-. Publications: Who Was Who in Egyptology, 3rd edition 1995; The Temples of Per Ramesses, 1984; Egyptian Towns and Cities, 1988, 2nd edition, 2001; Pharaoh's Gateway to Eternity The Hawara Labyrinth of King Amenemhat III, 2000; Contributions to: Great Tombs of First Dynasty, III, 1958; MacDonald Library History Civilization From its Beginnings, 1962; Man Settlement and Urbanism, 1972; The Fortress of Buhen: The Archaeological Report, 1979; Articles in Journal of Egyptian Archaeology; Tell el-Amarna City in: Encyclopaedia of the Archaeology of Ancient Egypt, 1999; The Ancient Egyptian View of World History in: Never Had the Like Occurred: Egypt's View of Its Past. Honour: Honorary Research Fellow, Department of Egyptology, University College London. Memberships: Egypt Exploration Society, 1953-. Address: Department of Egyptology, University College London, Gower Street, London WC1E 6BT, England.

URBACH Hansjoerg, b. 26 June 1940, Prenzlau, Germany. Chemist. m. Renate, 2 daughters. Education: Diploma in Chemistry, 1961-67; PhD, Organic Chemistry, 1967-69 and Post Doctoral Research with Professor Kirmse, 1969-70, University of Marburg, Germany. Appointments: Researcher in Medicinal Chemistry, Hoechst Pharmaceuticals, Frankfurt/Main, Germany, 1970-74; Research Delegation to Hoechst-Roussel Pharmaceuticals, Bridgewater, New Jersey, USA, 1974-75; Group-Leader, Medicinal Chemistry Research, 1975-77, Assistant of the Pharmaceutical Board, Research and Production, 1977-79, Main Group-Leader, Medicinal Chemistry Research, 1980-88, Deputy Head, Cardio Vascular Research, 1989-91, Head of General Pharmaceutical Research, 1992-96, Hoechst AG, Frankfurt/Main, Germany; Lecturer, Medicinal Chemistry, University of Mainz, Germany, 1992-. Publications: Author and co-author of 38 publications; Inventor and co-inventor of 65 patents/applications; Researches resulted in 3 products as drugs on the world-wide market: Ramipril (trade-names Delix®, Altace®, Tritace®), trandolapril and quinapril (licensed out). Honour: Honorary Professor, University of Mainz, Germany, 1995. Membership: Society of German Chemists, Medicinal Chemistry. Address: Oberhoechstaedter Strasse 54, 61476 Kronberg/TS, Germany. E-mail: hansjoerg.urbach@aranea.de

URBAN Stan, b. 10 January 1944, Dundee, Scotland. Musician (piano); Singer. m. (1) Erika Kuhnert, 3 September 1963, divorced 1984, 2 sons, (2) Annette Wetterberg, 29 March 1986, deceased 1987, 1 adopted son, (3) Evelyn Jetzschmann, 15 April 1996. Musical Education: Self-taught. Career: Rock'n'roll pianist; Formed own band of German musicians, following tour of Germany with Long John Baldry, 1962; Lived and played in Ibiza, late 60s to 1984; Scandinavia recommended by Robert Plant; Tours of Scandinavia, 1981-. Recordings: Single: Little Queenie, 1982; Albums: Rock 'N' Roll Cocktail, 1982; M'Roccan Rollers, 1986; Live, 1988; Through My Door, 1992; Can't Hold On Can't Let Go, 1995; The Devil Made the Boogie, 1997; Dundee Jivin', 2002. Address: Skaering Sandager 18, 8250 Egå, Denmark.

URBANI Carlo Enrico, b. 1 June 1961, Milan, Italy. Dermatologist. m. Paola Quinteri, 7 May 1988, separated February 1999. Education: Liceo Scientifico Diploma, 1980; Degree, Medicine and Surgery, summa cum laude, University Milan, 1986; Specialisation in Dermatology with full marks, University Milan, 1989; Specialisation in Chemotherapy with full marks, University Milan, 1993. Appointments: Research Department, Internal Medicine, H Sacco, Milan, 1983-86; Fellow Research, Department Dermatology, H S Paolo, Milan, 1986-89; Consultant Dermatology, Scientific Institute for Hospitalisation and Treatment, Hospital San Raffaele-Resnati, Milan, 1989-; Medical Practitioner, Immigration Medical Examination of Health Programmes for Canadian Embassy, 1990-; Consultant Dermatology, Hospital Center Multimedica, Sesto San Giovanni, Milan, 1998-. Publications: Over 116 in science journals, both dermatologic and internal medical genetics; Author: Accessory Mammary Tissue in Clinical Practice, 1995; Complementary Medicine in Dermatology (with others), 1998; Reviewer for: Dermatology; European Journal of Paediatrics. Honours: Distinguished Leadership Award in the field of Dermatology and Medical Genetics, 2000. Memberships: Fellow, American Academy of Dermatology; International Society of Dermatology; Dermatology Foundation; New York Academy of Sciences; Italian Society of Dermatology and Venereology; Italian Society of Dermatology Surgery and Oncology; National Task Force for "Melanoma Prevention Program"; Italian Medical Association; Italian Association for Atopic Eczema; European Academy of Dermatology and Venereology; International Society of Plastic and Aesthetic Dermatology; Italian Society of Chemotherapy; Member IBC Advisory Council; Honorary Member ABI Research Board of Advisors. Address: via G Frua 11, 20146 Milan, Italy.

USHAKOV Nickolai N, b. 8 January 1942, Russia. Metallurgical Engineer. m. Tatyana A, 1 daughter. Education: Graduated, Metallurgy Faculty, Kazakhstan Polytechnical Institute, 1966; Candidate of Technical Science, 1979. Appointments: Director, Eastern Mining and Metallurgical Research Institute for Non-Ferrous Metals; Honourable Professor, East Kazakhstan Technical University; Corresponding Member of Mineral Resources International Academy and Kazakhstan Republic Mineral Resources Academy. Publications: More than 100 publications on science; Author of 36 inventions. Honours: Certificate of the Soviet Union Non-ferrous Metallurgy Ministry for Successful developments in the field of non-ferrous metallurgy sector, 1987; Winner, Prize of the Soviet Union Council of Minister, 1989; One gold, two silver, three bronze medals, Achievements of the Soviet Union National Economy exhibition. Address: VNIItsvetmet 1, Promyshlennaya St, Ust-Kamenogorsk 492020, Kazakhstan Republic.

UYSAL Ilhan, b. 10 January 1968, Cankiri, Turkey. Naval Officer. m. Yesim Uysal, 1 son, 1 daughter. Education: Degree, Electronics, Control Systems, Naval War School, 1990; MSc, Computer Engineering, Bilkent University, 2000. Appointments: Weapons Officer on Warships, 1990-94; Automatic Data processing Officer, Turkish General Staff, 1995-97; Communications and Information Systems Requirements and Concepts Officer, Turkish General Staff, 2000-. Publications: An overview of regression techniques for knowledge recovery, 1999; Regression on Feature Projections, 2000; Instance-based Regression by Partitioning Feature Projections, forthcoming. Honours: MSc and PhD, Scholarships from Bilkent University; Publication Awards, Bilkent University and National Science Council. Address: Akdeniz Cad. 49/1 (Akedeniz 2 Lojmani), Bahcelievler 06490 Ankara, Turkey.

UZUNIDIS Dimitri Nicolas, b. 24 May 1960, Alexandropolis, Greece. Professor; Economist. m. Sophie Boutillier, 1 son, 1 daughter. Education: Diploma, Journalism, Athens, Greece, 1979; Master in Sociology, 1985, PhD, Economics, 1987, University of Paris 10. Appointments: Associate Professor, Institute of political Studies, Lille, France, 1991-96; Assistant Professor, University of Littoral, Dunkirque, France, 1992-; Professor, Postgraduate School, University of Littoral, Invited professor, Institute of Social Management, Paris, 2002-; Director, Research Unit: Innovation and Industrial Redeployment; Editor: Innovations, Economie et Innovation. Publications: Le Travail brade, 1997; La Legende de l'entrepreneur, 1999; Mondialisation et Citoyennete, 1999; L'histoire des entrepreneurs, 2002. Honours: Ministry of Industry, Athens, Greece, 1989; Ministry of National Education, Paris, 1999. Memberships: French Council of Universities; Association of French Economists; The Society of Advancement of Socio-Economics; Observatory of Globalization. Address: Lab RII, 21 Quai de la Citadelle, F-59140 Dunkirque, France.

Dictionary of International Biography

V

VADON Lehel, b. 23 February 1942, Debrecen, Hungary. Professor. m. Márta Tóth, 1 daughter. Education: MA, Hungarian and English Literature and Linguistics, Kossuth Lajos University, Debrecen, Hungary, 1968; Dr Univ., American Literature, 1979, PhD, American Literature, 1994, Dr Habil., American Literature, University of Debrecen, Hungary. Appointments: High School Teacher, Dobó István Grammar School, 1968-73; Assistant Professor, 1973-84, Associate Professor, 1984-96, Eszterházy Károly College; Vice President, Eszterházy Károly Teacher Training College, 1989-94; Founder and Head, Department of American Studies, Hungary, 1990; Founder and Editor, Eger Journal of American Studies, 1993; Director of International Relations, 1994; Professor, 1996, Director, 1998-, Institute of English and American Studies. Publications include: An Anthology of American Prose, 1989; Upton Sinclair in Hungary, 1993; Országh László, 1994; Masterpieces of American Drama: An Anthology and Introduction, 1994; An American Poetry Anthology. The Colonial Period – The Nineteenth Century, 1995; An American Poetry Anthology. The Twentieth Century, 1995; A Bibliography of American Literature and Literary Scholarship in Hungarian Periodicals till 1990, 1997. Honours: Award for Hungarian Higher Education, Pro Academia Paedagogica Agriensi, Outstanding Professional Award. Memberships: Vice President, Hungarian Society for the Study of English; Hungarian Association for American Studies; European Association for American Studies; Chairman, Board of Trustees Országh László Award, 2001-; Hungarian Accreditation Committee, 2001-. Address: 33 Zöldfa Street, Eger 3300, Hungary. E-mail: lvadon@ektf.hu

VADUS Gloria A, b. Forrestville, Pennsylvania, USA. Scientific Document Examiner. Education: Diploma, Cole School of Graphology, California, 1978; Certificate in American College of Graphology, Washington, 1978; BA, Psychology Counselling, Columbia Pacific University, 1981; MA, Psychology, 1982; Diploma, Handwriting Expert, Edith Eisenberg, Bethesda, Maryland, 1991; Certificate, Behavioural Profiling and Certificate, Questioned Documents, American Board of Forensic Examiners. Appointments: Certified Scientific Document Examiner, Registered Graphologist, 1978; President, Owner, Graphinc, Inc, 1985-; Accredited Instructor, Graphology, Montgomery County Schools, Maryland, 1978-79; Instructor: Psychogram Centre, 1978-85, Council Graphological Societies, 1989; Testifier, Superior and Probate Courts; Public Forum Panellist, Lecturer, Researcher, Script Therapist, Personnel Selection Specialist, Writer in field; Consultant Graphologist; Developed Trilogy base for research, American Handwriting Analysis Foundation. Publications: Numerous studies and papers in field; Environmental papers. Honours include: Gold Nib Analyst of the Year Award, American Handwriting Analysis Federation, 1982; Dancing Fan Award, Marine Technology Society, Tokyo Chapter, 1991; Bronze American Honor Medal, ABI, 2001; Meritorious Award, 1994, Outstanding Contribution Certificate, American Board of Forensic Examiners; American Medal of Honor for Contribution to Handwriting, ABI, 2001; Medal of Honour, IBC, 2004; Order of Excellence, IBC, 2004. Memberships include: Fellow, Diplomate, American Board of Forensic Examiners; Council Graphological Societies; National Association of Document Examiners; National Forensic Center; Numerous official positions, American Handwriting Analysis Foundation; Nature Conservancy; Charles F Menninger Society; IEEE Distaff; Soroptomist. Address: 8500 Timber Hill Lane, Potomac, MD20854-4237, USA. E-mail: fvadus@erols.com

VAHABZADEH Abdolvahab, b. 2 October 1952, Ardabil, Iran. Neuroscientist. Education: BSc, Biology, Mashhad University, Iran, 1975; MSc, Physiology, Beheshti University, Iran, 1988; MBBS, Medicine, King's College London, UK, 1991; DPhil, Neuroscience, Oxford University, UK, 1993. Appointments: 2nd Lieutenant, Military Academy, Military Service, Tehran, Iran, 1975-77; Instructor of Physiology, Beheshti University of Medical Science, 1977-88; Student, Oxford University, 1988-93; Vice Chancellor, Ardabil University of Medical Science, 1993-94; Lecturer, Head of Neuroscience Division, Iran University of Medical Science, 1994-2000. Publications: Over 60 books, papers and abstracts. Honours: Scholarship, Iranian Ministry of Health; Honorary Member, Azerbaijan Academy of Science; Member, Green College, Oxford University; Member, New York Academy of Science. Memberships: British Neuroscience Association; Federation of European Neuroscience Society; International Brain Research Organisation; International Organisation of Psychophysiology; American Physiological Society. Address: PO Box 19395-3598, Tehran, Iran. E-mail: vahabzadeha@hotmail.com

VAIDYA Sadashiv Satish, b. 13 October 1961, Chalisgaon (MS), India. Electrical Engineer. m. Pushpalata, 1 son, 1 daughter. Education: HSS, Daly College, Indore (MP), India, 1979; BE, VRCE, Nagpur University, India, 1983. Appointments: Senior Design Engineer (Offshore Projects), Mazagon Dock Ltd, Mumbai, India, 1983-90; Electrical Design Engineer, M/S NPCC, Abu Dhabi, United Arab Emirates, 1991; Electrical Design Engineer, Offshore Engineering, M/S Abu Dhabi Marine Operating Company (ADMA-OPCO Oil and Gas Producing Company), 1992-; Associated with "Sri Sathya Sai Baba", India; Voluntarily building a school for poor students in Bhopal for higher secondary level education, fund-raising. Honours: Recognition Award for Y2K Project, ADMA-OPCO; Spot Recognition Award, ADMA-OPCO, 2001; Listed in Who's Who publications and biographical dictionaries. Address: ADMA-OPCO, ZKAU, 13E-1, PO Box 303, Abu Dhabi, United Arab Emirates. E-mail: vaidya@adma.co.ae

VAJPAYEE Atal Bihari, b. 25 December 1924, Gwalior, Madhya Pradesh, India. Prime Minister of India. Education: Student of political science and law. Career: Journalist; Joined Bharatiya Jana Sangh, now Bharatiya Janata Party, 1951-; Elected to the Lok Sabha, House of the People, 9 times; Elected to the Rajya Sabha, House of the States, twice; Foreign Minister; Leader of the Opposition; Prime Minister of India, 1996, 1998-2004; Minister of Health and Family Welfare, Atomic Energy and Agriculture, 1998-. Publications: New Dimensions of India's Foreign Policy; Jan Sangh Aur Musalmans; Three Decades in Parliament; collections of poems and numerous articles. Honours: Hon PhD, Kanpur University, 1993; Padma Vibhushan; Best Parliamentarian, 1994. Memberships: Chair, National Security Council, 1998-; Member, National Integration Council, 1961-. Address: 7 Race Course Road, New Delhi 110011, India.

VALENTINE Jean, b. 27 April 1934, Chicago, Illinois, USA. Poet; Teacher. m. James Chace, 1957, divorced 1968, 2 daughters. Education: BA, Radcliffe College, 1956. Appointments: Teacher, Swarthmore College, 1968-70; Barnard College, 1968, 1970; Yale University, 1970, 1973-74; Hunter College of the City University of New York, 1970-75; Sarah Lawrence College, 1974-. Publications: Poetry: Dream Barker and Other Poems, 1965; Pilgrims, 1969; Ordinary Things, 1974; Turn, 1977; The Messenger, 1979; Home, Deep, Blue: New and Selected Poems, 1988; Night Lake, 1992; The River at Wolf, 1992; Growing Darkness, Growing Light, 1997; The Cradle of the Real Life, 2000; Door in the Mountain, Collected and New Poems, 2004. Honours:

Yale Series of Younger Poets Award, 1965; National Endowment for the Arts Grant, 1972; Guggenheim Fellowship, 1976. Address: 527 West 110th Street, #81, New York, NY 10025, USA.

VALLBONA Rima-Gretchen Rothe, b. 15 March 1931, San José, Costa Rica, Central America. m. Carlos, 1 son, 3 daughters. Education: BA, BS, Colegio Superior de Senoritas, 1948; Diploma, Professor of French in a Foreign Country, University of Paris Sorbonne, 1953; Diploma in Spanish Philology, University of Salamanca, Spain, 1954; MA, University of Costa Rica, 1962; Doctor in Modern Languages, Middlebury College, USA, 1981. Appointments: Liceo J J Vargas Calvo, Costa Rica, 1955-56; Faculty Member, 1964-, Professor of Spanish, 1978-, Head of Spanish Department, 1966-71, Chairman, Modern Language Department, 1978-80, Cullen Foundation Professor of Spanish, 1989-, Emeritus Professor, 1995-, University of St Thomas, Houston, Texas; Visiting Professor, University of Houston, 1975-76; Visiting Professor, Rice University, 1980-83; University of St Thomas Summer Program in Argentina, 1972; Rice University Summer Program in Spain, 1974. Publications: Numerous short stories and literary essays; 3 novels. Honours: Aquileo J Echeverria Novel Prize, 1968; Agripina Montes de Valle Novel Prize, 1978; Jorge Luis Borges Short Stories Prize, 1977; Southwest Conference of Latin American Studies Literary Award, 1982; Constantin Foundation Grantee for Research, 1981; Ancora Award for Best Book in Costa Rica, 1983-84; Contantion Grant to write dissertation, 1980; Medal of Civil Service for cultural work in the Hispanic World, King Juan Carlos of Spain, 1989; Prize in an Open Contest of Bay Area Writers League, 2003. Memberships: Academia Noreamericana de la Lengua Espanola; Academia Costarricense de la Lengua; Pan American Round Table of Houston. Address: 3706 Lake Street, Houston, TX 77098, USA.

VALNERE Rita, b. 21 September 1929, Bene, Latvia. Painter. m. Eduards Kalnins, 1 daughter. Education: Graduate, J Rozentala Art School, Riga, 1949; Graduate, Latvian Academy of Arts, Painting Department, under leadership of E Kalnins with diploma work, Puku Veikala, 1949-56; Professor, 1985; MA, 1992. Appointments: Exhibitions in Latvia and abroad, 1955-; Creative trip to France, 1965; Pedagogue, 1967-, Assistant Professor, 1978-, Professor, 1985-, Latvian Academy of Arts; Creative trip to Italy, 1970; Recent exhibitions include: One-man shows in Riga, 1977, 1980, Lapmezciema (Tukuma district), 1983, Auce, 1985, Moscow, Artists of USSR Union House, 1987, "Nepartrauktiba", Riga Museum of Arts, 1996-97; Gallery M6 and Gallery Lita, Riga, 2000; Group exhibitions include: Moscow, 1980, Bremen (Germany), 1981, Luxembourg, 1983, Moscow, 1984, Berlin, 1984, Latvian Academy of Arts, Cologne, Dusseldorf, 1990; Works collected in State Art Museum of Latvia, Latvian Artists Union, Gekosso Gallery in Japan, Tretiakov Gallery in Moscow, Ministry of Culture of Russia, Tukums Art Museum and many private collections in Latvia, India, Germany, USA, Japan. Publications: Work appears in monographs, catalogues, books, albums, journals; Honours: Laureate, Baltics 2nd Painting triennial, Vilnius, 1972; Honorary Title of Latvia SSR, 1977; Diploma Latvian Artists Union, Medal and Prize, 1986; Peoples Artist of Latvia, 1987. Memberships: Latvian Artists Union, 1957; International Association of Arts B-13. Address: A Caka iela 67/69, App 1, Riga, Latvia, LV 1001.

VAN ALLEN James Alfred, b. 7 September 1914, Mount Pleasant, Iowa, USA. Physicist. Education: BS, Iowa Wesleyan College, 1935; MS, 1936, PhD, 1939, University of Iowa. Appointments: Research Fellow, Department of Terrestrial Magnetism, Carnegie Institute, Washington, DC, 1939-42; Ordnance and Gunnery Officer, US Navy, 1942-46; Supervisor, High Altitude Research Group and Proximity Fuse Unit, Applied Physics Department, Johns Hopkins University, 1946-50; Organised and led scientific expeditions to Peru, 1949, Gulf of Alaska, 1950, Greenland, 1952, 1957, Antarctica, 1957, to study cosmic radiation; Professor of Physics, Head of Physics Department, University of Iowa, 1951; Project Matterhorn, 1953-54; Research Associate, Princeton University, 1954; Helped organise International Geophysical Year, 1957-58; Professor of Physics, Head of Department, 1951-85, Carver Professor of Physics, 1985-92, Regent Distinguished Professor 1992-, Professor Emeritus, University of Iowa; Key figure in the development of the US space programme; Discovered the earth's magnetosphere, named the "Van Allen Belt". Publications: Physics and Medicine of the Upper Atmosphere; Rocket Exploration of the Upper Atmosphere; Origins of Magnetospheric Physics, 1983; 225 scientific papers. Honours: Numerous honorary DSc degrees; Distinguished Civilian Service Medal, US Army, 1959; NASA Medal for Exceptional Scientific Achievement, 1974; Distinguished Public Service Award, US Navy, 1976; Award of Merit, American Consulting Engineers Council, 1978; Space Science Award, American Institute of Aeronautics and Astronautics, 1982; Crawford Prize, Swedish Royal Academy of Sciences, 1989. Address: Department of Physics and Astronomy, 701 Van Allen Hall, University of Iowa, Iowa City, IA 52242, USA.

VAN BLARICOM Richard, b. 19 July 1937, Hood River, Oregon, USA. Geophysicist. m. Jeanne, 2 sons, 2 daughters. Education: BS, Geology, Portland State College, 1965; MS, Geophysics, University of Arizona, 1967; PhD, Geology, Geophysics, Geoelectrochemistry, Hydrology, University of Idaho, 1999. Appointments: Electronic Instructor US Army, Electronic Technician, RCA, 1957-62; Crew Chief, MaPhar Geophysics, 1963-67; Division Geophysicist, ASARCO, 1967-74; Chief Geophysicist, Cominco America Inc, 1976-98, retired; Consulting Geophysicist, Paterson Grant and Watson, 1998-2000; Chief Geophysicist, Principal, VGS, 1974-76, 1998-; Adjunct Professor, University of Idaho, 2001-. Publications: Numerous papers in scientific journals including most recently: Interpretation of the Magnetics and the Mid-continent of the US, 1998; Dissertation The Principles and Application of Geoelectrochemical Sampling for Mineral Exploration and Environmental Testing, 1999; Ultra-High Resolution Shallow Resistivity Survey Using Corrected Resistivity, 2002. Honours: Undergraduate Award, Sigma Xi, 1965; American Men and Women in Science. 1997. Memberships: American Association for the Advancement of Science; Society of Exploration Geophysicists; American Geophysicists Union; International Association of Geomagnetism and Aeronomy. Address: N 22710 Perry Road, Colbert, WA 99005, USA. E-mail: geodutch@attbi.com

VAN DE KAMP Alexandra, b. 23 April 1965, Portchester, New York, USA. Poet; Editor; Professor. m. William D Glenn III. Education: BA, English, University College, London, Johns Hopkins University, Baltimore, USA, 1987; Master of Fine Arts, Poetry, University of Washington, Seattle, 1991. Appointments: Teaching Assistant, University of Washington, 1989-91; Reading Series Organiser, The Watermark Series, Seattle, 1990-91; Office Manager, Kaplan Educational Center, Seattle, 1992-93; Full-time ESL Instructor, Linguacenter, Madrid, Spain, 1993-94; Director of Studies, ESL Instructor, Linford Academy, Madrid, 1994-98; Founder, Madrid Writers Group, Spain, 1995-97; ESL Instructor, Eco 3, Madrid, 1998-99; Editor and co-founder, Terra Incognita magazine, Brooklyn, 1998-; ESL Instructor, Training Express, Madrid, 1999-2000; Adjunct Professor, English Language Center, New School University, New York, 2001; Adjunct Professor, Intensive English Program, Long Island University, 2000-; Curator, Latino and Latin American Reading Series, Cornelia Street Café, New York, 2003-. Publications: Prose, numerous poems and translations. Honours: Nominated, Pushcart Prize for Essay, 1994; 2001 Quentin R Howard Poetry Prize; Nominated, 2003 Pushcart Prize in Poetry. Memberships: Council of Literary Magazines and Presses, Terra Incognita. Address: 469 47th Street, Brooklyn, NY 11220, USA. E-mail: avandekamp65@yahoo.com

VAN DEN BERGHE Pierre Louis, b. 30 January 1933, Lubumbashi, Congo. Professor Emeritus of Sociology and Anthropology. m. Irmgard Cornelia Niehuis, 3 sons. Education: BA, Distinction, Political Science, 1952, MA, Sociology, 1953, Stanford University, USA; Elève Titulaire de l'Ecole Pratique des Hautes Etudes, Sorbonne, France, 1957; MA, Sociology, 1959, PhD, Sociology, 1960, Harvard University, USA. Appointments: Teaching Fellow, Harvard University, USA, 1957-60; Ford Foundation Research Fellow, Lecturer, University of Natal, South Africa, 1960-61; Visiting Lecturer, Sorbonne, France, 1962; Assistant Professor, Wesleyan University, USA, 1962-63; Associate Professor, State University of New York at Buffalo, 1963-65; Associate Professor, University of Washington, USA, 1965-67; Visiting Rockefeller Professor, University of Nairobi, Kenya and University of Ibadan, Nigeria, 1967-69; Professor, University of Washington, USA, 1967-98; Visiting Professor, University of Haifa, Israel, 1976; Senior Fulbright Fellow, University of New South Wales, Australia, 1982; Visiting Professor, Université Louis Pasteur, Strasbourg, France, 1983; Fellow, Center for Advanced Study in the Behavioral Sciences, Stanford University, USA, 1984-85; Visiting Professor, University of Tuebingen, Germany, 1986, University of Tel Aviv, Israel, 1988, University of Cape Town, South Africa, 1989; Professor Emeritus, University of Washington, USA, 1998-. Publications: 22 books and numerous articles in professional journals. Address: University of Washington, Department of Sociology, Seattle, WA 98195-3340, USA.

VAN DEN BROEK Gerard J, b. 18 July 1953, Netherlands. Director. m. Claudia Weertman, 1 son, 1 daughter. Education: BA, 1977, MA, 1980, Anthropology, Doctor of Social Sciences, 1986, Leiden University. Appointments: Director, Management, Moscow, St Petersburg Exhibitions and Conferences, 1993; Senior Consultant, Major Financial Institution; Account Manager, Public Relations; Science Journalist, Publicist, numerous periodicals; Research Associate, Leiden University; Managing Director, Bibliotheca Philosophica Hermetica, 1991-93; Director, Provincial Library of Friesland, 1996-2001; Director, Central Archives Selection Services, Home Office, 2001-. Publications: Numerous articles in professional international journals. Honours include: Grants, Netherlands Organization for Pure Scientific Research, 1983, 1984; Fulbright Grant, Netherlands-America Commission for Educational Exchange, 1984. Memberships include: American Board of Investigation, American Biographical Center; Netherlands Semiotic Society, Chair, 1991-94; Chair, Communal Commission of the Arts, 1997-2001; Board Member, Oldambt Historiography Foundation, 2001-; Board Member, Memorial Foundation, Winschoten, 2004-. Address: Rijkstraatweg 124, 9752 BK Haren, The Netherlands.

VAN DUYN Mona (Jane), b. 9 May 1921, Waterloo, Iowa, USA. Poet; Writer; Critic; Editor; Reviewer; Lecturer. m. Jarvis A Thurston, 31 August 1943. Education: BA, Iowa State Teachers College, 1942; MA, State University of Iowa, 1943. Appointments: Reviewer, Poetry magazine, 1944-70; Instructor in English, State University of Iowa, 1945, University of Louisville, 1946-50; Founder-Editor (with Jarvis A Thurston), Perspective: A Quarterly of Literature, 1947-67; Lecturer in English, 1950-67, Adjunct Professor, 1983, Visiting Hurst Professor, 1987, Washington University, St Louis; Poetry Advisor, College English, 1955-57; Lecturer, Salzburg Seminar in American Studies, 1973; Poet-in-Residence, Bread Loaf Writing Conferences, 1974, 1976; Poet

Laureate of the USA, 1992-93; Numerous poetry readings. Publications: Valentines to the Wide World: Poems, 1959; A Time of Bees, 1964; To See, To Take, 1970; Bedtime Stories, 1972; Merciful Disguises: Poems Published and Unpublished, 1973; Letters From a Father and Other Poems, 1982; Near Changes: Poems, 1990; Lives and Deaths of the Poets and Non-Poets, 1991; If It Be Not I: Collected Poems, 1993; Firefall, 1993; Selected Poems, 2002. Contributions to: Many anthologies; Poems, criticism, reviews, and short stories in various periodicals. Honours: Eunice Tietjens Memorial Prize, 1956; National Endowment for the Arts Grants, 1966-67, 1985; Harriet Monroe Memorial Prize, 1968; Hart Crane Memorial Award, 1968; 1st Prize, Borestone Mountain Awards, 1968; Bollingen Prize, 1970; National Book Award for Poetry, 1971; Guggenheim Fellowship, 1972-73; Loines Prize, National Institute of Arts and Letters, 1976; Fellow, Academy of American Poets, 1981; Sandburg Prize, Cornell College, 1982; Shelley Memorial Award, Poetry Society of America, 1987; Ruth Lilly Prize, 1989; Pulitzer Prize in Poetry, 1991. Memberships: Academy of American Poets, chancellor, 1985; National Institute of Arts and Letters. Address: 7505 Teasdale Avenue, St Louis, MO 63130, USA.

VAN DYCK Stephan, b. Brussels. Singer (Tenor); Voice Teacher. Education: Diplome Superieur for voice, CRBM, Brussels; First prize, CNSSM, Paris; Licenc es Lettres, Musicology, ULB, Brussels. Debut: Weihnachts Oratorium, Brussels, 1985. Career: Baroque opera and oratorio, recital French cantatas and lieder; Many performances for TV and radio. Recordings: More than 60 CD's. Address: 29 Rue Picolome, 6238 Luttre, Belgium.

VAN GINNEKEN Andreas Johannes, b. 1 January 1935, Wynegem, Belgium. Scientist. m. Lydia D Thompson, 1 son. Education: MSc, 1960, PhD, 1966, Chemistry, University of Chicago, USA. Appointments: Postdoctoral Fellow, Physics Department, McGill University, 1966-70; Staff Member, Fermilab, 1970-. Publications: Numerous articles in journals such as Physical Review and Physical Review Letters, Nuclear Instruments and Methods; Numerous presentations to conferences and workshops. Memberships: American Physical Society. Address: Fermilab, Box 500, Batavia, IL 60510, USA. E-mail: vangin@fnal.gov

VAN KHACHATUR (Vanik Khachaturyan), b. 1926, Baku, Azerbaijan. Architect; Sculptor; Artist; Scientist; Poet. m. Arpenik Gazaryan, 1 son. Education: Yerevan Institute of Fine Arts, Armenia, 1954; PhD in Art Criticism, 1966. Career: Senior Scientific Worker of the Institute of Art, Academy of Sciences in Armenia, 1957-; Doctor of Architecture, "Color in Architecture of Armenia from IV to XIX AD", 2001; A series of paintings: "The Terrible World" (0.4-6)sqm, "The World of Ancestors" (0.8-24)sqm, "Cosmic Symphony" (0.4-2.56)sqm, "Geometrical World" (0.4-3)sqm, "Apocalypse" (0.4-16.2)sqm; Relief of red and black stone on the wall of Olympic Centre in Tsakhkadzor (238sqm), 1967; Front wall of Spendiarov Music school from white and black stone (150sqm), Yerevan, 1970; Monument to "Yeghern", abstract geometrical sculpture, pink tufa Nor-Kharberrd, 1964 (5x2.5x2.5); Architecture: Designs of towns of Future "Dynamically Developing in the Air", author's technique, certificate N1178889, Moscow, 1985; Participant in exhibitions in Armenia and abroad; Main works: Matenadaran, "History of Armenia Culture", (fresco, plaster, tempera), Ancient Period (4.5x2) 9sqm, Hellenistic Period (4.5x2) 9sqm, Medieval Period (7x2) 14sqm, 1956-59; Matenadaran, "Avarayr Battle", mosaic with smelt (7x3.5) 24.5sqm, 1956-60; Central Building of the Presidium of the Academy of Sciences of the Republic of Armenia, Mesrop Mashtots, author's technique (6x8) 48sqm, Movses Khorenatsi, author's technique (6x8) 48sqm, 1958; Architectural construction, concrete: Sea-Gull, Entrance to Yerevan, 1960;

Architectural construction, concrete basalt, Monument-ensemble devoted to the Victims of Genocide in "Yeghern", Tsitsernakaberd, monumental tectonic work, black and white tufa, author's technique, 1964-67; Front Wall of a house near the hotel "Ani" in Yerevan (225sqm), 1965; Sculptural relief, copper chasing (44x3), "2000 Years of Armenian Theatre", Dramatic Theatre, Leninakan, 1964-74. Publications: 90 scientific articles; Books: "Urartians, Who are They?", 1991; A volume of poetry, 1998; 2600 paintings given as a gift to the Armenian people. Memberships: Founder, Modern Monumental Art in Armenia, 1956; Union of Architects of Armenia, 1963; Union of Painters of Armenia, 1984. Address: Apt 29, Yeznik Koghbatsi 42, 375002, Yerevan, Armenia. E-mail: anararka-89@rambler.ru Website: www.geocities.com/vankhachatour

VAN PRAAG Herman Meir, b. 17 October 1929, Schiedam, The Netherlands. Psychiatrist. m. Cornelia Eikens, 3 sons, 1 daughter. Education: MD, State University, Leiden, The Netherlands, 1948-56; PhD, University of Utrecht, 1958-62; 4 years Psychiatry and Psychotherapy, 1 year, Neurobiology, Foundation for Advanced Clinical Training, Rotterdam, 1958-63. Appointments: Chief of Staff, Department of Psychiatry, Dijkzigt Hospital, Rotterdam, 1963-66; Founder, 1st Head of Department of Biological Psychiatry State University of Gronigen, 1966-77; Associate Professor, 1968, Professor, 1970, Biological Psychiatry, State University Groningen; Lady Davis Visiting Professor, Hebrew University, Jerusalem, Israel, 1976-77; Professor and Head of Department of Psychiatry, Academic Hospital, State University, Utrecht, 1977-82; Professor, Chairman, Department of Psychiatry, Albert Einstein College of Medicine, Bronx, New York; Psychiatrist-in-Chief, Montefiore Medical Center, Bronx, 1982-92; Professor and Chairman, Department of Psychiatry and Neuropsychology, Maastricht University, 1992-97; Interim Head of Department of Psychiatry and Neuropsychology, Academic Hospital, Maastricht, 1997-99; Scientific Advisor, Department of Psychiatry and Neuropsychology, Academic Hospital, Maastricht, 1999-. Publications: 600 in international professional journals. Honours: Recipient of many honours and distinctions; Knighted by Queen Beatrix of the Netherlands, 1989; Guest speaker, lecturer, in many countries; Visiting professorships including: H B Williams Travelling Professor of the Royal Australian and New Zealand College of Psychiatrists, 1997. Memberships include: Fellow, New York Academy of Medicine, 1983; Fellow, American Psychopathological Association, 1984; Fellow, American College of Neuropsychopharmacology, 1987; Fellow, American Psychiatric Association, 1992; Member, Royal Society of Arts and Scientists of the Netherlands, 1996; Founding Member, Foundation for Psychiatry and Religion; Chairman, Section Religion, Spirituality and Psychiatry, World Psychiatric Association. Address: University Hospital Maastricht, Department of Psychiatry, PO Box 5800, 6202 AZ Maastricht, The Netherlands.

VAN SANT Gus Jr, b. 1952, Louisville, Kentucky, USA. Film Director; Screenwriter. Education: Rhode Island School of Design. Appointments: Former Production Assistant to Ken Shapiro. Films include: Mala Noche; Drugstore Cowboy, 1989; My Own Private Idaho, 1991; Even Cowgirls Get the Blues, 1993; To Die For, 1995; Kids, 1995; Ballad of the Skeletons, 1996; Good Will Hunting, 1997; Psycho, 1998; Finding Forrester, 2000. Publications: 108 Portraits, 1995; Pink, 1997. Honours: National Society of Film Critics Awards for Best Director and Screenplay, 1990; New York Film Critics and Los Angeles Film Critics Award for Best Screenplay, 1989; PEN Literary Award for Best Screenplay Adaptation, 1989. Address: c/o William Morris Agency Inc, 151 South El Camino Drive, Beverly Hills, CA 90212, USA.

VANAHALLI Umesh, b. 1 June 1962, Byadagi. Medical Homeopathic Doctor. m. Vandana, 1 son. Education: Medical Laboratory Technologist, 1981; Homeopathic Doctor, 1985. Appointments: President, Dr HRH MP Association; Former Founder, Managing Director, Gold Pharma, Proprietor, Mahesh Homeopathic Drug House; Founder, Homeopathic Research Centre for Aids Cancer and Chronic Diseases; Proprietor, Dr Vanahalli Homoeo Pharmaceuticals. Publications: Homeoking, Monthly Kannada Magazine; Articles: Cancer, Cancer, Cancer; Immuninum New Medicine for Aids Research Articles; Organising Secretary, National Homeopathic Conference, Belgaum, India, 2000. Honours: Best Promoter of Homeopathy in Rural Places; Winner, Dr Hahnemann's Award. Memberships: National and International Homeo Conferences; Speaker, World Homeopathic Conference on Cancer, Culcutta. Address: PO Mahalingpur, Dt Bagalkot, Karnatak, India 587312.

VANDE KEMP Hendrika, b. 13 December 1948, Voorthuizen, Gelderland, The Netherlands. Clinical Psychologist; Educator. Education: BA, Hope College, 1971; MS, 1974, PhD, 1977, University of Massachusetts/Amherst. Appointments: Internship, Clinical Psychology, Topeka State Hospital, 1975-76; Instructor in Psychology, 1976-77, Assistant Professor in Psychology, 1977-81, Associate Professor of Psychology, 1982-91, Professor of Psychology, 1992-2001, Graduate School of Psychology, Fuller Theological Seminary. Publications: Co-author: Femininity and Shame: Women and men giving voice to the feminine, 1997; Humanistic Psychology and Feminist Psychology, 1999; Introduction to the special issue on historical aspects of dreaming, 2000; Author: Christian Psychologies for the 21st Century: Lessons from History, 1998; Grieving the death of a sibling or the death of a friend, 1999; Mentoring as a witness to the way of exchange, 2000; Author and co-author of numerous articles. Honours include: National Honor Society, 1966; Valedictorian, Lakewood Public Schools, 1967; Eta Sigma Phi, National Honorary Classical Fraternity, 1968; Psi Chi, National Honor Society in Psychology, 1969; Pi Sigma Alpha, 1970; Phi Beta Kappa, Zeta of Michigan, 1971; Hope College Scholarship, Michigan Competitive Scholarship, Michigan Tuition Grant, 1967-1971; Fellow, American Psychological Association, Division 26, 1989; William Bier Award, 1990; C Davis Weyerhaeuser Award for Excellence, 1996; John Templeton Foundation Award, 1996; Distinguished Service Award, Theoretical and Philosophical Psychology, 2000; Distinguished Service Award, Psychology of Religion, 2001. Memberships: International Society for the History of the Behavioural and Social Sciences; American Psychological Association; American Association for Marriage and Family Therapy. E-mail: hendrika@earthlink.net

VANDEN DRIESEN Cynthia Anne, b. Sri Lanka. University Lecturer. m. Ian Vanden Driesen, 1 son, 3 daughters. Education: BA (Hons) English, University of Ceylon; MA, English, 1972, PhD, English, 1980, University of Western Australia; Dip Ed, Murdoch University, Western Australia, 1978. Appointments: Lecturer, University of Ceylon, 1968; Lecturer, University of Ile-Ife, Nigeria, 1974; Australian Commonwealth Public Service Senior Lecturer, Edith Cowan University, Western Australia, 1981-. Publications: Numerous articles in journals on Australian and post-colonial literature; 3 authored books; 3 co-edited books. Honours: University of Ceylon Entrance Scholarship, University of Ceylon; Pettah Library Prize for English, University of Ceylon; Australian Commonwealth Government Scholarship for PhD. Memberships: Australian President, Association for Study of Australia in Asia; Founder Member, Western Australian Women Against War. Address: School of International Community & Cultural Studies, Edith Cowan University, 2 Bradford Street, Mt Lawley, Perth, Western Australia.

Dictionary of International Biography

VANDIVER Frank Everson, b. 9 December 1925, Austin, Texas, USA. Historian; Educator. m. (1) Carol Sue Smith, 19 April 1952, deceased 1979, 1 son, 2 daughters, (2) Renee Aubry, 21 March 1980. Education: MA, University of Texas, 1949; PhD, Tulane University, 1951; MA hons, University of Oxford, 1963. Appointments: Assistant Professor of History, Washington University, St Louis, 1952-55; Professor of History, Louisiana State University, 1953-57; Assistant Professor of History, 1955-56, Associate Professor, 1956-58, Professor of History, 1958-65, Harris Masterson Jr Professor of History, 1965-79, Acting President, 1969-70, Provost, 1970-79, Vice President, 1975-79, Rice University; Harmsworth Professor of American History, University of Oxford, 1963-64; President and Chancellor, North Texas State University at Denton and Texas College of Osteopathic Medicine, 1979-81; President, 1981-88, President Emeritus and Distinguished University Professor, 1988-, Texas A & M University at College Station; Chairman of the Board, 1992-97, Acting President, 1997-98, American University, Cairo; Various visiting lectureships and professorships. Publications: Ploughshares Into Swords: Josiah Gorgas and the Confederate Command System, 1956; Mighty Stonewall, 1957; Fields of Glory (with W H Nelson), 1960; Jubal's Raid, 1960; Basic History of the Confederacy, 1962; Jefferson Davis and the Confederate State, 1964; Their Tattered Flags: The Epic of the Confederacy, 1970; The Southwest: South or West?, 1975; Black Jack: The Life and Times of John J Pershing, 1977; The Long Loom of Lincoln, 1986; Blood Brothers: A Short History of the Civil War, 1992; Shadows of Vietnam: Lyndon Johnson's Wars, 1997; 1001 Things Everyone Should Know About the Civil War, 1999, paperback 2000; 1001 Things Everyone Should Know About World War II, 2002, paperback 2003. Editor: Several volumes. Contributions to: Oxford Book of United States Military History; Facing Armageddon (chapters); Passchendaele in Perspective (chapters). Honours: Many honorary doctorates; Guggenheim Fellowship, 1955-56; Carr P Collins Prize, Texas Institute of Letters, 1958; Harry S Truman Award, Kansas City Civil War Round Table, 1970; Fletcher Pratt Award, New York Civil War Round Table, 1970; Outstanding Civilian Service Medal, Department of the Army, 1974; Nevins-Freeman Award, Chicago Civil War Round Table, 1982; T Harry Williams Memorial Award, 1985; Honorary Knight of San Jacinto, 1993. Memberships: American Historical Association; Jefferson Davis Association; Organization of American Historians; Phi Beta Kappa; Society of American Historians; Southern Historical Association, president, 1975-76; Texas Historical Association, fellow; Texas Institute of Letters; Texas Philosophical Society, president, 1978; Salado Centre for the Humanities, director. Address: A & M University, College Station, TX 77843, USA.

VANDROSS Luther, b. 20 April 1951, New York, USA. Singer; Songwriter; Arranger; Producer. Career: Member, Listen My Brother (musical theatre workshop), Harlem, 1973; Session singer (recordings and commercials), arranger, 1974-80; Leader, own group, Luther, 1976-77; Solo artiste, 1980-; Regular international concerts. Compositions include: Fascination, David Bowie; You Stopped Lovin' Me, Roberta Flack; Recordings: Albums: Luther, 1976; This Close To You, 1977; Solo albums: Never Too Much, 1981; Forever For Always For Love, 1982; Busy Body, 1984; Give Me The Reason, 1986; Any Love, 1988; The Best Of Luther Vandross, 1989; Power Of Love, 1991; Never Let Me Go, 1993; Songs, 1994; This is Christmas, 1995; Your Secret Love, 1996; I Know, 1998; Hit singles include: The Night I Fell In Love, 1985; Give Me The Reason, from film Ruthless People, 1986; Stop To Love, 1987; There's Nothing Better Than Love, duet with Gregory Hines, 1987; Any Love, 1989; She Won't Talk To Me, 1989; Here And Now, 1990; Power Of Love/Love Power, 1991; Don't Want To Be A Fool, 1991; The Best Things In Life Are Free, duet with Janet Jackson, from film Mo' Money, 1992; Love The One You're

With, 1995; Going in Circles, 1995; I Can Make It Better, 1996; Are You Using Me?, 1998; Heart of a Hero, 1999; Sessions as backing singer include: Young Americans, David Bowie, 1974; Songs For The New Depression, Bette Midler, 1975; Sounds And Stuff Like That, Quincy Jones, 1978; Le Freak, Chic, 1978; We Are Family, Sister Sledge, 1978; Other sessions for Ringo Starr; Carly Simon; Chaka Khan; Average White Band; Vocal arranger, No More Tears, Donna Summer and Barbra Streisand, 1979; Producer, recordings by Aretha Franklin; Dionne Warwick; Diana Ross; Whitney Houston; Contributor, Voices That Care (Red Cross charity record), 1991; The Heart Of A Hero (AIDS research benefit record), 1992. Honours include: MVP Background Singer, 1977-80; Grammy Awards: Best R&B Vocal Performance, 1991, 1992; Best R&B Song, 1992; Grammy Nomination, Best R&B Vocal, 1987; Soul Train Music Awards: Best Male R&B Album, 1987, 1992; Best Male R&B Single, 1990; American Music Awards: Favourite Soul/R&B Male Artist, 1988, 1990, 1992; Favourite Soul/R&B Album, 1992; NAACP Image Awards: Best Male Artist, 1990; Best Male Vocalist, Best Album, 1992; Luther Vandross Day, Los Angeles, 1991. Address: Epic Records, 550 Madison Avenue, New York, NY 10022, USA..

VANDVIK Bodvar, b. 1 August 1937, Oslo, Norway. Physician. m. Inger Helene, 17 June 1971, 2 sons, 1 daughter. Education: MD, School of Medicine, University of Oslo, 1962; Certificate of Speciality, Neurology, 1970; Doctor of Medicine, 1977. Appointments: Consultant, Department of Neurology, National Hospital, 1979-88; Professor of Medicine, University of Oslo, 1979-2003; Chief Consultant, Director, Department of Neurology, Oslo City Hospital, 1989-95; Director, Centre of Medical Ethics, 1995-96; Consultant, Department of Neurology, Oslo City Hospitals, 1997-2003; Retired, 2003. Publications: Over 100 articles in professional national and international medicine journals. Honours: Reberg's Legacy Prize, University of Oslo, 1975; Monrad-Krohn's Legacy Prize, University of Oslo, 1977. Memberships: Norwegian Medical Association; Norwegian Neurology Association; World Federation of Neurology; Scandinavian Society of Immunology. Address: Staverbakken 8, 1341 Slependen, Norway.

VANYUSHIN Boris, b. 16 February 1935, Tula, Russia. Professor. m. Abrosimova Valeria Ivanovna. Education: MS, Biology Department, Moscow State University, 1957; PhD, Bakh Biochemistry Institute, Academy of Sciences, Moscow, 1961; DSci, Biology Department, Moscow State University, 1973. Appointments: Junior Research Scientist, Plant Biochemistry Department, 1960-64, Senior Research Scientist, Laboratory of Bio-organic Chemistry, 1965-73, Moscow State University; Postdoctoral Research Fellow, Virus Research Unit ARC, Cambridge, England, 1964-65; Head, Department of Molecular Bases of Ontogenesis, Belozersky Institute, Moscow State University, 1973-; Regent's Lecturer, Department of Biochemistry, University of California, USA, 1976; UNESCO Expert in Molecular Biology, Lucknow University, India, 1978; Head, Laboratory of Hormonal Regulation of Plant Ontogenesis, Institute of Agricultural Biotechnology, Moscow, 1985-96; Visiting Professor, University of Catania, Italy, 1990; Visiting Research Fellow, National Centre for Toxicology Research, Arkansas, USA, 1994-95. Publications: Book, Molecular and Genetic Mechanisms of Ageing, 1977; Author of more than 400 papers in various journals. Honours: Award, Lomonosov Prize, 2002; Grants, International Science Foundation, 1994-95; Russian Foundation of Fundamental Research, 1993-95, 1996-98, 1999-. Memberships: Russian Biochemical Society; Russian Society of Plant Physiologists; DNA Methylation Society; Corresponding Member,

Russian Academy of Sciences. Address: Belozersky Institute of Physico-Chemical Biology, Moscow State University, 119992 Moscow, Russia. E-mail: vanyush@belozersky.msu.ru

VARGA László, b. 17 April 1927, Békéscsaba, Hungary. Engineer; Professor of Geotechnics. m. Maria Wellmann, 1 son, 1 daughter. Education: BS, Engineering, 1950; University Doctorate, 1960; Candidate of Technical Science (PhD equivalent), Hungarian Academy of Sciences, 1964. Appointments: Assistant Professor, 1950-59, Adjunct, 1959-65, Associate Professor, 1965-72, Technical University Budapest; Professor, Head of Department of Geotechnics, 1972-90, Technical College of Győr. Publications: 65 papers, reports; 23 lecture notes; Textbooks and 17 (mostly as co-author) technical books. Honours: Order of Labour, 1981; Pro Universitate Győr, 1995; Széchy Prize, 2000; Zielinski Prize, 2000. Memberships: International Society for Soil Mechanics and Geotechnical Engineering, 1966-; Hungarian Chamber of Engineers, 1990-. Address: H-9023 Győr, Tihanyi Árpád Street 58, Hungary.

VARGAS-HERNÁNDEZ José Guadalupe, b. 8 November 1951, Zapotiltic, Jalisco, México. Economist. m. Maria Elba González, 6 May 1976, 3 sons. Education: MBA, 1980; PhD, Economics, 1992; PhD, Public Management, 1998. Appointments: Professor, Instituto Tecnológico de Cd Guzmán, 1974-94; Director, Mass Media Communication, Presidencia Municipal Cd Guzmán, Jalisco, 1985-1990; Director, Patronato Instituto Tecnológico de Cd Guzmán, 1983-93; General Manager, Consejo de Colaboración Ciudadana, Cd Guzman, 1992-94; CEO, Novacal, 1994-95; Independent Consultant, 1980-2000; Research Professor, Instituto Tecnológico de Colima, 1994-2000; Research Professor, Universidad de Colima, 1994-2000; Research Professor, Instituto Tecnológico de Cd Guzmán, 2000-; Research Professor, Centro Universiario del Sur, Universidad de Guadalajara, 2000-; Research Professor, Doctorate in Management Studies, UASLP. Publications: Over 300 essays and articles in professional scientific journals and reviews in the field of organisational economics; Books A Challenge to the Quest for Leadership and Managerial Effectiveness, 1980; La Culturo craziz en México;. Honours include: Sommer Al Mérito; CONACYT Award; PSU Award; British Council Award, 1982. Memberships: Academy of Management; British Academy of Management; Eastern Region of Organisation of Public Administrators. Address: Cerrada Petronilo López 31, Cd Guzmán, Jalisco 49000, México. E-mail: jvargas@cusur.udg.mx

VARMAN Arumugam Raghu, b. 1 July 1941, Aruppukottai, India. Scientist. m. Amirtha Raghu Varman, 1 daughter. Education: BSc, 1961, MSc, 1963, PhD, 1969, University of Madras, Madras; Postdoctoral Research Fellow, Department of Entomology, University of Georgia, Athens, USA, 1968-70; Alexander von Humboldt Fellow, Institut für Physiologische Chemie, Philipps Universität, Marburg, Germany, 1971-74. Appointments: Council of Scientific and Industrial Research Pool Officer, Biochemistry Department, A 11 MS, New Delhi, 1974-75; Reader, Professor, Department of Zoology, North-Eastern Hill University, Shillong, 1975-. Publications: Curr Sci, India, vol 36: 436-437, 1967; Ent exp and appl, vol 12: 183-190, 1969; Nature, vol 237: 457, 1972; Indian Zoologist, vol 17: 1-5, 1993; Annals Ent, India, vol 11: 43-46, 1993, vol 14: 79-81, 1996; J Endo Reprod, Vol 1: 22-26, 1997. Honours: Alexander von Humboldt Fellow, Germany, 1971-73; Gold Medallist, Zoological Society of India, 1999. Memberships: Life Member, Indian Science Congress; Life Member, Indian Society of Radiation Biology. Address: Department of Zoology, North-Eastern Hill University, Shillong 793022, Meghalaya, India. E-mail: arvnchu@hotmail.com

VARNIK Airi, b. 26 October 1939, Estonia. Psychiatrist. m. Tõnis Varnik, 1 son. Education: Psychiatrist MD, Tartu University, Estonia, 1969; MD, PhD, Geriatric Psychiatry, Leningrad Bechterev Institute, Russia, 1973; MD, PhD, Psychiatry, Suicidology, Karolinska Institute, Sweden, 1997. Appointments: Chief Forensic Psychiatrist of Estonia, 1987-93; Director, Estonian-Swedish Institute of Suicidology, 1993-; Professor, Tartu University, Estonia, 1998-. Publications: Book: Suicide in the Baltic Countries and in the Former Republic of the USSR; Numerous articles in international scientific journals on suicide research and prevention. Honours: Golden Medal, High School Graduation; Award from Estonian Ministry of Foreign Affairs for Scientific Collaboration over the World, 2003. Memberships: President, Internet Network of Survivors of Suicide; National Representative, JASP; Member of Steering Group, WHO/Ewes Network of Suicide Prevention; WPA. Address: Vabaduse Pst 90, Tallinn 11619, Estonia. E-mail: airiv@online.ee

VASILAKAKOS John, b. 3 December 1951, Greece. Lecturer; Writer; Literary Translator. m. Mary Mylonas, 12 December 1982, 2 daughters. Education: BA, University of Melbourne, 1979; BLitt, University of New England, 1982; RMIT Assoc DIPL, Interpreting and Translating, 1982; MA (Hons), 1984, PhD, 1994, University of Melbourne. Appointments include: Lecturer, Modern Greek, Deakin University, 1990; PhD Researcher, 1991-93; Lecturer, Modern Greek, Deakin University, 1994; Full-time Literary Translator, Writer and Freelance Book Reviewer, 1995-2000; Lecturer, Interpreting and Translating, RMIT University, 2000-04. Publications include: Studies in Modern Greek Literature, 1980; The Identity, 1982; The Set-Up, 1987; Modern Greek Literature of the Diaspora: Australia, 1997; The Greek Civil War in Post-War Greek Prose 1946-58, 2000; 7 translations of books into Greek, 1976-2001. Contributions: Articles published in magazines and journals in Australia, Greece and USA. Honours include: Travel research grants to Canada and Greece, University of Melbourne, 1990, 1991; Award, Australian-Greek Hellenic Association, 1991; Honorary plaque, Laconians of Montreal, Canada, 1991; Honorary diploma, Greek-Australian Cultural League of Melbourne and Cultural Association for Hellenic Women of Victoria, 2000; Honorary diploma, International Society of Greek Writers (Athens), 2001; Special edition of Athenian literary journal Eolika Grammata, 2001; Honorary Diploma, American Biographical Institute, 2001. Memberships: Society of Greek Men of Letters (Athens); Greek-Australian Cultural League of Melbourne and Victoria; Australian Society of Authors. Address: 33 Woodfull St, Prahran Vic, Melbourne 3181, Australia.

VASILE Cornelia, b. 12 September 1942, Homoraciu, Prahova, Romania. Chemist. Education: Chemist Degree, Bucharest University, 1965; PhD, Physical Chemistry, 1971. Appointments: Assistant Professor, Medicine and Pharmacy University, 1965-66; Researcher, Senior Researcher, P Poni Institute, 1965-; Associate Professor, Laval University, Quebec, Gh ASACHI, Technical University, Iasi and Al I Cuza University, 1995-. Publications: 250 scientific papers, 7 books. Honours: Prize, Romanian Academy, 1971. Memberships: Planetary Society; IUPAC; Fulbright Association. Address: P Poni Institute of Macromolecular Chemistry, 41A Gr G Voda Alley, RO 700487 Iasi, Romania.

VASILE Tomiţa-Constantin, b. 28 December 1954, Drobeta Turnu Severin, Romania. Professor. 1 son. Education: Diploma, University of Mathematics, 1978; University Lecturer, 1994; Diploma, Doctor in Science, 2002. Appointment: University Lecturer, Dobeta Turnu Severin Mathematics College, Romania. Publications: Special Mathematics, 1999; Applied Mathematics, 2002; Flows and Energies on Riemann Manifolds. Honours: First

Dictionary of International Biography

Degree in Mathematics; Doctoral Degree, Studies in Computational Geometry. Address: 1, Călugăreni Street, 1500 Drobeta Turnu Severin, Romania. E-mail: vasiletomita@yahoo.com

VASILIEV Sergei Aleksandrovich, b. 8 June 1957, Leningrad, Russia. Politician. m. 2 daughters. Education: Institute of Economy and Finance, Leningrad, Russia, 1979; Postdoctoral, Economics, 1997; Professor, University of Economy and Finance, St Petersburg. Appointments: Head, Research Laboratory, Institute of Finance and Economy, took part in activities of Moscow-Leningrad Group of Young Economists, Member, Leningrad Political Club "Perestroika", 1985-90; Chairman, Committee for Economic Reform under the Leningrad City Soviet, 1990-91; Head, Working Centre for Economic Reform under the Russian Government, 1991-94; Deputy Minister of Economy of the Russian Federation, 1994-97; Deputy Head, Office of Russian Government, 1997-98; Chairman of the Board, International Investment Bank, Moscow, 1998-99; President, International Centre for Social and Economic Research "Leontief Centre", St Petersburg, 1999-2001; Representative of Leningrad Regional Government to Council of Federation, Chairman of the Committee on Financial Markets, 2001-. Publications: Economics and Power, 1998; Ten years of Russian Economic Reform – A Collection of Papers, 1999; Comparative Analysis of Stabilizations Programs of the 90's, 2003. Address: Council of Federation, Bolshaya Dmitrovka 26, 103426 Moscow, Russia. E-mail: SAVasilev@council.gov.ru

VASILIEV Vitali Nicolaevich, b. 14 September 1938, Samarkand, Uzbekistan. Medical Neuroendocrinologist. m. Faina Vasilieva. Education: Faculty of Physiology, Institute of Biology, Rostov-on-Don, 1960; Candidate of Biology Sciences, Institute of Geochemistry, 1967, Doctorate, Laboratory of Neurohumoral Regulation of Human and Animal Functions, 1975, USSR Academy of Sciences, Moscow; Doctor of Biology Sciences, Aerospace Medicine, Moscow, 1982; Professor of Sports Medicine Chair, Central Institute of Physical Culture and Sports, Moscow, 1985; Professor of Chair, CPSU Central Committee High Party School, 1989. Appointments include: Senior Staff Scientist, Head, Neurohormonal Laboratory, All-Union Research Institute of Hygiene, 1069; Research Assistant, Institute of Psychiatry, USSR Academy of Medical Sciences, 1977; Head, Neurohormonal Laboratory, Psycho-neurological Hospital No 8, Moscow, 1979; Scientific Adviser Central Administrative Board, USSR Ministry of Health, 1980; Head Neuro-hormonal Laboratory, All-Union Scientific Centre of Medico-Biologic Problems of Narcology, Moscow, 1987; Director, All-Union Centre of Medical Care of Paralytic Patients, USSR Ministry of health, 1990; Chief Scientific Advisor for biocorrection of patients with paralyses of dopamine aetology including Shoshina and Vasilyev Syndrome at clinical and medical centres in Bulgaria, Italy and Ukraine, 1993-2003. Publications: About 400 scientific works including article, monographs, books, textbooks and methodic handbooks including: Application of Adrenograms in Neuroses Clinics, 1984; Diagnostics and Treatment of Motor Disorders Caused by Dopamine Metabolism (Shoshina – Vasilyev Syndrome), 1987; 11 patents. Honours: USSR Worker of public Health with Honours, 1982; Il Carro d'Oro for Original Developments in Medicine, Mirabella, Italy, 1994 Laureat of European Trade Unions premium in the Field of Medicine, 1996; Man of the Year 2003, ABI, USA; listed in Who's Who publications and biographical dictionaries. Memberships: Editorial Boards: International Journal of Clinical Investigation, 1999 and Likarska Sprava-Vrachebnoye Delo (Medical Science), 1999; Founding Member, Pharmaceutical Medical Scientific International Ethical Committee, International Association Catholic Apostolate, Italy, 2002. Address: S. Ignazio di Loyola, 280, 80131, Naples, Italy.

VASILJEVA Ludmila J, b. 5 August 1945, Narophominsk, Russia. Biophysical and Physico-Chemical Educator. 1 son, 1 daughter. Education: Graduate, Physics, State Pedagogical Institute, Kalinin, 1963; Postgraduate, Polytechnical Institute, Kalinin, 1973; Candidate of Physics, Mathematical Science, 1975; Doctor of Physics, Mathematical Science, 1998. Appointments: Engineer, Radio-Chemical Labor, Polytechnical Institute, 1973-74; Senior Researcher, Pedagogical Institute, 1974-78; Science Researcher, Institute of Synthetic Fiber, Kalinin, 1978; Assistant Professor, 1979-99, Professor, 1999-, State University, Tver, Russia; Professor, Moscow State University of Printing Arts; Professor, Moscow State University of Technology, Stankin. Publications include: Physiology of Plants and Metal's Role, 1989; Quantum-chemical models of the structure and the functions of the active centres of the polynuclear complexes in Mathematical Modeling, 2001; Some aspects of electromagnetic field interaction with ferroporpherin active centres in Fundamental physiocomathematical problems and modeling of technicotechnological systems, 2004. Address: 6-1-28 Molodjoschnj Bulvar, 170039 Tver, Russia.

VASSILEV Hristo Stoynov, b. 21 March 1969, Troyan, Bulgaria. Engineer. Education: Dip Eng; D Mitropolia, Bulgaria. Appointments: Served Bulgarian Air Force, 1993-94; Self-employed Engineer, 1995-99; Flight Navigator on AN-12 Air Sofia, 1999-. Address: Hristo Botev = 9, Troyan 5600, Bulgaria. E-mail: hristo_vassilev@yahoo.com

VASTRUP Claus, b. 24 March 1942, Copenhagen, Denmark. Economist. m. Lis Werdelin, 1 son, 1 daughter. Education: Cand Polit, Economics, University of Copenhagen, 1966; Dr OECon, University of Aarhus, 1983. Appointments: Economist, Denmark's National Bank, 1966-69; Economist, University of Copenhagen, 1969-72; Economist, 1972-, Professor of Economics, 1983-, University of Aarhus. Memberships: Danish Economic Council; Danish Schedule of International Affairs; Board of Directors, Danske Bank. Address: Department of Economics, University of Aarhus, 8000 Aarhus, Denmark.

VAUGHAN Dindy Belinda, b. 26 December 1938, Kogarah, New South Wales, Australia. Consultant in Arts Education and Environment. 1 daughter. Education: BA (honours), University of Sydney, Australia, 1968; MA, Flinders University, South Australia, 1970. Appointments: Tertiary Lecturer, Royal Melbourne Institute of Technology and Footscray Institute (now Victoria University of Technology); Academic Assessor, Deakin University; Community Arts Officer; Frequent contracts and commissions for music composition; Consultant in arts, education and environment; Established Gallery Without Walls. Publications: By-line Correspondent for local paper, 1979-81; Books and articles on environment and the arts; Musical composition scores including tutoring books. Honours: University of Sydney Alumni Association Award for achievements in community service; Listed in several biographical dictionaries. Memberships: Life Member, University of Sydney Alumni Association; Life Member, Sydney University Arts Association; Melbourne Composer's League; Australian Geographic; Candlebark Community Nursery; Life Member, Croydon Conservation Society; Life Member, Dandenong Ranges Community and Cultural Centre; Greenpeace; Australian Conservation Foundation; Australians for Native Title and Reconciliation (ANTAR). Address: PO 668 Ringwood, VIC 3134, Australia. E-mail: rondaf@vicnet.net.au

VAVRINECZ Béla, b. 18 November 1925, Budapest, Hungary. Composer; Conductor. m. Amalia Endrey, 1950, 1 son, 6 daughters. Education: Diploma in Composition, 1950, Diploma in Conducting, 1952, Budapest Academy of Music. Debut: Budapest Academy of Music, 1949. Career: First Conductor, Philharmonic Orchestra, Györ, 1957-58; Chief Conductor, Ministry of Home Affairs Symphony Orchestra, Budapest, 1961-73; Artistic Director, Dance Ensemble Budapest, 1974-83; Artistic Director, Ensemble Duna Budapest, 1983-85; Works frequently performed on radio and television. Compositions: 2 operas; 2 ballets; 112 musical pieces for dance theatre; 12 incidental works; 4 oratoria; Gisela, 1991; Chronicle of Somogy, 1999; 6 cantatas; 18 works for choir and orchestra; 20 works for symphony orchestra, including Symphonie, 1955; 6 works for chamber orchestra; 7 concerts; 45 chamber music works; Solo pieces; 33 choral works; 1 Mass; Songs; Arrangements; Music for windbands. Recordings: Numerous. Publication: Kodály Memorial Book, 1953. Address: Cinkotai utca 39, H-1141 Budapest, Hungary.

VEERAKYATHIAH V D, b. 25 June 1926, Vaddagere, India. Retired. m. V Rajamma, 25 June 1955, 2 sons. Education: BSc, Agriculture. Appointments: Village Level Worker, 1954-55; Agricultural Extension Officer, 1955-57; Block Development Officer, 1957-65; Principal, State Level Young Farmers Training Centre, 1 year; Instructor, Orientation and Study Centre, Government of India, Poona, 1 year; Assistant Development Commissioner, 1967-71; Assistant Director, Land Army, 1971-72; Principal, Rural Development Training Centre, Mandya, Karnataka, 1972-75; Secretary, Chief Executive Officer, State Khadi and Village Industries Board, Bangalore, 1976-77; Project Director, SFDA, Government of Karnataka, 1977-80; Selected for Indian Administrative Service, Government of India; Director, Special Economic Programmes, IRDP, Government of Karnataka, 1980-82; Director, Backward Classes and Other Weaker Sections, 1982-84. Publications: 3 professional papers in the Indian Science Congress Sessions. Memberships: Honorary Director, Asian Institute for Urban Development; Advisor, Ganga Rural Development Trust; Bangalore Zilla Aadhar Member, Age Foundation, Ministry of Social Welfare, Government of India; Honorary President, Vaddagere Temple Development Committee; Founder-President, Akhila Kunchitigara Mahal Mardal, Bangalore. Address: 596 IInd Stage 1 E Block, Rajajinagar, Bangalore 560010, India.

VEEREMAN Genevieve, b. 9 June 1957, Schoten, Belgium. Paediatric Gastroenterologist. m. Dirk Wauters, 3 sons, 1 daughter. Education: Medical Doctor, 1982, Paediatrician, 1987, University of Antwerp, Belgium; Paediatric Gastroenterology and Nutrition, University of California, San Francisco, USA, 1990; PhD, Catholic University of Leuven, Belgium, 1995. Appointments: Attending Physician, University of California San Francisco, USA, 1990-91; Attending Physician, UZ Leuven, Belgium, 1992-2002; Professor, Catholic University Leuven, Belgium, 1996-2002; Consultant, AZ Middelheim, Antwerp, Belgium, 2002-. Publications: Related to gastrointestinal motility in children and paediatric gastroenterology, including: Aspects of the Development of Gastrointestinal Function, 1995. Memberships: Espghan; AGA; Bespghan; BVK; AMS. Address: Bovenbosstraat 17, 3052 Blanden, Belgium. E-mail: gveereman@skynet.be

VEGA FELICIANO Edwin D, b. 25 May 1945, Bayamon, Puerto Rico. Medical Doctor; Specialist in Obstetrics and Gynaecology. 1 son, 3 daughters. Education: BSc, 1966, MD, 1970, Speciality in Obstetrics and Gynaecology, 1974, University of Puerto Rico. Appointments: Private Practice, Obstetrics and Gynaecology; Active Staff, Pavia Hospital, San Juan, Puerto Rico. Honours: Most Distinguished Professionals, 1984; Listed in Who's Who publications and biographical dictionaries. Memberships: American Medical Association; American College of Obstetrics and Gynecology; Interamerican College of Physicians and Surgeons; International College of Surgeons; American Fertility

Society; Royal Society of Medicine; Phi Chi Medical Fraternity; Medical Surgeons College of Puerto Rico. Address: Arzuaga 112, Medina Center 1102, San Juan, PR 00928, USA.

VÉGH Johan Alexander Sándor, b. 11 February 1953, Sneek, The Netherlands. Clergyman. m. Els Jansma, 2 sons, 2 daughters. Education: Master's Degree, Theology, Vrije Universiteit, Amsterdam, The Netherlands. Appointments: Minister of the Reformed Church: Schoonrewoerd, 1981-86; Middenmeer, 1986-91; Amsterdam, 1991-2000; Bunschoten-Spakenburg, 2000- Publications: Most recent articles include: Wat zoekt gij de levende bij de doden? Enkele gedachten over Lk. 24: 1-12, 2003; Kracht uit de hoge. Enkele gedachten over Lk. 24:49, 2003; Ben ik mijns broeders hoeder? Enkele gedachten over Gen. 4:9, 2003; Johannes Hus: een voorloper van de Reformatie, 2003. Memberships: Stichting Oudchristelijke Studien; Christen-Democratisch Appel; Joods Historisch Museum. Address: Koningin Wilhelminastraat 27, NL-3751 DE, Bunschoten-Spakenburg, The Netherlands. Website: www.vegh.tk

VELASCO BELMONT Rosa María, b. 2 November 1946, Mexico, Distrito Federal. Physicist. m. Juan Varela Ham, 1 son. Education: BSc, Physics, 1969, MSc, Physics, 1971, PhD, Sciences, 1973, Faculty of Sciences, Universidad Nacional Autónoma de México; Postdoctoral Fellow, College de France, 1974-76. Lecturer, Faculty of Sciences, 1968-73, 1979, 1983; Mexican Petroleum Institute, 1972-74; Lecturer, School of Physics and Mathematics, National Polytechnic Institute, 1973-74; Physics Department UAM-Iztapalapa, 1977-. Publications: Articles in scientific journals as co-author include: The maximum entropy formalism in kinetic theory, 2000; Inconsistency in the Moments Method, 2002. Honour: National Researcher in the National Research System Level III. Membership: Mexican Physics Society. Address: San Rafael Atlixo 186, 09340 Iztapalapa, Mexico D F. E-mail: rmvb@xanum.uam.mx

VELTCHEVA Albena Dimitrova, b. 5 January 1964, Vabel, Bulgaria. Research Scientist. m. Lyoubomir Petkov Veltchev, 1 son, 1 daughter. Education: MSc, Physical Faculty, Sofia University, Sofia, Bulgaria. 1987. Appointments: Researcher, 1988-94, Junior Researcher, 1995-97, Institute of Oceanology, Bulgarian Academy of Sciences, Varna, Bulgaria; Fellow, Japan, Science and Technology Agency, 1998-2000; Transport Technical Researcher, Corporation for Advanced Transport and Technology, 2000-2002; Visiting Researcher, Port and Airport Research Institute, Japan, 2002-. Publications: Articles in scientific journals and papers presented at conferences as author and co-author include: Wave groupiness in the nearshore area by Hilbert spectrum, 2001; Wave and group transformation by a Hilbert spectrum, 2002; Effect of the distortion of typhoon pressure distribution on the storm surge estimation, 2002; Comparison of methods for calculation of wave envelope, 2003. Honours: Gold Medal, Mathematical High School Diploma, 1982; Listed in Who's Who publications and biographical dictionaries. Address: Port and Airport Research Institute, Nagase 3-1-1, Yokosuka 239-0826, Japan. E-mail: velchevi@bigfoot.com

VENDLER Helen, (Helen Hennessy), b. 30 April 1933, Boston, Massachusetts, USA. Professor; Poetry Critic. 1 son. Education: AB, Emmanuel College, 1954; PhD, Harvard University, 1960. Appointments: Instructor, Cornell University, 1960-63; Lecturer, Swarthmore College and Haverford College, Pennsylvania, 1963-64; Associate Professor, 1966-68, Professor, 1968-85, Boston University; Fulbright Lecturer, University of Bordeaux, 1968-69; Poetry Critic, The New Yorker, 1978-; Overseas Fellow, Churchill College, Cambridge, 1980; Senior Fellow, Harvard Society of Fellows, 1981-93; Visiting Professor, 1981-85, Kenan Professor,

1985-, Associate Academic Dean, 1987-92, Porter University Professor, 1990-, Harvard University; Charles Stewart Parnell Fellow, 1996, Honorary Fellow, 1996-, Magdalene College, Cambridge. Publications: Yeat's Vision and the Later Plays, 1963; On Extended Wings: Wallace Stevens' Longer Poems, 1969; The Poetry of George Herbert, 1975; Part of Nature, Part of Us: Modern American Poets, 1980; The Odes of John Keats, 1983; Wallace Stevens: Words Chosen Out of Desire, 1984; The Harvard Book of Contemporary American Poetry (editor), 1985; Voices and Visions: The Poet in America, 1987; The Music of What Happens, 1988; Soul Says, 1995; The Given and the Made, 1995; The Breaking of Style, 1995; Poems, Poets, Poetry, 1995; The Art of Shakespeare's Sonnets, 1997; Seamus Heaney, 1998. Contributions to: Professional journals. Honours: Lowell Prize, 1969; Guggenheim Fellowship, 1971-72; American Council of Learned Societies Fellow, 1971-72; National Institute of Arts and Letters Award, 1975; Radcliffe College Graduate Society Medal, 1978; National Book Critics Award, 1980; National Endowment for the Humanities Fellowships, 1980, 1985, 1994; Keats-Shelley Association Award, 1994; Truman Capote Award, 1996; Many honorary doctorates; Phi Beta Kappa. Memberships: American Academy of Arts and Letters; American Academy of Arts and Sciences, vice-president, 1992-95; American Philosophical Society; English Institute; Modern Language Association, president, 1980. Address: Harvard University, Department of English, Barker Center, Cambridge, MA 02138, USA..

VENN George Andrew Fyfe, b. 12 October 1943, Tacoma, Washington, USA. Professor; Writer; Editor; Poet; Critic. m. Elizabeth Cheney, divorced, 1 son, 1 daughter. Education: BA, College of Idaho, 1967; MFA, Creative Writing, University of Montana, 1970; Central University, Quito, Ecuador; University of Salamanca, Spain; City Literary Institute, London. Appointments: Writer-on-Tour, Western States Arts Foundation, 1977; Foreign Expert, Changsha Railway University, Hunan, China, 1981-82; General Editor, Oregon Literature Series, 1989-94; Writer-in-Residence, Eastern Oregon University. Publications: Sunday Afternoon: Grande Ronde, 1975; Off the Main Road, 1978; Marking the Magic Circle, 1988; Oregon Literature Series, 1992-94; West of Paradise: New Poems, 1999; many poems, essays, stories. Contributions to: Oregon Humanities; Writer's Northwest Handbook; North West Review; Northwest Reprint Series; Poetry Northwest; Willow Springs; Clearwater Journal; Oregon East; Portland Review; Worldviews and the American West (book). Honours: Pushcart Prize, 1980; Oregon Book Award, 1988; Stewart Holbrook Award, 1994; Andres Berger Poetry Prize, Northwest Writers, 1995. Memberships: Oregon Council of Teachers of English; Pen West; Western American Literature; Fishtrap Gathering; National Council of Teachers of English. Address: Department of English, Eastern Oregon University, La Grande, OR 97850, USA.

VERDIJK Gerard, b. 1 September 1934, Boxmeer, The Netherlands. Artist; Painter; Sculptor. m. Josephine, Baroness van den Clooster, 1 son. Education: Canisius College, Nymegen; Academie de la Grande Chaumiere, Paris; Academie Andre Lhote, Paris; Vrije Academie, Den Haag. Career: Solo exhibitions include: Paris; Copenhagen; Dusseldorf; The Hague; Brussels; Rotterdam; Wuppertal; Berlin, with Yayoi Kusama; Amsterdam; Cologne; Zurich; Basel; Vienna; Livorno; Genova; Verona; Geneva; Munich; Antwerp, 1988; Marseille, with Daniel Dezeuze; Toulouse; New York, with Josephine Sloet; Cape Town, with Josephine Sloet; Cobra Museum, Amstelveen, Amsterdam, 2004; Group exhibitions include: Biennale de Paris; Contemporary Dutch Art, London; Liverpool and Dublin; Expo Montreal; Holland Fair, Tokyo; Dutch Graphics, Cologne; Arteder, Bilbao; Plein Feu, Paris; Der Freie Raum, Munich; Visions in Dutch Art, Prague; The Reach of

Abstraction, New York; Spring Collection, Santa Fe, New Mexico, USA; Presentation, curated by H M Beatrix the Queen of the Netherlands, Amsterdam; Kobo Gallery, Tokyo. Publications: Artwork appears in several professional and popular publications. Honours: Jacob Maris Material Prize, 1964; 2nd Hartog Prize, 1965; Jacob Maris Prize, 1967; Silver Medal Prix d'Europe, Ostend, 1966; Grantee, Dutch Government, 1965 and Dutch Government, 1969-71; Grantee, van Gogh Foundation, 1991. Memberships: Member, Soutien Musee Barbier-Muller, Geneva. Address: Les Places, Marcillac St Quentin, Par 24200 Sarlat, Dordogne, France.

VERE HODGE (Richard) Anthony, b. 27 December 1943, Burnham-on-Sea, England. Biochemist. m. 1 son, 2 daughters. Education: BA, Trinity College, Dublin, Ireland, 1962-66; D Phil, Worcester College, Oxford, England, 1966-69. Appointments: Employee, 1969-96, Beecham Pharmaceuticals (then SmithKline Beecham Pharmaceuticals, now GlaxoSmithKline), 1969-96 (Project Manager, Interferon Inducers, Human Interferon, 1974-76; Chief Biochemist, Antiviral Chemotherapy Project which discovered penciclovir, 1983, famciclovir, 1985, 1981-92; Seconded as Expert on famciclovir, 1993-94, Associate Director, Anti-Infectives Section, World-wide Strategic Development Project, 1995-96); Director, Vere Hodge Antivirals Ltd, 2000-; Consultant to Pharmasset Inc, Atlanta, Georgia, USA, 2000-. Publications in professional journals include: Mode of action of 9-(4-Hydroxy-3-Hydroxymethylbut-1-yl)Guanine (BRL 39123) against herpes simplex virus in MRC-5 cells, 1989; Famciclovir and penciclovir. The mode of action of famciclovir including its conversion to penciclovir, 1993; Chirality presents a challenge: Famciclovir – a case study, 1995; Book Chapter, Famciclovir: Discovery and development of a novel antiherpesvirus agent, 1998; Numerous papers presented at international conferences. Memberships: Royal Society of Chemistry, 1968; The Chromatographic Society, 1989; International Society for Antiviral Research, 1990; American Society for Microbiology, 1997. Address: Old Denshott, Leigh, Reigate, Surrey RH2 8RD, England. E-mail: averehodge@aol.com

VEREKER John (Michael Medlicott) (Sir), b. 9 August 1944, UK. Governor of Bermuda. m. Judith Diane Rowen, 1 son, 1 daughter. Education: BA (Hons), University of Keele, 1967. Appointments: World Bank, Washington, 1970-72; Principal, Ministry of Overseas Development, 1972; Private Secretary to successive Ministers of Overseas Development, 1977-78; Prime Minister's Office, 1980-83; Under Secretary, 1983-88, Principal Finance Officer, 1986-88, Overseas Development Administration, Foreign and Commonwealth Office; Deputy Secretary, Department for Education, 1988-93; Permanent Secretary, Department for International Development, 1994-2002; Governor and Commander-in-Chief of Bermuda, 2002-. Publication: Blazing the Trail (Journal of Development Studies), 2002. Honours: CB, 1992; CIMgt, 1995; Hon D Litt, University of Keele; KCB, 1999; FRSA, 1999, KStJ, 2001. Memberships: Chairman, Student Loans Co Ltd, 1989-91; Board Member, British Council, 1994-2001; Board Member, Institute of Development Studies, 1994-2000. Address: Government House, Hamilton, Bermuda.

VERKHIVKER Grygoriy, b. 19 April 1928, Odessa, Ukraine. Nuclear Engineer; Educator. m. Lyudmila Balaban, 1 son. Education: Engineer of Electric Station, 1949; Bachelor of Science, 1962; Associate Professor, 1964; Professor, 1990. Appointments: Power Plant Engineer, 1949-53; Engineer, Project Office, Odessa, Ukraine, 1957-57; Assistant, Odessa Food Institute, 1957-62; Associate Professor, Odessa Polytechnic University, 1963-88; Professor, Odessa National Polytechnic University, 1988-. Publications: 5 books and 150 articles in the field of power plants and energetics. Honours: Honour Worker of Nuclear Energetics; Honour Worker of Energetics of Ukraine. Membership: Energetic Union of Ukraine. Address: Apt 32, B Hmelnizkiy St 15/19, Odessa, Ukraine 65028. E-mail: yaverkhivker@upk.od.ua

VERLOREN VAN THEMAAT Pieter, b. 16 March 1916, Rotterdam, Netherlands. m. Maria, 3 sons, 1 daughter. Education: Master of Law, University of Leiden, 1939; Doctor of Law, 1946. Appointments: Director-General Competition, EEC Commission, 1958-67; Professor of National, European and International Economic Law, University of Utrecht, 1967-81; Advocate General, European Court of Justice, 1981-86; Co Editor, Introduction To The Law of The European Communities, 1970-98. Publications: Co-author, Introduction To The Law of The European Communities, 3 editions; The Changing Structure of International Economic Law, 1981; International Fiscal Law, 1946; 1990-2002: many articles and papers in English, French and Dutch languages on European and international economic law and its future development. Honours: Knight, Order of The Netherlands Lion; Listed in Biographical Publications. Membership: Royal Netherland Academy of Arts And Science. Address: Mozartlaan 4, 3723 J M Bilthoven, Netherlands.

VERMA Chaman Lal, b. 22 October 1944, Ludhiana (PB), India. Senior Director Grade Scientist. m. Raji, 1 son, 1 daughter. Education: B Tech, Chemical Engineering, Indian Institute of Technology, Kanpur, India, 1967; M Tech, Chemical Engineering, Indian Institute of Technology, Bombay, India, 1969; PhD, Chemical Engineering, University of Roorkee (IIT), Roorkee, India, 1987. Appointments: Lecturer, Department of Chemical Engineering, University of Roorkee, Roorkee, India, 1970-73; Scientist C, 1973-81; Scientist E-I, 1981-87; Scientist E-II, 1987-93; Scientist F, 1993-98; Scientist G, 1998-, Central Building Research Institute, Roorkee, India; Areas of work and expertise: Building Materials and Chemical Process Technologies; Environmental Studies and Pollution Abatement; R&D Management; Travelled to numerous countries including Cuba, Denmark, Germany, Japan, Norway, Poland, Singapore, Sri Lanka, Thailand and USA. Publications: 65 research and technical papers; 85 papers presented in seminars, conferences, symposia; 105 technical reports; 5 patents filed. Honours include: National Merit Scholarship, Government of India, 1962-67; Technical Teachers Training Fellowship, Government of India, 1967-70; Khosla Research Commendation Certificate, University of Roorkee, 1989; Numerous Commendation Certificates and cash prizes for technical writing and research papers; R B Hajela Award, Central Building Research Institute, 1997-98; Honorary Member, Research Board of Advisors, American Biographical Institute, USA, 1999; CBRI Foundation Day Award, 2001; National NRDC Invention Award, 2001; Excellence Award, Institute of Economic Studies, 2001; Gem of India Award-2001, All India Achievers' Conference, 2001; Listed in numerous Who's Who publications and biographical dictionaries. Memberships: Fellow, Institution of Engineers, India; Life Member, Indian Institute of Chemical Engineers; Life Member, Material Research Society of India; Life Member, Loss Prevention Association of India; Corporate Member, Indian Buildings Congress; Life Member, Indian Concrete Institute; Life Member, Indian Society for Construction Materials and Structures; Corporate Member, Indian Association for Environmental Management. Address: Environmental Science and Technology Division, Central Building Research Institute, Roorkee 247667, Uttaranchal, India.

VERSACE Donatella, b. 1955, Reggio Calabria, Italy. Designer. m. Paul Back, 1 son, 1 daughter. Appointments: Joined Versace, 1978; Formerly overseer of advertising and public relations, accessories designer, children's collection designer, solo designer,

Versus and Isante Lines; Creative Director, Gianni Versace Group, 1997-. Address: c/o Keeble Cavaco and Duka Inc, 450 West 15th Street, Suite 604, New York, NY 10011, USA.

VIDAL Gore, (Edgar Box), b. 3 October 1925, West Point, New York, USA. Writer. Education: Graduate, Phillips Exeter Academy, 1943. Publications: Novels: Williwaw, 1946; In a Yellow Wood, 1947; The City and the Pillar, 1948; The Season of Comfort, 1949; A Search for the King, 1950; Dark Green, Bright Red, 1950; The Judgment of Paris, 1952; Messiah, 1954; Julian, 1964; Washington, DC, 1967; Myra Breckinridge, 1968; Two Sisters, 1970; Burr, 1973; Myron, 1974; Kalki, 1978; Creation, 1981; Duluth, 1983; Lincoln, 1984; Empire, 1987; The Smithsonian Institution, 1998; The Golden Age, 2000. Stories: A Thirsty Evil, 1956. Play: Visit to a Small Planet, 1957. Television and Broadway productions: The Best Man, 1960; Romulus, 1966; Weekend, 1968; An Evening with Richard Nixon, 1972; Gore Vidal's Lincoln, 1988. Essays: Rocking the Boat, 1962; Reflections upon a Sinking Ship, 1969; Homage to Daniel Shays, 1973; Matters of Fact and of Fiction, 1977; The Second American Revolution, 1982; Armageddon?, 1987; United States: Essays 1952-1992, 1993. Memoir: Palimpsest, 1995. Films: The Catered Affair, 1956; The Left-Handed Gun, 1958; The Best Man, 1964. Teleplays: The Death of Billy the Kid, 1958; Dress Gray, 1986. Honour: National Book Award, 1993. Membership: American Academy of Arts and Letters. Address: 84010 Ravello, Italy.

VIDANES Fred, b. 25 April 1944, Philippines. Chemical Engineer. m. Elsie M Vidanes, 1 son, 1 daughter. Education: Bachelor of Science, Chemical Engineering, 1969. Appointments: Staff Engineer, Sugeco, 1970; Quality Control, Ablestik Laboratories, 1972; Research Associate, National Institute of Science and Technology, 1975; Quality Control Manager, Environmental Manager, LPS Laboratories Inc, 1976-. Publication: Immigrants Contributions to US Economic Success. Honours: Listed in Who's Who publications and biographical dictionaries. Memberships: American Society for Quality; American Chemical Society; Philippines Institute of Chemical Engineers; National Association of Mapua Alumni. Address: 4957 Castlewood Drive, Lilburn, GA 30047, USA. E-mail: fvidanes@yahoo.com

VIDLÁKOVÁ Olga Anna, b. 17 January 1928, Duchcov, Czech Republic. Associate Professor. m. Lubor Vidlák, 2 daughters. Education: LLD, Charles University, Prague, 1951; Candidate, Science in Administrative Law, Czechoslovak Academy of Sciences, 1975; Associate Professor of Environmental Law and Administrative Law, Charles University, 1988. Appointments: Research Group Leader, Institute of Landscape Ecology, Czechoslovak Academy of Sciences; Chief Resident Fellow, Deputy Director, Institute of State Administration; Director of Department, PMO, Czech Government, 1991-92; Director, Department of Public Administration, Office for Legislation and Public Administration of the Czech Republic, 1992-96; Senior Advisor to Deputy Minister of Interior, 1997-99; Head, Department of Law and Administrative Science, University Pardubice, 2000-01; Independent consultant in Public Administration, Partner, Institute for Legal Education and Information, Praha, Head of Public Administration Section, 2002-. Publications: Author, 15 books; Contributor, 37 books; over 350 articles in national and international professional journals. Honours: Plaques, 1981, Golden Bage, 1988, Council for Environment, Czech Government; Commemorative Medals from Masaryk University, Brno, 1996 and Universitas Pardubiciensis, 2001. Memberships: IUSSP, 1968-88; IIAS; Czech Demographic Association; Legislative Council of Czech Government, 1991-98; Delegate to PUMA Com/OECD, 1995-99. Address: Na Zvoničce 32, 147 00 Prague 4, Czech Republic.

Dictionary of International Biography

VIEIRA Carlos José, b. 3 April 1937, Aveiro, Portugal. Business Entrepreneur. m. Maria Elisa. Education: Specialised Course in Marketing, Executive Top Management, Company Planning, International Investments, Instituto Comercial do Porto, Portugal. Appointments: Shareholder and Executive Director, Ernesto Vieira & Filhos, SA – Aveiro (Portugal), 1964-; Shareholder and Chief Executive Officer of the Group Auto-Sueco (Coimbra) Ldª (Portugal); Chairman, Volvo Maquinaria de Constuccion de España, SA – Madrid (Spain); Executive Manager, Sociedade de Construções do Arnado – Coimbra (Portugal); Executive Manager, Sicolipo- Soc. Imobiliária do Colipo, Ldª – Leiria (Portugal); Shareholder, Agroturismo Serrana do Olival, Ldª – Ourém (Portugal). Publications: Various articles published in papers concerning humanity, senior compassion houses; Opinion maker in various economic reviews and newspapers. Honours: Recipient thankfulness, Red Cross, 1987; Merit Medal, Portuguese Red Cross, 1988; Lions, President and Awards, 1985, 1986, 1988, 1989, 1990; Merit Medal, Lions International, 1998. Memberships: Literary Association (Grémio Literário) , Lisbon, Portugal; Chamber of Commerce Portugal – Sweden; Portuguese Automobile Association; Portuguese Red Cross, Regional Vice-President; Nerlei Trade Association, Leiria; Catholic House Compassion, Leiria, Portugal. Address: Rua Coronel Pinheiro Correia No 3, 2400-211 Leiria, Portugal. E-mail: cvieira@ascoimbra.pt

VIEIRA Waldo, b. 12 April 1932, Monte Carmelo, Minas Gerais, Brazil. Physician; Dentist; Consciousness and Out of Body Experience Researcher; Lexicographer. Education: Postgraduate Degree in Plastic Surgery, Japan. Appointments: Independent research of consciousness and its manifestations outside the human body for over 40 years; Founder: International Institute of Projectiology and Conscientiology, Center of Higher Studies of Conscientiology, International Academy of Consciousness, International Association for the Evolution of Consciousness; International Organisation of Conscientiotherapy. Publications: Author of 18 books in the field of consciousness research including: Homo sapiens reurbanisatus, 2004; Encyclopaedia of Conscientology, in progress. Memberships include: American Society for Psychical Research New York, USA; The Society for Psychical Research, London, England; The Brazilian Association of Parapsychology, Rio de Janeiro, Brazil. Address: CEAEC – Caixa Postal 1027, Centro, Foz do Iguaçu, PR, Brazil, Cep: 85.851-970.

VIERECK Peter (Robert Edwin), b. 5 August 1916, New York, New York, USA. Historian; Poet; Professor. m. (1) Aanya de Markov, June 1945, divorced May 1970, 1 son, 1 daughter, (2) Betty Martin Falkenberg, 30 August 1972. Education: BS, 1937, MA, 1939, PhD, 1942, Harvard University; Graduate Study as a Henry Fellow, Christ Church, Oxford, 1937-38. Appointments: Instructor, Tutor, Harvard University, 1946-47; Assistant Professor of History, 1947-48, Visiting Lecturer in Russian History, 1948-49, Smith College, Northampton, Massachusetts; Associate Professor, 1948-55, Professor of Modern European and Russian History, 1955-65, Mount Holyoke Alumnae Foundation Chair of Interpretative Studies, 1965-79, William R Kenan Chair of History, 1979-, Mount Holyoke College; Whittal Lecturer in Poetry, Library of Congress, Washington, DC, 1954, 1963; Fulbright Professor in American Poetry and Civilization, University of Florida, 1955; Elliston Chair and Poetry Lecturer, University of Cincinnati, 1956; Visiting Lecturer, University of California at Berkeley, 1957, 1964; City College of the City University of New York, 1964; Visiting Research Scholar in Russian for the Twentieth Century Fund, 1962-63; Director, Poetry Workshop, New York Writers Conferences, 1965-67. Publications: History: Metapolitics: From the Romantics to Hitler, 1941, revised edition as Metapolitics: The Roots of the Nazi Mind, 1961, 2nd revised edition, 1965, updated edition, 1982;

Conservatism Revisited: The Revolt Against Revolt, 1815-1949, 1949, 2nd edition as Conservatism Revisited and the New Conservatism: What Went Wrong?, 1962, 3rd edition, 1972; Shame and Glory of the Intellectuals: Babbitt, Jr Versus the Rediscovery of Values, 1953; The Unadjusted Man: A New Hero for Americans: Reflections on the Distinction Between Conserving and Conforming, 1956; Conservatism: From John Adams to Churchill, 1956, revised edition, 1962; Inner Liberty: The Stubborn Grit in the Machine, 1957; Conservatism from Burke and John Adams till 1982: A History and an Anthology, 1982. Poetry: Terror and Decorum: Poems 1940-1948, 1948; Strike Through Mask: Lyrical Poems, 1950; The First Morning: New Poems, 1952; Dream and Responsibility: The Tension Between Poetry and Society, 1953; The Persimmon Tree, 1956; The Tree Witch: A Poem and a Play (First of All a Poem), 1961; New and Selected Poems, 1932-1967, 1967; Archer in the Marrow: The Applewood Cycles of 1967-1987, 1987; Tide and Continuities: Last and First Poems, 1995-1938, 1995; Metapolitics from Wagner to Hitler, 2002. Play: Opcomp: A Modern Medieval Miracle Play, 1993. Contributions to: Monographs, essays, reviews and poems to numerous periodicals. Honours: Pulitzer Prize in Poetry, 1949; Guggenheim Fellowship, 1959-60; Rockefeller Foundation Research Grant, 1958; National Endowment for the Humanities Senior Research Fellowship, 1969; Poetry Award, Massachusetts Artists Foundation, 1978; Sadin Prize, New York Quarterly, 1980; Golden Rose Award, 1981, Varoujan Poetry Prize, 1983, New England Poetry Club; Ingram Merrill Foundation Fellowship in Poetry, 1985. Memberships: American Committee for Cultural Freedom, executive committee; American Historical Association; Committee for Basic Education, charter member; Oxford Society; PEN; Phi Beta Kappa; Poetry Society of America. Address: 12 Silver Street, South Hadley, MA 01075, USA.

VIERTL Reinhard, b. 25 March 1946, Hall in Tirol, Austria. Professor of Applied Statistics. m. Dorothea, 2 sons. Education: Dipl Ing, 1972; Dr techn. 1974. Appointments: Assistant, 1972-79; University Docent, 1979-80; Research Fellow, University of California, Berkeley, 1980-81; Visiting Docent, University of Klagenfurt, 1981-82; Full Professor, Vienna University of Technology, 1982-; Visiting Professor, University of Innsbruck, 1991-93; Seasonal Instructor, University of Calgary, summer 2003. Publications: 7 books, including Statistical Methods for Non-Precise Data, 1996; Over 90 scientific papers in mathematics, probability theory, life testing, regional statistics, Bayesian statistics, and statistics with non-precise data. Honours: Max Kade Fellow, 1980. Memberships: Royal Statistical Society, London; Austrian Statistical Society; International Statistical Institute; German Statistical Society; New York Academy of Sciences; Austrian Mathematical Society. Address: Department of Statistics, Vienna University of Technology, Wiedner Hauptstr 8/107, A-1040 Vienna, Austria. E-mail: r.viertl@tuwien.ac.at

VIJAYARATNAM Kanapathipillai, b. 10 May 1948, Analaitivu, Ceylon (Sri Lanka). Chartered Civil, Water, Environmental Engineer and Manager; Consultant; Educator. m. Sakuntala Mylwaganam, 31 October 1979. Education: BSc (Engineering), Honours (Ceylon), 1971; MEng (AIT), 1977; MSc, Eng (London), 1982; DIC (Imperial College, London), 1982; Certificate, Sustainable Business, World Business Council on Sustainable Development, 1999. Appointments: Instructor Civil Engineering, University of Ceylon, 1972; Civil Engineer Mahaveli (River) Development Board, 1972-75; Postgraduate Engineering Studies, Asian Institute of Technology, 1976-77; Civil Engineer, Renardet Engineering, Singapore, 1977-80; Postgraduate Engineering Studies, Imperial College, London, 1981-82; Engineer, Chanton Engineering Ltd, Middlesex, England, 1984-85; Engineer, S P Collins & Associates, Consulting Engineers, Cambridge, 1985-

86; Consulting Engineer, 1986-88; Senior Engineer, Neilcot Construction, 1988-90; Engineer, Clean Water Department, Binnie & Partners Consulting Engineers, 1990-94; Senior Engineer, Gr I, SMHB, Consulting Engineers, KL Malaysia, 1995-96; Principal Engineer (Deputy Project Manager), Resident Engineer, SSP Consulting Engineers, Malaysia, 1996-97; Engineering Consultant, England, 1998; Director, Rosebury Consulting Ltd, Engineering Consultants, 1999-; Director, AITA – NET (Europe) Ltd, 2001-; Distinguished Participant, World Summit on Sustainable Development, South Africa, 2002; World Water Forum and Ministerial Conference, The Netherlands, 2000, Japan, 2003; Stockholm Water Symposium, 2002; Entrepreneur Workshop, Singapore, 2004; Adjunct Faculty, Professor and Dean, School of Engineering Management, Sustainable Development and Public Policy, American University of London, 2003; Original contributions to Integrated water resources development of river basins, World Water Resources Congress, 1977; Mathematical modelling, optimisation and simulation of water treatment systems, Dissertation/Thesis to Imperial College, London, 1982 and Conferences in USA (1986) and UK (1987); Sustainable development of dams and hydropower, 1995, 1998; Sustainable urban environmental management, 1999; Re-engineering of water supply organisations, 1996; Sustainable water supply system planning for Cities, 2001, Making waste work, UK, 2000; Sustainable Waste Management, USA, 2001; Broader education of civil, water resources and environmental engineers, 1986, 1995. Publications: Conference Proceedings and Technical Reports, USA, England, Malaysia, Switzerland, Sweden and Egypt. Honours: UK Government Scholar, 1976-77; NATO - Advanced Study Institute Grantee, 1981; Grantee, UNESCO/Colorado State University, 1981; Cricket team Champions, UK Engineering Consultants Tournament, 1993; Elected as one of top 500 Leaders of 21st Century; Vijayaratnam's paper on Engineering Education for Sustainable Development in New Millennium on MIT website, 2000-; Listed in numerous biographical publications; Pilgrimage to 7 Hindu temples in South India, 1988 and 2004, and Varanasi, East India, 1988; Pilgrimage to 11 Hindu temples in Singapore, Sivarathri night, 2004. Memberships: CEng, MICE, 1977; MCIWEM, 1979; MASCE, 1986; MIWRA, 1992; MIAHR, 1993; MIWA, 1993; MIHA, 1998. Address: 1 Ashcroft Rise, Coulsdon Woods, Coulsdon, Surrey CR5 2SS, England. E-mail: vijay@aitanet.co.uk

VILLENEUVE Jacques, b. 9 April 1971, Canada. Racing Car Driver. Appointments: Started racing in Italian Touring Car Championship Italian Formula 3, 1989, 1990; With Reynaud and Alfa Romeo, 1992; Japanese Formula 3, 1993; Formula Atlantic, 1993; IndyCar Driver, 1994-95; IndyCar Racing Champion, 1995; Drove Formula One Cars with Williams Renault Team, then British American Racing team, now with BAR-Honda; Grand Prix Winner, Britain, 1996, 1997, Brazil, 1997; Argentina, 1997; Spain, 1997; Hungary, 1997, Austria, 1997; Luxembourg, 1997; Formula One Champion, 1997.

VINCENT Olatunde Olabode, b. 16 May 1925. Banker. Education: CIS, London, 1951-53; BA, Com, University of Manchester, 1956; Administrative Staff College, Henley, England, 1961. Appointments: Nigerian Army, 1942-46; Financial Secretary's Office, 1947-56; Federal Ministry of Finance, 1956-61; Member, Lagos Executive Development Board, 1957-60; Assistant General Manager, 1961, Deputy General, 1962, General Manager, 1963-66, Advisor, 1973-75, Deputy Governor, 1975-77, Governor, 1977-82, Central Bank of Nigeria; Member, Committee of 9 which set up African Development Bank; Vice-President, 1966-73, African Development Bank, Abidjan, Cote d'Ivoire; Director, Nigerian Security Printing and Mining Co. Ltd, 1975-77; Chairman, Capital Issues Committee, 1975-77;

Chairman, Committee on Motor Vehicle Advs and Basic Allowance, 1978-; National Economic Council, 1979-82; Chairman, City Business Computers Ltd; Chairman, Equity and Trust Ltd, 1987-2003; Chairman Lagos State University Visitation Panel, 1993; Chairman, Governing Board, Centre for Environmental Science Education, Lagos State University, 1996-; Chairman Board of Trustees, Nigerian Lions Charity Foundation, 1993-; Trustee, Cancer Aid Foundation; Patron Lagos State Chapter, Spinal Cord Injuries Association of Nigeria; President African Church Lads and Lasses Brigade, 1984-; Grand Patron, African Church, Lagos Diocese. Honours: Commander, Order of the Federal Republic, 1982; DSc (Honoris Causa) by Lagos State University, Lagos, 2000. Memberships: Life Fellow, IBA; Life Member, Nigerian Economic Society; Life Member, Society for International Development; Cath Youngmen Friendly Society, African Church Cath (Bethel), Lagos; Nigerian Conservative Foundation; Victoria Island Lions Club; President, Metropolitan Club, Lagos 1997-2002; Island Club, Lagos; Fellow, Nigerian Institute of Bankers; Fellow, Institute of Directors; Fellow, Nigerian Institute of Management; Member, Order of International Fellowship, 1996; Charter Member, International Honour Society, 2003; World Peace and Diplomacy Forum. Listed in: Who's Who in the Commonwealth; Who's Who in the World. Address: 8 Balarabe Musa Crescent, Victoria Island, PO Box 8780, Lagos, Nigeria

VISWESWARA Channarayapatna Sreekantaiah, b. 27 November 1936, Mysore City, India. Chartered Engineer; Consultant. m. K Sudhamani, 3 daughters. Education: Intermediate Science, The Vijaya College, University of Mysore, 1953; BSc, The National College, University of Mysore, 1955; BE, Civil, The National Institute of Engineering, University of Mysore, 1959. Appointments: Junior Engineer, PWD, Mysore State; Assistant Inspecting Officer, DGS & D, India Government, 1963-66; Design Engineer, Chief Design Engineer, Metallurgical and Engineering Consultants Ltd, India, 1967-95; Consultant, Assistant Chief Consultant, Ajaokuta Steel Plant, Nigeria, 1988-90; Consultant, Advisor, Simplex Castings (Pvt) Ltd, Bangalore, 1996-97; Consultant, Civil and Structural works, Mysore, 1997-; Resident Engineer, Techno Arts Construction (Pvt) Ltd, Bangalore, Mysore, 2000-01; Consultant, Dalal Matt Macdonald (Pvt) Ltd, Mumbai, Mysore, 2003-. Publications: Several articles for professional Seminars. Honours: Fellow of the Institute of Engineers, Civil Section, India, 1981; Best Citizen of India Award, 1998; Numerous entries in British and American biographical dictionaries. Address: No 163/74, 2nd Main, 8th Cross Road, Vidyaranyapuram, Mysore, 570 008, Karnataka, India.

VITKIENE Elena, b. 1939, Kursenai, Lithuania. Economist. m. Benediktas, 1 son, 1 daughter. Education: Diploma of Economist, Faculty of Economics, Vilnius State University, Lithuania,1974; Postgraduate Studies, Diploma of Doctor of Social Sciences, St Petersburg Culture Institute, Russia, 1983. Appointments: Head, Kursenai Club Reading Room; Production Manager, Klaipeda Merger of Restaurants and Cafes; Teacher, Klaipeda Trade School, 1978-83; Head Teacher, Klaipeda Faculties, Lithuanian State Conservatory, 1983; Associate Professor, Klaipeda University, 1991-. Publications: Monographs: Service Marketing, 1999; Recreation. Recreation Marketing Research, 2002; Books: Personality and Activities of Culture Worker, 1989; Analysis of Club Institution Activities, 1989; About 160 scientific publications and presentations in countries including: Italy, Poland, USA, UK and Portugal. Honours: Helen Prize for Humanitarian Works for Women, 2001; Medal commemorating the XIII World Congress of the International Economic Association, Portugal, 2002. Memberships: European Union for Coastal Conservation; Lithuanian Economic Association; Lithuanian Folk Art Society;

Vice-President, Lithuanian National Coastal Association. Address: K Manto 84 str, Klaipeda 92294, Lithuania. E-mail: rekkat@gmf.ku.lt

VIZINCZEY Stephen, b. 12 May 1933, Kaloz, Hungary. Writer. m. September 1963, 3 daughters. Education: University of Budapest, 1949-50; Academy of Theatre Arts, Budapest, 1951-56. Appointments: Editor, Exchange Magazine, 1960-61; Producer, Canadian Broadcasting Corporation, 1962-65. Publications: In Praise of Older Women, 1965; The Rules of Chaos, 1969; An Innocent Millionaire, 1983; Truth and Lies in Literature, 1986; The Man with the Magic Touch, 1994; Be Faithful unto Death (translation), 1995; Wishes, 2001. Contributions to: Currently; The Los Angeles Times Book Review. Memberships: PEN; Society of Authors; ALCS. Address: 70 Coleherne Court, Old Brompton Road, London SW5 0EF, England.

VLAMOS Panayiotis, b. 3 March 1970, Athens, Greece. Educator; Research Mathematician. Education: BSc, Mathematics, Mathematics Department, University of Athens, Greece, 1991; PhD, Science of Mathematics, School of Sciences, Mathematics Department, National Technical University of Athens, 1997. Appointments: Instructor, General Mathematics, Hellenic Open University, 2000, 2001; Associate Professor, Department of Algebra and Geometry, Centre of Applied Mathematics and Informatics, Pedagogical Faculty, University of Rousse, Bulgaria, 2000-. Publications: 20 publications in international journals; 10 publications in proceedings of international conferences; 12 publications in Greek journals; 9 publications in proceedings of Greek conferences; Author of 7 books; Co-author of 6 books. Honours: Participations, Awards and Distinctions in National Mathematical Competitions and in the 26th and 27th IMO, Scholarships for Postgraduate Studies from the Bodosakis Foundation, 1991-92 and the National Technical University, 1993-97. Memberships: Hellenic Mathematical Society; American Mathematical Society; European Mathematical Society; Mathematical Society of Edinburgh. Address: 40 Riga Ferraiou str, 18344 Moschato, Athens, Greece. E-mail: vlamos@vlamos.com

VLASSOV Vasiliy V, b. 15 June 1953, Novosibirsk, USSR. Physician. m. Irina, 23 November 1973, 1 daughter. Education: MD, Military Medical Academy, St Petersburg, Russia; Dr Medical Science; Professor. Appointments: Air Surgeon, 1976-79; Clinical Physiology Department Head, Irkutsk, Aviation Hospital, 1980-88; Professor, Head Department, Aerospace Medicine Saratov Military Medical Institute; Professor, Head Department, Social Science Saratov Medical University, 1995-2001; Professor, Moscow Physics-Technical University, 2001-; Chief Editor, Media Sphera Publishing Group, Moscow. Publications: Effectiveness of diagnostic tests; Aviat Space Environmental Medicine; Military Medicine. Memberships: Russian Medical Association, Cochrane Collaboration, Director of Russian Branch, 2001-. Address: PO Box 13, Moscow 109451, Russia.

VOINEA Silvia, b. 1 November 1942, Bacau, Romania. Lyrical Artist; Professor. 1 son. Education: Voice and Opera, Ciprian Porumbescu Conservatoire, Bucharest, 1961-66; Special Training in Mozart Repertoire, Germany, 1968; PhD in Musicology, University of Music, Bucharest, 1998-2000, first lyrical woman artist to achieve this title. Career: Coloratura Soprano, Romanian National Opera, Bucharest, 1968-98, Opera Comique, Bucharest, 1998-; Voice Teacher, National University of Music, Bucharest, 1990-; Appearances throughout Europe, 18 countries; Permanent Guest, 15 years, Opera Comique, Berlin, 5 years, Semper Oper, Desden, 3 years, Theatre Royal de Liege, Belgium, 4 years, Klagenfurt, Austria; Participated in 11 international festivals in

Europe; Filmed 2 operas, Les folies d'Offenbach, with the roll of Olympia from Offenbach's The Tales of Hoffmann, Olympia, and Lucia di Lammermoor; Numerous recordings for radio and TV in Romania, Switzerland, Germany and UK; Sang over 33 leading roles; Member of numerous international and national juries. Publications: A Journey in the History of Singing Art and Vocal Aesthetics; Voice Performance – history, technique expression: A view upon the methods in the art of chant, 2002. Honours: Prize of Flacara (Flame) magazine, 1987; Nomination in bicentennial Donizetti, role of Lucia, Opera International, Paris, 1997; Prize of Performance in Lyric Art, Actualitatea Muzicala, 1997; Excellence Prizes, Oedip Foundation, 1997, 1998, 1999; Prize, Musical Critics, Glorie in arta lirica, 1999; Diploma, George Stephanescu, Opera Nationala Roama, 2002; Excellence Prize, The National Romanian Opera, 2004; Romanian State Order, The Cultural Merit, Commander Degree, President of the Republic. Memberships: National Union of Theatric Performers of Romania; Union of Musical Critics, Mihail Jora; Directorial Collegiate of Opera Comique, Bucharest; Numerous national and international juries. Address: C A Rossetti str, No 7 Sector 1, Bucharest, Romania.

VOLLMAR James Anthony, b. 8 January 1952, Wellingborough, Northamptonshire, England. Writer; Poet; Playwright. Education: Queen Mary College, University of London, 1970-72. Appointment: Founder, Editor, Greylag Press, 1977-. Publications: Circles and Spaces; Orkney Poems; Hoy: The Seven Postcards; Warming the Stones; Explorers Log Book. Contributions to: Agenda; Iron; Oasis; Joe Soaps Canoe; Ally; Pacific Quarterly; Ambit. Memberships: Writers' Guild of Great Britain. Address: 7 Moreton Way, Kingsthorpe. Northampton, NN2 8PD

VOLPOV Evgeni, b. 20 February 1959, Donetzk Region, Ukraine. Electrical Research Engineer. m. Irena Volpov, 2 sons. Education: Masters Degree, St Petersburg State Technical University, 1976-82; PhD, Electrotechnical Institute of Russia, 1986-89. Appointments: R&D and Failure Analysis Engineer, Planning, Development and Technology Division, Israel Electric Corporation, Haifa, Israel; Specialising in electric field modelling, insulation co-ordination, and diagnostics of HV power apparatus. Publications: Articles in scientific journals include: HVDC Gas Insulated Apparatus: Electric Field Specificity and Insulation Design Concept, 2002; Electric Field Modeling and Field Formation Mechanism, 2003. Honours: Listed in Who's Who publications and biographical dictionaries. Address: Israel Electric Co, Planning, Development and Technology Division, Haifa 31000, Israel. E-mail: evgeni.volpov@gmx.net Website: http://www.geocities.com/evgeni_volpov

VOLTTI Hilkka Annikki, b. 6 December 1944, Mikkeli, Finland. Chemist. Education: MSc, Biochemistry, 1970; PhD, Biochemistry, 1974; Clinical Chemist, Clinical Chemistry, 1983. Appointments: Assistant, Department of Biochemistry, University Oulu, Finland; Research Assistant, Finnish National Research Council, Oulu, 1969-72; Reader, Associate Professor, Medical Biochemistry, University of Oulu, 1973-79; Lecturer, Biochemistry, 1980-81; Chemist, University Hospital, Oulu, 1982-84; Clinical Chemist, Central Hospital, Kymenlaakso, Kotka, 1985-2001; Retired, 2001. Publications: Contributions to professional journals. Honours: International Scientist of the Year, IBC, 2002; Woman of Achievement, IBC, 2002; Most Influential Scientist of the Decade, ABI, 2002; Woman of the Year, ABI, 2002, 2003; Universal Award of Accomplishment, ABI, 2002; Nomination to both the Companion of Honour Awards and the Honours List of 500 Founders of the 21st Century, IBC, 2002; The Global Award of Accomplishment, BWW, 2000; Listed in numerous biographical reference books. Memberships: Fellowship of the International Biographical Association, Cambridge, England; Member, Scientific

Advisor to the President and Director of the BWW Society, USA; Member, ABI Research Association's Board of Governors, USA. Address: Tallinnankatu 6-8 A 3, 48100 Kotka, Finland.

VOORHEES Stephanie Robin, b. 18 December 1951, Indianapolis, Indiana, USA. Artist. m. James Voorhees. Education: BA, Fine Arts Education, Montclair State University, New Jersey, USA; Postgraduate work, 32 credits. Appointments: Secretary to the Producer of the Foreign Broadcast Service, Democratic and Republican National Conventions in Miami, Florida, 1972; Art Teacher, K-12, Woodbridge, New Jersey; Professional Artist, Bradenton, Florida. Honours: State of New Jersey Governor's Teachers Award; Chamber of Commerce Excellence in Education Award; Listed in Who's Who publications and biographical dictionaries. Memberships: American Legion Auxiliary; Life Member, Ladies Auxiliary VFW. Address: 4212 Chinaberg Road, Bradenton, FL 34208, USA. E-mail: stpvoorhs6@aol.com

VORA Bipin, b. 1 April 1943, Harij, Gujarat, India. Chemical Engineer. m. Kalpi, 1 son, 2 daughters. Education: BSc honours, Chemistry, University of Mumbai, 1963; BS, 1965, MS, 1967, Chemical Engineering, University of New Mexico, USA. Appointments: Various Research and Development and Technical Services positions, UOP LLC, 1967-90; Associate Director, Olefins and Detergents Research and Development, 1990-94; Director, Olefins and Detergents Research and Development, 1994-2000; Senior Corporate Fellow, Development, UOP LLC, 2001-. Publications: Over 100 publications; Numerous international patents. Honours: Distinguished Alumni, University of New Mexico, 1999; ACS National Award of Industrial Chemistry, 2002. Memberships: American Institute of Chemical Engineer; Fellow Member, American Chemical Society. Address: 1324 Kallien Court, Naperville, IL 60540, USA. E-mail: bipin.vora@uop.com

VORECHOVSKY Igor, b. February 8 1958, Brno, Czechoslovakia. Research Scientist; Lecturer. 1 son, 1 daughter. Education: MD, Brno University, Czechoslovakia, 1983; PhD, Charles University, Prague, Czechoslovakia, 1989. Appointments: Research Fellow, Institute of Child Health, Brno, Czechoslovakia, 1983-89; Research Fellow, Paterson Institute, Manchester, England, 1989-91; Postdoctoral Scientist Karolinska Institute, Stockholm, Sweden, 1991-95; Lecturer, University College, London, 1995; Currently Research Scientist, Southampton University Medical School. Publications: articles in scientific journals include: Discoverer of the human gene for X-linked agammaglobulinaemia (Bruton's disease), the first described immunodeficiency, 1992, mouse homolog, 1993; Developed DNA-based diagnostic assay for X-linked agammaglobulinaemia, 1995. Honour: European BIOMED Award, European Community, 1995. Membership: Human Genome Organisation. Address: University of Southampton, Medical School, Division of Human Genetics, Southampton SO16 6YD, England. E-mail iguo@soton.ac.uk

VUKASOVIĆ Ante, b. 9 January 1929, Osijek, Croatia. University Professor. m. Nada Vukasović, 1 son, 1 daughter. Education: Teachers' Academy Degree, Osijek, Croatia, 1950; Faculty of Philosophy, Department of Pedagogy, 1956, PhD, Scientific Degree, Faculty of Philosophy, 1965, Doctorate and Honorary Title of Scientific Advisor, 1979, University of Zagreb. Appointments: Teacher, Šestanovac Primary School near Split, 1950-51; Student, University of Zagreb, 1951-56; Teachers' Academy Professor, 1956-57; Director, Pedagogical Centre for primary and secondary school teacher training for the region of Eastern Slavonia, Osijek, 1957-60; Assistant Lecturer, 1960-66, Senior Lecturer, 1966-73, Associate Professor, 1973-78, Professor, 1978-93, Department of Pedagogy, Faculty of Philosophy, University of Zagreb; Director of Centre for Education and

Research, 1971-79; Director, Scientific Research Project: System and programme of pre-service and in-service training of teachers for work in the field of family planning, UN Fund for Population Activity, 1979-83. Publications: Over 1400 publications including books as author, editor and co-author, scientific dissertations in conference proceedings and journals, newspaper articles and reviews, most notably: The Influence of the Contemporary Technology on the Concept of General Education (doctoral dissertation), 1964; Vocational and Technical Education, 1972; Moral Education, 1974; Intellectual Education, 1976; Moral Qualities of Our Students, 1977; Training Teachers for Educational Work in the Area of Humanization of Relations between the Sexes, 1982; Education for Humane Relationships and Responsible Parenthood, 1984; Pedagogy, 1990; Ethics – Morality – Personality, 1993; Family – the Source and Bearer of Life, 1999. Honours include: National Decoration: Work Medal with a Gold Wreath, 1971; Award for Improvement of Scientific Research Work, 1971; Several Jan Amos Komenský Medals, Danica Hrvatska Order of Merit, Republic of Croatia, 1996; National "Ivan Filipović Award" for lifetime achievement, 2002. Memberships include: Chairman, Society of Croatian-Slovakian Friendship, 1993-2003; World Association for Educational Research; Academy of Humanities, St Petersburg, Russia; Management Board, Croatian Victimological Society; Croatian Pedagogical Literary Association; Croatian Pedagogical Society; Croatian Society for Life and Family. Address: Gjure Szaba 13, 10 000 Zagreb, Croatia. E-mail: hkz@hkz-mi.hr

W

WABARA Marc Inyanagbo, b. 26 February 1951, Lagos, Nigeria. Banker. m. Ngozi, 2 sons, 2 daughters. Education: BSc, Finance (Banking), University of Lagos, Nigeria, 1977; MBA, Finance, Adelphi University, Garden City New York, USA, 1983. Appointments: Accountant, Mobil Producing Nigeria, 1979-81; Manager-in-Training, Metropolitan Life Insurance Company, New York, USA, 1982-83; SM Banking, International Merchant Bank Limited, 1984-88; SM, Banking, International Treasury Department, ACB Ltd, 1988-89; SM, Credit and Marketing, Chartered Bank Ltd, 1981-91; General Manager, Treasury, International Operations, Manufacturers Merchant Bank, 1991-93; Chairman, Chief Executive, Hallmark Bank PLC, 1999-Honours: National Award in Business Administration, Beta Xi Chapter of Deltamu Delta; Financial Post Award, Banker of the Year, 1994; University of Lagos Alumni Achievers Award, 2003. Memberships: University of Lagos Alumni Association; Chartered Institute of Bankers of Nigeria; Institute of Management Consultants. Address: Hallmark Bank PLC, Hallmark Bank Plaza, 137/139 Broad Street, PMB 12917, Marina, Lagos, Nigeria. E-mail: ceo@hallmarkbankplc.com

WADE (Sarah) Virginia, b. 10 July 1945, Bournemouth, England. Tennis Player. Education: University of Sussex. Appointments: Amateur player, 1962-68, professional, 1968-; British Hard Court Champion, 1967, 1968, 1973, 1974; USA Champion, 1968 (singles) 1973, 1975 (doubles); Italian Champion, 1971; Australian Champion, 1972; Wimbledon Ladies Champion, 1977; Played Wightman Cup for Great Britain, 1965-81, Captain 1973-80; Played Federation Cup for Great Britain, 1967-81, Captain, 1973-81; Commentator, BBC, 1980-. Publications: Courting Triumph (with Mary Lou Mellace), 1978; Ladies of the Court, 1984. Honours include: LLD, Sussex, 1985; International Tennis Hall of Fame, 1989. Membership: Committee, All England Lawn Tennis Club, 1983-91. Address: c/o International Management Group, Pier House, Strand on the Green, London W4 3NN, England.

WADE David, b. 2 December 1929, Edinburgh, Scotland. Writer. Education: Queen's College, Cambridge, 1952. Appointments: Radio Critic, The Listener, 1965-67, The Times, 1967-89. Publications: Trying to Connect You; The Cooker; The Guthrie Process; The Gold Spinners; Three Blows in Anger; The Ogden File; The Carpet Maker of Samarkand; The Nightingale; Summer of 39; The Facts of Life; A Rather Nasty Crack; On Detachment; The Tree of Strife; Power of Attorney; Alexander. Membership: Society of Authors. Address: Willow Cottage, Stockland Green Road, Southborough, Kent TN3 0TL, England.

WAETZMAN Larry Samuel, b. 11 December 1945, Reading, Pennsylvania, USA. Urban Planner. m. Bonnie Waetzman, 2 sons, 1 daughter. Education: BA, Franklin & Marshall College, 1967; MA, University of Wisconsin (Madison), 1969. Appointments: 1st Lieutenant, US Army, 1969-71; Borough Planner, Borough of Morristown, Pennsylvania, 1972-74; Director of Community Development, Haverford Township, Pennsylvania, 1974-78; Planner, Government Studies and Systems Inc., 1978-81; Partner, Tredinnick Waetzman Associates, 1981-87; Owner, Waetzman Planning Group, 1987-2000; President, Waetzman Planning Group Inc., 2000-. Publications: Various articles: Pennsylvania Department of Community Affairs Reports; New Jersey Municipalities; 8 professional education seminars: Corman Educational Services, Pennsylvania Bar Institute, International Council of Shopping Centers. Memberships: Practising Planner, American Institute of Certified Planners; Licensed Professional Planner, New Jersey; American Planning Association; New Jersey

Planning Officials. Address: 1230 County Line Road, Bryn Mawr, PA 19010, USA. E-mail: lsw@waetzmanplanning.com Website: www.waetzmanplanning.com

WAGNER Hugh McKinlay, b. 5 March 1948, Danville, Pennsylvania, USA. Palaeontologist. Education: BA, Palaeontology, 1971, MA, Palaeontology, 1974, University California at Berkeley; PhD, Geology, University California Riverside, 1981. Appointments: Lecturer, University California at Irvine, 1979-1984; Lecturer, Saddleback Community College, 1980-1992; Lecturer, Shasta College, 1994-1996; Collections Manager, Department of Palaeontology, San Diego Natural History Museum, 1997-2003. Publications: Numerous articles in professional journals. Honours: Sigma Xi, 1973. Memberships: Society of Vertebrate Palaeontology; Geological Society of America; Geological Association of Canada. Address: San Diego Natural History Museum, PO Box 121390, San Diego, CA 72112-1930, USA. E-mail: hwagner@sdnhm.org

WAGONER David (Russell), b. 5 June 1926, Massillon, Ohio, USA. Professor of English; Poet; Author. m. (1) Patricia Parrott, 1961, divorced 1982, (2) Robin Heather Seyfried, 1982, 2 daughters. Education: BA, Pennsylvania State University, 1947; MA, Indiana University, 1949. Appointments: Instructor, DePauw University, 1949-50, Pennsylvania State University, 1950-53; Assistant Professor, 1954-57, Associate Professor, 1958-66, Professor of English, 1966-, University of Washington, Seattle; Editor, Poetry Northwest, 1966-; Elliston Professor of Poetry, University of Cincinnati, 1968. Publications: Poetry: Dry Sun, Dry Wind, 1953; A Place to Stand, 1958; Poems, 1959; The Nesting Ground, 1963; Staying Alive, 1966; New and Selected Poems, 1969; Working Against Time, 1970; Riverbed, 1972; Sleeping in the Woods, 1974; A Guide to Dungeness Spit, 1975; Travelling Light, 1976; Collected Poems, 1956-1976, 1976; Who Shall be the Sun?: Poems Based on the Love, Legends, and Myths of Northwest Coast and Plateau Indians, 1978; In Broken Country, 1979; Landfall, 1981; First Light, 1983; Through the Forest: New and Selected Poems, 1977-1987, 1987; Traveling Light: Collected and New Poems, 1999. Fiction: The Man in the Middle, 1954; Money, Money, Money, 1955; Rock, 1958; The Escape Artist, 1965; Baby, Come on Inside, 1968; Where Is My Wandering Boy Tonight?, 1970; The Road to Many a Wonder, 1974; Tracker, 1975; Whole Hog, 1976; The Hanging Garden, 1980. Editor: Straw for the Fire: From the Notebooks of Theodore Roethke 1943-1963, 1972. Honours: Guggenheim Fellowship, 1956; Ford Foundation Fellowship, 1964; American Academy of Arts and Letters Grant, 1967; National Endowment for the Arts Grant, 1969; Morton Dauwen Zabel Prize, 1967; Oscar Blumenthal Prize, 1974; Fels Prize, 1975; Eunice Tietjens Memorial Prize, 1977; English-Speaking Union Prize, 1980; Sherwood Anderson Prize, 1980; Pacific Northwest Booksellers Award, 2000. Membership: Academy of American Poets, chancellor, 1978. Address: University of Washington, 4045 Brooklyn Avenue NE, Seattle, WA 98105, USA.

WAINWRIGHT Geoffrey, b. 16 July 1939, Yorkshire, England. Professor of Systematic Theology; Methodist Minister. m. Margaret Wiles, 20 April 1965, 1 son, 2 daughters. Education: BA, 1960, MA, 1964, BD, 1972, DD, 1987, University of Cambridge; DrThéol, University of Geneva, 1969. Appointments: Editor, Studia Liturgica, 1974-87; Professor of Systematic Theology, The Divinity School, Duke University, Durham, North Carolina, 1983-. Publications: Christian Initiation, 1969; Eucharist and Eschatology, 1971, 2nd edition, 1981; The Study of Liturgy (co-editor), 1978, 2nd edition, 1992; Doxology, 1980; The Ecumenical Moment, 1983; The Study of Spirituality (co-editor), 1986; On Wesley and Calvin, 1987; Keeping the Faith: Essays to Mark the Centenary of

Lux Mundi (editor), 1989; The Dictionary of the Ecumenical Movement (co-editor), 1991; Methodists in Dialogue, 1995; Worship With One Accord, 1997; For Our Salvation, 1997; Is the Reformation Over? Catholics and Protestants at the Turn of the Millennia, 2000; Lesslie Newbigin: A Theological Life, 2000. Contributions to: Reference books and theological journals. Honours: Numerous named lectureships world-wide; Berakah Award, North American Academy of Liturgy, 1999; Received a Festschrift: Ecumenical Theology in Worship, Doctrine, and Life: Essays Presented to Geoffrey Wainwright on his 60th Birthday, 1999; Outstanding Ecumenist Award, Washington Theological Consortium, 2003. Memberships: American Theological Society, secretary, 1988-95, president, 1996-97; International Dialogue Between the World Methodist Council and the Roman Catholic Church, chairman; Societas Liturgica, president, 1983-85; World Council of Churches Faith and Order Commission, 1976-91. Address: The Divinity School, Duke University, Durham, NC 27708, USA.

WAITE Terence Hardy, b. 31 May 1939, Bollington, England. Writer and Broadcaster. m. Helen Frances Watters, 1964, 1 son, 3 daughters. Education: Church Army College, London. Appointments: Lay Training Advisor to Bishop and Diocese of Bristol, 1964-68; Advisor to Archbishop of Uganda, Rwanda and Burundi, 1968-71; International Consultant with Roman Catholic Church, 1972-79; Advisor, Archbishop of Canterbury on Anglican Communion Affairs, 1980-92; Iranian Hostages Mission, 1981; Libyan Hostages Mission, 1985; Kidnapped in Beirut, 1987, Released, 1991. Publications: Taken on Trust, 1993; Footfalls in Memory, 1995; Travels with a Primate, 2000. Honours include: Hon DCL, Kent, 1986, City of London, Durham, 1992; Hon DLL, Liverpool; Hon LLD, Sussex, 1992; Hon LHD, Wittenberg University, 1992; Hon Dr International Law, Florida Southern University, 1992; Dr hc, Yale University Divinity School, 1992; Roosevelt Freedom Medal, 1992; Man of the Year, England, 1985; Freeman, City of Canterbury, 1992, Borough of Lewisham, 1992; Hon DPhil, Anglia Polytechnic, 2001; Hon DLitt, Nottingham Trent, 2001. Memberships: Church of England National Association, 1966-68; Co-ordinator, Southern Sudan Relief Project, 1969-71; Royal Institute of International Affairs, 1980-; Butler Trust, Prison Officers Award Programme; President, Y-Care International (YMCA International Development Committee); UK President, Emmaus Appeal Committee; Cambridge (for the Homeless), 1996-; Founder Chair, Friends of Victim Support, 1992-; Patron, Strode Park Foundation for the Disabled; Rainbow Trust; Fellow Commoner, Trinity Hall, Cambridge, 1992-; Honorary Chancellor, Florida Southern University, 1992; Chairman, Prison Video Trust; Trustee Freeplay Foundation. Address: Trinity Hall, Cambridge, CB2 1TJ, England.

WAKEHAM John (Baron Wakeham of Malden), b. 1932. Chartered Accountant; Politician. m. Alison Bridget, 3 sons. Appointments: Chartered Accountant with own practice; Retired from business, 1977; Elected Conservative Member of Parliament for Maldon and Rochford, 1974, South Colchester and Maldon, 1983; Ministerial Appointments: Assistant Government Whip, 1979; Lord Commissioner of the Treasury, 1981; Parliamentary Under Secretary of State, Department of Industry, 1981; Minister of State, Treasury, 1982; Government Chief Whip, 1983; Appointed Member of the Privy Council, Lord Privy Seal and Leader of the House of Commons, 1987; Lord President of the Council and Leader of the House of Commons, 1988; Secretary of State for Energy, 1989; Lord Privy Seal and Leader of the House of Lords, 1992; Retired from Government, 1994; 6 Non-Executive Directorships; Chairman, Cothill House, 1998; Chairman, Alexandra Rose Day, 1998; Chairman, Vosper Thorneycroft Holdings Plc, 1995; Chairman, Press Complaints Commission,

1995-2002; Non-Executive Director, Enron Corporation, 1994-2002; Bristol and West PLC, 1995-2002; NM Rothschild & Sons Ltd, 1995-2002; Chairman, Royal Commission on House of Lords Reform, 1999-2000; Chairman, Michael Page International Plc, 2001-02;. Honours: JP; DL; FLA; Honorary PhD; Honorary D Univ. Memberships: Director, National Association for Gambling Care, Educational Resources and Training; Trustee and Committee of Management, RNLI; Trustee, HMS Warrior 1860; Clubs: Garrick, Carlton, Royal Yacht Squadron, Royal Southern Yacht Club. Address: House of Lords, London SW1, England.

WAKELEY Amanda, b. 15 September 1962, England. Fashion Designer. m. Neil David Gillon, 1992. Appointments: Fashion industry, New York, 1983-85; Designing, private clients, England, 1986; Launched own label, 1990; Retail, wholesale world-wide, bridal, high street brand Amanda Wakeley for Principles and corporate-wear consultancy. Honours: Glamour Award, British Fashion Awards, 1992, 1993, 1996. Membership: Co-Chair, Fashion Targets Breast Cancer Campaign, 1996, 1998, 2000, 2002. Address: Amanda Wakeley Ltd, 26-28 Conway Street, London, W1T 6BQ, England. Website: www.amandawakeley.com

WAKOSKI Diane, b. 3 August 1937, Whittier, California, USA. Poet; Professor of English. m. Robert J Turney, 14 February 1982. Education: BA, English, University of California at Berkeley, 1960. Appointments: Poet-in-Residence, Professor of English, 1975-, University Distinguished Professor, 1990-, Michigan State University; Many visiting writer-in-residencies. Publications: Poetry: Coins and Coffins, 1962; Discrepancies and Apparitions, 1966; The George Washington Poems, 1967; Inside the Blood Factory, 1968; The Magellanic Clouds, 1970; The Motorcycle Betrayal Poems, 1971; Smudging, 1972; Dancing on the Grave of a Son of a Bitch, 1973; Virtuoso Literature for Two and Four Hands, 1975; Waiting for the King of Spain, 1976; The Man Who Shook Hands, 1978; Cap of Darkness, 1980; The Magician's Feastletters, 1982; The Collected Greed, 1984; The Rings of Saturn, 1986; Emerald Ice: Selected Poems 1962-1987, 1988; Medea the Sorceress, 1991; Jason the Sailor, 1993; The Emerald City of Las Vegas, 1995; Argonaut Rose, 1998; The Butcher's Apron: New and Selected Poems, 2000. Criticism: Towards a New Poetry, 1980. Contributions to: Anthologies and other publications. Honours: Cassandra Foundation Grant, 1970; Guggenheim Fellowship, 1972; National Endowment for the Arts Grant, 1973; CAPS Grant, 1988, New York State, 1974; Writer's Fulbright Award, 1984; Michigan Arts Council Grant, 1988; William Carlos Williams Prize, 1989; Distinguished Artist Award, Michigan Arts Foundation, 1989. Memberships: Author's Guild; PEN; Poetry Society of America. Address: 607 Division Street, East Lansing, MI 48823, USA.

WALCOTT Derek (Alton), b. 23 January 1930, Castries, St Lucia, West Indies. Poet; Dramatist; Visiting Professor. m. (1) Fay Moyston, 1954, divorced 1959, 1 son, (2) Margaret Ruth Maillard, 1962, divorced, 2 daughters, (3) Norline Metivier, 1982, divorced 1993. Education: St Mary's College, Castries, 1941-47; BA, University College of the West Indies, Mona, Jamaica, 1953. Appointments: Teacher, St Mary's College, Castries, 1947-50, 1954, Grenada Boy's Secondary School, St George's, 1953-54, Jamaica College, Kingston, 1955; Feature Writer, Public Opinion, Kingston, 1956-57; Founder-Director, Little Carib Theatre Workshop, later Trinidad Theatre Workshop, 1959-76; Feature Writer, 1960-62, Drama Critic, 1963-68, Trinidad Guardian, Port-of-Spain; Visiting Professor, Columbia University, 1981, Harvard University, 1982, 1987; Assistant Professor of Creative Writing, 1981, Visiting Professor, 1985-, Brown University. Publications: Poetry: 25 Poems, 1948; Epitaph for the Young: XII Cantos, 1949; Poems, 1951; In a Green Night: Poems 1948-1960, 1962; Selected Poems, 1964; The Castaway and Other Poems, 1965; The Gulf and Other Poems, 1969; Another Life, 1973; Sea Grapes, 1976; The Star-Apple Kingdom, 1979; Selected Poems, 1981; The Fortunate Traveller, 1981; The Caribbean Poetry of Derek Walcott and the Art of Romare Bearden, 1983; Midsummer, 1984; Collected Poems 1948-1984, 1986; The Arkansas Testament, 1987; Omeros, 1989; Collected Poems, 1990; Poems 1965-1980, 1992; Derek Walcott: Selected Poems, 1993. Plays: Cry for a Leader, 1950; Senza Alcun Sospetto or Paolo and Francesca, 1950; Henri Christophe: A Chronicle, 1950; Robin and Andrea or Bim, 1950; Three Assassins, 1951; The Price of Mercy, 1951; Harry Dernier, 1952; The Sea at Dauphin, 1954; Crossroads, 1954; The Charlatan, 1954, 4th version, 1977; The Wine of the Country, 1956; The Golden Lions, 1956; Ione: A Play with Music, 1957; Ti-Jear and His Brothers, 1957; Drums and Colours, 1958; Malcochon, or, The Six in the Rain, 1959; Jourmard, or, A Comedy till the Last Minute, 1959; Batai, 1965; Dream on Monkey Mountain, 1967; Franklin: A Tale of the Islands, 1969, 2nd version, 1973; In a Fine Castle, 1970; The Joker of Seville, 1974; O Babylon!, 1976; Remembrance, 1977; The Snow Queen, 1977; Pantomime, 1978; Marie Laveau, 1979; The Isle is Full of Noises, 1982; Beef, No Chicken, 1982; The Odyssey: A Stage Version, 1993; Tiepolo's Hound, 2000. Non-Fiction: The Antilles: Fragments of Epic Memory: The Nobel Lecture, 1993; What the Twilight Says (essays), 1998. Honours: Rockefeller Foundation Grants, 1957, 1966, and Fellowship, 1958; Arts Advisory Council of Jamaica Prize, 1960; Guinness Award, 1961; Ingram Merrill Foundation Grant, 1962; Borestone Mountain Awards, 1964, 1977; Heinemann Awards, Royal Society of Literature, 1966, 1983; Cholmondeley Award, 1969; Eugene O'Neill Foundation Fellowship, 1969; Gold Hummingbird Medal, Trinidad, 1969; Obie Award, 1971; Officer of the Order of the British Empire, 1972; Guggenheim Fellowship, 1977; Welsh Arts Council International Writers Prize, 1980; John D and Catharine T MacArthur Foundation Fellowship, 1981; Los Angeles Times Book Prize, 1986; Queen's Gold Medal for Poetry, 1988; Nobel Prize for Literature, 1992. Memberships: American Academy of Arts and Letters, honorary member; Royal Society of Literature, fellow. Address: c/o Faber & Faber, 3 Queen Square, London, WC1N 3AU, England.

WALDEN Henry Russell, b. 28 November 1934, Timaru, New Zealand. Architect; Academic. m. Helen Elizabeth Green, 2 sons, 1 daughter. Education: BArch (Hons), New Zealand, 1962; MArch (distinction), Auckland, New Zealand, 1965; PhD, University of Birmingham, England, 1978; FNZIA, 1987. Appointments: Private Practice, England and New Zealand, 1962-72; Senior Lecturer, Birmingham School of Architecture, University of Central England in Birmingham, 1972-78; Associate Professor, Victoria University of Wellington, New Zealand, 1978-2002. Publications: Editor: The Open Hand, Essays on Le Corbusier, 1982; Author: Voices of Silence, New Zealand's Chapel of Futuna, 1987; Finnish Harvest, Chapel in Otaniemi, 1998. Honours: National Award for Architecture, NZIA, 1993. Memberships: Fellow, New Zealand Institute of Architects (FNZIA). Address: c/o School of Architecture, Victoria University of Wellington, New Zealand. E-mail: russell.walden@vuw.ac.nz

WALKER Alice (Malsenior), b. 9 February 1944, Eatonton, Georgia, USA. Author; Poet. m. Melvyn R Leventhal, 17 March 1967, divorced 1976, 1 daughter. Education: BA, Sarah Lawrence College, 1966. Appointments: Writer-in-Residence and Teacher of Black Studies, Jackson State College, 1968-69, Tougaloo College, 1970-71; Lecturer in Literature, Wellesley College, 1972-73, University of Massachusetts at Boston, 1972-73; Distinguished Writer, Afro-American Studies Department, University of California at Berkeley, 1982; Fannie Hurst Professor of Literature, Brandeis University, 1982; Co-Founder and Publisher, Wild Trees Press, Navarro, California, 1984-88. Publications: Once, 1968;

The Third Life of Grange Copeland, 1970; Five Poems, 1972; Revolutionary Petunias and Other Poems, 1973; In Love and Trouble, 1973; Langston Hughes: American Poet, 1973; Meridian, 1976; Goodnight, Willie Lee, I'll See You in the Morning, 1979; You Can't Keep a Good Woman Down, 1981; The Color Purple, 1982; In Search of Our Mother's Gardens, 1983; Horses Make a Landscape Look More Beautiful, 1984; To Hell With Dying, 1988; Living by the Word: Selected Writings, 1973-1987, 1988; The Temple of My Familiar, 1989; Her Blue Body Everything We Know: Earthling Poems, 1965-1990, 1991; Finding the Green Stone, 1991; Possessing the Secret of Joy, 1992; Warrior Marks (with Pratibha Parmar), 1993; Double Stitch: Black Women Write About Mothers and Daughters (with others), 1993; Everyday Use, 1994; By the Light of My Father's Smile, 1998; The Way Forward is with a Broken heart, 2000. Editor: I Love Myself When I'm Laughing... And Then Again When I'm Looking Mean and Impressive, 1979. Honours: Bread Loaf Writer's Conference Scholar, 1966; Ingram Merrill Foundation Fellowship, 1967; McDowell Colony Fellowships, 1967, 1977-78; National Endowment for the Arts Grants, 1969, 1977; Richard and Hinda Rosenthal Pound Award, American Academy and Institute of Arts and Letters, 1974; Guggenheim Fellowship, 1977-78; Pulitzer Prize for Fiction, 1983; American Book Award, 1983; O Henry Award, 1986; Nora Astorga Leadership Award, 1989; Freedom to Write Award, PEN Center, West, 1990; Honorary doctorates. Address: c/o Random House, 201 E 50th Street, New York, NY 10022, USA.

WALKER Catherine, b. 27 June 1945, Pas de Calais, France. Couturier. m. John Walker, deceased, 2 daughters. Education: University of Lille; University of Aix-en-Provence. Appointments: Director, Film Department, French Institute, London, 1970; Lecturer, French Embassy, London, 1971, The Chelsea Design Company Ltd, 1978-; Founder Sponsor, Honorary Member of Board, Gilda's Club; Founder Sponsor, Haven Trust. Publication: Catherine Walker, an Autobiography by the Private Couturier to Diana Princess of Wales, 1998; Catherine Walker, Twenty Five Years 1977-2002. Honours: Designer of the Year for British Couture, 1990-91; Designer of the Year for Glamour Award, 1991-92. Address: 65 Sydney Street, Chelsea, London SW3 6PX, England.

WALKER Miles Rawstron, b. 13 November 1940, Colby, Isle of Man. Politician; Company Director. m. Mary L Cowell, 11 October 1966, 1 son, 1 daughter. Education: Shropshire College of Agriculture, 1959-60. Appointments: Member and Chairman, Arbory Parish Commissioners, 1970-76; Member of House of Keys, Isle of Man Government, 1976-; Elected to Chief Ministry, 1986-96, Member of Treasury, 1996-, Isle of Man Government. Publications: Isle of Man Government Policy Documents, 1987-96. Honours: CBE, 1991; Awarded LLD, Liverpool University, 1994; KB, 1997. Memberships: Member, Isle of Man Treasury, 1996-2000; Chair, Isle of Man Swimming Association; President, Rotary Club, 2000-01; Port St Mary Rifle Club. Address: Magher Feailley, Main Road, Colby, IM9 4AD, Isle of Man. E-mail: miles.walker@talk21.com

WALKER Richard K, b. 21 October 1948, Knoxville, Tennessee, USA. Attorney. m. Beverley F Walker, 1 son, 1 daughter. Education: Bachelor of Arts Degree (Hons), Psychology, 1970, Juris Doctor Degree, 1975, University of Kansas; Universität Bonn, Germany, 1968-69; Universität Tübingen, Germany, 1971-72. Appointments: Assistant Professor of Law, 1977-80, Associate Professor of Law, 1980-82, University of South Carolina; Partner, Bishop, Cook, Purcell & Reynolds, 1981-90; Partner, Winston & Strawn, 1990-93; Partner, Streich Lang P.A., 1993-2000; Partner, Quarles & Brady Streich Lang LLP, 2000-. Publications: Articles

Dictionary of International Biography

in learned journals include: Court Awarded Attorneys Fees Under the Private Attorney General Concept – A Defense Perspective, 1975; The Exorbitant Cost of Redistributing Injustice: A Critical View of United Steel Workers of America v Weber and the Misguided Policy of Numerical Employment, 1979; Book chapter in Arizona Employment Law Handbook re Whistleblower Protection Law. Honours: ALCOA Scholar; Kimball Foundation Scholar; Fulbright Direct Exchange Fellow; Samuel Mellinger Leadership Award; Order of the Barristers; Scribes. Memberships: American Bar Association (Labor and Employment Law Section and Litigation Section); Arizona Bar; District of Columbia Bar; Maricopa County Bar Association. Address: Quarles & Brady Streich Lang LLP, Renaissance One, Two North Central Avenue, Phoenix, AZ 85004-2391, USA. E-mail: rwalker@quarles.com

WALLACE Robert Kimball, b. 2 August 1944, Seattle, Washington, USA. Professor; Author. m. Joan Ferrante. Education: BA, English, Whitman College; MA, English, Columbia University; PhD. Appointments: Assistant Professor, Northern Kentucky University, 1972-; Associate Professor; Professor; Regents Professor; Fulbright Professor, University of Deusto, Bilbao, Spain, 1976-77. Publications: Author of books on Josef and Rosina Lhevinne; Jane Austen and Mozart; Melville and Turner; Frank Stella's Moby-Dick. Honours: Midwest Book Award; Woodrow Wilson Fellowship; 2 NEH Fellowships for College Teachers. Memberships: Melville Society; Turner Society; Modern Language Association. Address: Literature and Language, Northern Kentucky University, Highland Heights, Kentucky 41076, USA.

WALLACE-BRUCE Nii Lante, b. 25 November 1953, Accra, Ghana. Lawyer. Education: PhD, University of Sydney, 1986; M International Law, Australian National University. Appointments: Practising Lawyer in Australia, 1985-91; University of Western Australia, 1992-2003; United Nations, 2003. Publications: More than 50 publications; 5 books; Articles in international refereed journals including: The Netherlands Journal of International Law; The Comparative and International Journal of Southern Africa. Honour: LLB Hons, University of Ghana, 1979. Membership: American Society of International Law. Address: ESPD, United Nations ECA, PO Box 3005, Addis Ababa, Ethiopia. E-mail: wallace-bruce@un.org

WALLACE-CRABBE Chris(topher Keith), b. 6 May 1934, Richmond, Victoria, Australia. Professor of English; Poet; Writer. m. (1) Helen Margaret Wiltshire, 1957, 1 son, 1 daughter, (2) Sophie Feil, 2 sons. Education: BA, 1956, MA, 1964, University of Melbourne; Reader in English, 1976-88, Professor of English, 1987-, Personal Chair, 1987-97, University of Melbourne; Visiting Chair in Australian Studies, Harvard University, USA. Publications: Poetry: No Glass Houses, 1956; The Music of Division, 1959; Eight Metropolitan Poems, 1962; In Light and Darkness, 1964; The Rebel General, 1967; Where the Wind Came, 1971; Act in the Noon, 1974; The Shapes of Gallipoli, 1975; The Foundations of Joy, 1976; The Emotions Are Not Skilled Workers, 1979; The Amorous Cannibal and Other Poems, 1985; I'm Deadly Serious, 1988; For Crying out Loud, 1990; Falling into Language, 1990; From the Republic of Conscience, 1992; Rungs of Time, 1993; Whirling, 1998; By and Large, 2001; Selected Poems 1956-1994, 1995. Novel: Splinters, 1981. Other: Melbourne or the Bush: Essays on Australian Literature and Society, 1973; Author! Author!, 1999. Editor: Volumes of Australian poetry. Honour: Masefield Prize for Poetry, 1957; Farmer's Poetry Prize, 1964; Grace Leven Prize, 1986; Dublin Prize, 1987; Christopher Brennan Award, 1990; Age Book of the Year Prize, 1995. Address: c/o Department of English, University of Melbourne, Melbourne, Victoria 3052, Australia.

WALSH Mary, b. 30 October 1933, Peoria, Illinois, USA. Artist; Curator. Education: Tutored in drawing and painting at the age of 9 years, Illinois Wesleyan University; BA, Marymount College, Tarrytown, New York. Career: Lifelong studio artist; Participated in 40 regional and national shows; Solo exhibitions at the Strasenburg Planetarium and the National Women's Hall of Fame; Instructor of Adult Continuing Education; Promoter of artwork of talented artists through newspapers, radio and television; Arranged ten exhibitions for PASTEL ARTISTS GROUP sponsored by the Cooperstown Art Association. Address: 1572 Tracy Drive, Skaneateles, NY 13152, USA.

WALSHAM Bruce Taylor, b. 28 February 1936, Grimsby, England. Mining Executive. m. Carole Moore, 3 January 1998. 2 daughters. Education: BSc, Birmingham University, England, 1958. Appointments: Geologist, Union Corporation, South Africa, 1958-62; Geologist, Mackay and Schnellmann Ltd, London, 1962-64; Geologist in Charge, Union Corp, London, 1964-71; Director, Mackay and Schnellmann Ltd, Brisbane, Australia, 1971; Vice-President, Freeport of Australia Incorporated, Melbourne, 1971-76; Vice-President, Freeport Exploration Co, Reno, USA, 1976-79; President, Freeport of Australia Inc, Melbourne, 1979-89; Vice-President, Freeport QNL, 1979-87; Deputy Chairman, Managing Director, Freeport McMoran Australia, 1987-89; Vice-President, Freeport Minerals Company, Freeport Sulphur Company, New Orleans, USA, 1986-89; President, Pittston Minerals International, Stamford, Melbourne, Australia, 1989-93; Executive Chairman, Panorama Resources, Perth, Australia, 1993-97; Chairman, President, Chief Executive Officer, Diamond Works Ltd, Vancouver, Canada, 1997-1999; President and Chief Executive Officer, Kansai Mining Corporation, Vancouver, 2000-. Publications: articles in various journals. Memberships: IMM; AUSIMM; MSEG; MAIME; MGSSA; MGSA; MAEG. Address: Carrswood, Fortescue Road, Salcombe TQ8 8AP, England

WALSS-RODRIGUEZ Rodolfo Jesus, b. 13 June 1945, Monclova, Mexico. Gynaecologist. m. Maria Eugenia, 17 December 1969, 2 sons, 3 daughters. Education: Medical School, University of Coahuila, 1962-70; MD, Research Obstetrics-Gynaecology, West Virginia University, 1973-77. Appointments: Professor, Obstetrics and Gynaecology, University of Coahuila, Mexico, 1978-92; Chief of Service, Obstetrics and Gynaecology, Mexican Institute of Social Security, 1985-89; Professor, Chairman, Obstetrics and Gynaecology, North Medical Center, Institute of Social Security, 1989-92; Private Practice, Brownsville, 1992-. Publications: 22 publications. Memberships: American College of Obstetrics and Gynaecology; American College of Surgery; American Society of Reproductive Medal. Address: 24 Summit Ct, Brownsville, TX 78521, USA.

WALTERS Barbara, b. 25 September 1931, Brookline, Massachusetts, USA. Television Broadcaster. m. (1) Lee Guber, 1963, divorced 1976, 1 adopted daughter, (2) Merv Adelson, 1986, divorced 1993. Education: Sarah Lawrence College, New York. Appointments: Writer, Producer, WNBC TV, Station WPIX, CBS TV Morning Broadcasts; Producer, NBC TV; Writer, Today Programme, NBC TV, 1961, Reporter, Panel Member, 1963-74, Co-Host, 1974-76; Moderator, Not for Women Only, 5 years; Correspondent, ABC News, Co-Anchor, Evening News Programme, 1976-78, Fascinating People, 1994-; Co-Executive Producer, The View ABC, New York, 1997-. Publications: How to Talk with Practically Anybody About Practically Anything, 1970; Contributor to several magazines. Honours include: Silver Satellite Award, American Women in Radio and TV, 1985; Named One of the 100 Most Important Women of the Century, Good Housekeeping, 1985; President Award, Overseas Press Club, 1988; Lowell Thomas Award for Journalism, 1990, 1994; Lifetime

Achievement Award, International Women's Media Foundation, 1992. Address: 20/20 147 Columbus Avenue, 10th Floor, New York, NY 10023, USA.

WALTERS Julie, b. 22 February 1950, Birmingham, England. Actress. m. Grant Roffey, 1998, 1 daughter. Education: Manchester Polytechnic; School Governor, Open University. Creative Works: Films include: Educating Rita, 1983; She'll Be Wearing Pink Pyjamas, 1984; Personal Services, 1986; Prick Up Your Ears, 1986; Buster, 1987; Mack the Knife, 1988; Killing Dad, 1989; Stepping Out, 1991; Just Like a Woman, 1992; Sister My Sister, 1994; Intimate Relations, 1996; Titanic Town, 1997; Girls Night, 1997; All Forgotten, 1999; Dancer, 1999; Billy Elliot, 2000; Harry Potter and the Philosopher's Stone, 2001; Before You Go, 2002; Harry Potter and the Chamber of Secrets, 2002; Calendar Girls, 2003; Harry Potter and the Prisoner of Azkaban, 2004; Mickybo and Me, 2004; TV includes: Talent, 1980; Wood and Walters, 1981; Boys From the Blackstuff, 1982; Say Something Happened, 1982; Victoria Wood as Seen on TV, 1984, 1986, 1987; The Birthday Party, 1986; Her Big Chance, 1987; GBH, 1991; Stepping Out, 1991; Julie Walters and Friends, 1991; Clothes in the Wardrobe, 1992; Wide Eyed and Legless, 1993; Bambino Mio, 1993; Pat and Margaret, 1994; Jake's Progress, 1995; Little Red Riding Hood, 1995; Intimate Relations, 1996; Julie Walters in an Alien, 1997; Dinner Ladies, 1998-99; Jack and the Beanstalk, 1998; Oliver Twist, 1999; My Beautiful Son, 2001; Murder, 2002; The Canterbury Tales, mini-series, 2003; The Return, 2003; Several stage appearances. Publication: Baby Talk, 1990. Honours: Variety Club Best Newcomer Award, 1980; Best Actress Award, 1984; British Academy Award for Best Actress, 1984; Golden Globe Award, 1984; Variety Club Award for Best Actress, 1991; Olivier Award, 2001. Address: c/o ICM, 76 Oxford Street, London W1N 0AX, England.

WALTERS Sherwood George, b. 9 May 1926, Detroit, USA. Professor; Consultant. m. Alexandra Sielcken, 4 September 1952, 1 son, 3 daughters. Education: BA cum laude, West Maryland College, 1949; MS, Columbia University, 1950; MBA with distinction, Columbia University Graduate School of Business, 1953; PhD honours scholar, New York University, 1960. Appointments: 1st Lieutenant, Infantry/Quartermaster Corps, 1944-47; Associate Professor of Economics and Sociology, College of Business Economics, Lehigh University, Bethlehem, Pennsylvania, 1950-60; Executive Vice President, Director of Centers, Retail Planning Manager, Mobil Oil, New York City, 1960-65; Executive Officer, Marketing Director, General Tire and Rubber International Plastics Co, Chemical Plastics Division, Akron, Ohio, 1965-70; Professor, Rutgers University, Newark, New Jersey, 1970-93; Professor Emeritus Management Studies, Rutgers University, Newark, 1993-; Founding Director, interfunctional management programme, 1970-88; Evaluator/ Emissary, Consultant in field, US NSF, 1980-. Publications: Co-author, Marketing Management Viewpoints, 2nd edition, 1970; Mandatory Housing Finance Programs, 1975; Managing the Industry University Co-operative Research Centers: A Guide for Directors and Other Stakeholders, 1998. Memberships: Chairman, New York Government Public Utility Commission Task Force, 1973-75; Chairman, University/Industrial Partnerships, John Von Neumann Center, Princeton, New Jersey, 1986; Newcomen Society. Address: 110 Topsail Watch Lane, Hampstead, NC 28443-2728, USA. Email: s.george.walters@worldnet.att.net

WALTON James Stephen, b. 27 November 1946, Kingston upon Thames, Surrey, England. Research Scientist. m. Dorcas Ann Graham, 1 son, one daughter. Education: Diploma in Physical Education, 1968, Certificate of Education, 1968, Carnegie College of Physical Education, Leeds, England; MA, Education, Michigan

State University, USA, 1970; MS, Applied Mechanics, Stanford University, California, USA, 1976; PhD, Physical Education, Biomechanics, Pennsylvania State University, USA, 1981. Appointments: Graduate Teaching Assistant, Michigan State University, 1968-69; Teacher, Gaynesford High School, Carshalton, Surrey, England, 1969-70; Graduate Teaching and Research Assistant, Pennsylvania State University, 1970-74; Graduate Teaching Assistant, Stanford University, California, 1974-76; Director of Engineering, Computerised Biomechanical Analysis, Amherst, Massachusetts, 1979; Associate Senior Research Scientist, 1979-81, Senior Research Scientist, 1981-85, Biomedical Science Department, General Motors Research Laboratories; Vice-President Applications Engineering, Motion Analysis Corporation, 1987-88; President/Owner, 4D Video, Sebastopol, California, 1988-. Publications: Numerous papers in scientific journals and presented at conferences including: Image-Based Motion Measurement: The Camera as a Transducer, 1997; Image-Based Motion Measurement: An Introduction to the Element of the Technology, 1998; Calibration and Processing of Image as an After Thought, 2000; A High-Speed Video Tracking System for Generic Applications, 2000; The Camera as a Transducer, 2000. Honours: Fellow, Society of Photo-optical Instrumentation Engineers (SPIE) Honorary Fellow, British Association for Physical Training. Memberships include: American Association for the Advancement of Science; American College of Sports Medicine; New York Academy of Sciences; Sigma Xi; Society of Photo-Optical Instrumentation Engineers Address: 4D Video, 825 Gravenstein Highway North, Suite #4, Sebastopol, California 95472-2844, USA.

WAN ISMAIL Wan Ishak, b. 13 May 1952, Terengganu, Malaysia. University Professor. m. Zanima, 2 sons, 2 daughters. Education: Bachelor of Science, 1974-77, Master of Science, 1977-79, in Agricultural Engineering, Louisiana State University, USA; Doctor of Philosophy in Agricultural Engineering, Michigan State University, USA, 1987-91. Appointments: Head, Department of Power and Machinery, Faculty of Engineering, Deputy Dean, Faculty of Engineering, University Putra Malaysia; Director, Consultancy Unit, University Business Center, Director, Institute of Advanced Technology, University Putra Malaysia. Publications: Published over 90 papers in Journals, Seminars and Proceedings. Memberships: Registered Professional Engineer (P.Eng); Fellow, Institution of Engineers, Malaysia. Address: Director, Institute of Advanced Technology, Universiti Putra Malaysia, 43400 Selangor, Malaysia. E-mail: wiwi@putra.upm.edu.my

WANAMAKER Zoë, b. New York, USA. Actress. m. Gawn Grainger, 7 November 1994, 1 stepson, 1 stepdaughter. Education: Hornsey College of Art; Central School of Speech and Drama. Appointments: Actor; Theatre: A Midsummer Night's Dream, 1970; Guys and Dolls, 1972; The Cherry Orchard, 1970-71; Dick Whittington, 1971-72; Tom Thumb, Much Ado About Nothing, 1974; A Streetcar Named Desire, Pygmalion, The Beggar's Opera, Trumpets and Drums, 1975-76; Wild Oats, 1977; Once in a Lifetime, 1970-80; The Devil's Disciple; Wild Oats; Ivanov; The Taming of the Shrew; Captain Swing; Piaf; A Comedy of Errors, Twelfth Night and The Time of Your Life, 1983-85; Mother Courage; Othello; The Importance of Being Earnest 1982-83; The Bay at Nice and Wrecked Eggs, 1986-87; Mrs Klein; The Crucible; Twelfth Night, 1973-74; Cabaret, 1974; Kiss Me Kate, 1974; The Taming of the Shrew, 1975; Loot; Made in Bangkok, 1988; The Last Yankee, 1993; Dead Funny, 1994; The Glass Menagerie; Sylvia, 1996; Electra, 1997; The Old Neighbourhood, 1998; Electra, New York, 1998; Battle Royal, 1999; Boston Marriage, Donmar Warehouse, 2001; Boston Marriage, New Ambassadors, 2002. TV: Sally for Keeps, 1970; The Eagle Has Landed, 1972; Between the Wars, 1973; The Silver Mask, 1973; Lorna and Ted,

Dictionary of International Biography

1973; The Confederacy of Wives, 1974; The Village Hall, 1975; Danton's Death, 1977; Beaux Stratagem, 1977; The Devil's Crown, 1978-79; Strike, 1981; Baal, 1981; All the World's A Stage, 1982; Richard III, 1982; Enemies of the State, 1982; Edge of Darkness, 1985; Paradise Postponed, 1985; Poor Little Rich Girl, 1987; Once in a Lifetime, 1987; The Dog It Was That Died, 1988; Ball Trap on the Cote Sauvage, 1989; Othello, 1989; Prime Suspect, 1990; Love Hurts, 1991-93; Dance to the Music of Time, 1997; Gormenghast, Leprechauns, David Copperfield, 1999. Radio including: The Golden Bowl, Plenty, 1979; Bay at Nice, 1987; A February Morning, 1990; Carol, book reading, 1990; Such Rotten Luck, 1991, series I and TV films: The Blackheath Poisonings, Central, 1991; Memento Mori, BBC, 1991; Countess Alice, BBC, 1991; The English Wife, 1994; The Widowing of Mrs Holroyd, BBC, 1995; Wilde; Swept in By the Sea; TV: Adrian Mole, The Cappuccino Years, 2001; My Family, BBC Series 1, 2 and 3, 2000-2003; Film: Harry Potter and the Philosopher's Stone, 2001. Honours: SWET Award, 1979; Numerous Tony nominations; Drama Award, Mother Courage, 1985; Honorary DLitt, Southbank University, 1995; Variety Club of Great Britain Award, Best Actress, Electra, 1997; Olivier Awards including Best Actress for Electra, 1997; Calaway Award, New York, Best Actress, Electra; Best Actress, BAFTA for Love Hurts, Prime Suspects and Wilde; Honorary Doctorate Richmond American University of London; CBE; Boston Marriage, Oliver Nomination, Best Actress, 2002. Membership: Honorary Member, Voluntary Euthanasia Society; Trustee, Shakespeares Globe. Address: c/o Conway Van Gelder, 18/21 Jermyn Street, London SW1Y 6HP, England.

WANG Fu Yu, b. 16 August 1952, Henan, China. Civil Servant. 1 son, 1 daughter. Education: Central South University; Master of Law, Doctor Degree of Management, Huazhong University of Science and Technology. Appointments: County Magistrate of Huo Lu County of Hebei Province, China; Executive Vice-Mayor of Shi Jia Zhuang of Hebei Province; Executive Vice-Mayor of Haikou City; Mayor of Qiongshan City of Hainan Province; Member, Standing Committee, Hainan Provincial Party Committee of the Communist Party of China; Secretary, Sanya Municipal Party Committee, Communist Party of China; Deputy Secretary, Hainan Provincial Party Committee, Communist Party of China; Secretary, Haikou Municipal Party Committee, Communist Party of China. Publications: Roads to the Development of Ecological City; On the Ways to the Development of International Tropical Coastal City; Many articles on city construction, environmental protection and business administration published in state publications. Honours: State awards for achievements in fields of city construction, environmental protection, macroeconomic management, business administration and tourism development; Prizes for articles in state publications. Address: No 49 Hai Fu Da Dao, Haiku City, Hainan, China.

WANG Jennie, (Lin Jian), b. 19 March 1952, Shanghai, China. Literature Educator. Education: BA, cum laude, San Francisco State University, California, USA, 1983; MA, English, Stanford University, California, USA, 1984; PhD, English, State University of New York at Buffalo, Buffalo, New York, USA, 1992. Appointments: Instructor of English, Department of Foreign Languages, Shanghai Jiao-Tong University, Shanghai, China, 1977-79; Teaching Fellow, Department of English, State University of New York at Buffalo, Buffalo, New York, 1987-91; Preceptor, Expository Writing Program, Harvard University, Cambridge, Massachusetts, 1992-93; Research Associate, Department of Ethnic Studies, University of California at Berkeley, Summer 1996; Assistant Professor, 1993-98, Associate Professor, 1998-, Department of English Language and Literature, University of Northern Iowa, Cedar Falls, Iowa; Visiting Scholar, Department of English, University of California at Berkeley, 2000-01, 2003-

04; Full Professor of Comparative Literature, Dissertation Director, Chinese Department, Fudan University, Shanghai, China, 2004-. Publications: Author: Novelistic Love in the Platonic Tradition: Fielding, Faulkner and the Postmodernists, 1997; Chinese Translator, Smiles on Washington Square: A Love Story of Sorts by Raymond Federman, 1999; The Iron Curtain of Language: Maxine Hong Kingston and American Orientalism, in progress; numerous articles on Postmodern fiction in literary journals. E-mail: linjian@fudan.edu.cn

WANG Liqian, b. 23 January 1933, Nanjing, China. Engineer; Scientific Researcher. m. Bentao Zhang, 1 son. Education: BSc, Nanjing University, 1952. Appointments: Professor, Heat Thermodynamic Department of South-East University, 2001; Research Fellow, Humanities Institute of China, Management and Administration Research Institute, 2003. Publications: Many articles in professional journals. Honours: Firmament Award, Chinese Society of Electrostatic Precipitation; Distinguished Reputation Honour, Chinese Association of Environmental Industry; First Class Research, Nanjing Municipal Government. Memberships: International Society of Electrostatic Precipitation; Chinese Society of Electrical Engineering. Address: 43 East Beijing Road, Nanjing 210008, Peoples Republic of China. E-mail: wanglq4602@163.com

WANG Yingxu, b. 21 June 1956, Xian, China. Professor. m. Ren Han, 1 daughter. Education: MSc, Shanghai Tiedao University, China, 1983; PhD, Nottingham Trent University, England, 1998. Appointments: Professor (and other ranks), Lanzhou Tiedao University, China, 1983-95; Visiting Professor, University of Oxford, Oxford, England; Senior Research Fellow, South Bank University, London, England, 1997-98; Professor, The Swedish Institute of Engineering, Sweden, 1998-2000; Professor, Director of Theoretical and Empirical Software Engineering Research Centre, University of Calgary, Canada, 2000-. Publications: As author and co-author: Software Engineering Processes, Principles and Applications, 2000; Software Engineering Foundations: A Transdisciplinary Perspective, 2004; Introduction to Cognitive Informatics: Transdisciplinary Research on the Natural and Artificial Intelligence, 2004. Honours: Fellow, WIF; Honorary Professor of Nanjing University and Tongji University; National Zhan Tianyou Young Scientist Award, 1994; EU and Canadian Research Awards. Memberships: AAAS; IEEE (Computer, TCSE, Communications and SMC Societies); ACM; APEGGA (PEng); The Canadian Advisory Committee for ISO/IEC. Address: Theoretical and Empirical Software Engineering Research Centre, Department of Electrical and Computer Engineering, University of Calgary, 2500 University Drive NW, Calgary, Alberta, T2N 1N4 Canada. E-mail: wangyx@enel.ucalgary.ca

WANNER Sonia Viktoria, AdVAH, b. 15 March 1931, Gothenburg, Sweden. Artist in Fine Arts. m. Sigvard Ulf, 2 sons. Appointments: Chalmers University of Technology and Architecture, Gothenburg, Sweden, 1976-94; More than 100 exhibitions in Sweden and Norway as well as in New York, Los Angeles, Paris, Geneva, Innsbrück, Vienna, Seoul, Beirut and St Raphael; Although best known for her marine oils of rough seas, also acclaimed for her well-balanced landscapes and still life paintings. Honour: Scholarship, Eva Ljungqvist's Scholarship Fund, 1992; Hall of Fame for Outstanding Achievements in the field of Fine Arts, 2000; Toile d'Or de l'Anné, Federation Nationale de la Culture Française, 2001. Honours: Biblio: Listed in numerous biographical publications. Memberships: Sweden: Swedish Art Corporation, Gothenburg, Westsweden Chamber of Commerce and Industry, Gothenburg, The Regional Resource Centre for Womens work and Development in Western Sweden, Gothenburg; Great Britain: Womens Art Library, London; USA: National

Museum of Women in the Arts, Washington, Metropolitan Museum of Arts, New York, Linos School of Art, New York and Verona, World Artists Directory. Address: Haljerod 620, 442 96 Kungalv, Sweden. E-mail: sonia@wanner.net

WARD Christopher Stephen, b. 25 December 1947, UK. Lecturer. Education: BA, Chinese Studies, 1969; Postgraduate Diploma in Teaching English as a Second Language, 1971; MA, Applied Linguistics, 1988; PhD, 1995. Appointments: Teacher, Bradford Education Authority, England, 1969-70, 1971-73; Teacher/Manager Testing, International Language Centre, 1973-83; School Director, International Language Centre, Singapore, 1983-84; Senior Teacher, Manager, British Council, Singapore, 1984-96; Head, Specialists Department, SEAMEO Regional Language Centre, Singapore, 1996-. Publications: Rainbow Kirihara Shoten, 1975; Contributed to: Language Testing (editor J B Heaton), 1982; Co-author, Focus on Fluency, 1997; Co-editor, Computers and Language Learning, 1998. Memberships: Singapore Tertiary English Teachers Society; Singapore Association for Applied Linguistics. Address: SEAMEO Regional Language Centre, 30 Orange Grove Rd, Singapore 258352. E-mail: chrisward@relc.org.sg

WARD David John, b. 4 November 1949, Northampton, England. Poet. m. Frieda Nyahoe, 26 May 1972, 3 sons, 1 daughter. Education: BA, Honours, English, University of Lancaster. Appointments: Coordinator, Windows Poetry Project; Editor, Smoke, poetry magazine. Publications: Jambo, 1993; Candy and Jazzz, 1994; Tracts, 1996. Contributions to: Poetry Review; Transatlantic Review; Poetry Wales; University of Toronto Review; Die Horen, Germany. Memberships: University of Lancaster Literary Society, chair; Nemo Poets, Northampton; John Clare Society; Halewood Arts Association, secretary. Address: 22 Roseheath Drive, Halewood, Merseyside L26 9UH, England.

WARD Simon, b. 19 October 1941, Beckenham, England. Actor. m. Alexandra Malcolm, 3 daughters. Education: Royal Academy of Dramatic Art. Creative Works: Stage appearances include: Konstantin in The Seagull, Birmingham Repertory, 1964; Abel Drugger in The Alchemist and Hippolytus in Phèdre, Playhouse, Oxford, 1965-66; Dennis in Loot, Jeannetta Cochrane and Criterion, 1966; The Unknown Soldier in the Unknown Soldier and His Wife, Ferdinand in The Tempest and Henry in The Skin of Our Teen, Chichester Festival, 1968; Donald in Spoiled, Haymarket, 1971; Romeo in Romeo and Juliet, Shaw, 1972; Troilus in Troilus and Cressida, Young Vic; Films include: I Start Counting, 1970; Young Winston, 1971; Hitler - The Last Ten Days, 1972; The Three Musketeers, 1973; The Four Musketeers, Deadly Strangers, All Creatures Great and Small, 1974-75; Aces High, 1975; Battle Flag, 1976; The Four Feathers, 1978; Zulu Dawn, 1979; Supergirl, Around the World in 80 Days, Double X, 1992; Wuthering Heights; Ghost Writers; TV includes: The Black Tulip; The Roads to Freedom; Holocaust (serial). Address: c/o Shepherd & Ford Associates Ltd, 13 Radner Walk, London SW3 4BP, England.

WARFIELD John N(elson), b. 21 November 1925, Sullivan, Missouri, USA. Researcher. m. Rosamond Howe, 2 sons, 1 daughter. Education: BA, Mathematics, 1948, BSc, Electrical Engineering, 1948, MSc, Electrical Engineering, 1949, University of Missouri; Army Specialised Training Program, 1944-46, Graduate Study, 1949-51, Pennsylvania State University; PhD, Electrical Engineering, Purdue University, 1952. Appointments: Instructor, Electrical Engineering, University of Missouri, 1949; Instructor, 1949-51, Assistant Professor, 1952-53, Associate Professor, 1953-55, Electrical Engineering, Pennsylvania State University; Assistant Professor, 1955-56, Associate Professor,

1956-57, University of Illinois, Urbana; Associate Professor, Associate Director of Computer Laboratory, Purdue University, Indiana, 1957-58; Associate Professor, 1958-59, Professor, 1959-66, University of Kansas; Visiting Professor, University of Colorado at Boulder, 1965; Adjunct Professor of Electrical Engineering, Ohio State University, Columbus, 1966-73; Senior Research Leader, Battelle Memorial Institute, 1966-74; Chairman, Department of Electrical Engineering, 1974-78, Harry Douglas Forsyth Professor of Electrical Engineering, 1974-83, Director, Centre for Interactive Management, 1980-81, University of Virginia at Charlottesville; Visiting Professor of Management, University of Northern Iowa, 1980-81; University Professor, 1984-2000, Emeritus, 2000-, George Mason University, Fairfax, Virginia. Publications: Co-translator, Synthesis of Linear Communications Networks; Introduction to Electronic Analog Computers, 1959; Principles of Logic Design, 1963; Societal Systems: Planning, Policy and Complexity, 1976; A Science of Generic Design: Managing Complexity Through Systems Design, 1994; Co-author, A Handbook of Interactive Management, 1994; Understanding Complexity: Thought and Behaviour, 2002; The Mathematics of Structure, 2003; Discovering Systems Science, 2003; Numerous articles in professional journals. Honours include: Western Electric Fund Award for Excellence in Instruction of Students, 1966; Eminent Scholar, University of Virginia, 1974-83, George Mason University, 1984-; Outstanding Contribution Award, IEEE Systems, Man and Cybernetics Society, 1977; Centennial Medal, IEEE, 1984; Peace Pipe Award, Americans for Indian Opportunity, 1987; Mayor's Certificate, City of Austin, Texas, 1993; Plaque of Recognition, Minister of Social Development, Governor of Guanajuato, 1994; Third Millennium Medal, IEEE, 2000. Memberships include: IEEE; Association for Integrative Studies; Charles S Peirce Society; Society for Design and Process Science; Tau Beta Pi; Eta Kappa Nu; Sigma Xi; Panetics Society; Board of Advisers, Magic Circle Chamber Opera Company, New York; President, Integrative Sciences, Inc, 2001; President, AJAR Publishing Company, 2002. Address: 2673 Westcott Circle, Palm Harbor, FL 34684, USA. E-mail: jnwarfield@aol.com Website: http://jnwarfield.com

WARNE Shane Keith, b. 13 September 1969, Ferntree Gully, Melbourne, Australia. Cricketer. m. Simone, 1 son, 2 daughters. Appointments: Leg-Break and Googly Bowler; Right-Hand Lower-Order Batsman; 183 first-class matches for Hampshire took 70 wickets (average 23.1), 2000; Highest ever Australian wicket taker in Tests; 107 Tests for Australia, 1991-92 to 2002, taking 491 wickets (average 25.71) and scoring 2,238 runs, took hat-trick v England, Melbourne, 1994; Took 850 wickets and scored 4,103 runs in 1st class cricket, to 2003; Toured England, 1993, 1997, 2001; 191 limited-overs internationals (11 as Captain), to 2003; Captain Victoria Sheffield Shield Team (Bushrangers), 1996-99; received 12 month ban for testing positive for a banned substance, 2003. Publications: Shane Warne: The Autobiography, 2001. Honours: Wisden Cricketer of the Year, 1994; Selected as one of five Wisden Cricketers of the Century, 2000. Address: c/o Victorian Cricket Association, 86 Jolimont Street, Victoria 3002, Australia.

WARNOCK Helen Mary, (Baroness), b. 14 April 1924, England. Philosopher; Writer. m. Sir Geoffrey Warnock, 1949, deceased 1995, 2 sons, 3 daughters. Education: MA, BPhil, Lady Margaret Hall, Oxford. Appointments: Fellow and Tutor in Philosophy, 1949-66, Senior Research Fellow, 1976-84, St Hugh's College, Oxford; Headmistress, Oxford High School, 1966-72; Talbot Research Fellow, Lady Margaret Hall, Oxford, 1972-76; Mistress, Girton College, Cambridge, 1985-91; Visiting Professor of Rhetoric, Gresham College, 2000-2001; Several visiting lectureships. Publications: Ethics Since 1900, 1960, 3rd edition, 1978; J-P Sartre, 1963; Existentialist Ethics, 1966; Existentialism, 1970;

Imagination, 1976; Schools of Thought, 1977; What Must We Teach? (with T Devlin), 1977; Education: A Way Forward, 1979; A Question of Life, 1985; Teacher Teach Thyself, 1985; Memory, 1987; A Common Policy for Education, 1988; Universities: Knowing Our Minds, 1989; The Uses of Philosophy, 1992; Imagination and Time, 1994; Women Philosophers (editor), 1996; An Intelligent Person's Guide to Ethics, 1998; A Memoir: People and Places, 2000; Making Babies, 2002; Nature and Mortality, 2003; Utilitarianism (editor), 2003. Honours: 15 honorary doctorates; Honorary Fellow, Lady Margaret Hall, Oxford, 1984, St Hugh's College, Oxford, 1985, Hertford College, Oxford, 1997; Dame Commander of the Order of the British Empire, 1984; Life Peer, 1985; Albert Medal, RSA; Honorary Fellowship, British Academy, 2000. Address: 60 Church Street, Great Bedwyn, Wiltshire SN8 3PE, England.

WARREN William Howard, b. 4 November 1951, Toronto, Canada. Thoracic Surgeon. m. Karen V Kole, 2 sons. Education: MD, 1976, FRCS(C), General Surgery, 1981, University of Toronto; Cardiothoracic Surgery, Rush-Presbyterian St Luke's Medical Center, 1981-85. Appointments: Chief, Division of Thoracic Surgery, Cook County Hospital; Chief, Division of General Thoracic Surgery, Rush-Presbyterian St Luke's Medical Center; Professor, Department of Cardiovascular Surgery, Professor, Department of Pathology, Rush Medical College. Publications: 5 articles in professional journals. Memberships: American Association for Thoracic Surgery; Society of Thoracic Surgery; American College of Surgeons; American College of Chest Physicians. Address: Ste 218, 1725 W Harrison St, Chicago, IL 60612, USA. E-mail: wwarren@rush.edu

WARWICK (Marie) Dionne, b. 12 December 1940, East Orange, New Jersey, USA. Singer. m. Bill Elliott, divorced 1975, 2 sons. Education: Hartt College of Music, Hartford, Connecticut; Masters Degree, Music. Appointments: Singer, Gospel Groups, The Drinkard Singers, The Gospelaires; Solo Singer, 1962-; Numerous concerts, tours and benefit shows worldwide. Creative Works: Singles: Anyone Who Had A Heart, 1964; Walk On By, 1964; A Message To Michael, 1966; Alfie, 1967; I Say A Little Prayer, 1967; Do You Know The Way To San José, 1968; This Girl's In Love With You, 1969; I'll Never Fall In Love Again, 1970; Then Came You, 1974; I'll Never Love This Way Again, 1979; Heartbreaker, 1982; All The Love In The World, 1983; That's What Friends Are For (AIDS charity record), 1985; Albums include: Greatest Hits, 1990; Dionne Warwick Sings Cole Porter, 1990; Hidden Gems: The Best of Dionne Warwick, Volume 2, 1992; Friends Can Be Lovers, with Whitney Houston, 1993; Dionne Warwick and Placido Domingo, 1994; Aquarela do Brasil, 1994; From the Vaults, 1995; Dionne Sings Dionne, 1998; I Say a Little Prayer For You, 2000. Honours: Top Selling Female Artist, NARM, 1964; Best Female Pop Vocal Performance, 1969, 1970, 1980; Best Contemporary Vocal Performance, 1971; Best Female R&B Vocal Performance, 1980; Best Pop Performance, Duo or Group, 1987; Song of the Year, 1987; Star on Hollywood's Walk of Fame, 1985; NAACP Key of Life Award, 1990; CORE Humanitarian Award, 1992; Nosotros Golden Eagle Humanitarian Award, 1992; City of New York Award, Contribution to AIDS Research, 1987; DIVA Award, 1992; Platinum and Gold Discs. Address: c/o Arista Records Inc, 6 West 57th Street, New York, NY 10019, USA.

WASHBURN Robert, b. 11 July 1928, Bouckville, New York, USA. Composer; Conductor; Dean. m. Beverly Darnell, 1 son, 1 daughter. Education: BS, Crane School of Music, 1949; MS, SUNY, Potsdam, 1956; PhD, Eastman School of Music, 1960; Aspen Music School, 1963. Career: USAF, 1950-54; Professor, Crane School of Music, 1954-; Frequent appearances as guest composer, conductor. Publications: Numerous articles to professional journals; 1 college music text. Compositions: Over 150 published compositions. Honours: Danforth Foundation, 1959; Annual ASCAP Awards since 1960; Ford Foundation Grant, 1960; Fulbright Grant, Cairo, Egypt, 1986; US Department of Education Grant, 2001. Memberships: MENC; NYSSMA; ASCAP. Address: 87 State Hwy 72, Potsdam, NY 13676. E-mail: Washburb@potsdam.edu

WASHINGTON Denzel, b. 28 December 1954, Mount Vernon, New York, USA. Film Actor. m. Pauletta Pearson, 1983, 2 sons, 2 daughters. Education: Fordham University; American Conservatory Theatre, San Francisco. Creative Works: Off-Broadway appearances include: Ceremonies in Dark Old Men; When the Chickens Come Home to Roost; A Soldier's Play; Films include: A Soldier's Story, 1984; The Mighty Quinn, 1987; Cry Freedom, 1987; Heart Condition, 1989; Glory, 1990; Love Supreme, 1990; Mo' Better Blues, 1990; Ricochet, 1991; Mississippi Masala, 1991; Much Ado About Nothing, 1992; Malcolm X, 1992; The Pelican Brief, 1993; Philadelphia, 1993; Devil in a Blue Dress, 1995; Courage Under Fire, 1996; The Preachers Wife, 1996; Fallen, 1997; He Got Game, 1998; The Siege, 1998; The Bone Collector, 1999; The Hurricane, 1999; Remember the Titans, 2001; John Q, 2002; Antwone Fisher, 2002; Out of Time, 2003; Man of Fire, 2004; Manchurian Candidate, in progress. Honours include: Academy Award, Best Supporting Actor, 1990; Awards for Best Actor, Supporting Actor and Director, National Association for the Advancement of Colored People Awards, 2003. Address: c/o ICM, 8942 Wilshire Boulevard, Beverly Hills, CA 90211, USA.

WASSERSTEIN Wendy, b. 18 October 1950, Brooklyn, New York, USA. Dramatist; Writer. Education: BA, Mount Holyoke College, 1971; MA, City College of the City University of New York, 1973; MFA, Yale University, 1976. Publications: Plays: Any Woman Can't, 1973; Happy Birthday, Montpelier Pizz-zazz, 1974; When Dinah Shore Ruled the Earth (with Christopher Durang), 1975; Uncommon Women and Others, 1975; Isn't it Romantic, 1981; Tender Offer, 1983; The Man in a Case, 1986; The Heidi Chronicles, 1988; The Sisters Rosensweig, 1992. Other: Miami (musical), 1986; Bachelor Girls (essays), 1990; Pamela's First Musical (children's picture book), 1996. Honours: Guggenheim Fellowship, 1983; American Playwrights Project Grant, 1988; Pulitzer Prize for Drama, 1989; Tony Award, 1989; New York Drama Critics Circle Award, 1989; Drama Desk Award, 1989; Outer Critics Circle Award, 1989; Susan Smith Blackburn Prize, 1989. Memberships: British American Arts Association; Dramatists Guild; Dramatists Guild for Young Playwrights. Address: c/o Royce Carlton Inc, 866 United Nations Plaza, Suite 4030, New York, NY 10017, USA.

WATANABE Hisao, b. 1 October 1937, Nagoya, Japan. Psychiatrist; Educator. m. Towako Sugiyama, 1 son, 2 daughters. Education: MB, School of Medicine, 1962, Master's Degree, Graduate School, 1967, PhD, 1969, Nagoya University, Japan. Appointments: Associate Professor, 1971-79, Director, Centre for Health Care, 1977-2001, Professor, 1979-01, Emeritus Professor, 2001-, Aichi National University of Education; Professor, Tokaigakuen University, 2001-. Publications: Mental Health for the Student I, 1985; Mental Health for the Student II, 1990; Hints for Well-being – Lessons from 45 cases, 2003. Honour: Honour for the contribution to corrective medical treatment, Minister of Justice, Japan. Memberships: Chairman, Japanese Association for University Mental Health, 1994-; New York Academy of Sciences. Address: 1-11-2-802 Kanayamacho Atsuta-Ku, Nagoya 4560002, Japan.

Dictionary of International Biography

WATKINS Karen Christna, (Catrin Collier, Katherine John), b. 30 May 1948, Pontypridd, Wales. Writer. m. Trevor John Watkins, 28 December 1968, 2 sons, 1 daughter. Education: Teaching Certificate, Swansea College, 1969. Publications: Without Trace, 1990; Hearts of Gold, 1992; One Blue Moon, 1993; Six Foot Under; A Silver Lining, 1994; Murder of a Dead Man, 1994; All That Glitters, 1995; By Any Other Name, 1995; Such Sweet Sorrow, 1996; Past Remembering, 1997; Broken Rainbows, 1998. Memberships: PEN; Society of Authors; Crime Writers Association; Welsh Academy, 1998. Address: c/o A M Heath and Co, 79 St Martin's Lane, London WC2N 4AA. England.

WATSON Emily, b. 14 January 1967, London, England. Actress. Creative Works: Films: Breaking the Waves; Mill on the Floss; Metroland; The Boxer; Hilary and Jackie; Angela's Ashes, 1991; The Cradle Will Rock; Trixie; The Luzhin Defense; Gosford Park, 2001; Equilibrium, 2002; Red Dragon, 2002; Punch-Drunk Love, 2002; In Search of the Assassin, 2002; Blossoms and Blood, 2003; Life and Death of Peter Sellers, 2004; Way Through the Woods, 2004; Theatre includes: Uncle Vanya; Twelfth Night. Honours include: New York Society of Film Critics Award; National Society of Film Critics Award. Address: c/o ICM Ltd, Oxford House, 76 Oxford Street, London W1N 0AX, England.

WATSON James Dewey, b. 6 April 1928, Chicago, Illinois, USA. m. Elizabeth Lewis, 1968, 2 sons. Education: Graduated, Zoology, University of Chicago, 1947; Postgraduate Research, University of Indiana, PhD, 1950. Appointments: Research into viruses, University of Copenhagen, 1950; Cavendish Laboratory, Cambridge University, 1951; Senior Research Fellow, Biology, California Institute of Technology, 1953-55; Several positions, Department of Biology, Harvard University; Assistant Professor, 1955-58, Associate Professor, 1958-61, Professor, 1961-68; Director, 1968, President, 1994-, Quantitative Biology, Cold Spring Harbor Laboratory; Associate Director, NIH (USA), 1988-89; Director, National Center for Human Genome Research, NIH, 1989-92; Newton Abraham Visiting Professor, Oxford University, England, 1994; Research to help determine the structure of DNA. Publications: Molecular Biology of the Gene, 1965, 1970, 1976; The Double Helix, 1968; The DNA Story, 1981; Recombinant DNA: A Short Course, 1983; The Molecular Biology of the Cell, 1986; Recombinant DNA, 1992; Papers on the structure of DNA, on protein synthesis and on the induction of cancer by viruses. Honours: Joint Winner, Nobel Prize for Physiology or Medicine, 1962; John J Carty Gold Medal, 1971; Medal of Freedom, 1977; Gold Medal Award, National Institute of Social Sciences, 1984; Kaul Foundation Award for Excellence, 1992; Capley Medal of Royal Society, 1993; National Biotechnology Venture Award, 1993; Lomosonov Medal, 1994; National Medal of Science, 1997; Liberty Medal Award, 2000; Benjamin Franklin Medal, 2001. Address: Cold Spring Harbor Laboratory, PO Box 100, Cold Spring Harbor, New York NY 11724, USA.

WATSON Thomas Sturges (Tom), b. 4 September 1949, Kansas City, USA. Golfer. m. Linda Tova Rubin, 1973, 1 son, 1 daughter. Education: Stanford University. Appointments: Professional, 1971-; British Open Champion, 1975, 1977, 1980, 1982, 1983; Record low aggregate for British Open of 268, record two single round scores of 65, lowest final 36-hole score of 130, Turnberry, 1977; Won US Masters Title, 1977, 1981; Won US Open, 1982; Won World Series, 1975, 1977, 1980; Winner, numerous other open championships, 1974-; First player ever to win in excess of $500,000 in prize money in one season, 1980; Ryder Cup Player, Captain, 1993-. Publication: Getting Back into Basics (jointly), 1992. Honours include: Top Money Winner on US PGA Circuit, 1977, 1978, 1979, 1980; US PGA Player of the Year, 1977, 1978,

1979, 1980, 1982; PGA World Golf Hall of Fame, 1988-. Address: PGA America, PO Box 109801, 100 Avenue of the Champions, Palm Beach Gardens, FL 33410, USA.

WATT Gilbert, b. Aberdeen Scotland. Sculptor. m. Irene Mae Petrie, deceased. Education: Diploma of Art, 1946, Post Diploma, 1947, studied under T. B. Huxley Jones, Grays School of Art, Aberdeen; Certificate of Merit, studied under Siegfried Charoux and Maurice Lambert, Royal Academy Schools of Art, London, 1952; Prix de Rome Scholarship, British School at Rome Italy, 1952-1954. Appointments: Freelance work for industrial firms in London, design and projects for promoting sales in the British Isles and abroad; Latterly private practice including private tuition. Exhibitions: Royal Academy; Royal Scottish Academy; Rome; Leicester Galleries; Royal Festival Hall; Arts Council Travelling Exhibition; Scone Palace; Shakespeare's Birthplace Trust Exhibition; Takesin Art Centre; Edinburgh Civic Centre; Swansea University; Aberdeen Art Gallery; Art Space Gallery. Works include: Bronze heraldic shield, Granholme Mills, Aberdeen; Portrait of former Director, Dr Alexander C West, Grays School of Art, Aberdeen; Limited edition of a meditation figure, Aberdeen, 1950; Portrait head in bronze for Dr Marriot, Harley Street Specialist; A sculpture purchased by Sir Alfred Munnings when President of the Royal Academy; Life size figure of Brigette Bardot for French film company and London cinema distributor; Garden sculpture for a London manufacturer; Stone carving for a director, Colorado Springs, USA; Life figure for a bank official, Germany; Heraldic sculpture, Peacock Printmakers Building, Aberdeen; Portrait head in bronze of the late Dr Ian Fleming, Royal Scottish Academician, Aberdeen Art Gallery. Honours: Landseer Bronze Medal, Royal Academy Schools of Art, London, 1948; Certificate of Merit, Royal Academy Schools of Art, London, 1952; Prix de Rome, Sculpture Scholarship, British School at Rome, 1952-54; Diploma, Royal Society of British Sculptors, London, 1982. Memberships: Associate Member, Royal Society of British Sculptors, London; Society of Rome Scholars; Grays Former Students Club. Address: Riverside, 4 Ellon Road, Bridge of Don, Aberdeen AB23 2EA, Scotland.

WATTERS David Allan Kilpatrick, b. 8 August 1952, South Africa. Surgeon. m. Helga Maria Watters-Koestonbauer, 4 sons, 2 daughters. Education: Edinburgh Academy, 1961-70; Edinburgh University, 1970-77; BSc (1st Class Honours), 1977; MBChB, 1977; FRCSEd, 1981; ChM, Edinburgh University, 1983; FRACS, 1996. Appointments: Lothian Registrar Rotation, 1979-81; Wolfson Research Fellow, Western General Hospital, 1981-82; Senior Registrar, King Edward VIII Hospital, Durban SA, 1982-85; McCard Hospital, 1984; Senior Lecturer, University of Zambra, 1985-90; Visiting Lecturer, Chinese University of Hong Kong, 1991; Professor of Surgery, University of Papua, New Guinea, 1992-2000; Professor of Surgery, University of Melbourne and Barwon Health, 2000-. Publications: Editor, Surgery in the Tropics (Beillieres Clinics in Tropical Medicine), 1988; Care of the Critically Ill in the Tropics, 1991; Gastroenteology in the Tropics, 1995; Neurosurgery in the Tropics, 2000; Over 80 articles in medical journals. Honours: Duke of Edinburgh Gold Award, 1970; Paul Harris Fellowship, Rotary, 2000. Memberships: Association of Surgeons of East Africa, 1982-; Association of Surgeons of Papua, New Guinea, 1992-; Fellow, Hong Kong College of Surgeons; General Surgeons, Australia; College of Surgeons of East Africa. Address: Department of Surgery, Geelong Hospital, Geelong, Victoria 3220, Australia. E-mail: davidw@barwonhealth.org.au

WATTS Charlie (Charles Robert), b. 2 June 1941, England. Musician. m. Shirley Anne Shepherd, 1964, 1 daughter. Appointments: Drummer, Rolling Stones, 1963-. Creative Works:

Albums with The Rolling Stones include: The Rolling Stones, 1964; The Rolling Stones No 2, 1965; Out of Our Heads, 1965; Aftermath, 1966; Big Hits, 1966; Got LIVE if You Want It!, 1967; Between the Buttons, 1967; Their Satanic Majesties Request, 1967; Beggars Banquet, 1968; Let it Bleed, 1969; Get Yer Ya-Ya's Out!, 1970; Stone Age, 1971; Sticky Fingers, 1971; Goats Head Soup, 1973; It's Only Rock 'N' Roll, 1974; Black and Blue, 1976; Love You Live, 1977; Some Girls, 1978; Emotional Rescue, 1980; Tattoo You, 1981; Still Life, 1981; Dirty Work, 1986; Steel Wheels, 1989; Flashpoint, 1991; Voodoo Lounge, 1994; Solo albums include: Charlie Watts Orchestra - Live at Fulham Town Hall, 1986; From One Charlie, 1992; Warm and Tender, 1993; From One Charlie, 1995; Long Ago and Far Away, 1996; Films include: Sympathy For the Devil, 1969; Gimme Shelter, 1970; Ladies and Gentlemen, The Rolling Stones, 1977; Let's Spend the Night Together, 1983; Flashpoint, 1991. Publication: Ode to a High Flying Bird, 1965. Address: c/o Munro Sounds, 5 Church Row, Wandsworth Plain, London SW18 1ES, England.

WAX Ruby, b. 19 April 1953, Illinois, USA. Comedienne; Actress. m. Edward Richard Morison Bye, 1988, 1 son, 2 daughters. Education: Berkeley University; Royal Scottish Academy of Music and Drama. Appointments: With Crucible Theatre, 1976, Royal Shakespeare Company, 1978-82. Creative Works: TV includes: Not the Nine O'Clock News, 1982-83; Girls on Top, 1983-85; Don't Miss Wax, 1985-87; Hit and Run, 1988; Full Wax, 1987-92; Ruby Wax Meets..., 1996, 1997, 1998, 1999; Ruby, 1997, 1998, 1999; Ruby's American Pie, 1999, 2000; Hot Wax, 2001; The Waiting Game, 2001, 2002; Ruby, 2002; Films include: Miami Memoirs, 1987; East Meets Wax, 1988; Class of '69; Ruby Takes a Trip, 1992; Plays include: Wax Acts (one woman show), 1992; Stressed (one woman show), 2000. Publication: How Do You Want Me? (autobiography), 2002. Address: c/o ICM, Oxford House, 76 Oxford Street, London, W1N 0AY, England.

WEAVER Sigourney, b. 8 October 1949, New York, USA. Actress. m. James Simpson, 1984, 1 daughter. Creative Works: Films include: Annie Hall, 1977; Tribute to a Madman, 1977; Camp 708, 1978; Alien, 1979; Eyewitness, 1981; The Year of Living Dangerously, 1982; Deal of the Century, 1983; Ghostbusters, 1984; Une Femme ou Deux, 1985; Half Moon Street, 1986; Aliens, 1986; Gorillas in the Mist, 1988; Ghostbusters II, 1989; Aliens 3, 1992; 1492: Conquest of Paradise, 1993; Dave, 1993; Death and the Maiden, 1994; Jeffrey, 1995; Copycat, 1996; Snow White in the Black Forest, 1996; Ice Storm, 1996; Alien Resurrection, 1997; A Map of the World, 1999; Galaxy Quest, 1999; Get Bruce, 1999; Company Man, 1999; Airframe, 1999; Heartbreakers, 2001. Honours include: Golden Globe Best Actress Award, 1988; Best Supporting Actress Golden Globe Award, 1988. Address: c/o ICM, 8942 Wilshire Boulevard, Beverly Hills, CA 90211, USA.

WEBB Robert Gravem, 18 February 1927, Long Beach, California, USA. Retired Professor of Biological Sciences. m. Patricia A (Peden) Webb, 1 son. Education: BS, 1950, MS, 1952, University of Oklahoma; PhD, University of Kansas, 1960. Appointments: University of Texas at El Paso, 1962-93; Retired, 1993. Publications: 1 book: Reptiles of Oklahoma; 113 publications dealing with amphibians and reptiles. Honours: Faculty Research Award, University of Texas at El Paso, 1978; President, Society for the Study of Amphibians and Reptiles, 1980. Memberships: Herpetologists' League; American Society of Ichthyologists and Herpetologists; Society for the Study of Amphibians and Reptiles; Societas Europeae Herpetologica; Southwestern Association of Naturalists. Address: Department of Biological Sciences, University of Texas at El Paso, El Paso, TX 79968-0519, USA. E-mail: rgwebb@utep.edu

WEDGE John Francis Newdigate, b. 13 July 1921, London, England. Retired; Poet. m. Laura Jacqueline Roberts, 10 October 1946, 1 son, 2 daughters. Contributions to: Anthologies: Poems from the Forces; Poems of the Second World War; The Terrible Rain; Verse of Valour; In Time of War; Poetry Pot Pourri; Echoes of War; Poetry Review; Literary Review etc. Address: 23 Talbot Road, Carshalton, Surrey SM5 3BP, England.

WEEDIN James Frank, b. 17 December 1949, San Antonio, Texas, USA. m. Teresa Johnson. Education: BA, Geography, University of Texas, Austin, Texas, 1975; MS, Biology, Sul Ross State University, Alpine, Texas, 1976; AS, Geology, San Antonio College, San Antonio, Texas, 1969. Appointments: Science Faculty, St John's School, Houston, Texas, 1978-81; Science Faculty, Community College of Denver, 1981-83; Science Instructor-Co-ordinator, Community College of Aurora, 1983-85; Science Faculty, Community College of Aurora, 1983-; Science Division Chair, Community College of Aurora, 1985-92; Geology Co-ordinator, Community College of Aurora, 1981-. Publications: Co-author: Chromosome numbers in Chihuahuan Desert Cactaceae, 1978; In IOPB chromosome number reports LXIX, 1980; Chromosome numbers in Compositae XII: Heliantheae, 1981; Chromosome numbers in Compositae XV: Liabeae, 1986; Chromosome numbers in Compositae XVI: Eupatorieae II, 1989; Chromosome numbers in Chihuahuan Desert Cactaceae II, 1989; Chromosome numbers in Chihuahuan Desert Cactaceae III, 2001; The Cacti of Trans-Pecos Texas and Adjacent Areas, in press. Honours: Chihuahuan Desert Research Institute Innovative Research Award, 1975; Outstanding Young Men of America, 1982; Community College of Aurora Faculty of the Year, 1990; National Institute for Staff and Organizational Development Excellence Award, 1991; Cactus named for Biographee, Echinocereus russanthus var. weedinii, 1998. Memberships: Chihuahuan Desert Research Institute; Southwestern Association of Naturalists; Cactus and Succulent Society of America; Paleobotanical Section, Botanical Society of America; Colorado Cactus and Succulent Society; Western Interior Paleontological Society. Address: Department of Science, Community College of Aurora, 16000 E Centre Tech Parkway, Aurora, CO 80011, USA. E-mail: jim.weedin@ccaurora.edu

WEILER Stephan, b. 2 December 1965, Palo Alto, California, USA. Professor. m. Becky Zerlentes. Education: BA honours, Economics, 1988, MA, Agricultural Economics, 1988, Stanford University; PhD, Economics, University of California at Berkeley, 1994. Appointments: Associate Professor, Economics and Real Estate/Finance; Co-director, Center for Research on the Colorado Economy; Editorial Board, Review of Regional Studies. Publications: 21 refereed journal articles; 3 book chapters; 17 other publications. Honours: Outstanding Instructor, University of California at Berkeley; Service Learning Scholar, Colorado State University. Memberships: American Economic Association; Regional Science Association International. Address: CSU Economics Department, Fort Collins, CO 80523-1771, USA.

WEIMANN Robert Karl, b. 18 November 1928, Magdeburg, Germany. Scholar; Critic; Teacher. m. Maja Weimann, 2 sons, 3 daughters. Education: PhD, 1955, Phil Habil, 1962, Humboldt University, Berlin; Full Professor, 1968. Appointments: Professor, Humboldt University, 1965-68; Faculty member, Academy of Sciences, Berlin, 1968-91; Visiting Professor, University of Virginia, 1974; Visiting Professor, Toronto, 1982; Visiting Professor, Harvard University, 1984, 1989; Visiting Professor, Berkeley, 1986; Vice President, Akademie der Künste, Berlin, 1979-90; President, German Shakespeare Society, Weimar, 1985-93; Chair, Literaturwissenschaft, Max Planck Society Associate Institute, 1992-94; Professor, University of California, Irvine, 1992-

2001. Publications: Books: New Criticism, 1962; Shakespeare und die Tradition des Volkstheaters, 1967; Literaturgeschichte und Mythologie, 1971; Structure and Society in Literary History, 1976, 1984; Shakespeare und die Macht der Mimesis, 1988; Authority and Representation in Early Modern Discourse, 1996; Author's Pen and Actor's Voice, 2000; More than 40 essays and articles; Part of works translated into more than a dozen languages. Honours: Honorary Doctorate, 1988; Honorary Member, MLA, 1985-; American Medal of Honor for Contributions to Theatre History, 2002; Listed in national and international biographical dictionaries. Memberships: MLA; Deutsche Shakespeare Gesellschaft; International Shakespeare Association; International PEN; Akademie der Künste, Berlin; Academy of Sciences, New York; American Association for the Advancement of Science. Address: Muhlenbecker Str 22, 16352 Basdorf, Germany.

WEINBERG Steven, b. 3 May 1933, New York, New York, USA. Professor of Science; Author. m. Louise Goldwasser, 6 July 1954, 1 daughter. Education: BA, Cornell University, 1954; Postgraduate Studies, Copenhagen Institute of Theoretical Physics, 1954-55; PhD, Princeton University, 1957. Appointments: Research Associate and Instructor, Columbia University, 1957-59; Research Physicist, Lawrence Radiation Laboratory, Berkeley, 1959-60; Faculty, 1960-64, Professor of Physics, 1964-69, University of California at Berkeley; Visiting Professor, 1967-69, Professor of Physics, 1979-83, Massachusetts Institute of Technology; Higgins Professor of Physics, Harvard University, 1973-83; Senior Scientist, Smithsonian Astrophysics Laboratory, 1973-83; Josey Professor of Science, University of Texas at Austin, 1982-; Senior Consultant, Smithsonian Astrophysics Observatory, 1983-; Various visiting professorships and lectureships. Publications: Gravitation and Cosmology: Principles and Application of the General Theory of Relativity, 1972; The First Three Minutes: A Modern View of the Origin of the Universe, 1977; The Discovery of Subatomic Particles, 1982; Elementary Particles and the Laws of Physics (with R Feynman), 1987; Dreams of a Final Theory, 1992; The Quantum Theory of Fields, Vol I, Foundations, 1995, Vol II, Modern Applications, 1996, Vol III, Supersymmetry, 2000; Facing Up, 2001. Contributions to: Books, periodicals and professional journals. Honours: J Robert Oppenheimer Memorial Prize, 1973; Dannie Heineman Prize in Mathematical Physics, 1977; American Institute of Physics-US Steel Foundation Science Writing Award, 1977; Nobel Prize in Physics, 1979; Elliott Cresson Medal, Franklin Institute, 1979; Madison Medal, Princeton University, 1991; National Medal of Science, National Science Foundation, 1991; Andrew Gemant Prize, American Institute of Physics, 1997; Piazzi Prize, Governments of Sicily and Palermo, 1998; Lewis Thomas Prize for the Scientist as Poet, Rockefeller University, 1999. Memberships: American Academy of Arts and Sciences; American Mediaeval Academy; American Philosophical Society; American Physical Society; Council on Foreign Relations; History of Science Society; International Astronomical Union; National Academy of Science; Phi Beta Kappa; Philosophical Society of Texas, president, 1994; Royal Society; Texas Institute of Letters. Address: c/o Department of Physics, University of Texas at Austin, Austin, TX 78712, USA.

WEINER Claire Muriel, b. 18 December 1951, Bronx, New York, USA. Writer. Education: BA, University of Miami, Florida, 1973; MA, University of Maryland, 1980. Appointments: Public relations Specialist, City of Hialeah, Florida, Recreation Division, 1974-1977; Freelance Writer, Editor, Researcher, 1980-; Acting Communications Director, Educational Information Services, 1998-. Publications: Numerous articles on travel and consumer topics in various specialised publications. Honours: Listed in several Who's Who publications. Memberships: World Literary

Academy; American Biographical Institute; International Biographical Centre; National Trust for Historic Preservation. Address: 18828 Sky Blue Circle, Germantown, MD 20874, USA.

WEINMANN Eric W, b. 29 July 1913, Teplice, Czech Republic. Attorney. m. (1) Camilla Behn, 1 son, 1 daughter, (2) Mary E de Limur. Education: International Administration, MA, LLB, Columbia University, New York, New York; LLM, Georgetown University Law School, Washington DC. Appointment: Deputy General Counsel, Small Business Administration (Retired). Publications: Articles in law journals include: This Small Business Went to Market. Memberships: DC Bar; New York City Bar; US Supreme Court Bar. Address: 3244 Nebraska Avenue NW, Washington DC 20016-2704, USA.

WEINSTEIN Harvey, b. USA. Film Company Executive. Appointment: Co-Chair, Miramax Films Corporation, New York. Creative Works: Films produced jointly include: Playing for Keeps, 1986; Scandal, 1989; Strike it Rich, 1990; Hardware, 1990; A Rage in Harlem, 1991; The Crying Game, 1992; The Night We Never Met, 1993; Benefit of the Doubt, 1993; True Romance, 1993; Mother's Boys, 1994; Like Water for Chocolate, 1994; Pulp Fiction, 1994; Pret-A-Porter, 1994; Smoke, 1995; A Month by the Lake, 1995; The Crossing Guard, 1995; The Journey of August King, 1995; Things To Do In Denver When You're Dead, 1995; The Englishman Who Went Up A Hill But Came Down A Mountain, 1995; Blue in the Face, 1995; Restoration, 1995; Scream, 1996; The Pallbearer, 1996; The Last of the High Kings, 1996; Jane Eyre, 1996; Flirting with Disaster, 1996; The English Patient, 1996; Emma, 1996; The Crow; City of Angels, 1996; Beautiful Girls, 1996; Addicted to Love, 1997; Shakespeare in Love, 1998; Allied Forces, She's All That, 1999; My Life So Far, 1999; The Yards, 1999; Bounce, 2000; Scary Movie, 2000; Boys and Girls, 2000; Love's Labour Lost, 2000; Scream 3, 2000; About Adam, 2000; Chocolat, 2000; Spy Kids, 2001; Scary Movie 2, 2001; The Others, 2001; Lord of the Rings: The Fellowship of the Ring, 2001; Iris, 2001; Halloween: Resurrection, 2002; Spy Kids 2: Island of Lost Dreams, 2002; Lord of the Rings: The Two Towers, 2002; Gangs of New York, 2002; Chicago, 2002; Spy Kids 3-D: Game Over, 2003; Kill Bill: Vol 1, 2003; Scary Movie 3, 2003; Lord of the Rings: Return of The King, 2003; Cold Mountain, 2003; Kill Bill: Vol 2, 2004; Numerous other films in progress. Address: Miramax Films Corporation, 375 Greenwich Street, New York, NY 10013, USA.

WEINSTEIN Michael Alan, b. 24 August 1942, Brooklyn, New York, USA. Political Philosopher. m. Deena Schneiweiss, 31 May 1964. Education: BA, summa cum laude, New York University, 1964; MA, 1965, PhD 1967, Western Reserve University. Appointments: Assistant Professor, Western Reserve University, 1967, Virginia Polytechnic Institute, 1967-68, Purdue University, 1972-; Distinguished Professor of Political Science, University of Wyoming, 1979. Publications: The Polarity of Mexican Thought: Instrumentalism and Finalism, 1976; The Tragic Sense of Political Life, 1977; Meaning and Appreciation: Time and Modern Political Life, 1978; The Structure of Human Life: A Vitalist Ontology, 1979; The Wilderness and the City: American Classical Philosophy as a Moral Quest, 1982; Unity and Variety in the Philosophy of Samuel Alexander, 1984; Finite Perfection: Reflections on Virtue, 1985; Culture Critique: Fernand Dumont and the New Quebec Sociology, 1985; Data Trash, 1994; Culture/Flesh: Explorations of Postcivilized Modernity, 1995. Contributions to: Magazines and journals. Honours: Best Paper Prize, Midwest Political Science Association, 1969; Guggengeim Fellowship, 1974-75; Rockefeller Foundation Humanities Fellowship, 1976. Address: Department of Political Science, Purdue University, West Lafayette, IN 47907, USA.

Dictionary of International Biography

WEINSTEIN Robert, b. 1954, USA. Film Producer; Executive. Appointment: Co-Chair, Miramax Films Corporation. Creative Works: Films produced include: Playing for Keeps (with Alan Brewer), 1986; Scandal (with Joe Boyd and Nik Powell), 1989; Strike it Rich, 1990; Hardware (with Nik Powell, Stephen Wooley, Trix Worrell), 1990; A Rage in Harlem (with Terry Glinwood, William Horberg, Nik Powell), 1991; The Night We Never Met (with Sidney Kimmel), 1993; Benefit of the Doubt, 1993; True Romance (with Gary Barber, Stanley Margolis, James G Robinson), 1993; Mother's Boys (with Randall Poster), 1994; Pulp Fiction (with Richard N Gladstein), 1994; Pret-A-Porter (with Ian Jessel), 1994; Smoke (with Satoru Iseki), 1995; A Month By the Lake (with Donna Gigliotti), 1995; The Crossing Guard (with Richard N Gladstein), 1995; The Journey of August King, 1995; Things To Do in Denver When You're Dead (with Marie Cantin), 1995; The Englishman Who Went Up a Hill But Came Down a Mountain (with Sally Hibbin, Robert Jones), 1995; Blue in the Face (with Harvey Keitel), 1995; Restoration (with Donna Gigliotti), 1995; Velvet Goldmine, 1998; Shakespeare in Love, 1998; Allied Forces, 1999; My Life So Far, 1999; The Yards, 1999; Music of the Heart, 1999; The Cider House Rules, 1999; Down To You, 2000; Boys and Girls, 2000; Scream 3, 2000; Love's Labour's Lost, 2000; Scary Movie, 2000; Chocolat, 2000; Spy Kids, 2001; Scary Movie 2, 2001; The Others, 2001; Lord of the Rings: The Fellowship of the Ring, 2001; Iris, 2001; Halloween: Resurrection, 2002; Spy Kids 2: Island of Lost Dreams, 2002; Lord of the Rings: The Two Towers, 2002; Gangs of New York, 2002; Chicago, 2002; Spy Kids 3-D: Game Over, 2003; Kill Bill: Vol 1, 2003; Scary Movie 2, 2003; Lord of the Rings: Return of the King, 2003; Cold Mountain, 2003; Kill Bill: Vol 2, 2004; Several other films in progress. Address: Miramax Films Corporation, 375 Greenwich Street, New York, NY 10013, USA.

WEIR Hugh William Lindsay, b. 29 August 1934. Writer; Publisher. m. The Honourable Grania O'Brien, 17 July 1973. Education: DLitt, History, Trinity College, UIC, 1994. Appointments: Managing Director, Weir Machinery Ltd, 1965-75; Environmental Correspondent, The Clare Champion; Correspondent, The Church of Ireland Gazette; Served in British Army, Far and Middle East; Worked for Harmsworth Press, London; Teacher, Hong Kong, Cork, Dublin; Director, Christian Training Institute Ltd; Director, The Hunt Museums Trust; Chairman, Clare County Council Heritage Forum; Onetime Member, Church of Ireland General Synod Standing Committee and Representative Body; Managing Director, Weir Publishing Group, Ballinakella Press and Bell'acards. Publications: Hall Craig - Words on an Irish House; O'Brien People and Places; Houses of Clare; Ireland - A Thousand Kings; O'Connor People and Places; One of Our Own – Memoirs of Change; The Clare Young Environmentalists – An Exercise; Trapa, An Adventure in Spanish and English; Brian Boru; Short stories, academic articles/essays and topographical/historical contributions made to various anthologies and books; Contributions to: The Other Clare; The Clare Champion; The Church of Ireland Gazette; The Catholic Twin Circle; English Digest. Honours: Oidhreacht Award for the environment, Ireland; Clare Environmentalists National Award; Jaume Roca Award, Spain; Founder and President, Young Environmentalist Federation; Vice-President, Clare Archaeological and Historical Society. Memberships: Irish Writers' Union; Irish Georgian Society; Clogher Historical Society; Irish Genealogical Research Society; East Clare Historical Society; Shannon Historical Society; Thomond Historical Society; Kerry Historical Society; Ulster Architectural Heritage Society; Federation of Ulster Local History Societies. Address: Ballinakella Lodge, Whitegate, Co Clare, Ireland. E-mail: hughweir@ballinakella.com

WEIR Peter Lindsay, b. 21 August 1944, Sydney, Australia. Film Director. m. Wendy Stites, 1966, 1 son, 1 daughter. Education: Sydney University. Appointments: Real Estate, 1965; Stagehand, TV, Sydney, 1967; Director, Film Sequences, Variety Show, 1968; Director, Amateur University Reviews, 1967-69; Director, Film Australia, 1969-73; Made Own Short Films, 1969-73; Independent Feature-Film Director, Writer, 1973-. Creative Works: Films: Cars That Ate Paris, 1973; Picnic at Hanging Rock, 1975; The Last Wave, 1977; The Plumber (TV), 1978; Gallipoli, 1980; The Year of Living Dangerously, 1982; Witness, 1985; The Mosquito Coast, 1986; The Dead Poets Society, 1989; Green Card, 1991; Fearless, 1994; The Truman Show, 1997; Master and Commander: The Far Side of the World, 2003. Honours include: BAFTA Award, Best Director, 1997; BAFTA Award, Best Director, 2004. Address: Salt Pan Films Pty Ltd, PO Box 29, Palm Beach, NSW 2108, Australia.

WEIZSÄCKER Carl Friedrich von, b. 28 June 1912, Kiel, Germany. Theoretical Physicist. Education: PhD, University of Leipzig, 1933. Appointments: Assistant, Institute of Theoretical Physics, University of Leipzig, 1934-36; Kaiser Wilhelm Institute of Physics, Berlin-Dahlem; Lecturer, University of Berlin, 1936-42; Chair, University of Strasbourg, 1942; Kaiser Wilhelm Institute, 1944; Member of German research team investigating feasibility of nuclear weapons, but feared that such weapons may be used by the Nazi government; Director, Department, Max Planck Institute of Physics, Göttingen, 1946, with Honorary Professorship; Professor of Philosophy, University of Hamburg, 1957-69; Honorary Chair, University of Munich, 1969; Director, Max Planck Institute, 1970; Investigated the way in which energy is generated in the centre of stars; Devised theory on the origin of the solar system. Publications include: Bedingungen der Freiheit, 1990; Der Mensch in seiner Geschichte, 1991; Zeit und Wissen, 1992; Der bedrohte Friede-heute, 1994; Wohin gehen wir?, 1997. Address: Alpenstrasse 15, 82319 Starnberg, Germany.

WELCH Richard LeRoy, b. 15 October 1939, USA. Chief Executive Officer and Founder, Educom Inc. m. Donna, 1 stepson, 2 daughters. Education: University of Nebraska, 1958-59; Honorary PhD, Devonshire University, 2000. Appointments: Chief Executive Officer and Founder, Educom Inc, Dynamic Brain Management and Mental Photography, Subliminal Dynamics, 1980-; President, International Speed Reading Institute and American Speed Reading Academy; General Agent, Branch Manager and Agent, Insurance Industry, 15 years. Publications: Brain Management; Numerous articles in journals. Honours: Known as The Father of Mental Photography. International Diploma of Honour, Outstanding Man of the 20th Century and numerous others all International Biographical Centre, England also Lifetime Deputy Governor and Lifetime Fellow of American Biographical Institute Research Board of Advisors; Listed in several biographical publications. Membership: Mason. Address: 19744 E Union Drive, Suite 400, Centennial, CO 80015, USA. E-mail: subdyn@subdyn.com

WELDON Fay, b. 22 September 1931, Alvechurch, Worcestershire, England. Writer. m. (1) Ron Weldon, 12 June 1961, 4 daughters, (2) Nick Fox, 1994. Education: MA, St Andrews University, 1952. Career: Numerous theatre plays and over 30 television plays, dramatizations and radio plays. Publications: Fat Woman's Joke, 1968; Down Among the Women, 1971; Female Friends, 1975; Remember Me, 1976; Praxis, 1978; Puffball, 1980; The President's Child, 1982; Letters to Alice, 1984; Life and Loves of a She Devil, 1984; Rebecca West, 1985; The Shrapnel Academy, 1986; The Hearts and Lives of Men, 1987; Leader of the Band, 1988; Wolf of the Mechanical Dog, 1989; The Cloning of Joanna May, 1989; Party Puddle, 1989; Moon Over Minneapolis or Why She Couldn't Stay, (short stories), 1991; Life Force, 1992; Growing

Rich, 1992; Affliction, 1994; Splitting, 1995; Worst Fears, 1996; Wicked Women, (short stories), 1996; Big Women, 1998; A Hard Time to be a Father (short stories), 1998; Rhode Island Blues, 2000; Godless in Eden (essays), 2000; Nothing to Wear, Nowhere to Hide, 2002; Auto-da-Fay (autobiography), 2002; Contributor to numerous journals and magazines. Honours: DLitt, Universities of Bath, 1989 and St Andrews, 1992; Women in Publishing, Pandora Award, 1997. Memberships: Royal Society of Authors; Writers Guild of Great Britain. Address: Casarotto Co Ltd, National House, 62/66 Wardour Street, London, W1V 3HP, England.

WELLER Elizabeth Boghossian, b. 7 August 1949, Beirut, Lebanon. Psychiatrist; Physician. m. Ronald A Weller, 1 son, 1 daughter. Education: BSc, 1971, MD, 1975; Resident in Psychiatry, Washington University, 1978; Fellow, Child Psychiatry, University of Kansas, 1979. Appointments: University of Kansas, 1979-85; OSU, 1985-96; Professor of Psychiatry and Pediatrics, University of Pennsylvania, 1996- Publications: Papers in refereed journals. Honours include: Alpha Omega Alpha, 1975; American Academy, Clinical Psychiatry Research Award, 1982, 1984, 1988; Outstanding Young Woman in Psychiatry, 1985; Professor of Year, Department of Psychiatry, 1990; Distinguished Award, Program Chair, American Academy of Clinical Psychiatry, 1992; Outstanding Mentor Award, presented at annual meeting, American Academy of Child and Adolescent Psychiatry, Toronto, Canada, 1997. Memberships: Fellow, Academy of Child and Adolescent Psychiatry; President, Society of Biological Psychiatry, 1995; American College of Psychiatrists, 1995; Director, American Board of Psychiatry and Neurology, 1996-; President, American Board of Psychiatry and Neurology, 2004. Address: Children's Hospital, 34th and Civic Center Blvd, Philadelphia, PA 19104, USA.

WELLER Paul, b. 25 May 1958, Woking, Surrey, England. Singer; Songwriter; Musician (guitar, piano). m. Dee C Lee, December 1986. Career: Founder, singer, guitarist, The Jam, 1976-1982; Concerts include: Reading Festival, 1978; Great British Music Festival, 1978; Pink Pop Festival, 1980; Loch Lomond Festival, 1980; Founder, The Style Council, 1983-89; Appearances include: Miners benefit concert, Royal Albert Hall, London, 1984; Live Aid, Wembley Arena, 1985; Film: JerUSAlem, 1987; Founder, The Paul Weller Movement, 1990; Solo artiste, 1990-; UK and international tours; Phoenix Festival, 1995; T In The Park Festival, Glasgow, 1995; Own record label, Freedom High. Creative works: Compositions include: My Ever Changing Moods; Shout To The Top; The Walls Come Tumbling Down; Have You Ever Had It Blue, for film Absolute Beginners; It Didn't Matter; Wanted; Sunflower; Wild Wood; The Weaver; Recordings: Albums: with The Jam: In The City, 1977; This Is The Modern World, 1977; All Mod Cons, 1978; Setting Sons, 1979; Sound Affects, 1980; The Gift, 1982; Dig The New Breed, 1982; Snap!, 1983; Greatest Hits, 1991; Extras, 1992; Live Jam, 1993; with Style Council: Introducing The Style Council, 1983; Café Bleu, 1984; Our Favourite Shop, 1985; Home And Abroad, 1986; The Cost Of Loving, 1987; Confessions Of A Pop Group, 1988; The Singular Adventures Of The Style Council, 1989; Here's Some That Got Away, 1993; Solo albums: Paul Weller, 1992; Wild Wood, 1993; Live Wood, 1994; Stanley Road, 1995; Heavy Soul, 1997; Modern Classics, 1998; Heliocentric, 2000; Illumination, 2002. Honours include: Ivor Novello Award; BRIT Awards, 1995, 1996. Address: c/o Go'Discs Ltd, 72 Black Lion Lane, Hammersmith, London W6 9BE, England. Website: www.paulweller.com

WELLINGTON Mary Boone, b. 21 November 1949, Washington, DC, USA. Sculptor. 1 son, 2 daughters. Education: BFA, University of the Arts, Philadelphia. Honours: Citation for Painting, Hood Museum, Dartmouth College, Hanover; New Hampshire Painting Award, Breneau College Georgia.

Memberships: New England Sculptors Association; International Sculpture Center, Washington, DC. Commissions and Creative Works: Solar Calendar, Alum and Lightblocks, City of Flagstaff, Arizona; Taking Off, Aluminium, City of Manchester; Mt Meru, Steel State of New Hampshire. Address: 141 Canal Street, Nashua, NH 03064, USA.

WELLIO John Skafturu, b. 23 April 1946, Maun, Botswana. Trader. m. Ikwathaeng, 3 daughters. Education: Diploma in Accountancy and Business Studies, 1968; Appointments: Assistant Accountant, 1968-70; Accountant, 1971-78; General Manager, 1979-84; Managing Director, 1985-. Honour: Presidential Order of Meritorious Service, Republic of Botswana. Membership: Vice-President, Botswana Confederation of Commerce and Manpower. Address: PO Box 59, Maun, Botswana.

WELLMAN Donald, b. 7 July 1944, Nashua, New Hampshire, USA. Poet; Teacher; Editor. m. (1), 1 son, (2) Irene Turner, 2 January 1982, 1 daughter. Education: BA, University of New Hampshire, 1967; MA, 1972, DA, 1974, University of Oregon. Appointments: Professor and Chair, Humanities Division, Daniel Webster College, Nashua, New Hampshire; Editor, OARS Inc. Publications: The House in the Fields, 1992; Fields, 1995. Contributions to: Tyuonyi; Puckerbruch Review; Interstate; Zone; Adz; Polis; Boundary-2; Tamarisk; Hyperion; MC; New Maine Writing; Main Review; Generator; Sagetrieb. Address: 21 Rockland Road, Weare, NH 03281, USA.

WELLS Alan Arthur, 1 May 1924, Goffs Oak, Hertfordshire, England. Professional Civil and Mechanical Engineer. m. Rosemary Edith Alice Mitchell, 4 sons, 1 daughter. Education: University College, Nottingham, 1941-43; Clare College, Cambridge, 1947-50. Appointments: British Welding Research Association, 1950-64, Deputy Director, 1963; Chair of Structural Science, Head, Civil Engineering, Dean, Applied Science, The Queens' University, Belfast, 1964-77; Visiting Professor, Mechanical Engineering, Imperial College, London; Director General, The Welding Institute, 1977-89; Technical Director, Applied Research and Technology Ltd, Inverness, 1991-96. Publications: Numerous papers in professional scientific journals; Co-author, book: The brittle fracture of welded plate, 1967. Honours include: Bayliss Prize, 1942, Miller Prize, 1946, Institution of Civil Engineers; President's Gold Medal, Society of Engineers, 1955; Houdremont Lecture, International Institute of Welding, 1961; Hadfield Medal, Iron and Steel Institute, 1966; Larke Medal, Institute of Welding, 1968; Honorary Doctorate, University of Ghent, 1973; Rupert H Myers Award, University of New South Wales, 1982; OBE, 1982; DSc, honoris causa, University of Glasgow, 1982, University of Belfast, 1986; Freedom of the City of London, 1984; Platinum Medal, Institute of Metals, 1986; Edstrom Medal, International Institute of Welding, 1987; Arata Gold Medal, International Institute of Welding; Professorial Fellow, Queens' University, Belfast; Esso Gold Medal, Royal Society, 1994; Honorary Fellowship, Institution of Mechanical Engineers, 1999. Memberships: Institute of Welding, 1955; Institution of Mechanical Engineers, 1956; Royal Irish Academy, 1975; Fellow, Royal Society of London, 1977; Fellow, Royal Academy of Engineering, 1979. Address: Grove House, 15 Bridge Road, Mepal, Ely, Cambridgeshire CB6 2AR, England.

WELLS Peter George, b. 27 April 1925, Sheffield, England. Medical Doctor. m. Finola Fidelma Ginty, deceased 2000, 1 son, 1 daughter. Education: University of Sheffield Medical School; Numerous Postgraduate Institutes from 1955-1970. Appointments: Sub-Lieutenant RNVR, Royal Navy, 1943-46; House Physician, Royal Postgraduate Medical School, Hammersmith Hospital; London Chest Hospital; Resident Medical Officer, Maida Vale Hospital for Nervous Diseases; RMO, National Heart Hospital;

Registrar, General Medical Unit, West Middlesex Hospital; General Practice, West Kirby, Cheshire; Registrar, 1963, Senior Registrar, 1966-69, Deva Hospital, Chester; Senior Registrar, United Liverpool Hospitals; Senior Registrar, Walton Hospital, Tavistock Clinic, London; Consultant, Adolescent Psychiatry, Mersey and NWRHA's, 1970-1992; Seconded to create a brief for services for disturbed adolescents in the Hunter Valley, New South Wales, Australia, 1980-81; Locum Consultant, Isle of Wight, 1992, 1993; Psychiatric Adviser to Visyon, 1994- Founder five mental after-care clubs and mental after-care home in Chester. Publications: Numerous articles in medical journals including: Are Adolescent Units Satisfactory, 1982; Cut Price Adolescent units that Meet All Needs and None?, 1986; Whatever Happened to the Nursing Process?, 1986; Another Big Bang, 1986; Management of The Disturbed Adolescent, 1987; Why admit to a bed? Disposal of 1000 referrals to a Regional Adolescent Service, 1989; Survival in a cold climate, 1992; Inpatient treatment of 165 adolescents with emotional and conduct disorders – a study of outcome, 1993; 4 Psychiatric Films. Honours: BMA Silver Medal for film, 1969; Fellow, Royal College of Psychiatrists, 1979; Fellow, Royal Australian and New Zealand College, 1983; 'C' Merit Award, 1979; Cheadle Royal Prize for Research Paper, 1992. Memberships: British Medical Association; Association for Professionals in Service for Adolescents. Address: High Trees, Dark Lane, Henbury, Macclesfield, SK11 9PE.

WELLS Roger, b. 30 January 1947, London, England. Professor in History; Writer. Divorced, 1 son, 1 daughter. Education: BA, 1969, Dphil, 1978, University of York. Appointments: Lecturer, University of Wales, 1972-73; University of Exeter, 1973-75; University of York, 1975-76; Senior Lecturer, University of Brighton, 1976-95; Professor of History, Christ Church University College, Canterbury, 1995-. Publications: Death and Distress in Yorkshire, 1793-1801, 1977; Riot and Political Disaffection in Nottinghamshire in the Age of Revolutions 1776-1803, 1983; Insurrection: The British Experience 1795-1803, 1983; Wretched Faces: Famine in Wartime England, 1793-1801, 1988; Class, Conflict and Protest in the English Countryside, 1700-1880, 1990; Victorian Village, 1992; Crime, Protest and Popular Politics in Southern England 1740-1850 (with J Rule). Contributions to: Social History; Rural History; Southern History; Northern History; Policing and Society; Journal of Peasant Studies; Journal of Historical Geography; Local Historian; English Historical Review; Agricultural History Review; London Journal; Labour History Bulletin; Journal of Social Policy. Membership: Royal Historical Society. Address: Christ Church University College, Canterbury, Kent CT1 1QU, England.

WELSH James Michael, b. 15 July 1938, Logansport, Indiana, USA. Professor; Editor. m. Anne Robison Welsh, 2 daughters. Education: BA, English, Indiana University, Bloomington, 1963; MA, 1965, PhD, 1996, English, University of Kansas. Appointments: Assistant Instructor, English, 1963-65, Research Fellow, Analytical Bibliography, 1966-71, University of Kansas; Teaching Associate, History, Indiana University, 1965-66; Instructor of English, 1971-74, Assistant Professor, 1974-84, Associate Professor, 1984-96, Professor, 1996-, Salisbury State University, Salisbury, Maryland. Publications: Abel Gance, 1978; Peter Watkins: A Guide to References and Resources, 1986; The Encyclopedia of Novels into Film, 1998, revised edition, 2005; The Cinema of Tony Richardson: Essays and Interviews, 1999; The Encyclopedia of Stageplays into Film, 2001; Video Versions: Film Adaptions of Plays on Video, 2000; Shakespeare into Film, 2002; Founding Editor, Literature/Film Quarterly, 1973-. Honours: Distinguished Faculty Award, Salisbury University, 1987, 2000; Fulbright Fellowships, 1994, 1998. Memberships: Literature/Film Association (Founding President); International Association for Media and History (IMHIST); Modern Language Association of America. Address: English Department, Salisbury University, Salisbury, MD 21801, USA.

WELTON Peter, b. 15 March 1933, Barnetby, Lincolnshire, England. Artist. m. Liza, 2 sons. Education: Leeds Teacher Training College, 1954-56; Fine Art, Durham University (Kings College, Newcastle upon Tyne), 1956-60. Appointments: Hospital Clerk, Grimsby General Hospital, 1949-51; Aircraft Radio Mechanic, RAF, 1951-54; Railway Shunter, Barnetby, Lincolnshire, 1954; Stage Designer, Playhouse Repertory Theatre, Newcastle upon Tyne, 1960; Teacher of Art, Kenton Comprehensive School, 1960-61; Lecturer in Painting, Salford School of Art, 1961-62; Lecturer in Foundation Studies, Newcastle College of Art, 1962-67; Head of Visual Communication, Sunderland Polytechnic, 1967-74; Dean of Arts, Crewe and Alsager College, 1974-87; Professor of Fine Art, Leicester Polytechnic, 1987-90; Full time Watercolour Painter, 1990-; Artist-on-Board, Cruise Liner Minerva, Swan Hellenic, 2000, 2002, Minerva II, 2004; One man exhibition, Slimbridge Art Gallery, 2003; Commissioned works include: Portrait of Garret Fitzgerald; Watercolour landscape for H M the Queen, 1992; Watercolour to celebrate the opening of the new Number 1 court at Wimbledon for All England Lawn Tennis Club, 1997; Painting, Flora and Fauna for London Transport, 1999; Painting of Kimbolton School for HRH the Duke of Gloucester, 1999; 14 watercolours for P & O as part of the permanent collection on board the Aurora, 1999; Portrait of Walker Cup golfer Gary Wolstenholme, 2000; 2 landscapes purchased by the House of Lords, 2000; Commission for the Maharajah of Udaipur, 2001; Celebratory portrait of Elizabeth Marchioness Conyngham, 2001; 12 covers for a new series of Miss Read books, Haughton Mifflin, publishers, New York, USA, 2001; Watercolour of a game reserve in Namibia, 2002; 8 watercolours of a 1953 Beetle for Volkswagen UK, 2003; portrait of the Sagrada Familia for Aventis Pharmaceuticals, Barcelona, Spain, 2004. Publications: See What I Mean/ An introduction to visual communication. (with John Morgan, 1986; How to Paint in Watercolour; 1995; Peter Welton's Sketchdiary, 1999; Many articles on watercolour painting and communication; Welton's Way with Watercolour, Video; many limited edition prints since, 1990. Honour: Emeritus Professor of Fine Art, De Montfort University, Leicester. Address: Orchard Cottage, Arnesby, Leicestershire LE8 5WG, England. E-mail: peterwelton@peterwelton.com

WELTY Eudora, b. 13 April 1909, Jackson, Mississippi, USA. Author. Education: Mississippi State College for Women; BA, University of Wisconsin, 1929; Postgraduate Studies, Columbia School of Advertising, 1930-31. Publications: A Curtain of Green, 1941; The Robber Bridegroom, 1942; The Wide Net, 1943; Delta Wedding, 1946; Music From Spain, 1948; Short Stories, 1949; The Golden Apples, 1949; The Ponder Heart, 1954; The Bride of the Innisfallen, 1955; Place in Fiction, 1957; The Shoe Bird, 1964; Thirteen Stories, 1965; A Sweet Devouring, 1969; Losing Battles, 1970; One Time, One Place, 1971; The Optimist's Daughter, 1972; The Eye of the Story, 1978; The Collected Stories of Eudora Welty, 1980; One Writer's Beginnings, 1985; Eudora Welty Photographs, 1989; The Norton Book of Friendship (editor with Ronald A Sharp), 1991; A Writer's Eye: Collected Book Reviews, 1994; Monuments to Interruption: Collected Book Reviews, 1994; The First Story, 1999. Contributions to: The New Yorker. Honours: Guggenheim Fellowship, 1942; O Henry Awards, 1942, 1943, 1968; National Institute of Arts and Letters Grant, 1944, and Gold Medal, 1972; William Dean Howells Medal, American Academy of Arts and Letters, 1955; Christopher Book Award, 1972; Pulitzer Prize in Fiction, 1973; Presidential Medal of Freedom, 1980; National Medal for Literature, 1980; Notable Book Award, American Library Association, 1980; American Book Awards,

1981, 1984; Commonwealth Medal, Modern Language Association, 1984; National Medal of Arts, 1987; Chevalier de l'Ordre des Arts et Lettres, France, 1987. Membership: American Academy of Arts and Letters. Address: 1119 Pinehurst Street, Jackson, MS 39202, USA.

WEMPLE-KINDER Suzanne, b. 1 August 1927, Veszprem, Hungary. Professor of History. m. (1) George B Wemple, deceased, (2) Gordon T Kinder, 2 sons, 1 daughter. Education: Bachelor, English Sisters, Budapest, 1945; BA, University of California, 1953; MLS, 1955, PhD, 1967, Columbia University. Appointments: Reference Assistant, Columbia Libraries, New York, 1955-57; Lecturer, Stern College for Women, New York, 1962-64; Assistant Professor, Teachers College, Columbia University, New York, 1964-66; Assistant Associate and Full Professor, Barnard College, Columbia University, 1966-92. Publications: Atto of Vercelli; Church, State and Society in the Tenth Century, 1979; Women in Frankish Society; Marriage and the Cloister, 1981; Co-editor: Women in Medieval Society, 1985; Contributor to essays, books and articles. Honours: Grantee, Spivak Summer Grant, Barnard College, 1970, 1981; NEH, 1974-75, 1980, 1981-86; Fulbright, 1982. Membership: AAUP. Address: 1285 Gulf Shore Blvd N, Naples, Florida 34102, USA.

WEN Sophia Ming-Lee, b. 3 June 1953, Taiwan. Professor . Education: PhD, Institute of Education, University of London, 1992; EdD, National Taiwan Normal University, Taiwan, 1995. Appointment: Professor of Education, 1998-; Dean, College of Humanities and Social Sciences, School of Education and Communication, Tzu-chi University. Memberships: Philosophy of Education Society, Great Britain; Teachers Education Society, Taiwan; Comparative Education Society, Taiwan. Address: Fl 21-6, No 93, Sec 2, Roosevelt Road, Taipei 10647, Taiwan.

WENDT Albert, b. 27 October 1939, Apia, Western Samoa. Professor of English; Writer; Poet; Dramatist. 1 son, 2 daughters. Education: MA, History, Victoria University, Wellington, 1964. Appointments: Professor of Pacific Literature, University of the South Pacific, Suva, Fiji, 1982-87; Professor of English, University of Auckland, 1988-. Publications: Fiction: Sons for the Return Home, 1973; Pouliuli, 1977; Leaves of the Banyan Tree, 1979; Ola, 1990; Black Rainbow, 1992. Short Stories: Flying-Fox in a Freedom Tree, 1974; The Birth and Death of the Miracle Man, 1986; The Best of Albert Wendt's Short Stories, 1999. Plays: Comes the Revolution, 1972; The Contract, 1972. Poetry: Inside Us the Dead: Poems 1961-74, 1975; Shaman of Visions, 1984; Photographs, 1995. Honours: Landfall Prize, 1963; Wattie Award, 1980; Commonwealth Book Prize, South East Asia and the Pacific, 1991; Companion of the New Zealand Order of Merit, 2001. Address: c/o Department of English, University of Auckland, Private Bag 92019, Auckland 1, New Zealand. Website: www.auckland.ac.nz

WENDT Vernon Carl, b. 26 March 1931, Cleveland, Ohio, USA. Physician; Cardiologist. m. Hildegard Moeller, 4 sons, 3 daughters. Education: BS cum laude, Baldwin-Wallace College, 1952; MD, Columbia University College of Physicians and Surgeons, 1956. Appointments: Captain, USAF, 1957-59; Resident, Internal Medicine, 1959, 1960, 1962; US Post Doctorate Fellow in Cardiology, Wayne State University, Detroit, Michigan, 1960-62; Assistant Professor of Medicine, Wayne State University, 1965-67; Director of Research, Blodgett Memorial Medical Center, Grand Rapids, Michigan, 1965-67; Private practice, International Medicine and Cardiology, 1967-2000. Memberships: Fellow, American College of Physicians, American College of Cardiology and College of Angiology; Diplomat, American Board of Internal Medicine; Michigan Society of Internal Medicine; Trustee,

American H T Association of Michigan; Michigan State Medical Society. Address: 1620 Andover SE, East Grand Rapids, MI 49506, USA.

WENNER Donald E, b. 23 December 1953, Philadelphia, Pennsylvania, USA. Surgeon. m. Laurie P Wenner, 3 sons, 1 daughter. Education: BS, New Mexico Institute of Mining and Technology, 1974; MD, University of New Mexico, 1979; General Surgery Residency, Maricopa Medical Center, Phoenix, Arizona, 1985. Appointments: Surgeon, Eastern New Mexico Medical Center, Roswell, New Mexico, 1985-; Clinical Volunteer faculty, University of New Mexico School of Medicine, 1986-; President, Lapsurgical Systems LLC, 2001-. Publication: Actual Time Required for Dynamic Fluoroscopic Intraoperative Cholangiography. Honours: Eastern New Mexico Medical Center Family Medicine Residency Program Faculty of the Year; 2 US Patents; Listed in Who's Who publications and biographical dictionaries. Memberships: Society of Laparoendoscopic Surgeons; American College of Surgeons, Society of Gastrointestinal Endoscopy. Address: 1600 SE Main Ste F, Roswell, NM 88023, USA. E-mail: wenner@lapsurgical.com Website: www.lapsurgical.com

WERNER Helmut, b. 19 April 1934, Mühlhausen, Germany. Professor of Chemistry. Widower, 1 son, 1 daughter. Education: Diploma, University of Jena, 1958; PhD, 1961, Habilitation, 1966, Technical University of Munich; Honorary Doctorate, University of Zaragoza, Spain, 2001. Appointments: Assistant Professor, 1968, Full Professor, 1970, University of Zürich, Switzerland; Full Professor, Head of Department, 1975, Dean of Faculty, 1987-89, Chairman Interdisciplinary Research Unit, 1990-2001, University of Würzburg. Publications: 630; 1 monograph; 4 books edited. Honours: Fellow Royal Society of Chemistry, 1987; Member of the Academy Leopoldina, 1988; Alfred-Stock-Award, German Chemical Society, 1988; Max-Planck-Research Award, 1994; Centenary Medal and Lecturership, 1994; Alexander-von-Humboldt Award, 1995. Memberships: Deutsche Chemische Gesellschaft; Swiss Chemical Society; Royal Society of Chemistry; American Chemical Society; Deutsche Gesellschaft für Naturforschung. Address: Institut für Anorganische Chemie, Am Hubland, D-97074 Würzburg, Germany. E-mail: helmut.werner@mail.uni-wuerzburg.de

WERNER Reiner, b. 22 February 1932, Zschopau, Erzgebirge, Germany. Professor of Forensic Psychology. 4 sons. Education: Diploma, Psychology, Humboldt University, Berlin, Germany, 1954-49; Dr rer nat, 1965; Dr rer nat habil, 1967. Appointments: Director of the main Psychological Counselling Centre, Berlin, Germany; Director, Combined Psychotherapy Home for Children and Young People, Berlin-Brandenburg, Germany; Professor of Forensic Psychology, Humboldt University Berlin, 1971-. Publications: Das Verhaltensgestörte Kind; Problemfamilien – Familienprobleme; Schwierige Charaktere; Homosexualität – Herausforderung an Wissen und Toleranz; Mein unruhiges Ich – Selbstfindung zwischen Vernunft und Illusion; 200 articles. Honours: Numerous state and society orders and honours. Address: Alpenrosenweg 91, 12437 Berlin, Germany.

WERTHEIM Sally H, b. 1 November 1931, Cleveland, Ohio, USA. Professor; University Administrator. m. Stanley Wertheim, 3 daughters. Education: BS, Flora Stone Mather College, 1953; MA, 1967, PhD, 1970, Case Western Reserve University. Appointments: Social Service Department, University Hospitals, 1953-54; Teacher, Fairmount Temple Religious School, 1957-72; Kindergarten Teacher, Beachwood Recreation Department, 1965; Graduate Assistant, Case Western Reserve University, 1966-70; Instructor, 1969-71, Assistant Professor, 1971-75, Co-ordinator of Teacher Education, 1973-77, Associate Professor, 1975-80, Chairman, Department of Education, 1977-86, Professor, Department of Education, 1980-, Dean of Graduate School, Grantsperson for Faculty, Co-ordinator of Research and Faculty Development, 1986-93, 1994-, 1996-99, Academic Vice President, 1993-94, Acting Academic Vice President, 1995-96, Director of Planning and Assessment, Secretary, Board of Trustees, 1999-2000, John Carroll University. Publications: Numerous articles and papers in professional journals. Honours: Martha Holden Jennings Foundation Grant; Cleveland and Gund Foundation Grants; Teacher Competency Model with Berea Schools; Lilly Endowment Foundation, John Carroll University Faculty Development Grant; Flora Stone Mather College Centennial Distinguished Alumna Award, 1988; Sally H Wertheim Leadership Educational Award and Scholarship, 1996; The Curtis W Miles Faculty Community Service Award, 1997; Cleveland Magazine, 100 Most Influential Women, 1983; 29 Most Influential Women, 1997; Listed in national and international biographical dictionaries. Memberships include: Committee on Cleveland Public Schools; History of Education Society; Institute for Educational Renewal; Jewish Community Federation; Jewish Family Service Association; County Board of Mental Health; Jewish Education Center of Cleveland; The Gerson Foundation; The Mount Sinai Health Care Foundation; The Mandel Foundation. Address: John Carroll University, 20700 North Park Blvd, Cleveland, OH 44118, USA. E-mail: wertheim@jcu.edu

WERTHEIMER Esther, b. Poland. Sculptor. Education: Student, Montreal Museum of Fine Arts, 1958-63; International Academy, Austria, 1966; Academy Belle Arte, Florence, Italy, 1967-68; BA Loyola of Montreal, 1973; MA, Goddard College, 1975. Career: Sculptures installed in: Maimonaides Hospital, Montreal Canada; Recreation Centre, Pt St Lucie, Florida, USA; Itami City Cultural Hall, Hyogo Prefecture, Japan; Okaloosa-Walton CC, Niceville, Florida, USA; Upper Iowa University, Fayette; Okayama Municipal Centre, Japan; Health Care Center, Kyoto Japan; Royal Palm Plaza, Boca Raton, Florida, USA; Hikifune Cultural Center, Sumida-ku, Tokyo, Japan; 21st Century Forest Park, Kukushima, Japan; Yemeji Museum, Okayama, Japan; Katsushika performing Art Center, Tokyo, Japan; City of Hamura, Tokyo, Japan; Fukuoka City Hall, Japan; Hakone Open Air Museum; Palm Springs, California, USA; North Miami Beach, Florida, USA; Atrium of Alcan Aluminium Ltd, Montreal, Canada; Glouster City Hall for Carling Park of Commerce, East Ottawa, Canada; Joliette Museum, Quebec, Canada; Carling Executive Park, Ottawa, Canada; Cote St-Luc City Hall and Library, Montreal, Canada; Conference Building of Canada, Ottawa; Douglas Hospital, Montreal, Canada among others. Honours include: Awards from Montreal Museum of Fine Art, 1956-63; Borsa di Studio, Italian Government, 1967-68; Government of Quebec Bource de l'Enseignement Superieur, 1974; Gold Medal INT Tourisma, Rome, Italy; EUR Europa Premio, Rome; B'nai B'rith International Arts Award, 1997. Address: 6507 Brava Way, Boca Raton, FL 33433-8239, USA. E-mail: wertheimer@ewertheimer.com

WESEMAN Vicki Kennedy, b. Hastings, Nebraska, USA. Elementary Teacher. 1 son. Education: Bachelor of Science, University of Nebraska at Lincoln, Nebraska; Master of Arts Degree, University of Nebraska at Kearney, Nebraska. Appointments: Elementary Teacher, Hanover School, Glenvil, Nebraska for 26 years; Currently, Elementary Teacher, Grand Island Public Schools, Grand Island, Nebraska. Publication: Co-author, Oregon Trail Rodeo Education Booklet, 2000. Honours: Miss Rodeo Nebraska, 1977; Top Ten Finalist, Miss Rodeo America, Oklahoma City, Oklahoma, 1977; Committee Person of the Year, Oregon Trail Rodeo, Hastings, Nebraska, 1999. Memberships: Hastings YMCA; Grand Island Public Schools Education Association; Nebraska Education Association; National

Education Association; Faith Lutheran Church, Hastings, Nebraska; Women's Professional Rodeo Association. Address: 835 Briggs Avenue, Hastings, NE 68901, USA. E-mail: vweseman@esu9.org

WESKER Arnold, b. 24 May 1932, London, England. Dramatist; Playwright; Director. m. Dusty Bicker, 2 sons, 2 daughters. Appointments: Founder-Director, Centre Fortytwo, 1961-70. Publications: Chicken Soup with Barley, 1959; Roots, 1959; I'm Talking About Jerusalem, 1960; The Wesker Trilogy, 1960; The Kitchen, 1961; Chips with Everything, 1962; The Four Seasons, 1966; Their Very Own and Golden City, 1966; The Friends, 1970; Fears of Fragmentation (essays), 1971; Six Sundays in January (stories), 1971; The Old Ones, 1972; The Journalists, 1974; Love Letters on Blue Paper (stories), 1974, 2nd edition, 1990; Say Goodbye!: You May Never See Them Again (with John Allin), 1974; Words—As Definitions of Experience, 1976; The Wedding Feast, 1977; Journey Into Journalism, 1977; Said the Old Man to the Young Man (stories), 1978; The Merchant (renamed Shylock), 1978; Fatlips, 1978; The Journalists: A Triptych, 1979; Caritas, 1981; Distinctions (essays), 1985; Yardsale, 1987; Whatever Happened to Betty Lemon, 1987; Little Old Lady, 1988; Shoeshine, 1989; Collected Plays, 7 volumes, 1989-97; As Much As I Dare (autobiography), 1994; Circles of Perception, 1996; Break, My Heart, 1997; Denial, 1997; The Birth of Shylock and the Death of Zero Mostel (diaries), 1997; The King's Daughters (stories), 1998; Barabbas (play for TV), 2000; Groupie (play for radio), 2001; The Wesker Trilogy, 2001; One Woman Plays, 2001. Contributions to: Stage, film, radio and television. Honours: Fellow, Royal Society of Literature, 1985; Honorary DLitt, University of East Anglia, 1989; Honorary Fellow, Queen Mary and Westfield College, London, 1995; Honorary DHL, Denison University, Ohio, 1997. Memberships: International Playwrights Committee, president, 1979-83; International Theatre Institute, chairman, British Centre, 1978-82. Address: Hay on Wye, Hereford HR3 5RJ, England. Website: www.arnoldwesker.com

WEST Timothy Lancaster, b. 20 October 1934. Actor; Director. m. (1) Jacqueline Boyer, 1956, dissolved, 1 daughter, (2) Prunella Scales, 1963, 2 sons. Education: Regent Street Polytechnic, London, 1951-52. Appointments: Freelance Actor and Director, 1956-, Member, various times, Royal Shakespeare Company, National Theatre, Old Vic Company and Prospect Theatre Company; Artistic Director, Billingham Theatre Company, 1974-76, Old Vic Company, 1980-82; Director in Residence, University of Washington, 1982; Associate Director, Bristol Old Vic, 1991-; Film appearances include: The Looking Glass War; The Day of the Jackal; Oliver Twist; Cry Freedom; 102 Dalmatians; The Fourth Angel; Villa des Roses; Iris; Beyond Borders; TV appearances include: Why Lockerbie?; Framed; Smokescreen; Reith to the Nation; Eleven Men Against Eleven; Cuts; Place of the Dear; Midsomer Murders; Murder in Mind; Bedtime; Numerous theatre appearances. Publications: I'm Here I Think, Where Are You? 1997; A Moment Towards the End of the Play, 2001; Various articles in national newspapers, National Trust magazine, Times Literary Supplement. Honours: CBE, 1984; Honorary DUniv, Bradford, 1993; Honorary DLitt, West of England, 1994; East Anglia, 1995; Honorary DLitt, University of Westminster, 1999. Memberships: FRSA, 1992-; Chairman, London Academy of Music and Dramatic Art, 1992-; Chairman, All Change Arts, 1986-99; At various times, member of Arts Council Drama and Touring Panels, various Theatre Boards; Director, National Student Drama Festival; President, Society for Theatrical Research. Address: c/o Gavin Barker Associates Ltd., 2D Wimpole Street, London W1M 7AA, England.

WEST-HILL Gwendolyn, b. 30 July 1951, Indianapolis, Indiana, USA. Poet; Artist; Evangelist; Educator. m. David Hill, 1 son, 1 daughter. Education: BA, Elementary Education, Indiana University, Bloomington, Indiana; BA, Business Administration, Butler University; Charles Wharton School of Art; Georgia Medical Institute. Appointments: Emory School/University, Atlanta, Georgia. Publications: Numerous poems, songs and tributes. Honours: Eubie Blake Award, Indiana Black Expo; Charles Wharton School of Art Award; Wendell Parker, Best Poet of the Year Award; Gwendolyn Brooks Best Poet of the Year Award; Famous Poets.com Award; Listed in national and international biographical dictionaries. Memberships: Delta Sigma Theta Sorority; Academy of American Poets, 2000-; Famous Poets.com, 2003-. Address: 4251 Parkview Court, Stone Mountain, Georgia 30083-1294, USA.

WESTCOTT Joan Clark. b. 8 February 1919, Union City, Pennsylvania, USA. Poet. Education: Graduated, Baldwin School, Bryn Mawr, Pennsylvania, 1937; Graduated, Vassar College, 1941; Graduated, Katherine Gibbs School, Boston, 1942. Appointments: Clerk, Typist, Boston Port of Embarkation; Secretary, Harvard College, Student Clinic; Secretary, Players Little Theater, Sarasota, Florida; Secretary, University of California Atomic Energy Research Project, Westwood, California; Secretary to John Loveton, TV producer, Hollywood, California; Office Manager, Architect, Jack West, Sarasota, Florida. Publications: 8 books of poetry. Honours: Listed in national and international biographical dictionaries. Memberships: Planetary Society; Women in Arts; Union of Concerned Scientists; Physicians for Social Responsibilities; National Trust for Historic Preservation. Address: John Knox Village, 4100 E Fletcher Avenue, Tampa, FL 33613, USA.

WESTIN Steinar, b. 21 June 1944, Oslo. Physician; Professor. m. (1) Rigmor Austgulen, 28 December 1970, divorced 1985, 1 son, 2 daughters, (2) Lise Skjaak Braek, 25 May 1991. Education: Medical School, University of Bergen, 1963-70; Wien/Fulbright Scholar, Brandeis University, Massachusetts, USA, 1966-67; MD, PhD, 1990, University Trondheim; Specialist of General Practice, 1986. Appointments: Junior Registrar, 1970-71, Research Fellow, 1972, Neevengaarden Psychiatric Hospital, Bergen; Intern, Haraldsplass Hospital, Bergen and Asköy district, 1973; General Practitioner, District Physician, Asköy district, 1973-78; Senior Lecturer, 1979-83, Associate Professor, 1983-90, Professor and Department Chairman, 1990-, Department of Community Medicine and General Practice, University Trondheim. Publications: Research in General Practice, 1983; The Educational Handbook for General Practitioners, 1985, 1996; Problem Solving in General Practice, 1987; Unemployment and Health, 1990; Becoming Disabled, 1990; Over 200 articles. Honours: Visiting Professor, Royal Australian College of General Practitioners, 1995. Memberships: Royal Norwegian Society of Sciences and Letters; Chairman Editorial Board, Journal of the Norwegian Medical Association; Editorial Board, British Medical Journal and European Journal of General Practice. Address: Department of Community Medicine and General Practice, Norwegian University of Science & Technology, Medisinsk Teknisk Senter, N-7489, Trondheim, Norway.

WESTON Joan Spencer, b. 11 August 1943, Barton, Vermont, USA. Production Director. Education: BA, University of Massachusetts, Amherst. Appointments: English Teacher, Gorham, Maine, 1965-66; English Teacher, Mansfield and Warsop, Nottingham, England, 1966-68; English Department Head, Teacher, Goffstown, New Hampshire, 1968-82; Circulation Director, T.H.E. Journal, Acton, Massachusetts, 1982-83; Production Director, Robb Report Magazine, Acton,

Massachusetts, 1983-87; Production Manager, LSM/The New England Group, Portland, Maine, 1987-88; Production Consultant, The Spencer Weston Group, Portland, Maine, 1988-93; Production Director, New Age Publishing, Watertown, Massachusetts, 1993-97; Editorial and Production Director, Private Colleges and Universities, Westford, Massachusetts, 1996-. Honours: Phi Beta Kappa, 1965; Broderson Award for Excellence in Advertising, 1988; Memberships: Executive Board Member, New Hampshire Association of Teachers of English, 1978; Charter Member, Boston Production Managers Group, 1996. Address: Private Colleges and Universities, 2 LAN Drive, Suite 100, Westford, MA 01886, USA

WESTROPP George Victor, b. 2 November 1943, Marlow, Buckinghamshire, England. Public Relations Director. Divorced, 2 sons. Appointments: Reporter, City Press, 1961-63; City Reporter, Sunday Express, 1963; Financial Journalist, Evening Standard, 1963-68; Assistant City Editor, Extel, 1968-69; Director, Shareholder Relations Ltd, 1969-73; Financial Public Relations Executive, PPR International Ltd, 1974-76; Managing Director, Hemingway Public Relations Ltd, 1977-79; National Director of Communications, Touche Ross, now Deloitte & and Touche, 1979-2000, Partner, 1985-2000. Publications: The Lake Vyrnwy Fishing Book, 1979; Lake Vyrnwy – The Story of a Sporting Hotel, 1992; The Westropp Family 1250-2000, 2000; Editor, Beauly News; Numerous articles on fly fishing for Trout & Salmon magazine, etc. Memberships: Institute of Public Relations; Vice Chairman, Salmon & Trout Association; Chairman, Three Shires Ltd; Director, Royal Horticultural Society Gala Board; Director, London Press Club; Fellow, Royal Society of Arts. Address: 36 Holley Road, London W3 7TS, England. E-mail: george.westropp@btinternet.com

WESTWOOD Vivienne Isabel, b. 8 April 1941, England. Fashion Designer. 2 sons. Career: Developed Punk fashion in partnership with Malcolm McLaren, Chelsea, London, 1970-83; Work produced for musicians including: Boy George; The Sex Pistols; Bananarama; Adam and the Ants; Bow Wow Wow; Solo avant-garde designer, 1984-; Also worked with S Galeotti, Italy, 1984; Launched Mini Crini, 1985; Produced collection featuring Harris tweed suits and princess coats; Pagan 5, 1989; Opened own shop in Mayfair, London, 1990; Launch of signature fragrance, Boudoir, 1998; Numerous fashion shows including: London; Paris Tokyo; New York. Honours: Professor of Fashion, Academy of Applied Arts, Vienna, 1989-91; Hochschule der Künste, Berlin, 1993-; Senior FRCA, 1992; British Designer of the Year, 1990, 1991; OBE, 1992; Queen's Award for Export, 1998. Address: Westwood Studios, 9-15 Elcho Street, London SW11 4AU, England.

WETZEL Stephen P, b. 4 February 1959, Brooklyn, New York. Investment Advisor; Professor. m. Christa McGlynn, 2 sons. Education: BA Honours, Economics, State University of New York, Stonybrook, 1981; MBA cum laude, Finance, International Business, New York University, 1983; CCM, Treasury Management, New York University, 1986; CFP, College Financial Planning, 1988; Advanced Accounting Certificate, New York University, 1991. Appointments: Professor of Financial Management, New York University, 1991-; President, Prometheus Capital Management, 1994 -. Publications: Numerous articles in professional journals; Book in progress. Honours: Award For Outstanding Service, New York University, 2000; Award For Teaching Excellence, New York University, 2002. Memberships: Secretary Board Member; Financial Planning Association; Philadelphia Chapter , 2001-. Address: 30 South Main Street, Yardley, PA 19067, USA. E-mail: pcmcorp@erols.com. Website: www.procap.net

WHALEN Norma Jean, b. 26 November 1936, Albuquerque, New Mexico, USA. Special Education Teacher. m. Thomas Whalen, 3 sons, 2 daughters. Education: BEd, Carson Newman College, Jefferson City, Tennessee, 1959; Certified Teacher of Secondary Education, Florida, 1959; Certified Teacher of History, Florida, 1959. Appointments: Secondary School Teacher, L Puente Junior High School, 1959-62; Teacher, Umatilla (Florida) Elementary School, 1969-70; Substitute Teacher, Lake County Schools, Leesburg, 1969-70; Board of Directors, Melon Patch Theater, Leesburg, 1976-81; Teacher, Evening Class, Lee Adult High School, Leesburg, Florida, 1979-70; Elementary School Teacher, St Paul's Catholic Church, Leesburg, Florida, 1980-81; Special Education Teacher, Lee Opportunity-Lifestream Behavioral Center, Leesburg, Florida, 1990-2003; Cons Curriculum de vel, St Paul's Catholic Church, Leesburg, 1986-89; Director, Learning Resource Center, St Paul's Catholic Church, Leesburg, 1986-89; Teacher, 1st Communion and Confession Classes, 1986-2004. Honours: Recipient, Best Supporting Actress Award, Melon Patch Theater, 1979; Distinguished Service Award, 1980; Service Award, Lake County Board of Education, 1999; National Association of Mentally Ill Parents Organisation, Service Awards, 2000, 2002 and 2003; Lifestream Behavioral Center Award from Full Circle Staff, 2003; Lake Technical Center Award for 15 years of dedicated service, 2003. Memberships: NEA; Leesburg Education Association; Roman Catholic. Address: 2904 Pecan Ave, Leesburg, FL 34748-4914, USA.

WHALEN-BRIDGE John, b. 8 May 1961, Stamford, Connecticut, USA. Educator. m. Helena Whalen, 2 children. Education: BA, Honours and Magna Cum Laude, University of Connecticut, 1985; MA, University of California, Davis, 1987; PhD, University of Southern California, 1993. Appointments: Teaching Assistant, University of California, Davis, 1985-88; Lecturer, Los Angeles Southwest College, 1991-92; Lecturer, California State University, Dominguez Hills, 1992-93; Visiting Professor, University of the Ryukyus, 1993-98; Lecturer, University of Maryland, Asian Division, 1994-97; Assistant Professor, 1998-2003, Associate Professor with tenure, 2003-, National University of Singapore. Publications: Book, Political Fiction and the American Self, 1998; Numerous articles in scholarly journals, book chapters and papers presented at conferences as author and co-author include most recently: Murderous Desire in Lolita in Nabukov Studies, 2003; Waking Cain: Buddhist-Christian Dialogue in Charles Johnson's Dreamer, 2003; Christopher Isherwood in Scribner's Great Writers Series, 2004, forthcoming; DeLillo and Disaster (with Valerie Wee), in Approaches to Teaching White Noise, 2004, forthcoming; Late Mailer: Literary Karma, Reincarnation and the Demands of Art, 2005. Honours: All-University Pre-Doctoral Funding, 1988-91, Feuchtwanger Fellow, 1991-92, University of Southern California; National University of Singapore Academic Research Grant, 1990-2000; Haynes Research Fellow, Huntington Library, 2001-2002; Sabatical Leave with funding to visit Princeton's Center for the Study of Religion, National University of Singapore, 2004. Address: English Language and Literature, National University of Singapore, 10 Kent Ridge Road, Singapore 117570. E-mail: elljwb@nus.edu.sg

WHALLEY Dorothy, (Dorothy Cowlin), b. 16 August 1911, Grantham, Lincolnshire, England. Retired Teacher; Writer. m. R H Whalley, 12 April 1941, 1 daughter. Education: BA, University of Manchester, 1929-31. Appointments: Assistant Teacher, St John's, Heaten Mersey, Stockport, and Junior School, Flixton, Lancashire. Publications: Novels: A Penny To Spend, 1941; Winter Solstice, 1942; The Holly and the Ivy, 1950; Slow Train Home, 1951; Rowanberry Wine, 1952; An End and a Beginning, 1954; Draw the Well Dry, 1955; The Pair of Them, 1956; The Sound of Rain, 1991; Do You Remember Pickering, 2000; Poetry: Winter Rooks, 1998; Pigeon Post, 2002; Biographies: Greenland Seas, 1965; A Woman In The Desert, 1967; Eliz Barrett Browning, 1968; Cleopatra, 1970. Contributions to: Envoi; Pennine Platform; Pennine Ink; Airings; Hybrid; Iota; Moonstone; Psychopoetica; New Hope International; Rialto. Honours: Yorkshire TV Competition, 1993. Membership: Scarborough Poetry Workshop. Address: 14 Littledale, Pickering, North Yorkshire YO18 8PS, England.

WHARTON Christopher Frederick Percy, b. 19 February 1937, Banbury, Oxfordshire, England. Consultant Physician. m. Pamela Mary Deane, 2 daughters. Education: Worcester College, Oxford; Guy's Hospital, London. Appointments: House Officer and Senior House Officer, Guy's and Lewisham Hospitals; Senior Registrar and Registrar, Medicine and Cardiology, Guy's Hospital, London; Consultant Physician and Cardiologist, Bromley Hospitals. Publications: Numerous journal articles on echocardiography and cardiology; Books: Author, Problems in Cardiology, 1981; Co-author, Cardiology – Management of Common Diseases, 1986. Honours: MA (Oxon); DM (Oxon); FRCP (London); British Heart Foundation Award, 1969. Memberships: Freeman City of London; Liveryman Worshipful Company of Gunmakers; Athenaeum Club; Chelsea Football Club. Address: 24-26 High Street, Chipstead, Nr Sevenoaks, Kent TN13 2RP, England.

WHEATLEY David Pearse, b. 25 May 1919, Exeter, England. Doctor of Medicine. m. Marta Susana, 2 sons, 2 daughters. Education: MD, Cambridge University, England, 1955; MRCPsych, 1976, FRCPsych, 1982, Royal College of Psychiatrists. Appointments: Founder, British Association for Psychopharmacology, 1954; Head, Psychopharmacology and General Practitioner Research Groups, 1958-; Editor, Journal of Pharmacotherapy, 1977-80; Editor, Stress Magazine, 1984-92; Director, Stress Clinic, Maudsley Hospital, London, 1985-92; President, International Society for the Investigation of Stress, 1988-92; Consultant Psychiatrist, Royal Masonic Hospital, London, 1990-98; Medical Consultant, Feighner Research Institute, London, 1996-99; Consultant Psychiatrist, Charter Clinic Chelsea, 1998-99; Currently Private Consultant Psychiatrist, Harley Street, London. Publications: Books include: Psychopharmacology in Family Practice, 1977; Stress and the Heart, 1977, 2nd edition, 1981; The Anxiolytic Jungle, 1990; Psychopharmacology of Cognitive and Psychiatric Disorders in the Elderly, 1997; Numerous articles in professional journals on depression, anxiety , sleep, stress, old age and psychosomatic disorders. Honours: Research Grants, National Institute of Mental Health, USA, 1964-76; Honorary Member, Turkish College of Neuropsychopharmacology; Fellow, Academy of Psychosomatic Medicine. Memberships: World Psychiatric Association; International College of Psychopharmacology; World Federation of Biological Psychiatry; Quebec Psychopharmacological Research Association; Past President: Anglo-American Medical Society; Section of General Practitioners, Royal Society of Medicine, London. Address: 15 Elizabeth Court, Lower Kings Road, Kingston-on-Thames, Surrey KT2 5HP, England. E-mail: wheatley@ukgateway.net

WHEELER (Henry) Neil George (Sir), b. 8 July 1917, Plymouth, Devon, England. Air Chief Marshal. m. Alice Elizabeth Weightman, 2 sons, 1 daughter. Education: RAF College Cranwell, 1935-37. Appointments: Royal Air Force, 1935-76; Retired as Air Chief Marshal; Director Rolls Royce Ltd, 1977-82; Director Flight Refuelling Ltd, 1977-85. Publications: Numerous articles on aeronautical matters mostly connected with operations during the 1939-45 war. Honours: DFC, 1941; Bar to DFC, 1943; DSO, 1943, OBE, 1949; AFC, 1954; CBE, 1957; ADC to H.M. The Queen, 1957-61; CB, 1967, KCB, 1969, GCB, 1975.

Memberships: Fellow of the Royal Aeronautical Society; Companion of the British Institute of Management; Vice-President of the Air League; Past Master of the Guild of Air Pilots and Air Navigators. Address: Boundary Hall, Cooksbridge, Lewes, East Sussex BN8 4PT, England.

WHELAN Peter, b. 3 October 1931, Newcastle-under-Lyme, England. Playwright. Education: Graduated, University of Keele, Staffordshire, 1955. Appointments: Advertising Copywriter and Director, 1959-90; Associate, Royal Shakespeare Company, 1998-. Plays produced and published: Double Edge (co-author), 1975; Captain Swing, 1978; The Accrington Pals, 1981; Clay, 1982; The Bright and Bold Design, 1991; The School of Night, 1992; Shakespeare Country, 1993; The Tinderbox, 1994; Divine Right, 1996; The Herbal Bed, 1997; Nativity, 1999; A Russian In The Woods, 2001. Honours: Writers Guild Best Play Nominations; Lloyds Private Banking Playwright of the Year, 1996; TMA Regional Theatre Awards, Best New Play, 1996; Nomination Best Play, Olivier Awards, 1997. Address: c/o The Agency, 24 Pottery Lane, Holland Park, London W11 4LZ, England.

WHIPPLE Fred Lawrence, b. 5 November 1906, Red Oak, Iowa, USA. Astronomer. m. (1) Dorothy Woods, 1 son, (2) Babette Frances Samelson, 2 daughters. Education: AB, University of California, Los Angeles, 1924-27; PhD, University of California, Berkeley, 1927-31; MS, honorary, Harvard University, 1945; DSc, honorary, American International College, 1958; DSc, honorary, Temple University, 1961; DLitt, honorary, Northeastern University, 1961; LLD, honorary, CW Post College of Long Island University, 1962; DSc, honorary, Univ Arizona. Appointments: Teaching Fellow, University of California, 1927-29; Instructor, Stanford University, 1929; Lick Observatory Fellow, 1930-31; Instructor, University of California, 1931; Staff Member, Harvard College Observatory, 1931-77; In Charge, Oak Ridge Station, Harvard College Observatory, 1932-37; Instructor, 1932-38, Lecturer, 1935-45, Harvard University; Research Associate, Radio Research Laboratory, OSRD, 1942-45; Associate Professor, 1945-50, Chairman, Committee on Concentration in the Physical Sciences, 1947-49, Chairman, Department of Astronomy, 1949-56, Professor, 1950-77, Harvard University; Director, Smithsonian Institution Astrophysical Observatory, 1955-73; Phillips Professor of Astronomy, 1968-77; Senior Scientist, Smithsonian Institution Astrophysical Observatory, 1973-; Phillips Professor of Astronomy, Emeritus, 1977-. Publications: Earth, Moon and Planets, 1942; Orbiting the Sun, 1981; The Mystery of Comets, 1985; Numerous scientific papers and several articles in professional journals. Honours include: Bruce Gold Medal, Astronomy Society of the Pacific, 1986; Phi Beta Kappa Award in Science, 1986; Henry Norris Russell Lecturer, 1988; Fred L Whipple Lecturer, American Geophysical Union, Planetary Division, 1990; Medal, University of California Los Angeles, 1997. Memberships include: American Astronomical Society; American Astronautical Society; American Geophysical Society; American Institute of Aeronautics & Astronautics. Address: Smithsonian Astrophysical Observatory, 60 Garden Street, Cambridge, MA 02138, USA.

WHIPPLE George, b. 24 May 1927, St John, New Brunswick, Canada. Retired. Education: Vancouver Teacher's College, 1953. Publication: Life Cycle, 1984; Passing Through Eden, 1991; Hats Off to the Sun, 1996; Carousel, 1999; Tom Thomson and Other Poems, 2000; Origins, 2003; Fanfares, 2003. Contributions to: Poetry Canada Review; Canadian Forum; Fiddlehead; Writers Market (USA); Candleabrum (UK); Antigonish Review. Memberships: League of Canadian Poets; The Writers Union of Canada. Address: 2004-4390 Grange Street, St Burnaby, BC, V5H 1P6, Canada.

WHITBREAD Fatima, b. 3 March 1961, Stoke Newington, England. Athlete. m. Andrew Norman, 1997, 1 son. Appointments: UK International Debut as Javelin Thrower, 1977; European Junior Champion, 1979; European Cup Champion, 1983; European Cup Silver Medallist, 1985; European Champion, 1986; Commonwealth Games Bronze Medallist, 1982, Silver Medallist, 1986; Olympic Games Bronze Medallist, 1984, Silver Medallist, 1988; World Championships Silver Medallist, 1983; World Record Holder, 1986; World Champion, 1987; Retired, 1990; Founder Member, President, Chafford Hundred A.C; Marketing Consultant. Honours include: BBC Sports Personality of the Year, 1987; British Sports Writers Sportswoman of the Year, 1986, 1987; British Athletic Writers Woman Athlete of the Year, 1986, 1987. Memberships include: Voluntary Service Overseas Ambassador, 1992-93; President, Thurrock Harriers Athletic Club, 1993-; Governor, King Edward Grammer School, Chelmsford, 2000-02. Address: Chafford Hundred Information Centre, Elizabeth Road, Chafford Hundred, Grays, Essex RM16 6QZ, England. E-mail: champinternational@tinyworld.co.uk

WHITE Edmund (Valentine III), b. 13 January 1940, Cincinnati, Ohio, USA. Writer. Education: BA, University of Michigan, 1962. Appointments: Writer, Time-Life Books, New York City, 1962-70; Senior Editor, Saturday Review, New York City, 1972-73; Assistant Professor of Writing Seminars, Johns Hopkins University, 1977-79; Adjunct Professor, Columbia University School of the Arts, 1981-83; Executive Director, New York Institute for the Humanities, 1982-83; Professor, Brown University, 1990-92; Professor of Humanities, Princeton University, 1999-. Publications: Fiction: Forgetting Elena, 1973; Nocturnes for the King of Naples, 1978; A Boy's Own Story, 1982; Aphrodisiac (with others), stories, 1984; Caracole, 1985; The Darker Proof: Stories from a Crisis (with Adam Mars-Jones), 1987; The Beautiful Room is Empty, 1988; Skinned Alive, stories, 1995; The Farewell Symphony, 1997; The Married Man, 2000. Non-Fiction: The Joy of Gay Sex: An Intimate Guide for Gay Men to the Pleasures of a Gay Lifestyle (with Charles Silverstein), 1977; States of Desire: Travels in Gay America, 1980; The Faber Book of Gay Short Fiction (editor), 1991; Genet: A Biography, 1993; The Selected Writings of Jean Genet (editor), 1993; The Burning Library, essays, 1994; Our Paris, 1995; Proust, 1998; The Flâneur, 2001. Contributions to: Many periodicals. Honours: Ingram Merrill Foundation Grants, 1973, 1978; Guggenheim Fellowship, 1983; American Academy and Institute of Arts and Letters Award, 1983; Chevalier de l'ordre des arts et lettres, France, 1993; Officier Ordre des Arts et des Lettres, 1999. Address: c/o Amanda Urban, International Creative Management, 40 West 57th Street, New York, NY 10019, USA.

WHITE George Edward, b. 19 March 1941, Northampton, Massachusetts, USA. Professor. m. Susan Davis White, 2 daughters. Education: BA, Amherst College, 1963; MA, PhD, Yale University, 1967; JD, Harvard Law School, 1970. Appointments: Law Clerk, Chief Justice Earl Warren, Supreme Court of United States, 1971-72; Assistant Professor of Law, University of Virginia Law School, 1972-74; Associate Professor, 1974-77; Professor, 1977-86; John B Minor Professor of Law and History, 1986-2003; University Professor, 1992-2003; David and Mary Harrison Distinguished Professor, 2003-. Publications: The Eastern Establishment and the Western Experience, 1968; The American Judicial Tradition, 1976; Patterns of American Legal Thought, 1978; Tort Law in America, 1980; Earl Warren: A Public Life, 1982; The Marshall Court and Cultural Change, 1987; Justice Oliver Wendell Holmes: Law and the Inner Self, 1993; Intervention and Detachment: Essays in Legal History and Jurisprudence, 1994; Creating the National Pastime, 1996; The Constitution and the New Deal, 2000; Alger Hiss's Looking-Glass Wars, 2004. Honours: Fellow, National Endowment for the Humanities, 1977-

78, 1982-83; Fellow, Guggenheim Foundation, 1982-83; Triennial Award for Distinguished Scholarship, Association of American Law Schools, 1996. Memberships: Phi Beta Kappa; American Academy of Arts and Sciences; Society of American Historians; American Law Institute. Address: School of Law, University of Virginia, 580 Massie Road, Charlottesville, VA 22903, USA.

WHITE Marco Pierre, b. 11 December 1961, Leeds, England. Chef; Restaurateur. m. (1) Alexandra McArthur, 1988, divorced 1990, 1 daughter, (2) Lisa Butcher, 1992, divorced 1994, (3) Matilda Conejero-Caldera, 2000, 2 sons, 1 daughter. Appointments: Commis Chef, The Box Tree, Ilkley, 1978; Commis Chef de Partie, Le Gavroche, 1981, Tante Claire, 1983; Sous Chef, Le Manoir aux Quat' Saisons, 1984; Chef, Proprietor, Harveys, 1987-, The Restaurant, 1993-; Co-Owner, The Canteen, 1992-96; Founder, Criterion Restaurant with Sir Rocco Forte, 1995-; Re-opened Quo Vadis, 1996-; Oak Room, Le Meridien, 1997-99; MPW Canary Wharf, 1997-; Café Royal Grill Room, 1997-; Mirabelle Restaurant, Curzon Street, 1998-; L'Escargot Belvedere, 1999; Wheeler of St James, 2002. Publications: White Heat, 1990; White Heat II, 1994; Wild Food From Land and Sea, 1994; Canteen Cuisine, 1995; The Mirabelle Cookbook, 1999. Honours include: Restaurant of the Year, Egon Ronay (for The Restaurant), 1997. Address: Mirabelle Restaurant, 56 Curson Street, London W1Y 7PF, England.

WHITE Susan Dorothea, b. 10 August 1941, Adelaide, South Australia. Visual Artist; Painter; Sculptor; Printmaker. m. Brian Freeman, 2 sons, 1 daughter. Education: Full-time studies, South Australian School of Art, Adelaide, 1959-60; Full-time studies, Julian Ashton Art School, Sydney, 1960-61; Additional studies in sculpture, 1959-61, 1985-89 and printmaking, 1972, 1975, 1978. Career: Solo exhibitions, Australia, Europe, USA, 1962-98; Group exhibitions, Australia, Europe, USA, Asia, South America, 1959-2004. Collections held in: Hechinger Collection, Washington DC; National Gallery of Australia, Canberra; Dr Ulla Mitzdorf Collection, Munich; Museum of International Contemporary Graphic Art, Lublin; FMK Gallery, Budapest; Gallery of Modern Art, Lublin; Mornington Peninsula Arts Centre, Victoria; Westmead Centre, Sydney. Publications: Artwork appears in numerous publications; Significant artwork: The First Supper, 1988; The Seven Deadly Isms, 1992; The Seven Deadly Sins of Modern Times, 1993; It Cuts Both Ways, 1998; Next-Door Neighbours, 2000; Menopausal Me in a Saucepan Lid, Warts 'n All, with Everything, including the Kitchen Sink, 2001. Memberships: International Association of Artists; Viscopy; National Association for the Visual Arts. Address: 278 Annandale St, Annandale (Sydney), NSW 2038, Australia. E-mail: studio@susandwhite.com.au Website: www.susandwhite.com.au

WHITEHURST Brooks Morris, b. 9 April 1930, Reading, Pennsylvania, USA. Chemical Engineer. m. Carolyn Boyer, 2 sons, 1 daughter. Education: BS, Chemical Engineering, Virginia Polytechnic Institute and State University, 1951. Appointments: Senior Process Assistant, American Enka Corporation, 1951-56; Process Research Engineer, Va-Cara Chemical Corporation, 1956-63; Project Engineering, Texaco Inc, 1963-66; Manager, Engineering Services, Special Project, Long-Range Planning, Texasgulf, 1967-81; President, Whitehurst Associates Inc, 1981-. Publications: Paper presented at Solar World Forum, Brighton, UK, 1981; Patents and current work on biodegradable chelate systems, development of environmentally friendly products for forest fertilization and seedling propagation, waste rubber recycling, micronutrients for agriculture. Honour: Recipient, Commendation from US President, 1981. Memberships: National Association of Professional Engineers; American Institute of Chemical Engineers. 1983 Hoods Creek Drive, New Bern, NC 28562, USA.

WHITNEY Stewart Bowman, b. 15 November 1938, Buffalo, New York, USA. Professor Emeritus. m. Joan Noel Conti, 2 sons, 4 daughters. Education: BA, University of Buffalo, 1961; MA, 1965, PhD, 1972, SUNY, Buffalo. Appointments: Study Director, SUNY, Buffalo, 1962-65; Assistant Professor, Ithaca College, 1965-69; Assistant Professor, Antioch College, 1970-73; Professor, Niagara University, 1973-. Publications: Several book and numerous articles in professional journals. Honours: Outstanding Achievement, International Wildlife; CFLE, National Council on Family Relations; FAACS, American Board of Sexology; Alpha Kappa Delta. Memberships: National Council on Family Relations; American Board of Sexology; American Sociological Association; World Future Society; Society for Scientific Study of Sexuality. Address: 73 Niagara Falls Boulevard, University Heights, Buffalo, NY 14214, USA.

WHITTINGDALE John, b. 1959. Member of Parliament. m. Ancilla, 2 children. Education: Economics Degree, University College, London. Appointments: Head, Political Section, Conservative Research Department, 1982-84; Special Advisor to three consecutive Secretaries of State for Trade and Industry, 1984-85; Political Secretary to the Prime Minister, 1988-90; Private Secretary to Baroness Thatcher, 1990-92; Elected Member of Parliament for South Colchester and Maldon, 1992; Member, House of Commons Select Committee on Health, 1993-97; Parliamentary Private Secretary to the Minister of State for Education and Employment, 1994-96; Elected Member of Parliament for Maldon and East Chelmsford, 1997; Opposition Whip, 1997; Frontbench Treasury Spokesman, 1998; Parliamentary Private Secretary to the Leader of the Opposition, 1999; Shadow Secretary of State for Trade and Industry, 2001; Shadow Secretary of State for Culture, Media and Sport, 2002; Shadow Secretary of State for Agriculture, Fisheries and Food, 2003-.

WHITTINGTON Robert W, b. 25 September 1934, Alabama, USA. Corporate Professional. 1 daughter. Education: BA, Auburn University, 1954; BS, University of Miami, 1956; MS, Cornell University, 1958. Appointments: President, Travel Centers Inc, 1959-70, Prestige Vacations, 1961-70; Service Centers Inc, 1970-85, Exotics SA, 1988-; Chairman, Travel USA, Department of Commerce, USA, 1962-64. Memberships: Board Director, Eastern Airlines Inc, 1962-64, ASTA, 1964-66. Address: PO Box 025292, Miami, FL 33101-5292, USA.

WICKER Franklin Michael, b. 3 June 1924, St Paul, Minnesota, USA. Senior Financial Advisor; Independent Analyst and Consultant. m. Alice M Wicker. Education: BA, Economics, Sub Major, Political Science, Macalester College, St Paul, Minnesota, USA, 1948. Appointments include: World War II Veteran, Fuel Co-ordinator, Central Pacific Theatre, USN NAS, 1943-46; Credit Analyst, Swift and Co, St Paul, 1953-60; Apartment house and commercial property owner, private investor, entrepreneur, 1953-; Financial Consultant, Independent Contractor, various firms including finance and construction, St Paul, 1960-64; Representative, Senior Accountant Executive, Waddell and Reed, Kansas City and Bloomington, Minnesota, 1964-97; Senior Financial Advisor, 1997-2001; Retired from Waddell and Reed, 2001; Involved in the indictment and impeachment of Presidents Nixon and Clinton; Creator and instructor of You and Your Money Class, local schools and colleges, 22 years. Publications: Weekly articles on economic and political science issues. Honours: Over 260 honour citations and awards; President of Waddell and Reed's Presidents Council Qualifier, 1981 and member of Council four times, 1981-86; Invited to the White House, USA, four times by Presidents Regan, Bush, George W Bush and Vice-President Quale, 1980-2000; Qualified for Waddell and Reed's Circle of Champions for 23rd time, 2000. Memberships: Senior Trustee, St James

Lutheran Church, Head Trustee for many years; Small Business Administration, US Government, 1979-; International Association of Financial Planners, 1979-2000; Big Brother and Mentor Programmes, 1950-; Currently working on a large church foundation, 2001 and in the real estate and tax fields; Worked on 2002 campaign election reform and mid term election victories to change Senate from Democrats to Republicans. Address: 9991 Oak Shore Dr, Lakerville, MN 55044, USA.

WIDMER Winifred Ruth, b. 25 January 1921, Herkimer, New York, USA. Law and Educational Research Administration. m. Francis E Downey, 1 step-son, 2 step-daughters. Education: LLB, cum laude, Albany Law School, Union University, 1954; BA, History and Government, Russell Sage College, 1958. Appointments: Admitted to practice, New York State Bar, 1954, United States Supreme Court, 1958; Officer, Assistant Director for Administration, Corporate Secretary, The Research Foundation of State University of New York, a non-profit educational corporation administering research and educational funds for the State University of New York, 1954-80; Retired, 1988. Honours: Honorary Juris Doctor, Albany Law School, Union University, 2003; Kate Stoneman Award, Albany Law School, 2003; Member, Justinian Society honorary legal society. Memberships: Former Member, Council on Governmental Relations, subcommittee of NACUBO, representing the Research Foundation; Former member, New York State Bar Association; Board of Trustees, Capital District Genealogical Society; The Essex Society for Family History; National Curtis/Curtiss Society. Address: 3 Colonial Avenue, Albany, New York 12203-2009, USA. E-mail: fnwdowney@worldnet.att.net

WIEDERKEHR Karl Heinrich, b. 1 February 1922, Oftersheim, Nr Mannheim, Germany. Teacher; Headmaster. m. Gisela Wiederkehr, 1 son. Education: Studies in Physics, Mathematics, Chemistry, Philosophy, University of Hamburg, Germany, 1945-49; Grammar School Teacher's Examination; Dr rer. nat., 1962, Habilitation and venia legendi, Privatdozent (university teacher), History of Sciences, 1974, University of Hamburg. Appointments: Engineering Officer, German Navy. 1941-45; Grammar School Teacher, 1950-84; Headmaster, 1974. Publications include: Wilhelm Webers Stellung in der Entwicklung der Elektrizitätslehre (Dissertation), 1960; Aus der Geschichte des Göttinger Magnetischen Vereins und seiner Resultate, 1964; Wilhelm Eduard Weber, Erforscher der Wellenbewegung und der Elektrizität, 1967; René Just Haüys Vorstellungen vom Kristallbau und einer chemischen Atomistik, 1977 and 1978; Über die Verleihung der Copley-Medaille an Gauss und die Mitarbeit Englands im Göttinger Magnetischen Verein, 1982; Wilhelm Weber und Maxwells elektromagnetische Lichttheorie, 1994; Geophysics Contributed to the Radical Change from Classical to Modern Physics, 100 Years Ago, 1998; Gauss and Weber's Creation of the Absolute System of Units in Physics, 2002; Many other articles; Numerous biographies of famous scientists; Books for television series. Honour: Physics and Geophysics with special historical case studies (A Festschrift in honour of Karl Heinrich Wiederkehr), collected and edited by Wilfried Schröder, 1997. Address: Birkenau 24, 22087 Hamburg, Germany.

WIENER Marvin S, b. 16 March 1925, New York City, USA. Rabbi; Editor; Executive. m. Sylvia Bodek, 1 son, 1 daughter. Education: BS, 1944; MS, 1945; BHL, 1947; MHL and Ordination, 1951; DD (Hon), 1977. Appointments: Registrar, Rabbinical School, Jewish Theological Seminary of America, 1951-57; Consultant, Frontiers of Faith, television series, NBC, 1951-57; Director, Instructor Liturgy, Cantors Institute-Seminary College Jewish Music, Jewish Theological Seminary of America, 1954-58; Faculty Co-ordinator, Seminary School and Womens Institute,

1958-64; Director, National Academy for Adult Jewish Studies, United Synagogue, New York City, 1958-78; Editor, Burning Bush Press, 1958-78, United Synagogue Review, 1978-86; Director, Committee on Congregational Standards, United Synagogue, 1976-86; Consultant, Community Relations and Social Action, 1981-82, Editor, Executive, Joint Retirement Board, 1986-. Publications: Editor of numerous volumes of Judaica; Author of articles in professional journals. Memberships include: American Academy of Jewish Research; Association of Jewish Studies. Address: 67-66 108th Street, Apt D-46, Forest Hills, NY 11375-2974, USA.

WIENER Valerie, b. 30 October 1948, Las Vegas, Nevada, USA. Positioning Strategist; Author; State Senator. Education: Bachelor of Journalism, 1971, Master of Arts, Broadcast Journalism, 1972, University of Missouri, Columbia, Missouri; Master of Arts, Contemporary Literature, University of Illinois, Springfield, 1974; Law studies, McGeorge School of Law, University of the Pacific, Sacramento, California, 1976-79. Appointments: Producer, Checkpoint, weekly TV series, KOMU-TV and Missouri School of Religion, 1972-73; Editor, Saturday, Illinois State Register, 1973; Public Affairs Director/Community Liaison, First Illinois Cable Television Inc, Springfield, 1973-74; Producer/Talent, Nevada Realities, KLVX-TV, Las Vegas, Nevada, 1974-75; Owner, Vice President, Broadcast Associates, Nevada, 1972-86; Press Secretary, US Congress, Washington DC, 1983-88; Nevada State Senator, 1996-2004; Senate Minority Whip, 2001-; Owner, President, Wiener Communications Group, Las Vegas, Nevada, 1988-; Owner, President, PowerMark Publishing, Las Vegas, Nevada, 1998-. Publications: Contributor to magazines, Columnist, Business to Business; Author, works including: Power Communications: Positioning Yourself for High Visibility, 1994; Gang Free: Influencing Friendship Choices in Today's World, 1995, 1996; The Nesting Syndrome: Grown Children Living at Home, 1997; Winning the War Against Youth Gangs, 1999; Power Positioning: Advancing Yourself as THE Expert, 2000; PowerMaster HandBooks (series of 15), 2000-. Honours include: 147 state and national communications awards, NFPW and Nevada Press Women, 1990-; Sweepstakes/Outstanding Achievement Award (US, Canada, Germany), National Federation of Press Women, 1991; Distinguished Leadership Award, National Association for Community Leadership, 1993; Circle of Excellence Award, 1993; Gold Medallist, Fitness and Weightlifting, Nevada Senior Olympics, 1998, 1999, 2000, 2001, 2002, 2003; Gold Medallist, Swimming, Nevada Senior Olympics, 2002, 2003; Distinguished Senior Athlete, Nevada, 2000; Outstanding Women Advocate for Education, Virginia Commonwealth University, 2000; Healthy School Hero (one of 27 in US), 2002; Nevada Women's Healthcare Policy Hero, 2003. Address: 3540 W Sahara Avenue #352, Las Vegas, NV 89102, USA.

WIERUSZEWSKA-ADAMCZYK Maria Jolanta, b. 15 February 1943, Lodz, Poland. Professor of Humanities. Education: Philosophy Doctor, 1970, Associate Professor, 1979, Lodz University; Professor of Humanities, conferred by Poland's President, 1992. Appointments: Assistant, Assistant Lecturer, Senior Lecturer, Ethnography Department, Lodz University, 1965-70; Senior Lecturer, 1971-78 Deputy Director for Scientific Affairs, 1986-90, Director in Warsaw, 1991-97, Institute of Rural and Agricultural Development, PAN; Scholarship to the University of Chicago, USA, The Kosciuszko Foundation, 1975-76. Publications: Sanction of the social system against rural family, 1971; Changes in rural community. Zaborow after 35 years, 1978; Rural community in search of socio-cultural whole, 1991; Renewal of rural community. Between myth and hope (co-author), 1992; Rural community and agriculture at cross-roads? (co-author), 1993; Polish rural community – context – contrasts – strategies, 1997; Self-organisation in rural communities: aspects, structures,

Dictionary of International Biography

differences (co-author), 2002. Honours: The Award of the Scientific Secretary, Polish Academy of Sciences, 1980; Gold Cross of Merit, 1995. Memberships: Presidential Council for Rural Community and Agriculture; Ethnological Sciences Committee, Polish Sociological Society. Address: ul Nowy Swiat 72, 00-330 Warsaw, Poland. E-mail: mwierusz@irwirpan.waw.pl

WIESEL Elie(zer), b. 30 September 1928, Sighet, Romania (US citizen, 1963). Author; Professor in the Humanities Religion and Philosophy. m. Marion Erster Rose, 1969, 1 son. Education: Sorbonne, University of Paris, 1948-51. Appointments: Distinguished Professor, City College of the City University of New York, 1972-76; Andrew W Mellon Professor in the Humanities, 1976-, Professor of Philosophy, 1988-, Boston University; Distinguished Visiting Professor of Literature and Philosophy, Florida International University, Miami, 1982; Henry Luce Visiting Scholar in the Humanities and Social Thought, Yale University, 1982-83. Publications: Un Di Velt Hot Geshvign, 1956, English translation as Night, 1960; L'Aube, 1961, English translation as Dawn, 1960; Le Jour, 1961, English translation as The Accident, 1962; La Ville de la chance, 1962, English translation as The Town Beyond the Wall, 1964; Les Portes de la foret, 1964, English translation as The Gates of the Forest, 1966; Le Chant des morts, 1966, English translation as Legends of Our Time, 1968; The Jews of Silence: A Personal Report on Soviet Jewry, 1966; Zalmen, ou, la Folie de Dieu, 1966, English translations as Zalmen, or, The Madness of God, 1974; And the Sea is Never Full: Memoirs, 1969-, English translation, 1999; Le Mendiant de Jerusalem, 1968, English translation as A Beggar in Jerusalem, 1970; Entre deux soleils, 1970, English translation as One Generation After, 1970; Célébration Hassidique: Portraits et légendes, 1972, English translation as Souls on Fire: Portraits and Legends of Haisdic Masters, 1972; Le Serment de Kolvillag, 1973, English translation as The Oath, 1973; Célébration Biblique: Portraits and Legends, 1975; Un Juif aujourd'hui: Recits, essais, dialogues, 1977, English translation as A Jew Today, 1978; Dimensions of the Holocaust (with others), 1977; Four Hasidic Masters and Their Struggle Against Melancholy, 1978; Le Proces de Shamgorod tel qu'il se droula le 25 fevrier 1649: Piéce en trois actes, 1979, English translation as The Trial of God (as It Was Held on February 25, 1649, in Shamgorod): A Play in Three Acts, 1979; Images from the Bible, 1980; Le Testament d'un poète Juif assassine, 1980, English translation as The Testament, 1981; Five Biblical Portraits, 1981; Somewhere a Master, 1982; Paroles d'étranger, 1982; The Golem: The Story of a Legend as Told by Elie Wiesel, 1983; Le Cinquieme Fils, 1983, English translation as The Fifth Son, 1985; Signes d'exode, 1985; Job ou Dieu dans la tempete, 1986; Le Crépuscule au loin, 1987, English translation as Twilight, 1988; The Six Days of Destruction (with Albert H Friedlander), 1989; L'Oublie: Roman, 1989; From the Kingdom of Memory, 1990; Evil and Exile (with Philippe-Michael de Saint-Cheron), 1990; The Forgotten, English translation, 1992; Monsieur Chouchani: L'enigme d'un Maitre du XX Siècle: Entretiens Avec Elie Wiesel, Suivis d'une Enquete, 1994; Tous les Fleuves Vont a la Mer: Mémoires, 1994, English translation as All Rivers Run to the Sea: Memoirs, 1995; Mémoire a Deux Voix (with Francois Mitterrand), 1995, English translation as Memoir in Two Voices, 1996; Et la mer n'est pas remplie, Memoirs Vol II, 1996; Celebration prophetique, 1998; King Solomon and his Magic Ring, 1999; The Judges, novel, 2002; After the Darkness, essays, 2002; Elie Wiesel: Conversation, 2002; Le temps des déracinés, novel, 2003; Wise Men and Their Tales (Portraits of Biblical, Talmudic and Hasidic Masters, 2003. Honours: Numerous, including: Prix Medicis, 1969; Prix Bordin, 1972; US Congressional Gold Medal, 1985; Nobel Prize for Peace, 1986; US Presidential Medal of Freedom, 1992; Grand-Croix of the French Legion of Honor, 2001. Memberships: American Academy of Arts and Sciences; Amnesty International; Author's Guild; European Academy of Arts and Sciences; Foreign Press Association, honorary lifetime member; Jewish Academy of Arts and Sciences; PEN; Writers Guild of America; The Royal Norwegian Society of Sciences and Letters; Founding President, Universal Academy of Cultures, Paris, 1993-; PEN New England Council, 1993-; Fellow, American Academy of Arts and Letters, Department of Literature, 1996-; Honorary Fellow, Modern Language Association of America, 1998; Honorary Member, Romanian Academy, 2001. Address: c/o University Professors, Boston University, 745 Commonwealth Avenue, Boston, MA 02215, USA.

WILBUR Richard (Purdy), b. 1 March 1921, New York, New York, USA. Poet; Writer; Translator; Editor; Professor. m. Mary Charlotte Hayes Ward, 20 June 1942, 3 sons, 1 daughter. Education: AB, Amherst College, 1942; AM, Harvard University, 1947. Appointments: Assistant Professor of English, Harvard University, 1950-54; Associate Professor of English, Wellesley College, 1955-57; Professor of English, Wesleyan University, 1957-77; Writer-in-Residence, Smith College, 1977-86; Poet Laureate of the USA, 1987-88; Visiting Lecturer at various colleges and universities. Publications: Poetry: The Beautiful Changes and Other Poems, 1947; Ceremony and Other Poems, 1950; Things of This World, 1956; Poems, 1943-1956, 1957; Advice to a Prophet and Other Poems, 1961; The Poems of Richard Wilbur, 1963; Walking to Sleep: New Poems and Translations, 1969; Digging to China, 1970; Seed Leaves: Homage to R F, 1974; The Mind-Reader: New Poems, 1976; Seven Poems, 1981; New and Collected Poems, 1988; Bone Key and other poems, 1998; Mayflies, 2000. For Children: Loudmouse, 1963; Opposites, 1973; More Opposites, 1991; A Game of Catch, 1994; Runaway Opposites, 1995; Opposites, More Opposites and Some Differences, 2000; The Pig in the Spigot, 2000. Non-Fiction: Anniversary Lectures (with Robert Hillyer and Cleanth Brooks), 1959; Emily Dickinson: Three Views (with Louise Bogan and Archibald MacLeish), 1960; Responses: Prose Pieces, 1953-1976, 1976. Editor: Modern American and Modern British Poetry (with Louis Untermeyer and Karl Shapiro), 1955; A Bestiary, 1955; Poe: Complete Poems, 1959; Shakespeare: Poems (with Alfred Harbage), 1966, revised edition, 1974; Poe: The Narrative of Arthur Gordon Pym, 1974; Witter Bynner: Selected Poems, 1978. Translator: Molière: The Misanthrope, 1955; Molière: Tartuffe, 1963; Molière: The School for Wives, 1971; Molière: The Learned Ladies, 1978; Racine: Andromache, 1982; Racine: Phaedra, 1986; Molière: The School for Husbands, 1992; Molière: The Imaginary Cuckold, 1993; Molière: Amphitryon, 1995; Molière: Don Juan, 2000; Molière: The Bungler, 2000. Honours: Harriet Monroe Memorial Prizes, 1948, 1978; Oscar Blumenthal Prize, 1950; Guggenheim Fellowships, 1952-53, 1963-64; Prix de Rome Fellowship, American Academy of Arts and Letters, 1954; Edna St Vincent Millay Memorial Award, 1957; Pulitzer Prizes in Poetry, 1957, 1989; National Book Award for Poetry, 1957; Ford Foundation Fellowship, 1960; Bollingen Prizes, 1963, 1971; Brandeis University Creative Arts Award, 1971; Shelley Memorial Award, 1973; Drama Desk Award, 1983; Chevalier, Ordre des Palmes Academiques, 1983; Los Angeles Times Books Prize, 1988; Gold Medal for Poetry, American Academy and Institute of Arts and Letters, 1991; Edward Mac Dowell Medal, 1991; National Medal of Arts, 1994. Memberships: Academy of American Poets, chancellor; American Academy of Arts and Letters, president, 1974-76, chancellor, 1976-78, 1980-81; American Academy of Arts and Sciences; American Society of Composers, Authors and Publishers; Authors League of America; Dramatists Guild; Modern Language Association, honorary fellow. Address: 87 Dodwells Road, Cummington, MA 01206, USA.

WILCHEK Meir, b. 17 October 1935, Warsaw, Poland. Biochemist. m. Esther Edlis, 1 son, 2 daughters. Education: BS, Bar-Ilan University, Ramat Gan, Israel, 1960; PhD, Weizmann Institute of Science, Rehovot, 1965. Appointments: Chief Chemist, Yeda Co, Rehovot, Israel, 1960-62; Chief Consultant, Miles-Yeda (Bio Makor), Rehovot, 1960-87; Research Associate, Department of Biophysics, 1965-66, Senior Scientist, 1968-71, Associate Professor, 1971-74, Professor, 1974-, Department Head, 1977-78, 1983-87, Dean of Biochemistry, 1995-99, Weizmann Institute of Science, Rehovot; Visiting Fellow, 1966-67, Research Associate, 1967-68, Visiting Scientist, 1972, 1974-75, Fogarty Scholar, 1981-82, National Institutes of Health, USA. Publications: 400 articles in professional journals. Honours: Rothschild Prize for Chemistry, Israel, 1984; Wolf Prize for Medicine, Israel, 1987; Pierce Prize, Rockford, Illinois, USA, 1987; Honorary DSc, University of Waterloo, Canada, 1989; Israel Prize in Biotechnology, Israeli Government, 1990; Sarstedt Prize for Analytical Biochemistry, 1990; Honorary PhD, Bar-Ilan University, Ramat Gan, 1995; Distinguished Clinical Chemist Award, International Federation of Clinical Chemistry, 1996; Honorary PhD, University of Jyvaskyla, Finland, 2000; Honorary PhD, Ben-Gurion University, Beer-Sheva, Israel, 2000; Anfinsen Award, Protein Society, USA, 2004. Memberships: Honorary Member, American Society of Biological Chemists; American Chemical Society; Foreign Associate, Institute of Medicine, National Academy of Sciences, USA; European Molecular Biology Organisation; Israel Biochemistry Society; Israel Chemical Society; Israel Immunological Society; Israeli Academy of Sciences. Address: Ha-Avoda St 3Bm Rehovot, Israel.

WILCOX Violet Gaynell, b. 31 October 1923, Richmond, Virginia, USA. m. Richard, 10 March 1957, divorced, 1 son, 3 daughters. Education: Washington School of Art, Port Washington, New York, 1948. Appointments: Thalhimers Inc, 1946-57; Seamstress, Hub Uniform, 1977-92. Contributions to: Lone Stars; Smile, Omnific; Sunflower Dream. Honours: 1st Prize, Aztec Peak, 1986; 1st Prize, Writer's Exchange, 1987; 1st Prize, Poets at Work, 1988, 1989; 3rd Prize, International Contest; 1st for drawing, Psych It; Special Award, Lines N'Rhymes; Joint Winner, Song Contest. Address: 208 Newbridge Circle, Apt D, Richmond, VA 23223-6265, USA.

WILDER Gene, b. 11 June 1935, Milwaukee, Wisconsin, USA. Film Actor; Director; Producer. m. (1) Mary Joan Schutz, 1967, divorced 1974, 1 daughter, (2) Gilda Radner, 1984, deceased, (3) Karen Boyer, 1991. Education: University of Iowa; Bristol Old Vic Theatre School. Appointment: US Army, 1956-58. Creative Works: Films include: Bonnie and Clyde, 1966; The Producers, 1967; Start the Revolution Without Me, 1968; Quackser Fortune Has a Cousin in the Bronx, 1969; Willy Wonka and the Chocolate Factory, 1970; The Scarecrow, 1972; Everything You Always Wanted to Know About Sex, But Were Afraid to Ask, 1971; Rhinoceros, 1972; Blazing Saddles, 1973; Young Frankenstein, 1974; The Little Prince, 1974; Thursday's Game, 1974; The Adventure of Sherlock Holmes's Smarter Brother, 1975; Silver Streak, 1976; The World's Greatest Lover, 1977; The Frisco Kid, 1979; Stir Crazy, 1980; Sunday Lovers, 1980; Hanky Panky, 1982; The Woman in Red, 1984; Haunted Honeymoon, 1986; See No Evil, Hear No Evil, 1989; Funny About Love, 1990; Another You, 1991; Stuart Little (voice), 1999; Murder in a Small Town, 1999; TV appearances include: The Scarecrow, 1972; The Trouble With People, 1973; Marlo Thomas Special, 1973; Thursday's Games, 1973; Something Wilder, 1994-; Alice in Wonderland (film), 1999; The Lady in Question (film), 1999. Address: Ames Cushing, William Morris Agency, 151 El Camino Drive, Beverly Hills, CA 90212, USA.

WILDER Virginia, b. 5 February 1963, Orleans, Indiana, USA. Real Estate Agent. m. Danny Ray Wilder, 1 son, 1 daughter. Education: Stenography, Lee County Vocational School, Virginia, 1981; Real Estate Licence, Virginia, Tennessee and Kentucky, 2000; Appraisal School, 2002. Appointments: Branch Manager, Loan Officer, Peoples Bank, 1983-2000; Real Estate Agent, 2000-. Honours: Library Club Service Award; Highest Grade in Stenography Award; Best Dressed of Senior Class; Most Courteous of Senior Class; Real Estate Agent of the Year; Best of the Best Award in Real Estate; Centurion Producer, Century 21, 2 consecutive years; Premier Agent, Century 21 Mortgage; #1 Premier Agent with Century 21 Mortgage; Listed in national and international biographical dictionaries. Memberships: Bell County Chamber of Commerce; Lee County Virginia Chamber of Commerce; Pentecostal Tabernacle Church. Address: Route 1, Box 72, Rose Hill, VA 24281, USA. E-mail: wilder@mounet.com

WILFORD John Noble, b. 4 October 1933, Murray, Kentucky, USA. Journalist; Writer. m. Nancy Watts Paschall, 25 December 1966, 1 daughter. Education: BS, Journalism, University of Tennessee, 1955; MA, Political Science, Syracuse University, 1956; International Reporting Fellow, Columbia University, 1961-62. Appointments: Science Reporter, 1965-73, 1979-, Assistant National Editor, 1973-75, Director of Science News, 1975-79, Science Correspondent, 1979-, New York Times, New York City; Mc Graw Distinguished Lecturer in Writing, Princeton University, 1985; Professor of Science Journalism, University of Tennessee, 1989-90. Publications: We Reach the Moon, 1969; The Mapmakers, 1981; The Riddle of the Dinosaur, 1985; Mars Beckons, 1990; The Mysterious History of Columbus, 1991; Cosmic Dispatches, 2000. Contributions to: Nature; Wilson Quarterly; New York Times Magazine; Science Digest; Popular Science. Honours: Westinghouse-American Association for the Advancement of Science Writing Award, 1983; Pulitzer Prizes for National Reporting, 1984, shared 1987; Ralph Coats Roe Medal, American Society of Mechanical Engineers, 1995; American Acsademy of Arts and Sciences, fellow, 1998. Memberships: Century Club, New York City; National Association of Science Writers; American Geographical Society, council member, 1994-. Address: New York Times, 229 West 43rd Street, New York, NY 10036, USA.

WILHELM Laura Marie, b. 17 May 1965, Philadelphia, Pennsylvania, USA. Russian Translator; Scholar; Instructor. m. Chris Wilhelm. Education: BA, Russian, Reed College, 1988; MA, Russian Language and Literature, 1990, PhD, 1994, University of Kansas. Appointments: US Co-ordinator, Pushkin House Study Programme (part-time), 1993-95; Russian Translator, Transportation Assistant, City of West Hollywood, 1995-; Recording Secretary, Russian Advisory Board, 2001; Instructor, Russian Life and Language, Beverly Hills Adult School, 2003-; Independent Living Specialist, Accessible Design and Counseling Inc. Publications: Pornography and the Politics of Oppression in the Russian Aesopian Tradition in Eros and Pornography in Russian Culture, 1999. Honours: Graduate School Honours Fellowship, University of Kansas, 1988-92; City of West Hollywood Employee of the Quarter, 1997. Memberships: Phi Beta Kappa; Dobro Slovo; AAUW; Beast Fable Society; Los Angeles World Affairs Council; Los Angeles/St Petersburg Sister City Committee. Address: 1236 N. Sweetzer Ave, No. 19, West Hollywood, CA 90069, USA. E-mail: laurawilhelm2003@yahoo.com

WILHELMI Cynthia Joy, b. 12 September 1946, Marshaltown, Iowa, USA. Information Technology Consultant. 1 son, 1 daughter. Education: BA, Art, University of Iowa, 1969; BA, Equivalent Degree in Journalism, 1993, MA, Communication, 1996, University of Nebraska. Appointments include: Editor, Publisher,

Dictionary of International Biography

Contributing Author, Salaam, Omaha, Nebraska, 1985-86; Master Artist-in-Residence, Nebraska Arts Council, 1985-91; Graduate Teaching Assistant, University of Nebraska, 1993-95; Program Co-ordinator, Family Friends of Easter Nebraska, Visiting Nurse Association, 1996-97; College Instructor, Midland Lutheran College, Fremont, 1997-99; Information Technology Consultant, Inacom Headquarters, Omaha, 1998; Information Technology Consultant, Bass and Associates, Omaha, 1999-2000; Information Technology Consultant, RHI Consulting, Omaha, 2000; Information Technology Consultant, TEKsystems, Omaha, 2000-; IT Business Analyst, Alegent Health, Omaha; Test Engineer, Regression Test Development, Project Leader, IT Consultant, Ameritrade (Securities Trading); Senior Test Engineer, Third Party Vendor Interface Management, Lincoln Benefit Life Insurance Company, Lincoln, Nebraska; Senior Test Engineer, Ameritas Life Insurance Corporation, Omaha, Nebraska; US Airforce Data Manager (Contractor), Air Force Weather Agency (Secret Clearance), Bellvue Airforce Base, Nebraska. Publications: Numerous articles in professional journals. Honours: Outstanding Graduate Teaching Assistant Award, University of Nebraska at Omaha, 1995; Admiral in the Great Navy of Nebraska; Honorary Member, Society of Collegiate Journalists; Nebraska Republican Gubernatorial Re-election Campaign Committee; One Thousand Great Scientists, IBC, Cambridge, England; Listed in Who's Who publications and Biographical Dictionaries. Memberships: Phi Delta Gamma; Nebraska Admirals' Association; American Association of University Women; Advisory Council, Foster Grandparents; Society for Technical Communication; Friends of Art, University of Nebraska; Mensa (Nebraska-Western Iowa Executive Committee). Address: 13516 Redwood Street, Omaha, NE 68138, USA. E-mail: cwi813@earthlink.net

WILKES Maurice Vincent, b. 26 June 1913, England. Mathematician. Education: Graduated, Mathematics, St John's College, Cambridge. Appointments: University Demonstrator, 1937; Radar and Operational Research, World War II; Lecturer, Acting Director, Mathematical Laboratory, Cambridge University, 1945, Director of Laboratory, 1946-70; Head, Computer Laboratory, 1970; Professor of Computer Technology, University of Cambridge, 1965-80; Staff Consultant, Digital Equipment Corporation, 1980-86; Adjunct Professor, MIT, 1981-85; Research Strategy, Olivetti Research Board, 1986-96; Adviser on Research Strategy, Olivetti and Oracle Research Laboratory, 1996-99; Staff Consultant, AT&T Laboratories, Cambridge, 1999-2002. Publications: Oscillations of the Earth's Atmosphere, 1949; Preparation of Programs for an Electronic Digital Computer, 1951, 1957; Automatic Digital Computers, 1956; A Short Introduction to Numerical Analysis, 1966; Time-Sharing Computer Systems, 1968; The Cambridge CAP Computer and its Operating System, 1979; Memoirs of a Computer Pioneer, 1985; Computing Perspectives, 1995. Honours: 9 honorary degrees; Harry Goode Memorial Award, 1968; Eckert-Mauchly Award, 1980; McDowell Award, 1981; Faraday Medal, 1981; Pender Award, 1982; C and C Prize, 1988; Italgas Prize, 1991; Kyoto Prize, 1992; John von Neumann Medal, 1997; Mountbatten Medal, 1997. Memberships include: Fellow, St John's College, Cambridge, 1950; Fellow, Royal Society, 1956; First President, British Computer Society, 1957; American Academy of Arts and Sciences; US National Academy of Engineering. Address: Computer Laboratory, University of Cambridge, William Gates Building, J J Thomson Road, Cambridge, Cb3 0FD, England.

WILKINS Maurice Hugh Frederick, b. 15 December 1916, Pongaroa, New Zealand. m. Patricia Chidgey, 1959, 2 sons, 2 daughters. Education: Graduated, Physics, St John's College, Cambridge, 1938; Doctorate, University of Birmingham, 1940. Appointments: Ministry of Home Security and Aircraft Production;

Manhattan Project, development of atomic bomb, University of California; Biophysics project, St Andrews University, Scotland, 1945; Biophysics Research Unit, King's College, London, 1946, Assistant Director, 1950, Deputy Director, 1955, Director, 1970-72; Professor of Biophysics, Head of Department, 1970-82, Fellow, 1973-, Professor Emeritus, 1981-, King's College. Publications: Papers on luminescence and topics in biophysics, eg, molecular structure of nucleic acids and structure of nerve membranes. Honours: Albert Lasker Award, American Public Health Association, 1960; Joint Winner, Nobel Prize for Physiology or Medicine, 1962; Honorary LLD, Glasgow, 1972; Honorary ScD, Birmingham, 1992; Honorary DSc, London, 1998. Memberships: Honorary Member, American Society of Biological Chemists, 1964; President, British Society for Social Responsibility in Science, 1969-91; Foreign Honorary Member, American Academy of Arts and Sciences, 1970; Russell Committee against Chemical Weapons, 1981; Food and Disarmament International, 1984-. Address: 30 St John's Park, London, SE3 7JH, England.

WILKS Dina Marie, b. 18 June 1959, Houston, Texas, USA. Writer; Film Maker. 1 son, 1 daughter. Education: Psychology, Texas A&M, 1977-79, 2003-05; Psychology, University of Houston, 1998; Screenwriting, University of California at Los Angeles, 2001. Appointments: Staff Writer, Houston Theater Monthly; Novelist; Poet; Film Maker; Writer; Director; Production Crew Member, Warner Bros, Charter Films, Touchstone. Publications: Poems in professional journals and magazines; Novel, Gonna Lay Down My Burdens, 1997; Film Maker, documentaries and short film; Several articles. Honours: Mary Gibbs Jones Scholarship, 1977-79; Texas A&M Scholarship, 1977-78; Mary Harding Hoffman Scholarship, 1997; Gulf Coast Award; Country Club Women's Scholarship. Memberships: Dramatist Guild; Authors League; Women in Film and Television; TSEU; National Association of Female Executives; National Museum for Women in the Arts. Address: MSM, PO Box 1516, College Station, TX 77841-1516, USA. E-mail: dinawilks@hotmail.com

WILLAMOWSKI Michael, b. 23 November 1939, Brno, Czech Republic. Academic Librarian. m. Sibylle Zwirner-Willamowski, 2 sons, 1 daughter. Education: Degree in Physics, 1972; Doctor rerum naturalium, 1975. Appointments: Captain, German Airforce, 1961-62; Teacher, Hamburg, Germany, 1966-70; Information Broker, Universität der Bundeswehr, Hamburg, 1976-. Publications: Achievements include: Invention of semipermeable membranes for reverse osmosis. Memberships: Deutsche Gesellschaft für Schiffahrt-und Marinegeschichte; Verband der Elekrotechnik. Address: Gruener Bogen 10, D-22113 Oststeinbek, Germany. E-mail: tuscade@hotmail.com Website: www.topsurfen.de

WILLCOCKS Michael (Sir), b. 27 July 1944, Kent, England. Lieutenant General Retired; Black Rod. m. Jean, 1 son, 2 daughters. Education: Royal Military Academy, Sandhurst, 1962-64; BSc (Hons), London University, 1965-68; Army Staff College, 1975-76; Higher Command and Staff Course, 1988; Royal College of Defence Studies, 1991. Appointments: Regimental and Staff Appointments, 1965-83; Commanding Officer, 1st Regiment Royal Horse Artillery, 1983-85; Staff Posts, UK, 1985-89; Commander, Royal Artillery 4th Armoured Division, 1989-90; Chief of Staff, Land Operations, Gulf War, 1991; Director, Army Plans and Programme, 1991-93; Director General, Land Warfare, 1993-94; Chief of Staff, Allied Command Europe Rapid Reaction Corps, 1994-96; Chief of Staff, Land Component Implementation Force, Bosnia-Herzegovina, 1995-96; Assistant Chief, UK Army, 1996-99; Deputy Commander (Operations) Stabilisation Force, Bosnia-Herzegovina, 1999-2000; UK Military Representative to NATO, the EU and WEU, 2000-2001; Retired 2001; Gentleman Usher of the Black Rod, Secretary to the Lord Great Chamberlain and Serjeant at Arms of the House of Lords, 2001-. Publication: Airmobility and the Armoured Experience, 1989. Honours: Meritorious Service Medal (USA), 1996, 2000; CB (Companion Order of Bath), 1997; KCB (Knight Commander Order of Bath), 2000. Memberships: Pilgrims; European Atlantic Group; Honourable Artillery Company; Honorary Colonel 1st Regiment Royal Horse Artillery; Colonel Commandant Royal Artillery; Commissioner, Royal Hospital Chelsea, 1996-99; Clubs: National Liberal, Pitt. Address: House of Lords, London SW1A 0PW, England. E-mail: willcocksm@parliament.uk

WILLETT Anna Hart, b. 18 June 1931, Barttesville, Oklahoma, USA. Composer. 1 son, 1 daughter. Education: Bachelor of Music Education, Piano and Voice Major, University of Southern Louisiana, Lafayette, 1954; Master of Arts, Music History, Louisiana State University, Baton Rouge, 1964; Scholar, Loyala University, New Orleans, 1972; Postgraduate, Composition, 1977-84. Appointments: Public School Music Teacher, Iberville Parish, Plaquemine, Louisiana, 1954-55; Library and Listening Room Supervisor, Louisiana State University, 1960-64; Ininerant Vocal Music Teacher, Orleans Paris, 1966-71; Music Pedagogy Teacher, St Mary's Dominican College, 1972-. Publications include: A Treatise on the Mathematical Recurring of the Sine Wave, 1999. Honours: LSU Delta Literary Annual Staff Editor and Contributor, 1957, 1958, 1959; Juried Student Art Show, 1977, 1978. Memberships: New Orleans Concert Choir, 1966-71; St Louis Cathedral Choir, 1972-73; St Alban's Chapel Choir, 1977-. Address: 2244 Ferndale Avenue, Baton Rouge, LA 70808, USA.

WILLIAM SCOTT Seann, b. 3 October 1976, Cottage Grove, Minnesota. Actor. Films include: Born into Exile, 1997; American Pie, 1999; Final Destination, 2000; Road Trip, 2000; Dude, where's my car?, 2000; Evolution, 2001; American Pie 2, 2001; Jay and Silent Bob Strike Back; 2001; Stark Raving Mad, 2002; Old School, 2003; Bulletproof Monk, 2003; American Wedding, 2003; The Rundown, 2003. TV Appearences include: Unhappily Ever After, 1996; Something so Right, 1998; The Big Breakfast, 2001; The Tonight Show with Jay Leno, 2001; Diary, 2003. Honours: MTV Movie Award, 2002; MTV Movie Award, 2004.

WILLIAMES Lee, b. 4 July 1942, Darby, Pennsylvania, USA. University Administrator; Professor. m. Frances Williams, 2 sons, 1 daughter. Education: BA, La Salle University, 1964; MA, European History, Niagara University, New York, 1966; Area Certificate, Soviet and East European Affairs, Soviet Institute, 1966; PhD, Russian and European History, State University of New York, Binghamton, 1981. Appointments: Professor of History, Director, Honours Program, College Misericordia, 1966-86; Professor, Assistant Provost for Academic Affairs, University of Scranton, Pennsylvania, 1986-92; Professor, Vice President for Academic Affairs, Secretary of the Board of Directors, University of St Thomas, Houston, 1992-2000; Secretary General, International Council Universities of St Thomas Aquinas, 1995-97; Acting President, summer 1997, currently Vice President, Academic Affairs Emeritus and Professor of History, University of St Thomas. Publications: Numerous articles on European/Russian History; Author, Anton Chekhov The Iconoclast. Honours: Jubilarian Medal, La Salle University; Centenial Medal, University of Scranton; Fellow, American Council on Education. Memberships: American Association for the Advancement of Slavic Studies; American Council on Education. Address: University of St Thomas, 3800 Montrose Boulevard, Houston, TX 77006, USA.

WILLIAMS Bernard Arthur Owen (Sir), b. 21 September 1929, Southend, Essex, England. Professor of Philosophy; Writer. m. (1) Shirley Vivienne Teresa Brittain Catlin, 1955, divorced 1974,

1 daughter, (2) Patricia Law Skinner, 1974, 2 sons. Education: BA, 1951, MA, 1954, Balliol College, Oxford. Appointments: Fellow, All Souls College, Oxford, 1951-54, 1997-; Fellow and Tutor in Philosophy, New College, Oxford, 1954-59; Lecturer in Philosophy, University College, London, 1959-64; Visiting Professor, 1963; Senior Fellow in the Humanities, 1978, Princeton University; Professor of Philosophy, Bedford College, London University, 1964-67; Knightbridge Professor of Philosophy, Cambridge University, 1967-79; Fellow, 1967-79, 1988-, Provost, 1979-87, King's College, Cambridge; Visiting Professor, Harvard University, 1973; Visiting Professor, 1986, Monroe Deutsch Professor of Philosophy, 1988-, Sather Professor of Classics, 1989, University of California at Berkeley; White's Professor of Moral Philosophy, Oxford University, and Fellow, Corpus Christi College, Oxford, 1990-96; Visiting Fellow, Wissenschaftskolleg, Berlin, 1997. Publications: British Analytical Philosophy (editor with A C Montefiore), 1966; Morality, 1972; Utilitarianism: For and Against (with J J C Smart), 1973; Problems of the Self, 1973; Descartes: The Project of Pure Enquiry, 1978; Moral Luck, 1981; Utilitarianism and Beyond, (editor with A K Sen), 1982; Ethics and the Limits of Philosophy, 1985; Shame and Necessity, 1993; Making Sense of Humanity, 1995; Plato, 1998; Der Wert der Wahrheit, 1998; Truth and Truthfulness, 2002. Other: What is Truth? (writer and presenter), Channel 4 TV, UK, 1988. Contributions to: Scholarly books and journals. Honours: Honorary Fellow, Balliol College, Oxford, 1984, Corpus Christi College, Oxford, 1996; Dr Margrit Egner Stiftung Prize, Zürich, 1997; Knight, 1999; Hon DLitt, Yale, 2001; Hon DHL, Chicago, 1999; Hon LLD, Harvard, 2002. Memberships: American Academy of Arts and Sciences, honorary foreign member; Sadler's Wells Opera, later English National Opera, board, 1968-86; Chairman, Government Committee on Obscenity and Film Censorship, 1977-79; British Academy, fellow; Commission on Social Justice, Labour Party, 1992-94. Address: All Souls College, Oxford, OX1 4AL, England.

WILLIAMS C(harles) K(enneth), b. 4 November 1936, Newark, New Jersey, USA. Poet; Professor. m. (1) Sarah Dean Jones, 1966, divorced 1975, 1 daughter, (2) Catherine Justine Mauger, April 1975, 1 son. Education: BA, University of Pennsylvania, 1959. Appointments: Visiting Professor, Franklin and Marshall College, Lancaster, Pennsylvania, 1977, University of California at Irvine, 1978, Boston University, 1979-80; Professor of English, George Mason University, 1982; Visiting Professor, Brooklyn College, 1982-83; Lecturer, Columbia University, 1982-85; Holloway Lecturer, University of California at Berkeley, 1986; Professor, Princeton University, 1996-. Publications: A Day for Anne Frank, 1968; Lies, 1969; I Am the Bitter Name, 1972; The Sensuous President, 1972; With Ignorance, 1977; The Women of Trachis (co-translator), 1978; The Lark, the Thrush, the Starling, 1983; Tar, 1983; Flesh and Blood, 1987; Poems 1963-1983, 1988; The Bacchae of Euripides (translator), 1990; A Dream of Mind, 1992; Selected Poems, 1994; The Vigil, 1997; Poetry and Consciousness (selected essays), 1998; Repair (poems), 1999; Misgivings, A Memoir, 2000; Love About Love, 2001. Contributions to: Akzent; Atlantic; Carleton Miscellany; Crazyhorse; Grand Street; Iowa Review; Madison Review; New England Review; New Yorker; Seneca Review; Transpacific Review; TriQuarterly; Yale Review; Threepenny Review. Honours: Guggenheim Fellowship; Pushcart Press Prizes, 1982, 1983, 1987; National Book Critics Circle Award, 1983; National Endowment for the Arts Fellowship, 1985; Morton Dawen Zabel Prize, 1988; Lila Wallace Writers Award, 1993; Berlin Prize Fellowship, 1998; PEN Voelker Prize, 1998; Pulitzer Prize, 2000; Los Angeles Times Book Prize, 2000. Memberships: PEN; American Academy of Arts and Science. Address: 82 Rue d'Hauteville, 75010 Paris, France.

WILLIAMS Christopher Maxwell John, b. 25 September 1948, Sydney, Australia. Agricultural Scientist. m. Judith Barbara Spall, 1 daughter. Education: BScAgric Hons, Agriculture, University of Sydney 1970; PhD, Agronomy, University of Adelaide, 1978. Appointments: Senior Research Officer, South Australia Department of Agriculture, Naracoorte, South Australia 1975-79; Senior Lecturer, Massey University, Palmerston North, New Zealand 1979-81; Senior Agronomist, Department of Agriculture, Walpeup, Victoria, Australia 1981-82; Senior Research Scientist, Horticulture, South Australian Research and Development Institute, Adelaide, 1982-, including Convenor, Potatoes 2000, Australian Potato Research and Development conference in Adelaide July 2000. Publications: Author or co-author of over 100 articles on potato and horticulture crop agronomy; Potato Varieties for South Australia. Honours: Recipient, Howard Memorial Trust Scholarship 1977; Best Paper Award, Australian Potato Industry Conference 1990; Convenor, Australian Potatoes 2000 Conference, Adelaide, July 2000. Memberships: Australian Institute of Agricultural Science and Technology; International and Australian Societies for Horticultural Science. Address: South Australian Research and Development Institute, Waite Precinct, GPO Box 397, Adelaide, SA 5001, Australia. E-mail williams.chrism@saugov.sa.gov.au

WILLIAMS Filomena, b. 4 August 1951, Italy. Executive Director. 1 son, 1 daughter. Education: SWWD, Social Work, Seneca College, 1982. Appointments: Co-operative College student, 1980, Second Stage Housing Co-ordinator, 1982, Shelter Worker with Human Resources responsibility, Public Education Co-ordinator, Executive Director, 1990-, Yellow Brick House Women's Shelter, Aurora, Ontario, Canada; Executive Director, Pathway of Peace Foundation (awareness and fundraising project); Implemented counselling service in Rita's Place (8 apartment interim residency), Aurora, Ontario and a multicultural counselling service in Thornhill, Ontario; Worked with York Regional Police in educating officers on how to intervene efficiently in domestic disputes. Publications: Yellow Brick House Dating Manual; Information Manual. Honours: Certificates of Appreciation for launching pathway of Peace, MPP Al Palladini and Aurora Mayor Tim Jones, 2000; Queens Jubilee Medal, 2002; Certificate in Domestic Violence, Ministry of the Attorney General, 2003; International Peace Award, Cultural Universal Convention, 2003; Featured in the international book, Beacon of Hope by Marion Verweij, Amsterdam; Listed in Who's Who publications and biographical dictionaries. Memberships: Death Review Committee, Ministry of the Attorney General, Ontario, Canada; Canadian Public Relations Society. Address: Yellow Brick House, 37 Wellington Street East, Aurora, Ontario, L4G 1H6 Canada. E-mail: info@yellowbrickhouse.org Website: www.yellowbrickhouse.org

WILLIAMS Herbert Lloyd, b. 8 September 1932, Aberystwyth, Wales. Writer; Poet; Dramatist. m. Dorothy Maud Edwards, 13 November 1954, 4 sons, 1 daughter. Publications: The Trophy, 1967; A Lethal Kind of Love, 1968; Battles in Wales, 1975; Come Out Wherever You Are, 1976; Stage Coaches in Wales, 1977; The Welsh Quiz Book, 1978; Railways in Wales, 1981; The Pembrokeshire Coast National Park, 1987; Stories of King Arthur, 1990; Ghost Country, 1991; Davies the Ocean, 1991; The Stars in Their Courses, 1992; John Cowper Powys, 1997; Looking Through Time, 1998; A Severe Case of Dandruff, 1999; Voices of Wales, 1999; The Woman in Back Row, 2000; Punters, 2002. Television Dramas and Documentaries: Taff Acre, 1981; A Solitary Mister, 1983; Alone in a Crowd, 1984; Calvert in Camera, 1990; The Great Powys, 1994; Arouse All Wales, 1996. Radio Dramas: Doing the Bard, 1986; Bodyline, 1991; Adaptations: A Child's Christmas in Wales, 1994; The Citadel, 1997. Contributions to: Reviews and journals. Honours: Welsh Arts Council Short Story Prize, 1972, and Bursary, 1988; Aberystwyth Open Poetry Competition, 1990; Hawthornden Poetry Fellowship, 1992; Rhys Davies Short Story Award, 1995. Memberships: Welsh Academy, fellow; The Powys Society; The William Barnes Society; The Society of Authors. Address: 63 Bwlch Road, Fairwater, Cardiff CF5 3BX, Wales

WILLIAMS Lawrence A D, b. 5 October 1962, St Elizabeth, Jamaica. Lecturer; Researcher. m. Lisa Simone Caleb-Williams. Education: BS, Chemistry and Zoology, 1987, PhD, Insect Toxicology, 1992, both degrees from the University of the West Indies, Jamaica, West Indies. Appointments: Scientific/Senior Research Officer, 1987-91, Project Supervisor, 1992, Scientific Research Council of Jamaica Post Doctoral Research Fellow, 1993, Assistant Lecturer, 1994-95, Lecturer, Examiner, 1995-99, University of the West Indies. Publications: In professional journals, 2001-. Honours: DAAD Research Fellow, Germany; Caribbean Academy Award Sciences, 1998; Alexander von Humboldt Scholar, 1999, 2001; International Order of Merit for Excellence, 1999; Five Hundred Leaders of Influence, 1999. Memberships: Fellow, International Biographical Research Association (FIBA); New York Academy of Sciences, 1994; International Society for Invertebrate Reproduction. Address: Scientific Research Council, Hope Gardens, PO Box 350, Kingston 6, Jamaica, West Indies.

WILLIAMS Malcolm David, b. 9 April 1939, South Wales. Author. Widower, 1 daughter. Education: Birmingham University Institute of Education, 1959-61. Publications: Yesterday's Secret, 1980; Poor Little Rich Girl, 1981; Debt of Friendship, 1981; Another Time, Another Place, 1982; Mr Brother's Keeper, 1982; The Stuart Affair, 1983; The Cordillera Conspiracy, 1983; The Girl from Derry's Bluff, 1983; A Corner of Eden, 1984; Sorrow's End, 1984; A Stranger on Trust, 1987; Shadows From the Past, 1989. Contributions to: Various publications, two Poetry Collections, 1998 and 2003. Honours: 1st Prize, Short Story Competition, 1961, 1969. Memberships: Society of Authors; West Country Writers Association; World Literary Academy, fellow. Address:17 Beaumont Road, Cheltenham, Glos, GL51 0LP, England.

WILLIAMS Marcia Dorothy, b. 8 August 1945, White Lackington, England. Children's Author; Illustrator. 1 son, 1 daughter. Education: Surrey University,Roehampton, MA course in Children's Literature. Publications: The First Christmas, 1987; Noah's Ark, 1989; Jonah and the Whale, 1990; Joseph and His Amazing Coat of Many Colours, 1990; When I Was Little, 1991; Not a Worry in the World, 1991; Don Quixote, 1992; Greek Myths, 1993; Sinbad the Sailor, 1994; King Arthur, 1995; Robin Hood, 1996; The Odyssey and the Iliad, 1997; Mr William Shakespeare, 1998; Plays, Fabulous Monsters, 1999; Bravo, Mr William Shakespeare!, 2000; Charles Dickens and Friends, 2002; God and His Creations, 2004. Address: Walker Books Ltd, 87 Vauxhall Walk, SE11 5HJ, England.

WILLIAMS Patricia Ann, b. 18 September 1950, Houston, Texas, Professor; Director. Education: Postdoctoral work, University of Houston and Sam Houston State University; BAT, Sam Houston State University, 1973; MA, English, Sam Houston State University, 1974; EdD, University of Houston, 1979. Appointments: Chair, English Department, Klein High School, 1976-78; Assistant Professor, 1979-85; Associate Professor, 1985-91; Professor of Education, 1992-; Director, Across-the-University Writing Program, 1989-2002; Executive Director, Academic Enrichment Center, Sam Houston State University, 1999-2002. Publications: Co-author of several books; Secondary Classroom Management; Why Didn't I Think of That?; Responsibilities of the Professional Educator. Honours: Phi Delta Kappa Service Key;

Dictionary of International Biography

International Woman of the Year; Sam Houston State University Alumni Outstanding Service Award, 2004; Inclusion into many Who's Who publications. Memberships: Alpha Chi National College Honor Scholarship Society, Immediate Past National President; Sam Houston State University Alumni Advisory Board, Past President; Delta Kappa Gamma, Past President of SHSU Chapter; Phi Delta Kappa, Past President of Chapter; Association of Teacher Educators; Vice-Chair, Classroom Management Special Interest Group.

WILLIAMS Robbie (Robert Peter), b. 13 February 1974, Stoke-on-Trent, Staffordshire, England. Singer. Career: Member, UK all-male vocal group Take That, 1990-95; Solo artiste, 1995-; Television includes: Take That And Party, C4, 1993; Take That Away documentary, BBC2, 1993; Take That In Berlin, 1994. Recordings: Albums: Take That And Party, 1992; Everything Changes, 1993; Greatest Hits, 1996; Solo album: Life Thru A Lens, 1997; I've Been Expecting You, 1998; The Ego Has Landed, 1999; Sing When You're Winning, 2000; Swing When You're Winning, 2001; Escapology, 2002; Hit singles: with Take That: It Only Takes A Minute, 1992; I Found Heaven, 1992; A Million Love Songs, 1992; Could It Be Magic, 1993; Why Can't I Wake Up With You, 1993; Love Ain't Here Anymore, 1994; Never Forget, 1995; Pray, 1993; Relight My Fire (with Lulu), 1993; Babe, 1993; Everything Changes, 1994; Sure, 1994; Back For Good, 1995; Solo hit singles: Freedom, 1996; Old Before I Die, 1997; Lazy Days, 1997; South of the Border, 1997; Angels, 1997; I've Been Expecting You, 1998; Millennium, 1998; Let Me Entertain You, 1998; No Regrets, 1999; She's The One/It's Only Us, 1999; Strong, 1999; Rock DJ, 2000; Kids, with Kylie Minogue, 2000; Supreme, 2000; Let Love Be Your Energy, 2001; Eternity/Road To Mandalay, 2001; Better Man, 2001; Somethin' Stupid (with Nicole Kirman), 2001; Feel, 2002; My Culture, 2002; Come Undone, 2003; Something Beautiful, 2003; Sexed Up, 2003. Publications: F for English, 2000; Numerous videos, books, magazines. Honours include: 7 Smash Hit Awards, 1992; 1 Smash Hit Award, 1996; BRIT Awards: Best Male Artist, Best Single, Best Video, 1998; MTV Award, Best Male, 1998; Smash Hits, Best Male, 1998; Nordoff-Robbins Music Therapy Original Talen Award, 1998; BRIT Awards: Best Video, Best Single, 1999. Memberships: Equity; Musicians' Union; MCPS; PRS; ADAMI; GVC; AURA. Address: c/o IE Music Ltd, 59 A Chesson Road, London, W14 9QS, England,

WILLIAMS Robert Joseph Paton, b. 25 February 1926, Wallasey, Cheshire, England. Scientist; Academic. m. Jelly Klara Büchli, 2 sons. Education: BA, 1948, DPhil, 1951, Chemistry, Merton College, Oxford University. Appointments: Tutor, Chemistry, Wadham College, Oxford, 1955-66; Lecturer, Chemistry, Oxford University, 1955-72; Commonwealth Fellow, Harvard Medical School, USA, 1965-66; Tutor, Biochemistry, Wadham College Oxford, 1966-72; Reader, Chemistry, 1972-74, Royal Society Napier Research Professor, 1974-91; Senior Research Fellow, 1991-93, Emeritus Fellow, 1993- Wadham College, Oxford; Visiting Professor, Royal Free Hospital, London University, 1991-95. Publications: Books: Inorganic Chemistry (with C S G Phillips) volume 1 and 2, 1966; The Natural Selection of the Chemical Elements (with J R R Fràusto da Silva), 1996; Bringing Chemistry to Life (with J R R Fràusto da Silva), 1999; The Biological Chemistry of the Elements (with J R R Fràusto da Silva), 2nd edition, 2001; Editor of several books; Over 600 articles in chemical and biological journals. Honours include: Fellow of the Royal Society, 1972; Twice Medallist of the Biochemical Society; Twice Medallist of the Royal Society; Three times Medallist of the Royal Chemical Society; Twice Medallist of the European Biochemical Societies and the International Union of Biochemistry; Named Lecturer at Numerous colleges and universities in the UK, USA and Europe. Memberships: Fellow

Royal Society of Chemistry; Honorary Member, British Biophysics Society, Society for Biological Inorganic Chemistry, Society for the Study of Calcium Proteins; Member, Biochemical Society; Editor of several journals. Inorganic Chemistry Laboratory, Oxford University, South Parks Road, Oxford, OX1 3QR. E-mail: bob.williams@chem.ox.ac.uk

WILLIAMS Robin, b. 21 July 1951, Chicago, USA. Actor; Comedian. m. (1) Valerie Velardi, 1978, 1 son, (2) Marsha Garces, 1989, 1 son, 1 daughter. Education: Juillard School, New York. Creative Works: TV appearances include: Laugh-In; The Richard Pryor Show; America 2-Night; Happy Days; Mork and Mindy, 1978-82; Carol and Carl and Whoopi and Robin; Stage appearances include: Waiting for Godot; Films include: Popeye, 1980; The World According to Garp, 1982; The Survivors, 1983; Moscow on the Hudson, 1984; Club Paradise, 1986; Good Morning Vietnam, 1987; Dead Poets' Society, 1989; Awakenings, 1990; The Fisher King, 1991; Hook, 1991; Dead Again, 1991; Toys, 1992; Being Human, 1993; Aladdin (voice), 1993; Mrs Doubtfire, 1993; Jumanji, 1996; The Birdcage, 1996; Jack, Hamlet, Joseph Conrad's The Secret Agent, 1996; Good Will Hunting, 1997; Flubber, 1997; What Dreams May Come, 1998; Patch Adams, 1998; Jakob the Liar, 1999; Bicentennial Man, 1999; Get Bruce, 1999; One Hour Photo, 2001; Insomnia, 2002; Death to Smoochy, 2002; The Final Cut, 2004; House of D, 2004; Recordings: Reality, What a Concept, 1979; Throbbing Python of Love; A Night at the Met. Honours include: Several Emmy Awards; Several Grammy Awards; Golden Globe Award, 1988, 1991. Address: CAA, Creative Artists Agency, 9830 Wilshire Boulevard, Beverly Hills, CA 90212, USA.

WILLIAMS Steven D, b. 19 April 1956, Minneapolis, Minnesota, USA. Plastic Surgeon. m. Yvonne Christian-Williams. Education: Bachelor of Arts, University of Chicago, 1979; Doctorate of Medicine, Loyola University, Stritch School of Medicine, 1985. Appointments: Resident, Intern, General Surgery, The University of Illinois, Cook County Hospital Program, 1985-89; Chief Resident, General Surgery, 1989-90, Fellow, Staff Attending, Burn Fellowship, Director, Intensive Care Unit, 1990-91, Cook County Hospital; Attending Clinical Instructor, Department of Surgery, Cook County Hospital, 1990-91; Resident, Plastic and Reconstructive Surgery, 1991-92, Chief Resident, Plastic and Reconstructive Surgery, 1992-93, Assistant Clinical Instructor, Department of Surgery, 1991-93, The Medical College of Ohio at Toledo; Attending Physician, Plastic Surgeon, Private Practice, Center for Reconstructive Surgery, Oak Lawn, Illinois, 1993-95; Attending Physician, Plastic Surgeon, Private Practice, Community Health Center of Bourbonnais, Illinois, 1995-; Co-Chairman, Department of Surgery, Riverside Medical Center and St Mary's Hospital. Publications: Numerous articles and papers, abstracts and presentations. Honours: Listed in many national and international biographical dictionaries; Listed in America's Top Surgeons, 2002-03; Man of the Year, ABI, 2003; Nominated for Great Minds of the 21st Century, ABI, 2003; Nominated for Outstanding Intellectuals of the 21st Century, IBC, 2003; Fellowship, American College of Surgeons, 2002. Memberships: Fellow, American College of Surgeons; American Society of Plastic Surgeons; Midwest Association of Plastic Surgeons; Chicago Society of Plastic Surgeons; American Burn Association; American Medical Association; Illinois State Medical Society; Chicago Medical Society; Kankakee County Medical Society; Karl A Meyer Surgical Society of Cook County Hospital. Address: 338 Power Road, Bourbonnais, IL 60914, USA.

WILLIAMS-BLANGERO Sarah, b. 26 April 1962, Greenwich, England. Scientist. m. John Blangero. Education: BA, Anthropology, 1984, MA, Anthropology, 1984, PhD,

Anthropology, 1987, Case Western Reserve University. Appointments: Postdoctoral Scientist, 1987-90, Assistant Scientist, Genetics, 1990-93, Associate Scientist, Genetics, 1993-96, Scientist, Department of Genetics, 1996-99, Chair, Department of Genetics, 1999-, Southwest Foundation Biomed Research. Publications: Numerous articles. Honours: BA, magna cum laude, (Hons) Anthropology; Phi Beta Kappa; Sigma Xi. Memberships: American Association of Physical Anthropologists; American Society of Human Genetics; American Society for Tropical Medicine and Hygiene. Address: Department of Genetics, Southwest Foundation for Biomedical Research, PO Box 760549, San Antonio, TX 78245, USA. E-mail: sarah@darwin.sfbr.org

WILLIAMSEN Dannye Sue, b. 26 March 1949, Memphis, Tennessee, USA; Publisher; Writer. m. John Dean Williamsen. Education: Bachelor of Arts, Psychology, cum laude, University of Memphis, Tennessee, USA. Appointments: Administrator, Security Investments Inc, 1972-75; Investor, Owner, 2 night-clubs, 1976-78; International Technical Analyst for Financial Instruments, ContiCommodity Inc, 1977-80; Owner, Technical Analyst, Commodity Consultant Inc, 1981; Project Manager, B&P Development Co, Austin, Texas, 1982-84; Assistant to President, Memphis Area Chamber of Commerce, 1984-86; Owner, Dental Technician, Williamsen Dental Laboratory, 1986-; Partner, Personal Education Network, 2001-; Owner, Publisher, Networx Publishing, 2002-. Publications: Novel: Illusions, 1998; E-Newsletter: Creative Living, 2001; E-Newsletter, Metaphysical Minute: Philosophy on the Run, 2003; CD Audiobook: It's Your Move! Transform Your Dreams from Wishful Thinking to Reality, 2003. Honours: Balfour Award; Chi Beta Phi National Honor Society in the Sciences; Psi Chi, National Honor Society in Psychology; Golden Web Award for Design, Content, Creativity for www.penetwork.org; Listed in Who's Who publications and biographical dictionaries. Memberships: American Association of University Women; American Business Women's Association; National Organization of Women; National Association of Female Executives; American Psychological Association; Association of Humanistic Psychology; Small Publishers Association of North America; Publishers Marketing Association; Association for Global New Thought; National Women's History Museum; National Association of Women Writers. Address: 13299 Blackhawk Road, Prophetstown, IL 61277-9725, USA. E-mail: dannyew@penetwork.org

WILLIAMSON Jack, (John Stewart Williamson), b. 29 April 1908, Bisbee, Arizona, USA. Writer. m. Blanche Slaten Harp, 15 August 1947, deceased 1985, 2 stepchildren. Education: BA, MA, 1957, Eastern New Mexico University; PhD, University of Colorado, 1964. Appointment: Professor of English, Eastern New Mexico University, Portales, 1960-77. Publications: Science Fiction: The Legion of Space, 1947; Darker Than You Think, 1948; The Humanoids, 1949; The Green Girl, 1950; The Cometeers, 1950; One Against the Legion, 1950; Seetee Shock, 1950; Seetee Ship, 1950; Dragon's Island, 1951; The Legion of Time, 1952; Dome Around America, 1955; The Trial of Terra, 1962; Golden Blood, 1964; The Reign of Wizardry, 1965; Bright New Universe, 1967; Trapped in Space, 1968; The Pandora Effect, 1969; People Machines, 1971; The Moon Children, 1972; H G Wells: Critic of Progress, 1973; Teaching Science Fiction, 1975; The Early Williamson, 1975; The Power of Blackness, 1976; The Best of Jack Williamson, 1978; Brother to Demons, Brother to Gods, 1979; Teaching Science Fiction: Education for Tomorrow, 1980; The Alien Intelligence, 1980; The Humanoid Touch, 1980; Manseed, 1982; The Queen of a Legion, 1983; Wonder's Child: My Life in Science Fiction, 1984; Lifeburst, 1984; Firechild, 1986; Mazeway, 1990; Beachhead, 1992; Demon Moon, 1994; The Black Sun, 1997; The Fortress of Utopia, 1998; The Silicon Dagger, 1999. With Frederik Pohl: Undersea Quest, 1954; Undersea Fleet, 1955;

Undersea City, 1956; The Reefs of Space, 1964; Starchild, 1965; Rogue Star, 1969; The Farthest Star, 1975; Wall Around a Star, 1983; Land's End, 1988. With James Gunn: Star Bridge, 1955. With Miles J Breuer: The Birth of a New Republic, 1981. Honours: Pilgrim Award, Science Fiction Research Association, 1968; Grand Master Nebula Award, 1976; Hugo Award, 1985. Memberships: Science Fiction Writers of America, president 1978-80; Science Fiction Research Association; World Science Fiction Planetary Society. Address: PO Box 761, Portales, NM 88130, USA.

WILLIAMSON Joel R, b. 27 October 1929, Anderson County, South Carolina, USA. Professor; Writer. m. Anna Woodson, 18 November 1986, 1 son, 2 daughters. Education: AB, 1949, MA, 1951, University of South Carolina; PhD, University of California, Berkeley, 1964. Appointments: Instructor, 1950-64, Assistant Professor, 1964-66, Associate Professor, 1966-69, Professor, 1969-85, Lineberger Professor in Humanities, 1985-, Department of History, University of North Carolina, Chapel Hill. Publications: After Slavery: The Negro in South Carolina During Reconstruction, 1965; Origins of Segregation, 1968; New People: Miscegenation and Mulattoes in the US, 1980; The Crucible of Race, 1984; A Rage for Order, 1986; William Faulkner and Southern History, 1993. Honours: Parkman, Emerson, Owsley, Kennedy, Mayflower Awards; Mayflower Cup, 1994; Finalist, Pulitzer Prize in History, 1985, 1994. Memberships: Society of American Historians; Southern Historical Association; Organisation of American Historians; American Historical Society. Address: 211 Hillsborough Street, Chapel Hill, NC 27514, USA. E-mail: william@email.unc.edu

WILLIS Bruce Walter, b. 19 March 1955, Germany. Actor; Singer. m. Demi Moore, divorced 2000, 3 daughters. Education: Montclair State College; Moved to USA, 1957; Studied with Stella Adler. Creative Works: Stage appearances: (off Broadway): Heaven and Earth, 1977; Fool for Love, 1984; The Bullpen; The Bayside Boys; The Ballad of Railroad William; Films: Prince of the City, 1981; The Verdict, 1982; Blind Date, 1987; Sunset, 1988; Die Hard, 1988; In Country, 1989; Die Hard 2: Die Harder, 1990; Bonfire of the Vanities, 1990; Hudson Hawk, 1991; The Last Boy Scout, 1991; Death Becomes Her, 1994; Distance, 1994; Color of Night, 1994; North, 1994; Nobody's Fool, 1994; Pulp Fiction, 1994; Die Hard with a Vengeance, 1995; 12 Monkeys, 1995; Four Rooms, 1996; Last Man Standing, 1996; The Jackal, 1997; The Fifth Element, 1997; Mercury Rising, 1998; Armageddon, 1998; Breakfast of Champions, 1998; The Story of US, 1999; The Sixth Sense, 1999; Unbreakable, 2000; Disneys' The Kid, 2000; Bandits, 2001; Hart's War, 2002; Grand Champion, 2002; True West, 2002; Tears of the Sun, 2003; Rugrats Go Wild! (voice), 2003; Charlie's Angels: Full Throttle, 2003; The Whole Ten Yards, 2004; TV: Trackdown (film); Miami Vice (series); The Twilight Zone (series); Moonlighting (series), 1985-89; Friends (guest), 2000; Recordings: The Return of Bruno, 1987; If It Don't Kill You, It Just Makes You Stronger, 1989. Honours include: People's Choice Award, 1986; Emmy Award, 1987; Golden Globe Award, 1987.

WILLIS Gladden Williams, b. 26 March 1939, Minden, Louisiana, USA. Pathologist; Tree Farmer; Photographer. m. Lydia Hall, 2 sons. Education: BS, Centenary College, Shreveport, Louisiana, USA, 1957-60; MD, Tulane University School of Medicine, New Orleans, Louisiana, USA, 1960-64; Pathology Residency, LSU Medical Center, Shreveport, Louisiana, USA, 1964-69; Surgical Pathology Fellowship, Memorial Sloan-Kettering, New York, USA, 1969-71. Appointments: Private Practice Pathology, 1971-73; Pathologist, 1973-, Director, Anatomic Pathology, 1976-2003, Vice-Chair, Laboratory Medicine, 1996-2003, Ochsner Clinic Foundation, New Orleans, Louisiana, USA. Publications: 28 scientific papers and presentations; 1093 scientific photographs in biology and other textbooks. Honours: George Washington Honor Medal, Valley Forge Foundation; Listed in several Who's Who publications and biographical dictionaries. Memberships: Association of Directors of Anatomic Pathology; Arthur Purdy Stout Society; Royal Microscopical Society; International Academy of Pathology; New York Academy of Sciences; American Society of Media Photographers. Address: Ochsner Clinic Foundation, 1516 Jefferson Highway, New Orleans, LA 70121, USA. E-mail: qwillis@ochsner.org

WILLIS Meredith Sue, b. 31 May 1946, West Virginia, USA. Writer; Educator. m. Andrew B Weinberger, 9 May 1982, 1 son. Education: BA, Barnard College, 1969; MFA, Columbia University, 1972. Publications: A Space Apart, 1979; Higher Ground, 1981; Only Great Changes, 1985; Personal Fiction Writing, 1984; Quilt Pieces, 1990; Blazing Pencils, 1990; Deep Revision, 1993; The Secret Super Power of Marco, 1994; In the Mountains of America, 1994; Marco's Monster, 1996; Trespassers, 1997; Oradell at Sea, 2002. Honours: National Endowment for the Arts Fellowship, 1978; New Jersey Arts Fellowship, 1995; Honoree, Emory and Henry Literary Festival, 1995. Address: 311 Prospect Street, South Orange, NJ 07079, USA.

WILSNACK Sharon Carlson, b. 31 July 1943, Manhattan, Kansas, USA. Professor. m. Richard William Wilsnack, 4 sons, 1 daughter. Education: BA, Kansas State University, 1965; Fulbright Fellow, Albert-Ludwigs University, Germany, 1965-66; MA, 1968, PhD, 1972, Clinical Psychology, Harvard University. Appointments: Research and Teaching Fellow, Harvard University, 1966-71; Clinical Psychology Intern, Harvard Medical School, 1968-69; Supervising Psychologist, Massachusetts Mental Health Center, Boston, 1971-74; Associate in Psychology, Harvard Medical School, 1972-74; Director, Regional Alcoholism Rehabilitation Programme, Indiana, 1974-78; Adjunct Assistant Professor, Psychology, Indiana University, 1975-78; Co-director, Clinical Research Training Program in Alcoholism, Indiana University, 1975-78; Associate Professor, Director, 1978-85, Professor and Director, 1985-, Preclinical Curriculum in Psychiatry and Behavioral Science, Chester Fritz Distinguished Professor, Department of Neuroscience, 1989-, University of North Dakota School of Medicine; Adjunct Professor, Psychology, University of North Dakota, 1989-. Publications: Many articles and papers in scientific journals. Honours include: President's Advisory Council on Women Award, University of North Dakota, 1997; Terry McGovern Award for Excellence in Research, Terry McGovern Family Foundation, 1999; H David Wilson MD, Award for Excellence in Neuroscience Research, University of North Dakota School of Medicine and Health Sciences, 2002. Memberships: American Psychological Association; American Psychological Society; Research Society on Alcoholism; North Dakota Psychological Association; Kettil Bruun International Society for Social and Epidemiological Research on Alcohol; American Public Health Association; Society for the Psychological Study of Social Issues; American Association for the Advancement of Science; Psychologists for Social Responsibility; National Organization for Women. Address: Department of Neuroscience, University of North Dakota, School of Medicine & Health Sciences, PO Box 9037, Grand Forkes, ND 58202-9037, USA. E-mail: swilsnac@medicine.nodak.edu

WILSON Andrew Bray Cameron (Hon), b. 3 June 1936, Adelaide, South Australia. Former Justice of the High Court of Fiji. m. Julie Elizabeth Pearce, 11 April 1987. 2 son, 6 daughters. Education: LLB, University of Adelaide, 1959. Appointments: Barrister and Solicitor, 1960-72; Judge, Adelaide Juvenile Court, 1972-76; Judge District Court of South Australia, 1972-99; Acting

Justice of the Supreme Court of Papua New Guinea, 1973; Lecturer, Criminology, University of Adelaide, 1973; Justice of the National and Supreme Courts, Papua New Guinea, 1978-80; Justice of the Supreme Court of Samoa, 1999-2000; Justice of the High Court of Fiji, 2002-03. Honours: Churchill Fellowship, 1972; AM, 1998. Memberships: Member, Council, Law Society, South Australia, 1961-72; Chairman, Prisoners Aid Association, South Australia, 1966-73; Member, Social Welfare Advisory Council, 1970-72; Member, Australia and New Zealand Society of Criminology, 1971-; Member, Law Reform Committee, South Australia, 1972; Member Coalition Against Crime, 1990-94; Vice-President, 1973-77, 1991-93, President, 1993-95, Australian Crime Prevention Council; Chairman, McDouall Stuart Board, Burra Art Gallery, South Australia, 1995-97; President, Offenders Aid and Rehabilitation Services, South Australia, 1997-99. Address: 114 Allinga Avenue, Glenunga, SA 5064, Australia.

WILSON A(ndrew) N(orman), b. 27 October 1950, England. Author. m. (1) Katherine Duncan-Jones, 2 daughters, (2) Ruth Alexander Guilding, 1991, 1 daughter. Education: MA, New College, Oxford. Appointments: Lecturer, St Hugh's College and New College, Oxford, 1976-81; Literary Editor, The Spectator, 1981-83. Publications: The Sweets of Pimlico (novel), 1977; Unguarded Hours (novel), 1978; Kindly Light (novel), 1979; The Laird of Abbotsford, 1980; The Healing Art (novel), 1980; Who Was Oswald Fish (novel), 1981; Wise Virgin (novel), 1982; A Life of John Milton, 1983; Scandal (novel), 1983; Hilaire Belloc, 1984; Gentlemen in England (novel), 1985; Love Unknown (novel), 1986; The Church in Crisis (co-author), 1986; Stray (novel), 1987; Landscape in France, 1987; Incline Our Hearts (novel), 1987; Penfriends from Porlock: Essays and Reviews, 1977-86, 1988; Tolstoy: A Biography, 1988; Eminent Victorians, 1989; C S Lewis: A Biography, 1990; A Bottle in the Smoke (novel), 1990; Against Religion, 1991; Daughters of Albion (novel), 1991; Jesus, 1992; The Vicar of Sorrows (novel), 1993; The Faber Book of Church and Clergy, 1992; The Rise and Fall of the House of Windsor, 1993; The Faber Book of London (editor), 1993; Hearing Voices (novel), 1995; Paul: The Mind of the Apostle, 1997; Dream Children (novel), 1998; God's Funeral, 1999; The Victorians, 2002. Honours: Royal Society of Literature, fellow, 1981; Whitbread Biography Award, 1988. Address: 5 Regent's Park Terrace, London, NW1 7EE, England.

WILSON August, b. 27 April 1945, Pittsburgh, Pennsylvania, USA. Dramatist. 1 daughter. Appointment: Founder, Black Horizons Theatre Co, Pittsburgh, 1968. Publications: The Homecoming, 1979; The Coldest Day of the Year, 1979; Fullerton Street, 1980; Black Bart and the Sacred Hills, 1981; Jitney, 1982; Ma Rainey's Black Bottom, 1984; Fences, 1985; Joe Turner's Come and Gone, 1986; The Piano Lesson, 1987; Two Trains Running, 1990; Seven Guitars, 1995. Honours: New York Drama Critics Circle Awards, 1985, 1986, 1988, 1990, 1996; Whiting Writer's Award, 1986; American Theatre Critics Outstanding Play Awards, 1986, 1990, 1992; Drama Desk Awards, 1986, 1990; Pulitzer Prizes for Drama, 1987, 1990; Tony Award, 1987; Outer Critics' Circle Award, 1987; Literary Lion Award, New York Public Library, 1988. Membership: American Academy of Arts and Letters. Address: c/o John Breglio, Paul, Weiss, Rifkind, Wharton & Garrison, 1285 Avenue of the Americas, New York, NY 10019, USA.

WILSON Catherine Thelma, b. 9 June 1929, Ashington, Northumberland, England. Academic. m. Noel Wilson, deceased, 2 sons. Education: BA, (Dunelm) (Hons), Social Studies, Durham University, 1951; MSc, Gerontology, Kings College London, 1998. Appointments: Social Work with Family Welfare Association and Wimbledon Guild of Social Welfare, Lecturer, Economics, Social

Policy and Social Administration, Further Education Colleges in London, 1952-65; Senior Lecturer, Principal Lecturer, Special Course Organiser, Acting Head of Department of Social Work, Health and Nursing, University of East London, 1965-94; Consultant, Bray Leino Training for Change, 1995-; Consultant Research Associates, 1995; Consultant on Preparation for Retirement for clients including: Ford Motor Company, Shell Oil Company, Tate and Lyle Refineries Ltd, Distillers Company Ltd; Short term assignment to United Nations Development Fund, 1973; Expert Assignment, Regional Office for Europe, World Health Organisation, Copenhagen, 1981; British Council Links Scheme, UK-US, 1990-91. Publications: Over 40 publications. Honours: Fellow, Institute of Chartered Secretaries and Administrators, 1974; Liveryman, Worshipful Company of Secretaries and Administrators, 1984; Fellow, Royal Society of Arts, 1990. Memberships: Committee Member, Conference Organising Committee, International Round Table for the Advancement of Counselling; International Committee, European Regional Clearing House for Community Work; Social Administration and Social Work Committees, Joint University Council for Social and Public Administration; The Council for Education and Training of Health Visitors; Examination Committee, Local Government Management Board; Course Committees and Examination Boards for courses in several aspects of community nursing and health promotion; NHS Manager, Goodmayes Hospital; Livery Company, WCCSA; Chairman, Livery Liaison Committee, 1998-2001; Deputy Chairman, Patient Partnership Group, Marylebone H C. Address: 163 Clarence Gate Gardens, Glentworth Street, London NW1 6AP, England.

WILSON Colin Henry, b. 26 July 1931, Leicester, England. Author. m. (1) Dorothy Betty Troop, 1 son, (2) Joy Stewart, 2 sons, 1 daughter. Appointments: Visiting Professor, Hollins College, Virginia, 1966-67, University of Washington, Seattle, 1967, Dowling College, Majorca, 1969, Rutgers University, New Jersey, 1974. Publications: The Outsider, 1956; Religion and the Rebel, 1957; The Age of Defeat, 1959; Ritual in the Dark, 1960; The Strength to Dream, 1962; Origins of the Sexual Impulse, 1963; Necessary Doubt, 1964; Eagle and the Earwig, 1965; The Glass Cage, 1966; Sex and the Intelligent Teenager, 1966; Voyage to a Beginning, 1969; Hermann Hesse, 1973; Strange Powers, 1973; The Space Vampires, 1976; Mysteries, 1978; Starseekers, 1980; Access to Inner Worlds, 1982; Psychic Detectives, 1983; The Essential Colin Wilson, 1984; Rudolf Steiner: The Man and His Work, 1985; An Encyclopedia of Scandal (with Donald Seaman), 1986; Spider World: The Tower, 1987; Aleister Crowley - The Man and the Myth, 1987; An Encyclopedia of Unsolved Mysteries (with Damon Wilson), 1987; Marx Refuted, 1987; Written in Blood (with Donald Seaman), 1989; The Misfits - A Study of Sexual Outsiders, 1988; Beyond the Occult, 1988; The Serial Killers, 1990; Spiderworld: The Magician, 1991; The Strange Life of P D Ouspensky, 1993; Unsolved Mysteries Past and Present (with Damon Wilson), 1993; Atlas of Holy Places and Sacred Sites, 1996; From Atlantis to the Sphinx, 1996; Alien Dawn, 1998; The Devil's Party, 2000; Atlantis Blueprint (with Rand Fle'math), 2000; Spiderworld: Shadowland, 2003; Autobiography Dreaming to some Purpose, 2004. Contributions to: The Times; The Gramophone; Daily Mail. Membership: Society of Authors. Address: Tetherdown, Trewallock Lane, Gorran Haven, Cornwall, PL26 6NT, England.

WILSON OF TILLYORN, Baron (Life Peer) of Finzean in the District of Kincardine and Deeside and of Fanling in Hong Kong, Sir David Clive Wilson, b. 14 February 1935. m. Natasha Helen Mary Alexander, 2 sons. Education: Scholar, MA, Keble College, Oxford; University of Hong Kong; Visiting Scholar, Columbia University New York, USA; PhD, University of London.

Appointments: HM Diplomatic Service: Joined SE Asia Department, Foreign Office, 1958; Third Secretary, Vientiane, 1959-60; Language Student, Hong Kong, 1960-62; Third then Second Secretary, Peking, 1963-65; First Secretary, Far Eastern Department, 1965-68, resigned 1968; Editor, The China Quarterly, Contemporary China Institute SOAS, University of London, 1968-74; Rejoined HM Diplomatic Service, 1974; Cabinet Office, 1974-77; Political Adviser, Hong Kong, 1977-81; Head, Southern European Department, Foreign and Commonwealth Office 1981-84; Assistant Under Secretary of State responsible for Asia and the Pacific, Foreign and Commonwealth Office, 1984-87; Governor and Commander in Chief of Hong Kong, 1987-92; Member of the Board, British Council, 1993-2002, Chairman, Scottish Committee, 1993-2002; Council, CBI Scotland, 1993-92; Prime Minister's Advisory Committee on Business Appointments, 2000-; Chairman, Scottish and Southern Energy (formerly Scottish Hydro-Electric), 1993-2000; Director, Martin Currie Pacific Trust plc, 1993-2003; Chancellor, University of Aberdeen, 1997-; Master, Peterhouse, Cambridge, 2002-. Honours: CMG, 1985; KCMG, 1987; GCMG, 1991; Life Peer, 1992; KT, 2000; Honorary Fellow, Keble College, Oxford, 1987; KStJ, 1987; Honorary LLD, University of Aberdeen, 1990, University of Abertay Dundee, 1995, Chinese University of Hong Kong, 1996; Honorary DLitt, University of Sydney, 1991; FRSE, 2000; Burgess of Guild, City of Aberdeen, 2003. Memberships: President: Bhutan Society of the UK, 1993-, Hong Kong Society, 1994-, Hong Kong Association, 1994-; Vice-President, RSGS, 1996; Chairman of Trustees, National Museums of Scotland, 2002-; Chairman, Council of Glenalmond College, 2000-, Scottish Peers' Association, 2000-2002; Member, Carnegie Trust for the Universities of Scotland, 2000-; Registrar, Order of St Michael and St George, 2001-. Address: House of Lords, London SW1A 0PW, England or The Master's Lodge, Peterhouse, Cambridge, CB2 1QY, England.

WILSON Eldon Ray, b. 16 April 1931, Washington, USA. Clergyman. m. 2 sons. Education: BTH, 1967; PhD, 1972; Diploma, Spanish Language, 1987. Appointments: Founder, Pastor, Emmanuel Tabernacle, Port Arthur, Texas, 1958-63; Evangelist, Canada and USA, 1963-65; Founder, Pastor, Gospel Tabernacle, Ilion, New York, 1965-70, New Covenant Church, Columbus, Ohio, 1977-84; Missionary, New Covenant Ministries, 1977-98; Dean, City Bible College, New York, 1998-2001. Publications: The New Creation, 1975. Address: PO Box 317, Newport, NY 13416, USA.

WILSON Jim C, b. 16 July 1948, Edinburgh, Scotland. Writer; Poet. m. Mik Kerr, 21 August 1971. Education: MA, Honours, English Language and Literature, University of Edinburgh, 1971. Appointments: Lecturer, English Telford College, Edinburgh, 1972-81; Writer-in-Residence, Stirling District, 1989-91; Creative Writing Tutor, University of Edinburgh, 1994-. Publications: The Loutra Hotel, 1988; Six Twentieth Century Poets; Cellos in Hell, 1993. Contributions to: Scotsman; Chapman; Lines Review; Radical Scotland; Times Educational Supplement; Cencrastus; Outposts; Orbis; Acumen; Rialto; Poetry Canada Review; Envoi; 2 Plus 2; Poet's Voice; Iron; Stand; Encounter; Literary Review; Imaga (Australia). Honours: Scottish Arts Council Writer's Bursary, 1987, 1994; Scottish International Open Poetry Award, 1987; 1st Prize, Swanage Arts Festival Literary Competition, 1988, 1989, 1997; Hugh MacDiarmid Trophy for Poetry, 1997. Address: 25 Muirfield Park, Gullane, East Lothian EH31 2DY, Scotland.

WILSON Lois M, b. 8 April 1927, Winnipeg, Canada. Minister of Religion; Senator. m. Roy Wilson, 2 sons, 2 daughters. Education: BA, 1947; MDiv, 1965. Appointments: Past President, Canadian Council of Churches, 1976-79; Past Moderator, United Church of Canada, 1980-82; Past President, World Council of

Churches, 1983-91; Pastor on team ministry with husband for 17 years; Chancellor, Lakehead University, 1991-2000; Canadian Senator, 1998-2002. Publications: Author, 6 books: Like a Mighty River, 1981; Telling Her Story, 1990; Turning the World Upside Down, 1989; Miriam, Mary and Me, 1991; Stories Seldom Told, 1993; Nuclear Waste – Exploring the Ethical Options, 1999. Honours: McGeachy Senior Scholar, United Church of Canada, 1989-91; Order of Canada, 1984; Companion of the Order of Canada, 2003; UN Pearson Peace Prize, 1984; Order of Ontario, 1991; 11 honorary degrees from universities. Memberships: Chair, Canada-Democratic Peoples Republic of Korea Association; Advisory Board, Across Boundaries, a multi-faith journal; Vice President, Canadian Civil Liberties; Advisory Board, Center for Study of Religions and Society; Public Review Board of Canadian Automobile Workers. Address: 40 Glen Road # 310, Toronto, Ontario M4W 2V1, Canada.

WILSON Lorraine Margaret, b. 18 May 1939, Echuca, Victoria, Australia. Education Consultant. Education: Trained Infant Teacher's Certificate, 1956-58; Certificate A Victoria Education Department, 1974. Appointments: Teacher with Victoria Education Department, 1959-77, including Vice Principal, Helen Street Northcote Primary School, 1973-77; Lecturer (part-time), Language and Literature Department, Coburg Teachers College, 1978; Lecturer (part-time), Curriculum Studies Department, Melbourne State College, 1979-82; Educational Consultancy, 1978-2004; Consultant to schools in Colorado, USA, 1989; Consultant to schools, Washington DC, USA, 1992; Consultant to schools in Virginia, USA, 1993. Publications: Numerous papers at international, national and state conferences; Journal articles; Reference books including: Getting Started, series of titles, 1978-83; (co-author) An Integrated Approach To Learning, 1991; (author) Write Me a Poem, 1994; Children's books: City Kids (60 titles), 1978, 1979, 1980, 1981, 1986; Country Kids (48 titles), 1982, 1983, 1985, 1987; Footy Kids (24 titles), 1982, 1984; Champions (6 titles), 1984; Firefighters (6 titles), 1986; Police (10 titles), 1989; My Mum has False Teeth and Other Stories, 1990; The Lift-Off Kids (4 titles), 1992; I Have Two Dads, 1995; I Speak Two Languages, 1995; Footy Kids, 1995; James and Jessie Books, 1995, 1996; The Best of City Kids (20 titles), 1997; New City Kids (10 titles), 1997; Reading to Live: How to Teach Reading for Today's World, 2002. Honours; ALEA Medal, Australian Literacy Educators' Association, 1996. Memberships: Author Representative, Federal Government Public Lending Right Committee, 1995-2001; Public Lending Right Committee Representative, Steering Committee for Evaluation of the Public Lending Right Scheme, 1998; Australian Literacy Educators Association; International Reading Association; Australian Society of Authors; National Council for Teachers of English; Whole Language Umbrella, Society of Children's Book Writers and Illustrators. Address: 81 Amess St North Carlton, Victoria, Australia, 3054.

WILSON Michael George Carey, b. 4 December 1954, Harare, Zimbabwe. Economic Geologist. m. Heather Patricia Duff, 1 son, 1 daughter. Education: BSc, Geology and Geography, University of Natal, Durban, South Africa, 1972-75; Graduate Certificate, Education, University of Zimbabwe, 1976; MSc, Economic Geology, Rhodes University, Grahamstown, South Africa, 1987-90 (part-time). Appointments: Geography Teacher, Prince Edward High School, Harare, Zimbabwe, 1977-78; Acting Chief Geologist, Lomgundi Smelting and Mining, 1979-80; Mine Geologist, 1980-81; Gravelotte Emeralds (Pty) Ltd; Project Geologist, Witwatersrand Exploration, African Selection Trust Exploration, 1982-83; Chief Geologist, Gravelotte Emeralds (Pty) Ltd, 1983-86; Divisional Geologist, South African Development Trust Corporation, 1987-93; Geological Consultant, 1993-94; Deputy

Manager, Metallogenic Mapping Section, Council for Geoscience, 1994-98; Manager, Pretoria Mapping Services Unit, Council for Geoscience, 1998-2002, Senior Economic Geologist, Council for Geoscience, 2002-. Publications: Books: Chief Compiler and Editor-in-Chief, The Mineral Resources of South Africa (M G C Wilson and C R Anhaeusser, eds), 1998; Articles: The South African Minerals Industry: The Geological Background. 1995; Diamonds through the decades: A review of South African production, 1997; Numerous book chapters. Honours: Merit Awards for Outstanding Achievements in Physics, IT and Geology , University of Natal, Durban, South Africa; Special Merit Award for Exceptional Achievement in Geoscience, Council for Geoscience, 1998; Listed in Who's Who publications and biographical dictionaries. Memberships: Vice President, Member of Management Committee and Council, Geological Society of South Africa; Botanical Society of South Africa; Trustee: Geological Society of South Africa Trust; Council for Geoscience Pension and Provident Funds; St Albans College Trust. Address: PO Box 987, Irene, Centurion, South Africa 0062. E-mail: mwilson@geoscience.org.za

WILSON Robert Woodrow, b. 10 January 1936, USA. Radioastronomer. m. Elizabeth Rhoads Sawin, 1958, 2 sons, 1 daughter. Education: Bachelor's Degree, Rice University, 1957; PhD, California Institute of Technology, 1962. Appointments: Technical Staff, Bell Telephone Laboratory, Holmdel, New Jersey, 1963, Head, Radiophysics Department, 1976-94; Senior Scientist, Harvard-Smithsonian Center for Astrophysics, 1994-; Detected cosmic microwave background radiation, supposedly a residue of the Big Bang. Publications: Numerous articles in scientific journals. Memberships: NAS; American Astronomical Society; American Physical Society; International Astronomical Union. Honours: Henry Draper Award, National Academy of Sciences, 1977; Herschel Award, Royal Astronomical Society, 1977; Joint Winner, Nobel Prize for Physics, 1978. Address: Harvard-Smithsonian Center for Astrophysics, 60 Garden Street #42, Cambridge, MA 02138, USA.

WILSON Schrena, b. 14 November 1963, Antlers, Oklahoma, USA. Writer; Childcare Worker. Education: Associate Degree, Journalism, Eastern Oklahoma State College, 1985; Vo-Tech Childcare Certificates, 1990-92; Laureate Certificate, International Library of Poetry, 2002. Career: Poet and childcare worker. Publications: Numerous poems published in books, chapbooks and anthologies. Address: HC 67, Box 1060, Antlers, OK 74523, USA.

WINCH Donald Norman, b. 15 April 1935, London, England. Professor of the History of Economics. m. Doreen Lidster, 5 August 1983. Education: BSc, London School of Economics and Political Science, 1956; PhD, Princeton University, 1960. Appointments: Visiting Lecturer, University of California, Berkeley, 1959-60; Lecturer in Economics, University of Edinburgh, 1960-63; Lecturer, 1963-66, Reader, 1966-69, Dean, School of Social Sciences, 1968-74, Professor of the History of Economics, 1969-, Pro-Vice-Chancellor, Arts and Social Studies, 1986-89, University of Sussex; Publications Secretary, Royal Economic Society, 1971-; Visiting Fellow, Institute for Advanced Study, Princeton, New Jersey, 1974-75; King's College, Cambridge, 1983, Australian National University, 1983, St Catharine's College, Cambridge, 1989, All Souls College, Oxford, 1994; Review Editor, Economic Journal, 1976-83; British Council Distinguished Visiting Fellow, Kyoto University, 1992; Carlyle Lecturer, University of Oxford, 1995. Publications: Classical Political Economy and Colonies, 1965; James Mill: Selected Economic Writings (editor), 1966; Economics and Policy, 1969; The Economic Advisory Council 1930-1939 (with S K Howson), 1976; Adam Smith's Politics, 1978; That Noble Science of Politics (with S Collini and J W Burrow),

1983; Malthus, 1987; Riches and Poverty, 1996. Contributions to: Many learned journals. Honours: British Academy, fellow, 1986-, vice president, 1993-94; Royal Historical Society, fellow, 1987-. Address: c/o Arts B, University of Sussex, Brighton BN1 9QN, England.

WINE Sherwin Theodore, b. 25 January 1928m Detroit, Michigan, USA. Clergyman; Rabbi. Education: AB, 1950, AM, 1951, University of Michigan; BHL, 1953, MHL, 1956, Hebrew Union College. Appointments: Founder, Rabbi, The Birmingham Temple, 1963-2003; Founder, Director, Center for New Thinking, 1976-; Founder, Dean, International Institute for Secular Humanistic Judaism, 1985-. Publications: Books: Humanistic Judaism, 1976; Judaism Beyond God, 1985; Celebration, 1990; Staying Sane in a Crazy World, 1995; Over 600 articles. Memberships: International Federation of Secular Humanistic Jews, Co-Chair; Founder, Society for Humanistic Judaism; Founder, Association of Humanistic Rabbis. Address: 28611 W Twelve Mile Road, Farmington Hills, MI 48334, USA.

WINEGARTEN Renee, b. 23 June 1922, London, England. Literary Critic; Author. m. Asher Winegarten, deceased 1946. Education: BA, 1943, PhD, 1950, Girton College, Cambridge. Publications: French Lyric Poetry in the Age of Malherbe, 1954; Writers and Revolution, 1974; The Double Life of George Sand, 1978; Madame de Staël, 1985; Simone de Beauvoir: A Critical View, 1988; Accursed Politics: Some French Women Writers and Political Life 1715-1850, 2003 Contributions to: Journals. Memberships: Friends of George Sand Association; Society of Authors; Authors Guild. Address: 12 Heather Walk, Edgware, Middlesex HA8 9TS, England.

WINFREY Oprah, b. 29 January 1954, Missouri, USA. Talk Show Host; Actress. Education: Tennessee State University. Career: Radio WVOL while at University in Tennessee, then on TV Stations: WTVF-TV Nashville as Reporter and Anchor, WJZ-TV Balt News, Co-anchor, 1976; People are Talking, Co-host, 1978; AM Chicago, Host, show re-named The Oprah Winfrey Show, 1985-; formed Harpo Productions, Owner/Producer, 1986; Founder, Editing Director, The Oprah Magazines, 2000-; Partner, Oxygen Media, 2000-; Producer of several TV films; Actress: The Color Purple, 1985; Native Son, 1986; The Woman of Brewster Place, TV, 1989; Throw Momma From the Train, 1988; Listen Up: The Lives of Quincy Jones, 1990; Beloved, 1998. Publications: Oprah, 1993; In the Kitchen with Rosie, 1996; Make the Connection, 1996. Honours: Numerous awards including: International Radio and Television Society's Broadcaster of the Year Award, 1988; Lifetime Achievement Award, National Academy of TV Arts and Sciences, 1998. Address: Harpo Productions, 110 N Carpenter Street, Chicago, IL 60607, USA.

WINGER Debra, b. 16 May 1955, Cleveland, USA. Actress. m. Timothy Hutton, 1986, divorced, 1 son. Education: California University, Northridge. Appointments: Served, Israel Army, 1972; First Professional Appearance, Wonder Woman, tv series, 1976-77. Creative Works: Films include: Thank God Its Friday, 1978; French Postcards, 1979; Urban Cowboy, 1980; Cannery Row, 1982; An Officer and a Gentleman, 1982; Terms of Endearment, 1983; Mike's Murder, 1984; Legal Eagles, 1986; Black Widow, 1987; Made in Heaven, 1987; Betrayed, 1988; The Sheltering Sky, 1990; Everybody Wins, 1990; Leap of Faith, 1992; Shadowlands, 1993; A Dangerous Women, 1993; Forget Paris, 1995; Big Bad Love, 2002; Radio, 2003; Eulogy, 2004. Address: c/o CAA, 9830 Wilshire Boulevard, Beverly Hills, CA 90212, USA.

WINKEL Wolfgang, b. 15 June 1941, Danzig, Germany. Zoologist. m. Doris Laux, 1 daughter. Education: Graduation (Dr rer nat), University Brunswick, 1968. Scientific Assistant, Institute of Avian Research, Wilhelmshaven, Germany, 1970-77; Head, working group population ecology of Vogelwarte Helgoland, Brunswick, 1978-. Publications: Over 150 in scientific journals; Co-author, Eco-ornithological Glossary, 1983; Co-author, Die Vogelfamilien der Westpaläarktis, 1995; Editor-in-Chief, Die Vogelwelt, 1971-87; Co-editor, Die Vogelwarte, 1972-. Honours: Silberne Ehrennadel, Deutscher Bund für Vogelschutz, 1984; Förderpreis der Werner-Sunkel-Stiftung, Deutsche Ornithologen-Gesellschaft, 2001. Memberships: Deutsche Ornithologen-Gesellschaft; British Ornithologists' Union; American Ornithologists' Union. Address: Institut für Vogelforschung, Vogelwarte Helgoland, Arbeitsgruppe Populationsökologie, Bauernstr 14, D-38162 Cremlingen-Weddel, Germany.

WINNER Michael Robert, b. 30 October 1935, London, England. Producer; Director; Writer. Education: Downing College, Cambridge University. Appointments: Film Critic and Fleet Street Journalist; Contributor to: The Spectator, Daily Express, London Evening Standard; Columnist, The Sunday Times, The News of the World; Panellist on Any Questions, BBC Radio; Presenter, Michael Winner's True Crimes; Entered motion pictures, 1956 as Screen Writer, Assistant Director, Editor; Member of the Council and Trustee, Director's Guild of Great Britain, 1983-; Founder and Chairman, The Police Memorial Trust, 1984; Director, Scimitar Films Ltd. Films include: Play it Cool, 1962; The Cool Mikado, 1962; West Eleven, 1963; The System, 1963; You Must Be Joking, 1965; The Jokers, 1966; I'll Never Forget What's 'isname, 1967; Hannibal Brooks, 1968; The Games, 1969; Lawman, 1970; The Nightcomers, 1971; Chato's Land, 1971; The Mechanic, 1972; Scorpio, 1972; The Stone Killer, 1973; Death Wish, 1974; Won Ton Ton The Dog That Saved Hollywood, 1975; The Sentinel, 1976; The Big Sleep, 1977; Firepower, 1978; Death Wish Two, 1981; The Wicked Lady 1982; Scream for Help, 1984; Death Wish Three, 1985; Appointment with Death, 1988; A Chorus of Disapproval, 1989; Bullseye!, 1990; Dirty Weekend, 1993; Parting Shots, 1999; Actor: For the Greater Good, 1990; Decadence, 1993; Radio Play: The Flump, 2000; Theatre Productions: The Tempest, Wyndhams, 1974; A Day in Hollywood A Night in Ukraine, 1978. Publications: Winner's Dinners, 1999, revised edition, 2000; Winner Guide, 2002; Biography: Winner Takes All, 2004. Honour: MA (Cantab). Address: 219 Kensington High Street, London W8 6BD, England. E-mail: winner@ftech.co.uk

WINSLET Kate, b. October 1975, Reading, England. Actress. m. Jim Threapleton, 1998, 1 daughter. Education: Theatre School, Maidenhead. Creative Works: TV appearances: Get Back; Casualty; Anglo-Saxon Attitudes; Films: A Kid in King Arthur's Court; Heavenly Creatures, 1994; Sense and Sensibility, 1996; Jude, 1996; Hamlet, 1996; Titanic, 1997; Hideous Kinky, 1997; Holy Smoke, 1998; Quills, 1999; Enigma, 2000; Iris, 2001; The Life of David Gale, 2002; Plunge: The Movie, 2003; Eternal Sunshine of the Spotless Mine, 2004; J M Barrie's Neverland, 2004. Honours include: BAFTA Award; Best European Actress, European Film Academy, 1998; Film Actress of the Year, Variety Club of Great Britain, 1998. Address: c/o Dallas Smith, Peters Fraser & Dunlop Ltd, 503 The Chambers, Chelsea Harbour, Lots Road, London SW10 0XF, England.

WINTERS Shelley, b. 18 August 1922, St Louis, USA. Actress. m. (1) Vittorio Gassmann, 1 daughter, (2) Anthony Franciosa, 1957, divorced 1960. Education: Wayne University. Creative Works: Films include: A Thousand and One Nights; A Place in the Sun; Playgirl; Executive Suite; The Diary of Anne Frank, 1958; Odds Against Tomorrow; Let No Man Write My Epitaph; Lolita, 1962; Wives and Lovers, 1963; The Balcony, 1964; A House is Not A Home, 1964; A Patch of Blue, 1965; Time of Indifference, 1965; Alfie, 1965; The Moving Target, 1965; The Poseidon Adventure,

1972; Cleopatra Jones, 1973; Blume in Love, 1974; Whoever Slew Auntie Roo, 1974; Heaven Save Us From Our Friends, 1975; Diamonds, 1975; That Lucky Touch, 1975; Next Stop Greenwich Village, 1976; The Tenant, 1976; Pete's Dragon, 1977; The Magician, 1979; The Visitor, 1980; Over the Brooklyn Bridge, 1983; The Delta Force, 1985; Awakenings, 1990; Stepping Out, 1991; The Pickle, 1996; Portrait of a Lady, 1996; Gideon's Webb, 1998; La Bamba, 1999; Stage appearances include: A Hatful of Rain, 1955; Girls of Summer, 1957; The Night of the Iguana; Cages; Who's Afraid of Virginia Wolf?; Minnie's Boys; Marlon Brando: The Wild One, 1996; TV appearances include: The Vamp, 1972-73; Roseanne (TV series). Publications: Shelley also Known as Shirley (autobiography); One Night Stands of a Noisy Passenger (play), 1971; Shelley II: The Middle of My Century, 1989. Honours include: Academy Awards; Emmy Award, Best Actress, 1964; Monte Carlo Golden Nymph Award, 1964; International TV Award, Cannes Festival, 1965. Address: c/o Jack Gilliardi, ICM, 8942 Wilshire Boulevard, Beverly Hills, CA 90211, USA.

WINTERTON Rosie, b. 10 August 1958, Leicester, England. Member of Parliament. Education: BA (Hons), History 2:1, University of Hull, England, 1979. Appointments: Assistant to John Prescott MP, 1980-86; Parliamentary Officer, London Borough of Southwark, 1986-88; Parliamentary Officer, Royal College of Nursing, 1988-90; Managing Director, Connect Public Affairs, 1990-94; Head of Private office of John Prescott MP, Deputy Leader of the Labour Party; Entered Parliament as MP for Doncaster Central, 1997; Elected representative of Parliamentary Labour Party on the National Policy Forum of the Labour Party, 1997-2001; Chair of Transport and General Worker's Parliamentary Group, 1998-99; Leader of Leadership Campaign Team, 1998-99; Member on Standing Committee of Transport Bill, 2000; Intelligence and Security Committee, 2000; Member on Standing Committee of Finance Bill, 2000; Standing Committee of the Local Government Finance (Supplementary Credit Approvals) Bill and the Regional Development Agencies Bill; Member of the Labour Party Strategic Campaign; Parliamentary Secretary, Lord Chancellor's Office, 2001. Address: Guildhall Advice Centre, Old Guildhall Yard, Doncaster, South Yorkshire, DN1 1OW.

WINWOOD Stephen Lawrence, Birmingham, England. Musician; Composer. m. Eugenia Crafton, 1987, 1 son, 3 daughters. Career: Singer, Musician, Spencer Davis Group, 1964-67, Traffic, 1967-74, Blind Faith, 1970; Solo Artist, 1974-; Director, F S Ltd. Creative Works: Albums include: Arc of a Diver, 1980; Talking Back to the Night, 1982; Back in the Highlife, 1986; Roll With It, 1988; Chronicles, 1990; Refugees of the Heart, 1991; Traffic, Far From Home, 1994; Junction 7, 1997. Honours: 14 Gold Records; 4 Platinum Record Awards; 2 Grammy Awards. Address: c/o Trinity Cottage, Tirley, Gloucs GL19 4EU, England.

WIRSIG Woodrow Marohn, b. 28 June 1916, Spokane, Washington, USA. Journalist; Consultant; Consumer Affairs Executive. m. (1) Jean Pollard, 1939, deceased; (2) Jane Daley, 1942, deceased; (3) Milrae Nelson, 1990, deceased; 3 sons. Education: Kearney State Teachers' College, 1933-35; Los Angeles City College, 1936-38; University of California at Los Angeles, 1939; AB Degree, Occidental College, 1941; Master of Arts, Journalism, Columbia College, New York, 1942. Appointments include: Radio Newswriter, WQXR, New York City, 1941-42; News Writer, Propaganda Analyst, CBS Shortwave, 1942-43; Reporter Re-write, Los Angeles Times, 1943-44; Assistant Editor, This Week Magazine, 1944-45; Staff Writer,1946, Assistant Managing Editor, 1946-49, Executive Editor (Editor-in-Chief), 1950-52, LOOK Magazine; Creator, Managing Editor QUICK Magazine, 1949-50; Associate Editor, Newsweek, Ladies Home Journal, 1952; Editor-in-Chief, Woman's Home Companion, 1952-56; Editor, Consultant, Educational Testing Service, Princeton, 1957-67; TV Consultant, NBC-TV, ABC-TV, Creator, National Daytime Programmes, 1957-60; President, communications firm Wirsig, Gordon and O'Connor, Inc. 1956-58; Editor, Printer's Ink Magazine, 1958-65, Salesweek Magazine, 1959-60; President, Better Business Bureau Metropolitan New York Inc, President, BBB Education Research Foundation, 1966-77; Founder, Business Advocacy Center Inc, 1977-; Consultant to the Office of the Secretary of Health, Education and Welfare, Washington DC, 1965-66; Pioneer of consumer/business arbitration; Key figure in fighting Food and Drug Administration to approve Cognex the first drug approved for Alzheimer's Disease. Publications: I Love You, Too, about the effects of Alzheimer's Disease; Co-author, You and Your Diabetes; Editor: Advertising Today-Yesterday-Tomorrow; New products Marketing; Principles of Advertising; Numerous articles to magazines and periodicals. Honours: Gold medal, Benjamin Franklin Magazine Award (equivalent to Pulitzer Prize); Listed in numerous Who's Who publications and biographical dictionaries. Memberships include: Society of Consumer Affairs Professionals; Journalism Fraternity Gamma delta Upsilon; Overseas Press Club; National Press Club; Press Club of New York; New York Advertising Club; Sigma Delta Chi; Phi Gamma Delta; Newcomen Society. Address: Mt San Antonio Gardens, B-39, 900 East Harrison Avenue, Pomona, CA 91767, USA.

WIRTZ Dorothy Marie, b. 9 March 1915, Keokuk, Iowa, USA. Professor of French. Education: BA, University of Iowa, Iowa City, USA; MA, PhD, University of Wisconsin, Madison, Wisconsin, USA. Appointments: Secretary, Keokuk Coal Company; Secretary State Tax Commission, Arizona; Secretary to the Democratic Whip of the State Legislature; Graduate Assistant and Instructor of French, University of Wisconsin; Professor of French University of Minnesota, Minneapolis; Deputy State Treasurer of Arizona; Professor of French, Arizona State University, Tempe, Arizona. Publications: Articles include: Teaching Literature; The Literate Delacroix; Graphic Illustration of Literature; Denis Diderot on Women; Poetry in magazines including: Poetry Magazine, Perspective, Latitude, Moon, Reader; Book of Poems: Evolution. Honours: Vachel Lindsay Poetry Prize, Culver-Stockton; Phi Beta Kappa, University of Iowa; Listed in Who's who publications and biographical dictionaries. Membership: Delta Kappa Gamma; Phi Beta Kappa; American Association of University Women. Address: 1711 W State Avenue, Phoenix, AZ 85021-7955, USA.

WISEMAN James Anthony, b. 19 February 1942, Louisville, Kentucky, USA. Benedictine Monk; University Professor. Education: BA, Georgetown University; MA, The Catholic University of America, 1970; STD, The Catholic University of America, 1979. Appointments: Abbot, St Anselm's Abbey, Washington, DC, 1975-83; Professor of Theology, Catholic University of America, 1985-; Chairman, Monastic Interreligious Dialogue, North America, 1994-99. Publications: Theology and Modern Science; Co-editor, Transforming Suffering; Co-editor, The Gethsemani Encounter; Co-editor, Light from Light; John Ruusbroec: The Spiritual Espousals. Honours: Winner, Award from the Templeton Foundation's Science and Religion Course Program Competition; Alumni Achievement Award in Education from the Catholic University of America. Memberships: The Catholic Theological Society of America; The American Academy of Religion. Address: St Anselm's Abbey, 4501 South Dakota Ave NE, Washington, DC 20017, USA.

WISLER Darla Lee, b. 14 May 1940, Baltimore, Maryland, USA. Senior Pastor; Dean. m. Norman Wisler, 1 son, 1 daughter. Education: Associate, Biblical Studies, 1982, Bachelor of

Theology, 1984, Christian International School of Theology; Master of Divinity, 1990, Doctor of Ministry, 1993, Christian International Graduate School of Theology. Appointments: Founder, Senior Pastor, Dean, Living Water Church, Living Water Bible College; Midweek Devotions, NHC Healthcare, Anderson, 1980-; Prinicpal, Living Water Christian School, 1983-88; Regular Co-Host, TV-16, Greenville, South Carolina, 1984-; President, NHC Healthcare, Anderson Advisory Board, 1986-; President, Clergy Staff Executive Committee, Anderson Area Medical Center, 1993-94; Co-ordinator, Christian International Network of Churches, Mid-East Region, 1994-96; Chaplain, Board Member, 1996-, President of Board, 2002-, Anderson County Sheriff's Officer; On Call Chaplain, Anderson Area Medical Center, 2003-. Publications: Author, teaching manuals: Basic Christian Teaching Made Plain and Clear, 1994; Advanced Christian Teaching Made Plain and Clear, 1995. Honours: Volunteer of the Year Award, NHC Healthcare. Memberships: Listed in national and international biographical dictionaries. Address: 8 Harbor Gate, Anderson, SC 29625, USA.

WISSE Eduard, b. 4 May 1938, The Hague. University Professor. Education: State University, Biology, Leiden, 1956-64; Candidate in Experimental Biology (great distinction), 1960; Doctorandus in Biology, (Distinction), 1964; Doctor, Faculty of Science/Biology, 1974. Appointments: Senior Research Fellow, Laboratory for Electron Microscopy, Medical Faculty, Leiden, 1964-79; Advisor, Academic Hospital, Department of Pathology, Leiden (NL), 1969-78; Full Professor in Cell Biology and Histology, Chairman of the Laboratory for Cell Biology and Histology, 1978-, Dean, Faculty of Medicine and Pharmacy, 1991-93, Free University of Brussels; Visiting Research Professor, University of Arizona, Tucson, USA, 1997-. Publications: 229 articles in professional journals or proceedings, as author or co-author; Co-editor or publisher several books. Memberships: Belgian Society for Microscopy; Belgian Society for Cell Biology; Dutch Society for Microscopy; Dutch Society for Cell Biology; Dutch Society for Hepatology; Deutsche Gesellschaft fur Elektronenmikroskopie; European Association for Study of the Liver (EASL); International Association for the Study of the Liver (IASL); Royal Microscopial Society (RMS); Microscopy Society of America; American Association for Cancer Research (AACR); Association for the Advancement of Computing in Education (AACE). Address: Laboratory for Cell Biology and Histology, Free University Brussels, Laarbeeeklaan 103, A-1090 Brussels Lake, Belgium.

WITTSTADT Thomas Peter, b. 21 September 1967, Muenster, Germany. Entrepreneur. Education: University of Muenster, 1987-90; Studium Generale, 1990-92. Career: Various activities as Manager, Consultant, Partner, Advisor, Initiator with corporations, governments, personalities, special legal entities. Publications: Various publications in print, television and general media world-wide. Honours: Special private awards and honours; one of youngest German Citizens to be listed in Who's Who in the World. Address: Angelstrasse 22, 48167 Muenster, Germany.

WOGAN Michael Terence (Terry), b. 3 August 1938, Ireland. Broadcaster. m. Helen Joyce, 1965, 2 sons, 1 daughter. Education: Crescent College, Limerick; Belvedere College, Dublin. Appointments: Announcer, RTE, 1963, Senior Announcer, 1964-66; Various programmes for BBC Radio, 1965-67; Late Night Extra, BBC Radio, 1967-69; The Terry Wogan Show, BBC Radio 1, 1969-72, BBC Radio 2, 1972-84, 1993; Wake Up to Wogan, BBC Radio 2, 1995-. Creative Works: TV shows include: Lunchtime with Wogan, ATV; BBC: Come Dancing; Song for Europe; The Eurovision Song Contest; Children in Need; Wogan's Guide to the BBC; Blankety Blank; Wogan; Terry Wogan's Friday Night; Auntie's Bloomers; Wogan's Web; Points of View, 2000-01. Publications: Banjaxed, 1979; The Day Job, 1981; To Horse, To Horse, 1982; Wogan on Wogan, 1987; Wogan's Ireland, 1988; Bumper Book of Togs, 1995; Is It Me?, autobiography, 2000. Honours include: Radio Award, 1980; Radio Industry Award, 1982, 1985, 1987; Carl Alan Award, 3 times; Variety Club of Britain Special Award, 1982; Showbusiness Personality, 1984; Radio Personality of Last 21 years, Daily Mail National Radio Awards, 1988; Sony Radio Award, Barcelona Olympics, 1993; Best Breakfast Show, 1994. Address: c/o Jo Gurnett, 2 New Kings Road, London SW6 4SA, England.

WOLFE Darlene, b. 4 June 1944, Washington DC. Educator and Consultant. m. Lawrence E Wolfe. Education: BS, Psychology, University of Maryland, 1966; MA, University of Iowa; Certified Camp Director, George Williams College and American Camping Association, 1974; PhD, Community Education Administration, George Peabody College, Vanderbilt University, 1979; Courses for personal interest and recertification at University of South Florida, 1979-. Appointments: Youth and Camp Director, Community Centers for Baltimore, 1966-71, and Nashville, 1972-75; Consultant, 1968-; Mayor's Office of Community Services and Urban Observatory, Jewish Community Center of Nashville, 1975-80; Teacher, TV Production, Science, Psychology, 1981-. Publications: Video Bulletin Boards; Leadership and Technology Development Newsletters; Florida Scholaristic Press Association Today, Merging Technologies. Honour: Digital Media Alliance Florida Education Chair; Listed in numerous Who's Who and biographical publications. Memberships: SIGGRAPH; DMAF; FMAC; AFT/NEA; FEMEC; FSPA; PTSA. Address: 5144 Barnegat Point Road, Orlando, FL 32808, USA. E-mail: wolfed@ocps.net

WOLFE Elaine Claire Daughetee, b. 29 May 1940, Indianapolis, Indiana, USA. Educator; Professional Artist. m. (1) Stephen Roger Allen, deceased, (2) Howard Evans Wolfe, divorced, 1 son, 1 daughter. Education: BS, Biological Sciences, Purdue University, 1962; MA, Vertebrate Zoology, UCLA, 1964; EdS, 1994, EdD, 1997, School Administration and Curriculum Instruction, Indiana University. Appointments: Biology Teacher, Canoga Park, California, 1963-64; Biology Instructor, Purdue University, West Lafayette, Indiana, 1964-65; Science, Education Instructor, Texas Christian University, Fort Worth, Texas, 1965-66; Science Teacher, Fort Worth Public Schools, Fort Worth, Texas, 1966-67; Biology Teacher, Upper Merion High School, King of Prussia, Pennsylvania, 1967-71; Science Teacher, Fulton Junior High School, Wayne Twp Schools, Indianapolis, 1982; Science Department Chair and Science Teacher, Guion Creek Middle School, Indianapolis, 1982-. Publications: 3 articles in scientific journals; Published Dissertation, An Ethnographic Study of How One School District and Its Mobil Low Socioeconomic Status Students Perceive and Respond to the Problem of Acclimation into New School Setting, 1997; Poem, Vision – Whispers at Dusk; Poem, Windows, 1998. Honours include: Finalist, Indiana State Teacher, 1992; NSF Grant, Finalist Presidential Award for Excellence in Science Teaching, 1993, 1997; Golden Apple Award, 1995; Distinguished Alumni Award, Purdue University, 1998; Subaru Middle School, midwestern Regional Winner for Excellence in Science Teaching, 2003. Memberships include: Kappa Delta Pi; Phi Lambda Theta; National Science Teachers Association; Hoosier Association of Science Teachers; National Middle School Association; Purdue University Alumni Association; National Wildlife Association; National Geographic Society; National Parks Association; Smithsonian Institute; Indianapolis Purdue Alumni Association. Address: 3541 Windham Lake Trace, Indianapolis, IN 46214-1400, USA. E-mail: ewolfe@pike.k12.in.us

Dictionary of International Biography

WOLFE John Henry Nicholas, b. 4 June 1947, Cardiff, Wales. Vascular Surgeon. m. Dorothy, 3 sons, 2 daughters. Education: St Thomas's Hospital Medical School; London University. Appointments: Senior House Officer, St James's Hospital, Balham; Surgical Registrar, Salisbury Infirmary; Lecturer in Surgery, St Thomas's Hospital; Research Fellow, Brigham and Women's Hospital, Harvard Medical School; Senior Surgical Registrar, St Thomas's Hospital; Honorary Senior Lecturer, Imperial College School of Medicine; Honorary Consultant Vascular Surgeon, Royal Brompton Hospital; Honorary Consultant Vascular Surgeon, Edward VII Hospital for Officers; Consultant Vascular Surgeon, St Mary's Hospital; Honorary Vascular Surgeon, Great Ormond Street Hospital for Children. Publications: 300 articles in professional journals; Associate Editor, Rutherfords Vascular Surgery, 1984; Editor, Author, ABC Vascular Disease, 1992; Associate Editor, Year Book of Vascular Surgery, 2001. Honours: Hunterian Professor, Royal College of Surgeons of England, 1982; Moynihan Fellow, Association of Surgeons of Great Britain and Ireland; Honorary Member, Society of Vascular Technologists; Honorary Member, Vascular Society of India; Editorial Board, European Journal of Vascular and Endovascular Surgery; Chairman, CME Committee for Vascular Surgery in UEMS; Vice President, Division of Vascular Surgery, UEMS; President, Board of Vascular Surgery, UEMS; Chairman, Vascular Advisory Committee of Great Britain and Ireland; Council of the Association of Surgeons of Great Britain and Ireland; Trustee, British Vascular Foundation. Memberships: Surgical Research Society; Association of Great Britain and Ireland; Vascular Society of Great Britain and Ireland; European Cardio-Vascular Society and European Chapter of the International Cardiovascular Society; European Vascular Society; Honorary Corresponding of the Society of Vascular Surgery; Fellow, Royal Geographic Society; Member, Medical Arts Society; Member, Royal Ocean Racing Club. Address: 66 Harley Street, London W19 7HD, England.

WOLFE Tom, (Thomas Kennerly Wolfe Jr), b. 2 March 1930, Richmond, Virginia, USA. Writer; Journalist; Artist. m. Sheila Berger, 1 son, 1 daughter. Education: AB, Washington and Lee University, 1951; PhD, American Studies, Yale University, 1957. Appointments: Reporter, Springfield Union, Massachusetts, 1956-59; Reporter and Latin American Correspondent, Washington Post, 1959-62; Writer, New York Sunday Magazine, 1962-66; City Reporter, New York Herald Tribune, 1962-66; Magazine Writer, New York World Journal Tribune, 1966-67; Contributing Editor, New York magazine, 1968-76, Esquire magazine, 1977-; Contributing Artist, Harper's magazine, 1978-81. Publications: The Kandy-Kolored Tangerine-Flake Streamline Baby, 1965; The Electric Kool-Aid Acid Test, 1968; The Pump House Gang, 1968; Radical Chic and Mau-mauing the Flak Catchers, 1970; The Painted Word, 1975; Mauve Gloves and Madmen, Clutter and Vine, 1976; The Right Stuff, 1979; In Our Time, 1980; From Bauhaus to Our House, 1981; The Purple Decades: A Reader, 1982; The Bonfire of the Vanities, 1987; A Man in Full, 1998; Hooking Up, 2000. Contributions to: Newspapers and magazines. Honours: Various honorary doctorates; American Book Award, 1980; Harold D Vursell Memorial Award, American Academy of Arts and Letters, 1980; John Dos Passos Award, 1984; Theodore Roosevelt Medal, Theodore Roosevelt Association, 1990; St Louis Literary Award, 1990; Membership: American Academy of Arts and Letters. Address: c/o Farrar Straus & Giroux Inc, 19 Union Square West, Floor 11, New York, NY 10003, USA.

WOLFERS Michael, b. 28 September 1938, London, England. Writer; Translator. Education: Wadham College, Oxford, 1959-62; South Bank Polytechnic, 1990-91. Appointments: Journalist, The Times, London, 1965-72; Visiting Senior Lecturer, African Politics and Government, University of Juba, 1979-82.

Publications: Black Man's Burden Revisited, 1974; Politics in the Organisation of African Unity, 1976; Luandino Vieira: The Real Life of Domingos Xavier, 1978; Poems from Angola, 1979; Samir Amin, Delinking: Towards a Polycentric World, 1990; Hamlet and Cybernetics, 1991; Thomas Hodgkin: Letters from Africa, 2000. Contributions to: Numerous publications. Memberships: Royal Institute of International Affairs; Gyosei Institute of Management. Address: 66 Roupell Street, London SE1 8SS, England.

WOLFF Tobias J A, b. 19 June 1945, Birmingham, USA. Writer. m. Catherine Dolores Spohn, 1975, 2 sons, 1 daughter. Education: Oxford University; Stanford University. Appointments: US Army, 1964-68; Reporter, Washington Post, 1972; Writing Fellow, Stanford University, 1975-78; Writer-in-Residence, Arizona State University, 1978-80, Syracuse University, 1980-97, Stanford University, 1997-. Publications: Hunters in the Snow, 1981; The Barracks Thief, 1984; Back in the World, 1985; This Boy's Life, 1989; In Pharaoh's Army: Memories of a Lost War, 1994; The Vintage Book of Contemporary American Short Stories, 1994; The Best American Short Stories, 1994; The Night in Question, 1996. Honours include: Guggenheim Fellow, 1983; National Endowment Fellow, 1978, 1984; PEN/Faulkner Award for Fiction, 1985; Rea Award, 1989; Whiting Foundation Award, 1989; Los Angeles Times Book Prize, 1989; Ambassador Book Award, 1990; Lila Wallace/Readers Digest Award, 1993; Esquire-Volvo-Waterstone Award for Non-Fiction, 1994; Exceptional Achievement Award, American Academy of Arts and Letters, 2001. Address: English Department, Stanford University, CA 94305, USA.

WOLFHARD Hans Georg, b. 2 April 1912, Basel, Switzerland. Research Scientist. m. (1) Adelheid Rohde, 1940, deceased 1995, 3 sons, (2) Clara Ralston, 1997. Education: Student, University of Berlin, 1934-35; Dr rer nat, University of Goettingen, 1938. Appointments: Scientist, Aeronautical Research Station, Brunswick, Germany, 1939-46; Research Scientist, Imperial College, London; Senior Principal Scientific Officer, Royal Aircraft Establishment, England, 1946-56; Bureau Mines, Pittsburgh, 1956-59; Head Department of Physics Reaction Motors Division, Thiokol Chemical Corporation, Denville, New Jersey, 1959-63; Member, Senior Research Staff Institute, Defence Analyses, Alexandria, Virginia, 1963-96; Consultant, Sverdrup Technology, AECD-Arnold AFB, Tennessee, 1995-. Publications: Co-author, Flames: their structure radiation and temperature, 4th edition, 1979, Chinese translation, 1990; More than 60 published papers. Honours: Senior Principal Scientist, Great Britain, 1955; 1st General Goodpastor award for Excellence in Research, 1983; Several Pentagon Awards; Awards from the Institute for Defense Analyses; Fellow, American Optical Society; Military Sensor Symposium (First Jamieson Award). Memberships: Numerous scientific societies include: AIAA; Combustion Institute. Address: 711 Bright Avenue, Fayetteville, TN 37334-2255, USA.

WOLFINGER Bernd E, b. 5 February 1951, Pforzheim, Germany. University Professor. m. Gabriele, 1 son, 1 daughter. Education: Maîtrise de Mathématiques et Applications Fondamentales, Université Claude-Bernard, Lyon, France, 1974; Diplom-Mathematiker, University Fridericiana, Karlsruhe, 1975; PhD, Dr rer nat, Computer Science, University Fridericiana, Karlsruhe, 1979. Appointments: Scientific Staff Member, Nuclear Research Centre, Karlsruhe, 1975-80; Assistant Professor, Department of Computer Science, Karlsruhe University, 1981; University Professor, Telecommunications and Computer Networks, Department of Computer Science, Hamburg University, 1981-; Sabbaticals at IBM, Th J Watson Research Centre, Yorktown Heights, USA, 1985, International Computer Science Institute, Berkeley, California, 1991 and 1996, and at Université

Pierre et Marie Curie, Paris, France, 2001. Publications: Author, numerous scientific publications within computer science; Editor, books and conference proceedings. Honours: International Cultural Diploma of Honour, 1995; Listed in numerous international biographical publications. Memberships: New York Academy of Sciences; Association for Computing Machinery; Gesellschaft fuer Informatik; IEEE; Fellow, ABI; Deputy Governor, ABI Research Association. Address: Ahornweg 98, D-25469 Halstenbek, Germany. E-mail: wolfinger@informatik.uni-hamburg.de

WONDER Stevie (Steveland Morris), b. 13 May 1950, Saginaw, Michigan, USA. Singer; Musician; Composer. m. Syreeta Wright, 1970, divorced 1972, (2) Yolanda Simmons, 3 children. Education: Michigan School for the Blind, 1963-68; Self-taught, harmonica and piano. Appointments: Motown Recording Artist, 1963-70; Founder, President, Black Bull Music Inc; Founder, Wonderdirection Records Inc and Taurus Productions; Numerous concerts worldwide. Creative Works: Fingertips Part 2, 1963; Uptight (Everything's Alright), 1966; I Was Made to Love Her, 1967; For Once in My Life, 1968; My Cherie Amour, 1969; Yester-Me, Yester-You, Yesterday, 1969; Signed Sealed Delivered I'm Yours, 1970; Superstition, 1973; You Are the Sunshine of My Life, 1973; Higher Ground, 1974; Living For the City, 1974; You Haven't Done Nothin', 1974; Boogie On Reggae Woman, 1975; I Wish, 1977; Sir Duke, 1977; Master Blaster, 1980; Lately, 1981; Happy Birthday, 1981; Ebony and Ivory, 1982; I Just Called To Say I Love You, 1984; Part-Time Lover, 1985; Don't Drive Drunk, 1985; Albums include: Music of My Mind, 1972; Innervisions, 1973; Songs in the Key of Life, 1976; Journey Through the Secret Life of Plants, 1979; Hotter than July, 1980; Original Musiquarium, 1981; Woman in Red, 1984; In Square Circle, 1986; Characters, 1987; Jungle Fever, 1991; Inner Peace, 1995; Motown Legends, 1995. Honours: Edison Award, 1973; Songwriters Hall of Fame, 1983; Numerous American Music Awards; Oscar, Best Song, 1984; Gold Ticket, Madison Square Garden, 1986; Soul Train Heritage Award, 1987; Rock'n'Roll Hall of Fame, 1989; Nelson Mandella Courage Award, 1991; IAAAM Diamond Award for Excellence, 1991; Lifetime Achievement Award, National Academy of Songwriters, 1992; NAACP Image Award, 1992; Numerous Grammy, Charity and Civil Rights Awards. Address: c/o Steveland Morris Music, 4616 W Magnolia Blvd, Burbank, CA 91505, USA.

WONG Baron C K W, b. 1 December 1970, Hawaii, USA. Physician. Education: BS, Biology, University of Hawaii, 1988-92; MD, Medicine, John A Burns School of Medicine, University of Hawaii, 1993-97; Internal Medicine Residency Programme, 1997-2000, Geriatric Medicine Fellowship Programme, 2000-2001, University of Hawaii. Appointments: Clinical Teaching Assistant, Internal Medicine Residency Programme, 1997-2000, Clinical Teaching Assistant, Geriatric Medicine Fellowship Programme, 2000-2001, Assistant Professor of Medicine, Geriatric Programme, 2001-2002, Clinical Instructor, Geriatric Medicine Fellowship Programme, 2002-; Currently: Geriatric/Internal Medicine Physician, The Queen Emma Outpatient Center, The Queen's Health Care Center-Hawaii Kai Facility; Staff Physician (Clinical Instructor), University of Hawaii Geriatrics Programme, Continuity Clinic for the Geriatric Medicine Fellows; Hospitalist, St Francis Medical Center-West, Ewa Beach, Hawaii; House Physician, Castle Medical Center, Kailua, Hawaii; Emergency Room Physician, St Francis Medical Center-West, Ewa Beach, Hawaii; Internal Medicine Physician, Kalihi-Palama Health Center, Honolulu, Hawaii. Publications: Over 15 publications in scientific journals and presented as lectures include most recently: The Role of Geriatrics and Gero-Psychiatry in Medical Education, 2002; Geriatric Rehabilitation, 2002; A 76 year old Man with Anemia, Lymphadenopathy and Pericarditis, 2003. Honours: Golden Key National Honor Society, Dean's List, Bachelor of Science Degree

with Distinction, University of Hawaii; James A Orbison Resident of the Year Award, 1999-2000; The Queen's Medical Center Ke Kauka Po'okela 2000 Physician of the Year Nominee; America's Top Physicians Award, State Licence Documentation, 2003. Memberships include: Alpha Omega Alpha Medical Honor Society; American Medical Association; American College of Physicians-American Society of Internal Medicine; Hawaii Medical Association; American Geriatrics Society; American Association of Family Physicians; Honolulu Chinese Jaycees. Address: 45-708 Kuakua Place, Kaneohe, HI 96744, USA. E-mail: baronwong@hotmail.com

WONG Chau Tung, 9 July 1944, Guang Dong, China. Artist. m. Wai Kuen Lam, 1 son, 1 daughter. Graduate, Guang Tung, 1959. Appointments: Artist; Managing Director and Owner of Wong's Art Limited, Hong Kong. Honours: Honourable Research Fellow, European International Academy of Oriental Fine Arts; "After Rainfall" selected for 9th National Fine Arts and won Outstanding Prize; "At the Bottom of Tai Ping Shan" selected for 200 Hong Kong-Macau-Taiwan Fine Arts Show and won a Gold Medal; "Tai Pin Shan" was selected for European International Exposition of Oriental Fine Arts in Amsterdam and won a Silver Medal; "As Splendid Lighting On" selected for 21st Century Traditional Chinese Painting in Australia and won a Bronze Medal. Memberships: Vice Chairman, Asian Artist Association of Hong Kong; Chairman, Hong Kong Academy of Fine Arts. Address: 1/F, 31 Main Street, Stanley, Hong Kong. E-mail: www.wongsart@yahoo.com.hk

WONG Jean, b. 14 April 1949, Hong Kong. Professor of Medicine. m. Chee Ming Wong, 2 daughters. Education: BA (Cantab) 1st Class Honours, 1971; MBBChir (Cantab), 1974; MA (Cantab), 1975; MCRP (UK), 1976; MD (Cantab), 1988; FRCP (Lond), 1991; FRCP (Edin), 1991; FRACP, 1995, FFPHM, 2003. Appointments: Chairman, Department of Medicine, 1993-99, Professor of Medicine, 1994-, Chairman, Department of Community and Family Medicine, 2000-, Director, School of Public Health, 2001-, The Chinese University of Hong Kong; Chief of Service (General), Shatin Hospital, Hospital Authority, Hong Kong, 1994-. Publications: Articles in medical journals as co-author include: Is waist circumference a useful measure in predicting health outcomes in the elderly?; Ageing in China: Health and social consequences and responses, 2002; Socioeconomic impact of arthritis in Hong Kong Chinese, 2003. Honour: Croucher Senior Clinical Research Fellowship, 1999-2002. Memberships: Fellow, Hong Kong Academy of Medicine; Fellow, Royal College of Physicians (London and Edinburgh); Fellow, Royal Australasian College of Physicians. Address: Department of Medicine and Therapeutics, The Chinese University of Hong Kong; Prince of Wales Hospital, Shatin, NT, Hong Kong. E-mail: jeanwoowong@cuhk.edu.hk

WOO John, b. 1948, Guangzhou, China. Film Director. Education: Matteo Ricci College, Hong Kong. Appointments: Production Assistant, Assistant Director, Cathay Film Co, 1971; Assistant Director to Zhang Che, Shaw Bros. Creative Works: Films: The Young Dragons, 1973; The Dragon Tamers; Countdown in Kung Fu; Princess Chang Ping; From Riches to Rags; Money Crazy; Follow the Star; Last Hurrah for Chivalry; To Hell with the Devil; Laughing Times; Plain Jane to the Rescue; Sunset Warriors (Heroes Shed No Tears); The Time You Need a Friend; Run Tiger Run; A Better Tomorrow; A Better Tomorrow II; Just Heroes; The Killer; Bullet in the Head; Once a Thief; Hard Boiled; Hard Target; Broken Arrow; Face/Off; Kings Ransom; Mission Impossible II; The Last Word (producer); Windtalkers, 2000; The Hire: Hostage, 2002; Red Skies (producer), 2002; Paycheck, 2003; Bullet Proof Monk (producer), 2003. Address: c/o MGM Studios Inc, 2500 Broadway Street, Santa Monica, CA 90404, USA.

Dictionary of International Biography

WOO Sung-Il, b. 23 January 1959, Seoul, Korea. Professor; Physician. m. Hwa-Sook Lee, 1 son, 1 daughter. Education: MD, Seoul National University, Korea, 1977-83; PhD, Seoul National University Graduate School, Korea, 1998. Appointments: Intern, Resident, Seoul National University Hospital, Korea, 1986-90; Lecturer, 1990-92, Assistant Professor, 1992-96, Associate Professor, 1996-2001, Gyeongsang National University Medical College, Korea; Associate Professor, 2001-2004, Chief, Department of Neuropsychiatry, 2002-, Professor, 2004-, Soonchunhyang University Hospital, Seoul, Korea. Publications: Books as co-author: Dementia, let's talk about hopes (in Korean), 2002; CERAD-K (in Korean), 2003; Articles in medical journals as first author include: Alternative splicing patterns of CYP2D6 genes in human brain and neurodegenerative disorders, 1999; CPY2D6*4 polymorphism in not associated with Parkinson's disease and has no protective role against Alzheimer's disease in the Korean population, 2001; Association of the Ser9Gly polymorphism in the dopamine D3 receptor gene with tardive dyskinesia in Korean Schizophrenics, 2002. Honour: Rakcheon Academic Award, 2003. Memberships: Korean Association of Medicine; Korean Association of Neuropsychiatry; Korean Association of Biological Psychiatry; Korean Association of Geriatric Psychoneuropharmacology. Address: Soonchunhyang University Hospital, Department of Neuropsychiatry, 657, Han-Nam Dong, Seoul 140-743, Republic of Korea. E-mail: siwoo@hosp.sch.ac.kr

WOOD Christopher John, b. 18 August 1939, London. Consultant Geologist. m. Jenny Lennon. Education: BSc, Geology, 1961, University of Reading, 1957-61. Appointments: Scientific Officer, 1961, Senior Scientific Officer 1967, Principal Scientific Officer, 1973-86, Voluntary Premature Retirement, 1986, British Geological Survey; Self-employed Consultant Geologist, 1986-88; Director own consultancy, Scops Geological Services Ltd, 1988-; Member, Editorial Board of Acta Geologica Polonica, Warsaw, Poland, 2004; Associate Editor, Cretaceous Research, Amsterdam, The Netherlands, 2004; Numerous lectures and tutorials. Publications: 47 articles on various aspects of geology in learned journals; 1 article on English medieval coinage; Co-author, 6 British Geological Survey geological sheet memoirs; Contributions to and chapters in books: The scientific study of flint and chert, 1986; Sylloge of Coins of the British Isles, The J J North Collection, Edwardian English Silver Coins 1279-1351, 1989; Engineering Geology of the Channel Tunnel, 1996; Key localities of the northwest European Cretaceous, editor and contributor, 1998; Die Kreide der Bundesrepublik Deutschland, 2000; British Upper Cretaceous Stratigraphy, joint author, 2001. Honours: Franklin Sibly Prize, Geology, University of Reading, 1961; Halstead Medal, Geologists' Association, 1993; Joint winner, Richardson Award, Geologists' Association, 1998. Memberships: Secretary, Cretaceous Working Party, Mesozoic Era Subcommittee, Geological Society, 1968-78; UK Convenor, Coniacian-Maastrichtian Working Party, IUGS Subcommission on Cretaceous Stratigraphy, 1978-84; Palaeontographical Society, Council, 1987-92; Palaeontological Association; Geologists' Association, Council, 1988-91, 1999-2002; Hertfordshire RIGS Group, 1990-; Buckinghamshire RIGS Group, 1991-; German Subcommission for Cretaceous Stratigraphy, 1992-; Fellow, Geological Society, elected to Chartered Geologist, 1992; Six Working Parties, IUGS Subcommission on Cretaceous Stratigraphy, 1995-; Deutsche Paläontologische Gesellschaft; Geological Society of Norfolk. Address: 20 Temple Road, Croydon, Surrey, CR0 1HT. E-mail: chrisjwood@btopenworld.com

WOOD Cynthia L, b. 13 November 1957, Wichita, Kansas, USA. Educator. m. Richard, 1 son, 1 daughter. Education: BSEd, English, Spanish, University of Missouri-Columbia, 1976-80; MA, Curriculum and Instruction English, University of Missouri, Kansas City, 1980-90. Appointments: Teacher: English, Spanish, Ervin Junior High, 1980-82; Teacher: English, Spanish, Hickman Mills High School, 1982-83; Teacher: English, Spanish, Blue Springs Junior High, 1983-88; Teacher: English, Spanish, Yearbook, Video Yearbook, Blue Springs High School,, Vesper Campus, 1988-92; Teacher: English, Yearbook, Video Yearbook, Blue Springs South High School, 1992-. Honours: Selected by seniors to walk at graduation; Employee of the Month, October, 1998; Excellence in Teaching; Scholarship to Writing Project in Journalism; Teacher Appreciation Award; Teacher of the Year, Blue Springs South, 1999-2000; Yearbook: First Honors (NSPA); All-Missouri (MIPA); others. Memberships: Parent Teacher Student Association; Missouri State Teachers Association; Community Educators Association; National Council Teachers of English; Journalism Educators Association; Missouri Intersholastic Press Association; Journalism Educators of Metropolitan Kansas City; National Scholastic Press Association. Address: 1200 Taylor Road, Blue Springs, MO 64014, USA.

WOOD Elijah, b. 28 January 1981, Ceder Rapids, Iowa, USA. Actor. Education: Avent Studios, Modelling school. Films include: Back to the Future Part II, 1989; Internal Affairs, 1990; The Adventures of Huck Finn, 1993; The War, 1994; The Ice Storm, 1997; Oliver Twist, 1997; Deep Impact, 1998; The Faculty, 1998; Chains of Fools, 2000; The Lord of the Rings: The Fellowship of the Ring, 2001; The Adventures of Tom Thumb and Thumbelina, 2002; The Lord of the Rings: The Two Towers, 2002; The Lord of the Rings: The Return of the King, 2003; Eternal Sunshine of the Spotless Mind, 2004. TV Appearances include: Frasier, 1994; Adventures from the Book of Virtues, 1996; SM:TV Live, 2001; The Osbournes, 2002; The Buzz, 2002; Player$, 2002; The Tonight Show with Jay Leno, 2003; Saturday Night Live, 2003; NY Graham Norton, 2004; King of the Hill (voice), 2004. Honours: Young Artist Award, 1991; Saturn Award, 1994; Young Star Award, 1998; Empire Award, 2002; Young Hollywood Award, 2002. MTV Movie Award, 2003; National Board of Review, USA, 2003; Saturn Award, 2004; Broadcast Film Critics Association Award, 2004; Screen Actors Guild Award, 2004; Visual Effects Society Awards, 2003. Address: c/o Nicole David 151 S El Camino Drive, Beverly Hills, CA 90212-2775, USA.

WOOD James Albert, b. 9 November 1949, Enterprise, Oregon, USA. Professor. m. Maritza Alvarez, 1 daughter. Education: BS, David Lipscomb University, 1975; BA, MA, Southern Oregon University, 1979; EdD, Texas A&M University, 1986; Postgraduate Studies, University of Tennessee and Sul Ross State University Rio Grande College. Appointments: Graduate Teaching Assistant, Texas A&M University at Kingsville, and University of Tennessee; Spanish ESL Teacher, Sheldon ISD, Texas, Galena Park, ISD, Texas, Rice Consolidated ISD, Texas, Jefferson Co ISD, Madras, Oregon; Senior Program Development Specialist, University of Oklahoma; Full Professor, Sul Ross State University Rio Grande College. Publications: 41 articles in refereed journals. Honour: Dean's Grant, Bilingual Fellowship; Listed in national and international biographical dictionaries. Memberships: National Association for Bilingual Education; Texas Association for Bilingual Education; TESOL; ASCD; TTE; Life Member, Non-Commissioned Officers Association; American Legion; Life Member, VFW; Masonic Lodge 472. Address: PO Box 1415, Uvalde, TX 78802, USA. E-mail: jawood@sulross.edu

WOOD Renate, b. 5 February 1938, Berlin, Germany. Poet. m. William B Wood, 30 June 1961, 2 sons. Education: PhD, Stanford University, 1970; MFA Program for Writers, Warren Wilson College, North Carolina, 1985. Appointments: Lecturer, University of Colorado, Boulder, 1985-91; Faculty, Program for Writers,

Warren Wilson College, North Carolina. Publications: Points of Entry, 1981; Raised Underground, 1991; The Patience of Ice, 2000. Contributions to: American Poetry Review; Massachusetts Review; New England Review; TriQuarterly; Virginia Review; Seneca Review; Prairie Schooner; Ploughshares. Honours: Nominee, Colorado Governor's Award for Excellence in the Arts, 1982; Grant, Colorado Council on the Arts, 1995. Memberships: Associated Writing Programs; Academy of American Poets. Address: 1900 King Avenue, Boulder, CO 80302, USA.

WOOD Roger Holmes, b. 26 April 1920, Corning, New York, USA. Educator; Financial Planner. m. Phyllis Anderson, 2 sons, 1 daughter. Education: AB, University of Pittsburgh, 1944; MS, Columbia University Graduate School of Journalism, 1945; MA, San Francisco State University, 1951; PhD, International College, 1978; American College CLU, ChFC, College of Financial Planning, CFP. Appointments: Educator, schools and colleges, 1947-; Agent, New York Life, 1954-; Journalist, 1944-47. Publications: When Tankers Collide, novel; A Forgiving at Assisi, autobiography; Life is a Four Letter Word. Memberships include: Numerous professional, historical, genealogical and learned affiliations, including, Sons of the American Revolution; Society of Genealogists, London; First Families of Ohio; San Francisco Estate Planning Council; Society of Financial Service Professionals; Chartered Life Underwriter (CLU); Chartered Financial Consultant (ChFC); College for Financial Planning; Certified Financial Planner (CFP); Accredited Estate Planner (AEP). Address: 65 Capay Circle, San Francisco, CA 94080, USA.

WOOD Ronnie (Ronald), b. 1 June 1947, England. Musician. m. (1) 1 son, (2) Jo Howard, 1985, 1 son, 1 daughter. Appointments: Guitarist, Jeff Beck Group, 1968-69, The Faces, 1969-75, The Rolling Stones, 1975-. Creative Works: Albums with Jeff Beck Group: Truth, 1968; Beck-Ola, 1969; with The Faces: First Step, 1970; Long Player, 1971; A Nod's As Good As A Wink...To A Blind Horse, 1971; Ooh La La, 1973; Coast to Coast Overtures and Beginners, 1974; with The Rolling Stones: Black and Blue, 1976; Love You Live, 1977; Some Girls, 1978; Emotional Rescue, 1980; Tattoo You, 1981; Still Life, 1981; Undercover, 1983; Rewind 1971-1984, 1984; Dirty Work, 1986; Steel Wheels, 1989; Flashpoint, 1991; Voodoo Lounge, 1994; Solo albums including: Slide on This, 1992; Films include: Let's Spend the Night Together, 1983; Flashpoint, 1991; Also played with Bo Diddley, Rod Stewart, Jerry Lee Lewis. Address: c/o Monroe Sounds, 5 Church Row, Wandsworth Plain, London SW18 1ES, England. Website: www.ronniewood.com

WOODBURY Marda, b. 20 September 1925, New York, New York, USA. Retired Librarian; Author. m. (1) Philip J Evans, 1 son (2) Mark Lee Woodbury, 1 son, 1 daughter. Education: BA, Chemistry and Political Science, Bard College, 1946; BS, Library Science, Columbia University, 1948; Studies in Education and Journalism, 1955-56, 1960-61, MJ, 1995, University of California, Berkeley. Appointments: Librarian, Special, Medical and Public Libraries, 1946-60; High School Librarian, Mt Diablo, California, 1962-67; Elementary School Librarian, Oakland and Berkeley, California, 1967-69; Head of Research Library, Far West Laboratory of Educational Research and Development, 1969-73; Librarian, Editor and Resource Consultant, Gifted Resource Center of San Mateo, California, 1974-75; Research Ventures (Information Consultants), Oakland, California, 1975-; Library Director, Life Chiropractic College West, 1980-95; Retired, 1995. Publications: A Guide to Sources of Educational Information, 1976, 2nd edition, 1982; Selecting Instructional Materials, 1978 ; Selecting Materials for Instruction, volume I: Issues and Policies, 1979, volume II: Media and the Curriculum, 1980, volume III: Subject Areas and Implementation, 1980; Childhood Information Resources, 1985;

Youth Information Resources, 1987; Stopping the Presses: The Murder of Walter W Liggett, 1997. Memberships: Investigative Reporters and Editors; Minnesota Historical Society. Address: 145 Monte Cresta Avenue, # 402, Oakland, CA 94611, USA. E-mail: mardawoodbury@msn.com

WOODFORD F Peter, b. 8 November 1930, Portland, Oregon, USA. Retired Biochemist. m. Susan Woodford, 1 daughter. Education: BA Honours, 1952, MA, 1955, Balliol College, Oxford University; PhD, Components of Wool Wax, Leeds University, 1955; Classical Greek, City Literary Institute, London, 1993-. Appointments: Docent, Lector, Medical Chemistry, Gaubius Institute, University of Leiden, The Netherlands, 1958-63; Visiting Professor, University of Tennessee Medical School, USA, 1964; Visiting Scientist, National Heart Institute, Bethesda, USA, 1964; Guest Investigator, Rockefeller Institute/University, New York, USA, 1964-71; Head, Biochemistry, Physiology and European Programmes, Wellcome Trust, London, 1971-74; Scientific Historian, Ciba Foundation, London, 1971-74; Executive Director, Institute for Research into Mental and Multiple Handicap, London, 1974-77; Principal Scientific Officer, Department of Health (UK clinical chemistry services), London, 1977-84; Chief Scientific Officer to the Department of Health, London, 1984-93; In retirement: Editorial Secretary, Clinical Sciences Reviews Committee, Association of Clinical Biochemists, 1994-2002; Editor of Publications, Camden History Society, 1994-; Distinguished Visitor and Honorary Senior Lecturer, Royal Free Hospital Medical School, London, 1994-; Chairman, Hampstead Music Club, 1996-99; Student Governor, City Literary Institute, 1999-2001. Publications: 60 articles on biochemistry applied to medicine, organisation of clinical chemistry, other pathology services, local history; 44 written or edited books on the above subjects include: Medical Research Systems in Europe, 1973; From hospital to home care: the potential for acute service provision in the home, 1992; How to teach scientific communication, 1999; Streets of Camden Town, 2003. Honours: Domus Exhibitioner, Balliol College, Oxford, 1948-52; Proxime accessit Gibbs Prize in Chemistry, Oxford University, 1950; Waverley Gold Medal for scientific writing for laymen, Royal Society of Arts, 1955; Meritorious Award, Council of Biology Editors, USA, 1984; Woolmer Memorial Lecturer, Biological Engineering Society, 1992; Honorary Doctor of Science, Salford University, 1993; First non-medical Affiliate, Royal College of Physicians, 2000. Memberships: Fellow, Royal College of Pathologists, 1984; Fellow, Royal Society of Chemistry, 1990; Fellow, Biological Engineering Society, 1991; Fellow, Institute of Physics and Engineering in Medicine, 1995. Address: 1 Akenside Road, London NW3 5BS, England. E-mail: drswoodford@blueyonder.co.uk

WOODRING Carl, b. 29 August 1919, Terrell, Texas, USA. Educator. m. Mary Frances Ellis, 24 December 1942. Education: BA, 1940, MA, 1942, Rice University; AM, 1947, PhD, 1949, Harvard University. Publications: Victorian Samplers, 1952; Virginia Woolf, 1966; Wordsworth, 1965, revised edition, 1968; Politics in English Romantic Poetry, 1970; Nature into Art, 1989; Table Talk of Samuel Taylor Coleridge (editor), 1990; Columbia History of British Poetry (editor), 1993; Columbia Anthology of British Poetry (co-editor), 1995; Literature: An Embattled Profession, 1999; Lucky Thirteen: USS Hopkins, DD 249, DMS 13 (co-author), 2000. Contributions to: Western Review; Virginia Quarterly Review; Keats-Shelley Journal; Comparative Drama. Honours: Guggenheim Fellowship, 1955; American Council of Learned Societies, Fellow, 1965; Phi Beta Kappa Gauss Prize, 1971; PKB Visiting Scholar, 1974-75; Senior Mellon Fellow, 1987-88. Memberships: American Academy of Arts and Sciences; International Association of University Professors of English; Grolier Club. Address: 1034 Liberty Park Drive, Austin, TX 78746, USA.

Dictionary of International Biography

WOODS James, b. 18 April 1947, Vernal, Utah, USA. Actor. m. (1) Kathryn Greko, 1980, (2) Sarah Owen, 1989. Education: University of California, Los Angeles; Massachusetts Institute of Technology. Creative Works: Films include: The Visitors, 1971; The Way We Were, 1972; The Gambler, 1974; Distance, 1975; Alex and the Gipsy, 1976; The Choirboys, 1977; The Onion Field, 1979; Black Marble, 1980; Fast Walking, 1982; Split Image, 1982; Videodrome, 1983; Once Upon a Time in America, 1984; Against All Odds, 1984; Joshua Then and Now, 1985; Best Seller, 1987; Cop, 1987; The Boost, 1989; True Believer, 1989; Immediate Family, 1989; Straight Talk, 1992; Diggstown Chaplin, 1992; The Gateway, 1994; Curse of the Starving Class, 1994; Casino, 1995; Nixon, 1996; Killer: A Journal of Murder, 1966; Ghosts of Mississippi, 1996; Hercules (voice), 1997; Contact, 1997; Vampires, 1998; True Crime, 1999; Virgin Suicides, 2000; Race to Space, 2001; John Q, 2001; Riding in Cars with Boys, 2001; Scary Movie 2, 2001; Rudy: The Rudy Giuliani Story, 2003; TV films include: Holocaust, 1978; Promise, 1986; My Name is Bill W, 1989; Next Door, 1994; The Summer of Ben Tyler, 1996; Dirty Pictures, 2000; Showtime, 2000. Honours include: Emmy Award, 1989. Address: c/o Guttman Associates, 118 South Beverly Drive, Beverly Hills, CA 90212, USA.

WOODS Philip Wells, b. 2 November 1931, Springfield, Massachusetts, USA. Musician (Alto Saxophone, Clarinet); Composer. m. Jill Goodwin, 20 December 1985, 1 son, 2 daughters. Education: Lessons with Harvey Larose, Springfield; Manhattan School, New York, 1948; Juilliard Conservatory, 1948-52. Career: Appearances with Benny Goodman, Buddy Rich, Quincy Jones, Thelonious Monk, Michel Legrand, Dizzy Gillespie and others; Appearing with own bands, Phil Woods Quintet, Phil Woods Little Big Band, Phil Woods Big Band; Featured, soundtracks of films including It's My Turn; Bandleader, Composer, Arranger and Soloist. Compositions include: Three Improvisations for Saxophone Quartet; Sonata for Alto and Piano; Rights of Swing; The Sun Suite; Fill the Woods with Light; I Remember; Deer Head Sketches. Recordings include: Images, with Michel Legrand, 1976; I Remember, Phil Woods Quartet, 1979; Dizzy Gillespie Meets Phil Woods Quintet; Evolution, Phil Woods Little Big Band; An Affair to Remember, Phil Woods Quintet; The Rev & I, with Johnny Griffin; Elsa, 1998; Porgy and Bess, 1999. Honours: Down Beat Magazine New Star Award, 1956, Critics' Poll Winner, alto saxophone, 1975-79, 1981-90, 1992, Readers' Poll Winner, alto saxophone, 1976-95; Grammy Award, Images with Michel Legrand, 1976, for More Live, Phil Woods Quartet, 1982, 1983; National Association of Jazz Educators Poll Winner, alto saxophone, 1987, Phil Woods Quintet, 1987; East Stroudsburg University Honorary Degree, 1994; Induction into American Jazz Hall of Fame, 1994; Officier des Arts et des Lettres; Beacon Jazz Award, 2001. Memberships: Delaware Water Gap Celebration of the Arts; Board of Directors, Al Cohn Memorial Jazz Collection; American Federation of Musicians; International Association of Jazz Educators. Address: Box 278, Delaware Water Gap, PA 18327, USA.

WOODS Tiger (Eldrick), b. 30 December 1975, Cypress, California, USA. Golfer. Education: Stanford University. Appointments: Winner: International Junior World Championship, 1984-91; National Youth Classic, 1990; US Junior Championships, 1991 (youngest winner), 1992, 1993; US Amateur Championships 1994 (youngest winner), 1995, 1996; Las Vegas Invitational Competition, 1996; Walt Disney Classic, 1996; Honda Asian Classic, 1997; Mercedes Championships, 1997, 2000; US Masters, 1997 (youngest winner, broke records for lowest score and greatest margin of victory), 2001, 2002; Bell S Classic, 1998; US PGA Championship, 1999, 2000; National Car Rental Golf Classic, 1999; WGC American Express Championship, 1999; AT&T

Pebble Beach National Pro-Am, 2000; Bay Hill Invitational, 2000, 2001, 2002; US Open, 2000, 2002; British Open, 2000; Winner, numerous other titles; Contract with Nike, 1999-. Memberships: Member, US Team World Amateur Team Championship, 1994, US Walker Cup Team, 1995. Honours include: Golf World Player of the Year, 1992; Man of the Year, 1994; Sports Illustrated Sportsman of the Year, 1996, 2000; PGA Tour Player of the Year, 1997, 1999-2002. Address: PGA, PO Box 109601, 100 Avenue of the Champions, Palm Beach Gardens, FL 33418, USA.

WOODWARD Edward, b. 1 June 1930, Croydon, Surrey, England. Actor; Singer. m. (1) Venetia Mary Collett, 1952, 2 sons, 1 daughter, (2) Michele Dotrice, 1987, 1 daughter. Education: Kingston College; Royal Academy of Dramatic Art. Creative Works: Stage appearances include: Mercutio in Romeo and Juliet, Laertes in Hamlet, Stratford, 1958; Rattle of a Simple Man, Garrick, 1962; Two Cities (musical), 1968, Cyrano in Cyrano de Bergerac; Flamineo in The White Devil, National Theatre Company, 1971; The Wolf, Apollo, 1973; Male of the Species, Piccadilly, 1975; On Approval, Theatre Royal, Haymarket, 1976; The Dark Horse, Comedy, 1978; Beggar's Opera, 1980; The Assassin, 1982; Richard III, 1982; The Dead Secret, 1992; 3 productions, New York; Films include: Becket, 1966; The File on the Golden Goose, 1968; Hunted, 1973; Sitting Target, 1974; Young Winston, 1974; The Wicker Man, 1974; Stand Up Virgin Soldiers, 1977; Breaker Morant, 1980; The Appointment, 1981; Comeback, 1982; Merlin and the Sword, 1982; Champions, 1983; A Christmas Carol, 1984; King David, 1984; Uncle Tom's Cabin, 1989; Mister Johnson, 1990; Deadly Advice, 1993; A Christmas Reunion, 1994; Gulliver's Travels, 1995-96; The Abduction Club, 2002; Over 2000 TV productions including title role in Callan, 1966-71; The New Professionals, 1998-99; Night Flight, 2002; 12 LP records as singer, 3 as poetry; 14 talking book recordings. Honours: Numerous international and national acting awards. Address: c/o Janet Glass, Eric Glass Ltd, 28 Berkeley Square, London, W1X 6HD, England.

WOOSNAM Ian Harold, b. 2 March 1958, England. Golfer. m. Glendryth Pugh, 1983, 1 son, 2 daughters. Education: St Martin's Modern School. Appointments: Professional Golfer, 1976-. Creative Works: Tournament Victories: News of the World Under-23 Matchplay, 1979; Cacharel Under-25 Championship, 1982; Swiss Open, 1982; Silk Cut Masters, 1983; Scandinavian Enterprise Open, 1984; Zambian Open, 1985; Lawrence Batley TPC, 1986; 555 Kenya Open, 1986; Hong Kong Open, 1987; Jersey Open, 1987; Cepsa Madrid Open, 1987; Bell's Scottish Open, 1987, 1990; Lancome Trophy, 1987; Suntory World Match-Play Championship, 1987, 1990; Volvo PGA Championship, 1988; Million Dollar Challenge, 1988; Carrolls Irish Open, 1988, 1989; Panasonic Euro Open, 1988; Welsh Pro Championship, 1988; American Express Mediterranean Open, 1990; Torras Monte Carlo Open, 1990; Epson Grand Prix, 1990; World Cup Team and Individual Winner, 1987; World Cup Individual Winner, 1991; US Masters, 1991; USF+G Lassic, 1991; PGA Grand Slam, 1991; Fujitsu Mediterranean Open, 1991; Torras Monte Carlo Open, 1991; European Monte Carlo Open, 1992; Lancome Trophy, 1993; Murphy's English Open, 1993; British Masters, 1994; Cannes Open, 1994; Heineken Classic, 1996; Scottish Open, 1996; German Open, 1996; Johnnie Walker Classic, 1996; Volvo PGA Championships, 1997; Hyundai Motor Masters, 1997; Ryder Cup Member, 1983, 1985, 1987, 1989, 1991, 1993, 1995, 1997; Numerous team events. Publications: Ian Woosnam's Golf Masterpieces (with Peter Grosvenor), 1991; Golf Made Simple: The Woosie Way, 1997. Membership: President, World Snooker Associate, 2000-. Address: c/o IMG, Pier House, Strand on the Green, London W4 3NN, England. Website: www.woosie.com

Dictionary of International Biography

WORKMAN Jerome James, b. 6 August 1952, Northfield, Minnesota, USA. Chemist. m. Rebecca M, 2 sons, 3 daughters. Education: BA, Natural Sciences, St Mary's University, 1976; MA, Biological Sciences, Genetics, 1980; PhD, Biological Chemistry, Columbia Pacific University, 1984; EPM, Executive Programmes in Management, Columbia University Graduate School of Business, 1990, 1991, 1999, 2000; MIT Sloan, 2001; CSEP, Columbia Graduate School of Business, 2004. Appointments: Research Chemist, Laboratory Manager, Watkins Products Inc, 1978-80; Spectroscopy Consultant, Graduate Student, 1980-84; Supervising Scientist, Senior Application Chemist, Technicon/Bran and Luebbe, 1984-87; Senior Scientist, Hitachi Instruments, 1987-89; Director, Technical Support and Marketing, Perstorp Analytical Inc, 1989-93; Principal Scientist, Perkin-Elmer Corp, 1993-96; Senior Research Fellow, Kimberly Clark Corp, 1996-2002; Chief Technical Officer, Vice President of Research and Engineering, Argose Inc, Waltham, Massachusetts, 2002-. Publications: 300 scientific papers, abstracts and book chapters; Statistics in Spectroscopy; Applied Spectroscopy; A Compact Reference for Practitioners; The Academic Press Handbook of Ultraviolet-Visible-Near-Infrared-Infrared-Raman Spectroscopy; Introduction to Near Infrared Spectroscopy; UV-VIS Spectroscopy; Near Infrared Reflectance Spectroscopy. Honours: Fellow and Chartered Chemist, Royal Society of Chemistry; Fellow, American Institute of Chemists; Fellow, American Society for Testing and Materials; Silver Anniversary Member, American Chemical Society; Outstanding People of the 20th Century; Sigma Xi; National Science Foundation Study Grants; ASTM Award of Merit; EAS Award for Outstanding Achievements in Near Infrared Spectroscopy; US National Academies NRC Panel; US FDA Visiting Scientist; National Wrestling Champion of United States Catholic Colleges and Universities; Others. Memberships: New York Academy of Sciences; American Chemical Society; ASTM; Council for Near Infrared Spectroscopy; Coblentz Society; Others. Address: Argose, Inc, 230 Second Avenue, Waltham, MA 02451, USA.

WORSLEY, Sir (William) Marcus John, b. 6 April 1925, Hovingham, Yorkshire, England. Retired Landowner. m. Bridget Assheton, 3 sons, 1 daughter. Education: New College Oxford. Appointments: JP, 1957-90 (Chairman, Malton Bench 1983-90); Member of Parliament for Keighley, 1959-64; Member of Parliament for Chelsea, 1966-74; Second Church Estates Commissioner, 1970-74; Church Commissioner, 1976-84; Deputy Chairman, National Trust, 1986-92; High Sheriff, North Yorkshire, 1982; Lord Lieutenant, North Yorkshire,1987-99. Address: Park House, Hovingham, York, YO62 4JZ, England.

WORSLEY William Ralph, 12 September 1956, York, England. Chartered Surveyor. m. Marie-Noelle Dreesmann, 1 son, 2 daughters. Education: Royal Agricultural College. Appointments: Chairman, Hovingham Estates; Vice-Chairman, Scarborough Building Society; Director, The Brunner Investment Trust plc; Member, Executive Committee, Country Land and Business Association; Member, Forestry Commission's Advisory Panel; Vice-Chairman, Howardian Hills AONB JAC. Honour: Fellow, Royal Institution of Chartered Surveyors. Address: Hovingham Hall, York, England. E-mail: office@hovingham.co.uk.

WORSTHORNE Sir Peregrine (Gerard), b. 22 December 1923, London, England. Journalist; Editor; Writer. m. (1) Claude Bertrand de Colasse, 1950, deceased 1990, 1 daughter, (2) Lady Lucinda Lambton, 1991. Education: BA, Peterhouse, Cambridge; Magdalen College, Oxford. Appointments: Sub-editor, Glasgow Herald, 1946; Editorial Staff, The Times, 1948-53; Daily Telegraph, 1953-61; Deputy Editor, 1961-76, Associate Editor, 1976-86, Editor, 1986-89, Editor, Comment Section, 1989-91, Sunday Telegraph.

Publications: The Socialist Myth, 1972; Peregrinations: Selected Pieces, 1980; By the Right, 1987; Tricks of Memory (autobiography), 1993. Contributions to: Newspapers and journals. Honours: Granada Columnist of the Year, 1980; Knighted, 1991. Address: The Old Rectory, Hedgerley, Buckinghamshire SL2 3VY, England.

WOSCHNI Eugen-Georg, b. 18 February 1929, Berlin, Germany. Professor. 3 sons. Education: Teacher, 1946; Dipl-Ing, Technical University Dresden, 1951; Dr-Ing Technical University, Dresden, 1953; Habilitation, 1956. Appointments: Assistant Professor, Technical University, Dresden, 1952-56; Head of Institute of Electrical Engineering, 1957-90; Vice Chancellor, 1959-62; Dean of Faculty of Electrical Engineering, 1965-69; Head of Institute of Telecommunication, Technical University, Chemnitz, 1990-98; Head of Technology Class and Member of Presidiúm, Saxonia Academy of Science, 1995-2001. Publications: 12 monographs and over 250 papers and contributions to international congresses in the fields of communication and measurement. Honours: Dr-Ing E h, honorary doctor, Technical University, Dresden, 1981; Distinguished Leadership Award, 1999; Deputy Director General, International Biographical Institute, Cambridge, 2000; Fellow, American Biographical Institute, 2000. Memberships: Academy of Science, Berlin, 1973; Saxonia Academy of Science, Leipzig, 1985; VDI, 1990; Senate of Union of German Academy of Science, Mainz, 1996-2001; Member, TC1 (Education), TC7 (Theory), IMEKO; Konvent für Technikwissemschaften, München, 2002. Address: Sonnenleite 4, D-01324 Dresden, Germany.

WRATNY Jerzy, b. 1 November 1943, Warsaw, Poland. Lawyer; Professor. m. Jadwiga Maria Wratny, 2 sons, 1 daughter. Education: Master in Law, 1966, Faculty of Law, Warsaw University; PhD, 1974, Dr habil., 1983, Professor, 1984; Graduate, Popish Theological Faculty, Warsaw, 1992. Appointments: Assistant Professor, 1966-68, Financial Law Chair, Warsaw University; Postgraduate Doctor's Degree in Economy, Warsaw School of Economics, 1970-73; Assistant Professor, 1968-80, Privatdocent, 1980-84, Professor, 1984-, Manager of Department of Labour Law and Social Security, Institute of Labour (now Institute of Labour and Social Studies), 1975-; Professor of Labour Law and Social Insurance, Catholic University of Lublin, 1984-94; Chair of Labour Law, Rzeszów University,1995-. Visiting Professorships include Canada and Germany. Publications: Nearly 200 publications; 22 monographs in the field of labour law, especially industrial relations, European law and its application in Poland, social security and social ethics. Honours: Second Prize for best doctoral dissertation, State and Law Journal, Academy of Sciences. Listed in Who's Who publications and biographical dictionaries. Memberships include: International Society for Labour Law and Social Security, Polish Section; International Committee of Industrial Relations, Polish Section; Business Ethics Association; Association des Amies de la Culture Juridique Française-Henri Capitant. Address: ul Bagatela 15 m 76, 00-585 Warsaw, Poland. E-mail: jerzy_wratny@poczta.onet.pl

WRIGHT Evelyn Louise, b. 2 August 1913, Odessa, Missouri, USA. Artist. m. Douglas Wright, 1 son, 2 daughters. Education: University of the Pacific, 1958-60; Merced College, 1960-61, California, USA Columbia College, 1962-64. Appointments: Employed by Graphic Arts, Independence, Missouri, USA, 1938-34; Assistant Manager and Bookkeeper, Wrights, 1984-86; Art Instructor, Ripona School, 1992-94, Owner and Instructor of Evelyn's Watercolour Classes and Workshops; At age of 90 still teaching 11 classes a week and conducting 3 major workshops a year. Publications: Several TV Tapes for local showing. Honours: Best of Show, Richard Yip Art, several years; Sonora National,

1980, 1984; Lodi Grape Festival, 1982, 1986; Chosen to hang paintings for Governor. Membership: Stockton Art League. Address: 508 W Morada Lane, Stockton, CA 95210, USA.

WRIGHT George T(haddeus), b. 17 December 1925, New York, New York, USA. Professor Emeritus; Author; Poet. m. Jerry Honeywell, 28 April 1955. Education: BA, Columbia College, 1946; MA, Columbia University, 1947; University of Geneva, 1947-48; PhD, University of California, 1957. Appointments: Teaching Assistant, 1954-55, Lecturer, 1956-57, University of California; Visiting Assistant Professor, New Mexico Highlands University, 1957; Instructor, Assistant Professor, University of Kentucky, 1957-60; Assistant Professor, San Francisco State College, 1960-61; Associate Professor, University of Tennessee, 1961-68; Fulbright Lecturer, University of Aix-Marseilles, 1964-66, University of Thessaloniki, 1977-78; Visiting Lecturer, University of Nice, 1965; Professor, 1968-89, Chairman, English Department, 1974-77, Regents' Professor, 1989-93, Regents' Professor Emeritus, 1993-, University of Minnesota. Publications: The Poet in the Poem: The Personae of Eliot, Yeats and Pound, 1960; W H Auden, 1969, revised edition, 1981; Shakespeare's Metrical Art, 1988; Aimless Life: Poems 1961-1995, 1999; Hearing the Measures: Shakespearean and Other Inflections, 2002. Editor: Seven American Literary Stylists from Poe to Mailer: An Introduction, 1973. Contributions to: Articles, reviews, poems and translations in many periodicals and books. Honours: William Riley Parker Prize, Modern Language Association, 1974, 1981; Guggenheim Fellowship, 1981-82; National Endowment for the Humanities Fellowship, 1984-85. Memberships: Minnesota Humanities Commission, 1985-88; Modern Language Association; Shakespeare Association of America; Phi Kappa Phi. Address: 2617 West Crown King Drive, Tucson, AZ 85741, USA.

WRIGHT John MacNair Jr, b. 14 April 1916, Los Angeles, California, USA. United States Army. m. Helene Tribit, 28 June 1940, 2 sons. Education: BSc, US Military Academy, West Point, New York, 1940; MBA, University Southern California, Los Angeles, California 1956; MSc, International Affairs, George Washington University, Washington DC, 1973. Appointments: Battery Executive Officer, Battery Sunset, 91st Coast Artillery, Corregidor, Philippine Islands, 1940-42; Battery Commander, Battery Wright, 1942; Prisoner of War of Japan, Philippine Islands, Japan, Korea, 1942-45; Intelligence Division, War Department General Staff, Washington, 1946-48; Military Attaché, US Embassy, Asuncion, Paraguay, 1948-50; Executive Officer, 30th Infantry Regiment, Fort Benning, Georgia, 1950; Student Advanced Course, Infantry School, Fort Benning, Georgia, 1950-51; Commander, 3rd Battalion, 508th Airborne Regimental Combat Team, Fort Benning, Georgia, 1951-52; Student, Command and General Staff College, Fort Leavenworth, Kansas, 1952-53; Assistant Chief of Staff for Personnel, Assistant Chief of Staff for Logistics, 7th Infantry Division, Korea, 1953-54; Office of Deputy Chief of Staff, Logistics, Department of the Army, Washington, 1956-58; Office of Chief of Staff, US Army, Washington, 1958-60; Student, National War College, Washington, 1960-61; Chief of Staff, 8th Infantry Division, Bad Kreuznach, Germany, 1961-62; Assistant Chief of Staff, Plans and Operations, VII Corps, Stuttgart, 1962-63; Assistant Chief of Staff, Plans and Operations, Seventh Army, Stuttgart, 1963; Assistant Division Commander, 11th Air Assault Division, Fort Benning, Georgia, 1963-65; Assistant Division Commander, 1st Cavalry Division, Vietnam, 1965-66; Office of Assistant Chief of Staff, Force Development, Department of the Army, Washington, 1966-67; Commanding General, US Army Infantry Center and Commandant, US Army Infantry School, Fort Benning, Georgia, 1967-69; Commanding General, 101st Airborne Division, Vietnam, 1969-70; Comptroller of the Army, Washington, 1970-72; Retired, 1972; National

Director of Research and Development, National Director of Programs, National Director of Exploring, Boy Scouts of America, N Brunswick, New Jersey and Irving, Texas, 1973-81; Retired, 1981. Publication: Captured on Corregidor, 1988. Honours include: Distinguished Service Medal with two Oak Leaf Clusters; Silver Star with Oak Leaf Cluster; Legion of Merit with Oak Leaf Cluster; Distinguished Flying Cross; Bronze Star Medal with Oak Leaf Cluster; Purple Heart with Oak Leaf Cluster; Air Medal with 59 Oak Leaf Clusters; Army Commendation Medal; Prisoner of War Medal; American Defense Service Medal; Asiatic Pacific Campaign Medal; World War II Victory Medal; US Presidential Unit Citation with three Oak Leaf Clusters; National Defense Service Medal with Oak Leaf Cluster; Korea Service Medal; United Nations Service Medal; Republic of Korea Presidential Unit Citation; Vietnam Service Medal; Philippine Defense Medal; Philippine Liberation Medal; Philippine Independence Medal; Philippine Presidential Unit Citation; Paraguayan Order of National Merit; Vietnamese Gallantry Cross with three Palms and Gold Star; Vietnamese Commendation Medal; Vietnamese National Order, 5th Class; Vietnamese Civic Actions Medal, 1st Class; Vietnamese Armed Forces Honor Medal, 1st Class; Vietnamese Rural Revolutionary Development Medal with Palm; Vietnamese National Police Honor Medal, 1st Class; Combat Infantryman Badge; Master Parachutist Badge (US, German and Vietnamese); Senior Army Aviator Badge; Freedoms Foundation at Valley Forge: George Washington Honour Medal; America's Freedom Festival: Freedom Award; Boy Scouts of America: Distinguished Eagle Scout Award; Silver Antelope; Silver Beaver. Memberships include: National Eagle Scout Association; Kentucky Colonels; National Flag Foundation; National Congress of Patriotic Organisations; Society of the Cincinnati; Baronial Order of Magna Charta; Order of the Crown of Charlemagne; many others. Address: 21227 George Brown Avenue, Riverside, CA 92518-2881, USA.

WRIGHT John Robert, b. 20 October 1936, Carbondale, Illinois, USA. Priest; Professor. Education: BA optime merens, University of the South, Sewanee, Tennessee, 1958; MA Honours, Mediaeval History, Emory University, Atlanta, Georgia, 1959; MDiv cum laude, General Theological Seminary, New York City, 1963; DPhil, Oxford University, England, 1967. Appointments: Ordained, 1963; Instructor in Church History, Episcopal Divinity School, Cambridge, Massachusetts, 1966-68; Assistant Professor of Church History, 1968-71, Professor of Church History, 1971-, St Mark's Professor of Ecclesiastical History, 1974-, General Theological Seminary, New York City; Several visiting positions including Visiting Professor, St George's College, Jerusalem, 1982, 1992, 1995, 1996; Provost's Visiting Professor in Divinity, Trinity College, University of Toronto, 1989. Publications: Author, co-author, editor, co-author, 16 books including: Episcopalians and Roman Catholics: Can They Ever Get Together?, 1972; Handbook of American Orthodoxy, 1972; A Communion of Communions: One Eucharistic Fellowship, 1979; The Church and the English Crown, 1305-1334: A Study based on the Register of Archbishop Walter Reynolds, 1980; Called to Full Unity: Documents on Anglican-Roman Catholic Relations 1966-1983, 1986; Prayer Book Spirituality, 1989; Readings for the Daily Office from the Early Church, 1991; The Anglican Tradition: A Handbook of Sources, 1991; On Being a Bishop: Papers on Episcopacy from the Moscow Consultation 1992, 1993; Saint Thomas Church Firth Avenue, 2001; Russo-Greek papers 1863-1874, 2002; Forthcoming: Anglican Commentaries on the 39 Articles; The Privilege of England 1231-1530; 3 booklets; 169 papers and articles. Honours include: Phi Beta Kappa, Pi Gamma Mu and Omicron Delta Kappa, 1958; Life Fellow, Royal Historical Society, London, 1981-; DD hc, Episcopal Theological Seminary of the Southwest, Austin, Texas, 1983; Honorary Canon Theologian to Bishop of New York, 1990-; DD hc, Trinity Lutheran Seminary,

1991; DCnL hc, University of the South, 1996; Dr. Theol. hc, University of Bern (Switzerland), 2000; Holy Crosses of the Orthodox Patriarchs of Constantinople, Jerusalem, Antioch and Moscow; Historiographer of the Episcopal Church, 2000-; Life Fellow, Society of Antiquaries, London, 2001. Memberships include: The Anglican Society, President, 1994-; North American Academy of Ecumenists, President, 1989-91; Conference of Anglican Church Historians, Convenor, 1995-; American Catholic Historical Association; American Society of Church History; Medieval Academy of America. Address: c/o General Theological Seminary, 175 Ninth Avenue, New York, NY10011, USA. E-mail: wright@gts.edu

WRIGHT Paul (Hervé Giraud), b. 12 May 1915. Retired. m. Beatrice Frederika Rathbone, 1 daughter. Appointments: John Lewis Partnership Ltd, 1933-39; Served in HM Forces, 1939-45; Major, KRRC; HQ 21 Army Group, 1944-45 (despatches); Contested (L) NE Bethnal Green, 1945; Assistant Director, Public Relations, National Coal Board, 1946-48; Director, Public Relations, Festival of Britain, 1948-51; HM Foreign Service: Paris and New York, 1951-54; Foreign Office, 1954-56; The Hague, 1956-57; Head of Information, Policy Department in Foreign Office, 1957-60; Cairo, 1960-61; UK Delegation to North Atlantic Council, 1961-64; Minister for Information, Washington, 1965-68; Director General, British Information Services, New York, 1964-68; Ambassador to Congo (Kinshasa) and to Republic of Burundi, 1969-71; Ambassador to the Lebanon, 1971-75; Special Representative of the Secretary of State for Foreign and Commonwealth Affairs, 1975-78; Chairman, Irvin Great Britain Ltd, 1979-88; Chairman, British American Arts Association, 1983-88; Chairman, British Lebanese Association , 1987-90; Chairman, Member Council, Forte plc, 1987-97. Publications: A Brittle Glory, autobiography, 1986. Honours: OBE, 1952; CMG, 1960; KCMG, 1975; Honorary Secretary General, London Celebrations Committee for Queen's Silver Jubilee, 1977; Knight of the Order of the Cedar of Lebanon, 1990; Honorary RCM, 1990; KCSG, 1996; GCSG, 2000. Memberships: Vice Chairman, The American Festival, 1985; President, Elizabethan Club, 1988-95; Governor, 1981-2000, (Chairman, 1993-2000), Westminster Cathedral Choir School; Chairman, Westminster School Development Council, 1994-97; Trustee, Trusthouse Charitable Foundation, 1996-2000; Life Vice President, Hearing Dogs for Deaf People. Address: 62 Westminster Gardens, Marsham Street, London SW1P 4JG, England.

WRIGHT Theodore Paul Jr, b. 12 April 1926, Port Washington, New York, USA. Professor. m. Susan J Standfast, 1 son, 2 daughters. Education: BA, Swarthmore College, 1949; MA, 1951, PhD, 1957, Yale University. Appointments: Instructor to Associate Professor, Bates College, Lewiston, Maine, USA, 1955-65; Associate Professor, Professor, Graduate School of Public Affairs, State University of New York at Albany, Albany, New York, 1965-95; Emeritus Professor, 1995-. Publications: American Support of Free Elections Abroad, 1963; 67 articles on Muslim politics, India and Pakistan, 1963-2004. Memberships: Association for Asian Studies; Board Member, American Council for the Study of Islamic Society; Past President, now Newsletter Editor, South Asian Muslim Studies Association; Columbia University Faculty Seminar on South Asia, 1967-; Past President, New York Conference on Asian Studies; European Conference on Modern South Asian Studies, 1979-; Board Member, New Netherland Institute. Address: 17 Wellington Way, Niskayana, NY 12309, USA. E-mail: wright15@Juno.com

WU Dar Ching, b. 15 July 1945, Singapore. Cardiothoracic Surgeon. m. Lorna, 3 daughters. Education: Bachelor of Medicine, Bachelor of Surgery, Singapore, 1970; Fellow, Royal Australasian College of Surgeons, 1974; Fellow, Academy of Medicine, 1977; Fellow, American College of Cardiology, 1984. Appointments: Consultant Cardiothoracic and Vascular Surgeon, Mount Elizabeth Hospital, Singapore; Visiting Consultant: National Heart Centre, Changi General Hospital, Beijing Friendship Hospital, Fujian CV Research Institute, Xiamen 1st Hospital; Honorary Medical Director, Wuhan Asia Heart Hospital; Vice-President, Trinity Annual Conference, Singapore; Assistant Governor, District 3301, Rotary International. Publications: 42 scientific articles. Honours: Performed first cardiomyoplasty surgery in South East Asia. Memberships: Society of Thoracic Surgeons, USA. Address: 3 Mount Elizabeth, #17-17/18 Mount Elizabeth Medical Centre, Singapore 228510. E-mail: heartctr@singnet.com.sg

WU He, b. 20 January 1924, Beijing, China. Doctor of Specialised Medicine. m. Zhu Yimin, 1 son, 2 daughters. Education: Bachelor, Medical Doctor, Shanghai Medical University, China, 1948; Visiting Doctor, Beijing Union Medical College, China, 1956-60; 1979-80; Visiting Doctor, Ames Laboratory, Biochemistry Department, University of California, Berkeley, USA, 1980-81. Appointments: Medical Doctor of Zhong-San Hospital, Red Cross Hospital, Affiliated Hospitals of Shanghai Medical University of China; Chief Doctor of Medical and Allergic, Department of Central Construction Friendship Hospital of Shaanxi; Allergic Department of Xi'an Medical University, Stomatological Hospital. Publications: Thesis for, Immune Therapy for Vascular Edema; Relation between Environment with Immune Functions and Allergic Diseases, 1999; Immune Therapy of Senile Bronchial Asthma, US Chinese Health and Hygiene Journal, 1999. Honours: First Grade Award of Chinese Special Effect Medical Treatise for Immune Treatment for Allergic Diseases by the Combination of Chinese Traditional Medicine and Western Medicine, 1998; First Grade Award of National Hua Tuo Cup. Memberships include: Vice President, Modern Medical Association of China, 1998-. Address: 277 You-Yi West Road, Xi'an, Shaanxi 710 068, China. E-mail: wuhe80@sohu.com

WU Jiann-Kuo, b. 25 February 1950, Taipei, Taiwan. University President. m. Li-Hwa, 1 son, 2 daughters. Education: Diploma, National Taipei Institute of Technology, 1971; PhD, University of Nebraska, 1984. Appointments: Professor, 1989-; Dean, Academic Affairs, 1993-97; President, National Taiwan Ocean University, 1997-2003; Board Chairman, Metal Industries Research and Development Centre, 2003-. Publications: Over 200 papers, materials science. Memberships: The Minerals, Metals and Materials Society. Address: National Taiwan Ocean University, 2 Pei-Ning Road, Keelung, Taiwan 20024, China.

WU Ming-Lu, b. 3 March 1963, Nanzhao County, Henan Province, China. Management Consultant. m. Chung Shing, 1 son. Education: BEng, Applied Mathematics, Jihin University of Technology, Changchun, China, 1983; MSc, Operations Research and Cybernetics, 1986, PhD, Probability and Mathematical Statistics, 1994, Academia Sinica, Beijing, China. Appointments: Assistant Professor, 1986-91, Associate Professor, 1994-95, National Research Centre for Science and Technology for Development, Beijing; Research Fellow, Department of Management Sciences, City University of Hong Kong, 1995-. Publications: 13 papers for internationally refereed journals; Co-authored 2 books: China's Economic Development and Some Related Factors' Analysis, 1991; International Competitiveness, 1992. Address: Department of Management Sciences, City University of Hong Kong, 83 Tat Chee Avenue, Kowloon, Hong Kong. E-mail: msminglu@cityu.edu.hk

WU Ning, b. 6 December 1967, Hubei Province, Peoples Republic of China. Researcher. Education: BS, 1991, MA, 1994, PhD, 1997, University of Science and Technology of China. Appointments:

Postdoctoral, 1997-99, Associate Professor, 1999-, Institute of High Energy Physics, Beijing, China. Publications: Articles in the scientific journal, Communications in Theoretical Physics, 2002, 2002, 2003. Honours: Guang Hua Scholarship, 1991, 1994. Address: Division 1, PO Box 918-1, Institute of High Energy Physics, Beijing 10039, Peoples Republic of China.

WULFF Günter, b. 19 February 1935, Hamburg, Germany. Professor of Chemistry. m. Gertraud Zaake, 2 sons, 1 daughter. Education: Study of Chemistry, University of Hamburg, 1954-60; Diploma in Chemistry, Hamburg, 1960; PhD, Natural Products Chemistry, with Professor Dr R Tschesche, University of Bonn, 1963. Appointments: Research Group Leader, University of Bonn, 1963-70; Habilitation and Privatdozent, 1970; Guest Professor, Ateneo-de-Manila University, Philippines, 1970; Associate Professor, H-3, University of Bonn, 1972; Full Professor, Organic and Macromolecular Chemistry, University of Düsseldorf, 1979; Dean, 1991-92; Retired, 2000-. Publications: Over 200 original publications and reviews in different scientific journals and books; 10 patents in the field; Co-editor, 2 books. Honours: Dozentenpreis, Fonds Chem Industrie, 1973; Honorary Member, Azerbaijan Academy of Sciences, 1993; Prix Céréalier, Europe, 1996; Havinga Medal, Netherlands, 1997. Memberships: Gesellschaft Deutscher Chemiker; American Chemical Society; Member, Editorial Board, Angew Chem and Advisory Board, Starch/Stärke. Address: Institute of Organic and Macromolecular Chemistry, Heinrich-Heine University Duesseldorf, Universitaetsstr 1, 40225 Duesseldorf, Germany. E-mail: wulffg@uni-duesseldorf.de Website: www.oc2.uni-duesseldorf.de

WYMAN Bill (William George), b. 24 October 1941, London, England. Musician. m. (1) Diane Cory, divorced 1968, 1 son, (2) Mandy Smith, 1989, divorced 1991, (3) Suzanne Accosta, 1993, 2 daughters. Appointments: Bass-Player, The Rolling Stones, 1962-93; Owner, Ripple Records, Ripple Music, Ripple Publications, Ripple Productions. Creative Works: Albums include: 12 x 5, 1964; New, 1965; Big Hits, 1966; Got Live If You Want It, 1967; Flowers, 1967; Sucking in the 70's, 1981; Still Life, 1981; Rewind, Dirty Work, 1986; Emotional Rescue, 1988; Steel Wheels, 1989; Flashpoint, 1991; Voodoo Lounge, 1994; Solo recordings include: Stone Alone; Monkey Grip; Bill Wyman; Groovin', 2000; Double Bill, 2001; Blues Odyssey, 2001; Singles: Films: Sympathy for the Devil, 1970; Gimme Shelter, 1970; Ladies and Gentlemen the Rolling Stones, 1974; Let's Spend the Night Together, 1982; Digital Dreams, 1983. Publications: Stone Alone: The Story of a Rock and Roll Band (with Ray Coleman), 1990; Wyman Shoots Chagall, 2000; Bill Wyman's Blues Odyssey (with Richard Havers), 2001; Rolling With The Stones (with Richard Havers), 2002. Honours include: Prince's Trust Award, 1991; Ivor Novello Award for Outstanding Contribution to British Music, 1991; Blues Foundation, Memphis Literary Award, 2002. Address: c/o Ripple Productions Ltd, 344 Kings Road, London SW3 5UR, England.

X

XIA Jisong, b. 15 May 1925. Professor in Modern Philosophy. m. 1 April 1956, 1 son, 1 daughter. Education: Bachelor in Politics, National Central University, Nanjing, 1943-48; MPhil, People's University of China, Beijing, 1952-54. Appointments: Assistant Lecturer, Department of Politics, National Central University, 1948-52; Lecturer, Department of Politics, Nanjing University, 1954-78; Associate Professor and Deputy Head of Department, Department of Philosophy, Nanjing University, 1978-82; Professor and Head of Department, Department of Philosophy, Nanjing University, 1982-90; Professor, Department of Philosophy, Hangzhou University and Zhejiang University, Hangzhou, 1990-. Publications: More than 10 books including: Course of the Modern Philosophy in the West, 1985; Mathematics Philosophy in the West, 1986; Review on Existentialism, 1987; Philosophy of Science in the West. Honour: Honorary Head of the Philosophy Department, Nanjing University. Memberships: Philosophy Division of the State Council's Academic Degree Committee in China; Vice Chairman, Society of Modern Foreign Philosophy Study in China; Chairman of the Society of Foreign Philosophy Study in China. Address: Department of Philosophy, College of Humanities, Zhejiang University, Hangzhou 310028, China.

XIAO Da Zhun, b. 25 December 1938, Pingxiang City, Jiangxi, China. Professor of Mechanical Engineering. m. Shu Yuan Chen. Education: Graduate, Power Engineering Department, Huazhong University of Science and Technology, Wuhan, China, 1955-60. Appointments: Teaching Assistant, Lecturer, Associate Professor, Professor, Dalian University of Technology, Dalian, China, 1960-80, 1983-; Visiting Assistant Professor, University of California, Davis, USA, 1981-82. Publications: 4 books include: Mechanism Design, 1993, 1998; Solution Guide and Problem Collections for Mechanism Design, 1996; over 50 papers. Honours: Honour Graduate Award, HUST, 1960; Advanced Faculty Member Award, DUT, 1978, 1987; Active Member Award, Liaoning Mechanical Transmission Society, 1984, 1987; Science and Technology Progress Award, Liaoning Education Commission, 1996; Excellent Teacher Award, Bao Steel Education Fund, 1997; Model Worker, Dalian Municipal Government, 1998; Memberships: Senior Member, CMES, 1986-; Teaching Directing Committee on Theory of Machines and Mechanisms (TMM), 1990-2000; Deputy Chief of Council, Chinese Education Society for TMM, 1992-2000; China Committee, IFToMM, 1998-. Address: School of Mechanical Engineering, Dalian University of Technology, Dalian 116024, China.

Dictionary of International Biography

Y

YAGI Tamotsu, b. 8 November 1933, Tokyo, Japan. Professor. m. Masumi Segawa, 1 daughter. Education: Bachelor, Pedagogy, University of Tokyo, 1957; DMedSci, Kyoto University, 1990. Appointments: Member, Counselling Room, University of Tokyo, 1957-62; Instructor, 1962-74, Associate Professor, 1974-92, Professor, 1992-97, Head of Counselling Room for Physically-handicapped Students, 1995-97, Emeritus Professor, 1997-, Kyoto University; Member, Kinki Society of School Health, President, 1993-94; ICHPER-SD Health Education Commission, 1995-. Publications: Secular Trends in Physique and Physical Fitness in Japanese Students during the last 20 years. Honours: Sports Award (for scientific contribution), Kyoto Prefecture, 1997; 20th Century Award, IBC, 1998. Memberships; Human Biology Association; ICHPER-SD. Address: 2-14 Kamitakano Santandacho, Sakyoku, Kyoto 606-0054, Japan.

YAKOVLEV Valery Petrovitch, b. 28 September 1940, Volgograd, Russia. Physicist. m. Margarita Yakovleva, 2 daughters. Education: MS, Distinction, 1963, PhD, 1967, DSc, 1987, Moscow Engineering Physics Institute. Appointments: Assistant Professor, 1967-69, Senior Lecturer, 1969-75, Associate Professor, 1975-88, Full Professor, 1988-, Moscow Engineering Physics Institute; Heraeus Professor, Universität Ulm, Germany, 1994-1996. Publications: Over 170 scientific papers on quantum electrodynamics of strong fields, physics of semiconductors, interferometry of atomic states and matter waves, subrecoil laser cooling and atom optics and strange kinetics; Monograph, Mechanical Action of Light on Atoms, 1990. Address: Theoretical Nuclear Physics Department, Moscow Engineering Physics Institute, Kashirskoe shosse 31, 115409 Moscow, Russia. E-mail: yakovlev@theor.mephi.ru

YALOW Rosalyn, b. 19 July 1921, New York, New York, USA. Medical Physicist. m. Aaron Yalow, 1943, 1 son, 1 daughter. Education: Graduated, Physics, Hunter College, New York, 1941; PhD, Experimental Nuclear Physics, University of Illinois, 1945. Appointments: Assistant in Physics, University of Illinois, 1941-43; Instructor, 1944-45; Lecturer and temporary Assistant Professor in Physics, Hunter College, New York, 1946-50; Physicist and Assistant Chief, 1950-70, Acting Chief, 1968-70, Chief Radioimmunoassay Reference Laboratory, 1969, Chief Nuclear Medicine Service, 1970-80, Senior Medical Investigator, 1972-92, Senior Medical Investigator Emeritus, 1992-, Director, Solomon A Berson Research Laboratory, Veterans Administration Medical Center, 1973-92, Radioisotope Service, Veterans Administration Hospital, Bronx, New York; Research Professor, 1968-74, Distinguished Service Professor, 1974-79, Department of Medicine, Mount Sinai School of Medicine, New York; Distinguished Professor at Large, 1979-85, Professor Emeritus, 1985-, Albert Einstein College of Medicine, Yeshiva University; Chair, Department of Clinical Sciences, Montefiore Hospital, Bronx, 1980-85; Solomon A Berson Distinguished Professor at Large, Mt Sinai School of Medicine, New York, 1986-; Harvey Lecturer, 1966; American Gastroenterology Association Memorial Lecturer, 1972; Joslyn Lecturer, New England Diabetes Association, 1972; Franklin I Harris Memorial Lecturer, 1973; 1st Hagedorn Memorial Lecturer, Acta Endocrinologia Congress, 1973; President, Endocrine Society, 1978-79; Honours: Over 60 honorary doctorates; Joint Winner, Nobel Prize for Physiology or Medicine, 1977; More than 30 other awards. Memberships: NAS; American Physics Society; Radiation Research Society; American Association of Physicists in Medicine; Biophysics Society; American Academy of Arts and Sciences; American Physiology Society; Foreign Associate, French Academy of Medicine; Fellow,

New York Academy of Science; Radiation Research Society; American Association of Physicists in Medicine; Associate Fellow in Physics, American College of Radiology; American Diabetes Association; Endocrine Society; Society of Nuclear Medicine. Address: Veterans Administration Medical Center, 130 West Kingsbridge Road, Bronx, New York, NY 10468, USA.

YAMAGISHI Katsuei, b. 22 September 1944, Yamaguchi Prefecture, Japan. University Professor; Lexicographer. m. Sayoko Kamakura, 1 son, 1 daughter. Education: BA, First Class Honours, Hosei University; MA, Distinction, Hosei University Graduate School, Tokyo, Japan. Appointments: Lecturer, 1970-72, Senior Lecturer, 1972-76, Associate Professor, 1976-85, Director of London Office, 1981-82, Professor, 1985-88, Hosei University; Professor, Meikai University and Meikai University Graduate School, Chiba, Japan, 1988-. Publications include: Aspects of Japanese-English Languages and Cultures; Aspects of Modern British and American English, 3 volumes; A Theory and its Practice of Compiling Japanese-English Dictionaries for Japanese Learners; English Language Teaching and Dictionaries; English Language Teaching and Dictionary Philosophy and Practice; Language and Society of Britain; Editor-in Chief: The Gakken New Anchor Japanese-English Dictionary, The Gakken Super-Anchor Japanese-English Dictionary, The Gakken Super-Anchor English-Japanese Dictionary; The Japanese-English Ways of Thinking; The Romance of English Expressions. Honours: Three First Prizes at Three All-Hosei English Oratorical Contests; Distinguished Service Award, Hosei University Second High School; Best Undergraduates 2nd Year Student Award, Hosei University; Best MA Course Student Award, Hosei University Graduate School. Memberships: Advisor, Council of International Education; Advisor, International Institute of Education; English Language Teaching Consultant, Cambridge International Dictionary of English, 1st edition; First President, Fujimi Society of Language and Literature. Address: 7-20-24 Tomioka-Nishi, Kanazawa-ku, Yokohama 236-0052, Japan.

YAMAGUCHI Masashi, b. 1 September 1948, Yamagata, Japan. Associate Professor. m. Naoko Terakawa, 2 sons, 1 daughter. Education: BS, Yamagata University, Yamagata, Japan, 1971; MS, Tokyo Metropolitan University, Tokyo, Japan, 1974; DSc, 1978. Appointments: Visiting Research Fellow, Memorial Sloane-Kettering Cancer Center, New York, USA 1979; Associate Researcher, 1980; Staff Scientist, Monell Chemical Senses Center, Philadelphia, USA, 1980-81; Research Associate, The Jikei University School of Medicine, Tokyo, Japan, 1981-88; Lecturer, 1988-96, Associate Professor, 1996-, Chiba University, Chiba, Japan. Publications: Articles in medical journals include: Dynamics of hepatitis B virus core antigen in a transformed yeast cell, 1994; The spindle pole body duplicates in early G1 phase in a pathogenic yeast Exophiala dermatitidis, 2002. Honours: Best Paper Award, Japanese Society of Electron Microscopy, 1996. Memberships: Japanese Society of Microscopy; Japanese Society of Medical Mycology; Mycological Society of Japan. Address: Research Centre for Pathogenic Fungi and Microbial Toxicores, 1-8-1 Inohama, Chuo-ku, Chiba 260-8673, Japan. Website: http://www.pf.chiba-u.ac.jp/

YAMAMOTO Irwin Toraki, b. 5 April 1955, Wailuku, Maui, Hawaii. Editor; Publisher. Education: YB, Business Administration, Marketing, Chaminade University, 1977. Appointments: President, Editor, Publisher, The Yamamoto Forecast, Kahului, Hawaii, 1977-. Publications: Book: Profit Making in the Stock Market, 1983; Columnist, The Hawaii Herald, 1978-. Honours: Named: Top Market Timer; Top Gold Timer; Top Bond Timer; Timer Digest Honor Roll, Timer Digest; Also honors by: Select Information Exchange; Rating the Stock Selectors. Address: PO Box 573, Kahului Hl, 96733-7073, Hawaii.

Dictionary of International Biography

YAMAMOTO Kentaro, b. 12 November 1969, Yokohama, Japan. Researcher. Education: Bachelor of Engineering, 1993, Master of Engineering, 1995, Doctor of Engineering, 1998, Kumamoto University, Japan. Appointments: Consulting Engineer, Kokusai Kogyo Co, Amagasaki, Japan, 1990-91; Research Associate, Kagoshima University, Kagoshima, Japan, 1998-. Publications: Articles in scientific journals including: Geotextiles and Geomembranes; Soils and Foundations. Memberships: Japan Society of Civil Engineers; Japanese Geotechnical Society. Address: Department of Ocean Civil Engineering, 1-21-40, Korimoto, Kagoshima, 890-0065 Japan. E-mail: yamaken@oce.kagoshima-u.ac.jp

YAMANAKA Masami, b. 29 January 1929, Tokyo, Japan. Professor. m. Hiroko, 1 son, 1 daughter. Education: Bachelor of Medicine, 1953, Dr Medical Science, 1960, University of Tokyo. Appointments: Full-time Physician, Faculty of Medicine, University of Tokyo, 1954-70; Assistant Professor, 1970-71, Associate Professor, 1971-77, Professor, 1977-99, Teikyo University; Director, Teikyo University Hospital, 1996-99; Professor Emeritus, Teikyo University, 1999-; President Emeritus, Ageo Chuo General Hospital, 1999-. Publications: Cellular and Molecular Biology, 1995, Interferon Therapy on Chronic Hepatitis C, 1996; Hepatocellular Carcinoma, 1997; Liver Cirrhosis Update, 1998; Liver and Immunology, 1999, in Hepatology, vols 1-5. Honours: Director General, Japan Society of Hepatology (JSH), 1992-96; President, 32nd Annual Meeting of JSH, 1996. Memberships: Member Emeritus, JSH; Member Emeritus, Japanese Society of Gastroenterology; Asian-Pacific Association for Study of the Liver; World Society of Gastroenterology. Address: 34-10 Oyamacho, Shibuya-ku, Tokyo, Japan 151-0065.

YAMASHITA Hitoshi, b. 30 December 1964, Ehime, Japan. Acupuncturist. m. Atsuko Tanaka, 2 sons. Education: BS, Acupuncture, Meiji University of Oriental Medicine, 1987; PhD, Health Sciences, University of Tokyo, 2002. Appointments: Technician, Ehime Prefectural Institute of Oriental Medicine, 1987-92, Instructor, Tsukuba College of Technology Clinic, 1992-; Honorary Research Fellow, Complementary Medicine, University of Exeter, England, 1999-2002; Visiting Research Fellow, Department of Family Nursing, University of Tokyo, 1999-2004. Publications: 9 books, first author, 2 books including: Acupuncture a scientific appraisal (Japanese version); 165 articles, first author, 114 articles including: Adverse events related to acupuncture, 1998; Incidence of adverse reactions associated with acupuncture, 2000; Safety of acupuncture: Incident reporting and feedback may reduce risks, 2002; Popularity of complementary and alternative medicine in Japan: a telephone survey, 2002. Honours: President's Award, Meiji University of Oriental Medicine, 1987; Ibaraki Foundation for International Conference, 1996; Grants for Scientific Research, 2001. Memberships: Chairman, Committee for Safety of Acupuncture, Japan Society of Acupuncture and Moxibustion; Member, Executive Committee, Japanese Association for Alternative, Complementary and Traditional Medicine; Founding Member, Japanese Society of Integrative Medicine; International Editorial Board Member, Focus on Alternative and Complementary Therapies; Founding Member, International Society of Complementary Medicine Research. Address: Tsukuba College of Technology Clinic, 4-12-7 Kasuga, Tsukuba, 305-0821, Japan.

YANAKA Kiyoyuki, b. 5 September 1961, Yuki City, Ibaraki, Japan. Neurosurgeon. m. Kumiko Suzuki, 1 daughter. Education: MD, 1986, PhD, 1993, University of Tsukuba, Tsukuba, Japan. Appointments: Junior and Senior resident, 1986-89, Chief Resident, Neurosurgery, 1990-91, University of Tsukuba, Japan; Chief Neurosurgeon, Soujinkai Hospital, Kitasouma, Japan, 1992-93; Assistant Professor, Neurosurgery, University of Minnesota,

Minneapolis, USA, 1994-96; Staff Neurosurgeon, Tsukuba Medical Centre, Tsukuba, Japan, 1996-98; Chief Neurosurgeon, Satte General Hospital, Satte, Japan, 1998-99; Assistant Professor, Neurosurgery, University of Tsukuba, Tsukuba, Japan, 1999-. Publications: Articles as co-author in international medical journals include most recently: Postoperative brainstem high intensity is correlated with poor outcomes for patients with cerebellar hemorrhage, 1999; Intraoperative angiography evaluation of the microsurgical clipping of unruptured cerebral aneurysms, 2002; Small unruptured cerebral aneurysms presenting with oculomotor nerve palsy, 2003; Intraoperative angiography in the surgical treatment of cerebral arteriovenous malformations and fistulas, 2003. Honours: Grant-in-Aid Research Award, American Heart Association, USA, 1995; Research Awards (Japan): Matsuoka Memorial Foundation, 1999; Mitsui Life Social Welfare Foundation, 2000, 2002; Japan Heart Association, 2000, Mishima Kaiun Memorial Foundation, 2001; Takeda Science Foundation, 2001; Japan Atherosclerosis Association, 2002; Mitsui Sumimoto Social Welfare Foundation, 2002; Sagawa Science Foundation, 2003. Memberships: American Association of Neurological Surgeons; Congress of Neurological Surgeons; American Heart Association, Stroke Council; Japan Neurosurgical Society; Japanese Congress of Neurological Surgeons. Address: Department of Neurosurgery, Institute of Clinical Medicine, University of Tsukuba, Tsukuba, Ibaraki, 305-8575, Japan. E-mail: kyanaka@md.tsukuba.ac.jp

YANG Chen-Chung, b. 15 July 1927, Taipei. Chair Professor. m. Yeh-Shiang Lin, 2 sons, 3 daughters. Education: MD, National Taiwan University, Taipei, 1950; DMed Science, Tokyo Jikei University, 1956. Appointments: Associate Professor, Kaohsiung Medical University, 1956-58; Professor, Biochemistry, 1958-73; President, 1967-73; Concurrent Research Fellow, Zoology Academia Sinica, Taipei, 1964-87; National Research Chair Professor, National Science Council, Republic of China, 1964-67; Founding Director, Institute Molecular Biology, National Tsing Hua University, Taiwan, 1973-85; Professor, Institute of Life Science, 1985-94; Distinguished Chair Professor, 1994-; Research Associate, University of Wisconsin, Madison; Chairman, Commission Inquiry of Division Life Sciences, National Science Council. Publications: More than 150 articles on snake venom proteins to professional journals. Honours: Premir's Award, Outstanding Scientists; Outstanding Research Award, National Science Council; Named, Distinguished Research Chair; Javits Neuroscience Investigator Award (NIH); One of Ten Outstanding Young Men. Memberships: AAAS (life); International Society on Toxicology; American Chemical Society (Emeritus, Life); Protein Society; Taiwan Society for Biochemistry and Molecular Biology (Emeritus Director, life president, 1979-81); Chinese Chemical Society; Japanese Biochemical Society; Formosan Medical Association; Asia-Pacific International Molecular Biology Network; Academician, Academia Sinica Taipei (elected member, life). Address: National Tsing Hua University, 61-5F West Compund, Hsinchu 300, Taiwan.

YANG Chih-Ping, b. 5 July 1959, Taipei, Taiwan. Pharmaceutical Executive. m. Professor Shir-ly Huang, 1 daughter. Education: BS, Chemistry, National Taiwan University, 1982; PhD, Organic Chemistry, University of Texas at Austin, 1990; EMBA, General Management, National Cheng-Chi University, 1998. Appointments: Research Scientist, Upjohn, USA, 1990-92; Research Fellow, Development Center for Biotechnology, Taiwan, 1992-96; Medical Department Manager, Bayer Taiwan, 1996-99; Medical Director, Schering-Plough, Taiwan, 1999-2000; Vice President, 2000-2001, Chief Executive Officer, 2001-, Caleb Pharmaceuticals Inc; Chief Executive Officer, General Biotherapeutics, USA, 2002-; Chief Executive Officer, CytoPharm,

Taiwan, 2003-. Publications: 30 in journals; 6 patents. Memberships: AAAS; ACS; DIA; IRPMA; AmCham. Address: 7F-2 #8, Lane 280, Section 6, Min-Chuan East Road, Nei-Hu, Taipei, Taiwan 114.

YANG Chunghai, b. 4 November 1928, Shanghai, China. Chemist; Researcher. m. Wenyou Sha, 1 son. Education: BSc, Tangshan Jiaotung University, China, 1952. Appointments: Lecturer, Anshan Institute of Iron and Steel, 1952-56, Southeast University, 1957-58; Senior Researcher, Institute of Atomic Energy, Chinese Academy of Sciences, Beijing, 1958-61, Nanjing, 1961-73; Professor of Physical Chemistry, Nanjing Institute of Chemical Technology, 1973-. Publications: Several articles in professional journals. Memberships: American Chemical Society; American Association for the Advancement of Science; New York Academy of Sciences; Chinese Chemical Society. Address: Department of Applied Chemistry, Nanjing Institute of Chemical Technology, 5 New Model Road, Nanjing, Jiangsu 210009, China.

YANG Czau-Siung, b. 28 January 1922, Nan-You, Taiwan. Professor. Medical Microbiologist. m. Pi-Yun Lin, 1 son, 2 daughters. Education: MD, Imperial University College, Taihoku, Japan, 1945; D M Sc, Masumoto Medical School, Japan, 1960. Appointments: Fellow in Virology, Baylor College of Medicine, Houston, Texas, USA, 1961-63; Professor of Microbiology, College of Medicine, National Taiwan University, Taipei, 1963-92, Professor Emeritus, College of Medicine, 1992-; Director, Institute of Microbiology, 1969-75; Fellow, International Union Against Cancer, 1972-73; Consultant, USN Medical Research Unit #2 Taipei, 1974-77; Director, National Institute of Preventive Medicine, Department of Health, Taipei, 1977-81; Dean, College of Medicine, National Taiwan University, 1985-87; President, Ching-Hsing Medical Foundation, 1988-; President, National Taiwan University Medical College Alumni Association, 2000-. Publications: Co-editor, Human Tumor Immunology, 1984; Epstein-Barr Virus and Human Diseases, 1990; Publisher, Journal of Microbiology, Immunology and Infection, 1998-2001; Contributor of articles to professional journals. Memberships: Chinese Society of Microbiology; Chinese Society of Immunology; Formosan Medical Association; American Society of Microbiology; New York Academy of Sciences. Address: 2F #38 Yun-Ho St., Taipei, 106 Taiwan. E-mail: csyang@ha.mc.ntu.edu.tw

YANG Hyungjae, b. 25 August 1954, Koje, Republic of Korea. Environmental Engineer. m. June Youngsuk, 2 daughters. Education: BS, Environmental Engineering, Dong-A University, Pusan, Korea; MS, Environmental Engineering, Polytechnic University, New York, USA; PhD, Environmental Engineering, Hanyang University, Seoul, Korea. Appointments: Senior Researcher, National Institute of Environmental Research, Ministry of Environment, 1991-; Environmental Expert, Commission on Protection of the Quality of Freshwater Resources, 2003-. Publications: Assessment and Promotion of Human Resources for River Water Quality Management, 1996; Sequencing Batch Reactor A/S Process, 1997; Simultaneous Biological Removal of N&P using the SBR Process, 1999. Honours: Listed in Who's Who publications and biographical dictionaries. Memberships: Water Environment Federation; Korean Society of Water Quality. Address: National Institute of Environmental Research, Kyungseo-dong, Seo-gu, Inchon, Korea 404-170. E-mail: hyungyang@hanmail.net

YANG Jin-Gang, b. 30 June 1925, Shanghai, China. m. Zhang Qi-Shu, 1 son, 1 daughter. Electroacoustic engineer; Audio engineer. Education: BSc, Physics, University of Shanghai, 1948; Diploma in English; Diploma in Chinese. Appointments: Designer, 500W loudspeaker system, 1961; Research and development, long-

distance high-power electrodynamic wired broadcast system, 1984; Professor, Senior Engineer, Ministry of Machinery and Electronics, 1988. Publications: Articles: Design of stereo loudspeaker systems used in 10,000-seat Peking auditorium, 1959; Study on optimum frequency response of high-power loudspeakers and sound system for outdoor use, 1992; Research progress in microminiaturisation of silicon microphone, 1999; Book: Audio Dictionary, 1993. Honours: National Award of Science and Technology of China, 1985; Distinguished Contribution Expert, State Council, 1993. Memberships: Fellow, China Institute of Electronics; Member, Committee of Audio Engineering Society of China; Member, Committee of China Standardisation on Acoustics; Editor, Chinese Journal of Acoustics. Address: PO Box 743, Beijing 100015, China.

YANG Shang-Kuo, b. 10 September 1960, Tainan City, Taiwan. Professor. m. Mei-Hwei Horng, 1 son, 1 daughter. Education: Bachelor of Engineering, 1982; Master of Science, 1985; Doctor of Philosophy, 1999. Appointments: Assistant Researcher, Chung Shan Institute of Science and Technology, Taiwan; Director of Library, Director of Incubation Centre, National Chin-Yi Institute of Technology, Taiwan; Assistant Preacher, Free Methodist Church, Taiwan. Publications: Articles in scientific journals as author and co-author include: Implementation of Petri nets using a Field-Programmable Gate Array, 2000; A temperature measuring method for a thermocouple with varied reference-junction temperature, 2002; An experiment of state estimation for predictive maintenance using Kalman filter on a DC motor, 2002; A Petri-net approach to remote diagnosis for failures of cardiac pacemakers, 2003; A condition-based failure-prediction and processing-scheme for preventive maintenance, 2003. Honours: A-class Award, National Science Council, Taiwan; Meritorious Award, Chung Shan Institute of Science and Technology. Address: # 117-38, Bu-Tz Lane, Taichung City, 406 Taiwan. E-mail: skyang@chinyi.ncit.edu.tw

YANG Sien-Sing, b. 26 November 1953, Taiwan. Hepatologist; Professor of Medicine. m. Su-Jen, 9 April 1981, 1 son, 1 daughter. Education: BMed, Medical Faculty, China Medicine College, Taiwan, 1972-79; Diploma, Chelsea College, London, 1985-86. Appointments: Professor of Medicine, China Medicine College; Director, Liver Unit, Cathay General Hospital, Taipei; Director, Voluntary Medical Service, Dharma DM Foundation, Taipei; Vice Chairman, East Valley Glendora Hospital LP, Glendora, California. Publications: Several articles in professional medical journals. Honours: Poster Prize, Taiwan Gastroenterological Association, 1991, 1992; Best Science Award, National Science Committee, Taiwan, 1998. Memberships: American Association for the Study of Liver Diseases; Asian Pacific Association for the Study of Liver; Taiwan Gastroenterological Association. Address: Liver Unit, Director, Cathay General Hospital, 280 Sec 4 Jen-Ai Road, Taipei 10650, Taiwan.

YANG Xiao-Qi, b. 24 April, Sichuan, China. Scientist. m. Qiong Tang, 2 daughters. Education: Bachelor of Science, Chongqing Jianzhu University, China, 1982; Master of Science, Chinese Academy of Sciences, 1987; Doctor of Philosophy, University of New South Wales, Australia, 1994. Appointments: Research Associate, 1994-96, ARC Postdoctoral Fellow, 1997, Lecturer, 1998, University of Western Australia; Assistant Professor, 1999-2000, Associate Professor, 2001-, Hong Kong Polytechnic University. Publications: Mathematical Programming; Siam J Optimisation; Management Science; Nonlinear Analysis; Over 100 articles in professional journals. Honours: Overseas Postgraduate Research Scholarship, Australia, 1991-94; Glenden Travel Award, University of Western Australia, 1996; ISI Citation Award, 2000; The President's Awards, Hong Kong Polytechnic University, 2000. Memberships: Mathematical Programming Society; Hong Kong

Dictionary of International Biography

Mathematical Society. Address: Department of Applied Mathematics, Hong Kong Polytechnic University, Hung Hum, Kowloon, Hong Kong. E-mail: mayangxq@polyu.edu.hk

YANOFF Arthur, b. 9 May 1939, Boston, Massachusetts, USA. Artist. Divorced, 2 daughters. Education: MA, Museum School of Fine Arts, Boston, 1958-61; Private Study with Jason Berger, 1961-65; Seminars, Psychology and Art, 1970-71. Appointments: Exhibitions: Museum of Fine Arts, Boston, Massachusetts; Yeshiva University Museum, New York City; Addison Gallery of American Art, Andover, Massachusetts; The Currier Gallery of Art, Manchester, New Hampshire; Wade Gallery, Los Angeles; Public Collections: MFA, Boston; MFA, Santa Fe, Rose Art Museum, Brandeis University; Detroit Institute of Arts, Detroit, Michigan; Museum of Art, Fort Lauderdale, Florida; Le Centre D'Art, Baie-St-Paul, Quebec, Canada. Publications: Waiting to Freeze; Paste Up Autobiography, A Visual Memoir. Honours: Prix Rene Richard; Memorial Foundation Grant; The Max and Anna Levinson Foundation Grant; Listed in national and international biographical dictionaries. Memberships: American Working Terrier Association; Greater Boston Kerry Blue Terrier Club's Livestock Protection Committee. Address: 624 South Egremont Road, Great Barrington, MA 01230, USA.

YAO Kui, b. 14 October 1967, Huainan, China. Senior Scientist. Education: BS, Xi'an Jiaotong University, China, 1989; MS, Xidian University, China, 1992; PhD, Xi'an Jiaotong University, China, 1995. Appointments: Post Doctoral Fellow, 1995-97, Research Fellow, assigned by Institute of Materials Research and Engineering, 1997-98, Nanyang Technological University, Singapore; Research Associate, Pennsylvania State University, USA, 1998-99; Research Fellow, 1997-2001, Senior Research Fellow, 2002-2003, Senior Scientist, 2003-, Institute of Materials Research and Engineering (IMRE), Singapore. Publications: Many invention patents and technical publications in scientific journals. Memberships: IEEE; MRS. Address: Institute of Materials Research and Engineering, 3 Research Link, Singapore 117602, Singapore.

YAO Ming-Jong, b. 21 April 1966, Changhwa County, Taiwan. Professor. m. Ling-Kuan Lin, 1 son, 1 daughter. Education: BS, Tunghai University, Taichung City, Taiwan, 1988; MS, Iowa State University, Ames City, Iowa, USA, 1994; PhD, North Carolina State University, Raleigh, North Carolina, USA, 1999. Appointments: Research Assistant, Yuan-Ze Institute of Technology, Taoyuan, Taiwan, 1990-91; Research Assistant, Electric Power Research Center, Ames, Iowa, USA, 1992-94; Teaching Assistant, North Carolina State University, Raleigh, North Carolina, 1994-96; Consultant, World-Class Manufacturing Team, Raleigh, North Carolina, USA, 1996-98; Assistant Professor, 1999-2003, Associate Professor, 2003-, Tunghai University, Taichung City, Taiwan; Chair of Academic Division, INFORMS Taiwan Chapter, Taiwan, 2003-; Vice-Chair of Academic Division, Operations Research Society of Taiwan. Publications: Book: Introduction to Industrial Engineering and Management (co-author), 2004; 13 referred papers in scientific journals include: On the Feasibility Testing of the Economic Lot Scheduling Problem using the Extended Base Period Approach, 2003; Critical Evaluation on the Search Algorithms for the Joint Replenishment Problem, 2003; 8 journal articles in Chinese. Honours include: Omega Ro Honor Society, 1995; Outstanding Teaching Assistant Award, Department of Industrial Engineering, North Carolina State University, 1997; Class A Research Award, National Science Council, 2000, 2001; Creative Teaching Award, 2003; Listed in Who's Who publications and biographical dictionaries. Memberships: Operations Research Society of Taiwan; Operations Research Society of America and the Institute of Management

Science (INFORMS); Chinese Institute of Industrial Engineers; Chinese Society for Quality. Address: 181 3rd Sec. Taichung Kang Road, Department of Industrial Engineering and Enterprise Information, PO Box 985, Tunghai University, 407 Taichung City, Taiwan. E-mail: myao@ie.thu.edu.tw

YAP Yee Guan, b. 19 December 1967, Malaysia. Cardiologist; Scientist. m. Wendy, 2 sons. Education: B. Med. Sci. Hons (Nottm.), 1990, MBBS, 1992 (Nottm.), University of Nottingham Medical School, England; MCRP (UK), 1996; MD (London), 2004. Appointments include: Junior House Officer, General Surgery, Gynaecology, University Hospital, Nottingham, 1992-93; Senior House Officer, Cardiology, CCU and Chest Medicine, The Cardiothoracic Centre, Liverpool, 1993-94; Senior House Officer, General Medicine, Cardiology, Neurology, Diabetes and Endocrinology, Ashford Hospital, Middlesex, 1994-95; Senior House Officer, Neurology, Atkinson Moreley Hospital, London, 1995-96; Senior house Officer, Gastroenterology and General Medicine, St George's, 1996; British Heart Foundation Research Fellow in Cardiology and Honorary Registrar in Cardiology, St George's Hospital Medical School, London and Mayday University Hospital, Croydon, 1997-2000; Specialist Registrar, Cardiology, General Internal Medicine, St Peter's Hospital, Chertsey, Surrey, 2000-2001, Frimley Park Hospital, Camberley, Surrey, 2001-2002; Specialist Registrar in Cardiology, Mayday University Hospital, Thornton Heath, Surrey, 2002-2003, St George's Hospital, Tooting, London, 2003-. Publications: Books as co-author: Drug-induced Long QT Syndrome. Clinical Approaches to Tachyarrhythmias, 2002; Acquired Long QT Syndrome (in press) 2003; 11 book chapters; 12 review articles; 7 original scientific papers; 80 abstracts. Honours: Vale of Trent Faculty of the Royal College of General Practitioners Student Audit Prize, 1992; British Heart Foundation Research Fellowship, 1997-99, Project Grants, 1998-99, 2000-2001; Listed in Who's Who publications and biographical dictionaries. Memberships: Royal College of Physicians of the United Kingdom; Fellow, Royal Society of Medicine. Address: Department of Cardiological Sciences, St George's Hospital Medical School, Cranmer Terrace, London SW17 0RE, England. E-mail: ygyap@aol.com

YAQUB Pervez Raziq, b. 15 December 1961, Peshawar, Pakistan. Engineer. m. Kiran Raziq, 2 daughters. Education: BSc, University of Peshawar, 1981; BSc Engineering with honours, 1985, MSc Engineering with honours, University of Engineering and Technology, Peshawar; PhD, Keio University, Tokyo, Japan, 1998. Appointments: Aircraft Engineer, Pakistan International Airlines, 1986-87; Shift Engineer, Pakistan Water and Power Development Authority, 1987-88; Assistant Divisional Engineer, Pakistan Telecommunication Corporation, 1988-93; English Teacher, YMCA and Minami Junior High School, Tsurugashima, Saitama, Japan, 1995-98; Research Engineer, NOKIA, 1998-99; Assistant Manager, DDI Corporation, Japan, 1999-2001; Research Director, Toshiba America Research Inc, 2001-. Publications: Research papers in professional journals, transactions and international conference proceedings; Editor, Writer, English Newspaper, Keio University. Honours: Scholarship, Rikkyo University, Tokyo, 1993-95; Scholarship, Keio University, 1995-96; Scholarship, Ministry of Education, Government of Japan, 1996-98; Principal Nominee as Visiting Researcher, Rikkyo University. Memberships: IEICE; Christian Students Fellowship Pakistan; Anglican Church Peshawar; Operation Committee and Session Chair, IWDCCA; Chairman, Mobile Wireless Internet Forum, 2000-. Address: 15 Cook Court, Stewartsville, NJ 08886, USA.

YASSUKOVICH Stanislas Michael, b. 5 February 1935, Paris, France. Banker. m. Diana V Obre Townsend, 2 sons, 1 daughter. Education: Deerfield Academy, Deerfield, Massachusetts, USA;

Dictionary of International Biography

Harvard College, Cambridge, Massachusetts, USA; US Marine Corps. Appointments: Partner, White, Weld and Co; Deputy Chairman, European Banking Group; Deputy Chairman, Bristol and West plc; Deputy Chairman, Pennon Group plc; Chairman, Merrill Lynch, Europe and Middle East; Chairman, The Securities Association; Deputy Chairman, London Stock Exchange; Chairman, EASDAQ; Non Executive Director, Telewest Communication plc, Atlas Capital Ltd; Chairman, Park Place Capital; Chairman, Manek Investment Management; Chairman, Henderson Euro-Trust Co plc; Deputy Chairman, ABC International Bank, London. Honours: Commander, Order of the British Empire. Memberships: Fellow, RSA; Whites; Buck's; Brook, New York; Travellers, Paris. Address: 42 Berkeley Square, London W1J 5AW, England. E-mail: smycolto@aol.com

YASUHARA Michiru, b. 22 March 1928, Taiwan. Educator (Aerospace and Mechanical). m. Yumiko Shinohara, 1 son. Education: Bachelor Degree, Engineering, 1951, Dr Engrg, 1962, Department of Applied Mathematics, University Tokyo. Appointments: Research Associate, University of Tokyo, 1954-58; Associate Professor, 1958-67, Professor, 1967-91, Nagoya University; Professor, Aichi Institute of Technology, 1991-; Research Associate: Cornell University, 1963-65; Associate Professor, University Southern California, 1965; Managing Committee Member, Institute of Space and Astronautical Science, 1987-91. Publications: The Day Japanese Space Shuttle Flies, 1984; Computational Fluid Dynamics, co-ed, 1992. Honours: Professor Emeritus, Nagoya University, 1991; Paper Awards, 1993; Honorary member, Japan Society for Aeronautical and Space Science (JSASS), 1997-; World Lifetime Achievement Award, ABI, 1999; Listing in several biographical publications. Memberships: JSASS; Japan Society for Mechanical Engineers. Address: 34-18 Neura Iwasaki, 470-0131 Nissin Aichi, Japan.

YATUSSEVICH Anton Ivanovich, b. 2 January 1947, Brest Region, Belarus. Veterinary Surgeon. m. Valentina, 1 son, 1 daughter. Education: Vitebsk Veterinary Institute, 1972; PhD, Veterinary Science, 1978; Veterinary Science Doctorate, 1989; Associate Professor, 1980; Professor, 1990. Appointments: Farm Veterinary Surgeon, 1972-73; Assistant, 1973-80, Associate Professor, 1980-84, Pro-rector for Academic Affairs, 1984-89, Parasitology Department, Vitebsk Veterinary Medicine Academy; Head, Parasitology Department, 1990-; Rector, Vitebsk Veterinary Medicine Academy, 1998-; Chief Editor, Veterinarnaya Gazeta, 1995-99; Chief Editor, Veterinary Medicine, 2001-. Publications: 26 textbooks and monographs; 12 invention patents; 452 articles. Honours: Honorary Badge, Inventor of the USSR; Silver Medal of the Exhibition of National Economic Achievements of the USSR; Letters of Honour of Vitebsk Region Executive Committee; Letters of Honour by the Ministry of Agriculture; Honourable Scientist of Belarus; Memorable Medal, Christianity 2000. Memberships: Petrovskaya Academy of Sciences and Arts; International Academy of Agrarian Education; International Academy of Information Technologies; International Parasitocenologists Association; Belarusian Society of Protozoologists; Scandinavian Society of Parasitologists. Address: Dovatora Street 7/11, Vitebsk 210026, Republic of Belarus. E-mail: vet@lib.belpak.vitebsk.by

YAZDANI Nur, b. 15 January 1955, Dhaka, Bangladesh. Professor; Graduate Co-ordinator. m. Kelly, 2 sons. Education: BSc, University of Engineering and Technology, Dhaka, Bangladesh, 1977; BS, University of Oklahoma, School of Civil Engineering and Environmental Science, 1981; PhD, Structural Engineering, University of Maryland, 1984. Appointments: Professor and Graduate Co-ordinator, Department of Civil and Environmental Engineering, FAMU-FSU College of Engineering, Tallahassee, Florida, USA. Publications: 47 articles. Honours:

University Service Award, 1990-2001; University Superior Achievement Award, 2003. Memberships: ASCE; ACI. Address: 2525 Pottsdamer Street, Tallahassee, FL 32310, USA. E-mail: yazdan@eng.fsu.edu

YE Minglu, b. 13 April 1936, Fujian Province, China. Professor of Chemistry. m. Jingjuan Tang, 1 son, 1 daughter. Education: Graduated, Chemistry Department, Fudan University, Shanghai, China, 1958. Appointments: Worked in Department of Nuclear Science, 1958-96, then Department of Environmental Science and Engineering, 1996-98, Fudan University, Shanghai, 1958-98; Professor and Director of the Nuclear Chemistry Section, Fudan University; Lectures, Nuclear Chemistry and Application of Nuclear Technology and completed many science research projects; Visiting Scholar, Freie Universitat Berlin (Free University, Berlin), West Germany, 1984-85; Visiting Researcher, Japan Atomic Energy Research Institute, 1994; Retired, 1998. Publications: 5 books include: Radiochemistry Experiments, 1991; Introduction of Environmental Chemistry, 1997; 62 scientific papers. Honours: 5 science and technology prizes awarded by Shanghai Science Commission and Ministry of Nuclear Industry of China, 1984-96; Biography listed in several national and international biographical publications. Memberships: Council Member: Isotope Society of China, 1985-98, Nuclear and Radiochemistry Society of China, 1991-98. Address: Department of Environmental Science and Engineering, Fudan University, Shanghai, 200433, China. E-mail: mingluye@yahoo.com.au

YEAGER Anson Anders, b. 5 June 1919, Salt Lake City, Utah, USA. Newspaper Editor; Writer. m. Ada May Bidwell, 3 sons, 2 daughters. Education: BS, Printing and Rural Journalism, 1947, Honorary Doctor of Public Service, 1991, South Dakota State University; Honorary Doctor of Letters, Dakota State University, 1972. Appointments: Reporter, 1947-55, Sunday Editor, 1955-60, Executive Editor, 1961-77, Editor of Editorial Page, 1961-84, Associate Editor, 1977-84, Contributing Columnist and Writer, 1984-98, Argus Leader, Sioux Falls, South Dakota; Commanding Officer of the 3rd and 1st Battalions of the 147th Field Artillery of the South Dakota Army National Guard, Lieutenant Colonel, 1961-64; Retired, Lieutenant Colonel, US Army, 1979. Publications: Various editor's notebooks and columns in Argus Leader; Book in 2 volumes, Anson Yeager's Stories, 2000. Honours: South Dakota Sigma Delta Chi Award, 1956; Editorial Excellence Award, 1976; Newsman of the Year Award, 1978; Ralph D Casey Minnesota Award for Distinguished Service in Journalism, 1981; Eminent Service Award, 1984; Mass Communications Award, 1985; Les Helgeland Community Service Award, 1985; South Dakota Press Association Distinguished Service Award, 1988; A H Pankow Award, 1995; Jerome J Lohr Award, 1995; Elected to South Dakota Hall of Fame, 1998; Western America Award, 2000. Memberships: American Society of Newspaper Editors; Sigma Delta Chi; Downtown Rotary Club, Sioux Falls; American Legion; Veterans of Foreign Wars; Methodist Church; Sioux Falls Area Chamber of Commerce. Address: 2204 West 28th Street, Sioux Falls, SD 57105-2404, USA.

YEGOROV Vladimir Grigoryevich, b. 26 November 1938, Moscow, Russia. Regional Governor. m. Lyudmila Yegorova, 1 son, 1 daughter. Education: Higher Naval College with distinction, 1962; Naval Academy with distinction, 1984; Degree with honours, Academy of the General Staff of the Russian Armed Forces; Candidate of Military Sciences. Appointments: Officer in the Northern Fleet, 1962; Officer in the Baltic Fleet, 1964; Executive Officer on antisubmarine warfare ship Obraztsovy, 1967; Executive Officer on antisubmarine warfare ship Bditelny, Commanding Officer of the Obraztsovy, 1971; Head of the Staff, Vice-commander of the Destroyer Brigade, 1974-76; Commander of the Guided Missile Ships Brigade 1976-83; Commander, Guided Missile Fast Boats Brigade, 1983-85; Commander, Baltijsk Naval Base, 1985-86; Commander, 5th Mediterranean Flotilla of the Black Sea Fleet, 1986-88; Deputy Commander of the Baltic Fleet, 1988-91; Commander of the Baltic Fleet with military rank of Admiral, 1991-2000; Elected Head of the Administration (Governor) of Kaliningrad Oblast, 2000. Publications: Chief of Authors Collective and Author of monographs of the 6 language edition of History of the Baltic Fleet. Honours: Rank III Orders For Service to the Fatherland; Rank II and III orders For Military Merits and for Service to the Fatherland in the Armed Forces; Rank I for Combat Training (Syria); 23 medals and arms of honour; Laureate of the State Prize of the Russian Federation in the field of science and technology; Honourable Citizen of Kaliningrad; Honorary Member, Swedish Royal Naval Society; Honorary Member, St Petersburg Naval Assembly. Memberships: Honorary Member, Royal Swedish Society of Naval Sciences; Russian Academy of Military and Historical Sciences. Address: ul DM Donskogo 1, Regional Administration, 236007 Kaliningrad, Russia. E-mail: first@gov.kaliningrad.ru Website: www.gov.kaliningrad.ru

YELTSIN Boris Nikolayevich, b. 1 February 1931, Sverdlovsk, Russia. Politician (Retired). Education: Urals Polytech Institute. Appointments: Foreman, Chief of Works, Chief Engineer, Head, Construction Administration, Yushgorstvoy Trust, 1955-63; Chief Engineer, Director, Sverdlovsk House Building Complex, 1963-68; Member, CPSU, 1961-90; Secretary, Sverdlovsk Provincial Committee, 1968-76; 1st Secretary, District Central Committee, Sverdlovsk, 1976-85; Member, Party Central Committee, 1981; Secretary, Central Committee, 1985-86; 1st Secretary, Moscow Party Committee, 1985-87; Candidate Member, Politburo, 1986-88; 1st Deputy Chairman, State Committee for Construction, 1987-89; Chairman, Committee for Construction and Architecture, 1989-90; Member, Congress of People's Deputies, 1989-91; Chairman, Supreme Soviet, RSFSR, 1990-91; President, Russian Federation, 1991-99; Resigned, 1999; Acting Head, Russian Federation Defence Ministry, 1992; Supreme Commander of Russian Army, 1992-99. Publications: Against the Grain, autobiography, 1990; Three Days, 1992; Memoirs: The View from the Kremlin, 1990, 1994, 2000. Honours: Olympic Gold Order, 1992; German Press Award, 1996.

YENTOB Alan, b. 11 March 1947, England. Television Administrator. 1 son, 1 daughter, by Philippa Walker. Education: University of Grenoble, France; University of Leeds. Appointments: BBC General Trainee, 1968; Producer, Director, 1970-, Head of Music & Arts, 1985-88, BBC TV; Controller, BBC 2, 1988-93, BBC 1, 1993-96, BBC Director of Programmes, 1996-97; BBC Director of TV, 1997-2000, of Drama, Entertainment and Children's Programmes, 2000-. Honours: Fellow, RCA, RIBA. Memberships: Board of Directors, Riverside Studios, 1984-88, British Film Institute Production Board, 1985-93; British Screen Advisory Council; Advisory Committee, Institute of Contemporary Arts; Council, Royal Court Theatre; Governor, National Film School, 1998-; South Bank Board, 1999-. Address: BBC Television, Television Centre, Wood Lane, London W12 7RJ, England.

YEO Jung-Sou, b. 10 May 1950, Gimcheon, Korea. Professor. m. Taesun Kim, 1 son, 1 daughter. Education: BS, Department of Animal Science, Yeungnam University, Korea, 1973; MS, 1978, PhD, 1981, Department of Animal Science, Seoul National University. Appointments: Postdoctoral, University of Minnesota, USA, 1984-85; Concurrent, Researcher, Rural Development Organisation, Korea, 1988-92, Director, Biotechnology Institute, Yeungnam University, Korea, 1987-99; Dean of Natural Resources

College, Yeungnam University, Korea, 2001-. Publications: Animal Biotechnology and another 10 publications; Linkage Mapping and QTL on Chromosome 6 in Korean Cattle (Hanwoo) and another 80 articles. Honours: The Best Agricultural Research, Minister of Agriculture, Korea; The Best Researcher, Korean Society of Animal Science and Technology, Korea. Memberships: Korean Society of Animal Science and Technology; American Poultry Science. Address: School of Biotechnology, Yeungnam University, Gyeongsan, Gyeongbuk, 712-749 Korea. E-mail: jsyeo@yu.ac.kr

YESUFU Momoh Lawani, b. 22 June 1947, Agbede, Nigeria. Brigadier General (Retired); Academic; Sociologist; Defence Consultant. m. Amina Yesufu, deceased 22 April 2003, 5 sons, 3 daughters. Education: Graduate, Nigerian Defence Academy, Class 1970-71; Basic Officers Armour Course, Armoured Corps Centre and School, India, 1974; Gunnery, Royal Armoured Corps Centre, UK, 1975; US Army Armor School Officers Advanced Course, Fort Knox, 1980; psc (CSC), 1983; Graduate Certificate in Faculty Development, Fort Leavenworth, USA, 1985; Master of Military Art and Science (MMAS), Fort Leavenworth, USA, 1985; psc(+), Nigeria, 1987, psc(+)Ghana, 1989; PhD, Sociology, University of Jos, Nigeria, 2001. Appointments: Primary School Teacher, 1967; Tutor, Western Boys High School, Benin, 1968-69; Platoon Commander, 1969-70, 1971-72; Grade 3 Staff Officer, 1972-75; Squadron Leader, 1975-77; Commanding Officer, 1972-86; Peace Keeping Company Commander, Chad, 1978; Staff Officer Grade I Policy, Army Headquarters; Directing Staff, 1986-89, 1990-91; Colonel Policy, Army Headquarters, 1991-93; Colonel General Staff, 1993-96, Brigade Commander, 1996, 1997-99; Corps Commander, 1999-2000; Directing Staff, War College, 2000-2001; Senior Fellow/Moderator, National Institute for Policy and Strategic Studies, Kuru, Nigeria, 2002-; Chairman and Member of various Committees, 1991-2003. Publications: Combat Readiness for the Nigerian Army, 1983; The Essence of Good Teaching, 1988; Contribution of Individual Personnel Replacement System to Unit Cohesion, 1990; The Main Battle Tank: Its Implications for Training in the Nigerian Army, 1992; The Effects of Crises on Women and Children, 1999; Manoeuvrability of Armoured Formation in Limited Warfare, 2000; Pensions and Post Service Life in Nigeria, 2002; Post Service and Housing Scheme in Nigeria, 2002. Honours: Distinguished Service Star; Meritorious Service Star; Forces Service Star; Defence Service Medal; National Service Medal; Republic Medal; Silver Jubilee Medal; Recognised Service to the Nation Medal. Memberships: Fellow, War College; Fellow, Nigerian Institute of Management; Member, Institute of Personnel Development, UK; Nigerian Institute of International Affairs; IBB International Golf and Country Club, Abuja; Rayfield Golf Club, Jos. Address: Plot 6 Army Vacated Area, Rayfield, Jos, PO Box 8401 Anglo Jos Post Office, Jos, 930007, Nigeria. E-mail: lawyesufu@yahoo.com

YIH Kuang-Hway, b. 28 August 1967, Taichung, Taiwan, Republic of China. Chemist; Educator. m. Jia-Ling Chu, 1 son, 1 daughter. Education: BS, Chemistry, 1989, MS, Chemistry, 1991, National Chengjung University, Tainan, Taiwan; PhD, National Taiwan University, Taipei, Taiwan, 1995; Exchange Student, Tübingen University, Germany, 1994-95. Appointments: Assistant Professor, 1997-2000, Director of Personnel, 1997-2000, Associate Professor, 2000-2003, Professor, 2003-, Dean of Academic Affairs, 2000-2001, 2003-, Hungkuang University, Taiwan. Publications: Organic Chemistry, 2001; Synoptic Chemistry, 2001; Thiazoliumyldiphenylphosphine Tungsten: Trigonal Twist rotational behavior of allyldithio Molybdenum Complexes; Phosphine Transfer from Tungsten to Palladium; 1,3-dithiolliumyldiphenylphosphine Tungsten Complexes; Endo-exo Allyl rotational behavior; Sulfur-Assisted Dissociation of Phosphine of Chloride in Palladium Complex; Palladium and

Dictionary of International Biography

Platinum carbene complexes. Honours: Publication Grade A Award, National Science Council, Taipei, 2001; Exemplary Teacher Award, China National Education Association, 2002. Membership: Chinese Chemical Society, Member of Editorial Board, 1997-. Address: No 73, Alley 41, Lane 93, Sec 3 Zoho Road, Taichung 406, Taiwan, Republic of China. E-mail: khyih@sunrise.hk.edu.tw

YING Mingde, b. 26 February 1929, Wuxi, Jiangsu. Medical Doctor and Professor. m. Jianming Bei, 1 son. Education: MB. Nanjing Medical University (former National Jiangsu Medical College), 1946-52; MD, Beijing Medical University (former Beijing University Medical College), 1951-53. Appointments: Assistant, Resident Doctor, 1955-56; Visiting Doctor, Lecturer, 1956-81; Associate Professor, Vice Chief, 1981-86; Chief, Professor, 1986-; Retirement, 1995; Member, Medical Councillors Office, 1995; Member, Senior Experts Consultation Centre, 1997; Emeritus Professor, 2000-; Honorary Member, International Biographical Centre Advisory Council; Honorary Member, American Biographical Association Board of Advisors. Publications: Fundamentals of Otolaryngology; Dizziness; Emergency Otolaryngology; Otolaryngology - Head and Neck Surgery; Chapters in 15 medical books; 150 medical articles in professional journals. Honours: 3rd municipal and 4th provincial science and technology award; Central People's Government allowance. Memberships: Chairman, Society of Otolaryngology, CMA, Nanjing and Jiangsu Branches; Otolaryngology Committee, Chinese Association of Integration of TCM and Western Medicine, Jiangsu Branch; Member, Allergy Committee, Chinese Society of Microbiology and Immunology; ARS; AAO-HNS; ACAAI; ISOAI; IAACI. Address: Department of Otolaryngology, First Affiliated Hospital of Nanjing Medical University, Jiangsu Province Hospital, 300 Guangzhou Road, 210029 Nanjing, PR China.

YOCUM Harrison Gerald, 2 April 1923, Bethlehem, Pennsylvania, USA. Horticulturalist; Botanist. Education: BS, Pennsylvania State University, 1955; MS, Rutgers University, 1961. Appointments: Horticulture Instructor, University of Tennessee, 1957-59; Research Assistant, Geochronology, 1960-68, Environmental Research Laboratory, 1969-76, University of Arizona; Superintendent of Landscaping, Tucon Airport Authority, 1976-82; Instructor, Pima Community College, 1976-. Publications: Articles for professional journals. Honours: Life Member, Pennsylvania State Alumni; Life Member, Ancient and Accepted Scottish Rite of Freemasonry; Founder, Tucson Botanical Garden; Many awards from the Gardeners of Tucson. Memberships: American Horticultural Society; Men's Garden Club, Tucson; Tucson Cactus and Succulent Society; International Palm Society; El Paso Cactus and Rock Club; Tucson Gem and Mineral Society; Old Pueblo Lapidary Club; Deming Mineral Society; National Geographic Society; Arizona-Sonora Desert Museum; Huachuca Vigilantes; Life Member, Pennsylvania State Alumni Association; Pennsylvania Club, Tucson; Fraternal Order of Police Associates; Life Member, North American Hunting Club; Boyce-Thompson Arboretum; Shriners; Masons; Scottish Rite; Lutheran; National Trust for Historic Preservation; Arizona Preservation Foundation. Address: 1628 N Jefferson Ave, Tucson, AZ 85712-4204, USA.

YOELIN Sherwin D, b. 25 February 1935, Denver, Colorado, USA. Petroleum Engineer. m. Rochelle, 2 sons, 1 daughter. Education: BS, Petroleum Engineering, University of Oklahoma, 1957; MS, Petroleum Engineering, Colorado School of Mines, 1963. Appointments: Petroleum Engineer, several companies, 1957-74; Consulting Petroleum Engineer, Oil and Gas Operator, 1974-. Publications: Numerous articles in Journal of Petroleum Technology. Honours: Sigma Tau; Pi Epsilon Tau; Tau Beta Pi; Scabbard and Blade. Memberships: Society of Petroleum

Evaluation Engineers; Society of Petroleum Engineers; CIPA; IOPA. Address: 6389 Ebb Tide Way, Carlsbad, CA 92009, USA. E-mail: sdyengr@pacbell.net

YONEI Yoshikazu, b. 18 January 1958, Tokyo, Japan. Gastroenterologist. m. Keiko Nakatani, 1 son, 1 daughter. Education: MD, 1982, PhD, 1986, Keio University. Appointments: Visiting Researcher, Center for Ulcer Research and Education, University of California Los Angeles, 1986-89; Attending Physician, Nippon Kokan Hospital, 1989-; Board of Directors, Shushin Kai Medical Foundation, 1996-2002; Consultant, Asakusa Police Station, 1997-2001; Reviewer, Journal of Gastroenterology and Hepatology, 1997-; Chairman of Board of Directors, Keiyo Kai Medical Foundation, 1997-2002; President, Mind Works Inc, 1999-2001; President, Cenegenics Japan, 2000-02; Secretary General, Association of Anti-Aging Medicine Japan, 2001. Publication: Mast Cell, 1990. Honours: Named Honorary Citizenship, Botucatu City, Sao Paulo. Memberships: Keio Sakura Reunion; Keio Medical School Yacht Club; Sympathy for H Pylori Association. Address: 5-21-26 Ryokuen Izumi-ku, Yokohama, Kanagawa 245-0002, Japan.

YONG Suzanne, b. 3 December 1961, California, USA. Systems Consultant. Education: BSc, Computer Information Systems, Arizona State University, 1979-82, 1983-84; Certificate in Chinese Language Studies, National Taiwan Normal University, 1982-83; Continuing Extension, Advances in Software Engineering, University of California at Irvine, 1988. Appointments: Technical Writer, Multitech; Acceptance Tester, Prudential; Associate Programmer Analyst, Avco Financial Services; Systems Analyst, Douglas Aircraft Company; Systems Consultant, Owner, InfoSolutions International, 1990-. Honours: Listed in national and international biographical dictionaries. Memberships: Association for Systems Management; Quantitative Systems Club; Alpha Mu Gamma; French Club; Civil Air Patrol. Address: PO Box 26226, San Francisco, CA 94126-6226, USA. E-mail: suzanne_yong@usa.net

YOO Vak Yeong, b. 28 June 1947, Seoul. Physician. Education: EWHA Women's Medical University, 1968-74. Appointments: Director of Hospital, Cheongvak Primebeyond Hospital; YVY-QOL Meno-Osteoporosis Group President. Publications: Quality of Midbeyonds Women's Life; Phytoestrogen; How to Manage a Menopause Clinic; Aging and Gender Specific Quality of Life; Journal of the Korean Geriatrics Society; Journal YVY-QOL Meno/Osteoporosis. Memberships: North American Menopause Society; The Endocrine Society; International Menopause Society; American Society of Bone Mineral Research; National Osteoporosis Foundation Professional Partner Network. Address: 582 Shinsa Dong Kangnam Ku Seoul 135-120, Korea.

YOON Seung Kew, b. 12 April 1959, Kyungki-do, Korea. Professor; Physician. m. So-Hyun Kim, 1 son, 1 daughter. Education: MD, Catholic University of Korea, 1985; Postgraduate Training, Internal Medicine and Hepatology, Catholic University Hospital; PhD, Catholic University Graduate School, 1995. Appointments: Clinical Instructor, 1992-94, Full Time Teaching Staff, 1994-96, Assistant Professor, 1996-2000, Associate Professor of Medicine and Hepatology, 2000-, Kangnam St Mary's Hospital, Seoul, Korea. Publications: Over 100 papers and abstracts on various topics in liver diseases. Honours: Listed in Who's Who publications and biographical dictionaries. Memberships: Korean Association of Internal Medicine; Korean Association of Hepatology; American Association for the Study of Liver Disease. Address: Department of Internal Medicine, Kangnam St Mary's Hospital, #505 Banpo-dong, Seocho-ku, Seoul 137-701, Republic of Korea. E-mail: yoonsk@catholic.ac.kr

YOON Tae Ki, b. 11 June 1951, Kyungnam, Korea. Physician. m. Kyung Ae Jun-Yoon, 1 son, 1 daughter. Education: MD, Yonsei University College of Medicine, 1975; Resident, Severance Hospital, Department of Obstetrics and Gynaecology, 1983; Diplomate, Korean Board of Obstetrics and Gynaecology, 1983; Postdoctoral Fellow, Reproductive Endocrinology and Infertility, Yale University, Connecticut, USA, 1989. Appointments: Director, Infertility, Medical Centre, CHA, General Hospital, Seoul, Korea, 1990; Associate professor, Department of Obstetrics and Gynaecology, Yonsei University, Seoul, Korea, 1994; Associate Professor, Department of Obstetrics and Gynaecology, Kyung Hee University, Seoul, Korea, 1994; Professor, Department of Obstetrics and Gynaecology, College of Medicine, Pochon CHA University, 1997-. Publications: Laparoscopic Tubal Anastomosis, Fertility Outcome, 1997; Pregnancy and delivery underwent on oocyte bank program, 2000; Laparoscopic Tubal Anastomosis, 2000; Live Births after Vitrification of oocytes, 2003. Honours: The Prize Paper, Korea Federation of Science and Technology, 1997; The Plenary Prize Paper, IFFS '98/ASRM, 1998; The Best Video Award of ASRM, 2000. Memberships: Korean Society of Obstetricians and Gynaecologists; Korean Fertility Society; ASRM; SSR; ESHRE. Address: Sampoong Apt #12-606, Seocho-dong, Seocho-gu, Seoul, Korea 137-799. E-mail: tkyoon@cha.ac.kr

YORK Michael (Michael York-Johnson), b. 27 March 1942, Fulmer, England, Actor. m. Patricia McCallum, 1968. Education: University College, Oxford. Appointments: Dundee Repertory Co, 1964, National Theatre Company, 1965; Guest Lecturer, Chair, CA Youth Theatre. Creative Works: TV appearances include: The Forsyte Saga; Rebel in the Grave; True Patriot; Much Ado About Nothing; Jesus of Nazareth; A Man Called Intrepid; For Those I Loved; The Weather in The Streets; The Master of Ballantrae; Space; The Far Country; Are You My Mother, 1986; Ponce de Leon, 1987; Knot's Landing, 1987; The Four Minute Mile, 1988; The Lady and the Highwayman, 1988; The Heat of the Day, 1988; A Duel of Love, 1990; The Road to Avonlea, 1990; Teklab, 1994; September, 1995; A Young Connecticut Yankee in King Arthur's Court, 1995; Not of This Earth, 1995; The Ring, 1996; True Women, 1996; The Haunting of Hall House, 2000; The Lot, 2001; Founding Fathers, Founding Brothers; Films include: The Return of the Musketeers, 1988; Till We Meet Again, 1989; The Heat of the Day, 1989; The Night of the Fox, 1990; Eline Vere, 1990; Duel of Hearts, 1990; The Wanderer, 1991; The Long Shadow, 1991; Wide Sargasso Sea, 1991; Rochade, 1991; Discretion Assured, 1993; The Shadow of a Kiss, 1994; Fall From Grace, 1994; Gospa, 1995; Goodbye America, 1996; Austin Powers, 1996; Dark Planet, 1996; The Ripper, 1997; A Knight in Camelot, 1998; Perfect Little Angels, 1998; Wrongfully Accused, 1998; One Hell of a Guy, 1998; The Omega Code, 1999; Borstal boy, 2000; Megiddo, 2001; Austin Powers in Goldmember, 2002. Publications: The Courage of Conviction, 1986; Voices of Survival, 1987; Travelling Player (autobiography), 1991; Accidentally on Purpose (autobiography), 1992; A Shakespearian Actor Prepares, 2000; Dispatches From Armageddon, 2002. Honours: Numerous. Address: c/o Andrew Manson, 288 Munster Road, London SW6 6BQ, England. Website: www.michaelyork.net

YORK Susannah, b. 9 January 1942, London, England. Actress. m. Michael Wells, 1960, divorced 1976, 1 son, 1 daughter. Education: Royal Academy of Dramatic Art. Creative Works: Films include: Tunes of Glory, 1960; The Greengage Summer, 1961; Freud, 1962; Tom Jones, 1963; The Seventh Dawn, 1964; Act One Scene Nun, 1964; Sands of the Kalahari, 1965; Scruggs, 1966; Kaleidoscope, 1966; A Man for All Seasons, 1966; Sebastian, 1967; The Killing of Sister George, 1968; Duffy, 1968; Lock Up Your Daughters, 1969; They Shoot Horses, Don't They?, 1969;

Country Dance, 1970; Jane Eyre, 1970; Zee and Co, 1971; Happy Birthday Wanda June, 1971; Images, 1972; The Maids, Gold, 1974; Conduct Unbecoming, 1974; That Lucky Touch, 1975; Skyriders, 1976; Eliza Fraser, 1976; The Shout, 1977; The Silent Partner, Superman II, 1980; Yellowbeard, Fatal Attraction, 1985; A Summer Story, 1987; Melancholia, 1988; Just Ask for Diamond, 1988; Princess, 1993; TV appearances: The Crucible; Fallen Angels; Second Chance; We'll Meet Again; The Other Side of Me; Macho; Trainer; Devices and Desires; Producer, The Big One, 1983; Numerous stage appearances. Publications: Childrens books: In Search of Unicorns; Larks Castle. Honours include: Best Actress Award, Cannes Film Festival. Address: c/o Peters Fraser & Dunlop, 34-43 Russell Street, Drury House, London WC2B 5HA, England.

YORKE Margaret, (Margaret Beda Nicholson), b. 30 January 1924, Surrey, England. Writer. m. Basil Nicholson, 1945, divorced 1957, 1 son, 1 daughter. Appointments: Assistant Librarian, St Hilda's College, Oxford, 1959-60; Library Assistant, Christ Church, Oxford, 1963-65; Chairman, Crime Writers Association, 1979-80. Publications: Summer Flight, 1957; Pray Love Remember, 1958; Christopher, 1959; Deceiving Mirror, 1960; The China Doll, 1961; Once a Stranger, 1962; The Birthday, 1963; Full Circle, 1965; No Fury, 1967; The Apricot Bed, 1968; The Limbo Ladies, 1969; Dead in the Morning, 1970; Silent Witness, 1972; Grave Matters, 1973; No Medals for the Major, 1974; Mortal Remains, 1974; The Small Hours of the Morning, 1975; Cast for Death, 1976; The Cost of Silence, 1977; The Point of Murder, 1978; Death on Account, 1979; The Scent of Fear, 1980; The Hand of Death, 1981; Devil's Work, 1982; Find Me a Villain, 1983; The Smooth Face of Evil, 1984; Intimate Kill, 1985; Safely to the Grave, 1986; Evidence to Destroy, 1987; Speak for the Dead, 1988; Crime in Question, 1989; Admit to Murder, 1990; A Small Deceit, 1991; Criminal Damage, 1992; Dangerous to Know, 1993; Almost the Truth, 1994; Pieces of Justice, 1994; Serious Intent, 1995; A Question of Belief, 1996; Act of Violence, 1997; False Pretences, 1998; The Price of Guilt, 1999; A Case to Answer, 2000; Cause for Concern, 2001. Honours: Swedish Academy of Detection, 1982; Cartier Diamond Dagger, Crime Writers Association, 1999 Address: c/o Curtis Brown Ltd, Haymarket House, 28/29 Haymarket, London SW1Y 4SP, England.

YOSHIDA Fumitake, b. 20 March 1913, Saitama, Japan. Professor Emeritus, Kyoto University. m. Kazuko, deceased, 1 son, 1 daughter. Education: BEng, 1937, Dr Eng, 1951, Kyoto University. Appointments; Chemical Engineer, Hitachi Ltd, 1937-45; Assistant Professor, 1945-51, Professor, 1951-76, Professor emeritus, 1976-, Kyoto University; Visiting Professor, University of California, Berkeley, 1963; Visiting Professor, University of Pennsylvania, 1970; Guest Professor, University of Dortmund, 1987. Publications: Around 60 research papers; Book: Chemical Engineering and Artificial Organs, with Sakai, in Japanese, 1993. Honours: Distinguished Service Citation, University Wisconsin, 1988; Honorary Dr Ing, University of Dortmund, 1992. Memberships: National Academy of Engineering, USA; American Institute of Chemical Engineers; American Chemical Society; Society Chemical Engineers, Japan; Japanese Society of Artificial Organs. Address: 2 Matsugasaki-Yobikaeshi, Sakyo-ku, Kyoto 606-0912, Japan.

YOSHIDA Kohei, b. 1 May 1919, Gifu, Japan. University Professor. m. 1 son, 2 daughters. Education: Graduate, Faculty of Economics, Keio University, Tokyo, Japan, 1929; Master of Business Administration (Management), Meijo University, Nagoya, Japan, 1929-31; Doctoral Course, Freedom of Religion and State Power, Newport University, California, USA, 1977-81; Doctoral Course, Cultural Anthropology, Oriental University, Los Angeles, USA, 1980-85. Appointments: President, Japanese

Armour Institute, Japan, 1950; Chairman, Board of Directors, Japanese Museum Association, Gifu, Japan, 1965; Director, International Conference of Museums, Japan, 1970; President, Japanese Armour Museum, Sekigahara, Japan, 1970; Professor, Chubu-Gakuin University, Japan, 1975; Director, Society of Aesthetic Buddhist Monks, Japan, 1975; Professor, Ohgaki Women's College, Japan, 1975; Representative Director, Coterie Magazine "Bungei-Nagara", 1984-; Director, Society of Christian Studies, Newport University, 2001. Publications: Freedom of Religion and State Power- Mino's Christian Mission in Japan during WWII (doctoral dissertation); A Study of Iron in Mountain Worship in Mount Hakusan, Gifu, Japan; Christian Studies in Edo Period, Gifu Area, Japan; 30 other books. Honours: MBA, Business Administration Management; PhD, Literature; PhD, Philosophy; PhD, Christian Studies, University of Newport, USA. Memberships include: Japan Society of Sentiment and Culture; Japan Institute of Sentiment and Culture; Japanese Armour Association; Japanese Society of Aesthetic Buddhist Monks; Gifu 1.8 Association; Japanese Museum Association; International Conference of Museums, Paris, France. Address: 2-48 Shio-machi, Gifu, Gifu Prefecture, Japan 500-8127.

YOSHIHARA Hiroshi, b. 16 October 1963, Tokyo, Japan. Associate Professor. Education: Bachelor of Agriculture, 1987, Doctor of Philosophy, 1995, Forest Products Department, Faculty of Agriculture, University of Tokyo, Japan. Appointments: Research Associate, Faculty of Agriculture, University of Tokyo, Japan, 1988-96; Associate Professor, Faculty of Science and Engineering, Shimane University, Japan, 1996-. Publications: Articles in scientific journals include: Resistance curve for the mode II fracture toughness of wood obtained by end-notched flexure test under the constant loading point displacement condition, 2003. Honours: Progress Award, 1994, Prize, 2001, Japan Wood Research Society. Memberships: Japan Wood Research Society; Wood Technological Association of Japan; Society of Materials Science, Japan. Address: Department of Natural Resources Process Engineering, Faculty of Science and Engineering, Shimane University, Nishikawazu-cho 1060, Matsue, Shimane, 690-8504, Japan. E-mail: yosihara@riko.shimane-u.ac.jp

YOSHIOKA Shoichi, b. 3 November 1962, Okayama, Japan. Geophysicist. m. Masako Kunita. Education: BSc, Kobe University, Japan, 1985; MSc, 1987, PhD, 1990, Kyoto University, Japan. Appointments: Postdoctoral Fellow, Kyoto University, Japan, 1990-91; Postdoctoral Fellow, University of Tokyo, 1991-92; Postdoctoral Fellow, Utrecht University, The Netherlands, 1992-94; Assistant Professor, Ehime University, Matsuyama, Japan, 1994-97; Associate Professor, Kyushu University, 1997-. Publications: Contributor of numerous articles to professional journals. Memberships: American Geophysical Union; Seismological Society of Japan. Address: Aquitaine 203, Maimatsubara 5-12-5, Higashi Ward, Fukuoka 813-0042, Japan.

YOSHIYAMA Mitsuharu, b. 26 August 1964, Sawara, Chiba, Japan. Physician. Education: MD, Showa University School of Medicine, 1989; PhD, Showa University Graduate School of Medicine, 1993. Appointments: Research Associate, Department of Pharmacology, University of Pittsburgh School of Medicine, 1989-98; Instructor, 1998, Research Assistant Professor, 1998-2004, Department of Pharmacology, University of Pittsburgh, School of Medicine, USA; Showa University, Fujigaoka Hospital, 2000; Department of Neurology, Chiba University Graduate School of Medicine, 2000-2003; Asahi Hospital for Neurological Diseases, 2001-2003; Yamanashi Onsen Hospital, 2003; Adjunct Professor, Department of Urology, University of Yamanashi Interdisciplinary Graduate School of Medicine and Engineering, 2003. Memberships: Society for Neuroscience, 1990-; International Brain

Research Organisation, 1990-; International Continence Society, 2004. Address: Yamanashi Onsen Hospital, 855 Komatsu, Kasugai-cho, Higashi-Yamanashi-gun, Yamanashi, 406-0004 Japan. E-mail: pxn15164@nifty.com

YOUNG Ian George, b. 5 January 1945, London, England. Poet; Writer; Editor. Appointments: Director, Catalyst Press, 1969-80, Director, TMW Communications, 1990-. Publications: Poetry: White Garland, 1969; Year of the Quiet Sun, 1969; Double Exposure, 1970; Cool Fire, 1970; Lions in the Stream, 1971; Some Green Moths, 1972; The Male Muse, 1973; Invisible Words, 1974; Common-or-Garden Gods, 1976; The Son of the Male Muse, 1983; Sex Magick, 1986. Fiction: On the Line, 1981. Non-Fiction: The Male Homosexual in Literature, 1975, 2nd edition, 1982; Overlooked and Underrated, 1981; Gay Resistance, 1985; The AIDS Dissidents, 1993; The Stonewall Experiment, 1995; The Aids Cult, 1997. Honours: Several Canada Council and Ontario Arts Council Awards. Membership: International Psychohistory Association. Address: 2483 Gerrard Street East, Scarborough, Ontario M1N 1W7, Canada.

YOUNG John McIntosh (Sir), b. 17 December 1919, Melbourne, Australia. Lawyer; Barrister. m. Elisabeth Mary Twining, 1 son, 2 daughters. Education: MA, Brasenose College, Oxford (Hon Fellow, 1991); LLB, Melbourne University. Appointments: Barrister, 1949-1974; QC, 1961; Chief Justice, Supreme Court of Victoria, 1974-91; Lieutenant Governor of Victoria, 1974-95; Chancellor, Order of St John in Australia, 1982-91; Chief Scout of Australia, 1989-96; Chairman, Police Board of Victoria, 1992-98. Publications: Australian Company Law and Practice (jointly); Articles in legal journals. Honours: KCMG, 1975; K St J, 1977; Hon LLD (Monash), 1986; AC, 1989; GC St J, 1991; Hon LLD (Melbourne) 1989. Address: 2/18 Huntingtower Road, Armadale 3143, Australia.

YOUNG Raymond James, b. 2 November 1922, Howard, Kansas. Retired Education Educator. m. (1) Blenda E Thompson, deceased, 1 son, 1 daughter, (2) Ruby I Wright, 2 daughters. Education: BS, Kansas State Teachers College, 1948; MS, 1949; EdD, University Colorado, 1950; Post-graduate, University Idaho, 1986. Appointments: Teacher, Principal, Elk County School, Howard, Kansas, 1941-42; U.S. Army, 1943-45, WWII ETO; Assistant Professor, Oklahoma State University, Stillwater, 1950-54; Associate Professor, University Oklahoma, Norman, 1954-55; University Illinois, Champaign 1955-59; Professor, University Michigan, Ann Arbor, 1959-69, Washington State University, Pullman, 1976-89; Professor Emeritus 1990; Senior Consultant Education, Arthur D Little Inc, Cambridge, Massachusetts, major projects in Algiers, Greece and Holland in addition to USA, 1969-75; Principal Associate, McMannis Associates Inc. Washington, DC, 1975-76; developed citizens participatory process for starting new 2 year colleges. Publications: Major co-author: The School and The Community, 1955; Summer Sessions in Colleges and Universities, 1991; Contribution of over 150 articles to professional journals. Honours: A number over a Lifetime. Memberships: VFW, DAV and American Legion, post Commander, 1997-2000; District Commander, 1998-99, Elks, Ind Order of Odd Fellows; Phi Delta Kappa, NEA, Kappa Delta Phi. Address: PO Box 4573, East Lansing, MI 48826, USA.

YU Bao Ming, b. 1934, Shanghai, China. Colorectal Surgeon. Education: MD, Shanghai Second Medical College, 1956. Appointments: Chief Surgeon, Professor of Surgery, Rui Jun Hospital, Shanghai, 1990-; Teacher of doctoral degree level, 1995-. Publications: Numerous articles in professional journals. Honours: Third Prize, Scientific and Technological Progress, Ministry of Hygiene, 1994; Second Prize, Scientific and Technological

Progress, Shanghai, 1994; Third Prize, National Education Committee, 1996. Memberships: Chairman, Division of Anorectal Surgery, Chinese Surgical Association; Member, Chinese Medical Association; Board Member, Oncology and General Surgery Association; China Ostomy Society; Shanghai Branch, Chinese Medical Association; International Gastro-Surgical Club. Address: Department of Surgery, Rui Jin Hospital, 197 Rui Jin Er Road, Shanghai 200025, China.

YU Chunghsun, b. 8 October 1932, Taibei, Taiwan, China. University Professor. m. Huie Zhang, 2 daughters. Education: Doctor of Economics, School of Economics, Kobe University, Japan. Appointments: Professor, Faculty of Management, Toho University, Nagoya, Japan. Publications: Overseas Ethnic Chinese Economy, 1996; Ethnic Chinese: Their Economy, Politics and Culture, 2000. Memberships: President, Japan Society of Overseas Ethnic Studies. Address: 1-378-1-A508 Mukaikogane, Nagareyamashi, Chiba 270-0143, Japan.

YUAN Yi Quan, b. 27 July 1938, Wu Xi, China. Physician. m. Liu Xuefen, 1 daughter. Education: Southeast University, Nanjing, China. Appointments: Joined Communist Party of China, 1961; Bachelor, Southeast University of Nanjing, China, 1961; Lecturer, Department of Radio, Southeast University, Nanjing, China, 1987-91; Professor, 1992-. Publications: Papers: IEEE Transactions on UFFC, 1991, 1992, 1995, 1997; Sensors and Actuators, 1993; Book: Ultrasonic Transducer, 1992; Lately Acoustic Principle and Its Application, 1994; Lately Ultrasonic Principle and its Application, 1996; Patents. Honours: Second Class Awards for Science and Technology: State Education Committee, 1987; China State Shipbuilding Corporation, 1992; State Education Committee, 1996. Memberships: Visiting Research Fellow, Shanghai Institute Ceramics Chinese Academy of Science, 1984-90; Key Opening Key-Opening Laboratory Sensor, 1990-94; Modern Acoustics Laboratory, Nanjing V, 1994-96; Glacier Frozen Chinese Association Technology (Electronics Institute, Acoustics Institute). Address: Southeast University, Si Pai Lou 2, Nanjing 21008, China.

YULMETYEV Renat, b. 14 December 1940, Kazan, Russia. Physicist; Educator. m. Dinara Yulmetyeva, 1 son. Education: MSc, 1962, PhD, 1966, Kazan State University, Russia. Appointments: Associate Professor, 1965-70, Docent, 1970-83, Professor of Physics, 1983-, Dean of Physical Mathematical Faculty, 1971-72, 1978-86, Head of the Chair of Theoretical Physics, 1984-, Kazan State Pedagogical University. Publications: Articles in international journals including: Physical Review E; Physica A; Physics Letters A; Journal of Physics; Acta Physica Polonica; Physica Status Solidi; JETP; JETP Letters; Non-Linear Phenomena and Complex Systems; Soviet Physics-Uspekhi; 104 papers. Honour: Soros Professor, 1994-2001. Memberships: Active Member, Russian Academy of Nature, 1997-; Russian Physical Society; International Advisory Board of "Nonlin.phen@compl.syst". Address: Department of Physics, Kazan State Pedagogical University, Mezhlauk Str 1, 420021 Kazan, Russia. E-mail: rmy@theory.kazan.spu.ry

YUN Soo In, b. 6 November 1937, Gyungju, Korea. Professor Emeritus. m. Hyun Young Heo, 1 son, 2 daughters. Education: BS, Physics, 1960, MS, Physics, 1962, Pusan National University, Korea; MS, Physics, Carnegie-Mellon University, USA, 1970; PhD, Physics, Oklahoma State University, USA, 1972. Appointments: Professor, President, Chairman of Physics Department, Dean of Academic Affairs, Pusan National University, Korea; Visiting Assistant Professor, Oklahoma State University, USA; Honorary Fellow, University of Wisconsin, USA; Visiting Scholar, University of Alabama; Vice President, Korean Physical Society. Publications: Articles in scientific journals include:

Enhancement of 3d impurity-ion spin-forbidden absorption by color centers in MgF_2, 1972; Mechanism of upconverted fluorescence in an Er^{3+} doped $LiNbO_3$ single crystal, 1996; Where they go – 21st Century Universities. Honours: Research Award, Korean Physical Society; Cultural Award, Nulwon Foundation; Blue Stripes Order of Service Merit, Republic of Korea. Memberships: Korean Physical Society; Korean Optical Society; American Physical Society; Optical Society of America. Address: 208-903 Hyundai 2nd Apt, 2307 Hwamyung-Dong, Busan 616-120, Republic of Korea. E-mail: yunsi@pusan.ac.kr

YURTOGLU B Burcin, b. 21 April 1968, Istanbul, Turkey. Economist. m. Aylin. Education: BA, Economics, Bogazici University, 1991; MA, 1993, PhD, 1997, Economics, University of Vienna. Appointments: Research and Teaching Assistant, Assistant Professor, Department of Economics, University of Vienna; Visiting Fellow, Centre for Business Research, University of Cambridge. Publications: 10 articles in professional journals. Honours: Vienna Stock Exchange Research Stipend; Nestle Prize in Economics, 1997; Honourable Mention, Istanbul Stock Exchange Best Paper Award; IVA Corporate Governance Award, 2000. Memberships: American Economic Association; European Economic Association; Verein fuer Socialpolitik; EARIE. Address: University of Vienna, Department of Economics, BWZ, Bruennerstr 72, A-1210 Vienna, Austria. E-mail: burcin.yurtoglu@univie.ac.at

YUS Miguel, b. 11 September 1947, Saragossa, Spain. Chemist. m. Carmen, 1 son, 1 daughter. Education: BSc, 1969, MSc, 1971, PhD, 1973, University of Saragossa. Appointments: Associate Professor, 1978, Professor, 1987, Organic Chemistry, University of Oviedo; Professor, Organic Chemistry, University of Alicante, 1988-. Publications: Numerous papers in professional journals. Honours include: Prize of JSPS, Japan, 1999; French-Spanish Prize of SFC, France, 1999. Memberships: Fellow or Member of Chemical Societies of Spain, Switzerland, Germany, Japan, UK, USA, Argentina. Address: Departmento de Quimica Organica, Facultad de Ciencias, Universidad de Alicante, Apdo 99, 03080 Alicante, Spain. E-mail: yus@ua.es

Dictionary of International Biography

Z

ZACHARIASSON Toini Maria, b. 14 March 1943, Hedenaeset, Sweden. Director; Business Owner. Education: Computer Degree, Scandinavian School, Gothenburg, Sweden, 1974; Degree, Philosophy, Stockholm University, Sweden, 1980. Appointments: Clerk, Executive, The Defence Office, Stockholm, 1962-64; Secretary of Business, Eriksson, Stockholm, 1964-79; Secretary of Parliament, 1979-82; Director of Business, Hedenaeset, Norrbotten, Sweden, 1982-88, 1988-; Taxation Professional, The Central Party, Stockholm, 1977-88. Memberships: Volunteer, Marine Defence, Sweden; Member, The Central Party. Address: Lasarettsgatan 55B, S-98234 Gallivare, Norrbotten, Sweden.

ZAKHARCHENKO Irina, b. 19 July 1946, Rostov-on-Don, Russia. X-ray Physicist. m. Krivitskii V V, 2 sons. Education: Graduate, Department of Physics, Rostov State University, 1969; PhD, Physics and Mathematics, Rostov State University, 1978. Appointments: Junior Researcher, 1969-77; Senior Researcher, 1978-92; Leading Researcher, Laboratory of Ferroelectric Thin Films, Institute of Physics, Rostov State University, 1993-. Publications: Several articles for professional journals. Memberships: International Union of Crystallography. Address: Institute of Physics, Rostov State University, Pr Stachky 194, Rostov-on-Don 344090, Russia. E-mail: zin@ip.rsu.ru

ZALUSKY Deborah, b. 27 September 1959, USA. Ordained Minister. Education: Associate of Arts in Accounting, 1981; Bachelor of Arts in Accounting, 1985; Master of Divinity, 1993; Doctor of Ministry, 1995. Appointments: Ordained Minister, various churches in midwest USA, 1995-2004; Public Accountant in CPA Firms for last 27 years to supplement the ministry; Numerous public speaking engagements, radio interviews and newspaper articles; Unique internet ministry. Special interests: Worship, prayer, preaching, healing and deliverance; Dealing with theological questions submitted by e-mail; Musician, organ keyboard, guitar and clarinet; Composer and singer. Publications include: The Proverbs of the Bible: How Can They be Used Today?, 1997; Thank God for Women Preachers, 1998; Bible Memorization Plan for a Year, 2000; Living in the Presence of God, 2000; Discernment for Christians, 2000; and numerous other publications. Honours: Key Award for Religious Leadership; Key Award for Excellence in Teaching; Key Award as a Notable Author; Key Award for Community Leadership; Woman of the Year, 2000, 2002, 2003; Nominated Woman of the Year, 2001; Nominated for Noble Prize for outstanding achievements and contributions towards humanity; Listed in several biographical titles. Memberships: Illinois Society of CPA's. Address: Sacramento, California, USA. E-mail: revdrdeb@hotmail.com

ZAMAN Agha Sher Hamid, b. 10 January 1947, Hoshiarpur, India. Petroleum Exploration and Development. m. Anjam Agha. Education: BSc honours, Geology, 1968, MSc, Geology, Geophysics, 1970, Punjab University, Lahore, Pakistan. Appointments: Junior Geophysicist, Water and Power Development Authority, 1970; Geophysicist, 1971-74, Senior Geophysicist, 1974-79, Deputy Chief Geophysicist/Chief Geophysicist Interpreter, 1979-88, Chief Geophysicist, 1988-90, Senior Chief, Deputy Manager, 1990-93, Manager Exploitation and Reservoir Engineering, 1995-96, Manager Exploration, 1993-95, 1996-97, General Manager, 1997, Oil and Gas Development Corporation, Pakistan; Explorationist, Senior Seismologist, Geophysical Service Inc, England, 1981; Senior Geophysicist, Saudi Aramco, Schlumberger, 1997-2001; Technical Director, Government Holdings Ltd, 2001-. Publications: 8 articles in professional journals. Honours: Several cash awards for new

discoveries by Oil and Gas Development Corporation, Pakistan; Listed in national and international biographical directories. Memberships: American Association of Petroleum Geologists; Society of Exploration Geophysicists; Society of Petroleum Engineers; and others. Address: House No 382, Street 14, Sector G-10/2, Islamabad 44000, Pakistan. E-mail: ashz@isb.paknet.com.pk

ZAMBARAS Vassilis, b. 1 May 1944, Revmatia, Messenias, Greece. Teacher of English as a Second Language; Poet. m. Eleni Nezi, October 1980, 1 son, 1 daughter. Education: BA, English, 1970, MA, English, 1972, University of Washington, Seattle. Publications: Sentences, 1976; Aural, 1984. Contributions to: How the Net is Gripped: Selection of Contemporary American Poetry, 1992; Chiron Review; Karer Murr's Press; Maverick Magazine; Poetry Salzburg Review; The London Magazine; The Salt River Review; Tattoo Highway; Fine-Words.com; Poetry Northwest; Madrona; West Coast Review; Wisconsin Review; Assay; Edge; Text; Smoot Drive Press; Rialto; Shearsman; Southeastern Review; Southern Poetry Review; Longhouse; Intermedio; Workshop; Falcon; Klinamen; Apopeira. Honours: Harcourt, Brace and Jovanovich Poetry Fellowship to the University of Colorado, Boulder, 1970; University of Washington Poetry Prizewinner, 1972. Address: 21 K Fotopoulou, Meligalas 24002, Messenias, Greece.

ZAMBITO Peter J, b. 14 September 1935, New York, USA. Attorney. m. Marguerite, 1 son, 1 daughter. Education: BA, St Bonaventure University, 1957; LLB, Fordham Law School, 1961. Appointments: Associate, Haight Gardner Poor and Havens, 1961-67; Partner, Practice Admiralty Law, Dougherty Ryan Giuffra Zambito and Hession, 1967-; Admitted to Bar, New York, 1961; Admitted to Second Circuit Court, 1963; Admitted to Supreme Court of United States of America, 1974. Memberships: Maritime Law Association of the United States. Address: 131 E 38th Street, New York, NY 10016, USA. E-mail: peterzambito@aol.com

ZAPF Hermann, b. 8 November 1918, Nuremberg, Germany. Designer. m. Gudrun Zapf von Hesse, 1 son. Education: D in Fine Arts (Hon), University of Illinois, USA. Appointments: Freelance designer, 1938-; Type Director, D Stempel AG, type foundry, Frankfurt, 1947-56; Design Consultant, Mergenthaler Linotype Co, New York and Frankfurt, 1957-74; Consultant, Hallmark International, Kansas City, Missouri, 1966-73; Vice President, Design Processing International Inc, New York, 1977-86; Professor, typographic computer programs, Rochester Institute of Technology, New York, 1977-87; Chairman, Zapf, Burns and Co, New York City, 1987-91; Instructor, Lettering Werkkunstschule, Offenbach, Germany, 1948-50; Professor, Graphic Design, Carnegie Institute of Technology, 1960; Instructor, Typography Technische Hochschule, Darmstadt, Germany, 1972-81. Publications: Author: William Morris, 1948; Pen and Graver, 1952; Manuale Typographicum, 1954, 1968; About Alphabets, 1960, 1970; Typographic Variations, 1964; Orbis Typographicus, 1980; Hora fugit/Carpe diem, 1984; Hermann Zapf and His Design Philosophy, 1987; ABC-XYZapf, 1989; Poetry Through Typography, 1993; August Rosenberger, 1996; CD-ROM, The World of Alphabets, 2001; Film, The Art of Hermann Zapf; Designer of over 180 typefaces. Honours: Honorary President, Edward Johnston Foundation, England; Honorary Curator, Computer Museum, Boston; Silver Medal, Brussels, 1962; 1st Prize Typography Biennale, Brno, Czechoslovakia, 1966; Gold Medal, Type Directors Club, New York; Frederic W Goudy Award, Institute of Technology, Rochester, 1969; Silver Medal, International Book Exhibition, Leipzig, 1971; Gold Medal, 1989; Johannes Gutenberg Prize, Mainz, Germany, 1974; Gold Medal, Museo Bodoniano, Parma, Italy, 1975; J H Merck Award, Darmstadt, 1978; Robert Hunter Middleton Award, 1987; Euro

Dictionary of International Biography

Design Award, 1994; Wadim Lazursky Award, Academy of Graphic Arts, Moscow, 1996; Named Honorary Citizen, State of Texas, 1970; Honorary Royal Designer for Industry, 1985; Listed in national and international biographical dictionaries. Memberships: Royal Society of Arts; American Mathematical Society; Alliance Graphique Internationale; Bund Deutscher Grafik Designer; International Gutenberg Gessellschaft; Honorary Member, Type Directors Club, New York City; Sociéte Typographique de France, Paris; Society of Typographic Arts, Chicago; Double Crown Club, London; Letter Exchange, London; Society of Scribes and Illuminators, London; Friends of Calligraphy, San Francisco; Society of Printers, Boston; Society of Graphic Designers, Canada; Bund Deutscher Buchkünstler; Grafiska Institute, Stockholm; Typophiles, New York; Alpha Beta Club, Hong Kong; Society of Calligraphy, Los Angeles; Wynkyn de Worde Society, London; Monterey Calligrapher's Guild; Washington Calligraphers Guild; Eesti Kalligraafide Koondis, Tallinn, Estonia; Chicago Calligraphers Guild; Caxton Club, Chicago; Typographers International Association; Art Directors Club, Kansas City; Associates of Stanford University Libraries; Alcuin Society, Vancouver; Goudy International Centre; Brno Biennale Association; Society of Scribes, New York; Grolier Club, New York; Dante e V, German TEX Group, Heidelberg; Gamma Epsilon Tau. Address: D-64287 Darmstadt, Seitersweg 35, Germany.

ZAREMBKA Paul, b. 17 April 1942, St Louis, Missouri, USA. Economist. m. Beata Banas, 1 daughter. Education: BS, Mathematics, Purdue University, 1964; MS, PhD, Economics, 1967, University of Wisconsin. Appointments: Assistant Professor, Department of Economics, University of California, Berkeley, 1967-72; Visiting Professorships: Heidelberg University, 1970-71; Goettingen University, 1971-72; Associate Professor, Professor, Department of Economics, State University of New York at Buffalo, 1973-; Senior Research Officer, World Employment Program, International Labor Office, Geneva, Switzerland, 1974-77; Researcher, Group For Research on Science, Louis Pasteur University, Strasbourg, 1978-79. Publications: Author, Toward a Theory of Economic Development, 1972; Editor, Frontiers in Econometrics, 1974; Co-editor with M Brown and K Sato, Essays in Modern Capital Theory, 1976; General Editor, Research in Political Economy, 21 volumes to date, 1977-; Numerous articles and book chapters. Honours: Fulbright-Hayes Lecturer, Poznan, Poland, 1979; Listed in numerous biographical dictionaries. Address: Department of Economics, 415 Fronczak Hall, State University of New York at Buffalo, Buffalo, New York 14260. E-mail: zarembka@buffalo.edu. Website: http://ourworld.compuserve.com/homepages/PZarembka

ZAVATI Constantin C, b. 7 July 1923, Bacau, Romania. Teacher. m. Iulia Bucur, 1 daughter. Education: Scoala de Baieti No 2; Scholarship, Stefan Cel Mare Military Boarding College; Baccalauréat, Distinction, 1942; Private Merit Regiment 10; Chemistry Faculty, University Alexandru Ioan Cuza, 1947-51; MSc, honours. Appointments: Various Military Positions; Assistant Lecturer, University and Academy in Iasi; Teacher, Chemistry and Physics, Ferdinand I Boarding College, Bacau, Romania; Teacher, Chemistry and Physics, Head of Chemistry, Vasile Alecsandri Boarding College, Bacau, Romania; Schools Inspector for Chemistry. Publications: Numerous papers at various national conferences; Many scientific articles in newspapers and magazines; Co-author, 1 book; Organised the first science laboratories in the county of Bacau. Honours: Citation for great bravery during the Second World War; Several Orders and Medals for Bravery in War; Professor Fruntas, 1964; Professor Grade 1, 1972; Advanced Captain, Major and Colonel in the Army Reserves. Memberships: Societatea De Stiinte Fizice Si Chimice; Societatea Stiintelor

Medicale; First President, Radio Club, Bacau, Romania. Address: c/o Mariana Zavati Gardner, 14 Andrew Goodall Close, East Dereham, Norfolk, NR19 1SR, England.

ZAVATI Iulia Bucur, b. 19 July 1921, Racova-Bacau, Romania. Pharmacist. m. Constantin C Zavati, 26 January 1947, 1 daughter. Education: Baccalauréat with Distinct; MSc, Pharmacy, 1st class honours, University of Bucharest, Romania. Appointments: Opened own pharmacy at Valea Rea-Târgu Ocna, Romania; Pharmacist, State Pharmacy in Bacau, Romania; Appointed Principal Pharmacist; Deputy Director, Director, Oficiul Farmaceutic, City and Region of Bacau-Romania; Directed, re-organised and modernised all pharmacies in Bacau; Established links with western pharmacy companies; Lecturer, Scoala Sanitara for nurses and pharmacy assistants in Bacau. Honours: Medals and Orders for modernising and re-organising pharmacies in Bacau. Membership: Romanian Society of Pharmacists. Address: c/o Andrew Goodall Close, East Dereham, Norfolk NR19 1SR, England.

ZAVODNIK Ilya, b. 23 June 1956, Grodno, Soviet Union. Researcher; Educator. Education: MSc, Physics, Grodno Pedagogic Institute, 1977; PhD, Biophysics, 1985; DSc, Biophysics, 1997. Appointments: Institute of Biochemistry, Academy of Sciences, Belarus, 1977-; Researcher, Institute of Biophysics, Puschino, 1977-78; Guest Adjunct, University of Lodz, Poland, 1995; Professor, Grodno State University, Grodno Agricultural University, 2000-. Publications: Several articles in professional journals. Honours: Grants, European Fellowship Fund, 1994, 1999; Grants, Mianowski Fund, Warsaw, 1996, 1998; Award, President of the Republic of Belarus, 1999; Grant, NATO Science program, 2003; Listed in national and international biographical dictionaries. Memberships: Society of Photobiology and Biophysics of Belarus. Address: Institute of Biochemistry, National Academy of Sciences of Belarus, BLK-50, 230017 Grodno, Belarus.

ZAYATS Nikolai E, b. 4 January 1943, Stradechi, Brest Region, Belarus. Professor; Economist. m. Glafira Bondar, 2 sons. Education: Graduate, Belarusian State Economic University, 1969; Postgraduate studies, 1973-78. Appointments: Budget Department, Ministry of Finance of Belarus, 1969-73; Academic Staff, 1978-91, Vice-Rector and Chief of Finance Chair, 1991-, Belarusian State Economic University. Publications: More than 130 articles in economic and financial journals; Textbooks on the theory of finance, taxes, the theory of taxation, the state budget, international economy and managerial accounting on agriculture entities. Honours: Honoured Economist of the Republic of Belarus, 1998; Medal of Honour in Education, 1999; Medal of Honour of the Ministry of Finance of Belarus, 2003. Membership: Corresponding Member, Agricultural Science Academy of Belarus. Address: Smorgovski Trakt 10-84, Minsk 220068, Belarus. E-mail: azayats@softhome.net

ZDARZIL Herbert, b. 1 October 1928, Vienna, Austria. Professor. m. Traute Pistulka, 2 daughters. Education: Philosophy, History, Education, Teacher's Qualification, 1950, Doctor of Philosophy, 1953, University of Vienna; Habilitation, University of Bonn, Germany, 1970. Appointments: Librarian, University Library, Vienna, 1954; Lecturer, Adult Education, University of Vienna, 1961, Associate Professor, Education, University of Bonn, Germany, 1963; Professor of Education, 1971-, Dean, 1977-79, University of Vienna. Publications: Lebendiger Geist, 1963; Pädagogische Anthropologie, 2nd edition, 1978; Several book chapters as co-author include: Anthropologie, 1976; Die pädagogische Frage nach dem Menschen, 1997; La mia pedagogia, 2001. Honour: Promoting Prize for Adult Education, Austrian

Dictionary of International Biography

Ministry of Education, 1960. Membership: Corresponding Member, Austrian Society of Science, 1981. Address: Wallrißstraße 62, A-1180 Vienna, Austria.

ZECCHINO Vincent, b. 15 May 1909, Brooklyn, New York, USA. Medical Doctor; Orthopaedic Surgeon. m. Julia M Pilkanis, 1 son. Education: MD, University of Bologna, Italy, 1936; Resident, Orthopaedic surgery, Rhode Island Hospital, 1936-38; Resident, Orthopaedic Surgery, Boston Children's Hospital and Massachusetts General Hospital, 1938-41. Appointments: Lieutenant Colonel, US Army, Chief Orthopaedic Surgeon, Hospitals in India and Burma (48th General Hospital); Diplomate American Board of Orthopaedic Surgery, FACS, AAOS; Chairman, Department of Orthopaedic Surgery, Brown University Medical School and Rhode Island Hospital; Visiting Professor: Colombia, Tunisia, Sri Lanka, Italy, Canada; Now retired and Emeritus. Publications: Numerous publications on topic including plastic surgery, thumb reconstruction, hip prosthesis. Honour: Julia and Vincent Zecchino Pavilion, Rhode Island Hospital. Memberships: AAOS; FICS; FACS; Rhode Island Medical Society; Boston Orthopaedic Club; Boston Children's Hospital Alumni Association; International Scientific Society. Address: 530 S Collier Blvd, Apt 202, Marco Island, FL 34145-5514, USA.

ZEFFIRELLI G Franco, b. 12 February 1923, Florence, Italy. Opera & Film Producer; Designer. Education: Liceo Artistico, Florence; School of Agriculture, Florence. Appointments: Designer, University Productions, Florence; Actor, Morelli Stoppa Co; Collaborated with Salvador Dali on sets for As You Like It, 1948; Designed sets for A Streetcar Named Desire, Troilus, Cressida, Three Sisters; Producer, Designer, numerous operas. Creative Works: Theatre: Romeo and Juliet, Old Vic, London, 1960; Othello, Stratford, 1961; Amleto, National Theatre, London, 1964; After the Fall, Rome, 1964; Who's Afraid of Virginia Woolf, Paris, 1964, Milan, 1965, La Lupa, Rome, 1965; Much Ado About Nothing, National Theatre, London, 1966; Black Comedy, Rome, 1967; A Delicate Balance, Rome, 1967; Saturday, Sunday, Monday, National Theatre, London, 1973; Filumena, Lyric, London, 1977; Six Characters in Search of an Author, London, 1992; Films: The Taming of the Shrew, 1966; Florence, Days of Destruction, 1966; Romeo and Juliet, 1967; Brother Sun and Sister Moon, 1973; Jesus of Nazareth, 1977; The Champ, 1979; Endless Love, 1981; La Traviata, 1983; Cavalleria Rusticana, 1983; Otello, 1986; The Young Toscanini, 1987; Hamlet, 1990; Sparrow, 1994; Jane Eyre, 1995; Tea With Mussolini, 1998; Callas Forever, 2002; Ballet: Swan Lake, 1985; Producer, Beethoven's Missa Solemnis, San Pietro, Rome, 1971. Publication: Zeffirelli by Zeffirelli (autobiog), 1986.

ZELASKIEWICZ Jozef Jan, b. 21 February 1929, Ksiaz Wielki, Poland. Building and Electrical Assembly Organisation Manager. m. Jadwiga, 1 son, 2 daughters. Education: Electrical Engineer Diploma, Electrical Engineering Faculty, Mining and Metallurgy Academy, Krakow, 1952-56; MSc, Organisation and Economics of the Building Industry, Civil Engineering Department, University of Technology, Poznan, 1970-73; Certificate, Social Organisation and Communication, Social Science Academy, Moscow, 1979; Attestation, Foreign Trade Organisation, Postgraduate Course, Ministry of Foreign Trade High School, 1980. Appointments: Manager Electrical Projects, Sendzimir Steel Plant, Nowa Huta, 1952-61; Chief of Engineers, Electrical Section, Building Complex, Glogow, Power Plant, Turoszow, Cooper Plant Legnica, 1961-65; Managing Director, PPiMUEB Electromontaz, Poznan, 1965-73; General Director, Company of Sixteen State Enterprises "Elmont" to reorganise methods of management in the Polish Building Industry, 1973-77; Under Secretary of State, Ministry of Building and Constructional Materials Industry, Warsaw, 1977-

80; Counsellor for Building Engineering, Polish Embassy in Baghdad, 1980-84; Director, Board Member, IDM Corporation, Elektromontaz Export, Elektrim SA, 1984-94; Vice-Chairman of Supervisory Council PRE Bydgoszcz, Director of Emerging Markets, Comber Engineering, Warsaw, 1995-2003-. Publications: Several pamphlets and books on building industry economics; Numerous articles in professional journals. Honours include: Many awards for bravery during the Second World War; Polonia Restituta: Knight's Cross, 1967, Officer's Cross, 1975; Golden Order of Banner of Work, 1984; Commander's Cross with Star of the Sovereign Order of St Stanislaw, 1990. Memberships include: Scientific Council of the Organisation and Management Institute of the Building Industry; Leading Technical Organisation, Polish Arabic Friendship Society; Home Army Soldiers, AK Veterans of War Society. Address: ul Nowiniarska 1/22, 00-235 Warsaw, Poland. E-mail: zelaskiewicz@poczta.onet.pl

ZELDIS Jerome Bernard, b. 6 April 1950, Waterbury, Connecticut. Clinical Professor of Medicine; Chief Medical Officer. m. Sharon Winston Stamm, 1 son, 2 daughters. Education: AB MS, Brown University, 1972; MPhil, Yale University, 1977; MD, 1978; PhD, 1978. Appointments: Instructor, Medicine, Harvard Medical School, 1984-87; Tutor, Medical Sciences, 1985-87; Assistant Professor, Medicine, 1987-88; Assistant Professor, University of California, 1988-90; Clinical Research Physician, Sacramento Medical Foundation, 1990-94; Associate Professor, University of California, 1990-94; Clinical Assistant Professor, Cornell University, 1995-; Clinical Associate Professor, 1996-2003; Clinical Professor of Medicine, Robert Wood Johnson Medical School, 2003-. Publications: 65 original reports; 24 reviews, chapters, editorials; 42 abstracts; 8 book reviews; 4 letters; 3 commentaries. Honours: Phi Beta Kappa; Sigma Xi; Barry Rosen Memorial Award; Fulton Award 2; Mosby Award for Scholastic Achievement; American Liver Foundation Post-doctoral Training Award; Pfizer Post-doctoral Research Fellowship Award; AGA Travel Award; Hans Popper Faculty Scholar Award. Memberships: American College of Physicians; American Association of Immunologists; American Gastroenterlogical Association; American Association for the Study of Liver Disease; American Gastroenterological Association; American Association for Advancement of Science; European Association for the Study of Liver Disease; American Federation for Clinical Research; American College of Physicians; Western Society of Clinical Investigations. Address: Celgene Corp, 7 Powder Horn Dr, Warren, NJ 07059, USA.

ZELIAŚ Aleksander Józef, b. 14 September 1939, Oleśnica. Full Professor of Economics. m. Jadwiga Kurowska, 1 son, 1 daughter. Education: MSc, Economics, 1962, DSc, Economics, 1966, Cracow School of Economics; DSc Habilit, Statistics, Poznań School of Economics, 1970; Nomination for degrees of Professor, 1977, Full Professor, 1982, State Council for the Polish People's Republic. Appointments include: Assistant Lecturer to Associate Professor, Statistics, 1963-77; Full Professor of Economics, Cracow Academy of Economics, 1982-; Visiting Professor: Pittsburgh University, 1982, Bonn University, Marburg University, Göttingen University, 1986, Tilburg University, Netherlands, 1988, Al-Mustansiryah University, Iraq, 1989, Pittsburgh University, 1991, Konstanz University, 2000; Member of editorial staffs of several professional journals. Publications: Over 290 papers and reports; Numerous books as author or co-author. Honours: Golden Cross of Merit, 1979; Medal, Committee of National Education, 1982; Knight Cross of the Order of Polonia Restituta, 1984, Gold Mark of Distinction, Social Activities, Kraków City, 1984, Kraków District, 1985; Bronze Medal, Country's Defenses, 1988; Officer's Cross of the Order of Polonia Restituta, 1999; 20th Century Award for Achievement, IBC; 2000

Dictionary of International Biography

Millennium Medal of Honour, ABI, 1998; Doctor honoris causa, Wrocław University of Economics, 1996; Doctor honoris causa, Bratislava University of Economics, 2002. Memberships: Polish Economic Association; Polish Statistical Association; Deputy President, Committee of Mathematics of the Central Statistical Office in Warsaw; Polish Cybernetics Association; Committee of Economics, Cracow Branch, Polish Academy of Sciences; Honorary Advisor, Research Board of Advisors, American Biographical Institute; International Statistical Institute; Econometric Society; Deputy President, Polish Statistical Association; German Statistical Association; Academician, International Academy of Computer Sciences and Systems; Chairman, Committee of Statistics and Econometrics of the Polish Academy of Sciences in Warsaw. Address: Kowalskiego 1, 30 147 Kraków, Poland.

ZELLWEGER Renée, b. 25 April 1969, Katy, Texas, USA. Actress. Education: University of Texas at Austin. Appointments: Films: Dazed and Confused, 1993; Reality Bites, 1994; Love and a .45, 1994; 8 Seconds, 1994; The Low Life, 1995; Empire Records, 1995; The Whole Wide World, 1996; Jerry Maguire, 1996; Texas Chainsaw Massacre: The Next Generation, 1997; Deceiver, 1997; One True Thing, 1998; A Price Above Rubies, 1998; The Bachelor, 1999; Me, Myself and Irene, 2000; Nurse Betty, 2000; Bridget Jones' Diary, 2001; Chicago, 2002; Down With Love, 2003; Cold Mountain, 2003; TV: Shake, Rattle and Rock Movie, 1993; Murder in the Heartland, 1994. Honours: Golden Globe Best Comedy Film Actress Award for Nurse Betty, 2001; Golden Globe Best Actress in a Musical for Chicago, 2003; Screen Actors Guild Award for Best Actress for Chicago, 2003; BAFTA Award for Best Supporting Actress, 2004; Best Supporting Actress Oscar for Cold Mountain, 2004. Address: c/o United Talent Agency, 9560 Wilshire Boulevard, Suite 500, Beverly Hills, CA 90212, USA.

ZEMECKIS Robert, b. May 1952, Chicago, USA. Film Director; Writer. m. Mary Ellen Trainor. Education: University South California. Creative Works: Films include: I Wanna Hold Your Hand (co-screenplay writer), 1978; Romancing the Stone; Back to the Future (co-screenplay writer), II, III; Death Becomes Her (also co-producer); Trespass (co-screenplay writer); Forest Gump; Who Framed Roger Rabbit?; Contact; The House on Haunted Hill; Cast Away; What Lies Beneath; Ghost Ship; Several TV Films. Address: c/o CAA, 9830 Wilshire Boulevard, Beverly Hills, CA 90212, USA.

ZEMSKOV Andrei Il'ich, b. 2 January 1939, Moscow Region, Russia. Librarian. m. Irina Zemskova, 1 son. Education: Explorer on Nuclear Physics, Institute of Technical Physics, 1956-65; PhD, Low Temperature Plasma Physics, 1965. Appointments: Researcher, Kurchatov Atomic Energy Institute, 1965-81; Supervisor, Plasma Physics Programs, CPSU CC, 1981-90; Director, Russian National Public Library for Science and Technology, 1990-. Publications: Over 70 on Plasma Physics, Library Management, CD-ROM applications; Editor-in-Chief of SciTech Libraries Journal. Honours: Order of Merit, 1976; Silver Medal of All Union Exhibition, 1983; Order of Friendship, 1998. Memberships: Vice President, Russian Library Association; President, International Association of Research and Sci-Tech Libraries. Address: 12 Kuznetski most, 107996 Moscow, Russia.

ZERBIN-RÜDIN Edith, b. 2 May 1921, Munich, Germany. Physician; University Professor. m. Adolf Zerbin. Education: Medical Doctor, Ludwig-Maximilian-University, 1947; Dr Med, magna cum laude, 1950. Appointments: Clinical Assistant, Psychiatric University Hospital, Munich, 1950-51; Research Worker, 1947-58, Head of Research Group, Psychiatric Genetics,

1958-86, Max-Planck-Institut for Psychiatry, Munich; Lecturer, Medical Genetics, 1972-86, Extraordinary Professor, Medical Genetics, 1978-, Ludwig-Maximilian-University; Retired, 1986. Publications: About 145 publications in medical, psychiatric and human genetic journals; Chapters in handbooks, textbooks, multi-author books, medical encyclopaedias. Honours: Scholarship, Galton Laboratory, London, British Council, 1955-56; Invited lectures at national and international congresses, Germany, USA, Switzerland, Norway, Denmark, Netherlands, France, Japan, Austria. Memberships: American Society of Human Genetics; Behaviour Genetics Association; Society for the Study of Social Biology. Address: Besselstr 1A, 81679, Munich, Germany.

ZHANG Jingguo, b. 7 October 1940, Shanghai, China. Materials Scientist; Engineer. m. Ninghua Zhu, 1 son. Education: Graduate, Department of Physical Metallurgy, University of Science and Technology, Beijing, China, 1964. Appointments: Research Assistant, 1964-74, Research Engineer, 1974-83, Director of Testing Centre, 1983-84, Deputy Director of Institute, Senior Engineer, 1984-87, Vice-President, Academic Committee, Associate Chief Engineer, Professor of Materials Science and Engineering, 1987-2000, Shanghai Iron and Steel Research Institute; Senior Specialist, Professor of Materials Science and Engineering, Shanghai Bao Steel Research Institute, 2000-; Visiting Scholar, Columbia University, USA, 1980; Assistant Professor, University of Connecticut, USA, 1980-82. Publications: 34 and 48 papers published in scientific and engineering journals in English and Chinese respectively; Co-author 2 books in Chinese; Recently published papers: Structure of Amorphous Fe-Zr-B powders obtained by chemical reduction, 2002; Microstructure and CCT Thermograms of Spray Formed G Cr15 Steel, 2002; Superplastic Ultra-high Carbon Steels Processed by Spray Forming, 2003. Honours: Honours and Prize for distinct achievements and contribution in engineering, The State Council of China, 1993; Li Xun Prize, Acta Metallurgica Sinica, 1993; Special Prize for Scientists in the fields of applied basic research, Science and Technology Commission of Shanghai Municipality, 1994-95, 1998-99. Memberships: Institute of Materials Science, University of Connecticut, USA, 1980-82; SAMPE, Japan, 1993-95; Board of Directors: Chinese Society of Metals, 1991-94, Chinese Materials Research Society, 1991-, Chinese Stereology Society, 1991. Address: Room 2603, No 12, Lane 300, Wu Ning Road, Shanghai 200063, PR China.

ZHANG Luqian, b. 1 March 1926, China. Professor. m. Li Bowei, 2 daughters. Education: Tsinghua University, 1951. Appointment: Chief Designer, China Aerospace Corporation, 1979-. Honours: Microwave Satellite TTC Radar, National Top Award, Beijing, 1985; Ho Leung Ho Lee Foundation Award, Hong Kong, 1997. Memberships: AIAA, USA; CSA; CAE, China. Address: China Aerospace Corporation, PO Box 849-1, 100830 Beijing, China.

ZHANG Zhibo, b. 23 April 1968, Sichuan, China. College Professor. Education: BS, Tsinghua University, China, 1990; MS, Chinese Academy of Sciences, 1993; PhD, Massachusetts Institute of Technology, 1998. Appointments: Member of Technical Staff, Lucent Technologies, Bell Laboratories, 1998-2000; Assistant Professor, Department of Electrical and Computer Engineering, North Carolina State University, 2000-. Publications: More than 20 articles in research journals and conferences including as co-author: Journal of Physical Chemistry, 1998; Chemistry of Materials, 1999; Journal of the Electrochemical Society, 2002. Honours: Outstanding Graduate Student Award, Chinese Academy of Sciences; Honoured Member, Strathmore's Who's Who, 2001-2002. Memberships: IEEE; Materials Research Society; American Physical Society. Address: North Carolina State University, Department of Electrical and Computer Engineering, Raleigh, NC 27695-7564, USA. Website: http://www4.ncsu.edu/~zzhang4/

ZHAO Gong Yun, b. 5 March 1955, China. Associate Professor. m. Zhi Quian Wan, 1 son. Education: PhD, Würzburg University, Germany, 1991. Appointments: Teaching Fellow, Lecturer, Senior Lecturer, Associate Professor, National University of Singapore, 1992-. Publications: More than 20 articles published in journals including: Mathematical Programming; Mathematics of Operations Research; SIAM Journal on Optimization. Honour: Award of Commonwealth Fellowship, 2000-2001. Membership: International Advisory Committee, 15th International Symposium on Mathematical Programming. Address: Department of Mathematics, National University of Singapore, Republic of Singapore. E-mail: matzgy@nus.edu.sg Website: www.math.nus.edu.sg/~matzgy

ZHAO Zhijian, b. 12 April 1957, Yiyang City, China. Senior Systems Analyst. m. Huiru Li, 2 sons. Education: BS, Mechanical Engineering, 1982, MS, Mechanical Engineering, 1984, PhD, Mechanical Engineering, 1988, Nanjing University of Science and Technology, Nanjing, China; PhD Candidate, Mechanical Engineering, The City College of the City University of New York, USA, 1994-97. Appointments: Research Assistant, Nanjing University of Science and Technology, Nanjing, China, 1983-88; Lecturer, Changsha Institute of Technology, Changsha, China, 1988-91; Research Fellow, Nanjing University of Science and Technology, Nanjing, China, 1991-93; Tutor, Hunter College, The City University of New York, USA, 1994-95; Visiting Scientist, Sibley School of Mechanical and Aerospace Engineering, Cornell University, 1995-96; Research Assistant, Levich Institute, The City College of the City University of New York, 1993-96; Analysis Engineer, 1997-99, Senior Systems Analyst, 1999-, Automotive Systems Laboratory, Inc., Farmington Hills, Michigan, USA. Publications: Co-author book: Dynamics and Control of Large Spacecraft, 1990; 21 articles in scientific journals and conference proceedings as co-author include: On the correlation between the Burning and Thermal Decomposition Characteristics of Nitramine Propellants, 1994; Criteria for Transition to Turbulence Induced by the Richtmyer-Meshkov and Rayleigh-Taylor Instabilities, 1996; Scaling in Wall-bounded Shear Turbulence, 1998; 14 presentations at conferences and seminars; 12 degree theses and technical reports. Honours include: Excellent Paper Awards, Nanjing University of Science and Technology, 1986, 1990; Humboldt Research Fellowship Award, 1990; Outstanding Tutoring Performance Award, Hunter College, 1994-95; Special Achievement Award, Automotive Systems Laboratory Inc, 1999. Memberships: American Society of Mechanical Engineers; The Society of Automotive Engineers; Executive Committee of Dynamics and Control, Chinese Society of Theoretical and Applied Mechanics, 1990-93. Address: Automotive Systems Laboratory, Inc., 27200 Haggerty Road, Farmington Hills, MI 48331, USA. E-mail: zhijian.zhao@asl-tk.com

ZHAO Zhong Wei, b. 29 September 1954, Beijing, China. Researcher. m. Yan Ping Zhang, 1 daughter. Education: BA, Peking University, 1979-83; MA, Exeter University, 1986-87; PhD, Cambridge University, 1988-93. Appointments: Senior Fellow, Program of Demography and Sociology, RSSS, Australian National University; Senior Research Associate, Cambridge Group for the History of Population and Social Structure, University of Cambridge; Fellow, Demography Program, RSSS, Australian National University; Post-doctoral Fellow, Department of Sociology, University of New South Wales; Post-doctoral Fellow, East-West Centre, Hawaii. Publications: Many articles in professional journals. Honours: Biographical listing in Who's Who in the World. Memberships: International Union for the Scientific Study of Population. Address: Program of Demography and Sociology, RSSS, The Australian National University, ACT 0200, Australia.

ZHELUDEV Nikolay, b. 23 April 1955, Moscow, Russia. University Professor; Physicist; Educator. m. Tanya Nousinova, 2 sons. Education: MSc, 1978, PhD, 1981, DSc, 1992, Moscow State University. Appointments: Research Fellow, Senior Research Fellow (Faculty), Department of Physics and International Laser Centre, Moscow State University, Moscow, Russia, 1981-91; Lecturer in Physics, 1991-94, Reader in Physics, 1994-2000, Professor of Physics and Astronomy, 2000-, University of Southampton, England; Engineering and Physical Sciences Research Council, UK, Senior Research Professor, 2002-; Creator and manager of several international research projects funded by the Royal Society, British Council, NATO, EPSRC, JSPS, Air Force Research Office, which include projects with: Catholic University, Leuven, Belgium; Moscow State University and General Physics Institute, Russia; University of Tokyo, Japan; Australian National University, Australia; Ecole Nationale Superieure, ENSSAT, France; US Air Force Academy, USA. Publications: More than 200 articles in professional journals; Co-author 3 research books: Susceptibility Tensors for Non-Linear Optics, 1995; Polarization of Light in Non-Linear Optics, 1998; Encyclopaedia of Material Tensors, 1999. Honours: Grantee: EPSRC, Royal Society, NATO, R W Paul Instrument Fund, Leverhulme Trust; Leverhulme Senior Research Fellow, 2000. Memberships: Fellow, Institute of Physics, London; Member, Steering Committees, Quantum Electronics and Photonics Group and Applied Optics Group, Institute of Physics; Optical Society of America; Member, Programme and Organising Committees of numerous international conferences. Address: School of Physics & Astronomy, University of Southampton, Southampton SO17 1BJ. E-mail: nikolay@zheludev.net

ZHENG Kaiqi, b. 4 February 1929, Jiansu Province, China. Scientific Researcher. m. Yu Ren, 2 daughters. Education: Graduated Beijing Russian College, 1957. Appointments: Translator, Shanghai Sino-Soviet Friendship Association, 1951; Editor, Contemporary Foreign Philosophy and Social Sciences Digest, 1961; Teacher, Aiguo Middle School, 1970; Research Fellow, Director, Information Research Institute, Shanghai Academy of Social Sciences, 1978. Publications: Social Science Information: Theory and Methods; Meaning and Usage of the Cases of Nouns in German; Handbook of the Usage of German Preposition; Translations from Russian, German and English, 13 books in all; Chief Editor of 13 books. Memberships: Shanghai Assessment Committee for Senior Professional Titles in Social Sciences, 1987, for Titles in Translation, 1987. Address: Information Research Institute of Shanghai Academy of Social Sciences, Huaihai Road, Shanghai 200020, China.

ZHIRABOK Alexey, b. 27 November 1946, Khabarovsk. Radio and Electrical Educator. m. Nina, 1 daughter. Education: Engineer Degree, 1970; PhD, Radio Engineering, 1978; Dr Sc Degree, Control Engineering, 1996. Appointments: Assistant Professor, Far Eastern State Technical University, 1970-75; Associate Professor, 1979-83; Head of Department, 1983-92; Postdoctoral Trainee, 1992-95; Professor, 1996-. Publications: 2 books; 4 booklets; More than 140 articles. Honours: Soros Professor; Award of Soros Foundation; Honoured Higher School Worker of Russia; Listed in national and international biographical dictionaries. Memberships: IEEE; Russian Academy of Engineering. Address: Far Eastern State Technical University, Pushkinskaya Street 10, Vladivostok 690950, Russia.

ZHOU Erfu, b. 3 January 1914, Nanjing, China. Author; Calligrapher. 2 sons. Education: Bachelor of English Literature, Guanghua University, China, 1938. Appointments include: Eighth Army, Northern China, 1939-42; Editor, Mass magazine,

Chongqing City, 1944-46; Deputy Secretary, Culture Commission, Hong Kong Working Committee, CPC South Bureau, 1946-49; Secretary General, United Front Work Department, CPC East China Bureau, 1949-59; Deputy Director of Propaganda & the United Front Work Department, CPC Shanghai Committee, 1949-59; Secretary General of China Foreign Culture Liaison Commission, 1959-77; Deputy Secretary General of the 5th and Member of the 6th and 7th sessions of China People's Political Consultative Conference, 1978-92; Deputy Minister of Culture, 1978-80; Deputy Director of China Foreign Culture Liaison Commission, 1981; Vice-Chairman of Shanghai Branch; Consultant, China Writers' Association, 1950-; Standing Director, International Pen Club, China Centre, 1979-; Vice President and Consultant, China Calligraphers Association, 1980-. Publications: Numerous works include: Poetry: Night Stroll; Novels: Dr Norman Bethune; The Morning in Shanghai (4 volumes) which depicts the buy-out policy initiated unprecedly by CPC over private-owned capitals in the early stage of New China; Panorama of the Great Wall (6 volumes), a work of 16 years hardwork and worldwide data collection, which is the only river novel with panoramic views in China focusing on nationwide Anti-Japanese by both KMT and CPC armies, plus international allied countries participation; Collection of Zhou Erfu's Prose (4 volumes) Great Man Zhou Enlai (4 volumes, 57,000-line long poetry), which is the longest and rarely seen epic in China Han Nationality; Calligraphy works include: Zhou Erfu's Handscript on the Pipa Canto; Collection of Zhou Erfu's Calligraphy; Zhou Erfu's Handscript on Quyuan's Song of Parting. Honours: Listed in Who's Who publications and biographical dictionaries. Address: The Ministry of Culture of the People's Republic of China, 100020 Beijing, China. E-mail: zhouyankang@yahoo.com

ZHOU Kang-Wei, b. 21 June 1935, Zhongxian, Chongqing, China. Professor. m. Dai Shi-Fang, 1 daughter. Education: Graduate Physics, Sichuan University, 1961. Appointment: Physics Professor, Sichuan University, 1993-. Publications: Over 60 papers in professional journals. Honours: Science and Technology Award, National Education Commission, China, 1990, Sichuan, 1993. Memberships: AAAS; American Physical Society. Address: Department of Physics, Sichuan University, Chengdu 610065, China.

ZHOU Yuming, b. 23 June 1934, Hebei, China. Senior Translator. m. Shuying Li, 2 sons. Education: Graduate, Faculty of Foreign Languages and Literature, University of Central China, 1956. Appointments: Assistant Professor, University of Central China, 1956; English Translator, Chinese Ministry of the Petroleum Industry, 1974; Senior Translator, China National Offshore Oil Corporation, 1984; Retired 1994; Senior Translator, Enron Oil and Gas China Ltd, 1994-1999; Retired from Enron Oil and Gas, China, 1999. Publications: Books of modern lyrics: Flowing Bunch of Flowers; Kiss of Wings; Love of Dolphin; The Tenderly Grown Green; Selected Poems of Yuming; Earth Newborn; Selected Verses by Yuming; Books of long epic poems: Liang Shanbo and Zhu Yingtai – Chinese Romeo and Juliet; Love Between a Human Being and a Serpentine Being. Honours: Gold Prize of the Chinese Long "Dragon" Culture; Award, International Poet of Merit, International Society of Poets, America; Honorary Doctor of Literature of the World Academy of Arts and Culture; Distinguished Leadership Award, American Biographical Institute; Man of the Year 2002, ABI; The Founders Award, IBC; Universal Award of Accomplishment; American Medal of Honor; ABI World Laureate of China; Worldwide Honours List, IBC. Memberships: China Poetry Association; Member and Membership Director, World Congress of Poets; Distinguished Member, International Society of Poets. Address: 233, Building 7, Ruyili, Western District, Beijing 100035, China.

ZHU Bao-Ting, b. 20 January 1962, Shanghai, China. Professor. m. Karen Xiaomeng Xu, 1 daughter. Education: MB, 1985, MS, 1988, Shanghai Medical University; PhD, University of Texas Medical Branch, 1992. Appointments: Assistant Professor, Associate Professor, Full Professor, University of South Carolina, 1996-. Publications: Over 50 articles in professional journals. Honours: Burroughs Wellcome Toxicology-Teratology Award, 1992; Shirley Patricia Parker Memorial Award, 1993. Memberships: American Association for Cancer Research; The American Society for Pharmacology and Experimental Therapeutics. Address: University of South Carolina, College of Pharmacy, 700 Sumter Street, Columbia, SC 29208, USA. E-mail: btzhu@cop.sc.edu

ZHU Hong, b. 1 March 1960, Guiyang, China. Musician. m. Lu Deng, 1 son, 1 daughter. Education: BA, Central Conservatory of Music, Beijing, 1982; MM, Michigan State University, 1990; DMA, Michigan State University, 1995. Appointments: Assistant Professor, Central Conservatory of Music, Beijing, 1982-87; Instructor, Flint Institute of Music, 1989-94; Adjunct Instructor, University of Michigan-Flint, 1991-93; Murray State University, 1994-96; Instructor, Concert Master, Colorado Music Festival, 1996-; Associate Professor, Violin, University of Central Oklahoma, 1996-. Honours: Yehudi Menuhin Prize. Memberships: Chamber Music America; American Federation of Musicians; American String Teachers Association. Address: 1125 Bradford Place, Edmond, OK 73003, USA. E-mail: hzhu@ucok.edu

ZHU Yilin, b. 17 August 1934, Shanghai, China. Research Professor. m. Ye Bihua, 1 son, 1 daughter. Education: Bachelor, Nanjing Institute of Technology, 1953; Postgraduate Study, Harbin Institute of Technology, 1955; Postgraduate Study, Tsinghua University, 1959. Appointments: Engineer, 1958-65; Vice Director of Research Division, 1965-85; Vice Director, Science and Technology Commission, Institute of Spacecraft System Engineering, 1985-89; Secretary General, Science and Technology Commission, Chinese Academy of Space Technology, 1989-2000; Consultant, Beijing Institute of Space Science and Technology Information, 2000-. Publications: Space Technology Elementary; Flight to the Stars; Versatile in Space; Flight to Space; Space Time; An Introduction to China's Space Endeavour, in English; Over 150 academic papers and around 500 articles in Chinese and international journals, magazines and 6 other treatises. Honours: Second State Prize, State Council, 1985; Merit Citation Class II, Ministry of Aerospace of China; Government Special Subsidy, State Council. Memberships: Corresponding Member, International Academy of Astronautics, 1999-; Standing Committee, Chinese Society of Space Science, 1980-96; Councils of Chinese Society of Space Science and Chinese Society of Science Writers. Address: Room 502, Building 11, 31 Zhongguencun Nandajie, Haidian District, Beijing, 100081, China.

ZHURAVLEV Sergei, b. 30 November 1936, Ural'sk, Russia. Mathematician; Educator. m. Irina Grishko, 1 son, 1 daughter. MSc, Mechanics, Moscow Aviation Institute, Moscow, Russia, 1962; PhD, Mathematics and Physics, Patrice Lumumba University, Moscow, Russia, 1970; DrSc, Mathematics and Physics, Lomonosov State University, Moscow, Russia, 1983. Senior Engineer, Research Bureau, Moscow, Russia, 1962-65; Assistant, Lumumba University, Moscow, Russia, 1969-73; Lecturer, Dar-Es-Salaam Technical College, Tanzania, 1973-75; Professor, Technical University, Moscow, Russia, 1975-. Publications: The Asteroids: A History of Origin, Statistics and Evolution, 1979; Artificial Satellites of Earth, 1980; Method of Investigation of Sharp Resonant Problem of Celestial Mechanics and Astrodynamics part 1: Orbital Motion, 2000, part 2: Transitory-rotary Motion, 2002.

Dictionary of International Biography

Membership: AMS. Address: Technical University (MADI), Leningradsky pr 64, 125829 Moscow, Russia. E-mail: zhur@umat.madi.ru

ZIELINSKI Andrzej, b. 14 November 1939, Poznan, Poland. Lawyer. Education: Master in Law, Faculty of Law, Adam Mickiewicz University, Poznan, Poland, 1962; Doctor of Law, 1976; Assistant Professor, 1994; Professor, 1995. Appointments: Apprenticeship in Judicial Profession, 1962-64; Apprenticeship in Attorney Profession, 1966-69; Attorney; Tutoring and Scientific Employee, Faculty of Law, University of Szczecin, 1969-; Head of Civil Proceeding Cathedra, High School of Trade and Law, Warsaw, 1997-. Publications: 14 scientific books of civil proceedings and family law; 120 scientific articles. Honours: Gold Cross of Merit; Silver Cross of Merit. Membership: Scientific Association in Szczecin, branch of National Academy of Science. Address: ul Dabrowskiego 12 c/7, 70-100 Szczecin, Poland.

ZIMIN Sergey Pavlovich, b. 18 June 1954, Yaroslavl, Russia. Physicist; Educator; Researcher. m. Olga Kuzikova, 10 April 1976, 1 son, 2 daughters. Education: Diploma as Physicist, Yaroslavl State University, 1976; DSc, Physics, Mathematics, 1989. Appointments: Engineer, Electronpribor, Yaroslavl, 1976-77; Senior Researcher, 1977-90, Associate Professor, 1990-, Yaroslavl State University. Publications: More than 200 scientific publications. Honour: Honorary Title, Soros Associate Professor, 1999, 2000, 2001. Membership: Active Member, New York Academy of Sciences. Address: Komsomolskaya 10-3, Yaroslavl 150000, Russia. E-mail: zimin@univ.uniyar.ac.ru

ZIVELONGHI Kurt, b. 3 October 1960, Barstow, California, USA. Designer; Painter. Education: Art Students League, New York, 1988-89; Studies with Ted Seth Jacobs, Ecole D'Albert Defois, Anger, France, 1989; BFA, Art Center College of Design, Pasadena, California, 1990-93. Career: Independent Artist and Painter, 1993-; Exhibitions across USA, Spain, and Bosnia and Herzegovina. Publications: Illustration for Potpourri Magazine, Summer Edition, 2002; Editorial Cartoon, University of North Carolina Monitor, 2002. Honours: Listed in international biographical dictionaries; Exhibited at EuroArt '99 III Salo Internacional d'Artistes Contemporanis Independents, Barcelona, 1999. Memberships: American Academy of Poets. Address: 960 E Bonita Ave #55, Pomona, CA 91767, USA. E-mail: kzivelonghi@earthlink.net

ZLOCHEVSKAYA Alla, b. 10 November 1951, Moscow, Russia. Literary Critic; Researcher. Education: MA, Philology, Moscow State University; Defended and published 2 literary research theses: PhD equivalent, 1982 and 2002. Appointments: Research Worker, 1985-2000, Senior Researcher, 2000-, Department of Philology, Moscow State University, Russia. Publications: Published about 70 research articles concerning Russian literature of XIX-XX centuries and Czech and Slovak Rusistik; In-depth study of F Dostoyevsky, V Nabokov, M Bulgakov; Monograph: Artistic World of V Nabokov and Russian Literature of XIX Century, 2002. Membership: F M Dostoyevsky Society, Moscow. Address: Olympic Village 8, Flat 153, Mitchurinsky Pr. Moscow 119602, Russia. E-mail: zlocevskaya@mail.ru

ZOLBERG Vera L, b. 22 September 1932, Vienna, Austria. Sociology Professor. m. Aristide R Zolberg, 1 son, 1 daughter. Education: AB, Hunter College, 1950; MA, Boston University, 1956; PhD, University of Chicago, 1974. Appointments: Edgewood College, Madison, Wisconsin, 1962-64; St Xavier College, Chicago, 1964-71; Purdue University, 1974-84; Professor, New School for Social Research, 1984-. Publications include:

Outsider Art: Contested Boundaries in Contemporary Culture; The Happy Few-en Masse: Franco-American Comparisons in Cultural Democratization; Constructing a Sociology of the Arts. Honours: Rockefeller Humanities Fellowship; ACLS Fellowship; Several travel grants. Memberships: American Sociological Association; Society for Social Theory, Politics and the Arts; International Sociological Association; Association Internationale des Sociologues de Langue Francaise; Eastern Sociological Society; American Council for the Arts. Address: New School for Social Research, 65th Avenue, New York City, NY 10003, USA.

ZUBOVICH Stanislav Francevich, b. 12 July 1937, Ukraine. m. Natalia, 1 son. Education: Technical College, Department of Cartography, Kiev, 1956-59; Faculty of Geography, Belarusian State University, 1963-69; Aspiranture of Laboratory of Geochemical Problems, Academy of Sciences, Minsk, 1969-72; Medical College, Minsk, 1993-96. Appointments: Technician of Topography, 1959; Geography Assistant, 1969; Scientific Worker, 1972; Doctor of Sciences, Geology and Mineralogy, 1973; Senior Scientific Worker, 1973; Professor, Belarusian State Pedagogical Institute, 1986-. Publications include: 14 monographs; 3 popular books, 204 science articles; 73 new taxons of fossils and recent ostracodas; Author, theoretical basis and creation of Ostracodology of Plaistocaen as a separate scientific trend. Honours: 1 Silver and 3 Bronze Medals, Exhibition of National Economics of the USSR; Medals, International Man of the Year, 1999-2000, 2000-01, 2003, 20th Century Award for Achievement, 21st Century Award for Achievement, International Intellectual of the Year, 2001, International Scientists of the Year, 2003; International Educator of the year 2003; One-in-a-Million, One Thousand Great Intellectuals, 2000 Outstanding People, International Educator of the Year, 2003, International Order of Merit, IBC, England; Diploma, 1000 Leaders of World of Influence, 500 Leaders of Influence, Commemorative Medal, Man of Year, 2001, ABI, USA; The Honoured Master of Education of Belarus; Medal for Sports Achievement of Trade Union of the USSR; Medal for Development of Youth Tourism in the USSR. Memberships: Geographical Society of Belarus; Society of Country Sciences; International Academy of Ecology and Natural Employment; Deputy Director General, IBC. Address: Belarusian State Pedagogical University, Str Sovetskaya 18, 220809 Minsk, Belarus.

ZUBRITSKY Alexander, b. 14 March 1949, Severo-Kurilsk, Sakhalin Region, Russia. Pathologist. Education: Curative and Preventative Faculty, Sverdlovsk Medical Institute, 1968-74; I year specialism in Pathological Anatomy, Sverdlovsk Regional Clinical Hospital No 1, 1975; Advanced Training Course for Pathological Anatomy, Kharkov, Ukraine Institute of Advanced Medical Studies, 1977; Advanced Training Course for Perinatal Pathology, Moscow Institute for Postgraduate Medical Training, 1986; PhD, 1991; Advanced Training Course for Cytology, Moscow Regional Research Clinical Institute, 1994; Pathological Anatomy, Russian Medical Academy for Postgraduate Training, 2000. Appointments: Hospital Attendant, Department of Pathology, City Hospital No 21, Sverdlovsk, 1965-67; Hospital Attendant, Medico-Legal Morgue No 1, Sverdlovsk, 1967-68; Chief of Pathology Department, Central Regional Hospital in Neviyansk, Sverdlovsk Region, 1975-76; Chief of Pathology Department, Head Pathologist, Sverdlovsk Road, 1976-83; Lecturer, Pathological Anatomy, Medical School of Sverdlovsk Road, 1976-77; Chief of Department of Pathology, Municipal Institution, Taldom Central Regional Hospital, Taldom, Moscow Region, 1983-. Publications: 4 rationalisation proposals; 165 published works as sole author. Honours: Certificate, A Finalist, Marvin I Dunn Award, Best Poster Presentation in Cardiology, American College of Chest Physicians, 1990; Pathology Research Practice Award for the Expert Quiz, Innsbruck, MD Taldom, 1993; International Man of the Year, 1994-

95; Certificate, Researcher of the Year, ABI, 2001; International Peace Prize Winner, UCC, 2003; 21st Century Award for Achievement, IBC, 2003; Listed in Several Biographical Publications. Memberships: European Society of Pathology 1989; International Union Against Tuberculosis and Lung Disease, 1990; European Section, International Society for Heart Research, 1992; International Society on Diagnostic Quantitative Pathology, 1994; New York Academy of Sciences, 1995; Research Board of Advisors, ABI, 2000; Honorary Member, IBC Advisory Council, 2000; American Association for the Advancement of Science, 2003. Address: Prospekt Mira101 B/79, Moscow 129085, Russia.

ZUK-HRYSKIEVIC Raisa, b. 22 October 1919, Belarus. Dental Surgeon. m. Vincent, 4 September 1953, 1 daughter. Education: Law, Steven Batory University, Vilna, 1938-39; Faculty of Dentistry, University Marburg, Germany, 1948; Student, Faculty of Dentistry, University of Toronto, Canada, 1951-54; DDS, Senat, University of Toronto, Canada, 1954. Appointments: General Practice, Toronto, Barrie, Ontario, Canada, 1954-90; Member, Belarus Republic, Canadian Consultative Council on Multiculturalism, 1973-78 Retired. Publications: Articles in Belarusan Newspapers; Book, The Life of Vincent Zuk-Hryskievic. Honour: Volunteer Service Award, 1986. Memberships: Belarusan Study Association; Canadian Dental Association; Ontario Dental Association; Simcoe Dental Association; University Womens' Club; Soroptimist Club of Barrie; Belarusan Canadian Alliance; Belarusan Canadian Womens' Association; Belarusan Canadian Co-ordinating Committee; Institute of Arts and Science, Canana; Belarusan Democratic Republic in Exile. Address: 54 Mary Street, Barrie, Ontario, Canada, L4N 1T1.

ZUTSHI Derek Wyndham Hariram, b. 26 April 1930, London, England. Consultant Rheumatologist. m. Dr Marguerite Elizabeth Smith. Education: MBChB, University of Bristol, England; Fellow, Royal College of Physicians, London, (FRCP). Appointments: Houseman Professional, Medical Unit and casualty/Orthopaedic Departments, Bristol Royal Infirmary, 1957-58; Houseman Professional, Obstetric and Paediatric Units, Southmead Hospital, Bristol 1958-59; Senior House Officer, Llandough Hospital, Cardiff, 1959-61; Medical Registrar,1963-65; Medical Registrar, MRC Rheumatism Research Unit, 1966-68, Canadian Red Cross Memorial Hospital, Taplow; Senior Registrar, Rheumatology, and Clinical Tutor, Medicine, The London Hospital, 1968-73; Consultant Rheumatologist, Prince of Wales's and St Ann's General Hospitals, Tottenham, London, 1973-77; Medical Director, School of Physiotherapy, Prince of Wales's General Hospital, 1973-77; Examiner, Chartered Society of Physiotherapy, 1974-78; Senior Medical Officer, Medicines and Communicable Disease Divisions, DHSS, 1976-86; Examiner, College of Occupational Therapists, 1980-89; Temporary Advisor, WHO, 1981-82; Disability Appeal Tribunals, Independent Tribunal Service, 1992-99; Consultant Rheumatologist, 1973-. Publications: Papers on medical, rheumatological and immunological subjects and Sumerian medicine. Honours: Honorary Fellow, The Hunterian Society, 1991; Honorary LLD, University of Bristol, 1999. Memberships include: President, Students Union, 1953; Member Court, 1958-, Member, Council, 1988-2000, Member, Standing Committee of Convocation, 1981-, Chairman, 1988-98, University of Bristol; Chairman, Federal Council of Indian Organisations, 1994-95; Council Member, Section of Rheumatology, Royal Society of Medicine, 1973-76; Councillor and Honorary Secretary, British Association for Rheumatology and Rehabilitation, 1974-78; Member of Council, Medical Society of London, 1977-80; Member of Council, The Hunterian Society, 1978-96, Honorary Treasurer, 1979-93, President, 1993-94, Vice-President, 1994-96; Member, Board of Trustees, The Hindu Centre, London, 1962-95, Chairman, 1984-95, Patron, 1996-; Member Board of Governors, Tottenham

College of Further Education, 1974-90, Vice Chairman, 1978-87; National Rubella Council (National Council for Child Health), Member, Management Committee, 1983-86, 1989-90; Founder Director, Eton Court Ltd, 1980-, Secretary, 1982-86, Chairman, 1996-; Founder, Director, Freehold of Eton Court, Ltd, 1994-2003, Secretary, 1995-96, Chairman, 1996-2003; Freeman City of London; Liveryman, Worshipful Company of Apothecaries; Fellow, Royal Society of Arts; Fellow Royal Society of Medicine; Athenaeum. Address: 36 Eton Court, Eton Avenue, Hampstead, London NW3 3HJ, England.

ZWEIFLER Richard, b. 7 December 1964, New York. Neurologist. m. Kim, 3 daughters. Education: BSE, Bioengineering, University of Pennsylvania, 1982-1986; MD, Tulane Medical School, 1986-1990; Internship, Internal Medicine, Ochsner Foundation Hospital, 1990-1991; Neurology Residency, University of California at San Diego, 1991-1994; Cerebrovascular Disease Fellowship, University of California at San Diego, 1994-95; Clinical Instructor in Neurosciences, University of California at San Diego, 1994-1995; Assistant Professor of Neurology, 1995-1999, Associate Professor of Neurology, 1999-, University of South Alabama. Publications: 4 book chapters; 32 abstract and minor publications; 18 manuscripts. Honours: Scarlet Sash Teaching Award, USA, 2003; Golden Neuron Award, Most Outstanding Resident, UCSD, 1994; Chief Neurology Resident UCSD, 1993-1994; Golden Diaper Award in Paediatric Neurology, UCSD, 1993; Hyman S Myerson Award in Physiology Research, Tulane, 1990; Herman P Schwarn Bioengineering Award, University of Pennsylvania, 1986; Tau Beta Pi Engineering Honor Society, 1985; Listed in national and international biographical dictionaries. Memberships: American Academy of Neurology; Fellow, American Stroke Association; National Stroke Association. Address: USA Stroke Center, 2451 Fillingim Street, Mobile, AL 36617, USA. E-mail: rzweifle@usouthal.edu

ZWILLENBERG Lutz Oscar, b. 9 December 1925, Berlin-Charlottenburg, Germany. Biologist. m. Dr Celia Fridman, 2 daughters. Education: Graduated, Gymnasium, Hilversum and Amsterdam, 1940-43; Baccalaureate, Barlaeus Gymnasium, Amsterdam, 1946; PhD, Natural Sciences, University of Amsterdam, 1959. Appointments: Assistant, Department of Anatomy, 1959-63, Senior Research Assistant, Department of Hygiene and Medical Microbiology, 1963-67, University of Bern; Founder, Proprietor, Biologisches Forschungslaboratorium, Dres. Zwillenberg, Bern, 1970-; President, ZW Biomedical Research AG, Bern, 1994-2002; Main research interests: Histology; Microbiology; Virology; Electron microscopy; Ectocervical epithelium; Gynaecology; Pharmacology; Philosophy of Science. Publications: Numerous papers and articles contributed to conferences and specialist peer-reviewed journals; 2 books, Woher und Wozu, 1980; Zwischen Bit und Bibel 1986, 1987; Editor, Tradition und Erneuerung (journal of the Swiss Association for Progressive Judaism) Translator Prayerbook, Gottesdienst im Herzen (Avodah Shebalev). Memberships: American Association for the Advancement of Science; New York Academy of Sciences; Swiss Association of Anatomists; Swiss Association of Biochemistry; Swiss Association of Natural Science. Address: Holligenstrasse 93 CH-3008 Bern, Switzerland.

ZYUNG Taehyoung, b. 24 September 1954, Republic of Korea. Research Scientist. m. Sangsub Yoon, 1 son, 1 daughter. Education: BS, Seoul National University, Korea, 1977; PhD, Texas Tech University, USA, 1986. Appointments: Researcher, KIST, 1978-81; Research Assistant, Texas Tech University, 1981-86; Postdoctoral Research Associate, University of Illinois, 1986-89; Principal Member of Research Staff, 1989-2000, Director, 2001-, ETRI, Korea. Publications: Electrical and Optical Polymer

Systems, 1998; Display Engineering, 2000; Advanced Functional Molecules and Polymers, 2001. Honours: ISI Citation Classic Award, 2000; Songkok Award, 2001. Memberships: Korean Chemical Society; Polymer Society of Korea. Address: 109-1504 Hanwood Apt, Sinsung-dong, Yusong-gu, Taejon, Korea.

20TH CENTURY HONOURS LIST

NAME: Dr Farid A Akasheh LFIBA

ADDRESS: PO Box 2173
Amman
Jordan

OCCUPATION: Doctor (Consultant Obstetrician and Gynaecologist)

YEAR OF ENTRY: 1986

CITATION: For your Outstanding Contribution to Medicine

NAME: Dr Farouk M Akhdar LFIBA

ADDRESS: The Economic Bureau
PO Box 86619
Riyadh 11632
Kingdom of Saudi Arabia

OCCUPATION: President of the Economic Bureau

YEAR OF ENTRY: 1989

CITATION: For your Outstanding Contribution to Economics and to the development of Saudi Arabia

NAME: Abdullatif A R Al-Bahar

ADDRESS: PO Box 89
Safat
13001 Kuwait City
Kuwait

OCCUPATION: Director General, Office of H H The Crown Prince & Prime Minister - Kuwait

YEAR OF ENTRY: 1989

CITATION: For you Outstanding Contribution to his present position within the field of Political & Economics Institutions

NAME: Ahmad Mohamad Ali

ADDRESS: Islamic Development Bank
PO Box 5925
Jeddah 21432
Saudi Arabia

OCCUPATION: President, Islamic Development Bank

YEAR OF ENTRY: 1990

CITATION: For your Outstanding Contribution to the Banking Business

NAME: Jacob Oladele Amao DDG LFIBA

ADDRESS: PO Box 51722
Ikoyi
Lagos
Nigeria

OCCUPATION: Company President - Executive

YEAR OF ENTRY: 1990

CITATION: For your Outstanding Contribution to the Banking Business

NAME: Professor Basile Angelopoulos MD PhD LPIBA DDG

ADDRESS: Ipsilantou Str 37
Athens 106-76
Greece

OCCUPATION: Professor in Pathologic Physiology

YEAR OF ENTRY: 1986

CITATION: For your Outstanding Contribution to Medicine

NAME: Kathlyn Ballard LPIBA

ADDRESS: 40 Mont Victor Road
Kew
3101 Melbourne
Australia

OCCUPATION: Artist

YEAR OF ENTRY: 1986

CITATION: For your Outstanding Contribution to Art

NAME: Abdul Rahman Batal LPIBA LFWLA DDG AdVBus

ADDRESS: Chairman, Hannibal Tourism & Transport Co
PO Box 4088
Damascus
Syria

OCCUPATION: Company Chairman

YEAR OF ENTRY: 1986

CITATION: For your Outstanding Contribution to Tourism and
Transport

NAME: Shauna D Boulton LFIBA DDG

ADDRESS: 1516 Glen Arbor
Salt Lake City
UT 84105
USA

OCCUPATION: Educator

YEAR OF ENTRY: 1986

CITATION: For your Outstanding Contribution to Education

NAME: Richard E Butler LFIBA

ADDRESS: 40 Barrington Avenue
Kew
Victoria 3101
Australia

OCCUPATION: International Official

YEAR OF ENTRY: 1990

CITATION: For your Outstanding Contribution to International Cooperation and to World-wide Telecommunication Development

NAME: Professor Chen Jian Hong

ADDRESS: Gansu University of Tech
Lanzhou
Gansu
China

OCCUPATION: President, Professor

YEAR OF ENTRY: 1989

CITATION: For your Outstanding Contribution to the Science and Education of China

NAME: Thomas J Cleary

ADDRESS: 933 Kiowa
Burkburnett
TX 76354
USA

OCCUPATION: Clinical Social Worker, Teaching Assistant, Graduate Student US History MSU

YEAR OF ENTRY: 1989

CITATION: For your Outstanding Contribution to Social Work Service

NAME: The Hon Dame Dr Joy Beaudette Cripps N.H DGC
DCMSS IOM LFWLA MOIF LDAF

ADDRESS: 3 Mill Street
Aspendale
Victoria 3195
Australia

OCCUPATION: Publisher, Poet, Photographer

YEAR OF ENTRY: 1988

CITATION: For your Outstanding Contribution to Literature

NAME: Basil V Damalas

ADDRESS: Parission 171
Athens 112 52
Greece

OCCUPATION: Publicist and Economist

YEAR OF ENTRY: 1986

CITATION: For your Outstanding Contribution to Economics

NAME: Dr J Edward Dealy MS PhD

ADDRESS: 1040 W Rio Guaymas
Green Valley
AZ 85614-4026
USA

OCCUPATION: Forestry

YEAR OF ENTRY: 1986

CITATION: For your Outstanding Contribution to Forestry

NAME: Thaneswari De Silva LPIBA

ADDRESS: 148/2A Kynsey Road
Colombo 8
Sri Lanka

OCCUPATION: Estate Proprietoress and Directress 'Leighton Park'
Montessori and Junior School

YEAR OF ENTRY: 1986

CITATION: For your Outstanding Contribution as Montessori and
Junior School Directress

NAME: Howard M Dupuy Jr BA LLP

ADDRESS: 465 NE 181st Avenue = 110
Portland
OR 97230
USA

OCCUPATION: Lawyer

YEAR OF ENTRY: 1986

CITATION: For your Outstanding Contribution to The Law

NAME: Chris Economides

ADDRESS: 6 Dositheos
PO Box 1632
Nicosia
Cyprus

OCCUPATION: Director

YEAR OF ENTRY: 1988

CITATION: For your Outstanding Contribution to Economics

NAME: Professor M Gembicki MD

ADDRESS: Department of Endocrinology
University School of Medicine in Poznan
Al Przybyszewskiego 49
PL-60 355, Poland

OCCUPATION: Doctor

YEAR OF ENTRY: 1986

CITATION: For your Outstanding Contribution to Medicine

NAME: Dr Richard Sherwin Gothard

ADDRESS: Gothard House
Henley-on-Thames
Oxon RE9 1AJ
England

OCCUPATION: Information Scientist

YEAR OF ENTRY: 1986

CITATION: For your Outstanding Contribution to Information
Science

NAME: Violet Edna Hobbs Hain

ADDRESS: 3530 Raymoor Road
Kensington
MD 20895
USA

OCCUPATION: Artist

YEAR OF ENTRY: 1986

CITATION: For your Outstanding Contribution to Art

NAME:	Dr Paul L C Hao

ADDRESS:	10FI No 116
	Nanking East Road, Sec 2
	Taipei
	Taiwan

OCCUPATION:	Biochemist

YEAR OF ENTRY:	1986

CITATION:	For your Outstanding Contribution to Science

NAME:	Dr Kazuyuki Hatada DDG LFIBA IOM

ADDRESS:	Department of Mathematics
	Faculty of Education, Gifu University
	1-1 Yanagido, Gifu City
	Gifu Prefecture 501-1193, Japan

OCCUPATION:	Mathematician

YEAR OF ENTRY:	1990

CITATION:	For your Outstanding Contribution to Pure Mathematics, especially to the Theory of Modular Forms

NAME:	Professor Zuey-Shin Hsu MD LFIBA DDG IOM MOIF

ADDRESS:	Department of Physiology
	Kaohsiung Medical College
	No 100 Shih-Chuan 1st Road, Kaohsiung
	Taiwan

OCCUPATION:	Professor of Physiology

YEAR OF ENTRY:	1989

CITATION:	For your Outstanding Contribution to Medical Science and the Teaching Profession

NAME:

John Chih-An Hu

ADDRESS:

2813 Whitworth Avenue
Renton
WA 98055
USA

OCCUPATION:

Chemist and Chemical Engineer

YEAR OF ENTRY:

1986

CITATION:

For your Outstanding Contribution to Chemistry

NAME:

Professor Dr Kazuyosi Ikeda DSc DLitt LPIBA DDG
IOM LFWLA MOIF CH DO

ADDRESS:

Nisi - 7 - 7 - 11 Aomadani
Minoo-Si
Osaka 562-0023
Japan

OCCUPATION:

Professor of Theoretical Physics and Poet

YEAR OF ENTRY:

1989

CITATION:

For your Outstanding Contribution to Theoretical
Physics and Poetry

NAME:

Dr Drago Ikic LFIBA

ADDRESS:

Croation Academy of Sciences and Arts
Gunduliceva 24/11
Zagreb 10000
Croatia

OCCUPATION:

Doctor

YEAR OF ENTRY:

1986

CITATION:

For your Outstanding Contribution to Medicine

NAME: Hazel Emma Jones FIBA

ADDRESS: 35 Greer Street
Bardon
Queensland 4065
Australia

OCCUPATION: Librarian

YEAR OF ENTRY: 1986

CITATION: For your Outstanding Contribution to Librarianship

NAME: Kristjan G Kjartansson

ADDRESS: Einimelur 7
107 Reykjavik
Iceland

OCCUPATION: Company Vice President

YEAR OF ENTRY: 1986

CITATION: For your Outstanding Contribution to Commerce

NAME: Professor Lidia Agnes Kozubek

ADDRESS: ul J Dabrowskiego 77m.9
02-503 Warsaw
Poland

OCCUPATION: Pianist, Educator and Musicologist

YEAR OF ENTRY: 1986

CITATION: For your Outstanding Contribution to Music

NAME: Dr Vernette Landers LPIBA LFWLA DDG MOIF IOM DO

ADDRESS: PO Box 3839
Landers
CA 92285
USA

OCCUPATION: Educator

YEAR OF ENTRY: 1986

CITATION: For your Outstanding Contribution to Education and
Community

NAME: Dato Dr Sip Hon Lew

ADDRESS: 15 Jalan 12
Taman Tun Abdul Razak
Ampang Jaya
Selangor, Malaysia

OCCUPATION: Company Director, Retired Ambassador

YEAR OF ENTRY: 1988

CITATION: For your Outstanding Contribution to the economic,
political and cultural life of Malaysia and to your role
in the larger world community

NAME: Anneliese List LFWLA LFIBA IOM MOIF HE

ADDRESS: Fuenfbronn 27
91174 Spalt
Germany

OCCUPATION: Soubrette

YEAR OF ENTRY: 1986

CITATION: For your Outstanding Contribution to Literature

NAME: Konstantin Mandic IOM

ADDRESS: PO Box 672
Gaborone
Botswana
Africa

OCCUPATION: Architect

YEAR OF ENTRY: 1989

CITATION: For your Outstanding Contribution to Architecture

NAME: Professor Dr Mitsuo Masai

ADDRESS: Faculty of Engineering
Kobe University
Rokkadai-Cho, Nada-Ku
Kobe 657
Japan

OCCUPATION: University Professor

YEAR OF ENTRY: 1986

CITTION: For your Outstanding Contribution to Catalysis

NAME: Emeritus Professor Junji Matsumoto LFIBA IOM

ADDRESS: 2-3-14 Asukano Minami
Ikoma City
630-01 Japan

OCCUPATION: Neuroscientist

YEAR OF ENTRY: 1988

CITATION: For your Outstanding Contribution to Science

NAME: Professor Seiichi Matsumoto

ADDRESS: Yuigahama 1-11-17
Kamakura 248-0014
Japan

OCCUPATION: Director and Professor

YEAR OF ENTRY: 1986

CITATION: For your Outstanding Contribution to Medicine

NAME: Ralph E Montijo DDG IOM LPIBA

ADDRESS: 7811 E Edison St
Tucson
AZ 85715-4255

OCCUPATION: Company President, Executive

YEAR OF ENTRY: 1987

CITATION: For your Outstanding Contribution to Business

NAME: Peggy Jean Mueller IOM

ADDRESS: PO Box 5868
Austin
TX 78763
USA

OCCUPATION: Dance Teacher/Choreographer

YEAR OF ENTRY: 1990

CITATION: For your Outstanding Contribution to Dancing,
Ranching and Trail Riding

NAME: Hassenally Nanuck LFIBA

ADDRESS: PO Box 40346
Gaborone
Botswana

OCCUPATION: Auto Body Mechanic and Panel Beater

YEAR OF ENTRY: 1992

CITATION: For your Outstanding Contribution to Auto Body
Mechanics and Panel Beating

NAME: Professor Henry Ian A Nowik DDG

ADDRESS: 1250 Merchant Lane
McLean
VA 22101
USA

OCCUPATION: Education

YEAR OF ENTRY: 1990

CITATION: For your Outstanding Contribution to Education

NAME: Dr Wilson Reid Ogg LPIBA LFWLA DDG MOIF

ADDRESS: Pinebrook at Bret Harte Way
1104 Keith Avenue
Berkeley
CA 94708
USA

OCCUPATION: Poet, Graphic Illustrator, Publisher,
Retired Lawyer and Educator

YEAR OF ENTRY: 1991

CITATION: For your Outstanding Contribution to the Legal
Profession

NAME: Masa Aki Oka DDG

ADDRESS: 3-24-15-401
Tsurumaki
Setagaya-ku
Tokyo 154
Japan

OCCUPATION: Businessman

YEAR OF ENTRY: 1991

CITATION: For your Outstaniding Contribution to Finance and
Banking

NAME: Dr Irene M K Ovenstone LFIBA

ADDRESS: 10 Moor Road
Calverton
Nottingham
NG14 6FW
England

OCCUPATION: Consultant Psychiatrist

YEAR OF ENTRY: 1986

CITATION: For your Outstanding Contribution to Psychiatry

NAME: Dr Pritam Singh Panesar LFIBA DDG

ADDRESS: PO Box 46235
Nairobi
Kenya

OCCUPATION: Engineer and Pilot

YEAR OF ENTRY: 1986

CITATION: For your Outstanding Contribution to Engineering

NAME:　　　　　　　　Dr Lucy T Parker LPIBA DDG IOM

ADDRESS:　　　　　　205 Harbor Drive
Sitka
AK 99835-7552
USA

OCCUPATION:　　　　Director, The Parker Academy

YEAR OF ENTRY:　　1986

CITATION:　　　　　　For your Outstanding Contribution to Education

NAME:　　　　　　　　Robert Al Serlippens LPIBA IOM

ADDRESS:　　　　　　c/o Vanderbeck
2 Chemin Coparty Bte 5
B1400 Nivelles
Belgium

OCCUPATION:　　　　Attorney at Law

YEAR OF ENTRY:　　1986

CITATION:　　　　　　For your Outstanding Contribution to The Law

NAME:　　　　　　　　Dr Isadore Shapiro BChE PhD DDG IOM

ADDRESS:　　　　　　5624 West 62nd Street
Los Angeles
CA 90056
USA

OCCUPATION:　　　　Material Scientist

YEAR OF ENTRY:　　1990

CITATION:　　　　　　For your Outstanding Contribution to Science

NAME: Carolyn Juanita Shearer LFIBA

ADDRESS: 205 South Tucson Circle
Aurora
CO 80012
USA

OCCUPATION: Educator

YEAR OF ENTRY: 1990

CITATION: For your Outstanding Contribution to Education

NAME: Dr Muhammad M Mukram Sheikh PhD HLFIBA DDG

ADDRESS: PO Box 1974
Gaborone
Botswana

OCCUPATION: Government Official, Marketing Executive, Public
Relations Specialist

YEAR OF ENTRY: 1992

CITATION: For your Outstanding Contribution to Trade Journalism

NAME: Daphne Marjorie Sheldrick

ADDRESS: David Sheldrick Wildlife Trust
Box 15555
Nairobi
Kenya

OCCUPATION: Authoress and Wildlife Specialist

YEAR OF ENTRY: 1989

CITATION: For your Outstanding Contribution to Wildlife
Conservation

NAME:	Professor Koki Shimoji MD DDG LFIBA
ADDRESS:	2-808 Suido-cho Niigata 951-2181 Japan
OCCUPATION:	Professor and Chairman
YEAR OF ENTRY:	1986
CITATION:	For your Outstanding Contribution to Medicine

NAME:	Kathleen Stuart Strehlow LFIBA
ADDRESS:	30 Da Costa Avenue Prospect SA 5082 Australia
OCCUPATION:	Research Director
YEAR OF ENTRY:	1986
CITATION:	For your Outstanding Contribution to Education

NAME:	Dr Srikanta M N Swamy LFIBA DDG IOM
ADDRESS:	H961-49 Concordia University, Montreal Quebec H3G 1M8 Canada
OCCUPATION:	Electrical Engineer
YEAR OF ENTRY:	1986
CITATION:	For your Outstanding Contribution to Engineering

NAME: Dr Vern William Urry PhD LPABI LFIBA LFWLA

ADDRESS: 806 Tepic Drive
El Paso
TX 79912
USA

OCCUPATION: Personnel Research Psychologist

YEAR OF ENTRY: 1986

CITATION: For your Outstanding Contribution to Research
Psychology

NAME: Professor R F Vliegen LFIBA DDG IOM

ADDRESS: Residentie Seniorum
Koniriksemsteenweg 66.6.110
3700 Tongeren
Belgium

OCCUPATION: Honorary Consul of Belgium

YEAR OF ENTRY: 1991

CITATION: For your Outstanding Contribution to Musicology
Related Education and International Exchange

NAME: M R Wiemann LPIBA LFWLA DDG IOM MOIF

ADDRESS: 418 South 9th Street
PO Box 1016
Chesterton
IN 46304
USA

OCCUPATION: Biologist, Microscopist

YEAR OF ENTRY: 1991

CITATION: For your Outstanding Contribution to Theoretical and
Applied Biology

NAME: Dr Azi Wolfenson U PhD LPIBA DDG

ADDRESS:
3781 NE 208 Terr
N Miami Beach
FL 33180
USA

OCCUPATION: Engineer

YEAR OF ENTRY: 1986

CITATION: For your Outstanding Contribution to Engineering and Development

NAME: Professor Dr Ken-ichi Yoshihara LPIBA DDG IOM MOIF AdVAh

ADDRESS:
2-9-26 Yamanone
Zushi
Kanagawa 249-0002
Japan

OCCUPATION: Professor of Engineering

YEAR OF ENTRY: 1988

CITATION: For your Outstanding Contribution to Mathematical Statistics

NAME: Professor Zhang Shi-ding LFIBA IOM

ADDRESS:
1911-43-401 Caobao Road
Shanghai 201101
China

OCCUPATION: Teacher

YEAR OF ENTRY: 1991

CITATION: For your Outstanding Contribution to Education

21ST CENTURY HONOURS LIST

NAME: Edmund Norwood Bacon

ADDRESS: 2117 Locust Street
Philadelphia
PA 19103
USA

OCCUPATION: City Planner

YEAR OF ENTRY: 2001

CITATION: For your Outstanding Contribution to City Planning

NAME: Daniel D Brunda DDG LPIBA MOIF IOM AdVSci

ADDRESS: 106 West Upper Ferry Road
Ewing
NJ 08628
USA

OCCUPATION: Consultant: Mechanical/Electromagnetic Powerline
Radiation/Engineer/Scientist

YEAR OF ENTRY: 2002

CITATION: For your Outstanding Contribution to the Design and
Control of Electrical Transmission, Distribution and
Service Lines

NAME: Dr C Juliana Ching LPIBA DDG IOM MOIF AdVBus

ADDRESS: 4 Mount Butler Drive
Jardine's Lookout
Hong Kong

OCCUPATION: Businesswoman

YEAR OF ENTRY: 2000

CITATION: For your Outstanding Contribution to Business &
Medicine

NAME: Donald Mercer Cormie LLM. Q.C. IOM

ADDRESS: 5101 N Casa Bianca = 314
Scottsdale
AZ 85253
USA

OCCUPATION: Barrister

YEAR OF ENTRY: 2001

CITATION: For your Outstanding Contribution to Law

NAME: Dr Tarun Kumar De, Scientific (H) VECC DAE

ADDRESS: 22a Motilal Nehru Road
Calcutta
700029
India

OCCUPATION: Scientist, Engineer & Researcher

YEAR OF ENTRY: 2000

CITATION: For your Outstanding Contribution to Engineering
Research

NAME: Joan E Hirsh Emma

ADDRESS: 23 Pheasant Lane
E Setauket
NY 11733
USA

OCCUPATION: Teacher, Writer

YEAR OF ENTRY: 2000

CITATION: For your Outstanding Contribution to College Teaching
and Manuscript Development

NAME: Bruce Alan Grindley LFIBA

ADDRESS: Tenerife Property Shop S.L.
117 Puerto Colon
Playa De Las Americas, Adeje, Tenerife
Canary Islands
Spain

OCCUPATION: Estate Agent

YEAR OF ENTRY: 2001

CITATION: For your Outstanding Contribution to International
Business Integrity in Property Conveyancing

NAME: Prof E Hanaoka-Kawamura IOM AdVAh DDG LPIBA
CH

ADDRESS: Higashitakenosatocho 2-1
1-607 Oharano
Nishikyoku
Kyoto 610-1144
Japan

OCCUPATION: University Professor

YEAR OF ENTRY: 2000

CITATION: For your Outstanding Contribution to Philosophy of
Religion

NAME: Eleanor May Cash Harwood

ADDRESS: 10 Maple Street
Box 255
Chester
CT 06412
USA

OCCUPATION: Librarian

YEAR OF ENTRY: 2002

CITATION: For your Outstanding Contribution to Library Services

NAME: Professor Shinji Itoh IOM DDG LPIBA AdVMed
MOIF CH

ADDRESS: 2-6-31 Nishikoori
Otsu 520 0027
Japan

OCCUPATION: University Professor

YEAR OF ENTRY: 2000

CITATION: For your Outstanding Contribution to Medical Research

NAME: Neil Herman Jacoby Jr LPIBA IOM AdVSci CH

ADDRESS: 1434 Midvale Avenue
Los Angeles
CA 90024
USA

OCCUPATION: Astrodynamic Scientist

YEAR OF ENTRY: 2000

CITATION: For your Outstanding Contribution to Astrodynamics

NAME: Dr Tien-Ming Jen MD

ADDRESS: Clinical Mycology Study
No 24-5 3rd Floor
Lane 24 Kinmen Road
Taipei 100-17
Taiwan
Republic of China

OCCUPATION: Educator, Consultant and Physician

YEAR OF ENTRY: 2002

CITATION: For your Outstanding Contribution to Medical Research

NAME: Dr Nella Kacergiene MOIF DDG FIBA

ADDRESS: Virsuliskiu 89-22
Vilnius
LT-2056
Lithuania

OCCUPATION: Physician, Paediatrician

YEAR OF ENTRY: 2000

CITATION: For your Outstanding Contribution to Paediatrics and Human Ecology

NAME: Tetsuo Kaneko LPIBA DDG AdVSci IOM

ADDRESS: Kogane Kazusacho 16-1
Matsudo-shi
270-0015
Japan

OCCUPATION: Physicist

YEAR OF ENTRY: 2000

CITATION: For your Outstanding Contribution to Scientific Research

NAME: Dr Khoo Boo-Chai AdVMed DDG IOM MOIF

ADDRESS: Parkway Parade Medical Centre # 05-12
80 Marine Parade
Singapore 449269

OCCUPATION: Medical Doctor

YEAR OF ENTRY: 2001

CITATION: For your Outstanding Contribution to Reconstructive Plastic Surgery

NAME: Professor Doo-Hie Kim

ADDRESS: Na-101 Lombard Apt
1-3 Sooseong 2-Ga
Sooseong-Gu
Taegu 706-032
Korea

OCCUPATION: Educator

YEAR OF ENTRY: 2000

CITATION: For your Outstanding Contribution to Environmental
Health and Preventative Medicine

NAME: Professor Pill Soo Kim LPIBA DDG IOM AdVSci CH

ADDRESS: Dept of Automotive Engineering
Daelim College
526-9 Bisan-dong, Dongan-ku
Anyang-si. Kyunggi-do
431-715 Korea

OCCUPATION: Professor

YEAR OF ENTRY: 2001

CITATION: For your Outstanding Contribution to Engineering

NAME: Professor Eliezer I Klainman LPIBA IOM AdVMed DDG

ADDRESS: 86 Pardess-Meshutaf St
Raanana
Israel 43350

OCCUPATION: Cardiologist

YEAR OF ENTRY: 2000

CITATION: For your Outstanding Contribution to Cardiology

NAME:
Professor Distinguished Soji Kurimoto IOM AdVMed DDG

ADDRESS:
650-353 Koyoen Honjocho
Nishinomiya 662-0015
Japan

OCCUPATION:
Physician

YEAR OF ENTRY:
2000

CITATION:
For your Outstanding Contribution to Education and Professional Training in Medicine

NAME:
Professor Chul Lee IOM

ADDRESS:
Department of Chemistry
Hanyang University
133-791 Seoul
Korea

OCCUPATION:
Professor

YEAR OF ENTRY:
2000

CITATION:
For your Outstanding Contribution to Chemistry

NAME:
Associate Professor Cornelis A Los

ADDRESS:
Block B Nanyang Avenue
10-04 Singapore
639611
Singapore

OCCUPATION:
Economist

YEAR OF ENTRY:
2000

CITATION:
For your Outstanding Contribution to Financial Economics

NAME: Dr Virendra B Mahesh LPIBA DDG IOM MOIF

ADDRESS:
Medical College of Georgia
1120 15th Street
Augusta
GA 30912-3000
USA

OCCUPATION: Endocrinologist

YEAR OF ENTRY: 2001

CITATION: For your Outstanding Contribution to Physiology and Endocrinology

NAME: Dr Ivka Maria Munda AdVSci DDG

ADDRESS:
Centre for Scientific Research
Slovene Academy of Science & Arts
Nori trg 2
1000 Ljubljana
Slovenia

OCCUPATION: Marine Biologist, Phycologist

YEAR OF ENTRY: 2002

CITATION: For your Outstanding Contribution to Marine Biology

NAME: Dr Tadeusz K Murawski DDG MOIF LFIBA IOM

ADDRESS:
ul Marszalkowska 27/35
Apt 102
00-639 Warsaw
Poland

OCCUPATION: Economist

YEAR OF ENTRY: 2001

CITATION: For your Outstanding Contribution to Environmental Economics

NAME: Dr Tanya Niyamapa

ADDRESS: Agricultural Machinery & Management
Dept of Agricultural Eng
Kasetsart Univ Kampaeng Saen
Campus Nakornpathom 73140
Thailand

OCCUPATION: Agricultural Engineer

YEAR OF ENTRY: 2000

CITATION: For your Outstanding Contribution to Agricultural
Engineering

NAME: Joyce A. Oliver IOM

ADDRESS: J.A. Oliver Associates
2045 Fullerton Road
PO Box 2607 La Habra Heights
CA 90631-8213
USA

OCCUPATION: Author/Journalist

YEAR OF ENTRY: 2001

CITATION: For your Outstanding Contribution to Commercial
Journalism

NAME: Eugene T Ouzts LFIBA

ADDRESS: 739E Cottonwood Road
Duncan
AZ 85534-8108
USA

OCCUPATION: Minister

YEAR OF ENTRY: 2001

CITATION: For your Outstanding Contribution to Education and
Religion

NAME: Dr Roland Peter

ADDRESS: Schwesternweg 11/74
A-5020 Salzburg
Austria

OCCUPATION: Biologist, Educator

YEAR OF ENTRY: 2001

CITATION: For your Outstanding Contribution to Biology, Science and Education

NAME: Thresia Pierce LFIBA DDG AdVAh

ADDRESS: 3105 Cardinal Dr
Las Vegas
NV 89121
USA

OCCUPATION: Teacher

YEAR OF ENTRY: 2001

CITATION: For your Outstanding Contribution to Teaching and Writing

NAME: Professor Dr Desider A Pragay FIBA IOM

ADDRESS: C/O Dr G Roland
Hauzenberger Strasse 13
D 80687 Munchen
Germany

OCCUPATION: Scientist

YEAR OF ENTRY: 2001

CITATION: For your Outstanding Contribution to Biochemistry and Education

NAME: Professor Naseem Rahman

ADDRESS: Department of Chemistry
University of Trieste
Via Giogieri No 1
34100 Trieste
Italy

OCCUPATION: Professor

YEAR OF ENTRY: 2001

CITATION: For your Outstanding Contribution to Chemistry

NAME: Luis B Rosario MD, FESC

ADDRESS: R Quinta Grande 8 r/c
2780-156 Oeiras
Portugal

OCCUPATION: Physician

YEAR OF ENTRY: 2001

CITATION: For your Outstanding Contribution to Cardiology

NAME: Honorable Dr Kazuo Sato DDG

ADDRESS: 3-11-21 Yabe
Sagamihara-shi
Kanagawa-ken 229-0032
Japan

OCCUPATION: University Professor

YEAR OF ENTRY: 2001

CITATION: For your Outstanding Contribution to Engineering

NAME:	Dr Mika Sato-Ilic
ADDRESS:	Institute of Policy & Planning Sciences University of Tsukuba Tenodai 1-1-1 Tsukuba, Ibaraki 305-8573 Japan
OCCUPATION:	Assistant Professor
YEAR OF ENTRY:	2000
CITATION:	For your Outstanding Contribution to Engineering

NAME:	Count Hans C von Seherr-Thoss LFIBA AdVSci
ADDRESS:	Habichtstr 39 D 82008 Unterhaching Germany
OCCUPATION:	Mechanical Engineer
YEAR OF ENTRY:	2000
CITATION:	For your Outstanding Contribution to Mechanical Engineering

NAME:	Dr Ingeborg Hildegard Solbrig
ADDRESS:	1126 Pine Street Iowa City IA 52240 USA
OCCUPATION:	Educator
YEAR OF ENTRY:	2004
CITATION:	For your Outstanding Contribution to Writing, Education and Research

NAME: Mary Goldacre Spencer

ADDRESS: Tenerife Property Shop SL
117 Puerto Colon
Playas De Las Americas
Adeje Tenerife
Canary Islands, Spain

OCCUPATION: Real Estate Agent

YEAR OF ENTRY: 2001

CITATION: For your Outstanding Contribution to International
Business Integrity

NAME: Professor Dr Andy Sun IOM MOIF LPIBA DDG CH
AdVMed

ADDRESS: National Taiwan University Hospital
Taipei
Taiwan
Republic of China

OCCUPATION: Immunologist

YEAR OF ENTRY: 2001

CITATION: For your Outstanding Contribution to Immunology and
Medical Science

NAME: Thomas H Syddall IOM MOIF

ADDRESS: C/O A J Park
P O Box 949
Wellington
New Zealand

OCCUPATION: Patent Attorney

YEAR OF ENTRY: 2003

CITATION: For your Outstanding Contribution to Patent Law

NAME: Dr Manfred Thiel IOM LPIBA DDG MOIF AAAS CH DO

ADDRESS: Rohrbacherstr 20
69115 Heidelberg
Germany

OCCUPATION: Philosopher, Poet

YEAR OF ENTRY: 2000

CITATION: For your Outstanding Contribution to Philosophy and
Poetry

NAME: J E Vander Naald LFIBA DDG IOM

ADDRESS: 36047 Palomino Way
Palm Desert
CA 92211
USA

OCCUPATION: Educator

YEAR OF ENTRY: 2000

CITATION: For your Outstanding Contribution to Education

NAME: Dr Ruslana Vernickaite DDG LFIBA IOM

ADDRESS: Rambyno 7-5
LT-5810 Klaipeda
Lithuania

OCCUPATION: Physician, Obstetrician-Gynaeologist

YEAR OF ENTRY: 2000

CITATION: For your Outstanding Contribution to Obstetrics,
Gynaecology and Ecology

NAME: Professor Hugo Walter

ADDRESS: 157 Loomis Court
Princeton
NJ 08540
USA

OCCUPATION: College Professor

YEAR OF ENTRY: 2000

CITATION: For your Outstanding Contribution to Humanities and Poetry

NAME: Lt Gen John MacNair Wright, Jr

ADDRESS: 21227 George Brown Avenue
Riverside
CA 92518-2881
USA

OCCUPATION: Lieutenant General, U.S. Army (Retired)

YEAR OF ENTRY: 2002

CITATION: For your Outstanding Contribution to the Military

NAME: Professor Michiru Yasuhara LFIBA IOM AdVSci

ADDRESS: 34-18 Neura Iwasaki
Nissin-city
Aichi 470-0131
Japan

OCCUPATION: Professor

YEAR OF ENTRY: 2000

CITATION: For your Outstanding Contribution to Education

NAME: Dr Vak Yeong Yoo MOIF DDG LPIBA AdVMed IOM

ADDRESS: Cheong-Vak Antiaging Hospital
582 Shinsa Dong Kangnam Ku
Seoul 135-120
Korea

OCCUPATION: Physician

YEAR OF ENTRY: 2001

CITATION: For your Outstanding Contribution to Medicine